Here's where to find whatever you are looking for in the 720 pages of British Hit Singles & Albums

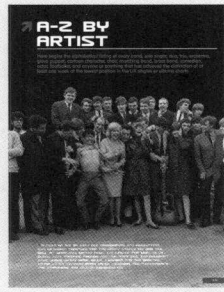

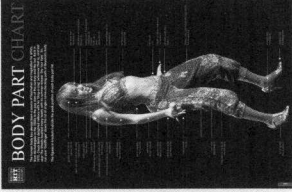

This year's book (our 18th edition since 1977) gives you a triple whammy, if such a thing exists. Our recent introduction of Hit Albums and Hit Singles in one volume is further boosted by the addition of more than 70 pages devoted to the 1,000 No.1 hits. This special supplement, which celebrates half a century of chart-toppers, can be found at the back of the book.

The other big change to the book is its size. Rather than continuing to grow fatter, this year we have grown taller to enable us to squeeze in more hits and features. Also, in order to capture all 1,000 No.1 hits, we are more up to date than usual. Although all our basic A-Z act information still stretches up to the last chart of 2004, we have extended our printing deadlines for the No.1s section to include everything from the first chart-topper, Al Martino's 'Here in My Heart' in 1952, to the 1,000th, Elvis Presley's 'One Night' / 'I Got Stung' in 2005.

Downloads can breathe new life into the singles chart. Someday, all music may be paid for this way, but in the meantime the inclusion of downloaded tracks, CDs and vinyl in the same Top 75 will be a boost.

The alterations to this book reflect the major changes in the way in which Britain's music lovers are buying their records these days. In the first week of 2005 there were more sales of downloads than physical CD singles for the first time. Just as vinyl and cassette were displaced as the format of choice, now the CD seems to be going the same way. No need to panic just yet, though. CD and even vinyl to a certain extent, will still be around for years. However, legal computer downloads have an important part to play in contributing healthy sales figures for the single and its continued life as a well-loved national institution. Downloads can breathe new life into the singles chart. Someday, all music may be paid for this way, but in the meantime the inclusion of downloaded tracks, alongside CDs and vinyl in the same Top 75, will boost the disappointing singles sales figures of the past couple of years. If this comes to pass we should be able to look forward to the next 1,000 No.1 hits.

David Roberts
Editor: British Hit Singles & Albums

1000 NUMBER ONE SINGLES

1952 - 2005

↗ THE 1,000 NO.1S SECTION BEGINS ON PAGE 643

 WRITE TO US...

Send   Chat   Attach   Address   Fonts   Colors   Save As Draft

To: editor@bibleofpop.com

Subject: WRITE TO US...

We thrive on your feedback about the book or music in general. So, write to us at

The Editor, British Hit Singles & Albums, Guinness World Records, 338 Euston Road, London NW1 3BD.

Or email editor@bibleofpop.com

VISIT OUR WEBSITE

Go to www.bibleofpop.com for more information about the book. The website brings you pop history from the past six decades courtesy of our chart consultant Dave McAleer, together with reviews of some the best new releases, a forum for discussing chart-related issues and the No.1 calculator for discovering what was top of the charts on any day you care to select. You can also pit your pop wits against our weekly pop genius quiz, devised by Matthew White. Why not send in your own articles and charts? If we like what we see, we'll include them on the site or maybe even publish them in the book.

↗ JANUARY

January 2004 becomes the best ever post-Christmas month for UK album sales; in broader terms, Elvis Presley's total US LP sales are certified at 117.5 million, and Michael Jackson's 'Number Ones' becomes the 50th UK million-selling album of the 21st century. Less noteworthy is the Cheeky Girls' achievement. They top a list of the 100 worst pop records voted for by Channel 4 viewers with 'Cheeky Song (Touch My Bum)'. Kink Ray Davies is shot in the leg in a New Orleans street as he defends his girlfriend from armed muggers, and, to the dismay of thousands of teenage boys, Britney Spears marries teenage sweetheart Jason Alexander, wearing a baseball cap, ripped jeans and a garter. Boys needn't have worried: Britney files for divorce just 55 hours later. Pop Idol 2 winner Michelle McManus tops the singles chart with her debut. 'All This Time' is the 13th No.1 from a reality TV contestant.

Number of US albums sold by Elvis Presley … 117.5m

Number of hours Britney was married … 55

↗ FEBRUARY

The superstar story of the month is undoubtedly Janet Jackson and Justin Timberlake's half-time appearance at the American Super Bowl, broadcast to hundreds of millions across the US and worldwide. While performing Justin's 'Rock Your Body', JT seems to rip off a section of Janet's costume, exposing her right breast. TV executives and the artists themselves try to dismiss the incident as a "wardrobe malfunction", though the song lyric "I'm gonna have you naked by the end of this song" seems to suggest otherwise. British award winners in February include Annie Lennox, who wins an Oscar for 'Into the West', and Coldplay's 'Clocks', which takes the prestigious Grammy for Record of the Year. Beyoncé takes home four more awards than they did and signs a multimillion-dollar sponsorship deal with Tommy Hilfiger. The Darkness, Daniel Bedingfield, Lemar and Duran Duran are all Brit winners. Outkast spends a record eight weeks occupying the top two spots of the US chart and Elton John opens in Vegas at the start of a three-year deal which will net him a cool $50m. Digital downloads in the States pass the two-million mark in a week for the first time.

Number of seconds Janet Jackson's breast was exposed … 1.7

Number of Super Bowl viewers who saw it … almost one billion

← BRITNEY SPEARS GETS HITCHED TWICE IN 2004. HUSBAND NO.1, JASON ALEXANDER, LASTS LESS THAN THREE DAYS. HUSBAND NO.2, DANCER KEVIN FEDERLINE, IS PICTURED HERE WITH BRITNEY ON SANTA MONICA BEACH FIVE MONTHS BEFORE THEIR 8 SEPTEMBER WEDDING

→ PETER ANDRE BAGS A BRITISH HIT SINGLES NO.1 AWARD AT THE MTV STUDIOS IN MARCH. 'MYSTERIOUS GIRL' IS THE FIRST SINGLE TO TOP THE CHART AFTER PREVIOUSLY PEAKING AT NO.2

↗ MARCH

In a good month for Radio 2 listeners, the first week of March sees three Terry Wogan-championed jazz artists dominate the album chart: Katie Melua, Norah Jones and Jamie Cullum take No.1, No.2 and No.3, respectively. After his controversial, Bush-baiting 'Shoot the Dog' single, George Michael returns to the top of the UK albums chart with 'Patience', selling a sizeable 274,816 copies in its first week. After a dozen chart-toppers, Westlife are reduced from a quintet to a quartet when Bryan McFadden leaves to grow a beard, change the spelling of Bryan to Brian, split up with Kerry and start a solo career as a sensitive singer-songwriter. Peter Andre becomes a TV jungle survivor alongside John Lydon, and turns tabloid man-eater Jordan into the demure Katie Price. His 'Mysterious Girl' is the first record to top the chart after previously peaking at No.2. On its third chart entry it becomes the third No.1 for the personality who came third in the third series of I'm a Celebrity… Portugal becomes the first major country to stop compiling a singles chart and WH Smith announces it will stop selling singles. There's better news from the US where paid downloads total 24 million for the first three months of 2004.

First-week sales of 'Mysterious Girl' …107,870

#1
BRITISH HIT SINGLES

The 973rd UK No.1 He is recorded in
Guinness World Records book of
British Hit Singles
PETER ANDRE
'Mysterious Girl'
'Warner Bros' etc.
6th March 2004

>> SINGLES 2004

SINGLES SOLD IN 2004
26,490,000

BIGGEST-SELLING SINGLES ACT OF 2004
BAND AID 20 1,065,749 SINGLES

TOP 10 SINGLES OF 2004
1. DO THEY KNOW IT'S CHRISTMAS?
   BAND AID 20 1,065,749
2. F**K IT (I DON'T WANT YOU BACK)
   EAMON 552,628
3. CHA CHA SLIDE DJ CASPER 352,367
4. CALL ON ME ERIC PRYDZ 316,869
5. YEAH! USHER FEATURING
   LIL' JON & LUDACRIS 300,740
6. ALL THIS TIME MICHELLE 291,427
7. LEFT OUTSIDE ALONE ANASTACIA 275,296
8. MYSTERIOUS GIRL PETER ANDRE 259,691
9. TOXIC BRITNEY SPEARS 258,604
10. F.U.R.B. - F U RIGHT BACK
    FRANKEE 245,964

>> ALBUMS 2004

ARTIST ALBUMS SOLD IN 2004
124,446,753

COMPILATION ALBUMS SOLD IN 2004
38,958,904

BIGGEST-SELLING ALBUMS ACT OF 2004
ROBBIE WILLIAMS 1,830,000 ALBUMS

TOP 10 ALBUMS OF 2004
1. SCISSOR SISTERS SCISSOR SISTERS 1,594,259
2. HOPES AND FEARS KEANE 1,593,677
3. GREATEST HITS ROBBIE WILLIAMS 1,530,788
4. SONGS ABOUT JANE MAROON5 1,490,117
5. CALL OFF THE SEARCH KATIE MELUA 1,356,962
6. ANASTACIA ANASTACIA 1,115,928
7. CONFESSIONS USHER 1,108,590
8. FEELS LIKE HOME NORAH JONES 993,632
9. FINAL STRAW SNOW PATROL 991,219
10. IL DIVO IL DIVO 968,460

↗ APRIL

Eamon's debut single 'F**k It (I Don't Want You Back)', with its record 33 expletives, gives the New York newcomer the biggest seller of the year after Band Aid 20, shifting 153,287 in the first week. Frankee's response record, 'F.U.R.B. - F U Right Back', replaces the record that inspired it at No.1, turning the spat into a chart first. Usher simultaneously tops the UK singles and albums charts, becoming the first American male to achieve this since Meat Loaf in 1993. His Confessions album sells an incredible 1.1 million in its first week in the US. A survey shows that the most-played artist on British radio in the past 20 years is George Michael. Elton John takes second place and Robbie Williams is third. Anastacia's self-titled album enters at No.1 around Europe, and goes on to become her third multi-platinum album in a row in the UK. The latest instalment of the never-ending compilation series, Now! 57, sells 334,345 in its first week – a record for a compilation album, and more than the rest of the Top 40 compilation albums combined.

> **Number of expletives in Eamon's debut single … 33**

↗ MAY

After years of being chased through the courts by the major labels, Napster finally goes legit and is launched in the UK, stealing a march on iTunes. Usher continues his stellar year, matching the US success of The Bee Gees and The Beatles by having three singles simultaneously in the Top 10 of the Billboard Hot 100 chart. The R&B heart-throb occupies the No.1 spot with 'Burn', while 'Yeah!' is at No.4 and 'Confessions' climbs to No.9. Madonna kicks off her Reinvention tour in California. It proceeds to attract 880,000 fans and grosses $124.5m, selling out 54 of 55 shows. Morrissey sells out the 15,000-seat MEN Arena in Manchester in just 90 minutes, and his No.3 hit 'Irish Blood, English Heart' gives him his highest ever position in the UK singles chart. About 385,000 people watch the star-studded Rock in Rio festival in Lisbon, Portugal, and stadium rockers par excellence, The Darkness, are named Songwriters of the Year at the Ivor Novello awards. A record 36 countries participate in the Eurovision Song Contest, which is won by the Ukrainian entry, 'Wild Dances' by Ruslana. The UK's James Fox comes 16th. Back across the pond, our American cousins show that the reality pop format is far from dead when a record 71 million votes are cast in the final of American Idol 3, which is won by Fantasia Barrino.

> **Number of minutes taken for 15,000 Morrissey tickets to sell out … 90**

↗ JUNE

In a month of bans, Pop!'s single, 'Heaven and Earth', is banned from the chart for being 26 seconds too long - thereby breaking chart rules - and Tony Blackburn is suspended from duty on Classic Gold Digital for playing Cliff Richard records on his radio show. Cliff's old mates The Shadows play their final gig, witnessed by Cliff and Cilla Black. In the same month the Shads' Bruce Welch and Brian Bennett receive OBEs but Hank Marvin declines his for personal reasons. Legendary stadium live act The Who return to what they do best with a triumphant sun-kissed performance at the Isle of Wight festival. In a strong month for festivals, Glastonbury returns with one of its most successful weekends ever. Tens of thousands arrive at the site on the Thursday to watch England crash out of Euro 2004 on the big screens and end the weekend muddy and emotional after witnessing Muse steal the show from fellow headliners Oasis and Paul McCartney. The Glasto stats are as follows: 112,500 tickets sold, 25,000 staff employed, 25 stages, 2,000 acts, 296 people evicted, 90,000 tents, 36,000 vehicles parked, 205 crimes reported, 106 arrests, 1,560 injuries or medical conditions treated, one death. The Red Hot Chili Peppers' gigs in Hyde Park are seen by a total of 258,000 fans, the year's biggest attendance worldwide, and gross $17.2m. Four of the band's albums make the Top 75 during their tour. Other high achievers this month include James Brown, who bags a Lifetime Achievement award at the Mobos, Stevie Wonder, who is inducted into the US Songwriters' Hall of Fame, Dido, who receives a plaque for eight million sales worldwide of Life for Rent, Eamon, who tops the first UK ring tone chart by selling 170,000 tones, and the Pixies, who are No.1 in the first unofficial downloads chart.

Number of acts performing at Glastonbury ... 2,000

>> TOP 10 DOWNLOADS OF 2004

1. VERTIGO U2
2. WHAT YOU WAITING FOR? GWEN STEFANI
3. LOSE MY BREATH DESTINY'S CHILD
4. AMERICAN IDIOT GREEN DAY
5. DO THEY KNOW IT'S CHRISTMAS? BAND AID 20
6. THESE WORDS NATASHA BEDINGFIELD
7. SHE WILL BE LOVED MAROON5
8. JUST LOSE IT EMINEM
9. I BELIEVE IN YOU KYLIE
10. CAR WASH CHRISTINA AGUILERA FEATURING MISSY ELLIOTT

>> RADIO PLAY

MOST PLAYED TRACK ON RADIO IN 2004
HEY YA! OUTKAST 53,634 PLAYS

>> TOP 10 MUSIC DVDS OF 2004

1. LIVE AID VARIOUS 280,256
2. ON FIRE - LIVE AT THE BOWL QUEEN 108,703
3. DEFINITELY MAYBE OASIS 105,602
4. DREAM CAST - LES MISERABLES IN CONCERT - CAST RECORDING VARIOUS 99,626
5. CASTLES IN THE AIR CLIFF RICHARD 83,931
6. WHAT WE DID LAST SUMMER ROBBIE WILLIAMS 83,330
7. WELCOME TO THE VIDEOS GUNS N' ROSES 78,430
8. '68 COMEBACK SPECIAL ELVIS PRESLEY 75,449
9. LIVE AT WEMBLEY STADIUM QUEEN 74,471
10. ALOHA FROM HAWAII ELVIS PRESLEY 72,035

← THE YEAR'S BIGGEST ATTENDANCE FOR A LIVE GIG ANYWHERE IN THE WORLD IS SET BY THE RED HOT CHILI PEPPERS

↗ JULY

'I Believe' by American Idol winner Fantasia becomes only the 13th single to enter the US Hot 100 at No.1 and the first debut single ever to achieve the feat, despite the lowest reported radio play of any US No.1 in history. Usher continues his incredible year when he replaces himself at the top of the US chart for the second time in 2004 and becomes the first artist in history to have three consecutive No.1s on the US airplay chart. A record 13 albums pass the 500,000 sales mark in the UK in the first 31 weeks of 2004, and Katie Melua's Call off the Search becomes the first to pass the million mark. Swedish group The Hives sign to Universal for a reported $10m deal; Jamie Cullum and Massive Attack earn European platinum albums; Abba members Benny and Agnetha have solo top five albums in Sweden; and The Cure's eponymous comeback album tops the European chart and makes the US Top 10. Back home, Top of the Pops goes 100 per cent live for the first time (from Baltic Square in Gateshead). Blue reveal they are taking a break from music and Jay-Z announces his retirement.

↗ AUGUST

Germany leads the way in recognising legal downloads by becoming the first European country to include download sales in its physical singles chart. Meanwhile the UK registers the lowest weekly singles sales since records began in 1969. The total of 365,382 was one-third of the 1.2 million registered just four years ago, with cassette sales reaching an all-time low of 200 copies in a week. More positively, it is announced that more than two million tracks have been legally downloaded in the UK since January. Elvis replicates his 2000 success on the singles chart by topping the UK music DVD sales chart, holding the top three places with Aloha from Hawaii, '68 Comeback Special and Elvis 56. Fulfilling their early promise, Busted score their fourth No.1 in 15 months with 'Thunderbirds' / '3AM'. Very heavy metallers Megadeth begin suing each other over a reported $200m in royalties. Outkast continue their success story by winning four MTV Video awards. A crowd of 65,000 Phish-heads turn up to watch American rock band Phish's last ever show – the group notched up 28 US album entries, but none in the UK. Red Hot Chili Peppers' rush-release Live in Hyde Park, which tops the UK albums chart, and Anthrax, Green Day and Ash are among the Kerrang! award winners.

THE MANTELPIECE
IN THE USHER CRIB
NEEDS EXTENDING
BY THE END OF 2004

Singles sold in the lowest week since records began ... 365,382

→ WITH LITTLE NEW PRODUCT TO SHOUT ABOUT, 2004 IS A COMPARATIVELY QUIET YEAR FOR ROBBIE WILLIAMS. HE NEVERTHELESS STILL MANAGES TO BE THE BIGGEST-SELLING ALBUM ACT OF THE YEAR, CREATE THE VOICE OF DOUGAL FOR THE MAGIC ROUNDABOUT MOVIE, ENTER THE UK MUSIC HALL OF FAME AND CONTRIBUTE TO THE BEST-SELLING SINGLE OF 2004

↗ SEPTEMBER

The first Official UK Chart Company download chart is revealed at a launch party at the Marquee Club, Leicester Square, London, on 1 September. The countdown is broadcast live on BBC Radio 1. Digital single sales for the first week total 132,000 compared with 374,000 physical sales in the same week. Nearly 90 per cent of the sales of the first chart-topper, a live version of 'Flying Without Wings' by Westlife, are achieved through downloads from the band's official website. Franz Ferdinand finally breaks a tradition of bookies' favourites not winning the Mercury Music Prize by collecting the 2004 award for their self-titled debut album. Smash Hits readers' most fanciable female, Rachel Stevens, adds another prize to her CV when she breaks a Guinness World Record for the greatest number of public appearances by a pop artist in 24 hours in different cities, visiting seven cities across the UK on 8 and 9 September. Further afield, Alicia Keys is joined by Cyndi Lauper and Boyz II Men, who play the first gig ever to be staged on the Great Wall of China for the Wall of Hope, a China 2004 charity concert for the China Children's and Teenagers' Fund. As a final sign that CD singles are dying a death in the States, 'Dreams' by American Idol contestant Diana Degarmo becomes the lowest-selling US No.1 in history with a week's sale below 3,000. Interestingly, this sale would not have been sufficient for the track to make the paid downloads Top 50 stateside.

↗ OCTOBER

The month kicks off in bizarre fashion as the city of Melbourne honours AC/DC by renaming Corporation Lane AC/DC Lane. Back in the UK, Joss Stone, at 17, becomes the youngest female solo artist to have a No.1 album. The soulful teenager grew up in the Devon village of Ashill, and co-wrote most of the tracks on Mind Body & Soul, which sells 75,092 copies in its first week. More noisily, Elton John launches a four-letter tirade at Madonna at the Q awards. The knight of the realm takes exception to Madge being nominated for best live act (a category won by Muse), accusing her of miming on stage during her Reinvention tour. In a political month in pop, Mattie from Busted decides that "From the financial position I am in now, I'm a f****** Tory boy too", but he is unlikely to have the same impact as Bono's endorsement of the government's policy on debt relief. It is later reported that Conservative leader Michael Howard hadn't heard of the band. It's the time of year when the big guns release their album offerings for the Christmas market and Robbie Williams's Greatest Hits gets off to a flying start with 320,081 copies crossing UK record shop counters in its first week on sale. Not so impressive is the smallest recorded sale of 'Call on Me'; this Eric Prydz single goes to the top of the UK chart on sales of only 21,749. Once again the download chart shows encouraging signs of growth, with U2's Vertigo racking up 30,000 sales in a week that sees the top three downloads all managing sales of more than 20,000. Stateside, Nelly becomes the first artist to have two albums simultaneously enter at No.1 and No.2, with Suit and Sweat sweeping all before them. More modestly, but long awaited, Brian Wilson's re-recorded Smile album hits the UK charts and Donny Osmond achieves his highest ever UK singles chart entry position, when 'Breeze on By' debuts at No.8.

Number of copies sold of Robbie Williams's Greatest Hits in week of release … 320,081

→ DEVONIAN TEENAGE SOUL SENSATION JOSS STONE BREAKS A RECORD HELD BY AVRIL LAVIGNE IN OCTOBER AND, COINCIDENTALLY, DUETS WITH STONE MICK JAGGER ON A TRACK FOR THE MOVIE ALFIE

↗ NOVEMBER

On 11 November, the first acts are inducted into the new UK Music Hall of Fame in a Channel 4 broadcast from London's Hackney Empire. On the same Sunday, 21st-century pop stars attempt to reproduce the charitable effort Band Aid created by the original 'Do They Know It's Christmas?' single released 20 years earlier, and the long-awaited release of the Live Aid TV coverage enters the DVD chart at No.1. More charity news, as the Girls Aloud cover of The Pretenders' 'I'll Stand by You' tops the singles chart in aid of Children in Need. In an outstanding month for old-timers, Rod Stewart manages a US No.1 album – the first solo Brit to do so since Eric Clapton in 1994; 70-year-old Leonard Cohen adds another UK chart album to his list and Tom Waits performs a rare gig at the Hammersmith Apollo, where tickets change hands for more than £400 a seat. Lawyers are busy as the R Kelly and Jay-Z US tour ends early over an alleged pepper spray attack and Badly Drawn Boy sues his record label over £300,000 royalties. More positively, Usher mops up at the American Music Awards with four awards, just ahead of Outkast on three. Shania Twain sets a US Greatest Hits category record for a female, shifting 529,000 copies of her Greatest Hits in the first week of release.

↗ UK MUSIC HALL OF FAME

FOUNDING MEMBERS:
1950s ELVIS PRESLEY
1960s THE BEATLES
1970s BOB MARLEY
1980s MADONNA
1990s U2

INDUCTEES VOTED FOR BY THE PUBLIC:
1950s CLIFF RICHARD
1960s THE ROLLING STONES
1970s QUEEN
1980s MICHAEL JACKSON
1990s ROBBIE WILLIAMS

> THE SUN HELPS TO KICK-START BAND AID 20 AND SUCCESSFULLY PREDICTS THE 2004 CHRISTMAS NO.1 AS EARLY AS THIS EDITION OF THE NEWSPAPER ON 15 NOVEMBER

↗ DECEMBER

Usher is at it again, bagging 11 trophies at the 2004 Billboard magazine awards, beating Outkast (again) who, nevertheless, grab five. Outkast's André 3000 is cast as Jimi Hendrix in a forthcoming movie about the legendary guitarist. Strangely, Irishman Daniel O'Donnell ends the year with a record-breaking nine albums in the US World Music Top 15. Back at home, 'Thunderbirds' is voted not the best movie but the Record of the Year when ITV viewers text and phone for the Busted single. The long-awaited U2 album sets cash registers ringing as it establishes first-week sales of 200,863 in the UK and more than 840,000 in the US. How to Dismantle an Atomic Bomb also tops the charts in 30 countries. In the UK singles chart, 'Do They Know It's Christmas?', by Band Aid 20, duly fights off all contenders for the coveted Christmas No.1 slot after notching up 72,491 sales on day one and easily becomes the year's best-seller. On Boxing Day the singles chart shows Steve Brookstein's 'Against All Odds' as the post-Christmas No.1. Steve, who had beaten the distinctive pop operatic group G4 in the final of ITV's The X Factor, promptly donates proceeds from the single to the tsunami disaster appeal.

Number of copies of the Band Aid 20 single sold on its first day in the shops … 72,491

CHART MILESTONES

What follows is a history of the charts used to compile this book and some significant changes to the way in which we have listened to music down the years.

1952 – First UK singles chart launched by New Musical Express. No.1 in the first Top 12 on Friday 14 November 1952 was Al Martino with 'Here in My Heart'.

1953 – Seven-inch vinyl 45rpm pop singles introduced.

1954 – The singles chart became a Top 20 on 1 October.

1956 – Top 30 singles chart established on 13 April and the albums chart used by this book began with a Record Mirror Top 5 on 28 July.

1958 – Albums chart extended to a Top 10 using Melody Maker on 8 November.

1959 – Sales of vinyl 45s overtook 78s. A newspaper strike prevented the albums chart publication between 27 June and 8 August, with the 20 June chart repeated during this period.

1960 – For the purposes of this book, a larger Top 50 Record Retailer chart replaced NME singles listings on 5 March, and a Record Retailer Top 20 albums chart replaced the Melody Maker version on 26 March. On 10 March the date of the chart changed to a Thursday.

1963 – The singles chart was independently audited for Record Retailer.

1966 – The albums chart became a Top 30 on 14 April and Top 40 on 8 December.

1967 – On 5 July the date of the chart changed to a Wednesday.

1969 – The date of the chart changed to a Saturday on 9 August. The albums chart decreased to a Top 15 on 12 February, rose to a Top 20 on 11 June, back up to a Top 40 on 25 June, became a Top 32 for one week on 9 August and dropped to a Top 25 on 11 October. Then it varied from a Top 20 to a Top 24 until January 1970. The singles Top 50 now compiled for Record Retailer and the BBC by the British Market Research Bureau. Note that Record Retailer printed an incorrect albums chart on 9 March 1969, containing both budget and full-price LPs. For this book, we have replaced it with the correct full-price albums chart data for the purposes of our listings.

1970 – The albums chart varied from 47 to 77 entries from 31 January to 9 January 1971.

1971 – Record Retailer became Record and Tape Retailer. The albums chart stabilised as a Top 50 on 16 January. A postal strike resulted in no Record and Tape Retailer albums charts from 6 February to 3 April, and as a result this book returned to Melody Maker chart listings for this eight-week period. On 7 August the Record and Tape Retailer full-price chart was combined with the previously separate budget chart.

1972 – The albums chart reverted to a full-price listing only on 8 January. Record and Tape Retailer changed its name to Music Week.

1973 – On the chart date 18 August, the minimum dealer price for albums was changed to qualify for the chart, removing and excluding mostly cheaper compilation releases. The first year of BPI trade delivery figures showed 54.6 million singles sold, compared to 96.5 million LPs. The albums chart was a Top 24 for one week on 13 January.

1974 – The albums chart was a Top 42 for one week on 5 January.

1975 – The albums chart became a Top 60 on 5 July.

1977 – The first edition of The Guinness Book of British Hit Singles was published. Singles sold in the year totalled 62.1 million.

1978 – The singles chart expanded to a Top 75. The albums chart was a Top 30 for one week on 14 January. Singles sold in the year totalled 88.1 million.

1979 – The highest yearly figure for singles sales to date: 89.1 million. Two consecutive weeks' albums charts were published simultaneously as a result of a new faster chart compilation system which enabled Music Week to catch up a week.

1980 – The first cassette single released: 'C-30, C-60, C-90' by Bow Wow Wow. Singles sales dropped by 10 million.

1981 – The albums chart became a Top 100.

1983 – Chart compilation taken over by Gallup, with 500 record stores used. The first edition of The Guinness Book of British Hit Albums was published.

1986 – Sales of singles totalled 67.4 million, the first dip below 70 million in nine years.

1987 – The first CD singles released. Singles chart announcement day changed from Tuesday lunchtime to Sunday teatime on 4 October.

1989 – The albums chart split in two, with an Artists Top 75 and a Compilations Top 20.

1992 – CD singles outsold vinyl and cassette for the first time, with sales dropping to 52.9 million. The chart, in association with the BPI and Bard, became the copyright of Chart Information Network Co Ltd (CIN).

1994 – Millward Brown took over the chart compilation from Gallup using a sample of 1,000 record stores.

1995 – Singles sales rose to more than 70 million for the year.

1996 – Album sales topped the 200-million mark for the first time.

1997 – Total sales of singles for the year totalled 87 million, boosted by the UK's biggest best-seller ever, 'Candle in the Wind 1997' by Elton John.

2000 – Sales of singles dropped to 66.1 million.

2001 – CIN changed its name to The Official UK Charts Company.

2003 – Plans for the official UK singles and albums charts to be sponsored by Coca-Cola were announced.

2004 – The first Official UK Charts Company downloads chart was launched.

2005 – In the first week of the year, download singles sales (312,290) outperformed CD singles sales (282,399) for the first time.

TODAY'S CHART

The Official UK Charts Company is responsible for the commissioning, marketing, distribution and management of the UK's official music charts. Sales information is supplied by more than 5,600 retailers including all the major high street music retail chains, supermarkets, a number of internet retailers and approximately 600 independent record stores. This market research sample equates to 99 per cent of the total UK singles market. The week's sales which contribute to the official charts are collated after the close of business on Saturday for release from noon the following day. The chart rundown at 4pm on Sundays is still the most listened-to programme on BBC Radio 1.

Here begins the alphabetical listing of every band, solo singer, duo, trio, orchestra, glove puppet, cartoon character, choir, marching band, brass band, comedian, actor, footballer, and anyone or anything that has achieved the distinction of at least one week at the lowest position in the UK singles or albums charts.

▸ ALMOST AN A-Z OF 1964 POP PERFORMERS AND PRESENTERS, WHO GATHERED TOGETHER FOR THE READY STEADY GO! MAD MOD BALL AT WEMBLEY'S EMPIRE POOL. THE LINE-UP FEATURES CILLA BLACK, KEITH FORDYCE, FREDDIE AND THE DREAMERS, THE FOURMOST, BRIAN JONES, KATHY KIRBY, BILLY J KRAMER AND THE DAKOTAS, KENNY LYNCH, MANFRED MANN, CATHY MCGOWAN, THE MERSEYBEATS, THE SEARCHERS AND SOUNDS INCORPORATED

↗ HOW TO USE THE A-Z

First note that all **SINGLES** in this section of the book are printed in **BLACK** and all **ALBUMS** in **RED**. Now use this key to establish what refers to what on the following pages, which list, in alphabetical order, every act that has ever made the charts.

447 *Top 500*	= act's position in the British Hit Singles & Albums Top 500 list, calculated by total weeks on the singles and albums charts
(see also DIVE)	= act connected to the entry that is also listed in its own right elsewhere in the A-Z
22 Apr 89	= date record first entered the chart. Since 1969 this date has been the Saturday following the new chart revealed the previous Tuesday and more recently the Sunday
pos/wks	= first column equals peak position of record and the second the total weeks on chart
★	= No.1 single
★	= No.1 album
●	= Top 10 single
●	= Top 10 album
+	= single still on chart at end of 2004
+	= album still on chart at end of 2004
■	= single entered at No.1
■	= album entered at No.1
▲	= US No.1 single
▲	= US No.1 album
◆	= UK million-selling single
2	= Footnote indicates a change to the name of the act for a particular
2	single /album or a collaboration with another artist

BIOGRAPHICAL INFORMATION
Abbreviations: b. – born, d. – died, b – bass guitar, d – drums, fl – flute, g – guitar, k – keyboards, prc – percussion, prog – programming, s – saxophone, syn – synthesizer, t – trumpet, v – vocals. Act biographies include real names of all solo artists and duos who have scored a Top 40 single or album entry and the birth and death dates of any deceased solo artist or duo member.

ALPHABETICAL ORDERING
In keeping with traditional alphabetical ordering, artist names consisting of initials [e.g. AC/DC, KLF] are dealt with at the beginning of each letter's section, except when the names have become acronyms [i.e. pronounceable as one word such as for Abba]. The only exceptions to this rule are for acts appearing as DJs and MCs where their actual names are listed in alphabetical order.

RE-ENTRIES, RE-MIXES, RE-ISSUES and RE-RECORDINGS
All singles that have re-entered the chart at some point are indicated by (re) which shows that the single has re-entered once and (2re), (3re), etc for twice and three times. Where a re-entry on the chart has outperformed the original hit, you will find the relevant information as an act's footnote. All the weeks on chart for re-entries are added together with those of the original listing for that single. There is no re-entry data in the albums listings. Albums re-entries are too numerous to record and all re-entry weeks on chart are given with the one original chart entry.

Re-mixes are updated different versions of a previous hit with a completely new catalogue number. Re-issues are new releases of an unaltered previous hit on a completely new catalogue number. Re-recordings are re-workings of a previous hit by the same act.

A *UK, male vocal / instrumental group (Singles: 18 Weeks, Albums: 10 Weeks)* pos/wks

7 Feb 98	FOGHORN *Tycoon TYCD 5*	63 1
11 Apr 98	NUMBER ONE *Tycoon TYCD 6*	47 1
27 Jun 98	SING-A-LONG *Tycoon TYCD 7*	57 1
24 Oct 98	SUMMER ON THE UNDERGROUND *Tycoon TYCD 8*	72 1
5 Jun 99	OLD FOLKS *Tycoon TYCD 9*	54 1
21 Aug 99	I LOVE LAKE TAHOE *Tycoon TYCD 10*	59 1
2 Mar 02	● NOTHING *London LONCD 463*	9 6
1 Jun 02	STARBUCKS *London LONCD 467*	20 3
30 Nov 02	SOMETHING'S GOING ON *London LONCD 471*	51 1
13 Sep 03	GOOD TIME *London LONCD 480*	23 2
28 Aug 99	MONKEY KONG *Tycoon 3984276952*	62 1
16 Mar 02	HI-FI SERIOUS *London 927447762*	18 9

ABC (368) *Top 500*

Glossy but witty pop group formed in 1980 in Sheffield, South Yorkshire, UK. Led by stylish vocalist Martin Fry, b. 9 Mar 1959. First UK group of the 1980s to prise four Top 20 hits off their debut album (1982's 'The Lexicon of Love') and they were equally successful Stateside (Singles: 93 Weeks, Albums: 91 Weeks) pos/wks

31 Oct 81	TEARS ARE NOT ENOUGH *Neutron NT 101*	19 8
20 Feb 82	● POISON ARROW *Neutron NT 102*	6 11
15 May 82	● THE LOOK OF LOVE (re) *Neutron NT 103*	4 12
4 Sep 82	● ALL OF MY HEART *Neutron NT 104*	5 8
5 Nov 83	THAT WAS THEN THIS IS NOW *Neutron NT 105*	18 4
21 Jan 84	S.O.S. *Neutron NT 106*	39 5
10 Nov 84	HOW TO BE A MILLIONAIRE *Neutron NT 107*	49 4
6 Apr 85	BE NEAR ME *Neutron NT 108*	26 4
15 Jun 85	VANITY KILLS *Neutron NT 109*	70 1
16 Jan 86	OCEAN BLUE *Neutron NT 110*	51 3
6 Jun 87	WHEN SMOKEY SINGS *Neutron NT 111*	11 10
5 Sep 87	THE NIGHT YOU MURDERED LOVE *Neutron NT 112*	31 8
28 Nov 87	KING WITHOUT A CROWN *Neutron NT 113*	44 3
27 May 89	ONE BETTER WORLD *Neutron NT 114*	32 4
23 Sep 89	THE REAL THING *Neutron NT 115*	68 1
14 Apr 90	THE LOOK OF LOVE (re-mix) *Neutron NT 116*	68 1
27 Jul 91	LOVE CONQUERS ALL *Parlophone R 6292*	47 2
11 Jan 92	SAY IT *Parlophone R 6298*	42 3
22 Mar 97	STRANGER THINGS *Blatant / Deconstruction 453632*	57 1
3 Jul 82	★ THE LEXICON OF LOVE *Neutron NTRS 1* ■	1 50
26 Nov 83	BEAUTY STAB *Neutron NTRL 2*	12 13
26 Oct 85	HOW TO BE A ZILLIONAIRE *Neutron NTRH 3*	28 3
24 Oct 87	● ALPHABET CITY *Neutron NTRH 4*	7 10
28 Oct 89	UP *Neutron 8386461*	58 1
21 Apr 90	● ABSOLUTELY *Neutron 8429671*	7 12
24 Aug 91	ABRACADABRA *Parlophone PCS 7355*	50 1
4 Aug 01	LOOK OF LOVE – THE VERY BEST OF ABC *Mercury 5862372*	69 1

The act was a UK, male vocal / instrumental group for first six hits, a UK / US, male / female vocal / instrumental group for the next four, a male duo from 1987-1992 and Martin Fry alone for 'Stranger Things'

A.B.'S *Japan, instrumental group (Albums: 2 weeks)* pos/wks

14 Apr 84	DÉJÀ VU *Street Sounds XKHAN 503*	80 2

AC/DC (129) *Top 500*

Internationally acclaimed Australia-based quintet: Angus Young (g), Malcolm Young (g), Bon Scott (v) (d. 1980), Cliff Williams (b), Phillip Rudd (d). Brian Johnson (ex-Geordie) replaced Scott in 1980. No act has had more hits (28) without a Top 10 than AC/DC. Inducted into the Rock and Roll Hall of Fame in 2003 (Singles: 126 Weeks, Albums: 255 Weeks) pos/wks

10 Jun 78	ROCK 'N' ROLL DAMNATION *Atlantic K 11142*	24 9
1 Sep 79	HIGHWAY TO HELL *Atlantic K 11321*	56 4
2 Feb 80	TOUCH TOO MUCH *Atlantic K 11435*	29 9
28 Jun 80	DIRTY DEEDS DONE DIRT CHEAP *Atlantic HM 2*	47 3
28 Jun 80	HIGH VOLTAGE (LIVE VERSION) *Atlantic HM 1*	48 3
28 Jun 80	IT'S A LONG WAY TO THE TOP (IF YOU WANNA ROCK 'N' ROLL) *Atlantic HM 3*	55 3
28 Jun 80	WHOLE LOTTA ROSIE *Atlantic HM 4*	36 8
13 Sep 80	YOU SHOOK ME ALL NIGHT LONG *Atlantic K 11600*	38 6
29 Nov 80	ROCK 'N' ROLL AIN'T NOISE POLLUTION *Atlantic K 11630*	15 8
6 Feb 82	LET'S GET IT UP *Atlantic K 11706*	13 6
3 Jul 82	FOR THOSE ABOUT TO ROCK (WE SALUTE YOU) *Atlantic K 11721*	15 6
29 Oct 83	GUNS FOR HIRE *Atlantic A 9774*	37 4
4 Aug 84	NERVOUS SHAKEDOWN *Atlantic A 9651*	35 4
6 Jul 85	DANGER *Atlantic A 9532*	48 4
18 Jan 86	SHAKE YOUR FOUNDATIONS *Atlantic A 9474*	24 5
24 May 86	WHO MADE WHO *Atlantic A 9425*	16 5
30 Aug 86	YOU SHOOK ME ALL NIGHT LONG (re-issue) *Atlantic A 9377*	46 4
16 Jan 88	HEATSEEKER *Atlantic A 9136*	12 6
2 Apr 88	THAT'S THE WAY I WANNA ROCK 'N' ROLL *Atlantic A 9098*	22 5
22 Sep 90	THUNDERSTRUCK *Atco B 8907*	13 5
24 Nov 90	MONEYTALKS *Atco B 8886*	36 3
27 Apr 91	ARE YOU READY *Atco B 8830*	34 3
17 Oct 92	HIGHWAY TO HELL (LIVE) *Atco B 8479*	14 4
6 Mar 93	DIRTY DEEDS DONE DIRT CHEAP (LIVE) *Atco B 6073CD*	68 1
10 Jul 93	BIG GUN *Atco B 8396CD*	23 3
30 Sep 95	HARD AS A ROCK *Atlantic A 4368CD*	33 2
11 May 96	HAIL CAESAR *East West 7559660512*	56 1
15 Apr 00	STIFF UPPER LIP *EMI CDSTIFF 100*	65 1
5 Nov 77	LET THERE BE ROCK *Atlantic K 50366*	17 5
20 May 78	POWERAGE *Atlantic K 50483*	26 9
28 Oct 78	IF YOU WANT BLOOD YOU'VE GOT IT *Atlantic K 50532*	13 58
18 Aug 79	● HIGHWAY TO HELL *Atlantic K 50628*	8 32
9 Aug 80	★ BACK IN BLACK *Atlantic K 50735* ■	1 40
5 Dec 81	● FOR THOSE ABOUT TO ROCK (WE SALUTE YOU) *Atlantic K 50851* ▲	3 29
3 Sep 83	● FLICK OF THE SWITCH *Atlantic 7801001*	4 9
13 Jul 85	● FLY ON THE WALL *Atlantic 781263..*	7 10
7 Jun 86	WHO MADE WHO *Atlantic WX 57*	11 12
13 Feb 88	● BLOW UP YOUR VIDEO *Atlantic WX 144*	2 14
6 Oct 90	● THE RAZOR'S EDGE *Atco WX 364*	4 18
7 Nov 92	● AC/DC LIVE *Atco 7567922152*	5 7
7 Oct 95	● BALLBREAKER *East West 7559617802*	6 8
11 Mar 00	STIFF UPPER LIP *EMI 5256672*	12 4

A CAMP *Sweden / US, female / male vocal / instrumental group – leader Nina Persson (Singles: 1 Week)* pos/wks

1 Sep 01	I CAN BUY YOU *Stockholm 0152162*	46 1

A CERTAIN RATIO, A FLOCK OF SEAGULLS, A GUY CALLED GERALD, A HOME BOY A HIPPIE AND A FUNKY DREDD, A LOVE SUPREME, A TASTE OF HONEY, A TRIBE CALLED QUEST, A VERY GOOD FRIEND OF MINE, A WAY OF LIFE, ETC – *See SECOND LETTER OF EACH ACT NAME TO LOCATE THESE ENTRIES*

A.D.A.M. featuring AMY *France, male / female vocal / instrumental duo – Andrea Bellicapelli and Amy (Singles: 11 Weeks)* pos/wks

1 Jul 95	ZOMBIE *Eternal YZ 951CD*	16 11

AFI *US, male vocal / instrumental group (Singles: 4 Weeks, Albums: 1 Week)* pos/wks

21 Jun 03	GIRL'S NOT GREY *Dreamworks / Polydor 4504600*	22 3
20 Sep 03	THE LEAVING SONG PT.2 *Dreamworks / Polydor 4504625*	43 1
22 Mar 03	SING THE SORROW *Dreamworks / Polydor 04504482*	52 1

AFX (see also APHEX TWIN; POLYGON WINDOW) *UK, male instrumentalist / producer – Richard James (Singles: 1 Week)* pos/wks

11 Aug 01	2 REMIXES BY AFX *MEN1 MEN1CD*	69 1

A FLUX OF PINK INDIANS
UK, male vocal / instrumental group (Albums: 2 Weeks) pos/wks

| 5 Feb 83 | STRIVE TO SURVIVE CAUSING LEAST SUFFERING POSSIBLE | | |
| | *Spiderleg SDL 8* .... | 79 | 2 |

A HOUSE
Ireland, male vocal / instrumental group (Singles: 8 Weeks) pos/wks

13 Jun 92	ENDLESS ART *Setanta AHOU 1*	46	3
8 Aug 92	TAKE IT EASY ON ME *Setanta AHOU 2*	55	1
25 Jun 94	WHY ME *Setanta CDAHOU 4*	52	1
1 Oct 94	HERE COME THE GOOD TIMES *Setanta CDAHOUS 5*	37	2

AKA *UK, male vocal group (Singles: 2 Weeks)* pos/wks

| 12 Oct 96 | WARNING *RCA 74321360662* .... | 43 | 2 |

a1 *UK, male vocal group (Singles: 91 Weeks, Albums: 19 Weeks)* pos/wks

3 Jul 99	● BE THE FIRST TO BELIEVE *Columbia 6674222*	6	9
11 Sep 99	● SUMMERTIME OF OUR LIVES *(re) Columbia 6678322* ...	5	8
20 Nov 99	● EVERYTIME / READY OR NOT *Columbia 6681872* ...	3	11
4 Mar 00	● LIKE A ROSE *Columbia 6689032*	6	12
9 Sep 00	★ TAKE ON ME *Columbia 6695902* ■	1	11
18 Nov 00	● SAME OLD BRAND NEW YOU *Columbia 6705202* ■ ...	1	10
3 Mar 01	● NO MORE *(re) Columbia 6708742*	6	13
2 Feb 02	● CAUGHT IN THE MIDDLE *Columbia 6722322*	2	12
25 May 02	MAKE IT GOOD *(re) Columbia 6726182*	11	5
4 Dec 99	HERE WE COME *Columbia 4961362*	20	8
2 Dec 00	THE A LIST *Columbia 5011952*	14	9
8 Jun 02	MAKE IT GOOD *Columbia 5082212*	15	2

A PERFECT CIRCLE *US, male vocal / instrumental group (Singles: 2 Weeks, Albums: 2 Weeks)* pos/wks

18 Nov 00	THE HOLLOW *Virgin VUSCD 181*	72	1
13 Jan 01	3 LIBRAS *Virgin VUSCD 184*	49	1
3 Jun 00	MER DE NOMS *Virgin CDVUS 173*	55	1
27 Sep 03	THIRTEENTH STEP *Virgin CDVUS 247*	37	1

A+ *US, male rapper – Andre Levins (Singles: 9 Weeks)* pos/wks

| 13 Feb 99 | ● ENJOY YOURSELF *Universal UND 56230* .... | 5 | 9 |

A.R.E. WEAPONS
US, male vocal / insrumental group (Singles: 1 Week) pos/wks

| 4 Aug 01 | STREET GANG *Rough Trade RTRADECD 022* ..... | 72 | 1 |

ASAP *UK, male vocal / instrumental group (Singles: 4 Weeks, Albums: 1 Week)* pos/wks

14 Oct 89	SILVER AND GOLD *EMI EM 107*	60	2
3 Feb 90	DOWN THE WIRE *EMI EM 131*	67	2
4 Nov 89	SILVER AND GOLD *EMI EMC 3566*	70	1

ATB *Germany, male producer – Andre Tanneberger (Singles: 52 Weeks, Albums: 3 Weeks)* pos/wks

13 Mar 99	(9PM) TILL I COME *Ministry of Sound DATA 1*	68	1
22 May 99	(9PM) TILL I COME *(German import) (re)*		
	Club Tools CLU 66066	47	5
19 Jun 99	(9PM) TILL I COME *(Australian import) Dancenet DNET 131* ...	63	1
3 Jul 99	★ 9PM (TILL I COME) *Sound of Ministry MOSCDS 132* ■ ...	1	15
9 Oct 99	DON'T STOP *(import) Club Tools CLU 66406* ...	61	2
23 Oct 99	● DON'T STOP *(re) Sound of Ministry MOSCDS 134* ...	3	13
25 Mar 00	● KILLER *(re) Sound of Ministry MOSCDS 138* ...	4	9
27 Jan 01	THE FIELDS OF LOVE *Club Tools / Edel 0124095 CLU* [1] ...	16	4
30 Jun 01	LET U GO *Kontour 0117335 KTR*	34	2
8 Apr 00	MOVIN MELODIES *Sound of Ministry ATBCDZ 1* ...	32	3

[1] ATB featuring York

ATC *Italy / New Zealand / UK / Australia, male / female vocal group (Singles: 4 Weeks)* pos/wks

| 17 Aug 02 | AROUND THE WORLD (LA LA LA LA LA) | | |
| | *EMI / Liberty CDATC 001* .... | 15 | 4 |

A.T.F.C. *UK, male producer – Aydin Hasirci (Singles: 10 Weeks)* pos/wks

| 30 Oct 99 | IN AND OUT OF MY LIFE *Defected DEFECT 8CDS* [1] ... | 11 | 5 |
| 16 Sep 00 | BAD HABIT *Defected DFECT 19CDS* [2] .... | 17 | 3 |

| 9 Feb 02 | SLEEP TALK *Defected DFECT 43CDS* [3] ...... | 33 | 2 |

[1] A.T.F.C. presents Onephatdeeva [2] A.T.F.C. presents Onephatdeeva featuring Lisa Millett [3] A.T.F.C. featuring Lisa Millett

A.T.G.O.C. *Italy, male instrumentalist / producer – Andrea Mazzali (Singles: 2 Weeks)* pos/wks

| 21 Nov 98 | REPEATED LOVE *Wonderboy WBOYD 012* ...... | 38 | 2 |

A*TEENS *Sweden, male / female vocal group (Singles: 19 Weeks)* pos/wks

4 Sep 99	MAMMA MIA *Stockholm 5613432*	12	5
11 Dec 99	SUPER TROUPER *Stockholm 5615002*	21	5
26 May 01	● UPSIDE DOWN *Stockholm 1588492*	10	7
27 Oct 01	HALFWAY AROUND THE WORLD *Stockholm 0153612* ...	30	2

ATL *US, male vocal group (Singles: 9 Weeks)* pos/wks

| 29 May 04 | CALLING ALL GIRLS *Epic 6748272* .... | 12 | 5 |
| 28 Aug 04 | MAKE IT UP WITH LOVE *Epic 6751102* ...... | 21 | 4 |

A vs B *UK, male production duo (Singles: 1 Week)* pos/wks

| 9 May 98 | RIPPED IN 2 MINUTES *Positiva CDTIV 89* ..... | 49 | 1 |

AALIYAH *US, female vocalist – Aaliyah Haughton, b. 16 Jan 1979, d. 25 Aug 2001 (Singles: 72 Weeks, Albums: 56 Weeks)* pos/wks

2 Jul 94	BACK AND FORTH *Jive JIVECD 357*	16	5
15 Oct 94	(AT YOUR BEST) YOU ARE LOVE *Jive JIVECD 359* ...	27	2
11 Mar 95	AGE AIN'T NOTHING BUT A NUMBER *Jive JIVECD 369* ...	32	2
13 May 95	DOWN WITH THE CLIQUE *Jive JIVECD 377* ..	33	2
9 Sep 95	THE THING I LIKE *Jive JIVECD 382*	33	2
3 Feb 96	I NEED YOU TONIGHT *Big Beat A 8130CD* [1] ...	66	1
24 Aug 96	IF YOUR GIRL ONLY KNEW *Atlantic A 5669CD* ...	21	2
23 Nov 96	GOT TO GIVE IT UP *Atlantic A 5632CD*	37	2
24 May 97	IF YOUR GIRL ONLY KNEW / ONE IN A MILLION *(re-issue)*		
	Atlantic A 5610CD	15	3
30 Aug 97	4 PAGE LETTER *Atlantic A 0010CD1*	24	2
22 Nov 97	THE ONE I GAVE MY HEART TO / HOT LIKE FIRE		
	Atlantic AT 0017CD	30	2
18 Apr 98	JOURNEY TO THE PAST *Atlantic AT 0026CD* ...	23	1
12 Sep 98	ARE YOU THAT SOMEBODY? *Atlantic AT 0047CD* ...	11	4
22 Jul 00	● TRY AGAIN *(re) Virgin VUSCD 167* ▲	5	12
21 Jul 01	WE NEED A RESOLUTION *(re) Blackground VUSCD 206* [2] ...	20	6
19 Jan 02	★ MORE THAN A WOMAN *Blackground / Virgin VUSCD 230* ■ ...	1	12
18 May 02	ROCK THE BOAT *Blackground / Virgin VUSCD 243* ...	12	7
26 Apr 03	DON'T KNOW WHAT TO TELL YA		
	Independiente / Blackground / Unique ISOM 73MS ...	22	3
23 Jul 94	AGE AIN'T NOTHING BUT A NUMBER *Jive CHIP 149* ...	23	6
7 Sep 96	ONE IN A MILLION *Atlantic 7567927152* ...	33	3
28 Jul 01	● AALIYAH *Virgin CDVUS 199* ▲	5	31
15 Feb 03	● I CARE 4 U		
	Independiente / Blackground / Unique ISOM 37CDL ...	4	16

[1] Junior M.A.F.I.A. featuring Aaliyah [2] Aaliyah featuring Timbaland

ABBA (17 Top 500)
The most successful Swedish recording act ever amassed nine No.1 singles and eight successive chart-topping albums: Bjorn Ulvaeus (g/v), Benny Andersson (k/v), Agnetha Faltskog (v), Anni-Frid (Frida) Lyngstad (v). The video-genic quartet's 'Waterloo' was the first No.1 by a Scandinavian act in the UK and the biggest ever Eurovision Song Contest hit in the US. Their 'Gold – Greatest Hits' topped the chart on two separate occasions – six years apart – selling over one million copies in 1999 alone. It returned to the top on its 218th chart week – a longevity record – and was the only album in the UK's Top 100 sellers every year between 1992 and 2000. Long after the group split in 1982 (following the divorces of Bjorn and Agnetha and Benny and Frida) they continued to collect awards and gold records on every continent, and their influence was still heard in countless acts around the globe. They have sold more than 300 million records, all except one track – 'Medley' – self-penned, and many feature in the Abba-based hit musical 'Mamma Mia'. They were given a star-studded tribute at the 1999 Brit awards, which resulted in the hit single 'Thank Abba for the Music'. They were the first act from mainland Europe to become chart regulars in both the UK and US, and as such opened the doors to many later European artists. Total UK single sales: 10,004,039 (Singles: 255 Weeks, Albums: 882 Weeks) pos/wks

20 Apr 74	★ WATERLOO *Epic EPC 2240*	1	9
13 Jul 74	RING RING *Epic EPC 2452*	32	5
12 Jul 75	I DO, I DO, I DO, I DO, I DO *Epic EPC 3229* ...	38	6

20 Sep 75 ●	S.O.S. *Epic EPC 3576*	6	10
13 Dec 75 ★	MAMMA MIA *Epic EPC 3790*	1	14
27 Mar 76 ★	FERNANDO *Epic EPC 4036*	1	15
21 Aug 76 ★	DANCING QUEEN *Epic EPC 4499* ▲	1	15
20 Nov 76 ●	MONEY, MONEY, MONEY *Epic EPC 4713*	3	12
26 Feb 77 ★	KNOWING ME, KNOWING YOU *Epic EPC 4955*	1	13
22 Oct 77 ★	THE NAME OF THE GAME *Epic EPC 5750*	1	12
4 Feb 78 ★	TAKE A CHANCE ON ME *Epic EPC 5950*	1	10
16 Sep 78 ●	SUMMER NIGHT CITY *Epic EPC 6595*	5	9
3 Feb 79 ●	CHIQUITITA *Epic EPC 7030*	2	9
5 May 79 ●	DOES YOUR MOTHER KNOW *Epic EPC 7316*	4	9
14 Jul 79 ●	ANGELEYES / VOULEZ-VOUS *Epic EPC 7499*	3	11
20 Oct 79 ●	GIMME, GIMME, GIMME (A MAN AFTER MIDNIGHT) *Epic EPC 7914*	3	12
15 Dec 79 ●	I HAVE A DREAM *Epic EPC 8088*	2	10
2 Aug 80 ★	THE WINNER TAKES IT ALL *Epic EPC 8835*	1	10
15 Nov 80 ★	SUPER TROUPER *Epic EPC 9089*	1	12
18 Jul 81 ●	LAY ALL YOUR LOVE ON ME *Epic EPC A 131456*	7	7
12 Dec 81 ●	ONE OF US *Epic EPC A 1740*	3	10
20 Feb 82	HEAD OVER HEELS *Epic EPC A 2037*	25	7
23 Oct 82	THE DAY BEFORE YOU CAME *Epic EPC A 2847*	32	6
11 Dec 82	UNDER ATTACK *Epic EPC A 2971*	26	8
12 Nov 83	THANK YOU FOR THE MUSIC *CBS A 3894*	33	6
5 Sep 92	DANCING QUEEN (re-issue) *Polydor PO 231*	16	5
29 May 04	WATERLOO (re-issue) *Polydor 9820539*	20	3
8 Jun 74	WATERLOO *Epic EPC 80179*	28	2
31 Jan 76	ABBA *Epic EPC 80835*	13	10
10 Apr 76 ★	GREATEST HITS *Epic EPC 69218*	1	130
27 Nov 76 ★	ARRIVAL *Epic EPC 86018*	1	92
4 Feb 78 ★	THE ALBUM *Epic EPC 86052* ■	1	61
19 May 79 ★	VOULEZ-VOUS *Epic EPC 86086* ■	1	43
10 Nov 79 ★	GREATEST HITS VOLUME 2 *Epic EPC 10017*	1	63
22 Nov 80 ★	SUPER TROUPER *Epic EPC 10022* ■	1	43
19 Dec 81 ★	THE VISITORS *Epic EPC 10032*	1	21
20 Nov 82 ★	THE SINGLES – THE FIRST TEN YEARS *Epic ABBA 10*	1	22
19 Nov 83	THANK YOU FOR THE MUSIC *Epic EPC 10043*	17	12
19 Nov 88	ABSOLUTE ABBA *Telstar STAR 2329*	70	7
3 Oct 92 ★	GOLD – GREATEST HITS *Polydor 5170072* ■	1	343+
5 Jun 93	MORE ABBA GOLD – MORE ABBA HITS *Polydor 5193532*	13	23
7 Nov 98	LOVE STORIES *Polydor 5592212*	51	2
10 Nov 01	THE DEFINITIVE COLLECTION *Polydor 5499742*	17	8

'Lay All Your Love on Me' was available only on 12-inch vinyl in the UK 'Gold – Greatest Hits' peaked at No.4 when it re-entered the chart in Apr 2004 and was issued with a new catalogue number for this chart run – Polydor 9818754

ABBACADABRA
UK, male / female vocal / instrumental group (Singles: 1 Week) pos/wks

5 Sep 92	DANCING QUEEN *PWL International PWL 246*	57	1

Russ ABBOT *UK, male comedian / vocalist –*
Russell Roberts (Singles: 22 Weeks, Albums: 16 Weeks) pos/wks

6 Feb 82	A DAY IN THE LIFE OF VINCE PRINCE (re) *EMI 5249*	61	2
29 Dec 84	ATMOSPHERE *Spirit FIRE 4*	7	13
13 Jul 85	ALL NIGHT HOLIDAY *Spirit FIRE 6*	20	7
5 Nov 83	RUSS ABBOT'S MADHOUSE *Ronco RTL 2096*	41	7
23 Nov 85	I LOVE A PARTY *K-Tel ONE 1313*	12	9

Gregory ABBOTT
US, male vocalist (Singles: 13 Weeks, Albums: 5 Weeks) pos/wks

22 Nov 86 ●	SHAKE YOU DOWN *CBS A 7326* ▲	6	13
10 Jan 87	SHAKE YOU DOWN *CBS 4500611*	53	5

Paula ABDUL
US, female vocalist (Singles: 67 Weeks, Albums: 51 Weeks) pos/wks

4 Mar 89 ●	STRAIGHT UP *Siren SRN 111* ▲	3	13
3 Jun 89	FOREVER YOUR GIRL *Siren SRN 112* ▲	24	6
19 Aug 89	KNOCKED OUT *Siren SRN 92*	45	3
2 Dec 89	(IT'S JUST) THE WAY THAT YOU LOVE ME *Siren SRN 101*	74	1
7 Apr 90 ●	OPPOSITES ATTRACT *Siren SRN 124* [1] ▲	2	13
21 Jul 90	KNOCKED OUT (re-mix) *Virgin America VUS 23*	21	5
29 Sep 90	COLD HEARTED *Virgin America VUS 27* ▲	46	3
22 Jun 91 ●	RUSH RUSH *Virgin America VUS 38* ▲	6	11
31 Aug 91	THE PROMISE OF A NEW DAY *Virgin America VUS 44* ▲	52	2
18 Jan 92	VIBEOLOGY *Virgin America VUS 53*	19	6
8 Aug 92	WILL YOU MARRY ME *Virgin America VUS 58*	73	1
17 Jun 95	MY LOVE IS FOR REAL *Virgin America VUSCD 91* [2]	28	3

15 Apr 89 ●	FOREVER YOUR GIRL *Siren SRNLP 19* ▲	3	39
10 Nov 90	SHUT UP AND DANCE (THE DANCE MIXES) *Virgin America VUSLP 28*	40	2
27 Jul 91 ●	SPELLBOUND *Virgin America VUSLP 33* ▲	4	9
1 Jul 95	HEAD OVER HEELS *Virgin America CDVUS 90*	61	1

[1] Paula Abdul with the Wild Pair [2] Paula Abdul featuring Ofra Haza

ABERFELDY
UK, male / female vocal / instrumental group (Singles: 1 Week) pos/wks

28 Aug 04	HELIOPOLIS BY NIGHT *Rough Trade RTRADECD 192*	66	1

ABI *UK, male vocalist (Singles: 2 Weeks)* pos/wks

13 Jun 98	COUNTING THE DAYS *Kuku CDKUKU 1*	44	2

ABIGAIL *UK, female vocalist – Gayle Zsigmond (Singles: 4 Weeks)* pos/wks

16 Jul 94	SMELLS LIKE TEEN SPIRIT *Klone CDKLONE 25*	29	4

ABNEA See Johan GIELEN presents ABNEA

Colonel ABRAMS *US, male vocalist (Singles: 35 Weeks)* pos/wks

17 Aug 85 ●	TRAPPED *MCA MCA 997*	3	23
7 Dec 85	THE TRUTH *MCA MCA 1022*	53	3
8 Feb 86	I'M NOT GONNA LET YOU *MCA MCA 1031*	24	7
15 Aug 87	HOW SOON WE FORGET *MCA MCA 1179*	75	2

ABS (see also FIVE) *UK, male vocalist / rapper –*
Richard Breen (Singles: 24 Weeks, Albums: 2 Weeks) pos/wks

31 Aug 02 ●	WHAT YOU GOT *S 74321957192*	4	8
7 Jun 03	STOP SIGN *BMG 82876530392*	10	9
6 Sep 03 ●	MISS PERFECT *BMG 82876556742* [1]	5	7
13 Sep 03	ABSTRACT THEORY *BMG 82876538802*	29	2

[1] Abs featuring Nodesha

ABSOLUTE *US, male production / instrumental*
duo – Mark Picchiotti and Craig Snider (Singles: 3 Weeks) pos/wks

18 Jan 97	I BELIEVE *AM:PM 5820752* [1]	38	2
14 Mar 98	CATCH ME *AM:PM 5825032*	69	1

[1] Absolute featuring Suzanne Palmer

ABSOLUTELY FABULOUS See PET SHOP BOYS

ACADEMY OF ST MARTIN IN THE FIELDS See Neville MARRINER and the ACADEMY OF ST MARTIN IN THE FIELDS; Christopher HOGWOOD

Marc ACARDIPANE See SCOOTER

ACCEPT
Germany, male vocal / instrumental group (Albums: 5 Weeks) pos/wks

7 May 83	RESTLESS AND WILD *Heavy Metal Worldwide HMILP 6*	98	2
30 Mar 85	METAL HEART *Portrait PRT 26358*	50	1
15 Feb 86	KAIZOKU-BAN *Portrait PRT 5916*	91	1
3 May 86	RUSSIAN ROULETTE *Portrait PRT 26893*	80	1

ACE *UK, male vocal / instrumental group –*
includes Paul Carrack (Singles: 10 Weeks) pos/wks

9 Nov 74	HOW LONG *Anchor ANC 1002*	20	10

Richard ACE *Jamaica, male vocalist (Singles: 2 Weeks)* pos/wks

2 Dec 78	STAYIN' ALIVE *Blue Inc. INC 2*	66	2

ACE OF BASE 494 Top 500
Swedish pop-reggae outfit comprising three Berggren family members, Linn (v), Jenny (v), Jonas, 'Joker' (k) and Ulf 'Buddha' Ekberg (k), all from Gothenburg. Only Swedish act to top the US album chart with 'The Sign' (titled 'Happy Nation' outside US) in 1994. Best-selling single: 'All That She Wants' 603,900 (Singles: 100 Weeks, Albums: 45 Weeks) pos/wks

8 May 93 ★	ALL THAT SHE WANTS *London 8612702*	1	16
28 Aug 93	WHEEL OF FORTUNE *London 8615452*	20	6
13 Nov 93	HAPPY NATION *London 8619272*	42	3
26 Feb 94 ●	THE SIGN *London ACECD 1* ▲	2	16
11 Jun 94 ●	DON'T TURN AROUND *London ACECD 2*	5	11

Date	Title	Pos	Wks
15 Oct 94	HAPPY NATION (re-issue) *London 8610972*	40	3
14 Jan 95	LIVING IN DANGER *London ACECD 3*	18	4
11 Nov 95	LUCKY LOVE *London ACECD 4*	20	5
27 Jan 96	BEAUTIFUL LIFE *London ACECD 5*	15	6
25 Jul 98 ●	LIFE IS A FLOWER *London ACECD 7*	5	11
10 Oct 98 ●	CRUEL SUMMER *London ACECD 8*	8	5
19 Dec 98	ALWAYS HAVE. ALWAYS WILL *London ACECD 9*	12	10
17 Apr 99	EVERYTIME IT RAINS *London ACECD 10*	22	4
19 Jun 93 ★	HAPPY NATION *London 5177492* ▲	1	38
2 Dec 95	THE BRIDGE *London 5296552*	66	1
22 Aug 98	FLOWERS *London 5576912*	15	5
27 Nov 99	SINGLES OF THE 90'S *Polydor 5432272*	62	1

'Happy Nation' changed its catalogue number to 5214722 during its chart run

ACEN *UK, male producer – Syed Ahsen Razvi (Singles: 4 Weeks)* pos/wks

8 Aug 92	TRIP II THE MOON *Production House PNT 042*	38	3
10 Oct 92	TRIP II THE MOON (re-mix) *Production House PNT 042RX*	71	1

ACES See Desmond DEKKER and the ACES

Tracy ACKERMAN See Q

ACT *UK / Germany, male / female vocal / instrumental group (Singles: 2 Weeks)* pos/wks

23 May 87	SNOBBERY AND DECAY *ZTT ZTAS 28*	60	2

ACT ONE
US, male / female vocal / instrumental group (Singles: 6 Weeks) pos/wks

18 May 74	TOM THE PEEPER *Mercury 6008 005*	40	6

ACZESS *UK, male producer – Dave Birchard (Singles: 1 Week)* pos/wks

27 Oct 01	DO WHAT WE WOULD *INCredible 6719782*	65	1

ADAM and the ANTS `251` `Top 500`
Warpaint-wearing, colourfully-costumed 'Antmusic' innovators: included Stuart (Adam Ant) Goddard (v) and Marco Pirroni (g). The London-based act was 1981's top chart act with nine hits. Also in that year, they amassed 91 chart weeks – a total not bettered until 1996. Best-selling single: 'Stand and Deliver' 985,000 (Singles: 130 Weeks, Albums: 121 Weeks) pos/wks

2 Aug 80 ●	KINGS OF THE WILD FRONTIER (re) *CBS 8877*	2	18
11 Oct 80 ●	DOG EAT DOG *CBS 9039*	4	16
6 Dec 80 ●	ANTMUSIC *CBS 9352*	2	18
27 Dec 80	YOUNG PARISIANS *Decca F13803*	9	13
24 Jan 81	CARTROUBLE *Do It DUN 10*	33	9
24 Jan 81	ZEROX *Do It DUN 8*	45	9
9 May 81 ★	STAND AND DELIVER *CBS A 1065* ■	1	15
12 Sep 81 ●	PRINCE CHARMING *CBS A 1408*	1	12
12 Dec 81	ANT RAP *CBS A 1738*	3	10
27 Feb 82	DEUTSCHER GIRLS *Ego 5*	13	9
13 Mar 82	THE ANTMUSIC EP (THE B-SIDES) *Do It DUN 20*	46	4
15 Nov 80 ★	KINGS OF THE WILD FRONTIER *CBS 84549*	1	66
17 Jan 81	DIRK WEARS WHITE SOX *Do It RIDE 3*	16	29
14 Nov 81 ●	PRINCE CHARMING *CBS 85268*	2	21
3 Apr 99	THE VERY BEST OF ADAM AND THE ANTS *Columbia 4942292*	33	4

'Kings of the Wild Frontier' reached No.48 on its first visit to the chart, peaking at No.2 as a re-entry in Feb 1981. Tracks on The Antmusic EP (The B-sides): Friends / Kick / Physical 'The Very Best of Adam and the Ants' did not reach its peak position until 2004

Arthur ADAMS *US, male vocalist (Singles: 5 Weeks)* pos/wks

24 Oct 81	YOU GOT THE FLOOR *RCA 146*	38	5

Bryan ADAMS `52` `Top 500`
Globally successful rock singer / songwriter / guitarist, b. 5 Nov 1959, Kingston, Ontario, Canada. He has had more UK hits than any other Canadian artist and was the biggest-selling singles artist in the UK in 1991 when he hogged the No.1 spot for a record 16 consecutive weeks. Biggest-selling single: '(Everything I Do) I Do It for You' 1,527,824 (Singles: 248 Weeks, Albums: 404 Weeks) pos/wks

12 Jan 85	RUN TO YOU *A&M AM 224*	11	12
16 Mar 85	SOMEBODY *A&M AM 236*	35	7
25 May 85	HEAVEN *A&M AM 256* ▲	38	5
10 Aug 85	SUMMER OF '69 *A&M AM 267*	42	7
2 Nov 85	IT'S ONLY LOVE *A&M AM 285* [1]	29	6

21 Dec 85	CHRISTMAS TIME *A&M AM 297*	55	2
22 Feb 86	THIS TIME *A&M AM 295*	41	7
12 Jul 86	STRAIGHT FROM THE HEART *A&M AM 322*	51	3
28 Mar 87	HEAT OF THE NIGHT *A&M ADAM 2*	50	2
20 Jun 87	HEARTS ON FIRE *A&M ADAM 3*	57	3
17 Oct 87	VICTIM OF LOVE *A&M AM 407*	68	2
29 Jun 91 ★	(EVERYTHING I DO) I DO IT FOR YOU (re) *A&M AM 789* ◆ ▲	1	25
14 Sep 91	CAN'T STOP THIS THING WE STARTED *A&M AM 612*	12	6
23 Nov 91	THERE WILL NEVER BE ANOTHER TONIGHT *A&M AM 838*	32	3
22 Feb 92 ●	THOUGHT I'D DIED AND GONE TO HEAVEN *A&M AM 848*	8	7
18 Jul 92	ALL I WANT IS YOU *A&M AM 879*	22	5
26 Sep 92	DO I HAVE TO SAY THE WORDS *A&M AM 0068*	30	3
30 Oct 93 ●	PLEASE FORGIVE ME *A&M 5804232*	2	16
15 Jan 94 ●	ALL FOR LOVE *A&M 5804772* [2] ▲	2	13
22 Apr 95 ●	HAVE YOU EVER REALLY LOVED A WOMAN *A&M 5810282* ▲	4	9
11 Nov 95	ROCK STEADY *Capitol CDCL 763* [3]	50	2
1 Jun 96 ●	THE ONLY THING THAT LOOKS GOOD ON ME IS YOU *A&M 5813692*	6	7
24 Aug 96 ●	LET'S MAKE A NIGHT TO REMEMBER *A&M 5815672*	10	8
23 Nov 96	STAR *A&M 5820252*	13	4
8 Feb 97 ●	I FINALLY FOUND SOMEONE *A&M 5820832* [4]	10	7
19 Apr 97	18 TIL I DIE *A&M 5821852*	22	3
20 Dec 97	BACK TO YOU *A&M 5824752*	18	7
21 Mar 98	I'M READY *A&M 5825352*	20	4
10 Oct 98	ON A DAY LIKE TODAY *Mercury MERCD 516*	13	5
12 Dec 98 ●	WHEN YOU'RE GONE *A&M 5828212* [5]	3	19
15 May 99 ●	CLOUD NUMBER 9 *A&M / Mercury 5828492*	6	9
18 Dec 99	THE BEST OF ME (re) *Mercury / A&M 4971952*	47	3
18 Mar 00 ●	DON'T GIVE UP *Xtravaganza XTRAV 9CDS* [6] ■	1	14
20 Jul 02	HERE I AM *A&M 4977442*	5	8
25 Sep 04	OPEN ROAD *Polydor 9869053*	21	3
11 Dec 04	FLYING *Polydor 9869276*	39	2
2 Mar 85 ●	RECKLESS *A&M AMA 5013* ▲	7	115
24 Aug 85	YOU WANT IT YOU GOT IT *A&M AMLH 64864*	78	5
15 Mar 86	CUTS LIKE A KNIFE *A&M AMLH 64919*	21	6
11 Apr 87 ●	INTO THE FIRE *A&M AMA 3907*	10	21
5 Oct 91 ★	WAKING UP THE NEIGHBOURS *A&M 3971641* ■	1	54
20 Nov 93 ★	SO FAR SO GOOD *A&M 5401572*	1	55
6 Aug 94	LIVE! LIVE! LIVE! *A&M 3970942*	17	4
22 Jun 96 ★	18 TIL I DIE *A&M 5405512* ■	1	40
13 Dec 97	UNPLUGGED *A&M 5408312*	19	19
31 Oct 98	ON A DAY LIKE TODAY *Mercury / A&M 5410162*	11	35
27 Nov 99	THE BEST OF ME *Mercury / A&M 4905222*	12	39
27 Jul 02 ●	SPIRIT – STALLION OF THE CIMARRON (FILM SOUNDTRACK) *A&M 4933042*	8	5
2 Oct 04 ●	ROOM SERVICE *Polydor 9868245*	4	6

[1] Bryan Adams and Tina Turner [2] Bryan Adams, Rod Stewart and Sting [3] Bonnie Raitt and Bryan Adams [4] Barbra Streisand and Bryan Adams [5] Bryan Adams featuring Melanie C [6] Chicane featuring Bryan Adams

Gayle ADAMS *US, female vocalist (Singles: 1 Week)* pos/wks

26 Jul 80	STRETCHIN' OUT *Epic EPC 8791*	64	1

Marie ADAMS See Johnny OTIS SHOW

Oleta ADAMS
US, female vocalist / instrumentalist – keyboards (Singles: 36 Weeks, Albums: 34 Weeks) pos/wks

24 Mar 90	RHYTHM OF LIFE (re) *Fontana OLETA 1*	52	5
12 Jan 91 ●	GET HERE *Fontana OLETA 3*	4	12
13 Apr 91	YOU'VE GOT TO GIVE ME ROOM / RHYTHM OF LIFE (re-issue) *Fontana OLETA 4*	49	3
29 Jun 91	CIRCLE OF ONE *Fontana OLETA 5*	73	1
28 Sep 91	DON'T LET THE SUN GO DOWN ON ME *Fontana TRIBO 1*	33	5
25 Apr 92	WOMAN IN CHAINS (re-issue) *Fontana IDEA 16* [1]	57	1
10 Jul 93	I JUST HAD TO HEAR YOUR VOICE *Fontana OLECD 6*	42	3
7 Oct 95	NEVER KNEW LOVE *Fontana OLECD 9*	22	3
16 Dec 95	RHYTHM OF LIFE (re-mix) *Fontana OLECD 10*	38	2
10 Feb 96	WE WILL MEET AGAIN *Mercury OLECD 11*	51	1
26 May 90 ★	CIRCLE OF ONE *Fontana 8427441*	1	26
7 Aug 93	EVOLUTION *Fontana 5149652*	10	7
4 Nov 95	MOVING ON *Fontana 5285302*	59	1

[1] Tears for Fears featuring Oleta Adams

The original release of 'Woman in Chains' credits Tears for Fears only

Ryan ADAMS
US, male vocalist (Singles: 8 Weeks, Albums: 14 Weeks) pos/wks

8 Dec 01	**NEW YORK NEW YORK** *Lost Highway 1722232*	**53**	1
20 Apr 02	**ANSWERING BELL** *Lost Highway 1722392*	**39**	2
28 Sep 02	**NUCLEAR** *Lost Highway 1722592*	**37**	1
31 Jan 04	**SO ALIVE** *Lost Highway 9861610*	**21**	2
10 Jul 04	**WONDERWALL** *Lost Highway 9863098*	**27**	2
6 Oct 01	**GOLD** *Lost Highway 1702622*	**20**	9
5 Oct 02	**DEMOLITION** *Lost Highway 1703332*	**22**	2
15 Nov 03	**ROCK N ROLL** *Lost Highway 9861324*	**41**	1
15 Nov 03	**LOVE IS HELL PT.1 (EP)** *Lost Highway 9813666*	**62**	1
15 May 04	**LOVE IS HELL** *Lost Highway 9862325*	**68**	1

'Love is Hell Pt.1' is an eight-track EP. 'Love is Hell' features tracks from 'Love is Hell Pt.1' and 'Love is Hell Pt.2', which failed to chart

Cliff ADAMS SINGERS
UK, male / female vocal group – leader b. 21 Aug 1923, d. 22 Oct 2001 (Singles: 2 Weeks, Albums: 20 Weeks) pos/wks

28 Apr 60	**THE LONELY MAN THEME** *Pye International 7N 25056* [1]	**39**	2
16 Apr 60	**SING SOMETHING SIMPLE** *Pye MPL 28013*	**15**	4
24 Nov 62	**SING SOMETHING SIMPLE** *Pye Golden Guinea GGL 0150*	**15**	2
20 Nov 76	**SING SOMETHING SIMPLE '76** *Warwick WW 5016/17*	**23**	8
25 Dec 82	**SING SOMETHING SIMPLE** *Ronco RTD 2087*	**39**	6

ADAMSKI
UK, male instrumentalist / producer – Adam Tinley (Singles: 39 Weeks, Albums: 16 Weeks) pos/wks

20 Jan 90	**N-R-G** *MCA MCA 1386*	**12**	6
7 Apr 90 ★	**KILLER** *MCA MCA 1400*	**1**	18
8 Sep 90 ●	**THE SPACE JUNGLE** *MCA MCA 1435*	**7**	8
17 Nov 90	**FLASHBACK JACK** *MCA MCA 1459*	**46**	2
9 Nov 91	**NEVER GOIN' DOWN / BORN TO BE ALIVE** *MCA MCS 1578* [1]	**51**	2
4 Apr 92	**GET YOUR BODY** *MCA MCS 1613* [2]	**68**	1
4 Jul 92	**BACK TO FRONT** *MCA MCS 1644*	**63**	1
11 Jul 98	**ONE OF THE PEOPLE** *ZTT ZTT 101CD* [3]	**56**	1
9 Dec 89	**LIVEANDIRECT** *MCA MCL 1900*	**47**	11
13 Oct 90 ●	**DOCTOR ADAMSKI'S MUSICAL PHARMACY** *MCA MCG 6107*	**8**	5

[1] Adamski featuring Jimi Polo / Adamski featuring Soho [2] Adamski featuring Nina Hagen [3] Adamski's Thing

Featured vocalist on 'Killer' was Seal

Barry ADAMSON
UK, male producer / instrumentalist – bass (Albums: 1 Week) pos/wks

10 Aug 96	**OEDIPUS SCHMOEDIPUS** *Mute CDSTUMM 134*	**51**	1

ADDAMS and GEE
UK, male instrumental duo (Singles: 1 Week) pos/wks

20 Apr 91	**CHUNG KUO (REVISITED)** *Debut DEBT 3108*	**72**	1

ADDIS BLACK WIDOW
US, male rap duo (Singles: 2 Weeks) pos/wks

3 Feb 96	**INNOCENT** *Mercury Black Vinyl MBVCD 1*	**42**	2

ADDRISI BROTHERS
US, male vocal duo – Don, b. 14 Dec 1938, d. 13 Nov 1984, and Richard Addrisi (Singles: 3 Weeks) pos/wks

6 Oct 79	**GHOST DANCER** *Scotti Brothers K 11361*	**57**	3

King Sunny ADE and his AFRICAN BEATS
Nigeria, male vocalist and male vocal / instrumental group (Albums: 1 Week) pos/wks

9 Jul 83	**SYNCHRO SYSTEM** *Island ILPS 9737*	**93**	1

ADEMA
US, male vocal / instrumental group (Singles: 3 Weeks) pos/wks

16 Mar 02	**GIVING IN** *Arista 74321924022*	**62**	1
10 Aug 02	**THE WAY YOU LIKE IT** *Arista 74321954712*	**61**	1
23 Aug 03	**UNSTABLE** *Arista 82876534512*	**46**	1

ADEVA
US, female vocalist – Patricia Daniels (Singles: 66 Weeks, Albums: 24 Weeks) pos/wks

14 Jan 89	**RESPECT** *Cooltempo COOL 179*	**17**	9
25 Mar 89	**MUSICAL FREEDOM (MOVING ON UP)** *Cooltempo COOL 182* [1]	**22**	8
12 Aug 89	**WARNING** *Cooltempo COOL 185*	**17**	8
21 Oct 89	**I THANK YOU** *Cooltempo COOL 192*	**17**	7
16 Dec 89	**BEAUTIFUL LOVE** *Cooltempo COOL 195*	**57**	5
28 Apr 90	**TREAT ME RIGHT** *Cooltempo COOL 200*	**62**	2
6 Apr 91	**RING MY BELL** *Cooltempo COOL 224* [2]	**20**	5
19 Oct 91	**IT SHOULD'VE BEEN ME** *Cooltempo COOL 236*	**48**	3
29 Feb 92	**DON'T LET IT SHOW ON YOUR FACE** *Cooltempo COOL 248*	**34**	4
6 Jun 92	**UNTIL YOU COME BACK TO ME** *Cooltempo COOL 254*	**45**	3
17 Oct 92	**I'M THE ONE FOR YOU** *Cooltempo COOL 264*	**51**	2
11 Dec 93	**RESPECT (re-mix)** *Network NWKCD 79*	**65**	1
27 May 95	**TOO MANY FISH** *Virgin America VUSCD 89* [3]	**34**	2
18 Nov 95	**WHADDA U WANT (FROM ME)** *Virgin America VUSCD 98* [3]	**36**	2
6 Apr 96	**DO WATCHA DO** *Avex UK AVEXCD 24* [4]	**54**	1
4 May 96	**I THANK YOU (re-mix)** *Cooltempo CDCOOLS 318*	**37**	2
12 Apr 97	**DO WATCHA DO (re-mix)** *Distinctive DISNCD 28* [4]	**60**	1
26 Jul 97	**WHERE IS THE LOVE? / THE WAY THAT YOU FEEL** *Distinctive DISNCD 31*	**54**	1
9 Sep 89 ●	**ADEVA** *Cooltempo ICTLP 13*	**6**	24

[1] Paul Simpson featuring Adeva [2] Monie Love vs Adeva [3] Frankie Knuckles featuring Adeva [4] Hyper Go Go and Adeva

The ADICTS
UK, male vocal / instrumental group (Singles: 1 Week, Albums: 1 Week) pos/wks

14 May 83	**BAD BOY** *Razor RZS 104*	**75**	1
4 Dec 82	**SOUND OF MUSIC** *Razor RAZ 2*	**99**	1

ADIEMUS
UK, male instrumental duo – Karl Jenkins and Mark Ratledge (Singles: 2 Weeks, Albums: 23 Weeks) pos/wks

14 Oct 95	**ADIEMUS** *Venture VEND 4*	**48**	2
1 Jul 95	**SONGS OF SANCTUARY** *Virgin CDVE 925*	**35**	13
1 Mar 97	**CANTATA MUNDI** *Venture CDVE 932* [1]	**15**	9
24 Oct 98	**DANCES OF TIME** *Venture CDVE 940* [2]	**58**	1

[1] Adiemus II [2] Adiemus III

All tracks on 'Songs of Sanctuary' feature Miriam Stockley and the London Philharmonic Orchestra. The sleeve of 'Cantata Mundi' contains the credit: Composed by Karl Jenkins

Larry ADLER
US, male instrumentalist – harmonica, b. 10 Feb 1914, d. 7 Aug 2001 (Singles: 2 Weeks, Albums: 18 Weeks) pos/wks

30 Jul 94	**THE MAN I LOVE** *Mercury MERCD 408* [1]	**27**	2
6 Aug 94 ●	**THE GLORY OF GERSHWIN** *Mercury 5227272*	**2**	18

[1] Kate Bush and Larry Adler

ADONIS featuring 2 PUERTO RICANS, A BLACK MAN AND A DOMINICAN
US, male vocal / instrumental group (Singles: 4 Weeks) pos/wks

13 Jun 87	**DO IT PROPERLY ('NO WAY BACK') / NO WAY BACK** *London LON 136*	**47**	4

ADORABLE
UK, male vocal / instrumental group (Albums: 1 Week) pos/wks

13 Mar 93	**AGAINST PERFECTION** *Creation CRECD 138*	**70**	1

ADRENALIN M.O.D.
UK, male instrumental / production group (Singles: 5 Weeks) pos/wks

8 Oct 88	**O-O-O** *MCA RAGAT 2*	**49**	5

ADULT NET
UK / US, male / female vocal / instrumental group (Singles: 2 Weeks) pos/wks

10 Jun 89	**WHERE WERE YOU** *Fontana BRX 2*	**66**	2

The ADVENTURES
UK, male vocal / instrumental group (Singles: 24 Weeks, Albums: 11 Weeks) pos/wks

15 Sep 84	**ANOTHER SILENT DAY** *Chrysalis CHS 2000*	**71**	2
1 Dec 84	**SEND MY HEART** *Chrysalis CHS 2001*	**62**	4
13 Jul 85	**FEEL THE RAINDROPS** *Chrysalis AD 1*	**58**	3
9 Apr 88	**BROKEN LAND** *Elektra EKR 69*	**20**	10
2 Jul 88	**DROWNING IN THE SEA OF LOVE** *Elektra EKR 76*	**44**	4
13 Jun 92	**RAINING ALL OVER THE WORLD** *Polydor PO 211*	**68**	1
21 May 88	**THE SEA OF LOVE** *Elektra EKT 45*	**30**	10
17 Mar 90	**TRADING SECRETS WITH THE MOON** *Elektra EKT 63*	**64**	1

The ADVENTURES OF STEVIE V
UK, male / female vocal / production group (Singles: 22 Weeks) pos/wks

21 Apr 90 ●	**DIRTY CASH** *Mercury MER 311*	**2**	13
29 Sep 90	**BODY LANGUAGE** *Mercury MER 331*	**29**	5

			pos/wks
2 Mar 91	JEALOUSY *Mercury MER 337*	...............**58**	3
27 Sep 97	DIRTY CASH (re-mix) *Avex Trax AVEXCDX 57*	...............**69**	1

The ADVERTS UK, male / female vocal / instrumental
group (Singles: 11 Weeks, Albums: 1 Week) pos/wks

27 Aug 77	GARY GILMORE'S EYES *Anchor ANC 1043*	...............**18**	7
4 Feb 78	NO TIME TO BE 21 *Bright BR 1*	...............**34**	4
11 Mar 78	CROSSING THE RED SEA WITH THE ADVERTS *Bright BRL 201*	**38**	1

AEROSMITH 285 Top 500
*Godfathers of the contemporary heavy rock scene, formed 1970, New
Hampshire, US. Multi-platinum album act's UK success came only after
frontmen Steven Tyler (v) and Joe Perry (g) teamed with rappers Run-DMC
on 'Walk This Way' (1986). Group's first US No.1 single (1998) came 25 years
after chart debut. Best-selling single: 'I Don't Want to Miss a Thing' 572,900
(Singles: 92 Weeks, Albums: 137 Weeks)* pos/wks

17 Oct 87	DUDE (LOOKS LIKE A LADY) *Geffen GEF 29*	...............**45**	5
16 Apr 88	ANGEL *Geffen GEF 34*	...............**69**	2
9 Sep 89	LOVE IN AN ELEVATOR *Geffen GEF 63*	...............**13**	8
24 Feb 90	DUDE (LOOKS LIKE A LADY) (re-issue) *Geffen GEF 72*	...............**20**	5
14 Apr 90	RAG DOLL *Geffen GEF 76*	...............**42**	4
1 Sep 90	THE OTHER SIDE *Geffen GEF 79*	...............**46**	2
10 Apr 93	LIVIN' ON THE EDGE *Geffen GFSTD 35*	...............**19**	4
3 Jul 93	EAT THE RICH *Geffen GFSTD 46*	...............**34**	3
30 Oct 93	CRYIN' *Geffen GFSTD 56*	...............**17**	6
18 Dec 93	AMAZING *Geffen GFSTD 63*	...............**57**	2
2 Jul 94	SHUT UP AND DANCE *Geffen GFSTD 75*	...............**24**	4
20 Aug 94	SWEET EMOTION *Columbia 6604492*	...............**74**	1
5 Nov 94	CRAZY / BLIND MAN *Geffen GFSTD 80*	...............**23**	4
8 Mar 97	FALLING IN LOVE (IS HARD ON THE KNEES) *Columbia 6640752*	...............**22**	4
21 Jun 97	HOLE IN MY SOUL *Columbia 66645012*	...............**29**	2
27 Dec 97	PINK *Columbia 6648722*	...............**38**	2
12 Sep 98 ●	I DON'T WANT TO MISS A THING *Columbia 6664082* ▲	...............**4**	20
26 Jun 99	PINK (re-issue) *Columbia 6675342*	...............**13**	6
17 Mar 01	JADED *Columbia 6709312*	...............**13**	7
5 Sep 87	PERMANENT VACATION *Geffen WX 126*	...............**37**	14
23 Sep 89 ●	PUMP *Geffen WX 304*	...............**3**	26
1 May 93 ●	GET A GRIP *Geffen GED 24444* ▲	...............**2**	38
12 Nov 94 ●	BIG ONES *Geffen GED 24546*	...............**7**	16
22 Mar 97 ●	NINE LIVES *Columbia 4850206* ▲	...............**4**	11
31 Oct 98	A LITTLE SOUTH OF SANITY *Geffen GED 25221*	...............**36**	2
24 Mar 01 ●	JUST PUSH PLAY *Columbia 5015352*	...............**7**	5
8 Dec 01	YOUNG LUST – THE AEROSMITH ANTHOLOGY *UMTV 4931192*	**32**	14
3 Aug 02 ●	O YEAH – ULTIMATE HITS *Columbia / UMTV 5084672*	...............**6**	8
10 Apr 04	HONKIN' ON BOBO *Columbia CK 92079*	...............**28**	3

'Pump' changed its catalogue number to GEF 24245 during its chart run

The AFGHAN WHIGS
US, male vocal / instrumental group (Albums: 3 Weeks) pos/wks

16 Oct 93	GENTLEMEN *Blast First BFFP 90CD*	...............**58**	1
23 Mar 96	BLACK LOVE *Mute CDSTUMM 143*	...............**41**	2

AFRICAN BEATS See King Sunny ADE and his AFRICAN BEATS

AFRICAN BUSINESS
Italy, male vocal / instrumental group (Singles: 1 Week) pos/wks

17 Nov 90	IN ZAIRE *Urban URB 64*	...............**73**	1

AFRO CELT SOUND SYSTEM UK / Ireland / France / Guinea, male
vocal / instrumental group (Singles: 1 Week, Albums: 5 Weeks) pos/wks

29 Apr 00	RELEASE *Realworld RWSCD 10*	...............**71**	1
27 Jul 96	VOLUME 1 – SOUND MAGIC *Realworld CDRW 61*	...............**59**	2
8 May 99	VOLUME 2 – RELEASE *Realworld CDRW 76*	...............**38**	3

AFRO MEDUSA UK, male production duo – Patrick Cole and Nick Benneti
and Spain, female vocalist – Isabel Fructuoso (Singles: 2 Weeks) pos/wks

28 Oct 00	PASILDA *Rulin RULIN 6CDS*	...............**31**	2

AFROMAN
US, male vocalist – Joseph Foreman (Singles: 30 Weeks) pos/wks

6 Oct 01	BECAUSE I GOT HIGH (import) *Universal 0152822*	...............**45**	3
27 Oct 01 ★	BECAUSE I GOT HIGH (re) *Universal MCSTD 40266* ■	...............**1**	19
2 Feb 02 ●	CRAZY RAP *Universal MCSTD 40273*	...............**10**	8

AFTER DARK UK, male instrumentalist –
saxophone – Mornington Lockett (Albums: 5 Weeks) pos/wks

3 Feb 96	LATE NIGHT SAX *EMI TV CDEMTV 108*	...............**18**	5

AFTER 7 US, male vocal group (Singles: 3 Weeks) pos/wks

3 Nov 90	CAN'T STOP *Virgin America VUS 31*	...............**54**	3

AFTER THE FIRE UK, male vocal /
instrumental group (Singles: 12 Weeks, Albums: 4 Weeks) pos/wks

9 Jun 79	ONE RULE FOR YOU *CBS 7025*	...............**40**	6
8 Sep 79	LASER LOVE *CBS 7769*	...............**62**	2
9 Apr 83	DER KOMMISSAR *CBS A 2399*	...............**47**	4
13 Oct 79	LASER LOVE *CBS 83795*	...............**57**	1
1 Nov 80	80 F *Epic 84545*	...............**69**	1
3 Apr 82	BATTERIES NOT INCLUDED *CBS 85566*	...............**82**	2

AFTERNOON BOYS See Steve WRIGHT

AFTERSHOCK US, male vocal / instrumental
duo – Frost Rivera and Guy Routte (Singles: 8 Weeks) pos/wks

21 Aug 93	SLAVE TO THE VIBE *Virgin America VUSCD 75*	...............**11**	8

AGE OF CHANCE
UK, male / female vocal / instrumental group (Singles: 13 Weeks) pos/wks

17 Jan 87	KISS *Fon AGE 5*	...............**50**	6
30 May 87	WHO'S AFRAID OF THE BIG BAD NOISE! *Fon VS 962*	...............**65**	2
20 Jan 90	HIGHER THAN HEAVEN *Virgin VS 1228*	...............**53**	5

AGE OF LOVE
Italy, male instrumental / production trio (Singles: 6 Weeks) pos/wks

5 Jul 97	THE AGE OF LOVE – THE REMIXES *React CDREACT 100*	...............**17**	4
19 Sep 98	AGE OF LOVE *React CDREACT 135*	...............**38**	2

AGENT BLUE
UK, male vocal / instrumental group (Singles: 2 Weeks) pos/wks

29 May 04	SEX, DRUGS AND ROCKS THROUGH YOUR WINDOW *Fierce Panda NING 153CD*	...............**71**	1
21 Aug 04	SOMETHING ELSE *Island TEMPTCD 001*	...............**59**	1

AGENT 00 UK, male production duo (Singles: 1 Week) pos/wks

7 Mar 98	THE MAGNIFICENT *Inferno CDFERN 002*	...............**65**	1

AGENT PROVOCATEUR
UK, male / female vocal / production group (Singles: 1 Week) pos/wks

22 Mar 97	AGENT DAN *Epic AGENT 3CD*	...............**49**	1

AGENT SUMO UK, male production duo –
Steven Halliday and Martin Cole (Singles: 4 Weeks) pos/wks

9 Jun 01	24 HOURS *Virgin VSCDT 1806*	...............**44**	2
20 Apr 02	WHY *Virgin VSCDT 1819*	...............**40**	2

AGNELLI & NELSON UK, male DJ duo –
Chris Agnelli and Robbie Nelson (Singles: 17 Weeks) pos/wks

15 Aug 98	EL NINO *Xtravaganza 0091575 EXT*	...............**21**	4
11 Sep 99	EVERYDAY *Xtravaganza XTRAV 2CDS*	...............**17**	4
17 Jun 00	EMBRACE *Xtravaganza XTRAV 11CDS*	...............**35**	2
9 Sep 00	HUDSON STREET *Xtravaganza XTRAV 13CDS*	...............**29**	2
7 Apr 01	VEGAS *Xtravaganza XTRAV 23CDS*	...............**48**	1
15 Jun 02	EVERYDAY (re-mix) *Xtravaganza XTRAV 31CDS*	...............**33**	2
3 Apr 04	HOLDING ON TO NOTHING *Xtravaganza XTRAV 43CX* [1]	......**41**	2

[1] Agnelli & Nelson featuring Aureus

Christina AGUILERA 240 Top 500
*Internationally successful photogenic pop vocalist, b. 18 Dec 1980, New York,
US. She has four US chart-toppers, was a winner of World Music Awards in
2000 and 2001 and won a Grammy in 2004 for 'Beautiful'. Best-selling single:
'Genie in a Bottle' 626,741 (Singles: 143 Weeks, Albums: 114 Weeks)* pos/wks

11 Sep 99	GENIE IN A BOTTLE (import) *RCA 701062*	...............**50**	5
16 Oct 99 ★	GENIE IN A BOTTLE *RCA 74321705482* ■ ▲	...............**1**	19
26 Feb 00 ●	WHAT A GIRL WANTS *RCA 74321737522* ▲	...............**3**	13
22 Jul 00	I TURN TO YOU *RCA 74321765472*	...............**19**	6

		pos/wks
11 Nov 00 ●	COME ON OVER BABY (ALL I WANT IS YOU) (re) *RCA 74321799912* ▲	8 8
10 Mar 01 ●	NOBODY WANTS TO BE LONELY *Columbia 6709462* [1]	4 12
30 Jun 01 ★	LADY MARMALADE *Interscope / Polydor 4975612* [2] ■ ▲	1 16
23 Nov 02 ★	DIRRTY *RCA 74321962702* [3] ■	1 9
22 Feb 03	BEAUTIFUL (import) *Arista 74321983642*	51 2
8 Mar 03 ★	BEAUTIFUL *RCA 82876502462* ■	1 10
21 Jun 03 ●	FIGHTER *RCA 82876524292*	3 13
20 Sep 03 ●	CAN'T HOLD US DOWN *RCA 87876556332* [4]	6 9
20 Dec 03 ●	THE VOICE WITHIN *RCA 82876584292*	9 10
13 Nov 04 ●	CAR WASH *Dreamworks 986430* [5]	4 7+
4 Dec 04 ●	TILT YA HEAD BACK *Universal MCSTD 40396* [6]	5 4+
30 Oct 99	CHRISTINA AGUILERA *RCA 7863676902* ▲	14 26
9 Nov 02 ●	STRIPPED *RCA 74321961252*	4 88

[1] Ricky Martin and Christina Aguilera [2] Christina Aguilera, Lil' Kim, Mya and Pink [3] Christina Aguilera featuring Redman [4] Christina Aguilera featuring Lil' Kim [5] Christina Aguilera featuring Missy Elliott [6] Nelly & Christina Aguilera

A-HA ⬭218 *Top 500* *Norway's biggest-selling act: Morten Harket (v), Pal Waaktaar (g), Magna Furuholmen (k). This globally popular teen-targeted trio was noted for its innovative videos and stage shows (Singles: 133 Weeks, Albums: 148 Weeks)*

		pos/wks
28 Sep 85 ●	TAKE ON ME *Warner Bros. W 9006* ▲	2 19
28 Dec 85 ★	THE SUN ALWAYS SHINES ON TV *Warner Bros. W 8846*	1 12
5 Apr 86 ●	TRAIN OF THOUGHT *Warner Bros. W 8736*	8 8
14 Jun 86 ●	HUNTING HIGH AND LOW *Warner Bros. W 6663*	5 10
4 Oct 86 ●	I'VE BEEN LOSING YOU *Warner Bros. W 8594*	8 7
6 Dec 86 ●	CRY WOLF *Warner Bros. W 8500*	5 9
28 Feb 87	MANHATTAN SKYLINE *Warner Bros. W 8405*	13 6
4 Jul 87 ●	THE LIVING DAYLIGHTS *Warner Bros. W 8305*	5 9
26 Mar 88 ●	STAY ON THESE ROADS *Warner Bros. W 7936*	5 9
18 Jun 88	THE BLOOD THAT MOVES THE BODY *Warner Bros. W 7840*	25 4
27 Aug 88	TOUCHY! *Warner Bros. W 7749*	11 7
3 Dec 88 ●	YOU ARE THE ONE *Warner Bros. W 7636*	13 10
13 Oct 90	CRYING IN THE RAIN *Warner Bros. W 9547*	13 7
15 Dec 90	I CALL YOUR NAME *Warner Bros. W 9462*	44 5
26 Oct 91	MOVE TO MEMPHIS *Warner Bros. W 0070*	47 2
5 Jun 93	DARK IS THE NIGHT *Warner Bros. W 0175CD*	19 4
18 Sep 93	ANGEL *Warner Bros. W 0195CD*	41 3
26 Mar 94	SHAPES THAT GO TOGETHER *Warner Bros. W 0236CD*	27 4
3 Jun 00	SUMMER MOVED ON *WEA WEA 275CD*	33 2
9 Nov 85 ●	HUNTING HIGH AND LOW *Warner Bros. WX 30*	2 78
18 Oct 86 ●	SCOUNDREL DAYS *Warner Bros. WX 62*	2 19
14 May 88 ●	STAY ON THESE ROADS *Warner Bros. WX 166*	2 19
2 Nov 90	EAST OF THE SUN WEST OF THE MOON *Warner Bros. WX 378*	12 4
16 Nov 91	HEADLINES AND DEADLINES – THE HITS OF A-HA *Warner Bros. WX 450*	12 12
26 Jun 93	MEMORIAL BEACH *Warner Bros. 9362452292*	17 3
17 Jun 00	MINOR EARTH MAJOR SKY *WEA 8573821832*	27 4
22 Jun 02	LIFELINES *WEA 927448492*	67 1

AHMAD *US, male rapper – Ahmad Lewis (Singles: 2 Weeks)* pos/wks

9 Jul 94	BACK IN THE DAY *Giant 74321212042*	64 2

AIDA *Holland, male production duo (Singles: 1 Week)* pos/wks

19 Feb 00	FAR AND AWAY *48K / Perfecto SPECT 03CDS*	58 1

AIM *UK, male DJ / producer – Andy Turner (Albums: 1 week)* pos/wks

9 Mar 02	HINTERLAND *Grand Central GCCD 112*	47 1

AIR *France, male instrumental / production duo – Jean-Benoît Dunckel and Nicolas Godin (Singles: 16 Weeks, Albums: 85 Weeks)* pos/wks

21 Feb 98	SEXY BOY *Virgin VSCDT 1672*	13 4
16 May 98	KELLY WATCH THE STARS *Virgin VSCDT 1690*	18 3
21 Nov 98	ALL I NEED *Virgin VSCDT 1702*	29 3
26 Feb 00	PLAYGROUND LOVE *Virgin VSCDT 1764* [1]	25 2
2 Jun 01	RADIO #1 *Virgin VSCDT 1803*	31 2
21 Aug 04	ALPHA BETA GAGA *Source VSCDX 1880*	44 2
31 Jan 98 ●	MOON SAFARI *Virgin CDV 2848*	6 61
18 Sep 99	PREMIERS SYMPTOMES *Virgin CDV 2895*	12 7
11 Mar 00	THE VIRGIN SUICIDES (FILM SOUNDTRACK) *Virgin CDV 2910*	14 4
9 Jun 01 ●	10000 HZ LEGEND *Virgin CDV 2945*	7 5
2 Mar 02	EVERYBODY HERTZ *Virgin CDV 2956*	67 1
7 Feb 04 ●	TALKIE WALKIE *Virgin CDVX 2980*	2 7

[1] Air – sung by Gordon Tracks

The CD sleeve credits 'Moon Safari' to Air – French Band

AIR SUPPLY *Australia, male vocal / instrumental duo – Russell Hitchcock and Graham Russell (b. UK) (Singles: 17 Weeks)* pos/wks

27 Sep 80	ALL OUT OF LOVE *Arista ARIST 362*	11 11
2 Oct 82	EVEN THE NIGHTS ARE BETTER *Arista ARIST 474*	44 4
20 Nov 93	GOODBYE *Giant 74321153462*	66 2

AIRHEAD *UK, male vocal / instrumental group (Singles: 10 Weeks, Albums: 7 Weeks)* pos/wks

5 Oct 91	FUNNY HOW *Korova KOW 47*	57 3
21 Dec 91	COUNTING SHEEP *Korova KOW 48*	35 5
7 Mar 92	RIGHT NOW *Korova KOW 49*	50 2
1 Feb 92	BOING! *Korova 9031746792*	29 7

AIRHEADZ (see also DOUBLE TROUBLE) *UK, male DJ / production duo – Leigh Guest and Andrew Peach (Singles: 2 Weeks)* pos/wks

28 Apr 01	STANLEY (HERE I AM) *AM:PM CDAMPM 145*	36 2

AIRSCAPE (see also BLUE BAMBOO; CUBIC 22; TRANSFORMER 2; BALEARIC BILL; Johan GIELEN presents ABNEA; SVENSON and GIELEN) *Belgium / Holland, male instrumental / production duo – Johann Gielen and Sven Maes (Singles: 5 Weeks)* pos/wks

9 Aug 97	PACIFIC MELODY *Xtravaganza 0091165*	27 2
29 Aug 98	AMAZON CHANT *Xtravaganza 0091605 EXT*	46 1
4 Dec 99	L'ESPERANZA *Xtravaganza EXTRAV 7CD*	33 2

Laurel AITKEN and the UNITONE *Jamaica / Cuba, male vocal / instrumental group (Singles: 3 Weeks)* pos/wks

17 May 80	RUDI GOT MARRIED *I-Spy SEE 6*	60 3

AKABU featuring Linda CLIFFORD (see also HED BOYS; Li KWAN; RAVEN MAIZE; Joey NEGRO; JAKATTA; PHASE II; IL PADRINOS featuring Jocelyn BROWN) *UK, male producer – Dave Lee and US, female vocalist (Singles: 1 Week)* pos/wks

15 Sep 01	RIDE THE STORM *NRK Sound Division NRKCD 053*	69 1

Jewel AKENS *US, male vocalist (Singles: 8 Weeks)* pos/wks

25 Mar 65	THE BIRDS AND THE BEES *London HLN 9954*	29 8

AKIL See JURASSIC 5; DJ FORMAT featuring Chali 2NA & AKIL

AKIN *UK, female vocal duo (Singles: 1 Week)* pos/wks

14 Jun 97	STAY RIGHT HERE *WEA WEA 117CD*	60 1

AKON featuring STYLES P *US, male rappers (Singles: 1 Week)* pos/wks

25 Dec 04	LOCKED UP *Universal AAB 224511*	74 1+

ALABAMA 3 *UK, male vocal / instrumental group (Singles: 3 Weeks)* pos/wks

22 Nov 97	SPEED AT THE SOUND OF LONELINESS *Elemental ELM 42CDS 1721*	72 1
11 Apr 98	AIN'T GOIN' TO GOA *Elemental ELM 45CDS 1*	40 2

Roberto ALAGNA / Angela GHEORGIU *France, male opera singer and Romania, female vocalist (Albums: 5 Weeks)* pos/wks

18 May 96	DUETS & ARIAS *EMI Classics CDC 5561172*	42 5

ALANA See MK

The ALARM (see also The POPPY FIELDS) *UK, male vocal / instrumental group (Singles: 65 Weeks, Albums: 29 Weeks)* pos/wks

24 Sep 83	68 GUNS *IRS PFP 1023*	17 7
21 Jan 84	WHERE WERE YOU HIDING WHEN THE STORM BROKE *IRS IRS 101*	22 6
31 Mar 84	THE DECEIVER *IRS IRS 103*	51 4
3 Nov 84	THE CHANT HAS JUST BEGUN *IRS IRS 104*	48 4
2 Mar 85	ABSOLUTE REALITY *IRS ALARM 1*	35 6
28 Sep 85	STRENGTH *IRS IRM 104*	40 4
18 Jan 86	SPIRIT OF '76 *IRS IRM 109*	22 5
26 Apr 86	KNIFE EDGE *IRS IRM 112*	43 3
17 Oct 87	RAIN IN THE SUMMERTIME *IRS IRM 144*	18 5
12 Dec 87	RESCUE ME *IRS IRM 150*	48 4

20 Feb 88	PRESENCE OF LOVE *IRS IRM 155*	44	3
16 Sep 89	SOLD ME DOWN THE RIVER *IRS EIRS 123*	43	3
4 Nov 89	A NEW SOUTH WALES / THE ROCK *IRS EIRS 129*	31	5
3 Feb 90	LOVE DON'T COME EASY *IRS EIRS 134*	48	3
27 Oct 90	UNSAFE BUILDING 1990 *IRS ALARM 2*	54	2
13 Apr 91	RAW *IRS ALARM 3*	51	2
3 Jul 04	NEW HOME NEW LIFE *Snapper Music SMASCD 061*	45	1
25 Feb 84 ●	DECLARATION *IRS IRSA 7044*	6	11
26 Oct 85	STRENGTH *IRS MIRF 1004*	18	6
14 Nov 87	EYE OF THE HURRICANE *IRS MIRG 1023*	23	4
5 Nov 88	ELECTRIC FOLKLORE LIVE *IRS MIRMC 5001*	62	2
30 Sep 89	CHANGE *IRS EIRSAX 1020*	13	3
24 Nov 90	STANDARDS *IRS EIRSA 1043*	47	1
4 May 91	RAW *IRS EIRSA 1055*	33	2

'Sold Me Down the River' was joined by 'Yn Gymreag' for the first week on chart.
'A New South Wales' features Morriston Orpheus Male Voice Choir.

Morris ALBERT
Brazil, male vocalist – Morris Kaisermann (Singles: 10 Weeks)   pos/wks

27 Sep 75 ●	FEELINGS *Decca F 13591*	4	10

ALBERTA
Sierra Leone, female vocalist – Alberta Sheriff (Singles: 3 Weeks)   pos/wks

26 Dec 98	YOYO BOY *RCA 74321640602*	48	3

ALBERTO Y LOS TRIOS PARANOIAS
UK, male vocal / instrumental group (Singles: 5 Weeks)   pos/wks

23 Sep 78	HEADS DOWN NO NONSENSE MINDLESS BOOGIE *Logo GO 323*	47	5

Al ALBERTS See FOUR ACES

ALBION
(see also MOONMAN; SYSTEM F; VERACOCHA; GOURYELLA; STARPARTY)
Holland, male producer – Ferry Corsten (Singles: 1 Week)   pos/wks

3 Jun 00	AIR 2000 *Platipus PLATCD 73*	59	1

ALCATRAZ
*US, male instrumental / production duo –
Jean-Philippe Aviance and Victor Imbres (Singles: 4 Weeks)*   pos/wks

17 Feb 96	GIV ME LUV *AM:PM 5814332*	12	4

ALCAZAR
Sweden, male / female vocal trio (Singles: 18 Weeks)   pos/wks

8 Dec 01	CRYING AT THE DISCOTEQUE *Arista 74321893432*	13	11
16 Mar 02	SEXUAL GUARANTEE *Arista 74321920252*	30	2
2 Oct 04	THIS IS THE WORLD WE LIVE IN *RCA 82876652372*	15	5

ALDA
Iceland, female vocalist – Alda Olafsdottir (Singles: 14 Weeks)   pos/wks

29 Aug 98 ●	REAL GOOD TIME *Wildstar CDWILD 7*	7	7
26 Dec 98	GIRLS NIGHT OUT *Wildstar CDWILD 10*	20	7

John ALDISS See LONDON PHILHARMONIC CHOIR

Cali ALEMAN See Tito PUENTE Jr and The LATIN RHYTHM featuring Tito PUENTE, INDIA and Cali ALEMAN

ALENA
Jamaica, female vocalist – Alena Lova (Singles: 5 Weeks)   pos/wks

13 Nov 99	TURN IT AROUND *Wonderboy WBOYD 16*	14	5

Hannah ALETHEA See SODA CLUB

ALESSI
US, male vocal duo – Billy and Bobby Alessi (Singles: 11 Weeks)   pos/wks

11 Jun 77 ●	OH, LORI *A&M AMS 7289*	8	11

ALEX PARTY (see also LIVIN' JOY) *Italy / UK, male / female vocal /
instrumental group – leader Paolo Visnadi (Singles: 28 Weeks)*   pos/wks

18 Dec 93	SATURDAY NIGHT PARTY (READ MY LIPS) (re) *Cleveland City Imports CCICD 17000*	29	10
18 Feb 95 ●	DON'T GIVE ME YOUR LIFE *Systematic SYSCD 7*	2	13
18 Nov 95	WRAP ME UP *Systematic SYSCD 22*	17	3
19 Oct 96	READ MY LIPS (re-mix) *Systematic SYSCD 30*	28	2

ALEXANDER BROTHERS
UK, male vocal duo – Tom and Jack Alexander (Albums: 1 Week)   pos/wks

10 Dec 66	THESE ARE MY MOUNTAINS *Pye GGL 0375*	29	1

ALEXIA
Italy, female vocalist – Alessia Aquilani (Singles: 15 Weeks)   pos/wks

21 Mar 98	UH LA LA LA *Dance Pool ALEX 1CD*	10	9
13 Jun 98	GIMME LOVE *Dance Pool ALEX 2CDZ*	17	4
10 Oct 98	THE MUSIC I LIKE *Dance Pool ALEX 3CD*	31	2

ALEXIA *UK, female vocalist (Singles: 1 Week)*   pos/wks

22 Feb 03	RING *Virgin VSCDT 1836*	48	1

ALFI and HARRY (see also The CHIPMUNKS; David SEVILLE)
*US, male vocalist / instumentalist – David Seville, b. 27 Jan 1919,
d. 16 Jan 1972 under two false names (Singles: 5 Weeks)*   pos/wks

23 Mar 56	TROUBLE WITH HARRY *London HLU 8242*	15	5

ALFIE *UK, male vocal / instrumental
group (Singles: 5 Weeks, Albums: 1 Week)*   pos/wks

8 Sep 01	YOU MAKE NO BONES *Twisted Nerve TN 033CD*	61	1
16 Mar 02	A WORD IN YOUR EAR *Twisted Nerve TN 037CD*	66	1
21 Jun 03	PEOPLE *Regal REG 84CD*	53	1
13 Sep 03	STUNTMAN *Regal REG 87CDS*	51	1
28 Feb 04	NO NEED *Regal REG 99CD*	66	1
7 Apr 01	IF YOU HAPPY WITH YOU NEED DO NOTHING *Twisted Nerve TN 026CD*	62	1

John ALFORD
UK, male actor / vocalist – John Shannon (Singles: 12 Weeks)   pos/wks

17 Feb 96	SMOKE GETS IN YOUR EYES *Love This LUVTHISCD 7*	13	5
25 May 96 ●	BLUE MOON / ONLY YOU *Love This LUVTHISCD 9*	9	4
23 Nov 96	IF / KEEP ON RUNNING *Love This LUVTHISCD 15*	24	3

ALI *UK, male vocalist – Ali Tennant (Singles: 2 Weeks)*   pos/wks

23 May 98	LOVE LETTERS *Wild Card 5698092*	63	1
24 Oct 98	FEELIN' YOU *Wild Card 5676992*	63	1

Tatyana ALI
US, female vocalist (Singles: 18 Weeks, Albums: 4 Weeks)   pos/wks

14 Nov 98 ●	DAYDREAMIN' *Epic 6665462*	6	5
13 Feb 99 ●	BOY YOU KNOCK ME OUT (re) *MJJ / Epic 6669372* [1]	3	9
19 Jun 99	EVERYTIME *Epic / MJJ 674742*	20	4
20 Feb 99	KISS THE SKY *Epic 4916519*	41	4

[1] Tatyana Ali featuring Will Smith

ALI and FRAZIER *UK, female vocal duo –
Kirsty Ali and Natasha Frazier (Singles: 4 Weeks)*   pos/wks

7 Aug 93	UPTOWN TOP RANKING *Arista 74321158842*	33	4

ALIBI *UK, male vocal duo (Singles: 2 Weeks)*   pos/wks

15 Feb 97	I'M NOT TO BLAME *Urgent 74321434762*	51	1
7 Feb 98	HOW MUCH I FEEL *Urgent 74321548472*	58	1

The ALICE BAND *UK / Ireland / US, female vocal /
instrumental group (Singles: 2 Weeks, Albums: 1 Week)*   pos/wks

23 Jun 01	ONE DAY AT A TIME *Instant Karma KARMA 5CD*	52	1
27 Apr 02	NOW THAT YOU LOVE ME *Instant Karma KARMA 17CD*	44	1
25 May 02	THE LOVE JUNK STORE *Instant Karma KARMACD 4*	55	1

ALICE DEEJAY
*Holland, male / female production / vocal group
(Singles: 50 Weeks, Albums: 11 Weeks)*   pos/wks

31 Jul 99 ●	BETTER OFF ALONE *Positiva CDTIV 113* [1]	2	16
4 Dec 99 ●	BACK IN MY LIFE *Positiva CDTIV 121*	4	15
15 Jul 00 ●	WILL I EVER *Positiva CDTIV 134*	7	10
21 Oct 00	THE LONELY ONE *Positiva CDTIV 145*	16	5
10 Feb 01	CELEBRATE OUR LOVE *Positiva CDTIV 149*	17	4
29 Jul 00 ●	WHO NEEDS GUITARS ANYWAY? *Positiva 5270010*	8	11

[1] DJ Jurgen presents Alice Deejay

Singles re-entries are listed as (re), (2re), (3re).... which signifies that the hit re-entered the chart once, twice or three times...

ALICE IN CHAINS
US, male vocal / instrumental group (Singles: 14 Weeks, Albums: 22 Weeks) pos/wks

23 Jan 93	WOULD *Columbia 6588882*	19	3
20 Mar 93	THEM BONES *Columbia 6590902*	26	3
5 Jun 93	ANGRY CHAIR *Columbia 6593652*	33	2
23 Oct 93	DOWN IN A HOLE *Columbia 6597512*	36	2
11 Nov 95	GRIND *Columbia 6626232*	23	2
10 Feb 96	HEAVEN BESIDE YOU *Columbia 6628935*	35	2
24 Oct 92 ●	DIRT *Columbia 4723302*	42	13
5 Feb 94 ●	JAR OF FLIES / SAP *Columbia 4757132* ▲	4	5
18 Nov 95	ALICE IN CHAINS *Columbia 4811149* ▲	37	2
10 Aug 96	MTV UNPLUGGED *Columbia 4843002*	20	2

ALIEN ANT FARM
US, male vocal / instrumental group (Singles: 25 Weeks, Albums: 24 Weeks) pos/wks

30 Jun 01	MOVIES *Dreamworks / Polydor 4508992*	53	1
8 Sep 01	SMOOTH CRIMINAL (import) *Dreamworks / Polydor 4508852*	74	2
29 Sep 01 ●	SMOOTH CRIMINAL (re) *Dreamworks / Polydor DRMDM 50887*	3	13
16 Feb 02 ●	MOVIES *Dreamworks / Polydor 4508492*	5	8
25 May 02	ATTITUDE *Dreamworks / New Noize 4508292*	66	1
18 Aug 01	ANTHOLOGY *Dreamworks 4502932*	11	23
30 Aug 03	TRUANT *Dreamworks / Polydor 4505014*	68	1

ALIEN SEX FIEND
UK, male / female vocal / instrumental group (Albums: 1 Week) pos/wks

12 Oct 85	MAXIMUM SECURITY *Anagram GRAM 24*	100	1

ALIEN VOICES featuring The THREE DEGREES
(see also BOOGIE BOX HIGH: Andy G's STARSKY & HUTCH ALL STARS)
UK, male producer – Andros Georgiou and
US, female vocal trio (Singles: 2 Weeks) pos/wks

26 Dec 98	LAST CHRISTMAS *Wildstar CDWILD 15*	54	2

ALISHA
US, female vocalist (Singles: 2 Weeks) pos/wks

25 Jan 86	BABY TALK *Total Control TOCO 6*	67	2

ALISHA'S ATTIC
UK, female vocal duo – Shellie and Karen Poole (Singles: 47 Weeks, Albums: 47 Weeks) pos/wks

3 Aug 96	I AM I FEEL *Mercury AATCD 1*	14	10
2 Nov 96	ALISHA RULES THE WORLD *Mercury AATCD 2*	12	6
15 Mar 97	INDESTRUCTIBLE *Mercury AATCD 3*	12	6
12 Jul 97	AIR WE BREATHE *Mercury AATCD 4*	12	6
19 Sep 98	THE INCIDENTALS *Mercury AATCD 5*	13	7
9 Jan 99	WISH I WERE YOU *Mercury AATCD 6*	29	5
17 Apr 99	BARBARELLA *Mercury AATCD 7*	34	2
24 Mar 01	PUSH IT ALL ASIDE *Mercury AATCD 8*	24	4
28 Jul 01	PRETENDER GOT MY HEART *Mercury AATCD 9*	43	1
23 Nov 96	ALISHA RULES THE WORLD *Mercury 5340272*	14	43
17 Oct 98	ILLUMINA *Mercury 5589912*	15	3
4 Aug 01	THE HOUSE WE BUILT *Mercury 5428542*	55	1

ALIVE featuring D.D. KLEIN
Italy, male production trio and Antigua, female vocalist (Singles: 1 Week) pos/wks

27 Jul 02	ALIVE *Serious / Universal CDAMPM 153*	49	1

ALIZÉE
France, female vocalist – Alizée Jacotet (Singles: 9 Weeks) pos/wks

23 Feb 02 ●	MOI ... LOLITA *Polydor 5705952*	9	9

ALKALINE TRIO
US, male vocal / instrumental trio (Singles: 4 Weeks, Albums: 1 Week) pos/wks

2 Feb 02	PRIVATE EYE *B Unique / Vagrant BUN 013CDS*	51	1
30 Mar 02	STUPID KID *B Unique / Vagrant BUN 016CD*	53	1
26 Jul 03	WE'VE HAD ENOUGH *Vagrant 9809023*	50	1
18 Oct 03	ALL ON BLACK *Interscope 9811506*	60	1
24 May 03	GOOD MOURNING *Vagrant 9801238*	32	1

ALL ABOUT EVE
UK, female / male vocal / instrumental group (Singles: 48 Weeks, Albums: 37 Weeks) pos/wks

31 Oct 87	IN THE CLOUDS *Mercury EVEN 5*	47	5
23 Jan 88	WILD HEARTED WOMAN *Mercury EVEN 6*	33	4
9 Apr 88	EVERY ANGEL *Mercury EVEN 7*	30	5
30 Jul 88 ●	MARTHA'S HARBOUR *Mercury EVEN 8*	10	8
12 Nov 88	WHAT KIND OF FOOL *Mercury EVEN 9*	29	4
30 Sep 89	ROAD TO YOUR SOUL *Mercury EVEN 10*	37	4
16 Dec 89	DECEMBER *Mercury EVEN 11*	34	5
28 Apr 90	SCARLET *Mercury EVEN 12*	34	2
15 Jun 91	FAREWELL MR SORROW *Mercury EVEN 14*	36	2
10 Aug 91	STRANGE WAY *Vertigo EVEN 15*	50	3
19 Oct 91	THE DREAMER *Vertigo EVEN 16*	41	2
10 Oct 92	PHASED (EP) *MCA MCS 1688*	38	2
28 Nov 92	SOME FINER DAY *MCA MCS 1706*	57	1
5 Jun 04	LET ME GO HOME *Voiceprint AAEVP 10CD1*	52	1
27 Feb 88 ●	ALL ABOUT EVE *Mercury MERH 119*	7	29
28 Oct 89 ●	SCARLET AND OTHER STORIES *Mercury 838965 1*	9	4
7 Sep 91	TOUCHED BY JESUS *Vertigo 510461*	17	3
7 Nov 92	ULTRAVIOLET *MCA MCD 10712*	46	1

Tracks on Phased (EP): Phased / Mine / Infra Red / Ascent-Descent

The ALL-AMERICAN REJECTS
US, male vocal / instrumental group (Singles: 6 Week, Albums: 5 Weeks) pos/wks

2 Aug 03	SWING, SWING *Dreamworks 4504616*	13	5
22 Nov 03	THE LAST SONG *Dreamworks 4504641*	69	1
9 Aug 03	THE ALL-AMERICAN REJECTS *Dreamworks / Polydor 4504606*	50	5

ALL BLUE
UK, male vocal duo (Singles: 1 Week) pos/wks

21 Aug 99	PRISONER *WEA WEA 213CD1*	73	1

ALL EYES
UK, male vocal group (Singles: 1 Week) pos/wks

13 Nov 04	SHE'S A VISION *Specsavers CXSPECS 1*	65	1

ALL-4-ONE
US, male vocal group (Singles: 23 Weeks, Albums: 5 Weeks) pos/wks

2 Apr 94	SO MUCH IN LOVE *Atlantic A 7261CD*	60	1
18 Jun 94 ●	I SWEAR *Atlantic A 7255CD* ▲	2	18
19 Nov 94	SO MUCH IN LOVE (re-mix) *Atlantic A 7216CD*	49	2
15 Jul 95	I CAN LOVE YOU LIKE THAT *Atlantic A 8193CD*	33	2
23 Jul 94	ALL-4-ONE *Atlantic 7567825882*	25	5

ALL SAINTS   325 Top 500
(see also ARTFUL DODGER: OUTSIDAZ featuring Rah DIGGA and Melanie BLATT; APPLETON) *From All Saints Road, London, a cooler, R&B-motivated vocal girl group in the wake of the Spice Girls. Melanie Blatt, London, Shaznay Lewis, London, Nicole Appleton, Canada, Natalie Appleton, Canada. Crowned Best Breakthrough Artists in the 1998 MTV Europe Music Awards. Group split in 2001. Biggest-selling single: 'Never Ever' 1,254,604 (Singles: 109 Weeks, Albums: 96 Weeks)* pos/wks

6 Sep 97 ●	I KNOW WHERE IT'S AT *London LONCD 398*	4	8
22 Nov 97 ★	NEVER EVER *London LONCD 407* ◆	1	24
9 May 98 ★	UNDER THE BRIDGE / LADY MARMALADE *London LONCD 408* ■	1	14
12 Sep 98 ★	BOOTIE CALL *London LONCD 415* ■	1	11
5 Dec 98 ●	WAR OF NERVES *London LONCD 421*	7	11
26 Feb 00 ★	PURE SHORES *London LONCD 444* ■	1	16
14 Oct 00 ●	BLACK COFFEE (2re) *London LONCD 454* ■	1	18
27 Jan 01 ●	ALL HOOKED UP (re) *London LONCD 456*	7	7
6 Dec 97 ●	ALL SAINTS *London 8289792*	2	71
28 Oct 00 ★	SAINTS & SINNERS *London 8573852952* ■	1	21
17 Nov 01	ALL HITS *London 927421522*	18	4

From 29 Apr 00 'All Saints' changed catalogue number to 3984291362

The ALL SEEING I
UK, male vocal / instrumental group (Singles: 17 Weeks, Albums: 1 Week) pos/wks

28 Mar 98	BEAT GOES ON *ffrr FCD 334*	11	7
23 Jan 99 ●	WALK LIKE A PANTHER '98 *ffrr FCD 351* 1	10	7
18 Sep 99	1ST MAN IN SPACE *ffrr FCD 370* 2	28	3
2 Oct 99	PICKLED EGGS & SHERBET *ffrr 3984292412*	45	1

1 The All Seeing I featuring Tony Christie 2 The All Seeing I featuring Phil Oakey

ALL STAR CHOIR *See Donna SUMMER*

ALL-STARS *See Louis ARMSTRONG*

ALL-STARS *See Jr WALKER & the ALL-STARS*

ALL SYSTEMS GO
UK, male vocal / instrumental group (Singles: 2 Weeks) pos/wks

18 Jun 88	POP MUZIK *Unique NIQ 03*	63	2

Richard ALLAN *UK, male vocalist (Singles: 1 Week)*   pos/wks

24 Mar 60	**AS TIME GOES BY** *Parlophone R 4634*		43	1

Steve ALLAN *UK, male vocalist (Singles: 2 Weeks)*   pos/wks

27 Jan 79	**TOGETHER WE ARE BEAUTIFUL (re)** *Creole CR 164*		67	2

Donna ALLEN *US, female vocalist (Singles: 27 Weeks)*   pos/wks

18 Apr 87 ●	**SERIOUS** *Portrait 650744 7*		8	12
3 Jun 89 ●	**JOY AND PAIN** *BCM BCM 257*		10	10
21 Jan 95	**REAL** *Epic 6610992*		34	2
11 Oct 97	**SATURDAY** *AM:PM 5823752* 1		29	3

1 East 57th Street featuring Donna Allen

Keith ALLEN See BLACK GRAPE; FAT LES; Joe STRUMMER

Ed ALLEYNE-JOHNSON
UK, male instrumentalist – violin (Albums: 1 Week)   pos/wks

18 Jun 94	**ULTRAVIOLET** *Equation EQCD 002*		68	1

Dot ALLISON *(see also ONE DOVE)*
UK, female vocalist (Singles: 1 Week)   pos/wks

17 Aug 02	**STRUNG OUT** *Mantra MNT 74CD*		67	1

Mose ALLISON
US, male vocalist / instrumentalist – piano (Albums: 1 Week)   pos/wks

4 Jun 66	**MOSE ALIVE** *Atlantic 587007*		30	1

The ALLISONS *UK, male vocal / instrumental duo – John Allison (Brian Alford) and Bob Allison (Colin Day) (Singles: 27 Weeks)*   pos/wks

23 Feb 61 ●	**ARE YOU SURE** *Fontana H 294*		2	16
18 May 61	**WORDS** *Fontana H 304*		34	5
15 Feb 62	**LESSONS IN LOVE** *Fontana H 362*		30	6

The ALLMAN BROTHERS BAND
US, male vocal / instrumental group (Albums: 4 Weeks)   pos/wks

6 Oct 73	**BROTHERS AND SISTERS** *Warner Bros. K 47507* ▲		42	3
6 Mar 76	**THE ROAD GOES ON FOREVER** *Capricorn 2637 101*		54	1

ALLNIGHT BAND
UK, male instrumental group (Singles: 3 Weeks)   pos/wks

3 Feb 79	**THE JOKER (THE WIGAN JOKER)** *Casino Classics CC 6*		50	3

ALLSTARS
UK, female / male vocal group (Singles: 22 Weeks, Albums: 2 Weeks)   pos/wks

23 Jun 01	**BEST FRIENDS (re)** *Island CID 775*		20	7
22 Sep 01	**THINGS THAT GO BUMP IN THE NIGHT / IS THERE SOMETHING I SHOULD KNOW** *Island CID 783*		12	4
26 Jan 02 ●	**THE LAND OF MAKE BELIEVE (re)** *Island CID 791*		9	8
11 May 02	**BACK WHEN / GOING ALL THE WAY** *Island CID 796*		19	3
25 May 02	**ALLSTARS** *Island CID 8116*		43	2

ALLURE *US, female vocal group (Singles: 8 Weeks)*   pos/wks

14 Jun 97	**HEAD OVER HEELS** *Epic 6645942* 1		18	3
10 Jan 98	**ALL CRIED OUT** *Epic 6652715* 2		12	5

1 Allure featuring Nas 2 Allure featuring 112

The ALMIGHTY *UK, male vocal / instrumental group (Singles: 22 Weeks, Albums: 13 Weeks)*   pos/wks

30 Jun 90	**WILD AND WONDERFUL** *Polydor PO 75*		50	2
2 Mar 91	**FREE 'N' EASY** *Polydor PO 127*		35	2
11 May 91	**DEVIL'S TOY** *Polydor PO 144*		36	2
29 Jun 91	**LITTLE LOST SOMETIMES** *Polydor PO 151*		42	2
3 Apr 93	**ADDICTION** *Polydor PZCD 261*		38	2
29 May 93	**OUT OF SEASON** *Polydor PZCD 266*		41	2
30 Oct 93	**OVER THE EDGE** *Polydor PZCD 298*		26	2
24 Sep 94	**WRENCH** *Chrysalis CDCHS 5014*		26	2
14 Jan 95	**JONESTOWN MIND** *Chrysalis CDCHS 5017*		26	3
16 Mar 96	**ALL SUSSED OUT** *Chrysalis CDCHS 5030*		28	2
25 May 96	**DO YOU UNDERSTAND** *Raw Power RAWX 1022*		38	1
20 Oct 90	**BLOOD FIRE AND LIVE** *Polydor 8471071*		62	1

30 Mar 91	**SOUL DESTRUCTION** *Polydor 8479611*		22	4
17 Apr 93 ●	**POWERTRIPPIN'** *Polydor 5191042*		5	4
8 Oct 94	**CRANK** *Chrysalis CDCHRZ 6086*		15	2
30 Mar 96	**JUST ADD LIFE** *Chrysalis CDCHR 6112*		34	2

Marc ALMOND (see also SOFT CELL)
UK, male vocalist (Singles: 112 Weeks, Albums: 26 Weeks)   pos/wks

2 Jul 83	**BLACK HEART** *Some Bizzare BZS 19* 1		49	3
2 Jun 84	**THE BOY WHO CAME BACK** *Some Bizzare BZS 23*		52	5
1 Sep 84	**YOU HAVE** *Some Bizzare BZS 24*		57	3
20 Apr 85 ●	**I FEEL LOVE (MEDLEY)** *Forbidden Fruit BITE 4* 2		3	12
24 Aug 85	**STORIES OF JOHNNY** *Some Bizzare BONK 1*		23	5
26 Oct 85	**LOVE LETTER** *Some Bizzare BONK 2*		68	1
4 Jan 86	**THE HOUSE IS HAUNTED (BY THE ECHO OF YOUR LAST GOODBYE)** *Some Bizzare GLOW 1*		55	3
7 Jun 86	**A WOMAN'S STORY** *Some Bizzare GLOW 2* 3		41	5
18 Oct 86	**RUBY RED** *Some Bizzare GLOW 3*		47	3
14 Feb 87	**MELANCHOLY ROSE** *Some Bizzare GLOW 4*		71	1
3 Sep 88	**TEARS RUN RINGS** *Parlophone R 6186*		26	7
5 Nov 88	**BITTER SWEET** *Some Bizzare R 6194*		40	3
14 Jan 89 ★	**SOMETHING'S GOTTEN HOLD OF MY HEART** *Parlophone R 6201* 4		1	12
8 Apr 89	**ONLY THE MOMENT** *Parlophone R 6210*		45	2
3 Mar 90	**A LOVER SPURNED** *Some Bizzare R 6229*		29	4
19 May 90	**THE DESPERATE HOURS** *Some Bizzare R 6252*		45	2
23 Mar 91	**SAY HELLO WAVE GOODBYE '91 (re-recording)** *Mercury SOFT 1* 5		38	3
18 May 91 ●	**TAINTED LOVE (re-issue)** *Mercury SOFT 2* 5		5	8
28 Sep 91	**JACKY** *Some Bizzare YZ 610*		17	6
11 Jan 92	**MY HAND OVER MY HEART** *Some Bizzare YZ 633*		33	5
25 Apr 92 ●	**THE DAYS OF PEARLY SPENCER** *Some Bizzare YZ 638*		4	7
27 Mar 93	**WHAT MAKES A MAN A MAN (LIVE)** *Some Bizzare YZ 720CD*		60	2
13 May 95	**ADORED AND EXPLORED** *Some Bizzare MERCD 431*		25	3
29 Jul 95	**THE IDOL** *Some Bizzare MERCD 437*		44	2
30 Dec 95	**CHILD STAR** *Some Bizzare MERCD 450*		41	1
28 Dec 96	**YESTERDAY HAS GONE (re)** *EMI Premier CDPRESX 13* 6		58	2
16 Oct 82	**UNTITLED** *Some Bizzare BZA 13* 1		42	4
20 Aug 83	**TORMENT & TOREROS** *Some Bizzare BIZL 4* 1		28	5
10 Nov 84	**VERMIN IN ERMINE** *Some Bizzare BIZL 8*		36	2
5 Oct 85	**STORIES OF JOHNNY** *Some Bizzare FAITH 1*		22	3
18 Apr 87	**MOTHER FIST AND HER FIVE DAUGHTERS** *Some Bizzare FAITH 2* 2		41	2
8 Oct 88	**THE STARS WE ARE** *Parlophone PCS 7324*		41	5
16 Jun 90	**ENCHANTED** *Some Bizzare PCS 7344*		52	1
26 Oct 91	**TENEMENT SYMPHONY** *Some Bizzare WX 442*		39	3
9 Mar 96	**FANTASTIC STAR** *Some Bizzare 5286592*		54	1

1 Marc and the Mambas 2 Bronski Beat and Marc Almond 3 Marc Almond and the Willing Sinners 4 Marc Almond featuring special guest star Gene Pitney 5 Soft Cell / Marc Almond 6 PJ Proby and Marc Almond featuring the My Life Story Orchestra 1 Marc and the Mambas 2 Marc Almond and the Willing Sinners

I Feel Love (medley) comprises: I Feel Love / Love to Love You Baby / Johnny Remember Me. Original hit versions of 'Tainted Love' (1981) and 'Say Hello Wave Goodbye' (1982) credited to Soft Cell alone

ALOOF *UK, male vocal / instrumental group (Singles: 6 Weeks)*   pos/wks

19 Sep 92	**ON A MISSION** *Cowboy RODEO 5*		64	1
18 May 96	**WISH YOU WERE HERE ...** *East West EW 038CD*		61	1
30 Nov 96	**ONE NIGHT STAND** *East West EW 067CD*		30	2
1 Mar 97	**WISH YOU WERE HERE ... (re-mix)** *East West EW 083CD1*		43	1
29 Aug 98	**WHAT I MISS THE MOST** *East West EW 179CD1*		70	1

Herb ALPERT and the TIJUANA BRASS `109` `Top 500`
Leader of the US's biggest-selling instrumental act, The Tijuana Brass, b. 31 Mar 1935, Los Angeles. The multi-talented trumpet-toting star's band had four albums simultaneously in the US Top 10 in the mid-1960s. He sold his A&M label for $300m in 1989 and his publishing company for $350m in 2000 (Singles: 106 Weeks, Albums: 312 Weeks)   pos/wks

3 Jan 63	**THE LONELY BULL (EL SOLO TORRO)** *Stateside SS 138* 1		22	9
9 Dec 65 ●	**SPANISH FLEA** *Pye International 7N 25335*		3	20
24 Mar 66	**TIJUANA TAXI** *Pye International 7N 25352*		37	4
27 Apr 67	**CASINO ROYALE** *A&M AMS 700*		27	14
3 Jul 68	**THIS GUY'S IN LOVE WITH YOU (3re)** *A&M AMS 727* 2 ▲		3	19
18 Jun 69	**WITHOUT HER** *A&M AMS 755*		36	4
12 Dec 70	**JERUSALEM (re)** *A&M AMS 810*		42	3
13 Oct 79	**RISE** *A&M AMS 7465* 2 ▲		13	13
19 Jan 80	**ROTATION** *A&M AMS 7500* 2		46	3

21 Mar 87	KEEP YOUR EYE ON ME *Breakout USA 602* [2]	**19**	9
6 Jun 87	DIAMONDS *Breakout USA 605* [2]	**27**	7
29 Jan 66 ●	GOING PLACES *Pye NPL 28065* ▲	**4**	138
23 Apr 66 ●	WHIPPED CREAM AND OTHER DELIGHTS *Pye NPL 28058* ▲	**2**	42
28 May 66	WHAT NOW MY LOVE *Pye NPL 28077* ▲	**18**	17
11 Feb 67 ●	SRO *Pye NSPL 28088*	**5**	26
15 Jul 67	SOUNDS LIKE *A&M AMLS 900* ▲	**21**	10
3 Feb 68	NINTH *A&M AMLS 905*	**26**	9
29 Jun 68 ●	BEAT OF THE BRASS *A&M AMLS 916* ▲	**4**	21
9 Aug 69	WARM *A&M AMLS 937*	**30**	4
14 Mar 70	THE BRASS ARE COMIN' *A&M AMLS 962*	**40**	1
30 May 70 ●	GREATEST HITS *A&M AMLS 980*	**8**	27
27 Jun 70	DOWN MEXICO WAY *A&M AMLS 974*	**64**	1
13 Nov 71	AMERICA *A&M AMLB 1000*	**45**	1
12 Nov 77	40 GREATEST *K-Tel NE 1005*	**45**	2
17 Nov 79	RISE *A&M AMLH 64790* [1]	**37**	7
4 Apr 87	KEEP YOUR EYE ON ME *Breakout AMA 5125* [1]	**79**	3
28 Sep 91	THE VERY BEST OF HERB ALPERT *A&M 3971651* [1]	**34**	3

[1] The Tijuana Brass [2] Herb Alpert [1] Herb Alpert

Alpert provides vocals on 'This Guy's in Love with You' and 'Without Her'. Janet Jackson and Lisa Keith provide uncredited vocals on 'Diamonds' On 29 Jun 67 'Going Places' and 'What Now My Love' changed labels and numbers to A&M AMLS 965 and AMLS 977 respectively

ALPHA-BETA See Izhar COHEN and the ALPHA-BETA

ALPHAVILLE
Germany, male vocal / instrumental group (Singles: 13 Weeks) pos/wks

18 Aug 84 ●	BIG IN JAPAN *WEA Int. X 9505*	**8**	13

ALPINESTARS featuring Brian MOLKO
UK, male production duo and US, male vocalist (Singles: 1 Week) pos/wks

22 Jun 02	CARBON KID *Riverman RMR 11CDS*	**63**	1

ALSOU
Russia, female vocalist – Alsou Tenisheva (Singles: 3 Weeks) pos/wks

12 May 01	BEFORE YOU LOVE ME *Mercury 1589142*	**27**	3

Gerald ALSTON *US, male vocalist (Singles: 1 Week)* pos/wks

15 Apr 89	ACTIVATED *RCA ZB 42681*	**73**	1

ALT *Ireland / New Zealand / UK, male
vocal / instrumental group (Albums: 1 Week)* pos/wks

24 Jun 95	ALTITUDE *Parlophone CDPCS 7377*	**67**	1

ALTER EGO *Germany, male production duo –
Roman Flugel and Jorn Elling Wuttke (Singles: 3 Weeks)* pos/wks

11 Dec 04	ROCKER *Skint SKINT 103CD*	**32**	3+

ALTERED IMAGES *UK, male / female vocal /
instrumental group (Singles: 60 Weeks, Albums: 40 Weeks)* pos/wks

28 Mar 81	DEAD POP STARS *Epic EPC A 1023*	**67**	2
26 Sep 81 ●	HAPPY BIRTHDAY *Epic EPC A 1522*	**2**	17
12 Dec 81 ●	I COULD BE HAPPY *Epic EPC A 1834*	**7**	12
27 Mar 82	SEE THOSE EYES *Epic EPC A 2198*	**11**	7
22 May 82	PINKY BLUE *Epic EPC A 2426*	**35**	6
19 Mar 83 ●	DON'T TALK TO ME ABOUT LOVE *Epic EPC A 3083*	**7**	7
28 May 83	BRING ME CLOSER *Epic EPC A 3398*	**29**	6
16 Jul 83	LOVE TO STAY *Epic EPC A 3582*	**46**	3
19 Sep 81	HAPPY BIRTHDAY *Epic EPC 84893*	**26**	21
15 May 82	PINKY BLUE *Epic EPC 85665*	**12**	10
25 Jun 83	BITE *Epic EPC 25413*	**16**	9

ALTERN 8 *UK, male instrumental / production duo –
Mark Archer and Chris Peat (Singles: 34 Weeks, Albums: 4 Weeks)* pos/wks

13 Jul 91	INFILTRATE 202 *Network NWK 24*	**28**	7
16 Nov 91 ●	ACTIV 8 (COME WITH ME) *Network NWK 34*	**3**	9
8 Feb 92	FREQUENCY *Network NWKT 37*	**41**	1
11 Apr 92 ●	EVAPOR 8 *Network NWK 38* [1]	**6**	6
4 Jul 92	HYPNOTIC ST-8 *Network NWK 49*	**16**	4
10 Oct 92	SHAME *Network NWKTEN 56* [2]	**74**	1
12 Dec 92	BRUTAL-8-E *Network NWK 59*	**43**	5
3 Jul 93	EVERYBODY *Network NWKCD 73*	**58**	1

25 Jul 92	FULL ON ... MASK HYSTERIA *Network TOPCD 1*	**11**	4

[1] Guest vocal PP Arnold [2] Altern 8 vs Evelyn King

ALTHIA and DONNA *Jamaica, female vocal
duo – Althea Forrest and Donna Reid (Singles: 11 Weeks)* pos/wks

24 Dec 77 ★	UPTOWN TOP RANKING *Lightning LIG 506*	**1**	11

ALVIN and the CHIPMUNKS See CHIPMUNKS

ALY-US *US, male vocal / instrumental group (Singles: 3 Weeks)* pos/wks

21 Nov 92	FOLLOW ME *Cooltempo COOL 266*	**43**	2
25 May 02	FOLLOW ME (re-mix) *Strictly Rhythm SRUKCD 05*	**54**	1

Shola AMA *UK, female vocalist – Mathurin
Campbell (Singles: 58 Weeks, Albums: 32 Weeks)* pos/wks

19 Apr 97 ●	YOU MIGHT NEED SOMEBODY *WEA WEA 097CD1*	**4**	14
30 Aug 97 ●	YOU'RE THE ONE I LOVE *WEA WEA 121CD1*	**3**	8
29 Nov 97	WHO'S LOVING MY BABY *WEA WEA 145CD1*	**13**	7
21 Feb 98	MUCH LOVE *WEA WEA 154CD1*	**17**	3
11 Apr 98	SOMEDAY I'LL FIND YOU / I'VE BEEN TO A MARVELLOUS PARTY *EMI CDTCB 001* [1]	**28**	3
17 Apr 99 ●	TABOO *WEA WEA 203CD* [2]	**10**	8
6 Nov 99	STILL BELIEVE *WEA WEA 239CD1*	**26**	3
29 Apr 00	IMAGINE *WEA WEA 252CD*	**24**	4
11 Sep 04 ●	YOU SHOULD REALLY KNOW *Relentless RELCD 9* [3]	**8**	8
13 Sep 97 ●	MUCH LOVE *WEA 3984200202*	**6**	32

[1] Shola Ama and Craig Armstrong / The Divine Comedy [2] Glamma Kid featuring Shola Ama [3] Pirates featuring Enya, Shola Ama, Naila Boss & Ishani

Eddie AMADOR
US, male DJ / producer (Singles: 5 Weeks) pos/wks

24 Oct 98	HOUSE MUSIC *Pukka CDPUKKA 18*	**37**	2
22 Jan 00	RISE *Defected DEFECT 9CDS*	**19**	3

Ruby AMANFU *US, female vocalist (Singles: 2 Weeks)* pos/wks

15 Mar 03	SUGAH *Polydor 0658302*	**32**	2

AMAR
UK, female vocalist / instrumentalist – Amar Nagi (Singles: 1 Week) pos/wks

9 Sep 00	SOMETIMES IT SNOWS IN APRIL *Blanco Y Negro NEG 129CD*	**48**	1

AMAZULU *UK, female / male vocal /
instrumental group (Singles: 57 Weeks, Albums: 1 Week)* pos/wks

6 Jul 85	EXCITABLE *Island IS 201*	**12**	13
23 Nov 85	DON'T YOU JUST KNOW IT *Island IS 233*	**15**	11
15 Mar 86	THE THINGS THE LONELY DO *Island IS 267*	**43**	6
31 May 86 ●	TOO GOOD TO BE FORGOTTEN *Island IS 284*	**5**	13
13 Sep 86	MONTEGO BAY *Island IS 293*	**16**	9
10 Oct 87	MONY MONY *EMI EM 32*	**38**	5
6 Dec 88	AMAZULU *Island ILPS 9851*	**97**	1

AMBASSADOR
Holland, male DJ / production group (Singles: 1 Week) pos/wks

12 Feb 00	ONE OF THESE DAYS *Platipus PLATCD 69*	**67**	1

AMBASSADORS OF FUNK featuring MC MARIO *UK, male
DJ and rapper – Simon Harris and Einstein (Singles: 8 Weeks)* pos/wks

31 Oct 92 ●	SUPERMARIOLAND *Living Beat SMASH 23*	**8**	8

AMBER
Holland, female vocalist – Marie Cremers (Singles: 2 Weeks) pos/wks

24 Jun 00	SEXUAL *Substance SUBS 2CDS*	**34**	2

AMBUSH See RMXCRW featuring EBON-E plus AMBUSH

AMEN
US, male vocal / instrumental group (Singles: 3 Weeks) pos/wks

17 Feb 01	TOO HARD TO BE FREE *Virgin VUSCD 191*	**72**	1
21 Jul 01	THE WAITING 18 *Virgin VUSCD 207*	**61**	1
3 Apr 04	CALIFORNIA'S BLEEDING *Columbia 6746162*	**52**	1

AMEN CORNER (see also FAIR WEATHER)
UK, male vocal / instrumental group – lead vocal Andy Fairweather-Low (Singles: 67 Weeks, Albums: 8 Weeks) pos/wks

26 Jul 67	GIN HOUSE BLUES *Deram DM 136*	**12**	10
11 Oct 67	THE WORLD OF BROKEN HEARTS *Deram DM 151*	**24**	6
17 Jan 68 ●	BEND ME, SHAPE ME *Deram DM 172*	**3**	12
31 Jul 68 ●	HIGH IN THE SKY *Deram DM 197*	**6**	13
29 Jan 69 ★	(IF PARADISE IS) HALF AS NICE *Immediate IM 073*	**1**	11
25 Jun 69 ●	HELLO SUZIE *Immediate IM 081*	**4**	10
14 Feb 76	(IF PARADISE IS) HALF AS NICE (re-issue) *Immediate IMS 103*	**34**	5
30 Mar 68	ROUND AMEN CORNER *Deram SML 1021*	**26**	7
1 Nov 69	EXPLOSIVE COMPANY *Immediate IMSP 023*	**19**	1

AMEN UK
UK , male / female vocal / production group (Singles: 8 Weeks) pos/wks

8 Feb 97	PASSION *Feverpitch CDFVR 1015*	**15**	4
28 Jun 97	PEOPLE OF LOVE *Feverpitch CDFVR 18*	**36**	2
6 Sep 03	PASSION (re-mix) *Positiva CDTIV 195* [1]	**40**	2

[1] Amen! UK

AMERICA *US / UK, male vocal / instrumental trio (Singles: 20 Weeks, Albums: 22 Weeks)* pos/wks

18 Dec 71 ●	A HORSE WITH NO NAME (re) *Warner Bros. K 16128* ▲	**3**	13
25 Nov 72	VENTURA HIGHWAY *Warner Bros. K 16219*	**43**	4
6 Nov 82	YOU CAN DO MAGIC *Capitol CL 264*	**59**	3
22 Jan 72	AMERICA *Warner Bros. K 46093* ▲	**14**	13
9 Dec 72	HOMECOMING *Warner Bros. K 46180*	**21**	5
10 Nov 73	HAT TRICK *Warner Bros. K 56016*	**41**	3
7 Feb 76	HISTORY – AMERICA'S GREATEST HITS *Warner Bros. K 56169*	**60**	1

The AMERICAN BREED
US, male vocal / instrumental group (Singles: 6 Weeks) pos/wks

7 Feb 68	BEND ME SHAPE ME *Stateside SS 2078*	**24**	6

AMERICAN HEAD CHARGE
US, male vocal / instrumental group (Singles: 1 Week) pos/wks

8 Jun 02	JUST SO YOU KNOW *Mercury 5829622*	**52**	1

AMERICAN HI-FI
US, male vocal / instrumental group (Singles: 4 Weeks) pos/wks

8 Sep 01	FLAVOR OF THE WEAK *Mercury 5886722*	**31**	3
26 Apr 03	THE ART OF LOSING *Mercury 0779152*	**75**	1

AMERICAN MUSIC CLUB *US, male vocal / instrumental group (Singles: 4 Weeks, Albums: 3 Weeks)* pos/wks

24 Apr 93	JOHNNY MATHIS' FEET *Virgin VSCDG 1445*	**58**	2
10 Sep 94	WISH THE WORLD AWAY *Virgin VSCDX 1512*	**46**	2
27 Mar 93	MERCURY *Virgin CDV 2708*	**41**	2
24 Sep 94	SAN FRANCISCO *Virgin CDV 2752*	**72**	1

AMERIE *US, female vocalist – Amerie Rogers (Singles: 7 Weeks)* pos/wks

9 Nov 02	WHY DON'T WE FALL IN LOVE *Columbia 6732212* [1]	**40**	2
22 Feb 03	PARADISE *Def Jam 0637032* [2]	**18**	5

[1] Amerie featuring Ludacris [2] LL Cool J featuring Amerie

AMES BROTHERS *US, male vocal group (Singles: 6 Weeks)* pos/wks

4 Feb 55 ●	THE NAUGHTY LADY OF SHADY LANE *HMV B 10800*	**6**	6

With Hugo Winterhalter and his Orchestra

AMICI FOREVER *UK / South Africa / New Zealand, male / female vocal group (Albums: 9 Weeks)* pos/wks

27 Sep 03	THE OPERA BAND *Victor / Arista Assoc 828765822*	**39**	9

AMIL See JAY-Z

AMILLIONSONS
UK, male production trio (Singles: 2 Weeks) pos/wks

24 Aug 02	MISTI BLU *London LONCD 468*	**39**	2

Includes vocal by Taka Boom

AMIRA
US, female vocalist – Amira McNiel (Singles: 7 Weeks) pos/wks

13 Dec 97	MY DESIRE *VC VCRD 27*	**51**	1
8 Aug 98	MY DESIRE (re-mix) *VC Recordings VCRD 36*	**46**	2
10 Feb 01	MY DESIRE (2nd re-mix) *VC Recordings VCRD 71*	**20**	4

AMNESIA See Frank'o MOIRAGHI featuring AMNESIA

Cherie AMORE *France, female vocalist (Singles: 2 Weeks)* pos/wks

15 Apr 00	I DON'T WANT NOBODY (TELLIN' ME WHAT TO DO) *Eternal / WEA WEA 262CD*	**33**	2

Vanessa AMOROSI *Australia, female vocalist (Singles: 10 Weeks)* pos/wks

23 Sep 00 ●	ABSOLUTELY EVERYBODY *Mercury 1582972*	**7**	10

AMORPHOUS ANDROGYNOUS
(see also FUTURE SOUND OF LONDON) UK, male instrumental / production duo – Brian Dougans and Gary Cobain (Albums: 1 Week) pos/wks

17 Aug 02	FSOL PRESENTS AMORPHOUS ANDROGYNOUS: THE ISNESS *Artful FSOLCD 101*	**68**	1

Amorphous Androgynous is Future Sound Of London under a different name

AMOS (see also Jeremy HEALY and AMOS) *UK, male vocalist / rapper / producer – Amos Pizzey (Singles: 12 Weeks)* pos/wks

3 Sep 94	ONLY SAW TODAY – INSTANT KARMA *Positiva CDTIV 16*	**48**	2
25 Mar 95	LET LOVE SHINE *Positiva CDTIV 24*	**31**	2
7 Oct 95	CHURCH OF FREEDOM *Positiva CDTIV 38*	**54**	1
12 Oct 96	STAMP! *Positiva CDTIV 65* [1]	**11**	5
31 May 97	ARGENTINA *Positiva CDTIV 74* [1]	**30**	2

[1] Jeremy Healy & Amos

Tori AMOS *US, female vocalist / instrumentalist – piano – Myra Amos (Singles: 66 Weeks, Albums: 53 Weeks)* pos/wks

23 Nov 91	SILENT ALL THESE YEARS *East West YZ 618*	**51**	3
1 Feb 92	CHINA *East West YZ 7531*	**51**	2
21 Mar 92	WINTER *East West A 7504*	**25**	4
20 Jun 92	CRUCIFY *East West A 7479*	**15**	6
22 Aug 92	SILENT ALL THESE YEARS (re-issue) *East West A 7433*	**26**	4
22 Jan 94 ●	CORNFLAKE GIRL *East West A 7281CD*	**4**	6
19 Mar 94 ●	PRETTY GOOD YEAR *East West A 7263CD*	**7**	4
28 May 94	PAST THE MISSION *East West YZ 7257CD*	**31**	3
15 Oct 94	GOD *East West A 7251CD*	**44**	2
13 Jan 96	CAUGHT A LITE SNEEZE *East West A 5524CD1*	**20**	3
23 Mar 96	TALULA *East West A 8512CD1*	**22**	2
3 Aug 96	HEY JUPITER / PROFESSIONAL WIDOW *East West A 5494CD*	**20**	9
9 Nov 96	BLUE SKIES *Perfecto PERF 130CD1* [1]	**26**	2
11 Jan 97 ★	PROFESSIONAL WIDOW (IT'S GOT TO BE BIG) (re-mix) *East West A 5450CD*	**1**	10
2 May 98	SPARK *Atlantic AT 0031CD*	**16**	3
13 Nov 99	GLORY OF THE 80'S *Atlantic AT 0077CD1*	**46**	1
26 Oct 02	A SORTA FAIRYTALE *Epic 6730432*	**41**	2
18 Jan 92	LITTLE EARTHQUAKES *East West 7567823582*	**14**	23
12 Feb 94 ★	UNDER THE PINK *East West 7567825672* ■	**1**	13
3 Feb 96 ●	BOYS FOR PELE *East West 7567828622*	**2**	6
16 May 98 ●	FROM THE CHOIRGIRL HOTEL *Atlantic 7567830952*	**6**	5
2 Oct 99	TO VENUS AND BACK *Atlantic 7567832422*	**22**	2
29 Sep 01	STRANGE LITTLE GIRLS *Atlantic 7567834862*	**16**	2
9 Nov 02	SCARLET'S WALK *Epic 5087829*	**26**	1
29 Nov 03	TALES OF A LIBRARIAN *Atlantic 7567932232*	**74**	1

[1] BT featuring Tori Amos

'Past the Mission' features guest vocals by Trent Reznor of Nine Inch Nails

AMOURE *UK, male production duo – Rod Edwards and Nick Magnus (Singles: 2 Weeks)* pos/wks

27 May 00	IS THAT YOUR FINAL ANSWER? (WHO WANTS TO BE A MILLIONAIRE – THE SINGLE) *Celador MILLION 2*	**33**	2

AMP FIDDLER *US, male producer / instrumentalist – Joseph 'Amp' Fiddler (Singles: 2 Weeks)* pos/wks

20 Mar 04	I BELIEVE IN YOU *Genuine GEN 022CD*	**72**	1
19 Jun 04	DREAMIN' *Genuine GEN 025CDM*	**71**	1

Singles re-entries are listed as (re), (2re), (3re)…. which signifies that the hit re-entered the chart once, twice or three times…

The AMPS
US, male / female vocal / instrumental group (Singles: 1 Week, Albums: 1 Week) pos/wks

21 Oct 95	**TIPP CITY** *4AD BAD 5015CD*	**61**	1
11 Nov 95	**PACER** *4AD CAD 5016CD*	**60**	1

AMY See A.D.A.M. featuring AMY

AN EMOTIONAL FISH
Ireland, male vocal / instrumental group (Singles: 5 Weeks, Albums: 3 Weeks) pos/wks

23 Jun 90	**CELEBRATE** *East West YZ 489*	**46**	5
25 Aug 90	**AN EMOTIONAL FISH** *East West WX 359*	**40**	3

ANASTACIA (271) Top 500
Unique, powerhouse vocalist who has sold more than six million albums in Europe but remains little known in her homeland, b. Anastacia Newkirk, 17 Sep 1975, Chicago, US. Her first two albums went double-platinum in the UK (Singles: 95 Weeks, Albums: 145 Weeks) pos/wks

30 Sep 00 ●	**I'M OUTTA LOVE** *Epic 6695782*	**6**	17
3 Feb 01	**NOT THAT KIND (re)** *Epic 6707632*	**11**	8
2 Jun 01	**COWBOYS & KISSES** *Epic 6712622*	**28**	5
25 Aug 01	**MADE FOR LOVIN' YOU** *Epic 6717172*	**27**	3
1 Dec 01	**PAID MY DUES** *Epic 6721252*	**14**	9
6 Apr 02	**ONE DAY IN YOUR LIFE** *Epic 6724562*	**11**	9
21 Sep 02	**WHY'D YOU LIE TO ME (re)** *Epic 6731112*	**25**	5
7 Dec 02	**YOU'LL NEVER BE ALONE** *Epic 6733802*	**31**	3
3 Apr 04 ●	**LEFT OUTSIDE ALONE** *Epic 6747482*	**3**	20
14 Aug 04 ●	**SICK AND TIRED** *Epic 6751092*	**4**	11
27 Nov 04	**WELCOME TO MY TRUTH** *Epic 6754922*	**25**	5+
14 Oct 00 ●	**NOT THAT KIND** *Epic 4974122*	**2**	65
8 Dec 01 ●	**FREAK OF NATURE** *Epic 5047572*	**4**	42
10 Apr 04 ★	**ANASTACIA** *Epic 5134717* ■	**1**	38+

Andrea ANATOLA See SODA CLUB

AND WHY NOT?
UK, male vocal / instrumental group (Singles: 18 Weeks, Albums: 3 Weeks) pos/wks

14 Oct 89	**RESTLESS DAYS (SHE CRIES OUT LOUD)** *Island IS 426*	**38**	7
13 Jan 90	**THE FACE** *Island IS 444*	**13**	8
21 Apr 90	**SOMETHING YOU GOT** *Island IS 452*	**39**	4
10 Mar 90	**MOVE YOUR SKIN** *Island ILPS 9935*	**24**	3

... AND YOU WILL KNOW US BY THE TRAIL OF DEAD
US, male vocal / instrumental group (Singles: 2 Weeks, Albums: 1 Week) pos/wks

11 Nov 00	**MISTAKES AND REGRETS** *Domino RUG 114CD*	**69**	1
11 May 02	**ANOTHER MORNING STONER** *Interscope / Polydor 4977162*	**54**	1
16 Mar 02	**SOURCE TAGS AND CODES** *Interscope 4932492*	**73**	1

Angry ANDERSON
Australia, male vocalist – Gary Anderson (Singles: 13 Weeks) pos/wks

19 Nov 88 ●	**SUDDENLY** *Food For Thought YUM 113*	**3**	13

Carl ANDERSON
US, male vocalist (Singles: 4 Weeks) pos/wks

8 Jun 85	**BUTTERCUP** *Streetwave KHAN 45*	**49**	4

Carleen ANDERSON
(see also The BRAND NEW HEAVIES; Paul WELLER) *US, female vocalist (Singles: 17 Weeks, Albums: 7 Weeks)* pos/wks

12 Feb 94	**NERVOUS BREAKDOWN** *Circa YRCDG 112*	**27**	4
28 May 94	**MAMA SAID** *Circa YRCD 114*	**26**	4
13 Aug 94	**TRUE SPIRIT** *Circa YRCD 118*	**24**	3
14 Jan 95	**LET IT LAST** *Circa YRCD 119*	**16**	3
7 Feb 98	**MAYBE I'M AMAZED** *Circa YRCD 128*	**24**	2
25 Apr 98	**WOMAN IN ME** *Circa YRCD 129*	**74**	1
13 Nov 93	**DUSKY SAPPHO (EP)** *Circa YRCDG 108*	**38**	1
18 Jun 94	**TRUE SPIRIT** *Circa CIRCDX 30*	**12**	4
2 May 98	**BLESSED BURDEN** *Circa CIRCD 35*	**51**	2

Gillian ANDERSON See HAL featuring Gillian ANDERSON

Ian ANDERSON
(see also JETHRO TULL) *UK, male vocalist / instrumentalist – flute (Albums: 1 Week)* pos/wks

26 Nov 83	**WALK INTO LIGHT** *Chrysalis CDL 1443*	**78**	1

Jon ANDERSON
(see also YES: ANDERSON BRUFORD WAKEMAN HOWE; JON AND VANGELIS) *UK, male vocalist (Albums: 19 Weeks)* pos/wks

24 Jul 76 ●	**OLIAS OF SUNHILLOW** *Atlantic K 50261*	**8**	10
15 Nov 80	**SONG OF SEVEN** *Atlantic K 50756*	**38**	3
5 Jun 82	**ANIMATION** *Polydor POLD 5044*	**43**	6

Laurie ANDERSON
US, female vocalist / multi-instrumentalist (Singles: 6 Weeks, Albums: 8 Weeks) pos/wks

17 Oct 81 ●	**O SUPERMAN** *Warner Bros. K 17870*	**2**	6
1 May 82	**BIG SCIENCE** *Warner Bros. K 57002*	**29**	6
10 Mar 84	**MISTER HEARTBREAK** *Warner Bros. 9250771*	**93**	2

LC ANDERSON vs PSYCHO RADIO
UK, male vocalist and Italy, male production duo (Singles: 2 Weeks) pos/wks

26 Jul 03	**RIGHT STUFF** *Faith & Hope FHCD 039*	**45**	2

Leroy ANDERSON and his POP CONCERT ORCHESTRA
US, orchestra – leader b. 29 Jun 1908, d. 18 May 1975 (Singles: 4 Weeks) pos/wks

28 Jun 57	**FORGOTTEN DREAMS (2re)** *Brunswick 05485*	**24**	4

Lynn ANDERSON
US, female vocalist (Singles: 20 Weeks, Albums: 1 Week) pos/wks

20 Feb 71 ●	**ROSE GARDEN** *CBS 5360*	**3**	20
17 Apr 71	**ROSE GARDEN** *CBS 64333*	**45**	1

Moira ANDERSON
UK, female vocalist (Singles: 2 Weeks, Albums: 6 Weeks) pos/wks

27 Dec 69	**THE HOLY CITY** *Decca F 12989*	**43**	2
20 Jun 70	**THESE ARE MY SONGS** *Decca SKL 5016*	**50**	1
5 Dec 81	**GOLDEN MEMORIES** *Warwick WW 5107* [1]	**46**	5

[1] Harry Secombe and Moira Anderson

Sunshine ANDERSON
US, female vocalist (Singles: 8 Weeks, Albums: 6 Weeks) pos/wks

2 Jun 01 ●	**HEARD IT ALL BEFORE** *Atlantic AT 0100CD*	**9**	7
22 Sep 01	**LUNCH OR DINNER** *Atlantic AT 0109CD*	**57**	1
26 May 01	**YOUR WOMAN** *Atlantic 7567930112*	**39**	6

John ANDERSON BIG BAND
UK, big band (Singles: 5 Weeks) pos/wks

21 Dec 85	**GLENN MILLER MEDLEY (re)** *Modern GLEN 1*	**61**	5

Glenn Miller Medley comprises the following tracks: In the Mood / American Patrol / Little Brown Jug / Pennsylvania 65000

John ANDERSON ORCHESTRA
Ireland, orchestra (Albums: 5 Weeks) pos/wks

25 Nov 95	**PAN PIPES – ROMANCE OF IRELAND** *MCA MCD 60004*	**56**	5

ANDERSON BRUFORD WAKEMAN HOWE
(see also Jon ANDERSON; Rick WAKEMAN; Steve HOWE; YES) *UK, male vocal / instrumental group (Singles: 2 Weeks, Albums: 6 Weeks)* pos/wks

24 Jun 89	**BROTHER OF MINE** *Arista 112379*	**63**	2
8 Jul 89	**ANDERSON BRUFORD WAKEMAN HOWE** *Arista 209970*	**14**	6

ANDRÉ 3000 See KELIS; OUTKAST

Peter ANDRE
UK, male vocalist – Peter Andrea (Singles: 106 Weeks, Albums: 28 Weeks) pos/wks

10 Jun 95	**TURN IT UP** *Mushroom D 1000*	**64**	1
16 Sep 95	**MYSTERIOUS GIRL** *Mushroom D 11921*	**53**	2
16 Mar 96	**ONLY ONE (re)** *Mushroom D 1307*	**16**	4
1 Jun 96 ●	**MYSTERIOUS GIRL (re-issue)** *Mushroom D 2000* [1]	**2**	18
14 Sep 96 ★	**FLAVA** *Mushroom D 2003* ■	**1**	9
7 Dec 96 ★	**I FEEL YOU (2re)** *Mushroom D 1521* ■	**1**	11
8 Mar 97 ●	**NATURAL (2re)** *Mushroom DX 1577*	**6**	11
9 Aug 97 ●	**ALL ABOUT US (re)** *Mushroom MUSH 5CD*	**3**	9
8 Nov 97 ●	**LONELY (re)** *Mushroom MUSH 16CD*	**6**	9
24 Jan 98	**ALL NIGHT ALL RIGHT** *Mushroom MUSH 21CD* [2]	**16**	4
25 Jul 98 ●	**KISS THE GIRL** *Mushroom MUSH 34CDSX*	**9**	5
6 Mar 04 ★	**MYSTERIOUS GIRL (2nd re-issue)** *A&E PA 01CD* ■	**1**	11
12 Jun 04 ●	**INSANIA (re)** *East West PA 0002CD*	**3**	7
18 Sep 04	**THE RIGHT WAY** *Atlantic ATUK 001CD*	**14**	5

		pos/wks
12 Oct 96 ★	NATURAL *Mushroom D 2005* ■	1 23
29 Nov 97	TIME *Mushroom MUSH 18CD*	28 4
19 Jun 04	THE LONG ROAD BACK *East West 5046738102*..........	44 1

1 Peter Andre featuring Bubbler Ranx 2 Peter Andre featuring Warren G

Chris ANDREWS *UK, male vocalist (Singles: 36 Weeks)* pos/wks

7 Oct 65 ●	YESTERDAY MAN *Decca F 12236*	3 15
2 Dec 65	TO WHOM IT CONCERNS *Decca F 22285*	13 10
14 Apr 66	SOMETHING ON MY MIND (re) *Decca F 22365*	41 3
2 Jun 66	WHAT'CHA GONNA DO NOW? *Decca F 22404*	40 4
25 Aug 66	STOP THAT GIRL *Decca F 22472*	36 4

Eamonn ANDREWS *Ireland, male vocalist / TV presenter, b. 19 Dec 1922, d. 5 Nov 1987 (Singles: 3 Weeks)* pos/wks

20 Jan 56	THE SHIFTING WHISPERING SANDS (PARTS 1 & 2) *Parlophone R 4106*	18 3

Hit is credited: 'with Ron Goodwin and his Orchestra and Chorus'

Julie ANDREWS *UK, female vocalist / actor (Albums: 5 Weeks)* pos/wks

16 Jul 83	LOVE ME TENDER *Peach River JULIE 1*	63 5

Michael ANDREWS featuring Gary JULES
US, male producer and male vocalist (Singles: 15 Weeks) pos/wks

27 Dec 03 ★	MAD WORLD *Adventures in Music / Sanctuary SANXD 250* ■ ..1 15

The ANDROIDS *Australia, male vocal / instrumental group (Singles: 5 Weeks)* pos/wks

17 May 03	DO IT WITH MADONNA *Universal MCSTD 40321*	15 5

ANEKA *UK, female vocalist – Mary Sandeman (Singles: 16 Weeks)* pos/wks

8 Aug 81 ★	JAPANESE BOY *Hansa HANSA 5*	1 12
7 Nov 81	LITTLE LADY *Hansa HANSA 8*	50 4

Dave ANGEL *UK, male DJ / producer (Singles: 1 Week)* pos/wks

2 Aug 97	TOKYO STEALTH FIGHTER *Fourth & Broadway BRCD 355*	58 1

Simone ANGEL *Holland, female vocalist (Singles: 1 Week)* pos/wks

13 Nov 93	LET THIS FEELING *A&M 5803652*	60 1

ANGEL CITY
(see also NIGHTBREED) *Holland, male production duo – Aldwin Oomen and Hugo Zentveld (Singles: 19 Weeks)* pos/wks

8 Nov 03	LOVE ME RIGHT (OH SHEILA) (re) *Data DATA 59CDS* 1 ......11 8
3 Jul 04	TOUCH ME *Data DATA 73CDS* 18 4
16 Oct 04	DO YOU KNOW (I GO CRAZY) *Data DATA 76CDS* 8 7

1 Angel City featuring Lara McAllen

Lara McAllen is the uncredited vocalist on the last two singles

The ANGELETTES *UK, female vocal group (Singles: 5 Weeks)* pos/wks

13 May 72	DON'T LET HIM TOUCH YOU *Decca F 13284*	35 5

ANGELHEART
UK, female DJ / producer – Angel Johnson (Singles: 2 Weeks) pos/wks

6 Apr 96	COME BACK TO ME *Hi-Life 5776312* 1	68 1
22 Mar 97	I'M STILL WAITING *Hi-Life 5735452* 2	74 1

1 Angelheart featuring Rochelle Harris 2 Angelheart featuring Aletia Bourne

ANGELIC (see also CITIZEN CANED; DT8 PROJECT; Jurgen VRIES; ORION)
UK, male / female production / vocal duo – Amanda O'Riordan and Darren Tate (Singles: 16 Weeks) pos/wks

17 Jun 00	IT'S MY TURN *Serious MCSTD 40235* 11 10
24 Feb 01	CAN'T KEEP ME SILENT *Serious SERR 023CD* 12 4
10 Nov 01	STAY WITH ME *Serious SERR 35CD* 36 2

ANGELIC UPSTARTS *UK, male vocal / instrumental group (Singles: 30 Weeks, Albums: 20 Weeks)* pos/wks

21 Apr 79	I'M AN UPSTART *Warner Bros. K 17354*	31 8

11 Aug 79	TEENAGE WARNING *Warner Bros. K 17426*	29 6
3 Nov 79	NEVER 'AD NOTHIN' *Warner Bros. K 17476*	52 4
9 Feb 80	OUT OF CONTROL *Warner Bros. K 17558*	58 3
22 Mar 80	WE GOTTA GET OUT OF THIS PLACE *Warner Bros. K 17576*	65 2
2 Aug 80	LAST NIGHT ANOTHER SOLDIER *Zonophone Z 7*	51 4
7 Feb 81	KIDS ON THE STREET *Zonophone Z 16*	57 3
18 Aug 79	TEENAGE WARNING *Warner Bros. K 50634*	25 7
12 Apr 80	WE'VE GOTTA GET OUT OF THIS PLACE *Warner Bros. K 56806*..54 3
7 Jun 81	2000000 VOICES *Zonophone ZONO 104*	32 3
26 Sep 81	ANGELIC UPSTARTS *Zonophone ZEM 102*	27 7

ANGELLE *UK, female vocalist – Sarah Davies (Singles: 1 Week)* pos/wks

17 Aug 02	JOY AND PAIN *Innovation CDINNOV 1*	43 1

Steve ANGELLO *See Eric PRYDZ*

Bobby ANGELO and the TUXEDOS
UK, male vocal / instrumental group (Singles: 6 Weeks) pos/wks

10 Aug 61	BABY SITTIN' *HMV POP 892*	30 6

The ANGELS *US, female vocal trio (Singles: 1 Week)* pos/wks

3 Oct 63	MY BOYFRIEND'S BACK *Mercury AMT 1211* ▲	50 1

ANGELS OF LIGHT *See PSYCHIC TV*

ANGELS REVERSE
Germany, male production duo (Singles: 1 Week) pos/wks

31 Aug 02	DON'T CARE *Inferno CDFERN 46*	71 1

ANGELWITCH
UK, male vocal / instrumental group (Singles: 1 Week) pos/wks

7 Jun 80	SWEET DANGER *EMI 5064*	75 1

ANIMAL (see also The MUPPETS)
US, male puppet vocalist / instrumentalist – drums (Singles: 3 Weeks) pos/wks

23 Jul 94	WIPE OUT *BMG Kidz 74321219532*	38 3

ANIMAL NIGHTLIFE *UK, male / female vocal / instrumental group (Singles: 22 Weeks, Albums: 6 Weeks)* pos/wks

13 Aug 83	NATIVE BOY (UPTOWN) *Innervision A3584*	60 3
18 Aug 84	MR SOLITAIRE *Island IS 193*	25 12
6 Jul 85	LOVE IS JUST THE GREAT PRETENDER *Island IS 200*	28 6
5 Oct 85	PREACHER, PREACHER *Island IS 245*	67 1
24 Aug 85	SHANGRI-LA *Island ILPS 9830*	36 6

ANIMALHOUSE
UK, male vocal / instrumental group (Singles: 1 Week) pos/wks

15 Jul 00	READY TO RECEIVE *Boilerhouse / Arista 74321771072*	61 1

The ANIMALS (279) *Top 500*
Ground-breaking Newcastle band: Eric Burdon (v), Alan Price (k), Brian 'Chas' Chandler (b) (d. 1996), Hilton Valentine (g), John Steel (d). They were the first hit act produced by Mickie Most, who reportedly helped them to record 'The House of the Rising Sun' in 15 minutes at a cost of £1 10 shillings. After The Tornados and The Beatles, they were the third UK group to top the US singles chart (Singles: 146 Weeks, Albums: 86 Weeks) pos/wks

16 Apr 64	BABY LET ME TAKE YOU HOME *Columbia DB 7247*	21 8
25 Jun 64 ★	THE HOUSE OF THE RISING SUN *Columbia DB 7301* ▲	1 12
17 Sep 64 ●	I'M CRYING *Columbia DB 7354*	8 10
4 Feb 65 ●	DON'T LET ME BE MISUNDERSTOOD *Columbia DB 7445*	3 9
8 Apr 65 ●	BRING IT ON HOME TO ME *Columbia DB 7539*	7 11
15 Jul 65 ●	WE'VE GOTTA GET OUT OF THIS PLACE *Columbia DB 7639*	2 12
28 Oct 65 ●	IT'S MY LIFE *Columbia DB 7741*	7 11
17 Feb 66	INSIDE – LOOKING OUT *Decca F 12332*	12 8
2 Jun 66 ●	DON'T BRING ME DOWN *Decca F 12407*	6 8
27 Oct 66	HELP ME GIRL *Decca F 12502* 1	14 9
15 Jun 67	WHEN I WAS YOUNG *MGM 1340* 2	45 3
6 Sep 67	GOOD TIMES *MGM 1344* 2	20 11
18 Oct 67	SAN FRANCISCAN NIGHTS *MGM 1359* 2	7 10
14 Feb 68	SKY PILOT *MGM 1373* 2	40 3
15 Jan 69	RING OF FIRE *MGM 1461* 2	35 5
7 Oct 72	THE HOUSE OF THE RISING SUN (re) (re-issue) *RAK RR 1* ...11 16
14 Nov 64 ●	THE ANIMALS *Columbia 33SX 1669*	6 20

Singles re-entries are listed as (re), (2re), (3re).... which signifies that the hit re-entered the chart once, twice or three times...

22 May 65 ●	**ANIMAL TRACKS** *Columbia 33SX 1708*	**6**	26
16 Apr 66 ●	**THE MOST OF THE ANIMALS** *Columbia 33SX 6035*	**4**	20
28 May 66 ●	**ANIMALISMS** *Decca LK 4797*	**4**	17
25 Sep 71	**THE MOST OF THE ANIMALS (re-issue)** *MFP 5218*	**18**	3

[1] Eric Burdon and session musicians billed as The Animals [2] Eric Burdon and The Animals

'The House of the Rising Sun' (re-issue) peaked at No.11 as a re-entry in 1982

ANIMOTION
US / UK, male / female vocal / instrumental group (Singles: 12 Weeks) pos/wks

11 May 85 ●	**OBSESSION** *Mercury PH 34*	**5**	12

Paul ANKA *Canada, male vocalist (Singles: 134 Weeks)* pos/wks

9 Aug 57 ★	**DIANA** *Columbia DB 3980* ◆ ▲	**1**	25
8 Nov 57 ●	**I LOVE YOU, BABY** *Columbia DB 4022*	**3**	15
8 Nov 57	**TELL ME THAT YOU LOVE ME** *Columbia DB 4022*	**25**	2
31 Jan 58 ●	**YOU ARE MY DESTINY** *Columbia DB 4063*	**6**	13
30 May 58	**CRAZY LOVE** *Columbia DB 4110*	**26**	1
26 Sep 58	**MIDNIGHT** *Columbia DB 4172*	**26**	1
30 Jan 59 ●	**(ALL OF A SUDDEN) MY HEART SINGS** *Columbia DB 4241*	**10**	13
10 Jul 59	**LONELY BOY** *Columbia DB 4324* ▲	**3**	17
30 Oct 59 ●	**PUT YOUR HEAD ON MY SHOULDER** *Columbia DB 4355*	**7**	12
26 Feb 60	**IT'S TIME TO CRY (re)** *Columbia DB 4390*	**28**	2
31 Mar 60	**PUPPY LOVE (re)** *Columbia DB 4434*	**33**	7
15 Sep 60	**HELLO YOUNG LOVERS** *Columbia DB 4504*	**44**	1
15 Mar 62	**LOVE ME WARM AND TENDER** *RCA 1276*	**19**	11
26 Jul 62	**A STEEL GUITAR AND A GLASS OF WINE** *RCA 1292*	**41**	4
28 Sep 74 ●	**(YOU'RE) HAVING MY BABY** *United Artists UP 35713* [1] ▲	**6**	10

[1] Paul Anka featuring Odia Coates

Ana ANN *UK, female vocalist – Ana Petrovic (Singles: 3 Weeks)* pos/wks

23 Feb 02	**RIDE** *LL RIDELLR 100*	**24**	2
6 Mar 04	**CHILDREN OF THE WORLD** *Century Vista LLR 104* [1]	**44**	1

[1] Ana Ann and the London Community Choir

ANNIA See XTM & DJ CHUCKY presents ANNIA

ANNIE *Norway, female vocalist –*
Annie Lilia Berge Strand (Singles: 3 Weeks) pos/wks

25 Sep 04	**CHEWING GUM** *679 Recordings 679L 075CD1*	**25**	3

ANNIHILATOR
Canada, male vocal / instrumental group (Albums: 1 Week) pos/wks

11 Aug 90	**NEVER NEVERLAND** *Roadrunner RR 93741*	**48**	1

ANOTHER LEVEL
UK, male vocal group (Singles: 81 Weeks, Albums: 40 Weeks) pos/wks

28 Feb 98 ●	**BE ALONE NO MORE** *Northwestside 74321551982*	**6**	9
18 Jul 98 ★	**FREAK ME** *Northwestside 74321582362* ■	**1**	12
7 Nov 98 ●	**GUESS I WAS A FOOL** *Northwestside 74321621202*	**5**	13
23 Jan 99 ●	**I WANT YOU FOR MYSELF** *Northwestside 743216446332* [1]	**2**	8
10 Apr 99	**BE ALONE NO MORE** *Northwestside 74321658472* [2]	**11**	9
12 Jun 99 ●	**FROM THE HEART (re)** *Northwestside 74321673012*	**6**	11
4 Sep 99 ●	**SUMMERTIME** *Northwestside 74321694672* [3]	**7**	7
13 Nov 99 ●	**BOMB DIGGY** *Northwestside 74321712212*	**6**	12
21 Nov 98 ●	**ANOTHER LEVEL** *Northwestside 74321582412*	**13**	25
25 Sep 99 ●	**NEXUS ...** *Northwestside 74321694572*	**7**	15

[1] Another Level / Ghostface Killah [2] Another Level featuring Jay-Z [3] Another Level featuring TQ

ANOTHERSIDE (see also HONEYZ)
UK, female duo – Alani Gibbon and Celena Cherry (Singles: 1 Week) pos/wks

5 Jul 03	**THIS IS YOUR NIGHT** *V2 / J-Did JAD 5023293*	**41**	1

ANOUCHKA See Terry HALL

Adam ANT (see also ADAM and the ANTS) *UK, male*
vocalist – Stuart Goddard (Singles: 69 Weeks, Albums: 39 Weeks) pos/wks

22 May 82 ★	**GOODY TWO SHOES** *CBS A 2367*	**1**	11
18 Sep 82 ●	**FRIEND OR FOE** *CBS A 2736*	**9**	8
27 Nov 82	**DESPERATE BUT NOT SERIOUS** *CBS A 2892*	**33**	7

29 Oct 83 ●	**PUSS 'N BOOTS** *CBS A 3614*	**5**	11
10 Dec 83	**STRIP** *CBS A 3589*	**41**	6
22 Sep 84	**APOLLO 9** *CBS A 4719*	**13**	8
13 Jul 85	**VIVE LE ROCK** *CBS A 6367*	**50**	4
17 Feb 90	**ROOM AT THE TOP** *MCA MCA 1387*	**13**	7
28 Apr 90	**CANT SET RULES ABOUT LOVE** *MCA MCA 1404*	**47**	2
11 Feb 95	**WONDERFUL** *EMI CDEMS 366*	**32**	3
3 Jun 95	**GOTTA BE A SIN** *EMI CDEMS 379*	**48**	2
23 Oct 82 ●	**FRIEND OR FOE** *CBS 25040*	**5**	12
19 Nov 83	**STRIP** *CBS 25705*	**20**	8
14 Sep 85	**VIVE LE ROCK** *CBS 26583*	**42**	3
24 Mar 90	**MANNERS AND PHYSIQUE** *MCA MCG 6068*	**19**	3
28 Aug 93 ●	**ANTMUSIC – THE VERY BEST OF ADAM ANT** *Arcade ARC 3100052*	**6**	11
15 Apr 95	**WONDERFUL** *EMI CDEMC 3687*	**24**	2

ANT & DEC *UK, male actors / TV presenters / vocal duo – Anthony McPartlin*
and Declan Donnelly (aka PJ & Duncan) (Singles: 92 Weeks) pos/wks

18 Dec 93	**TONIGHT I'M FREE** *Telstar CDSTAS 2706*	**62**	3
23 Apr 94	**WHY ME** *Telstar CDSTAS 2719*	**27**	4
23 Jul 94 ●	**LET'S GET READY TO RHUMBLE** *XSrhythm CDANT 1*	**9**	11
8 Oct 94 ●	**IF I GIVE YOU MY NUMBER** *XSrhythm CDANT 2*	**15**	7
3 Dec 94	**ETERNAL LOVE** *XSrhythm CDANT 3*	**12**	9
25 Feb 95	**OUR RADIO ROCKS** *XSrhythm CDANT 4*	**15**	5
29 Jul 95	**STUCK ON U** *XSrhythm CDANT 5*	**12**	5
14 Oct 95	**U KRAZY KATZ** *XSrhythm CDANT 6*	**15**	4
2 Dec 95	**PERFECT** *Telstar CDANT 7*	**16**	7
20 Mar 96	**STEPPING STONE** *Telstar CDANT 8*	**11**	5
24 Aug 96 ●	**BETTER WATCH OUT** *Telstar CDANT 9*	**10**	4
23 Nov 96	**WHEN I FALL IN LOVE** *Telstar CDANT 10*	**12**	8
15 Mar 97 ●	**SHOUT** *Telstar CDDEC 11*	**10**	5
10 May 97	**FALLING** *Telstar CDDEC 12*	**14**	4
8 Jun 02 ●	**WE'RE ON THE BALL** *Columbia 6727312*	**3**	11

All hits up to and including 20 Mar 96 credited to PJ & Duncan

ANTARCTICA
Australia, male producer – Steve Gibbs (Singles: 2 Weeks) pos/wks

29 Jan 00	**RETURN TO REALITY** *React CDREACT 173*	**53**	1
8 Jul 00	**ADRIFT (CAST YOUR MIND)** *React CDREACT 172*	**72**	1

Mark ANTHONI See FIRE ISLAND

Billie ANTHONY *UK, female vocalist –*
Philomena Brown, b. 1933, d. 1991 (Singles: 16 Weeks) pos/wks

15 Oct 54 ●	**THIS OLE HOUSE** *Columbia DB 3519*	**4**	16

This release was 'with Eric Jupp and his Orchestra'

Marc ANTHONY (see also Louie VEGA)
US, male vocalist – Marco Antonio Muniz (Singles: 3 Weeks) pos/wks

13 Nov 99	**I NEED TO KNOW** *Columbia 6683612*	**28**	3

Miki ANTHONY *UK, male vocalist (Singles: 7 Weeks)* pos/wks

3 Feb 73	**IF IT WASN'T FOR THE REASON THAT I LOVE YOU** *Bell 1275*	**27**	7

Ray ANTHONY & his ORCHESTRA
US, orchestra – leader Ray Antonini (Singles: 2 Weeks) pos/wks

4 Dec 53 ●	**DRAGNET (re)** *Capitol CL 13983*	**7**	2

Richard ANTHONY
France, male vocalist – Richard Anthony Bush (Singles: 15 Weeks) pos/wks

12 Dec 63	**WALKING ALONE** *Columbia DB 7133*	**37**	5
2 Apr 64	**IF I LOVED YOU (re)** *Columbia DB 7235*	**18**	10

ANTHRAX *US, male vocal / instrumental*
group (Singles: 37 Weeks, Albums: 23 Weeks) pos/wks

28 Feb 87	**I AM THE LAW** *Island IS LAW 1*	**32**	5
27 Jun 87	**INDIANS** *Island IS 325*	**44**	4
5 Dec 87	**I'M THE MAN** *Island IS 338*	**20**	6
10 Sep 88	**MAKE ME LAUGH** *Island IS 379*	**26**	3
18 Mar 89	**ANTI-SOCIAL** *Island IS 409*	**44**	3
1 Sep 90	**IN MY WORLD** *Island IS 470*	**29**	2
5 Jan 91	**GOT THE TIME** *Island IS 476*	**16**	4
6 Jul 91	**BRING THE NOISE** *Island IS 490* [1]	**14**	5

8 May 93	**ONLY** Elektra EKR 166CD	**36**	3
11 Sep 93	**BLACK LODGE** Elektra EKR 171CD	**53**	2
18 Apr 87	**AMONG THE LIVING** Island ILPS 9865	**18**	5
24 Sep 88	**STATE OF EUPHORIA** Island ILPS 9916	**12**	4
8 Sep 90	**PERSISTENCE OF TIME** Island ILPS 9967	**13**	5
20 Jul 91	**ATTACK OF THE KILLER B'S** Island ILPS 9980	**13**	5
29 May 93	**SOUND OF WHITE NOISE** Elektra 7559614302	**14**	3
1 Aug 98	**VOLUME 8 – THE THREAT IS REAL!** Ignition IGN 740343	**73**	1

1 Anthrax featuring Chuck D

ANTI-NOWHERE LEAGUE UK, male vocal /
instrumental group (Singles: 10 Weeks, Albums: 12 Weeks) pos/wks

23 Jan 82	**STREETS OF LONDON** WXYZ ABCD 1	**48**	5
20 Mar 82	**I HATE ... PEOPLE** WXYZ ABCD 2	**46**	3
3 Jul 82	**WOMAN** WXYZ ABCD 4	**72**	2
22 May 82	**WE ARE ... THE LEAGUE** WXYZ LMNOP 1	**24**	11
5 Nov 83	**LIVE IN YUGOSLAVIA** I.D. NOSE 3	**88**	1

ANTI-PASTI (see also EXPLOITED)
UK, male vocal / instrumental group (Albums: 7 Weeks) pos/wks

15 Aug 81	**THE LAST CALL** Rondelet ABOUT 5	**31**	7

ANTICAPPELLA Italy / UK, male / female
vocal / instrumental group (Singles: 12 Weeks) pos/wks

16 Nov 91	**THE SQUARE ROOT OF 231** PWL Continental PWL 205	**24**	4
18 Apr 92	**EVERY DAY** PWL Continental PWL 220	**45**	2
25 Jun 94	**MOVE YOUR BODY** Media MCSTD 1980 1	**21**	3
1 Apr 95	**EXPRESS YOUR FREEDOM** Media MCSTD 2048	**31**	2
25 May 96	**THE SQUARE ROOT OF 231 / MOVE YOUR BODY (re-mix)** Media MCSTD 40037	**54**	1

1 Anticappella featuring MC Fixx It

ANTONIA See BOMB THE BASS

ANTS See ADAM and the ANTS

ANUNA See Bill WHELAN

APACHE INDIAN UK, male vocalist – Steven
Kapur (Singles: 33 Weeks, Albums: 2 Weeks) pos/wks

28 Nov 92	**FE' REAL** Ten TEN 416 1	**33**	3
2 Jan 93	**ARRANGED MARRIAGE** Island CID 544	**16**	6
27 Mar 93	**CHOK THERE** Island CID 555	**30**	4
14 Aug 93 ●	**NUFF VIBES (EP)** Island CID 560	**5**	10
23 Oct 93	**MOVIN' ON** Island CID 580	**48**	2
7 May 94	**WRECKX SHOP** MCA MCSTD 1969 2	**26**	2
11 Feb 95	**MAKE WAY FOR THE INDIAN** Island CID 586 3	**29**	2
22 Apr 95	**RAGGAMUFFIN GIRL** Island CID 606 4	**31**	2
29 Mar 97	**LOVIN' (LET ME LOVE YOU)** Coalition COLA 002CD	**53**	1
18 Oct 97	**REAL PEOPLE** Coalition COLA 019CD	**66**	1
6 Feb 93	**NO RESERVATIONS** Island CID 8001	**36**	2

1 Maxi Priest featuring Apache Indian 2 Wreckx-N-Effect featuring Apache Indian 3 Apache Indian and Tim Dog 4 Apache Indian with Frankie Paul

The listed flip side of 'Fe' Real' was 'Just Wanna Know' by Maxi Priest. Tracks on Nuff Vibes (EP): Boom Shack a Lak / Fun / Caste System / Warning

APHEX TWIN (see also POLYGON WINDOW; AFX)
UK, male instrumentalist / producer –
Richard James (Singles: 12 Weeks, Albums: 11 Weeks) pos/wks

9 May 92	**DIGERIDOO** R&S RSUK 12	**55**	2
27 Nov 93	**ON** Warp WAP 39CD	**32**	3
8 Apr 95	**VENTOLIN** Warp WAP 60CD	**49**	1
26 Oct 96	**GIRL / BOY (EP)** Warp WAP 78CD	**64**	1
18 Oct 97	**COME TO DADDY** Warp WAP 94CD	**36**	2
3 Apr 99	**WINDOWLICKER** Warp WAP 105CD	**16**	3
19 Mar 94	**SELECTED AMBIENT WORKS VOLUME II** Warp WARPCD 21 ..	**11**	2
11 Feb 95	**CLASSICS** R&S RS 94035CD	**24**	2
6 May 95	**... I CARE BECAUSE YOU DO** Warp WARPCD 30	**24**	1
16 Nov 96	**RICHARD D JAMES ALBUM** Warp WARPCD 43	**62**	1
3 Nov 01	**DRUKQS** Warp WARPCD 2	**22**	2
5 Apr 03	**26 MIXES FOR CASH** Warp WARPCD 102	**63**	1

Tracks on Girl / Boy (EP): Girl / Boy Song / Milkman / Inkey $ / Beatles Under My Carpet. The EP was incorrectly listed in the chart and, because of its length, should have been considered an album

APHRODITE featuring WILDFLOWER
UK, male producer and female rapper / vocalist (Singles: 1 Week) pos/wks

16 Nov 02	**SEE THRU IT** V2 VVR 5020983	**68**	1

APHRODITE'S CHILD Greece, male vocal / instrumental
group – includes Demis Roussos and Vangelis (Singles: 7 Weeks) pos/wks

6 Nov 68	**RAIN AND TEARS** Mercury MF 1039	**29**	7

APOLLO presents HOUSE OF VIRGINISM
Sweden, male instrumentalist and male
vocal / instrumental group (Singles: 1 Week) pos/wks

17 Feb 96	**EXCLUSIVE** Logic 74321324102	**67**	1

APOLLO FOUR FORTY UK, male instrumental /
production group (Singles: 53 Weeks, Albums: SSXCD 2) pos/wks

22 Jan 94	**ASTRAL AMERICA** Stealth Sonic SSXCD 2 1	**36**	2
5 Nov 94	**LIQUID COOL** Stealth Sonic SSXCD 3 1	**35**	2
25 Mar 95	**(DON'T FEAR) THE REAPER** Stealth Sonic SSXCD 4 1	**35**	2
27 Jul 96	**KRUPA (re)** Stealth Sonic SSXCD 5	**23**	8
15 Feb 97 ●	**AIN'T TALKIN' 'BOUT DUB** Stealth Sonic SSXCDX 6 ●	**7**	7
5 Jul 97	**RAW POWER** Stealth Sonic SSXCD 7	**32**	3
11 Jul 98	**RENDEZ-VOUS '98** Epic 6661102 2	**12**	6
8 Aug 98 ●	**LOST IN SPACE** Stealth Sonic SSX 9CD	**4**	9
28 Aug 99 ●	**STOP THE ROCK** Epic SSX 10CD	**10**	6
27 Nov 99	**HEART GO BOOM** Epic SSX 11CD	**57**	1
9 Dec 00	**CHARLIE'S ANGELS 2000** Epic SSX 13CD	**29**	6
21 Jun 03	**DUDE DESCENDING A STAIRCASE** Stealth / SONY SSX 14CD 3	**58**	1
15 Mar 97	**ELECTRO GLIDE IN BLUE** Stealth Sonic SSX 2440CD	**62**	1
18 Sep 99	**GETTIN' HIGH ON YOUR OWN SUPPLY** Epic SSX 3440CD	**20**	3

1 Apollo 440 2 Jean-Michel Jarre and Apollo 440 3 Apollo 440 featuring The Beatnuts

APOLLO 2000 UK, male instrumentalist /
producer – Gordon Smith (Albums: 3 Weeks) pos/wks

27 Apr 96	**OUT OF THIS WORLD** Telstar TCD 2816	**43**	3

Carmine APPICE See Jeff BECK and Tim BOGERT

Fiona APPLE US, female vocalist – Fiona
Apple Maggart (Singles: 2 Weeks, Albums: 1 Week) pos/wks

26 Feb 00	**FAST AS YOU CAN** Columbia 6689962	**33**	2
11 Mar 00	**WHEN THE PAWN HITS THE CONFLICTS HE THINKS LIKE A KING WHAT HE KNOWS THROWS THE BLOWS WHEN HE GOES TO THE FIGHT AND HE'LL WIN THE WHOLE THING 'FORE HE ENTERS THE RING THERE'S NOBODY TO BATTER WHEN YOUR MIND IS YOUR MIGHT SO WHEN YOU GO SOLO, YOU HOLD YOUR OWN HAND AND REMEMBER THAT DEPTH IS THE GREATEST OF HEIGHTS AND IF YOU KNOW WHERE YOU STAND, THEN YOU KNOW WHERE TO LAND AND IF YOU FALL IT WON'T MATTER, CUZ YOU'LL KNOW THAT YOU'RE RIGHT** Columbia 4964282	**46**	1

Kim APPLEBY (see also MEL and KIM)
UK, female vocalist (Singles: 31 Weeks, Albums: 13 Weeks) pos/wks

3 Nov 90 ●	**DON'T WORRY** Parlophone R 6272	**2**	10
9 Feb 91 ●	**G.L.A.D.** Parlophone R 6281	**10**	6
29 Jun 91	**MAMA** Parlophone R 6291	**19**	8
19 Oct 91	**IF YOU CARED** Parlophone R 6297	**44**	3
31 Jul 93	**LIGHT OF THE WORLD** Parlophone CDR 6352	**41**	2
13 Nov 93	**BREAKAWAY** Parlophone CDR 6362	**56**	1
12 Nov 94	**FREE SPIRIT** Parlophone CDR 6397	**51**	1
8 Dec 90	**KIM APPLEBY** Parlophone PCS 7348	**23**	13

The APPLEJACKS
UK, male / female vocal / instrumental group (Singles: 29 Weeks) pos/wks

5 Mar 64 ●	**TELL ME WHEN** Decca F 11833	**7**	13
11 Jun 64	**LIKE DREAMERS DO** Decca F 11916	**20**	11
15 Oct 64	**THREE LITTLE WORDS (I LOVE YOU)** Decca F 11981	**23**	5

APPLES UK, male vocal / instrumental group (Singles: 1 Week) pos/wks

23 Mar 91	**EYE WONDER** Epic 6566717	**75**	1

APPLETON (see also ALL SAINTS) Canada, female vocal duo – Nicole and Natalie Appleton (Singles: 22 Weeks, Albums: 6 Weeks)

		pos/wks
14 Sep 02 ●	FANTASY Polydor 5709842	2 10
22 Feb 03 ●	DON'T WORRY Polydor 0658182	5 10
26 Jul 03	EVERYTHING EVENTUALLY Polydor 9808278	38 2
8 Mar 03 ●	EVERYTHING'S EVENTUAL Polydor 0651992	9 6

Charlie APPLEWHITE
US, male vocalist, b. 1933, d. 27 Apr 2001 (Singles: 1 Week)

		pos/wks
23 Sep 55	BLUE STAR Brunswick 05416	20 1

'With Victor Young his Orchestra and Chorus'

Helen APRIL See John DUMMER and Helen APRIL

APRIL WINE Canada, male vocal / instrumental group (Singles: 9 Weeks, Albums: 8 Weeks)

		pos/wks
15 Mar 80	I LIKE TO ROCK Capitol CL 16121	41 5
11 Apr 81	JUST BETWEEN YOU AND ME Capitol CL 16184	52 4
15 Mar 80	HARDER ... FASTER Capitol EST 12013	34 5
24 Jan 81	THE NATURE OF THE BEAST Capitol EST 12125	48 3

AQUA Denmark / Norway, male / female vocal / production group (Singles: 85 Weeks, Albums: 49 Weeks)

		pos/wks
25 Oct 97 ★	BARBIE GIRL (re) Universal UMD 80413 ◆	1 26
7 Feb 98 ★	DOCTOR JONES Universal UMD 80457 ■	1 14
16 May 98 ★	TURN BACK TIME Universal UMD 80490 ■	1 10
1 Aug 98 ●	MY OH MY (re) Universal UMD 85058	6 11
26 Dec 98	GOOD MORNING SUNSHINE Universal UMD 85086	18 7
26 Feb 00 ●	CARTOON HEROES (re) Universal MCSTD 40226	7 11
10 Jun 00	AROUND THE WORLD Universal MCSTD 40234	26 6
15 Nov 97 ●	AQUARIUM Universal UMD 85020	6 47
11 Mar 00	AQUARIUS Universal 1538102	24 2

AQUA MARINA See FAB

AQUAGEN Germany, male production duo – Olaf Dieckman and Gino Montesano (Singles: 11 Weeks)

		pos/wks
9 Dec 00 ●	PHATT BASS Nulife / Arista 74321817102 [1]	9 8
1 Mar 03	HARD TO SAY I'M SORRY All Around the World CDGLOBE 265	33 3

[1] Warp Brothers vs Aquagen

AQUALUNG UK, male vocalist / instrumentalist / producer – Matt Hales (Singles: 10 Weeks, Albums: 6 Weeks)

		pos/wks
28 Sep 02 ●	STRANGE AND BEAUTIFUL (I'LL PUT A SPELL ON YOU) B Unique BUN 032CDS	7 6
14 Dec 02	GOOD TIMES GONNA COME B Unique BUN 043CDS	71 1
25 Oct 03	BRIGHTER THAN SUNSHINE B Unique BUN 072CDS	37 2
27 Mar 04	EASIER TO LIE B Unique WEA 373CD	60 1
12 Oct 02	AQUALUNG B Unique 5046606982	15 6

AQUANUTS
US / Argentina, male production / instrumental duo (Singles: 1 Week)

		pos/wks
4 May 02	DEEP SEA Data DATA 34T	74 1

AQUARIAN DREAM
US, male / female vocal / instrumental group (Singles: 1 Week)

		pos/wks
24 Feb 79	YOU'RE A STAR Elektra LV 7	67 1

ARAB STRAP UK, male vocal / instrumental duo – Aiden Moffat and Malcolm Middleton (Singles: 4 Weeks, Albums: 2 Weeks)

		pos/wks
13 Sep 97	THE GIRLS OF SUMMER (EP) Chemikal Underground CHEM 017CD	74 1
4 Apr 98	HERE WE GO / TRIPPY Chemikal Underground CHEM 20CD	48 1
10 Oct 98	(AFTERNOON) SOAPS Chemikal Underground CHEM 27CD	74 1
10 Feb 01	LOVE DETECTIVE Chemikal Underground CHEM 049CD	66 1
2 May 98	PHILOPHOBIA Chemikal Underground CHEM 21CD	37 2

Tracks on The Girls of Summer (EP): Hey! Fever / Girls of Summer / The Beautiful Barmaids of Dundee / One Day After School

ARCADIA (see also DURAN DURAN) UK, male vocal / instrumental group (Singles: 13 Weeks, Albums: 10 Weeks)

		pos/wks
26 Oct 85 ●	ELECTION DAY Odeon NSR 1	7 7
25 Jan 86	THE PROMISE Odeon NSR 2	37 4
26 Jul 86	THE FLAME Odeon NSR 3	58 2
7 Dec 85	SO RED THE ROSE Parlophone Odeon PCSD 101	30 10

Arcadia was Duran Duran sideline band featuring Simon Le Bon, Nick Rhodes and Roger Taylor

Tasmin ARCHER
UK, female vocalist (Singles: 37 Weeks, Albums: 42 Weeks)

		pos/wks
12 Sep 92 ★	SLEEPING SATELLITE (re) EMI EM 233	1 17
20 Feb 93	IN YOUR CARE EMI CDEMS 260	16 6
29 May 93	LORDS OF THE NEW CHURCH EMI CDEM 266	26 4
21 Aug 93	ARIENNE EMI CDEM 275	30 4
8 Jan 94	SHIPBUILDING EMI CDEM 302	40 4
23 Mar 96	ONE MORE GOOD NIGHT WITH THE BOYS EMI CDEM 401	45 2
31 Oct 92 ●	GREAT EXPECTATIONS EMI CDEMC 3624	8 42

The ARCHIES (see also The CUFFLINKS) US, male / female cartoon vocal group – lead vocal Ron Dante (Singles: 26 Weeks)

		pos/wks
11 Oct 69 ★	SUGAR, SUGAR RCA 1872 ▲	1 26

ARCHITECHS
UK, male production duo and female vocalist (Singles: 19 Weeks)

		pos/wks
7 Oct 00 ●	BODY GROOVE Go Beat / Polydor GOBCD33 [1]	3 14
7 Apr 01	SHOW ME THE MONEY (re) Go Beat GOBCD 38	20 5

[1] Architechs featuring Nana

Jann ARDEN
Canada, female vocalist – Jann Arden Richards (Singles: 2 Weeks)

		pos/wks
13 Jul 96	INSENSITIVE A&M 5812652	40 2

Tina ARENA Australia, female vocalist – Philopina Arena (Singles: 33 Weeks, Albums: 15 Weeks)

		pos/wks
15 Apr 95 ●	CHAINS Columbia 6611255	6 11
12 Aug 95	HEAVEN HELP MY HEART Columbia 6620975	25 5
2 Dec 95	SHOW ME HEAVEN Columbia 6626975	29 3
3 Aug 96	SORRENTO MOON (I REMEMBER) Columbia 6635435	22 4
27 Jun 98	WHISTLE DOWN THE WIND Really Useful 5672192	24 5
24 Oct 98	IF I WAS A RIVER Columbia 6665605	43 2
13 Mar 99	BURN Columbia 6667442	47 1
20 May 00	LIVE FOR THE ONE I LOVE Columbia 6691332	63 1
12 Apr 03	NEVER (PAST TENSE) Illustrious CDILL 010 [1]	42 1
20 May 95	DON'T ASK Columbia 4778862	11 15

[1] ROC Project featuring Tina Arena

ARGENT
(see also SAN JOSÉ featuring RODRIGUEZ; SILSOE; The ZOMBIES) UK, male vocal / instrumental group (Singles: 27 Weeks, Albums: 9 Weeks)

		pos/wks
4 Mar 72 ●	HOLD YOUR HEAD UP Epic EPC 7786	5 12
10 Jun 72	TRAGEDY Epic EPC 8115	34 7
24 Mar 73	GOD GAVE ROCK AND ROLL TO YOU Epic EPC 1243	18 8
29 Apr 72	ALL TOGETHER NOW Epic EPC 64962	13 8
31 Mar 73	IN DEEP Epic EPC 65475	49 1

india.arie US, female vocalist – India.Arie Simpson (Singles: 6 Weeks, Albums: 3 Weeks)

		pos/wks
30 Jun 01	VIDEO Motown TMGCD 1505	32 3
20 Oct 01	BROWN SKIN Motown TMGCD 1507	29 2
12 Apr 03	LITTLE THINGS Motown TMGCD 1509	62 1
7 Jul 01	ACOUSTIC SOUL Motown 137702	55 3

ARIEL UK, male production group (Singles: 2 Weeks)

		pos/wks
27 Mar 93	LET IT SLIDE Deconstruction 74321134512	57 2

ARIEL
Argentina, male DJ / producer – Ariel Belloso (Singles: 4 Weeks)

		pos/wks
21 Jun 97	DEEP (I'M FALLING DEEPER) Wonderboy WBOYD 005	47 1
17 Jun 00	A9 Essential Recordings ESCD 15	28 3

ARIZONA featuring ZEITIA UK, male production / instrumental duo and female vocalist (Singles: 1 Week)

		pos/wks
12 Mar 94	I SPECIALIZE IN LOVE Union City UCRCD 27	74 1

Ship's Company and Royal Marine Band of HMS ARK ROYAL
UK, male choir and marine band (Singles: 6 Weeks) pos/wks

23 Dec 78	THE LAST FAREWELL *BBC RESL 61*	46	6

ARKARNA
UK, male vocal / instrumental / production group (Singles: 3 Weeks) pos/wks

25 Jan 97	HOUSE ON FIRE *WEA WEA 088CD1*	33	2
2 Aug 97	SO LITTLE TIME *WEA WEA 108CD1*	46	1

Joan ARMATRADING `258` `Top 500`
Highly acclaimed singer-songwriter / instrumentalist – guitar, b. 9 Dec 1950, St. Kitts, West Indies. Raised in Birmingham, UK, her debut album was issued in 1972. Twice nominated at both Brit and Grammy Awards, and won an Ivor Novello award in 1996 (Singles: 53 Weeks, Albums: 196 Weeks) pos/wks

16 Oct 76 ●	LOVE AND AFFECTION *A&M AMS 7249*	10	9
23 Feb 80	ROSIE *A&M AMS 7506*	49	5
14 Jun 80	ME MYSELF I *A&M AMS 7527*	21	11
6 Sep 80	ALL THE WAY FROM AMERICA *A&M AMS 7552*	54	3
12 Sep 81	I'M LUCKY *A&M AMS 8163*	46	5
16 Jan 82	NO LOVE *A&M AMS 8179*	50	5
19 Feb 83	DROP THE PILOT *A&M AMS 8306*	11	10
16 Mar 85	TEMPTATION *A&M AM 238*	65	2
26 May 90	MORE THAN ONE KIND OF LOVE *A&M AM 561*	75	1
23 May 92	WRAPPED AROUND HER *A&M AM 877*	56	2
4 Sep 76	JOAN ARMATRADING *A&M AMLH 64588*	12	27
1 Oct 77 ●	SHOW SOME EMOTION *A&M AMLH 68433*	6	11
14 Oct 78	TO THE LIMIT *A&M AMLH 64732*	13	10
24 May 80	ME MYSELF I *A&M AMLH 64809*	5	23
12 Sep 81 ●	WALK UNDER LADDERS *A&M AMLH 64876*	6	29
12 Mar 83 ●	THE KEY *A&M AMLX 64912*	10	14
26 Nov 83	TRACK RECORD *A&M JA 2001*	18	32
16 Feb 85	SECRET SECRETS *A&M AMA 5040*	14	12
24 May 86	SLEIGHT OF HAND *A&M AMA 5130*	34	6
16 Jul 88	THE SHOUTING STAGE *A&M AMA 5211*	28	10
16 Jun 90	HEARTS AND FLOWERS *A&M 3952981*	29	4
16 Mar 91 ●	THE VERY BEST OF JOAN ARMATRADING *A&M 3971221*	9	11
20 Jun 92	SQUARE THE CIRCLE *A&M 3953882*	34	2
10 Jun 95	WHAT'S INSIDE *RCA 74321272692*	48	2
4 Sep 04	LOVE AND AFFECTION: JOAN ARMATRADING CLASSICS (1975-1983) *Universal TV 9823506*	24	3

ARMIN See Armin VAN BUUREN

ARMOURY SHOW *UK, male vocal / instrumental group (Singles: 6 Weeks, Albums: 1 Week)* pos/wks

25 Aug 84	CASTLES IN SPAIN *Parlophone R 6079*	69	2
26 Jan 85	WE CAN BE BRAVE AGAIN *Parlophone R 6087*	66	1
17 Jan 87	LOVE IN ANGER *Parlophone R 6149*	63	3
21 Sep 85	WAITING FOR THE FLOODS *Parlophone ARM 1*	57	1

Craig ARMSTRONG
(see also Shola AMA) *UK, male musical director (Albums: 1 Week)* pos/wks

27 Apr 02	AS IF TO NOTHING *Melankolic CDSAD 13*	61	1

Louis ARMSTRONG
Best known jazz artist of the 20th century, b. 4 Aug 1901, New Orleans, US (not 4 Jul 1900 according to previous claims by the man himself), d. Jul 6 1971. This ground-breaking, trumpet-playing gravel-voiced vocalist, known as 'Satchmo', is the oldest performer to top either the UK or US charts (Singles: 93 Weeks, Albums: 32 Weeks) pos/wks

19 Dec 52 ●	TAKES TWO TO TANGO *Brunswick 04995*	6	10
13 Apr 56 ●	A THEME FROM THE THREEPENNY OPERA (MACK THE KNIFE) *Philips PB 574* [1]	8	11
15 Jun 56	TAKE IT SATCH (EP) *Philips BBE 12035* [1]	29	1
13 Jul 56	THE FAITHFUL HUSSAR *Philips PB 604* [1]	27	2
6 Nov 59	MACK THE KNIFE (A THEME FROM THE THREEPENNY OPERA) *Philips PB 967* [1]	24	1
4 Jun 64 ●	HELLO, DOLLY! *London HLR 9878* [2] ▲	4	14
7 Feb 68 ★	WHAT A WONDERFUL WORLD / CABARET *HMV POP 1615* [3]	1	29
26 Jun 68	THE SUNSHINE OF LOVE *Stateside SS 2116*	41	7
16 Apr 88	WHAT A WONDERFUL WORLD (re-issue) *A&M AM 435* [3]	53	5
19 Nov 94 ●	WE HAVE ALL THE TIME IN THE WORLD (re) *EMI CDEM 357*	3	13
28 Jul 56 ●	AT THE CRESCENDO *Brunswick LAT 8084*	4	1
22 Oct 60	SATCHMO PLAYS KING OLIVER *Audio Fidelity AFLP 1930*	20	1
28 Oct 61	JAZZ CLASSICS *Ace of Hearts AH 7*	20	1
27 Jun 64	HELLO, DOLLY! *London HAR 8190* ▲	11	6
16 Nov 68	WHAT A WONDERFUL WORLD *Stateside SSL 10247*	37	3
20 Feb 82	THE VERY BEST OF LOUIS ARMSTRONG *Warwick WW 5112*	30	3
21 May 94	THE ULTIMATE COLLECTION *Bluebird 74321197062*	48	3
17 Dec 94 ●	WE HAVE ALL THE TIME IN THE WORLD – THE VERY BEST OF LOUIS ARMSTRONG *EMI CDEMTV 89*	10	12
25 Oct 03	AT HIS VERY BEST *UCJ 9812425*	75	1
18 Sep 04	ELLA AND LOUIS TOGETHER ... *UCJ 9867768* [1]	43	1

[1] Louis Armstrong and his All-Stars [2] Louis Armstrong and the All Stars
[3] Louis Armstrong Orchestra & Chorus [1] Ella Fitzgerald and Louis Armstrong

Take It Satch (EP) tracks: Tiger Rag / Mack the Knife / The Faithful Hussar / Back O'Town Blues. 'Mack the Knife' is a re-issue of 'Theme from the Threepenny Opera' under a different title. 'Cabaret' was not listed with 'What a Wonderful World' until 14 Feb 1968

ARMY OF LOVERS
Sweden / France, male / female vocal group (Singles: 12 Weeks) pos/wks

17 Aug 91	CRUCIFIED *Ton Son Ton WOK 2007*	47	5
28 Dec 91	OBSESSION *Ton Son Ton WOK 2009*	67	1
15 Feb 92	CRUCIFIED (re-issue) *Ton Son Ton WOK 2017*	31	5
18 Apr 92	RIDE THE BULLET *Ton Son Ton WOK 2018*	67	1

ARNEE and the TERMINATERS
UK, male vocal / instrumental group (Singles: 7 Weeks) pos/wks

24 Aug 91 ●	I'LL BE BACK *Epic 6574177*	5	7

ARNIE'S LOVE
US, male / female vocal / instrumental group (Singles: 3 Weeks) pos/wks

26 Nov 83	I'M OUT OF YOUR LIFE *Streetwave WAVE 9*	67	3

David ARNOLD (see also BJÖRK; David McALMONT; PROPELLERHEADS; Nina PERSSON) *UK, male composer (Albums: 10 Weeks)* pos/wks

17 Aug 96	INDEPENDENCE DAY (FILM SOUNDTRACK) *RCA Victor 9026685642*	71	1
1 Nov 97	SHAKEN AND STIRRED *East West 3984207382*	11	9

Eddy ARNOLD *US, male vocalist (Singles: 21 Weeks)* pos/wks

17 Feb 66 ●	MAKE THE WORLD GO AWAY *RCA 1496*	8	17
26 May 66	I WANT TO GO WITH YOU (re) *RCA 1519*	46	3
28 Jul 66	IF YOU WERE MINE MARY *RCA 1529*	49	1

PP ARNOLD
US, female vocalist – Patricia Arnold (Singles: 37 Weeks) pos/wks

4 May 67	THE FIRST CUT IS THE DEEPEST *Immediate IM 047*	18	10
2 Aug 67	THE TIME HAS COME *Immediate IM 055*	47	2
24 Jan 68	(IF YOU THINK YOU'RE) GROOVY *Immediate IM 061*	41	4
10 Jul 68	ANGEL OF THE MORNING *Immediate IM 067*	29	11
24 Sep 88	BURN IT UP *Rhythm King LEFT 27* [1]	14	10

[1] The Beatmasters with PP Arnold

ARPEGGIO *US, male / female vocal group (Singles: 3 Weeks)* pos/wks

31 Mar 79	LOVE AND DESIRE (PART 1) *Polydor POSP 40*	63	3

ARRESTED DEVELOPMENT *US, male / female vocal / instrumental / rap group (Singles: 39 Weeks, Albums: 40 Weeks)* pos/wks

16 May 92	TENNESSEE (re) *Cooltempo COOL 253*	46	7
24 Oct 92 ●	PEOPLE EVERYDAY *Cooltempo COOL 265*	2	14
9 Jan 93 ●	MR WENDAL / REVOLUTION *Cooltempo CDCOOL 268*	4	9
3 Apr 93	TENNESSEE (re-issue) *Cooltempo CDCOOL 270*	18	6
28 May 94	EASE MY MIND *Cooltempo COOL 293*	33	3
31 Oct 92 ●	3 YEARS 5 MONTHS AND 2 DAYS IN THE LIFE OF ... *Cooltempo CCD 1929*	3	34
10 Apr 93	UNPLUGGED *Cooltempo CTCD 33*	40	3
18 Jun 94	ZINGALAMDUNI *Cooltempo CTCD 42*	16	3

Steve ARRINGTON
US, male vocalist (Singles: 19 Weeks, Albums: 11 Weeks) pos/wks

27 Apr 85 ●	FEEL SO REAL *Atlantic A 9576*	5	10
6 Jul 85	DANCIN' IN THE KEY OF LIFE (re) *Atlantic A 9534*	21	9
13 Apr 85	DANCIN' IN THE KEY OF LIFE *Atlantic 781245*	41	11

ARRIVAL
UK, male / female vocal / instrumental group (Singles: 20 Weeks)   pos/wks

10 Jan 70 ●	FRIENDS *Decca F 12986*	......8 9
6 Jun 70 ●	I WILL SURVIVE *Decca F 13026*	.....16 11

ARROLA See RUFF DRIVERZ

ARROW
Montserrat, male vocalist – Alphonsus Cassell (Singles: 15 Weeks)   pos/wks

28 Jul 84	HOT HOT HOT *Cooltempo ARROW 1*	.....59 5
13 Jul 85	LONG TIME *London LON 70*	.....30 7
3 Sep 94	HOT HOT HOT (re-mix) *The Hit Label HLC 7*	.....38 3

The ARROWS
US / UK, male vocal / instrumental trio (Singles: 16 Weeks)   pos/wks

25 May 74 ●	A TOUCH TOO MUCH *RAK 171*	......8 9
1 Feb 75	MY LAST NIGHT WITH YOU *RAK 189*	.....25 7

ARSENAL FC
UK, male football team vocal group (Singles: 16 Weeks)   pos/wks

8 May 71	GOOD OLD ARSENAL *Pye 7N 45067* [1]	.....16 7
15 May 93	SHOUTING FOR THE GUNNERS *London LONCD 342* [2]	....34 3
23 May 98 ●	HOT STUFF *Grapevine AFCCD 1*	......9 5
3 Jun 00	ARSENAL NUMBER ONE / OUR GOAL *Grapevine CDGPS 280*	..46 1

[1] Arsenal FC First Team Squad [2] Arsenal FA Cup Squad featuring Tippa Irie and Peter Hunnigale

ART BRUT
UK, male vocal / instrumental group (Singles: 2 Weeks)   pos/wks

10 Apr 04	FORMED A BAND *Rough Trade RTRADSCD 174*	.....52 1
18 Dec 04	MODERN ART / MY LITTLE BROTHER *Fierce Panda NING 164CD*	.....49 1

ART COMPANY
Holland, male vocal / instrumental group (Singles: 11 Weeks)   pos/wks

26 May 84	SUSANNA *Epic A 4174*	.....12 11

ART OF NOISE
UK, male / female instrumental / production trio (Singles: 65 Weeks, Albums: 37 Weeks)   pos/wks

24 Nov 84 ●	CLOSE (TO THE EDIT) *ZTT ZTPS 01*	......8 19
13 Apr 85	MOMENTS IN LOVE / BEAT BOX *ZTT ZTPS 02*	.....51 4
9 Nov 85	LEGS *China WOK 5*	.....69 1
22 Mar 86 ●	PETER GUNN (re-recording) *China WOK 6* [1]	......8 9
21 Jun 86	PARANOIMIA *China WOK 9* [2]	.....12 9
18 Jul 87	DRAGNET *China WOK 14*	.....60 4
29 Oct 88 ●	KISS *China CHINA 11* [3]	......5 7
12 Aug 89	YEBO *China CHINA 18* [4]	.....63 3
16 Jun 90	ART OF LOVE *China CHINA 23*	.....67 1
11 Jan 92	INSTRUMENTS OF DARKNESS (ALL OF US ARE ONE PEOPLE) *China WOK 2012*	.....45 5
29 Feb 92	SHADES OF PARANOIMIA *China WOK 2014*	.....53 1
26 Jun 99	METAFORCE *ZTT ZTT 129CD*	.....53 1
3 Nov 84	(WHO'S AFRAID OF?) THE ART OF NOISE! *ZTT ZTTIQ 2*	....27 14
26 Apr 86	IN VISIBLE SILENCE *Chrysalis WOL 2*	.....18 15
10 Oct 87	IN NO SENSE/NONSENSE *China WOL 4*	.....55 2
3 Dec 88	THE BEST OF THE ART OF NOISE *China 837 367 1*	.....55 3

[1] Art of Noise featuring Duane Eddy [2] Art of Noise featuring Max Headroom [3] Art of Noise featuring Tom Jones [4] Art of Noise featuring Mahlathini and the Mahotella Queens

Act was a male / female instrumental group for first two albums

ART OF TRANCE
UK, male instrumentalist / producer – Simon Berry (Singles: 6 Weeks)   pos/wks

31 Oct 98	MADAGASCAR *Platipus PLAT 43CD*	.....69 1
7 Aug 99	MADAGASCAR (re-mix) *Platipus PLAT 58CD*	.....48 2
15 Jun 02	MADAGASCAR (2nd re-mix) *Platipus PLATCD 102*	.....41 2
10 Aug 02	LOVE WASHES OVER *Platipus PLATCD 98*	.....60 1

ARTEMESIA (see also ETHICS; MOVIN' MELODIES; SUBLIMINAL CUTS)
Holland, male producer – Patrick Prinz (Singles: 4 Weeks)   pos/wks

15 Apr 95	BITS + PIECES (re) *Hooj Choons HOOJ 31CD*	.....46 3
12 Aug 00	BITS AND PIECES (re-mix) *Tidy Trax TIDT 141CD*	.....51 1

ARTFUL DODGER
UK, male production / instrumental duo – Mark Hill and Peter Devereux (Singles: 71 Weeks, Albums: 27 Weeks)   pos/wks

11 Dec 99 ●	RE-REWIND THE CROWD SAY BO SELECTA *Public Demand / Relentless RELENT 1CDS* [1]	.....2 17
4 Mar 00 ●	MOVIN TOO FAST (re) *Locked On XLLOX 117CD* [2]	.....2 12
15 Jul 00 ●	WOMAN TROUBLE *Public Demand / ffrr FCD 380* [3]	.....6 10
25 Nov 00 ●	PLEASE DON'T TURN ME ON *Public Demand / ffrr FCD 388* [4]	.....4 10
17 Mar 01	THINK ABOUT ME *ffrr FCD 394* [5]	.....11 8
15 Sep 01 ●	TWENTYFOURSEVEN *ffrr / Public Demand FCD 400* [6]	.....6 9
15 Dec 01	IT AIN'T ENOUGH *ffrr / Public Demand FCD 401* [7]	.....20 5
2 Dec 00	IT'S ALL ABOUT THE STRAGGLERS *ffrr 8573859092*	.....18 27

[1] Artful Dodger featuring Craig David [2] Artful Dodger and Romina Johnson [3] Artful Dodger and Robbie Craig featuring Craig David [4] Artful Dodger featuring Lifford [5] Artful Dodger featuring Michelle Escoffery [6] Artful Dodger featuring Melanie Blatt [7] Dreem Teem vs Artful Dodger featuring MZ May and MC Alistair

Davey ARTHUR See The FUREYS with Davey ARTHUR

Neil ARTHUR (see also BLANCMANGE)
UK, male vocalist (Singles: 2 Weeks)   pos/wks

5 Feb 94	I LOVE I HATE *Chrysalis CDCHSS 5005*	.....50 2

ARTIFICIAL FUNK featuring Nellie ETTISON
Denmark, male producer – Rune Kolsch and female vocalist (Singles: 1 Week)   pos/wks

22 Mar 03	TOGETHER *Skint SKINT 82CD*	.....40 1

ARTIFICIAL INTELLIGENCE
UK, production duo (Singles: 1 Week)   pos/wks

21 Aug 04	UPRISING / THROUGH THE GATE *V Recordings VRECS 001UK*	..73 1

ARTIST See PRINCE

ARTISTS AGAINST AIDS WORLDWIDE
US / Ireland, all-star male / female vocal ensemble (Singles: 12 Weeks)   pos/wks

17 Nov 01 ●	WHAT'S GOING ON *Columbia 6721172*	.....6 12

ARTISTS UNITED AGAINST APARTHEID
International, male / female vocal / instrumental charity assembly (Singles: 8 Weeks)   pos/wks

23 Nov 85	SUN CITY *Manhattan MT 7*	.....21 8

ASCENSION (see also CHAKRA; ESSENCE; LUSTRAL; SPACE BROTHERS; OXYGEN featuring Andrea BRITTON)
UK, male production duo – Ricky Simmons and Steve Jones (Singles: 4 Weeks)   pos/wks

5 Jul 97	SOMEONE *Perfecto PERF 141CD*	.....55 1
15 Jul 00	SOMEONE (re-mix) *Code Blue BLU 011CD1*	.....43 2
23 Mar 02	FOR A LIFETIME *Xtravaganza XTRAV 20CDS* [1]	.....45 1

[1] Ascension featuring Erin Lordan

ASH (see also Charlotte HATHERLEY)
Premier pop-punk trio from Northern Island formed in 1992 and fronted by Tim Wheeler, b. 4 Jan 1977, Downpatrick. The chart-topping album act became a quartet when they added London born female vocalist Charlotte Hatherley (Singles: 69 Weeks, Albums: 73 Weeks)   pos/wks

1 Apr 95	KUNG FU *Infectious INFECT 21CD*	.....57 1
12 Aug 95	GIRL FROM MARS *Infectious INFECT 24CD*	.....11 5
21 Oct 95	ANGEL INTERCEPTOR *Infectious INFECT 27CD*	.....14 4
27 Apr 96 ●	GOLDFINGER *Infectious INFECT 39CD*	.....5 5
6 Jul 96 ●	OH YEAH (re) *Infectious INFECT 41CD*	.....6 8
25 Oct 97 ●	A LIFE LESS ORDINARY *Infectious INFECT 50CD*	.....10 5
3 Oct 98	JESUS SAYS *Infectious INFECT 59CD*	.....15 4
5 Dec 98	WILD SURF *Infectious INFECT 61CDS*	.....31 2
10 Feb 01 ●	SHINING LIGHT *Infectious INFECT 98CD*	.....8 4
14 Apr 01	BURN BABY BURN *Infectious INFECT 99CDS*	.....13 6
21 Jul 01	SOMETIMES *Infectious INFECT 101CDS*	.....21 6
13 Oct 01	CANDY *Infectious INFECT 106CDS*	.....20 3
12 Jan 02	THERE'S A STAR *Infectious INFECT 112CDS*	.....13 3
7 Sep 02	ENVY *Infectious INFECT 119CDS*	.....21 2
15 May 04	ORPHEUS *Infectious ASH 01CD*	.....13 4
31 Jul 04	STARCROSSED *Infectious ASH 02CD*	.....22 4
18 Dec 04	RENEGADE CAVALCADE *Infectious ASH 03CD*	.....33 2+
18 May 96 ★	1977 *Infectious INFECT 40CD* ■	.....1 27
17 Oct 98 ●	NU-CLEAR SOUNDS *Infectious INFECT 60CD*	.....7 4

		pos/wks
5 May 01 ★	**FREE ALL ANGELS** *Infectious INFECT 100CD* ■	**1** 28
21 Sep 02 ●	**INTERGALACTIC SONIC 7'S – SINGLES COLLECTION**	
	1994-2002 *Infectious INFEC 120CDB*	**3** 6
29 May 04 ●	**MELTDOWN** *Infectious 5046732462*	**5** 8

Act was a male trio before 1997 hit

ASHA *Italy, female vocalist (Singles: 2 Weeks)*

		pos/wks
8 Jul 95	**JJ TRIBUTE** *Ffrreedom TABCD 228*	**38** 2

ASHANTI *US, female vocalist – Ashanti*
Douglas (Singles: 82 Weeks, Albums: 44 Weeks)

		pos/wks
2 Feb 02 ●	**ALWAYS ON TIME** *Def Jam 5889462* [1] ▲	**6** 13
25 May 02 ●	**WHAT'S LUV?** *Atlantic AT 0128CD* [2]	**4** 8
8 Jun 02	**FOOLISH (IMPORT) (re)** *Mercury 5829362*	**68** 3
20 Jul 02 ●	**FOOLISH** *Murder Inc / Mercury 0639942* ▲	**4** 10
12 Oct 02 ●	**DOWN 4 U (2re)** *Murder Inc 0639002* [3]	**4** 10
23 Nov 02	**HAPPY** *Murder Inc / Mercury 0638242*	**13** 8
29 Mar 03	**MESMERIZE** *Murder Inc / Mercury 0779582* [1]	**12** 8
28 Jun 03 ●	**ROCK WIT U (AWWW BABY)** *Murder Inc / Mercy 9808431* ▲	**7** 10
1 Nov 03	**RAIN ON ME** *Murder Inc / Mercury 9813176*	**19** 4
6 Nov 04 ★	**WONDERFUL** *Def Jam 9864605* [4] ■	**1** 8+
20 Apr 02 ●	**ASHANTI** *Mercury 5868302* ▲	**3** 36
12 Jul 03 ●	**CHAPTER II** *Murder Inc / Mercury 9808434* ▲	**5** 8

[1] Ja Rule featuring Ashanti [2] Fat Joe featuring Ashanti [3] Irv Gotti presents Ja Rule, Ashanti, Charli Baltimore and Vita [4] Ja Rule featuring R Kelly & Ashanti

ASHAYE *UK, male vocalist – Trevor Ashaye (Singles: 3 Weeks)*

		pos/wks
15 Oct 83	**MICHAEL JACKSON MEDLEY** *Record Shack SOHO 10*	**45** 3

Tracks on Michael Jackson medley: Don't Stop Til You Get Enough / Wanna Be Startin' Something / Shake Your Body Down to the Ground / Blame It on the Boogie

Richard ASHCROFT (see also The VERVE)
UK, male vocalist (Singles: 30 Weeks, Albums: 30 Weeks)

		pos/wks
15 Apr 00 ●	**A SONG FOR THE LOVERS (re)** *Hut / Virgin HUTCD 128*	**3** 11
24 Jun 00	**MONEY TO BURN** *Hut / Virgin HUTCD 136*	**17** 4
23 Sep 00	**C'MON PEOPLE (WE'RE MAKING IT NOW)**	
	Hut / Virgin HUTCD 138	**21** 3
19 Oct 02	**CHECK THE MEANING (re)** *Hut / Virgin HUTCD 161*	**11** 6
18 Jan 03	**SCIENCE OF SILENCE** *Hut / Virgin HUTCD 163*	**14** 4
19 Apr 03	**BUY IT IN BOTTLES** *Hut / Virgin HUTCD 167*	**26** 2
8 Jul 00 ★	**ALONE WITH EVERYBODY** *Hut CDHUTX 63* ■	**1** 20
2 Nov 02 ●	**HUMAN CONDITIONS** *Hut / Virgin CDHUT 77*	**3** 10

John ASHER *UK, male vocalist / TV presenter (Singles: 6 Weeks)* pos/wks

15 Nov 75	**LET'S TWIST AGAIN** *Creole CR 112*	**14** 6

ASHFORD and SIMPSON *US, male / female vocal duo – Nickolas*
Ashford and Valerie Simpson (Singles: 22 Weeks, Albums: 6 Weeks) pos/wks

18 Nov 78	**IT SEEMS TO HANG ON** *Warner Bros. K 17237*	**48** 4
5 Jan 85 ●	**SOLID** *Capitol CL 345*	**3** 15
20 Apr 85	**BABIES** *Capitol CL 355*	**56** 3
16 Feb 85	**SOLID** *Capitol SASH 1*	**42** 6

ASHTON, GARDNER AND DYKE
UK, male vocal / instrumental trio (Singles: 14 Weeks) pos/wks

16 Jan 71 ●	**THE RESURRECTION SHUFFLE** *Capitol CL 15665*	**3** 14

ASIA (see also Steve HOWE) *UK, male vocal /*
instrumental group (Singles: 13 Weeks, Albums: 50 Weeks) pos/wks

3 Jul 82	**HEAT OF THE MOMENT** *Geffen GEF A2494*	**46** 5
18 Sep 82	**ONLY TIME WILL TELL** *Geffen GEF A2228*	**54** 3
13 Aug 83	**DON'T CRY** *Geffen A 3580*	**33** 5
10 Apr 82	**ASIA** *Geffen GEF 85577* ▲	**11** 38
20 Aug 83 ●	**ALPHA** *Geffen GEF 25508*	**5** 11
14 Dec 85	**ASTRA** *Geffen GEF 26413*	**68** 1

ASIA BLUE *UK, female vocal group (Singles: 2 Weeks)* pos/wks

27 Jun 92	**ESCAPING** *Atomic WNR 882*	**50** 2

ASIAN DUB FOUNDATION *UK, male vocal /*
instrumental group (Singles: 8 Weeks, Albums: 6 Weeks) pos/wks

21 Feb 98	**FREE SATPAL RAM** *ffrr FCD 326*	**56** 1

		pos/wks
2 May 98	**BUZZIN'** *ffrr FCD 335*	**31** 2
4 Jul 98	**BLACK WHITE** *ffrr FCD 337*	**52** 1
18 Mar 00	**REAL GREAT BRITAIN** *ffrr FCD 376*	**41** 2
3 Jun 00	**NEW WAY, NEW LIFE** *ffrr FCD 378*	**49** 1
1 Feb 03	**FORTRESS EUROPE** *Virgin DINSDX 253*	**57** 1
23 May 98	**RAFI'S REVENGE** *ffrr 5560062*	**20** 3
1 Apr 00	**COMMUNITY MUSIC** *ffrr 8573820422*	**20** 3

ASSEMBLY (see also ERASURE; The UNDERTONES; YAZOO)
UK, male vocal / instrumental group – includes
Fergal Sharkey and Vince Clarke (Singles: 10 Weeks) pos/wks

12 Nov 83 ●	**NEVER NEVER** *Mute TINY 1*	**4** 10

ASSOCIATES
UK, male vocal / instrumental group – leader Billy MacKenzie, b. 27
Mar 1957, d. 22 Jan 1997 (Singles: 47 Weeks, Albums: 28 Weeks) pos/wks

20 Feb 82 ●	**PARTY FEARS TWO** *Associates ASC 1*	**9** 10
8 May 82	**CLUB COUNTRY** *Associates ASC 2*	**13** 10
7 Aug 82	**LOVE HANGOVER / 18 CARAT LOVE AFFAIR** *Associates ASC 3*	**21** 8
16 Jun 84	**THOSE FIRST IMPRESSIONS** *WEA YZ 6*	**43** 6
1 Sep 84	**WAITING FOR THE LOVEBOAT** *WEA YZ 16*	**53** 4
19 Jan 85	**BREAKFAST** *WEA YZ 28*	**49** 6
17 Sep 88	**HEART OF GLASS** *WEA YZ 310*	**56** 3
22 May 82 ●	**SULK** *Associates ASCL 1*	**10** 20
16 Feb 85	**PERHAPS** *WEA WX 9*	**23** 7
31 Mar 90	**WILD AND LONELY** *Circa CIRCA 11*	**71** 1

'18 Carat Love Affair' listed until 28 Aug only. The act was a duo on their 1982 hits. Act was a duo for the first album

The ASSOCIATION
US, male vocal / instrumental group (Singles: 8 Weeks) pos/wks

22 May 68	**TIME FOR LIVIN'** *Warner Bros. WB 7195*	**23** 8

Rick ASTLEY ⊂448 Top 500⊃ *Soulful-voiced pop vocalist, b. 6 Feb 1966,*
Warrington, UK. Brit award-winning, US chart-topping debut hit was 1987's
best-selling UK single. No British solo male can match his seven consecutive
(mostly Stock Aitken Waterman produced) Top 10 hits in the 1980s (Singles:
91 Weeks, Albums: 66 Weeks) pos/wks

8 Aug 87 ★	**NEVER GONNA GIVE YOU UP** *RCA PB 41447* ▲	**1** 18
31 Oct 87 ●	**WHENEVER YOU NEED SOMEBODY** *RCA PB 41567*	**3** 12
12 Dec 87 ●	**WHEN I FALL IN LOVE / MY ARMS KEEP MISSING YOU**	
	RCA PB 41683	**2** 10
27 Feb 88 ●	**TOGETHER FOREVER** *RCA PB 41817* ▲	**2** 9
24 Sep 88 ●	**SHE WANTS TO DANCE WITH ME** *RCA PB 42189*	**6** 10
26 Nov 88 ●	**TAKE ME TO YOUR HEART** *RCA PB 42573*	**8** 10
11 Feb 89 ●	**HOLD ME IN YOUR ARMS** *RCA PB 42615*	**10** 8
26 Jan 91 ●	**CRY FOR HELP** *RCA PB 44247*	**7** 7
30 Mar 91	**MOVE RIGHT OUT** *RCA PB 44407*	**58** 2
29 Jun 91	**NEVER KNEW LOVE** *RCA PB 44737*	**70** 1
4 Sep 93	**THE ONES YOU LOVE** *RCA 74321160142*	**48** 2
13 Nov 93	**HOPELESSLY** *RCA 74321175642*	**33** 2
28 Nov 87 ★	**WHENEVER YOU NEED SOMEBODY** *RCA PL 71529* ■	**1** 34
10 Dec 88 ●	**HOLD ME IN YOUR ARMS** *RCA PL 71932*	**8** 19
2 Mar 91 ●	**FREE** *RCA PL 74896*	**9** 9
14 Sep 02	**GREATEST HITS** *BMG 74321955122*	**16** 4

Before 9 Jan 1988, 'When I Fall in Love' was listed by itself. After that date 'My Arms Keep Missing You' was the side listed

ASTRO TRAX
UK, male / female vocal / production trio (Singles: 1 Week) pos/wks

24 Oct 98	**THE ENERGY (FEEL THE VIBE)** *Satellite 74321622052*	**74** 1

ASWAD *UK, male vocal / instrumental group – leader*
Brinsley Forde (Singles: 81 Weeks, Albums: 61 Weeks) pos/wks

3 Mar 84	**CHASING FOR THE BREEZE** *Island IS 160*	**51** 3
6 Oct 84	**54-46 (WAS MY NUMBER)** *Island IS 170*	**70** 3
27 Feb 88 ★	**DON'T TURN AROUND** *Mango IS 341*	**1** 12
21 May 88	**GIVE A LITTLE LOVE** *Mango IS 358*	**11** 8
24 Sep 88	**SET THEM FREE** *Mango IS 383*	**70** 6
1 Apr 89	**BEAUTY'S ONLY SKIN DEEP** *Mango MNG 105*	**31** 6
22 Jul 89	**ON AND ON** *Mango MNG 708*	**25** 8
18 Aug 90	**NEXT TO YOU** *Mango MNG 753*	**24** 6
17 Nov 90	**SMILE** *Mango MNG 767* [1]	**53** 3
30 Mar 91	**TOO WICKED (EP)** *Mango MNG 771*	**61** 2

Singles re-entries are listed as (re), (2re), (3re).... which signifies that the hit re-entered the chart once, twice or three times...

		pos	wks
31 Jul 93	HOW LONG *Polydor PZCD 252* [2]	31	5
9 Oct 93	DANCEHALL MOOD *Bubblin' CDBUBB 1*	48	2
18 Jun 94 ●	SHINE *Bubblin' CDBUBB 3*	5	14
17 Sep 94	WARRIORS *Bubblin' CDBUBB 4*	33	3
18 Feb 95	YOU'RE NO GOOD *Bubblin' CDBUBB 5*	35	3
5 Aug 95	IF I WAS *Bubblin' CDBUBB 6*	58	1
31 Aug 02	SHY GUY *Universal TV 0192632* [3]	62	1
24 Jul 82	NOT SATISFIED *CBS 85666*	50	6
10 Dec 83	LIVE AND DIRECT *Island IMA 6*	57	16
3 Nov 84	REBEL SOULS *Island ILPS 9780*	48	2
28 Jun 86	TO THE TOP *Simba SIMBALP 2*	71	3
9 Apr 88 ●	DISTANT THUNDER *Mango ILPS 9895*	10	15
3 Dec 88	RENAISSANCE *Stylus SMR 866*	52	8
22 Sep 90	TOO WICKED *Mango MLPS 1054*	51	2
9 Jul 94	RISE AND SHINE *Bubblin' BUBBCD 1*	38	5
12 Aug 95	GREATEST HITS *Bubblin' BUBBCD 4*	20	3
24 Aug 02	COOL SUMMER REGGAE *UMTV 643762*	54	1

[1] Aswad featuring Sweetie Irie [2] Yazz and Aswad [3] Aswad featuring
Easther Bennett

*Tracks on Too Wicked (EP): Best of My Love / Warrior Re-Charge / Fire / I Shot
the Sheriff*

AT THE DRIVE-IN *US, male vocal / instrumental*
group (Singles: 3 Weeks, Albums: 2 Weeks) pos/wks

		pos	wks
19 Aug 00	ONE ARMED SCISSOR *Grand Royal GR 091CD*	64	1
16 Dec 00	ROLODEX PROPAGANDA *Grand Royal / Virgin VUSCD 189*	54	1
24 Mar 01	INVALID LITTER DEPT *Grand Royal / Virgin VUSCD 193*	50	1
30 Sep 00	RELATIONSHIP OF COMMAND *Grand Royal CDVUS 184*	33	2

Gali ATARI *See MILK AND HONEY featuring Gali ATARI*

The ATARIS *US, male vocal / instrumental group (Singles: 1 Week)* pos/wks

		pos	wks
11 Oct 03	THE BOYS OF SUMMER *Columbia 6743402*	49	1

ATEED *Germany, female vocalist (Singles: 1 Week)* pos/wks

		pos	wks
4 Oct 03	COME TO ME *Better the Devil BTD 4CD*	56	1

ATHLETE *UK, male vocal / instrumental*
group (Singles: 7 Weeks, Albums: 21 Weeks) pos/wks

		pos	wks
29 Jun 02	YOU GOT THE STYLE *Parlophone CDATH 001*	37	2
16 Nov 02	BEAUTIFUL *Parlophone CDATH 002*	41	1
5 Apr 03	EL SALVADOR *Parlophone CDATHS 003*	31	2
5 Jul 03	WESTSIDE *Parlophone CDATHS 005*	42	1
4 Oct 03	YOU GOT THE STYLE (re-issue) *Parlophone CDATH 006*	42	1
19 Apr 03	VEHICLES & ANIMALS *Parlophone 5842112*	19	21

ATHLETICO SPIZZ 80
UK, male vocal / instrumental group (Albums: 5 Weeks) pos/wks

		pos	wks
26 Jul 80	DO A RUNNER *A&M AMLE 68514*	27	5

Chet ATKINS *US, male instrumentalist – guitar – Chester Atkins, b. 20*
Jun 1924, d. 30 Jun 2001 (Singles: 2 Weeks, Albums: 16 Weeks) pos/wks

		pos	wks
17 Mar 60	TEENSVILLE (re) *RCA 1174*	46	2
18 Mar 61	THE OTHER CHET ATKINS *RCA RD 27194*	20	1
17 Jun 61	CHET ATKINS' WORKSHOP *RCA RD 27214*	19	1
20 Feb 63	CARIBBEAN GUITAR *RCA RD 7519*	17	3
24 Nov 90	NECK AND NECK *CBS 4674351* [1]	41	11

[1] Chet Atkins and Mark Knopfler

Rowan ATKINSON (see also NOT THE NINE O'CLOCK NEWS;
MR BEAN) *UK, male comedian / actor (Albums: 9 Weeks)* pos/wks

		pos	wks
7 Feb 81	LIVE IN BELFAST *Arista SPART 1150*	44	9

ATLANTA RHYTHM SECTION
US, male vocal / instrumental group (Singles: 4 Weeks) pos/wks

		pos	wks
27 Oct 79	SPOOKY *Polydor POSP 74*	48	4

ATLANTIC OCEAN *Holland, male instrumental duo –*
Rene van der Weyde and Lex van Coeverden (Singles: 14 Weeks) pos/wks

		pos	wks
19 Feb 94	WATERFALL *Eastern Bloc BLOCCD 001*	22	6
2 Jul 94	BODY IN MOTION *Eastern Bloc BLOCCD 009*	15	4
26 Nov 94	MUSIC IS A PASSION *Eastern Bloc BLOCCDX 017*	59	1
30 Nov 96	WATERFALL (re-mix) *Eastern Bloc BLOC 104CD*	21	3

ATLANTIC STARR *US, male / female vocal /*
instrumental group (Singles: 48 Weeks, Albums: 15 Weeks) pos/wks

		pos	wks
9 Sep 78	GIMME YOUR LUVIN' *A&M AMS 7380*	66	3
29 Jun 85	SILVER SHADOW *A&M AM 260*	41	6
7 Sep 85	ONE LOVE *A&M AM 273*	58	4
15 Mar 86 ●	SECRET LOVERS *A&M AM 307*	10	12
24 May 86	IF YOUR HEART ISN'T IN IT *A&M AM 319*	48	4
13 Jun 87 ●	ALWAYS *Warner Bros. W 8455* ▲	3	14
12 Sep 87	ONE LOVER AT A TIME *Warner Bros. W 8327*	57	3
27 Aug 94	EVERYBODY'S GOT SUMMER *Arista 74321228072*	36	2
15 Jun 85	AS THE BAND TURNS *A&M AMA 5019*	64	3
11 Jul 87	ALL IN THE NAME OF LOVE *WEA WX 115*	48	12

ATLANTIS vs AVATAR *UK, male production group*
featuring female vocalist – Miriam Stockley (Singles: 2 Weeks) pos/wks

		pos	wks
28 Oct 00	FIJI *Inferno CDFERN 34*	52	2

Natacha ATLAS *See Jean-Michel JARRE*

ATMOSFEAR *UK, male instrumental group (Singles: 7 Weeks)* pos/wks

		pos	wks
17 Nov 79	DANCING IN OUTER SPACE *MCA 543*	46	7

ATOMIC KITTEN [288] [Top 500] *The Liverpool ladies were the first*
female trio to amass three No.1 singles. Line-up is Natasha Hamilton,
Elizabeth McClarnon and Jenny Frost (who replaced Kerry Katona in
2001). 'Eternal Flame' and 'The Tide Is High' are the only songs to top the
chart twice by two different female-fronted acts. Best-selling single: 'Whole
Again' 940,000 (Singles: 144 Weeks, Albums: 83 Weeks) pos/wks

		pos	wks
11 Dec 99 ●	RIGHT NOW *Innocent SINCD 15*	10	9
8 Apr 00 ●	SEE YA (re) *Innocent SINCD 17*	6	7
15 Jul 00 ●	I WANT YOUR LOVE *Innocent SINCD 18*	10	5
21 Oct 00	FOLLOW ME *Innocent SINCD 22*	20	5
10 Feb 01 ★	WHOLE AGAIN (re) *Innocent SINDX 24* ■	1	23
4 Aug 01 ★	ETERNAL FLAME *Innocent SINCD 27* ■	1	15
1 Jun 02 ●	IT'S OK! *Innocent SINCD 36*	3	13
7 Sep 02 ★	THE TIDE IS HIGH (GET THE FEELING) *Innocent SINCD 38* ■	1	16
7 Dec 02 ●	THE LAST GOODBYE / BE WITH YOU *Innocent SINDX 42*	2	12
12 Apr 03 ●	LOVE DOESN'T HAVE TO HURT *Innocent SINCD 45*	4	10
8 Nov 03 ●	IF YOU COME TO ME *Innocent SINCD 50*	3	10
27 Dec 03 ●	LADIES NIGHT *Innocent SINCD 53* [1]	8	11
10 Apr 04 ●	SOMEONE LIKE ME / RIGHT NOW 2004 (re-recording) *Innocent SINDX 60*	8	8
4 Nov 00 ●	RIGHT NOW *Innocent CDSIN 6* ■	1	37
21 Sep 02 ★	FEELS SO GOOD *Innocent CDSIN 10* ■	1	27
22 Nov 03 ●	LADIES NIGHT *Innocent CDSIN 14*	5	11
17 Apr 04 ●	THE GREATEST HITS *Innocent CDSIN 16*	5	8

[1] Atomic Kitten featuring Kool and the Gang

*'Right Now' peaked at No.39 in 2000 and reached No.1 in 2001 after it was
repackaged with three new tracks*

ATOMIC ROOSTER *UK, male vocal / instrumental*
group (Singles: 25 Weeks, Albums: 13 Weeks) pos/wks

		pos	wks
6 Feb 71	TOMORROW NIGHT *B&C CB 131*	11	12
10 Jul 71 ●	DEVIL'S ANSWER *B&C CB 157*	4	13
13 Jun 70	ATOMIC ROOSTER *B&C CAS 1010*	49	1
16 Jan 71	DEATH WALKS BEHIND YOU *Charisma CAS 1026*	12	8
21 Aug 71	IN HEARING OF ATOMIC ROOSTER *Pegasus PEG 1*	18	4

ATTRACTIONS *See Elvis COSTELLO*

Winifred ATWELL *Trinidad, female instrumentalist –*
piano, b. 27 Apr 1914, d. 28 Feb 1983 (Singles: 117 Weeks) pos/wks

		pos	wks
12 Dec 52 ●	BRITANNIA RAG (re) *Decca F 10015*	5	6
15 May 53 ●	CORONATION RAG (re) *Decca F 10110*	5	6
25 Sep 53 ●	FLIRTATION WALTZ (2re) *Decca F 10161*	10	3
4 Dec 53 ●	LET'S HAVE A PARTY (re) *Philips PB 213*	2	15
23 Jul 54 ●	RACHMANINOFF'S 18TH VARIATION ON A THEME BY PAGANINI (THE STORY OF THREE LOVES) (re) *Philips PB 234*	9	9
26 Nov 54 ★	LET'S HAVE ANOTHER PARTY *Philips PB 268*	1	8
4 Nov 55 ●	LET'S HAVE A DING DONG *Decca F 10634*	3	10
16 Mar 56 ★	THE POOR PEOPLE OF PARIS *Decca F 10681*	1	16
18 May 56	PORT-AU-PRINCE *Decca F 10727* [1]	18	6
20 Jul 56	LEFT BANK (C'EST A HAMBOURG) *Decca F 10762*	14	7
26 Oct 56 ●	MAKE IT A PARTY *Decca F 10796*	7	12

22 Feb 57	LET'S ROCK 'N' ROLL (re) *Decca F 10852*	24	4
6 Dec 57 ●	LET'S HAVE A BALL *Decca F 10956*	4	6
7 Aug 59	THE SUMMER OF THE SEVENTEENTH DOLL *Decca F 11143*	24	2
27 Nov 59 ●	PIANO PARTY *Decca F 11183*	10	7

1 Winifred Atwell and Frank Chacksfield

Various hits listed above were medleys as follows: Let's Have a Party: If You Knew Suzie / The More We Are Together / That's My Weakness Now / Knees Up Mother Brown / Daisy Bell / Boomps a Daisy / She Was One of the Early Birds / Three O'Clock in the Morning. Let's Have Another Party: Somebody Stole My Gal / I Wonder Where My Baby Is Tonight / When the Red Red Robin / Bye Bye Blackbird / Sheik of Araby / Another Little Drink / Lilly of Laguna / Honeysuckle and the Bee / Broken Doll / Nellie Dean. Let's Have a Ding Dong: Ain't She Sweet / Oh Johnny Oh Johnny Oh / Oh You Beautiful Doll / Yes We Have No Bananas / Happy Days Are Here Again / I'm Forever Blowing Bubbles / I'll Be Your Sweetheart / If These Lips Could Only Speak / Who's Taking You Home Tonight. Make It a Party: Who Were You With Last Night / Hello Hello Who's Your Lady Friend / Yes Sir That's My Baby / Don't Dilly Dally on the Way / Beer Barrel Polka / After the Ball / Peggy O'Neil / Meet Me Tonight in Dreamland / I Belong to Glasgow / Down at the Old Bull and Bush. Let's Rock 'n' Roll: Singin' The Blues / Green Door / See You Later Alligator / Shake Rattle and Roll / Rock Around the Clock / Razzle Dazzle. Let's Have a Ball: Music Music Music / This Ole House / Heartbreaker / Woody Woodpecker / Last Train to San Fernando / Bring a Little Water Sylvie / Puttin' on the Style / Don't You Rock Me Daddy-O. Piano Party: Baby Face / Comin' Thru' The Rye / Annie Laurie / Little Brown Jug / Let Him Go Let Him Tarry / Put Your Arms Around Me Honey / I'll Be With You in Apple Blossom Time / Shine on Harvest Moon / Blue Skies / I'll Never Say 'Never Again' Again / I'll See You in My Dreams. 'Let's Have A Party' re-entered for a second visit peaking at No.14 in Nov 1954

AU PAIRS
UK, female / male vocal / instrumental group (Albums: 10 Weeks)   pos/wks

6 Jun 81	PLAYING WITH A DIFFERENT SEX *Human HUMAN 1*	33	7
4 Sep 82	SENSE AND SENSUALITY *Kamera KAM 010*	79	3

THE AUDIENCE See THEAUDIENCE

AUDIO BULLYS
UK, male vocal / production group (Singles: 8 Weeks, Albums: 3 Weeks)   pos/wks

18 Jan 03	WE DON'T CARE *Source SOURCD 061*	15	3
31 May 03	THE THINGS / TURNED AWAY *Source SOURCD 084*	22	3
26 Jun 04	BREAK DOWN THE DOORS *Subliminal SUB 124CD* 1	44	2
14 Jun 03	EGO WAR *Source CD SOUR 073*	19	3

1 Morillo featuring Audio Bullys

AUDIOSLAVE
US, male vocal / instrumental group (Singles: 3 Weeks, Albums: 20 Weeks)   pos/wks

1 Feb 03	COCHISE *Epic / Interscope 6732762*	24	3
30 Nov 02	AUDIOSLAVE *Epic / Interscope 5101302*	19	20

AUDIOWEB
UK, male vocal / instrumental group (Singles: 12 Weeks, Albums: 1 Week)   pos/wks

14 Oct 95	SLEEPER *Mother MUMCD 69*	74	1
9 Mar 96	YEAH *Mother MUMCD 72*	73	1
15 Jun 96	INTO MY WORLD *Mother MUMCD 76*	42	1
19 Oct 96	SLEEPER (re-mix) *Mother MUMCD 78*	50	2
15 Feb 97	BANKROBBER *Mother MUMCD 85*	19	2
24 May 97	FAKER *Mother MUMCD 91*	70	1
25 Apr 98	POLICEMAN SKANK ... (THE STORY OF MY LIFE) *Mother MUMCD 100*	21	2
4 Jul 98	PERSONAL FEELING *Mother MUMCD 104*	65	1
20 Feb 99	TEST THE THEORY *Mother MUMCD 110*	56	1
9 Nov 96	AUDIOWEB *Mother MUMXD 9604*	70	1

AUF DER MAUR
Canada, female vocalist – Melissa Auf Der Maur (Singles: 5 Weeks, Albums: 2 Weeks)   pos/wks

28 Feb 04	FOLLOWED THE WAVES *EMI CDEM 635*	35	2
15 May 04	REAL A LIE *EMI CDEMS 642*	33	2
9 Oct 04	TASTE YOU *EMI CDEM 650*	51	1
13 Mar 04	AUF DER MAUR *EMI 5943082CD*	31	2

Brian AUGER TRINITY See Julie DRISCOLL, Brian AUGER and the TRINITY

AURA See POPPERS presents AURA

AUREUS See AGNELLI & NELSON

AURORA (see also DIVE)
UK, male production duo – Sacha Collisson and Simon Greenaway (Singles: 19 Weeks)   pos/wks

5 Jun 99	HEAR YOU CALLING *Additive 12AD 040*	71	1
5 Feb 00	HEAR YOU CALLING (re-issue) *Positiva CDTIV 124*	17	4
23 Sep 00 ●	ORDINARY WORLD *Positiva CDTIV 139* 1	5	7
13 Apr 02	DREAMING *EMI CDEM 611*	24	4
6 Jul 02	THE DAY IT RAINED FOREVER *EMI CDEMS 613*	29	3

1 Aurora featuring Naimee Coleman

AURRA
US, male / female vocal / instrumental group (Singles: 18 Weeks)   pos/wks

4 May 85	LIKE I LIKE IT *10 TEN 45*	51	5
19 Apr 86	YOU AND ME TONIGHT *10 TEN 71*	12	8
21 Jun 86	LIKE I LIKE IT (re-issue) *10 TEN 126*	43	5

Adam AUSTIN
UK, male vocalist (Singles: 1 Week)   pos/wks

13 Feb 99	CENTERFOLD *Media PSRCA 0107*	41	1

David AUSTIN
UK, male vocalist (Singles: 3 Weeks)   pos/wks

21 Jul 84	TURN TO GOLD *Parlophone R 6068*	68	3

Patti AUSTIN
US, female vocalist (Singles: 11 Weeks, Albums: 1 Week)   pos/wks

12 Feb 83	BABY COME TO ME *Qwest K 15005* 1 ▲	11	10
5 Sep 92	I'LL KEEP YOUR DREAMS ALIVE *Ammi AMMI 101* 2	68	1
26 Sep 81	EVERY HOME SHOULD HAVE ONE *Qwest K 56931*	99	1

1 Patti Austin and James Ingram 2 George Benson and Patti Austin

AUTECHRE
UK, male instrumental duo (Singles: 1 Week)   pos/wks

7 May 94	BASSCADET (EP) *Warp WAP 44CD*	56	1

The AUTEURS
UK, male / female vocal / instrumental group (Singles: 9 Weeks, Albums: 4 Weeks)   pos/wks

27 Nov 93	LENNY VALENTINO *Hut HUTCD 36*	41	2
23 Apr 94	CHINESE BAKERY *Hut HUTDX 41*	42	2
6 Jan 96	BACK WITH THE KILLER AGAIN *Hut HUTCD 65*	45	3
24 Feb 96	LIGHT AIRCRAFT ON FIRE *Hut HUTCD 66*	58	1
3 Jul 99	THE RUBETTES *Hut HUTCD 113*	66	1
6 Mar 93	NEW WAVE *Hut CDHUT 7*	35	2
21 May 94	NOW I'M A COWBOY *Hut CDHUT 16*	27	1
16 Mar 96	AFTER MURDER PARK *Hut CDHUT 33*	53	1

AUTUMN
UK, male vocal / instrumental group (Singles: 6 Weeks)   pos/wks

16 Oct 71	MY LITTLE GIRL *Pye 7N 45090*	37	6

Peter AUTY and the SINFONIA OF LONDON conducted by Howard BLAKE (see also DIGITAL DREAM BABY)
UK, male vocalist with orchestra (Singles: 9 Weeks)   pos/wks

14 Dec 85	WALKING IN THE AIR *Stiff LAD 1*	42	5
19 Dec 87	WALKING IN THE AIR (re-issue) *CBS GA 3950*	37	4

The AVALANCHES
Australia, male production group (Singles: 12 Weeks, Albums: 25 Weeks)   pos/wks

7 Apr 01	SINCE I LEFT YOU *XL Recordings XLS 128CD*	16	7
21 Jul 01	FRONTIER PSYCHIATRIST *XL Recordings XLS 134CD*	18	5
28 Apr 01 ●	SINCE I LEFT YOU *XL Recordings XLCD 138*	8	25

Frankie AVALON
US, male vocalist – Francis Avallone (Singles: 15 Weeks)   pos/wks

10 Oct 58	GINGERBREAD *HMV POP 517*	30	1
24 Apr 59	VENUS *HMV POP 603* ▲	16	6
22 Jan 60	WHY *HMV POP 688* ▲	20	4
28 Apr 60	DON'T THROW AWAY ALL THOSE TEARDROPS *HMV POP 727*	37	4

AVALON BOYS See LAUREL and HARDY with the AVALON BOYS featuring Chill WILLS

AVERAGE WHITE BAND
UK, male vocal / instrumental group (Singles: 47 Weeks, Albums: 50 Weeks)   pos/wks

22 Feb 75 ●	PICK UP THE PIECES *Atlantic K 10489* ▲	6	9
26 Apr 75	CUT THE CAKE *Atlantic K 10605*	31	4

			pos/wks
9 Oct 76	QUEEN OF MY SOUL Atlantic K 10825	**23**	7
28 Apr 79	WALK ON BY RCA XC 1087	**46**	5
25 Aug 79	WHEN WILL YOU BE MINE RCA XB 1096	**49**	5
26 Apr 80	LET'S GO ROUND AGAIN PT.1 RCA AWB 1	**12**	11
26 Jul 80	FOR YOU FOR LOVE RCA AWB 2	**46**	4
26 Mar 94	LET'S GO ROUND AGAIN (re-mix) The Hit Label HLC 5	**56**	2
1 Mar 75 ●	AVERAGE WHITE BAND Atlantic K 50058 ▲	**6**	14
5 Jul 75	CUT THE CAKE Atlantic K 50146	**28**	4
31 Jul 76	SOUL SEARCHING TIME Atlantic K 50272	**60**	1
10 Mar 79	I FEEL NO FRET RCA XL 13063	**15**	15
31 May 80	SHINE RCA XL 13123	**14**	13
2 Apr 94	LET'S GO ROUND AGAIN – THE BEST OF THE AVERAGE WHITE BAND The Hit Label AHLCD 15	**38**	3

Kevin AVIANCE US, male vocalist (Singles: 1 Week)

			pos/wks
13 Jun 98	DIN DA DA Distinctive DISNCD 42	**65**	1

The AVONS UK, male / female vocal trio (Singles: 22 Weeks)

			pos/wks
13 Nov 59 ●	SEVEN LITTLE GIRLS SITTING IN THE BACK SEAT Columbia DB 4363	**3**	13
7 Jul 60	WE'RE ONLY YOUNG ONCE (re) Columbia DB 4461	**45**	2
27 Oct 60	FOUR LITTLE HEELS (re) Columbia DB 4522	**45**	3
26 Jan 61	RUBBER BALL Columbia DB 4569	**30**	4

AWESOME UK, male vocal group (Singles: 2 Weeks)

			pos/wks
8 Nov 97	RUMOURS Universal MCSTD 40145	**58**	1
21 Mar 98	CRAZY Universal MCSTD 40195	**63**	1

AWESOME 3
UK, male / female vocal / instrumental group (Singles: 8 Weeks)

			pos/wks
8 Sep 90	HARD UP A&M AM 591	**55**	3
3 Oct 92	DON'T GO Citybeat CBE 1271	**75**	1
4 Jun 94	DON'T GO (re-mix) XL Recordings CBX 771CD	**45**	2
26 Oct 96	DON'T GO (2nd re-mix) XL Recordings XLS 78CD [1]	**27**	2

[1] Awesome 3 featuring Julie McDermott

Hoyt AXTON
US, male vocalist, b. 25 Mar 1938, d. 26 Oct 1999 (Singles: 4 Weeks)

			pos/wks
7 Jun 80	DELLA AND THE DEALER Young Blood YB 82	**48**	4

AXUS UK, male / female vocal / production duo (Singles: 1 Week)

			pos/wks
26 Sep 98	ABACUS (WHEN I FALL IN LOVE) INCredible INCRL 8CD	**62**	1

Roy AYERS US, male vocalist / instrumentalist –
vibraphone (Singles: 13 Weeks, Albums: 2 Weeks)

			pos/wks
21 Oct 78	GET ON UP, GET ON DOWN Polydor AYERS 7	**41**	4
13 Jan 79	HEAT OF THE BEAT Polydor POSP 16 [1]	**43**	5
2 Feb 80	DON'T STOP THE FEELING Polydor STEP 6	**56**	3
16 May 98	EXPANSIONS Soma Recordings SOMA 65CDS [2]	**68**	1
26 Oct 85	YOU MIGHT BE SURPRISED CBS 26653	**91**	2

[1] Roy Ayers and Wayne Henderson [2] Scott Grooves featuring Roy Ayers

AYLA Germany, male producer – Ingo Kunzi (Singles: 3 Weeks)

			pos/wks
4 Sep 99	AYLA Positiva CDTIV 117	**22**	3

Pam AYRES UK, female poet (Albums: 29 Weeks)

			pos/wks
27 Mar 76	SOME OF ME POEMS AND SONGS Galaxy GAL 6003	**13**	23
11 Dec 76	SOME MORE OF ME POEMS AND SONGS Galaxy GAL 6010	**23**	6

AZ US, male rapper – Anthony Cruz (Singles: 1 Week)

			pos/wks
30 Mar 96	SUGARHILL Cooltempo CDCOOL 315	**67**	1

AZ YET US, male vocal group (Singles: 10 Weeks)

			pos/wks
1 Mar 97	LAST NIGHT LaFace 74321423202	**21**	3
21 Jun 97 ●	HARD TO SAY I'M SORRY LaFace 74321481482 [1]	**7**	7

[1] Az Yet featuring Peter Cetera

Charles AZNAVOUR France, male vocalist –
Shanaur Aznavourian (Singles: 29 Weeks, Albums: 21 Weeks)

			pos/wks
22 Sep 73	THE OLD FASHIONED WAY (LES PLAISIRS DÉMODÉS) (2re) Barclay BAR 20	**38**	15
22 Jun 74 ★	SHE Barclay BAR 26	**1**	14
29 Jun 74	AZNAVOUR SINGS AZNAVOUR VOLUME 3 Barclay 80472	**23**	7
7 Sep 74 ●	A TAPESTRY OF DREAMS Barclay 90003	**9**	13
2 Aug 80	HIS GREATEST LOVE SONGS K-Tel NE 1078	**73**	1

'The Old Fashioned Way (Les Plaisirs Démodés' re-entered the chart in Oct 1973 (at its peak position) and Jul 1974)

AZTEC CAMERA (468 Top 500)
Sensitive, tuneful pop band formed in 1980 and centred around teenage singer / songwriter Roddy Frame, b. 29 Jan 1964, East Kilbride, Scotland. Album 'Love' was among the nominations for Best British Album at the 1989 Brit awards (Singles: 74 Weeks, Albums: 80 Weeks)

			pos/wks
19 Feb 83	OBLIVIOUS Rough Trade RT 122	**47**	6
4 Jun 83	WALK OUT TO WINTER Rough Trade RT 132	**64**	4
5 Nov 83	OBLIVIOUS (re-issue) WEA AZTEC 1	**18**	11
1 Sep 84	ALL I NEED IS EVERYTHING / JUMP WEA AC 1	**34**	6
13 Feb 88	HOW MEN ARE WEA YZ 168	**25**	9
23 Apr 88 ●	SOMEWHERE IN MY HEART WEA YZ 181	**3**	14
6 Aug 88	WORKING IN A GOLDMINE WEA YZ 199	**31**	5
8 Oct 88	DEEP AND WIDE AND TALL WEA YZ 154	**55**	3
7 Jul 90	THE CRYING SCENE WEA YZ 492	**70**	3
6 Oct 90	GOOD MORNING BRITAIN WEA YZ 521 [1]	**19**	8
18 Jul 92	SPANISH HORSES WEA YZ 688	**52**	3
1 May 93	DREAM SWEET DREAMS WEA YZ 740CD1	**67**	2
23 Apr 83	HIGH LAND HARD RAIN Rough Trade ROUGH 47	**22**	18
29 Sep 84	KNIFE WEA WX 8	**14**	6
21 Nov 87 ●	LOVE WEA WX 128	**10**	43
16 Jun 90	STRAY WEA WX 350	**22**	7
29 May 93	DREAMLAND WEA 4509924922	**21**	2
7 Aug 99	THE BEST OF AZTEC CAMERA Warner.esp 3984289842	**36**	4

[1] Aztec Camera and Mick Jones

'Jump' listed only from 22 Sep 1984 to end of chart run

AZTEC MYSTIC See DJ ROLANDO AKA AZTEC MYSTIC

AZURE Italy / US, male / female vocal / DJ duo (Singles: 1 Week)

			pos/wks
25 Apr 98	MAMA USED TO SAY Inferno CDFERN 005	**56**	1

AZYMUTH Brazil, male instrumental group (Singles: 8 Weeks)

			pos/wks
12 Jan 80	JAZZ CARNIVAL Milestone MRC 101	**19**	8

Bob AZZAM and his ORCHESTRA and CHORUS
Egypt, bandleader and his orchestra (Singles: 14 Weeks)

			pos/wks
26 May 60	MUSTAPHA Decca F 21235	**23**	14

Derek B UK, male rapper – Derek Boland
(Singles: 15 Weeks, Albums: 9 Weeks)

			pos/wks
27 Feb 88	GOODGROOVE Music of Life 7NOTE 12	**16**	6
7 May 88	BAD YOUNG BROTHER Tuff Audio DRKB 1	**16**	6
2 Jul 88	WE'VE GOT THE JUICE Tuff Audio DRKB 2	**56**	3
28 May 88	BULLET FROM A GUN Tuff Audio DRKLP 1	**11**	9

Emma B See NU CIRCLES featuring Emma B

Eric B and RAKIM
US, male DJ / rap duo – Eric Barrier and William Griffin Jr (Singles: 26 Weeks, Albums: 10 Weeks) pos/wks

7 Nov 87	**PAID IN FULL** *Fourth & Broadway BRW 78*	**15**	6
20 Feb 88	**MOVE THE CROWD** *Fourth & Broadway BRW 88*	**53**	2
12 Mar 88	**I KNOW YOU GOT SOUL** *Cooltempo COOL 146*	**13**	6
2 Jul 88	**FOLLOW THE LEADER** *MCA MCA 1256*	**21**	5
19 Nov 88	**THE MICROPHONE FIEND** *MCA MCA 1300*	**74**	1
12 Aug 89	**FRIENDS** *MCA MCA 1352* [1]	**21**	6
12 Sep 87	**PAID IN FULL** *Fourth & Broadway BRLP 514*	**85**	4
6 Aug 88	**FOLLOW THE LEADER** *MCA MCG 6031*	**25**	4
7 Jul 90	**LET THE RHYTHM HIT 'EM** *MCA MCG 6097*	**58**	1
11 Jul 92	**DON'T SWEAT THE TECHNIQUE** *MCA MCAD 10594*	**73**	1

[1] Jody Watley with Eric B and Rakim

Howie B
UK, male instrumentalist / producer – Howard Bernstein (Singles: 4 Weeks, Albums: 1 Week) pos/wks

19 Jul 97	**ANGELS GO BALD: TOO** *Polydor 5711672*	**36**	2
18 Oct 97	**SWITCH** *Polydor 5717112*	**62**	1
11 Apr 98	**TAKE YOUR PARTNER BY THE HAND** *Polydor 5693272* [1]	**74**	1
9 Aug 97	**TURN THE DARK OFF** *Polydor 5379342*	**58**	1

[1] Howie B featuring Robbie Robertson

Jazzie B *See Maxi PRIEST; SOUL II SOUL*

John B
UK, male producer (Singles: 1 Week) pos/wks

22 Jun 02	**UP ALL NIGHT / TAKE CONTROL** *Metalheadz METH 041CD*	**58**	1

Jon B
US, male vocalist – Jonathan Buck (Singles: 5 Weeks) pos/wks

17 Oct 98	**THEY DON'T KNOW** *Epic 6663975*	**32**	2
26 May 01	**DON'T TALK** *Epic 6712792*	**29**	3

Lisa B
US, female vocalist – Lisa Barbuscia (Singles: 9 Weeks) pos/wks

12 Jun 93	**GLAM** *ffrr FCD 210*	**49**	2
25 Sep 93	**FASCINATED** *ffrr FCD 218*	**35**	3
8 Jan 94	**YOU AND ME** *ffrr FCD 226*	**39**	4

Lorna B
UK, female vocalist – Lorna Bannon (Singles: 6 Weeks) pos/wks

28 Jan 95	**DO YOU WANNA PARTY** *Steppin' Out SPONCD 2* [1]	**36**	3
1 Apr 95	**SWEET DREAMS** *Steppin' Out SPONCD 3* [1]	**37**	2
15 Mar 97	**FEELS SO GOOD** *Avex UK AVEXCD 53*	**69**	1

[1] DJ Scott featuring Lorna B

Mark B & BLADE
UK, male producer – Mark Barnes (Singles: 4 Weeks) pos/wks

10 Feb 01	**THE UNKNOWN** *Wordplay WORDCDS 011* [1]	**49**	1
26 May 01	**YA DON'T SEE THE SIGNS** *Wordplay WORDCDSE 019* [1]	**23**	3
25 Sep 04	**MOVE NOW** *Genuine GEN 033CD* [2]	**61**	1

[1] Mark B and Blade [2] Mark B featuring Tommy Evans

Melanie B (see also SPICE GIRLS)
UK, female vocalist – Melanie Brown (Singles: 36 Weeks, Albums: 2 Weeks) pos/wks

26 Sep 98	★ **I WANT YOU BACK** *Virgin VSCDT 1716* [1] ■	**1**	9
10 Jul 99	**WORD UP (re)** *Virgin VSCDT 1735* [2]	**14**	8
7 Oct 00	● **TELL ME** *Virgin VSCDT 1777*	**4**	7
3 Mar 01	● **FEELS SO GOOD** *Virgin VSCDT 1787*	**5**	8
16 Jun 01	**LULLABY** *Virgin VSCDT 1798*	**13**	4
21 Oct 00	**HOT** *Virgin CDVX 2918*	**28**	2

[1] Melanie B featuring Missy 'Misdemeanor' Elliott [2] Melanie G

Sandy B
US, female vocalist – Sandy Barber (Singles: 10 Weeks) pos/wks

20 Feb 93	**FEEL LIKE SINGIN'** *Nervous SANCD 1*	**60**	1
18 May 96	**MAKE THE WORLD GO ROUND** *Champion CHAMPCD 322*	**73**	1
24 May 97	**MAKE THE WORLD GO ROUND (re-mix)** *Champion CHAMPCD 327*	**35**	2
8 Nov 97	**AIN'T NO NEED TO HIDE** *Champion CHAMPCD 331*	**60**	1
28 Feb 98	**MAKE THE WORLD GO ROUND (2nd re-mix)** *Champion CHAMPCD 333*	**20**	3
1 May 04	**MAKE THE WORLD GO ROUND 2004 (re) (3rd re-mix)** *Champion CHAMPCD 780*	**51**	2

Stevie B
US, male vocalist – Steven Hill (Singles: 9 Weeks) pos/wks

23 Feb 91	● **BECAUSE I LOVE YOU (THE POSTMAN SONG)** *Polydor PO 126* ▲	**6**	9

Tairrie B
US, female rapper (Singles: 2 Weeks) pos/wks

1 Dec 90	**MURDER SHE WROTE** *MCA MCA 1455*	**71**	2

B B and Q BAND
US, male vocal / instrumental group (Singles: 15 Weeks) pos/wks

18 Jul 81	**ON THE BEAT** *Capitol CL 202*	**41**	5
6 Jul 85	**GENIE** *Cooltempo COOL 110* [1]	**40**	4
20 Sep 86	**(I'M A) DREAMER** *Cooltempo COOL 132*	**35**	5
17 Oct 87	**RICOCHET** *Cooltempo COOL 154*	**71**	1

[1] Brooklyn Bronx and Queens

BBC CONCERT ORCHESTRA, BBC SYMPHONY CHORUS cond. Stephen JACKSON
UK, orchestra, chorus and conductor (Singles: 3 Weeks) pos/wks

22 Jun 96	**ODE TO JOY (FROM BEETHOVEN'S SYMPHONY NO.9)** *Virgin VSCDT 1591*	**36**	3

BBC SYMPHONY ORCHESTRA SINGERS and CHORUS
UK, orchestra / choir and audience (Albums: 7 Weeks) pos/wks

4 Oct 69	**LAST NIGHT OF THE PROMS** *Philips SFM 23033* [1]	**36**	1
11 Dec 82	**HIGHLIGHTS – LAST NIGHT OF THE PROMS '82** *K-Tel NE 1198* [2]	**69**	5
28 Feb 98	**ELGAR/PAYNE – SYMPHONY NO.3** *NMCD 053* [3]	**44**	1

[1] BBC Symphony Orchestra Singers and Chorus conducted by Colin Davis [2] BBC Symphony Orchestra Singers and Symphony Chorus conducted by James Loughran [3] BBC Symphony Orchestra conducted by Andrew Davis

BBC WELSH CHORUS *See Aled JONES*

B.B.E.
France / Italy, male instrumental group (Singles: 20 Weeks, Albums: 2 Weeks) pos/wks

28 Sep 96	● **SEVEN DAYS AND ONE WEEK** *Positiva CDTIV 67*	**3**	9
29 Mar 97	● **FLASH** *Positiva CDTIV 73*	**5**	5
14 Feb 98	**DESIRE** *Positiva CDTIV 87*	**19**	3
30 May 98	**DEEPER LOVE (SYMPHONIC PARADISE)** *Positiva CDTIV 93*	**19**	3
28 Dec 98	**GAMES** *Positiva 4934932*	**60**	2

BBG
UK, male vocal / instrumental trio (Singles: 10 Weeks) pos/wks

28 Apr 90	**SNAPPINESS** *Urban URB 54* [1]	**28**	5
11 Aug 90	**SOME KIND OF HEAVEN** *Urban URB 59*	**65**	2
23 Mar 96	**LET THE MUSIC PLAY** *MCA MCSTD 40029* [2]	**46**	1
18 May 96	**SNAPPINESS (re-mix)** *Hi-Life 5762072*	**50**	1
5 Jul 97	**JUST BE TONIGHT** *Hi-Life 5738972* [2]	**45**	1

[1] BBG featuring Dina Taylor [2] BBG featuring Erin

BBM
(see also GINGER BAKER'S AIR FORCE; BAKER-GURVITZ ARMY; Gary MOORE) UK, male vocal / instrumental trio (Singles: 2 Weeks, Albums: 4 Weeks) pos/wks

6 Aug 94	**WHERE IN THE WORLD** *Virgin VSCD 1495*	**57**	2
18 Jun 94	● **AROUND THE NEXT DREAM** *Virgin CDV 2745*	**9**	4

BBMAK
UK, male vocal trio (Singles: 18 Weeks, Albums: 3 Weeks) pos/wks

28 Aug 99	**BACK HERE** *Telstar CDSTAS 3053*	**37**	2
24 Feb 01	● **BACK HERE (re-issue)** *Telstar CDSTAS 3166*	**5**	10
26 May 01	● **STILL ON YOUR SIDE** *Telstar CDSTAS 3185*	**8**	4
16 Nov 02	**OUT OF MY HEART** *Telstar CDSTAS 3281*	**36**	2
9 Jun 01	**SOONER OR LATER** *Telstar TCD 3179*	**16**	3

B BOYS
US, male vocal / instrumental group (Albums: 1 Week) pos/wks

28 Jan 84	**CUTTIN' HERBIE** *Streetwave X KHAN 501*	**90**	1

BEF featuring Lalah HATHAWAY
US, male production duo – Martyn Ware and Ian Craig Marsh and female vocalist (Singles: 5 Weeks) pos/wks

27 Jul 91	**FAMILY AFFAIR** *Ten TEN 369*	**37**	5

B-15 PROJECT featuring Crissy D and Lady G UK / Jamaica,
male production duo and female vocalists (Singles: 10 Weeks) pos/wks

17 Jun 00 ●	GIRLS LIKE US (re) *Ministry of Sound RELENT 3CDS*	7	10

The B-52's US, male / female vocal / instrumental
group (Singles: 61 Weeks, Albums: 69 Weeks) pos/wks

11 Aug 79		ROCK LOBSTER *Island WIP 6506*	37	5
9 Aug 80		GIVE ME BACK MY MAN *Island WIP 6579*	61	3
7 May 83		(SONG FOR A) FUTURE GENERATION *Island IS 107*	63	2
10 May 86		ROCK LOBSTER / PLANET CLAIRE (re-issue) *Island BFT 1*	12	7
3 Mar 90	●	LOVE SHACK *Reprise W 9917*	2	13
19 May 90		ROAM *Reprise W 9827*	17	7
18 Aug 90		CHANNEL Z *Reprise W 9737*	61	2
20 Jun 92		GOOD STUFF *Reprise W 0109*	21	6
12 Sep 92		TELL IT LIKE IT T-I-IS *Reprise W 0130*	61	3
9 Jul 94	●	(MEET) THE FLINTSTONES *MCA MCSTD 1986* [1]	3	12
30 Jan 99		LOVE SHACK 99 *Reprise W 0461CD*	66	1
4 Aug 79		B-52'S *Island ILPS 9580*	22	12
13 Sep 80		WILD PLANET *Island ILPS 9622*	18	4
11 Jul 81		THE PARTY MIX ALBUM *Island IPM 1001*	36	5
27 Feb 82		MESOPOTAMIA *EMI ISSP 4006*	18	6
21 May 83		WHAMMY! *Island ILPS 9759*	33	4
8 Aug 87		BOUNCING OFF THE SATELLITES *Island ILPS 9871*	74	2
29 Jul 89	●	COSMIC THING *Reprise WX 283*	8	27
14 Jul 90		THE BEST OF THE B-52'S – DANCE THIS MESS AROUND *Island ILPS 9959*	36	3
11 Jul 92	●	GOOD STUFF *Reprise 7599269432*	8	6

[1] BC-52's

'Planet Claire' listed only from 17 May 1986

BG THE PRINCE OF RAP
Germany (b. US), male rapper – Bernard Greene (Singles: 2 Weeks) pos/wks

18 Jan 92	TAKE CONTROL OF THE PARTY *Columbia 6576330*	71	2

BK UK, male producer – Ben Keen (Singles: 11 Weeks) pos/wks

25 Nov 00	HOOVERS AND HORNS *Nukleuz NUKC 0185* [1]	57	2
8 Dec 01	FLASH *Nukleuz NUKP 0361* [2]	67	1
26 Jan 02	ERECTION (TAKE IT TO THE TOP) *Nukleuz NUKC 0352* [3]	48	1
9 Feb 02	FLASH (re-mix) *Nukleuz NUKC 0361* [2]	61	1
7 Dec 02	REVOLUTION *Nukleuz NUKC 0437*	42	2
16 Aug 03	KLUB KOLLABORATIONS (re) *Nukleuz 0524 FNUK*	43	4

[1] Fergie and BK [2] BK and Nick Sentience [3] Cortina featuring BK and Madam Friction

BM DUBS present MR RUMBLE featuring BRASSTOOTH and KEE UK, male production group (Singles: 2 Weeks) pos/wks

17 Mar 01	WHOOMP THERE IT IS *Incentive CENT 16CDS*	32	2

B M EX
UK, male production / instrumental group (Albums: 2 Weeks) pos/wks

30 Jan 93	APPOLONIA *Union City UCRCD 14*	17	2

B.M.R. featuring FELICIA Germany, male producer –
Michi Lange and female vocalist (Singles: 2 Weeks) pos/wks

1 May 99	CHECK IT OUT (EVERYBODY) *AM:PM CDAMPM 120*	29	2

B.M.U. US / UK, male vocal group (Singles: 2 Weeks) pos/wks

18 Feb 95	U WILL KNOW *Mercury MERCD 420*	23	2

B REAL / BUSTA RHYMES / COOLIO / LL COOL J / METHOD MAN US, male rappers (Singles: 6 Weeks) pos/wks

5 Apr 97	●	HIT 'EM HIGH (MONSTARS' ANTHEM) *Atlantic A 5449CD*	8	6

BT US, male producer – Brian Transeau
(Singles: 29 Weeks, Albums: 5 Weeks) pos/wks

18 Mar 95	EMBRACING THE SUNSHINE *East West YZ 895CD*	34	2
16 Sep 95	LOVING YOU MORE *Perfecto PERF 110CD* [1]	28	2
10 Feb 96	LOVING YOU MORE (re-mix) *Perfecto PERF 117CD* [1]	14	3
9 Nov 96	BLUE SKIES *Perfecto PERF 130CD1* [2]	26	2
19 Jul 97	FLAMING JUNE *Perfecto PERF 145CD1*	19	4
29 Nov 97	LOVE, PEACE & GREASE *Perfecto PERF 153CD1*	41	1
10 Jan 98	FLAMING JUNE (re-mix) *Perfecto PERF 157CD1*	28	4
18 Apr 98	REMEMBER *Perfecto PERF 160CD1*	27	2
21 Nov 98	GODSPEED *Renaissance RENCD 002*	54	1
9 Oct 99	MERCURY AND SOLACE *Headspace HEDSCD 001*	38	2
24 Jun 00	DREAMING *Headspace HEDSCD 002* [3]	38	2
23 Jun 01	NEVER GONNA COME BACK DOWN *Ministry of Sound MOSBT CDS1*	51	1
15 May 04	LOVE COMES AGAIN *Nebula NEBCD 058* [4]	30	3
21 Oct 95	IMA *Perfecto 0630123452*	45	4
4 Oct 97	ESCM *Perfecto 3984200652*	35	1

[1] BT featuring Vincent Covello [2] BT featuring Tori Amos [3] BT featuring Kirsty Hawkshaw [4] Tiësto featuring BT

BT EXPRESS
US, male instrumental / vocal group (Singles: 11 Weeks) pos/wks

29 Mar 75	EXPRESS *Pye International 7N 25674*	34	6
26 Jul 80	DOES IT FEEL GOOD / GIVE UP THE FUNK (LET'S DANCE) *Calibre CAB 503*	52	4
23 Apr 94	EXPRESS (re-mix) *PWL International PWCD 285*	67	1

B BUMBLE and the STINGERS
US, male instrumental group (Singles: 26 Weeks) pos/wks

19 Apr 62	★	NUT ROCKER *Top Rank JAR 611*	1	15
3 Jun 72		NUT ROCKER (re-issue) *Stateside SS 2203*	19	11

B-CREW US, female vocal group (Singles: 1 Week) pos/wks

20 Sep 97	PARTAY FEELING *Positiva CDTIV 78*	45	1

B-MOVIE UK, male vocal / instrumental group (Singles: 7 Weeks) pos/wks

18 Apr 81	REMEMBRANCE DAY *Deram DM 437*	61	3
27 Mar 82	NOWHERE GIRL *Some Bizzare B258*	67	4

B-TRIBE
Spain, male / female vocal / instrumental group (Singles: 4 Weeks) pos/wks

25 Sep 93	!FIESTA FATAL! *East West YZ 770CD*	64	4

B2K
US, male vocal group (Singles: 20 Weeks, Albums: 12 Weeks) pos/wks

24 Aug 02		UH HUH *Epic 6729512*	35	2
29 Mar 03		BUMP, BUMP, BUMP *Epic 6732762* [1] ▲	24	3
21 Jun 03	●	GIRLFRIEND *Epic 6739332*	10	8
18 Oct 03		UH HUH 2003 (re-mix) *Epic 6744012*	31	2
20 Mar 04		BADABOOM *Epic 6747512* [2]	26	5
5 Apr 03		PANDEMONIUM *Epic 5105342*	35	12

[1] B2K featuring P Diddy [2] B2K featuring Fabolous

BVSMP US, male rap / vocal group (Singles: 12 Weeks) pos/wks

23 Jul 88	●	I NEED YOU *Debut DEBT 3044*	3	12

B*WITCHED 492 Top 500 Ireland's most successful female group:
sisters Edele and Keavy Lynch, Sinead O'Carroll and Lindsay Armaou. Youngest girl group to top the chart. They sold more than one million copies of their debut album in the US and were the first act to enter at No.1 with their first four singles. Group split in Sept 2002. Best-selling single: 'C'est la Vie' 852,923 (Singles: 98 Weeks, Albums: 48 Weeks) pos/wks

6 Jun 98	★	C'EST LA VIE *Glow Worm / Epic 6660532* ■	1	19
3 Oct 98	★	ROLLERCOASTER *Glow Worm / Epic 6664752* ■	1	15
19 Dec 98	★	TO YOU I BELONG (re) *Glow Worm / Epic 6667712* ■	1	14
27 Mar 99	★	BLAME IT ON THE WEATHERMAN *Glow Worm / Epic 6670335* ■	1	9
10 Apr 99	●	THANK ABBA FOR THE MUSIC *Epic ABCD 1* [1]	4	13
16 Oct 99	●	JESSE HOLD ON (re) *Glow Worm / Epic 6679612*	4	12
18 Dec 99		I SHALL BE THERE *Glow Worm / Epic 683332* [2]	13	9
8 Apr 00		JUMP DOWN (re) *Glow Worm / Epic 6691282*	16	7
24 Oct 98	●	B*WITCHED *Epic 4917042*	3	36
30 Oct 99	●	AWAKE AND BREATHE *Epic 4960792*	5	12

[1] Steps, Tina Cousins, Cleopatra, B*Witched, Billie [2] B*Witched featuring Ladysmith Black Mambazo

BABE INSTINCT
UK, female vocal group (Singles: 2 Weeks) pos/wks

16 Jan 99	DISCO BABES FROM OUTER SPACE *Positiva CDTIV 103*	21	2

BABE TEAM
UK, female vocal group (Singles: 2 Weeks)

		pos/wks
8 Jun 02	**OVER THERE** Edel 0140655 ERE	**45** 2

BABES IN TOYLAND
US, female vocal / instrumental group (Albums: 3 Weeks)

		pos/wks
5 Sep 92	**FONTANELLE** Southern 185012	**24** 2
3 Jul 93	**PAINKILLERS** Southern 185122	**53** 1

Alice BABS
Sweden, female vocalist – Alice Nilsson (Singles: 1 Week)

		pos/wks
15 Aug 63	**AFTER YOU'VE GONE** Fontana TF 409	**43** 1

BABY ANIMALS
Australia, male vocal / instrumental group (Albums: 1 Week)

		pos/wks
14 Mar 92	**BABY ANIMALS** Imago PD 90580	**70** 1

BABY BUMPS
UK, male / female vocal / instrumental
duo – Sean Casey and Lisa Millett (Singles: 6 Weeks)

		pos/wks
8 Aug 98	**BURNING** Delirious DELICD 10	**17** 4
26 Feb 00	**I GOT THIS FEELING** Sound of Ministry MOSCDS 137	**22** 2

BABY D
UK, male / female vocal / instrumental
group (Singles: 45 Weeks, Albums: 5 Weeks)

		pos/wks
18 Dec 93	**DESTINY** Production House PNC 057	**69** 1
23 Jul 94	**CASANOVA** Production House PNC 065	**67** 1
19 Nov 94 ★	**LET ME BE YOUR FANTASY** Systematic SYSCD 4	**1** 14
3 Jun 95 ●	**(EVERYBODY'S GOT TO LEARN SOMETIME) I NEED YOUR**	
	LOVING Systematic SYSCD 11	**3** 12
13 Jan 96 ●	**SO PURE** Systematic SYSCD 21	**3** 7
6 Apr 96	**TAKE ME TO HEAVEN** Systematic SYSCD 26	**15** 5
2 Sep 00	**LET ME BE YOUR FANTASY (re-mix)** Systematic SYSCD 35	..16 5
10 Feb 96 ●	**DELIVERANCE** Systematic 8287202	**5** 5

BABY DC featuring IMAJIN
US, male rapper –
Derrick Coleman Jr and vocal group (Singles: 1 Week)

		pos/wks
24 Apr 99	**BOUNCE, ROCK, SKATE, ROLL** Jive 0522142	**45** 1

BABY FORD
UK, male instrumentalist –
keyboards – Peter Ford (Singles: 16 Weeks)

		pos/wks
10 Sep 88	**OOCHY KOOCHY (F.U. BABY YEAH YEAH)**	
	Rhythm King 7BFORD 1	**58** 6
24 Dec 88	**CHIKKI CHIKKI AHH AHH (re)** Rhythm King 7BFORD 2	**54** 4
17 Jun 89	**CHILDREN OF THE REVOLUTION** Rhythm King 7BFORD 4	**53** 4
17 Feb 90	**BEACH BUMP** Rhythm King 7BFORD 6	**68** 2

BABY JUNE
UK, male vocalist – Tim Hegarty (Singles: 1 Week)

		pos/wks
15 Aug 92	**HEY! WHAT'S YOUR NAME** Arista 115271	**75** 1

BABY O
US, male / female vocal / instrumental group (Singles: 5 Weeks)

		pos/wks
26 Jul 80	**IN THE FOREST** Calibre CAB 505	**46** 5

BABY ROOTS
UK, male vocalist (Singles: 1 Week)

		pos/wks
1 Aug 92	**ROCK ME BABY** ZYX ZYX 68027	**71** 1

BABY SHAMBLES
(see also The LIBERTINES)
UK, male / female vocal / instrumental group –
leader Peter Doherty (Singles: 3 Weeks)

		pos/wks
11 Dec 04 ●	**KILLAMANGIRO** Rough Trade RTRADSCD 201	**8** 3+

BABYBIRD
UK, male vocal / instrumental
group (Singles: 35 Weeks, Albums: 14 Weeks)

		pos/wks
10 Aug 96	**GOODNIGHT** Echo ECSCD 24	**28** 2
12 Oct 96 ●	**YOU'RE GORGEOUS** Echo ECSCD 26	**3** 16
1 Feb 97	**CANDY GIRL** Echo ECSCD 31	**14** 3
17 May 97	**CORNERSHOP** Echo ECSCD 33	**37** 2
9 May 98	**BAD OLD MAN** Echo ECSCD 60	**31** 2
22 Aug 98	**IF YOU'LL BE MINE** Echo ECSCX 65	**28** 4
27 Feb 99	**BACK TOGETHER** Echo ECSCD 73	**22** 3
25 Mar 00	**THE F-WORD** Echo ECSCD 92	**35** 2
3 Jun 00	**OUT OF SIGHT** Echo ECSCD 97	**58** 1

2 Nov 96 ●	**UGLY BEAUTIFUL** Echo ECHCD 11	**9** 12
5 Sep 98	**THERE'S SOMETHING GOING ON** Echo ECHCD 24	**28** 2

BABYFACE
US, male vocalist / producer –
Kenneth Edmonds (Singles: 23 Weeks, Albums: 5 Weeks)

		pos/wks
9 Jul 94	**ROCK BOTTOM** Epic 6601832	**50** 4
1 Oct 94	**WHEN CAN I SEE YOU** Epic 6606592	**35** 3
9 Nov 96	**THIS IS FOR THE LOVER IN YOU** Epic 6639352	**12** 5
8 Mar 97	**EVERYTIME I CLOSE MY EYES** Epic 6642492	**13** 4
19 Jul 97 ●	**HOW COME, HOW LONG** Epic 6646202 [1]	**10** 5
25 Oct 97	**SUNSHINE** Northwestside 74321528702 [2]	**25** 2
16 Nov 96	**THE DAY** Epic 4853682	**34** 5

[1] Babyface featuring Stevie Wonder [2] Jay-Z featuring Babyface and Foxy Brown

BABYLON ZOO
UK, male vocalist / multi-instrumentalist –
Jas Mann (Singles: 20 Weeks, Albums: 5 Weeks)

		pos/wks
27 Jan 96 ★	**SPACEMAN** EMI CDEM 416 ◆ ■	**1** 14
27 Apr 96	**ANIMAL ARMY** EMI CDEM 425	**17** 3
5 Oct 96	**THE BOY WITH THE X-RAY EYES** EMI CDEMS 440	**32** 2
6 Feb 99	**ALL THE MONEY'S GONE** EMI CDEM 519	**46** 1
17 Feb 96 ●	**THE BOY WITH THE X-RAY EYES** EMI CDEMC 3742	**6** 5

The BABYS
US / UK, male / instrumental
group – includes John Waite (Singles: 3 Weeks)

		pos/wks
21 Jan 78	**ISN'T IT TIME** Chrysalis CHS 2173	**45** 3

BACCARA
Spain, female vocal duo – Maria Mendiola
and Mayte Mateos (Singles: 25 Weeks, Albums: 6 Weeks)

		pos/wks
17 Sep 77 ★	**YES SIR, I CAN BOOGIE** RCA PB 5526	**1** 16
14 Jan 78 ●	**SORRY I'M A LADY** RCA PB 5555	**8** 9
4 Mar 78	**BACCARA** RCA PL 28316	**26** 6

Burt BACHARACH
US, male instrumentalist –
piano (Singles: 12 Weeks, Albums: 46 Weeks)

		pos/wks
20 May 65 ●	**TRAINS AND BOATS AND PLANES** London HL 9968 [1] **4** 11
1 May 99	**TOLEDO** Mercury 8709652 [2]	**72** 1
22 May 65 ●	**HIT MAKER – BURT BACHARACH** London HAR 8233 .....**3** 18
28 Nov 70	**REACH OUT** A&M AMLS 908	**52** 3
27 Mar 71 ●	**PORTRAIT IN MUSIC** A&M AMLS 2010	**5** 23
10 Oct 98	**PAINTED FROM MEMORY** Mercury 5380022 [1]	**32** 2

[1] Burt Bacharach, his Orchestra and Chorus [2] Elvis Costello / Burt Bacharach
[1] Elvis Costello with Burt Bacharach

The BACHELORS
205 **Top 500** Irish vocal / instrumental trio
from Dublin who were one of the few popular non-rock groups of the 1960s:
brothers Declan and Con Cluskey and John Stokes. The first trio to top the
UK singles chart, they had hits on both sides of the Atlantic with revivals of
popular pre-rock ballads (Singles: 187 Weeks, Albums: 102 Weeks) pos/wks

24 Jan 63 ●	**CHARMAINE** Decca F 11559	**6** 19
4 Jul 63	**FARAWAY PLACES** Decca F 11666	**36** 3
29 Aug 63	**WHISPERING** Decca F 11712	**18** 10
23 Jan 64 ★	**DIANE** Decca F 11799	**1** 19
19 Mar 64 ●	**I BELIEVE** Decca F 11857	**2** 17
4 Jun 64 ●	**RAMONA** Decca F 11910	**4** 13
13 Aug 64 ●	**I WOULDN'T TRADE YOU FOR THE WORLD** Decca F 11949 .....**4** 13
3 Dec 64 ●	**NO ARMS CAN EVER HOLD YOU** Decca F 12034 ....**7** 12
1 Apr 65	**TRUE LOVE FOR EVER MORE** Decca F 12108	**34** 6
20 May 65 ●	**MARIE** Decca F 12156	**9** 12
28 Oct 65	**IN THE CHAPEL IN THE MOONLIGHT** Decca F 12256	**27** 10
6 Jan 66	**HELLO, DOLLY!** Decca F 12309	**38** 4
17 Mar 66 ●	**THE SOUND OF SILENCE** Decca F 12351	**3** 13
7 Jul 66	**CAN I TRUST YOU** Decca F 12417	**26** 4
1 Dec 66	**WALK WITH FAITH IN YOUR HEART** Decca F 22523	**21** 9
6 Apr 67	**OH HOW I MISS YOU** Decca F 22592	**30** 8
5 Jul 67	**MARTA** Decca F 22634	**20** 9
27 Jun 64 ●	**THE BACHELORS AND 16 GREAT SONGS** Decca LK 4614.........**2** 44
9 Oct 65	**MORE GREAT SONG HITS FROM THE BACHELORS**	
	Decca LK 4721	**15** 6
9 Jul 66	**HITS OF THE SIXTIES** Decca TXL 102	**12** 9
5 Nov 66	**BACHELORS' GIRLS** Decca LK 4827	**24** 7
1 Jul 67	**GOLDEN ALL TIME HITS** Decca SKL 4849	**19** 7
14 Jun 69 ●	**WORLD OF THE BACHELORS** Decca SPA 2	**8** 18
23 Aug 69	**WORLD OF THE BACHELORS VOLUME 2** Decca SPA 22 ......**11** 7
22 Dec 79	**25 GOLDEN GREATS** Warwick WW 5068	**38** 4

Randy BACHMAN See BUS STOP

Singles re-entries are listed as (re), (2re), (3re)…. which signifies that the hit re-entered the chart once, twice or three times…

Tal BACHMAN
Canada, male vocalist / instrumentalist – guitar (Singles: 2 Weeks)   pos/wks

| 30 Oct 99 | SHE'S SO HIGH *Columbia 6679932* | 30 | 2 |

BACHMAN-TURNER OVERDRIVE (see also Randy BACHMAN)
Canada, male vocal / instrumental group
(Singles: 18 Weeks, Albums: 13 Weeks)   pos/wks

16 Nov 74	YOU AIN'T SEEN NOTHING YET *Mercury 6167 025* ▲	2	12
1 Feb 75	ROLL ON DOWN THE HIGHWAY *Mercury 6167 071*	22	6
14 Dec 74	NOT FRAGILE *Mercury 9100 007* ▲	12	13

BACK TO THE PLANET
UK, male / female vocal / instrumental group (Singles: 2 Weeks, Albums: 2 Weeks)   pos/wks

10 Apr 93	TEENAGE TURTLES *Parallel LLLCD 3*	52	1
4 Sep 93	DAYDREAM *Parallel LLLCD 8*	52	1
18 Sep 93	MIND AND SOUL COLLABORATORS *Parallel ALLCD 2*	32	2

BACKBEAT BAND
US, male vocal / instrumental group (Singles: 5 Weeks, Albums: 2 Weeks)   pos/wks

26 Mar 94	MONEY (re) *Virgin VSCDX 1489*	48	4
14 May 94	PLEASE MR POSTMAN *Virgin VSCDX 1502*	69	1
16 Apr 94	BACKBEAT (FILM SOUNDTRACK) *Virgin CDV 2729*	39	2

BACKBEAT DISCIPLES See Arthur BAKER

BACKROOM BOYS See Frank IFIELD

BACKSTREET BOYS `183` `Top 500` *American boy band vocal quintet (Brian Littrell, Nick Carter, A J McLean, Howie Dorough, Kevin Richardson) created teen hysteria in Europe before becoming 1999's top-selling act in their homeland. Their 13 consecutive UK Top 10 entries are a record for a US group (Singles: 161 Weeks, Albums: 146 Weeks)*   pos/wks

28 Oct 95	WE'VE GOT IT GOIN' ON *Jive JIVECD 386*	54	1
16 Dec 95	I'LL NEVER BREAK YOUR HEART *Jive JIVECD 389*	42	3
1 Jun 96	GET DOWN (YOU'RE THE ONE FOR ME) *Jive JIVECD 394*	14	8
24 Aug 96 ●	WE'VE GOT IT GOIN' ON (re-issue) *Jive JIVECD 400*	3	7
16 Nov 96 ●	I'LL NEVER BREAK YOUR HEART (re-issue) *Jive JIVERCD 406*	8	8
18 Jan 97 ●	QUIT PLAYING GAMES (WITH MY HEART) *Jive JIVECD 409*	2	10
29 Mar 97 ●	ANYWHERE FOR YOU (2re) *Jive JIVECD 416*	4	8
2 Aug 97 ●	EVERYBODY (BACKSTREET'S BACK) *Jive JIVECD 426*	3	11
11 Oct 97 ●	AS LONG AS YOU LOVE ME *Jive JIVECD 434*	3	19
14 Feb 98 ●	ALL I HAVE TO GIVE *Jive JIVECD 445*	2	12
15 May 99 ★	I WANT IT THAT WAY *Jive 0523392* ■	1	14
30 Oct 99 ●	LARGER THAN LIFE *Jive 0550562*	5	14
26 Feb 00	SHOW ME THE MEANING OF BEING LONELY (IMPORT) *Jive IMPORT 9250082*	66	1
4 Mar 00 ●	SHOW ME THE MEANING OF BEING LONELY (re) *Jive 9250082*	3	11
24 Jun 00 ●	THE ONE (re) *Jive 9250662*	8	8
18 Nov 00 ●	SHAPE OF MY HEART *Jive 9251442*	4	9
24 Feb 01 ●	THE CALL *Jive 9251702*	8	5
7 Jul 01	MORE THAN THAT *Jive 9252342*	12	5
12 Jan 02 ●	DROWNING *Jive 9252882*	4	7
21 Sep 96	BACKSTREET BOYS *Jive CHIP 169*	12	19
23 Aug 97 ●	BACKSTREET'S BACK *Jive CHIP 186*	2	44
29 May 99 ●	MILLENNIUM *Jive 523222* ▲	2	56
2 Dec 00	BLACK & BLUE *Jive 9221172* ▲	13	9
10 Nov 01 ●	GREATEST HITS – CHAPTER ONE *Jive 9222672*	5	18

BACKYARD DOG
UK, male vocal / production group (Singles: 6 Weeks)   pos/wks

| 7 Jul 01 | BADDEST RUFFEST (re) *East West EW 233CD* | 15 | 6 |

BAD ANGEL See BOOTH and the BAD ANGEL

BAD BOYS INC
UK, male vocal group (Singles: 31 Weeks, Albums: 6 Weeks)   pos/wks

14 Aug 93	DON'T TALK ABOUT LOVE *A&M 5803412*	19	5
2 Oct 93	WHENEVER YOU NEED SOMEONE *A&M 5804032*	26	3
11 Dec 93	WALKING ON AIR *A&M 5804692*	24	6
21 May 94 ●	MORE TO THIS WORLD *A&M 5806072*	8	8
23 Jul 94	TAKE ME AWAY (I'LL FOLLOW YOU) *A&M 5806912*	15	6
17 Sep 94	LOVE HERE I COME *A&M 5807752*	26	4
18 Jun 94	BAD BOYS INC *A&M 5402002*	13	6

BAD COMPANY
UK, male vocal / instrumental group (Singles: 23 Weeks, Albums: 87 Weeks)   pos/wks

1 Jun 74	CAN'T GET ENOUGH *Island WIP 6191*	15	8
22 Mar 75	GOOD LOVIN' GONE BAD *Island WIP 6223*	31	6
30 Aug 75	FEEL LIKE MAKIN' LOVE *Island WIP 6242*	20	9
15 Jun 74 ●	BAD COMPANY *Island ILPS 9279* ▲	3	25
12 Apr 75 ●	STRAIGHT SHOOTER *Island ILPS 9304*	3	27
21 Feb 76 ●	RUN WITH THE PACK *Island ILPS 9346*	4	12
19 Mar 77	BURNIN' SKY *Island ILPS 9441*	17	8
17 Mar 79 ●	DESOLATION ANGELS *Swansong SSK 59408*	10	9
28 Aug 82	ROUGH DIAMONDS *Swansong SSK 59419*	15	6

BAD COMPANY (see also DJ FRESH; FRESH BC; FRESH)
UK, male production group (Singles: 5 Weeks)   pos/wks

9 Mar 02	SPACEHOPPER / TONIGHT *Ram RAMM 37*	56	1
4 May 02	RUSH HOUR / BLIND *BC Recordings BCRUK 002CD*	59	1
15 Mar 03	MO' FIRE *BC Recordings BCRUK 003CD*	24	3

BAD ENGLISH
UK / US, male vocal / instrumental group (Singles: 3 Weeks, Albums: 2 Weeks)   pos/wks

25 Nov 89	WHEN I SEE YOU SMILE *Epic 6553471* ▲	61	3
16 Sep 89	BAD ENGLISH *Epic 4634471*	74	1
19 Oct 91	BACKLASH *Epic 4685691*	64	1

BAD HABIT BOYS
Germany, male production duo (Singles: 1 Week)   pos/wks

| 1 Jul 00 | WEEKEND *Inferno CDFERN 28* | 41 | 1 |

BAD MANNERS `461` `Top 500`
Good-time ska band fronted by shaven-headed Buster Bloodvessel (b. Douglas Trendle, 6 Sep 1958, London). Spent more weeks on UK chart in 1980 (45) than anyone bar Madness. Even after the hits, they remained a popular live attraction (Singles: 111 Weeks, Albums: 44 Weeks)   pos/wks

1 Mar 80	NE-NE NA-NA NA-NA NU-NU *Magnet MAG 164*	28	14
14 Jun 80	LIP UP FATTY *Magnet MAG 175*	15	14
27 Sep 80 ●	SPECIAL BREW *Magnet MAG 180*	3	13
6 Dec 80	LORRAINE *Magnet MAG 181*	21	12
28 Mar 81	JUST A FEELING *Magnet MAG 187*	13	9
27 Jun 81 ●	CAN CAN *Magnet MAG 190*	3	13
26 Sep 81 ●	WALKING IN THE SUNSHINE *Magnet MAG 197*	10	9
21 Nov 81	BUONA SERA *Magnet MAG 211*	34	9
1 May 82	GOT NO BRAINS *Magnet MAG 216*	44	5
31 Jul 82 ●	MY GIRL LOLLIPOP (MY BOY LOLLIPOP) *Magnet MAG 232*	9	7
30 Oct 82	SAMSON AND DELILAH *Magnet MAG 236*	58	3
14 May 83	THAT'LL DO NICELY *Magnet MAG 243*	49	3
26 Apr 80	SKA 'N' B *Magnet MAG 5033*	34	13
29 Nov 80	LOONEE TUNES *Magnet MAG 5038*	36	12
24 Oct 81	GOSH IT'S BAD MANNERS *Magnet MAGL 5043*	18	12
27 Nov 82	FORGING AHEAD *Magnet MAGL 5050*	78	1
7 May 83	THE HEIGHT OF BAD MANNERS *Telstar STAR 2229*	23	6

BAD MEETS EVIL featuring EMINEM & ROYCE DA 5'9 (see also EMINEM)
US, male producer and male rappers (Singles: 1 Week)   pos/wks

| 1 Sep 01 | SCARY MOVIES *Mole UK MOLEUK 045* | 63 | 1 |

BAD NEWS
UK, male vocal group (Singles: 5 Weeks, Albums: 1 Week)   pos/wks

| 12 Sep 87 | BOHEMIAN RHAPSODY *EMI EM 24* | 44 | 5 |
| 24 Oct 87 | BAD NEWS *EMI EMC 3535* | 69 | 1 |

BAD RELIGION
US, male vocal / instrumental group (Singles: 3 Weeks)   pos/wks

| 11 Feb 95 | 21ST CENTURY (DIGITAL BOY) *Columbia 6611435* | 41 | 2 |
| 21 Aug 04 | LOS ANGELES IS BURNING *Epitaph 11692* | 67 | 1 |

BAD SEEDS See Nick CAVE and the BAD SEEDS

BAD YARD CLUB See David MORALES

Angelo BADALAMENTI with Julee CRUISE and VARIOUS ARTISTS
(see also BOOTH and the BAD ANGEL; ORBITAL)
US, male composer and female vocalist (Albums: 25 weeks)   pos/wks

| 17 Nov 90 | MUSIC FROM 'TWIN PEAKS' *Warner Bros. 7599263161* | 27 | 25 |

Shanin BADAR *See Tim DELUXE*

Wally BADAROU
France, male instrumentalist – keyboards (Singles: 6 Weeks) pos/wks

19 Oct 85   CHIEF INSPECTOR *Fourth & Broadway BRW 37* 46 6

BADDIEL and SKINNER and The LIGHTNING SEEDS
UK, male vocal group – David Baddiel, Frank Skinner –
Christopher Collins and The Lightning Seeds (Singles: 34 Weeks) pos/wks

1 Jun 96 ★	THREE LIONS (THE OFFICIAL SONG OF THE ENGLAND FOOTBALL TEAM) *Epic 6632732* [1] ■	1 15
20 Jun 98 ★	THREE LIONS '98 *Epic 6660982* [1] ■	1 13
15 Jun 02	THREE LIONS '98 (re) (re-issue) *Epic 6728152* [2]	16 6

[1] Baddiel and Skinner and The Lightning Seeds [2] Baddiel, Skinner and
The Lightning Seeds

BADFELLAS featuring CK *UK, male production*
group and Kenya, female vocalist (Singles: 1 Week) pos/wks

15 Feb 03   SOC IT TO ME *Serious SER 053CD* 55 1

BADFINGER
UK, male vocal / instrumental group (Singles: 34 Weeks) pos/wks

10 Jan 70 ●	COME AND GET IT *Apple 20*	4 11
9 Jan 71 ●	NO MATTER WHAT *Apple 31*	5 12
29 Jan 72 ●	DAY AFTER DAY *Apple 40*	10 11

BADLANDS
UK, male vocal / instrumental group (Albums: 3 Weeks) pos/wks

24 Jun 89	BADLANDS *WEA 7819661*	39 2
22 Jun 91	VOODOO HIGHWAY *Atlantic 7567822511*	74 1

BADLY DRAWN BOY
UK, male vocalist / producer / instrumentalist – Damon Gough
(Singles: 28 Weeks, Albums: 89 Weeks) pos/wks

4 Sep 99	ONCE AROUND THE BLOCK *Twisted Nerve / XL Recordings TNXL 003CD*	46 2
17 Jun 00	ANOTHER PEARL *Twisted Nerve / XL Recordings TNXL 004CD*	41 1
16 Sep 00	DISILLUSION *Twisted Nerve / XL Recordings TNXL 005CD*	26 2
25 Nov 00	ONCE AROUND THE BLOCK (re-issue) *Twisted Nerve / XL Recordings TNXL 009CD*	27 2
19 May 01	PISSING IN THE WIND *Twisted Nerve / XL Recordings TNXL 010CD*	22 2
6 Apr 02	SILENT SIGH *Twisted Nerve / XL Recordings TNXL 012CD*	16 7
22 Jun 02	SOMETHING TO TALK ABOUT *Twisted Nerve / XL Recordings TNXL 014CD*	28 2
26 Oct 02 ●	YOU WERE RIGHT *Twisted Nerve / XL Recordings TNXL 015CD*	9 3
18 Jan 03	BORN AGAIN *Twisted Nerve / XL Recordings TNXL 016CD*	16 3
3 May 03	ALL POSSIBILITIES *Twisted Nerve / XL Recordings TNXL 017CD*	24 2
31 Jul 04	YEAR OF THE RAT *XL Recordings TNXL 018CD*	38 2
8 Jul 00	THE HOUR OF BEWILDERBEAST *XL Recordings TNXLCD 133*	13 47
20 Apr 02 ●	ABOUT A BOY – ORIGINAL SOUNDTRACK *Twisted Nerve TNXLCD 152*	6 18
16 Nov 02 ●	HAVE YOU FED THE FISH? *XL TNXLCD 156*	10 20
3 Jul 04 ●	ONE PLUS ONE IS ONE *Twisted Nerve / XL TNXLCD 179*	9 4

BADMAN
UK, male producer – Julian Brettle (Singles: 3 Weeks) pos/wks

2 Feb 91   MAGIC STYLE *Citybeat CBE 759* 61 3

Erykah BADU *US, female vocalist – Erica*
Wright (Singles: 17 Weeks, Albums: 25 Weeks) pos/wks

19 Apr 97	ON & ON *Universal UND 561117*	12 4
14 Jun 97	NEXT LIFETIME *Universal UND 56132*	30 3
29 Nov 97	APPLE TREE *Universal UND 56150*	47 1
11 Jul 98	ONE *Elektra E 3833CD1* [1]	23 3
6 Mar 99	YOU GOT ME *MCA MCSTD 48110* [2]	31 2
15 Sep 01	SWEET BABY *Epic 6718822* [3]	23 4
1 Mar 97	BADUIZM *MCA UD 530272*	17 25

[1] Busta Rhymes featuring Erykah Badu [2] Roots featuring Erykah Badu [3] Macy
Gray featuring Erykah Badu

Joan BAEZ *US, female vocalist / instrumentalist –*
guitar (Singles: 47 Weeks, Albums: 88 Weeks) pos/wks

6 May 65	WE SHALL OVERCOME *Fontana TF 564*	26 10
8 Jul 65 ●	THERE BUT FOR FORTUNE *Fontana TF 587*	8 12
2 Sep 65	IT'S ALL OVER NOW, BABY BLUE *Fontana TF 604*	22 8
23 Dec 65	FAREWELL ANGELINA (re) *Fontana TF 639*	35 4
28 Jul 66	PACK UP YOUR SORROWS *Fontana TF 727*	50 1
9 Oct 71 ●	THE NIGHT THEY DROVE OLD DIXIE DOWN *Vanguard VS 35138*	6 12
18 Jul 64 ●	JOAN BAEZ IN CONCERT VOLUME 2 *Fontana TFL 6033*	8 19
15 May 65 ●	JOAN BAEZ 5 *Fontana TFL 6043*	3 27
19 Jun 65 ●	JOAN BAEZ *Fontana TFL 6002*	9 13
27 Nov 65 ●	FAREWELL ANGELINA *Fontana TFL 6058*	5 23
19 Jul 69	JOAN BAEZ ON VANGUARD *Vanguard SVXL 100*	15 5
3 Apr 71	FIRST TEN YEARS *Vanguard 6635 003*	41 1

BAHA MEN
Bahamas, male vocal group (Singles: 35 Weeks) pos/wks

14 Oct 00 ●	WHO LET THE DOGS OUT *Edel 0115425 ERE*	2 23
3 Feb 01	YOU ALL DAT *Edel 0124855 ERE*	14 5
13 Jul 02	MOVE IT LIKE THIS *S-Curve / EMI CDEM 615*	16 7

'You All Dat' features vocal by Imani Coppola

Carol BAILEY
UK, female vocalist (Singles: 2 Weeks) pos/wks

25 Feb 95   FEEL IT *Multiply CDMULTY 3* 41 2

Philip BAILEY (see also EARTH WIND AND FIRE)
US, male vocalist (Singles: 20 Weeks, Albums: 17 Weeks) pos/wks

9 Mar 85 ★	EASY LOVER *CBS A 4915* [1]	1 12
18 May 85	WALKING ON THE CHINESE WALL *CBS A 6202*	34 8
30 Mar 85	CHINESE WALL *CBS 26161*	29 17

[1] Philip Bailey (duet with Phil Collins)

Merril BAINBRIDGE *Australia, female vocalist (Singles: 1 Week)* pos/wks

7 Dec 96   MOUTH *Gotham 74321431012* 51 1

Adrian BAKER and the TONICS (see also GIDEA PARK)
UK, male vocalist (Singles: 8 Weeks) pos/wks

19 Jul 75 ● SHERRY *Magnet MAG 34* 10 8

Anita BAKER
US, female vocalist (Singles: 22 Weeks, Albums: 83 Weeks) pos/wks

15 Nov 86	SWEET LOVE *Elektra EKR 44*	13 10
31 Jan 87	CAUGHT UP IN THE RAPTURE *Elektra EKR 49*	51 5
8 Oct 88	GIVING YOU THE BEST THAT I GOT *Elektra EKR 79*	55 3
30 Jun 90	TALK TO ME *Elektra EKR 111*	68 2
17 Sep 94	BODY & SOUL *Elektra EKR 190CD*	48 2
3 May 86	RAPTURE *Elektra EKT 37*	13 47
29 Oct 88	GIVING YOU THE BEST THAT I GOT *Elektra EKT 49* ▲	9 20
14 Jul 90 ●	COMPOSITIONS *Elektra EKT 72*	7 9
24 Sep 94	RHYTHM OF LOVE *Elektra 7559615552*	14 5
1 Jun 02	SWEET LOVE – THE VERY BEST OF ANITA BAKER *Atlantic 8122736032*	49 2

Arthur BAKER (see also Wally JUMP Jr and the CRIMINAL ELEMENT)
US, male producer / multi-instrumentalist (Singles: 8 Weeks) pos/wks

20 May 89	IT'S YOUR TIME *Breakout USA 654* [1]	64 2
21 Oct 89	THE MESSAGE IS LOVE *Breakout USA 668* [2]	38 5
30 Nov 02	CONFUSION (re-mix) *Whacked WACKT 002CD* [3]	64 1

[1] Arthur Baker featuring Shirley Lewis [2] Arthur Baker and the Backbeat
Disciples featuring Al Green [3] Arthur Baker vs New Order

Hylda BAKER and Arthur MULLARD
UK, female, b. 4 Feb 1905, d. 1 May 1986 / male, b. 10 Nov 1913,
d. 11 Dec 1995, actors / vocal duo (Singles: 6 Weeks) pos/wks

9 Sep 78   YOU'RE THE ONE THAT I WANT *Pye 7N 46121* 22 6

George BAKER SELECTION *Holland, male /*
female vocal / instrumental group (Singles: 10 Weeks) pos/wks

6 Sep 75 ● PALOMA BLANCA *Warner Bros. K 16541* 10 10

Ginger BAKER'S AIR FORCE (see also BAKER-GURVITZ ARMY; BBM; BLIND FAITH) UK, male vocal / instrumental group (Albums: 1 Week) pos/wks

13 Jun 70	GINGER BAKER'S AIR FORCE Polydor 266 2001	37	1

BAKER-GURVITZ ARMY (see also GINGER BAKER'S AIR FORCE; BBM; BLIND FAITH) UK, male vocal / instrumental group (Albums: 5 Weeks) pos/wks

22 Feb 75	BAKER-GURVITZ ARMY Vertigo 9103 201	22	5

BAKSHELF DOG
UK, male bulldog vocalist – Churchill (Singles: 2 Weeks) pos/wks

21 Dec 02	NO LIMITS WVC CDCHURCH 1	51	2

BALAAM AND THE ANGEL UK, male vocal / instrumental group (Singles: 2 Weeks, Albums: 2 Weeks) pos/wks

29 Mar 86	SHE KNOWS Virgin VS 842	70	2
16 Aug 86	THE GREATEST STORY EVER TOLD Virgin V 2377	67	2

Long John BALDRY UK, male vocalist (Singles: 36 Weeks) pos/wks

8 Nov 67 ★	LET THE HEARTACHES BEGIN Pye 7N 17385	1	13
28 Aug 68	WHEN THE SUN COMES SHINING THRU Pye 7N 17593	29	7
23 Oct 68	MEXICO Pye 7N 17563	15	8
29 Jan 69	IT'S TOO LATE NOW Pye 7N 17664	21	8

BALEARIC BILL (see also AIRSCAPE; BLUE BAMBOO; CUBIC 22; TRANSFORMER 2; SVENSON and GIELEN) Belgium / Holland, male production duo – Johan Gielen and Sven Maes (Singles: 2 Weeks) pos/wks

2 Oct 99	DESTINATION SUNSHINE Xtravaganza XTRAV 3CDS	36	2

Edward BALL UK, male vocalist (Singles: 2 Weeks) pos/wks

20 Jul 96	THE MILL HILL SELF HATE CLUB Creation CRESCD 233	57	1
22 Feb 97	LOVE IS BLUE Creation CRESCD 244	59	1

Kenny BALL and his JAZZMEN 362 Top 500
Top UK trad jazz bandleader, b. 22 May 1930, Essex, UK. His Dixieland band was at the forefront of the early 1960s jazz revival. Their biggest hit, 'Midnight in Moscow', reached the runner-up spot on both sides of the Atlantic (Singles: 136 Weeks, Albums: 50 Weeks) pos/wks

23 Feb 61	SAMANTHA Pye Jazz Today 7NJ 2040 [1]	13	15
11 May 61	I STILL LOVE YOU ALL Pye Jazz 7NJ 2042	24	6
31 Aug 61	SOMEDAY (YOU'LL BE SORRY) Pye Jazz 7NJ 2047	28	6
9 Nov 61 ●	MIDNIGHT IN MOSCOW Pye Jazz 7NJ 2049	2	21
15 Feb 62 ●	MARCH OF THE SIAMESE CHILDREN Pye Jazz 7NJ 2051	4	13
17 May 62 ●	THE GREEN LEAVES OF SUMMER Pye Jazz 7NJ 2054	7	14
23 Aug 62	SO DO I Pye Jazz 7NJ 2056	14	8
18 Oct 62	THE PAY-OFF (AMOI DE PAYER) Pye Jazz 7NJ 2061 [2]	23	6
17 Jan 63 ●	SUKIYAKI Pye Jazz 7NJ 2062	10	13
25 Apr 63	CASABLANCA Pye Jazz 7NJ 2064	21	11
13 Jun 63	RONDO Pye Jazz 7NJ 2065	24	8
22 Aug 63	ACAPULCO 1922 Pye Jazz 7NJ 2067	27	6
11 Jun 64	HELLO, DOLLY! Pye Jazz 7NJ 2071	30	7
19 Jul 67	WHEN I'M SIXTY FOUR Pye 7N 17348	43	2
25 Aug 62 ★	THE BEST OF BALL, BARBER AND BILK Pye Golden Guinea GGL 0131 [1]	1	24
7 Sep 63 ●	KENNY BALL'S GOLDEN HITS Pye Golden Guinea GGL 0209 [2]	4	26

[1] Lonnie Donegan presents Kenny Ball and his Jazz Band [2] Clarinet – Dave Jones [1] Kenny Ball, Chris Barber and Acker Bilk [2] Kenny Ball

Michael BALL
UK, male vocalist / actor (Singles: 39 Weeks, Albums: 98 Weeks) pos/wks

28 Jan 89 ●	LOVE CHANGES EVERYTHING Really Useful RUR 3	2	14
28 Oct 89	THE FIRST MAN YOU REMEMBER Really Useful RUR 6 [1]	68	2
10 Aug 91	IT'S STILL YOU Polydor PO 160	58	2
25 Apr 92	ONE STEP OUT OF TIME Polydor PO 206	20	7
12 Dec 92	IF I CAN DREAM (EP) (re) Polydor PO 248	51	2
11 Sep 93	SUNSET BOULEVARD Polydor PZCD 293	72	1
30 Jul 94	FROM HERE TO ETERNITY Columbia 6606905	36	3
17 Sep 94	THE LOVERS WE WERE Columbia 6607972	63	2
9 Dec 95	THE ROSE Columbia 6614535	42	4
17 Feb 96	(SOMETHING INSIDE) SO STRONG Columbia 6629005	40	2
30 May 92 ★	MICHAEL BALL Polydor 5113302 ■	1	10
17 Jul 93 ●	ALWAYS Polydor 5196662	3	11

13 Aug 94 ●	ONE CAREFUL OWNER Columbia 4772802	7	6
19 Nov 94	THE BEST OF MICHAEL BALL PolyGram TV 5238912	25	7
27 Jan 96 ●	FIRST LOVE Columbia 4835992	4	6
16 Nov 96	THE MUSICALS Columbia 5338922	20	10
7 Nov 98	THE MOVIES PolyGram TV 5592412	13	17
20 Nov 99	THE VERY BEST OF MICHAEL BALL – IN CONCERT AT THE ROYAL ALBERT HALL / CHRISTMAS Universal Music TV 5421952	18	7
11 Nov 00	THIS TIME ... IT'S PERSONAL Universal Music TV 1597282	20	8
29 Sep 01	CENTRE STAGE Universal Music TV 160712	11	7
1 Nov 03	A LOVE STORY Liberty 5919492	41	1
6 Nov 04	LOVE CHANGES EVERYTHING – THE ESSENTIAL MICHAEL BALL Universal Music TV 9825039	21	8+

[1] Michael Ball and Diana Morrison

Tracks on If I Can Dream (EP): If I Can Dream / You Don't Have to Say You Love Me / Always on My Mind / Tell Me There's a Heaven

Steve BALSAMO UK, male vocalist (Singles: 2 Weeks) pos/wks

16 Mar 02	SUGAR FOR THE SOUL Columbia 6718552	32	2

BALTIMORA Ireland, male vocalist – Jimmy McShane, b. 23 May 1957, d. 14 Dec 2002 (Singles: 12 Weeks) pos/wks

10 Aug 85 ●	TARZAN BOY Columbia DB 9102	3	12

Charli BALTIMORE
US, female rapper – Tiffany Lane (Singles: 14 Weeks) pos/wks

1 Aug 98	MONEY Epic 6662272	12	4
12 Oct 02 ●	DOWN 4 U (2re) Murder Inc 0639002 [1]	4	10

[1] Irv Gotti presents Ja Rule, Ashanti, Charli Baltimore and Vita

BAM BAM US, male vocalist / instrumentalist – Chris Westbrook (Singles: 2 Weeks) pos/wks

19 Mar 88	GIVE IT TO ME Serious 7OUS 10	65	2

Afrika BAMBAATAA
US, male DJ / producer / rapper – Kevin Donovan (Singles: 34 Weeks) pos/wks

28 Aug 82	PLANET ROCK 21 POSP 497 [1]	53	3
10 Mar 84	RENEGADES OF FUNK Tommy Boy AFR 1 [1]	30	4
1 Sep 84	UNITY (PART 1 – THE THIRD COMING) Tommy Boy AFR 2 [2]	49	5
27 Feb 88	RECKLESS EMI EM 41 [3]	17	8
12 Oct 91	JUST GET UP AND DANCE EMI USA MT 100	45	3
17 Oct 98	GOT TO GET UP Multiply CDMULTY 42	22	4
18 Sep 99 ●	AFRIKA SHOX Hard Hands HAND 057CD1 [4]	7	5
25 Aug 01	PLANET ROCK Tommy Boy TBCD 2266 [5]	47	1
13 Mar 04	D-FUNKTIONAL Wall of Sound WALLD 092 [6]	72	1

[1] Afrika Bambaataa and the Soul Sonic Force [2] Afrika Bambaataa and James Brown [3] Afrika Bambaataa and Family featuring UB40 [4] Leftfield / Bambaataa [5] Paul Oakenfold presents Afrika Bambaataa and Soulsonic Force [6] Mekon featuring Afrika Bambaataa

BAMBOO
UK, male producer – Andrew Livingstone (Singles: 12 Weeks) pos/wks

17 Jan 98 ●	BAMBOOGIE VC Recordings VCRD 29	2	10
4 Jul 98	THE STRUTT VC Recordings VCRD 35	36	2

BANANARAMA 192 Top 500
Britain's most charted female group: Sarah Dallin, Keren Woodward, Siobhan Fahey. The London-based trio was also a best-selling act in the US, where 'Venus' topped the chart. Fahey, who married Eurythmic Dave Stewart, left in 1988 to form Shakespear's Sister and was replaced by Jacqui O'Sullivan (Singles: 202 Weeks, Albums: 99 Weeks) pos/wks

13 Feb 82	IT AIN'T WHAT YOU DO IT'S THE WAY THAT YOU DO IT Chrysalis CHS 2570 [1]	4	10
10 Apr 82 ●	REALLY SAYING SOMETHING Deram NANA 1 [2]	5	10
3 Jul 82	SHY BOY London NANA 2	4	11
4 Dec 82	CHEERS THEN London NANA 3	45	7
26 Feb 83 ●	NA NA HEY HEY KISS HIM GOODBYE London NANA 4	5	10
9 Jul 83	CRUEL SUMMER London NANA 5	8	10
3 Mar 84 ●	ROBERT DE NIRO'S WAITING London NANA 6	3	11
26 May 84	ROUGH JUSTICE London NANA 7	23	7
24 Nov 84	HOTLINE TO HEAVEN London NANA 8	58	2
24 Aug 85	DO NOT DISTURB London NANA 9	31	6

CONFESSIONS OF A POP STAR

– an experience of a lifetime

This book concentrates on the facts and statistics behind thousands of chart acts. So, just for a change, we decided to uncover the glamorous (and sometimes unglamorous) truth behind what it's like to strive for pop stardom. About 10 years ago, Bryn Downing was working as a picture researcher for The European newspaper when he spotted an intriguing advert in the Daily Star. Bryn, who would go on to hit the charts with the band Optimystic, takes up the story.

The advert in the Daily Star asked for all budding wannabes to send in a tape of them singing, and the winner would be offered a recording contract with the well-known producer Ian Levine, who was working with stars like Bad Boys Inc, Take That, etc. How could I resist?

I was in a band called World and had put together a couple of tracks. We managed to produce a pop video for our song 'Fight for Your Planet' with the help of another good friend, William Green, who is now producing promos for Outkast and 50 Cent. The video was entered into a competition looking for new talent on BBC2; though we didn't win, we did get the video played on TV. I thought the video would be a good way to get Ian Levine's attention and possibly an audition for the Daily Star competition, so I sent it off.

The audition
A week later Ian Levine called me to say he was impressed with the video and could I please meet him at his studios in Ealing for a chat. I was obviously delighted and made arrangements to meet up. When I arrived at Tropicana studios, which weren't as nice as they sound, we chatted about my experience of performing in front of crowds. I sang 'Fight for Your Planet' a capella and he asked about my dancing and guitar playing.

Two weeks later he rang me up to arrange a photo shoot and the following day he told me I was in! I'd be joining a band with two brothers from Newcastle, Ian and Stuart McKeith, and two girls, Shola and Selina, who were picked at a later date when Ian decided he wanted to try something different, rather than just put together another boy band. Bad move!

The line-up
I met the brothers at Ian's house and we immediately hit it off. We became mates very quickly and found a house to share in Surrey. We went out for dinner with Shola and Selina and we all got on so well that the line-up was decided there and then. That night we were also introduced to Carolyn and Alwyn, who would become our publicists.

Recording an album started shortly afterwards. The next six months were spent in the studio, resulting in about 16 songs to take to the record companies. We produced two pop promos and created a portfolio of pictures of the band. While Ian was pitching this package to the record companies we began intense dance rehearsals at Pineapple Studios in Covent Garden. We soon realised that the boys were no match for Selina and Shola. The girls were professional dancers and it was decided then that the rest of the band should stick to playing their instruments. That sorted out, the line-up looked like this: Ian – lead singer and keyboards; Stuart – backing vocals, keyboards, saxophone; me – backing vocals and guitar; Shola and Selina – backing vocals and dancing. Throughout our rehearsals, the buzz of what the future held was too great for any problems or rivalry to surface.

> "Although we were only on the C list (at Radio 1), that still meant four plays a day and at the time it seemed a huge achievement, despite one of those plays coming at 3am."

The contract
We had very little say in the creative side of the business. Ian Levine had already made us all sign contracts that pretty much said: "I am your producer. I am your manager and you will sing and perform all of my songs and will have no input whatsoever when it comes to the music unless I say so, and then if you do I will take the majority of the writers' and producers' royalties." He had allegedly been stung previously by Bad Boys Inc walking out on him and going to 1st Avenue management because they didn't want to sing his music any more. Our solicitor said the contract was so over the top that it wouldn't stand up in court; nonetheless, when you are in a position to sign a contract with a major label and told "I will make you a star", quibbles about the contract go out the window.

The money
The financial side was a complete joke. While recording and rehearsing for about nine months we were paid nothing. I had to give up my job and sold my car to finance myself, and the boys were on housing benefit so we could pay the rent. When we finally signed to Warner Brothers it was for a £5m, five-album deal. This doesn't mean you get £5m; it just means you'd receive £5m if you had five albums out. For our first album we received £125,000. Out of this, our manager and producer Ian Levine, plus lawyers, agents and God knows who else, took £100,000. The band was left with £5,000 each. This was then taken by our accountants who told us it would have to last us until we have a hit and can pay off the £125,000 advance. Five thousand pounds doesn't go very far, and we were given a grand total of £50 per week until the funds ran out. The only other money we received was £10 per day

The subject of this story, Bryn Downing, is pictured in the centre, flanked by other Optimystic group members who are, left to right, Ian, Shola, Bryn, Selina, and Stuart.

subsistence for food, but only when on tour, and performance fees if you were on TV, which was a godsend because it was usually about £200-250 per performance. That was four weeks' wages!

The record company paid for a tour manager, hotels and a tour van. Then we three boys were investigated by the fraud department of the DSS because they had seen a piece in the Daily Express saying "new band sign £5m deal to Warner Bros" and wanted to know why we were claiming housing benefit. It would have been funny if they hadn't been so serious. Fortunately for us, we arranged for the record company to write to them and explain the deal and they let us off the hook. They even sent us a good luck card.

The breakthrough
Smash Hits had to be one of the first real breakthroughs we had. It was THE magazine to get into if you wanted to make it, and they wrote a piece on us when we released our first single 'Caught Up in My Heart'. The other major break was that we were Radio 1 playlisted. Although we were only on the C list, that still meant four plays a day and at the time it seemed a huge achievement, despite one of those plays coming at 3am.

The one TV show that really sticks in my memory as big is the Des O'Connor Christmas special. It was a major coup for us to get on the show, particularly as we hadn't yet broken the Top 40. I will always remember our fellow guests, Arnold Schwarzenegger, Sylvester Stallone and Jim Davidson. Arnie was great – he was smoking a massive cigar and wished us luck before we went on to perform 'Nothing But Love'. We really felt like we had made it

> "We really felt like we had made it when we were picked to be a warm-up act for the Smash Hits Poll Winners' Party."

when we were picked to be a warm-up act for the Smash Hits Poll Winners' Party and nationwide tour. Suddenly we were performing in front of tens of thousands of people at huge venues such as Manchester G-Mex and Docklands London Arena. We were mixing with the absolute cream of the pop industry: Take That, Eternal, East 17, M People, Boyzone and Let Loose. The best feeling of all was seeing posters and banners with our name on them.

One of our best gigs was at the Point in Dublin. We met Boyzone on tour and they became good friends, particularly Keith Duffy and Ronan Keating. We used to borrow each other's clothes, sit on the coach together, go for after-gig drinks and practise singing harmonies. It was an adventure for all of us. At one memorable gig, Ronan got on the mic and said: "I want all of you out there to give a special Irish welcome to some very good friends of ours from England, Optimystic." The gig was awesome after that introduction.

The groupies
It's safe to say there was a huge amount of "attention" if you wanted it. We had a large group of about 30 young girls that used to come to most gigs and my God were they dedicated. One group from Scotland travelled down to see us at the Hippodrome in Leicester Square. They didn't even go to the concert; they just sat outside the back entrance. I felt terrible because we had time to chat to them for only about 30 seconds before we raced off to our next venue.

Most of the older girls would hang around at hotels after gigs. I actually found one girl in my room after a gig. She had rung every hotel in the area saying she was from

Warner Bros and needed to speak to Optimystic. Her dedication paid off and she found the hotel, and was waiting for me in my bed when I returned! It's actually pretty scary when you think about it, but at the time it was a laugh, and made a good story for the lads. A few of the more interesting fans knocking on my hotel room door in the middle of the night included a girl with no top on, a girl naked underneath a long coat, two sisters asking if I would like to see their tattoos, a group of girls asking if we would like to have a private room party, and the hotel receptionist asking if she could have an autograph at 3am! We also had visits from a drunken nutter asking us to sing our latest single a capella, because he had heard we weren't all that, and a bloke asking to see my guitar.

The other famous pop cliché is knickers being thrown on stage and I can categorically say I have a fabulous collection from those years, combined with about 5,000 love letters containing all sorts of weird and wonderful things. At one stage I was getting about 100 letters a week from fans and they would always include badges, bracelets, necklaces, rings, hair, underwear and even semi-naked photos with mobile numbers on the back. Amazing!

The chart debut
We were sitting in the tour van in Chancery Lane, waiting to go to a gig in a club nearby, when we heard we had made No.40 on Radio 1. We went absolutely berserk. Some of our fans were outside the venue listening on a small radio and saw us all jumping up and down in the van. We had a bit of a celebration right there on the street.

The end
The band eventually split up when our A&R man Clive Black at Warner Bros was headhunted to go to EMI. We weren't yet well established so the record label was pretty uninterested in continuing with us. With Clive gone and 'Best Thing in the World' stalling at No.65, it was pretty much all over. Us boys stuck together and we spent about a year writing a variety of tracks hoping to get another contract. After that I decided I had to get a proper job or I was going to be a poor musician for the rest of my life, so I moved out on amicable terms and we have kept in contact ever since.

There were no hard feelings, just disappointment really. Nobody realises how hard it is and how much of your life you have to dedicate to becoming a pop star. The rewards are huge but, when it doesn't work out it can be pretty hard on everyone, because you give so much up.

Would I do it all again? Of course I would. It was an experience of a lifetime. **Bryn Downing**

> "The other famous pop cliché is knickers being thrown on stage and I can categorically say I have a fabulous collection from those years, combined with about 5,000 love letters containing all sorts of weird and wonderful things."

Optimystic strut their stuff on stage at a mid-1990s Radio 1 Roadshow in baking hot Blackpool

For the full low-down on Optimystic's chart career, turn to page 374

			pos/wks
31 May 86 ●	**VENUS** *London NANA 10* ▲	8	13
16 Aug 86	**MORE THAN PHYSICAL** *London NANA 11*	41	5
14 Feb 87	**TRICK OF THE NIGHT** *London NANA 12*	32	5
11 Jul 87	**I HEARD A RUMOUR** *London NANA 13*	14	9
10 Oct 87 ●	**LOVE IN THE FIRST DEGREE** *London NANA 14*	3	12
9 Jan 88	**I CAN'T HELP IT** *London NANA 15*	20	6
9 Apr 88 ●	**I WANT YOU BACK** *London NANA 16*	5	10
24 Sep 88	**LOVE, TRUTH AND HONESTY** *London NANA 17*	23	8
19 Nov 88	**NATHAN JONES** *London NANA 18*	15	9
25 Feb 89 ●	**HELP** *London LON 222* ③	3	9
10 Jun 89	**CRUEL SUMMER (re-mix)** *London NANA 19*	19	6
28 Jul 90	**ONLY YOUR LOVE** *London NANA 21*	27	4
5 Jan 91	**PREACHER MAN** *London NANA 23*	20	6
20 Apr 91	**LONG TRAIN RUNNING** *London NANA 24*	30	5
29 Aug 92	**MOVIN' ON** *London NANA 25*	24	5
28 Nov 92	**LAST THING ON MY MIND** *London NANA 26*	71	2
20 Mar 93	**MORE MORE MORE** *London NACPD 27*	24	4
19 Mar 83 ●	**DEEP SEA SKIVING** *London RAMA 1*	7	16
28 Apr 84	**BANANARAMA** *London RAMA 2*	16	11
19 Jul 86	**TRUE CONFESSIONS** *London RAMA 3*	46	5
19 Sep 87	**WOW!** *London RAMA 4*	26	6
22 Oct 88 ●	**THE GREATEST HITS COLLECTION** *London RAMA 5*	3	37
25 May 91	**POP LIFE** *London 8282461*	42	1
10 Apr 93	**PLEASE YOURSELF** *London 8283572*	46	1
10 Nov 01 ●	**THE VERY BEST OF BANANARAMA** *London 927414992*	43	2

① Fun Boy Three and Bananarama ② Bananarama with Fun Boy Three
③ Bananarama / La Na Nee Nee Noo Noo

The listed flip side of 'Love in the First Degree' was 'Mr Sleaze' by Stock Aitken Waterman. Act was a duo for last three hits

BANCO DE GAIA
UK, male multi-instrumentalist – Toby Marks (Albums: 4 Weeks)   pos/wks

12 Mar 94	**MAYA** *Planet Dog BARKCD 3*	34	2
13 May 95	**LAST TRAIN TO LHASA** *Planet Dog BARKCD 0115*	31	2

The BAND (see also Bob DYLAN; Robbie ROBERTSON) *Canada / US, male vocal / instrumental group (Singles: 18 Weeks, Albums: 26 Weeks)*   pos/wks

18 Sep 68	**THE WEIGHT** *Capitol CL 15559*	21	9
4 Apr 70	**RAG MAMA RAG** *Capitol CL 15629*	16	9
31 Jan 70	**THE BAND** *Capitol EST 132*	25	12
3 Oct 70	**STAGE FRIGHT** *Capitol EA SW 425*	15	6
27 Nov 71	**CAHOOTS** *Capitol EAST 651*	41	1
13 Jul 74 ●	**BEFORE THE FLOOD** *Asylum IDBD 1* ①	8	7

① Bob Dylan / The Band

BAND AID *International, male / female vocal / instrumental charity assembly (Singles: 29 Weeks)*   pos/wks

15 Dec 84 ★	**DO THEY KNOW IT'S CHRISTMAS? (re)** *Mercury FEED 1* ◆ ■	...1	20
23 Dec 89 ★	**DO THEY KNOW IT'S CHRISTMAS?** *PWL / Polydor FEED 2* ① ■	...1	6
11 Dec 04 ★	**DO THEY KNOW IT'S CHRISTMAS?** *Mercury 9869413* ② ◆ ■	...1	3+

① Band Aid II ② Band Aid 20

BAND AID: Adam Clayton, Bono (U2); Bob Geldof, Johnny Fingers, Simon Crowe, Peter Briquette (Boomtown Rats); David Bowie; Paul McCartney; Holly Johnson (Frankie Goes To Hollywood); Midge Ure, Chris Cross (Ultravox); Simon Le Bon, Nick Rhodes, Andy Taylor, John Taylor, Roger Taylor (Duran Duran); Paul Young; Tony Hadley, Martin Kemp, John Keeble, Gary Kemp, Steve Norman (Spandau Ballet); Martyn Ware, Glenn Gregory (Heaven 17); Francis Rossi, Rick Parfitt (Status Quo); Sting; Boy George, Jon Moss (Culture Club); Marilyn; Keren Woodward, Sarah Dallin, Siobhan Fahey (Bananarama); Jody Watley (Shalamar); Paul Weller; Robert "Kool" Bell, James Taylor, Dennis Thomas (Kool and the Gang); George Michael and Phil Collins. Band Aid's 1984 'Do They Know It's Christmas?' re-entered the chart and peaked at No.3 in Dec 1985.

BAND AID II: Bananarama, Big Fun, Bros, Cathy Dennis, D Mob, Jason Donovan, Kevin Godley, Glen Goldsmith, Kylie Minogue, The Pasadenas, Chris Rea, Cliff Richard, Jimmy Somerville, Sonia, Lisa Stansfield, Technotronic, Wet Wet Wet.

BAND AID 20: Keane, Sir Paul McCartney, Sugababes, Skye, Robbie Williams, Dido, Bono, Jamelia, Justin Hawkins, Chris Martin, Fran Healy, Beverley Knight, Busted, Ms Dynamite, Danny Goffey, Katie Melua, Will Young, Natasha Bedingfield, Snow Patrol, Shaznay Lewis, Joss Stone, Daniel Bedingfield, Rachel Stevens, The Thrills, Roisin Murphy, Lemar, Estelle, Neil Hannon, Feeder, Dizzee Rascal.

BAND AKA *US, male vocal / instrumental group (Singles: 12 Weeks)*   pos/wks

15 May 82	**GRACE** *Epic EPC A 2376*	41	5
5 Mar 83	**JOY** *Epic EPC A 3145*	24	7

BAND OF GOLD *Holland, male / female vocal / instrumental group (Singles: 11 Weeks)*   pos/wks

14 Jul 84	**LOVE SONGS ARE BACK AGAIN (MEDLEY)** *RCA 428*	24	11

BAND OF THIEVES *See Luke GOSS and the BAND OF THIEVES*

BANDA SONORA
UK, male producer – Gerald Elms (Singles: 3 Weeks)   pos/wks

6 Oct 01	**GUITARRA G** *Defected DFECT 36CDS*	50	2
19 Oct 02	**PRESSURE COOKER** *Defected DFTD 060CDS* ①	46	1

① G Club Presents Banda Sonora

BANDERAS *UK, female vocal / instrumental duo – Sally Herbert and Caroline Buckley (Singles: 16 Weeks, Albums: 3 Weeks)*   pos/wks

23 Feb 91	**THIS IS YOUR LIFE** *London LON 290*	16	10
15 Jun 91	**SHE SELLS** *London LON 298*	41	6
13 Apr 91	**RIPE** *London 8282471*	40	3

The BANDITS
UK, male vocal / instrumental group (Singles: 2 Weeks)   pos/wks

28 Jun 03	**TAKE IT AND RUN** *B Unique BUN 055CDS*	32	1
20 Sep 03	**2 STEP ROCK** *B Unique BUN 065CDS*	35	1

BANDWAGON *See Johnny JOHNSON and the BANDWAGON*

Honey BANE
UK, female vocalist – Donna Boylan (Singles: 8 Weeks)   pos/wks

24 Jan 81	**TURN ME ON TURN ME OFF** *Zonophone Z 15*	37	5
18 Apr 81	**BABY LOVE** *Zonophone Z 19*	58	3

BANG *UK, male vocal duo (Singles: 2 Weeks)*   pos/wks

6 May 89	**YOU'RE THE ONE** *RCA PB 42715*	74	2

The BANGLES   335   Top 500
Originally named The Supersonic Bangs, then Bangs, melodic pop-rock quartet formed 1981, Los Angeles, California, US. Comprised Susanna Hoffs (v), sisters Vicki (g) and Debbi Peterson (d) and Michael Steele (b). Split 1989, having become the most successful all-female rock band in chart history, then reformed for a tour in 2000. 'Eternal Flame' returned to the top in 2001 by Atomic Kitten (Singles: 96 Weeks, Albums: 105 Weeks)   pos/wks

15 Feb 86 ●	**MANIC MONDAY** *CBS A 6796*	2	12
26 Apr 86	**IF SHE KNEW WHAT SHE WANTS** *CBS A 7062*	31	7
5 Jul 86	**GOING DOWN TO LIVERPOOL** *CBS A 7255*	56	3
13 Sep 86 ●	**WALK LIKE AN EGYPTIAN** *CBS 6500717* ▲	3	19
10 Jan 87	**WALKING DOWN YOUR STREET** *CBS BANGS 1*	16	6
18 Apr 87	**FOLLOWING** *CBS BANGS 2*	55	3
6 Feb 88	**HAZY SHADE OF WINTER** *Def Jam BANGS 3*	11	10
5 Nov 88	**IN YOUR ROOM** *CBS BANGS 4*	35	6
18 Feb 89 ★	**ETERNAL FLAME** *CBS BANGS 5* ▲	1	18
10 Jun 89	**BE WITH YOU** *CBS BANGS 6*	23	8
14 Oct 89	**I'LL SET YOU FREE** *CBS BANGS 7*	74	1
9 Jun 90	**WALK LIKE AN EGYPTIAN (re-issue)** *CBS BANGS 8*	73	1
15 Mar 03	**SOMETHING THAT YOU SAID** *Down Kiddie / EMI / Liberty BANGLES 003*	38	2
16 Mar 85	**ALL OVER THE PLACE** *CBS 26015*	86	1
15 Mar 86 ●	**DIFFERENT LIGHT** *CBS 26659*	3	47
10 Dec 88 ●	**EVERYTHING** *CBS 4629791*	5	26
9 Jun 90 ●	**GREATEST HITS** *CBS 4667691*	4	23
4 Aug 01	**ETERNAL FLAME – THE BEST OF THE BANGLES** *Columbia STVCD 121*	15	7
29 Mar 03	**DOLL REVOLUTION** *EMI / Liberty 5815102*	62	1

Lloyd BANK$ (see also G-UNIT)
US, male rapper (Singles: 6 Weeks, Albums: 10 Weeks)   pos/wks

21 Aug 04	**ON FIRE** *Interscope 9863485*	19	6
10 Jul 04	**THE HUNGER FOR MORE** *Interscope 9863026* ▲	15	10

Tony BANKS (see also FISH; GENESIS) *UK, male vocal / instrumentalist – keyboards (Singles: 1 Week, Albums: 7 Weeks)*   pos/wks

18 Oct 86	**SHORT CUT TO SOMEWHERE** *Charisma CB 426* ①	75	1
20 Oct 79	**A CURIOUS FEELING** *Charisma CAS 1148*	21	5
25 Jun 83	**THE FUGITIVE** *Charisma TBLP 1*	50	2

① Fish and Tony Banks

BANNED UK, male vocal / instrumental group (Singles: 6 Weeks) pos/wks

17 Dec 77	LITTLE GIRL Harvest HAR 5145	36	6

BANSHEES See SIOUXSIE and the BANSHEES

Buju BANTON Jamaica, male vocalist (Singles: 1 Week) pos/wks

7 Aug 93	MAKE MY DAY Mercury BUJCD 2	72	1

Pato BANTON
UK, male vocalist – Patrick Murray (Singles: 37 Weeks) pos/wks

1 Oct 94 ★	BABY COME BACK Virgin VSCDT 1522	1	18
11 Feb 95	THIS COWBOY SONG A&M 5809652 [1]	15	6
8 Apr 95	BUBBLING HOT Virgin VSCDT 1530 [2]	15	7
20 Jan 96	SPIRITS IN THE MATERIAL WORLD MCA MCSTD 2113 [3]	36	2
27 Jul 96	GROOVIN' IRS CDEIRS 195 [4]	14	4

[1] Sting featuring Pato Banton [2] Pato Banton with Ranking Roger [3] Pato Banton with Sting [4] Pato Banton and the Reggae Revolution

The sleeve of 'Baby Come Back' credits Ali and Robin Campbell

BAR CODES featuring Alison BROWN
UK, male / female vocal group (Singles: 1 Week) pos/wks

17 Dec 94	SUPERMARKET SWEEP Blanca Casa BC 101CD	72	1

Chris BARBER UK, male jazz band – leader
Chris Barber – trombone (Singles: 30 Weeks, Albums: 91 Weeks) pos/wks

13 Feb 59 ●	PETITE FLEUR (re) Pye Nixa NJ 2026 [1]	3	24
9 Oct 59	LONESOME (SI TU VOIS MA MERE) Columbia DB 4333 [2]	27	4
4 Jan 62	REVIVAL (re) Columbia SCD 2166 [3]	43	4
24 Sep 60	CHRIS BARBER BAND BOX NO. 2 Columbia 33SCX 3277	17	1
5 Nov 60	ELITE SYNCOPATIONS Columbia 33SX 1245	18	1
12 Nov 60	THE BEST OF CHRIS BARBER Ace of Clubs ACL 1037	17	1
27 May 61 ●	THE BEST OF BARBER AND BILK VOLUME 1 Pye Golden Guinea GGL 0075 [1]	4	43
11 Nov 61 ●	THE BEST OF BARBER AND BILK VOLUME 2 Pye Golden Guinea GGL 0096 [1]	8	18
25 Aug 62 ★	THE BEST OF BALL, BARBER AND BILK Pye Golden Guinea GGL 0131 [2]	1	24
29 Jan 00	THE SKIFFLE SESSIONS – LIVE IN BELFAST Venture CDVE 945 [3]	14	3

[1] Clarinet solo – Monty Sunshine [2] Chris Barber featuring Monty Sunshine [3] Chris Barber's Jazz Band [1] Chris Barber and Acker Bilk [2] Kenny Ball, Chris Barber and Acker Bilk [3] Van Morrison / Lonnie Donegan / Chris Barber

BARBRA and NEIL See Neil DIAMOND; Barbra STREISAND

BARCLAY JAMES HARVEST UK, male vocal /
instrumental group (Singles: 9 Weeks, Albums: 42 Weeks) pos/wks

2 Apr 77	LIVE (EP) (re) Polydor 2229 198	49	2
26 Jan 80	LOVE ON THE LINE Polydor POSP 97	63	2
22 Nov 80	LIFE IS FOR LIVING Polydor POSP 195	61	3
21 May 83	JUST A DAY AWAY Polydor POSP 585	68	2
14 Dec 74	BARCLAY JAMES HARVEST LIVE Polydor 2683 052	40	2
18 Oct 75	TIME HONOURED GHOST Polydor 2383 361	32	3
23 Oct 76	OCTOBERON Polydor 2442 144	19	4
1 Oct 77	GONE TO EARTH Polydor 2442 148	30	7
21 Oct 78	BARCLAY JAMES HARVEST XII Polydor POLD 5006	31	2
23 May 81	TURN OF THE TIDE Polydor POLD 5040	55	2
24 Jul 82	A CONCERT FOR THE PEOPLE (BERLIN) Polydor POLD 5052	15	11
28 May 83	RING OF CHANGES Polydor POLH 3	36	4
14 Apr 84	VICTIMS OF CIRCUMSTANCE Polydor POLD 5135	33	6
14 Feb 87	FACE TO FACE Polydor POLD 5209	65	1

Tracks on Live (EP): Rock 'n' Roll Star / Medicine Man (Parts 1 & 2)

BARDO UK, male / female vocal duo – Sally Ann
Triplett and Stephen Fischer (Singles: 8 Weeks) pos/wks

10 Apr 82 ●	ONE STEP FURTHER Epic EPC A2265	2	8

BARDOT Australia, female vocal group (Singles: 1 Week) pos/wks

14 Apr 01	POISON East West EW 229CD	45	1

BAREFOOT MAN
Germany, male vocalist – George Nowak (Singles: 7 Weeks) pos/wks

5 Dec 98	BIG PANTY WOMAN Plaza PZACD 082	21	7

BARENAKED LADIES Canada, male vocal /
instrumental group (Singles: 12 Weeks, Albums: 18 Weeks) pos/wks

20 Feb 99 ●	ONE WEEK Reprise W 468CD ▲	5	8
15 May 99	IT'S ALL BEEN DONE Reprise W 476CD	28	2
24 Jul 99	CALL AND ANSWER Reprise W 498CD1	52	1
11 Dec 99	BRIAN WILSON Reprise W 511CD1	73	1
27 Aug 94	MAYBE YOU SHOULD DRIVE Reprise 9362457092	57	1
6 Mar 99	STUNT Reprise 9362469632	20	16
30 Sep 00	MAROON Reprise 9362478912	64	1

Daniel BARENBOIM See John WILLIAMS

The BAR-KAYS
US, male vocal / instrumental group (Singles: 15 Weeks) pos/wks

23 Aug 67	SOUL FINGER Stax 601 014	33	7
22 Jan 77	SHAKE YOUR RUMP TO THE FUNK Mercury 6167 417	41	4
12 Jan 85	SEXOMATIC Club JAB 10	51	4

BARKIN BROTHERS featuring Johnnie FIORI
UK, male production group and US, female vocalist (Singles: 2 Weeks) pos/wks

15 Apr 00	GONNA CATCH YOU Brothers Organisation BRUVCD 15	51	2

Gary BARLOW (see also TAKE THAT)
UK, male vocalist (Singles: 47 Weeks, Albums: 27 Weeks) pos/wks

20 Jul 96 ★	FOREVER LOVE RCA 74321397922 ■	1	16
10 May 97 ★	LOVE WON'T WAIT (2re) RCA 74321470842 ■	1	9
26 Jul 97	SO HELP ME GIRL (re) RCA 74321501202	11	11
15 Nov 97 ●	OPEN ROAD RCA 74321518292	7	5
17 Jul 99	STRONGER RCA 74321682002	16	4
9 Oct 99	FOR ALL THAT YOU WANT RCA 74321701012	24	2
7 Jun 97 ●	OPEN ROAD RCA 74321417202 ■	1	26
23 Oct 99	TWELVE MONTHS ELEVEN DAYS RCA 74321707662	35	1

Gary BARNACLE See BIG FUN; SONIA

BARNBRACK
UK, male vocal / instrumental group (Singles: 7 Weeks) pos/wks

16 Mar 85	BELFAST Homespun HS 092	45	7

BARNDANCE BOYS UK, male production duo –
John Matthews and Darren Simpson (Singles: 2 Weeks) pos/wks

13 Sep 03	YIPPIE-I-OH Concept CDCON 41	32	2

Jimmy BARNES and INXS
Australia (b. UK), male vocalist – James Swan
and vocal / instrumental group (Singles: 8 Weeks) pos/wks

26 Jan 91	GOOD TIMES Atlantic A 7751	18	8

Richard BARNES UK, male vocalist (Singles: 10 Weeks) pos/wks

23 May 70	TAKE TO THE MOUNTAINS Philips BF 1840	35	6
24 Oct 70	GO NORTH (re) Philips 6006 039	38	4

BARON UK, male producer – Piers Bailey (Singles: 1 Week) pos/wks

7 Feb 04	THE WAY IT WAS / REDHEAD Virus VRS 012	71	1

The BARRACUDAS
UK / US, male vocal / instrumental group (Singles: 6 Weeks) pos/wks

16 Aug 80	SUMMER FUN Zonophone Z 5	37	6

Syd BARRETT (see also PINK FLOYD)
UK, male vocalist / instrumentalist – guitar (Albums: 1 Week) pos/wks

7 Feb 70	THE MADCAP LAUGHS Harvest SHVL 765	40	1

Wild Willy BARRETT See John OTWAY and Wild Willy BARRETT

Amanda BARRIE and Johnny BRIGGS
UK, female / male actors vocal duo (Singles: 3 Weeks) pos/wks

16 Dec 95	SOMETHING STUPID EMI Premier CDEMS 411	35	3

The listed flip side of 'Something Stupid' was 'Always Look on the Bright Side of Life' by the Coronation Street Cast

JJ BARRIE
Canada, male vocalist – Barrie Authors (Singles: 11 Weeks) pos/wks

24 Apr 76 ★ **NO CHARGE** *Power Exchange PX 209* 1 11

Featured vocalist is Vicki Brown

Ken BARRIE
UK, male vocalist (Singles: 15 Weeks) pos/wks

10 Jul 82 **POSTMAN PAT (2re)** *Post Music PP 001* 44 15

Re-entries at Christmas 1982 and 1983

The BARRON KNIGHTS
UK, male vocal / instrumental group – leader Duke D'Mond (Richard Palmer) (Singles: 94 Weeks, Albums: 22 Weeks) pos/wks

9 Jul 64 ● **CALL UP THE GROUPS** *Columbia DB 7317* [1] 3 13
22 Oct 64 **COME TO THE DANCE** *Columbia DB 7375* [1] 42 2
25 Mar 65 ● **POP GO THE WORKERS** *Columbia DB 7525* [1] 5 13
16 Dec 65 ● **MERRY GENTLE POPS** *Columbia DB 7780* [1] 9 7
1 Dec 66 **UNDER NEW MANAGEMENT** *Columbia DB 8071* [1] 15 9
23 Oct 68 **AN OLYMPIC RECORD** *Columbia DB 8485* 35 4
29 Oct 77 ● **LIVE IN TROUBLE** *Epic EPC 5752* 7 10
2 Dec 78 ● **A TASTE OF AGGRO** *Epic EPC 6829* 3 10
8 Dec 79 **FOOD FOR THOUGHT** *Epic EPC 8011* 46 6
4 Oct 80 **THE SIT SONG** *Epic EPC 8994* 44 4
6 Dec 80 **NEVER MIND THE PRESENTS** *Epic EPC 9070* 17 8
5 Dec 81 **BLACKBOARD JUMBLE** *CBS A 1795* 52 5
19 Mar 83 **BUFFALO BILL'S LAST SCRATCH** *Epic EPC A 3208* ...49 3
2 Dec 78 **NIGHT GALLERY** *Epic EPC 83221* 15 13
1 Dec 79 **TEACH THE WORLD TO LAUGH** *Epic EPC 83891* 51 4
13 Dec 80 **JUST A GIGGLE** *Epic EPC 84550* 45 5

[1] The Barron Knights with Duke D'Mond

Joe BARRY
US, male vocalist – Joe Barrios (Singles: 1 Week) pos/wks

24 Aug 61 **I'M A FOOL TO CARE** *Mercury AMT 1149* 49 1

John BARRY
UK, male composer – John Prendergast (Singles: 79 Weeks, Albums: 18 Weeks) pos/wks

4 Mar 60 ● **HIT AND MISS (re)** *Columbia DB 4414* [1] 10 14
28 Apr 60 **BEAT FOR BEATNIKS** *Columbia DB 4446* [2] 40 2
14 Jul 60 **NEVER LET GO** *Columbia DB 4480* [2] 49 1
18 Aug 60 **BLUEBERRY HILL** *Columbia DB 4480* [2] 34 3
8 Sep 60 **WALK DON'T RUN (re)** *Columbia DB 4505* [3] 11 14
8 Dec 60 **BLACK STOCKINGS** *Columbia DB 4554* [3] 27 3
2 Mar 61 **THE MAGNIFICENT SEVEN (3re)** *Columbia DB 4598* [3] 45 5
26 Apr 62 **CUTTY SARK** *Columbia DB 4806* [3] 35 2
1 Nov 62 **THE JAMES BOND THEME** *Columbia DB 4898* [2] 13 11
21 Nov 63 **FROM RUSSIA WITH LOVE (re)** *Ember S 181* [2] 39 3
11 Dec 71 **THEME FROM 'THE PERSUADERS'** *CBS 7469* 13 15
29 Jan 72 **THE PERSUADERS** *CBS 64816* 18 9
20 Apr 91 **DANCES WITH WOLVES (FILM SOUNDTRACK)** *Epic 4675911*..45 8
8 May 99 **THE BEYONDNESS OF THINGS** *Decca 4600092* [1] 67 1

[1] John Barry Seven plus Four [2] John Barry Orchestra [3] John Barry Seven [1] English Chamber Orchestra conducted by John Barry

Len BARRY
US, male vocalist – Leonard Borisoff (Singles: 24 Weeks) pos/wks

4 Nov 65 ● **1-2-3** *Brunswick 05942* 3 14
13 Jan 66 ● **LIKE A BABY** *Brunswick 05949* 10 10

Michael BARRYMORE
UK, male vocalist / comedian – Michael Parker (Singles: 4 Weeks) pos/wks

16 Dec 95 **TOO MUCH FOR ONE HEART** *EMI CDEM 412* 25 4

Lionel BART
UK, male vocalist, b. 1 Aug 1930, d. 3 Apr 1999 (Singles: 3 Weeks) pos/wks

25 Nov 89 **HAPPY ENDINGS (GIVE YOURSELF A PINCH) (re)** *EMI EM 121* ..68 3

Bart and Homer See The SIMPSONS

BARTHEZZ
Holland, male producer – Bart Claessen (Singles: 8 Weeks) pos/wks

22 Sep 01 **ON THE MOVE** *Positiva CDTIV 158* 18 4
20 Apr 02 **INFECTED** *Positiva CDTIVS 168* 25 4

BAS NOIR
US, female vocal duo (Singles: 1 Week) pos/wks

11 Feb 89 **MY LOVE IS MAGIC** *10 TEN 257* 73 1

Rob BASE and D.J. E-Z ROCK
US, male rap / DJ duo – Robert Ginyard and Rodney Bryce (Singles: 19 Weeks) pos/wks

16 Apr 88 **IT TAKES TWO (re)** *Citybeat CBE 724* 24 9
14 Jan 89 **GET ON THE DANCE FLOOR** *Supreme SUPE 139* 14 7
22 Apr 89 **JOY AND PAIN** *Supreme SUPE 143* 47 3

The BASEMENT
UK, male vocal / instrumental group (Singles: 1 Week) pos/wks

14 Jun 03 **SLAIN THE TRUTH (AT THE ROADHOUSE)** *Deltasonic DLTCD 012* 48 1

BASEMENT BOYS present Ultra NATÉ
US, male production group and female vocalist (Singles: 1 Week) pos/wks

23 Feb 91 **IS IT LOVE?** *Eternal YZ 509* 71 1

BASEMENT JAXX [425] [Top 500]
Boundary-stretching "punk garage" production duo from South London, Felix Buxton and Simon Ratcliffe. They surfaced from the underground house scene, are regular transatlantic club chart-toppers and won the Brit award for Best Dance Act in 2002 and 2004 (Singles: 78 Weeks, Albums: 87 Weeks) pos/wks

31 May 97 **FLY LIFE** *Multiply CDMULTY 21* 19 3
1 May 99 ● **RED ALERT** *XL Recordings XLS 100CD* 5 10
14 Aug 99 ● **RENDEZ-VU** *XL Recordings XLS 110CD* 4 8
6 Nov 99 **JUMP 'N SHOUT** *XL Recordings XLS 116CD* 12 5
15 Apr 00 **BINGO BANGO** *XL Recordings XLS 120CD* 13 4
16 Jun 01 ● **ROMEO** *XL Recordings XLS 132CD* 6 10
6 Oct 01 **JUS 1 KISS (re)** *XL Recordings XLS 136CD* 23 4
8 Dec 01 **WHERE'S YOUR HEAD AT?** *XL Recordings XLS 140CD* 9 8
29 Jun 02 **GET ME OFF** *XL Recordings XLS 146CD* 22 3
22 Nov 03 **LUCKY STAR** *XL Recordings XLS 172CD* [1] 23 4
17 Jan 04 **GOOD LUCK** *XL Recordings XLS 178CD* [2] 12 8
10 Apr 04 **PLUG IT IN** *XL Recordings XLS 180CD* [3] 22 4
10 Jul 04 **GOOD LUCK (re-mix)** *XL Recordings XLS 190CD* [2] ...14 7
22 May 99 ● **REMEDY** *XL Recordings XLCD 129* 4 45
7 Jul 01 ● **ROOTY** *XL Recordings XLCD 143* 5 26
1 Nov 03 **KISH KASH** *XL Recordings XLCD 174* 17 16

[1] Basement Jaxx featuring Dizzee Rascal [2] Basement Jaxx featuring Lisa Kekaula [3] Basement Jaxx featuring JC Chasez

'Good Luck' was re-issued after the BBC adopted it for their coverage of the Euro 2004 football championships

BASIA (see also MATT BIANCO)
Poland, female vocalist – Basia Trzetrzelewska (Singles: 9 Weeks, Albums: 4 Weeks) pos/wks

23 Jan 88 **PROMISES** *Epic BASH 4* 48 4
28 May 88 **TIME AND TIDE** *Epic BASH 5* 61 3
14 Jan 95 **DRUNK ON LOVE** *Epic 6611582* 41 2
13 Feb 88 **TIME AND TIDE** *Portrait 4502631* 61 3
3 Mar 90 **LONDON WARSAW NEW YORK** *Epic 4632821* 68 1

Count BASIE
US, orchestra leader – William Basie, b. 21 Aug 1904, d. 26 Mar 1984 (Albums: 24 Weeks) pos/wks

16 Apr 60 **CHAIRMAN OF THE BOARD** *Columbia 33SX 1209* 17 1
23 Feb 63 ● **SINATRA – BASIE** *Reprise R 1008* [1] 2 23

[1] Frank Sinatra and Count Basie

Toni BASIL
US, female vocalist – Antonia Basilotta (Singles: 16 Weeks, Albums: 16 Weeks) pos/wks

6 Feb 82 ● **MICKEY** *Radialchoice TIC 4* ▲ 2 12
1 May 82 **NOBODY** *Radialchoice TIC 2* 52 4
6 Feb 82 **WORD OF MOUTH** *Radialchoice BASIL 1* 15 16

Olav BASOSKI
Holland, male producer (Singles: 1 Week) pos/wks

26 Aug 00 **OPIUM SCUMBAGZ** *Defected DFECT 20CDS* 56 1

Alfie BASS See Michael MEDWIN, Bernard BRESSLAW, Alfie BASS and Leslie FYSON

Fontella BASS
US, female vocalist (Singles: 15 Weeks) pos/wks

2 Dec 65 **RESCUE ME** *Chess CRS 8023* 11 10
20 Jan 66 **RECOVERY** *Chess CRS 8027* 32 5

Norman BASS *Germany, male producer (Singles: 4 Weeks)* pos/wks

21 Apr 01	**HOW U LIKE BASS** *Substance SUBS 10CDS*	**17** 4

BASS BOYZ (see also PIANOMAN)
UK, male producer – James Sammon (Singles: 1 Week) pos/wks

28 Sep 96	**GUNZ AND PIANOZ** *Polydor 5753432*	**74** 1

BASS BUMPERS *Germany / UK, male / female vocal / instrumental group (Singles: 4 Weeks)* pos/wks

25 Sep 93	**RUNNIN'** *Vertigo VERCD 78*	**68** 1
5 Feb 94	**THE MUSIC'S GOT ME** *Vertigo VERCD 84*	**25** 3

BASS JUMPERS
Holland, male producer and female vocalist (Singles: 1 Week) pos/wks

13 Feb 99	**MAKE UP YOUR MIND** *Pepper 0530112*	**44** 1

Shirley BASSEY `57` `Top 500` *Internationally acclaimed vocalist and cabaret entertainer, b. 8 Jan 1937, Cardiff, Wales. With 31 hit singles (spanning a record 42-year period for a female) and 36 hit albums, she is Britain's most successful female chart artist. Honoured with a damehood in 2000 (Singles: 326 Weeks, Albums: 294 Weeks)* pos/wks

15 Feb 57 ●	**THE BANANA BOAT SONG** *Philips PB 668*	**8** 10
23 Aug 57	**FIRE DOWN BELOW** *Philips PB 723*	**30** 1
6 Sep 57	**YOU YOU ROMEO** *Philips PB 723*	**29** 2
19 Dec 58 ★	**AS I LOVE YOU** (re) *Philips PB 845*	**1** 19
26 Dec 58 ●	**KISS ME, HONEY HONEY, KISS ME** *Philips PB 860*	**3** 17
31 Mar 60	**WITH THESE HANDS** (2re) *Columbia DB 4421*	**38** 14
4 Aug 60 ●	**AS LONG AS HE NEEDS ME** *Columbia DB 4490*	**2** 30
11 May 61 ●	**YOU'LL NEVER KNOW** *Columbia DB 4643*	**6** 17
27 Jul 61 ★	**REACH FOR THE STARS / CLIMB EV'RY MOUNTAIN** (re) *Columbia DB 4685*	**1** 18
23 Nov 61 ●	**I'LL GET BY (AS LONG AS I HAVE YOU)** *Columbia DB 4737*	**10** 8
15 Feb 62	**TONIGHT** *Columbia DB 4777*	**21** 8
26 Apr 62	**AVE MARIA** *Columbia DB 4816*	**31** 4
31 May 62	**FAR AWAY** *Columbia DB 4836*	**24** 13
30 Aug 62 ●	**WHAT NOW MY LOVE** *Columbia DB 4882*	**5** 17
28 Feb 63	**WHAT KIND OF FOOL AM I?** *Columbia DB 4974*	**47** 2
26 Sep 63 ●	**I (WHO HAVE NOTHING)** *Columbia DB 7113*	**6** 20
23 Jan 64	**MY SPECIAL DREAM** *Columbia DB 7185*	**32** 7
9 Apr 64	**GONE** *Columbia DB 7248*	**36** 5
15 Oct 64	**GOLDFINGER** *Columbia DB 7360*	**21** 9
20 May 65	**NO REGRETS** *Columbia DB 7535*	**39** 4
11 Oct 67	**BIG SPENDER** *United Artists UP 1192*	**21** 15
20 Jun 70 ●	**SOMETHING** (re) *United Artists UP 35125*	**4** 22
2 Jan 71	**THE FOOL ON THE HILL** *United Artists UP 35156*	**48** 1
27 Mar 71	**(WHERE DO I BEGIN) LOVE STORY** *United Artists UP 35194*	**34** 9
7 Aug 71 ●	**FOR ALL WE KNOW** (re) *United Artists UP 35267*	**6** 24
15 Jan 72	**DIAMONDS ARE FOREVER** *United Artists UP 35293*	**38** 6
3 Mar 73 ●	**NEVER, NEVER, NEVER (GRANDE, GRANDE, GRANDE)** (re) *United Artists UP 35490*	**8** 19
22 Aug 87	**THE RHYTHM DIVINE** *Mercury MER 253* `1`	**54** 2
16 Nov 96	**'DISCO' LA PASSIONE** *East West EW 072CD* `2`	**41** 1
20 Dec 97	**HISTORY REPEATING** *Wall of Sound WALLD 036* `3`	**19** 7
23 Oct 99	**WORLD IN UNION** *Universal TV 4669402* `4`	**35** 3
28 Jan 61	**FABULOUS SHIRLEY BASSEY** *Columbia 33SX 1178*	**12** 2
25 Feb 61 ●	**SHIRLEY** *Columbia 33SX 1286*	**9** 10
17 Feb 62	**SHIRLEY BASSEY** *Columbia 33SX 1382*	**14** 11
15 Dec 62	**LET'S FACE THE MUSIC** *Columbia 33SX 1454* `1`	**12** 7
4 Dec 65	**SHIRLEY BASSEY AT THE PIGALLE** *Columbia 33SX 1787*	**15** 7
27 Aug 66	**I'VE GOT A SONG FOR YOU** *United Artists ULP 1142*	**26** 1
17 Feb 68	**TWELVE OF THOSE SONGS** *Columbia SCX 6204*	**38** 3
7 Dec 68	**GOLDEN HITS OF SHIRLEY BASSEY** *Columbia SCX 6294*	**28** 40
11 Jul 70	**LIVE AT THE TALK OF THE TOWN** *United Artists UAS 29095*	**38** 6
29 Aug 70 ●	**SOMETHING** *United Artists UAS 29100*	**5** 20
15 May 71 ●	**SOMETHING ELSE** *United Artists UAG 29149*	**7** 9
2 Oct 71	**BIG SPENDER** *Sunset SLS 50262*	**27** 8
30 Oct 71	**IT'S MAGIC** *Starline SRS 5082*	**32** 1
6 Nov 71	**THE FABULOUS SHIRLEY BASSEY** *MFP 1398*	**48** 1
4 Dec 71	**WHAT NOW MY LOVE** *MFP 5230*	**17** 5
8 Jan 72	**THE SHIRLEY BASSEY COLLECTION** *United Artists UAD 60013/4*	**37** 2
19 Feb 72	**I CAPRICORN** *United Artists UAS 29246*	**13** 11
29 Nov 72	**AND I LOVE YOU SO** *United Artists UAS 29385*	**24** 9
2 Jun 73 ●	**NEVER NEVER NEVER** *United Artists UAG 29471*	**10** 10
15 Mar 75 ●	**THE SHIRLEY BASSEY SINGLES ALBUM** *United Artists UAS 29728*	**2** 23
1 Nov 75	**GOOD BAD BUT BEAUTIFUL** *United Artists UAS 29881*	**13** 7
15 May 76	**LOVE LIFE AND FEELINGS** *United Artists UAS 29944*	**13** 5
4 Dec 76	**THOUGHTS OF LOVE** *United Artists UAS 30011*	**15** 9
25 Jun 77	**YOU TAKE MY HEART AWAY** *United Artists UAS 30037*	**34** 5
4 Nov 78 ●	**25TH ANNIVERSARY ALBUM** *United Artists SBTV 601 4748*	**3** 12
12 May 79	**THE MAGIC IS YOU** *United Artists UATV 30230*	**40** 5
17 Jul 82	**LOVE SONGS** *Applause APKL 1163*	**48** 5
20 Oct 84	**I AM WHAT I AM** *Towerbell TOWLP 7*	**25** 18
18 May 91	**KEEP THE MUSIC PLAYING** *Dino DINTV 21*	**25** 7
5 Dec 92	**THE BEST OF SHIRLEY BASSEY** *Dino DINCD 49*	**27** 5
4 Dec 93	**SHIRLEY BASSEY SINGS ANDREW LLOYD WEBBER** *Premier CDDPR 114*	**34** 5
11 Nov 95	**SHIRLEY BASSEY SINGS THE MOVIES** *PolyGram TV 5293992*	**24** 9
9 Nov 96	**THE SHOW MUST GO ON** *PolyGram TV 5337122*	**47** 8
9 Sep 00	**THE REMIX ALBUM ... DIAMONDS ARE FOREVER** *EMI 5258732*	**62** 1
25 Nov 00	**THE GREATEST HITS – THIS IS MY LIFE** *Liberty 5258742*	**54** 4
7 Jun 03	**THANK YOU FOR THE YEARS** *Citrus 5122722*	**19** 4

`1` Yello featuring Shirley Bassey `2` Chris Rea and Shirley Bassey
`3` Propellerheads featuring Miss Shirley Bassey `4` Shirley Bassey / Bryn Terfel
`1` Shirley Bassey with the Nelson Riddle Orchestra

BASSHEADS
UK, male / female vocal / instrumental group (Singles: 19 Weeks) pos/wks

16 Nov 91 ●	**IS THERE ANYBODY OUT THERE?** *Deconstruction R 6303*	**5** 8
30 May 92	**BACK TO THE OLD SCHOOL** *Deconstruction R 6310*	**12** 4
28 Nov 92	**WHO CAN MAKE ME FEEL GOOD** *Deconstruction R 6326*	**38** 2
28 Aug 93	**START A BRAND NEW LIFE (SAVE ME)** *Deconstruction CDR 6353*	**49** 2
15 Jul 95	**IS THERE ANYBODY OUT THERE?** (re-mix) *Deconstruction 74321293882*	**24** 3

BASS-O-MATIC *UK, male multi-instrumentalist / producer – William Orbit (Singles: 19 Weeks, Albums: 2 Weeks)* pos/wks

12 May 90	**IN THE REALM OF THE SENSES** *Virgin VS 1265*	**66** 3
1 Sep 90 ●	**FASCINATING RHYTHM** *Virgin VS 1274*	**9** 11
22 Dec 90	**EASE ON BY** *Virgin VS 1295*	**61** 4
3 Aug 91	**FUNKY LOVE VIBRATIONS** *Virgin VS 1355*	**71** 1
13 Oct 90	**SET THE CONTROLS FOR THE HEART OF THE BASS** *Virgin V 2641*	**57** 2

BASSTOY (see also ABSOLUTE)
US, male producer – Mark Picchiotti (Singles: 6 Weeks) pos/wks

27 May 00	**RUNNIN'** *Neo NEOCD 029*	**62** 1
19 Jan 02	**RUNNIN'** (re-recording) *Black & White NEOCD 073* `1`	**13** 5

`1` Mark Picchiotti presents Basstoy featuring Dana

BATES
Germany, male vocal / instrumental group (Singles: 1 Week) pos/wks

3 Feb 96	**BILLIE JEAN** *Virgin International DINSD 151*	**67** 1

Mike BATT with the NEW EDITION
(see also Justin HAYWARD; The WOMBLES) *UK, male vocalist and male / female vocal group (Singles: 8 Weeks, Albums: 7 Weeks)* pos/wks

16 Aug 75 ●	**SUMMERTIME CITY** *Epic EPC 3460*	**4** 8
28 Oct 89	**CLASSIC BLUE** *Trax MODEM 1040* `1`	**47** 7

`1` Justin Hayward, Mike Batt and the London Philharmonic Orchestra

BAUHAUS (see also Peter MURPHY) *UK, male vocal / instrumental group (Singles: 35 Weeks, Albums: 24 Weeks)* pos/wks

18 Apr 81	**KICK IN THE EYE** *Beggars Banquet BEG 54*	**59** 3
4 Jul 81	**THE PASSION OF LOVERS** *Beggars Banquet BEG 59*	**56** 2
6 Mar 82	**KICK IN THE EYE (EP)** *Beggars Banquet BEG 74*	**45** 4
19 Jun 82	**SPIRIT** *Beggars Banquet BEG 79*	**42** 5
9 Oct 82	**ZIGGY STARDUST** *Beggars Banquet BEG 83*	**15** 7
22 Jan 83	**LAGARTIJA NICK** *Beggars Banquet BEG 88*	**44** 4
9 Apr 83	**SHE'S IN PARTIES** *Beggars Banquet BEG 91*	**26** 6
29 Oct 83	**THE SINGLES 1981-83** *Beggars Banquet BEG 100E*	**52** 4
15 Nov 80	**IN THE FLAT FIELD** *4AD CAD 13*	**72** 1
24 Oct 81	**MASK** *Beggars Banquet BEGA 29*	**30** 5
30 Oct 82 ●	**THE SKY'S GONE OUT** *Beggars Banquet BEGA 42*	**4** 6
23 Jul 83	**BURNING FROM THE INSIDE** *Beggars Banquet BEGA 45*	**13** 10
30 Nov 85	**1979-1983** *Beggars Banquet BEGA 64*	**36** 2

Tracks on Kick in the Eye (EP): Kick in the Eye (Searching for Satori) / Harry / Earwax. The Singles 1981-83 was an EP: The Passion of Lovers / Kick in the Eye / Spirit / Ziggy Stardust / Lagartija Nick / She's in Parties

Les BAXTER, his Chorus and Orchestra
US, chorus and orchestra – leader b. 14 Mar 1922, d. 15 Jan 1996 (Singles: 9 Weeks) pos/wks

13 May 55 ●	UNCHAINED MELODY *Capitol CL 14257*	**10** 9

Tasha BAXTER *See Roger GOODE featuring Tasha BAXTER*

Tom BAXTER
UK, male vocalist (Singles: 1 Week, Albums: 3 Weeks) pos/wks

31 Jul 04	THIS BOY *Sony Music 6751692*	**65** 1
14 Aug 04	FEATHER & STONE *Columbia 5174689*	**65** 3

BAY CITY ROLLERS 〈245 Top 500〉 *Tartan teen sensations from*
Edinburgh: Leslie McKeown (v), Eric Faulkner (g), Stuart Wood (g), Alan Longmuir (b), Derek Longmuir (d). They were the first of many acts heralded as the 'Biggest Group Since The Beatles' and one of the most screamed-at teeny-bopper acts of the 1970s (Singles: 117 Weeks, Albums: 136 Weeks) pos/wks

18 Sep 71 ●	KEEP ON DANCING *Bell 1164*	**9** 13
9 Feb 74 ●	REMEMBER (SHA-LA-LA) *Bell 1338*	**6** 12
27 Apr 74 ●	SHANG-A-LANG *Bell 1355*	**2** 10
27 Jul 74 ●	SUMMERLOVE SENSATION *Bell 1369*	**3** 10
12 Oct 74 ●	ALL OF ME LOVES ALL OF YOU *Bell 1382*	**4** 10
8 Mar 75 ★	BYE BYE BABY *Bell 1409*	**1** 16
12 Jul 75 ★	GIVE A LITTLE LOVE *Bell 1425*	**1** 9
22 Nov 75 ●	MONEY HONEY *Bell 1461*	**3** 9
10 Apr 76 ●	LOVE ME LIKE I LOVE YOU *Bell 1477*	**4** 10
11 Sep 76 ●	I ONLY WANNA BE WITH YOU *Bell 1493*	**4** 9
7 May 77	IT'S A GAME *Arista 108*	**16** 6
30 Jul 77	YOU MADE ME BELIEVE IN MAGIC *Arista 127*	**34** 3
12 Oct 74 ●	ROLLIN' *Bell BELLS 244* ■	**1** 62
3 May 75 ★	ONCE UPON A STAR *Bell SYBEL 8001* ■	**1** 37
13 Dec 75 ●	WOULDN'T YOU LIKE IT *Bell SYBEL 8002*	**3** 12
25 Sep 76 ●	DEDICATION *Bell SYBEL 8005*	**4** 12
13 Aug 77	IT'S A GAME *Arista SPARTY 1009*	**18** 4
17 Apr 04	THE VERY BEST OF BAY CITY ROLLERS *Bell / Arista 82876608192*	**11** 9

Duke BAYSEE *UK, male vocalist – Kevin Rowe (Singles: 6 Weeks)* pos/wks

3 Sep 94	SUGAR SUGAR *Bell 74321228702*	**30** 4
21 Jan 95	DO YOU LOVE ME *Double Dekker CDDEK 1*	**46** 2

BAZ *UK, female vocalist – Baz Gooden (Singles: 3 Weeks)* pos/wks

15 Dec 01	BELIEVERS *One Little Indian 313TP 7CD1*	**36** 2
30 Mar 02	SMILE TO SHINE *One Little Indian 316TP 7CD*	**58** 1

BC-52's *See The B-52's*

BE BOP DELUXE (see also Bill NELSON) *UK, male vocal / instrumental group (Singles: 13 Weeks, Albums: 28 Weeks)* pos/wks

21 Feb 76	SHIPS IN THE NIGHT *Harvest HAR 5104*	**23** 8
13 Nov 76	HOT VALVES (EP) *Harvest HAR 5117*	**36** 5
31 Jan 76	SUNBURST FINISH *Harvest SHSP 4053*	**17** 12
25 Sep 76	MODERN MUSIC *Harvest SHSP 4058*	**12** 6
6 Aug 77 ●	LIVE! IN THE AIR AGE *Harvest SHVL 816*	**10** 5
25 Feb 78	DRASTIC PLASTIC *Harvest SHSP 4091*	**22** 5

Tracks on Hot Valves (EP): Maid in Heaven / Blazing Apostles / Jet Silver and the Dolls of Venus / Bring Back the Spark

The BEACH BOYS 〈27 Top 500〉
California family band famous for their harmonies. The most successful and consistently popular US group of the rock era: Brian Wilson (b/k/v), Mike Love (v), Carl Wilson (g/v) (d. 1998), Al Jardine (g/v), Dennis Wilson (d/v) (d. 1983) (Singles: 281 Weeks, Albums: 564 Weeks) pos/wks

1 Aug 63	SURFIN' U.S.A. *Capitol CL 15305*	**34** 7
9 Jul 64 ●	I GET AROUND *Capitol CL 15350* ▲	**7** 13
29 Oct 64	WHEN I GROW UP (TO BE A MAN) (re) *Capitol CL 15361*	**27** 7
21 Jan 65	DANCE, DANCE, DANCE *Capitol CL 15370*	**24** 6
3 Jun 65	HELP ME, RHONDA *Capitol CL 15392* ▲	**27** 10
2 Sep 65	CALIFORNIA GIRLS *Capitol CL 15409*	**26** 8
17 Feb 66 ●	BARBARA ANN *Capitol CL 15432*	**3** 10
21 Apr 66 ●	SLOOP JOHN B *Capitol CL 15441*	**2** 15

28 Jul 66 ●	GOD ONLY KNOWS *Capitol CL 15459*	**2** 14
3 Nov 66 ★	GOOD VIBRATIONS *Capitol CL 15475* ▲	**1** 13
4 May 67 ●	THEN I KISSED HER *Capitol CL 15502*	**4** 11
23 Aug 67 ●	HEROES AND VILLAINS *Capitol CL 15510*	**8** 9
22 Nov 67	WILD HONEY *Capitol CL 15521*	**29** 6
17 Jan 68	DARLIN' *Capitol CL 15527*	**11** 14
8 May 68	FRIENDS *Capitol CL 15545*	**25** 7
24 Jul 68 ★	DO IT AGAIN *Capitol CL 15554*	**1** 14
25 Dec 68	BLUEBIRDS OVER THE MOUNTAIN *Capitol CL 15572*	**33** 5
26 Feb 69 ●	I CAN HEAR MUSIC *Capitol CL 15584*	**10** 13
11 Jun 69 ●	BREAK AWAY *Capitol CL 15598*	**6** 11
16 May 70 ●	COTTONFIELDS *Capitol CL 15640*	**5** 17
3 Mar 73	CALIFORNIA SAGA – CALIFORNIA *Reprise K 14232*	**37** 5
3 Jul 76	GOOD VIBRATIONS (re-issue) *Capitol CL 15875*	**18** 7
10 Jul 76	ROCK AND ROLL MUSIC *Reprise K 14440*	**36** 4
31 Mar 79	HERE COMES THE NIGHT *Caribou CRB 7204*	**37** 8
16 Jun 79 ●	LADY LYNDA *Caribou CRB 7427*	**6** 11
29 Sep 79	SUMAHAMA *Caribou CRB 7846*	**45** 4
29 Aug 81	THE BEACH BOYS MEDLEY *Capitol CL 213*	**47** 4
22 Aug 87 ●	WIPEOUT *Urban URB 5* [1]	**2** 12
19 Nov 88	KOKOMO *Elektra EKR 85* ▲	**25** 9
2 Jun 90	WOULDN'T IT BE NICE *Capitol CL 579*	**58** 1
29 Jun 91	DO IT AGAIN (re-issue) *Capitol EMCT 1*	**61** 2
2 Mar 96	FUN FUN FUN *PolyGram TV 5762972* [2]	**24** 4
25 Sep 65	SURFIN' USA *Capitol T 1890*	**17** 7
19 Feb 66 ●	BEACH BOYS PARTY *Capitol T 2398*	**3** 14
16 Apr 66 ●	BEACH BOYS TODAY *Capitol T 2269*	**6** 25
9 Jul 66 ●	PET SOUNDS *Capitol T 2458*	**2** 39
16 Jul 66 ●	SUMMER DAYS (AND SUMMER NIGHTS!!) *Capitol T 2354*	**4** 22
12 Nov 66 ●	BEST OF THE BEACH BOYS *Capitol T 20865*	**2** 142
11 Mar 67	SURFER GIRL *Capitol T 1981*	**13** 14
21 Oct 67 ●	BEST OF THE BEACH BOYS VOLUME 2 *Capitol ST 20956*	**3** 39
18 Nov 67 ●	SMILEY SMILE *Capitol ST 9001*	**9** 8
16 Mar 68 ●	WILD HONEY *Capitol ST 2859*	**7** 15
21 Sep 68	FRIENDS *Capitol ST 2895*	**13** 8
23 Nov 68 ●	BEST OF THE BEACH BOYS VOLUME 3 *Capitol ST 21142*	**9** 12
29 Mar 69 ●	20/20 *Capitol EST 133*	**3** 10
19 Sep 70 ●	GREATEST HITS *Capitol T 21628*	**5** 22
5 Dec 70	SUNFLOWER *Stateside SSL 8251*	**29** 6
27 Nov 71	SURF'S UP *Stateside SLS 10313*	**15** 7
24 Jun 72	CARL AND THE PASSIONS / SO TOUGH *Reprise K 44184*	**25** 1
17 Feb 73	HOLLAND *Reprise K 54008*	**20** 7
10 Jul 76 ★	20 GOLDEN GREATS *Capitol EMTV 1*	**1** 86
24 Jul 76	15 BIG ONES *Reprise K 54079*	**31** 3
7 May 77	THE BEACH BOYS LOVE YOU *Reprise K 54087*	**28** 1
21 Apr 79	LA (LIGHT ALBUM) *Caribou CRB 86081*	**32** 6
12 Apr 80	KEEPING THE SUMMER ALIVE *Caribou CRB 86109*	**54** 3
30 Jul 83 ★	THE VERY BEST OF THE BEACH BOYS *Capitol BBTV 1867193*	**1** 17
22 Jun 85	THE BEACH BOYS *Caribou CRB 26378*	**60** 2
23 Jun 90 ●	SUMMER DREAMS – 28 CLASSIC TRACKS *Capitol EMTVD 51*	**2** 27
1 Jul 95	THE BEST OF THE BEACH BOYS *Capitol CDESTVD 3*	**25** 6
16 Sep 95	PET SOUNDS (re-issue) *Fame CDFA 3298*	**59** 4
11 Jul 98	GREATEST HITS *EMI 4956962*	**28** 4
19 Sep 98	ENDLESS HARMONY SOUNDTRACK *Capitol 4963912*	**56** 1
21 Jul 01	THE VERY BEST OF THE BEACH BOYS *Capitol 5326152*	**31** 6

[1] Fat Boys and The Beach Boys [2] Status Quo with The Beach Boys

The Beach Boys Medley comprised Good Vibrations / Help Me, Rhonda / I Get Around / Shut Down / Surfin' Safari / Barbara Ann / Surfin' USA / Fun, Fun, Fun
The two 'Best of The Beach Boys', 'Greatest Hits' and 'The Very Best of The Beach Boys' albums are different

BEAR WHO? *See DJ SNEAK featuring BEAR WHO?*

Walter BEASLEY *US, male vocalist (Singles: 3 Weeks)* pos/wks

23 Jan 88	I'M SO HAPPY *Urban URB 14*	**70** 3

BEASTIE BOYS 〈421 Top 500〉 *Scourge of the tabloids in the late 1980s: MCA (Adam Yauch, v/b), Mike D (Michael Diamond, v/d) and Ad-Rock (Adam Horowitz, v/g). This New York rap trio turned their backs on their early image to become dedicated campaigners for a free Tibet. Known for their innovative videos, they founded a record label and magazine, both called Grand Royal (Singles: 71 Weeks, Albums: 94 Weeks)* pos/wks

28 Feb 87	(YOU GOTTA) FIGHT FOR YOUR RIGHT (TO PARTY) *Def Jam 650418 7*	**11** 11
30 May 87	NO SLEEP TILL BROOKLYN *Def Jam BEAST 1*	**14** 7
18 Jul 87	SHE'S ON IT *Def Jam BEAST 2*	**10** 8
3 Oct 87	GIRLS / SHE'S CRAFTY *Def Jam BEAST 3*	**34** 4

11 Apr 92		PASS THE MIC *Capitol 12CL 653*	47	2
4 Jul 92		FROZEN METAL HEAD (EP) *Capitol 12CL 665*	55	1
9 Jul 94		GET IT TOGETHER / SABOTAGE *Capitol CDCL 716*	19	4
26 Nov 94		SURE SHOT *Capitol CDCL 726*	27	3
4 Jul 98	●	INTERGALACTIC *Grand Royal CDCL 803*	5	7
7 Nov 98		BODY MOVIN' (re) *Grand Royal CDCL 809*	15	5
29 May 99		REMOTE CONTROL / 3 MCS & 1 DJ *Grand Royal CDCL 812*	21	3
18 Dec 99		ALIVE *Grand Royal CDCL 818*	28	4
12 Jun 04	●	CH-CHECK IT OUT *Capitol CDCLS 857*	8	7
25 Sep 04		TRIPLE TROUBLE *Capitol CDCLS 859*	37	3
18 Dec 04		AN OPEN LETTER TO NYC *Capitol CDCLS 867*	38	2+
31 Jan 87	●	LICENCE TO ILL *Def Jam 450062* ▲	7	40
5 Aug 89		PAUL'S BOUTIQUE *Capitol EST 2102*	44	2
4 Jun 94		ILL COMMUNICATION *Capitol CDEST 2229* ▲	10	15
10 Jun 95		ROOT DOWN EP *Capitol CDEST 2262*	23	2
6 Apr 96		THE IN SOUND FROM WAY OUT! *Grand Royal CDEST 2281*	45	1
18 Jul 98	★	HELLO NASTY *Grand Royal 4957232* ■ ▲	1	21
4 Dec 99		ANTHOLOGY – THE SOUNDS OF SCIENCE		
		Grand Royal 5236642	36	7
26 Jun 04	●	TO THE 5 BOROUGHS *Capitol 4733390* ▲	2	6

Tracks on Frozen Metal Head (EP): Jimmy James / Jimmy James (Original) / Drinkin'
Wine / The Blue Nun

The BEAT 424 Top 500 *Birmingham, UK-based band that married ska*
and new wave influences, formed 1978; Dave Wakeling (v/g), Ranking Roger
(v), Andy Cox (g) and David Steele (b). After 1983 break-up, former two
launched General Public and latter pair formed Fine Young Cannibals
(Singles: 92 Weeks, Albums: 73 Weeks) pos/wks

8 Dec 79	●	TEARS OF A CLOWN / RANKING FULL STOP *2 Tone CHSTT 6*	6	11
23 Feb 80	●	HANDS OFF – SHE'S MINE *Go Feet FEET 1*	9	9
3 May 80	●	MIRROR IN THE BATHROOM *Go Feet FEET 2*	4	9
16 Aug 80		BEST FRIEND / STAND DOWN MARGARET (DUB)		
		Go Feet FEET 3	22	9
13 Dec 80	●	TOO NICE TO TALK TO *Go Feet FEET 4*	7	11
18 Apr 81		DROWNING / ALL OUT TO GET YOU *Go Feet FEET 6*	22	8
20 Jun 81		DOORS OF YOUR HEART *Go Feet FEET 9*	33	6
5 Dec 81		HIT IT *Go Feet FEET 11*	70	2
17 Apr 82		SAVE IT FOR LATER *Go Feet FEET 333*	47	5
18 Sep 82		JEANETTE *Go Feet FEET 15*	45	3
4 Dec 82		I CONFESS *Go Feet FEET 16*	54	3
30 Apr 83	●	CAN'T GET USED TO LOSING YOU *Go Feet FEET 17*	3	11
2 Jul 83		ACKEE 1-2-3 *Go Feet FEET 18*	54	4
27 Jan 96		MIRROR IN THE BATHROOM (re-mix) *Go Feet 74321232062*	44	2
31 May 80	●	I JUST CAN'T STOP IT *Go Feet BEAT 001*	3	32
16 May 81	●	WHA'PPEN *Go Feet BEAT 3*	3	18
9 Oct 82		SPECIAL BEAT SERVICE *Go Feet BEAT 5*	21	6
11 Jun 83	●	WHAT IS BEAT? (THE BEST OF THE BEAT) *Go Feet BEAT 6*	10	13
10 Feb 96		B.P.M. ... THE VERY BEST OF THE BEAT		
		Go Feet 74321231952	13	4

BEAT BOYS *See Gene VINCENT*

BEAT RENEGADES (see also DREAM FREQUENCY;
QUAKE featuring Marcia RAE; RED) *UK, male production*
duo – Ian Bland and Paul Fitzpatrick (Singles: 1 Week) pos/wks

19 May 01		AUTOMATIK *Slinky Music SLINKY 014CD*	73	1

BEAT SYSTEM
UK, male vocal / instrumental group (Singles: 3 Weeks) pos/wks

3 Mar 90		WALK ON THE WILD SIDE *Fourth & Broadway BRW 163*	63	2
18 Sep 93		TO A BRIGHTER DAY (O' HAPPY DAY) *ffrr FCD 217*	70	1

The BEAT UP (see also The BEATINGS)
UK, male vocal / instrumental group (Singles: 1 Week) pos/wks

4 Dec 04		MESSED UP *Fantastic Plastic FPS 043*	62	1

The Beat Up are The Beatings under a different name

BEATCHUGGERS featuring Eric CLAPTON
Denmark, male producer – Michael Linde and UK,
male vocalist / instrumentalist (Singles: 2 Weeks) pos/wks

18 Nov 00		FOREVER MAN (HOW MANY TIMES) *ffrr FCD 386*	26	2

The BEATINGS (see also The BEAT UP)
UK, male vocal / instrumental group (Singles: 1 Week) pos/wks

26 Oct 02		BAD FEELING *Fantastic Plastic FPS 034*	68	1

The Beatings changed their name to The Beat Up

The BEATLES 3 Top 500
World's most successful group: John Lennon (v/g), b. 9 Oct 1940, Liverpool,
d. 8 Dec 1980, New York, Paul McCartney (v/b), b. 18 Jun 1942, Liverpool,
George Harrison (v/g), b. 24 Feb 1943, Liverpool, d. 29 Nov 2001, Ringo Starr
(Richard Starkey) (v/d), b. 7 Jul 1940, Liverpool. This legendary group
changed the face of popular music. Achievements include most No.1 albums
in the UK and US. Within three months of their US chart debut in 1964, they
held all the Top 5 single chart places, had a record 14 simultaneous entries in
the Billboard Top 100 and had the two top-selling albums. During those 12
weeks they earned six gold singles and sold four million albums. Their
album 'Sgt. Pepper's Lonely Hearts Club Band' is the biggest seller ever in
the UK, and the group is the No.1 all-time US best-selling album act. They
split on 9 Apr 1970, since when Lennon, McCartney and Harrison have all had
No.1 singles. (Starr reached No.2.) Their '1' collection (2000) is the world's
fastest selling album with 23.5 million copies shipped in the first month and was
the top-selling album of 2000 in the UK. The Beatles, who were made MBEs in
1965 and in 2004, were honoured as founder members of the UK Music Hall of
Fame (representing the 1960s) and have sold an estimated one billion records,
including 20,799,632 UK singles. Best-selling single: 'She Loves You' 1,890,000
(Singles: 456 Weeks, Albums: 1293 Weeks) pos/wks

11 Oct 62	●	LOVE ME DO (re) *Parlophone R 4949* ▲	4	26
17 Jan 63	●	PLEASE PLEASE ME (re) *Parlophone R 4983*	2	22
18 Apr 63	★	FROM ME TO YOU (re) *Parlophone R 5015*	1	25
6 Jun 63		MY BONNIE *Polydor NH 66833* ①	48	1
29 Aug 63	★	SHE LOVES YOU (2re) *Parlophone R 5055* ◆ ▲	1	36
5 Dec 63	★	I WANT TO HOLD YOUR HAND (re) *Parlophone R 5084* ◆ ▲	1	24
26 Mar 64	★	CAN'T BUY ME LOVE (2re) *Parlophone R 5114* ◆ ▲	1	17
11 Jun 64		AIN'T SHE SWEET *Polydor 52 317*	29	6
16 Jul 64	★	A HARD DAY'S NIGHT (re) *Parlophone R 5160* ▲	1	15
3 Dec 64	★	I FEEL FINE (re) *Parlophone R 5200* ◆ ▲	1	14
15 Apr 65	★	TICKET TO RIDE (re) *Parlophone R 5265* ▲	1	14
29 Jul 65	★	HELP! (re) *Parlophone R 5305* ▲	1	17
9 Dec 65	★	DAY TRIPPER / WE CAN WORK IT OUT		
		Parlophone R 5389 ◆ ▲	1	12
16 Jun 66	★	PAPERBACK WRITER (re) *Parlophone R 5452* ▲	1	16
11 Aug 66	★	YELLOW SUBMARINE / ELEANOR RIGBY (re)		
		Parlophone R 5493	1	14
23 Feb 67	●	PENNY LANE / STRAWBERRY FIELDS FOREVER (2re)		
		Parlophone R 5570	2	16
12 Jul 67	★	ALL YOU NEED IS LOVE (re) *Parlophone R 5620* ▲	1	16
29 Nov 67	★	HELLO, GOODBYE (re) *Parlophone R 5655* ▲	1	13
13 Dec 67	●	MAGICAL MYSTERY TOUR (DOUBLE EP)		
		Parlophone SMMT / MMT 1	2	12
20 Mar 68	★	LADY MADONNA (re) *Parlophone R 5675*	1	9
4 Sep 68	★	HEY JUDE (2re) *Apple R 5722* ▲	1	25
23 Apr 69	★	GET BACK (2re) *Apple R 5777* ② ■ ▲	1	23
4 Jun 69	★	THE BALLAD OF JOHN AND YOKO *Apple R 5786*	1	14
8 Nov 69	●	SOMETHING / COME TOGETHER *Apple R 5814* ▲	4	12
14 Mar 70	●	LET IT BE (re) *Apple R 5833* ▲	2	10
13 Mar 76	●	YESTERDAY *Apple R 6013* ▲	8	7
10 Jul 76		BACK IN THE U.S.S.R. *Apple R 6016*	19	6
7 Oct 78		SGT. PEPPER'S LONELY HEARTS CLUB BAND – WITH		
		A LITTLE HELP FROM MY FRIENDS *Parlophone R 6022*	63	3
5 Jun 82	●	BEATLES MOVIE MEDLEY *Parlophone R 6055*	10	9
1 Apr 95	●	BABY IT'S YOU (re) *Apple CDR 6406*	7	7
16 Dec 95	●	FREE AS A BIRD *Apple CDR 6422*	2	8
16 Mar 96	●	REAL LOVE *Apple CDR 6425*	4	7
6 Apr 63	★	PLEASE PLEASE ME *Parlophone PMC 1202*	1	70
30 Nov 63	★	WITH THE BEATLES *Parlophone PMC 1206*	1	51
18 Jul 64	★	A HARD DAY'S NIGHT *Parlophone PMC 1230* ▲	1	38
12 Dec 64	★	BEATLES FOR SALE *Parlophone PMC 1240*	1	46
14 Aug 65	★	HELP! *Parlophone PMC 1255* ■ ▲	1	37
11 Dec 65	★	RUBBER SOUL *Parlophone PMC 1267* ▲	1	42
13 Aug 66	★	REVOLVER *Parlophone PMC 7009* ▲	1	34
10 Dec 66	●	A COLLECTION OF BEATLES OLDIES *Parlophone PMC 7016*	7	34
3 Jun 67	★	SGT. PEPPER'S LONELY HEARTS CLUB BAND		
		Parlophone PCS 7027 ▲	1	149
13 Jan 68		MAGICAL MYSTERY TOUR (IMPORT) *Capitol SMAL 2835* ▲	31	4
7 Dec 68	●	THE BEATLES (WHITE ALBUM) *Apple PCS 7067/8* ■ ▲	1	22
1 Feb 69	●	YELLOW SUBMARINE *Apple PCS 7070*	3	10
4 Oct 69	★	ABBEY ROAD *Apple PCS 7088* ■ ▲	1	81
23 May 70	★	LET IT BE *Apple PCS 7096* ■ ▲	1	59
16 Jan 71		A HARD DAY'S NIGHT (re-issue) *Parlophone PCS 3058*	30	1
24 Jul 71		HELP! (re-issue) *Parlophone PCS 3071*	33	2
5 May 73	●	THE BEATLES 1962-1966 *Apple PCSP 717*	3	148
5 May 73	●	THE BEATLES 1967-1970 *Apple PCSP 718* ▲	2	115

26 Jun 76	ROCK 'N' ROLL MUSIC *Parlophone PCSP 719*	11	15
21 Aug 76	THE BEATLES TAPES *Polydor 2683 068*	45	1
21 May 77 ★	THE BEATLES AT THE HOLLYWOOD BOWL *Parlophone EMTV 4*	1	17
17 Dec 77 ●	LOVE SONGS *Parlophone PCSP 721*	7	17
3 Nov 79	RARITIES *Parlophone PCM 1001*	71	1
15 Nov 80	BEATLES BALLADS *Parlophone PCS 7214*	17	16
30 Oct 82 ●	20 GREATEST HITS *Parlophone PCTC 260*	10	30
7 Mar 87	A HARD DAY'S NIGHT (2nd re-issue) *Parlophone CDP 746 4372*	30	4
7 Mar 87	WITH THE BEATLES (re-issue) *Parlophone CDP 746 4362*	40	3
7 Mar 87	BEATLES FOR SALE (re-issue) *Parlophone CDP 746 4382*	45	2
7 Mar 87	PLEASE PLEASE ME (re-issue) *Parlophone CDP 746 4352*	32	4
9 May 87	REVOLVER (re-issue) *Parlophone CDP 746 4412*	46	12
9 May 87	RUBBER SOUL (re-issue) *Parlophone CDP 746 4402*	60	5
9 May 87	HELP! (2nd re-issue) *Parlophone CDP 746 4392*	61	2
6 Jun 87 ●	SGT. PEPPER'S LONELY HEARTS CLUB BAND (re-issue) *Parlophone CDP 746 4422*	3	49
5 Sep 87	THE BEATLES (re-issue) *Parlophone CDS 746 4439*	18	2
5 Sep 87	YELLOW SUBMARINE (re-issue) *Parlophone CDP 746 4452*	60	1
3 Oct 87	MAGICAL MYSTERY TOUR (re-issue) *Parlophone PCTC 255*	52	1
31 Oct 87	ABBEY ROAD (re-issue) *Parlophone CDP 746 4462*	30	11
31 Oct 87	LET IT BE (re-issue) *Parlophone CDP 746 4472*	50	1
19 Mar 88	PAST MASTERS – VOLUME TWO *Parlophone CDBPM 2*	46	1
19 Mar 88	PAST MASTERS – VOLUME ONE *Parlophone CDBPM 1*	49	1
2 Oct 93 ●	THE BEATLES 1962-1966 (re-issue) *Parlophone BEACD 2511*	3	24
2 Oct 93 ●	THE BEATLES 1967-1970 (re-issue) *Parlophone BEACD 2512*	4	21
10 Dec 94 ★	LIVE AT THE BBC *Apple CDS 8317962* ■	1	20
2 Dec 95 ●	ANTHOLOGY 1 *Apple CDPCSP 727* ▲	2	10
30 Mar 96 ●	ANTHOLOGY 2 *Apple CDPCSP 728* ■ ▲	1	12
9 Nov 96 ●	ANTHOLOGY 3 *Apple CDPCSP 729* ▲	4	11
25 Sep 99 ●	YELLOW SUBMARINE – SONGTRACK (FILM SOUNDTRACK) *Parlophone 5214812*	8	5
25 Nov 00 ★	1 *Apple 5299702* ■ ▲	1	46
29 Nov 03 ●	LET IT BE – NAKED *Apple 5957132*	7	7

1 Tony Sheridan and The Beatles 2 The Beatles with Billy Preston

Tracks on Magical Mystery Tour (EP): Magical Mystery Tour / Your Mother Should Know / I Am the Walrus / Fool on the Hill / Flying / Blue Jay Way. 'We Can Work It Out', 'Come Together' and 'Penny Lane' were the tracks from the double A-sides that topped the US chart. The 1982 'Beatles Movie Medley' comprised (A-side) Magical Mystery Tour / All You Need Is Love / You've Got To Hide Your Love Away / I Should Have Known Better / A Hard Day's Night / Ticket To Ride / Get Back and (B-side) I'm Happy Just To Dance With You. Many Beatles hits re-entered the chart, including a large number on the original Parlophone label between 1982 and 1992. The best performing re-entry was 'Love Me Do', which made No.4 in 1982 but only peaked at No.17 on its release in 1962

The BEATMASTERS *UK, male / female production group (Singles: 47 Weeks, Albums: 10 Weeks)* pos/wks

9 Jan 88 ●	ROK DA HOUSE *Rhythm King LEFT 11* 1	5	11
24 Sep 88	BURN IT UP *Rhythm King LEFT 27* 2	14	10
22 Apr 89 ●	WHO'S IN THE HOUSE *Rhythm King LEFT 31* 3	8	9
12 Aug 89 ●	HEY DJ – I CAN'T DANCE (TO THAT MUSIC YOU'RE PLAYING) / SKA TRAIN *Rhythm King LEFT 34* 4	7	11
2 Dec 89 ●	WARM LOVE *Rhythm King LEFT 37* 5	51	2
21 Sep 91	BOULEVARD OF BROKEN DREAMS *Rhythm King 6573617*	62	1
16 May 92	DUNNO WHAT IT IS (ABOUT YOU) *Rhythm King 6580017* 6	43	3
1 Jul 89	ANYWAYAWANNA *Rhythm King LEFTLP 10*	30	10

1 The Beatmasters featuring the Cookie Crew 2 The Beatmasters with PP Arnold 3 The Beatmasters with Merlin 4 The Beatmasters featuring Betty Boo 5 The Beatmasters featuring Claudia Fontaine 6 The Beatmasters featuring Elaine Vassell

The BEATNUTS *US, male rap duo (Singles: 2 Weeks)* pos/wks

14 Jul 01	NO ESCAPIN' THIS *Epic 6713412*	47	1
21 Jun 03	DUDE DESCENDING A STAIRCASE *Stealth / SONY SSX 14CD* 1	58	1

1 Apollo 440 featuring The Beatnuts

BEATRICE See Mike KOGLIN

BEATS INTERNATIONAL (see also Norman COOK; FATBOY SLIM; FREAKPOWER; The HOUSEMARTINS; MIGHTY DUB KATZ; PIZZAMAN) *UK, male / female vocal / instrumental group – leader Norman Cook (Singles: 30 Weeks, Albums: 15 Weeks)* pos/wks

10 Feb 90 ★	DUB BE GOOD TO ME *Go Beat GOD 39* 1	1	13
12 May 90 ●	WON'T TALK ABOUT IT *Go Beat GOD 43*	9	7
15 Sep 90	BURUNDI BLUES *Go Beat GOD 45*	51	3
2 Mar 91	ECHO CHAMBER *Go Beat GOD 51*	60	2
21 Sep 91	THE SUN DOESN'T SHINE *Go Beat GOD 59*	66	2
23 Nov 91	IN THE GHETTO *Go Beat GOD 64*	44	3
14 Apr 90	LET THEM EAT BINGO *Go Beat 8421961*	17	15

1 Beats International featuring Lindy Layton

India BEAU See Basil BRUSH featuring India BEAU

BEAUTIFUL PEOPLE *UK, male instrumental / production group (Singles: 1 Week)* pos/wks

28 May 94	IF 60S WERE 90S *Essential ESSX 2037*	74	1

The BEAUTIFUL SOUTH 93 Top 500

Ex-Housemartins Paul Heaton (v/g) and Dave Hemingway (v) (from the beautiful north of England) formed the band that featured Briana Corrigan (v) (replaced by Jacqui Abbot 1994-2000). Heaton and Dave Rotheray (g) write the witty and ironic songs (Singles: 159 Weeks, Albums: 291 Weeks) pos/wks

3 Jun 89 ●	SONG FOR WHOEVER *Go Discs GOD 32*	2	11
23 Sep 89 ●	YOU KEEP IT ALL IN *Go Discs GOD 35*	8	8
2 Dec 89 ●	I'LL SAIL THIS SHIP ALONE *Go Discs GOD 38*	31	8
6 Oct 90 ★	A LITTLE TIME *Go Discs GOD 47*	1	14
8 Dec 90	MY BOOK *Go Discs GOD 48*	43	6
16 Mar 91	LET LOVE SPEAK UP ITSELF *Go Discs GOD 53*	51	2
11 Jan 92	OLD RED EYES IS BACK *Go Discs GOD 66*	22	6
14 Mar 92	WE ARE EACH OTHER *Go Discs GOD 71*	30	3
13 Jun 92	BELL BOTTOMED TEAR *Go Discs GOD 78*	16	5
26 Sep 92	36D *Go Discs GOD 88*	46	2
12 Mar 94	GOOD AS GOLD *Go Discs GODCD 110*	23	5
4 Jun 94	EVERYBODY'S TALKIN' *Go Discs GODCD 113*	12	8
3 Sep 94	PRETTIEST EYES *Go Discs GODCD 119*	37	3
12 Nov 94	ONE LAST LOVE SONG *Go Discs GODCD 122*	14	5
18 Nov 95	PRETENDERS TO THE THRONE *Go Discs GODCD 134*	18	4
12 Oct 96 ●	ROTTERDAM *Go Discs GODCD 155*	5	9
14 Dec 96 ●	DON'T MARRY HER *Go Discs GODCD 158*	8	10
29 Mar 97	BLACKBIRD ON THE WIRE *Go Discs 5821252*	23	5
5 Jul 97	LIARS' BAR *Go Discs 5822492*	43	1
3 Oct 98 ●	PERFECT 10 *Go Discs 5664832*	2	14
19 Dec 98	DUMB (re) *Go Discs 5667532*	16	8
20 Mar 99	HOW LONG'S A TEAR TAKE TO DRY? *Go Discs 8708212*	12	6
10 Jul 99	THE TABLE *Go Discs 5621652*	47	2
7 Oct 00	CLOSER THAN MOST *Go Discs / Mercury 5629672*	22	4
23 Dec 00	THE RIVER / JUST CHECKIN' *Go Discs / Mercury 5727552*	59	1
17 Nov 01	THE ROOT OF ALL EVIL *Go Discs / Mercury 5888702*	50	1
25 Oct 03	JUST A FEW THINGS THAT I AIN'T *Go Discs / Mercury 981308*	30	2
13 Dec 03	LET GO WITH THE FLOW *Go Discs / Mercury 9815083*	47	2
23 Oct 04	LIVIN' THING *Sony Music 6753712*	24	2
18 Dec 04	THIS OLD SKIN *Sony Music 6756842*	43	2+
4 Nov 89 ●	WELCOME TO THE BEAUTIFUL SOUTH *Go Discs AGOLP 16*	2	26
10 Nov 90 ●	CHOKE *Go Discs 8282331*	2	22
11 Apr 92 ●	0898 BEAUTIFUL SOUTH *Go Discs 8283102*	4	17
9 Apr 94 ●	MIAOW *Go Discs 8285072*	6	24
19 Nov 94 ★	CARRY ON UP THE CHARTS – THE BEST OF THE BEAUTIFUL SOUTH *Go Discs 8285722*	1	89
2 Nov 96 ★	BLUE IS THE COLOUR *Go Discs 8288452* ■	1	46
24 Oct 98 ★	QUENCH *Go Discs 5381662* ■	1	37
21 Oct 00 ●	PAINTING IT RED *Go Discs / Mercury 5483352*	2	11
24 Nov 01 ●	SOLID BRONZE – GREAT HITS *Go Discs / Mercury 5864442*	10	13
8 Nov 03 ●	GAZE *Go Discs 9865694*	14	3
6 Nov 04	GOLDDIGGAS HEADNODDERS & PHOLK SONGS *Sony Music 5186329*	11	3

BEAVIS and BUTT-HEAD See CHER

Gilbert BECAUD *France, male vocalist – François Silly, b. 24 Oct 1927, d. 18 Dec 2001 (Singles: 12 Weeks)* pos/wks

29 Mar 75 ●	A LITTLE LOVE AND UNDERSTANDING *Decca F 13537*	10	12

BECK *US, male vocalist – David Campbell (Singles: 27 Weeks, Albums: 78 Weeks)* pos/wks

5 Mar 94	LOSER *Geffen GFSTD 67*	15	6
29 Jun 96	WHERE IT'S AT *Geffen GFSTD 22156*	35	2
16 Nov 96	DEVIL'S HAIRCUT *Geffen GFSTD 22183*	22	2
8 Mar 97	THE NEW POLLUTION *Geffen GFSTD 22205*	14	5
24 May 97	SISSYNECK *Geffen GFSTD 22253*	30	2

		pos/wks
8 Nov 97	**DEADWEIGHT** *Geffen GFSTD 22293*	23 3
19 Dec 98	**TROPICALIA** *Geffen GFSTD 22365*	39 2
20 Nov 99	**SEXX LAWS** *Geffen 4971812*	27 3
8 Apr 00	**MIXED BIZNESS** *Geffen 4973002*	34 2
2 Apr 94	**MELLOW GOLD** *Geffen GED 24634*	41 4
6 Jul 96	**ODELAY** *Geffen GED 24926*	17 51
14 Nov 98	**MUTATIONS** *Geffen GED 25184*	24 6
4 Dec 99	**MIDNITE VULTURES** *Geffen 4905272*	19 14
5 Oct 02	**SEA CHANGE** *Geffen / Polydor 4933932*	20 3

Jeff BECK (see also The YARDBIRDS) UK, male vocalist / instrumentalist – guitar (Singles: 57 Weeks, Albums: 15 Weeks)

		pos/wks
23 Mar 67	**HI-HO SILVER LINING** *Columbia DB 8151*	14 14
2 Aug 67	**TALLYMAN** *Columbia DB 8227*	30 3
28 Feb 68	**LOVE IS BLUE (L'AMOUR EST BLEU)** *Columbia DB 8359*	23 7
9 Jul 69	**GOO GOO BARABAJAGAL (LOVE IS HOT)** *Pye 7N 17778* [1]	12 9
4 Nov 72	**HI-HO SILVER LINING (re) (re-issue)** *RAK RR 3*	17 15
5 May 73	**I'VE BEEN DRINKING** *RAK RR 4* [2]	27 6
7 Mar 97	**PEOPLE GET READY** *Epic 6577567* [2]	49 3
13 Sep 69	**BECK-OLA** *Columbia SCX 6351*	39 1
28 Apr 73	**JEFF BECK TIM BOGERT AND CARMINE APPICE** *Epic EPC 65455* [1]	28 3
24 Jul 76	**WIRED** *CBS 86012*	38 5
19 Jul 80	**THERE AND BACK** *Epic EPC 83288*	38 4
17 Aug 85	**FLASH** *Epic EPC 26112*	83 1
27 Mar 99	**WHO ELSE!** *Epic 4930412*	74 1

[1] Donovan with the Jeff Beck Group [2] Jeff Beck and Rod Stewart
[1] Jeff Beck, Tim Bogert and Carmine Appice

Robin BECK
US, female vocalist (Singles: 13 Weeks)

		pos/wks
22 Oct 88	★ **THE FIRST TIME** *Mercury MER 270*	1 13

Peter BECKETT See Barry GRAY ORCHESTRA

Victoria BECKHAM (see also SPICE GIRLS) UK, female vocalist – Victoria Adams (Singles: 46 Weeks, Albums: 3 Weeks)

		pos/wks
26 Aug 00	● **OUT OF YOUR MIND (re)** *Nulife 74321782942* [1]	2 20
29 Sep 01	● **NOT SUCH AN INNOCENT GIRL (2re)** *Virgin VSCDT 1816*	6 11
23 Feb 02	● **A MIND OF ITS OWN** *Virgin VSCDT 1824*	6 7
10 Jan 04	● **THIS GROOVE / LET YOUR HEAD GO** *19 / Telstar CDVB 1*	3 8
13 Oct 01	● **VICTORIA BECKHAM** *Virgin CDV 2942*	10 3

[1] True Steppers and Dane Bowers featuring Victoria Beckham

BEDAZZLED
UK, male vocal / instrumental group (Singles: 1 Week)

		pos/wks
4 Jul 92	**SUMMER SONG** *Columbia 6581627*	73 1

Daniel BEDINGFIELD (429) Top 500
Highly talented musical chameleon, b. 3 Dec 1979, New Zealand, and raised in South London. This singer / songwriter / producer, who recorded his first hits in his bedroom, was voted Best British Male Solo Artist at the 2004 Brits. (Singles: 78 Weeks, Albums: 85 Weeks)

		pos/wks
8 Dec 01	★ **GOTTA GET THRU THIS** *Relentless RELENT 27CD* ■	1 18
24 Aug 02	● **JAMES DEAN (I WANNA KNOW)** *Polydor 5709342*	4 8
7 Dec 02	★ **IF YOU'RE NOT THE ONE** *Polydor 0658632* ■	1 21
19 Apr 03	● **I CAN'T READ YOU** *Polydor 0657132*	6 11
2 Aug 03	★ **NEVER GONNA LEAVE YOU** *Polydor CDATH 006* ■	1 11
1 Nov 03	**FRIDAY** *Polydor 9812919*	28 2
6 Nov 04	● **NOTHING HURTS LIKE LOVE** *Polydor 9868820*	3 7
7 Sep 02	● **GOTTA GET THRU THIS** *Polydor 651252*	2 79
20 Nov 04	● **SECOND FIRST IMPRESSION** *Polydor 9868637*	8 6+

Natasha BEDINGFIELD
UK, female vocalist (Singles: 26 Weeks, Albums: 15 Weeks)

		pos/wks
15 May 04	● **SINGLE** *Phonogenic / BMG 82876615232*	3 10
28 Aug 04	★ **THESE WORDS** *Phonogenic / BMG 82876639182* ■	1 13
11 Dec 04	★ **UNWRITTEN** *Phonogenic / BMG 82876663522*	6 3+
18 Sep 04	★ **UNWRITTEN** *Phonogenic / BMG 82876637022* ■	1 15+

BEDLAM (see also DIDDY) UK, male DJ / production duo – Alan Thomson and Richard 'Diddy' Dearlove (Singles: 1 Week)

		pos/wks
6 Feb 99	**DA-FORCE** *Playola 0091695 PLA*	68 1

BEDLAM AGO GO
UK, male vocal / instrumental group (Singles: 1 Week)

		pos/wks
4 Apr 98	**SEASON NO.5** *Sony S2 BDLM 2CD*	57 1

BEDROCK UK, male vocal / instrumental duo – John Digweed and Nick Muir (Singles: 9 Weeks)

		pos/wks
1 Jun 96	**FOR WHAT YOU DREAM OF** *Stress CDSTR 23* [1]	25 3
12 Jul 97	**SET IN STONE / FORBIDDEN ZONE** *Stress CDSTR 80*	71 1
6 Nov 99	**HEAVEN SCENT** *Bedrock BEDRCDS 001*	35 3
8 Jul 00	**VOICES** *Bedrock BEDRCDS 005*	44 2

[1] Bedrock featuring KYO

BEDROCKS
UK, male vocal / instrumental group (Singles: 7 Weeks)

		pos/wks
18 Dec 68	**OB-LA-DI, OB-LA-DA** *Columbia DB 8516*	20 7

Celi BEE and the BUZZY BUNCH
US, male / female vocal / instrumental group (Singles: 1 Week)

		pos/wks
17 Jun 78	**HOLD YOUR HORSES, BABE** *TK TKR 6032*	72 1

The BEE GEES (31) Top 500
All-time top family recording act, who are members of the exclusive 100 million-plus sales club, are Isle of Man, UK-born and Australian raised Barry, Robin and Maurice Gibb (b. 22 Dec 1949, d. 12 Jan 2003). As composers, they have penned hits for many top acts and had 10 UK No.1s. In 1978 they wrote four consecutive US chart-toppers (three of which they also produced). Their 'Saturday Night Fever' album is the world's biggest selling soundtrack and they were the first group to have UK Top 20s in five decades. Distinctive trio has won countless trophies including the World Music Legend Award (1997) and Brits Outstanding Contribution to British Music (1997) (Singles: 354 Weeks, Albums: 413 Weeks)

		pos/wks
27 Apr 67	**NEW YORK MINING DISASTER 1941** *Polydor 56 161*	12 10
12 Jul 67	**TO LOVE SOMEBODY (re)** *Polydor 56 178*	41 5
20 Sep 67	★ **(THE NIGHT THE LIGHTS WENT OUT IN) MASSACHUSETTS** *Polydor 56 192*	1 17
22 Nov 67	● **WORLD** *Polydor 56 220*	9 16
31 Jan 68	● **WORDS** *Polydor 56 229*	8 10
27 Mar 68	**JUMBO / THE SINGER SANG HIS SONG** *Polydor 56 242*	25 7
7 Aug 68	★ **I'VE GOTTA GET A MESSAGE TO YOU** *Polydor 56 273*	1 15
19 Feb 69	● **FIRST OF MAY** *Polydor 56 304*	6 11
4 Jun 69	● **TOMORROW, TOMORROW** *Polydor 56 331*	23 8
16 Aug 69	● **DON'T FORGET TO REMEMBER** *Polydor 56 343*	2 15
28 Mar 70	**I.O.I.O.** *Polydor 56 377*	49 1
5 Dec 70	**LONELY DAYS** *Polydor 2001 104*	33 9
29 Jan 72	**MY WORLD** *Polydor 2058 185*	16 9
22 Jul 72	**RUN TO ME** *Polydor 2058 255*	9 10
28 Jun 75	● **JIVE TALKIN'** *RSO 2090 160* ▲	5 11
31 Jul 76	● **YOU SHOULD BE DANCING** *RSO 2090 195* ▲	5 10
13 Nov 76	**LOVE SO RIGHT** *RSO 2090 207*	41 4
29 Oct 77	● **HOW DEEP IS YOUR LOVE** *RSO 2090 259* ▲	3 15
4 Feb 78	● **STAYIN' ALIVE (re)** *RSO 2090 267* ▲	4 18
15 Apr 78	★ **NIGHT FEVER** *RSO 002* ▲	1 20
25 Nov 78	● **TOO MUCH HEAVEN** *RSO 25* ▲	3 13
17 Feb 79	● **TRAGEDY** *RSO 27* ▲	1 10
14 Apr 79	**LOVE YOU INSIDE OUT** *RSO 31* ▲	13 9
5 Jan 80	**SPIRITS (HAVING FLOWN)** *RSO 52*	16 7
17 Sep 83	**SOMEONE BELONGING TO SOMEONE** *RSO 96*	49 4
26 Sep 87	★ **YOU WIN AGAIN** *Warner Bros. W 8351*	1 15
12 Dec 87	**E.S.P.** *Warner Bros. W 8139*	51 5
15 Apr 89	**ORDINARY LIVES** *Warner Bros. W 7523*	54 4
24 Jun 89	**ONE** *Warner Bros. W 2916*	71 1
2 Mar 91	● **SECRET LOVE** *Warner Bros. W 0014*	5 11
21 Aug 93	**PAYING THE PRICE OF LOVE** *Polydor PZCD 284*	23 5
27 Nov 93	● **FOR WHOM THE BELL TOLLS** *Polydor PZCD 299*	4 14
16 Apr 94	**HOW TO FALL IN LOVE PART 1** *Polydor PZDD 311*	30 4
1 Mar 97	● **ALONE** *Polydor 5735272*	5 9
21 Jun 97	**I COULD NOT LOVE YOU MORE** *Polydor 5712232*	14 3
8 Nov 97	**STILL WATERS (RUN DEEP)** *Polydor 5718892*	18 3
18 Jul 98	● **IMMORTALITY** *Epic 6661682* [1]	5 12
7 Apr 01	**THIS IS WHERE I CAME IN** *Polydor 5879772*	18 5
12 Aug 67	● **BEE GEES FIRST** *Polydor 583012*	8 27
24 Feb 68	**HORIZONTAL** *Polydor 582020*	16 15
28 Sep 68	● **IDEA** *Polydor 583036*	4 18
5 Apr 69	● **ODESSA** *Polydor 583049/50*	10 1
8 Nov 69	● **BEST OF THE BEE GEES** *Polydor 583063*	7 22

9 May 70	CUCUMBER CASTLE *Polydor 2383010*	**57**	2
17 Feb 79 ★	SPIRITS HAVING FLOWN *RSO RSBG 001* ▲	**1**	33
10 Nov 79 ●	BEE GEES GREATEST *RSO RSDX 001* ▲	**6**	25
7 Nov 81	LIVING EYES *RSO RSBG 002*	**73**	8
3 Oct 87 ●	E.S.P. *Warner Bros. WX 83*	**5**	24
29 Apr 89	ONE *Warner Bros. WX 252*	**29**	3
17 Nov 90 ●	THE VERY BEST OF THE BEE GEES *Polydor 8473391*	**6**	108
6 Apr 91	HIGH CIVILISATION *Warner Bros. WX 417*	**24**	5
25 Sep 93	SIZE ISN'T EVERYTHING *Polydor 5199452*	**23**	13
22 Mar 97 ●	STILL WATERS *Polydor 5373022*	**2**	19
19 Sep 98 ●	ONE NIGHT ONLY *Polydor 5592202*	**4**	44
14 Apr 01 ●	THIS IS WHERE I CAME IN *Polydor 5494582*	**6**	6
24 Nov 01 ●	THEIR GREATEST HITS – THE RECORD *Polydor 5894492*	**5**	33
13 Nov 04 ●	NUMBER ONES *Polydor 9868840*	**7**	7+

1 Celine Dion with special guests The Bee Gees

Sir Thomas BEECHAM
UK, conductor, b. 29 Apr 1879, d. 8 Mar 1961 (Albums: 2 Weeks) pos/wks

26 Mar 60	CARMEN *HMV ALP 1762/4*	**18**	2

Full credit on sleeve reads 'Orchestre National de la Radio Diffusion Française conducted by Sir Thomas Beecham'

BEENIE MAN *Jamaica, male vocalist / toaster / rapper – Anthony Moses David (Singles: 51 Weeks)* pos/wks

20 Sep 97	DANCEHALL QUEEN *Island Jamaica IJCD 2018* 1	**70**	1
7 Mar 98	WHO AM I *Greensleeves GRECD 588*	**10**	5
8 Aug 98	FOUNDATION *Shocking Vibes SVJCDS1*	**69**	1
4 Mar 00 ●	MONEY *Parlophone Rhythm Series CDRHYTHM 27* 2	**5**	9
24 Mar 01	GIRLS DEM SUGAR *Virgin VUSCD 173* 3	**13**	5
28 Sep 02	FEEL IT BOY (re) *Virgin VUSCD 258* 4	**9**	7
14 Dec 02	DIRTY HARRY'S REVENGE *Kaos KAOS 004* 5	**50**	5
8 Feb 03	STREET LIFE *Virgin VUSCD 260*	**13**	5
13 Mar 04 ●	DUDE *Virgin VUSCD 282* 6	**7**	11
21 Aug 04	KING OF THE DANCEHALL *Virgin VUSCD 293*	**14**	5

1 Chevelle Franklyn / Beenie Man 2 Jamelia featuring Beenie Man 3 Beenie Man featuring Mya 4 Beenie Man featuring Janet 5 Adam F featuring Beenie Man 6 Beenie Man featuring Ms Thing

The BEES *UK, male vocal / instrumental group (Singles: 5 Weeks, Albums: 3 Weeks)* pos/wks

1 May 04	WASH IN THE RAIN *Virgin VSCDT 1868*	**31**	3
26 Jun 04	HORSEMEN *Virgin VSCDX 1869*	**41**	2
10 Jul 04	FREE THE BEES *Virgin CDV 2983*	**26**	3

Lou BEGA *Germany, male vocalist – David Lubega (Singles: 21 Weeks, Albums: 2 Weeks)* pos/wks

7 Aug 99	MAMBO NO.5 (A LITTLE BIT OF ...) (IMPORT) *Ariola 74321658012*	**31**	4
4 Sep 99 ★	MAMBO NO.5 (A LITTLE BIT OF ...) *RCA 74321696722* ■	**1**	15
18 Dec 99	I GOT A GIRL *RCA 74321720642*	**55**	2
18 Sep 99	A LITTLE BIT OF MAMBO *RCA 74321688612*	**50**	2

BEGGAR and CO
UK, male vocal / instrumental group (Singles: 15 Weeks) pos/wks

7 Feb 81	(SOMEBODY) HELP ME OUT *Ensign ENY 201*	**15**	10
12 Sep 81	MULE (CHANT NO.2) *RCA 130*	**37**	5

BEGINERZ *UK, male production duo – Ibi Tijani and Euen MacNeil (Singles: 3 Weeks)* pos/wks

13 Jul 02	RECKLESS GIRL *Cheeky / Arista 74321942232*	**28**	3

BEGINNING OF THE END
US, male vocal / instrumental group (Singles: 6 Weeks) pos/wks

23 Feb 74	FUNKY NASSAU *Atlantic K 10021*	**31**	6

BEIJING SPRING *UK, female vocal duo (Singles: 5 Weeks)* pos/wks

23 Jan 93	I WANNA BE IN LOVE AGAIN *MCA MCSTD 1709*	**43**	3
8 May 93	SUMMERLANDS *MCA MCSTD 1761*	**53**	2

BEJAY *See 56K featuring BEJAY*

BEL AMOUR
France, male / female vocal / production trio (Singles: 3 Weeks) pos/wks

12 May 01	BEL AMOUR *Credence CDCRED 010*	**23**	3

BEL CANTO *UK, male vocal / instrumental group (Singles: 1 Week)* pos/wks

14 Oct 95	WE'VE GOT TO WORK IT OUT *Good Groove CDGG 2*	**65**	1

Harry BELAFONTE *US, male vocalist / actor (Singles: 87 Weeks)* pos/wks

1 Mar 57 ●	BANANA BOAT SONG (DAY-O) *HMV POP 308* 1	**2**	18
14 Jun 57 ●	ISLAND IN THE SUN *RCA 1007*	**3**	25
6 Sep 57	SCARLET RIBBONS *HMV POP 360*	**18**	6
1 Nov 57 ★	MARY'S BOY CHILD (2re) *RCA 1022* ◆	**1**	19
22 Aug 58	LITTLE BERNADETTE *RCA 1072* 3	**16**	7
12 Dec 58	THE SON OF MARY *RCA 1084*	**18**	4
21 Sep 61	THERE'S A HOLE IN MY BUCKET (re) *RCA 1247* 4	**32**	8

1 Harry Belafonte with Tony Scott's Orchestra and Chorus and Millard Thomas, Guitar 2 Harry Belafonte and Millard Thomas 3 Belafonte 4 Harry Belafonte and Odetta

'Mary's Boy Child' re-entered twice, peaking at No.10 in 1958 and at No.30 in 1959

Archie BELL and the DRELLS
US, male vocal / instrumental group (Singles: 33 Weeks) pos/wks

7 Oct 72	HERE I GO AGAIN *Atlantic K 10210*	**11**	10
27 Jan 73	(THERE'S GONNA BE A) SHOWDOWN *Atlantic K 10263*	**36**	5
8 May 76	THE SOUL CITY WALK *Philadelphia International PIR 4250*	**13**	10
11 Jun 77	EVERYBODY HAVE A GOOD TIME *Philadelphia International PIR 5179*	**43**	4
28 Jun 86	DON'T LET LOVE GET YOU DOWN *Portrait A 7254*	**49**	4

Freddie BELL and the BELLBOYS
US, male vocal / instrumental group (Singles: 10 Weeks) pos/wks

28 Sep 56 ●	GIDDY-UP-A DING DONG *Mercury MT 122*	**4**	10

Maggie BELL *(see also STONE THE CROWS)*
UK, female vocalist (Singles: 12 Weeks) pos/wks

15 Apr 78	HAZELL (re) *Swansong SSK 19412*	**37**	4
17 Oct 81	HOLD ME *Swansong BAM 1* 1	**11**	8

1 B A Robertson and Maggie Bell

William BELL
US, male vocalist – William Yarborough (Singles: 22 Weeks) pos/wks

29 May 68	A TRIBUTE TO A KING *Stax 601 038*	**31**	7
20 Nov 68 ●	PRIVATE NUMBER *Stax 101* 1	**8**	14
26 Apr 86	HEADLINE NEWS *Absolute LUTE 1*	**70**	1

1 Judy Clay and William Bell

BELL and JAMES *US, male vocal duo (Singles: 3 Weeks)* pos/wks

31 Mar 79	LIVIN' IT UP (FRIDAY NIGHT) (re) *A&M AMS 7424*	**59**	3

BELL & SPURLING *UK, male vocal duo – Martin Bellamy and John Spurling (Singles: 10 Weeks)* pos/wks

13 Oct 01 ●	SVEN SVEN SVEN *Eternal WEA 336CD*	**7**	6
8 Jun 02	GOLDENBALLS (MR BECKHAM TO YOU) *Eternal WEA 350CD*	**25**	4

BELL BIV DEVOE *(see also NEW EDITION)*
US, male vocal group (Singles: 29 Weeks, Albums: 5 Weeks) pos/wks

30 Jun 90	POISON *MCA MCA 1414*	**19**	11
22 Sep 90	DO ME *MCA MCA 1440*	**56**	3
15 Aug 92 ●	THE BEST THINGS IN LIFE ARE FREE *Perspective PERSS 7400* 1	**2**	13
9 Oct 93	SOMETHING IN YOUR EYES *MCA MCSTD 1934*	**60**	2
1 Sep 90	POISON *MCA MCG 6094*	**35**	5

1 Luther Vandross and Janet Jackson with special guests BBD and Ralph Tresvant

BELL BOOK & CANDLE
Germany, male / female vocal / instrumental group (Singles: 1 Week) pos/wks

17 Oct 98	RESCUE ME *Logic 74321616882*	**63**	1

BELL X1 *Ireland, male vocal / instrumental group (Singles: 1 Week)* pos/wks

26 Jun 04	EVE, THE APPLE OF MY EYE *Island CID 856*	**65**	1

The BELLAMY BROTHERS *US, male vocal duo – Howard and David Bellamy (Singles: 29 Weeks, Albums: 6 Weeks)* pos/wks

17 Apr 76 ●	LET YOUR LOVE FLOW *Warner Bros. / Curb K 16690* ▲	**7**	12
21 Aug 76	SATIN SHEETS *Warner Bros. / Curb K 16775*	**43**	3

		pos/wks
11 Aug 79 ●	IF I SAID YOU HAVE A BEAUTIFUL BODY WOULD YOU	
	HOLD IT AGAINST ME *Warner Bros. / Curb K 17405* **3** 14	
19 Jun 76	BELLAMY BROTHERS *Warner Bros. K 56242* **21** 6	

BELLATRIX
Iceland, male / female vocal / instrumental group (Singles: 1 Week) pos/wks

16 Sep 00	JEDI WANNABE *Fierce Panda NING 101CD* **65** 1

BELLBOYS See Freddie BELL and the BELLBOYS

Regina BELLE
US, female vocalist (Singles: 13 Weeks, Albums: 5 Weeks) pos/wks

21 Oct 89	GOOD LOVIN' *CBS 655230* **73** 1
11 Dec 93	A WHOLE NEW WORLD (ALADDIN'S THEME)
	Columbia 6599002 [1] ▲ **12** 12
1 Aug 87	ALL BY MYSELF *CBS 4509981* **53** 4
16 Sep 89	STAY WITH ME *CBS 465132 1* **62** 1

[1] Regina Belle and Peabo Bryson

BELLE & SEBASTIAN
UK, male / female vocal / instrumental group (Singles: 21 Weeks, Albums: 18 Weeks) pos/wks

24 May 97	DOG ON WHEELS *Jeepster JPRCDS 001* **59** 1
9 Aug 97	LAZY LINE PAINTER JANE *Jeepster JPRCDS 002* **41** 2
25 Oct 97 ●	3 ... 6 ... 9 SECONDS OF LIGHT (EP) *Jeepster JPRCDS 003* **32** 2
3 Jun 00	LEGAL MAN *Jeepster JPRCD 018* **15** 3
30 Jun 01	JONATHAN DAVID *Jeepster JPRCDS 022* **31** 2
8 Dec 01	I'M WAKING UP TO US *Jeepster JPRCDS 023* **39** 2
29 Nov 03	STEP INTO MY OFFICE, BABY *Rough Trade RTRADSCD 128* ..**32** 2
28 Feb 04	I'M A CUCKOO *Rough Trade RTRADSCD 157* **14** 4
3 Jul 04	BOOKS *Rough Trade RTRADSCD 180* **20** 3
19 Sep 98	THE BOY WITH THE ARAB STRAP *Jeepster JPRCD 003* **12** 6
24 Jul 99	TIGERMILK *Jeepster JPRCD 007* **13** 4
17 Jun 00 ●	FOLD YOUR HANDS CHILD YOU WALK LIKE A PEASANT
	Jeepster JPRMD 010 ....**10** 3
15 Jun 02	STORYTELLING *Jeepster JPRCD 014* **26** 2
18 Oct 03	DEAR CATASTROPHE WAITRESS
	Rough Trade RTRADSCD 080 ....**21** 3

Tracks on 3... 6... 9 Seconds of Light (EP): A Century of Fakers / Le Pastie de la Bourgeoisie / Beautiful / Put the Book Back on the Shelf. The album track 'Wrapped Up in Books' was abbreviated to 'Books' for the single release
Group billed as Belle and Sebastian on 'Tigermilk' and 'Storytelling'

BELLE and the DEVOTIONS
UK, female vocal group (Singles: 8 Weeks) pos/wks

21 Apr 84	LOVE GAMES *CBS A 4332* **11** 8

THE BELLE STARS
UK, female vocal / instrumental group (Singles: 42 Weeks, Albums: 12 Weeks) pos/wks

5 Jun 82	IKO IKO *Stiff BUY 150* **35** 6
17 Jul 82	THE CLAPPING SONG *Stiff BUY 155* **11** 9
16 Oct 82	MOCKINGBIRD *Stiff BUY 159* **51** 3
15 Jan 83 ●	SIGN OF THE TIMES *Stiff BUY 167* **3** 11
16 Apr 83	SWEET MEMORY *Stiff BUY 174* **22** 9
13 Aug 83	INDIAN SUMMER *Stiff BUY 185* **52** 3
14 Jul 84	80S ROMANCE *Stiff BUY 200* **71** 1
5 Feb 83	THE BELLE STARS *Stiff SEEZ 45* **15** 12

BELLEFIRE
Ireland, female vocal group (Singles: 12 Weeks) pos/wks

14 Jul 01	PERFECT BLISS *Virgin VSCDT 1807* **18** 4
18 May 02	ALL I WANT IS YOU *Virgin VSCDT 1820* **18** 4
24 Apr 04	SAY SOMETHING ANYWAY *East West EW 287CD* **26** 3
16 Oct 04	SPIN THE WHEEL *East West EW 293CD1* **67** 1

BELLINI
Germany, male vocal / production group (Singles: 7 Weeks) pos/wks

27 Sep 97 ●	SAMBA DE JANEIRO *Virgin DINSD 165* **8** 7

The BELLRAYS
US, male / female vocal / instrumental group (Singles: 1 Week, Albums: 1 Week) pos/wks

20 Jul 02	THEY GLUED YOUR HEAD ON UPSIDE DOWN
	Poptones MC 5073SCD **75** 1
18 May 02	MEET THE BELLRAYS *Poptones MC 5069CD* **73** 1

Louis BELLSON See Duke ELLINGTON

BELLY (see also Tanya DONELLY)
US, male / female vocal / instrumental group (Singles: 9 Weeks, Albums: 13 Weeks) pos/wks

23 Jan 93	FEED THE TREE *4AD BAD 3001CD* **32** 3
10 Apr 93	GEPETTO *4AD BAD 2018CD* **49** 2
4 Feb 95	NOW THEY'LL SLEEP *4AD BAD 5003CD* **28** 2
22 Jul 95	SEAL MY FATE *4AD BAD 5007CD* **35** 2
13 Feb 93 ●	STAR *4AD 3002CD* **2** 10
25 Feb 95 ●	KING *4AD CADD 5004CD* **6** 3

Pierre BELMONDE
France, male instrumentalist – panpipes – Jeff Jarrett (Albums: 10 Weeks) pos/wks

7 Jun 80	THEMES FOR DREAMS *K-Tel ONE 1077* **13** 10

BELMONTS See DION

The BELOVED
UK, male / female vocal / instrumental duo (Singles: 47 Weeks, Albums: 31 Weeks) pos/wks

21 Oct 89	THE SUN RISING *WEA YZ 414* **26** 7
27 Jan 90	HELLO *WEA YZ 426* **19** 7
24 Mar 90	YOUR LOVE TAKES ME HIGHER *East West YZ 463* **39** 3
9 Jun 90	TIME AFTER TIME *East West YZ 482* **46** 4
10 Nov 90	IT'S ALRIGHT NOW *East West YZ 541* **48** 3
23 Jan 93 ●	SWEET HARMONY *East West YZ 709CD* **8** 10
10 Apr 93	YOU'VE GOT ME THINKING *East West YZ 709CD* **23** 4
14 Aug 93	OUTERSPACE GIRL *East West YZ 726CD* **38** 2
30 Mar 96	SATELLITE *East West EW 034CD* **19** 3
10 Aug 96	EASE THE PRESSURE *East West EW 058CD* **43** 2
30 Aug 97	THE SUN RISING (re-issue) *East West EW 122CD1* **31** 2
3 Mar 90	HAPPINESS *East West WX 299* **14** 14
1 Dec 90	BLISSED OUT *East West WX 383* **38** 2
20 Feb 93 ●	CONSCIENCE *East West 4509914832* **2** 12
20 Apr 96	X *East West 630133162* **25** 3

The act was male only before 1993

BELTRAM
US, male producer – Joey Beltram (Singles: 4 Weeks) pos/wks

28 Sep 91	ENERGY FLASH (EP) *R&S RSUK 3* **52** 2
7 Dec 91	THE OMEN *R&S RSUK 7* [1] **53** 2

[1] Program 2 Beltram

Tracks on Energy Flash (EP): Energy Flash / Psycho Bass / My Sound / Sub-Base Experience

Benny BENASSI presents the BIZ
Italy, male producer (Singles: 13 Weeks) pos/wks

26 Jul 03 ●	SATISFACTION *Data / MoS DATA 58CDS* **2** 11
14 Feb 04	NO MATTER WHAT YOU DO *Data / MoS DATA 66CDS* **40** 2

Pat BENATAR
US, female vocalist – Patricia Andrzejewski (Singles: 53 Weeks, Albums: 84 Weeks) pos/wks

21 Jan 84	LOVE IS A BATTLEFIELD *Chrysalis CHS 2747* **49** 5
12 Jan 85	WE BELONG *Chrysalis CHS 2821* **22** 9
23 Mar 85	LOVE IS A BATTLEFIELD (re-issue) *Chrysalis PAT 1* **17** 10
15 Jun 85	SHADOWS OF THE NIGHT *Chrysalis PAT 2* **50** 4
19 Oct 85	INVINCIBLE (THEME FROM 'THE LEGEND OF BILLIE JEAN')
	Chrysalis PAT 3 ....**53** 3
15 Feb 86	SEX AS A WEAPON *Chrysalis PAT 4* **67** 3
2 Jul 88	ALL FIRED UP *Chrysalis PAT 5* **19** 10
1 Oct 88	DON'T WALK AWAY *Chrysalis PAT 6* **42** 5
14 Jan 89	ONE LOVE *Chrysalis PAT 7* **59** 3
30 Oct 93	SOMEBODY'S BABY *Chrysalis CDCHS 5001* **48** 1
25 Jul 81	PRECIOUS TIME *Chrysalis CHR 1346* ▲ **30** 7
13 Nov 82	GET NERVOUS *Chrysalis CHR 1396* **73** 6
15 Oct 83	LIVE FROM EARTH *Chrysalis CHR 1451* **60** 5
17 Nov 84	TROPICO *Chrysalis CHR 1471* **31** 25
24 Aug 85	IN THE HEAT OF THE NIGHT *Chrysalis CHR 1236* **98** 1
7 Dec 85	SEVEN THE HARD WAY *Chrysalis CHR 1507* **69** 4
7 Nov 87 ●	BEST SHOTS *Chrysalis PATV 1* **6** 15
16 Jul 88	WIDE AWAKE IN DREAMLAND *Chrysalis CDL 1628* **11** 14
4 May 91	TRUE LOVE *Chrysalis CHR 1805* **40** 3

David BENDETH
Canada, male vocalist / multi-instrumentalist (Singles: 5 Weeks) pos/wks

8 Sep 79	FEEL THE REAL *Sidewalk SID 113* **44** 5

Singles re-entries are listed as (re), (2re), (3re).... which signifies that the hit re-entered the chart once, twice or three times...

BENELUX and Nancy DEE *Belgium / Holland /*
Luxembourg, female vocal group (Singles: 4 Weeks) pos/wks

25 Aug 79	SWITCH *Scope SC 4*	52	4

Eric BENET *US, male vocalist – Eric Bennet*
Jordan (Singles: 5 Weeks, Albums: 1 Week) pos/wks

22 Mar 97	SPIRITUAL THANG *Warner Bros. W 0390CD*	62	1
1 May 99	GEORGY PORGY *Warner Bros. W 478CD2* [1]	28	3
5 Feb 00	WHY YOU FOLLOW ME *Warner Bros. W 491CD*	48	1
15 May 99	A DAY IN THE LIFE *Warner Bros. 9362473702*	67	1

[1] Eric Benet featuring Faith Evans

Nigel BENN *See PACK featuring Nigel BENN*

Simone BENN *See VOLATILE AGENTS featuring Simone BENN*

BENNET *UK, male vocal / instrumental group (Singles: 3 Weeks)* pos/wks

22 Feb 97	MUM'S GONE TO ICELAND *Roadrunner RR 22853*	34	2
3 May 97	SOMEONE ALWAYS GETS THERE FIRST *Roadrunner RR 22983*	69	1

Boyd BENNETT and his ROCKETS *US, male vocalist, b. 7 Dec 1924, d. 2 Jun 2002, and male vocal / instrumental group (Singles: 2 Weeks)* pos/wks

23 Dec 55	SEVENTEEN *Parlophone R 4063*	16	2

Chris BENNETT *See MUNICH MACHINE*

Cliff BENNETT and the REBEL ROUSERS *UK, male*
vocal / instrumental group (Singles: 23 Weeks, Albums: 3 Weeks) pos/wks

1 Oct 64 ●	ONE WAY LOVE *Parlophone R 5173*	9	9
4 Feb 65	I'LL TAKE YOU HOME *Parlophone R 5229*	42	3
11 Aug 66 ●	GOT TO GET YOU INTO MY LIFE *Parlophone R 5489*	6	11
22 Oct 66	DRIVIN' ME WILD *MFP 1121*	25	3

Easther BENNETT *See ASWAD; ETERNAL*

Peter E BENNETT with the CO-OPERATION CHOIR
UK, male vocalist and choir (Singles: 1 Week) pos/wks

7 Nov 70	THE SEAGULL'S NAME WAS NELSON *RCA 1991*	45	1

Tony BENNETT *US, male vocalist – Anthony*
Benedetto (Singles: 61 Weeks, Albums: 70 Weeks) pos/wks

15 Apr 55 ★	STRANGER IN PARADISE *Philips PB 420*	1	16
16 Sep 55	CLOSE YOUR EYES *Philips PB 445*	18	1
13 Apr 56	COME NEXT SPRING *Philips PB 537*	29	1
5 Jan 61	TILL *Philips PB 1079*	35	2
18 Jul 63	THE GOOD LIFE *CBS AAG 153*	27	13
6 May 65	IF I RULED THE WORLD *CBS 201735*	40	5
27 May 65	(I LEFT MY HEART) IN SAN FRANCISCO (2re) *CBS 201730*	25	14
23 Dec 65	THE VERY THOUGHT OF YOU *CBS 202021*	21	9
29 May 65	I LEFT MY HEART IN SAN FRANCISCO *CBS BPG 62201*	13	14
19 Feb 66 ●	A STRING OF TONY'S HITS *CBS DP 66010*	9	13
10 Jun 67	TONY'S GREATEST HITS *CBS SBPG 62821*	14	24
23 Sep 67	TONY MAKES IT HAPPEN *CBS SBPG 63055*	31	3
23 Mar 68	FOR ONCE IN MY LIFE *CBS SBPG 63166*	29	5
26 Feb 77	THE VERY BEST OF TONY BENNETT – 20 GREATEST HITS *Warwick PA 5021*	23	4
28 Nov 98	THE ESSENTIAL TONY BENNETT *Columbia 4928222*	49	4
5 Jul 03	A WONDERFUL WORLD *Columbia 5098702* [1]	33	3

[1] Tony Bennett & kd lang

Gary BENSON
UK, male vocalist – Harry Hyams (Singles: 8 Weeks) pos/wks

9 Aug 75	DON'T THROW IT ALL AWAY *State STAT 10*	20	8

George BENSON 98 Top 500

Grammy-winning guitarist / vocalist, b. 22 Mar 1943, Pennsylvania, US. This one-time child prodigy topped the US chart in 1976 with the triple-platinum album 'Breezin''. He was also a major live attraction in Britain during the 1980s (Singles: 143 Weeks, Albums: 299 Weeks) pos/wks

25 Oct 75	SUPERSHIP *CTI CTSP 002* [1]	30	6
4 Jun 77	NATURE BOY *Warner Bros. K 16921*	26	6

24 Sep 77	THE GREATEST LOVE OF ALL *Arista 133*	27	7
31 Mar 79	LOVE BALLAD *Warner Bros. K 17333*	29	9
26 Jul 80 ●	GIVE ME THE NIGHT *Warner Bros. K 17673*	7	10
4 Oct 80 ●	LOVE X LOVE *Warner Bros. K 17699*	10	8
7 Feb 81	WHAT'S ON YOUR MIND *Warner Bros. K 17748*	45	5
19 Sep 81	LOVE ALL THE HURT AWAY *Arista ARIST 428* [2]	49	3
14 Nov 81	TURN YOUR LOVE AROUND *Warner Bros. K 17877*	29	11
23 Jan 82	NEVER GIVE UP ON A GOOD THING *Warner Bros. K 17902*	14	10
21 May 83	LADY LOVE ME (ONE MORE TIME) *Warner Bros. W 9614*	11	10
16 Jul 83	FEEL LIKE MAKIN' LOVE *Warner Bros. W 9551*	28	7
24 Sep 83 ●	IN YOUR EYES *Warner Bros. W 9487*	7	10
17 Dec 83	INSIDE LOVE (SO PERSONAL) *WEA Int. W 9427*	57	5
19 Jan 85	20 / 20 *Warner Bros. W 9120*	29	9
20 Apr 85	BEYOND THE SEA (LA MER) *Warner Bros. W 9014*	60	3
16 Aug 86	KISSES IN THE MOONLIGHT *Warner Bros. W 8640*	60	4
29 Nov 86	SHIVER *Warner Bros. W 8523*	19	9
14 Feb 87	TEASER *Warner Bros. W 8437*	45	4
27 Aug 88	LET'S DO IT AGAIN *Warner Bros. W 7780*	56	3
5 Sep 92	I'LL KEEP YOUR DREAMS ALIVE *Ammi AMMI 101* [3]	68	1
11 Jul 98	SEVEN DAYS *MCA MCSTD 48083* [4]	22	3
19 Mar 77	IN FLIGHT *Warner Bros. K 56237*	19	23
18 Feb 78	WEEKEND IN L.A. *Warner Bros. K 66074*	47	1
24 Mar 79	LIVING INSIDE YOUR LOVE *Warner Bros. K 66085*	24	14
26 Jul 80 ●	GIVE ME THE NIGHT *Warner Bros. K 56823*	3	40
14 Nov 81	THE GEORGE BENSON COLLECTION *Warner Bros. K 66107*	19	35
11 Jun 83 ●	IN YOUR EYES *Warner Bros. 9237441*	3	53
26 Jan 85 ●	20/20 *Warner Bros. 9251781*	9	19
19 Oct 85 ★	THE LOVE SONGS *K-Tel NE 1308*	1	26
6 Sep 86	WHILE THE CITY SLEEPS ... *Warner Bros. WX 55*	13	27
11 Jul 87	COLLABORATION *Warner Bros. WX 91* [1]	47	6
10 Sep 88	TWICE THE LOVE *Warner Bros. WX 160*	16	10
8 Jul 89	TENDERLY *Warner Bros. WX 263*	52	3
26 Oct 91	MIDNIGHT MOODS – THE LOVE COLLECTION *Telstar STAR 2450*	25	12
29 Jun 96	THAT'S RIGHT *GRP GRP 98242*	61	1
25 Apr 98 ●	ESSENTIALS ... THE VERY BEST OF GEORGE BENSON *Warner.esp / Jive 9548362292*	8	10
5 Jul 03 ●	THE VERY BEST OF GEORGE BENSON – THE GREATEST HITS OF ALL *WSM 8122736932*	4	18
27 Mar 04	IRREPLACEABLE *GRP 9861996*	58	1

[1] George "Bad" Benson [2] Aretha Franklin and George Benson [3] George Benson and Patti Austin [4] Mary J Blige featuring George Benson [1] George Benson and Earl Klugh

Rhian BENSON
Ghana, female vocalist (Singles: 2 Weeks) pos/wks

23 Oct 04	SAY HOW I FEEL *DKG 10071002*	27	2

BENT *UK, male production duo (Singles: 1 Week)* pos/wks

12 Jul 03	STAY THE SAME *Sport SPORT 9CDS*	59	1

BENTLEY RHYTHM ACE *UK, male instrumental duo – Mike*
Stokes and Richard March (Singles: 7 Weeks, Albums: 6 Weeks) pos/wks

6 Sep 97	BENTLEY'S GONNA SORT YOU OUT! *Parlophone CDRS 6476*	17	4
27 May 00	THEME FROM GUTBUSTER *Parlophone CDRS 6537*	29	2
2 Sep 00	HOW'D I DO DAT *Parlophone CDRS 6543*	57	1
24 May 97	BENTLEY RHYTHM ACE *Skint BRASSIC 5CD*	13	5
10 Jun 00	FOR YOUR EARS ONLY *Parlophone 5257322*	48	1

Brook BENTON *US, male vocalist – Benjamin*
Peay, b. 19 Sep 1931, d. 9 Apr 1988 (Singles: 18 Weeks) pos/wks

10 Jul 59	ENDLESSLY *Mercury AMT 1043*	28	2
6 Oct 60	KIDDIO (re) *Mercury AMT 1109*	41	6
16 Feb 61	FOOLS RUSH IN *Mercury AMT 1121*	50	1
13 Jul 61	THE BOLL WEEVIL SONG *Mercury AMT 1148*	30	9

BENZ *UK, male rap / vocal group (Singles: 9 Weeks)* pos/wks

16 Dec 95	BOOM ROCK SOUL *Hacktown 74321329652*	62	2
16 Mar 96	URBAN CITY GIRL *Hacktown 74321348732*	31	3
25 May 96	MISS PARKER *Hacktown 74321377292*	35	2
29 Mar 97	IF I REMEMBER *Hendricks CDBENZ 1*	59	1
9 Aug 97	ON A SUN-DAY *Hendricks CDBENZ 2*	73	1

Ingrid BERGMAN *See Dooley WILSON*

BERLIN
US, male / female vocal / instrumental group –
lead vocal Terri Nunn (Singles: 39 Weeks, Albums: 11 Weeks)   pos/wks

25 Oct 86	★ TAKE MY BREATH AWAY (LOVE THEME FROM 'TOP GUN') (re)		
	CBS A 7320 ▲	1	18
17 Jan 87	YOU DON'T KNOW *Mercury MER 237*	39	6
14 Mar 87	LIKE FLAMES *Mercury MER 240*	47	3
13 Oct 90	● TAKE MY BREATH AWAY (re-issue) *CBS 656361 7*	3	12
17 Jan 87	COUNT THREE AND PRAY *Mercury MER 101*	32	11

'Take My Breath Away' re-entered the chart in 1988, when it peaked at No.52

BERLIN PHILHARMONIC ORCHESTRA / Herbert Von KARAJAN
Germany, orchestra and Austria, male conductor (Albums: 1 Week) pos/wks

13 Apr 96	ADAGIO 2 *Deutsche Grammophon 4495152*	63	1

Shelley BERMAN
US, male comedian (Albums: 4 Weeks)   pos/wks

19 Nov 60	INSIDE SHELLEY BERMAN *Capitol CLP 1300*	12	4

Elmer BERNSTEIN
US, orchestra – leader
b. 4 Apr 1922, d. 19 Aug 2004 (Singles: 11 Weeks)   pos/wks

18 Dec 59	● STACCATO'S THEME (re) *Capitol CL 15101*	4	11

Leonard BERNSTEIN
US, orchestra and chorus – leader
b. 25 Aug 1918, d. 14 Oct 1990 (Singles: 4 Weeks, Albums: 2 Weeks) pos/wks

2 Jul 94	AMERICA – WORLD CUP THEME 1994		
	Deutsche Grammophon USACD 1 [1]	44	4
10 Feb 90	BERNSTEIN IN BERLIN – BEETHOVEN'S 9TH		
	Deutsche Grammophon 42986	54	2

[1] Leonard Bernstein, Orchestra and Chorus

Leonard BERNSTEIN'S WEST SIDE STORY *See STUDIO CAST RECORDINGS*

BERRI
UK, female vocalist – Rebecca Sleight (Singles: 22 Weeks)   pos/wks

26 Nov 94	THE SUNSHINE AFTER THE RAIN *Ffrreedom TABCD 223* [1] ..26		6
2 Sep 95	● THE SUNSHINE AFTER THE RAIN (re-mix)		
	Ffrreedom TABCD 232	4	11
2 Dec 95	SHINE LIKE A STAR *Ffrreedom TABCD 239*	20	5

[1] New Atlantic / U4EA featuring Berri

LaKiesha BERRI
US, female vocalist (Singles: 1 Week)   pos/wks

5 Jul 97	LIKE THIS AND LIKE THAT *Adept ADPTCD 7*	54	1

Chuck BERRY   498 Top 500
First guitar-playing rock star, b. 18 Oct 1926, Missouri, US. Often called rock
'n' roll's premier poet and most influential instrumentalist. 'Duck walking'
legend was among the first acts inducted into the Rock and Roll Hall of Fame
(Singles: 91 Weeks, Albums: 53 Weeks)   pos/wks

21 Jun 57	SCHOOL DAY (re) *Columbia DB 3951*	24	4
25 Apr 58	SWEET LITTLE SIXTEEN *London HLM 8585*	16	5
11 Jul 63	GO GO GO *Pye International 7N 25209*	38	6
10 Oct 63	● LET IT ROCK / MEMPHIS TENNESSEE		
	Pye International 7N 25218	6	13
19 Dec 63	RUN RUDOLPH RUN *Pye International 7N 25228*	36	6
13 Feb 64	NADINE (IS IT YOU) (re) *Pye International 7N 25236* ..	27	7
7 May 64	● NO PARTICULAR PLACE TO GO *Pye International 7N 25242* ..3		12
20 Aug 64	YOU NEVER CAN TELL *Pye International 7N 25257* ...	23	8
14 Jan 65	THE PROMISED LAND *Pye International 7N 25285*	26	6
28 Oct 72	★ MY DING-A-LING *Chess 6145 019* ▲	1	17
3 Feb 73	REELIN' AND ROCKIN' *Chess 6145 020*	18	7
25 May 63	CHUCK BERRY *Pye International NPL 28024*	12	16
5 Oct 63	● CHUCK BERRY ON STAGE *Pye International NPL 28027* ..6		11
7 Dec 63	MORE CHUCK BERRY *Pye International NPL 28028*	9	8
30 May 64	● THE LATEST AND THE GREATEST – YOU NEVER CAN TELL		
	Pye NPL 28037	8	7
3 Oct 64	YOU NEVER CAN TELL *Pye NPL 29039*	18	2
12 Feb 77	● MOTORVATIN' *Chess 9288 690*	7	9

Dave BERRY
UK, male vocalist – Dave Grundy (Singles: 77 Weeks)   pos/wks

19 Sep 63	MEMPHIS TENNESSEE *Decca F 11734* [1]	19	13
9 Jan 64	MY BABY LEFT ME (re) *Decca F 11803* [1]	37	9
30 Apr 64	BABY IT'S YOU *Decca F 11876*	24	6
6 Aug 64	● THE CRYING GAME *Decca F 11937*	5	12

26 Nov 64	ONE HEART BETWEEN TWO (re) *Decca F 12020*	41	3
25 Mar 65	● LITTLE THINGS *Decca F 12103*	5	12
22 Jul 65	THIS STRANGE EFFECT *Decca F 12188*	37	6
30 Jun 66	MAMA *Decca F 12435*	5	16

[1] Dave Berry and the Cruisers

Mike BERRY
UK, male vocalist – Michael
Bourne (Singles: 51 Weeks, Albums: 3 Weeks)   pos/wks

12 Oct 61	TRIBUTE TO BUDDY HOLLY *HMV POP 912* [1]	24	6
3 Jan 63	● DON'T YOU THINK IT'S TIME *HMV POP 1105* [2] ...	6	12
11 Apr 63	MY LITTLE BABY *HMV POP 1142* [2]	34	7
2 Aug 80	● THE SUNSHINE OF YOUR SMILE *Polydor 2059 261* ..	9	12
29 Nov 80	IF I COULD ONLY MAKE YOU CARE *Polydor POSP 202* .	37	9
5 Sep 81	MEMORIES *Polydor POSP 287*	55	5
24 Jan 81	THE SUNSHINE OF YOUR SMILE *Polydor 2383 592*	63	3

[1] Mike Berry and the Outlaws [2] Mike Berry and the Outlaws

Nick BERRY
UK, male actor / vocalist (Singles: 24 Weeks, Albums: 8 Weeks) pos/wks

4 Oct 86	★ EVERY LOSER WINS (re) *BBC RESL 204*	1	13
13 Jun 92	● HEARTBEAT *Columbia 6581517*	2	8
31 Oct 92	LONG LIVE LOVE *Columbia 6587597*	47	3
20 Dec 86	NICK BERRY *BBC REB 618*	99	1
21 Nov 92	NICK BERRY *Columbia 4727182*	28	7

The two identically titled albums are different

Adele BERTEI *See JELLYBEAN*

BEST COMPANY
UK, male vocal duo (Singles: 1 Week)   pos/wks

27 Mar 93	DON'T YOU FORGET ABOUT ME *ZYX ZYX 69468*	65	1

BEST SHOT
UK, male rap group (Singles: 2 Weeks)   pos/wks

5 Feb 94	UNITED COLOURS *East West YZ 795CD*	64	2

The BETA BAND
UK, male vocal /
instrumental group (Singles: 7 Weeks, Albums: 9 Weeks)   pos/wks

14 Jul 01	BROKE / WON *Regal Recordings REG 60CD*	30	2
27 Oct 01	HUMAN BEING *Regal Recordings REG 65CD*	57	1
16 Feb 02	SQUARES *Regal Recordings REG 69CD*	42	1
24 Apr 04	ASSESSMENT *Regal Recordings REG 012CDS*	31	2
24 Jul 04	OUT-SIDE *Regal Recordings REG 110CDS*	54	1
10 Oct 98	THE THREE EP'S *Regal Recordings 4973852*	35	1
3 Jul 99	THE BETA BAND *Regal Recordings REG 30CD*	18	2
28 Jul 01	HOT SHOTS II *Regal Recordings REG 59CD*	13	6
8 May 04	HEROES TO ZEROS *Regal Recordings REG 101CD*	18	3

Martin BETTINGHAUS *See Timo MAAS*

Frankie BEVERLY *See MAZE featuring Frankie BEVERLY*

The BEVERLEY SISTERS
UK, female vocal trio (Singles: 34 Weeks) pos/wks

27 Nov 53	● I SAW MOMMY KISSING SANTA CLAUS (re) *Philips PB 188* ..6		5
13 Apr 56	WILLIE CAN *Decca F 10705*	23	4
1 Feb 57	I DREAMED *Decca F 10832*	24	2
13 Feb 59	● LITTLE DRUMMER BOY *Decca F 11107*	6	13
20 Nov 59	LITTLE DONKEY *Decca F 11172*	14	7
23 Jun 60	GREEN FIELDS (re) *Columbia DB 4444*	29	3

BEVERLEY-PHILLIPS ORCHESTRA
UK, orchestra (Albums: 9 Weeks)   pos/wks

9 Oct 76	GOLD ON SILVER *Warwick WW 5018*	22	9

BEYONCÉ (see also DESTINY'S CHILD) US, female vocalist –
Beyoncé Knowles (Singles: 64 Weeks, Albums: 48 Weeks)   pos/wks

27 Jul 02	WORK IT OUT (re) *Columbia 6729822*	7	11
1 Feb 03	● '03 BONNIE & CLYDE *Roc-A-Fella 0770102* [1]	2	12
12 Jul 03	★ CRAZY IN LOVE *Columbia 6740672* ■ ▲	1	15
18 Oct 03	● BABY BOY (re) *Columbia 6744082* [2] ▲	2	11
24 Jan 04	ME, MYSELF AND I *Columbia 6745442*	11	7
17 Apr 04	● NAUGHTY GIRL *Columbia 6748282*	10	8
5 Jul 03	★ DANGEROUSLY IN LOVE *Columbia 5093952* ■ ▲	1	48

[1] Jay-Z featuring Beyoncé Knowles [2] Beyoncé featuring Sean Paul

Singles re-entries are listed as (re), (2re), (3re).... which signifies that the hit re-entered the chart once, twice or three times...

BEYOND UK, male vocal / instrumental group (Singles: 1 Week)
pos/wks

| 21 Sep 91 | RAGING (EP) Harvest HARS 530 | 68 | 1 |

Tracks on Raging (EP): Great Indifference / Nail / Eve of My Release

BHANGRA KNIGHTS vs HUSAN UK, male production trio –
Jack Berry, Jules Spinner and Raul and Holland, male production duo – Jeroen Den Hengst and Niels Zuiderhoek (Singles: 7 Weeks) pos/wks

| 17 May 03 ● | HUSAN Positiva CDTIV 188 | 7 | 7 |

BHOYS FROM PARADISE
UK, male vocal group – Celtic fans (Singles: 2 Weeks) pos/wks

| 3 Jul 04 | DIRTY OLD TOWN / THE ROAD TO PARADISE Lord of the Wing LWSP 7 | 46 | 2 |

The BIBLE UK, male vocal / instrumental
group (Singles: 8 Weeks, Albums: 2 Weeks) pos/wks

20 May 89	GRACELAND Chrysalis BIB 4	51	4
26 Aug 89	HONEY BE GOOD Ensign BIB 5	54	4
2 Jan 88	EUREKA Cooltempo CHR 1646	71	1
7 Oct 89	THE BIBLE Ensign CHEN 12	67	1

BIBLE OF DREAMS See Johnny PANIC and the BIBLE OF DREAMS

BIDDU ORCHESTRA
UK, orchestra – leader Biddu Appaiah (Singles: 13 Weeks) pos/wks

2 Aug 75	SUMMER OF '42 Epic EPC 3318	14	8
17 Apr 76	RAIN FOREST Epic EPC 4084	39	4
11 Feb 78	JOURNEY TO THE MOON Epic EPC 5910	41	1

BIFFY CLYRO UK, male vocal / instrumental
trio (Singles: 9 Weeks, Albums: 2 Weeks) pos/wks

16 Feb 02	57 Beggars Banquet BBQ 358CD	61	1
5 Apr 03	THE IDEAL HEIGHT Beggars Banquet BBQ 365CD	46	1
7 Jun 03	QUESTIONS & ANSWERS Beggars Banquet BBQ 368CD	26	2
21 Aug 04	GLITTER AND TRAUMA Beggars Banquet BBQ 377CD	21	3
2 Oct 04	MY RECOVERY INJECTION Beggars Banquet BBQ 379CD	24	2
28 Jun 03	THE VERTIGO OF BLISS Beggars Banquet BBQCD 233	48	1
16 Oct 04	INFINITY LAND Beggars Banquet BBQCD 238	47	1

BIG APPLE BAND See Walter MURPHY and the BIG APPLE BAND

BIG AUDIO DYNAMITE UK / US, male vocal /
instrumental group (Singles: 27 Weeks, Albums: 43 Weeks) pos/wks

22 Mar 86	E=MC2 CBS A 6963	11	9
7 Jun 86	MEDICINE SHOW CBS A 7181	29	5
18 Oct 86	C'MON EVERY BEATBOX CBS 650147	51	3
21 Feb 87	V THIRTEEN CBS BAAD 2	49	5
28 May 88	JUST PLAY MUSIC CBS BAAD 4	51	3
12 Nov 94	LOOKING FOR A SONG Columbia 6610182 [1]	68	2
16 Nov 85	THIS IS BIG AUDIO DYNAMITE CBS 26714	27	27
8 Nov 86	NO. 10 UPPING STREET CBS 4501371	11	8
9 Jul 88	TIGHTEN UP VOL. 88 CBS 4611991	33	3
16 Sep 89	MEGATOP PHOENIX CBS 4657901	26	3
2 Nov 90	KOOL-AID CBS 4674661	55	1
17 Aug 91	THE GLOBE Columbia 4677061	63	1

[1] Big Audio

BIG BAD HORNS See LITTLE ANGELS

BIG BAM BOO
UK / Canada, male vocal / instrumental duo (Singles: 2 Weeks) pos/wks

| 28 Jan 89 | SHOOTING FROM MY HEART MCA MCA 1281 | 61 | 2 |

BIG BAND UK, male instrumental group (Albums: 1 Week)
pos/wks

| 16 Nov 02 | SWINGIN' WITH THE BIG BAND Columbia STVCD 157 | 62 | 1 |

BIG BANG THEORY
UK, male producer – Seamus Haji (Singles: 1 Week) pos/wks

| 2 Mar 02 | GOD'S CHILD Defected DFECT 45CDS | 51 | 1 |

BIG BASS vs Michelle NARINE
Canada, male production group and female vocalist (Singles: 1 Week) pos/wks

| 2 Sep 00 | WHAT YOU DO Stonebridge / Edel 0110965 ERE | 67 | 1 |

BIG BEN UK, clock (Singles: 2 Weeks)
pos/wks

| 1 Jan 00 | MILLENNIUM CHIMES London BIGONE 2000 | 53 | 2 |

BIG BEN BANJO BAND UK, male instrumental group – Norrie
Paramor, b. 1913, d. 9 Sep 1979 (Singles: 6 Weeks, Albums: 1 Week) pos/wks

10 Dec 54 ●	LET'S GET TOGETHER NO.1 Columbia DB 3549	6	4
9 Dec 55	LET'S GET TOGETHER AGAIN NO.1 (re) Columbia DB 3676	18	2
17 Dec 60	MORE MINSTREL MELODIES Columbia 33SX 1254	20	1

Both singles were medleys as follows: Let's Get Together No.1: I'm Just Wild About Harry / April Showers / Rock-a-Bye Your Baby / Swanee / Darktown Strutters Ball / For Me and My Gal / Oh You Beautiful Doll / Yes Sir That's My Baby / Let's Get Together

BIG BOI See KILLER MIKE

The BIG BOPPER US, male vocalist – JP Richardson,
b. 24 Oct 1930, d. 3 Feb 1959 (Singles: 8 Weeks) pos/wks

| 26 Dec 58 | CHANTILLY LACE (re) Mercury AMT 1002 | 12 | 8 |

BIG BOSS STYLUS presents RED VENOM UK, male
production duo and male rapper – Mike Neilson (Singles: 1 Week) pos/wks

| 31 Jul 99 | LET'S GET IT ON All Around the World CDGLOBE 195 | 72 | 1 |

BIG BROVAZ UK, male / female vocal / rap /
production group (Singles: 65 Weeks, Albums: 35 Weeks) pos/wks

26 Oct 02 ●	NU FLOW (re) Epic 6730282	3	18
15 Feb 03 ●	OK Epic 6735212	7	9
17 May 03 ●	FAVOURITE THINGS Epic 6738072	2	11
13 Sep 03 ●	BABY BOY Epic 6743092	4	12
20 Dec 03	AIN'T WHAT YOU DO Epic 6745102	15	7
17 Apr 04	WE WANNA THANK YOU (THE THINGS YOU DO) Epic 6748602	17	4
9 Oct 04	YOURS FATALLY Epic 6753542	15	4
16 Nov 02 ●	NU FLOW Epic 5099402	6	35

BIG C See Alex WHITCOMBE & BIG C

BIG COUNTRY 249 Top 500 Distinctively Scottish-sounding rock
quartet from Dunfermline, Scotland: Stuart Adamson, b. 11 Apr 1958, d. 16 Dec 2001 (v/g, ex-Skids), Bruce Watson (g), Tony Butler (b), Mark Brzezicki (d). These frequent early-1980s chart visitors achieved five Top 10 albums including the 1984 No.1 'Steeltown', and were well known for Watson's bagpipe-like guitar sound (Singles: 103 Weeks, Albums: 149 Weeks) pos/wks

26 Mar 83 ●	FIELDS OF FIRE (400 MILES) Mercury COUNT 2	10	12
28 May 83	IN A BIG COUNTRY Mercury COUNT 3	17	7
3 Sep 83 ●	CHANCE Mercury COUNT 4	9	9
21 Jan 84 ●	WONDERLAND Mercury COUNT 5	8	8
29 Sep 84	EAST OF EDEN Mercury MER 175	17	6
1 Dec 84	WHERE THE ROSE IS SOWN Mercury MER 185	29	7
19 Jan 85	JUST A SHADOW Mercury BCO 8	26	4
12 Apr 86 ●	LOOK AWAY Mercury BIGC 1	7	8
21 Jun 86	THE TEACHER Mercury BIGC 2	28	4
20 Sep 86	ONE GREAT THING Mercury BIGC 3	19	6
29 Nov 86	HOLD THE HEART Mercury BIGC 4	55	2
20 Aug 88	KING OF EMOTION (re) Mercury BIGC 5	16	6
5 Nov 88	BROKEN HEART (THIRTEEN VALLEYS) Mercury BIGC 6	47	4
4 Feb 89	PEACE IN OUR TIME Mercury BIGC 7	39	3
12 May 90	SAVE ME Mercury BIGC 8	41	3
21 Jul 90	HEART OF THE WORLD Mercury BIGC 9	50	2
31 Aug 91	REPUBLICAN PARTY REPTILE (EP) Vertigo BIC 1	37	2
19 Oct 91	BEAUTIFUL PEOPLE Vertigo BIC 2	72	1
13 Mar 93	ALONE Compulsion CDPULSS 4	24	3
1 May 93	SHIPS (WHERE WERE YOU) Compulsion CDPULSS 6	29	3
10 Jun 95	I'M NOT ASHAMED Transatlantic TRAX 1009	69	1
9 Sep 95	YOU DREAMER Transatlantic TRAD 1012	68	1
21 Aug 99	FRAGILE THING Track TRACK 0004A [1]	69	1
6 Aug 83 ●	THE CROSSING Mercury MERH 27	3	80
27 Oct 84 ★	STEELTOWN Mercury MERH 49 ■	1	21
12 Jul 86 ●	THE SEER Mercury MERH 87	2	16
8 Oct 88 ●	PEACE IN OUR TIME Mercury MERH 130	9	6
26 May 90 ●	THROUGH A BIG COUNTRY – GREATEST HITS Mercury 8460221	2	17
28 Sep 91	NO PLACE LIKE HOME Vertigo 5102301	28	2
3 Apr 93	THE BUFFALO SKINNERS Compulsion CDNOIS 2	25	2
18 Jun 94	WITHOUT THE AID OF A SAFETY NET (LIVE) Compulsion CDNOIS 5	35	1

24 Jun 95	WHY THE LONG FACE *Transatlantic TRACD 109*	48	2
24 Aug 96	ECLECTIC *Transatlantic TRACD 234*	41	1
8 Jun 02	THE GREATEST HITS OF BIG COUNTRY AND THE SKIDS – THE BEST OF STUART ADAMSON *UMTV 5869892* [1]	71	1

[1] Big Country featuring Eddi Reader [1] Big Country and The Skids

Tracks on Republican Party Reptile (EP): Republican Party Reptile / Comes a Time / You Me and the Truth

BIG DADDY
US, male vocal group (Singles: 8 Weeks) pos/wks

9 Mar 85	DANCING IN THE DARK *Making Waves SURF 1033*	21	8

BIG DADDY KANE *US, male rapper –*
Antonio Hardy (Singles: 6 Weeks, Albums: 3 Weeks) pos/wks

13 May 89	RAP SUMMARY / WRATH OF KANE *Cold Chillin' W 2973*	52	2
26 Aug 89	SMOOTH OPERATOR *Cold Chillin' W 2804*	65	1
13 Jan 90	AIN'T NO STOPPIN' US NOW *Cold Chillin' W 2635*	44	3
30 Sep 89	IT'S A BIG DADDY THING *Cold Chillin' WX 305*	37	3

BIG DISH *UK, male vocal / instrumental*
group (Singles: 5 Weeks, Albums: 3 Weeks) pos/wks

12 Jan 91	MISS AMERICA *East West YZ 529*	37	5
11 Oct 86	SWIMMER *Virgin V 2374*	85	1
23 Feb 91	SATELLITES *East West WX 400*	43	2

BIG FAMILY See JT and the BIG FAMILY

BIG FUN
UK, male vocal group (Singles: 33 Weeks, Albums: 11 Weeks) pos/wks

12 Aug 89 ●	BLAME IT ON THE BOOGIE *Jive JIVE 217*	4	11
25 Nov 89 ●	CAN'T SHAKE THE FEELING *Jive JIVE 234*	8	9
17 Mar 90	HANDFUL OF PROMISES *Jive JIVE 243*	21	6
23 Jun 90	YOU'VE GOT A FRIEND *Jive CHILD 90* [1]	14	6
4 Aug 90	HEY THERE LONELY GIRL *Jive JIVE 251*	62	1
12 May 90 ●	A POCKETFUL OF DREAMS *Jive FUN 1*	7	11

[1] Big Fun and Sonia featuring Gary Barnacle

BIG MOUNTAIN
US, male / female vocal / instrumental group (Singles: 15 Weeks) pos/wks

4 Jun 94 ●	BABY I LOVE YOUR WAY *RCA 74321198062*	2	14
24 Sep 94	SWEET SENSUAL LOVE *Giant 74321234642*	51	1

BIG PUN See Jennifer LOPEZ

BIG ROLL BAND See Zoot MONEY and the BIG ROLL BAND

BIG RON
UK, male producer – Aaron Gilbert (aka Jules Verne) (Singles: 1 Week) pos/wks

11 Mar 00	LET THE FREAK *48k SPECT 06CDS*	57	1

BIG ROOM GIRL featuring Darryl PANDY (see also RHYTHM
MASTERS) *UK, male production / instrumental duo – Robert Chetcutti and Steve McGuinness and US, male vocalist (Singles: 2 Weeks)* pos/wks

20 Feb 99	RAISE YOUR HANDS *VC Recordings VCRD 44*	40	2

BIG SOUND See Simon DUPREE and the BIG SOUND

BIG SOUND AUTHORITY
UK, male / female vocal / instrumental group (Singles: 12 Weeks) pos/wks

19 Jan 85	THIS HOUSE (IS WHERE YOUR LOVE STANDS) *Source BSA1*	21	9
8 Jun 85	A BAD TOWN *Source BSA 2*	54	3

BIG SUPREME *UK, male vocal group (Singles: 5 Weeks)* pos/wks

20 Sep 86	DON'T WALK *Polydor POSP 809*	58	3
14 Mar 87	PLEASE YOURSELF *Polydor POSP 840*	64	2

The BIG THREE *UK, vocal / instrumental group (Singles: 17 Weeks)* pos/wks

11 Apr 63	SOME OTHER GUY *Decca F 11614*	37	7
11 Jul 63	BY THE WAY *Decca F 11689*	22	10

BIG TIGGER See R KELLY

BIG TIME CHARLIE (see also BIG RON) *UK, male DJ /*
production duo – Aaron Gilbert and Les Sharma (Singles: 4 Weeks) pos/wks

23 Oct 99	ON THE RUN *Inferno CDFERN 18*	22	2
18 Mar 00	MR DEVIL *Inferno CDFERN 24* [1]	39	2

[1] Big Time Charlie featuring Soozy Q

BIGFELLA featuring Noel McCALLA
US, male production duo and UK, male vocalist (Singles: 1 Week) pos/wks

17 Aug 02	BEAUTIFUL *Nulife 74321942282*	52	1

Barry BIGGS *Jamaica, male vocalist (Singles: 46 Weeks)* pos/wks

28 Aug 76	WORK ALL DAY *Dynamic DYN 101*	38	5
4 Dec 76 ●	SIDESHOW *Dynamic DYN 118*	3	16
23 Apr 77	YOU'RE MY LIFE *Dynamic DYN 127*	36	4
9 Jul 77	THREE RING CIRCUS *Dynamic DYN 128*	22	8
15 Dec 79	WHAT'S YOUR SIGN GIRL *Dynamic DYN 150*	55	7
20 Jun 81	WIDE AWAKE IN A DREAM *Dynamic DYN 10*	44	6

Ronald BIGGS See The SEX PISTOLS

Ivor BIGGUN *UK, male vocalist – Doc Cox (Singles: 15 Weeks)* pos/wks

2 Sep 78	THE WINKER'S SONG (MISPRINT) *Beggars Banquet BOP 1* [1]	22	12
12 Sep 81	BRAS ON 45 (FAMILY VERSION) *Dead Badger BOP 6* [2]	50	3

[1] Ivor Biggun & the Red-Nosed Burglars [2] Ivor Biggun and the D Cups

BILBO *UK, male vocal / instrumental group (Singles: 7 Weeks)* pos/wks

26 Aug 78	SHE'S GONNA WIN *Lightning LIG 548*	42	7

Acker BILK   165 Top 500
First UK act to top the US chart in 1960s, b. 28 Jan 1929, Somerset, UK. Band leader / clarinettist / vocalist was at the forefront of the UK trad-jazz revival. 'Stranger on the Shore' spent more than one year on the chart, selling 1,130,000, and was voted No.1 instrumental of 1962 in the US. Made an MBE in the 2001 honours list (Singles: 172 Weeks, Albums: 161 Weeks) pos/wks

22 Jan 60 ●	SUMMER SET *Columbia DB 4382* [1]	5	20
9 Jun 60	GOODNIGHT SWEET PRINCE *Melodisc MEL 1547* [1]	50	1
18 Aug 60	WHITE CLIFFS OF DOVER *Columbia DB 4492* [1]	30	9
8 Dec 60 ●	BUONA SERA *Columbia DB 4544* [1]	7	18
13 Jul 61 ●	THAT'S MY HOME *Columbia DB 4673* [1]	7	17
2 Nov 61	STARS AND STRIPES FOREVER / CREOLE JAZZ *Columbia SCD 2155* [1]	22	10
30 Nov 61	STRANGER ON THE SHORE *Columbia DB 4750* [2] ◆ ▲	2	55
15 Mar 62	FRANKIE AND JOHNNY *Columbia DB 4795* [1]	42	2
26 Jul 62	GOTTA SEE BABY TONIGHT *Columbia SCD 2176* [1]	24	9
27 Sep 62	LONELY *Columbia DB 4897* [2]	14	11
24 Jan 63	A TASTE OF HONEY *Columbia DB 4949* [2]	16	9
21 Aug 76 ●	ARIA *Pye 7N 45607* [3]	5	11
19 Mar 60 ●	SEVEN AGES OF ACKER *Columbia 33SX 1205*	6	6
9 Apr 60	ACKER BILK'S OMNIBUS *Pye NJL 22*	14	3
4 Mar 61	ACKER *Columbia 33SX 1248*	17	1
1 Apr 61	GOLDEN TREASURY OF BILK *Columbia 33SX 1304*	11	6
27 May 61 ●	THE BEST OF BARBER AND BILK VOLUME 1 *Pye Golden Guinea GGL 0075* [1]	4	43
11 Nov 61 ●	THE BEST OF BARBER AND BILK VOLUME 2 *Pye Golden Guinea GGL 0096* [1]	8	18
26 May 62 ●	STRANGER ON THE SHORE *Columbia 33SX 1407*	6	28
25 Aug 62 ★	THE BEST OF BALL, BARBER AND BILK *Pye Golden Guinea GGL 0131* [2]	1	24
4 May 63	A TASTE OF HONEY *Columbia 33SX 1493*	17	4
9 Oct 76	THE ONE FOR ME *Pye NSPX 41052*	38	6
4 Jun 77 ●	SHEER MAGIC *Warwick WW 5028*	5	8
11 Nov 78	EVERGREEN *Warwick PW 5045*	17	14

[1] Mr Acker Bilk and his Paramount Jazz Band [2] Mr Acker Bilk with the Leon Young String Chorale [3] Acker Bilk, his Clarinet and Strings [1] Chris Barber and Acker Bilk [2] Kenny Ball, Chris Barber and Acker Bilk

BILL *UK, male vocalist (Singles: 1 Week)* pos/wks

23 Oct 93	CAR BOOT SALE *Mercury MINCD 1*	73	1

BILL & BEN *UK, male flowerpot-dwelling*
vocalists – voiced by John Thomson (Singles: 4 Weeks) pos/wks

13 Jul 02	FLOBBADANCE *BBC Music WMSS 60552*	23	4

BILLIE See Billie PIPER

BILLY TALENT
Canada, male vocal / instrumental group (Singles: 3 Weeks)   pos/wks

13 Sep 03	**TRY HONESTLY** *Atlantic AT 0160CD*	**68** 1
10 Apr 04	**THE EX** *Atlantic AT 0173CD*	**61** 1
17 Jul 04	**RIVER BELOW** *Atlantic AT 0178CD*	**70** 1

BIMBO JET
France, male / female vocal / instrumental group (Singles: 10 Weeks)   pos/wks

26 Jul 75	**EL BIMBO** *EMI 2317*	**12** 10

BINARY FINARY *UK, male production duo –*
Matt Lawes and Ricky Grant (Singles: 9 Weeks)   pos/wks

10 Oct 98	**1998** *Positiva CDTIV 98*	**24** 3
28 Aug 99	**1999** *Positiva CDTIV 118*	**11** 6

Umberto BINDI
Italy, male vocalist, b. 12 May 1933, d. May 2002 (Singles: 1 Week)   pos/wks

10 Nov 60	**IL NOSTRO CONCERTO** *Oriole CB 1577*	**47** 1

BINI & MARTINI *(see also ECLIPSE;*
HOUSE OF GLASS; GOODFELLAS featuring Lisa MILLETT)
Italy, male production duo (Singles: 2 Weeks)   pos/wks

4 Mar 00	**HAPPINESS (MY VISION IS CLEAR)** *Azuli AZNYCDX 113* ...**53** 1
10 Mar 01	**BURNING UP** *Azuli AZNY 137*	**65** 1

BIOHAZARD *US, male vocal / instrumental*
group (Singles: 4 Weeks, Albums: 2 Weeks)   pos/wks

9 Jul 94	**TALES FROM THE HARD SIDE** *Warner Bros. W 0254CD* **47** 2
20 Aug 94	**HOW IT IS** *Warner Bros. W 0259CD*	**62** 2
14 May 94	**STATE OF THE WORLD ADDRESS** *Warner Bros. 9362455952*..**72** 1
8 Jun 96	**MATA LEAO** *Warner Bros. 9362462082*	**72** 1

La BIONDA *Italy, male / female vocal group (Singles: 4 Weeks)*   pos/wks

7 Oct 78	**ONE FOR YOU ONE FOR ME** *Philips 6198 227*	**54** 4

BIOSPHERE *Norway, male instrumentalist –*
keyboards – Ger Jenssen (Singles: 2 Weeks, Albums: 1 Week)   pos/wks

29 Apr 95	**NOVELTY WAVES** *Apollo APOLLO 20CDX*	**51** 2
5 Mar 94	**PATASHNIK** *Apollo AMB 3927CDX*	**50** 1

BIRDLAND *UK, male vocal / instrumental*
group (Singles: 7 Weeks, Albums: 1 Week)   pos/wks

1 Apr 89	**HOLLOW HEART** *Lazy LAZY 13*	**70** 1
8 Jul 89	**PARADISE** *Lazy LAZY 14*	**70** 1
3 Feb 90	**SLEEP WITH ME** *Lazy LAZY 17*	**32** 3
22 Sep 90	**ROCK 'N' ROLL NIGGER** *Lazy LAZY 20*	**47** 1
2 Feb 91	**EVERYBODY NEEDS SOMEBODY** *Lazy LAZY 24*	**44** 1
2 Mar 91	**BIRDLAND** *Lazy LAZY 25*	**44** 1

The BIRDS
UK, male vocal / instrumental group (Singles: 1 Week)   pos/wks

27 May 65	**LEAVING HERE** *Decca F 12140*	**45** 1

Zoe BIRKETT *UK, female vocalist (Singles: 6 Weeks)*   pos/wks

25 Jan 03	**TREAT ME LIKE A LADY (re)** *19 / Universal 0196822* ...**12** 6

Jane BIRKIN and Serge GAINSBOURG
UK / France, female / male vocal duo – Serge Gainsbourg
(Lucien Ginsberg), b. 2 Apr 1928, d. 2 Mar 1991 (Singles: 34 Weeks)   pos/wks

30 Jul 69	● **JE T'AIME ... MOI NON PLUS** *Fontana TF 1042* **2** 11
4 Oct 69	★ **JE T'AIME ... MOI NON PLUS (re-issue)**
	Major Minor MM 645 ....**1** 14
7 Dec 74	**JE T'AIME ... MOI NON PLUS (2nd re-issue)**
	Antic K 11511 ....**31** 9

BIRTHDAY PARTY *(see also Nick CAVE)*
Australia, male vocal / instrumental group (Albums: 3 Weeks)   pos/wks

24 Jul 82	**JUNKYARD** *4AD CAD 207* **73** 3

BIS *UK, male / female vocal / instrumental*
group (Singles: 9 Weeks, Albums: 1 Week)   pos/wks

30 Mar 96	**THE SECRET VAMPIRE SOUNDTRACK (EP)**
	Chemikal Underground CHEM 003CD **25** 2
22 Jun 96	**BIS VS THE DIY CORPS (EP)** *Teen-C SKETCH 001CD* **45** 1
9 Nov 96	**ATOM POWERED ACTION (EP)** *Wiiija WIJ 55CD* **54** 1
15 Mar 97	**SWEET SHOP AVENGERZ** *Wiiija WIJ 67CD* **46** 1
10 May 97	**EVERYBODY THINKS THAT THEY'RE GOING TO GET THEIRS**
	Wiiija WIJ 69CD **64** 1
14 Nov 98	**EURODISCO** *Wiiija WIJ 86CD* **37** 2
27 Feb 99	**ACTION AND DRAMA** *Wiiija WIJ 95CD* **50** 1
19 Apr 97	**THE NEW TRANSISTOR HEROES** *Wiiija WIJCD 1064* **55** 1

Tracks on The Secret Vampire Soundtrack (EP): Kandy Pop / Secret Vampires / Teen-C Power / Diska. Tracks on Bis vs the DIY Corps (EP): This Is Fake DIY / Burn the Suit / Dance to the Disco Beat. Tracks on Atom Powered Action (EP): Starbright Boy / Wee Love / Team Theme / Cliquesuck

BISCUIT BOY *UK, male vocal / instrumental trio (Singles: 1 Week)*   pos/wks

15 Sep 01	**MITCH** *Mercury 5887582* **75** 1

Elvin BISHOP *US, male instrumentalist – guitar (Singles: 4 Weeks)*   pos/wks

15 May 76	**FOOLED AROUND AND FELL IN LOVE** *Capricorn 2089 024* **34** 4

Hit has uncredited vocal by Mickey Thomas of Starship

Stephen BISHOP
US, male instrumentalist – piano (Albums: 3 Weeks)   pos/wks

1 Apr 72	**GRIEG AND SCHUMANN PIANO CONCERTOS** *Philips 6500 166* ..**34** 3

BITI See DEGREES OF MOTION featuring BITI

BIZ See Benny BENASSI presents the BIZ

BIZZ NIZZ *US / Belgium, male / female*
vocal / instrumental group (Singles: 11 Weeks)   pos/wks

31 Mar 90	● **DON'T MISS THE PARTYLINE** *Cooltempo COOL 203* **7** 11

BIZARRE INC *UK, male / female vocal /*
instrumental group (Singles: 49 Weeks, Albums: 2 Weeks)   pos/wks

16 Mar 91	**PLAYING WITH KNIVES** *Vinyl Solution STORM 25R* **43** 5
14 Sep 91	**SUCH A FEELING** *Vinyl Solution STORM 32S* **13** 9
23 Nov 91	● **PLAYING WITH KNIVES (re-issue)**
	Vinyl Solution STORM 38S **4** 8
3 Oct 92	● **I'M GONNA GET YOU (re)** *Vinyl Solution STORM 46S* [1] ...**3** 13
27 Feb 93	**TOOK MY LOVE** *Vinyl Solution STORM 60CD* [1] **19** 5
23 Mar 96	**KEEP THE MUSIC STRONG** *Some Bizzare MERCD 451* **33** 2
6 Jul 96	**SURPRISE** *Some Bizzare MERCD 462* **21** 3
14 Sep 96	**GET UP SUNSHINE STREET** *Some Bizzare MERCD 471* **45** 2
13 Mar 99	**PLAYING WITH KNIVES (re-mix)** *Vinyl Solution VC01CD1* ..**30** 2
7 Nov 92	**ENERGIQUE** *Vinyl Solution STEAM 47CD* **41** 2

[1] Bizarre Inc featuring Angie Brown

BIZZI *UK, male vocalist – Basil Dixon (Singles: 1 Week)*   pos/wks

6 Dec 97	**BIZZI'S PARTY** *Parlophone Rhythm CDRHYTHM 7* **62** 1

BJÖRK 317 Top 500
Captivating, eccentric, uncompromising female singer / songwriter, b. Björk Gudmundsdottir, 21 Nov 1965, Reykjavik, Iceland. Formerly a member of The Sugarcubes, she was a double Brits winner in 1994 (Best International Female and Best International Newcomer) and sang at the 2004 Olympics opening ceremony (Singles: 79 Weeks, Albums: 130 Weeks)   pos/wks

27 Apr 91	**OOOPS** *ZTT ZANG 19* [1] **42** 3
19 Jun 93	**HUMAN BEHAVIOUR** *One Little Indian 112TP 7CD* **36** 2
4 Sep 93	**VENUS AS A BOY** *One Little Indian 122TP 7CD* **29** 4
23 Oct 93	**PLAY DEAD** *Island CID 573* [2] **12** 6
4 Dec 93	**BIG TIME SENSUALITY** *One Little Indian 132TP 7CD* **17** 8
19 Mar 94	**VIOLENTLY HAPPY** *One Little Indian 142TP 7CD* **13** 4
6 May 95	**ARMY OF ME** *One Little Indian 162TP 7CD* **10** 5
26 Aug 95	**ISOBEL** *One Little Indian 172TP 7CD* **23** 3
25 Nov 95	● **IT'S OH SO QUIET** *One Little Indian 182TP 7CD* **4** 15
24 Feb 96	● **HYPERBALLAD** *One Little Indian 192TP 7CD* **8** 4
9 Nov 96	**POSSIBLY MAYBE** *One Little Indian 193TP 7CD* **13** 3
1 Mar 97	**I MISS YOU** *One Little Indian 194TP 7CDL* **36** 2

			pos/wks
20 Dec 97	**BACHELORETTE** *One Little Indian 212TP 7CD*	**21**	5
17 Oct 98	**HUNTER** *One Little Indian 222TP 7CD*	**44**	1
12 Dec 98	**ALARM CALL** *One Little Indian 232TP 7CDL*	**33**	2
19 Jun 99	**ALL IS FULL OF LOVE** *One Little Indian 242TP 7CD*	**24**	2
18 Aug 01	**HIDDEN PLACE** *One Little Indian 332TP 7CD*	**21**	2
17 Nov 01	**PAGAN POETRY** *One Little Indian 352TP 7CD*	**38**	2
23 Mar 02	**COCOON** *One Little Indian 322TP 7CD*	**35**	2
7 Dec 02	**IT'S IN OUR HANDS** *One Little Indian 366TP 7CD*	**37**	2
30 Oct 04	**WHO IS IT** *One Little Indian 446TP T7CD2*	**26**	2
17 Jul 93 ●	**DEBUT** *One Little IndianTPLP 31CD*	**3**	69
24 Jun 95 ●	**POST / TELEGRAM** *One Little IndianTPLP 51CD*	**2**	38
4 Oct 97 ●	**HOMOGENIC** *One Little IndianTPLP 71CD*	**4**	13
30 Sep 00	**SELMA SONGS (FILM SOUNDTRACK)** *One Little IndianTPLP 151CD*	**34**	1
8 Sep 01 ●	**VESPERTINE** *One Little IndianTPLP 101CD*	**8**	4
16 Nov 02	**GREATEST HITS** *One Little IndianTPLP 359CD*	**53**	2
11 Sep 04	**MEDULLA** *One Little IndianTPLP 358CD*	**9**	3

[1] 808 State featuring Björk [2] Björk and David Arnold

'Telegram', a re-mix album, was listed with 'Post' from 7 Dec 96 and sales were combined

BJÖRN AGAIN *Australia, male / female vocal / instrumental group (Singles: 8 Weeks)*

			pos/wks
24 Oct 92	**ERASURE-ISH (A LITTLE RESPECT / STOP!)** *M&G MAGS 32*	**25**	3
12 Dec 92	**SANTA CLAUS IS COMING TO TOWN** *M&G MAGS 35*	**55**	4
27 Nov 93	**FLASHDANCE ... WHAT A FEELING** *M&G MAGCD 50*	**65**	1

BLACK *UK, male vocalist – Colin Vearncombe (Singles: 35 Weeks, Albums: 29 Weeks)*

			pos/wks
27 Sep 86	**WONDERFUL LIFE** *Ugly Man JACK 71*	**72**	1
27 Jun 87	**SWEETEST SMILE** *A&M AM 394*	**8**	10
22 Aug 87 ●	**WONDERFUL LIFE (re-recording)** *A&M AM 402*	**8**	9
16 Jan 88	**PARADISE** *A&M AM 422*	**38**	3
24 Sep 88	**THE BIG ONE** *A&M AM 468*	**54**	4
21 Jan 89	**NOW YOU'RE GONE** *A&M AM 491*	**66**	2
4 May 91	**FEEL LIKE CHANGE** *A&M AM 780*	**56**	2
15 Jun 91	**HERE IT COMES AGAIN** *A&M AM 753*	**70**	2
5 Mar 94	**WONDERFUL LIFE (re-issue)** *PolyGram TV 5805552*	**42**	3
26 Sep 87 ●	**WONDERFUL LIFE** *A&M AMA 5165*	**3**	23
29 Oct 88	**COMEDY** *A&M AMA 5222*	**32**	4
1 Jun 91	**BLACK** *A&M 3971261*	**42**	2

'Wonderful Life' on A&M is a re-recording. It was re-issued on Polygram TV in 1994

Cilla BLACK ⟨238⟩ ⟨Top 500⟩

Undoubtedly one of Britain's favourite female vocalists / entertainers of the past 50 years, b. Priscilla White, 27 May 1943, Liverpool, UK. After handing in her Top 20 season ticket, she has become an award-winning and extremely popular TV presenter (Singles: 194 Weeks, Albums: 64 Weeks)

			pos/wks
17 Oct 63	**LOVE OF THE LOVED** *Parlophone R 5065*	**35**	6
6 Feb 64 ★	**ANYONE WHO HAD A HEART** *Parlophone R 5101*	**1**	17
7 May 64 ★	**YOU'RE MY WORLD** *Parlophone R 5133*	**1**	17
6 Aug 64 ●	**IT'S FOR YOU** *Parlophone R 5162*	**7**	10
14 Jan 65 ●	**YOU'VE LOST THAT LOVIN' FEELIN'** *Parlophone R 5225*	**2**	9
22 Apr 65	**I'VE BEEN WRONG BEFORE** *Parlophone R 5269*	**17**	8
13 Jan 66 ●	**LOVE'S JUST A BROKEN HEART** *Parlophone R 5395*	**5**	11
31 Mar 66 ●	**ALFIE** *Parlophone R 5427*	**9**	12
9 Jun 66 ●	**DON'T ANSWER ME** *Parlophone R 5463*	**6**	10
20 Oct 66	**A FOOL AM I (DIMMELO PARLAME)** *Parlophone R 5515*	**13**	9
8 Jun 67	**WHAT GOOD AM I?** *Parlophone R 5608*	**24**	7
29 Nov 67	**I ONLY LIVE TO LOVE YOU** *Parlophone R 5652*	**26**	11
13 Mar 68 ●	**STEP INSIDE LOVE** *Parlophone R 5674*	**8**	9
12 Jun 68	**WHERE IS TOMORROW** *Parlophone R 5706*	**39**	3
12 Feb 69 ●	**SURROUND YOURSELF WITH SORROW** *Parlophone R 5759*	**3**	12
9 Jul 69 ●	**CONVERSATIONS** *Parlophone R 5785*	**7**	12
13 Dec 69	**IF I THOUGHT YOU'D EVER CHANGE YOUR MIND** *Parlophone R 5820*	**20**	9
20 Nov 71 ●	**SOMETHING TELLS ME (SOMETHING IS GONNA HAPPEN TONIGHT)** *Parlophone R 5924*	**3**	14
2 Feb 74	**BABY WE CAN'T GO WRONG** *EMI 2107*	**36**	6
18 Sep 93	**THROUGH THE YEARS** *Columbia 6596982*	**54**	1
30 Oct 93	**HEART AND SOUL** *Columbia 6598562* [1]	**75**	1
13 Feb 65 ●	**CILLA** *Parlophone PMC 1243*	**5**	11
14 May 66 ●	**CILLA SINGS A RAINBOW** *Parlophone PMC 7004*	**4**	15
13 Apr 68 ●	**SHER-OO** *Parlophone PCS 7041*	**7**	11
30 Nov 68	**THE BEST OF CILLA BLACK** *Parlophone PCS 7065*	**21**	11

			pos/wks
25 Jul 70	**SWEET INSPIRATION** *Parlophone PCS 7103*	**42**	4
29 Jan 83	**THE VERY BEST OF CILLA BLACK** *Parlophone EMTV 38*	**20**	9
2 Oct 93	**THROUGH THE YEARS** *Columbia 4746502*	**41**	2
4 Oct 03	**BEGINNINGS ... GREATEST HITS AND NEW SONGS** *EMI 5931812*	**68**	1

[1] Cilla Black with Dusty Springfield

Frank BLACK *US, male vocalist – Charles Thompson (Singles: 4 Weeks, Albums: 8 Weeks)*

			pos/wks
21 May 94	**HEADACHE** *4AD BAD 4007CD*	**53**	1
20 Jan 96	**MEN IN BLACK** *Dragnet 6627862*	**37**	2
27 Jul 96	**I DON'T WANT TO HURT YOU (EVERY SINGLE TIME)** *Dragnet 6634635*	**63**	1
20 Mar 93 ●	**FRANK BLACK** *4AD CAD 3004CD*	**9**	3
4 Jun 94	**TEENAGER OF THE YEAR** *4AD CAD 4009CD*	**21**	2
3 Feb 96	**THE CULT OF RAY** *Dragnet 481472*	**39**	2
16 May 98	**FRANK BLACK AND THE CATHOLICS** *Play It Again Sam BIAS 370CD* [1]	**61**	1

[1] Frank Black and the Catholics

Jeanne BLACK *US, female vocalist – Gloria Jeanne Black (Singles: 4 Weeks)*

			pos/wks
23 Jun 60	**HE'LL HAVE TO STAY** *Capitol CL 15131*	**41**	4

Mary BLACK *Ireland, female vocalist (Albums: 10 Weeks)*

			pos/wks
3 Jul 93	**THE HOLY GROUND** *Grapevine GRACD 11*	**58**	2
16 Sep 95	**CIRCUS** *Grapevine GRACD 014*	**16**	4
29 Mar 97	**SHINE** *Grapevine GRACD 015*	**33**	3
28 Aug 99	**SPEAKING WITH THE ANGEL** *Grapevine GRACD 264*	**63**	1

BLACK & WHITE ARMY *UK, 250 Newcastle United football fan vocalists (Singles: 2 Weeks)*

			pos/wks
23 May 98	**BLACK & WHITE ARMY** *Toon TOON 1CD*	**26**	2

BLACK BOX *Italy, male / female vocal / instrumental production trio – Mirko Limoni, Valerio Semplici and Daniele Davoli (Singles: 74 Weeks, Albums: 30 Weeks)*

			pos/wks
12 Aug 89 ★	**RIDE ON TIME** *Deconstruction PB 43055*	**1**	22
17 Feb 90 ●	**I DON'T KNOW ANYBODY ELSE** *Deconstruction PB 43479*	**4**	8
2 Jun 90	**EVERYBODY EVERYBODY** *Deconstruction PB 43715*	**16**	5
3 Nov 90 ●	**FANTASY** *Deconstruction PB 43895*	**5**	11
15 Dec 90	**THE TOTAL MIX** *Deconstruction PB 44235*	**12**	8
6 Apr 91	**STRIKE IT UP** *Deconstruction PB 44459*	**16**	8
14 Dec 91	**OPEN YOUR EYES** *Deconstruction PB 45053*	**48**	4
14 Aug 93	**ROCKIN' TO THE MUSIC** *Deconstruction 74321158122*	**39**	2
24 Jun 95	**NOT ANYONE** *Mercury MERCD 434*	**31**	2
20 Apr 96	**I GOT THE VIBRATION / A POSITIVE VIBRATION** *Manifesto MERCD 459* [1]	**21**	3
22 Feb 97	**NATIVE NEW YORKER** *Manifesto FESCD 18* [1]	**46**	1
5 May 90	**DREAMLAND** *Deconstruction PL 74572*	**14**	30

[1] Blackbox

BLACK BOX RECORDER *UK, male / female vocal / instrumental group (Singles: 4 Weeks, Albums: 1 Week)*

			pos/wks
22 Apr 00	**THE FACTS OF LIFE** *Nude NUD 48CD1*	**20**	3
15 Jul 00	**THE ART OF DRIVING** *Nude NUD 51CD1*	**53**	1
13 May 00	**THE FACTS OF LIFE** *Nude NUDE 16CD*	**37**	1

BLACK CONNECTION *Italy, male / female vocal / production group (Singles: 3 Weeks)*

			pos/wks
14 Mar 98	**GIVE ME RHYTHM** *Xtravaganza / Edel 0091465 EXT*	**32**	2
24 Oct 98	**I'M GONNA GET YA BABY** *Xtravaganza 0091615 EXT*	**62**	1

The BLACK CROWES *US, male vocal / instrumental group (Singles: 28 Weeks, Albums: 33 Weeks)*

			pos/wks
1 Sep 90	**HARD TO HANDLE** *Def American DEFA 6*	**45**	5
12 Jan 91	**TWICE AS HARD** *Def American DEFA 7*	**47**	3
22 Jun 91	**JEALOUS AGAIN / SHE TALKS TO ANGELS** *Def American DEFA 8*	**70**	1
24 Aug 91	**HARD TO HANDLE (re-issue)** *Def American DEFA 10*	**39**	4
26 Oct 91	**SEEING THINGS** *Def American DEFA 13*	**72**	1
2 May 92	**REMEDY** *Def American DEFA 16*	**24**	3

26 Sep 92	STING ME *Def American DEFA 21*	42	2
28 Nov 92	HOTEL ILLNESS *Def American DEFA 23*	47	3
11 Feb 95	HIGH HEAD BLUES / A CONSPIRACY *American 74321258492*	25	2
22 Jul 95	WISER TIME *American 74321298272*	34	2
27 Jul 96	ONE MIRROR TOO MANY *American 74321398572*	51	1
7 Nov 98	KICKING MY HEART AROUND *American Recordings 6666665*	55	1
24 Aug 91	SHAKE YOUR MONEY MAKER *American 8425151*	36	11
23 May 92 ●	THE SOUTHERN HARMONY AND MUSICAL COMPANION *Def American 5122632* ▲	2	7
12 Nov 94 ●	AMORICA *American 74321241942*	8	4
3 Aug 96	THREE SNAKES AND ONE CHARM *American Recordings 74321384842*	17	3
23 Jan 99	BY YOUR SIDE *Columbia 4916992*	34	2
22 Jul 00	LIVE AT THE GREEK *SPV Recordings SPV 09172022* [1]	39	4
19 May 01	LIONS *V2 VVR 1015672*	37	2

[1] Jimmy Page and the Black Crowes

BLACK DIAMOND
US, male vocalist – Charles Diamond (Singles: 1 Week) pos/wks

17 Sep 94	LET ME BE *Systematic SYSCD 1*	56	1

BLACK DOG
UK, male instrumentalist / producer – Ken Downie (Singles: 1 Week, Albums: 2 Weeks) pos/wks

3 Apr 99	BABYLON *Warner.esp WESP 006 CD1* [1]	65	1
28 Jan 95	SPANNERS *Warp PUPCD 1*	30	2

[1] Black Dog featuring Ofra Haza

BLACK DUCK (see also BLAIR)
UK, male rapper – Blair Mackichan (Singles: 5 Weeks) pos/wks

17 Dec 94	WHIGGLE IN LINE *Flying South CDDUCK 1*	33	5

BLACK EYED PEAS *US, male / female vocal / rap / production group (Singles: 55 Weeks, Albums: 56 Weeks)* pos/wks

10 Oct 98	JOINTS & JAMS *Interscope IND 95604*	53	1
12 May 01	REQUEST LINE *Interscope 4970532* [1]	31	3
13 Sep 03 ★	WHERE IS THE LOVE? *A&M 9810996* ■	1	19
13 Dec 03 ●	SHUT UP *A&M 9814501*	2	12
20 Mar 04 ●	HEY MAMA *A&M 9861976*	6	10
10 Jul 04	LET'S GET IT STARTED *A&M 9863032*	11	10
30 Aug 03 ●	ELEPHUNK *A&M / Mercury 9860365*	3	56

[1] Black Eyed Peas featuring Macy Gray

BLACK GORILLA
UK, male / female vocal / instrumental group (Singles: 6 Weeks) pos/wks

27 Aug 77	GIMME DAT BANANA *Response SR 502*	29	6

BLACK GRAPE *UK, male vocal / instrumental group (Singles: 25 Weeks, Albums: 46 Weeks)* pos/wks

10 Jun 95 ●	REVEREND BLACK GRAPE *Radioactive RAXTD 16*	9	5
5 Aug 95 ●	IN THE NAME OF THE FATHER *Radioactive RAXTD 19*	8	4
2 Dec 95	KELLY'S HEROES *Radioactive RAXTD 22*	17	5
25 May 96 ●	FAT NECK *Radioactive RAXTD 24*	10	3
29 Jun 96 ●	ENGLAND'S IRIE *Radioactive RAXTD 25* [1]	6	4
1 Nov 97	GET HIGHER *Radioactive RAXTD 32*	24	3
7 Mar 98	MARBLES *Radioactive RAXTD 33*	46	1
19 Aug 95 ★	IT'S GREAT WHEN YOU'RE STRAIGHT ... YEAH *Radioactive RAD 11224*	1	39
22 Nov 97	STUPID STUPID STUPID *Radioactive RARD 11716*	11	7

[1] Black Grape featuring Joe Strummer and Keith Allen

The BLACK KEYS *US, male vocal / instrumental duo (Singles: 2 Weeks, Albums: 1 Week)* pos/wks

11 Sep 04	10 A.M. AUTOMATIC *Epitaph 11732*	66	1
11 Dec 04	TILL I GET MY WAY / GIRL IS ON MY MIND *Fat Possum 11832*	62	1
18 Sep 04	RUBBER FACTORY *Fat Possum 03792*	62	1

BLACK LACE *UK, male vocal / instrumental duo – Alan Barton, b. 16 Sep 1953, d. 23 Mar 1995, and Colin Routh (Singles: 83 Weeks, Albums: 26 Weeks)* pos/wks

31 Mar 79	MARY ANN *EMI 2919*	42	4
24 Sep 83 ●	SUPERMAN (GIOCA JOUER) *Flair FLA 105*	9	18

30 Jun 84 ●	AGADOO *Flair FLA 107*	2	30
24 Nov 84 ●	DO THE CONGA *Flair FLA 108*	10	9
1 Jun 85	EL VINO COLLAPSO *Flair LACE 1*	42	5
7 Sep 85	I SPEAKA DA LINGO *Flair LACE 2*	49	4
7 Dec 85	HOKEY COKEY *Flair LACE 3*	31	6
20 Sep 86	WIG WAM BAM *Flair LACE 5*	63	3
26 Aug 89	I AM THE MUSIC MAN *Flair LACE 10*	52	3
22 Aug 98	AGADOO (re-recording) *NOW CDWAG 260*	64	1
8 Dec 84 ●	PARTY PARTY – 16 GREAT PARTY ICEBREAKERS *Telstar STAR 2250*	4	14
7 Dec 85	PARTY PARTY 2 *Telstar STAR 2266*	18	6
6 Dec 86	PARTY CRAZY *Telstar STAR 2288*	58	6

Black Lace was a group for their first hit

BLACK LEGEND *Italy, male production duo – J Reverse and Ferrari (Singles: 22 Weeks)* pos/wks

20 May 00	YOU SEE THE TROUBLE WITH ME (IMPORT) *Rise RISECD 072*	52	5
24 Jun 00 ★	YOU SEE THE TROUBLE WITH ME *Eternal WEA 282CD* ■	1	15
4 Aug 01	SOMEBODY *WEA WEA 328CD* [1]	37	2

[1] Shortie vs Black Legend

No.1 version features a 'karaoke' re-recording of the original Barry White vocal by UK vocalist Spoonface

BLACK MACHINE *France / Nigeria, male vocal / instrumental duo – Herry Iyere Innocent and Alasson Wat (Singles: 5 Weeks)* pos/wks

9 Apr 94	HOW GEE *London LONCD 348*	17	5

BLACK MAGIC (see also LIL' LOUIS)
US, male producer – Marvin Burns (Singles: 2 Weeks) pos/wks

1 Jun 96	FREEDOM (MAKE IT FUNKY) *Positiva CDTIV 51*	41	2

BLACK REBEL MOTORCYCLE CLUB *US, male vocal / instrumental group (Singles: 10 Weeks, Albums: 21 Weeks)* pos/wks

2 Feb 02	LOVE BURNS *Virgin VUSCD 234*	37	2
1 Jun 02	SPREAD YOUR LOVE *Virgin VUSCD 245*	27	2
28 Sep 02	WHATEVER HAPPENED TO MY ROCK 'N' ROLL (PUNK SONG) *Virgin VUSCD 257*	46	2
30 Aug 03	STOP *Virgin VUSCD 273*	19	3
29 Nov 03	WE'RE ALL IN LOVE *Virgin VUSCDX 279*	45	1
26 Jan 02	B.R.M.C. *Virgin CDVUS 207*	25	17
6 Sep 03 ●	TAKE THEM ON, ON YOUR OWN *Virgin CDVUS 245*	3	4

BLACK RIOT (see also GYPSYMEN; ROYAL HOUSE; SWAN LAKE; Todd TERRY PROJECT) *US, male producer – Todd Terry (Singles: 3 Weeks)* pos/wks

3 Dec 88	WARLOCK / A DAY IN THE LIFE *Champion CHAMP 75*	68	3

'A Day in the Life' listed only from 17 Dec 1988

BLACK ROB *US, male rapper – Robert Ross (Singles: 8 Weeks)* pos/wks

12 Aug 00	WHOA *Puff Daddy / Arista 74321782732*	44	2
6 Oct 01	BAD BOY FOR LIFE *Bad Boy / Arista 74321889982* [1]	13	6

[1] P Diddy, Black Rob and Mark Curry

BLACK, ROCK and RON *US, male rap group (Albums: 1 Week)* pos/wks

22 Apr 89	STOP THE WORLD *Supreme SU 5*	72	1

BLACK SABBATH 210 Top 500 (see also GILLAN)
Macabre Birmingham, UK-based seminal heavy metal outfit first fronted by Ozzy (John) Osbourne (v) and Tommy Iommi (g). Later vocalists included Ronnie James Dio and Ian Gillan. Voted Best Band in the World and Act of The Millennium by Kerrang! magazine in 1999 (Singles: 70 Weeks, Albums: 214 Weeks) pos/wks

29 Aug 70 ●	PARANOID *Vertigo 6059 010*	4	18
3 Jun 78	NEVER SAY DIE *Vertigo SAB 001*	21	8
14 Oct 78	HARD ROAD *Vertigo SAB 002*	33	4
5 Jul 80	NEON KNIGHTS *Vertigo SAB 3*	22	9
16 Aug 80	PARANOID (re-issue) *Nems BSS 101*	14	12
6 Dec 80	DIE YOUNG *Vertigo SAB 4*	41	7
7 Nov 81	MOB RULES *Vertigo SAB 5*	46	4
13 Feb 82	TURN UP THE NIGHT *Vertigo SAB 6*	37	5
15 Apr 89	HEADLESS CROSS *IRS EIRS 107*	62	1
13 Jun 92	TV CRIMES *IRS EIRSP 178*	33	2

		pos/wks
7 Mar 70 ●	BLACK SABBATH *Vertigo VO 6*	8 42
26 Sep 70 ★	PARANOID *Vertigo 6360 011*	1 20
21 Aug 71 ●	MASTER OF REALITY *Vertigo 6360 050*	5 13
30 Sep 72 ●	BLACK SABBATH VOL 4 *Vertigo 6360 071*	8 10
8 Dec 73 ●	SABBATH BLOODY SABBATH *WWA WWA 005*	4 11
27 Sep 75 ●	SABOTAGE *NEMS 9119 001*	7 7
7 Feb 76	WE SOLD OUR SOUL FOR ROCK 'N' ROLL *NEMS 6641 335*	35 5
6 Nov 76	TECHNICAL ECSTASY *Vertigo 9102 750*	13 6
14 Oct 78	NEVER SAY DIE *Vertigo 9102 751*	12 6
26 Apr 80 ●	HEAVEN AND HELL *Vertigo 9102 752*	9 22
5 Jul 80 ●	BLACK SABBATH LIVE AT LAST *NEMS BS 001*	5 15
27 Sep 80	PARANOID (re-issue) *NEMS NEL 6003*	54 2
14 Nov 81	MOB RULES *Mercury 6V02119*	12 14
22 Jan 83	LIVE EVIL *Vertigo SAB 10*	13 11
24 Sep 83 ●	BORN AGAIN *Vertigo VERL 8*	4 7
1 Mar 86	SEVENTH STAR *Vertigo VERH 29* [1]	27 5
28 Nov 87	THE ETERNAL IDOL *Vertigo VERH 51*	66 1
29 Apr 89	HEADLESS CROSS *IRS EIRSA 1002*	31 2
1 Sep 90	TYR *IRS EIRSA 1038*	24 3
4 Jul 92	DEHUMANIZER *IRS EIRSCD 1064*	28 2
12 Feb 94	CROSS PURPOSES *IRS EIRSCD 1067*	41 1
17 Jun 95	FORBIDDEN *IRS EIRSCD 1072*	71 1
31 Oct 98	REUNION *Epic 4919549*	41 1
17 Jun 00	THE BEST OF BLACK SABBATH *Metal Is RAWDD 145*	24 6
6 Jul 02	PARANOID (2ND re-issue) *Castle Music CMTCD 004*	63 1

[1] Black Sabbath featuring Tony Iommi

Group UK only for first three hits and re-issue of 'Paranoid'

BLACK SCIENCE ORCHESTRA
UK, male production group (Albums: 1 Week)

		pos/wks
3 Aug 96	WALTERS ROOM *Junior Boy's Own JBOCD 5*	68 1

BLACK SHEEP
US, male rap duo (Singles: 1 Week)

		pos/wks
19 Nov 94	WITHOUT A DOUBT *Mercury MERCD 417*	60 1

BLACK SLATE
UK / Jamaica, male vocal / instrumental group (Singles: 15 Weeks)

		pos/wks
20 Sep 80 ●	AMIGO *Ensign ENY 42*	9 9
6 Dec 80	BOOM BOOM *Ensign ENY 47*	51 6

BLACK STAR LINER
UK, male / female vocal / instrumental group (Albums: 1 Week)

		pos/wks
7 Sep 96	YEMEN CUTTA CONNECTION *EXP EXPCD 006*	66 1

BLACK UHURU
Jamaica, male vocal / instrumental group (Singles: 9 Weeks, Albums: 22 Weeks)

		pos/wks
8 Sep 84	WHAT IS LIFE? *Island IS 150*	56 6
31 May 86	THE GREAT TRAIN ROBBERY *Real Authentic Sound RAS 7018*	62 3
13 Jun 81	RED *Island ILPS 9625*	28 13
22 Aug 81	BLACK UHURU *Virgin VX 1004*	81 2
19 Jun 82	CHILL OUT *Island ILPS 9701*	38 6
25 Aug 84	ANTHEM *Island ILPS 9773*	90 1

Band of the BLACK WATCH
UK, military band (Singles: 22 Weeks, Albums: 13 Weeks)

		pos/wks
30 Aug 75 ●	SCOTCH ON THE ROCKS *Spark SRL 1128*	8 14
13 Dec 75	DANCE OF THE CUCKOOS (THE 'LAUREL AND HARDY' THEME) *Spark SRL 1135*	37 8
7 Feb 76	SCOTCH ON THE ROCKS *Spark SRLM 503*	11 13

BLACK WIDOW
UK, male vocal / instrumental group (Albums: 2 Weeks)

		pos/wks
4 Apr 70	SACRIFICE *CBS 63948*	32 2

Tony BLACKBURN
UK, male DJ / vocalist – Kenneth Blackburn (Singles: 7 Weeks)

		pos/wks
24 Jan 68	SO MUCH LOVE *MGM 1375*	31 4
26 Mar 69	IT'S ONLY LOVE *MGM 1467*	42 3

The BLACKBYRDS
US, male vocal / instrumental group (Singles: 6 Weeks)

		pos/wks
31 May 75	WALKING IN RHYTHM *Fantasy FTC 114*	23 6

BLACKFOOT
US, male vocal / instrumental group (Singles: 5 Weeks, Albums: 22 Weeks)

		pos/wks
6 Mar 82	DRY COUNTY *Atco K 11686*	43 4
18 Jun 83	SEND ME AN ANGEL *Atco B 9880*	66 1
18 Jul 81	MARAUDER *Atco K 50799*	38 12
11 Sep 82	HIGHWAY SONG BLACKFOOT LIVE *Atco K 50910*	14 6
21 May 83	SIOGO *Atco 7900801*	28 3
29 Sep 84	VERTICAL SMILES *Atco 790218*	82 1

J BLACKFOOT
US, male vocalist – John Colbert (Singles: 4 Weeks)

		pos/wks
17 Mar 84	TAXI *Allegiance ALES 2*	48 4

BLACKFOOT SUE
UK, male vocal / instrumental group (Singles: 15 Weeks)

		pos/wks
12 Aug 72 ●	STANDING IN THE ROAD *Jam 13*	4 10
16 Dec 72	SING DON'T SPEAK *Jam 29*	36 5

BLACKGIRL
US, female vocal group (Singles: 3 Weeks)

		pos/wks
16 Jul 94	90S GIRL *RCA 74321217882*	23 3

BLACKHEARTS See Joan JETT and the BLACKHEARTS

Honor BLACKMAN See Patrick MacNEE and Honor BLACKMAN

Ritchie BLACKMORE'S RAINBOW See RAINBOW

BLACKNUSS
Sweden, male / female vocal / instrumental group (Singles: 1 Week)

		pos/wks
28 Jun 97	DINAH *Arista 74321479762*	56 1

BLACKOUT
UK, male production / instrumental duo – Marc Dillon and Pat Dickins (Singles: 1 Week)

		pos/wks
27 Mar 99	GOTTA HAVE HOPE *Multiply CDMULTY 47*	46 1

BLACKOUT
UK, male / female / rap group (Singles: 8 Weeks)

		pos/wks
31 Mar 01	MR DJ *Independiente ISOM 48MS*	19 7
6 Oct 01	GET UP *Independiente ISOM 52MS*	67 1

Bill BLACK'S COMBO
US, male instrumental group – leader b. 17 Sep 1926, d. 21 Oct 1965 (Singles: 8 Weeks)

		pos/wks
8 Sep 60	WHITE SILVER SANDS *London HLU 9090*	50 1
3 Nov 60	DON'T BE CRUEL *London HLU 9212*	32 7

BLACKSTREET
US, male vocal group – includes Teddy Riley (Singles: 80 Weeks, Albums: 36 Weeks)

		pos/wks
19 Jun 93	BABY BE MINE *MCA MCSTD 1772* [1]	37 3
13 Aug 94	BOOTI CALL *Interscope A 8250CD*	56 1
11 Feb 95	U BLOW MY MIND *Interscope A 8222CD*	39 2
27 May 95	JOY *Interscope A 8195CD*	56 2
19 Oct 96 ●	NO DIGGITY *Interscope IND 95003* [2] ▲	9 7
8 Mar 97	GET ME HOME *Def Jam DEFCD 32* [3]	11 5
26 Apr 97 ●	DON'T LEAVE ME *Interscope IND 95534*	6 10
27 Sep 97 ●	FIX *Interscope IND 97521*	7 5
13 Dec 97	(MONEY CAN'T) BUY ME LOVE *Interscope IND 95563*	18 6
4 Apr 98 ●	I GET LONELY *Virgin VSCDT 1683* [4]	5 7
27 Jun 98	THE CITY IS MINE *Northwestside 74321588012* [5]	38 2
12 Dec 98	TAKE ME THERE *Interscope IND 95620* [6]	7 9
17 Apr 99	GIRLFRIEND / BOYFRIEND *Interscope IND 95640* [7]	11 7
10 Jul 99	GET READY *Puff Daddy / Arista 74321682602* [8]	32 4
8 Feb 03	WIZZY WOW *Dreamworks 4507902*	37 2
22 Feb 03 ●	REMINISCE / WHERE THE STORY ENDS *East West SQUAD 003CD1*	8 8
9 Jul 94	BLACKSTREET *Interscope 6544923512*	35 6
21 Sep 96	ANOTHER LEVEL *Interscope INTD 90071*	26 26
3 Apr 99	FINALLY *Interscope IND 90323*	27 4

[1] BLACKstreet featuring Teddy Riley [2] BLACKstreet featuring Dr Dre [3] Foxy Brown featuring BLACKstreet [4] Janet featuring BLACKstreet [5] Jay-Z featuring BLACKstreet [6] BLACKstreet and Mya featuring Ma$e and Blinky Blink [7] BLACKstreet with Janet [8] Ma$e featuring BLACKstreet

The BLACKWELLS
US, male vocal duo – Dewayne and Ronald Blackwell (Singles: 2 Weeks)

		pos/wks
18 May 61	LOVE OR MONEY *London HLW 9334*	46 2

Richard BLACKWOOD
UK, male comedian / rapper (Singles: 16 Weeks, Albums: 2 Weeks) pos/wks

17 Jun 00	● MAMA – WHO DA MAN? *East West MICKY 01CD1*	3	7
16 Sep 00	● 1.2.3.4. GET WITH THE WICKED *East West MICKY 05CD1*	10	6
25 Nov 00	SOMEONE THERE FOR ME *Hopefield / East West MICKY 06CD*	23	3
30 Sep 00	YOU'LL LOVE TO HATE THIS *Hopefield / East West 8573844882*	35	2

BLADE See Mark B & BLADE

BLAGGERS I.T.A.
UK, male vocal / instrumental group (Singles: 7 Weeks) pos/wks

12 Jun 93	STRESS *Parlophone CDITA 1*	56	2
9 Oct 93	OXYGEN *Parlophone CDITA 2*	51	2
8 Jan 94	ABANDON SHIP *Parlophone CDITA 3*	48	3

BLAHZAY BLAHZAY
US, male rap duo (Singles: 1 Week) pos/wks

2 Mar 96	DANGER *Mercury Black Vinyl MBVCD 2*	56	1

Vivian BLAINE
US, female actor / vocalist – Vivienne Stapleton, b. 21 Nov 1921, d. 13 Dec 1995 (Singles: 1 Week) pos/wks

10 Jul 53	BUSHEL AND A PECK *Brunswick 05100*	12	1

BLAIR (see also BLACK DUCK)
UK, male vocalist – Blair Mackichan (Singles: 5 Weeks) pos/wks

2 Sep 95	HAVE FUN GO MAD *Mercury MERCD 443*	37	3
6 Jan 96	LIFE *Mercury MERCD 447*	44	2

BLAIR See Terry HALL

BLAK TWANG *UK, male rapper – Tony Rotton (Singles: 2 Weeks)* pos/wks

29 Jun 02	TRIXSTAR *Bad Magic MAGICD 24* 1	54	1
26 Oct 02	SO ROTTEN *Bad Magic MAGICD 25* 2	48	1

1 Blak Twang featuring Est'Elle 2 Blak Twang featuring Jahmali

Howard BLAKE conducting the SINFONIA OF LONDON
UK, conductor and orchestra (Albums: 12 Weeks) pos/wks

22 Dec 84	THE SNOWMAN *CBS 71116*	54	12

Narration by Bernard Cribbins

Peter BLAKE *UK, male vocalist (Singles: 4 Weeks)* pos/wks

8 Oct 77	LIPSMACKIN' ROCK 'N' ROLLIN' *Pepper UP 36295*	40	4

BLAME *UK, male instrumental / production duo (Singles: 2 Weeks)* pos/wks

11 Apr 92	MUSIC TAKES YOU *Moving Shadow SHADOW 11*	48	2

BLAMELESS
UK, male vocal / instrumental group (Singles: 5 Weeks) pos/wks

4 Nov 95	TOWN CLOWNS *China WOKCD 2046*	56	1
23 Mar 96	BREATHE (A LITTLE DEEPER) *China WOKCD 2070*	27	3
1 Jun 96	SIGNS ... *China WOKCD 2077*	49	1

BLANCMANGE (see also Neil ARTHUR) *UK, vocal / instrumental duo (Singles: 71 Weeks, Albums: 57 Weeks)* pos/wks

17 Apr 82	GOD'S KITCHEN / I'VE SEEN THE WORD *London BLANC 1*	65	2
31 Jul 82	FEEL ME *London BLANC 2*	46	5
30 Oct 82	● LIVING ON THE CEILING *London BLANC 3*	7	14
19 Feb 83	WAVES *London BLANC 4*	19	9
7 May 83	● BLIND VISION *London BLANC 5*	10	8
26 Nov 83	THAT'S LOVE, THAT IT IS *London BLANC 6*	33	8
14 Apr 84	● DON'T TELL ME *London BLANC 7*	8	10
21 Jul 84	THE DAY BEFORE YOU CAME *London BLANC 8*	22	8
7 Sep 85	WHAT'S YOUR PROBLEM *London BLANC 9*	40	5
10 May 86	I CAN SEE IT *London BLANC 11*	71	2
9 Oct 82	HAPPY FAMILIES *London SH 8552*	30	38
26 May 84	● MANGE TOUT *London SH 8554*	8	17
26 Oct 85	BELIEVE YOU ME *London LONLP 10*	54	2

Bobby BLANCO & Mikki MOTO
UK, male production duo (Singles: 1 Week) pos/wks

29 May 04	3 AM *Defected DFTD 088*	70	1

Billy BLAND *US, male vocalist (Singles: 10 Weeks)* pos/wks

19 May 60	LET THE LITTLE GIRL DANCE *London HL 9096*	15	10

BLANK & JONES *Germany, male production duo –*
Piet Blank and Jaspa Jones (Singles: 9 Weeks) pos/wks

26 Jun 99	CREAM *Devia DVNT 31CDS*	24	3
27 May 00	AFTER LOVE *Nebula NEBCDS 3*	57	1
30 Sep 00	THE NIGHTFLY *Nebula NEBCD 010*	55	1
3 Mar 01	BEYOND TIME *Gang Go / Edel 01245115 GAG*	53	2
29 Jun 02	DJS FANS & FREAKS *Incentive CENT 42CDS*	45	2

BLAQUE IVORY *US, female vocal group (Singles: 3 Weeks)* pos/wks

3 Jul 99	808 *Columbia 6674962*	31	3

BLAST featuring VDC
Italy, male / female vocal / instrumental group (Singles: 5 Weeks) pos/wks

18 Jun 94	CRAYZY MAN *UMM MCSTD 1982*	22	3
12 Nov 94	PRINCES OF THE NIGHT *UMM MCSTD 2011*	40	2

Melanie BLATT (see also ALL SAINTS; ARTFUL DODGER; OUTSIDAZ featuring Rah DIGGA and Melanie BLATT)
UK, female vocalist (Singles: 3 Weeks) pos/wks

6 Sep 03	DO ME WRONG *London LONCD 479*	18	3

BLAZE featuring Palmer BROWN
US, male production duo and male vocalist (Singles: 3 Weeks) pos/wks

10 Mar 01	MY BEAT *Black & Blue / Kickin' NEOCD 053*	53	2
21 Sep 02	DO YOU REMEMBER HOUSE *Slip 'n' Slide SLIPCD 151*	55	1

BLAZIN' SQUAD
UK, male vocal / rap group (Singles: 50 Weeks, Albums: 8 Weeks) pos/wks

31 Aug 02	★ CROSSROADS *East West SQUAD 01CD* ■	1	13
23 Nov 02	● LOVE ON THE LINE *East West SQUAD 02CD1*	6	13
5 Jul 03	● WE JUST BE DREAMIN' *East West SQUAD 04CD*	3	9
15 Nov 03	● FLIP REVERSE *East West SQUAD 05CD1*	2	10
14 Feb 04	● HERE 4 ONE *East West SQUAD 06CD*	6	5
7 Dec 02	IN THE BEGINNING *East West 5046610792*	33	6
29 Nov 03	NOW OR NEVER *East West 5046703662*	37	2

BLEACHIN'
UK, male vocal / instrumental group (Singles: 4 Weeks) pos/wks

22 Jul 00	PEAKIN' (re) *Boiler House / Arista 74321774812*	32	4

BLESSID UNION OF SOULS
US, male vocal / instrumental group (Singles: 6 Weeks) pos/wks

27 May 95	I BELIEVE *EMI CDEM 374*	29	5
23 Mar 96	LET ME BE THE ONE *EMI CDEM 387*	74	1

The BLESSING
UK, male vocal / instrumental group (Singles: 13 Weeks) pos/wks

11 May 91	HIGHWAY 5 *MCA MCS 1509*	42	6
18 Jan 92	HIGHWAY 5 (re-mix) *MCA MCS 1603*	30	6
19 Feb 94	SOUL LOVE *MCA MCSTD 1940*	73	1

Mary J BLIGE [270] Top 500 *Original queen of hip hop and R&B, b. 11 Jan 1971, the Bronx, New York, US. Transatlantic chart regular since platinum-selling debut album 'What's the 411?'. She won Grammy Awards in both 2003 and 2004 (Singles: 136 Weeks, Albums: 105 Weeks)* pos/wks

28 Nov 92	REAL LOVE *Uptown MCS 1721*	68	2
27 Feb 93	REMINISCE *Uptown MCSTD 1731*	31	4
12 Jun 93	YOU REMIND ME *Uptown MCSTD 1770*	48	3
28 Aug 93	REAL LOVE (re-mix) *Uptown MCSTD 1922*	26	4
4 Dec 93	YOU DON'T HAVE TO WORRY *Uptown MCSTD 1948*	36	2
14 May 94	MY LOVE *Uptown MCSTD 1972*	29	3
10 Dec 94	BE HAPPY *Uptown MCSTD 2033*	30	4
15 Apr 95	I'M GOIN' DOWN *Uptown MCSTD 2053*	12	4
29 Jul 95	● I'LL BE THERE FOR YOU – YOU'RE ALL I NEED TO GET BY *Def Jam DEFDX 11* 1	10	5
30 Sep 95	MARY JANE (ALL NIGHT LONG) *Uptown MCSTD 2088*	17	4
16 Dec 95	(YOU MAKE ME FEEL LIKE A) NATURAL WOMAN *Uptown MCSTD 2108*	23	3
30 Mar 96	NOT GON' CRY *Arista 74321358252*	39	2
1 Mar 97	CAN'T KNOCK THE HUSTLE *Northwestside 74321447192* 2	30	2

17 May 97	LOVE IS ALL WE NEED *Uptown MCSTD 48053*	15	4
16 Aug 97 ●	EVERYTHING *MCA MCSTD 48059*	6	9
29 Nov 97	MISSING YOU (2re) *MCA MCSTD 48071*	19	5
11 Jul 98	SEVEN DAYS *MCA MCSTD 48083* ③	22	3
13 Mar 99 ●	AS *Epic 6670122* ④	4	10
21 Aug 99	ALL THAT I CAN SAY *MCA MCSTD 40215*	29	3
11 Dec 99	DEEP INSIDE *MCA MCSTD 40224*	42	2
29 Apr 00	GIVE ME YOU *MCA MCSTD 40230*	19	4
16 Dec 00 ●	911 *Columbia 6706122* ⑤	9	10
6 Oct 01 ●	FAMILY AFFAIR *MCA MCSTD 40267* ▲	8	16
9 Feb 02	DANCE FOR ME *MCA MCSTD 40274* ⑥	13	7
11 May 02 ●	NO MORE DRAMA *MCA MCSTD 40281*	9	7
24 Aug 02	RAINY DAYZ *MCA MCSTD 40288* ⑦	17	5
27 Sep 03	LOVE @ 1ST SIGHT *Geffen / Island MCSTD 40338* ⑧	18	5
6 Dec 03	NOT TODAY *Geffen MCSTD 40349* ⑨	40	2
20 Dec 03	WHENEVER I SAY YOUR NAME *A&M 9815394* ⑩	60	1
18 Dec 04	I TRY *Island MCSTD 40390* ⑪	59	1
20 Mar 93	WHAT'S THE 411? *Uptown UPTD 10681*	53	1
17 Dec 94	MY LIFE *Uptown UPTD 11156*	59	1
26 Apr 97 ●	SHARE MY WORLD *MCA MCD 11619* ▲	8	32
28 Aug 99 ●	MARY *MCA MCD 11976*	5	6
8 Sep 01 ●	NO MORE DRAMA *MCA 1126322*	4	58
6 Sep 03 ●	LOVE & LIFE *Geffen / Island 9860700* ▲	8	5

① Method Man featuring Mary J Blige ② Jay-Z featuring Mary J Blige ③ Mary
J Blige featuring George Benson ④ George Michael and Mary J Blige ⑤ Wyclef
Jean featuring Mary J Blige ⑥ Mary J Blige featuring Common ⑦ Mary J Blige
featuring Ja Rule ⑧ Mary J Blige featuring Method Man ⑨ Mary J Blige featuring Eve ⑩ Sting and Mary J Blige ⑪ Talib Kweli featuring Mary J Blige

BLIND FAITH
UK, male vocal / instrumental group (Albums: 10 Weeks) pos/wks

13 Sep 69 ★	BLIND FAITH *Polydor 583059* ▲	1	10

BLIND MELON *US, male vocal / instrumental*
group (Singles: 13 Weeks, Albums: 4 Weeks) pos/wks

12 Jun 93	TONES OF HOME *Capitol CDCL 687*	62	2
11 Dec 93	NO RAIN *Capitol CDCL 699*	17	6
9 Jul 94	CHANGE *Capitol CDCL 717*	35	3
5 Aug 95	GALAXIE *Capitol CDCLS 755*	37	2
22 Jan 94	BLIND MELON *Capitol CDEST 2188*	53	3
19 Aug 95	SOUP *Capitol CDEST 2261*	48	1

BLINK *Ireland, male vocal / instrumental group (Singles: 1 Week)* pos/wks

16 Jul 94	HAPPY DAY *Lime CDR 6385*	57	1

BLINK-182 *US, male vocal / instrumental*
group (Singles: 48 Weeks, Albums: 83 Weeks) pos/wks

2 Oct 99	WHAT'S MY AGE AGAIN? *MCA MCSTD 40219*	38	2
25 Mar 00 ●	ALL THE SMALL THINGS *MCA MCSTD 40223*	2	10
8 Jul 00	WHAT'S MY AGE AGAIN? (re-issue) *MCA MCSZD 40219*	17	6
14 Jul 01	THE ROCK SHOW *MCA MCSTD 40259*	14	7
6 Oct 01	FIRST DATE (re) *MCA MCSTD 40264*	31	4
6 Dec 03	FEELING THIS *Geffen MCSTD 40347*	15	5
13 Mar 04 ●	I MISS YOU *Geffen MCSTD 40359*	8	10
3 Jul 04	DOWN *Geffen MCSTD 40366*	24	3
25 Dec 04	ALWAYS *Geffen MCSTD 40400*	36	1+
11 Mar 00	ENEMA OF THE STATE *MCA MCD 11950*	15	32
18 Nov 00	THE MARK, TOM & TRAVIS SHOW – THE ENEMA STRIKES BACK *MCA 1123792*	69	1
23 Jun 01 ●	TAKE OFF YOUR PANTS AND JACKET *MCA 1126712* ▲	4	24
29 Nov 03	BLINK-182 *Geffen / Polydor 9861408*	22	26

BLINKY BLINK See BLACKSTREET

BLITZ *UK, male vocal / instrumental group (Albums: 3 Weeks)* pos/wks

6 Nov 82	VOICE OF A GENERATION *No Future PUNK 1*	27	3

BLIZZARD OF OZ See Ozzy OSBOURNE

BLOC PARTY
UK, male vocal / instrumental group (Singles: 5 Weeks) pos/wks

15 May 04	BANQUET / STAYING FAT *Moshi Moshi MOSH 10CD*	51	1
24 Jul 04	LITTLE THOUGHTS / TULIPS *Wichita Recordings WEBB 067SCD*	38	2
6 Nov 04	HELICOPTER *Wichita Recordings WEBB 070SCD*	26	2

The BLOCKHEADS *(see also Ian DURY and The BLOCKHEADS)*
UK, male vocal / instrumental group (Albums: 3 Weeks) pos/wks

21 Apr 01	BRAND NEW BOOTS AND PANTIES *East Central One NEWBOOTS 2CD*	44	3

BLOCKSTER
UK / Italy, male production group (Singles: 11 Weeks) pos/wks

16 Jan 99 ●	YOU SHOULD BE ... *Sound of Ministry MOSCDS 128*	3	9
24 Jul 99	GROOVELINE *Sound of Ministry MOSCDS 131*	18	2

BLODWYN PIG
UK, male vocal / instrumental group (Albums: 11 Weeks) pos/wks

16 Aug 69 ●	AHEAD RINGS OUT *Island ILPS 9101*	9	4
25 Apr 70 ●	GETTING TO THIS *Island ILPS 9122*	8	7

BLOKES See Billy BRAGG

Kristine BLOND *Denmark, female vocalist (Singles: 7 Weeks)* pos/wks

11 Apr 98	LOVE SHY *Reverb BNOISE 1CD*	22	3
11 Nov 00	LOVE SHY (re-mix) *Relentless RELENT 4CDS*	28	2
4 May 02	YOU MAKE ME GO OOOH *WEA WEA 343CD*	35	2

BLONDIE 75 Top 500

Influential New York-based quintet, fronted by ex-Bunny Girl Deborah Harry
(v) (b. 1 Jul 1945, Miami) and fiancé Chris Stein (g). Few acts can match their
20-year span of No.1 hits. Best-selling single: 'Heart Of Glass' 1,180,000
(Singles: 172 Weeks, Albums: 351 Weeks) pos/wks

18 Feb 78 ●	DENIS (DENEE) *Chrysalis CHS 2204*	2	14
6 May 78 ●	(I'M ALWAYS TOUCHED BY YOUR) PRESENCE DEAR *Chrysalis CHS 2217*	10	9
26 Aug 78	PICTURE THIS *Chrysalis CHS 2242*	12	11
11 Nov 78 ●	HANGING ON THE TELEPHONE *Chrysalis CHS 2266*	5	12
27 Jan 79 ★	HEART OF GLASS *Chrysalis CHS 2275* ◆ ▲	1	12
19 May 79 ★	SUNDAY GIRL *Chrysalis CHS 2320*	1	13
29 Sep 79 ●	DREAMING *Chrysalis CHS 2350*	2	8
24 Nov 79	UNION CITY BLUE *Chrysalis CHS 2400*	13	10
23 Feb 80 ★	ATOMIC *Chrysalis CHS 2410*	1	9
12 Apr 80 ★	CALL ME *Chrysalis CHS 2414* ▲	1	9
8 Nov 80 ★	THE TIDE IS HIGH *Chrysalis CHS 2465* ▲	1	12
24 Jan 81 ●	RAPTURE *Chrysalis CHS 2485* ▲	5	8
8 May 82	ISLAND OF LOST SOULS *Chrysalis CHS 2608*	11	9
24 Jul 82	WAR CHILD *Chrysalis CHS 2624*	39	4
3 Dec 88	DENIS (re-mix) *Chrysalis CHS 3328*	50	3
11 Feb 89	CALL ME (re-mix) *Chrysalis CHS 3342*	61	2
10 Sep 94	ATOMIC (re-mix) *Chrysalis CDCHS 5013*	19	4
8 Jul 95	HEART OF GLASS (re-mix) *Chrysalis CSCHS 5023*	15	3
28 Oct 95	UNION CITY BLUE (re-mix) *Chrysalis CDCHS 5027*	31	2
13 Feb 99 ★	MARIA *Beyond 74321645632* ■	1	12
12 Jun 99	NOTHING IS REAL BUT THE GIRL *Beyond 74321669472*	26	3
18 Oct 03	GOOD BOYS *Epic 6743992*	12	3
4 Mar 78 ●	PLASTIC LETTERS *Chrysalis CHR 1166*	10	54
23 Sep 78 ★	PARALLEL LINES *Chrysalis CDL 1192*	1	108
10 Mar 79	BLONDIE *Chrysalis CHR 1165*	75	1
13 Oct 79 ●	EAT TO THE BEAT *Chrysalis CDL 1225* ■	1	38
29 Nov 80 ●	AUTOAMERICAN *Chrysalis CDL 1290*	3	16
31 Oct 81 ●	THE BEST OF BLONDIE *Chrysalis CDLTV 1*	4	40
5 Jun 82 ●	THE HUNTER *Chrysalis CDL 1384*	9	12
17 Dec 88	ONCE MORE INTO THE BLEACH *Chrysalis CJB 2* ①	50	4
16 Mar 91 ●	THE COMPLETE PICTURE – THE VERY BEST OF DEBORAH HARRY AND BLONDIE *Chrysalis CHR 1817* ①	3	22
29 Jul 95	BEAUTIFUL – THE REMIX ALBUM *Chrysalis CDCHR 6105*	25	2
25 Jul 98	ATOMIC – THE VERY BEST OF BLONDIE / ATOMIX *EMI 4949962*	12	34
27 Feb 99 ●	NO EXIT *Beyond Music 74321641142*	3	15
2 Nov 02	GREATEST HITS *Chrysalis 5431052*	38	4
25 Oct 03	THE CURSE OF BLONDIE *Epic 5119219*	36	1

① Deborah Harry and Blondie

The re-mix album 'Atomix' was listed with 'Atomic – The Very Best of Blondie'
from 20 Feb 99. 'Parallel Lines' changed catalogue number to Fame CD 25CR 01
when it charted in 2004

BLOOD SWEAT & TEARS *US / Canada, male vocal /*
instrumental group (Singles: 6 Weeks, Albums: 21 Weeks) pos/wks

30 Apr 69	YOU'VE MADE ME SO VERY HAPPY *CBS 4116*	35	6
13 Jul 68	CHILD IS FATHER TO THE MAN *CBS 63296*	40	1

| 12 Apr 69 | BLOOD SWEAT & TEARS *CBS 63504* ▲ | 15 | 8 |
| 8 Aug 70 | BLOOD SWEAT & TEARS 3 *CBS 64024* ▲ | 14 | 12 |

The BLOODHOUND GANG
US, male vocal / instrumental group (Singles: 21 Weeks, Albums: 7 Weeks)   pos/wks

23 Aug 97	WHY'S EVERYBODY ALWAYS PICKIN' ON ME? *Geffen GFSTD 22252*	56	1
15 Apr 00 ●	THE BAD TOUCH *Geffen 4972672*	4	14
2 Sep 00	THE BALLAD OF CHASEY LAIN *Geffen 4973812*	15	6
6 May 00	HOORAY FOR BOOBIES *Geffen 4904552*	37	7

Male / female act for 1997 debut hit

BLOODSTONE
US, male vocal / instrumental group (Singles: 4 Weeks)   pos/wks

| 18 Aug 73 | NATURAL HIGH *Decca F 13382* | 40 | 4 |

Bobby BLOOM
US, male vocalist, b. 1945, d. 28 Feb 1974 (Singles: 24 Weeks)   pos/wks

| 29 Aug 70 ● | MONTEGO BAY (2re) *Polydor 2058 051* | 3 | 19 |
| 9 Jan 71 | HEAVY MAKES YOU HAPPY *Polydor 2001 122* | 31 | 5 |

BLOOMSBURY SET
UK, male vocal / instrumental group (Singles: 3 Weeks)   pos/wks

| 25 Jun 83 | HANGING AROUND WITH THE BIG BOYS *Stiletto STL 13* | 56 | 3 |

Tanya BLOUNT *US, female vocalist (Singles: 1 Week)*   pos/wks

| 11 Jun 94 | I'M GONNA MAKE YOU MINE *Polydor PZCD 315* | 69 | 1 |

Kurtis BLOW
US, male rapper – Kurtis Walker (Singles: 23 Weeks)   pos/wks

15 Dec 79	CHRISTMAS RAPPIN' *Mercury BLOW 7*	30	6
11 Oct 80	THE BREAKS *Mercury BLOW 8*	47	4
16 Mar 85	PARTY TIME (THE GO-GO EDIT) *Club JAB 12* [1]	67	1
15 Jun 85	SAVE YOUR LOVE (FOR NUMBER 1) *Club JAB 14* [1]	66	2
18 Jan 86	IF I RULED THE WORLD *Club JAB 26*	24	8
8 Nov 86	I'M CHILLIN' *Club JAB 42*	64	2

[1] René and Angela featuring Kurtis Blow

The BLOW MONKEYS *UK, male vocal / instrumental group (Singles: 46 Weeks, Albums: 27 Weeks)*   pos/wks

1 Mar 86	DIGGING YOUR SCENE *RCA PB 40599*	12	10
17 May 86	WICKED WAYS *RCA MONK 2*	60	2
31 Jan 87 ●	IT DOESN'T HAVE TO BE THIS WAY *RCA MONK 4*	5	8
28 Mar 87	OUT WITH HER *RCA MONK 5*	30	6
30 May 87	(CELEBRATE) THE DAY AFTER YOU *RCA MONK 6* [1]	52	1
15 Aug 87	SOME KIND OF WONDERFUL *RCA MONK 7*	67	1
6 Aug 88	THIS IS YOUR LIFE *RCA PB 42149*	70	2
8 Apr 89	THIS IS YOUR LIFE (re-mix) *RCA PB 42695*	32	5
15 Jul 89	CHOICE? *RCA PB 42885* [2]	22	6
14 Oct 89	SLAVES NO MORE *RCA PB 43201* [2]	73	2
26 May 90	SPRINGTIME FOR THE WORLD *RCA PB 43623*	69	2
19 Apr 86	ANIMAL MAGIC *RCA PL 70910*	21	8
25 Apr 87	SHE WAS ONLY A GROCER'S DAUGHTER *RCA PL 71245*	20	8
11 Feb 89	WHOOPS! THERE GOES THE NEIGHBOURHOOD *RCA PL 71858*	46	2
26 Aug 89 ●	CHOICES – THE SINGLES COLLECTION *RCA PL 74191*	5	9

[1] The Blow Monkeys with Curtis Mayfield [2] The Blow Monkeys featuring Sylvia Tella

BLOWING FREE *UK, male instrumental duo – Stewart and Bradley Palmer (Albums: 14 Weeks)*   pos/wks

| 29 Jul 95 ● | SAX MOODS *Dino DINCD 106* | 6 | 13 |
| 30 Nov 96 | SAX MOODS – VOLUME 2 *Dino DINCD 118* | 70 | 1 |

Angel BLU See JAIMESON

BLU PETER
UK, male DJ / producer – Peter Harris (Singles: 1 Week)   pos/wks

| 21 Mar 98 | TELL ME WHAT YOU WANT / JAMES HAS KITTENS *React CDREACT 285* | 70 | 1 |

BLUE *UK, male vocal / instrumental group (Singles: 8 Weeks)*   pos/wks

| 30 Apr 77 | GONNA CAPTURE YOUR HEART *Rocket ROKN 522* | 18 | 8 |

BLUE ⟨253⟩ Top 500
One of Britain's top global sellers this century: Duncan James, Anthony Costa, Lee Ryan and Simon Webbe. The London based boy band, who have won countless awards, including Best Pop Act at the 2003 Brits, saw their first two albums go quadruple platinum in the UK (Singles: 137 Weeks, Albums: 113 Weeks)   pos/wks

2 Jun 01 ●	ALL RISE *Innocent SINCD 28*	4	13
8 Sep 01 ★	TOO CLOSE *Innocent SINCD 30* ■	1	13
24 Nov 01 ★	IF YOU COME BACK *Innocent SINCD 32* ■	1	13
30 Mar 02 ●	FLY BY II *Innocent SINCD 33*	6	12
2 Nov 02 ●	ONE LOVE *Innocent SINCD 41*	3	12
21 Dec 02 ★	SORRY SEEMS TO BE THE HARDEST WORD (re-recording) *Innocent SINDX 43* [1] ■	1	17
29 Mar 03 ●	U MAKE ME WANNA *Innocent SINCD 44*	4	10
1 Nov 03 ●	GUILTY *Innocent SINCD 51*	2	11
27 Dec 03	SIGNED, SEALED, DELIVERED, I'M YOURS *Innocent SINCD 50* [2]	11	10
3 Apr 04 ●	BREATHE EASY *Innocent SINCD 58*	4	12
10 Jul 04 ●	BUBBLIN' *Innocent SINDX 64*	9	8
20 Nov 04 ●	CURTAIN FALLS *Innocent SINDX 67*	4	6+
8 Dec 01 ★	ALL RISE *Innocent CDSIN 8*	1	63
16 Nov 02 ★	ONE LOVE *Innocent CDSIN 11* ■	1	29
15 Nov 03 ★	GUILTY *Innocent CDSIN 13* ■	1	16
27 Nov 04 ●	BEST OF BLUE *Innocent CDSINX 18*	6	5+

[1] Blue featuring Elton John [2] Blue featuring Stevie Wonder and Angie Stone

Babbity BLUE *UK, female vocalist (Singles: 2 Weeks)*   pos/wks

| 11 Feb 65 | DON'T MAKE ME (FALL IN LOVE WITH YOU) *Decca F 12053* | 48 | 2 |

Barry BLUE (see also CRY SISCO!)
UK, male vocalist – Barry Green (Singles: 48 Weeks)   pos/wks

28 Jul 73 ●	DANCIN' (ON A SATURDAY NIGHT) *Bell 1295*	2	15
3 Nov 73 ●	DO YOU WANNA DANCE? *Bell 1336*	7	12
2 Mar 74	SCHOOL LOVE *Bell 1345*	11	9
3 Aug 74	MISS HIT AND RUN *Bell 1364*	26	7
26 Oct 74	HOT SHOT *Bell 1379*	23	5

BLUE ADONIS featuring LIL' MISS MAX
Belgium, male production duo – Dirk de Boeck and Wim Perdaen and female vocalist (Singles: 3 Weeks)   pos/wks

| 17 Oct 98 | DISCO COP *Serious SERR 002CD* | 27 | 3 |

The BLUE AEROPLANES *UK, male / female vocal / instrumental group (Singles: 3 Weeks, Albums: 5 Weeks)*   pos/wks

17 Feb 90	JACKET HANGS *Ensign ENY 628*	72	1
26 May 90	... AND STONES *Ensign ENY 632*	63	2
24 Feb 90	SWAGGER *Ensign CHEN 13*	54	1
17 Aug 91	BEATSONGS *Ensign CHEN 21*	33	3
12 Mar 94	LIFE MODEL *Beggars Banquet BBQCD 143*	59	1

BLUE AMAZON
UK, male production duo and female vocalist (Singles: 2 Weeks)   pos/wks

| 17 May 97 | AND THEN THE RAIN FALLS *Sony S2 BAS 301CD* | 53 | 1 |
| 1 Jul 00 | BREATHE *Subversive SUB 61D* | 73 | 1 |

BLUE BAMBOO (see also AIRSCAPE; CUBIC 22; TRANSFORMER 2; BALEARIC BILL; Johan GIELEN presents ABNEA; SVENSON and GIELEN)
Belgium, male producer – Johan Gielen (Singles: 4 Weeks)   pos/wks

| 3 Dec 94 | ABC AND D ... *Escapade CDJAPE 6* | 23 | 4 |

BLUE BOY
UK, male producer – Alexis Blackmore (Singles: 16 Weeks)   pos/wks

| 1 Feb 97 ● | REMEMBER ME *Pharm CDPHARM 1* | 8 | 13 |
| 23 Aug 97 | SANDMAN *Sidewalk CDSWALK 001* | 25 | 3 |

BLUE CAPS See Gene VINCENT

BLUE FEATHER
Holland, male vocal / instrumental group (Singles: 4 Weeks)   pos/wks

| 3 Jul 82 | LET'S FUNK TONIGHT *Mercury MER 109* | 50 | 4 |

BLUE FLAMES See Georgie FAME

BLUE GRASS BOYS See Johnny DUNCAN and the BLUE GRASS BOYS

BLUE HAZE
UK, male vocal / instrumental group (Singles: 6 Weeks)   pos/wks

18 Mar 72	**SMOKE GETS IN YOUR EYES** *A&M AMS 891* **32** 6	

BLUE JEANS See Bob B SOXX and the BLUE JEANS

BLUE MELONS
UK, male / female vocal / instrumental group (Singles: 1 Week)   pos/wks

8 Jun 96	**DO WAH DIDDY DIDDY** *Fundamental FUNDCD 1* **70** 1	

BLUE MERCEDES *UK, male vocal / instrumental*
duo – Duncan Millar and David Titlow (Singles: 18 Weeks)   pos/wks

10 Oct 87	**I WANT TO BE YOUR PROPERTY** *MCA BONA 1* **23** 11	
13 Feb 88	**SEE WANT MUST HAVE** *MCA BONA 2* **57** 2	
23 Jul 88	**LOVE IS THE GUN** *MCA BONA 3* **46** 5	

BLUE MINK (see also DAVID and JONATHAN; PIPKINS)
UK / US, male vocal / instrumental group (Singles: 83 Weeks)   pos/wks

15 Nov 69 ●	**MELTING POT** *Philips BF 1818* **3** 15	
28 Mar 70 ●	**GOOD MORNING FREEDOM** *Philips BF 1838* **10** 10	
19 Sep 70	**OUR WORLD** *Philips 6006 042* **17** 9	
29 May 71 ●	**BANNER MAN** *Regal Zonophone RZ 3034* **3** 14	
11 Nov 72	**STAY WITH ME** (re) *Regal Zonophone RZ 3064* **11** 15	
3 Mar 73	**BY THE DEVIL (I WAS TEMPTED)** *EMI 2007* **26** 9	
23 Jun 73 ●	**RANDY** *EMI 2028* **9** 11	

BLUE MURDER
UK, male vocal / instrumental group (Albums: 3 Weeks)   pos/wks

6 May 89	**BLUE MURDER** *Geffen WX 245* **45** 3	

BLUE NILE *UK, male vocal / instrumental*
group (Singles: 5 Weeks, Albums: 13 Weeks)   pos/wks

30 Sep 89	**THE DOWNTOWN LIGHTS** *Linn LKS 3* **67** 1	
29 Sep 90	**HEADLIGHTS ON THE PARADE** *Linn LKS 4* **72** 1	
19 Jan 91	**SATURDAY NIGHT** *Linn LKS 5* **50** 2	
4 Sep 04	**I WOULD NEVER** *Sanctuary SANXD 305* **52** 1	
19 May 84	**A WALK ACROSS THE ROOFTOPS** *Linn LKH 1* ...**80** 2	
21 Oct 89	**HATS** *Linn LKH 2* **12** 4	
22 Jun 96	**PEACE AT LAST** *Warner Bros. 9362458482* **13** 4	
11 Sep 04 ●	**HIGH** *Sanctuary SANDP 285* **10** 3	

BLUE ÖYSTER CULT *US, male vocal /*
instrumental group (Singles: 14 Weeks, Albums: 40 Weeks)   pos/wks

20 May 78	**(DON'T FEAR) THE REAPER** *CBS 6333* **16** 14	
3 Jul 76	**AGENTS OF FORTUNE** *CBS 81385* **26** 10	
4 Feb 78	**SPECTRES** *CBS 86050* **60** 1	
28 Oct 78	**SOME ENCHANTED EVENING** *CBS 86074* **18** 4	
18 Aug 79	**MIRRORS** *CBS 86087* **46** 5	
19 Jul 80	**CULTOSAURUS ERECTUS** *CBS 86120* **12** 7	
25 Jul 81	**FIRE OF UNKNOWN ORIGIN** *CBS 85137* **29** 7	
22 May 82	**EXTRATERRESTRIAL LIVE** *CBS 22203* **39** 5	
19 Nov 83	**THE REVOLUTION BY NIGHT** *CBS 25686* **95** 1	

BLUE PEARL *UK / US, male / female vocal /*
instrumental group (Singles: 29 Weeks, Albums: 2 Weeks)   pos/wks

7 Jul 90 ●	**NAKED IN THE RAIN** *Big Life BLR 23* **4** 13	
3 Nov 90	**LITTLE BROTHER** *Big Life BLR 32* **31** 5	
11 Jan 92	**(CAN YOU) FEEL THE PASSION** *Big Life BLR 67* ...**14** 6	
25 Jul 92	**MOTHER DAWN** *Big Life BLR 73* **50** 2	
27 Nov 93	**FIRE OF LOVE** *Logic 74321170292* 1 ....**71** 1	
4 Jul 98	**NAKED IN THE RAIN '98** (re-recording) *Malarky MLKD 7* ...**22** 2	
1 Dec 90	**NAKED** *Big Life BLR LP4* **58** 2	

1 Jungle High with Blue Pearl

BLUE RONDO A LA TURK *UK, male vocal /*
instrumental group (Singles: 9 Weeks, Albums: 2 Weeks)   pos/wks

14 Nov 81	**ME AND MR SANCHEZ** *Virgin VS 463* **40** 4	
13 Mar 82	**KLACTOVEESEDSTEIN** *Diable Noir VS 476* **50** 5	
6 Nov 82	**CHEWING THE FAT** *Diable Noir V 2240* **80** 2	

BLUE ZOO
UK, male vocal / instrumental group (Singles: 17 Weeks)   pos/wks

12 Jun 82	**I'M YOUR MAN** *Magnet MAG 224* **55** 3	
16 Oct 82	**CRY BOY CRY** *Magnet MAG 234* **13** 10	
28 May 83	**I JUST CAN'T (FORGIVE AND FORGET)** *Magnet MAG 241* ...**60** 4	

The BLUEBELLS *UK, male vocal / instrumental*
group (Singles: 49 Weeks, Albums: 15 Weeks)   pos/wks

12 Mar 83	**CATH / WILL SHE ALWAYS BE WAITING** *London LON 20* ...**62** 2	
9 Jul 83	**SUGAR BRIDGE (IT WILL STAND)** *London LON 27* ...**72** 1	
24 Mar 84	**I'M FALLING** *London LON 45* **11** 12	
23 Jun 84 ●	**YOUNG AT HEART** *London LON 49* **8** 12	
1 Sep 84	**CATH** (re-issue) *London LON 54* **38** 7	
9 Feb 85	**ALL I AM (IS LOVING YOU)** *London LON 58* **58** 3	
27 Mar 93 ★	**YOUNG AT HEART** (re-issue) *London LONCD 338* **1** 12	
11 Aug 84	**SISTERS** *London LONLP 1* **22** 10	
17 Apr 93	**THE SINGLES COLLECTION** *London 8284052* **27** 5	

BLUENOTES See Harold MELVIN and the BLUENOTES

The BLUES BAND *UK, male vocal / instrumental*
group (Singles: 2 Weeks, Albums: 18 Weeks)   pos/wks

12 Jul 80	**BLUES BAND (EP)** *Arista BOOT 2* **68** 2	
8 Mar 80	**OFFICIAL BOOTLEG ALBUM** *Arista BBBP 101* **40** 9	
18 Oct 80	**READY** *Arista BB 2* **36** 6	
17 Oct 81	**ITCHY FEET** *Arista BB 3* **60** 3	

Tracks on The Blues Band (EP): Maggie's Farm / Ain't it Tuff / Diddy Wah Diddy / Back Door Man

BLUES BROTHERS
US / Canada, male actors / vocal duo – John Belushi, b. 24 Jan 1949, d. 5 Mar 1982, and Dan Ackroyd (Singles: 8 Weeks, Albums: 3 Weeks)   pos/wks

7 Apr 90	**EVERYBODY NEEDS SOMEBODY TO LOVE** *East West A 7591* 12 8	
4 Dec 04	**THE DEFINITIVE BLUES BROTHERS COLLECTION** *Atlantic 7567808405* ....**64** 3+	

For the first two weeks, the flip side of 'Everybody Needs Somebody to Love' – 'Think' by Aretha Franklin – was listed

The BLUESKINS
UK, male vocal / instrumental group (Singles: 2 Weeks)   pos/wks

21 Feb 04	**CHANGE MY MIND / I WANNA KNOW** *Domino RUG 174CD* ...**56** 1	
5 Jun 04	**THE STUPID ONES** *Domino RUG 175CD* **61** 1	

The BLUETONES *UK, male vocal / instrumental*
group (Singles: 46 Weeks, Albums: 50 Weeks)   pos/wks

17 Jun 95	**ARE YOU BLUE OR ARE YOU BLIND** *Superior Quality BLUE 001CD* **31** 2	
14 Oct 95	**BLUETONIC** *Superior Quality BLUE 002CD* **19** 3	
3 Feb 96 ●	**SLIGHT RETURN** *Superior Quality BLUE 003CD* **2** 8	
11 May 96 ●	**CUT SOME RUG / CASTLE ROCK** (re) *Superior Quality BLUE 005CD* **7** 6	
28 Sep 96 ●	**MARBLEHEAD JOHNSON** *Superior Quality BLUE 006CD* **7** 6	
21 Feb 98 ●	**SOLOMON BITES THE WORM** *Superior Quality BLUED 007* ...**10** 3	
9 May 98	**IF ...** *Superior Quality BLUED 009* **13** 5	
8 Aug 98	**SLEAZY BED TRACK** *Superior Quality BLUED 010* **35** 2	
4 Mar 00	**KEEP THE HOME FIRES BURNING** *Superior Quality BLUED 012* **13** 3	
20 May 00	**AUTOPHILIA** *Superior Quality BLUED 013* **18** 3	
6 Apr 02	**AFTER HOURS** *Superior Quality BLUED 016* **26** 2	
3 May 03	**FAST BOY / LIQUID LIPS** *Superior Quality BLUE 18CDS* ...**25** 2	
23 Aug 03	**NEVER GOING NOWHERE** *Superior Quality BLUE 020CDS* ...**40** 1	
24 Feb 96 ★	**EXPECTING TO FLY** *Superior Quality BLUECD 004* ■ **1** 25	
21 Mar 98 ●	**RETURN TO THE LAST CHANCE SALOON** *Superior Quality BLUED 008* **10** 16	
27 May 00 ●	**SCIENCE & NATURE** *Superior Quality BLUECD 014* **7** 4	
20 Apr 02	**THE SINGLES** *Superior Quality BLUECD 017* **14** 4	
24 May 03	**LUXEMBOURG** *Superior Quality BLUECD 019* **49** 1	

Colin BLUNSTONE (see also ARGENT; Neil MacARTHUR; The ZOMBIES)
UK, male vocalist (Singles: 30 Weeks)   pos/wks

12 Feb 72	**SAY YOU DON'T MIND** *Epic EPC 7765* **15** 9	
11 Nov 72	**I DON'T BELIEVE IN MIRACLES** *Epic EPC 8434* ...**31** 6	
17 Feb 73	**HOW COULD WE DARE TO BE WRONG** *Epic EPC 1197* ...**45** 2	
14 Mar 81	**WHAT BECOMES OF THE BROKEN HEARTED** *Stiff BROKEN 1* 1 ....**13** 10	
29 May 82	**TRACKS OF MY TEARS** *PRT 7P 236* **60** 2	
15 Jan 83	**OLD AND WISE** *Arista ARIST 494* 2 ....**74** 1	

1 Dave Stewart: Guest vocals: Colin Blunstone   2 Alan Parsons Project: Lead vocals by Colin Blunstone

BLUR `92` `Top 500` (see also FAT LES; Graham COXON)

Prime movers of Britpop: Damon Albarn (v/k), Graham Coxon (g), Alex James (b), Dave Rowntree (d). They won a record four Brit awards in 1995, and their first No.1 caused a media storm when it outpaced 'Roll With It' by Britpop rivals Oasis to become their best-selling single at 640,000 (Singles: 146 Weeks, Albums: 308 Weeks)

		pos/wks
27 Oct 90	SHE'S SO HIGH / I KNOW *Food FOOD 26*	48 3
27 Apr 91	THERE'S NO OTHER WAY *Food FOOD 29*	8 8
10 Aug 91	BANG *Food FOOD 31*	24 4
11 Apr 92	POPSCENE *Food FOOD 37*	32 2
1 May 93	FOR TOMORROW *Food CDFOODS 40*	28 4
10 Jul 93	CHEMICAL WORLD *Food CDFOODS 45*	28 4
16 Oct 93	SUNDAY SUNDAY *Food CDFOOD 46*	26 3
19 Mar 94 ●	GIRLS AND BOYS *Food CDFOODS 47*	5 7
11 Jun 94	TO THE END *Food CDFOODS 50*	16 5
3 Sep 94 ●	PARKLIFE *Food CDFOOD 53*	10 7
19 Nov 94	END OF A CENTURY *Food CDFOOD 56*	19 5
26 Aug 95 ★	COUNTRY HOUSE (re) *Food FOODS 63* ■	1 12
25 Nov 95 ●	THE UNIVERSAL *Food CDFOODS 69* ■	5 9
24 Feb 96 ●	STEREOTYPES *Food CDFOOD 73* ■	7 5
11 May 96 ●	CHARMLESS MAN *Food CDFOOD 77* ■	5 6
1 Feb 97 ★	BEETLEBUM (re) *Food CDFOODS 89* ■	1 7
19 Apr 97 ●	SONG 2 *Food CDFOODS 93*	2 5
28 Jun 97 ●	ON YOUR OWN *Food CDFOOD 98*	5 5
27 Sep 97	MOR *Food CDFOOD 107*	15 3
6 Mar 99 ●	TENDER *Food CDFOODS 117*	2 10
10 Jul 99	COFFEE + TV *Food CDFOODS 122*	11 7
27 Nov 99	NO DISTANCE LEFT TO RUN (re) *Food CDFOOD 123*	14 4
28 Oct 00 ●	MUSIC IS MY RADAR (re) *Food / Parlophone CDFOODS 135*	10 9
26 Apr 03 ●	OUT OF TIME *Parlophone CDR 6606*	5 9
19 Jul 03	CRAZY BEAT *Parlophone CDR 6610*	18 3
18 Oct 03	GOOD SONG *Parlophone CDR 6619*	22 2
7 Sep 91	LEISURE *Food FOODLP 6*	7 12
22 May 93	MODERN LIFE IS RUBBISH *Food FOODCD 9*	15 14
7 May 94 ★	PARKLIFE *Food FOODCD 10* ■	1 106
23 Sep 95 ★	THE GREAT ESCAPE *Food FOODCD 14* ■	1 47
22 Feb 97 ★	BLUR *Food FOODCD 19* ■	1 65
27 Mar 99 ★	13 *Food FOODCD 29* ■	1 27
11 Nov 00 ●	THE BEST OF *Food FOODCD 33*	3 29
17 May 03 ★	THINK TANK *Parlophone 5829972* ■	1 8

Chart rules allow for a maximum of three formats; the 7-inch of 'Country House', already available on two CDs and cassette, was therefore listed separately

BO SELECTA (see also MERRION, McCALL & KENSIT)

UK, male rubber-faced comedian / vocalist – Avid Merrion (Leigh Francis) (Singles: 9 Weeks)

		pos/wks
27 Dec 03 ●	PROPER CRIMBO *BMG 82876581412*	4 9

BOARDS OF CANADA

UK, male instrumental / production duo (Albums: 2 Weeks)

		pos/wks
2 Mar 02	GEOGADDI *Warp WARPCD 101*	21 2

BOB and EARL

US, male vocal duo – Bobby Relf and Earl Nelson (Singles: 13 Weeks)

		pos/wks
12 Mar 69 ●	HARLEM SHUFFLE *Island WIP 6053*	7 13

BOB and MARCIA *Jamaica, male / female vocal*

duo – Bob Andy and Marcia Griffiths (Singles: 25 Weeks)

		pos/wks
14 Mar 70 ●	YOUNG, GIFTED AND BLACK *Harry J HJ 6605*	5 12
5 Jun 71	PIED PIPER *Trojan TR 7818*	11 13

BOB THE BUILDER *UK, male silicone puppet building contractor –*

voiced by Neil Morrissey (Singles: 41 Weeks, Albums: 12 Weeks)

		pos/wks
16 Dec 00 ★	CAN WE FIX IT? (2re) *BBC Music WMSS 60372* ◆	1 22
15 Sep 01 ★	MAMBO NO.5 *BBC Music WMSS 60442* ■	1 19
13 Oct 01 ●	THE ALBUM *BBC Music WMSF 60472*	4 12

The BOBBYSOCKS

Norway / Sweden, female vocal duo (Singles: 4 Weeks)

		pos/wks
25 May 85	LET IT SWING *RCA PB 40127*	44 4

Su Su BOBIEN See MASS SYNDICATE featuring Su Su BOBIEN

Andrea BOCELLI `423` `Top 500` *Blind Italian operatic tenor who*

has sold more than 50 million albums worldwide, b. 22 Sep 1958, Lajatico. 'Romanza' sold 17 million copies worldwide, 'Sogno' topped the European chart and at times he held the top 3 places on the US classical chart (Singles: 24 Weeks, Albums: 141 Weeks)

		pos/wks
24 May 97 ●	TIME TO SAY GOODBYE (CON TE PARTIRO) [1] *Coalition COLA 003CD*	2 14
25 Sep 99	CANTO DELLA TERRA (re) *Polydor / Sugar 5613192*	24 9
18 Dec 99	AVE MARIA *Philips 4644852*	65 1
31 May 97 ●	ROMANZA *Philips 4564562*	6 25
9 May 98	ARIA – THE OPERA ALBUM *Philips 4620332*	33 5
13 Feb 99	VIAGGIO ITALIANO *Philips 4621962*	24 10
10 Apr 99 ●	SOGNO *Polydor 5472212*	4 42
20 Nov 99	SACRED ARIAS *Philips 4626002*	20 12
23 Sep 00	VERDI *Philips 4646002*	17 10
27 Oct 01 ●	CIELI DI TOSCANA *Polydor 5892452*	3 16
16 Nov 02	SENTIMENTO *Philips 4734102*	7 15
13 Nov 04	ANDREA *Universal 9867973*	19 6+

[1] Sarah Brightman and Andrea Bocelli

'Canto Della Terra' was originally No.25 before re-entering and peaking one place higher in Jul 2000 'Viaggio Italiano' stalled at No.55 in 1999 and reached its peak position in 2003 after the album was repackaged with bonus tracks. 'Sentimento' features the London Symphony Orchestra and Lorin Maazel

Karen BODDINGTON and Mark WILLIAMS

Australia / New Zealand, female / male vocal duo (Singles: 1 Week) pos/wks

2 Sep 89	HOME AND AWAY *First Night SCORE 19*	73 1

The BODINES

UK, male vocal / instrumental group (Albums: 1 Week) pos/wks

29 Aug 87	PLAYED *Pop BODL 2001*	94 1

BODY COUNT (see also ICE-T) *US, male rap /*

instrumental group (Singles: 4 Weeks, Albums: 2 Weeks) pos/wks

8 Oct 94	BORN DEAD *Rhyme Syndicate SYNDG 4*	28 2
17 Dec 94	NECESSARY EVIL *Virgin VSCDX 1529*	45 2
17 Sep 94	BORN DEAD *Rhyme Syndicate RSYND 2*	15 2

BODYSNATCHERS

UK, female vocal / instrumental group (Singles: 12 Weeks) pos/wks

15 Mar 80	LET'S DO ROCK STEADY *2 Tone CHSTT 9*	22 9
19 Jul 80	EASY LIFE *2 Tone CHSTT 12*	50 3

Humphrey BOGART See Dooley WILSON

Suzy BOGGUSS *US, female vocalist (Albums: 1 Week)* pos/wks

25 Sep 93	SOMETHING UP MY SLEEVE *Liberty CDEST 221*	69 1

Hamilton BOHANNON

US, male vocalist / instrumentalist – drums (Singles: 38 Weeks) pos/wks

15 Feb 75	SOUTH AFRICAN MAN *Brunswick BR 16*	22 8
24 May 75 ●	DISCO STOMP *Brunswick BR 19*	6 12
5 Jul 75	FOOT STOMPIN' MUSIC *Brunswick BR 21*	23 6
6 Sep 75	HAPPY FEELING *Brunswick BR 24*	49 3
26 Aug 78	LET'S START THE DANCE *Mercury 6167 700*	56 4
13 Feb 82	LET'S START TO DANCE AGAIN *London HL 10582*	49 5

BOILING POINT

US, male vocal / instrumental group (Singles: 6 Weeks) pos/wks

27 May 78	LET'S GET FUNKTIFIED *Bang BANG 1312*	41 6

Marc BOLAN See T. REX

CJ BOLLAND (see also RAVESIGNAL III) *Belgium, male producer –*

Christian Jay Bolland (Singles: 10 Weeks, Albums: 2 Weeks) pos/wks

5 Oct 96	SUGAR IS SWEETER *Internal LIECD 35*	11 5
17 May 97	THE PROPHET *ffrr FCD 300*	19 3
3 Jul 99	IT AIN'T GONNA BE ME *Essential Recordings ESCD 5*	35 2
26 Oct 96	THE ANALOGUE THEATRE *Internal TRUCD 13*	43 2

BOLSHOI *UK, male vocal / instrumental group (Albums: 1 Week)* pos/wks

3 Oct 87	LINDY'S PARTY *Beggars Banquet BEGA 86*	100 1

Michael BOLTON `159` `Top 500` *Soulful rock balladeer / songwriter who initially recorded under his real name, Michael Bolotin (b. 26 Feb 1953, Connecticut, US), and fronted recording groups The Nomads and Blackjack (Singles: 113 Weeks, Albums: 230 Weeks)*

pos/wks

17 Feb 90	● HOW AM I SUPPOSED TO LIVE WITHOUT YOU *CBS 6553977* ▲	3	10
28 Apr 90	● HOW CAN WE BE LOVERS *CBS 6559187*	10	10
21 Jul 90	WHEN I'M BACK ON MY FEET AGAIN *CBS 6560777*	44	5
20 Apr 91	LOVE IS A WONDERFUL THING *Columbia 6567717*	23	8
27 Jul 91	TIME LOVE AND TENDERNESS *Columbia 6569897*	28	7
9 Nov 91	● WHEN A MAN LOVES A WOMAN *Columbia 6574887* ▲	8	9
8 Feb 92	STEEL BARS *Columbia 6577257*	17	6
9 May 92	MISSING YOU NOW *Columbia 6579917* [1]	28	4
31 Oct 92	TO LOVE SOMEBODY *Columbia 6584557*	16	6
26 Dec 92	DRIFT AWAY *Columbia 6588657*	18	5
13 Mar 93	REACH OUT I'LL BE THERE *Columbia 6588972*	37	4
13 Nov 93	SAID I LOVED YOU BUT I LIED *Columbia 6598762*	15	8
26 Feb 94	SOUL OF MY SOUL *Columbia 6601772*	32	3
14 May 94	LEAN ON ME *Columbia 6604132*	14	7
9 Sep 95	● CAN I TOUCH YOU ... THERE *Columbia 6624385*	6	9
2 Dec 95	A LOVE SO BEAUTIFUL *Columbia 6627092*	27	5
16 Mar 96	SOUL PROVIDER *Columbia 6629812*	35	3
8 Nov 97	THE BEST OF LOVE / GO THE DISTANCE *Columbia 6652802*	14	4
17 Mar 90	● SOUL PROVIDER *CBS 4653431*	4	72
11 Aug 90	THE HUNGER *CBS 4601631*	44	1
18 May 91	● TIME, LOVE AND TENDERNESS *Columbia 4678121* ▲	2	57
10 Oct 92	● TIMELESS – THE CLASSICS *Columbia 4723022* ▲	3	24
27 Nov 93	● THE ONE THING *Columbia 4743552*	4	24
30 Sep 95	● GREATEST HITS 1985-1995 *Columbia 4810022*	2	30
22 Nov 97	ALL THAT MATTERS *Columbia 4885312*	20	7
2 May 98	MY SECRET PASSION – THE ARIAS *Sony Classical SK 63077*	25	5
4 Dec 99	TIMELESS – THE CLASSICS – VOL.2 *Columbia 4960782*	50	2
6 Apr 02	ONLY A WOMAN LIKE YOU *Jive 9223522*	19	2
27 Mar 04	VINTAGE *Universal TV 9817973*	23	2

[1] Michael Bolton featuring Kenny G

BOMB THE BASS *UK, male producer –*
Tim Simenon (Singles: 50 Weeks, Albums: 16 Weeks)

pos/wks

20 Feb 88	● BEAT DIS *Mister-ron DOOD 1*	2	9
27 Aug 88	● MEGABLAST / DON'T MAKE ME WAIT *Mister-ron DOOD 2* [1]	6	9
26 Nov 88	● SAY A LITTLE PRAYER *Rhythm King DOOD 3* [2]	10	10
27 Jul 91	● WINTER IN JULY *Rhythm King 6572757*	7	9
9 Nov 91	THE AIR YOU BREATHE *Rhythm King 6575387*	52	3
2 May 92	KEEP GIVING ME LOVE *Rhythm King 6579887*	62	2
1 Oct 94	BUG POWDER DUST *Stoned Heights BRCD 300* [3]	24	3
17 Dec 94	DARKHEART *Stoned Heights BRCD 305* [4]	35	3
1 Apr 95	1 TO 1 RELIGION *Stoned Heights BRCD 313* [5]	53	1
16 Sep 95	SANDCASTLES *Fourth & Broadway BRCD 324* [6]	54	1
22 Oct 88	INTO THE DRAGON *Rhythm King DOOD 1*	18	10
31 Aug 91	UNKNOWN TERRITORY *Rhythm King 4687740*	19	4
15 Apr 95	CLEAR *Fourth & Broadway BRCD 611*	22	2

[1] Bomb the Bass featuring Merlin and Antonia / Bomb the Bass featuring Lorraine and Lose [2] Bomb the Bass featuring Maureen [3] Bomb the Bass featuring Justin Warfield [4] Bomb the Bass featuring Spikey Tee [5] Bomb the Bass featuring Carlton [6] Bomb the Bass featuring Bernard Fowler

BOMBALURINA featuring Timmy MALLETT
UK, male / female vocal group and male TV presenter / vocalist (Singles: 20 Weeks, Albums: 5 Weeks)

pos/wks

28 Jul 90	★ ITSY BITSY TEENY WEENY YELLOW POLKA DOT BIKINI *Carpet CRPT 1* [1]	1	13
24 Nov 90	SEVEN LITTLE GIRLS SITTING IN THE BACKSEAT *Carpet CRPT 2* [2]	18	7
15 Dec 90	HUGGIN' AN' A KISSIN' *Polydor 8476481*	55	5

[1] Bombalurina [2] Bombalurina featuring Timmy Mallett

The BOMBERS
Canada, male / female vocal / instrumental group (Singles: 10 Weeks) pos/wks

5 May 79	(EVERYBODY) GET DANCIN' *Flamingo FM 1*	37	7
18 Aug 79	LET'S DANCE *Flamingo FM 4*	58	3

BOMFUNK MC'S *Finland, male DJ / rap duo – Raymond Ebanks and DJ Gismo (Singles: 21 Weeks, Albums: 2 Weeks)*

pos/wks

5 Aug 00	● FREESTYLER *Dancepool DPS 2CD*	2	12
2 Dec 00	UP ROCKING BEATS *INCredible 6706132*	11	9
26 Aug 00	IN STEREO *INCredible 4943092*	33	2

BON *Germany, male vocal duo – Guy Gross and Claus Capek (Singles: 5 Weeks)*

pos/wks

3 Feb 01	BOYS *Epic 6707092*	15	5

BON JOVI `50` `Top 500` *Globally popular New Jersey band: Jon Bon Jovi (Jon Bongiovi Jr. v), Richie Sambora (g), David Bryan (k), Alec John Such (b), Tico Torres (d). The UK's biggest-selling album act of 1994. They have sold 100 million albums worldwide. Legendary fact: At one of their gigs a pig's head was thrown on stage. Best-selling single: 'Always' 560,500 (Singles: 232 Weeks, Albums: 428 Weeks)*

pos/wks

31 Aug 85	HARDEST PART IS THE NIGHT *Vertigo VER 22*	68	1
9 Aug 86	YOU GIVE LOVE A BAD NAME *Vertigo VER 26* ▲	14	10
25 Oct 86	LIVIN' ON A PRAYER *Vertigo VER 28* ▲	4	15
11 Apr 87	WANTED DEAD OR ALIVE *Vertigo JOV 1*	13	7
15 Aug 87	NEVER SAY GOODBYE *Vertigo JOV 2*	21	5
24 Sep 88	BAD MEDICINE *Vertigo JOV 3* ▲	17	7
10 Dec 88	BORN TO BE MY BABY *Vertigo JOV 4*	22	7
29 Apr 89	I'LL BE THERE FOR YOU *Vertigo JOV 5* ▲	18	7
26 Aug 89	LAY YOUR HANDS ON ME *Vertigo JOV 6*	18	6
9 Dec 89	LIVING IN SIN *Vertigo JOV 7*	35	6
24 Oct 92	● KEEP THE FAITH *Jambco JOV 8*	5	6
23 Jan 93	BED OF ROSES *Jambco JOVCD 9*	13	6
15 May 93	● IN THESE ARMS *Jambco JOVCD 10*	9	7
7 Aug 93	I'LL SLEEP WHEN I'M DEAD *Jambco JOVCD 11*	17	5
2 Oct 93	I BELIEVE *Jambco JOVCD 12*	11	6
26 Mar 94	DRY COUNTY *Jambco JOVCD 13*	9	6
24 Sep 94	● ALWAYS *Jambco JOVCD 14*	2	18
17 Dec 94	● PLEASE COME HOME FOR CHRISTMAS (re) *Jambco JOVCD 16*	7	10
25 Feb 95	● SOMEDAY I'LL BE SATURDAY NIGHT *Jambco JOVDD 15*	7	7
10 Jun 95	● THIS AIN'T A LOVE SONG *Mercury JOVCD 17*	6	9
30 Sep 95	● SOMETHING FOR THE PAIN *Mercury JOVCD 18*	8	7
25 Nov 95	● LIE TO ME *Mercury JOVCD 19*	10	8
9 Mar 96	● THESE DAYS *Mercury JOVCD 20*	7	6
6 Jul 96	HEY GOD *Mercury JOVCD 21*	13	5
10 Apr 99	REAL LIFE *Reprise W 479CD*	21	5
3 Jun 00	● IT'S MY LIFE *Mercury 5627682*	3	13
9 Sep 00	● SAY IT ISN'T SO (re) *Mercury 5688972*	10	7
9 Dec 00	THANK YOU FOR LOVING ME *Mercury 5727302*	12	6
19 May 01	● ONE WILD NIGHT *Mercury 5729502*	10	7
28 Sep 02	● EVERYDAY (re) *Mercury 0639362*	5	6
21 Dec 02	MISUNDERSTOOD *Mercury 0638152*	21	5
24 May 03	● ALL ABOUT LOVIN' YOU (re) *Mercury 9800242*	9	6
28 Apr 84	BON JOVI *Vertigo VERL 14*	71	3
11 May 85	7800 FAHRENHEIT *Vertigo VERL 24*	28	12
20 Sep 86	● SLIPPERY WHEN WET *Vertigo VERH 38* ▲	6	123
1 Oct 88	★ NEW JERSEY *Vertigo VERH 62* ■	1	47
14 Nov 92	★ KEEP THE FAITH *Jambco 5141972* ■	1	70
22 Oct 94	★ CROSS ROAD – THE BEST OF BON JOVI *Jambco 5229362* ■...1	1	68
1 Jul 95	★ THESE DAYS *Mercury 5282482* ■	1	50
10 Jun 00	★ CRUSH *Mercury 5425622* ■	1	29
26 May 01	● ONE WILD NIGHT – LIVE 1985-2001 *Mercury 5488652*	2	9
5 Oct 02	● BOUNCE *Mercury 0633952*	2	9
15 Nov 03	● THIS LEFT FEELS RIGHT *Mercury 9861391*	4	8

Jon BON JOVI (see also BON JOVI) *US, male vocalist / instrumentalist – John Bongiovi Jr (Singles: 27 Weeks, Albums: 41 Weeks)*

pos/wks

4 Aug 90	● BLAZE OF GLORY *Vertigo JBJ 1* ▲	13	8
10 Nov 90	MIRACLE *Vertigo JBVJ 2*	29	5
14 Jun 97	● MIDNIGHT IN CHELSEA *Mercury MERCD 488*	4	7
30 May 97	● QUEEN OF NEW ORLEANS *Mercury MERCD 493*	10	4
15 Nov 97	JANIE, DON'T TAKE YOUR LOVE TO TOWN *Mercury 5749872*	13	3
25 Aug 90	● BLAZE OF GLORY / YOUNG GUNS II (FILM SOUNDTRACK) *Vertigo 8464731*	2	23
28 Jun 97	● DESTINATION ANYWHERE *Mercury 5360112*	2	18

BOND *Australia / UK, female string quartet (Albums: 23 Weeks)* pos/wks

14 Oct 00	BORN *Decca 4670912*	16	18
16 Nov 02	SHINE *Decca 4734602*	26	3
18 Sep 04	CLASSIFIED *Decca 4756301*	32	2

Graham BOND *UK, male vocalist / instrumentalist – keyboards, b. 28 Oct 1937, d. 8 May 1974 (Albums: 2 Weeks)*

pos/wks

20 Jun 70	SOLID BOND *Warner Bros. WS 3001*	40	2

Ronnie BOND *UK, male vocalist (Singles: 5 Weeks)* pos/wks

31 May 80	IT'S WRITTEN ON YOUR BODY *Mercury MER 13*	52	5

Gary 'U.S.' BONDS *US, male vocalist –*
Gary Anderson (Singles: 39 Weeks, Albums: 8 Weeks)   pos/wks

19 Jan 61	**NEW ORLEANS** *Top Rank JAR 527* [1]	16	11
20 Jul 61 ●	**QUARTER TO THREE** *Top Rank JAR 575* [2] ▲	7	13
30 May 81	**THIS LITTLE GIRL** *EMI America EA 122*	43	6
22 Aug 81	**JOLE BLON** *EMI America EA 127*	51	3
31 Oct 81	**IT'S ONLY LOVE** *EMI America EA 128*	43	3
17 Jul 82	**SOUL DEEP** *EMI America EA 140*	59	3
22 Aug 81	**DEDICATION** *EMI America AML 3017*	43	3
10 Jul 82	**ON THE LINE** *EMI America AML 3022*	55	5

[1] U.S. Bonds [2] US Bonds

BONE *UK, male vocal / instrumental duo (Singles: 1 Week)*   pos/wks

2 Apr 94	**WINGS OF LOVE** *Deconstruction 74321176282*	55	1

BONE THUGS-N-HARMONY
US, male rap group (Singles: 26 Weeks, Albums: 4 Weeks)   pos/wks

4 Nov 95	**1ST OF THA MONTH** *Epic 6625172*	32	2
10 Aug 96 ●	**THA CROSSROADS** *Epic 6635502* ▲	8	11
9 Nov 96	**1ST OF THA MONTH (re-issue)** *Epic 6638505*	15	4
15 Feb 97	**DAYS OF OUR LIVEZ** *East West A 3982CD*	37	3
26 Jul 97	**LOOK INTO MY EYES** *Epic 6647862*	16	3
24 May 03	**HOME** *Epic 6738302* [1]	19	4
31 Aug 96	**E.1999 ETERNAL** *Epic 4810382* ▲	39	3
9 Aug 97	**THE ART OF WAR** *Epic 4880802* ▲	42	1

[1] Bone Thugs-N-Harmony featuring Phil Collins

Elbow BONES and the RACKETEERS
US, male vocalist and female backing group (Singles: 9 Weeks)   pos/wks

14 Jan 84	**A NIGHT IN NEW YORK** *EMI America EA 165*	33	9

BONEY M | 178 | Top 500
Internationally successful West Indian vocal group: Bobby Farrell, Marcia Barrett, Liz Mitchell, Maisie Williams. This German-based quartet was assembled by producer Frank Farian (later behind controversial duo Milli Vanilli). Best-selling single: 'Rivers of Babylon' / 'Brown Girl in the Ring' 1,985,000 (Singles: 171 Weeks, Albums: 142 Weeks)   pos/wks

18 Dec 76 ●	**DADDY COOL** *Atlantic K 10827*	6	13
12 Mar 77 ●	**SUNNY** *Atlantic K 10892*	3	10
25 Jun 77 ●	**MA BAKER** *Atlantic K 10965*	2	13
29 Oct 77 ●	**BELFAST** *Atlantic K 11020*	8	13
29 Apr 78 ★	**RIVERS OF BABYLON / BROWN GIRL IN THE RING**		
	Atlantic / Hansa K 11120 ◆	1	40
7 Oct 78 ●	**RASPUTIN** *Atlantic / Hansa K 11192*	2	10
2 Dec 78 ★	**MARY'S BOY CHILD – OH MY LORD** *Atlantic / Hansa K 11221* ◆	1	8
3 Mar 79 ●	**PAINTER MAN** *Atlantic / Hansa K 11255*	10	6
28 Apr 79 ●	**HOORAY HOORAY, IT'S A HOLI-HOLIDAY**		
	Atlantic / Hansa K 11279	3	9
11 Aug 79	**GOTTA GO HOME / EL LUTE** *Atlantic / Hansa K 11351*	12	11
15 Dec 79	**I'M BORN AGAIN** *Atlantic / Hansa K 11410*	35	7
26 Apr 80	**MY FRIEND JACK** *Atlantic / Hansa K 11463*	57	5
14 Feb 81	**CHILDREN OF PARADISE** *Atlantic / Hansa K 11637*	66	2
21 Nov 81	**WE KILL THE WORLD (DON'T KILL THE WORLD)**		
	Atlantic / Hansa K 11689	39	5
24 Dec 88	**MEGAMIX / MARY'S BOY CHILD (re-mix)** *Ariola 111947*	52	3
5 Dec 92 ●	**BONEY M MEGAMIX** *Arista 74321125127*	7	9
17 Apr 93	**BROWN GIRL IN THE RING (re-mix)** *Arista 74321137052*	38	3
8 May 99	**MA BAKER (re-mix) – SOMEBODY SCREAMED**		
	Logic 74321653872 [1]	22	2
29 Dec 01	**DADDY COOL 2001 (re-mix)** *BMG 74321913512*	47	2
23 Apr 77	**TAKE THE HEAT OFF ME** *Atlantic K 50314*	40	5
6 Aug 77	**LOVE FOR SALE** *Atlantic K 50385*	13	10
29 Jul 78 ★	**NIGHT FLIGHT TO VENUS** *Atlantic / Hansa K 50498*	1	65
29 Sep 79 ★	**OCEANS OF FANTASY** *Atlantic / Hansa K 50610* ■	1	18
12 Apr 80 ★	**THE MAGIC OF BONEY M – 20 GOLDEN HITS**		
	Atlantic / Hansa BMTV 1	1	26
6 Sep 86	**THE BEST OF 10 YEARS – 32 SUPERHITS** *Stylus SMR 621*	35	5
27 Mar 93	**THE GREATEST HITS** *Telstar TCD 2656*	14	10
15 Dec 01	**THE GREATEST HITS** *BMG 74321896142*	66	3

[1] Boney M vs Horny United

'Brown Girl in the Ring' listed with 'Rivers of Babylon' only from 5 Aug 1978, peaking at No.2. 'El Lute' listed with 'Gotta Go Home' only from 29 Sep 1979. The 1988 and 1992 megamixes are different   The two 'The Greatest Hits' albums are different

BONFIRE
Germany, male vocal / instrumental group (Albums: 1 Week)   pos/wks

21 Oct 89	**POINT BLANK** *MSA ZL 74249*	74	1

BONIFACE
Seychelles, male vocalist – Bruce Boniface (Singles: 3 Weeks)   pos/wks

31 Aug 02	**CHEEKY** *Columbia 6729902*	25	3

Guest vocal by Lady Luck

Graham BONNET
UK, male vocalist (Singles: 15 Weeks, Albums: 3 Weeks)   pos/wks

21 Mar 81 ●	**NIGHT GAMES** *Vertigo VER 1*	6	11
13 Jun 81	**LIAR** *Vertigo VER 2*	51	4
7 Nov 81	**LINE UP** *Mercury 6302151*	62	3

Graham BONNEY
UK, male vocalist – Graham Bradley (Singles: 8 Weeks)   pos/wks

24 Mar 66	**SUPERGIRL** *Columbia DB 7843*	19	8

BONNIE *See DELANEY and BONNIE and FRIENDS*

BONNIE "PRINCE" BILLY *US, male vocalist / instrumentalist –*
guitar – Will Oldham (Singles: 1 Week, Albums: 2 Weeks)   pos/wks

4 Sep 04	**AGNES, QUEEN OF SORROW** *Domino RUG 185CD*	69	1
8 Feb 03	**MASTER AND EVERYONE** *Domino WIGCD 121*	48	1
3 Apr 04	**BONNIE 'PRINCE' BILLY SINGS GREATEST PALACE MUSIC**		
	Domino WIGCD 140	63	1

BONO (see also U2)
Ireland, male vocalist – Paul Hewson (Singles: 25 Weeks)   pos/wks

25 Jan 86	**IN A LIFETIME** *RCA PB 40535* [1]	20	5
10 Jun 89	**IN A LIFETIME (re-issue)** *RCA PB 42873* [1]	17	7
4 Dec 93 ●	**I'VE GOT YOU UNDER MY SKIN** *Island CID 578* [2]	4	9
9 Apr 94	**IN THE NAME OF THE FATHER** *Island CID 593* [3]	46	2
23 Oct 99	**NEW DAY** *Columbia 6682122* [4]	23	2

[1] Clannad featuring Bono [2] Frank Sinatra with Bono [3] Bono and Gavin Friday
[4] Wyclef Jean featuring Bono

'I've Got You Under My Skin' was the listed B-side of 'Stay (Faraway So Close)' by U2

The BONZO DOG DOO-DAH BAND *UK, male vocal /*
instrumental group (Singles: 14 Weeks, Albums: 4 Weeks)   pos/wks

6 Nov 68 ●	**I'M THE URBAN SPACEMAN** *Liberty LBF 15144*	5	14
18 Jan 69	**DOUGHNUT IN GRANNY'S GREENHOUSE** *Liberty LBS 83158*	40	1
30 Aug 69	**TADPOLES** *Liberty LBS 83257*	36	1
22 Jun 74	**THE HISTORY OF THE BONZOS** *United Artists UAD 60071*	41	2

Betty BOO *UK, female rapper – Alison*
Clarkson (Singles: 55 Weeks, Albums: 25 Weeks)   pos/wks

12 Aug 89 ●	**HEY DJ – I CAN'T DANCE (TO THAT MUSIC YOU'RE PLAYING) /**		
	SKA TRAIN *Rhythm King LEFT 34* [1]	7	11
19 May 90 ●	**DOIN' THE DO** *Rhythm King LEFT 39*	7	12
11 Aug 90 ●	**WHERE ARE YOU BABY?** *Rhythm King LEFT 43*	3	10
1 Dec 90	**24 HOURS** *Rhythm King LEFT 45*	25	8
8 Aug 92	**LET ME TAKE YOU THERE** *WEA YZ 677*	12	8
3 Oct 92	**I'M ON MY WAY** *WEA YZ 693*	44	3
10 Apr 93	**HANGOVER** *WEA YZ 719*	50	3
22 Sep 90	**BOOMANIA** *Rhythm King LEFTLP 12*	4	24
24 Oct 92	**GRRR! IT'S BETTY BOO** *WEA 4509909082*	62	1

[1] The Beatmasters featuring Betty Boo

The BOO RADLEYS *UK, male vocal / instrumental*
group (Singles: 27 Weeks, Albums: 29 Weeks)   pos/wks

20 Jun 92	**DOES THIS HURT / BOO! FOREVER** *Creation CRE 128*	67	1
23 Oct 93	**WISH I WAS SKINNY** *Creation 169*	75	1
12 Feb 94	**BARNEY (... & ME)** *Creation CRESCD 178*	48	2
11 Jun 94	**LAZARUS** *Creation CRESCD 187*	50	2
11 Mar 95 ●	**WAKE UP BOO!** *Creation CRESCD 191*	9	8
13 May 95	**FIND THE ANSWER WITHIN** *Creation CRESCD 202*	37	3
29 Jul 95	**IT'S LULU** *Creation CRESCD 211*	25	4
7 Oct 95	**FROM THE BENCH AT BELVIDERE** *Creation CRESCD 214*	24	2
17 Aug 96	**WHAT'S IN THE BOX (SEE WATCHA GOT)**		
	Creation CRESCD 220	25	2

		pos/wks
19 Oct 96	**C'MON KIDS** *Creation CRESCD 236*	**18** 2
1 Feb 97	**RIDE THE TIGER** *Creation CRESCD 248X*	**38** 1
17 Oct 98	**FREE HUEY** *Creation CRESCD 299X*	**54** 1
4 Apr 92	**EVERYTHING'S ALRIGHT FOREVER** *Creation CRECD 120*	**55** 1
28 Aug 93	**GIANT STEPS** *Creation CRECD 149*	**17** 4
8 Apr 95 ★	**WAKE UP!** *Creation CRECD 179* ■	**1** 21
21 Sep 96	**C'MON KIDS** *Creation CRECD 194*	**20** 2
31 Oct 98	**KINGSIZE** *Creation CRECD 228*	**62** 1

BOO-YAA T.R.I.B.E.
US, male rap group (Singles: 6 Weeks, Albums: 1 Week) pos/wks

		pos/wks
30 Jun 90	**PSYKO FUNK** *Fourth & Broadway BRW 179*	**43** 3
6 Nov 93	**ANOTHER BODY MURDERED** *Epic 6597942* 1	**26** 3
14 Apr 90	**NEW FUNKY NATION** *Fourth & Broadway BRCD 5448423962*	**74** 1

1 Faith No More and Boo-Yaa T.R.I.B.E.

BOOGIE BOX HIGH (see also Andy G's STARSKY & HUTCH ALL STARS)
UK, male vocal / instrumental group –
leader Andros Georgiou (Singles: 11 Weeks) pos/wks

		pos/wks
4 Jul 87 ●	**JIVE TALKIN'** *Hardback 7BOSS 4*	**7** 11

BOOGIE DOWN PRODUCTIONS
US, male rap / production group (Singles: 2 Weeks, Albums: 9 Weeks) pos/wks

		pos/wks
4 Jun 88	**MY PHILOSOPHY / STOP THE VIOLENCE** *Jive JIVEX 170*	**69** 2
18 Jan 88	**BY ALL MEANS NECESSARY** *Jive HIP 63*	**38** 3
22 Jul 89	**GHETTO MUSIC: THE BLUEPRINT OF HIP HOP** *Jive HIP 80*	**32** 4
25 Aug 90	**EDUTAINMENT** *Jive HIP 100*	**52** 2

BOOGIE PIMPS *Germany, male DJ / production / instrumental*
duo – Mark J. Klak and Mirko Jacob (Singles: 21 Weeks) pos/wks

		pos/wks
17 Jan 04 ●	**SOMEBODY TO LOVE** *Data DATA 61CDS*	**3** 15
8 May 04 ●	**SUNNY** *Data DATA 67CDX*	**10** 6

BOOKER T and the MG's
US, male instrumental group (Singles: 43 Weeks, Albums: 5 Weeks) pos/wks

		pos/wks
11 Dec 68	**SOUL LIMBO** *Stax 102*	**30** 9
7 May 69	**TIME IS TIGHT** *Stax 119*	**4** 18
30 Aug 69	**SOUL CLAP '69** *Stax 127*	**35** 4
15 Dec 79 ●	**GREEN ONIONS** *Atlantic K 10109*	**7** 12
25 Jul 64	**GREEN ONIONS** *London HAK 8182*	**11** 4
11 Jul 70	**MCLEMORE AVENUE** *Stax SXATS 1031*	**70** 1

BOOM! *UK, male / female vocal group (Singles: 5 Weeks)* pos/wks

		pos/wks
27 Jan 01	**FALLING** *London LONCD 458*	**11** 5

Taka BOOM See Joey NEGRO; EYE TO EYE featuring Taka BOOM

BOOM BOOM ROOM
UK, male vocal / instrumental group (Singles: 1 Week) pos/wks

		pos/wks
8 Mar 86	**HERE COMES THE MAN** *Fun After All FUN 101*	**74** 1

BOOMKAT *US, male / female vocal / instrumental /*
production duo – Kellin and Taryn Mann (Singles: 2 Weeks) pos/wks

		pos/wks
31 May 03	**THE WRECKONING** *Dreamworks 4504580*	**37** 2

The BOOMTOWN RATS 298 Top 500
New wave group named after a band in a Woody Guthrie novel. Fronted by charismatic Bob Geldof (b. 5 Oct 1954, Dublin, Ireland), who was later knighted for organising Live Aid and won an Outstanding Contribution to Music award at the 2005 Brits. The Mutt Lange-produced 'Rat Trap' was the first new wave No.1 (Singles: 123 Weeks, Albums: 98 Weeks) pos/wks

		pos/wks
27 Aug 77	**LOOKING AFTER NO.1** *Ensign ENY 4*	**11** 9
19 Nov 77	**MARY OF THE 4TH FORM** *Ensign ENY 9*	**15** 9
15 Apr 78	**SHE'S SO MODERN** *Ensign ENY 13*	**12** 11
17 Jun 78 ●	**LIKE CLOCKWORK** *Ensign ENY 14*	**6** 13
14 Oct 78 ★	**RAT TRAP** *Ensign ENY 16*	**1** 15
21 Jul 79 ★	**I DON'T LIKE MONDAYS** *Ensign ENY 30*	**1** 12
17 Nov 79	**DIAMOND SMILES** *Ensign ENY 33*	**13** 10
26 Jan 80 ●	**SOMEONE'S LOOKING AT YOU** *Ensign ENY 34*	**4** 9
22 Nov 80 ●	**BANANA REPUBLIC** *Mercury BONGO 1*	**3** 11
31 Jan 81	**THE ELEPHANT'S GRAVEYARD (GUILTY)** *Mercury BONGO 2*	**26** 6
12 Dec 81	**NEVER IN A MILLION YEARS** *Mercury MER 87*	**62** 4

		pos/wks
20 Mar 82	**HOUSE ON FIRE** *Mercury MER 91*	**24** 8
18 Feb 84	**TONIGHT** *Mercury MER 154*	**73** 1
19 May 84	**DRAG ME DOWN** *Mercury MER 163*	**50** 3
2 Jul 94	**I DON'T LIKE MONDAYS (re-issue)** *Vertigo VERCD 87*	**38** 2
17 Sep 77	**BOOMTOWN RATS** *Ensign ENVY 1*	**18** 11
8 Jul 78 ●	**A TONIC FOR THE TROOPS** *Ensign ENVY 3*	**8** 44
3 Nov 79 ●	**THE FINE ART OF SURFACING** *Ensign ENROX 11*	**7** 26
24 Jan 81 ●	**MONDO BONGO** *Mercury 6359 042*	**6** 7
3 Apr 82	**V DEEP** *Mercury 6359 082*	**64** 5
9 Jul 94 ●	**LOUDMOUTH – THE BEST OF BOB GELDOF & THE BOOMTOWN RATS** *Vertigo 5222852* 1	**10** 3
8 May 04	**BEST OF THE BOOMTOWN RATS** *Universal TV 9819145*	**44** 2

1 The Boomtown Rats and Bob Geldof

The Clint BOON EXPERIENCE
UK, male / female vocal / instrumental group (Singles: 3 Weeks) pos/wks

		pos/wks
6 Nov 99	**WHITE NO SUGAR** *Artful CDARTFUL 32*	**61** 1
5 Feb 00	**BIGGEST HORIZON** *Artful CDARTFUL 33*	**70** 1
5 Aug 00	**DO WHAT YOU DO (EARWORM SONG)** *Artful CDARTFUL 34*	**63** 1

Daniel BOONE
UK, male vocalist – Peter Lee Stirling (Singles: 25 Weeks) pos/wks

		pos/wks
14 Aug 71	**DADDY DON'T YOU WALK SO FAST** *Penny Farthing PEN 764*	**17** 15
1 Apr 72	**BEAUTIFUL SUNDAY (re)** *Penny Farthing PEN 781*	**21** 10

Debby BOONE *US, female vocalist (Singles: 2 Weeks)* pos/wks

		pos/wks
24 Dec 77	**YOU LIGHT UP MY LIFE** *Warner Bros. / Curb K 17043* ▲	**48** 2

Pat BOONE 171 Top 500
Major rival to Elvis in late 1950s, b. Charles Boone, 1 Jun 1934, Florida, US. This clean-cut vocalist was voted the World's Outstanding Male Singer in the UK in 1957. He was seldom absent from the UK or US charts during the early rock 'n' roll years (Singles: 311 Weeks, Albums: 12 Weeks) pos/wks

		pos/wks
18 Nov 55 ●	**AIN'T THAT A SHAME (re)** *London HLD 8172*	**7** 11
27 Apr 56 ★	**I'LL BE HOME (re)** *London HLD 8253*	**1** 24
27 Jul 56	**LONG TALL SALLY** *London HLD 8291*	**18** 7
17 Aug 56	**I ALMOST LOST MY MIND** *London HLD 8303*	**14** 7
7 Dec 56 ●	**FRIENDLY PERSUASION (THEE I LOVE)** *London HLD 8346*	**3** 21
1 Feb 57	**DON'T FORBID ME** *London HLD 8370*	**2** 16
26 Apr 57	**WHY BABY WHY** *London HLD 8404*	**17** 7
5 Jul 57 ●	**LOVE LETTERS IN THE SAND** *London HLD 8445* ▲	**2** 21
27 Sep 57	**REMEMBER YOU'RE MINE / THERE'S A GOLDMINE IN THE SKY** *London HLD 8479*	**5** 18
6 Dec 57 ●	**APRIL LOVE** *London HLD 8512* ▲	**7** 23
13 Dec 57	**WHITE CHRISTMAS** *London HLD 8520*	**29** 1
4 Apr 58 ●	**A WONDERFUL TIME UP THERE** *London HLD 8574 (A)*	**2** 17
11 Apr 58 ●	**IT'S TOO SOON TO KNOW** *London HLD 8574 (B)*	**7** 12
27 Jun 58 ●	**SUGAR MOON** *London HLD 8640*	**6** 12
29 Aug 58	**IF DREAMS CAME TRUE** *London HLD 8675*	**16** 11
5 Dec 58	**GEE, BUT IT'S LONELY** *London HLD 8739*	**30** 1
16 Jan 59	**I'LL REMEMBER TONIGHT (2re)** *London HLD 8775*	**18** 9
10 Apr 59	**WITH THE WIND AND THE RAIN IN YOUR HAIR** *London HLD 8824*	**21** 3
22 May 59	**FOR A PENNY (re)** *London HLD 8855*	**19** 9
31 Jul 59	**'TWIXT TWELVE AND TWENTY (re)** *London HLD 8910*	**18** 7
23 Jun 60	**WALKING THE FLOOR OVER YOU (re)** *London HLD 9138*	**39** 3
6 Jul 61	**MOODY RIVER** *London HLD 9350* ▲	**18** 10
7 Dec 61 ●	**JOHNNY WILL** *London HLD 9461*	**4** 13
15 Feb 62	**I'LL SEE YOU IN MY DREAMS** *London HLD 9504*	**27** 9
24 May 62	**QUANDO, QUANDO, QUANDO** *London HLD 9543*	**41** 4
12 Jul 62 ●	**SPEEDY GONZALES** *London HLD 9573*	**2** 19
15 Nov 62	**THE MAIN ATTRACTION** *London HLD 9620*	**12** 11
22 Nov 58 ●	**STARDUST** *London HAD 2127*	**10** 1
28 May 60	**HYMNS WE HAVE LOVED** *London HAD 2228*	**12** 2
25 Jun 60	**HYMNS WE LOVE** *London HAD 2092*	**14** 1
24 Apr 76	**PAT BOONE ORIGINALS** *ABC ABSD 301*	**16** 8

'There's a Goldmine in the Sky' was listed only for the week of 27 Sep 1957. It peaked at No.23. 'A Wonderful Time Up There' and 'It's Too Soon to Know' were both on the same single release

BOOOM See Boris DLUGOSCH

BOOT ROOM BOYZ See LIVERPOOL FC

Duke BOOTEE See GRANDMASTER FLASH

Tim BOOTH (see also BOOTH and the BAD ANGEL; JAMES)
UK, male vocalist (Singles: 1 Week) pos/wks

10 Jul 04	**DOWN TO THE SEA** Sanctuary SANXS 279 ....**68** 1

BOOTH and the BAD ANGEL (see also JAMES)
UK / US, male vocal / instrumental duo – Tim Booth and
Angelo Badalamenti (Singles: 4 Weeks, Albums: 2 Weeks) pos/wks

22 Jun 96	**I BELIEVE** Fontana BBCD 1 ....**25** 3
11 Jul 98	**FALL IN LOVE WITH ME** Mercury MERCD 503 ....**57** 1
13 Jul 96	**BOOTH AND THE BAD ANGEL** Fontana 5268522............**35** 2

Ken BOOTHE *Jamaica, male vocalist (Singles: 22 Weeks)* pos/wks

21 Sep 74 ★	**EVERYTHING I OWN** Trojan TR 7920 ....**1** 12
14 Dec 74	**CRYING OVER YOU** Trojan TR 7944 ....**11** 10

BOOTHILL FOOT-TAPPERS
UK, male / female vocal / instrumental group (Singles: 3 Weeks) pos/wks

14 Jul 84	**GET YOUR FEET OUT OF MY SHOES** Go Discs TAP 1 ....**64** 3

BOOTSY'S RUBBER BAND
US, male vocal / instrumental group (Singles: 3 Weeks) pos/wks

8 Jul 78	**BOOTZILLA** Warner Bros. K 17196 ....**43** 3

BOOTZILLA ORCHESTRA See Malcolm McLAREN

BOSS (see also David MORALES; PULSE featuring Antoinette ROBERSON)
US, male producer – David Morales (Singles: 1 Week) pos/wks

27 Aug 94	**CONGO** Cooltempo CDCOOL 296 ....**54** 1

Naila BOSS *UK, female rapper / vocalist (Singles: 16 Weeks)* pos/wks

22 May 04 ●	**IT CAN'T BE RIGHT** 2PSL / Inferno 2PSLCD 04 [1] **8** 7
10 Jul 04	**LA LA LA** LaBoss NBCD 1 ....**65** 1
11 Sep 04 ●	**YOU SHOULD REALLY KNOW** Relentless RELCD 9 [2] **8** 8

[1] 2Play featuring Raghav and Naila Boss [2] Pirates featuring Enya, Shola Ama, Naila Boss & Ishani

BOSTON *US, male vocal / instrumental*
group (Singles: 13 Weeks, Albums: 44 Weeks) pos/wks

29 Jan 77	**MORE THAN A FEELING** Epic EPC 4658 ....**22** 8
7 Oct 78	**DON'T LOOK BACK** Epic EPC 6653 ....**43** 5
5 Feb 77	**BOSTON** Epic EPC 81611 ....**11** 20
9 Sep 78 ●	**DON'T LOOK BACK** Epic EPC 86057 ▲ **9** 10
4 Apr 81	**BOSTON** Epic EPC 32038 ....**58** 2
18 Oct 86	**THIRD STAGE** MCA MCG 6017 ▲ **37** 11
25 Jun 94	**WALK ON** MCA MCD 10973 ....**56** 1

The two eponymous albums are different

Eve BOSWELL *Hungary, female vocalist – Eva Keleti,*
b. 11 May 1924, d. 13 Aug 1998 (Singles: 13 Weeks) pos/wks

30 Dec 55 ●	**PICKIN' A-CHICKEN (2re)** Parlophone R 4082..........................**9** 13

'with Glen Somers and his Orchestra'

Judy BOUCHER
St Vincent, female vocalist (Singles: 23 Weeks, Albums: 1 Week) pos/wks

4 Apr 87 ●	**CAN'T BE WITH YOU TONIGHT** Orbitone OR 721 ....**2** 14
4 Jul 87	**YOU CAUGHT MY EYE** Orbitone OR 722 ....**18** 9
25 Apr 87	**CAN'T BE WITH YOU TONIGHT** Orbitone OLP 024................**95** 1

Peter BOUNCER See SHUT UP AND DANCE

BOUNCING CZECKS
UK, male vocal / instrumental group (Singles: 1 Week) pos/wks

29 Dec 84	**I'M A LITTLE CHRISTMAS CRACKER** RCA 463 ....**72** 1

BOUNTY KILLER
Jamaica, male rapper – Rodney Price (Singles: 1 Week) pos/wks

27 Feb 99	**IT'S A PARTY** Edel 0066135 BLA **65** 1

BOURGEOIS TAGG *US, male vocal / instrumental*
duo – Brent Bourgeois and Larry Tagg (Singles: 6 Weeks) pos/wks

6 Feb 88	**I DON'T MIND AT ALL** Island IS 353 ....**35** 6

BOURGIE BOURGIE
UK, male vocal / instrumental group (Singles: 4 Weeks) pos/wks

3 Mar 84	**BREAKING POINT** MCA BOU 1 ....**48** 4

Toby BOURKE with George MICHAEL
UK, male vocalists (Singles: 4 Weeks) pos/wks

7 Jun 97 ●	**WALTZ AWAY DREAMING** Aegean AECD 01 ....**10** 4

Aletia BOURNE See ANGELHEART

BOW WOW *US, male rapper – Rashad Moss (Singles: 14 Weeks)* pos/wks

14 Apr 01 ●	**BOW WOW (THAT'S MY NAME)** So So Def / Columbia 6709832 [1] **6** 9
27 Nov 04 ●	**BABY IT'S YOU** Mercury 9869056 [2] ....**8** 5+

[1] Lil Bow Wow [2] JoJo featuring Bow Wow

BOW WOW WOW *UK / Burma, female / male vocal /*
instrumental group (Singles: 54 Weeks, Albums: 38 Weeks) pos/wks

26 Jul 80	**C'30, C'60, C'90, GO** EMI 5088 ....**34** 7
6 Dec 80	**YOUR CASSETTE PET** EMI WOW 1 ....**58** 6
28 Mar 81	**W.O.R.K. (N.O. NAH NO NO MY DADDY DON'T)** EMI 5153 ....**62** 3
15 Aug 81	**PRINCE OF DARKNESS** RCA 100 ....**58** 4
7 Nov 81	**CHIHUAHUA** RCA 144 ....**51** 4
30 Jan 82 ●	**GO WILD IN THE COUNTRY** RCA 175 ....**7** 13
1 May 82	**SEE JUNGLE (JUNGLE BOY) / TV SAVAGE** RCA 220 ....**45** 3
5 Jun 82	**I WANT CANDY** RCA 238 ....**9** 8
31 Jul 82	**LOUIS QUATORZE** RCA 263 ....**66** 2
12 Mar 83	**DO YOU WANNA HOLD ME?** RCA 314 ....**47** 4
24 Oct 81	**SEE JUNGLE! SEE JUNGLE! GO JOIN YOUR GANG YEAH! CITY ALL OVER GO APE CRAZY** RCA RCALP 00273000 ....**26** 32
7 Aug 82	**I WANT CANDY** EMI EMC 3416...............................**26** 6

'Your Cassette Pet' listed as 'Louis Quatorze' on 6 Dec 1980 only. Tracks on 'Your Cassette Pet' (available on cassette only): Louis Quatorze / Gold He Said / Umo-Sex-Al Apache / I Want My Baby on Mars / Sexy Eiffel Towers / Giant Sized Baby Thing / Fools Rush In / Radio G String. RCA 263 is disc version of track on EMI WOW 1

BOWA featuring MALA
US, male / female vocal / instrumental duo (Singles: 1 Week) pos/wks

7 Dec 91	**DIFFERENT STORY** Dead Dead Good GOOD 8 ....**64** 1

Dane BOWERS See TRUE STEPPERS; DANE

David BOWIE ⟨ 9 ⟩ Top 500 (see also TIN MACHINE)
Chameleon-like singer / songwriter / entertainer, b. David Jones, 8 Jan 1947, Brixton, London. Noted for his changes of character and fashion, he became Ziggy Stardust, Aladdin Sane and The Thin White Duke. His striking appearance was enhanced by an unfortunate school playground incident that changed the colour of one of his blue eyes to green after being stabbed by a compass. Voted most influential artist in an NME poll in 2000. Among his many accolades and awards, for both recording and songwriting, is the 1996 Brit Award for Outstanding Contribution to British Music. (He is the only act to reject induction into the Rock and Roll Hall of Fame.) No UK act can better the 10 albums he charted with simultaneously in the Top 100 in 1983, and no British male can match his eight No.1 albums. This often sampled performer has starred in movies, acted on Broadway, painted and recorded music with many of the world's leading acts. In 1999 he released the first virtual album and became the first major act to make a full album available for download, released the first enhanced CD single (1995) and became the first singer / songwriter to go to the stock market selling interest in his back catalogue, raising $55m in the process. Bowie, whose very succesful 2004 tour had to be interrupted by a heart operation, has sold more than nine million singles in the UK (Singles: 454 Weeks, Albums: 1005 Weeks) pos/wks

6 Sep 69 ●	**SPACE ODDITY (re)** Philips BF 1801 ....**5** 14
24 Jun 72 ●	**STARMAN** RCA 2199 ....**10** 11
16 Sep 72	**JOHN, I'M ONLY DANCING** RCA 2263 ....**12** 10
9 Dec 72 ●	**THE JEAN GENIE** RCA 2302 ....**2** 13
14 Apr 73	**DRIVE-IN SATURDAY** RCA 2352 ....**3** 10
30 Jun 73 ●	**LIFE ON MARS?** RCA 2316 ....**3** 13
15 Sep 73 ●	**THE LAUGHING GNOME** Deram DM 123 ....**6** 12
20 Oct 73	**SORROW** RCA 2424 ....**3** 15
23 Feb 74 ●	**REBEL REBEL** RCA LPBO 5009 ....**5** 7
20 Apr 74	**ROCK 'N' ROLL SUICIDE** RCA LPBO 5021 ....**22** 7
22 Jun 74	**DIAMOND DOGS** RCA APBO 0293 ....**21** 6

Date	Title	pos	wks
28 Sep 74 ●	KNOCK ON WOOD *RCA 2466*	10	6
1 Mar 75	YOUNG AMERICANS *RCA 2523*	18	7
2 Aug 75	FAME *RCA 2579* ▲	17	8
11 Oct 75 ★	SPACE ODDITY (re-issue) *RCA 2593*	1	10
29 Nov 75 ●	GOLDEN YEARS *RCA 2640*	8	10
22 May 76	TVC 15 *RCA 2682*	33	4
19 Feb 77 ●	SOUND AND VISION *RCA PB 0905*	3	11
15 Oct 77	HEROES *RCA PB 1121*	24	8
21 Jan 78	BEAUTY AND THE BEAST *RCA PB 1190*	39	3
2 Dec 78	BREAKING GLASS (EP) *RCA BOW 1*	54	7
5 May 79 ●	BOYS KEEP SWINGING *RCA BOW 2*	7	10
21 Jul 79	D.J. *RCA BOW 3*	29	5
15 Dec 79	JOHN I'M ONLY DANCING (AGAIN) (1975) / JOHN I'M ONLY DANCING (1972) *RCA BOW 4*	12	8
1 Mar 80	ALABAMA SONG *RCA BOW 5*	23	5
16 Aug 80 ★	ASHES TO ASHES *RCA BOW 6*	1	10
1 Nov 80 ●	FASHION *RCA BOW 7*	5	12
10 Jan 81	SCARY MONSTERS (AND SUPER CREEPS) *RCA BOW 8*	20	6
28 Mar 81	UP THE HILL BACKWARDS *RCA BOW 9*	32	6
14 Nov 81 ★	UNDER PRESSURE *EMI 5250* [1]	1	11
28 Nov 81	WILD IS THE WIND *RCA BOW 10*	24	10
6 Mar 82	BAAL (EP) *RCA BOW 11*	29	5
10 Apr 82	CAT PEOPLE (PUTTING OUT FIRE) *MCA 770*	26	6
27 Nov 82 ●	PEACE ON EARTH – LITTLE DRUMMER BOY *RCA BOW 12* [2]	3	8
26 Mar 83 ★	LET'S DANCE *EMI America EA 152* ▲	1	14
11 Jun 83 ●	CHINA GIRL *EMI America EA 157*	2	8
24 Sep 83 ●	MODERN LOVE *EMI America EA 158*	2	8
5 Nov 83	WHITE LIGHT, WHITE HEAT *RCA 372*	46	3
22 Sep 84 ●	BLUE JEAN *EMI America EA 181*	6	8
8 Dec 84	TONIGHT *EMI America EA 187*	53	4
9 Feb 85	THIS IS NOT AMERICA (THE THEME FROM 'THE FALCON AND THE SNOWMAN') *EMI America EA 190* [3]	14	7
8 Jun 85	LOVING THE ALIEN (re) *EMI America EA 195*	19	7
7 Sep 85 ★	DANCING IN THE STREET *EMI America EA 204* [4] ■	1	12
15 Mar 86 ●	ABSOLUTE BEGINNERS *Virgin VS 838*	2	9
21 Jun 86	UNDERGROUND *EMI America EA 216*	21	6
8 Nov 86	WHEN THE WIND BLOWS *Virgin VS 906*	44	6
4 Apr 87	DAY-IN DAY-OUT *EMI America EA 230*	17	6
27 Jun 87	TIME WILL CRAWL *EMI America EA 237*	33	4
29 Aug 87	NEVER LET ME DOWN *EMI America EA 239*	34	4
7 Apr 90	FAME (re-mix) *EMI-USA FAME 90*	28	4
22 Aug 92	REAL COOL WORLD *Warner Bros. W 0127*	53	1
27 Mar 93 ●	JUMP THEY SAY *Arista 74321139422*	9	6
12 Jun 93	BLACK TIE WHITE NOISE *Arista 74321148682* [5]	36	2
23 Oct 93	MIRACLE GOODNIGHT *Arista 74321162262*	40	2
4 Dec 93	BUDDHA OF SUBURBIA *Arista 74321177052* [6]	35	3
23 Sep 95	THE HEART'S FILTHY LESSON *RCA 74321307032*	35	2
2 Dec 95	STRANGERS WHEN WE MEET / THE MAN WHO SOLD THE WORLD (LIVE) *RCA 74321329402*	39	2
2 Mar 96	HALLO SPACEBOY *RCA 74321353842*	12	4
8 Feb 97	LITTLE WONDER *RCA 74321452072*	14	4
26 Apr 97	DEAD MAN WALKING *RCA 74321475852*	32	2
30 Aug 97	SEVEN YEARS IN TIBET *RCA 74321512542*	61	1
21 Feb 98	I CAN'T READ *Velvet ZYX 87578*	73	1
2 Oct 99	THURSDAY'S CHILD *Virgin VSCDT 1753*	16	2
18 Dec 99	UNDER PRESSURE (re-mix) *Parlophone CDQUEEN 28* [1]	14	7
5 Feb 00	SURVIVE *Virgin VSCDT 1767*	28	2
29 Jul 00	SEVEN *Virgin VSCDT 1776*	32	2
11 May 02	LOVING THE ALIEN *Positiva CDTIV 172* [7]	41	2
28 Sep 02	EVERYONE SAYS "HI" *Columbia 6731342*	20	3
12 Jul 03	JUST FOR ONE DAY (HEROES) *Virgin DINST 263* [8]	73	1
26 Jun 04	REBEL NEVER GETS OLD *Columbia 6750406*	47	2
1 Jul 72 ●	THE RISE AND FALL OF ZIGGY STARDUST AND THE SPIDERS FROM MARS *RCA Victor SF 8287*	5	106
23 Sep 72 ●	HUNKY DORY *RCA Victor SF 8244*	3	69
25 Nov 72 ●	THE MAN WHO SOLD THE WORLD *RCA Victor LSP 4816*	26	22
25 Nov 72	SPACE ODDITY *RCA Victor LSP 4813*	17	37
5 May 73 ★	ALADDIN SANE *RCA Victor RS 1001* ■	1	48
3 Nov 73 ★	PINUPS *RCA Victor RS 1003* ■	1	21
8 Jun 74 ●	DIAMOND DOGS *RCA Victor APL1 0576* ■	1	17
16 Nov 74 ●	DAVID LIVE *RCA Victor APL 2 0771*	2	12
5 Apr 75 ●	YOUNG AMERICANS *RCA Victor RS 1006*	2	12
7 Feb 76 ●	STATION TO STATION *RCA Victor APL1 1327*	5	16
12 Jun 76	CHANGESONEBOWIE *RCA Victor RS 1055*	2	28
29 Jan 77 ●	LOW *RCA Victor PL 12030*	2	18
29 Oct 77 ●	HEROES *RCA Victor PL 12522*	3	18
14 Oct 78 ●	STAGE *RCA Victor PL 02913*	5	10
9 Jun 79 ●	LODGER *RCA Victor BOW LP 1*	4	17

Date	Title	pos	wks
27 Sep 80 ★	SCARY MONSTERS AND SUPER CREEPS *RCA Victor BOW LP 2* ■	1	32
10 Jan 81 ●	THE VERY BEST OF DAVID BOWIE *K-Tel NE 1111*	3	20
17 Jan 81	HUNKY DORY (re-issue) *RCA International INTS 5064*	32	51
31 Jan 81	THE RISE AND FALL OF ZIGGY STARDUST AND THE SPIDERS FROM MARS (re-issue) *RCA International INTS 5063*	33	62
28 Nov 81	CHANGESTWOBOWIE *RCA BOW LP 3*	24	17
6 Mar 82	ALADDIN SANE (re-issue) *RCA International INTS 5067*	49	24
14 Jan 83	RARE *RCA PL 45406*	34	11
23 Apr 83 ★	LET'S DANCE *EMI America AML 3029* ■	1	56
30 Apr 83	PIN-UPS (re-issue) *RCA International INTS 5236*	57	15
30 Apr 83	THE MAN WHO SOLD THE WORLD (re-issue) *RCA International INTS 5237*	64	8
14 May 83	DIAMOND DOGS (re-issue) *RCA International INTS 5068*	60	14
11 Jun 83	LOW (re-issue) *RCA International INTS 5065*	75	8
11 Jun 83	HEROES (re-issue) *RCA International INTS 5066*	85	5
20 Aug 83	GOLDEN YEARS *RCA BOWLP 4*	33	5
5 Nov 83	ZIGGY STARDUST – THE MOTION PICTURE *RCA PL 84862*	17	6
28 Apr 84	FAME AND FASHION (BOWIE'S ALL TIME GREATEST HITS) *RCA PL 84919*	40	6
19 May 84	LOVE YOU TILL TUESDAY *Deram BOWIE 1*	53	4
6 Oct 84 ★	TONIGHT *EMI America DB 1* ■	1	19
2 May 87 ●	NEVER LET ME DOWN *EMI America AMLS 3117*	6	16
24 Mar 90 ★	CHANGESBOWIE *EMI DBTV 1*	1	29
14 Apr 90	HUNKY DORY (2nd re-issue) *EMI EMC 3572*	39	5
14 Apr 90	THE MAN WHO SOLD THE WORLD (2nd re-issue) *EMI EMC 3573*	64	1
14 Apr 90	SPACE ODDITY (re-issue) *EMI EMC 3571*	39	2
23 Jun 90	THE RISE AND FALL OF ZIGGY STARDUST AND THE SPIDERS FROM MARS (2nd re-issue) *EMI EMC 3577*	25	4
28 Jul 90	PIN-UPS (2nd re-issue) *EMI EMC 3580*	52	1
28 Jul 90	ALADDIN SANE (2nd re-issue) *EMI EMC 3579*	43	1
27 Oct 90	DIAMOND DOGS (2nd re-issue) *EMI EMC 3584*	67	3
4 May 91	STATION TO STATION (re-issue) *EMI EMD 1020*	54	1
4 May 91	YOUNG AMERICANS (re-issue) *EMI EMD 1021*	57	1
7 Sep 91	LOW (2nd re-issue) *EMI EMD 1027*	64	1
17 Apr 93 ★	BLACK TIE WHITE NOISE *Arista 74321136972* ■	1	11
20 Nov 93 ●	THE SINGLES COLLECTION *EMI CDEM 1512*	9	16
7 May 94	SANTA MONICA '72 *Trident GY 002*	74	1
7 Oct 95 ●	OUTSIDE *RCA 74321310662*	8	4
15 Feb 97 ●	EART HL I NG *RCA 74321449042*	6	4
8 Nov 97	THE BEST OF DAVID BOWIE 1969/1974 *EMI 8218492*	13	17
2 May 98	THE BEST OF DAVID BOWIE 1974/1979 *EMI 4943002*	39	2
16 Oct 99 ●	HOURS ... *Virgin CDV 2900*	5	5
7 Oct 00 ●	BOWIE AT THE BEEB – THE BEST OF THE BBC RADIO SESSIONS 68-72 *EMI 5289582*	7	4
22 Jun 02 ●	HEATHEN *Columbia 5082222*	5	18
20 Jul 02	THE RISE AND FALL OF ZIGGY STARDUST AND THE SPIDERS FROM MARS (3rd re-issue) *EMI 5398262*	36	2
16 Nov 02	BEST OF BOWIE *EMI 5398212*	11	36
27 Sep 03 ●	REALITY *Columbia 5125552*	3	4
9 Oct 04	THE RISE AND FALL OF ZIGGY STARDUST AND THE SPIDERS FROM MARS (4th re-issue) *EMI CDP 7944002*	17	2

[1] Queen and David Bowie [2] David Bowie and Bing Crosby [3] David Bowie and the Pat Metheny Group [4] David Bowie and Mick Jagger [5] David Bowie featuring Al B Sure! [6] David Bowie featuring Lenny Kravitz [7] Scumfrog vs Bowie [8] David Guetta vs Bowie

The 1975 reissue of 1969's Space Oddity was part of a three track single which also included 'Changes' and 'Velvet Goldmine'. Tracks on Breaking Glass (EP): Breaking Glass / Art Decade / Ziggy Stardust. All three versions of 'John I'm Only Dancing' are different. Tracks on Baal (EP): Baal's Hymn / Remembering Marie A. / Ballad of the Adventurers / The Drowned Girl / Dirty Song

BOWLING FOR SOUP *US, male vocal / instrumental group (Singles: 12 Weeks, Albums: 5 Weeks)*   pos/wks

Date	Title	pos	wks
17 Aug 02 ●	GIRL ALL THE BAD GUYS WANT *Music for Nations CDKUT 194*	8	8
16 Nov 02	EMILY *Music for Nations CDKUT 198*	67	1
6 Sep 03	PUNK ROCK 101 *Music for Nations CDKUT 203*	43	1
16 Oct 04	1985 *Jive 82876647472*	35	2
7 Sep 02	DRUNK ENOUGH TO DANCE *Music for Nations JIV 418192*	14	4
25 Sep 04	A HANGOVER YOU DON'T DESERVE *Jive 82876643652*	64	1

George BOWYER *UK, male vocalist (Singles: 2 Weeks)*   pos/wks

Date	Title	pos	wks
22 Aug 98	GUARDIANS OF THE LAND *Boys BYSCD 01*	33	2

BOX CAR RACER *US, male vocal / instrumental group (Singles: 1 Week, Albums: 3 Weeks)* pos/wks

6 Jul 02	I FEEL SO *MCA MCSTD 40290*	.41	1
8 Jun 02	BOX CAR RACER *MCA 1129472*	.27	3

The BOX TOPS *US, male vocal / instrumental group (Singles: 33 Weeks)* pos/wks

13 Sep 67 ●	THE LETTER *Stateside SS 2044* ▲	.5	12
20 Mar 68	CRY LIKE A BABY *Bell 1001*	.15	12
23 Aug 69	SOUL DEEP *Bell 1068*	.22	9

BOXCAR WILLIE *US, male vocalist – Lecil Martin, b. 1 Sep 1981, d. 12 Apr 1999 (Albums: 12 Weeks)* pos/wks

31 May 80 ●	KING OF THE ROAD *Warwick WW 5084*	.5	12

BOXER REBELLION *UK, male vocal / instrumental group (Singles: 2 Weeks)* pos/wks

10 Apr 04	IN PURSUIT *Poptones MC 5088SCD*	.57	1
9 Oct 04	CODE RED *Vertigo 9867001*	.61	1

BOY GEORGE *(see also CULTURE CLUB; JESUS LOVES YOU) UK, male vocalist – George O'Dowd (Singles: 46 Weeks, Albums: 15 Weeks)* pos/wks

7 Mar 87 ★	EVERYTHING I OWN *Virgin BOY 100*	.1	9
6 Jun 87	KEEP ME IN MIND *Virgin BOY 101*	.29	4
18 Jul 87	SOLD *Virgin BOY 102*	.24	5
21 Nov 87	TO BE REBORN *Virgin BOY 103*	.13	7
5 Mar 88	LIVE MY LIFE *Virgin BOY 105*	.62	2
18 Jun 88	NO CLAUSE 28 *Virgin BOY 106*	.57	3
8 Oct 88	DON'T CRY *Virgin BOY 107*	.60	2
4 Mar 89	DON'T TAKE MY MIND ON A TRIP *Virgin BOY 108*	.68	2
19 Sep 92	THE CRYING GAME *Spaghetti CIAO 6*	.22	4
12 Jun 93	MORE THAN LIKELY *Gee Street GESCD 49* [1]	.40	2
1 Apr 95	FUNTIME *Virgin VSCDG 1538*	.45	2
1 Jul 95	IL ADORE *Virgin VSCDX 1543*	.50	2
21 Oct 95	SAME THING IN REVERSE *Virgin VSCDT 1561*	.56	1
27 Jun 87	SOLD *Virgin V 2430*	.29	6
13 Apr 91	THE MARTYR MANTRAS *More Protein CUMLP 1* [1]	.60	1
2 Oct 93	AT WORST ... THE BEST OF BOY GEORGE AND CULTURE CLUB *Virgin VTCD 19* [2]	.24	5
12 Mar 94	THE DEVIL IN SISTER GEORGE *Virgin VSCDG 1490*	.26	2
3 Jun 95	CHEAPNESS AND BEAUTY *Virgin CDV 2780*	.44	1

[1] PM Dawn featuring Boy George [1] Jesus Loves You [2] Boy George and Culture Club

BOY MEETS GIRL *US, male / female vocal duo – Shannon Rubicam and George Merrill (Singles: 13 Weeks, Albums: 1 Week)* pos/wks

3 Dec 88 ●	WAITING FOR A STAR TO FALL *RCA PB 49519*	.9	13
4 Feb 89	REEL LIFE *RCA PL 88414*	.74	1

BOY WUNDA *See PROGRESS presents the BOY WUNDA*

MAX BOYCE *UK, male comedian / vocalist (Albums: 105 Weeks)* pos/wks

5 Jul 75	LIVE AT TREORCHY *One Up OU 2033*	.21	32
1 Nov 75 ★	WE ALL HAD DOCTORS' PAPERS *EMI MB 101*	.1	17
20 Nov 76 ●	THE INCREDIBLE PLAN *EMI MB 102*	.9	12
7 Jan 78	THE ROAD AND THE MILES *EMI MB 103*	.50	3
11 Mar 78	LIVE AT TREORCHY (re-issue) *One Up OU 54043*	.42	6
27 May 78 ●	I KNOW COS I WAS THERE *EMI MAX 1001*	.6	14
13 Oct 79	NOT THAT I'M BIASED *EMI MAX 1002*	.27	13
15 Nov 80	ME AND BILLY WILLIAMS *EMI MAX 1003*	.37	8

Jimmy BOYD *US, male vocalist (Singles: 22 Weeks)* pos/wks

8 May 53 ●	TELL ME A STORY (re) *Philips PB 126* [1]	.5	16
27 Nov 53 ●	I SAW MOMMY KISSING SANTA CLAUS *Columbia DB 3365* ▲	.3	6

[1] Jimmy Boyd – Frankie Laine

Jacqueline BOYER *France, female vocalist (Singles: 2 Weeks)* pos/wks

28 Apr 60	TOM PILLIBI *Columbia DB 4452*	.33	2

The BOYS *UK, male vocal group (Albums: 1 Week)* pos/wks

1 Oct 77	THE BOYS *NEMS NEL 6001*	.50	1

BOYS TOWN GANG *US, male / female vocal group (Singles: 20 Weeks)* pos/wks

22 Aug 81	AIN'T NO MOUNTAIN HIGH ENOUGH – REMEMBER ME (MEDLEY) *WEA DICK 1*	.46	6
31 Jul 82 ●	CAN'T TAKE MY EYES OFF YOU *ERC 101*	.4	11
9 Oct 82	SIGNED SEALED DELIVERED (I'M YOURS) *ERC 102*	.50	3

BOYSTEROUS *UK, male vocal group (Singles: 1 Week)* pos/wks

22 Nov 03	UP & DOWN *Square Biz SBR 4*	.53	1

BOYZ *See HEAVY D and the BOYZ*

BOYZ II MEN *US, male vocal quartet – brothers Nathan and Wanya Morris, Shawn Stockman, Michael McCary (Singles: 81 Weeks, Albums: 46 Weeks)* pos/wks

5 Sep 92 ★	END OF THE ROAD *Motown TMG 1411* ▲	.1	21
19 Dec 92	MOTOWNPHILLY *Motown TMG 1402*	.23	6
27 Feb 93	IN THE STILL OF THE NITE (I'LL REMEMBER) *Motown TMGCD 1415*	.27	4
3 Sep 94 ●	I'LL MAKE LOVE TO YOU (re) *Motown TMGCD 1431* ▲	.5	15
26 Nov 94	ON BENDED KNEE *Motown TMGCD 1433* ▲	.20	3
22 Apr 95	THANK YOU *Motown TMGCD 1438*	.26	3
8 Jul 95	WATER RUNS DRY *Motown TMGCD 1443*	.24	3
9 Dec 95 ●	ONE SWEET DAY *Columbia 6626035* [1] ▲	.6	11
20 Jan 96	HEY LOVER *Def Jam DEFCD 14* [2]	.17	4
20 Sep 97 ●	4 SEASONS OF LONELINESS *Motown 8606992* ▲	.10	6
6 Dec 97	A SONG FOR MAMA *Motown 8607372*	.34	2
25 Jul 98	CAN'T LET HER GO *Motown 8607952*	.23	3
31 Oct 92 ●	COOLEYHIGHHARMONY *Motown 5300892*	.7	18
24 Sep 94	II *Motown 5304312* ▲	.17	5
4 Oct 97	EVOLUTION *Motown 5308222*	.12	5
23 Sep 00	NATHAN MICHAEL SHAWN WANYA *Universal 1592812*	.54	1
16 Feb 02 ●	LEGACY – THE GREATEST HITS COLLECTION *UMTV 168882*	.2	15
3 Aug 02	FULL CIRCLE *Arista 7822147412*	.56	2

[1] Mariah Carey and Boyz II Men [2] LL Cool J featuring Boyz II Men

BOYZONE `110` `Top 500` *(see also KEITH 'n' SHANE) Irish boy band vocal quintet who became international teen idols and the UK's best-selling boyband with total single sales of 6,435,711: Ronan Keating, Stephen Gately, Mikey Graham, Keith Duffy, Shane Lynch. They achieved the best ever start to a UK singles career with 16 consecutive Top 5 singles. Best-selling single: 'No Matter What' 1,074,192 (Singles: 213 Weeks, Albums: 203 Weeks)* pos/wks

10 Dec 94 ●	LOVE ME FOR A REASON *Polydor 8512802*	.2	13
29 Apr 95 ●	KEY TO MY LIFE *Polydor PZCD 342*	.3	8
12 Aug 95 ●	SO GOOD *Polydor 5797732*	.3	6
25 Nov 95 ●	FATHER AND SON *Polydor 5775762*	.2	16
9 Mar 96 ●	COMING HOME NOW *Polydor 5775702*	.4	9
19 Oct 96 ★	WORDS *Polydor 5755372* ■	.1	14
14 Dec 96 ★	A DIFFERENT BEAT (2re) *Polydor 5732052* ■	.1	15
22 Mar 97 ●	ISN'T IT A WONDER (re) *Polydor 5735472*	.2	14
2 Aug 97 ●	PICTURE OF YOU *Polydor 5713112*	.2	18
6 Dec 97 ●	BABY CAN I HOLD YOU / SHOOTING STAR *Polydor 5691672*	.2	14
2 May 98 ★	ALL THAT I NEED (re) *Polydor 5698732* ■	.1	14
15 Aug 98 ★	NO MATTER WHAT *Polydor 5675672* ◆ ■	.1	15
5 Dec 98 ●	I LOVE THE WAY YOU LOVE ME *Polydor 5631992*	.2	13
13 Mar 99 ★	WHEN THE GOING GETS TOUGH *Polydor 5699132* ■	.1	16
22 May 99 ★	YOU NEEDED ME (re) *Polydor 5639332* ■	.1	15
4 Dec 99 ●	EVERY DAY I LOVE YOU *Polydor 5615802*	.3	13
2 Sep 95 ★	SAID AND DONE *Polydor 5278012* ■	.1	58
9 Nov 96 ★	A DIFFERENT BEAT *Polydor 5337422* ■	.1	24
6 Jun 98 ★	WHERE WE BELONG *Polydor 5573982* ■	.1	55
12 Jun 99 ★	... BY REQUEST *Polydor 5475992* ■	.1	57
29 Mar 03 ●	BALLADS – THE LOVE SONG COLLECTION *Universal TV 0760742*	.6	9

BRAD *US, male vocal / instrumental group (Singles: 1 Week, Albums: 1 Week)* pos/wks

26 Jun 93	20TH CENTURY *Epic 6592482*	.64	1
15 May 93	SHAME *Epic 4735962*	.72	1

Scott BRADLEY *UK, male vocalist (Singles: 1 Week)* pos/wks

15 Oct 94	ZOOM *Hidden Agenda HIDDCD 1*	.61	1

Paul BRADY *UK, male vocalist (Singles: 1 Week, Albums: 1 Week)* pos/wks

13 Jan 96	THE WORLD IS WHAT YOU MAKE IT *Mercury PBCD 5*	.67	1
6 Apr 91	TRICK OR TREAT *Fontana 8484541*	.62	1

Billy BRAGG
UK, male vocalist / instrumentalist – guitar (Singles: 53 Weeks, Albums: 89 Weeks)

		pos/wks
16 Mar 85	BETWEEN THE WARS (EP) *Go Discs AGOEP 1*	15 6
28 Dec 85	DAYS LIKE THESE *Go Discs GOD 8*	43 5
28 Jun 86	LEVI STUBBS' TEARS *Go Discs GOD 12*	29 6
15 Nov 86	GREETINGS TO THE NEW BRUNETTE *Go Discs GOD 15* [1]	58 7
14 May 88 ★	SHE'S LEAVING HOME *Childline CHILD 1* [2]	1 11
10 Sep 88	WAITING FOR THE GREAT LEAP FORWARDS	
	Go Discs GOD 23	52 3
8 Jul 89	WON'T TALK ABOUT IT *Go Beat GOD 33* [3]	29 6
6 Jul 91	SEXUALITY *Go Discs GOD 56*	27 5
7 Sep 91	YOU WOKE UP MY NEIGHBOURHOOD *Go Discs GOD 60*	54 2
29 Feb 92	ACCIDENT WAITING TO HAPPEN (EP) *Go Discs GOD 67*	33 3
31 Aug 96	UPFIELD *Cooking Vinyl FRYCD 051*	46 1
17 May 97	THE BOY DONE GOOD *Cooking Vinyl FRYCD 064*	55 1
1 Jun 02	TAKE DOWN THE UNION JACK *Cooking Vinyl FRYCD 131* [4]	22 2
21 Jan 84	LIFE'S A RIOT WITH SPY VS SPY *Utility UTIL 1*	30 30
20 Oct 84	BREWING UP WITH BILLY BRAGG *Go Discs AGOLP 4*	16 21
4 Oct 86 ●	TALKING WITH THE TAXMAN ABOUT POETRY	
	Go Discs AGOLP 6	8 8
13 Jun 87	BACK TO BASICS *Go Discs AGOLP 8*	37 4
1 Oct 88	WORKERS PLAYTIME *Go Discs AGOLP 15*	17 4
12 May 90	THE INTERNATIONALE *Utility UTIL 11*	34 4
28 Sep 91 ●	DON'T TRY THIS AT HOME *Go Discs 8282791*	8 6
21 Sep 96	WILLIAM BLOKE *Cooking Vinyl COOKCD 100*	16 1
28 Jun 97	BLOKE ON BLOKE *Cooking Vinyl COOKCD 127*	72 1
11 Jul 98	MERMAID AVENUE *Elektra 7559622042* [1]	34 2
11 Sep 99	REACHING TO THE CONVERTED *Cooking Vinyl COOKCD 186*	41 2
10 Jun 00	MERMAID AVENUE – VOL. 2 *Elektra 7559625222* [1]	61 1
16 Mar 02	ENGLAND HALF ENGLISH *Cooking Vinyl COOKCD 222* [2]	51 2
18 Oct 03	MUST I PAINT YOU A PICTURE *Cooking Vinyl COOKCD 266X*	49 1

[1] Billy Bragg with Johnny Marr and Kirsty MacColl [2] Billy Bragg with Cara Tivey [3] Norman Cook featuring Billy Bragg [4] Billy Bragg and the Blokes [1] Billy Bragg and Wilco [2] Billy Bragg and the Blokes

Tracks on Between the Wars (EP): Between the Wars / Which Side Are You On / World Turned Upside Down / It Says Here. Tracks on Accident Waiting to Happen (EP): Accident Waiting to Happen / Revolution / Sulk / The Warmest Room. 'She's Leaving Home' was listed with the flip side 'With a Little Help from My Friends' by Wet Wet Wet. 'Won't Talk About It' was listed with the flip side 'Blame It on the Bassline' by Norman Cook featuring MC Wildski.

The BRAIDS
US, female vocal duo – Zoe Ellis and Caitlin Cornwell (Singles: 3 Weeks) pos/wks

2 Nov 96	BOHEMIAN RHAPSODY *Atlantic A 5640CD*	21 3

BRAIN BASHERS
UK, male / female DJ / production duo (Singles: 1 Week)

		pos/wks
1 Jul 00	DO IT NOW *Tidy Trax TIDY 137CD*	64 1

BRAINBUG
Italy, male producer – Alberto Bertapelle (Singles: 8 Weeks)

		pos/wks
3 May 97	NIGHTMARE *Positiva CDTIV 76*	11 5
22 Nov 97	BENEDICTUS / NIGHTMARE (re-mix) *Positiva CDTIV 86*	24 2
4 Sep 04	NIGHTMARE (2nd re-mix) *Positiva 12TIV 200*	63 1

BRAINCHILD
Germany, male producer – Matthias Hoffmann (Singles: 2 Weeks)

		pos/wks
30 Oct 99	SYMMETRY C *Multiply CDMULTY 55*	31 2

Wilfrid BRAMBELL and Harry H. CORBETT
UK, male vocal / TV comedy duo – Wilfrid Brambell, b. 22 Mar 1912, d 18 Jan 1985, and Harry Corbett, b. 28 Feb 1925 d. 21 Mar 1982 (Singles: 12 Weeks, Albums: 34 Weeks)

		pos/wks
28 Nov 63	STEPTOE AND SON AT BUCKINGHAM PALACE	
	(PARTS 1 & 2) *Pye 7N 15588*	25 12
23 Mar 63 ●	STEPTOE AND SON *Pye NPL 18081*	4 28
11 Jan 64	STEPTOE AND SON *Pye GGL 0217*	14 5
14 Mar 64	MORE JUNK *Pye NPL 18090*	19 1

The two 'Steptoe and Son' albums are different

Bekka BRAMLETT See Joe COCKER

BRAN VAN 3000
Canada, male / female vocal / instrumental group (Singles: 15 Weeks)

		pos/wks
6 Jun 98	DRINKING IN L.A. *Capitol CDCL 802*	34 2
21 Aug 99 ●	DRINKING IN L.A. (re-issue) *Capitol CDCL 811*	3 11
16 Jun 01	ASTOUNDED *Virgin VUSCD 194* [1]	40 2

[1] Bran Van 3000 featuring Curtis Mayfield

BRANCACCIO & AISHER
UK, male production duo – Luke Brancaccio and Bruce Aisher (Singles: 2 Weeks)

		pos/wks
16 Mar 02	IT'S GONNA BE ... (A LOVELY DAY) *Credence CDCRED 017*	40 2

Michelle BRANCH
US, female vocalist (Singles: 18 Weeks, Albums: 5 Weeks)

		pos/wks
13 Apr 02	EVERYWHERE *Maverick W 577CDX*	18 6
3 Aug 02	ALL YOU WANTED *Maverick W 585CDX*	33 2
23 Nov 02	THE GAME OF LOVE *Arista 74321959442* [1]	16 8
12 Jul 03	ARE YOU HAPPY NOW? *Maverick W 613CD*	31 2
27 Apr 02	THE SPIRIT ROOM *Maverick 9362480972*	54 2
19 Jul 03	HOTEL PAPER *Maverick / Warner Bros. MAV 484262*	35 3

[1] Santana featuring Michelle Branch

BRAND NEW
US, male vocal / instrumental group (Singles: 3 Weeks)

		pos/wks
14 Feb 04	SIC TRANSIT GLORIA GLORY FADES	
	Sore Point SORE 011CDS	37 2
29 May 04	THE QUIET THINGS THAT NO ONE EVER KNOWS	
	Sore Point SORE 014CDS	39 1

The BRAND NEW HEAVIES   `401` `Top 500`
Sophisticated funk / 'acid jazz' band, formed 1985 in London, UK. Remaining original members Simon Bartholomew (g), Andrew Levy (b) and Jan Kincaid (d/v) had vocal assistance on their hits from US females N'dea Davenport (1991-95), Siedah Garrett (1997-98) and Carleen Anderson (1999-2000) (Singles: 69 Weeks, Albums: 103 Weeks)

		pos/wks
5 Oct 91	NEVER STOP *ffrr F 165*	43 3
15 Feb 92	DREAM COME TRUE *ffrr F 180*	24 4
18 Apr 92	ULTIMATE TRUNK FUNK (EP) *ffrr F 185*	19 6
1 Aug 92	DON'T LET IT GO TO YOUR HEAD *ffrr BNH 1*	24 4
19 Dec 92	STAY THIS WAY *ffrr BNH 2*	40 5
26 Mar 94	DREAM ON DREAMER *ffrr BNHCD 3*	15 4
11 Jun 94	BACK TO LOVE *ffrr BNHCD 4*	23 4
13 Aug 94	MIDNIGHT AT THE OASIS *ffrr BNHCD 5*	13 6
5 Nov 94	SPEND SOME TIME *ffrr BNHCD 6*	26 4
11 Mar 95	CLOSE TO YOU *ffrr BNHCD 7*	38 3
12 Apr 97	SOMETIMES *ffrr BNHCD 8*	11 5
28 Jun 97	YOU ARE THE UNIVERSE *ffrr GNHCD 9*	21 4
18 Oct 97 ●	YOU'VE GOT A FRIEND *London BNHCD 10*	9 8
10 Jan 98	SHELTER *London BNHCD 11*	31 4
11 Sep 99	SATURDAY NITE *ffrr BNHCD12*	35 2
29 Jan 00	APPARENTLY NOTHING *ffrr BNHCD 13*	32 2
23 Oct 04	BOOGIE *Onetwo TBNHCDS 001* [1]	66 1
14 Mar 92	BRAND NEW HEAVIES *London 8283002*	25 16
5 Sep 92	HEAVY RHYME EXPERIENCE: VOL.1 *Acid Jazz 8283352*	38 2
16 Apr 94 ●	BROTHER SISTER *ffrr 8284902*	4 48
12 Nov 94	ORIGINAL FLAVA *Acid Jazz JAZIDCD 114*	64 1
3 May 97 ●	SHELTER *ffrr 8288872*	5 33
25 Sep 99	TRUNK FUNK – THE BEST OF THE BRAND NEW HEAVIES	
	ffrr 3984291642	13 3

[1] The Brand New Heavies featuring Nicole Russo

The first 10 hits are credited 'featuring N'Dea Davenport' on either the sleeve or the label. Tracks on Ultimate Trunk Funk (EP): Never Stop / Stay This Way / Mr Tanaka. BNH 2 is a re-mixed version of the track on the Ultimate Trunk Funk EP. Nicole Russo took over as lead vocalist in 2004

BRAND X
UK, male vocal / instrumental group (Albums: 6 Weeks)

		pos/wks
21 May 77	MOROCCAN ROLL *Charisma CAS 1126*	37 5
11 Sep 82	IS THERE ANYTHING ABOUT? *CBS 85967*	93 1

Johnny BRANDON with the PHANTOMS
UK, male vocalist and male instrumental group (Singles: 12 Weeks) pos/wks

		pos/wks
11 Mar 55 ●	TOMORROW (re) *Polygon P 1131* [1]	8 8
1 Jul 55	DON'T WORRY *Polygon P 1163*	18 4

[1] Johnny Brandon with the Phantoms and the Norman Warren Music

BRANDY 479 Top 500

Grammy-winning vocalist / actor who had her first hit aged 15, b. Brandy Norwood, 2 Nov 1979, McComb, Mississippi. 'The Boy Is Mine' spent a record (for a duo) 13 weeks at No.1 in the US (Singles: 101 Weeks, Albums: 50 Weeks)

		pos/wks
10 Dec 94	I WANNA BE DOWN *Atlantic A 7217CD*	44 3
3 Jun 95	I WANNA BE DOWN (re-mix) *Atlantic A 7186CD*	36 3
3 Feb 96	SITTIN' UP IN MY ROOM *Arista 74321344012*	30 4
6 Jun 98 ●	THE BOY IS MINE *Atlantic AT 0036CD* [1] ▲	2 20
10 Oct 98 ●	TOP OF THE WORLD (re) *Atlantic AT 0046CD* [2]	2 9
12 Dec 98	HAVE YOU EVER? *Atlantic AT 0058CD* ▲	13 8
19 Jun 99	ALMOST DOESN'T COUNT *Atlantic AT 0068CD1*	15 5
16 Jun 01 ●	ANOTHER DAY IN PARADISE *WEA WEA 327CD1* [3]	5 10
23 Feb 02 ●	WHAT ABOUT US? (re) *Atlantic AT 0125CD*	4 11
15 Jun 02	FULL MOON (IMPORT) *Atlantic 7567853092*	72 1
29 Jun 02	FULL MOON *Atlantic AT 130CD*	15 9
26 Jun 04 ●	TALK ABOUT OUR LOVE *Atlantic AT 017CD* [4]	6 10
16 Oct 04	AFRODISIAC *Atlantic AT 0183CD*	11 8
20 Jun 98	NEVER S-A-Y NEVER *Atlantic 7567830392*	19 31
9 Mar 02 ●	FULL MOON *Atlantic 7567931102*	9 15
10 Jul 04	AFRODISIAC *Atlantic 7567836332*	32 4

[1] Brandy and Monica [2] Brandy featuring Ma$e [3] Brandy and Ray J [4] Brandy featuring Kanye West

Laura BRANIGAN *US, female vocalist, b. 3 Jul 1957, d. 26 Aug 2004 (Singles: 33 Weeks, Albums: 18 Weeks)*

		pos/wks
18 Dec 82 ●	GLORIA *Atlantic K 11759*	6 13
7 Jul 84 ●	SELF CONTROL *Atlantic A 9676*	5 17
6 Oct 84	THE LUCKY ONE *Atlantic A 9636*	56 3
18 Aug 84	SELF CONTROL *Atlantic 780147*	16 14
24 Aug 85	HOLD ME *Atlantic 7812651*	64 4

BRASS CONSTRUCTION *US, male vocal / instrumental group (Singles: 35 Weeks, Albums: 12 Weeks)*

		pos/wks
3 Apr 76	MOVIN' *United Artists UP 36090*	23 6
5 Feb 77	HA CHA CHA (FUNKTION) *United Artists UP 36205*	37 5
26 Jan 80	MUSIC MAKES YOU FEEL LIKE DANCING *United Artists UP 615*	39 6
28 May 83	WALKIN' THE LINE *Capitol CL 292*	47 3
16 Jul 83	WE CAN WORK IT OUT *Capitol CL 299*	70 2
7 Jul 84	PARTYLINE *Capitol CL 335*	56 4
27 Oct 84	INTERNATIONAL *Capitol CL 341*	70 2
9 Nov 85	GIVE AND TAKE *Capitol CL 377*	62 3
28 May 88	MOVIN' 1988 (re-mix) *Syncopate SY 11*	24 4
20 Mar 76 ●	BRASS CONSTRUCTION *United Artists UAS 29923*	9 11
30 Jun 84	RENEGADES *Capitol EJ 24 0160*	94 1

BRASSTOOTH See BM DUBS present MR RUMBLE featuring BRASSTOOTH and KEE

BRAT *UK, male vocalist – Roger Kitter (Singles: 8 Weeks)*

		pos/wks
10 Jul 82	CHALK DUST – THE UMPIRE STRIKES BACK *Hansa SMASH 1*	19 8

BRAVADO *UK, male / female vocal / instrumental group (Singles: 3 Weeks)*

		pos/wks
18 Jun 94	HARMONICA MAN *Peach PEACHCD 5*	37 3

BRAVEHEARTS See QB FINEST featuring NAS & BRAVEHEARTS

BRAVO ALL STARS *UK / US, male / female vocal / instrumental group (Singles: 2 Weeks)*

		pos/wks
29 Aug 98	LET THE MUSIC HEAL YOUR SOUL *Edel 0039335 ERE*	36 2

Artists featured: Backstreet Boys, Aaron Carter, Scooter, 'N Sync, Caught in the Act, The Boyz, Blumchen, Gil, Squeezer, Mr President, Touche, R'N'G and The Moffatts

Alan BRAXE and Fred FALKE *France, male production duo (Singles: 3 Weeks)*

		pos/wks
25 Nov 00	INTRO *Vulture / Credence CDCRED 006*	35 3

Dhar BRAXTON *US, female vocalist (Singles: 8 Weeks)*

		pos/wks
31 May 86	JUMP BACK (SET ME FREE) *Fourth & Broadway BRW 47*	32 8

Toni BRAXTON 297 Top 500

Sultry, sexy soul / R&B vocalist, b. 7 Oct 1968, Maryland, US, who won Best New Artist Grammy in 1993 and was one of America's top-selling pop and R&B artists of the 1990s. Her biggest hits have been ballads from the pens of top writers Babyface, Diane Warren, R Kelly and Rodney Jerkins. Biggest-selling single: 'Un-Break My Heart' 770,000 (Singles: 86 Weeks, Albums: 136 Weeks)

		pos/wks
18 Sep 93	ANOTHER SAD LOVE SONG *LaFace 74321163502*	51 2
15 Jan 94 ●	BREATHE AGAIN *LaFace 74321185442*	2 12
2 Apr 94	ANOTHER SAD LOVE SONG (re-issue) *LaFace 74321196682*	15 8
9 Jul 94	YOU MEAN THE WORLD TO ME *LaFace 74321214702*	30 5
3 Dec 94	LOVE SHOULDA BROUGHT YOU HOME *LaFace 74321249412*	33 3
13 Jul 96	YOU'RE MAKIN' ME HIGH *LaFace 74321395402* ▲	7 11
2 Nov 96 ●	UN-BREAK MY HEART *LaFace 74321410632* ▲	2 19
24 May 97	I DON'T WANT TO *LaFace 74321468612*	9 8
8 Nov 97	HOW COULD AN ANGEL BREAK MY HEART *LaFace 74321531982* [1]	22 4
29 Apr 00 ●	HE WASN'T MAN ENOUGH *LaFace 74321757852*	5 11
8 Mar 03	HIT THE FREEWAY *LaFace / Arista 82876506372*	29 3
29 Jan 94	TONI BRAXTON *LaFace 74321162682* ▲	4 33
29 Jun 96 ●	SECRETS *LaFace 73008260202*	10 81
6 May 00 ●	THE HEAT *LaFace 73008260692*	3 19
15 Nov 03	ULTIMATE *Arista 82876574852*	23 3

[1] Toni Braxton with Kenny G

The BRAXTONS *US, female vocal group (Singles: 7 Weeks)*

		pos/wks
1 Feb 97	SO MANY WAYS *Atlantic A 5469CD*	32 2
29 Mar 97	THE BOSS *Atlantic A 5441CD*	31 3
19 Jul 97	SLOW FLOW *Atlantic AT 0001CD*	26 2

BREAD 264 Top 500

Internationally popular soft-rock group whose initial line-up was David Gates (v/g/k), James Griffin (g), Robb Royner (g) and Jim Gordon (d). Los Angeles formed quartet wrote and orignally recorded No.1 hits 'If' and 'Everything I Own' (Singles: 46 Weeks, Albums: 198 Weeks)

		pos/wks
1 Aug 70 ●	MAKE IT WITH YOU *Elektra 2101 010* ▲	5 14
15 Jan 72	BABY I'M-A WANT YOU *Elektra K 12033*	14 10
29 Apr 72	EVERYTHING I OWN *Elektra K 12041*	32 6
30 Sep 72	THE GUITAR MAN *Elektra K 12066*	16 9
25 Dec 76	LOST WITHOUT YOUR LOVE *Elektra K 12241*	27 7
26 Sep 70	ON THE WATERS *Elektra 2469005*	34 5
18 Mar 72	BABY I'M-A WANT YOU *Elektra K 42100*	9 19
28 Oct 72	THE BEST OF BREAD *Elektra K 42115*	7 100
27 Jul 74	THE BEST OF BREAD VOLUME 2 *Elektra K 42161*	48 1
29 Jan 77	LOST WITHOUT YOUR LOVE *Elektra K 52044*	17 6
5 Nov 77 ★	THE SOUND OF BREAD *Elektra K 52062*	1 46
28 Nov 87	THE VERY BEST OF BREAD *Telstar STAR 2303*	84 2
5 Jul 97	ESSENTIALS *Jive 9548354082* [1]	9 19

[1] David Gates and Bread

BREAK MACHINE *US, male vocal group (Singles: 32 Weeks, Albums: 16 Weeks)*

		pos/wks
4 Feb 84 ●	STREET DANCE *Record Shack SOHO 13*	3 14
12 May 84 ●	BREAK DANCE PARTY (re) *Record Shack SOHO 20*	9 10
11 Aug 84	ARE YOU READY? *Record Shack SOHO 24*	27 8
9 Jun 84	BREAK MACHINE *Record Shack SOHOLP 3*	17 16

BREAKBEAT ERA *UK, male / female drum and bass trio (Singles: 5 Weeks, Albums: 2 Weeks)*

		pos/wks
18 Jul 98	BREAKBEAT ERA *XL Recordings XLS 95CD*	38 2
21 Aug 99	ULTRA – OBSCENE *XL Recordings XLS 107CD*	48 2
11 Mar 00	BULLITPROOF *XL Recordings XLS 115CD*	65 1
11 Sep 99	ULTRA OBSCENE *XL Recordings XLCD 130*	31 2

BREAKFAST CLUB *US, male vocal / instrumental group (Singles: 3 Weeks)*

		pos/wks
27 Jun 87	RIGHT ON TRACK *MCA MCA 1146*	54 3

Julian BREAM *UK, male instrumentalist – guitar / lute (Albums: 2 Weeks)*

		pos/wks
27 Apr 96	THE ULTIMATE GUITAR COLLECTION *RCA Victor 74321337052*	66 2

BREATHE
UK, male vocal / instrumental group (Singles: 27 Weeks, Albums: 5 Weeks) — pos/wks

30 Jul 88 ●	HANDS TO HEAVEN *Siren SRN 68*	4	12
22 Oct 88	JONAH *Siren SRN 95*	60	3
3 Dec 88	HOW CAN I FALL? *Siren SRN 102*	48	7
11 Mar 89	DON'T TELL ME LIES *Siren SRN 109*	45	5
8 Oct 88	ALL THAT JAZZ *Siren SRNLP 12*	22	5

Freddy BRECK
Germany, male vocalist (Singles: 4 Weeks) — pos/wks

13 Apr 74	SO IN LOVE WITH YOU *Decca F 13481*	44	4

BRECKER BROTHERS
US, male vocal / instrumental duo – Randy and Michael Brecker (Singles: 5 Weeks) — pos/wks

4 Nov 78	EAST RIVER *Arista ARIST 211*	34	5

BREED 77
Gibraltar, male vocal / instrumental group (Singles: 4 Weeks, Albums: 1 Week) — pos/wks

1 May 04	THE RIVER *Albert Productions JASCDUK 007*	39	2
7 Aug 04	WORLD'S ON FIRE *Albert Productions JASCDUK 011*	43	2
15 May 04	CULTURA *Albert Productions JASCDUK 008*	61	1

The BREEDERS
(see also PIXIES; THROWING MUSES) *US / UK, female / male vocal / instrumental group (Singles: 7 Weeks, Albums: 9 Weeks)* — pos/wks

18 Apr 92	SAFARI (EP) *4AD BAD 2003*	69	1
21 Aug 93	CANNONBALL (EP) *4AD BAD 3011CD*	40	3
6 Nov 93	DIVINE HAMMER *4AD BAD 3017CD*	59	1
23 Jul 94	HEAD TO TOE (EP) *4AD BADD 4012*	68	1
14 Sep 02	SON OF THREE *4AD BAD 2213CD*	72	1
9 Jun 90	POD *4AD CAD 0006*	22	3
11 Sep 93 ●	LAST SPLASH *4AD CAD 3014CD*	5	5
1 Jun 02	TITLE TK *4AD CAD 2205CD*	51	1

Tracks on Safari (EP): Do You Love Me Now / Don't Call Home / Safari / So Sad About Us. Tracks on Cannonball (EP): Cannonball / Cro-Aloha / Lord of the Thighs / 900. Tracks on Head to Toe (EP): Head to Toe / Shocker in Gloom Town / Freed Pig

BREEKOUT KREW
US, male vocal duo (Singles: 3 Weeks) — pos/wks

24 Nov 84	MATT'S MOOD *London LON 59*	51	3

Ann BREEN
Ireland, female vocalist (Singles: 2 Weeks) — pos/wks

19 Mar 83	PAL OF MY CRADLE DAYS (re) *Homespun HS 052*	69	2

Mark BREEZE See Darren STYLES & Mark BREEZE present INFEXTIOUS

Jo BREEZER
UK, female vocalist (Singles: 2 Weeks) — pos/wks

13 Oct 01	VENUS AND MARS *Columbia 6717612*	27	2

BRENDON
UK, male vocalist – Brendon Dunning (Singles: 9 Weeks) — pos/wks

19 Mar 77	GIMME SOME *Magnet MAG 80*	14	9

Maire BRENNAN
(see also CLANNAD) *Ireland, female vocalist – now records as Moya Brennan (Singles: 12 Weeks, Albums: 2 Weeks)* — pos/wks

16 May 92	AGAINST THE WIND *RCA PB 45399*	64	2
5 Jun 99 ●	SALTWATER *Xtravaganza XTRAV 1CDS* [1]	6	10
13 Jun 92	MAIRE *RCA PD 75358*	53	2

[1] Chicane featuring Maire Brennan of Clannad

Rose BRENNAN
Ireland, female vocalist (Singles: 9 Weeks) — pos/wks

7 Dec 61	TALL DARK STRANGER *Philips PB 1193*	31	9

Walter BRENNAN
US, male vocalist, b. 25 Jul 1894, d. 21 Sep 1974 (Singles: 3 Weeks) — pos/wks

28 Jun 62	OLD RIVERS *Liberty LIB 55436*	38	3

Tony BRENT
UK, male vocalist – Reginald Bretagne, b. 26 Aug 1927, d. 19 Jun 1993 (Singles: 52 Weeks) — pos/wks

19 Dec 52 ●	WALKIN' TO MISSOURI (re) *Columbia DB 3147*	7	7
2 Jan 53 ●	MAKE IT SOON (re) *Columbia DB 3187*	9	7
23 Jan 53	GOT YOU ON MY MIND *Columbia DB 3226*	12	1
30 Nov 56	CINDY, OH CINDY (re) *Columbia DB 3844*	16	7
28 Jun 57	DARK MOON *Columbia DB 3950*	17	14
28 Feb 58	THE CLOUDS WILL SOON ROLL BY (re) *Columbia DB 4066*	20	5
5 Sep 58	GIRL OF MY DREAMS *Columbia DB 4177*	16	7
24 Jul 59	WHY SHOULD I BE LONELY? *Columbia DB 4304*	24	4

Bernard BRESSLAW
(see also Michael MEDWIN, Bernard BRESSLAW, Alfie BASS and Leslie FYSON) *UK, male comedian / actor / vocalist, b. 25 Feb 1934, d. 11 Jun 1993 (Singles: 11 Weeks)* — pos/wks

5 Sep 58 ●	MAD PASSIONATE LOVE *HMV POP 522*	6	11

Adrian BRETT
UK, male instrumentalist – flute (Albums: 11 Weeks) — pos/wks

10 Nov 79	ECHOES OF GOLD *Warwick WW 5062*	19	11

Paul BRETT
UK, male instrumentalist – guitar (Albums: 7 Weeks) — pos/wks

19 Jul 80	ROMANTIC GUITAR *K-Tel ONE 1079*	24	7

Teresa BREWER
US, female vocalist – Theresa Breuer (Singles: 53 Weeks) — pos/wks

11 Feb 55 ●	LET ME GO LOVER *Vogue / Coral Q 72043* [1]	9	10
13 Apr 56 ●	A TEAR FELL *Vogue / Coral Q 72146*	2	15
13 Jul 56 ●	A SWEET OLD FASHIONED GIRL *Vogue / Coral Q 72172*	3	15
10 May 57	NORA MALONE *Vogue / Coral Q 72224*	26	2
23 Jun 60	HOW DO YOU KNOW IT'S LOVE *Coral Q 72396*	21	11

[1] Teresa Brewer with the Lancers

BRIAN and MICHAEL
UK, male vocal duo – Kevin Parrott and Michael Coleman (Singles: 19 Weeks) — pos/wks

25 Feb 78 ★	MATCHSTALK MEN AND MATCHSTALK CATS AND DOGS (LOWRY'S SONG) *Pye 7N 46035*	1	19

BRICK
US, male vocal / instrumental group (Singles: 4 Weeks) — pos/wks

5 Feb 77	DAZZ *Bang 004*	36	4

Edie BRICKELL and the NEW BOHEMIANS
US, female / male vocal / instrumental group (Singles: 10 Weeks, Albums: 19 Weeks) — pos/wks

4 Feb 89	WHAT I AM *Geffen GEF 49*	31	7
27 May 89	CIRCLE *Geffen GEF 51*	74	1
1 Oct 94	GOOD TIMES *Geffen GFSTD 78* [1]	40	2
4 Feb 89	SHOOTING RUBBERBANDS AT THE STARS *Geffen WX 215*	25	17
10 Nov 90	GHOST OF A DOG *Geffen WX 386*	63	1
3 Sep 94	PICTURE PERFECT MORNING *Geffen GED 24715* [1]	59	1

[1] Edie Brickell [1] Edie Brickell

Alicia BRIDGES
US, female vocalist (Singles: 11 Weeks) — pos/wks

11 Nov 78	I LOVE THE NIGHTLIFE (DISCO 'ROUND) *Polydor 2066 936*	32	10
8 Oct 94	I LOVE THE NIGHTLIFE (DISCO 'ROUND) (re-mix) *Mother MUMCD 57*	61	1

Johnny BRIGGS See Amanda BARRIE and Johnny BRIGGS

The BRIGHOUSE AND RASTRICK BRASS BAND
UK, male brass band (Singles: 13 Weeks, Albums: 11 Weeks) — pos/wks

12 Nov 77 ●	THE FLORAL DANCE *Transatlantic BIG 548*	2	13
28 Jan 78 ●	FLORAL DANCE *Logo 1001*	10	11

Bette BRIGHT
UK, female vocalist (Singles: 5 Weeks) — pos/wks

8 Mar 80	HELLO, I AM YOUR HEART *Korova KOW 3*	50	5

Sarah BRIGHTMAN
(see also Andrew LLOYD WEBBER) *UK, female vocalist (Singles: 98 Weeks, Albums: 31 Weeks)* — pos/wks

11 Nov 78 ●	I LOST MY HEART TO A STARSHIP TROOPER *Ariola / Hansa AHA 527* [1]	6	14
7 Apr 79	THE ADVENTURES OF THE LOVE CRUSADER *Ariola / Hansa AHA 538* [2]	53	5
30 Jul 83	HIM *Polydor POSP 625* [3]	55	4
23 Mar 85 ●	PIE JESU *HMV WEBBER 1* [4]	3	8

ASH TOP 10

The gospel according to Ash, who choose their favourite albums

Tim Wheeler, Mark Hamilton, Richard McMurray and
Charlotte Hatherley select the LPs that rock their world.

album – act – (peak position)

APPETITE FOR DESTRUCTION
Guns N' Roses (5)

BLOOD ON THE TRACKS
Bob Dylan (4)

IS THIS IT
The Strokes (2)

LIVE AND DANGEROUS
Thin Lizzy (2)

NEVERMIND
Nirvana (7)

PET SOUNDS
The Beach Boys (2)

RITUAL DE LO HABITUAL
Jane's Addiction (37)

SONGS FOR THE DEAF
Queens of the Stone Age (4)

SURFER ROSA *
Pixies

THE RISE AND FALL OF ZIGGY STARDUST
AND THE SPIDERS FROM MARS
David Bowie (5)

* Did not chart

					pos/wks
11 Jan 86	●	THE PHANTOM OF THE OPERA *Polydor POSP 800* [5]	**7**	10
4 Oct 86	●	ALL I ASK OF YOU *Polydor POSP 802* [6]	**3**	16
10 Jan 87	●	WISHING YOU WERE SOMEHOW HERE AGAIN *Polydor POSP 803*	**7**	11
11 Jul 92		AMIGOS PARA SIEMPRE (FRIENDS FOR LIFE) *Really Useful RUR 10* [7]	**11**	11
24 May 97	●	TIME TO SAY GOODBYE (CON TE PARTIRO) *Coalition COLA 003CD* [8]	**2**	14
23 Aug 97		WHO WANTS TO LIVE FOREVER *Coalition COLA 014CD*	**45**	1
6 Dec 97		JUST SHOW ME HOW TO LOVE YOU *Coalition COLA 035CD* [9]	**54**	2
14 Feb 98		STARSHIP TROOPERS *Coalition COLA 040CD*	**58**	1
13 Feb 99		EDEN *Coalition COLA 065CD*	**68**	1
17 Jun 89		THE SONGS THAT GOT AWAY *Really Useful 839116 1*	**48**	2
8 Aug 92		AMIGOS PARA SIEMPRE *East West 4509902562* [1]	**53**	4
11 Nov 95		THE UNEXPECTED SONGS – SURRENDER *Really Useful 5277022*	**45**	2
14 Jun 97	●	TIMELESS *Coalition 630191812*	**2**	21
20 Jan 01		LA LUNA *East West 8573859152*	**37**	2

[1] Sarah Brightman and Hot Gossip [2] Sarah Brightman and the Starship Troopers [3] Sarah Brightman and the London Philharmonic [4] Sarah Brightman and Paul Miles-Kingston [5] Sarah Brightman and Steve Harley [6] Cliff Richard and Sarah Brightman [7] José Carreras and Sarah Brightman [8] Sarah Brightman and Andrea Bocelli [9] Sarah Brightman and the LSO featuring José Cura [1] José Carreras and Sarah Brightman

The listed flip side of 'Wishing You Were Somehow Here Again' was 'The Music of the Night' by Michael Crawford. COLA 040CD is a dance re-mix of AHA 527

BRIGHTON AND HOVE ALBION FC
UK, male football team vocalists (Singles: 2 Weeks) pos/wks

28 May 83	THE BOYS IN THE OLD BRIGHTON BLUE *Energy NRG 2*	**65**	2

BRILLIANT
UK, male / female vocal / instrumental group (Singles: 13 Weeks, Albums: 1 Week) pos/wks

19 Oct 85	IT'S A MAN'S MAN'S MAN'S WORLD *Food FOOD 5*	**58**	5
22 Mar 86	LOVE IS WAR *Food FOOD 6*	**64**	4
2 Aug 86	SOMEBODY *Food FOOD 7*	**67**	4
20 Sep 86	KISS THE LIPS OF LIFE *Food BRILL 1*	**83**	1

Danielle BRISEBOIS
US, female vocalist (Singles: 1 Week) pos/wks

9 Sep 95	GIMME LITTLE SIGN *Epic 6610782*	**75**	1

Johnny BRISTOL
US, male vocalist, b. 3 Feb 1939, d. 21 Mar 2004 (Singles: 16 Weeks, Albums: 7 Weeks) pos/wks

24 Aug 74	●	HANG ON IN THERE BABY *MGM 2006 443*	**3**	11
19 Jul 80		MY GUY – MY GIRL (MEDLEY) *Atlantic / Hansa K 11550* [1]	**39**	5
5 Oct 74		HANG ON IN THERE BABY *MGM 2315 303*	**12**	7

[1] Amii Stewart and Johnny Bristol

BRIT PACK
UK / Ireland, male vocal group (Singles: 2 Weeks) pos/wks

12 Feb 00	SET ME FREE *When! WENX 2000*	**41**	2

BRITISH SEA POWER
UK, male vocal / instrumental group (Singles: 3 Weeks, Albums: 1 Week) pos/wks

12 Jul 03	CARRION / APOLOGIES TO INSECT LIFE *Rough Trade RTRADSCD 092*	**36**	1
1 Nov 03	REMEMBER ME *Rough Trade RTRADSCD 125*	**30**	2
14 Jun 03	THE DECLINE OF BRITISH SEA POWER *Rough Trade RTRADSCD 065*	**54**	1

BRITS *See VARIOUS ARTISTS (MONTAGES)*

Andrea BRITTON *See Jurgen VRIES; OXYGEN featuring Andrea BRITTON*

BROCK LANDARS
UK, male vocal / production duo (Singles: 2 Weeks) pos/wks

11 Jul 98	S.M.D.U. *Parlophone CDBLUE 001*	**49**	2

BROCKIE & ED SOLO
UK, male producers (Singles: 1 Week) pos/wks

24 Apr 04	SYSTEM CHECK *Undiluted UD 010*	**68**	1

BRODSKY QUARTET *See Elvis COSTELLO*

BROKEN ENGLISH
UK, male vocal / instrumental group (Singles: 13 Weeks) pos/wks

30 May 87	COMIN' ON STRONG *EMI EM 5*	**18**	10
3 Oct 87	LOVE ON THE SIDE *EMI EM 55*	**69**	3

June BRONHILL and Thomas ROUND
Australia / UK, female / male vocal duo (Albums: 1 Week) pos/wks

18 Jun 60	LILAC TIME *HMV CLP 1248*	**17**	1

BRONSKI BEAT `490` `Top 500`

Electronic dance trio formed in 1984 in London, UK; Steve Bronski (k), Larry Steinbachek (k) and the plaintive falsetto of Jimmy Somerville (v), who left in 1985 for The Communards (replaced by John Foster). The first openly gay hit pop group, split in 1989 (Singles: 78 Weeks, Albums: 69 Weeks)   pos/wks

2 Jun 84 ●	SMALLTOWN BOY *Forbidden Fruit BITE 1*	.3 13
22 Sep 84	WHY? *Forbidden Fruit BITE 2*	.6 10
1 Dec 84	IT AIN'T NECESSARILY SO *Forbidden Fruit BITE 3*	.16 11
20 Apr 85	I FEEL LOVE (MEDLEY) *Forbidden Fruit BITE 4* [1]	.3 12
30 Nov 85	HIT THAT PERFECT BEAT *Forbidden Fruit BITE 6*	.3 14
29 Mar 86	COME ON, COME ON *Forbidden Fruit BITE 7*	.20 7
1 Jul 89	CHA CHA HEELS *Arista 112331* [2]	.32 7
2 Feb 91	SMALLTOWN BOY (re-mix) *London LON 287* [3]	.32 4
20 Oct 84 ●	THE AGE OF CONSENT *Forbidden Fruit BITLP 1*	.4 53
21 Sep 85	HUNDREDS AND THOUSANDS *Forbidden Fruit BITLP 2*	.24 6
10 May 86	TRUTHDARE DOUBLEDARE *Forbidden Fruit BITLP 3*	.18 6
22 Sep 01	THE VERY BEST OF JIMMY SOMERVILLE BRONSKI BEAT AND THE COMMUNARDS *London 927412582* [1]	.29 4

[1] Bronski Beat and Marc Almond [2] Eartha Kitt and Bronski Beat [3] Jimmy Somerville with Bronski Beat [1] Jimmy Somerville, Bronski Beat and The Communards

Tracks on I Feel Love (medley): I Feel Love / Love to Love You Baby / Johnny Remember Me

The BRONX

US, male vocal / instrumental group (Singles: 2 Weeks)   pos/wks

24 Apr 04	THEY WILL KILL US ALL *Wichita Recordings WEBB 0603CD*	65 1
17 Jul 04	FALSE ALARM *Wichita Recordings WEBB 062SCD*	73 1

Jet BRONX and the FORBIDDEN *UK, male vocal / instrumental group – featuring TV presenter Loyd Grossman (Singles: 1 Week)*   pos/wks

17 Dec 77	AIN'T DOIN' NOTHIN' *Lightning LIG 50*	.49 1

The BROOK BROTHERS

UK, male vocal duo – Geoff and Ricky Brook (Singles: 35 Weeks)   pos/wks

30 Mar 61 ●	WARPAINT *Pye 7N 15333*	.5 14
24 Aug 61	AIN'T GONNA WASH FOR A WEEK *Pye 7N 15369*	.13 10
25 Jan 62	HE'S OLD ENOUGH TO KNOW BETTER *Pye 7N 15409*	.37 1
16 Aug 62	WELCOME HOME BABY *Pye 7N 15453*	.33 6
21 Feb 63	TROUBLE IS MY MIDDLE NAME *Pye 7N 15498*	.38 4

Michael BROOK *See Nusrat Fateh Ali KHAN / Michael BROOK*

Bruno BROOKES *See Liz KERSHAW and Bruno BROOKES*

BROOKLYN BOUNCE *Germany, male production duo and male / female vocal group (Singles: 1 Week)*   pos/wks

30 May 98	THE MUSIC'S GOT ME *Club Tools 0064795 CLU*	.67 1

BROOKLYN, BRONX and QUEENS *See B B and Q BAND*

Elkie BROOKS `177` `Top 500` *Husky-voiced female vocalist, professional at age 15, b. Elaine Bookbinder, 25 Feb 1945, Salford, UK. Blues, jazz then rock phases (in Vinegar Joe with Robert Palmer) followed by a solo career which featured an impressive 20-year run of 15 hit albums from 1977 (Singles: 91 Weeks, Albums: 223 Weeks)*   pos/wks

2 Apr 77 ●	PEARL'S A SINGER *A&M AMS 7275*	.8 9
20 Aug 77 ●	SUNSHINE AFTER THE RAIN *A&M AMS 7306*	.10 9
25 Feb 78	LILAC WINE *A&M AMS 7333*	.16 7
3 Jun 78	ONLY LOVE CAN BREAK YOUR HEART *A&M AMS 7353*	.43 5
11 Nov 78	DON'T CRY OUT LOUD *A&M AMS 7395*	.12 11
5 May 79	THE RUNAWAY *A&M AMS 7428*	.50 5
16 Jan 82	FOOL IF YOU THINK IT'S OVER *A&M AMS 8187*	.17 10
1 May 82	OUR LOVE *A&M AMS 8214*	.43 5
17 Jul 82	NIGHTS IN WHITE SATIN *A&M AMS 8235*	.33 5
22 Jan 83	GASOLINE ALLEY *A&M AMS 8305*	.52 5
22 Nov 86 ●	NO MORE THE FOOL *Legend LM 4*	.5 16
4 Apr 87	BREAK THE CHAIN *Legend LM 8*	.55 3
11 Jul 87	WE'VE GOT TONIGHT *Legend LM 9*	.69 1
18 Jun 77	TWO DAYS AWAY *A&M AMLH 68409*	.16 20
13 May 78	SHOOTING STAR *A&M AMLH 64695*	.20 13
13 Oct 79	LIVE AND LEARN *A&M AMLH 68509*	.34 6
14 Nov 81 ●	PEARLS *A&M ELK 1981*	.2 79

13 Nov 82 ●	PEARLS II *A&M ELK 1982*	.5 25
14 Jul 84	MINUTES *A&M AML 68565*	.35 7
8 Dec 84	SCREEN GEMS *EMI SCREEN 1*	.35 11
6 Dec 86 ●	NO MORE THE FOOL *Legend LMA 1*	.5 23
27 Dec 86 ●	THE VERY BEST OF ELKIE BROOKS *Telstar STAR 2284*	.10 18
11 Jun 88	BOOKBINDER'S KID *Legend LMA 3*	.57 3
18 Nov 89	INSPIRATIONS *Telstar STAR 2354*	.58 3
13 Mar 93	ROUND MIDNIGHT *Castle Communications CTVCD 113*	.27 4
16 Apr 94	NOTHIN' BUT THE BLUES *Castle Communications CTVCD 127*	.58 2
13 Apr 96	AMAZING *Carlton Premiere 3036000282* [1]	.49 2
15 Mar 97	THE VERY BEST OF ELKIE BROOKS *PolyGram TV 5407122*	.23 7

[1] Elkie Brooks with the Royal Philharmonic Orchestra

The two 'The Very Best of Elkie Brooks' albums are different

Garth BROOKS *US, male vocalist – Troyal Brooks (Singles: 15 Weeks, Albums: 48 Weeks)*   pos/wks

1 Feb 92	SHAMELESS *Capitol CL 646*	.71 1
22 Jan 94	THE RED STROKES / AIN'T GOING DOWN *Liberty CDCLS 704*	.13 5
16 Apr 94	STANDING OUTSIDE THE FIRE *Liberty CDCL 712*	.28 4
18 Feb 95	THE DANCE / FRIENDS IN LOW PLACES *Capitol CDCL 735*	.36 3
17 Feb 96	SHE'S EVERY WOMAN *Capitol CDCL 767*	.55 1
13 Nov 99	LOST IN YOU *Capitol CDCL 814*	.70 1
15 Feb 92	ROPIN' THE WIND *Capitol CDESTU 2162* ▲	.41 2
12 Feb 94 ●	IN PIECES *Capitol CDEST 2212* ▲	.2 11
24 Dec 94	THE HITS *Capitol CDP 8320812* ▲	.11 21
2 Dec 95	FRESH HORSES *Capitol CDGB 1*	.22 6
13 Dec 97	SEVENS *Capitol 8565992* ▲	.34 7
28 Nov 98	DOUBLE LIVE *Capitol 4974242* ▲	.57 1

Harry BROOKS *See STUDIO B / ROMEO and Harry BROOKS*

Mel BROOKS

US, male actor / rapper – Melvin Kaminsky (Singles: 10 Weeks)   pos/wks

18 Feb 84	TO BE OR NOT TO BE (THE HITLER RAP) *Island IS 158*	.12 10

Meredith BROOKS *US, female vocal / instrumentalist (Singles: 13 Weeks, Albums: 10 Weeks)*   pos/wks

2 Aug 97 ●	BITCH *Capitol CDCL 790*	.6 10
6 Dec 97	I NEED *Capitol CDCLS 794*	.28 2
7 Mar 98	WHAT WOULD HAPPEN *Capitol CDCL 798*	.49 1
23 Aug 97 ●	BLURRING THE EDGES *Capitol CDEST 2298*	.5 10

Norman BROOKS

Canada, male vocalist – Norman Arie (Singles: 1 Week)   pos/wks

12 Nov 54	A SKY-BLUE SHIRT AND A RAINBOW TIE *London L 1228*	.17 1

Nigel BROOKS SINGERS

UK, male / female vocal choir (Albums: 17 Weeks)   pos/wks

29 Nov 75 ●	SONGS OF JOY *K-Tel NE 706*	.5 16
5 Jun 76	20 ALL TIME EUROVISION FAVOURITES *K-Tel NE 712*	.44 1

BROS `471` `Top 500`

Top teen appeal act; photogenic twins Matt (v) and Luke Goss (d), b. 29 Sep 1968, London, UK, and Craig Logan (b), who left in 1989. Sold out tours, broke sales records, created hysteria and won Brits Best Newcomer of 1988 award. Matt had some solo success in the 21st century. (Singles: 84 Weeks, Albums: 69 Weeks)   pos/wks

5 Dec 87 ●	WHEN WILL I BE FAMOUS? (re) *CBS ATOM 2*	.2 15
19 Mar 88 ●	DROP THE BOY *CBS ATOM 3*	.2 10
18 Jun 88 ★	I OWE YOU NOTHING *CBS ATOM 4*	.1 11
17 Sep 88 ●	I QUIT *CBS ATOM 5*	.4 8
3 Dec 88 ●	CAT AMONG THE PIGEONS / SILENT NIGHT *CBS ATOM 6*	.2 8
29 Jul 89 ●	TOO MUCH *CBS ATOM 7*	.2 7
7 Oct 89 ●	CHOCOLATE BOX *CBS ATOM 8*	.9 6
16 Dec 89 ●	SISTER *CBS ATOM 9*	.10 6
10 Mar 90	MADLY IN LOVE *CBS ATOM 10*	.14 4
13 Jul 91	ARE YOU MINE? *Columbia 6569707*	.12 5
21 Sep 91	TRY *Columbia 6574047*	.27 4
9 Apr 88 ●	PUSH *CBS 460629 1*	.2 54
28 Oct 89 ●	THE TIME *CBS 465918 1*	.4 13
12 Oct 91	CHANGING FACES *Columbia 4688171*	.18 2

Act was duo for last six hits and last two albums

BROTHER BEYOND UK, male vocal / instrumental group (Singles: 58 Weeks, Albums: 24 Weeks)

pos/wks

4 Apr 87	HOW MANY TIMES *EMI EMI 5591*	62	3
8 Aug 87	CHAIN-GANG SMILE *Parlophone R 6160*	57	3
23 Jan 88	CAN YOU KEEP A SECRET? *Parlophone R 6174*	56	4
30 Jul 88 ●	THE HARDER I TRY *Parlophone R 6184*	2	14
5 Nov 88 ●	HE AIN'T NO COMPETITION *Parlophone R 6193*	6	10
21 Jan 89	BE MY TWIN *Parlophone R 6195*	14	6
1 Apr 89	CAN YOU KEEP A SECRET (re-mix) *Parlophone R 6197*	.22	5
28 Oct 89	DRIVE ON *Parlophone R 6233*	39	4
9 Dec 89	WHEN WILL I SEE YOU AGAIN *Parlophone R 6239*	43	5
10 Apr 90	TRUST *Parlophone R 6245*	53	2
19 Jan 91	THE GIRL I USED TO KNOW *Parlophone R 6265*	48	2
26 Nov 88 ●	GET EVEN *Parlophone PCS 7327*	9	23
25 Nov 89	TRUST *Parlophone PCS 7337*	60	1

BROTHER BROWN featuring FRANK'EE Denmark, male DJ / production duo and female vocalist (Singles: 5 Weeks)

pos/wks

| 2 Oct 99 | UNDER THE WATER *ffrr FCD 367* | .....18 | 4 |
| 24 Nov 01 | STAR CATCHING GIRL *Rulin / MoS RULIN 21CDS* | .....51 | 1 |

BROTHER LOVE See PRATT and McCLAIN with BROTHERLOVE

The BROTHERHOOD
UK, male rap group (Singles: 1 Week, Albums: 1 Week)

pos/wks

| 27 Jan 96 | ONE SHOT / NOTHING IN PARTICULAR *Bite It BHOODD 3* | .....55 | 1 |
| 17 Feb 96 | ELEMENTALZ *Bite It BHOODCD 1* | .....50 | 1 |

BROTHERHOOD OF MAN
UK, male vocal quartet (Singles: 97 Weeks, Albums: 40 Weeks)

pos/wks

14 Feb 70 ●	UNITED WE STAND *Deram DM 284*	10	9
4 Jul 70	WHERE ARE YOU GOING TO MY LOVE *Deram DM 298*	...22	10
13 Mar 76 ★	SAVE YOUR KISSES FOR ME *Pye 7N 45569* ◆	1	16
19 Jun 76	MY SWEET ROSALIE *Pye 7N 45602*	30	7
26 Feb 77 ●	OH BOY (THE MOOD I'M IN) *Pye 7N 45656*	8	12
9 Jul 77	ANGELO *Pye 7N 45699*	1	12
14 Jan 78 ★	FIGARO *Pye 7N 46037*	1	11
27 May 78	BEAUTIFUL LOVER *Pye 7N 46071*	15	12
30 Sep 78	MIDDLE OF THE NIGHT *Pye 7N 46117*	41	6
3 Jul 82	LIGHTNING FLASH *EMI 5309*	67	2
24 Apr 76	LOVE AND KISSES FROM *Pye NSPL 18490*	20	8
12 Aug 78	B FOR BROTHERHOOD *Pye NSPL 18567*	18	9
7 Oct 78 ●	BROTHERHOOD OF MAN *K-Tel BML 7980*	6	15
29 Nov 80	SING 20 NUMBER ONE HITS *Warwick WW 5087*	14	8

BROTHERLOVE See PRATT and McCLAIN with BROTHERLOVE

The BROTHERS UK, male vocal group (Singles: 9 Weeks)

pos/wks

| 29 Jan 77 ● | SING ME *Bus Stop Bus 1054* | .....8 | 9 |

The BROTHERS FOUR US, male vocal group (Singles: 2 Weeks)

pos/wks

| 23 Jun 60 | GREENFIELDS (re) *Philips PB 1009* | .....40 | 2 |

BROTHERS GRIMM See JAZZ and the BROTHERS GRIMM

BROTHERS IN RHYTHM UK, male instrumental / production duo – Dave Seaman and Steve Anderson (Singles: 12 Weeks)

pos/wks

16 Mar 91	SUCH A GOOD FEELING *Fourth & Broadway BRW 228*	64	2
14 Sep 91	SUCH A GOOD FEELING (re-issue) *Fourth & Broadway BRW 228 210*	14	8
30 Apr 94	FOREVER AND A DAY *Stress CDSTR 36* [1]	51	2

[1] Brothers in Rhythm present Charvoni

The BROTHERS JOHNSON US, male vocal / instrumental duo – George and Louis Johnson (Singles: 34 Weeks, Albums: 22 Weeks)

pos/wks

9 Jul 77	STRAWBERRY LETTER 23 *A&M AMS 7297*	35	5
2 Sep 78	AIN'T WE FUNKIN' NOW *A&M AMS 7379*	43	6
4 Nov 78	RIDE-O-ROCKET *A&M AMS 7400*	50	4
23 Feb 80 ●	STOMP *A&M AMS 7509*	6	12
31 May 80	LIGHT UP THE NIGHT *A&M AMS 7526*	47	4
25 Jul 81	THE REAL THING *A&M AMS 8149*	50	3
19 Aug 78	BLAM!! *A&M AMLH 64714*	48	8
23 Feb 80	LIGHT UP THE NIGHT *A&M AMLK 63716*	22	12
18 Jul 81	WINNERS *A&M AMLK 63724*	42	2

BROTHERS LIKE OUTLAW featuring Alison EVELYN
UK, male / female vocal group (Singles: 1 Week)

pos/wks

| 23 Jan 93 | GOOD VIBRATIONS *Gee Street GESCD 44* | .....74 | 1 |

Edgar BROUGHTON BAND UK, male vocal / instrumental group (Singles: 10 Weeks, Albums: 6 Weeks)

pos/wks

18 Apr 70	OUT DEMONS OUT *Harvest HAR 5015*	39	5
23 Jan 71	APACHE DROPOUT (3re) *Harvest HAR 5032*	33	5
20 Jun 70	SING BROTHER SING *Harvest SHVL 772*	18	4
5 Jun 71	THE EDGAR BROUGHTON BAND *Harvest SHVL 791*	28	2

Alison BROWN See BAR CODES featuring Alison BROWN

Angie BROWN See BIZARRE INC; MOTIV 8

Andrea BROWN See GOLDTRIX presents Andrea BROWN

Bobby BROWN ⟨ 347 ⟩ Top 500
Energetic swingbeat superstar, b. 5 Feb 1969, Massachusetts, US, who married Whitney Houston in 1992. He joined a re-formed New Edition in 1996, the vocal group in which he topped the chart with 'Candy Girl' as a 14-year-old (Singles: 131 Weeks, Albums: 65 Weeks)

pos/wks

6 Aug 88	DON'T BE CRUEL *MCA MCA 1268*	42	7
17 Dec 88 ●	MY PREROGATIVE *MCA MCA 1299* ▲	6	17
25 Mar 89	DON'T BE CRUEL (re-issue) *MCA MCA 1310*	13	8
20 May 89 ●	EVERY LITTLE STEP *MCA MCA 1338*	6	9
15 Jul 89 ●	ON OUR OWN (FROM GHOSTBUSTERS II) *MCA MCA 1350*	4	9
23 Sep 89	ROCK WIT'CHA *MCA MCA 1367*	33	6
25 Nov 89	RONI *MCA MCA 1384*	21	7
9 Jun 90	THE FREE STYLE MEGA-MIX *MCA MCA 1421*	14	7
30 Jun 90	SHE AIN'T WORTH IT *London LON 265* [1] ▲	12	9
22 Aug 92	HUMPIN' AROUND *MCA MCS 1680*	19	6
17 Oct 92	GOOD ENOUGH *MCA MCS 1704*	41	4
19 Jun 93	THAT'S THE WAY LOVE IS *MCA MCSTD 1783*	56	2
22 Jan 94	SOMETHING IN COMMON *MCA MCSTD 1957* [2]	16	5
25 Jun 94 ●	TWO CAN PLAY THAT GAME (re) *MCA MCSTD 1973*	3	15
8 Jul 95 ●	HUMPIN' AROUND (re-mix) *MCA MCSTD 2073*	8	6
14 Oct 95	MY PREROGATIVE (re-mix) *MCA MCSTD 2094*	17	3
3 Feb 96	EVERY LITTLE STEP (re-mix) *MCA MCSTD 48004*	25	2
22 Nov 97	FEELIN' INSIDE *MCA MCSTD 48067*	40	1
21 Dec 02	THUG LOVIN' *Def Jam 0637872* [3]	15	8
28 Jan 89 ●	DON'T BE CRUEL *MCA MCF 3425* ▲	3	41
5 Aug 89	KING OF STAGE *MCA MCL 1886*	40	6
2 Dec 89	DANCE! ... YA KNOW IT! *MCA MCG 6074*	26	10
5 Sep 92	BOBBY *MCA MCAD 10695*	11	5
5 Aug 95	TWO CAN PLAY THAT GAME *MCA MCD 11334*	24	3

[1] Glenn Medeiros featuring Bobby Brown [2] Bobby Brown and Whitney Houston [3] Ja Rule featuring Bobby Brown

'Two Can Play That Game' reached its peak position of No.3 only on its re-entry in Apr 1995

Carl BROWN See DOUBLE TROUBLE

Crazy World of Arthur BROWN
UK, male vocal / instrumental group – leader Arthur Wilton (Singles: 14 Weeks, Albums: 16 Weeks)

pos/wks

| 26 Jun 68 ★ | FIRE *Track 604022* | .....1 | 14 |
| 6 Jul 68 ● | THE CRAZY WORLD OF ARTHUR BROWN *Track 612005* | .....2 | 16 |

Dennis BROWN
Jamaica, male vocalist – Clarence Brown, b. 1 Feb 1957, d. 1 Jul 1999 (Singles: 18 Weeks, Albums: 6 Weeks)

pos/wks

3 Mar 79	MONEY IN MY POCKET *Lightning LV 5*	14	9
3 Jul 82	LOVE HAS FOUND ITS WAY *A&M AMS 8226*	47	6
11 Sep 82	HALFWAY UP HALFWAY DOWN *A&M AMS 8250*	56	3
26 Jun 82	LOVE HAS FOUND ITS WAY *A&M AMLH 64886*	72	6

Diana BROWN and Barrie K SHARPE
UK, female / male vocal duo (Singles: 11 Weeks)

pos/wks

2 Jun 90	THE MASTERPLAN *ffrr F 133*	39	6
1 Sep 90	SUN WORSHIPPERS (POSITIVE THINKING) *ffrr F 144*	61	2
23 Mar 91	LOVE OR NOTHING *ffrr F 152*	71	1
27 Jun 92	EATING ME ALIVE *ffrr F 190*	53	2

Errol BROWN (see also HOT CHOCOLATE)
UK, male vocalist (Singles: 13 Weeks, Albums: 2 Weeks)   pos/wks

4 Jul 87	**PERSONAL TOUCH** *WEA YZ 130*	**25** 8
28 Nov 87	**BODY ROCKIN'** *WEA YZ 162*	**51** 2
14 Feb 98	**IT STARTED WITH A KISS** *EMI CDHOT 101* [1]	**18** 3
9 Jun 01	**STILL SEXY – THE ALBUM** *Universal Music TV 138162*	**44** 2

[1] Hot Chocolate featuring Errol Brown

Foxy BROWN
US, female rapper –
Inga Marchand (Singles: 25 Weeks, Albums: 1 Week)   pos/wks

21 Sep 96	**TOUCH ME TEASE ME** *Def Jam DEFCD 18* [1]	**26** 3
8 Mar 97	**GET ME HOME** *Def Jam DEFCD 32* [2]	**11** 5
10 May 97	**AIN'T NO PLAYA** *Northwestside 74321474842* [3]	**31** 2
21 Jun 97 ●	**I'LL BE** *Def Jam 5710432* [4]	**9** 5
11 Oct 97	**BIG BAD MAMMA** *Def Jam 5749792* [5]	**12** 3
25 Oct 97	**SUNSHINE** *Northwestside 74321528702* [6]	**25** 2
13 Mar 99	**HOT SPOT** *Def Jam 8708352*	**31** 2
8 Sep 01	**OH YEAH** *Def Jam 5887312*	**27** 3
6 Feb 99	**CHYNA DOLL** *Def Jam 5589332* ▲	**51** 1

[1] Case featuring Foxxy Brown [2] Foxy Brown featuring BLACKstreet [3] Jay-Z featuring Foxy Brown [4] Foxy Brown featuring Jay-Z [5] Foxy Brown featuring Dru Hill [6] Jay-Z featuring Babyface and Foxy Brown

Gloria D BROWN
US, female vocalist (Singles: 3 Weeks)   pos/wks

8 Jun 85	**THE MORE THEY KNOCK, THE MORE I LOVE YOU** *10 TEN 52*	**57** 3

Horace BROWN
US, male vocalist (Singles: 7 Weeks, Albums: 1 Week)   pos/wks

25 Feb 95	**TASTE YOUR LOVE** *Uptown MCSTD 2026*	**58** 1
18 May 96	**ONE FOR THE MONEY** *Motown 8605232*	**12** 4
12 Oct 96	**THINGS WE DO FOR LOVE** *Motown 8605712*	**27** 2
6 Jul 96	**HORACE BROWN** *Motown 5306942*	**48** 1

Ian BROWN (see also The STONE ROSES) *UK, male*
vocalist / instrumentalist (Singles: 37 Weeks, Albums: 41 Weeks)   pos/wks

24 Jan 98 ●	**MY STAR** *Polydor 5719872*	**5** 4
4 Apr 98	**CORPSES** *Polydor 5696552*	**14** 4
20 Jun 98	**CAN'T SEE ME** *Polydor 5440452*	**21** 3
20 Feb 99 ●	**BE THERE** *Mo Wax MW 108CD1* [1]	**8** 6
6 Nov 99	**LOVE LIKE A FOUNTAIN** *Polydor 5615162*	**23** 3
19 Feb 00 ●	**DOLPHINS WERE MONKEYS** *Polydor 5616372*	**5** 4
17 Jun 00	**GOLDEN GAZE** *Polydor 5618442*	**29** 2
29 Sep 01	**F.E.A.R.** *Polydor 5872842*	**13** 4
23 Feb 02	**WHISPERS** *Polydor 5705382*	**33** 2
2 Oct 04	**KEEP WHAT YA GOT** *Fiction 9868284*	**18** 3
27 Nov 04	**REIGN** *Mo Wax GUSIN 007CDS* [1]	**40** 2
14 Feb 98 ●	**UNFINISHED MONKEY BUSINESS** *Polydor 5395652*	**4** 24
20 Nov 99	**GOLDEN GREATS** *Polydor 5431412*	**14** 6
13 Oct 01 ●	**MUSIC OF THE SPHERES** *Polydor 5891262*	**3** 5
25 Sep 04 ●	**SOLARIZED** *Fiction 9867772*	**7** 6

[1] Unkle featuring Ian Brown

"Keep What Ya Got' features an uncredited Noel Gallagher

James BROWN 447 Top 500
'Soul Brother No.1', b. 3 May 1928, South Carolina, US. The most charted R&B performer of all time has influenced numerous musical styles since the mid-1950s. Only Elvis Presley has enjoyed more US pop chart entries (Singles: 104 Weeks, Albums: 54 Weeks)   pos/wks

23 Sep 65	**PAPA'S GOT A BRAND NEW BAG** *London HL 9990* [1]	**25** 7
24 Feb 66	**I GOT YOU (I FEEL GOOD)** *Pye International 7N 25350* [1]	**29** 6
16 Jun 66	**IT'S A MAN'S MAN'S MAN'S WORLD** *Pye International 7N 25371* [1]	**13** 9
10 Oct 70	**GET UP I FEEL LIKE BEING A SEX MACHINE** *Polydor 2001 071*	**32** 7
27 Nov 71	**HEY AMERICA** *Mojo 2093 006*	**47** 3
18 Sep 76	**GET UP OFFA THAT THING** *Polydor 2066 687*	**22** 6
29 Jan 77	**BODY HEAT** *Polydor 2066 763*	**36** 4
10 Jan 81	**RAPP PAYBACK (WHERE IZ MOSES?)** *RCA 28*	**39** 5
2 Jul 83	**BRING IT ON ... BRING IT ON** *Sonet SON 2258*	**45** 4
1 Sep 84	**UNITY (PART 1 – THE THIRD COMING)** *Tommy Boy AFR 2* [2]	**49** 5
27 Apr 85	**FROGGY MIX** *Boiling Point FROG 1*	**50** 3
1 Jun 85	**GET UP I FEEL LIKE BEING A SEX MACHINE (re) (re-issue)** *Boiling Point POSP 751*	**46** 9

25 Jan 86 ●	**LIVING IN AMERICA** *Scotti Brothers A 6701*	**5** 10
18 Oct 86	**GRAVITY** *Scotti Brothers 650059 7*	**65** 2
30 Jan 88	**SHE'S THE ONE** *Urban URB 13*	**45** 3
23 Apr 88	**THE PAYBACK MIX** *Urban URB 17*	**12** 6
4 Jun 88	**I'M REAL** *Scotti Brothers JSB 1* [3]	**31** 4
23 Jul 88	**I GOT YOU (I FEEL GOOD) (re-issue)** *A&M AM 444*	**52** 3
16 Nov 91	**GET UP (I FEEL LIKE BEING A) SEX MACHINE (2nd re-issue)** *Polydor PO 185*	**69** 2
24 Oct 92	**I GOT YOU (I FEEL GOOD) (re-mix)** *FBI FBI 9* [4]	**72** 1
17 Apr 93	**CAN'T GET ANY HARDER** *Polydor PZCD 262*	**59** 2
17 Apr 99	**FUNK ON AH ROLL** *Inferno / Eagle EAGXA 073*	**40** 2
22 Apr 00	**FUNK ON AH ROLL (re-mix)** *Eagle EAGXS 127*	**63** 1
18 Oct 86	**GRAVITY** *Scotti Brothers SCT 57108*	**85** 3
25 Jun 88	**I'M REAL** *Scotti Brothers POLD 5230*	**27** 5
10 Oct 88	**THE BEST OF JAMES BROWN – GODFATHER OF SOUL** *K-Tel NE 1376*	**17** 21
16 Nov 91	**SEX MACHINE – THE VERY BEST OF JAMES BROWN** *Polydor 8458281*	**19** 22
11 May 02	**THE GODFATHER – THE VERY BEST OF JAMES BROWN** *UMTV 5898412*	**30** 3

[1] James Brown and the Famous Flames [2] Afrika Bambaataa and James Brown [3] James Brown featuring Full Force [4] James Brown vs Dakeyne

'Froggy Mix' is a medley of 12 James Brown songs. The listed flip side of 'I Got You (I Feel Good)' was 'Nowhere to Run' by Martha Reeves and the Vandellas

Jennifer BROWN
Sweden, female vocalist (Singles: 1 Week)   pos/wks

1 May 99	**TUESDAY AFTERNOON** *RCA 74321604092*	**57** 1

Joanne BROWN See Tony OSBORNE SOUND

Jocelyn BROWN
US, female vocalist (Singles: 79 Weeks)   pos/wks

21 Apr 84	**SOMEBODY ELSE'S GUY** *Fourth & Broadway BRW 5*	**13** 9
22 Sep 84	**I WISH YOU WOULD** *Fourth & Broadway BRW 14*	**51** 3
15 Mar 86	**LOVE'S GONNA GET YOU** *Warner Bros. W 8889*	**70** 1
29 Jun 91 ●	**ALWAYS THERE** *Talkin Loud TLK 10* [1]	**6** 9
14 Sep 91	**SHE GOT SOUL** *A&M AM 819* [2]	**57** 3
7 Dec 91	**DON'T TALK JUST KISS** *Tug SNOG 2* [3]	**3** 11
20 Mar 93	**TAKE ME UP** *A&M AMCD 210* [4]	**61** 1
11 Jun 94	**NO MORE TEARS (ENOUGH IS ENOUGH)** *Bell 74321209032* [5]	**13** 7
8 Oct 94	**GIMME ALL YOUR LOVIN'** *Bell 74321231322* [6]	**22** 3
13 Jul 96 ●	**KEEP ON JUMPIN'** *Manifesto FESCD 11* [7]	**8** 6
10 May 97	**IT'S ALRIGHT, I FEEL IT!** *Talkin Loud TLCD 22* [8]	**26** 2
12 Jul 97 ●	**SOMETHING GOIN' ON** *Manifesto FESCD 25* [7]	**5** 10
25 Oct 97	**I AM THE BLACK GOLD OF THE SUN** *Talkin Loud TLCD 26* [8]	**31** 2
22 Nov 97	**HAPPINESS** *Sony S3 KAMCD 2* [9]	**45** 1
2 May 98	**FUN** *INCredible INCRL 2CD* [10]	**33** 2
29 Aug 98	**AIN'T NO MOUNTAIN HIGH ENOUGH** *INCredible INCRL 7CD* [2]	**35** 2
27 Mar 99	**I BELIEVE** *Playola 0091705 PLA* [2]	**62** 1
3 Jul 99	**IT'S ALL GOOD** *INCredible INCRL 14CD* [10]	**54** 1
11 Mar 00	**BELIEVE** *Defected DFECT 14CD3* [11]	**45** 2
27 Jan 01	**BELIEVE (re-mix)** *Defected DFECT 26CDS* [11]	**42** 2
7 Sep 02	**THAT'S HOW GOOD YOUR LOVE IS** *Defected DFTD 057CDS* [12]	**54** 1

[1] Incognito featuring Jocelyn Brown [2] Jamestown featuring Jocelyn Brown [3] Right Said Fred. Guest vocals: Jocelyn Brown [4] Sonic Surfers featuring Jocelyn Brown [5] Kym Mazelle and Jocelyn Brown [6] Jocelyn Brown and Kym Mazelle [7] Todd Terry featuring Martha Wash and Jocelyn Brown [8] Nuyorican Soul featuring Jocelyn Brown [9] Kamasutra featuring Jocelyn Brown [10] Da Mob featuring Jocelyn Brown [11] Ministers De La Funk featuring Jocelyn Brown [12] Il Padrinos featuring Jocelyn Brown

Joe BROWN and the BRUVVERS *UK, male vocalist / instrumentalist –*
guitar and vocal group (Singles: 92 Weeks, Albums: 47 Weeks)   pos/wks

17 Mar 60	**THE DARKTOWN STRUTTERS' BALL** *Decca F 11207*	**34** 6
26 Jan 61	**SHINE** *Pye 7N 15322* [1]	**33** 6
11 Jan 62	**WHAT A CRAZY WORLD WE'RE LIVING IN** *Piccadilly 7N 35024* [1]	**37** 2
17 May 62 ●	**A PICTURE OF YOU** *Piccadilly 7N 35047*	**2** 19
13 Sep 62	**YOUR TENDER LOOK** *Piccadilly 7N 35058*	**31** 6
15 Nov 62 ●	**IT ONLY TOOK A MINUTE (re)** *Piccadilly 7N 35082*	**6** 14
7 Feb 63 ●	**THAT'S WHAT LOVE WILL DO** *Piccadilly 7N 35106*	**3** 14
27 Jun 63	**NATURE'S TIME FOR LOVE** *Piccadilly 7N 35129*	**26** 6
26 Sep 63	**SALLY ANN** *Piccadilly 7N 35138*	**28** 9
29 Jun 67	**WITH A LITTLE HELP FROM MY FRIENDS** *Pye 7N 17339* [1]	**32** 4
14 Apr 73	**HEY MAMA** *Ammo AMO 101* [1]	**33** 6
1 Sep 62 ●	**A PICTURE OF YOU** *Pye Golden Guinea GGL 0146* [1]	**3** 39
25 May 63	**JOE BROWN – LIVE** *Piccadilly NPL 38006* [1]	**14** 8

[1] Joe Brown [1] Joe Brown

Karen BROWN See DJ's RULE

Kathy BROWN US, female vocalist (Singles: 9 Weeks)
pos/wks

25 Nov 95	TURN ME OUT Stress CDSTR 40		**44**	2
20 Sep 97	TURN ME OUT (TURN TO SUGAR) (re-mix) ffrr FCD [1]		**35**	3
10 Apr 99	JOY Azuli AZNYCDX 094		**63**	1
5 May 01	LOVE IS NOT A GAME Defected DFECT 31CDS [2]		**34**	2
2 Jun 01	OVER YOU Defected DFECT 28CDS [3]		**42**	1

[1] Praxis featuring Kathy Brown [2] J Majik featuring Kathy Brown [3] Warren Clarke featuring Kathy Brown

Miquel BROWN US, female vocalist (Singles: 7 Weeks)
pos/wks

18 Feb 84	HE'S A SAINT, HE'S A SINNER Record Shack SOHO 15		**68**	4
24 Aug 85	CLOSE TO PERFECTION Record Shack SOHO 48		**63**	3

Palmer BROWN See BLAZE featuring Palmer BROWN

Peter BROWN US, male vocalist (Singles: 9 Weeks)
pos/wks

11 Feb 78	DO YA WANNA GET FUNKY WITH ME TK TKR 6009 [1]		**43**	4
17 Jun 78	DANCE WITH ME TK TKR 6027		**57**	5

[1] special background vocals: Betty Wright

Polly BROWN (see also PICKETTYWITCH; SWEET DREAMS)
UK, female vocalist (Singles: 5 Weeks)
pos/wks

14 Sep 74	UP IN A PUFF OF SMOKE GTO GT 2		**43**	5

Roy 'Chubby' BROWN UK, male comedian / vocalist –
Royston Vasey (Singles: 22 Weeks, Albums: 8 Weeks)
pos/wks

13 May 95 ●	LIVING NEXT DOOR TO ALICE (WHO THE F**K IS ALICE) (re) N.O.W. CDWAG 245 [1]		**3**	19
21 Dec 96	ROCKIN' GOOD CHRISTMAS PolyStar 5732612		**51**	3
25 Nov 95	TAKE FAT AND PARTY PolyStar 5297842		**29**	7
7 Dec 96	FAT OUT OF HELL PolyStar 5370602		**67**	1

[1] Smokie featuring Roy 'Chubby' Brown

Sam BROWN
UK, female vocalist (Singles: 35 Weeks, Albums: 30 Weeks)
pos/wks

11 Jun 88 ●	STOP (re) A&M AM 440		**4**	15
13 May 89	CAN I GET A WITNESS A&M AM 509		**15**	7
3 Mar 90	WITH A LITTLE LOVE A&M AM 539		**44**	4
5 May 90	KISSING GATE A&M AM 549		**23**	8
26 Aug 95	JUST GOOD FRIENDS Dick Bros. DDICK 014CD1 [1]		**63**	1
11 Mar 89 ●	STOP! A&M AMA 5195		**4**	18
14 Apr 90	APRIL MOON A&M AMA 9014		**38**	12

[1] Fish featuring Sam Brown

'Stop' reached its peak position of No.4 only on its re-entry in Feb 1989

Sharon BROWN US, female vocalist (Singles: 11 Weeks)
pos/wks

17 Apr 82	I SPECIALIZE IN LOVE Virgin VS 494		**38**	9
26 Feb 94	I SPECIALIZE IN LOVE (re-mix) Deep Distraxion OILYCD 025		**62**	2

Sleepy BROWN See OUTKAST

BROWN SAUCE
UK, male / female vocal group (Singles: 12 Weeks)
pos/wks

12 Dec 81	I WANNA BE A WINNER BBC RESL 101		**15**	12

BROWN SUGAR See SEX CLUB featuring BROWN SUGAR

Duncan BROWNE UK, male vocalist (Singles: 8 Weeks)
pos/wks

19 Aug 72	JOURNEY RAK 135		**23**	6
22 Dec 84	THEME FROM 'THE TRAVELLING MAN' Towerbell TOW 64		**68**	2

Jackson BROWNE
US, male vocalist (Singles: 14 Weeks, Albums: 41 Weeks)
pos/wks

1 Jul 78	STAY Asylum K 13128		**12**	11
18 Oct 86	IN THE SHAPE OF A HEART Elektra EKR 42		**66**	2
25 Jun 94	EVERYWHERE I GO Elektra EKR 184CD1		**67**	1
4 Dec 76	THE PRETENDER Asylum K 53048		**26**	5
21 Jan 78	RUNNING ON EMPTY Asylum K 53070		**28**	7
12 Jul 80	HOLD OUT Asylum K 52226 ▲		**44**	5
13 Aug 83	LAWYERS IN LOVE Asylum 9602681		**37**	7
8 Mar 86	LIVES IN THE BALANCE Asylum EKT 31		**36**	7
17 Jun 89	WORLD IN MOTION Elektra EKT 50		**39**	2
6 Nov 93	I'M ALIVE Elektra 7559615242		**35**	3
9 Mar 96	LOOKING EAST Elektra 7559618672		**47**	1
26 Oct 02	THE NAKED RIDE HOME Elektra EA 627932		**53**	1
16 Oct 04	THE VERY BEST OF JACKSON BROWNE Elektra / Rhino 8122780912		**53**	3

Ronnie BROWNE See SCOTTISH RUGBY TEAM with Ronnie BROWNE

Tom BROWNE
US, male instrumentalist – trumpet (Singles: 24 Weeks)
pos/wks

19 Jul 80 ●	FUNKIN' FOR JAMAICA (N.Y.) Arista ARIST 357		**10**	11
25 Oct 80	THIGHS HIGH (GRIP YOUR HIPS AND MOVE) Arista ARIST 367		**45**	5
30 Jan 82	FUNGI MAMA (BEBOPAFUNKADISCOLYPSO) Arista ARIST 450		**58**	4
11 Jan 92	FUNKIN' FOR JAMAICA (re-mix) Arista 114998		**45**	4

The BROWNS US, male / female vocal trio –
Jim Ed, Maxine and Bonnie Brown (Singles: 13 Weeks)
pos/wks

18 Sep 59 ●	THE THREE BELLS RCA 1140 ▲		**6**	13

BROWNSTONE
US, female vocal group (Singles: 24 Weeks, Albums: 16 Weeks)
pos/wks

1 Apr 95 ●	IF YOU LOVE ME MJJ 6614135		**8**	12
15 Jul 95	GRAPEVYNE MJJ 6620942		**16**	4
23 Sep 95	I CAN'T TELL YOU WHY MJJ 6623775		**27**	2
17 May 97	5 MILES TO EMPTY Epic 6640962		**12**	4
27 Sep 97	KISS AND TELL Epic 6649852		**21**	2
29 Apr 95	FROM THE BOTTOM UP MJJ 4773622		**18**	13
31 May 97	STILL CLIMBING Epic 4853882		**19**	3

BROWNSVILLE STATION
US, male vocal / instrumental group (Singles: 6 Weeks)
pos/wks

2 Mar 74	SMOKIN' IN THE BOYS' ROOM Philips 6073 834		**27**	6

Dave BRUBECK QUARTET US, male instrumental group –
leader David Warren (Singles: 30 Weeks, Albums: 17 Weeks)
pos/wks

26 Oct 61 ●	TAKE FIVE Fontana H 339		**6**	15
8 Feb 62	IT'S A RAGGY WALTZ Fontana H 352		**36**	3
17 May 62	UNSQUARE DANCE CBS AAG 102		**14**	12
25 Jun 60	TIME OUT Fontana TFL 5085		**11**	1
7 Apr 62	TIME FURTHER OUT Fontana TFL 5161 [1]		**12**	16

[1] Dave Brubeck

Jack BRUCE (see also CREAM) UK, male vocalist /
instrumentalist – bass – John Asher (Albums: 9 Weeks)
pos/wks

27 Sep 69 ●	SONGS FOR A TAILOR Polydor 583058		**6**	9

Tommy BRUCE and the BRUISERS
UK, male vocal / instrumental group (Singles: 21 Weeks)
pos/wks

26 May 60 ●	AIN'T MISBEHAVIN' Columbia DB 4453		**3**	16
8 Sep 60	BROKEN DOLL Columbia DB 4498		**36**	4
22 Feb 62	BABETTE Columbia DB 4776 [1]		**50**	1

[1] Tommy Bruce

Claudia BRÜCKEN Germany, female vocalist (Singles: 2 Weeks) pos/wks

11 Aug 90	ABSOLUT(E) Island IS 471		**71**	1
16 Feb 91	KISS LIKE ETHER Island IS 479		**63**	1

BRUFORD See ANDERSON BRUFORD WAKEMAN HOWE

The BRUISERS (see also Tommy BRUCE)
UK, male instrumental group (Singles: 7 Weeks)
pos/wks

8 Aug 63	BLUE GIRL (re) Parlophone R 5042		**31**	7

Frank BRUNO UK, male boxer / vocalist (Singles: 4 Weeks)
pos/wks

23 Dec 95	EYE OF THE TIGER RCA 74321336282		**28**	4

BRUNO and LIZ See Liz KERSHAW and Bruno BROOKES

Tyrone BRUNSON
US, male instrumentalist – bass (Singles: 5 Weeks)   pos/wks

25 Dec 82	THE SMURF *Epic EPC A 3024*	**52**	5

Basil BRUSH featuring India BEAU
UK, male fox vocalist and female vocalist (Singles: 3 Weeks)   pos/wks

27 Dec 03	BOOM BOOM / CHRISTMAS SLIDE *Right RRBB 001*	**44**	3

BRUVVERS See Joe BROWN and the BRUVVERS

Dora BRYAN
UK, female actor / vocalist – Dora Broadbent (Singles: 6 Weeks)   pos/wks

5 Dec 63	ALL I WANT FOR CHRISTMAS IS A BEATLE *Fontana TF 427*	**20**	6

Kéllé BRYAN (see also ETERNAL)
UK, female vocalist (Singles: 4 Weeks)   pos/wks

2 Oct 99	HIGHER THAN HEAVEN *1st Avenue / Mercury MERCD 522*	**14**	4

Anita BRYANT *US, female vocalist (Singles: 6 Weeks)*   pos/wks

26 May 60	PAPER ROSES (2re) *London HLL 9144*	**24**	4
6 Oct 60	MY LITTLE CORNER OF THE WORLD *London HLL 9171*	**48**	2

Peabo BRYSON
US, male vocalist – Robert Bryson (Singles: 35 Weeks)   pos/wks

20 Aug 83 ●	TONIGHT I CELEBRATE MY LOVE *Capitol CL 302* [1]	**2**	13
16 May 92 ●	BEAUTY AND THE BEAST *Epic 6576607* [2]	**9**	7
17 Jul 93	BY THE TIME THIS NIGHT IS OVER *Arista 74321157142* [3] ...**56**	3
11 Dec 93	A WHOLE NEW WORLD (ALADDIN'S THEME) *Columbia 6599002* [4] ▲ **12**	12

[1] Peabo Bryson and Roberta Flack [2] Celine Dion and Peabo Bryson
[3] Kenny G with Peabo Bryson [4] Regina Belle and Peabo Bryson

BUBBLEROCK See Jonathan KING

Michael BUBLÉ *Canada, male vocalist (Albums: 30 Weeks)* pos/wks

18 Oct 03 ●	MICHAEL BUBLÉ *Reprise 9362485352*	**6**	26
29 May 04	COME FLY WITH ME *Reprise 9362486832*	**52**	2
20 Nov 04	MICHAEL BUBLÉ *Reprise 9362489162*	**46**	4+

The second eponymous album was repacked as a "special Christmas limited edition" and was the original 'Michael Bublé' album with a bonus CD of classic Christmas songs. It was treated as a new album, with a different catalogue number from the original

Catherine BUCHANAN See JELLYBEAN

Roy BUCHANAN *US, male instrumentalist – guitar,*
b. 23 Sep 1939, d. 14 Aug 1988 (Singles: 3 Weeks)   pos/wks

31 Mar 73	SWEET DREAMS *Polydor 2066 307*	**40**	3

The BUCKETHEADS *US, male producer –*
Kenny Gonzalez (Singles: 16 Weeks, Albums: 1 Week)   pos/wks

4 Mar 95 ●	THE BOMB! (THESE SOUNDS FALL INTO MY MIND) *Positiva CDTIV 33*	**5**	13
20 Jan 96	GOT MYSELF TOGETHER *Positiva CDTIV 48*	**12**	3
27 Jan 96	ALL IN THE MIND *Positiva CDTIVA 1010*	**74**	1

Lindsey BUCKINGHAM (see also FLEETWOOD MAC)
US, male vocalist (Singles: 7 Weeks, Albums: 1 Week)   pos/wks

16 Jan 82	TROUBLE *Mercury MER 85*	**31**	7
8 Aug 92	OUT OF THE CRADLE *Mercury 5126582*	**51**	1

Jeff BUCKLEY *US, male vocalist, b. 17 Nov 1966,*
d. 29 May 1997 (Singles: 3 Weeks, Albums: 15 Weeks)   pos/wks

27 May 95	LAST GOODBYE *Columbia 6620422*	**54**	2
6 Jun 98	EVERYBODY HERE WANTS YOU *Columbia 6657912*	**43**	1
27 Aug 94	GRACE *Columbia 4759282*	**50**	7
23 May 98 ●	SKETCHES FOR MY SWEETHEART THE DRUNK *Columbia 4886616*	**7**	4
20 May 00 ●	MYSTERY WHITEBOY – LIVE '95-'96 *Columbia 4979722*...	**8**	2
4 Sep 04	GRACE – LEGACY EDITION (re-issue) *Columbia 5174603*	**44**	2

'Grace – Legacy Edition' is a repackaged three-disc CD and DVD set commemorating the 10th anniversary of the 'Grace' album

BUCKS FIZZ `280` `Top 500` *Chart-topping mixed quartet: Cheryl Baker, Mike Nolan, Jay Aston (replaced by Shelley Preston in 1985) and Bobby G (Gubby). Formed for the 1981 Eurovision Song Contest, they were the last UK winners for 16 years (Singles: 150 Weeks, Albums: 80 Weeks)*   pos/wks

28 Mar 81 ★	MAKING YOUR MIND UP *RCA 56*	**1**	12
6 Jun 81	PIECE OF THE ACTION *RCA 88*	**12**	9
15 Aug 81	ONE OF THOSE NIGHTS *RCA 114*	**20**	10
28 Nov 81 ★	THE LAND OF MAKE BELIEVE *RCA 163*	**1**	16
27 Mar 82 ★	MY CAMERA NEVER LIES *RCA 202*	**1**	8
19 Jun 82 ●	NOW THOSE DAYS ARE GONE *RCA 241*	**8**	9
27 Nov 82 ●	IF YOU CAN'T STAND THE HEAT *RCA 300*	**10**	11
12 Mar 83	RUN FOR YOUR LIFE *RCA FIZ 1*	**14**	7
18 Jun 83 ●	WHEN WE WERE YOUNG *RCA 342*	**10**	8
1 Oct 83	LONDON TOWN *RCA 363*	**34**	6
17 Dec 83	RULES OF THE GAME *RCA 380*	**57**	6
25 Aug 84	TALKING IN YOUR SLEEP *RCA FIZ 2*	**15**	9
27 Oct 84	GOLDEN DAYS *RCA FIZ 3*	**42**	6
29 Dec 84	I HEAR TALK *RCA FIZ 4*	**34**	8
22 Jun 85	YOU AND YOUR HEART SO BLUE *RCA PB 40233*	**43**	4
14 Sep 85	MAGICAL *RCA PB 40367*	**57**	3
7 Jun 86 ●	NEW BEGINNING (MAMBA SEYRA) *Polydor POSP 794*	**8**	10
30 Aug 86	LOVE THE ONE YOU'RE WITH *Polydor POSP 813*	**47**	3
15 Nov 86	KEEP EACH OTHER WARM *Polydor POSP 835*	**45**	4
5 Nov 88	HEART OF STONE *RCA PB 42035*	**50**	3
8 Aug 81	BUCKS FIZZ *RCA RCALP 5050*	**14**	28
18 May 82 ●	ARE YOU READY? *RCA RCALP 8000*	**10**	23
19 Mar 83	HAND CUT *RCA RCALP 6100*	**17**	13
3 Dec 83	GREATEST HITS *RCA RCA PL 70022*	**25**	13
24 Nov 84	I HEAR TALK *RCA PL 70397*	**66**	2
13 Dec 86	THE WRITING ON THE WALL *Polydor POHL 30*	**89**	1

BUCKSHOT LEFONQUE
US, male vocal / instrumental group (Singles: 1 Week)   pos/wks

6 Dec 97	ANOTHER DAY *Columbia 6653762*	**65**	1

Roy BUDD
UK, male instrumentalist – piano (Singles: 1 Week, Albums: 1 Week) pos/wks

10 Jul 99	GET CARTER *Cinephile CINX 1003*	**68**	1
19 Sep 98	GET CARTER (FILM SOUNDTRACK) *Cinephile CINCD 001*	**68**	1

Joe BUDDEN
US, male vocalist (Singles: 20 Weeks, Albums: 1 Week)   pos/wks

19 Jul 03	PUMP IT UP *Def Jam / Mercury 9808879*	**13**	7
20 Mar 04	CLUBBIN' *Elektra E 7544CD* [1]	**15**	6
16 Oct 04 ●	WHATEVER U WANT *Def Jam 9864266* [2]	**9**	7
28 Jun 03	JOE BUDDEN *Def Jam / Mercury 9807936*.....................	**55**	1

[1] Marques Houston featuring Joe Budden and Pied Piper [2] Christina Milian featuring Joe Budden

Harold Budd / Liz FRASER / Robin GUTHRIE / Simon RAYMONDE (see also COCTEAU TWINS)
UK, male / female vocal / instrumental group (Albums: 2 Weeks)   pos/wks

22 Nov 86	THE MOON AND THE MELODIES *4AD CAD 611*	**46**	2

BUDGIE *UK, male vocal / instrumental*
group (Singles: 2 Weeks, Albums: 10 Weeks)   pos/wks

3 Oct 81	KEEPING A RENDEZVOUS *RCA BUDGIE 3*	**71**	2
8 Jun 74	IN FOR THE KILL *MCA MCF 2546*	**29**	3
27 Sep 75	BANDOLIER *MCA MCF 2723*	**36**	4
31 Oct 81	NIGHT FLIGHT *RCA RCALP 6003*	**68**	2
23 Oct 82	DELIVER US FROM EVIL *RCA RCALP 6054*	**62**	1

BUFFALO G *Ireland, female vocal / rap duo –*
Olive Tucker and Naomi Lynch (Singles: 4 Weeks)   pos/wks

10 Jun 00	WE'RE REALLY SAYING SOMETHING (re) *Epic 6694182*	**17**	4

BUFFALO TOM *US, male vocal / instrumental*
group (Singles: 5 Weeks, Albums: 5 Weeks)   pos/wks

23 Oct 99 ●	GOING UNDERGROUND: CARNATION *Ignition IGNSCD 16*	**6**	5
14 Mar 92	LET ME COME OVER *Situation Two SITU 36CD*	**49**	1
9 Oct 93	(BIG RED LETTER DAY) *Beggars Banquet BBQCD 142*.....................	**17**	3
22 Jul 95	SLEEPY EYED *Beggars Banquet BBQCD 177*	**31**	1

BUG KANN and the PLASTIC JAM
UK, male / female vocal / instrumental group (Singles: 2 Weeks) pos/wks

31 Aug 91	MADE IN TWO MINUTES *Optimum Dance BKPJ 1S* [1]	70	1
26 Feb 94	MADE IN 2 MINUTES (re-mix) *PWL International PWCD 286*	64	1

[1] Bug Kann and the Plastic Jam featuring Patti Low and Doogie

The BUGGLES *UK, male vocal / instrumental duo – Trevor Horn and Geoff Downes (Singles: 28 Weeks, Albums: 6 Weeks)* pos/wks

22 Sep 79	★ VIDEO KILLED THE RADIO STAR *Island WIP 6524*	1	11
26 Jan 80	THE PLASTIC AGE *Island WIP 6540*	16	8
5 Apr 80	CLEAN, CLEAN *Island WIP 6584*	38	5
8 Nov 80	ELSTREE *Island WIP 6624*	55	4
16 Feb 80	THE AGE OF PLASTIC *Island ILPS 9585*	27	6

LTJ BUKEM
UK, male DJ / producer – Danny Williamson (Albums: 3 Weeks) pos/wks

8 Apr 00	JOURNEY INWARDS *Good Looking GLRAA 001*	40	3

James BULLER *UK, male vocalist (Singles: 1 Week)* pos/wks

6 Mar 99	CAN'T SMILE WITHOUT YOU *BBC Music WMSS 60092*	51	1

Silvah BULLET See Jonny L

BULLETPROOF
UK, male producer – Paul Chambers (Singles: 1 Week) pos/wks

10 Mar 01	SAY YEAH / DANCE TO THE RHYTHM *Tidy Trax TIDY 148CD*	62	1

BUMP *UK, male instrumental / production duo – Marc Auerbach and Steve Travell (Singles: 5 Weeks)* pos/wks

4 Jul 92	I'M RUSHING *Good Boy EDGE 71*	40	4
11 Nov 95	I'M RUSHING (re-mix) *Deconstruction 74321320692*	45	1

BUMP & FLEX
UK, male / female vocal / production duo (Singles: 1 Week) pos/wks

23 May 98	LONG TIME COMING *Heat Recordings HEATCD 014*	73	1

BUNKER KRU See HARLEQUIN 4s / BUNKER KRU

The BUNNYMEN See ECHO and the BUNNYMEN

Emma BUNTON (see also SPICE GIRLS)
UK, female vocalist (Singles: 68 Weeks, Albums: 23 Weeks) pos/wks

13 Nov 99	● WHAT I AM *VC Recordings VCRD 53* [1]	2	12
14 Apr 01	★ WHAT TOOK YOU SO LONG *Virgin VSCDT 1796* ■	1	12
8 Sep 01	● TAKE MY BREATH AWAY *Virgin VSCDT 1814*	5	9
22 Dec 01	WE'RE NOT GONNA SLEEP TONIGHT *Virgin VSCDT 1821*	20	5
7 Jun 03	● FREE ME *19 / Universal 9807472* [2]	5	9
25 Oct 03	● MAYBE *19 / Universal 9812785* [2]	6	9
7 Feb 04	● I'LL BE THERE (re) *19 / Universal 9816267* [2]	7	8
12 Jun 04	CRICKETS SING FOR ANAMARIA *19 9866826* [2]	15	4
28 Apr 01	● A GIRL LIKE ME *Virgin CDV 2935*	4	12
21 Feb 04	● FREE ME *19 / Universal 9866158* [1]	7	11

[1] Tin Tin Out featuring Emma Bunton [2] Emma [1] Emma

Eric BURDON and WAR (see also The ANIMALS; WAR) *UK, male vocalist and US, male vocal / instrumental group (Albums: 4 Weeks)* pos/wks

3 Oct 70	ERIC BURDON DECLARES WAR *Polydor 2310041*	50	2
20 Feb 71	BLACKMAN'S BURDON *Liberty LDS 8400*	25	2

Tim BURGESS
UK, male vocalist (Singles: 2 Weeks, Albums: 1 Week) pos/wks

6 Sep 03	I BELIEVE IN THE SPIRIT *PIAS Recordings PIASB 109CD*	44	1
15 Nov 03	ONLY A BOY *PIAS Recordings PIASB 119CD*	54	1
20 Sep 03	I BELIEVE *PIAS PIASB 099CD*	38	1

Geoffrey BURGON *UK, orchestra (Singles: 4 Weeks)* pos/wks

26 Dec 81	BRIDESHEAD THEME *Chrysalis CHS 2562*	48	4

Keni BURKE *US, male vocalist (Singles: 4 Weeks)* pos/wks

27 Jun 81	LET SOMEBODY LOVE YOU *RCA 93*	59	3
18 Apr 92	RISIN' TO THE TOP *RCA PB 49103*	70	1

Solomon BURKE See JUNKIE XL

BURN *UK, male vocal / instrumental group (Singles: 2 Weeks)* pos/wks

8 Jun 02	THE SMILING FACE *Hut / Virgin HUTCD 155*	72	1
29 Mar 03	DRUNKEN FOOL *Hut / Virgin HUTCD 166*	54	1

Jean-Jacques BURNEL
UK, male vocalist / instrumentalist – bass guitar (Albums: 6 Weeks) pos/wks

21 Apr 79	EUROMAN COMETH *United Artists UAG 30214*	40	5
3 Dec 83	FIRE AND WATER *Epic EPC 25707* [1]	94	1

[1] Dave Greenfield and Jean-Jacques Burnel

Hank C BURNETTE *Sweden, male multi-instrumentalist – Sven-Ake Hogberg (Singles: 8 Weeks)* pos/wks

30 Oct 76	SPINNING ROCK BOOGIE *Sonet SON 2094*	21	8

Johnny BURNETTE
US, male vocalist, b. 25 Mar 1934, d. 1 Aug 1964 (Singles: 48 Weeks) pos/wks

29 Sep 60	● DREAMIN' *London HLG 9172*	5	16
12 Jan 61	● YOU'RE SIXTEEN *London HLG 9254*	3	12
13 Apr 61	LITTLE BOY SAD *London HLG 9315*	12	12
10 Aug 61	GIRLS *London HLG 9388*	37	5
17 May 62	CLOWN SHOES *Liberty LIB 55416*	35	3

Rocky BURNETTE
US, male vocalist – Jonathan Burnette (Singles: 7 Weeks) pos/wks

17 Nov 79	TIRED OF TOEIN' THE LINE *EMI 2992*	58	7

Jerry BURNS *UK, female vocalist (Singles: 1 Week)* pos/wks

25 Apr 92	PALE RED *Columbia 6579467*	64	1

Pete BURNS (see also DEAD OR ALIVE)
UK, male vocalist (Singles: 1 Week) pos/wks

19 Jun 04	JACK AND JILL PARTY *Olde English UKCDS 02*	75	1

Ray BURNS *UK, male vocalist (Singles: 19 Weeks)* pos/wks

11 Feb 55	● MOBILE *Columbia DB 3563* [1]	4	13
26 Aug 55	THAT'S HOW A LOVE SONG WAS BORN *Columbia DB 3640* [2]	14	6

[1] Ray Burns with Eric Jupp and his Orchestra [2] Ray Burns with the Coronets

BURRELLS See RESONANCE featuring the BURRELLS

Malandra BURROWS
UK, female vocalist / actor (Singles: 10 Weeks) pos/wks

1 Dec 90	JUST THIS SIDE OF LOVE *Yorkshire Television DALE 1*	11	8
18 Oct 97	CARNIVAL IN HEAVEN *Warner.esp WESP 001CD*	49	1
29 Aug 98	DON'T LEAVE ME *Warner.esp WESP 004CD*	54	1

Jenny BURTON *US, female vocalist (Singles: 2 Weeks)* pos/wks

30 Mar 85	BAD HABITS *Atlantic A 9583*	68	2

BURUNDI STEIPHENSON BLACK
Burundi / France, drummers and chanters with orchestral additions by Mike Steiphenson (Singles: 14 Weeks) pos/wks

13 Nov 71	BURUNDI BLACK *Barclay BAR 3*	31	14

BUS 75 See WHALE

BUS STOP (see also FLIP & FILL)
UK, male production group (Singles: 19 Weeks) pos/wks

23 May 98	● KUNG FU FIGHTING *All Around the World CDGLOBE 173* [1]	8	11
24 Oct 98	YOU AIN'T SEEN NOTHIN' YET *All Around the World CDGLOBE 187* [2]	22	4
10 Apr 99	JUMP *All Around the World CDGLOBE 186*	23	3
7 Sep 00	GET IT ON *All Around the World CDGLOBE 225* [3]	59	1

[1] Bus Stop featuring Carl Douglas [2] Bus Stop featuring Randy Bachman [3] Bus Stop featuring T. Rex

Lou BUSCH and his Orchestra *US, orchestra and chorus – aka Joe 'Fingers' Carr, b. 18 Jul 1910, d. 19 Sep 1979 (Singles: 17 Weeks)* pos/wks

27 Jan 56	● ZAMBESI *Capitol CL 14504*	2	17

BUSH *UK, male vocal / instrumental group*
(Singles: 13 Weeks, Albums: 18 Weeks) pos/wks

8 Jun 96	**MACHINEHEAD** *Interscope IND 95505*	.48	2
1 Mar 97 ●	**SWALLOWED** *Interscope IND 95528*	.7	5
7 Jun 97	**GREEDY FLY** *Interscope IND 95536*	.22	2
1 Nov 97	**BONE DRIVEN** *Interscope IND 95553*	.49	1
4 Dec 99	**THE CHEMICALS BETWEEN US** *Trauma / Polydor 4972222*	.46	1
18 Mar 00	**WARM MACHINE** *Trauma / Polydor 4972752*	.45	1
3 Jun 00	**LETTING THE CABLES SLEEP** *Trauma / Polydor 4973352*	.51	1
15 Jun 96	**SIXTEEN STONE** *Interscope 6544925312*	.42	3
1 Feb 97 ●	**RAZORBLADE SUITCASE** *Interscope IND 90091* ▲	.4	12
6 Nov 99	**THE SCIENCE OF THINGS** *Trauma / Polydor 4904832*	.28	2
10 Nov 01	**GOLDEN STATE** *Atlantic 7567834882*	.53	1

Kate BUSH `96` `Top 500`
Unmistakable singer / songwriter with operatic vocal ability, b. 30 Jul 1958, Kent, UK. Discovered by Dave Gilmour of Pink Floyd. First British female to top the singles chart with a self-composed song and the first to have a UK No.1 album (Singles: 168 Weeks, Albums: 281 Weeks) pos/wks

11 Feb 78 ★	**WUTHERING HEIGHTS** (re) *EMI 2719*	.1	13
10 Jun 78 ●	**THE MAN WITH THE CHILD IN HIS EYES** *EMI 2806*	.6	11
11 Nov 78	**HAMMER HORROR** *EMI 2887*	.44	6
17 Mar 79	**WOW** *EMI 2911*	.14	10
15 Sep 79 ●	**ON STAGE (EP)** *EMI MIEP 2991*	.10	9
26 Apr 80	**BREATHING** *EMI 5058*	.16	7
5 Jul 80 ●	**BABOOSHKA** *EMI 5085*	.5	10
4 Oct 80	**ARMY DREAMERS** *EMI 5106*	.16	9
6 Dec 80	**DECEMBER WILL BE MAGIC AGAIN** *EMI 5121*	.29	7
11 Jul 81	**SAT IN YOUR LAP** *EMI 5201*	.11	7
7 Aug 82	**THE DREAMING** *EMI 5296*	.48	3
17 Aug 85 ●	**RUNNING UP THAT HILL** *EMI KB 1*	.3	11
26 Oct 85	**CLOUDBUSTING** *EMI KB 2*	.20	6
1 Mar 86	**HOUNDS OF LOVE** *EMI KB 3*	.18	5
10 May 86	**THE BIG SKY** *EMI KB 4*	.37	3
1 Nov 86 ●	**DON'T GIVE UP** *Virgin PGS 2* [1]	.9	11
8 Nov 86	**EXPERIMENT IV** *EMI KB 5*	.23	4
30 Sep 89	**THE SENSUAL WORLD** *EMI EM 102*	.12	5
2 Dec 89	**THIS WOMAN'S WORK** *EMI EM 119*	.25	5
10 Mar 90	**LOVE AND ANGER** *EMI EM 134*	.38	3
7 Dec 91	**ROCKET MAN (I THINK IT'S GOING TO BE A LONG LONG TIME)** *Mercury TRIBO 2*	.12	8
18 Sep 93	**RUBBERBAND GIRL** *EMI CDEM 280*	.12	5
27 Nov 93	**MOMENTS OF PLEASURE** *EMI CDEM 297*	.26	3
16 Apr 94	**THE RED SHOES** *EMI CDEMS 316*	.21	3
30 Jul 94	**THE MAN I LOVE** *Mercury MERCD 408* [2]	.27	2
19 Nov 94	**AND SO IS LOVE** *EMI CDEMS 355*	.26	2
11 Mar 78 ●	**THE KICK INSIDE** *EMI EMC 3223*	.3	70
25 Nov 78 ●	**LIONHEART** *EMI EMA 787*	.6	36
20 Sep 80 ★	**NEVER FOR EVER** *EMI EMA 7964* ■	.1	23
25 Sep 82 ●	**THE DREAMING** *EMI EMC 3419*	.3	10
28 Sep 85 ★	**HOUNDS OF LOVE** *EMI KAB 1* ■	.1	52
22 Nov 86 ★	**THE WHOLE STORY** *EMI KBTV 1*	.1	55
28 Oct 89 ●	**THE SENSUAL WORLD** *EMI EMD 1010*	.2	20
13 Nov 93 ●	**THE RED SHOES** *EMI CDEMD 1047*	.2	15

[1] Peter Gabriel and Kate Bush [2] Kate Bush and Larry Adler

Tracks on On Stage (EP): Them Heavy People / Don't Push Your Foot on the Heartbrake / James and the Cold Gun / L'Amour Looks Something Like You

BUSTED `307` `Top 500`
Talented pop punk trio who are the highest new entrants in the Top 500 acts; songwriter James Bourne (Southend), Charlie Simpson (Ipswich) and Mattie Jay (Surrey). Named Best Pop Act at the 2004 Brits and 'Thunderbirds' was the ITV 'Record of the Year' in 2004. Announced they were splitting up in early 2005 (Singles: 92 Weeks, Albums: 123 Weeks) pos/wks

28 Sep 02 ●	**WHAT I GO TO SCHOOL FOR** *Universal MCSTD 40294*	.3	12
25 Jan 03 ●	**YEAR 3000** *Universal MCSTD 40306*	.2	15
3 May 03 ★	**YOU SAID NO** *Universal MCSTD 40318* ■	.1	10
23 Aug 03 ●	**SLEEPING WITH THE LIGHT ON** *Universal MCSTD 40327*	.3	10
22 Nov 03 ★	**CRASHED THE WEDDING** *Universal MCSTD 40345* ■	.1	12
28 Feb 04 ★	**WHO'S DAVID** *Universal MCSTD 40355* ■	.1	10
8 May 04 ●	**AIR HOSTESS** *Universal MCSXD 40361*	.2	10
7 Aug 04 ★	**THUNDERBIRDS / 3AM** *Universal MCSXD 40375*	.1	13
12 Oct 02 ●	**BUSTED** *Universal MCD 60084*	.2	77
29 Nov 03 ●	**A PRESENT FOR EVERYONE** *Universal MCD 60090*	.2	39
13 Nov 04	**LIVE – A TICKET FOR EVERYONE** *Universal MCD 60096*	.11	7+

BUSTER *UK, male vocal / instrumental group (Singles: 1 Week)* pos/wks

19 Jun 76	**SUNDAY** *RCA 2678*	.49	1

Bernard BUTLER (see also SUEDE; McALMONT and BUTLER) *UK, male vocalist / instrumentalist (Singles: 9 Weeks, Albums: 9 Weeks)* pos/wks

17 Jan 98	**STAY** *Creation CRESCD 281*	.12	4
28 Mar 98	**NOT ALONE** *Creation CRESCD 289*	.27	3
27 Jun 98	**A CHANGE OF HEART** *Creation CRESCD 297*	.45	1
23 Oct 99	**YOU MUST GO ON** *Creation CRESCD 324*	.44	1
18 Apr 98	**PEOPLE MOVE ON** *Creation CCRE 221*	.11	8
6 Nov 99	**FRIENDS AND LOVERS** *Creation CRECD 248*	.43	1

Jonathan BUTLER *South Africa, male vocalist / instrumentalist – guitar (Singles: 18 Weeks, Albums: 14 Weeks)* pos/wks

25 Jan 86	**IF YOU'RE READY (COME GO WITH ME)** *Jive JIVE 109* [1]	.30	7
8 Aug 87	**LIES** *Jive JIVE 141*	.18	11
12 Sep 87	**JONATHAN BUTLER** *Jive HIP 46*	.12	11
4 Feb 89	**MORE THAN FRIENDS** *Jive HIP 70*	.29	3

[1] Ruby Turner featuring Jonathan Butler

BUTTERSCOTCH *UK, male vocal group (Singles: 11 Weeks)* pos/wks

2 May 70	**DON'T YOU KNOW (SHE SAID HELLO)** *RCA 1937*	.17	11

BUTTHOLE SURFERS *US, male vocal / instrumental group (Singles: 1 Week, Albums: 2 Weeks)* pos/wks

5 Oct 96	**PEPPER** *Capitol CDCL 778*	.59	1
16 Mar 91	**PIOUHGD** *Rough Trade R 20812601*	.68	1
3 Apr 93	**INDEPENDENT WORM SALOON** *Capitol CDEST 2192*	.73	1

The BUZZCOCKS *UK, male vocal / instrumental group (Singles: 53 Weeks, Albums: 23 Weeks)* pos/wks

18 Feb 78	**WHAT DO I GET?** *United Artists UP 36348*	.37	3
13 May 78	**I DON'T MIND** *United Artists UP 36386*	.55	2
15 Jul 78	**LOVE YOU MORE** *United Artists UP 36433*	.34	6
23 Sep 78	**EVER FALLEN IN LOVE (WITH SOMEONE YOU SHOULDN'T'VE)** *United Artists UP 36455*	.12	11
25 Nov 78	**PROMISES** *United Artists UP 36471*	.20	10
10 Mar 79	**EVERYBODY'S HAPPY NOWADAYS** *United Artists UP 36499*	.29	6
21 Jul 79	**HARMONY IN MY HEAD** *United Artists UP 36541*	.32	6
25 Aug 79	**SPIRAL SCRATCH (EP)** *New Hormones ORG 1*	.31	6
6 Sep 80	**ARE EVERYTHING / WHY SHE'S A GIRL FROM THE CHAINSTORE** *United Artists BP 365*	.61	3
25 Mar 78	**ANOTHER MUSIC IN A DIFFERENT KITCHEN** *United Artists UAG 30159*	.15	11
7 Oct 78	**LOVE BITES** *United Artists UAG 30184*	.13	9
6 Oct 79	**A DIFFERENT KIND OF TENSION** *United Artists UAG 30260*	.26	3

Tracks on Spiral Scratch (EP): Breakdown / Time's Up / Boredom / Friends of Mine. Sleeve of EP (not the label) credits The Buzzcocks with Howard Devoto. 'Why She's a Girl from the Chainstore' listed from 13 Sep 1980

BUZZY BUNCH *See Celi BEE and the BUZZY BUNCH*

BY ALL MEANS
US, male vocal group (Singles: 2 Weeks, Albums: 1 Week) pos/wks

18 Jun 88	**I SURRENDER TO YOUR LOVE** *Fourth & Broadway BRW 102*	65	2
16 Jul 88	**BY ALL MEANS** *Fourth & Broadway BRLP 520*	.80	1

Max BYGRAVES `184` `Top 500`
One of Britain's best-loved entertainers, b. Walter Bygraves, 16 Oct 1922, London, UK. The comedian / singer / songwriter was the only British male in the first UK singles chart. He had five Top 20 'sing-a-long' hit albums in just 15 months of the 1970s (Singles: 131 Weeks, Albums: 176 Weeks) pos/wks

14 Nov 52 ●	**COWPUNCHER'S CANTATA** (3re) *HMV B 10250*	.6	8
14 May 54 ●	**(THE GANG THAT SANG) HEART OF MY HEART** *HMV B 10654*	7	8
10 Sep 54 ●	**GILLY GILLY OSSENFEFFER KATZENELLEN BOGEN BY THE SEA** (re) *HMV B 10734*	.7	8
21 Jan 55	**MISTER SANDMAN** *HMV B 10801*	.16	1
18 Nov 55 ●	**MEET ME ON THE CORNER** *HMV POP 116*	.2	11
17 Feb 56	**THE BALLAD OF DAVY CROCKETT** *HMV POP 153*	.20	1
25 May 56	**OUT OF TOWN** *HMV POP 164*	.18	7
5 Apr 57	**HEART** *Decca F 10862* [1]	.14	8
2 May 58 ●	**YOU NEED HANDS / TULIPS FROM AMSTERDAM** *Decca F 11004* [2]	.3	25

22 Aug 58	LITTLE TRAIN / GOTTA HAVE RAIN *Decca F 11046*	28	2
2 Jan 59	(I LOVE TO PLAY) MY UKULELE *Decca F 11077*	19	4
18 Dec 59 ●	JINGLE BELL ROCK *Decca F 11176*	7	4
10 Mar 60 ●	FINGS AIN'T WOT THEY USED T'BE *Decca F 11214*	5	15
28 Jul 60	CONSIDER YOURSELF *Decca F 11251*	50	1
1 Jun 61	THE BELLS OF AVIGNON *Decca F 11350*	36	5
19 Feb 69	YOU'RE MY EVERYTHING (re) *Pye 7N 17705*	34	4
6 Oct 73	DECK OF CARDS *Pye 7N 45276*	13	15
9 Dec 89	WHITE CHRISTMAS *Parkfield PMS 5012*	71	4
23 Sep 72 ●	SING ALONG WITH MAX *Pye NSPL 18361*	4	44
2 Dec 72	SING ALONG WITH MAX VOLUME 2 *Pye NSPL 18383*	11	23
5 May 73 ●	SINGALONGAMAX VOLUME 3 *Pye NSPL 18401*	5	30
29 Sep 73	SINGALONGAMAX VOLUME 4 *Pye NSPL 18410*	7	12
15 Dec 73	SINGALONGPARTY SONG *Pye NSPL 18419*	15	6
12 Oct 74	YOU MAKE ME FEEL LIKE SINGING A SONG *Pye NSPL 18436*	39	3
7 Dec 74	SINGALONGAXMAS *Pye NSPL 18439*	21	6
13 Nov 76 ●	100 GOLDEN GREATS *Ronco RTDX 2019*	3	21
28 Oct 78	LINGALONGAMAX *Ronco RPL 2033*	39	5
16 Dec 78	THE SONG AND DANCE MEN *Pye NSPL 18574*	67	1
19 Aug 89 ●	SINGALONGAWARYEARS *Parkfield Music PMLP 5001*	5	19
25 Nov 89	SINGALONGAWARYEARS VOLUME 2 *Parkfield Music PMLP 5006*	33	6

[1] Max Bygraves with Malcolm Lockyer and his Orchestra [2] Max Bygraves with the Clark Bros and Eric Rodgers and his Orchestra / Max Bygraves with Eric Rodgers and his Orchestra

Cowpuncher's Cantata is a medley with the following songs: Cry of the Wild Goose / Riders in the Sky / Mule Train / Jezebel. 'Tulips from Amsterdam' was listed with 'You Need Hands' from 9 May 1958

BYKER GROOOVE!
UK, female actors / vocal group (Singles: 3 Weeks) pos/wks

24 Dec 94	LOVE YOUR SEXY ... !! *Groove GROVD 01*	48	3

Charlie BYRD *See Stan GETZ*

Debra BYRD *See Barry MANILOW*

Donald BYRD *US, male instrumentalist –*
trumpet (Singles: 6 Weeks, Albums: 3 Weeks) pos/wks

26 Sep 81	LOVING YOU / LOVE HAS COME AROUND *Elektra K 12559*	41	6
10 Oct 81	LOVE BYRD *Elektra K 52301*	70	3

Gary BYRD and the GB EXPERIENCE *US, male rapper*
and male / female vocal / instrumental group (Singles: 9 Weeks) pos/wks

23 Jul 83 ●	THE CROWN *Motown TMGT 1312*	6	9

Features uncredited vocals by Stevie Wonder

The BYRDS *US, male vocal / instrumental*
group (Singles: 52 Weeks, Albums: 42 Weeks) pos/wks

17 Jun 65 ★	MR TAMBOURINE MAN *CBS 201765* ▲	1	14
12 Aug 65 ●	ALL I REALLY WANT TO DO *CBS 201796*	4	10
11 Nov 65	TURN! TURN! TURN! (TO EVERYTHING THERE IS A SEASON) *CBS 202008* ▲	26	8
5 May 66	EIGHT MILES HIGH *CBS 202067*	24	9
5 Jun 68	YOU AIN'T GOING NOWHERE *CBS 3411*	45	3
13 Feb 71	CHESTNUT MARE *CBS 5322*	19	8
28 Aug 65 ●	MR. TAMBOURINE MAN *CBS BPG 62571*	7	12
9 Apr 66	TURN TURN TURN *CBS BPG 62652*	11	5
1 Oct 66	5TH DIMENSION *CBS BPG 62783*	27	2
22 Apr 67	YOUNGER THAN YESTERDAY *CBS SBPG 62988*	37	4
4 May 68	THE NOTORIOUS BYRD BROTHERS *CBS 63169*	12	11
24 May 69	DR. BYRDS AND MR. HYDE *CBS 63545*	15	1
14 Feb 70	BALLAD OF EASY RIDER *CBS 63795*	41	1
28 Nov 70	(UNTITLED) / (UNISSUED) *CBS 66253*	11	4
14 Apr 73	BYRDS *Asylum SYLA 8754*	31	1
19 May 73	HISTORY OF THE BYRDS *CBS 68242*	47	1

David BYRNE (see also TALKING HEADS) *UK, male vocalist /*
instrumentalist (Singles: 8 Weeks, Albums: 18 Weeks) pos/wks

20 Apr 02 ●	LAZY *Skint SKINT 74CD* [1]	2	13
21 Feb 81	MY LIFE IN THE BUSH OF GHOSTS *Polydor EGLP 48* [1]	29	8
21 Oct 89	REI MOMO *Warner Bros. WX 319*	52	2
14 Mar 92	UH-OH *Luaka Bop 7599267992*	26	5
4 Jun 94	DAVID BYRNE *Luaka Bop 9362455582*	44	2
19 May 01	LOOK INTO THE EYEBALL *Luaka Bop CDVUS 189*	58	1

[1] X-Press 2 featuring David Byrne [1] Brian Eno and David Byrne

Edward BYRNES and Connie STEVENS
US, male / female actors / vocal duo – Edward Brietenberger and Concetta Ingolia (Singles: 8 Weeks) pos/wks

5 May 60	KOOKIE KOOKIE (LEND ME YOUR COMB) *Warner Bros. WB 5*	27	8

The BYSTANDERS
UK, male vocal / instrumental group (Singles: 1 Week) pos/wks

9 Feb 67	98.6 *Piccadilly 7N 35363*	45	1

ANDY C *See SHIMON & Andy C*

Melanie C (427 Top 500) (see also SPICE GIRLS)
Former Sporty Spice (b. Melanie Chisholm, 12 Jan 1974, Liverpool, UK) has appeared on 11 No.1 hits – a total never bettered by any female artist. Only woman to top the UK chart solo and as part of a duo, quartet and quintet (Singles: 91 Weeks, Albums: 73 Weeks) pos/wks

12 Dec 98 ●	WHEN YOU'RE GONE *A&M 5828212* [1]	3	19
9 Oct 99 ●	GOIN' DOWN (re) *Virgin VSCDT 1744*	4	6
4 Dec 99 ●	NORTHERN STAR *Virgin VSCDT 1748*	4	11
1 Apr 00 ★	NEVER BE THE SAME AGAIN (re) *Virgin VSCDT 1762* [2] ■	1	16
19 Aug 00 ★	I TURN TO YOU *Virgin VSCDT 1772* ■	1	12
9 Dec 00	IF THAT WERE ME (re) *Virgin VSCDT 1786*	18	10
8 Mar 03 ●	HERE IT COMES AGAIN (re) *Virgin VSCDT 1842*	7	8
14 Jun 03	ON THE HORIZON (re) *Virgin VSCDT 1851*	14	7
22 Nov 03	MELT / YEH YEH YEH *Virgin VSCDX 1858*	27	2
30 Oct 99 ●	NORTHERN STAR *Virgin CDVX 2893*	4	69
22 Mar 03 ●	REASON *Virgin CDV 2969*	5	4

[1] Bryan Adams featuring Melanie C [2] Melanie C / Lisa 'Left Eye' Lopes

Roy C *US, male vocalist – Roy C Hammond (Singles: 24 Weeks)* pos/wks

21 Apr 66 ●	SHOTGUN WEDDING *Island WI 273*	6	11
25 Nov 72 ●	SHOTGUN WEDDING (re-issue) *UK 19*	8	13

C & C MUSIC FACTORY *US, male instrumental / production duo – Robert*
Clivilles and David Cole, b. 3 Jun 1962, d. 24 Jan 1995, featuring male / female vocalists / rappers (Singles: 53 Weeks, Albums: 14 Weeks) pos/wks

15 Dec 90 ●	GONNA MAKE YOU SWEAT (EVERYBODY DANCE NOW) *CBS 6564540* [1] ▲	3	12
30 Mar 91	HERE WE GO *Columbia 6567557* [1]	20	7
6 Jul 91 ●	THINGS THAT MAKE YOU GO HMMM ... *Columbia 6566907* [1]	4	11
23 Nov 91	JUST A TOUCH OF LOVE (EVERYDAY) *Columbia 6575247* [2]	31	3
18 Jan 92	PRIDE (IN THE NAME OF LOVE) *Columbia 6577017* [3]	15	5
14 Mar 92	A DEEPER LOVE *Columbia 6578497* [3]	15	5
3 Oct 92	KEEP IT COMIN' (DANCE TILL YOU CAN'T DANCE NO MORE) *Columbia 6584307* [4]	34	3
27 Aug 94	DO YOU WANNA GET FUNKY *Columbia 6607622*	27	3
18 Feb 95	I FOUND LOVE / TAKE A TOKE *Columbia 6612112* [5]	26	2
11 Nov 95	I'LL ALWAYS BE AROUND *MCA MCSTD 40001*	42	2
9 Feb 91 ●	GONNA MAKE YOU SWEAT *Columbia 4678141* [1]	8	13
28 Mar 92	GREATEST REMIXES VOLUME 1 *Columbia 4694462* [2]	45	1

[1] C & C Music Factory (featuring Freedom Williams) [2] C & C Music Factory featuring Zelma Davis [3] Clivilles and Cole [4] C & C Music Factory featuring Q Unique and Deborah Cooper [5] C & C Music Factory / C & C Music Factory featuring Martha Wash [1] C&C Music Factory [2] Clivilles and Cole

C.C.S. UK, male vocal / instrumental group
(Singles: 55 Weeks, Albums: 5 Weeks)

		pos/wks	
31 Oct 70	WHOLE LOTTA LOVE *RAK 104*	.13	13
27 Feb 71 ●	WALKIN' *RAK 109*	.7	16
4 Sep 71 ●	TAP TURNS ON THE WATER *RAK 119*	.5	13
4 Mar 72	BROTHER *RAK 126*	.25	8
4 Aug 73	THE BAND PLAYED THE BOOGIE *RAK 154*	.36	5
8 Apr 72	CCS *RAK SRAK 503*	.23	5

CJ & CO US, male vocal / instrumental group (Singles: 2 Weeks)

		pos/wks	
30 Jul 77	DEVIL'S GUN *Atlantic K 10956*	.43	2

CK See BADFELLAS featuring CK; JAIMESON

CK & SUPREME DREAM TEAM
Holland / Belgium / US, male production trio (Singles: 3 Weeks)

		pos/wks	
11 Jan 03	DREAMER *Multiply CDMULTY 96*	.23	3

CLS US, male vocal / production duo (Singles: 1 week)

		pos/wks	
30 May 98	CAN YOU FEEL IT *Satellite 74321580162*	.46	1

CMC See Charlotte CHURCH

CM2 featuring Lisa LAW
UK, male production group and female vocalist (Singles: 1 Week)

		pos/wks	
18 Jan 03	FALL AT YOUR FEET *Dance Pool 6732532*	.66	1

C.O.D US, male vocal / instrumental group (Singles: 2 Weeks)

		pos/wks	
14 May 83	IN THE BOTTLE *Streetwave WAVE 2*	.54	2

CRW Italy, male producer – Mauro Picotto (Singles: 8 Weeks)

		pos/wks	
26 Feb 00	I FEEL LOVE *VC Recordings VCRD 63*	.15	4
25 Nov 00	LOVIN' *VC Recordings VCRD 77*	.49	2
27 Apr 02	LIKE A CAT *BXR BXRC 0397* [1]	.57	1
26 Oct 02	PRECIOUS LIFE *BXR BXRC 0395* [2]	.57	1

[1] CRW featuring Veronika [2] CRW presents Veronika

CZR featuring DELANO
US, male production group and US, male vocalist (Singles: 1 Week)

		pos/wks	
30 Sep 00	I WANT YOU *Credence CDCRED 002*	.57	1

ÇA VA ÇA VA
UK, male vocal / instrumental group (Singles: 8 Weeks)

		pos/wks	
18 Sep 82	WHERE'S ROMEO *Regard RG 103*	.49	5
19 Feb 83	BROTHER BRIGHT *Regard RG 105*	.65	3

Montserrat CABALLÉ
Spain, female vocalist (Singles: 17 Weeks, Albums: 11 Weeks)

		pos/wks	
7 Nov 87 ●	BARCELONA *Polydor POSP 887* [1]	.8	9
8 Aug 92 ●	BARCELONA (re-issue) *Polydor PO 221* [1]	.2	8
22 Oct 88	BARCELONA *Polydor POLH 44* [1]	.15	8
8 Aug 92	FROM THE OFFICIAL BARCELONA GAMES CEREMONY *RCA Red Seal 09026612042* [2]	.41	3

[1] Freddie Mercury and Montserrat Caballé [1] Freddie Mercury and Montserrat Caballé [2] Placido Domingo, José Carreras and Montserrat Caballé

CABANA
Brazil, male / female vocal / instrumental duo (Singles: 1 Week)

		pos/wks	
15 Jul 95	BAILANDO CON LOBOS *Hi-Life 5792512*	.65	1

CABARET VOLTAIRE UK, male vocal /
instrumental group (Singles: 8 Weeks, Albums: 11 Weeks)

		pos/wks	
18 Jul 87	DON'T ARGUE *Parlophone R 6157*	.69	2
4 Nov 89	HYPNOTISED *Parlophone R 6227*	.66	2
12 May 90	KEEP ON *Parlophone R 6250*	.55	2
18 Aug 90	EASY LIFE *Parlophone R 6261*	.61	2
26 Jun 82	2 X 45 *Rough Trade ROUGH 42*	.98	1
13 Aug 83	THE CRACKDOWN *Some Bizzare CV 1*	.31	5

		pos/wks	
10 Nov 84	MICRO-PHONIES *Some Bizzare CV 2*	.69	1
3 Aug 85	DRINKING GASOLINE *Some Bizzare CVM 1*	.71	2
26 Oct 85	THE COVENANT THE SWORD AND THE ARM OF THE LORD *Some Bizzare CV 3*	.57	2

CABLE UK, male vocal / instrumental group (Singles: 2 Weeks)

		pos/wks	
14 Jun 97	FREEZE THE ATLANTIC *Infectious INFECT 38CD*	.44	2

Albert CABRERA See David MORALES

CACIQUE
UK, male / female vocal / instrumental group (Singles: 1 Week)

		pos/wks	
1 Jun 85	DEVOTED TO YOU *Diamond Duel DISC 1*	.69	1

CACTUS WORLD NEWS Ireland, male vocal /
instrumental group (Singles: 7 Weeks, Albums: 2 Weeks)

		pos/wks	
8 Feb 86	YEARS LATER *MCA MCA 1024*	.59	3
26 Apr 86	WORLDS APART *MCA MCA 1040*	.58	3
20 Sep 86	THE BRIDGE *MCA MCA 1080*	.74	1
24 May 86	URBAN BEACHES *MCA MCG 6005*	.56	2

CADETS with Eileen REID Ireland, male /
female vocal / instrumental group (Singles: 1 Week)

		pos/wks	
3 Jun 65	JEALOUS HEART *Pye 7N 15852*	.42	1

Susan CADOGAN
Jamaica, female vocalist – Alison Cadogan (Singles: 19 Weeks)

		pos/wks	
5 Apr 75 ●	HURT SO GOOD *Magnet MAG 23*	.4	12
19 Jul 75	LOVE ME BABY *Magnet MAG 36*	.22	7

CAESARS
Sweden, male vocal / instrumental group (Singles: 1 Week)

		pos/wks	
19 Apr 03	JERK IT OUT *Virgin DINSD 244*	.60	1

Athena CAGE See Keith SWEAT

Al CAIOLA US, orchestra leader – guitar (Singles: 6 Weeks)

		pos/wks	
15 Jun 61	THE MAGNIFICENT SEVEN *HMVPOP 889 / LONDON HLT 9294*	.34	6

CAKE US, male vocal / instrumental
group (Singles: 7 Weeks, Albums: 2 Weeks)

		pos/wks	
22 Mar 97	THE DISTANCE *Capricorn 5742212*	.22	3
31 May 97	I WILL SURVIVE *Capricorn 5744712*	.29	2
1 May 99	NEVER THERE *Capricorn 8708112*	.66	1
3 Nov 01	SHORT SKIRT LONG JACKET *Columbia 6720402*	.63	1
5 Apr 97	FASHION NUGGET *Capricorn 5328672*	.53	2

J.J. CALE US, male vocalist / instrumentalist –
guitar – Jean Jacques Cale (Albums: 24 Weeks)

		pos/wks	
2 Oct 76	TROUBADOUR *Island ISA 5011*	.53	1
25 Aug 79	5 *Shelter ISA 5018*	.40	6
21 Feb 81	SHADES *Shelter ISA 5021*	.44	7
20 Mar 82	GRASSHOPPER *Shelter IFA 5022*	.36	5
24 Sep 83	#8 *Mercury MERL 22*	.47	3
26 Sep 92	NUMBER 10 *Silvertone ORECD 523*	.58	2

John CALE See Lou REED

CALEXICO
US, male vocal / instrumental group (Albums: 2 Weeks)

		pos/wks	
20 May 00	HOT RAIL *City Slang 201532*	.57	1
22 Feb 03	FEAST OF WIRE *City Slang 5816932*	.71	1

CALIBRE CUTS See VARIOUS ARTISTS (MONTAGES)

CALIFORNIA SUNSHINE
Israel / Italy, male / female DJ / production group (Singles: 1 Week)

		pos/wks	
16 Aug 97	SUMMER '89 *Perfecto PERF 143CD*	.56	1

CALL US, male vocal / instrumental group (Singles: 6 Weeks)

		pos/wks	
30 Sep 89	LET THE DAY BEGIN *MCA MCA 1362*	.42	6

Maria CALLAS Greece, female vocalist – Cecilia
Kalogeropoulou, b. 2 Dec 1923, d. 16 Sep 1978 (Albums: 19 Weeks)

		pos/wks
20 Jun 87	THE MARIA CALLAS COLLECTION Stylus SMR 732 50	7
24 Feb 96	DIVA – THE ULTIMATE COLLECTION EMI CDEMTVD 113 61	1
11 Nov 00	POPULAR MUSIC FROM TV FILM AND OPERA EMI Classics CDC 5570502 45	8
27 Oct 01	THE BEST OF – ROMANTIC CALLAS – A COLLECTION OF ROMANTIC ARIAS AND DUETS EMI Classics CDC 5572112 .. 32	3

Terry CALLIER US, male vocalist (Singles: 4 Weeks)

		pos/wks
13 Dec 97	BEST BIT (EP) Heavenly HVN 72CD [1] 36	3
23 May 98	LOVE THEME FROM SPARTACUS Talkin Loud TLCD 32 57	1

[1] Beth Orton featuring Terry Callier

Tracks on Best Bit (EP): Best Bit / Skimming Stone / Dolphins / Lean On Me

The CALLING US, male vocal /
instrumental group (Singles: 21 Weeks, Albums: 29 Weeks)

		pos/wks
29 Jun 02	WHEREVER YOU WILL GO (IMPORT) RCA 74321912242 64	1
6 Jul 02 ●	WHEREVER YOU WILL GO RCA 74321947652 3	11
2 Nov 02	ADRIENNE RCA 74321968352 18	3
29 May 04	OUR LIVES RCA 82876618642 13	4
28 Aug 04	THINGS WILL GO MY WAY RCA 82876637362 34	2
29 Jun 02	CAMINO PALMERO RCA 74321916102 12	25
12 Jun 04 ●	II RCA 82876622622 9	4

Eddie CALVERT UK, male instrumentalist – trumpet,
b. 15 Mar 1922, d. 7 Aug 1978 (Singles: 80 Weeks)

		pos/wks
18 Dec 53 ★	OH, MEIN PAPA Columbia DB 3337 1	21
8 Apr 55 ★	CHERRY PINK AND APPLE BLOSSOM WHITE Columbia DB 3581 1	21
13 May 55	STRANGER IN PARADISE Columbia DB 3594 14	4
29 Jul 55 ●	JOHN AND JULIE Columbia DB 3624 6	11
9 Mar 56	ZAMBESI (re) Columbia DB 3747 13	7
7 Feb 58 ●	MANDY (LA PANSE) Columbia DB 3956 9	14
20 Jun 58	LITTLE SERENADE Columbia DB 4105 28	2

Donnie CALVIN See ROCKER'S REVENGE featuring Donnie CALVIN

CAMBRIDGE SINGERS See John RUTTER

CAMEL
UK, male vocal / instrumental group (Albums: 47 Weeks)

		pos/wks
24 May 75	THE SNOW GOOSE Decca SKL 5207 22	13
17 Apr 76	MOON MADNESS Decca TXS 115 15	6
17 Sep 77	RAIN DANCES Decca TXS 124 20	8
14 Oct 78	BREATHLESS Decca TXS 132 26	1
27 Oct 79	I CAN SEE YOUR HOUSE FROM HERE Decca TXS 137 45	3
31 Jan 81	NUDE Decca SKL 5323 34	7
15 May 82	THE SINGLE FACTOR Decca SKL 5328 57	5
21 Apr 84	STATIONARY TRAVELLER Decca SKL 5334 57	4

CAMEO US, male vocal / instrumental
group (Singles: 71 Weeks, Albums: 47 Weeks)

		pos/wks
31 Mar 84	SHE'S STRANGE Club JAB 2 37	8
13 Jul 85	ATTACK ME WITH YOUR LOVE Club JAB 16 65	2
14 Sep 85	SINGLE LIFE Club JAB 21 15	10
7 Dec 85	SHE'S STRANGE (re-issue) Club JAB 25 22	8
22 Mar 86	A GOODBYE Club JAB 28 65	2
30 Aug 86 ●	WORD UP Club JAB 38 3	13
29 Nov 86	CANDY Club JAB 43 27	9
25 Apr 87	BACK AND FORTH Club JAB 49 11	9
17 Oct 87	SHE'S MINE Club JAB 57 35	4
29 Oct 88	YOU MAKE ME WORK Club JAB 70 74	1
28 Jul 01	LOVERBOY (re) Virgin VUSCD 211 [1] 12	5
10 Aug 85	SINGLE LIFE Club JABH 11 66	12
18 Oct 86 ●	WORD UP Club JABH 19 7	34
26 Nov 88	MACHISMO Club 836002 1 86	1

[1] Mariah featuring Cameo

Andy CAMERON UK, male vocalist (Singles: 8 Weeks)

		pos/wks
4 Mar 78 ●	ALLY'S TARTAN ARMY Klub 03 6	8

CAMILLA See MOJOLATORS featuring CAMILLA

Tony CAMILLO'S BAZUKA
US, male instrumental / vocal group (Singles: 5 Weeks)

		pos/wks
31 May 75	DYNOMITE (PART 1) A&M AMS 7168 28	5

CAMISRA (see also ESCRIMA; The GRIFTERS) UK, male
DJ / producer – 'Tall Paul' Newman (Singles: 12 Weeks)

		pos/wks
21 Feb 98 ●	LET ME SHOW YOU VC Recordings VCRD 31 5	8
11 Jul 98	FEEL THE BEAT VC Recordings VCRD 39 32	2
22 May 99	CLAP YOUR HANDS VC Recordings VCRD 49 34	2

CAMOUFLAGE featuring MYSTI
UK, male / female vocal / instrumental group (Singles: 3 Weeks)

		pos/wks
24 Sep 77	BEE STING State STAT 58 48	3

CAMP LO US, male rap duo (Singles: 1 Week)

		pos/wks
16 Aug 97	LUCHINI AKA (THIS IS IT) ffrr FCD 305 74	1

CAMPAG VELOCET
UK, male / female vocal / instrumental group (Singles: 1 Week)

		pos/wks
19 Feb 00	VITO SATAN Pias Recordings PIASX 010CD 75	1

Ali CAMPBELL (see also Pato BANTON; UB40)
UK, male vocalist (Singles: 18 Weeks, Albums: 11 Weeks)

		pos/wks
20 May 95 ●	THAT LOOK IN YOUR EYE Kuff KUFFDG 1 5	10
26 Aug 95	LET YOUR YEAH BE YEAH Kuff KUFFD 2 25	4
9 Dec 95	SOMETHIN' STUPID Kuff KUFFDG 5 [1] 30	4
17 Jun 95 ●	BIG LOVE Kuff CDV 2783 6	11

[1] Ali and Kibibi Campbell

Danny CAMPBELL and SASHA
UK, male vocalist and male DJ / producer (Singles: 1 Week)

		pos/wks
31 Jul 93	TOGETHER ffrr FCD 212 57	1

Don CAMPBELL See GENERAL SAINT

Ellie CAMPBELL UK, female vocalist (Singles: 5 Weeks)

		pos/wks
3 Apr 99	SWEET LIES Jive / Eastern Bloc 0519222 42	1
14 Aug 99	SO MANY WAYS Jive / Eastern Bloc 0519362 26	3
9 Jun 01	DON'T WANT YOU BACK Jive 9201302 50	1

Ethna CAMPBELL UK, female vocalist (Singles: 11 Weeks)

		pos/wks
27 Dec 75	THE OLD RUGGED CROSS Philips 6006 475 33	11

Glen CAMPBELL 202 Top 500
Top session guitarist and singer who became one of the biggest selling country and easy listening artists of the 1960s, b. 22 Apr 1936, Arkansas, US. Other credits include part-time member of The Beach Boys and vocalist with The Crickets (Singles: 106 Weeks, Albums: 185 Weeks)

		pos/wks
29 Jan 69 ●	WICHITA LINEMAN Ember EMBS 261 7	13
7 May 69	GALVESTON Ember EMBS 263 14	10
6 Dec 69 ●	ALL I HAVE TO DO IS DREAM Capitol CL 15619 [1] 3	14
7 Feb 70	TRY A LITTLE KINDNESS Capitol CL 15622 45	2
9 May 70 ●	HONEY COME BACK Capitol CL 15638 4	19
26 Sep 70	EVERYTHING A MAN COULD EVER NEED Capitol CL 15653 .. 32	5
21 Nov 70 ●	IT'S ONLY MAKE BELIEVE Capitol CL 15663 4	14
27 Mar 71	DREAM BABY (HOW LONG MUST I DREAM) Capitol CL 15674 .. 39	3
4 Oct 75 ●	RHINESTONE COWBOY Capitol CL 15824 ▲ 4	12
26 Mar 77	SOUTHERN NIGHTS Capitol CL 15907 ▲ 28	6
30 Nov 02	RHINESTONE COWBOY (GIDDY UP GIDDY UP) Serious SER 059CD [2] 12	8
31 Jan 70	GLEN CAMPBELL LIVE Capitol SB 21444 16	14
28 Feb 70	BOBBIE GENTRY AND GLEN CAMPBELL Capitol ST 2928 [1] .. 50	1
30 May 70	TRY A LITTLE KINDNESS Capitol ESW 389 37	10
12 Dec 70	THE GLEN CAMPBELL ALBUM Capitol ST 22493 16	5
27 Nov 71 ●	GLEN CAMPBELL'S GREATEST HITS Capitol ST 21885 8	113
25 Oct 75	RHINESTONE COWBOY Capitol ESW 11430 38	9
20 Nov 76 ★	GLEN CAMPBELL'S TWENTY GOLDEN GREATS Capitol EMTV 2 .. 1	27
23 Apr 77	SOUTHERN NIGHTS Capitol EST 11601 51	1
22 Jul 89	THE COMPLETE GLEN CAMPBELL Stylus SMR 979 47	4
2 Oct 99	MY HITS AND LOVE SONGS Capitol 5223002 50	1

[1] Bobbie Gentry and Glen Campbell [2] Rikki and Daz featuring Glen Campbell
[1] Bobbie Gentry and Glen Campbell

Jo Ann CAMPBELL
US, female vocalist (Singles: 3 Weeks)   pos/wks

8 Jun 61	MOTORCYCLE MICHAEL *HMV POP 873* **41** 3

Junior CAMPBELL (see also MARMALADE)
UK, male vocalist – William Campbell (Singles: 18 Weeks)   pos/wks

| 14 Oct 72 ● | HALLELUJAH FREEDOM *Deram DM 364* .... **10** 9 |
| 2 Jun 73 | SWEET ILLUSION *Deram DM 387* .... **15** 9 |

Kibibi CAMPBELL See Ali CAMPBELL

Naomi CAMPBELL
UK, female vocalist (Singles: 3 Weeks)   pos/wks

| 24 Sep 94 | LOVE AND TEARS *Epic 6608352* .... **40** 3 |

Pat CAMPBELL
Ireland, male vocalist (Singles: 5 Weeks)   pos/wks

| 15 Nov 69 | THE DEAL *Major Minor MM 648* .... **31** 5 |

Stan CAMPBELL
UK, male vocalist (Singles: 3 Weeks)   pos/wks

| 6 Jun 87 | YEARS GO BY *WEA YZ 127* .... **65** 3 |

Tevin CAMPBELL
US, male vocalist (Singles: 2 Weeks)   pos/wks

| 18 Apr 92 | TELL ME WHAT YOU WANT ME TO DO *Qwest W 0102* .... **63** 2 |

Ian CAMPBELL FOLK GROUP
UK, male vocal / instrumental group (Singles: 5 Weeks)   pos/wks

| 11 Mar 65 | THE TIMES THEY ARE A-CHANGIN' (2re) *Transatlantic SP 5* .. **42** 5 |

CAM'RON
US, male rapper – Cameron Giles (Singles: 27 Weeks)   pos/wks

19 Sep 98	HORSE AND CARRIAGE *Epic 6662612* [1] **12** 4
17 Aug 02	OH BOY *Roc-A-Fella 0639642* [2] **13** 7
8 Feb 03 ●	HEY MA *Roc-A-Fella 0637242* [2] **8** 10
5 Apr 03	BOY (I NEED YOU) *Def Jam 0779282* [3] **17** 6

[1] Cam'ron featuring Ma$e [2] Cam'ron featuring Juelz Santana [3] Mariah Carey featuring Cam'ron

CAN
Germany, male vocal / instrumental group (Singles: 10 Weeks) pos/wks

| 28 Aug 76 | I WANT MORE *Virgin VS 153* .... **26** 10 |

CANDIDO
Cuba, male multi-instrumentalist – Candido Camero (Singles: 3 Weeks)   pos/wks

| 18 Jul 81 | JINGO *Excalibur EXC 102* .... **55** 3 |

CANDLEWICK GREEN
UK, male vocal / instrumental group (Singles: 8 Weeks)   pos/wks

| 23 Feb 74 | WHO DO YOU THINK YOU ARE? *Decca F 13480* .... **21** 8 |

CANDY FLIP
UK, male vocal / instrumental duo – Rick Peel and Danny 'Dizzy' Deo (Singles: 14 Weeks)   pos/wks

| 17 Mar 90 ● | STRAWBERRY FIELDS FOREVER *Debut DEBT 3092* ● .... **3** 10 |
| 14 Jul 90 | THIS CAN BE REAL *Debut DEBT 3099* .... **60** 4 |

CANDY GIRLS (see also DOROTHY; HI-GATE; CLERGY; Paul MASTERSON presents SUSHI)
UK, male / female instrumental / production duo – Rachel Auburn and Paul Masterson (Singles: 10 Weeks)   pos/wks

30 Sep 95	FEE FI FO FUM *VC VCRD 1* [1] **23** 4
24 Feb 96	WHAM BAM *VC VCRD 6* [1] **20** 4
7 Dec 96	I WANT CANDY *Feverpitch CDFVR 1013* [2] **30** 2

[1] Candy Girls featuring Sweet Pussy Pauline [2] Candy Girls featuring Valerie Malcolm

CANDYLAND
UK, male vocal / instrumental group (Singles: 1 Week)   pos/wks

| 9 Mar 91 | FOUNTAIN O' YOUTH *Non Fiction YES 4* .... **72** 1 |

The CANDYSKINS
UK, male vocal / instrumental group (Singles: 4 Weeks)   pos/wks

19 Oct 96	MRS HOOVER *Ultimate TOPP 051CD* **65** 1
8 Feb 97	MONDAY MORNING *Ultimate TOPP 055CD* **34** 2
3 May 97	HANG MYSELF ON YOU *Ultimate TOPP 059CD* **65** 1

CANIBUS
US, male rapper – Germaine Williams (Singles: 3 Weeks, Albums: 1 Week)   pos/wks

27 Jun 98	SECOND ROUND KO *Universal UND 56198* **35** 2
10 Oct 98	HOW COME *Interscope IND 95598* [1] **52** 1
19 Sep 98	CAN-I-BUS *Universal UND 53222* **43** 1

[1] Youssou N'Dour and Canibus

CANNED HEAT
US, male vocal / instrumental group (Singles: 41 Weeks, Albums: 40 Weeks)   pos/wks

24 Jul 68 ●	ON THE ROAD AGAIN *Liberty LBS 15090* **8** 15
1 Jan 69	GOING UP THE COUNTRY *Liberty LBF 15169* **19** 10
17 Jan 70 ●	LET'S WORK TOGETHER *Liberty LBF 15302* **2** 15
11 Jul 70	SUGAR BEE *Liberty LBF 15350* **49** 1
29 Jun 68 ●	BOOGIE WITH CANNED HEAT *Liberty LBL 83103* **5** 21
14 Feb 70 ●	CANNED HEAT COOKBOOK *Liberty LBS 83303* **8** 12
4 Jul 70	CANNED HEAT '70 CONCERT *Liberty LBS 83333* **15** 3
10 Oct 70	FUTURE BLUES *Liberty LBS 83364* **27** 4

Freddy CANNON
US, male vocalist – Freddy Picariello (Singles: 54 Weeks, Albums: 11 Weeks)   pos/wks

14 Aug 59	TALLAHASSEE LASSIE *Top Rank JAR 135* **17** 8
1 Jan 60 ●	WAY DOWN YONDER IN NEW ORLEANS *Top Rank JAR 247* .. **3** 18
4 Mar 60	CALIFORNIA HERE I COME (re) *Top Rank JAR 309* **25** 3
17 Mar 60	INDIANA *Top Rank JAR 309* **42** 1
19 May 60	THE URGE *Top Rank JAR 369* **18** 10
20 Apr 61	MUSKRAT RAMBLE *Top Rank JAR 548* **32** 5
28 Jun 62	PALISADES PARK *Stateside SS 101* **20** 9
27 Feb 60 ★	THE EXPLOSIVE FREDDY CANNON *Top Rank 25/108* **1** 11

Blu CANTRELL
US, female vocalist – Tiffany Cantrell (Singles: 33 Weeks, Albums: 11 Weeks)   pos/wks

24 Nov 01	HIT 'EM UP STYLE (OOPS!) *Arista 74321891632* **12** 9
19 Jul 03	BREATHE (IMPORT) *Arista 8788509842* [1] **59** 3
9 Aug 03 ★	BREATHE *Arista 82876545722* [1]■ **1** 18
13 Dec 03	MAKE ME WANNA SCREAM *Arista 82876573382* **24** 3
9 Aug 03	BITTERSWEET *Arista 82876534042* **20** 11

[1] Blu Cantrell featuring Sean Paul

Jim CAPALDI
UK, male vocalist, b. 2 Aug 1944, d. 28 Jan 2005 (Singles: 17 Weeks) pos/wks

| 27 Jul 74 | IT'S ALL UP TO YOU *Island WIP 6198* .... **27** 6 |
| 25 Oct 75 ● | LOVE HURTS *Island WIP 6246* .... **4** 11 |

CAPERCAILLIE
UK / Ireland, male / female vocal / instrumental group (Singles: 3 Weeks, Albums: 8 Weeks)   pos/wks

23 May 92	A PRINCE AMONG ISLANDS (EP) *Survival ZB 45393* **39** 2
17 Jun 95	DARK ALAN (AILEIN DUINN) *Survival SURCD 55* **65** 1
25 Sep 93	SECRET PEOPLE *Arista 74321162742* **40** 3
17 Sep 94	CAPERCAILLIE *Survival 74321229112* **61** 1
4 Nov 95	TO THE MOON *Survival SURCD 019* **41** 2
20 Sep 97	BEAUTIFUL WASTELAND *Survival SURCD 021* **55** 2

Tracks on A Prince Among Islands (EP): Coisich a Ruin (Walk My Beloved) / Fagail Bhearnaraid (Leaving Bernaray) / The Lorn Theme / Gun Teann Mi Ris Na Ruinn Tha Seo (Remembrance)

CAPPADONNA (see also WU-TANG CLAN)
US, male rapper – Daryl Hill (Albums: 1 Week)   pos/wks

| 4 Apr 98 | THE PILLAGE *Epic 4888502* .... **43** 1 |

CAPPELLA (see also 49ers)
Italy, male / female production / vocal group (Singles: 68 Weeks, Albums: 9 Weeks)   pos/wks

9 Apr 88	PUSH THE BEAT / BAUHAUS *Fast Globe FGL 1* **60** 2
6 May 89	HELYOM HALIB *Music Man MMPS 7004* **11** 9
23 Sep 89	HOUSE ENERGY REVENGE *Music Man MMPS 7009* **73** 1
27 Apr 91	EVERYBODY *ffrr F158* **66** 1
18 Jan 92	TAKE ME AWAY *PWL Continental PWL 210* [1] **25** 5
3 Apr 93 ●	U GOT 2 KNOW *Internal Dance IDC 1* **6** 11
14 Aug 93	U GOT 2 KNOW (re-mix) *Internal Dance IDC 1* **43** 3
23 Oct 93 ●	U GOT 2 LET THE MUSIC *Internal Dance IDC 3* **2** 12
19 Feb 94 ●	MOVE ON BABY *Internal Dance IDC 4* **7** 7
18 Jun 94 ●	U & ME *Internal Dance IDCC 6* **10** 7
15 Oct 94	MOVE IT UP / BIG BEAT *Internal Dance IDC 7* **16** 6

Singles re-entries are listed as (re), (2re), (3re).... which signifies that the hit re-entered the chart once, twice or three times...

16 Sep 95		TELL ME THE WAY *Systematic SYSCD 17*	**17**	3
6 Sep 97		BE MY BABY *Nukleuz PSNC 0072*	**53**	1
26 Mar 94	●	U GOT 2 KNOW *Internal Dance CAPPC 1*	**10**	9

[1] Cappella featuring Loleatta Holloway

CAPRICCIO *UK, production duo (Singles: 2 Weeks)* pos/wks

27 Mar 99	EVERYBODY GET UP *Defected DEFECT 2CDS*	**44**	2

CAPRICE *US, female vocalist – Caprice Bourret (Singles: 5 Weeks)* pos/wks

4 Sep 99	OH YEAH *Virgin VSCDT 1745*	**24**	3
10 Mar 01	ONCE AROUND THE SUN *Virgin VSCDT 1750*	**24**	2

CAPRICORN *Belgium, male DJ – Hans Weekhout (Singles: 1 Week)* pos/wks

29 Nov 97	20 HZ (NEW FREQUENCIES) *R&S RS 97126CD*	**73**	1

Tony CAPSTICK and the CARLTON MAIN / FRICKLEY COLLIERY BAND *UK, male vocalist, b. 27 Jul 1944, d. 23 Oct 2003, and male instrumental band (Singles: 8 Weeks)* pos/wks

21 Mar 81	●	THE SHEFFIELD GRINDER / CAPSTICK COMES HOME *Dingles SID 27*	**3** 8

CAPTAIN BEAKY See Keith MICHELL

CAPTAIN BEEFHEART and his MAGIC BAND *US, male vocal / instrumental group – leader Don Van Vliet (Albums: 8 Weeks)* pos/wks

6 Dec 69	TROUT MASK REPLICA *Straight STS 1053*	**21**	1
23 Jan 71	LICK MY DECALS OFF BABY *Straight STS 1063*	**20**	2
29 May 71	MIRROR MAN *Buddah 2365 002*	**49**	1
19 Feb 72	THE SPOTLIGHT KID *Reprise K 44162*	**44**	2
18 Sep 82	ICE CREAM FOR CROW *Virgin V 2337*	**90**	2

CAPTAIN HOLLYWOOD PROJECT *US / Germany, male / female vocal / instrumental group (Singles: 31 Weeks)* pos/wks

22 Sep 90	●	I CAN'T STAND IT *BCM BCMR 395* [1]	**7** 10
24 Nov 90		ARE YOU DREAMING *BCM BCM 07504* [1]	**17** 10
27 Mar 93		ONLY WITH YOU *Pulse 8 CDLOSE 40*	**67** 1
6 Nov 93		MORE AND MORE *Pulse 8 CDLOSE 50*	**23** 5
5 Feb 94		IMPOSSIBLE *Pulse 8 CDLOSE 54*	**29** 3
11 Jun 94		ONLY WITH YOU (re-issue) *Pulse 8 CDLOSE 62*	**61** 1
1 Apr 95		FLYING HIGH *Pulse 8 CDLOSE 82*	**58** 1

[1] Twenty 4 Seven featuring Captain Hollywood

CAPTAIN SENSIBLE (see also The DAMNED) *UK, male vocalist – Ray Burns (Singles: 31 Weeks, Albums: 3 Weeks)* pos/wks

26 Jun 82	★	HAPPY TALK *A&M CAP 1*	**1** 8
14 Aug 82		WOT! *A&M CAP 2*	**26** 7
24 Mar 84	●	GLAD IT'S ALL OVER / DAMNED ON 45 *A&M CAP 6*	**6** 10
28 Jul 84		THERE ARE MORE SNAKES THAN LADDERS *A&M CAP 7*	**57** 1
10 Dec 94		THE HOKEY COKEY *Have a Nice Day CDHOKEY 1*	**71** 1
11 Sep 82		WOMEN AND CAPTAIN FIRST *A&M AMLH 68548*	**64** 3

CAPTAIN and TENNILLE *US, male instrumentalist – keyboards, Daryl Dragon, and female vocalist, Toni Tennille (Singles: 24 Weeks, Albums: 6 Weeks)* pos/wks

2 Aug 75		LOVE WILL KEEP US TOGETHER *A&M AMS 7165* ▲	**32** 5
24 Jan 76		THE WAY I WANT TO TOUCH YOU *A&M AMS 7203*	**28** 6
4 Nov 78		YOU NEVER DONE IT LIKE THAT *A&M AMS 7384*	**63** 3
16 Feb 80	●	DO THAT TO ME ONE MORE TIME *Casablanca CAN 175* ▲	**7** 10
22 Mar 80		MAKE YOUR MOVE *Casablanca CAL 2060*	**33** 1

Irene CARA *US, female actor / vocalist (Singles: 33 Weeks)* pos/wks

3 Jul 82	★	FAME *RSO 90*	**1** 16
4 Sep 82		OUT HERE ON MY OWN *RSO 66*	**58** 3
4 Jun 83	●	FLASHDANCE ... WHAT A FEELING *Casablanca CAN 1016* ▲	**2** 14

CARAMBA *Sweden, male vocalist / multi-instrumentalist / dog impersonator – Michael Tretow (Singles: 6 Weeks)* pos/wks

12 Nov 83	FEDORA (I'LL BE YOUR DAWG) *Billco BILL 101*	**56**	6

CARAVAN *UK, male vocal / instrumental group (Albums: 2 Weeks)* pos/wks

30 Aug 75	CUNNING STUNTS *Decca SKL 5210*	**50**	1
15 May 76	BLIND DOG AT ST. DUNSTAN'S *BTM BTM 1007*	**53**	1

The CARAVELLES *UK, female vocal duo – Lois Wilkinson and Andrea Simpson (Singles: 13 Weeks)* pos/wks

8 Aug 63	●	YOU DON'T HAVE TO BE A BABY TO CRY *Decca F 11697*	**6** 13

CARCASS *UK, male vocal / instrumental group (Albums: 2 Weeks)* pos/wks

6 Nov 93	HEARTWORK *Earache MOSH 097CD*	**67**	1
6 Jul 96	SWANSONG *Earache MOSH 160CD*	**68**	1

The CARDIGANS (see also A CAMP) *Sweden, female / male vocal / instrumental group (Singles: 67 Weeks, Albums: 70 Weeks)* pos/wks

17 Jun 95		CARNIVAL (re) *Trampolene PZCD 345*	**35** 3
30 Sep 95		SICK AND TIRED *Stockholm 5773112*	**34** 3
17 Feb 96		RISE AND SHINE *Trampolene 5778252*	**29** 2
21 Sep 96		LOVEFOOL *Stockholm 5752952*	**21** 4
7 Dec 96		BEEN IT *Stockholm 5759672*	**56** 1
3 May 97	●	LOVEFOOL (re-issue) *Stockholm 5710502*	**2** 13
6 Sep 97		YOUR NEW CUCKOO *Stockholm 5716632*	**35** 2
17 Oct 98		MY FAVOURITE GAME *Stockholm 5679912*	**14** 18
6 Mar 99	●	ERASE / REWIND *Stockholm 5635332*	**7** 9
24 Jul 99		HANGING AROUND *Stockholm 5612682*	**17** 4
25 Sep 99	●	BURNING DOWN THE HOUSE *Gut CDGUT 26* [1]	**7** 7
26 Jul 03		YOU'RE THE STORM *Stockholm 9809673*	**74** 1
8 Jul 95		LIFE *Stockholm 5235562*	**51** 9
12 Oct 96		FIRST BAND ON THE MOON *Stockholm 5331172*	**18** 10
31 Oct 98	●	GRAN TURISMO *Stockholm 5590812*	**8** 49
5 Apr 03		LONG GONE BEFORE MIDNIGHT *Stockholm 381092*	**47** 2

[1] Tom Jones and The Cardigans

CARE *UK, male vocal / instrumental duo (Singles: 4 Weeks)* pos/wks

12 Nov 83	FLAMING SWORD *Arista KBIRD 2*	**48**	4

Mariah CAREY `60` `Top 500` *Record-shattering vocalist / songwriter, b. 27 Mar 1970, New York, US. Since her 1990 chart debut she has sold more than 120 million albums worldwide and has topped the US singles chart 15 times – only Elvis Presley has spent longer at the top. She had a brief, and much publicised, $20m an album deal with Virgin in 2001. Best-selling UK single: 'Without You' 559,200 (Singles: 282 Weeks, Albums: 306 Weeks)* pos/wks

4 Aug 90	●	VISION OF LOVE *CBS 6559320* ▲	**9** 12
10 Nov 90		LOVE TAKES TIME *CBS 6563647* ▲	**37** 8
26 Jan 91		SOMEDAY *Columbia 6565837* ▲	**38** 5
1 Jun 91		THERE'S GOT TO BE A WAY *Columbia 6569317*	**54** 3
5 Oct 91		EMOTIONS *Columbia 6574037* ▲	**17** 9
11 Jan 92		CAN'T LET GO *Columbia 6576627*	**20** 7
18 Apr 92		MAKE IT HAPPEN *Columbia 6579417*	**17** 5
27 Jun 92	●	I'LL BE THERE *Columbia 6581377* ▲	**2** 9
21 Aug 93	●	DREAMLOVER *Columbia 6594445* ▲	**9** 10
6 Nov 93	●	HERO *Columbia 6598122* ▲	**7** 15
19 Feb 94	●	WITHOUT YOU *Columbia 6599192* ■	**1** 14
18 Jun 94	●	ANYTIME YOU NEED A FRIEND *Columbia 6603542*	**8** 10
17 Sep 94	●	ENDLESS LOVE (2re) *Epic 6608062* [1]	**3** 16
10 Dec 94	●	ALL I WANT FOR CHRISTMAS IS YOU (re) *Columbia 6610702*	**2** 8
23 Sep 95	●	FANTASY *Columbia 6624952* ▲	**4** 11
9 Dec 95	●	ONE SWEET DAY *Columbia 6626035* [2] ▲	**6** 11
17 Feb 96	●	OPEN ARMS *Columbia 6629772*	**4** 6
22 Jun 96	●	ALWAYS BE MY BABY *Columbia 6633345* ▲	**3** 8
6 Sep 97	●	HONEY *Columbia 6650192* ▲	**3** 8
13 Dec 97		BUTTERFLY *Columbia 6653365*	**22** 6
13 Jun 98	●	MY ALL *Columbia 6660592* ▲	**4** 8
19 Dec 98	●	WHEN YOU BELIEVE (re) *Columbia 6667522* [3]	**4** 13
10 Apr 99		I STILL BELIEVE *Columbia 6670732*	**16** 7
6 Nov 99	●	HEARTBREAKER *Columbia 6683012* [4] ▲	**5** 13
11 Mar 00	●	THANK GOD I FOUND YOU (re) *Columbia 6690582* [5] ▲	**10** 10
30 Sep 00	★	AGAINST ALL ODDS (re) *Columbia 6698872* [6] ■	**1** 12
28 Jul 01		LOVERBOY (re) *Virgin VUSCD 211* [7]	**12** 5
29 Dec 01		NEVER TOO FAR / DON'T STOP (FUNKIN' 4 JAMAICA) *Virgin VUSCD 228* [8]	**32** 4
30 Nov 02	●	THROUGH THE RAIN *Mercury 0638072*	**8** 8
5 Apr 03		BOY (I NEED YOU) *Def Jam 0779282* [9]	**17** 6
7 Jun 03	●	I KNOW WHAT YOU WANT *J 82876528292* [10]	**3** 13
15 Sep 90	●	MARIAH CAREY *CBS 4668151* ▲	**6** 40
26 Oct 91	●	EMOTIONS *Columbia 4688511* ▲	**4** 40
18 Jul 92	●	MTV UNPLUGGED EP *Columbia 4718692*	**3** 10
11 Sep 93	★	MUSIC BOX *Columbia 4742702* ■ ▲	**1** 77
19 Nov 94		MERRY CHRISTMAS *Columbia 4773422*	**32** 7
7 Oct 95	★	DAYDREAM *Columbia 4813672* ■ ▲	**1** 46

20 Sep 97 ●	BUTTERFLY *Columbia 4885372* ▲	2	27
28 Nov 98 ●	#1'S *Columbia 4926042*	10	32
13 Nov 99 ●	RAINBOW *Columbia 4950652*	8	5
22 Sep 01 ●	GLITTER *Virgin CDVUS 201*	10	3
15 Dec 01	GREATEST HITS *Columbia 5054612*	46	4
14 Dec 02	CHARMBRACELET *Island US / Mercury 0633842*	52	3
18 Oct 03	THE REMIXES *Columbia 5107542*	35	2

[1] Luther Vandross and Mariah Carey [2] Mariah Carey and Boyz II Men [3] Mariah Carey & Whitney Houston [4] Mariah Carey featuring Jay-Z [5] Mariah Carey featuring Joe and 98 Degrees [6] Mariah Carey featuring Westlife [7] Mariah featuring Cameo [8] Mariah Carey / Mariah Carey featuring Mystikal [9] Mariah Carey featuring Cam'ron [10] Busta Rhymes and Mariah Carey featuring The Flipmode Squad

Although he is uncredited, 'I'll Be There' is a duet with Trey Lorenz

CARL *See CLUBHOUSE*

Belinda CARLISLE 186 Top 500
Lead vocalist of the first really successful all-girl rock group, The Go-Go's; b. 17 Aug 1958, Hollywood. She married the son of British-born film star James Mason in 1992 and her career fared even better in the UK than in her homeland. Joined a re-formed Go-Go's in 2001 (Singles: 145 Weeks, Albums: 160 Weeks) pos/wks

12 Dec 87 ★	HEAVEN IS A PLACE ON EARTH *Virgin VS 1036* ▲	1	14
27 Feb 88 ●	I GET WEAK *Virgin VS 1046*	10	9
7 May 88 ●	CIRCLE IN THE SAND *Virgin VS 1074*	4	11
6 Aug 88	MAD ABOUT YOU *IRS IRM 118*	67	3
10 Sep 88	WORLD WITHOUT YOU *Virgin VS 1114*	34	5
10 Dec 88	LOVE NEVER DIES ... *Virgin VS 1150*	54	5
7 Oct 89 ●	LEAVE A LIGHT ON *Virgin VS 1210*	4	10
9 Dec 89	LA LUNA *Virgin VS 1230*	38	6
24 Feb 90	RUNAWAY HORSES *Virgin VS 1244*	40	5
26 May 90	VISION OF YOU (re) *Virgin VS 1264*	41	5
13 Oct 90 ●	(WE WANT) THE SAME THING *Virgin VS 1319*	6	10
22 Dec 90	SUMMER RAIN *Virgin VS 1323*	23	10
28 Sep 91	LIVE YOUR LIFE BE FREE *Virgin VS 1370*	12	7
16 Nov 91	DO YOU FEEL LIKE I FEEL *Virgin VS 1383*	29	4
11 Jan 92	HALF THE WORLD *Virgin VS 1388*	35	4
29 Aug 92	LITTLE BLACK BOOK *Virgin VS 1428*	28	5
25 Sep 93	BIGSCARYANIMAL *Virgin VSCDT 1472*	12	6
27 Nov 93	LAY DOWN YOUR ARMS *Virgin VSCDG 1476*	27	6
13 Jul 96 ●	IN TOO DEEP *Chrysalis CDCHS 5033*	6	6
21 Sep 96 ●	ALWAYS BREAKING MY HEART *Chrysalis CDCHS 5037*	8	6
30 Nov 96	LOVE IN THE KEY OF C *Chrysalis CDCHS 5044*	20	3
1 Mar 97	CALIFORNIA *Chrysalis CDCHSS 5047*	31	2
27 Nov 99	ALL GOD'S CHILDREN *Virgin VSCDT 1756*	66	1
2 Jan 88 ●	HEAVEN ON EARTH *Virgin V 2496*	4	54
4 Nov 89 ●	RUNAWAY HORSES *Virgin V 2599*	4	39
26 Oct 91	LIVE YOUR LIFE BE FREE *Virgin V 2680*	7	16
19 Sep 92 ★	THE BEST OF BELINDA VOLUME 1 *Virgin BELCD 1*	1	35
23 Oct 93 ●	REAL *Virgin CDV 2725*	9	5
5 Oct 96	A WOMAN & A MAN *Chrysalis CDCHR 6115*	12	5
13 Nov 99	A PLACE ON EARTH – THE GREATEST HITS *Virgin CDV 2901*	15	6

Bob CARLISLE US, male vocalist (Singles: 2 Weeks) pos/wks

30 Aug 97	BUTTERFLY KISSES *Jive JIVECD 249*	56	2

Don CARLOS *See SINGING DOGS*

Sara CARLSON *See MANIC MCs featuring Sara CARLSON*

CARLTON UK, male vocalist – Carlton McCarthy (Singles: 3 Weeks) pos/wks

16 Feb 91	LOVE AND PAIN *Smith & Mighty SNM 4*	56	2
1 Apr 95	1 TO 1 RELIGION *Stoned Heights BRCD 313* [1]	53	1

[1] Bomb the Bass featuring Carlton

Carl CARLTON US, male vocalist (Singles: 8 Weeks) pos/wks

18 Jul 81	SHE'S A BAD MAMA JAMA (SHE'S BUILT, SHE'S STACKED) *20th Century TC 2488*	34	8

Larry CARLTON *See Mike POST*

CARLTON MAIN / FRICKLEY COLLIERY BAND *See Tony CAPSTICK and the CARLTON MAIN / FRICKLEY COLLIERY BAND*

Vanessa CARLTON US, female vocalist (Singles: 14 Weeks, Albums: 15 Weeks) pos/wks

3 Aug 02 ●	A THOUSAND MILES *A&M 4977542*	6	13
30 Nov 02	ORDINARY DAY *A&M 4978132*	53	1
27 Jul 02 ●	BE NOT NOBODY *A&M 4933672*	7	15

CARMEL UK, female / male vocal / instrumental group (Singles: 19 Weeks, Albums: 11 Weeks) pos/wks

6 Aug 83	BAD DAY *London LON 29*	15	9
11 Feb 84	MORE, MORE, MORE *London LON 44*	23	7
14 Jun 86	SALLY *London LON 90*	60	3
1 Oct 83	CARMEL *Red Flame RFM 9*	94	2
24 Mar 84	THE DRUM IS EVERYTHING *London SH 8555*	19	8
27 Sep 86	THE FALLING *London LONLP 17*	88	1

Eric CARMEN US, male vocalist (Singles: 7 Weeks, Albums: 1 Week) pos/wks

10 Apr 76	ALL BY MYSELF *Arista 42*	12	7
15 May 76	ERIC CARMEN *Arista ARTY 120*	58	1

Tracey CARMEN *See RUTHLESS RAP ASSASSINS*

Jean CARN *See Bobby M featuring Jean CARN*

Kim CARNEGIE UK, female vocalist (Singles: 1 Week) pos/wks

19 Jan 91	JAZZ RAP *Best ZB 44085*	73	1

Kim CARNES US, female vocalist (Singles: 15 Weeks, Albums: 16 Weeks) pos/wks

9 May 81 ●	BETTE DAVIS EYES *EMI America EA 121* ▲	10	9
8 Aug 81	DRAW OF THE CARDS *EMI America EA 125*	49	4
9 Oct 82	VOYEUR *EMI America EA 143*	68	2
20 Jun 81	MISTAKEN IDENTITY *EMI America AML 3018* ▲	26	16

CARNIVAL featuring RIP vs RED RAT
(see also RIP PRODUCTIONS) UK, male production duo and Jamaica, male vocalist (Singles: 1 Week) pos/wks

12 Sep 98	ALL OF THE GIRLS (ALL AI-DI GIRL DEM) *Pepper 0530072*	51	1

Renato CAROSONE and his SEXTET Italy, male vocalist, b. 2 Jan 1920, d. 27 Apr 2001, and instrumental backing group (Singles: 1 Week) pos/wks

4 Jul 58	TORERO – CHA CHA CHA *Parlophone R 4433*	25	1

Mary-Chapin CARPENTER US, female vocalist / instrumentalist – guitar (Singles: 6 Weeks, Albums: 9 Weeks) pos/wks

20 Nov 93	HE THINKS HE'LL KEEP HER *Columbia 6598632*	71	1
7 Jan 95	ONE COOL REMOVE *Columbia 6611342* [1]	40	3
3 Jun 95	SHUT UP AND KISS ME *Columbia 6613675*	35	2
29 Oct 94	STONES IN THE ROAD *Columbia CK 64327*	26	5
2 Nov 96	A PLACE IN THE WORLD *Columbia 4851822*	36	2
5 Jun 99	PARTY DOLL AND OTHER FAVOURITES *Columbia 4886592*	65	1
26 May 01	TIME*SEX*LOVE *Columbia 5023542*	57	1

[1] Shawn Colvin with Mary-Chapin Carpenter

The CARPENTERS 30 Top 500
All-time biggest-selling brother / sister duo: Karen Carpenter (v/d), b. 2 Mar 1950, d. 4 Feb 1983, Richard Carpenter (k/v). This Connecticut couple were among the world's most popular pop / MOR acts of the 1970s before Karen's anorexia-associated death (Singles: 173 Weeks, Albums: 603 Weeks) pos/wks

5 Sep 70 ●	(THEY LONG TO BE) CLOSE TO YOU *A&M AMS 800* ▲	6	18
9 Jan 71	WE'VE ONLY JUST BEGUN *A&M AMS 813*	28	7
18 Sep 71	SUPERSTAR / FOR ALL WE KNOW *A&M AMS 864*	18	13
1 Jan 72	MERRY CHRISTMAS DARLING *A&M AMS 601*	45	1
23 Sep 72 ●	I WON'T LAST A DAY WITHOUT YOU / GOODBYE TO LOVE *A&M AMS 7023*	9	16
7 Jul 73 ●	YESTERDAY ONCE MORE *A&M AMS 7073*	2	17
20 Oct 73 ●	TOP OF THE WORLD *A&M AMS 7086*	5	18
2 Mar 74	JAMBALAYA (ON THE BAYOU) / MR GUDER *A&M AMS 7098*	12	11
8 Jun 74	I WON'T LAST A DAY WITHOUT YOU (re-issue) *A&M AMS 7111*	32	5
18 Jan 75 ●	PLEASE MR POSTMAN *A&M AMS 7141* ▲	2	12
19 Apr 75 ●	ONLY YESTERDAY *A&M AMS 7159*	7	10

		pos/wks
30 Aug 75	SOLITAIRE *A&M AMS 7187* **32**	5
20 Dec 75	SANTA CLAUS IS COMIN' TO TOWN *A&M AMS 7144* **37**	4
27 Mar 76	THERE'S A KIND OF HUSH (ALL OVER THE WORLD)	
	A&M AMS 7219 ....**22**	6
3 Jul 76	I NEED TO BE IN LOVE *A&M AMS 7238* **36**	5
8 Oct 77 ●	CALLING OCCUPANTS OF INTERPLANETARY CRAFT	
	(THE RECOGNISED ANTHEM OF WORLD CONTACT DAY)	
	A&M AMS 7318 ....**9**	9
11 Feb 78	SWEET, SWEET SMILE *A&M AMS 7327* **40**	4
22 Oct 83	MAKE BELIEVE IT'S YOUR FIRST TIME *A&M AM 147* **60**	3
8 Dec 90	MERRY CHRISTMAS DARLING / (THEY LONG TO BE)	
	CLOSE TO YOU (re-issue) *A&M AM 716* **25**	5
13 Feb 93	RAINY DAYS AND MONDAYS *A&M AMCD 0180* **63**	2
24 Dec 94	TRYIN' TO GET THE FEELING AGAIN *A&M 5807612* **44**	2
23 Jan 71	CLOSE TO YOU *A&M AMLS 998* **23**	75
30 Oct 71	CARPENTERS *A&M AMLS 63502* **12**	36
15 Apr 72	TICKET TO RIDE *A&M AMLS 64342* **20**	3
23 Sep 72	A SONG FOR YOU *A&M AMLS 63511* **13**	37
7 Jul 73 ●	NOW & THEN *A&M AMLH 63519* **2**	65
26 Jan 74 ★	THE SINGLES 1969–1973 *A&M AMLH 63601* ▲ **1**	125
28 Jun 75 ★	HORIZON *A&M AMLH 64530* **1**	27
23 Aug 75	TICKET TO RIDE (re-issue) *Hamlet AMLP 8001* **35**	2
3 Jul 76 ●	A KIND OF HUSH *A&M AMLK 64581* **3**	15
8 Jan 77	LIVE AT THE PALLADIUM *A&M AMLS 68403* **28**	3
8 Oct 77	PASSAGE *A&M AMLK 64703* **12**	12
2 Dec 78 ●	THE SINGLES 1974–1978 *A&M AMLT 19748* **2**	27
27 Jun 81	MADE IN AMERICA *A&M AMLK 63723* **12**	10
15 Oct 83 ●	VOICE OF THE HEART *A&M AMLX 64954* **6**	19
20 Oct 84 ●	YESTERDAY ONCE MORE *EMI / A&M SING 1* **10**	26
13 Jan 90	LOVELINES *A&M AMA 3931* **73**	1
31 Mar 90 ★	ONLY YESTERDAY – THEIR GREATEST HITS *A&M AMA 1990* **1**	82
15 Oct 94	INTERPRETATIONS *A&M 5402512* **29**	10
22 Nov 97	LOVE SONGS *A&M 5408382* **47**	5
9 Dec 00	GOLD – GREATEST HITS *A&M 4908652* **21**	20

'I Won't Last A Day Without You' AMS 7023 listed by itself 23 Sep 1972 at No.49. 'Goodbye to Love', the other side, listed by itself from 30 Sep 1972, until the end of the record's chart run. 'Mr Guder' listed with 'Jambalaya' from 16 Mar 1974, until the end of its chart run

CARPET BOMBERS FOR PEACE
UK / US, male / female vocal / instrumental group (Singles: 1 Week) pos/wks

5 Apr 03	SALT IN THE WOUND *Jungle JUNG 066CD* **67**	1

Dick CARR *See Slim DUSTY*

Joe 'Fingers' CARR
US, male instrumentalist – piano – Lou Busch under a false name, b. 18 Jul 1910, d. 19 Sep 1979 (Singles: 5 Weeks) pos/wks

29 Jun 56	PORTUGUESE WASHERWOMAN *Capitol CL 14587* **20**	5

Linda CARR
US, female vocalist (Singles: 12 Weeks) pos/wks

12 Jul 75	HIGHWIRE *Chelsea 2005 025* [1] **15**	8
5 Jun 76	SOLD MY ROCK 'N' ROLL (GAVE IT FOR FUNKY SOUL)	
	Spark SRL 1139 [2] **36**	4

[1] Linda Carr and the Love Squad [2] Linda and the Funky Boys

Lucy CARR
UK, female vocalist (Singles: 3 Weeks) pos/wks

25 Jan 03	MISSING YOU *Lickin LICKINCD 001* **28**	2
9 Aug 03	THIS IS GOODBYE *Lickin LICKINCD 002* **41**	1

Pearl CARR and Teddy JOHNSON
UK, female / male vocal duo (Singles: 19 Weeks) pos/wks

20 Mar 59	SING LITTLE BIRDIE *Columbia DB 4275* **12**	8
6 Apr 61	HOW WONDERFUL TO KNOW *Columbia DB 4603* [1] **23**	11

[1] Teddy Johnson and Pearl Carr

Suzi CARR *US, female vocalist (Singles: 1 Week)* pos/wks

8 Oct 94	ALL OVER ME *Cowboy RODEO 947CD* **45**	1

Valerie CARR *US, female vocalist (Singles: 2 Weeks)* pos/wks

4 Jul 58	WHEN THE BOYS TALK ABOUT THE GIRLS (re)	
	Columbia DB 4131 ....**29**	2

Vikki CARR
US, female vocalist – Florencia Bisenta de Casillas Martinez Cardona (Singles: 26 Weeks, Albums: 12 Weeks) pos/wks

1 Jun 67 ●	IT MUST BE HIM (SEUL SUR SON ETOILE)	
	Liberty LIB 55917 ....**2**	20
30 Aug 67	THERE I GO *Liberty LBF 15022* **50**	1
12 Mar 69	WITH PEN IN HAND (2re) *Liberty LBF 15166* **39**	5
22 Jul 67	WAY OF TODAY *Liberty SLBY 1331* **31**	2
12 Aug 67	IT MUST BE HIM *Liberty LBS 83037* **12**	10

Raffaella CARRA
Italy, female vocalist – Raffaella Pelloni (Singles: 12 Weeks) pos/wks

15 Apr 78 ●	DO IT, DO IT AGAIN *Epic EPC 6094* **9**	12

Paul CARRACK (see also ACE; MIKE and the MECHANICS; SQUEEZE)
UK, male vocalist (Singles: 18 Weeks, Albums: 9 Weeks) pos/wks

16 May 87	WHEN YOU WALK IN THE ROOM *Chrysalis CHS 3109* **48**	5
18 Mar 89	DON'T SHED A TEAR *Chrysalis CHS 3164* **60**	3
6 Jan 96	EYES OF BLUE *IRS CDEIRS 192* **40**	4
6 Apr 96	HOW LONG *IRS CDEIRS 193* **32**	5
24 Aug 96	EYES OF BLUE (re-mix) *IRS CDEIRS 194* **45**	1
3 Feb 96	BLUE VIEWS *IRS EIRSCD 1075* **55**	7
24 Jun 00	SATISFY MY SOUL *Carrack-UK PCARCD 1* **63**	1
19 Jun 04	REWIRED *Virgin CDVX 2984* [1] **61**	1

[1] Mike and the Mechanics & Paul Carrack

CARRAPICHO *See CHILLI featuring CARRAPICHO*

José CARRERAS (403 | Top 500)
One of the world's foremost opera singers, b. 5 Dec 1946, Barcelona, Spain. He is one of the world-acclaimed Three Tenors, the only chart-topping opera act. His duet with Sarah Brightman was a No.1 single in Australia (Singles: 19 Weeks, Albums: 152 Weeks) pos/wks

11 Jul 92	AMIGOS PARA SIEMPRE (FRIENDS FOR LIFE)	
	Really Useful RUR 10 [1] **11**	11
30 Jul 94	LIBIAMO / LA DONNA E MOBILE *Teldec YZ 843CD* [2] **21**	4
25 Jul 98	YOU'LL NEVER WALK ALONE *Decca 4607982* [3] **35**	4
1 Oct 88	JOSE CARRERAS COLLECTION *Stylus SMR 860* **90**	4
23 Dec 89	JOSE CARRERAS SINGS ANDREW LLOYD WEBBER	
	WEA WX 325 ....**42**	6
1 Sep 90 ★	IN CONCERT *Decca 4304331* [1] **1**	78
23 Feb 91	THE ESSENTIAL JOSE CARRERAS *Philips 4326921* **24**	9
6 Apr 91	HOLLYWOOD GOLDEN CLASSICS *East West WX 416* **47**	3
8 Aug 92	FROM THE BARCELONA GAMES CEREMONY	
	RCA Red Seal 09026612042 ....**41**	3
8 Aug 92	AMIGOS PARA SIEMPRE (FRIENDS FOR LIFE)	
	East West 4509902562 [3] **53**	4
16 Oct 93	WITH A SONG IN MY HEART *Teldec 450923692* **73**	1
25 Dec 93	CHRISTMAS IN VIENNA *Sony Classical SK 53358* [4] **71**	2
10 Sep 94 ★	THE THREE TENORS IN CONCERT 1994 *Teldec 4509962002* [5] **1**	26
3 Feb 96	PASSION *Erato 630125962* **21**	8
29 Aug 98	THE THREE TENORS IN PARIS 1998 *Decca 4605002* [1] **14**	6
23 Dec 00	THE THREE TENORS CHRISTMAS	
	Sony Classical SK 89131 [6] **57**	2

[1] José Carreras and Sarah Brightman [2] José Carreras featuring Placido Domingo and Luciano Pavarotti with Mehta [3] José Carreras, Placido Domingo and Luciano Pavarotti with Mehta [1] José Carreras, Placido Domingo and Luciano Pavarotti [2] Placido Domingo, José Carreras and Montserrat Caballé [3] José Carreras and Sarah Brightman [4] Placido Domingo, Diana Ross and José Carreras [5] José Carreras, Placido Domingo and Luciano Pavarotti conducted by Zubin Mehta [6] José Carreras, Placido Domingo and Luciano Pavarotti featuring Zubin Mehta

Tia CARRERE
US, female actor / vocalist – Althia Janairo (Singles: 6 Weeks) pos/wks

30 May 92	BALLROOM BLITZ *Reprise W 0105* **26**	6

Jim CARREY *Canada, male actor / vocalist (Singles: 3 Weeks)* pos/wks

21 Jan 95	CUBAN PETE *Columbia 6606625* **31**	3

CARRIE
US / UK, male vocal / instrumental group (Singles: 2 Weeks) pos/wks

14 Mar 98	MOLLY *Island CID 687* **56**	1
9 May 98	CALIFORNIA SCREAMIN' *Island CID 694* **55**	1

Dina CARROLL `383` `Top 500` Brit award-winning Best Female
Vocalist of 1994, b. 21 Aug 1968, Newmarket, UK. Soul / dance vocalist's 'So Close' was the biggest-selling debut album by a British female artist in the 1990s, and she was the only UK woman to have two simultaneous Top 10 singles that decade (in 1993) (Singles: 99 Weeks, Albums: 80 Weeks)   pos/wks

2 Feb 91 ●	IT'S TOO LATE Mercury ITM 3 [1]	8	14
15 Jun 91	NAKED LOVE (JUST SAY YOU WANT ME) Mercury ITM 4 [2]	39	3
11 Jul 92	AIN'T NO MAN A&M AM 0001	16	8
10 Oct 92	SPECIAL KIND OF LOVE A&M AM 0088	16	5
5 Dec 92	SO CLOSE A&M AM 0101	20	8
27 Feb 93	THIS TIME A&M AMCD 0184	23	6
15 May 93	EXPRESS A&M 580262-7	12	6
16 Oct 93 ●	DON'T BE A STRANGER A&M 5803892	3	13
11 Dec 93 ●	THE PERFECT YEAR A&M 5804812	5	11
28 Sep 96 ●	ESCAPING Mercury / First Avenue DCCD 1	3	8
21 Dec 96	ONLY HUMAN Mercury / First Avenue DCCD 2	33	4
24 Oct 98	ONE, TWO, THREE Mercury / First Avenue MERCD 514	16	4
24 Jul 99	WITHOUT LOVE Manifesto / First Avenue FESCD 57	13	7
16 Jun 01	SOMEONE LIKE YOU Mercury / First Avenue 5689062	38	2
30 Jan 93 ●	SO CLOSE A&M 5400342	2	63
26 Oct 96 ●	ONLY HUMAN Mercury 5340962	2	13
23 Jun 01	THE VERY BEST OF DINA CARROLL Mercury 5489182	15	4

[1] Quartz introducing Dina Carroll [2] Quartz and Dina Carroll

Ron CARROLL See SUPERFUNK; KLUSTER featuring Ron CARROLL; HARDSOUL featuring Ron CARROLL

Ronnie CARROLL
Ireland, male vocalist – Ronald Cleghorn (Singles: 50 Weeks)   pos/wks

27 Jul 56	WALK HAND IN HAND Philips PB 605	13	8
29 Mar 57	THE WISDOM OF A FOOL Philips PB 667	20	2
31 Mar 60	FOOTSTEPS Philips PB 1004	36	3
22 Feb 62	RING-A-DING GIRL Philips PB 1222	46	3
2 Aug 62 ●	ROSES ARE RED Philips 326532 BF	3	16
15 Nov 62	IF ONLY TOMORROW Philips 326550 BF	33	4
7 Mar 63 ●	SAY WONDERFUL THINGS Philips 326574 BF	6	14

Jasper CARROTT UK, male comedian / vocalist –
Bob Davies (Singles: 15 Weeks, Albums: 66 Weeks)   pos/wks

16 Aug 75 ●	FUNKY MOPED / MAGIC ROUNDABOUT DJM DJS 388	5	15
18 Oct 75 ●	RABBITS ON AND ON DJM DJLPS 462	10	7
6 Nov 76	CARROTT IN NOTTS DJM DJ 20482	56	1
25 Nov 78	THE BEST OF JASPER CARROTT DJM DJF 20549	38	13
20 Oct 79	THE UNRECORDED JASPER CARROTT DJM DJF 20560	19	15
19 Sep 81	BEAT THE CARROTT DJM DJF 20575	13	16
25 Dec 82	CARROTT'S LIB DJM DJ 20580	80	3
19 Nov 83	THE STUN (CARROTT TELLS ALL) DJF 20582	57	8
7 Feb 87	COSMIC CARROTT Portrait LAUGH 1	66	3

The CARS US, male vocal / instrumental
group (Singles: 51 Weeks, Albums: 72 Weeks)   pos/wks

11 Nov 78 ●	MY BEST FRIEND'S GIRL Elektra K 12301	3	10
17 Feb 79	JUST WHAT I NEEDED Elektra K 12312	17	10
28 Jul 79	LET'S GO Elektra K 12371	51	4
5 Jun 82	SINCE YOU'RE GONE Elektra K 13177	37	4
29 Sep 84 ●	DRIVE (re) Elektra E 9706	4	23
2 Dec 78	CARS Elektra K 52088	29	15
7 Jul 79	CANDY-O Elektra K 52148	30	6
6 Oct 84	HEARTBEAT CITY Elektra 960296	25	30
9 Nov 85	THE CARS GREATEST HITS Elektra EKT 25	27	19
5 Sep 87	DOOR TO DOOR Elektra EKT 42	72	2

'My Best Friend's Girl' was the first picture disc to make the singles chart. 'Drive', originally a No.5 hit, re-entered and peaked one place higher in Aug 1985

Alex CARTAÑA
Spain (b. UK), female vocalist (Singles: 2 Weeks)   pos/wks

8 May 04	HEY PAPI EMI PAP 1CDS	34	2

Aaron CARTER
US, male vocalist (Singles: 33 Weeks, Albums: 8 Weeks)   pos/wks

29 Nov 97 ●	CRUSH ON YOU Ultra Pop 0099605 ULT	9	8
7 Feb 98 ●	CRAZY LITTLE PARTY GIRL Ultra Pop 0099645 ULT	7	6
28 Mar 98	I'M GONNA MISS YOU FOREVER Ultra Pop 0099725 ULT	24	5
4 Jul 98	SURFIN' USA Ultra Pop 0099805 ULT	18	5
16 Sep 00	I WANT CANDY Jive 9250892	31	3
28 Oct 00	AARON'S PARTY (COME GET IT) Jive 9251272	51	2
13 Apr 02	LEAVE IT UP TO ME Jive 9253262	22	4
28 Feb 98	AARON CARTER Ultra Pop 0099572 ULT	12	8

Brad CARTER (see also RUFF DRIVERZ)
UK, male producer / vocalist (Singles: 1 Week)   pos/wks

23 Oct 04	MORNING ALWAYS COMES TOO SOON Positiva CDTIVS 210	48	1

Clarence CARTER US, male vocalist (Singles: 13 Weeks)   pos/wks

10 Oct 70 ●	PATCHES Atlantic 2091 030	2	13

Nick CARTER (see also BACKSTREET BOYS)
US, male vocalist (Singles: 3 Weeks)   pos/wks

19 Oct 02	HELP ME Jive 9254332	17	3

CARTER – THE UNSTOPPABLE SEX MACHINE
UK, male / instrumental duo – James 'Jim Bob' Morrison and Leslie 'Fruitbat' Carter (Singles: 46 Weeks, Albums: 40 Weeks) pos/wks

26 Jan 91	BLOODSPORT FOR ALL Rough Trade R 20112687	48	2
22 Jun 91	SHERIFF FATMAN Big Cat USM 1	23	7
26 Oct 91	AFTER THE WATERSHED Big Cat USM 2	11	5
11 Jan 92	RUBBISH Big Cat USM 3	14	5
25 Apr 92 ●	THE ONLY LIVING BOY IN NEW CROSS Big Cat USM 4	7	4
4 Jul 92	DO RE ME SO FAR SO GOOD Chrysalis USM 5	22	3
28 Nov 92	THE IMPOSSIBLE DREAM Chrysalis USM 6	21	3
4 Sep 93	LEAN ON ME I WON'T FALL OVER Chrysalis CDUSM 7	16	3
16 Oct 93	LENNY AND TERENCE Chrysalis CDUSM 8	40	2
12 Mar 94	GLAM ROCK COPS Chrysalis CDUSM 10	24	3
19 Nov 94	LET'S GET TATTOOS Chrysalis CDUSMS 30	30	3
4 Feb 95	THE YOUNG OFFENDER'S MUM Chrysalis CDUSMS 12	34	3
30 Sep 95	BORN ON THE 5TH OF NOVEMBER Chrysalis CDUSM 13	35	2
2 Mar 91	30 SOMETHING Rough Trade R 20112702	8	9
21 Sep 91	101 DAMNATIONS Big Cat ABB 101	29	6
1 Feb 92	30 SOMETHING (re-issue) Chrysalis CHR 1897	21	4
16 May 92 ★	1992 – THE LOVE ALBUM Chrysalis CCD 1946 ■	1	9
18 Sep 93	POST HISTORIC MONSTERS Chrysalis CDCHR 7090	5	4
26 Mar 94	STARRY EYED AND BOLLOCK NAKED Chrysalis CDCHR 6069	22	2
18 Feb 95 ●	WORRY BOMB Chrysalis CDCHRX 6096	9	3
14 Oct 95	STRAW DONKEY ... THE SINGLES Chrysalis CDCHR 6110	37	2
5 Apr 97	A WORLD WITHOUT DAVE Cooking Vinyl COOKCD 120	73	1

CARTER TWINS Ireland, male vocal duo (Singles: 1 Week)   pos/wks

8 Mar 97	THE TWELFTH OF NEVER / TOO RIGHT TO BE RCA 74321453082	61	1

Junior CARTIER
UK, male producer – Jon Carter (Singles: 1 Week)   pos/wks

6 Nov 99	WOMEN BEAT THEIR MEN Nucamp CAMPD 3X	70	1

CARTOONS Denmark, male / female vocal /
instrumental group (Singles: 30 Weeks, Albums: 14 Weeks)   pos/wks

3 Apr 99 ●	WITCH DOCTOR Flex / EMI CDTOONS 001	2	13
19 Jun 99 ●	DOODAH! (re) Flex / EMI CDTOON 002	7	12
4 Sep 99	AISY WAISY Flex/ EMI CDTOONS 003	16	5
17 Apr 99	TOONAGE EMI 4966922	17	14

Richard CARTRIDGE UK, male vocalist (Singles: 1 Week)   pos/wks

25 Sep 04	I'VE FOUND LOVE AGAIN Springboard Media SMCDSRC 001	50	1

Sam CARTWRIGHT See VOLCANO

CARVELLS
UK, male vocalist / instrumentalist – Alan Carvell (Singles: 4 Weeks) pos/wks

26 Nov 77	THE L.A. RUN Creole CR 143	31	4

The CASCADES US, male vocal group (Singles: 16 Weeks)   pos/wks

28 Feb 63 ●	RHYTHM OF THE RAIN Warner Bros. WB 88	5	16

CASE US, male rapper – Case Woodard (Singles: 15 Weeks)   pos/wks

21 Sep 96	TOUCH ME TEASE ME Def Jam DEFCD 18 [1]	26	3

10 Nov 01	LIVIN' IT UP *Def Jam 5888142* [2]	27	4
3 Aug 02 ●	LIVIN' IT UP (re-issue) *Def Jam 0639782* [2]	5	8

[1] Case featuring Foxxy Brown [2] Ja Rule featuring Case

Ed CASE
UK, male producer – Edward Makromallies (Singles: 5 Weeks)   pos/wks

21 Oct 00	SOMETHING IN YOUR EYES *Red Rose CDRROSE 003*	38	2
15 Sep 01	WHO? *Columbia 6718302* [1]	29	2
20 Jul 02	GOOD TIMES *Columbia 6727672* [2]	49	1

[1] Ed Case and Sweetie Irie [2] Ed Case featuring Skin

Brian and Brandon CASEY See NIVEA

Natalie CASEY
UK, female actor / vocalist – youngest ever chart entrant at three years of age (Singles: 1 Week)   pos/wks

7 Jan 84	CHICK CHICK CHICKEN *Polydor CHICK 1*	72	1

Johnny CASH   163   Top 500
Worldwide country music giant, b. 26 Feb, 1932, Arkansas, US, d. 12 Sep 2003. He scored 136 country hits between 1956–2003. Elected to the Country Music Hall of Fame (1980) and R'n'R equivalent (1992) and enjoyed a renaissance late in his career, culminating in an MTV award for his version of Nine Inch Nails' 'Hurt' (Singles: 62 Weeks, Albums: 275 Weeks)   pos/wks

3 Jun 65		IT AIN'T ME BABE *CBS 201760*	28	8
6 Sep 69 ●		A BOY NAMED SUE *CBS 4460*	4	19
23 May 70		WHAT IS TRUTH *CBS 4934*	21	11
15 Apr 72 ●		A THING CALLED LOVE (re) *CBS 7797* [1]	4	14
3 Jul 76		ONE PIECE AT A TIME *CBS 4287* [2]	32	7
10 May 03		HURT / PERSONAL JESUS (re) *American / Lost Highway 0779982*	39	3
23 Jul 66		EVERYBODY LOVES A NUT *CBS BPG 62717*	28	1
4 May 68		FROM SEA TO SHINING SEA *CBS 62972*	40	1
6 Jul 68		OLD GOLDEN THROAT *CBS 63316*	37	2
24 Aug 68 ●		JOHNNY CASH AT FOLSOM PRISON *CBS 63308*	8	45
23 Aug 69		JOHNNY CASH AT SAN QUENTIN *CBS 63629* ▲	2	106
4 Oct 69		GREATEST HITS VOLUME 1 *CBS 63062*	23	25
7 Mar 70 ●		HELLO I'M JOHNNY CASH *CBS 63796*	6	16
15 Aug 70 ●		THE WORLD OF JOHNNY CASH *CBS 66237*	5	25
12 Dec 70		THE JOHNNY CASH SHOW *CBS 64089*	18	6
18 Sep 71		MAN IN BLACK *CBS 64331*	18	7
13 Nov 71		JOHNNY CASH *Hallmark SHM 739*	43	2
20 May 72 ●		A THING CALLED LOVE *CBS 64898*	8	11
14 Oct 72		STAR PORTRAIT *CBS 67201*	16	7
10 Jul 76		ONE PIECE AT A TIME *CBS 81416*	49	3
9 Oct 76		THE BEST OF JOHNNY CASH *CBS 10000*	48	2
2 Sep 78		ITCHY FEET *CBS 10009*	36	4
27 Aug 94		THE MAN IN BLACK – THE DEFINITIVE COLLECTION *Columbia MOODCD 35*	15	5
9 Mar 02		MAN IN BLACK – THE VERY BEST OF JOHNNY CASH *Columbia 5063452*	39	4
6 Mar 04		AMERICAN RECORDINGS IV – THE MAN COMES AROUND *Lost Highway 0633392*	40	3

[1] Johnny Cash with the Evangel Temple Choir [2] Johnny Cash with the Tennessee Three

Pat CASH See John McENROE and Pat CASH with the FULL METAL RACKETS

CA$HFLOW
US, male vocal / instrumental group (Singles: 8 Weeks, Albums: 3 Weeks)   pos/wks

24 May 86	MINE ALL MINE / PARTY FREAK *Club JAB 30*	15	8
28 Jun 86	CASHFLOW *Club JABH 17*	33	3

CASHMERE
US, male vocal / instrumental group (Singles: 11 Weeks, Albums: 5 Weeks)   pos/wks

19 Jan 85	CAN I *Fourth & Broadway BRW 19*	29	8
23 Mar 85	WE NEED LOVE *Fourth & Broadway BRW 22*	52	3
2 Mar 85	CASHMERE *Fourth & Broadway BRLP 503*	63	5

CASINO
UK, male vocal / production group (Singles: 2 Weeks)   pos/wks

17 May 97	SOUND OF EDEN *Worx WORXCD 005*	52	1
10 Jul 99	ONLY YOU *Pow! CDPOW 006*	72	1

The CASINOS *US, male vocal group (Singles: 7 Weeks)*   pos/wks

23 Feb 67	THEN YOU CAN TELL ME GOODBYE *President PT 123*	28	7

CASSANDRA See Rui DA SILVA featuring CASSANDRA

CASSIDY *US, male rapper – Barry Reese (Singles: 18 Weeks)*   pos/wks

29 May 04 ●	HOTEL *J 82876618532* [1]	3	14
25 Sep 04	GET NO BETTER *J 82876649282* [2]	24	4

[1] Cassidy featuring R Kelly [2] Cassidy featuring Mashonda

David CASSIDY   300   Top 500
Top teen idol of the 1970s, b. 12 Apr 1950, New York, US. This photogenic singer / actor first found fame via the TV series The Partridge Family. His UK chart career took off as his US sales slowed down. Returned to Top 5 album chart in 2001 (Singles: 109 Weeks, Albums: 110 Weeks)   pos/wks

8 Apr 72 ●		COULD IT BE FOREVER / CHERISH *Bell 1224*	2	17
16 Sep 72 ★		HOW CAN I BE SURE *Bell 1258*	1	11
25 Nov 72		ROCK ME BABY *Bell 1268*	11	9
24 Mar 73 ●		I'M A CLOWN / SOME KIND OF A SUMMER *Bell MABEL 4*	3	12
13 Oct 73 ★		DAYDREAMER / THE PUPPY SONG *Bell 1334*	1	15
11 May 74 ●		IF I DIDN'T CARE *Bell 1350*	9	8
27 Jul 74		PLEASE PLEASE ME *Bell 1371*	16	6
5 Jul 75		I WRITE THE SONGS / GET IT UP FOR LOVE *RCA 2571*	11	8
25 Oct 75		DARLIN' *RCA 2622*	16	8
23 Feb 85 ●		THE LAST KISS *Arista ARIST 589*	6	9
11 May 85		ROMANCE (LET YOUR HEART GO) *Arista ARIST 620*	54	4
20 May 72		CHERISH *Bell BELLS 210*	2	43
24 Feb 73		ROCK ME BABY *Bell BELLS 218*	2	20
24 Nov 73 ★		DREAMS ARE NOTHIN' MORE THAN WISHES *Bell BELLS 231*	1	13
3 Aug 74 ●		CASSIDY LIVE *Bell BELLS 243*	9	7
9 Aug 75		THE HIGHER THEY CLIMB *RCA Victor RS 1012*	22	5
8 Jun 85		ROMANCE *Arista 206 983*	20	6
13 Oct 01 ●		THEN AND NOW *Universal Music TV 160822*	5	15
15 Nov 03		A TOUCH OF BLUE *Universal TV 9812859*	61	1

Eva CASSIDY   432   Top 500
Unique singer / songwriter / instrumentalist – guitar, whose recording fame came after her death, b. 2 Feb 1963, Maryland, US, d. 2 Nov 1996. Worldwide success started when fourth album, 'Songbird', was 'discovered' by the BBC. Only female singer to score two posthumous No.1 albums in UK. (Singles: 10 Weeks, Albums: 152 Weeks)   pos/wks

21 Apr 01		OVER THE RAINBOW (3re) *Blix Street / Hot HIT 16*	42	9
11 Oct 03		YOU TAKE MY BREATH AWAY *Blix Street / Hot HIT 27*	54	1
3 Jun 00		TIME AFTER TIME *Blix Street G 210073*	25	14
10 Feb 01 ★		SONGBIRD *Blix Street G 210045*	1	101
31 Aug 02 ★		IMAGINE *Blix Street / Hot G 210075* ■	1	20
23 Aug 03 ★		AMERICAN TUNE *Blix Street / Hot G 210079* ■	1	11
24 Jul 04		WONDERFUL WORLD *Blix Street G 210082*	11	6

CASSIUS
France, DJ / production duo – Philippe Zdar and Hubert Blanc-Francart (Singles: 13 Weeks, Albums: 2 Weeks)   pos/wks

23 Jan 99 ●	CASSIUS 1999 *Virgin DINSD 177*	7	7
15 May 99	FEELING FOR YOU *Virgin DINSD 181*	16	4
20 Nov 99	LA MOUCHE *Virgin DINSD 188*	53	1
5 Oct 02	THE SOUND OF VIOLENCE *Virgin DINSD 241*	49	1
6 Feb 99	1999 *Virgin CDVIR 76*	28	2

CAST   404   Top 500
The La's guitarist John Power, b. 14 Sep 1967, Liverpool, fronted this retro sounding Merseyside Brit pop quartet with Liam Tyson (g), Peter Wilkinson (b) and Keith O'Neill (d). Nominated for Best Newcomers at the 1995 Brit Awards (Singles: 55 Weeks, Albums: 116 Weeks)   pos/wks

15 Jul 95	FINETIME *Polydor 5795072*	17	4
30 Sep 95	ALRIGHT *Polydor 5799272*	13	4
20 Jan 96 ●	SANDSTORM *Polydor 5778732*	8	5
30 Mar 96 ●	WALKAWAY *Polydor 5762852*	9	7
26 Oct 96 ●	FLYING *Polydor 5754772*	4	5
5 Apr 97 ●	FREE ME (re) *Polydor 5736512*	7	7
28 Jun 97 ●	GUIDING STAR *Polydor 5711732*	9	6
13 Sep 97 ●	LIVE THE DREAM *Polydor 5716852*	7	5
15 Nov 97	I'M SO LONELY *Polydor 5690592*	14	3
8 May 99 ●	BEAT MAMA *Polydor 5635932*	9	5
7 Aug 99	MAGIC HOUR *Polydor 5612072*	28	3
28 Jul 01	DESERT DROUGHT *Polydor 5871752*	45	1
28 Oct 95 ●	ALL CHANGE *Polydor 5293122*	7	67
26 Apr 97 ●	MOTHER NATURE CALLS *Polydor 5375672*	3	42
29 May 99 ●	MAGIC HOUR *Polydor 5471762*	6	7

CAST FROM CASUALTY
UK, male / female actors / vocal group (Singles: 6 Weeks)   pos/wks

| 14 Mar 98 ● | EVERLASTING LOVE *Warner.esp WESP 003CD* ....**5** | 6 |

CAST OF THE NEW ROCKY HORROR SHOW
UK, male / female vocal group (Singles: 1 Week)   pos/wks

| 12 Dec 98 | THE TIMEWARP *Damn It Janet DAMJAN 1CD* ....**57** | 1 |

Roy CASTLE
UK, male vocalist, b. 31 Aug 1932, d. 2 Sep 1994 (Singles: 3 Weeks) pos/wks

| 22 Dec 60 | LITTLE WHITE BERRY *Philips PB 1087* ....**40** | 3 |

The CASUALS
UK, male vocal / instrumental group (Singles: 26 Weeks)   pos/wks

| 14 Aug 68 ● | JESAMINE *Decca F 22784* ....**2** | 18 |
| 4 Dec 68 | TOY *Decca F 22852* ....**30** | 8 |

The CAT *UK, male vocalist – Danny John-Jules (Singles: 4 Weeks)* pos/wks

| 23 Oct 93 | TONGUE TIED *EMI CDEM 286* ....**17** | 4 |

CATATONIA 387 Top 500 (see also SPACE) *Brit-nominated, chart-topping gregarious Welsh indie-pop band formed Cardiff, Wales 1991: Cerys Matthews (v) b. 11 Apr 1969, Swansea, Mark Roberts (g), Paul Jones (b), Owen Powell (g) and Aled Richards (d). Group split in 2001 and Matthews launched solo career (Singles: 50 Weeks, Albums: 125 Weeks)* pos/wks

3 Feb 96	SWEET CATATONIA *Blanco Y Negro NEG 85CD* **61**	1
4 May 96	LOST CAT *Blanco Y Negro NEG 88CD1* **41**	1
7 Sep 96	YOU'VE GOT A LOT TO ANSWER FOR	
	Blanco Y Negro NEG 93CD1 ....**35**	2
30 Nov 96	BLEED *Blanco Y Negro NEG 97CD1* **46**	1
18 Oct 97	I AM THE MOB *Blanco Y Negro NEG 107CD* **40**	2
31 Jan 98 ●	MULDER AND SCULLY *Blanco Y Negro NEG 109CD* **3**	10
2 May 98 ●	ROAD RAGE *Blanco Y Negro NEG 112CD* **5**	8
1 Aug 98	STRANGE GLUE *Blanco Y Negro NEG 113CD* **11**	6
7 Nov 98	GAME ON *WEA NEG 114CD* **33**	2
10 Apr 99 ●	DEAD FROM THE WAIST DOWN *Blanco Y Negro NEG 115CD* ..**7**	8
24 Jul 99	LONDINIUM *Blanco Y Negro NEG 117CD* **20**	3
13 Nov 99	KARAOKE QUEEN *Blanco Y Negro NEG 119CD* **36**	2
4 Aug 01	STONE BY STONE (re) *Blanco Y Negro NEG 134CD* **19**	4
12 Oct 96	WAY BEYOND BLUE *Blanco Y Negro 630163052*.......**32**	3
14 Feb 98 ★	INTERNATIONAL VELVET *Blanco Y Negro 3984208342* **1**	93
24 Apr 99 ★	EQUALLY CURSED AND BLESSED	
	Blanco Y Negro 3984270942 ■ **1**	23
18 Aug 01 ●	PAPER SCISSORS STONE *Blanco Y Negro 8573888482*....**6**	4
14 Sep 02	GREATEST HITS *Blanco Y Negro 0927941942* **24**	2

CATCH
UK, male vocal / instrumental group (Singles: 6 Weeks)   pos/wks

| 11 Oct 97 | BINGO *Virgin VSCDT 1656* ....**23** | 4 |
| 21 Feb 98 | DIVE IN *Virgin VSCDT 1665* ....**44** | 2 |

CATCH *UK, male vocal / instrumental group (Singles: 1 Week)*   pos/wks

| 17 Nov 90 | FREE (C'MON) *ffrr F 147* ....**70** | 1 |

CATHERINE WHEEL *UK, male vocal / instrumental group (Singles: 12 Weeks, Albums: 3 Weeks)*   pos/wks

23 Nov 91	BLACK METALLIC (EP) *Fontana CW 1* **68**	1
8 Feb 92	BALLOON *Fontana CW 2* **59**	1
18 Apr 92	I WANT TO TOUCH YOU *Fontana CW 3* **35**	2
9 Jan 93	30TH CENTURY MAN *Fontana CWCD 4* **47**	2
10 Jul 93	CRANK *Fontana CWCD 5* **66**	1
16 Oct 93	SHOW ME MARY *Fontana CWCDA 6* **62**	1
5 Aug 95	WAYDOWN *Fontana CWCD 7* **67**	1
13 Dec 97	DELICIOUS *Chrysalis CDCHS 5071* **53**	1
28 Feb 98	MA SOLITUDA *Chrysalis CDCHS 5077* **53**	1
2 May 98	BROKEN NOSE *Chrysalis CDCHS 5086* **48**	1
29 Feb 92	FERMENT *Fontana 5109032* **36**	1
31 Jul 93	CHROME *Fontana 5180392* **58**	1
16 May 98	ADAM AND EVE *Chrysalis 4930992* **53**	1

Tracks on Black Metallic (EP): Black Metallic / Crawling Over Me / Let Me Down Again / Saccharine

CATHOLICS *See Frank BLACK*

Lorraine CATO *UK, female vocalist (Singles: 3 Weeks)*   pos/wks

| 6 Feb 93 | HOW CAN YOU TELL ME IT'S OVER *Columbia 6587662* ....**46** | 2 |
| 3 Aug 96 | I WAS MADE TO LOVE YOU *MCA MCSTD 40055* ....**41** | 1 |

The CATS *UK, male instrumental group (Singles: 2 Weeks)*   pos/wks

| 9 Apr 69 | SWAN LAKE (re) *BAF 1* ....**48** | 2 |

CATS U.K. *UK, male instrumental group (Singles: 8 Weeks)*   pos/wks

| 6 Oct 79 | LUTON AIRPORT *WEA K 18075* ....**22** | 8 |

Nick CAVE and the BAD SEEDS (see also BIRTHDAY PARTY)
Australia / Germany, male vocal / instrumental group (Singles: 16 Weeks, Albums: 32 Weeks)   pos/wks

11 Apr 92	STRAIGHT TO YOU / JACK THE RIPPER *Mute MUTE 140* ..**68**	1
12 Dec 92	WHAT A WONDERFUL WORLD *Mute MUTE 151* [1] **72**	1
9 Apr 94	DO YOU LOVE ME *Mute CDMUTE 160* **68**	1
14 Oct 95	WHERE THE WILD ROSES GROW *Mute CDMUTE 185* [2] ...**11**	4
9 Mar 96	HENRY LEE *Mute CDMUTE 189* [3] **36**	1
22 Feb 97	INTO MY ARMS *Mute CDMUTE 192* **53**	1
31 May 97	(ARE YOU) THE ONE THAT I'VE BEEN ... *Mute CDMUTE 206* ..**67**	1
31 Mar 01	AS I SAT SADLY BY HER SIDE *Mute CDMUTE 249* **42**	1
2 Jun 01	FIFTEEN FEET OF PURE WHITE SNOW *Mute CDMUTE 262* ..**52**	1
8 Mar 03	BRING IT ON *Mute CDMUTE 265* **58**	1
18 Sep 04	NATURE BOY *Mute CDMUTE 324* **37**	2
27 Nov 04	BREATHLESS / THERE SHE GOES, MY BEAUTIFUL WORLD	
	Mute CDMUTE 329 ....**45**	1
2 Jun 84	FROM HER TO ETERNITY *Mute STUMM 17* **40**	3
15 Jun 85	THE FIRST BORN IS DEAD *Mute STUMM 21* **53**	1
30 Aug 86	KICKING AGAINST THE PRICKS *Mute STUMM 28* **89**	1
1 Oct 88	TENDER PREY *Mute STUMM 52* **67**	1
28 Apr 90	THE GOOD SON *Mute STUMM 76* **47**	1
9 May 92	HENRY'S DREAM *Mute CDSTUMM 92* **29**	2
18 Sep 93	LIVE SEEDS *Mute CDSTUMM 122* **67**	1
30 Apr 94	LET LOVE IN *Mute LCDSTUMM 123* **12**	2
17 Feb 96 ●	MURDER BALLADS *Mute CDSTUMM 138*...............**8**	5
15 Mar 97	THE BOATMAN'S CALL *Mute CDSTUMM 142* **22**	3
23 May 98	THE BEST OF NICK CAVE AND THE BAD SEEDS	
	Mute LCDMUTEL 4 ....**11**	4
14 Apr 01	NO MORE SHALL WE PART *Mute CDSTUMM 164* **15**	3
15 Feb 03	NOCTURAMA *Mute LCDSTUMM 207*...............**20**	2
2 Oct 04	ABATTOIR BLUES / THE LYRE OF ORPHEUS	
	Mute CDSTUMM 233 ....**11**	3

[1] Nick Cave and Shane MacGowan [2] Nick Cave and the Bad Seeds + Kylie Minogue [3] Nick Cave and the Bad Seeds and PJ Harvey

CAVE IN *US, male vocal / instrumental group (Singles: 1 Week, Albums: 1 Week)*   pos/wks

| 31 May 03 | ANCHOR *RCA 82876522982* ....**42** | 1 |
| 29 Mar 03 | ANTENNA *RCA 82876515552* ....**67** | 1 |

CAVEMAN
UK, male rap group (Singles: 2 Weeks, Albums: 2 Weeks)   pos/wks

| 9 Mar 91 | I'M READY *Profile PROF 330* ....**65** | 2 |
| 13 Apr 91 | POSITIVE REACTION *Profile FILER 406* ....**43** | 2 |

CECIL *UK, male vocal / instrumental group (Singles: 2 Weeks)*   pos/wks

| 25 Oct 97 | HOSTAGE IN A FROCK *Parlophone CDRS 6471* ....**68** | 1 |
| 28 Mar 98 | THE MOST TIRING DAY *Parlophone CDR 6490* ....**69** | 1 |

CELEDA *US, female vocalist (Singles: 5 Weeks)*   pos/wks

5 Sep 98	MUSIC IS THE ANSWER (DANCIN' AND PRANCIN)	
	Twisted UK TWCD 10038 [1] **36**	3
12 Jun 99	BE YOURSELF *Twisted UK TWCD 10049* **61**	1
23 Oct 99	MUSIC IS THE ANSWER (DANCIN' AND PRANCIN)	
	Twisted UK TWCD 10052 [2] **50**	1

[1] Danny Tenaglia and Celeda [2] Celeda with Danny Tenaglia

CELETIA *UK, female vocalist – Celetia Martin (Singles: 3 Weeks)*   pos/wks

| 11 Apr 98 | REWIND *Big Life BLRD 142* ....**29** | 2 |
| 8 Aug 98 | RUNAWAY SKIES *Big Life BLRD 144* ....**66** | 1 |

CELTIC CHORUS *See LISBON LIONS featuring Martin O'NEILL & CELTIC CHORUS*

CELTIC SPIRIT
Ireland / UK, male vocal / instrumental group (Albums: 1 Week)   pos/wks

31 Jan 98	CELTIC DREAMS *PolyGram TV 5399992*	62 1

CENOGINERZ
Holland, male producer – Michel Pollen (Singles: 1 Week)   pos/wks

2 Feb 02	GIT DOWN *Tripoli Trax TTRAX 081CD*	75 1

CENTORY
US, male rapper – Turbo B (Durron Butler) (Singles: 1 Week)   pos/wks

17 Dec 94	POINT OF NO RETURN *EMI CDEM 354*	67 1

CENTRAL LINE
UK, male vocal / instrumental group (Singles: 30 Weeks, Albums: 5 Weeks)   pos/wks

31 Jan 81	(YOU KNOW) YOU CAN DO IT *Mercury LINE 7*	67 3
15 Aug 81	WALKING INTO SUNSHINE *Mercury MER 78*	42 10
30 Jan 82	DON'T TELL ME *Mercury MER 90*	55 3
20 Nov 82	YOU'VE SAID ENOUGH *Mercury MER 117*	58 3
22 Jan 83	NATURE BOY *Mercury MER 131*	21 8
11 Jun 83	SURPRISE SURPRISE *Mercury MER 133*	48 3
13 Feb 82	BREAKING POINT *Mercury MERA 001*	64 5

CERRONE
France, male producer / multi-instrumentalist – Jean-Marc Cerrone (Singles: 21 Weeks, Albums: 1 Week)   pos/wks

5 Mar 77	LOVE IN C MINOR *Atlantic K 10895*	31 4
29 Jul 78 ●	SUPERNATURE *Atlantic K 11089*	8 12
13 Jan 79	JE SUIS MUSIC *CBS 6918*	39 4
10 Aug 96	SUPERNATURE (re-mix) *Encore CDCOR 013*	66 1
30 Sep 78	SUPERNATURE *Atlantic K 50431*	60 1

A CERTAIN RATIO
UK, male vocal / instrumental group (Singles: 3 Weeks, Albums: 3 Weeks)   pos/wks

16 Jun 90	WON'T STOP LOVING YOU *A&M ACR 540*	55 3
30 Jan 82	SEXTET *Factory FACT 55*	53 3

Peter CETERA (see also CHICAGO)
US, male vocalist (Singles: 20 Weeks, Albums: 4 Weeks)   pos/wks

2 Aug 86 ●	GLORY OF LOVE *Full Moon W 8662* ▲	3 13
21 Jun 97 ●	HARD TO SAY I'M SORRY *LaFace 74321481482* [1]	7 7
13 Sep 86	SOLITUDE/SOLITAIRE *Full Moon 9254741*	56 4

[1] Az Yet featuring Peter Cetera

Frank CHACKSFIELD and his ORCHESTRA
UK, orchestra leader, b. 9 May 1914, d. 9 Jun 1995 (Singles: 41 Weeks)   pos/wks

3 Apr 53 ●	LITTLE RED MONKEY *Parlophone R 3658* [1]	10 3
22 May 53 ●	TERRY'S THEME FROM 'LIMELIGHT' *Decca F 10106*	2 24
12 Feb 54 ●	EBB TIDE *Decca F 10122*	9 2
24 Feb 56	IN OLD LISBON *Decca F 10689*	15 4
18 May 56	PORT-AU-PRINCE *Decca F 10727* [2]	18 6
31 Aug 56	DONKEY CART *Decca F 10743*	26 2

[1] Frank Chacksfield's Tunesmiths, featuring Jack Jordan – clavioline [2] Winifred Atwell and Frank Chacksfield

The CHAIRMEN OF THE BOARD
US, male vocal / instrumental quartet – leader Norman (General) Johnson (Singles: 77 Weeks)   pos/wks

22 Aug 70 ●	GIVE ME JUST A LITTLE MORE TIME *Invictus INV 501*	3 13
14 Nov 70 ●	YOU'VE GOT ME DANGLING ON A STRING *Invictus INV 504*	5 13
20 Feb 71	EVERYTHING'S TUESDAY *Invictus INV 507*	12 9
15 May 71	PAY TO THE PIPER *Invictus INV 511*	34 7
4 Sep 71	CHAIRMAN OF THE BOARD *Invictus INV 516*	48 2
15 Jul 72	WORKING ON A BUILDING OF LOVE *Invictus INV 519*	20 8
7 Oct 72	ELMO JAMES *Invictus INV 524*	21 7
16 Dec 72	I'M ON MY WAY TO A BETTER PLACE (re) *Invictus INV 527*	30 6
23 Jun 73	FINDERS KEEPERS *Invictus INV 530*	21 9
13 Sep 86	LOVER BOY *EMI EMI 5585* [1]	56 3

[1] Chairmen of the Board featuring General Johnson

The CHAKACHAS
Belgium, male / female vocal / instrumental group (Singles: 8 Weeks)   pos/wks

11 Jan 62	TWIST TWIST *RCA 1264*	48 1
27 May 72	JUNGLE FEVER *Polydor 2121 064*	29 7

George CHAKIRIS
US, male vocalist / actor (Singles: 1 Week)   pos/wks

2 Jun 60	HEART OF A TEENAGE GIRL *Triumph RGM 1010*	49 1

CHAKKA BOOM BANG
Holland, male instrumental / production group (Singles: 1 Week)   pos/wks

20 Jan 96	TOSSING AND TURNING *Hooj Choons HOOJCD 39*	57 1

CHAKRA
(see also ASCENSION; ESSENCE; LUSTRAL; SPACE BROTHERS; OXYGEN featuring Andrea BRITTON) *UK, male production duo – Ricky Simmons and Steve Jones and female vocalist (Singles: 5 Weeks)*   pos/wks

18 Jan 97	I AM *WEA WEA 091CD*	24 2
23 Aug 97	HOME *WEA WEA 116CD2*	46 1
23 Oct 99	LOVE SHINES THROUGH *WEA WEA 227CD*	67 1
26 Aug 00	HOME (re-mix) *WEA WEA 266CD*	47 1

CHALI 2NA See JURASSIC 5; DJ FORMAT featuring Chali 2NA & AKIL

Sue CHALONER
UK, female vocalist (Singles: 1 Week)   pos/wks

22 May 93	MOVE ON UP *Pulse 8 CDLOSE 41*	64 1

Richard CHAMBERLAIN
US, male actor / vocalist – George Chamberlain (Singles: 36 Weeks, Albums: 8 Weeks)   pos/wks

7 Jun 62	THEME FROM 'DR KILDARE' (THREE STARS WILL SHINE TONIGHT) *MGM 1160*	12 10
1 Nov 62	LOVE ME TENDER *MGM 1173*	15 11
21 Feb 63	HI-LILI, HI-LO *MGM 1189*	20 9
18 Jul 63	TRUE LOVE *MGM 1205*	30 6
16 Mar 63 ●	RICHARD CHAMBERLAIN SINGS *MGM C 923*	8 8

Bryan CHAMBERS See CLEPTOMANIACS featuring Bryan CHAMBERS

CHAMELEON
UK, male vocal / instrumental group (Singles: 2 Weeks)   pos/wks

18 May 96	THE WAY IT IS *Stress CDSTR 65*	34 2

CHAMELEONS
UK, male vocal / instrumental group (Albums: 4 Weeks)   pos/wks

25 May 85	WHAT DOES ANYTHING MEAN? BASICALLY *Statik STATLP 22*	60 2
20 Sep 86	STRANGE TIMES *Geffen 9241191*	44 2

CHAMELEONS See LORI and the CHAMELEONS

CHAMONIX See Kurtis MANTRONIK

CHAMPAIGN
US, male / female vocal / instrumental group (Singles: 13 Weeks, Albums: 4 Weeks)   pos/wks

9 May 81 ●	HOW 'BOUT US *CBS A 1046*	5 13
27 Jun 81	HOW 'BOUT US *CBS 84927*	38 4

CHAMPIONSHIP LEGEND See RAZE

The CHAMPS
US, male instrumental group (Singles: 10 Weeks)   pos/wks

4 Apr 58 ●	TEQUILA *London HLU 8580* ▲	5 9
17 Mar 60	TOO MUCH TEQUILA *London HLH 9052*	49 1

CHAMPS BOYS
France, male instrumental group (Singles: 6 Weeks)   pos/wks

19 Jun 76	TUBULAR BELLS *Philips 6006 519*	41 6

CHANCE See SUNKIDS featuring CHANCE

Gene CHANDLER
US, male vocalist – Eugene Dixon (Singles: 29 Weeks)   pos/wks

5 Jun 68	NOTHING CAN STOP ME *Soul City SC 102*	41 4
3 Feb 79	GET DOWN *20th Century BTC 1040*	11 11
1 Sep 79	WHEN YOU'RE NUMBER 1 *20th Century TC 2411*	43 5
28 Jun 80	DOES SHE HAVE A FRIEND? *20th Century TC 2451*	28 9

CHANELLE
US, female vocalist – Charlene Munford (Singles: 9 Weeks)   pos/wks

11 Mar 89	ONE MAN *Cooltempo COOL 183*	16 8
10 Dec 94	ONE MAN (re-mix) *Deep Distraxion OILYCD 031*	50 1

CHANGE (see also Luther VANDROSS) *US, male / female vocal / instrumental group (Singles: 43 Weeks, Albums: 23 Weeks)* pos/wks

28 Jun 80	A LOVER'S HOLIDAY / THE GLOW OF LOVE *WEA K 79141*	14 8
6 Sep 80	SEARCHING *WEA K 79156*	11 10
2 Jun 84	CHANGE OF HEART *WEA YZ 7*	17 10
11 Aug 84	YOU ARE MY MELODY *WEA YZ 14*	48 4
16 Mar 85	LET'S GO TOGETHER *Cooltempo COOL 107*	37 7
25 May 85	OH WHAT A FEELING *Cooltempo COOL 109*	56 2
13 Jul 85	MUTUAL ATTRACTION *Cooltempo COOL 111*	60 2
19 May 84	CHANGE OF HEART *WEA WX 5*	34 17
27 Apr 85	TURN ON THE RADIO *Cooltempo CHR 1504*	39 6

CHANGING FACES *US, female vocal duo – Cassandra Lucas and Charisse Rose (Singles: 12 Weeks)* pos/wks

24 Sep 94	STROKE YOU UP *Big Beat A 8251CD*	43 3
26 Jul 97 ●	G.H.E.T.T.O.U.T. *Atlantic AT 0003CD*	10 5
1 Nov 97	I GOT SOMEBODY ELSE *Atlantic AT 0014CD*	42 1
4 Apr 98	TIME AFTER TIME *Atlantic AT 0027CD* [1]	35 2
1 Aug 98	SAME TEMPO *A&M 5826952*	53 1

[1] Changing Faces featuring Jay-Z

Bruce CHANNEL *US, male vocalist (Singles: 28 Weeks)* pos/wks

22 Mar 62 ●	HEY! BABY *Mercury AMT 1171* ▲	2 12
26 Jun 68	KEEP ON *Bell 1010*	12 16

CHANNEL X *Belgium, male / female vocal / instrumental group (Singles: 1 Week)* pos/wks

14 Dec 91	GROOVE TO MOVE *PWL Continental PWL 209*	67 1

CHANSON *US, male / female vocal group (Singles: 7 Weeks)* pos/wks

13 Jan 79	DON'T HOLD BACK *Ariola ARO 140*	33 7

CHANTAL See MOONMAN

The CHANTAYS *US, male instrumental group (Singles: 14 Weeks)* pos/wks

18 Apr 63	PIPELINE *London HLD 9696*	16 14

CHANTER SISTERS *UK, female vocal group (Singles: 5 Weeks)* pos/wks

17 Jul 76	SIDESHOW *Polydor 2058 735*	43 5

CHAOS *UK, male vocal group (Singles: 2 Weeks)* pos/wks

3 Oct 92	FAREWELL MY SUMMER LOVE *Arista 74321116397*	55 2

Harry CHAPIN *US, male vocalist, b. 7 Dec 1942, d. 16 Jul 1981 (Singles: 5 Weeks)* pos/wks

11 May 74	W.O.L.D. *Elektra K 12133*	34 5

Beth Nielsen CHAPMAN *US, female vocalist (Albums: 1 Week)* pos/wks

12 Jun 04	LOOK *Sanctuary SANCD 269*	63 1

Michael CHAPMAN *UK, male vocalist (Albums: 1 Week)* pos/wks

21 Mar 70	FULLY QUALIFIED SURVIVOR *Harvest SHVL 764*	45 1

Simone CHAPMAN See ILLEGAL MOTION featuring Simone CHAPMAN

Tracy CHAPMAN 269 Top 500
Modern folk vocalist / instrumentalist – guitar, whose socially conscious songs scored internationally, b. 20 Mar 1964, Ohio, US. Boosted by her appearance at Nelson Mandela's 70th Birthday Tribute show, her eponymous debut album sold more than 10 million copies and won the Grammy for Best New Act of 1988 (Singles: 15 Weeks, Albums: 227 Weeks) pos/wks

11 Jun 88 ●	FAST CAR *Elektra EKR 73*	5 12
30 Sep 89	CROSSROADS *Elektra EKR 95*	61 3
21 May 88 ★	TRACY CHAPMAN *Elektra EKT 44* ▲	1 188
14 Oct 89 ★	CROSSROADS *Elektra EKT 61*	1 16
9 May 92	MATTERS OF THE HEART *Elektra 7559612152*	19 3
6 Oct 01 ●	COLLECTION *Elektra 7559627002*	3 18
2 Nov 02	LET IT RAIN *Elektra 7559628362*	36 2

CHAPTERHOUSE *UK, male vocal / instrumental group (Singles: 3 Weeks, Albums: 3 Weeks)* pos/wks

30 Mar 91	PEARL *Dedicated STONE 003*	67 1
12 Oct 91	MESMERISE *Dedicated HOUSE 001*	60 2
11 May 91	WHIRLPOOL *Dedicated DEDLP 001*	23 3

CHAQUITO ORCHESTRA *UK, orchestra – arranged and conducted by Johnny Gregory (Singles: 1 Week, Albums: 2 Weeks)* pos/wks

27 Oct 60	NEVER ON SUNDAY *Fontana H 265*	50 1
24 Feb 68	THIS IS CHAQUITO *Fontana SFXL 50* [1]	36 1
4 Mar 72	THRILLER THEMES *Philips 6308 087*	48 1

[1] Chaquito and Quedo Brass

CHARGE GBH *UK, male vocal / instrumental group (Albums: 6 Weeks)* pos/wks

14 Aug 82	CITY BABY ATTACKED BY RATS *Clay CLAYLP 4*	17 6

The CHARLATANS 341 Top 500
North country boys from Northwich, Cheshire, UK, who came to prominence as part of the 'Madchester' scene – includes Tim Burgess (v) b. 30 May 1968, Manchester, UK, and Rob Collins (k) b. 23 Feb 1963, d. 23 Jul 1996 (Singles: 83 Weeks, Albums: 114 Weeks) pos/wks

2 Jun 90 ●	THE ONLY ONE I KNOW *Situation Two SIT 70T*	9 9
22 Sep 90	THEN *Situation Two SIT 74T*	12 5
9 Mar 91	OVER RISING *Situation Two SIT 76*	15 5
17 Aug 91	INDIAN ROPE *Dead Dead Good GOOD 1T*	57 1
9 Nov 91	ME. IN TIME *Situation Two SIT 84*	28 3
7 Mar 92	WEIRDO *Situation Two SIT 88*	19 4
18 Jul 92	TREMELO SONG (EP) *Situation Two SIT 97T*	44 2
5 Feb 94	CAN'T GET OUT OF BED *Beggars Banquet BBQ 27CD*	24 3
19 Mar 94	I NEVER WANT AN EASY LIFE IF ME AND HE WERE EVER TO GET THERE *Beggars Banquet BBQ 31CD*	38 1
2 Jul 94	JESUS HAIRDO *Beggars Banquet BBQ 32CD1*	48 2
7 Jan 95	CRASHIN' IN *Beggars Banquet BBQ 44CD*	31 2
27 May 95	JUST LOOKIN' / BULLET COMES *Beggars Banquet BBQ 55CD*	32 3
26 Aug 95	JUST WHEN YOU'RE THINKIN' THINGS OVER *Beggars Banquet BBQ 60CD*	12 3
7 Sep 96 ●	ONE TO ANOTHER *Beggars Banquet BBQ 301CD*	3 6
5 Apr 97 ●	NORTH COUNTRY BOY (re) *Beggars Banquet BBQ 309CD*	4 6
21 Jun 97	HOW HIGH *Beggars Banquet BBQ 312CD*	6 5
1 Nov 97	TELLIN' STORIES *Beggars Banquet BBQ 318CD*	16 3
16 Oct 99	FOREVER *Universal MCSTD 40220*	12 3
18 Dec 99	MY BEAUTIFUL FRIEND *Universal MCSTD 40225*	31 3
27 May 00	IMPOSSIBLE *Universal MCSTD 40231*	15 3
8 Sep 01	LOVE IS THE KEY *Universal MCSTD 40262*	16 3
1 Dec 01	A MAN NEEDS TO BE TOLD *Universal MCSTD 40271*	31 2
22 May 04	UP AT THE LAKE *Universal MCSTD 40363*	23 3
7 Aug 04	TRY AGAIN TODAY *Universal MCSTD 40370*	24 3
20 Oct 90 ★	SOME FRIENDLY *Situation Two SITU 30* ■	1 17
4 Apr 92	BETWEEN 10TH AND 11TH *Situation Two SITU 37CD*	21 4
2 Apr 94 ●	UP TO OUR HIPS *Beggars Banquet BBQ 147*	8 3
9 Sep 95 ★	THE CHARLATANS *Beggars Banquet BBQCD 174* ■	1 13
3 May 97 ★	TELLIN' STORIES *Beggars Banquet BBQCD 190* ■	1 28
7 Mar 98 ●	MELTING POT *Beggars Banquet BBQCD 198*	4 25
30 Oct 99 ●	US AND US ONLY *Universal MCD 60069*	2 10
22 Sep 01 ●	WONDERLAND *Universal MCD 60076*	2 5
1 Jun 02	SONGS FROM THE OTHER SIDE *Beggars Banquet BEGL 2032CD*	55 1
3 Aug 02	LIVE IT LIKE YOU LOVE IT *Universal MCD 60079*	40 2
29 May 04	UP AT THE LAKE *Universal MCD 60093*	13 6

Tracks on Tremelo Song (EP): Tremelo Song / Happen to Die / Normality Swing

CHARLENE *US, female vocalist – Charlene Duncan (Singles: 12 Weeks, Albums: 4 Weeks)* pos/wks

15 May 82 ★	I'VE NEVER BEEN TO ME *Motown TMG 1260*	1 12
17 Jul 82	I'VE NEVER BEEN TO ME *Motown STML 12171*	43 4

Alex CHARLES See DJ INNOCENCE featuring Alex CHARLES

Don CHARLES *UK, male vocalist (Singles: 5 Weeks)* pos/wks

22 Feb 62	WALK WITH ME MY ANGEL *Decca F 11424*	39 5

Ray CHARLES `351` `Top 500` (see also INXS)

Rock era's first 'genius'. b. Ray Charles Robinson, 23 Sep 1930, Georgia, US, d. 10 Jun 2004. This blind singer / songwriter / pianist and band leader had a US R&B chart career spanning seven decades. In 1994 he received a prestigious National Medal of Arts from US President Clinton. His posthumous album was a global hit and the 2004 bio-pic, 'Ray', a box office success (Singles: 130 Weeks, Albums: 63 Weeks) pos/wks

Date	Title	pos	wks
1 Dec 60	GEORGIA ON MY MIND (re) *HMV POP 792* ▲	24	8
19 Oct 61 ●	HIT THE ROAD JACK *HMV POP 935* ▲	6	12
14 Jun 62 ★	I CAN'T STOP LOVING YOU *HMV POP 1034* ▲	1	17
13 Sep 62 ●	YOU DON'T KNOW ME *HMV POP 1064*	9	13
13 Dec 62	YOUR CHEATING HEART *HMV POP 1099*	13	8
28 Mar 63	DON'T SET ME FREE *HMV POP 1133*	37	3
16 May 63 ●	TAKE THESE CHAINS FROM MY HEART *HMV POP 1161*	5	20
12 Sep 63	NO ONE *HMV POP 1202*	35	7
31 Oct 63	BUSTED *HMV POP 1221*	21	10
24 Sep 64	NO ONE TO CRY TO *HMV POP 1333*	38	3
21 Jan 65	MAKIN' WHOOPEE *HMV POP 1383*	42	4
10 Feb 66	CRYIN' TIME *HMV POP 1502* [1]	50	1
21 Apr 66	TOGETHER AGAIN *HMV POP 1519*	48	1
5 Jul 67	HERE WE GO AGAIN (re) *HMV POP 1595*	38	3
20 Dec 67	YESTERDAY *Stateside SS 2071*	44	4
31 Jul 68	ELEANOR RIGBY *Stateside SS 2120*	36	9
13 Jan 90	I'LL BE GOOD TO YOU *Qwest W 2697* [2]	21	7
28 Jul 62 ●	MODERN SOUNDS IN COUNTRY AND WESTERN MUSIC *HMV CLP 1580* ▲	6	16
23 Feb 63	MODERN SOUNDS IN COUNTRY AND WESTERN MUSIC VOLUME 2 *HMV CLP 1613*	15	5
20 Jul 63	GREATEST HITS *HMV CLP 1626*	16	5
5 Oct 68	GREATEST HITS VOLUME 2 *Stateside SSL 10241*	24	5
19 Jul 80	HEART TO HEART – 20 HOT HITS *London RAY TV 1*	29	5
24 Mar 90	THE COLLECTION *Arcade RCLP 101*	36	3
13 Mar 93	RAY CHARLES – THE LIVING LEGEND *Arcade ARC 94642*	48	3
25 Aug 01	THE DEFINITIVE RAY CHARLES *WSM 0122735562*	13	12
11 Sep 04	GENIUS LOVES COMPANY *Liberty 8665402*	18	6

[1] With the Jack Halloran Singers and the Ray Charles Orchestra with the Raeletts [2] Quincy Jones featuring Ray Charles and Chaka Khan

Suzette CHARLES *US, female vocalist (Singles: 2 Weeks)* pos/wks

Date	Title	pos	wks
21 Aug 93	FREE TO LOVE AGAIN *RCA 74321158372*	58	2

Tina CHARLES (see also 5000 VOLTS) *UK, female vocalist – Tina Hoskins (Singles: 63 Weeks, Albums: 7 Weeks)* pos/wks

Date	Title	pos	wks
7 Feb 76 ★	I LOVE TO LOVE (BUT MY BABY LOVES TO DANCE) *CBS 3937*	1	12
1 May 76	LOVE ME LIKE A LOVER *CBS 4237*	28	7
21 Aug 76 ●	DANCE LITTLE LADY DANCE *CBS 4480*	6	13
4 Dec 76 ●	DR LOVE *CBS 4779*	4	10
14 May 77	RENDEZVOUS *CBS 5174*	27	6
29 Oct 77	LOVE BUG – SWEETS FOR MY SWEET (MEDLEY) *CBS 5680*	26	4
11 Mar 78	I'LL GO WHERE YOUR MUSIC TAKES ME *CBS 6062*	27	8
30 Aug 86	I LOVE TO LOVE (re-mix) *DMC DECK 1*	67	3
3 Dec 77	HEART 'N' SOUL *CBS 82180*	35	7

CHARLES and EDDIE

US, male vocal duo – Charles Pettigrew, b. 12 May 1963, d. 6 Apr 2001 and Eddie Chacon (Singles: 30 Weeks, Albums: 15 Weeks) pos/wks

Date	Title	pos	wks
31 Oct 92 ★	WOULD I LIE TO YOU *Capitol CL 673*	1	17
20 Feb 93	N.Y.C. (CAN YOU BELIEVE THIS CITY) *Capitol CDCL 681*	33	5
22 May 93	HOUSE IS NOT A HOME *Capitol CDCLS 688*	29	4
13 May 95	24-7-365 *Capitol CDCLS 747*	38	4
12 Dec 92	DUOPHONIC *Capitol CDESTU 2186*	19	15

Dick CHARLESWORTH and his CITY GENTS *UK, male jazz band group – Dick Charlesworth – clarinet (Singles: 1 Week)* pos/wks

Date	Title	pos	wks
4 May 61	BILLY BOY *Top Rank JAR 558*	43	1

CHARLISE *See KID CREME*

CHARLOTTE

UK, female vocalist – Charlotte Kelly (Singles: 4 Weeks) pos/wks

Date	Title	pos	wks
12 Mar 94	QUEEN OF HEARTS *Big Life BLRD 106*	54	1
2 May 98	BE MINE *Parlophone Rhythm CDRHYTHM 10*	59	1
29 May 99	SKIN *Parlophone Rhythm Series CDRHYTHM 20*	56	1
4 Sep 99	SOMEDAY *Parlophone Rhythm Series CDRHYTHM 23*	74	1

CHARME *US, male / female vocal group (Singles: 2 Weeks)* pos/wks

Date	Title	pos	wks
17 Nov 84	GEORGY PORGY *RCA 464*	68	2

CHARO and the SALSOUL ORCHESTRA *US, female vocalist – Maria Martinez and orchestra (Singles: 4 Weeks)* pos/wks

Date	Title	pos	wks
29 Apr 78	DANCE A LITTLE BIT CLOSER *Salsoul SSOL 101*	44	4

CHARVONI *See BROTHERS IN RHYTHM*

CHAS and DAVE `415` `Top 500` (see also TOTTENHAM HOTSPUR FA CUP FINAL SQUAD) *Goodtime 'rockney' music duo; Chas Hodges (k/v) and Dave Peacock (b/v). Lovable Londoners who provide a mix of music hall, humorous 'knees-up' songs and early rock 'n' roll, which are ideal for pubs and parties (Singles: 66 Weeks, Albums: 101 Weeks)* pos/wks

Date	Title	pos	wks
11 Nov 78	STRUMMIN' / I'M IN TROUBLE *EMI 2874* [1]	52	3
26 May 79	GERTCHA *EMI 2947*	20	8
1 Sep 79	THE SIDEBOARD SONG (GOT MY BEER IN THE SIDEBOARD HERE) *EMI 2986*	55	3
29 Nov 80 ●	RABBIT *Rockney 9*	8	11
12 Dec 81	STARS OVER 45 *Rockney KOR 12*	21	8
13 Mar 82 ●	AIN'T NO PLEASING YOU *Rockney KOR 14*	2	11
17 Jul 82	MARGATE *Rockney KOR 15*	46	4
19 Mar 83	LONDON GIRLS *Rockney KOR 17*	63	3
3 Dec 83	MY MELANCHOLY BABY *Rockney KOR 21*	51	6
3 May 86 ●	SNOOKER LOOPY *Rockney POT 147* [2]	6	9
5 Dec 81	CHAS AND DAVE'S CHRISTMAS JAMBOREE BAG *Warwick WW 5166*	25	15
17 Apr 82	MUSTN'T GRUMBLE *Rockney 909*	35	11
8 Jan 83	JOB LOT *Rockney ROC 910*	59	15
15 Oct 83 ●	CHAS AND DAVE'S KNEES UP – JAMBOREE BAG NO. 2 *Rockney / Towerbell Roc 911*	7	17
11 Aug 84	WELL PLEASED *Rockney ROC 912*	27	10
17 Nov 84	CHAS AND DAVE'S GREATEST HITS *Rockney ROC 913*	16	10
15 Dec 84	CHAS AND DAVE'S CHRISTMAS JAMBOREE BAG (re-issue) *Rockney ROCM 001*	87	1
9 Nov 85	JAMBOREE BAG NUMBER 3 *Rockney ROC 914*	15	13
13 Dec 86	CHAS AND DAVE'S CHRISTMAS CAROL ALBUM *Telstar STAR 2293*	37	4
29 Apr 95 ●	STREET PARTY *Telstar TCD 2765*	3	5

[1] Chas and Dave with Rockney [2] Matchroom Mob with Chas and Dave

Tara CHASE *See Sonny JONES featuring Tara CHASE*

JC CHASEZ (see also 'N SYNC) *US, male vocalist (Singles: 10 Weeks, Albums: 2 Weeks)* pos/wks

Date	Title	pos	wks
10 Apr 04	PLUG IT IN *XL Recordings XLS 180CD* [1]	22	4
24 Apr 04	SOME GIRLS (DANCE WITH WOMEN) / BLOWIN' ME UP (WITH HER LOVE) *Jive 82876605302*	13	6
8 May 04	SCHIZOPHRENIC *Jive JIV537242*	46	2

[1] Basement Jaxx featuring JC Chasez

CHEAP TRICK *US, male vocal / instrumental group (Singles: 14 Weeks, Albums: 15 Weeks)* pos/wks

Date	Title	pos	wks
5 May 79	I WANT YOU TO WANT ME *Epic EPC 7258*	29	9
2 Feb 80	WAY OF THE WORLD *Epic EPC 8114*	73	2
31 Jul 82	IF YOU WANT MY LOVE *Epic EPC A 2406*	57	3
24 Feb 79	CHEAP TRICK AT BUDOKAN *Epic EPC 86083*	29	9
6 Oct 79	DREAM POLICE *Epic EPC 83522*	41	5
5 Jun 82	ONE ON ONE *Epic EPC 85740*	95	1

Oliver CHEATHAM *US, male vocalist (Singles: 22 Weeks)* pos/wks

Date	Title	pos	wks
2 Jul 83	GET DOWN SATURDAY NIGHT *MCA 828*	38	5
5 Apr 03 ★	MAKE LUV *Positiva CDTIV 187* [1] ■	1	15
6 Dec 03	MUSIC & YOU *Positiva CDTIV 197* [1]	38	2

[1] Room 5 featuring Oliver Cheatham

CHECK 1-2 *See Craig McLACHLAN*

Chubby CHECKER *US, male vocalist – Ernest Evans (Singles: 112 Weeks, Albums: 7 Weeks)* pos/wks

Date	Title	pos	wks
22 Sep 60	THE TWIST (2re) *Columbia DB 4503* ▲	14	12
30 Mar 61	PONY TIME *Columbia DB 4591* ▲	27	6
17 Aug 61 ●	LET'S TWIST AGAIN (3re) *Columbia DB 4691*	2	34
5 Apr 62	SLOW TWISTIN' *Columbia DB 4808*	23	8

		pos/wks
19 Apr 62	TEACH ME TO TWIST *Columbia DB 4802* [1]	**45** 1
9 Aug 62	DANCIN' PARTY *Columbia DB 4876*	**19** 13
1 Nov 62	LIMBO ROCK *Cameo Parkway P 849*	**32** 10
20 Dec 62	JINGLE BELL ROCK *Cameo Parkway C 205* [1]	**40** 3
31 Oct 63	WHAT DO YA SAY *Cameo Parkway P 806*	**37** 4
29 Nov 75 ●	LET'S TWIST AGAIN / THE TWIST (re-issue)	
	London HLU 10512	**5** 10
18 Jun 88 ●	THE TWIST (YO, TWIST) *Urban URB 20* [2]	**2** 11
27 Jan 62	TWIST WITH CHUBBY CHECKER *Columbia 33SX 1315*	**13** 4
3 Mar 62	FOR TWISTERS ONLY *Columbia 33SX 1341*	**17** 3

[1] Chubby Checker and Bobby Rydell [2] Fat Boys and Chubby Checker

'The Twist' first charted in Sep 1960 peaking at No.49, then re-entered making No.44 a month later and No.14 in Jan 1962. 'Let's Twist Again' first charted in Aug 1961 peaking at No.37, then No.2 in Dec 1961, No.46 in Aug 1962 and No.49 a month later

CHECKMATES *See Emile FORD and the CHECKMATES*

CHECKMATES LTD
US, male vocal / instrumental group (Singles: 8 Weeks) pos/wks

15 Nov 69	PROUD MARY *A&M AMS 769*	**30** 8

Judy CHEEKS *US, female vocalist (Singles: 15 Weeks)* pos/wks

13 Nov 93	SO IN LOVE (THE REAL DEAL) *Positiva CDTIV 6*	**27** 3
7 May 94	REACH *Positiva CDTIV 12*	**17** 4
4 Mar 95	THIS TIME / RESPECT *Positiva CDTIV 28*	**23** 2
17 Jun 95	YOU'RE THE STORY OF MY LIFE / AS LONG AS YOU'RE	
	GOOD TO ME *Positiva CDTIV 34*	**30** 3
13 Jan 96	REACH (re-mix) *Positiva CDTIV 42*	**22** 3

The CHEEKY GIRLS *Romania, female vocal duo – Monica and Gabriella Irimia (Singles: 40 Weeks, Albums: 6 Weeks)* pos/wks

14 Dec 02 ●	CHEEKY SONG (TOUCH MY BUM) *Multiply CDMULTY 97*	**2** 14
24 May 03 ●	TAKE YOUR SHOES OFF *Multiply CDMULTY 101*	**3** 10
16 Aug 03 ●	HOORAY HOORAY (IT'S A CHEEKY HOLIDAY)	
	Multiply CDMULTY 106	**3** 7
20 Dec 03 ●	HAVE A CHEEKY CHRISTMAS *Multiply CDMULTY 110*	**10** 5
9 Oct 04	CHEEKY FLAMENCO *XBN XBNCD 1*	**29** 2
18 Dec 04	BOYS AND GIRLS *XBN XBNCDS 001* [1]	**50** 2+
23 Aug 03	PARTYTIME *Multiply MULTYCD 13*	**14** 6

[1] Cheeky Girls with Andy Newton-Lee

The CHEETAHS
UK, male vocal / instrumental group (Singles: 6 Weeks) pos/wks

1 Oct 64	MECCA *Philips BF 1362*	**36** 3
21 Jan 65	SOLDIER BOY *Philips BF 1383*	**39** 3

CHEF *US, male cartoon vocalist – Isaac Hayes (Singles: 13 Weeks)* pos/wks

26 Dec 98 ★	CHOCOLATE SALTY BALLS (PS I LOVE YOU)	
	Columbia 6667985	**1** 13

CHELSEA FC *UK, male football team vocalists (Singles: 22 Weeks)* pos/wks

26 Feb 72 ●	BLUE IS THE COLOUR *Penny Farthing PEN 782*	**5** 12
14 May 94	NO ONE CAN STOP US NOW *RCA 74321210452*	**23** 3
17 May 97	BLUE DAY *WEA WEA 112CD* [1]	**22** 5
27 May 00	BLUE TOMORROW *Telstar TV CFCCD 2000*	**22** 2

[1] Suggs & Co featuring Chelsea Team

The CHEMICAL BROTHERS (337 Top 500)
Internationally successful, Manchester formed (1992), dance production duo Tom Rowlands and Ed Simons, originally named The Dust Brothers (after their production heroes, who forced a name change). These Brit and Grammy winners are the first contemporary dance act to achieve three successive No.1 albums (Singles: 68 Weeks, Albums: 132 Weeks) pos/wks

17 Jun 95	LEAVE HOME *Junior Boy's Own CHEMSD 1*	**17** 4
9 Sep 95	LIFE IS SWEET *Junior Boy's Own CHEMSD 2*	**25** 3
27 Jan 96	LOOPS OF FURY (EP) *Junior Boy's Own CHEMSD 3*	**13** 1
12 Oct 96 ★	SETTING SUN *Junior Boy's Own CHEMSD 4* ■	**1** 7
5 Apr 97 ★	BLOCK ROCKIN' BEATS (re) *Virgin CHEMSD 5* ■	**1** 7
20 Sep 97	ELEKTROBANK *Virgin CHEMSD 6*	**17** 4
12 Jun 99 ●	HEY BOY HEY GIRL *Virgin CHEMSD 8*	**3** 10
14 Aug 99	LET FOREVER BE *Virgin CHEMSD 9*	**9** 7
23 Oct 99	OUT OF CONTROL *Virgin CHEMSD 10*	**21** 4
22 Sep 01 ●	IT BEGAN IN AFRIKA (re) *Virgin CHEMSD 12*	**8** 6

26 Jan 02 ●	STAR GUITAR (re) *Virgin CHEMSD 14*	**8** 8
4 May 02	COME WITH US / THE TEST *Virgin CHEMSD 15*	**14** 3
27 Sep 03	THE GOLDEN PATH *Virgin CHEMSD 18* [1]	**17** 4
8 Jul 95 ●	EXIT PLANET DUST *Junior Boy's Own XDUSTCD 1*	**9** 41
19 Apr 97 ★	DIG YOUR OWN HOLE *Virgin XDUSTCD 2* ■	**1** 27
3 Jul 99 ★	SURRENDER *Virgin XDUSTCD 4* ■	**1** 47
9 Feb 02 ★	COME WITH US *Virgin XDUSTCD 5* ■	**1** 11
4 Oct 03 ●	SINGLES 93-03 *Virgin XDUSTCDX 6*	**9** 6

[1] The Chemical Brothers / The Flaming Lips

Tracks on Loops of Fury (EP): Loops of Fury / (The Best Part of) Breaking Up / Get Upon it Like This / Chemical Beats. Uncredited vocals on 'Setting Sun' and 'Let Forever Be' by Noel Gallagher and on 'Out of Control' by Bernard Sumner

CHEQUERS
UK, male vocal / instrumental group (Singles: 10 Weeks) pos/wks

18 Oct 75	ROCK ON BROTHER *Creole CR 111*	**21** 5
28 Feb 76	HEY MISS PAYNE *Creole CR 116*	**32** 5

CHER (68 Top 500) (see also MEAT LOAF)
Perennially popular vocalist, b. Cherilyn Sarkisian LaPierre, 20 May 1946, California, US, is one of the world's top earning live performers. She was half of the most successful husband / wife duo ever, Sonny and Cher, and had an even more stunning run of solo smashes. In 1998, at the age of 52, she became the oldest female solo singer to top the chart. Best-selling single: 'Believe' 1,672,108 (Singles: 229 Weeks, Albums: 310 Weeks) pos/wks

19 Aug 65 ●	ALL I REALLY WANT TO DO *Liberty LIB 66114*	**9** 10
31 Mar 66 ●	BANG BANG (MY BABY SHOT ME DOWN) *Liberty LIB 66160*	**3** 12
4 Aug 66	I FEEL SOMETHING IN THE AIR *Liberty LIB 12034*	**43** 2
22 Sep 66	SUNNY *Liberty LIB 12083*	**32** 5
6 Nov 71	GYPSYS, TRAMPS AND THIEVES *MCA MU 1142* ▲	**4** 13
16 Feb 74	DARK LADY (re) *MCA 101* ▲	**36** 4
19 Dec 87 ●	I FOUND SOMEONE *Geffen GEF 31*	**5** 10
2 Apr 88	WE ALL SLEEP ALONE *Geffen GEF 35*	**47** 5
2 Sep 89 ●	IF I COULD TURN BACK TIME *Geffen GEF 59*	**6** 14
13 Jan 90	JUST LIKE JESSE JAMES *Geffen GEF 69*	**11** 11
7 Apr 90	HEART OF STONE *Geffen GEF 75*	**43** 5
11 Aug 90	YOU WOULDN'T KNOW LOVE *Geffen GEF 77*	**55** 3
13 Apr 91 ★	THE SHOOP SHOOP SONG (IT'S IN HIS KISS) *Epic 6566737*	**1** 15
13 Jul 91	LOVE AND UNDERSTANDING *Geffen GFS 5*	**10** 8
12 Oct 91	SAVE UP ALL YOUR TEARS *Geffen GFS 11*	**37** 5
7 Dec 91	LOVE HURTS *Geffen GFS 16*	**43** 5
18 Apr 92	COULD'VE BEEN YOU *Geffen GFS 19*	**31** 4
14 Nov 92	OH NO NOT MY BABY *Geffen GFS 29*	**33** 4
16 Jan 93	MANY RIVERS TO CROSS *Geffen GFSTD 31*	**37** 3
6 Mar 93	WHENEVER YOU'RE NEAR *Geffen GFSTD 32*	**72** 1
15 Jan 94	I GOT YOU BABE *Geffen GFSTD 64* [1]	**35** 3
18 Mar 95 ★	LOVE CAN BUILD A BRIDGE *London COCD 1* [2]	**1** 8
28 Oct 95	WALKING IN MEMPHIS *WEA WEA 021CD1*	**11** 7
20 Jan 96 ●	ONE BY ONE *WEA WEA 032CD*	**7** 9
27 Apr 96	NOT ENOUGH LOVE IN THE WORLD *WEA WEA 052CD*	**31** 2
17 Aug 96	THE SUN AIN'T GONNA SHINE ANYMORE *WEA WEA 071CD*	**26** 3
31 Oct 98 ★	BELIEVE (re) *WEA WEA 175CD* ◆ ■ ▲	**1** 28
6 Mar 99 ●	STRONG ENOUGH *WEA WEA 201CD1*	**5** 10
19 Jun 99	ALL OR NOTHING *WEA WEA 212CD1*	**12** 7
6 Nov 99	DOVE L'AMORE *WEA WEA 230CD1*	**21** 3
17 Nov 01 ●	THE MUSIC'S NO GOOD WITHOUT YOU *WEA WEA 337CD*	**8** 10
2 Oct 65 ●	ALL I REALLY WANT TO DO *Liberty LBY 3058*	**7** 9
7 May 66	SONNY SIDE OF CHER *Liberty LBY 3072*	**11** 11
16 Jan 88	CHER *Geffen WX 132*	**26** 22
22 Jul 89 ●	HEART OF STONE *Geffen GEF 24239*	**7** 82
29 Jun 91 ★	LOVE HURTS *Geffen GEF 24427* ■	**1** 51
21 Nov 92 ★	GREATEST HITS 1965-1992 *Geffen GED 24439* ■	**1** 33
18 Nov 95 ●	IT'S A MAN'S WORLD *WEA 0630126702*	**10** 18
7 Nov 98 ●	BELIEVE *WEA 3984253192*	**7** 44
20 Nov 99 ●	THE GREATEST HITS *WEA / Universal TV 8573804202*	**7** 24
1 Dec 01	LIVING PROOF *WEA 927424632*	**46** 2
6 Dec 03	THE VERY BEST OF CHER *UMTV / WSM 5046685862*	**17** 14

[1] Cher with Beavis and Butt-Head [2] Cher, Chrissie Hynde and Neneh Cherry with Eric Clapton

The catalogue number for 'Heart Of Stone' changed from WX 262 during the album's chart run

CHERI *Canada, female vocal duo – Rosalind Hunt and Lyn Cullerier (Singles: 9 Weeks)* pos/wks

19 Jun 82	MURPHY'S LAW *Polydor POSP 459*	**13** 9

The CHEROKEES
UK, male vocal / instrumental group (Singles: 5 Weeks) pos/wks

3 Sep 64	**SEVEN DAFFODILS** *Columbia DB 7341*	**33** 5

CHERRELLE
US, female vocalist – Cheryl Norton (Singles: 26 Weeks, Albums: 9 Weeks) pos/wks

28 Dec 85 ●	**SATURDAY LOVE** *Tabu A 6829* [1]	**6** 11
1 Mar 86	**WILL YOU SATISFY?** *Tabu A 6927*	**57** 3
6 Feb 88	**NEVER KNEW LOVE LIKE THIS** *Tabu 6513827* [2]	**26** 7
6 May 89	**AFFAIR** *Tabu 654673 7*	**67** 2
24 Mar 90	**SATURDAY LOVE (re-mix)** *Tabu 6558007* [1]	**55** 2
2 Aug 97	**BABY COME TO ME** *One World OWECD 1* [2]	**56** 1
25 Jan 86	**HIGH PRIORITY** *Tabu TBU 26699*	**17** 9

[1] Cherrelle with Alexander O'Neal [2] Alexander O'Neal featuring Cherrelle

Don CHERRY
US, male vocalist, b. 11 Jan 1924, d. 19 Oct 1995 (Singles: 11 Weeks) pos/wks

10 Feb 56 ●	**BAND OF GOLD** *Philips PB 549*	**6** 11

Eagle-Eye CHERRY
Sweden, male vocalist (Singles: 28 Weeks, Albums: 32 Weeks) pos/wks

4 Jul 98 ●	**SAVE TONIGHT** *Polydor 5695952*	**6** 13
14 Nov 98	**FALLING IN LOVE AGAIN** *Polydor 5630252*	**8** 8
20 Mar 99	**PERMANENT TEARS** *Polydor 5636752*	**43** 1
29 Apr 00	**ARE YOU STILL HAVING FUN** *Polydor 5618032*	**21** 4
11 Nov 00	**LONG WAY AROUND** *Polydor 5677812* [1]	**48** 2
1 Aug 98 ●	**DESIRELESS** *Polydor 5372262*	**3** 29
20 May 00	**LIVING IN THE PRESENT FUTURE** *Polydor 5437442*	**12** 3

[1] Eagle-Eye Cherry featuring Neneh Cherry

Neneh CHERRY `488` `Top 500` (see also RIP RIG and PANIC)
Sassy, strident rapper-singer, b. Neneh Mariann Karlsson, 10 Mar 1964, Stockholm, Sweden, raised in New York and relocated to UK early 1980s. Stepdaughter of jazz trumpeter Don Cherry and sister of Eagle-Eye Cherry. Winner of 1990 Best New Female award in Rolling Stone and at the Brits (Singles: 98 Weeks, Albums: 49 Weeks) pos/wks

10 Dec 88 ●	**BUFFALO STANCE** *Circa YR 21*	**3** 13
20 May 89 ●	**MANCHILD** *Circa YR 30*	**5** 10
12 Aug 89	**KISSES ON THE WIND** *Circa YR 33*	**20** 6
23 Dec 89	**INNA CITY MAMMA** *Circa YR 42*	**31** 7
29 Sep 90	**I'VE GOT YOU UNDER MY SKIN** *Circa YR 53*	**25** 5
3 Oct 92	**MONEY LOVE** *Circa YR 83*	**23** 4
16 Jan 93	**BUDDY X** *Circa YRCD 98*	**35** 3
25 Jun 94 ●	**7 SECONDS (re)** *Columbia 6605082* [1]	**3** 25
18 Mar 95 ★	**LOVE CAN BUILD A BRIDGE** *London COCD 1* [2]	**1** 8
3 Aug 96 ●	**WOMAN** *Hut HUTCD 70*	**9** 7
14 Dec 96	**KOOTCHI** *Hut HUTDG 75*	**38** 2
22 Feb 97	**FEEL IT** *Hut HUTCD 79*	**68** 1
6 Nov 99	**BUDDY X 99 (re-mix)** *4 Liberty LIBTCD 33* [3]	**15** 5
11 Nov 00	**LONG WAY AROUND** *Polydor 5677812* [4]	**48** 2
17 Jun 89 ●	**RAW LIKE SUSHI** *Circa CIRCA 8*	**2** 43
7 Nov 92	**HOMEBREW** *Circa CIRCD 25*	**27** 2
14 Sep 96	**MAN** *Hut CDHUT 38*	**16** 4

[1] Youssou N'Dour (featuring Neneh Cherry) [2] Cher, Chrissie Hynde and Neneh Cherry with Eric Clapton [3] Dreem Teem vs Neneh Cherry [4] Eagle-Eye Cherry featuring Neneh Cherry

CHERRYFALLS
UK, male vocal / instrumental group (Singles: 1 Week) pos/wks

14 Aug 04	**STANDING WATCHING** *Island CID 868*	**64** 1

Cody CHESNUTT See ROOTS

The CHI-LITES *US, male vocal / instrumental group – leader Eugene Record (Singles: 89 Weeks)* pos/wks

28 Aug 71	**(FOR GOD'S SAKE) GIVE MORE POWER TO THE PEOPLE** *MCA MU 1138*	**32** 6
15 Jan 72 ●	**HAVE YOU SEEN HER** *MCA MU 1146*	**3** 12
27 May 72	**OH GIRL** *MCA MU 1156* ▲	**14** 9
23 Mar 74	**HOMELY GIRL** *Brunswick BR 9*	**5** 13
20 Jul 74	**I FOUND SUNSHINE** *Brunswick BR 12*	**35** 5
2 Nov 74 ●	**TOO GOOD TO BE FORGOTTEN** *Brunswick BR 13*	**10** 11
21 Jun 75 ●	**HAVE YOU SEEN HER / OH GIRL (re-issue)** *Brunswick BR 20*	**5** 9

13 Sep 75 ●	**IT'S TIME FOR LOVE** *Brunswick BR 25*	**5** 10
31 Jul 76 ●	**YOU DON'T HAVE TO GO** *Brunswick BR 34*	**3** 11
13 Aug 83	**CHANGING FOR YOU** *R & B RBS 215*	**61** 3

CHIC
US, male / female vocal / instrumental group – leaders Nile Rodgers and Bernard Edwards, b. 31 Oct 1952, d. 18 Apr 1996 (Singles: 90 Weeks, Albums: 47 Weeks) pos/wks

26 Nov 77 ●	**DANCE, DANCE, DANCE (YOWSAH, YOWSAH, YOWSAH)** *Atlantic K 11038*	**6** 12
1 Apr 78 ●	**EVERYBODY DANCE** *Atlantic K 11097*	**9** 11
18 Nov 78 ●	**LE FREAK** *Atlantic K 11209* ▲	**7** 16
24 Feb 79 ●	**I WANT YOUR LOVE** *Atlantic LV 16*	**4** 11
30 Jun 79 ●	**GOOD TIMES** *Atlantic K 11310* ▲	**5** 11
13 Oct 79	**MY FORBIDDEN LOVER** *Atlantic K 11385*	**15** 8
8 Dec 79	**MY FEET KEEP DANCING** *Atlantic K 11415*	**21** 9
12 Mar 83	**HANGIN'** *Atlantic A 9898*	**64** 1
19 Sep 87	**JACK LE FREAK** *Atlantic A 9198*	**19** 6
14 Jul 90	**MEGACHIC – CHIC MEDLEY** *East West A 7949*	**58** 2
15 Feb 92	**CHIC MYSTIQUE** *Warner Bros. W 0083*	**48** 3
3 Feb 79 ●	**C'EST CHIC** *Atlantic K 50565*	**2** 24
18 Aug 79	**RISQUE** *Atlantic K 50634*	**29** 12
15 Dec 79	**THE BEST OF CHIC** *Atlantic K 50686*	**30** 8
5 Dec 87	**FREAK OUT** *Telstar STAR 2319* [1]	**72** 3

[1] Chic and Sister Sledge

Megachic was a medley of Le Freak / Everybody Dance / Good Times / I Want Your Love See also Compilation Albums – Dino

CHICAGO `313` `Top 500` *Pioneering jazz-rock group included Peter Cetera (v/b). Group relocated from city of the same name to California, US, in 1967. Released longest numerical sequence of album titles (majority going platinum in the US) – the most recent being Chicago 26 (1999) (Singles: 81 Weeks, Albums: 132 Weeks)* pos/wks

10 Jan 70 ●	**I'M A MAN** *CBS 4715* [1]	**8** 11
18 Jul 70	**25 OR 6 TO 4** *CBS 5076*	**7** 13
9 Oct 76 ★	**IF YOU LEAVE ME NOW** *CBS 4603* ▲	**1** 16
5 Nov 77	**BABY, WHAT A BIG SURPRISE** *CBS 5672*	**41** 3
21 Aug 82 ●	**HARD TO SAY I'M SORRY** *Full Moon K 79301* ▲	**4** 15
27 Oct 84	**HARD HABIT TO BREAK** *Full Moon W 9214*	**8** 13
26 Jan 85	**YOU'RE THE INSPIRATION** *Warner Bros. W 9126*	**14** 10
27 Sep 69 ●	**CHICAGO TRANSIT AUTHORITY** *CBS 66221* [1]	**9** 14
4 Apr 70 ●	**CHICAGO** *CBS 66233*	**6** 27
6 Mar 71 ●	**CHICAGO 3** *CBS 66260*	**9** 5
30 Sep 72	**CHICAGO 5** *CBS 69108* ▲	**24** 2
23 Oct 76	**CHICAGO X** *CBS 86010*	**21** 11
2 Oct 82	**CHICAGO 16** *Full Moon K 99235*	**44** 9
4 Dec 82	**LOVE SONGS** *TV TVA 6*	**42** 8
1 Dec 84	**CHICAGO 17** *Full Moon 925040*	**24** 20
25 Nov 89	**THE HEART OF CHICAGO** *Reprise WX 328*	**6** 25
13 Feb 99	**THE HEART OF CHICAGO – 1967-1997** *Reprise 9362465542*	**21** 4
14 Sep 02	**THE COMPLETE GREATEST HITS – THE CHICAGO STORY** *Rhino 8122736302*	**11** 7

[1] Chicago Transit Authority [1] Chicago Transit Authority

CHICANE *UK, male producer / instrumentalist – Nick Bracegirdle (Singles: 53 Weeks, Albums: 9 Weeks)* pos/wks

21 Dec 96	**OFFSHORE** *Xtravaganza 0091005*	**14** 7
14 Jun 97	**SUNSTROKE** *Xtravaganza 0091125*	**21** 3
13 Sep 97	**OFFSHORE '97 (re-mix)** *Xtravaganza 0091255 EXT* [1]	**17** 4
20 Dec 97	**LOST YOU SOMEWHERE** *Xtravaganza 0091415*	**35** 3
10 Oct 98	**STRONG IN LOVE** *Xtravaganza 0091675 EXT* [2]	**32** 2
5 Jun 99 ●	**SALTWATER** *Xtravaganza 0091675* [3]	**6** 10
18 Mar 00 ★	**DON'T GIVE UP** *Xtravaganza XTRAV 9CDS* [4] ■	**1** 14
22 Jul 00	**NO ORDINARY MORNING / HALCYON** *Xtravaganza XTRAV 12CDS*	**28** 3
28 Oct 00	**AUTUMN TACTICS** *Xtravaganza XTRAV 17CDS*	**44** 2
8 Feb 03	**SALTWATER (re-mix)** *Xtravaganza XTRAV 35CDS*	**43** 2
8 Mar 03	**LOVE ON THE RUN** *WEA WEA 361CD* [5]	**33** 2
14 Feb 04	**DON'T GIVE UP 2004 (re-mix)** *Xtravaganza XTRAV 44CDS*	**43** 1
1 Nov 97	**FAR FROM THE MADDENING CROWDS** *Xtravaganza 0093172 EXT*	**49** 1
8 Apr 00 ●	**BEHIND THE SUN** *Xtravaganza XTRAV 10CD*	**10** 8

[1] Chicane with Power Circle [2] Chicane featuring Mason [3] Chicane featuring Maire Brennan of Clannad [4] Chicane featuring Bryan Adams [5] Chicane featuring Peter Cunnah

CHICKEN SHACK (see also FLEETWOOD MAC)
*UK, male / female vocal / instrumental group – includes Christine
Perfect (aka Christine McVie) (Singles: 19 Weeks, Albums: 9 Weeks)* pos/wks

7 May 69	I'D RATHER GO BLIND *Blue Horizon 57-3153*	14	13
6 Sep 69	TEARS IN THE WIND *Blue Horizon 57-3160*	29	6
22 Jul 68	40 BLUE FINGERS FRESHLY PACKED *Blue Horizon 763203*	12	8
15 Feb 69 ●	OK KEN? *Blue Horizon 763209*	9	1

CHICKEN SHED *UK, youth theatre company (Singles: 6 Weeks)* pos/wks

27 Dec 97	I AM IN LOVE WITH THE WORLD *Columbia 6654172*	15	6

CHICKS ON SPEED See Dave CLARKE

CHICORY TIP
UK, male vocal / instrumental group (Singles: 34 Weeks) pos/wks

29 Jan 72 ★	SON OF MY FATHER *CBS 7737*	1	13
20 May 72	WHAT'S YOUR NAME *CBS 8021*	13	8
31 Mar 73	GOOD GRIEF CHRISTINA *CBS 1258*	17	13

The CHIEFTAINS *Ireland, male vocal / instrumental
group (Singles: 4 Weeks, Albums: 27 Weeks)* pos/wks

18 Mar 95	HAVE I TOLD YOU LATELY THAT I LOVE YOU *RCA 74321271702* [1]	71	1
12 Jun 99	I KNOW MY LOVE *RCA Victor 74321670622* [2]	37	3
28 Mar 87	JAMES GALWAY AND THE CHIEFTAINS IN IRELAND *RCA Red Seal RL 85798* [1]	32	5
2 Jul 88	IRISH HEARTBEAT *Mercury MERH 124* [2]	18	7
4 Feb 95	THE LONG BLACK VEIL *RCA 74321251672*	17	9
6 Mar 99	TEARS OF STONE *RCA Victor 9026689682*	36	4
23 Mar 02	THE WIDE WORLD OVER *RCA Victor 9026639172*	37	2

[1] The Chieftains with Van Morrison [2] The Chieftains featuring The Corrs
[1] James Galway and The Chieftains [2] Van Morrison and The Chieftains

The CHIFFONS *US, female vocal group (Singles: 40 Weeks)* pos/wks

11 Apr 63	HE'S SO FINE *Stateside SS 172* ▲	16	12
18 Jul 63	ONE FINE DAY *Stateside SS 202*	29	6
26 May 66	SWEET TALKIN' GUY *Stateside SS 512*	31	8
18 Mar 72 ●	SWEET TALKIN' GUY (re-issue) *London HL 10271*	4	14

CHIKINKI *UK, male vocal / instrumental group (Singles: 4 Weeks)* pos/wks

29 Nov 03	ASSASSINATOR 13 *Island CID 834*	72	1
27 Mar 04	LIKE IT OR LEAVE IT *Island CID 848*	65	1
19 Jun 04	ETHER RADIO *Island CID 860*	50	1
6 Nov 04	ALL EYES *Island CIDX 875*	74	1

CHILD *UK, male vocal / instrumental group (Singles: 22 Weeks)* pos/wks

29 Apr 78	WHEN YOU WALK IN THE ROOM *Ariola Hansa AHA 511*	38	5
22 Jul 78 ●	IT'S ONLY MAKE BELIEVE *Ariola Hansa AHA 522*	10	12
28 Apr 79	ONLY YOU (AND YOU ALONE) *Ariola Hansa AHA 536*	33	5

Jane CHILD *Canada, female vocalist (Singles: 8 Weeks)* pos/wks

12 May 90	DON'T WANNA FALL IN LOVE *Warner Bros. W 9817*	22	8

CHILDLINERS
UK / Australia, male / female vocal group (Singles: 6 Weeks) pos/wks

16 Dec 95 ●	THE GIFT OF CHRISTMAS *London LONCD 376*	9	6

CHILDREN FOR RWANDA
UK, male / female choir (Singles: 2 Weeks) pos/wks

10 Sep 94	LOVE CAN BUILD A BRIDGE *East West YZ 849CD*	57	2

CHILDREN OF THE NIGHT
UK, male vocalist / producer (Singles: 2 Weeks) pos/wks

26 Nov 88	IT'S A TRIP (TUNE IN, TURN ON, DROP OUT) *Jive JIVE 189*	52	2

CHILDREN OF THE REVOLUTION See The KLF

Toni CHILDS
US, female vocalist (Singles: 4 Weeks, Albums: 1 Week) pos/wks

25 Mar 89	DON'T WALK AWAY *A&M AM 462*	53	4
29 Apr 89	UNION *A&M AMA 5175*	73	1

CHILI HI FLY *Australia, male DJ / production duo –
Simon Lewicki and Noel Burgess (Singles: 2 Weeks)* pos/wks

18 Mar 00	IS IT LOVE *Ministry of Sound MOSCDS 141*	37	2

CHILL FAC-TORR
US, male vocal / instrumental group (Singles: 8 Weeks) pos/wks

2 Apr 83	TWIST (ROUND 'N' ROUND) *Phillyworld PWS 109*	37	8

CHILLI featuring CARRAPICHO *US / Ghana / Brazil,
male / female vocal / instrumental group (Singles: 1 Week)* pos/wks

20 Sep 97	TIC, TIC TAC *Arista 74321511332*	59	1

The CHIMES *UK, male / female vocal / instrumental
group (Singles: 28 Weeks, Albums: 19 Weeks)* pos/wks

19 Aug 89	1-2-3 *CBS 655166 7*	60	3
2 Dec 89	HEAVEN (re) *CBS 655432 7*	66	5
19 May 90 ●	I STILL HAVEN'T FOUND WHAT I'M LOOKING FOR *CBS CHIM 1 6*		9
28 Jul 90	TRUE LOVE *CBS CHIM 2*	48	3
29 Sep 90	HEAVEN (re-issue) *CBS CHIM 3*	24	6
1 Dec 90	LOVE COMES TO MIND *CBS CHIM 4*	49	2
23 Jun 90	THE CHIMES *CBS 4664811*	17	19

CHIMIRA *South Africa, female vocalist (Singles: 1 Week)* pos/wks

6 Dec 97	SHOW ME HEAVEN *Neoteric NRDCD 11*	70	1

CHINA BLACK *UK, male vocal / instrumental duo – Errol
Reid and Simon Fung (Singles: 35 Weeks, Albums: 4 Weeks)* pos/wks

16 Jul 94 ●	SEARCHING (re) *Wild Card CARDD 7*	4	20
29 Oct 94	STARS *Wild Card CARDD 9*	19	7
11 Feb 95	ALMOST SEE YOU (SOMEWHERE) *Wild Card CARDW 15*	31	2
3 Jun 95	SWING LOW SWEET CHARIOT *PolyGram TV SWLOW 2* [1]	15	6
11 Mar 95	BORN *Wild Card 5237552*	27	4

[1] Ladysmith Black Mambazo featuring China Black

CHINA CRISIS *UK, male vocal / instrumental
group (Singles: 66 Weeks, Albums: 68 Weeks)* pos/wks

7 Aug 82	AFRICAN AND WHITE *Inevitable INEV 011*	45	5
22 Jan 83	CHRISTIAN *Virgin VS 562*	12	9
21 May 83	TRAGEDY AND MYSTERY *Virgin VS 587*	46	6
15 Oct 83	WORKING WITH FIRE AND STEEL *Virgin VS 620*	48	5
14 Jan 84 ●	WISHFUL THINKING *Virgin VS 647*	9	8
10 Mar 84	HANNA HANNA *Virgin VS 665*	44	3
30 Mar 85	BLACK MAN RAY *Virgin VS 752*	14	9
1 Jun 85	KING IN A CATHOLIC STYLE (WAKE UP) *Virgin VS 765*	19	9
7 Sep 85	YOU DID CUT ME *Virgin VS 799*	54	3
8 Nov 86	ARIZONA SKY *Virgin VS 898*	47	4
24 Jan 87	BEST KEPT SECRET *Virgin VS 926*	36	5
20 Nov 82	DIFFICULT SHAPES & PASSIVE RHYTHMS SOME PEOPLE THINK IT'S FUN TO ENTERTAIN *Virgin V 2243*	21	18
12 Nov 83	WORKING WITH FIRE AND STEEL – POSSIBLE POP SONGS VOLUME TWO *Virgin V 2286*	20	16
11 May 85 ●	FLAUNT THE IMPERFECTION *Virgin V 2342*	9	22
6 Dec 86	WHAT PRICE PARADISE *Virgin V 2410*	63	6
13 May 89	DIARY OF A HOLLOW HORSE *Virgin V 2567*	58	2
15 Sep 90	CHINA CRISIS COLLECTION *Virgin V 2613*	32	4

CHINA DRUM *UK, male vocal / instrumental
group (Singles: 4 Weeks, Albums: 1 Week)* pos/wks

2 Mar 96	CAN'T STOP THESE THINGS *Mantra MNT 8CD*	65	1
20 Apr 96	LAST CHANCE *Mantra MNT 10CD*	60	1
9 Aug 97	FICTION OF LIFE *Mantra MNT 21CD*	65	1
27 Sep 97	SOMEWHERE ELSE *Mantra MNT 022CD1*	74	1
11 May 96	GOOSEFAIR *Mantra MNTCD 1002*	53	1

Jonny CHINGAS
US, male instrumentalist (Singles: 6 Weeks) pos/wks

19 Feb 83	PHONE HOME *CBS A 3121*	43	6

CHINGY *US, male rapper –
Howard Bailey Jr. (Singles: 21 Weeks, Albums: 1 Week)* pos/wks

25 Oct 03	RIGHT THURR *Capitol CDCLS 849*	17	5
21 Feb 04	HOLIDAE IN *Capitol CDCL 852* [1]	35	3

29 May 04	ONE CALL AWAY *Capitol CDCL 856* [2]		26	4
18 Sep 04	I LIKE THAT *Capitol CDCL 861* [3]		11	6
13 Nov 04	BALLA BABY *Parlophone CDCLS 865*		34	3
29 May 04	JACKPOT *Capitol 5818270*		73	1

[1] Chingy featuring Ludacris and Snoop Dogg [2] Chingy featuring J Weav
[3] Houston featuring Chingy, Nate Dogg & I-20

The CHIPMUNKS
US, chipmunk vocal trio – David Seville (Singles: 12 Weeks) pos/wks

24 Jul 59	RAGTIME COWBOY JOE *London HLU 8916* [1]		11	8
19 Dec 92	ACHY BREAKY HEART *Epic 6588837* [2]		53	3
14 Dec 96	MACARENA *Sony Wonder 6639981* [3]		65	1

[1] David Seville and The Chipmunks [2] Alvin and The Chipmunks featuring Billy Ray Cyrus [3] Los Del Chipmunks

The Chipmunk characters were created by David Seville, who died in 1972. His son resurrected the act in 1980

The CHIPPENDALES
UK / US, male vocal group (Singles: 4 Weeks) pos/wks

31 Oct 92	GIVE ME YOUR BODY *XSrhythm XSR 3*		28	4

!!! (CHK CHK CHK)
US, male vocal / instrumental group (Singles: 1 Week) pos/wks

21 Aug 04	HELLO? IS THIS THING ON? *Warp WAP 176CD*		74	1

George CHISHOLM See JOHNSTON BROTHERS

CHOCOLATE PUMA (see also GOODMEN; JARK PRONGO;
RHYTHMKILLAZ; RIVA featuring DANNI MINOGUE; TOMBA VIRA)
*Holland, male production duo – DJ Dobri and DJ Zki
(Rene ter Horst and Gaston Steenkist) (Singles: 9 Weeks)* pos/wks

24 Mar 01	● I WANNA BE U (re) *Cream / Parlophone CREAM 13CD*		6	9

CHOO CHOO PROJECT (see also José NUNEZ featuring OCTAVIA;
Harry 'Choo-Choo' ROMERO) *US, male / female production / instrumental / vocal duo – Harry Romero and Octahvia Lambert (Singles: 3 Weeks)* pos/wks

15 Jan 00	HAZIN' & PHAZIN' *Defected DEFECT 10CDS*		21	3

CHOPS-EMC + EXTENSIVE
UK, male instrumental group and rapper (Singles: 1 Week) pos/wks

8 Aug 92	ME' ISRAELITES *Faze 2 FAZE 6*		60	1

The CHORDETTES
US, female vocal group (Singles: 25 Weeks) pos/wks

17 Dec 54	MR SANDMAN *Columbia DB 3553* ▲		11	8
31 Aug 56	● BORN TO BE WITH YOU *London HLA 8302*		8	9
18 Apr 58	● LOLLIPOP *London HLD 8584*		6	8

The CHORDS *UK, male vocal / instrumental
group (Singles: 17 Weeks, Albums: 3 Weeks)* pos/wks

6 Oct 79	NOW IT'S GONE *Polydor 2059 141*		63	2
2 Feb 80	MAYBE TOMORROW *Polydor POSP 101*		40	5
26 Apr 80	SOMETHING'S MISSING *Polydor POSP 146*		55	3
12 Jul 80	THE BRITISH WAY OF LIFE *Polydor 2059 258*		54	3
18 Oct 80	IN MY STREET *Polydor POSP 185*		50	4
24 May 80	SO FAR AWAY *Polydor POLS 1019*		30	3

CHRIS and JAMES
UK, male instrumental / production duo (Singles: 3 Weeks) pos/wks

17 Sep 94	CALM DOWN (BASS KEEPS PUMPIN') *Stress 12STR 38*		74	1
4 Nov 95	FOX FORCE FIVE *Stress CDSTR 61*		71	1
7 Nov 98	CLUB FOR LIFE '98 *Stress CDSTR 85*		66	1

Neil CHRISTIAN
UK, male vocalist – Christopher Tidmarsh (Singles: 10 Weeks) pos/wks

7 Apr 66	THAT'S NICE *Strike JH 301*		14	10

Roger CHRISTIAN
UK, male vocalist (Singles: 3 Weeks) pos/wks

30 Sep 89	TAKE IT FROM ME *Island IS 427*		63	3

The CHRISTIANS (379) (Top 500) *Soul / gospel-influenced UK pop
group; vocalist brothers Russell, Roger (who went solo in 1986) and Garry Christian plus Henry Priestman (k/v). In 1974, the brothers appeared on TV talent show Opportunity Knocks. Their self-titled debut album went double platinum (Singles: 84 Weeks, Albums: 96 Weeks)* pos/wks

31 Jan 87	FORGOTTEN TOWN *Island IS 291*		22	11
13 Jun 87	HOOVERVILLE (AND THEY PROMISED US THE WORLD) *Island IS 326*		21	10
26 Sep 87	WHEN THE FINGERS POINT *Island IS 335*		34	7
5 Dec 87	IDEAL WORLD *Island IS 347*		14	13
23 Apr 88	BORN AGAIN *Island IS 365*		25	7
15 Oct 88	● HARVEST FOR THE WORLD *Island IS 395*		8	7
20 May 89	★ FERRY 'CROSS THE MERSEY *PWL PWL 41* [1] ■		1	7
23 Dec 89	WORDS *Island IS 450*		18	8
7 Apr 90	I FOUND OUT *Island IS 453*		56	2
15 Sep 90	GREENBANK DRIVE *Island IS 466*		63	2
5 Sep 92	WHAT'S IN A WORD *Island IS 536*		33	5
14 Nov 92	FATHER *Island IS 543*		55	2
6 Mar 93	THE BOTTLE *Island CID 549*		39	3
31 Oct 87	● THE CHRISTIANS *Island ILPS 9876*		2	68
27 Jan 90	★ COLOUR *Island ILPS 9948*		1	17
10 Oct 92	HAPPY IN HELL *Island CID 9996*		18	3
20 Nov 93	THE BEST OF THE CHRISTIANS *Island CIDTV 6*		22	8

[1] The Christians, Holly Johnson, Paul McCartney, Gerry Marsden and Stock Aitken Waterman

CHRISTIE
UK, male vocal / instrumental group (Singles: 37 Weeks) pos/wks

2 May 70	★ YELLOW RIVER *CBS 4911*		1	22
10 Oct 70	● SAN BERNADINO (re) *CBS 5169*		7	14
25 Mar 72	IRON HORSE *CBS 7747*		47	1

David CHRISTIE *France, male vocalist (Singles: 12 Weeks)* pos/wks

14 Aug 82	● SADDLE UP *KR KR 9*		9	12

John CHRISTIE *Australia, male vocalist (Singles: 6 Weeks)* pos/wks

25 Dec 76	HERE'S TO LOVE (AULD LANG SYNE) *EMI 2554*		24	6

Lou CHRISTIE
US, male vocalist – Lugee Sacco (Singles: 35 Weeks) pos/wks

24 Feb 66	LIGHTNIN' STRIKES *MGM 1297* ▲		11	8
28 Apr 66	RHAPSODY IN THE RAIN *MGM 1308*		37	2
13 Sep 69	● I'M GONNA MAKE YOU MINE *Buddah 201 057*		2	17
27 Dec 69	SHE SOLD ME MAGIC *Buddah 201 073*		25	8

Tony CHRISTIE *UK, male vocalist – Tony
Fitzgerald (Singles: 54 Weeks, Albums: 10 Weeks)* pos/wks

9 Jan 71	LAS VEGAS *MCA MK 5058*		21	9
8 May 71	● I DID WHAT I DID FOR MARIA *MCA MK 5064*		2	17
20 Nov 71	(IS THIS THE WAY TO) AMARILLO *MCA MKS 5073*		18	13
10 Feb 73	AVENUES AND ALLEYWAYS *MCA MKS 5101*		37	4
17 Jan 76	DRIVE SAFELY DARLIN' *MCA 219*		35	4
23 Jan 99	● WALK LIKE A PANTHER '98 *ffrr FCD 351* [1]		10	7
24 Jul 71	I DID WHAT I DID FOR MARIA *MCA MKPS 2016*		37	1
17 Feb 73	WITH LOVING FEELING *MCA MUPS 468*		19	2
31 May 75	TONY CHRISTIE – LIVE *MCA MCF 2703*		33	3
6 Nov 76	BEST OF TONY CHRISTIE *MCA MCF 2769*		28	4

[1] The All Seeing I featuring Tony Christie

Shawn CHRISTOPHER
US, female vocalist (Singles: 10 Weeks) pos/wks

4 May 91	ANOTHER SLEEPLESS NIGHT *Arista 114186*		50	4
21 Mar 92	DON'T LOSE THE MAGIC *Arista 115097*		30	5
2 Jul 94	MAKE MY LOVE *BTB BTBCD 502*		57	1

CHRON GEN
UK, male vocal / instrumental group (Albums: 3 Weeks) pos/wks

3 Apr 82	CHRONIC GENERATION *Secret SEC 3*		53	3

The CHUCKS *UK, male / female vocal group (Singles: 7 Weeks)* pos/wks

24 Jan 63	LOO-BE-LOO *Decca F 11569*		22	7

CHUMBAWAMBA UK, male / female vocal / instrumental group (Singles: 31 Weeks, Albums: 10 Weeks)

			pos/wks
18 Sep 93	ENOUGH IS ENOUGH One Little Indian 79TP 7CD [1]	56	2
4 Dec 93	TIMEBOMB One Little Indian 89TP 7CD	59	1
23 Aug 97 ●	TUBTHUMPING EMI CDEM 486	2	20
31 Jan 98 ●	AMNESIA EMI CDEM 498	10	5
13 Jun 98	TOP OF THE WORLD (OLE, OLE, OLE) EMI CDEM 511	21	3
7 May 94	ANARCHY One Little Indian TPLP 46CD	29	2
4 Nov 95	SWINGIN' WITH RAYMOND One Little Indian TPLP 66CDS	70	1
13 Sep 97	TUBTHUMPER EMI CDEMC 3773	19	7

[1] Chumbawamba and Credit to the Nation

Chubby CHUNKS UK, male instrumentalist / producer – Scott Tinsley (Singles: 2 Weeks)

			pos/wks
4 Jun 94	TESTAMENT 4 Cleveland City CLECD 13017 [1]	52	1
29 May 99	I'M TELLIN YOU (re-mix) Cleveland City CLECD 13052 [2]	61	1

[1] Chubby Chunks Volume II [2] Chubby Chunks featuring Kim Ruffin

'I'm Tellin You' is a re-mix of 'Testament 4' with a new title

CHUPITO Spain, male vocalist (Singles: 2 Weeks)

			pos/wks
23 Sep 95	AMERICAN PIE Eternal WEA 018CD	54	2

Charlotte CHURCH UK, female vocalist (Singles: 14 Weeks, Albums: 45 Weeks)

			pos/wks
25 Dec 99	JUST WAVE HELLO Sony Classical 6685312	31	4
1 Feb 03 ●	THE OPERA SONG (BRAVE NEW WORLD) (re) Direction 6734642 [1]	3	10
21 Nov 98 ●	VOICE OF AN ANGEL Sony Classical SK 60957	4	20
27 Nov 99 ●	CHARLOTTE CHURCH Sony Classical SK 89003	8	10
2 Dec 00	DREAM A DREAM Sony Classical SK 89459	30	6
3 Nov 01	ENCHANTMENT Sony Classical SK 89710	24	9

[1] Jurgen Vries featuring CMC

Sir Winston CHURCHILL UK, male statesman, b. 30 Nov 1874, d. 24 Feb 1965 (Albums: 8 Weeks)

			pos/wks
13 Feb 65 ●	THE VOICE OF CHURCHILL Decca LXT 6200	6	8

CHYNA See INCOGNITO

CICA See PQM featuring CICA

CICCONE YOUTH See SONIC YOUTH

CICERO UK, male vocalist – Dave Cicero (Singles: 12 Weeks)

			pos/wks
18 Jan 92	LOVE IS EVERYWHERE Spaghetti CIAO 3	19	8
18 Apr 92	THAT LOVING FEELING Spaghetti CIAO 4	46	3
1 Aug 92	HEAVEN MUST HAVE SENT YOU BACK Spaghetti CIAO 5	70	1

CINDERELLA US, male vocal / instrumental group (Singles: 7 Weeks, Albums: 8 Weeks)

			pos/wks
6 Aug 88	GYPSY ROAD Vertigo VER 40	54	2
4 Mar 89	DON'T KNOW WHAT YOU GOT (TILL IT'S GONE) Vertigo VER 43	54	2
17 Nov 90	SHELTER ME Vertigo VER 51	55	2
27 Apr 91	HEARTBREAK STATION Vertigo VER 53	63	1
23 Jul 88	LONG COLD WINTER Vertigo VERH 59	30	6
1 Dec 90	HEARTBREAK STATION Vertigo 8480181	36	2

CINDY and the SAFFRONS UK, female vocal group (Singles: 3 Weeks)

			pos/wks
15 Jan 83	PAST, PRESENT AND FUTURE Stiletto STL 9	56	3

CINEMATIC ORCHESTRA UK, male orchestra (Albums: 2 Weeks)

			pos/wks
25 May 02	EVERY DAY Ninja Tune ZENCD 59	54	2

CINERAMA (see also The WEDDING PRESENT) UK, male / female vocal / instrumental duo – David Gedge and Sally Murrell (Singles: 1 Week)

			pos/wks
18 Jul 98	KERRY KERRY Cooking Vinyl FRYCD 072	71	1

Gigliola CINQUETTI Italy, female vocalist (Singles: 27 Weeks)

			pos/wks
23 Apr 64	NON HO L'ETA PER AMARTI Decca F 21882	17	17
4 May 74 ●	GO (BEFORE YOU BREAK MY HEART) CBS 2294	8	10

CIRCA featuring DESTRY UK, male production group and US, male vocalist (Singles: 1 Week)

			pos/wks
27 Nov 99	SUN SHINING DOWN Inferno CDFERN 22	70	1

CIRCUIT UK, male / female vocal / instrumental group (Singles: 3 Weeks)

			pos/wks
20 Jul 91	SHELTER ME Cooltempo COOL 237	44	2
1 Apr 95	SHELTER ME (re-issue) Pukka CDPUKA 2	50	1

CIRCULATION UK, male production duo (Singles: 1 Week)

			pos/wks
1 Sep 01	TURQUOISE Hooj Choons HOOJ 109	64	1

CIRRUS UK, male vocal group (Singles: 1 Week)

			pos/wks
30 Sep 78	ROLLIN' ON Jet 123	62	1

CITIZEN CANED (see also ANGELIC; ORION; Jurgen VRIES; DT8 PROJECT) UK, male producer – Darren Tate (Singles: 2 Weeks)

			pos/wks
7 Apr 01	THE JOURNEY Serious SERR 029CD	41	2

CITY BEAT BAND See PRINCE CHARLES and the CITY BEAT BAND

CITY BOY UK, male vocal / instrumental group (Singles: 20 Weeks)

			pos/wks
8 Jul 78	5.7.0.5. Vertigo 6059 207	8	12
28 Oct 78	WHAT A NIGHT Vertigo 6059 211	39	5
15 Sep 79	THE DAY THE EARTH CAUGHT FIRE Vertigo 6059 238	67	3

CITY GENTS See Dick CHARLESWORTH and his CITY GENTS

CITY HIGH US, male / female vocal / rap trio (Singles: 27 Weeks)

			pos/wks
6 Oct 01 ●	WHAT WOULD YOU DO? Interscope / Polydor IND 97617	3	17
16 Mar 02 ●	CARAMEL Interscope / Polydor 4976742 [1]	9	10

[1] City High featuring Eve

CITY OF LONDON SINFONIA See John RUTTER

CITY SPUD See NELLY

CK See BADFELLAS featuring CK

Gary CLAIL ON-U SOUND SYSTEM (see also PRIMAL SCREAM) UK, male vocal / instrumental group (Singles: 19 Weeks, Albums: 2 Weeks)

			pos/wks
14 Jul 90	BEEF RCA PB 43843 [1]	64	2
30 Mar 91 ●	HUMAN NATURE Perfecto PB 44401	10	9
8 Jun 91	ESCAPE Perfecto PB 44563	44	3
14 Nov 92	WHO PAYS THE PIPER Perfecto 74321117017	31	3
22 May 93	THESE THINGS ARE WORTH FIGHTING FOR Perfecto 74321147222	45	2
4 May 91	THE EMOTIONAL HOOLIGAN Perfecto PL 74965	35	2

[1] Gary Clail On-U Sound System featuring Bim Sherman

CLAIRE and FRIENDS UK, female vocalist and young male / female friends (Singles: 11 Weeks)

			pos/wks
7 Jun 86	IT'S 'ORRIBLE BEING IN LOVE (WHEN YOU'RE 8 1/2) BBC RESL 189	13	11

CLANCY BROTHERS and Tommy MAKEM Ireland, male vocal / instrumental group and male vocalist (Albums: 5 Weeks)

			pos/wks
16 Apr 66	ISN'T IT GRAND BOYS CBS BPG 62674	22	5

CLANNAD 374 Top 500 Grammy-winning folk / new age / world music mainstays formed 1970, Northern Ireland, included Brennan siblings Maire [Moya] (v / harp / k), Ciaran (g / k), Pol (k) and Ethne O'Bhraonain [Enya] (v/k) (1979-82). Gaelic speaking group won a BAFTA for Best Soundtrack in 1985 for 'Robin of Sherwood' (Singles: 29 Weeks, Albums: 154 Weeks)

			pos/wks
6 Nov 82 ●	THEME FROM 'HARRY'S GAME' RCA 292	5	10
2 Jul 83	NEW GRANGE RCA 340	65	1

12 May 84	ROBIN (THE HOODED MAN) *RCA HOOD 1*	**42**	5
25 Jan 86	IN A LIFETIME *RCA PB 40535* [1]	**20**	5
10 Jun 89	IN A LIFETIME (re-issue) *RCA PB 42873* [1]	**17**	7
10 Aug 91	BOTH SIDES NOW *MCA MCS 1546* [2]	**74**	1
2 Apr 83	MAGICAL RING *RCA RCALP 6072*	**26**	21
12 May 84	LEGEND (MUSIC FROM ROBIN OF SHERWOOD) *RCA PL 70188*	**15**	40
2 Jun 84	MAGICAL RING (re-issue) *RCA PL 70003*	**91**	1
26 Oct 85	MACALLA *RCA PL 70894*	**33**	24
7 Nov 87	SIRIUS *RCA PL 71513*	**34**	4
11 Feb 89	ATLANTIC REALM *BBC REB 727*	**41**	3
6 May 89 ●	PASTPRESENT *RCA PL 74074*	**5**	26
20 Oct 90	ANAM *RCA PL 74762*	**14**	7
15 May 93 ●	BANBA *RCA 74321139612*	**5**	11
6 Apr 96	LORE *RCA 74321300802*	**14**	7
31 May 97	THE ULTIMATE COLLECTION *RCA 74321486742*	**46**	4
11 Apr 98	LANDMARKS *RCA 74321560072*	**34**	2
11 Oct 03	THE BEST OF – IN A LIFETIME *RCA 82876564022*	**23**	4

[1] Clannad featuring Bono [2] Clannad and Paul Young

'Pastpresent' changed its catalogue number to 74321289812 during its chart run

Jimmy CLANTON *US, male vocalist (Singles: 1 Week)*   pos/wks

21 Jul 60	ANOTHER SLEEPLESS NIGHT *Top Rank JAR 382*	**50**	1

Eric CLAPTON (39) Top 500

Rock and blues guitar player and vocalist, b. Eric Clapp, 30 Mar 1945, Surrey, UK, "Clapton is God" was a description bestowed by fans and media alike in the 60s and 70s – also nicknamed 'Slowhand'. Prior to long and lucrative solo career he recorded with hitmakers The Yardbirds, Cream, Blind Faith and Derek and the Dominoes. Multi-Grammy-winning singer-guitarist and mega-grossing live performer (Singles: 150 Weeks, Albums: 555 Weeks)   pos/wks

20 Dec 69	COMIN' HOME *Atlantic 584 308* [1]	**16**	9
12 Aug 72 ●	LAYLA *Polydor 2058 130* [2]	**7**	11
27 Jul 74 ●	I SHOT THE SHERIFF *RSO 2090 132* ▲	**9**	9
10 May 75	SWING LOW SWEET CHARIOT *RSO 2090 158*	**19**	9
16 Aug 75	KNOCKIN' ON HEAVEN'S DOOR *RSO 2090 166*	**38**	4
24 Dec 77	LAY DOWN SALLY *RSO 2090 264*	**39**	6
21 Oct 78	PROMISES *RSO 21*	**37**	7
6 Mar 82 ●	LAYLA (re-issue) *RSO 87* [2]	**4**	10
5 Jun 82	I SHOT THE SHERIFF (re-issue) *RSO 88*	**64**	2
23 Apr 83	THE SHAPE YOU'RE IN *Duck W 9701*	**75**	1
16 Mar 85	FOREVER MAN *Warner Bros. W 9069*	**51**	4
4 Jan 86	EDGE OF DARKNESS *BBC RESL 178* [3]	**65**	3
17 Jan 87	BEHIND THE MASK *Duck W 8461*	**15**	11
20 Jun 87	TEARING US APART *Duck W 8299* [4]	**56**	3
27 Jan 90	BAD LOVE *Duck W 2644*	**25**	7
14 Apr 90	NO ALIBIS *Duck W 9981*	**53**	3
16 Nov 91	WONDERFUL TONIGHT (LIVE) *Duck W 0069*	**30**	7
8 Feb 92 ●	TEARS IN HEAVEN (re) *Reprise W 0081*	**5**	12
1 Aug 92	RUNAWAY TRAIN *Rocket EJS 29* [5]	**31**	4
29 Aug 92	IT'S PROBABLY ME *A&M AM 883* [6]	**30**	5
3 Oct 92	LAYLA (ACOUSTIC) (re-recording) *Duck W 0134*	**45**	3
15 Oct 94	MOTHERLESS CHILD *Duck W 0271CD*	**63**	1
18 Mar 95 ★	LOVE CAN BUILD A BRIDGE *London COCD 1* [7]	**1**	8
20 Jul 96	CHANGE THE WORLD *Reprise W 0358CD*	**18**	5
4 Apr 98	MY FATHER'S EYES *Duck W 0443CD*	**33**	2
4 Jul 98	CIRCUS *Duck W 0447CD*	**39**	2
18 Nov 00	FOREVER MAN (HOW MANY TIMES) *ffrr FCD 386* [8]	**26**	2
30 Jul 66 ●	BLUES BREAKERS *Decca LK 4804* [1]	**6**	17
5 Sep 70	ERIC CLAPTON *Polydor 2383021*	**17**	8
26 Aug 72	HISTORY OF ERIC CLAPTON *Polydor 2659 2478 027*	**20**	6
24 Mar 73	IN CONCERT *RSO 2659020* [2]	**36**	1
3 Nov 73	ERIC CLAPTON'S RAINBOW CONCERT *RSO 2394 116*	**19**	4
24 Aug 74 ●	461 OCEAN BOULEVARD *RSO 2479 118* ▲	**3**	19
12 Apr 75	THERE'S ONE IN EVERY CROWD *RSO 2479 132*	**15**	8
13 Sep 75	E.C. WAS HERE *RSO 2394 160*	**14**	6
11 Sep 76 ●	NO REASON TO CRY *RSO 2479 179*	**8**	7
26 Nov 77	SLOWHAND *RSO 2479 201*	**23**	13
9 Dec 78	BACKLESS *RSO RSD 5001*	**18**	12
10 May 80 ●	JUST ONE NIGHT *RSO RSDX 2*	**3**	12
7 Mar 81	ANOTHER TICKET *RSO RSD 5008*	**18**	8
24 Apr 82	TIMEPIECES – THE BEST OF ERIC CLAPTON *RSO RSD 5010*	**20**	14
19 Feb 83	MONEY & CIGARETTES *Duck W 3773*	**13**	17
9 Jun 84	BACKTRACKIN' *Starblend ERIC 1*	**29**	16
23 Mar 85 ●	BEHIND THE SUN *Duck 9251661*	**8**	14
6 Dec 86 ●	AUGUST *Duck WX 71*	**3**	46
26 Sep 87 ●	THE CREAM OF ERIC CLAPTON *Polydor ECTV 1* [3]	**3**	109
18 Nov 89 ●	JOURNEYMAN *Duck WX 322*	**2**	32

26 Oct 91	24 NIGHTS *Duck WX 373*	**17**	7
12 Sep 92 ●	UNPLUGGED *Duck 9362450242* ▲	**2**	90
24 Sep 94 ★	FROM THE CRADLE *Duck 9362457352* ■ ▲	**1**	18
21 Mar 98	PILGRIM *Duck 9362465772*	**6**	15
26 Jun 99	BLUES *Polydor 5471782*	**52**	2
30 Oct 99 ●	CLAPTON CHRONICLES – THE BEST OF ERIC CLAPTON *Duck 9362475642*	**6**	21
24 Jun 00	RIDING WITH THE KING *Reprise 9362476122* [4]	**15**	15
15 Jul 00	TIME PIECES – THE BEST OF ERIC CLAPTON (re-issue) *Polydor 8000142*	**73**	2
17 Mar 01 ●	REPTILE *Reprise 9362479662*	**7**	7
16 Nov 02	LIVE ON TOUR 2001 – ONE MORE CAR ONE MORE RIDER *Reprise 9362483542*	**69**	1
3 Apr 04 ●	ME AND MR JOHNSON *Reprise 9362487302*	**10**	8

[1] Delaney and Bonnie and Friends featuring Eric Clapton [2] Derek and the Dominoes [3] Eric Clapton featuring Michael Kamen [4] Eric Clapton and Tina Turner [5] Elton John and Eric Clapton [6] Sting with Eric Clapton [7] Cher, Chrissie Hynde and Neneh Cherry with Eric Clapton [8] Beatchuggers featuring Eric Clapton [1] John Mayall and Eric Clapton [2] Derek and the Dominos [3] Eric Clapton and Cream [4] B.B. King and Eric Clapton

From 9 Jul 93 'The Cream of Eric Clapton' was repackaged and was available as 'The Best of Eric Clapton'

CLARISSA See DJ VISAGE featuring CLARISSA

The Dave CLARK FIVE (327) Top 500

Beat Boom superstars from Tottenham, London, UK: Dave Clark (d), Mike Smith (v/k), Lenny Davidson (g), Denis Payton (s), Rick Huxley (g). In the first years of the 'British Invasion', this foot-stomping quintet was second only to The Beatles in the US (Singles: 174 Weeks, Albums: 31 Weeks)   pos/wks

3 Oct 63	DO YOU LOVE ME *Columbia DB 7112*	**30**	6
21 Nov 63 ★	GLAD ALL OVER *Columbia DB 7154*	**1**	19
20 Feb 64 ●	BITS AND PIECES *Columbia DB 7210*	**2**	11
28 May 64 ●	CAN'T YOU SEE THAT SHE'S MINE *Columbia DB 7291*	**10**	11
13 Aug 64	THINKING OF YOU BABY *Columbia DB 7335*	**26**	4
22 Oct 64	ANYWAY YOU WANT IT *Columbia DB 7377*	**25**	5
14 Jan 65	EVERYBODY KNOWS *Columbia DB 7453*	**37**	4
11 Mar 65	REELIN' AND ROCKIN' *Columbia DB 7503*	**24**	8
27 May 65	COME HOME *Columbia DB 7580*	**16**	8
15 Jul 65 ●	CATCH US IF YOU CAN *Columbia DB 7625*	**5**	11
11 Nov 65	OVER AND OVER *Columbia DB 7744* ▲	**45**	4
19 May 66	LOOK BEFORE YOU LEAP *Columbia DB 7909*	**50**	1
16 Mar 67	YOU GOT WHAT IT TAKES *Columbia DB 8152*	**28**	8
1 Nov 67 ●	EVERYBODY KNOWS *Columbia DB 8286*	**2**	14
28 Feb 68	NO ONE CAN BREAK A HEART LIKE YOU *Columbia DB 8342*	**28**	7
18 Sep 68 ●	THE RED BALLOON *Columbia DB 8465*	**7**	11
27 Nov 68	LIVE IN THE SKY *Columbia DB 8505*	**39**	6
25 Jun 69	PUT A LITTLE LOVE IN YOUR HEART *Columbia DB 8624*	**31**	4
6 Dec 69 ●	GOOD OLD ROCK 'N' ROLL *Columbia DB 8638*	**7**	12
7 Mar 70 ●	EVERYBODY GET TOGETHER *Columbia DB 8660*	**8**	8
4 Jul 70	HERE COMES SUMMER *Columbia DB 8689*	**44**	3
7 Nov 70	MORE GOOD OLD ROCK 'N' ROLL *Columbia DB 8724*	**34**	6
1 May 93	GLAD ALL OVER (re-issue) *EMI CDEMCT 8*	**37**	3
18 Apr 64 ●	A SESSION WITH THE DAVE CLARK FIVE *Columbia 33SX 1598*	**3**	8
14 Aug 65 ●	CATCH US IF YOU CAN *Columbia 33SX 1756*	**8**	8
4 Mar 78	25 THUMPING GREAT HITS *Polydor POLTV 7*	**7**	10
17 Apr 93	GLAD ALL OVER AGAIN *EMI CDEMTV 75*	**28**	5

'Everybody Knows' on DB 7453 and 'Everybody Knows' on DB 8286 are two different songs. The two Rock 'n' Roll titles are medleys as follows: Good Old Rock 'n' Roll: Sweet Little Sixteen / Long Tall Sally / Whole Lotta Shakin' Goin' On / Blue Suede Shoes / Lucille / Reelin' and Rockin' / Memphis Tennessee. More Good Old Rock 'n' Roll Music: Blueberry Hill / Good Golly Miss Molly / My Blue Heaven / Keep a Knockin' / Loving You / One Night / Lawdy Miss Clawdy

Dee CLARK *US, male vocalist – Delecta Clark. b. 7 Nov 1938, d. 7 Dec 1990 (Singles: 9 Weeks)*   pos/wks

2 Oct 59	JUST KEEP IT UP (AND SEE WHAT HAPPENS) *London HL 8915*	**26**	1
11 Oct 75	RIDE A WILD HORSE *Chelsea 2005 037*	**16**	8

Gary CLARK *UK, male vocalist (Singles: 8 Weeks, Albums: 2 Weeks)*   pos/wks

30 Jan 93	WE SAIL ON THE STORMY WATERS *Circa YRCDX 93*	**34**	4
3 Apr 93	FREEFLOATING *Circa YRCDX 94*	**50**	3
19 Jun 93	MAKE A FAMILY *Circa YRCDX 105*	**70**	1
8 May 93	TEN SHORT SONGS ABOUT LOVE *Circa CIRCD 23*	**25**	2

Loni CLARK
US, female vocalist (Singles: 6 Weeks) pos/wks

5 Jun 93	RUSHING *A&M 5802862*	37 2
22 Jan 94	U *A&M 5804752*	28 3
17 Dec 94	LOVE'S GOT ME ON A TRIP SO HIGH *A&M 5808872*	59 1

Louis CLARK *See ROYAL PHILHARMONIC ORCHESTRA*

Petula CLARK (199) Top 500
Britain's most consistently successful female vocalist, b. 15 Nov 1932, Surrey. Before her 47-year chart span, she starred in movies and was voted Britain's Top TV Personality. First UK female to win a Grammy and to be named Top Female Vocalist of the Year in the US in 1966 (Singles: 247 Weeks, Albums: 47 Weeks) pos/wks

11 Jun 54 ●	THE LITTLE SHOEMAKER (re) *Polygon P 1117*	7 10
18 Feb 55	MAJORCA (re) *Polygon P 1146*	12 5
25 Nov 55 ●	SUDDENLY THERE'S A VALLEY *Pye Nixa N 15013*	7 10
26 Jul 57 ●	WITH ALL MY HEART *Pye Nixa N 15096*	4 18
15 Nov 57 ●	ALONE *Pye Nixa N 15112*	8 12
28 Feb 58	BABY LOVER *Pye Nixa N 15126*	12 7
26 Jan 61 ★	SAILOR *Pye 7N 15324*	1 15
13 Apr 61	SOMETHING MISSING *Pye 7N 15337*	44 1
13 Jul 61 ●	ROMEO *Pye 7N 15361*	3 15
16 Nov 61 ●	MY FRIEND THE SEA *Pye 7N 15389*	7 13
8 Feb 62	I'M COUNTING ON YOU *Pye 7N 15407*	41 2
28 Jun 62	YA YA TWIST (re) *Pye 7N 15448*	14 13
2 May 63	CASANOVA / CHARIOT *Pye 7N 15522*	39 7
12 Nov 64 ●	DOWNTOWN *Pye 7N 15722* ▲	2 15
11 Mar 65	I KNOW A PLACE *Pye 7N 15772*	17 8
12 Aug 65	YOU BETTER COME HOME *Pye 7N 15864*	44 3
14 Oct 65	ROUND EVERY CORNER *Pye 7N 15945*	43 3
4 Nov 65	YOU'RE THE ONE *Pye 7N 15991*	23 9
10 Feb 66 ●	MY LOVE *Pye 7N 17038* ▲	4 9
21 Apr 66	A SIGN OF THE TIMES *Pye 7N 17071*	49 1
30 Jun 66 ●	I COULDN'T LIVE WITHOUT YOUR LOVE *Pye 7N 17133* ...	6 11
2 Feb 67 ★	THIS IS MY SONG *Pye 7N 17258*	1 14
25 May 67	DON'T SLEEP IN THE SUBWAY *Pye 7N 17325*	12 11
13 Dec 67	THE OTHER MAN'S GRASS (IS ALWAYS GREENER) *Pye 7N 17416*	20 9
6 Mar 68	KISS ME GOODBYE *Pye 7N 17466*	50 1
30 Jan 71	THE SONG OF MY LIFE (re) *Pye 7N 45026*	32 12
15 Jan 72	I DON'T KNOW HOW TO LOVE HIM (re) *Pye 7N 45112* ...	47 2
19 Nov 88 ●	DOWNTOWN '88 (re-mix) *PRT PYS 19*	10 11
30 Jul 66	I COULDN'T LIVE WITHOUT YOUR LOVE *Pye NPL 18148* ...	11 10
4 Feb 67	HIT PARADE *Pye NPL 18159*	18 13
18 Feb 67	COLOUR MY WORLD *Pye NSPL 18171*	16 9
7 Oct 67	THESE ARE MY SONGS *Pye NSPL 18197*	38 3
6 Apr 68	THE OTHER MAN'S GRASS IS ALWAYS GREENER *Pye NSPL 18211*	37 1
5 Feb 77	20 ALL TIME GREATEST *K-Tel NE 945*	18 7
27 Apr 02	THE ULTIMATE COLLECTION *Sanctuary SANDD 111*	18 4

Roland CLARK *See Armand VAN HELDEN; Azzido DA BASS*

Dave CLARKE
UK, male producer (Singles: 10 Weeks, Albums: 2 Weeks) pos/wks

30 Sep 95	RED THREE: THUNDER / STORM *Deconstruction 74321306992*	45 2
3 Feb 96	SOUTHSIDE *Bush 74321335382*	34 2
15 Jun 96	NO ONE'S DRIVING *Bush 74321380162*	37 2
8 Dec 01	THE COMPASS *Skint SKINT 73CD*	46 1
28 Dec 02	THE WOLF *Skint SKINT 78*	66 1
25 Oct 03	WAY OF LIFE *Skint SKINT 93CD*	59 1
21 Feb 04	WHAT WAS HER NAME? *Skint SKINT 94CD* [1]	50 1
17 Feb 96	ARCHIVE ONE *Bush 74321320672*	36 2

[1] Dave Clarke featuring Chicks On Speed

Gilby CLARKE (see also GUNS N' ROSES)
US, male instrumentalist – guitar (Albums: 1 Week) pos/wks

6 Aug 94	PAWNSHOP GUITARS *Virgin America CDVUS 76*	39 1

John Cooper CLARKE
UK, male vocalist (Singles: 3 Weeks, Albums: 9 Weeks) pos/wks

10 Mar 79	GIMMIX! PLAY LOUD *Epic EPC 7009*	39 3
19 Apr 80	SNAP CRACKLE AND BOP *Epic EPC 84083*	26 7
5 Jun 82	ZIP STYLE METHOD *Epic EPC 85667*	97 2

Rick CLARKE *UK, male vocalist (Singles: 2 Weeks)* pos/wks

30 Apr 88	I'LL SEE YOU ALONG THE WAY *WA WA 1*	63 2

Sharon D CLARKE *See FPI PROJECT; SERIOUS ROPE*

Stanley CLARKE
US, male vocalist / instrumentalist – bass (Albums: 2 Weeks) pos/wks

12 Jul 80	ROCKS PEBBLES AND SAND *Epic EPC 84342*	42 2

Warren CLARKE featuring Kathy BROWN
UK, male producer and US, female vocalist (Singles: 1 Week) pos/wks

2 Jun 01	OVER YOU *Defected DFECT 28CDS*	42 1

CLARKESVILLE
UK, male vocalist – Michael Clarke (Singles: 1 Week) pos/wks

7 Feb 04	SPINNING *Wildstar CDWILD 53*	72 1

Kelly CLARKSON
US, female vocalist (Singles: 13 Weeks, Albums: 4 Weeks) pos/wks

6 Sep 03 ●	MISS INDEPENDENT *S 82876553642*	6 10
29 Nov 03	LOW / THE TROUBLE WITH LOVE IS *S 82876570702* ...	35 3
6 Sep 03	THANKFUL *S 82876540882* ▲	52 4

Julian CLARY *See JOAN COLLINS FAN CLUB*

The CLASH (252) Top 500
Leading lights of the UK punk rock explosion: Joe Strummer, b. John Mellor, 21 Aug 1952, d. 23 Dec 2002 (v/g), Mick Jones (g/v), Paul Simonon (b), Topper Headon (d). Their third LP, 'London Calling' (first released 1979), was voted Best Album of the 1980s by Rolling Stone magazine. Inducted into the Rock and Roll Hall of Fame in 2003 (Singles: 135 Weeks, Albums: 116 Weeks) pos/wks

2 Apr 77	WHITE RIOT *CBS 5058*	38 3
8 Oct 77	COMPLETE CONTROL *CBS 5664*	28 2
4 Mar 78	CLASH CITY ROCKERS *CBS 5834*	35 4
24 Jun 78	(WHITE MAN) IN HAMMERSMITH PALAIS *CBS 6383* ...	32 7
2 Dec 78	TOMMY GUN *CBS 6788*	19 10
3 Mar 79	ENGLISH CIVIL WAR (JOHNNY COMES MARCHING HOME) *CBS 7082*	25 6
19 May 79	THE COST OF LIVING (EP) *CBS 7324*	22 8
15 Dec 79	LONDON CALLING *CBS 8087*	11 10
9 Aug 80	BANKROBBER *CBS 8323*	12 10
6 Dec 80	THE CALL UP *CBS 9339*	40 6
24 Jan 81	HITSVILLE UK *CBS 9480*	56 4
25 Apr 81	THE MAGNIFICENT SEVEN *CBS 1133*	34 5
28 Nov 81	THIS IS RADIO CLASH *CBS A 1797*	47 6
1 May 82	KNOW YOUR RIGHTS *CBS A 2309*	43 3
26 Jun 82	ROCK THE CASBAH *CBS A 2429*	30 10
25 Sep 82	SHOULD I STAY OR SHOULD I GO / STRAIGHT TO HELL *CBS A 2646*	17 9
12 Oct 85	THIS IS ENGLAND *CBS A 6122*	24 5
12 Mar 88	I FOUGHT THE LAW *CBS CLASH 1*	29 5
7 May 88	LONDON CALLING (re-issue) *CBS CLASH 2*	46 3
21 Jul 90	RETURN TO BRIXTON *CBS 656072 7*	57 2
2 Mar 91 ★	SHOULD I STAY OR SHOULD I GO (re-issue) *Columbia 6566677*	1 9
13 Apr 91	ROCK THE CASBAH (re-issue) *Columbia 6568147*	15 6
8 Jun 91	LONDON CALLING (re-issue) *Columbia 6569467*	64 2
30 Apr 77	THE CLASH *CBS 82000*	12 16
25 Nov 78 ●	GIVE 'EM ENOUGH ROPE *CBS 82431*	2 14
22 Dec 79 ●	LONDON CALLING *CBS CLASH 3*	9 21
20 Dec 80	SANDINISTA! *CBS FSLN 1*	19 9
22 May 82 ●	COMBAT ROCK *CBS FMLN 2*	2 23
16 Nov 85	CUT THE CRAP *CBS 26601*	16 3
2 Apr 88 ●	THE STORY OF THE CLASH – VOLUME 1 *CBS 4602441* ...	7 21
16 Nov 91	THE SINGLES *Columbia 4689461*	68 2
16 Oct 99	FROM HERE TO ETERNITY *Columbia 4961832*	13 3
22 Mar 03	THE ESSENTIAL CLASH *Columbia 05109982*	18 3
2 Oct 04	LONDON CALLING – 25TH ANNIVERSARY EDITION *Columbia 5179283*	26 1

Tracks on The Cost of Living (EP): I Fought the Law / Groovy Times / Gates of the West / Capital Radio. CBS CLASH 1 is a re-issue of a track from The Cost of Living (EP)

CLASS ACTION featuring Chris WILTSHIRE
US, female vocal group (Singles: 3 Weeks) pos/wks

7 May 83	WEEKEND *Jive JIVE 35*	49 3

The CLASSICS IV
US, male vocal / instrumental group (Singles: 1 Week) pos/wks

28 Feb 68	SPOOKY *Liberty LBS 15051*	46 1

CLASSIX NOUVEAUX (see also Sal SOLO) *UK, male vocal / instrumental group (Singles: 34 Weeks, Albums: 6 Weeks)* pos/wks

28 Feb 81	**GUILTY** *Liberty BP 388*	43	7
16 May 81	**TOKYO** *Liberty BP 397*	67	3
8 Aug 81	**INSIDE OUTSIDE** *Liberty BP 403*	45	5
7 Nov 81	**NEVER AGAIN (THE DAYS TIME ERASED)** *Liberty BP 406*	44	4
13 Mar 82	**IS IT A DREAM** *Liberty BP 409*	11	9
29 May 82	**BECAUSE YOU'RE YOUNG** *Liberty BP 411*	43	4
30 Oct 82	**THE END ... OR THE BEGINNING** *Liberty BP 414*	60	2
30 May 81	**NIGHT PEOPLE** *Liberty LBG 30325*	66	2
24 Apr 82	**LA VERITE** *Liberty LBG 30346*	44	4

CLAWFINGER *Norway / Sweden, male vocal / instrumental group (Singles: 1 Week)* pos/wks

19 Mar 94	**WARFAIR** *East West YZ 804CD1*	54	1

Judy CLAY and William BELL *US, female / male vocal duo – Clay, b. 12 Sep 1938, d.19 Jul 2001 (Singles: 14 Weeks)* pos/wks

20 Nov 68 ●	**PRIVATE NUMBER** *Stax 101*	8	14

Richard CLAYDERMAN `315` `Top 500`

'The world's most successful pianist' according to Guinness World Records, b. Philippe Pagès (adopted great grandmother's surname), 28 Dec 1953, Paris, France. He has sold in excess of 70 million albums and earned over 250 gold and 70 platinum albums (Albums: 211 Weeks) pos/wks

13 Nov 82 ●	**RICHARD CLAYDERMAN** *Decca SKL 5329*	2	64
8 Oct 83	**THE MUSIC OF RICHARD CLAYDERMAN** *Decca SKL 5333*	21	28
24 Nov 84	**THE MUSIC OF LOVE** *Decca SKL 5340*	28	21
1 Dec 84	**CHRISTMAS** *Decca SKL 5337*	53	5
23 Nov 85	**THE CLASSIC TOUCH** *Decca SKL 5343*	17	18
22 Nov 86	**HOLLYWOOD AND BROADWAY** *Decca SKL 5344*	28	9
28 Nov 87	**SONGS OF LOVE** *Decca SKL 5345*	19	13
3 Dec 88	**A LITTLE NIGHT MUSIC** *Decca Delphine 8281251*	52	5
25 Nov 89	**THE LOVE SONGS OF ANDREW LLOYD WEBBER** *Decca Delphine 8281751*	18	10
24 Nov 90	**MY CLASSIC COLLECTION** *Decca Delphine 8282281*	29	7
9 Nov 91	**TOGETHER AT LAST** *Delphine / Polydor 5115251* [1]	14	15
14 Nov 92	**THE VERY BEST OF RICHARD CLAYDERMAN** *Decca Delphine 8283362* [2]	47	5
19 Nov 94	**IN HARMONY** *Polydor 5238242* [1]	28	7
25 Nov 95	**THE CARPENTERS COLLECTION** *PolyGram TV 8286882*	65	2
20 Dec 97	**THE BEST OF RICHARD CLAYDERMAN** *Delphine DTVCD 700*	73	1
18 Sep 99	**... WITH LOVE** *Music Club MCTVCD 002*	62	1

[1] Richard Clayderman and James Last [2] Richard Clayderman with the Royal Philharmonic Orchestra

Adam CLAYTON and Larry MULLEN (see also U2) *Ireland, male instrumental duo (Singles: 12 Weeks)* pos/wks

15 Jun 96 ●	**THEME FROM 'MISSION: IMPOSSIBLE'** *Mother MUMCD 75*	7	12

Merry CLAYTON *US, female vocalist – Mary Clayton (Singles: 1 Week)* pos/wks

21 May 88	**YES** *RCA PB 49563*	70	1

CLAYTOWN TROUPE *UK, male vocal / instrumental group (Singles: 3 Weeks, Albums: 1 Week)* pos/wks

16 Jun 90	**WAYS OF LOVE** *Island IS 464*	57	2
14 Mar 92	**WANTED IT ALL** *EMI USA MT 102*	74	1
21 Oct 89	**THROUGH THE VEIL** *Island ILPS 9933*	72	1

CLEA *UK, female vocal group (Singles: 5 Weeks)* pos/wks

4 Oct 03	**DOWNLOAD IT** *1967 CLEA 01CD*	21	3
28 Feb 04	**STUCK IN THE MIDDLE** *1967 CLEA 02CD*	23	2

Johnny CLEGG and SAVUKA (see also JULUKA) *UK / South Africa, male vocal / instrumental group (Singles: 1 Week)* pos/wks

16 May 87	**SCATTERLINGS OF AFRICA** *EMI EMI 5605*	75	1

CLEOPATRA *UK, female vocal trio – (Singles: 44 Weeks, Albums: 4 Weeks)* pos/wks

14 Feb 98 ●	**CLEOPATRA'S THEME** *WEA WEA 133CD*	3	10
16 May 98 ●	**LIFE AIN'T EASY** *WEA WEA 159CD1*	4	7
22 Aug 98 ●	**I WANT YOU BACK** *WEA WEA 172CD1*	4	7
6 Mar 99	**A TOUCH OF LOVE** *WEA WEA 199CD1*	24	4
10 Apr 99 ●	**THANK ABBA FOR THE MUSIC** *Epic ABCD 1* [1]	4	13
29 Jul 00	**COME AND GET ME** *WEA WEA 216CD1*	29	3
6 Jun 98	**COMIN' ATCHA!** *WEA 3984233562*	20	4

[1] Steps, Tina Cousins, Cleopatra, B*Witched, Billie

CLEPTOMANIACS featuring Bryan CHAMBERS *UK, male production group and vocalist (Singles: 3 Weeks)* pos/wks

3 Feb 01	**ALL I DO** *Defected DFECT 27CDS*	23	3

CLERGY (see also CANDY GIRLS; DOROTHY; HI-GATE; Paul MASTERSON presents SUSHI; SLEAZE SISTERS; YOMANDA) *UK, male production duo – Paul Masterson and Judge Jules (Singles: 1 Week)* pos/wks

20 Jul 02	**THE OBOE SONG** *ffrr DFCD 005*	50	1

CLICK *US, male rap group (Singles: 1 Week)* pos/wks

29 Jun 96	**SCANDALOUS** *Jive JIVECD 393*	54	1

CLIENT *UK, female vocal duo (Singles: 2 Weeks)* pos/wks

26 Jun 04	**IN IT FOR THE MONEY** *Toast Hawaii CDTH 005*	51	1
2 Oct 04	**RADIO** *Toast Hawaii CDTH 006*	68	1

Jimmy CLIFF *Jamaica, male vocalist – James Chambers (Singles: 33 Weeks)* pos/wks

25 Oct 69 ●	**WONDERFUL WORLD, BEAUTIFUL PEOPLE** *Trojan TR 690*	6	13
14 Feb 70	**VIETNAM (re)** *Trojan TR 7722*	46	3
8 Aug 70	**WILD WORLD** *Island WIP 6087*	8	12
19 Mar 94	**I CAN SEE CLEARLY NOW** *Columbia 6601982*	23	5

Buzz CLIFFORD *US, male vocalist – Reese Clifford III (Singles: 13 Weeks)* pos/wks

2 Mar 61	**BABY SITTIN' BOOGIE** *Fontana H 297*	17	13

Linda CLIFFORD *US, female vocalist (Singles: 13 Weeks)* pos/wks

10 Jun 78	**IF MY FRIENDS COULD SEE ME NOW** *Curtom K 17163*	50	5
5 May 79	**BRIDGE OVER TROUBLED WATER** *RSO 30*	28	7
15 Sep 01	**RIDE THE STORM** *NRK Sound Division NRKCD 053* [1]	69	1

[1] Akabu featuring Linda Clifford

The CLIMAX BLUES BAND *UK, male vocal / instrumental group (Singles: 9 Weeks, Albums: 1 Week)* pos/wks

9 Oct 76 ●	**COULDN'T GET IT RIGHT** *BTM SBT 105*	10	9
13 Nov 76	**GOLD PLATED** *BTM 1009*	56	1

Simon CLIMIE (see also CLIMIE FISHER) *UK, male vocalist (Singles: 2 Weeks)* pos/wks

19 Sep 92	**SOUL INSPIRATION** *Epic 6582837*	60	2

CLIMIE FISHER (see also NAKED EYES) *UK, male vocal / instrumental duo – Simon Climie and Rob Fisher, b. 5 Nov 1959, d. 25 Aug 1999 (Singles: 44 Weeks, Albums: 38 Weeks)* pos/wks

5 Sep 87	**LOVE CHANGES (EVERYTHING)** *EMI EM 15*	67	2
12 Dec 87 ●	**RISE TO THE OCCASION** *EMI EM 33*	10	11
12 Mar 88 ●	**LOVE CHANGES (EVERYTHING) (re-mix)** *EMI EM 47*	2	12
21 May 88	**THIS IS ME** *EMI EM 58*	22	5
20 Aug 88	**I WON'T BLEED FOR YOU** *EMI EM 66*	35	4
24 Dec 88	**LOVE LIKE A RIVER** *EMI EM 81*	22	7
23 Sep 89	**FACTS OF LOVE** *EMI EM 103*	50	3
13 Feb 88	**EVERYTHING** *EMI EMC 3538*	14	36
21 Oct 89	**COMING IN FOR THE KILL** *EMI EMC 3565*	35	2

Patsy CLINE *US, female vocalist – Virginia Hensley, b. 8 Sep 1932, d. 5 Mar 1963 (Singles: 17 Weeks, Albums: 28 Weeks)* pos/wks

26 Apr 62	**SHE'S GOT YOU** *Brunswick 05866*	43	1
29 Nov 62	**HEARTACHES** *Brunswick 05878*	31	5
8 Dec 90	**CRAZY** *MCA MCA 1465*	14	11
19 Jan 91	**DREAMING** *Platinum Music PLAT 303*	55	4
19 Jan 91	**SWEET DREAMS** *MCA MCG 6003*	18	10
5 Sep 92	**THE DEFINITIVE PATSY CLINE** *Arcade ARC 94992*	11	8
6 Jul 96	**THE VERY BEST OF PATSY CLINE** *MCA MCD 11483*	21	6

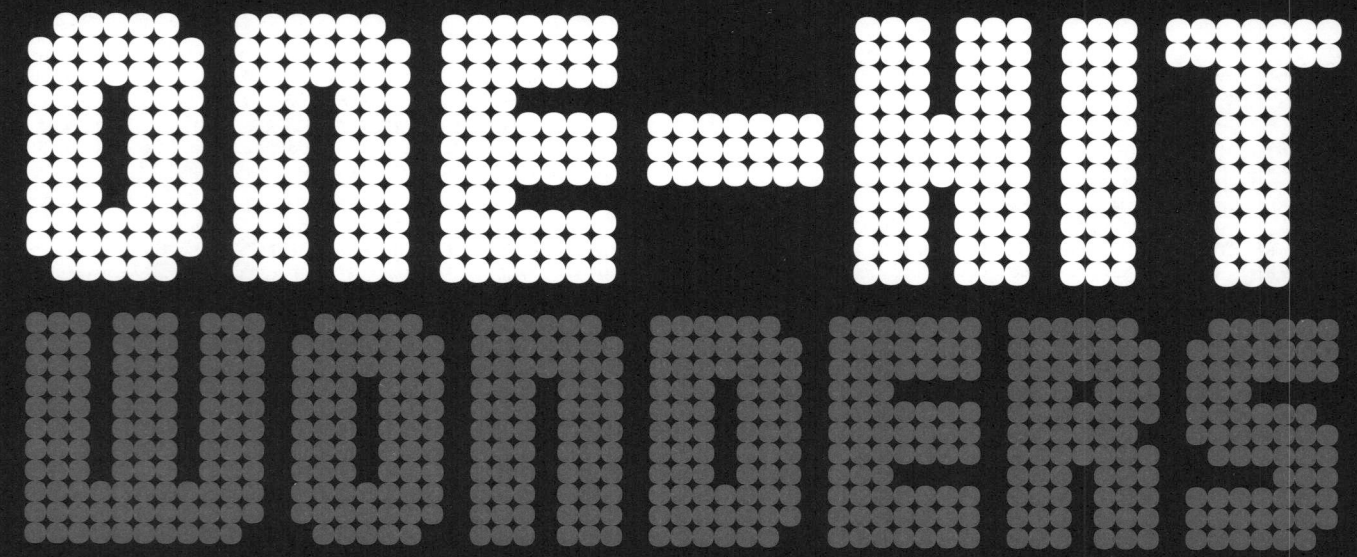

ONE-HIT WONDERS

Are there more one-hit wonders today than ever before? Is this really the era of the flash-in-the-pan pop star who is here today and gone tomorrow? To find out, our chart expert Dave McAleer undertook the truly mammoth task of checking every single chart entry to determine the facts.

Before plunging headlong into the information provided by the graph below, let's define "one-hit wonder". The ultimate one-hit wonder is undoubtedly an act's only chart appearance resulting in a No.1 hit and nothing else, before or after. However, far more revealing is an in-depth study of every act that has had, just the once, a hit in any chart position.

Our graph includes one-hit wonders created by any act that has one solitary chart entry. To clarify who is included and who isn't, here are some handy examples. LMC vs U2 may have charted only once, but since parts of that named act, U2, have charted previously in their own right, then the act LMC vs U2 would not be considered one-hit wonders for our purposes. On the other hand, an act such as Oris Jay presents Delsena would be included, as neither Oris nor Delsena has had any other chart entries. Also note that acts that changed

their name midstream, but still had the same line-up; eg Martha and the Vandellas and Martha Reeves and the Vandellas, are counted as one act, and therefore Martha Reeves and the Vandellas are not one-hit wonders.

Bear in mind that when the chart was a Top 12, Top 20, Top 30 or Top 50, naturally there were fewer chart entries, and therefore fewer one-hit wonders. If you want to compare like with like, then perhaps you should focus your attention on totals for the years 1978 to 2002, which are all based on Top 75 entries. This graph ends in 2002, as some acts who made their chart debut after that year may still have a hit or two left in them.

We'll let the graph speak for itself and leave you to draw your own conclusions. But, not surprisingly, it does appear that we could be living in the era of the one-hit wonder.

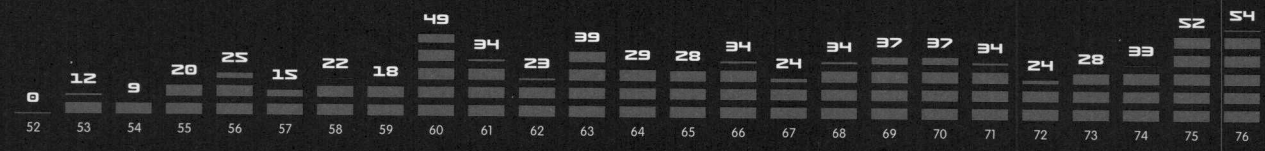

Year by year totals of one-hits wonders from 1952-2002

ULTIMATE ONE-HIT WONDERS

Acts with just one hit, but what a hit! It's astonishing that no follow-up of any description could penetrate even the lower reaches of the chart for any of these mighty chart-toppers.

1. THE ARCHIES
Sugar, Sugar
1969 (26 weeks on chart / 8 at No.1)

2. THE KALIN TWINS
When
1958 (18 weeks on chart / 5 at No.1)

3. THE SIMON PARK ORCHESTRA
Eye Level (Theme from the TV Series 'Van Der Valk')
1972 (24 weeks on chart / 4 at No.1)

4. PARTNERS IN KRYME
Turtle Power
1990 (10 weeks on chart / 4 at No.1)

5. CLIVE DUNN
Grandad
1970 (28 weeks on chart / 3 at No.1)

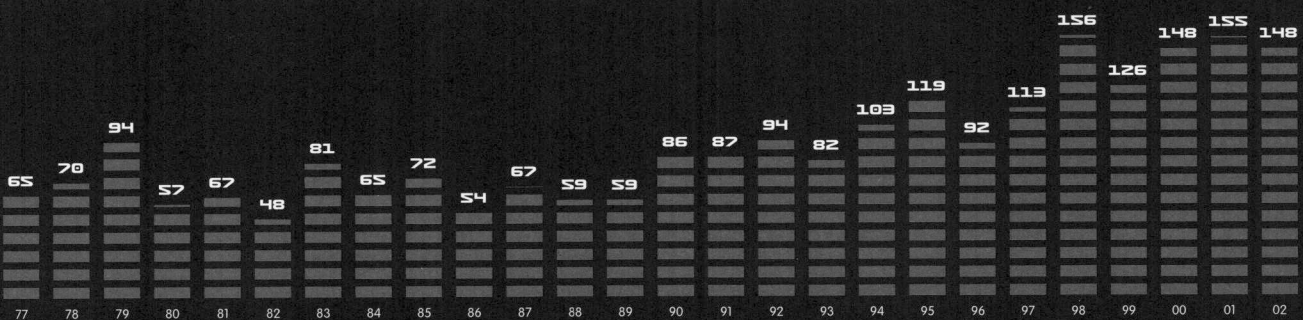

CLINIC
UK, male vocal / instrumental group (Singles: 3 Weeks)   pos/wks

22 Apr 00	THE RETURN OF EVIL BILL *Domino RUG 093CD*	**70**	1
4 Nov 00	THE SECOND LINE *Domino RUG 116CD*	**56**	1
2 Mar 02	WALKING WITH THEE *Domino RUG 134CD*	**65**	1

George CLINTON (see also FUNKADELIC)
US, male vocalist (Singles: 10 Weeks)   pos/wks

4 Dec 82	LOOPZILLA *Capitol CL 271*	**57**	5
26 Apr 86	DO FRIES GO WITH THAT SHAKE *Capitol CL 402*	**57**	2
27 Aug 94	BOP GUN (ONE NATION) *Fourth & Broadway BRCD 308* [1]	**22**	3

[1] Ice Cube featuring George Clinton

CLIPSE
US, male rap duo – Gene and Terence Thornton (Singles: 5 Weeks) pos/wks

22 Feb 03	WHEN THE LAST TIME *Arista 82876502212*	**41**	2
24 May 03	MA, I DON'T LOVE HER *Arista 82876526482* [1]	**38**	3

[1] Clipse featuring Faith Evans

CLIPZ *UK, male producer (Singles: 1 Week)*
pos/wks

6 Mar 04	COCOA / JIGGY *Full Cycle FCY 064*	**71**	1

CLIVILLES & COLE See C & C MUSIC FACTORY

CLOCK *UK, male production / vocal /*
instrumental duo (Singles: 70 Weeks, Albums: 4 Weeks)   pos/wks

30 Oct 93	HOLDING ON *Media MRLCD 007*	**66**	1
21 May 94	THE RHYTHM *Media MCSTD 1971*	**28**	2
10 Sep 94	KEEP THE FIRES BURNING *Media MCSTD 1998*	**36**	3
4 Mar 95 ●	AXEL F / KEEP PUSHIN' *Media MCSTD 2041*	**7**	9
1 Jul 95 ●	WHOOMPH! (THERE IT IS) *Media MCSTD 2059*	**4**	9
26 Aug 95 ●	EVERYBODY *Media MCSTD 2077*	**6**	5
18 Nov 95	IN THE HOUSE *Media MCSTD 40005*	**23**	3
24 Feb 96	HOLDING ON 4 U (re-mix) *Media MCSTD 40019*	**27**	2
7 Sep 96	OH WHAT A NIGHT *Power Station MCSTD 40057*	**13**	10
22 Mar 97 ●	IT'S OVER *Media MCSTD 40100*	**10**	5
18 Oct 97	U SEXY THING *Media MCSTD 40138*	**11**	9
17 Jan 98	THAT'S THE WAY (I LIKE IT) *Media MCSTD 40148*	**11**	4
11 Jul 98	ROCK YOUR BODY *Media MCSTD 40160*	**30**	3
28 Nov 98	BLAME IT ON THE BOOGIE *Media MCSTD 40191*	**16**	4
31 Jul 99	SUNSHINE DAY *Media MCSTD 40208*	**58**	1
23 Sep 95	IT'S TIME ... *Media MCD 11355*	**27**	2
5 Apr 97	ABOUT TIME 2 *Media MCD 60032*	**56**	2

Rosemary CLOONEY *US, female vocalist,*
b. 23 May 1928, d. 29 Jun 2002 (Singles: 81 Weeks)   pos/wks

14 Nov 52 ●	HALF AS MUCH *Columbia DB 3129*	**3**	9
5 Feb 54 ●	MAN (UH-HUH) *Philips PB 220*	**7**	5
8 Oct 54 ★	THIS OLE HOUSE *Philips PB 336* ▲	**1**	18
17 Dec 54 ★	MAMBO ITALIANO *Philips PB 382* [1]	**1**	16
20 May 55 ●	WHERE WILL THE DIMPLE BE? *Philips PB 428* [1]	**6**	13
30 Sep 55 ●	HEY THERE *Philips PB 494* ▲	**4**	11
29 Mar 57	MANGOS (re) *Philips PB 671*	**17**	9

[1] Rosemary Clooney and the Mellomen

From 19 Feb 1954, the flip side of 'Man (Uh-Huh)', 'Woman (Uh-Huh)', by Jose Ferrer, was also credited

CLOUD *UK, male instrumental group (Singles: 1 Week)*
pos/wks

31 Jan 81	ALL NIGHT LONG / TAKE IT TO THE TOP *UK Champagne FUNK 1*	**72**	1

CLOUDBURST See DISCO TEX presents CLOUDBURST

CLOUT
South Africa, female vocal / instrumental
group (Singles: 15 Weeks)   pos/wks

17 Jun 78 ●	SUBSTITUTE *Carrere EMI 2788*	**2**	15

CLUB NOUVEAU
US, male / female vocal / instrumental group (Singles: 12 Weeks)   pos/wks

21 Mar 87 ●	LEAN ON ME *King Jay W 8430* ▲	**3**	12

CLUB 69 *Austria / US, male producer /*
instrumentalist – Peter Rauhofer (Singles: 6 Weeks)   pos/wks

5 Dec 92	LET ME BE YOUR UNDERWEAR *ffrr F 204*	**33**	5
14 Nov 98	ALRIGHT *Twisted UK TWCD 10039* [1]	**70**	1

[1] Club 69 featuring Suzanne Palmer

CLUBHOUSE
Italy, male vocal / instrumental group (Singles: 40 Weeks)   pos/wks

23 Jul 83	DO IT AGAIN – BILLIE JEAN (MEDLEY) *Island IS 132*	**11**	6
3 Dec 83	SUPERSTITION – GOOD TIMES (MEDLEY) *Island IS 147*	**59**	3
1 Jul 89	I'M A MAN – YEKE YEKE (MEDLEY) *Music Man MMPS 7003*	**69**	3
20 Apr 91	DEEP IN MY HEART (re) *ffrr F 157*	**55**	4
4 Sep 93	LIGHT MY FIRE (2re) *PWL Continental PWCD 272* [1]	**45**	12
30 May 94 ●	LIGHT MY FIRE (re-mix) *PWL Continental PWCD 288* [1]	**7**	8
23 Jul 94	LIVING IN THE SUNSHINE *PWL Continental PWCD 309* [1]	**21**	3
11 Mar 95	NOWHERE LAND *PWL International PWCD 318* [1]	**56**	1

[1] Clubhouse featuring Carl

CLUBZONE
UK / Germany, male vocal / instrumental group (Singles: 1 Week)   pos/wks

19 Nov 94	HANDS UP *Logic 74321236982*	**50**	1

CLUELESS
US, male / female vocal / production group (Singles: 1 Week)   pos/wks

5 Apr 97	DON'T SPEAK *ZYX ZYX 660738*	**61**	1

Jeremy CLYDE See Chad STUART and Jeremy CLYDE

CLYDE VALLEY STOMPERS
UK, male instrumental group (Singles: 8 Weeks)   pos/wks

9 Aug 62	PETER AND THE WOLF *Parlophone R 4928*	**25**	8

CO-CO
UK, male / female vocal / instrumental group (Singles: 7 Weeks)   pos/wks

22 Apr 78	BAD OLD DAYS *Ariola Hansa AHA 513*	**13**	7

CO-OPERATION CHOIR See Peter E BENNETT with the CO-OPERATION CHOIR

COAL CHAMBER
US, male vocal / instrumental group (Albums: 4 Weeks)   pos/wks

18 Sep 99	CHAMBER MUSIC *Roadrunner RR 86592*	**21**	2
18 May 02	DARK DAYS *Roadrunner RR 84842*	**43**	2

COAST TO COAST
UK, male vocal / instrumental group (Singles: 22 Weeks)   pos/wks

31 Jan 81 ●	(DO) THE HUCKLEBUCK *Polydor POSP 214*	**5**	15
23 May 81	LET'S JUMP THE BROOMSTICK *Polydor POSP 249*	**28**	7

COAST 2 COAST featuring DISCOVERY
Ireland, male production duo and female vocalist (Singles: 1 Week) pos/wks

16 Jun 01	HOME *Religion RLG 0126955*	**44**	1

The COASTERS *US, male vocal group (Singles: 32 Weeks)* pos/wks

27 Sep 57	SEARCHIN' *London HLE 8450*	**30**	1
15 Aug 58	YAKETY YAK *London HLE 8665*	**12**	8
27 Mar 59 ●	CHARLIE BROWN *London HLE 8819*	**6**	12
30 Oct 59	POISON IVY *London HLE 8938*	**15**	7
9 Apr 94	SORRY BUT I'M GONNA HAVE TO PASS *Rhino A 4519CD*	**41**	4

Odia COATES See Paul ANKA

Luis COBOS *Spain, male orchestra*
conductor (Singles: 2 Weeks, Albums: 1 Week)   pos/wks

16 Jun 90	NESSUN DORMA FROM 'TURANDOT' *Epic 656005 7* [1]	**59**	2
21 Apr 90	OPERA EXTRAVAGANZA *Epic MOOD 12*	**72**	1

[1] Luis Cobos featuring Placido Domingo

Eddie COCHRAN *US, male vocalist / instrumentalist,*
b. 3 Oct 1938, d. 17 Apr 1960 (Singles: 90 Weeks, Albums: 47 Weeks) pos/wks

7 Nov 58	SUMMERTIME BLUES *London HLU 8702*	**18**	6
13 Mar 59 ●	C'MON EVERYBODY *London HLU 8792*	**6**	13

Singles re-entries are listed as (re), (2re), (3re)…. which signifies that the hit re-entered the chart once, twice or three times…

16 Oct 59	SOMETHIN' ELSE *London HLU 8944*	**22** 3
22 Jan 60	HALLELUJAH, I LOVE HER SO (re) *London HLW 9022*	**22** 4
12 May 60 ★	THREE STEPS TO HEAVEN *London HLG 9115*	**1** 15
6 Oct 60	SWEETIE PIE *London HLG 9196*	**38** 3
3 Nov 60	LONELY *London HLG 9196*	**41** 1
15 Jun 61	WEEKEND *London HLG 9362*	**15** 16
30 Nov 61	JEANNIE, JEANNIE, JEANNIE *London HLG 9460*	**31** 4
25 Apr 63	MY WAY *London LIB 10088*	**23** 10
24 Apr 68	SUMMERTIME BLUES (re-issue) *Liberty LBF 15071*	**34** 8
13 Feb 88	C'MON EVERYBODY (re-issue) *Liberty EDDIE 501*	**14** 7
30 Jul 60	SINGING TO MY BABY *London HAU 2093*	**19** 1
1 Oct 60 ●	EDDIE COCHRAN MEMORIAL ALBUM *London HAG 2267*	**9** 12
12 Jan 63	CHERISHED MEMORIES *Liberty LBY 1109*	**15** 3
20 Apr 63	EDDIE COCHRAN MEMORIAL ALBUM (re-issue) *Liberty LBY 1127*	**11** 18
19 Oct 63	SINGING TO MY BABY (re-issue) *Liberty LBY 1158*	**20** 1
9 May 70	VERY BEST OF EDDIE COCHRAN *Liberty LBS 83337*	**34** 3
18 Aug 79	THE EDDIE COCHRAN SINGLES ALBUM *United Artists UAK 30244*	**39** 6
16 Apr 88	C'MON EVERYBODY *Liberty ECR 1*	**53** 3

Brenda COCHRANE *Ireland, female vocalist (Albums: 14 Weeks)* pos/wks

14 Apr 90	THE VOICE *Polydor 8431411*	**14** 11
6 Apr 91	IN DREAMS *Polydor 8490341*	**55** 3

Tom COCHRANE *Canada, male vocalist (Singles: 2 Weeks)* pos/wks

27 Jun 92	LIFE IS A HIGHWAY *Capitol CL 660*	**62** 2

COCK ROBIN
US, male / female vocal / instrumental group (Singles: 12 Weeks) pos/wks

31 May 86	THE PROMISE YOU MADE *CBS A 6764*	**28** 12

Joe COCKER ⟨ 451 Top 500 ⟩

Throaty, emotive pop / rock singer b. 20 May 1944, Sheffield, UK, whose first single was released in 1964. Remembered for a memorable performance at Woodstock, Cocker is still scoring Top 20 albums across Europe in the 21st century (Singles: 89 Weeks, Albums: 68 Weeks) pos/wks

22 May 68	MARJORINE *Regal-Zonophone RZ 3006*	**48** 1
2 Oct 68 ★	WITH A LITTLE HELP FROM MY FRIENDS *Regal-Zonophone RZ 3013*	**1** 13
27 Sep 69 ●	DELTA LADY *Regal-Zonophone RZ 3024*	**10** 11
4 Jul 70	THE LETTER *Regal-Zonophone RZ 3027*	**39** 6
26 Sep 81	I'M SO GLAD I'M STANDING HERE TODAY *MCA 741* [1]	**61** 3
15 Jan 83 ●	UP WHERE WE BELONG *Island WIP 6830* [2] ▲	**7** 13
14 Nov 87	UNCHAIN MY HEART *Capitol CL 465*	**46** 4
13 Jan 90	WHEN THE NIGHT COMES *Capitol CL 535*	**65** 2
7 Mar 92	(ALL I KNOW) FEELS LIKE FOREVER *Capitol CL 645*	**25** 5
9 May 92	NOW THAT THE MAGIC HAS GONE *Capitol CL 657*	**28** 6
4 Jul 92	UNCHAIN MY HEART (re-issue) *Capitol CL 664*	**17** 6
21 Nov 92	WHEN THE NIGHT COMES (re-issue) *Capitol CL 674*	**61** 3
13 Aug 94	THE SIMPLE THINGS *Capitol CDCLS 722*	**17** 5
22 Oct 94	TAKE ME HOME *Capitol CDCLS 729* [3]	**41** 3
17 Dec 94	LET THE HEALING BEGIN *Capitol CDCLS 727*	**32** 5
23 Sep 95	HAVE A LITTLE FAITH *Capitol CDCLS 744*	**67** 2
12 Oct 96	DON'T LET ME BE MISUNDERSTOOD *Parlophone CDCLS 779*	**53** 1
26 Sep 70	MAD DOGS AND ENGLISHMEN *A&M AMLS 6002*	**16** 8
6 May 72	JOE COCKER / WITH A LITTLE HELP FROM MY FRIENDS *Double Back TOOFA 1/2*	**29** 4
30 Jun 84	A CIVILISED MAN *Capitol EJ 240139 1*	**100** 1
11 Apr 92	NIGHT CALLS *Capitol CDESTU 2167*	**25** 14
27 Jun 92 ●	THE ESSENTIAL COLLECTION – THE LEGEND *PolyGram TV 5154112*	**4** 20
17 Sep 94 ●	HAVE A LITTLE FAITH *Capitol CDEST 2233*	**9** 15
26 Oct 96	ORGANIC *Parlophone CDESTD 6*	**49** 1
20 Feb 99	GREATEST HITS *EMI 4977192*	**24** 2
23 Oct 99	NO ORDINARY WORLD *Parlophone 5230912*	**63** 1
15 Jun 02	RESPECT YOURSELF *Parlophone 5396432*	**51** 2

[1] The Crusaders, featured vocalist Joe Cocker [2] Joe Cocker and Jennifer Warnes [3] Joe Cocker featuring Bekka Bramlett

COCKEREL CHORUS *UK, male Tottenham Hotspur Football Club supporters vocal group (Singles: 12 Weeks)* pos/wks

24 Feb 73	NICE ONE CYRIL *Youngblood YB 1017*	**14** 12

COCKNEY REBEL See Steve HARLEY and COCKNEY REBEL

COCKNEY REJECTS *UK, male vocal / instrumental group (Singles: 22 Weeks, Albums: 17 Weeks)* pos/wks

1 Dec 79	I'M NOT A FOOL *EMI 5008*	**65** 2
16 Feb 80	BADMAN *EMI 5035*	**65** 3
26 Apr 80	THE GREATEST COCKNEY RIP-OFF *Zonophone Z 2*	**21** 7
17 May 80	I'M FOREVER BLOWING BUBBLES *Zonophone Z 4*	**35** 5
12 Jul 80	WE CAN DO ANYTHING *Zonophone Z 6*	**65** 2
25 Oct 80	WE ARE THE FIRM *Zonophone Z 10*	**54** 3
15 Mar 80	GREATEST HITS VOLUME 1 *Zonophone ZONO 101*	**22** 11
25 Oct 80	GREATEST HITS VOLUME 2 *Zonophone ZONO 102*	**23** 3
18 Apr 81	GREATEST HITS VOLUME 3 (LIVE AND LOUD) *Zonophone ZEM 101*	**27** 3

COCO (see also FRAGMA) *UK, female vocalist (Singles: 2 Weeks)* pos/wks

8 Nov 97	I NEED A MIRACLE *Positiva CDTIV 81*	**39** 2

The COCONUTS
US, female vocal group (Singles: 61 Weeks) pos/wks

13 Jun 81	ME NO POP I *Ze WIP 6711* [1]	**32** 7
15 May 82 ●	I'M A WONDERFUL THING, BABY *Ze WIP 6756* [2]	**4** 11
24 Jul 82 ●	STOOL PIGEON *Ze WIP 6793* [2]	**7** 9
9 Oct 82 ●	ANNIE I'M NOT YOUR DADDY *Ze WIP 6801* [2]	**2** 8
11 Dec 82	DEAR ADDY *Ze WIP 6840* [2]	**29** 7
11 Jun 83	DID YOU HAVE TO LOVE ME LIKE YOU DID *EMI America EA 156*	**60** 3
10 Sep 83	THERE'S SOMETHING WRONG IN PARADISE *Island IS 130* [2]	**35** 5
19 Nov 83	THE LIFEBOAT PARTY *Island IS 142* [2]	**49** 4
14 Apr 90	THE SEX OF IT *CBS 655698 7* [2]	**29** 5
10 Apr 93	I'M A WONDERFUL THING BABY *Island CID 551* [2]	**60** 2

[1] Kid Creole and the Coconuts present Coati Mundi [2] Kid Creole and the Coconuts

COCTEAU TWINS (see also Harold BUDD / Liz FRASER / Robin GUTHRIE / Simon RAYMONDE) *UK, male / female vocal / instrumental group (Singles: 25 Weeks, Albums: 46 Weeks)* pos/wks

28 Apr 84	PEARLY-DEWDROPS' DROPS *4AD 405*	**29** 5
30 Mar 85	AIKEA-GUINEA *4AD AD 501*	**41** 3
23 Nov 85	TINY DYNAMINE (EP) *4AD BAD 510*	**52** 2
7 Dec 85	ECHOES IN A SHALLOW BAY (EP) *4AD BAD 511*	**65** 1
25 Oct 86	LOVE'S EASY TEARS *4AD AD 610*	**53** 1
8 Sep 90	ICEBLINK LUCK *4AD AD 0011*	**38** 3
2 Oct 93	EVANGELINE *Fontana CTCD 1*	**34** 2
18 Dec 93	WINTER WONDERLAND / FROSTY THE SNOWMAN *Fontana COCCD 1*	**58** 1
26 Feb 94	BLUEBEARD *Fontana CTCD 2*	**33** 2
7 Oct 95	TWINLIGHTS (EP) *Fontana CTCD 3*	**59** 1
4 Nov 95	OTHERNESS (EP) *Fontana CTCD 4*	**59** 1
30 Mar 96	TISHBITE *Fontana CTCD 5*	**34** 2
20 Jul 96	VIOLAINE *Fontana CTCD 6*	**56** 1
29 Oct 83	HEAD OVER HEELS *4AD CAD 313*	**51** 15
24 Nov 84	TREASURE *4AD CAD 412*	**29** 8
26 Apr 86 ●	VICTORIALAND *4AD CAD 602*	**10** 7
1 Oct 88	BLUE BELL KNOLL *4AD CAD 808*	**15** 4
22 Sep 90 ●	HEAVEN OR LAS VEGAS *4AD CAD 0012*	**7** 5
30 Oct 93	FOUR-CALENDAR CAFÉ *Fontana 5182592*	**13** 3
27 Apr 96	MILK & KISSES *Fontana 5145012*	**17** 3
28 Oct 00	STARS AND TOPSOIL – A COLLECTION (1982-1990) *4AD CAD 2K 019CD*	**63** 1

Tracks on Tiny Dynamine (EP): Pink Orange Red / Ribbed and Veined / Plain Tiger / Sultitan Itan. Tracks on Echoes in a Shallow Bay (EP): Great Spangled Fritillary / Melonella / Pale Clouded White / Eggs and Their Shells. Tracks on Twinlights (EP): Golden-Vein / Half-Gifts / Pink Orange Red / Rilkean Heart. Tracks on Otherness (EP): Cherry Coloured Funk / Feet Like Fins / Seekers Who Are Lovers / Violaine

CODE RED *UK, male vocal group (Singles: 7 Weeks)* pos/wks

6 Jul 96	I GAVE YOU EVERYTHING *Polydor 5763992*	**50** 1
16 Nov 96	THIS IS OUR SONG *Polydor 5756332*	**59** 1
14 Jun 97	CAN WE TALK *Polydor 5710992*	**29** 2
9 Aug 97	IS THERE SOMEONE OUT THERE? *Polydor 5714652*	**34** 2
4 Jul 98	WHAT WOULD YOU DO IF ...? *Polydor 569932*	**55** 1

COFFEE *US, female vocal group (Singles: 13 Weeks)* pos/wks

27 Sep 80	CASANOVA *De-Lite MER 38*	**13** 10
6 Dec 80	SLIP AND DIP / I WANNA BE WITH YOU *De-Lite DE 1*	**57** 3

Alma COGAN
UK, female vocalist,
b. 19 May 1932, d. 26 Oct 1966 (Singles: 110 Weeks) pos/wks

19 Mar 54 ●	BELL BOTTOM BLUES *HMV B 10653*	4 9
27 Aug 54	LITTLE THINGS MEAN A LOT (2re) *HMV B 10717*	11 5
3 Dec 54 ●	I CAN'T TELL A WALTZ FROM A TANGO *HMV B 10786*	6 11
27 May 55 ★	DREAMBOAT *HMV B 10872*	1 16
23 Sep 55	THE BANJO'S BACK IN TOWN *HMV B 10917 (A)*	17 1
14 Oct 55	GO ON BY *HMV B 10917 (B)*	16 4
16 Dec 55	TWENTY TINY FINGERS *HMV POP 129 (A)*	17 1
23 Dec 55 ●	NEVER DO A TANGO WITH AN ESKIMO *HMV POP 129 (B)*	6 5
30 Mar 56	WILLIE CAN *HMV POP 187* [1]	13 8
13 Jul 56	THE BIRDS AND THE BEES *HMV POP 223*	25 4
10 Aug 56	WHY DO FOOLS FALL IN LOVE *HMV POP 223*	22 3
2 Nov 56	IN THE MIDDLE OF THE HOUSE (re) *HMV POP 261*	20 4
18 Jan 57	YOU, ME AND US *HMV POP 284*	18 6
29 Mar 57	WHATEVER LOLA WANTS (LOLA GETS) *HMV POP 317*	26 2
31 Jan 58	THE STORY OF MY LIFE *HMV POP 433*	25 2
14 Feb 58	SUGARTIME (re) *HMV POP 450*	16 11
23 Jan 59	LAST NIGHT ON THE BACK PORCH *HMV POP 573*	27 2
18 Dec 59	WE GOT LOVE *HMV POP 670*	26 4
12 May 60	DREAM TALK *HMV POP 728*	48 1
11 Aug 60	TRAIN OF LOVE *HMV POP 760*	27 5
20 Apr 61	COWBOY JIMMY JOE *Columbia DB 4607*	37 6

[1] Alma Cogan with Desmond Lane – penny whistle

Shaye COGAN
US, female vocalist (Singles: 1 Week) pos/wks

24 Mar 60	MEAN TO ME *MGM 1063*	40 1

Izhar COHEN and the ALPHA-BETA
Israel, male / female vocal group (Singles: 7 Weeks) pos/wks

13 May 78	A-BA-NI-BI *Polydor 2001 781*	20 7

Leonard COHEN 454 Top 500
Singer-songwriter and poet with a reputation for dark humour, b. 21 Sep 1934, Montreal, Canada, was still charting worldwide at 70. Jennifer Warnes devoted her 1987 set 'Famous Blue Raincoat' entirely to his compositions (Albums: 156 Weeks) pos/wks

31 Aug 68	SONGS OF LEONARD COHEN *CBS 63241*	13 71
3 May 69 ●	SONGS FROM A ROOM *CBS 63587*	2 26
24 Apr 71 ●	SONGS OF LOVE AND HATE *CBS 69004*	4 18
28 Sep 74	NEW SKIN FOR THE OLD CEREMONY *CBS 69087*	24 3
10 Dec 77	DEATH OF A LADIES' MAN *CBS 86042*	35 5
16 Feb 85	VARIOUS POSITIONS *CBS 26222*	52 6
27 Feb 88	I'M YOUR MAN *CBS 4606421*	48 13
6 Aug 88	GREATEST HITS *CBS 32644*	99 1
5 Dec 92	THE FUTURE *Columbia 4724982*	36 3
6 Aug 94	COHEN LIVE – LEONARD COHEN IN CONCERT *Columbia 4771712*	35 4
20 Oct 01	TEN NEW SONGS *Columbia 5012022*	26 3
1 Feb 03	THE ESSENTIAL LEONARD COHEN *Columbia 4979952*	70 1
6 Nov 04	DEAR HEATHER *Columbia 5147682*	34 2

COHEN vs DELUXE (see also Tim DELUXE) *Brazil / UK, male producers – Renato Cohen and Tim Liken (Singles: 1 Week)* pos/wks

13 Mar 04	JUST KICK *Intec INTEC 24XXX*	70 1

Marc COHN
US, male vocalist (Singles: 15 Weeks, Albums: 23 Weeks) pos/wks

25 May 91	WALKING IN MEMPHIS *Atlantic A 7747*	66 4
10 Aug 91	SILVER THUNDERBIRD *Atlantic A 7657*	54 3
12 Oct 91	WALKING IN MEMPHIS (re-issue) *Atlantic A 7585*	22 5
29 May 93	WALK THROUGH THE WORLD *Atlantic A 7340CD*	37 3
29 Jun 91	MARC COHN *Atlantic 7567821781*	27 20
12 Jun 93	THE RAINY SEASON *Atlantic 7567824912*	24 3

COLA BOY *UK, male / female vocal / instrumental duo – Andrew Midgely and Janey Lee Grace (Singles: 7 Weeks)* pos/wks

6 Jul 91 ●	7 WAYS TO LOVE *Arista 114526*	8 7

COLD JAM featuring GRACE
US, male / female vocal / instrumental group (Singles: 2 Weeks) pos/wks

28 Jul 90	LAST NIGHT A DJ SAVED MY LIFE *Big Wave BWR 39*	64 2

COLDCUT *UK, male production duo – Matt Black and Jonathan Moore (Singles: 39 Weeks, Albums: 5 Weeks)* pos/wks

20 Feb 88 ●	DOCTORIN' THE HOUSE *Ahead of Our Time CCUT 27* [1]	6 9
10 Sep 88	STOP THIS CRAZY THING *Ahead of Our Time CCUT 4* [2]	21 7
25 Mar 89	PEOPLE HOLD ON *Ahead of Our Time CCUT 5* [3]	11 9
3 Jun 89	MY TELEPHONE *Ahead of Our Time CCUT 6*	52 2
16 Dec 89	COLDCUT'S CHRISTMAS BREAK *Ahead of Our Time CCUT 7*	67 3
26 May 90	FIND A WAY *Ahead of Our Time CCUT 8* [4]	52 2
4 Sep 93	DREAMER *Arista 74321156642*	54 2
22 Jan 94	AUTUMN LEAVES *Arista 74321171052*	50 2
16 Aug 97	MORE BEATS & PIECES *Ninja Tune ZENCDS 58*	37 2
16 Jun 01	REVOLUTION *Ninja Tune ZENCDS 88*	67 1
29 Apr 89	WHAT'S THAT NOISE *Ahead of Our Time CCUTLP 1*	20 4
20 Sep 97	LET US PLAY! *Ninja Tune ZENCD 30*	33 1

[1] Coldcut featuring Yazz and the Plastic Population [2] Coldcut featuring Junior Reid and the Ahead of Our Time Orchestra [3] Coldcut featuring Lisa Stansfield [4] Coldcut featuring Queen Latifah

COLDPLAY 254 Top 500
Anthemic rock group with a social conscience. Chris Martin (v/k), Jonny Buckland (g), Guy Berryman (b) and Will Champion (d) formed while attending University College, London. The only act to have won both a Brit and a Grammy for each of their first two albums also won a Record of the Year Grammy in 2004 for 'Clocks'. (Singles: 50 Weeks, Albums: 200 Weeks) pos/wks

18 Mar 00	SHIVER *Parlophone CDR 6536*	35 3
8 Jul 00 ●	YELLOW *Parlophone CDR 6538*	4 11
4 Nov 00	TROUBLE *Parlophone CDR 6549*	10 9
17 Aug 02 ●	IN MY PLACE *Parlophone CDRS 6579*	2 10
23 Nov 02 ●	THE SCIENTIST *Parlophone CDR 6588*	10 9
5 Apr 03 ●	CLOCKS *Parlophone CDR 6594*	9 8
22 Jul 00 ★	PARACHUTES *Parlophone 5277832* ■	1 111
7 Sep 02 ★	A RUSH OF BLOOD TO THE HEAD *Parlophone 5405042* ■	1 89

Andy COLE *UK, male footballer / vocalist (Singles: 1 Week)* pos/wks

18 Sep 99	OUTSTANDING *WEA WEA 224CD*	68 1

Cozy COLE *US, male instrumentalist – drums – William Cole, b. 17 Oct 1909, d. 9 Jan 1981 (Singles: 1 Week)* pos/wks

5 Dec 58	TOPSY (PARTS 1 AND 2) *London HL 8750*	29 1

George COLE See Dennis WATERMAN

Lloyd COLE 470 Top 500
Introspective and inventive indie singer / songwriter / guitarist, b. 31 Jan 1961, Derbyshire, UK. Had most success with Glasgow-based band The Commotions before he relocated to the US in 1990 (Singles: 62 Weeks, Albums: 92 Weeks) pos/wks

26 May 84	PERFECT SKIN (re) *Polydor COLE 1* [1]	26 9
25 Aug 84	FOREST FIRE *Polydor COLE 2* [1]	41 6
17 Nov 84	RATTLESNAKES *Poldor COLE 3* [1]	65 2
14 Sep 85	BRAND NEW FRIEND *Polydor COLE 4* [1]	19 8
9 Nov 85	LOST WEEKEND *Polydor COLE 5* [1]	17 7
18 Jan 86	CUT ME DOWN *Polydor COLE 6* [1]	38 4
3 Oct 87	MY BAG *Polydor COLE 7* [1]	46 4
9 Jan 88	JENNIFER SHE SAID *Polydor COLE 8* [1]	31 5
23 Apr 88	FROM THE HIP (EP) *Polydor COLE 9* [1]	59 2
3 Feb 90	NO BLUE SKIES *Polydor COLE 11*	42 4
7 Apr 90	DON'T LOOK BACK *Polydor COLE 12*	59 3
31 Aug 91	SHE'S A GIRL AND I'M A MAN *Polydor COLE 14*	55 2
25 Sep 93	SO YOU'D LIKE TO SAVE THE WORLD *Fontana VIBE D1*	72 2
16 Sep 95	LIKE LOVERS DO *Fontana LCDD 1*	24 3
2 Dec 95	SENTIMENTAL FOOL *Fontana LCDD 2*	73 1
20 Oct 84	RATTLESNAKES *Polydor LCLP 1* [1]	13 30
30 Nov 85 ●	EASY PIECES *Polydor LCLP 2* [1]	5 18
7 Nov 87 ●	MAINSTREAM *Polydor LCLP 3* [1]	9 20
8 Apr 89	19841989 *Polydor 8377361* [1]	14 7
3 Mar 90	LLOYD COLE *Polydor 8419071*	11 6
28 Sep 91	DON'T GET WEIRD ON ME BABE *Polydor 5110931*	21 3
23 Oct 93	BAD VIBES *Fontana 5183182*	38 2
7 Oct 95	LOVE STORY *Fontana 5285292*	27 2
23 Jan 99	THE COLLECTION *Mercury 5381042*	24 4

[1] Lloyd Cole and the Commotions [1] Lloyd Cole and the Commotions

Tracks on From the Hip (EP): From the Hip / Please / Lonely Mile / Love Your Wife

Singles re-entries are listed as (re), (2re), (3re).... which signifies that the hit re-entered the chart once, twice or three times...

MJ COLE UK, male producer –
Matt Coleman (Singles: 19 Weeks, Albums: 4 Weeks)

		pos/wks
23 May 98	SINCERE AM:PM 5826912	**38** 2
6 May 00 ●	CRAZY LOVE Talkin Loud TLCD 59	**10** 7
12 Aug 00	SINCERE (re-mix) Talkin Loud TLCD 60	**13** 5
2 Dec 00	HOLD ON TO ME Talkin Loud TLCD 62 [1]	**35** 2
29 Mar 03	WONDERING WHY Talkin Loud 0779522	**30** 3
19 Aug 00	SINCERE Talkin Loud 5425792	**14** 4

[1] MJ Cole featuring Elizabeth Troy

Nat 'King' COLE ⟨116⟩ Top 500
One of the 20th century's most distinctive song stylists, b. Nathaniel Adams Coles, 17 Mar 1917, Montgomery, Alabama, US, d. 15 Feb 1965. His 50-year chart span is proof that the highly regarded vocalist's recordings are timeless (Singles: 249 Weeks, Albums: 150 Weeks)

		pos/wks
14 Nov 52 ●	SOMEWHERE ALONG THE WAY Capitol CL 13774	**3** 7
19 Dec 52 ●	BECAUSE YOU'RE MINE (2re) Capitol CL 13811	**6** 4
2 Jan 53 ●	FAITH CAN MOVE MOUNTAINS (2re) Capitol CL 13811	**10** 4
24 Apr 53 ●	PRETEND Capitol CL 13878	**2** 18
14 Aug 53 ●	CAN'T I (2re) Capitol CL 13937	**6** 8
18 Sep 53 ●	MOTHER NATURE AND FATHER TIME Capitol CL 13912	**7** 7
16 Apr 54 ●	TENDERLY Capitol CL 14061	**10** 1
10 Sep 54 ●	SMILE Capitol CL 14149	**2** 14
8 Oct 54	MAKE HER MINE Capitol CL 14149	**11** 2
25 Feb 55 ●	A BLOSSOM FELL Capitol CL 14235	**3** 10
26 Aug 55	MY ONE SIN (re) Capitol CL 14327	**17** 2
27 Jan 56 ●	DREAMS CAN TELL A LIE Capitol CL 14513	**10** 9
11 May 56 ●	TOO YOUNG TO GO STEADY Capitol CL 14573	**8** 14
14 Sep 56	LOVE ME AS THOUGH THERE WERE NO TOMORROW (re) Capitol CL 14621	**11** 15
19 Apr 57 ●	WHEN I FALL IN LOVE Capitol CL 14709	**2** 20
5 Jul 57	WHEN ROCK AND ROLL CAME TO TRINIDAD Capitol CL 14733	28 1
18 Oct 57	MY PERSONAL POSSESSION Capitol CL 14765 [1]	**21** 2
25 Oct 57	STARDUST Capitol CL 14787	**24** 2
29 May 59	YOU MADE ME LOVE YOU Capitol CL 15017	**22** 3
4 Sep 59	MIDNIGHT FLYER (re) Capitol CL 15056	**23** 4
12 Feb 60	TIME AND THE RIVER (2re) Capitol CL 15111	**23** 5
26 May 60 ●	THAT'S YOU Capitol CL 15129	**10** 8
10 Nov 60	JUST AS MUCH AS EVER Capitol CL 15163	**18** 10
2 Feb 61	THE WORLD IN MY ARMS Capitol CL 15178	**36** 10
16 Nov 61	LET TRUE LOVE BEGIN Capitol CL 15224	**29** 10
22 Mar 62	BRAZILIAN LOVE SONG (ANDORHINA PRETA) Capitol CL 15241	**34** 4
31 May 62	THE RIGHT THING TO SAY Capitol CL 15250	**42** 4
19 Jul 62	LET THERE BE LOVE Capitol CL 15257 [2]	**11** 14
27 Sep 62 ●	RAMBLIN' ROSE Capitol CL 15270	**5** 14
20 Dec 62	DEAR LONELY HEARTS Capitol CL 15280	**37** 3
12 Dec 87 ●	WHEN I FALL IN LOVE (re-issue) Capitol CL 15975	**4** 7
22 Jun 91	UNFORGETTABLE Elektra EKR 128 [3]	**19** 8
14 Dec 91	THE CHRISTMAS SONG Capitol CL 641	**69** 2
19 Mar 94	LET'S FACE THE MUSIC AND DANCE EMI CDEM 312	**30** 3
18 May 57 ★	LOVE IS THE THING Capitol LCT 6129 ▲	**1** 14
19 Aug 61	STRING ALONG WITH NAT 'KING' COLE Encore ENC 102	**12** 9
20 Oct 62 ●	NAT 'KING' COLE SINGS AND THE GEORGE SHEARING QUINTET PLAYS Capitol W 1675 [1]	**8** 7
27 Mar 65	UNFORGETTABLE NAT 'KING' COLE Capitol W 20664	**11** 8
7 Dec 68 ●	THE BEST OF NAT 'KING' COLE Capitol ST 21139	**5** 18
5 Dec 70	THE BEST OF NAT 'KING' COLE VOLUME 2 Capitol ST 21687	**39** 2
27 Nov 71	WHITE CHRISTMAS MFP 5224 [2]	**45** 1
8 Apr 78 ★	20 GOLDEN GREATS Capitol EMTV 9	**1** 37
20 Nov 82 ●	GREATEST LOVE SONGS Capitol EMTV 35	**7** 26
26 Nov 88	CHRISTMAS WITH NAT 'KING' COLE Stylus SMR 868	**25** 9
23 Nov 91	UNFORGETTABLE NAT 'KING' COLE EMI EMTV 61	**23** 9
20 Nov 99	THE ULTIMATE COLLECTION EMI 4995752	**26** 7
15 Feb 03	LOVE SONGS Capitol 05815132	**20** 3

[1] Nat 'King' Cole and the Four Knights [2] Nat 'King' Cole with George Shearing [3] Natalie Cole and Nat 'King' Cole [1] Nat 'King' Cole and the George Shearing Quintet [2] Nat 'King' Cole and Dean Martin

The two 'Unforgettable Nat 'King' Cole' albums are different

Natalie COLE ⟨474⟩ Top 500
Daughter of the legendary Nat 'King' Cole who has a 20-year Grammy-winning span of her own, b. 6 Feb 1950, Los Angeles, US. 'Unforgettable' was an electronically recorded duet with her late father. Nat and Natalie are the only dad and daughter who both have No.1 US albums (Singles: 87 Weeks, Albums: 66 Weeks)

		pos/wks
11 Oct 75	THIS WILL BE Capitol CL 15834	**32** 5
8 Aug 87	JUMP START Manhattan MT 22	**44** 8

		pos/wks
26 Mar 88 ●	PINK CADILLAC Manhattan MT 35	**5** 12
25 Jun 88	EVERLASTING Manhattan MT 46	**28** 6
20 Aug 88	JUMP START (re-issue) Manhattan MT 50	**36** 5
26 Nov 88	I LIVE FOR YOUR LOVE Manhattan MT 57	**23** 14
15 Apr 89 ●	MISS YOU LIKE CRAZY EMI-USA MT 63	**2** 15
22 Jul 89	REST OF THE NIGHT EMI-USA MT 69	**56** 2
16 Dec 89	STARTING OVER AGAIN EMI-USA MT 77	**56** 4
21 Apr 90	WILD WOMEN DO EMI-USA MT 81	**16** 7
22 Jun 91	UNFORGETTABLE Elektra EKR 128 [1]	**19** 8
16 May 92	THE VERY THOUGHT OF YOU Elektra EKR 147	**71** 1
17 Sep 83 ●	UNFORGETTABLE: A MUSICAL TRIBUTE TO NAT 'KING' COLE CBS 10042 [1] ▲	**5** 16
7 May 88	EVERLASTING Manhattan MTL 1012	**62** 4
20 May 89 ●	GOOD TO BE BACK EMI-USA MTL 1042	**10** 12
27 Jul 91	UNFORGETTABLE – WITH LOVE Elektra EKT 91	**11** 29
26 Jun 93	TAKE A LOOK Elektra 7559614962	**16** 4
30 Nov 02	ASK A WOMAN WHO KNOWS Verve AA 3145897742	**63** 1

[1] Natalie Cole and Nat 'King' Cole [1] Johnny Mathis and Natalie Cole

Paula COLE
US, female vocalist (Singles: 9 Weeks, Albums: 1 Week)

		pos/wks
28 Jun 97	WHERE HAVE ALL THE COWBOYS GONE? Warner Bros. W 0406CD	**15** 8
1 Aug 98	I DON'T WANT TO WAIT Warner Bros. W 0422CD	**43** 1
26 Jul 97	THIS FIRE Warner Bros. 9362464242	**60** 1

Naimee COLEMAN See AURORA

COLETTE See SISTER BLISS

John Ford COLEY See ENGLAND DAN and John Ford COLEY

COLLAGE US / Canada / Philippines, male
vocal / instrumental group (Singles: 5 Weeks)

		pos/wks
21 Sep 85	ROMEO WHERE'S JULIET? MCA MCA 1006	**46** 5

COLLAPSED LUNG
UK, male vocal / instrumental group (Singles: 8 Weeks)

		pos/wks
22 Jun 96	LONDON TONIGHT / EAT MY GOAL Deceptive BLUFF 029CD	31 3
30 May 98	EAT MY GOAL (re-issue) Deceptive BLUFF 060CD	**18** 5

Dave and Ansil COLLINS Jamaica, male vocal / instrumental duo –
Dave Barker and Ansil Collins (Singles: 27 Weeks, Albums: 2 Weeks) pos/wks

		pos/wks
27 Mar 71 ★	DOUBLE BARREL Technique TE 901	**1** 15
26 Jun 71 ●	MONKEY SPANNER Technique TE 914 [1]	**7** 12
7 Aug 71	DOUBLE BARREL Trojan TBL 162	**41** 2

[1] Dave and Ansel Collins

Edwyn COLLINS (see also ORANGE JUICE) UK, male
vocalist / instrumentalist (Singles: 25 Weeks, Albums: 9 Weeks) pos/wks

		pos/wks
11 Aug 84	PALE BLUE EYES Swamplands SWP 1 [1]	**72** 2
12 Nov 94	EXPRESSLY (EP) Setanta ZOP 001CD1	**42** 3
17 Jun 95 ●	A GIRL LIKE YOU (re-issue) Setanta ZOP 003CD	**4** 14
2 Mar 96	KEEP ON BURNING Setanta ZOP 004CD1	**45** 2
2 Aug 97	THE MAGIC PIPER (OF LOVE) Setanta SETCDA 041	**32** 3
18 Oct 97	ADIDAS WORLD Setanta SETCDB 045	**71** 1
22 Jul 95 ●	GORGEOUS GEORGE Setanta AHOAON 058	**8** 8
13 Sep 97	I'M NOT FOLLOWING YOU Setanta SETCD 039	**55** 1

[1] Paul Quinn and Edwyn Collins

The only track on all formats of Expressly (EP) was 'A Girl Like You'

Felicia COLLINS See LUKK featuring Felicia COLLINS

Jeff COLLINS UK, male vocalist (Singles: 8 Weeks) pos/wks
		pos/wks
18 Nov 72	ONLY YOU Polydor 2058 287	**40** 8

Joan COLLINS See Anthony NEWLEY

Judy COLLINS
US, female vocalist (Singles: 86 Weeks, Albums: 23 Weeks) pos/wks

		pos/wks
17 Jan 70	BOTH SIDES NOW Elektra EKSN 45043	**14** 11
5 Dec 70 ●	AMAZING GRACE (7re) Elektra 2101 020	**5** 67

		pos/wks
17 May 75 ●	SEND IN THE CLOWNS *Elektra K 12177*	6 8
27 Feb 71	WHALES AND NIGHTINGALES *Elektra EKS 75010*	16 7
31 May 75	JUDITH *Elektra K 52019*	7 12
14 Dec 85	AMAZING GRACE *Telstar STAR 2265*	34 4

'Amazing Grace' re-entered in Jul, Sep, Nov, Dec 1971 and Apr, Sep, Dec 1972

Michelle COLLINS
UK, female actor / singer (Singles: 3 Weeks) pos/wks

27 Feb 99	SUNBURN *BBC Music WMSS 60082*	28 3

Phil COLLINS `19` `Top 500`

Continually popular singer / songwriter / drummer / actor, b. 31 Jan 1951, Chiswick, London, UK. While at stage school he played the Artful Dodger in the West End production 'Oliver' and was an extra in The Beatles' film 'A Hard Day's Night'. He first recorded with art rock band Flaming Youth before joining Genesis in 1970 (taking over lead vocals when Peter Gabriel left in 1975). He first recorded solo in 1981 and until 1996 combined a successful solo career with fronting the hit group. He was one of the world's top artists in the 1980s and 1990s, during which time he collected numerous singing and songwriting awards, had transatlantic album chart-toppers 'No Jacket Required' and '... But Seriously' (which sold in excess of 13 million globally) and scored seven US No.1 singles. Known for his charitable work, he was the only act to appear on stage in both London and Philadelphia at Live Aid, and played and sung on the Band Aid single. The multi-talented artist became a household name, selling over 80 million copies of his first six albums by the time he left stadium-fillers Genesis in 1996. Only members of The Beatles have appeared on more UK No.1 albums than this Songwriters Hall of Fame member, who won an Oscar in 2000 for his music in Disney's 'Tarzan', and is one of the few British acts still selling well Stateside in the 21st century (Singles: 235 Weeks, Albums: 827 Weeks) pos/wks

		pos/wks
17 Jan 81 ●	IN THE AIR TONIGHT *Virgin VS102*	2 10
7 Mar 81	I MISSED AGAIN *Virgin VS 402*	14 8
30 May 81	IF LEAVING ME IS EASY *Virgin VS 423*	17 8
23 Oct 82	THRU' THESE WALLS *Virgin VS 524*	56 2
4 Dec 82 ★	YOU CAN'T HURRY LOVE *Virgin VS 531*	1 16
19 Mar 83	DON'T LET HIM STEAL YOUR HEART AWAY *Virgin VS 572*	45 5
7 Apr 84 ●	AGAINST ALL ODDS (TAKE A LOOK AT ME NOW) *Virgin VS 674* ▲	2 14
26 Jan 85	SUSSUDIO *Virgin VS 736* ▲	12 9
9 Mar 85 ★	EASY LOVER *CBS A 4915* [1]	1 12
13 Apr 85 ●	ONE MORE NIGHT *Virgin VS 755* ▲	4 9
27 Jul 85	TAKE ME HOME *Virgin VS 777*	19 9
23 Nov 85 ●	SEPARATE LIVES *Virgin VS 818* [2] ▲	4 13
18 Jun 88 ●	IN THE AIR TONIGHT (re-mix) *Virgin VS 102*	4 9
3 Sep 88 ★	A GROOVY KIND OF LOVE *Virgin VS 1117* ▲	1 13
26 Nov 88 ●	TWO HEARTS *Virgin VS 1141* ▲	6 11
4 Nov 89 ●	ANOTHER DAY IN PARADISE *Virgin VS 1234* ▲	2 11
27 Jan 90 ●	I WISH IT WOULD RAIN DOWN *Virgin VS 1240*	7 9
28 Apr 90	SOMETHING HAPPENED ON THE WAY TO HEAVEN *Virgin VS 1251*	15 7
28 Jul 90	THAT'S JUST THE WAY IT IS *Virgin VS 1277*	26 5
6 Oct 90	HANG IN LONG ENOUGH *Virgin VS 1300*	34 3
8 Dec 90	DO YOU REMEMBER (LIVE) *Virgin VS 1305*	57 5
15 May 93	HERO *Atlantic A 7360* [3]	56 3
30 Oct 93 ●	BOTH SIDES OF THE STORY (re) *Virgin VSCDT 1500*	7 6
15 Jan 94	EVERYDAY *Virgin VSCDT 1505*	15 5
7 May 94	WE WAIT AND WE WONDER *Virgin VSCDT 1510*	45 2
5 Oct 96 ●	DANCE INTO THE LIGHT *Face Value EW 066CD*	9 4
14 Dec 96	IT'S IN YOUR EYES *Face Value EW 076CD1*	30 4
12 Jul 97	WEAR MY HAT *Face Value EW 113CD*	43 2
7 Nov 98	TRUE COLORS *Virgin VSCDT 1715*	26 4
6 Nov 99	YOU'LL BE IN MY HEART *Edel / Walt Disney 0100735 DNY*	17 6
22 Sep 01	IN THE AIR TONITE *WEA WEA 331CD* [4]	26 2
16 Nov 02	CAN'T STOP LOVING YOU *Face Value EW 254CD*	28 2
24 May 03	HOME *Epic 6738302* [5]	19 4
29 Nov 03	LOOK THROUGH MY EYES *Walt Disney DISNEY 001*	61 1
21 Feb 81 ★	FACE VALUE *Virgin V 2185*	1 274
13 Nov 82 ●	HELLO I MUST BE GOING *Virgin V 2252*	2 163
2 Mar 85 ★	NO JACKET REQUIRED *Virgin V 2345* ■ ▲	1 176
2 Dec 89 ★	... BUT SERIOUSLY *Virgin V 2620* ■ ▲	1 72
17 Nov 90 ●	SERIOUS HITS ... LIVE! *Virgin PCLP 1*	2 50
20 Nov 93 ★	BOTH SIDES *Virgin CDV 2800* ■	1 21
2 Nov 96 ●	DANCE INTO THE LIGHT *Face Value 630160002* ■	4 13
17 Oct 98 ★	... HITS *Virgin CDV 2870* ■	1 27
23 Nov 02	TESTIFY *Face Value / East West 5046614842*	15 7

		pos/wks
12 Jun 04 ●	THE PLATINUM COLLECTION *Virgin PHILCD 1*	4 17
13 Nov 04 ●	LOVE SONGS – A COMPILATION ... OLD AND NEW *Virgin PHILCDX 2*	10 7+

[1] Philip Bailey (duet with Phil Collins) [2] Phil Collins and Marilyn Martin [3] David Crosby featuring Phil Collins [4] Lil' Kim featuring Phil Collins [5] Bone Thugs-N-Harmony featuring Phil Collins

Rodger COLLINS
US, male vocalist (Singles: 6 Weeks) pos/wks

3 Apr 76	YOU SEXY SUGAR PLUM (BUT I LIKE IT) *Fantasy FTC 132*	22 6

Willie COLLINS
US, male vocalist (Singles: 4 Weeks, Albums: 1 Week) pos/wks

28 Jun 86	WHERE YOU GONNA BE TONIGHT? *Capitol CL 410*	46 4
14 Jun 86	WHERE YOU GONNA BE TONIGHT? *Capitol EST 2012*	97 1

Willie COLON
US, male vocalist (Singles: 7 Weeks) pos/wks

28 Jun 86	SET FIRE TO ME *A&M AM 330*	41 7

COLOR ME BADD
US, male vocal group (Singles: 31 Weeks, Albums: 22 Weeks) pos/wks

18 May 91 ★	I WANNA SEX YOU UP *Giant W 0036*	1 14
3 Aug 91 ●	ALL 4 LOVE *Giant W 0053* ▲	5 10
12 Oct 91	I ADORE MI AMOR *Giant W 0067* ▲	44 2
9 Nov 91	I ADORE MI AMOR (re-issue) *Giant W 0076*	59 2
22 Feb 92	HEARTBREAKER *Giant W 0078*	58 1
20 Nov 93	TIME AND CHANCE *Giant 74321168992*	62 1
16 Apr 94	CHOOSE *Giant 74321199432*	65 1
24 Aug 91 ●	CMB *Giant WX 425*	3 22

COLORADO
UK, female vocal group (Singles: 3 Weeks) pos/wks

21 Oct 78	CALIFORNIA DREAMING *Pinnacle PIN 67*	45 3

COLOSSEUM
UK, male vocal / instrumental group (Albums: 14 Weeks) pos/wks

17 May 69	THOSE WHO ARE ABOUT TO DIE *Fontana STL 5510*	15 1
22 Nov 69	VALENTYNE SUITE *Vertigo VO 1*	15 2
5 Dec 70	DAUGHTER OF TIME *Vertigo 6360 017*	23 5
26 Jun 71	COLOSSEUM LIVE *Bronze ICD 1*	17 6

COLOUR GIRL
UK, female vocalist – Rebecca Skingley (Singles: 5 Weeks) pos/wks

11 Mar 00	CAN'T GET USED TO LOSING YOU *4 Liberty LIBTCD 037*	31 3
9 Sep 00	JOYRIDER (YOU'RE PLAYING WITH FIRE) *4 Liberty LIBTCD 039*	51 1
3 Feb 01	MAS QUE NADA *4 Liberty LIBTCD 040* [1]	57 1

[1] Colour Girl featuring PSG

COLOURBOX
UK, male vocal / instrumental group (Albums: 2 Weeks) pos/wks

24 Aug 85	COLOURBOX *4AD CAD 508*	67 2

The COLOURFIELD *UK, male vocal / instrumental group (Singles: 18 Weeks, Albums: 8 Weeks)* pos/wks

21 Jan 84	THE COLOURFIELD *Chrysalis COLF 1*	43 4
28 Jul 84	TAKE *Chrysalis COLF 2*	70 1
26 Jan 85	THINKING OF YOU *Chrysalis COLF 3*	12 10
13 Apr 85	CASTLES IN THE AIR *Chrysalis COLF 4*	51 3
4 May 85	VIRGINS AND PHILISTINES *Chrysalis CHR 1480*	12 7
4 Apr 87	DECEPTION *Chrysalis CDL 1546*	95 1

COLOURS featuring EMMANUEL & ESKA (see also EN-CORE featuring Stephen EMMANUEL & ESKA; Nitin SAWHNEY) *UK, male instrumentalist / producer and female vocalist (Singles: 1 Week)* pos/wks

27 Feb 99	WHAT U DO *Inferno CDFERN 12*	51 1

COLOURSOUND
UK, male production duo (Singles: 2 Weeks) pos/wks

28 Sep 02	FLY WITH ME *City Rockers ROCKERS 20CD*	49 2

COLUMBO featuring OOE
UK, male production duo (Singles: 1 Week)   pos/wks

| 15 May 99 | ROCKABILLY BOB *V2 / Milkgems VVR 5006903* | **59** 1 |

Shawn COLVIN
US, female vocalist (Singles: 12 Weeks, Albums: 1 Week)   pos/wks

27 Nov 93	I DON'T KNOW WHY *Columbia 6598272*	**62** 1
12 Feb 94	ROUND OF BLUES *Columbia 6594282*	**73** 1
3 Sep 94	EVERY LITTLE THING HE DOES IS MAGIC *Columbia 6607742*	**65** 2
7 Jan 95	ONE COOL REMOVE *Columbia 6611342* [1]	**40** 3
12 Aug 95	I DON'T KNOW WHY (re-issue) *Columbia 6622725*	**52** 1
15 Mar 97	GET OUT OF THIS HOUSE *Columbia 6638522*	**70** 1
30 May 98	SUNNY CAME HOME *Columbia 6648022*	**29** 3
17 Sep 94	COVER GIRL *Columbia 4772402*	**67** 1

[1] Shawn Colvin with Mary-Chapin Carpenter

COMETS *See Bill HALEY and his COMETS*

COMIC RELIEF
UK, charity ensemble of comedians (Albums: 8 Weeks)   pos/wks

| 10 May 86 | ● UTTERLY UTTERLY LIVE! *WEA WX 51* | **10** 8 |

COMING OUT CREW
US, male / female vocal duo (Singles: 1 Week)   pos/wks

| 18 Mar 95 | FREE, GAY AND HAPPY *Out on Vinyl CDOOV 002* | **50** 1 |

COMMANDER TOM
Germany, male producer – Tom Weyer (Singles: 1 Week)   pos/wks

| 23 Dec 00 | EYE BEE M *Tripoli Trax TTRAX 069CD* | **75** 1 |

The COMMENTATORS
UK, male impressionist – Rory Bremner (Singles: 7 Weeks)   pos/wks

| 22 Jun 85 | N-N-NINETEEN NOT OUT *Oval 100* | **13** 7 |

The COMMITMENTS 487 Top 500
Irish band formed especially for Alan Parker's 1991 film of the same name. Led by vocalist Andrew Strong, with Angelina Ball, Maria Doyle, Bronagh Gallagher and Robert Arkins, their revivals of 1960s soul favourites became briefly, but hugely popular (Singles: 1 Week, Albums: 147 Weeks) pos/wks

30 Nov 91	MUSTANG SALLY *MCA MCS 1598*	**63** 1
26 Oct 91	● THE COMMITMENTS (FILM SOUNDTRACK) *MCA MCA 10286*	...**4** 136
25 Apr 92	THE COMMITMENTS VOLUME 2 *MCA MCAD 10506*	...**13** 11

The COMMODORES 228 Top 500 Top-notch US R&B combo:
Lionel Richie (v/k), William King (t), Thomas McClary (g), Milan Williams (var), Ronald LaPread (b), Walter Orange (d). They were among the 1970s' biggest-selling groups, but lost ground when songwriter Richie went solo in 1982 (Singles: 121 Weeks, Albums: 149 Weeks) pos/wks

24 Aug 74	MACHINE GUN *Tamla Motown TMG 902*	**20** 11
23 Nov 74	THE ZOO (THE HUMAN ZOO) *Tamla Motown TMG 924*	**44** 2
2 Jul 77	● EASY *Motown TMG 1073*	**9** 10
8 Oct 77	SWEET LOVE / BRICK HOUSE *Motown TMG 1086*	**32** 6
11 Mar 78	TOO HOT TA TROT / ZOOM *Motown TMG 1096*	**38** 4
24 Jun 78	FLYING HIGH *Motown TMG 1111*	**37** 7
5 Aug 78	★ THREE TIMES A LADY *Motown TMG 1113* ▲	**1** 14
25 Nov 78	JUST TO BE CLOSE TO YOU *Motown TMG 1127*	**62** 4
25 Aug 79	● SAIL ON *Motown TMG 1155*	**8** 10
3 Nov 79	● STILL *Motown TMG 1166* ▲	**4** 11
19 Jan 80	WONDERLAND *Motown TMG 1172*	**40** 4
1 Aug 81	LADY (YOU BRING ME UP) *Motown TMG 1238*	**56** 5
21 Nov 81	OH NO *Motown TMG 1245*	**44** 3
26 Jan 85	● NIGHTSHIFT *Motown TMG 1371*	**3** 14
11 May 85	ANIMAL INSTINCT *Motown ZB 40097*	**74** 1
25 Oct 86	GOIN' TO THE BANK *Polydor POSPA 826*	**43** 4
13 Aug 88	EASY (re-issue) *Motown ZB 41793*	**15** 11
13 May 78	LIVE! *Motown TMSP 6007*	**60** 1
10 Jun 78	● NATURAL HIGH *Motown STML 12087*	**8** 23
2 Dec 78	GREATEST HITS *Motown STML 12100*	**19** 16
18 Aug 79	MIDNIGHT MAGIC *Motown STMA 8032*	**15** 25
28 Jun 80	HEROES *Motown STMA 8034*	**50** 5
18 Jul 81	IN THE POCKET *Motown STML 12156*	**69** 5
14 Aug 82	● LOVE SONGS *K-Tel NE 1171*	**5** 28

23 Feb 85	NIGHTSHIFT *Motown ZL 72343*	**13** 10
9 Nov 85	THE VERY BEST OF THE COMMODORES *Telstar STAR 2249*	...**25** 13
6 May 95	THE VERY BEST *Motown 5305472*	**26** 3
22 Nov 03	● THE DEFINITIVE COLLECTION *Universal TV 9861394* [1]	...**10** 20

[1] Lionel Richie / The Commodores

The group was US / UK for their 1985 and 1986 hits The group was US only for
their first seven albums

COMMON *US, male rapper – Rasheed Lynn (Singles: 10 Weeks)*   pos/wks

8 Nov 97	REMINDING ME (OF SEF) *Relativity 6560762* [1]	**59** 1
14 Oct 00	THE LIGHT / THE 6TH SENSE (SOMETHING U FEEL) *MCA MCSTD 40237*	**56** 1
28 Apr 01	GETO HEAVEN *MCA MCSTD 40246* [2]	**48** 1
9 Feb 02	DANCE FOR ME *MCA MCSTD 40274* [3]	**13** 7

[1] Common featuring Chantay Savage [2] Common featuring Macy Gray [3] Mary
J Blige featuring Common

COMMOTIONS *See Lloyd COLE*

The COMMUNARDS 466 Top 500
Controversial, melodic pop duo consisted of Bronski Beat's Jimmy Somerville (v), b. 22 Jun 1961, Glasgow, Scotland, and Richard Coles (k), b. 23 Jun 1962, Northampton, UK. Their No.1 cover marked the song's third Top 20 reading within a decade (Singles: 76 Weeks, Albums: 78 Weeks) pos/wks

12 Oct 85	YOU ARE MY WORLD *London LON 77*	**30** 8
24 May 86	DISENCHANTED *London LON 89*	**29** 5
23 Aug 86	★ DON'T LEAVE ME THIS WAY *London LON 103* [1]	**1** 14
29 Nov 86	SO COLD THE NIGHT *London LON 110*	**8** 10
21 Feb 87	YOU ARE MY WORLD (87) (re-mix) *London LON 123*	**21** 6
12 Sep 87	TOMORROW *London LON 143*	**23** 7
7 Nov 87	● NEVER CAN SAY GOODBYE *London LON 158*	**4** 11
20 Feb 88	FOR A FRIEND *London LON 166*	**28** 7
11 Jun 88	THERE'S MORE TO LOVE *London LON 173*	**20** 8
2 Aug 86	● COMMUNARDS *London LONLP 18*	**7** 45
17 Oct 87	● RED *London LONLP 39*	**4** 29
22 Sep 01	THE VERY BEST OF JIMMY SOMERVILLE, BRONSKI BEAT AND THE COMMUNARDS *London 927412582* [1]	...**29** 4

[1] The Communards with Sarah Jane Morris [1] Jimmy Somerville, Bronski Beat
and The Communards

Perry COMO 73 Top 500 One of the 20th century's most enduring
entertainers, b. 18 May 1912, Pennsylvania, US, d. 12 May 2001. This easy-on-the-ear relaxed balladeer launched his career in 1933, collected 150 US chart entries, hosted an Emmy-winning TV series and continued to score hits past the age of 60 (Singles: 323 Weeks, Albums: 203 Weeks) pos/wks

16 Jan 53	★ DON'T LET THE STARS GET IN YOUR EYES *HMV B 10400* [1] ▲	**1** 15
4 Jun 54	● WANTED (re) *HMV B 10691* ▲	**4** 15
25 Jun 54	● IDLE GOSSIP *HMV B 10667*	**3** 15
10 Dec 54	PAPA LOVES MAMBO *HMV B 10776*	**16** 1
30 Dec 55	TINA MARIE *HMV POP 103*	**24** 1
27 Apr 56	JUKE BOX BABY *HMV POP 191*	**22** 6
25 May 56	● HOT DIGGITY (DOG ZIGGITY BOOM) *HMV POP 212*	**4** 13
21 Sep 56	● MORE (re) *HMV POP 240*	**10** 12
28 Sep 56	GLENDORA *HMV POP 240*	**18** 6
7 Feb 58	★ MAGIC MOMENTS *RCA 1036*	**1** 17
7 Mar 58	● CATCH A FALLING STAR *RCA 1036*	**9** 10
9 May 58	● KEWPIE DOLL *RCA 1055*	**9** 7
30 May 58	I MAY NEVER PASS THIS WAY AGAIN *RCA 1062*	**15** 8
5 Sep 58	MOON TALK *RCA 1071*	**17** 11
7 Nov 58	● LOVE MAKES THE WORLD GO ROUND *RCA 1086*	**6** 14
21 Nov 58	MANDOLINS IN THE MOONLIGHT *RCA 1086*	**13** 12
27 Feb 59	● TOMBOY *RCA 1111*	**10** 12
10 Jul 59	I KNOW *RCA 1126* [2]	**13** 16
26 Feb 60	● DELAWARE *RCA 1170*	**3** 14
10 May 62	CATERINA (re) *RCA 1283*	**37** 6
30 Jan 71	● IT'S IMPOSSIBLE *RCA 2043*	**4** 23
15 May 71	I THINK OF YOU *RCA 2075*	**14** 11
21 Apr 73	● AND I LOVE YOU SO (re) *RCA 2346*	**3** 35
25 Aug 73	● FOR THE GOOD TIMES *RCA 2402*	**7** 27
8 Dec 73	WALK RIGHT BACK *RCA 2432*	**33** 10
25 May 74	I WANT TO GIVE *RCA LPBO 7518*	**31** 6
28 Jun 58	● WE GET LETTERS (VOL.2) *RCA RD 27070*	**4** 7
8 Nov 58	● DEAR PERRY *RCA RD 27078*	**6** 5
31 Jan 59	● COMO'S GOLDEN RECORDS *RCA RD 27100*	**4** 5

10 Apr 71	IT'S IMPOSSIBLE *RCA Victor SF 8175*........................	13	13
7 Jul 73	★ AND I LOVE YOU SO *RCA Victor SF 8360*	1	109
24 Aug 74	PERRY *RCA Victor APLI 0585*..............................	26	3
19 Apr 75	MEMORIES ARE MADE OF HITS *RCA Victor RS 1005*......	14	16
25 Oct 75	★ 40 GREATEST HITS *K-Tel NE 700*	1	34
3 Dec 83	FOR THE GOOD TIMES *Telstar STAR 2235*	41	6
17 Nov 01	GOLD – GREATEST HITS *RCA 74321865542*.............	55	2
4 Oct 03	THE ESSENTIAL PERRY COMO *Jive / RCA 82876560172*	54	2
5 Jun 04	THE VERY BEST OF PERRY COMO – PAPA LOVES MAMBO *RCA 82876616572*	63	1

[1] Perry Como with the Ramblers [2] Perry Como with the Mitchell Ayers Orchestra and the Ray Charles Singers

LES COMPAGNONS DE LA CHANSON
France, male vocal group (Singles: 3 Weeks) pos/wks

9 Oct 59	THE THREE BELLS (THE JIMMY BROWN SONG) (re) *Columbia DB 4358*	21	3

COMPILATION ALBUMS *See VARIOUS ARTISTS (EPs and LPs)*

COMPULSION
Ireland / Holland, male vocal / instrumental group (Albums: 1 Week) pos/wks

9 Apr 94	COMFORTER *One Little Indian TPLP 59CDL*	59	1

COMSAT ANGELS
UK, male vocal / instrumental group (Singles: 2 Weeks, Albums: 9 Weeks) pos/wks

21 Jan 84	INDEPENDENCE DAY (re) *Jive JIVE 54*	71	2
5 Sep 81	SLEEP NO MORE *Polydor POLS 1038*...................	51	5
18 Sep 82	FICTION *Polydor POLS 1075*	94	2
8 Oct 83	LAND *Jive HIP 8*	91	2

CON FUNK SHUN
US, male vocal / instrumental group (Singles: 2 Weeks) pos/wks

19 Jul 86	BURNIN' LOVE *Club JAB 32*	68	2

CONCEPT
US, male vocalist / instrumentalist – Eric Reed (Singles: 6 Weeks) pos/wks

14 Dec 85	MR DJ *Fourth & Broadway BRW 40*	27	6

The CONCRETES
Sweden, male / female vocal / instrumental group (Singles: 2 Weeks) pos/wks

26 Jun 04	YOU CAN'T HURRY LOVE *EMI LFS 011*	55	1
2 Oct 04	SEEMS FINE *EMI LFS 013*	52	1

CONDUCTOR & THE COWBOY
UK, male production duo – Lee Hallett and Adam Pracy (Singles: 2 Weeks) pos/wks

20 May 00	FEELING THIS WAY *Serious SERR 016CD*	35	2

CONFEDERATES *See Elvis COSTELLO*

CONGREGATION
UK, male / female choir (Singles: 14 Weeks) pos/wks

27 Nov 71	● SOFTLY WHISPERING I LOVE YOU *Columbia DB 8830*	4	14

CONGRESS
UK, male / female vocal / instrumental group (Singles: 4 Weeks) pos/wks

26 Oct 91	40 MILES *Inner Rhythm 7HEART 01*	26	4

CONJURE ONE
Canada, male producer – Rhys Fulber (Singles: 1 Week) pos/wks

15 Feb 03	SLEEP / TEARS FROM THE MOON *Nettwerk 331792*	42	1

'Tears from the Moon' features uncredited vocalist Sinead O'Connor

Arthur CONLEY
US, male vocalist, b. 4 Jan 1946, d. 17 Nov 2003 (Singles: 15 Weeks) pos/wks

27 Apr 67	● SWEET SOUL MUSIC *Atlantic 584 083*	7	14
10 Apr 68	FUNKY STREET *Atlantic 583 175*	46	1

The CONNELLS
US, male vocal / instrumental group (Singles: 11 Weeks, Albums: 2 Weeks) pos/wks

12 Aug 95	74–75 (re) *TVT LONCD 369*	14	11
9 Sep 95	RING *London 8286602*.................................	36	2

Harry CONNICK, Jr
US, male vocalist / instrumentalist – keyboards (Singles: 11 Weeks, Albums: 73 Weeks) pos/wks

25 May 91	RECIPE FOR LOVE / IT HAD TO BE YOU *Columbia 6568907* 32		6
3 Aug 91	WE ARE IN LOVE *Columbia 6572847* 62		2
23 Nov 91	BLUE LIGHT RED LIGHT (SOMEONE'S THERE) *Columbia 6575367*	54	3
22 Sep 90	● WE ARE IN LOVE *CBS 4667361*	7	46
26 Oct 91	BLUE LIGHT *Columbia 4690871*.......................	16	11
30 Jan 93	25 *Columbia 4728092*	35	2
12 Jun 93	FOREVER FOR NOW *Columbia 4738732*..............	32	5
27 Aug 94	SHE *Columbia 4768162*................................	21	3
20 Mar 04	● ONLY YOU *Columbia 5150462*	6	6

Ray CONNIFF
US, male orchestra leader, b. 6 Nov 1916, d. 12 Oct 2002 (Albums: 100 Weeks) pos/wks

28 May 60	IT'S THE TALK OF THE TOWN *Philips BBL 7354*	15	1
25 Jun 60	S'AWFUL NICE *Philips BBL 7281*	13	1
26 Nov 60	● HI-FI COMPANION ALBUM *Philips BET 101*	3	44
20 May 61	MEMORIES ARE MADE OF THIS *Philips BBL 7439*	14	4
29 Dec 62	S WONDERFUL 'S MARVELLOUS *CBS DPG 66001*	18	3
29 Dec 62	WE WISH YOU A MERRY CHRISTMAS *CBS BPG 62092* ...	12	1
16 Apr 66	HI-FI COMPANION ALBUM (re-issue) *CBS DP 66011*	24	4
9 Sep 67	SOMEWHERE MY LOVE *CBS SBPG 62740*	34	3
21 Jun 69	★ HIS ORCHESTRA HIS CHORUS HIS SINGERS HIS SOUND *CBS SPR 27* ■	1	16
23 May 70	BRIDGE OVER TROUBLED WATER *CBS 64020*	30	14
12 Jun 71	LOVE STORY *CBS 64294*	34	1
19 Feb 72	I'D LIKE TO TEACH THE WORLD TO SING *CBS 64449*	17	4
27 Oct 73	HARMONY *CBS 65792*	24	4

Billy CONNOLLY
UK, male comedian / vocalist / instrumentalist (Singles: 31 Weeks, Albums: 108 Weeks) pos/wks

1 Nov 75	★ D.I.V.O.R.C.E. *Polydor 2058 652*	1	10
17 Jul 76	NO CHANCE (NO CHARGE) *Polydor 2058 748*	24	5
25 Aug 79	IN THE BROWNIES *Polydor 2059 160*	38	7
9 Mar 85	SUPER GRAN *Stiff BUY 218*	32	9
20 Jul 74	● SOLO CONCERT *Transatlantic TRA 279*	8	33
18 Jan 75	● COP YER WHACK OF THIS *Polydor 2383 310*.........	10	29
20 Sep 75	WORDS AND MUSIC *Transatlantic TRA SAM 32*	34	10
6 Dec 75	● GET RIGHT INTAE HIM *Polydor 2383 368*	6	14
11 Dec 76	ATLANTIC BRIDGE *Polydor 2383 419*	20	9
28 Jan 78	RAW MEAT FOR THE BALCONY *Polydor 2383 463* ...	57	3
5 Dec 81	THE PICK OF BILLY CONNOLLY *Polydor POLTV 15*	23	8
5 Dec 87	BILLY AND ALBERT *10 DIX 65*..........................	81	2

Sarah CONNOR (see also TQ)
Germany, female vocalist (Singles: 10 Weeks) pos/wks

13 Oct 01	LET'S GET BACK TO BED ... BOY *Epic 6718662* [1]	16	5
5 Jun 04	BOUNCE *Epic 6749001*	14	5

[1] Sarah Connor featuring TQ

CONQUERING LION
UK, male vocal group (Singles: 1 Week) pos/wks

8 Oct 94	CODE RED *Mango CIDM 821*	53	1

Leena CONQUEST and HIP HOP FINGER
US, female vocalist and male rapper (Singles: 1 Week) pos/wks

18 Jun 94	BOUNDARIES *Natural Response 74321208522*	67	1

Jess CONRAD
UK, male vocalist / actor – Gerald James (Singles: 13 Weeks) pos/wks

30 Jun 60	CHERRY PIE *Decca F 1123*	39	1
26 Jan 61	MYSTERY GIRL (re) *Decca F 11315*	18	10
11 Oct 62	PRETTY JENNY *Decca F 11511*	50	2

CONSOLIDATED
US, male vocal / instrumental group (Albums: 1 Week) pos/wks

30 Jul 94	BUSINESS OF PUNISHMENT *London 8285142*	53	1

CONSORTIUM
UK, male vocal group (Singles: 9 Weeks) pos/wks

12 Feb 69	ALL THE LOVE IN THE WORLD *Pye 7N 17635*	22	9

Ann CONSUELO *See SUBTERRANIA featuring Ann CONSUELO*

Singles re-entries are listed as (re), (2re), (3re).... which signifies that the hit re-entered the chart once, twice or three times...

The CONTOURS US, male vocal group (Singles: 6 Weeks)

			pos/wks
24 Jan 70	**JUST A LITTLE MISUNDERSTANDING** Tamla Motown TMG 723	**31**	6

CONTRABAND Germany / US, male / female vocal / instrumental group (Singles: 2 Weeks)

			pos/wks
20 Jul 91	**ALL THE WAY FROM MEMPHIS** Impact American EM 195	**65**	2

CONTROL
UK, male / female vocal / instrumental group (Singles: 5 Weeks)

			pos/wks
2 Nov 91	**DANCE WITH ME (I'M YOUR ECSTASY)** All Around the World GLOBE 105	**17**	5

CONVERT (see also TRANSFORMER 2) Belgium, male instrumental / production duo – Peter Ramson and Danny Van Wauwe (Singles: 7 Weeks)

			pos/wks
11 Jan 92	**NIGHTBIRD** A&M AM 845	**39**	4
29 May 93	**ROCKIN' TO THE RHYTHM** A&M 5802532	**42**	2
31 Jan 98	**NIGHTBIRD (re-issue)** Wonderboy WBOYD 008	**45**	1

CONWAY BROTHERS US, male vocal group (Singles: 10 Weeks)

			pos/wks
22 Jun 85	**TURN IT UP** 10 TEN 57	**11**	10

Raz CONWAY See MORJAC featuring Raz CONWAY

Russ CONWAY 259 Top 500 Popular pianist and composer, b. Trevor Stanford, 2 Sep 1925, Bristol, UK, d. 16 Nov 2000. Against the trends of the day, this MOR piano player was the UK's top-selling artist in 1959 (Singles: 179 Weeks, Albums: 69 Weeks)

			pos/wks
29 Nov 57	**PARTY POPS** Columbia DB 4031	**24**	5
29 Aug 58	**GOT A MATCH** Columbia DB 4166	**30**	1
28 Nov 58 ●	**MORE PARTY POPS** Columbia DB 4204	**10**	7
23 Jan 59	**THE WORLD OUTSIDE (re)** Columbia DB 4234	**24**	4
20 Feb 59 ★	**SIDE SADDLE** Columbia DB 4256	**1**	30
15 May 59 ★	**ROULETTE** Columbia DB 4298	**1**	19
21 Aug 59 ●	**CHINA TEA** Columbia DB 4337	**5**	13
13 Nov 59 ●	**SNOW COACH** Columbia DB 4368	**7**	9
20 Nov 59 ●	**MORE AND MORE PARTY POPS** Columbia DB 4373	**5**	8
4 Mar 60	**ROYAL EVENT** Columbia DB 4418	**15**	8
21 Apr 60	**FINGS AIN'T WOT THEY USED T'BE** Columbia DB 4422	**47**	1
19 May 60	**LUCKY FIVE** Columbia DB 4457	**14**	9
29 Sep 60	**PASSING BREEZE** Columbia DB 4508	**16**	10
24 Nov 60	**EVEN MORE PARTY POPS** Columbia DB 4535	**27**	9
19 Jan 61	**PEPE** Columbia DB 4564	**19**	9
25 May 61	**PABLO** Columbia DB 4649	**45**	2
24 Aug 61	**SAY IT WITH FLOWERS** Columbia DB 4665 [1]	**23**	10
30 Nov 61 ●	**TOY BALLOONS** Columbia DB 4738	**7**	11
22 Feb 62	**LESSON ONE** Columbia DB 4784	**21**	7
29 Nov 62	**ALWAYS YOU AND ME (re)** Columbia DB 4934	**33**	7
22 Nov 58 ●	**PACK UP YOUR TROUBLES** Columbia 33SX 1120	**9**	5
2 May 59 ●	**SONGS TO SING IN YOUR BATH** Columbia 33SX 1149	**8**	10
19 Sep 59 ●	**FAMILY FAVOURITES** Columbia 33SX 1169	**3**	16
19 Dec 59 ●	**TIME TO CELEBRATE** Columbia 33SX 1197	**3**	7
26 Mar 60 ●	**MY CONCERTO FOR YOU** Columbia 33SX 1214	**5**	17
17 Dec 60 ●	**PARTY TIME** Columbia 33SX 1279	**7**	11
23 Apr 77	**RUSS CONWAY PRESENTS 24 PIANO GREATS** Ronco RTL 2022	**25**	3

[1] Dorothy Squires and Russ Conway

'Always You and Me' featured Russ Conway talking as well as playing piano. Several of the discs were medleys as follows: Party Pops: When You're Smiling / I'm Looking over a Four-Leafed Clover / When You Wore a Tulip / Row Row Row / For Me and My Girl / Shine on Harvest Moon / By the Light of the Silvery Moon / Side By Side. More Party Pops: Music Music Music / If You Were the Only Girl in the World / Nobody's Sweetheart / Yes Sir That's My Baby / Some of these Days / Honeysuckle and the Bee / Hello Hello Who's Your Lady Friend / Shanty in Old Shanty Town. More and More Party Pops: Sheik of Araby / Who Were You With Last Night / Any Old Iron / Tiptoe Through the Tulips / If You Were the Only Girl in the World / When I Leave the World Behind. Even More Party Pops: Ain't She Sweet / I Can't Give You Anything But Love / Yes We Have No Bananas / I May Be Wrong / Happy Days And Lonely Nights / Glad Rag Doll

Ry COODER US, male vocalist / instrumentalist – guitar – Ryland Cooder (Albums: 49 Weeks)

			pos/wks
11 Aug 79	**BOP TILL YOU DROP** Warner Bros. K 56691	**36**	9
18 Oct 80	**BORDER LINE** Warner Bros. K 56864	**35**	6
24 Apr 82	**THE SLIDE AREA** Warner Bros. K 56976	**18**	12
14 Nov 87	**GET RHYTHM** Warner Bros. WX 121	**75**	3
9 Apr 94	**TALKING TIMBUKTU** World Circuit WCD 040 [1]	**44**	3

5 Jul 97	**BUENA VISTA SOCIAL CLUB** World Circuit WCD 050	**44**	15
8 Feb 03	**MAMBO SINUENDO** Nonesuch 75597969612	**40**	1

[1] Ali Farka Touri and Ry Cooder

Martin COOK See Richard DENTON and Martin COOK

Norman COOK (see also BEATS INTERNATIONAL; FATBOY SLIM; FREAKPOWER; The HOUSEMARTINS; MIGHTY DUB KATZ; PIZZAMAN)
UK, male producer / multi-instrumentalist – Quentin Cook (Singles: 10 Weeks)

			pos/wks
8 Jul 89	**WON'T TALK ABOUT IT / BLAME IT ON THE BASSLINE** Go Beat GOD 33 [1]	**29**	6
21 Oct 89	**FOR SPACIOUS LIES** Go Beat GOD 37 [2]	**48**	4

[1] Norman Cook featuring Billy Bragg / Norman Cook featuring MC Wildski
[2] Norman Cook featuring Lester

Peter COOK and Dudley MOORE
(see also Dudley MOORE; Sir George SOLTI) UK, male comedy / vocal duo – Peter Cook, b. 17 Nov 1937, d. 9 Jan 1995, and Dudley Moore, b. 19 Apr 1935, d. 28 Mar 2002 (Singles: 15 Weeks, Albums: 34 Weeks)

			pos/wks
17 Jun 65	**GOODBYE-EE** Decca F 12158	**18**	10
15 Jul 65	**THE BALLAD OF SPOTTY MULDOON** Decca F 12182 [1]	**34**	5
21 May 66	**ONCE MOORE WITH COOK** Decca LK 4785	**25**	1
18 Sep 76	**DEREK AND CLIVE LIVE** Island ILPS 9434 [1]	**12**	25
24 Dec 77	**DEREK AND CLIVE COME AGAIN** Virgin V 2094 [1]	**18**	8

[1] Peter Cook [1] Derek and Clive

Brandon COOKE featuring Roxanne SHANTE
UK, male producer and US, female rapper (Singles: 3 Weeks)

			pos/wks
29 Oct 88	**SHARP AS A KNIFE** Club JAB 73	**45**	3

Sam COOKE US, male vocalist, b. 22 Jan 1931, d. 11 Dec 1964 (Singles: 82 Weeks, Albums: 32 Weeks)

			pos/wks
17 Jan 58	**YOU SEND ME** London HLU 8506 ▲	**29**	1
14 Aug 59	**ONLY SIXTEEN** HMV POP 642	**23**	4
7 Jul 60	**WONDERFUL WORLD** HMV POP 754	**27**	8
29 Sep 60 ●	**CHAIN GANG** RCA 1202	**9**	11
27 Jul 61 ●	**CUPID** RCA 1242	**7**	14
8 Mar 62 ●	**TWISTIN' THE NIGHT AWAY** RCA 1277	**6**	14
16 May 63	**ANOTHER SATURDAY NIGHT** RCA 1341	**23**	12
5 Sep 63	**FRANKIE AND JOHNNY** RCA 1361	**30**	6
22 Mar 86 ●	**WONDERFUL WORLD (re-issue)** RCA PB 49871	**2**	11
10 May 86	**ANOTHER SATURDAY NIGHT (re-issue)** RCA PB 49849	**75**	1
26 Apr 86 ●	**THE MAN AND HIS MUSIC** RCA PL 87127	**8**	27
25 Oct 03	**PORTRAIT OF A LEGEND** Universal TV 9807446	**30**	5

The COOKIE CREW UK, female rap duo – Susie Banfield and Debbie Pryce (Singles: 31 Weeks, Albums: 4 Weeks)

			pos/wks
9 Jan 88 ●	**ROK DA HOUSE** Rhythm King LEFT 11 [1]	**5**	11
7 Jan 89	**BORN THIS WAY (LET'S DANCE)** ffrr FFR 19	**23**	5
1 Apr 89	**GOT TO KEEP ON** ffrr F 110	**17**	9
15 Jul 89	**COME AND GET SOME** ffrr F 110	**42**	3
27 Jul 91	**SECRETS (OF SUCCESS)** ffrr F159 [2]	**53**	3
6 May 89	**BORN THIS WAY!** London 828134 1	**24**	4

[1] The Beatmasters featuring The Cookie Crew [2] The Cookie Crew featuring Danny D

The COOKIES US, female vocal group (Singles: 1 Week)

			pos/wks
10 Jan 63	**CHAINS** London HLU 9634	**50**	1

COOL DOWN ZONE
UK, male / female vocal / instrumental group (Singles: 4 Weeks)

			pos/wks
30 Jun 90	**HEAVEN KNOWS** 10 TEN 309	**52**	4

COOL, the FAB, and the GROOVY present Quincy JONES
UK, male production duo, US, male band and US, male producer / instrumentalist (Singles: 1 Week)

			pos/wks
1 Aug 98	**SOUL BOSSA NOVA** Manifesto FESCD 48	**47**	1

COOL JACK
Italy, male instrumental / production duo (Singles: 1 Week)

			pos/wks
9 Nov 96	**JUS' COME** AM:PM 5819892	**44**	1

The COOL NOTES
UK, male / female vocal / instrumental group (Singles: 28 Weeks, Albums: 2 Weeks) pos/wks

18 Aug 84	**YOU'RE NEVER TOO YOUNG** *Abstract Dance AD 1*	42	5
17 Nov 84	**I FORGOT** *Abstract Dance AD 2*	63	2
23 Mar 85	**SPEND THE NIGHT** *Abstract Dance AD 3*	11	9
13 Jul 85	**IN YOUR CAR** *Abstract Dance AD 4*	13	9
19 Oct 85	**HAVE A GOOD FOREVER** *Abstract Dance AD 5*	73	1
17 May 86	**INTO THE MOTION** *Abstract Dance AD 8*	66	2
9 Nov 85	**HAVE A GOOD FOREVER** *Abstract Dance ADLP 1*	66	2

Rita COOLIDGE
US, female vocalist (Singles: 24 Weeks, Albums: 44 Weeks) pos/wks

25 Jun 77 ●	**WE'RE ALL ALONE** *A&M AMS 7295*	6	13
15 Oct 77	**(YOUR LOVE HAS LIFTED ME) HIGHER AND HIGHER (re)** *A&M AMS 7315*	48	2
4 Feb 78	**WORDS** *A&M AMS 7330*	25	8
25 Jun 83	**ALL TIME HIGH** *A&M AM 007*	75	1
6 Aug 77 ●	**ANYTIME ANYWHERE** *A&M AMLH 64616*	6	28
6 May 78	**NATURAL ACT** *A&M AMLH 64690* [1]	35	4
8 Jul 78	**LOVE ME AGAIN** *A&M AMLH 64699*	51	1
14 Mar 81 ●	**THE VERY BEST OF RITA COOLIDGE** *A&M AMLH 68520*	6	11

[1] Kris Kristofferson and Rita Coolidge

COOLIO
US, male rapper – Artis Ivey Jr (Singles: 62 Weeks, Albums: 27 Weeks) pos/wks

23 Jul 94	**FANTASTIC VOYAGE** *Tommy Boy TB 0617CD*	41	2
15 Oct 94	**I REMEMBER** *Tommy Boy TBXCD 635*	73	1
28 Oct 95 ★	**GANGSTA'S PARADISE** *Tommy Boy MCSTD 2104* [1] ◆ ■ ▲	1	20
20 Jan 96 ●	**TOO HOT** *Tommy Boy TBCD 718*	9	6
6 Apr 96	**1234 (SUMPIN' NEW)** *Tommy Boy TBCD 7721*	13	7
17 Aug 96	**IT'S ALL THE WAY LIVE (NOW)** *Tommy Boy TBCD 7731*	34	2
5 Apr 97 ●	**HIT EM HIGH (THE MONSTARS' ANTHEM)** *Atlantic A 5449CD* [2]	8	6
7 Jun 97	**THE WINNER** *Atlantic A 5433CD*	53	1
19 Jul 97 ●	**C U WHEN U GET THERE** *Tommy Boy TBCD 785* [3]	3	12
11 Oct 97	**OOH LA LA** *Tommy Boy TBCD 799*	14	5
29 Oct 94	**IT TAKES A THIEF** *Tommy Boy TBCD 1083*	67	1
18 Nov 95	**GANGSTA'S PARADISE** *Tommy Boy TBCD 1141*	18	24
13 Sep 97	**MY SOUL** *Tommy Boy TBCD 1180*	28	2

[1] Coolio featuring LV [2] B Real / Busta Rhymes / Coolio / LL Cool J / Method Man [3] Coolio featuring 40 Thevz

COOLY'S HOT BOX *See Roger SANCHEZ*

COOPER
Holland, male production trio (Singles: 2 Weeks) pos/wks

11 Jan 03	**I BELIEVE IN LOVE** *Product PDT 05CDS*	50	2

Alice COOPER `262` `Top 500`
The alter ego of shock-rock vocalist Vincent Furnier, b. 4 Feb 1948, Detroit, US. Transatlantic chart-topper whose group was voted World's Top Band in 1972 in UK. In 2001 he received Living Legend Award from International Horror Guild (Singles: 104 Weeks, Albums: 141 Weeks) pos/wks

15 Jul 72 ★	**SCHOOL'S OUT** *Warner Bros. K 16188*	1	12
7 Oct 72 ●	**ELECTED** *Warner Bros. K 16214*	4	10
10 Feb 73 ●	**HELLO HURRAY** *Warner Bros. K 16248*	6	10
21 Apr 73 ●	**NO MORE MR NICE GUY** *Warner Bros. K 16262*	10	10
19 Jan 74	**TEENAGE LAMENT '74** *Warner Bros. K 16345*	12	7
21 May 77	**(NO MORE) LOVE AT YOUR CONVENIENCE** *Warner Bros. K 16935*	44	2
23 Dec 78	**HOW YOU GONNA SEE ME NOW** *Warner Bros. K 17270*	61	6
6 Mar 82	**SEVEN AND SEVEN IS (LIVE VERSION)** *Warner Bros. K 17924*	62	3
8 May 82	**FOR BRITAIN ONLY / UNDER MY WHEELS** *Warner Bros. K 17940*	66	2
18 Oct 86	**HE'S BACK (THE MAN BEHIND THE MASK)** *MCA MCA 1090*	61	2
9 Apr 88	**FREEDOM** *MCA MCA 1241*	50	3
29 Jul 89 ●	**POISON** *Epic 655061 7*	2	11
7 Oct 89	**BED OF NAILS** *Epic ALICE 3*	38	5
2 Dec 89	**HOUSE OF FIRE** *Epic ALICE 4*	65	2
22 Jun 91	**HEY STOOPID** *Epic 6569837*	21	6
5 Oct 91	**LOVE'S A LOADED GUN** *Epic 6574387*	38	3
6 Jun 92	**FEED MY FRANKENSTEIN** *Epic 6580927*	27	3
28 May 94	**LOST IN AMERICA** *Epic 6603472*	22	3
23 Jul 94	**IT'S ME** *Epic 6605632*	34	2
5 Feb 72	**KILLER** *Warner Bros. K 56005*	27	18
22 Jul 72 ●	**SCHOOL'S OUT** *Warner Bros. K 56007*	4	20
9 Sep 72	**LOVE IT TO DEATH** *Warner Bros. K 46177*	28	7
24 Mar 73 ★	**BILLION DOLLAR BABIES** *Warner Bros. K 56013* ■ ▲	1	23
4 Aug 73	**SCHOOL DAYS** *Warner Bros. 66021*	13	8
12 Jan 74	**MUSCLE OF LOVE** *Warner Bros. K 56018*	34	4
15 Mar 75	**WELCOME TO MY NIGHTMARE** *Anchor ANCL 2011*	19	8
24 Jul 76	**ALICE COOPER GOES TO HELL** *Warner Bros. K 56171*	23	7
28 May 77	**LACE AND WHISKY** *Warner Bros. K 56365*	33	3
23 Dec 78	**FROM THE INSIDE** *Warner Bros. K 56577*	68	3
17 May 80	**FLUSH THE FASHION** *Warner Bros. K 56805*	56	3
12 Sep 81	**SPECIAL FORCES** *Warner Bros. K 56927*	96	1
12 Nov 83	**DADA** *Warner Bros. 9239691*	93	1
1 Nov 86	**CONSTRICTOR** *MCA MCF 3341*	41	2
7 Nov 87	**RAISE YOUR FIST AND YELL** *MCA MCF 3392*	48	3
26 Aug 89 ●	**TRASH** *Epic 465130 1*	2	12
13 Jul 91 ●	**HEY STOOPID** *Epic 4684161*	4	7
18 Jun 94 ●	**THE LAST TEMPTATION** *Epic 4765949*	6	5
24 Jun 00	**BRUTAL PLANET** *Eagle EAGCD 115*	38	1
10 Mar 01	**THE DEFINITIVE ALICE COOPER** *Rhino 8122735342*	33	5

For the first five hits, 'Alice Cooper' was the name of the entire group, not just of the lead vocalist Alice Cooper was a US, male vocal / instrumental group for the first five albums. Album 'School Days' is a double re-issue of earlier albums 'Pretties for You' and 'Easy Action'

Deborah COOPER *See C & C MUSIC FACTORY*

Tommy COOPER
UK, male comedian / vocalist, b. 19 Mar 1923, d. 15 Apr 1984 (Singles: 3 Weeks) pos/wks

29 Jun 61	**DON'T JUMP OFF THE ROOF DAD (re)** *Palette PG 9019*	40	3

The COOPER TEMPLE CLAUSE
UK, male vocal / instrumental group (Singles: 10 Weeks, Albums: 5 Weeks) pos/wks

29 Sep 01	**LET'S KILL MUSIC** *Morning MORNING 9*	41	1
9 Feb 02	**FILM MAKER / BEEN TRAINING DOGS** *Morning MORNING 15*	20	3
18 May 02	**WHO NEEDS ENEMIES?** *Morning MORNING 23*	22	2
13 Sep 03	**PROMISES PROMISES** *Morning MORNING 30*	19	2
22 Nov 03	**BLIND PILOTS** *Morning MORNING 38*	37	2
23 Feb 02	**SEE THIS THROUGH AND LEAVE** *Morning MORNING 18*	27	3
20 Sep 03 ●	**KICK UP THE FIRE, AND LET THE FLAMES BREAK LOOSE** *Morning MORNING 36*	5	2

CO-ORDINATE *See PESHAY*

Julian COPE (see also The TEARDROP EXPLODES)
UK, male vocalist (Singles: 59 Weeks, Albums: 35 Weeks) pos/wks

19 Nov 83	**SUNSHINE PLAYROOM** *Mercury COPE 1*	64	1
31 Mar 84	**THE GREATNESS AND PERFECTION OF LOVE** *Mercury MER 155*	52	5
27 Sep 86	**WORLD SHUT YOUR MOUTH** *Island IS 290*	19	8
17 Jan 87	**TRAMPOLENE** *Island IS 305*	31	6
11 Apr 87	**EVE'S VOLCANO (COVERED IN SIN)** *Island IS 318*	41	5
24 Sep 88	**CHARLOTTE ANNE** *Island IS 368*	35	6
21 Jan 89	**5 O'CLOCK WORLD** *Island IS 399*	42	4
24 Jun 89	**CHINA DOLL** *Island IS 406*	53	2
9 Feb 91	**BEAUTIFUL LOVE** *Island IS 483*	32	6
20 Apr 91	**EAST EASY RIDER** *Island IS 492*	51	3
3 Aug 91	**HEAD** *Island IS 497*	57	2
8 Aug 92	**WORLD SHUT YOUR MOUTH (re-issue)** *Island IS 534*	44	3
17 Oct 92	**FEAR LOVES THIS PLACE** *Island IS 545*	42	2
12 Aug 95	**TRY TRY TRY** *Echo ECSCD 11*	24	3
27 Jul 96	**I COME FROM ANOTHER PLANET BABY** *Echo ECSCD 22*	34	2
5 Oct 96	**PLANETARY SIT-IN (EVERY GIRL HAS YOUR NAME)** *Echo ECSCD 25*	34	1
3 Mar 84	**WORLD SHUT YOUR MOUTH** *Mercury MERL 37*	40	4
24 Nov 84	**FRIED** *Mercury MERL 48*	87	1
14 Mar 87	**SAINT JULIAN** *Island ILPS 9861*	11	10
29 Oct 88	**MY NATION UNDERGROUND** *Island ILPS 9918*	42	2
16 Mar 91	**PEGGY SUICIDE** *Island ILPSD 9977*	23	7
15 Aug 92	**FLOORED GENIUS – THE BEST OF JULIAN COPE AND THE TEARDROP EXPLODES 1979-91** *Island CID 8000* [1]	22	3
31 Oct 92	**JEHOVAHKILL** *Island 5140522*	20	2
16 Jul 94	**AUTOGEDDON** *Echo ECHCD 1*	16	3
9 Sep 95	**JULIAN COPE PRESENTS 20 MOTHERS** *Echo ECHCD 5*	20	2
26 Oct 96	**INTERPRETER** *Echo ECHCD 12*	39	1

[1] Julian Cope and The Teardrop Explodes

Imani COPPOLA (see also BAHA MEN)
US, female vocalist / instrumentalist (Singles: 3 Weeks) pos/wks

28 Feb 98	**LEGEND OF A COWGIRL** *Columbia 6656015*	32	3

The CORAL
UK, male vocal / instrumental group (Singles: 22 Weeks, Albums: 46 Weeks)   pos/wks

		pos/wks
27 Jul 02	GOODBYE *Deltasonic DLTCD 2005*	**21** 2
19 Oct 02	DREAMING OF YOU *Deltasonic DLTCD 2008*	**13** 5
15 Mar 03 ●	DON'T THINK YOU'RE THE FIRST (re) *Deltasonic DLTCDC 010*	**10** 4
26 Aug 03 ●	PASS IT ON *Deltasonic DLTCD 013*	**5** 7
18 Oct 03	SECRET KISS *Deltasonic DLTCD 015*	**25** 2
6 Dec 03	BILL MCCAI *Deltasonic DLTCD 017*	**23** 2
10 Aug 02 ●	THE CORAL *Deltasonic DLTCD 006*	**5** 34
9 Aug 03 ★	MAGIC AND MEDICINE *Deltasonic DLTCDPS 014* ■	**1** 9
7 Feb 04 ●	NIGHTFREAK AND THE SONS OF BECKER *Deltasonic DLTCD 018*	**5** 3

Harry H CORBETT See Wilfrid BRAMBELL and Harry H. CORBETT

Frank CORDELL and his ORCHESTRA
UK, orchestra – leader b. 1918, d. 6 Jul 1980 (Singles: 4 Weeks)   pos/wks

		pos/wks
24 Aug 56	SADIE'S SHAWL *HMV POP 229*	**29** 2
16 Feb 61	THE BLACK BEAR *HMV POP 824*	**44** 2

Louise CORDET
UK, female vocalist – Louise Boisot (Singles: 13 Weeks)   pos/wks

		pos/wks
5 Jul 62	I'M JUST A BABY *Decca F 11476*	**13** 13

CORDUROY
UK, male vocal / instrumental group (Albums: 1 Week)   pos/wks

		pos/wks
8 Oct 94	OUT OF HERE *Acid Jazz JAZIDCD 107*	**73** 1

COREE See DAMAGE; ICEBERG SLIMM

Chris CORNELL (see also SOUNDGARDEN)
US, male vocalist (Singles: 1 Week, Albums: 1 Week)   pos/wks

		pos/wks
23 Oct 99	CAN'T CHANGE ME *A&M 4971732*	**62** 1
2 Oct 99	EUPHORIA MORNING *A&M 4904222*	**31** 1

Don CORNELL
US, male vocalist – Luigi Varlaro, b. 21 Apr 1919, d. 23 Feb 2004 (Singles: 23 Weeks)   pos/wks

		pos/wks
3 Sep 54 ★	HOLD MY HAND *Vogue Q 2013*	**1** 21
22 Apr 55	STRANGER IN PARADISE *Vogue Q 72073*	**19** 2

Lynn CORNELL (see also The PEARLS)
UK, female vocalist (Singles: 9 Weeks)   pos/wks

		pos/wks
20 Oct 60	NEVER ON SUNDAY *Decca F 11277*	**30** 9

CORNERSHOP
UK, male vocal / instrumental duo (Singles: 19 Weeks, Albums: 18 Weeks)   pos/wks

		pos/wks
30 Aug 97	BRIMFUL OF ASHA *Wiiija WIJ 75CD*	**60** 1
28 Feb 98 ★	BRIMFUL OF ASHA (re-mix) *Wiiija WIJ 81CD* ■	**1** 12
16 May 98	SLEEP ON THE LEFT SIDE *Wiiija WIJ 80CD*	**23** 3
16 Mar 02	LESSONS LEARNED FROM ROCKY I TO ROCKY III *Wiiija WIJ 129CD*	**37** 2
7 Aug 04	TOPKNOT *Rough Trade RTRADSCD 168* [1]	**53** 1
20 Sep 97	WHEN I WAS BORN FOR THE 7TH TIME *Wiiija WIJCD 1065* ...	**17** 15
13 Apr 02	HANDCREAM FOR A GENERATION *Wiiija WIJCD 1115*	**30** 3

[1] Cornershop presents Bubbley Kaur

Charlotte CORNWELL See Julie COVINGTON, Rula LENSKA, Charlotte CORNWELL and Sue JONES-DAVIES

Hugh CORNWELL
(see also The STRANGLERS) UK, male vocalist / instrumentalist – guitar (Singles: 3 Weeks, Albums: 1 Week)   pos/wks

		pos/wks
24 Jan 87	FACTS + FIGURES *Virgin VS 922*	**61** 2
7 May 88	ANOTHER KIND OF LOVE *Virgin VS 945*	**71** 1
18 Jun 88	WOLF *Virgin V 2420*	**98** 1

CORO DE MUNJES DEL MONASTERIO BENEDICTINO DE SANTO DOMINGO DE SILOS
Spain, monastic choir (Albums: 28 Weeks)   pos/wks

		pos/wks
5 Mar 94 ●	CANTO GREGORIANO *EMI Classics CMS 5652172*	**7** 25
17 Dec 94	CANTO NOEL *EMI Classics CDC 5552172*	**53** 3

CO-RO featuring TARLISA
Germany, male / female vocal / production group (Singles: 1 Week) pos/wks

		pos/wks
12 Dec 92	BECAUSE THE NIGHT *ZYX ZYX 68227*	**61** 1

CORONA
Brazil, male producer and female vocalist – Francesco Bontempi and Olga de Souza (Singles: 44 Weeks, Albums: 7 Weeks) pos/wks

		pos/wks
10 Sep 94 ●	THE RHYTHM OF THE NIGHT (re) *WEA YZ 837CD1*	**2** 18
8 Apr 95 ●	BABY BABY *Eternal YZ 919CD*	**5** 8
22 Jul 95 ●	TRY ME OUT *Eternal YZ 955CD*	**6** 10
23 Dec 95	I DON'T WANNA BE A STAR *Eternal WEA 029CD*	**22** 6
22 Feb 97	MEGAMIX *Eternal WEA 092CD*	**36** 2
20 May 95	THE RHYTHM OF THE NIGHT *Eternal 0630103312*	**18** 7

CORONATION STREET CAST featuring Bill WADDINGTON
UK, male / female actors / vocal group and male actor / vocalist, b. 10 Jun 1916, d. 11 Sep 2000 (Singles: 3 Weeks)   pos/wks

		pos/wks
16 Dec 95	ALWAYS LOOK ON THE BRIGHT SIDE OF LIFE *EMI Premier CDEMS 411*	**35** 3

The listed flip side of 'Always Look on the Bright Side of Life' was 'Something Stupid' by Amanda Barrie and Johnny Briggs

The CORONETS
UK, male / female vocal group (Singles: 7 Weeks) pos/wks

		pos/wks
26 Aug 55	THAT'S HOW A LOVE SONG WAS BORN *Columbia DB 3640* [1]	**14** 6
25 Nov 55	TWENTY TINY FINGERS *Columbia DB 3671*	**20** 1

[1] Ray Burns with the Coronets

The CORRIES
UK, male vocal / instrumental duo – Ronnie Browne and Roy Williamson (Albums: 5 Weeks)   pos/wks

		pos/wks
9 May 70	SCOTTISH LOVE SONGS *Fontana 6309004*	**46** 4
16 Sep 72	SOUND OF PIBROCH *Columbia SCX 6511*	**39** 1

Briana CORRIGAN (see also The BEAUTIFUL SOUTH)
UK, female vocalist (Singles: 2 Weeks)   pos/wks

		pos/wks
11 May 96	LOVE ME NOW *East West EW 041CD1*	**48** 2

CORROSION OF CONFORMITY
US, male vocal / instrumental group (Albums: 1 Week)   pos/wks

		pos/wks
14 Sep 96	WISEBLOOD *Columbia 4843282*	**43** 1

The CORRS 89 *Top 500*
Internationally successful Irish sisters and brother group: Andrea, Caroline, Sharon and Jim Corr. The quartet, which has sold more than five million albums in the UK, was voted Best International Group at the 1999 Brits. 'Talk on Corners' was the top UK album in 1998 (Singles: 106 Weeks, Albums: 361 Weeks)   pos/wks

		pos/wks
17 Feb 96	RUNAWAY (re) *Atlantic A 5727CD*	**49** 3
1 Feb 97	LOVE TO LOVE YOU / RUNAWAY (re-issue) *Atlantic A 5621CD*	**62** 1
25 Oct 97	ONLY WHEN I SLEEP *Atlantic AT 0015CD*	**58** 1
20 Dec 97	I NEVER LOVED YOU ANYWAY *Atlantic AT 0018CD*	**43** 2
28 Mar 98	WHAT CAN I DO *Atlantic AT 0029CD*	**53** 1
16 May 98 ●	DREAMS *Atlantic AT 0032CD*	**6** 10
29 Aug 98 ●	WHAT CAN I DO (re-mix) *Atlantic AT 0044CD*	**3** 11
28 Nov 98 ●	SO YOUNG *Atlantic AT 0057CD1*	**6** 13
27 Feb 99 ●	RUNAWAY (re-mix) *Atlantic AT 0062CD*	**2** 11
12 Jun 99	I KNOW MY LOVE *RCA Victor 74321670622* [1]	**37** 3
11 Dec 99	RADIO *Atlantic AT 0079CD*	**18** 9
15 Jul 00 ★	BREATHLESS *Atlantic AT 0084CD* ■	**1** 13
11 Nov 00	IRRESISTIBLE (re) *Atlantic AT 0089CD*	**20** 7
28 Apr 01	GIVE ME A REASON *Atlantic AT 0097CD*	**27** 2
10 Nov 01	WOULD YOU BE HAPPIER? *Atlantic AT 0115CD*	**14** 5
29 May 04 ●	SUMMER SUNSHINE *Atlantic AT 0179CD1*	**6** 8
25 Sep 04	ANGEL *Atlantic AT 0182CD2*	**16** 4
18 Dec 04	LONG NIGHT *Atlantic AT 0190CD*	**31** 2+
2 Mar 96 ●	FORGIVEN NOT FORGOTTEN *Atlantic 7567926122*	**2** 113
1 Nov 97 ★	TALK ON CORNERS *Atlantic 7567830512*	**1** 142
27 Nov 99 ●	UNPLUGGED *Atlantic 7567809862*	**7** 26
29 Jul 00 ★	IN BLUE *Atlantic 7567833522* ■	**1** 45
17 Nov 01 ●	THE BEST OF THE CORRS *Atlantic 7567930732*	**6** 21
12 Jun 04 ●	BORROWED HEAVEN *Atlantic 7567932432*	**2** 14

[1] The Chieftains featuring The Corrs

CORRUPTED CRU featuring MC NEAT
(see also Scott GARCIA featuring MC STYLES) *UK, male rap / production duo –*
Scott Garcia and Michael Wood and male rapper (Singles: 1 Week)   pos/wks

2 Mar 02	**G.A.R.A.G.E.** *Red Rose CDRRROSE 011*	**59** 1

Ferry CORSTEN (see also ALBION; GOURYELLA; MOONMAN; STARPARTY;
SYSTEM F; VERACOCHA) *Holland, male producer (Singles: 11 Weeks)* pos/wks

8 Jun 02	**PUNK** *Positiva CDTIV 173*	**29** 3
21 Feb 04	**ROCK YOUR BODY ROCK (re)** *Positiva CDTIV 202* ...	**11** 6
10 Jul 04	**IT'S TIME** *Positiva CDTIVS 206*	**51** 2

CORTINA (see also BK)
UK, male producer – Ben Keen (Singles: 3 Weeks)   pos/wks

24 Mar 01	**MUSIC IS MOVING** *Nukleuz NUKC 0159*	**42** 2
26 Jan 02	**ERECTION (TAKE IT TO THE TOP)** *Nukleuz NUKC 0352* [1] **48** 1

[1] Cortina featuring BK and Madam Friction

Vladimir COSMA *Hungary, orchestra (Singles: 1 Week)*   pos/wks

14 Jul 79	**DAVID'S SONG (MAIN THEME FROM 'KIDNAPPED')** *Decca FR 13841*	**64** 1

COSMIC BABY
Germany, male producer (Singles: 1 Week, Albums: 1 Week)   pos/wks

26 Feb 94	**LOOPS OF INFINITY** *Logic 74321191432*	**70** 1
23 Apr 94	**THINKING ABOUT MYSELF** *Logic 74321196052*	**60** 1

COSMIC GATE *Germany, male production trio (Singles: 12 Weeks)* pos/wks

4 Aug 01 ●	**FIRE WIRE** *Data DATA 24CDS*	**9** 7
11 May 02	**EXPLORATION OF SPACE** *Data DATA 30CDS*	**29** 3
25 Jan 03	**THE WAVE / RAGING** *Nebula NEBCD 036*	**48** 2

COSMIC ROUGH RIDERS
UK, male vocal / instrumental group (Singles: 4 Weeks)   pos/wks

4 Aug 01	**REVOLUTION (IN THE SUMMERTIME)** *Poptones MC 5047SCD* ..**35** 1
29 Sep 01	**THE PAIN INSIDE** *Poptones MC 5052SCD* **36** 1
21 Jun 03	**BECAUSE YOU** *Measured MRCOSMIC 2SC* **34** 1
20 Sep 03	**JUSTIFY THE RAIN** *Measured MRCOSMIC 3SCD* **39** 1

COSMOS (see also GLOBAL COMMUNICATION) *UK, male*
producer / instrumentalist – Tom Middleton (Singles: 3 Weeks)   pos/wks

18 Sep 99	**SUMMER IN SPACE** *Island Blue PFACD 3* **49** 1
5 Oct 02	**TAKE ME WITH YOU** *Polydor 659952* **32** 2

Don COSTA *US, orchestra – leader*
b. 10 Jun 1925, d. 19 Jan 1983 (Singles: 10 Weeks)   pos/wks

13 Oct 60	**NEVER ON SUNDAY (re)** *London HLT 9195* **27** 10

Nikka COSTA *US, female vocalist (Singles: 1 Week)*   pos/wks

11 Aug 01	**LIKE A FEATHER** *Virgin VUSCD 199* **53** 1

Elvis COSTELLO `113` `Top 500`
ASCAP (US songwriter's body) Founders Award winner in 2003, b. Declan
McManus, 25 Aug 1955, Liverpool, UK. He emerged during the punk explosion
of 1976, but was soon accepted as a mainstream artist. Has clocked up 13 US
Top 40 albums (Singles: 180 Weeks, Albums: 228 Weeks)   pos/wks

5 Nov 77	**WATCHING THE DETECTIVES** *Stiff BUY 20* **15** 11
11 Mar 78	**(I DON'T WANT TO GO TO) CHELSEA** *Radar ADA 3* [1] **16** 10
13 May 78	**PUMP IT UP** *Radar ADA 10* [1] **24** 10
28 Oct 78	**RADIO RADIO** *Radar ADA 24* [1] **29** 7
10 Feb 79 ●	**OLIVER'S ARMY** *Radar ADA 31* [1] **2** 12
12 May 79	**ACCIDENTS WILL HAPPEN** *Radar ADA 35* [1] **28** 8
16 Feb 80 ●	**I CAN'T STAND UP FOR FALLING DOWN** *F. Beat XX 1* [1] **4** 8
12 Apr 80	**HIGH FIDELITY** *F. Beat XX 3* **30** 5
7 Jun 80	**NEW AMSTERDAM** *F. Beat XX 5* **36** 6
20 Dec 80	**CLUBLAND** *F. Beat XX 12* [1] **60** 4
3 Oct 81 ●	**A GOOD YEAR FOR THE ROSES** *F. Beat XX 17* [1] **6** 11
12 Dec 81	**SWEET DREAMS** *F. Beat XX 19* **42** 8
10 Apr 82	**I'M YOUR TOY** *F. Beat XX 21* [2] **51** 3
19 Jun 82	**YOU LITTLE FOOL** *F. Beat XX 26* **52** 3
31 Jul 82	**MAN OUT OF TIME** *F. Beat XX 28* **58** 2
25 Sep 82	**FROM HEAD TO TOE** *F. Beat XX 30* **43** 4

11 Dec 82	**PARTY PARTY** *A&M AMS 8267* [3] **48** 6
11 Jun 83	**PILLS AND SOAP** *Imp IMP 001* [4] **16** 4
9 Jul 83	**EVERYDAY I WRITE THE BOOK** *F. Beat XX 32* **28** 8
17 Sep 83	**LET THEM ALL TALK** *F. Beat XX 33* **59** 2
28 Apr 84	**PEACE IN OUR TIME** *Imposter TRUCE 1* [4] **48** 3
16 Jun 84	**I WANNA BE LOVED / TURNING THE TOWN RED** *F. Beat XX 35* **25** 6
25 Aug 84	**THE ONLY FLAME IN TOWN** *F. Beat XX 37* **71** 2
4 May 85	**GREEN SHIRT (re)** *F. Beat ZB 40085* **68** 2
1 Feb 86	**DON'T LET ME BE MISUNDERSTOOD** *F. Beat ZB 40555* [5] ...**33** 4
30 Aug 86	**TOKYO STORM WARNING** *Imp IMP 007* **73** 1
4 Mar 89	**VERONICA** *Warner Bros. W 7558* **31** 6
20 May 89	**BABY PLAYS AROUND (EP)** *Warner Bros. W 2949* ...**65** 1
4 May 91	**THE OTHER SIDE OF SUMMER** *Warner Bros. W 0025* **43** 4
5 Mar 94	**SULKY GIRL** *Warner Bros. W 0234CD* [1] **22** 3
30 Apr 94	**13 STEPS LEAD DOWN** *Warner Bros. W 0245CD* [1] **59** 1
26 Nov 94	**LONDON'S BRILLIANT PARADE** *Warner Bros. W 0270CD1* [1] 48 2
11 May 96	**IT'S TIME** *Warner Bros. W 0348CD* [1] **58** 1
1 May 99	**TOLEDO** *Mercury 8709652* [6] **72** 1
31 Jul 99	**SHE (re)** *Mercury MERCD 521* **19** 10
20 Apr 02	**TEAR OFF YOUR OWN HEAD (IT'S A DOLL REVOLUTION)** *Mercury 5828872* **58** 1
6 Aug 77	**MY AIM IS TRUE** *Stiff SEEZ 3* **14** 12
1 Apr 78 ●	**THIS YEAR'S MODEL** *Radar RAD 3* [1] **4** 14
20 Jan 79 ●	**ARMED FORCES** *Radar RAD 14* [1] **2** 28
23 Feb 80 ●	**GET HAPPY!!** *F-Beat XXLP 1* **2** 14
31 Jan 81 ●	**TRUST** *F-Beat XXLP 11* [1] **9** 7
31 Oct 81 ●	**ALMOST BLUE** *F-Beat XXLP 13* **7** 18
10 Jul 82 ●	**IMPERIAL BEDROOM** *F-Beat XXLP 17* [1] **6** 12
6 Aug 83 ●	**PUNCH THE CLOCK** *F-Beat XXLP 19* [1] **3** 13
7 Jul 84 ●	**GOODBYE CRUEL WORLD** *F-Beat ZL 70317* [1] **10** 10
20 Apr 85 ●	**THE BEST OF ELVIS COSTELLO – THE MAN** *Telstar STAR 2247* [1] **8** 25
1 Mar 86	**KING OF AMERICA** *F-Beat ZL 70496* [2] **11** 9
27 Sep 86	**BLOOD AND CHOCOLATE** *Imp XFIEND 80* **16** 5
18 Feb 89	**SPIKE** *Warner Bros. WX 238* **5** 16
28 Oct 89	**GIRLS GIRLS GIRLS** *Demon DFIEND 160* [1] **67** 1
25 May 91 ●	**MIGHTY LIKE A ROSE** *Warner Bros. WX 419* **5** 6
30 Jan 93	**THE JULIET LETTERS** *Warner Bros. 9362451802* [3] **18** 3
19 Mar 94	**BRUTAL YOUTH** *Warner Bros. 9362455352* [1] **2** 5
12 Nov 94	**THE VERY BEST OF ELVIS COSTELLO AND THE ATTRACTIONS** *Demon DPAM 13* [1] **57** 2
27 May 95	**KOJAK VARIETY** *Warner Bros. 9362459032* **21** 2
12 Aug 95	**KING OF AMERICA (re-issue)** *Demon DPAM 11* ...**71** 1
25 May 96	**ALL THIS USELESS BEAUTY** *Warner Bros. 9362461982* ...**28** 3
10 Oct 98	**PAINTED FROM MEMORY** *Mercury 5380022* [4] **32** 2
14 Aug 99 ●	**THE VERY BEST OF ELVIS COSTELLO** *Universal Music TV 5464902* **4** 13
31 Mar 01	**FOR THE STARS** *Deutsche Grammophon 4695302* [5] **67** 1
27 Apr 02	**WHEN I WAS CRUEL** *Mercury 5868292* **17** 4
27 Sep 03	**NORTH** *Deutsche Grammophon 9809656* **44** 1
2 Oct 04	**THE DELIVERY MAN** *Lost Highway 9863727* [6] **73** 1

[1] Elvis Costello and the Attractions [2] Elvis Costello and the Attractions with the
Royal Philharmonic Orchestra [3] Elvis Costello and the Attractions with the Royal
Horn Guards [4] Imposter [5] The Costello Show featuring the Confederates [6] Elvis
Costello / Burt Bacharach [1] Elvis Costello and the Attractions [2] Costello Show
[3] Elvis Costello and the Brodsky Quartet [4] Elvis Costello with Burt Bacharach
[5] Anne von Otter Meets Elvis Costello [6] Elvis Costello & the Imposters

Tracks on Baby Plays Around (EP): Baby Plays Around / Poisoned Rose / Almost
Blue / My Funny Valentine

COTTAGERS See Tony REES and the COTTAGERS

Billy COTTON and his BAND *UK, male bandleader / vocalist, b. 6 May
1899, d. 25 Mar 1969, with band and chorus (Singles: 25 Weeks)*   pos/wks

1 May 53 ●	**IN A GOLDEN COACH (THERE'S A HEART OF GOLD)** *Decca F 10058* [1] **3** 10
18 Dec 53	**I SAW MOMMY KISSING SANTA CLAUS** *Decca F 10206* [2] **11** 3
30 Apr 54 ●	**FRIENDS AND NEIGHBOURS (re)** *Decca F 10299* [3] **3** 12

[1] Billy Cotton and his Band, vocals by Doreen Stephens [2] Billy Cotton and his
Band, vocals by the Mill Girls and the Bandits [3] Billy Cotton and his Band, vocals
by the Bandits

Mike COTTON'S JAZZMEN *UK, male instrumental
band – Mike Cotton – trumpet (Singles: 4 Weeks)*   pos/wks

20 Jun 63	**SWING THAT HAMMER** *Columbia DB 7029* **36** 4

John COUGAR See John Cougar MELLENCAMP

The COUGARS
UK, male instrumental group (Singles: 8 Weeks)   pos/wks

| 28 Feb 63 | SATURDAY NITE AT THE DUCK-POND Parlophone R 4989 | 33 | 8 |

Phil COULTER Ireland, male orchestra leader / instrumentalist – piano (Albums: 15 Weeks)   pos/wks

| 13 Oct 84 | SEA OF TRANQUILITY K-Tel Ireland KLP 185 | 46 | 14 |
| 18 May 85 | PHIL COULTER'S IRELAND K-Tel ONE 1296 | 86 | 1 |

COUNCIL COLLECTIVE
UK / US, male / female vocal / instrumental group (Singles: 6 Weeks) pos/wks

| 22 Dec 84 | SOUL DEEP (PART 1) Polydor MINE 1 | 24 | 6 |

COUNT INDIGO
UK, male vocalist – Bruce Marcus (Singles: 1 Week)   pos/wks

| 9 Mar 96 | MY UNKNOWN LOVE Cowboy RODEO 952CD | 59 | 1 |

COUNTING CROWS US, male vocal / instrumental group (Singles: 29 Weeks, Albums: 64 Weeks)   pos/wks

30 Apr 94	MR JONES Geffen GFSTD 69	28	2
9 Jul 94	ROUND HERE Geffen GFSTD 74	70	1
15 Oct 94	RAIN KING Geffen GFSTD 82	49	3
19 Oct 96	ANGELS OF THE SILENCES Geffen GFSTD 22182	41	1
14 Dec 96	A LONG DECEMBER (re) Geffen GFSTD 22190	62	2
31 May 97	DAYLIGHT FADING Geffen GFSTD 22247	54	1
30 Oct 99	HANGINAROUND Geffen 4971842	46	1
29 Jun 02	AMERICAN GIRLS Geffen 4977402	33	2
15 Feb 03	BIG YELLOW TAXI Geffen 4978302 [1]	16	9
21 Jun 03	IF I COULD GIVE ALL MY LOVE Geffen GED 9806830	50	1
27 Mar 04	HANGINAROUND (re-recording) Geffen 9861994	68	1
24 Jul 04	ACCIDENTALLY IN LOVE Dreamworks 9862881	28	5
12 Mar 94	AUGUST AND EVERYTHING AFTER Geffen GED 24528	16	38
26 Oct 96 ●	RECOVERING THE SATELLITES Geffen GED 24975 ▲	4	4
25 Jul 98	ACROSS A WIRE – LIVE IN NEW YORK Geffen GED 25226	27	4
13 Nov 99	THIS DESERT LIFE Geffen 4904152	19	3
20 Jul 02 ●	HARD CANDY Geffen 4933662	9	11
7 Feb 04	FILMS ABOUT GHOSTS – THE BEST OF … Geffen / Polydor 9861505	15	5

[1] Counting Crows featuring Vanessa Carlton

The COUNTRYMEN UK, male vocal group (Singles: 2 Weeks)   pos/wks

| 3 May 62 | I KNOW WHERE I'M GOING Piccadilly 7N 35029 | 45 | 2 |

COURSE Holland, male / female vocal / DJ / production group (Singles: 15 Weeks)   pos/wks

19 Apr 97 ●	READY OR NOT The Brothers Organisation CDBRUV 2	5	7
5 Jul 97 ●	AIN'T NOBODY The Brothers Organisation CDBRUV 3	8	6
20 Dec 97	BEST LOVE The Brothers Organisation CDBRUV 6	51	2

Michael COURTNEY See LINCOLN CITY FC featuring Michael COURTNEY

Tina COUSINS
UK, female vocalist (Singles: 42 Weeks, Albums: 1 Week)   pos/wks

15 Aug 98 ●	MYSTERIOUS TIMES Multiply CDMULTY 40 [1]	2	12
21 Nov 98	PRAY Jive 0519162	20	3
27 Mar 99	KILLIN' TIME Jive / Eastern Bloc 0519232	15	4
10 Apr 99 ●	THANK ABBA FOR THE MUSIC ABCD 1 Epic [2]	4	13
10 Jul 99	FOREVER Jive 0519332	45	2
9 Oct 99	ANGEL Ebul / Jive 0519432	46	1
22 Apr 00 ●	JUST AROUND THE HILL Multiply CDMULTY 62 [1]	8	7
24 Jul 99	KILLING TIME Jive / Eastern Bloc 519342	50	1

[1] Sash! featuring Tina Cousins [2] Steps, Tina Cousins, Cleopatra, B*Witched, Billie

Don COVAY
US, male vocalist (Singles: 6 Weeks)   pos/wks

| 7 Sep 74 | IT'S BETTER TO HAVE (AND DON'T NEED) Mercury 6052 634 | 29 | 6 |

Vincent COVELLO See BT

COVENTRY CITY CUP FINAL SQUAD
UK, male football team vocalists (Singles: 2 Weeks)   pos/wks

| 23 May 87 | GO FOR IT! Sky Blue SKB 1 | 61 | 2 |

The COVER GIRLS
US, female vocal group (Singles: 4 Weeks)   pos/wks

| 1 Aug 92 | WISHING ON A STAR Epic 6581437 | 38 | 4 |

David COVERDALE (see also COVERDALE PAGE; DEEP PURPLE; WHITESNAKE) UK, male vocalist (Singles: 1 Week, Albums: 2 Weeks) pos/wks

7 Jun 97	TOO MANY TEARS EMI CDEM 471 [1]	46	1
27 Feb 82	NORTHWINDS Purple TTS 3513	78	1
7 Oct 00	INTO THE LIGHT EMI 5281242	75	1

[1] David Coverdale and Whitesnake

COVERDALE PAGE (see also David COVERDALE; Jimmy PAGE) UK, male vocal / instrumental duo – David Coverdale and Jimmy Page (Singles: 3 Weeks, Albums: 8 Weeks)   pos/wks

3 Jul 93	TAKE ME FOR A LITTLE WHILE EMI CDEM 270	29	2
23 Oct 93	TAKE A LOOK AT YOURSELF EMI CDEM 279	43	1
27 Mar 93 ●	COVERDALE PAGE EMI CDEMD 1041	4	8

Julie COVINGTON
UK, female actor / vocalist (Singles: 29 Weeks)   pos/wks

25 Dec 76 ★	DON'T CRY FOR ME ARGENTINA (re) MCA 260	1	18
3 Dec 77	ONLY WOMEN BLEED Virgin VS 196	12	11
21 May 77 ●	OK? Polydor 2001 714 [1]	10	6

[1] Julie Covington, Rula Lenska, Charlotte Cornwell and Sue Jones-Davies

Warren COVINGTON See Tommy DORSEY ORCHESTRA starring Warren COVINGTON

COWBOY See CONDUCTOR and the COWBOY

COWBOY JUNKIES
US, male / female vocal / instrumental group (Albums: 7 Weeks)   pos/wks

| 24 Mar 90 | THE CAUTION HORSES RCA PL 90450 | 33 | 4 |
| 15 Feb 92 | BLACK EYED MAN RCA PD 90620 | 21 | 3 |

Patrick COWLEY See SYLVESTER

Carl COX
UK, male producer (Singles: 19 Weeks, Albums: 4 Weeks)   pos/wks

28 Sep 91	I WANT YOU (FOREVER) Perfecto PB 44885 [1]	23	7
8 Aug 92	DOES IT FEEL GOOD TO YOU Perfecto PB 74321102877 [1]	35	3
6 Nov 93	THE PLANET OF LOVE Perfecto 74321161772	44	2
9 Mar 96	TWO PAINTINGS AND A DRUM (EP) Edel 0090715 COX	24	2
8 Jun 96	SENSUAL SOPHIS-TI-CAT / THE PLAYER Ultimatum 0090875 COX	25	2
12 Dec 98	THE LATIN THEME Edel 0091685 COX	52	1
22 May 99	PHUTURE 2000 Worldwide Ultimatum / Edel 0091715 COX	40	2
15 Jun 96	AT THE END OF THE CLICHÉ Ultimatum 0090752 COX	23	4

[1] DJ Carl Cox

Tracks on Two Paintings and a Drum (EP): Phoebus Apollo / Yum Yum / Siberian Snow Storm

Deborah COX Canada, female vocalist (Singles: 8 Weeks)   pos/wks

11 Nov 95	SENTIMENTAL Arista 74321324962	34	3
24 Feb 96	WHO DO U LOVE Arista 74321337942	31	3
31 Jul 99	IT'S OVER NOW Arista 74321686942	49	1
9 Oct 99	NOBODY'S SUPPOSED TO BE HERE Arista 74321702102	55	1

Michael COX UK, male vocalist (Singles: 15 Weeks)   pos/wks

| 9 Jun 60 ● | ANGELA JONES Triumph RGM 1011 | 7 | 13 |
| 20 Oct 60 | ALONG CAME CAROLINE HMV POP 789 | 41 | 2 |

Peter COX (see also GO WEST)
UK, male vocalist (Singles: 6 Weeks, Albums: 1 Week)   pos/wks

2 Aug 97	AIN'T GONNA CRY AGAIN Chrysalis CDCHS 5056	37	2
15 Nov 97	IF YOU WALK AWAY Chrysalis CDCHS 5069	24	2
20 Jun 98	WHAT A FOOL BELIEVES Chrysalis CDCHS 5089	39	2
29 Nov 97	PETER COX Chrysalis CDCHR 6130	64	1

Graham COXON (see also BLUR) UK, male vocalist / instrumentalist – guitar (Singles: 9 Weeks, Albums: 5 Weeks)

		pos/wks
20 Mar 04	FREAKIN' OUT Transcopic R 6632	37 1
15 May 04	BITTERSWEET BUNDLE OF MISERY Transcopic CDRS 6637	22 3
7 Aug 04	SPECTACULAR Transcopic CDRS 6643	32 2
6 Nov 04	FREAKIN' OUT (re-issue) / ALL OVER ME Transcopic CDRS 6652	19 3
22 Aug 98	THE SKY IS TOO HIGH Transcopic TRAN 005CD	31 2
29 May 04	HAPPINESS IN MAGAZINES Transcopic / Parlophone 5775192	19 3

CRACKER US, male vocal / instrumental group (Singles: 9 Weeks, Albums: 2 Weeks)

		pos/wks
28 May 94	LOW (re) Virgin America VUSDG 80	43 6
23 Jul 94	GET OFF THIS Virgin America VUSCD 83	41 3
25 Jun 94	KEROSENE HAT Virgin America CDVUS 67	44 2

Sarah CRACKNELL (see also SAINT ETIENNE) UK, female vocalist (Singles: 1 Week)

		pos/wks
14 Sep 96	ANYMORE Gut CDGUT 3	39 1

CRACKOUT UK, male vocal / instrumental group (Singles: 3 Weeks)

		pos/wks
22 Jun 02	I AM THE ONE Hut / Virgin HUTCD 156	72 1
9 Aug 03	OUT OF OUR MINDS Hut / Virgin HUTCD 170	63 1
13 Mar 04	THIS IS WHAT WE DO Hut / Virgin HUTCD 174	65 1

CRADLE OF FILTH UK, male vocal / instrumental group (Singles: 2 Weeks, Albums: 4 Weeks)

		pos/wks
15 Mar 03	BABALON A.D. (SO GLAD FOR THE MADNESS) Epic 6735549	35 2
16 May 98	CRUELTY AND THE BEAST Music For Nations CDMFN 242	48 1
11 Nov 00	MIDIAN Music For Nations CDMFN 666	63 1
30 Jun 01	BITTER SUITES TO SUCCUBI Snapper Music COF 001CD	63 1
22 Mar 03	DAMNATION AND A DAY Epic 5109632	44 1

'Babalon A.D. (So Glad for the Madness)' was the first DVD-only single to reach the Top 40

STEVE CRADOCK See OCEAN COLOUR SCENE; BUFFALO TOM

CRAIG UK, male vocalist – Craig Phillips (Singles: 6 Weeks)

		pos/wks
23 Dec 00	AT THIS TIME OF YEAR (re) WEA WEA 321CD	14 6

Robbie CRAIG See ARTFUL DODGER

Floyd CRAMER US, male instrumentalist – piano, b. 27 Oct 1933, d. 31 Dec 1997 (Singles: 24 Weeks)

		pos/wks
13 Apr 61	★ ON THE REBOUND RCA 1231	1 14
20 Jul 61	SAN ANTONIO ROSE RCA 1241	36 8
23 Aug 62	HOT PEPPER RCA 1301	46 2

The CRAMPS US, male / female vocal / instrumental group (Singles: 4 Weeks, Albums: 13 Weeks)

		pos/wks
9 Nov 85	CAN YOUR PUSSY DO THE DOG? Big Beat NS 110	68 1
10 Feb 90	BIKINI GIRLS WITH MACHINE GUNS Enigma ENV 17	35 3
25 Jun 83	OFF THE BONE Illegal ILP 012	44 4
26 Nov 83	SMELL OF FEMALE Big Beat NED 6	74 2
1 Mar 86	A DATE WITH ELVIS Big Beat WIKA 46	34 6
24 Feb 90	STAY SICK! Enigma ENVLP 1001	62 1

The CRANBERRIES 267 Top 500 Irish rock quartet with a feverish international following, formed County Limerick, 1991, fronted by Dolores O'Riordan (v). The group, who have sold over 40 million albums worldwide, spent longer on the UK chart in 1995 (96 weeks) than any other act (Singles: 50 Weeks, Albums: 193 Weeks)

		pos/wks
27 Feb 93	LINGER Island CID 556	74 1
12 Feb 94	LINGER (re-issue) Island CID 559	14 11
7 May 94	DREAMS Island CIDX 594	27 5
1 Oct 94	ZOMBIE Island CID 600	14 6
3 Dec 94	ODE TO MY FAMILY Island CIDX 601	26 6
11 Mar 95	I CAN'T BE WITH YOU Island CID 605	23 4
12 Aug 95	RIDICULOUS THOUGHTS Island CID 616	20 3
20 Apr 96	SALVATION Island CID 633	13 5
13 Jul 96	FREE TO DECIDE Island CID 637	33 3
17 Apr 99	PROMISES Island US / Mercury 5725912	13 4
17 Jul 99	ANIMAL INSTINCT Island US / Mercury 5621972	54 1

		pos/wks
13 Mar 93	★ EVERYBODY ELSE IS DOING IT SO WHY CAN'T WE? Island CID 8003	1 86
15 Oct 94	● NO NEED TO ARGUE Island CID 8029	2 78
11 May 96	● TO THE FAITHFUL DEPARTED Island CID 8048	2 19
1 May 99	● BURY THE HATCHET Island US / Mercury 5246442	7 5
3 Nov 01	WAKE UP AND SMELL THE COFFEE MCA 1127062	61 1
28 Sep 02	STARS – THE BEST OF 1992-2002 Universal TV 0633862	20 4

Les CRANE US, male vocalist (Singles: 14 Weeks)

		pos/wks
19 Feb 72	● DESIDERATA Warner Bros. K 16119	7 14

Whitfield CRANE See ICE-T; MOTORHEAD

The CRANES UK, male / female vocal / instrumental group (Singles: 2 Weeks, Albums: 2 Weeks)

		pos/wks
25 Sep 93	JEWEL Dedicated CRANE 007CD	29 1
3 Sep 94	SHINING ROAD Dedicated CRANE 008CD1	57 1
28 Sep 91	WINGS OF JOY Dedicated DEDLP 003	52 1
8 May 93	FOREVER Dedicated DEDCD 009	40 1

CRASH TEST DUMMIES Canada, male / female vocal / instrumental group (Singles: 20 Weeks, Albums: 23 Weeks)

		pos/wks
23 Apr 94	● MMM MMM MMM MMM RCA 74321201512	2 11
16 Jul 94	AFTERNOONS & COFFEESPOONS RCA 74321219622	23 5
15 Apr 95	THE BALLAD OF PETER PUMPKINHEAD RCA 74321276772 [1]	30 4
14 May 94	● GOD SHUFFLED HIS FEET RCA 74321201522	2 23

[1] Crash Test Dummies featuring Ellen Reid

CRASS UK, male vocal / instrumental group (Albums: 2 Weeks)

		pos/wks
28 Aug 82	CHRIST THE ALBUM Crass BOLLOX 2U2	26 2

Beverley CRAVEN UK, female vocalist / instrumentalist – keyboards (Singles: 33 Weeks, Albums: 67 Weeks)

		pos/wks
20 Apr 91	● PROMISE ME Epic 6559437	3 13
20 Jul 91	HOLDING ON Epic 6565507	32 7
5 Oct 91	WOMAN TO WOMAN Epic 6574647	40 5
7 Dec 91	MEMORIES Epic 6576617	68 2
25 Sep 93	LOVE SCENES Epic 6595952	34 4
20 Nov 93	MOLLIE'S SONG Epic 6598132	61 2
2 Mar 91	● BEVERLEY CRAVEN Columbia 4670531	3 52
9 Oct 93	● LOVE SCENES Epic 4745172	4 13
12 Jun 99	MIXED EMOTIONS Epic 4941502	46 2

Billy CRAWFORD US, male vocalist (Singles: 5 Weeks)

		pos/wks
10 Oct 98	URGENTLY IN LOVE V2 VVR 5003063	48 2
3 May 03	YOU DIDN'T EXPECT THAT V2 VVR 5022083	35 2
30 Aug 03	TRACKIN' V2 VVR 5021753	55 1

Jimmy CRAWFORD
UK, male vocalist – Ronald Lindsey (Singles: 11 Weeks)

		pos/wks
8 Jun 61	LOVE OR MONEY Columbia DB 4633	49 1
16 Nov 61	I LOVE HOW YOU LOVE ME Columbia DB 4717	18 10

Michael CRAWFORD UK, male actor / vocalist – Michael Dumble-Smith (Singles: 14 Weeks, Albums: 76 Weeks)

		pos/wks
10 Jan 87	● THE MUSIC OF THE NIGHT Polydor POSP 803 [1]	7 11
15 Jan 94	THE MUSIC OF THE NIGHT Columbia 6597382 [2]	54 3
28 Nov 87	SONGS FROM THE STAGE AND SCREEN Telstar STAR 2308 [1]	12 13
2 Dec 89	WITH LOVE Telstar STAR 2340	31 7
9 Nov 91	● MICHAEL CRAWFORD PERFORMS ANDREW LLOYD WEBBER Telstar STAR 2544	3 36
13 Nov 93	A TOUCH OF MUSIC IN THE NIGHT Telstar TCD 2676	12 11
19 Nov 94	THE LOVE SONGS ALBUM Telstar STAR 2748	64 3
21 Nov 98	ON EAGLE'S WINGS Atlantic 7567830762	65 2
25 Dec 99	THE MOST WONDERFUL TIME OF THE YEAR Telstar TV TTVCD 3111	69 1
4 Dec 04	THE VERY BEST OF MICHAEL CRAWFORD Virgin / EMI VTCD 685	54 3

[1] Michael Crawford with the Royal Philharmonic Orchestra, conducted by David Caddick [2] Barbra Streisand (duet with Michael Crawford) [1] Michael Crawford with the London Symphony Orchestra

The flip side of POSP 803 – 'Wishing You Were Somehow Here Again' by Sarah Brightman – was also listed

Singles re-entries are listed as (re), (2re), (3re).... which signifies that the hit re-entered the chart once, twice or three times...

Randy CRAWFORD (282) Top 500 (see also The CRUSADERS)

Soulful jazz-slanted song stylist – Veronica Crawford, b. 18 Feb 1952, Georgia, US. Has surprisingly proved more successful in Europe than her homeland, where she has yet to crack the pop Top 100. Winner of Brits Best Female Artist award in 1982 (Singles: 75 Weeks, Albums: 155 Weeks)   pos/wks

		pos	wks
21 Jun 80	LAST NIGHT AT DANCELAND *Warner Bros. K 17631*	61	2
30 Aug 80 ●	ONE DAY I'LL FLY AWAY *Warner Bros. K 17680*	2	11
30 May 81	YOU MIGHT NEED SOMEBODY *Warner Bros. K 17803*	11	13
8 Aug 81	RAINY NIGHT IN GEORGIA *Warner Bros. K 17840*	18	9
31 Oct 81	SECRET COMBINATION *Warner Bros. K 17872*	48	3
30 Jan 82	IMAGINE (re) *Warner Bros. K 17906*	60	2
5 Jun 82	ONE HELLO *Warner Bros. K 17948*	48	4
19 Feb 83	HE REMINDS ME *Warner Bros. K 17970*	65	2
8 Oct 83	NIGHT LINE *Warner Bros. W 9530*	51	4
29 Nov 86 ●	ALMAZ *Warner Bros. W 8583*	4	17
18 Jan 92	DIAMANTE *London LON 313* [1]	44	2
15 Nov 97	GIVE ME THE NIGHT *WEA WEA 142CD*	60	1
28 Jun 80 ●	NOW WE MAY BEGIN *Warner Bros. K 56791*	10	16
16 May 81 ●	SECRET COMBINATION *Warner Bros. K 56904*	2	60
12 Jun 82 ●	WINDSONG *Warner Bros. K 57011*	7	17
22 Oct 83	NIGHTLINE *Warner Bros. K 57212*	37	4
13 Oct 84 ●	MISS RANDY CRAWFORD – THE GREATEST HITS *K-Tel NE 1281*	10	17
28 Jun 86	ABSTRACT EMOTIONS *Warner Bros. WX 46*	14	10
10 Oct 87	THE LOVE SONGS *Telstar STAR 2299*	27	13
21 Oct 89	RICH AND POOR *Warner Bros. WX 308*	63	1
27 Mar 93 ●	THE VERY BEST OF RANDY CRAWFORD *Dino DINCD 58*	8	13
12 Feb 00	LOVE SONGS – THE VERY BEST OF RANDY CRAWFORD *Warner.esp WMMCD 002*	22	4

[1] Zucchero with Randy Crawford

Robert CRAY BAND *US, male vocal / instrumental group (Singles: 5 Weeks, Albums: 53 Weeks)*   pos/wks

		pos	wks
20 Jun 87	RIGHT NEXT DOOR (BECAUSE OF ME) *Mercury CRAY 3*	50	4
20 Apr 96	BABY LEE *Silvertone ORECD 81* [1]	65	1
12 Oct 85	FALSE ACCUSATIONS *Demon FIEND 43*	68	1
15 Nov 86	STRONG PERSUADER *Mercury MERH 97*	34	28
3 Sep 88	DON'T BE AFRAID OF THE DARK *Mercury MERH 129*	13	12
22 Sep 90	MIDNIGHT STROLL *Mercury 8466521*	19	7
12 Sep 92	I WAS WARNED *Mercury 5127212*	29	3
16 Oct 93	SHAME AND SIN *Mercury 5185172*	48	1
20 May 95	SOME RAINY MORNING *Mercury 5269282* [1]	63	1

[1] John Lee Hooker with Robert Cray [1] Robert Cray

CRAZY ELEPHANT *US, male vocal group (Singles: 13 Weeks)*   pos/wks

		pos	wks
21 May 69	GIMME GIMME GOOD LOVIN' *Major Minor MM 609*	12	13

CRAZY HORSE See Neil YOUNG

CRAZY TOWN (see also SHIFTY) *US, male vocal / rap / instrumental group (Singles: 19 Weeks, Albums: 9 Weeks)*   pos/wks

		pos	wks
7 Apr 01 ●	BUTTERFLY *Columbia 6710012*	3	13
11 Aug 01	REVOLVING DOOR *Columbia 6714942*	23	5
30 Nov 02	DROWNING *Columbia 6733262*	50	1
21 Apr 01	THE GIFT OF GAME *Columbia 4952972*	15	9

CRAZYHEAD
UK, male vocal / instrumental group (Singles: 4 Weeks)   pos/wks

		pos	wks
16 Jul 88	TIME HAS TAKEN ITS TOLL ON YOU *Food FOOD 12*	65	2
25 Feb 89	HAVE LOVE, WILL TRAVEL (EP) *Food SGE 2025*	68	2

Tracks on Have Love, Will Travel (EP): Have Love, Will Travel / Out on a Limb (Live) / Baby Turpentine (Live) / Snake Eyes (Live)

CREAM (154) Top 500 *The first real 'supergroup' performed 1966-1968; Eric Clapton (g/v), Jack Bruce (b/v), Ginger Baker (d). Loud innovative blues-based trio, who introduced long solos to popular music, were prototype for 1970s progressive rock bands. Inducted into Rock and Roll Hall of Fame 1993 (Singles: 59 Weeks, Albums: 290 Weeks)*   pos/wks

		pos	wks
20 Oct 66	WRAPPING PAPER *Reaction 591 007*	34	6
15 Dec 66	I FEEL FREE *Reaction 591 011*	11	12
8 Jun 67	STRANGE BREW *Reaction 591 015*	17	9
5 Jun 68	ANYONE FOR TENNIS (THE SAVAGE SEVEN THEME) *Polydor 56 258*	40	3
9 Oct 68	SUNSHINE OF YOUR LOVE *Polydor 56 286*	25	7
15 Jan 69	WHITE ROOM *Polydor 56 300*	28	8
9 Apr 69	BADGE *Polydor 56 315*	18	10
28 Oct 72	BADGE (re-issue) *Polydor 2058 285*	42	4
24 Dec 66 ●	FRESH CREAM *Reaction 593001*	6	16
18 Nov 67 ●	DISRAELI GEARS *Reaction 594003*	5	42
17 Aug 68 ●	WHEELS OF FIRE (DOUBLE) *Polydor 583-031/2* ▲	3	26
17 Aug 68 ●	WHEELS OF FIRE (SINGLE) *Polydor 583033*	7	13
8 Feb 69 ●	FRESH CREAM (re-issue) *Reaction 594001*	7	2
8 Mar 69 ★	GOODBYE *Polydor 583053* ■	1	28
8 Nov 69 ●	THE BEST OF CREAM *Polydor 583060*	6	34
4 Jul 70 ●	LIVE CREAM *Polydor 2383016*	4	15
24 Jun 72	LIVE CREAM VOLUME 2 *Polydor 2383 119*	15	5
26 Sep 87 ●	THE CREAM OF ERIC CLAPTON *Polydor ECTV* [1]	3	109

[1] Eric Clapton and Cream

From 9 Jul 93 'The Cream of Eric Clapton' was repackaged and was available as 'The Best of Eric Clapton'

CREATION *UK, male vocal / instrumental group (Singles: 3 Weeks)*   pos/wks

		pos	wks
7 Jul 66	MAKING TIME *Planet PLF 116*	49	1
3 Nov 66	PAINTER MAN *Planet PLF 119*	36	2

The CREATURES (see also SIOUXSIE and the BANSHEES) *UK, male / female vocal / instrumental group (Singles: 28 Weeks, Albums: 9 Weeks)*   pos/wks

		pos	wks
3 Oct 81	MAD EYED SCREAMER *Polydor POSPD 354*	24	7
23 Apr 83	MISS THE GIRL *Wonderland SHE 1*	21	7
16 Jul 83	RIGHT NOW *Wonderland SHE 2*	14	10
14 Oct 89	STANDING THERE *Wonderland SHE 17*	53	2
27 Mar 99	SAY *Sioux SIOUX 6CD*	72	1
25 Oct 03	GODZILLA *Sioux SIOUX 14CD1*	53	1
28 May 83	FEAST *Wonderland SHELP 1*	17	9

CREDIT TO THE NATION
UK, male rap group (Singles: 11 Weeks, Albums: 3 Weeks)   pos/wks

		pos	wks
22 May 93	CALL IT WHAT YOU WANT *One Little Indian 94TP 7CD*	57	3
18 Sep 93	ENOUGH IS ENOUGH *One Little Indian 79TP 7CD* [1]	56	2
12 Mar 94	TEENAGE SENSATION *One Little Indian 124TP 7CD*	24	3
14 May 94	SOWING THE SEEDS OF HATRED *One Little Indian 134TP 7CD*	72	1
22 Jul 95	LIAR LIAR *One Little Indian 144TP 7CD*	60	1
12 Sep 98	TACKY LOVE SONG *Chrysalis CDCHS 5097*	60	1
9 Apr 94	TAKE DIS *One Little Indian TPLP 44CDH*	20	3

[1] Chumbawamba and Credit to the Nation

CREED *US, male vocal / instrumental group (Singles: 13 Weeks, Albums: 21 Weeks)*   pos/wks

		pos	wks
15 Jan 00	HIGHER *Epic 6683152*	47	1
20 Jan 01	WITH ARMS WIDE OPEN *Epic 6706952* ▲	13	5
29 Sep 01	HIGHER (re-issue) *Epic 6710642*	64	1
16 Mar 02	MY SACRIFICE *Epic 6723162*	18	5
3 Aug 02	ONE LAST BREATH / BULLETS *Epic 6728262*	47	1
3 Feb 01	HUMAN CLAY *Epic 4950276* ▲	29	4
1 Dec 01	WEATHERED *Epic 5049792* ▲	44	17

CREEDENCE CLEARWATER REVIVAL (441) Top 500

Internationally successful combo which cleverly created original songs with 50s rock 'n' roll feel, fronted by John Fogerty, b. 28 May 1945, California, US. Voted World's Top Group in UK Polls 1970/71 (beating The Beatles and The Rolling Stones) (Singles: 94 Weeks, Albums: 65 Weeks)   pos/wks

		pos	wks
28 May 69 ●	PROUD MARY *Liberty LBF 15223*	8	13
16 Aug 69 ★	BAD MOON RISING *Liberty LBF 15230*	1	15
15 Nov 69	GREEN RIVER *Liberty LBF 15250*	19	11
14 Feb 70	DOWN ON THE CORNER *Liberty LBF 15283*	31	6
4 Apr 70 ●	TRAVELLIN' BAND (re) *Liberty LBF 15310*	8	13
20 Jun 70	UP AROUND THE BEND *Liberty LBF 15354*	3	12
5 Sep 70	LONG AS I CAN SEE THE LIGHT *Liberty LBF 15384*	20	9
20 Mar 71	HAVE YOU EVER SEEN THE RAIN *Liberty LBF 15440*	36	6
24 Jul 71	SWEET HITCH-HIKER *United Artists UP 35261*	36	8
2 May 92	BAD MOON RISING (re-issue) *Epic 6580047*	71	1
24 Jan 70	GREEN RIVER *Liberty LBS 83273* ▲	20	6
28 Mar 70 ●	WILLY AND THE POOR BOYS *Liberty LBS 83338*	10	24
2 May 70	BAYOU COUNTRY *Liberty LBS 83261*	62	1
12 Sep 70 ●	COSMO'S FACTORY *Liberty LBS 83388* ■ ▲	1	15
23 Jan 71	PENDULUM *Liberty LBG 83400*	8	12
30 Jun 79	GREATEST HITS *Fantasy FT 558*	35	5
19 Oct 85	THE CREEDENCE COLLECTION *Impression IMDP 3*	68	2

Kid CREOLE and the COCONUTS US, male vocalist and
female vocal group (Singles: 58 Weeks, Albums: 54 Weeks)   pos/wks

13 Jun 81	ME NO POP I Ze WIP 6711 [1]	32	7
15 May 82 ●	I'M A WONDERFUL THING, BABY Ze WIP 6756	4	11
24 Jul 82 ●	STOOL PIGEON Ze WIP 6793	7	9
9 Oct 82 ●	ANNIE I'M NOT YOUR DADDY Ze WIP 6801	2	8
11 Dec 82	DEAR ADDY Ze WIP 6840	29	7
10 Sep 83	THERE'S SOMETHING WRONG IN PARADISE Island IS 130	35	5
19 Nov 83	THE LIFEBOAT PARTY Island IS 142	49	4
14 Apr 90	THE SEX OF IT CBS 655698 7	29	5
10 Apr 93	I'M A WONDERFUL THING BABY (re-mix) Island CID 551	60	2
22 May 82 ●	TROPICAL GANGSTERS Ze ILPS 7016	3	40
26 Jun 82	FRESH FRUIT IN FOREIGN PLACES Ze ILPS 7014	99	1
17 Sep 83	DOPPELGANGER Island ILPS 9743	21	6
15 Sep 84	CRE-OLE (THE BEST OF KID CREOLE AND THE COCONUTS) Island IMA 13	21	7

[1] Kid Creole and the Coconuts present Coati Mundi

CRESCENDO UK / US, male / female vocal / instrumental
duo – Serena and Steve Hitchcock (Singles: 5 Weeks)   pos/wks

23 Dec 95	ARE YOU OUT THERE ffrr FCD 270	20	5

The CRESCENT
UK, male vocal / instrumental group (Singles: 3 Weeks)   pos/wks

18 May 02	ON THE RUN Hut / Virgin HUTCD 153	49	1
27 Jul 02	TEST OF TIME Hut / Virgin HUTCD 157	60	1
28 Sep 02	SPINNIN' WHEELS Hut / Virgin HUTCD 160	61	1

CRESTERS See Mike SAGAR and the CRESTERS

The CREW CUTS Canada, male vocal group (Singles: 29 Weeks)   pos/wks

1 Oct 54	SH-BOOM Mercury MB 3140 ▲	12	9
15 Apr 55 ●	EARTH ANGEL Mercury MB 3202	4	20

Bernard CRIBBINS (see also Howard BLAKE conducting the
SINFONIA OF LONDON) UK, male actor / vocalist (Singles: 29 Weeks) pos/wks

15 Feb 62 ●	HOLE IN THE GROUND Parlophone R 4869	9	13
5 Jul 62 ●	RIGHT, SAID FRED Parlophone R 4923	10	10
13 Dec 62	GOSSIP CALYPSO Parlophone R 4961	25	6

The CRIBS UK, male vocal / instrumental trio (Singles: 2 Weeks) pos/wks

6 Mar 04	YOU WERE ALWAYS THE ONE Wichita Recordings WEBB 059SCD	66	1
29 May 04	WHAT ABOUT ME Wichita Recordings WEBB 061SCD	75	1

The CRICKETS (426) Top 500
Band that originally featured Buddy Holly formed in Lubbock, Texas, US, best
known members being Jerry Allison (d), Joe B Mauldin (b) and Sonny Curtis
(g/v). Without Holly they recorded original versions of Top 10 hits 'I Fought the
Law', 'Someone Someone', 'When You Ask About Love' and 'More Than I Can
Say' (Singles: 97 Weeks, Albums: 67 Weeks)   pos/wks

27 Sep 57 ★	THAT'LL BE THE DAY (re) Vogue Coral Q 72279 ▲	1	15
27 Dec 57 ●	OH BOY Coral Q 72298	3	15
14 Mar 58 ●	MAYBE BABY Coral Q 72307	4	10
25 Jul 58	THINK IT OVER Coral Q 72329	11	7
24 Apr 59	LOVE'S MADE A FOOL OF YOU (re) Coral Q 72365	26	2
15 Jan 60	WHEN YOU ASK ABOUT LOVE Coral Q 72382	27	1
12 May 60	MORE THAN I CAN SAY Coral Q 72395	42	1
26 May 60	BABY MY HEART Coral Q 72395	33	4
21 Jun 62 ●	DON'T EVER CHANGE Liberty LIB 55441	5	13
24 Jan 63	MY LITTLE GIRL Liberty LIB 10067	17	9
6 Jun 63	DON'T TRY TO CHANGE ME Liberty LIB 10092	37	4
14 May 64	YOU'VE GOT LOVE Liberty LIB 72472	40	6
2 Jul 64	(THEY CALL HER) LA BAMBA Liberty LIB 55696	21	10
19 Apr 58	THE "CHIRPING" CRICKETS Coral LVA 9081	5	1
25 Mar 61	IN STYLE WITH THE CRICKETS Coral LVA 9142	13	7
27 Oct 62 ●	BOBBY VEE MEETS THE CRICKETS Liberty LBY 1086 [1]	2	27
11 Mar 78 ★	20 GOLDEN GREATS MCA EMTV 8 [2]	1	20
20 Feb 93 ★	WORDS OF LOVE PolyGram TV 5144872 [2]	1	9
28 Aug 99	THE VERY BEST OF BUDDY HOLLY AND THE CRICKETS Universal Music TV 1120462 [2]	25	3

[1] Buddy Holly and The Crickets [1] Bobby Vee and The Crickets [2] Buddy Holly
and The Crickets

Although not credited on the records, Buddy Holly was featured on the first four hits

CRIMINAL ELEMENT ORCHESTRA See Wally JUMP Jr and the CRIMINAL ELEMENT

CRISPY AND COMPANY
US, male vocal / instrumental group (Singles: 11 Weeks)   pos/wks

16 Aug 75	BRAZIL Creole CR 109	26	5
27 Dec 75	GET IT TOGETHER Creole CR 114 [1]	21	6

[1] Crispy & Co

The CRITTERS
US, male vocal / instrumental group (Singles: 5 Weeks)   pos/wks

30 Jun 66	YOUNGER GIRL London HL 10047	38	5

Tony CROMBIE and his ROCKETS
UK, male vocal / instrumental group – Tony Crombie –
drums, b. 27 Aug 1925, d. 18 Oct 1999 (Singles: 2 Weeks)   pos/wks

19 Oct 56	TEACH YOU TO ROCK / SHORT'NIN' BREAD Columbia DB 3822	25	2

CROOKLYN CLAN See FATMAN SCOOP featuring the CROOKLYN CLAN

Bing CROSBY US, male vocalist – Harry
Lillis Crosby (Singles: 97 Weeks, Albums: 45 Weeks)   pos/wks

14 Nov 52 ●	THE ISLE OF INNISFREE Brunswick 04900	3	12
5 Dec 52 ●	ZING A LITTLE ZONG Brunswick 04981 [1]	10	2
19 Dec 52 ●	SILENT NIGHT, HOLY NIGHT Brunswick 03929	8	2
19 Mar 54 ●	CHANGING PARTNERS (2re) Brunswick 05244	9	3
7 Jan 55	COUNT YOUR BLESSINGS INSTEAD OF SHEEP (re) Brunswick 05339	11	3
29 Apr 55	STRANGER IN PARADISE Brunswick 05410	17	2
27 Apr 56	IN A LITTLE SPANISH TOWN Brunswick 05543	22	3
23 Nov 56 ●	TRUE LOVE Capitol CL 14645 [2]	4	27
24 May 57 ●	AROUND THE WORLD Brunswick 05674	5	15
9 Aug 75	THAT'S WHAT LIFE IS ALL ABOUT United Artists UP 35852	41	4
3 Dec 77 ●	WHITE CHRISTMAS MCA 111 ▲	5	7
27 Nov 82 ●	PEACE ON EARTH – LITTLE DRUMMER BOY RCA BOW 12 [3]	3	8
17 Dec 83	TRUE LOVE (re-issue) Capitol CL 315 [2]	70	3
21 Dec 85	WHITE CHRISTMAS (re-issue) MCA BING 1	69	2
19 Dec 98	WHITE CHRISTMAS (2nd re-issue) MCA MCSRD 48105	29	4
8 Oct 60 ●	JOIN BING AND SING ALONG Warner Bros. WM 4021	7	11
21 Dec 74	WHITE CHRISTMAS MCA MCF 2568	45	3
20 Sep 75	THAT'S WHAT LIFE IS ALL ABOUT United Artists UAG 2973	28	6
5 Nov 77	THE BEST OF BING MCA MCF 2540	41	7
5 Nov 77 ●	LIVE AT THE LONDON PALLADIUM K-Tel NE 951	9	2
17 Dec 77	SEASONS Polydor 2442 151	25	7
5 May 79	SONGS OF A LIFETIME Philips 6641 923	29	3
14 Dec 91	CHRISTMAS WITH BING CROSBY Telstar STAR 2468	66	3
23 Nov 96	THE BEST OF BING CROSBY MCA MCD 11561	59	3

[1] Bing Crosby and Jane Wyman [2] Bing Crosby and Grace Kelly [3] David Bowie
and Bing Crosby

David CROSBY (see also CROSBY, STILLS, NASH and YOUNG) US, male
vocalist / instrumentalist (Singles: 3 Weeks, Albums: 12 Weeks)   pos/wks

15 May 93	HERO Atlantic A 7360 [1]	56	3
24 Apr 71	IF I COULD ONLY REMEMBER MY NAME Atlantic 2401005	12	7
13 May 72	GRAHAM NASH DAVID CROSBY Atlantic K 50011 [1]	13	5

[1] David Crosby featuring Phil Collins [1] Graham Nash David Crosby

CROSBY, STILLS, NASH and YOUNG (see also Stephen STILLS;
Graham NASH; Neil YOUNG; David CROSBY) US / UK / Canada, male
vocal / instrumental group (Singles: 12 Weeks, Albums: 93 Weeks)   pos/wks

16 Aug 69	MARRAKESH EXPRESS Atlantic 584 283 [1]	17	9
21 Jan 89	AMERICAN DREAM Atlantic A 9003	55	3
23 Aug 69	CROSBY, STILLS & NASH Atlantic 588189 [1]	25	5
30 May 70 ●	DEJA VU Atlantic 2401001 [2]	5	60
22 May 71	4 WAY STREET Atlantic 2956 004 ▲	5	12
21 May 74	SO FAR Atlantic K 50023 ▲	25	6
9 Jul 77	CSN Atlantic K 50369 [1]	23	9
6 Nov 99	LOOKING FORWARD Reprise 9362474362	54	1

[1] Crosby, Stills and Nash [1] Crosby, Stills & Nash [2] Crosby, Stills, Nash & Young.
Dallas Taylor & Greg Reeves

CROSS UK / US, male vocal / instrumental
group (Singles: 1 Week, Albums: 2 Weeks)   pos/wks

17 Oct 87	COWBOYS AND INDIANS Virgin VS 1007	74	1
6 Feb 88 ●	SHOVE IT Virgin V 2477	58	2

Christopher CROSS *US, male vocalist –*
Christopher Geppert (Singles: 27 Weeks, Albums: 93 Weeks)   pos/wks

19 Apr 80	RIDE LIKE THE WIND *Warner Bros. K 17582* **69** 1
14 Feb 81	SAILING *Warner Bros. K 17695* ▲ **48** 6
17 Oct 81	● ARTHUR'S THEME (BEST THAT YOU CAN DO) (re) *Warner Bros. K 17847* ▲ **7** 15
5 Feb 83	ALL RIGHT *Warner Bros. W 9843* **51** 5
21 Feb 81	CHRISTOPHER CROSS *Warner Bros. K 56789*...............**14** 77
19 Feb 83	● ANOTHER PAGE *Warner Bros. W 3757* **4** 16

It was not until 'Arthur's Theme' re-entered in Jan 1982 that it reached the peak position of No.7

CROW *Germany, male production duo –*
David Rzenno and David Nothroff (Singles: 1 Week)   pos/wks

19 May 01	WHAT YA LOOKIN' AT *Tidy Trax TIDY 153CD* **60** 1

Sheryl CROW (226 Top 500) *Multi-Grammy-winning pop singer / songwriter / instrumentalist – guitar, b. 11 Feb 1962, Missouri, US. The one-time backing singer for Michael Jackson and George Harrison became the first US female soloist to score six UK hits off a debut LP (1993's Tuesday Night Music Club) (Singles: 90 Weeks, Albums: 181 Weeks)*   pos/wks

18 Jun 94	LEAVING LAS VEGAS *A&M 5806472* **66** 1
5 Nov 94	● ALL I WANNA DO *A&M 5808452* **4** 13
11 Feb 95	STRONG ENOUGH *A&M 5809212* **33** 4
27 May 95	CAN'T CRY ANYMORE *A&M 5810552* **33** 3
29 Jul 95	RUN BABY RUN *A&M 5811492* **24** 4
11 Nov 95	WHAT I CAN DO FOR YOU *A&M 5812292* **43** 1
21 Sep 96	● IF IT MAKES YOU HAPPY *A&M 5819032* **9** 6
30 Nov 96	EVERYDAY IS A WINDING ROAD *A&M 5820232* **12** 6
29 Mar 97	HARD TO MAKE A STAND *A&M 5821492* **22** 3
12 Jul 97	● A CHANGE WOULD DO YOU GOOD *A&M 5822092* **8** 5
18 Oct 97	HOME *A&M 0440312* **25** 2
13 Dec 97	TOMORROW NEVER DIES *A&M 5824572* **12** 9
12 Sep 98	● MY FAVORITE MISTAKE *Polydor 5827632* **9** 6
5 Dec 98	THERE GOES THE NEIGHBORHOOD *A&M 5828092* **19** 7
6 Mar 99	ANYTHING BUT DOWN *A&M / Polydor 5828272* **19** 4
11 Sep 99	SWEET CHILD O' MINE *Columbia 6678882* **30** 3
13 Apr 02	SOAK UP THE SUN *A&M 4977042* **16** 8
13 Jul 02	STEVE MCQUEEN *A&M 4977042* **44** 1
1 Nov 03	THE FIRST CUT IS THE DEEPEST *A&M 9813556* **37** 3
3 Jul 04	LIGHT IN YOUR EYES *A&M 9862700* **73** 1
12 Feb 94	● TUESDAY NIGHT MUSIC CLUB *A&M 5401262* **8** 55
12 Oct 96	● SHERYL CROW *A&M 5405902* **5** 70
3 Oct 98	● THE GLOBE SESSIONS *A&M 5409742* **2** 32
20 Apr 02	● C'MON C'MON *A&M 4932622* **2** 8
25 Oct 03	● THE VERY BEST OF SHERYL CROW *A&M / Mercury 9861092*....**2** 16

The CROWD *International, male / female vocal / instrumental charity assembly (Singles: 11 Weeks)*   pos/wks

1 Jun 85	★ YOU'LL NEVER WALK ALONE *Spartan BRAD 1* **1** 11

CROWDED HOUSE (256 Top 500)
(see also FINN) Top Antipodean group evolved from Split Enz, and featured New Zealanders Neil and Tim Finn (v/g & k). Formed 1986, they received Best International Group award at 1993 Brits, and played their last show (1996) to over 100,000 on the steps of Sydney Opera House (Singles: 64 Weeks, Albums: 186 Weeks)   pos/wks

6 Jun 87	DON'T DREAM IT'S OVER *Capitol CL 438* **27** 8
22 Jun 91	CHOCOLATE CAKE *Capitol CL 618* **69** 2
2 Nov 91	FALL AT YOUR FEET *Capitol CL 626* **17** 7
29 Feb 92	● WEATHER WITH YOU *Capitol CL 643* **7** 9
20 Jun 92	FOUR SEASONS IN ONE DAY *Capitol CL 655* **26** 5
26 Sep 92	IT'S ONLY NATURAL *Capitol CL 661* **24** 4
2 Oct 93	DISTANT SUN *Capitol CDCLS 697* **19** 6
20 Nov 93	NAILS IN MY FEET *Capitol CDCLS 701* **22** 4
19 Feb 94	LOCKED OUT *Capitol CDCLS 707* **12** 4
11 Jun 94	FINGERS OF LOVE *Capitol CDCLS 715* **25** 3
24 Sep 94	PINEAPPLE HEAD *Capitol CDCLS 723* **27** 3
22 Jun 96	INSTINCT *Capitol CDCLS 774* **12** 4
17 Aug 96	NOT THE GIRL YOU THINK YOU ARE *Capitol CDCLS 776* **20** 3
9 Nov 96	DON'T DREAM IT'S OVER (re-issue) *Capitol CDCL 780* **25** 2
13 Jul 91	● WOODFACE *Capitol EST 2144* **6** 86
23 Oct 93	● TOGETHER ALONE *Capitol CDESTU 2215* **4** 32
6 Jul 96	★ RECURRING DREAM – THE VERY BEST OF CROWDED HOUSE *Capitol CDEST 2283* ■ **1** 66
19 Feb 00	AFTERGLOW *Capitol 5237222* **18** 2

CROWN HEIGHTS AFFAIR *US, male vocal / instrumental group (Singles: 34 Weeks, Albums: 3 Weeks)*   pos/wks

19 Aug 78	GALAXY OF LOVE *Mercury 6168 801* **24** 10
11 Nov 78	I'M GONNA LOVE YOU FOREVER *Mercury 6168 803* **47** 4
14 Apr 79	DANCE LADY DANCE *Mercury 6168 804* **44** 4
3 May 80	● YOU GAVE ME LOVE *De-Lite MER 9* **10** 12
9 Aug 80	YOU'VE BEEN GONE *De-Lite MER 28* **44** 4
23 Sep 78	DREAM WORLD *Philips 6372 754* **40** 3

Julee CRUISE *US, female vocalist (Singles: 14 Weeks)*   pos/wks

10 Nov 90	● FALLING *Warner Bros. W 9544* **7** 11
2 Mar 91	ROCKIN' BACK INSIDE MY HEART *Warner Bros. W 0004* **66** 2
11 Sep 99	IF I SURVIVE *Distinctive DISNCD 55* [1] **52** 1

[1] Hybrid featuring Julee Cruise

CRUISERS *See Dave BERRY*

The CRUSADERS *US, male vocal / instrumental group – includes Wilton Felder (Singles: 16 Weeks, Albums: 30 Weeks)*   pos/wks

18 Aug 79	● STREET LIFE *MCA 513* **5** 11
26 Sep 81	I'M SO GLAD I'M STANDING HERE TODAY *MCA 741* [1] **61** 3
7 Apr 84	NIGHT LADIES *MCA MCA 853* **55** 2
21 Jul 79	STREET LIFE *MCA MCF 3008* **10** 16
19 Jul 80	RHAPSODY AND BLUE *MCA MCG 4010* **40** 5
12 Sep 81	STANDING TALL *MCA MCF 3122* **47** 5
7 Apr 84	GHETTO BLASTER *MCA MCF 3176* **46** 4

[1] The Crusaders, featured vocalist Joe Cocker

Uncredited vocalist on 'Street Life' was Randy Crawford

CRUSH *UK, female vocal duo (Singles: 3 Weeks)*   pos/wks

24 Feb 96	JELLYHEAD *Telstar CDSTAS 2809* **50** 2
3 Aug 96	LUV'D UP *Telstar CDSTAS 2833* **45** 1

Bobby CRUSH *UK, male instrumentalist – piano (Singles: 4 Weeks, Albums: 12 Weeks)*   pos/wks

4 Nov 72	BORSALINO *Philips 6006 248* **37** 4
25 Nov 72	BOBBY CRUSH *Philips 6308 135* **15** 7
18 Dec 82	THE BOBBY CRUSH INCREDIBLE DOUBLE DECKER *Warwick WW 5126/7* **53** 5

CRY BEFORE DAWN
Ireland, male vocal / instrumental group (Singles: 2 Weeks)   pos/wks

17 Jun 89	WITNESS FOR THE WORLD *Epic GONE 3* **67** 2

CRY OF LOVE
US, male / female vocal / instrumental group (Singles: 1 Week)   pos/wks

15 Jan 94	BAD THING *Columbia 6600462* **60** 1

CRY SISCO!
UK, male producer – Barry Blue (Singles: 9 Weeks)   pos/wks

2 Sep 89	AFRO DIZZI ACT (re) *Escape AWOL 1* **42** 9

The CRYAN' SHAMES
UK, male vocal / instrumental group (Singles: 7 Weeks)   pos/wks

31 Mar 66	PLEASE STAY *Decca F 12340* **26** 7

CRYPT-KICKERS *See Bobby 'Boris' PICKETT and the CRYPT-KICKERS*

The CRYSTAL METHOD
US, male instrumental duo (Singles: 4 Weeks)   pos/wks

11 Oct 97	(CAN'T YOU) TRIP LIKE I DO *Epic 6650862* [1] **39** 2
7 Mar 98	KEEP HOPE ALIVE *Sony S2CM 3CD* **71** 1
8 Aug 98	COMIN' BACK *Sony S2CM 4CD* **73** 1

[1] Filter and The Crystal Method

CRYSTAL PALACE with the FAB FOUR *UK, male football team vocalists and UK, male group (Singles: 2 Weeks)*   pos/wks

12 May 90	GLAD ALL OVER / WHERE EAGLES FLY *Parkfield PMS 5019* **50** 2

The CRYSTALS
US, female vocal group – includes Darlene Love (Singles: 54 Weeks) pos/wks

22 Nov 62		HE'S A REBEL *London HLU 9611* ▲	...19 13
20 Jun 63	●	DA DOO RON RON *London HLU 9732*	...5 16
19 Sep 63	●	THEN HE KISSED ME *London HLU 9773*	...2 14
5 Mar 64		I WONDER *London HLU 9852*	...36 3
19 Oct 74		DA DOO RON RON (re-issue) *Warner Spector K 19010*	...15 8

CSILLA *Hungary, female vocalist (Singles: 1 Week)* pos/wks

13 Jul 96	MAN IN THE MOON *Worx WORXCD 001*	...69 1

Alex CUBA BAND featuring Ron SEXSMITH *Cuba, male instrumental group and Canada, male vocalist (Singles: 1 Week)* pos/wks

6 Nov 04	LO MISMO QUE YO (IF ONLY) *Shell GET 2CD*	...52 1

CUBAN BOYS
UK, male / female production group (Singles: 9 Weeks) pos/wks

25 Dec 99	●	COGNOSCENTI VS INTELLIGENTSIA (re) *EMI CDCUBAN 001*	...4 9

CUBIC 22 (see also AIRSCAPE; BLUE BAMBOO; TRANSFORMER 2; BALEARIC BILL; Johan GIELEN presents ABNEA; SVENSON and GIELEN)
Belgium, male instrumental / production duo – Peter Ramson and Danny Van Wauwe (Singles: 7 Weeks) pos/wks

22 Jun 91	NIGHT IN MOTION *XL Recordings XLS 20*	...15 7

CUD *UK, male vocal / instrumental group (Singles: 16 Weeks, Albums: 2 Weeks)* pos/wks

19 Oct 91	OH NO WON'T DO (EP) *A&M AMB 829*	...49 2
28 Mar 92	THROUGH THE ROOF *A&M AM 857*	...44 2
30 May 92	RICH AND STRANGE *A&M AM 871*	...24 3
15 Aug 92	PURPLE LOVE BALLOON *A&M AM 0024*	...27 3
10 Oct 92	ONCE AGAIN *A&M AM 0081*	...45 1
12 Feb 94	NEUROTICA *A&M 5805172*	...37 2
2 Apr 94	STICKS AND STONES *A&M 5805472*	...68 1
3 Sep 94	ONE GIANT LOVE *A&M 5807292*	...52 2
11 Jul 92	ASQUARIUS *A&M 3953902*	...30 1
23 Apr 94	SHOWBIZ *A&M 5402112*	...46 1

Tracks on Oh No Won't Do (EP): Oh No Won't Do / Profession / Ariel / Price of Love

The CUFF LINKS (see also The ARCHIES)
US, male vocal group – leader Ron Dante (Singles: 30 Weeks) pos/wks

29 Nov 69	●	TRACY *MCA MU 1101*	...4 16
14 Mar 70	●	WHEN JULIE COMES AROUND *MCA MU 1112*	...10 14

Jamie CULLUM *UK, male vocalist / instrumentalist – piano (Singles: 11 Weeks, Albums: 44 Weeks)* pos/wks

20 Mar 04		THESE ARE THE DAYS / FRONTIN' *UCJ 9866211*	...12 5
20 Nov 04		EVERLASTING LOVE *UCJ 9865574*	...20 6+
1 Nov 03	●	TWENTYSOMETHING *UCJ 9865574*	...3 42+
13 Mar 04		POINTLESS NOSTALGIC *Candid CCD 79782*	...55 2

The CULT ⟨ 417 ⟩ **Top 500**
UK gothic rock stars who became US heavy rock heroes, previously recorded as Southern Death Cult and Death Cult. West Yorkshire band's constant members were Ian Astbury (v) and Billy Duffy (g). The group, who relocated to the US in 1988, topped the UK album chart with hits collection in 1993 (Singles: 80 Weeks, Albums: 86 Weeks) pos/wks

22 Dec 84	RESURRECTION JOE *Beggars Banquet BEG 122*	...74 2
25 May 85	SHE SELLS SANCTUARY (re) *Beggars Banquet BEG 135*	...15 19
5 Oct 85	RAIN *Beggars Banquet BEG 147*	...17 8
30 Nov 85	REVOLUTION *Beggars Banquet BEG 152*	...30 7
28 Feb 87	LOVE REMOVAL MACHINE *Beggars Banquet BEG 182*	...18 7
2 May 87	LIL' DEVIL *Beggars Banquet BEG 188*	...11 7
22 Aug 87	WILD FLOWER (DOUBLE SINGLE) *Beggars Banquet BEG 195D*	24 2
29 Aug 87	WILD FLOWER *Beggars Banquet BEG 195*	...30 4
1 Apr 89	FIRE WOMAN *Beggars Banquet BEG 228*	...15 4
8 Jul 89	EDIE (CIAO BABY) *Beggars Banquet BEG 230*	...32 5
18 Nov 89	SUN KING / EDIE (CIAO BABY) (re-issue) *Beggars Banquet BEG 235*	...39 2
10 Mar 90	SWEET SOUL SISTER *Beggars Banquet BEG 241*	...42 4
14 Sep 91	WILD HEARTED SON *Beggars Banquet BEG 255*	...40 2
29 Feb 92	HEART OF SOUL *Beggars Banquet BEG 260*	...51 1

30 Jan 93		SHE SELLS SANCTUARY (re-mix) *Beggars Banquet BEG 253CD*	...15 4
8 Oct 94		COMING DOWN *Beggars Banquet BBQ 40CD*	...50 1
7 Jan 95		STAR *Beggars Banquet BBQ 45CD*	...65 1
18 Jun 83		THE SOUTHERN DEATH CULT *Beggars Banquet BEGA 46* [1]	...43 3
8 Sep 84		DREAMTIME *Beggars Banquet BEGA 57*	...21 8
26 Oct 85	●	LOVE *Beggars Banquet BEGA 65*	...4 22
18 Apr 87	●	ELECTRIC *Beggars Banquet BEGA 80*	...4 27
22 Apr 89	●	SONIC TEMPLE *Beggars Banquet BEGA 98*	...3 11
5 Oct 91	●	CEREMONY *Beggars Banquet BEGA 122*	...9 4
13 Feb 93	★	PURE CULT *Beggars Banquet BEGACD 130* ■	...1 8
22 Oct 94		THE CULT *Beggars Banquet BBQCD 164*	...21 2
23 Jun 01		BEYOND GOOD AND EVIL *Atlantic 7567834402*	...69 1

[1] Southern Death Cult

Tracks on Wild Flower (double single): Love Trooper / Outlaw (live) / Horse Nation (live)

CULT JAM *See LISA LISA*

Smiley CULTURE
UK, male vocalist – David Emanuel (Singles: 13 Weeks) pos/wks

15 Dec 84	POLICE OFFICER *Fashion FAD 7012*	...12 10
6 Apr 85	COCKNEY TRANSLATION *Fashion FAD 7028*	...71 1
13 Sep 86	SCHOOLTIME CHRONICLE *Polydor POSP 815*	...59 2

CULTURE
Jamaica, male vocal / instrumental group (Albums: 1 Week) pos/wks

1 Apr 78	TWO SEVENS CLASH *Lightning LIP 1*	...60 1

CULTURE BEAT *UK / US / Germany, male / female vocal / instrumental group (Singles: 47 Weeks, Albums: 10 Weeks)* pos/wks

3 Feb 90		CHERRY LIPS (DER ERDBEERMUND) *Epic 6556337*	...55 3
7 Aug 93	★	MR VAIN *Epic 6594682*	...1 15
6 Nov 93	●	GOT TO GET IT *Epic 6597212*	...4 11
15 Jan 94	●	ANYTHING *Epic 6600252*	...5 8
2 Apr 94		WORLD IN YOUR HANDS *Epic 6602292*	...20 4
27 Jan 96		INSIDE OUT *Epic 6625562*	...32 2
15 Jun 96		CRYING IN THE RAIN *Epic 6633582*	...29 2
28 Sep 96		TAKE ME AWAY *Epic 6637552*	...52 1
20 Sep 03		MR VAIN RECALL *East West EW 270CD*	...51 1
25 Sep 93		SERENITY *Dance Pool 4741012*	...13 10

CULTURE CLUB ⟨ 212 ⟩ **Top 500**
Internationally successful London-based quartet, whose flamboyant lead singer, Boy George (b. George O'Dowd, 14 Jun 1961, Kent), attracted considerable media attention. In 1984, they won both Brit (Best Group) and Grammy Awards (Best New Artist). Original members reunited for late 1990s tours. Best-selling single: 'Karma Chameleon' 1,405,000 (Singles: 119 Weeks, Albums: 163 Weeks) pos/wks

18 Sep 82	★	DO YOU REALLY WANT TO HURT ME *Virgin VS 518*	...1 18
27 Nov 82	●	TIME (CLOCK OF THE HEART) *Virgin VS 558*	...3 12
9 Apr 83	●	CHURCH OF THE POISON MIND *Virgin VS 571*	...2 9
17 Sep 83	★	KARMA CHAMELEON *Virgin VS 612* ◆ ▲	...1 20
10 Dec 83	●	VICTIMS *Virgin VS 641*	...3 10
24 Mar 84	●	IT'S A MIRACLE *Virgin VS 662*	...4 9
6 Oct 84	●	THE WAR SONG *Virgin VS 694*	...2 8
1 Dec 84		THE MEDAL SONG (re) *Virgin VS 730*	...32 5
15 Mar 86		MOVE AWAY *Virgin VS 845*	...7 7
31 May 86		GOD THANK YOU WOMAN *Virgin VS 861*	...31 5
31 Oct 98	●	I JUST WANNA BE LOVED *Virgin VSCDT 1710*	...4 10
7 Aug 99		YOUR KISSES ARE CHARITY *Virgin VSCDT 1736*	...25 4
27 Nov 99		COLD SHOULDER / STARMAN *Virgin VSCDT 1758*	...43 2
16 Oct 82	●	KISSING TO BE CLEVER *Virgin V 2232*	...5 59
22 Oct 83	★	COLOUR BY NUMBERS *Virgin V 2285* ■	...1 56
3 Nov 84	●	WAKING UP WITH THE HOUSE ON FIRE *Virgin V 2330*	...2 13
12 Apr 86	●	FROM LUXURY TO HEARTACHE *Virgin V 2380*	...10 6
18 Apr 87		THIS TIME *Virgin VTV 1*	...8 10
2 Oct 93		AT WORST ... THE BEST OF BOY GEORGE AND CULTURE CLUB *Virgin VYCD 19* [1]	...24 5
21 Nov 98		GREATEST MOMENTS *Virgin CDVX 2865*	...15 13
4 Dec 99		DON'T MIND IF I DO *Virgin CDV 2887*	...64 1

[1] Boy George and Culture Club

Peter CUNNAH *See CHICANE; D:REAM*

Larry CUNNINGHAM and the MIGHTY AVONS
Ireland, male vocal / instrumental group (Singles: 11 Weeks) pos/wks

10 Dec 64	TRIBUTE TO JIM REEVES (re) *King KG 1016*	.40 11

CUPID'S INSPIRATION
UK, male vocal / instrumental group (Singles: 19 Weeks) pos/wks

19 Jun 68 ●	YESTERDAY HAS GONE *Nems 56 3500*	.4 11
2 Oct 68 ●	MY WORLD *Nems 56 3702*	.33 8

Jose CURA See Sarah BRIGHTMAN

Mike CURB CONGREGATION See Little Jimmy OSMOND

The CURE `143` `Top 500` (see also GLOVE)
Influential goth rock giants: Robert Smith (v/g), Lol Tolhurst (k), Simon Gallup (b), Porl Thompson, Boris Williams (d), who went from UK cult heroes to stadium-packing supergroup. Voted Best Group at 1991 Brit Awards (Singles: 149 Weeks, Albums: 212 Weeks) pos/wks

12 Apr 80	A FOREST *Fiction FICS 10*	.31 8
4 Apr 81	PRIMARY *Fiction FICS 12*	.43 6
17 Oct 81	CHARLOTTE SOMETIMES *Fiction FICS 14*	.44 4
24 Jul 82	HANGING GARDEN *Fiction FICS 15*	.34 4
27 Nov 82	LET'S GO TO BED (re) *Fiction FICS 17*	.44 5
9 Jul 83	THE WALK *Fiction FICS 18*	.12 8
29 Oct 83 ●	THE LOVE CATS *Fiction FICS 19*	.7 11
7 Apr 84	THE CATERPILLAR *Fiction FICS 20*	.14 7
27 Jul 85	IN BETWEEN DAYS *Fiction FICS 22*	.15 10
21 Sep 85	CLOSE TO ME *Fiction FICS 23*	.24 8
3 May 86	BOYS DON'T CRY *Fiction FICS 24*	.22 6
18 Apr 87	WHY CAN'T I BE YOU? *Fiction FICS 25*	.21 5
4 Jul 87	CATCH *Fiction FICS 26*	.27 6
17 Oct 87	JUST LIKE HEAVEN *Fiction FICS 27*	.29 5
20 Feb 88	HOT HOT HOT!!! *Fiction FICSX 28*	.45 3
22 Apr 89 ●	LULLABY *Fiction FICS 29*	.5 6
2 Sep 89	LOVESONG *Fiction FICS 30*	.18 7
31 Mar 90	PICTURES OF YOU *Fiction FICS 34*	.24 6
29 Sep 90	NEVER ENOUGH *Fiction FICS 35*	.13 5
3 Nov 90	CLOSE TO ME (re-mix) *Fiction FICS 36*	.13 5
28 Mar 92 ●	HIGH *Fiction FICS 39*	.8 3
11 Apr 92	HIGH (re-mix) *Fiction FICSX 41*	.44 1
23 May 92 ●	FRIDAY I'M IN LOVE *Fiction FICS 42*	.6 7
17 Oct 92	A LETTER TO ELISE *Fiction FICS 46*	.28 2
4 May 96	THE 13TH *Fiction 5764692*	.15 2
29 Jun 96	MINT CAR *Fiction FISCD 52*	.31 2
14 Dec 96	GONE *Fiction FICD 53*	.60 1
29 Nov 97	WRONG NUMBER *Fiction FICD 54*	.62 1
10 Nov 01	CUT HERE *Fiction 5873892*	.54 1
31 Jul 04	THE END OF THE WORLD *Geffen 9862976*	.25 3
30 Oct 04	TAKING OFF *Geffen 9864491*	.39 1
2 Jun 79	THREE IMAGINARY BOYS *Fiction FIX 001*	.44 3
3 May 80	17 SECONDS *Fiction FIX 004*	.20 10
25 Apr 81	FAITH *Fiction FIX 6*	.14 9
15 May 82 ●	PORNOGRAPHY *Fiction FIX D7*	.8 9
3 Sep 83	BOYS DON'T CRY *Fiction SPELP 26*	.71 7
24 Dec 83	JAPANESE WHISPERS *Fiction FIXM 8*	.26 14
12 May 84 ●	THE TOP *Fiction FIXS 9*	.10 10
3 Nov 84	CONCERT – THE CURE LIVE *Fiction FIXH 10*	.26 4
7 Sep 85 ●	THE HEAD ON THE DOOR *Fiction FIXH 11*	.7 13
31 May 86 ●	STANDING ON A BEACH – THE SINGLES *Fiction FIXH 12*	.4 35
6 Jun 87 ●	KISS ME KISS ME KISS ME *Fiction FIXH 13*	.6 15
13 May 89 ●	DISINTEGRATION *Fiction FIXH 14*	.3 26
17 Nov 90 ●	MIXED UP *Fiction 8470991*	.8 17
6 Apr 91 ●	ENTREAT *Fiction FIXH 17*	.10 5
2 May 92 ★	WISH *Fiction FIXCD 20* ■	.1 13
25 Sep 93	SHOW *Fiction FIXCD 25*	.29 2
6 Nov 93	PARIS *Fiction FIXCD 26*	.56 1
18 May 96 ●	WILD MOOD SWINGS *Fiction FIXCD 28*	.9 6
15 Nov 97	GALORE – THE SINGLES 1987-1997 *Fiction FIXCD 30*	.37 2
26 Feb 00	BLOODFLOWERS *Fiction FIXCD 31*	.14 2
24 Nov 01	GREATEST HITS *Fiction 5894352*	.33 5
10 Jul 04 ●	THE CURE */ Am / Geffen 9862890*	.8 5

The CD version of FIXH 12 was titled 'Staring at the Sea'

CURIOSITY KILLED THE CAT
UK, male vocal / instrumental group (Singles: 58 Weeks, Albums: 27 Weeks) pos/wks

13 Dec 86 ●	DOWN TO EARTH *Mercury CAT 2*	.3 18
4 Apr 87	ORDINARY DAY *Mercury CAT 3*	.11 7
20 Jun 87 ●	MISFIT *Mercury CAT 4*	.7 9
19 Sep 87	FREE *Mercury CAT 5*	.56 2
16 Sep 89	NAME AND NUMBER *Mercury CAT 6* [1]	.14 9
25 Apr 92 ●	HANG ON IN THERE BABY *RCA PB 45377* [1]	.3 10
29 Aug 92	I NEED YOUR LOVIN' *RCA 74321111377* [1]	.47 2
30 Oct 93	GIMME THE SUNSHINE *RCA 74321168602* [1]	.73 1
9 May 87 ★	KEEP YOUR DISTANCE *Mercury CATLP 1* ■	.1 24
4 Oct 89	GETAHEAD *Mercury 842010 1*	.29 3

[1] Curiosity

CURLS See Paul EVANS

Mark CURRY See P DIDDY

Chantal CURTIS
France, female vocalist (Singles: 3 Weeks) pos/wks

14 Jul 79	GET ANOTHER LOVE *Pye 7P 5003*	.51 3

TC CURTIS
Jamaica, male vocalist / instrumentalist (Singles: 4 Weeks) pos/wks

23 Feb 85	YOU SHOULD HAVE KNOWN BETTER *Hot Melt VS 754*	.50 4

CURVE
UK, male / female vocal / instrumental duo – Toni Halliday and Dean Garcia (Singles: 14 Weeks, Albums: 6 Weeks) pos/wks

16 Mar 91	THE BLINDFOLD (EP) *AnXious ANX 27*	.68 1
25 May 91	COAST IS CLEAR *AnXious ANX 30*	.34 3
9 Nov 91	CLIPPED *AnXious ANX 35*	.36 2
7 Mar 92	FAIT ACCOMPLI *AnXious ANXT 36*	.22 3
18 Jul 92	HORROR HEAD (EP) *AnXious ANXT 38*	.31 2
4 Sep 93	BLACKERTHREETRACKER (EP) *AnXious ANXCD 42*	.39 2
16 May 98	COMING UP ROSES *Universal UND 80489*	.51 1
21 Mar 92	DOPPELGANGER *AnXious ANXCD 77*	.11 3
19 Jun 93	RADIO SESSIONS *AnXious ANXCD 80*	.72 1
25 Sep 93	CUCKOO *AnXious ANXCD 81*	.23 2

Tracks on The Blindfold (EP): Ten Little Girls / I Speak Your Every Word / Blindfold / No Escape from Heaven. Tracks on Horror Head (EP): Horror Head / Falling Free / Mission from God / Today Is Not the Day. Tracks on Blackerthreetracker (EP): Missing Link (only track available on all formats of EP) / On The Wheel / Triumph

CURVED AIR
UK, male / female vocal / instrumental group (Singles: 12 Weeks, Albums: 32 Weeks) pos/wks

7 Aug 71 ●	BACK STREET LUV *Warner Bros. K 16092*	.4 12
5 Dec 70 ●	AIR CONDITIONING *Warner Bros. WSX 3012*	.8 21
9 Oct 71	CURVED AIR *Warner Bros. K 46092*	.11 6
13 May 72	PHANTASMAGORIA *Reprise K 46158*	.20 5

Malachi CUSH See MALACHI

CUT 'N' MOVE
Denmark, male / female vocal / instrumental group (Singles: 4 Weeks) pos/wks

2 Oct 93	GIVE IT UP *EMI CDEM 273*	.61 2
9 Sep 95	I'M ALIVE *EMI CDEM 375*	.49 2

Frankie CUTLASS
US, male rapper – Francis Parker (Singles: 1 Week) pos/wks

5 Apr 97	THE CYPHER: PART 3 *Epic 6641445*	.59 1

Adge CUTLER See The WURZELS

Jon CUTLER featuring E-MAN
US, male producer and male vocalist – Eric Clark (Singles: 2 Weeks) pos/wks

19 Jan 02	IT'S YOURS *Direction 6720532*	.38 2

CUTTING CREW
UK / Canada, male vocal / instrumental group (Singles: 37 Weeks, Albums: 6 Weeks) pos/wks

16 Aug 86 ●	(I JUST) DIED IN YOUR ARMS *Siren SIREN 21* ▲	.4 12
25 Oct 86	I'VE BEEN IN LOVE BEFORE (re) *Siren SIREN 29*	.31 10
7 Mar 87	ONE FOR THE MOCKINGBIRD *Siren SIREN 40*	.52 5
21 Nov 87	I'VE BEEN IN LOVE BEFORE (re-mix) *Siren SRN 29*	.24 8
22 Jul 89	(BETWEEN A) ROCK AND A HARD PLACE *Siren SRN 108*	.66 2
29 Nov 86	BROADCAST *Siren SIRENLP 7*	.41 6

CYBERSONIK
US, male instrumentalist / producer (Singles: 1 Week) pos/wks

10 Nov 90	TECHNARCHY *Champion CHAMP 264*	.73 1

CYCLEFLY
Ireland, male vocal / instrumental group (Singles: 1 Week) pos/wks

| 6 Apr 02 | **NO STRESS** *Radioactive RAXTD 41* ...... | .68 | 1 |

CYGNUS X
Germany, male producer – A C Bousten (Singles: 5 Weeks) pos/wks

| 11 Mar 00 | **THE ORANGE THEME** *Hooj Choons HOOJ 88CD* | .43 | 2 |
| 18 Aug 01 | **SUPERSTRING** *Xtravaganza XTRAV 28CDS* | .33 | 3 |

Johnny CYMBAL *Canada (b. UK), male vocalist,*
b. 3 Feb 1945, d. 16 Mar 1993 (Singles: 10 Weeks) pos/wks

| 14 Mar 63 | **MR BASS MAN** *London HLR 9682* | .24 | 10 |

CYPRESS HILL
US, male rap group (Singles: 46 Weeks, Albums: 68 Weeks) pos/wks

31 Jul 93	**INSANE IN THE BRAIN** *Ruff House 6595332*	.32	4
2 Oct 93	**WHEN THE SH.. GOES DOWN** *Ruff House 6596702*	.19	4
11 Dec 93	**I AIN'T GOIN' OUT LIKE THAT** *Ruff House 6596902*	.15	7
26 Feb 94	**INSANE IN THE BRAIN** (re-issue) (re-mix) *Ruff House 6601762*	.21	4
7 May 94	**LICK A SHOT** *Ruff House 6603192*	.20	3
7 Oct 95	**THROW YOUR SET IN THE AIR** *Ruff House 6623542*	.15	3
17 Feb 96	**ILLUSIONS** *Columbia 6629052*	.23	2
10 Oct 98	**TEQUILA SUNRISE** *Columbia 6664935*	.23	2
10 Apr 99	**DR GREENTHUMB** *Columbia 6671202*	.34	2
26 Jun 99	**INSANE IN THE BRAIN** (re-mix) *INCredible INCRL 17CD* [1]	19	3
29 Apr 00	**(RAP) SUPERSTAR / (ROCK) SUPERSTAR** *Columbia 6692642*	13	5
16 Sep 00	**HIGHLIFE / CAN'T GET THE BEST OF ME** *Columbia 6697892*	.35	2
8 Dec 01	**LOWRIDER / TROUBLE** (re) *Columbia 6721662*	.33	3
27 Mar 04	**WHAT'S YOUR NUMBER?** *Columbia 6746172*	.44	2
7 Aug 93	**BLACK SUNDAY** *Ruff House 4740752* ▲	.13	49
11 Nov 95	**CYPRESS HILL III (TEMPLES OF BOOM)** *Columbia 4781279*	.11	5
24 Aug 96	**UNRELEASED & REVAMPED (EP)** *Columbia 4852302*	.29	4
17 Oct 98	**IV** *Columbia 4916046*	.25	3
6 May 00 ●	**SKULL & BONES** *Columbia 4951832*	.6	5
15 Dec 01	**STONED RAIDERS** *Columbia 5041719*	.71	1
3 Apr 04	**TILL DEATH DO U$ PART** *Columbia 5150292*	.53	1

[1] Jason Nevins vs Cypress Hill

Billy Ray CYRUS
US, male vocalist (Singles: 18 Weeks, Albums: 10 Weeks) pos/wks

25 Jul 92 ●	**ACHY BREAKY HEART** *Mercury MER 373*	.3	10
10 Oct 92	**COULD'VE BEEN ME** *Mercury MER 378*	.24	4
28 Nov 92	**THESE BOOTS ARE MADE FOR WALKIN'** *Mercury MER 384*	.63	1
19 Dec 92	**ACHY BREAKY HEART** *Epic 6588837* [1]	.53	3
29 Aug 92 ●	**SOME GAVE ALL** *Mercury 5106352* ▲	.9	10

[1] Alvin and the Chipmunks featuring Billy Ray Cyrus

Holgar CZUKAY *See David SYLVIAN*

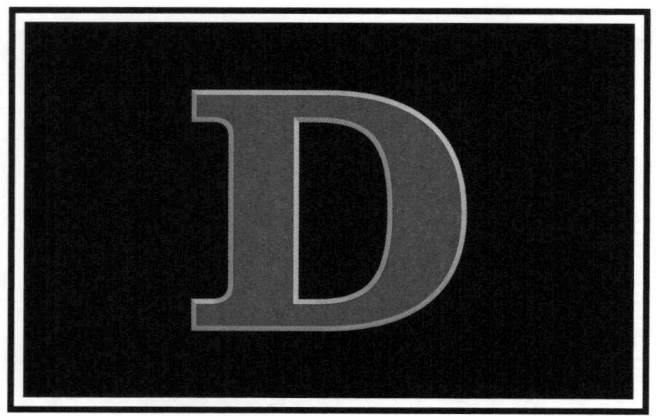

Asher D (see also SO SOLID CREW)
UK, male rapper – Ashley Walters (Singles: 2 Weeks) pos/wks

| 4 Aug 01 | **BABY, CAN I GET YOUR NUMBER** *East West EW 235CD* | .75 | 1 |
| 8 Jun 02 | **BACK IN THE DAY / WHY ME** *Independiente ISOM 57MS* | .43 | 1 |

Chuck D (see also PUBLIC ENEMY)
US, male rapper – Carlton Ridenhour (Singles: 9 Weeks) pos/wks

6 Jul 91	**BRING THE NOISE** *Island IS 490* [1]	.14	5
26 Oct 96	**NO** *Mercury MERCD 476*	.55	1
23 Jun 01	**ROCK DA FUNKY BEATS** *Xtrahard / Xtravaganza X2H 3CDS* [2]	.19	3

[1] Anthrax featuring Chuck D [2] Public Domain featuring Chuck D

Crissy D *See B-15 PROJECT featuring Crissy D and Lady G*

Danny D *See The COOKIE CREW*

Dimples D *US, female rapper – Crystal Smith (Singles: 10 Weeks)* pos/wks

| 17 Nov 90 | **SUCKER DJ** *FBI FBI 11* | .17 | 10 |

Juggy D *UK, male vocalist (Albums: 1 Week)* pos/wks

| 4 Sep 04 | **JUGGY D** *2point9 2POINT9 100CD* | .70 | 1 |

Longsy D *UK, male instrumentalist / producer (Singles: 7 Weeks)* pos/wks

| 4 Mar 89 | **THIS IS SKA** *Big One VBIG 13* | .56 | 7 |

Maxwell D
UK, male rapper – Maxwell Donaldson (Singles: 2 Weeks) pos/wks

| 15 Sep 01 | **SERIOUS** *4 Liberty LIBTCD 046* | .38 | 2 |

Nikki D *US, female rapper – Nichelle Strong (Singles: 6 Weeks)* pos/wks

| 6 May 89 | **MY LOVE IS SO RAW** *Def Jam 6548987* [1] | .34 | 5 |
| 30 Mar 91 | **DADDY'S LITTLE GIRL** *Def Jam 6567347* | .75 | 1 |

[1] Alyson Williams featuring Nikki D

Vicky D *US, female vocalist (Singles: 6 Weeks)* pos/wks

| 13 Mar 82 | **THIS BEAT IS MINE** *Virgin VS 486* | .42 | 6 |

DB BOULEVARD
Italy, male production trio and female vocalist (Singles: 12 Weeks) pos/wks

| 23 Feb 02 ● | **POINT OF VIEW** *Illustrious CDILL 002* | .3 | 12 |

DBM
Germany, male / female vocal / instrumental group (Singles: 3 Weeks) pos/wks

| 12 Nov 77 | **DISCO BEATLEMANIA** *Atlantic K 11027* | .45 | 3 |

D, B, M and T (see also Dave DEE, DOZY, BEAKY, MICK and TICH)
UK, male vocal / instrumental group (Singles: 8 Weeks) pos/wks

| 1 Aug 70 | **MR PRESIDENT** *Fontana 6007 022* | .33 | 8 |

D BO GENERAL *See URBAN SHAKEDOWN*

The D4 *New Zealand, male vocal /*
instrumental group (Singles: 3 Weeks) pos/wks

28 Sep 02	**GET LOOSE** *Infectious INFEC 117CDS*	.64	1
7 Dec 02	**COME ON!** *Infectious INFEC 121CDS*	.50	1
29 Mar 03	**LADIES MAN** *Infectious INFECT 122CDS*	.41	1

D.H.S. *UK, male producer – Ben Stokes (Singles: 1 Week)* pos/wks

| 9 Feb 02 | **HOUSE OF GOD** *Club Tools 0135825 CLU* | .72 | 1 |

D KAY & EPSILON featuring STAMINA MC
Austria / UK, production / vocal trio (Singles: 5 Weeks) pos/wks

| 30 Aug 03 | **BARCELONA** *Alphamagic / BC / BMG BCAU 001CD* | .14 | 5 |

DMX *US, male rapper – Earl Simmons*
(Singles: 27 Weeks, Albums: 11 Weeks) pos/wks

15 May 99	**SLIPPIN'** *Def Jam 8707552*	.30	2
15 Dec 01	**WHO WE BE** *Def Jam 5888512*	.34	4
3 May 03 ●	**X GON' GIVE IT TO YA** *Def Jam 0779042*	.6	12
11 Oct 03	**WHERE THE HOOD AT?** *Def Jam 9811251*	.16	5
10 Jan 04	**GET IT ON THE FLOOR** *Def Jam 9815206* [1]	.34	4
3 Nov 01	**THE GREAT DEPRESSION** *Def Jam 5864502* ▲	.20	3
27 Sep 03 ●	**GRAND CHAMP** *Def Jam / Mercury 9861021* ▲	.6	8

[1] DMX featuring Swizz Beatz

Singles re-entries are listed as (re), (2re), (3re).... which signifies that the hit re-entered the chart once, twice or three times...

D MOB UK, male producer – Danny Poku
(Singles: 48 Weeks, Albums: 11 Weeks)   pos/wks

15 Oct 88	● WE CALL IT ACIEED ffrr FFR 13 [1]	3 12
3 Jun 89	● IT IS TIME TO GET FUNKY ffrr F 107 [2]	9 10
21 Oct 89	C'MON AND GET MY LOVE ffrr F 117 [3]	15 10
6 Jan 90	● PUT YOUR HANDS TOGETHER ffrr F 124 [4]	7 8
7 Apr 90	THAT'S THE WAY OF THE WORLD ffrr F 132 [3]	48 3
12 Feb 94	WHY ffrr FCD 227	23 3
3 Sep 94	ONE DAY ffrr FCDP 239	41 2
11 Nov 89	A LITTLE BIT OF THIS A LITTLE BIT OF THAT ffrr 8281591	46 11

[1] D Mob featuring Gary Haisman [2] D Mob featuring LRS [3] D Mob with Cathy Dennis [4] D Mob featuring Nuff Juice

DNA UK, male production duo –
Neal Slateford and Nick Bett (Singles: 29 Weeks)   pos/wks

28 Jul 90	● TOM'S DINER (re-mix) A&M AM 592 [1]	2 10
18 Aug 90	LA SERENISSIMA Raw Bass RBASS 006	34 8
3 Aug 91	REBEL WOMAN DNA 7DNA 001 [2]	42 4
1 Feb 92	CAN YOU HANDLE IT (re-recording) EMI EM 219 [3]	17 5
9 May 92	BLUE LOVE (CALL MY NAME) EMI EM 226 [4]	66 2

[1] DNA featuring Suzanne Vega [2] DNA featuring Jazzi P [3] DNA featuring Sharon Redd [4] DNA featuring Joe Nye

D*NOTE UK, male producer – Matt Winn (Singles: 3 Weeks)   pos/wks

12 Jul 97	WAITING HOPEFULLY A&M 5822792	46 1
15 Nov 97	LOST AND FOUND VC VCRD 25	59 1
27 Apr 02	SHED MY SKIN Channel 4 Music C4M 00182	73 1

D.O.P. UK, male instrumental / production duo (Singles: 2 Weeks)   pos/wks

3 Feb 96	STOP STARTING TO START STOPPING (EP) Hi-Life 5779472	58 1
13 Jul 96	GROOVY BEAT Hi-Life 5750652	54 1

Tracks on Stop Starting to Start Stopping (EP): Gusta / Dance to the House / Can You Feel It / How Do Y'All Feel

D.O.S.E. See Mark E SMITH

D:REAM UK, male vocal / instrumental /
production duo (Singles: 74 Weeks, Albums: 41 Weeks)   pos/wks

4 Jul 92	U R THE BEST THING FXU FXU 3	72 1
30 Jan 93	THINGS CAN ONLY GET BETTER Magnet MAG 1010CD	24 5
24 Apr 93	U R THE BEST THING (re-issue) Magnet MAG 1011CD	19 8
31 Jul 93	UNFORGIVEN Magnet MAG 1016CD	29 3
2 Oct 93	STAR / I LIKE IT Magnet MAG 1019CD	26 4
8 Jan 94	★ THINGS CAN ONLY GET BETTER (re-issue) Magnet MAG 1020CD	1 16
26 Mar 94	U R THE BEST THING (re-mix) Magnet MAG 1021CD	4 10
18 Jun 94	TAKE ME AWAY Magnet MAG 1025CD	18 5
10 Sep 94	BLAME IT ON ME Magnet MAG 1027CD	25 5
8 Jul 95	● SHOOT ME WITH YOUR LOVE Magnet MAG 1034CD	7 7
9 Sep 95	PARTY UP THE WORLD Magnet MAG 1037CD	20 6
11 Nov 95	THE POWER (OF ALL THE LOVE IN THE WORLD) Magnet MAG 1039CD	40 1
3 May 97	THINGS CAN ONLY GET BETTER (2nd re-issue) Magnet MAG 1050CD	19 3
30 Oct 93	● D:REAM ON VOLUME 1 Magnet 4509933712	5 37
30 Sep 95	● WORLD Magnet 0630117962	5 4

For second album D:Ream was just Peter Cunnah

DSK UK, male / female vocal / instrumental /
production group (Singles: 4 Weeks)   pos/wks

31 Aug 91	WHAT WOULD WE DO / READ MY LIPS Boy's Own BOI 6	46 3
22 Nov 97	WHAT WOULD WE DO (re-mix) Fresh FRSHD 63	55 1

DSM US, male rap group (Singles: 4 Weeks)   pos/wks

7 Dec 85	WARRIOR GROOVE 10 DAZZ 45-7	68 4

DSP See Matt DAREY

D-SHAKE
Holland, male producer – Adrianus De Mooy (Singles: 8 Weeks)   pos/wks

2 Jun 90	YAAAH / TECHNO TRANCE Cooltempo COOL 213	20 6
2 Feb 91	MY HEART THE BEAT Cooltempo COOL 228	42 2

D-SIDE
Ireland, male vocal group (Singles: 25 Weeks, Albums: 1 Week)   pos/wks

26 Apr 03	● SPEECHLESS WEA WEA 366CD1	9 8
26 Jul 03	● INVISIBLE Blacklist / Edsel / WEA WEA 369CD1	7 6
13 Dec 03	REAL WORLD Blacklist / Edel 9814017	9 8
12 Jun 04	PUSHIN' ME OUT Blacklist / Edel 0155825 ERE	21 3
17 Jan 04	STRONGER TOGETHER Blacklist / Edel 9866006	62 1

DT8 PROJECT (see also ANGELIC; ORION; CITIZEN CANED; Jurgen VRIES) UK, male producer – Darren Tate (Singles: 6 Weeks) pos/wks

3 May 03	DESTINATION ffrr DFCD 007 [1]	23 3
14 Aug 04	THE SUN IS SHINING (DOWN ON ME) Mondo MNDO 19CD	17 3

[1] DT8 featuring Roxanne Wilde

DTI US, male vocal / instrumental group (Singles: 1 Week)   pos/wks

16 Apr 88	KEEP THIS FREQUENCY CLEAR Premiere UK ERE 501	73 1

D-TEK UK, male instrumental / production group (Singles: 1 Week)   pos/wks

6 Nov 93	DROP THE ROCK (EP) Positiva 12TIV 5	70 1

Tracks on Drop the Rock (EP): Drop the Rock / Chunkafunk / Drop the Rock (re-mix) / Don't Breathe

D TRAIN US, male vocal / instrumental duo – James Williams and Hubert
Eaves III (Singles: 36 Weeks, Albums: 4 Weeks)   pos/wks

6 Feb 82	YOU'RE THE ONE FOR ME Epic EPC A 2016	30 8
8 May 82	WALK ON BY Epic EPC A 2298	44 6
7 May 83	MUSIC PART 1 Prelude A 3332	23 7
16 Jul 83	KEEP GIVING ME LOVE Prelude A 3497	65 2
27 Jul 85	YOU'RE THE ONE FOR ME (re-mix) Prelude ZB 40302	15 11
12 Oct 85	MUSIC (re-mix) Prelude ZB 40431	62 2
8 May 82	D-TRAIN Epic EPC 85683	72 4

D12 (see also EMINEM)
US, male rap group (Singles: 46 Weeks, Albums: 37 Weeks)   pos/wks

17 Mar 01	● SHIT ON YOU (re) Interscope 4974962	10 8
21 Jul 01	● PURPLE PILLS Shady / Interscope 4975692	2 12
17 Nov 01	FIGHT MUSIC Shady / Interscope 4976522	11 5
24 Apr 04	● MY BAND Shady / Interscope 9862352	2 13
7 Aug 04	HOW COME Shady / Interscope 9863318	4 8
30 Jun 01	● DEVILS NIGHT Interscope 4930792 ▲	2 17
8 May 04	★ D12 WORLD Interscope 9862431 ■ ▲	1 20

Azzido DA BASS
Germany, male DJ / producer – Ingo Martens (Singles: 13 Weeks)   pos/wks

4 Mar 00	DOOMS NIGHT (re) Club Tools 0067285 CLU	46 3
21 Oct 00	● DOOMS NIGHT (re) (re-mix) Club Tools 0120285 CLU	8 9
23 Mar 02	SPEED (CAN YOU FEEL IT) Club Tools 0135815 CLU [1]	68 1

[1] Azzido Da Bass featuring Roland Clark

DA BRAT US, female rapper – Shawntae Harris (Singles: 3 Weeks)   pos/wks

22 Oct 94	FUNKDAFIED Columbia 6609212	65 1
29 Nov 97	SOCKIT2ME East West E 3890CD [1]	33 2

[1] Missy Elliott featuring Da Brat

DA CLICK
UK, male rap group and female vocalist (Singles: 8 Weeks)   pos/wks

16 Jan 99	GOOD RHYMES ffrr FCD 353	14 6
29 May 99	WE ARE DA CLICK ffrr FCD 363	38 2

DA FOOL
US, male DJ / producer – Mike Stewart (Singles: 2 Weeks)   pos/wks

16 Jan 99	NO GOOD ffrr FCD 352	38 2

Ricardo DA FORCE (see also N-TRANCE)
UK, male rapper – Ricardo Lyte (Singles: 14 Weeks)   pos/wks

18 Mar 95	PUMP UP THE VOLUME Stress CDSTR 49 [1]	51 2
16 Sep 95	● STAYIN' ALIVE All Around the World CDGLOBE 131 [2]	2 11
31 Aug 96	WHY ffrr FCD 280	58 1

[1] Greed featuring Ricardo Da Force [2] N-Trance featuring Ricardo Da Force

DA HOOL *Germany, male instrumentalist /*
producer – Frank Tomiczek (Singles: 13 Weeks) pos/wks

14 Feb 98	**MEET HER AT THE LOVE PARADE** *Manifesto FESCD 39*	**15** 4
22 Aug 98	**BORA BORA** *Manifesto FESCD 47*	**35** 3
28 Jul 01	**MEET HER AT THE LOVE PARADE 2001** *Manifesto FESCD 85*	11 6

DA LENCH MOB *US, male rap group (Singles: 2 Weeks)* pos/wks

20 Mar 93	**FREEDOM GOT AN A.K.** *East West America A 8431CD*	**51** 2

DA MOB featuring JOCELYN BROWN
US, male / female vocal / instrumental group (Singles: 3 Weeks) pos/wks

2 May 98	**FUN** *INCredible INCR1 2CD*	**33** 2
3 Jul 99	**IT'S ALL GOOD** *INCredible INCR1 14CD*	**54** 1

DA MUTTZ (see also SHAFT) *UK, male production*
duo – Elliot Ireland and Alex Rizzo (Singles: 10 Weeks) pos/wks

9 Dec 00	**WASSUUP** *Eternal WEA 319CD*	11 10

Rui DA SILVA featuring CASSANDRA *Portugal, male producer*
and UK, female vocalist – Cassandra Fox (Singles: 14 Weeks) pos/wks

13 Jan 01	★ **TOUCH ME** *Kismet / Arista 74321823992* ■	1 14

DA SLAMMIN' PHROGZ
France, male production duo (Singles: 1 Week) pos/wks

29 Apr 00	**SOMETHING ABOUT THE MUSIC** *WEA WEA 251CD*	**53** 1

DA TECHNO BOHEMIAN
(see also KLUBHEADZ; DRUNKENMONKEY; ITTY BITTY BOOZY WOOZY)
Holland, male production trio (Singles: 1 Week) pos/wks

25 Jan 97	**BANGIN' BASS** *Hi-Life 5731772*	**63** 1

Paul DA VINCI (see also The RUBETTES)
UK, male vocalist – Paul Prewer (Singles: 8 Weeks) pos/wks

20 Jul 74	**YOUR BABY AIN'T YOUR BABY ANYMORE**	
	Penny Farthing PEN 843	**20** 8

Terry DACTYL and the DINOSAURS
UK, male vocalist and instrumental group (Singles: 16 Weeks) pos/wks

15 Jul 72	● **SEASIDE SHUFFLE** *UK 5*	**2** 12
13 Jan 73	**ON A SATURDAY NIGHT** *UK 21*	**45** 4

Terry Dactyl is Jona Lewie

DADA *US, male vocal / instrumental group (Singles: 1 Week)* pos/wks

4 Dec 93	**DOG** *IRS CDEIRSS 185*	**71** 1

DADDY FREDDY *See Simon HARRIS*

DADDY'S FAVOURITE
UK, male DJ / producer – DJ Harri (Singles: 3 Weeks) pos/wks

21 Nov 98	**I FEEL GOOD THINGS FOR YOU** *Go Beat GONCD 12*	**44** 2
9 Oct 99	**I FEEL GOOD THINGS FOR YOU** (re-issue) *Go Beat GOBCD 22*	**50** 1

DAFFY DUCK featuring the GROOVE GANG
Germany, male instrumental / production group (Singles: 3 Weeks) pos/wks

6 Jul 91	**PARTY ZONE** *East West YZ 592*	**58** 3

DAFT PUNK
France, male instrumental / production duo – Thomas Bangalter and Guy
Manuel de Homem-Christo (Singles: 35 Weeks, Albums: 54 Weeks) pos/wks

22 Feb 97	● **DA FUNK / MUSIQUE** *Soma / Virgin VSCDT 1625*	**7** 5
26 Apr 97	● **AROUND THE WORLD** *Virgin VSCDT 1633*	**5** 5
4 Oct 97	**BURNIN'** *Virgin VSCDT 1649*	**30** 2
28 Feb 98	**REVOLUTION 909** *Virgin VSCDT 1682*	**47** 1
25 Nov 00	● **ONE MORE TIME** *Virgin VSCDT 1791*	**2** 12
23 Jun 01	**DIGITAL LOVE** *Virgin VSCDT 1810*	14 7
17 Nov 01	**HARDER BETTER FASTER STRONGER** *Virgin VSCDT 1822*	**25** 3
1 Feb 97	● **HOMEWORK** *Virgin CDV 2821*	**8** 17
24 Mar 01	● **DISCOVERY** *Virgin CDVX 2940*	**2** 37

Etienne DAHO *See SAINT ETIENNE*

DAINTEES *See Martin STEPHENSON and the DAINTEES*

DAISY CHAINSAW *UK, male / female vocal /*
instrumental group (Singles: 6 Weeks, Albums: 1 Week) pos/wks

18 Jan 92	**LOVE YOUR MONEY** *Deva DEVA 001*	**26** 5
28 Mar 92	**PINK FLOWER / ROOM ELEVEN** *Deva 82TP 7*	**65** 1
10 Oct 92	**ELEVENTEEN** *Deva TPLP 100CD*	**62** 1

The first week on chart for 'Love Your Money' was listed under EP title 'Lovesick Pleasure'

DAJAE *See Junior SANCHEZ featuring DAJAE*

DAKEYNE *See James BROWN; TINMAN*

The DAKOTAS (see also Billy J KRAMER and the DAKOTAS)
UK, male instrumental group (Singles: 13 Weeks) pos/wks

11 Jul 63	**THE CRUEL SEA** *Parlophone R 5044*	**18** 13

Jim DALE *UK, male vocalist – James Smith (Singles: 22 Weeks)* pos/wks

11 Oct 57	● **BE MY GIRL** *Parlophone R 4343*	**2** 16
10 Jan 58	**JUST BORN (TO BE MY BABY)** *Parlophone R 4376*	**27** 1
17 Jan 58	**CRAZY DREAM** *Parlophone R 4376*	**24** 2
7 Mar 58	**SUGARTIME** *Parlophone R 4402*	**25** 3

DALE and GRACE
US, male / female vocal duo (Singles: 2 Weeks) pos/wks

9 Jan 64	**I'M LEAVING IT UP TO YOU** *London HL 9807* ▲	**42** 2

DALE SISTERS *UK, female vocal trio –*
Julie, Hazel and Betty Dunderdale (Singles: 7 Weeks) pos/wks

17 Mar 60	**HEARTBEAT** *HMV POP 710* [1]	**33** 1
23 Nov 61	**MY SUNDAY BABY** *Ember S 140*	**36** 6

[1] England Sisters

DALEK I *UK, male vocal / instrumental group (Albums: 2 Weeks)* pos/wks

9 Aug 80	**COMPASS KUMPAS** *Backdoor OPEN 1*	**54** 2

DALI'S CAR *UK, male vocal / instrumental*
duo (Singles: 2 Weeks, Albums: 1 Week) pos/wks

3 Nov 84	**THE JUDGEMENT IS THE MIRROR** *Paradox DOX 1*	**66** 2
1 Dec 84	**THE WAKING HOUR** *Paradox DOXLP 1*	**84** 1

DALLAS SUPERSTARS *Finland, male production duo –*
Heikki Liimatainen and Jaakko Slovaara (Singles: 1 Week) pos/wks

27 Oct 03	**HELIUM** *All Around the World CDGLOBE 289*	**64** 1

Roger DALTREY (see also The WHO)
UK, male vocalist (Singles: 46 Weeks, Albums: 30 Weeks) pos/wks

14 Apr 73	● **GIVING IT ALL AWAY** *Track 2094 110*	**5** 11
4 Aug 73	**I'M FREE** *Ode ODS 66302* [1]	**13** 10
14 May 77	**WRITTEN ON THE WIND** *Polydor 2121 319*	**46** 2
2 Aug 80	**FREE ME** *Polydor 2001 980*	**39** 6
11 Oct 80	**WITHOUT YOUR LOVE** *Polydor POSP 181*	**55** 4
3 Mar 84	**WALKING IN MY SLEEP** *WEA U 9686*	**56** 3
5 Oct 85	**AFTER THE FIRE** *10 TEN 69*	**50** 5
8 Mar 86	**UNDER A RAGING MOON** *10 TEN 81*	**43** 5
26 May 73	● **DALTREY** *Tracks 2406 107*	**6** 6
26 Jul 75	**RIDE A ROCK HORSE** *Polydor 2660 111*	**14** 10
4 Jun 77	**ONE OF THE BOYS** *Polydor 2442 146*	**45** 1
23 Aug 80	**MCVICAR (FILM SOUNDTRACK)** *Polydor POLD 5034*	**39** 11
2 Nov 85	**UNDER A RAGING MOON** *10 DIX 17*	**52** 2

[1] With London Symphony Orchestra and English Chamber Orchestra and English
Chamber Choir – conducted by David Measham

Glen DALY *UK, male vocalist (Albums: 2 Weeks)* pos/wks

20 Nov 71	**GLASGOW NIGHT OUT** *Golden Guinea GGL 0479*	**28** 2

DAMAGE
UK, male vocal group (Singles: 59 Weeks, Albums: 22 Weeks) pos/wks

20 Jul 96	**ANYTHING** *Big Life BLRD 129*	**68** 1
12 Oct 96	**LOVE II LOVE** *Big Life BLRD 131*	**12** 6

Singles re-entries are listed as (re), (2re), (3re)…. which signifies that the hit re-entered the chart once, twice or three times…

14 Dec 96 ●	**FOREVER** *Big Life BLRD 132* 6	9
22 Mar 97 ●	**LOVE GUARANTEED (re)** *Big Life BLRDA 133* 7	7
17 May 97 ●	**WONDERFUL TONIGHT** *Big Life BLRDA 134* 3	8
9 Aug 97	**LOVE LADY** *Big Life BLRDB 137* 33	2
1 Jul 00 ●	**GHETTO ROMANCE** *Cooltempo CDCOOL 347* 7	7
28 Oct 00	**RUMOURS** *Cooltempo CDCOOLS 352* 22	4
31 Mar 01	**STILL BE LOVIN' YOU (re)** *Cooltempo CDCOOLS 355* 11	7
14 Jul 01	**SO WHAT IF I (re)** *Cooltempo CDCOOLS 357* 12	6
15 Dec 01	**AFTER THE LOVE HAS GONE** *Cooltempo CDCOOL 360* 42	2
19 Apr 97	**FOREVER** *Big Life BLRCD 31* 13	12
14 Apr 01	**SINCE YOU'VE BEEN GONE** *Cooltempo 5289592* 16	10

Carolina DAMAS See SUENO LATINO

Bobby D'AMBROSIO featuring Michelle WEEKS
US, male DJ / producer and female vocalist (Singles: 3 Weeks)　pos/wks

2 Aug 97	**MOMENT OF MY LIFE** *Ministry of Sound MOSCDS 1* 23	3

DAMIAN *UK, male vocalist – Damian Davis (Singles: 26 Weeks)*　pos/wks

26 Dec 87	**THE TIME WARP 2** *Jive JIVE 160* 51	6
27 Aug 88	**THE TIME WARP 2 (re-issue)** *Jive JIVE 182* 64	4
19 Aug 89 ●	**THE TIME WARP (re-mix)** *Jive JIVE 209* 7	13
16 Dec 89	**WIG WAM BAM** *Jive JIVE 236* 49	4

'The Time Warp' is a re-mix of 'The Time Warp 2'

The DAMNED
UK, male vocal / instrumental group – includes Captain Sensible
(Ray Burns) (Singles: 77 Weeks, Albums: 54 Weeks)　pos/wks

5 May 79	**LOVE SONG** *Chiswick CHIS 112* 20	8
20 Oct 79	**SMASH IT UP** *Chiswick CHIS 116* 35	5
1 Dec 79	**I JUST CAN'T BE HAPPY TODAY** *Chiswick CHIS 120* 46	5
4 Oct 80	**HISTORY OF THE WORLD (PART 1)** *Chiswick CHIS 135* ...51	4
28 Nov 81	**FRIDAY 13TH (EP)** *Stiff One TRY 1* 50	4
10 Jul 82	**LOVELY MONEY** *Bronze BRO 149* 42	4
9 Jun 84	**THANKS FOR THE NIGHT** *Damned DAMNED 1* 43	4
30 Mar 85	**GRIMLY FIENDISH** *MCA GRIM 1* 21	7
22 Jun 85	**THE SHADOW OF LOVE (EDITION PREMIERE)** *MCA GRIM 2* ...25	8
21 Sep 85	**IS IT A DREAM** *MCA GRIM 3* 34	4
8 Feb 86 ●	**ELOISE (re)** *MCA GRIM 4* 3	10
22 Nov 86	**ANYTHING** *MCA GRIM 5* 32	4
7 Feb 87	**GIGOLO** *MCA GRIM 6* 29	3
25 Apr 87	**ALONE AGAIN OR** *MCA GRIM 7* 27	6
28 Nov 87	**IN DULCE DECORUM** *MCA GRIM 8* 72	1
12 Mar 77	**DAMNED DAMNED DAMNED** *Stiff SEEZ 1* 36	10
17 Nov 79	**MACHINE GUN ETIQUETTE** *Chiswick CWK 3011* ...31	5
29 Nov 80	**THE BLACK ALBUM** *Chiswick CWK 3015* 29	3
28 Nov 81	**THE BEST OF THE DAMNED** *Chiswick DAM 1* 43	12
23 Oct 82	**STRAWBERRIES** *Bronze BRON 542* 15	4
27 Jul 85	**PHANTASMAGORIA** *MCA MCF 3275* 11	17
13 Dec 86	**ANYTHING** *MCA MCG 6015* 40	2
12 Dec 87	**LIGHT AT THE END OF THE TUNNEL** *MCA MCSP 312* ...87	1

Tracks on Friday 13th (EP): Disco Man / Limit Club / Billy Bad Breaks / Citadel

Kenny DAMON *US, male vocalist (Singles: 1 Week)*　pos/wks

19 May 66	**WHILE I LIVE** *Mercury MF 907* 48	1

Vic DAMONE *US, male vocalist –*
Vito Farinola (Singles: 22 Weeks, Albums: 8 Weeks)　pos/wks

6 Dec 57	**AN AFFAIR TO REMEMBER (OUR LOVE AFFAIR) (re)**	
	Philips PB 745 29	2
9 May 58 ★	**ON THE STREET WHERE YOU LIVE** *Philips PB 819* 1	17
1 Aug 58	**THE ONLY MAN ON THE ISLAND** *Philips PB 837* 24	3
25 Apr 81	**NOW!** *RCA INTS 5080* 28	7
2 Apr 83	**VIC DAMONE SINGS THE GREAT SONGS** *CBS 32261* ...87	1

Richie DAN
UK, male DJ / producer – Richard Gittens (Singles: 3 Weeks)　pos/wks

12 Aug 00	**CALL IT FATE** *Pure Silk CDPSR 1* 34	3

DANA *Ireland, female vocalist – Rosemary Brown*
(later Scallon) (Singles: 75 Weeks, Albums: 2 Weeks)　pos/wks

4 Apr 70 ★	**ALL KINDS OF EVERYTHING (re)** *Rex R 11054* 1	16
13 Feb 71	**WHO PUT THE LIGHTS OUT** *Rex R 11062* 14	11

25 Jan 75 ●	**PLEASE TELL HIM THAT I SAID HELLO** *GTO GT 6* 8	14
13 Dec 75 ●	**IT'S GONNA BE A COLD COLD CHRISTMAS** *GTO GT 45* 4	6
6 Mar 76	**NEVER GONNA FALL IN LOVE AGAIN** *GTO GT 55* 31	4
16 Oct 76	**FAIRYTALE** *GTO GT 66* 13	16
31 Mar 79	**SOMETHING'S COOKIN' IN THE KITCHEN** *GTO GT 243* ...44	5
15 May 82	**I FEEL LOVE COMIN' ON** *Creole CR 32* 66	3
27 Dec 80	**EVERYTHING IS BEAUTIFUL** *Warwick WW 5099* 43	2

DANA See Mark PICCHIOTTI presents BASSTOY featuring DANA

DANA INTERNATIONAL
Israel, transgender vocalist – Yaron Cohen (Singles: 4 Weeks)　pos/wks

27 Jun 98	**DIVA** *Dance Pool DANA 1CD* 11	4

DANCE CONSPIRACY
UK, male instrumental / production duo (Singles: 1 Week)　pos/wks

3 Oct 92	**DUB WAR** *XL Recordings XLT 34* 72	1

DANCE FLOOR VIRUS
Italy, male vocal / instrumental group (Singles: 2 Weeks)　pos/wks

21 Oct 95	**MESSAGE IN A BOTTLE** *Epic 6623742* 49	2

DANCE TO TIPPERARY
UK, male vocal / instrumental group (Singles: 2 Weeks)　pos/wks

24 May 03	**THE BHOYS ARE BACK IN TOWN** *Nede NRCD 2105* 44	2

DANCE 2 TRANCE (see also JAM and SPOON featuring PLAVKA)
Germany, male instrumental / production duo –
Rolf Ellmer and Dag Lerner (Singles: 8 Weeks)　pos/wks

24 Apr 93	**P.OWER OF A.MERICAN N.ATIVES** *Logic 74321139582* 25	4
24 Jul 93	**TAKE A FREE FALL** *Logic 74321153602* 36	3
4 Feb 95	**WARRIOR** *Logic 74321257722* 56	1

Evan DANDO (see also The LEMONHEADS)
US, male vocalist (Singles: 2 Weeks, Albums: 1 Week)　pos/wks

24 Jun 95	**PERFECT DAY** *Virgin VSCDT 1552* [1] 75	1
31 May 03	**STOP MY HEAD** *Setanta SETCDA 127* 38	1
29 Mar 03	**BABY I'M BORED** *Setanta SETCD 114* 30	1

[1] Kirsty MacColl and Evan Dando

Suzanne DANDO
UK, female exercise instructor (Albums: 1 Week)　pos/wks

17 Mar 84	**SHAPE UP AND DANCE WITH SUZANNE DANDO**	
	Lifestyle LEG 21 87	1

The DANDY WARHOLS *US, male / female vocal /*
instrumental group (Singles: 30 Weeks, Albums: 20 Weeks)　pos/wks

28 Feb 98	**EVERY DAY SHOULD BE A HOLIDAY** *Capitol CDCL 797* 29	2
2 May 98	**NOT IF YOU WERE THE LAST JUNKIE ON EARTH**	
	Capitol CDCL 800 13	4
8 Aug 98	**BOYS BETTER** *Capitol CDCL 805* 36	2
10 Jun 00	**GET OFF** *Capitol CDCLS 821* 38	2
9 Sep 00	**BOHEMIAN LIKE YOU** *Capitol CDCLS 823* 42	1
7 Jul 01	**GODLESS** *Capitol CDCL 829* 66	1
10 Nov 01 ●	**BOHEMIAN LIKE YOU (re-issue)**	
	Parlophone / Capitol CDCLX 823 5	10
16 Mar 02	**GET OFF (re-issue)** *Parlophone / Capitol CDCL 835* ...34	2
17 May 03	**WE USED TO BE FRIENDS** *Capitol CDCL 843* 18	3
9 Aug 03	**YOU WERE THE LAST HIGH** *Parlophone CDCL 845* ...34	2
6 Dec 03	**PLAN A** *Parlophone CDCLS 851* 66	1
16 May 98	**COME DOWN** *Capitol 8365052* 16	8
24 Jun 00	**THIRTEEN TALES FROM URBAN BOHEMIA** *Capitol 8577872* ...32	9
31 May 03	**WELCOME TO THE MONKEYHOUSE** *Parlophone 5901232* 20	3

The DANDYS *UK, male vocal / instrumental group (Singles: 2 Weeks)*　pos/wks

14 Mar 98	**YOU MAKE ME WANT TO SCREAM** *Artificial ATFCD 3* 71	1
30 May 98	**ENGLISH COUNTRY GARDEN** *Artificial ATFCD 4* 57	1

DANE (see also ANOTHER LEVEL)
UK, male vocalist – Dane Bowers (Singles: 38 Weeks)　pos/wks

29 Apr 00 ●	**BUGGIN'** *Nulife 74321753342* [1] 6	8
26 Aug 00 ●	**OUT OF YOUR MIND (re)** *Nulife 74321782942* [2] 2	20

		pos/wks
3 Mar 01 ●	SHUT UP AND FORGET ABOUT IT *Arista 74321835342*	**9** 5
7 Jul 01 ●	ANOTHER LOVER *Arista 74321863412*	**9** 5

[1] True Steppers featuring Dane Bowers [2] True Steppers and Dane Bowers featuring Victoria Beckham

D'ANGELO *US, male vocalist – Michael*
D'Angelo (Singles: 11 Weeks, Albums: 5 Weeks) pos/wks

28 Oct 95	BROWN SUGAR *Cooltempo CDCOOL 307*	**24** 3
2 Mar 96	CRUISIN' *Cooltempo CDCOOL 316*	**31** 2
2 Mar 96	COLD WORLD *Geffen GFSTD 22114* [1]	**40** 2
15 Jun 96	LADY *Cooltempo CDCOOLS 323*	**21** 2
22 May 99	BREAK UPS 2 MAKE UPS *Def Jam 8709272* [2]	**33** 2
28 Oct 95	BROWN SUGAR *Cooltempo CTCD 46*	**57** 2
26 Feb 00	VOODOO *EMI 5250712* ▲	**21** 3

[1] Genius / GZA featuring D'Angelo [2] Method Man featuring D'Angelo

DANGER DANGER
US, male vocal / instrumental group (Singles: 5 Weeks) pos/wks

8 Feb 92	MONKEY BUSINESS *Epic 6577517*	**42** 2
28 Mar 92	I STILL THINK ABOUT YOU *Epic 6578387*	**46** 2
13 Jun 92	COMIN' HOME *Epic 6581337*	**75** 1

DAN-I *UK, male vocalist – Selmore Lewinson (Singles: 9 Weeks)* pos/wks

10 Nov 79	MONKEY CHOP *Island WIP 6520*	**30** 9

Charlie DANIELS BAND *US, male vocal / instrumental group (Singles: 10 Weeks, Albums: 1 Week)* pos/wks

22 Sep 79	THE DEVIL WENT DOWN TO GEORGIA *Epic EPC 7737*	**14** 10
10 Nov 79	MILLION MILE REFLECTIONS *Epic EPC 83446*	**74** 1

Johnny DANKWORTH and his ORCHESTRA *UK, male orchestra leader / instrumentalist – alto sax (Singles: 33 Weeks)* pos/wks

22 Jun 56 ●	EXPERIMENTS WITH MICE *Parlophone R 4185*	**7** 12
23 Feb 61 ●	AFRICAN WALTZ *Columbia DB 4590*	**9** 21

DANNII *See Dannii MINOGUE*

DANNY and the JUNIORS *US, male vocal group – leader*
Danny Rapp, b. 10 May 1941, d. 5 Apr 1983 (Singles: 19 Weeks) pos/wks

17 Jan 58 ●	AT THE HOP *HMV POP 436* ▲	**3** 14
10 Jul 76	AT THE HOP (re-issue) *ABC 4123*	**39** 5

DANNY WILSON *UK, male vocal / instrumental group (Singles: 28 Weeks, Albums: 11 Weeks)* pos/wks

22 Aug 87 ●	MARY'S PRAYER (re) *Virgin VS 934*	**3** 18
17 Jun 89	THE SECOND SUMMER OF LOVE *Virgin VS 1186*	**23** 9
16 Sep 89	NEVER GONNA BE THE SAME *Virgin VS 1203*	**69** 1
30 Apr 88	MEET DANNY WILSON *Virgin V 2419*	**65** 5
29 Jul 89	BEEBOP MOPTOP *Virgin V 2594*	**24** 5
31 Aug 91	SWEET DANNY WILSON *Virgin V 2669*	**54** 1

It was not until 'Mary's Prayer' re-entered in Apr 1988 that it reached its peak position of No.3

The DANSE SOCIETY *UK, male vocal / instrumental group (Singles: 5 Weeks, Albums: 4 Weeks)* pos/wks

27 Aug 83	WAKE UP *Society SOC 5*	**61** 3
5 Nov 83	HEAVEN IS WAITING *Society SOC 6*	**60** 2
11 Feb 84	HEAVEN IS WAITING *Society 205 972*	**39** 4

Steven DANTE *UK, male vocalist –*
Steven Dennis (Albums: 1 Week, Singles: 16 Weeks) pos/wks

26 Sep 87	THE REAL THING *Chrysalis CHS 3167* [1]	**13** 10
9 Jul 88	I'M TOO SCARED *Cooltempo DANTE 1*	**34** 6
3 Sep 88	FIND OUT *Cooltempo CTLP 6*	**87** 1

[1] Jellybean featuring Steven Dante

Tonja DANTZLER *US, female vocalist (Singles: 1 Week)* pos/wks

17 Dec 94	IN AND OUT OF MY LIFE *ffrr FCD 246*	**66** 1

DANY *See DOUBLE DEE*

DANZEL
Belgium, male producer – Johan Waem (Singles: 5 Weeks) pos/wks

6 Nov 04	PUMP IT UP *Data DATA 75CDS*	**11** 5

DANZIG *US, male vocal / instrumental group (Singles: 1 Week)* pos/wks

14 May 94	MOTHER *American MOMDD 1*	**62** 1

DAPHNE *US, female vocalist (Singles: 1 Week)* pos/wks

9 Dec 95	CHANGE *Stress CDSTR 54*	**71** 1

DAPHNE & CELESTE *US, female vocal duo –*
Daphne DeConcetto and Celeste Cruz (Singles: 28 Weeks) pos/wks

5 Feb 00 ●	OOH STICK YOU! *Universal MCSTD 40209*	**8** 12
17 Jun 00	UGLY *Universal MCSTD 40232*	**18** 12
2 Sep 00	SCHOOL'S OUT *Universal MCSTD 40238*	**12** 4

Olu DARA *See NAS*

Terence Trent D'ARBY `398` `Top 500`
Unpredictable US pop / soul singer / songwriter, b. 15 Mar 1962, New York, US, whose success came after relocating to the UK. Multi-million-selling, Grammy-winning debut album, 'Introducing the Hardline...', was a worldwide hit. Winner of 1988 Brit award for Best International Newcomer (Singles: 77 Weeks, Albums: 96 Weeks) pos/wks

14 Mar 87 ●	IF YOU LET ME STAY *CBS TRENT 1*	**7** 13
20 Jun 87 ●	WISHING WELL *CBS TRENT 2* ▲	**4** 11
10 Oct 87	DANCE LITTLE SISTER (PART ONE) *CBS TRENT 3*	**20** 7
9 Jan 88	SIGN YOUR NAME *CBS TRENT 4*	**2** 10
20 Jan 90	TO KNOW SOMEONE DEEPLY IS TO KNOW SOMEONE SOFTLY *CBS TRENT 6*	**55** 3
17 Apr 93	DO YOU LOVE ME LIKE YOU SAY *Columbia 6590732*	**14** 6
19 Jun 93	DELICATE *Columbia 6593312* [1]	**14** 6
28 Aug 93	SHE KISSED ME *Columbia 6595922*	**16** 7
20 Nov 93	LET HER DOWN EASY *Columbia 6598642*	**18** 7
8 Apr 95	HOLDING ON TO YOU *Columbia 6614235*	**20** 6
5 Aug 95	VIBRATOR *Columbia 6622585*	**57** 1
25 Jul 87 ★	INTRODUCING THE HARDLINE ACCORDING TO TERENCE TRENT D'ARBY *CBS 4509111* ■	**1** 67
4 Nov 89	NEITHER FISH NOR FLESH *CBS 4658091*	**12** 5
15 May 93 ●	SYMPHONY OR DAMN *Columbia 4735612*	**4** 19
29 Apr 95	TERENCE TRENT D'ARBY'S VIBRATOR *Columbia 4785052*	**11** 5

[1] Terence Trent D'Arby featuring Des'ree

Richard DARBYSHIRE *(see also LIVING IN A BOX)*
UK, male vocalist (Singles: 7 Weeks) pos/wks

20 Aug 88	COMING BACK FOR MORE *Chrysalis JEL 4* [1]	**41** 3
24 Jul 93	THIS I SWEAR *Dome CDDOME 1003*	**50** 3
12 Feb 94	WHEN ONLY LOVE WILL DO *Dome CDDOME 1008*	**54** 1

[1] Jellybean featuring Richard Darbyshire

DARE *UK, male vocal / instrumental group (Singles: 7 Weeks, Albums: 1 Week)* pos/wks

29 Apr 89	THE RAINDANCE *A&M AM 483*	**62** 2
29 Jul 89	ABANDON *A&M AM 519*	**71** 2
10 Aug 91	WE DON'T NEED A REASON *A&M AM 755*	**52** 2
5 Oct 91	REAL LOVE *A&M AM 824*	**67** 1
14 Sep 91	BLOOD FROM STONE *A&M 3953601*	**48** 1

DARE *Holland, female vocal duo (Singles: 1 Week)* pos/wks

13 Sep 03	CHIHUAHUA *All Around the World CDGLOBE 311*	**45** 1

Matt DAREY *(see also SPACE BABY; LOST TRIBE; MELT featuring LITTLE MS MARCIE; SUNBURST; MDM)*
UK, male producer / instrumentalist (Singles: 17 Weeks) pos/wks

9 Oct 99	LIBERATION (TEMPTATION – FLY LIKE AN ANGEL) *Incentive CENT 1CDS* [1]	**19** 3
22 Apr 00	FROM RUSSIA WITH LOVE *Liquid Asset ASSETCD 003* [2]	**40** 1
15 Jul 00	BEAUTIFUL *Incentive CENT 7CDS* [3]	**21** 4
20 Apr 02 ●	BEAUTIFUL (re-mix) *Incentive CENT 38CDS* [4]	**10** 6
14 Dec 02	U SHINE ON *Incentive CENT 50CDS* [5]	**34** 2

[1] Matt Darey presents Mash Up [2] Matt Darey presents DSP [3] Matt Darey's Mash Up presents Marcella Woods [4] Matt Darey featuring Marcella Woods [5] Matt Darey and Marcella Woods

Bobby DARIN 367 Top 500

Singer / songwriter / actor and multi-instrumentalist who had pop, rock, R&B, country and MOR hits, b. Walden Robert Cassotto, 14 May 1936, New York, US, d. 20 Dec 1973. This Grammy winner was posthumously inducted into the Rock and Roll Hall of Fame in 1990. His 2004 bio-pic 'Beyond the Sea' starred Kevin Spacey (Singles: 162 Weeks, Albums: 22 Weeks)   pos/wks

1 Aug 58	SPLISH SPLASH (re) *London HLE 8666*	18 7
9 Jan 59	QUEEN OF THE HOP *London HLE 8737*	24 2
29 May 59 ★	DREAM LOVER *London HLE 8867*	1 19
25 Sep 59 ★	MACK THE KNIFE (2re) *London HLK 8939* ▲	1 18
29 Jan 60 ●	LA MER (BEYOND THE SEA) (re) *London HLK 9034*	8 13
31 Mar 60 ●	CLEMENTINE *London HLK 9086*	8 12
30 Jun 60	BILL BAILEY (re) *London HLK 9142*	34 2
16 Mar 61 ●	LAZY RIVER *London HLK 9303*	2 13
6 Jul 61	NATURE BOY *London HLK 9375*	24 7
12 Oct 61 ●	YOU MUST HAVE BEEN A BEAUTIFUL BABY *London HLK 9429*	10 11
26 Oct 61	THEME FROM 'COME SEPTEMBER' *London HLK 9407* [1]	50 1
21 Dec 61 ●	MULTIPLICATION *London HLK 9474*	5 13
19 Jul 62 ●	THINGS *London HLK 9575*	2 17
4 Oct 62	IF A MAN ANSWERS *Capitol CL 15272*	24 6
29 Nov 62	BABY FACE *London HLK 9624*	40 4
25 Jul 63	EIGHTEEN YELLOW ROSES *Capitol CL 15306*	37 4
13 Oct 66 ●	IF I WERE A CARPENTER *Atlantic 584 051*	9 12
14 Apr 79	DREAM LOVER / MACK THE KNIFE (re-issue) *Lightning LIG 9017*	64 1
19 Mar 60 ●	THIS IS DARIN *London HA 2235*	4 8
9 Apr 60	THAT'S ALL *London HAE 2172*	15 1
5 Oct 85	THE LEGEND OF BOBBY DARIN – HIS GREATEST HITS *Stylus SMR 8504*	39 6
24 Jul 04	BEYOND THE SEA – THE VERY BEST OF BOBBY DARIN *Warner.esp WSMCD 183*	26 7

[1] Bobby Darin Orchestra

DARIO G

UK, male DJ / production trio (Singles: 44 Weeks, Albums: 4 Weeks)   pos/wks

27 Sep 97 ●	SUNCHYME *Eternal WEA 130CD*	2 18
20 Jun 98 ●	CARNAVAL DE PARIS *Eternal WEA 162CD*	5 9
12 Sep 98	SUNMACHINE *Eternal WEA 173CD*	17 4
25 Mar 00	VOICES *Eternal WEA 256CD*	37 2
3 Feb 01 ●	DREAM TO ME *Manifesto FESCD 79*	9 6
8 Jun 02	CARNAVAL 2002 (re-mix) *Eternal WEA 349CD*	34 3
25 Jan 03	HEAVEN IS CLOSER (FEELS LIKE HEAVEN) *Serious SER 61CD*	39 2
11 Jul 98	SUNMACHINE *Eternal 3984233782*	26 4

DARIUS *UK, male vocalist –*

Darius Danesh (Singles: 46 Weeks, Albums: 21 Weeks)   pos/wks

10 Aug 02 ★	COLOURBLIND *Mercury 639652* ■	1 16
7 Dec 02 ●	RUSHES (re) *Mercury 0638042*	5 12
15 Mar 03	INCREDIBLE (WHAT I MEANT TO SAY) (re) *Mercury 0779772*	9 8
21 Jun 03	GIRL IN THE MOON (re) *Fontana 9808233*	21 3
30 Oct 04 ●	KINDA LOVE *Mercury 9868349*	8 7
14 Dec 02 ●	DIVE IN *Mercury 635922*	6 19
6 Nov 04	LIVE TWICE *Mercury 9868263*	36 2

DARK GLOBE featuring Amanda GHOST

UK, male production duo and female vocalist (Singles: 1 Week)   pos/wks

1 May 04	BREAK MY WORLD *Island CID 853*	52 1

DARK MONKS *UK, male production duo (Singles: 1 Week)*   pos/wks

14 Sep 02	INSANE *Incentive CENT 45CDS*	62 1

DARK STAR

UK, male vocal / instrumental group (Singles: 6 Weeks)   pos/wks

26 Jun 99	ABOUT 3AM *Harvest CDEM 545*	50 1
15 Jan 00	GRACEADELICA *Harvest CDEMS 556*	25 3
13 May 00	I AM THE SUN *Harvest CDEMS 566*	31 2

DARKMAN

UK, male rapper – Brian Mitchell (Singles: 7 Weeks)   pos/wks

14 May 94	YABBA DABBA DOO *Wild Card CARDD 6*	49 2
20 Aug 94	WHO'S THE DARKMAN *Wild Card CARDD 8*	46 2

3 Dec 94	YABBA DABBA DOO (re-issue) *Wild Card CARDD 11*	37 2
21 Oct 95	BRAND NEW DAY *Wild Card 5771892*	74 1

The DARKNESS *UK, male vocal / instrumental*

group (Singles: 33 Weeks, Albums: 46 Weeks)   pos/wks

8 Mar 03	GET YOUR HANDS OFF MY WOMAN *Must Destroy DUSTY 006CD*	43 2
28 Jun 03	GROWING ON ME *Must Destroy DUSTY 010CD*	11 5
4 Oct 03 ●	I BELIEVE IN A THING CALLED LOVE *Must Destroy DARK 01CD*	2 11
27 Dec 03 ●	CHRISTMAS TIME (DON'T LET THE BELLS END) *Must Destroy DARK 02CD*	2 7
3 Apr 04 ●	LOVE IS ONLY A FEELING *Must Destroy DARK 03CD*	5 8
19 Jul 03 ★	PERMISSION TO LAND *Must Destroy 5046674522*	1 46

DARLING BUDS *UK, male / female vocal /*

instrumental group (Singles: 20 Weeks, Albums: 3 Weeks)   pos/wks

8 Oct 88	BURST *Epic BLOND 1*	50 5
7 Jan 89	HIT THE GROUND *CBS BLOND 2*	27 5
25 Mar 89	LET'S GO ROUND THERE *CBS BLOND 3*	49 4
22 Jul 89	YOU'VE GOT TO CHOOSE *CBS BLOND 4*	45 3
2 Jun 90	TINY MACHINE *CBS BLOND 5*	60 2
12 Sep 92	SURE THING *Epic 6582157*	71 1
18 Feb 89	POP SAID *Epic 462894 1*	23 3

Guy DARRELL *UK, male vocalist (Singles: 13 Weeks)*   pos/wks

18 Aug 73	I'VE BEEN HURT *Santa Ponsa PNS 4*	12 13

James DARREN

US, male vocalist – James Ercolani (Singles: 25 Weeks)   pos/wks

11 Aug 60	BECAUSE THEY'RE YOUNG *Pye International 7N 25059*	29 7
14 Dec 61	GOODBYE CRUEL WORLD *Pye International 7N 25116*	28 9
29 Mar 62	HER ROYAL MAJESTY *Pye International 7N 25125*	36 3
21 Jun 62	CONSCIENCE *Pye International 7N 25138*	30 6

The DARTS 392 Top 500

Britain's best-known doo-wop vocal group; line-up included Den Hegarty, Griff Fender, Rita Ray and Bob Fish. The popular London-based eight-piece band had three successive No.2 hits with revivals of early US rock 'n' roll and R&B songs (Singles: 117 Weeks, Albums: 57 Weeks)   pos/wks

5 Nov 77 ●	DADDY COOL / THE GIRL CAN'T HELP IT *Magnet MAG 100*	6 13
28 Jan 78 ●	COME BACK MY LOVE *Magnet MAG 110*	2 12
6 May 78 ●	THE BOY FROM NEW YORK CITY *Magnet MAG 116*	2 13
5 Aug 78 ●	IT'S RAINING *Magnet MAG 126*	2 11
11 Nov 78	DON'T LET IT FADE AWAY *Magnet MAG 134*	18 11
10 Feb 79	GET IT *Magnet MAG 140*	10 9
21 Jul 79	DUKE OF EARL *Magnet MAG 147*	6 11
20 Oct 79	CAN'T GET ENOUGH OF YOUR LOVE *Magnet MAG 156*	43 6
1 Dec 79	REET PETITE *Magnet MAG 160*	51 7
31 May 80	LET'S HANG ON *Magnet MAG 174*	11 14
6 Sep 80	PEACHES *Magnet MAG 179*	66 3
29 Nov 80	WHITE CHRISTMAS / SH-BOOM (LIFE COULD BE A DREAM) *Magnet MAG 184*	48 7
3 Dec 77 ●	DARTS *Magnet MAG 5020*	9 22
3 Jun 78	EVERYONE PLAYS DARTS *Magnet MAG 5022*	12 18
18 Nov 78 ●	AMAZING DARTS *K-Tel / Magnet DLP 7981*	8 13
6 Oct 79	DART ATTACK *Magnet MAG 5030*	38 4

DARUDE

Finland, male producer – Ville Virtanen (Singles: 29 Weeks)   pos/wks

24 Jun 00 ●	SANDSTORM *Neo NEOCD 033*	3 15
25 Nov 00 ●	FEEL THE BEAT *Neo NEOCD 045*	5 10
15 Sep 01	OUT OF CONTROL (BACK FOR MORE) *Neo NEOCD 067*	13 4

DAS EFX *US, male production / rap duo –*

Andre Weston and Willie Hines (Singles: 5 Weeks)   pos/wks

7 Aug 93	CHECK YO SELF *Fourth & Broadway BRCD 283* [1]	36 4
25 Apr 98	RAP SCHOLAR *East West E 3853CD* [2]	42 1

[1] Ice Cube featuring Das EFX [2] Das EFX featuring Redman

DASHBOARD CONFESSIONAL

US, male vocalist – Chris Carrabba (Singles: 2 Weeks)   pos/wks

25 Oct 03	HANDS DOWN *Vagrant 9813790*	60 1
27 Mar 04	RAPID HOPE LOSS *Vagrant 9861991*	75 1

The DATSUNS *New Zealand, male vocal /*
instrumental group (Singles: 7 Weeks, Albums: 4 Weeks)   pos/wks

5 Oct 02	IN LOVE *V2 VVR 5020953*	25	2
22 Feb 03	HARMONIC GENERATOR *V2 VVR 5021223*	33	2
6 Sep 03	MF FROM HELL *V2 5021753*	55	1
12 Jun 04	BLACKEN MY THUMB *V2 VVR 5026953*	48	1
23 Oct 04	GIRLS BEST FRIEND *V2 VVR 5028893*	71	1
19 Oct 02	THE DATSUNS *V2 VVR 1020962*	17	3
19 Jun 04	OUTTA SIGHT / OUTTA MIND *V2 VVR 1026942*	58	1

N'Dea DAVENPORT (see also The BRAND NEW HEAVIES)
US, female vocalist (Singles: 7 Weeks)   pos/wks

11 Sep 93	TRUST ME *Cooltempo CDCOOL 278* [1]	34	2
20 Jun 98	BRING IT ON *Gee Street VVR 5002033*	52	1
15 Dec 01	YOU CAN'T CHANGE ME *Defected DFECT 41CDS* [2]	25	4

[1] Guru featuring N'Dea Davenport [2] Roger Sanchez featuring Armand Van Helden and N'Dea Davenport

Anne-Marie DAVID *France, female vocalist (Singles: 9 Weeks)* pos/wks

| 28 Apr 73 | WONDERFUL DREAM *Epic EPC 1446* | 13 | 9 |

Craig DAVID (332) **Top 500**
Critically lauded singer / songwriter, b. 5 May 1981, Southampton, UK.
At 18 years, 11 months and 10 days he was the youngest British male to
write and sing a No.1. Won numerous awards for his songs, records and
videos. Debut album 'Born to Do It' went gold in 24 countries with UK sales
exceeding 1.5 million (Singles: 117 Weeks, Albums: 85 Weeks)   pos/wks

11 Dec 99	● RE-REWIND THE CROWD SAY BO SELECTA		
	Public Demand / Relentless RELENT 1CDS [1]	2	17
15 Apr 00	★ FILL ME IN *Wildstar CDWILD 28* ■	1	14
15 Jul 00	● WOMAN TROUBLE *Public Demand / ffrr FCD 380* [2]	6	10
5 Aug 00	★ 7 DAYS (re) *Wildstar CDWILD 30* ■	1	15
2 Dec 00	● WALKING AWAY *Wildstar CDWILD 35*	3	10
31 Mar 01	● RENDEZVOUS *Wildstar CDWILD 36*	8	10
9 Nov 02	● WHAT'S YOUR FLAVA? *Wildstar CDWILD 43*	8	10
1 Feb 03	● HIDDEN AGENDA *Wildstar CDWILD 44*	10	6
10 May 03	● RISE & FALL *Wildstar CDWILD 45* [3]	2	10
9 Aug 03	● SPANISH (re) *Wildstar CDWILD 49*	8	6
25 Oct 03	WORLD FILLED WITH LOVE *Wildstar CDWILD 51*	15	4
10 Jan 04	YOU DON'T MISS YOUR WATER ('TIL THE WELL RUNS DRY)		
	Wildstar CDWILD 52	43	2
26 Aug 00	★ BORN TO DO IT *Wildstar CDWILD 32* ■	1	50
23 Nov 02	● SLICKER THAN YOUR AVERAGE *Wildstar TWR 00252*	4	35

[1] Artful Dodger featuring Craig David [2] Artful Dodger and Robbie Craig featuring Craig David [3] Craig David featuring Sting

FR DAVID *France, male vocalist –*
Robert Fitoussi (Singles: 13 Weeks, Albums: 6 Weeks)   pos/wks

2 Apr 83	● WORDS *Carrere CAR 248*	2	12
18 Jun 83	MUSIC *Carrere CAR 282*	71	1
7 May 83	WORDS *Carrere CAL 145*	46	6

DAVID and JONATHAN (see also BLUE MINK; The PIPKINS) *UK, male*
vocal duo – Roger Greenaway and Roger Cook (Singles: 22 Weeks) pos/wks

| 13 Jan 66 | MICHELLE *Columbia DB 7800* | 11 | 6 |
| 7 Jul 66 | ● LOVERS OF THE WORLD UNITE *Columbia DB 7950* | 7 | 16 |

Jim DAVIDSON *UK, male vocalist (Singles: 4 Weeks)*   pos/wks

| 27 Dec 80 | WHITE CHRISTMAS / TOO RISKY *Scratch SCR 001* | 52 | 4 |

Paul DAVIDSON *Jamaica, male vocalist (Singles: 10 Weeks)*   pos/wks

| 27 Dec 75 | ● MIDNIGHT RIDER *Tropical ALO 56* | 10 | 10 |

Dave DAVIES (see also The KINKS)
UK, male vocalist (Singles: 17 Weeks)   pos/wks

| 19 Jul 67 | ● DEATH OF A CLOWN *Pye 7N 17356* | 3 | 10 |
| 6 Dec 67 | SUZANNAH'S STILL ALIVE *Pye 7N 17429* | 20 | 7 |

Windsor DAVIES See Don ESTELLE and Windsor DAVIES

Andrew DAVIS See BBC SYMPHONY ORCHESTRA SINGERS and CHORUS

Billie DAVIS
UK, female vocalist – Carol Hedges (Singles: 33 Weeks)   pos/wks

30 Aug 62	WILL I WHAT *Parlophone R 4932* [1]	18	10
7 Feb 63	● TELL HIM *Decca F 11572*	10	12
30 May 63	HE'S THE ONE *Decca F 11658*	40	3
9 Oct 68	I WANT YOU TO BE MY BABY *Decca F 12823*	33	8

[1] Mike Sarne with Billie Davis

Billy DAVIS Jr See 5TH DIMENSION; Marilyn McCOO and Billy DAVIS Jr

**Carl DAVIS and the ROYAL LIVERPOOL PHILHARMONIC
ORCHESTRA** *US, male conductor and orchestra (Albums: 4 Weeks)* pos/wks

| 19 Oct 91 | PAUL McCARTNEY'S LIVERPOOL ORATORIO | | |
| | *EMI Classics PAUL 1* | 36 | 4 |

Colin DAVIS See BBC SYMPHONY ORCHESTRA SINGERS and CHORUS

Darlene DAVIS *US, female vocalist (Singles: 5 Weeks)*   pos/wks

| 7 Feb 87 | I FOUND LOVE *Serious 7OUS 1* | 55 | 5 |

John DAVIS and the MONSTER ORCHESTRA
US, male vocal / instrumental group (Singles: 2 Weeks)   pos/wks

| 10 Feb 79 | AIN'T THAT ENOUGH FOR YOU *Miracle M 2* | 70 | 2 |

Mac DAVIS *US, male vocalist (Singles: 22 Weeks)*   pos/wks

| 4 Nov 72 | BABY DON'T GET HOOKED ON ME *CBS 8250* ▲ | 29 | 6 |
| 15 Nov 80 | IT'S HARD TO BE HUMBLE *Casablanca CAN 210* | 27 | 16 |

Miles DAVIS *US, male instrumentalist – trumpet,*
b. 26 May 1926, d. 28 Sep 1991 (Albums: 9 Weeks)   pos/wks

11 Jul 70	BITCHES BREW *CBS 66236*	71	1
15 Jun 85	YOU'RE UNDER ARREST *CBS 26447*	88	1
18 Oct 86	TUTU *Warner Bros. 925490 1*	74	2
3 Jun 89	AMANDLA *Warner Bros. WX 250*	49	2
5 Oct 96	THE VERY BEST OF MILES DAVIS *Columbia SONYTV 17CD*	64	1
28 Apr 01	KIND OF BLUE *Columbia CK 64935*	63	2

Richie DAVIS See SHUT UP AND DANCE

Roy DAVIS Jr
US, male DJ / producer (Singles: 5 Weeks)   pos/wks

| 1 Nov 97 | GABRIEL *XL XLS 88CD* [1] | 22 | 4 |
| 31 Jan 04 | ABOUT LOVE *Classic CMC 21* | 70 | 1 |

[1] Roy Davis Jr featuring Peven Everett

Ruth DAVIS See Bo KIRKLAND and Ruth DAVIS

Sammy DAVIS Jr (see also The RATPACK) *US, male vocalist,*
b. 8 Dec 1925, d. 16 May 1990 (Singles: 37 Weeks, Albums: 1 Week) pos/wks

29 Jul 55	SOMETHING'S GOTTA GIVE (re) *Brunswick LAT 8296*	11	7
9 Sep 55	● LOVE ME OR LEAVE ME (re) *Brunswick 05428*	8	8
30 Sep 55	THAT OLD BLACK MAGIC *Brunswick 05450*	16	1
7 Oct 55	HEY THERE *Brunswick 05469*	19	1
20 Apr 56	IN A PERSIAN MARKET *Brunswick 05518*	28	1
28 Dec 56	ALL OF YOU *Brunswick 05629*	28	1
16 Jun 60	HAPPY TO MAKE YOUR ACQUAINTANCE *Brunswick 05830* [1]	46	1
22 Mar 62	WHAT KIND OF FOOL AM I? / GONNA BUILD A MOUNTAIN		
	Reprise R 20048	26	8
13 Dec 62	ME AND MY SHADOW (re) *Reprise R 20128* [2]	20	9
13 Apr 63	SAMMY DAVIS JR AT THE COCONUT GROVE *Reprise R 6063/2*	19	1

[1] Sammy Davis Jr and Carmen McRae [2] Frank Sinatra and Sammy Davis Jr

Skeeter DAVIS *US, female vocalist – Mary Penick,*
b. 30 Dec 1931, d. 19 Sep 2004 (Singles: 13 Weeks)   pos/wks

| 14 Mar 63 | THE END OF THE WORLD *RCA 1328* | 18 | 13 |

TJ DAVIS *UK, female vocalist (Singles: 4 Weeks)*   pos/wks

| 27 Jul 96 | BRILLIANT FEELING *Arista 74321380902* [1] | 72 | 1 |
| 29 Dec 01 | WONDERFUL LIFE *Melting Pot MPRCD 20* | 42 | 3 |

[1] Full Monty Allstars featuring TJ Davis

Zelma DAVIS See C & C MUSIC FACTORY

Spencer DAVIS GROUP (see also Steve WINWOOD) *UK, male vocal / instrumental group (Singles: 71 Weeks, Albums: 47 Weeks)* pos/wks

5 Nov 64	I CAN'T STAND IT *Fontana TF 499*	.....47 3
25 Feb 65	EVERY LITTLE BIT HURTS (re) *Fontana TF 530*	.....41 3
10 Jun 65	STRONG LOVE (re) *Fontana TF 571*	.....44 4
2 Dec 65 ★	KEEP ON RUNNING *Fontana TF 632*	.....1 14
24 Mar 66 ★	SOMEBODY HELP ME *Fontana TF 679*	.....1 10
1 Sep 66	WHEN I COME HOME *Fontana TF 739*	.....12 9
3 Nov 66 ●	GIMME SOME LOVING *Fontana TF 762*	.....2 12
26 Jan 67 ●	I'M A MAN *Fontana TF 785*	.....9 7
9 Aug 67	TIME SELLER *Fontana TF 854*	.....30 5
10 Jan 68	MR SECOND CLASS *United Artists UP 1203*	.....35 4
8 Jan 66 ●	THEIR 1ST LP *Fontana TL 5242*	.....6 9
22 Jan 66 ●	THE 2ND LP *Fontana TL 5295*	.....3 18
11 Sep 66 ●	AUTUMN '66 *Fontana TL 5359*	.....4 20

DAVIS PINCKNEY PROJECT *See GO GO LORENZO and the DAVIS PINCKNEY PROJECT*

DAWN *US, male / female vocal group – leader Tony Orlando (Michael Cassavitis) (Singles: 109 Weeks, Albums: 2 Weeks)* pos/wks

16 Jan 71 ●	CANDIDA *Bell 1118*	.....9 11
10 Apr 71 ★	KNOCK THREE TIMES *Bell 1146* ▲	.....1 27
31 Jul 71 ●	WHAT ARE YOU DOING SUNDAY *Bell 1169* [1]	.....3 12
10 Mar 73 ★	TIE A YELLOW RIBBON ROUND THE OLE OAK TREE (re) *Bell 1287* [1] ▲	.....1 40
4 Aug 73	SAY, HAS ANYBODY SEEN MY SWEET GYPSY ROSE *Bell 1322* [1]	.....12 15
9 Mar 74	WHO'S IN THE STRAWBERRY PATCH WITH SALLY *Bell 1343* [2]	.....37 4
4 May 74	GOLDEN RIBBONS *Bell BELLS 236*	.....46 2

[1] Dawn featuring Tony Orlando [2] Tony Orlando and Dawn

Julie DAWN *See Cyril STAPLETON and his ORCHESTRA*

Liz DAWN *See Joe LONGTHORNE*

DAWN OF THE REPLICANTS *UK, male vocal / instrumental group (Singles: 2 Weeks, Albums: 1 Week)* pos/wks

7 Feb 98	CANDLEFIRE *East West EW 147CD1*	.....52 1
4 Apr 98	HOGWASH FARM (THE DIESEL HANDS EP) *East West EW 157CD*	.....65 1
28 Feb 98	ONE HEAD TWO ARMS TWO LEGS *East West 630196002*	.....62 1

Tracks on Hogwash Farm (The Diesel Hands EP): Hogwash Farm (re-built) / Night Train to Lichtenstein / The Duchess of Surin / Crow Valley

Dana DAWSON *US, female vocalist (Singles: 14 Weeks)* pos/wks

15 Jul 95 ●	3 IS FAMILY *EMI CDEM 378*	.....9 8
28 Oct 95	GOT TO GIVE ME LOVE *EMI CDEM 392*	.....27 2
4 May 96	SHOW ME *EMI CDEMS 423*	.....28 3
20 Jul 96	HOW I WANNA BE LOVED *EMI CDEMS 432*	.....42 1

Bobby DAY *US, male vocalist – Robert Byrd, b. 1 Jul 1930, d. 15 Jul 1990 (Singles: 2 Weeks)* pos/wks

7 Nov 58	ROCKIN' ROBIN *London HL 8726*	.....29 2

Darren DAY *UK, male vocalist (Singles: 7 Weeks, Albums: 1 Week)* pos/wks

8 Oct 94	YOUNG GIRL *Bell 74321231082*	.....42 2
8 Jun 96	SUMMER HOLIDAY MEDLEY *RCA 74321384472*	.....17 4
9 May 98	HOW CAN I BE SURE? *Eastcoast DDCD 001*	.....71 1
18 Apr 98	DARREN DAY *Eastcoast DAYCD 01*	.....62 1

Doris DAY `373` **Top 500** *The fifties' favourite singer / actress, b. Doris Kappelhoff, 3 Apr 1924, Cincinnati, US. The No.1 female movie star of that era, she also had numerous British hits (not to mention 25 US bestsellers) before the UK chart first started (Singles: 146 Weeks, Albums: 37 Weeks)* pos/wks

14 Nov 52 ●	SUGARBUSH (re) *Columbia DB 3123* [1]	.....8 8
21 Nov 52 ●	MY LOVE AND DEVOTION *Columbia DB 3157*	.....10 2
3 Apr 53	MA SAYS, PA SAYS *Columbia DB 3242* [2]	.....12 1
17 Apr 53	FULL TIME JOB *Columbia DB 3242* [2]	.....11 1
24 Jul 53 ●	LET'S WALK THAT-A-WAY *Philips PB 157* [2]	.....4 14
2 Apr 54 ★	SECRET LOVE *Philips PB 230* ▲	.....1 29
27 Aug 54 ●	THE BLACK HILLS OF DAKOTA *Philips PB 287*	.....7 8
1 Oct 54 ●	IF I GIVE MY HEART TO YOU *Philips PB 325* [3]	.....4 11
8 Apr 55 ●	READY, WILLING AND ABLE *Philips PB 402*	.....7 9

9 Sep 55	LOVE ME OR LEAVE ME *Philips PB 479*	.....20 1
21 Oct 55	I'LL NEVER STOP LOVING YOU (re) *Philips PB 497*	.....17 3
29 Jun 56 ★	WHATEVER WILL BE, WILL BE (QUE SERA, SERA) *Philips PB 586*	.....1 22
13 Jun 58	A VERY PRECIOUS LOVE *Philips PB 799*	.....16 11
15 Aug 58	EVERYBODY LOVES A LOVER (re) *Philips PB 843*	.....25 4
12 Mar 64 ●	MOVE OVER DARLING *CBS AAG 183*	.....8 16
18 Apr 87	MOVE OVER DARLING (re-issue) *CBS LEGS 1*	.....45 6
6 Jan 79	20 GOLDEN GREATS *Warwick PR 5053*	.....12 11
11 Nov 89	A PORTRAIT OF DORIS DAY *Stylus SMR 984*	.....32 9
6 Nov 93	GREATEST HITS *Telstar TCD 2659*	.....14 12
10 Dec 94	THE LOVE ALBUM *Vision VIS CD2*	.....64 3
20 Nov 99	THE MAGIC OF THE MOVIES *Columbia SONYTV 79CD*	.....63 1
20 Apr 02	THE BEST OF DORIS DAY – 41 HOLLYWOOD GREATS *Columbia 5079632*	.....73 1

[1] Doris Day and Frankie Laine [2] Doris Day and Johnnie Ray [3] Doris Day with the Mellomen

Inaya DAY (see also Boris DLUGOSCH) *US, female vocalist – Inaya Davis (Singles: 3 Weeks)* pos/wks

22 May 99	JUST CAN'T GET ENOUGH *AM:PM CDAMPM 121* [1]	.....39 2
7 Oct 00	FEEL IT *Positiva CDTIV 141*	.....51 1

[1] Harry 'Choo Choo' Romero presents Inaya Day

DAY ONE *UK, male vocal / instrumental duo (Singles: 1 Week, Albums: 1 Week)* pos/wks

13 Nov 99	I'M DOIN' FINE *Melankolic / Virgin SADD 6*	.....68 1
25 Mar 00	ORDINARY MAN *Melankolic CDSAD 8*	.....70 1

Patti DAY *US, female vocalist (Singles: 1 Week)* pos/wks

9 Dec 89	RIGHT BEFORE MY EYES *Debut DEBT 3080*	.....69 1

DAYEENE *Sweden, female vocal duo (Singles: 1 Week)* pos/wks

17 Jul 99	AND IT HURTS *Pukka CDPUKKA 20*	.....63 1

Taylor DAYNE *US, female vocalist – Leslie Wundermann (Singles: 54 Weeks, Albums: 17 Weeks)* pos/wks

23 Jan 88 ●	TELL IT TO MY HEART *Arista 109616*	.....3 13
19 Mar 88 ●	PROVE YOUR LOVE *Arista 109830*	.....8 10
11 Jun 88	I'LL ALWAYS LOVE YOU *Arista 111536*	.....41 7
18 Nov 89	WITH EVERY BEAT OF MY HEART *Arista 112760*	.....53 2
14 Apr 90	I'LL BE YOUR SHELTER *Arista 112996*	.....43 5
4 Aug 90	LOVE WILL LEAD YOU BACK *Arista 113277* ▲	.....69 1
3 Jul 93	CAN'T GET ENOUGH OF YOUR LOVE *Arista 74321147852*	.....14 8
16 Apr 94	I'LL WAIT *Arista 74321203472*	.....29 3
4 Feb 95	ORIGINAL SIN (THEME FROM 'THE SHADOW') *Arista 74321223462*	.....63 1
18 Nov 95	SAY A PRAYER *Arista 74321324292*	.....58 1
13 Jan 96	TELL IT TO MY HEART (re-mix) *Arista 74321335962*	.....23 3
5 Mar 88	TELL IT TO MY HEART *Arista 208898*	.....24 17

DAYTON *US, male vocal group (Singles: 1 Week)* pos/wks

10 Dec 83	THE SOUND OF MUSIC *Capitol CL 318*	.....75 1

DAZZ BAND *US, male vocal / instrumental group (Singles: 12 Weeks)* pos/wks

3 Nov 84	LET IT ALL BLOW *Motown TMG 1361*	.....12 12

Darryl D'BONNEAU *See Barbara TUCKER*

D'BORA *US, female vocalist – Deborah Walker (Singles: 4 Weeks)* pos/wks

14 Sep 91	DREAM ABOUT YOU *Polydor PO 161*	.....75 1
1 Jul 95	GOING ROUND *Vibe MCSTD 2055*	.....40 2
30 Mar 96	GOOD LOVE REAL LOVE *Music Plant MCSTD 40023*	.....58 1

Nino DE ANGELO *Germany, male vocalist (Singles: 5 Weeks)* pos/wks

21 Jul 84	GUARDIAN ANGEL *Carrere CAR 335*	.....57 5

DE BOS *Holland, male DJ / producer – Andre Van Den Bosch (Singles: 1 Week)* pos/wks

25 Oct 97	ON THE RUN *Jive JIVECD 433*	.....51 1

Chris DE BURGH `149` `Top 500`

Irish singing / songwriting son of a diplomat, b. Christopher Davidson, 15 Oct 1948, Argentina. The first act to enter the Swiss album chart at No.1. Despite his international album success, he will be remembered for the No.1 he reportedly wrote for and about his wife. Daughter Rosanna was crowned Miss World in 2003 (Singles: 71 Weeks, Albums: 282 Weeks)

pos/wks

23 Oct 82	DON'T PAY THE FERRYMAN *A&M AMS 8256*	48	5
12 May 84	HIGH ON EMOTION *A&M AM 190*	44	5
12 Jul 86 ★	THE LADY IN RED (re) *A&M AM 331*	1	15
20 Sep 86	FATAL HESITATION *A&M AM 346*	44	4
13 Dec 86	A SPACEMAN CAME TRAVELLING / THE BALLROOM OF ROMANCE *A&M AM 365*	40	5
12 Dec 87	THE SIMPLE TRUTH (A CHILD IS BORN) (re) *A&M AM 427*	55	3
29 Oct 88 ●	MISSING YOU *A&M AM 474*	3	12
7 Jan 89	TENDER HANDS *A&M AM 486*	43	6
14 Oct 89	THIS WAITING HEART *A&M AM 528*	59	3
25 May 91	THE SIMPLE TRUTH (A CHILD IS BORN) (re-issue) *A&M RELF 1*	36	2
11 Apr 92	SEPARATE TABLES *A&M AM 863*	30	4
21 May 94	BLONDE HAIR BLUE JEANS *A&M 5805932*	51	1
9 Dec 95	THE SNOWS OF NEW YORK *A&M 5813132*	60	1
27 Sep 97	SO BEAUTIFUL *A&M 5823932*	29	4
18 Sep 99	WHEN I THINK OF YOU *A&M / Mercury 4971302*	59	1
12 Sep 81	BEST MOVES *A&M AMLH 68532*	65	4
9 Oct 82	THE GETAWAY *A&M AMLH 68549*	30	16
19 May 84	MAN ON THE LINE *A&M AMLX 65002*	11	24
29 Dec 84 ●	THE VERY BEST OF CHRIS DE BURGH *Telstar STAR 2248*	6	70
24 Aug 85	SPANISH TRAIN AND OTHER STORIES *A&M AMLH 68343*	78	3
7 Jun 86 ●	INTO THE LIGHT *A&M AM 5121*	2	59
4 Oct 86	CRUSADER *A&M AMLH 64746*	72	1
15 Oct 88 ★	FLYING COLOURS *A&M AMA 5224* ■	1	30
4 Nov 89 ●	SPARK TO A FLAME – THE VERY BEST OF CHRIS DE BURGH *A&M CDBLP 100*	4	29
22 Sep 90	HIGH ON EMOTION – LIVE FROM DUBLIN! *A&M 3970861*	15	14
9 May 92 ●	POWER OF TEN *A&M 3971882*	3	10
28 May 94 ●	THIS WAY UP *A&M 5402332*	5	6
18 Nov 95	BEAUTIFUL DREAMS *A&M 5404322*	33	8
11 Oct 97 ●	THE LOVE SONGS *A&M 5407942*	8	7
2 Oct 99	QUIET REVOLUTION *Mercury / A&M 4904462*	23	3
31 Mar 01	THE ULTIMATE COLLECTION – NOTES FROM PLANET EARTH *Mercury / A&M 4908992*	19	4
28 Sep 02 ●	TIMING IS EVERYTHING ... *Mercury / A&M 4934292*	41	1
27 Mar 04	THE ROAD TO FREEDOM *Ferryman FERRY 888*	75	1

DE CASTRO SISTERS *Cuba, female vocal group (Singles: 1 Week)* pos/wks

11 Feb 55	TEACH ME TONIGHT *London HL 8104*	20	1

'with Skip Martin and his Orchestra'

DE-CODE featuring Beverli SKEETE
UK, male / female vocal / instrumental group (Singles: 1 Week) pos/wks

18 May 96	WONDERWALL / SOME MIGHT SAY *Neoteric NRCD 2*	69	1

Etienne DE CRECY
France, male DJ / producer (Singles: 3 Weeks) pos/wks

28 Mar 98	PRIX CHOC REMIXES *Different DIF 007CD*	60	1
20 Jan 01	AM I WRONG *XL Recordings XLS 127CD*	44	2

DE FUNK featuring F45
Italy / UK, male production / vocal group (Singles: 1 Week) pos/wks

25 Sep 99	PLEASURE LOVE *INCredible INCS 3CD*	49	1

Lennie DE ICE *UK, male producer (Singles: 1 Week)* pos/wks

17 Apr 99	WE ARE I. E. *Distinctive DISNCD 50*	61	1

DE LA SOUL `480` `Top 500` (see also The JUNGLE BROTHERS)

Brooklyn, New York vocal / production trio that replaced bitches and firearms with beads and flowers. Posdnous (Kelvin Mercer), Trugoy the Dove (David Joliceur) and Mase (Vincent Mason). '3 Feet High and Rising', produced by Prince Paul, spawned four hit singles and was one of the most influential rap LPs of all time (Singles: 63 Weeks, Albums: 88 Weeks)

pos/wks

8 Apr 89	ME MYSELF AND I *Big Life BLR 7*	22	8
8 Jul 89	SAY NO GO *Big Life BLR 10*	18	7
21 Oct 89	EYE KNOW *Big Life BLR 13*	14	7
23 Dec 89 ●	THE MAGIC NUMBER / BUDDY *Big Life BLR 14*	7	8
24 Mar 90	MAMA GAVE BIRTH TO THE SOUL CHILDREN *Gee Street GEE 26* [1]	14	7
27 Apr 91 ●	RING RING RING (HA HA HEY) *Big Life BLR 42*	10	7
3 Aug 91	A ROLLER SKATING JAM NAMED 'SATURDAYS' *Big Life BLR 55*	22	5
23 Nov 91	KEEPIN' THE FAITH *Big Life BLR 64*	50	2
18 Sep 93	BREAKADAWN *Big Life BLRD 103*	39	3
2 Apr 94	FALLIN' *Epic 6602622* [2]	59	1
29 Jun 96	STAKES IS HIGH *Tommy Boy TBCD 7730*	55	1
8 Mar 97	4 MORE *Tommy Boy TBCD 7779A* [3]	52	1
22 Jul 00	OOOH *Tommy Boy TBCD 2102* [4]	29	2
11 Nov 00	ALL GOOD *Tommy Boy TBCD 2154B* [5]	33	3
2 Mar 02	BABY PHAT *Tommy Boy TBCD 2359*	55	1
25 Mar 89	3 FEET HIGH AND RISING *Big Life DLSLP 1*	13	56
25 May 91 ●	DE LA SOUL IS DEAD *Big Life BLRLP 8*	7	11
9 Oct 93	BUHLOONE MINDSTATE *Big Life BLRCD 25*	37	2
13 Jul 96	STAKES IS HIGH *Tommy Boy TBCD 1149*	42	1
9 Oct 99	3 FEET HIGH AND RISING (re-issue) *Tommy Boy TBCD 1019*	17	2
19 Aug 00	ART OFFICIAL INTELLIGENCE: MOSAIC THUMP *Tommy Boy TBCD 1348*	22	4
14 Jun 03	THE BEST OF *Rhino / Tommy Boy 8122736652*	17	12

[1] Queen Latifah + De La Soul [2] Teenage Fanclub and De La Soul [3] De La Soul featuring Zhané [4] De La Soul featuring Redman [5] De La Soul featuring Chaka Khan

'Buddy' listed only until 6 Jan 1990, peaking at No.8

Donna DE LORY *US, female vocalist (Singles: 1 Week)* pos/wks

24 Jul 93	JUST A DREAM *MCA MCSTD 1750*	71	1

Vincent DE MOOR (see also VERACOCHA)
Holland, male producer (Singles: 4 Weeks) pos/wks

16 Aug 97	FLOWTATION *XL Recordings XLS 89CD*	54	1
7 Apr 01	FLY AWAY *VC Recordings VCRD 87*	30	3

DE NADA
UK, male / female production / vocal group (Singles: 7 Weeks) pos/wks

25 Aug 01	LOVE YOU ANYWAY *Wildstar CDWILD 37*	15	4
9 Feb 02	BRING IT ON TO MY LOVE *Wildstar CDWILD 39*	24	3

DE NUIT *Italy, male production duo –*
Fabio Seveso and Francesco de Leo (Singles: 2 Weeks) pos/wks

23 Nov 02	ALL THAT MATTERED (LOVE YOU DOWN) *Credence CDCRED 029*	38	2

Lynsey DE PAUL
UK, female vocalist / instrumentalist – keyboards – Lynsey Rubin (Singles: 54 Weeks) pos/wks

19 Aug 72 ●	SUGAR ME *MAM 81*	5	11
2 Dec 72	GETTING A DRAG *MAM 88*	18	8
27 Oct 73	WON'T SOMEBODY DANCE WITH ME *MAM 109*	14	7
8 Jun 74	OOH I DO *Warner Bros. K 16401*	25	6
2 Nov 74	NO HONESTLY *Jet 747*	7	11
22 Mar 75	MY MAN AND ME *Jet 750*	40	4
26 Mar 77	ROCK BOTTOM *Polydor 2058 859* [1]	19	7

[1] Lynsey De Paul and Mike Moran

Tullio DE PISCOPO *Italy, male vocalist (Singles: 4 Weeks)* pos/wks

28 Feb 87	STOP BAJON ... PRIMAVERA *Greyhound GREY 9*	58	4

Manitas DE PLATA *France, male*
instrumentalist – guitar – Ricardo Baliardo (Albums: 1 Week) pos/wks

29 Jul 67	FLAMENCO GUITAR *Philips SBL 7786*	40	1

Rebecca DE RUVO *Sweden, female vocalist (Singles: 1 Week)* pos/wks

1 Oct 94	I CAUGHT YOU OUT *Arista 74321230782*	72	1

Teri DE SARIO *US, female vocalist (Singles: 5 Weeks)* pos/wks

2 Sep 78	AIN'T NOTHING GONNA KEEP ME FROM YOU *Casablanca CAN 128*	52	5

Stephanie DE SYKES
UK, female vocalist – Stephanie Ryton (Singles: 17 Weeks) pos/wks

20 Jul 74 ●	BORN WITH A SMILE ON MY FACE		
	Bradley's BRAD 7409 [1] **2**	10
19 Apr 75	WE'LL FIND OUR DAY *Bradley's BRAD 7509* **17**	7

[1] Stephanie De Sykes with Rain

Tony DE VIT
UK, male DJ / producer,
b. 12 Sep 1957, d. 2 Jul 1998 (Singles: 13 Weeks) pos/wks

4 Mar 95	BURNING UP *Icon ICONCD 001* **25**	3
12 Aug 95	HOOKED *Labello Dance LAD 18CD* [1] **28**	2
9 Sep 95	TO THE LIMIT *X:Plode BANG 1CD* **44**	2
30 May 96	I'LL BE THERE *Labello Dance LAD 25CD1* [1] **37**	2
28 Oct 00	DAWN *Tidy Trax TIDY 140CD* **56**	2
21 Dec 02	I DON'T CARE *Tidy Trax TIDY 181T* **65**	1
12 Jul 03	GIVE ME A REASON *Tidy Trax TIDYTWO 123CD* [2] ...**53**	1

[1] 99th Floor Elevators featuring Tony De Vit [2] Tony De Vit featuring Niki Mak

DEACON BLUE `167` `Top 500`
Scottish sextet with fervent following, led by singer / songwriter Ricky Ross (v) and featuring his wife Lorraine McIntosh (v). Named after a Steely Dan song, they achieved five Top 5 albums, including the million-selling 'When the World Knows Your Name' (Singles: 112 Weeks, Albums: 217 Weeks) pos/wks

23 Jan 88	DIGNITY *CBS DEAC 4* **31**	8
9 Apr 88	WHEN WILL YOU MAKE MY TELEPHONE RING	
	CBS DEAC 5 ....**34**	7
16 Jul 88	CHOCOLATE GIRL *CBS DEAC 6* **43**	7
15 Oct 88 ●	REAL GONE KID *CBS DEAC 7* **8**	13
4 Mar 89	WAGES DAY *CBS DEAC 8* **18**	6
20 May 89	FERGUS SINGS THE BLUES *CBS DEAC 9* **14**	6
16 Sep 89	LOVE AND REGRET *CBS DEAC 10* **28**	5
6 Jan 90	QUEEN OF THE NEW YEAR *CBS DEAC 11* **21**	5
25 Aug 90 ●	FOUR BACHARACH AND DAVID SONGS (EP) *CBS DEAC 12* ...**2**	9
25 May 91	YOUR SWAYING ARMS *Columbia 6568937* **23**	4
27 Jul 91 ●	TWIST AND SHOUT *Columbia 6573027* **10**	9
12 Oct 91	CLOSING TIME *Columbia 6575027* **42**	3
14 Dec 91	COVER FROM THE SKY *Columbia 6576737* **31**	4
28 Nov 92	YOUR TOWN *Columbia 6587867* **14**	8
13 Feb 93	WILL WE BE LOVERS *Columbia 6589732* **31**	4
24 Apr 93	ONLY TENDER LOVE *Columbia 6591842* **22**	4
17 Jul 93	HANG YOUR HEAD *Columbia 6594602* **21**	3
2 Apr 94	I WAS RIGHT AND YOU WERE WRONG *Columbia 6602222* ...**32**	3
28 May 94	DIGNITY (re-issue) *Columbia 6604485* **20**	3
28 Apr 01	EVERYTIME YOU SLEEP *Papillon BTFLY 0011* **64**	1
6 Jun 87	RAINTOWN *CBS 4505491* **14**	77
15 Apr 89 ★	WHEN THE WORLD KNOWS YOUR NAME *CBS 4633211* ■ **1**	54
22 Sep 90 ●	OOH LAS VEGAS *CBS 4672421* **3**	8
15 Jun 91 ●	FELLOW HOODLUMS *Columbia 4685501* **2**	27
13 Mar 93 ●	WHATEVER YOU SAY SAY NOTHING *Columbia 4735272* ...**4**	10
16 Apr 94 ★	OUR TOWN – THE GREATEST HITS *Columbia 4766422* ...**1**	38
23 Oct 99	WALKING BACK HOME *Columbia 4963802* **39**	2
12 May 01	HOMESICK *Papillon BTFLYCD 0014* **59**	1

Tracks on Four Bacharach and David Songs (EP): I'll Never Fall in Love Again / The Look of Love / Message to Michael / Are You There (With Another Girl). 'Dignity' in 1994 was the original recording of the song first issued in 1987, when it failed to chart

The DEAD 60S
UK, male vocal / instrumental group (Singles: 2 Weeks) pos/wks

16 Oct 04	RIOT RADIO *Deltasonic DLTCD 025* **30**	2

DEAD CAN DANCE *Australia, male /*
female vocal / instrumental duo (Albums: 3 Weeks) pos/wks

25 Sep 93	INTO THE LABYRINTH *4AD CAD 3013CD* **47**	1
29 Jun 96	SPIRITCHASER *4AD CAD 6008CD* **43**	2

DEAD DRED
UK, male instrumental / production duo (Singles: 2 Weeks) pos/wks

5 Nov 94	DRED BASS *Moving Shadow SHADOW 50CD* **60**	2

The DEAD END KIDS
UK, male vocal / instrumental group (Singles: 10 Weeks) pos/wks

26 Mar 77 ●	HAVE I THE RIGHT *CBS 4972* **6**	10

DEAD KENNEDYS *US, male vocal /*
instrumental group (Singles: 9 Weeks, Albums: 8 Weeks) pos/wks

1 Nov 80	KILL THE POOR *Cherry Red CHERRY 16* **49**	3
30 May 81	TOO DRUNK TO FUCK *Cherry Red CHERRY 24* **36**	6
13 Sep 80	FRESH FRUIT FOR ROTTING VEGETABLES	
	Cherry Red BRED 10 ....**33**	6
4 Jul 87	GIVE ME CONVENIENCE *Alternative Tentacles VIRUS 5* ...**84**	2

DEAD OR ALIVE (see also Pete BURNS) *UK, male vocal /*
instrumental group (Singles: 73 Weeks, Albums: 22 Weeks) pos/wks

24 Mar 84	THAT'S THE WAY (I LIKE IT) *Epic A 4271* **22**	9
1 Dec 84 ★	YOU SPIN ME ROUND (LIKE A RECORD) *Epic A 4861* **1**	23
20 Apr 85	LOVER COME BACK TO ME *Epic A 6086* **11**	8
29 Jun 85	IN TOO DEEP *Epic A 6360* **14**	8
21 Sep 85	MY HEART GOES BANG (GET ME TO THE DOCTOR)	
	Epic A 6571 ....**23**	6
20 Sep 86	BRAND NEW LOVER *Epic A 650075 7* **31**	4
10 Jan 87	SOMETHING IN MY HOUSE *Epic BURNS 1* **12**	7
4 Apr 87	HOOKED ON LOVE *Epic BURNS 2* **69**	2
3 Sep 88	TURN AROUND AND COUNT 2 TEN *Epic BURNS 4* ...**70**	1
22 Jul 89	COME HOME WITH ME BABY *Epic BURNS 5* **62**	2
17 May 03	YOU SPIN ME ROUND (re-mix) *Epic 6735782* **23**	3
28 Apr 84	SOPHISTICATED BOOM BOOM *Epic EPC 25835* **29**	3
25 May 85 ●	YOUTHQUAKE *Epic EPC 26420* **9**	15
14 Feb 87	MAD BAD AND DANGEROUS TO KNOW *Epic 450 2571* ...**27**	4

DEAD PREZ *US, male rap duo (Singles: 2 Weeks)* pos/wks

11 Mar 00	HIP HOP *Epic 6689862* **41**	2

DEADLY SINS
UK / Italy, male vocal / instrumental duo (Singles: 2 Weeks) pos/wks

30 Apr 94	WE ARE GOING ON DOWN *Ffrreedom TABCD 220* ...**45**	2

Hazell DEAN
UK, female vocalist (Singles: 71 Weeks, Albums: 3 Weeks) pos/wks

18 Feb 84	EVERGREEN / JEALOUS LOVE *Proto ENA 114* **63**	3
21 Apr 84 ●	SEARCHIN' (I GOTTA FIND A MAN) *Proto ENA 109* ...**6**	15
28 Jul 84 ●	WHATEVER I DO (WHEREVER I GO) *Proto ENA 119* ...**4**	11
3 Nov 84	BACK IN MY ARMS (ONCE AGAIN) *Proto ENA 122* ...**41**	4
2 Mar 85	NO FOOL (FOR LOVE) *Proto ENA 123* **41**	5
12 Oct 85	THEY SAY IT'S GONNA RAIN *Parlophone R 6107* ...**58**	4
2 Apr 88 ●	WHO'S LEAVING WHO *EMI EM 45* **4**	11
25 Jun 88	MAYBE (WE SHOULD CALL IT A DAY) *EMI EM 62* ...**15**	6
24 Sep 88	TURN IT INTO LOVE *EMI EM 71* **21**	7
26 Aug 89	LOVE PAINS *Lisson DOLE 12* **48**	4
23 Mar 91	BETTER OFF WITHOUT YOU *Lisson DOLE 19* **72**	1
22 Oct 88	ALWAYS *EMI EMC 3546* **38**	3

Jimmy DEAN
US, male vocalist – Seth Ward (Singles: 17 Weeks) pos/wks

26 Oct 61 ●	BIG BAD JOHN *Philips PB 1187* ▲ **2**	13
8 Nov 62	LITTLE BLACK BOOK *CBS AAG 122* **33**	4

Letitia DEAN and Paul MEDFORD
UK, female / male vocal / actor duo (Singles: 7 Weeks) pos/wks

25 Oct 86	SOMETHING OUTA NOTHING *BBC RESL 203* **12**	7

Sheryl DEANE See THRILLSEEKERS

DEANNA See David MORALES

DEAR JON
UK, female / male vocal / instrumental group (Singles: 1 Week) pos/wks

22 Apr 95	ONE GIFT OF LOVE *MDMC DEVCS 2* **68**	1

The DEARS
Canada, male / female vocal / instrumental group (Singles: 1 Week) pos/wks

20 Nov 04	LOST IN THE PLOT *Bella Union BELLACD 86* **49**	1

DEATH FROM ABOVE 1979
Canada, male vocal / instrumental duo (Singles: 1 Week) pos/wks

13 Nov 04	ROMANTIC RIGHTS *679 Recordings 679L 090CD* ...**57**	1

DEATH IN VEGAS
*UK, male instrumental / production duo – Richard Fearless
and Tim Holmes (Singles: 17 Weeks, Albums: 16 Weeks)*   pos/wks

2 Aug 97	DIRT *Concrete HARD 27CD*	61	1
1 Nov 97	ROCCO *Concrete HARD 29CD*	51	1
12 Feb 00 ●	AISHA *Concrete HARD 43CD*	9	4
6 May 00	DIRGE *Concrete HARD 44CD*	24	2
21 Sep 02	HANDS AROUND MY THROAT *Concrete HARD 48CD*	36	1
28 Dec 02	SCORPIO RISING (re) *Concrete HARD 54CD1* [1]	14	8
29 Mar 97	DEAD ELVIS *Concrete HARD 22LPCD*	52	1
25 Sep 99	THE CONTINO SESSIONS *Concrete HARD 41CDU*	19	12
28 Sep 02	SCORPIO RISING *Concrete / BMG HARD 53CD2*	19	3

[1] Death In Vegas with Liam Gallagher

Uncredited vocal on 'Aisha' by Iggy Pop

DeBARGE (see also Chico DeBARGE; El DeBARGE)
US, male / female vocal group (Singles: 17 Weeks, Albums: 2 Weeks) pos/wks

6 Apr 85 ●	RHYTHM OF THE NIGHT *Gordy TMG 1376*	4	14
21 Sep 85	YOU WEAR IT WELL *Gordy ZB 40345* [1]	54	3
25 May 85	RHYTHM OF THE NIGHT *Gordy ZL 72340*	94	2

[1] El DeBarge with DeBarge

Chico DeBARGE (see also DeBARGE)
US, male vocalist (Singles: 1 Week)   pos/wks

14 Mar 98	IGGIN' ME *Universal UND 56170*	50	1

El DeBARGE (see also DeBARGE)
US, male vocalist (Singles: 3 Weeks)   pos/wks

28 Jun 86	WHO'S JOHNNY ('SHORT CIRCUIT' THEME) *Gordy ELD 1*	60	2
31 Mar 90	SECRET GARDEN *Qwest W 9992* [1]	67	1

[1] Quincy Jones featuring Al B Sure!, James Ingram, El DeBarge and Barry White

Diana DECKER
US, female actor / vocalist (Singles: 10 Weeks)   pos/wks

23 Oct 53 ●	POPPA PICCOLINO (re) *Columbia DB 3325*	2	10

DECLAN *UK, male vocalist –*
Declan Galbraith (Singles: 4 Weeks, Albums: 3 Weeks)   pos/wks

21 Dec 02	TELL ME WHY *EMI / Liberty CDDECS 004* [1]	29	4
5 Oct 02	DECLAN *EMI / Liberty 5416012*	44	3

[1] Declan featuring Young Voices Choir

DECOY AND ROY
*Belgium, male production duo – Danny Van Wauwe
and Roy Van Luffelen (Singles: 1 Week)*   pos/wks

1 Feb 03	INNER LIFE *Ministry of Sound / Data DATA 43CDS*	45	1

Dave DEE (see also Dave DEE, DOZY, BEAKY, MICK and TICH)
UK, male vocalist – David Harman (Singles: 4 Weeks)   pos/wks

14 Mar 70	MY WOMAN'S MAN *Fontana TF 1074*	42	4

Joey DEE and the STARLITERS
US, male vocal / instrumental group (Singles: 8 Weeks)   pos/wks

8 Feb 62	PEPPERMINT TWIST *Columbia DB 4758* ▲	33	8

Kiki DEE
*UK, female vocalist – Pauline Matthews
(Singles: 79 Weeks, Albums: 11 Weeks)*   pos/wks

10 Nov 73	AMOUREUSE *Rocket PIG 4*	13	13
7 Sep 74	I'VE GOT THE MUSIC IN ME *Rocket PIG 12* [1]	19	8
12 Apr 75	(YOU DONT KNOW) HOW GLAD I AM *Rocket PIG 16* [1]	33	4
3 Jul 76 ★	DON'T GO BREAKING MY HEART *Rocket ROKN 512* [2] ▲	1	14
11 Sep 76	LOVING AND FREE / AMOUREUSE (re-issue) *Rocket ROKN 515*	13	8
19 Feb 77	FIRST THING IN THE MORNING *Rocket ROKN 520*	32	5
11 Jun 77	CHICAGO *Rocket ROKN 526*	28	4
21 Feb 81	STAR *Ariola ARO 251*	13	10
23 May 81	PERFECT TIMING *Ariola ARO 257*	66	3
20 Nov 93 ●	TRUE LOVE *Rocket EJSCX 32* [2]	2	10
26 Mar 77	KIKI DEE *Rocket ROLA 3*	24	5

18 Jul 81	PERFECT TIMING *Ariola ARL 5050*	47	4
9 Apr 94	THE VERY BEST OF KIKI DEE *PolyGram TV 516728*	62	2

[1] Kiki Dee Band [2] Elton John and Kiki Dee

*On 18 Sep, 25 Sep and 2 Oct 1976, 'Loving and Free' was listed by itself. 'Chicago'
was one side of a double-sided chart entry, the other being 'Bite Your Lip (Get Up
and Dance)' by Elton John*

Nancy DEE *See BENELUX and Nancy DEE*

Suzanna DEE *See SAINT featuring Suzanna DEE*

DEE DEE (see also IAN VAN DAHL) *Belgium, male production
trio – Christophe Chantzis and Eric Vanspauwen (Ian Van Dahl)
and female vocalist – Diana Trippaers (Singles: 9 Weeks)*   pos/wks

20 Jul 02	FOREVER *Incentive CENT 43CDS*	12	7
1 Mar 03	THE ONE *Incentive CENT 52CDS*	28	2

Dave DEE, DOZY, BEAKY, MICK and TICH `452` `Top 500`
*Quirkily named UK quintet was very popular in late 1960s: Dave Dee
(David Harman) (v), Dozy (Trevor Davies) (b), Beaky (John Dymond) (g),
Mick (Michael Wilson) (d), Tich (Ian Amey) (g). Catchy productions and
ultra-commercial songs (penned by managers Howard and Blaikley)
ensured a string of hits (Singles: 141 Weeks, Albums: 15 Weeks)*   pos/wks

23 Dec 65	YOU MAKE IT MOVE *Fontana TF 630*	26	8
3 Mar 66 ●	HOLD TIGHT! *Fontana TF 671*	4	17
9 Jun 66 ●	HIDEAWAY *Fontana TF 711*	10	11
15 Sep 66 ●	BEND IT! *Fontana TF 746*	2	12
8 Dec 66 ●	SAVE ME *Fontana TF 775*	3	10
9 Mar 67	TOUCH ME, TOUCH ME *Fontana TF 798*	13	9
18 May 67 ●	OKAY! *Fontana TF 830*	4	11
11 Oct 67 ●	ZABADAK! *Fontana TF 873*	3	14
14 Feb 68 ★	THE LEGEND OF XANADU *Fontana TF 903*	1	12
3 Jul 68 ●	LAST NIGHT IN SOHO *Fontana TF 953*	8	11
2 Oct 68	THE WRECK OF THE 'ANTOINETTE' *Fontana TF 971*	14	9
5 Mar 69	DON JUAN *Fontana TF 1000*	23	9
14 May 69	SNAKE IN THE GRASS *Fontana TF 1020*	23	9
2 Jul 66	DAVE DEE DOZY BEAKY MICK AND TICH *Fontana STL 5350*	11	10
7 Jan 67	IF MUSIC BE THE FOOD OF LOVE ... PREPARE FOR INDIGESTION *Fontana STL 5388*	27	5

DEEE-LITE
*US / Russia / Japan, male / female vocal / instrumental
group (Singles: 30 Weeks, Albums: 19 Weeks)*   pos/wks

18 Aug 90 ●	GROOVE IS IN THE HEART / WHAT IS LOVE *Elektra EKR 114*	2	13
24 Nov 90	POWER OF LOVE / DEEE-LITE THEME *Elektra EKR 117*	25	7
23 Feb 91	HOW DO YOU SAY ... LOVE / GROOVE IS IN THE HEART (re-mix) *Elektra EKR 118*	52	2
27 Apr 91	GOOD BEAT *Elektra EKR 122*	53	3
13 Jun 92	RUNAWAY *Elektra EKR 148*	45	3
30 Jul 94	PICNIC IN THE SUMMERTIME *Elektra EKR 186CD1*	43	2
8 Sep 90	WORLD CLIQUE *Elektra EKT 77*	14	18
4 Jul 92	INFINITY WITHIN *Elektra 7559613132*	37	1

'What Is Love' listed only from 25 Aug 1990

DEEJAY PUNK-ROC *US, male DJ / producer –*
Charles Gettis (Singles: 5 Weeks, Albums: 1 Week)   pos/wks

21 Mar 98	DEAD HUSBAND *Independiente ISOM 9MS*	71	1
9 May 98	MY BEATBOX *Independiente ISOM 12MS*	43	1
8 Aug 98	FAR OUT *Independiente ISOM 17MS*	43	2
20 Feb 99	ROC-IN-IT *Independiente ISOM 21MS* [1]	59	1
30 May 98	CHICKENEYE *Independiente ISOM 5CD*	47	1

[1] Deejay Punk-Roc vs Onyx

DEEJAY SVEN *See MC MIKER 'G' and Deejay SVEN*

Carol DEENE
UK, female vocalist – Carole Carver (Singles: 25 Weeks)   pos/wks

26 Oct 61	SAD MOVIES (MAKE ME CRY) *HMV POP 922*	44	3
25 Jan 62	NORMAN *HMV POP 973*	24	8
5 Jul 62	JOHNNY GET ANGRY *HMV POP 1027*	32	4
23 Aug 62	SOME PEOPLE *HMV POP 1058*	25	10

Scotti DEEP
US, male producer / instrumentalist – Scott Kinchen (Singles: 1 Week) pos/wks

15 Mar 97	BROOKLYN BEATS *Xtravaganza 0090095*	**67** 1

DEEP BLUE
UK, male producer – Sean O'Keefe (Singles: 2 Weeks) pos/wks

16 Apr 94	HELICOPTER TUNE *Moving Shadow SHADOW 41CD*	**68** 2

DEEP BLUE SOMETHING
US, male vocal / instrumental group (Singles: 17 Weeks, Albums: 5 Weeks) pos/wks

6 Jul 96	★ BREAKFAST AT TIFFANY'S (re) *Interscope IND 80032*	**1** 14
7 Dec 96	JOSEY *Interscope IND 95518*	**27** 3
5 Oct 96	HOME *Interscope IND 90002*	**24** 5

DEEP C
UK, male / female vocal / instrumental group (Singles: 3 Weeks) pos/wks

19 Jan 91	AFRICAN REIGN *M&G MAGS 4*	**75** 1
8 Jun 91	CHILL TO THE PANIC *M&G MAGS 10*	**73** 2

DEEP COVER (see also TRU FAITH & DUB CONSPIRACY; SCOTT & LEON)
UK, male production group (Singles: 1 Week) pos/wks

11 May 02	SOUNDS OF EDEN (EVERYTIME I SEE THE GIRL) *Attitude! 0158392*	**63** 1

Title on the label was incorrect. Should have read 'The Sound Of Eden'

DEEP CREED '94
US, male producer – Armand van Helden (Singles: 1 Week) pos/wks

7 May 94	CAN U FEEL IT *Eastern Bloc BLOCCD 005*	**59** 1

DEEP DISH
Iran, male instrumental / production duo – Ali 'Dubfire' Shirazinia and Sharam Tayebi (Singles: 16 Weeks, Albums: 2 Weeks) pos/wks

26 Oct 96	STAY GOLD *Deconstruction 74321418222*	**41** 1
1 Nov 97	STRANDED *Deconstruction 74321512232*	**60** 1
3 Oct 98	THE FUTURE OF THE FUTURE (STAY GOLD) *Deconstruction 74321616252* [1]	**31** 2
9 Oct 04	● FLASHDANCE *Positiva CDTIVS 211*	**3** 12+
18 Jul 98	JUNK SCIENCE *Deconstruction 74321580342*	**37** 2

[1] Deep Dish with Everything but the Girl

DEEP FEELING
UK, male vocal / instrumental group (Singles: 5 Weeks) pos/wks

25 Apr 70	DO YOU LOVE ME (re) *Page One POF 165*	**34** 5

DEEP FOREST
France, male instrumental duo – Eric Mouquet and Michel Sanchez (Singles: 14 Weeks, Albums: 17 Weeks) pos/wks

5 Feb 94	● SWEET LULLABY *Columbia 6599242*	**10** 6
21 May 94	DEEP FOREST *Columbia 6604115*	**20** 4
23 Jul 94	SAVANNA DANCE *Columbia 6606355*	**28** 2
24 Jun 95	MARTA'S SONG *Columbia 6621402*	**26** 2
26 Feb 94	DEEP FOREST *Columbia 4741782*	**15** 11
3 Jun 95	BOHEME *Columbia 4786232*	**12** 5
31 Jan 98	COMPARSA *Columbia 4887252* [1]	**60** 1

[1] Deep Forest III

DEEP PURPLE 139 Top 500
Long-running legendary heavy rock group. London band's ever-changing line-up ensured many spin-off groups, among them Rainbow (founded by ex-guitarist Ritchie Blackmore), Whitesnake (featuring ex-vocalist David Coverdale) and Gillan (started by ex-vocalist Ian Gillan) (Singles: 85 Weeks, Albums: 278 Weeks) pos/wks

15 Aug 70	● BLACK NIGHT *Harvest HAR 5020*	**2** 21
27 Feb 71	● STRANGE KIND OF WOMAN *Harvest HAR 5033*	**8** 12
13 Nov 71	FIREBALL *Harvest HAR 5045*	**15** 13
1 Apr 72	NEVER BEFORE *Purple PUR 102*	**35** 6
16 Apr 77	SMOKE ON THE WATER *Purple PUR 132*	**21** 7
15 Oct 77	NEW LIVE AND RARE (EP) *Purple PUR 135*	**31** 4
7 Oct 78	NEW LIVE AND RARE II (EP) *Purple PUR 137*	**45** 3
2 Aug 80	BLACK NIGHT (re-issue) *Harvest HAR 5210*	**43** 6
1 Nov 80	NEW LIVE AND RARE III (EP) *Harvest SHEP 101*	**48** 3
26 Jan 85	PERFECT STRANGERS *Polydor POSP 719*	**48** 3
15 Jun 85	KNOCKING AT YOUR BACK DOOR / PERFECT STRANGERS *Polydor POSP 749*	**68** 1
18 Jun 88	HUSH *Polydor PO 4*	**62** 2

20 Oct 90	KING OF DREAMS *RCA PB 49247*	**70** 1
2 Mar 91	LOVE CONQUERS ALL *RCA PB 49225*	**57** 2
24 Jun 95	BLACK NIGHT (re-mix) *EMI CDEM 382*	**66** 1
24 Jan 70	CONCERTO FOR GROUP AND ORCHESTRA *Harvest SHVL 767*	**26** 4
20 Jun 70	● DEEP PURPLE IN ROCK *Harvest SHVL 777*	**4** 68
18 Sep 71	★ FIREBALL *Harvest SHVL 793*	**1** 25
15 Apr 72	★ MACHINE HEAD *Purple TPSA 7504*	**1** 24
6 Jan 73	MADE IN JAPAN *Purple TPSP 351*	**16** 14
17 Feb 73	● WHO DO WE THINK WE ARE *Purple TPSA 7508*	**4** 11
2 Mar 74	● BURN *Purple TPA 3505*	**3** 21
23 Nov 74	STORM BRINGER *Purple TPS 3508*	**6** 12
5 Jul 75	24 CARAT PURPLE *Purple TPSM 2002*	**14** 17
22 Nov 75	COME TASTE THE BAND *Purple TPSA 7515*	**19** 4
27 Nov 76	DEEP PURPLE LIVE *Purple TPSA 7517*	**12** 6
21 Apr 79	THE MARK II PURPLE SINGLES *Purple TPS 3514*	**24** 6
19 Jul 80	★ DEEPEST PURPLE *Harvest EMTV 25*	**1** 15
13 Dec 80	IN CONCERT *Harvest SHDW 4121/4122*	**30** 8
4 Sep 82	DEEP PURPLE LIVE IN LONDON *Harvest SHSP 4124*	**23** 5
10 Nov 84	● PERFECT STRANGERS *Polydor POLH 16*	**5** 15
29 Jun 85	THE ANTHOLOGY *Harvest PUR 1*	**50** 3
24 Jan 87	● THE HOUSE OF BLUE LIGHT *Polydor POLH 32*	**10** 9
16 Jul 88	NOBODY'S PERFECT *Polydor PODV 10*	**38** 2
2 Nov 90	SLAVES AND MASTERS *RCA PL 90535*	**45** 2
7 Aug 93	THE BATTLE RAGES ON ... *RCA 74321154202*	**21** 3
17 Feb 96	PURPENDICULAR *RCA 74321338022*	**58** 1
31 Jan 98	MADE IN JAPAN (re-issue) *EMI 8578642*	**73** 1
24 Oct 98	30: VERY BEST OF DEEP PURPLE *EMI 4968072*	**39** 2

Tracks on New Live and Rare (EP): Black Night (Live) / Painted Horse / When a Blind Man Cries. Tracks on New Live and Rare II (EP): Burn (Edited Version) / Coronarias Redig / Mistreated (Interpolating Rock Me Baby). Tracks on New Live and Rare III (EP): Smoke on the Water / Bird Has Flown / Grabsplatter

The DEEP RIVER BOYS
US, male vocal group (Singles: 1 Week) pos/wks

7 Dec 56	THAT'S RIGHT *HMV POP 263*	**29** 1

DEEP SENSATION
UK, male production duo (Singles: 1 Week) pos/wks

4 Sep 04	SOMEHOW SOMEWHERE *In the House ITHS 07*	**74** 1

DEEPEST BLUE
Israel / UK, male production / vocal duo – Matti Schwartz and Joel Edwards (Singles: 19 Weeks, Albums: 3 Weeks) pos/wks

2 Aug 03	● DEEPEST BLUE *Data / MoS DATA 55CDS*	**7** 8
28 Feb 04	● GIVE IT AWAY *Data / MoS DATA 65CDS*	**9** 8
5 Jun 04	IS IT A SIN *Open OPEN 3CDS*	**24** 2
4 Sep 04	SHOOTING STAR *Open OPEN 05CDS*	**57** 1
19 Jun 04	LATE SEPTEMBER *Open OPENCD 3*	**22** 3

Rick DEES and his CAST OF IDIOTS
US, male DJ / vocalist – Rigdon Dees and male / female vocal / instrumental group (Singles: 9 Weeks) pos/wks

18 Sep 76	● DISCO DUCK (PART ONE) *RSO 2090 204* ▲	**6** 9

DEETAH
Chile, female vocalist – Claudia Ogalde (Singles: 10 Weeks) pos/wks

26 Sep 98	RELAX *ffrr FCDP 345*	**11** 8
1 May 99	EL PARAISO RICO *ffrr FCD 356*	**39** 2

DEF LEPPARD 179 Top 500
(see also Mick RONSON with Joe ELLIOTT) Mainstream UK rock stalwarts who wooed the US before their homeland: Joe Elliott (v), Phil Collen (g from 1983), Steve Clark (g) (d. 1991), Rick Savage (b), Rick Allen (d). In the US they achieved the feat of two consecutive albums selling more than eight million (Singles: 116 Weeks, Albums: 197 Weeks) pos/wks

17 Nov 79	WASTED *Vertigo 6059 247*	**61** 3
23 Feb 80	HELLO AMERICA *Vertigo LEPP 1*	**45** 4
5 Feb 83	PHOTOGRAPH *Vertigo VER 5*	**66** 3
27 Aug 83	ROCK OF AGES *Vertigo VER 6*	**41** 4
1 Aug 87	● ANIMAL *Bludgeon Riffola LEP 1*	**6** 9
19 Sep 87	POUR SOME SUGAR ON ME *Bludgeon Riffola LEP 2*	**18** 6
28 Nov 87	HYSTERIA (re) *Bludgeon Riffola LEP 3*	**26** 6
9 Apr 88	ARMAGEDDON IT *Bludgeon Riffola LEP 4*	**20** 5
16 Jul 88	LOVE BITES *Bludgeon Riffola LEP 5* ▲	**11** 8
11 Feb 89	ROCKET *Bludgeon Riffola LEP 6*	**15** 7
28 Mar 92	● LET'S GET ROCKED *Bludgeon Riffola DEF 7*	**2** 7
27 Jun 92	MAKE LOVE LIKE A MAN *Bludgeon Riffola LEP 7*	**12** 5
12 Sep 92	HAVE YOU EVER NEEDED SOMEONE SO BAD *Bludgeon Riffola LEP 8*	**16** 5

TIM RICE TOP 10

The gospel according to Tim Rice, who chooses his favourite singles and albums

Sir Tim is one of the founding fathers of The Guinness Book of British Hit Singles (& Albums), an Oscar-winning lyricist and the producer of the biggest-selling single by a UK female vocalist (Julie Covington) back in 1977. He insists that the records that rock his boat are favourites only at the time of asking and that his choices change on a daily basis.

SINGLES
single – act – (peak position)

ALBUMS
album – act – (peak position)

SINGLES	ALBUMS
CATHY'S CLOWN The Everly Brothers (1)	BRIDGE OVER TROUBLED WATER Simon and Garfunkel (1)
EIGHTEEN YELLOW ROSES Bobby Darin (37)	BRINGING IT ALL BACK HOME Bob Dylan (1)
GIRLS JUST WANT TO HAVE FUN Cyndi Lauper (2)	COSMO'S FACTORY Creedence Clearwater Revival (1)
HELP! The Beatles (1)	IT'S EVERLY TIME The Everly Brothers (2)
IT'S NOW OR NEVER Elvis Presley with the Jordanaires (1)	ROCK 'N ROLL (NO.2) Elvis Presley (3)
THE LAST TIME The Rolling Stones (1)	RUBBER SOUL The Beatles (1)
MEMORIES ARE MADE OF THIS Dean Martin (1)	STICKY FINGERS The Rolling Stones (1)
RUNAWAY Del Shannon (1)	THE TOMMY STEELE STORY Tommy Steele (1)
STAYIN' ALIVE The Bee Gees (4)	TUNNEL OF LOVE Bruce Springsteen (1)
SUMMERTIME BLUES Eddie Cochran (18)	WHAT'D I SAY * Ray Charles

* Did not chart

			pos	wks
30 Jan 93	**HEAVEN IS** *Bludgeon Riffola LEPCD 9*		13	5
1 May 93	**TONIGHT** *Bludgeon Riffola LEPCD 10*		34	3
18 Sep 93	**TWO STEPS BEHIND** *Bludgeon Riffola LEPCD 12*		32	4
15 Jan 94	**ACTION** *Bludgeon Riffola LEPCD 13*		14	5
14 Oct 95 ●	**WHEN LOVE AND HATE COLLIDE** *Bludgeon Riffola LEPCD 14*		2	10
4 May 96	**SLANG** *Bludgeon Riffola LEPCD 15*		17	5
13 Jul 96	**WORK IT OUT** *Bludgeon Riffola LEPCD 16*		22	3
28 Sep 96	**ALL I WANT IS EVERYTHING** *Bludgeon Riffola LEPCD 17*		38	2
30 Nov 96	**BREATHE A SIGH** *Bludgeon Riffola LEPCD 18*		43	1
24 Jul 99	**PROMISES** *Bludgeon Riffola 5621362*		41	1
9 Oct 99	**GOODBYE** *Bludgeon Riffola 5622892*		54	1
17 Aug 02	**NOW** *Bludgeon Riffola / Mercury 0639692*		23	2
26 Apr 03	**LONG LONG WAY TO GO** *Bludgeon Riffola 9800024*		40	2
22 Mar 80	**ON THROUGH THE NIGHT** *Vertigo 9102 040*		15	8
25 Jul 81	**HIGH 'N' DRY** *Vertigo 6359 045*		26	8
12 Mar 83	**PYROMANIA** *Vertigo VERS 2*		18	8
29 Aug 87 ★	**HYSTERIA** *Bludgeon Riffola HYSLP 1* ■ ▲		1	101
11 Apr 92 ★	**ADRENALIZE** *Bludgeon Riffola 5109782* ■ ▲		1	30
16 Oct 93 ●	**RETRO ACTIVE** *Bludgeon Riffola 5183052*		6	5
4 Nov 95 ●	**DEF LEPPARD GREATEST HITS 1980-1995 – VAULT** *Bludgeon Riffola 5286572*		3	14
25 May 96 ●	**SLANG** *Bludgeon Riffola 5324932*		5	8
26 Jun 99	**EUPHORIA** *Bludgeon Riffola 5462442*		11	5
24 Aug 02	**X** *Bludgeon Riffola 631202*		14	3
6 Nov 04 ●	**BEST OF** *Bludgeon Riffola 9868512*		6	7

DEFAULT

US, male vocal / instrumental group (Singles: 1 Week)   pos/wks

			pos	wks
8 Feb 03	**WASTING MY TIME** *TVT / Island CID 809*		73	1

DEFINITION OF SOUND *UK, male rap duo – Donald*
Weekes and Kevin Clark (Singles: 25 Weeks, Albums: 3 Weeks)   pos/wks

			pos	wks
9 Mar 91	**WEAR YOUR LOVE LIKE HEAVEN** *Circa YR 61*		17	9
1 Jun 91	**NOW IS TOMORROW** *Circa YR 66*		46	4
8 Feb 92	**MOIRA JANE'S CAFE** *Circa YR 80*		34	4
19 Sep 92	**WHAT ARE YOU UNDER** *Circa YR 95*		68	1
14 Nov 92	**CAN I GET OVER** *Circa YR 97*		61	2
20 May 95	**BOOM BOOM** *Fontana DOSCD 1*		59	1
2 Dec 95	**PASS THE VIBES** *Fontana DOSCD 2*		23	3
24 Feb 96	**CHILD** *Fontana DOSCD 3*		48	1
29 Jun 91	**LOVE AND LIFE** *Circa CIRCA 14*		38	3

Singles re-entries are listed as (re), (2re), (3re).... which signifies that the hit re-entered the chart once, twice or three times...

DEFTONES *US, male vocal / instrumental group (Singles: 9 Weeks, Albums: 8 Weeks)* pos/wks

21 Mar 98	MY OWN SUMMER (SHOVE IT) *Maverick W 0432CD*	29	2
11 Jul 98	BE QUIET AND DRIVE (FAR AWAY) *Maverick W 0445CD*	50	1
26 Aug 00	CHANGE (IN THE HOUSE OF FLIES) *Maverick W 531CD*	53	1
24 May 03	MINERVA *Maverick W 605CD*	15	3
4 Oct 03	HEXAGRAM *Maverick W 623CD*	68	2
8 Nov 97	AROUND THE FUR *Maverick 9362468102*	56	1
1 Jul 00	WHITE PONY *Maverick 9362477972*	13	2
24 Mar 01	BACK TO SCHOOL (MINI MAGGIT) *WEA 9362480822*	35	2
31 May 03 ●	DEFTONES *Maverick 9362483912*	7	3

DEGREES OF MOTION featuring BITI *US, female vocal group (Singles: 21 Weeks)* pos/wks

25 Apr 92	DO YOU WANT IT RIGHT NOW *ffrr F 184*	31	5
18 Jul 92	SHINE ON *ffrr F 192* [1]	43	3
7 Nov 92	SOUL FREEDOM – FREE YOUR SOUL *ffrr FX 201*	64	1
19 Mar 94 ●	SHINE ON (re-mix) *ffrr FCD 229*	8	8
25 Jun 94	DO YOU WANT IT RIGHT NOW (re-mix) *ffrr FCD 236* [2]	26	4

[1] Degrees of Motion featuring Biti with Kit West [2] Degrees of Motion

DEICIDE *US, male vocal / instrumental group (Albums: 1 Week)* pos/wks

13 May 95	ONCE UPON THE CROSS *Roadrunner RR 89492*	66	1

DEJA *US, male / female vocal duo (Singles: 1 Week)* pos/wks

29 Aug 87	SERIOUS *10 TEN 132*	75	1

DEJA VU *UK, male vocal / instrumental duo (Singles: 1 Week)* pos/wks

5 Feb 94	WHY WHY WHY *Cowboy CDRODEO 941*	57	1

DEJURE (see also DREAM FREQUENCY; RED) *UK, male production duo – Ian Bland and Paul Fitzpatrick (Singles: 1 Week)* pos/wks

23 Aug 03	SANCTUARY *Nebula NEBT 032*	62	1

Desmond DEKKER and the ACES *Jamaica, male vocalist – Desmond Dacres and male vocal group (Singles: 71 Weeks, Albums: 4 Weeks)* pos/wks

12 Jul 67	007 (SHANTY TOWN) *Pyramid PYR 6004*	14	11
19 Mar 69 ★	ISRAELITES (re) *Pyramid PYR 6058*	1	15
25 Jun 69	IT MIEK *Pyramid PYR 6068*	7	11
10 Jan 70	PICKNEY GAL *Pyramid PYR 6078*	42	3
22 Aug 70 ●	YOU CAN GET IT IF YOU REALLY WANT *Trojan TR 7777* [1]	2	15
10 May 75 ●	ISRAELITES (re-recording) *Cactus CT 57* [1]	10	9
30 Aug 75	SING A LITTLE SONG *Cactus CT 73* [1]	16	7
5 Jul 69	THIS IS DESMOND DEKKER *Trojan TTL 4* [1]	27	4

[1] Desmond Dekker [1] Desmond Dekker

DEL AMITRI `384` `Top 500`

Stylish soft-rock band whose name is Greek for 'from the womb'. Core members Justin Currie (v/b) and Iain Harvie (g) formed the band in Glasgow, Scotland, 1983. 'Roll to Me' was one of the few UK records to reach the US Top 10 in the late 1990s (Singles: 71 Weeks, Albums: 108 Weeks) pos/wks

19 Aug 89	KISS THIS THING GOODBYE *A&M AM 515*	59	2
13 Jan 90	NOTHING EVER HAPPENS *A&M AM 536*	11	9
24 Mar 90	KISS THIS THING GOODBYE (re-issue) *A&M AM 551*	43	4
16 Jun 90	MOVE AWAY JIMMY BLUE *A&M AM 555*	36	6
3 Nov 90	SPIT IN THE RAIN *A&M AM 589*	21	6
9 May 92	ALWAYS THE LAST TO KNOW *A&M AM 870*	13	7
11 Jul 92	BE MY DOWNFALL *A&M AM 884*	30	4
12 Sep 92	JUST LIKE A MAN *A&M AM 0057*	25	4
23 Jan 93	WHEN YOU WERE YOUNG *A&M AMCD 0132*	20	3
18 Feb 95	HERE AND NOW *A&M 5809692*	21	4
29 Apr 95	DRIVING WITH THE BRAKES ON *A&M 5810072*	18	4
8 Jul 95	ROLL TO ME *A&M 5811312*	22	4
28 Oct 95	TELL HER THIS *A&M 5812172*	32	2
21 Jun 97	NOT WHERE IT'S AT *A&M 5822532*	21	3
6 Dec 97	SOME OTHER SUCKER'S PARADE *A&M 5824352*	46	1
13 Jun 98	DON'T COME HOME TOO SOON *A&M 5827052*	15	4
5 Sep 98	CRY TO BE FOUND *A&M MERCD 513*	40	2
13 Apr 02	JUST BEFORE YOU LEAVE *Mercury 4976972*	37	2
24 Feb 90 ●	WAKING HOURS *A&M AMA 9006*	6	44
13 Jun 92 ●	CHANGE EVERYTHING *A&M 3953852*	2	20
11 Mar 95 ●	TWISTED *A&M 5403112*	3	25

12 Jul 97 ●	SOME OTHER SUCKER'S PARADE *A&M 5407052*	6	5
19 Sep 98 ●	THE BEST OF DEL AMITRI – HATFUL OF RAIN *Mercury / A&M 5409402*	5	11
20 Apr 02	CAN YOU DO ME GOOD? *Mercury / A&M 4932162*	30	3

DE'LACY *US, male / female vocal / instrumental group (Singles: 16 Weeks, Albums: 1 Week)* pos/wks

2 Sep 95	HIDEAWAY *Slip 'N' Slide 74321310472*	9	10
31 Aug 96	THAT LOOK *Slip 'N' Slide 74321398322*	19	4
14 Feb 98	HIDEAWAY 1998 (re-mix) *Slip 'N' Slide 74321561052*	21	2
1 Jul 95	HIDEAWAY *Slip 'N' Slide SLIP 023*	53	1

DELAGE *UK, female vocal group (Singles: 2 Weeks)* pos/wks

15 Dec 90	ROCK THE BOAT *PWL / Polydor PO 113*	63	2

DELAKOTA *UK, male vocal / instrumental duo (Singles: 3 Weeks, Albums: 1 Week)* pos/wks

18 Jul 98	THE ROCK *Go Beat GOBCD 10*	60	1
19 Sep 98	C'MON CINCINNATI *Go Beat GOBCD 11* [1]	55	1
13 Feb 99	555 *Go Beat GOBCD 14*	42	1
3 Oct 98	ONE LOVE *Go Beat 5578612*	58	1

[1] Delakota featuring Rose Smith

DELANEY and BONNIE and FRIENDS *US, male / female vocal duo – Delaney and Bonnie Bramlett and instrumental group (Singles: 9 Weeks, Albums: 3 Weeks)* pos/wks

20 Dec 69	COMIN' HOME *Atlantic 584 308* [1]	16	9
6 Jun 70	ON TOUR *Atlantic 2400013*	39	3

[1] Delaney and Bonnie and Friends featuring Eric Clapton

DELANO *See CZR featuring DELANO*

The DELAYS *UK, male vocal / instrumental group (Singles: 10 Weeks, Albums: 4 Weeks)* pos/wks

2 Aug 03	HEY GIRL *Rough Trade RTRADSCD 102*	40	1
31 Jan 04	LONG TIME COMING *Rough Trade RTRADSCD 136*	16	4
3 Apr 04	NEARER THAN HEAVEN *Rough Trade RTRADSCD 175*	21	3
4 Dec 04	LOST IN A MELODY / WANDERLUST *Rough Trade RTRADSCD 197*	28	2
17 Apr 04	FADED SEASIDE GLAMOUR *Rough Trade RTRADDVCD 114*	17	4

DELEGATION *UK, male vocal / instrumental group (Singles: 7 Weeks)* pos/wks

23 Apr 77	WHERE IS THE LOVE (WE USED TO KNOW) *State STAT 40*	22	6
20 Aug 77	YOU'VE BEEN DOING ME WRONG *State STAT 55*	49	1

DELERIUM *Canada, male production duo – Rhys Fulber and Bill Leeb (Singles: 30 Weeks)* pos/wks

12 Jun 99	SILENCE *Nettwerk 398152*	73	1
5 Feb 00	HEAVEN'S EARTH *Nettwerk 331032*	44	1
14 Oct 00 ●	SILENCE (re-mix) *Nettwerk 331072*	3	16
7 Jul 01	INNOCENTE (FALLING IN LOVE) *Nettwerk 331172* [1]	32	3
24 Nov 01	UNDERWATER *Nettwerk 331422* [2]	33	2
12 Jul 03	AFTER ALL *Nettwerk 332012*	46	1
28 Feb 04	TRULY *Nettwerk 332202* [3]	54	2
27 Nov 04	SILENCE 2004 (re-mix) *Nettwerk 332422* [4]	38	4

[1] Delerium featuring Leigh Nash [2] Delerium featuring Rani [3] Delerium featuring Nerina Pallot [4] Delerium featuring Sarah McLachlan

Sarah McLachlan is also the uncredited vocalist on the original version and re-mix of 'Silence'

The DELFONICS *US, male vocal group (Singles: 23 Weeks)* pos/wks

10 Apr 71	DIDN'T I (BLOW YOUR MIND THIS TIME) (re) *Bell 1099*	22	9
10 Jul 71	LA-LA MEANS I LOVE YOU *Bell 1165*	19	10
16 Oct 71	READY OR NOT HERE I COME (CAN'T HIDE FROM LOVE) *Bell 1175*	41	4

The DELGADOS *UK, male / female vocal / instrumental group (Singles: 4 Weeks, Albums: 3 Weeks)* pos/wks

23 May 98	PULL THE WIRES FROM THE WALL *Chemikal CHEM 023CD*	69	1
3 Jun 00	AMERICAN TRILOGY *Chemikal Underground CHEM 039CD*	61	1

			pos/wks
1 Mar 03	ALL YOU NEED IS HATE *Mantra MNT 79CD*	...72	1
18 Sep 04	EVERYBODY COME DOWN	...67	1
	Chemikal Underground CHEM 073CD		
20 Jun 98	PELOTON *Chemikal Underground CHEM 024CD*	...56	1
29 Apr 00	THE GREAT EASTERN *Chemikal Underground CHEM 040CD*..72		1
26 Oct 02	HATE *Mantra / Beggars Banquet MNTCD 1031*	...57	1

DELIRIOUS? *UK, male vocal / instrumental group (Singles: 17 Weeks, Albums: 6 Weeks)*

			pos/wks
1 Mar 97	WHITE RIBBON DAY *Furious? CDFURY 1*	...41	2
17 May 97	DEEPER *Furious? CDFURY 2*	...20	3
26 Jul 97	PROMISE *Furious? CDFURY 3*	...20	2
15 Nov 97	DEEPER (EP) *Furious? CXFURY 4*	...36	2
27 Mar 99	SEE THE STAR *Furious? CDFURY 5*	...16	2
4 Mar 00	IT'S OK *Furious? CDFURY 6*	...18	2
16 Jun 01	WAITING FOR THE SUMMER *Furious? CDFURY 7*	...26	2
22 Dec 01	I COULD SING OF YOUR LOVE FOREVER *Furious? CDFURY 9* 40		2
28 Jun 97	KING OF FOOLS *Furious? FURYCD 1*	...13	3
24 Apr 99	MEZZAMORPHIS *Furious? FURYCD 2*	...25	2
18 Aug 01	AUDIO LESSONOVER? *Furious? FURYCD 4*	...58	1

Tracks on Deeper (EP): Deeper / Summer of Love / Touch / Sanctify

'DELIVERANCE' SOUNDTRACK *US, male instrumental duo – Eric Weissberg – banjo and Steve Mandell – guitar (Singles: 7 Weeks)*

			pos/wks
31 Mar 73	DUELLING BANJOS *Warner Bros. K 16223*	...17	7

The DELLS *US, male vocal group (Singles: 9 Weeks)*

			pos/wks
16 Jul 69	I CAN SING A RAINBOW – LOVE IS BLUE (MEDLEY) *Chess CRS 8099*	...15	9

DELORES See MONOBOY featuring DELORES

DELRONS See REPARATA and The DELRONS

DELSENA See Oris JAY presents DELSENA

DELTA See David MORALES; Crystal WATERS

DELUXE *US, female vocalist – Delores Springer (Singles: 1 Week)* pos/wks

18 Mar 89	JUST A LITTLE MORE *Unyque UNQ 5*	...74	1

Tim DELUXE (see also COHEN vs DELUXE) *UK, male DJ / producer – Tim Liken (Singles: 11 Weeks)*

			pos/wks
20 Jul 02	IT JUST WON'T DO *Underwater H2O 016CD* [1]	...14	7
4 Oct 03	LESS TALK MORE ACTION *Underwater H2O 928CD*	...45	2
7 Feb 04	MUNDAYA (THE BOY) *Underwater H2O 040CD* [2]	...61	1
13 Mar 04	JUST KICK *Intec INTEC 24XXX* [3]	...70	1

[1] Tim Deluxe featuring Sam Obernik [2] Tim Deluxe featuring Shahin Badar [3] Cohen vs Deluxe

DEM 2 *UK, male production duo (Singles: 2 Weeks)*

			pos/wks
24 Oct 98	DESTINY *Locked On LOX 101CD*	...58	2

DEMETREUS See Christian FALK featuring DEMETREUS

DEMOLITION MAN See PRIZNA featuring DEMOLITION MAN

DEMON *UK, male vocal / instrumental group (Albums: 5 Weeks)*

			pos/wks
14 Aug 82	THE UNEXPECTED GUEST *Carrere CAL 139*	...47	3
2 Jul 83	THE PLAGUE *Clay CLAYLP 6*	...73	2

DEMON vs HEARTBREAKER *France, male production group (Singles: 1 Week)*

			pos/wks
19 May 01	YOU ARE MY HIGH *Source SOURCDSE 1032*	...70	1

D'EMPRESS See 187 LOCKDOWN

Chaka DEMUS and PLIERS *Jamaica, male vocal duo – John Taylor and Everton Bonner (Singles: 55 Weeks, Albums: 30 Weeks)*

			pos/wks
12 Jun 93	● TEASE ME *Mango CIDM 806*	...3	15
18 Sep 93	● SHE DON'T LET NOBODY *Mango CIDM 810*	...4	10
18 Dec 93	★ TWIST AND SHOUT (re) *Mango CIDM 814* [1]	...1	14

12 Mar 94	MURDER SHE WROTE *Mango CIDM 812*	...27	4
18 Jun 94	I WANNA BE YOUR MAN *Mango CIDM 817*	...19	6
27 Aug 94	GAL WINE *Mango CIDM 818*	...20	4
31 Aug 96	EVERY KINDA PEOPLE *Island Jamaica IJCD 2005*	...47	1
30 Aug 97	EVERY LITTLE THING SHE DOES IS MAGIC *Virgin VSCDT 1654* 51		1
10 Jul 93	★ TEASE ME *Mango CIDM 1102*	...1	30

[1] Chaka Demus and Pliers featuring Jack Radics and Taxi Gang

Terry DENE *UK, male vocalist – Terry Williams (Singles: 20 Weeks)*

			pos/wks
7 Jun 57	A WHITE SPORT COAT (re) *Decca F 10895*	...18	7
19 Jul 57	START MOVIN' *Decca F 10914*	...15	8
16 May 58	STAIRWAY OF LOVE *Decca F 11016*	...16	5

DENISE and JOHNNY (see also THOSE 2 GIRLS; Andy WILLIAMS) *UK, male / female TV presenters / vocal duo – Denise Van Outen and Johnny Vaughan (Singles: 12 Weeks)*

			pos/wks
26 Dec 98	● ESPECIALLY FOR YOU (re) *RCA 74321644722*	...3	12

Cathy DENNIS *UK, female vocalist / songwriter (Singles: 68 Weeks, Albums: 35 Weeks)*

			pos/wks
21 Oct 89	C'MON AND GET MY LOVE *ffrr F 117* [1]	...15	10
7 Apr 90	THAT'S THE WAY OF THE WORLD *ffrr F 132* [1]	...48	3
4 May 91	● TOUCH ME (ALL NIGHT LONG) *Polydor CATH 3*	...5	10
20 Jul 91	JUST ANOTHER DREAM *Polydor CATH 2*	...13	7
5 Oct 91	TOO MANY WALLS *Polydor CATH 4*	...17	7
7 Dec 91	EVERYBODY MOVE *Polydor CATH 5*	...25	8
29 Aug 92	YOU LIED TO ME *Polydor CATH 6*	...34	4
21 Nov 92	IRRESISTIBLE *Polydor CATH 7*	...24	4
6 Feb 93	FALLING *Polydor CATHD 8*	...32	2
12 Feb 94	WHY *ffrr FCD 227* [1]	...23	3
10 Aug 96	WEST END PAD *Polydor 5752812*	...25	2
1 Mar 97	WATERLOO SUNSET *Polydor 5759612*	...11	5
21 Jun 97	WHEN DREAMS TURN TO DUST *Polydor 5711852*	...43	1
10 Aug 91	● MOVE TO THIS *Polydor 8495031*	...3	31
23 Jan 93	● INTO THE SKYLINE *Polydor 5139352*	...8	4

[1] D Mob with Cathy Dennis

Jackie DENNIS *UK, male vocalist (Singles: 10 Weeks)*

			pos/wks
14 Mar 58	● LA DEE DAH *Decca F 10992*	...4	9
27 Jun 58	THE PURPLE PEOPLE EATER *Decca F 11033*	...29	1

Stefan DENNIS *Australia, male actor / vocalist (Singles: 8 Weeks)* pos/wks

6 May 89	DON'T IT MAKE YOU FEEL GOOD *Sublime LIME 105*	...16	7
7 Oct 89	THIS LOVE AFFAIR *Sublime LIME 113*	...67	1

The DENNISONS *UK, male vocal / instrumental group (Singles: 13 Weeks)*

			pos/wks
15 Aug 63	BE MY GIRL *Decca F 11691*	...46	6
7 May 64	WALKING THE DOG *Decca F 11880*	...36	7

Sandy DENNY (see also FAIRPORT CONVENTION) *UK, female vocalist, b. 6 Jan 1947, d. 21 Apr 1978 (Albums: 2 Weeks)* pos/wks

2 Oct 71	THE NORTH STAR GRASSMAN AND THE RAVENS *Island ILPS 9165*	...31	2

Richard DENTON and Martin COOK *UK, male orchestra leaders – instrumental duo – guitar and keyboards (Singles: 7 Weeks)* pos/wks

15 Apr 78	THEME FROM 'HONG KONG BEAT' *BBC RESL 52*	...25	7

John DENVER 〔219〕 Top 500
Unmistakable light tenor singer / songwriter / instrumentalist – guitar, with pop, country, folk and easy listening appeal, b. Henry John Deutschendorf, 31 Dec 1943, Roswell, New Mexico, US, d. 12 Oct 1997. One of America's top sellers in the 1970s amassed 19 platinum albums and four No.1 singles there (Singles: 22 Weeks, Albums: 256 Weeks) pos/wks

17 Aug 74	★ ANNIE'S SONG *RCA APBO 0295* ▲	...1	13
12 Dec 81	PERHAPS LOVE *CBS A 1905* [1]	...46	9
17 Mar 73	ROCKY MOUNTAIN HIGH *RCA SF 2308*	...11	15
2 Jun 73	POEMS PRAYERS AND PROMISES *RCA SF 8219*	...19	5
23 Jun 73	RHYMES AND REASONS *RCA Victor SF 8348*	...21	5
30 Mar 74	● THE BEST OF JOHN DENVER *RCA Victor APL1 0374*	...7	69

Singles re-entries are listed as (re), (2re), (3re).... which signifies that the hit re-entered the chart once, twice or three times...

7 Sep 74 ●	BACK HOME AGAIN *RCA Victor APLI 0548* ▲	3	29
22 Mar 75	AN EVENING WITH JOHN DENVER *RCA Victor LSA 3211/12*	31	4
11 Oct 75	WIND SONG *RCA Victor APLI 1183* ▲	14	21
15 May 76 ●	LIVE IN LONDON *RCA Victor RS 1050*	2	29
4 Sep 76 ●	SPIRIT *RCA Victor APLI 1694*	9	11
19 Mar 77 ●	BEST OF JOHN DENVER VOLUME 2 *RCA Victor PL 42120*	9	9
11 Feb 78	I WANT TO LIVE *RCA PL 12561*	25	5
21 Apr 79	JOHN DENVER *RCA Victor PL 13075*	68	1
28 Nov 81	PERHAPS LOVE *CBS 73592* [1]	17	21
22 Oct 83	IT'S ABOUT TIME *RCA RCALP 6087*	90	2
1 Dec 84	JOHN DENVER – THE COLLECTION *Telstar STAR 2253*	20	11
23 Aug 86	ONE WORLD *RCA PL 85811*	91	3
22 Mar 97	THE ROCKY MOUNTAIN COLLECTION *RCA 7863668372*	19	9
2 Oct 04	A SONG'S BEST FRIEND – THE VERY BEST OF JOHN DENVER *RCA 82876652742*	18	7

[1] Placido Domingo with John Denver [1] Placido Domingo and John Denver

Karl DENVER (469 Top 500)

Versatile Scottish singer with multi-octave vocal range, b. Angus McKenzie, 16 Dec 1934, Glasgow, Scotland, d. 21 Dec 1998. This unique artist, whose yodel-laced style added colour and contrast to the charts, reached the Top 20 with his first five singles (Singles: 127 Weeks, Albums: 27 Weeks) pos/wks

22 Jun 61 ●	MARCHETA *Decca F 11360*	8	20
19 Oct 61 ●	MEXICALI ROSE *Decca F 11395*	8	11
25 Jan 62 ●	WIMOWEH *Decca F 11420*	4	17
22 Feb 62 ●	NEVER GOODBYE *Decca F 11431*	9	18
7 Jun 62	A LITTLE LOVE A LITTLE KISS *Decca F 11470*	19	10
20 Sep 62	BLUE WEEK-END *Decca F 11505*	33	5
21 Mar 63	CAN YOU FORGIVE ME *Decca F 11608*	32	8
13 Jun 63	INDIAN LOVE CALL *Decca F 11674*	32	8
22 Aug 63	STILL *Decca F 11720*	13	15
5 Mar 64	MY WORLD OF BLUE *Decca F 11828*	29	6
4 Jun 64	LOVE ME WITH ALL YOUR HEART *Decca F 11905*	37	6
9 Jun 90	LAZYITIS – ONE ARMED BOXER *Factory FAC 2227* [1]	46	3
23 Dec 61 ●	WIMOWEH *Ace of Clubs ACL 1098*	7	27

[1] Happy Mondays and Karl Denver

DENZIE *See MONSTA BOY featuring DENZIE*

DEODATO

US, male multi-instrumentalist – Eumir Deodato (Singles: 9 Weeks) pos/wks

5 May 73 ●	ALSO SPRACH ZARATHUSTRA (2001) *Creed Taylor CTI 4000*	7	9

DEPARTMENT S

UK, male vocal / instrumental group (Singles: 13 Weeks) pos/wks

4 Apr 81	IS VIC THERE? *RCA 1003*	22	10
11 Jul 81	GOING LEFT RIGHT *Stiff BUY 118*	55	3

The DEPARTURE

UK, male vocal / instrumental group (Singles: 3 Weeks) pos/wks

14 Aug 04	ALL MAPPED OUT *Parlophone CDR 6642*	30	2
30 Oct 04	BE MY ENEMY *Parlophone CDRS 6653*	41	1

DEPECHE MODE (103 Top 500)

Consistently successful synth-led Essex band: Dave Gahan (v), Martin Gore (syn), Andy Fletcher (b/syn), Vince Clarke (syn, replaced 1982 by Alan Wilder). One of the world's best-selling groups, who reached the UK Top 10 with their first 13 albums (Singles: 246 Weeks, Albums: 183 Weeks) pos/wks

4 Apr 81	DREAMING OF ME *Mute MUTE 013*	57	4
13 Jun 81	NEW LIFE *Mute MUTE 014*	11	15
19 Sep 81 ●	JUST CAN'T GET ENOUGH *Mute MUTE 016*	8	10
13 Feb 82 ●	SEE YOU *Mute MUTE 018*	6	10
8 May 82	THE MEANING OF LOVE *Mute MUTE 022*	12	8
28 Aug 82	LEAVE IN SILENCE *Mute BONG 1*	18	10
12 Feb 83	GET THE BALANCE RIGHT *Mute 7BONG 2*	13	8
23 Jul 83 ●	EVERYTHING COUNTS *Mute 7BONG 3*	6	11
1 Oct 83	LOVE IN ITSELF *Mute 7BONG 4*	21	7
24 Mar 84 ●	PEOPLE ARE PEOPLE *Mute 7BONG 5*	4	10
1 Sep 84 ●	MASTER AND SERVANT *Mute 7BONG 6*	9	9
10 Nov 84	SOMEBODY / BLASPHEMOUS RUMOURS *Mute 7BONG 7*	16	6
11 May 85	SHAKE THE DISEASE *Mute BONG 8*	18	9
28 Sep 85	IT'S CALLED A HEART *Mute BONG 9*	18	4
22 Feb 86	STRIPPED *Mute BONG 10*	15	10
26 Apr 86	A QUESTION OF LUST *Mute BONG 11*	28	5

23 Aug 86	A QUESTION OF TIME *Mute BONG 12*	17	6
9 May 87	STRANGELOVE *Mute BONG 13*	16	5
5 Sep 87	NEVER LET ME DOWN AGAIN *Mute BONG 14*	22	4
9 Jan 88	BEHIND THE WHEEL *Mute BONG 15*	21	5
28 May 88	LITTLE 15 (IMPORT) *Mute LITTLE 15*	60	2
25 Feb 89	EVERYTHING COUNTS *Mute BONG 16*	22	7
9 Sep 89	PERSONAL JESUS *Mute BONG 17*	13	8
17 Feb 90 ●	ENJOY THE SILENCE *Mute BONG 18*	6	9
19 May 90	POLICY OF TRUTH *Mute BONG 19*	16	6
29 Sep 90	WORLD IN MY EYES *Mute BONG 20*	17	6
27 Feb 93 ●	I FEEL YOU *Mute CDBONG 21*	8	7
8 May 93	WALKING IN MY SHOES *Mute CDBONG 22*	14	4
25 Sep 93 ●	CONDEMNATION *Mute CDBONG 23*	9	4
22 Jan 94 ●	IN YOUR ROOM *Mute CDBONG 24*	8	4
15 Feb 97 ●	BARREL OF A GUN *Mute CDBONG 25*	4	4
12 Apr 97 ●	IT'S NO GOOD *Mute CDBONG 26*	5	5
28 Jun 97	HOME *Mute CDBONG 27*	23	4
1 Nov 97	USELESS *Mute CDBONG 28*	28	2
19 Sep 98	ONLY WHEN I LOSE MYSELF *Mute CDBONG 29*	17	3
5 May 01 ●	DREAM ON (re) *Mute CDBONG 30*	6	5
11 Aug 01	I FEEL LOVED *Mute CDBONG 31*	12	6
17 Nov 01	FREELOVE *Mute CDBONG 32*	19	3
30 Oct 04 ●	ENJOY THE SILENCE 04 (re-mix) *Mute LCDBONG 34*	7	5
4 Dec 04	SOMETHING TO DO *Mute L12BONG 34*	75	1
14 Nov 81 ●	SPEAK AND SPELL *Mute STUMM 5*	10	33
9 Oct 82 ●	A BROKEN FRAME *Mute STUMM 9*	8	11
3 Sep 83 ●	CONSTRUCTION TIME AGAIN *Mute STUMM 13*	6	12
6 Sep 84 ●	SOME GREAT REWARD *Mute STUMM 19*	5	12
26 Oct 85 ●	THE SINGLES 81–85 *Mute MUTEL 1*	6	22
29 Mar 86 ●	BLACK CELEBRATION *Mute STUMM 26*	4	11
10 Oct 87 ●	MUSIC FOR THE MASSES *Mute STUMM 47*	10	4
25 Mar 89 ●	101 *Mute STUMM 101*	5	8
31 Mar 90 ●	VIOLATOR *Mute STUMM 64*	2	30
3 Apr 93 ★	SONGS OF FAITH AND DEVOTION *Mute CDSTUMM 106* ■ ▲	1	16
26 Apr 97 ★	ULTRA *Mute CDSTUMM 148* ■	1	11
10 Oct 98 ●	THE SINGLES 86–98 *Mute CDMUTEL 5*	5	6
7 Nov 98	THE SINGLES 81–85 *Mute LCDMUTEL 1*	57	1
26 May 01 ●	EXCITER *Mute CDSTUMM 190*	9	4
6 Nov 04	REMIXES 81–04 *Mute XLCDMUTEL 8*	24	2

BONG 16 is a live version of BONG 3

DEPTH CHARGE

UK, male producer – Jonathan Kane (Singles: 1 Week) pos/wks

29 Jul 95	LEGEND OF THE GOLDEN SNAKE *DC DC 01CD*	75	1

DER DRITTE RAUM

Germany, male producer – Andreas Kruger (Singles: 1 Week) pos/wks

4 Sep 99	HALLE BOPP *Additive 12AD 042*	75	1

DEREK AND CLIVE *See Peter COOK and Dudley MOORE*

DEREK and the DOMINOES *See Eric CLAPTON*

Yves DERUYTER

Belgium, male DJ / producer (Singles: 3 Weeks) pos/wks

14 Apr 01	BACK TO EARTH *UK Bonzai UKBONZAICD 01*	63	1
19 Jan 02	BACK TO EARTH (re-mix) *UK Bonzai UKBONZAI 109CD*	56	2

DESERT *UK, male production duo (Singles: 1 Week)* pos/wks

20 Oct 01	LETTIN' YA MIND GO *Future Groove CDFGR 017*	74	1

DESERT EAGLE DISCS featuring Keisha WHITE

UK, male / female production / vocal group (Singles: 1 Week) pos/wks

1 Mar 03	BIGGER BETTER DEAL *Echo ECSCD 129*	67	1

DESERT SESSIONS *US / UK, male / female vocal / instrumental group (Singles: 2 Weeks)* pos/wks

15 Nov 03	CRAWL HOME *Island 9812964*	41	2

DESIDERIO *UK / Holland, male production duo and female vocalist (Singles: 1 Week)* pos/wks

3 Jun 00	STARLIGHT *Code Blue BLU 010CD*	57	1

Kevin DESIMONE *See Barry MANILOW*

DESIRELESS
France, female vocalist – Claudie Fritsch (Singles: 19 Weeks) pos/wks

31 Oct 87	**VOYAGE VOYAGE** *CBS DESI 1*	53	6
14 May 88 ●	**VOYAGE VOYAGE (re-mix)** *CBS DESI 2*	5	13

DESIYA featuring Melissa YIANNAKOU
UK, male / female vocal / instrumental duo (Singles: 1 Week) pos/wks

1 Feb 92	**COMIN' ON STRONG** *Black Market 12MKT 2*	74	1

DESKEE
UK, male instrumentalist – Derek Crumpley (Singles: 3 Weeks) pos/wks

3 Feb 90	**LET THERE BE HOUSE** *Big One VBIG 19*	52	2
8 Sep 90	**DANCE, DANCE** *Big One VBIG 22*	74	1

DES'REE *UK, female vocalist –*
Desiree Weekes (Singles: 73 Weeks, Albums: 27 Weeks) pos/wks

31 Aug 91	**FEEL SO HIGH** *Dusted Sound 6573667*	51	5
11 Jan 92	**FEEL SO HIGH (re-issue)** *Dusted Sound 6576897*	13	7
21 Mar 92	**MIND ADVENTURES** *Dusted Sound 6578637*	43	3
27 Jun 92	**WHY SHOULD I LOVE YOU** *Dusted Sound 6580917*	44	3
19 Jun 93	**DELICATE** *Columbia 6593312* [1]	14	6
9 Apr 94	**YOU GOTTA BE** *Dusted Sound 6601342*	20	7
18 Jun 94	**I AIN'T MOVIN'** *Dusted Sound 6604672*	44	3
3 Sep 94	**LITTLE CHILD** *Dusted Sound 6604515*	69	1
11 Mar 95	**YOU GOTTA BE (re-mix)** *Dusted Sound 6613215*	14	8
20 Jun 98 ●	**LIFE** *Sony S2 6659302*	8	15
7 Nov 98	**WHAT'S YOUR SIGN?** *Sony S2 6665162*	19	4
3 Apr 99 ●	**YOU GOTTA BE (2nd re-mix)**		
	Dusted Sound / Sony S2 6668935	10	8
16 Oct 99	**AIN'T NO SUNSHINE** *Universal Music TV 1564332* [2]	42	2
5 Apr 03	**IT'S OKAY** *Sony S2 6736492*	69	1
29 Feb 92	**MIND ADVENTURES** *Dusted Sound 4712632*	26	5
21 May 94	**I AIN'T MOVIN'** *Dusted Sound 4758432*	13	6
11 Jul 98	**SUPERNATURAL** *Sony S2 4897192*	16	16

[1] Terence Trent D'Arby featuring Des'ree [2] Ladysmith Black Mambazo featuring Des'ree

DESTINY'S CHILD 237 Top 500
(see also BEYONCÉ) *Texas-based US female R&B quartet turned trio, fronted by co-writer and co-producer Beyoncé Knowles with Kelly Rowland and Michelle Williams. Responsible for four US No.1 singles. The only US girl group to top the UK chart twice. Beyoncé won a Brit and four Grammy awards in 2004 (Singles: 117 Weeks, Albums: 143 Weeks)* pos/wks

28 Mar 98 ●	**NO, NO, NO** *Columbia 6656592* [1]	5	8
11 Jul 98	**WITH ME** *Columbia 6661472*	19	3
7 Nov 98	**SHE'S GONE** *Columbia 6664915* [2]	24	3
23 Jan 99	**GET ON THE BUS** *East West E 3780CD* [3]	15	5
24 Jul 99 ●	**BILLS, BILLS, BILLS** *Columbia 6676902* ▲	6	9
30 Oct 99 ●	**BUG A BOO** *Columbia 6681882*	9	7
8 Apr 00 ●	**SAY MY NAME** *Columbia 6691882* ▲	3	11
29 Jul 00 ●	**JUMPIN' JUMPIN'** *Columbia 6696292*	5	11
2 Dec 00 ★	**INDEPENDENT WOMEN PART 1** *Columbia 6705932* ■ ▲	1	15
28 Apr 01 ★	**SURVIVOR** *Columbia 6711732* ■	1	13
4 Aug 01 ●	**BOOTYLICIOUS** *Columbia 6717382* ▲	2	11
24 Nov 01 ●	**EMOTION** *Columbia 6721112*	3	14
13 Nov 04 ●	**LOSE MY BREATH** *Columbia 6754912*	2	7+
14 Mar 98	**DESTINY'S CHILD** *Columbia 4885352*	45	4
7 Aug 99	**THE WRITING'S ON THE WALL** *Columbia 4943942*	10	87
12 May 01 ★	**SURVIVOR** *Columbia 5017832* ■ ▲	1	44
30 Mar 02	**THIS IS THE REMIX** *Columbia 5076272*	25	3
27 Nov 04 ●	**DESTINY FULFILLED** *Columbia 5179162*	5	5+

[1] Destiny's Child featuring Wyclef Jean [2] Matthew Marsden featuring Destiny's Child [3] Destiny's Child featuring Timbaland

DESTROYERS *See George THOROGOOD and the DESTROYERS*

DESTRY *See ZOO EXPERIENCE featuring DESTRY; CIRCA featuring DESTRY*

Marcella DETROIT (see also SHAKESPEAR'S SISTER) *US, female vocalist – Marcella Levy (Singles: 16 Weeks, Albums: 5 Weeks)* pos/wks

12 Mar 94	**I BELIEVE** *London LONCD 347*	11	8
14 May 94	**AIN'T NOTHING LIKE THE REAL THING**		
	London LONCD 350 [1]	24	4

16 Jul 94	**I'M NO ANGEL** *London LOCDP 351*	33	4
9 Apr 94	**JEWEL** *London 8284912*	15	5

[1] Marcella Detroit and Elton John

DETROIT COBRAS
US, male / female vocal / instrumental group (Singles: 1 Week) pos/wks

25 Sep 04	**CHA CHA TWIST** *Rough Trade RTRADSCD 189*	59	1

DETROIT EMERALDS
US, male vocal group (Singles: 44 Weeks) pos/wks

10 Feb 73 ●	**FEEL THE NEED IN ME** *Janus 6146 020*	4	15
5 May 73	**YOU WANT IT YOU GOT IT** *Westbound 6146 103*	12	9
11 Aug 73	**I THINK OF YOU** *Westbound 6146 104*	27	9
18 Jun 77	**FEEL THE NEED (re-recording)** *Atlantic K 10945*	12	11

DETROIT GRAND PU BAHS
US, male production / vocal group (Singles: 3 Weeks) pos/wks

8 Jul 00	**SANDWICHES** *Jive Electro 9230252*	29	3

The DETROIT SPINNERS
US, male vocal group (Singles: 93 Weeks, Albums: 3 Weeks) pos/wks

14 Nov 70	**IT'S A SHAME** *Tamla Motown TMG 755* [1]	20	11
21 Apr 73	**COULD IT BE I'M FALLING IN LOVE** *Atlantic K 10283*	11	11
29 Sep 73 ●	**GHETTO CHILD** *Atlantic K 10359*	7	10
19 Oct 74	**THEN CAME YOU** *Atlantic K 10495* [2] ▲	29	6
11 Sep 76	**THE RUBBERBAND MAN** *Atlantic K 10807*	16	11
29 Jan 77	**WAKE UP SUSAN** *Atlantic K 10799*	29	6
7 May 77	**COULD IT BE I'M FALLING IN LOVE (EP)** *Atlantic K 10935*	32	3
23 Feb 80 ★	**WORKING MY WAY BACK TO YOU – FORGIVE ME GIRL**		
	(MEDLEY) *Atlantic K 11432*	1	14
10 May 80	**BODY LANGUAGE** *Atlantic K 11392*	40	7
28 Jun 80 ●	**CUPID – I'VE LOVED YOU FOR A LONG TIME (MEDLEY)**		
	Atlantic K 11498	4	10
24 Jun 95	**I'LL BE AROUND** *Cooltempo CDCOOL 306* [3]	30	4
14 May 77	**DETROIT SPINNERS' SMASH HITS** *Atlantic K 50363*	37	3

[1] Motown Spinners [2] Dionne Warwicke and the Detroit Spinners [3] Rappin' 4-Tay featuring the Spinners

Tracks on Could It Be I'm Falling in Love (EP): Could It Be I'm Falling in Love / You're Throwing a Good Love Away / Games People Play / Lazy Susan

DETROIT WHEELS *See Mitch RYDER and the DETROIT WHEELS*

DEUCE *UK, male / female vocal group*
(Singles: 23 Weeks, Albums: 2 Weeks) pos/wks

21 Jan 95	**CALL IT LOVE** *London LONCD 355*	11	10
22 Apr 95 ●	**I NEED YOU** *London LONCD 365*	10	5
19 Aug 95	**ON THE BIBLE** *London LONCD 368*	13	6
29 Jun 96	**NO SURRENDER** *Love This LUVTHISCD 10*	29	2
9 Sep 95	**ON THE LOOSE!** *London 8286642*	18	2

dEUS *Belgium, male vocal / instrumental*
group (Singles: 7 Weeks, Albums: 1 Week) pos/wks

11 Feb 95	**HOTEL LOUNGE (BE THE DEATH OF ME)** *Island CID 603*	55	1
13 Jul 96	**THEME FROM TURNPIKE (EP)** *Island CID 630*	68	1
19 Oct 96	**LITTLE ARITHMETICS** *Island CID 643*	44	2
15 Mar 97	**ROSES** *Island CID 645*	56	1
24 Apr 99	**INSTANT STREET** *Island CID 742*	49	1
3 Jul 99	**SISTER DEW** *Island CID 750*	62	1
3 Apr 99	**THE IDEAL CRASH** *Island 5246432*	64	1

Tracks on Theme from Turnpike (EP): Theme from Turnpike / Worried About Satan / Overflow / My Little Contessa

David DEVANT & HIS SPIRIT WIFE *UK, male vocal /*
instrumental group (Singles: 2 Weeks, Albums: 1 Week) pos/wks

5 Apr 97	**GINGER** *Rhythm King KIND 4CD*	54	1
21 Jun 97	**THIS IS FOR REAL** *Rhythm King KIND 5CD*	61	1
5 Jul 97	**WORK LOVELIFE MISCELLANEOUS**		
	Rhythm King KINDCD 1	70	1

William DEVAUGHN *US, male vocalist (Singles: 10 Weeks)* pos/wks

6 Jul 74	**BE THANKFUL FOR WHAT YOU'VE GOT** *Chelsea 2005 002*	31	5
20 Sep 80	**BE THANKFUL FOR WHAT YOU'VE GOT (re-recording)**		
	EMI 5101	44	5

Sidney DEVINE
UK, male vocalist (Singles: 1 Week, Albums: 11 Weeks)   pos/wks

1 Apr 78	**SCOTLAND FOREVER (EP)** *Philips SCOT 1* **48** 1
10 Apr 76	**DOUBLE DEVINE** *Philips 6625 019* **14** 10
11 Dec 76	**DEVINE TIME** *Philips 6308 283*....................**49** 1

Tracks on Scotland Forever (EP): Scotland Forever / Scots Wha' Hae / Flower of Scotland / Scottish Trilogy

DEVO *US, male vocal / instrumental*
group (Singles: 23 Weeks, Albums: 22 Weeks)   pos/wks

22 Apr 78	**(I CAN'T ME GET NO) SATISFACTION** *Stiff BOY 1* **41** 8
13 May 78	**JOCKO HOMO** *Stiff DEV 1* **62** 3
12 Aug 78	**BE STIFF** *Stiff BOY 2* **71** 1
2 Sep 78	**COME BACK JONEE** *Virgin VS 223* **60** 4
22 Nov 80	**WHIP IT** *Virgin VS 383* **51** 7
16 Sep 78	**Q: ARE WE NOT MEN? A: NO WE ARE DEVO!** *Virgin V 2106* ...**12** 7
23 Jun 79	**DUTY NOW FOR THE FUTURE** *Virgin V 2125* **49** 6
24 May 80	**FREEDOM OF CHOICE** *Virgin V 2162* **47** 5
5 Sep 81	**NEW TRADITIONALISTS** *Virgin V 2191* **50** 4

DEVOTIONS *See BELLE and the DEVOTIONS*

Howard DEVOTO (see also The BUZZCOCKS; MAGAZINE)
UK, male vocalist (Albums: 2 Weeks)   pos/wks

| 6 Aug 83 | **JERKY VERSIONS OF THE DREAM** *Virgin V 2272* ....**57** 2 |

DEXY'S MIDNIGHT RUNNERS ⟨394 ⟩ Top 500
Maverick Birmingham, UK-based post-punk group which split up in 1987. Led throughout radical personnel and stylistic changes by Kevin Rowland (v/g). Transatlantic No.1 'Come on Eileen' was the top selling UK single of 1982 – 1,201,000 (Singles: 93 Weeks, Albums: 80 Weeks)   pos/wks

19 Jan 80	**DANCE STANCE** *Oddball Productions R 6028* **40** 6
22 Mar 80	★ **GENO** *Late Night Feelings R 6033* **1** 14
12 Jul 80	● **THERE THERE MY DEAR** *Late Night Feelings R 6038* **7** 9
21 Mar 81	**PLAN B** *Parlophone R 6046* **58** 2
11 Jul 81	**SHOW ME** *Mercury DEXYS 6* **16** 9
20 Mar 82	**THE CELTIC SOUL BROTHERS** *Mercury DEXYS 8* ⟨1⟩ **45** 4
3 Jul 82	★ **COME ON EILEEN** *Mercury DEXYS 9* ⟨1⟩ ◆ ▲ **1** 17
2 Oct 82	**JACKIE WILSON SAID (I'M IN HEAVEN WHEN YOU SMILE)** *Mercury DEXYS 10* ⟨2⟩ **5** 7
4 Dec 82	**LET'S GET THIS STRAIGHT (FROM THE START) / OLD** *Mercury DEXYS 11* ⟨2⟩ **17** 9
2 Apr 83	**THE CELTIC SOUL BROTHERS** *Mercury DEXYS 12* ⟨2⟩ **20** 6
22 Nov 86	**BECAUSE OF YOU** *Mercury BRUSH 1* **13** 10
26 Jul 80	● **SEARCHING FOR THE YOUNG SOUL REBELS** *Parlophone PCS 7213* **6** 10
7 Aug 82	● **TOO-RYE-AY** *Mercury MERS 5* **2** 46
26 Mar 83	**GENO** *EMI EMS 1007* **79** 2
21 Sep 85	**DON'T STAND ME DOWN** *Mercury MERH 56* **22** 6
8 Jun 91	**THE VERY BEST OF DEXY'S MIDNIGHT RUNNERS** *Mercury 8464601* **12** 15
4 Oct 03	**LET'S MAKE THIS PRECIOUS – THE BEST OF DEXY'S MIDNIGHT RUNNERS** *EMI 5926802* **75** 1

⟨1⟩ Dexy's Midnight Runners with the Emerald Express ⟨2⟩ Kevin Rowland and Dexy's Midnight Runners

DEXYS 8 and DEXYS 12 are different   The group was all male for first album

DHANY *See KMC featuring DHANY*

DI *See SHY FX; T-POWER*

Tony DI BART
UK, male vocalist – Tony Di Bartholomew (Singles: 19 Weeks)   pos/wks

9 Apr 94	★ **THE REAL THING** *Cleveland City Blues CCBCD 15001* **1** 12
20 Aug 94	**DO IT** *Cleveland City Blues CCBCD 15003* **21** 4
20 May 95	**WHY DID YA** *Cleveland City Blues CCBCD 15004* **46** 1
2 Mar 96	**TURN YOUR LOVE AROUND** *Cleveland City Blues CCBCD 15006* **66** 1
17 Oct 98	**THE REAL THING (re-mix)** *Cleveland City CLECD 13050* **51** 1

Jim DIAMOND (see also PhD)
UK, male vocalist (Singles: 30 Weeks, Albums: 5 Weeks)   pos/wks

| 3 Nov 84 | ★ **I SHOULD HAVE KNOWN BETTER** *A&M AM 220* ....**1** 13 |
| 2 Feb 85 | **I SLEEP ALONE AT NIGHT** *A&M AM 229* ....**72** 1 |

18 May 85	**REMEMBER I LOVE YOU** *A&M AM 247* **42** 5
22 Feb 86	● **HI HO SILVER** *A&M AM 296* **5** 11
22 May 93	**JIM DIAMOND** *PolyGram TV 8438472* **16** 5

Neil DIAMOND ⟨37⟩ Top 500
World-renowned singer / guitarist / songwriter, b. 24 Jan 1941, Brooklyn, US. First found fame as writer of 'I'm a Believer' (The Monkees), before going on to become one of the world's most popular live artists and biggest-selling album acts, with 110 million sales. In 2004 he received a Lifetime Achievement Award from US Songwriters Hall of Fame (Singles: 121 Weeks, Albums: 606 Weeks)   pos/wks

7 Nov 70	● **CRACKLIN' ROSIE** *Uni UN 529* ▲ **3** 17
20 Feb 71	● **SWEET CAROLINE** *Uni UN 531* **8** 11
8 May 71	● **I AM ... I SAID** *Uni UN 532* **4** 12
13 May 72	**SONG SUNG BLUE** *Uni UN 538* ▲ **14** 13
14 Aug 76	**IF YOU KNOW WHAT I MEAN** *CBS 4398* **35** 4
23 Oct 76	**BEAUTIFUL NOISE** *CBS 4601* **13** 9
24 Dec 77	**DESIREE** *CBS 5869* **39** 6
25 Nov 78	● **YOU DON'T BRING ME FLOWERS** *CBS 6803* ⟨1⟩ ▲ **5** 12
3 Mar 79	**FOREVER IN BLUE JEANS** *CBS 7047* **16** 12
15 Nov 80	**LOVE ON THE ROCKS** *Capitol CL 16173* **17** 12
14 Feb 81	**HELLO AGAIN** *Capitol CL 16176* **51** 4
20 Nov 82	**HEARTLIGHT** *CBS A 2814* **47** 7
21 Nov 92	**MORNING HAS BROKEN** *Columbia 6588267* **36** 2
13 Mar 71	**GOLD** *Uni UNLS 116* **23** 13
20 Mar 71	**TAP ROOT MANUSCRIPT** *Uni UNLS 117* **19** 14
11 Dec 71	**STONES** *Uni UNLS 121* **18** 14
5 Aug 72	● **MOODS** *Uni UNLS 128* **7** 19
17 Feb 73	**HOT AUGUST NIGHT** *Uni ULD 1* **21** 20
16 Feb 74	**JONATHAN LIVINGSTON SEAGULL** *CBS 69047* **35** 1
9 Mar 74	**RAINBOW** *MCA MCF 2529* **39** 5
29 Jul 74	**HIS 12 GREATEST HITS** *MCA MCF 2550* **13** 78
9 Nov 74	**SERENADE** *CBS 69067* **11** 14
10 Jul 76	● **BEAUTIFUL NOISE** *CBS 86004* **10** 26
12 Mar 77	● **LOVE AT THE GREEK – RECORDED LIVE AT THE GREEK THEATRE** *CBS 95001* **3** 32
6 Aug 77	**HOT AUGUST NIGHT (re-issue)** *MCA MCSP 255* **60** 1
17 Dec 77	**I'M GLAD YOU'RE HERE WITH ME TONIGHT** *CBS 86044* **16** 12
25 Nov 78	● **20 GOLDEN GREATS** *MCA EMTV 14* **2** 29
6 Jan 79	**YOU DON'T BRING ME FLOWERS** *CBS 86077* **15** 23
19 Jan 80	**SEPTEMBER MORN** *CBS 86096* **14** 11
22 Nov 80	● **THE JAZZ SINGER (FILM SOUNDTRACK)** *Capitol EAST 12120* ...**3** 110
28 Feb 81	**LOVE SONGS** *MCA MCF 3092* **43** 6
5 Dec 81	**THE WAY TO THE SKY** *MCA MCF 3090* **39** 13
19 Jun 82	**12 GREATEST HITS VOLUME 2** *CBS 85844* **32** 8
13 Nov 82	**HEARTLIGHT** *CBS 25073* **43** 10
10 Dec 83	**THE VERY BEST OF NEIL DIAMOND** *K-Tel NE 1265* **33** 11
28 Jul 84	● **PRIMITIVE** *CBS 86306* **7** 10
24 May 86	**HEADED FOR THE FUTURE** *CBS 26952* **36** 8
28 Nov 87	**HOT AUGUST NIGHT II** *CBS 460 4081* **74** 4
25 Feb 89	**THE BEST YEARS OF OUR LIVES** *CBS 463201 1* **42** 6
9 Nov 91	**LOVESCAPE** *Columbia 4688901* **36** 13
4 Jul 92	★ **THE GREATEST HITS 1966–1992** *Columbia 4715022* **1** 30
28 Nov 92	**THE CHRISTMAS ALBUM** *Columbia 4724102* **50** 6
9 Oct 93	**UP ON THE ROOF – SONGS FROM THE BRILL BUILDING** *Columbia 4743562* **28** 10
17 Feb 96	**TENNESSEE MOON** *Columbia 4813782* **13** 13
25 May 96	**THE BEST OF NEIL DIAMOND** *MCA MCD 11452* **68** 1
31 Aug 96	● **THE ULTIMATE COLLECTION** *Sony TV / Universal MOODCD 45* ...**5** 20
14 Nov 98	**THE MOVIE ALBUM – AS TIME GOES BY** *Columbia 4916552* **68** 2
15 Sep 01	**THREE CHORD OPERA** *Columbia 5024932* **49** 1
16 Mar 02	**THE ESSENTIAL COLLECTION** *Columbia 5010662* **11** 12

⟨1⟩ Barbra and Neil *(Barbra was Barbra Streisand)*

Gregg DIAMOND BIONIC BOOGIE *US, male / female vocal*
group leader b. 4 May 1949, d. 14 Mar 1999 (Singles: 3 Weeks)   pos/wks

| 20 Jan 79 | **CREAM (ALWAYS RISES TO THE TOP)** *Polydor POSP 18* ....**61** 3 |

DIAMOND HEAD *UK, male vocal /*
instrumental group (Singles: 2 Weeks, Albums: 9 Weeks)   pos/wks

11 Sep 82	**IN THE HEAT OF THE NIGHT** *MCA DHM 102* **67** 2
23 Oct 82	**BORROWED TIME** *MCA DH 1001* **24** 5
24 Sep 83	**CANTERBURY** *MCA DH 1002* **32** 4

The DIAMONDS *Canada / US, male vocal group (Singles: 17 Weeks)* pos/wks

| 31 May 57 | ● **LITTLE DARLIN'** *Mercury MT 148* ....**3** 17 |

DICK and DEEDEE
US, male / female vocal duo – Dick St John (Richard Gosting),
b. 1940, d. 27 Dec 2003, and Deedee Sperling (Singles: 3 Weeks)   pos/wks

26 Oct 61	THE MOUNTAIN'S HIGH *London HLG 9408*	**37** 3

Charles DICKENS
UK, male vocalist – David Anthony (Singles: 8 Weeks)   pos/wks

1 Jul 65	THAT'S THE WAY LOVE GOES *Pye 7N 15887*	**37** 8

Gwen DICKEY (see also ROSE ROYCE)
US, female vocalist (Singles: 13 Weeks)   pos/wks

27 Jan 90	CAR WASH *Swanyard SYR 7*	**72** 2
2 Jul 94	AIN'T NOBODY (LOVES ME BETTER) *X-clusive XCLU 010CD* [1]	**21** 4
14 Feb 98	WISHING ON A STAR *Northwestside 74321554632* [2]	**13** 4
31 Oct 98	CAR WASH (re-recording) *MCA MCSTD 48096* [3]	**18** 3

[1] KWS and Gwen Dickey [2] Jay-Z featuring Gwen Dickey [3] Rose Royce featuring Gwen Dickey

Neville DICKIE
UK, male instrumentalist – piano (Singles: 10 Weeks)   pos/wks

25 Oct 69	ROBIN'S RETURN (re) *Major Minor MM 644*	**33** 10

The DICKIES *US, male vocal / instrumental*
group (Singles: 28 Weeks, Albums: 19 Weeks)   pos/wks

16 Dec 78	SILENT NIGHT *A&M AMS 7403*	**47** 4
21 Apr 79 ●	BANANA SPLITS (THE TRA LA LA SONG) *A&M AMS 7431*	**7** 8
21 Jul 79	PARANOID *A&M AMS 7368*	**45** 6
15 Sep 79	NIGHTS IN WHITE SATIN *A&M AMS 7469*	**39** 5
16 Feb 80	FAN MAIL *A&M AMS 7504*	**57** 3
19 Jul 80	GIGANTOR *A&M AMS 7544*	**72** 2
17 Feb 79	THE INCREDIBLE SHRINKING DICKIES *A&M AMLE 64742*	**18** 17
24 Nov 79	DAWN OF THE DICKIES *A&M AMLE 68510*	**60** 2

Bruce DICKINSON (see also IRON MAIDEN)
UK, male vocalist – Paul Dickinson
(Singles: 23 Weeks, Albums: 15 Weeks)   pos/wks

28 Apr 90	TATTOOED MILLIONAIRE *EMI EM 138*	**18** 5
23 Jun 90	ALL THE YOUNG DUDES *EMI EM 142*	**23** 5
25 Aug 90	DIVE! DIVE! DIVE! *EMI EM 151*	**45** 2
4 Apr 92 ●	(I WANT TO BE) ELECTED *London LON 319* [1]	**9** 5
28 May 94	TEARS OF THE DRAGON *EMI CDEM 322*	**28** 2
8 Oct 94	SHOOT ALL THE CLOWNS *EMI CDEMS 341*	**37** 2
13 Apr 96	BACK FROM THE EDGE *Raw Power RAWX 1012*	**68** 1
3 May 97	ACCIDENT OF BIRTH *Raw Power RAWX 1042*	**54** 1
19 May 90	TATTOOED MILLIONAIRE *EMI EMC 3574*	**14** 9
18 Jun 94	BALLS TO PICASSO *EMI CDEMX 1057*	**21** 3
9 Mar 96	SKUNKWORKS *Raw Power RAWCD 106*	**41** 1
24 May 97	ACCIDENT OF BIRTH *Raw Power RAWCD 124*	**53** 1
26 Sep 98	THE CHEMICAL WEDDING *Air Raid AIRCD 1*	**55** 1

[1] Mr Bean and Smear Campaign featuring Bruce Dickinson

Barbara DICKSON (350 Top 500)
Noted folk-inflected pop singer, b. 27 Sep 1947, Dunfermline, Scotland. A familiar
face on 1970s and 1980s TV who later received acclaim for theatrical forays
(notably Willy Russell's 'Blood Brothers') and TV acting roles ('Band of Gold').
Awarded an OBE in 2002 (Singles: 49 Weeks, Albums: 144 Weeks)   pos/wks

17 Jan 76 ●	ANSWER ME *RSO 2090 174*	**9** 7
26 Feb 77	ANOTHER SUITCASE IN ANOTHER HALL *MCA 266*	**18** 7
19 Jan 80	CARAVAN SONG *Epic EPC 8103*	**41** 7
15 Mar 80	JANUARY FEBRUARY *Epic EPC 8115*	**11** 10
14 Jun 80	IN THE NIGHT *Epic EPC 8593*	**48** 2
5 Jan 85 ★	I KNOW HIM SO WELL *RCA CHESS 3* [1]	**1** 16
18 Jun 77	MORNING COMES QUICKLY *RSO 2394 188*	**58** 1
12 Apr 80 ●	THE BARBARA DICKSON ALBUM *Epic EPC 84088*	**7** 12
16 May 81	YOU KNOW IT'S ME *Epic EPC 84551*	**39** 6
6 Feb 82 ●	ALL FOR A SONG *Epic 10030*	**3** 37
24 Sep 83	TELL ME IT'S NOT TRUE *Legacy LLM 101*	**100** 1
23 Jun 84	HEARTBEATS *Epic EPC 25706*	**21** 8
12 Jan 85 ●	THE BARBARA DICKSON SONGBOOK *K-Tel NE 1287*	**5** 19
23 Nov 85	GOLD *K-Tel ONE 1312*	**11** 18
15 Nov 86	THE VERY BEST OF BARBARA DICKSON *Telstar STAR 2276*	**78** 8
29 Nov 86	THE RIGHT MOMENT *K-Tel ONE 1335*	**39** 8

6 May 89	COMING ALIVE AGAIN *Telstar STAR 2349*	**30** 7
15 Aug 92	DON'T THINK TWICE IT'S ALL RIGHT *Columbia MOODCD 25*	**32** 5
28 Nov 92	THE BEST OF ELAINE PAIGE AND BARBARA DICKSON *Telstar TCD 2632* [1]	**22** 9
5 Mar 94	PARCEL OF ROGUES *Castle Communications CTVCD 126*	**30** 3
20 Mar 04	THE PLATINUM COLLECTION *Sony Music TV 5161092*	**35** 2

[1] Elaine Paige and Barbara Dickson [1] Elaine Paige and Barbara Dickson

'Tell Me It's Not True' is a mini-album featuring songs from the musical
Blood Brothers

The DICTATORS
US, male vocal / instrumental group (Singles: 2 Weeks)   pos/wks

17 Sep 77	SEARCH AND DESTROY (re) *Asylum K 13091*	**49** 2

Bo DIDDLEY *US, male vocalist / instrumentalist – guitar –*
Ellas McDaniel (Singles: 10 Weeks, Albums: 16 Weeks)   pos/wks

10 Oct 63	PRETTY THING *Pye International 7N 25217*	**34** 6
18 Mar 65	HEY GOOD LOOKIN' *Chess CRS 8000*	**39** 4
5 Oct 63	BO DIDDLEY *Pye International NPL 28026*	**11** 8
9 Oct 63	BO DIDDLEY IS A GUNSLINGER *Pye NJL 33*	**20** 1
30 Nov 63	BO DIDDLEY RIDES AGAIN *Pye International NPL 28029*	**19** 1
15 Jun 64	BO DIDDLEY'S BEACH PARTY *Pye NPL 28032*	**13** 6

DIDDY (see also BEDLAM)
UK, male producer – Richard 'Diddy' Dearlove (Singles: 3 Weeks)   pos/wks

19 Feb 94	GIVE ME LOVE *Positiva CDTIV 8*	**52** 1
12 Jul 97	GIVE ME LOVE (re-mix) *Feverpitch CDFVR 19*	**23** 2

DIDO (257 Top 500) (see also FAITHLESS)
Record-breaking singer / songwriter and double Brit award winner in 2004,
b. Florian Cloud de Bounevialle Armstrong, 25 Dec 1971, London. 'No Angel'
(including the Eminem sampled 'Thank You') was the world's top selling
album in 2001 (8.6 million) and is the UK's biggest selling debut album by a
female artist (Singles: 64 Weeks, Albums: 185 Weeks)   pos/wks

24 Apr 01 ●	HERE WITH ME *Cheeky / Arista 74321832732*	**4** 12
2 Jun 01 ●	THANK YOU *Cheeky / Arista 74321853042*	**3** 10
22 Sep 01	HUNTER *Cheeky / Arista 74321885452*	**17** 8
20 Apr 02 ●	ONE STEP TOO FAR *Cheeky / Arista 74321926412* [1]	**6** 3
13 Sep 03 ●	WHITE FLAG *Cheeky / Arista 82876546022*	**2** 13
13 Dec 03 ●	LIFE FOR RENT *Cheeky / Arista 82876579462*	**8** 9
24 Apr 04	DON'T LEAVE HOME *Cheeky / Arista 82876611722*	**25** 6
25 Sep 04	SAND IN MY SHOES *Cheeky / Arista 82876626922*	**29** 3
28 Oct 00 ★	NO ANGEL *Cheeky / Arista 74321802682*	**1** 133
11 Oct 03 ★	LIFE FOR RENT *Cheeky / Arista 82876545982* ■	**1** 52

[1] Faithless featuring Dido

DIE *See Roni SIZE / REPRAZANT*

DIESEL PARK WEST *UK, male vocal / instrumental*
group (Singles: 15 Weeks, Albums: 3 Weeks)   pos/wks

4 Feb 89	ALL THE MYTHS ON SUNDAY *Food FOOD 17*	**66** 2
1 Apr 89	LIKE PRINCES DO *Food FOOD 19*	**58** 3
5 Aug 89	WHEN THE HOODOO COMES *Food FOOD 20*	**62** 2
18 Jan 92	FALL TO LOVE *Food FOOD 35*	**48** 3
21 Mar 92	BOY ON TOP OF THE NEWS *Food FOOD 36*	**58** 2
5 Sep 92	GOD ONLY KNOWS *Food FOOD 39*	**57** 3
11 Feb 89	SHAKESPEARE ALABAMA *Food FOODLP 2*	**55** 2
15 May 92	DECENCY *Food FOODCD 7*	**57** 1

DIFFERENT GEAR vs POLICE *UK / Italy, male production group*
and UK / US, male vocal / instrumental trio (Singles: 3 Weeks)   pos/wks

5 Aug 00	WHEN THE WORLD IS RUNNING DOWN *Pagan PAGAN 039CDS*	**28** 3

DIFFORD and TILBROOK (see also SQUEEZE) *UK, male*
vocal / instrumental duo (Singles: 2 Weeks, Albums: 3 Weeks)   pos/wks

30 Jun 84	LOVE'S CRASHING WAVES *A&M AM 193*	**57** 2
14 Jul 84	DIFFORD AND TILBROOK *A&M AMLX 64985*	**47** 3

DIFF'RENT DARKNESS
UK, male vocal / instrumental group (Singles: 1 Week)   pos/wks

27 Dec 03	ORCHESTRAL MANOEUVRES IN THE DARKNESS *Guided Missile GUIDE 49CD*	**66** 1

Singles re-entries are listed as (re), (2re), (3re).... which signifies that the hit re-entered the chart once, twice or three times...

DIGABLE PLANETS
US, male / female vocal / instrumental group (Singles: 2 Weeks)   pos/wks

| 13 Feb 93 | **REBIRTH OF SLICK (COOL LIKE DAT)** *Pendulum EKR 159CD* **67** | 2 |

Rah DIGGA See JAMELIA; OUTSIDAZ featuring Rah DIGGA and Melanie BLATT

DIGITAL DREAM BABY (see also Peter AUTY
and the SINFONIA OF LONDON conducted by Howard BLAKE)
UK, male producer – Steven Teear (Singles: 4 Weeks)   pos/wks

| 14 Dec 91 | **WALKING IN THE AIR** *Columbia 6576067* **49** | 4 |

Hit is a dance re-mix of 'Walking in the Air' by vocalist Peter Auty

DIGITAL EXCITATION
Belgium, male producer – Frank de Wulf (Singles: 2 Weeks)   pos/wks

| 29 Feb 92 | **PURE PLEASURE** *R&S RSUK 10* **37** | 2 |

DIGITAL ORGASM *Belgium, male / female*
vocal / instrumental group (Singles: 14 Weeks)   pos/wks

7 Dec 91	**RUNNING OUT OF TIME** *Dead Dead Good GOOD 009* **16**	9
18 Apr 92	**STARTOUCHERS** *DDG International GOOD 13* **31**	3
25 Jul 92	**MOOG ERUPTION** *DDG International GOOD 17* **62**	2

DIGITAL UNDERGROUND
US, male rap group (Singles: 4 Weeks, Albums: 2 Weeks)   pos/wks

16 Mar 91	**SAME SONG** *Big Life BLR 40* **52**	4
7 Apr 90	**SEX PACKETS** *BCM BCM 377LP* **59**	1
30 Jun 90	**DOOWUTCHYALIKE / PACKET MAN** *BCM BCM 463X* **59**	1

DILATED PEOPLES *US, male vocal / DJ /*
production group (Singles: 6 Weeks, Albums: 1 Week)   pos/wks

23 Feb 02	**WORST COMES TO WORST** *Capitol CDCL 834* **29**	3
10 Apr 04	**THIS WAY** *Capitol CDCL 854* **35**	3
2 Mar 02	**EXPANSION TEAM** *Capitol 5314772* **55**	1

DILEMMA
Italy, male instrumental / production group (Singles: 1 Week)   pos/wks

| 6 Apr 96 | **IN SPIRIT** *ffrr FCD 274* **42** | 1 |

Ricky DILLARD See Farley 'Jackmaster' FUNK

DILLINJA *UK, male producer – Karl Francis (Singles: 9 Weeks)*   pos/wks

9 Nov 02	**TWIST 'EM OUT** *Renegade Hardware RH 40* **50**	1
21 Dec 02	**LIVE OR DIE / SOUTH MANZ** *Valve VLV 007* **53**	1
10 May 03	**THIS IS A WARNING / SUPER DJ** *Valve VLV 008* **47**	1
28 Jul 03	**TWIST 'EM OUT** *Trouble on Vinyl TOV 56CD* [1] **35**	3
27 Sep 03	**FAST CAR** *Valve VLV 011* **56**	2
12 Jun 04	**ALL THE THINGS / FORSAKEN DREAMS** *Valve VLV 012* **71**	1
10 Jul 04	**IN THE GRIND / ACID TRAK** *Valve VLV 013* **71**	1

[1] Dillinja featuring Skibadee

Richard DIMBLEBY *UK, male broadcaster,*
b. 25 May 1913, d. 22 Dec 1965 (Albums: 5 Weeks)   pos/wks

| 4 Jun 66 | **THE VOICE OF RICHARD DIMBLEBY** *MFP 1087* **14** | 5 |

DIMESTARS
UK, male / female vocal / instrumental group (Singles: 1 Week)   pos/wks

| 16 Jun 01 | **MY SUPERSTAR** *Polydor 5870912* **72** | 1 |

D'INFLUENCE *UK, male / female vocal /*
instrumental group (Singles: 10 Weeks, Albums: 1 Week)   pos/wks

20 Jun 92	**GOOD LOVER** *East West A 8573* [1] **46**	2
27 Mar 93	**GOOD LOVER (re-mix)** *East West America A 8439CD* [1] **61**	1
24 Jun 95	**MIDNITE** *East West A 4418CD* [2] **58**	1
16 Aug 97	**HYPNOTIZE** *Echo ECSCD 41* **33**	2
11 Oct 97	**MAGIC** *Echo ECSCD 45* **45**	1
5 Sep 98	**ROCK WITH YOU** *Echo ECSCD 56* **30**	3
25 Oct 97	**LONDON** *Echo ECHCD 16* **56**	1

[1] D-Influence [2] D*Influence

Paolo DINI See FPI PROJECT

Mark DINNING
US, male vocalist, b. 17 Aug 1933, d. 22 Mar 1986 (Singles: 4 Weeks) pos/wks

| 10 Mar 60 | **TEEN ANGEL (re)** *MGM 1053* ▲ **37** | 4 |

DINOSAUR JR *US, male vocal /*
instrumental group (Singles: 13 Weeks, Albums: 7 Weeks)   pos/wks

2 Feb 91	**THE WAGON** *Blanco Y Negro NEG 48* **49**	2
14 Nov 92	**GET ME** *Blanco Y Negro NEG 60* **44**	1
30 Jan 93	**START CHOPPIN'** *Blanco Y Negro NEG 61CD* **20**	3
12 Jun 93	**OUT THERE** *Blanco Y Negro NEG 63CD* **44**	2
27 Aug 94	**FEEL THE PAIN** *Blanco Y Negro NEG 74CD* **25**	3
11 Feb 95	**I DON'T THINK SO** *Blanco Y Negro NEG 77CD* **67**	1
5 Apr 97	**TAKE A RUN AT THE SUN** *Blanco Y Negro NEG 103CD* **53**	1
2 Mar 91	**GREEN MIND** *Blanco Y Negro BYN 24* **36**	2
20 Feb 93	● **WHERE YOU BEEN** *Blanco Y Negro 4509916272* **10**	3
10 Sep 94	**WITHOUT A SOUND** *Blanco Y Negro 4509969332* **24**	2

DINOSAURS See Terry DACTYL and the DINOSAURS

DIO *UK / US, male vocal /*
instrumental group (Singles: 22 Weeks, Albums: 48 Weeks)   pos/wks

20 Aug 83	**HOLY DIVER** *Vertigo DIO 1* **72**	2
29 Oct 83	**RAINBOW IN THE DARK** *Vertigo DIO 2* **46**	3
11 Aug 84	**WE ROCK** *Vertigo DIO 3* **42**	3
29 Sep 84	**MYSTERY** *Vertigo DIO 4* **34**	4
10 Aug 85	**ROCK 'N' ROLL CHILDREN** *Vertigo DIO 5* **26**	6
2 Nov 85	**HUNGRY FOR HEAVEN** *Vertigo DIO 6* **72**	1
17 May 86	**HUNGRY FOR HEAVEN (re-issue)** *Vertigo DIO 7* **56**	2
1 Aug 87	**I COULD HAVE BEEN A DREAMER** *Vertigo DIO 8* **69**	1
11 Jun 83	**HOLY DIVER** *Vertigo VERS 5* **13**	15
21 Jul 84	● **THE LAST IN LINE** *Vertigo VERL 16* **4**	14
7 Sep 85	● **SACRED HEART** *Vertigo VERH 30* **4**	5
5 Jul 86	**INTERMISSION** *Vertigo VERB 40* **22**	5
22 Aug 87	● **DREAM EVIL** *Vertigo VERH 46* **8**	5
26 May 90	**LOCK UP THE WOLVES** *Vertigo 8460331* **28**	3

DION
US, male vocalist – Dion DiMucci
(Singles: 35 Weeks, Albums: 5 Weeks)   pos/wks

26 Jun 59	**A TEENAGER IN LOVE** *London HLU 8874* [1] **28**	2
19 Jan 61	**LONELY TEENAGER** *Top Rank JAR 521* **47**	1
2 Nov 61	**RUNAROUND SUE** *Top Rank JAR 586* ▲ **11**	9
15 Feb 62	● **THE WANDERER** *HMV POP 971* **10**	12
22 May 76	**THE WANDERER (re-issue)** *Philips 6146 700* **16**	9
19 Aug 89	**KING OF THE NEW YORK STREETS** *Arista 112556* **74**	2
12 Apr 80	**20 GOLDEN GREATS** *K-Tel NE 1057* [1] **31**	5

[1] Dion and the Belmonts   [1] Dion and the Belmonts

Celine DION   49 Top 500
French-Canadian vocalist who won the 1988 Eurovision Song Contest
(for Switzerland), b. 30 Mar 1968, Quebec, Canada. She has sold a reported
155 million albums worldwide and is the only female with two UK million-
selling singles as a solo artist. Best-selling single: 'My Heart Will Go On'
1,312,551 (Singles: 250 Weeks, Albums: 411 Weeks)   pos/wks

16 May 92	● **BEAUTY AND THE BEAST** *Epic 6576607* [1] **9**	7
4 Jul 92	**IF YOU ASKED ME TO (re)** *Epic 6581927* **57**	5
14 Nov 92	**LOVE CAN MOVE MOUNTAINS** *Epic 6587787* **46**	2
3 Apr 93	**WHERE DOES MY HEART BEAT NOW** *Epic 6563265* **72**	1
29 Jan 94	● **THE POWER OF LOVE** *Epic 6597992* ▲ **4**	10
23 Apr 94	**MISLED** *Epic 6602922* **40**	3
22 Oct 94	★ **THINK TWICE** *Epic 6606422* ◆ **1**	31
20 May 95	● **ONLY ONE ROAD** *Epic 6613535* **8**	8
9 Sep 95	● **TU M'AIMES ENCORE (TO LOVE ME AGAIN)** *Epic 6624255* **7**	9
2 Dec 95	**MISLED (re-issue)** *Epic 6626495* **15**	6
2 Mar 96	● **FALLING INTO YOU** *Epic 6629795* **10**	10
1 Jun 96	● **BECAUSE YOU LOVED ME (THEME FROM 'UP CLOSE AND PERSONAL')** *Epic 6632282* ▲ **5**	16
5 Oct 96	● **IT'S ALL COMING BACK TO ME NOW** *Epic 6637112* **3**	14
21 Dec 96	● **ALL BY MYSELF (re)** *Epic 6640622* **6**	13
28 Jun 97	**CALL THE MAN** *Epic 6646922* **11**	6
15 Nov 97	● **TELL HIM** *Epic 6653052* [2] **3**	15
20 Dec 97	**THE REASON** *Epic 6653812* **11**	8
21 Feb 98	★ **MY HEART WILL GO ON** *Epic 6655472* ◆ ■ ▲ **1**	20
18 Jul 98	● **IMMORTALITY** *Epic 6661682* [3] **5**	12
28 Nov 98	● **I'M YOUR ANGEL** *Epic 6666282* [4] ▲ **3**	13

		pos	wks
10 Jul 99	TREAT HER LIKE A LADY *Epic 6675522*	29	3
11 Dec 99	THAT'S THE WAY IT IS *Epic 6684622*	12	11
8 Apr 00	THE FIRST TIME EVER I SAW YOUR FACE (re) *Epic 6691942*	19	7
23 Mar 02 ●	A NEW DAY HAS COME *Epic 6725032*	7	10
31 Aug 02	I'M ALIVE *Epic 6730652*	17	6
7 Dec 02	GOODBYE'S (THE SADDEST WORD) *Epic 6733732*	38	2
20 Sep 03	ONE HEART *Columbia 6743482*	27	2
5 Mar 94 ★	THE COLOUR OF MY LOVE *Epic 4747432*	1	109
16 Sep 95	UNISON *Epic 472032*	55	3
7 Oct 95	D'EUX *Epic 4802862*	7	9
23 Mar 96 ★	FALLING INTO YOU *Epic 4837928* ■ ▲	1	113
9 Nov 96	LIVE A PARIS *Epic 4866062*	53	1
15 Mar 97	C'EST POUR VIVRE *Nectar Masters NTRCD 076*	49	2
29 Nov 97 ★	LET'S TALK ABOUT LOVE *Epic 4891592* ■ ▲	1	73
19 Sep 98	S'IL SUFFISAIT D'AIMER *Epic 4918592*	17	4
26 Sep 98	CELINE DION *Epic 4715089*	70	2
14 Nov 98	THESE ARE SPECIAL TIMES *Epic 4927302*	20	10
27 Nov 99 ★	ALL THE WAY ... A DECADE OF SONG *Epic 4960942* ■ ▲	1	40
11 Nov 00	THE COLLECTOR'S SERIES – VOLUME ONE *Epic 5009952*	30	3
6 Apr 02 ★	A NEW DAY HAS COME *Epic 5062262* ■ ▲	1	23
5 Apr 03 ●	ONE HEART *Columbia 5108772*	4	9
26 Jun 04	A NEW DAY – LIVE IN LAS VEGAS *Columbia 5152253*	22	4
23 Oct 04	MIRACLE – A CELEBRATION OF NEW LIFE *Columbia 5187487* [1]	5	5

[1] Celine Dion and Peabo Bryson [2] Barbra Streisand and Celine Dion [3] Celine Dion with special guests The Bee Gees [4] Celine Dion and R Kelly [1] Celine Dion & Anne Geddes

Kathryn DION *See 2 FUNKY 2 starring Kathryn DION*

DIONNE
Canada, female vocalist (Singles: 2 Weeks) pos/wks

		pos	wks
23 Sep 89	COME GET MY LOVIN' *Citybeat CBC 745*	69	2

Wasis DIOP featuring Lena FIAGBE
Senegal, male producer and UK, female singer (Singles: 2 Weeks) pos/wks

		pos	wks
10 Feb 96	AFRICAN DREAM *Mercury MERCD 453*	44	2

DIRE STRAITS `14` `Top 500`
(see also David KNOPFLER; NOTTING HILLBILLIES) *Internationally acclaimed, album-oriented rock group fronted by Mark Knopfler (g/v), b. 12 Aug 1949, Glasgow, Scotland. The London-based band was discovered after a demo tape was played on Charlie Gillett's Radio London show in 1977. Eponymous Knopfler-penned debut album (total cost just £12,500) was a transatlantic million-seller and, like their first single, 'Sultans of Swing', was even more successful in the US. By the early 1980s, they were global chart regulars, selling out shows across the USA and Europe and attracting record-breaking crowds in Australasia. In 1983, they were voted Best British Group for the first time at the Brit Awards, and during that decade picked up countless other trophies. They released their most successful album, the Grammy and Brit-winning 'Brothers in Arms', in 1985 – it topped the chart in 22 countries (as did 'On Every Street'), sold over nine million Stateside and nearly four million in the UK. The album included the US No.1 single 'Money for Nothing' (which featured co-writer Sting), the first video seen on MTV Europe. In 1991, the group started a record-shattering world tour, which was seen by over seven million people in 25 countries and grossed around £70 million. In total, Dire Straits have sold in excess of 100 million albums around the globe (Singles: 119 Weeks, Albums: 1136 Weeks)* pos/wks

		pos	wks
10 Mar 79 ●	SULTANS OF SWING *Vertigo 6059 206*	8	11
28 Jul 79	LADY WRITER *Vertigo 6059 230*	51	6
17 Jan 81 ●	ROMEO AND JULIET *Vertigo MOVIE 1*	8	11
4 Apr 81	SKATEAWAY *Vertigo MOVIE 2*	37	5
10 Oct 81	TUNNEL OF LOVE *Vertigo MUSIC 3*	54	3
4 Sep 82 ●	PRIVATE INVESTIGATIONS *Vertigo DSTR 1*	2	8
22 Jan 83	TWISTING BY THE POOL *Vertigo DSTR 2*	14	7
18 Feb 84	LOVE OVER GOLD (LIVE) / SOLID ROCK (LIVE) *Vertigo DSTR 6*	50	3
20 Apr 85	SO FAR AWAY *Vertigo DSTR 9*	20	6
6 Jul 85 ●	MONEY FOR NOTHING *Vertigo DSTR 10* ▲	4	16
26 Oct 85	BROTHERS IN ARMS *Vertigo DSTR 11*	16	13
11 Jan 86 ●	WALK OF LIFE *Vertigo DSTR 12*	2	11
3 May 86	YOUR LATEST TRICK *Vertigo DSTR 13*	26	6
5 Nov 88	SULTANS OF SWING (re-issue) *Vertigo DSTR 15*	62	1
31 Aug 91	CALLING ELVIS *Vertigo DSTR 16*	21	4
2 Nov 91	HEAVY FUEL *Vertigo DSTR 17*	55	2
29 Feb 92	ON EVERY STREET *Vertigo DSTR 18*	42	2

		pos	wks
27 Jun 92	THE BUG *Vertigo DSTR 19*	67	1
22 May 93	ENCORES (EP) *Vertigo DSCD 20*	31	3
22 Jul 78 ●	DIRE STRAITS *Vertigo 9102 021*	5	132
23 Jun 79 ●	COMMUNIQUE *Vertigo 9102 031*	5	32
25 Oct 80 ●	MAKING MOVIES *Vertigo 6359 034*	4	251
2 Oct 82 ★	LOVE OVER GOLD *Vertigo 6359 109* ■	1	200
24 Mar 84 ●	ALCHEMY – DIRE STRAITS LIVE *Vertigo VERY 11*	3	163
25 May 85 ★	BROTHERS IN ARMS *Vertigo VERH 25* ■ ▲	1	228
29 Oct 88 ●	MONEY FOR NOTHING *Vertigo VERH 64* ■	1	64
21 Sep 91 ★	ON EVERY STREET *Vertigo 5101601* ■	1	35
22 May 93 ●	ON THE NIGHT *Vertigo 5147662*	4	7
8 Jul 95	LIVE AT THE BBC *Windsong WINDCD 072X*	71	1
31 Oct 98 ●	SULTANS OF SWING – THE VERY BEST OF DIRE STRAITS *Vertigo 5586582*	6	23

Tracks on Encores (EP): Your Latest Trick / The Bug / Solid Rock / Local Hero (Wild Theme)

DIRECKT (see also E-LUSTRIOUS)
UK, male instrumental / production duo – Mike 'E-Bloc' Kirwin and Danny 'Hibrid' Bennett (Singles: 2 Weeks) pos/wks

		pos	wks
13 Aug 94	TWO FATT GUITARS (REVISITED) *UFG UFG 7CD*	36	2

DIRECT DRIVE
UK, male / female vocal / instrumental group (Singles: 3 Weeks) pos/wks

		pos	wks
26 Jan 85	ANYTHING? *Polydor POSP 728*	67	2
4 May 85	A.B.C. (FALLING IN LOVE'S NOT EASY) *Boiling Point POSP 742*	75	1

DIRT DEVILS
UK / Finland, male production duo – Jon Grant and Paavo Siljamaki (Singles: 8 Weeks) pos/wks

		pos	wks
2 Feb 02	THE DRILL *Nulife / Arista 74321915262*	15	6
6 Dec 03	MUSIC IS LIFE *Nulife 82876571412*	53	2

DIRTY ROTTEN SCOUNDRELS *See Lisa STANSFIELD*

DIRTY VEGAS
UK, male production trio (Singles: 12 Weeks, Albums: 3 Weeks) pos/wks

		pos	wks
19 May 01	DAYS GO BY *Credence CDCRED 011*	27	4
3 Aug 02	GHOSTS *Credence CDCRED 028*	31	3
12 Oct 02	DAYS GO BY (re-issue) *Credence CDCRED 030*	16	4
23 Oct 04	WALK INTO THE SUN *Parlophone CDRS 6647*	54	1
17 Aug 02	DIRTY VEGAS *Credence 5399852*	40	3

DISCHARGE
UK, male vocal / instrumental group (Singles: 3 Weeks, Albums: 5 Weeks) pos/wks

		pos	wks
24 Oct 81	NEVER AGAIN *Clay CLAY 6*	64	3
15 May 82	HEAR NOTHING SEE NOTHING SAY NOTHING *Clay CLAYLP 3*	40	5

DISCIPLES OF SOUL *See LITTLE STEVEN*

DISCO ANTHEM
Holland, male producer – Lex van Coeverden (Singles: 2 Weeks) pos/wks

		pos	wks
18 Jun 94	SCREAM *Sweat MCSTD 1977*	47	2

DISCO CITIZENS (see also CHICANE)
UK, male producer – Nick Bracegirdle (Singles: 5 Weeks) pos/wks

		pos	wks
22 Jul 95	RIGHT HERE RIGHT NOW *Deconstruction 74321293872*	40	2
12 Apr 97	FOOTPRINT *Xtravaganza 0091115*	34	2
4 Jul 98	NAGASAKI BADGER *Xtravaganza 0091595 EXT*	56	1

Disco Citizens are Chicane under another name

DISCO EVANGELISTS
UK, male instrumental / production group (Singles: 2 Weeks) pos/wks

		pos	wks
8 May 93	DE NIRO *Positiva CDTIV 2*	59	2

DISCO TEX and the SEX-O-LETTES
US, male vocalist and female vocal group (Singles: 22 Weeks) pos/wks

		pos	wks
23 Nov 74 ●	GET DANCING *Chelsea 2005 013*	8	12
26 Apr 75 ●	I WANNA DANCE WIT CHOO (DOO DAT DANCE) – PART 1 *Chelsea 2005 024* [1]	6	10

[1] Disco Tex and the Sex-O-Lettes featuring Sir Monti Rock III

DISCO TEX presents CLOUDBURST
(see also FULL INTENTION; HUSTLERS CONVENTION featuring
Dave LAUDAT and Ondrea DUVERNEY; SEX-O-SONIQUE; Michael GRAY)
UK, male / female production / vocal group (Singles: 2 Weeks) pos/wks

24 Mar 01	**I CAN CAST A SPELL** *Absolution CDABSOL 1*	35	2

DISCOVERY *See COAST 2 COAST featuring DISCOVERY*

The DISPOSABLE HEROES OF HIPHOPRISY
US, male rap / instrumental duo – Michael Franti
and Rono Tse (Singles: 7 Weeks, Albums: 3 Weeks) pos/wks

4 Apr 92	**TELEVISION THE DRUG OF THE NATION (re)** *Fourth & Broadway BRW 241*	44	6
30 May 92	**LANGUAGE OF VIOLENCE** *Fourth & Broadway 12BRW 248*	68	1
16 May 92	**HYPOCRISY IS THE GREATEST LUXURY** *Fourth & Broadway BRCD 584*	40	3

DISTANT SOUNDZ *UK, male production / vocal trio –*
Jack Berry, Mark Shrimpton and Rob Beaumont (Singles: 4 Weeks) pos/wks

9 Mar 02	**TIME AFTER TIME** *W10 / Incentive CENT 36CDS*	20	4

Sacha DISTEL *France, male vocalist, b. 29 Jan 1933,*
d. 22 Jul 2004 (Singles: 27 Weeks, Albums: 14 Weeks) pos/wks

10 Jan 70 ●	**RAINDROPS KEEP FALLING ON MY HEAD (4re)** *Warner Bros. WB 7345*	10	27
2 May 70	**SACHA DISTEL** *Warner Bros. WS 3003*	21	14

The DISTILLERS *Australia / US, male / female*
vocal / instrumental group (Singles: 3 Weeks, Albums: 1 Week) pos/wks

15 Nov 03	**DRAIN THE BLOOD** *Sire W 628CD*	51	1
10 Apr 04	**THE HUNGER** *Sire W 636CD1*	48	1
19 Jun 04	**BEAT YOUR HEART OUT** *Sire W 644CD*	74	1
25 Oct 03	**CORAL FANG** *Sire 9362484202*	46	1

DISTORTED MINDS *UK, male production duo (Singles: 3 Weeks)* pos/wks

29 Mar 03	**T-10 / THE TENTH PLANET (re)** *Kaos KAOSCD 006*	43	4

DISTURBED *US, male vocal / instrumental*
group (Singles: 4 Weeks, Albums: 1 Week) pos/wks

7 Apr 01	**VOICES** *Giant 74321848962*	52	1
28 Sep 02	**PRAYER** *Reprise W 591CD1*	31	2
14 Dec 02	**REMEMBER** *Reprise W 596CD1*	56	1
5 Oct 02	**BELIEVE** *Reprise WB 483202* ▲	41	1

DIVA *Norway, female vocal duo (Singles: 2 Weeks)* pos/wks

7 Oct 95	**THE SUN ALWAYS SHINES ON TV** *East West YZ 947CD*	53	1
20 Jul 96	**EVERYBODY (MOVE YOUR BODY)** *East West EW 035CD*	44	1

DIVA SURPRISE featuring Georgia JONES (see also ORIGINAL)
US / Spain, male production duo – Walter Taieb and
Giuseppe Nuzzo and US, female vocalist (Singles: 2 Weeks) pos/wks

14 Nov 98	**ON THE TOP OF THE WORLD** *Positiva CDTIV 100*	29	2

Terra DIVA *See WHO DA FUNK*

DIVE (see also AURORA) *UK, male production duo –*
Sacha Collisson and Simon Greenaway (Singles: 1 Week) pos/wks

21 Feb 98	**BOOGIE** *WEA WEA 147CD1*	35	1

Hit features vocalist Nasreen Shah

The DIVERSIONS
UK, male / female vocal / instrumental group (Singles: 3 Weeks) pos/wks

20 Sep 75	**FATTIE BUM BUM** *Gull GULS 18*	34	3

DIVINE *US, male vocalist – Harris Milstead,*
b. 19 Oct 1945, d. 7 Mar 1988 (Singles: 24 Weeks) pos/wks

15 Oct 83	**LOVE REACTION** *Design Communication DES 4*	65	2
14 Jul 84	**YOU THINK YOU'RE A MAN** *Proto ENA 118*	16	10
20 Oct 84	**I'M SO BEAUTIFUL** *Proto ENA 121*	52	2
27 Apr 85	**WALK LIKE A MAN** *Proto ENA 125*	23	7
20 Jul 85	**TWISTIN' THE NIGHT AWAY** *Proto ENA 127*	47	3

DIVINE *US, female vocal group (Singles: 1 Week)* pos/wks

16 Oct 99	**LATELY** *Mushroom / Red Ant RA 002CDS* ▲	52	1

The DIVINE COMEDY *UK, male vocalist / instrumentalist –*
Neil Hannon (Singles: 42 Weeks, Albums: 46 Weeks) pos/wks

29 Jun 96	**SOMETHING FOR THE WEEKEND** *Setanta SETCD 26*	14	5
24 Aug 96	**BECOMING MORE LIKE ALFIE** *Setanta SETCD 27*	27	2
16 Nov 96	**THE FROG PRINCESS** *Setanta SETCD 32*	15	2
22 Mar 97	**EVERYBODY KNOWS (EXCEPT YOU)** *Setanta SETCDA 038*	14	4
11 Apr 98	**SOMEDAY I'LL FIND YOU / I'VE BEEN TO A MARVELLOUS PARTY** *EMI CDTCB 001* [1]	28	3
26 Sep 98	**GENERATION SEX** *Setanta SETCDA 050*	19	3
28 Nov 98	**THE CERTAINTY OF CHANCE** *Setanta SETCDA 067*	49	1
6 Feb 99 ●	**NATIONAL EXPRESS** *Setanta SETCDA 069*	8	7
21 Aug 99	**THE POP SINGER'S FEAR OF THE POLLEN COUNT** *Setanta SETCDA 070*	17	4
13 Nov 99	**GIN SOAKED BOY** *Setanta SETCDA 071*	38	2
10 Mar 01	**LOVE WHAT YOU DO** *Parlophone CDRS 6554*	26	2
26 May 01	**BAD AMBASSADOR** *Parlophone CRDS 6558*	34	2
10 Nov 01	**PERFECT LOVESONG** *Parlophone CDR 6561*	42	1
3 Apr 04	**COME HOME BILLY BIRD** *Parlophone CDRS 6630*	25	2
26 Jun 04	**ABSENT FRIENDS** *Parlophone CDRS 6641*	38	2
11 May 96	**CASANOVA** *Setanta SETCD 25*	48	9
22 Feb 97	**A SHORT ALBUM ABOUT LOVE** *Setanta SETCD 036*	13	6
12 Sep 98 ●	**FIN DE SIECLE** *Setanta SETCD 057*	9	14
11 Sep 99 ●	**A SECRET HISTORY – THE BEST OF THE DIVINE COMEDY** *Setanta SETCD 100*	3	11
24 Mar 01	**REGENERATION** *Parlophone 5317612*	14	3
10 Apr 04	**ABSENT FRIENDS** *Parlophone 5962802*	23	3

[1] Shola Ama and Craig Armstrong / The Divine Comedy

DIVINE INSPIRATION
UK, male / female production / vocal group (Singles: 8 Weeks) pos/wks

18 Jan 03 ●	**THE WAY (YOU PUT YOUR HAND IN MY HAND)** *Data / MoS DATA 42CDS*	5	7
15 Nov 03	**WHAT WILL BE WILL BE (DESTINY)** *Heat Recordings HEATCD 036*	55	1

DIVINE WORKS (see also SACRED SPIRIT)
Germany, male producer – Claus Zundel (Albums: 2 Weeks) pos/wks

16 Aug 97	**DIVINE WORKS – SOUNDTRACK TO THE NEW MILLENNIUM** *Virgin VTCD 119*	43	2

DIVINYLS *Australia, male / female vocal /*
instrumental duo (Singles: 12 Weeks, Albums: 1 Week) pos/wks

18 May 91 ●	**I TOUCH MYSELF** *Virgin America VUS 36*	10	12
20 Jul 91	**DIVINYLS** *Virgin America VUSLP 30*	59	1

DIXIE CHICKS
US, female vocal / instrumental trio – Natalie Maines, Emily Erwin
and Martie Seidel (Singles: 7 Weeks, Albums: 20 Weeks) pos/wks

3 Jul 99	**THERE'S YOUR TROUBLE** *Epic 6675162*	26	5
6 Nov 99	**READY TO RUN** *Epic 6682472*	53	1
19 Apr 03	**LANDSLIDE** *Columbia 6737392*	55	1
3 Jul 99	**WIDE OPEN SPACES** *Epic 4898422*	26	6
11 Sep 99	**FLY** *Epic 4951512* ▲	38	2
22 Mar 03	**HOME** *Epic 5096032* ▲	33	12

The DIXIE CUPS *US, female vocal group (Singles: 16 Weeks)* pos/wks

18 Jun 64	**CHAPEL OF LOVE** *Pye International 7N 25245* ▲	22	8
13 May 65	**IKO IKO** *Red Bird RB 10024*	23	8

DIZZEE RASCAL
UK, male rapper / producer (Singles: 27 Weeks, Albums: 26 Weeks) pos/wks

7 Jun 03	**I LUV U** *XL Recordings XLS 165CD*	29	3
30 Aug 03	**FIX UP LOOK SHARP** *XL Recordings XLS 167CD*	17	5
22 Nov 03	**LUCKY STAR** *XL Recordings XLS 172CD* [1]	23	4
6 Dec 03	**JUS' A RASCAL** *XL Recordings XLS 175CD*	30	3
4 Sep 04 ●	**STAND UP TALL** *XL Recordings XLS 198CD1*	10	6
20 Nov 04	**DREAM** *XL Recordings XKLS 204CD*	14	6+
2 Aug 03	**BOY IN DA CORNER** *XL XLCD 170*	23	15
18 Sep 04 ●	**SHOWTIME** *XL XLCD 181*	8	11

[1] Basement Jaxx featuring Dizzee Rascal

DIZZY HEIGHTS
UK, male rapper (Singles: 4 Weeks) pos/wks
18 Dec 82	**CHRISTMAS RAPPING** *Polydor WRAP 1* 49	4

DJ ALIGATOR PROJECT
Denmark, male producer – Aliasghar Movasat (Singles: 11 Weeks) pos/wks
7 Sep 00	**THE WHISTLE SONG** *EMI CDBLOW 001* 57	1
19 Jan 02 ●	**THE WHISTLE SONG (BLOW MY WHISTLE BITCH) (re-mix)** *All Around the World CDGLOBE 247* 5	10

DJ ARABESQUE *See Mario PIU*

DJ BADMARSH and SHRI featuring UK APACHE
India / Yemen, male instrumental / production duo and UK, male rapper (Singles: 1 Week) pos/wks
28 Jul 01	**SIGNS** *Outcaste OUT 38CD1* 63	1

DJ BOBO
Switzerland, male DJ / producer – Rene Baumann (Singles: 7 Weeks) pos/wks
24 Sep 94	**EVERYBODY** *PWL Continental PWCD 312* 47	2
17 Jun 95	**LOVE IS ALL AROUND** *Avex UK AXEXCD 7* 49	2
25 Oct 03	**CHIHUAHUA** *Fuelin 82876559422* 36	3

DJ CASPER
US, male DJ / producer – Willie Perry (Singles: 24 Weeks) pos/wks
13 Mar 04 ★	**CHA CHA SLIDE** *All Around the World CDGLOBE 329* 1	18
16 Oct 04	**OOPS UPSIDE YOUR HEAD** *All Around the World CDGLOBE 376* [1] 16	6

[1] DJ Casper featuring The Gap Band

DJ CHUCKY *See XTM & DJ CHUCKY presents ANNIA*

DJ CHUS presents GROOVE FOUNDATION
Spain, male DJ / production duo (Singles: 1 Week) pos/wks
2 Nov 02	**THAT FEELING** *Defected DFTD 055R* 65	1

DJ DADO
Italy, male producer – Roberto Gallo (Singles: 9 Weeks) pos/wks
6 Apr 96 ●	**X-FILES** *ZYX ZYX 8065R8* 8	6
14 Mar 98	**COMING BACK** *ffrr TABCD 247* 63	1
11 Jul 98	**GIVE ME LOVE** *VC Recordings VCRD 37* [1] 59	1
8 May 99	**READY OR NOT** *Chemistry CDKEM 006* [2] 51	1

[1] DJ Dado vs Michelle Weeks [2] DJ Dado and Simone Jay

DJ DAN presents NEEDLE DAMAGE
US, male DJ / production group (Singles: 1 Week) pos/wks
5 May 01	**THAT ZIPPER TRACK** *Duty Free DF 026CD* 53	1

DJ DEE KLINE
UK, male DJ / producer – Nick Annand (Singles: 6 Weeks) pos/wks
3 Jun 00	**I DON'T SMOKE** *East West EW 213CD* 11	6

DJ DISCIPLE
US, male DJ / producer – David Banks (Singles: 1 Week) pos/wks
12 Nov 94	**ON THE DANCEFLOOR** *Mother MUMCD 55* 67	1

DJ DUKE
Denmark, male producer – Ken Larson (Singles: 7 Weeks) pos/wks
8 Jan 94	**BLOW YOUR WHISTLE** *ffrr FCD 228* 15	5
16 Jul 94	**TURN IT UP (SAY YEAH)** *ffrr FCD 235* 31	2

DJ E-Z ROCK *See Rob BASE and DJ E-Z ROCK*

DJ EMPIRE presents Giorgio MORODER
Germany, male producer – Alexander Wilkie (Singles: 1 Week) pos/wks
12 Feb 00	**THE CHASE** *Logic 731482* 46	1

DJ ERIC
UK, male vocal / production trio (Singles: 3 Weeks) pos/wks
13 Feb 99	**WE ARE LOVE** *Distinctive DISNCD 49* 37	2
10 Jun 00	**DESIRE** *Distinctive DISNCD 56* 67	1

DJ FALCON *See TOGETHER*

DJ 'FAST' EDDIE
US, male producer – Eddie Smith (Singles: 15 Weeks) pos/wks
11 Apr 87	**CAN U DANCE (re)** *Champion CHAMP 41* [1] 67	4
21 Jan 89	**HIP HOUSE / I CAN DANCE** *DJ International DJIN 5* 47	4
11 Mar 89	**YO YO GET FUNKY** *DJ International DJIN 7* 54	3
28 Oct 89	**GIT ON UP** *DJ International 655366 7* [2] 49	4

[1] Kenny 'Jammin' Jason and 'Fast' Eddie Smith [2] 'Fast' Eddie featuring Sundance

DJ FLAVOURS
UK, male producer – Neil Rumney (Singles: 4 Weeks) pos/wks
11 Oct 97	**YOUR CARESS (ALL I NEED)** *All Around the World CDGLOBE 160* 19	4

DJ FORMAT featuring Chali 2NA & AKIL
UK, male DJ / producer – Matt Ford and US, male rappers (Singles: 1 Week) pos/wks
22 Mar 03	**WE KNOW SOMETHING YOU DON'T KNOW** *Genuine GEN 004CDX* 73	1

DJ FRESH (see also BAD COMPANY; FRESH BC; FRESH)
UK, male producer – Dan Stein (Singles: 3 Weeks) pos/wks
1 Nov 03	**DALICKS / TEMPLE OF DOOM** *Breakbeat Kaos BBK 001* 60	1
31 Jul 04	**SUBMARINES** *Breakbeat Kaos BBK 004* 73	1
30 Oct 04	**WHEN THE SUN GOES DOWN** *Breakbeat Kaos BBK 005* [1] 68	1

[1] DJ Fresh featuring Adam F

DJ GARRY
Belgium, male producer – Marino Stephano (Singles: 2 Weeks) pos/wks
19 Jan 02	**DREAM UNIVERSE** *Xtravaganza XTRAV 32CDS* 36	2

DJ GERT
Belgium, male DJ / producer – Gert Rossenbacker (Singles: 1 Week) pos/wks
26 May 01	**GIVE ME SOME MORE** *Mostika 23200253* 50	1

DJ GREGORY
France, male producer – Gregory Darsa (Singles: 2 Weeks) pos/wks
9 Nov 02	**TROPICAL SOUNDCLASH** *Defected DFTD 061CD* 59	1
11 Oct 03	**ELLE / TROPICAL SOUNDCLASH (re-mix)** *Defected DFTD 077* 73	1

DJ HYPE
UK, male producer – Kevin Ford (Singles: 2 Weeks) pos/wks
20 Mar 93	**SHOT IN THE DARK** *Suburban Base SUBBASE 20CD* 63	1
2 Jun 01	**CASINO ROYALE / DEAD A'S** *True Playaz TPRCD 004* [1] 58	1

[1] DJ Zinc / DJ Hype

DJ HYPE presents GANJA KRU
UK, male producer (Albums: 1 Week) pos/wks
30 Aug 97	**NEW FRONTIERS (EP)** *Parousia 74321501072* 56	1

DJ INNOCENCE featuring Alex CHARLES
UK, male producer – Gary Booker and male vocalist (Singles: 1 Week) pos/wks
6 Apr 02	**SO BEAUTIFUL** *Echo ECSCD 119* 51	1

DJ JAZZY JEFF and the FRESH PRINCE
US, male rap / DJ duo – Jeff Townes and Will Smith (Singles: 49 Week, Albums: 15 Weeks) pos/wks
4 Oct 86	**GIRLS AIN'T NOTHING BUT TROUBLE** *Champion Champ 18* 21	8
3 Aug 91 ●	**SUMMERTIME (re)** *Jive JIVECD 279* 8	12
9 Nov 91	**RING MY BELL** *Jive JIVECD 288* 53	2
11 Sep 93 ★	**BOOM! SHAKE THE ROOM** *Jive JIVECD 335* [1] 1	13
20 Nov 93	**I'M LOOKING FOR THE ONE (TO BE WITH ME)** *Jive JIVECD 345* [1] 24	4
19 Feb 94	**CAN'T WAIT TO BE WITH YOU** *Jive JIVECD 348* [1] 29	4
4 Jun 94	**TWINKLE TWINKLE (I'M NOT A STAR)** *Jive JIVECD 354* [1] 62	2
2 Dec 95	**BOOM! SHAKE THE ROOM (re-mix)** *Jive JIVECD 387* [1] 40	2
11 Jul 98	**LOVELY DAZE** *Jive 0518902* 37	2
28 Feb 87	**ROCK THE HOUSE** *Champion CHAMP 1004* 97	1
21 May 88	**HE'S THE DJ I'M THE RAPPER** *Jive HIP 61* 68	2
14 Sep 91	**HOMEBASE** *Jive HIP 116* 69	1
11 Dec 93	**CODE RED** *Jive CHIP 140* [1] 50	6
16 May 98	**GREATEST HITS** *Jive 518482* [1] 20	5

[1] Jazzy Jeff & the Fresh Prince [1] Jazzy Jeff and the Fresh Prince

'Summertime' re-entered the chart and peaked at No.29 in Aug 1994

DJ JEAN
Holland, DJ / producer – Jan Engelaar (Singles: 11 Weeks) pos/wks

11 Sep 99 ●	THE LAUNCH *AM:PM CDAMPM 123*	**2**	11

DJ JURGEN presents Alice DEEJAY *Holland, male DJ /*
production group and female vocalist (Singles: 16 Weeks) pos/wks

31 Jul 99 ●	BETTER OFF ALONE *Positiva CDTIV 113*	**2**	16

DJ KOOL
US, male rapper / DJ / producer – John Bowman (Singles: 7 Weeks) pos/wks

22 Feb 97 ●	LET ME CLEAR MY THROAT *American 74321452092*	**8**	7

DJ KRUSH *Japan, male producer –*
Hideaki Ishi (Singles: 2 Weeks, Albums: 2 Weeks) pos/wks

16 Mar 96	MEISO *Mo Wax MW 042CD*	**52**	1
12 Oct 96	ONLY THE STRONG SURVIVE *Mo Wax MW 060CD*	**71**	1
3 Sep 94	BAD BROTHERS *Island IMCD 8024* [1]	**58**	1
11 Nov 95	MEISO *Mo Wax MW 039CD*	**64**	1

[1] Ronny Jordan meets DJ Krush

DJ LUCK & MC NEAT *UK, male DJs / producers – Joel*
Samuels and Michael Rose (Singles: 44 Weeks, Albums: 2 Weeks) pos/wks

25 Dec 99 ●	A LITTLE BIT OF LUCK *Red Rose CORROSE 1*	**9**	15
27 May 00 ●	MASTERBLASTER 2000 *Red Rose RROSE 002CD* [1]	**5**	8
7 Oct 00 ●	AIN'T NO STOPPIN' US *Red Rose CDRROSE 004* [1]	**8**	6
17 Mar 01	PIANO LOCO *Island CID 773*	**12**	8
8 Sep 01	I'M ALL ABOUT YOU (re) *Island CID 781* [2]	**18**	5
25 May 02	IRIE *Island CID 795* [3]	**31**	2
8 Jun 02	IT'S ALL GOOD *Island CIDD 8117* [1]	**34**	2

[1] DJ Luck & MC Neat featuring JJ [2] DJ Luck and MC Neat featuring Ari Gold
[3] Luck & Neat [1] Luck & Neat

DJ MANTA
Holland, male / female DJ / production trio (Singles: 1 Week) pos/wks

9 Oct 99	HOLDING ON *AM:PM CDAMPM 125*	**47**	1

DJ MARKY & XRS featuring STAMINA MC *Brazil, male DJ / produc-*
tion duo – Marco da Silva and Michael Nicassio (Singles: 8 Weeks) pos/wks

20 Jul 02	LK 'CAROLINA CAROL BELA' *V Recordings V 035*	**17**	6
16 Nov 02	LK (re-mix) *V Recordings V 038*	**45**	2

DJ MIKO
Italy, male producer – Quartobaro Manier (Singles: 10 Weeks) pos/wks

13 Aug 94 ●	WHAT'S UP *Systematic SYSCD 2*	**6**	10

DJ MILANO featuring SAMANTHA FOX *Italy, male DJ /*
producer – Mirko Milano and UK, female vocalist (Singles: 2 Weeks) pos/wks

28 Mar 98	SANTA MARIA *All Around the World CDGLOBE 163*	**31**	2

DJ MISJAH and DJ TIM *Holland, male instrumental / production duo –*
Misjah Van Der Heiden and Tim Hoogestegger (Singles: 4 Weeks) pos/wks

23 Mar 96	ACCESS *Ffrreedom TABCD 240*	**16**	3
27 May 00	ACCESS (re-mix) *Tripoli Trax TTRAXCD 063*	**45**	1

DJ MUGGS *See TRICKY*

DJ NATION (see also NUKLEUZ DJS)
UK, male DJ / production collective (Singles: 5 Weeks) pos/wks

9 Aug 03	SUMMER EDITION *Nukleuz 0542 FNUK*	**59**	2
27 Mar 04	X-RATED *Nukleuz 0501 FNUK*	**52**	3

'X-Rated' is a set of three 12" various artist singles with one common track,
DJ Nation's 'X-Rated'

DJ OTZI
Austria, male DJ / producer – Gerry Friedle (Singles: 48 Weeks) pos/wks

18 Aug 01	HEY BABY (IMPORT) *EMI 8892462*	**41**	5
22 Sep 01 ★	HEY BABY (UHH, AHH) (re) *EMI CDOTZI 001* ■	**1**	24
1 Dec 01 ●	DO WAH DIDDY *EMI CDOTZI 002*	**9**	9
29 Dec 01	X-MAS TIME *EMI CDOTZI 003*	**51**	2

8 Jun 02 ●	HEY BABY (THE UNOFFICIAL WORLD CUP REMIX) (2re)		
	EMI Austria / Liberty CDOTZI 004	**10**	7
28 Dec 02	LIVE IS LIFE *EMI / Liberty CDLIVE 001* [1]	**50**	1

[1] Hermes House Band and DJ Otzi

DJ PIED PIPER and the MASTERS OF CEREMONIES
UK, male rap / production group (Singles: 14 Weeks) pos/wks

2 Jun 01 ★	DO YOU REALLY LIKE IT *Relentless MOS RELMOS 1CDS* ■	**1**	14

DJ POWER
Italy, male producer – Steve Gambaroli (Singles: 2 Weeks) pos/wks

7 Mar 92	EVERYBODY PUMP *Cooltempo COOL 252*	**46**	2

DJ PROFESSOR
Italy, male producer – Luca Lauri (Singles: 6 Weeks) pos/wks

10 Aug 91	WE GOTTA DO IT *Fourth & Broadway BRW 225* [1]	**57**	2
28 Mar 92	ROCK ME STEADY *PWL Continental PWL 219*	**49**	2
8 Oct 94	ROCKIN' ME *Citra CITRA 1CD* [2]	**56**	1
1 Mar 97	WALKIN' ON UP *Nukleuz MCSTD 40098* [3]	**64**	1

[1] DJ Professor featuring Francesco Zappala [2] Professor [3] DJ Prof-x-or

DJ QUICKSILVER
Turkey / Belgium, male DJ / production duo – Ohran Terzi and
Tomasso De Donatis (Singles: 29 Weeks, Albums: 3 Weeks) pos/wks

5 Apr 97 ●	BELLISSIMA *Positiva CDTIV 72*	**4**	17
6 Sep 97 ●	FREE *Positiva CDTIVS 77*	**7**	7
21 Feb 98	PLANET LOVE *Positiva CDTIV 88*	**12**	5
7 Mar 98	QUICKSILVER *Positiva 4934942*	**26**	3

DJ QUICK *See TONY TONI TONÉ*

DJ RAP *UK, female vocalist / DJ /*
producer – Charissa Saverio (Singles: 5 Weeks) pos/wks

4 Jul 98	BAD GIRL *Higher Ground HIGHS 8CD*	**32**	2
17 Oct 98	GOOD TO BE ALIVE *Higher Ground HIGHS 14CD*	**36**	2
3 Apr 99	EVERYDAY GIRL *Higher Ground HIGHS 19CD*	**47**	1

DJ ROLANDO AKA AZTEC MYSTIC
US, male DJ / producer – Rolando Rocha (Singles: 2 Weeks) pos/wks

21 Oct 00	JAGUAR *430 West 430WUKTCD 1*	**43**	2

DJ SAKIN & FRIENDS
Germany, DJ / producer – Sakin Botzkurt (Singles: 18 Weeks) pos/wks

20 Feb 99 ●	PROTECT YOUR MIND (FOR THE LOVE OF A PRINCESS) (re)		
	Positiva CDTIV 107	**4**	11
5 Jun 99	NOMANSLAND (DAVID'S SONG) *Positiva CDTIV 112*	**14**	7

DJ SAMMY *Spain, male DJ / producer –*
Samuel Bouriah (Singles: 41 Weeks, Albums: 9 Weeks) pos/wks

9 Nov 02 ★	HEAVEN *Data / MoS DATA 45CDS* [1] ■	**1**	19
8 Mar 03 ●	THE BOYS OF SUMMER *Data / MoS DATA 49CDS*	**2**	13
21 Jun 03 ●	SUNLIGHT *Data / MoS DATA 54CDS*	**8**	9
22 Mar 03	HEAVEN *Ministry of Sound DATACD 01X*	**14**	9

[1] DJ Sammy and Yanou featuring Do

DJ SANDY vs HOUSETRAP *Germany, female DJ /*
producer – Sande de Sutter and vocalist (Singles: 2 Weeks) pos/wks

1 Jul 00	OVERDRIVE *Positiva CDTIV 133*	**32**	2

DJ SCOT PROJECT
Germany, male DJ / producer – Frank Zenker (Singles: 2 Weeks) pos/wks

27 Jul 96	U (I GOT THE FEELING) *Positiva CDTIV 55* [1]	**66**	1
14 Feb 98	Y (HOW DEEP IS YOUR LOVE) *Perfecto PERF 158CD1*	**57**	1

[1] Scot Project

DJ Doc SCOTT
UK, male producer – Scott McIlroy (Singles: 2 Weeks) pos/wks

1 Feb 92	NHS (EP) *Absolute 2ABS 001DJ*	**64**	2

Tracks on NHS (EP): Surgery / Night Nurse

DJ SCOTT featuring Lorna B *UK, male DJ –*
Scott Robertson and female vocalist (Singles: 5 Weeks) pos/wks

28 Jan 95	**DO YOU WANNA PARTY** *Steppin' Out SPONCD 2*	36	3
1 Apr 95	**SWEET DREAMS** *Steppin' Out SPONCD 3*	37	2

DJ SEDUCTION
UK, male producer – John Kallum (Singles: 8 Weeks) pos/wks

22 Feb 92	**HARDCORE HEAVEN / YOU AND ME** *Ffrreedom TAB 103*	26	5
11 Jul 92	**COME ON** *Ffrreedom TAB 111*	37	3

DJ SHADOW *US, male producer –*
Josh Davis (Singles: 11 Weeks, Albums: 6 Weeks) pos/wks

25 Mar 95	**WHAT DOES YOUR SOUL LOOK LIKE** *Mo Wax MW 027CD*	59	1
14 Sep 96	**MIDNIGHT IN A PERFECT WORLD** *Mo Wax MW 057CD*	54	1
9 Nov 96	**STEM** *Mo Wax MW 058CD*	74	1
11 Oct 97	**HIGH NOON** *Mo Wax MW 063CD*	22	2
20 Dec 97	**CAMEL BOBSLED RACE** *Mo Wax MW 084CD*	62	1
24 Jan 98	**WHAT DOES YOUR SOUL LOOK LIKE (PART 1)** *Mo Wax MW 087*	54	1
1 Jun 02	**YOU CAN'T GO HOME AGAIN** *Mo Wax CID 797*	30	2
2 Nov 02	**SIX DAYS** *Island CID 807*	28	2
28 Sep 96	**ENDTRODUCING ...** *Mo Wax MW 059CD*	17	3
15 Jun 02	● **THE PRIVATE PRESS** *Island CID 8118*	8	3

DJ SHOG
Germany, male DJ / producer – Sven Greiner (Singles: 2 Weeks) pos/wks

20 Jul 02	**THIS IS MY SOUND** *Nulife 74321942272*	40	2

DJ SHORTY See Lenny FONTANA

DJ SKRIBBLE See MR REDS vs DJ SKRIBBLE

DJ SNEAK featuring BEAR WHO? *Puerto Rico, male DJ / producer –*
Carlos Sosa and US, male DJ / producer (Singles: 3 Weeks) pos/wks

1 Feb 03	**FIX MY SINK** *Credence CDCREDS 033*	26	3

DJ SS *UK, male DJ / producer – Leroy Small (Singles: 1 Week)* pos/wks

20 Apr 02	**THE LIGHTER** *Formation FORM 12093*	63	1

DJ SUPREME
UK, male producer – Nick Destri (Singles: 11 Weeks) pos/wks

5 Oct 96	**THA WILD STYLE** *Distinctive DISNCD 19*	39	2
3 May 97	**THA WILD STYLE (re-issue)** *Distinctive DISNCD 29*	24	2
6 Dec 97	**ENTER THE SCENE** *Distinctive DISNCD 40* [1]	49	1
21 Feb 98	**THA HORNS OF JERICHO** *All Around the World CDGLOBE 164*	29	2
16 Jan 99	● **UP TO THE WILDSTYLE** *All Around the World CDGLOBE 170* [2]	10	4

[1] DJ Supreme vs The Rhythm Masters [2] Porn Kings vs DJ Supreme

DJ TAUCHER
Germany, male DJ / producer – Ralf Armand Beck (Singles: 1 Week) pos/wks

8 May 99	**CHILD OF THE UNIVERSE** *Additive 12AD 037*	74	1

DJ TIËSTO (see also GOURYELLA) *Holland, male*
producer – Tijs Verwest (Singles: 17 Weeks, Albums: 2 Weeks) pos/wks

12 May 01	**FLIGHT 643** *Nebula NEBCD 016*	56	1
29 Sep 01	**URBAN TRAIN** *Nebula VCRD 95* [1]	22	3
13 Apr 02	**LETHAL INDUSTRY** *Nebula VCRD 103*	25	3
29 Jun 02	**643 (LOVE'S ON FIRE) (re-recording)** *Nebula VCRD 106* [2]	36	2
30 Nov 02	**OBSESSION** *Nebula NEBCD 029* [3]	56	1
11 Oct 03	**TRAFFIC** *Nebula NEBCD 052* [4]	48	2
15 May 04	**LOVE COMES AGAIN** *Nebula NEBCD 058* [5]	30	3
23 Oct 04	**JUST BE** *Nebula NEBCD 062* [6]	43	2
29 May 04	**JUST BE** *Nebula NEBCD 9010* [1]	54	2

[1] DJ Tiësto featuring Kirsty Hawkshaw [2] DJ Tiësto featuring Suzanne Palmer [3] Tiësto and Junkie XL [4] Tiësto [5] Tiësto featuring BT [6] Tiësto featuring Kirsty Hawkshaw [1] Tiësto

DJ TIM See DJ MISJAH and DJ TIM

DJ TOUCHÉ (see also The WISEGUYS)
UK, male DJ / producer – Theo Keating (Singles: 1 Week) pos/wks

31 Jan 04	**THE PADDLE / THE GIRL'S A FREAK** *Southern Fried ECB 60*	65	1

DJ VISAGE featuring CLARISSA *Denmark, male DJ / producer –*
Martin Sig and Germany, female vocalist (Singles: 1 Week) pos/wks

10 Jun 00	**THE RETURN (TIME TO SAY GOODBYE)** *One Step Music OSMCDS 13*	58	1

DJ WHAT? See OBI PROJECT featuring HARRY, ASHER D and DJ WHAT?

DJ ZINC
UK, male DJ / producer – Benjamin Pettit (Singles: 8 Weeks) pos/wks

18 Nov 00	**138 TREK** *Phaze One PHAZE CDX 03*	27	3
2 Jun 01	**CASINO ROYALE / DEAD A'S** *True Playaz TPRCD 004* [1]	58	1
13 Apr 02	**REACHOUT** *True Playaz TPR 12039*	73	1
21 Sep 02	**FAIR FIGHT / AS WE DO** *Bingo Beats BING 008*	72	1
13 Mar 04	**SKA** *True Playaz TPR 12051*	54	1
15 May 04	**STEPPIN STONES / SOUTH PACIFIC** *Bingo Beats BING 012*	62	1

[1] DJ Zinc / DJ Hype

DJAIMIN
Switzerland, male producer – Dario Mancini (Singles: 2 Weeks) pos/wks

19 Sep 92	**GIVE YOU** *Cooltempo COOL 262*	45	2

DJD presents HYDRAULIC DOGS
UK, male production duo (Singles: 1 Week) pos/wks

8 Jun 02	**SHAKE IT BABY** *Direction 6721812*	56	1

DJH featuring STEFY
Italy, male instrumental / production group (Singles: 14 Weeks) pos/wks

16 Feb 91	**THINK ABOUT ...** *RCA PB 44385*	22	6
13 Jul 91	**I LIKE IT** *RCA PB 44741*	16	7
19 Oct 91	**MOVE YOUR LOVE** *RCA PB 44965*	73	1

DJPC *Belgium, male producer – Patrick Cools (Singles: 5 Weeks)* pos/wks

26 Oct 91	**INSSOMNIAK** *Hype 7PUM 005*	62	4
29 Feb 92	**INSSOMNIAK (re-issue)** *Hype PUMR 005*	64	1

DJ's RULE
Canada, male instrumental / production duo (Singles: 2 Weeks) pos/wks

2 Mar 96	**GET INTO THE MUSIC** *Distinctive DISNCD 9*	72	1
5 Apr 97	**GET INTO THE MUSIC (re-mix)** *Distinctive DISNCDD 27* [1]	65	1

[1] DJ's Rule featuring Karen Brown

DJUM DJUM See LEFTFIELD

Boris DLUGOSCH *Germany, male producer (Singles: 8 Weeks)* pos/wks

7 Dec 96	**KEEP PUSHIN'** *Manifesto FESCD 17* [1]	41	2
13 Sep 97	**HOLD YOUR HEAD UP HIGH** *Positiva CDTIV 79* [1]	23	2
16 Jun 01	**NEVER ENOUGH** *Positiva CDTIV 156* [2]	16	4

[1] Boris Dlugosch presents Booom!: Vocals by Inaya Davis (aka Inaya Day)
[2] Boris Dlugosch featuring Roisin Murphy

D'LUX
UK, male / female vocal / instrumental group (Singles: 1 Week) pos/wks

22 Jun 96	**LOVE RESURRECTION** *Logic 74321371012*	58	1

DMAC *UK, male vocalist – Derek McDonald (Singles: 2 Weeks)* pos/wks

27 Jul 02	**THE WORLD SHE KNOWS** *Chrysalis CDCHS 5140*	33	2

D'MENACE *UK, male production duo –*
Sandy Rivera and John Alvarez (Singles: 3 Weeks) pos/wks

8 Aug 98	**DEEP MENACE (SPANK)** *Inferno CDFERN 8*	20	3

DO See DJ SAMMY

DO ME BAD THINGS
UK, male / female vocal / instrumental group (Singles: 1 Week) pos/wks

6 Nov 04	**TIME FOR DELIVERANCE** *Must Destroy MJDA 002CD*	57	1

Carl DOBKINS Jr *US, male vocalist (Singles: 1 Week)* pos/wks

31 Mar 60	**LUCKY DEVIL** *Brunswick 05817*	44	1

Anita DOBSON UK, female actor / vocalist (Singles: 13 Weeks)
pos/wks

9 Aug 86 ●	ANYONE CAN FALL IN LOVE BBC RESL 191 [1]	4	9
18 Jul 87	TALKING OF LOVE Parlophone R 6159	43	4

[1] Anita Dobson featuring the Simon May Orchestra

Fefe DOBSON US, female vocalist (Singles: 2 Weeks)
pos/wks

8 May 04	EVERYTHING Mercury 9862501	42	2

DR ALBAN
Nigeria, male vocalist – Alban Nwapa (Singles: 28 Weeks)
pos/wks

5 Sep 92 ●	IT'S MY LIFE Logic 115330	2	12
14 Nov 92	ONE LOVE Logic 74321108727	45	2
10 Apr 93	SING HALLELUJAH! Logic 74321136202	16	8
26 Mar 94	LOOK WHO'S TALKING Logic 74321195342	55	3
13 Aug 94	AWAY FROM HOME Logic 74321222682	42	2
29 Apr 95	SWEET DREAMS Logic 74321251552 [1]	59	1

[1] Swing featuring Dr Alban

DOCTOR and the MEDICS
UK, male / female vocal / instrumental group –
lead vocal Clive Jackson (Singles: 25 Weeks, Albums: 3 Weeks)
pos/wks

10 May 86 ★	SPIRIT IN THE SKY IRS IRM 113	1	15
9 Aug 86	BURN IRS IRM 119	29	6
22 Nov 86	WATERLOO IRS IRM 125 [1]	45	4
21 Jun 86	LAUGHING AT THE PIECES MCA MIRG 1010	25	3

[1] Doctor and the Medics featuring Roy Wood

DR DRE (443) Top 500
Controversial rapper / producer and architect of West Coast gangsta rap, b. Andre Young, 18 Feb 1965, Los Angeles, US. Former member of rap group NWA and founder of the Death Row record label, whose disciples include Snoop Dogg and Eminem (Singles: 79 Weeks, Albums: 80 Weeks)
pos/wks

22 Jan 94	NUTHIN' BUT A 'G' THANG / LET ME RIDE Death Row A 8328CD	31	3
3 Sep 94	DRE DAY Death Row A 8292CD	59	2
15 Apr 95	NATURAL BORN KILLAZ Death Row A 8197CD [1]	45	2
10 Jun 95	KEEP THEIR HEADS RINGIN' Priority PTYCD 103	25	4
13 Apr 96 ●	CALIFORNIA LOVE Death Row DRWCD 3 [2]	6	8
19 Oct 96 ●	NO DIGGITY Interscope IND 95003 [3] ▲	9	7
11 Jul 98	ZOOM Interscope IND 95594 [4]	15	3
14 Aug 99 ●	GUILTY CONSCIENCE Interscope IND 4971282 [5]	5	8
25 Mar 00 ●	STILL D.R.E. Interscope 4972742 [6]	6	10
10 Jun 00	FORGOT ABOUT DRE Interscope 4973142 [7]	7	9
3 Feb 01	THE NEXT EPISODE (re) Interscope 4974762 [6]	3	12
19 Jan 02 ●	BAD INTENTIONS (re) Interscope 4973932 [8]	4	11
27 Nov 99 ●	2001 Interscope 4904862	4	76
9 Sep 00	THE CHRONIC Interscope 7567922332	43	4

[1] Dr Dre and Ice Cube [2] 2Pac featuring Dr Dre [3] BLACKstreet featuring Dr Dre [4] Dr Dre and LL Cool J [5] Eminem featuring Dr Dre [6] Dr Dre featuring Snoop Dogg [7] Dr Dre featuring Eminem [8] Dr Dre featuring Knoc-Turn'al

DR FEELGOOD UK, male vocal / instrumental
group (Albums: 33 Weeks, Singles: 29 Weeks)
pos/wks

11 Jun 77	SNEAKIN' SUSPICION United Artists UP 36255	47	3
24 Sep 77	SHE'S A WIND UP United Artists UP 36304	34	5
30 Sep 78	DOWN AT THE DOCTORS United Artists UP 36444	48	5
20 Jan 79 ●	MILK AND ALCOHOL United Artists UP 36468	9	9
5 May 79	AS LONG AS THE PRICE IS RIGHT United Artists YUP 36506	40	6
8 Dec 79	PUT HIM OUT OF YOUR MIND United Artists BP 306	73	1
18 Oct 75	MALPRACTICE United Artists UAS 29880	17	6
2 Oct 76 ★	STUPIDITY United Artists UAS 29990	1	9
4 Jun 77 ●	SNEAKIN' SUSPICION United Artists UAS 30075	10	6
8 Oct 77	BE SEEING YOU United Artists UAS 30123	55	3
7 Oct 78	PRIVATE PRACTICE United Artists UAG 30184	41	5
2 Jun 79	AS IT HAPPENS United Artists UAK 30239	42	4

DR HOOK (236) Top 500
Distinctive group, fronted by vocalists Dennis Locorriere and Ray Sawyer, had eight years of regular UK / US hits. Early recordings often featured humorous, anarchic Shel Silverstein songs, but this good-time New Jersey act had greater success with later, gentler material (Singles: 104 Weeks, Albums: 157 Weeks)
pos/wks

24 Jun 72 ●	SYLVIA'S MOTHER CBS 7929 [1]	2	13
26 Jun 76 ●	A LITTLE BIT MORE Capitol CL 15871	2	14
30 Oct 76 ●	IF NOT YOU Capitol CL 15885	5	10
25 Mar 78	MORE LIKE THE MOVIES Capitol CL 15967	14	10
22 Sep 79 ★	WHEN YOU'RE IN LOVE WITH A BEAUTIFUL WOMAN Capitol CL 16039	1	17
5 Jan 80 ●	BETTER LOVE NEXT TIME Capitol CL 16112	8	8
29 Mar 80 ●	SEXY EYES Capitol CL 16127	4	9
23 Aug 80	YEARS FROM NOW Capitol CL 16154	47	6
8 Nov 80	SHARING THE NIGHT TOGETHER Capitol CL 16171	43	4
22 Nov 80	GIRLS CAN GET IT Mercury MER 51	40	5
1 Feb 92	WHEN YOU'RE IN LOVE WITH A BEAUTIFUL WOMAN (re-issue) Capitol EMCT 4	44	4
6 Jun 92	A LITTLE BIT MORE (re-issue) EMI EMCT 6	47	4
25 Jun 76 ●	A LITTLE BIT MORE Capitol EST 23795	5	42
29 Oct 77	MAKING LOVE AND MUSIC Capitol EST 11632	39	4
27 Oct 79	PLEASURE AND PAIN Capitol EAST 11859	47	6
17 Nov 79	SOMETIMES YOU WIN Capitol EST 12018	14	44
29 Nov 80	RISING Mercury 6302 076	44	5
6 Dec 80 ●	DR HOOK GREATEST HITS Capitol EST 26037	2	28
14 Nov 81	DR HOOK LIVE IN THE UK Capitol EST 26706	90	1
13 Jun 92 ●	COMPLETELY HOOKED – THE BEST OF DR HOOK Capitol CDESTV 2	3	19
13 Feb 99 ●	LOVE SONGS EMI 4979432	8	8

[1] Dr Hook and the Medicine Show

DR JOHN US, male vocalist / instrumentalist –
piano – Malcolm Rebennack (Albums: 3 Weeks)
pos/wks

27 Jun 98	ANUTHA ZONE Parlophone 4954902	33	3

DR MOUTHQUAKE See E-ZEE POSSEE

DR OCTAGON
US, male producer – Keith Thornton (Singles: 1 Week)
pos/wks

7 Sep 96	BLUE FLOWERS Mo Wax MW 055CD	66	1

DOCTOR SPIN UK, male instrumental / production duo –
Nigel Wright and Andrew Lloyd Webber (Singles: 8 Weeks)
pos/wks

3 Oct 92 ●	TETRIS Carpet CRPT 4	6	8

Ken DODD (231) Top 500
Seasoned stand-up comedian-cum-balladeer, b. 8 Nov 1929, Liverpool, UK. The tickling-stick-wielding troubadour was one of the most successful Merseyside acts in the mid-1960s, at times enjoying two Top 10 singles simultaneously. Biggest-selling single: 'Tears' 1,521,000 (Singles: 233 Weeks, Albums: 36 Weeks)
pos/wks

7 Jul 60 ●	LOVE IS LIKE A VIOLIN Decca F 11248	8	18
15 Jun 61	ONCE IN EVERY LIFETIME (2re) Decca F 11355	28	18
1 Feb 62	PIANISSIMO Decca F 11422	21	15
29 Aug 63	STILL Columbia DB 7094	35	10
6 Feb 64	EIGHT BY TEN Columbia DB 7191	22	11
23 Jul 64	HAPPINESS Columbia DB 7325	31	13
26 Nov 64	SO DEEP IS THE NIGHT Columbia DB 7398	31	7
2 Sep 65 ★	TEARS Columbia DB 7659 ◆	1	24
18 Nov 65 ●	THE RIVER (LE COLLINE SONO IN FIORO) Columbia DB 7750	3	14
12 May 66 ●	PROMISES Columbia DB 7914	6	14
4 Aug 66	MORE THAN LOVE Columbia DB 7976	14	11
27 Oct 66	IT'S LOVE Columbia DB 8031	36	7
19 Jan 67	LET ME CRY ON YOUR SHOULDER Columbia DB 8101	11	10
30 Jul 69	TEARS WON'T WASH AWAY THESE HEARTACHES Columbia DB 8600	22	11
5 Dec 70	BROKEN HEARTED (re) Columbia DB 8725	15	10
10 Jul 71	WHEN LOVE COMES ROUND AGAIN (L'ARCA DI NOE) Columbia DB 8796	19	16
18 Nov 72	JUST OUT OF REACH (OF MY TWO EMPTY ARMS) Columbia DB 8947	29	11
29 Nov 75	THINK OF ME (WHEREVER YOU ARE) EMI 2342	21	8
26 Dec 81	HOLD MY HAND Images IMGS 0002	44	5
25 Dec 65 ●	TEARS OF HAPPINESS Columbia 33SX 1793	6	11
23 Jul 66	HITS FOR NOW AND ALWAYS Columbia SX 6060	14	11
14 Jan 67	FOR SOMEONE SPECIAL Columbia SCX 6224	40	1
29 Nov 80 ●	20 GOLDEN GREATS OF KEN DODD Warwick WW 5098	8	12

Rory DODD See Jim STEINMAN

DODGY UK, male vocal / instrumental
group (Singles: 41 Weeks, Albums: 54 Weeks)
pos/wks

8 May 93	LOVEBIRDS A&M AMCD 0177	65	2

3 Jul 93	I NEED ANOTHER (EP) *A&M 5803172*		67	2
6 Aug 94	THE MELOD-EP *Bostin 5806772*		53	1
1 Oct 94	STAYING OUT FOR THE SUMMER *Bostin 5807972*		38	2
7 Jan 95	SO LET ME GO FAR *Bostin 5809032*		30	3
11 Mar 95	MAKING THE MOST OF *Bostin 5809892*	[1]	22	3
10 Jun 95	STAYING OUT FOR THE SUMMER (re-mix) *Bostin 5810952*		19	5
8 Jun 96	IN A ROOM *A&M 5816252*		12	6
10 Aug 96 ●	GOOD ENOUGH *A&M 5818152*		4	8
16 Nov 96	IF YOU'RE THINKING OF ME *A&M 5819992*		11	4
15 Mar 97	FOUND YOU *A&M 5821332*		19	1
26 Sep 98	EVERY SINGLE DAY *A&M MERCD 512*		32	2
5 Jun 93	THE DODGY ALBUM *5400822*		75	1
5 Nov 94	HOMEGROWN *A&M 5402822*		28	14
29 Jun 96 ●	FREE PEACE SWEET *A&M 5405732*		7	38
17 Oct 98	ACE A'S + KILLER B'S *Mercury / A&M 5410182*		55	1

[1] Dodgy with the Kick Horns

Tracks on I Need Another (EP): I Need Another / If I Fall / Hendre DDU. Tracks on The Melod-EP: Melodies Haunt You / The Snake / Don't Go / Summer Fayre

Tim DOG *US, male rapper – Timothy Blair (Singles: 3 Weeks)*   pos/wks

29 Oct 94	BITCH WITH A PERM *Dis-stress DISCD 1*		49	1
11 Feb 95	MAKE WAY FOR THE INDIAN *Island CID 586*	[1]	29	2

[1] Apache Indian and Tim Dog

DOG EAT DOG *US, male vocal / instrumental group (Singles: 7 Weeks, Albums: 2 Weeks)*   pos/wks

19 Aug 95 ●	NO FRONTS (re) *Roadrunner RR 23312*		9	6
13 Jul 96	ISMS *Roadrunner RR 23083*		43	1
27 Jul 96	PLAY GAMES *Roadrunner RR 88762*		40	2

It was not until the Apr 1996 re-entry that 'No Fronts' reached its peak position of No.9

Nate DOGG *US, male rapper – Nathan Hale (Singles: 54 Weeks)*   pos/wks

23 Jul 94 ●	REGULATE *Death Row A 8290CD* [1]		5	14
3 Feb 01	OH NO *Rawkus RWK 302* [2]		24	4
25 Aug 01	WHERE I WANNA BE (re) *London LONCD 461* [3]		14	7
29 Sep 01	AREA CODES *Def Jam 5887722* [4]		25	3
1 Mar 03	THE STREETS *Def Jam 0779852* [5]		48	2
12 Jul 03	21 QUESTIONS *Interscope 9807195* [6] ▲		6	8
1 Nov 03	OOH WEE *Elektra E 7490CD* [7]		15	7
14 Feb 04	THE SET UP (YOU DON'T KNOW) *Interscope 9815333* [8]		32	3
18 Sep 04	I LIKE THAT *Capitol CDCL 861* [9]		11	6

[1] Warren G and Nate Dogg [2] Mos Def and Nate Dogg featuring Pharoahe Monch [3] Shade Sheist featuring Nate Dogg and Kurupt [4] Ludacris featuring Nate Dogg [5] WC featuring Snoop Dogg and Nate Dogg [6] 50 Cent featuring Nate Dogg [7] Mark Ronson featuring Ghostface Killah and Nate Dogg [8] Obie Trice featuring Nate Dogg [9] Houston featuring Chingy, Nate Dogg & I-20

DOGS D'AMOUR *UK, male vocal / instrumental group (Singles: 15 Weeks, Albums: 12 Weeks)*   pos/wks

4 Feb 89	HOW COME IT NEVER RAINS *China CHINA 13*		44	3
5 Aug 89	SATELLITE KID *China CHINA 17*		26	3
14 Oct 89	TRAIL OF TEARS *China CHINA 20*		47	3
23 Jun 90	VICTIMS OF SUCCESS *China CHINA 24*		36	3
15 Sep 90	EMPTY WORLD *China CHINA 27*		61	2
19 Jun 93	ALL OR NOTHING *China WOKCD 2033*		53	1
22 Oct 88	IN THE DYNAMITE JET SALOON *China WOL 8*		97	1
25 Mar 89	A GRAVEYARD OF EMPTY BOTTLES *China 8390740*		16	4
30 Sep 89	ERROL FLYNN *China 8397001*		22	3
6 Oct 90	STRAIGHT *China 8437961*		32	2
7 Sep 91	DOG'S HITS AND THE BOOTLEG ALBUM *China WOL 1020*		58	1
15 May 93	... MORE UNCHARTED HEIGHTS OF DISGRACE *China WOLCD 1032*		30	1

DOGS DIE IN HOT CARS *UK, male / female vocal / instrumental group (Singles: 5 Weeks, Albums: 2 Weeks)*   pos/wks

8 May 04	GODHOPPING *V2 VVR 5025863*		24	2
17 Jul 04	I LOVE YOU 'CAUSE I HAVE TO *V2 VVR 5025873*		32	2
16 Oct 04	LOUNGER *V2 VVR 5028213*		43	1
24 Jul 04	PLEASE DESCRIBE YOURSELF *V2 VVR 1027142*		44	2

Ken DOH *UK, male producer – Michael Devlin (Singles: 7 Weeks)*   pos/wks

30 Mar 96 ●	NAKASAKI (EP) *ffrr FCD 272*		7	7

Tracks on Nakasaki (EP): Nakasaki (2 mixes) / I Need A Lover Tonight (2 mixes) / Kaki Traki

PETER DOHERTY (see also The LIBERTINES; BABY SHAMBLES)
UK, male vocalist / instrumentalist (Singles: 7 Weeks)   pos/wks

24 Apr 04 ●	FOR LOVERS *Rough Trade TRADSCD 177* [1]		7	6
22 May 04	BABYSHAMBLES *High Society HSCDS 003*		32	1

[1] Wolfman featuring Peter Doherty

DOKKEN *US, male vocal / instrumental group (Albums: 1 Week)*   pos/wks

21 Nov 87	BACK FOR THE ATTACK *Elektra EKT 43*		96	1

Joe DOLAN *Ireland, male vocalist (Singles: 40 Weeks)*   pos/wks

25 Jun 69 ●	MAKE ME AN ISLAND (re) *Pye 7N 17738*		3	19
1 Nov 69	TERESA *Pye 7N 17833*		20	7
28 Feb 70	YOU'RE SUCH A GOOD LOOKING WOMAN *Pye 7N 17891*		17	13
17 Sep 77	I NEED YOU *Pye 7N 45702*		43	1

Thomas DOLBY *UK, male vocalist / multi-instrumentalist – Thomas Robertson (Singles: 51 Weeks, Albums: 29 Weeks)*   pos/wks

3 Oct 81	EUROPA AND THE PIRATE TWINS *Parlophone R 6051*		48	3
14 Aug 82	WINDPOWER *Venice in Peril VIPS 103*		31	8
6 Nov 82	SHE BLINDED ME WITH SCIENCE *Venice in Peril VIPS 104*		49	4
16 Jul 83	SHE BLINDED ME WITH SCIENCE (re-issue) *Venice in Peril VIPS 105*		56	4
21 Jan 84	HYPERACTIVE *Parlophone Odeon R 6065*		17	9
31 Mar 84	I SCARE MYSELF *Parlophone Odeon R 6067*		46	5
16 Apr 88	AIRHEAD *Manhattan MT 38*		53	3
9 May 92	CLOSE BUT NO CIGAR *Virgin VS 1410*		22	5
11 Jul 92	I LOVE YOU GOODBYE *Virgin VS 1417*		36	4
26 Sep 92	SILK PYJAMAS *Virgin VS 1430*		62	2
22 Jan 94	HYPERACTIVE! (re-mix) *Parlophone CDEMCTS 10*		23	4
22 May 82	THE GOLDEN AGE OF WIRELESS *Venice in Peril VIP 1001*		65	10
18 Feb 84	THE FLAT EARTH *Parlophone Odeon PCS 2400341*		14	14
7 May 88	ALIENS ATE MY BUICK *Manhattan MTL 1020*		30	3
8 Aug 92	ASTRONAUTS AND HERETICS *Virgin CDV 2701*		35	2

Joe DOLCE MUSIC THEATRE
US, male vocalist (Singles: 10 Weeks)   pos/wks

7 Feb 81 ★	SHADDAP YOU FACE *Epic EPC 9518*		1	10

DOLL
UK, male / female vocal / instrumental group (Singles: 8 Weeks)   pos/wks

13 Jan 79	DESIRE ME *Beggars Banquet BEG 11*		28	8

DOLLAR   456   Top 500
Photogenic teen-targeted UK vocal duo, who were originally one third of Guys 'n' Dolls: David Van Day and Thereze Bazar. Their Top 10 hits came from writers as diverse as John Lennon, Paul McCartney, Trevor Horn, Erasure and themselves (Singles: 128 Weeks, Albums: 28 Weeks)   pos/wks

11 Nov 78	SHOOTING STAR *Carrere EMI 2871*		14	12
19 May 79	WHO WERE YOU WITH IN THE MOONLIGHT *Carrere CAR 110*		14	12
18 Aug 79 ●	LOVE'S GOTTA HOLD ON ME *Carrere CAR 122*		4	13
24 Nov 79 ●	I WANNA HOLD YOUR HAND *Carrere CAR 131*		9	14
25 Oct 80	TAKIN' A CHANCE ON YOU *WEA K 18353*		62	3
15 Aug 81	HAND HELD IN BLACK AND WHITE *WEA BUCK 1*		19	12
14 Nov 81 ●	MIRROR MIRROR (MON AMOUR) *WEA BUCK 2*		4	17
20 Mar 82	RING RING *Carrere CAR 225*		61	2
27 Mar 82 ●	GIVE ME BACK MY HEART *WEA BUCK 3*		4	9
19 Jun 82	VIDEOTHEQUE *WEA BUCK 4*		17	10
18 Sep 82	GIVE ME SOME KINDA MAGIC *WEA BUCK 5*		34	6
16 Aug 86	WE WALKED IN LOVE *Arista DIME 1*		61	4
26 Dec 87 ●	O L'AMOUR *London LON 146*		7	11
16 Jul 88	IT'S NATURE'S WAY (NO PROBLEM) *London LON 179*		58	3
15 Sep 79	SHOOTING STARS *Carrere CAL 111*		36	8
24 Apr 82	THE VERY BEST OF DOLLAR *Carrere CAL 3001*		31	9
30 Oct 82	THE DOLLAR ALBUM *WEA DTV 1*		18	11

Placido DOMINGO   289   Top 500   (see also Andrew LLOYD WEBBER)
Perennially popular tenor, b. 21 Jan 1941, Madrid, Spain, who brought an operatic quality to the pop charts, most successfully as one of The Three Tenors with a series of football World Cup tie-in concerts. Received an honorary knighthood in 2002 (Singles: 28 Weeks, Albums: 199 Weeks)   pos/wks

12 Dec 81	PERHAPS LOVE *CBS A 1905* [1]		46	9
27 May 89	TILL I LOVED YOU *CBS 654843 7* [2]		24	9
16 Jun 90	NESSUN DORMA FROM 'TURANDOT' *Epic 656005 7* [3]		59	2

30 Jul 94	LIBIAMO / LA DONNA E MOBILE *Teldec YZ 843CD* [4]	.21	4
25 Jul 98	YOU'LL NEVER WALK ALONE *Decca 4607982* [5]	.35	4
28 Nov 81	PERHAPS LOVE *CBS 73592* [1]	.17	21
21 May 83	MY LIFE FOR A SONG *CBS 73683*	.31	8
27 Dec 86	PLACIDO DOMINGO COLLECTION *Stylus SMR 625*	.30	14
23 Apr 88	GREATEST LOVE SONGS *CBS 44701*	.63	2
17 Jun 89	GOYA ... A LIFE IN A SONG *CBS 463294 1*	.36	4
17 Jun 89	THE EESENTIAL DOMINGO *Deutsche Grammophon PDTV 1* [20]		8
1 Sep 90	★ IN CONCERT *Decca 4304331* [2]	.1	78
24 Nov 90	BE MY LOVE ... AN ALBUM OF LOVE *EMI EMTV 54* [3]	.14	12
7 Dec 91	THE BROADWAY I LOVE *East West 9031755901*	.45	6
13 Jun 92	DOMINGO: ARIAS AND SPANISH SONGS *Deutsche Grammophon 4371122*	.47	3
8 Aug 92	FROM THE OFFICIAL BARCELONA GAMES CEREMONY *RCA Red Seal 09026612042* [4]	.41	3
25 Dec 93	CHRISTMAS IN VIENNA *Sony Classical SK 53358* [5]	.71	2
10 Sep 94	★ THE THREE TENORS IN CONCERT 1994 *Teldec 4509962002* [6]	.1	26
10 Dec 94	CHRISTMAS IN VIENNA II *Sony Classical SK 64304* [7]	.60	2
29 Aug 98	THE THREE TENORS IN PARIS 1998 *Decca 4605002* [2]	.14	6
28 Oct 00	SONGS OF LOVE *EMI CDC 5571042*	.53	2
23 Dec 00	THE THREE TENORS CHRISTMAS *Sony Classical SK 89131* [8]	.57	2

[1] Placido Domingo with John Denver [2] Placido Domingo and Jennifer Rush [3] Luis Cobos featuring Placido Domingo [4] José Carreras featuring Placido Domingo and Luciano Pavarotti with Mehta [5] José Carreras, Placido Domingo and Luciano Pavarotti with Mehta [1] Placido Domingo and John Denver [2] José Carreras, Placido Domingo and Luciano Pavarotti [3] Placido Domingo featuring the London Symphony Orchestra [4] Placido Domingo, José Carreras and Montserrat Caballé [5] Placido Domingo, Diana Ross and José Carreras [6] José Carreras, Placido Domingo and Luciano Pavarotti conducted by Zubin Mehta [7] Dionne Warwick and Placido Domingo [8] José Carreras, Placido Domingo and Luciano Pavarotti featuring Zubin Mehta

DOMINO *US, male rapper / vocalist – Shawn Ivy (Singles: 6 Weeks)* pos/wks

22 Jan 94	GETTO JAM *Chaos 6600402*	.33	4
14 May 94	SWEET POTATOE PIE *Chaos 6603292*	.42	2

Fats DOMINO *US, male vocalist / instrumentalist – piano – Antoine Domino (Singles: 111 Weeks, Albums: 3 Weeks)* pos/wks

27 Jul 56	I'M IN LOVE AGAIN (re) *London HLU 8280*	.12	14
30 Nov 56	● BLUEBERRY HILL (re) *London HLU 8330*	.6	15
25 Jan 57	AIN'T THAT A SHAME *London HLU 8173*	.23	2
1 Feb 57	HONEY CHILE *London HLU 8356*	.29	1
29 Mar 57	BLUE MONDAY (re) *London HLP 8377*	.23	2
19 Apr 57	I'M WALKIN' *London HLP 8407*	.19	7
19 Jul 57	VALLEY OF TEARS *London HLP 8449*	.25	1
28 Mar 58	THE BIG BEAT *London HLP 8575*	.20	4
4 Jul 58	SICK AND TIRED *London HLP 8628*	.26	1
22 May 59	MARGIE *London HLP 8865*	.18	5
16 Oct 59	I WANT TO WALK YOU HOME *London HLP 8942*	.14	5
18 Dec 59	BE MY GUEST (re) *London HLP 9005*	.11	13
17 Mar 60	COUNTRY BOY *London HLP 9073*	.19	11
21 Jul 60	WALKING TO NEW ORLEANS *London HLP 9163*	.19	10
10 Nov 60	THREE NIGHTS A WEEK *London HLP 9198*	.45	2
5 Jan 61	MY GIRL JOSEPHINE *London HLP 9244*	.32	4
27 Jul 61	IT KEEPS RAININ' *London HLP 9374*	.49	1
30 Nov 61	WHAT A PARTY *London HLP 9456*	.43	1
29 Mar 62	JAMBALAYA *London HLP 9520*	.41	1
31 Oct 63	RED SAILS IN THE SUNSET *HMV POP 1219*	.34	6
24 Apr 76	BLUEBERRY HILL (re-issue) *United Artists UP 35797*	.41	5
16 May 70	VERY BEST OF FATS DOMINO *Liberty LBS 83331*	.56	1
6 Mar 04	THE BEST OF FATS DOMINO *EMI 5964972*	.58	2

DON PABLO'S ANIMALS
Italy, male production group (Singles: 10 Weeks) pos/wks

19 May 90	● VENUS *Rumour RUMA 18*	.4	10

Siobhan DONAGHY (see also SUGABABES)
UK, female vocalist (Singles: 5 Weeks) pos/wks

5 Jul 03	OVERRATED *London LONCD 476*	.19	4
27 Sep 03	TWIST OF FATE *London LONCD 481*	.52	1

DON-E *UK, male vocalist – Donald McLean (Singles: 8 Weeks)* pos/wks

9 May 92	LOVE MAKES THE WORLD GO ROUND *Fourth & Broadway BRW 242*	.18	6

25 Jul 92	PEACE IN THE WORLD *Fourth & Broadway BRW 256*	.41	1
28 Feb 98	DELICIOUS *Mushroom MUSH 20CD* [1]	.52	1

[1] Deni Hines featuring Don-E

Lonnie DONEGAN   [121]   Top 500
The 'King of Skiffle'. b. Anthony Donegan, 29 Apr 1931, Glasgow, Scotland, d. 3 Nov 2002. Britain's most successful and influential recording artist before The Beatles. Chalked up 24 successive Top 30 hits, and was the first UK male to score two US Top 10s. Album with Van Morrison and Chris Barber reached the Top 20 in 2000 (Singles: 326 Weeks, Albums: 68 Weeks) pos/wks

6 Jan 56	● ROCK ISLAND LINE (2re) *Decca F 10647* [1]	.8	22
20 Apr 56	● LOST JOHN / STEWBALL (re) *Pye Nixa N 15036* [1]	.2	18
6 Jul 56	SKIFFLE SESSION (EP) *Pye Nixa NJE 1017* [1]	.20	2
7 Sep 56	● BRING A LITTLE WATER, SYLVIE / DEAD OR ALIVE (re) *Pye Nixa N 15071* [1]	.7	13
21 Dec 56	LONNIE DONEGAN SHOWCASE (LP) *Pye Nixa NPT 19012* [2]	.26	3
18 Jan 57	● DON'T YOU ROCK ME DADDY-O *Pye Nixa N 15080* [2]	.4	17
5 Apr 57	★ CUMBERLAND GAP *Pye Nixa N 15087* [2]	.1	12
7 Jun 57	★ GAMBLIN' MAN / PUTTIN' ON THE STYLE *Pye Nixa N 15093* [2]	.1	19
11 Oct 57	● MY DIXIE DARLING *Pye Nixa N 15108* [2]	.10	15
20 Dec 57	JACK O' DIAMONDS *Pye Nixa 7N 15116* [2]	.14	7
11 Apr 58	● THE GRAND COOLIE DAM *Pye Nixa 7N 15129* [2]	.6	15
11 Jul 58	SALLY DON'T YOU GRIEVE / BETTY, BETTY, BETTY *Pye Nixa 7N 15148* [2]	.11	7
26 Sep 58	LONESOME TRAVELLER *Pye Nixa 7N 15158* [2]	.28	1
14 Nov 58	LONNIE'S SKIFFLE PARTY *Pye Nixa 7N 15165* [2]	.23	5
21 Nov 58	● TOM DOOLEY *Pye Nixa 7N 15172* [2]	.3	14
6 Feb 59	● DOES YOUR CHEWING GUM LOSE ITS FLAVOUR (ON THE BEDPOST OVERNIGHT) *Pye Nixa 7N 15181* [2]	.3	12
8 May 59	FORT WORTH JAIL *Pye Nixa 7N 15198* [2]	.14	5
26 Jun 59	● BATTLE OF NEW ORLEANS *Pye Nixa 7N 15206* [2]	.2	16
11 Sep 59	SAL'S GOT A SUGAR LIP *Pye 7N 15223* [2]	.13	4
2 Oct 59	HOLD BACK TOMORROW *Pye 7N 15213* [3]	.26	2
4 Dec 59	SAN MIGUEL *Pye 7N 15237* [2]	.19	4
24 Mar 60	★ MY OLD MAN'S A DUSTMAN *Pye 7N 15256* [4]	.1	13
26 May 60	● I WANNA GO HOME (THE WRECK OF THE 'JOHN B') *Pye 7N 15267* [5]	.5	17
25 Aug 60	● LORELEI *Pye 7N 15275*	.10	8
13 Oct 60	ROCKIN' ALONE *Pye 7N 15296* [6]	.44	3
24 Nov 60	LIVELY *Pye 7N 15312* [4]	.13	9
8 Dec 60	VIRGIN MARY *Pye 7N 15315*	.27	5
11 May 61	● HAVE A DRINK ON ME *Pye 7N 15354* [4]	.8	15
31 Aug 61	● MICHAEL, ROW THE BOAT / LUMBERED *Pye 7N 15371* [4]	.6	11
18 Jan 62	THE COMANCHEROS *Pye 7N 15410*	.14	10
5 Apr 62	● THE PARTY'S OVER *Pye 7N 15424*	.9	12
16 Aug 62	PICK A BALE OF COTTON *Pye 7N 15455* [4]	.11	10
17 Nov 56	● LONNIE DONEGAN SHOWCASE *Pye Nixa NPT 19012*	.2	21
12 Jul 58	● LONNIE *Pye Nixa NPT 19027*	.3	13
1 Sep 62	● GOLDEN AGE OF DONEGAN *Pye Golden Guinea GGL 0135*	.3	23
9 Feb 63	GOLDEN AGE OF DONEGAN VOLUME 2 *Pye Golden Guinea GGL 0170*	.15	3
25 Feb 78	PUTTING ON THE STYLE *Chrysalis CHR 1158*	.51	3
29 Jan 00	THE SKIFFLE SESSIONS – LIVE IN BELFAST *Venture CDVE 945* [1]	.14	3
8 Mar 03	PUTTIN' ON THE STYLE – THE GREATEST HITS *Castle Music TVSAN 002*	.45	2

[1] Lonnie Donegan Skiffle Group [2] Lonnie Donegan and his Skiffle Group [3] Lonnie Donegan presents Miki and Griff with the Lonnie Donegan Group [4] Lonnie Donegan and his Group [5] Lonnie Donegan and Wally Stott's Orchestra [6] Miki and Griff with the Lonnie Donegan Group [1] Van Morrison / Lonnie Donegan / Chris Barber

'Stewball' had one week on the chart by itself on 20 Apr 1956. 'Lost John', the other side, replaced it on 27 Apr 1956, but 'Stewball' was given co-billing with 'Lost John' for the weeks of 11, 18 and 25 May 1956, peaking only at No.7. 'Dead or Alive' was not listed with 'Bring a Little Water Sylvie' for the week 7 Sep 1956. 'Putting on the Style' was not listed with 'Gamblin' Man' for the weeks of 7 and 14 Jun 1956. Tracks on Skiffle Session (EP): Railroad Bill / Stockalee / Ballad of Jesse James / Ol' Riley. Tracks on Lonnie Donegan Showcase (LP): Wabash Cannonball / How Long / How Long Blues / Nobody's Child / I Shall Not Be Moved / I'm Alabammy Bound / I'm a Rambling Man / Wreck of the Old '97 / Frankie and Johnny

Tanya DONELLY (see also BELLY) *US, female vocalist / instrumentalist (Singles: 2 Weeks, Albums: 1 Week)* pos/wks

30 Aug 97	PRETTY DEEP *4AD BAD 7007CD*	.55	1
6 Dec 97	THE BRIGHT LIGHT *4AD BAD 7012CD*	.64	1
20 Sep 97	LOVESONGS FOR UNDERDOGS *4AD CAD 7008CD*	.36	1

The DONNAS
US, female vocal / instrumental group (Singles: 4 Weeks) pos/wks

12 Apr 03	**TAKE IT OFF** *Atlantic AT 0148CD* **38**	2
5 Jul 03	**WHO INVITED YOU?** *Atlantic AT 0156CD* **61**	1
23 Oct 04	**FALL BEHIND ME** *Atlantic AT 0186CD* **55**	1

Ral DONNER
US, male vocalist, b. 10 Feb 1943, d. 6 Apr 1984 (Singles: 10 Weeks) pos/wks

21 Sep 61	**YOU DON'T KNOW WHAT YOU'VE GOT (UNTIL YOU LOSE IT)** *Parlophone R 4820* **25**	10

DONOVAN `399` `Top 500`
Acclaimed Celtic singer / songwriter, b. Donovan Leitch, 10 May 1946, Glasgow, Scotland. Initially dubbed the British version of Bob Dylan, he enjoyed massive appeal on both sides of the Atlantic in the 'flower power' years of the late 1960s (Singles: 100 Weeks, Albums: 73 Weeks) pos/wks

25 Mar 65	● **CATCH THE WIND** *Pye 7N 15801* **4**	13	
3 Jun 65	● **COLOURS** *Pye 7N 15866* **4**	12	
11 Nov 65	**TURQUOISE** *Pye 7N 15984* **30**	6	
8 Dec 66	● **SUNSHINE SUPERMAN** *Pye 7N 17241* ▲ **2**	11	
9 Feb 67	● **MELLOW YELLOW** *Pye 7N 17267* **8**	8	
25 Oct 67	● **THERE IS A MOUNTAIN** *Pye 7N 17403* **8**	11	
21 Feb 68	● **JENNIFER JUNIPER** *Pye 7N 17457* **5**	11	
29 May 68	● **HURDY GURDY MAN** *Pye 7N 17537* **4**	10	
4 Dec 68	**ATLANTIS** *Pye 7N 17660* **23**	8	
9 Jul 69	**GOO GOO BARABAJAGAL (LOVE IS HOT)** *Pye 7N 17778* [1] ..**12**	9	
1 Dec 90	**JENNIFER JUNIPER** *Fontana SYP 1* [2] **68**	1	
5 Jun 65	**WHAT'S BIN DID AND WHAT'S BIN HID** *Pye NPL 18117* **3**	16	
6 Nov 65	**FAIRY TALE** *Pye NPL 18128* **20**	2	
8 Jul 67	**SUNSHINE SUPERMAN** *Pye NPL 18181* **25**	7	
14 Oct 67	● **UNIVERSAL SOLDIER** *Marble Arch MAL 718* **5**	18	
11 May 68	**A GIFT FROM A FLOWER TO A GARDEN** *Pye NSPL 20000* **13**	14	
12 Sep 70	**OPEN ROAD** *Dawn DNLS 3009* **30**	4	
24 Mar 73	**COSMIC WHEELS** *Epic EPC 65450* **15**	12	

[1] Donovan with the Jeff Beck Group [2] Singing Corner meets Donovan

Jason DONOVAN `274` `Top 500`
The top teen idol of the late 1980s, b. 1 Jun 1968, Melbourne, Australia. The actor turned singer had an impressive array of UK hits after leaving TV soap 'Neighbours'. His debut LP, 'Ten Good Reasons', was the UK's top-selling album of 1989 (Singles: 137 Weeks, Albums: 99 Weeks) pos/wks

10 Sep 88	● **NOTHING CAN DIVIDE US** *PWL PWL 17* **5**	12
10 Dec 88	★ **ESPECIALLY FOR YOU** *PWL PWL 24* [1] **1**	14
4 Mar 89	★ **TOO MANY BROKEN HEARTS** *PWL PWL 32* **1**	13
10 Jun 89	● **SEALED WITH A KISS** *PWL PWL 39* ■ **1**	10
9 Sep 89	● **EVERY DAY (I LOVE YOU MORE)** *PWL PWL 43* **2**	9
9 Dec 89	● **WHEN YOU COME BACK TO ME** *PWL PWL 46* **2**	11
7 Apr 90	● **HANG ON TO YOUR LOVE** *PWL PWL 51* **8**	7
30 Jun 90	**ANOTHER NIGHT** *PWL PWL 58* **18**	5
1 Sep 90	● **RHYTHM OF THE RAIN** *PWL PWL 60* **9**	6
27 Oct 90	**I'M DOING FINE** *PWL PWL 69* **22**	6
18 May 91	**RSVP** *PWL PWL 80* **17**	5
22 Jun 91	★ **ANY DREAM WILL DO** *Really Useful RUR 7* **1**	12
24 Aug 91	● **HAPPY TOGETHER** *PWL PWL 203* **10**	6
7 Dec 91	**JOSEPH MEGA REMIX** *Really Useful RUR 9* [2] **13**	8
18 Jul 92	**MISSION OF LOVE** *Polydor PO 222* **26**	4
28 Nov 92	**AS TIME GOES BY** *Polydor PO 245* **26**	6
7 Aug 93	**ALL AROUND THE WORLD** *Polydor PZCD 278* **41**	3
13 May 89	★ **TEN GOOD REASONS** *PWL HF 7* **1**	54
9 Jun 90	● **BETWEEN THE LINES** *PWL HF 14* **2**	26
28 Sep 91	● **GREATEST HITS** *PWL HF 20* **9**	17
11 Sep 93	**ALL AROUND THE WORLD** *Polydor 8477452* **27**	2

[1] Kylie Minogue and Jason Donovan [2] Jason Donovan and Original London Cast featuring Linzi Hately, David Easter and Johnny Amobi

The DOOBIE BROTHERS (see also Michael McDONALD) *US, male vocal / instrumental group (Singles: 45 Weeks, Albums: 33 Weeks)* pos/wks

9 Mar 74	**LISTEN TO THE MUSIC** *Warner Bros. K 16208* **29**	7
7 Jun 75	**TAKE ME IN YOUR ARMS (ROCK ME A LITTLE WHILE)** *Warner Bros. K 16559* **29**	5
17 Feb 79	**WHAT A FOOL BELIEVES (re)** *Warner Bros. K 17314* ▲ **31**	11
14 Jul 79	**MINUTE BY MINUTE** *Warner Bros. K 17411* **47**	4
24 Jan 87	**WHAT A FOOL BELIEVES (re-issue)** *Warner Bros. W 8451* [1] **57**	3
29 Jul 89	**THE DOCTOR** *Capitol CL 536* **73**	2
27 Nov 93	● **LONG TRAIN RUNNIN'** *Warner Bros. W 0217CD* **7**	10

14 May 94	**LISTEN TO THE MUSIC (re-mix)** *Warner Bros. W 0228CD* **37**	3
30 Mar 74	**WHAT WERE ONCE VICES ARE NOW HABITS** *Warner Bros. K 56206* **19**	10
17 May 75	**STAMPEDE** *Warner Bros. K 56094* **14**	11
10 Apr 76	**TAKIN' IT TO THE STREETS** *Warner Bros. K 56196* **42**	2
19 Sep 77	**LIVING ON THE FAULT LINE** *Warner Bros. K 56383* **25**	5
11 Oct 80	**ONE STEP CLOSER** *Warner Bros. K 56824* **53**	2
10 Jul 04	**GREATEST HITS** *WSM 8122765112* **45**	3

[1] The Doobie Brothers featuring Michael McDonald

DOOGIE *See BUG KANN and the PLASTIC JAM*

DOOLALLY (see also SHANKS & BIGFOOT) *UK, male production duo – Stephen Meade and Daniel Langsman (Singles: 16 Weeks)* pos/wks

14 Nov 98	**STRAIGHT FROM THE HEART (re)** *Locked On LOX 104CD* **20**	10
7 Aug 99	● **STRAIGHT FROM THE HEART (re-issue)** *Chocolate Boy / Locked On LOX 112CD* **9**	6

The DOOLEYS *UK, male vocal / instrumental group (Singles: 83 Weeks, Albums: 27 Weeks)* pos/wks

13 Aug 77	**THINK I'M GONNA FALL IN LOVE WITH YOU** *GTO GT 95* **13**	10
12 Nov 77	● **LOVE OF MY LIFE** *GTO GT 110* **9**	11
13 May 78	**DON'T TAKE IT LYIN' DOWN** *GTO GT 220* **60**	3
2 Sep 78	**A ROSE HAS TO DIE** *GTO GT 229* **11**	11
10 Feb 79	**HONEY I'M LOST** *GTO GT 242* **24**	9
16 Jun 79	● **WANTED** *GTO GT 249* **3**	14
22 Sep 79	● **THE CHOSEN FEW** *GTO GT 258* **7**	11
8 Mar 80	**LOVE PATROL** *GTO GT 260* **29**	7
6 Sep 80	**BODY LANGUAGE** *GTO GT 276* **46**	4
10 Oct 81	**AND I WISH** *GTO GT 300* **52**	3
30 Jun 79	● **THE BEST OF THE DOOLEYS** *GTO GTTV 038* **6**	21
3 Nov 79	**THE CHOSEN FEW** *GTO GTLP 040* **56**	4
25 Oct 80	**FULL HOUSE** *GTO GTTV 050* **54**	2

Val DOONICAN `180` `Top 500`
Popular balladeer and TV host, b. Michael Doonican, 3 Feb 1928, Waterford, Ireland. This relaxed crooner, who was known for his rocking chair and multicoloured jumpers, had five successive Top 10 albums in the Swinging Sixties (Singles: 143 Weeks, Albums: 170 Weeks) pos/wks

15 Oct 64	● **WALK TALL** *Decca F 11982* **3**	21
21 Jan 65	● **THE SPECIAL YEARS (re)** *Decca F 12049* **7**	13
8 Apr 65	**I'M GONNA GET THERE SOMEHOW** *Decca F 12118* **25**	5
17 Mar 66	● **ELUSIVE BUTTERFLY** *Decca F 12358* **5**	12
3 Nov 66	● **WHAT WOULD I BE** *Decca F 12505* **2**	17
23 Feb 67	**MEMORIES ARE MADE OF THIS** *Decca F 12566* **11**	12
25 May 67	**TWO STREETS** *Decca F 12608* **39**	4
18 Oct 67	● **IF THE WHOLE WORLD STOPPED LOVIN'** *Pye 7N 17396* **3**	19
21 Feb 68	**YOU'RE THE ONLY ONE** *Pye 7N 17465* **37**	4
12 Jun 68	**NOW** *Pye 7N 17534* **43**	2
23 Oct 68	**IF I KNEW THEN WHAT I KNOW NOW** *Pye 7N 17616* **14**	13
23 Apr 69	**RING OF BRIGHT WATER** *Pye 7N 17713* **48**	1
4 Dec 71	**MORNING** *Philips 6006 177* **12**	13
10 Mar 73	**HEAVEN IS MY WOMAN'S LOVE (re)** *Philips 6028 031* **34**	7
12 Dec 64	● **THE LUCKY 13 SHADES OF VAL DOONICAN** *Decca LK 4648* **2**	27
3 Dec 66	● **GENTLE SHADES OF VAL DOONICAN** *Decca LK 4831* **5**	52
2 Dec 67	★ **VAL DOONICAN ROCKS BUT GENTLY** *Pye NSPL 18204* **1**	23
30 Nov 68	● **VAL** *Pye NSPL 18236* **6**	11
14 Jun 69	● **THE WORLD OF VAL DOONICAN** *Decca SPA 3* **2**	31
13 Dec 69	**SOUNDS GENTLE** *Pye NSPL 18321* **22**	9
19 Dec 70	**THE MAGIC OF VAL DOONICAN** *Philips 6642 003* **34**	3
27 Nov 71	**THIS IS VAL DOONICAN** *Philips 6382 017* **40**	1
22 Feb 75	**I LOVE COUNTRY MUSIC** *Philips 9299261* **37**	2
21 May 77	**SOME OF MY BEST FRIENDS ARE SONGS** *Philips 6641 607* **29**	5
24 Mar 90	**SONGS FROM MY SKETCH BOOK** *Parkfield PMLP 5014* **33**	6

DOOP *Holland, male instrumental duo – Ferry Ridderhof and Peter Garnefski (Singles: 12 Weeks)* pos/wks

12 Mar 94	★ **DOOP** *Citybeat CBE 774CD* **1**	12

The DOORS `485` `Top 500` *Controversial, uncompromising rock band. Formed 1965 in Los Angeles. 'Lizard King' Jim Morrison (v), d. 1971, Ray Manzarek (k), Robby Krieger (g) and John Densmore (d) were 1993 Rock and Roll Hall of Fame inductees but did not score a UK Top 10 single until 1991 and album until 2000 (Singles: 42 Weeks, Albums: 108 Weeks)* pos/wks

16 Aug 67	**LIGHT MY FIRE** *Elektra EKSN 45014* ▲ **49**	1
28 Aug 68	**HELLO, I LOVE YOU** *Elektra EKSN 45037* ▲ **15**	12
16 Oct 71	**RIDERS ON THE STORM (re)** *Elektra K 12021* **22**	11

Date	Title	pos	wks
20 Mar 76	RIDERS ON THE STORM (re-issue) *Elektra K 12203*	33	5
3 Feb 79	HELLO I LOVE YOU (re-issue) *Elektra K 12215*	71	2
27 Apr 91	BREAK ON THROUGH *Elektra EKR 121*	64	2
1 Jun 91 ●	LIGHT MY FIRE (re-issue) *Elektra EKR 125*	7	8
10 Aug 91	RIDERS ON THE STORM (2nd re-issue) *Elektra EKR 131*	68	1
28 Sep 68	WAITING FOR THE SUN *Elektra EKS 74024* ▲	16	10
11 Apr 70	MORRISON HOTEL *Elektra EKS 75007*	12	8
26 Sep 70	ABSOLUTELY LIVE *Elektra 2665 002*	69	2
31 Jul 71	L.A. WOMAN *Elektra K 42090*	28	4
1 Apr 72	WEIRD SCENES INSIDE THE GOLD MINE *Elektra K 62009*	50	1
29 Oct 83	ALIVE SHE CRIED *Elektra 9602691*	36	5
4 Jul 87	LIVE AT THE HOLLYWOOD BOWL *Elektra EKT 40*	51	3
6 Apr 91	THE DOORS (FILM SOUNDTRACK) *Elektra EKT 85*	11	17
20 Apr 91	THE BEST OF THE DOORS *Elektra EKT 21*	17	18
20 Apr 91	THE DOORS *Elektra K 42012*	43	13
1 Jun 91	IN CONCERT *Elektra EKT 88*	24	5
21 Mar 98	THE BEST OF THE DOORS (re-issue) *Elektra K 9603452*	37	8
23 Sep 00 ●	THE BEST OF THE DOORS *Elektra 7559624682*	9	15

'The Best of The Doors' (2000) has a different track listing to the 1991/8 album

DOPE SMUGGLAZ
UK, male DJ / production trio (Singles: 5 Weeks) — pos/wks

| 5 Dec 98 | THE WORD *Mushroom PERFCDS 1* | 62 | 1 |
| 7 Aug 99 | DOUBLE DOUBLE DUTCH *Perfecto PERF 2CDS* | 15 | 4 |

Charlie DORE UK, female vocalist (Singles: 2 Weeks) — pos/wks

| 17 Nov 79 | PILOT OF THE AIRWAVES *Island WIP 6526* | 66 | 2 |

Andrea DORIA
Italy, male producer / instrumentalist (Singles: 1 Week) — pos/wks

| 26 Apr 03 | BUCCI BAG *Southern Fried ECB 38CDS* | 57 | 1 |

DOROTHY (see also The CANDY GIRLS; CLERGY; HI-GATE; Paul MASTERSON presents SUSHI; SLEAZE SISTERS) UK, male producer / instrumentalist – Paul Masterson (Singles: 5 Weeks) — pos/wks

| 9 Dec 95 | WHAT'S THAT TUNE (DOO DOO DOO DOO DOO-DOO-DOO-DOO-DOO-DOO) *RCA 74321330912* | 31 | 5 |

Lee DORSEY US, male vocalist – Irving Dorsey, b. 24 Dec 1924, d. 1 Dec 1986 (Singles: 36 Weeks, Albums: 3 Weeks) — pos/wks

3 Feb 66	GET OUT OF MY LIFE, WOMAN *Stateside SS 485*	22	7
5 May 66	CONFUSION *Stateside SS 506*	38	6
11 Aug 66 ●	WORKING IN THE COALMINE *Stateside SS 528*	8	11
27 Oct 66 ●	HOLY COW *Stateside SS 552*	6	12
17 Dec 66	NEW LEE DORSEY *Stateside SSL 10192*	34	3

Marc DORSEY US, male vocalist (Singles: 1 Week) — pos/wks

| 19 Jun 99 | IF YOU REALLY WANNA KNOW *Jive 0522592* | 58 | 1 |

Tommy DORSEY ORCHESTRA starring Warren COVINGTON
US, orchestra – leader Tommy Dorsey, b. 19 Nov 1905, d. 26 Nov 1956, and male instrumentalist – trombone (Singles: 19 Weeks) — pos/wks

| 17 Oct 58 ● | TEA FOR TWO CHA CHA *Brunswick 05757* | 3 | 19 |

DOUBLE Switzerland, male vocal / instrumental duo – Kurt Maloo and Felix Haug (Singles: 10 Weeks, Albums: 4 Weeks) — pos/wks

25 Jan 86 ●	THE CAPTAIN OF HER HEART *Polydor POSP 779*	8	9
5 Dec 87	DEVIL'S BALL *Polydor POSP 888*	71	1
8 Mar 86	BLUE *Polydor POLD 5187*	69	4

DOUBLE DEE
Italy, male producer – Davide Domenella (Singles: 5 Weeks) — pos/wks

1 Dec 90	FOUND LOVE *Epic 6563766* [1]	63	2
25 Nov 95	FOUND LOVE (re-mix) *Sony S3 DANUCD 1* [1]	33	2
27 Sep 03	SHINING *Positiva CDTIV 194*	58	1

[1] Double Dee featuring Dany

DOUBLE 99 (see also RIP PRODUCTIONS) UK, male instrumental / production duo – Tim Liken and Omar Adimora (Singles: 9 Weeks) — pos/wks

| 31 May 97 | RIPGROOVE *Satellite 74321485132* | 31 | 3 |
| 1 Nov 97 | RIPGROOVE (re-mix) *Satellite 74321529322* | 14 | 6 |

007 See RED RAW featuring 007

DOUBLE SIX
UK, male vocal / instrumental group (Singles: 2 Weeks) — pos/wks

| 19 Sep 98 | REAL GOOD *Multiply CDMULTY 39* | 66 | 1 |
| 12 Jun 99 | BREAKDOWN *Multiply CDMULTY 50* | 59 | 1 |

DOUBLE TROUBLE (see also AIRHEADZ)
UK, male instrumental / production duo – Leigh Guest and Michael Menson (Singles: 35 Weeks, Albums: 1 Week) — pos/wks

27 May 89	JUST KEEP ROCKIN' *Desire WANT 9* [1]	11	12
7 Oct 89	STREET TUFF *Desire WANT 18* [2]	3	14
12 May 90	TALK BACK *Desire WANT 27* [3]	71	1
30 Jun 90	LOVE DON'T LIVE HERE ANYMORE *Desire WANT 32* [4]	21	6
15 Jun 91	RUB-A-DUB *Desire WANT 41*	66	2
4 Aug 90	AS ONE *Desire LULP 6*	73	1

[1] Double Trouble and the Rebel MC [2] Rebel MC and Double Trouble [3] With vocals by Janette Sewell [4] Double Trouble featuring Janette Sewell and Carl Brown

DOUBLE TROUBLE See Stevie Ray VAUGHAN and DOUBLE TROUBLE

DOUBLE YOU?
Italy, male vocalist – Willie Morales (Singles: 3 Weeks) — pos/wks

| 2 May 92 | PLEASE DON'T GO *ZYX ZYX 67487* | 41 | 3 |

Rob DOUGAN (see also OUR TRIBE / ONE TRIBE; SPHINX) Australia, male vocalist / instrumentalist / producer (Singles: 4 Weeks) — pos/wks

| 4 Apr 98 | FURIOUS ANGELS *Cheeky CHEKCD 025* | 62 | 1 |
| 6 Jul 02 | CLUBBED TO DEATH *Cheeky / Arista 74321941702* | 24 | 3 |

Carl DOUGLAS Jamaica, male vocalist (Singles: 39 Weeks) — pos/wks

17 Aug 74 ★	KUNG FU FIGHTING *Pye 7N 45377* ▲	1	13
30 Nov 74	DANCE THE KUNG FU *Pye 7N 45418*	35	5
3 Dec 77	RUN BACK *Pye 7N 46018*	25	10
23 May 98	KUNG FU FIGHTING *All Around the World CDGLOBE 173* [1]	8	11

[1] Bus Stop featuring Carl Douglas
Second listing for Kung Fu Fighting was not a re-mix of the original but Douglas's 1974 hit vocal sampled and used in a new recording by Bus Stop

Carol DOUGLAS US, female vocalist (Singles: 4 Weeks) — pos/wks

| 22 Jul 78 | NIGHT FEVER *Gull GULS 61* | 66 | 4 |

Craig DOUGLAS UK, male vocalist – Terence Perkins (Singles: 113 Weeks, Albums: 2 Weeks) — pos/wks

12 Jun 59	A TEENAGER IN LOVE *Top Rank JAR 133*	13	11
7 Aug 59 ★	ONLY SIXTEEN *Top Rank JAR 159*	1	15
22 Jan 60 ●	PRETTY BLUE EYES *Top Rank JAR 195*	4	15
28 Apr 60 ●	THE HEART OF A TEENAGE GIRL *Top Rank JAR 340*	10	9
11 Aug 60	OH! WHAT A DAY *Top Rank JAR 406*	43	1
20 Apr 61 ●	A HUNDRED POUNDS OF CLAY *Top Rank JAR 556*	9	9
29 Jun 61 ●	TIME *Top Rank JAR 569*	9	14
22 Mar 62 ●	WHEN MY LITTLE GIRL IS SMILING *Top Rank JAR 610*	9	13
28 Jun 62 ●	OUR FAVOURITE MELODIES *Columbia DB 4854*	9	10
18 Oct 62	OH, LONESOME ME *Decca F 11523*	15	12
28 Feb 63	TOWN CRIER *Decca F 11575*	36	4
6 Aug 60	CRAIG DOUGLAS *Top Rank BUY 049*	17	2

DOVE Ireland, male / female vocal group (Singles: 2 Weeks) — pos/wks

| 11 Sep 99 | DON'T DREAM *ZTT 135CD* | 37 | 2 |

DOVES UK, male vocal / instrumental group (Singles: 15 Weeks, Albums: 40 Weeks) — pos/wks

14 Aug 99	HERE IT COMES *Casino CHIP 003CD*	73	1
1 Apr 00	THE CEDAR ROOM *Heavenly HVN 95CD*	33	2
10 Jun 00	CATCH THE SUN *Heavenly HVN 96CD*	32	2
11 Nov 00	THE MAN WHO TOLD EVERYTHING *Heavenly HVN 98CD*	32	2
27 Apr 02 ●	THERE GOES THE FEAR *Heavenly HVN 111CD*	3	3
3 Aug 02	POUNDING *Heavenly HVN 116CD*	21	3
26 Oct 02	CAUGHT BY THE RIVER *Heavenly HVN 126CDS*	29	2
15 Apr 00	LOST SOULS *Heavenly HVNLP 26CD*	16	16
11 May 02 ★	THE LAST BROADCAST *Heavenly HVNLP 35CD* ■	1	23
11 Oct 03	LOST SIDES *Heavenly HVNLP 46CDX*	50	1

The DOWLANDS UK, male vocal group (Singles: 7 Weeks) — pos/wks

| 9 Jan 64 | ALL MY LOVING *Oriole CB 1897* | 33 | 7 |

DOWN US, male vocal / instrumental group (Albums: 1 Week) pos/wks

30 Sep 95	NOLA Atlantic 7559618302	68	1

Robert DOWNEY Jr US, male actor / vocalist (Singles: 1 Week) pos/wks

30 Jan 93	SMILE Epic 6589052	68	1

Don DOWNING US, male vocalist (Singles: 10 Weeks) pos/wks

10 Nov 73	LONELY DAYS, LONELY NIGHTS People PEO 102	32	10

Will DOWNING
US, male vocalist (Singles: 35 Weeks, Albums: 28 Weeks) pos/wks

2 Apr 88	A LOVE SUPREME Fourth & Broadway BRW 90	14	10
25 Jun 88	IN MY DREAMS Fourth & Broadway BRW 104	34	6
1 Oct 88	FREE Fourth & Broadway BRW 112	58	5
21 Jan 89	WHERE IS THE LOVE Fourth & Broadway BRW 122 [1]	19	7
28 Oct 89	TEST OF TIME Fourth & Broadway BRW 146	67	2
24 Feb 90	COME TOGETHER AS ONE Fourth & Broadway BRW 159	48	4
18 Sep 93	THERE'S NO LIVING WITHOUT YOU Fourth & Broadway BRCD 278	67	1
26 Mar 88	WILL DOWNING Fourth & Broadway BRLP 518	20	23
18 Nov 89	COME TOGETHER AS ONE Fourth & Broadway BRLP 538	36	2
6 Apr 91	A DREAM FULFILLED Fourth & Broadway BRLP 565	43	3

[1] Mica Paris and Will Downing

Jason DOWNS featuring MILK US, male vocalist
and US, male rapper (Singles: 6 Weeks, Albums: 1 Week) pos/wks

12 May 01	WHITE BOY WITH A FEATHER Pepper 9230412	19	5
14 Jul 01	CATS IN THE CRADLE Pepper 9230442	65	1
28 Jul 01	WHITE BOY WITH A FEATHER Pepper 9230452	64	1

Lamont DOZIER See HOLLAND-DOZIER featuring Lamont DOZIER

DRAGONHEART UK, female vocal group (Singles: 1 Week) pos/wks

27 Nov 04	VIDEO KILLED THE RADIO STAR Lipstick 6150304	74	1

Charlie DRAKE
UK, male comedian / vocalist – Charles Sprigall (Singles: 37 Weeks) pos/wks

8 Aug 58 ●	SPLISH SPLASH Parlophone R 4461	7	11
24 Oct 58	VOLARE Parlophone R 4478	28	2
27 Oct 60	MR CUSTER Parlophone R 4701	12	12
5 Oct 61	MY BOOMERANG WON'T COME BACK Parlophone R 4824	14	11
1 Jan 72	PUCKWUDGIE Columbia DB 8829	47	1

Nick DRAKE UK, male vocalist, b. 19 Jun 1948,
d. 25 Nov 1974 (Singles: 3 Weeks, Albums: 2 Weeks) pos/wks

29 May 04	MAGIC Island CID 854	32	2
25 Sep 04	RIVER MAN Island CID 871	48	1
5 Jun 04	MADE TO LOVE MAGIC Island CID 8141	27	2

DRAMATIS
UK, male vocal / instrumental group (Singles: 8 Weeks) pos/wks

5 Dec 81	LOVE NEEDS NO DISGUISE Beggars Banquet BEG 68 [1]	33	7
13 Nov 82	I CAN SEE HER NOW Rocket XPRES 83	57	1

[1] Gary Numan and Dramatis

Rusty DRAPER US, male vocalist – Farrell H Draper,
b. 25 Jan 1923, d. 29 Mar 2003 (Singles: 4 Weeks) pos/wks

11 Aug 60	MULE SKINNER BLUES Mercury AMT 1101	39	4

DREAD ZEPPELIN US, male vocal /
instrumental group (Singles: 3 Weeks, Albums: 2 Weeks) pos/wks

1 Dec 90	YOUR TIME IS GONNA COME IRS DREAD 1	59	1
13 Jul 91	STAIRWAY TO HEAVEN IRS DREAD 2	62	2
11 Aug 90	UN-LED-ED IRS EIRSA 1042	71	2

DREADZONE
UK, male instrumental group (Singles: 15 Weeks, Albums: 5 Weeks) pos/wks

6 May 95	ZION YOUTH Virgin VSCDG 1537	49	2
29 Jul 95	CAPTAIN DREAD Virgin VSCDG 1541	49	2
23 Sep 95	MAXIMUM (EP) Virgin VSCDT 1555	56	2

6 Jan 96	LITTLE BRITAIN Virgin VSCDG 1565	20	6
30 Mar 96	LIFE LOVE AND UNITY Virgin VSCDT 1583	56	1
10 May 97	EARTH ANGEL Virgin VSCDT 1593	51	1
26 Jul 97	MOVING ON Virgin VSCDT 1635	58	1
10 Jun 95	SECOND LIGHT Virgin CDV 2778	37	4
9 Aug 97	BIOLOGICAL RADIO Virgin CDV 2808	45	1

Tracks on Maximum (EP): Maximum / Fight the Power 95 / One Way

DREAM US, female vocal group (Singles: 7 Weeks) pos/wks

17 Mar 01	HE LOVES U NOT Puff Daddy / Arista 74321823542	17	7

DREAM ACADEMY UK, male / female vocal /
instrumental group (Singles: 10 Weeks, Albums: 2 Weeks) pos/wks

30 Mar 85	LIFE IN A NORTHERN TOWN Blanco Y Negro NEG 10	15	8
14 Sep 85	THE LOVE PARADE Blanco Y Negro NEG 16	68	2
12 Oct 85	THE DREAM ACADEMY Blanco Y Negro BYN 6	58	2

DREAM FREQUENCY
(see also QUAKE featuring Marcia RAE; RED; BEAT RENEGADES)
UK, male producer – Ian Bland (Singles: 12 Weeks) pos/wks

12 Jan 91	LOVE PEACE AND HARMONY Citybeat CBE 756	71	2
25 Jan 92	FEEL SO REAL Citybeat CBE 763 [1]	23	5
25 Apr 92	TAKE ME Citybeat CBE 768	39	3
21 May 94	GOOD TIMES / THE DREAM Citybeat CBE 773CD	67	1
10 Sep 94	YOU MAKE ME FEEL MIGHTY REAL Citybeat CBE 775CD	65	1

[1] Dream Frequency featuring Debbie Sharp

DREAM THEATER
US, male vocal / instrumental group (Albums: 1 Week) pos/wks

15 Oct 94	AWAKE East West 7567901262	65	1

DREAM WARRIORS
Canada, male rap group (Singles: 19 Weeks, Albums: 7 Weeks) pos/wks

14 Jul 90	WASH YOUR FACE IN MY SINK Fourth & Broadway BRW 183	16	8
24 Nov 90	MY DEFINITION OF A BOOMBASTIC JAZZ STYLE Fourth & Broadway BRW 197	13	8
2 Mar 91	LUDI Fourth & Broadway BRW 206	39	3
16 Feb 91	AND NOW THE LEGACY BEGINS Fourth & Broadway BRLP 560	18	7

DREAMCATCHER
UK, male / female production / vocal trio (Singles: 4 Weeks) pos/wks

12 Jan 02	I DON'T WANNA LOSE MY WAY Positiva CDTIVS 157	14	4

DREAMERS See FREDDIE and the DREAMERS

DREAMHOUSE
UK, male vocal / instrumental group (Singles: 2 Weeks) pos/wks

3 Jun 95	STAY Chase CDPALACE 1	62	2

DREAMKEEPER
UK, female vocal duo – Nines and Aleesha (Albums: 1 Week) pos/wks

9 Aug 97	SPIRIT OF RELAXATION Flute SPIRICD 1	71	1

The DREAMWEAVERS
US, male / female vocal group (Singles: 18 Weeks) pos/wks

10 Feb 56 ★	IT'S ALMOST TOMORROW Brunswick 05515	1	18

DREEM TEEM
UK, male DJ / production trio (Singles: 14 Weeks) pos/wks

13 Dec 97	THE THEME 4 Liberty 74321542032	34	4
6 Nov 99	BUDDY X 99 4 Liberty LIBTCD 33 [1]	15	5
15 Dec 01	IT AIN'T ENOUGH ffrr / Public Demand FCD 401 [2]	20	5

[1] Dreem Teem vs Neneh Cherry [2] Dreem Teem vs Artful Dodger featuring MZ May and MC Alistair

DRELLS See Archie BELL and the DRELLS

Eddie DRENNON and B.B.S. UNLIMITED
US, male vocal / instrumental group (Singles: 6 Weeks) pos/wks

28 Feb 76	LET'S DO THE LATIN HUSTLE Pye International 7N 25702	20	6

Alan DREW *UK, male vocalist (Singles: 2 Weeks)*   pos/wks

26 Sep 63	**ALWAYS THE LONELY ONE** *Columbia DB 7090*	48	2

DRIFTERS *See The SHADOWS; Cliff RICHARD*

The DRIFTERS (209 Top 500)

Ever-changing, ever-popular US group, founded in 1953 by Clyde McPhatter (d. 1972) and still active today, with erstwhile members including Ben E King, Johnny Moore (d. 1998) and Rudy Lewis (d. 1964). Inducted into Rock and Roll Hall of Fame in 1988 (Singles: 176 Weeks, Albums: 109 Weeks)   pos/wks

8 Jan 60	**DANCE WITH ME (re)** *London HLE 8988*	17	5
3 Nov 60 ●	**SAVE THE LAST DANCE FOR ME** *London HLK 9201* ▲	2	18
16 Mar 61	**I COUNT THE TEARS** *London HLK 9287*	28	6
5 Apr 62	**WHEN MY LITTLE GIRL IS SMILING** *London HLK 9522*	31	3
10 Oct 63	**I'LL TAKE YOU HOME** *London HLK 9785*	37	5
24 Sep 64	**UNDER THE BOARDWALK** *Atlantic AT 4001*	45	4
8 Apr 65	**AT THE CLUB** *Atlantic AT 4019*	35	4
29 Apr 65	**COME ON OVER TO MY PLACE** *Atlantic AT 4023*	40	5
2 Feb 67	**BABY WHAT I MEAN** *Atlantic 584 065*	49	1
25 Mar 72 ●	**AT THE CLUB / SATURDAY NIGHT AT THE MOVIES (re) (re-issue)** *Atlantic K 10148*	3	20
26 Aug 72 ●	**COME ON OVER TO MY PLACE (re-issue)** *Atlantic K 10216*	9	11
4 Aug 73 ●	**LIKE SISTER AND BROTHER** *Bell 1313*	7	12
15 Jun 74 ●	**KISSIN' IN THE BACK ROW OF THE MOVIES** *Bell 1358*	2	13
12 Oct 74 ●	**DOWN ON THE BEACH TONIGHT** *Bell 1381*	7	9
8 Feb 75	**LOVE GAMES** *Bell 1396*	33	6
6 Sep 75 ●	**THERE GOES MY FIRST LOVE** *Bell 1433*	3	12
29 Nov 75 ●	**CAN I TAKE YOU HOME LITTLE GIRL** *Bell 1462*	10	10
13 Mar 76	**HELLO HAPPINESS** *Bell 1469*	12	8
11 Sep 76	**EVERY NITE'S A SATURDAY NIGHT WITH YOU** *Bell 1491*	29	7
18 Dec 76 ●	**YOU'RE MORE THAN A NUMBER IN MY LITTLE RED BOOK** *Arista 78*	5	12
14 Apr 79	**SAVE THE LAST DANCE FOR ME / WHEN MY LITTLE GIRL IS SMILING (re-issue)** *Lightning LIG 9014*	69	2
18 May 68	**GOLDEN HITS** *Atlantic 588103*	27	7
10 Jun 72	**GOLDEN HITS (re-issue)** *Atlantic K 40018*	26	8
8 Nov 75 ●	**24 ORIGINAL HITS** *Atlantic K 60106*	2	34
13 Dec 75	**LOVE GAMES** *Bell BELLS 246*	51	1
18 Oct 86	**THE VERY BEST OF THE DRIFTERS** *Telstar STAR 2280*	24	15
14 Mar 87	**STAND BY ME (THE ULTIMATE COLLECTION)** *Atlantic WX 90* [1]	14	8
20 Oct 90	**THE VERY BEST OF BEN E. KING & THE DRIFTERS** *Telstar STAR 2373* [1]	15	16
7 Nov 98	**THE VERY BEST OF BEN E. KING & THE DRIFTERS** *Warner.esp / Global TV RADCD 108* [1]	41	3
17 May 03 ●	**THE DEFINITIVE DRIFTERS** *Atlantic WSMCD 137*	8	17

[1] Ben E. King & The Drifters

'Saturday Night at the Movies' received chart credit with 'At the Club' only after the re-issue's return to the chart on 8 Apr 1972 The two albums entitled 'The Very Best of Ben E. King & The Drifters' are different

DRIFTWOOD *Holland, male production trio (Singles: 2 Weeks)*   pos/wks

1 Feb 03	**FREELOADER** *Positiva CDTIV 185*	32	2

Julie DRISCOLL, Brian AUGER and the TRINITY
UK, female vocalist and male instrumental group (Singles: 16 Weeks, Albums: 13 Weeks)   pos/wks

17 Apr 68 ●	**THIS WHEEL'S ON FIRE** *Marmalade 598006*	5	16
8 Jun 68	**OPEN** *Marmalade 608002*	12	13

Minnie DRIVER
UK, female actor / vocalist (Singles: 2 Weeks, Albums: 1 Week)   pos/wks

9 Oct 04	**EVERYTHING I'VE GOT IN MY POCKET** *Liberty 8674202*	34	2
30 Oct 04	**EVERYTHING I'VE GOT IN MY POCKET** *Liberty 8742702*	44	1

DRIVER 67 *UK, male vocalist – Paul Phillips (Singles: 12 Weeks)*   pos/wks

23 Dec 78 ●	**CAR 67** *Logo GO 336*	7	12

DRIZABONE *UK / US, male / female vocal / instrumental group (Singles: 18 Weeks, Albums: 1 Week)*   pos/wks

22 Jun 91	**REAL LOVE** *Fourth & Broadway BRW 223* [1]	16	8
26 Oct 91	**CATCH THE FIRE** *Fourth & Broadway BRW 232* [1]	54	2
23 Apr 94	**PRESSURE** *Fourth & Broadway BRCD 264*	33	2
15 Oct 94	**BRIGHTEST STAR** *Fourth & Broadway BRCD 293*	45	2

4 Mar 95	**REAL LOVE (re-recording)** *Fourth & Broadway BRCD 311*	24	4
19 Nov 94	**CONSPIRACY** *Fourth & Broadway BRCD 593*	72	1

[1] Driza Bone

Frank D'RONE *US, male vocalist (Singles: 6 Weeks)*   pos/wks

22 Dec 60	**STRAWBERRY BLONDE (THE BAND ROCKED ON)** *Mercury AMT 1123*	24	6

DROWNING POOL *US, male vocal / instrumental group (Singles: 3 Weeks, Albums: 2 Weeks)*   pos/wks

27 Apr 02	**BODIES** *Epic 6723172*	34	2
10 Aug 02	**TEAR AWAY** *Epic 6729832*	65	1
16 Feb 02	**SINNER** *Epic 5040912*	70	1
1 May 04	**DESENSITIZED** *Epic 5154112*	66	1

DRU HILL (see also SISQO)
US, male vocal group (Singles: 42 Weeks, Albums: 7 Weeks)   pos/wks

15 Feb 97	**TELL ME** *Fourth & Broadway BRCD 342*	30	3
10 May 97	**IN MY BED** *Fourth & Broadway BRCD 353*	16	3
11 Oct 97	**BIG BAD MAMMA** *Def Jam 5749792* [1]	12	3
6 Dec 97	**5 STEPS** *Island Black Music CID 675*	22	3
24 Oct 98 ●	**HOW DEEP IS YOUR LOVE (re)** *Island Black Music CID 725* [2] 9	8
6 Feb 99 ●	**THESE ARE THE TIMES** *Island Black Music CID 733*	4	6
10 Jul 99 ●	**WILD WILD WEST** *Columbia 6675962* [3] ▲	2	16
7 Nov 98	**ENTER THE DRU** *Island Black Music 5245422*	42	7

[1] Foxy Brown featuring Dru Hill [2] Dru Hill featuring Redman [3] Will Smith featuring Dru Hill – additional vocals Kool Moe Dee

DRUGSTORE *UK / US / Brazil, male / female vocal / instrumental group (Singles: 5 Weeks, Albums: 3 Weeks)*   pos/wks

10 Jun 95	**FADER** *Honey HONCD 7*	72	1
2 May 98	**EL PRESIDENT** *Roadrunner RR 22369*	20	3
4 Jul 98	**SOBER** *Roadrunner RR 22303*	68	1
8 Apr 95	**DRUGSTORE** *Honey 8286170*	31	2
16 May 98	**WHITE MAGIC FOR LOVERS** *Roadrunner RR 87112*	45	1

'El Presidente' includes additional vocals by Radiohead's Thom Yorke

DRUM CLUB *UK, male instrumental / production duo (Singles: 1 Week, Albums: 1 Week)*   pos/wks

6 Nov 93	**SOUND SYSTEM** *Butterfly BFLD 10*	62	1
20 Aug 94	**DRUMS ARE DANGEROUS** *Butterfly BFLCD 10*	53	1

DRUM THEATRE
UK, male vocal / instrumental group (Singles: 8 Weeks)   pos/wks

15 Feb 86	**LIVING IN THE PAST** *Epic A 6798*	67	2
17 Jan 87	**ELDORADO** *Epic EMU 1*	44	6

DRUMSOUND & Simon 'BASSLINE' SMITH *UK, male production duo – Andy Wright and Simon Smith (Singles: 2 Weeks)*   pos/wks

26 Jul 03	**JUNGLIST** *Technique TECH 021*	67	1
12 Jun 04	**THE ODYSSEY / BODY MOVIN'** *Prototype PROUK 004*	66	1

DRUNKENMUNKY
(see also KLUBHEADS; DA TECHNO BOHEMIAN, ITTY BITTY BOOZY WOOZY)
Holland, male production group (Singles: 2 Weeks)   pos/wks

4 Oct 03	**E** *All Around the World CDGLOBE 285*	41	2

DRUPI *Italy, male vocalist – Giampiero Anelli (Singles: 12 Weeks)*   pos/wks

1 Dec 73	**VADO VIA** *A&M AMS 7083*	17	12

DTOX
UK, male / female vocal / instrumental group (Singles: 1 Week)   pos/wks

21 Nov 92	**SHATTERED GLASS** *Vitality VITal 1*	75	1

John DU CANN *UK, male vocalist (Singles: 6 Weeks)*   pos/wks

22 Sep 79	**DON'T BE A DUMMY** *Vertigo 6059 241*	33	6

John DU PREZ *See MODERN ROMANCE*

The DUALERS *UK, male vocal / instrumental duo – Si Christone and Tyber O'Neil (Singles: 2 Weeks)*   pos/wks

30 Oct 04	**KISS ON THE LIPS** *Galley Music GALLEY 1003*	21	2

DUB CONSPIRACY See TRU FAITH & DUB CONSPIRACY

DUB PISTOLS
UK, male vocal / instrumental / production group (Singles: 2 Weeks) pos/wks

10 Oct 98	**CYCLONE** Concrete HARD 36CD	63	1
18 Oct 03	**PROBLEM IS** Distinctive DISNCD 107 [1]	66	1

[1] Dub Pistols featuring Terry Hall

DUB WAR
UK, male vocal / instrumental group (Singles: 5 Weeks) pos/wks

3 Jun 95	**STRIKE IT** Earache MOSH 138CD	70	1
27 Jan 96	**ENEMY MAKER** Earache MOSH 147CD	41	2
24 Aug 96	**CRY DIGNITY** Earache MOSH 163CDD	59	1
29 Mar 97	**MILLION DOLLAR LOVE** Earache MOSH 170CD1	73	1

The DUBLINERS
Ireland, male vocal / instrumental group (Singles: 45 Weeks, Albums: 91 Weeks) pos/wks

30 Mar 67 ●	**SEVEN DRUNKEN NIGHTS** Major Minor MM 506	7	17
30 Aug 67	**BLACK VELVET BAND** Major Minor MM 530	15	15
20 Dec 67	**MAIDS, WHEN YOU'RE YOUNG NEVER WED AN OLD MAN** Major Minor MM 551	43	3
28 Mar 87 ●	**THE IRISH ROVER** Stiff BUY 258 [1]	8	8
16 Jun 90	**JACK'S HEROES / WHISKEY IN THE JAR** Pogue Mahone YZ 500 [1]	63	2
13 May 67 ●	**A DROP OF THE HARD STUFF** Major Minor MMLP 3	5	41
9 Sep 67	**BEST OF THE DUBLINERS** Transatlantic TRA 158	25	11
7 Oct 67 ●	**MORE OF THE HARD STUFF** Major Minor MMLP 5	8	23
2 Mar 68	**DRINKIN' AND COURTIN'** Major Minor SMLP 14	31	3
25 Apr 87	**THE DUBLINERS 25 YEARS CELEBRATION** Stylus SMR 731	43	10
22 Mar 03	**SPIRIT OF THE IRISH** Sanctuary TVSAN 003	19	3

[1] The Pogues and The Dubliners

DUBSTAR
UK, female / male vocal / instrumental group (Singles: 26 Weeks, Albums: 20 Weeks) pos/wks

8 Jul 95	**STARS** Food CDFOOD 61	40	3
30 Sep 95	**ANYWHERE** Food CDFOOD 67	37	3
6 Jan 96	**NOT SO MANIC NOW** Food CDFOOD 71	18	5
30 Mar 96	**STARS (re-issue)** Food CDFOODS 75	15	6
3 Aug 96	**ELEVATOR SONG** Food CDFOOD 80	25	2
19 Jul 97	**NO MORE TALK** Food CDFOOD 96	20	3
20 Sep 97	**CATHEDRAL PARK** Food CDFOOD 104	41	1
7 Feb 98	**I WILL BE YOUR GIRLFRIEND** Food CDFOODS 108	28	2
27 May 00	**I (FRIDAY NIGHT)** Food CDFOODS 128	37	1
21 Oct 95	**DISGRACEFUL** Food FOODCDX 13	30	18
4 Oct 97	**GOODBYE** Food FOODCD 23	18	2

Ricardo 'Rikrok' DUCENT
Jamaica, male vocalist (Singles: 24 Weeks) pos/wks

17 Feb 01	**IT WASN'T ME (IMPORT)** MCA 1558032 [1]	31	3
10 Mar 01 ★	**IT WASN'T ME** MCA 1558022 [1] ◆ ■ ▲	1	20
3 Jul 04	**YOUR EYES** VP VPCD 6415 [2]	57	1

[1] Shaggy featuring Ricardo 'Rikrok' Ducent [2] Rik Rok featuring Shaggy

DUEL
UK, male instrumental duo - violins (Albums: 2 Weeks) pos/wks

28 Feb 04	**DUEL** Decca 4739992	47	2

Hilary DUFF
US, female vocalist / actor (Singles: 12 Weeks, Albums: 1 Week) pos/wks

1 Nov 03 ●	**SO YESTERDAY (re)** Hollywood HOL 003CD1	9	8
24 Apr 04	**COME CLEAN** Hollywood HOL 005CD1	18	4
15 Nov 03	**METAMORPHOSIS** Hollywood 5046692682 ▲	69	1

Mary DUFF See Daniel O'DONNELL

DUFFO
Australia, male vocalist - Jeff Duff (Singles: 2 Weeks) pos/wks

24 Mar 79	**GIVE ME BACK ME BRAIN** Beggars Banquet BEG 15	60	2

Stephen 'Tin Tin' DUFFY
UK, male vocalist (Singles: 24 Weeks, Albums: 7 Weeks) pos/wks

9 Jul 83	**HOLD IT** Curve X 9763 [1]	55	4
2 Mar 85 ●	**KISS ME** 10 TIN 2	4	11
18 May 85	**ICING ON THE CAKE** 10 TIN 3	14	9
20 Apr 85	**THE UPS AND DOWNS** 10 DIX 5	35	7

[1] Tin Tin

DUKE
UK, male vocalist (Singles: 6 Weeks) pos/wks

25 May 96	**SO IN LOVE WITH YOU** Encore CDCOR 009	66	1
26 Oct 96	**SO IN LOVE WITH YOU (re-issue)** Pukka CDPUKKA 11	22	4
11 Nov 00	**SO IN LOVE WITH YOU (re-mix)** 48k / Perfecto SPECT 08CDS	65	1

George DUKE
US, male vocalist / instrumentalist – keyboards (Singles: 6 Weeks, Albums: 4 Weeks) pos/wks

12 Jul 80	**BRAZILIAN LOVE AFFAIR** Epic EPC 8751	36	6
26 Jul 80	**BRAZILIAN LOVE AFFAIR** Epic EPC 84311	33	4

DUKE SPIRIT
UK, male / female vocal / instrumental group (Singles: 1 Week) pos/wks

12 Jun 04	**DARK IS LIGHT ENOUGH** Loog 9866673	55	1
16 Oct 04	**CUTS ACROSS THE LAND** Loog 9868119	45	1

DUKES (see also Steve EARLE)
UK, male vocal duo (Singles: 13 Weeks) pos/wks

17 Oct 81	**MYSTERY GIRL** WEA K 18867	47	7
1 May 82	**THANK YOU FOR THE PARTY** WEA K 19136	53	6

Candy DULFER
Holland, female instrumentalist – saxophone (Singles: 14 Weeks, Albums: 11 Weeks) pos/wks

24 Feb 90 ●	**LILY WAS HERE** RCA ZB 43045 [1]	6	12
4 Aug 90	**SAXUALITY** RCA PB 43769	60	2
18 Aug 90	**SAXUALITY** RCA PL 74661	27	9
13 Mar 93	**SAX-A-GO-GO** Ariola 4321111812	56	2

[1] David A Stewart featuring Candy Dulfer

Thuli DUMAKUDE
South Africa, female vocalist (Singles: 1 Week) pos/wks

2 Jan 88	**THE FUNERAL (SEPTEMBER 25, 1977)** MCA MCA 1228	75	1

The listed flip side of 'The Funeral' was 'Cry Freedom' by George Fenton and Jonas Gwangwa

DUMDUMS
UK, male vocal / instrumental group (Singles: 15 Weeks, Albums: 2 Weeks) pos/wks

11 Mar 00	**EVERYTHING** Good Behaviour CDGOOD 1	21	5
8 Jul 00	**CAN'T GET YOU OUT OF MY THOUGHTS** Good Behaviour GD OOD 2	18	5
23 Sep 00	**YOU DO SOMETHING TO ME** Good Behaviour CDGOLD 3	27	3
17 Feb 01	**ARMY OF TWO** Good Behaviour CDGOOD 5	27	2
30 Sep 00	**IT GOES WITHOUT SAYING** Good Behaviour CDGOOD 4	27	2

John DUMMER and Helen APRIL
UK, male / female vocal duo (Singles: 3 Weeks) pos/wks

28 Aug 82	**BLUE SKIES** Speed SPEED 8	54	3

DUMONDE
Germany, male / female production / vocal group (Singles: 3 Weeks) pos/wks

27 Jan 01	**TOMORROW** Variation VART 6	60	1
19 May 01	**NEVER LOOK BACK** Manifesto FESCD 83	36	2

DUNBLANE
UK, male / female vocal / instrumental group (Singles: 15 Weeks) pos/wks

21 Dec 96 ★	**KNOCKIN' ON HEAVEN'S DOOR / THROW THESE GUNS AWAY** BMG 74321442182 ■	1	15

Johnny DUNCAN and the BLUE GRASS BOYS
US, male vocalist, b. 7 Sep 1931, d. 15 Jul 2000, and UK, instrumental group (Singles: 20 Weeks) pos/wks

26 Jul 57 ●	**LAST TRAIN TO SAN FERNANDO** Columbia DB 3959	2	17
25 Oct 57	**BLUE, BLUE HEARTACHES** Columbia DB 3996	27	1
29 Nov 57	**FOOTPRINTS IN THE SNOW (re)** Columbia DB 4029	27	2

David DUNDAS
UK, male vocalist (Singles: 14 Weeks) pos/wks

24 Jul 76 ●	**JEANS ON** Air CHS 2094	3	9
9 Apr 77	**ANOTHER FUNNY HONEYMOON** Air CHS 2136	29	5

Errol DUNKLEY
Jamaica, male vocalist (Singles: 14 Weeks) pos/wks

22 Sep 79	**OK FRED** Scope SC 6	11	11
2 Feb 80	**SIT DOWN AND CRY** Scope SC 11	52	3

Clive DUNN
UK, male actor / vocalist (Singles: 28 Weeks)   pos/wks

28 Nov 70 ★ **GRANDAD** (re) *Columbia DB 8726* **1** 28

Simon DUPREE and the BIG SOUND *UK, male*
vocal / instrumental group (Singles: 16 Weeks, Albums: 1 Week)   pos/wks

22 Nov 67 ● **KITES** *Parlophone R 5646* **9** 13
3 Apr 68   **FOR WHOM THE BELL TOLLS** *Parlophone R 5670* **43** 3
16 Aug 67   **WITHOUT RESERVATIONS** *Parlophone PCS 7029*..............**39** 1

Jermaine 'JD' DUPRI *See Marques HOUSTON*

DURAN DURAN   (53   Top 500)
(see also ARCADIA; POWER STATION)
*New Romantics turned teen idols: Simon Le Bon (v), Nick Rhodes (k), John Taylor (b), Andy Taylor (g), Roger Taylor (d). The Birmingham band's successive Top 10 hits included 'A View to a Kill', the best-selling James Bond theme ever in the UK and the US. Group received MTV Lifetime Achievement award (2003), outstanding Contribution to British Music award at the 2004 Brits and returned to the Top 5 of the Singles and Albums charts in Oct 2004 (Singles: 226 Weeks, Albums: 422 Weeks)*pos/wks

21 Feb 81   **PLANET EARTH** *EMI 5137* **12** 11
9 May 81   **CARELESS MEMORIES** *EMI 5168* **37** 7
25 Jul 81 ● **GIRLS ON FILM** *EMI 5206* **5** 11
28 Nov 81   **MY OWN WAY** *EMI 5254* **14** 11
15 May 82 ● **HUNGRY LIKE THE WOLF** *EMI 5295* **5** 12
21 Aug 82 ● **SAVE A PRAYER** *EMI 5327* **2** 9
13 Nov 82 ● **RIO** *EMI 5346* **9** 11
26 Mar 83 ★ **IS THERE SOMETHING I SHOULD KNOW?** *EMI 5371* ■ **1** 9
29 Oct 83 ● **UNION OF THE SNAKE** (re) *EMI 5429* **3** 11
4 Feb 84 ● **NEW MOON ON MONDAY** *EMI DURAN 1* **9** 7
28 Apr 84 ★ **THE REFLEX** *EMI DURAN 2* ▲ **1** 14
3 Nov 84 ● **THE WILD BOYS** *Parlophone DURAN 3* **2** 14
18 May 85 ● **A VIEW TO A KILL** *Parlophone DURAN 007* ▲ **2** 16
1 Nov 86 ● **NOTORIOUS** (re) *EMI DDN 45* **7** 7
21 Feb 87   **SKIN TRADE** *EMI TRADE 1* **22** 6
25 Apr 87   **MEET EL PRESIDENTE** *EMI TOUR 1* **24** 5
1 Oct 88 ● **I DON'T WANT YOUR LOVE** *EMI YOUR 1* **14** 5
7 Jan 89 ● **ALL SHE WANTS IS** *EMI DD 11* **9** 5
22 Apr 89   **DO YOU BELIEVE IN SHAME?** *EMI DD 12* **30** 4
16 Dec 89   **BURNING THE GROUND** *EMI DD 13* **31** 5
4 Aug 90   **VIOLENCE OF SUMMER (LOVE'S TAKING OVER)**
       Parlophone DD 14 ....**20** 4
17 Nov 90   **SERIOUS** *Parlophone DD 15* **48** 3
30 Jan 93 ● **ORDINARY WORLD** *Parlophone CDDDS 16* **6** 9
10 Apr 93   **COME UNDONE** *Parlophone CDDDS 17* **13** 8
4 Sep 93   **TOO MUCH INFORMATION** *Parlophone CDDDS 18* **35** 3
25 Mar 95   **PERFECT DAY** *Parlophone CDDDS 20* **28** 4
17 Jun 95   **WHITE LINES (DON'T DO IT)** *Parlophone CDDD 19* [1] **17** 5
24 May 97   **OUT OF MY MIND** *Virgin VSCDT 1639* **21** 2
30 Jan 99   **ELECTRIC BARBARELLA** *EMI CDELEC 2000* **23** 3
10 Jun 00   **SOMEONE ELSE NOT ME** *Hollywood / Edel 0108845 HWR* **53** 1
16 Oct 04 ● **(REACH UP FOR THE) SUNRISE** *Epic 6753532* **5** 4
27 Jun 81 ● **DURAN DURAN** *EMI EMC 3372* **3** 118
22 May 82 ● **RIO** *EMI EMC 3411* **2** 109
3 Dec 83 ★ **SEVEN AND THE RAGGED TIGER** *EMI DD 1* ■ **1** 47
24 Nov 84 ● **ARENA** *Parlophone DD 2* **6** 31
6 Dec 86   **NOTORIOUS** *EMI DDN 331* **16** 16
29 Oct 88   **BIG THING** *EMI DDB 33*..**15** 5
25 Nov 89 ● **DECADE** *EMI DDX 10*...................................**5** 16
1 Sep 90   **LIBERTY** *Parlophone PCSD 112*................................**8** 4
27 Feb 93 ● **DURAN DURAN (THE WEDDING ALBUM)** *Parlophone CDDB 34* ..**4** 23
8 Apr 95   **THANK YOU** *Parlophone CDDDB 36* **12** 3
21 Nov 98 ● **GREATEST** *EMI 4962392* **4** 44
27 Mar 99   **STRANGE BEHAVIOUR** *EMI 4939722*...........................**70** 1
1 Jul 00   **POP TRASH** *Hollywood 0107512 HWR* **53** 1
23 Oct 04 ● **ASTRONAUT** *Epic 5179208*.............................**3** 4

[1] Duran Duran featuring Melle Mel and Grandmaster Flash and the Furious Five

Group was UK / US from 'Burning the Ground' Group were billed as Duranduran on EMI DDB 33. 'Greatest' peaked at No.15 on its original chart run and reached its new peak position in 2004

Jimmy DURANTE *US, male vocalist / comedian,*
b. 10 Feb 1893, d. 29 Jan 1980 (Singles: 1 Week)   pos/wks

14 Dec 96   **MAKE SOMEONE HAPPY** *Warner Bros. W 0385CD* **69** 1

Deanna DURBIN *Canada, female vocalist (Albums: 4 Weeks)*   pos/wks

30 Jan 82   **THE BEST OF DEANNA DURBIN** *MCA International MCL 1634* ..**84** 4

Judith DURHAM (see also The SEEKERS)
Australia, female vocalist (Singles: 5 Weeks, Albums: 16 Weeks)   pos/wks

15 Jun 67   **THE OLIVE TREE** *Columbia DB 8207* **33** 5
23 Apr 94 ● **A CARNIVAL OF HITS** *EMI CDEMTV 83* [1] **7** 14
30 Mar 96   **MONA LISAS** *EMI Premier CDJDTV 1*..........................**46** 2

[1] Judith Durham and The Seekers

Ian DURY and the BLOCKHEADS   (382   Top 500)
Art college lecturer-turned witty vocalist / songwriter, b. 12 May 1942, Billericay, Essex, UK, d. 27 Mar 2000. Ex-Kilburn & The High Roads member (1970-76) played his final show at the prestigious London Palladium. A 2001 tribute album included Paul McCartney and Robbie Williams (Singles: 56 Weeks, Albums: 123 Weeks)   pos/wks

29 Apr 78 ● **WHAT A WASTE!** *Stiff BUY 27* **9** 12
9 Dec 78 ★ **HIT ME WITH YOUR RHYTHM STICK** *Stiff BUY 38* [1] **1** 15
4 Aug 79 ● **REASONS TO BE CHEERFUL (PT. 3)** *Stiff BUY 50* **3** 8
30 Aug 80   **I WANT TO BE STRAIGHT** *Stiff BUY 90* **22** 7
15 Nov 80   **SUPERMAN'S BIG SISTER** *Stiff BUY 100* **51** 3
25 May 85   **HIT ME WITH YOUR RHYTHM STICK (re-mix)** *Stiff BUY 214* ..**55** 4
26 Oct 85   **PROFOUNDLY IN LOVE WITH PANDORA** *EMI EMI 5534* [2] ..**45** 5
27 Jul 91   **HIT ME WITH YOUR RHYTHM STICK '91** *Flying FLYR 1* **73** 1
11 Mar 00   **DRIP FED FRED** *Virgin VSCDT 1768* [3] **55** 1
22 Oct 77 ● **NEW BOOTS AND PANTIES!!** *Stiff SEEZ 4* [1] **5** 90
2 Jun 79 ● **DO IT YOURSELF** *Stiff SEEZ 14* **2** 18
6 Dec 80   **LAUGHTER** *Stiff SEEZ 30* **48** 4
10 Oct 81   **LORD UPMINSTER** *Polydor POLD 5042* **53** 4
4 Feb 84   **4000 WEEKS HOLIDAY** *Polydor POLD 5112* [2] **54** 2
11 Jul 98   **MR. LOVE PANTS** *Ronnie Harris DUR 1*........................**57** 2
9 Oct 99   **THE VERY BEST OF IAN DURY AND THE BLOCKHEADS –**
       REASONS TO BE CHEERFUL *EMI 5228882* **40** 2
30 Mar 02   **TEN MORE TURNIPS FROM THE TIP** *Ronnie Harris DUR 2*......**60** 1

[1] Ian and the Blockheads [2] Ian Dury [3] Madness featuring Ian Dury
[1] Ian Dury [2] Ian Dury and the Music Students

DUST BROTHERS
US, male production duo (Singles: 1 Week)   pos/wks

11 Dec 99   **THIS IS YOUR LIFE** *Restless 74321713962* **60** 1

DUST JUNKYS *UK, male vocal /*
instrumental group (Singles: 5 Weeks, Albums: 2 Weeks)   pos/wks

15 Nov 97   **(NONSTOPOPERATION)** *Polydor 5719732* **47** 2
28 Feb 98   **WHAT TIME IS IT?** *Polydor 5694912* **39** 2
16 May 98   **NOTHIN' PERSONAL** *Polydor 5699092* **62** 1
21 Mar 98   **DONE AND ... DUSTED** *Polydor 5570432* **35** 2

DUSTED (see also FAITHLESS; OUR TRIBE / ONE TRIBE; ROLLO; SPHINX)
UK, male production / instrumental duo –
Roland Armstrong and Mark Bates (Singles: 2 Weeks)   pos/wks

20 Jan 01   **ALWAYS REMEMBER TO RESPECT AND HONOUR YOUR**
       MOTHER PART ONE *Go Beat / Polydor GOBCD 36* **31** 2

Vocal by 12-year-old choirboy Alan Young

Slim DUSTY *Australia, male vocalist – David Kirkpatrick,*
b. 13 Jun 1927, d. 19 Sep 2003 (Singles: 15 Weeks)   pos/wks

30 Jan 59 ● **A PUB WITH NO BEER** *Columbia DB 4212*...................**3** 15

with Dick Carr and his Bushlanders

DUTCH featuring CRYSTAL WATERS
Holland, male producer and US, female vocalist (Singles: 4 Weeks) pos/wks

20 Sep 03   **MY TIME** *Illustrious / Epic CDILL 018* **22** 4

DUTCH FORCE
Holland, male producer – Benno De Goeij (Singles: 2 Weeks)   pos/wks

6 May 00   **DEADLINE** *Inferno CDFERN 27* **35** 2

Ondrea DUVERNEY *See HUSTLERS CONVENTION featuring Dave LAUDAT and Ondrea DUVERNEY*

DWEEB

UK, male / female vocal / instrumental trio (Singles: 2 Weeks) pos/wks

| 22 Feb 97 | SCOOBY DOO *Blanco Y Negro NEG 100CD* | **63** 1 |
| 7 Jun 97 | OH YEAH, BABY *Blanco Y Negro NEG 102CD1* | **70** 1 |

Sarah DWYER *See LANGE*

Bob DYLAN ⟨ 33 ⟩ [Top 500] (see also TRAVELING WILBURYS)

The most influential folk / rock vocalist / guitarist ever, b. Robert Zimmerman, 24 May 1941, Minnesota, US. The legendary performer, who led the 1960s folk music movement, redefined the term and, indeed, the image of the singer / songwriter. He was still adding to his impressive tally of Top 5 UK and US albums in 2001 (Singles: 137 Weeks, Albums: 618 Weeks) pos/wks

25 Mar 65	● TIMES THEY ARE A-CHANGIN' *CBS 201751*	**9** 11
29 Apr 65	● SUBTERRANEAN HOMESICK BLUES *CBS 201753*	**9** 9
17 Jun 65	MAGGIE'S FARM *CBS 201781*	**22** 8
19 Aug 65	● LIKE A ROLLING STONE *CBS 201811*	**4** 12
28 Oct 65	● POSITIVELY 4TH STREET *CBS 201824*	**8** 12
27 Jan 66	CAN YOU PLEASE CRAWL OUT YOUR WINDOW *CBS 201900*	**17** 5
14 Apr 66	ONE OF US MUST KNOW (SOONER OR LATER) *CBS 202053*	**33** 5
12 May 66	● RAINY DAY WOMEN NOS. 12 & 35 *CBS 202307*	**7** 8
21 Jul 66	I WANT YOU *CBS 202258*	**16** 9
14 May 69	I THREW IT ALL AWAY *CBS 4219*	**30** 6
13 Sep 69	● LAY LADY LAY *CBS 4434*	**5** 12
10 Jul 71	WATCHING THE RIVER FLOW *CBS 7329*	**24** 9
6 Oct 73	KNOCKIN' ON HEAVEN'S DOOR *CBS 1762*	**14** 9
7 Feb 76	HURRICANE *CBS 3878*	**43** 4
29 Jul 78	BABY STOP CRYING *CBS 6499*	**13** 11
28 Oct 78	IS YOUR LOVE IN VAIN *CBS 6718*	**56** 3
20 May 95	DIGNITY *Columbia 6620762*	**33** 2
11 Jul 98	LOVE SICK *Columbia 6659972*	**64** 1
14 Oct 00	THINGS HAVE CHANGED *Columbia 6693792*	**58** 1
23 May 64	★ THE FREEWHEELIN' BOB DYLAN *CBS BPG 62193*	**1** 49
11 Jul 64	● THE TIMES THEY ARE A-CHANGIN' *CBS BPG 62251*	**4** 20
21 Nov 64	● ANOTHER SIDE OF BOB DYLAN *CBS BPG 62429*	**8** 19
8 May 65	BOB DYLAN *CBS BPG 62022*	**13** 6
15 May 65	★ BRINGING IT ALL BACK HOME *CBS BPG 62515*	**1** 29
9 Oct 65	● HIGHWAY 61 REVISITED *CBS BPG 62572*	**4** 15
20 Aug 66	● BLONDE ON BLONDE *CBS DDP 66012*	**3** 15
14 Jan 67	● GREATEST HITS *CBS SBPG 62847*	**6** 82
2 Mar 68	★ JOHN WESLEY HARDING *CBS SBPG 63252*	**1** 29
17 May 69	★ NASHVILLE SKYLINE *CBS 63601*	**1** 42
11 Jul 70	★ SELF PORTRAIT *CBS 66250* ■	**1** 15
28 Nov 70	★ NEW MORNING *CBS 69001* ■	**1** 11
25 Dec 71	MORE BOB DYLAN GREATEST HITS *CBS 67238/9*	**12** 15
29 Sep 73	PAT GARRETT & BILLY THE KID (FILM SOUNDTRACK) *CBS 69042*	**29** 11
23 Feb 74	● PLANET WAVES *Island ILPS 9261* ▲	**7** 8
13 Jul 74	● BEFORE THE FLOOD *Asylum IDBD 1* [1]	**8** 7
15 Feb 75	● BLOOD ON THE TRACKS *CBS 69097* ▲	**4** 16
26 Jul 75	● THE BASEMENT TAPES *CBS 88147*	**8** 10
31 Jan 76	● DESIRE *CBS 86003* ▲	**3** 35
9 Oct 76	● HARD RAIN *CBS 86016*	**3** 7
1 Jul 78	● STREET LEGAL *CBS 86067*	**2** 20
26 May 79	● BOB DYLAN AT BUDOKAN *CBS 96004*	**4** 19
8 Sep 79	● SLOW TRAIN COMING *CBS 86095*	**2** 13
28 Jun 80	● SAVED *CBS 86113*	**3** 8
29 Aug 81	● SHOT OF LOVE *CBS 85178*	**6** 8
12 Nov 83	● INFIDELS *CBS 25539*	**9** 12
15 Dec 84	REAL LIVE *CBS 26334*	**54** 1
22 Jun 85	EMPIRE BURLESQUE *CBS 86313*	**11** 6
2 Aug 86	KNOCKED OUT LOADED *CBS 86326*	**35** 5
23 Apr 88	GREATEST HITS VOLUME 3 *CBS 4609071*	**47** 3
25 Jun 88	DOWN IN THE GROOVE *CBS 4602671*	**32** 3
18 Feb 89	DYLAN & THE DEAD *CBS 4633811* [2]	**38** 3
14 Oct 89	● OH MERCY *CBS 4658001*	**6** 7
22 Sep 90	UNDER THE RED SKY *CBS 4671881*	**13** 3
13 Apr 91	THE BOOTLEG SERIES VOLUMES 1-3 *Columbia 4680861*	**32** 5
14 Nov 92	GOOD AS I BEEN TO YOU *Columbia 4727102*	**18** 3
20 Nov 93	WORLD GONE WRONG *Columbia 4748572*	**35** 2
29 Apr 95	● UNPLUGGED *Columbia 4783742*	**10** 5
14 Jun 97	● THE BEST OF BOB DYLAN *Columbia SONYTV 28CD*	**6** 18
11 Oct 97	● TIME OUT OF MIND *Columbia 4869362*	**10** 4
24 Oct 98	LIVE AT THE ROYAL ALBERT HALL *Legacy 4914852*	**19** 2
20 May 00	THE BEST OF BOB DYLAN – VOLUME 2 *Columbia 4983612*	**22** 2
2 Jun 01	● THE ESSENTIAL BOB DYLAN *Columbia STVCD 116*	**9** 15
22 Sep 01	● LOVE AND THEFT *Columbia 5043642*	**3** 5

| 7 Dec 02 | LIVE 1975 – THE ROLLING THUNDER REVUE *Columbia 5101403* | **69** 1 |
| 10 Apr 04 | THE BOOTLEG SERIES VOL. 6 – BOB DYLAN LIVE 1964 – CONCERT AT PHILHARMONIC HALL *Columbia 5123582* | **33** 1 |

[1] Bob Dylan / The Band [2] Bob Dylan and The Grateful Dead

DYNAMITE MC

UK, male rapper – Dominic Smith (Singles: 2 Weeks) pos/wks

| 27 Sep 03 | HOTNESS *Ram RAMM 45* [1] | **66** 1 |
| 5 Jun 04 | RIDE *Ultimate Dilemma EW 288CD* | **54** 1 |

[1] Dynamite MC and Origin Unknown

DYNAMIX II featuring TOO TOUGH TEE

US, male vocal / instrumental group and rapper (Singles: 4 Weeks) pos/wks

| 8 Aug 87 | JUST GIVE THE DJ A BREAK *Cooltempo COOL 151* | **50** 4 |

DYNASTY

US, male / female vocal / instrumental group (Singles: 20 Weeks) pos/wks

13 Oct 79	I DON'T WANT TO BE A FREAK (BUT I CAN'T HELP MYSELF) *Solar FB 1694*	**20** 13
9 Aug 80	I'VE JUST BEGUN TO LOVE YOU *Solar SO 10*	**51** 4
21 May 83	DOES THAT RING A BELL *Solar E 9911*	**53** 3

Ronnie DYSON

US, male vocalist, b. 5 Jun 1950, d. 10 Nov 1990 (Singles: 6 Weeks) pos/wks

| 4 Dec 71 | WHEN YOU GET RIGHT DOWN TO IT *CBS 7449* | **34** 6 |

DYVERSE

UK, female vocal group (Singles: 1 Week) pos/wks

| 31 Jan 04 | MISGUIDED *Chilli Discs CCHIL 002* | **71** 1 |

Katherine E

US, female vocalist – Katherine Ellis (Singles: 7 Weeks) pos/wks

| 6 Apr 91 | I'M ALRIGHT *Dead Dead Good GOOD 2* | **41** 5 |
| 18 Jan 92 | THEN I FEEL GOOD *PWL Continental PWL 13* | **56** 2 |

Lizz E *See FRESH 4 featuring Lizz E*

Sheila E *US, female vocalist / instrumentalist / percussion – Sheila Escovedo (Singles: 9 Weeks)*

pos/wks

| 23 Feb 85 | THE BELLE OF ST MARK *Warner Bros. W 9180* | **18** 9 |

E-LUSTRIOUS (see also DIRECKT) *UK, male instrumental / production duo – Mike Kirwin and Danny Bennett (Singles: 2 Weeks)*

pos/wks

| 15 Feb 92 | DANCE NO MORE *MOS MOS 001T* [1] | **58** 1 |
| 2 Jul 94 | IN YOUR DANCE *UFG UFG 6CD* | **69** 1 |

[1] E-Lustrious featuring Deborah French

E-MALE *UK, male vocal / instrumental group (Singles: 1 Week)* pos/wks

| 31 Jan 98 | WE ARE E-MALE *East West EW 137CD* | **44** 1 |

E-MAN *See Jon CUTLER featuring E-MAN*

EMF *UK, male vocal / instrumental group*
(Singles: 50 Weeks, Albums: 22 Weeks)   pos/wks

3 Nov 90	●	UNBELIEVABLE *Parlophone R 6273* ▲	**3** 13
2 Feb 91	●	I BELIEVE *Parlophone R 6279*	**6** 7
27 Apr 91		CHILDREN *Parlophone R 6288*	**19** 5
31 Aug 91		LIES *Parlophone R 6295*	**28** 3
2 May 92		UNEXPLAINED (EP) *Parlophone SGE 2026*	**18** 4
19 Sep 92		THEY'RE HERE *Parlophone R 6321*	**29** 3
21 Nov 92		IT'S YOU *Parlophone R 6327*	**23** 3
25 Feb 95		PERFECT DAY *Parlophone CDRS 6401*	**27** 3
8 Jul 95	●	I'M A BELIEVER *Parlophone CDR 6412* [1]	**3** 8
28 Oct 95		AFRO KING *Parlophone CDRS 6416*	**51** 1
18 May 91	●	SCHUBERT DIP *Parlophone PCS 7353*	**3** 19
10 Oct 92		STIGMA *Parlophone CDPCSD 122*	**19** 2
18 Mar 95		CHA CHA CHA *Parlophone CDPCSD 165*	**30** 1

[1] EMF and Reeves and Mortimer

Tracks on Unexplained (EP): Getting Through / Far From Me / The Same / Search and Destroy

E-MOTION *UK, male vocal / instrumental duo –*
Alan Angus and Justin Oliver (Singles: 7 Weeks)   pos/wks

3 Feb 96	THE NAUGHTY NORTH AND THE SEXY SOUTH *Soundproof MCSTD 40017*	**20** 3
17 Aug 96	I STAND ALONE *Soundproof MCSTD 40061*	**60** 1
26 Oct 96	THE NAUGHTY NORTH AND THE SEXY SOUTH (re-mix) *Soundproof MCSTD 40076*	**17** 3

EPMD (see also Kurtis MANTRONIK)
US, male rap / DJ duo (Singles: 1 Week, Albums: 1 Week)   pos/wks

15 Aug 98	STRICTLY BUSINESS *Parlophone CDR 6502* [1]	**43** 1
16 Feb 91	BUSINESS AS USUAL *Def Jam 4676971*	**69** 1

[1] Kurtis Mantronik vs EPMD

E-ROTIC *Germany / US, male / female*
vocal / instrumental group (Singles: 2 Weeks)   pos/wks

3 Jun 95	MAX DON'T HAVE SEX WITH YOUR EX *Stip CDSTIP 2*	**45** 2

E-SMOOVE featuring Latanza WATERS
(see also THICK D: The PRAISE CATS) US, male producer –
Eric Miller and US, female vocalist (Singles: 1 Week)   pos/wks

15 Aug 98	DEJA VU *AM:PM 5827671*	**63** 1

E STREET BAND *See Bruce SPRINGSTEEN*

E-TRAX *Germany, male production duo (Singles: 1 Week)*   pos/wks

9 Jun 01	LET'S ROCK *Tidy Trax TIDY 155CD*	**60** 1

E-TYPE *Sweden, male vocalist – Bo Eriksson (Singles: 2 Weeks)*   pos/wks

23 Sep 95	THIS IS THE WAY *Ffrreedom TABCD 237*	**53** 1
24 Jun 00	CAMPIONE 2000 *Polydor 1580822*	**58** 1

E.U. *See SALT-N-PEPA*

EYC *US, male vocal group (Singles: 36 Weeks, Albums: 5 Weeks)*   pos/wks

11 Dec 93	FEELIN' ALRIGHT *MCA MCSTD 1952*	**16** 8
5 Mar 94	THE WAY YOU WORK IT *MCA MCSTD 1963*	**14** 7
14 May 94	NUMBER ONE *MCA MCSTD 1976*	**27** 5
30 Jul 94	BLACK BOOK *MCA MCSTD 1987*	**13** 6
10 Dec 94	ONE MORE CHANCE *MCA MCSTD 2025*	**25** 2
23 Sep 95	OOH-AH-AA (I FEEL IT) *Gasoline Alley MCSTD 2096*	**33** 2
2 Dec 95	IN THE BEGINNING *Gasoline Alley MCSTD 2107*	**41** 2
16 Apr 94	EXPRESS YOURSELF CLEARLY *MCA MCD 11061*	**14** 5

E-Z ROLLERS
UK, male / female vocal / instrumental group (Singles: 4 Weeks)   pos/wks

24 Apr 99	WALK THIS LAND *Moving Shadow 130CD1*	**18** 3
8 Feb 03	BACK TO LOVE *Moving Shadow 159CD*	**61** 1

E-ZEE POSSEE
UK, male / female vocal / instrumental group (Singles: 16 Weeks)   pos/wks

26 Aug 89	EVERYTHING STARTS WITH AN 'E' (re) *More Protein PROT 1*	**15** 9
20 Jan 90	LOVE ON LOVE *More Protein PROT 3* [1]	**59** 3
30 Jun 90	THE SUN MACHINE *More Protein PROT 4*	**62** 3
21 Sep 91	BREATHING IS E-ZEE *More Protein PROT 12* [2]	**72** 1

[1] E-Zee Possee with Dr Mouthquake [2] E-Zee Possee featuring Tara Newley

'Everything Starts with an 'E' did not reach its peak position until it re-entered the chart in Mar 1990

The EAGLES [72] **Top 500**
Legendary west coast rock group, which includes Glenn Frey (v/g), Don Henley (v/d) and Joe Walsh (v/g). America's biggest-selling album group disbanded in 1982, but re-united over a decade later for the Hell Freezes Over tour. No album in the US has outsold 'Their Greatest Hits 1971-1975' (28 million) and their total worldwide album sales are reportedly over 100 million (Singles: 52 Weeks, Albums: 476 Weeks)   pos/wks

9 Aug 75		ONE OF THESE NIGHTS *Asylum AYM 543* ▲	**23** 7
1 Nov 75		LYIN' EYES *Asylum AYM 548*	**23** 7
6 Mar 76		TAKE IT TO THE LIMIT *Asylum K 13029*	**12** 7
15 Jan 77		NEW KID IN TOWN *Asylum K 13069*	**20** 7
16 Apr 77	●	HOTEL CALIFORNIA *Asylum K 13079* ▲	**8** 10
16 Dec 78		PLEASE COME HOME FOR CHRISTMAS *Asylum K 13145*	**30** 5
13 Oct 79		HEARTACHE TONIGHT *Asylum K 12394* ▲	**40** 5
1 Dec 79		THE LONG RUN *Elektra K 12404*	**66** 2
13 Jul 96		LOVE WILL KEEP US ALIVE *Geffen GFSTD 21980*	**52** 1
25 Oct 03		HOLE IN THE WORLD *Eagles 8122745472*	**69** 1
27 Apr 74		ON THE BORDER *Asylum SYL 9016*	**28** 9
12 Jul 75	●	ONE OF THESE NIGHTS *Asylum SYLA 8759* ▲	**8** 41
12 Jul 75		DESPERADO *Asylum SYLL 9011*	**39** 9
6 Mar 76	●	THEIR GREATEST HITS 1971-1975 *Asylum K 53017* ▲	**2** 118
25 Dec 76	●	HOTEL CALIFORNIA *Asylum K 53051* ▲	**2** 70
13 Oct 79	●	THE LONG RUN *Asylum K 52181* ▲	**4** 16
22 Nov 80		LIVE *Asylum K 62032*	**24** 13
18 May 85	●	THE BEST OF EAGLES *Asylum EKT 5*	**8** 74
23 Jul 94	●	THE VERY BEST OF THE EAGLES *Elektra 9548323752*	**4** 54
19 Nov 94		HELL FREEZES OVER *Geffen GED 24725* ▲	**18** 21
9 Jun 01	●	THE VERY BEST OF THE EAGLES *Elektra 7559626802*	**3** 47
1 Nov 03		THE COMPLETE GREATEST HITS *WSM 8122737312*	**27** 4

'The Very Best of The Eagles' (2001) was an expanded and repackaged version of the 1994 album of the same name

EAMON *US, male vocalist – Eamon Doyle*
(Singles: 26 Weeks, Albums: 9 Weeks)   pos/wks

3 Apr 04		F**K IT (I DON'T WANT YOU BACK) (Import) *Jive 82876604852*	**46** 3
24 Apr 04	★	F**K IT (I DON'T WANT YOU BACK) *Jive 82876608502* ■	**1** 19
16 Oct 04		LOVE THEM *Jive 8287663912* [1]	**27** 4
17 Apr 04	●	I DON'T WANT YOU BACK *Jive JIV 583702*	**6** 9

[1] Eamon featuring Ghostface

Ghostface appears on a B-side re-mix of 'Love Them' and not the main version, but is credited on the sleeve. The track's full title, 'Love Them Hos', was shortened to be radio friendly

Robert EARL *UK, male vocalist – Monty Leigh (Singles: 27 Weeks)*   pos/wks

25 Apr 58	I MAY NEVER PASS THIS WAY AGAIN *Philips PB 805*	**14** 13
24 Oct 58	MORE THAN EVER (COME PRIMA) (re) *Philips PB 867*	**26** 4
13 Feb 59	THE WONDERFUL SECRET OF LOVE *Philips PB 891*	**17** 10

Charles EARLAND *US, male instrumentalist –*
keyboards, b. 24 May 1941, d. 11 Dec 1999 (Singles: 5 Weeks)   pos/wks

19 Aug 78	LET THE MUSIC PLAY *Mercury 6167 703*	**46** 5

Steve EARLE *US, male vocalist /*
instrumentalist – guitar (Singles: 7 Weeks, Albums: 22 Weeks)   pos/wks

15 Oct 88	COPPERHEAD ROAD *MCA MCA 1280*	**45** 6
31 Dec 88	JOHNNY COME LATELY *MCA MCA 1301*	**75** 1
4 Jul 87	EXIT 0 *MCA MCF 3379*	**77** 2
19 Nov 88	COPPERHEAD ROAD *MCA MCF 3426*	**42** 8
7 Jul 90	THE HARD WAY *MCA MCG 6095* [1]	**22** 4
19 Oct 91	SHUT UP AND DIE LIKE AN AVIATOR *MCA MCA 10315* [1]	**62** 1
23 Mar 96	I FEEL ALRIGHT *Transatlantic TRACD 227*	**44** 3
18 Oct 97	EL CORAZON *Warner Bros. 9362467892*	**59** 1
6 Mar 99	THE MOUNTAIN *Grapevine GRACD 252* [2]	**51** 1
17 Jun 00	TRANSCENDENTAL BLUES *Epic 4980749*	**32** 1
4 Sep 04	THE REVOLUTION STARTS NOW *Rykodisc RCD 17023*	**66** 1

[1] Steve Earle and The Dukes [2] Steve Earle and the Del McCoury Band

The EARLIES
US / UK, male vocal / instrumental group (Singles: 1 Week) pos/wks

| 6 Nov 04 | MORNING WONDER *WEA IAMNAMES 07* | ..67 | 1 |

EARLY MUSIC CONSORT directed by David MUNROW
UK, male / female instrumental group (Singles: 1 Week) pos/wks

| 3 Apr 71 | HENRY VIII SUITE (EP) *BBC RESL 1* | ..49 | 1 |

Tracks on Henry VIII Suite (EP): Fanfare, Passomezo du Roy, Gaillarde d'Escosse / Pavane, Mille Ducats / Larocque Gaillarde / Allemande / Wedding March, La Mourisque / If Love Now Reigned / Ronde, Pourquoi

EARTH WIND AND FIRE (197) Top 500
Colourful, mystical, Los Angeles-based group noted for flamboyant stage performances. The band featured founding member Maurice White (d/v), Philip Bailey (v), Ronnie Laws (s/fl) and Verdine White (b). Few R&B acts outsold them in the late 1970s, when they achieved eight successive US Top 10 albums (Singles: 128 Weeks, Albums: 167 Weeks) pos/wks

12 Feb 77	SATURDAY NITE *CBS 4835*	..17	9
11 Feb 78	FANTASY *CBS 6056*	..14	10
13 May 78	JUPITER *CBS 6267*	..41	5
29 Jul 78	MAGIC MIND (re) *CBS 6490*	..54	5
7 Oct 78	GOT TO GET YOU INTO MY LIFE *CBS 6553*	..33	7
9 Dec 78 ●	SEPTEMBER *CBS 6922*	..3	13
12 May 79 ●	BOOGIE WONDERLAND *CBS 7292* [1]	..4	13
28 Jul 79 ●	AFTER THE LOVE HAS GONE *CBS 7721*	..4	10
6 Oct 79	STAR *CBS 7902*	..16	8
15 Dec 79	CAN'T LET GO *CBS 8077*	..46	7
8 Mar 80	IN THE STONE *CBS 8252*	..53	3
11 Oct 80	LET ME TALK *CBS 8982*	..29	5
20 Dec 80	BACK ON THE ROAD *CBS 9377*	..63	4
7 Nov 81 ●	LET'S GROOVE *CBS A 1679*	..3	13
6 Feb 82	I'VE HAD ENOUGH *CBS A 1959*	..29	6
5 Feb 83	FALL IN LOVE WITH ME *CBS A 2927*	..47	4
7 Nov 87	SYSTEM OF SURVIVAL *CBS EWF 1*	..54	3
31 Jul 99	SEPTEMBER (re-mix) *INCredible INCR 24CD*	..25	3
21 Jan 78	ALL 'N' ALL *CBS 86051*	..13	23
16 Dec 78	THE BEST OF EARTH WIND AND FIRE VOLUME 1 *CBS 83284* ..6	42
23 Jun 79 ●	I AM *CBS 86084*	..5	41
1 Nov 80 ●	FACES *CBS 88498*	..10	6
14 Nov 81	RAISE! *CBS 85272*	..14	22
19 Feb 83	POWERLIGHT *CBS 25120*	..22	7
10 May 86 ●	THE COLLECTION *K-Tel NE 1322*	..5	13
28 Nov 92	THE VERY BEST OF EARTH WIND AND FIRE *Telstar TCD 2631* ..40	6
28 Sep 96	BOOGIE WONDERLAND – THE VERY BEST OF EARTH WIND AND FIRE *Telstar TCD 2879*	..29	4
7 Aug 99	THE ULTIMATE COLLECTION *Columbia SONYTV 66CD*	..34	3

[1] Earth Wind and Fire with The Emotions

EARTHLING *UK, male vocal /*
instrumental duo (Singles: 2 Weeks, Albums: 1 Week) pos/wks

14 Oct 95	ECHO ON MY MIND PART II *Cooltempo CDCOOL 312*	..61	1
1 Jun 96	BLOOD MUSIC (EP) *Cooltempo CDCOOL 319*	..69	1
3 Jun 95	RADAR *Cooltempo CTCD 44*	..66	1

Tracks on Blood Music (EP): First Transmission / Because the Night / Soup or No Soup / Infinite M

EAST 57th STREET featuring Donna ALLEN
UK, male production trio and US, female vocalist (Singles: 3 Weeks) pos/wks

| 11 Oct 97 | SATURDAY *AM:PM 5823752* | ..29 | 3 |

EAST OF EDEN
UK, male instrumental group (Singles: 12 Weeks, Albums: 2 Weeks) pos/wks

| 17 Apr 71 ● | JIG-A-JIG *Deram DM 297* | ..7 | 12 |
| 14 Mar 70 | SNAFU *Deram SML 1050* | ..29 | 2 |

EAST 17 (225) Top 500
London-based singing, rapping and dancing lads with international teen appeal: Tony Mortimer (v/k), Brian Harvey (v), John Hendy (v), Terry Coldwell (v). Bad press and personal problems resulted in main songwriter Mortimer quitting, and a name change to E-17 for their short-lived 1998 comeback. Biggest-selling single: 'Stay Another Day' 910,000 (Singles: 170 Weeks, Albums: 102 Weeks) pos/wks

29 Aug 92 ●	HOUSE OF LOVE *London LON 325*	..10	9
14 Nov 92	GOLD (re) *London LON 331*	..28	8
30 Jan 93 ●	DEEP *London LOCDP 334*	..5	10

10 Apr 93	SLOW IT DOWN *London LONCD 339*	..13	7
26 Jun 93	WEST END GIRLS *London LONCD 344*	..11	7
4 Dec 93 ●	IT'S ALRIGHT *London LONCD 345*	..3	14
14 May 94 ●	AROUND THE WORLD *London LONCD 349*	..3	13
1 Oct 94 ●	STEAM *London LONCD 353*	..7	8
3 Dec 94 ★	STAY ANOTHER DAY (re) *London LONCD 354*	..1	16
25 Mar 95 ●	LET IT RAIN *London LONCD 363*	..10	7
17 Jun 95	HOLD MY BODY TIGHT *London LONCD 367*	..12	7
4 Nov 95 ●	THUNDER *London LONCD 373*	..4	14
10 Feb 96 ●	DO U STILL *London LONCD 379*	..7	7
10 Aug 96	SOMEONE TO LOVE *London LONCD 385*	..16	8
2 Nov 96 ●	IF YOU EVER *London LONCD 388* [1]	..2	15
18 Jan 97	HEY CHILD *London LONCD 390*	..3	5
14 Nov 98 ●	EACH TIME *Telstar CDSTAS 3017* [2]	..2	10
13 Mar 99	BETCHA CAN'T WAIT *Telstar CDSTAS 3031* [2]	..12	5
27 Feb 93 ★	WALTHAMSTOW *London 8283732* ■	..1	33
29 Oct 94	STEAM *London 8285422*	..3	36
25 Nov 95	UP ALL NIGHT *London 8286992*	..7	15
16 Nov 96 ●	AROUND THE WORLD – HIT SINGLES – THE JOURNEY SO FAR *London 8288522* [1]	..3	16
28 Nov 98	RESURRECTION *Telstar TCD 3015* [2]	..43	2

[1] East 17 featuring Gabrielle [2] E-17 [1] East Seventeen [2] E-17

'Walthamstow' changed its catalogue number to 8284262 during its chart run

EAST SIDE BEAT *Italy, male vocal / instrumental duo –*
Carl Fanini and Francesco Petrocchi (Singles: 18 Weeks) pos/wks

30 Nov 91 ●	RIDE LIKE THE WIND *ffrr F 176*	..3	11
19 Dec 92	ALIVE AND KICKING *ffrr F 206*	..26	6
29 May 93	YOU'RE MY EVERYTHING *ffrr FCD 207*	..65	1

EASTERHOUSE
UK, male vocal / instrumental group (Albums: 1 Week) pos/wks

| 28 Jun 86 | CONTENDERS *Rough Trade ROUGH 94* | ..91 | 1 |

EASTERN LANE
UK, male vocal / instrumental group (Singles: 3 Weeks) pos/wks

15 Nov 03	FEED YOUR ADDICTION *Rough Trade RTRADSCD 132*	..72	1
13 Mar 04	SAFFRON *Rough Trade RTRADSCD 156*	..55	1
6 Nov 04	I SAID PIG ON FRIDAY *Rough Trade RTRADSCD 199*	..65	1

Sheena EASTON (see also PRINCE)
UK, female vocalist (Singles: 104 Weeks, Albums: 37 Weeks) pos/wks

5 Apr 80 ●	MODERN GIRL (re) *EMI 5042*	..8	15
19 Jul 80 ●	9 TO 5 *EMI 5066* ▲	..3	15
25 Oct 80	ONE MAN WOMAN *EMI 5114*	..14	6
14 Feb 81	TAKE MY TIME *EMI 5135*	..44	5
2 May 81	WHEN HE SHINES *EMI 5166*	..12	8
27 Jun 81 ●	FOR YOUR EYES ONLY *EMI 5195*	..8	13
12 Sep 81	JUST ANOTHER BROKEN HEART *EMI 5232*	..33	8
5 Dec 81	YOU COULD HAVE BEEN WITH ME *EMI 5252*	..54	3
31 Jul 82	MACHINERY *EMI 5326*	..38	5
12 Feb 83	WE'VE GOT TONIGHT *Liberty UP 658* [1]	..28	7
21 Jan 89	THE LOVER IN ME *MCA MCA 1289*	..15	8
18 Mar 89	DAYS LIKE THIS *MCA MCA 1325*	..43	3
15 Jul 89	101 *MCA MCA 1348*	..54	2
18 Nov 89	THE ARMS OF ORION *Warner Bros. W 2757* [2]	..27	5
9 Dec 00	GIVING UP GIVING IN *Universal MCSTD 40244*	..54	1
31 Jan 81	TAKE MY TIME *EMI EMC 3354*	..17	19
3 Oct 81	YOU COULD HAVE BEEN WITH ME *EMI EMC 3378*	..33	4
25 Sep 82	MADNESS MONEY AND MUSIC *EMI EMC 3414*	..44	4
15 Oct 83	BEST KEPT SECRET *EMI EMC 1077951*	..99	1
4 Mar 89	THE LOVER IN ME *MCA MCG 6036*	..30	7

[1] Kenny Rogers and Sheena Easton [2] Prince with Sheena Easton

'Modern Girl' reached its peak position only on re-entry in Aug 1980

EASTSIDE CONNECTION
US, disco aggregation (Singles: 3 Weeks) pos/wks

| 8 Apr 78 | YOU'RE SO RIGHT FOR ME *Creole CR 149* | ..44 | 3 |

Clint EASTWOOD *US, male actor / vocalist (Singles: 2 Weeks)* pos/wks

| 7 Feb 70 | I TALK TO THE TREES *Paramount PARA 3004* | ..18 | 2 |

This is the flip side of 'Wand'rin Star' by Lee Marvin and was listed with Marvin's A-side for two weeks only

Clint EASTWOOD and GENERAL SAINT
UK, male vocal duo (Singles: 3 Weeks, Albums: 3 Weeks) pos/wks

29 Sep 84	LAST PLANE (ONE WAY TICKET) *MCA MCA 910* [1]	**51**	3
6 Feb 82	TWO BAD DJ *Greensleeves GREL 24*	**99**	2
28 May 83	STOP THAT TRAIN *Greensleeves GREL 53*	**98**	1

[1] Clint Eastwood and General Saint

EASY RIDERS *See Frankie LAINE*

The EASYBEATS *Australia / Holland / UK, male*
vocal / instrumental group (Singles: 24 Weeks) pos/wks

27 Oct 66 ●	FRIDAY ON MY MIND *United Artists UP 1157*	**6**	15
10 Apr 68	HELLO, HOW ARE YOU *United Artists UP 2209*	**20**	9

EASYWORLD
UK, male vocal / instrumental trio (Singles: 7 Weeks) pos/wks

1 Jun 02	BLEACH *Jive 9253552*	**67**	1
21 Sep 02	YOU & ME *Jive 9254092*	**57**	1
8 Feb 03	JUNKIES *Jive 9254522*	**40**	1
18 Oct 03	2ND AMENDMENT *Jive 82876554692*	**42**	1
31 Jan 04	'TIL THE DAY *Jive 82876585362*	**27**	2
11 Sep 04	HOW DID IT EVER COME TO THIS? *Jive 82876632102*	**50**	1

EAT *UK / US, male / female vocal /*
instrumental group (Singles: 1 Week) pos/wks

12 Jun 93	BLEED ME WHITE *Fiction FICCD 48*	**73**	1

EAT STATIC *UK, male production duo – Marv Pepler*
and Joie Hinton (Singles: 3 Weeks, Albums: 5 Weeks) pos/wks

22 Feb 97	HYBRID *Planet Dog BARK 024CD*	**41**	1
27 Sep 97	INTERCEPTOR *Planet Dog BARK 030CD*	**44**	1
27 Jun 98	CONTACT ... *Planet Dog BARK 033CD*	**67**	1
15 May 93	ABDUCTION *Planet Dog BARKCD 1*	**62**	1
25 Jun 94	IMPLANT *Planet Dog BARKCD 005*	**13**	3
25 Oct 97	SCIENCE OF THE GODS *Planet Dog BARKCD 029*	**60**	1

Cleveland EATON
US, male instrumentalist – keyboards (Singles: 6 Weeks) pos/wks

23 Sep 78	BAMA BOOGIE WOOGIE *Gull GULS 63*	**35**	6

EAV *Austria, male vocal / instrumental group (Singles: 4 Weeks)* pos/wks

27 Sep 86	BA-BA-BANKROBBERY (ENGLISH VERSION) *Columbia DB 9139*	**63**	4

EAZY-E (see also NWA) *US, male rapper – Eric Wright,*
b. 7 Sep 1964, d. 26 Mar 1995 (Singles: 3 Weeks, Albums: 1 Week) pos/wks

6 Jan 96	JUST TAH LET YOU KNOW *Epic 6628162*	**30**	3
10 Feb 96	STR8 OFF THA STREETZ OF MUTHAPHUKKIN COMPTON *Ruthless 4835762*	**66**	1

EBON-E *See RMXCRW featuring EBON-E plus AMBUSH*

EBONY DUBSTERS (see also SHY FX) *UK, male production*
duo – Andre Williams and Mark Royal (Singles: 3 Weeks) pos/wks

24 Jan 04	MURDERATION *Ebony EBR 029*	**59**	2
22 May 04	NUMBER 1 / THE RITUAL *Ebony EBR 030*	**58**	1

ECHELON *UK, male vocal / instrumental group (Singles: 1 Week)* pos/wks

20 Nov 04	PLUS *Poptones MC 5095SCD*	**57**	1

ECHO and the BUNNYMEN ⟨363 Top 500⟩
Cult alternative rock group originally from Liverpool, UK, who named
themselves after their drum machine. Ian McCulloch (v), b. 5 May 1959, front
man of this moody and atmospheric group, went solo in 1988. The original
line-up reformed in 1997 (Singles: 86 Weeks, Albums: 100 Weeks) pos/wks

17 May 80	RESCUE *Korova KOW 1*	**62**	1
18 Apr 81	SHINE SO HARD (EP) *Korova ECHO 1*	**37**	4
18 Jul 81	A PROMISE *Korova KOW 15*	**49**	4
29 May 82	THE BACK OF LOVE *Korova KOW 24*	**19**	7
22 Jan 83 ●	THE CUTTER *Korova KOW 26*	**8**	8
16 Jul 83	NEVER STOP *Korova KOW 28*	**15**	7
28 Jan 84 ●	THE KILLING MOON *Korova KOW 32*	**9**	6
21 Apr 84	SILVER *Korova KOW 34*	**30**	5
14 Jul 84	SEVEN SEAS *Korova KOW 35*	**16**	7
19 Oct 85	BRING ON THE DANCING HORSES *Korova KOW 43*	**21**	7
13 Jun 87	THE GAME *WEA YZ 134*	**28**	4
1 Aug 87	LIPS LIKE SUGAR *WEA YZ 144*	**36**	4
20 Feb 88	PEOPLE ARE STRANGE *WEA YZ 175*	**29**	5
2 Mar 91	PEOPLE ARE STRANGE (re-issue) *East West YZ 567*	**34**	4
28 Jun 97 ●	NOTHING LASTS FOREVER *London LOCDP 396*	**8**	6
13 Sep 97	I WANT TO BE THERE WHEN YOU COME *London LONCD 399*	**30**	2
8 Nov 97	DON'T LET IT GET YOU DOWN *London LOCDP 406*	**50**	1
27 Mar 99	RUST *London LONCD 424*	**23**	3
5 May 01	IT'S ALRIGHT *Cooking Vinyl FRYCD 104*	**41**	1
26 Jul 80 ●	CROCODILES *Korova KODE 1*	**17**	6
6 Jun 81 ●	HEAVEN UP HERE *Korova KODE 3*	**10**	16
12 Feb 83 ●	PORCUPINE *Korova KODE 6*	**2**	17
12 May 84 ●	OCEAN RAIN *Korova KODE 8*	**4**	26
23 Nov 85 ●	SONGS TO LEARN & SING *Korova KODE 13*	**6**	15
18 Jul 87 ●	ECHO AND THE BUNNYMEN *WEA WX 108*	**4**	9
21 Jun 97	BALLYHOO – THE BEST OF ECHO AND THE BUNNYMEN *Korova 630191032*	**59**	1
26 Jul 97 ●	EVERGREEN *London 8289052*	**8**	7
17 Apr 99	WHAT ARE YOU GOING TO DO WITH YOUR LIFE? *London 5560802*	**21**	2
26 May 01	FLOWERS *Cooking Vinyl COOKCD 208*	**56**	1

Tracks on Shine So Hard (EP): Crocodiles / All That Jazz / Zimbo / Over the Wall

ECHOBASS
UK, male producer – Simon Woodgate (Singles: 1 Week) pos/wks

14 Jul 01	YOU ARE THE WEAKEST LINK *House of Bush CDANNE 001*	**53**	1

ECHOBEATZ *UK, male DJ / production duo –*
Dave De Braie and Paul Moody (Singles: 5 Weeks) pos/wks

25 Jul 98 ●	MAS QUE NADA *Eternal WEA 176CD*	**10**	5

ECHOBELLY (see also LITHIUM and Sonya MADAN)
UK / Sweden, male / female vocal / instrumental
group (Singles: 16 Weeks, Albums: 28 Weeks) pos/wks

2 Apr 94	INSOMNIAC *Fauve FAUV 1CD*	**47**	1
2 Jul 94	I CAN'T IMAGINE THE WORLD WITHOUT ME *Fauve FAUV 2CD*	**39**	2
5 Nov 94	CLOSE...BUT *Fauve FAUV 4CD*	**59**	1
2 Sep 95	GREAT THINGS *Fauve FAUV 5CD*	**13**	3
4 Nov 95	KING OF THE KERB *Fauve FAUV 7CD*	**25**	3
2 Mar 96	DARK THERAPY *Fauve FAUV 8CD*	**20**	3
23 Aug 97	THE WORLD IS FLAT *Epic 6648152*	**31**	2
8 Nov 97	HERE COMES THE BIG RUSH *Epic 6652452*	**56**	1
3 Sep 94 ●	EVERYONE'S GOT ONE *Fauve FAUV 3CD*	**8**	3
30 Sep 95 ●	ON *Fauve FAUV 6CD*	**4**	24
22 Nov 97	LUSTRA *Epic 4889672*	**47**	1

Billy ECKSTINE
US, male vocalist, b. 8 Jul 1914, d. 8 Mar 1993 (Singles: 48 Weeks) pos/wks

12 Nov 54 ●	NO ONE BUT YOU *MGM 763*	**3**	17
27 Sep 57	PASSING STRANGERS *Mercury MT 164* [1]	**22**	2
13 Feb 59 ●	GIGI *Mercury AMT 1018*	**8**	14
12 Mar 69	PASSING STRANGERS (re-issue) *Mercury MF 1082* [1]	**20**	15

[1] Billy Eckstine and Sarah Vaughan

ECLIPSE (see also BINI & MARTINI; HOUSE OF GLASS; GOODFELLAS
featuring Lisa MILLETT) Italy, male producer /
instrumentalist – Gianni Bini (Singles: 4 Weeks) pos/wks

14 Aug 99	MAKES ME LOVE YOU *Azuli AZNYCDX 100*	**25**	4

Silvio ECOMO *Holland, male producer (Singles: 1 Week)* pos/wks

15 Jul 00	STANDING *Hooj Choons HOOJ 098CD*	**70**	1

EDDIE and the HOT RODS *UK, male vocal /*
instrumental group (Singles: 26 Weeks, Albums: 9 Weeks) pos/wks

11 Sep 76	LIVE AT THE MARQUEE (EP) *Island IEP 2*	**43**	5
13 Nov 76	TEENAGE DEPRESSION *Island WIP 6354*	**35**	4
23 Apr 77	I MIGHT BE LYING *Island WIP 6388*	**44**	3
13 Aug 77 ●	DO ANYTHING YOU WANNA DO *Island WIP 6401* [1]	**9**	10

21 Jan 78	QUIT THIS TOWN *Island WIP 6411*	36	4
18 Dec 76	TEENAGE DEPRESSION *Island ILPS 9457*	43	1
3 Dec 77	LIFE ON THE LINE *Island ILPS 9509*	27	3
24 Mar 79	THRILLER *Island ILPS 9563*	50	1
24 Jul 82	WILD DOGS *Arista SPART 1196* [1]	75	4

[1] The Rods [1] The Rods

Live at the Marquee (EP): 96 Tears / Get out of Denver / Medley: Gloria / Satisfaction

EDDY
UK, female vocalist – Edith Emenike (Singles: 2 Weeks) pos/wks

9 Jul 94	SOMEDAY *Positiva CDTIV 14*	49	2

EDDY and the SOUL BAND
US, male / female vocal / instrumental group (Singles: 7 Weeks) pos/wks

23 Feb 85	THE THEME FROM 'SHAFT' *Club JAB 11*	13	7

Duane EDDY `203` `Top 500`
Twangy guitar legend, b. 26 Apr 1938, New York, US. Early rock's No.1 solo instrumentalist assembled a long string of UK and US hit singles and was one of the first rock acts to score on the album charts (Singles: 202 Weeks, Albums: 88 Weeks) pos/wks

5 Sep 58	REBEL-ROUSER *London HL 8669* [1]	19	10
2 Jan 59	CANNONBALL *London HL 8764* [1]	22	4
19 Jun 59 ●	PETER GUNN (re) *London HLW 8879*	6	11
24 Jul 59	YEP! *London HLW 8879*	17	5
4 Sep 59	FORTY MILES OF BAD ROAD *London HLW 8929*	11	9
18 Dec 59	SOME KIND-A EARTHQUAKE *London HLW 9007*	12	5
19 Feb 60	BONNIE CAME BACK *London HLW 9050*	12	11
28 Apr 60 ●	SHAZAM! *London HLW 9104*	4	13
21 Jul 60 ●	BECAUSE THEY'RE YOUNG *London HLW 9162*	2	18
10 Nov 60	KOMMOTION *London HLW 9225*	13	10
12 Jan 61 ●	PEPE *London HLW 9257*	2	14
20 Apr 61 ●	THEME FROM DIXIE *London HLW 9324*	7	10
22 Jun 61	RING OF FIRE *London HLW 9370*	17	10
14 Sep 61	DRIVIN' HOME *London HLW 9406*	30	4
5 Oct 61	CARAVAN *Parlophone R 4826*	42	3
24 May 62	DEEP IN THE HEART OF TEXAS *RCA 1288*	19	8
23 Aug 62 ●	BALLAD OF PALADIN *RCA 1300* [3]	10	10
8 Nov 62 ●	(DANCE WITH THE) GUITAR MAN *RCA 1316* [4]	4	16
14 Feb 63	BOSS GUITAR *RCA 1329* [4]	27	8
30 May 63	LONELY BOY LONELY GUITAR *RCA 1344* [4]	35	4
29 Aug 63	YOUR BABY'S GONE SURFIN' *RCA 1357* [4]	49	1
8 Mar 75	PLAY ME LIKE YOU PLAY YOUR GUITAR *GTO GT 11* [4]	9	9
22 Mar 86	PETER GUNN (re-recording) *China WOK 6* [5]	8	9
6 Jun 59 ●	HAVE 'TWANGY' GUITAR WILL TRAVEL *London HAW 2160*	6	3
31 Oct 59 ●	SPECIALLY FOR YOU *London HAW 2191*	6	8
19 Mar 60 ●	THE TWANG'S THE THANG *London HAW 2236*	2	25
26 Nov 60	SONGS OF OUR HERITAGE *London HAW 2285*	13	5
1 Apr 61 ●	A MILLION DOLLARS' WORTH OF TWANG *London HAW 2325*	5	19
9 Jun 62	A MILLION DOLLARS' WORTH OF TWANG VOLUME 2 *London HAW 2435*	18	1
21 Jul 62	TWISTIN' AND TWANGIN' *RCA RD 27264*	8	12
8 Dec 62	TWANGY GUITAR – SILKY STRINGS *RCA RD 7510*	13	11
16 Mar 63	DANCE WITH THE GUITAR MAN *RCA RD 7545*	14	4

[1] Duane Eddy and his Twangy Guitar [2] Duane Eddy, his Twangy Guitar & The Rebels [3] Duane Eddy – Orchestra conducted by Bob Thompson [4] Duane Eddy and The Rebelettes [5] Art of Noise featuring Duane Eddy

Randy EDELMAN
US, male vocalist / instrumentalist – piano (Singles: 18 Weeks) pos/wks

6 Mar 76	CONCRETE AND CLAY *20th Century BTC 2261*	11	7
18 Sep 76	UPTOWN UPTEMPO WOMAN *20th Century BTC 2225*	25	7
15 Jan 77	YOU *20th Century BTC 2253*	49	2
17 Jul 82	NOBODY MADE ME *Rocket XPRES 81*	60	2

EDELWEISS
Austria, male / female vocal / instrumental group (Singles: 10 Weeks) pos/wks

29 Apr 89 ●	BRING ME EDELWEISS *WEA YZ 353*	5	10

EDEN
UK / Australia, male / female vocal / instrumental group (Singles: 2 Weeks) pos/wks

6 Mar 93	DO U FEEL 4 ME *Logic 74321135422*	51	2

Lyn EDEN See SMOKIN BEATS featuring Lyn EDEN

EDISON LIGHTHOUSE
UK, male vocal / instrumental group – lead vocal Tony Burrows (Singles: 13 Weeks) pos/wks

24 Jan 70 ★	LOVE GROWS (WHERE MY ROSEMARY GOES) *Bell 1091*	1	12
30 Jan 71	IT'S UP TO YOU PETULA *Bell 1136*	49	1

EDMONTON SYMPHONY ORCHESTRA See PROCOL HARUM

Dave EDMUNDS
UK, male vocalist / instrumentalist – guitar (Singles: 93 Weeks, Albums: 21 Weeks) pos/wks

21 Nov 70 ★	I HEAR YOU KNOCKING *MAM 1* [1]	1	14
20 Jan 73 ●	BABY I LOVE YOU *Rockfield ROC 1*	8	13
9 Jun 73 ●	BORN TO BE WITH YOU *Rockfield ROC 2*	5	12
2 Jul 77	I KNEW THE BRIDE *Swansong SSK 19411*	26	8
30 Jun 79 ●	GIRLS TALK *Swansong SSK 19418*	4	11
22 Sep 79	QUEEN OF HEARTS *Swansong SSK 19419*	11	9
24 Nov 79	CRAWLING FROM THE WRECKAGE *Swansong SSK 19420*	59	4
9 Feb 80	SINGING THE BLUES *Swansong SSK 19422*	28	8
28 Mar 81	ALMOST SATURDAY NIGHT *Swansong SSK 19424*	58	3
20 Jun 81	THE RACE IS ON *Swansong SSK 19425* [2]	34	6
26 Mar 83	SLIPPING AWAY *Arista ARIST 522*	60	4
7 Apr 90	KING OF LOVE *Capitol CL 568*	68	1
23 Jun 79	REPEAT WHEN NECESSARY *Swansong SSK 59409*	39	12
18 Apr 81	TWANGIN' *Swansong SSK 59411*	37	4
3 Apr 82	D.E. 7TH *Arista SPART 1184*	60	3
30 Apr 83	INFORMATION *Arista 205348*	92	2

[1] Dave Edmunds' Rockpile [2] Dave Edmunds and The Stray Cats

Alton EDWARDS
Zimbabwe, male vocalist (Singles: 9 Weeks) pos/wks

9 Jan 82	I JUST WANNA (SPEND SOME TIME WITH YOU) *Streetwave STRA 1897*	20	9

Dennis EDWARDS
US, male vocalist (Singles: 10 Weeks, Albums: 1 Week) pos/wks

24 Mar 84	DON'T LOOK ANY FURTHER (re) *Gordy TMG 1334* [1]	45	10
14 Apr 84	DON'T LOOK ANY FURTHER *Gordy ZL 72148*	91	1

[1] Dennis Edwards featuring Siedah Garrett

The re-entry peaked at No.55 in Jun 1987

Rupie EDWARDS
Jamaica, male vocalist (Singles: 16 Weeks) pos/wks

23 Nov 74 ●	IRE FEELINGS (SKANGA) *Cactus CT 38*	9	10
8 Feb 75	LEGO SKANGA *Cactus CT 51*	32	6

Todd EDWARDS
US, male DJ / producer (Albums: 1 Week) pos/wks

24 Aug 96	SAVED MY LIFE *ffrr FX 279*	69	1

Tommy EDWARDS
US, male vocalist, b. 17 Feb 1922, d. 23 Oct 1969 (Singles: 18 Weeks) pos/wks

3 Oct 58 ★	IT'S ALL IN THE GAME *MGM 989* ▲	1	17
7 Aug 59	MY MELANCHOLY BABY *MGM 1020*	29	1

EEK-A-MOUSE
Jamaica, male vocalist – Ripton Hylton (Albums: 3 Weeks) pos/wks

14 Aug 82	SKIDIP *Greensleeves GREL 41*	61	3

EELS
US, male vocal / instrumental group (Singles: 23 Weeks, Albums: 40 Weeks) pos/wks

15 Feb 97 ●	NOVOCAINE FOR THE SOUL *Dreamworks DRMCD 22174*	10	5
17 May 97	SUSAN'S HOUSE *Dreamworks DRMCD 22238*	9	5
13 Sep 97	YOUR LUCKY DAY IN HELL *Dreamworks DRMCD 22277*	35	2
26 Sep 98	LAST STOP: THIS TOWN *Dreamworks DRMCD 22346*	23	3
12 Dec 98	CANCER FOR THE CURE *Dreamworks DRMCD 22373*	60	1
26 Feb 00	MR E'S BEAUTIFUL BLUES *Dreamworks DRMCD 4509762*	11	4
24 Jun 00	FLYSWATTER *Dreamworks DRMCD 4509462*	55	1
22 Sep 01	SOULJACKER PART 1 *Dreamworks DRMCD 4508922*	30	2
8 Feb 97 ●	BEAUTIFUL FREAK *Dreamworks DRMCD 50001*	5	27
3 Oct 98	ELECTRO-SHOCK BLUES *Dreamworks DRMD 50052*	12	4
11 Mar 00 ●	DAISIES OF THE GALAXY *Dreamworks 4502182*	8	5
6 Oct 01	SOULJACKER *Dreamworks 4503462*	12	2
14 Jun 03	SHOOTENANNY *Dreamworks 4504588*	35	2

EFUA
UK, female vocalist – Efua Baker (Singles: 5 Weeks) pos/wks

3 Jul 93	SOMEWHERE *Virgin VSCDT 1463*	42	5

EGG *UK, male vocal / instrumental group (Singles: 1 Week)*   pos/wks

| 30 Jan 99 | **GETTING AWAY WITH IT** *Indochina ID 079CD* | **58** | 1 |

EGGS ON LEGS *UK, male vocalist (Singles: 1 Week)*   pos/wks

| 23 Sep 95 | **COCK A DOODLE DO IT** *Avex UK AVEXCD 18* | **42** | 1 |

EGYPTIAN EMPIRE
UK, male producer – Tim Taylor (Singles: 2 Weeks)   pos/wks

| 24 Oct 92 | **THE HORN TRACK** *Ffrreedom TAB 115* | **61** | 2 |

EIFFEL 65
Italy, male vocal trio (Singles: 36 Weeks, Albums: 4 Weeks)   pos/wks

21 Aug 99	**BLUE (DA BA DEE) (IMPORT)** *Logic 74321688212*	**39**	5
25 Sep 99	★ **BLUE (DA BA DEE)** *Eternal WEA 226CD1* ◆ ■	**1**	21
19 Feb 00	● **MOVE YOUR BODY** *Eternal WEA 255CD1*	**3**	10
4 Mar 00	**EUROPOP** *Eternal 8573814552*	**12**	4

18 WHEELER
UK, male vocal / instrumental group (Singles: 1 Week)   pos/wks

| 15 Mar 97 | **STAY** *Creation CRESCD 249* | **59** | 1 |

EIGHTH WONDER
(see also MERRION, McCALL & KENSIT) *UK, male / female vocal / instrumental group (Singles: 25 Weeks, Albums: 4 Weeks)*   pos/wks

2 Nov 85	**STAY WITH ME** *CBS A 6594*	**65**	2
20 Feb 88	● **I'M NOT SCARED** *CBS SCARE 1*	**7**	13
25 Jun 88	**CROSS MY HEART** *CBS 6515527*	**13**	8
1 Oct 88	**BABY BABY** *CBS BABE 1*	**65**	2
23 Jul 88	**FEARLESS** *CBS 460628 1*	**47**	4

801 *UK, male vocal / instrumental group (Albums: 2 Weeks)*   pos/wks

| 20 Nov 76 | **801 LIVE** *Island ILPS 9444* | **52** | 2 |

808 STATE *UK, DJ / production / instrumental group (Singles: 70 Weeks, Albums: 20 Weeks)*   pos/wks

18 Nov 89	● **PACIFIC** *ZTT Zang 1*	**10**	9
31 Mar 90	**THE EXTENDED PLEASURE OF DANCE (EP)** *ZTT ZANG 2*	**56**	1
2 Jun 90	**THE ONLY RHYME THAT BITES** *ZTT Zang 3* [1]	**10**	10
15 Sep 90	**TUNES SPLITS THE ATOM** *ZTT Zang 6* [1]	**18**	7
10 Nov 90	● **CUBIK / OLYMPIC** *ZTT Zang 5*	**10**	10
16 Feb 91	● **IN YER FACE** *ZTT ZANG 14*	**9**	6
27 Apr 91	**OOOPS** *ZTT Zang 19* [2]	**42**	3
17 Aug 91	**LIFT / OPEN YOUR MIND** *ZTT Zang 20*	**38**	4
29 Aug 92	**TIME BOMB / NIMBUS** *ZTT Zang 33*	**59**	1
12 Dec 92	**ONE IN TEN (re-mix)** *ZTT Zang 39* [3]	**17**	8
30 Jan 93	**PLAN 9** *ZTT Zang 38CD*	**50**	2
26 Jun 93	**10 X 10** *ZTT Zang 42CD*	**67**	1
13 Aug 94	**BOMBADIN** *ZTT Zang 54CD*	**67**	1
29 Jun 96	**BOND** *ZTT Zang 80CD*	**57**	1
8 Feb 97	**LOPEZ** *ZTT Zang 87CD*	**20**	2
16 May 98	**PACIFIC / CUBIK (re-mix)** *ZTT ZTT 98CD1*	**21**	3
6 Mar 99	**THE ONLY RHYME THAT BITES 99** *ZTT ZTT 125CD* [1]	**53**	1
16 Dec 89	**NINETY** *ZTT ZTT 2*	**57**	5
16 Mar 91	● **EX:EL** *ZTT ZTT 6*	**4**	10
13 Feb 93	**GORGEOUS** *ZTT 4509911002*	**17**	3
30 May 98	**808:88:98** *ZTT ZTT 100CD*	**40**	2

[1] MC Tunes versus 808 State [2] 808 State featuring Björk [3] 808 State vs UB40

Tracks on The Extended Pleasure of Dance (EP): Cobra Bora / Ancodia / Cubik.
'Cubik' is a re-issue of one of the tracks from The Extended Pleasure of Dance (EP).
'Lopez' features the uncredited vocals of James Dean Bradfield, lead singer of the Manic Street Preachers

The EIGHTIES MATCHBOX B-LINE DISASTER *UK, male vocal / instrumental group (Singles: 11 Weeks, Albums: 1 Week)*   pos/wks

28 Sep 02	**CELEBRATE YOUR MOTHER** *No Death / Island MCSTD 40296*	**66**	1
18 Jan 03	**PSYCHOSIS SAFARI** *No Death / Island MCSTD 40308*	**26**	2
24 May 03	**CHICKEN** *No Death / Island MCSTD 40317*	**30**	2
24 Jan 04	**MISTER MENTAL** *Universal MCSTD 40353*	**25**	2
10 Jul 04	**I COULD BE AN ANGLE** *Island MCSTD 40368*	**35**	2
23 Oct 04	**RISE OF THE EAGLES** *Universal MCSTD 40382*	**40**	2
6 Nov 04	**ROYAL SOCIETY** *Universal MCD 60097*	**68**	1

88.3 See Lisa MAY

Ludovico EINAUDI *Italy, male vocalist (Albums: 5 Weeks)*   pos/wks

| 13 Sep 03 | **ECHOES – THE COLLECTION** *BMG 82876550892* | **40** | 4 |
| 18 Sep 04 | **UNA MATTINA** *Decca 4756292* | **59** | 1 |

EINSTEIN (see also AMBASSADORS OF FUNK featuring MC MARIO) *UK, male rapper – Colin Case (Singles: 6 Weeks)*   pos/wks

18 Nov 89	**ANOTHER MONSTERJAM** *ffrr F 116* [1]	**65**	1
15 Dec 90	**TURN IT UP** *Swanyard SYD 9* [2]	**42**	4
24 Aug 96	**THE POWER 96** *Arista 74321398672* [3]	**42**	1

[1] Simon Harris featuring Einstein [2] Technotronic featuring Melissa and Einstein [3] Snap! featuring Einstein

EL COCO
US, male vocal / instrumental group (Singles: 4 Weeks)   pos/wks

| 14 Jan 78 | **COCOMOTION** *Pye International 7N 25761* | **31** | 4 |

EL MARIACHI (see also FUNK JUNKEEZ)
US, male producer – Roger Sanchez (Singles: 2 Weeks)   pos/wks

| 9 Nov 96 | **CUBA** *ffrr FCD 286* | **38** | 2 |

ELASTICA *UK, female / male vocal / instrumental group (Singles: 12 Weeks, Albums: 27 Weeks)*   pos/wks

12 Feb 94	**LINE UP** *Deceptive BLUFF 004CD*	**20**	3
22 Oct 94	**CONNECTION** *Deceptive BLUFF 010CD*	**17**	4
25 Feb 95	**WAKING UP** *Deceptive BLUFF 011CD*	**13**	4
24 Jun 00	**MAD DOG** *Deceptive BLUFF 077CD*	**44**	1
25 Mar 95	★ **ELASTICA** *Deceptive BLUFF 014CD* ■	**1**	25
15 Apr 00	**THE MENACE** *Deceptive BLUFF 075CD*	**24**	2

ELATE
UK, male / female vocal / instrumental trio (Singles: 2 Weeks)   pos/wks

| 26 Jul 97 | **SOMEBODY LIKE YOU** *VC VCRD 22* | **38** | 2 |

Donnie ELBERT
US, male vocalist, b. 25 May 1936, d. 26 Jan 1989 (Singles: 29 Weeks)   pos/wks

8 Jan 72	● **WHERE DID OUR LOVE GO?** *London HL 10352*	**8**	10
26 Feb 72	**I CAN'T HELP MYSELF** *Avco 6105009*	**11**	10
29 Apr 72	**A LITTLE PIECE OF LEATHER** *London HL 10370*	**27**	9

ELBOW *UK, male vocal / instrumental group (Singles: 10 Weeks, Albums: 9 Weeks)*   pos/wks

5 May 01	**RED** *V2 VVR 5016153*	**36**	1
21 Jul 01	**POWDER BLUE** *V2 VVR 5016163*	**41**	1
20 Oct 01	**NEWBORN** *V2 VVR 5016173*	**42**	1
16 Feb 02	**ASLEEP IN THE BACK / COMING SECOND** *V2 VVR 5018703*	**19**	3
16 Aug 03	**FALLEN ANGEL** *V2 VVR 5021803*	**19**	1
8 Nov 03	**FUGITIVE MOTEL** *V2 VVR 5021823*	**44**	1
6 Mar 04	**NOT A JOB** *V2 VVR 5024678*	**26**	2
19 May 01	**ASLEEP IN THE BACK** *V2 VVR 1015882*	**14**	5
30 Aug 03	● **CAST OF THOUSANDS** *V2 VVR 1021812*	**7**	4

ELECTRA
UK, male vocal / instrumental group (Singles: 7 Weeks)   pos/wks

| 6 Aug 88 | **JIBARO** *ffrr FFR 9* | **54** | 3 |
| 30 Dec 89 | **IT'S YOUR DESTINY / AUTUMN LOVE** *London F 121* | **51** | 4 |

ELECTRAFIXION
UK, male vocal / instrumental group (Singles: 6 Weeks, Albums: 2 Weeks)   pos/wks

19 Nov 94	**ZEPHYR** *WEA YZ 865CD*	**47**	2
9 Sep 95	**LOWDOWN** *WEA YZ 977CD*	**54**	2
4 Nov 95	**NEVER** *Spacejunk WEA 022CD*	**58**	1
16 Mar 96	**SISTER PAIN** *Spacejunk WEA 037CD1*	**27**	1
7 Oct 95	**BURNED** *Spacejunk 0630112482*	**38**	2

ELECTRASY *UK, male vocal / instrumental group (Singles: 7 Weeks, Albums: 1 Week)*   pos/wks

13 Jun 98	**LOST IN SPACE** *MCA MCSTD 40171*	**60**	1
5 Sep 98	**MORNING AFTERGLOW** *MCA MCSTD 40184*	**19**	4
28 Nov 98	**BEST FRIEND'S GIRL** *MCA MCSXD 40195*	**41**	2
26 Sep 98	**BEAUTIFUL INSANE** *MCA MCD 60051*	**48**	1

TOP 100 ACTS

BRITISH HIT SINGLES & ALBUMS

Our annual list of the Top 100 most successful acts of all time is based on the total number of weeks each contender has spent on the UK singles and albums charts.

This Top 100 reflects the achievements of the consistently great acts through more than 50 years of chart music from 1952 to the end of 2004. It is, therefore, a major achievement for any newcomer to enter this list. So let's hear it for the Red Hot Chili Peppers, who have amassed enough weeks on the UK charts to join the pantheon pop for the first time by entering our Top 100 at No.91.

Note that acts tied by the same number of weeks on chart are separated by the better chart positions for those weeks.

Pos / **ACT** / total weeks on the UK singles and albums charts / up or down from last year

Pos	Act	Weeks		Pos	Act	Weeks		Pos	Act	Weeks	
1.	ELVIS PRESLEY	2,463	□	11.	ROD STEWART	1,381	□	21.	PINK FLOYD	966	□
2.	CLIFF RICHARD	1,972	□	12.	FRANK SINATRA	1,332	□	22.	UB40	955	□
3.	THE BEATLES	1,749	□	13.	DIANA ROSS	1,303	□	23.	MEAT LOAF	941	□
4.	QUEEN	1,725	□	14.	DIRE STRAITS	1,255	□	24.	TOM JONES	915	□
5.	MADONNA	1,653	□	15.	SIMON AND GARFUNKEL	1,201	□	25.	STATUS QUO	890	□
6.	ELTON JOHN	1,615	□	16.	THE ROLLING STONES	1,173	□	26.	SIMPLY RED	849	⇑
7.	THE SHADOWS	1,578	□	17.	ABBA	1,137	□	27.	THE BEACH BOYS	845	⇓
8.	MICHAEL JACKSON	1,477	⇑	18.	FLEETWOOD MAC	1,103	□	28.	OASIS	836	⇓
9.	DAVID BOWIE	1,459	⇓	19.	PHIL COLLINS	1,062	□	29.	STEVIE WONDER	807	□
10.	U2	1,402	□	20.	PAUL McCARTNEY	983	□	30.	THE CARPENTERS	776	□
								31.	THE BEE GEES	767	□
								32.	R.E.M.	761	⇑
								33.	BOB DYLAN	755	⇓
								34.	TINA TURNER	755	⇓
								35.	PRINCE	748	⇓
								36.	JIM REEVES	730	□
								37.	NEIL DIAMOND	727	□
								38.	BOB MARLEY & THE WAILERS	713	□
								39.	ERIC CLAPTON	705	□
								40.	WHITNEY HOUSTON	698	□
								41.	ANDY WILLIAMS	685	□
								42.	EURYTHMICS	684	□
								43.	ROBBIE WILLIAMS	682	⇑
								44.	MADNESS	682	⇓
								45.	GENESIS	681	⇓
								46.	BARBRA STREISAND	678	⇑
								47.	BRUCE SPRINGSTEEN	670	⇓
								48.	MIKE OLDFIELD	664	⇓
								49.	CELINE DION	661	⇓
								50.	BON JOVI	660	⇓
								51.	LIONEL RICHIE	655	⇑
								52.	BRYAN ADAMS	652	⇓
								53.	DURAN DURAN	648	⇑
								54.	ELECTRIC LIGHT ORCHESTRA	648	⇓
								55.	KYLIE MINOGUE	646	⇑
								56.	GEORGE MICHAEL	627	⇑
								57.	SHIRLEY BASSEY	620	⇓
								58.	PET SHOP BOYS	596	⇑
								59.	ROY ORBISON	593	⇓

A NEW ENTRY AT 91: THE RED HOT CHILI PEPPERS ARE THE ONLY NEWCOMERS TO JOIN THE LEGENDARY ACTS THAT MAKE UP THE BRITISH HIT SINGLES AND ALBUMS TOP 100 ACTS OF ALL TIME

ELECTRIBE 101
UK / Germany, male / female vocal / instrumental group
(Singles: 15 Weeks, Albums: 3 Weeks) pos/wks

28 Oct 89	TELL ME WHEN THE FEVER ENDED *Mercury MER 310*	32	5
24 Feb 90	TALKING WITH MYSELF *Mercury MER 316*	23	5
22 Sep 90	YOU'RE WALKING *Mercury MER 328*	50	1
10 Oct 98	TALKING WITH MYSELF (re-mix) *Manifesto FESDD 49*	39	2
20 Oct 90	ELECTRIBAL MEMORIES *Mercury 8429651*	26	3

ELECTRIC BOYS
Sweden, male vocal / instrumental group (Albums: 1 Week) pos/wks

6 Jun 92	GROOVUS MAXIMUS *Vertigo 5122552*	61	1

ELECTRIC LIGHT ORCHESTRA ⬭ 54 ▮Top 500▮
Ground-breaking and innovative UK group, fronted by multi-talented Jeff Lynne (v/g) from Birmingham, that originally included Roy Wood (The Move). Their unique sound, which featured an orchestral string section, helped them to achieve numerous transatlantic hits (Singles: 255 Weeks, Albums: 393 Weeks) pos/wks

29 Jul 72 ●	10538 OVERTURE *Harvest HAR 5053*	9	8
27 Jan 73 ●	ROLL OVER BEETHOVEN *Harvest HAR 5063*	6	10
6 Oct 73	SHOWDOWN *Harvest HAR 5077*	12	10
9 Mar 74	MA-MA-MA-BELLE *Warner Bros. K 16349*	22	8
10 Jan 76 ●	EVIL WOMAN *Jet 764*	10	8
3 Jul 76	STRANGE MAGIC *Jet 779*	38	3
13 Nov 76 ●	LIVIN' THING *Jet UP 36184*	4	12
19 Feb 77 ●	ROCKARIA! *Jet UP 36209*	9	9
21 May 77 ●	TELEPHONE LINE *Jet UP 36254*	8	10
29 Oct 77	TURN TO STONE *Jet UP 36313*	18	12
28 Jan 78 ●	MR. BLUE SKY *Jet UP 36342*	6	11
10 Jun 78 ●	WILD WEST HERO *Jet JET 109*	6	14
7 Oct 78 ●	SWEET TALKIN' WOMAN *Jet 121*	6	9
9 Dec 78	THE ELO (EP) *Jet ELO 1*	34	8
19 May 79 ●	SHINE A LITTLE LOVE *Jet 144*	6	10
21 Jul 79 ●	THE DIARY OF HORACE WIMP *Jet 150*	8	9
1 Sep 79 ●	DON'T BRING ME DOWN *Jet 153*	3	9
17 Nov 79 ●	CONFUSION / LAST TRAIN TO LONDON *Jet 166*	8	10
24 May 80	I'M ALIVE *Jet 179*	20	9
21 Jun 80 ★	XANADU *Jet 185* [1]	1	11
2 Aug 80	ALL OVER THE WORLD *Jet 195*	11	8
22 Nov 80	DON'T WALK AWAY *Jet 7004*	21	10
1 Aug 81 ●	HOLD ON TIGHT *Jet 7011* [2]	4	12
24 Oct 81	TWILIGHT *Jet 7015* [2]	30	7
9 Jan 82	TICKET TO THE MOON / HERE IS THE NEWS *Jet 7018* [2]	24	8
18 Jun 83	ROCK 'N' ROLL IS KING *Jet A 3500* [2]	13	9
3 Sep 83	SECRET MESSAGES *Jet A 3720* [2]	48	3
1 Mar 86	CALLING AMERICA *Epic A 6844*	28	7
11 May 91	HONEST MEN PART ONE *Telstar ELO 100* [3]	60	1
12 Aug 72	ELECTRIC LIGHT ORCHESTRA *Harvest SHVL 797*	32	4
31 Mar 73	ELECTRIC LIGHT ORCHESTRA II *Harvest SHVL 806*	35	1
11 Dec 76 ●	A NEW WORLD RECORD *United Artists UAG 30017*	6	100
12 Nov 77 ●	OUT OF THE BLUE *United Artists UAR 100*	4	108
6 Jan 79	THREE LIGHT YEARS *Jet JETBX 1*	38	9
16 Jun 79 ★	DISCOVERY *Jet JETLX 500* ■	1	46
1 Dec 79 ●	ELO'S GREATEST HITS *Jet JETLX 525*	7	18
8 Aug 81 ★	TIME *Jet JETLP 236*	1	32
2 Jul 83	SECRET MESSAGES *Jet JETLX 527*	4	15
15 Mar 86 ●	BALANCE OF POWER *Epic EPC 26467*	9	12
16 Dec 89	THE GREATEST HITS *Telstar STAR 2370*	23	21
1 Jun 91	ELECTRIC LIGHT ORCHESTRA PART II *Telstar STAR 2503* [1]	34	4
2 Jul 94 ●	THE VERY BEST OF THE ELECTRIC LIGHT ORCHESTRA *Dino DINCD 90*	4	11
8 Nov 97	LIGHT YEARS – THE VERY BEST OF ELECTRIC LIGHT ORCHESTRA *Epic 4890392*	60	4
23 Jun 01	ZOOM *Epic 5025002*	34	2
3 Nov 01	THE ULTIMATE COLLECTION *Columbia STVCD 126*	18	6

[1] Olivia Newton-John and Electric Light Orchestra [2] ELO [3] Electric Light Orchestra Part 2 [1] ELO Part 2

'Here is the News' listed from 16 Jan 1982. Tracks on The ELO (EP): Can't Get it Out of My Head / Strange Magic / Ma-Ma-Ma-Belle / Evil Woman. 'A New World Record' changed label number to JET LP 200 and 'Out of the Blue' changed to JET DP 400 during their chart runs. 'The Greatest Hits' was also issued under the title 'The Very Best of Electric Light Orchestra' with the same tracklisting and catalogue number

The ELECTRIC PRUNES
US, male vocal / instrumental group (Singles: 5 Weeks) pos/wks

9 Feb 67	I HAD TOO MUCH TO DREAM (LAST NIGHT) *Reprise RS 20532*	49	1
11 May 67	GET ME TO THE WORLD ON TIME *Reprise RS 20564*	42	4

ELECTRIC SIX *US, male vocal / instrumental group (Singles: 23 Weeks, Albums: 10 Weeks)* pos/wks

18 Jan 03 ●	DANGER! HIGH VOLTAGE *XL Recordings XLS 151CD*	2	11
14 Jun 03 ●	GAY BAR *XL Recordings XLS 158CD*	5	10
25 Oct 03	DANCE COMMANDER *XL Recordings XLS 170CD*	40	1
25 Dec 04	RADIO GA GA *WEA WEA 381CD2*	21	1+
12 Jul 03 ●	FIRE *XL XLCD 169*	7	10

The ELECTRIC SOFT PARADE *UK, male vocal / instrumental group – led by Alex and Tom White (Singles: 5 Weeks, Albums: 3 Weeks)* pos/wks

4 Aug 01	EMPTY AT THE END / SUMATRAN *DB DB 006CD7* [1]	65	1
10 Nov 01	THERE'S A SILENCE *DB DB 007CD7*	52	1
16 Mar 02	SILENT TO THE DARK II *DB DB 008CD7*	23	2
1 Jun 02	EMPTY AT THE END (re-recording) / THIS GIVEN LINE *DB DB 009CD7*	39	1
16 Feb 02	HOLES IN THE WALL *DB DB 002CDLP*	35	2
25 Oct 03	THE AMERICAN ADVENTURE *BMG 82876563692*	45	1

[1] Soft Parade

ELECTRIC SUN *See Uli Jon ROTH and ELECTRIC SUN*

ELECTRIC WIND ENSEMBLE
UK, male instrumental group (Albums: 9 Weeks) pos/wks

18 Feb 84	HAUNTING MELODIES *Nouveau Music NML 1007*	28	9

ELECTRIQUE BOUTIQUE
UK / France, male production group (Singles: 2 Weeks) pos/wks

26 Aug 00	REVELATION *Data DATA 14CDS*	37	2

ELECTRONIC *UK, male vocal / instrumental group (Singles: 36 Weeks, Albums: 24 Weeks)* pos/wks

16 Dec 89	GETTING AWAY WITH IT *Factory FAC 2577*	12	9
27 Apr 91 ●	GET THE MESSAGE *Factory FAC 2877*	8	7
21 Sep 91	FEEL EVERY BEAT *Factory FAC 3287*	39	4
4 Jul 92 ●	DISAPPOINTED *Parlophone R 6311*	6	5
6 Jul 96	FORBIDDEN CITY *Parlophone CDR 6436*	14	4
28 Sep 96	FOR YOU *Parlophone CDR 6445*	16	2
15 Feb 97	SECOND NATURE *Parlophone CDR 6455*	35	2
24 Apr 99	VIVID *Parlophone CDR 6514*	17	3
8 Jun 91 ●	ELECTRONIC *Factory FACT 290*	2	16
20 Jul 96 ●	RAISE THE PRESSURE *Parlophone CDPCS 7382*	8	5
8 May 99 ●	TWISTED TENDERNESS *Parlophone 5201462*	9	3

ELECTRONICAS
Holland, male instrumental group (Singles: 8 Weeks) pos/wks

19 Sep 81	ORIGINAL BIRD DANCE *Polydor POSP 360*	22	8

ELECTROSET
UK, male instrumental / production group (Singles: 4 Weeks) pos/wks

21 Nov 92	HOW DOES IT FEEL *ffrr F 203*	27	3
15 Jul 95	SENSATION *Ffrreedom TABCD 231*	69	1

The ELEGANTS *US, male vocal group (Singles: 2 Weeks)* pos/wks

26 Sep 58	LITTLE STAR *HMV POP 520* ▲	25	2

ELEMENT FOUR (see also VIRUS) *UK, male production duo – Paul Oakenfold and Andy Gray (Singles: 11 Weeks)* pos/wks

9 Sep 00 ●	BIG BROTHER UK TV THEME (re) *Channel 4 Music C4M 00072*	4	11

ELEPHANT MAN
Jamaica, male vocalist – O'Neil Bryan (Singles: 5 Weeks) pos/wks

22 Nov 03	PON DE RIVER, PON DE BANK *Atlantic AT 0168CD*	29	3
4 Sep 04	JOOK GAL *VP VPCD 6416*	41	1

ELEVATION
UK, male instrumental / production duo (Singles: 1 Week) pos/wks

23 May 92	CAN U FEEL IT *Nova Mute 12NOMU 3*	62	1

ELEVATOR SUITE
UK, male production / instrumental trio (Singles: 1 Week) pos/wks

| 12 Aug 00 | BACK AROUND *Infectious INFECT 85CDS* | **71** 1 |

ELEVATORMAN
UK, male instrumental / production group (Singles: 4 Weeks) pos/wks

| 14 Jan 95 | FUNK AND DRIVE *Wired WIRED 211* | **37** 3 |
| 1 Jul 95 | FIRED UP *Wired WIRED 216* | **44** 1 |

Danny ELFMAN *US, male orchestra leader (Albums: 6 Weeks)* pos/wks

| 12 Aug 89 | BATMAN *Warner Bros. WX 287* | **45** 6 |

The ELGINS *US, male / female vocal group (Singles: 20 Weeks)* pos/wks

| 1 May 71 ● | HEAVEN MUST HAVE SENT YOU *Tamla Motown TMG 771* | **3** 13 |
| 9 Oct 71 | PUT YOURSELF IN MY PLACE *Tamla Motown TMG 787* | **28** 7 |

ELIAS and his ZIG-ZAG JIVE FLUTES
South Africa, male instrumental group (Singles: 14 Weeks) pos/wks

| 25 Apr 58 ● | TOM HARK *Columbia DB 4109* | **2** 14 |

Yvonne ELLIMAN *US, female vocalist (Singles: 44 Weeks)* pos/wks

29 Jan 72	I DON'T KNOW HOW TO LOVE HIM *MCA MMKS 5077*	**47** 1
6 Nov 76 ●	LOVE ME *RSO 2090205*	**6** 13
7 May 77	HELLO STRANGER *RSO 2090 36*	**26** 5
13 Aug 77	I CAN'T GET YOU OUT OF MY MIND *RSO 2090251*	**17** 13
6 May 78 ●	IF I CAN'T HAVE YOU *RSO 2090266* ▲	**4** 12

'I Don't Know How to Love Him' was one of four tracks on a maxi-single, two of which were credited during the disc's one week on the chart. The other track credited was 'Superstar' by Murray Head

Duke ELLINGTON
US, male band leader / instrumentalist – piano – Edward Ellington, b. 29 Apr 1899, d. 24 May 1974 (Singles: 4 Weeks, Albums: 2 Weeks) pos/wks

| 5 Mar 54 ● | SKIN DEEP *Philips PB 243* [1] | **7** 4 |
| 8 Apr 61 | NUT CRACKER SUITE *Philips BBL 7418* | **11** 2 |

[1] Duke Ellington and his Orchestra with Louis Bellson (drums)

Lance ELLINGTON *UK, male vocalist (Singles: 1 Week)* pos/wks

| 21 Aug 93 | LONELY (HAVE WE LOST OUR LOVE) *RCA 74321158332* | **57** 1 |

Ray ELLINGTON *UK, male vocal / instrumental group –
leader b. 17 Mar 1915, d. 27 Feb 1985 (Singles: 4 Weeks)* pos/wks

| 15 Nov 62 | THE MADISON (re) *Ember S 102* | **36** 4 |

Bern ELLIOTT and the FENMEN
UK, male vocal / instrumental group (Singles: 22 Weeks) pos/wks

| 21 Nov 63 | MONEY *Decca F 11770* | **14** 13 |
| 19 Mar 64 | NEW ORLEANS *Decca F 11852* | **24** 9 |

Joe ELLIOTT *See Mick RONSON with Joe ELLIOTT*

Missy 'Misdemeanor' ELLIOTT (389 | Top 500)
Leading female rapper / songwriter / producer / arranger and record label (Gold Mind) boss, b. Melissa Elliott, Virginia, US, 1 Jul 1972. This multi-award-winning hip hop / R&B legend, who first surfaced in the group Sista in 1992, has recorded with countless artists and charted with 17 of them (Singles: 121 Weeks, Albums: 54 Weeks) pos/wks

30 Aug 97	THE RAIN (SUPA DUPA FLY) *East West E 3919CD*	**16** 3
29 Nov 97	SOCKIT2ME *East West E 3890CD* [1]	**33** 2
25 Apr 98	BEEP ME 911 *East West E 3859CD*	**14** 3
22 Aug 98	MAKE IT HOT *East West E 3821CD* [2]	**22** 4
22 Aug 98	HIT 'EM WIT DA HEE *East West E 3824CD1* [3]	**25** 3
26 Sep 98 ★	I WANT YOU BACK *Virgin VSCDT 1716* [4] ■	**1** 9
21 Nov 98	5 MINUTES *Elektra E 3803CD* [5]	**72** 1
13 Mar 99	HERE WE COME *Virgin DINSD 179* [6]	**43** 1
25 Sep 99	ALL N MY GRILL *Elektra E 3742CD* [7]	**20** 4
22 Jan 00	HOT BOYZ *Elektra E 7002CD* [8]	**18** 3
28 Apr 01 ●	GET UR FREAK ON *East West / Elektra E 7206CD*	**4** 11
18 Aug 01 ●	ONE MINUTE MAN *Elektra E 7245CD* [9]	**10** 8
13 Oct 01	SUPERFREAKON *East West / Elektra 759672550*	**72** 1
22 Dec 01	SON OF A GUN (I BETCHA THINK THIS SONG IS ABOUT YOU) (re) *Virgin VUSCD 232* [10]	**13** 9

6 Apr 02 ●	4 MY PEOPLE *Goldmind / Elektra E 7286CD*	**5** 13
16 Nov 02 ●	WORK IT *Goldmind / Elektra E 7344CD* [11]	**6** 9
22 Mar 03 ●	GOSSIP FOLKS *Elektra E 7380CD* [12]	**9** 9
22 Nov 03 ●	PASS THAT DUTCH *East West E 7509CD*	**10** 11
13 Mar 04	COP THAT SH*T *Unique Corp TIMBACD 001* [13]	**22** 3
3 Apr 04	I'M REALLY HOT *Elektra E 7552CD* [11]	**22** 4
17 Jul 04	PUSH *Def Jam 9862837*	**34** 3
13 Nov 04 ●	CAR WASH *Dreamworks 986430* [15]	**4** 7+
10 Jul 99	DA REAL WORLD *Elektra 7559624362*	**40** 2
26 May 01 ●	MISS E ... SO ADDICTIVE *Elektra 7559626392*	**10** 26
23 Nov 02	UNDER CONSTRUCTION *Elektra 7559628132*	**24** 22
6 Dec 03	THIS IS NOT A TEST *Elektra 7559629052*	**49** 4

[1] Missy Elliott featuring Da Brat [2] Nicole featuring Missy 'Misdemeanor' Elliott and Mocha [3] Missy 'Misdemeanor' Elliott featuring Lil' Kim [4] Melanie B featuring Missy 'Misdemeanor' Elliott [5] Lil' Mo featuring Missy 'Misdemeanor' Elliott [6] Timbaland / Missy Elliott and Magoo [7] Missy 'Misdemeanor' Elliott featuring MC Solaar [8] Missy 'Misdemeanor' Elliott featuring Nas, Eve and Q Tip [9] Missy 'Misdemeanor' Elliott featuring Ludacris [10] Janet with Carly Simon featuring Missy Elliott [11] Missy Elliott [12] Missy Elliott featuring Ludacris [13] Timbaland & Magoo featuring Missy Elliott [14] Ghostface featuring Missy Elliott [15] Christina Aguilera featuring Missy Elliott

Greg ELLIS *See Reva RICE and Greg ELLIS*

Joey B ELLIS *US, male rapper (Singles: 10 Weeks)* pos/wks

| 16 Feb 91 | GO FOR IT (HEART AND FIRE) *Capitol CL 601* [1] | **20** 8 |
| 18 May 91 | THOUGHT U WERE THE ONE FOR ME *Capitol CL 614* | **58** 2 |

[1] Rocky V featuring Joey B Ellis and Tynetta Hare

Shirley ELLIS
US, female vocalist – Shirley Elliston (Singles: 17 Weeks) pos/wks

| 6 May 65 ● | THE CLAPPING SONG *London HLR 9961* | **6** 13 |
| 8 Jul 78 | THE CLAPPING SONG (EP) *MCA MCEP 1* | **59** 4 |

Tracks on The Clapping Song (EP): The Clapping Song / Ever See a Diver Kiss His Wife While the Bubbles Bounce Above the Water / The Name Game / The Nitty Gritty. 'The Clapping Song' itself qualifies as a re-issue

ELLIS, BEGGS and HOWARD
UK, male vocal / instrumental group (Singles: 8 Weeks) pos/wks

| 2 Jul 88 | BIG BUBBLES, NO TROUBLES (re) *RCA PB 42089* | **41** 8 |

Peak position reached on its re-entry in Mar 89

Sophie ELLIS-BEXTOR *(see also THEAUDIENCE; SPILLER)*
UK, female vocalist (Singles: 63 Weeks, Albums: 46 Weeks) pos/wks

25 Aug 01 ●	TAKE ME HOME (A GIRL LIKE ME) *Polydor 5872312*	**2** 12
15 Dec 01 ●	MURDER ON THE DANCEFLOOR *Polydor 5704942*	**2** 16
22 Jun 02 ●	GET OVER YOU / MOVE THIS MOUNTAIN *Polydor 5708332*	**3** 13
16 Nov 02 ●	MUSIC GETS THE BEST OF ME *Polydor 659222*	**14** 10
25 Oct 03 ●	MIXED UP WORLD *Polydor 9812108*	**7** 6
10 Jan 04 ●	I WON'T CHANGE YOU *Polydor 9815124*	**9** 6
15 Sep 01 ●	READ MY LIPS *Polydor 5891742*	**2** 44
8 Nov 03	SHOOT FROM THE HIP *Polydor 9865834*	**19** 2

Jennifer ELLISON *UK, female actor / vocalist (Singles: 14 Weeks)* pos/wks

| 28 Jun 03 ● | BABY I DON'T CARE *East West EW 268CD1* | **6** 10 |
| 7 Aug 04 | BYE BYE BOY *Sky-Rocket / Concept CDSKYCON 01* | **13** 4 |

Ben ELTON *UK, male comedian / vocalist (Albums: 2 Weeks)* pos/wks

| 14 Nov 87 | MOTORMOUTH *Mercury BENLP 1* | **86** 2 |

ELVIS vs JXL *See Elvis PRESLEY; JUNKIE XL*

ELWOOD
US, male rapper / vocalist – Elwood Strickland (Singles: 1 Week) pos/wks

| 26 Aug 00 | SUNDOWN *Palm Pictures PPCD 70342* | **72** 1 |

EMBRACE *UK, male vocal / instrumental
group (Singles: 50 Weeks, Albums: 53 Weeks)* pos/wks

17 May 97	FIREWORKS (EP) *Hut HUTCD 84*	**34** 2
19 Jul 97	ONE BIG FAMILY (EP) *Hut HUTCD 86*	**21** 3
8 Nov 97 ●	ALL YOU GOOD GOOD PEOPLE *Hut HUTCD 90*	**8** 4

			pos/wks
6 Jun 98	●	**COME BACK TO WHAT YOU KNOW** *Hut HUTCD 93* **6**	8
29 Aug 98	●	**MY WEAKNESS IS NONE OF YOUR BUSINESS** *Hut HUTCD 103* ..**9**	4
13 Nov 99		**HOOLIGAN** *Hut HUTCD 123* **18**	3
25 Mar 00		**YOU'RE NOT ALONE** *Hut / Virgin HUTCD 126* **14**	3
10 Jun 00		**SAVE ME (re)** *Hut / Virgin HUTCD 133* **29**	3
19 Aug 00		**I WOULDN'T WANNA HAPPEN TO YOU**	
		Hut / Virgin HUTCD 137 ....**23**	2
1 Sep 01		**WONDER (re)** *Hut / Virgin HUTCD 142* **14**	4
17 Nov 01		**MAKE IT LAST** *Hut / Virgin HUTCD 144* **35**	2
11 Sep 04	●	**GRAVITY** *Independiente ISOM 87SMS* **7**	7
27 Nov 04		**ASHES** *Independiente ISOM 89SMS* **11**	5+
20 Jun 98	★	**THE GOOD WILL OUT** *Hut CDHUT 46* ■ **1**	21
8 Apr 00	●	**DRAWN FROM MEMORY** *Hut CDHUT 60* **8**	13
15 Sep 01	●	**IF YOU'VE NEVER BEEN** *Hut CDHUT 68* **9**	3
6 Apr 02		**FIREWORKS (SINGLES 1997-2002)** *Hut CDHUT 74* **36**	2
25 Sep 04	★	**OUT OF NOTHING** *Independiente ISOM 45CD* ■ **1**	14+

Tracks on Fireworks (EP): The Last Gas / Now You're Nobody / Blind / Fireworks.
Tracks on One Big Family (EP): One Big Family / Dry Kids / You've Only Got to Stop
to Get Better / Butter Wouldn't Melt

EMERALD EXPRESS See *DEXY'S MIDNIGHT RUNNERS*

EMERSON See *SASHA*

Keith EMERSON (see also The NICE; EMERSON,
LAKE and PALMER; EMERSON, LAKE and POWELL)
UK, male instrumentalist – keyboards (Singles: 5 Weeks)   pos/wks

10 Apr 76	**HONKY TONK TRAIN BLUES** *Manticore K 13513* **21**	5

EMERSON, LAKE and PALMER `482` `Top 500`
(see also ASIA; Keith EMERSON; Greg LAKE; EMERSON, LAKE and POWELL)
Pioneering armour-plated progressive rock supertrio: Keith Emerson,
ex-Nice (k), Greg Lake, ex-King Crimson, (v/b/g) and Carl Palmer,
ex-Atomic Rooster and Crazy World of Arthur Brown (d). Their classical-
orientated rock helped change the face of 1970s music (Singles: 13 Weeks,
Albums: 137 Weeks)   pos/wks

4 Jun 77	●	**FANFARE FOR THE COMMON MAN** *Atlantic K 10946* **2**	13
5 Dec 70	●	**EMERSON LAKE AND PALMER** *Island ILPS 9132* **4**	28
19 Jun 71	★	**TARKUS** *Island ILPS 9155* **1**	17
4 Dec 71	●	**PICTURES AT AN EXHIBITION** *Island HELP 1* **3**	5
8 Jul 72	●	**TRILOGY** *Island ILPS 9186* **2**	29
22 Dec 73	●	**BRAIN SALAD SURGERY** *Manticore K 53501* **2**	17
24 Aug 74	●	**WELCOME BACK MY FRIENDS TO THE SHOW THAT NEVER**	
		ENDS – LADIES AND GENTLEMEN: EMERSON LAKE AND	
		PALMER *Manticore K 63500* **5**	5
9 Apr 77	●	**WORKS** *Atlantic K 80009* **9**	25
10 Dec 77		**WORKS VOLUME 2** *Atlantic K 50422* **20**	5
9 Dec 78		**LOVE BEACH** *Atlantic K 50552* **48**	4
26 Jun 04		**THE ULTIMATE COLLECTION** *Sanctuary TDSAN 009X* **43**	2

EMERSON, LAKE and POWELL (see also ASIA; Keith EMERSON;
Greg LAKE; COZY POWELL; EMERSON, LAKE and PALMER)
UK, male vocal / instrumental group (Albums: 5 Weeks)   pos/wks

14 Jun 86	**EMERSON LAKE AND POWELL** *Polydor POLD 5191* **35**	5

Dick EMERY *UK, male actor / vocalist,*
b. 7 Feb 1917, d. 2 Jan 1983 (Singles: 8 Weeks)   pos/wks

26 Feb 69	**IF YOU LOVE HER** *Pye 7N 17644* **32**	4
13 Jan 73	**YOU ARE AWFUL** *Pye 7N 45202* **43**	4

EMILIA *Sweden, female vocalist –*
Emilia Rydberg (Singles: 14 Weeks)   pos/wks

12 Dec 98	●	**BIG BIG WORLD** *Universal UMD 87190* **5**	13
1 May 99		**GOOD SIGN** *Universal UMD 87206* **54**	1

EMINEM `112` `Top 500`
Controversy-courting, chainsaw-wielding, multi-award-winning rap super-
star, b. Marshall Mathers (aka Slim Shady), 17 Oct 1974, Detroit, US. The four
time Brit Award winner and Oscar winner is the most successful rap artist in
UK chart history (Singles: 148 Weeks, Albums: 263 Weeks)   pos/wks

10 Apr 99	●	**MY NAME IS (re)** *Interscope IND 95638* **2**	12
14 Aug 99	●	**GUILTY CONSCIENCE** *Interscope IND 4971282* [1] **5**	8
10 Jun 00	●	**FORGOT ABOUT DRE** *Interscope 4973412* [2] **7**	9
8 Jul 00	★	**THE REAL SLIM SHADY (re)** *Interscope 4973792* ■ **1**	16
14 Oct 00	●	**THE WAY I AM** *Interscope 4974252* **8**	9
16 Dec 00	★	**STAN (re)** *Interscope IND 97470* ■ **1**	17
1 Sep 01		**SCARY MOVIES** *Mole UK MOLEUK 045* [3] **63**	1
1 Jun 02	★	**WITHOUT ME** *Interscope 4977282* ■ **1**	16
28 Sep 02	●	**CLEANIN' OUT MY CLOSET (2re)** *Interscope 4973942* **4**	13
14 Dec 02	★	**LOSE YOURSELF** *Interscope 4978282* ■ ▲ **1**	21
15 Mar 03	●	**SING FOR THE MOMENT** *Interscope 4978612* **6**	10
19 Jul 03	●	**BUSINESS** *Interscope 9809382* **6**	9
13 Nov 04	★	**JUST LOSE IT** *Interscope 2103183* ■ **1**	7+
24 Apr 99	●	**THE SLIM SHADY LP** *Interscope IND 90321* **10**	114
3 Jun 00	★	**THE MARSHALL MATHERS LP** *Interscope 4906292* ▲ **1**	74
8 Jun 02	★	**THE EMINEM SHOW** *Interscope 4932902* ■ ▲ **1**	69
20 Nov 04	★	**ENCORE** *Interscope 9864884* ■ ▲ **1**	6+

[1] Eminem featuring Dr Dre [2] Dr Dre featuring Eminem [3] Bad meets Evil
featuring Eminem & Royce Da 5'9"

'Stan' features uncredited vocalist Dido, sampling her single 'Thank You'

EMMA See *SPICE GIRLS; Emma BUNTON*

EMMA *UK, female vocalist – Emma Booth (Singles: 6 Weeks)*   pos/wks

28 Apr 90	**GIVE A LITTLE LOVE BACK TO THE WORLD** *Big Wave BWR 33* **33**	6

Brandi EMMA See *STELLAR PROJECT featuring Brandi EMMA*

EMMANUEL & ESKA See *COLOURS featuring EMMANUEL & ESKA; EN-CORE*
featuring Stephen EMMANUEL & ESKA

EMMIE (see also INDIEN)
UK, female vocalist – Emma Morton Smith (Singles: 9 Weeks)   pos/wks

23 Jan 99	●	**MORE THAN THIS** *Indirect / Manifesto FESCD 52* **5**	8
16 Feb 02		**I WON'T LET YOU DOWN** *Decode / Telstar CDSTAS 3210* [1] **53**	1

[1] W.I.P. featuring Emmie

The EMOTIONS *US, female vocal group (Singles: 28 Weeks)*   pos/wks

10 Sep 77	●	**BEST OF MY LOVE** *CBS 5555* ▲ **4**	10
24 Dec 77		**I DON'T WANNA LOSE YOUR LOVE** *CBS 5819* **40**	5
12 May 79		**BOOGIE WONDERLAND** *CBS 7292* [1] **4**	13

[1] Earth Wind and Fire with The Emotions

Alec EMPIRE
Germany, male producer (Singles: 1 Week, Albums: 1 Week)   pos/wks

13 Apr 02	**ADDICTED TO YOU** *Digital Hardcore DHRMCD 38* **64**	1
4 May 02	**INTELLIGENCE & SACRIFICE** *Digital Hardcore DHRCD 29* **71**	1

EMPIRION
UK, male instrumental / production group (Singles: 2 Weeks)   pos/wks

6 Jul 96	**NARCOTIC INFLUENCE** *XL XLS 72CD* **64**	1
21 Jun 97	**BETA** *XL XLS 77CD* **75**	1

EN VOGUE
US, female vocal group (Singles: 83 Weeks, Albums: 52 Weeks)   pos/wks

5 May 90	●	**HOLD ON** *East West America 7908* **5**	11
21 Jul 90		**LIES** *East West America 7893* **44**	4
4 Apr 92	●	**MY LOVIN' (re)** *East West America A 8578* **4**	12
15 Aug 92		**GIVING HIM SOMETHING HE CAN FEEL**	
		East West America A 8524 ....**44**	3
7 Nov 92		**FREE YOUR MIND / GIVING HIM SOMETHING HE CAN FEEL**	
		(re-issue) *East West America A 8468* **16**	8
16 Jan 93		**GIVE IT UP TURN IT LOOSE** *East West America A 8445CD* ...**22**	4
10 Apr 93		**LOVE DON'T LOVE YOU** *East West America A 8424CD* **64**	1
9 Oct 93		**RUNAWAY LOVE** *East West America A 8359CD* **36**	3
19 Mar 94	●	**WHATTA MAN** *ffrr FCD 222* [1] **7**	10
11 Jan 97	●	**DON'T LET GO (LOVE)** *East West A 3976CD* **5**	16
14 Jun 97		**WHATEVER** *East West E 3642CD* **14**	5
6 Sep 97		**TOO GONE, TOO LONG** *East West E 3908CD* **20**	3
28 Nov 98		**HOLD ON (re-mix)** *East West E 3796CD* **53**	1
1 Jul 00		**RIDDLE** *Elektra E 7053CD* **33**	2
2 Jun 90		**BORN TO SING** *Atlantic 7567820841* **23**	13
23 May 92	●	**FUNKY DIVAS** *East West America 7567921212* **4**	29
28 Jun 97	●	**EV3** *East West 7559620972* **9**	8
31 Oct 98		**BEST OF EN VOGUE** *East West 7559623222* **39**	2

[1] Salt-N-Pepa with En Vogue

ENCORE
France, female vocalist – Sabine Ohmes (Singles: 4 Weeks) pos/wks

| 14 Feb 98 | LE DISC JOCKEY *Sum CDSUM 2* ....**12** 4 |

EN-CORE featuring Stephen EMMANUEL & ESKA
UK, male producer – Stephen Boreland and
female vocalist – Eska Mtungwazi (Singles: 2 Weeks) pos/wks

| 9 Sep 00 | COOCHY COO *VC Recordings VCRD 72* ....**32** 2 |

ENERGISE
UK, male vocal / instrumental group (Singles: 1 Week) pos/wks

| 16 Feb 91 | REPORT TO THE DANCEFLOOR *Network NWKT 16* ....**69** 1 |

ENERGY 52
Germany, male DJ / producer –
Paul Schmitz-Moormann (Singles: 11 Weeks) pos/wks

8 Mar 97	CAFE DEL MAR *Hooj Choons HOOJCD 51* **51** 1
25 Jul 98	CAFE DEL MAR '98 (re-mix) *Hooj Choons HOOJ 64CD* **12** 6
12 Oct 02	CAFE DEL MAR (2nd re-mix) *Lost Language LOST 019CD* ...**24** 4

ENERGY ORCHARD
Ireland, male vocal /
instrumental group (Singles: 6 Weeks, Albums: 2 Weeks) pos/wks

27 Jan 90	BELFAST *MCA MCA 1392* **52** 4
7 Apr 90	SAILORTOWN *MCA MCA 1402* **73** 2
12 May 90	ENERGY ORCHARD *MCA MCG 6083* **53** 2

Harry ENFIELD
UK, male comedian / vocalist (Singles: 7 Weeks) pos/wks

| 7 May 88 ● | LOADSAMONEY (DOIN' UP THE HOUSE) *Mercury DOSH 1* .....**4** 7 |

ENGLAND BOYS
UK, male vocal group (Singles: 3 Weeks) pos/wks

| 8 Jun 02 | GO ENGLAND *Phonogram 5829592* ....**26** 3 |

ENGLAND DAN and John Ford COLEY
US, male vocal
duo – Dan Seals and John Ford Coley (Singles: 12 Weeks) pos/wks

| 25 Sep 76 | I'D REALLY LOVE TO SEE YOU TONIGHT *Atlantic K 10810* .....**26** 7 |
| 23 Jun 79 | LOVE IS THE ANSWER *Big Tree K 11296* ....**45** 5 |

ENGLAND FOOTBALL WORLD CUP SQUAD
UK, male football team vocalists (Albums: 18 Weeks) pos/wks

16 May 70 ●	THE WORLD BEATERS SING THE WORLD BEATERS
	Pye NSPL 18337 ....**4** 8
15 May 82	THIS TIME *K-Tel NE 1169* **37** 10

ENGLAND RUGBY WORLD CUP SQUAD See UNION featuring the ENGLAND WORLD CUP SQUAD

ENGLAND SISTERS See DALE SISTERS

ENGLAND SUPPORTERS' BAND
UK, male instrumental group (Singles: 4 Weeks) pos/wks

| 27 Jun 98 | THE GREAT ESCAPE *V2 VVR 5002163* ....**46** 2 |
| 24 Jun 00 | THE GREAT ESCAPE 2000 (re-recording) *V2 VVR 5014293* .....**26** 2 |

ENGLAND UNITED
UK, male / female
vocal / instrumental group (Singles: 11 Weeks) pos/wks

| 13 Jun 98 ● | (HOW DOES IT FEEL TO BE) ON TOP OF THE WORLD (re) |
| | *London LONCD 414* ....**9** 11 |

ENGLAND WORLD CUP SQUAD
UK, male football team vocalists (Singles: 48 Weeks) pos/wks

18 Apr 70 ★	BACK HOME (re) *Pye 7N 17920* **1** 17
10 Apr 82 ●	THIS TIME (WE'LL GET IT RIGHT) / ENGLAND, WE'LL
	FLY THE FLAG *England ER 1* **2** 13
19 Apr 86	WE'VE GOT THE WHOLE WORLD AT OUR FEET /
	WHEN WE ARE FAR FROM HOME *Columbia DB 9128* **66** 2
21 May 88	ALL THE WAY *MCA GOAL 1* [1] **64** 2
2 Jun 90 ★	WORLD IN MOTION ... *Factory / MCA FAC 2937* [2] **1** 12
15 Jun 02	WORLD IN MOTION ... (re-issue)
	London / MCA NUD 0CD 12 [2] **43** 2

[1] England Football Team and the 'sound' of Stock, Aitken and Waterman
[2] Englandneworder (New Order, Keith Allen, England footballer / rapper John Barnes and the rest of the England World Cup squad)

ENGLAND'S BARMY ARMY
UK, 5,000 male / female vocal cricket supporters (Singles: 1 Week) pos/wks

| 12 Jun 99 | COME ON ENGLAND! *Wildstar CDWILD 20* ....**45** 1 |

ENGLISH CHAMBER ORCHESTRA See Kiri TE KANAWA; John WILLIAMS; Nigel KENNEDY

Kim ENGLISH
US, female vocalist (Singles: 7 Weeks) pos/wks

23 Jul 94	NITE LIFE *Hi-Life PZCD 323* **35** 2
4 Mar 95	TIME FOR LOVE *Hi-Life HICD 8* **48** 1
9 Sep 95	I KNOW A PLACE *Hi-Life 5798072* **52** 1
30 Nov 96	NITE LIFE (re-mix) *Hi-Life 5755332* **35** 2
26 Apr 97	SUPERNATURAL *Hi-Life 5736972* **50** 1

Scott ENGLISH
US, male vocalist (Singles: 10 Weeks) pos/wks

| 9 Oct 71 | BRANDY *Horse HOSS 7* ....**12** 10 |

ENIAC See Tom NOVY

ENIGMA
UK, male / female vocal / instrumental
group (Singles: 15 Weeks, Albums: 3 Weeks) pos/wks

23 May 81	AIN'T NO STOPPING *Creole CR 9* **11** 8
8 Aug 81	I LOVE MUSIC *Creole CR 14* **25** 7
5 Sep 81	AIN'T NO STOPPIN' *Creole CRX 1* **80** 3

ENIGMA   359 Top 500
New-age, ambient and dance fusion sculpted by Michael Cretu, b. 18 May 1957, Bucharest, Romania, and initially aided by German wife Sandra Lauer and producer Frank Peterson. The title of Gregorian chant-sampling international debut hit 'Sadness Part 1' – referring to the Marquis de Sade – was shortened for the UK release (Singles: 45 Weeks, Albums: 142 Weeks) pos/wks

15 Dec 90 ★	SADNESS PART 1 *Virgin International DINS 101* **1** 12
30 Mar 91	MEA CULPA PART II *Virgin International DINS 104* **55** 3
10 Aug 91	PRINCIPLES OF LUST *Virgin International DINS 110* **59** 2
11 Jan 92	THE RIVERS OF BELIEF *Virgin International DINS 112* **68** 2
29 Jan 94 ●	RETURN TO INNOCENCE *Virgin International DINSD 123* **3** 14
14 May 94	THE EYES OF TRUTH *Virgin International DINSD 126* **21** 4
20 Aug 94	AGE OF LONELINESS *Virgin International DINSD 135* **21** 5
25 Jan 97	BEYOND THE INVISIBLE *Virgin International DINSD 155* [1] **26** 2
19 Apr 97	TNT FOR THE BRAIN *Virgin International DINSD 161* [1] **60** 1
22 Dec 90 ★	MCMXC A.D. – 'THE LIMITED EDITION'
	Virgin International VIR 11 ....**1** 83
19 Feb 94 ★	THE CROSS OF CHANGES *Virgin International CDVIR 20* [1] ■ ..**1** 35
7 Dec 96	LE ROI EST MORT VIVE LE ROI! *Virgin CDVIR 60* [2] **12** 12
29 Jan 00 ●	THE SCREEN BEHIND THE MIRROR *Virgin CDVIR 100* **7** 6
17 Nov 01	LOVE SENSUALITY DEVOTION – THE GREATEST HITS
	Virgin CDVIR 150 ....**29** 4
20 Sep 03	VOYAGEUR *Virgin CDVIRX 211* **46** 2

[1] Enigma 3 [1] Enigma 2 [2] Enigma 3

Brian ENO (see also ROXY MUSIC)
UK, male instrumentalist – keyboards (Albums: 16 Weeks) pos/wks

9 Mar 74	HERE COME THE WARM JETS *Island ILPS 9268* **26** 2
21 Oct 78	MUSIC FOR FILMS *Polydor 2310623* **55** 1
21 Feb 81	MY LIFE IN THE BUSH OF GHOSTS *Polydor EGLP 48* [1] **29** 8
8 May 82	AMBIENT 4 ON LAND *EG EGED 20* **93** 1
12 Sep 92	NERVE NET *Opal 9362450332* **70** 1
24 Sep 94	WAH WAH *Fontana 5228272* [2] **11** 2
14 Oct 95	SPINNER *All Saints ASCD 023* [3] **71** 1

[1] Brian Eno and David Byrne [2] James and Brian Eno [3] Brian Eno and Jah Wobble

ENTOMBED
Sweden, male vocal / instrumental group (Albums: 1 Week) pos/wks

| 15 Mar 97 | TO RIDE SHOOT STRAIGHT AND SPEAK THE TRUTH |
| | *Threeman Recordings CDMFN 216* ....**75** 1 |

ENUFF Z'NUFF
US, male vocal / instrumental group (Albums: 1 Week) pos/wks

| 13 Apr 91 | STRENGTH *Atco 7567916381* ....**56** 1 |

ENYA `142` `Top 500`
The world's top selling New Age artist, b. Eithne Ni Brennan, 17 May 1961, County Donegal, Ireland. The multi-award winning ex-Clannad member (1980-82), whose sales top 60 million, was the world's biggest selling female artist in 2001 (15 million albums) (Singles: 88 Weeks, Albums: 274 Weeks)

		pos/wks
15 Oct 88 ★	ORINOCO FLOW WEA YZ 312	1 13
24 Dec 88	EVENING FALLS WEA YZ 356	20 4
10 Jun 89	STORMS IN AFRICA (PART II) WEA YZ 368	41 4
19 Oct 91	CARIBBEAN BLUE WEA YZ 604	13 7
7 Dec 91	HOW CAN I KEEP FROM SINGING? WEA YZ 365	32 5
1 Aug 92 ●	BOOK OF DAYS WEA YZ 640	10 4
14 Nov 92	THE CELTS WEA YZ 705	29 4
18 Nov 95 ●	ANYWHERE IS WEA WEA 023CD	7 12
7 Dec 96	ON MY WAY HOME WEA WEA 047CD	26 2
13 Dec 97	ONLY IF ... WEA WEA 143CD	43 2
25 Nov 00	ONLY TIME WEA WEA 316CD	32 3
31 Mar 01	WILD CHILD WEA WEA 324CD	72 1
2 Feb 02	MAY IT BE WEA W 578CD	50 2
5 Jun 04	I DON'T WANNA KNOW (IMPORT) Universal 9862372 PMI [1]	71 1
12 Jun 04 ★	I DON'T WANNA KNOW Bad Boy MCSTD 40369 [1]	1 14
11 Sep 04	YOU SHOULD REALLY KNOW Relentless RELCD 9 [2]	8 8
6 Jun 87 ●	ENYA BBC REB 605	69 4
15 Oct 88 ●	WATERMARK WEA WX 199	5 92
16 Nov 91 ★	SHEPHERD MOONS WEA WX 431 ■	1 90
28 Nov 92 ●	THE CELTS WEA 4509911672	10 19
2 Dec 95 ●	THE MEMORY OF TREES WEA 0630128792	5 24
15 Nov 97 ●	PAINT THE SKY WITH STARS – THE BEST OF ENYA WEA 3984208952	4 28
2 Dec 00 ●	A DAY WITHOUT RAIN WEA 8573859862	6 17

[1] Mario Winans featuring Enya & P Diddy [2] Pirates featuring Enya, Shola Ama, Naila Boss & Ishani

'You Should Really Know' is a response to 'I Don't Wanna Know': both tracks sample Enya's Boadicea. 'The Celts' is a repackaged and re-issued version of 'Enya'

EON UK, male producer – Ian Bela (Singles: 1 Week)

		pos/wks
17 Aug 91	FEAR: THE MINDKILLER Vinyl Solution STORM 33	63 1

EPSILON See D KAY & EPSILON featuring STAMINA MC

The EQUALS (see also EDDY GRANT) UK, male vocal / instrumental group (Singles: 69 Weeks, Albums: 10 Weeks)

		pos/wks
21 Feb 68	I GET SO EXCITED President PT 180	44 4
1 May 68 ★	BABY COME BACK (re) President PT 135	1 18
21 Aug 68	LAUREL AND HARDY President PT 200	35 5
27 Nov 68	SOFTLY SOFTLY President PT 222	48 3
2 Apr 69	MICHAEL AND THE SLIPPER TREE President PT 240	24 7
30 Jul 69 ●	VIVA BOBBY JOE President PT 260	6 14
27 Dec 69	RUB A DUB DUB President PT 275	34 7
19 Dec 70 ●	BLACK SKIN BLUE EYED BOYS President PT 325	9 11
18 Nov 67 ●	UNEQUALLED EQUALS President PTL 1006	10 9
9 Mar 68	EQUALS EXPLOSION President PTLS 1015	32 1

ERASURE `69` `Top 500` (see also The ASSEMBLY)
Award-winning UK duo formed by Vince Clarke (k) and Andy Bell (v). After hits with Depeche Mode, Yazoo and The Assembly, this act was Clarke's greatest success, scoring 16 Top 10 singles and having five albums enter at No.1 (Singles: 212 Weeks, Albums: 323 Weeks)

		pos/wks
5 Oct 85	WHO NEEDS LOVE LIKE THAT Mute MUTE 40	55 2
25 Oct 86 ●	SOMETIMES Mute MUTE 51	2 17
28 Feb 87	IT DOESN'T HAVE TO BE Mute MUTE 56	12 9
30 May 87 ●	VICTIM OF LOVE Mute MUTE 61	7 9
3 Oct 87 ●	THE CIRCUS Mute MUTE 66	6 10
5 Mar 88 ●	SHIP OF FOOLS Mute MUTE 74	6 8
11 Jun 88	CHAINS OF LOVE Mute MUTE 83	11 7
1 Oct 88 ●	A LITTLE RESPECT Mute MUTE 85	4 10
10 Dec 88 ●	CRACKERS INTERNATIONAL (EP) Mute MUTE 93	2 13
30 Sep 89 ●	DRAMA! Mute MUTE 89	4 8
9 Dec 89	YOU SURROUND ME Mute MUTE 99	15 9
10 Mar 90 ●	BLUE SAVANNAH Mute MUTE 109	3 10
2 Jun 90	STAR Mute MUTE 111	11 7
29 Jun 91 ●	CHORUS Mute MUTE 125	3 9
21 Sep 91 ●	LOVE TO HATE YOU Mute MUTE 131	4 9
7 Dec 91	AM I RIGHT? (EP) Mute MUTE 134	15 6
11 Jan 92	AM I RIGHT? (EP) (re-mix) Mute L12MUTE 134	22 3
28 Mar 92 ●	BREATH OF LIFE Mute MUTE 142	8 6
13 Jun 92 ★	ABBA-ESQUE (EP) Mute MUTE 144 ■	1 12
7 Nov 92 ●	WHO NEEDS LOVE (LIKE THAT) (re-mix) Mute MUTE 150	10 4
23 Apr 94 ●	ALWAYS Mute CDMUTE 152	4 9
30 Jul 94 ●	RUN TO THE SUN Mute CDMUTE 153	6 5
3 Dec 94	I LOVE SATURDAY Mute CDMUTE 166	20 6
23 Sep 95	STAY WITH ME Mute CDMUTE 174	15 4
9 Dec 95	FINGERS AND THUMBS (COLD SUMMER'S DAY) Mute CDMUTE 178	20 3
18 Jan 97	IN MY ARMS Mute CDMUTE 190	13 4
8 Mar 97	DON'T SAY YOUR LOVE IS KILLING ME Mute CDMUTE 195	23 2
21 Oct 00	FREEDOM Mute CDMUTE 244	27 2
18 Jan 03	SOLSBURY HILL Mute CDMUTE 275	10 3
19 Apr 03	MAKE ME SMILE (COME UP AND SEE ME) Mute CDMUTE 292	14 3
25 Oct 03	OH L'AMOUR Mute CDMUTE 312	13 3
14 Jun 86	WONDERLAND Mute STUMM 25	71 7
11 Apr 87 ●	THE CIRCUS Mute STUMM 35	6 107
30 Apr 88 ●	THE INNOCENTS Mute STUMM 55 ■	1 78
28 Oct 89 ★	WILD! Mute STUMM 75 ■	1 48
26 Oct 91 ★	CHORUS Mute STUMM 95 ■	1 25
28 Nov 92 ★	POP! – THE FIRST 20 HITS Mute CDMUTEL 2 ■	1 26
28 May 94 ★	I SAY I SAY I SAY Mute LCDSTUMM 115 ■	1 15
4 Nov 95	ERASURE Mute CDSTUMM 145	14 5
12 Apr 97 ●	COWBOY Mute CDSTUMM 155	10 4
4 Nov 00	LOVEBOAT Mute CDSTUMM 175	45 1
8 Feb 03	OTHER PEOPLE'S SONGS Mute CDSTUMM 215	17 2
1 Nov 03	HITS! THE VERY BEST OF ERASURE Mute LCDMUTEL 10	15 5

Tracks on Crackers International (EP): Stop / The Hardest Part / Knocking on Your Door / She Won't Be Home. Tracks on Am I Right? (EP): Am I Right? / Carry On Clangers / Let It Flow / Waiting for Sex. Tracks on Am I Right? (EP) (re-mix): Am I Right? / Chorus / Love to Hate You / Perfect Stranger. Tracks on Abba-esque (EP): Lay All Your Love on Me / SOS / Take a Chance on Me / Voulez-Vous. 'Take a Chance on Me' credits MC Kinky

ERIC and the GOOD GOOD FEELING
UK, male / female vocal / instrumental group (Singles: 1 Week)

		pos/wks
3 Jun 89	GOOD GOOD FEELING Equinox EQN 1	73 1

ERIK UK, female vocalist (Singles: 5 Weeks)

		pos/wks
10 Apr 93	LOOKS LIKE I'M IN LOVE AGAIN PWL Sanctuary PWCD 252 [1]	46 2
29 Jan 94	GOT TO BE REAL PWL International PWCD 278	42 2
1 Oct 94	WE GOT THE LOVE PWL International PWCD 305	55 1

[1] Key West featuring Erik

ERIN See BBG; SHUT UP AND DANCE

ERIRE See SCIENCE DEPARTMENT featuring ERIRE; Danny HOWELLS & Dick TREVOR featuring ERIRE

EROTIC DRUM BAND
Canada, male / female vocal / instrumental group (Singles: 3 Weeks) pos/wks

9 Jun 79	LOVE DISCO STYLE Scope SC 1	47 3

ERUPTION Jamaica, male / female vocal / instrumental group (Singles: 21 Weeks)

		pos/wks
18 Feb 78 ●	I CAN'T STAND THE RAIN Atlantic K 11068 [1]	5 11
21 Apr 79 ●	ONE WAY TICKET Atlantic / Hansa K 11266	9 10

[1] Eruption featuring Precious Wilson

Michelle ESCOFFERY See ARTFUL DODGER

Shaun ESCOFFERY UK, male vocalist (Singles: 2 Weeks)

		pos/wks
10 Mar 01	SPACE RIDER Oyster Music OYSCD 4	52 1
20 Jul 02	DAYS LIKE THIS Oyster Music OYSCDS 8	53 1

The ESCORTS
UK, male vocal / instrumental group (Singles: 2 Weeks)

		pos/wks
2 Jul 64	THE ONE TO CRY Fontana TF 474	49 2

ESCRIMA (see also CAMISRA; The GRIFTERS; PARTIZAN; TALL PAUL)
UK, male producer – Paul Newman (Singles: 4 Weeks)

		pos/wks
11 Feb 95	TRAIN OF THOUGHT Ffrreedom TABCD 225	36 2
7 Oct 95	DEEPER Hooj Choons TABCD 236	27 2

ESKA See COLOURS featuring EMMANUEL & ESKA; EN-CORE featuring Stephen EMMANUEL & ESKA; Nitin SAWHNEY

Singles re-entries are listed as (re), (2re), (3re).... which signifies that the hit re-entered the chart once, twice or three times...

ESKIMOS & EGYPT
UK, male vocal / instrumental group (Singles: 4 Weeks)   pos/wks

13 Feb 93	**FALL FROM GRACE** *One Little Indian EEF 96CD*	**51**	2
29 May 93	**UK-USA** *One Little Indian 99TP7 CD*	**52**	2

ESPIRITU
UK / France, male / female vocal / instrumental duo – Vanessa Quinones and Chris Chaplin (Singles: 10 Weeks)   pos/wks

6 Mar 93	**CONQUISTADOR** *Heavenly HVN 28CD*	**47**	2
7 Aug 93	**LOS AMERICANOS** *Heavenly HVN 33CD*	**45**	2
20 Aug 94	**BONITA MANANA** *Columbia 6606925*	**50**	1
25 Mar 95	**ALWAYS SOMETHING THERE TO REMIND ME** *WEA YZ 911CD* [1]	**14**	5

[1] Tin Tin Out featuring Espiritu

ESSENCE
(see also CHAKRA; LUSTRAL; SPACE BROTHERS; ASCENSION; OXYGEN featuring ANDREA BRITTON) *UK, male production group – Ricky Simmonds and Stephen Jones and female vocalist (Singles: 2 Weeks)* pos/wks

21 Mar 98	**THE PROMISE** *Innocent SINCD 1*	**27**	2

The ESSEX
US, male / female vocal group (Singles: 5 Weeks)   pos/wks

8 Aug 63	**EASIER SAID THAN DONE** *Columbia DB 7077* ▲	**41**	5

David ESSEX 130 Top 500
(see also Frank FINLAY) *Actor / teeny-bop star turned popular entertainer, b. David Cook, 23 Jul 1947, London, UK. This singer / songwriter was voted No.1 British Male Vocalist (1974) and was a teen idol for more than a decade. He starred in the stage show 'Godspell' and graduated successfully to films (Singles: 199 Weeks, Albums: 178 Weeks)* pos/wks

18 Aug 73	● **ROCK ON** *CBS 1693*	**3**	11
10 Nov 73	● **LAMPLIGHT** *CBS 1902*	**7**	15
11 May 74	**AMERICA** *CBS 2176*	**32**	5
12 Oct 74	★ **GONNA MAKE YOU A STAR** *CBS 2492*	**1**	17
14 Dec 74	● **STARDUST** *CBS 2828*	**7**	10
5 Jul 75	● **ROLLING STONE** *CBS 3425*	**5**	7
13 Sep 75	★ **HOLD ME CLOSE** *CBS 3572*	**1**	10
6 Dec 75	**IF I COULD** *CBS 3776*	**13**	8
20 Mar 76	**CITY LIGHTS** *CBS 4050*	**24**	4
16 Oct 76	**COMING HOME** *CBS 4486*	**24**	6
17 Sep 77	**COOL OUT TONIGHT** *CBS 5495*	**23**	6
11 Mar 78	**STAY WITH ME BABY** *CBS 6063*	**45**	5
19 Aug 78	● **OH WHAT A CIRCUS** *Mercury 6007 185*	**3**	11
21 Oct 78	**BRAVE NEW WORLD** *CBS 6705*	**55**	3
3 Mar 79	**IMPERIAL WIZARD** *Mercury 6007 202*	**32**	8
5 Apr 80	● **SILVER DREAM MACHINE (PART 1)** *Mercury BIKE 1*	**4**	11
14 Jun 80	**HOT LOVE** *Mercury HOT 11*	**57**	4
26 Jun 82	**ME AND MY GIRL (NIGHT-CLUBBING)** *Mercury MER 107*	**13**	10
11 Dec 82	● **A WINTER'S TALE** *Mercury MER 127*	**2**	10
4 Jun 83	**THE SMILE** *Mercury ESSEX 1*	**52**	4
27 Aug 83	● **TAHITI (FROM 'MUTINY ON THE BOUNTY')** *Mercury BOUNT 1*	**8**	11
26 Nov 83	**YOU'RE IN MY HEART (re)** *Mercury ESSEX 2*	**59**	6
23 Feb 85	**FALLING ANGELS RIDING** *Mercury ESSEX 5*	**29**	7
18 Apr 87	**MYFANWY** *Arista RIS 11*	**41**	7
26 Nov 94	**TRUE LOVE WAYS** *PolyGram TV TLWCD 2* [1]	**38**	3
24 Nov 73	● **ROCK ON** *CBS 65823*	**7**	22
19 Oct 74	● **DAVID ESSEX** *CBS 69088*	**2**	24
27 Sep 75	● **ALL THE FUN OF THE FAIR** *CBS 69160*	**3**	20
5 Jun 76	**ON TOUR** *CBS 95000*	**51**	1
30 Oct 76	**OUT ON THE STREET** *CBS 86017*	**31**	9
8 Oct 77	**GOLD AND IVORY** *CBS 86038*	**29**	4
6 Jan 79	**THE DAVID ESSEX ALBUM** *CBS 10011*	**29**	7
31 Mar 79	**IMPERIAL WIZARD** *Mercury 9109616*	**12**	9
12 Jun 80	**HOT LOVE** *Mercury 6359017*	**75**	1
19 Jun 82	**STAGE-STRUCK** *Mercury MERS 4*	**31**	15
27 Nov 82	**THE VERY BEST OF DAVID ESSEX** *TV TVA 4*	**37**	11
15 Oct 83	**MUTINY** *Mercury MERH 30*	**39**	4
17 Dec 83	**THE WHISPER** *Mercury MERH 34*	**67**	6
6 Dec 86	**CENTRE STAGE** *K-Tel ONE 1333*	**82**	4
19 Oct 91	**HIS GREATEST HITS** *Mercury 5103081*	**13**	13
10 Apr 93	● **COVER SHOT** *PolyGram TV 5145632*	**3**	8
22 Oct 94	**BACK TO BACK** *PolyGram TV 5237902*	**33**	2
9 Dec 95	**MISSING YOU** *PolyGram TV 5295822*	**26**	9
17 May 97	**A NIGHT AT THE MOVIES** *PolyGram TV 5376082*	**14**	5
13 Jun 98	**GREATEST HITS** *PolyGram TV 5584842*	**31**	4

[1] David Essex and Catherine Zeta Jones

'Mutiny' is a studio recording of a musical that was not staged until 1985. Both this album and the eventual stage production starred David Essex and Frank Finlay

Gloria ESTEFAN 102 Top 500
(see also MIAMI SOUND MACHINE)
Latin music's leading lady, b. Gloria Fajardo, 1 Sep 1957, Havana, Cuba. Successes in the dance and MOR fields have pushed her total worldwide sales to a reported 70 million, with two of her albums passing the one-million sales mark in the UK (Singles: 182 Weeks, Albums: 247 Weeks) pos/wks

16 Jul 88	● **ANYTHING FOR YOU** *Epic 651673 7* [1] ▲	**10**	16
22 Oct 88	● **1-2-3 (re)** *Epic 652958 7* [1]	**9**	10
17 Dec 88	**RHYTHM IS GONNA GET YOU** *Epic 654514 7* [1]	**16**	9
11 Feb 89	● **CAN'T STAY AWAY FROM YOU** *Epic 651444 7* [1]	**7**	12
15 Jul 89	● **DON'T WANNA LOSE YOU** *Epic 655054 0* ▲	**6**	10
16 Sep 89	**OYE MI CANTO (HEAR MY VOICE)** *Epic 655287 7*	**16**	8
25 Nov 89	**GET ON YOUR FEET** *Epic 655450 7*	**23**	7
3 Mar 90	**HERE WE ARE** *Epic 6554737*	**23**	6
26 May 90	**CUTS BOTH WAYS** *Epic 655982 7*	**49**	5
26 Jan 91	**COMING OUT OF THE DARK** *Epic 6565747* ▲	**25**	5
6 Apr 91	**SEAL OUR FATE** *Epic 6567737*	**24**	7
8 Jun 91	**REMEMBER ME WITH LOVE** *Epic 6569687*	**22**	6
21 Sep 91	**LIVE FOR LOVING YOU** *Epic 6573827*	**33**	5
24 Oct 92	**ALWAYS TOMORROW** *Epic 6583977*	**24**	4
12 Dec 92	● **MIAMI HIT MIX / CHRISTMAS THROUGH YOUR EYES** *Epic 6588377*	**8**	9
13 Feb 93	**I SEE YOUR SMILE** *Epic 6589612*	**48**	2
3 Apr 93	**GO AWAY** *Epic 6590952*	**13**	6
3 Jul 93	**MI TIERRA** *Epic 6593512*	**36**	3
14 Aug 93	**IF WE WERE LOVERS / CON LOS AÑOS QUE ME QUEDAN** *Epic 6595702*	**40**	3
18 Dec 93	**MONTUNO** *Epic 6599972*	**55**	2
15 Oct 94	**TURN THE BEAT AROUND** *Epic 6606822*	**21**	6
3 Dec 94	**HOLD ME THRILL ME KISS ME (re)** *Epic 6610802*	**11**	11
18 Feb 95	**EVERLASTING LOVE** *Epic 6611595*	**19**	5
25 May 96	**REACH (2re)** *Epic 6632642*	**15**	8
24 Aug 96	**YOU'LL BE MINE (PARTY TIME)** *Epic 6636505*	**18**	3
14 Dec 96	**I'M NOT GIVING YOU UP** *Epic 6640222*	**28**	3
6 Jun 98	**HEAVEN'S WHAT I FEEL** *Epic 6660042*	**17**	4
10 Oct 98	**OYE** *Epic 6664645*	**33**	2
16 Jan 99	**DON'T LET THIS MOMENT END** *Epic 6667472*	**28**	2
8 Jan 00	**MUSIC OF MY HEART** *Epic 6685272* [2]	**34**	3
19 Nov 88	★ **ANYTHING FOR YOU** *Epic 4631251* [1]	**1**	54
5 Aug 89	★ **CUTS BOTH WAYS** *Epic 4651451* ■	**1**	64
16 Feb 91	● **INTO THE LIGHT** *Epic 4677821*	**2**	36
14 Nov 92	● **GREATEST HITS** *Epic 4723322*	**2**	47
10 Jul 93	**MI TIERRA** *Epic 4737992*	**11**	11
29 Oct 94	● **HOLD ME THRILL ME KISS ME** *Epic 4774162*	**5**	19
21 Oct 95	**ABRIENDO PUERTAS** *Epic 4809922*	**70**	1
15 Jun 96	**DESTINY** *Epic 4839322*	**12**	9
13 Jun 98	**GLORIA!** *Epic 4898502*	**16**	4
27 May 00	**ALMA CARIBENA – CARIBBEAN SOUL** *Epic 4976172*	**44**	1
24 Feb 01	**GREATEST HITS VOL. II** *Epic 5016372*	**60**	1

[1] Gloria Estefan & Miami Sound Machine [2] 'N Sync / Gloria Estefan [1] Gloria Estefan & Miami Sound Machine

'Christmas Through Your Eyes' was listed only from 19 Dec 1992

ESTELLE
UK, female rapper – Estelle Swaray (Singles: 13 Weeks, Albums: 2 Weeks) pos/wks

31 Jul 04	**1980** *V2 / J-Did JAD 5027813*	**14**	7
16 Oct 04	**FREE** *V2 / J-Did 5027843*	**15**	6
30 Oct 04	**THE 18TH DAY ...** *V2 JAD 1027838*	**35**	2

EST'ELLE *See BLAK TWANG*

Don ESTELLE and Windsor DAVIES
UK, male actors / vocal duo – Don Estelle, b. 22 May 1933, d. 2 Aug 2003 (Singles: 16 Weeks, Albums: 8 Weeks) pos/wks

17 May 75	★ **WHISPERING GRASS** *EMI 2290* [1]	**1**	12
25 Oct 75	**PAPER DOLL** *EMI 2361*	**41**	4
10 Jan 76	● **SING LOFTY** *EMI EMC 3102*	**10**	8

[1] Windsor Davies as BSM Williams and Don Estelle as Gunner Sugden (Lofty)

ESTHERO *See Ian POOLEY*

Deon ESTUS
US, male vocalist / instrumentalist – bass (Singles: 7 Weeks) pos/wks

25 Jan 86	**MY GUY – MY GIRL (MEDLEY)** *Sedition EDIT 3310* [1]	**63**	3
29 Apr 89	**HEAVEN HELP ME** *Mika MIKA 2*	**41**	4

[1] Amii Stewart and Deon Estus

ETA _Denmark, male instrumental group (Singles: 5 Weeks)_   pos/wks

28 Jun 97	**CASUAL SUB (BURNING SPEAR)** _East West EW 110CD_ **28** 3
31 Jan 98	**CASUAL SUB (BURNING SPEAR) (re-mix)**	
	East West Dance EW 145CD **28** 2

ETERNAL (195) (Top 500) _London-based vocal group with across-the-board appeal: sisters Easther and Vernett Bennett, Kéllé Bryan, and Louise Nurding. The first all-female act to shift more than one million copies of an album in the UK. Louise left for a successful solo career in 1995, followed by Kéllé four years later. Best-selling single: 'I Wanna Be the Only One' 601,132. (Singles: 134 Weeks, Albums: 163 Weeks)_   pos/wks

2 Oct 93	● **STAY** _EMI CDEM 283_ 4 4
15 Jan 94	● **SAVE OUR LOVE** _EMI CDEM 296_ 8 7
30 Apr 94	● **JUST A STEP FROM HEAVEN** _EMI CDEM 311_ 8 10
20 Aug 94	**SO GOOD** _EMI CDEMS 339_ 13 7
5 Nov 94	● **OH BABY I ...** _EMI CDEM 353_ 4 13
24 Dec 94	**CRAZY** _EMI CDEMX 364_ 15 7
21 Oct 95	● **POWER OF A WOMAN** _EMI CDEM 396_ 5 8
9 Dec 95	● **I AM BLESSED** _EMI CDEMS 408_ 7 12
9 Mar 96	● **GOOD THING** _EMI CDEM 419_ 8 6
17 Aug 96	● **SOMEDAY** _EMI CDEMS 439_ 4 9
7 Dec 96	● **SECRETS** _EMI CDEM 459_ 9 7
8 Mar 97	● **DON'T YOU LOVE ME** _EMI CDEMS 465_ 3 7
31 May 97	★ **I WANNA BE THE ONLY ONE** _EMI CDEM 472_ [1] ■..1 15
11 Oct 97	● **ANGEL OF MINE** _EMI CDEM 493_ 4 13
30 Oct 99	**WHAT 'CHA GONNA DO** _EMI CDEM 552_ 16 4
11 Dec 93	● **ALWAYS & FOREVER** _EMI CDEMD 1053_ 2 76
11 Nov 95	● **POWER OF A WOMAN** _EMI CDEMD 1090_ 6 31
29 Mar 97	● **BEFORE THE RAIN** _EMI CDEMD 1103_ 3 29
1 Nov 97	● **GREATEST HITS** _EMI 8217982_ 2 27

[1] Eternal featuring BeBe Winans

ETHER _UK, male vocal / instrumental group (Singles: 1 Week)_   pos/wks

28 Mar 98	**WATCHING YOU** _Parlophone CDR 6491_ 74 1

Melissa ETHERIDGE
US, female vocalist / instrumentalist – guitar (Albums: 2 Weeks)   pos/wks

30 Sep 89	**BRAVE AND CRAZY** _Island ILPS 9939_ 63 1
9 May 92	**NEVER ENOUGH** _Island CID 9990_ 56 1

ETHICS (see also ARTEMESIA; MOVIN' MELODIES; SUBLIMINAL CUTS)
Holland, male producer – Patrick Prinz (Singles: 5 Weeks)   pos/wks

25 Nov 95	**TO THE BEAT OF THE DRUM (LA LUNA)** _VC VCRD 5_ 13 5

The ETHIOPIANS
Jamaica, male vocal / instrumental group (Singles: 6 Weeks)   pos/wks

13 Sep 67	**TRAIN TO SKAVILLE** _Rio RIO 130_ 40 6

Tony ETORIA _UK, male vocalist (Singles: 8 Weeks)_   pos/wks

4 Jun 77	**I CAN PROVE IT** _GTO GT 89_ 21 8

Nellie ETTISON See ARTIFICIAL FUNK featuring Nellie ETTISON

EUROGROOVE _UK, male / female vocal group (Singles: 7 Weeks)_ pos/wks

20 May 95	**MOVE YOUR BODY** _Avex UK AVEXCD 4_ 29 2
5 Aug 95	**DIVE TO PARADISE** _Avex UK AVEXCD 10_ 31 2
21 Oct 95	**IT'S ON YOU (SCAN ME)** _Avex UK AVEXCD 17_ 25 2
3 Feb 96	**MOVE YOUR BODY (re-mix)** _Avex UK AVEXCD 22_ 44 1

EUROPE _Sweden, male vocal / instrumental group – lead vocal Joey Tempest (Singles: 50 Weeks, Albums: 43 Weeks)_   pos/wks

1 Nov 86	★ **THE FINAL COUNTDOWN** _Epic A 7127_ 1 15
31 Jan 87	**ROCK THE NIGHT** _Epic EUR 1_ 12 9
18 Apr 87	**CARRIE** _Epic EUR 2_ 22 8
20 Aug 88	**SUPERSTITIOUS** _Epic EUR 3_ 34 5
1 Feb 92	**I'LL CRY FOR YOU** _Epic 6576977_ 28 5
21 Mar 92	**HALFWAY TO HEAVEN** _Epic 6578517_ 42 4
25 Dec 99	**THE FINAL COUNTDOWN 2000 (re-recording)** _Epic 6685042_ ..36 4
22 Nov 86	● **THE FINAL COUNTDOWN** _Epic EPC 26808_ 9 37
17 Sep 88	**OUT OF THIS WORLD** _Epic 4624491_ 12 5
19 Oct 91	**PRISONERS IN PARADISE** _Epic 4687551_ 61 1

EUROPEANS
UK, male vocal / instrumental group (Albums: 1 Week)   pos/wks

11 Feb 84	**LIVE** _A&M SCOT 1_ 100 1

EURYTHMICS (42) (Top 500) _Innovative and internationally popular duo formed by Brit award-winning Scottish vocalist Annie Lennox and multi-instrumentalist / songwriter / producer Dave Stewart, formerly known as The Tourists. The most charted male / female duo in the UK saw their greatest hits album sell more than two million copies in the UK and in Europe (Singles: 208 Weeks, Albums: 476 Weeks)_   pos/wks

4 Jul 81	**NEVER GONNA CRY AGAIN** _RCA 68_ 63 3
20 Nov 82	● **LOVE IS A STRANGER (re)** _RCA DA 1_ 6 13
12 Feb 83	● **SWEET DREAMS (ARE MADE OF THIS)** _RCA DA 2_ ▲ ...2 14
9 Jul 83	● **WHO'S THAT GIRL?** _RCA DA 3_ 3 10
5 Nov 83	● **RIGHT BY YOUR SIDE** _RCA DA 4_ 10 11
21 Jan 84	● **HERE COMES THE RAIN AGAIN** _RCA DA 5_ 8 8
3 Nov 84	● **SEXCRIME (NINETEEN EIGHTY FOUR)** _Virgin VS 728_ 4 13
19 Jan 85	**JULIA** _Virgin VS 734_ 44 4
20 Apr 85	**WOULD I LIE TO YOU?** _RCA PB 40101_ 17 8
6 Jul 85	★ **THERE MUST BE AN ANGEL (PLAYING WITH MY HEART)**	
	RCA PB 40247 ....1 13
2 Nov 85	● **SISTERS ARE DOIN' IT FOR THEMSELVES** _RCA PB 40339_ [1] ..9 11
11 Jan 86	**IT'S ALRIGHT (BABY'S COMING BACK)** _RCA PB 40375_ ...12 8
14 Jun 86	**WHEN TOMORROW COMES** _RCA DA 7_ 30 6
6 Sep 86	● **THORN IN MY SIDE** _RCA DA 8_ 5 11
29 Nov 86	**THE MIRACLE OF LOVE** _RCA DA 9_ 23 9
28 Feb 87	**MISSIONARY MAN** _RCA DA 10_ 31 4
24 Oct 87	**BEETHOVEN (I LOVE TO LISTEN TO)** _RCA DA 11_ 25 5
26 Dec 87	**SHAME** _RCA DA 14_ 41 6
9 Apr 88	**I NEED A MAN** _RCA DA 15_ 26 5
11 Jun 88	**YOU HAVE PLACED A CHILL IN MY HEART** _RCA DA 16_ 16 8
26 Aug 89	**REVIVAL** _RCA DA 17_ 26 6
4 Nov 89	**DON'T ASK ME WHY** _RCA DA 19_ 25 6
3 Feb 90	**THE KING AND QUEEN OF AMERICA** _RCA DA 20_ 29 5
12 May 90	**ANGEL** _RCA DA 21_ 23 6
9 Mar 91	**LOVE IS A STRANGER (re-issue)** _RCA PB 44265_ 46 3
16 Nov 91	**SWEET DREAMS (ARE MADE OF THIS) '91** _RCA PB 45031_ 48 2
16 Oct 99	**I SAVED THE WORLD TODAY** _RCA 74321695632_ 11 6
5 Feb 00	**17 AGAIN** _RCA 74321726262_ 27 4
12 Feb 83	● **SWEET DREAMS (ARE MADE OF THIS)** _RCA RCALP 6063_ ...3 60
26 Nov 83	● **TOUCH** _RCA PL 70109_ 1 48
9 Jun 84	**TOUCH DANCE** _RCA PG 70354_ 31 5
24 Nov 84	**1984 (FOR THE LOVE OF BIG BROTHER)** _Virgin V 1984_ ...23 17
11 May 85	● **BE YOURSELF TONIGHT** _RCA PL 70711_ 3 80
12 Jul 86	● **REVENGE** _RCA PL 71050_ 3 52
21 Nov 87	● **SAVAGE** _RCA PL 71555_ 7 33
23 Sep 89	★ **WE TOO ARE ONE** _RCA PL 74251_ ■ 1 32
30 Mar 91	★ **GREATEST HITS** _RCA PL 74856_ ■ 1 122
27 Nov 93	**EURYTHMICS LIVE 1983-1989** _RCA 74321171452_ 22 7
30 Oct 99	● **PEACE** _RCA 74321695622_ 4 20

[1] Eurythmics and Aretha Franklin

'Love Is a Stranger' reached its peak position when it re-entered in Apr 1983

EUSEBE
UK, male / female vocal group (Singles: 3 Weeks)   pos/wks

26 Aug 95	**SUMMERTIME HEALING** _Mama's Yard CDMAMA 4_ 32 3

EVANESCENCE _US, male / female vocal / instrumental group (Singles: 37 Weeks, Albums: 69 Weeks)_   pos/wks

31 May 03	**BRING ME TO LIFE (IMPORT)** _Epic 8734881_ [1] 60 2
14 Jun 03	★ **BRING ME TO LIFE** _Epic 6739762_ [1] ■ 1 17
4 Oct 03	● **GOING UNDER** _Epic / Wind Up 6743522_ 8 6
20 Dec 03	● **MY IMMORTAL** _Epic 6745422_ 7 9
12 Jun 04	**EVERYBODY'S FOOL** _Epic 6747992_ 24 3
10 May 03	★ **FALLEN** _Epic 13063_ 1 69

[1] Evanescence featuring Paul McCoy

EVANGEL TEMPLE CHOIR See Johnny CASH

Faith EVANS (see also CLIPSE)
US, female vocalist (Singles: 43 Weeks, Albums: 1 Week)   pos/wks

14 Oct 95	**YOU USED TO LOVE ME** _Puff Daddy 74321299812_ 42 2
23 Nov 96	**STRESSED OUT** _Jive JIVECD 404_ [1] 33 2
28 Jun 97	● **I'LL BE MISSING YOU** _Puff Daddy 74321499102_ [2] ◆ ■ ▲..1 21
14 Nov 98	**LOVE LIKE THIS** _Puff Daddy 74321625592_ 24 4
1 May 99	**ALL NIGHT LONG** _Puff Daddy / Arista 74321665692_ [3] 23 3
1 May 99	**GEORGY PORGY** _Warner Bros. W 478CD2_ [4] 28 3
30 Dec 00	**HEARTBREAK HOTEL** _Arista 74321820572_ [5] 25 5

24 May 03	**MA, I DON'T LOVE HER** *Arista 82876526482* [6]	**38**	3
7 Nov 98	**KEEP THE FAITH** *Arista 74321614672*	**69**	1

[1] A Tribe Called Quest featuring Faith Evans and Raphael Saadiq [2] Puff Daddy and Faith Evans featuring 112 [3] Faith Evans featuring Puff Daddy [4] Eric Benet featuring Faith Evans [5] Whitney Houston featuring Faith Evans and Kelly Price [6] Clipse featuring Faith Evans

Maureen EVANS *UK, female vocalist (Singles: 37 Weeks)* pos/wks

22 Jan 60	**THE BIG HURT** *Oriole CB 1533*	**26**	2
17 Mar 60	**LOVE KISSES AND HEARTACHES** *Oriole CB 1540*	**44**	1
2 Jun 60	**PAPER ROSES** *Oriole CB 1550*	**40**	5
29 Nov 62 ●	**LIKE I DO** *Oriole CB 1760*	**3**	18
27 Feb 64	**I LOVE HOW YOU LOVE ME (re)** *Oriole CB 1906*	**34**	11

Paul EVANS *US, male vocalist (Singles: 14 Weeks)* pos/wks

27 Nov 59	**SEVEN LITTLE GIRLS SITTING IN THE BACK SEAT** *London HLL 8968* [1]	**25**	1
31 Mar 60	**MIDNITE SPECIAL** *London HLL 9045*	**41**	1
16 Dec 78 ●	**HELLO, THIS IS JOANNIE (THE TELEPHONE ANSWERING MACHINE SONG)** *Spring 2066932*	**6**	12

[1] Paul Evans and the Curls

Tommy EVANS See MARK B featuring Tommy EVANS

The EVASIONS *UK, male / female vocal / rap / instrumental group (Singles: 8 Weeks)* pos/wks

13 Jun 81	**WIKKA WRAP** *Groove GP 107*	**20**	8

E.V.E. *UK / US, female vocal group (Singles: 5 Weeks)* pos/wks

1 Oct 94	**GROOVE OF LOVE** *Gasoline Alley MCSTD 2007*	**30**	3
28 Jan 95	**GOOD LIFE** *Gasoline Alley MCSTD 2038*	**39**	2

EVE (see also Missy 'Misdemeanor' ELLIOTT) *US, female rapper – Eve Jeffers (Singles: 46 Weeks, Albums: 13 Weeks)* pos/wks

19 May 01 ●	**WHO'S THAT GIRL** *Interscope 4975572*	**6**	8
25 Aug 01 ●	**LET ME BLOW YA MIND** *Interscope / Polydor 4975932* [1]	**4**	12
9 Mar 02	**BROTHA PART II** *J 74321922142* [2]	**37**	2
16 Mar 02 ●	**CARAMEL** *Interscope / Polydor 4976742* [3]	**9**	10
5 Oct 02 ●	**GANGSTA LOVIN'** *Ruff Ryders / Interscope 4978042* [4]	**6**	8
12 Apr 03 ●	**SATISFACTION** *Ruff Ryders / Interscope 4978262*	**20**	4
6 Dec 03	**NOT TODAY** *Geffen MCSTD 40349* [5]	**40**	2
11 Aug 01	**SCORPION** *Interscope 4930212*	**22**	8
7 Sep 02	**EVE-OLUTION** *Interscope / Polydor 4934722*	**47**	5

[1] Eve featuring Gwen Stefani [2] Angie Stone featuring Alicia Keys and Eve [3] City High featuring Eve [4] Eve featuring Alicia Keys [5] Mary J Blige featuring Eve

Jessica EVE See WHO DA FUNK

Alison EVELYN See BROTHERS LIKE OUTLAW featuring Alison EVELYN

EVERCLEAR *US, male vocal / instrumental group (Singles: 7 Weeks, Albums: 3 Weeks)* pos/wks

1 Jun 96	**HEARTSPARK DOLLARSIGN** *Capitol CDCLS 773*	**48**	2
31 Aug 96	**SANTA MONICA (WATCH THE WORLD DIE)** *Capitol CDCL 775*	**40**	2
9 May 98	**EVERYTHING TO EVERYONE** *Capitol CDCL 799*	**41**	1
14 Oct 00	**WONDERFUL** *Capitol CDCLS 824*	**36**	2
14 Mar 98	**SO MUCH FOR THE AFTERGLOW** *Capitol 8365032*	**63**	1
19 Aug 00	**SONGS FROM AN AMERICAN MOVIE – VOL. ONE – LEARNING HOW TO SMILE** *Capitol 5278642*	**51**	1
28 Apr 01	**SONGS FROM AN AMERICAN MOVIE – VOL. TWO – GOOD TIME FOR A BAD ATTITUDE** *Capitol 5304192*	**69**	1

Betty EVERETT *US, female vocalist, b. 23 Nov 1939, d. 18 Aug 2001 (Singles: 14 Weeks)* pos/wks

14 Jan 65	**GETTING MIGHTY CROWDED** *Fontana TF 520*	**29**	7
30 Oct 68	**IT'S IN HIS KISS (THE SHOOP SHOOP SONG)** *President PT 215*	**34**	7

Kenny EVERETT *UK, male DJ / vocalist – Maurice Cole, b. 25 Dec 1948, d. 4 Apr 1995 (Singles: 12 Weeks)* pos/wks

12 Nov 77	**CAPTAIN KREMMEN (RETRIBUTION)** *DJM DJS 10810* [1]	**32**	4
26 Mar 83 ●	**SNOT RAP** *RCA KEN 1*	**9**	8

[1] Kenny Everett and Mike Vickers

Peven EVERETT See Roy DAVIS Jr

EVERLAST (see also HOUSE OF PAIN) *US, male vocalist – Erik Schrody (Singles: 5 Weeks, Albums: 1 Week)* pos/wks

27 Feb 99	**WHAT IT'S LIKE** *Tommy Boy TBCD 7470*	**34**	2
3 Jul 99	**ENDS** *Tommy Boy TBCD 7346*	**47**	1
20 Jan 01	**BLACK JESUS** *Tommy Boy TBCD 2180*	**37**	2
13 Mar 99	**WHITEY FORD SINGS THE BLUES** *Tommy Boy TBCD 1236*	**65**	1

Phil EVERLY (see also The EVERLY BROTHERS) *US, male vocalist (Singles: 24 Weeks, Albums: 1 Week)* pos/wks

6 Nov 82	**LOUISE** *Capitol CL 266*	**47**	6
19 Feb 83 ●	**SHE MEANS NOTHING TO ME** *Capitol CL 276* [1]	**9**	9
10 Dec 94	**ALL I HAVE TO DO IS DREAM (re)** *EMI CDEMS 359* [2]	**14**	9
7 May 83	**PHIL EVERLY** *Capitol EST 27670*	**61**	1

[1] Phil Everly and Cliff Richard [2] Cliff Richard and Phil Everly

'All I Have to Do Is Dream' was listed with its flip side, 'Miss You Nights' by Cliff Richard

The EVERLY BROTHERS   86 Top 500

Rock 'n' roll's foremost vocal duo: Don, b. 1 Feb 1937, and Phil Everly, b. 19 Jan 1939. The Kentucky-based brothers' distinctive harmony sound has influenced scores of later groups including The Beatles. The duo, voted the World's Top Group by NME readers in 1958, was supported by The Rolling Stones on its 1963 UK tour. They achieved a long string of transatlantic hits, many of which were self-composed, were the first duo / group inducted into the Rock and Roll Hall of Fame, and were awarded a Lifetime Grammy in 1997. In 2001 they were elected into the Country Music Hall of Fame and their home state erected statues in their honour. Total UK single sales: 4,827,957 (Singles: 344 Weeks, Albums: 130 Weeks) pos/wks

12 Jul 57 ●	**BYE BYE LOVE** *London HLA 8440*	**6**	16
8 Nov 57 ●	**WAKE UP LITTLE SUSIE** *London HLA 8498* ▲	**2**	13
23 May 58 ★	**ALL I HAVE TO DO IS DREAM / CLAUDETTE** *London HLA 8618* ▲	**1**	21
12 Sep 58 ●	**BIRD DOG** *London HLA 8685* ▲	**2**	16
23 Jan 59 ●	**PROBLEMS** *London HLA 8781*	**6**	12
22 May 59	**TAKE A MESSAGE TO MARY (2re)** *London HLA 8863*	**20**	10
29 May 59	**POOR JENNY** *London B-HLA 8863*	**14**	11
11 Sep 59 ●	**('TIL) I KISSED YOU** *London HLA 8934*	**2**	15
12 Feb 60	**LET IT BE ME (re)** *London HLA 9039*	**13**	10
14 Apr 60 ★	**CATHY'S CLOWN** *Warner Bros. WB 1* ▲	**1**	18
14 Jul 60 ●	**WHEN WILL I BE LOVED** *London HLA 9157*	**4**	16
22 Sep 60 ●	**LUCILLE / SO SAD (TO WATCH GOOD LOVE GO BAD)** *Warner Bros. WB 19*	**4**	15
15 Dec 60	**LIKE STRANGERS** *London HLA 9250*	**11**	10
9 Feb 61 ★	**WALK RIGHT BACK / EBONY EYES** *Warner Bros. WB 33*	**1**	16
15 Jun 61 ★	**TEMPTATION** *Warner Bros. WB 42*	**1**	15
5 Oct 61	**MUSKRAT / DON'T BLAME ME** *Warner Bros. WB 50*	**20**	6
18 Jan 62 ●	**CRYING IN THE RAIN** *Warner Bros. WB 56*	**6**	15
17 May 62	**HOW CAN I MEET HER** *Warner Bros. WB 67*	**12**	10
25 Oct 62	**NO ONE CAN MAKE MY SUNSHINE SMILE** *Warner Bros. WB 79*	**11**	11
21 Mar 63	**SO IT WILL ALWAYS BE** *Warner Bros. WB 94*	**23**	11
13 Jun 63	**IT'S BEEN NICE (GOODNIGHT)** *Warner Bros. WB 99*	**26**	5
17 Oct 63	**THE GIRL SANG THE BLUES** *Warner Bros. WB 109*	**25**	9
16 Jul 64	**THE FERRIS WHEEL** *Warner Bros. WB 135*	**22**	10
3 Dec 64	**GONE, GONE, GONE (re)** *Warner Bros. WB 146*	**36**	6
6 May 65	**THAT'LL BE THE DAY** *Warner Bros. WB 158*	**30**	4
20 May 65 ●	**THE PRICE OF LOVE** *Warner Bros. WB 161*	**2**	14
26 Aug 65	**I'LL NEVER GET OVER YOU** *Warner Bros. WB 5639*	**35**	5
21 Oct 65	**LOVE IS STRANGE** *Warner Bros. WB 5649*	**11**	9
8 May 68	**IT'S MY TIME** *Warner Bros. WB 7192*	**39**	6
22 Sep 84	**ON THE WINGS OF A NIGHTINGALE** *Mercury MER 170*	**41**	9
2 Jul 60 ●	**IT'S EVERLY TIME** *Warner Bros. WM 4006*	**2**	23
15 Oct 60 ●	**FABULOUS STYLE OF THE EVERLY BROTHERS** *London HAA 2266*	**4**	11
4 Mar 61 ●	**A DATE WITH THE EVERLY BROTHERS** *Warner Bros. WM 4028*	**3**	14
21 Jul 62	**INSTANT PARTY** *Warner Bros. WM 4061*	**20**	1
12 Sep 70 ●	**ORIGINAL GREATEST HITS** *CBS 66255*	**7**	16
8 Jun 74	**THE VERY BEST OF THE EVERLY BROTHERS** *Warner Bros. K46008*	**43**	1
29 Nov 75 ●	**WALK RIGHT BACK WITH THE EVERLYS** *Warner Bros. K56118*	**10**	10
9 Apr 77	**LIVING LEGENDS** *Warwick WW 5027*	**12**	10
18 Dec 82	**LOVE HURTS** *K-Tel NE 1197*	**22**	22
7 Jan 84	**EVERLY BROTHERS REUNION CONCERT** *Impression IMDP 1*	**47**	6

3 Nov 84	THE EVERLY BROTHERS *Mercury MERH 44*	36	4
29 May 93	THE GOLDEN YEARS OF THE EVERLY BROTHERS – THEIR 24 GREATEST HITS *Warner Bros. 9548319922*	26	5
1 Jun 02 ●	THE DEFINITIVE EVERLY BROTHERS *WSM 927473042*	10	7

'All I Have to Do Is Dream' was listed without 'Claudette' for its first week on the chart but, from 30 May 1958, both sides charted for 20 more weeks

EVERTON FOOTBALL CLUB
UK, male football team vocalists (Singles: 8 Weeks)   pos/wks

| 11 May 85 | HERE WE GO *Columbia DB 9106* 1 | ....14 | 5 |
| 20 May 95 | ALL TOGETHER NOW *MDMC DEVCS 3* | ....24 | 3 |

1 Everton 1985

EVERYTHING BUT THE GIRL   287   Top 500
Introspective pop duo formed in 1982, Hull, UK; Tracey Thorn (v), b. 26 Sep 1962, Ben Watt (k), b. 6 Dec 1962. They gained greatest popularity after mid-90s conversion to low-key dance music. The re-mix of 'Missing' was the first single to spend an uninterrupted year on the US chart. Best-selling single: 'Missing' 870,000 (Singles: 96 Weeks, Albums: 132 Weeks)   pos/wks

12 May 84	EACH AND EVERY ONE *Blanco Y Negro NEG 1*	28	7
21 Jul 84	MINE *Blanco Y Negro NEG 3*	58	2
6 Oct 84	NATIVE LAND *Blanco Y Negro NEG 6*	73	2
2 Aug 86	COME ON HOME *Blanco Y Negro NEG 21*	44	7
11 Oct 86	DON'T LEAVE ME BEHIND *Blanco Y Negro NEG 23*	72	2
13 Feb 88	THESE EARLY DAYS *Blanco Y Negro NEG 30*	75	1
9 Jul 88 ●	I DON'T WANT TO TALK ABOUT IT *Blanco Y Negro NEG 34*	3	9
27 Jan 90	DRIVING *Blanco Y Negro NEG 40*	54	2
22 Feb 92	COVERS (EP) *Blanco Y Negro NEG 54*	13	6
24 Apr 93	THE ONLY LIVING BOY IN NEW YORK (EP) *Blanco Y Negro NEG 62CD*	42	5
19 Jun 93	I DIDN'T KNOW I WAS LOOKING FOR LOVE (EP) *Blanco Y Negro NEG 64CD*	72	1
4 Jun 94	ROLLERCOASTER (EP) *Blanco Y Negro NEG 69CD*	65	1
20 Aug 94	MISSING *Blanco Y Negro NEG 71CD1*	69	1
28 Oct 95 ●	MISSING (re-mix) *Blanco Y Negro NEG 84CD*	3	22
20 Apr 96 ●	WALKING WOUNDED *Virgin VSCDT 1577*	6	6
29 Jun 96 ●	WRONG *Virgin VSCDT 1589*	8	7
5 Oct 96	SINGLE *Virgin VSCDT 1600*	20	3
7 Dec 96	DRIVING (re-mix) *Blanco Y Negro NEG 99CD1*	36	2
1 Mar 97	BEFORE TODAY *Virgin VSCDT 1624*	25	2
3 Oct 98	THE FUTURE OF THE FUTURE (STAY GOLD) *Deconstruction 74321616252* 1	31	2
25 Sep 99	FIVE FATHOMS *Virgin VSCDT 1742*	27	3
4 Mar 00	TEMPERAMENTAL *Virgin VSCDT 1761*	72	1
27 Jan 01	TRACEY IN MY ROOM *VC Recordings VCRD 78* 2	34	2
16 Jun 84	EDEN *Blanco Y Negro BYN 2*	14	22
27 Apr 85 ●	LOVE NOT MONEY *Blanco Y Negro BYN 3*	10	9
6 Sep 86	BABY THE STARS SHINE BRIGHT *Blanco Y Negro BYN 9*	22	9
12 Mar 88	IDLEWILD *Blanco Y Negro BYN 14*	13	9
6 Aug 88	IDLEWILD (re-issue) *Blanco Y Negro BYN 16*	21	6
17 Feb 90 ●	THE LANGUAGE OF LIFE *Blanco Y Negro BYN 21*	10	6
5 Oct 91	WORLDWIDE *Blanco Y Negro BYN 25*	29	5
22 May 93 ●	HOME MOVIES – THE BEST OF EVERYTHING BUT THE GIRL *Blanco Y Negro 4509923192*	5	8
25 Jun 94	AMPLIFIED HEART *Blanco Y Negro 4509964822*	20	15
18 May 96 ●	WALKING WOUNDED *Virgin CDV 2803*	4	27
9 Nov 96	THE BEST OF EVERYTHING BUT THE GIRL *Blanco Y Negro 630166372*	23	12
9 Oct 99	TEMPERAMENTAL *Virgin CDV 2892*	16	3
2 Nov 02	LIKE THE DESERTS MISS THE RAIN *Virgin CDV 2966*	58	1

1 Deep Dish with Everything but the Girl 2 EBTG vs Soul Vision

Tracks on Covers (EP): Love Is Strange / Tougher Than the Rest / Time After Time / Alison. Tracks on The Only Living Boy in New York (EP): The Only Living Boy in New York / Birds / Gabriel / Horses in the Room. Tracks on I Didn't Know I Was Looking for Love (EP): I Didn't Know I Was Looking for Love / My Head Is My Only House Unless It Rains / Political Science / A Piece of My Mind. Tracks on Rollercoaster (EP): Rollercoaster / Straight Back to You / Lights of Te Touan / I Didn't Know I Was Looking for Love (demo)

E'VOKE
UK, female vocal duo – Marlaine Gordon and Kerry Potter (Singles: 9 Weeks)   pos/wks

25 Nov 95	RUNAWAY *Ffrreedom TABCD 238*	30	3
24 Aug 96	ARMS OF LOREN *Manifesto FESCD 10*	25	3
2 Feb 02	ARMS OF LOREN (re-mix) *Inferno CDFERN 001*	31	3

EVOLUTION
UK, male / female vocal / instrumental group (Singles: 12 Weeks)   pos/wks

20 Mar 93	LOVE THING *Deconstruction 74321134272*	32	2
3 Jul 93	EVERYBODY DANCE *Deconstruction 74321152012*	19	5
8 Jan 94	EVOLUTIONDANCE PART ONE (EP) *Deconstruction 74321171912*	52	3
4 Nov 95	LOOK UP TO THE LIGHT *Deconstruction 74321318042*	55	1
19 Oct 96	YOUR LOVE IS CALLING *Deconstruction 74321422872*	60	1

Tracks on Evolutiondance Part One (EP): Escape 2 Alcatraz (re-mix) / Everybody / Don't Stop the Rain

EX PISTOLS
UK, male vocal / instrumental group (Singles: 2 Weeks)   pos/wks

| 2 Feb 85 | LAND OF HOPE AND GLORY *Virginia PISTOL 76* | ....69 | 2 |

The EXCITERS *US, male / female vocal group (Singles: 7 Weeks)* pos/wks

| 21 Feb 63 | TELL HIM *United Artists UP 1011* | ....46 | 1 |
| 4 Oct 75 | REACHING FOR THE BEST *20th Century BTC 1005* | ....31 | 6 |

EXETER BRAMDEAN BOYS' CHOIR
UK, male choir (Singles: 3 Weeks)   pos/wks

| 18 Dec 93 | REMEMBERING CHRISTMAS *Golden Sounds DSCC 1* | ....46 | 3 |

EXILE *US, male vocal / instrumental group (Singles: 18 Weeks)*   pos/wks

19 Aug 78 ●	KISS YOU ALL OVER *RAK 279* ▲	6	12
12 May 79	HOW COULD THIS GO WRONG *RAK 293*	67	2
12 Sep 81	HEART AND SOUL *RAK 333*	54	4

EXODUS *US, male vocal / instrumental group (Albums: 1 Week)*   pos/wks

| 11 Feb 89 | FABULOUS DISASTER *Music for Nations MFN 90* | ....67 | 1 |

EXOTERIX *UK, male producer – Duncan Millar (Singles: 2 Weeks)*   pos/wks

| 24 Apr 93 | VOID *Positiva CDTIV 1* | ....58 | 1 |
| 5 Feb 94 | SATISFY MY LOVE *Union UCRCD 26* | ....62 | 1 |

EXOTICA featuring Itsy FOSTER *UK / Italy, male / female vocal / instrumental group (Singles: 1 Week)*   pos/wks

| 16 Sep 95 | THE SUMMER IS MAGIC *Polydor 5798392* | ....68 | 1 |

EXPLOITED
UK, male vocal / instrumental group (Singles: 13 Weeks, Albums: 26 Weeks)   pos/wks

18 Apr 81	DOGS OF WAR *Secret SHH 110*	63	4
17 Oct 81	DEAD CITIES *Secret SHH 120*	31	5
5 Dec 81	DON'T LET 'EM GRIND YOU DOWN *Superville EXP 1003* 1	70	1
8 May 82	ATTACK *Secret SHH 130*	50	3
16 May 81	PUNK'S NOT DEAD *Secret SEC 1*	20	11
14 Nov 81	EXPLOITED LIVE *Superville EXPLP 2001*	52	3
19 Jun 82	TROOPS OF TOMORROW *Secret SEC 8*	17	12

1 Exploited and Anti-Pasti

EXPOSÉ *US, female vocal group (Singles: 1 Week)*   pos/wks

| 28 Aug 93 | I'LL NEVER GET OVER YOU (GETTING OVER ME) *Arista 74321158962* | ....75 | 1 |

EXPRESS OF SOUND
Italy, male instrumental / production group (Singles: 1 Week)   pos/wks

| 2 Nov 96 | REAL VIBRATION (WANT LOVE) *Positiva CDTIV 66* | ....45 | 1 |

EXPRESSOS
UK, male / female vocal / instrumental group (Singles: 5 Weeks)   pos/wks

| 21 Jun 80 | HEY GIRL *WEA K 18246* | ....60 | 3 |
| 14 Mar 81 | TANGO IN MONO *WEA K 18431* | ....70 | 2 |

EXTENSIVE See CHOPS-EMC + EXTENSIVE

EXTREME *US, male vocal / instrumental group (Singles: 46 Weeks, Albums: 75 Weeks)*   pos/wks

8 Jun 91	GET THE FUNK OUT *A&M AM 737*	19	7
27 Jul 91 ●	MORE THAN WORDS *A&M AM 792* ▲	2	11
12 Oct 91	DECADENCE DANCE *A&M AM 773*	36	3

			pos	wks
23 Nov 91	HOLE HEARTED *A&M AM 839*		12	7
2 May 92	SONG FOR LOVE *A&M AM 698*		12	6
5 Sep 92	REST IN PEACE *A&M AM 0055*		13	5
14 Nov 92	STOP THE WORLD *A&M AM 0096*		22	2
6 Feb 93	TRAGIC COMIC *A&M AMCD 0156*		15	4
11 Mar 95	HIP TODAY *A&M 5809932*		44	1
1 Jun 91	EXTREME II PORNOGRAFFITTI *A&M 3953131*		12	61
26 Sep 92 ●	III SIDES TO EVERY STORY *A&M 5400062*		2	11
11 Feb 95 ●	WAITING FOR THE PUNCHLINE *A&M 5403052*		10	3

EYE TO EYE featuring Taka BOOM (see also MUKKAA; UMBOZA)
UK, male producer – Stuart Crichton
and US, female vocalist (Singles: 2 Weeks) pos/wks

9 Jun 01	JUST CAN'T GET ENOUGH (NO NO NO NO) *Xtravaganza XTRAV 25CD*	36	2

EYEOPENER
UK, male / female production / vocal group (Singles: 6 Weeks) pos/wks

20 Nov 04	HUNGRY EYES *All Around the World CDGLOBE 363*	16	6+

EYES CREAM
Italy, male producer – Agostino Carollo (Singles: 1 Week) pos/wks

16 Oct 99	FLY AWAY (BYE BYE) *Accolade CDAC 001*	53	1

Adam F *UK, male producer – Adam*
Fenton (Singles: 23 Weeks, Albums: 3 Weeks) pos/wks

27 Sep 97	CIRCLES *Positiva CDFJ 002*		20	3
7 Mar 98	MUSIC IN MY MIND *Positiva CDFJ 003*		27	3
15 Sep 01	SMASH SUMTHIN' *Def Jam 5886932* [1]		11	7
1 Dec 01	STAND CLEAR *Chrysalis CDEM 597* [2]		43	1
6 Apr 02	WHERE'S MY ...? *EMI CDEMS 598* [3]		37	2
27 Apr 02	METROSOUND *Kaos KAOS 001P* [4]		54	1
8 Jun 02	STAND CLEAR (re-mix) *Kaos KAOSCD 002* [2]		50	1
31 Aug 02	SMASH SUMTHIN' (re-mix) *Kaos KAOSCD 003* [5]		47	2
14 Dec 02	DIRTY HARRY'S REVENGE *Kaos KAOS 004* [6]		50	2
30 Oct 04	WHEN THE SUN GOES DOWN *Breakbeat Kaos BBK 055CD* [7]		68	1
15 Nov 97	COLOURS *Positiva 8217252*		47	1
22 Sep 01	KAOS – THE ANTI-ACOUSTIC WARFARE *Chrysalis 5342502*		44	2

[1] Redman featuring Adam F [2] Adam F featuring M.O.P. [3] Adam F featuring Lil' Mo [4] Adam F and J Majik [5] Adam F featuring Redman [6] Adam F featuring Beenie Man [7] DJ Fresh featuring Adam F

F A B
UK, male producers (Singles: 11 Weeks, Albums: 3 Weeks) pos/wks

7 Jul 90 ●	THUNDERBIRDS ARE GO *Brothers Organisation FAB 1* [1]	5	8
20 Oct 90	THE PRISONER *Brothers Organisation FAB 6* [2]	56	2
1 Dec 90	THE STINGRAY MEGAMIX *Brothers Organisation FAB 2* [3]	66	1
10 Nov 90	POWER THEMES 90 *Telstar STAR 2430*	53	3

[1] F A B featuring MC Parker [2] F A B featuring MC Number 6 [3] F A B featuring Aqua Marina

FBI See REDHEAD KINGPIN and The FBI

FC KAHUNA *UK, male production duo (Singles: 3 Weeks)* pos/wks

6 Apr 02	GLITTERBALL *City Rockers ROCKERS 11CD*	64	1
20 Jul 02	MACHINE SAYS YES *City Rockers ROCKERS 18CD*	58	1
22 Mar 03	HAYLING *Skint SKINT 84CD*	49	1

F45 See DE FUNK featuring F45

FFWD
UK / Germany, male instrumental group (Albums: 1 Week) pos/wks

13 Aug 94	FFWD *Inter INTA 001CD*	48	1

FKW *UK, male vocal / instrumental group (Singles: 8 Weeks)* pos/wks

2 Oct 93	NEVER GONNA (GIVE YOU UP) *PWL International PWCD 273*	48	2
11 Dec 93	SEIZE THE DAY *PWL International PWCD 279*	45	2
5 Mar 94	JINGO *PWL International PWCD 283*	30	3
4 Jun 94	THIS IS THE WAY *PWL International PWCD 307*	63	1

FLB See FAT LARRY'S BAND

F.L.O. See Rahni HARRIS and F.L.O.

FM *UK, male vocal / instrumental*
group (Singles: 11 Weeks, Albums: 3 Weeks) pos/wks

31 Jan 87	FROZEN HEART *Portrait DIDGE 1*	64	2
20 Jun 87	LET LOVE BE THE LEADER *Portrait MERV 1*	71	2
5 Aug 89	BAD LUCK *Epic 6550317*	54	4
7 Oct 89	SOMEDAY (YOU'LL COME RUNNING) *CBS DINK 1*	64	2
10 Feb 90	EVERYTIME I THINK OF YOU *Epic DINK 2*	73	1
20 Sep 86	INDISCREET *Portrait PRT 26827*	76	1
14 Oct 89	TOUGH IT OUT *Epic 4655891*	34	2

FPI PROJECT *Italy, male instrumental /*
production group (Singles: 17 Weeks) pos/wks

9 Dec 89 ●	GOING BACK TO MY ROOTS / RICH IN PARADISE *Rumour RUMAT 9*	9	12
9 Mar 91	EVERYBODY (ALL OVER THE WORLD) *Rumour RUMA 29*	65	3
7 Aug 93	COME ON (AND DO IT) *Synthetic SYNTH 006CD*	59	1
13 Mar 99	EVERYBODY (ALL OVER) (re-mix) *99 North CDNTH 14*	67	1

'Going Back to My Roots' was a vocal track available in two formats and featured either Paolo Dini or Sharon Dee Clarke

FYC See FINE YOUNG CANNIBALS

FAB! *Ireland, female vocal group (Singles: 1 Week)* pos/wks

1 Aug 98	TURN AROUND *Break Records BRCX 107*	59	1

FAB FOUR featuring Robert OWENS *Germany / Italy*
male production duo and US, male vocalist (Singles: 1 Week) pos/wks

15 Feb 03	LAST NIGHT A DJ BLEW MY MIND *Illustrious CDILL 013*	34	1

Shelley FABARES
US, female vocalist / actor – Michelle Fabares (Singles: 4 Weeks) pos/wks

26 Apr 62	JOHNNY ANGEL *Pye International 7N 25132* ▲	41	4

FABIAN *US, male vocalist – Fabiano Forte (Singles: 1 Week)* pos/wks

10 Mar 60	HOUND DOG MAN *HMV POP 695*	46	1

Lara FABIAN
Canada (b. Belgium), female vocalist (Singles: 1 Week) pos/wks

28 Oct 00	I WILL LOVE AGAIN *Columbia 6694062*	63	1

FABOLOUS *US, male rapper – John*
Jackson (Singles: 21 Weeks, Albums: 11 Weeks) pos/wks

16 Aug 03	CAN'T LET YOU GO *Elektra E 7408CD* [1]	14	5
1 Nov 03	INTO YOU *Elektra E 7470CD* [2]	18	6
20 Mar 04	BADABOOM *Epic 6747512* [3]	26	5
27 Nov 04	BREATHE *Atlantic AT 0189CD*	28	5+
2 Aug 03	SWEET DREAMS *East West 7559627912*	59	10
20 Nov 04	REAL TALK *Atlantic 7567837542*	66	1

[1] Fabolous featuring Mike Shorey and Lil' Mo [2] Fabolous featuring Tamia [3] B2K featuring Fabolous

The FABULOUS BAKER BOYS
UK, male DJ / production trio (Singles: 2 Weeks) pos/wks

| 15 Nov 97 | OH BOY *Multiply CDMULTY 28* | .34 | 2 |

FACE *See David MORALES*

The FACES (see also Rod STEWART) *UK, male vocal / instrumental group (Singles: 46 Weeks, Albums: 62 Weeks)* pos/wks

18 Dec 71	●	STAY WITH ME *Warner Bros. K 16136*	.6	14
17 Feb 73	●	CINDY INCIDENTALLY *Warner Bros. K 16247*	.2	9
8 Dec 73	●	POOL HALL RICHARD / I WISH IT WOULD RAIN *Warner Bros. K 16341*	.8	11
7 Dec 74		YOU CAN MAKE ME DANCE SING OR ANYTHING (EVEN TAKE THE DOG FOR A WALK, MEND A FUSE, FOLD AWAY THE IRONING BOARD, OR ANY OTHER DOMESTIC SHORT COMINGS) *Warner Bros. K 16494* [1]	.12	9
4 Jun 77		THE FACES (EP) *Riva 8*	.41	3
4 Apr 70		FIRST STEP *Warner Bros. WS 3000*	.45	1
8 May 71		LONG PLAYER *Warner Bros. W 3011*	.31	7
25 Dec 71	●	A NOD IS AS GOOD AS A WINK ... TO A BLIND HORSE *Warner Bros. K 56006*	.2	22
21 Apr 73	★	OOH LA LA *Warner Bros. K 56011*	.1	13
26 Jan 74	●	OVERTURE AND BEGINNERS *Mercury 9100001* [1]	.3	7
21 May 77		THE BEST OF THE FACES *Riva RVLP 1*	.24	6
7 Nov 92		THE BEST OF ROD STEWART AND THE FACES 1971-1975 *Mercury 5141802* [1]	.58	1
1 Nov 03		CHANGING FACES – THE VERY BEST OF ROD STEWART & THE FACES – THE DEFINITIVE COLLECTION 1969-1974 *Universal TV 9812604*	.13	5

[1] The Faces / Rod Stewart [1] Rod Stewart and The Faces

Tracks on The Faces (EP): Memphis / You Can Make Me Dance Sing or Anything / Stay with Me / Cindy Incidentally

FACTORY OF UNLIMITED RHYTHM *Jamaica, male / female vocal / instrumental group (Singles: 1 Week)* pos/wks

| 1 Jun 96 | THE SWEETEST SURRENDER *Kuff KUFFD 6* | .59 | 1 |

Donald FAGEN (see also STEELY DAN) *US, male vocalist / instrumentalist - keyboard (Singles: 2 Weeks, Albums: 25 Weeks)* pos/wks

3 Jul 93		TOMORROW'S GIRLS *Reprise W 0180CDX*	.46	2
20 Oct 82		THE NIGHTFLY *Warner Bros. 923696*	.44	16
5 Jun 93	●	KAMAKIRIAD *Reprise 9362452302*	.3	9

Joe FAGIN *UK, male vocalist (Singles: 20 Weeks)* pos/wks

| 7 Jan 84 | ● | THAT'S LIVIN' ALRIGHT *Towerbell TOW 46* | .3 | 11 |
| 5 Apr 86 | | BACK WITH THE BOYS AGAIN / GET IT RIGHT *Towerbell TOW 84* | .53 | 9 |

Jad FAIR *See TEENAGE FANCLUB*

Yvonne FAIR
US, female vocalist, b. 1942, d. 6 Mar 1994 (Singles: 11 Weeks) pos/wks

| 24 Jan 76 | ● | IT SHOULD HAVE BEEN ME *Tamla Motown TMG 1013* | .5 | 11 |

FAIR WEATHER (see also AMEN CORNER) *UK, male vocal / instrumental group – leader Andy Fairweather-Low (Singles: 12 Weeks)* pos/wks

| 18 Jul 70 | ● | NATURAL SINNER *RCA 1977* | .6 | 12 |

FAIRGROUND ATTRACTION
UK, female / male vocal / instrumental group – lead vocal Eddi Reader (Singles: 27 Weeks, Albums: 54 Weeks) pos/wks

16 Apr 88	★	PERFECT *RCA PB 41845*	.1	13
30 Jul 88		FIND MY LOVE *RCA PB 42079*	.7	10
19 Nov 88		A SMILE IN A WHISPER *RCA PB 42249*	.75	1
28 Jan 89		CLARE *RCA PB 42607*	.49	3
28 May 88	●	THE FIRST OF A MILLION KISSES *RCA PL 71696*	.2	52
30 Jun 90		AY FOND KISS *RCA PL 74596*	.55	2

Group were male only on last album

FAIRPORT CONVENTION
UK, male / female vocal / instrumental group – includes Sandy Denny (Singles: 9 Weeks, Albums: 41 Weeks) pos/wks

| 23 Jul 69 | | SI TU DOIS PARTIR (re) *Island WIP 6064* | .21 | 9 |

2 Aug 69		UNHALFBRICKING *Island ILPS 9102*	.12	8
17 Jan 70		LIEGE & LIEF *Island ILPS 9115*	.17	15
18 Jul 70		FULL HOUSE *Island ILPS 9130*	.13	11
3 Jul 71	●	ANGEL DELIGHT *Island ILPS 9160*	.8	5
12 Jul 75		RISING FOR THE MOON *Island ILPS 9313*	.52	1
28 Jan 89		RED AND GOLD *New Routes RUE 002*	.74	1

Andy FAIRWEATHER-LOW (see also FAIR WEATHER: AMEN CORNER) *UK, male vocalist (Singles: 18 Weeks)* pos/wks

| 21 Sep 74 | ● | REGGAE TUNE *A&M AMS 7129* | .10 | 8 |
| 6 Dec 75 | ● | WIDE EYED AND LEGLESS *A&M AMS 7202* | .6 | 10 |

Adam FAITH (193) [Top 500]
Teen-idol vocalist turned top actor then financial wizard, b. Terence Nelhams, 23 Jun 1940, London, UK, d. 8 Mar 2003. One of the most charted acts of the 1960s, he became the first UK artist to lodge their initial seven hits in the Top 5. Also one of the first UK acts to record original songs regularly (Singles: 252 Weeks, Albums: 46 Weeks) pos/wks

20 Nov 59	★	WHAT DO YOU WANT? *Parlophone R 4591*	.1	19
22 Jan 60	★	POOR ME *Parlophone R 4623*	.1	18
14 Apr 60	●	SOMEONE ELSE'S BABY *Parlophone R 4643*	.2	13
30 Jun 60	●	JOHNNY COMES MARCHING HOME / MADE YOU *Parlophone R 4665* [1]	.5	13
15 Sep 60	●	HOW ABOUT THAT! *Parlophone R 4689* [1]	.4	14
17 Nov 60	●	LONELY PUP (IN A CHRISTMAS SHOP) *Parlophone R 4708*	.4	11
9 Feb 61	●	WHO AM I! / THIS IS IT! *Parlophone R 4735*	.5	14
27 Apr 61		EASY GOING ME *Parlophone R 4766*	.12	10
20 Jul 61		DON'T YOU KNOW IT *Parlophone R 4807*	.12	10
26 Oct 61	●	THE TIME HAS COME *Parlophone R 4837*	.4	14
18 Jan 62		LONESOME *Parlophone R 4864* [1]	.12	9
3 May 62	●	AS YOU LIKE IT *Parlophone R 4896* [1]	.5	15
30 Aug 62	●	DON'T THAT BEAT ALL *Parlophone R 4930* [2]	.8	11
13 Dec 62		BABY TAKE A BOW *Parlophone R 4964*	.22	6
31 Jan 63		WHAT NOW *Parlophone R 4990* [2]	.31	5
11 Jul 63		WALKIN' TALL *Parlophone R 5039*	.23	6
19 Sep 63	●	THE FIRST TIME *Parlophone R 5061* [3]	.5	13
12 Dec 63		WE ARE IN LOVE *Parlophone R 5091* [3]	.11	12
12 Mar 64		IF HE TELLS YOU *Parlophone R 5109* [3]	.25	9
28 May 64		I LOVE BEING IN LOVE WITH YOU *Parlophone R 5138* [3]	.33	6
26 Nov 64		A MESSAGE TO MARTHA (KENTUCKY BLUEBIRD) *Parlophone R 5201*	.12	11
11 Feb 65		STOP FEELING SORRY FOR YOURSELF *Parlophone R 5235*	.23	6
17 Jun 65		SOMEONE'S TAKEN MARIA AWAY *Parlophone R 5289*	.34	5
20 Oct 66		CHERYL'S GOIN' HOME *Parlophone R 5516*	.46	2
19 Nov 60	●	ADAM *Parlophone PMC 1128*	.6	36
11 Feb 61		BEAT GIRL (FILM SOUNDTRACK) *Columbia 33SX 1225*	.11	3
24 Mar 62		ADAM FAITH *Parlophone PMC 1162*	.20	1
25 Sep 65		FAITH ALIVE *Parlophone PMC 1249*	.19	1
19 Dec 81		20 GOLDEN GREATS *Warwick WW 5113*	.61	3
27 Nov 93		MIDNIGHT POSTCARDS *PolyGram TV 8213982*	.43	2

[1] Adam Faith with John Barry and his Orchestra [2] Adam Faith with Johnny Keating and his Orchestra [3] Adam Faith and The Roulettes

Horace FAITH
Jamaica, male vocalist – Horace Smith (Singles: 10 Weeks) pos/wks

| 12 Sep 70 | | BLACK PEARL *Trojan TR 7790* | .13 | 10 |

Percy FAITH *Canada, orchestra leader, b. 7 Apr 1908, d. 9 Feb 1976 (Singles: 31 Weeks)* pos/wks

| 4 Mar 60 | ● | THE THEME FROM 'A SUMMER PLACE' *Philips PB 989* ▲ | .2 | 31 |

FAITH BROTHERS *UK, male vocal / instrumental group (Singles: 6 Weeks, Albums: 1 Week)* pos/wks

13 Apr 85		THE COUNTRY OF THE BLIND *Siren SIREN 2*	.63	3
6 Jul 85		A STRANGER ON HOME GROUND *Siren SIREN 4*	.69	3
9 Nov 85		EVENTIDE *Siren SIRENLP 1*	.66	1

FAITH, HOPE AND CHARITY
US, male / female vocal group (Singles: 4 Weeks) pos/wks

| 31 Jan 76 | | JUST ONE LOOK *RCA 2632* | .38 | 4 |

FAITH, HOPE AND CHARITY
UK, female vocal group (Singles: 3 Weeks) pos/wks

| 23 Jun 90 | | BATTLE OF THE SEXES *WEA YZ 480* | .53 | 3 |

FAITH NO MORE US, male vocal / instrumental group –
leader Mike Patton (Singles: 65 Weeks, Albums: 74 Weeks)   pos/wks

6 Feb 88	WE CARE A LOT Slash LASH 17	53	3
10 Feb 90	EPIC Slash LASH 21	37	4
14 Apr 90	FROM OUT OF NOWHERE Slash LASH 24	23	6
14 Jul 90	FALLING TO PIECES Slash LASH 25	41	4
8 Sep 90	EPIC (re-issue) Slash LASH 26	25	5
6 Jun 92 ●	MIDLIFE CRISIS Slash LASH 37	10	5
15 Aug 92	A SMALL VICTORY Slash LASH 39	29	5
12 Sep 92	A SMALL VICTORY (re-mix) Slash LASHX 40	55	1
21 Nov 92	EVERYTHING'S RUINED Slash LASH 43	28	3
16 Jan 93 ●	I'M EASY / BE AGGRESSIVE (re) Slash LACDP 44	3	8
6 Nov 93	ANOTHER BODY MURDERED Epic 6597942 [1]	26	3
11 Mar 95	DIGGING THE GRAVE Slash LASCD 51	16	4
27 May 95	RICOCHET Slash LASCD 53	27	2
29 Jul 95	EVIDENCE Slash LASCD 54	32	3
31 May 97	ASHES TO ASHES Slash LASCD 61	15	3
16 Aug 97	LAST CUP OF SORROW Slash LASCD 62	51	1
13 Dec 97	THIS TOWN AIN'T BIG ENOUGH FOR BOTH OF US Roadrunner RR 22513 [2]	40	2
17 Jan 98	ASHES TO ASHES (re-issue) Slash LACDP 63	29	3
7 Nov 98	I STARTED A JOKE Slash LASCD 65	49	1
17 Feb 90	THE REAL THING Slash 8281541	30	35
16 Feb 91	LIVE AT THE BRIXTON ACADEMY Slash 8282381	20	4
20 Jun 92 ●	ANGEL DUST Slash 8283212	2	25
25 Mar 95 ●	KING FOR A DAY FOOL FOR A LIFETIME Slash 8285602	5	6
21 Jun 97 ●	ALBUM OF THE YEAR Slash 8289012	7	3
21 Nov 98	WHO CARES A LOT? – THE GREATEST HITS Slash 5560572	37	1

[1] Faith No More and Boo-Yaa T.R.I.B.E. [2] Sparks vs Faith No More

Marianne FAITHFULL
UK, female vocalist (Singles: 59 Weeks, Albums: 19 Weeks)   pos/wks

13 Aug 64 ●	AS TEARS GO BY Decca F 11923	9	13
18 Feb 65 ●	COME AND STAY WITH ME Decca F 12075	4	13
6 May 65 ●	THIS LITTLE BIRD Decca F 12162	6	11
22 Jul 65 ●	SUMMER NIGHTS Decca F 12193	10	10
4 Nov 65	YESTERDAY Decca F 12268	36	4
9 Mar 67	IS THIS WHAT I GET FOR LOVING YOU? Decca F 22524	43	4
24 Nov 79	THE BALLAD OF LUCY JORDAN Island WIP 6491	48	6
5 Jun 65	COME MY WAY Decca LK 4688	12	7
5 Jun 65	MARIANNE FAITHFULL Decca LK 4689	15	2
24 Nov 79	BROKEN ENGLISH Island M1	57	4
17 Oct 81	DANGEROUS ACQUAINTANCES Island ILPS 9648	45	4
26 Mar 83	A CHILD'S ADVENTURE Island ILPS 9734	99	1
8 Aug 87	STRANGE WEATHER Island ILPS 9874	78	2

FAITHLESS (see also OUR TRIBE / ONE TRIBE; ROLLO; SISTER BLISS;
SPHINX; DUSTED; DIDO; 1 GIANT LEAP) UK, male / female vocal /
instrumental group (Singles: 83 Weeks, Albums: 57 Weeks)   pos/wks

5 Aug 95	SALVA MEA (SAVE ME) Cheeky CHEKCD 008	30	2
9 Dec 95	INSOMNIA Cheeky CHEKCD 010	27	2
23 Mar 96	DON'T LEAVE Cheeky CHEKCD 012	34	2
26 Oct 96 ●	INSOMNIA (re-issue) Cheeky CHEKCD 017	3	13
21 Dec 96 ●	SALVA MEA (re-mix) Cheeky CHEKCD 018	9	7
26 Apr 97 ●	REVERENCE Cheeky CHEKCD 019	10	3
15 Nov 97	DON'T LEAVE (re-mix) Cheeky CHEKXCD 024	21	2
5 Sep 98 ●	GOD IS A DJ Cheeky CHEKCD 028	6	8
5 Dec 98	TAKE THE LONG WAY HOME Cheeky CHEKCD 031	15	4
1 May 99	BRING MY FAMILY BACK Cheeky CHEKCD 035	14	5
16 Jun 01 ●	WE COME 1 Cheeky 74321850842	3	10
29 Sep 01	MUHAMMAD ALI (re) Cheeky 74321886442	29	4
29 Dec 01	TARANTULA (re) Cheeky 74321903592	29	5
20 Apr 02 ●	ONE STEP TOO FAR Cheeky / Arista 74321926412 [1]	6	3
12 Jun 04 ●	MASS DESTRUCTION Cheeky / Arista 82876614912	7	8
4 Sep 04	I WANT MORE Cheeky / BMG 82876641742	22	3
23 Nov 96	REVERENCE Cheeky CHEKCD 500	26	14
3 Oct 98 ●	SUNDAY 8PM Cheeky CHEKCD 503	10	7
30 Jun 01 ●	OUTROSPECTIVE Cheeky 74321850832	4	22
19 Jun 04 ★	NO ROOTS Cheeky 82876618702 ■	1	14

[1] Faithless featuring Dido

FALCO Austria, male vocalist – Johann Holzel, b. 19 Feb 1957,
d. 6 Feb 1998 (Singles: 26 Weeks, Albums: 15 Weeks)   pos/wks

22 Mar 86 ★	ROCK ME AMADEUS A&M AM 278 ▲	1	15
31 May 86 ●	VIENNA CALLING A&M AM 318	10	8
2 Aug 86	JEANNY A&M AM 333	68	1
27 Sep 86	THE SOUND OF MUSIK WEA U 8591	61	2
26 Apr 86	FALCO 3 A&M AMA 5105	32	15

Christian FALK featuring DEMETREUS
Sweden, male producer and male vocalist (Singles: 3 Weeks)   pos/wks

26 Aug 00	MAKE IT RIGHT London LONCD 452	22	3

Fred FALKE See Alan BRAXE and Fred FALKE

The FALL UK, male / female vocal / instrumental group –
leader Mark E Smith (Singles: 27 Weeks, Albums: 32 Weeks)   pos/wks

13 Sep 86	MR PHARMACIST Beggars Banquet BEG 168	75	1
20 Dec 86	HEY! LUCIANI Beggars Banquet BEG 176	59	1
9 May 87	THERE'S A GHOST IN MY HOUSE Beggars Banquet BEG 187	30	4
31 Oct 87	HIT THE NORTH Beggars Banquet BEG 200	57	5
30 Jan 88	VICTORIA Beggars Banquet BEG 206	35	3
26 Nov 88	BIG NEW PRINZ / JERUSALEM (DOUBLE SINGLE) Beggars Banquet FALL 2/3	59	2
27 Jan 90	TELEPHONE THING Cog Sinister SIN 4	58	1
8 Sep 90	WHITE LIGHTNING Cog Sinister SIN 6	56	2
14 Mar 92	FREE RANGE Cog Sinister SINS 8	40	1
17 Apr 93	WHY ARE PEOPLE GRUDGEFUL Permanent CDSPERM 9	43	1
25 Dec 93	BEHIND THE COUNTER Permanent CDSPERM 13	75	1
30 Apr 94	15 WAYS Permanent CDSPERM 14	65	1
17 Feb 96	THE CHISELERS Jet JETSCD 500	60	1
21 Feb 98	MASQUERADE Artful CDARTFUL 1	69	1
14 Dec 02	THE FALL VS 2003 Action TAKE 020CD	64	1
10 Jul 04	THEME FROM SPARTA FC #2 Action TAKE 23CD	66	1
20 Mar 82	HEX ENDUCTION HOUR Kamera KAM 005	71	3
20 Oct 84	THE WONDERFUL AND FRIGHTENING WORLD OF … Beggars Banquet BEGA 58	62	2
5 Oct 85	THE NATION'S SAVING GRACE Beggars Banquet BEGA 67	54	2
11 Oct 86	BEND SINISTER Beggars Banquet BEGA 75	36	3
12 Mar 88	THE FRENZ EXPERIMENT Beggars Banquet BEGA 91	19	4
12 Nov 88	I AM KURIOUS ORANJ Beggars Banquet BEGA 96	54	2
8 Jul 89	SEMINAL LIVE Beggars Banquet BBL 102	40	2
3 Mar 90	EXTRICATE Cog Sinister 8422041	31	3
15 Sep 90	458489 B-SIDES Beggars Banquet BEGA 111	44	2
4 May 91	SHIFT WORK Cog Sinister 8485941	17	2
28 Mar 92	CODE: SELFISH Cog Sinister 5121622	21	1
8 May 93 ●	INFOTAINMENT SCAN Permanent PERMCD 12	9	3
14 May 94	MIDDLE CLASS REVOLT Permanent PERMCD 16	48	1
11 Mar 95	CEREBRAL CAUSTIC Permanent PERMCD 30	67	1
22 Jun 96	THE LIGHT USER SYNDROME Jet JETCD 1012	54	1

Tracks on Big New Prinz / Jerusalem (double single): Big New Prinz / Wrong Place Right Time Number Two / Jerusalem / Acid Priest 2088. Tracks on The Fall vs 2003: Susan vs Youthclub (and re-mix) / Janey vs Johnny

FALLACY
UK, male producer – Daniel Fahey (Singles: 4 Weeks)   pos/wks

22 Jun 02	THE GROUNDBREAKER Wordplay WORDCD 036 [1]	47	2
24 May 03	BIG N BASHY Virgin VSCDT 1847 [2]	45	2

[1] Fallacy and Fusion [2] Fallacy featuring Tubby T

Harold FALTERMEYER
Germany, male instrumentalist – keyboards (Singles: 23 Weeks)   pos/wks

23 Mar 85 ●	AXEL F (re) MCA MCA 949	2	22
24 Aug 85	FLETCH THEME MCA MCA 991	74	1

'Axel F' reached its peak position only in Jun 1985

Agnetha FÄLTSKOG (see also ABBA)
Sweden, female vocalist (Singles: 19 Weeks, Albums: 21 Weeks)   pos/wks

28 May 83	THE HEAT IS ON Epic A 3436	35	6
13 Aug 83	WRAP YOUR ARMS AROUND ME Epic A 3622	44	5
22 Oct 83	CAN'T SHAKE LOOSE Epic A 3812	63	1
24 Apr 04	IF I THOUGHT YOU'D EVER CHANGE YOUR MIND WEA WEA 375CD	11	5
26 Jun 04	WHEN YOU WALK IN THE ROOM WEA WEA 378CD1	34	2
11 Jun 83	WRAP YOUR ARMS AROUND ME Epic EPC 25505	18	13
4 May 85	EYES OF A WOMAN Epic EPC 26446	38	3
12 Mar 88	I STAND ALONE WEA WX 150	72	1
1 May 04	MY COLOURING BOOK WEA 5046731222	12	4

Georgie FAME `360` Top 500

Critically acclaimed R&B / jazz vocalist / keyboard player, b. Clive Powell, 26 Jun 1943, Lancashire, UK. The one-time rock 'n' roll tour musician, who had a string of sixties hits, is still a popular performer, often working with contemporaries such as Van Morrison and Bill Wyman (Singles: 115 Weeks, Albums: 72 Weeks).

		pos/wks
17 Dec 64	★ YEH, YEH *Columbia DB 7428* [1]	1 12
4 Mar 65	IN THE MEANTIME *Columbia DB 7494* [1]	22 8
29 Jul 65	LIKE WE USED TO BE *Columbia DB 7633* [1]	33 7
28 Oct 65	SOMETHING *Columbia DB 7727* [1]	23 7
23 Jun 66	★ GET AWAY *Columbia DB 7946* [1]	1 11
22 Sep 66	SUNNY *Columbia DB 8015*	13 8
22 Dec 66	SITTING IN THE PARK *Columbia DB 8096* [1]	12 10
23 Mar 67	BECAUSE I LOVE YOU *CBS 202587*	15 8
13 Sep 67	TRY MY WORLD *CBS 2945*	37 5
13 Dec 67	★ THE BALLAD OF BONNIE AND CLYDE *CBS 3124*	1 13
9 Jul 69	PEACEFUL *CBS 4295*	16 9
13 Dec 69	SEVENTH SON *CBS 4659*	25 7
10 Apr 71	ROSETTA *CBS 7108* [2]	11 8
17 Oct 64	FAME AT LAST *Columbia 33SX 1638*	15 8
14 May 66	● SWEET THINGS *Columbia SX 6043*	6 22
15 Oct 66	● SOUND VENTURE *Columbia SX 6076*	9 9
11 Mar 67	HALL OF FAME *Columbia SX 6120*	12 18
1 Jul 67	TWO FACES OF FAME *CBS SBPG 63018*	22 15

[1] Georgie Fame and the Blue Flames [2] Fame and Price Together

FAMILY UK, male vocal / instrumental

group (Singles: 44 Weeks, Albums: 41 Weeks)

		pos/wks
1 Nov 69	NO MULE'S FOOL *Reprise RS 27001*	29 7
22 Aug 70	STRANGE BAND *Reprise RS 27009*	11 12
17 Jul 71	● IN MY OWN TIME *Reprise K 14090*	4 13
23 Sep 72	BURLESQUE *Reprise K 14196*	13 12
10 Aug 68	MUSIC IN THE DOLLS HOUSE *Reprise RLP 6312*	35 3
22 Mar 69	● FAMILY ENTERTAINMENT *Reprise RSLP 6340*	6 3
7 Feb 70	● A SONG FOR ME *Reprise RSLP 9001*	4 13
28 Nov 70	● ANYWAY *Reprise RSX 9005*	7 7
20 Nov 71	FEARLESS *Reprise K 54003*	14 2
30 Sep 72	BANDSTAND *Reprise K 54006*	15 10
29 Sep 73	IT'S ONLY A MOVIE *Raft RA 58501*	30 3

The FAMILY CAT UK, male vocal / instrumental

group (Singles: 4 Weeks, Albums: 1 Week)

		pos/wks
28 Aug 93	AIRPLANE GARDENS / ATMOSPHERIC ROAD *Dedicated FCUK 003CD*	69 1
21 May 94	WONDERFUL EXCUSE *Dedicated 74321208432*	48 1
30 Jul 94	GOLDENBOOK *Dedicated 74321220072*	42 2
4 Jul 92	FURTHEST FROM THE SUN *Dedicated DEDCD 007*	55 1

FAMILY COOKIN' *See LIMMIE and the FAMILY COOKIN'*

FAMILY DOGG UK, male / female vocal group –

includes Albert Hammond (Singles: 14 Weeks)

		pos/wks
28 May 69	● A WAY OF LIFE *Bell 1055*	6 14

FAMILY FOUNDATION

UK, male / female vocal / instrumental group (Singles: 4 Weeks)

		pos/wks
13 Jun 92	XPRESS YOURSELF *380 PEW 1*	42 4

The FAMILY STAND US, male / female vocal /

instrumental group (Singles: 13 Weeks, Albums: 3 Weeks)

		pos/wks
31 Mar 90	GHETTO HEAVEN *East West A 7997*	10 11
17 Jan 98	GHETTO HEAVEN (re-mix) *Perfecto PERF 156CD1*	30 2
19 May 90	CHAIN *Atlantic WX 349*	52 3

FAMILY STONE *See SLY and the FAMILY STONE*

FAMOUS FLAMES *See James BROWN*

The FANTASTIC FOUR US, male vocal group (Singles: 4 Weeks)

		pos/wks
24 Feb 79	B.Y.O.F. (BRING YOUR OWN FUNK) *Atlantic LV 14*	62 4

FANTASTICS US, male vocal group (Singles: 12 Weeks)

		pos/wks
27 Mar 71	● SOMETHING OLD, SOMETHING NEW *Bell 1141*	9 12

FANTASY UFO

UK, male instrumental group (Singles: 6 Weeks)

		pos/wks
29 Sep 90	FANTASY *XL XLT 15*	56 3
10 Aug 91	MIND BODY SOUL *Strictly Underground YZ 591* [1]	50 3

[1] Fantasy UFO featuring Jay Groove

FAR CORPORATION UK / US / Germany / Switzerland,

male vocal / instrumental group (Singles: 11 Weeks)

		pos/wks
26 Oct 85	● STAIRWAY TO HEAVEN *Arista ARIST 639*	8 11

Don FARDON

UK, male vocalist – Donald Maughn (Singles: 22 Weeks)

		pos/wks
18 Apr 70	BELFAST BOY *Young Blood YB 1010*	32 5
10 Oct 70	● INDIAN RESERVATION *Young Blood YB 1015*	3 17

FARGETTA (see also TAMPERER featuring MAYA)

Italy / UK, male producer – Mario Fargetta (Singles: 3 Weeks)

		pos/wks
23 Jan 93	MUSIC *Synthetic CDR 6334* [1]	34 2
10 Aug 96	THE MUSIC IS MOVING *Arista 74321381572*	74 1

[1] Fargetta and Anne-Marie Smith

Chris FARLOWE UK, male vocalist – John

Deighton (Singles: 36 Weeks, Albums: 3 Weeks)

		pos/wks
27 Jan 66	THINK (re) *Immediate IM 023*	37 3
23 Jun 66	★ OUT OF TIME *Immediate IM 035* [1]	1 13
27 Oct 66	RIDE ON BABY *Immediate IM 038*	31 7
16 Feb 67	MY WAY OF GIVING IN *Immediate IM 041*	48 1
29 Jun 67	MOANIN' *Immediate IM 056*	46 2
13 Dec 67	HANDBAGS AND GLADRAGS *Immediate IM 065*	33 6
27 Sep 75	OUT OF TIME (re-issue) *Immediate IMS 101*	44 4
2 Apr 66	14 THINGS TO THINK ABOUT *Immediate IMLP 005*	19 1
10 Dec 66	THE ART OF CHRIS FARLOWE *Immediate IMLP 006*	37 2

[1] Chris Farlowe and The Thunderbirds

The FARM UK, male vocal / instrumental

group (Singles: 59 Weeks, Albums: 17 Weeks)

		pos/wks
5 May 90	STEPPING STONE / FAMILY OF MAN *Produce MILK 101*	58 4
1 Sep 90	● GROOVY TRAIN *Produce MILK 102*	6 10
8 Dec 90	● ALL TOGETHER NOW *Produce MILK 103*	4 12
13 Apr 91	SINFUL! (SCARY JIGGIN' WITH DR LOVE) *Siren SRN 138* [1]	28 5
4 May 91	DON'T LET ME DOWN *Produce MILK 104*	36 3
24 Aug 91	MIND *Produce MILK 105*	31 4
14 Dec 91	LOVE SEE NO COLOUR *Produce MILK 106*	58 4
4 Jul 92	RISING SUN *End Product 6581737*	48 3
17 Oct 92	DON'T YOU WANT ME *End Product 6584687*	18 5
2 Jan 93	LOVE SEE NO COLOUR (re-mix) *End Product 6588682*	35 4
12 Jun 04	● ALL TOGETHER NOW 2004 *DMG ENGLCD 2004* [2]	5 5
16 Mar 91	★ SPARTACUS *Produce MILKLP 1* ■	1 17

[1] Pete Wylie with The Farm [2] The Farm featuring S.F.X. Boys' Choir, Liverpool

FARMERS BOYS UK, male vocal /

instrumental group (Singles: 17 weeks, Albums: 1 week)

		pos/wks
9 Apr 83	MUCK IT OUT! *EMI 5380*	48 6
30 Jul 83	FOR YOU *EMI 5401*	66 3
4 Aug 84	IN THE COUNTRY *EMI FAB 2*	44 5
3 Nov 84	PHEW WOW *EMI FAB 3*	59 3
29 Oct 83	GET OUT AND WALK *EMI EMC 1077991*	49 1

John FARNHAM Australia (b. UK), male

vocalist (Singles: 17 Weeks, Albums: 9 Weeks)

		pos/wks
25 Apr 87	● YOU'RE THE VOICE *Wheatley PB 41093*	6 17
11 Jul 87	WHISPERING JACK *RCA PL 71224*	35 9

FARRAR *See MARVIN, WELCH and FARRAR*

Joanne FARRELL US, female vocalist (Singles: 2 Weeks)

		pos/wks
24 Jun 95	ALL I WANNA DO *Big Beat A 8194CD*	40 2

Joe FARRELL US, male instrumentalist – saxophone,

b. 16 Dec 1937, d. 10 Jan 1986 (Singles: 4 Weeks)

		pos/wks
16 Dec 78	NIGHT DANCING *Warner Bros. LV 2*	57 4

Singles re-entries are listed as (re), (2re), (3re)…. which signifies that the hit re-entered the chart once, twice or three times…

Dionne FARRIS US, female vocalist (Singles: 6 Weeks)

		pos/wks
18 Mar 95	I KNOW (re) Columbia 6613542	41 5
7 Jun 97	HOPELESS Columbia 6645165	42 1

Gene FARRIS US, male producer (Singles: 1 Week)

		pos/wks
20 Dec 03	WELCOME TO CHICAGO Defected DFTD 081	74 1

Gene FARROW with the GF BAND
UK, male vocal / instrumental group (Singles: 8 Weeks)

		pos/wks
1 Apr 78	MOVE YOUR BODY (re) Magnet MAG 109	33 6
5 Aug 78	DON'T STOP NOW (re) Magnet MAG 125	71 2

The FASCINATIONS US, female vocal group (Singles: 6 Weeks)

		pos/wks
3 Jul 71	GIRLS ARE OUT TO GET YOU Mojo 2092004	32 6

FASHION UK, male vocal / instrumental
group (Singles: 12 Weeks, Albums: 17 Weeks)

		pos/wks
3 Apr 82	STREETPLAYER (MECHANIK) Arista ARIST 456	46 5
21 Aug 82	LOVE SHADOW Arista ARIST 483	51 5
18 Feb 84	EYE TALK Epic A 4106	69 2
3 Jul 82 ●	FABRIQUE Arista SPART 1185	10 16
16 Jun 84	TWILIGHT OF IDOLS De Stijl EPC 25909	69 1

Susan FASSBENDER UK, female vocalist (Singles: 8 Weeks)

		pos/wks
17 Jan 81	TWILIGHT CAFE CBS 9468	21 8

FAST FOOD ROCKERS
UK, male / female vocal group (Singles: 24 Weeks)

		pos/wks
28 Jun 03 ●	FAST FOOD SONG Better the Devil BTD 1CD	2 14
18 Oct 03 ●	SAY CHEESE (SMILE PLEASE) Better the Devil BTD 5CD	10 7
27 Dec 03	I LOVE CHRISTMAS Better the Devil BTD 6CDX	25 3

FASTBALL US, male vocal / instrumental trio (Singles: 5 Weeks)

		pos/wks
3 Oct 98	THE WAY Polydor 5699472	21 5

FASTER PUSSYCAT
US, male vocal / instrumental group (Albums: 3 Weeks)

		pos/wks
16 Sep 89	WAKE ME WHEN IT'S OVER Elektra EKT 64	35 2
22 Aug 92	WHIPPED! Elektra 7559611242	58 1

FASTWAY UK, male vocal / instrumental
group (Singles: 1 Week, Albums: 2 Weeks)

		pos/wks
2 Apr 83	EASY LIVIN' CBS A 3196	74 1
30 Apr 83	FASTWAY CBS 25359	43 2

FAT BOYS
US, male rap group (Singles: 29 Weeks, Albums: 5 Weeks)

		pos/wks
4 May 85	JAIL HOUSE RAP Sutra U 9123	63 2
22 Aug 87 ●	WIPEOUT Urban URB 5 [1]	2 12
18 Jun 88 ●	THE TWIST (YO, TWIST) Urban URB 20 [2]	2 11
5 Nov 88	LOUIE LOUIE Urban URB 26	46 4
3 Oct 87	CRUSHIN' Urban URBLP 3	49 4
30 Jul 88	COMING BACK HARD AGAIN Urban URBLP 13	98 1

[1] Fat Boys and The Beach Boys [2] Fat Boys and Chubby Checker

FAT JOE (see also Jennifer LOPEZ) US, male rapper –
Joseph Cartagena (Singles: 22 Weeks, Albums: 10 Weeks)

		pos/wks
1 Apr 00	FEELIN' SO GOOD Columbia 6691972 [1]	15 6
30 Mar 02	WE THUGGIN' Atlantic AT 0124CD	48 1
25 May 02 ●	WHAT'S LUV? Atlantic AT 0128CD [2]	4 8
14 Dec 02	CRUSH TONIGHT Atlantic AT 0142CD [3]	42 2
16 Oct 04	LEAN BACK Universal MCSTD 40385 [4] ▲	24 5
27 Apr 02	JEALOUS ONES STILL ENVY (J.O.S.E.) Atlantic 7567834722	19 10

[1] Jennifer Lopez featuring Big Pun and Fat Joe [2] Fat Joe featuring Ashanti
[3] Fat Joe featuring Ginuwine [4] Terror Squad featuring Fat Joe (aka Joey
Crack) & Remy

Sleeve, not the label, of 'We Thuggin' has the credit: Fat Joe featuring R. Kelly

FAT LADY SINGS Ireland, male vocal /
instrumental group (Singles: 2 Weeks, Albums: 1 Week)

		pos/wks
17 Jul 93	DRUNKARD LOGIC East West YZ 756CD	56 2
18 May 91	TWIST East West WX 418	50 1

FAT LARRY'S BAND US, male vocal / instrumental
group – Larry James (Singles: 26 Weeks, Albums: 4 Weeks)

		pos/wks
2 Jul 77	CENTER CITY Atlantic K 10951	31 5
10 Mar 79	BOOGIE TOWN Fantasy FTC 168 [1]	46 4
18 Aug 79	LOOKING FOR LOVE TONIGHT Fantasy FTC 179 [2]	46 6
18 Sep 82 ●	ZOOM Virgin VS 546	2 11
9 Oct 82	BREAKIN' OUT Virgin V 2229	58 4

[1] FLB [2] Fat Larry's Band (FLB)

FAT LES (see also BLUR; ME ME ME) UK, male / female
vocal group – includes Alex James (Singles: 22 Weeks)

		pos/wks
20 Jun 98 ●	VINDALOO Telstar CDSTAS 2982	2 12
19 Dec 98	NAUGHTY CHRISTMAS (GOBLIN IN THE OFFICE) Turtleneck NECKCD 001	21 5
17 Jun 00 ●	JERUSALEM (re) Parlophone CDR 6540 [1]	10 5

[1] Fat Les 2000

The FATBACK BAND US, male vocal / instrumental
group (Singles: 67 Weeks, Albums: 7 Weeks)

		pos/wks
6 Sep 75	YUM, YUM (GIMME SOME) Polydor 2066590	40 6
6 Dec 75	(ARE YOU READY) DO THE BUS STOP Polydor 2066637	18 10
21 Feb 76	(DO THE) SPANISH HUSTLE Polydor 2066656	10 7
29 May 76	PARTY TIME Polydor 2066682	41 4
14 Aug 76	NIGHT FEVER Spring 2066706	38 4
12 Mar 77	DOUBLE DUTCH Spring 2066777	31 4
9 Aug 80	BACKSTROKIN' Spring POSP 149 [1]	41 9
23 Jun 84 ●	I FOUND LOVIN' (re) Master Mix CHE 8401	7 16
4 May 85	GIRLS ON MY MIND Atlantic / Cotillion FBACK 1 [1]	69 2
6 Sep 86	I FOUND LOVIN' (re-issue) Important TAN 10	55 5
6 Mar 76	RAISING HELL Polydor 2391203	19 6
4 Jul 87	FATBACK LIVE Start STL 12	80 1

[1] Fatback

FATBOY SLIM 353 Top 500 (see also Norman COOK; FREAKPOWER;
The HOUSEMARTINS; MIGHTY DUB KATZ; PIZZAMAN; URBAN ALL STARS)
Multi-aliased, superstar DJ / producer Norman Cook, (b. Quentin Cook, 31 Jul
1963, Bromley, Kent, UK). He finally achieved a solo No.1 in this guise, having
already topped the chart with the Housemartins and Beats International.
Famous for launching 'big beat', he DJed in front of a quarter of a million fans
on Brighton Beach in 2002 (Singles: 78 Weeks, Albums: 114 Weeks) pos/wks

		pos/wks
3 May 97	GOING OUT OF MY HEAD Skint SKINT 19CD	57 1
1 Nov 97	EVERYBODY NEEDS A 303 Skint SKINT 31CD	34 2
20 Jun 98 ●	THE ROCKAFELLER SKANK Skint SKINT 35CD	6 10
17 Oct 98 ●	GANGSTER TRIPPIN' Skint SKINT 39CD	3 8
16 Jan 99 ★	PRAISE YOU Skint SKINT 42CD ■	1 12
1 May 99 ●	RIGHT HERE RIGHT NOW Skint SKINT 46CD	2 10
1 May 99	BADDER BADDER SCHWING Eye Q EYEUK 040CD [1]	34 2
28 Oct 00 ●	SUNSET (BIRD OF PREY) (re) Skint SKINT 58CD	9 13
20 Jan 01	DEMONS Skint SKINT 60CD [2]	16 5
5 May 01 ●	STAR 69 Skint SKINT 64CD	10 7
15 Sep 01	YA MAMA / SONG FOR SHELTER Skint SKINT 71CD	30 2
26 Jan 02	RETOX Skint SKINT FAT 18	73 1
2 Oct 04	SLASHDOTDASH Skint SKINT 100CD	12 3
11 Dec 04	A WONDERFUL NIGHT Skint SKINT 104CD	51 2
28 Sep 96	BETTER LIVING THROUGH CHEMISTRY Skint BRASSIC 2CD	69 3
31 Oct 98 ★	YOU'VE COME A LONG WAY, BABY Skint BRASSIC 11CD	1 86
18 Nov 00 ●	HALFWAY BETWEEN THE GUTTER AND THE STARS Skint BRASSIC 20CD	8 22
16 Oct 04	PALOOKAVILLE Skint BRASSIC 29CD	14 3

[1] Freddy Fresh featuring Fatboy Slim [2] Fatboy Slim featuring Macy Gray

FATHER ABRAHAM See The SMURFS

FATHER ABRAPHART and the SMURPS See Jonathan KING

FATHER KILCOYNE See POPE JOHN PAUL II

FATIMA MANSIONS Ireland, male vocal /
instrumental group (Singles: 11 Weeks, Albums: 1 Week)

		pos/wks
23 May 92	EVIL MAN Radioactive SKX 56	59 1
1 Aug 92	1000% Radioactive SKX 59	61 3
19 Sep 92 ●	(EVERYTHING I DO) I DO IT FOR YOU Columbia 6583827	7 6

		pos/wks
6 Aug 94	**THE LOYALISER** *Kitchenware SKCD 67*	**58** 1
6 Jun 92	**VALHALLA AVENUE** *Radioactive KWCD 18*	**52** 1

'(Everything I Do) I Do It For You' was listed with 'Theme From M.A.S.H. (Suicide Is Painless)' by Manic Street Preachers

FATMAN SCOOP featuring the CROOKLYN CLAN
US, male DJ / rapper – Isaac Freeman III (Singles: 22 Weeks) pos/wks

1 Nov 03 ★	**BE FAITHFUL** *Def Jam 9812716* ■ 1 16
21 Feb 04 ●	**IT TAKES SCOOP** *Def Jam 9816983* 9 6

FEAR FACTORY
US, male vocal / instrumental group (Singles: 1 Week, Albums: 7 Weeks) pos/wks

9 Oct 99	**CARS** *Roadrunner RR 21893*	**57** 1
1 Jul 95	**DEMANUFACTURE** *Roadrunner RR 89565*	**27** 1
14 Jun 97	**REMANUFACTURE – CLONING TECHNOLOGY** *Roadrunner RR 88342*	**22** 1
8 Aug 98	**OBSOLETE** *Roadrunner RR 87522*	**20** 2
5 May 01	**DIGIMORTAL** *Roadrunner RR 85612*	**24** 2
1 May 04	**ARCHETYPE** *Roadrunner RR 83115*	**41** 1

Phil FEARON
UK, male vocalist (Singles: 63 Weeks, Albums: 9 Weeks) pos/wks

23 Apr 83 ●	**DANCING TIGHT** *Ensign ENY 501* [1] 4 11
30 Jul 83	**WAIT UNTIL TONIGHT (MY LOVE)** *Ensign ENY 503* [1] 20 8
22 Oct 83	**FANTASY REAL** *Ensign ENY 507* [2] 41 6
10 Mar 84 ●	**WHAT DO I DO** *Ensign ENY 510* [2] 5 10
14 Jul 84 ●	**EVERYBODY'S LAUGHING** *Ensign ENY 514* [2] 10 10
15 Jun 85	**YOU DON'T NEED A REASON** *Ensign ENY 517* [2] 42 4
27 Jul 85	**THIS KIND OF LOVE** *Ensign ENY 521* [3] 70 3
2 Aug 86 ●	**I CAN PROVE IT** *Ensign PF 1* 8 9
15 Nov 86	**AIN'T NOTHING BUT A HOUSEPARTY** *Ensign PF 2* 60 2
25 Aug 84 ●	**PHIL FEARON AND GALAXY** *Ensign ENCL 2* [1] 8 8
14 Sep 85	**THIS KIND OF LOVE** *Ensign ENCL 4* [1] 98 1

[1] Galaxy featuring Phil Fearon [2] Phil Fearon and Galaxy [3] Phil Fearon and Galaxy featuring Dee Galdes [1] Phil Fearon and Galaxy

FEEDER
UK, male vocal / instrumental group (Singles: 56 Weeks, Albums: 44 Weeks) pos/wks

8 Mar 97	**TANGERINE** *Echo ECSCD 32* 60 1
10 May 97	**CEMENT** *Echo ECSCX 36* 53 1
23 Aug 97	**CRASH** *Echo ECSCD 42* 48 1
18 Oct 97	**HIGH** *Echo ECSCD 44* 24 2
28 Feb 98	**SUFFOCATE** *Echo ECSCX 52* 37 1
3 Apr 99	**DAY IN DAY OUT** *Echo ECSCD 75* 31 2
12 Jun 99	**INSOMNIA** *Echo ECSCD 77* 22 3
21 Aug 99	**YESTERDAY WENT TOO SOON** *Echo ECSCD 79* 20 3
20 Nov 99	**PAPERFACES** *Echo ECSCD 85* 41 2
20 Jan 01 ●	**BUCK ROGERS** *Echo ECSCD 106* 5 6
14 Apr 01	**SEVEN DAYS IN THE SUN** (re) *Echo ECSCD 107* 14 6
14 Jul 01	**TURN** *Echo ECSCD 116* 27 2
22 Dec 01	**JUST A DAY (EP)** *Echo ECSCD 121* 12 7
12 Oct 02	**COME BACK AROUND** (re) *Echo ECSCD 130* 14 5
25 Jan 03 ●	**JUST THE WAY I'M FEELING** *Echo ECSCD 133* 10 8
17 May 03	**FORGET ABOUT TOMORROW** *Echo ECSCD 135* 12 4
4 Oct 03	**FIND THE COLOUR** *Echo ECSCD 145* 24 2
31 May 97	**POLYTHENE** *Echo ECHCD 15* 65 1
11 Sep 99 ●	**YESTERDAY WENT TOO SOON – LIMITED EDITION** *Echo ECHCD 28* 8 3
5 May 01 ●	**ECHO PARK** *Echo ECHCD 34* 5 9
2 Nov 02 ●	**COMFORT IN SOUND** *Echo ECHCD 43* 6 31

Tracks on Just a Day (EP) CD1: Just a Day / Can't Stand Losing You / Piece By Piece (video). CD2: Just a Day' (full version) / Emily / Slowburn / Just A Day (video)

Wilton FELDER (see also CRUSADERS)
US, male instrumentalist – tenor sax (Singles: 7 Weeks, Albums: 3 Weeks) pos/wks

1 Nov 80	**INHERIT THE WIND** *MCA 646* 39 5
16 Feb 85	**(NO MATTER HOW HIGH I GET) I'LL STILL BE LOOKIN' UP TO YOU** *MCA MCA 919* [1] 63 2
23 Feb 85	**SECRETS** *MCA MCF 3237* 77 3

[1] Featuring Bobby Womack and introducing Alltrina Grayson

Bobby Womack is the uncredited vocalist on 'Inherit the Wind'

FELICIA See B.M.R. featuring FELICIA

José FELICIANO
US, male vocalist / instrumentalist – guitar (Singles: 23 Weeks, Albums: 40 Weeks) pos/wks

18 Sep 68 ●	**LIGHT MY FIRE** *RCA 1715* 6 16
18 Oct 69	**AND THE SUN WILL SHINE** *RCA 1871* 25 7
2 Nov 68 ●	**FELICIANO** *RCA Victor SF 7946* 6 36
29 Nov 69	**JOSE FELICIANO** *RCA Victor SF 8044* 29 2
14 Feb 70	**10 TO 23** *RCA SF 7946* 38 1
22 Aug 70	**FIREWORKS** *RCA SF 8124* 65 1

FELIX
UK, male producer – Francis Wright (Singles: 29 Weeks, Albums: 4 Weeks) pos/wks

8 Aug 92 ●	**DON'T YOU WANT ME** *Deconstruction 74321110507* 6 11
24 Oct 92	**IT WILL MAKE ME CRAZY** *Deconstruction 74321118137* 11 6
22 May 93	**STARS** *Deconstruction 74321147102* 29 3
12 Aug 95 ●	**DON'T YOU WANT ME (re-mix)** *Deconstruction 74321293972* 10 5
19 Oct 96	**DON'T YOU WANT ME (2nd re-mix)** *Deconstruction 74321418142* 17 4
10 Apr 93	**#1** *Deconstruction 74321137002* 26 4

Gil FELIX See INFRARED vs Gil FELIX

Julie FELIX
US, female vocalist / instrumentalist – guitar (Singles: 19 Weeks, Albums: 4 Weeks) pos/wks

18 Apr 70	**IF I COULD (EL CONDOR PASA)** *RAK 101* 19 11
17 Oct 70	**HEAVEN IS HERE** *RAK 105* 22 8
11 Sep 66	**CHANGES** *Fontana TL 5368* 27 4

FELIX DA HOUSECAT
US, male producer – Felix Stallings Jr (Singles: 8 Weeks) pos/wks

6 Sep 97	**DIRTY MOTHA** *Manifesto FESCD 29* [1] 66 1
14 Jul 01	**SILVER SCREEN SHOWER SCENE** *City Rockers ROCKERS 1CD* 55 1
2 Mar 02	**WHAT DOES IT FEEL LIKE?** *City Rockers ROCKERS 8CD* 66 1
5 Oct 02	**SILVER SCREEN SHOWER SCENE (re-mix)** *City Rockers ROCKERS 19CD* 39 2
14 Aug 04	**ROCKET RIDE** *Rykodisc ENR 522* 55 1
27 Nov 04	**WATCHING CARS GO BY** *Emperor Norton ENR 532* [2] 49 2

[1] Qwilo and Felix Da Housecat [2] Felix Da Housecat vs Sasha and Armand Van Helden

FELLY See TECHNOTRONIC

FELON
UK, female vocalist – Simone Locker (Singles: 2 Weeks) pos/wks

23 Mar 02	**GET OUT** *Serious SERR 032CD* 31 2

FE-M@IL
UK, female vocal group (Singles: 2 Weeks) pos/wks

5 Aug 00	**FLEE FLY FLO** *Jive 9250592* 46 2

FEMME FATALE
US, male / female vocal / instrumental group (Singles: 2 Weeks) pos/wks

11 Feb 89	**FALLING IN AND OUT OF LOVE** *MCA MCA 1309* 69 2

The FENDERMEN
US, male vocal / instrumental duo – Phil Humphrey and Jim Sundquist – guitars (Singles: 9 Weeks) pos/wks

18 Aug 60	**MULE SKINNER BLUES (2re)** *Top Rank JAR 395* 32 9

FENIX TX
US, male vocal / instrumental group (Singles: 1 Week) pos/wks

11 May 02	**THREESOME** *MCA MCSTD 40279* 66 1

FENMEN See Bern ELLIOTT and the FENMEN

George FENTON and Jonas GWANGWA
UK / South Africa, male instrumental / production duo (Singles: 1 Week) pos/wks

2 Jan 88	**CRY FREEDOM** *MCA MCA 1228* 75 1

The listed flip side of 'Cry Freedom' was 'The Funeral' by Thuli Dumakude

Peter FENTON
UK, male vocalist (Singles: 3 Weeks) pos/wks

10 Nov 66	**MARBLE BREAKS IRON BENDS** *Fontana TF 748* 46 3

Shane FENTON and the FENTONES (see also Alvin STARDUST)
UK, male instrumental group (Singles: 32 Weeks) pos/wks

26 Oct 61	**I'M A MOODY GUY** *Parlophone R 4827* 22 8
1 Feb 62	**WALK AWAY** *Parlophone R 4866* 38 5

5 Apr 62	IT'S ALL OVER NOW *Parlophone R 4883*	**29**	7
19 Apr 62	THE MEXICAN *Parlophone R 4899* [1]	**41**	3
12 Jul 62	CINDY'S BIRTHDAY *Parlophone R 4921*	**19**	8
27 Sep 62	THE BREEZE AND I *Parlophone R 4937* [1]	**48**	1

[1] The Fentones

FERGIE
Ireland, male DJ / producer – Robert Ferguson (Singles: 5 Weeks) pos/wks

9 Sep 00	DECEPTION *Duty Free DF 020CD*	**47**	1
25 Nov 00	HOOVERS & HORNS *Nukleuz NUKC 0185* [1]	**57**	2
10 Aug 02	THE BASS EP *Duty Free / Decode DFTELCX 004*	**47**	2

[1] Fergie & BK

Tracks on The Bass EP: Bass Generator (mixes) / Bass Has Got Me On (mixes)

Sheila FERGUSON (see also The THREE DEGREES)
US, female vocalist (Singles: 1 Week) pos/wks

5 Feb 94	WHEN WILL I SEE YOU AGAIN *XSrhythm CDSTAS 2711*	**60**	1

FERKO STRING BAND
US, male instrumental group (Singles: 2 Weeks) pos/wks

12 Aug 55	ALABAMA JUBILEE *London HL 8140*	**20**	2

Luisa FERNANDEZ *Spain, female vocalist (Singles: 8 Weeks)* pos/wks

11 Nov 78	LAY LOVE ON YOU *Warner Bros. K 17061*	**31**	8

Pamela FERNANDEZ *US, female vocalist (Singles: 3 Weeks)* pos/wks

17 Sep 94	KICKIN' IN THE BEAT *Ore AG 5CD*	**43**	2
3 Jun 95	LET'S START OVER / KICKIN' IN THE BEAT (re-mix) *Ore AG 9CD*	**59**	1

FERRANTE and TEICHER *US, male instrumental duo –*
Arthur Ferrante and Louis Teicher – pianos (Singles: 18 Weeks) pos/wks

18 Aug 60	THEME FROM 'THE APARTMENT' *London HLT 9164*	**44**	1
9 Mar 61	● EXODUS (THEME FROM 'EXODUS') *London HLT 9298 and HMV POP 881*	**6**	17

'Exodus (Theme from 'Exodus')' was available first on London, then on HMV when the US label, United Artists, changed its UK outlet

Ibrahim FERRER
Cuba, male vocalist / instrumentalist – piano (Albums: 3 Weeks) pos/wks

5 Jun 99	BUENA VISTA SOCIAL CLUB PRESENTS IBRAHIM FERRER *World Circuit WCD 055*	**42**	3

José FERRER *US, male actor / vocalist – José Vicente*
Ferrer y Centron, b. 8 Jan 1912, d. 26 Jan 1992 (Singles: 3 Weeks) pos/wks

19 Feb 54	● WOMAN (UH-HUH) *Philips PB 220*	**7**	3

'Woman (Uh-Huh)' was coupled with 'Man (Uh-Huh)' by Rosemary Clooney

Tony FERRINO
UK, male vocalist – comedian Steve Coogan (Singles: 2 Weeks) pos/wks

23 Nov 96	HELP YOURSELF / BIGAMY AT CHRISTMAS *RCA 74321430302*	**42**	2

Bryan FERRY (90 Top 500) *Sophisticated and stylish UK vocalist /*
songwriter, b. 26 Sep 1945, Tyne and Wear, who split his time between a solo career and fronting the visually stimulating Roxy Music. He was still having Top 20 albums in 2004 (Singles: 133 Weeks, Albums: 329 Weeks) pos/wks

29 Sep 73	● A HARD RAIN'S A-GONNA FALL *Island WIP 6170*	**10**	9
25 May 74	THE 'IN' CROWD *Island WIP 6196*	**13**	6
31 Aug 74	SMOKE GETS IN YOUR EYES *Island WIP 6205*	**17**	8
5 Jul 75	YOU GO TO MY HEAD *Island WIP 6234*	**33**	3
12 Jun 76	● LET'S STICK TOGETHER (LET'S WORK TOGETHER) *Island WIP 6307*	**4**	10
7 Aug 76	● EXTENDED PLAY (EP) *Island IEP 1*	**7**	9
5 Feb 77	● THIS IS TOMORROW *Polydor 2001 704*	**9**	9
14 May 77	TOKYO JOE *Polydor 2001 711*	**15**	7
13 May 78	WHAT GOES ON *Polydor POSP 3*	**67**	2
5 Aug 78	SIGN OF THE TIMES *Polydor 2001 798*	**37**	8
11 May 85	● SLAVE TO LOVE *EG FERRY 1*	**10**	9
31 Aug 85	DON'T STOP THE DANCE *EG FERRY 2*	**21**	7
7 Dec 85	WINDSWEPT *EG FERRY 3*	**46**	3
29 Mar 86	IS YOUR LOVE STRONG ENOUGH? *EG FERRY 4*	**22**	7
10 Oct 87	THE RIGHT STUFF *Virgin VS 940*	**37**	6
13 Feb 88	KISS AND TELL *Virgin VS 1034*	**41**	5
29 Oct 88	LET'S STICK TOGETHER (re-mix) *EG EGO 44*	**12**	7
11 Feb 89	THE PRICE OF LOVE (re-mix) *EG EGO 46*	**49**	3
22 Apr 89	HE'LL HAVE TO GO *EG EGO 48*	**63**	1
6 Mar 93	I PUT A SPELL ON YOU *Virgin VSCDG 1400*	**18**	5
29 May 93	WILL YOU LOVE ME TOMORROW *Virgin VSCDG 1455*	**23**	5
4 Sep 93	GIRL OF MY BEST FRIEND *Virgin VSCDG 1488*	**57**	2
29 Oct 94	YOUR PAINTED SMILE *Virgin VSCDG 1508*	**52**	1
11 Feb 95	MAMOUNA *Virgin VSCDG 1528*	**57**	1
3 Nov 73	● THESE FOOLISH THINGS *Island ILPS 9249*	**5**	42
20 Jul 74	● ANOTHER TIME ANOTHER PLACE *Island ILPS 9284*	**4**	25
2 Oct 76	LET'S STICK TOGETHER *Island ILPSX 1*	**19**	5
5 Mar 77	● IN YOUR MIND *Polydor 2302055*	**5**	17
30 Sep 78	THE BRIDE STRIPPED BARE *Polydor POLD 5003*	**13**	5
15 Jun 85	★ BOYS AND GIRLS *EG EGLP 62* ■	**1**	44
26 Apr 86	★ STREET LIFE – 20 GREAT HITS *EG EGTV 1* [1] ■	**1**	77
14 Nov 87	● BETE NOIRE *Virgin V 2474*	**9**	16
19 Nov 88	● THE ULTIMATE COLLECTION *EG EGTV 2* [1]	**6**	35
3 Apr 93	● TAXI *Virgin CDV 2700*	**2**	14
17 Sep 94	● MAMOUNA *Virgin CDV 2751*	**11**	4
4 Nov 95	MORE THAN THIS – THE BEST OF BRYAN FERRY AND ROXY MUSIC *Virgin CDV 2791* [1]	**15**	15
6 Nov 99	AS TIME GOES BY *Virgin CDVIR 89*	**16**	10
22 Jul 00	SLAVE TO LOVE *Virgin CDV 2921*	**11**	11
11 May 02	● FRANTIC *Virgin CDVIR 167*	**6**	5
19 Jun 04	THE PLATINUM COLLECTION *Virgin BFRM 1* [1]	**17**	4

[1] Bryan Ferry and Roxy Music

Tracks on Extended Play (EP): Price of Love / Shame Shame Shame / Heart on My Sleeve / It's Only Love

FERRY AID
International, male / female charity ensemble (Singles: 7 Weeks) pos/wks

4 Apr 87	★ LET IT BE *The Sun AID 1* ■	**1**	7

FEVER featuring Tippa IRIE *UK, male production /*
instrumental group and male vocalist (Singles: 1 Week) pos/wks

8 Jul 95	STAYING ALIVE 95 *Telstar CDSTAS 2776*	**48**	1

Lena FIAGBE *UK, female vocalist (Singles: 13 Weeks)* pos/wks

24 Jul 93	YOU COME FROM EARTH *Mother MUMCD 42* [1]	**69**	1
23 Oct 93	GOTTA GET IT RIGHT *Mother MUMCD 44*	**20**	5
16 Apr 94	WHAT'S IT LIKE TO BE BEAUTIFUL *Mother MUMCD 49*	**52**	3
25 Jun 94	VISIONS *Mother MUMCD 53*	**48**	2
10 Feb 96	AFRICAN DREAM *Mercury MERCD 453* [2]	**44**	2

[1] Lena [2] Wasis Diop featuring Lena Fiagbe

Karel FIALKA
UK, male vocalist / multi-instrumentalist (Singles: 12 Weeks) pos/wks

17 May 80	THE EYES HAVE IT *Blueprint BLU 2005*	**52**	4
5 Sep 87	● HEY MATTHEW *IRS IRM 140*	**9**	8

FIAT LUX *UK, male vocal / instrumental group (Singles: 4 Weeks)* pos/wks

28 Jan 84	SECRETS *Polydor FIAT 2*	**65**	3
17 Mar 84	BLUE EMOTION *Polydor FIAT 3*	**59**	1

FICTION FACTORY
UK, male vocal / instrumental group (Singles: 11 Weeks) pos/wks

14 Jan 84	● (FEELS LIKE) HEAVEN *CBS A 3996*	**6**	9
17 Mar 84	GHOST OF LOVE *CBS A 3819*	**64**	2

FIDDLER'S DRAM
UK, male / female vocal / instrumental group (Singles: 9 Weeks) pos/wks

15 Dec 79	● DAYTRIP TO BANGOR (DIDN'T WE HAVE A LOVELY TIME) *Dingle's SID 211*	**3**	9

FIDELFATTI featuring RONNETTE *Italy, male producer –*
Piero Fidelfatti and female vocalist (Singles: 1 Week) pos/wks

27 Jan 90	JUST WANNA TOUCH ME *Urban URB 46*	**65**	1

Brad FIEDEL *US, male arranger (Albums: 7 Weeks)* pos/wks

31 Aug 91	TERMINATOR 2 (FILM SOUNDTRACK) *Vareses Sarabande VS 5335*	**26**	7

Billy FIELD *Australia, male vocalist (Singles: 3 Weeks)*

		pos/wks
12 Jun 82	**YOU WEREN'T IN LOVE WITH ME** *CBS A 2344*	**67** 3

Ernie FIELDS and his ORCHESTRA *US, orchestra –*
leader b. 26 Aug 1905, d. 11 May 1997 (Singles: 8 Weeks)

		pos/wks
25 Dec 59	**IN THE MOOD** *London HL 8985*	**13** 8

Gracie FIELDS *UK, female vocalist – Grace Stansfield,*
b. 9 Jan 1898, d. 27 Sep 1979 (Singles: 15 Weeks, Albums: 3 Weeks) pos/wks

		pos/wks
31 May 57 ●	**AROUND THE WORLD (re)** *Columbia DB 3953*	**8** 9
6 Nov 59	**LITTLE DONKEY (re)** *Columbia DB 4360*	**20** 6
20 Dec 75	**THE GOLDEN YEARS** *Warwick WW 5007*	**48** 3

Richard 'Dimples' FIELDS
US, male vocalist, b. 1942, d. 15 Jan 2000 (Singles: 4 Weeks) pos/wks

		pos/wks
20 Feb 82	**I'VE GOT TO LEARN TO SAY NO** *Epic EPC A 1918*	**56** 4

FIELDS OF THE NEPHILIM *UK, male vocal /*
instrumental group (Singles: 10 Weeks, Albums: 9 Weeks)

		pos/wks
24 Oct 87	**BLUE WATER** *Situation Two SIT 48*	**75** 1
4 Jun 88	**MOONCHILD** *Situation Two SIT 52*	**28** 3
27 May 89	**PSYCHONAUT** *Situation Two SIT 57*	**35** 3
4 Aug 90	**FOR HER LIGHT** *Beggars Banquet BEG 244T*	**54** 1
24 Nov 90	**SUMERLAND (DREAMED)** *Beggars Banquet BEG 250*	**37** 1
28 Sep 02	**FROM THE FIRE** *Jungle JUNG 65CD*	**62** 1
30 May 87	**DAWNRAZOR** *Situation 2 SITU 18*	**62** 2
17 Sep 88	**THE NEPHILIM** *Situation 2 SITU 22*	**14** 3
6 Oct 90	**ELIZIUM** *Beggars Banquet BEGA 115*	**22** 2
6 Apr 91	**EARTH INFERNO** *Beggars Banquet BEGA 120*	**39** 2

FIERCE
UK, female vocal group (Singles: 23 Weeks, Albums: 2 Weeks)

		pos/wks
9 Jan 99	**RIGHT HERE RIGHT NOW** *Wildstar CDWILD 13*	**25** 5
15 May 99	**DAYZ LIKE THAT** *Wildstar CDWILD 19*	**11** 5
14 Aug 99	**SO LONG** *Wildstar CDWILD 27*	**15** 5
12 Feb 00 ●	**SWEET LOVE 2K** *Wildstar CDWILD 34*	**3** 8
28 Aug 99	**RIGHT HERE RIGHT NOW** *Wildstar CDWILD 14*	**27** 2

FIERCE GIRL *UK, male vocal / rap duo (Singles: 1 Week)*

		pos/wks
11 Sep 04	**DOUBLE DROP** *Red Flag RF 012CDS*	**74** 1

The FIERY FURNACES *US, male / female production / vocal*
duo – Matthew and Eleanor Friedberger (Singles: 2 Weeks)

		pos/wks
6 Mar 04	**TROPICAL ICE-LAND** *Rough Trade RTRADSCD 152*	**52** 1
17 Jul 04	**SINGLE AGAIN** *Rough Trade RTRADSCD 190*	**49** 1

The 5TH DIMENSION (see also Billie DAVIS; Billy DAVIS Jr)
US, male / female vocal group (Singles: 21 Weeks)

		pos/wks
16 Apr 69	**AQUARIUS – LET THE SUNSHINE IN (MEDLEY)** *Liberty LBF 15193* ▲	**11** 12
17 Jan 70	**WEDDING BELL BLUES** *Liberty LBF 15288* ▲	**16** 9

50 CENT (see also G-UNIT) *US, male rapper –*
Curtis Jackson (Singles: 52 Weeks, Albums: 69 Weeks)

		pos/wks
22 Mar 03 ●	**IN DA CLUB** *Interscope 4978742* ▲	**3** 24
12 Jul 03 ●	**21 QUESTIONS** *Interscope 9807195* [1] ▲	**6** 8
18 Oct 03	**P.I.M.P. (IMPORT)** *Interscope 9811812CD*	**74** 1
25 Oct 03 ●	**P.I.M.P. (re)** *Interscope 9812333*	**5** 11
6 Mar 04 ●	**IF I CAN'T / ... THEM THANGS** *Interscope 9815279* [2]	**10** 8
1 Mar 03 ●	**GET RICH OR DIE TRYIN'** *Interscope ISC 4935442* ▲	**2** 68
18 Sep 04	**50 CENT IS THE FUTURE** *Street Dance SDR 0166752* [1]	**65** 1

[1] 50 Cent featuring Nate Dogg [2] 50 Cent & G-Unit [1] 50 Cent & G-Unit

5050 *UK, male production duo – Jason*
Powell and Andy Lysandrou (Singles: 2 Weeks)

		pos/wks
13 Oct 01	**WHO'S COMING ROUND** *Obsessive FIFTYCD 01*	**54** 1
23 Mar 02	**BAD BOYS HOLLER BOO** *Logic 74321910202*	**73** 1

50 GRIND featuring POKEMON ALLSTARS *UK, male vocal /*
instrumental group and Pokemon popsters (Singles: 1 Week)

		pos/wks
22 Dec 01	**GOTTA CATCH 'EM ALL** *Recognition CDREC 21*	**57** 1

52ND STREET *UK, male / female vocal /*
instrumental group (Singles: 13 Weeks, Albums: 1 Week)

		pos/wks
2 Nov 85	**TELL ME (HOW IT FEELS)** *10 TEN 74*	**54** 5
11 Jan 86	**YOU'RE MY LAST CHANCE** *10 TEN 89*	**49** 4
8 Mar 86	**I CAN'T LET YOU GO** *10 TEN 114*	**57** 4
19 Apr 86	**CHILDREN OF THE NIGHT** *10 DIX 25*	**71** 1

53RD & 3RD See Jonathan KING

56K featuring BEJAY
UK, male / female production / vocal group (Singles: 1 Week)

		pos/wks
19 Apr 03	**SAVE A PRAYER** *Kontor 0146495*	**46** 1

FIGHT CLUB featuring Laurent KONRAD
France, male producer and male vocalist (Singles: 1 Week)

		pos/wks
7 Feb 04	**SPREAD LOVE** *Nebula NEBCD 054*	**70** 1

FILTER *US, male vocal / instrumental duo – Richard Patrick*
and Brian Liesgang (Singles: 5 Weeks, Albums: 2 Weeks)

		pos/wks
11 Oct 97	**(CAN'T YOU) TRIP LIKE I DO** *Epic 6650862* [1]	**39** 2
18 Mar 00	**TAKE A PICTURE** *Reprise W 515CD*	**25** 3
4 Sep 99	**TITLE OF RECORD** *Reprise 9362473882*	**75** 1
10 Aug 02	**THE AMALGAMUT** *Reprise 9362479632*	**68** 1

[1] Filter and The Crystal Method

FINAL CUT See TRUE FAITH and Bridgette GRACE with FINAL CUT

FINCH *US, male vocal / instrumental group (Singles: 2 Weeks)*

		pos/wks
5 Apr 03	**LETTERS TO YOU** *Drive-Thru / MCA MCSTD 40310*	**39** 2

FINE YOUNG CANNIBALS (358 **Top 500**)
(see also FYC; TWO MEN, A DRUM MACHINE and A TRUMPET) *Politically
aware pop / soul trio from Birmingham, UK; Roland Gift (v) and ex-Beat
members Andy Cox (g) and David Steele (b). Unmistakable vocalist Gift also
acted in films, most notably 1989's Scandal. FYC, who were among 1989's
biggest selling acts worldwide, won (and returned) two Brit awards in 1990
(Singles: 81 Weeks, Albums: 107 Weeks)*

		pos/wks
8 Jun 85 ●	**JOHNNY COME HOME** *London LON 68*	**8** 13
9 Nov 85	**BLUE** *London LON 79*	**41** 6
11 Jan 86 ●	**SUSPICIOUS MINDS** *London LON 82*	**8** 9
12 Apr 86	**FUNNY HOW LOVE IS** *London LON 88*	**58** 4
21 Mar 87 ●	**EVER FALLEN IN LOVE** *London LON 121*	**9** 10
7 Jan 89	**SHE DRIVES ME CRAZY** *London LON 199* ▲	**5** 11
15 Apr 89 ●	**GOOD THING** *London LON 218* ▲	**7** 8
19 Aug 89	**DON'T LOOK BACK** *London LON 220*	**34** 4
18 Nov 89	**I'M NOT THE MAN I USED TO BE** *London LON 244*	**20** 8
24 Feb 90	**I'M NOT SATISFIED** *London LON 252*	**46** 3
16 Nov 96	**THE FLAME** *ffrr LONCD 389*	**17** 3
11 Jan 97	**SHE DRIVES ME CRAZY (re-mix)** *ffrr LONCD 391*	**36** 2
21 Dec 85	**FINE YOUNG CANNIBALS** *London LONLP 16*	**11** 27
18 Feb 89 ★	**THE RAW & THE COOKED** *London 828069 1* ■	**1** 66
15 Dec 90	**THE RAW AND THE REMIX** *London 8282211* [1]	**61** 1
23 Nov 96 ●	**THE FINEST** *ffrr 8288542*	**10** 13

[1] FYC

'The Raw and the Remix' is a re-mix album of 'The Raw and the Cooked'

FINITRIBE
UK, male instrumental / production group (Singles: 2 Weeks)

		pos/wks
11 Jul 92	**FOREVERGREEN** *One Little Indian 74TP 12F*	**51** 1
19 Nov 94	**BRAND NEW** *ffrr FCD 247*	**69** 1

FINK BROTHERS
UK, male vocal / instrumental duo (Singles: 4 Weeks)

		pos/wks
9 Feb 85	**MUTANTS IN MEGA CITY ONE** *Zarjazz JAZZ 2*	**50** 4

Frank FINLAY See David ESSEX

FINN (see also CROWDED HOUSE)
New Zealand, male vocal / instrumental duo –
Neil and Tim Finn (Singles: 8 Weeks, Albums: 6 Weeks)

		pos/wks
14 Oct 95	**SUFFER NEVER** *Parlophone CDRS 6417*	**29** 3
9 Dec 95	**ANGEL'S HEAP** *Parlophone CDRS 6421*	**41** 2

21 Aug 04	WON'T GIVE IN *Parlophone CDRS 6644* [1]	**26** 2
20 Nov 04	NOTHING WRONG WITH YOU *Parlophone CDRS 6655* [1]	**31** 1
28 Oct 95	FINN *Parlophone CDFINN 1*	**15** 3
4 Sep 04 ●	EVERYONE IS HERE *Parlophone 8647762* [1]	**8** 3

[1] The Finn Brothers [1] The Finn Brothers

Micky FINN *See* URBAN SHAKEDOWN

Neil FINN (see also CROWDED HOUSE; FINN) *New Zealand, male vocalist / instrumentalist (Singles: 6 Weeks, Albums: 15 Weeks)* pos/wks

13 Jun 98	SHE WILL HAVE HER WAY *Parlophone CDR 6495*	**26** 2
17 Oct 98	SINNER *Parlophone CDR 6505*	**39** 1
7 Apr 01	WHEREVER YOU ARE *Parlophone CDRS 6557*	**32** 1
22 Sep 01	HOLE IN THE ICE *Parlophone CDRS 6563*	**43** 1
27 Jun 98 ●	TRY WHISTLING THIS *Parlophone 4951392*	**5** 11
21 Apr 01	ONE NIL *Parlophone 5320392*	**14** 4

Tim FINN (see also CROWDED HOUSE; FINN) *New Zealand, male vocalist / instrumentalist (Singles: 6 Weeks, Albums: 2 Weeks)* pos/wks

26 Jun 93	PERSUASION *Capitol 6592482*	**43** 3
18 Sep 93	HIT THE GROUND RUNNING *Capitol CDCLS 694*	**50** 3
10 Jul 93	BEFORE AND AFTER *Capitol CDEST 2202*	**29** 2

Johnnie FIORI *See* BARKIN BROTHERS featuring Johnnie FIORI

Elisa FIORILLO *US, female vocalist (Singles: 14 Weeks)* pos/wks

28 Nov 87 ●	WHO FOUND WHO *Chrysalis CHS JEL 1* [1]	**10** 10
13 Feb 88	HOW CAN I FORGET YOU *Chrysalis ELISA 1*	**50** 4

[1] Jellybean featuring Elisa Fiorillo

FIRE INC *See* Jim STEINMAN

FIRE ISLAND (see also HELLER & FARLEY PROJECT; STYLUS TROUBLE) *UK, male instrumental / production group – includes Terry Farley and Pete Heller (Singles: 7 Weeks)* pos/wks

8 Aug 92	IN YOUR BONES / FIRE ISLAND *Boy's Own BOIX 11*	**66** 1
12 Mar 94	THERE BUT FOR THE GRACE OF GOD *Junior Boy's Own JBO 18CD* [1]	**32** 3
4 Mar 95	IF YOU SHOULD NEED A FRIEND *Junior Boy's Own JBO 26CDS* [2]	**51** 1
11 Apr 98	SHOUT TO THE TOP *JBO JNR 5001573* [3]	**23** 2

[1] Fire Island featuring Love Nelson [2] Fire Island featuring Mark Anthoni [3] Fire Island featuring Loleatta Holloway

The FIREBALLS *US, male vocal / instrumental group (Singles: 17 Weeks)* pos/wks

27 Jul 61	QUITE A PARTY *Pye International 7N 25092*	**29** 9
14 Nov 63	SUGAR SHACK (re) *London HLD 9789* [1] ▲	**45** 8

[1] Jimmy Gilmer and The Fireballs

FIREHOUSE *US, male vocal / instrumental group (Singles: 2 Weeks)* pos/wks

13 Jul 91	DON'T TREAT ME BAD *Epic 6567807*	**71** 1
19 Dec 92	WHEN I LOOK INTO YOUR EYES *Epic 6588347*	**65** 1

The FIRM *UK, male vocal / instrumental group (Singles: 21 Weeks)* pos/wks

17 Jul 82	ARTHUR DALEY ('E'S ALRIGHT) *Bark HID 1*	**14** 9
6 Jun 87 ★	STAR TREKKIN' *Bark TREK 1*	**1** 12

The FIRM (see also LED ZEPPELIN; FREE; COVERDALE / PAGE) *UK, male vocal / instrumental group – Jimmy Page and Paul Rodgers (Albums: 8 Weeks)* pos/wks

2 Mar 85	THE FIRM *Atlantic 7812391*	**15** 5
5 Apr 86	MEAN BUSINESS *Atlantic WX 35*	**46** 3

The FIRM featuring Dawn ROBINSON *US, male rap group and US, female vocalist (Singles: 3 Weeks)* pos/wks

29 Nov 97	FIRM BIZ *Columbia 6651612*	**18** 3

FIRST CHOICE *US, female vocal group (Singles: 21 Weeks)* pos/wks

19 May 73	ARMED AND EXTREMELY DANGEROUS *Bell 1297*	**16** 10
4 Aug 73 ●	SMARTY PANTS *Bell 1324*	**9** 11

FIRST CIRCLE *US, male vocal / instrumental group (Albums: 2 Weeks)* pos/wks

2 May 87	BOYS' NIGHT OUT *EMI America AML 3118*	**70** 2

FIRST CLASS *UK, male vocal group (Singles: 10 Weeks)* pos/wks

15 Jun 74	BEACH BABY *UK 66*	**13** 10

FIRST EDITION *See* Kenny ROGERS

FIRST LIGHT *UK, male vocal / instrumental duo (Singles: 5 Weeks)* pos/wks

21 May 83	EXPLAIN THE REASONS *London LON 26*	**65** 3
28 Jan 84	WISH YOU WERE HERE *London LON 43*	**71** 2

FIRSTBORN *Ireland, male producer – Oisin Lunny (Singles: 1 Week)* pos/wks

19 Jun 99	THE MOOD CLUB *Independiente ISOM 28MS*	**69** 1

FISCHER-Z *UK, male vocal / instrumental group (Singles: 7 Weeks, Albums: 1 Week)* pos/wks

26 May 79	THE WORKER *United Artists UP 36509*	**53** 5
3 May 80	SO LONG *United Artists BP 342*	**72** 2
23 Jun 79	WORD SALAD *United Artists UAG 30232*	**66** 1

FISCHERSPOONER *US, male vocal / instrumental duo – Warren Fischer and Casey Spooner (Singles: 3 Weeks)* pos/wks

20 Jul 02	EMERGE *Ministry of Sound FSMOS 1CDS*	**25** 3

FISH (see also MARILLION) *UK, male vocalist – Derek Dick (Singles: 20 Weeks, Albums: 17 Weeks)* pos/wks

18 Oct 86	SHORT CUT TO SOMEWHERE *Charisma CB 426* [1]	**75** 1
28 Oct 89	STATE OF MIND *EMI EM 109*	**32** 3
6 Jan 90	BIG WEDGE *EMI EM 125*	**25** 4
17 Mar 90	A GENTLEMAN'S EXCUSE ME *EMI EM 135*	**30** 3
28 Sep 91	INTERNAL EXILE *Polydor FISHY 1*	**37** 2
11 Jan 92	CREDO *Polydor FISHY 2*	**38** 2
4 Jul 92	SOMETHING IN THE AIR *Polydor FISHY 3*	**51** 2
16 Apr 94	LADY LET IT LIE *Dick Bros. DDICK 3CD1*	**46** 1
1 Oct 94	FORTUNES OF WAR *Dick Bros. DDICK 008CD1*	**67** 1
26 Aug 95	JUST GOOD FRIENDS *Dick Bros. DDICK 014CD1* [2]	**63** 1
10 Feb 90 ●	VIGIL IN A WILDERNESS OF MIRRORS *EMI EMD 1015*	**5** 6
9 Nov 91	INTERNAL EXILE *Polydor 5110491*	**21** 3
30 Jan 93	SONGS FROM THE MIRROR *Polydor 5174992*	**46** 2
11 Jun 94	SUITS *Dick Bros. DDICK 004CD*	**18** 2
16 Sep 95	YANG *Dick Bros. DDICK 012CD*	**52** 1
16 Sep 95	YIN *Dick Bros. DDICK 011CD*	**58** 1
31 May 97	SUNSETS ON EMPIRE *Dick Bros. DDICK 25CD*	**42** 1
1 May 99	RAINGODS WITH ZIPPOS *Roadrunner RR 86772*	**57** 1

[1] Fish and Tony Banks [2] Fish featuring Sam Brown

FISHBONE *US, male vocal / instrumental group (Singles: 3 Weeks, Albums: 1 Week)* pos/wks

1 Aug 92	EVERYDAY SUNSHINE / FIGHT THE YOUTH *Columbia 6581937*	**60** 2
28 Aug 93	SWIM *Columbia 6596252*	**54** 1
13 Jul 91	THE REALITY OF MY SURROUNDINGS *Columbia 4676151*	**75** 1

Cevin FISHER *US, male DJ / producer (Singles: 9 Weeks)* pos/wks

3 Oct 98	THE FREAKS COME OUT *Ministry of Sound MOSCDS 127* [1]	**34** 2
20 Feb 99	(YOU GOT ME) BURNING UP *Wonderboy WBOYD 013* [2]	**14** 4
7 Aug 99	MUSIC SAVED MY LIFE *Sm:)e Communications SM 90982*	**67** 1
20 Jan 01	IT'S A GOOD LIFE *Wonderboy WBOYD 022* [3]	**54** 1
24 Feb 01	LOVE YOU SOME MORE *Subversive SUB 68D* [4]	**60** 1

[1] Cevin Fisher's Big Break [2] Cevin Fisher / Loleatta Holloway [3] Cevin Fisher featuring Ramona Kelly [4] Cevin Fisher featuring Sheila Smith

Eddie FISHER *US, male vocalist (Singles: 105 Weeks)* pos/wks

2 Jan 53 ★	OUTSIDE OF HEAVEN (re) *HMV B 10362*	**1** 17
23 Jan 53 ●	EVERYTHING I HAVE IS YOURS (re) *HMV B 10398*	**8** 5
1 May 53 ●	DOWNHEARTED *HMV B 10450*	**3** 15
22 May 53 ★	I'M WALKING BEHIND YOU *HMV B 10489* [1] ▲	**1** 18
6 Nov 53 ●	WISH YOU WERE HERE *HMV B 10564*	**8** 9
22 Jan 54 ●	OH MY PAPA (O MEIN PAPA) (3re) *HMV B 10614* ▲	**9** 4

		pos/wks
29 Oct 54	**I NEED YOU NOW (2re)** *HMV B 10755* ▲	**13** 10
18 Mar 55 ●	**(I'M ALWAYS HEARING) WEDDING BELLS** *HMV B 10839*	**5** 11
23 Nov 56 ●	**CINDY, OH CINDY** *HMV POP 273*	**5** 16

1 Eddie Fisher with Sally Sweetland (soprano)

Mark FISHER featuring Dotty GREEN *UK, male*
instrumentalist – keyboards and female vocalist (Singles: 2 Weeks) pos/wks

29 Jun 85	**LOVE SITUATION** *Total Control TOCO 3*	**59** 2

Toni FISHER
US, female vocalist, b. 1931, d. 12 Feb 1999 (Singles: 1 Week) pos/wks

12 Feb 60	**THE BIG HURT** *Top Rank JAR 261*	**30** 1

FITS OF GLOOM *UK / Italy, male vocal duo (Singles: 4 Weeks)* pos/wks

4 Jun 94	**HEAVEN** *Media MCSTD 1981*	**47** 2
5 Nov 94	**THE POWER OF LOVE** *Media MCSTD 2016* 1	**49** 2

1 Fits of Gloom featuring Lizzy Mack

Ella FITZGERALD *US, female vocalist, b. 25 Apr 1918,*
d. 15 June 1996 (Singles: 29 Weeks, Albums: 58 Weeks) pos/wks

23 May 58	**THE SWINGIN' SHEPHERD BLUES** *HMV POP 486*	**15** 5
16 Oct 59	**BUT NOT FOR ME (re)** *HMV POP 657*	**25** 3
21 Apr 60	**MACK THE KNIFE** *HMV POP 736*	**19** 9
6 Oct 60	**HOW HIGH THE MOON** *HMV POP 782*	**46** 1
22 Nov 62	**DESAFINADO (re)** *Verve VS 502*	**38** 6
30 Apr 64	**CAN'T BUY ME LOVE** *Verve VS 519*	**34** 5
19 Jul 58 ●	**ELLA FITZGERALD SINGS THE IRVING BERLIN SONG BOOK** *HMV CLP 1183*	**5** 1
11 Jun 60	**ELLA SINGS GERSHWIN** *Brunswick LA 8648*	**13** 3
18 Jun 60	**ELLA AT THE OPERA HOUSE** *Columbia 3SX 10126*	**16** 1
23 Jul 60	**ELLA SINGS GERSHWIN VOLUME 5** *HMV CLP 1353*	**18** 2
10 May 80	**THE INCOMPARABLE ELLA** *Polydor POLTV 9*	**40** 7
27 Feb 88	**A PORTRAIT OF ELLA FITZGERALD** *Stylus SMR 847*	**42** 10
19 Nov 94	**ESSENTIAL ELLA – 21 ELLA FITZGERALD CLASSICS** *PolyGram TV 5239902*	**35** 14
23 Mar 96	**FOREVER ELLA – 21 ELLA FITZGERALD CLASSICS** *Verve / PolyGram TV 5293872*	**19** 6
15 Feb 03	**GOLD – ALL HER GREATEST HITS** *Verve 654842*	**15** 13
18 Sep 04	**ELLA AND LOUIS TOGETHER ...** *UCJ 9867768* 1	**43** 1

1 Ella Fitzgerald and Louis Armstrong

Scott FITZGERALD
UK, male vocalist – William McPhail (Singles: 12 Weeks) pos/wks

14 Jan 78 ●	**IF I HAD WORDS** *Pepper UP 36333* 1	**3** 10
7 May 88	**GO** *PRT PYS 10*	**52** 2

1 Scott Fitzgerald and Yvonne Keeley with the St Thomas More School Choir

FIVE (283) Top 500 (see also ABS)
Superior all-boy vocal group; 'Abs' Breen, 'J' Brown, Sean Conlon, Rich Neville, Scott Robinson. Eponymous debut album sold more than four million worldwide. The only UK act to reach the Top 10 with every one of their first 11 releases split in 2001 (Singles: 133 Weeks, Albums: 96 Weeks) pos/wks

13 Dec 97 ●	**SLAM DUNK (DA FUNK)** *RCA 74321537352*	**10** 9
14 Mar 98 ●	**WHEN THE LIGHTS GO OUT** *RCA 74321562312*	**4** 9
20 Jun 98 ●	**GOT THE FEELIN'** *RCA 74321584892*	**3** 13
12 Sep 98 ●	**EVERYBODY GET UP** *RCA 74321613752*	**2** 12
28 Nov 98 ●	**UNTIL THE TIME IS THROUGH** *RCA 74321632602*	**2** 12
31 Jul 99 ●	**IF YA GETTIN' DOWN** *RCA 74321689692*	**2** 12
6 Nov 99 ★	**KEEP ON MOVIN'** *RCA 74321709872* ■	**1** 17
18 Mar 00 ●	**DON'T WANNA LET YOU GO** *RCA 74321745292*	**9** 12
29 Jul 00 ★	**WE WILL ROCK YOU (re)** *RCA 74321774022* 1 ■	**1** 13
25 Aug 01 ★	**LET'S DANCE** *RCA 74321875962* ■	**1** 12
3 Nov 01 ●	**CLOSER TO ME (re)** *RCA 74321900742*	**4** 12
4 Jul 98 ★	**FIVE** *RCA 74321589762* ■	**1** 36
20 Nov 99 ●	**INVINCIBLE** *RCA 74321713922*	**4** 39
8 Sep 01 ●	**KINGSIZE** *RCA 74321875972*	**3** 11
1 Dec 01 ●	**GREATEST HITS** *RCA 74321913432*	**9** 10

1 Five and Queen

FIVE FOR FIGHTING *US, male vocalist /*
instrumentalist – John Ondrasik (Singles: 1 Week) pos/wks

1 Jun 02	**SUPERMAN (IT'S NOT EASY)** *Columbia 6727202*	**48** 1

FIVE PENNY PIECE
UK, male / female vocal / instrumental group (Albums: 6 Weeks) pos/wks

24 Mar 73	**MAKING TRACKS** *Columbia SCX 6536*	**37** 1
3 Jul 76 ●	**KING COTTON** *EMI EMC 3129*	**9** 5

The 5.6.7.8'S
Japan, female vocal / instrumental group (Singles: 3 Weeks) pos/wks

17 Jul 04	**WOO HOO** *Sweet Nothing CSSN 028*	**28** 2
18 Sep 04	**I'M BLUE** *Sweet Nothing CSSN 029*	**71** 1

FIVE SMITH BROTHERS
UK, male vocal group (Singles: 1 Week) pos/wks

22 Jul 55	**I'M IN FAVOUR OF FRIENDSHIP** *Decca F 10527*	**20** 1

FIVE STAR (200) Top 500
Britain's best known black family act: Deniece, Doris, Stedman, Lorraine and Delroy Pearson. The Essex-based group became the youngest act to top the LP chart with the UK million-seller 'Silk and Steel'. In 1987 they were voted Top British Group in Smash Hits and at the Brit Awards. Act relocated to US and had some R&B chart success (Singles: 140 Weeks, Albums: 153 Weeks) pos/wks

4 May 85	**ALL FALL DOWN** *Tent PB 40039*	**15** 12
20 Jul 85	**LET ME BE THE ONE** *Tent PB 40193*	**18** 9
14 Sep 85	**LOVE TAKE OVER** *Tent PB 40353*	**25** 9
16 Nov 85	**RSVP** *Tent PB 40445*	**45** 5
11 Jan 86 ●	**SYSTEM ADDICT** *Tent PB 40515*	**3** 11
12 Apr 86 ●	**CAN'T WAIT ANOTHER MINUTE** *Tent PB 40697*	**7** 10
26 Jul 86 ●	**FIND THE TIME** *Tent PB 40799*	**7** 10
13 Sep 86 ●	**RAIN OR SHINE** *Tent PB 40901*	**2** 11
22 Nov 86	**IF I SAY YES** *Tent PB 40981*	**15** 9
7 Feb 87 ●	**STAY OUT OF MY LIFE** *Tent PB 41131*	**9** 8
18 Apr 87 ●	**THE SLIGHTEST TOUCH** *Tent PB 41265*	**4** 9
22 Aug 87	**WHENEVER YOU'RE READY** *Tent PB 41477*	**11** 6
10 Oct 87	**STRONG AS STEEL** *Tent PB 41565*	**16** 7
5 Dec 87	**SOMEWHERE SOMEBODY** *Tent PB 41661*	**23** 6
4 Jun 88	**ANOTHER WEEKEND** *Tent PB 42081*	**18** 4
6 Aug 88	**ROCK MY WORLD** *Tent PB 42145*	**28** 4
17 Sep 88	**THERE'S A BRAND NEW WORLD** *Tent PB 42235*	**61** 2
19 Nov 88	**LET ME BE YOURS** *Tent PB 42343*	**51** 3
8 Apr 89	**WITH EVERY HEARTBEAT** *Tent PB 42693*	**49** 2
10 Mar 90	**TREAT ME LIKE A LADY** *Tent FIVE 1*	**54** 2
7 Jul 90	**HOT LOVE** *Tent FIVE 2*	**68** 1
3 Aug 85	**LUXURY OF LIFE** *Tent PL 70735*	**12** 70
30 Aug 86 ★	**SILK AND STEEL** *Tent PL 71100*	**1** 58
26 Sep 87 ●	**BETWEEN THE LINES** *Tent PL 71505*	**7** 17
27 Aug 88	**ROCK THE WORLD** *Tent PL 71747*	**17** 5
21 Oct 89	**GREATEST HITS** *Tent PL 74080*	**53** 3

FIVE THIRTY *UK, male vocal /*
instrumental group (Singles: 4 Weeks, Albums: 1 Week) pos/wks

4 Aug 90	**ABSTAIN** *East West YZ 530*	**75** 1
25 May 91	**13TH DISCIPLE** *East West YZ 577*	**67** 1
3 Aug 91	**SUPERNOVA** *East West YZ 594*	**75** 1
2 Nov 91	**YOU (EP)** *East West YZ 624*	**72** 1
31 Aug 91	**BED** *East West WX 530*	**57** 1

Tracks on You (EP): You / Cuddly Drug / Slow Train into the Ocean

5000 VOLTS
UK, male / female vocal / instrumental group (Singles: 18 Weeks) pos/wks

6 Sep 75 ●	**I'M ON FIRE** *Philips 6006 464*	**4** 9
24 Jul 76 ●	**DOCTOR KISS-KISS** *Philips 6006 533*	**8** 9

Tina Charles is the uncredited vocalist on 'I'm On Fire'

FIXATE *UK, male vocal group (Singles: 1 Week)* pos/wks

14 Jul 01	**24/7** *Epark EPKFIX CD1*	**42** 1

FIXX *UK, male vocal / instrumental*
group (Singles: 8 Weeks, Albums: 7 Weeks) pos/wks

24 Apr 82	**STAND OR FALL** *MCA FIXX 2*	**54** 4
17 Jul 82	**RED SKIES** *MCA FIXX 3*	**57** 4
22 May 82	**SHUTTERED ROOM** *MCA FX 1001*	**54** 6
21 May 83	**REACH THE BEACH** *MCA FX 1002*	**91** 1

Roberta FLACK
US, female vocalist (Singles: 79 Weeks, Albums: 50 Weeks) pos/wks

27 May 72	THE FIRST TIME EVER I SAW YOUR FACE *Atlantic K 10161* ▲	14	14
5 Aug 72	WHERE IS THE LOVE *Atlantic K 10202* [1]	29	7
17 Feb 73 ●	KILLING ME SOFTLY WITH HIS SONG *Atlantic K 10282* ▲	6	14
24 Aug 74	FEEL LIKE MAKIN' LOVE *Atlantic K 10467* ▲	34	7
6 May 78	THE CLOSER I GET TO YOU *Atlantic K 11099* [2]	42	4
17 May 80 ●	BACK TOGETHER AGAIN *Atlantic K 11481* [1]	3	11
30 Aug 80	DON'T MAKE ME WAIT TOO LONG *Atlantic K 11555*	44	7
20 Aug 83 ●	TONIGHT I CELEBRATE MY LOVE *Capitol CL 302* [3]	2	13
29 Jul 89	UH-UH OOH OOH LOOK OUT (HERE IT COMES) *Atlantic A 8941*	72	2
15 Jul 72	FIRST TAKE *Atlantic K 40040* ▲	47	2
13 Oct 73	KILLING ME SOFTLY *Atlantic K 50021*	40	2
7 Jun 80	ROBERTA FLACK AND DONNY HATHAWAY		
	Atlantic K 50696 [1]	31	7
17 Sep 83	BORN TO LOVE *Capitol EST 7122841* [2]	15	10
31 Mar 84	ROBERTA FLACK'S GREATEST HITS *K-Tel NE 1269*	35	14
19 Feb 94 ●	SOFTLY WITH THESE SONGS – THE BEST OF ROBERTA		
	FLACK *Atlantic 7567824982*	7	15

[1] Roberta Flack and Donny Hathaway [2] Roberta Flack with Donny Hathaway
[3] Peabo Bryson and Roberta Flack [1] Roberta Flack and Donny Hathaway [2]
Peabo Bryson and Roberta Flack

FLAJ *See GETO BOYS featuring FLAJ*

The FLAMING LIPS *US, male vocal / instrumental*
group (Singles: 15 Weeks, Albums: 17 Weeks) pos/wks

9 Mar 96	THIS HERE GIRAFFE *Warner Bros. W 0335CD*	72	1
26 Jun 99	RACE FOR THE PRIZE *Warner Bros. W 494CD1*	39	2
20 Nov 99	WAITIN' FOR A SUPERMAN *Warner Bros. W 505CD1*	73	1
31 Aug 02	DO YOU REALIZE?? *Warner Bros. WEA W 586CD*	32	2
25 Jan 03	YOSHIMI BATTLES THE PINK ROBOTS PT.1		
	Warner Bros. W 597CD1	18	3
5 Jul 03	FIGHT TEST *Warner Bros. W611 CD1*	28	2
27 Sep 03	THE GOLDEN PATH *Virgin CHEMSD 18* [1]	17	4
29 May 99	THE SOFT BULLETIN *Warner Bros. 9362473932*	39	2
27 Jul 02	YOSHIMI BATTLES THE PINK ROBOTS		
	Warner Bros. 9362481412	13	15

[1] The Chemical Brothers / The Flaming Lips

The FLAMINGOS *US, male vocal group (Singles: 5 Weeks)* pos/wks

4 Jun 69	THE BOOGALOO PARTY *Philips BF 1786*	26	5

Michael FLANDERS with the Michael SAMMES SINGERS
UK, male vocalist, b. 1 Mar 1922, d. 14 Apr 1975 (Singles: 3 Weeks) pos/wks

27 Feb 59	THE LITTLE DRUMMER BOY (re) *Parlophone R 4528*	20	3

FLASH and the PAN *Australia, male vocal /*
instrumental group (Singles: 15 Weeks, Albums: 2 Weeks) pos/wks

23 Sep 78	AND THE BAND PLAYED ON (DOWN AMONG THE DEAD MEN)		
	Ensign ENY 15	54	4
21 May 83 ●	WAITING FOR A TRAIN *Easy Beat EASY 1*	7	11
16 Jul 83	PAN-ORAMA *Easy Beat EASLP 100*	69	2

FLASH BROTHERS *Israel, male production trio (Singles: 1 Week)* pos/wks

6 Nov 04	AMEN (DON'T BE AFRAID) *Direction 6754362*	75	1

Lester FLATT and Earl SCRUGGS *US, male instrumental duo – banjos*
Lester Flatt, b. 28 Jun 1914, d. 11 May 1979 (Singles: 6 Weeks) pos/wks

15 Nov 67	FOGGY MOUNTAIN BREAKDOWN		
	CBS 3038 and Mercury MF 1007	39	6

The versions on the two labels were not the same cuts; CBS had a 1965 recording, Mercury a 1949 recording. The chart did not differentiate and listed both together

Fogwell FLAX and the ANKLEBITERS from FREEHOLD JUNIOR
SCHOOL *UK, male vocalist and school choir (Singles: 2 Weeks)* pos/wks

26 Dec 81	ONE NINE FOR SANTA *EMI 5255*	68	2

The FLEE-REKKERS
UK, male instrumental group (Singles: 13 Weeks) pos/wks

19 May 60	GREEN JEANS *Triumph RGM 1008*	23	13

FLEETWOOD MAC `18` `Top 500`

Record breaking, Anglo-American soft-rock superstars, who started as a British blues band. Members included Mick Fleetwood (d), John McVie (b), Peter Green (Peter Greenbaum g), Christine (Perfect) McVie (k/v), Lindsey Buckingham (g/v), Stevie Nicks (v). Group made live debut at 1967 Windsor Jazz & Blues Festival and by 1969 were one of Britain's most popular bands, thanks partly to Green's hypnotic composition 'Albatross' (which returned to the Top 3 in 1973). Green left shortly before McVie's future wife, Christine (voted Top British Female Singer in 1969 MM poll), joined from Chicken Shack. Group's Stateside breakthrough came with chart-topping second eponymous album, with featured new members, American singer / songwriters Buckingham and Nicks. Grammy Hall of Fame album 'Rumours' topped the US chart for a staggering 31 weeks. It has sold 19 million in America and is ten times platinum in the UK, where it has spent longer on the chart than any album. Group members concentrated on solo projects in the 1980s, reconvening in 1987 for the hit packed 'Tango in the Night'. They split again in 1990, reunited briefly for President Clinton's Inaugural concert in 1993 and in 1997, Fleetwood, Buckingham, Nicks and the McVie's live recording 'The Dance' topped the US chart. In 1998 they received the Outstanding Contribution to British Music Award at the Brits and were inducted into the Rock and Roll Hall of Fame (Singles: 223 Weeks, Albums: 880 Weeks) pos/wks

10 Apr 68	BLACK MAGIC WOMAN *Blue Horizon 573138*	37	7
17 Jul 68	NEED YOUR LOVE SO BAD *Blue Horizon 573139*	31	13
4 Dec 68 ★	ALBATROSS *Blue Horizon 573145*	1	20
16 Apr 69 ●	MAN OF THE WORLD *Immediate IM 080*	2	14
23 Jul 69	NEED YOUR LOVE SO BAD (re) (re-issue)		
	Blue Horizon 573157	32	9
4 Oct 69 ●	OH WELL *Reprise RS 27000*	2	16
23 May 70 ●	THE GREEN MANALISHI (WITH THE TWO-PRONG CROWN)		
	Reprise RS 27007	10	12
12 May 73 ●	ALBATROSS (re-issue) *CBS 8306*	2	15
13 Nov 76	SAY YOU LOVE ME *Reprise K 14447*	40	4
19 Feb 77	GO YOUR OWN WAY *Warner Bros. K 16872*	38	4
30 Apr 77	DON'T STOP *Warner Bros. K 16930*	32	5
9 Jul 77	DREAMS *Warner Bros. K 16969* ▲	24	9
22 Oct 77	YOU MAKE LOVING FUN *Warner Bros. K 17013*	45	2
11 Mar 78	RHIANNON *Reprise K 14430*	46	3
6 Oct 79 ●	TUSK *Warner Bros. K 17468*	6	10
22 Dec 79	SARA *Warner Bros. K 17533*	37	8
25 Sep 82	GYPSY *Warner Bros. K 17997*	46	3
18 Dec 82 ●	OH DIANE *Warner Bros. FLEET 1*	9	15
4 Apr 87 ●	BIG LOVE *Warner Bros. W 8398*	9	12
11 Jul 87	SEVEN WONDERS *Warner Bros. W 8317*	56	4
26 Sep 87 ●	LITTLE LIES *Warner Bros. W 8291*	5	12
26 Dec 87	FAMILY MAN *Warner Bros. W 8114*	54	5
2 Apr 88 ●	EVERYWHERE *Warner Bros. W 8143*	4	10
18 Jun 88	ISN'T IT MIDNIGHT *Warner Bros. W 7860*	60	2
17 Dec 88	AS LONG AS YOU FOLLOW *Warner Bros. W 7644*	66	3
5 May 90	SAVE ME *Warner Bros. W 9866*	53	3
25 Aug 90	IN THE BACK OF MY MIND *Warner Bros. W 9739*	58	3
2 Mar 68 ●	FLEETWOOD MAC *Blue Horizon BPG 763200*	4	37
7 Sep 68 ●	MR. WONDERFUL *Blue Horizon 763205*	10	11
30 Aug 69	THE PIOUS BIRD OF GOOD OMEN *Blue Horizon 763215*	18	4
4 Oct 69 ●	THEN PLAY ON *Reprise RSLP 9000*	6	11
10 Oct 70	KILN HOUSE *Reprise RSLP 9004*	39	2
19 Feb 72	GREATEST HITS *CBS 69011*	36	13
6 Nov 76	FLEETWOOD MAC *Reprise K 54043* ▲	23	19
26 Feb 77 ★	RUMOURS *Warner Bros. K 56344* ▲	1	477
27 Oct 79 ●	TUSK *Warner Bros. K 66088*	1	26
13 Dec 80	FLEETWOOD MAC LIVE *Warner Bros. K 66097*	31	9
10 Jul 82 ●	MIRAGE *Warner Bros. K 56592* ▲	5	39
25 Apr 87 ★	TANGO IN THE NIGHT *Warner Bros. WX 65*	1	115
3 Dec 88 ●	GREATEST HITS *Warner Bros. WX 221*	3	53
21 Apr 90 ★	BEHIND THE MASK *Warner Bros. WX 335* ■	1	21
23 Sep 95	LIVE AT THE BBC *Essential EDFCD 297*	48	2
21 Oct 95	TIME *Warner Bros. 9362459202*	47	1
6 Sep 97 ●	THE DANCE *Reprise 9362467022* ▲	15	10
26 Oct 02 ●	THE VERY BEST OF FLEETWOOD MAC		
	WSM 8122736352	7	22
10 May 03 ●	SAY YOU WILL *WEA WB 48467*	6	8

*Group was UK and male only up to and including the re-issue of 'Albatross'
Group were UK and male only for first six albums and for 'Live At The BBC'. All the above albums are different although some are identically titled. 'Greatest Hits' in 1972 changed its catalogue number to 4607041 during its chart run*

The FLEETWOODS
US, male / female vocal group (Singles: 8 Weeks)   pos/wks

24 Apr 59 ● COME SOFTLY TO ME *London HLU 8841* ▲	6	8

John 'OO' FLEMING *UK, male DJ / producer (Singles: 3 Weeks)* pos/wks

25 Dec 99	**LOST IN EMOTION** *React CDREACT 170*	74 1
12 Aug 00	**FREE** *React CDREACT 186*	61 1
2 Feb 02	**BELFAST TRANCE** *Nebula BELFCD 001* [1]	74 1

[1] John "OO" Fleming vs Simple Minds

FLESH & BONES
Belgium, male / female production / vocal trio (Singles: 1 Week)   pos/wks

10 Aug 02	**I LOVE YOU** *Multiply CDMULTY 86*	70 1

FLICKMAN *Italy, male production duo – Andreas*
Mazzali and Giuliano Orlandi (Singles: 6 Weeks)   pos/wks

4 Mar 00	**THE SOUND OF BAMBOO** *Inferno CDFERN 25*	11 5
28 Apr 01	**HEY! PARADISE** *Inferno CDFERN 37*	69 1

KC FLIGHTT *US, male rapper (Singles: 5 Weeks)*   pos/wks

1 Apr 89	**PLANET E** *RCA PT 49404*	48 4
12 May 01	**VOICES** *Hooj Choons HOOJ 106CD* [1]	59 1

[1] KC Flightt vs Funky Junction

Dread FLIMSTONE and the MODERN TONE AGE FAMILY
US, male vocal / instrumental group (Singles: 1 Week)   pos/wks

30 Nov 91	**FROM THE GHETTO** *Urban URB 87*	66 1

Berni FLINT
UK, male vocalist (Singles: 11 Weeks, Albums: 6 Weeks)   pos/wks

19 Mar 77 ●	**I DON'T WANT TO PUT A HOLD ON YOU** *EMI 2599*	3 10
23 Jul 77	**SOUTHERN COMFORT** *EMI 2621*	48 1
2 Jul 77	**I DON'T WANT TO PUT A HOLD ON YOU** *EMI EMC 3184*	37 6

FLINTLOCK
UK, male vocal / instrumental group (Singles: 5 Weeks)   pos/wks

29 May 76	**DAWN** *Pinnacle P 8419*	30 5

FLIP & FILL *(see also* BUS STOP*) UK, male production duo – Graham*
Turner and Mark Hall (Singles: 45 Weeks, Albums: 7 Weeks)   pos/wks

24 Mar 01	**TRUE LOVE NEVER DIES**	
	All Around the World CDGLOBE 240 [1]	34 3
2 Feb 02 ●	**TRUE LOVE NEVER DIES (re-mix)**	
	All Around the World CDGLOBE 248 [1]	7 10
27 Jul 02 ●	**SHOOTING STAR** *All Around the World CDGLOBE 258*	3 10
18 Jan 03	**I WANNA DANCE WITH SOMEBODY (re)**	
	All Around the World CDGLOBE 275	13 7
22 Mar 03	**SHAKE YA SHIMMY** *All Around the World CDGLOBE 213* [2]	28 2
28 Jun 03	**FIELD OF DREAMS** *All Around the World CDGLOBE 273* [3]	28 2
17 Jan 04	**IRISH BLUE** *All Around the World CXGLOBE 309* [4]	20 4
24 Jul 04	**DISCOLAND** *All Around the World CDGLOBE 346* [5]	11 7
19 Jul 03	**FLOOR FILLAS** *UMTV / AATW 0392192*	29 7

[1] Flip & Fill featuring Kelly Llorenna [2] Porn Kings vs Flip & Fill featuring 740 Boyz [3] Flip & Fill featuring Jo James [4] Flip & Fill featuring Junior [5] Flip & Fill featuring Karen Parry

'Shooting Star' features uncredited vocalist Karen Parry

The FLIPMODE SQUAD
US, male / female production / rap group (Singles: 14 Weeks)   pos/wks

31 Oct 98	**CHA CHA CHA** *Elektra E 3810CD*	54 1
7 Jun 03 ●	**I KNOW WHAT YOU WANT** *J 82876528292* [1]	3 13

[1] Busta Rhymes and Mariah Carey featuring the Flipmode Squad

The FLOATERS
US, male vocal group (Singles: 11 Weeks, Albums: 8 Weeks)   pos/wks

23 Jul 77 ★	**FLOAT ON** *ABC 4187*	1 11
20 Aug 77	**FLOATERS** *ABC ABCL 5229*	17 8

FLOCK *UK, male vocal / instrumental group (Albums: 2 Weeks)*   pos/wks

2 May 70	**FLOCK** *CBS 63733*	59 2

A FLOCK OF SEAGULLS *UK, male vocal /*
instrumental group (Singles: 46 Weeks, Albums: 59 Weeks)   pos/wks

27 Mar 82	**I RAN** *Jive JIVE 14*	43 6
12 Jun 82	**SPACE AGE LOVE SONG** *Jive JIVE 17*	34 6
6 Nov 82 ●	**WISHING (IF I HAD A PHOTOGRAPH OF YOU)** *Jive JIVE 25*	10 12
23 Apr 83	**NIGHTMARES** *Jive JIVE 33*	53 3
25 Jun 83	**TRANSFER AFFECTION** *Jive JIVE 41*	38 5
14 Jul 84	**THE MORE YOU LIVE, THE MORE YOU LOVE** *Jive JIVE 62*	26 11
19 Oct 85	**WHO'S THAT GIRL (SHE'S GOT IT)** *Jive JIVE 106*	66 3
17 Apr 82	**A FLOCK OF SEAGULLS** *Jive HOP 201*	32 44
7 May 83	**LISTEN** *Jive HIP 4*	16 10
1 Sep 84	**THE STORY OF A YOUNG HEART** *Jive HIP 14*	30 5

FLOETRY *UK, female vocal duo (Singles: 1 Week)*   pos/wks

26 Apr 03	**FLOETIC** *Dreamworks 4507752*	73 1

FLOORPLAY
UK, male instrumental / production duo (Singles: 1 Week)   pos/wks

27 Jan 96	**AUTOMATIC** *Perfecto PERF 115CD*	50 1

FLOWER POWER *See Dannii* MINOGUE

FLOWERED UP *UK, male vocal / instrumental*
group (Singles: 17 Weeks, Albums: 3 Weeks)   pos/wks

28 Jul 90	**IT'S ON** *Heavenly HVN 3*	54 4
24 Nov 90	**PHOBIA** *Heavenly HVN 7*	75 1
11 May 91	**TAKE IT** *Heavenly HVN 9*	34 4
17 Aug 91	**IT'S ON / EGG RUSH (re-recording)** *London FUP 2*	38 3
2 May 92	**WEEKENDER** *Heavenly HVN 16*	20 5
7 Sep 91	**A LIFE WITH BRIAN** *London 8282441*	23 3

FLOWERPOT MEN *UK, male vocal group (Singles: 12 Weeks)*   pos/wks

23 Aug 67 ●	**LET'S GO TO SAN FRANCISCO** *Deram DM 142*	4 12

Mike FLOWERS POPS
UK, male / female / vocal / instrumental group (Singles: 14 Weeks)   pos/wks

30 Dec 95 ●	**WONDERWALL (re)** *London LONCD 378*	2 9
8 Jun 96	**LIGHT MY FIRE / PLEASE RELEASE ME** *London LONCD 384*	39 2
28 Dec 96	**DON'T CRY FOR ME ARGENTINA** *Love This LUVTHIS 16*	30 3

Eddie FLOYD
US, male vocalist (Singles: 29 Weeks, Albums: 5 Weeks)   pos/wks

2 Feb 67	**KNOCK ON WOOD (re)** *Atlantic 584041*	19 18
16 Mar 67	**RAISE YOUR HAND** *Stax 601001*	42 3
9 Aug 67	**THINGS GET BETTER** *Stax 601016*	31 8
29 Apr 67	**KNOCK ON WOOD** *Stax 589006*	36 5

FLUFFY *UK, female vocal / instrumental group (Singles: 2 Weeks)* pos/wks

17 Feb 96	**HUSBAND** *Parkway PARK 006CD*	58 1
5 Oct 96	**NOTHING** *Virgin VSCDT 1614*	52 1

FLUKE *(see also* LUCKY MONKEYS*) UK, male instrumental /*
production group (Singles: 20 Weeks, Albums: 3 Weeks)   pos/wks

20 Mar 93	**SLID** *Circa YRCD 103*	59 1
19 Jun 93	**ELECTRIC GUITAR** *Circa YRCD 104*	58 2
11 Sep 93	**GROOVY FEELING** *Circa YRCD 106*	45 1
23 Apr 94	**BUBBLE** *Circa YRCD 110*	37 2
29 Jul 95	**BULLET** *Circa YRCD 121*	23 3
16 Dec 95	**TOSH** *Circa YRCD 122*	32 3
16 Nov 96	**ATOM BOMB** *Circa YRCD 125*	20 3
31 May 97	**ABSURD** *Virgin YRCD 126*	25 2
27 Sep 97	**SQUIRT** *Circa YRCD 127*	46 1
23 Oct 93	**SIX WHEELS ON MY WAGON** *Circa CIRCDX 27*	41 1
19 Aug 95	**OTO** *Circa CIRCD 31*	44 1
11 Oct 97	**RISOTTO** *Virgin CIRCD 33*	45 1

FLUSH *See* SLADE

The FLYING LIZARDS *UK, male / female vocal /*
instrumental group (Singles: 16 Weeks, Albums: 3 Weeks)   pos/wks

4 Aug 79 ●	**MONEY** *Virgin VS 276*	5 10
9 Feb 80	**TV** *Virgin VS 325*	43 6
16 Feb 80	**FLYING LIZARDS** *Virgin V 2150*	60 3

The FLYING PICKETS
UK, male vocal group (Singles: 20 Weeks, Albums: 22 Weeks) pos/wks

		pos	wks
26 Nov 83 ★	**ONLY YOU** *10 TEN 14*	**1**	11
21 Apr 84 ●	**WHEN YOU'RE YOUNG AND IN LOVE** *10 TEN 20*	**7**	8
8 Dec 84	**WHO'S THAT GIRL** *10 GIRL 1*	**71**	1
17 Dec 83	**LIVE AT THE ALBANY EMPIRE** *AVM AVMLP 0001*	**48**	11
9 Jun 84	**LOST BOYS** *10 DIX 4*	**11**	11

Jerome FLYNN *See ROBSON & JEROME*

FLYTRONIX *See PESHAY*

FOCUS
Holland, male instrumental group (Singles: 21 Weeks, Albums: 65 Weeks) pos/wks

		pos	wks
20 Jan 73	**HOCUS POCUS** *Polydor 2001211*	**20**	10
27 Jan 73 ●	**SYLVIA** *Polydor 2001422*	**4**	11
11 Nov 72 ●	**MOVING WAVES** *Polydor 2931002*	**2**	34
2 Dec 72 ●	**FOCUS 3** *Polydor 2383016*	**6**	15
20 Oct 73	**AT THE RAINBOW** *Polydor 2442118*	**23**	5
25 May 74	**HAMBURGER CONCERTO** *Polydor 2442124*	**20**	5
9 Aug 75	**FOCUS** *Polydor 2384070*	**23**	6

FOG (see also FUNKY GREEN DOGS)
US, male DJ / producer – Ralph Falcon (Singles: 4 Weeks) pos/wks

		pos	wks
19 Feb 94	**BEEN A LONG TIME** *Columbia 6601212*	**44**	2
6 Jun 98	**BEEN A LONG TIME (re-mix)** *Pukka CDPUKKA 16*	**27**	2

Dan FOGELBERG
US, male vocalist (Singles: 4 Weeks, Albums: 3 Weeks) pos/wks

		pos	wks
15 Mar 80	**LONGER** *Epic EPC 8230*	**59**	4
29 Mar 80	**PHOENIX** *Epic EPC 83317*	**42**	3

John FOGERTY (see also CREEDENCE CLEARWATER REVIVAL)
US, male vocalist / instrumentalist – guitar (Albums: 11 Weeks) pos/wks

		pos	wks
16 Feb 85	**CENTERFIELD** *Warner Bros. 9252031* ▲	**48**	11

Ben FOLDS FIVE
US, male vocal / instrumental group (Singles: 13 Weeks, Albums: 7 Weeks) pos/wks

		pos	wks
14 Sep 96	**UNDERGROUND** *Caroline CDCAR 008*	**37**	2
1 Mar 97	**BATTLE OF WHO COULD CARE LESS** *Epic 6642302*	**26**	3
7 Jun 97	**KATE** *Epic 6645365*	**39**	2
18 Apr 98	**BRICK** *Epic 6656612*	**26**	3
24 Apr 99	**ARMY** *Epic 6672182*	**28**	2
29 Sep 01	**ROCKIN' THE SUBURBS** *Epic 6718492* [1]	**53**	1
15 Mar 97	**WHATEVER AND EVER AMEN** *Epic 4866982*	**30**	3
24 Jan 98	**NAKED BABY PHOTOS** *Caroline CAR 7554*	**65**	1
8 May 99	**THE UNAUTHORIZED BIOGRAPHY OF REINHOLD MESSNER** *Epic 4933122*	**22**	2
6 Oct 01	**ROCKIN' THE SUBURBS** *Epic 5040632* [1]	**73**	1

[1] Ben Folds [1] Ben Folds

Ellen FOLEY
US, female vocalist (Albums: 3 Weeks) pos/wks

		pos	wks
17 Nov 79	**NIGHT OUT** *Epic EPC 83718*	**68**	1
4 Apr 81	**SPIRIT OF ST. LOUIS** *Epic EPC 84809*	**57**	2

FOLK IMPLOSION
US, male vocal / instrumental duo (Singles: 1 Week) pos/wks

		pos	wks
15 Jun 96	**NATURAL ONE** *London LONCD 382*	**45**	1

Jane FONDA
US, female exercise instructor (Albums: 51 Weeks) pos/wks

		pos	wks
29 Jan 83 ●	**JANE FONDA'S WORKOUT RECORD** *CBS 88581*	**7**	47
22 Sep 84	**JANE FONDA'S WORKOUT RECORD: NEW AND IMPROVED** *CBS 88640*	**60**	4

Claudia FONTAINE *See The BEATMASTERS*

Lenny FONTANA
US, male producer (Singles: 3 Weeks) pos/wks

		pos	wks
4 Mar 00	**CHOCOLATE SENSATION** *ffrr FCD 375* [1]	**39**	2
24 Mar 01	**POW POW POW** *Strictly Rhythm SRUKCD 01* [2]	**62**	1

[1] Fontana featuring Darryl D'Bonneau [2] Lenny Fontana and DJ Shorty

Wayne FONTANA
UK, male vocalist – Glyn Ellis (Singles: 76 Weeks, Albums: 1 Week) pos/wks

		pos	wks
11 Jul 63	**HELLO JOSEPHINE** *Fontana TF 404* [1]	**46**	2
28 May 64	**STOP LOOK AND LISTEN** *Fontana TF 451* [1]	**37**	4
8 Oct 64 ●	**UM, UM, UM, UM, UM, UM** *Fontana TF 497* [1]	**5**	15
4 Feb 65 ●	**GAME OF LOVE** *Fontana TF 535* [1] ▲	**2**	11
17 Jun 65	**JUST A LITTLE BIT TOO LATE** *Fontana TF 579* [1]	**20**	7
30 Sep 65	**SHE NEEDS LOVE** *Fontana TF 611* [1]	**32**	6
9 Dec 65	**IT WAS EASIER TO HURT HER** *Fontana TF 642*	**36**	6
21 Apr 66	**COME ON HOME** *Fontana TF 684*	**16**	12
25 Aug 66	**GOODBYE BLUEBIRD** *Fontana TF 737*	**49**	1
8 Dec 66	**PAMELA, PAMELA** *Fontana TF 770*	**11**	12
20 Feb 65	**WAYNE FONTANA AND THE MINDBENDERS** *Fontana TL 5230* [1]	**18**	1

[1] Wayne Fontana and The Mindbenders [1] Wayne Fontana and The Mindbenders

FOO FIGHTERS
US, male vocal / instrumental group (Singles: 50 Weeks, Albums: 86 Weeks) pos/wks

		pos	wks
1 Jul 95 ●	**THIS IS A CALL** *Roswell CDCL 753*	**5**	4
16 Sep 95	**I'LL STICK AROUND** *Roswell CDCL 757*	**18**	3
2 Dec 95	**FOR ALL THE COWS** *Roswell CDCL 762*	**28**	2
6 Apr 96	**BIG ME** *Roswell CDCL 768*	**19**	3
10 May 97	**MONKEY WRENCH** *Roswell CDCLS 788*	**12**	4
30 Aug 97	**EVERLONG** *Roswell CDCL 792*	**18**	3
31 Jan 98	**MY HERO** *Roswell CDCL 796*	**21**	2
29 Aug 98	**WALKING AFTER YOU: BEACON LIGHT** *Elektra E 4100CD* [1]	**20**	3
30 Oct 99	**LEARN TO FLY** *RCA 74321706622*	**21**	3
30 Sep 00	**BREAKOUT** *RCA 74321790102*	**29**	3
16 Dec 00	**NEXT YEAR** *RCA 74321809262*	**42**	2
18 Jan 01	**TIMES LIKE THESE** *RCA 74321989552*	**12**	5
19 Oct 02 ●	**ALL MY LIFE** *RCA 74321973152*	**5**	9
5 Jul 03	**LOW** *RCA 82876522562*	**21**	2
4 Oct 03	**HAVE IT ALL** *RCA 82876563702*	**37**	2
8 Jul 95 ●	**FOO FIGHTERS** *Roswell CDSET 2266*	**3**	17
24 May 97 ●	**THE COLOUR AND THE SHAPE** *Roswell CDEST 2295*	**3**	12
13 Nov 99 ●	**THERE IS NOTHING LEFT TO LOSE** *RCA 74321716992*	**10**	16
2 Nov 02 ★	**ONE BY ONE** *RCA 74321973482* ■	**1**	41

[1] Foo Fighters: Ween

FOOL BOONA
UK, male DJ / producer – Colin Tevendale (Singles: 1 Week) pos/wks

		pos	wks
10 Apr 99	**POPPED!!** *Virgin / VC Recordings / Uber Disko VCRD 46*	**52**	1

FOOLPROOF
US, male vocal / instrumental group (Singles: 1 Week) pos/wks

		pos	wks
26 Jun 04	**PAPER HOUSE** *Island CID 863*	**53**	1

FOOL'S GARDEN
Germany, male vocal / instrumental group (Singles: 4 Weeks) pos/wks

		pos	wks
25 May 96	**LEMON TREE** *Encore CDCOR 014*	**61**	1
3 Aug 96	**LEMON TREE (re-issue)** *Encore CDCOR 018*	**26**	3

FOR REAL
US, female vocal group (Singles: 2 Weeks) pos/wks

		pos	wks
1 Jul 95	**YOU DON'T KNOW NOTHIN'** *A&M 5811232*	**54**	1
12 Jul 97	**LIKE I DO** *Rowdy 74321486582*	**45**	1

Steve FORBERT
US, male vocalist (Albums: 3 Weeks) pos/wks

		pos	wks
9 Jun 79	**ALIVE ON ARRIVAL** *Epic EPC 83308*	**56**	1
24 Nov 79	**JACK RABBIT SLIM** *Epic EPC 83879*	**54**	2

Bill FORBES
UK, male vocalist (Singles: 1 Week) pos/wks

		pos	wks
15 Jan 60	**TOO YOUNG** *Columbia DB 4386*	**29**	1

David FORBES
UK (b. Singapore), male producer (Singles: 1 Week) pos/wks

		pos	wks
25 Aug 01	**QUESTIONS (MUST BE ASKED)** *Serious SERR 031CD*	**57**	1

FORBIDDEN *See Jet BRONX and the FORBIDDEN*

FORCE & STYLES featuring Kelly LLORENNA
UK, male DJ duo and female vocalist (Singles: 1 Week) pos/wks

		pos	wks
25 Jul 98	**HEART OF GOLD** *Diverse VERSE 2CD*	**55**	1

FORCE MD'S
US, male vocal group (Singles: 9 Weeks) pos/wks

		pos	wks
12 Apr 86	**TENDER LOVE** *Tommy Boy IS 269*	**23**	9

Clinton FORD
UK, male vocalist – Ian Stopford Harrison (Singles: 25 Weeks, Albums: 4 Weeks)

		pos/wks	
23 Oct 59	OLD SHEP *Oriole CB 1500*	27	1
17 Aug 61	TOO MANY BEAUTIFUL GIRLS *Oriole CB 1623*	48	1
8 Mar 62	FANLIGHT FANNY *Oriole CB 1706*	22	10
5 Jan 67	RUN TO THE DOOR *Piccadilly 7N 35361*	25	13
26 May 62	CLINTON FORD *Oriole PS 40021*	16	4

Emile FORD and the CHECKMATES
UK, male vocal / instrumental group – leader Emile Sweatman (Singles: 89 Weeks)

		pos/wks	
30 Oct 59 ★	WHAT DO YOU WANT TO MAKE THOSE EYES AT ME FOR? *Pye 7N 15225*	1	26
5 Feb 60 ●	ON A SLOW BOAT TO CHINA *Pye 7N 15245*	3	15
26 May 60	YOU'LL NEVER KNOW WHAT YOU'RE MISSING ('TIL YOU TRY) *Pye 7N 15268*	12	9
1 Sep 60	THEM THERE EYES *Pye 7N 15282* [1]	18	16
8 Dec 60 ●	COUNTING TEARDROPS *Pye 7N 15314*	4	12
2 Mar 61	WHAT AM I GONNA DO *Pye 7N 15331*	33	6
18 May 61	HALF OF MY HEART (re) *Piccadilly 7N 35003* [2]	42	4
8 Mar 62	I WONDER WHO'S KISSING HER NOW *Piccadilly 7N 35033* [2]	43	1

[1] Emile Ford: The Babs Knight Group and Johnny Keating Music [2] Emile Ford

Lita FORD
UK, female vocalist (Singles: 7 Weeks, Albums: 4 Weeks)

		pos/wks	
17 Dec 88	KISS ME DEADLY *RCA PB 49575*	75	1
20 May 89	CLOSE MY EYES FOREVER *Dreamland PB 49409* [1]	47	3
11 Jan 92	SHOT OF POISON *RCA PB 49145*	63	3
26 May 84	DANCIN' ON THE EDGE *Vertigo VERL 13*	96	1
23 Jun 90	STILETTO *RCA PL 82090*	66	1
25 Jan 92	DANGEROUS CURVES *RCA PD 90592*	51	2

[1] Lita Ford duet with Ozzy Osbourne

Martyn FORD ORCHESTRA *UK, orchestra (Singles: 3 Weeks)* pos/wks

14 May 77	LET YOUR BODY GO DOWNTOWN *Mountain TOP 26*	38	3

Mary FORD See Les PAUL and Mary FORD

Penny FORD (see also SNAP!)
US, female vocalist (Singles: 7 Weeks)

		pos/wks	
4 May 85	DANGEROUS *Total Experience FB 49975* [1]	43	5
29 May 93	DAYDREAMING *Columbia 6590592*	43	2

[1] Pennye Ford

Tennessee Ernie FORD
US, male vocalist, b. 13 Feb 1919, d. 17 Oct 1991 (Singles: 42 Weeks) pos/wks

21 Jan 55 ★	GIVE ME YOUR WORD *Capitol CL 14005*	1	24
6 Jan 56 ★	SIXTEEN TONS *Capitol CL 14500* ▲	1	11
13 Jan 56 ●	THE BALLAD OF DAVY CROCKETT *Capitol CL 14506*	3	7

Julia FORDHAM
UK, female vocalist (Singles: 32 Weeks, Albums: 36 Weeks)

		pos/wks	
2 Jul 88	HAPPY EVER AFTER *Circa YR 15*	27	9
25 Feb 89	WHERE DOES THE TIME GO? *Circa YR 23*	41	5
31 Aug 91	I THOUGHT IT WAS YOU *Circa YR 69*	64	2
18 Jan 92	LOVE MOVES (IN MYSTERIOUS WAYS) *Circa YR 73*	19	9
30 May 92	I THOUGHT IT WAS YOU (re-mix) *Circa YR 90*	45	3
30 Apr 94	DIFFERENT TIME DIFFERENT PLACE *Circa YRCD 111*	41	4
23 Jul 94	I CAN'T HELP MYSELF *Circa YRCD 116*	62	1
18 Jun 88	JULIA FORDHAM *Circa CIRCA 4*	20	22
21 Oct 89	PORCELAIN *Circa CIRCA 10*	13	5
2 Nov 91	SWEPT *Circa CIRCA 18*	33	6
21 May 94	FALLING FORWARD *Circa CIRCD 28*	21	3

FOREIGNER `328` `Top 500`
Melodic Anglo-American rock group which amassed six US Top 10 albums. Featured Londoner Mick Jones (g) and New York native Lou Gramm (v). 'Waiting for a Girl Like You' stayed at No.2 in the US for a record-breaking 10 weeks (Singles: 78 Weeks, Albums: 126 Weeks)

		pos/wks	
6 May 78	FEELS LIKE THE FIRST TIME *Atlantic K 11086*	39	6
15 Jul 78	COLD AS ICE *Atlantic K 10986*	24	10
28 Oct 78	HOT BLOODED *Atlantic K 11167*	42	3
24 Feb 79	BLUE MORNING, BLUE DAY *Atlantic K 11236*	45	4
29 Aug 81	URGENT *Atlantic K 11665*	54	4
10 Oct 81	JUKE BOX HERO *Atlantic K 11678*	48	4
12 Dec 81 ●	WAITING FOR A GIRL LIKE YOU *Atlantic K 11696*	8	13
8 May 82	URGENT (re-issue) *Atlantic K 11728*	45	5
8 Dec 84 ★	I WANT TO KNOW WHAT LOVE IS *Atlantic A 9596* ▲	1	16
6 Apr 85	THAT WAS YESTERDAY *Atlantic A 9571*	28	6
22 Jun 85	COLD AS ICE (re-mix) *Atlantic A 9539*	64	2
19 Dec 87	SAY YOU WILL *Atlantic A 9169*	71	4
22 Oct 94	WHITE LIE *Arista 74321232862*	58	1
26 Aug 78	DOUBLE VISION *Atlantic K 50476*	32	5
25 Jul 81 ●	4 *Atlantic K 50796* ▲	5	62
18 Dec 82	RECORDS *Atlantic A 0999*	58	11
22 Dec 84 ★	AGENT PROVOCATEUR *Atlantic 7819991*	1	32
19 Dec 87	INSIDE INFORMATION *Atlantic WX 143*	64	7
6 Jul 91	UNUSUAL HEAT *Atlantic WX 424*	56	1
2 May 92	THE VERY BEST OF FOREIGNER *Atlantic 7567805112*	19	7
12 Nov 94	MR. MOONLIGHT *Arista 74321232852*	59	1

The FORMATIONS
US, male vocal group (Singles: 11 Weeks) pos/wks

31 Jul 71	AT THE TOP OF THE STAIRS (re) *Mojo 2027 001*	28	11

George FORMBY (see also 2 IN A TENT)
UK, male vocalist / instrumentalist – ukulele – George Hoy Booth, b. 26 May 1904, d. 6 Mar 1961 (Singles: 3 Weeks) pos/wks

21 Jul 60	HAPPY GO LUCKY ME / BANJO BOY *Pye 7N 15269*	40	3

FORREST
US, male vocalist – Forrest M Thomas Jr (Singles: 20 Weeks) pos/wks

26 Feb 83 ●	ROCK THE BOAT *CBS A 3163*	4	10
14 May 83	FEEL THE NEED IN ME *CBS A 3411*	17	8
17 Sep 83	ONE LOVER (DON'T STOP THE SHOW) *CBS A 3734*	67	2

Sharon FORRESTER
Jamaica, female vocalist (Singles: 1 Week) pos/wks

11 Feb 95	LOVE INSIDE *ffrr FCD 253*	50	1

Lance FORTUNE
UK, male vocalist – Chris Morris (Singles: 18 Weeks) pos/wks

19 Feb 60 ●	BE MINE *Pye 7N 15240*	4	13
5 May 60	THIS LOVE I HAVE FOR YOU *Pye 7N 15260*	26	5

The FORTUNES
UK, male vocal / instrumental group – leader Rod Allen (Rod Bainbridge) (Singles: 65 Weeks) pos/wks

8 Jul 65 ●	YOU'VE GOT YOUR TROUBLES *Decca F 12173*	2	14
7 Oct 65 ●	HERE IT COMES AGAIN *Decca F 12243*	4	14
3 Feb 66	THIS GOLDEN RING *Decca F 12321*	15	9
11 Sep 71 ●	FREEDOM COME, FREEDOM GO *Capitol CL 15693*	6	17
29 Jan 72 ●	STORM IN A TEACUP *Capitol CL 15707*	7	11

45 KING (DJ MARK THE 45 KING)
US, male producer – Mark James (Singles: 6 Weeks) pos/wks

28 Oct 89	THE KING IS HERE / THE 900 NUMBER (re) *Dance Trax DRX 9*	60	6

49ers (see also CAPPELLA) *Italy, male producer – Gianfranco Bortolotti (Singles: 27 Weeks, Albums: 5 Weeks)* pos/wks

16 Dec 89 ●	TOUCH ME *Fourth & Broadway BRW 157*	3	13
17 Mar 90	DON'T YOU LOVE ME *Fourth & Broadway BRW 167*	12	6
9 Jun 90	GIRL TO GIRL *Fourth & Broadway BRW 174*	31	3
6 Jun 92	GOT TO BE FREE *Fourth & Broadway BRW 255*	46	2
29 Aug 92	THE MESSAGE *Fourth & Broadway BRW 257*	68	1
18 Mar 95	ROCKIN' MY BODY *Media MCSTD 2021* [1]	31	2
10 Mar 90	THE 49ERS *Fourth & Broadway BRLP 547*	51	5

[1] 49ers featuring Ann-Marie Smith

Itsy FOSTER See EXOTICA featuring Itsy FOSTER

Lawrence FOSTER See LONDON SYMPHONY ORCHESTRA

Penny FOSTER See STAGECOACH featuring Penny FOSTER

FOSTER and ALLEN `250` `Top 500`

Ever-popular Irish duo formed in 1975: Mike Foster (accordian/v), Tony Allen (g/v). The folk-based performers have sold a reported 20 million albums globally, and are the only act to have at least one hit album per year between 1983-1999 (Singles: 47 Weeks, Albums: 205 Weeks)   pos/wks

27 Feb 82	**A BUNCH OF THYME** *Ritz RITZ 5*	**18** 11
30 Oct 82	**OLD FLAMES** *Ritz RITZ 028*	**51** 8
19 Feb 83	**MAGGIE** *Ritz RITZ 025*	**27** 9
29 Oct 83	**I WILL LOVE YOU ALL MY LIFE** *Ritz RITZ 056*	**49** 6
30 Jun 84	**JUST FOR OLD TIME'S SAKE** *Ritz RITZ 066*	**47** 6
29 Mar 86	**AFTER ALL THESE YEARS** *Ritz RITZ 106*	**43** 7
14 May 83	**MAGGIE** *Ritz RITZLP 0012*	**72** 6
5 Nov 83	**I WILL LOVE YOU ALL OF MY LIFE** *Ritz RITZLP 0015*	**71** 6
17 Nov 84	**THE VERY BEST OF FOSTER AND ALLEN** *Ritz RITZLP TV 1*	**18** 18
29 Mar 86	**AFTER ALL THESE YEARS** *Ritz RITZLP 0032*	**82** 2
25 Oct 86	**REMINISCING** *Stylus SMR 623*	**11** 15
27 Jun 87	**LOVE SONGS – THE VERY BEST OF FOSTER AND ALLEN VOLUME 2** *Ritz RITZLP 0036*	**92** 1
10 Oct 87	**REFLECTIONS** *Stylus SMR 739*	**16** 16
30 Apr 88	**REMEMBER YOU'RE MINE** *Stylus SMR 853*	**16** 6
28 Oct 89	**THE MAGIC OF FOSTER AND ALLEN – THEIR GREATEST HITS** *Stylus SMR 989*	**29** 12
9 Dec 89	**FOSTER AND ALLEN'S CHRISTMAS COLLECTION** *Stylus SMR 995*	**40** 4
10 Nov 90	**SOUVENIRS** *Telstar STAR 2457*	**15** 12
8 Dec 90	**THE CHRISTMAS COLLECTION** *Telstar STAR 2459*	**44** 4
2 Nov 91	**MEMORIES** *Telstar STAR 2527*	**18** 11
31 Oct 92	**HEART STRINGS** *Telstar TCD 2608*	**37** 10
23 Oct 93	**BY REQUEST** *Telstar TCD 2670*	**14** 12
5 Nov 94	**SONGS WE LOVE TO SING** *Telstar TCD 2741*	**41** 9
4 Nov 95	**100 GOLDEN GREATS** *Telstar TCD 2791*	**30** 12
2 Nov 96	**SOMETHING SPECIAL – 100 GOLDEN LOVE SONGS** *Telstar TCD 2846*	**46** 10
26 Apr 97	**SHADES OF GREEN** *Telstar TCD 2899*	**55** 2
15 Nov 97	**BEST FRIENDS** *Telstar TV TTVCD 2935*	**36** 8
12 Dec 98	**GREATEST HITS** *Telstar TV TTVCD 3000*	**52** 4
25 Dec 99	**ONE DAY AT A TIME** *Telstar TV TTVCD 3090*	**61** 1
15 Nov 03	**BY SPECIAL REQUEST – THE VERY BEST OF … FOSTER & ALLEN** *DMG TV DMGTV 003*	**30** 8
13 Nov 04	**FOSTER & ALLEN SING THE SIXTIES** *DMG TV DMGTV 012*	**31** 7+

FOTHERINGAY

UK, male / female vocal / instrumental group (Albums: 6 Weeks)   pos/wks

11 Jul 70	**FOTHERINGAY** *Island ILPS 9125*	**18** 6

The FOUNDATION featuring Natalie ROSSI

Holland, male producers and UK female vocalist (Singles: 2 Weeks)   pos/wks

12 Jul 03	**ALL OUT OF LOVE** *Fuelin 82876513292*	**40** 2

The FOUNDATIONS *West Indies / UK / Sri Lanka,*
male vocal / instrumental group (Singles: 57 Weeks)   pos/wks

27 Sep 67	★ **BABY NOW THAT I'VE FOUND YOU** *Pye 7N 17366*	**1** 16
24 Jan 68	**BACK ON MY FEET AGAIN** *Pye 7N 17417*	**18** 10
1 May 68	**ANY OLD TIME (YOU'RE LONELY AND SAD) (re)** *Pye 7N 17503*	**48** 2
20 Nov 68	● **BUILD ME UP BUTTERCUP** *Pye 7N 17636*	**2** 15
12 Mar 69	● **IN THE BAD BAD OLD DAYS (BEFORE YOU LOVED ME)** *Pye 7N 17702*	**8** 10
13 Sep 69	**BORN TO LIVE, BORN TO DIE** *Pye 7N 17809*	**46** 3
12 Dec 98	**BUILD ME UP BUTTERCUP (re-issue)** *Castle NEEX 1001*	**71** 1

FOUNTAINS OF WAYNE *US, male vocal /*
instrumental group (Singles: 15 Weeks, Albums: 1 Week)   pos/wks

22 Mar 97	**RADIATION VIBE** *Atlantic 7567956262*	**32** 2
10 May 97	**SINK TO THE BOTTOM** *Atlantic A 5612CD*	**42** 1
26 Jul 97	**SURVIVAL CAR** *Atlantic AT 0004CD*	**53** 1
27 Dec 97	**I WANT AN ALIEN FOR CHRISTMAS** *Atlantic AT 0020CD*	**36** 2
20 Mar 99	**DENISE** *Atlantic AT 0053CD*	**57** 1
20 Mar 04	**STACY'S MOM** *Virgin VSCDX 1860*	**11** 7
18 Sep 04	**HEY JULIE** *Virgin VSCDX 1881*	**57** 1
7 Jun 97	**FOUNTAINS OF WAYNE** *Atlantic 7567927252*	**67** 1

The FOUR ACES *US, male vocal group (Singles: 40 Weeks)*   pos/wks

30 Jul 54	● **THREE COINS IN THE FOUNTAIN (re)** *Brunswick 05308* [1]	**5** 6
7 Jan 55	● **MISTER SANDMAN** *Brunswick 05355* [1]	**9** 5
20 May 55	● **STRANGER IN PARADISE** *Brunswick 05418*	**6** 6
18 Nov 55	● **LOVE IS A MANY SPLENDORED THING** *Brunswick 05480* [1] ▲	**2** 13
19 Oct 56	**A WOMAN IN LOVE** *Brunswick 05589* [1]	**19** 3
4 Jan 57	**FRIENDLY PERSUASION (THEE I LOVE)** *Brunswick 05623* [1]	**29** 1
23 Jan 59	**THE WORLD OUTSIDE** *Brunswick 05773*	**18** 6

[1] The Four Aces featuring Al Alberts

The FOUR BUCKETEERS
UK, male / female vocal group (Singles: 6 Weeks)   pos/wks

3 May 80	**THE BUCKET OF WATER SONG** *CBS 8393*	**26** 6

The FOUR ESQUIRES *US, male vocal group (Singles: 2 Weeks)*   pos/wks

31 Jan 58	**LOVE ME FOREVER** *London HLO 8533*	**23** 2

4-4-2 *UK, male vocal group – England fans (Singles: 5 Weeks)*   pos/wks

19 Jun 04	● **COME ON ENGLAND** *Gut CDGUT 58*	**2** 5

The single's sleeve credits 4-4-2 featuring Talksport 1089 / 1053AM Presenters

4 HERO
UK, male instrumental group (Singles: 6 Weeks, Albums: 7 Weeks)   pos/wks

24 Nov 90	**MR KIRK'S NIGHTMARE** *Reinforced RIVET 1203*	**73** 2
9 May 92	**COOKIN' UP YAH BRAIN** *Reinforced RIVET 1216*	**59** 2
15 Aug 98	**STAR CHASERS** *Talkin Loud TLCD 36*	**41** 1
3 Nov 01	**LES FLEUR** *Talkin Loud TLCD 66*	**53** 1
25 Jul 98	**TWO PAGES** *Talkin Loud 5584622*	**38** 6
10 Nov 01	**CREATING PATTERNS** *Talkin Loud 5860572*	**65** 1

'Mr Kirk's Nightmare' was titled 'Combat Dancing (EP)' in its first week on chart

FOUR JAYS See Billy FURY

FOUR KESTRELS See Billy FURY

The FOUR KNIGHTS *US, male vocal group (Singles: 13 Weeks)*   pos/wks

4 Jun 54	● **(OH BABY MINE) I GET SO LONELY (re)** *Capitol CL 14076*	**5** 11
18 Oct 57	**MY PERSONAL POSSESSION** *Capitol CL 14765* [1]	**21** 2

[1] Nat 'King' Cole and The Four Knights

The FOUR LADS *Canada, male vocal group (Singles: 23 Weeks)*   pos/wks

19 Dec 52	● **FAITH CAN MOVE MOUNTAINS (re)** *Columbia DB 3154* [1]	**7** 3
22 Oct 54	● **RAIN, RAIN, RAIN** *Philips PB 311* [2]	**8** 16
28 Apr 60	**STANDING ON THE CORNER** *Philips PB 1000*	**34** 4

[1] Johnnie Ray and The Four Lads [2] Frankie Laine and The Four Lads

4 NON BLONDES *US, female / male vocal /*
instrumental group (Singles: 19 Weeks, Albums: 18 Weeks)   pos/wks

19 Jun 93	● **WHAT'S UP** *Interscope A 8412CD*	**2** 17
16 Oct 93	**SPACEMAN** *Interscope A 8349CD*	**53** 2
17 Jul 93	● **BIGGER BETTER FASTER MORE!** *Interscope 7567921122*	**4** 18

The 4 OF US *Ireland, male vocal /*
instrumental group (Singles: 6 Weeks, Albums: 1 Week)   pos/wks

27 Feb 93	**SHE HITS ME** *Columbia 6589192*	**35** 4
1 May 93	**I MISS YOU** *Columbia 6591722*	**62** 2
20 Mar 93	**MAN ALIVE** *Columbia 4723262*	**64** 1

The 411
UK, female vocal group (Singles: 26 Weeks, Albums: 2 Weeks)   pos/wks

29 May 04	**ON MY KNEES (re)** *Sony Music 6749381* [1]	**4** 11
4 Sep 04	**DUMB** *Sony / Streetside 6752622*	**3** 10
27 Nov 04	**TEARDROPS** *Sony / Streetside 6754812*	**23** 5+
4 Dec 04	**BETWEEN THE SHEETS** *Sony Music 5190842*	**46** 2

[1] The 411 featuring Ghostface Killah

The FOUR PENNIES *UK, male vocal / instrumental group –*
lead vocal Lionel Morton (Singles: 56 Weeks, Albums: 5 Weeks)   pos/wks

16 Jan 64	**DO YOU WANT ME TO (re)** *Philips BF 1296*	**47** 2
2 Apr 64	★ **JULIET** *Philips BF 1322*	**1** 15
16 Jul 64	**I FOUND OUT THE HARD WAY** *Philips BF 1349*	**14** 11
29 Oct 64	**BLACK GIRL** *Philips BF 1366*	**20** 12
7 Oct 65	**UNTIL IT'S TIME FOR YOU TO GO** *Philips BF 1435*	**19** 11
17 Feb 66	**TROUBLE IS MY MIDDLE NAME** *Philips BF 1469*	**32** 5
7 Nov 64	**TWO SIDES OF FOUR PENNIES** *Philips BL 7642*	**13** 5

The FOUR PREPS US, male vocal group (Singles: 23 Weeks) pos/wks

13 Jun 58 ●	BIG MAN (re) *Capitol CL 14873*	2	14
26 May 60	GOT A GIRL (re) *Capitol CL 15128*	28	7
2 Nov 61	MORE MONEY FOR YOU AND ME (MEDLEY) *Capitol CL 15217*	39	2

Tracks on More Money for You and Me medley: Mr Blue / Alley Oop / Smoke Gets in Your Eyes / In This Whole Wide World / A Worried Man / Tom Dooley / A Teenager in Love – all songs feature new lyrics

The FOUR SEASONS 〔302 Top 500〕
No.1 US group of the early 1960s: Frankie Valli (v), Bob Gaudio (k/v), Nick Massi (b/v) (died 2000), Tommy DeVito (g/v). Falsetto-voiced Valli's quartet, the first group to score three US No.1s in succession, has a chart span there of almost 40 years (Singles: 151 Weeks, Albums: 68 Weeks) pos/wks

4 Oct 62 ●	SHERRY *Stateside SS 122* ▲	8	16
17 Jan 63	BIG GIRLS DON'T CRY *Stateside SS 145* ▲	13	10
28 Mar 63	WALK LIKE A MAN *Stateside SS 169* ▲	12	12
27 Jun 63	AIN'T THAT A SHAME *Stateside SS 194*	38	3
27 Aug 64 ●	RAG DOLL *Philips BF 1347* 1 ▲	2	13
18 Nov 65	LET'S HANG ON *Philips BF 1439* 1	4	16
31 Mar 66	WORKIN' MY WAY BACK TO YOU *Philips BF 1474* 2	50	3
2 Jun 66	OPUS 17 (DON'T YOU WORRY 'BOUT ME) *Philips BF 1493* 2	20	9
29 Sep 66	I'VE GOT YOU UNDER MY SKIN *Philips BF 1511* 2	12	11
12 Jan 67	TELL IT TO THE RAIN *Philips BF 1538* 2	37	5
19 Apr 75 ●	THE NIGHT *Mowest MW 3024* 3	7	9
20 Sep 75 ●	WHO LOVES YOU *Warner Bros. / Curb K 16602*	6	9
31 Jan 76 ★	DECEMBER, 1963 (OH, WHAT A NIGHT) *Warner Bros. / Curb K 16688* ▲	1	10
24 Apr 76 ●	SILVER STAR *Warner Bros. / Curb K 16742*	3	9
27 Nov 76	WE CAN WORK IT OUT *Warner Bros. / Curb K 16845*	34	4
18 Jun 77	RHAPSODY *Warner Bros. / Curb K 16932*	37	3
20 Aug 77	DOWN THE HALL *Warner Bros. / Curb K 16982*	34	5
29 Oct 88	DECEMBER, 1963 (OH, WHAT A NIGHT) (re-mix) *BR 45277* 3	49	4
6 Jul 63	SHERRY *Stateside SL 10033*	20	1
10 Apr 71	EDIZIONE D'ORO *Philips 6640002*	11	7
20 Nov 71	THE BIG ONES *Philips 6336208*	37	1
6 Mar 76	THE FOUR SEASONS STORY *Private Stock DAPS 1001*	20	8
6 Mar 76	WHO LOVES YOU *Warner Bros. K 56179*	12	17
20 Nov 76 ●	GREATEST HITS *K-Tel NE 942*	4	6
21 May 88	THE COLLECTION *Telstar STAR 2320* 1	38	9
7 Mar 92 ●	THE VERY BEST OF FRANKIE VALLI AND THE FOUR SEASONS *PolyGram TV 5131192* 1	7	15
13 Oct 01	THE DEFINITIVE FRANKIE VALLI AND THE FOUR SEASONS *WSM 8122735552* 1	26	4

1 The Four Seasons with the sound of Frankie Valli 2 The Four Seasons with Frankie Valli 3 Frankie Valli and The Four Seasons 1 Frankie Valli and The Four Seasons

The 4-SKINS
UK, male vocal / instrumental group (Albums: 4 Weeks) pos/wks

17 Apr 82	THE GOOD THE BAD AND THE 4-SKINS *Secret SEC 4*	80	4

4 STRINGS (see also MADELYNE)
Holland, male / female production / vocal duo (Singles: 15 Weeks) pos/wks

23 Dec 00	DAY TIME *AM:PM 139*	48	3
11 May 02	(TAKE ME AWAY) INTO THE NIGHT (re) *Nebula / Virgin CDRD 107*	15	7
14 Sep 02	DIVING *Nebula VCRD 108*	38	2
13 Sep 03	LET IT RAIN *Nebula NEBCD 049*	49	1
31 Jul 04	TURN IT AROUND *Nebula NEBCD 059*	50	2

FOUR TET
UK, male DJ / producer – Keiran Hebden (Albums: 1 Week) pos/wks

17 May 03	ROUNDS *Domino WIDCD 126*	60	1

4 THE CAUSE US, male / female vocal group (Singles: 9 Weeks) pos/wks

10 Oct 98	STAND BY ME *RCA 7432162442*	12	9

The FOUR TOPS 〔62 Top 500〕
Unmistakable R&B vocal group from Detroit: Levi Stubbs, Renaldo Benson, Lawrence Payton (d. 1997), Abdul Fakir. The legendary Motown act performed together for a record 44 years (until Payton's death) and were inducted into the Rock and Roll Hall of Fame in 1990 (Singles: 318 Weeks, Albums: 256 Weeks) pos/wks

1 Jul 65	I CAN'T HELP MYSELF *Tamla Motown TMG 515* ▲	23	9
2 Sep 65	IT'S THE SAME OLD SONG *Tamla Motown TMG 528*	34	8
21 Jul 66	LOVING YOU IS SWEETER THAN EVER *Tamla Motown TMG 568*	21	12
13 Oct 66 ★	REACH OUT I'LL BE THERE *Tamla Motown TMG 579* ▲	1	16
12 Jan 67 ●	STANDING IN THE SHADOWS OF LOVE *Tamla Motown TMG 589*	6	8
30 Mar 67 ●	BERNADETTE *Tamla Motown TMG 601*	8	10
15 Jun 67	SEVEN ROOMS OF GLOOM *Tamla Motown TMG 612*	12	9
11 Oct 67	YOU KEEP RUNNING AWAY *Tamla Motown TMG 623*	26	7
13 Dec 67 ●	WALK AWAY RENEE *Tamla Motown TMG 634*	3	11
13 Mar 68 ●	IF I WERE A CARPENTER *Tamla Motown TMG 647*	7	11
21 Aug 68	YESTERDAY'S DREAMS *Tamla Motown TMG 665*	23	15
13 Nov 68	I'M IN A DIFFERENT WORLD *Tamla Motown TMG 675*	27	13
28 May 69	WHAT IS A MAN *Tamla Motown TMG 698*	16	11
27 Sep 69	DO WHAT YOU GOTTA DO *Tamla Motown TMG 710*	11	11
21 Mar 70 ●	I CAN'T HELP MYSELF (re-issue) *Tamla Motown TMG 732*	10	11
30 May 70	IT'S ALL IN THE GAME (re) *Tamla Motown TMG 736*	5	16
3 Oct 70 ●	STILL WATER (LOVE) (re) *Tamla Motown TMG 752*	10	12
1 May 71	JUST SEVEN NUMBERS (CAN STRAIGHTEN OUT MY LIFE) *Tamla Motown TMG 770*	36	5
26 Jun 71	RIVER DEEP MOUNTAIN HIGH *Tamla Motown TMG 777* 1	11	10
25 Sep 71 ●	SIMPLE GAME *Tamla Motown TMG 785*	3	11
20 Nov 71	YOU GOTTA HAVE LOVE IN YOUR HEART *Tamla Motown TMG 793* 1	25	10
11 Mar 72	BERNADETTE (re-issue) *Tamla Motown TMG 803*	23	7
5 Aug 72	WALK WITH ME TALK WITH ME DARLING *Tamla Motown TMG 823*	32	6
18 Nov 72	KEEPER OF THE CASTLE *Probe PRO 575*	18	9
10 Nov 73	SWEET UNDERSTANDING LOVE *Probe PRO 604*	29	10
17 Oct 81 ●	WHEN SHE WAS MY GIRL *Casablanca CAN 1005*	3	10
19 Dec 81	DON'T WALK AWAY *Casablanca CAN 1006*	16	11
6 Mar 82	TONIGHT I'M GONNA LOVE YOU ALL OVER *Casablanca CAN 1008*	43	4
26 Jun 82	BACK TO SCHOOL AGAIN *RSO 89*	62	2
23 Jul 88	REACH OUT I'LL BE THERE (re-mix) *Motown ZB 41943*	11	9
17 Sep 88	INDESTRUCTIBLE *Arista 111717* 2	55	4
3 Dec 88 ●	LOCO IN ACAPULCO *Arista 111850*	7	13
25 Feb 89	INDESTRUCTIBLE *Arista 112074* 2	30	7
19 Nov 66 ●	FOUR TOPS ON TOP *Tamla Motown TML 11037*	9	23
11 Feb 67 ●	FOUR TOPS LIVE! *Tamla Motown STML 11041*	4	72
25 Nov 67 ●	REACH OUT *Tamla Motown STML 11056*	4	34
20 Jan 68 ★	GREATEST HITS *Tamla Motown STML 11061*	1	67
8 Feb 69	YESTERDAY'S DREAMS *Tamla Motown STML 11087*	37	1
27 Jun 70	STILL WATERS RUN DEEP *Tamla Motown STML 11149*	29	8
29 May 71 ●	MAGNIFICENT SEVEN *Tamla Motown STML 11179* 1	6	11
27 Nov 71	FOUR TOPS' GREATEST HITS VOLUME 2 *Tamla Motown STML 11195*	25	10
10 Nov 73	THE FOUR TOPS STORY 1964-72 *Tamla Motown TMSP 11241/2*	35	5
13 Feb 82	THE BEST OF THE FOUR TOPS *K-Tel NE 1160*	13	13
8 Dec 90	THEIR GREATEST HITS *Telstar STAR 2437*	47	6
19 Sep 92	THE SINGLES COLLECTION *PolyGram TV 5157102*	11	5
30 Mar 02	AT THEIR VERY BEST – TEMPTATIONS / FOUR TOPS *Universal TV 5830142*	18	1

1 The Supremes and The Four Tops 2 The Four Tops featuring Smokey Robinson 1 The Supremes and The Four Tops

The original US recording of 'Indestructible' was not issued until after the chart run of the UK-only mix 'At Their Very Best – Temptations / Four Tops' appeared only in the UK Compilation Chart and was not listed in the standard Top 75

4TUNE 500 UK, male / female production group (Singles: 1 Week) pos/wks

16 Aug 03	DANCING IN THE DARK *Black Gold BLGD 04CDC 01*	75	1

4 VINI featuring Elisabeth TROY UK, male vocal / production group and female vocalist (Singles: 1 Week) pos/wks

18 May 02	FOREVER YOUNG *Botchit & Scarper BOS 2CD 033*	75	1

4CLUBBERS (see also FUTURE BREEZE)
Germany, male production group (Singles: 1 Week) pos/wks

14 Sep 02	CHILDREN *Code Blue BLU 026CD*	45	1

4MANDU UK, male vocal group (Singles: 6 Weeks) pos/wks

29 Jul 95	THIS IS IT *Final Vinyl 74321291222*	45	3
17 Feb 96	DO IT FOR LOVE *Arista 74321343902*	45	2
15 Jun 96	BABY DON'T GO *Arista 74321375914*	47	1

400 BLOWS UK, male vocal / instrumental duo (Singles: 4 Weeks) pos/wks

29 Jun 85	MOVIN' *Illuminated ILL 61*	54	4

The FOURMOST
UK, male vocal / instrumental group (Singles: 64 Weeks)   pos/wks

12 Sep 63 ●	HELLO LITTLE GIRL *Parlophone R 5056*	9 17
26 Dec 63	I'M IN LOVE *Parlophone R 5078*	17 12
23 Apr 64 ●	A LITTLE LOVING *Parlophone R 5128*	6 13
13 Aug 64	HOW CAN I TELL HER *Parlophone R 5157*	33 4
26 Nov 64	BABY I NEED YOUR LOVIN' *Parlophone R 5194*	24 12
9 Dec 65	GIRLS, GIRLS, GIRLS *Parlophone R 5379*	33 6

14-18 (see also STOCK AITKEN WATERMAN)
UK, male vocalist – Pete Waterman (Singles: 4 Weeks)   pos/wks

1 Nov 75	GOODBYE-EE *Magnet MAG 48*	33 4

40 THEVZ See COOLIO

Bernard FOWLER See BOMB THE BASS

FOX
UK / US, male / female vocal / instrumental group –
includes Noosha Fox (Singles: 29 Weeks, Albums: 8 Weeks)   pos/wks

15 Feb 75 ●	ONLY YOU CAN *GTO GT 8*	3 11
10 May 75	IMAGINE ME IMAGINE YOU *GTO GT 21*	15 8
10 Apr 76 ●	S-S-S-SINGLE BED *GTO GT 57*	4 10
17 May 75 ●	FOX *GTO GTLP 001*	7 8

Gemma FOX featuring MC LYTE
UK, female vocalist and US, female rapper (Singles: 3 Weeks)   pos/wks

8 May 04	GIRLFRIEND'S STORY *Polydor 9866362*	38 3

James FOX UK, male vocalist (Singles: 7 Weeks)   pos/wks

1 May 04	HOLD ONTO OUR LOVE *Sony Music 6748732*	13 7

Noosha FOX (see also FOX) UK, female vocalist (Singles: 6 Weeks)   pos/wks

12 Nov 77	GEORGINA BAILEY *GTO GT 106*	31 6

Samantha FOX (see also SOX)
UK, female vocalist (Singles: 73 Weeks, Albums: 18 Weeks)   pos/wks

22 Mar 86 ●	TOUCH ME (I WANT YOUR BODY) *Jive FOXY 1*	3 10
28 Jun 86 ●	DO YA DO YA (WANNA PLEASE ME) *Jive FOXY 2*	10 7
6 Sep 86	HOLD ON TIGHT *Jive FOXY 3*	26 5
13 Dec 86	I'M ALL YOU NEED *Jive FOXY 4*	41 6
30 May 87 ●	NOTHING'S GONNA STOP ME NOW *Jive FOXY 5*	8 9
25 Jul 87	I SURRENDER (TO THE SPIRIT OF THE NIGHT) *Jive FOXY 6*	25 7
17 Oct 87	I PROMISE YOU (GET READY) *Jive FOXY 7*	58 3
19 Dec 87	TRUE DEVOTION *Jive FOXY 8*	62 3
21 May 88	NAUGHTY GIRLS (NEED LOVE TOO) *Jive FOXY 9*	31 5
19 Nov 88	LOVE HOUSE *Jive FOXY 10*	32 6
28 Jan 89	I ONLY WANNA BE WITH YOU *Jive FOXY 11*	16 8
17 Jun 89	I WANNA HAVE SOME FUN *Jive FOXY 12*	63 2
28 Mar 98	SANTA MARIA *All Around the World CDGLOBE 163*	31 2
26 Jul 86	TOUCH ME *Jive HIP 39*	17 10
1 Aug 87	SAMANTHA FOX *Jive HIP 48*	22 6
18 Feb 89	I WANNA HAVE SOME FUN *Jive HIP 72*	46 2

Bruce FOXTON (see also The JAM)
UK, male vocalist (Singles: 9 Weeks, Albums: 4 Weeks)   pos/wks

30 Jul 83	FREAK *Arista BFOX 1*	23 5
29 Oct 83	THIS IS THE WAY *Arista BFOX 2*	56 3
21 Apr 84	IT MAKES ME WONDER *Arista BFOX 3*	74 1
12 May 84	TOUCH SENSITIVE *Arista 206 251*	68 4

Inez FOXX US, female vocalist (Singles: 8 Weeks)   pos/wks

23 Jul 64	HURT BY LOVE *Sue WI 323*	40 3
19 Feb 69	MOCKINGBIRD (re) *United Artists UP 2269* [1]	33 5

[1] Inez and Charlie Foxx

John FOXX UK, male vocalist – Dennis
Leigh (Singles: 31 Weeks, Albums: 17 Weeks)   pos/wks

26 Jan 80	UNDERPASS *Virgin VS 318*	31 8
29 Mar 80	NO-ONE DRIVING (DOUBLE SINGLE) *Virgin VS 338*	32 4
19 Jul 80	BURNING CAR *Virgin VS 360*	35 7
8 Nov 80	MILES AWAY *Virgin VS 382*	51 3
29 Aug 81	EUROPE (AFTER THE RAIN) *Virgin VS 393*	40 5

2 Jul 83	ENDLESSLY *Virgin VS 543*	66 3
17 Sep 83	YOUR DRESS *Virgin VS 615*	61 1
2 Feb 80	METAMATIC *Metalbeat V 2146*	18 7
3 Oct 81	THE GARDEN *Virgin V 2194*	24 6
8 Oct 83	THE GOLDEN SECTION *Virgin V 2233*	27 3
5 Oct 85	IN MYSTERIOUS WAYS *Virgin V 2355*	85 1

Tracks on No-One Driving (double single): No-One Driving / Glimmer / This City / Mr No

The FRAGGLES UK / US, puppets from TV
series (Singles: 8 Weeks, Albums: 4 Weeks)   pos/wks

18 Feb 84	'FRAGGLE ROCK' THEME *RCA 389*	33 8
21 Apr 84	FRAGGLE ROCK *RCA PL 70221*	38 4

FRAGMA Germany / Spain, male / female production /
vocal group (Singles: 45 Weeks, Albums: 12 Weeks)   pos/wks

25 Sep 99	TOCA ME *Positiva CDTIV 120*	11 6
22 Apr 00 ★	TOCA'S MIRACLE (re) (re-mix) *Positiva CDTIV 128* [1] ■	1 17
13 Jan 01 ●	EVERYTIME YOU NEED ME *Positiva CDTIV 147* [2]	3 11
19 May 01 ●	YOU ARE ALIVE *Positiva CDTIVS 153*	4 9
8 Dec 01	SAY THAT YOU'RE HERE *Illustrious CDILLS 001*	25 2
27 Jan 01	TOCA *Positiva 8506770*	19 12

[1] Fragma: Vocals by Co Co [2] Fragma featuring Maria Rubia

Roddy FRAME (see also AZTEC CAMERA) UK, male
vocalist / instrumentalist (Singles: 2 Weeks, Albums: 1 Week)   pos/wks

19 Sep 98	REASON FOR LIVING *Independiente ISOM 18MS*	45 2
3 Oct 98	THE NORTH STAR *Independiente ISOM 7CD*	55 1

Peter FRAMPTON (see also The HERD; HUMBLE PIE)
UK, male vocalist (Singles: 24 Weeks, Albums: 49 Weeks)   pos/wks

1 May 76 ●	SHOW ME THE WAY *A&M AMS 7218*	10 12
11 Sep 76	BABY I LOVE YOUR WAY *A&M AMS 7246*	43 5
6 Nov 76	DO YOU FEEL LIKE WE DO *A&M AMS 7260*	39 4
23 Jul 77	I'M IN YOU *A&M AMS 7298*	41 3
22 May 76 ●	FRAMPTON COMES ALIVE! *A&M AMLM 63703* ▲	6 39
18 Jun 77	I'M IN YOU *A&M AMLK 64039*	19 10

Connie FRANCIS ⟨ 220 ⟩ Top 500
The original Italian-American queen of pop, b. Concetta Franconero, 12 Dec 1938, New Jersey, US. The most successful international female vocalist of the 1950s and 1960s, the first female teenager to register a UK No.1 single and the first female solo artist to top the UK album chart (Singles: 244 Weeks, Albums: 31 Weeks)   pos/wks

4 Apr 58 ★	WHO'S SORRY NOW *MGM 975*	1 25
27 Jun 58	I'M SORRY I MADE YOU CRY *MGM 982*	11 10
22 Aug 58 ★	CAROLINA MOON / STUPID CUPID *MGM 985*	1 19
31 Oct 58	I'LL GET BY *MGM 993*	19 6
21 Nov 58	FALLIN' *MGM 993*	20 5
26 Dec 58	YOU ALWAYS HURT THE ONE YOU LOVE *MGM 998*	13 7
13 Feb 59 ●	MY HAPPINESS (re) *MGM 1001*	4 15
3 Jul 59 ●	LIPSTICK ON YOUR COLLAR *MGM 1018*	3 16
11 Sep 59	PLENTY GOOD LOVIN' *MGM 1036*	18 6
4 Dec 59	AMONG MY SOUVENIRS *MGM 1046*	11 10
17 Mar 60	VALENTINO *MGM 1060*	27 8
19 May 60 ●	MAMA / ROBOT MAN *MGM 1076*	2 19
18 Aug 60 ●	EVERYBODY'S SOMEBODY'S FOOL *MGM 1086* ▲	5 13
3 Nov 60 ●	MY HEART HAS A MIND OF ITS OWN *MGM 1100* ▲	3 15
12 Jan 61	MANY TEARS AGO *MGM 1111*	12 9
16 Mar 61 ●	WHERE THE BOYS ARE / BABY ROO *MGM 1121*	5 14
15 Jun 61	BREAKIN' IN A BRAND NEW BROKEN HEART *MGM 1136*	12 11
14 Sep 61 ●	TOGETHER *MGM 1138*	6 11
14 Dec 61	BABY'S FIRST CHRISTMAS *MGM 1145*	30 4
26 Apr 62	DON'T BREAK THE HEART THAT LOVES YOU *MGM 1157* ▲	39 3
2 Aug 62 ●	VACATION *MGM 1165*	10 9
20 Dec 62	I'M GONNA BE WARM THIS WINTER *MGM 1185*	48 1
10 Jun 65	MY CHILD *MGM 1271*	26 6
20 Jan 66	JEALOUS HEART *MGM 1293*	44 2
26 Mar 60	ROCK 'N' ROLL MILLION SELLERS *MGM C 804*	12 1
11 Feb 61	CONNIE'S GREATEST HITS *MGM C 831*	16 3
18 Jun 77 ★	20 ALL TIME GREATS *Polydor 2391 290*	1 22
24 Apr 93	THE SINGLES COLLECTION *PolyGram TV 5191312*	12 5

'Baby Roo' listed with 'Where the Boys Are' for first eight weeks only

Jill FRANCIS UK, female vocalist (Singles: 1 Week)

		pos/wks
3 Jul 93	MAKE LOVE TO ME *Glady Wax GW 003CD* **70**	1

Claude FRANÇOIS France (b. Egypt), male vocalist,
b. 1 Feb 1939, d. 11 Mar 1978 (Singles: 4 Weeks)

		pos/wks
10 Jan 76	TEARS ON THE TELEPHONE *Bradley's BRAD 7528* **35**	4

Girl vocal: Kathy Barnet

Joe FRANK See HAMILTON, Joe FRANK and REYNOLDS

The FRANK AND WALTERS Ireland, male vocal /
instrumental group (Singles: 13 Weeks, Albums: 1 Week)

		pos/wks
21 Mar 92	HAPPY BUSMAN *Setanta HOO 2* **49**	2
12 Sep 92	THIS IS NOT A SONG *Setanta HOO 3* **46**	3
9 Jan 93	AFTER ALL *Setanta HOOCD 4* **11**	5
17 Apr 93	FASHION CRISIS HITS NEW YORK *Setanta HOOCD 5* **42**	3
7 Nov 92	TRAINS BOATS AND PLANES *Setanta 8283692* **36**	1

FRANKE UK, male vocalist – Franke Pharoah (Singles: 3 Weeks)

		pos/wks
7 Nov 92	UNDERSTAND THIS GROOVE *China WOK 2028* **60**	2
21 May 94	LOVE COME HOME *Triangle BLUESCD 001* [1] **73**	1

[1] Our Tribe with Franke Pharoah and Kristine W

FRANK'EE See BROTHER BROWN featuring FRANK'EE

FRANKEE
US, female vocalist (Singles: 19 Weeks, Albums: 2 Weeks)

		pos/wks
1 May 04	F.U.R.B. – F U RIGHT BACK (IMPORT)	
	All Around the World 560342CD **43**	3
22 May 04 ★	F.U.R.B. – F U RIGHT BACK	
	All Around the World CDGLOBE 355 ■ **1**	16
19 Jun 04	THE GOOD, THE BAD, THE UGLY *Universal TV 9867000* **51**	2

FRANKIE & CALVIN See S CLUB JUNIORS; I DREAM featuring FRANKIE & CALVIN

FRANKIE GOES TO HOLLYWOOD (268) Top 500
*Fiercely marketed, controversial and regularly re-mixed Merseyside-based
quintet fronted by Holly Johnson (b. 19 Feb 1960, Sudan). First act since Gerry
and the Pacemakers to hit No.1 with initial three releases. During July 1984,
'Two Tribes' and 'Relax' held top two places in the chart. Total UK single
sales: 5,008,067. Best-selling single: 'Relax' 1,910,000 (Singles: 147 Weeks,
Albums: 95 Weeks)*

		pos/wks
26 Nov 83 ★	RELAX (re) *ZTT ZTAS 1* ◆ **1**	52
16 Jun 84 ★	TWO TRIBES (re) *ZTT ZTAS 3* ◆ ■ **1**	21
1 Dec 84 ★	THE POWER OF LOVE (re) *ZTT ZTAS 5* **1**	12
30 Mar 85 ●	WELCOME TO THE PLEASURE DOME *ZTT ZTAS 7* **2**	11
6 Sep 86 ●	RAGE HARD *ZTT ZTAS 22* **4**	7
22 Nov 86	WARRIORS (OF THE WASTELAND) *ZTT ZTAS 25* **19**	8
7 Mar 87	WATCHING THE WILDLIFE *ZTT ZTAS 26* **28**	6
2 Oct 93 ●	RELAX (re-issue) *ZTT FGTH 1CD* **5**	7
20 Nov 93	WELCOME TO THE PLEASURE DOME (re-mix) *ZTT FGTH 2CD* ...**18**	3
18 Dec 93	THE POWER OF LOVE (re-issue) *ZTT FGTH 3CD* **10**	7
26 Feb 94	TWO TRIBES (re-mix) *ZTT FGTH 4CD* **16**	3
1 Jul 00 ●	THE POWER OF LOVE (re-mix) *ZTT ZTT 150CD* **6**	6
9 Sep 00	TWO TRIBES (2nd re-mix) *ZTT ZTT 154CD* **17**	3
18 Nov 00	WELCOME TO THE PLEASURE DOME (2nd re-mix) *ZTT 166CD* **45**	1
10 Nov 84 ★	WELCOME TO THE PLEASUREDOME *ZTT ZTTIQ 1* ■ **1**	66
1 Nov 86 ●	LIVERPOOL *ZTT ZTTIQ 8* **5**	13
30 Oct 93 ●	BANG! – THE GREATEST HITS OF FRANKIE GOES TO	
	HOLLYWOOD *ZTT 4509939122* **4**	15
7 Oct 00	MAXIMUM JOY *ZTT ZTT 165CD* **54**	1

Aretha FRANKLIN (234) Top 500
*The 'Queen of Soul Music', b. 25 Mar 1942, Tennessee, US. With six decades
of recording behind her, this legendary gospel-influenced vocalist has won
countless awards and amassed more R&B hits than any other female in her
homeland (Singles: 182 Weeks, Albums: 85 Weeks)*

		pos/wks
8 Jun 67 ●	RESPECT *Atlantic 584115* ▲ **10**	14
23 Aug 67	BABY I LOVE YOU *Atlantic 584127* **39**	4
20 Dec 67	CHAIN OF FOOLS / SATISFACTION (re) *Atlantic 584157* **37**	7
13 Mar 68	SINCE YOU'VE BEEN GONE (SWEET SWEET BABY)	
	Atlantic 584172 ......**47**	4
22 May 68	THINK *Atlantic 584186* **26**	9
7 Aug 68 ●	I SAY A LITTLE PRAYER *Atlantic 584206* **4**	14

		pos/wks
22 Aug 70	DON'T PLAY THAT SONG *Atlantic 2091027* **13**	11
2 Oct 71	SPANISH HARLEM *Atlantic 2091138* **14**	9
8 Sep 73	ANGEL *Atlantic K 10346* **37**	5
16 Feb 74	UNTIL YOU COME BACK TO ME (THAT'S WHAT I'M GONNA	
	DO) *Atlantic K 10399* **26**	8
6 Dec 80	WHAT A FOOL BELIEVES *Arista ARIST 377* **46**	7
19 Sep 81	LOVE ALL THE HURT AWAY *Arista ARIST 428* [1] **49**	3
4 Sep 82	JUMP TO IT *Arista ARIST 479* **42**	5
23 Jul 83	GET IT RIGHT *Arista ARIST 537* **74**	2
13 Jul 85	FREEWAY OF LOVE (re) *Arista ARIST 624* **51**	6
2 Nov 85 ●	SISTERS ARE DOIN' IT FOR THEMSELVES *RCA PB 40339* [2] ..**9**	11
23 Nov 85	WHO'S ZOOMIN' WHO *Arista ARIST 633* **11**	14
22 Feb 86	ANOTHER NIGHT *Arista ARIST 657* **54**	6
25 Oct 86	JUMPIN' JACK FLASH *Arista ARIST 678* **58**	3
31 Jan 87 ★	I KNEW YOU WERE WAITING (FOR ME) *Epic DUET 1* [3] ▲ **1**	9
14 Mar 87	JIMMY LEE *Arista RIS 6* **46**	4
6 May 89	THROUGH THE STORM *Arista 112185* [4] **41**	7
9 Sep 89	IT ISN'T, IT WASN'T, IT AIN'T NEVER GONNA BE	
	Arista 112545 [5] **29**	5
7 Apr 90	THINK *East West A 7951* **31**	2
27 Jul 91	EVERYDAY PEOPLE *Arista 114420* **69**	1
12 Feb 94 ●	A DEEPER LOVE *Arista 74321187022* **5**	7
25 Jun 94	WILLING TO FORGIVE *Arista 74321213342* **17**	7
9 May 98	A ROSE IS STILL A ROSE *Arista 74321569742* **22**	4
26 Sep 98	HERE WE GO AGAIN *Arista 74321612742* **68**	1
12 Aug 67	I NEVER LOVED A MAN THE WAY I LOVE YOU	
	Atlantic 587006 ......**36**	2
13 Apr 68	LADY SOUL *Atlantic 588099* **25**	18
14 Sep 68 ●	ARETHA NOW *Atlantic 588114* **6**	11
18 Jan 86	WHO'S ZOOMIN' WHO? *Arista 2072 02* **49**	12
24 May 86	THE FIRST LADY OF SOUL *Stylus SMR 8506* **89**	1
8 Nov 86	ARETHA *Arista 208020* **51**	13
3 Jun 89	THROUGH THE STORM *Arista 209842* **46**	1
19 Mar 94	GREATEST HITS 1980-1994 *Arista 74321162022* **27**	3
29 Oct 94	QUEEN OF SOUL – THE VERY BEST OF ARETHA FRANKLIN	
	Atlantic 8122713962 ......**20**	5
21 Nov 98	GREATEST HITS *Global Television RADCD 110* **38**	10
15 Jun 02	RESPECT – THE VERY BEST OF ARETHA FRANKLIN	
	BMG TV / WSM 927470542 ......**15**	9

[1] Aretha Franklin and George Benson [2] Eurythmics and Aretha Franklin
[3] Aretha Franklin and George Michael [4] Aretha Franklin and Elton John
[5] Aretha Franklin and Whitney Houston

*'Think' on East West is a re-recording. It was the flip side of 'Everybody Needs
Somebody to Love' by The Blues Brothers and was listed for the first two weeks of
that record's run*

Erma FRANKLIN US, female vocalist,
b. 13 Mar 1938, d. 7 Sep 2002 (Singles: 10 Weeks)

		pos/wks
10 Oct 92 ●	(TAKE A LITTLE) PIECE OF MY HEART *Epic 6583847* **9**	10

Rodney FRANKLIN US, male instrumentalist –
piano (Singles: 9 Weeks, Albums: 2 Weeks)

		pos/wks
19 Apr 80 ●	THE GROOVE *CBS 8529* **7**	9
24 May 80	YOU'LL NEVER KNOW *CBS 83812* **64**	2

Chevelle FRANKLYN / BEENIE MAN
Jamaica, female / male vocalists (Singles: 1 Week)

		pos/wks
20 Sep 97	DANCEHALL QUEEN *Island Jamaica IJCD 2018* **70**	1

FRANTIC FIVE See Don LANG

FRANTIQUE US, female vocal group (Singles: 12 Weeks)

		pos/wks
11 Aug 79 ●	STRUT YOUR FUNKY STUFF *Philadelphia Int. PIR 7728* **10**	12

FRANZ FERDINAND UK, male vocal / instrumental
group (Singles: 20 Weeks, Albums: 45 Weeks)

		pos/wks
20 Sep 03	DARTS OF PLEASURE *Domino RUG 164CD* **44**	1
21 Feb 04 ●	TAKE ME OUT *Domino RUG 172CD* **3**	9
1 May 04 ●	MATINEE *Domino RUG 176CD* **8**	6
28 Aug 04	MICHAEL *Domino RUG 184CD1* **17**	4
21 Feb 04 ●	FRANZ FERDINAND *Domino W1GCD 136X* **3**	45+

Elizabeth FRASER See COCTEAU TWINS; FUTURE SOUND OF LONDON;
Ian McCULLOCH; MASSIVE ATTACK

Wendy FRASER See Patrick SWAYZE featuring Wendy FRASER

FRASH
UK, male vocal / instrumental group (Singles: 1 Week) pos/wks

18 Feb 95	HERE I GO AGAIN *PWL International FLIPCD 1*	69	1

FRAZIER CHORUS
UK, male / female vocal / instrumental group (Singles: 14 Weeks, Albums: 2 Weeks) pos/wks

4 Feb 89	DREAM KITCHEN *Virgin VS 1145*	57	3
15 Apr 89	TYPICAL! *Virgin VS 1174*	53	2
15 Jul 89	SLOPPY HEART *Virgin VS 1192*	73	1
9 Jun 90	CLOUD 8 *Virgin VS 1252*	52	3
25 Aug 90	NOTHING *Virgin VS 1284*	51	3
16 Feb 91	WALKING ON AIR *Virgin VS 1330*	60	2
20 May 89	SUE *Virgin V 2578*	56	1
16 Mar 91	RAY *Virgin VFC 2654*	66	1

FREAK OF NATURE
US / Denmark, male vocal / instrumental group (Albums: 1 Week) pos/wks

1 Oct 94	GATHERING OF FREAKS *Music for Nations CDMFN 169*	66	1

FREAKPOWER
(see also Norman COOK; FATBOY SLIM; The HOUSE-MARTINS; MIGHTY DUB KATZ; PIZZAMAN; URBAN ALL STARS) UK / Canada, male vocal / instrumental group (Singles: 20 Week, Albums: 5 Weeks) pos/wks

16 Oct 93	TURN ON TUNE IN COP OUT *Fourth & Broadway BRCD 284* [1]	29	5
26 Feb 94	RUSH *Fourth & Broadway BRCD 291*	62	2
18 Mar 95 ●	TURN ON TUNE IN COP OUT (re-issue) *Fourth & Broadway BRCD 317*	3	9
8 Jun 96	NEW DIRECTION *Fourth & Broadway BRCD 331*	60	1
9 May 98	NO WAY *Deconstruction 74321578572*	29	3
15 Apr 95	DRIVE-THRU BOOTY *Fourth & Broadway BRCDX 606* [1]	11	5

[1] Freak Power [1] Freak Power

FREAKY REALISTIC
UK / Japan, male / female vocal / instrumental group (Singles: 3 Weeks) pos/wks

3 Apr 93	KOOCHIE RYDER *Frealism FRECD 2*	52	2
3 Jul 93	LEONARD NIMOY *Frealism FRECD 3*	71	1

FREAKYMAN
Holland, male producer – Andre Van Den Bosch (Singles: 1 Week) pos/wks

27 Sep 97	DISCOBUG '97 *Xtravaganza 0091285 EXT*	68	1

Stan FREBERG
US, male vocalist / comedian (Singles: 5 Weeks) pos/wks

19 Nov 54	SH-BOOM *Capitol CL 14187* [1]	15	2
27 Jul 56	ROCK ISLAND LINE / HEARTBREAK HOTEL (re) *Capitol CL 14608* [2]	24	2
12 May 60	THE OLD PAYOLA ROLL BLUES *Capitol CL 15122* [3]	40	1

[1] Stan Freberg with the Toads [2] Stan Freberg and his Sniffle Group [3] Stan Freberg with Jesse White

FRED & ROXY
UK, female vocal duo – Phaedra and Roxanna Aslami (Singles: 2 Weeks) pos/wks

5 Feb 00	SOMETHING FOR THE WEEKEND *Echo ECSCD 81*	36	2

John FRED and the PLAYBOY BAND
US, male vocal / instrumental group – John Fred Gourrier (Singles: 12 Weeks) pos/wks

3 Jan 68 ●	JUDY IN DISGUISE (WITH GLASSES) *Pye International 7N 25442* ▲	3	12

FREDDIE and the DREAMERS
UK, male vocal / instrumental group – leader Freddie Garrity (Singles: 85 Weeks, Albums: 26 Weeks) pos/wks

9 May 63 ●	IF YOU GOTTA MAKE A FOOL OF SOMEBODY *Columbia DB 7032*	3	14
8 Aug 63 ●	I'M TELLING YOU NOW *Columbia DB 7086* ▲	2	11
7 Nov 63 ●	YOU WERE MADE FOR ME *Columbia DB 7147*	3	15
20 Feb 64	OVER YOU *Columbia DB 7214*	13	11
14 May 64	I LOVE YOU BABY *Columbia DB 7286*	16	8
16 Jul 64	JUST FOR YOU *Columbia DB 7322*	41	3
5 Nov 64 ●	I UNDERSTAND *Columbia DB 7381*	5	15
22 Apr 65	A LITTLE YOU *Columbia DB 7526*	26	5
4 Nov 65	THOU SHALT NOT STEAL *Columbia DB 7720*	44	3
9 Nov 63 ●	FREDDIE AND THE DREAMERS *Columbia 33SX 1577*	4	26

Dee FREDRIX
UK, female vocalist (Singles: 5 Weeks) pos/wks

27 Feb 93	AND SO I WILL WAIT FOR YOU *East West YZ 725CD*	56	4
3 Jul 93	DIRTY MONEY *East West YZ 750CD*	74	1

FREE
(see also BAD COMPANY) UK, male vocal / instrumental group – leader Paul Rodgers (Singles: 75 Weeks, Albums: 63 Weeks) pos/wks

6 Jun 70 ●	ALL RIGHT NOW (re) *Island WIP 6082*	2	25
1 May 71 ●	MY BROTHER JAKE *Island WIP 6100*	4	11
27 May 72	LITTLE BIT OF LOVE *Island WIP 6129*	13	10
13 Jan 73 ●	WISHING WELL *Island WIP 6146*	7	10
18 Feb 78	FREE (EP) (re) *Island IEP 6*	11	10
9 Feb 91	ALL RIGHT NOW (re-mix) *Island IS 486*	8	9
11 Jul 70 ●	FIRE AND WATER *Island ILPS 9120*	2	18
23 Jan 71	HIGHWAY *Island ILPS 9138*	41	2
26 Jun 71 ●	FREE LIVE! *Island ILPS 9160*	4	12
17 Jun 72 ●	FREE AT LAST *Island ILPS 9192*	9	9
3 Feb 73 ●	HEARTBREAKER *Island ILPS 9217*	9	7
16 Mar 74 ●	THE FREE STORY *Island ISLD 4*	2	6
2 Mar 91 ●	THE BEST OF FREE – ALL RIGHT NOW *Island ILPTV 2*	9	9

'All Right Now' re-entry peaked at No.15 in Jul 1973 and the 'Free' (EP) re-entered in Oct 1982, peaking at No.57. Tracks on the Free (EP): All Right Now (long version) / My Brother Jake (re-issue) / Wishing Well (re-issue)

FREE See Wyclef JEAN; Pras MICHEL; QUEEN; QUEEN LATIFAH

The FREE ASSOCIATION
(see also DAVID HOLMES) UK, male / female vocal / instrumental group (Singles: 2 Weeks) pos/wks

12 Apr 03	EVERYBODY KNOWS *Ramp RAMP 001CDS*	74	1
13 Sep 03	SUGARMAN *13 Amp 9809471*	53	1

FREE SPIRIT
UK, male / female vocal duo (Singles: 1 Week) pos/wks

13 May 95	NO MORE RAINY DAYS *Columbia 6612822*	68	1

FREE THE SPIRIT
UK, male instrumental duo – Nick Magnus and Rono Tse (Albums: 42 Weeks) pos/wks

4 Feb 95 ●	PAN PIPE MOODS *PolyGram TV 5271972*	2	26
4 Nov 95	PAN PIPE MOODS TWO *PolyGram TV 5293952*	18	11
25 May 96	PAN PIPE MOODS IN PARADISE *PolyGram TV 5319612*	26	5

FREEEZ
UK, male vocal / instrumental group (Singles: 48 Weeks, Albums: 18 Weeks) pos/wks

7 Jun 80	KEEP IN TOUCH *Calibre CAB 103*	49	3
7 Feb 81 ●	SOUTHERN FREEZ *Beggars Banquet BEG 51* [1]	8	11
18 Apr 81	FLYING HIGH *Beggars Banquet BEG 55*	35	5
18 Jun 83 ●	I.O.U. *Beggars Banquet BEG 96*	2	15
1 Oct 83	POP GOES MY LOVE *Beggars Banquet BEG 98*	26	6
17 Jan 87	I.O.U. (re-mix) *Citybeat CBE 709* [2]	23	6
30 May 87	SOUTHERN FREEEZ (re-mix) *Total Control TOCO 14* [1]	63	2
7 Feb 81	SOUTHERN FREEEZ *Beggars Banquet BEGA 22*	17	15
22 Oct 83	GONNA GET YOU *Beggars Banquet BEGA 48*	46	3

[1] Freeez featuring Ingrid Mansfield Allman [2] Freeez featuring John Rocca

FREEFALL featuring Jan JOHNSTON
UK / Australia, male DJ / production duo – Alan Bremner and Anthony Pappalardo and female vocalist (Singles: 5 Weeks) pos/wks

28 Nov 98	SKYDIVE *Stress CDSTR 89* [1]	75	1
22 Jul 00	SKYDIVE (re-mix) *Renaissance Recordings RENCDS 002* [1]	43	2
8 Sep 01	SKYDIVE (I FEEL WONDERFUL) (2nd re-mix) *Incentive CENT 22CDS* [1]	35	2

[1] Freefall featuring Jan Johnston

FREEFALL featuring PSYCHOTROPIC
UK / US, male instrumental / production group (Singles: 1 Week) pos/wks

27 Jul 91	FEEL SURREAL *ffrr FX 160*	63	1

FREEHOLD JUNIOR SCHOOL See Fogwell FLAX and the ANKLEBITERS from FREEHOLD JUNIOR SCHOOL

FREELAND
UK / Chile, male / female production / vocal / instrumental group (Singles: 3 Weeks) pos/wks

13 Sep 03	WE WANT YOUR SOUL *Maximise Profit FREECDS 01*	35	2
17 Feb 04	SUPERNATURAL THING *Marine Parade MAPACDS 024*	65	1

Claire FREELAND
UK, female vocalist (Singles: 1 Week)   pos/wks

| 10 Jul 01 | | FREE *Statuesque CDSTATU 1* .... | 44 | 1 |

FREESTYLERS UK, male instrumental /
vocal group (Singles: 10 Weeks, Albums: 3 Weeks)   pos/wks

7 Feb 98		**B-BOY STANCE** *Freskanova FND 7* [1]	23	3
14 Nov 98		**WARNING** *Freskanova FND 14* [2]	68	1
24 Jul 99		**HERE WE GO** *Freskanova FND 19*	45	1
20 Mar 04		**GET A LIFE** *Against the Grain ATG 008R*	66	1
26 Jun 04		**PUSH UP** *Against the Grain ATG 009CD*	22	4
15 Aug 98		**WE ROCK HARD** *Freskanova FNTCD 4*	33	3

[1] Freestylers featuring Tenor Fly [2] Freestylers featuring Navigator

FREEWAY See Cassius HENRY

FREHLEY'S COMET (see also KISS)
US, male vocal / instrumental group (Albums: 1 Week)   pos/wks

| 18 Jun 88 | | **SECOND SIGHTING** *Atlantic 7818621* .... | 79 | 1 |

FREIHEIT
Germany, male vocal / instrumental group (Singles: 9 Weeks)   pos/wks

| 17 Dec 88 | | **KEEPING THE DREAM ALIVE** *CBS 6529897* .... | 14 | 9 |

Deborah FRENCH See E-LUSTRIOUS

Nicki FRENCH UK, female vocalist (Singles: 18 Weeks)   pos/wks

15 Oct 94	●	**TOTAL ECLIPSE OF THE HEART** (re) *Bags of Fun BAGSCD 1* ..	5	13
22 Apr 95		**FOR ALL WE KNOW** *Bags of Fun BAGSCD 4*	42	2
15 Jul 95		**DID YOU EVER REALLY LOVE ME** *Love This LUVTHISCD 2*	55	1
27 May 00		**DON'T PLAY THAT SONG AGAIN** *RCA 74321764572*	34	2

'Total Eclipse of the Heart' peaked at No.5 on re-entry in Jan 1995

FRENCH AFFAIR
France, male production duo and female vocalist (Singles: 3 Weeks) pos/wks

| 16 Sep 00 | | **MY HEART GOES BOOM** *Arista 74321780562* .... | 44 | 3 |

Freddy FRESH
US, male producer – Frederick Schmid (Singles: 3 Weeks)   pos/wks

| 1 May 99 | | **BADDER BADDER SCHWING** *Eye Q EYEUK 040CD* [1] .... | 34 | 2 |
| 31 Jul 99 | | **WHAT IT IS** *Eye Q EYEUK 043CD* .... | 63 | 1 |

[1] Freddy Fresh featuring Fatboy Slim

FRESH BC (see also BAD COMPANY; DJ FRESH)
UK, male production group (Singles: 3 Weeks)   pos/wks

25 Oct 03		**SIGNAL / BIG LOVE** *Ram RAMM 46*	58	1
18 Sep 04		**COLOSSUS / HOODED** *Ram RAMM 51*	74	1
25 Dec 04		**CAPTURE THE FLAG** *Ramm RAMM 53*	70	1+

Doug E FRESH and the GET FRESH CREW
US, male rapper – Douglas Davis and DJ group (Singles: 11 Weeks) pos/wks

| 9 Nov 85 | ● | **THE SHOW** *Cooltempo COOL 116* .... | 7 | 11 |

FRESH 4 featuring Lizz E UK, male DJ /
production group and female vocalist (Singles: 9 Weeks)   pos/wks

| 7 Oct 89 | ● | **WISHING ON A STAR** *10 TEN 287* .... | 10 | 9 |

FRESH PRINCE See DJ JAZZY JEFF and the FRESH PRINCE

The FRESHIES
UK, male vocal / instrumental group (Singles: 3 Weeks)   pos/wks

| 14 Feb 81 | | **I'M IN LOVE WITH THE GIRL ON A CERTAIN MANCHESTER MEGASTORE CHECKOUT DESK** *MCA 670* .... | 54 | 3 |

Matt FRETTON UK, male vocalist (Singles: 5 Weeks)   pos/wks

| 11 Jun 83 | | **IT'S SO HIGH** *Chrysalis MATT 1* .... | 50 | 5 |

FREUR UK, male vocal / instrumental group (Singles: 4 Weeks) pos/wks

| 23 Apr 83 | | **DOOT DOOT** *CBS A 3141* .... | 59 | 4 |

Glenn FREY (see also The EAGLES)
US, male vocalist (Singles: 20 Weeks, Albums: 9 Weeks)   pos/wks

2 Mar 85		**THE HEAT IS ON** *MCA MCA 941*	12	12
22 Jun 85		**SMUGGLER'S BLUES** *BBC RESL 170*	22	8
6 Jul 85		**THE ALLNIGHTER** *MCA MCF 3277*	31	9

FRIDA (see also ABBA) Norway, female vocalist –
Anni-Frid Lyngstad (Singles: 12 Weeks, Albums: 8 Weeks)   pos/wks

21 Aug 82		**I KNOW THERE'S SOMETHING GOING ON** *Epic EPC A 2603*	43	7
17 Dec 83		**TIME** *Epic A 3983* [1]	45	5
18 Sep 82		**SOMETHING'S GOING ON** *Epic EPC 85966*	18	7
20 Oct 84		**SHINE** *Epic EPC 26178*	67	1

[1] Frida and B A Robertson

Gavin FRIDAY See BONO

Ralph FRIDGE
Germany, male producer – Ralf Fritsch (Singles: 4 Weeks)   pos/wks

| 24 Apr 99 | | **PARADISE** *Additive 12AD 036* .... | 68 | 1 |
| 8 Apr 00 | | **ANGEL** *Incentive CENT 6CDS* .... | 20 | 3 |

Dean FRIEDMAN US, male vocalist / instrumentalist –
keyboards (Singles: 22 Weeks, Albums: 14 Weeks)   pos/wks

3 Jun 78		**WOMAN OF MINE** *Lifesong LS 401*	52	5
23 Sep 78	●	**LUCKY STARS** *Lifesong LS 402*	3	10
18 Nov 78		**LYDIA** *Lifesong LS 403*	31	7
21 Oct 78		**WELL WELL SAID THE ROCKING CHAIR** *Lifesong LSLP 6019* ..	21	14

'Lucky Stars' features uncredited vocalist Denise Marsa

FRIENDS AGAIN
UK, male vocal / instrumental group (Singles: 3 Weeks)   pos/wks

| 4 Aug 84 | | **THE FRIENDS AGAIN EP** *Mercury FA 1* .... | 59 | 3 |

Tracks on The Friends Again EP: Lullaby on Board / Wand You Wave / Thank You for Being an Angel

FRIENDS OF MATTHEW
UK, male / female vocal / instrumental group (Singles: 1 Week) pos/wks

| 10 Jul 99 | | **OUT THERE** *Serious SERR 007CD* .... | 61 | 1 |

FRIGID VINEGAR UK, male rap / production duo (Singles: 1 Week) pos/wks

| 21 Aug 99 | | **DOGMONAUT 2000 (IS THERE ANYONE OUT THERE?)** *Gut CDGUT 27* .... | 53 | 1 |

FRIJID PINK
US, male vocal / instrumental group (Singles: 16 Weeks)   pos/wks

| 28 Mar 70 | ● | **THE HOUSE OF THE RISING SUN** *Deram DMR 288* .... | 4 | 16 |

Robert FRIPP (see also KING CRIMSON)
UK, male instrumentalist (Albums: 3 Weeks)   pos/wks

| 12 May 79 | | **EXPOSURE** *Polydor EGLP 101* .... | 71 | 1 |
| 17 Jul 93 | | **THE FIRST DAY** *Virgin CDVX 2712* [1] .... | 21 | 2 |

[1] David Sylvian and Robert Fripp

Jane FROMAN US, female vocalist – Ellen Froman,
b. 10 Nov 1907, d. 22 Apr 1980 (Singles: 4 Weeks)   pos/wks

| 17 Jun 55 | | **I WONDER** *Capitol CL 14254* .... | 14 | 4 |

FRONT 242 Belgium / US, male vocal /
instrumental group (Singles: 1 Week, Albums: 3 Weeks)   pos/wks

1 May 93		**RELIGION** *RRE RRE 106CD*	46	1
2 Feb 91		**TYRANNY FOR YOU** *RRE RRE 011*	49	1
22 May 93		**06:21:03: 11 UP EVIL** *RRE RRE 021CD*	44	1
4 Sep 93		**05:22:09: 12 OFF** *RRE RRE 022CD*	46	1

FROU FROU
UK, male / female production / vocal duo (Singles: 1 Week)   pos/wks

| 6 Jul 02 | | **BREATHE IN** *Island CID 799* .... | 44 | 1 |

John FRUSCIANTE
US, male vocalist / instrumentalist (Albums: 1 Week)   pos/wks

| 13 Mar 04 | | **SHADOWS COLLIDE WITH PEOPLE** *Warner Bros. 9362486602* | 53 | 1 |

Singles re-entries are listed as (re), (2re), (3re).... which signifies that the hit re-entered the chart once, twice or three times...

Christian FRY *UK, male vocalist (Singles: 3 Weeks)*

		pos/wks
14 Nov 98	YOU GOT ME *Mushroom MUSH 33CDS* 45	2
3 Apr 99	WON'T YOU SAY *Mushroom MUSH 46CDS* 48	1

FUGAZI *US, male vocal / instrumental group (Singles: 1 Week, Albums: 7 Weeks)*

		pos/wks
20 Oct 01	FURNITURE *Dischord DIS 129CD* 61	1
21 Sep 91	STEADY DIET OF NOTHING *Dischord DISCHORD 60* 63	1
19 Jun 93	IN ON THE KILLTAKER *Dischord DIS 70CD* 24	2
13 May 95	RED MEDICINE *Dischord DIS 90CD* 18	2
25 Apr 98	END HITS *Dischord DIS 110CD* 47	1
20 Oct 01	THE ARGUMENT *Dischord DIS 130CD* 63	1

FUGEES
US / Haiti, male / female vocal / rap / production trio – Lauryn Hill, Wyclef Jean and Pras Michel (Singles: 65 Weeks, Albums: 72 Weeks)

		pos/wks
6 Apr 96	FU-GEE-LA *Columbia 6630662* 21	5
8 Jun 96	★ KILLING ME SOFTLY *Columbia 6633435* ◆ ■ 1	20
14 Sep 96	★ READY OR NOT *Columbia 6637215* 1	12
30 Nov 96	● NO WOMAN, NO CRY *Columbia 6639925* 2	9
15 Mar 97	● RUMBLE IN THE JUNGLE *Mercury 5740692* 3	8
28 Jun 97	WE TRYING TO STAY ALIVE *Columbia 6648815* [1] 13	4
6 Sep 97	THE SWEETEST THING *Columbia 6649785* [2] 18	5
27 Sep 97	GUANTANAMERA *Columbia 6650852* [1] 25	2
30 Mar 96	● THE SCORE *Columbia 4835492* ▲ 2	70
7 Dec 96	BOOTLEG VERSIONS *Columbia 4868242* 55	2

[1] Wyclef Jean and the Refugee Allstars [2] Refugee Camp Allstars featuring Lauryn Hill

Group billed as The Fugees (Refugee Camp) on both albums

FULL CIRCLE *US, male vocal group (Singles: 5 Weeks)*

		pos/wks
7 Mar 87	WORKIN' UP A SWEAT *EMI America EA 229* 41	5

FULL FORCE
US, male vocal / instrumental group (Singles: 37 Weeks)

		pos/wks
4 May 85	I WONDER IF I TAKE YOU HOME (re) *CBS A 6057* [1] 12	17
21 Dec 85	● ALICE I WANT YOU JUST FOR ME *CBS A 6640* 9	11
21 May 88	NAUGHTY GIRLS (NEED LOVE TOO) *Jive FOXY 9* 31	5
4 Jun 88	I'M REAL *Scotti Brothers JSB 1* [2] 31	4

[1] Lisa Lisa and Cult Jam with Full Force [2] James Brown featuring Full Force

FULL INTENTION (see also HUSTLERS CONVENTION
featuring Dave LAUDAT and Ondrea DUVERNEY; SHENA;
DISCO TEX presents CLOUDBURST; Michael GRAY)
UK, male instrumental / production group (Singles: 8 Weeks)

		pos/wks
6 Apr 96	AMERICA (I LOVE AMERICA) *Stress CDSTR 56* 32	2
10 Aug 96	UPTOWN DOWNTOWN *Stress CDSTR 67* 61	1
26 Jul 97	SHAKE YOUR BODY (DOWN TO THE GROUND) *Sugar Daddy CDSTR 82* 34	2
22 Nov 97	AMERICA (I LOVE AMERICA) (re-mix) *Sugar Daddy CDSTRX 56* 56	1
6 Jun 98	YOU ARE SOMEBODY *Sugar Daddy CDSD 001* 75	1
1 Sep 01	I'LL BE WAITING *Rulin RULIN 17CDS* [1] 44	1

[1] Full Intention presents Shena

FULL METAL RACKETS *See John McENROE and Pat CASH with the FULL METAL RACKETS*

FULL MONTY ALLSTARS featuring TJ DAVIS *UK, male vocal / instrumental group and female vocalist (Singles: 1 Week)*

		pos/wks
27 Jul 96	BRILLIANT FEELING *Arista 74321380902* 72	1

Bobby FULLER FOUR *US, male vocal / instrumental group – leader b. 22 Oct 1943, d. 18 Jul 1966 (Singles: 4 Weeks)*

		pos/wks
14 Apr 66	I FOUGHT THE LAW *London HL 10030* 33	4

FUN BOY THREE (see also The COLOURFIELD; The SPECIALS; VEGAS)
UK, male vocal / instrumental trio – leader Terry Hall (Singles: 70 Weeks, Albums: 40 Weeks)

		pos/wks
7 Nov 81	THE LUNATICS (HAVE TAKEN OVER THE ASYLUM) *Chrysalis CHS 2563* 20	12
13 Feb 82	● IT AIN'T WHAT YOU DO IT'S THE WAY THAT YOU DO IT *Chrysalis CHS 2570* [1] 4	10
10 Apr 82	● REALLY SAYING SOMETHING *Deram NANA 1* [2] 5	10
8 May 82	THE TELEPHONE ALWAYS RINGS *Chrysalis CHS 2609* 17	9
31 Jul 82	SUMMERTIME *Chrysalis CHS 2629* 18	8
15 Jan 83	THE MORE I SEE (THE LESS I BELIEVE) *Chrysalis CHS 2664* 68	1
5 Feb 83	● TUNNEL OF LOVE *Chrysalis CHS 2678* 10	10
30 Apr 83	● OUR LIPS ARE SEALED *Chrysalis FUNB 1* 7	10
20 Mar 82	● THE FUNBOY THREE *Chrysalis CHR 1383* 7	20
19 Feb 83	WAITING *Chrysalis CHR 1417* 14	20

[1] Fun Boy Three and Bananarama [2] Bananarama with Fun Boy Three

FUN DA MENTAL *UK, male rap group (Albums: 1 Week)*

		pos/wks
25 Jun 94	SEIZE THE TIME *Nation NATCD 33* 74	1

FUN LOVIN' CRIMINALS `478` `Top 500`
Hip-hop and funk-blending trio formed in New York City in 1993; Huey Morgan (v/g), Brian 'Fast' Leiser (b/k) and Steve Borgovini (d). Act, whose catalogue includes the Pulp Fiction sampling 'Scooby Snacks' and Barry White tribute 'Love Unlimited', are more popular in the UK than in their homeland (Singles: 32 Weeks, Albums: 120 Weeks)

		pos/wks
8 Jun 96	THE GRAVE AND THE CONSTANT *Chrysalis CDCHS 5031* 72	1
17 Aug 96	SCOOBY SNACKS *Chrysalis CDCHS 5034* 22	3
16 Nov 96	THE FUN LOVIN' CRIMINAL *Chrysalis CDCHS 5040* 26	3
29 Mar 97	KING OF NEW YORK *Chrysalis CDCHS 5049* 28	3
5 Jul 97	I'M NOT IN LOVE / SCOOBY SNACKS *Chrysalis CDCHS 5060* 12	5
15 Aug 98	LOVE UNLIMITED *Chrysalis CDCHS 5096* 18	4
17 Oct 98	BIG NIGHT OUT *Chrysalis CDCHSS 5101* 29	2
8 May 99	KOREAN BODEGA *Chrysalis CDCHS 5108* 15	3
17 Feb 01	● LOCO *Chrysalis CDCHSS 5121* 5	6
1 Sep 01	BUMP / RUN DADDY RUN *Chrysalis CDCHSS 5128* 50	1
13 Sep 03	TOO HOT *Sanctuary SANXD 205* 61	1
13 Jul 96	● COME FIND YOURSELF *Chrysalis CDCHR 6113* 7	71
5 Sep 98	● 100% COLOMBIAN *Chrysalis 4970562* 3	26
11 Dec 99	MIMOSA *Chrysalis 5234592* 37	9
10 Mar 01	● LOCO *Chrysalis 5314712* 5	6
3 Aug 02	BAG OF HITS – 15 INTERGLOBAL CHARTSTOPPERS *Chrysalis 5399542* 11	6
20 Sep 03	WELCOME TO POPPY'S *Sanctuary SANCD 187* 20	2

FUNERAL FOR A FRIEND *UK, male vocal / instrumental group (Singles: 8 Weeks, Albums: 3 Weeks)*

		pos/wks
9 Aug 03	JUNEAU *Infectious EW 269CD1* 19	3
18 Oct 03	SHE DROVE ME TO DAYTIME TELEVISION *Infectious / East West EW 274CD1* 20	2
14 Feb 04	ESCAPE ARTISTS NEVER DIE *Infectious EW 283CD* 19	3
25 Oct 03	CASUALLY DRESSED AND DEEP IN CONVERSATION *Infectious 2564609472* 12	3

Farley 'Jackmaster' FUNK
US, male producer – Farley Williams (Singles: 16 Weeks)

		pos/wks
23 Aug 86	● LOVE CAN'T TURN AROUND *DJ International LON 105* 10	12
11 Feb 89	AS ALWAYS *Champion CHAMP 90* [1] 49	2
14 Dec 96	LOVE CAN'T TURN AROUND *4 Liberty LIBTCD 27* [2] 40	2

[1] Farley 'Jackmaster' Funk presents Ricky Dillard [2] Farley 'Jackmaster' Funk with Darryl Pandy

'Love Can't Turn Around' in 1996 is a re-recording

FUNK D'VOID
Sweden, male producer – Lars Sandberg (Singles: 2 Weeks)

		pos/wks
20 Oct 01	DIABLA *Soma SOMA 112* 70	1
31 Jan 04	EMOTIONAL CONTENT *Soma SOMA 139* 74	1

FUNK FEDERATION *See Arlene PHILLIPS*

FUNK JUNKEEZ (see also EL MARIACHI)
US, male DJ / producer – Roger Sanchez (Singles: 1 Week)

		pos/wks
21 Feb 98	GOT FUNK *Evocative EVOKE 1CDS* 57	1

The FUNK MASTERS *UK, male / female vocal / instrumental group (Singles: 12 Weeks)*

		pos/wks
18 Jun 83	● IT'S OVER *Master Funk Records 7MP 004* 8	12

Features Gonzales on horns and uncredited vocals by Juliet Roberts

---

Obituaries

These are the hit-makers that passed away in 2004.

12 Jan **RANDY VANWARMER**
22 Jan **BILLY MAY**
 3 Feb **GENE HUGHES** (lead vocalist The CASINOS)
16 Feb **DORIS TROY**
21 Feb **LES GRAY** (lead vocalist MUD)
23 Feb **DON CORNELL**
 9 Mar **RUBY WRIGHT**
13 Mar **MAX HARRIS**
14 Mar **JOHNNY BRISTOL**
27 Mar **JAN BERRY** (JAN AND DEAN)
 1 Mar **PAUL ATKINSON** (guitarist The ZOMBIES)
 6 Apr **NIKI SULLIVAN** (guitarist The CRICKETS)
11 May **JOHN WHITEHEAD** (McFADDEN AND WHITEHEAD)
10 Jun **RAY CHARLES**
 6 Jul **SYREETA** (WRIGHT)
22 Jul **SACHA DISTEL**
 6 Aug **RICK JAMES**
19 Aug **ELMER BERNSTEIN**
26 Aug **LAURA BRANIGAN**
31 Aug **CARL WAYNE** (lead vocalist The MOVE)
15 Sep **JOHNNY RAMONE** (guitarist The RAMONES)
16 Sep **IZORA RHODES ARMSTEAD** (The WEATHER GIRLS)
19 Sep **SKEETER DAVIS**
13 Nov **OL' DIRTY BASTARD**

↓ JOHN PEEL (1939-2004) NEVER ACHIEVED IMMORTALITY AS A RECORDING ARTIST HIMSELF, BUT HE WAS INSTRUMENTAL IN ENCOURAGING SO MANY BUDDING MUSICIANS, WRITERS AND VOCALISTS TO HAVE A GO, MAKE THAT DEMO AND, IN SOME CASES, END UP WITH A RECORDING CONTRACT. A GUSHING TRIBUTE PROBABLY WOULDN'T HAVE APPEALED TO JOHN, SO LET'S GO NO FURTHER THAN TO SAY HE WAS A NICE MAN WHO LISTENED TO MORE MUSIC THAN PROBABLY ANY OTHER HUMAN BEING AND PRESENTED SOME OF IT TO US ON THE RADIO.

FUNKADELIC US, male vocal / instrumental group –
leader George Clinton (Singles: 13 Weeks, Albums: 5 Weeks) pos/wks

9 Dec 78 ●	ONE NATION UNDER A GROOVE (PART 1)		
	Warner Bros. K 17246	9	12
21 Aug 99	MOTHERSHIP RECONNECTION Virgin DINSD 185 [1]	55	1
23 Dec 78	ONE NATION UNDER A GROOVE Warner Bros. K 56539	56	5

[1] Scott Grooves featuring Parliament / Funkadelic

FUNKAPOLITAN
UK, male vocal / instrumental group (Singles: 7 Weeks) pos/wks

22 Aug 81	AS TIME GOES BY London LON 001	41	7

FUNKDOOBIEST
US, male rap group (Singles: 6 Weeks, Albums: 1 Week) pos/wks

11 Dec 93	WOPBABALUBOP Immortal 6597112	37	4
5 Mar 94	BOW WOW WOW Immortal 6594052	34	2
15 Jul 95	BROTHAS DOOBIE Epic 4783812	62	1

FUNKSTAR DE LUXE Denmark, male producer /
instrumentalist – Matt Ottesen (Singles: 18 Weeks) pos/wks

25 Sep 99 ●	SUN IS SHINING Club Tools / Edel 0066895 CLU [1]	3	10
22 Jan 00	RAINBOW COUNTRY Club Tools 0067225 CLU [1]	11	6
13 May 00	WALKIN IN THE NAME Club Tools 0067375 CLU [2]	42	1
25 Nov 00	PULL UP TO THE BUMPER Club Tools 0120375 CLU [3]	60	1

[1] Bob Marley vs Funkstar De Luxe [2] Funkstar De Luxe vs Terry Maxx [3] Grace Jones vs Funkstar De Luxe

FUNKY BOYS See Linda CARR

FUNKY BUNCH See MARKY MARK and the FUNKY BUNCH

FUNKY CHOAD featuring Nick SKITZ Australia / Italy,
male production duo and Australia, male vocalist (Singles: 1 Week) pos/wks

29 Aug 98	THE ULTIMATE ffrr FCD 341	51	1

FUNKY GREEN DOGS (see also FOG)
US, male / female vocal / production trio – Oscar
Gaetan, Ralph Falcon and Tamara (Singles: 6 Weeks) pos/wks

12 Apr 97	FIRED UP! Twisted UK TWCD 10016	17	3
28 Jun 97	THE WAY Twisted UK TWCD 10026	43	1
20 Jun 98	UNTIL THE DAY Twisted UK TWCD 10034	75	1
27 Feb 99	BODY Twisted UK TWCD 110041	46	1

FUNKY JUNCTION See KC FLIGHTT

FUNKY POETS US, male vocal group (Singles: 1 Week) pos/wks

7 May 94	BORN IN THE GHETTO Epic 6603522	72	1

FUNKY WORM
UK, male / female vocal / instrumental group (Singles: 14 Weeks) pos/wks

30 Jul 88	HUSTLE! (TO THE MUSIC ...) Fon FON 15	13	8
26 Nov 88	THE SPELL! Fon FON 16	61	3
20 May 89	U + ME = LOVE Fon FON 19	46	3

The FUREYS with Davey ARTHUR
Ireland, male vocal duo – Finbar and Eddie Fury and UK,
male vocalist (Singles: 14 Weeks, Albums: 38 Weeks) pos/wks

10 Oct 81	WHEN YOU WERE SWEET SIXTEEN Ritz RITZ 003	14	11
3 Apr 82	I WILL LOVE YOU (EV'RY TIME WHEN WE ARE GONE)		
	Ritz RITZ 012 [1]	54	3
8 May 82	WHEN YOU WERE SWEET SIXTEEN Ritz RITZLP 0004	99	1
10 Nov 84	GOLDEN DAYS K-Tel ONE 1283	17	19
26 Oct 85	AT THE END OF THE DAY K-Tel ONE 1310	35	11
21 Nov 87	FUREYS FINEST Telstar HSTAR 2311	65	7

[1] The Fureys

FURIOUS FIVE See GRANDMASTER FLASH

FURNITURE
UK, male / female vocal / instrumental group (Singles: 10 Weeks) pos/wks

14 Jun 86	BRILLIANT MIND Stiff BUY 251	21	10

Nelly FURTADO
Canada, female vocalist (Singles: 52 Weeks, Albums: 61 Weeks) pos/wks

10 Mar 01 ●	I'M LIKE A BIRD Dreamworks 4509192	5	16
1 Sep 01 ●	TURN OFF THE LIGHT Dreamworks DRMDM 50891	4	10
19 Jan 02	... ON THE RADIO (REMEMBER THE DAYS) (re)		
	Dreamworks DRMDM 50856	18	6
20 Dec 03	POWERLESS (SAY WHAT YOU WANT) Dreamworks 4504645	13	10
27 Mar 04	TRY Dreamworks 4505113	15	7
24 Jul 04	FORÇA Dreamworks 9862823	40	3
24 Mar 01 ●	WHOA NELLY! Dreamworks 4502852	2	47
6 Dec 03	FOLKLORE Dreamworks / Polydor 4505089	11	14

Billy FURY 166 Top 500
Early British rock 'n' roll (and film) star, b. Ronald Wycherley, 17 Apr 1940,
Liverpool, UK, d. 28 Jan 1983. He has equalled The Beatles' record of 24 hits
in the 1960s, and spent 332 weeks on the chart but without a chart-topping
single or album. In 2003 a bronze statue of Fury was unveiled at the National
Museum of Liverpool Life (Singles: 281 Weeks, Albums: 51 Weeks) pos/wks

27 Feb 59	MAYBE TOMORROW (re) Decca F 11102	18	9
26 Jun 59	MARGO Decca F 11128	28	1
10 Mar 60 ●	COLETTE Decca F 11200	9	10
26 May 60	THAT'S LOVE Decca F 11237 [1]	19	11
22 Sep 60	WONDROUS PLACE Decca F 11267	25	9
19 Jan 61	A THOUSAND STARS Decca F 11311	14	10
27 Apr 61	DON'T WORRY Decca F 11334 [2]	40	2
11 May 61 ●	HALFWAY TO PARADISE Decca F 11349	3	23
7 Sep 61	JEALOUSY Decca F 11384	2	12
14 Dec 61 ●	I'D NEVER FIND ANOTHER YOU Decca F 11409	5	15
15 Mar 62	LETTER FULL OF TEARS Decca F 11437	32	6
3 May 62 ●	LAST NIGHT WAS MADE FOR LOVE Decca F 11458	4	16
19 Jul 62 ●	ONCE UPON A DREAM Decca F 11485	7	13
25 Oct 62	BECAUSE OF LOVE Decca F 11508	18	14
14 Feb 63 ●	LIKE I'VE NEVER BEEN GONE Decca F 11582	3	15
16 May 63 ●	WHEN WILL YOU SAY I LOVE YOU Decca F 11655	3	12
25 Jul 63 ●	IN SUMMER Decca F 11701	5	11
3 Oct 63	SOMEBODY ELSE'S GIRL Decca F 11744	18	7
2 Jan 64	DO YOU REALLY LOVE ME TOO? (FOOLS ERRAND)		
	Decca F 11792	13	10
30 Apr 64	I WILL Decca F 11888	14	12
23 Jul 64 ●	IT'S ONLY MAKE BELIEVE Decca F 11939	10	10
14 Jan 65	I'M LOST WITHOUT YOU Decca F 12048	16	10
22 Jul 65 ●	IN THOUGHTS OF YOU Decca F 12178	9	11
16 Sep 65	RUN TO MY LOVIN' ARMS Decca F 12230	25	7
10 Feb 66	I'LL NEVER QUITE GET OVER YOU Decca F 12325	35	5
4 Aug 66	GIVE ME YOUR WORD Decca F 12459	27	7
4 Sep 82	LOVE OR MONEY Polydor POSP 488	57	5
13 Nov 82	DEVIL OR ANGEL Polydor POSP 528	58	4
4 Jun 83	FORGET HIM Polydor POSP 558	59	4
4 Jun 60	THE SOUND OF FURY Decca LF 1329	18	2
23 Sep 61 ●	HALFWAY TO PARADISE Ace of Clubs ACL 1083	5	9
11 May 63	BILLY Decca LK 4533	6	21
26 Oct 63	WE WANT BILLY Decca LK 4548	14	2
19 Feb 83	THE BILLY FURY HIT PARADE Decca TAB 37	44	15
26 Mar 83	THE ONE AND ONLY BILLY FURY Polydor POLD 5069	54	2

[1] Billy Fury with The Four Jays [2] Billy Fury with The Four Kestrels

FUSE (see also PLASTIK MAN) Canada, male
instrumentalist – keyboards – Richie Hawtin (Albums: 1 Week) pos/wks

19 Jun 93	DIMENSION INTRUSION Warp WARPCD 12	63	1

FUSED Sweden, male instrumental /
production duo and female vocalist (Singles: 1 Week) pos/wks

20 Mar 99	THIS PARTY SUCKS! Columbia 6669302	64	1

FUTURE BREEZE (see also 4CLUBBERS) Germany, male production
duo – Markus Boehme and Martin Hensing (Singles: 11 Weeks) pos/wks

6 Sep 97	WHY DON'T YOU DANCE WITH ME AM:PM 5823312	50	1
20 Jan 01	SMILE Nebula NEBCD 014	67	1
13 Apr 02	TEMPLE OF DREAMS Ministry of Sound / DATA 31CDS	21	6
28 Dec 02	OCEAN OF ETERNITY Ministry of Sound / DATA 44CDS	46	3

FUTURE FORCE
UK / US, male / female vocal / instrumental duo (Singles: 1 Week) pos/wks

17 Aug 96	WHAT YOU WANT AM:PM 5816592	47	1

FUTURE SOUND OF LONDON (see also HUMANOID: AMORPHOUS
ANDROGYNOUS) *UK, male instrumental / production duo – Brian
Dougans and Gary Cobain (Singles: 25 Weeks, Albums: 10 Weeks)*   pos/wks

23 May 92	**PAPUA NEW GUINEA** *Jumpin' & Pumpin' TOT 17*	**22**	6
6 Nov 93	**CASCADE** *Virgin VSCDT 1478*	**27**	3
30 Jul 94	**EXPANDER** *Jumpin' & Pumpin' CDTOT 37*	**72**	1
13 Aug 94	**LIFEFORMS** *Virgin VSCDT 1484* [1]	**14**	3
27 May 95	**FAR-OUT SON OF LUNG AND THE RAMBLINGS**		
	OF A MADMAN *Virgin VSCDT 1540*	**22**	3
26 Oct 96	**MY KINGDOM** *Virgin VSCDT 1605*	**13**	3
12 Apr 97	**WE HAVE EXPLOSIVE** *Virgin VSCDX 1616*	**12**	3
29 Sep 01	**PAPUA NEW GUINEA 2001 (re-mix)**		
	Jumpin' & Pumpin' CDSTOT 44	**28**	3
18 Jul 92	**ACCELERATOR** *Jumpin' & Pumpin' CDTOT 2*	**75**	1
4 Jun 94	● **LIFEFORMS** *Virgin CDV 2722*	**6**	5
17 Dec 94	**ISDN** *Virgin CDV 2755*	**62**	1
17 Jun 95	**ISDN (REMIX)** *Virgin CDVX 2755*	**44**	1
9 Nov 96	**DEAD CITIES** *Virgin CDVX 2814*	**26**	2

[1] F.S.O.L.: vocals by Elizabeth Fraser

The FUTUREHEADS
UK, male vocal / instrumental group (Singles: 4 Weeks)   pos/wks

9 Aug 03	**FIRST DAY** *Fantastic Plastic FPS 036*	**58**	1
7 Aug 04	**DECENT DAYS AND NIGHTS** *679 Recordings 679L 080CD*	**26**	2
30 Oct 04	**MEANTIME** *679 Recordings 679L 088CD2*	**49**	1

FUTURESHOCK
UK, male production duo and male vocalist (Singles: 3 Weeks)   pos/wks

15 Mar 03	**ON MY MIND** *Junior / Parlophone CDR 6595* [1]	**51**	1
16 Aug 03	**PRIDE'S PARANOIA** *Junior / Parlophone CDR 6616*	**60**	1
1 Nov 03	**LATE AT NIGHT** *Parlophone CDR 6617*	**73**	1

[1] Futureshock featuring Ben Onono

FUZZBOX See WE'VE GOT A FUZZBOX AND WE'RE GONNA USE IT

FYA (see also SMUJJI) *UK, female vocal trio (Singles: 9 Weeks)*   pos/wks

13 Mar 04	**MUST BE LOVE** *Def Jam 9817508* [1]	**13**	7
24 Jul 04	**TOO HOT** *Def Jam 9867145*	**49**	2

[1] Fya featuring Smujji

Leslie FYSON See Michael MEDWIN, Bernard BRESSLAW, Alfie BASS and
Leslie FYSON

Ali G and SHAGGY *UK, male comedian / rapper – Sacha Baron Cohen
and Jamaica, male vocalist – Orville Burrell (Singles: 14 Weeks)*   pos/wks

23 Mar 02	● **ME JULIE** *Island CID 793*	**2**	14

Bobby G (see also BUCKS FIZZ)
UK, male vocalist – Robert Gubby (Singles: 12 Weeks)   pos/wks

1 Dec 84	**BIG DEAL (2re)** *BBC RESL 151*	**46**	12

Dennis G See WIDEBOYS featuring Dennis G

Gina G *Australia, female vocalist –
Gina Gardiner (Singles: 51 Weeks, Albums: 4 Weeks)*   pos/wks

6 Apr 96	★ **OOH AAH … JUST A LITTLE BIT (2re)** *Eternal WEA 041CD*	**1**	25
9 Nov 96	● **I BELONG TO YOU** *Eternal WEA 081CD*	**6**	11
22 Mar 97	● **FRESH!** *Eternal WEA 095CD*	**6**	7
7 Jun 97	**TI AMO** *Eternal WEA 107CD1*	**11**	5
6 Sep 97	**GIMME SOME LOVE** *Eternal WEA 101CD1*	**25**	2
15 Nov 97	**EVERY TIME I FALL** *Eternal WEA 134CD*	**52**	1
5 Apr 97	**FRESH!** *Eternal 630178402*	**12**	4

Hurricane G See P DIDDY

Kenny G *US, male instrumentalist – saxophone –
Kenny Gorelick (Singles: 26 Weeks, Albums: 62 Weeks)*   pos/wks

21 Apr 84	**HI! HOW YA DOIN'?** *Arista ARIST 561*	**70**	3
30 Aug 86	**WHAT DOES IT TAKE (TO WIN YOUR LOVE)** *Arista ARIST 672*	**64**	2
4 Jul 87	**SONGBIRD** *Arista RIS 18*	**22**	7
9 May 92	**MISSING YOU NOW** *Columbia 6579917* [1]	**28**	4
24 Apr 93	**FOREVER IN LOVE** *Arista 74321145552*	**47**	3
17 Jul 93	**BY THE TIME THIS NIGHT IS OVER** *Arista 74321157142* [2]	**56**	3
8 Nov 97	**HOW COULD AN ANGEL BREAK MY HEART**		
	LaFace 74321531982 [3]	**22**	4
17 Mar 84	**G FORCE** *Arista 206 168*	**56**	5
8 Aug 87	**DUOTONES** *Arista 207 792*	**28**	5
14 Apr 90	**MONTAGE** *Arista 210621*	**32**	7
15 May 93	● **BREATHLESS** *Arista 07822186462*	**4**	27
19 Oct 96	**THE MOMENT** *Arista 7822189352*	**19**	9
13 Dec 97	**GREATEST HITS** *Arista 7822189912*	**38**	5
14 Aug 04	**SONGBIRD – THE ULTIMATE COLLECTION**		
	Arista 82876625622	**24**	4

[1] Michael Bolton featuring Kenny G [2] Kenny G with Peabo Bryson [3] Toni
Braxton with Kenny G

Warren G *US, male rapper – Warren Griffin
(Singles: 60 Weeks, Albums: 10 Weeks)*   pos/wks

23 Jul 94	● **REGULATE** *Death Row A 8290CD* [1]	**5**	14
12 Nov 94	**THIS DJ (re)** *RAL RALCD 1*	**12**	7
25 Mar 95	**DO YOU SEE** *RAL RALCD 3*	**29**	2
23 Nov 96	● **WHAT'S LOVE GOT TO DO WITH IT** *Interscope IND 97008* [2]	**2**	12
22 Feb 97	● **I SHOT THE SHERIFF** *Mercury DEFCD 31*	**2**	8
31 May 97	**SMOKIN' ME OUT** *Def Jam 5744432* [3]	**14**	5
10 Jan 98	**PRINCE IGOR** *Def Jam 5749652* [4]	**15**	7
24 Jan 98	**ALL NIGHT ALL RIGHT** *Mushroom MUSH 21CD* [5]	**16**	4
16 Mar 02	**LOOKIN' AT YOU** *Universal MCSTD 40275* [6]	**60**	1
6 Aug 94	**REGULATE … G FUNK ERA** *RAL 5233352*	**25**	6
8 Mar 97	**TAKE A LOOK OVER YOUR SHOULDER (REALITY)**		
	Def Jam 5334842	**20**	4

[1] Warren G and Nate Dogg [2] Warren G featuring Adina Howard [3] Warren G
featuring Ron Isley [4] Warren G featuring Sissel [5] Peter Andre featuring Warren
G [6] Warren G featuring Toi

Andy G's STARSKY & HUTCH ALL STARS
UK, male producer – Andros Georgiou (Singles: 1 Week)   pos/wks

3 Oct 98	**STARSKY & HUTCH – THE THEME** *Virgin VSCDT 1708*	**51**	1

GBH *UK, male vocal / instrumental group (Singles: 5 Weeks)*   pos/wks

6 Feb 82	**NO SURVIVORS** *Clay CLAY 8*	**63**	2
20 Nov 82	**GIVE ME FIRE** *Clay CLAY 16*	**69**	3

The G-CLEFS *US, male vocal group (Singles: 12 Weeks)*   pos/wks

30 Nov 61	**I UNDERSTAND** *London HLU 9433*	**17**	12

G CLUB presents BANDA SONORA
UK, male producer – Gerald Elms (Singles: 1 Week)   pos/wks

19 Oct 02	**PRESSURE COOKER** *Defected DFTD 060CDS*	**46**	1

G NATION featuring ROSIE
*UK, male production duo – Jake Moses
and Mark Smith and female vocalist (Singles: 1 Week)*   pos/wks

9 Aug 97	**FEEL THE NEED** *Cooltempo CDCOOL 327*	**58**	1

G.O.S.H. *UK, male / female charity ensemble (Singles: 11 Weeks)*   pos/wks

28 Nov 87	**THE WISHING WELL** *MBS GOSH 1*	**22**	11

G.Q. *US, male vocal / instrumental group (Singles: 6 Weeks)* pos/wks

10 Mar 79	DISCO NIGHTS – (ROCK FREAK) *Arista ARIST 245* **42** 6	

GSP *UK, male instrumental / production duo –*
Ian Gallivan and Justin Stride (Singles: 3 Weeks) pos/wks

3 Oct 92	THE BANANA SONG *Yoyo YOYO 1* **37** 3	

GTO (see also TECHNOHEAD; TRICKY DISCO)
UK, male / female instrumental / production duo –
Lee Newman and Michael Wells (Singles: 7 Weeks) pos/wks

4 Aug 90	PURE *Cooltempo COOL 218* **57** 3	
7 Sep 91	LISTEN TO THE RHYTHM FLOW / BULLFROG	
	React REACT 7001 ....**72** 2	
2 May 92	ELEVATION *React REACT 4* **59** 2	

GTR (see also Steve HACKETT; Steve HOWE)
UK, male vocal / instrumental group (Albums: 4 Weeks) pos/wks

19 Jul 86	GTR *Arista 207 716* **41** 4	

G Tom MAC *See LOST BROTHERS featuring G Tom MAC*

G-UNIT (see also Lloyd BANK$) *US, male rap*
trio – leader 50 Cent (Singles: 27 Weeks, Albums: 12 Weeks) pos/wks

27 Dec 03	STUNT 101 *Interscope 9815335* **25** 7	
6 Mar 04 ●	IF I CAN'T / ... THEM THANGS *Interscope 9815279* [1] **10** 8	
17 Apr 04	WANNA GET TO KNOW YOU *Interscope 9862268* **27** 5	
24 Apr 04	RIDE WIT U / MORE & MORE *Jive 82876609212* [2] **12** 7	
29 Nov 03	BEG FOR MERCY *Interscope / Polydor 9861498* **13** 11	
18 Sep 04	50 CENT IS THE FUTURE *Street Dance SDR 0166752* [1] **65** 1	

[1] 50 Cent & G-Unit [2] Joe featuring G-Unit [1] 50 Cent & G-Unit

Eric GABLE *US, male vocalist (Singles: 1 Week)* pos/wks

19 Mar 94	PROCESS OF ELIMINATION *Epic 6602282* **63** 1	

Peter GABRIEL ⟨168⟩ Top 500
Award-winning singer / songwriter, b. 13 Feb 1950, Surrey, UK. Fronted
Genesis until 1975, when replaced by Phil Collins. He broke through interna-
tionally with 'Sledgehammer', which also made him a video innovator. He is
the driving force behind the Womad festival and is a tireless Amnesty
International supporter (Singles: 114 Weeks, Albums: 215 Weeks) pos/wks

9 Apr 77	SOLSBURY HILL *Charisma CB 301* **13** 9
9 Feb 80 ●	GAMES WITHOUT FRONTIERS *Charisma CB 354* **4** 11
10 May 80	NO SELF CONTROL *Charisma CB 360* **33** 6
23 Aug 80	BIKO *Charisma CB 370* **38** 3
25 Sep 82	SHOCK THE MONKEY *Charisma SHOCK 1* **58** 5
9 Jul 83	I DON'T REMEMBER *Charisma GAB 1* **62** 3
2 Jun 84	WALK THROUGH THE FIRE *Virgin VS 689* **69** 3
26 Apr 86 ●	SLEDGEHAMMER *Virgin PGS 1* ▲ **4** 16
1 Nov 86 ●	DON'T GIVE UP *Virgin PGS 2* [1] **9** 11
28 Mar 87	BIG TIME *Charisma PGS 3* **13** 7
11 Jul 87	RED RAIN *Charisma PGS 4* **46** 3
21 Nov 87	BIKO (LIVE) *Charisma PGS 6* **49** 6
3 Jun 89	SHAKIN' THE TREE *Virgin VS 1167* [2] **61** 3
22 Dec 90	SOLSBURY HILL / SHAKING THE TREE (re-issue)	
	Virgin VS 1322 [3] **57** 4
19 Sep 92	DIGGING IN THE DIRT *Realworld PGS 7* **24** 4
16 Jan 93 ●	STEAM *Realworld PGSDG 8* **10** 7
3 Apr 93	BLOOD OF EDEN *Realworld PGSDG 9* **43** 4
25 Sep 93	KISS THAT FROG *Realworld PGSDG 10* **46** 3
25 Jun 94	LOVETOWN *Epic 6604802* **49** 2
3 Sep 94	SW LIVE (EP) *Realworld PGSCD 11* **39** 2
11 Jan 03	MORE THAN THIS *Realworld PGSCD 14* **47** 2
12 Mar 77 ●	PETER GABRIEL *Charisma CDS 4006* **7** 19
17 Jun 78 ●	PETER GABRIEL *Charisma CDS 4013* **10** 8
7 Jun 80 ★	PETER GABRIEL *Charisma CDS 4019* **1** 18
18 Sep 82 ●	PETER GABRIEL *Charisma PG 4* **6** 16
18 Jun 83 ●	PETER GABRIEL PLAYS LIVE *Charisma PGDL 1* **8** 9
30 Apr 85	BIRDY (FILM SOUNDTRACK) *Charisma CAS 1167* **51** 3
31 May 86 ★	SO *Virgin PG 5* ■ **1** 76
17 Jun 89	PASSION *Virgin RWLP 1* **29** 5
1 Dec 90	SHAKING THE TREE – 16 GOLDEN GREATS *Virgin PGTV 6* ...**11** 18
10 Oct 92 ●	US *Realworld PGCD 7* **2** 29
10 Sep 94 ●	SECRET WORLD LIVE *Realworld PGDCD 8* **10** 4

24 Jun 00	OVO *Realworld PGCD 9* **24** 2
5 Oct 02	UP *Realworld PGCD 11* **11** 4
15 Nov 03	HIT *Realworld 5952372* **29** 4

[1] Peter Gabriel and Kate Bush [2] Youssou N'Dour and Peter Gabriel [3] Peter Gabriel / Youssou N'Dour and Peter Gabriel

Tracks available on all formats of SW Live (EP): Red Rain / San Jacinto *First four*
albums are different

GABRIELLE ⟨170⟩ Top 500
Eyepatch-wearing soul / pop vocalist, b. Louisa Gabrielle Bobb, 16 May 1970,
London, UK. Broke record for highest chart debut when 'Dreams' entered at
No.2. Voted Best British Newcomer at 1994 BRIT Awards and Best British
Female Vocalist in 1997. Best-selling single: 'Dreams' 513,200 (Singles: 148
Weeks, Albums: 175 Weeks) pos/wks

19 Jun 93 ★	DREAMS *Go Beat GODCD 99* **1** 15
2 Oct 93 ●	GOING NOWHERE *Go Beat GODCD 106* **9** 7
11 Dec 93	I WISH *Go Beat GODCD 108* **26** 5
26 Feb 94	BECAUSE OF YOU *Go Beat GODCD 109* **24** 5
24 Feb 96 ●	GIVE ME A LITTLE MORE TIME *Go Beat GODCD 139* **5** 18
22 Jun 96	FORGET ABOUT THE WORLD *Go Beat GODCD 146* **23** 5
5 Oct 96	IF YOU REALLY CARED *Go Beat GODCD 153* **15** 5
2 Nov 96 ●	IF YOU EVER *London LONCD 388* [1] **2** 15
1 Feb 97 ●	WALK ON BY *Go Beat GODCD 159* **7** 8
9 Oct 99 ●	SUNSHINE *Go Beat GOBCD 23* **9** 8
5 Feb 00 ★	RISE *Go Beat / Polydor GOBCD 25* ■ **1** 15
17 Jun 00	WHEN A WOMAN *Go Beat / Polydor GOBCD 27* **6** 8
4 Nov 00	SHOULD I STAY *Go Beat / Polydor GOBCD 32* **13** 7
21 Apr 01 ●	OUT OF REACH *Go Beat / Polydor GOLCD 39* **4** 16
3 Nov 01 ●	DON'T NEED THE SUN TO SHINE (TO MAKE ME SMILE)	
	Go Beat / Polydor GOBCD 47 ....**9** 7
15 May 04	STAY THE SAME *Go Beat / Polydor 9866529* **20** 3
14 Aug 04	TEN YEARS TIME *Go Beat 9867550* **43** 1
30 Oct 93 ●	FIND YOUR WAY *Go Beat 8284412* **9** 22
8 Jun 96 ●	GABRIELLE *Go Beat 8287242* **11** 30
30 Oct 99 ★	RISE *Go Beat 5477682* **1** 87
24 Nov 01 ●	DREAMS CAN COME TRUE – GREATEST HITS VOL. 1	
	Go Beat 5893742 ....**2** 26
29 May 04 ●	PLAY TO WIN *Go Beat / Island 9866530* **10** 10

[1] East 17 featuring Gabrielle

Yvonne GAGE *US, female vocalist (Singles: 4 Weeks)* pos/wks

16 Jun 84	DOIN' IT IN A HAUNTED HOUSE *Epic A 4519* **45** 4

Danni'elle GAHA *Australia, female vocalist (Singles: 7 Weeks)* pos/wks

1 Aug 92	STUCK IN THE MIDDLE *Epic 6581247* **68** 2
27 Feb 93	DO IT FOR LOVE *Epic 6584612* **52** 2
12 Jun 93	SECRET LOVE *Epic 6592212* **41** 3

Dave GAHAN (see also DEPECHE MODE)
UK, male vocalist (Singles: 4 Weeks, Albums: 2 Weeks) pos/wks

7 Jun 03	DIRTY STICKY FLOORS *Mute CDMUTE 294* **18** 2
8 Nov 03	BOTTLE LIVING *Mute CDMUTE 310* **36** 2
14 Jun 03	PAPER MONSTERS *Mute CDSTUMM 216* **36** 2

Billy and Sarah GAINES
US, male / female vocal duo (Singles: 1 Week) pos/wks

14 Jun 97	I FOUND SOMEONE *Expansion CDEXP 27* **48** 1

Rosie GAINES (see also PRINCE)
US, female vocalist (Singles: 15 Weeks) pos/wks

11 Nov 95	I WANT U *Motown 8604852* **70** 1
31 May 97 ●	CLOSER THAN CLOSE *Big Bang CDBBANG 1* **4** 12
29 Nov 97	I SURRENDER *Big Bang CDBBANG 2* **39** 2

Serge GAINSBOURG *See Jane BIRKIN and Serge GAINSBOURG*

GALA *Italy, female vocalist – Gala Rizzatto (Singles: 24 Weeks)* pos/wks

19 Jul 97 ●	FREED FROM DESIRE *Big Life BLRD 135* **2** 14
6 Dec 97	LET A BOY CRY *Big Life BLRD 140* **11** 8
22 Aug 98	COME INTO MY LIFE *Big Life BLRD 147* **38** 2

GALAXY *See Phil FEARON*

Dee GALDES *See Phil FEARON*

Eve GALLAGHER UK, female vocalist (Singles: 8 Weeks)

		pos/wks
1 Dec 90	**LOVE COME DOWN (re)** More Protein PROT 6 ....**61** 4
15 Apr 95	**YOU CAN HAVE IT ALL** Cleveland City CLECD 13023 ....**43** 2
28 Oct 95	**LOVE COME DOWN (re-recording)** Cleveland City CLECD 13028 ....**57** 1
6 Jul 96	**HEARTBREAK** React CDREACT 78 [1] **44** 1

[1] Mrs Wood featuring Eve Gallagher

Liam GALLAGHER See DEATH IN VEGAS; OASIS; BUFFALO TOM

Rory GALLAGHER (see also TASTE) Ireland, male vocalist / instrumentalist – guitar, b. 2 Mar 1949, d. 14 Jun 1995 (Albums: 43 Weeks)

		pos/wks
29 May 71	**RORY GALLAGHER** Polydor 2383044 ....**32** 2
4 Dec 71	**DEUCE** Polydor 2383076 ....**39** 1
20 May 72 ●	**LIVE! IN EUROPE** Polydor 2383112 ....**9** 15
24 Feb 73	**BLUE PRINT** Polydor 2383189 ....**12** 7
17 Nov 73	**TATTOO** Polydor 2383 30 ....**32** 3
27 Jul 74	**IRISH TOUR '74** Polydor 2659031 ....**36** 2
30 Oct 76	**CALLING CARD** Chrysalis CHR 1124 ....**32** 1
22 Sep 79	**TOP PRIORITY** Chrysalis CHR 1235 ....**56** 4
8 Nov 80	**STAGE STRUCK** Chrysalis CHR 1280 ....**40** 3
8 May 82	**JINX** Chrysalis CHR 1359 ....**68** 5

GALLAGHER and LYLE
UK, male vocal / instrumental duo – Benny Gallagher and Graham Lyle (Singles: 27 Weeks, Albums: 44 Weeks)

		pos/wks
28 Feb 76 ●	**I WANNA STAY WITH YOU** A&M AMS 7211 ....**6** 10
22 May 76 ●	**HEART ON MY SLEEVE** A&M AMS 7227 ....**6** 10
11 Sep 76	**BREAKAWAY** A&M AMS 7245 ....**35** 4
29 Jan 77	**EVERY LITTLE TEARDROP** A&M AMS 7274 ....**32** 4
28 Feb 76 ●	**BREAKAWAY** A&M AMLH 68348 ....**6** 35
29 Jan 77	**LOVE ON THE AIRWAYS** A&M AMLH 64620 ....**19** 9

Patsy GALLANT Canada, female vocalist (Singles: 9 Weeks)

		pos/wks
10 Sep 77 ●	**FROM NEW YORK TO L.A.** EMI 2620 ....**6** 9

GALLEON France, male vocal / production trio (Singles: 2 Weeks)

		pos/wks
20 Apr 02	**SO I BEGIN** Epic 6724102 ....**36** 2

Luke GALLIANA UK, male vocalist (Singles: 1 Week)

		pos/wks
12 May 01	**TO DIE FOR** Jive 9201272 ....**42** 1

GALLIANO UK, male / female vocal / instrumental group (Singles: 14 Weeks, Albums: 15 Weeks)

		pos/wks
30 May 92	**SKUNK FUNK** Talkin Loud TLK 23 ....**41** 2
1 Aug 92	**PRINCE OF PEACE** Talkin Loud TLK 24 ....**47** 3
10 Oct 92	**JUS' REACH (RECYCLED)** Talkin Loud TLK 29 ....**66** 2
28 May 94	**LONG TIME GONE** Talkin Loud TLKCD 48 ....**15** 3
30 Jul 94	**TWYFORD DOWN** Talkin Loud TLKCD 49 ....**37** 2
27 Jul 96	**EASE YOUR MIND** Talkin Loud TLCD 10 ....**45** 2
20 Jun 92	**A JOYFUL NOISE UNTO THE CREATOR** Talkin Loud 8480802 ....**28** 3
11 Jun 94 ●	**THE PLOT THICKENS** Talkin Loud 5224522 ....**7** 12

GALLON DRUNK
UK, male vocal / instrumental group (Albums: 1 Week)

		pos/wks
13 Mar 93	**FROM THE HEART OF TOWN** Clawfist HUNKACDL 005 ....**67** 1

James GALWAY UK, male instrumentalist – flute (Singles: 13 Weeks, Albums: 102 Weeks)

		pos/wks
27 May 78 ●	**ANNIE'S SONG** RCA Red Seal RB 5085 [1] **3** 13
27 May 78	**THE MAGIC FLUTE OF JAMES GALWAY** RCA Red Seal LRL1 5131 ....**43** 6
1 Jul 78	**THE MAN WITH THE GOLDEN FLUTE** RCA Red Seal LRL1 5127 ....**52** 3
9 Sep 78 ●	**JAMES GALWAY PLAYS SONGS FOR ANNIE** RCA Red Seal RL 25163 ....**7** 40
15 Dec 79	**SONGS OF THE SEASHORE** Solar RL 25253 ....**39** 6
31 May 80	**SOMETIMES WHEN WE TOUCH** RCA PL 25296 [1] **15** 14
18 Dec 82	**THE JAMES GALWAY COLLECTION** Telstar STAR 2224 ....**41** 8
8 Dec 84	**IN THE PINK** RCA Red Seal RL 85315 [2] **62** 6
28 Mar 87	**JAMES GALWAY AND THE CHIEFTAINS IN IRELAND** RCA Red Seal RL 85798 [3] **32** 5
17 Apr 93	**THE ESSENTIAL FLUTE OF JAMES GALWAY** RCA Victor 74321133852 ....**30** 5

		pos/wks
18 Feb 95	**I WILL ALWAYS LOVE YOU** RCA Victor 74321262212 ....**59** 2
20 Jul 96	**CLASSICAL MEDITATIONS** RCA Victor 74321377312 ....**45** 5
25 Sep 04	**WINGS OF SONG** Deutsche Grammophon 4775236 ....**45** 2

[1] James Galway, flute, National Philharmonic Orchestra; Charles Gerhart, conductor [1] Cleo Laine and James Galway [2] James Galway and Henry Mancini with the National Philharmonic Orchestra [3] James Galway and The Chieftains

GAMBAFREAKS Italy, male production duo (Singles: 2 Weeks)

		pos/wks
12 Sep 98	**INSTANT REPLAY** Evocative EVOKE 7CDS [1] **57** 1
13 May 00	**DOWN DOWN DOWN** Azuli AZNYCDX 116 ....**57** 1

[1] Gambafreaks featuring Paco Rivaz

GANG OF FOUR UK, male vocal / instrumental group (Singles: 5 Weeks, Albums: 9 Weeks)

		pos/wks
16 Jun 79	**AT HOME HE'S A TOURIST** EMI 2956 ....**58** 3
22 May 82	**I LOVE A MAN IN UNIFORM** EMI 5299 ....**65** 3
13 Oct 79	**ENTERTAINMENT** EMI EMC 3313 ....**45** 3
21 Mar 81	**SOLID GOLD** EMI EMC 3364 ....**52** 2
29 May 82	**SONGS OF THE FREE** EMI EMC 3412 ....**61** 4

GANG STARR (see also GURU) US, male rap duo – Christopher Martin and Keith Elam (Singles: 8 Weeks, Albums: 10 Weeks)

		pos/wks
13 Oct 90	**JAZZ THING** CBS 3563777 ....**66** 2
23 Feb 91	**TAKE A REST** Cooltempo COOL 230 ....**63** 1
25 May 91	**LOVESICK** Cooltempo COOL 234 ....**50** 3
13 Jun 92	**2 DEEP** Cooltempo COOL 256 ....**67** 2
26 Jan 91	**STEP IN THE ARENA** Cooltempo ZCTLP 21 ....**36** 3
12 Mar 94	**HARD TO EARN** Cooltempo CTCD 38 ....**29** 3
11 Apr 98	**MOMENT OF TRUTH** Cooltempo 8590322 ....**43** 1
7 Aug 99	**FULL CLIP: A DECADE OF GANG STARR** Cooltempo 5211892 ....**47** 2
5 Jul 03	**THE OWNERZ** Virgin CDVUS 235 ....**74** 1

GANJA KRU See DJ HYPE presents GANJA KRU

GANT UK, production duo – Julian Jonah and Danny Harrison (Singles: 1 Week)

		pos/wks
27 Dec 97	**SOUND BWOY BURIAL / ALL NIGHT LONG** Positiva CDTIV 85 ..**67** 1

The GAP BAND US, male vocal / instrumental trio (Singles: 88 Weeks, Albums: 3 Weeks)

		pos/wks
12 Jul 80 ●	**OOPS UP SIDE YOUR HEAD** Mercury MER 22 ....**6** 14
27 Sep 80	**PARTY LIGHTS** Mercury MER 37 ....**30** 8
27 Dec 80	**BURN RUBBER ON ME (WHY YOU WANNA HURT ME)** Mercury MER 52 ....**22** 11
11 Apr 81	**HUMPIN'** Mercury MER 63 ....**36** 6
27 Jun 81	**YEARNING FOR YOUR LOVE** Mercury MER 73 ....**47** 4
5 Jun 82	**EARLY IN THE MORNING** Mercury MER 97 ....**55** 3
19 Feb 83	**OUTSTANDING** Total Experience TE 001 ....**68** 2
31 Mar 84	**SOMEDAY** Total Experience TE 5 ....**17** 8
23 Jun 84	**JAMMIN' IN AMERICA** Total Experience TE 6 ....**64** 2
13 Dec 86 ●	**BIG FUN** Total Experience FB 49779 ....**4** 12
14 Mar 87	**HOW MUSIC CAME ABOUT (BOP B DA B DA DA)** Total Experience FB 49755 ....**61** 2
11 Jul 87	**OOPS UP SIDE YOUR HEAD (re-mix)** Club JAB 54 ....**20** 8
18 Feb 89	**I'M GONNA GIT YOU SUCKA** Arista 112016 ....**63** 2
16 Oct 04	**OOPS UPSIDE YOUR HEAD (re-mix)** All Around the World CDGLOBE 376 [1] **16** 6
7 Feb 87	**GAP BAND 8** Total Experience FL 89992 ....**47** 3

[1] DJ Casper featuring The Gap Band

GARBAGE (276 Top 500) The missing link between techno and grunge, formed Madison, Wisconsin, US, 1993: includes Shirley Manson (b. Edinburgh, Scotland, v/g) and Butch Vig (d), who produced Nirvana and Smashing Pumpkins (Singles: 66 Weeks, Albums: 169 Weeks)

		pos/wks
19 Aug 95	**SUBHUMAN** Mushroom D 1138 ....**50** 1
30 Sep 95	**ONLY HAPPY WHEN IT RAINS** Mushroom D 1199 ....**29** 3
2 Dec 95	**QUEER** Mushroom D 1237 ....**13** 4
23 Mar 96 ●	**STUPID GIRL** Mushroom D 1271 ....**4** 7
23 Nov 96 ●	**MILK (re)** Mushroom D 1494 [1] **10** 8
9 May 98 ●	**PUSH IT** Mushroom MUSH 28CDS **9** 5
18 Jul 98 ●	**I THINK I'M PARANOID** Mushroom MUSH 35CDS **9** 5
17 Oct 98 ●	**SPECIAL** Mushroom MUSH 39CDS **15** 4
6 Feb 99 ●	**WHEN I GROW UP** Mushroom MUSH 43CDS **9** 7

Singles re-entries are listed as (re), (2re), (3re).... which signifies that the hit re-entered the chart once, twice or three times...

		pos/wks
5 Jun 99	YOU LOOK SO FINE *Mushroom MUSH 49CDS*	**19** 4
27 Nov 99	THE WORLD IS NOT ENOUGH *Radioactive RAXTD 40*	**11** 9
6 Oct 01	ANDROGYNY *Mushroom MUSH 94CDS*	**24** 2
2 Feb 02	CHERRY LIPS (GO BABY GO!) *Mushroom MUSH 98CDS*	**22** 4
20 Apr 02	BREAKING UP THE GIRL *Mushroom MUSH 101CDS*	**27** 2
5 Oct 02	SHUT YOUR MOUTH *Mushroom MUSH 106CDS*	**20** 1
14 Oct 95 ●	GARBAGE *Mushroom D 31450*	**6** 100
23 May 98 ★	VERSION 2.0 *Mushroom MUSH 29CD* ■	**1** 65
13 Oct 01 ●	BEAUTIFUL GARBAGE *Mushroom MUSH 95CD*	**6** 4

1 Garbage featuring Tricky

Jan GARBAREK
Norway, male instrumentalist – saxophone (Albums: 1 Week) pos/wks

4 May 96	VISIBLE WORLD *ECM 5290862*	**69** 1

Adam GARCIA *Australia, male vocalist (Singles: 5 Weeks)* pos/wks

16 May 98	NIGHT FEVER *Polydor 5697972*	**15** 5

Scott GARCIA featuring MC STYLES
(see also CORRUPTED CRU featuring MC NEAT) *UK, male
producer and male rapper – Daryl Turner (Singles: 3 Weeks)* pos/wks

1 Nov 97	A LONDON THING *Connected CDCONNECT 1*	**29** 3

Boris GARDINER
Jamaica, male vocalist / instrumentalist (Singles: 38 Weeks) pos/wks

17 Jan 70	ELIZABETHAN REGGAE (re) *Duke DU 39*	**14** 14
26 Jul 86 ★	I WANT TO WAKE UP WITH YOU *Revue REV 733*	**1** 15
4 Oct 86	YOU'RE EVERYTHING TO ME *Revue REV 735*	**11** 8
27 Dec 86	THE MEANING OF CHRISTMAS *Revue REV 740*	**69** 1

*The first copies of 'Elizabethan Reggae', an instrumental, were printed with the
label incorrectly crediting Byron Lee as the performer. The charts for the first
entry, and the first four weeks of the re-entry, all reprinted this error. All charts
and discs printed after 28 Feb 1970 gave Boris Gardiner the credit he deserved*

Paul GARDINER
UK, male instrumentalist – bass (Singles: 4 Weeks) pos/wks

25 Jul 81	STORMTROOPER IN DRAG *Beggars Banquet BEG 61*	**49** 4

Uncredited vocalist is Gary Numan

Art GARFUNKEL (see also SIMON and GARFUNKEL)
US, male vocalist (Singles: 37 Weeks, Albums: 64 Weeks) pos/wks

13 Sep 75 ★	I ONLY HAVE EYES FOR YOU *CBS 3575*	**1** 11
3 Mar 79 ★	BRIGHT EYES *CBS 6947* ◆	**1** 19
7 Jul 79	SINCE I DON'T HAVE YOU *CBS 7371*	**38** 7
13 Oct 73	ANGEL CLARE *CBS 69021*	**14** 7
1 Nov 75 ●	BREAKAWAY *CBS 86002*	**7** 10
18 Mar 78	WATER MARK *CBS 86054*	**25** 5
21 Apr 79 ●	FATE FOR BREAKFAST *CBS 86082*	**2** 20
19 Sep 81	SCISSORS CUT *CBS 85259*	**51** 3
17 Nov 84	THE ART GARFUNKEL ALBUM *CBS 10046*	**12** 13
14 Dec 96	THE VERY BEST OF ART GARFUNKEL – ACROSS AMERICA *Virgin VTCD 113*	**35** 6

Judy GARLAND *US, female vocalist – Frances Gumm,
b. 10 Jun 1922, d. 22 Jan 1969 (Singles: 2 Weeks, Albums: 3 Weeks)* pos/wks

10 Jun 55	THE MAN THAT GOT AWAY *Philips PB 366*	**18** 2
3 Mar 62	JUDY AT CARNEGIE HALL *Capitol W 1569* ▲	**13** 3

Jessica GARLICK *UK, female vocalist (Singles: 6 Weeks)* pos/wks

25 May 02	COME BACK *Columbia 6725662*	**13** 6

Errol GARNER *US, male instrumentalist –
piano, b. 15 Jun 1923, d. 2 Jan 1977 (Albums: 1 Week)* pos/wks

14 Jul 62	CLOSE UP IN SWING *Philips BBL 7579*	**20** 1

Laurent GARNIER
France, male DJ / producer (Singles: 4 Weeks) pos/wks

15 Feb 97	CRISPY BACON *F Communications F 055CD*	**60** 1
22 Apr 00	MAN WITH THE RED FACE *F Communications F 119CD*	**65** 1
11 Nov 00	GREED / THE MAN WITH THE RED FACE (re-issue) *F Communications F 127CDUK*	**36** 2

Lee GARRETT *US, male vocalist (Singles: 7 Weeks)* pos/wks

29 May 76	YOU'RE MY EVERYTHING *Chrysalis CHS 2087*	**15** 7

Leif GARRETT *US, male vocalist (Singles: 14 Weeks)* pos/wks

20 Jan 79 ●	I WAS MADE FOR DANCIN' *Scotti Brothers K 11202*	**4** 10
21 Apr 79	FEEL THE NEED *Scotti Brothers K 11274*	**38** 4

Lesley GARRETT
UK, female vocalist (Singles: 10 Weeks, Albums: 44 Weeks) pos/wks

6 Nov 93	AVE MARIA *Internal Affairs KGBD 012* 1	**16** 10
12 Feb 94	THE ALBUM *Telstar TCD 2709*	**25** 7
18 Nov 95	SOPRANO IN RED *Silva Classics SILKTVCD 1*	**59** 8
19 Oct 96	SOPRANO IN HOLLYWOOD *Silva Classics SILKTVCD 2*	**53** 4
18 Oct 97	THE SOPRANO'S GREATEST HITS *Silva Classics SILKTVCD 3*	**53** 2
22 Nov 97	A SOPRANO INSPIRED *Conifer Classics 75605513292*	**48** 7
14 Nov 98	LESLEY GARRETT *BBC / BMG Conifer 75605513382*	**34** 8
27 May 00	I WILL WAIT FOR YOU *BBC / BMG Conifer 75605513542*	**28** 7
24 Nov 01	TRAVELLING LIGHT *EMI Classics CDC 5572512*	**75** 1

1 Lesley Garrett and Amanda Thompson

Siedah GARRETT *See The BRAND NEW HEAVIES; Dennis EDWARDS*

David GARRICK
UK, male vocalist – Philip Core (Singles: 16 Weeks) pos/wks

9 Jun 66	LADY JANE *Piccadilly 7N 35317*	**28** 7
22 Sep 66	DEAR MRS APPLEBEE *Piccadilly 7N 35335*	**22** 9

GARY'S GANG
US, male vocal / instrumental group (Singles: 18 Weeks) pos/wks

24 Feb 79 ●	KEEP ON DANCIN' *CBS 7109*	**8** 10
2 Jun 79	LET'S LOVEDANCE TONIGHT *CBS 7328*	**49** 4
6 Nov 82	KNOCK ME OUT *Arista ARIST 499*	**45** 4

Barbara GASKIN *See Dave STEWART*

GAT DECOR (see also PHUNKY PHANTOM; REST ASSURED)
UK, male instrumental / production group (Singles: 10 Weeks) pos/wks

16 May 92 ●	PASSION *Effective EFFS 1*	**29** 4
9 Mar 96 ●	PASSION (re-mix) *Way of Life WAYDA 1*	**6** 6

Stephen GATELY (see also BOYZONE)
Ireland, male vocalist (Singles: 19 Weeks, Albums: 4 Weeks) pos/wks

10 Jun 00 ●	NEW BEGINNING / BRIGHT EYES *A&M / Polydor 5618192*	**3** 11
14 Oct 00	I BELIEVE *Polydor 5877472*	**11** 4
12 May 01	STAY *A&M / Mercury 5870672*	**13** 4
1 Jul 00 ●	NEW BEGINNING *A&M 5439102*	**9** 4

David GATES (see also BREAD)
US, male vocalist (Singles: 2 Weeks, Albums: 30 Weeks) pos/wks

22 Jul 78	TOOK THE LAST TRAIN *Elektra K 12307*	**50** 2
31 May 75	NEVER LET HER GO *Elektra K 52012*	**32** 1
29 Jul 78	GOODBYE GIRL *Elektra K 52091*	**28** 3
5 Jul 97 ●	ESSENTIALS *Jive 9548354082* 1	**9** 19
12 Oct 02	THE DAVID GATES SONGBOOK – A LIFETIME OF MUSIC *Jive 0927491402*	**11** 7

1 David Gates and Bread

Gareth GATES
UK, male vocalist (Singles: 109 Weeks, Albums: 21 Weeks) pos/wks

30 Mar 02 ★	UNCHAINED MELODY (2re) *S 74321930882* ◆ ■	**1** 30
20 Jul 02 ★	ANYONE OF US (STUPID MISTAKE) *S 74321950602* ■	**1** 15
5 Oct 02 ★	THE LONG AND WINDING ROAD / SUSPICIOUS MINDS *S 74321965972* 1 ■	**1** 18
21 Dec 02 ●	WHAT MY HEART WANTS TO SAY (re) *S 743211985592*	**5** 13
22 Mar 03 ★	SPIRIT IN THE SKY *S 82876511202* 2 ■	**1** 10
20 Sep 03 ●	SUNSHINE (re) *S 82876560032*	**3** 15
13 Dec 03 ●	SAY IT ISN'T SO *S 82876583412*	**4** 8
9 Nov 02 ●	WHAT MY HEART WANTS TO SAY *S 74321975172*	**2** 17
4 Oct 03	GO YOUR OWN WAY *S 82876557452*	**11** 4

1 Will Young and Gareth Gates / Gareth Gates 2 Gareth Gates featuring
The Kumars

GAY DAD *UK, male / female vocal / instrumental*
group (Singles: 10 Weeks, Albums: 3 Weeks) pos/wks

30 Jan 99 ●	TO EARTH WITH LOVE *London LONCD 413*	10	4
5 Jun 99	JOY! *London LONCD 428*	22	3
14 Aug 99	OH JIM *London LONCD 437*	47	1
31 Mar 01	NOW ALWAYS AND FOREVER *B Unique BUN 004CD*	41	1
22 Sep 01	TRANSMISSION *B Unique BUN 009CD*	58	1
19 Jun 99	LEISURE NOISE *London 5561032*	14	3

GAY GORDON and the MINCE PIES
UK, male / female vocal / instrumental group (Singles: 5 Weeks) pos/wks

6 Dec 86	THE ESSENTIAL WALLY PARTY MEDLEY *Lifestyle XY 2*	60	5

Marvin GAYE 122 Top 500 *One of soul's most innovative and suc-cessful singer / songwriters, b. 2 Apr 1939, Washington DC, US, d. 1 Apr 1984. He went from doo-wop group member and session drummer to superstar. Posthumously awarded a Lifetime Achievement Grammy Award in 1996 (Singles: 202 Weeks, Albums: 190 Weeks)* pos/wks

30 Jul 64	ONCE UPON A TIME *Stateside SS 316* [1]	50	1
10 Dec 64	HOW SWEET IT IS *Stateside SS 360*	49	1
29 Sep 66	LITTLE DARLIN' (I NEED YOU) *Tamla Motown TMG 574*	50	1
26 Jan 67	IT TAKES TWO *Tamla Motown TMG 590* [2]	16	11
17 Jan 68	IF I COULD BUILD MY WHOLE WORLD AROUND YOU *Tamla Motown TMG 635* [3]	41	7
12 Jun 68	AIN'T NOTHIN' LIKE THE REAL THING *Tamla Motown TMG 655* [3]	34	7
2 Oct 68	YOU'RE ALL I NEED TO GET BY *Tamla Motown TMG 668* [3]	19	19
22 Jan 69	YOU AIN'T LIVIN' TILL YOU'RE LOVIN' *Tamla Motown TMG 681* [3]	21	8
12 Feb 69 ★	I HEARD IT THROUGH THE GRAPEVINE *Tamla Motown TMG 686* ▲	1	15
4 Jun 69	GOOD LOVIN' AIN'T EASY TO COME BY (re) *Tamla Motown TMG 697* [3]	26	8
23 Jul 69 ●	TOO BUSY THINKING 'BOUT MY BABY *Tamla Motown TMG 705*	5	16
15 Nov 69	ONION SONG *Tamla Motown TMG 715* [3]	9	12
9 May 70 ●	ABRAHAM, MARTIN AND JOHN *Tamla Motown TMG 734*	9	14
11 Dec 71	SAVE THE CHILDREN *Tamla Motown TMG 796*	41	6
22 Sep 73	LET'S GET IT ON *Tamla Motown TMG 868* ▲	31	7
23 Mar 74 ●	YOU ARE EVERYTHING *Tamla Motown TMG 890* [4]	5	12
20 Jul 74	STOP LOOK LISTEN (TO YOUR HEART) *Tamla Motown TMG 906* [4]	25	8
7 May 77 ●	GOT TO GIVE IT UP (PT.1) *Motown TMG 1069* ▲	7	10
24 Feb 79	POPS, WE LOVE YOU *Motown TMG 1136* [5]	66	5
30 Oct 82 ●	(SEXUAL) HEALING *CBS A 2855*	4	14
8 Jan 83	MY LOVE IS WAITING *CBS A 3048*	34	4
18 May 85	SANCTIFIED LADY *CBS A 4894*	51	4
26 Apr 86 ●	I HEARD IT THROUGH THE GRAPEVINE (re-issue) *Tamla Motown ZB 40701*	8	8
14 May 94	LUCKY LUCKY ME *Motown TMGCD 1426*	67	1
6 Oct 01	MUSIC *Polydor 4976222* [6]	36	2
16 Mar 68	GREATEST HITS *Tamla Motown STML 11065*	40	1
22 Aug 70	GREATEST HITS *Tamla Motown STML 11153* [1]	60	4
19 Jan 71 ●	DIANA&MARVIN *Tamla Motown STMA 8015* [2]	6	43
10 Nov 73	LET'S GET IT ON *Tamla Motown STMA 8013*	39	1
15 May 76	I WANT YOU *Tamla Motown STML 12025*	22	5
30 Oct 76	THE BEST OF MARVIN GAYE *Tamla Motown STML 12042*	56	1
28 Feb 81	IN OUR LIFETIME *Motown STML 12149*	48	4
29 Aug 81	DIANA AND MARVIN (re-issue) *Motown STMS 5001* [2]	78	2
20 Nov 82 ●	MIDNIGHT LOVE *CBS 85977*	10	16
12 Nov 83	GREATEST HITS *Telstar STAR 2234*	13	61
15 Jun 85	DREAM OF A LIFETIME *CBS 26239*	46	4
12 Nov 88	LOVE SONGS *Telstar STAR 2331* [3]	69	9
2 Nov 90	LOVE SONGS *Telstar STAR 2427*	39	5
9 Apr 94 ●	THE VERY BEST OF MARVIN GAYE *Motown 5302922*	3	19
24 Jul 99	WHAT'S GOING ON *Motown 5308832*	56	4
19 Feb 00 ●	THE LOVE SONGS *UMTV / Motown 5454702*	8	7
1 Sep 01	THE VERY BEST OF MARVIN GAYE *Motown 143672*	15	4

[1] Marvin Gaye and Mary Wells [2] Marvin Gaye and Kim Weston [3] Marvin Gaye and Tammi Terrell [4] Diana Ross and Marvin Gaye [5] Diana Ross, Marvin Gaye, Smokey Robinson and Stevie Wonder [6] Erick Sermon featuring Marvin Gaye [1] Marvin Gaye and Tammi Terrell [2] Diana Ross and Marvin Gaye [3] Marvin Gaye and Smokey Robinson

The two 'Greatest Hits' and 'The Very Best of Marvin Gaye' albums are different

GAYE BYKERS ON ACID *UK, male vocal /*
instrumental group (Singles: 2 Weeks, Albums: 1 Week) pos/wks

31 Oct 87	GIT DOWN (SHAKE YOUR THANG) *Purple Fluid VS 1008*	54	2
14 Nov 87	DRILL YOUR OWN HOLE *Virgin V 2478*	95	1

Crystal GAYLE *US, female vocalist – Brenda*
Gail Webb (Singles: 28 Weeks, Albums: 25 Weeks) pos/wks

12 Nov 77 ●	DON'T IT MAKE MY BROWN EYES BLUE *United Artists UP 36307*	5	14
26 Aug 78	TALKING IN YOUR SLEEP *United Artists UP 36422*	11	14
21 Jan 78	WE MUST BELIEVE IN MAGIC *United Artists UAG 30108*	15	7
23 Sep 78	WHEN I DREAM *United Artists UAG 30169*	25	8
22 Mar 80 ●	THE CRYSTAL GAYLE SINGLES ALBUM *United Artists UAG 30287*	7	10

Michelle GAYLE
UK, female actor / vocalist (Singles: 52 Weeks, Albums: 13 Weeks) pos/wks

7 Aug 93	LOOKING UP *RCA 74321154532*	11	6
24 Sep 94 ●	SWEETNESS *RCA 74321230192*	4	16
17 Dec 94	I'LL FIND YOU *RCA 74321247762*	26	7
27 May 95	FREEDOM *RCA 74321284692*	16	6
26 Aug 95	HAPPY JUST TO BE WITH YOU *RCA 74321302692*	11	7
8 Feb 97 ●	DO YOU KNOW *RCA 74321419282*	6	6
26 Apr 97	SENSATIONAL *RCA 74321419302*	14	4
22 Oct 94	MICHELLE GAYLE *RCA 74321234122*	30	10
10 May 97	SENSATIONAL *RCA 74321419322*	17	3

Roy GAYLE *See MIRAGE*

GAYLE & GILLIAN
Australia, female vocal / actor duo (twins) –
Gayle and Gillian Blakeney (Singles: 2 Weeks) pos/wks

3 Jul 93	MAD IF YA DON'T *Mushroom CDMUSH 1*	75	1
19 Mar 94	WANNA BE YOUR LOVER *Mushroom D 11598*	62	1

Gloria GAYNOR *US, female vocalist –*
Gloria Fowles (Singles: 73 Weeks, Albums: 17 Weeks) pos/wks

7 Dec 74 ●	NEVER CAN SAY GOODBYE *MGM 2006463*	2	13
8 Mar 75	REACH OUT, I'LL BE THERE *MGM 2006499*	14	8
9 Aug 75	ALL I NEED IS YOUR SWEET LOVIN' *MGM 2006531*	44	3
17 Jan 76	HOW HIGH THE MOON *MGM 2006558*	33	4
3 Feb 79 ★	I WILL SURVIVE *Polydor 2095017* ▲	1	15
6 Oct 79	LET ME KNOW (I HAVE A RIGHT) *Polydor STEP 5*	32	7
24 Dec 83	I AM WHAT I AM (FROM 'LA CAGE AUX FOLLES') *Chrysalis CHS 2765*	13	12
26 Jun 93 ●	I WILL SURVIVE (re-mix) *Polydor PZCD 270*	5	10
3 Jun 00	LAST NIGHT *Logic 74321738082*	67	1
8 Mar 75	NEVER CAN SAY GOODBYE *MGM 2315 321*	32	8
24 Mar 79	LOVE TRACKS *Polydor 2391 385*	31	7
16 Aug 86	THE POWER OF GLORIA GAYNOR *Stylus SMR 618*	81	2

GAZ
US, male vocal / instrumental group (Singles: 4 Weeks) pos/wks

24 Feb 79	SING SING *Salsoul SSOL 116*	60	4

GAZZA
UK, male footballer / vocalist – Paul Gascoigne (Singles: 14 Weeks) pos/wks

10 Nov 90 ●	FOG ON THE TYNE (REVISITED) *Best ZB 44083* [1]	2	9
22 Dec 90	GEORDIE BOYS (GAZZA RAP) *Best ZB 44229*	31	5

[1] Gazza and Lindisfarne

Anne GEDDES *See Celine DION*

Nigel GEE *UK, male producer (Singles: 1 Week)* pos/wks

27 Jan 01	HOOTIN' *Neo NEOCD 040*	57	1

J GEILS BAND *US, male vocal / instrumental group –*
leader Jerome Geils (Singles: 20 Weeks, Albums: 15 Weeks) pos/wks

9 Jun 79	ONE LAST KISS *EMI America AM 507*	74	1
13 Feb 82 ●	CENTERFOLD *EMI America EA 135* ▲	3	9
10 Apr 82	FREEZE-FRAME *EMI America EA 134*	27	7
26 Jun 82	ANGEL IN BLUE *EMI America EA 138*	55	3
27 Feb 82	FREEZE-FRAME *EMI America AML 3020* ▲	12	15

Bob GELDOF
(see also The BOOMTOWN RATS) *Ireland, male vocalist*
(Singles: 15 Weeks, Albums: 10 Weeks) pos/wks

1 Nov 86	THIS IS THE WORLD CALLING *Mercury BOB 101*	25	5
21 Feb 87	LOVE LIKE A ROCKET *Mercury BOB 102*	61	3
23 Jun 90	THE GREAT SONG OF INDIFFERENCE *Mercury BOB 104*	15	6
7 May 94	CRAZY *Vertigo VERCX 85*	65	1
6 Dec 86	DEEP IN THE HEART OF NOWHERE *Mercury BOBLP 1*	79	1
4 Aug 90	THE VEGETARIANS OF LOVE *Mercury 8462501*	21	6
9 Jul 94 ●	LOUDMOUTH – THE BEST OF BOB GELDOF & THE BOOMTOWN RATS *Vertigo 5222832* [1]	10	3

[1] The Boomtown Rats and Bob Geldof

GEM *See OUR TRIBE / ONE TRIBE*

GEMINI
UK, male vocal duo (twins) – Michael and David Smallwood (Singles: 7 Weeks) pos/wks

30 Sep 95	EVEN THOUGH YOU BROKE MY HEART *EMI CDEMS 391*	40	3
10 Feb 96	STEAL YOUR LOVE AWAY *EMI CDEMS 407*	37	2
29 Jun 96	COULD IT BE FOREVER *EMI CDEMS 426*	38	2

GEMS FOR JEM
UK, male instrumental / production duo – Steve McCutcheon and Darren Pearce (Singles: 2 Weeks) pos/wks

6 May 95	LIFTING ME HIGHER *Box 21 CDSBOKS 3*	28	2

GENE
UK, male vocal / instrumental group (Singles: 23 Weeks, Albums: 14 Weeks) pos/wks

13 Aug 94	BE MY LIGHT BE MY GUIDE *Costermonger COST 002CD*	54	1
12 Nov 94	SLEEP WELL TONIGHT *Costermonger COST 003CD*	36	2
4 Mar 95	HAUNTED BY YOU *Costermonger COST 004CD*	32	2
22 Jul 95	OLYMPIAN *Costermonger COST 005CD*	18	2
13 Jan 96	FOR THE DEAD *Costermonger COST 006CD*	14	3
2 Nov 96	FIGHTING FIT *Costermonger COST 009CD*	22	2
1 Feb 97	WE COULD BE KINGS *Polydor COSCD 10*	17	2
10 May 97	WHERE ARE THEY NOW? *Polydor COSCD 11*	22	2
9 Aug 97	SPEAK TO ME SOMEONE *Polydor COSCD 12*	30	2
27 Feb 99	AS GOOD AS IT GETS *Polydor COSCD 14*	23	2
24 Apr 99	FILL HER UP *Polydor COSCD 15*	36	2
25 Dec 04	LET ME MOVE ON *Costermonger COST 10CD1*	69	1+
1 Apr 95 ●	OLYMPIAN *Costermonger 5274462*	8	6
3 Feb 96	TO SEE THE LIGHTS *Costermonger GENE 002CD*	11	3
1 Mar 97 ●	DRAWN TO THE DEEP END *Polydor GENEC 3*	8	3
13 Mar 99	REVELATIONS *Polydor GENEC 4*	25	2

GENE AND JIM ARE INTO SHAKES
UK, male vocal / instrumental duo (Singles: 2 Weeks) pos/wks

19 Mar 88	SHAKE! (HOW ABOUT A SAMPLING, GENE?) *Rough Trade RT 216*	68	2

GENE LOVES JEZEBEL
UK, male vocal / instrumental group (Singles: 7 Weeks, Albums: 5 Weeks) pos/wks

29 Mar 86	SWEETEST THING *Beggars Banquet BEG 156*	75	1
14 Jun 86	HEARTACHE *Beggars Banquet BEG 161*	71	2
5 Sep 87	THE MOTION OF LOVE *Beggars Banquet BEG 192*	56	3
5 Dec 87	GORGEOUS *Beggars Banquet BEG 202*	68	1
19 Jul 87	DISCOVER *Beggars Banquet BEGA 73*	32	4
24 Oct 87	HOUSE OF DOLLS *Beggars Banquet BEGA 87*	81	1

GENERAL DEGREE *See Richie STEPHENS*

GENERAL LEVY
UK, male vocalist – Paul Levy (Singles: 14 Weeks) pos/wks

4 Sep 93	MONKEY MAN *ffrr FCD 214*	75	1
18 Jun 94	INCREDIBLE *Renk RENK 42 CD* [1]	39	2
10 Sep 94 ●	INCREDIBLE (re-mix) *Renk CD RENK 44* [1]	8	9
13 Mar 04	SHAKE (WHAT YA MAMA GAVE YA) *East West EW 281CD* [2]	51	1

[1] M-Beat featuring General Levy [2] General Levy vs Zeus featuring Bally Jagpal

GENERAL PUBLIC (see also The BEAT)
UK, male vocal / instrumental group (Singles: 4 Weeks) pos/wks

10 Mar 84	GENERAL PUBLIC *Virgin VS 659*	60	3
2 Jul 94	I'LL TAKE YOU THERE *Epic 6605532*	73	1

GENERAL SAINT (see also Clint EASTWOOD and GENERAL SAINT)
UK, male vocalist (Singles: 4 Weeks) pos/wks

29 Sep 84	LAST PLANE (ONE WAY TICKET) *MCA MCA 910* [1]	51	3
6 Aug 94	SAVE THE LAST DANCE FOR ME *Copasetic COPCD 12* [2]	75	1

[1] Clint Eastwood and General Saint [2] General Saint featuring Don Campbell

GENERATION X
(see also Billy IDOL) *UK, male vocal / instrumental group (Singles: 31 Weeks, Albums: 9 Weeks)* pos/wks

17 Sep 77	YOUR GENERATION *Chrysalis CHS 2165*	36	4
11 Mar 78	READY STEADY GO *Chrysalis CHS 2207*	47	3
20 Jan 79	KING ROCKER *Chrysalis CHS 2261*	11	9
7 Apr 79	VALLEY OF THE DOLLS *Chrysalis CHS 2310*	23	7
30 Jun 79	FRIDAY'S ANGELS *Chrysalis CHS 2330*	62	2
18 Oct 80	DANCING WITH MYSELF *Chrysalis CHS 2444* [1]	62	2
24 Jan 81	DANCING WITH MYSELF (EP) *Chrysalis CHS 2488* [1]	60	4
8 Apr 78	GENERATION X *Chrysalis CHR 1169*	29	4
17 Feb 79	VALLEY OF THE DOLLS *Chrysalis CHR 1193*	51	5

[1] Gen X

Tracks on Dancing With Myself (EP): Dancing With Myself / Untouchables / Rock On / King Rocker. 'Dancing With Myself' was a re-issue of their 1980 hit

GENERATOR
Holland, male producer – Robert Smit (Singles: 1 Week) pos/wks

23 Oct 99	WHERE ARE YOU NOW? *Tidy Trax TIDY 130CD*	60	1

GENESIS (45 Top 500) (see also FISH; MIKE and the MECHANICS)
Perennially popular UK group. Stalwart members are Tony Banks (k) and Mike Rutherford (g); others included Peter Gabriel (v), Phil Collins (v/d), Steve Hackett (g). These progressive 1970s rockers became a major act in the 1980s and had 10 consecutive newly recorded Top 3 albums (Singles: 187 Weeks, Albums: 494 Weeks) pos/wks

6 Apr 74	I KNOW WHAT I LIKE (IN YOUR WARDROBE) *Charisma CB 224*	21	7
26 Feb 77	YOUR OWN SPECIAL WAY *Charisma CB 300*	43	3
28 May 77	SPOT THE PIGEON (EP) *Charisma GEN 001*	14	7
11 Mar 78 ●	FOLLOW YOU FOLLOW ME *Charisma CB 309*	7	13
8 Jul 78	MANY TOO MANY *Charisma CB 315*	43	5
15 Mar 80 ●	TURN IT ON AGAIN *Charisma CB 356*	8	10
17 May 80	DUCHESS *Charisma CB 363*	46	5
13 Sep 80	MISUNDERSTANDING *Charisma CB 369*	42	5
22 Aug 81 ●	ABACAB *Charisma CB 388*	9	8
31 Oct 81	KEEP IT DARK *Charisma CB 391*	33	4
13 Mar 82	MAN ON THE CORNER *Charisma CB 393*	41	5
22 May 82 ●	3 X 3 (EP) *Charisma GEN 1*	10	8
3 Sep 83	MAMA *Virgin / Charisma MAMA 1*	4	10
12 Nov 83	THAT'S ALL *Charisma / Virgin TATA 1*	16	11
11 Feb 84	ILLEGAL ALIEN (re) *Charisma / Virgin AL1*	46	4
31 May 86	INVISIBLE TOUCH *Virgin GENS 1* ▲	15	8
30 Aug 86	IN TOO DEEP *Virgin GENS 2*	19	9
22 Nov 86	LAND OF CONFUSION *Virgin GENS 3*	14	12
14 Mar 87	TONIGHT TONIGHT TONIGHT *Virgin GENS 4*	18	6
20 Jun 87	THROWING IT ALL AWAY *Virgin GENS 5*	22	8
2 Nov 91	NO SON OF MINE (re) *Virgin GENS 6*	6	7
11 Jan 92 ●	I CAN'T DANCE *Virgin GENS 7*	7	9
18 Apr 92	HOLD ON MY HEART *Virgin GENS 8*	16	5
25 Jul 92	JESUS HE KNOWS ME *Virgin GENS 9*	20	7
21 Nov 92	INVISIBLE TOUCH (LIVE) *Virgin GENS 10*	7	4
20 Feb 93	TELL ME WHY *Virgin GENDG 11*	40	3
27 Sep 97	CONGO *Virgin GENSD 12*	29	2
13 Dec 97	SHIPWRECKED *Virgin GENDX 14*	54	1
7 Mar 98	NOT ABOUT US *Virgin GENSD 15*	66	1
14 Oct 72	FOXTROT *Charisma CAS 1058*	12	7
11 Aug 73 ●	GENESIS LIVE *Charisma CLASS 1*	9	10
20 Oct 73 ●	SELLING ENGLAND BY THE POUND *Charisma CAS 1074*	3	21
11 May 74	NURSERY CRYME *Charisma CAS 1052*	39	1
7 Dec 74 ●	THE LAMB LIES DOWN ON BROADWAY *Charisma CGS 101*	10	6
28 Feb 76 ●	A TRICK OF THE TAIL *Charisma CDS 4001*	3	39
15 Jan 77 ●	WIND AND WUTHERING *Charisma CDS 4005*	7	22
29 Oct 77 ●	SECONDS OUT *Charisma GE 2001*	4	17
15 Apr 78 ●	AND THEN THERE WERE THREE *Charisma CDS 4010*	3	32
5 Apr 80 ★	DUKE *Charisma CBR 101* ■	1	30
26 Sep 81 ★	ABACAB *Charisma CBR 102* ■	1	27
12 Jun 82 ●	THREE SIDES LIVE *Charisma GE 2002*	2	19
15 Oct 83 ★	GENESIS *Charisma GENLP 1* ■	1	51

		pos/wks
31 Mar 84	NURSERY CRYME (re-issue) *Charisma CHC 22*	68 1
21 Apr 84	TRESPASS *Charisma CHC 12*	98 1
21 Jun 86 ★	INVISIBLE TOUCH *Charisma GENLP 2* ■	1 96
23 Nov 91 ★	WE CAN'T DANCE *Virgin GENLP 3* ■	1 61
28 Nov 92 ●	LIVE – THE WAY WE WALK VOLUME ONE: THE SHORTS *Virgin GENCD 4*	3 18
23 Jan 93 ★	LIVE – THE WAY WE WALK VOLUME TWO: THE LONGS *Virgin GENCD 5* ■	1 9
13 Sep 97 ●	CALLING ALL STATIONS *Virgin GENCD 6*	2 7
4 Jul 98	ARCHIVE 1967-75 *Virgin CDBOX 6*	35 1
6 Nov 99 ●	TURN IT ON AGAIN – THE HITS *Virgin GENCDX 8*	4 15
11 Dec 04	PLATINUM COLLECTION *Virgin GENCDX 9*	21 3+

Tracks on Spot the Pigeon (EP): Match of the Day / Pigeons / Inside and Out. Tracks on 3 x 3 (EP): Paperlate / You Might Recall / Me and Virgil 'Platinum Collection' is a three-CD box set

Lee A GENESIS *See Bob SINCLAR*

GENEVA *UK, male vocal / instrumental group (Singles: 9 Weeks, Albums: 2 Weeks)* pos/wks

		pos/wks
26 Oct 96	NO ONE SPEAKS *Nude NUD 22CD*	32 2
8 Feb 97	INTO THE BLUE *Nude NUD 25CD*	26 2
31 May 97	TRANQUILIZER *Nude NUD 28CD1*	24 2
16 Aug 97	BEST REGRETS *Nude NUD 31CD1*	38 1
27 Nov 99	DOLLARS IN THE HEAVENS *Nude NUD 46CD1*	59 1
11 Mar 00	IF YOU HAVE TO GO *Nude NUD 49CD1*	69 1
21 Jun 97	FURTHER *Nude NUDE 7CD*	20 2

GENEVIEVE *UK, female vocalist – Susan Hunt (Singles: 1 Week)* pos/wks

		pos/wks
5 May 66	ONCE *CBS 202061*	43 1

GENIUS / GZA (see also WU-TANG CLAN) *US, male rapper – Gary Grice (Singles: 2 Weeks, Albums: 2 Weeks)* pos/wks

		pos/wks
2 Mar 96	COLD WORLD *Geffen GFSTD 22114* [1]	40 2
2 Dec 95	LIQUID SWORDS *Geffen GED 24813*	73 1
10 Jul 99	BENEATH THE SURFACE *MCA MCD 11969*	56 1

[1] Genius / GZA featuring D'Angelo

GENIUS CRU *UK, male production group (Singles: 7 Weeks)* pos/wks

		pos/wks
3 Feb 01	BOOM SELECTION *Incentive CENT 17CDS*	12 5
27 Oct 01	COURSE BRUV *Incentive CENT 28CDS*	39 2

Jackie GENOVA
UK, female exercise instructor (Albums: 2 Weeks) pos/wks

		pos/wks
21 May 83	WORK THAT BODY *Island ILPS 9732*	74 2

Bobbie GENTRY *US, female vocalist – Roberta Streeter (Singles: 48 Weeks, Albums: 2 Weeks)* pos/wks

		pos/wks
13 Sep 67	ODE TO BILLIE JOE *Capitol CL 15511* ▲	13 11
30 Aug 69 ★	I'LL NEVER FALL IN LOVE AGAIN *Capitol CL 15606*	1 19
6 Dec 69 ●	ALL I HAVE TO DO IS DREAM *Capitol CL 15619* [1]	3 14
21 Feb 70	RAINDROPS KEEP FALLING ON MY HEAD *Capitol CL 15626*	40 4
25 Oct 69	TOUCH 'EM WITH LOVE *Capitol EST 155*	21 1
28 Feb 70	BOBBIE GENTRY AND GLEN CAMPBELL *Capitol ST 2928* [1]	50 1

[1] Bobbie Gentry and Glen Campbell [1] Bobbie Gentry and Glen Campbell

GEORDIE *UK, male vocal / instrumental group (Singles: 35 Weeks)* pos/wks

		pos/wks
2 Dec 72	DON'T DO THAT *Regal Zonophone RZ 3067*	32 7
17 Mar 73 ●	ALL BECAUSE OF YOU *EMI 2008*	6 13
16 Jun 73	CAN YOU DO IT *EMI 2031*	13 9
25 Aug 73	ELECTRIC LADY *EMI 2048*	32 6

Lowell GEORGE (see also LITTLE FEAT) *US, male vocalist / instrumentalist – guitar, b. 13 Apr 1945, d. 29 Jun 1979 (Albums: 1 Week)* pos/wks

		pos/wks
21 Apr 79	THANKS BUT I'LL EAT IT HERE *Warner Bros. K 56487*	71 1

Robin GEORGE
UK, male vocalist (Singles: 2 Weeks, Albums: 3 Weeks) pos/wks

		pos/wks
27 Apr 85	HEARTLINE *Bronze BRO 191*	68 2
2 Mar 85	DANGEROUS MUSIC *Bronze BRON 554*	65 3

Sophia GEORGE *Jamaica, female vocalist (Singles: 11 Weeks)* pos/wks

		pos/wks
7 Dec 85 ●	GIRLIE GIRLIE *Winner WIN 01*	7 11

The GEORGIA SATELLITES *US, male vocal / instrumental group (Singles: 8 Weeks, Albums: 9 Weeks)* pos/wks

		pos/wks
7 Feb 87	KEEP YOUR HANDS TO YOURSELF *Elektra EKR 50*	69 1
16 May 87	BATTLESHIP CHAINS *Elektra EKR 58*	44 4
21 Jan 89	HIPPY HIPPY SHAKE *Elektra EKR 86*	63 3
7 Feb 87	GEORGIA SATELLITES *Elektra 9804961*	52 7
2 Jul 88	OPEN ALL NIGHT *Elektra EKT 47*	39 2

GEORGIE PORGIE
US, male producer – George Andros (Singles: 3 Weeks) pos/wks

		pos/wks
12 Aug 95	EVERYBODY MUST PARTY *Vibe MCSTD 2068*	61 1
4 May 96	TAKE ME HIGHER *Music Plant MCSTD 40031*	61 1
26 Aug 00	LIFE GOES ON *Neo NEOCD 039*	54 1

GEORGIO *US, male vocalist – Georgio Allentin (Singles: 3 Weeks)* pos/wks

		pos/wks
20 Feb 88	LOVER'S LANE *Motown ZB 41611*	54 3

Danyel GÉRARD *France, male vocalist – Gérard Daniel Kherlakian (Singles: 12 Weeks)* pos/wks

		pos/wks
18 Sep 71	BUTTERFLY *CBS 7454*	11 12

GERIDEAU *US, male vocalist – Theo Gerideau (Singles: 2 Weeks)* pos/wks

		pos/wks
27 Aug 94	BRING IT ALL BACK 2 LUV *Fruittree FTREE 10CD* [1]	65 1
4 Jul 98	MASQUERADE *Inferno CDFERN 7*	63 1

[1] Project featuring Gerideau

GERRY and the PACEMAKERS
Record-breaking Merseybeat band: Gerry Marsden (v/g), Les Chadwick (b), Les McGuire (p), Freddie Marsden (d). Second Liverpool group to chart (after The Beatles), but first to reach No.1 and first act ever to top UK chart with their initial three singles (Singles: 114 Weeks, Albums: 29 Weeks) pos/wks

		pos/wks
14 Mar 63 ★	HOW DO YOU DO IT? *Columbia DB 4987*	1 18
30 May 63 ★	I LIKE IT *Columbia DB 7041*	1 15
10 Oct 63 ★	YOU'LL NEVER WALK ALONE *Columbia DB 7126*	1 19
16 Jan 64 ●	I'M THE ONE *Columbia DB 7189*	2 15
16 Apr 64 ●	DON'T LET THE SUN CATCH YOU CRYING *Columbia DB 7268*	6 11
3 Sep 64	IT'S GONNA BE ALL RIGHT *Columbia DB 7353*	24 7
17 Dec 64 ●	FERRY 'CROSS THE MERSEY *Columbia DB 7437*	8 13
25 Mar 65	I'LL BE THERE *Columbia DB 7504*	15 9
18 Nov 65	WALK HAND IN HAND *Columbia DB 7738*	29 7
26 Oct 63 ●	HOW DO YOU LIKE IT? *Columbia 33SX 1546*	2 28
6 Feb 65	FERRY CROSS THE MERSEY *Columbia 33SX 1676*	19 1

GET FRESH CREW *See Doug E FRESH and the GET FRESH CREW*

GET READY *UK, male vocal group (Singles: 1 Week)* pos/wks

		pos/wks
3 Jun 95	WILD WILD WEST *Mega GACXCD 2698*	65 1

GETO BOYS featuring FLAJ
US, male rap group (Singles: 1 Week) pos/wks

		pos/wks
11 May 96	THE WORLD IS A GHETTO *Virgin America VUSCD 104*	49 1

Stan GETZ *US, male instrumentalist – tenor sax – Stanley Gayetzsky, b. 2 Feb 1927, d. 6 Jun 1991 (Singles: 29 Weeks, Albums: 7 Weeks)* pos/wks

		pos/wks
8 Nov 62	DESAFINADO *HMV POP 1061* [1]	11 13
23 Jul 64	THE GIRL FROM IPANEMA (GAROTA DE IPANEMA) *Verve VS 520* [2]	29 10
25 Aug 84	THE GIRL FROM IPANEMA (re-issue) *Verve IPA 1* [3]	55 6
23 Feb 63	JAZZ SAMBA *Verve SULP 9013* [1]	15 7

[1] Stan Getz and Charlie Byrd [2] Stan Getz and Joao Gilberto [3] Astrud Gilberto
[1] Stan Getz and Charlie Byrd

The re-issue of 'The Girl from Ipanema' was credited only to Astrud Gilberto, the vocalist, even though it was exactly the same recording as the original hit

Angela GHEORGIU *See Roberto ALAGNA / Angela GHEORGIU*

Amanda GHOST *UK, female vocalist (Singles: 2 Weeks)* pos/wks

		pos/wks
8 Apr 00	IDOL *Warner Bros. W 518CD*	63 1
1 May 04	BREAK MY WORLD *Island CID 853* [1]	52 1

[1] Dark Globe featuring Amanda Ghost

GHOST DANCE
UK, male vocal / instrumental group (Singles: 2 Weeks)   pos/wks

17 Jun 89	**DOWN TO THE WIRE** *Chrysalis CHS 3376*	66	2

GHOSTFACE KILLAH (see also WU-TANG CLAN) *US, male rapper – Dennis Coles (Singles: 38 Weeks, Albums: 2 Weeks)*   pos/wks

12 Jul 97	**ALL THAT I GOT IS YOU** *Epic 6646842*	11	4
23 Jan 99 ●	**I WANT YOU FOR MYSELF** *Northwestside 74321643632* [1]	2	8
4 Nov 00	**MISS FAT BOOTY – PART II** *Rawkus RWK 282CD* [2]	64	1
1 Nov 03	**OOH WEE** *Elektra E 7490CD* [3]	15	7
29 May 04 ●	**ON MY KNEES (re)** *Sony Music 6749381* [4]	4	11
17 Jul 04	**PUSH** *Def Jam 9862837* [5]	34	3
16 Oct 04	**LOVE THEM** *Jive 8287663912* [6]	27	4
9 Nov 96	**IRONMAN** *Epic 4853892*	38	2

[1] Another Level / Ghostface Killah [2] Mos Def featuring Ghostface Killah
[3] Mark Ronson featuring Ghostface Killah and Nate Dogg [4] The 411 featuring Ghostface Killah [5] Ghostface featuring Missy Elliott [6] Eamon featuring Ghostface

Andy GIBB *UK, male vocalist, b. 5 Mar 1958, d. 10 Mar 1988 (Singles: 30 Weeks, Albums: 9 Weeks)*   pos/wks

25 Jun 77	**I JUST WANNA BE YOUR EVERYTHING** *RSO 2090 237* ▲	26	7
13 May 78	**SHADOW DANCING** *RSO 001* ▲	42	6
12 Aug 78 ●	**AN EVERLASTING LOVE** *RSO 015*	10	10
27 Jan 79	**(OUR LOVE) DON'T THROW IT ALL AWAY** *RSO 26*	32	7
19 Aug 78	**SHADOW DANCING** *RSO RSS 0001*	15	9

Barry GIBB (see also The BEE GEES) *UK, male vocalist (Singles: 10 Weeks, Albums: 2 Weeks)*   pos/wks

6 Dec 80	**GUILTY** *CBS 9315* [1]	34	10
20 Oct 84	**NOW VOYAGER** *Polydor POLH 14*	85	2

[1] Barbra Streisand and Barry Gibb

Robin GIBB (see also The BEE GEES) *UK, male vocalist (Singles: 25 Weeks, Albums: 1 Week)*   pos/wks

9 Jul 69 ●	**SAVED BY THE BELL (re)** *Polydor 56337*	2	17
7 Feb 70	**AUGUST OCTOBER** *Polydor 56371*	45	3
11 Feb 84	**ANOTHER LONELY NIGHT IN NEW YORK** *Polydor POSP 668*	71	1
1 Jan 03	**PLEASE** *SPV Recordings SPV 05571463*	23	4
15 Feb 03	**MAGNET** *SPV Recordings SPV 08571472*	43	1

Beth GIBBONS & RUSTIN' MAN
(see also PORTISHEAD; TALK TALK) *UK, female vocalist and male producer / instrumentalist – Paul Webb (Singles: 1 Week, Albums: 2 Weeks)*   pos/wks

15 Mar 03	**TOM THE MODEL** *Go Beat GOBCD 55*	70	1
9 Nov 02	**OUT OF SEASON** *Go Beat 665742*	28	2

Steve GIBBONS BAND *UK, male vocal / instrumental group (Singles: 14 Weeks, Albums: 3 Weeks)*   pos/wks

6 Aug 77	**TULANE** *Polydor 2058 889*	12	10
13 May 78	**EDDY VORTEX** *Polydor 2059 017*	56	4
22 Oct 77	**CAUGHT IN THE ACT** *Polydor 2478 112*	22	3

Georgia GIBBS
US, female vocalist – Freda Gibbons (Singles: 2 Weeks)   pos/wks

22 Apr 55	**TWEEDLE DEE** *Mercury MB 3196*	20	1
13 Jul 56	**KISS ME ANOTHER** *Mercury MT 110*	25	1

Debbie GIBSON *US, female vocalist / producer (Singles: 70 Weeks, Albums: 52 Weeks)*   pos/wks

26 Sep 87	**ONLY IN MY DREAMS (re)** *Atlantic A 9322*	11	12
23 Jan 88 ●	**SHAKE YOUR LOVE** *Atlantic A 9187*	7	8
7 May 88	**OUT OF THE BLUE** *Atlantic A 9091*	19	7
9 Jul 88 ●	**FOOLISH BEAT** *Atlantic A 9059* ▲	9	9
15 Oct 88	**STAYING TOGETHER** *Atlantic A 9020*	53	2
28 Jan 89	**LOST IN YOUR EYES** *Atlantic A 8970* ▲	34	7
29 Apr 89	**ELECTRIC YOUTH** *Atlantic A 8919*	14	8
19 Aug 89	**WE COULD BE TOGETHER** *Atlantic A 8896*	22	8
9 Mar 91	**ANYTHING IS POSSIBLE** *Atlantic A 7735*	51	2
3 Apr 93	**SHOCK YOUR MAMA** *Atlantic A 7386CD*	74	1
24 Jul 93	**YOU'RE THE ONE THAT I WANT** *Epic 6595222* [1]	13	6
30 Jan 88	**OUT OF THE BLUE** *Atlantic WX 139*	26	35

11 Feb 89 ●	**ELECTRIC YOUTH** *Atlantic WX 231* ▲	8	16
30 Mar 91	**ANYTHING IS POSSIBLE** *Atlantic WX 399*	69	1

[1] Craig McLachlan and Debbie Gibson

'Only In My Dreams' made its peak position on re-entry in Mar 1988

Don GIBSON *US, male vocalist / instrumentalist – guitar, b. 3 Apr 1928, d. 17 Nov 2003 (Singles: 16 Weeks, Albums: 10 Weeks)*   pos/wks

31 Aug 61	**SEA OF HEARTBREAK** *RCA 1243*	14	13
1 Feb 62	**LONESOME NUMBER ONE** *RCA 1272*	47	3
22 Mar 80	**COUNTRY NUMBER ONE** *Warwick WW 5079*	13	10

Wayne GIBSON *UK, male vocalist (Singles: 13 Weeks)*   pos/wks

3 Sep 64	**KELLY** *Pye 7N 15680*	48	2
23 Nov 74	**UNDER MY THUMB** *Pye Disco Demand DDS 2001*	17	11

The GIBSON BROTHERS *Martinique, male vocal / instrumental group (Singles: 54 Weeks, Albums: 3 Weeks)*   pos/wks

10 Mar 79	**CUBA** *Island WIP 6483*	41	9
21 Jul 79 ●	**OOH! WHAT A LIFE** *Island WIP 6503*	10	12
17 Nov 79 ●	**QUE SERA MI VIDA (IF YOU SHOULD GO)** *Island WIP 6525*	5	11
23 Feb 80	**CUBA / BETTER DO IT SALSA (re-issue)** *Island WIP 6561*	12	9
12 Jul 80	**MARIANA** *Island WIP 6617*	11	10
9 Jul 83	**MY HEART'S BEATING WILD (TIC TAC TIC TAC)** *Stiff BUY 184*	56	3
30 Aug 80	**ON THE RIVIERA** *Island ILPS 9620*	50	3

GIDEA PARK
UK, male vocal group – includes Adrian Baker (Singles: 19 Weeks)   pos/wks

4 Jul 81	**BEACH BOY GOLD** *Sonet SON 2162*	11	13
12 Sep 81	**SEASONS OF GOLD** *Polo POLO 14*	28	6

Johan GIELEN presents ABNEA
(see also AIRSCAPE; BLUE BAMBOO; BALEARIC BILL; SVENSON and GIELEN) *Belgium, male producer (Singles: 1 Week)*   pos/wks

18 Aug 01	**VELVET MOODS** *Data DATA 17T*	74	1

GIFTED *UK, male vocal / instrumental duo (Singles: 1 Week)*   pos/wks

23 Aug 97	**DO I** *Perfecto PERF 140CD*	60	1

GIGOLO AUNTS
US, male vocal / instrumental group (Singles: 4 Weeks)   pos/wks

23 Apr 94	**MRS WASHINGTON** *Fire BLAZE 68CD*	74	1
13 May 95	**WHERE I FIND MY HEAVEN** *Fire BLAZE 87CD*	29	3

Astrud GILBERTO *See Stan GETZ*

Bebel GILBERTO *Brazil, female vocalist (Albums: 8 Weeks)*   pos/wks

31 Aug 02	**TANTO TEMPO** *East West 0927474072*	49	5
19 Jun 04	**BEBEL GILBERTO** *East West 5046732665*	49	3

Joao GILBERTO *See Stan GETZ*

Donna GILES *US, female vocalist (Singles: 4 Weeks)*   pos/wks

13 Aug 94	**AND I'M TELLING YOU I'M NOT GOING** *Ore AG 4CD*	43	2
10 Feb 96	**AND I'M TELLING YOU I'M NOT GOING (re-mix)** *Ore AGR 4CD*	27	2

Johnny GILL (see also NEW EDITION) *US, male vocalist (Singles: 12 Weeks, Albums: 3 Weeks)*   pos/wks

23 Feb 91	**WRAP MY BODY TIGHT** *Motown ZB 44271*	57	2
28 Nov 92	**SLOW AND SEXY** *Epic 6587727* [1]	17	7
17 Jul 93	**THE FLOOR** *Motown TMGCD 1416*	53	1
29 Jan 94	**A CUTE SWEET LOVE ADDICTION** *Motown TMGCD 1420*	46	2
19 Jun 93	**PROVOCATIVE** *Motown 5302062*	41	3

[1] Shabba Ranks featuring Johnny Gill

Vince GILL *See Amy GRANT; Barbra STREISAND*

GILLAN (see also DEEP PURPLE, BLACK SABBATH) *UK, male vocal / instrumental group – leader Ian Gillan, group includes Bernie Torme (Singles: 46 Weeks, Albums: 54 Weeks)*   pos/wks

14 Jun 80	**SLEEPING ON THE JOB** *Virgin VS 355*	55	3
4 Oct 80	**TROUBLE** *Virgin VS 377*	14	6

14 Feb 81	MUTUALLY ASSURED DESTRUCTION *Virgin VSK 103*	**32**	5
21 Mar 81	NEW ORLEANS *Virgin VS 406*	**17**	10
20 Jun 81	NO LAUGHING IN HEAVEN *Virgin VS 425*	**31**	6
10 Oct 81	NIGHTMARE *Virgin VS 441*	**36**	6
23 Jan 82	RESTLESS *Virgin VS 465*	**25**	7
4 Sep 82	LIVING FOR THE CITY *Virgin VS 519*	**50**	3
17 Jul 76	CHILD IN TIME *Polydor 2490136* [1]	**55**	1
20 Oct 79	MR. UNIVERSE *Acrobat ACRO 3*	**11**	6
16 Aug 80 ●	GLORY ROAD *Virgin V 2171*	**3**	12
25 Apr 81 ●	FUTURE SHOCK *Virgin VK 2196*	**2**	13
7 Nov 81	DOUBLE TROUBLE *Virgin VGD 3506*	**12**	15
2 Oct 82	MAGIC *Virgin V 2238*	**17**	6
28 Jul 90	NAKED THUNDER *Teldec 9031718991* [2]	**63**	1

[1] Ian Gillan Band [2] Ian Gillan

GILLETTE *See 20 FINGERS*

Stuart GILLIES *UK, male vocalist (Singles: 10 Weeks)*
pos/wks

31 Mar 73	AMANDA *Philips 6006293*	**13**	10

Jimmy GILMER *See The FIREBALLS*

Thea GILMORE
UK, female vocalist (Singles: 2 Weeks, Albums: 1 Week)
pos/wks

16 Aug 03	JULIET (KEEP THAT IN MIND) *Hungry Dog YRGNUHS 1*	**35**	1
8 Nov 03	MAINSTREAM *Hungry Dog YRGNUH 53*	**50**	1
23 Aug 03	AVALANCHE *Hungry Dog YRGNUHA 1*	**63**	1

David GILMOUR *(see also PINK FLOYD)*
UK, male instrumentalist – guitar (Albums: 18 Weeks)
pos/wks

10 Jun 78	DAVID GILMOUR *Harvest SHVL 817*	**17**	9
17 Mar 84	ABOUT FACE *Harvest SHSP 2400791*	**21**	9

James GILREATH *US, male vocalist (Singles: 10 Weeks)*
pos/wks

2 May 63	LITTLE BAND OF GOLD *Pye International 7N 25190*	**29**	10

Jim GILSTRAP *US, male vocalist (Singles: 11 Weeks)*
pos/wks

15 Mar 75 ●	SWING YOUR DADDY *Chelsea 2005021*	**4**	11

Gordon GILTRAP *UK, male instrumentalist –*
guitar (Singles: 10 Weeks, Albums: 7 Weeks)
pos/wks

14 Jan 78	HEARTSONG *Electric WOT 19*	**21**	7
28 Apr 79	FEAR OF THE DARK *Electric WOT 29* [1]	**58**	3
18 Feb 78	PERILOUS JOURNEY *Electric TRIX 4*	**29**	7

[1] Gordon Giltrap Band

GIN BLOSSOMS *US, male vocal / instrumental*
group (Singles: 12 Weeks, Albums: 6 Weeks)
pos/wks

5 Feb 94	HEY JEALOUSY *Fontana GINCD 3*	**24**	5
16 Apr 94	FOUND OUT ABOUT YOU *Fontana GINCD 4*	**40**	3
10 Feb 96	TIL I HEAR IT FROM YOU *A&M 5812272*	**39**	2
27 Apr 96	FOLLOW YOU DOWN *A&M 5815512*	**30**	2
26 Feb 94	NEW MISERABLE EXPERIENCE *Fontana 3954032*	**53**	4
24 Feb 96	CONGRATULATIONS I'M SORRY *A&M 5404702*	**42**	2

GINGERBREADS *See GOLDIE and the GINGERBREADS*

GINUWINE *US, male rapper –*
Elgin Lumpkin (Singles: 27 Weeks, Albums: 2 Weeks)
pos/wks

25 Jan 97	PONY *Epic 6641282*	**16**	6
24 May 97	TELL ME DO U WANNA *Epic 6645272*	**16**	3
6 Sep 97	WHEN DOVES CRY *Epic 6649245*	**10**	5
14 Mar 98	HOLLER *Epic 6653372*	**13**	4
13 Mar 99 ●	WHAT'S SO DIFFERENT? *Epic 6670522*	**10**	4
14 Dec 02	CRUSH TONIGHT *Atlantic AT 0142CD* [1]	**42**	2
7 Jun 03	HELL YEAH *Epic 6739242*	**27**	3
28 Mar 98	GINUWINE ... THE BACHELOR *Epic 4853912*	**74**	1
27 Mar 99	100% GINUWINE *Epic 4919922*	**42**	1

[1] Fat Joe featuring Ginuwine

GIPSY KINGS *France, male vocal /*
instrumental group (Singles: 2 Weeks, Albums: 65 Weeks)
pos/wks

3 Sep 94	HITS MEDLEY *Columbia 6606022*	**53**	2
15 Apr 89	GIPSY KINGS *Telstar STAR 2355*	**16**	29

25 Nov 89	MOSAÏQUE *Telstar STAR 2398*	**27**	13
13 Jul 91	ESTE MUNDO *Columbia 4686481*	**19**	7
6 Aug 94	GREATEST HITS *Columbia 4772422*	**11**	11
24 Jul 99	VOLARE – THE VERY BEST OF THE GIPSY KINGS *Columbia SONYTV 69CD*	**20**	5

Martine GIRAULT *UK, female vocalist (Singles: 7 Weeks)*
pos/wks

29 Aug 92	REVIVAL *ffrr FX 195*	**53**	2
30 Jan 93	REVIVAL (re-issue) *ffrr FCD 205*	**37**	3
28 Oct 95	BEEN THINKING ABOUT YOU *RCA 74321316142*	**63**	1
1 Feb 97	REVIVAL (re-mix) *RCA 74321432162*	**61**	1

GIRESSE *UK, male DJ / production duo (Singles: 1 Week)*
pos/wks

14 Apr 01	MON AMI *Inferno CDFERN 36*	**61**	1

GIRL *UK, male vocal / instrumental*
group (Singles: 3 Weeks, Albums: 6 Weeks)
pos/wks

12 Apr 80	HOLLYWOOD TEASE *Jet 176*	**50**	3
9 Feb 80	SHEER GREED *Jet JETLP 224*	**33**	5
23 Jan 82	WASTED YOUTH *Jet JETLP 238*	**92**	1

GIRL NEXT DOOR *See M&S presents GIRL NEXT DOOR*

GIRL THING *UK / Holland, female vocal group (Singles: 13 Weeks)*
pos/wks

1 Jul 00 ●	LAST ONE STANDING (re) *RCA 74321762412*	**8**	13
18 Nov 00	GIRLS ON TOP *RCA 74321801162*	**25**	3

GIRLFRIEND *Australia, female vocal group (Singles: 6 Weeks)*
pos/wks

30 Jan 93	TAKE IT FROM ME *Arista 74321114252*	**47**	4
15 May 93	GIRL'S LIFE *Arista 74321138452*	**68**	2

GIRLS ALOUD
UK, female vocal group (Singles: 83 Weeks, Albums: 21 Weeks)
pos/wks

28 Dec 02 ★	SOUND OF THE UNDERGROUND *Polydor 0658272* ■	**1**	21
24 May 03 ●	NO GOOD ADVICE *Polydor 9800051*	**2**	14
30 Aug 03 ●	LIFE GOT COLD *Polydor 9810656*	**3**	9
29 Nov 03 ●	JUMP *Polydor 9814103*	**2**	14
10 Jul 04 ●	THE SHOW *Polydor 9867040*	**2**	10
25 Sep 04 ●	LOVE MACHINE *Polydor 9867984*	**2**	10
27 Nov 04 ★	I'LL STAND BY YOU *Polydor 9869130* ■	**1**	5+
7 Jun 03	SOUND OF THE UNDERGROUND *Polydor 9865315*	**2**	18
11 Dec 04 ●	WHAT WILL THE NEIGHBOURS SAY? *Polydor 9868948*	**6**	3+

GIRLS AT OUR BEST
UK, male / female vocal / instrumental group (Albums: 3 Weeks)
pos/wks

7 Nov 81	PLEASURE *Happy Birthday RVLP 1*	**60**	3

GIRLS @ PLAY
UK, female vocal group (Singles: 7 Weeks)
pos/wks

24 Feb 01	AIRHEAD *GSM GSMCDR 1*	**18**	5
13 Oct 01	RESPECTABLE *Redbus RBMCD 101*	**29**	2

GIRLS OF FHM
UK, female models / vocalists (Singles: 5 Weeks)
pos/wks

3 Jul 04 ●	DA YA THINK I'M SEXY? *2PSL 2PSLCD 5*	**10**	5

GIRLSCHOOL *UK, female vocal / instrumental*
group (Singles: 25 Weeks, Albums: 23 Weeks)
pos/wks

2 Aug 80	RACE WITH THE DEVIL *Bronze BRO 100*	**49**	6
21 Feb 81 ●	ST VALENTINE'S DAY MASSACRE (EP) *Bronze BRO 116* [1]	**5**	8
11 Apr 81	HIT AND RUN *Bronze BRO 118*	**32**	6
11 Jul 81	C'MON LET'S GO *Bronze BRO 126*	**42**	3
3 Apr 82	WILDLIFE (EP) *Bronze BRO 144*	**58**	2
5 Jul 80	DEMOLITION *Bronze BRON 525*	**28**	10
25 Apr 81 ●	HIT 'N' RUN *Bronze BRON 534*	**5**	6
12 Jun 82	SCREAMING BLUE MURDER *Bronze BRON 541*	**27**	6
12 Nov 83	PLAY DIRTY *Bronze BRON 548*	**66**	1

[1] Motörhead and Girlschool (also known as Headgirl)

Tracks on St Valentine's Day Massacre (EP): Please Don't Touch / Emergency / Bomber. Tracks on Wildlife (EP): Don't Call It Love / Wildlife / Don't Stop

Junior GISCOMBE *See JUNIOR*

GITTA *Denmark / Italy, male / female*
vocal / instrumental group (Singles: 1 Week) pos/wks

19 Aug 00	**NO MORE TURNING BACK** *Pepper 9230302*	**54**	1

GLADIATOR featuring IZZY
UK, male DJ / production duo – Bobak Rembrandt and Dave
Lambert and female instrumentalist – violin (Singles: 4 Weeks) pos/wks

29 May 04	**NOW WE ARE FREE** *Universal TV 9866813*	**19**	4

The GLADIATORS
UK, male / female TV Gladiators / vocal group (Singles: 1 Week) pos/wks

30 Nov 96	**THE BOYS ARE BACK IN TOWN** *RCA 74321417002*	**70**	1

GLADIATORS See NERO and the GLADIATORS

GLAM
Italy, male instrumental / production group (Singles: 2 Weeks) pos/wks

1 May 93	**HELL'S PARTY** *Six6 SIXCD 001*	**42**	2

GLAM METAL DETECTIVES
UK, male / female vocal group (Singles: 2 Weeks) pos/wks

11 Mar 95	**EVERYBODY UP!** *ZTT ZANG 62CD*	**29**	2

GLAMMA KID *UK, male vocalist / rapper –*
Lyael Constable (Singles: 25 Weeks, Albums: 1 Week) pos/wks

21 Nov 98	**FASHION '98** *WEA WEA 179CD*	**49**	1
17 Apr 99 ●	**TABOO** *WEA WEA 203CD* [1]	**10**	8
27 Nov 99 ●	**WHY** *WEA WEA 229CD1*	**10**	10
2 Sep 00	**BILLS 2 PAY (re)** *WEA WEA 268CD*	**17**	6
16 Sep 00	**KIDOLOGY** *WEA 3984298572*	**66**	1

[1] Glamma Kid featuring Shola Ama

GLASS TIGER
Canada, male vocal / instrumental group (Singles: 18 Weeks) pos/wks

18 Oct 86	**DON'T FORGET ME (WHEN I'M GONE)** *Manhattan MT 13*	**29**	9
31 Jan 87	**SOMEDAY** *Manhattan MT 17*	**66**	2
26 Oct 91	**MY TOWN** *EMI EM 212*	**33**	7

'My Town' features the uncredited vocals of Rod Stewart

Mayson GLEN ORCHESTRA See Paul HENRY and the Mayson GLEN ORCHESTRA

GLENN and CHRIS
UK, male footballers / vocal duo – Glenn Hoddle
and Chris Waddle (Singles: 8 Weeks) pos/wks

18 Apr 87	**DIAMOND LIGHTS** *Record Shack KICK 1*	**12**	8

Gary GLITTER (227) **Top 500**
Glitter rock giant, b. Paul Gadd, 8 May 1940, Oxfordshire, UK. Started record-
ing in 1960 (as Paul Raven), and was the first act to put his first 11 hits into
the Top 10. This singer / songwriter remained a popular live performer until
he was jailed in 1999. Biggest-selling single: 'I Love You Love Me Love'
1,140,000 (Singles: 170 Weeks, Albums: 100 Weeks) pos/wks

10 Jun 72 ●	**ROCK AND ROLL (PARTS 1 & 2)** *Bell 1216*	**2**	15
23 Sep 72	**I DIDN'T KNOW I LOVED YOU (TILL I SAW YOU ROCK 'N' ROLL** *Bell 1259*	**4**	11
20 Jan 73 ●	**DO YOU WANNA TOUCH ME? (OH YEAH)** *Bell 1280*	**2**	11
7 Apr 73 ●	**HELLO! HELLO! I'M BACK AGAIN** *Bell 1299*	**2**	14
21 Jul 73 ★	**I'M THE LEADER OF THE GANG (I AM!)** *Bell 1321*	**1**	12
17 Nov 73 ★	**I LOVE YOU LOVE ME LOVE** *Bell 1337* ◆ ■	**1**	14
30 Mar 74 ●	**REMEMBER ME THIS WAY** *Bell 1349*	**3**	8
15 Jun 74 ★	**ALWAYS YOURS** *Bell 1359*	**1**	9
23 Nov 74 ●	**OH YES! YOU'RE BEAUTIFUL** *Bell 1391*	**2**	10
3 May 75 ●	**LOVE LIKE YOU AND ME** *Bell 1423*	**10**	6
21 Jun 75 ●	**DOING ALRIGHT WITH THE BOYS** *Bell 1429*	**6**	7
8 Nov 75	**PAPA OOM MOW MOW** *Bell 1451*	**38**	5
13 Mar 76	**YOU BELONG TO ME** *Bell 1473*	**40**	5
22 Jan 77	**IT TAKES ALL NIGHT LONG** *Arista 85*	**25**	6
16 Jul 77	**A LITTLE BOOGIE WOOGIE IN THE BACK OF MY MIND** *Arista 112*	**31**	5
20 Sep 80	**GARY GLITTER (EP)** *GTO GT 282*	**57**	3
10 Oct 81	**AND THEN SHE KISSED ME** *Bell BELL 1497*	**39**	5
5 Dec 81	**ALL THAT GLITTERS** *Bell BELL 1498*	**48**	5
23 Jun 84	**DANCE ME UP** *Arista ARIST 570*	**25**	5
1 Dec 84 ●	**ANOTHER ROCK AND ROLL CHRISTMAS** *Arista ARIST 592*	**7**	7

10 Oct 92	**AND THE LEADER ROCKS ON (MEGAMIX / MEDLEY)** *EMI EM 252*	**58**	2
21 Nov 92	**THROUGH THE YEARS** *EMI EM 256*	**49**	3
16 Dec 95	**HELLO! HELLO! I'M BACK AGAIN (AGAIN!)** *Carlton Sounds 3036000192* (re-recording)	**50**	2
21 Oct 72 ●	**GLITTER** *Bell BELLS 216*	**8**	40
16 Jun 73 ●	**TOUCH ME** *Bell BELLS 222*	**2**	33
29 Jun 74 ●	**REMEMBER ME THIS WAY** *Bell BELLS 237*	**5**	14
27 Mar 76	**GARY GLITTER'S GREATEST HITS** *Bell BELLS 262*	**33**	5
14 Nov 92	**MANY HAPPY RETURNS – THE HITS** *EMI CDEMTV 68*	**35**	8

'Rock and Roll Part 1' not listed with 'Part 2' for weeks of 10 and 17 Jun 1972.
Tracks on Gary Glitter (EP): I'm the Leader of the Gang (I Am!) / Rock and Roll
(Part 2) / Hello! Hello! I'm Back Again / Do You Wanna Touch Me? (Oh Yeah). All
were re-issues. All That Glitters was a medley of re-recordings: I'm The Leader Of
The Gang (I Am!) / Do You Wanna Touch Me (Oh Yeah) / Doing Alright with the
Boys / I Didn't Know I Loved You (Till I Saw You Rock 'n' Roll) / Rock and Roll (Part
2). And the Leader Rocks On was a medley of I'm The Leader Of The Gang (I Am!)
/ Come On, Come In, Get On / Rock On / I Didn't Know I Loved You (Till I Saw You
Rock 'n' Roll) / Do You Wanna Touch Me? (Oh Yeah) / Hello! Hello! I'm Back Again

The GLITTER BAND (see also Gary GLITTER) *UK, male vocal /*
instrumental group (Singles: 60 Weeks, Albums: 17 Weeks) pos/wks

23 Mar 74 ●	**ANGEL FACE** *Bell 1348*	**4**	10
3 Aug 74 ●	**JUST FOR YOU** *Bell 1368*	**10**	8
19 Oct 74 ●	**LET'S GET TOGETHER AGAIN** *Bell 1383*	**8**	8
18 Jan 75 ●	**GOODBYE MY LOVE** *Bell 1395*	**2**	9
12 Apr 75 ●	**THE TEARS I CRIED** *Bell 1416*	**8**	8
9 Aug 75	**LOVE IN THE SUN** *Bell 1437*	**15**	8
28 Feb 76 ●	**PEOPLE LIKE YOU AND PEOPLE LIKE ME** *Bell 1471*	**5**	9
14 Sep 74	**HEY!** *Bell BELLS 241*	**13**	12
3 May 75	**ROCK 'N' ROLL DUDES** *Bell BELLS 253*	**17**	4
19 Jun 76	**GREATEST HITS** *Bell BELLS 264*	**52**	1

GLOBAL COMMUNICATION (see also COSMOS)
UK, male instrumental / production duo – Tom
Middleton and Mark Pritchard (Singles: 1 Week) pos/wks

11 Jan 97	**THE WAY / THE DEEP** *Dedicated GLOBA 002CD*	**51**	1

GLOVE (see also The CURE; SIOUXSIE and the BANSHEES) *UK, male*
vocal / instrumental group (Singles: 3 Weeks, Albums: 3 Weeks) pos/wks

20 Aug 83	**LIKE AN ANIMAL** *Wonderland SHE 3*	**52**	3
17 Sep 83	**BLUE SUNSHINE** *Wonderland SHELP 2*	**35**	3

Dana GLOVER
US, female vocalist (Singles: 1 Week, Albums: 2 Weeks) pos/wks

10 May 03	**THINKING OVER** *Dreamworks 4507762*	**38**	1
17 May 03	**TESTIMONY** *Dreamworks / Polydor 04504522*	**43**	2

GLOWORM
UK / US, male vocal / instrumental group (Singles: 17 Weeks) pos/wks

6 Feb 93	**I LIFT MY CUP** *Pulse 8 CDLOSE 37*	**20**	4
14 May 94 ●	**CARRY ME HOME** *Go Beat GODCD 112*	**9**	11
6 Aug 94	**I LIFT MY CUP (re-issue)** *Pulse 8 CDLOSE 67*	**46**	2

GO GO LORENZO and the DAVIS PINCKNEY PROJECT
US, male vocal / instrumental group (Singles: 8 Weeks) pos/wks

6 Dec 86	**YOU CAN DANCE IF YOU WANT TO** *Boiling Point POSP 836*	**46**	8

GO-GO's
(see also Belinda CARLISLE; Jane WIEDLIN) *US, female vocal /*
instrumental group (Singles: 10 Weeks, Albums: 4 Weeks) pos/wks

15 May 82	**OUR LIPS ARE SEALED** *IRS GDN 102*	**47**	6
26 Jan 91	**COOL JERK** *IRS AM 712*	**60**	1
18 Feb 95	**THE WHOLE WORLD LOST ITS HEAD** *IRS CDEIRS 190*	**29**	3
21 Aug 82	**VACATION** *IRS SP 70031*	**75**	3
18 Mar 95	**RETURN TO THE VALLEY OF THE GO-GO'S** *IRS EIRSCD 1071*	**52**	1

GO WEST (330) **Top 500**
Songwriting duo specialising in radio-friendly white soul sounds: Peter Cox
(v) and Richard Drummie (g/k/v). Best Newcomers at the 1986 Brit awards
had a US Top 10 hit with 'King of Wishful Thinking', from the soundtrack of
Pretty Woman (Singles: 85 Weeks, Albums: 119 Weeks) pos/wks

23 Feb 85 ●	**WE CLOSE OUR EYES** *Chrysalis CHS 2850*	**5**	14
11 May 85	**CALL ME** *Chrysalis GOW 1*	**12**	10

3 Aug 85	GOODBYE GIRL *Chrysalis GOW 2*	**25** 7
23 Nov 85	DON'T LOOK DOWN – THE SEQUEL *Chrysalis GOW 3*	**13** 10
29 Nov 86	TRUE COLOURS *Chrysalis GOW 4*	**48** 7
9 May 87	I WANT TO HEAR IT FROM YOU *Chrysalis GOW 5*	**43** 3
12 Sep 87	THE KING IS DEAD *Chrysalis GOW 6*	**67** 2
28 Jul 90	THE KING OF WISHFUL THINKING *Chrysalis GOW 8*	**18** 10
17 Oct 92	FAITHFUL *Chrysalis GOW 9*	**13** 6
16 Jan 93	WHAT YOU WON'T DO FOR LOVE *Chrysalis CDGOWS 10*	**15** 5
27 Mar 93	STILL IN LOVE *Chrysalis CDGOWS 11*	**43** 3
2 Oct 93	TRACKS OF MY TEARS *Chrysalis CDGOWS 12*	**16** 5
4 Dec 93	WE CLOSE OUR EYES (re-mix) *Chrysalis CDGOWS 13*	**40** 3
13 Apr 85 ●	GO WEST / BANGS AND CRASHES *Chrysalis CHR 1495*	**8** 83
6 Jun 87	DANCING ON THE COUCH *Chrysalis CDL 1550*	**19** 5
14 Nov 92	INDIAN SUMMER *Chrysalis CDCHR 1964*	**13** 16
16 Oct 93 ●	ACES AND KINGS – THE BEST OF GO WEST *Chrysalis CDCHR 6050*	**5** 15

'Bangs and Crashes' is an album of re-mixed versions of Go West tracks and some new material. From 31 May 1986 both records were available together as a double album

The GO! TEAM
UK, male / female vocal / instrumental group (Singles: 1 Week) pos/wks

4 Dec 04	LADYFLASH *Memphis Industries MI 041CDS*	**68** 1

The GO-BETWEENS *Australia, male / female*
vocal / instrumental group (Albums: 2 Weeks) pos/wks

13 Jun 87	TALLULAH *Beggars Banquet BEGA 81*	**91** 1
10 Sep 88	16 LOVERS LANE *Beggars Banquet BEGA 95*	**81** 1

GOATS *US, male rap group (Singles: 2 Weeks, Albums: 1 Week)* pos/wks

29 May 93	AAAH D YAAA / TYPICAL AMERICAN *Ruff House 6593032*	**53** 2
27 Aug 94	NO GOATS NO GLORY *Columbia 4769372*	**58** 1

'Typical American' listed only from 5 Jun 1993, peaking at No.65

GOD MACHINE *US, male vocal / instrumental*
group (Singles: 2 Weeks, Albums: 1 Week) pos/wks

30 Jan 93	HOME *Fiction FICCD 47*	**65** 2
20 Feb 93	SCENES FROM THE SECOND STOREY *Fiction 5171562*	**55** 1

The GODFATHERS
UK, male vocal / instrumental group (Albums: 3 Weeks) pos/wks

13 Feb 88	BIRTH SCHOOL WORK DEATH *Epic 4602631*	**80** 2
20 May 89	MORE SONGS ABOUT LOVE AND HATE *Epic 4633941*	**49** 1

GODIEGO
Japan / US, male vocal / instrumental group (Singles: 11 Weeks) pos/wks

15 Oct 77	THE WATER MARGIN *BBC RESL 50*	**37** 4
16 Feb 80	GANDHARA *BBC RESL 66*	**56** 7

'The Water Margin' is the English version of the song, which shared chart credit with the Japanese language version by Pete Mac Jr

GODLEY and CREME (see also 10cc; HOTLEGS)
UK, male vocal / instrumental duo – Kevin Godley and
Lol Creme (Singles: 36 Weeks, Albums: 34 Weeks) pos/wks

12 Sep 81 ●	UNDER YOUR THUMB *Polydor POSP 322*	**3** 11
21 Nov 81 ●	WEDDING BELLS *Polydor POSP 369*	**7** 11
30 Mar 85	CRY (re) *Polydor POSP 732*	**19** 14
19 Nov 77	CONSEQUENCES *Mercury CONS 017*	**52** 1
9 Sep 78	L *Mercury 9109 611*	**47** 2
17 Oct 81	ISMISM *Polydor POLD 5043*	**29** 13
29 Aug 87 ●	CHANGING FACES – THE VERY BEST OF 10CC AND GODLEY AND CREME *ProTV TGCLP 1* [1]	**4** 18

[1] 10cc and Godley and Creme

GOD'S PROPERTY
US, male / female gospel choir (Singles: 1 Week) pos/wks

22 Nov 97	STOMP *B-rite Music IND 95559*	**60** 1

GODSPEED YOU BLACK EMPEROR!
Canada, male instrumental ensemble (Albums: 1 Week) pos/wks

21 Oct 00	LIFT YOUR SKINNY FISTS LIKE ANTENNAS TO HEAVEN *Kranky KRANK 043*	**66** 1

Alex GOLD featuring Philip OAKEY (see also HUMAN LEAGUE)
UK, male producer and male vocalist (Singles: 1 Week) pos/wks

26 Apr 03	L.A. TODAY *Xtravaganza XTRAV 37CDS*	**68** 1

Andrew GOLD (see also WAX) *US, male vocalist /*
instrumentalist – piano (Singles: 36 Weeks, Albums: 7 Weeks) pos/wks

2 Apr 77	LONELY BOY *Asylum K 13076*	**11** 9
25 Mar 78 ●	NEVER LET HER SLIP AWAY *Asylum K 13112*	**5** 13
24 Jun 78	HOW CAN THIS BE LOVE *Asylum K 13126*	**19** 10
14 Oct 78	THANK YOU FOR BEING A FRIEND *Asylum K 13135*	**42** 4
15 Apr 78	ALL THIS AND HEAVEN TOO *Asylum K 53072*	**31** 7

Ari GOLD *See DJ LUCK & MC NEAT*

GOLD BLADE
UK, male vocal / instrumental group (Singles: 1 Week) pos/wks

22 Mar 97	STRICTLY HARDCORE *Ultimate TOPP 056CD*	**64** 1

Brian and Tony GOLD *See RED DRAGON with Brian and Tony GOLD; SHAGGY*

GOLDBUG
UK, male / female vocal / instrumental group (Singles: 5 Weeks) pos/wks

27 Jan 96 ●	WHOLE LOTTA LOVE *Acid Jazz JAZID 125CD*	**3** 5

GOLDEN BOY with MISS KITTIN *Germany, male*
producer and France, female vocalist (Singles: 1 Week) pos/wks

7 Sep 02	RIPPIN KITTEN *Illustrious CDILL 007*	**67** 1

GOLDEN EARRING *Holland, male vocal /*
instrumental group (Singles: 16 Weeks, Albums: 4 Weeks) pos/wks

8 Dec 73 ●	RADAR LOVE *Track 2094116*	**7** 13
8 Oct 77	RADAR LOVE *Polydor 2121335*	**44** 3
2 Feb 74	MOONTAN *Track 2406112*	**24** 4

The 8 Oct 1977 version of Radar Love credits Golden Earring 'Live'

GOLDEN GIRLS *UK, male producer /*
instrumentalist – Mike Hazell (Singles: 3 Weeks) pos/wks

3 Oct 98	KINETIC *Distinctive DISNCD 46*	**38** 2
4 Dec 99	KINETIC (re-mix) *Distinctive DISNCD 59*	**56** 1

GOLDENSCAN *UK, male DJ / production duo (Singles: 1 Week)* pos/wks

11 Nov 00	SUNRISE *VC Recordings VCRD 79*	**52** 1

GOLDFINGER
US, male vocal / instrumental group (Singles: 1 Week) pos/wks

22 Jun 02	OPEN YOUR EYES *Jive 9270052*	**75** 1

GOLDFRAPP *UK, male / female vocal / instrumental*
group (Singles: 15 Weeks, Albums: 25 Weeks) pos/wks

23 Jun 01	UTOPIA *Mute CDMUTE 264*	**62** 1
17 Nov 01	PILOTS *Mute CDMUTE 267*	**68** 1
26 Apr 03	TRAIN *Mute CDMUTE 291*	**23** 3
2 Aug 03	STRICT MACHINE *Mute CDMUTE 295*	**25** 3
15 Nov 03	TWIST *Mute CDMUTE 311*	**31** 2
13 Mar 04	BLACK CHERRY *Mute CDMUTE 320*	**28** 2
22 May 04	STRICT MACHINE (re-issue) *Mute LCDMUTE 335*	**20** 3
25 Aug 01	FELT MOUNTAIN *Mute CDSTUMM 188*	**57** 5
10 May 03	BLACK CHERRY *Mute CDSTUMM 196*	**19** 20

GOLDIE
UK, male vocal / instrumental group (Singles: 11 Weeks) pos/wks

27 May 78 ●	MAKING UP AGAIN *Bronze BRO 50*	**7** 11

GOLDIE *UK, male producer – Clifford Price*
(Singles: 16 Weeks, Albums: 16 Weeks) pos/wks

3 Dec 94	INNER CITY LIFE *ffrr FCD 251* [1]	**49** 2
9 Sep 95	ANGEL *ffrr FCD 266*	**41** 3
11 Nov 95	INNER CITY LIFE (re-mix) *ffrr FCD 267*	**39** 2
1 Nov 97	DIGITAL *ffrr FCD 316* [2]	**13** 3
24 Jan 98	TEMPERTEMPER *ffrr FCD 325* [2]	**13** 4
18 Apr 98	BELIEVE *ffrr FCD 332*	**36** 2

		pos/wks
19 Aug 95 ●	**TIMELESS** *ffrr 8286142*	**7** 12
14 Feb 98	**SATURNZ RETURN** *ffrr 8289902*	**15** 4

[1] Goldie presents Metalheadz [2] Goldie featuring KRS One

GOLDIE and the GINGERBREADS
US, female vocal / instrumental group (Singles: 5 Weeks) pos/wks

25 Feb 65	**CAN'T YOU HEAR MY HEART BEAT?** *Decca F 12070*	**25** 5

GOLDIE LOOKIN CHAIN *UK, male rap /*
production group (Singles: 17 Weeks, Albums: 11 Weeks) pos/wks

1 May 04	**HALF MAN HALF MACHINE / SELF SUICIDE** *Must Destroy DUSTY 019CD*	**32** 4
28 Aug 04 ●	**GUNS DON'T KILL PEOPLE, RAPPERS DO** *Atlantic GLC 01CD*	**3** 9
6 Nov 04	**YOUR MOTHER'S GOT A PENIS** *East West GLC 02CD*	**14** 3
25 Dec 04	**YOU KNOWS I LOVES YOU BABY** *Atlantic GLC 03CD*	**22** 1+
25 Sep 04 ●	**GREATEST HITS** *Atlantic 5046748802*	**5** 11+

GOLDRUSH
UK, male vocal / instrumental group (Singles: 2 Weeks) pos/wks

22 Jun 02	**SAME PICTURE** *Virgin VSCDT 1833*	**64** 1
7 Sep 02	**WIDE OPEN SKY** *Virgin VSCDT 1834*	**70** 1

Bobby GOLDSBORO *US, male vocalist (Singles: 47 Weeks)* pos/wks

17 Apr 68 ●	**HONEY** *United Artists UP 2215* ▲	**2** 15
4 Aug 73 ●	**SUMMER (THE FIRST TIME)** *United Artists UP 35558*	**9** 10
3 Aug 74	**HELLO, SUMMERTIME** *United Artists UP 35705*	**14** 10
29 Mar 75 ●	**HONEY (re-issue)** *United Artists UP 35633*	**2** 12

Glen GOLDSMITH
UK, male vocalist (Singles: 24 Weeks, Albums: 9 Weeks) pos/wks

7 Nov 87	**I WON'T CRY** *Reproduction PB 41493*	**34** 7
12 Mar 88	**DREAMING** *Reproduction PB 41711*	**12** 11
11 Jun 88	**WHAT YOU SEE IS WHAT YOU GET** *Reproduction PB 42075*	**33** 5
3 Sep 88	**SAVE A LITTLE BIT** *Reproduction PB 42147*	**73** 1
23 Jul 88	**WHAT YOU SEE IS WHAT YOU GET** *RCA PL 71750*	**14** 9

GOLDTRIX presents Andrea BROWN *UK, male production /*
instrumental duo and US, female vocalist (Singles: 9 Weeks) pos/wks

19 Jan 02 ●	**IT'S LOVE (TRIPPIN') (re)** *AM:PM / Serious / Evolve CDAMPM 152*	**6** 9

GOMEZ *UK, male vocal /*
instrumental group (Singles: 17 Weeks, Albums: 101 Weeks) pos/wks

11 Apr 98	**78 STONE WOBBLE** *Hut HUTCD 95*	**44** 1
13 Jun 98	**GET MYSELF ARRESTED** *Hut HUTCD 97*	**45** 1
12 Sep 98	**WHIPPIN' PICCADILLY** *Hut HUTCD 105*	**35** 3
10 Jul 99	**BRING IT ON** *Hut HUTCD 112*	**21** 3
11 Sep 99	**RHYTHM & BLUES ALIBI** *Hut HUTCD 114*	**18** 3
27 Nov 99	**WE HAVEN'T TURNED AROUND** *Hut HUTCD 117*	**38** 2
16 Mar 02	**SHOT SHOT** *Hut / Virgin HUTCD 149*	**28** 2
15 Jun 02	**SOUND OF SOUNDS / PING ONE DOWN** *Hut / Virgin HUTCD 154*	**48** 1
20 Mar 04	**CATCH ME UP** *Hut / Virgin HUTDX 175*	**36** 2
22 May 04	**SILENCE** *Hut / Virgin HUTDX 178*	**41** 1
25 Apr 98	**BRING IT ON** *Hut CDHUTX 49*	**11** 60
25 Sep 99 ●	**LIQUID SKIN** *Hut CDHUT 54*	**2** 28
7 Oct 00 ●	**ABANDONED SHOPPING TROLLEY HOTLINE** *Hut CDHUTX 64*	**10** 4
30 Mar 02 ●	**IN OUR GUN** *Hut CDHUT 72*	**8** 7
29 May 04	**SPLIT THE DIFFERENCE** *Hut / Virgin CDHUT 84*	**35** 2

Leroy GOMEZ See SANTA ESMERALDA and Leroy GOMEZ

GOMPIE
Holland, male vocal / instrumental group (Singles: 12 Weeks) pos/wks

20 May 95	**ALICE (WHO THE X IS ALICE) (LIVING NEXT DOOR TO ALICE) (re)** *Habana HABSCD 5*	**17** 12

GONZALES See FUNK MASTERS

GONZALEZ
UK / US, male vocal / instrumental group (Singles: 11 Weeks) pos/wks

31 Mar 79	**HAVEN'T STOPPED DANCING YET** *Sidewalk SID 102*	**15** 11

GOO GOO DOLLS *US, male vocal /*
instrumental trio (Singles: 4 Weeks, Albums: 2 Weeks) pos/wks

1 Aug 98	**IRIS** *Reprise W 0449CD*	**50** 1
27 Mar 99	**SLIDE** *Edel / Hollywood / Third Rail 0102035 HWR*	**43** 1
17 Jul 99	**IRIS (re-issue)** *Hollywood 0102035 HWR*	**26** 2
31 Jul 99	**DIZZY UP THE GIRL** *Hollywood 0102042 HWR*	**47** 1
4 May 02	**GUTTERFLOWER** *Warner Bros. 9362483112*	**56** 1

GOOD CHARLOTTE *US, male vocal /*
instrumental group (Singles: 31 Weeks, Albums: 43 Weeks) pos/wks

15 Feb 03 ●	**LIFESTYLES OF THE RICH AND FAMOUS** *Epic 6735562*	**8** 10
17 May 03 ●	**GIRLS AND BOYS** *Epic 6738772*	**6** 9
30 Aug 03 ●	**THE ANTHEM** *Epic 6742555*	**10** 4
20 Dec 03	**THE YOUNG AND THE HOPELESS / HOLD ON** *Epic 6745432*	**34** 4
16 Oct 04	**PREDICTABLE** *Epic 6753882*	**12** 4
25 Jan 03	**THE YOUNG AND THE HOPELESS** *Epic 5094889*	**15** 39
23 Oct 04 ●	**THE CHRONICLES OF LIFE AND DEATH** *Epic 5176859*	**8** 4

GOOD GIRLS *US, female vocal group (Singles: 1 Week)* pos/wks

24 Jul 93	**JUST CALL ME** *Motown TMGCD 1417*	**75** 1

GOODBYE MR MACKENZIE
UK, male / female vocal / instrumental group – includes
Shirley Manson (Singles: 13 Weeks, Albums: 4 Weeks) pos/wks

20 Aug 88	**GOODBYE MR MACKENZIE** *Capitol CL 501*	**62** 2
11 Mar 89	**THE RATTLER** *Capitol CL 522*	**37** 6
29 Jul 89	**GOODWILL CITY / I'M SICK OF YOU** *Capitol CL 538*	**49** 2
21 Apr 90	**LOVE CHILD** *Parlophone R 6247*	**52** 2
23 Jun 90	**BLACKER THAN BLACK** *Parlophone R 6257*	**61** 1
22 Apr 89	**GOOD DEEDS AND DIRTY RAGS** *Capitol EST 2089*	**26** 3
16 Mar 91	**HAMMER AND TONGS** *Radioactive RAR 10227*	**61** 1

Roger GOODE featuring Tasha BAXTER *South Africa,*
male DJ / producer and female vocalist (Singles: 2 Weeks) pos/wks

13 Apr 02	**IN THE BEGINNING** *ffrr DFCD 004*	**33** 2

GOODFELLAS featuring Lisa MILLETT (see also ECLIPSE;
BINI & MARTINI; HOUSE OF GLASS) *Italy, male production duo – Paolo*
Martini and Gianni Bini and UK, female vocalist (Singles: 2 Weeks) pos/wks

21 Jul 01	**SOUL HEAVEN** *Direction 6713852*	**27** 2

GOODFELLAZ *US, male vocal trio (Singles: 2 Weeks)* pos/wks

10 May 97	**SUGAR HONEY ICE TEA** *Wild Card 5736132*	**25** 2

The GOODIES *UK, male comedy / vocal*
group (Singles: 38 Weeks, Albums: 11 Weeks) pos/wks

7 Dec 74 ●	**THE INBETWEENIES / FATHER CHRISTMAS DO NOT TOUCH ME** *Bradley's BRAD 7421*	**7** 9
15 Mar 75 ●	**FUNKY GIBBON / SICK-MAN BLUES** *Bradley's BRAD 7504*	**4** 10
21 Jun 75	**BLACK PUDDING BERTHA (THE QUEEN OF NORTHERN SOUL)** *Bradley's BRAD 7517*	**19** 7
27 Sep 75	**NAPPY LOVE / WILD THING** *Bradley's BRAD 7524*	**21** 6
13 Dec 75	**MAKE A DAFT NOISE FOR CHRISTMAS** *Bradley's BRAD 7533*	**20** 6
8 Nov 75	**THE NEW GOODIES LP** *Bradley's BRADL 1010*	**25** 11

Cuba GOODING (see also MAIN INGREDIENT)
US, male vocalist (Singles: 2 Weeks) pos/wks

19 Nov 83	**HAPPINESS IS JUST AROUND THE BEND** *London LON 41*	**72** 2

Benny GOODMAN *US, male instrumentalist –*
clarinet, b. 30 May 1909, d. 13 Jun 1986 (Albums: 1 Week) pos/wks

3 Apr 71	**BENNY GOODMAN TODAY** *Decca DDS 3*	**49** 1

GOODMEN (see also CHOCOLATE PUMA; TOMBA VIRA;
JARK PRONGO; RHYTHMKILLAZ; RIVA featuring Dannii MINOGUE)
Holland, male instrumental / production duo –
Rene Terhorst and Gaston Steenkist (Singles: 19 Weeks) pos/wks

7 Aug 93 ●	**GIVE IT UP (re)** *Fresh Fruit TABCD 118*	**5** 19

Delta GOODREM
Australia, female vocalist (Singles: 45 Weeks, Albums: 37 Weeks) pos/wks

22 Mar 03	● BORN TO TRY *Epic 6736342* 3	13
28 Jun 03	● LOST WITHOUT YOU *Epic 6739555* 4	11
4 Oct 03	● INNOCENT EYES *Epic 6743152* 9	9
13 Dec 03	NOT ME, NOT I *Epic 6745372* 18	6
20 Nov 04	● OUT OF THE BLUE *Epic 6754732* 9	6+
12 Jul 03	● INNOCENT EYES *Epic 5109512* 2	33
4 Dec 04	MISTAKEN IDENTITY *Epic 5189159* 25	4+

Ron GOODWIN and his ORCHESTRA
(see also Eamonn ANDREWS) *UK, orchestra leader,*
b. 17 Feb 1925, d. 8 Jan 2003 (Singles: 24 Weeks, Albums: 1 Week) pos/wks

15 May 53	● TERRY'S THEME FROM 'LIMELIGHT' *Parlophone R 3686* 3	23
28 Oct 55	BLUE STAR (THE MEDIC THEME) *Parlophone R 4074* 20	1
2 May 70	LEGEND OF THE GLASS MOUNTAIN *Studio Two TWO 220* 49	1

GOODY GOODY
US, female vocal duo (Singles: 5 Weeks) pos/wks

2 Dec 78	NUMBER ONE DEE JAY *Atlantic LV 3* 55	5

GOOMBAY DANCE BAND
Germany / Montserrat, male / female
vocal / instrumental group (Singles: 16 Weeks, Albums: 9 Weeks) pos/wks

27 Feb 82	★ SEVEN TEARS *Epic EPC A 1242* 1	12
15 May 82	SUN OF JAMAICA *Epic EPC A 2345* 50	4
10 Apr 82	SEVEN TEARS *Epic EPC 85702* 16	9

The GOONS
(see also Peter SELLERS; Harry SECOMBE; Spike MILLIGAN) *UK, male*
comedy / vocal group (Singles: 30 Weeks, Albums: 31 Weeks) pos/wks

29 Jun 56	● I'M WALKING BACKWARDS FOR CHRISTMAS / BLUEBOTTLE BLUES *Decca F 10756* 4	10
14 Sep 56	● BLOODNOK'S ROCK 'N' ROLL CALL / THE YING TONG SONG *Decca E 10780* 3	10
21 Jul 73	● YING TONG SONG (re-issue) *Decca F 13414* 9	10
28 Nov 59	● BEST OF THE GOON SHOWS *Parlophone PMC 1108* 8	14
17 Dec 60	BEST OF THE GOON SHOWS VOLUME 2 *Parlophone PMC 1129*..12	6
4 Nov 72	● LAST GOON SHOW OF ALL *BBC Radio Enterprise REB 142* 8	11

'Bluebottle Blues' listed only from 13 Jul 1956. It peaked at No.5

GORDON See PETER and GORDON

Lonnie GORDON
US, female vocalist (Singles: 23 Weeks) pos/wks

24 Jun 89	(I'VE GOT YOUR) PLEASURE CONTROL *ffrr F 106* [1] 60	3
27 Jan 90	● HAPPENIN' ALL OVER AGAIN *Supreme SUPE 159* 4	10
11 Aug 90	BEYOND YOUR WILDEST DREAMS *Supreme SUPE 167* 48	2
17 Nov 90	IF I HAVE TO STAND ALONE *Supreme SUPE 181* 68	1
4 May 91	GONNA CATCH YOU *Supreme SUPE 185* 32	5
7 Oct 95	LOVE EVICTION *X:Plode BANG 2CD* [2] 32	2

[1] Simon Harris featuring Lonnie Gordon [2] Quartz Lock featuring Lonnie Gordon

Lesley GORE
US, female vocalist – Lesley Goldstein (Singles: 20 Weeks) pos/wks

20 Jun 63	● IT'S MY PARTY *Mercury AMT 1205* ▲ 9	12
24 Sep 64	MAYBE I KNOW *Mercury MF 829* 20	8

Martin L GORE (see also DEPECHE MODE)
UK, male vocalist (Singles: 1 Week, Albums: 1 Week) pos/wks

26 Apr 03	STARDUST *Mute CDMUTE 296* 44	1
24 Jun 89	COUNTERFEIT E.P. *Mute STUMM 67* 51	1

GORILLAZ
UK / US, animated male vocal / instrumental / production
group (Singles: 39 Weeks, Albums: 53 Weeks) pos/wks

17 Mar 01	● CLINT EASTWOOD *Parlophone CDR 6552* 4	17
7 Jul 01	● 19/2000 *Parlophone CDR 6559* 6	10
3 Nov 01	ROCK THE HOUSE *Parlophone CDRS 6565* 18	8
9 Mar 02	TOMORROW COMES TODAY (re) *Parlophone CDR 6573* 33	3
3 Aug 02	LIL' DUB CHEFIN' *Parlophone CDR 6584* [1] 73	1
7 Apr 01	● GORILLAZ *Parlophone 5311380* 3	52
23 Mar 02	G SIDES *Parlophone 536942* 65	1

[1] Space Monkeyz vs Gorillaz

GORKY'S ZYGOTIC MYNCI
UK, male / female vocal /
instrumental group (Singles: 8 Weeks, Albums: 2 Weeks) pos/wks

9 Nov 96	PATIO SONG *Fontana GZMCD 1* 41	1
29 Mar 97	DIAMOND DEW *Fontana GZMCD 2* 42	1
21 Jun 97	YOUNG GIRLS & HAPPY ENDINGS / DARK NIGHT *Fontana GZMCD 3* 49	1
6 Jun 98	SWEET JOHNNY *Fontana GZMCD 4* 60	1
29 Aug 98	LET'S GET TOGETHER (IN OUR MINDS) *Fontana GZMCD 5* 43	1
2 Oct 99	SPANISH DANCE TROUPE *Mantra / Beggars Banquet MNT 47CD* 47	1
4 Mar 00	POODLE ROCKIN' *Mantra / Beggars Banquet MNT 52CD* 52	1
15 Sep 01	STOOD ON GOLD *Mantra / Beggars Banquet MNT 64CD* 65	1
19 Apr 97	BARAFUNDLE *Fontana 5347692* 46	1
12 Sep 98	GORKY 5 *Fontana 5588222* 67	1

Eydie GORME
US, female vocalist (Singles: 33 Weeks) pos/wks

24 Jan 58	LOVE ME FOREVER *HMV POP 432* 21	5
21 Jun 62	● YES MY DARLING DAUGHTER *CBS AAG 105* 10	9
31 Jan 63	BLAME IT ON THE BOSSA NOVA *CBS AAG 131* 32	6
22 Aug 63	● I WANT TO STAY HERE *CBS AAG 163* [1] 3	13

[1] Steve and Eydie

Matt GOSS (see also BROS)
UK, male vocalist (Singles: 10 Weeks) pos/wks

26 Aug 95	THE KEY *Atlas 5811532* 40	2
27 Apr 96	IF YOU WERE HERE TONIGHT *Atlas 5762932* 23	3
15 Nov 03	I'M COMING WITH YA *Concept CDCON 49* 22	2
31 Jul 04	FLY *Concept CDCON 57* 31	2
2 Oct 04	I NEED THE KEY (re-recording) *Inferno CDFERN 63* [1] 54	1

[1] Minimal Chic featuring Matt Goss

Luke GOSS and the BAND OF THIEVES (see also BROS)
UK, male vocal / instrumental group (Singles: 3 Weeks) pos/wks

12 Jun 93	SWEETER THAN THE MIDNIGHT RAIN *Sabre CDSAB 1* 52	2
21 Aug 93	GIVE ME ONE MORE CHANCE *Sabre CDSAB 2* 68	1

Irv GOTTI
US, male producer / rapper (Singles: 10 Weeks, Albums: 3 Weeks) pos/wks

12 Oct 02	● DOWN 4 U (2re) *Murder Inc 0639002* [1] 4	10
20 Jul 02	IRV GOTTI PRESENTS THE INC *Murder Inc / Mercury 630332* [1] 68	3

[1] Irv Gotti presents Ja Rule, Ashanti, Charli Baltimore and Vita [1] Irv Gotti presents the Inc

Nigel GOULDING See Abigail MEAD and Nigel GOULDING

Graham GOULDMAN (see also 10CC; WAX)
UK, male vocalist (Singles: 4 Weeks) pos/wks

23 Jun 79	SUNBURN *Mercury SUNNY 1* 52	4

GOURYELLA (see also ALBION; MOONMAN; SYSTEM F;
VERACOCHA; STARPARTY) *Holland, male production duo –*
Tijs Verwest and Ferry Corsten (Singles: 11 Weeks) pos/wks

10 Jul 99	GOURYELLA *Code Blue BLU 001CD* 15	7
4 Dec 99	WALHALLA *Code Blue BLU 006CD* 27	2
23 Dec 00	TENSHI *Code Blue BLU 017CD* 45	2

GRACE *UK, female vocalist – Dominique Atkins (Singles: 24 Weeks)* pos/wks

8 Apr 95	● NOT OVER YET *Perfecto PERF 104CD* 6	8
23 Sep 95	I WANT TO LIVE *Perfecto PERF 109CD* 30	2
24 Feb 96	SKIN ON SKIN *Perfecto PERF 116CD* 21	3
1 Jun 96	DOWN TO EARTH *Perfecto PERF 120CD* 20	2
28 Sep 96	IF I COULD FLY *Perfecto PERF 127CD* 29	2
3 May 97	HAND IN HAND *Perfecto PERF 129CD* 38	1
26 Jul 97	DOWN TO EARTH (re-mix) *Perfecto PERF 142CD1* 29	2
14 Aug 99	NOT OVER YET 99 *Code Blue BLU 004CD1* [1] 16	4

[1] Planet Perfecto featuring Grace

Bridgette GRACE See TRUE FAITH and Bridgette GRACE with FINAL CUT

GRACE BROTHERS *UK, male instrumental duo (Singles: 1 Week)* pos/wks

20 Apr 96	ARE YOU BEING SERVED *EMI Premier PRESCD 1* 51	1

Charlie GRACIE US, male vocalist / instrumentalist – guitar – Charlie Graci (Singles: 41 Weeks)
pos/wks

19 Apr 57		BUTTERFLY Parlophone R 4290	12	8
14 Jun 57	●	FABULOUS Parlophone R 4313	8	16
23 Aug 57	●	I LOVE YOU SO MUCH IT HURTS / WANDERIN' EYES (2re) London HLU 8467	6	16
10 Jan 58		COOL BABY London HLU 8521	26	1

'I Love You So Much It Hurts' and 'Wanderin' Eyes' were listed together for two weeks, then listed separately for a further two and 12 weeks respectively

GRAFITI (see also The STREETS)
UK, male producer – Mike Skinner (Singles: 2 Weeks)
pos/wks

30 Aug 03	WHAT IS THE PROBLEM? 679 Recordings 679L 021CD	37	2

Eve GRAHAM See The NEW SEEKERS

Jaki GRAHAM
UK, female vocalist (Singles: 75 Weeks, Albums: 10 Weeks)
pos/wks

23 Mar 85	●	COULD IT BE I'M FALLING IN LOVE Chrysalis GRAN 6 [1]	5	11
29 Jun 85	●	ROUND AND ROUND EMI JAKI 4	9	11
31 Aug 85		HEAVEN KNOWS EMI JAKI 5	59	3
16 Nov 85		MATED EMI JAKI 6 [1]	20	10
3 May 86	●	SET ME FREE EMI JAKI 7	7	12
9 Aug 86		BREAKING AWAY EMI JAKI 8	16	8
15 Nov 86		STEP RIGHT UP EMI JAKI 9	15	12
9 Jul 88		NO MORE TEARS EMI JAKI 12	60	2
24 Jun 89		FROM NOW ON EMI JAKI 15	73	2
16 Jul 94		AIN'T NOBODY Pulse 8 CDLOSE 64	44	2
4 Feb 95		YOU CAN COUNT ON ME Avex UK AVEXCD 1	62	1
8 Jul 95		ABSOLUTE E-SENSUAL Avex UK AVEXCD 5	69	1
14 Sep 85		HEAVEN KNOWS EMI JK 1	48	5
20 Sep 86		BREAKING AWAY EMI EMC 3514	25	5

[1] David Grant and Jaki Graham

Larry GRAHAM (see also SLY and the FAMILY STONE)
US, male vocalist / instrumentalist – bass (Singles: 4 Weeks)
pos/wks

3 Jul 82	SOONER OR LATER Warner Bros. K 17925	54	4

Mikey GRAHAM (see also BOYZONE)
Ireland, male vocalist (Singles: 6 Weeks)
pos/wks

10 Jun 00	YOU'RE MY ANGEL Public PR 001CDS	13	5
14 Apr 01	YOU COULD BE MY EVERYTHING Public PR 003CDS	62	1

Ron GRAINER ORCHESTRA UK, orchestra – leader b. 11 Aug 1922, d. 21 Feb 1981 (Singles: 7 Weeks)
pos/wks

9 Dec 78	A TOUCH OF VELVET – A STING OF BRASS Casino Classics CC 5	60	7

GRAM'MA FUNK See GROOVE ARMADA; ILLICIT featuring GRAM'MA FUNK

GRAND FUNK RAILROAD US, male vocal / instrumental group (Singles: 1 Week, Albums: 1 Week)
pos/wks

6 Feb 71	INSIDE LOOKING OUT Capitol CL 15668	40	1
13 Feb 71	GRAND FUNK LIVE Capital E-STDW 1/2	29	1

GRAND PLAZ
UK, male instrumental / production group (Singles: 4 Weeks)
pos/wks

8 Sep 90	WOW WOW – NA NA Urban URB 60	41	4

GRAND PRIX UK, male vocal / instrumental group (Singles: 1 Week, Albums: 2 Weeks)
pos/wks

27 Feb 82	KEEP ON BELIEVING RCA 162	75	1
18 Jun 83	SAMURAI Chrysalis CHR 1430	65	2

GRAND PUBA
US, male rapper – Maxwell Dixon (Singles: 6 Weeks)
pos/wks

13 Jan 96	WHY YOU TREAT ME SO BAD Virgin VSCDT 1566 [1]	11	5
30 Mar 96	WILL YOU BE MY BABY GHQ 74321339092 [2]	53	1

[1] Shaggy featuring Grand Puba [2] Infiniti featuring Grand Puba

GRAND THEFT AUDIO
UK, male vocal / instrumental group (Singles: 1 Week)
pos/wks

24 Mar 01	WE LUV U Sci-Fi SCIFI 1CD	70	1

GRANDAD ROBERTS AND HIS SON ELVIS
UK, male vocal duo (Singles: 1 Week)
pos/wks

20 Jun 98	MEAT PIE SAUSAGE ROLL WEA WEA 160CD	67	1

GRANDADDY US, male vocal / instrumental group (Singles: 6 Weeks, Albums: 6 Weeks)
pos/wks

2 Sep 00	HEWLETT'S DAUGHTER V2 VVR 5014333	71	1
10 Feb 01	THE CRYSTAL LAKE V2 VVR 5015153	38	2
14 Jun 03	NOW IT'S ON V2 VVR 25022243	23	2
6 Sep 03	EL CAMINOS IN THE WEST V2 VVR 5023663	48	1
20 May 00	THE SOPHTWARE SLUMP V2 VVR 1012252	36	4
21 Jun 03	SUMDAY V2 VVR 1022238	22	2

GRANDMASTER FLASH
(see also DURAN DURAN) US, male vocal / rap / DJ – Joseph Saddler (Singles: 61 Weeks, Albums: 20 Weeks)
pos/wks

28 Aug 82	●	THE MESSAGE Sugarhill SHL 117	8	9
19 Nov 83	●	WHITE LINES (DON'T DON'T DO IT) (3re) Sugarhill SH 130 [1]	7	43
16 Feb 85		SIGN OF THE TIMES Elektra E 9677 [2]	72	1
8 Jan 94		WHITE LINES (DON'T DO IT) (re-mix) WGAF WGAFCD 103 [1]	59	3
17 Jun 95		WHITE LINES (DON'T DO IT) Parlophone CDDD 19 [3]	17	5
23 Oct 82		THE MESSAGE Sugarhill SHLP 1007	77	3
23 Jan 84		GREATEST MESSAGES Sugarhill SHLP 5552	41	16
23 Feb 85		THEY SAID IT COULDN'T BE DONE Elektra 9603891	95	1

[1] Grandmaster and Melle Mel [2] Grandmaster Flash [3] Duran Duran featuring Melle Mel and Grandmaster Flash and the Furious Five

'White Lines (Don't Don't Do It)' re-entered in 1984 (twice), 1985 and 1994

GRANDMASTER MELLE MEL US, male vocalist – Melvin Glover (Singles: 70 Weeks, Albums: 5 Weeks)
pos/wks

22 Jan 83		MESSAGE II (SURVIVAL) Sugarhill SH 119 [1]	74	2
19 Nov 83	●	WHITE LINES (DON'T DO IT) (3RE) Sugarhill SH 130 [2]	7	43
30 Jun 84		BEAT STREET BREAKDOWN Atlantic A 9659 [3]	42	7
22 Sep 84		WE DON'T WORK FOR FREE Sugarhill SH 136 [3]	45	4
16 Mar 85		PUMP ME UP Sugarhill SH 141 [3]	45	6
8 Jan 94		WHITE LINES (DON'T DO IT) (re-mix) WGAF WGAFCD 103 [2]	59	3
17 Jun 95		WHITE LINES (DON'T DO IT) Parlophone CDDD 19 [4]	17	5
20 Oct 84		WORK PARTY Sugarhill SHLP 5553	45	5

[1] Melle Mel and Duke Bootee [2] Grandmaster and Melle Mel [3] Grandmaster Melle Mel and the Furious Five [4] Duran Duran featuring Melle Mel and Grandmaster Flash and the Furious Five

GRANDMIXER D.ST.
US, male DJ / producer – Derek Howells (Singles: 3 Weeks)
pos/wks

24 Dec 83	CRAZY CUTS (re) Island IS 146	71	3

GRANGE HILL CAST UK, male / female vocal charity assembly / TV show cast (Singles: 6 Weeks)
pos/wks

19 Apr 86	●	JUST SAY NO BBC RESL 183	5	6

Gerri GRANGER
US, female vocalist (Singles: 3 Weeks)
pos/wks

30 Sep 78	I GO TO PIECES (EVERYTIME) Casino Classics CC3	50	3

Amy GRANT
US, female vocalist (Singles: 39 Weeks, Albums: 15 Weeks)
pos/wks

11 May 91	●	BABY BABY A&M AM 727 ▲	2	13
3 Aug 91		EVERY HEARTBEAT A&M AM 783	25	7
2 Nov 91		THAT'S WHAT LOVE IS FOR A&M AM 666	60	3
15 Feb 92		GOOD FOR ME A&M AM 810	60	1
13 Aug 94		LUCKY ONE A&M 5807322	60	1
22 Oct 94		SAY YOU'LL BE MINE A&M 5808292	41	2
24 Jun 95		BIG YELLOW TAXI A&M 5809972	20	10
14 Oct 95		HOUSE OF LOVE A&M 5812332 [1]	46	2
22 Jun 91		HEART IN MOTION A&M 3953211	25	15

[1] Amy Grant with Vince Gill

Andrea GRANT UK, female vocalist (Singles: 1 Week)
pos/wks

14 Nov 98	REPUTATIONS (JUST BE GOOD TO ME) WEA WEA 192CD	75	1

Boysie GRANT See Ezz RECO and The LAUNCHERS with Boysie GRANT

David GRANT (see also LINX)
UK, male vocalist (Singles: 59 Weeks, Albums: 7 Weeks)   pos/wks

30 Apr 83	STOP AND GO *Chrysalis GRAN 1*	19	9
16 Jul 83 ●	WATCHING YOU WATCHING ME *Chrysalis GRAN 2*	10	13
8 Oct 83	LOVE WILL FIND A WAY *Chrysalis GRAN 3*	24	6
26 Nov 83	ROCK THE MIDNIGHT *Chrysalis GRAN 4*	46	4
23 Mar 85 ●	COULD IT BE I'M FALLING IN LOVE *Chrysalis GRAN 6* [1]	5	11
16 Nov 85	MATED *EMI JAKI 6* [1]	20	10
1 Aug 87	CHANGE *Polydor POSP 871*	55	4
12 May 90	KEEP IT TOGETHER *Fourth & Broadway BRW 169*	56	2
5 Nov 83	DAVID GRANT *Chrysalis CHR 1448*	32	6
18 May 85	HOPES AND DREAMS *Chrysalis CHR 1483*	96	1

[1] David Grant and Jaki Graham

Eddy GRANT `409` `Top 500`
Former lead guitarist and songwriter for UK group The Equals, b. 5 Mar 1948, Plaisance, Guyana. Left group 1972, went into production and formed own label, Ice. Re-mix of transatlantic No.2 'Electric Avenue' returned him to the Top 5 in 2001 (Singles: 107 Weeks, Albums: 62 Weeks)   pos/wks

2 Jun 79	LIVING ON THE FRONT LINE *Ensign ENY 26*	11	11
15 Nov 80 ●	DO YOU FEEL MY LOVE? *Ensign ENY 45*	8	11
4 Apr 81	CAN'T GET ENOUGH OF YOU *Ensign ENY 207*	13	10
25 Jul 81	I LOVE YOU, YES I LOVE YOU *Ensign ENY 216*	37	6
16 Oct 82 ★	I DON'T WANNA DANCE *Ice ICE 56*	1	15
15 Jan 83 ●	ELECTRIC AVENUE *Ice ICE 57*	2	9
19 Mar 83	LIVING ON THE FRONT LINE / DO YOU FEEL MY LOVE (re-issue) *Mercury MER 135*	47	4
23 Apr 83	WAR PARTY *Ice ICE 58*	42	4
29 Oct 83	TILL I CAN'T TAKE LOVE NO MORE *Ice ICE 60*	42	7
19 May 84	ROMANCING THE STONE *Ice ICE 61*	52	3
23 Jan 88 ●	GIMME HOPE JO'ANNA *Ice ICE 78701*	7	12
27 May 89	WALKING ON SUNSHINE *Blue Wave R 6217*	63	2
9 Jun 01 ●	ELECTRIC AVENUE (re) *Ice / East West EW 232CD*	5	12
24 Nov 01	WALKING ON SUNSHINE (re-mix) *Ice / East West EW 242CD*	57	1
30 May 81	CAN'T GET ENOUGH *Ice ICELP 21*	39	6
27 Nov 82 ●	KILLER ON THE RAMPAGE *Ice ICELP 3023*	7	23
17 Nov 84	ALL THE HITS *K-Tel NE 1284*	23	10
1 Jul 89	WALKING ON SUNSHINE (THE BEST OF EDDY GRANT) *Parlophone PCSD 108*	20	8
19 May 01 ●	THE GREATEST HITS *East West 8573885972*	3	15

Gogi GRANT
US, female vocalist – Audrey Arinsberg (Singles: 11 Weeks)   pos/wks

29 Jun 56 ●	THE WAYWARD WIND *London HLB 8282* ▲	9	11

Julie GRANT
UK, female vocalist – Vivienne Foreman (Singles: 17 Weeks)   pos/wks

3 Jan 63	UP ON THE ROOF *Pye 7N 15483*	33	3
28 Mar 63	COUNT ON ME *Pye 7N 15508*	24	9
24 Sep 64	COME TO ME *Pye 7N 15684*	31	5

Rudy GRANT (see also The EQUALS)
Guyana, male vocalist (Singles: 3 Weeks)   pos/wks

14 Feb 81	LATELY *Ensign ENY 202*	58	3

GRANT LEE BUFFALO
US, male vocal / instrumental group (Albums: 5 Weeks)   pos/wks

10 Jul 93	FUZZY *Slash 8283892*	74	1
1 Oct 94	MIGHTY JOE MOON *Slash 8285412*	24	2
15 Jun 96	COPPEROPOLIS *Slash 8287602*	34	2

GRAPEFRUIT
UK, male vocal / instrumental group (Singles: 19 Weeks)   pos/wks

14 Feb 68	DEAR DELILAH *RCA 1656*	21	9
14 Aug 68	C'MON MARIANNE *RCA 1716*	31	10

GRASS-SHOW
Sweden, male vocal / instrumental group (Singles: 2 Weeks)   pos/wks

22 Mar 97	1962 *Food CDFOOD 90*	53	1
23 Aug 97	OUT OF THE VOID *Food CDFOOD 103*	75	1

GRATEFUL DEAD
US, male vocal / instrumental group (Albums: 14 Weeks)   pos/wks

19 Sep 70	WORKINGMAN'S DEAD *Warner Bros. WS 1869*	69	2
20 Feb 71	AMERICAN BEAUTY *Warner Bros. WS 1893*	27	2
3 Aug 74	GRATEFUL DEAD FROM THE MARS HOTEL *Atlantic K 59302*	47	1
1 Nov 75	BLUES FOR ALLAH *United Artists UAS 29895*	45	1
4 Sep 76	STEAL YOUR FACE *United Artists UAS 60131/2*	42	1
20 Aug 77	TERRAPIN STATION *Arista SPARTY 1016*	30	1
19 Sep 87	IN THE DARK *Arista 208 564*	57	3
18 Feb 89	DYLAN AND THE DEAD *CBS 4633811* [1]	38	3

[1] Bob Dylan and The Grateful Dead

GRAVEDIGGAZ
(see also RZA; WU-TANG CLAN; DE LA SOUL; STETSASONIC)
US, male rap group (Singles: 6 Weeks, Albums: 1 Week)   pos/wks

11 Mar 95	SIX FEET DEEP (EP) *Gee Street GESCD 62*	64	1
5 Aug 95	THE HELL (EP) *Fourth & Broadway BRCD 326* [1]	12	3
24 Jan 98	THE NIGHT THE EARTH CRIED *Gee Street GEE 5001013*	44	1
25 Apr 98	UNEXPLAINED *Gee Street GEE 5001623*	48	1
4 Oct 97	THE PICK THE SICKLE AND THE SHOVEL *Gee Street GEE 1000562*	24	1

[1] Tricky vs The Gravediggaz

Tracks on Six Feet Deep (EP): Bang Your Head / Mommy / Suicide. Tracks on The Hell (EP): Hell Is Round the Corner / Hell Is Round the Corner (re-mix) / Psychosis / Tonite Is a Special Nite

David GRAY `260` `Top 500` (see also ORBITAL) *Acoustic singer / songwriter sensation, b. 13 Jun 1968, Manchester, UK. Ivor Novello award winning modern day troubadour took 66 weeks to top UK album chart with his two million selling 'White Ladder'. One of few new UK acts to score Stateside in 21st century (Singles: 40 Weeks, Albums: 207 Weeks)*   pos/wks

4 Dec 99	PLEASE FORGIVE ME *IHTCDS 003*	72	1
1 Jul 00 ●	BABYLON *IHT / East West EW 215CD1*	5	12
28 Oct 00	PLEASE FORGIVE ME (re-issue) *IHT / East West EW 219CD*	18	6
17 Mar 01	THIS YEAR'S LOVE *IHT / East West EW 228CD1*	20	5
28 Jul 01	SAIL AWAY *IHT / East West EW 234CD*	26	6
29 Dec 01	SAY HELLO WAVE GOODBYE *IHT / East West EW 244CD*	26	4
21 Dec 02	THE OTHER SIDE *IHT / East West EW 259CD*	35	3
19 Apr 03	BE MINE *IHT / East West EW 264CD*	23	3
13 May 00 ★	WHITE LADDER *East West 8573829832*	1	148
12 Aug 00	LOST SONGS 95-98 *IHT IHTCD 002*	7	11
14 Jul 01	THE EP'S 92-94 *Hut CDHUT 67*	68	1
9 Nov 02 ★	A NEW DAY AT MIDNIGHT *East West 5046616582* ■	1	47

David GRAY and Tommy TYCHO
UK, male vocalist and Australia, orchestra leader (Albums: 6 Weeks)   pos/wks

16 Oct 76	ARMCHAIR MELODIES *K-Tel NE 927*	21	6

Dobie GRAY
US, male vocalist – Lawrence Brown (Singles: 11 Weeks)   pos/wks

25 Feb 65	THE 'IN' CROWD *London HL 9953*	25	7
27 Sep 75	OUT ON THE FLOOR *Black Magic BM 107*	42	4

Dorian GRAY *UK, male vocalist (Singles: 7 Weeks)*   pos/wks

27 Mar 68	I'VE GOT YOU ON MY MIND *Parlophone R 5667*	36	7

Les GRAY (see also MUD)
UK, male vocalist, b. 9 Apr 1946, d. 21 Feb 2004 (Singles: 5 Weeks)   pos/wks

26 Feb 77	A GROOVY KIND OF LOVE *Warner Bros. K 16883*	32	5

Macy GRAY *US, female vocalist – Natalie McIntyre (Singles: 52 Weeks, Albums: 82 Weeks)*   pos/wks

3 Jul 99	DO SOMETHING *Epic 6675932*	51	1
9 Oct 99 ●	I TRY *Epic 6681832*	6	22
25 Mar 00	STILL (re) *Epic 6689822*	18	9
5 Aug 00	WHY DIDN'T YOU CALL ME (re) *Epic 6696682*	38	3
20 Jan 01	DEMONS *Skint SKINT 60CD* [1]	16	5
28 Apr 01	GETO HEAVEN *MCA MCSTD 40246* [2]	48	3
12 May 01	REQUEST LINE *Interscope 4970532* [3]	31	3
15 Sep 01	SWEET BABY *Epic 6718822* [4]	23	4
8 Dec 01	SEXUAL REVOLUTION *Epic 6721462*	45	1
3 May 03	WHEN I SEE YOU *Epic 6738402*	26	3

			pos/wks
17 Jul 99	●	**ON HOW LIFE IS** *Epic 4944232*	**3** 67
29 Sep 01	★	**THE ID** *Epic 5040892* ■	**1** 8
10 May 03		**THE TROUBLE WITH BEING MYSELF** *Epic 5108102*	**17** 5
11 Sep 04		**THE VERY BEST OF MACY GRAY** *Epic 5179132*	**36** 2

1 Fatboy Slim featuring Macy Gray 2 Common featuring Macy Gray 3 Black Eyed Peas featuring Macy Gray 4 Macy Gray featuring Erykah Badu

Michael GRAY (see also FULL INTENTION; HUSTLERS CONVENTION featuring Dave LAUDAT and Ondrea DUVERNEY; SEX-O-SONIQUE; DISCO TEX presents CLOUDBURST) *UK, male producer (Singles: 7 Weeks)* pos/wks

13 Nov 04	●	**THE WEEKEND** *Eye Industries / UMTV 9828865*	**7** 7+

Barry GRAY ORCHESTRA *UK, orchestra (Singles: 8 Weeks)* pos/wks

11 Jul 81	**THUNDERBIRDS** *PRT 7P 216*	**61** 2
14 Jun 86	**JOE 90 (THEME) / CAPTAIN SCARLET THEME** *PRT 7PX 354* 1	**53** 6

1 Barry Gray Orchestra with Peter Beckett – keyboards

Alltrina GRAYSON *See Wilton FELDER*

GREASE *See TRICKY*

GREAT WHITE *US, male vocal / instrumental group (Singles: 5 Weeks, Albums: 1 Week)* pos/wks

24 Feb 90	**HOUSE OF BROKEN LOVE** *Capitol CL 562*	**44** 2
16 Feb 91	**CONGO SQUARE** *Capitol CL 605*	**62** 1
7 Sep 91	**CALL IT ROCK 'N' ROLL** *Capitol CL 625*	**67** 2
9 Mar 91	**HOOKED** *Capitol EST 2138*	**43** 1

Martin GRECH *UK, male vocalist (Singles: 1 Week, Albums: 2 Weeks)* pos/wks

12 Oct 02	**OPEN HEART ZOO** *DTOX / Island CID 811*	**68** 1
3 Aug 02	**OPEN HEART ZOO** *Island CID 8119*	**54** 2

Buddy GRECO *US, male vocalist – Armando Greco (Singles: 8 Weeks)* pos/wks

7 Jul 60	**THE LADY IS A TRAMP** *Fontana H 255*	**26** 8

GREED featuring Ricardo DA FORCE *UK, male instrumental duo and male rapper (Singles: 2 Weeks)* pos/wks

18 Mar 95	**PUMP UP THE VOLUME** *Stress CDSTR 49*	**51** 2

The GREEDIES *Ireland / UK / US, male vocal / instrumental group (Singles: 5 Weeks)* pos/wks

15 Dec 79	**A MERRY JINGLE** *Vertigo GREED 1*	**28** 5

Adam GREEN *US, male vocalist (Singles: 1 Week)* pos/wks

3 Apr 04	**JESSICA / KOKOMO** *Rough Trade RTRADSCD 112*	**63** 1

Al GREEN *US, male vocalist – Al Greene (Singles: 68 Weeks, Albums: 31 Weeks)* pos/wks

9 Oct 71	●	**TIRED OF BEING ALONE** *London HLU 10337*	**4** 13
8 Jan 72	●	**LET'S STAY TOGETHER** *London HLU 10348* ▲	**7** 12
20 May 72		**LOOK WHAT YOU DONE FOR ME** *London HLU 10369*	**44** 4
19 Aug 72		**I'M STILL IN LOVE WITH YOU** *London HLU 10382*	**35** 5
16 Nov 74		**SHA-LA-LA (MAKE ME HAPPY)** *London HLU 10470*	**20** 11
15 Mar 75		**L.O.V.E. (LOVE)** *London HLU 10482*	**24** 8
3 Dec 88		**PUT A LITTLE LOVE IN YOUR HEART** *A&M AM 484* 1	**28** 4
21 Oct 89		**THE MESSAGE IS LOVE** *Breakout USA 668* 2	**38** 5
2 Oct 93		**LOVE IS A BEAUTIFUL THING** *Arista 74321162692*	**56** 2
26 Apr 75		**AL GREEN'S GREATEST HITS** *London SHU 8481*	**18** 16
1 Oct 88		**HI LIFE – THE BEST OF AL GREEN** *K-Tel NE 1420*	**34** 7
24 Oct 92		**AL** *Beechwood AGREECD 1*	**41** 2
16 Feb 02		**L-O-V-E: THE ESSENTIAL AL GREEN** *Hi ALTV 2002*	**18** 6

1 Annie Lennox and Al Green 2 Arthur Baker and The Backbeat Disciples featuring Al Green

Dotty GREEN *See Mark FISHER featuring Dotty GREEN*

Jesse GREEN *Jamaica, male vocalist (Singles: 26 Weeks)* pos/wks

7 Aug 76	**NICE AND SLOW** *EMI 2492*	**17** 12
18 Dec 76	**FLIP** *EMI 2564*	**26** 8
11 Jun 77	**COME WITH ME** *EMI 2615*	**29** 6

Peter GREEN (see also FLEETWOOD MAC) *UK, male vocalist / instrumentalist – guitar – Peter Greenbaum (Albums: 19 Weeks)* pos/wks

9 Jul 79	**IN THE SKIES** *Creole PULS 101*	**32** 13
24 May 80	**LITTLE DREAMER** *PUK PULS 102*	**34** 4
24 May 97	**SPLINTER GROUP** *Artisan SARCD 101*	**71** 1
30 May 98	**THE ROBERT JOHNSON SONGBOOK** *Artisan SARCD 002* 1	**57** 1

1 Peter Green with Nigel Watson and the Splinter Group

Robson GREEN (see also ROBSON & JEROME) *UK, male actor / vocalist (Albums: 4 Weeks)* pos/wks

14 Dec 02	**MOMENT IN TIME** *T2 TCD 3300*	**54** 4

GREEN DAY 422 *Top 500*

Superior US punk pop trio, formed California, US, in 1989: Billie Joe Armstrong (v/g), Mike Dirnt (d) and Tre Cool (Frank Wright III). Grammy winners were Top Modern Rock act in US in 1995 and 'Dookie' earned US diamond album status (10 million sales) *(Singles: 53 Weeks, Albums: 112 Weeks)* pos/wks

20 Aug 94		**BASKET CASE** *Reprise W 0257CD*	**55** 2
29 Oct 94		**WELCOME TO PARADISE** *Reprise W 0269CDX*	**20** 3
28 Jan 95	●	**BASKET CASE (re-issue)** *Reprise W 0279CD*	**7** 6
18 Mar 95		**LONGVIEW** *Reprise W 0278CD*	**30** 3
20 May 95		**WHEN I COME AROUND** *Reprise W 0294CD*	**27** 3
7 Oct 95		**GEEK STINK BREATH** *Reprise W 0320CD*	**16** 2
6 Jan 96		**STUCK WITH ME** *Reprise W 0327CD*	**24** 3
6 Jul 96		**BRAIN STEW / JADED** *Reprise W 0339CD*	**28** 2
11 Oct 97		**HITCHIN' A RIDE** *Reprise W 0424CD*	**25** 2
31 Jan 98		**TIME OF YOUR LIFE (GOOD RIDDANCE)** *Reprise W 0430CD1*	**11** 11
9 May 98		**REDUNDANT** *Reprise W 0438CD1*	**27** 2
30 Sep 00		**MINORITY** *Reprise W 532CD*	**18** 3
23 Dec 00		**WARNING** *Reprise W 548CD1*	**27** 4
10 Nov 01		**WAITING** *Reprise W 570CD*	**34** 2
25 Sep 04	●	**AMERICAN IDIOT** *Reprise W 652CD1*	**3** 7
11 Dec 04	●	**BOULEVARD OF BROKEN DREAMS** *Reprise W 659CD*	**5** 3+
5 Nov 94		**DOOKIE** *Reprise 9362457952*	**13** 55
21 Oct 95	●	**INSOMNIAC** *Reprise 936240462*	**8** 5
25 Oct 97		**NIMROD** *Reprise 9362467942*	**11** 11
14 Oct 00	●	**WARNING** *Reprise 9362480302*	**4** 11
24 Nov 01		**INTERNATIONAL SUPERHITS!** *Reprise 9362481452*	**15** 11
13 Jul 02		**SHENANIGANS** *Reprise 9362482082*	**32** 3
2 Oct 04	★	**AMERICAN IDIOT** *Reprise 9362488502* ■ ▲	**1** 13+

GREEN JELLY *US, male vocal / instrumental group (Singles: 15 Weeks, Albums: 10 Weeks)* pos/wks

5 Jun 93	●	**THREE LITTLE PIGS** *Zoo 74321151422*	**5** 8
14 Aug 93		**ANARCHY IN THE UK** *Zoo 74321159052*	**27** 3
25 Dec 93		**I'M THE LEADER OF THE GANG** *Arista 74321174892* 1	**25** 4
3 Jul 93		**CEREAL KILLER SOUNDTRACK** *Zoo 72445110382*	**18** 10

1 Hulk Hogan with Green Jelly

GREEN ON RED *US, male vocal / instrumental group (Albums: 1 Week)* pos/wks

26 Oct 85	**NO FREE LUNCH** *Mercury MERM 78*	**99** 1

GREEN VELVET *US, male DJ / producer – Curtis Jones (Singles: 2 Weeks)* pos/wks

25 May 02	**LA LA LAND** *Credence CDCRED 025*	**29** 2

Gavin GREENAWAY *See Hans ZIMMER*

Norman GREENBAUM *US, male vocalist (Singles: 20 Weeks)* pos/wks

21 Mar 70	★	**SPIRIT IN THE SKY** *Reprise RS 20885*	**1** 20

Lorne GREENE *Canada, male actor / vocalist, b. 12 Feb 1914, d. 11 Sep 1987 (Singles: 8 Weeks)* pos/wks

17 Dec 64	**RINGO** *RCA 1428* ▲	**22** 8

Dave GREENFIELD *See Jean-Jacques BURNEL*

GREENSLADE *UK, male vocal / instrumental group (Albums: 3 Weeks)* pos/wks

14 Sep 74	**SPYGLASS GUEST** *Warner Bros. K 56055*	**34** 3

Lee GREENWOOD
US, male vocalist (Singles: 6 Weeks) pos/wks

| 19 May 84 | THE WIND BENEATH MY WINGS *MCA 877* | 49 | 6 |

Christina GREGG
UK, female exercise instructor (Albums: 1 Week) pos/wks

| 27 May 78 | MUSIC 'N' MOTION *Warwick WW 5041* | 51 | 1 |

Iain GREGORY *UK, male vocalist (Singles: 2 Weeks)* pos/wks

| 4 Jan 62 | CAN'T YOU HEAR THE BEAT OF A BROKEN HEART *Pye 7N 15397* | 39 | 2 |

Johnny GREGORY *See CHAQUITO ORCHESTRA; Russ HAMILTON*

Band of the GRENADIER GUARDS *See ST JOHN'S COLLEGE SCHOOL CHOIR and the Band of the GRENADIER GUARDS*

GREYHOUND
Jamaica, male vocal / instrumental group (Singles: 33 Weeks) pos/wks

26 Jun 71	● BLACK AND WHITE *Trojan TR 7820*	6	13
8 Jan 72	MOON RIVER *Trojan TR 7848*	12	11
25 Mar 72	I AM WHAT I AM *Trojan TR 7853*	20	9

GRID *UK, male instrumental / production duo – Richard
Norris and Dave Ball (Singles: 47 Weeks, Albums: 4 Weeks)* pos/wks

7 Jul 90	FLOATATION *East West YZ 475*	60	2
29 Sep 90	A BEAT CALLED LOVE *East West YZ 498*	64	4
25 Jul 92	FIGURE OF 8 *Virgin VSTG 1421*	50	3
3 Oct 92	HEARTBEAT *Virgin VST 1427*	72	2
13 Mar 93	CRYSTAL CLEAR *Virgin VSCDT 1442*	27	4
30 Oct 93	TEXAS COWBOYS *Deconstruction 74321167762*	21	3
4 Jun 94	● SWAMP THING *Deconstruction 74321205842*	3	17
17 Sep 94	ROLLERCOASTER *Deconstruction 74321230772*	19	4
3 Dec 94	TEXAS COWBOYS (re-issue) *Deconstruction 74321244032*	17	6
23 Sep 95	DIABLO *Deconstruction 74321308402*	32	2
1 Oct 94	EVOLVER *Deconstruction 74321227182*	14	3
14 Oct 95	MUSIC FOR DANCING *Deconstruction 74321276702*	67	1

Zaine GRIFF *New Zealand, male vocalist (Singles: 6 Weeks)* pos/wks

| 16 Feb 80 | TONIGHT *Automatic K 17547* | 54 | 3 |
| 31 May 80 | ASHES AND DIAMONDS *Automatic K 17610* | 68 | 3 |

Alistair GRIFFIN
UK, male vocalist (Singles: 8 Weeks, Albums: 3 Weeks) pos/wks

17 Jan 04	● BRING IT ON / MY LOVER'S PRAYER *UMTV 9815673*	5	5
27 Mar 04	YOU AND ME (TONIGHT) *Universal TV 981776*	18	3
24 Jan 04	BRING IT ON *Universal TV 9816116*	12	3

'My Lover's Prayer' features Robin Gibb

Billy GRIFFIN (see also The MIRACLES)
US, male vocalist (Singles: 12 Weeks) pos/wks

| 8 Jan 83 | HOLD ME TIGHTER IN THE RAIN *CBS A 2935* | 17 | 9 |
| 14 Jan 84 | SERIOUS *CBS A 4053* | 64 | 3 |

Clive GRIFFIN *UK, male vocalist (Singles: 5 Weeks)* pos/wks

| 24 Jun 89 | HEAD ABOVE WATER *Mercury STEP 4* | 60 | 2 |
| 11 May 91 | I'LL BE WAITING *Mercury STEP 6* | 56 | 3 |

Nanci GRIFFITH
US, female vocalist / instrumentalist – guitar (Albums: 27 Weeks) pos/wks

28 Mar 88	LITTLE LOVE AFFAIRS *MCA MCF 3413*	78	1
23 Sep 89	STORMS *MCA MCG 6066*	38	3
28 Sep 91	LATE NIGHT GRANDE HOTEL *MCA MCA 10306*	40	5
20 Mar 93	OTHER VOICES / OTHER ROOMS *MCA MCD 10796*	18	6
13 Nov 93	THE BEST OF NANCI GRIFFITH *MCA MCD 10966*	27	4
1 Oct 94	FLYER *MCA MCD 11155*	20	4
5 Apr 97	BLUE ROSES FROM THE MOONS *Elektra 7559620152*	64	3
11 Aug 01	CLOCK WITHOUT HANDS *Elektra 7559626602*	61	1

Roni GRIFFITH *US, female vocalist (Singles: 4 Weeks)* pos/wks

| 30 Jun 84 | (THE BEST PART OF) BREAKING UP *Making Waves SURF 101* | 63 | 4 |

The GRIFTERS
(see also CAMISRA; ESCRIMA; PARTIZAN; TALL PAUL) *UK, male production
duo – Paul Newman and Brandon Block (Singles: 1 Week)* pos/wks

| 20 Feb 99 | FLASH *Duty Free DF 004CD* | 63 | 1 |

GRIM NORTHERN SOCIAL
UK, male vocal / instrumental group (Singles: 1 Week) pos/wks

| 6 Sep 03 | URBAN PRESSURE *One Little Indian 353TP 7CD* | 60 | 1 |

GRIMETHORPE COLLIERY BAND (see also Peter SKELLERN)
UK, male brass band (Albums: 5 Weeks) pos/wks

| 6 Jun 98 | BRASSED OFF (FILM SOUNDTRACK) *RCA Victor 9026687572* | 36 | 4 |
| 11 Sep 04 | THE VERY BEST OF THE GRIMETHORPE COLLIERY (UK COAL) BAND *BMG 82876637222* | 59 | 1 |

Josh GROBAN *US, male vocalist (Albums: 8 Weeks)* pos/wks

| 15 Feb 03 | JOSH GROBAN *Reprise 9362481542* | 28 | 8 |

Jay GROOVE *See FANTASY UFO*

GROOVE ARMADA (see also WEEKEND PLAYERS)
*UK, male production / instrumental duo – Andy Cato
and Tom Findlay (Singles: 32 Weeks, Albums: 38 Weeks)* pos/wks

8 May 99	IF EVERYBODY LOOKED THE SAME *Pepper 0530292*	25	2
7 Aug 99	AT THE RIVER *Pepper 0530062*	19	5
27 Nov 99	I SEE YOU BABY (re) *Pepper 9230002* [1]	17	6
25 Aug 01	SUPERSTYLIN' (re) *Pepper 9230472*	12	7
17 Nov 01	MY FRIEND *Pepper 9230532*	36	2
2 Nov 02	PURPLE HAZE *Pepper 9230642*	36	2
17 May 03	EASY *Pepper 9230712*	31	2
6 Sep 03	BUT I FEEL GOOD *Pepper 82876551792*	50	1
2 Oct 04	I SEE YOU BABY (re-mix) *Jive 82876649982*	11	5
5 Jun 99	VERTIGO *Pepper 530332*	23	19
6 May 00	THE REMIXES *Pepper 9230102*	68	1
22 May 01	● GOODBYE COUNTRY (HELLO NIGHTCLUB) *Pepper 9230492*	5	8
16 Nov 02	LOVEBOX *Pepper 9230682*	41	2
9 Oct 04	● THE BEST OF *Jive 82876652562*	6	8

[1] Groove Armada featuring Gram'ma Funk

GROOVE CONNEKTION 2 *UK, male producer /
instrumentalist – Jeremy Sylvester (Singles: 1 Week)* pos/wks

| 11 Apr 98 | CLUB LONELY *XL Recordings XLT 94CD* | 54 | 1 |

GROOVE CORPORATION *UK / Italy, male /
female vocal / instrumental group (Singles: 1 Week)* pos/wks

| 16 Apr 94 | RAIN *Six6 SIXCD 109* | 71 | 1 |

GROOVE FOUNDATION *See DJ CHUS presents GROOVE FOUNDATION*

GROOVE GANG *See DAFFY DUCK featuring The GROOVE GANG*

GROOVE GENERATION featuring Leo SAYER
UK, male production group (Singles: 3 Weeks) pos/wks

| 8 Aug 98 | YOU MAKE ME FEEL LIKE DANCING *Brothers Org. CDBRUV 8* | 32 | 3 |

GROOVE THEORY (see also MANTRONIX) *US, male / female production
vocal duo – Bryce Wilson and Amel Larrieux (Singles: 3 Weeks)* pos/wks

| 18 Nov 95 | TELL ME *Epic 6623882* | 31 | 3 |

GROOVERIDER *UK, male DJ / producer –
Ray Bingham (Singles: 3 Weeks, Albums: 1 Week)* pos/wks

26 Sep 98	RAINBOWS OF COLOUR *Higher Ground HIGHS 13CD*	40	2
19 Jun 99	WHERE'S JACK THE RIPPER *Higher Ground HIGHS 20CD*	61	1
10 Oct 98	MYSTERIES OF FUNK *Higher Ground HIGH 6CD*	50	1

Scott GROOVES
US, male DJ / producer – Patrick Scott (Singles: 3 Weeks) pos/wks

16 May 98	EXPANSIONS *Soma Recordings SOMA 65CDS* [1]	68	1
28 Nov 98	MOTHERSHIP RECONNECTION *Soma Recordings SOMA 71CDS*	55	1
21 Aug 99	MOTHERSHIP RECONNECTION *Virgin DINSD 185* [2]	55	1

[1] Scott Grooves featuring Roy Ayers [2] Scott Grooves featuring Parliament / Funkadelic

Singles re-entries are listed as (re), (2re), (3re).... which signifies that the hit re-entered the chart once, twice or three times...

Henry GROSS
US, male vocalist (Singles: 4 Weeks) pos/wks
28 Aug 76 **SHANNON** *Life Song ELS 45002* **32** 4

GROUND LEVEL
Australia, male instrumental / production group (Singles: 2 Weeks) pos/wks
30 Jan 93 **DREAMS OF HEAVEN** *Faze2 CDFAZE 14* **54** 2

The GROUNDHOGS
UK, male vocal / instrumental group (Albums: 51 Weeks) pos/wks
6 Jun 70 ● **THANK CHRIST FOR THE BOMB** *Liberty LBS 83295* **9** 13
27 Mar 71 ● **SPLIT** *Liberty LBG 83401* **5** 28
18 Mar 72 ● **WHO WILL SAVE THE WORLD** *United Artists UAG 29237* **8** 9
13 Jul 74 **SOLID** *WWA WWA 004* **31** 1

GROUP THERAPY
US, male rap group (Singles: 1 Week) pos/wks
30 Nov 96 **EAST COAST / WEST COAST KILLAS**
Interscope IND 95516 ....**51** 1

Boring Bob GROVER See The PIRANHAS

Sir Charles GROVES See ROYAL PHILHARMONIC ORCHESTRA

The GUESS WHO
Canada, male vocal / instrumental group (Singles: 14 Weeks) pos/wks
16 Feb 67 **HIS GIRL** *King KG 1044* **45** 1
9 May 70 **AMERICAN WOMAN (re)** *RCA 1943* ▲ **19** 13

David GUETTA
France, male producer (Singles: 6 Weeks) pos/wks
31 Aug 02 **LOVE, DON'T LET ME GO** *Virgin DINSD 243* [1] **46** 1
12 Jul 03 **JUST FOR ONE DAY (HEROES)** *Virgin DINST 263* [2] **73** 1
25 Oct 03 **JUST A LITTLE MORE LOVE** *Virgin DINSD 250* [1] **19** 4

[1] David Guetta featuring Chris Willis [2] David Guetta vs Bowie

The GUILDFORD CATHEDRAL CHOIR
UK, male / female choir (Albums: 4 Weeks) pos/wks
10 Dec 66 **CHRISTMAS CAROLS FROM GUILDFORD CATHEDRAL**
MFP 1104 ....**23** 4

Record credits Barry Rose as conductor

GUITAR CORPORATION
UK, male instrumental group (Albums: 5 Weeks) pos/wks
15 Feb 92 **IMAGES** *Quality Television QTVCD 002* **41** 5

GUN (see also BAKER-GURVITZ ARMY; Adrian GURVITZ)
UK, male vocal / instrumental trio (Singles: 11 Weeks) pos/wks
20 Nov 68 ● **RACE WITH THE DEVIL** *CBS 3734* **8** 11

GUN *UK, male vocal / instrumental*
group (Singles: 46 Weeks, Albums: 23 Weeks) pos/wks
1 Jul 89 **BETTER DAYS** *A&M AM 505* **33** 9
16 Sep 89 **MONEY (EVERYBODY LOVES HER)** *A&M AM 520* **73** 2
11 Nov 89 **INSIDE OUT** *A&M AM 531* **57** 2
10 Feb 90 **TAKING ON THE WORLD** *A&M AM 541* **50** 3
14 Jul 90 **SHAME ON YOU** *A&M AM 573* **33** 4
14 Mar 92 **STEAL YOUR FIRE** *A&M AM 851* **24** 4
2 May 92 **HIGHER GROUND** *A&M AM 869* **48** 2
4 Jul 92 **WELCOME TO THE REAL WORLD** *A&M AM 885* **43** 2
9 Jul 94 ● **WORD UP** *A&M 5806672* **8** 7
24 Sep 94 **DON'T SAY IT'S OVER** *A&M 5807572* **19** 3
25 Feb 95 **THE ONLY ONE** *A&M 5809552* **29** 3
15 Apr 95 **SOMETHING WORTHWHILE** *A&M 5810452* **39** 2
26 Apr 97 **CRAZY YOU** *A&M 5821932* [1] **21** 2
12 Jul 97 **MY SWEET JANE** *A&M 5822792* [1] **51** 1
22 Jul 89 **TAKING ON THE WORLD** *A&M AMA 7007* **44** 10
18 Apr 92 **GALLUS** *A&M 3953832* **14** 4
13 Aug 94 ● **SWAGGER** *A&M 5402542* **5** 7
24 May 97 **0141 632 6326** *A&M 5407232* **32** 2

[1] G.U.N.

GUNS N' ROSES (74) Top 500
(see also SLASH'S SNAKEPIT; DUFF McKAGAN; GILBY CLARKE)
Often controversial Los Angeles-based band. Best known line-up included Axl Rose (b. William Bailey) (v), Slash (b. Saul Hudson) (g), Izzy Stradlin (b. Jeffrey Isbell) (g). The only act to hold the top two album spots in both the UK and the US on the week of releasing both records: Use Your Illusion I and II in 1991 (Singles: 107 Weeks, Albums: 418 Weeks) pos/wks
3 Oct 87 **WELCOME TO THE JUNGLE** *Geffen GEF 30* **67** 2
20 Aug 88 **SWEET CHILD O' MINE** *Geffen GEF 43* ▲ **24** 8
29 Oct 88 **WELCOME TO THE JUNGLE / NIGHTRAIN (re-issue)**
Geffen GEF 47 ....**24** 5
18 Mar 89 ● **PARADISE CITY** *Geffen GEF 50* **6** 9
3 Jun 89 ● **SWEET CHILD O' MINE (re-issue)** *Geffen GEF 55* **6** 9
1 Jul 89 ● **PATIENCE** *Geffen GEF 56* **10** 9
2 Sep 89 **NIGHTRAIN (re-issue)** *Geffen GEF 60* **17** 5
13 Jul 91 ● **YOU COULD BE MINE** *Geffen GFS 6* **3** 10
21 Sep 91 ● **DON'T CRY** *Geffen GFS 9* **8** 4
21 Dec 91 ● **LIVE AND LET DIE** *Geffen GFS 17* **5** 7
7 Mar 92 ● **NOVEMBER RAIN** *Geffen GFS 18* **4** 5
23 May 92 ● **KNOCKIN' ON HEAVEN'S DOOR** *Geffen GFS 21* **2** 9
21 Nov 92 ● **YESTERDAYS / NOVEMBER RAIN (re-issue)** *Geffen GFS 27* **8** 9
29 May 93 **THE CIVIL WAR (EP)** *Geffen GFSTD 43* **11** 3
20 Nov 93 ● **AIN'T IT FUN** *Geffen GFSTD 62* **9** 3
4 Jun 94 ● **SINCE I DON'T HAVE YOU** *Geffen GFSTD 70* **10** 6
14 Jan 95 ● **SYMPATHY FOR THE DEVIL** *Geffen GFSTD 86* **9** 6
1 Aug 87 ● **APPETITE FOR DESTRUCTION** *Geffen WX 125* ▲ **5** 161
17 Dec 88 **G N' R LIES** *Geffen WX 218* **22** 41
28 Sep 91 ● **USE YOUR ILLUSION I** *Geffen GEF 24415* **2** 84
28 Sep 91 ★ **USE YOUR ILLUSION II** *Geffen GEF 24420* ■ ▲ **1** 84
4 Dec 93 ● **THE SPAGHETTI INCIDENT?** *Geffen GED 24617* **2** 10
11 Dec 99 **LIVE – ERA '87-'93** *Geffen 4905142* **45** 2
27 Mar 04 ★ **GREATEST HITS** *Geffen / Polydor 9862108* **1** 36

The re-issue of 'November Rain' was listed only from 28 Nov 1992. Tracks on The Civil War (EP): Civil War / Garden of Eden / Dead Horse / Interview 'Appetite for Destruction' changed catalogue number to Geffen / Polydor GEFD 24148 when it charted in 2004

GUNSHOT *UK, male rap group (Albums: 1 Week)* pos/wks
19 Jun 93 **PATRIOT GAMES** *Vinyl Solution STEAM 43CD* **60** 1

David GUNSON *UK, male after dinner speaker (Albums: 2 Weeks)* pos/wks
25 Dec 82 **WHAT GOES UP MIGHT COME DOWN** *Big Ben BB 0012* **92** 2

GÜNTHER & The SUNSHINE GIRLS
Sweden, male / female vocal group (Singles: 4 Weeks) pos/wks
15 May 04 **DING DONG SONG** *WEA WEA 376CD1* **14** 4

Peter GUNZ See LORD TARIQ and Peter GUNZ

GURU (see also GANG STARR) *US, male rapper /*
producer – Keith Allam (Singles: 12 Weeks, Albums: 12 Weeks) pos/wks
11 Sep 93 **TRUST ME** *Cooltempo CDCOOL 278* [1] **34** 2
13 Nov 93 **NO TIME TO PLAY** *Cooltempo CDCOOL 282* [2] **25** 3
19 Aug 95 **WATCH WHAT YOU SAY** *Cooltempo CDCOOL 308* [3] **28** 3
18 Nov 95 **FEEL THE MUSIC** *Cooltempo CDCOOLS 313* **34** 2
13 Jul 96 **LIVIN' IN THIS WORLD / LIFESAVER** *Cooltempo CDCOOL 320* **61** 1
16 Dec 00 **KEEP YOUR WORRIES** *Virgin VUSCD 177* [4] **57** 1
29 May 93 **JAZZMATAZZ** *Cooltempo CTCD 34* **58** 2
15 Jul 95 **JAZZMATAZZ VOLUME II – THE NEW REALITY**
Cooltempo CTCD 47 ....**12** 9
14 Oct 00 **STREETSOUL** *Virgin CDVUS 178* [1] **74** 1

[1] Guru featuring N'Dea Davenport [2] Guru featuring Dee C Lee [3] Guru featuring Chaka Khan [4] Guru's Jazzmatazz featuring Angie Stone [1] Guru's Jazzmatazz

GURU JOSH *UK, male producer – Paul*
Walden (Singles: 14 Weeks, Albums: 2 Weeks) pos/wks
24 Feb 90 ● **INFINITY** *Deconstruction PB 43475* **5** 10
16 Jun 90 **WHOSE LAW (IS IT ANYWAY?)** *Deconstruction PB 43647* **26** 4
14 Jul 90 **INFINITY** *Deconstruction PL 74701* **41** 2

Adrian GURVITZ (see also BAKER-GURVITZ ARMY; GUN)
UK, male vocalist – Adrian Curtis (Singles: 16 Weeks) pos/wks
30 Jan 82 ● **CLASSIC** *RAK 339* **8** 13
12 Jun 82 **YOUR DREAM** *RAK 343* **61** 3

G.U.S. (FOOTWEAR) BAND and the MORRISTOWN ORPHEUS CHOIR
UK, male instrumental group and male / female vocal group (Albums: 1 Week) pos/wks

3 Oct 70	LAND OF HOPE AND GLORY *Columbia SCX 6406*	54	1

GUSGUS
Iceland, male / female vocal / instrumental group (Singles: 5 Weeks) pos/wks

21 Feb 98	POLYESTERDAY *4AD BAD 8002CD*	55	1
13 Mar 99	LADYSHAVE *4AD BAD 9001CD*	64	1
24 Apr 99	STARLOVERS *4AD BADD 9004CD*	62	1
8 Feb 03	DAVID (I STILL HAVE LAST NIGHT IN MY BODY ...) *Underwater H2O 022CD*	52	1
28 Jun 03	CALL OF THE WILD *Underwater H2O 032CD*	75	1
10 Apr 04	DAVID (I STILL HAVE LAST NIGHT IN MY BODY ...) (re-mix) *Underwater H2O 042P*	72	1

GUSTO
US, male producer – Edward Green (Singles: 8 Weeks) pos/wks

2 Mar 96 ●	DISCO'S REVENGE *Manifesto FESCD 6*	9	5
7 Sep 96	LET'S ALL CHANT *Manifesto FESCD 13*	21	3

Arlo GUTHRIE
US, male vocalist (Albums: 1 Week) pos/wks

7 Mar 70	ALICE'S RESTAURANT *Reprise RSLP 6267*	44	1

Gwen GUTHRIE
(see also LIMIT) US, female vocalist, b. 9 Jul 1950, d. 3 Feb 1999 (Singles: 25 Weeks, Albums: 14 Weeks) pos/wks

19 Jul 86 ●	AIN'T NOTHIN' GOIN' ON BUT THE RENT *Boiling Point POSP 807*	5	12
11 Oct 86	(THEY LONG TO BE) CLOSE TO YOU *Boiling Point POSP 822*	25	7
14 Feb 87	GOOD TO GO LOVER / OUTSIDE IN THE RAIN *Boiling Point POSP 841*	37	4
4 Sep 93	AIN'T NOTHIN' GOIN' ON BUT THE RENT (re-mix) *Polydor PZCD 276*	42	2
23 Aug 86	GOOD TO GO LOVER *Boiling Point POLD 5201*	42	14

GUY
US, male vocal group (Singles: 4 Weeks, Albums: 1 Week) pos/wks

4 May 91	HER *MCA MCS 1575*	58	4
5 Feb 00	III *MCA 1121702*	55	1

Buddy GUY
US, male vocalist / instrumentalist – guitar (Albums: 9 Weeks) pos/wks

22 Jun 91	DAMN RIGHT I'VE GOT THE BLUES *Silvertone ORELP 516*	43	5
13 Mar 93	FEELS LIKE RAIN *Silvertone ORECD 525*	36	4

A GUY CALLED GERALD
UK, male producer – Gerald Simpson (Singles: 23 Weeks, Albums: 2 Weeks) pos/wks

8 Apr 89	VOODOO RAY (re) *Rham! RS 804*	12	18
16 Dec 89	FX / EYES OF SORROW *Subscape AGCG 1*	52	5
14 Apr 90	AUTOMANIKK *Subscape 4664821*	68	1
1 Apr 95	BLACK SECRET TECHNOLOGY *Juice Box JBCD 25*	64	1

GUYS 'N' DOLLS
UK, male / female vocal group (Singles: 33 Weeks, Albums: 1 Week) pos/wks

1 Mar 75 ●	THERE'S A WHOLE LOT OF LOVING *Magnet MAG 20* [1]	2	11
17 May 75	HERE I GO AGAIN *Magnet MAG 30*	33	5
21 Feb 76 ●	YOU DON'T HAVE TO SAY YOU LOVE ME *Magnet MAG 50*	5	8
6 Nov 76	STONEY GROUND *Magnet MAG 76*	38	4
13 May 78	ONLY LOVING DOES IT *Magnet MAG 115*	42	5
31 May 75	GUYS 'N' DOLLS *Magnet MAG 5005*	43	1

[1] Guys & Dolls

GUYVER
UK, male producer – Guy Mearns (Singles: 1 Week) pos/wks

29 Mar 03	TRAPPED / DIFFERENCES *Tidy Two TIDYTWO 118*	72	1

Jonas GWANGWA See George FENTON and Jonas GWANGWA

GYPSYMEN
(see also BLACK RIOT; ROYAL HOUSE; SWAN LAKE; TODD TERRY PROJECT) US, male producer – Todd Terry (Singles: 2 Weeks) pos/wks

11 Aug 01	BABARABATIRI *Sound Design SDES 09CDS*	32	2

The GYRES
UK, male vocal / instrumental group (Singles: 2 Weeks) pos/wks

13 Apr 96	POP COP *Sugar SUGA 9CD*	71	1
6 Jul 96	ARE YOU READY *Sugar SUGA 11CD*	71	1

GZA See GENIUS / GZA

H & CLAIRE
(see also STEPS) UK, male / female vocal duo – Ian Watkins and Claire Richards (Singles: 25 Weeks, Albums: 1 Week) pos/wks

18 May 02 ●	DJ *WEA WEA 347CD*	3	11
24 Aug 02 ●	HALF A HEART (re) *WEA WEA 359CDX*	8	6
16 Nov 02 ●	ALL OUT OF LOVE (re) *WEA WEA 360CD*	10	8
30 Nov 02	ANOTHER YOU ANOTHER ME *WEA 0927494622*	58	1

'All Out of Love' was a double A-side with 'Beauty and the Beast', although not listed as such on the chart

HHC
UK, male DJ / production duo (Singles: 1 Week) pos/wks

19 Apr 97	WE'RE NOT ALONE *Perfecto PERF 138CD*	44	1

H 20
UK, male vocal / instrumental group (Singles: 16 Weeks) pos/wks

21 May 83	DREAM TO SLEEP *RCA 330*	17	10
13 Aug 83	JUST OUTSIDE OF HEAVEN *RCA 349*	38	6

H20
(see also Billie PIPER) US / Switzerland, male / female vocal / instrumental group (Singles: 4 Weeks) pos/wks

14 Sep 96	NOBODY'S BUSINESS *AM:PM 5818832* [1]	19	3
30 Aug 97	SATISFIED (TAKE ME HIGHER) *AM:PM 5823252*	66	1

[1] H20 featuring Billie

HWA featuring SONIC THE HEDGEHOG
(see also Jeremy HEALY and AMOS; HAYSI FANTAYZEE) UK, male producer – Jeremy Healy (Singles: 6 Weeks) pos/wks

5 Dec 92	SUPERSONIC *Internal Affairs KGB 008*	33	6

HABIT
UK, male vocal / instrumental group (Singles: 2 Weeks) pos/wks

30 Apr 88	LUCY *Virgin VS 1063*	56	2

Steve HACKETT
(see also GENESIS; GTR) UK, male vocalist / instrumentalist – guitar (Singles: 2 Weeks, Albums: 38 Weeks) pos/wks

2 Apr 83	CELL 151 *Charisma CELL 1*	66	2
1 Nov 75	VOYAGE OF THE ACOLYTE *Charisma CAS 1111*	26	4
6 May 78	PLEASE DON'T TOUCH *Charisma CDS 4012*	38	5
26 May 79	SPECTRAL MORNINGS *Charisma CDS 4017*	22	11
21 Jun 80 ●	DEFECTOR *Charisma CDS 4018*	9	7
29 Aug 81	CURED *Charisma CDS 4021*	15	5
30 Apr 83	HIGHLY STRUNG *Charisma HACK 1*	16	3
19 Nov 83	BAY OF KINGS *Lamborghini LMGLP 3000*	70	1
22 Sep 84	TILL WE HAVE FACES *Lamborghini LMGLP 4000*	54	2

HADDAWAY
Trinidad and Tobago, male vocalist – Nester Haddaway (Singles: 52 Weeks, Albums: 16 Weeks) pos/wks

5 Jun 93 ●	WHAT IS LOVE *Logic 74321148502*	2	15
25 Sep 93 ●	LIFE *Logic 74321164212*	6	9
18 Dec 93 ●	I MISS YOU *Logic 74321181522*	9	14
2 Apr 94 ●	ROCK MY HEART *Logic 74321194122*	9	9
24 Jun 95	FLY AWAY *Logic 74321286942*	20	3
23 Sep 95	CATCH A FIRE *Logic 74321306652*	39	2
23 Oct 93 ●	HADDAWAY – THE ALBUM *Logic 74321169222*	9	16

Tony HADLEY (see also SPANDAU BALLET)
UK, male vocalist (Singles: 9 Weeks, Albums: 6 Weeks) pos/wks

7 Mar 92	LOST IN YOUR LOVE *EMI EM 222*	**42** 4
29 Aug 92	FOR YOUR BLUE EYES ONLY *EMI EM 234*	**67** 2
16 Jan 93	THE GAME OF LOVE *EMI CDEM 254*	**72** 1
10 May 97	DANCE WITH ME *VC VCRD 17* [1]	**35** 2
20 Sep 97	TONY HADLEY *PolyGram TV 5393012*	**45** 3
10 May 03	TRUE BALLADS *Universal TV 382882*	**31** 3

[1] Tin Tin Out featuring Tony Hadley

Sammy HAGAR (see also MONTROSE; VAN HALEN;
HAGAR SCHON AARONSON SHRIEVE) *US, male vocalist /
instrumentalist – guitar (Singles: 15 Weeks, Albums: 19 Weeks)* pos/wks

15 Dec 79	THIS PLANET'S ON FIRE (BURN IN HELL) / SPACE STATION NO.5 *Capitol CL 16114*	**52** 5
16 Feb 80	I'VE DONE EVERYTHING FOR YOU *Capitol CL 16120*	**36** 5
24 May 80	HEARTBEAT / LOVE OR MONEY *Capitol RED 1*	**67** 2
16 Jan 82	PIECE OF MY HEART (re) *Geffen GEFA 1884*	**67** 3
29 Sep 79	STREET MACHINE *Capitol EST 11983*	**38** 4
22 Mar 80	LOUD AND CLEAR *Capitol EST 25330*	**12** 8
7 Jun 80	DANGER ZONE *Capitol EST 12069*	**25** 3
13 Feb 82	STANDING HAMPTON *Geffen GEF 85456*	**84** 2
4 Jul 87	SAMMY HAGAR *Geffen WX 114*	**86** 2

HAGAR SCHON AARONSON SHRIEVE (see also Sammy HAGAR)
US, male vocal / instrumental group (Albums: 1 Week) pos/wks

19 May 84	THROUGH THE FIRE *Geffen GEF 25893*	**92** 1

Paul HAIG *UK, male vocalist (Singles: 3 Weeks, Albums: 2 Weeks)* pos/wks

28 May 83	HEAVEN SENT *Island IS 111*	**74** 3
22 Oct 83	RHYTHM OF LIFE *Crepuscule ILPS 9742*	**82** 2

HAIRCUT 100 *UK, male vocal / instrumental group –*
includes Nick Heyward *(Singles: 47 Weeks, Albums: 34 Weeks)* pos/wks

24 Oct 81	● FAVOURITE SHIRTS (BOY MEETS GIRL) *Arista CLIP 1*	**4** 14
30 Jan 82	● LOVE PLUS ONE *Arista CLIP 2*	**3** 12
10 Apr 82	● FANTASTIC DAY *Arista CLIP 3*	**9** 9
21 Aug 82	● NOBODY'S FOOL *Arista CLIP 4*	**9** 7
6 Aug 83	PRIME TIME *Polydor HC 1*	**46** 5
6 Mar 82	● PELICAN WEST *Arista HCC 100*	**2** 34

Curtis HAIRSTON *US, male vocalist.*
b. 10 Oct 1961, d. 18 Jan 1996 *(Singles: 16 Weeks)* pos/wks

15 Oct 83	I WANT YOU (ALL TONIGHT) *RCA 368*	**44** 5
27 Apr 85	I WANT YOUR LOVIN' (JUST A LITTLE BIT) *London LON 66*	**13** 7
6 Dec 86	CHILLIN' OUT *Atlantic A 9335*	**57** 4

Gary HAISMAN See D MOB

Seamus HAJI *UK, male producer (Singles: 1 Week)* pos/wks

18 Dec 04	LAST NIGHT A DJ SAVED MY LIFE *Big Love BL 013*	**69** 1

HAL *Ireland, male vocal / instrumental group (Singles: 1 Week)* pos/wks

8 May 04	WORRY ABOUT THE WIND *Rough Trade RTRADSCD 172*	**53** 1

HAL featuring Gillian ANDERSON *UK, male production
trio and US, female actor / vocalist (Singles: 3 Weeks)* pos/wks

24 May 97	EXTREMIS *Virgin VSCDT 1636*	**23** 3

HALE and PACE and The STONKERS *UK, male comedy duo – Gareth
Hale and Norman Pace and backing group (Singles: 7 Weeks)* pos/wks

9 Mar 91	★ THE STONK *London LON 296*	**1** 7

Bill HALEY and his COMETS 281 `Top 500` Original 'King of Rock
'n' Roll', b. 6 Jul 1925, Detroit, d. 9 Feb 1981. The kiss-curl hairstyled frontman introduced rock to the world via a string of 1950s smashes, including
'Rock Around the Clock', the only record to return to the Top 20 on five
occasions, selling 1,392,000 *(Singles: 199 Weeks, Albums: 31 Weeks)* pos/wks

17 Dec 54	● SHAKE, RATTLE AND ROLL *Brunswick 05338*	**4** 14
7 Jan 55	★ ROCK AROUND THE CLOCK (5re) *Brunswick 05317* ◆ ▲	**1** 36
15 Apr 55	MAMBO ROCK *Brunswick 05405*	**14** 2
30 Dec 55	● ROCK-A-BEATIN' BOOGIE *Brunswick 05509*	**4** 9
9 Mar 56	● SEE YOU LATER, ALLIGATOR (re) *Brunswick 05530*	**7** 21
25 May 56	● THE SAINTS ROCK 'N ROLL *Brunswick 05565*	**5** 24
17 Aug 56	● ROCKIN' THROUGH THE RYE (re) *Brunswick 05582*	**3** 23
14 Sep 56	RAZZLE DAZZLE *Brunswick 05453*	**13** 8
9 Nov 56	● RIP IT UP *Brunswick 05615*	**4** 18
9 Nov 56	ROCK 'N' ROLL STAGE SHOW (LP) *Brunswick LAT 8139*	**30** 1
23 Nov 56	RUDY'S ROCK (re) *Brunswick 05616*	**26** 5
1 Feb 57	ROCK THE JOINT *London HLF 8371*	**20** 4
8 Feb 57	● DON'T KNOCK THE ROCK *Brunswick 05640*	**7** 8
3 Apr 68	ROCK AROUND THE CLOCK (re-issue) *MCA MU 1013*	**20** 11
16 Mar 74	ROCK AROUND THE CLOCK (2nd re-issue) *MCA 128*	**12** 10
25 Apr 81	HALEY'S GOLDEN MEDLEY *MCA 694*	**50** 5
4 Aug 56	★ ROCK AROUND THE CLOCK *Brunswick LAT 8117*	**2** 17
20 Oct 56	★ ROCK 'N' ROLL STAGE SHOW *Brunswick LAT 8139*	**1** 8
16 Feb 57	● ROCK THE JOINT *London HAF 2037*	**5** 1
18 May 68	ROCK AROUND THE CLOCK (re-issue) *Ace of Hearts AH 13*	**34** 5

'Rock Around the Clock' peaked at No.17 on its first visit to the chart, then
re-entered peaking at No.1 in Oct 1955, No.5 in Sep 1956, No.24 in Dec 1956,
No.25 in Jan 1957 and No.22 later that same month. Tracks on Rock 'n' Roll Stage
Show (LP): Calling All Comets / Rockin' Through the Rye / A Rockin' Little Tune /
Hide and Seek / Hey There Now / Goofin' Around / Hook Line and Sinker / Rudy's
Rock / Choo Choo Ch'Boogie / Blue Comets Rock / Hot Dog Buddy Buddy /
Tonight's the Night. Occasionally, some of the 'Rock Around the Clock' labels
billed the song as '(We're Gonna) Rock Around the Clock'. Haley's Golden Medley
comprised: Rock Around the Clock / Rock-A-Beatin' Boogie / Shake, Rattle and Roll
/ Choo Choo Ch'Boogie / See You Later Alligator.

HALF MAN HALF BISCUIT
UK, male vocal / instrumental group (Albums: 14 Weeks) pos/wks

8 Feb 86	BACK IN THE D.H.S.S. *Probe Plus PROBE 4*	**60** 9
21 Feb 87	BACK AGAIN IN THE D.H.S.S. *Probe Plus PROBE 8*	**59** 5

Aaron HALL (see also GUY) *US, male vocalist (Singles: 3 Weeks)* pos/wks

13 Jun 92	DON'T BE AFRAID *MCA MCS 1632*	**56** 2
23 Oct 93	GET A LITTLE FREAKY WITH ME *MCA MCSTD 1936*	**66** 1

Audrey HALL *Jamaica, female vocalist (Singles: 20 Weeks)* pos/wks

25 Jan 86	ONE DANCE WON'T DO *Germain DG7-1985*	**20** 11
5 Jul 86	SMILE *Germain DG 15*	**14** 9

Daryl HALL (see also Daryl HALL and John OATES)
US, male vocalist – Daryl Hohl (Singles: 26 Weeks, Albums: 9 Weeks) pos/wks

2 Aug 86	DREAMTIME *RCA HALL 1*	**28** 8
25 Sep 93	I'M IN A PHILLY MOOD (re) *Epic 6595555*	**52** 4
8 Jan 94	STOP LOVING ME STOP LOVING YOU *Epic 6599982*	**30** 6
14 May 94	HELP ME FIND A WAY TO YOUR HEART *Epic 6604102*	**70** 1
2 Jul 94	GLORYLAND *Mercury MERCD 404* [1]	**36** 4
10 Jun 95	WHEREVER WOULD I BE *Columbia 6620592* [2]	**44** 3
23 Aug 86	THREE HEARTS IN THE HAPPY ENDING MACHINE *RCA PL 87196*	**26** 5
23 Oct 93	SOUL ALONE *Epic 4732912*	**55** 4

[1] Daryl Hall and The Sounds of Blackness [2] Dusty Springfield and Daryl Hall

Daryl HALL and John OATES 273 `Top 500`
White, soul-influenced US duo: Daryl Hall (v), b. Daryl Hohl, 11 Oct 1948,
Philadelphia, and John Oates (g), b. 7 Apr 1949, New York. Met at university in
1967, eventually becoming the most successful duo in US singles chart history,
with 16 Top 10s and six No.1s *(Singles: 84 Weeks, Albums: 154 Weeks)* pos/wks

16 Oct 76	SHE'S GONE *Atlantic K 10828*	**42** 4
14 Jun 80	RUNNING FROM PARADISE *RCA RUN 1*	**41** 6
20 Sep 80	YOU'VE LOST THAT LOVIN' FEELIN' *RCA 1*	**55** 3
15 Nov 80	KISS ON MY LIST *RCA 15* ▲	**33** 4
23 Jan 82	● I CAN'T GO FOR THAT (NO CAN DO) *RCA 172* ▲	**8** 10
10 Apr 82	PRIVATE EYES *RCA 134* ▲	**32** 7
30 Oct 82	● MANEATER *RCA 290* ▲	**6** 11
22 Jan 83	ONE ON ONE *RCA 305*	**63** 3
30 Apr 83	FAMILY MAN *RCA 323*	**15** 7
12 Nov 83	SAY IT ISN'T SO *RCA 375*	**69** 3
10 Mar 84	ADULT EDUCATION *RCA 396*	**63** 2
20 Oct 84	OUT OF TOUCH *RCA 449* ▲	**48** 5
9 Feb 85	METHOD OF MODERN LOVE *RCA 472*	**21** 8
22 Jun 85	OUT OF TOUCH (re-mix) *RCA PB 49967*	**62** 3
21 Sep 85	A NIGHT AT THE APOLLO LIVE! *RCA PB 49935* [1]	**58** 2
29 Sep 90	SO CLOSE *Arista 113600* [2]	**69** 1

		pos/wks
26 Jan 91	EVERYWHERE I LOOK *Arista 113980*	**74** 1
3 Jul 76	HALL AND OATES *RCA Victor APLI 1144*	**56** 1
18 Sep 76	BIGGER THAN BOTH OF US *RCA Victor APLI 1467*	**25** 7
15 Oct 77	BEAUTY ON A BACK STREET *RCA PL 12300*	**40** 2
6 Feb 82 ●	PRIVATE EYES *RCA RCALP 6001*	**8** 21
23 Oct 82	H2O *RCA RCALP 6056*	**24** 35
29 Oct 83	ROCK 'N' SOUL PART 1 *RCA PL 84858*	**16** 45
27 Oct 84	BIG BAM BOOM *RCA PL 85309*	**28** 13
28 Sep 85	HALL & OATES LIVE AT THE APOLLO WITH DAVID RUFFIN AND EDDIE KENDRICK *RCA PL 87035*	**32** 5
18 Jun 88	OOH YEAH! *RCA 208895*	**52** 3
27 Oct 90	CHANGE OF SEASON *Arista 210548*	**44** 2
19 Oct 91 ●	THE BEST OF DARYL HALL AND JOHN OATES – LOOKING BACK *Arista PL 90388*	**9** 16
6 Oct 01	THE ESSENTIAL COLLECTION *RCA 74321886972*	**26** 2
12 Apr 03	DO IT FOR LOVE *Sanctuary SANCD 166*	**37** 2

[1] Daryl Hall and John Oates featuring David Ruffin and Eddie Kendrick
[2] Hall and Oates

'A Night at the Apollo Live!' is a medley of 'The Way You Do the Things You Do' and 'My Girl'

Lynden David HALL *UK, male vocalist / instrumentalist (Singles: 12 Weeks, Albums: 4 Weeks)*

		pos/wks
25 Oct 97	SEXY CINDERELLA *Cooltempo CDCOOL 328*	**45** 2
14 Mar 98	DO I QUALIFY? *Cooltempo CDCOOLS 331*	**26** 2
4 Jul 98	CRESCENT MOON *Cooltempo CDCOOL 333*	**45** 1
31 Oct 98	SEXY CINDERELLA (re-issue) *Cooltempo CDCOOLS 340*	**17** 3
11 Mar 00	FORGIVE ME *Cooltempo CDCOOLS 346*	**30** 2
27 May 00	SLEEPING WITH VICTOR *Cooltempo CDCOOL 348*	**49** 1
23 Sep 00	LET'S DO IT AGAIN *Cooltempo CDCOOL 351*	**69** 1
14 Nov 00	MEDICINE 4 MY PAIN *Cooltempo 4959952*	**43** 2
10 Jun 00	THE OTHER SIDE *Cooltempo 5261492*	**36** 2

Pam HALL *Jamaica, female vocalist (Singles: 4 Weeks)*

		pos/wks
16 Aug 86	DEAR BOOPSIE *Bluemountain BM 027*	**54** 4

Terry HALL
(see also FUN BOY THREE; The SPECIALS; STARVING SOULS; VEGAS)
UK, male vocalist (Singles: 7 Weeks, Albums: 1 Week)

		pos/wks
11 Nov 89	MISSING *Chrysalis CHS 3381*	**75** 1
27 Aug 94	FOREVER J *AnXious ANX 1024CDX*	**67** 1
12 Nov 94	SENSE *AnXious ANX 1027CD*	**54** 2
28 Oct 95	RAINBOWS (EP) *AnXious ANX 1033CD1*	**62** 1
14 Jun 97	BALLAD OF A LANDLORD *Southsea Bubble CDBUBBLE 1*	**50** 1
18 Oct 03	PROBLEM IS *Distinctive DISNCD 107* [1]	**66** 1
18 Oct 97	LAUGH *Southsea Bubble CDBUBBLE 3*	**50** 1

[1] Dub Pistols featuring Terry Hall

The sleeve, not the label, of 'Missing' credits Terry, Blair and Anouchka. Tracks on Rainbows (EP) CD1: Chasing a Rainbow / Mistakes / See No Evil (live) / Ghost Town (live). CD2: Chasing a Rainbow / Our Lips are Sealed (live) / Thinking of You (live) / Ghost Town (live)

Toni HALLIDAY See LEFTFIELD; Paul VAN DYK

Geri HALLIWELL (457) Top 500
Headline-grabbing former Ginger Spice, b. 6 Aug 1972, Watford, UK, sang on seven Spice Girls chart-toppers before achieving more solo No.1s than any other UK female. She is the only person to score as many as four consecutive No.1s both as a solo artist and as part of group (Singles: 97 Weeks, Albums: 58 Weeks)

		pos/wks
22 May 99 ●	LOOK AT ME (re) *EMI CDEM 542*	**2** 14
28 Aug 99 ★	MI CHICO LATINO *EMI CDEM 548* ■	**1** 13
13 Nov 99 ★	LIFT ME UP (re) *EMI CDEM 554* ■	**1** 17
25 Mar 00 ★	BAG IT UP (re) *EMI CDEMS 560* ■	**1** 13
12 May 01 ★	IT'S RAINING MEN *EMI CDEMS 584* ■	**1** 15
11 Aug 01 ●	SCREAM IF YOU WANNA GO FASTER (re) *EMI CDEMS 595*	**8** 11
8 Dec 01 ●	CALLING *EMI CDEMS 606*	**7** 10
4 Dec 04 ●	RIDE IT *Innocent SINDX 69* [1]	**4** 4+
19 Jun 99 ●	SCHIZOPHONIC *EMI 5210092*	**4** 43
26 May 01 ●	SCREAM IF YOU WANNA GO FASTER *EMI 5333692*	**5** 15

[1] Geri

HALO *UK, male vocal / instrumental group (Singles: 3 Weeks)*

		pos/wks
16 Feb 02	COLD LIGHT OF DAY *S2 6723072*	**49** 1

		pos/wks
1 Jun 02	SANCTIMONIOUS *S2 6725962*	**44** 1
7 Sep 02	NEVER ENDING *S2 6730125*	**56** 1

HALO JAMES *UK, male vocal / instrumental group (Singles: 24 Weeks, Albums: 4 Weeks)*

		pos/wks
7 Oct 89	WANTED *Epic HALO 1*	**45** 5
23 Dec 89 ●	COULD HAVE TOLD YOU SO *Epic HALO 2*	**6** 12
17 Mar 90	BABY *Epic HALO 3*	**43** 4
19 May 90	MAGIC HOUR *Epic HALO 4*	**59** 3
14 Apr 90	WITNESS *Epic 466761*	**18** 4

The HAMBURG STUDENTS' CHOIR
Germany, male vocal group (Albums: 6 Weeks)

		pos/wks
17 Dec 60	HARK THE HERALD ANGELS SING *Pye GGL 0023*	**11** 6

Anthony HAMILTON See TWISTA

Ashley HAMILTON *US, male vocalist (Singles: 4 Weeks)*

		pos/wks
14 Jun 03	WIMMIN' (re) *Columbia 673902*	**27** 4

George HAMILTON IV
US, male vocalist (Singles: 13 Weeks, Albums: 11 Weeks)

		pos/wks
7 Mar 58	WHY DON'T THEY UNDERSTAND *HMV POP 429*	**22** 9
18 Jul 58	I KNOW WHERE I'M GOIN' *HMV POP 505*	**23** 4
10 Apr 71	CANADIAN PACIFIC *RCA SF 8062*	**45** 1
10 Feb 79	REFLECTIONS *Lotus WH 5008*	**25** 2
13 Nov 82	SONGS FOR A WINTER'S NIGHT *Ronco RTL 2082*	**94** 1

Lynne HAMILTON
Australia (b. UK), female vocalist (Singles: 11 Weeks)

		pos/wks
29 Apr 89 ●	ON THE INSIDE (THEME FROM 'PRISONER: CELL BLOCK H') *A1 A1 311*	**3** 11

Russ HAMILTON
UK, male vocalist – Ronald Hulme (Singles: 26 Weeks)

		pos/wks
24 May 57 ●	WE WILL MAKE LOVE *Oriole CB 1359*	**2** 20
27 Sep 57	WEDDING RING *Oriole CB 1388* [1]	**20** 6

[1] Russ Hamilton with Johnny Gregory and his Orchestra with The Tonettes

HAMILTON, Joe FRANK and REYNOLDS
US, male vocal group (Singles: 6 Weeks)

		pos/wks
13 Sep 75	FALLIN' IN LOVE *Pye International 7N 25690* ▲	**33** 6

Marvin HAMLISCH
US, male instrumentalist – piano (Singles: 13 Weeks)

		pos/wks
30 Mar 74	THE ENTERTAINER *MCA 121*	**25** 13

Jan HAMMER *Czech Republic, male instrumentalist – keyboards (Singles: 26 Weeks, Albums: 12 Weeks)*

		pos/wks
12 Oct 85 ●	MIAMI VICE THEME *MCA MCA 1000* ▲	**5** 8
19 Sep 87 ●	CROCKETT'S THEME *MCA MCA 1193*	**2** 12
1 Jun 91	CROCKETT'S THEME (re-issue) / CHANCER *MCA MCS 1541*	**47** 6
14 Nov 87	ESCAPE FROM TV *MCA MCF 3407*	**34** 12

Albert HAMMOND (see also FAMILY DOGG)
Gibraltar, male vocalist (Singles: 11 Weeks)

		pos/wks
30 Jun 73	FREE ELECTRIC BAND *Mums 1494*	**19** 11

Beres HAMMOND See Maxi PRIEST

HAMPENBERG *Denmark, male / female vocal / instrumental / production group (Singles: 2 Weeks)*

		pos/wks
21 Sep 02	DUCKTOY *Serious SERR 49CD*	**30** 2

Herbie HANCOCK *US, male vocalist / instrumentalist – keyboards (Singles: 41 Weeks, Albums: 24 Weeks)*

		pos/wks
26 Aug 78	I THOUGHT IT WAS YOU *CBS 6530*	**15** 9
3 Feb 79	YOU BET YOUR LOVE *CBS 7010*	**18** 10
30 Jul 83 ●	ROCKIT *CBS A 3577*	**8** 12
8 Oct 83	AUTODRIVE *CBS A 3802*	**33** 4
21 Jan 84	FUTURE SHOCK *CBS A 4075*	**54** 3

4 Aug 84	HARDROCK CBS A 4616	65 3
9 Sep 78	SUNLIGHT CBS 82240..................	27 6
24 Feb 79	FEETS DON'T FAIL ME NOW CBS 83491	28 8
27 Aug 83	FUTURE SHOCK CBS 25540	27 10

Tony HANCOCK UK, male comedian,
b. 12 May 1924, d. 25 Jun 1968 (Albums: 51 Weeks)   pos/wks

9 Apr 60 ●	THIS IS HANCOCK Pye NPL 10845	2 22
12 Nov 60	PIECES OF HANCOCK Pye NPL 18054	17 2
3 Mar 62	HANCOCK Pye NPL 18068	12 23
14 Sep 63	THIS IS HANCOCK (re-issue) Pye Golden Guinea GGL 0206 ..16 4

The HANDBAGGERS
UK, male / female vocal / instrumental group (Singles: 1 Week)   pos/wks

15 Jun 96	U FOUND OUT Tidy Trax TIDY 104CD	55 1

HANDLEY FAMILY
UK, male / female vocal group (Singles: 7 Weeks)   pos/wks

7 Apr 73	WAM BAM GL 100	30 7

HANI US, male DJ / producer –
Hani Adnan Al-Bader (Singles: 1 Week)   pos/wks

11 Mar 00	BABY WANTS TO RIDE Neo NEOCD 025	70 1

Jayn HANNA UK, female vocalist (Singles: 2 Weeks)   pos/wks

13 Apr 96	LOVELIGHT (RIDE ON A LOVE TRAIN) VC VCRD 10	42 1
1 Feb 97	LOST WITHOUT YOU VC VCRD 16	44 1

HANNAH
UK, female vocalist – Hannah Waddingham (Singles: 2 Weeks)   pos/wks

21 Oct 00	OUR KIND OF LOVE Telstar CDSTAS 3149	41 2

HANNAH See MAN WITH NO NAME

HANNAH and her SISTERS See Hannah JONES

Bo HANNSON Sweden, multi-instrumentalist (Albums: 7 Weeks) pos/wks

18 Nov 72	LORD OF THE RINGS Charisma CAS 1059	32 7

HANOI ROCKS Finland / UK, male vocal /
instrumental group (Singles: 2 Weeks, Albums: 4 Weeks)   pos/wks

7 Jul 84	UP AROUND THE BEND CBS A 4513	61 2
11 Jun 83	BACK TO MYSTERY CITY Lick LICLP 1	87 1
20 Oct 84	TWO STEPS FROM THE MOVE CBS 26066	28 3

HANSON US, male vocal / instrumental
group (Singles: 47 Weeks, Albums: 31 Weeks)   pos/wks

7 Jun 97 ★	MMMBOP Mercury 5745012 ■ ▲	1 13
13 Sep 97 ●	WHERE'S THE LOVE Mercury 5749032	4 9
22 Nov 97 ●	I WILL COME TO YOU Mercury 5680672	5 9
28 Mar 98	WEIRD Mercury 5685412	19 5
4 Jul 98	THINKING OF YOU (re) Mercury 5688132	23 7
29 Apr 00	IF ONLY Mercury 5627502	15 4
21 Jun 97 ★	MIDDLE OF NOWHERE Mercury 5346152 ■	1 29
13 Jun 98	3 CAR GARAGE – INDIE RECORDINGS 95–96 Mercury 5583992...39 1
13 May 00	THIS TIME AROUND Mercury 5427212	33 1

John HANSON UK, male vocalist (Albums: 12 Weeks)   pos/wks

23 Apr 60	THE STUDENT PRINCE Pye NPL 18046	17 1
2 Sep 61 ●	THE STUDENT PRINCE / THE VAGABOND KING Pye GGL 0086 ..9 7
10 Dec 77	JOHN HANSON SINGS 20 SHOWTIME GREATS K-Tel NE 1002 16 4

The two albums entitled 'The Student Prince' are different, although some tracks
are repeated

The HAPPENINGS US, male vocal group (Singles: 14 Weeks)   pos/wks

18 May 67	I GOT RHYTHM Stateside SS 2013	28 9
16 Aug 67	MY MAMMY
	Pye International 7N 25501 and BT Puppy BTS 45530 ....34 5

Pye gave the US BT Puppy label its own identification halfway through the success
of 'My Mammy'

HAPPY CLAPPERS
UK, male / female vocal / instrumental group (Singles: 19 Weeks)   pos/wks

3 Jun 95	I BELIEVE Shindig SHIN 4CD	21 3
26 Aug 95	HOLD ON Shindig SHIN 7CD	27 2
18 Nov 95 ●	I BELIEVE (re-issue) Shindig SHIN 9CD	7 8
15 Jun 96	CAN'T HELP IT Coliseum TOGA 004CD	18 3
21 Dec 96	NEVER AGAIN Coliseum TOGA 012CD	49 1
22 Nov 97	I BELIEVE (re-mix) Coalition COLA 027CD	28 2

HAPPY MONDAYS (see also BLACK GRAPE) UK, male vocal /
instrumental group – leader Shaun Ryder, includes Bez (dancer), winner of
Celebrity Big Brother 2005 (Singles: 53 Weeks, Albums: 57 Weeks)   pos/wks

30 Sep 89	WFL Factory FAC 2327	68 2
25 Nov 89	MADCHESTER RAVE ON (EP) Factory FAC 2427	19 14
7 Apr 90 ●	STEP ON Factory FAC 2727	5 11
9 Jun 90	LAZYITIS – ONE ARMED BOXER Factory FAC 2227 [1]	46 3
20 Oct 90	KINKY AFRO Factory FAC 3027	5 7
9 Mar 91	LOOSE FIT Factory FAC 3127	17 7
30 Nov 91	JUDGE FUDGE Factory FAC 3327	24 3
19 Sep 92	STINKIN THINKIN Factory FAC 3627	31 3
21 Nov 92	SUNSHINE AND LOVE Factory FAC 3727	62 1
22 May 99	THE BOYS ARE BACK IN TOWN London LONCD 432	24 2
27 Jan 90	BUMMED Factory FACT 220	59 14
17 Nov 90 ●	PILLS 'N' THRILLS AND BELLYACHES Factory FACT 320..........4 29
12 Oct 91	LIVE Factory FACT 322	21 3
10 Oct 92	... YES PLEASE! Factory FACD 420	14 3
18 Nov 95	LOADS – THE BEST OF THE HAPPY MONDAYS
	Factory Once 5203432..........	41 2
5 Jun 99	GREATEST HITS London 5561052	11 4
6 Jul 02	PILLS 'N' THRILLS AND BELLYACHES (re-issue)
	London 3984282512..........	47 2

[1] Happy Mondays and Karl Denver

Tracks on Madchester Rave On (EP): Hallelujah / Holy Ghost / Clap Your Hands /
Rave On

HAPPYLIFE UK, male vocal / instrumental group (Singles: 1 Week) pos/wks

9 Oct 04	SILENCE WHEN YOU'RE BURNING
	Albert Productions JASCDVUK 012	73 1

HAR MAR SUPERSTAR US, male vocalist –
Sean Tillman (Singles: 3 Weeks, Albums: 1 Week)   pos/wks

5 Jul 03	EZ PASS B Unique BUN 054CDS	59 1
4 Sep 04	DUI Record Collection W 651CD	46 2
18 Sep 04	THE HANDLER Record Collection 9362488102	68 1

Ed HARCOURT
UK, male vocalist (Singles: 4 Weeks, Albums: 2 Weeks)   pos/wks

2 Feb 02	APPLE OF MY EYE Heavenly HVN 107CDS	61 1
15 Feb 03	ALL OF YOUR DAYS WILL BE BLESSED
	Heavenly HVN 127CDS	35 1
11 Sep 04	THIS ONE'S FOR YOU Heavenly HVN 140CD	41 1
13 Nov 04	BORN IN THE 70S Heavenly HVN 146	61 1
1 Mar 03	FROM EVERY SPHERE Heavenly HVNLP 39CD	39 1
25 Sep 04	STRANGERS Heavenly HVNLP 49CD	57 1

Paul HARDCASTLE (see also SILENT UNDERDOG)
UK, male producer (Singles: 66 Weeks, Albums: 5 Weeks)   pos/wks

7 Apr 84	YOU'RE THE ONE FOR ME – DAYBREAK – AM
	Total Control TOCO 1	41 4
28 Jul 84	GUILTY Total Control TOCO 2	55 3
22 Sep 84	RAIN FOREST Bluebird BR 8	41 5
17 Nov 84	EAT YOUR HEART OUT Cooltempo COOL 102	59 4
4 May 85 ★	19 Chrysalis CHS 2860	1 16
15 Jun 85	RAIN FOREST (re-issue) Bluebird / 10BR 15	53 4
9 Nov 85	JUST FOR MONEY Chrysalis CASH 1	19 5
1 Feb 86 ●	DON'T WASTE MY TIME Chrysalis PAUL 1	8 11
21 Jun 86	FOOLIN' YOURSELF Chrysalis PAUL 2	51 3
11 Oct 86	THE WIZARD Chrysalis PAUL 3	15 6
9 Apr 88	WALK IN THE NIGHT Chrysalis PAUL 4	54 3
4 Jun 88	40 YEARS Chrysalis PAUL 5	53 2
30 Nov 85	PAUL HARDCASTLE Chrysalis CHR 1517..........	53 5

'Just for Money' features the voices of Laurence Olivier, Bob Hoskins, Ed O'Ross
and Alan Talbot, who are credited on the sleeve only. 'Don't Waste My Time'
features uncredited vocalist Carol Kenyon

HARDCORE RHYTHM TEAM
UK, male vocal / production group (Singles: 1 Week) pos/wks

| 14 Mar 92 | HARDCORE – THE FINAL CONFLICT *Furious FRUT 001* ....**69** 1 |

Duane HARDEN See POWERHOUSE; Armand VAN HELDEN

HARDFLOOR
Germany, male instrumental / production group (Singles: 6 Weeks, Albums: 1 Week) pos/wks

26 Dec 92	HARDTRANCE ACPERIENCE *Harthouse UK HARTUK 1* **56** 4
10 Apr 93	TRANCESCRIPT *Harthouse UK HARTUK 5CD* **72** 1
25 Oct 97	ACPERIENCE (re-mix) *Eye-q EYEUK 018CD1* **60** 1
29 Jun 96	HOME RUN *Harthouse HHCD 019* **68** 1

Ronan HARDIMAN
Ireland, male composer (Albums: 8 Weeks) pos/wks

| 2 Nov 96 | MICHAEL FLATLEY'S LORD OF THE DANCE *PolyGram TV 5337572* ....**37** 8 |

Tim HARDIN
US, male vocalist, b. 23 Dec 1941, d. 29 Dec 1980 (Singles: 1 Week) pos/wks

| 5 Jan 67 | HANG ON TO A DREAM *Verve VS 1504* ....**50** 1 |

Carolyn HARDING See PROSPECT PARK / Carolyn HARDING

Mike HARDING
UK, male vocalist / radio DJ / novelist / comedian (Singles: 8 Weeks, Albums: 24 Weeks) pos/wks

2 Aug 75	ROCHDALE COWBOY *Rubber ADUB 3* **22** 8
30 Aug 75	MRS 'ARDIN'S KID *Rubber RUB 011* **24** 6
10 Jul 76	ONE MAN SHOW *Philips 6625 022* **19** 10
11 Jun 77	OLD FOUR EYES IS BACK *Philips 6308 290* **31** 6
24 Jun 78	CAPTAIN PARALYTIC AND THE BROWN ALE COWBOY *Philips 6641 798* **60** 2

HARDSOUL featuring Ron CARROLL
Holland, male DJ / production duo – Rogier and Gregor Van Bueren and US, male vocalist (Singles: 1 Week) pos/wks

| 12 Jun 04 | BACKTOGETHER *In the House ITH 02CDS* ....**60** 1 |

Françoise HARDY
France, female vocalist (Singles: 27 Weeks) pos/wks

25 Jun 64	TOUS LES GARCONS ET LES FILLES *Pye 7N 15653* **36** 7
31 Dec 64	ET MEME *Pye 7N 15740* **31** 5
25 Mar 65	ALL OVER THE WORLD *Pye 7N 15802* **16** 15

Tynetta HARE See Joey B ELLIS

NIKI HARIS See SNAP!

Morten HARKET (see also A-HA)
Norway, male vocalist (Singles: 1 Week) pos/wks

| 19 Aug 95 | A KIND OF CHRISTMAS CARD *Warner Bros. W 0304CD* ....**53** 1 |

HARLEM COMMUNITY CHOIR See John LENNON

HARLEQUIN 4s / BUNKER KRU
US, male / female vocal / instrumental group and UK, male production duo (Singles: 4 Weeks) pos/wks

| 19 Mar 88 | SET IT OFF *Champion CHAMP 64* ....**55** 4 |

Steve HARLEY and COCKNEY REBEL
UK, male vocal / instrumental group – leader Steve Nice (Singles: 69 Weeks, Albums: 52 Weeks) pos/wks

11 May 74 ●	JUDY TEEN *EMI 2128* [1] **5** 11
10 Aug 74 ●	MR SOFT *EMI 2191* [1] **8** 9
8 Feb 75 ★	MAKE ME SMILE (COME UP AND SEE ME) *EMI 2263* [1] **1** 9
7 Jun 75	MR RAFFLES (MAN, IT WAS MEAN) *EMI 2299* **13** 6
31 Jul 76 ●	HERE COMES THE SUN *EMI 2505* [2] **10** 7
6 Nov 76	(I BELIEVE) LOVE'S A PRIMA DONNA *EMI 2539* [2] **41** 4
20 Oct 79	FREEDOM'S PRISONER *EMI 2994* [2] **58** 3
13 Aug 83	BALLERINA (PRIMA DONNA) *Stiletto STL 14* [2] **51** 5
11 Jan 86 ●	THE PHANTOM OF THE OPERA *Polydor POSP 800* [3] **7** 10
25 Apr 92	MAKE ME SMILE (COME UP AND SEE ME) (re-issue) *EMI EMCT 5* [2] **46** 1
30 Dec 95	MAKE ME SMILE (COME UP AND SEE ME) (2nd re-issue) *EMI CDHARLEY 1* **33** 3
22 Jun 74 ●	THE PSYCHOMODO *EMI EMC 3033* [1] **8** 20

22 Mar 75 ●	THE BEST YEARS OF OUR LIVES *EMI EMC 3068* **4** 19
14 Feb 76	TIMELESS FLIGHT *EMI EMA 775* **18** 6
27 Nov 76	LOVE'S A PRIMA DONNA *EMI EMC 3156* **28** 3
30 Jul 77	FACE TO FACE – A LIVE RECORDING *EMI EMSP 320* **40** 4

[1] Cockney Rebel [2] Steve Harley [3] Sarah Brightman and Steve Harley
[1] Cockney Rebel

HARLEY QUINNE
UK, male vocal group (Singles: 8 Weeks) pos/wks

| 14 Oct 72 | NEW ORLEANS *Bell 1255* ....**19** 8 |

HARMONIUM
(see also BLOWING FREE; HYPNOSIS; IN TUNE; JAMES BOYS; RAINDANCE; SCHOOL OF EXCELLENCE) *UK, male production / instrumental duo – Stewart and Bradley Palmer (Albums: 4 Weeks)* pos/wks

| 21 Mar 98 | SPIRIT OF TRANQUILITY *Global Television RADCD 79* ....**25** 4 |

HARMONIX
UK, male producer – Hamish Brown (Singles: 2 Weeks) pos/wks

| 30 Mar 96 | LANDSLIDE *Deconstruction 74321330762* ....**28** 2 |

HARMONY GRASS
UK, male vocal / instrumental group (Singles: 7 Weeks) pos/wks

| 29 Jan 69 | MOVE IN A LITTLE CLOSER BABY *RCA 1772* ....**24** 7 |

Ben HARPER
US, male vocalist / instrumentalist (Singles: 1 Week) pos/wks

| 4 Apr 98 | FADED *Virgin VUSCD 134* ....**54** 1 |

Charlie HARPER (see also UK SUBS)
UK, male vocalist – David Perez (Singles: 1 Week) pos/wks

| 19 Jul 80 | BARMY LONDON ARMY *Gem GEMS 35* ....**68** 1 |

Roy HARPER
UK, male vocalist / instrumentalist – guitar (Albums: 9 Weeks) pos/wks

9 Mar 74	VALENTINE *Harvest SHSP 4027* **27** 1
21 Jun 75	H.Q. *Harvest SHSP 4046* **31** 2
12 Mar 77	BULLINAMINGVASE *Harvest SHSP 4060* **25** 2
16 Mar 85	WHATEVER HAPPENED TO JUGULA? *Beggars Banquet BEGA 60* [1] **44** 4

[1] Roy Harper and Jimmy Page

HARPERS BIZARRE
US, male vocal group (Singles: 13 Weeks) pos/wks

| 30 Mar 67 | 59TH STREET BRIDGE SONG (FEELIN' GROOVY) *Warner Bros. WB 5890* ....**34** 7 |
| 4 Oct 67 | ANYTHING GOES *Warner Bros. WB 7063* ....**33** 6 |

HARPO
Sweden, male vocalist – Jan Svensson (Singles: 6 Weeks) pos/wks

| 17 Apr 76 | MOVIE STAR *DJM DJS 400* ....**24** 6 |

T HARRINGTON See Rahni HARRIS and F.L.O.

Anita HARRIS
UK, female vocalist (Singles: 50 Weeks, Albums: 5 Weeks) pos/wks

29 Jun 67 ●	JUST LOVING YOU *CBS 2724* **6** 30
11 Oct 67	THE PLAYGROUND *CBS 2991* **46** 3
24 Jan 68	ANNIVERSARY WALTZ *CBS 3211* **21** 9
14 Aug 68	DREAM A LITTLE DREAM OF ME *CBS 3637* **33** 8
27 Jan 68	JUST LOVING YOU *CBS SBPG 63182* **29** 5

Emmylou HARRIS
US, female vocalist / instrumentalist – guitar (Singles: 6 Weeks, Albums: 37 Weeks) pos/wks

6 Mar 76	HERE, THERE & EVERYWHERE *Reprise K 14415* **30** 6
14 Feb 76	ELITE HOTEL *Reprise K 54060* **17** 11
29 Jan 77	LUXURY LINER *Warner Bros. K 56344* **17** 6
4 Feb 78	QUARTER MOON IN A TEN CENT TOWN *Warner Bros. K 56433* **40** 5
29 Mar 80	HER BEST SONGS *K-Tel NE 1058* **36** 3
14 Feb 81	EVANGELINE *Warner Bros. K 56880* **53** 4
14 Mar 87	TRIO *Warner Bros. 9254911* [1] **60** 4
7 Oct 95	WRECKING BALL *Grapevine GRACD 102* **46** 1
29 Aug 98	SPYBOY *Grapevine GRACD 241* **57** 1
30 Sep 00	RED DIRT GIRL *Grapevine GRACD 103* **45** 1
4 Oct 03	STUMBLE INTO GRACE *Nonesuch 7559798052* **52** 1

[1] Dolly Parton / Emmylou Harris / Linda Ronstadt

Singles re-entries are listed as (re), (2re), (3re)…. which signifies that the hit re-entered the chart once, twice or three times…

Jet HARRIS and Tony MEEHAN

(see also The SHADOWS) *UK, male instrumental duo*
– Jet Harris (Terence Harris) – bass and Tony Meehan
(Daniel Meehan) – drums (Singles: 57 Weeks)   pos/wks

24 May 62	BESAME MUCHO *Decca F 11466* [1]	22	7
16 Aug 62	MAIN TITLE THEME (FROM 'THE MAN WITH THE GOLDEN ARM') *Decca F 11488* [1]	12	11
10 Jan 63	★ DIAMONDS *Decca F 11563*	1	13
25 Apr 63	● SCARLETT O'HARA *Decca F 11644*	2	13
5 Sep 63	● APPLEJACK *Decca F 11710*	4	13

[1] Jet Harris

Keith HARRIS and ORVILLE

UK, male ventriloquist vocalist and duck (Singles: 20 Weeks)   pos/wks

18 Dec 82	● ORVILLE'S SONG *BBC RESL 124*	4	11
24 Dec 83	COME TO MY PARTY *BBC RESL 138* [1]	44	4
14 Dec 85	WHITE CHRISTMAS *Columbia DB 9121*	40	5
4 Jun 83	AT THE END OF THE RAINBOW *BBC REH 465* [1]	92	1

[1] Keith Harris and Orville with Dippy   [1] Keith Harris, Orville and Cuddles

Major HARRIS *US, male vocalist (Singles: 9 Weeks)*   pos/wks

9 Aug 75	LOVE WON'T LET ME WAIT *Atlantic K 10585*	37	7
5 Nov 83	ALL MY LIFE *London LON 37*	61	2

Max HARRIS *UK, orchestra leader, b. 15*
Sep 1918, d. 13 Mar 2004 (Singles: 10 Weeks)   pos/wks

1 Dec 60	GURNEY SLADE *Fontana H 282*	11	10

Rahni HARRIS and F.L.O.

US, male instrumental group (Singles: 7 Weeks)   pos/wks

16 Dec 78	SIX MILLION STEPS (WEST RUNS SOUTH) *Mercury 6007 198*	43	7

Hit has credit 'vocals by T Harrington and O Rasbury'

Richard HARRIS *Ireland, male actor / vocalist,*
b. 1 Oct 1930, d. 25 Oct 2002 (Singles: 18 Weeks)   pos/wks

26 Jun 68	● MACARTHUR PARK *RCA 1699*	4	12
8 Jul 72	MACARTHUR PARK (re-issue) *Probe GFF 101*	38	6

Rochelle HARRIS *See ANGELHEART*

Rolf HARRIS *Australia, male artist / TV presenter /*
vocalist (Singles: 77 Weeks, Albums: 1 Week)   pos/wks

21 Jul 60	● TIE ME KANGAROO DOWN, SPORT *Columbia DB 4483* [1]	9	13
25 Oct 62	● SUN ARISE *Columbia DB 4888*	3	16
28 Feb 63	JOHNNY DAY *Columbia DB 4979*	44	2
16 Apr 69	BLUER THAN BLUE *Columbia DB 8553*	30	8
22 Nov 69	★ TWO LITTLE BOYS (re) *Columbia DB 8630*	1	25
13 Feb 93	STAIRWAY TO HEAVEN *Vertigo VERCD 73*	7	6
1 Jun 96	BOHEMIAN RHAPSODY *Living Beat LBECD 41*	50	1
25 Oct 97	SUN ARISE (re-recording) *EMI CDROO 001*	26	3
14 Oct 00	FINE DAY *Tommy Boy TBCD 2155*	24	3
1 Nov 97	CAN YOU TELL WHAT IT IS YET? *EMI 8218802*	70	1

[1] Rolf Harris with his wobble board and The Rhythm Spinners

Ronnie HARRIS *UK, male vocalist (Singles: 3 Weeks)*   pos/wks

24 Sep 54	THE STORY OF TINA *Columbia DB 3499*	12	3

Sam HARRIS *US, male vocalist (Singles: 2 Weeks)*   pos/wks

9 Feb 85	HEARTS ON FIRE / OVER THE RAINBOW *Motown TMG 1370*	67	2

Simon HARRIS

(see also AMBASSADORS OF FUNK featuring MC MARIO)
UK, male / DJ producer (Singles: 17 Weeks)   pos/wks

19 Mar 88	BASS (HOW LOW CAN YOU GO) *ffrr FFR 4*	12	6
29 Oct 88	HERE COMES THAT SOUND *ffrr FFR 12*	38	4
24 Jun 89	(I'VE GOT YOUR) PLEASURE CONTROL *ffrr F 106* [1]	60	3
18 Nov 89	ANOTHER MONSTERJAM *ffrr F 116* [2]	65	1
10 Mar 90	RAGGA HOUSE (ALL NIGHT LONG) *Living Beat 7SMASH 9* [3]	56	3

[1] Simon Harris featuring Lonnie Gordon [2] Simon Harris featuring Einstein [3] Simon Harris featuring Daddy Freddy

George HARRIS 385 Top 500 (see also TRAVELING WILBURYS)

Former Beatles guitarist, much inspired by Eastern musicians, b. 25 Feb 1943, Liverpool, UK, d. 29 Nov 2001. First ex-Beatle to score a solo UK No.1 single and only soloist to top chart twice with the same single. Although not credited as a George Harrison album, the triple disc Concert For Bangladesh was instigated and performed by him and star guests such as Ravi Shankar, Bob Dylan, Eric Clapton and Ringo Starr. In 2004, he won a Grammy for Best Instrumental ('Marwa Blues'), and was added to the Rock and Roll Hall of Fame (Singles: 94 Weeks, Albums: 82 Weeks)   pos/wks

23 Jan 71	★ MY SWEET LORD *Apple R 5884* ▲	1	17
14 Aug 71	● BANGLA-DESH *Apple R 5912*	10	9
2 Jun 73	● GIVE ME LOVE (GIVE ME PEACE ON EARTH) *Apple R 5988* ▲	8	10
21 Dec 74	DING DONG *Apple R 6002*	38	5
11 Oct 75	YOU *Apple R 6007*	38	5
10 Mar 79	BLOW AWAY *Dark Horse K 17327*	51	5
23 May 81	ALL THOSE YEARS AGO *Dark Horse K 17807*	13	7
24 Oct 87	● GOT MY MIND SET ON YOU *Dark Horse W 8178* ▲	2	14
6 Feb 88	WHEN WE WAS FAB *Dark Horse W 8131*	25	7
25 Jun 88	THIS IS LOVE *Dark Horse W 7913*	55	3
26 Jan 02	★ MY SWEET LORD (re-issue) *Parlophone CDR 6571* ■	1	10
24 May 03	ANY ROAD *Parlophone CDRS 6601*	37	2
26 Dec 70	★ ALL THINGS MUST PASS *Apple STCH 639* ▲	1	24
7 Jul 73	● LIVING IN THE MATERIAL WORLD *Apple PAS 10006* ▲	2	12
18 Oct 75	EXTRA TEXTURE (READ ALL ABOUT IT) *Apple PAS 10009*	16	4
18 Dec 76	THIRTY THREE AND A THIRD *Dark Horse K 56319*	35	4
17 Mar 79	GEORGE HARRISON *Dark Horse K 56562*	39	5
13 Jun 81	SOMEWHERE IN ENGLAND *Dark Horse K 56870*	13	4
14 Nov 87	● CLOUD NINE *Dark Horse WX 123*	10	23
3 Feb 01	ALL THINGS MUST PASS (re-issue) *Parlophone 5304742*	68	2
30 Nov 02	BRAINWASHED *Parlophone 5803450*	29	4

Jane HARRISON *UK, female vocalist (Albums: 1 Week)*   pos/wks

4 Feb 89	NEW DAY *Stylus SMR 869*	70	1

Noel HARRISON *UK, male vocalist (Singles: 14 Weeks)*   pos/wks

26 Feb 69	● THE WINDMILLS OF YOUR MIND *Reprise RS 20758*	8	14

HARRY

UK, female vocalist – Victoria Harrison (Singles: 2 Weeks)   pos/wks

2 Nov 02	SO REAL *Dirty Word DWRCD 003*	53	1
19 Apr 03	UNDER THE COVERS EP *Dirty Word DWRCD 005*	43	1

Tracks on Under the Covers EP: Imagination / Push It (Real Good) / She's in Parties

HARRY *See OBI PROJECT featuring HARRY, ASHER D and DJ WHAT?*

Deborah HARRY (see also BLONDIE)

US, female vocalist (Singles: 52 Weeks, Albums: 53 Weeks)   pos/wks

1 Aug 81	BACKFIRED *Chrysalis CHS 2526* [1]	32	6
15 Nov 86	● FRENCH KISSIN' IN THE USA *Chrysalis CHS 3066* [1]	8	10
28 Feb 87	FREE TO FALL *Chrysalis CHS 3093* [1]	46	4
9 May 87	IN LOVE WITH LOVE *Chrysalis CHS 3128* [1]	45	5
7 Oct 89	I WANT THAT MAN *Chrysalis CHS 3369*	13	10
2 Dec 89	BRITE SIDE *Chrysalis CHS 3452*	59	4
31 Mar 90	SWEET AND LOW *Chrysalis CHS 3491*	57	3
5 Jan 91	WELL DID YOU EVAH! *Chrysalis CHS 3646* [2]	42	4
3 Jul 93	I CAN SEE CLEARLY NOW *Chrysalis CDCHSS 4900*	23	4
18 Sep 93	STRIKE ME PINK *Chrysalis CDCHSS 5000*	46	2
8 Aug 81	● KOO KOO *Chrysalis CHR 1347* [1]	6	7
29 Nov 86	ROCKBIRD *Chrysalis CHR 1540* [1]	31	11
17 Dec 88	ONCE MORE INTO THE BLEACH *Chrysalis CJB 2* [2]	50	4
28 Oct 89	DEF DUMB AND BLONDE *Chrysalis CHR 1650*	12	7
16 Mar 91	● THE COMPLETE PICTURE – THE VERY BEST OF DEBORAH HARRY AND BLONDIE *Chrysalis CHR 1817* [2]	3	22
31 Jul 93	DEBRAVATION *Chrysalis CDCHR 6033*	24	2

[1] Debbie Harry [2] Deborah Harry and Iggy Pop [1] Debbie Harry [2] Deborah Harry and Blondie

HARRY J ALL STARS *Jamaica, male instrumental*
group – leader Harry Johnson (Singles: 25 Weeks)   pos/wks

25 Oct 69	● LIQUIDATOR *Trojan TR 675*	9	20
29 Mar 80	LIQUIDATOR (re-issue) *Trojan TRO 9063*	42	5

Re-issue of 'Liquidator' was coupled with re-issue of 'Long Shot Kick De Bucket' by The Pioneers

Keef HARTLEY BAND
UK, male vocal / instrumental group (Albums: 3 Weeks)   pos/wks

5 Sep 70	THE TIME IS NEAR *Deram SML 1071* 41	3

Richard HARTLEY / Michael REED ORCHESTRA *UK, male*
instrumentalist – synthesizer and orchestra (Singles: 10 Weeks)   pos/wks

25 Feb 84 ●	THE MUSIC OF TORVILL AND DEAN (EP) *Safari SKATE 1* 9	10

Tracks on EP: Bolero / Capriccio Espagnole Opus 34 (Nos. 4 and 5) – Richard Hartley; Barnum on Ice / Discoskate – Michael Reed Orchestra

Dan HARTMAN
US, male vocalist, b. 8 Dec 1950, d. 22 Mar 1994 (Singles: 34 Weeks) pos/wks

21 Oct 78 ●	INSTANT REPLAY *Blue Sky SKY 6706* 8	15
13 Jan 79	THIS IS IT *Blue Sky SKY 6999* 17	8
18 May 85	SECOND NATURE *MCA MCA 957* 66	2
24 Aug 85	I CAN DREAM ABOUT YOU *MCA MCA 988* 12	8
1 Apr 95	KEEP THE FIRE BURNIN' *Columbia 6611552* [1] 49	1

[1] Dan Hartman starring Loleatta Holloway

HARVEY (see also SO SOLID CREW)
UK, male rapper – Michael Harvey (Singles: 2 Weeks)   pos/wks

7 Sep 02	GET UP AND MOVE *Go Beat GOBCD 52* 24	2

Alex HARVEY *See SENSATIONAL ALEX HARVEY BAND*

Brian HARVEY (see also EAST 17; TRUE STEPPERS)
UK, male vocalist (Singles: 5 Weeks)   pos/wks

28 Apr 01	STRAIGHT UP NO BENDS *Edel 0126605 ERE* 26	2
27 Oct 01	LOVING YOU (OLE OLE OLE) *Blacklist 0132325 ERE* [1] 20	3

[1] Brian Harvey and The Refugee Crew

Lee HARVEY *See N*E*R*D*

PJ HARVEY (see also John PARISH)
UK, female vocalist – Polly Jean Harvey
(Singles: 27 Weeks, Albums: 36 Weeks)   pos/wks

29 Feb 92	SHEELA-NA-GIG *Too Pure PURE 008* 69	1
1 May 93	50 FT QUEENIE *Island CID 538* 27	2
17 Jul 93	MAN-SIZE *Island CID 569* 42	2
18 Feb 95	DOWN BY THE WATER *Island CID 607* 38	2
22 Jul 95	C'MON BILLY *Island CID 614* 29	2
28 Oct 95	SEND HIS LOVE TO ME *Island CID 610* 34	2
9 Mar 96	HENRY LEE *Mute CDMUTE 189* [1] 36	1
23 Nov 96	THAT WAS MY VEIL *Island CID 648* [2] 75	1
26 Sep 98	A PERFECT DAY ELISE *Island CID 718* 25	2
23 Jan 99	THE WIND *Island CID 730* 29	2
25 Nov 00	GOOD FORTUNE *Island CID 769* 41	2
10 Mar 01	A PLACE CALLED HOME *Island CID 771* 43	2
20 Oct 01	THIS IS LOVE *Island CID 785* 41	1
29 May 04	THE LETTER *Island CIDX 861* 28	2
31 Jul 04	YOU COME THROUGH *Island CIDX 869* 41	2
2 Oct 04	SHAME *Island CID 873* 45	1
11 Apr 92	DRY *Too Pure PURECD 10* 11	5
8 May 93 ●	RID OF ME *Island CID 8002* 3	4
30 Oct 93	4-TRACK DEMOS *Island IMCD 170* 19	2
11 Mar 95	TO BRING YOU MY LOVE *Island CID 8035* 12	6
5 Oct 96	DANCE HALL AT LOUSE POINT *Island CID 8051* [1] 46	1
10 Oct 98	IS THIS DESIRE? *Island CID 8076* 17	2
4 Nov 00	STORIES FROM THE CITY STORIES FROM THE SEA *Island CID 8099* 23	13
12 Jun 04	UH HUH HER *Island CIDX 8143* 12	3

[1] Nick Cave and the Bad Seeds and PJ Harvey [2] John Parish and Polly Jean Harvey [1] John Parish / Polly Jean Harvey

For the first three singles and albums PJ Harvey was the name of the entire group, not just the lead singer

Steve HARVEY *UK, male vocalist (Singles: 6 Weeks)*   pos/wks

28 May 83	SOMETHING SPECIAL *London LON 25* 46	4
29 Oct 83	TONIGHT *London LON 36* 63	2

Richard HARVEY and FRIENDS
UK, male instrumental group (Albums: 1 Week)   pos/wks

6 May 89	EVENING FALLS *Telstar STAR 2350* 72	1

HARVEY DANGER
US, male vocal / instrumental group (Singles: 1 Week)   pos/wks

1 Aug 98	FLAGPOLE SITTA *Slash LASCD 64* 57	1

Gordon HASKELL
UK, male vocalist (Singles: 6 Weeks, Albums: 11 Weeks)   pos/wks

29 Dec 01 ●	HOW WONDERFUL YOU ARE *Flying Sparks TDBCDS 04* 2	6
19 Jan 02 ●	HARRY'S BAR *East West 927439762* 2	10
26 Oct 02	SHADOWS ON THE WALL *Flying Sparks TDBCD 068* 44	1

Lee HASLAM *UK, male DJ / producer (Singles: 1 Week)*   pos/wks

14 Aug 04	LIBERATE / HERE COMES THE PAIN *Tidy Trax TIDTRWO 135* ..71	1

David HASSELHOFF *US, male vocalist / actor (Singles: 2 Weeks)*   pos/wks

13 Nov 93	IF I COULD ONLY SAY GOODBYE *Arista 74321172262* 35	2

Tony HATCH *UK, orchestra (Singles: 1 Week)*   pos/wks

4 Oct 62	OUT OF THIS WORLD *Pye 7N 15460* 50	1

Juliana HATFIELD *US, female vocalist /*
instrumentalist – guitar (Singles: 2 Weeks, Albums: 3 Weeks)   pos/wks

11 Sep 93	MY SISTER *Mammoth YZ 767CD* [1] 71	1
18 Mar 95	UNIVERSAL HEART-BEAT *East West YZ 916CD* 65	1
14 Aug 93	BECOME WHAT YOU ARE *Mammoth 4509935292* [1] 44	2
8 Apr 95	ONLY EVERYTHING *East West 4509998862* 59	1

[1] Juliana Hatfield Three [1] Juliana Hatfield Three

HATFIELD AND THE NORTH (see also Dave STEWART)
UK, male / female vocal / instrumental group (Albums: 1 Week)   pos/wks

29 Mar 75	ROTTERS CLUB *Virgin V 2030* 43	1

Donny HATHAWAY *See Roberta FLACK*

Lalah HATHAWAY *US, female vocalist (Singles: 10 Weeks)*   pos/wks

1 Sep 90	HEAVEN KNOWS *Virgin America VUS 28* 66	2
2 Feb 91	BABY DON'T CRY *Virgin America VUS 35* 54	3
27 Jul 91	FAMILY AFFAIR *Ten TEN 369* 37	5

Charlotte HATHERLEY (see also ASH) *UK, female vocalist /*
instrumentalist – guitar (Singles: 2 Weeks, Albums: 1 Week)   pos/wks

21 Aug 04	SUMMER *Double Dragon DD 2014CD* 31	2
28 Aug 04	GREY WILL FADE *Double Dragon DD 2015CD* 51	1

HATIRAS featuring SLARTA JOHN *Canada, male producer – George*
Hatiris and UK, male rapper – Mark James (Singles: 5 Weeks)   pos/wks

27 Jan 01	SPACED INVADER *Defected DFECT 25CDS* 14	5

HAVANA
UK, male instrumental / production group (Singles: 1 Week)   pos/wks

6 Mar 93	ETHNIC PRAYER *Limbo LIMBO 007CD* 71	1

HAVEN *UK, male vocal / instrumental*
group (Singles: 7 Weeks, Albums: 3 Weeks)   pos/wks

22 Sep 01	LET IT LIVE *Radiate RDT 3* 72	1
2 Feb 02	SAY SOMETHING *Radiate RDT 4* 24	1
4 May 02	TIL THE END *Radiate RDT 6* 28	2
27 Mar 04	WOULDN'T CHANGE A THING *Radiate RDTCD 14* 57	1
16 Feb 02	BETWEEN THE SENSES *Radiate RDTCD 1* 26	3

Nic HAVERSON *UK, male vocalist (Singles: 3 Weeks)*   pos/wks

30 Jan 93	HEAD OVER HEELS *Telstar CDHOH 1* 48	3

Chesney HAWKES
UK, male vocalist (Singles: 26 Weeks, Albums: 8 Weeks)   pos/wks

23 Feb 91 ★	THE ONE AND ONLY *Chrysalis CHS 3627* 1	16
22 Jun 91	I'M A MAN NOT A BOY *Chrysalis CHS 3708* 27	5
28 Sep 91	SECRETS OF THE HEART *Chrysalis CHS 3681* 57	3
29 May 93	WHAT'S WRONG WITH THIS PICTURE *Chrysalis CDCHS 3969* ..63	1
12 Jan 02	STAY AWAY BABY JANE *Arc DSART 13* 74	1
13 Apr 91	BUDDY'S SONG (FILM SOUNDTRACK) *Chrysalis CHR 1812* 18	8

Screamin' Jay HAWKINS *US, male vocalist – Jalacy*
Hawkins, b. 18 Jul 1929, d. 12 Feb 2000 (Singles: 3 Weeks) pos/wks

3 Apr 93	HEART ATTACK AND VINE *Columbia 6591092*	.....42 3

Sophie B HAWKINS
US, female vocalist (Singles: 37 Weeks, Albums: 6 Weeks) pos/wks

4 Jul 92	DAMN I WISH I WAS YOUR LOVER *Columbia 6581077*	.....14 9
12 Sep 92	CALIFORNIA HERE I COME *Columbia 6583177*	.....53 3
6 Feb 93	I WANT YOU *Columbia 6587772*	.....49 2
13 Aug 94	RIGHT BESIDE YOU *Columbia 6606915*	.....13 12
26 Nov 94	DON'T DON'T TELL ME NO *Columbia 6610152*	.....36 5
11 Mar 95	AS I LAY ME DOWN *Columbia 6612125*	.....24 6
1 Aug 92	TONGUES AND TAILS *Columbia 4688232*	.....46 2
3 Sep 94	WHALER *Columbia 4765122*	.....46 4

Ted HAWKINS *US, male vocalist / instrumentalist –*
guitar, b. 28 Oct 1936, d. 1 Jan 1995 (Albums: 1 Week) pos/wks

18 Apr 87	HAPPY HOUR *Windows on the World WOLP 2*	.....82 1

Edwin HAWKINS SINGERS
US, male / female vocal group (Singles: 13 Weeks) pos/wks

21 May 69	● OH HAPPY DAY (re) *Buddah 201 048*	.....2 13

Kirsty HAWKSHAW (see also OPUS III)
UK, female vocalist (Singles: 9 Weeks) pos/wks

24 Jun 00	DREAMING *Headspace HEDSCD 002* [1]	.....38 2
29 Sep 01	URBAN TRAIN *Nebula VCRD 95* [2]	.....22 3
21 Sep 02	STEALTH *Distinctive Breaks DISNCD 90* [3]	.....67 1
23 Nov 02	FINE DAY *Mainline CDMAIN 002*	.....62 1
23 Oct 04	JUST BE *Nebula NEBCD 062* [4]	.....43 2

[1] BT featuring Kirsty Hawkshaw [2] DJ Tiësto featuring Kirsty Hawkshaw [3]
Way Out West featuring Kirsty Hawkshaw [4] Tiësto featuring Kirsty Hawkshaw

HAWKWIND *UK, male vocal / instrumental group and*
female dancer (Singles: 28 Weeks, Albums: 101 Weeks) pos/wks

1 Jul 72	● SILVER MACHINE (2re) *United Artists UP 35381*	.....3 22
11 Aug 73	URBAN GUERRILLA *United Artists UP 35566*	.....39 3
19 Jul 80	SHOT DOWN IN THE NIGHT *Bronze BRO 98*	.....59 3
6 Nov 71	IN SEARCH OF SPACE *United Artists UAS 29202*	.....18 19
23 Dec 72	DOREMI FASOL LATIDO *United Artists UAS 29364*	.....14 5
2 Jun 73	● SPACE RITUAL ALIVE *United Artists UAD 60037/8*	.....9 5
21 Sep 74	HALL OF THE MOUNTAIN GRILL *United Artists UAG 29672*	.....16 5
31 May 75	WARRIOR ON THE EDGE OF TIME *United Artists UAG 29766*	.....13 7
24 Apr 76	ROAD HAWKS *United Artists UAK 29919*	.....34 4
18 Sep 76	ASTONISHING SOUNDS AMAZING MUSIC *Charisma CDS 4004*	.....33 5
9 Jul 77	QUARK STRANGENESS AND CHARM *Charisma CDS 4008*	.....30 6
21 Oct 78	25 YEARS ON *Charisma CD 4014* [1]	.....48 3
30 Jun 79	PXR 5 *Charisma CDS 4016*	.....59 5
9 Aug 80	LIVE 1979 *Bronze BRON 527*	.....15 7
8 Nov 80	LEVITATION *Bronze BRON 530*	.....21 4
24 Oct 81	SONIC ATTACK *RCA RCALP 5004*	.....19 5
22 May 82	CHURCH OF HAWKWIND *RCA RCALP 9004*	.....26 6
23 Oct 82	CHOOSE YOUR MASQUES *RCA RCALP 6055*	.....29 5
5 Nov 83	ZONES *Flicknife SHARP 014*	.....57 2
25 Feb 84	HAWKWIND *Liberty SLS 1972921*	.....75 1
16 Nov 85	CHRONICLE OF THE BLACK SWORD *Flicknife SHARP 033*	.....65 2
14 May 88	THE XENON CODEX *GWR GWLP 26*	.....79 2
6 Oct 90	SPACE BANDITS *GWR GWLP 103*	.....70 1
23 May 92	ELECTRIC TEPEE *Essential ESSCD 181*	.....53 1
6 Nov 93	IT IS THE BUSINESS OF THE FUTURE TO BE DANGEROUS *Essential ESCDCD 196*	.....75 1

[1] Hawklords

'Silver Machine' re-entries were in 1978 and 1983

Bill HAYES with Archie BLEYER'S ORCHESTRA
US, male vocalist (Singles: 9 Weeks) pos/wks

6 Jan 56	● THE BALLAD OF DAVY CROCKETT *London HLA 8220* ▲	.....2 9

Darren HAYES (see also SAVAGE GARDEN)
Australia, male vocalist (Singles: 35 Weeks, Albums: 30 Weeks) pos/wks

30 Mar 02	● INSATIABLE *Columbia 6723995*	.....8 14

20 Jul 02	STRANGE RELATIONSHIP *Columbia 6728685*	.....15 8
16 Nov 02	I MISS YOU (re) *Columbia 6733312*	.....20 5
1 Feb 03	CRUSH (1980 ME) *Columbia 6734902*	.....19 3
11 Sep 04	POP!ULAR *Columbia 6751112*	.....12 5
13 Apr 02	● SPIN *Columbia 5053192*	.....2 28
25 Sep 04	THE TENSION AND THE SPARK *Columbia 5154312*	.....13 2

Gemma HAYES
Ireland, female vocalist (Singles: 2 Weeks, Albums: 1 Week) pos/wks

25 May 02	HANGING AROUND *Source SOURCD 046*	.....62 1
10 Aug 02	LET A GOOD THING GO *Source SOURCD 051*	.....54 1
8 Jun 02	NIGHT ON MY SIDE *Source CDSOUR 049*	.....52 1

Isaac HAYES *US, male vocalist /*
multi-instrumentalist (Singles: 35 Weeks, Albums: 14 Weeks) pos/wks

4 Dec 71	● THEME FROM 'SHAFT' *Stax 2025 069* ▲	.....4 12
3 Apr 76	DISCO CONNECTION *ABC 4100* [1]	.....10 9
26 Dec 98	★ CHOCOLATE SALTY BALLS (PS I LOVE YOU) *Columbia 6667985* [2]	.....1 13
30 Sep 00	THEME FROM SHAFT (re-recording) *LaFace / Arista 74321792582*	.....53 1
18 Dec 71	SHAFT (FILM SOUNDTRACK) *Polydor 2659 007* ▲	.....17 13
12 Feb 72	BLACK MOSES *Stax 2628 004*	.....38 1

[1] Isaac Hayes Movement [2] Chef

HAYSI FANTAYZEE (see also HWA featuring SONIC THE HEDGEHOG)
UK, male / female production / vocal duo – Jeremy Healy
and Kate Garner (Singles: 25 Weeks, Albums: 5 Weeks) pos/wks

24 Jul 82	JOHN WAYNE IS BIG LEGGY *Regard RG 100*	.....11 10
13 Nov 82	HOLY JOE *Regard RG 104*	.....51 3
22 Jan 83	SHINY SHINY *Regard RG 106*	.....16 10
25 Jun 83	SISTER FRICTION *Regard RG 108*	.....62 2
26 Feb 83	BATTLE HYMNS FOR CHILDREN SINGING *Regard RGLP 6000*	.....53 5

Justin HAYWARD (see also The MOODY BLUES) *UK, male*
vocalist – David Hayward (Singles: 20 Weeks, Albums: 35 Weeks) pos/wks

25 Oct 75	● BLUE GUITAR *Threshold TH 21* [1]	.....8 7
8 Jul 78	● FOREVER AUTUMN *CBS 6368* [2]	.....5 13
29 Mar 75	● BLUE JAYS *Threshold THS 12* [1]	.....4 18
5 Mar 77	SONGWRITER *Deram SDL 15*	.....28 5
19 Jul 80	NIGHT FLIGHT *Decca TXS 138*	.....41 4
19 Oct 85	MOVING MOUNTAINS *Towerbell TOWLP 15*	.....78 1
28 Oct 89	CLASSIC BLUE *Trax MODEM 1040* [2]	.....47 7

[1] Justin Hayward and John Lodge [2] From Jeff Wayne's 'War of the Worlds'
featuring Justin Hayward [1] Justin Hayward and John Lodge [2] Justin Hayward,
Mike Batt and the London Philharmonic Orchestra

Leon HAYWOOD *US, male vocalist (Singles: 11 Weeks)* pos/wks

15 Mar 80	DON'T PUSH IT DON'T FORCE IT *20th Century Fox TC 2443*	.....12 11

HAYWOODE
UK, female vocalist – Sharon Haywoode (Singles: 31 Weeks) pos/wks

17 Sep 83	A TIME LIKE THIS *CBS A 3651*	.....48 7
29 Sep 84	I CAN'T LET YOU GO *CBS A 4664*	.....63 4
13 Apr 85	ROSES *CBS A 6069*	.....65 3
5 Oct 85	GETTING CLOSER *CBS A 6582*	.....67 2
21 Jun 86	ROSES (re-issue) *CBS A 7224*	.....11 11
13 Sep 86	I CAN'T LET YOU GO (re-issue) *CBS 650076 7*	.....50 4

Ofra HAZA *Israel, female vocalist,*
b. 19 Nov 1959, d. 23 Feb 2000 (Singles: 12 Weeks) pos/wks

30 Apr 88	IM NIN'ALU *WEA YZ 190*	.....15 8
17 Jun 95	MY LOVE IS FOR REAL *Virgin America VUSCD 91* [1]	.....28 3
3 Apr 99	BABYLON *Warner.esp WESP 006CD1* [2]	.....65 1

[1] Paula Abdul featuring Ofra Haza [2] Black Dog featuring Ofra Haza

HAZE See KINGS OF TOMORROW; Sandy RIVERA

HAZIZA *Sweden, male production duo (Singles: 1 Week)* pos/wks

28 Apr 01	ONE MORE *Tidy Trax TIDY 152T*	.....75 1

Lee HAZLEWOOD See Nancy SINATRA

The HAZZARDS US, female vocal duo – Sydney
Maresca and Anne Harris (Singles: 1 Week)   pos/wks

| 22 Nov 03 | GAY BOYFRIEND Better the Devil BTD 3CD | 67 | 1 |

Murray HEAD UK, male vocalist (Singles: 15 Weeks)   pos/wks

| 29 Jan 72 | SUPERSTAR MCA MMKS 5077 [1] | 47 | 1 |
| 10 Nov 84 | ONE NIGHT IN BANGKOK (re) RCA CHESS 1 | 12 | 14 |

[1] Murray Head with The Trinidad Singers

'Superstar' was one of four tracks on a maxi single, two of which were credited during the disc's one week on the chart. The other track credited was 'I Don't Know How to Love Him' by Yvonne Elliman

Roy HEAD US, male vocalist (Singles: 5 Weeks)   pos/wks

| 4 Nov 65 | TREAT HER RIGHT Vocalion V-P 9248 | 30 | 5 |

The HEADBANGERS
UK, male vocal / instrumental group (Singles: 3 Weeks)   pos/wks

| 10 Oct 81 | STATUS ROCK Magnet MAG 206 | 60 | 3 |

The HEADBOYS
UK, male vocal / instrumental group (Singles: 8 Weeks)   pos/wks

| 22 Sep 79 | THE SHAPE OF THINGS TO COME RSO 40 | 45 | 8 |

HEADGIRL See GIRLSCHOOL; MOTORHEAD

Max HEADROOM See ART OF NOISE

HEADS UK, male instrumental group (Singles: 4 Weeks)   pos/wks

| 21 Jun 86 | AZTEC LIGHTNING (THEME FROM BBC WORLD CUP GRANDSTAND) BBC RESL 184 | 45 | 4 |

HEADS with Shaun RYDER
US / UK, male / female vocal / instrumental group (Singles: 1 Week)   pos/wks

| 9 Nov 96 | DON'T TAKE MY KINDNESS FOR WEAKNESS Radioactive MCSTD 48024 | 60 | 1 |

Heads are Talking Heads minus lead singer David Byrne

HEADSWIM UK, male vocal / instrumental
group (Singles: 5 Weeks, Albums: 2 Weeks)   pos/wks

25 Feb 95	CRAWL Epic 6612252	64	1
14 Feb 98	TOURNIQUET Epic 6650442	30	3
16 May 98	BETTER MADE Epic 6658402	42	1
30 May 98	DESPITE YOURSELF Epic 4877262	24	2

Jeff HEALEY BAND
US, male vocal / instrumental group (Albums: 16 Weeks)   pos/wks

14 Jan 89	SEE THE LIGHT Arista 209441	58	7
9 Jun 90	HELL TO PAY Arista 210815	18	6
28 Nov 92	FEEL THIS Arista 74321120872	72	1
18 Mar 95	COVER TO COVER Arista 74321238882	50	2

Jeremy HEALY and AMOS (see also HAYSI FANTAYZEE;
HWA featuring SONIC THE HEDGEHOG) UK, male production / vocal duo – Jeremy Healy and Amos Pizzey (Singles: 7 Weeks)   pos/wks

| 12 Oct 96 | STAMP! Positiva CDTIV 65 | 11 | 5 |
| 31 May 97 | ARGENTINA Positiva CDTIV 74 | 30 | 2 |

Imogen HEAP See URBAN SPECIES

HEAR 'N' AID International, male / female vocal /
instrumental charity assembly (Singles: 6 Weeks)   pos/wks

| 19 Apr 86 | STARS Vertigo HEAR 1 | 26 | 6 |

HEAR'SAY (see also Myleene KLASS; Kym MARSH)
UK, male / female vocal group (Singles: 60 Weeks, Albums: 32 Weeks)   pos/wks

24 Mar 01	★ PURE AND SIMPLE Polydor 5870069 ◆ ■	1	25
7 Jul 01	★ THE WAY TO YOUR LOVE (re) Polydor 5871482 ■	1	17
8 Dec 01	● EVERYBODY Polydor 5705122	4	11
24 Aug 02	● LOVIN' IS EASY (re) Polydor 5708542	6	7

| 7 Apr 01 | ★ POPSTARS Polydor 5498212 ■ | 1 | 27 |
| 15 Dec 01 | EVERYBODY Polydor 5895412 | 24 | 5 |

HEART (304) Top 500 Giants of Stateside AOR,
who first tasted success in Canada and are regarded as key players on the Seattle music scene. Fronted by Californian-born Wilson sisters Ann (v/g/f), b. 19 Jun 1951, and Nancy (g/v), b. 16 Mar 1954. UK chart career began a full decade after their US debut (Singles: 76 Weeks, Albums: 143 Weeks)   pos/wks

29 Mar 86	THESE DREAMS Capitol CL 394 ▲	62	4
13 Jun 87	● ALONE Capitol CL 448 ▲	3	16
19 Sep 87	WHO WILL YOU RUN TO Capitol CL 457	30	7
12 Dec 87	THERE'S THE GIRL Capitol CL 473	34	7
5 Mar 88	● NEVER / THESE DREAMS (re-issue) Capitol CL 482	8	9
14 May 88	WHAT ABOUT LOVE Capitol CL 487	14	6
22 Oct 88	NOTHIN' AT ALL Capitol CL 507	38	3
24 Mar 90	● ALL I WANNA DO IS MAKE LOVE TO YOU Capitol CL 569	8	13
28 Jul 90	I DIDN'T WANT TO NEED YOU Capitol CL 580	47	3
17 Nov 90	STRANDED Capitol CL 595	60	2
14 Sep 91	YOU'RE THE VOICE Capitol CLS 624	56	2
20 Nov 93	WILL YOU BE THERE (IN THE MORNING) Capitol CDCLS 700	19	4
22 Jan 77	DREAMBOAT ANNIE Arista ARTY 139	36	8
23 Jul 77	LITTLE QUEEN Portrait PRT 82075	34	4
19 Jun 82	PRIVATE AUDITION Epic EPC 85792	77	2
26 Oct 85	HEART Capitol EJ 2403721 ▲	19	43
6 Jun 87	● BAD ANIMALS Capitol ESTU 2032	7	56
14 Apr 90	● BRIGADE Capitol ESTU 2121	3	20
28 Sep 91	ROCK THE HOUSE 'LIVE' Capitol ESTU 2154	45	2
11 Dec 93	DESIRE WALKS ON Capitol CDEST 2216	32	2
19 Apr 97	THESE DREAMS – GREATEST HITS Capitol CDEMC 3765	33	6

'Heart' changed label number during its chart run to Capitol LOVE 1

HEARTBEAT
UK, male / female vocal / instrumental group (Singles: 5 Weeks)   pos/wks

| 24 Oct 87 | TEARS FROM HEAVEN Priority P 17 | 32 | 4 |
| 23 Apr 88 | THE WINNER Priority P 19 | 70 | 1 |

HEARTBEAT COUNTRY
UK, male vocalist / actor – Bill Maynard (Singles: 1 Week)   pos/wks

| 31 Dec 94 | HEARTBEAT MMM MMM 01CD | 75 | 1 |

HEARTBREAKER See DEMON vs HEARTBREAKER

The HEARTBREAKERS (see also TELEVISION)
US, male vocal / instrumental group (Albums: 1 Week)   pos/wks

| 5 Nov 77 | L.A.M.F. Track 2409 218 | 55 | 1 |

HEARTBREAKERS See Tom PETTY and the HEARTBREAKERS

The HEARTISTS
Italy, male DJ / production trio (Singles: 5 Weeks)   pos/wks

| 9 Aug 97 | BELO HORIZONTI VC VCRD 23 | 42 | 3 |
| 31 Jan 98 | BELO HORIZONTI (re-mix) VC VCRD 28 | 40 | 2 |

HEARTLESS CREW
UK, male DJ / production trio (Singles: 3 Weeks, Albums: 2 Weeks) pos/wks

| 25 May 02 | THE HEARTLESS THEME AKA 'THE SUPERGLUE RIDDIM' East West HEART 02CD | 21 | 3 |
| 18 May 02 | ● HEARTLESS CREW PRESENTS CRISP BISCUIT VOL.1 East West 927460172 | 10 | 2 |

Ted HEATH and his MUSIC
UK, orchestra, leader b. 30 Mar 1900, d. 18 Nov 1969 (Singles: 56 Weeks, Albums: 5 Weeks)   pos/wks

16 Jan 53	VANESSA Decca F 9983	11	1
3 Jul 53	● HOT TODDY Decca F 10093	6	11
23 Oct 53	● DRAGNET (4re) Decca F 10176	9	5
12 Feb 54	● SKIN DEEP Decca F 10246	9	3
6 Jul 56	THE FAITHFUL HUSSAR Decca F 10746	18	9
14 Mar 58	● SWINGIN' SHEPHERD BLUES Decca F 11000	3	14
11 Apr 58	TEQUILA Decca F 11003	21	6
4 Jul 58	TOM HARK Decca F 11025	24	2
5 Oct 61	SUCU SUCU (re) Decca F 11392	36	5
21 Apr 62	BIG BAND PERCUSSION Decca PFM 24004	17	5

Singles re-entries are listed as (re), (2re), (3re).... which signifies that the hit re-entered the chart once, twice or three times...

HEATWAVE *UK / US, male vocal / instrumental group (Singles: 80 Weeks, Albums: 27 Weeks)* pos/wks

22 Jan 77 ●	BOOGIE NIGHTS *GTO GT 77*	2	14
7 May 77	TOO HOT TO HANDLE / SLIP YOUR DISC TO THIS *GTO GT 91*	15	11
14 Jan 78	THE GROOVE LINE *GTO GT 115*	12	8
3 Jun 78	MIND BLOWING DECISIONS *GTO GT 226*	12	11
4 Nov 78 ●	ALWAYS AND FOREVER / MIND BLOWING DECISIONS (re-mix) *GTO GT 236*	9	14
26 May 79	RAZZLE DAZZLE *GTO GT 248*	43	5
17 Jan 81	GANGSTERS OF THE GROOVE *GTO GT 285*	19	8
21 Mar 81	JITTERBUGGIN' *GTO GT 290*	34	7
1 Sep 90	MIND BLOWING DECISIONS (re-recording) *Brothers Organisation HW 1*	65	2
11 Jun 77	TOO HOT TO HANDLE *GTO GTLP 013*	46	2
6 May 78	CENTRAL HEATING *GTO GTLP 027*	26	15
14 Feb 81	CANDLES *GTO GTLP 047*	29	9
23 Feb 91	GANGSTERS OF THE GROOVE – 90'S MIX *Telstar STAR 2434*	56	1

HEAVEN 17 (309 Top 500)
Politically astute electronic pop trio from Sheffield, UK; Martyn Ware (k), Ian Craig Marsh (k) (both previously in Human League) and Glenn Gregory (v). Act, named after a fictional band in cult film A Clockwork Orange, reunited and played first ever gigs in 1997 (Singles: 87 Weeks, Albums: 128 Weeks) pos/wks

21 Mar 81	(WE DON'T NEED THIS) FASCIST GROOVE THANG *Virgin VS 400*	45	5
5 Sep 81	PLAY TO WIN *Virgin VS 433*	46	7
14 Nov 81	PENTHOUSE AND PAVEMENT *Virgin VS 455*	57	3
30 Oct 82	LET ME GO *Virgin VS 532*	41	6
16 Apr 83 ●	TEMPTATION *Virgin VS 570*	2	13
25 Jun 83	COME LIVE WITH ME *Virgin VS 607*	5	11
10 Sep 83	CRUSHED BY THE WHEELS OF INDUSTRY *Virgin VS 628*	17	7
1 Sep 84	SUNSET NOW *Virgin VS 708*	24	6
27 Oct 84	THIS IS MINE *Virgin VS 722*	23	7
19 Jan 85	... (AND THAT'S NO LIE) *Virgin VS 740*	52	5
17 Jan 87	TROUBLE *Virgin VS 920*	51	3
21 Nov 92 ●	TEMPTATION (re-mix) *Virgin VS 1446*	4	11
27 Feb 93	(WE DON'T NEED THIS) FASCIST GROOVE THANG (re-recording) *Virgin VSCDT 1451*	40	2
10 Apr 93	PENTHOUSE AND PAVEMENT (re-mix) *Virgin VSCDT 1457*	54	1
26 Sep 81	PENTHOUSE AND PAVEMENT *Virgin V 2208*	14	76
7 May 83 ●	THE LUXURY GAP *Virgin V 2253*	4	36
6 Oct 84	HOW MEN ARE *B.E.F. Virgin V 2326*	12	11
12 Jul 86	ENDLESS *Virgin TCVB / CDV 2383*	70	2
29 Nov 86	PLEASURE ONE *Virgin V 2400*	78	1
20 Mar 93	HIGHER AND HIGHER – THE BEST OF HEAVEN 17 *Virgin CDV 2717*	31	2

Carol Kenyon is the uncredited vocalist on 'Temptation'

HEAVENS CRY *Holland, male production duo (Singles: 2 Weeks)* pos/wks

6 Oct 01	TILL TEARS DO US PART (re) *Tidy Trax 158CD*	68	2

HEAVY D and the BOYZ *Jamaica / US, male rap / vocal duo (Singles: 28 Weeks, Albums: 3 Weeks)* pos/wks

6 Dec 86	MR BIG STUFF *MCA MCA 1106*	61	8
15 Jul 89	WE GOT OUR OWN THANG *MCA MCA 23942*	69	2
6 Jul 91 ●	NOW THAT WE FOUND LOVE *MCA MCS 1550*	2	12
28 Sep 91	IS IT GOOD TO YOU *MCA MCS 1564*	46	3
8 Oct 94	THIS IS YOUR NIGHT *MCA MCSTD 2010*	30	3
10 Aug 91	PEACEFUL JOURNEY *MCA MCA 10289*	40	3

HEAVY PETTIN' *UK, male vocal / instrumental group (Singles: 2 Weeks, Albums: 4 Weeks)* pos/wks

17 Mar 84	LOVE TIMES LOVE *Polydor HEP 3*	69	2
29 Oct 83	LETTIN' LOOSE *Polydor HEPLP 1*	55	2
13 Jul 85	ROCK AIN'T DEAD *Polydor HEPLP 2*	81	2

HEAVY STEREO *UK, male vocal / instrumental group (Singles: 4 Weeks)* pos/wks

22 Jul 95	SLEEP FREAK *Creation CRESCD 203*	46	1
28 Oct 95	SMILER *Creation CRESCD 213*	46	1
10 Feb 96	CHINESE BURN *Creation CRESCD 218*	45	1
24 Aug 96	MOUSE IN A HOLE *Creation CRESCD 230*	53	2

HEAVY WEATHER *US, male vocalist – Peter Lee (Singles: 1 Week)* pos/wks

29 Jun 96	LOVE CAN'T TURN AROUND *Pukka CDPUKKA 6*	56	1

Bobby HEBB *US, male vocalist (Singles: 15 Weeks)* pos/wks

8 Sep 66	SUNNY *Philips BF 1503*	12	9
19 Aug 72	LOVE LOVE LOVE *Philips 6051 023*	32	6

Sharlene HECTOR with the NEW INSPIRATIONAL CHOIR *UK, female vocalist and choir (Singles: 4 Weeks)* pos/wks

17 Apr 04	I WISH I KNEW HOW IT WOULD FEEL TO BE FREE *Radar RAD 006CD*	28	4

HED BOYS (see also AKABU featuring Linda Clifford; IL PADRINOS featuring Jocelyn BROWN; Li KWAN; JAKATTA; Joey NEGRO; PHASE II; RAVEN MAIZE; Z FACTOR) *UK, male instrumental / production duo – Dave Lee and Andrew Livingstone (Singles: 6 Weeks)* pos/wks

6 Aug 94	GIRLS + BOYS *Deconstruction 74321322322*	21	4
4 Nov 95	GIRLS + BOYS (re-mix) *Deconstruction 74321322032*	36	2

(HED) PLANET EARTH *US, male rap / vocal / instrumental group (Albums: 1 Week)* pos/wks

2 Sep 00	BROKE *Music for Nations CDMFN 262*	73	1

HEDGEHOPPERS ANONYMOUS *UK, male vocal / instrumental group (Singles: 12 Weeks)* pos/wks

30 Sep 65 ●	IT'S GOOD NEWS WEEK *Decca F 12241*	5	12

HEFNER *UK, male vocal / instrumental group (Singles: 3 Weeks)* pos/wks

26 Aug 00	GOOD FRUIT *Too Pure PURE 108CDS*	50	1
14 Oct 00	THE GREEDY UGLY PEOPLE *Too Pure PURE 111CDS*	64	1
8 Sep 01	ALAN BEAN *Too Pure PURE 118CDS*	58	1

Neal HEFTI *US, male orchestra (Singles: 4 Weeks)* pos/wks

9 Apr 88	BATMAN THEME *RCA PB 49571*	55	4

Den HEGARTY (see also The DARTS) *UK, male vocalist (Singles: 2 Weeks)* pos/wks

31 Mar 79	VOODOO VOODOO *Magnet MAG 143*	73	2

Anita HEGERLAND *See Mike OLDFIELD*

HEINZ (see also The TORNADOS) *UK (b. Germany), male vocalist – Heinz Burt, b. 24 Jul 1942, d. 7 Apr 2000 (Singles: 35 Weeks)* pos/wks

8 Aug 63 ●	JUST LIKE EDDIE *Decca F 11693*	5	15
28 Nov 63	COUNTRY BOY *Decca F 11768*	26	9
27 Feb 64	YOU WERE THERE *Decca F 11831*	26	8
15 Oct 64	QUESTIONS I CAN'T ANSWER *Columbia DB 7374*	39	7
18 Mar 65	DIGGIN' MY POTATOES *Columbia DB 7482* [1]	49	1

[1] Heinz and The Wild Boys

HELICOPTER (see also MUTINY UK) *UK, male instrumental / production duo – Dylan Barnes and Rob Davy (Singles: 4 Weeks)* pos/wks

27 Aug 94	ON YA WAY *Helicopter TIG 007CD*	32	2
22 Jun 96	ON YA WAY (re-mix) *Systematic SYSCD 27*	37	2

HELIOCENTRIC WORLD *UK, male / female vocal / instrumental group (Singles: 2 Weeks)* pos/wks

14 Jan 95	WHERE'S YOUR LOVE BEEN *Talkin Loud TLKCD 51*	71	2

HELIOTROPIC featuring Verna V *UK, male production duo – Nick Hale and Gez Dewar and female vocalist (Singles: 2 Weeks)* pos/wks

16 Oct 99	ALIVE *Multiply CDMULTY 52*	33	2

HELL IS FOR HEROES (see also SYMPOSIUM) *UK, male vocal / instrumental group (Singles: 9 Weeks, Albums: 2 Weeks)* pos/wks

9 Feb 02	YOU DROVE ME TO IT *Wishakismo CDWISH 003*	63	1
17 Aug 02	I CAN CLIMB MOUNTAINS *Chrysalis CDCHS 5143*	41	2
2 Nov 02	NIGHT VISION *Chrysalis CDCHSS 5147*	38	1
1 Feb 03	YOU DROVE ME TO IT (re-issue) *EMI CDCHSS 5149*	28	2

17 May 03	**RETREAT** *EMI CDEMS 619*	......	**39**	1
28 Aug 04	**ONE OF US** *Captains of Industry CAPT 008*	......	**71**	1
27 Nov 04	**KAMICHI** *Factotum TUM 001CD*	......	**72**	1
15 Feb 03	**THE NEON HANDSHAKE** *EMI 5409232*	......	**16**	2

Pete HELLER (see also HELLER & FARLEY PROJECT)
UK, male DJ / producer (Singles: 7 Weeks) pos/wks

15 May 99	**BIG LOVE** *Essential Recordings ESCD 4*	......	**12**	7

HELLER & FARLEY PROJECT
(see also FIRE ISLAND; STYLUS TROUBLE) *UK, male instrumental / production duo – Pete Heller and Terry Farley (Singles: 7 Weeks)* pos/wks

24 Feb 96	**ULTRA FLAVA** *AM:PM 5814372*	......	**22**	3
28 Dec 96	**ULTRA FLAVA (re-mix)** *AM:PM 5820552*	......	**32**	4

HELLO *UK, male vocal / instrumental group (Singles: 21 Weeks)* pos/wks

9 Nov 74 ●	**TELL HIM** *Bell 1377*	......	**6**	12
18 Oct 75 ●	**NEW YORK GROOVE** *Bell 1438*	......	**9**	9

HELLOWEEN *US, male vocal / instrumental group (Singles: 7 Weeks, Albums: 9 Weeks)* pos/wks

27 Aug 88	**DR STEIN** *Noise International 7HELLO 1*	......	**57**	3
12 Nov 88	**I WANT OUT** *Noise International 7HELLO 2*	......	**69**	2
2 Mar 91	**KIDS OF THE CENTURY** *EMI EM 178*	......	**56**	2
17 Sep 88	**KEEPER OF THE SEVEN KEYS PART 2** *Noise International NUK 117*	......	**24**	5
15 Apr 89	**LIVE IN THE UK** *EMI EMC 3558*	......	**26**	2
23 Mar 91	**PINK BUBBLES GO APE** *EMI EMC 3588*	......	**41**	2

HELMET *US, male vocal / instrumental group (Albums: 1 Week)* pos/wks

2 Jul 94	**BETTY** *Interscope 6544924042*	......	**38**	1

Bobby HELMS
US, male vocalist, b. 15 Aug 1935, d. 19 Jul 1997 (Singles: 7 Weeks) pos/wks

29 Nov 57	**MY SPECIAL ANGEL** *Brunswick 05721* [1]	......	**22**	3
21 Feb 58	**NO OTHER BABY** *Brunswick 05730*	......	**30**	1
1 Aug 58	**JACQUELINE** *Brunswick 05748* [1]	......	**20**	3

[1] Bobby Helms with The Anita Kerr Singers

Jimmy HELMS (see also LONDONBEAT)
US, male vocalist (Singles: 10 Weeks) pos/wks

24 Feb 73 ●	**GONNA MAKE YOU AN OFFER YOU CAN'T REFUSE** *Cube BUG 27*	......	**8**	10

HELTAH SKELTAH and ORIGINOO GUNN CLAPPAZ as the FABULOUS FIVE
US, male rap / vocal / production group (Singles: 1 Week) pos/wks

1 Jun 96	**BLAH** *Priority PTYCD 117*	......	**60**	1

HEMSTOCK See Paul VAN DYK

Ainslie HENDERSON *UK, male vocalist (Singles: 7 Weeks)* pos/wks

8 Mar 03 ●	**KEEP ME A SECRET (re)** *Mercury 0779812*	......	**5**	7

Eddie HENDERSON
US, male instrumentalist – trumpet (Singles: 6 Weeks) pos/wks

28 Oct 78	**PRANCE ON** *Capitol CL 16015*	......	**44**	6

Joe 'Mr Piano' HENDERSON *UK, male instrumentalist – piano, b. 2 May 1920, d. 4 May 1980 (Singles: 23 Weeks)* pos/wks

3 Jun 55	**SING IT WITH JOE** *Polygon P 1167*	......	**14**	4
2 Sep 55	**SING IT AGAIN WITH JOE** *Polygon P 1184*	......	**18**	3
25 Jul 58	**TRUDIE (re)** *Pye Nixa N 15147*	......	**14**	14
23 Oct 59	**TREBLE CHANCE** *Pye 7N 15224*	......	**28**	1
24 Mar 60	**OOH! LA! LA!** *Pye 7N 15257*	......	**44**	1

First two hits are medleys as follows: Sing It with Joe: Margie / I'm Nobody's Sweetheart / Somebody Stole My Gal / Moonlight Bay / By the Light of the Silvery Moon / Cuddle Up a Little Closer. Sing It Again with Joe: Put Your Arms Around Me Honey / Ain't She Sweet / When You're Smiling / Shine on Harvest Moon / My Blue Heaven / Show Me the Way to Go Home

---

Wayne HENDERSON See Roy AYERS

Billy HENDRIX (see also THREE 'N ONE)
Germany, male producer – Sharam Khososi (Singles: 2 Weeks) pos/wks

12 Sep 98	**THE BODY SHINE (EP)** *Hooj Choons HOOJ 65CD*	......	**55**	2

Tracks on The Body Shine (EP): The Body Shine / Funky Shine / Colour Systems Inc's Amber Dub / Timewriter (re-mix)

Jimi HENDRIX EXPERIENCE 〔141〕 Top 500
Guitar ace and hugely influential 20th-century icon, b. Johnny Allen Hendrix (renamed James Marshall Hendrix), 27 Nov 1942, Seattle, US, d. 18 Sep 1970, London. After being 'discovered' and then managed by Animals' bassist Chas Chandler, the left-handed guitarist and vocalist formed The Jimi Hendrix Experience, featuring Mitch Mitchell (d) and Noel Redding (b). His timeless appeal consistently generates annual global sales of about three million albums (Singles: 88 Weeks, Albums: 275 Weeks) pos/wks

29 Dec 66 ●	**HEY JOE** *Polydor 56 139*	......	**6**	11
23 Mar 67 ●	**PURPLE HAZE** *Track 604 001*	......	**3**	14
11 May 67 ●	**THE WIND CRIES MARY** *Track 604 004*	......	**6**	11
30 Aug 67	**BURNING OF THE MIDNIGHT LAMP** *Track 604 007*	......	**18**	9
23 Oct 68 ●	**ALL ALONG THE WATCHTOWER** *Track 604 025*	......	**5**	11
16 Apr 69	**CROSSTOWN TRAFFIC** *Track 604 029*	......	**37**	3
7 Nov 70 ★	**VOODOO CHILE** *Track 2095 001*	......	**1**	13
30 Oct 71	**GYPSY EYES / REMEMBER** *Track 2094 010*	......	**35**	5
12 Feb 72	**JOHNNY B GOODE** *Polydor 2001 277* [1]	......	**35**	5
21 Apr 90	**CROSSTOWN TRAFFIC (re-issue)** *Polydor PO 71* [1]	......	**61**	3
20 Oct 90	**ALL ALONG THE WATCHTOWER (EP)** *Polydor PO 100* [1]	......	**52**	3
27 May 67 ●	**ARE YOU EXPERIENCED** *Track 612001* [1]	......	**2**	33
16 Dec 67 ●	**AXIS: BOLD AS LOVE** *Track 613003* [1]	......	**5**	16
27 Apr 68 ●	**SMASH HITS** *Track 613004* [1]	......	**4**	25
18 May 68	**GET THAT FEELING** *London HA 8349* [2]	......	**39**	2
16 Nov 68 ●	**ELECTRIC LADYLAND** *Track 613008/9* [1] ▲	......	**6**	12
4 Jul 70 ●	**BAND OF GYPSIES** *Track 2406001*	......	**6**	22
3 Apr 71 ●	**CRY OF LOVE** *Track 2408101*	......	**2**	14
28 Aug 71 ●	**EXPERIENCE** *Ember NR 5057*	......	**9**	6
20 Nov 71	**JIMI HENDRIX AT THE ISLE OF WIGHT** *Track 2302 016*	......	**17**	2
4 Dec 71	**RAINBOW BRIDGE** *Reprise K 44159*	......	**16**	8
5 Feb 72 ●	**HENDRIX IN THE WEST** *Polydor 2302 018*	......	**7**	14
11 Nov 72	**WAR HEROES** *Polydor 2302 020*	......	**23**	3
21 Jul 73	**SOUNDTRACK RECORDINGS FROM THE FILM 'JIMI HENDRIX'** *Warner Bros. K 64017*	......	**37**	1
29 Mar 75	**JIMI HENDRIX** *Polydor 2343 080*	......	**35**	4
30 Aug 75	**CRASH LANDING** *Polydor 2310 398*	......	**35**	3
29 Nov 75	**MIDNIGHT LIGHTNING** *Polydor 2310 415*	......	**46**	1
14 Aug 82	**THE JIMI HENDRIX CONCERTS** *CBS 88592*	......	**16**	11
19 Feb 83	**THE SINGLES ALBUM** *Polydor PODV 6*	......	**77**	4
11 Mar 89	**RADIO ONE** *Castle Collectors CCSLP 212*	......	**30**	6
3 Nov 90 ●	**CORNERSTONES 1967-1970** *Polydor 8472311*	......	**5**	16
14 Nov 92	**THE ULTIMATE EXPERIENCE** *PolyGram TV 5172352*	......	**25**	26
30 Apr 94	**BLUES** *Polydor 5210372*	......	**10**	3
13 Aug 94	**WOODSTOCK** *Polydor 5233842*	......	**32**	3
10 May 97	**FIRST RAYS OF THE NEW RISING SUN** *MCA MCD 11599*	......	**37**	2
2 Aug 97	**ELECTRIC LADYLAND (re-issue)** *MCA MCD 11600*	......	**47**	1
13 Sep 97	**EXPERIENCE HENDRIX – THE BEST OF JIMI HENDRIX** *Telstar TV TTVCD 2930*	......	**18**	15
13 Jun 98	**BBC SESSIONS** *MCA MCD 11742* [1]	......	**42**	2
23 Sep 00 ●	**EXPERIENCE HENDRIX – THE BEST OF JIMI HENDRIX** *Universal TV 1123832*	......	**10**	7
20 Jul 02 ●	**VOODOO CHILD – THE JIMI HENDRIX COLLECTION** *UMTV 1703222*	......	**10**	13

[1] Jimi Hendrix [1] The Jimi Hendrix Experience [2] Jimi Hendrix and Curtis Knight

Tracks on All Along the Watchtower (EP): All Along the Watchtower / Voodoo Chile / Hey Joe (re-issues) 'Experience Hendrix – The Best of Jimi Hendrix' (2000) had a different track listing to the 1997 album of the same name and was repackaged with a bonus disc

Nona HENDRYX (see also LaBELLE)
US, female vocalist (Singles: 2 Weeks) pos/wks

16 May 87	**WHY SHOULD I CRY** *EMI America EA 234*	......	**60**	2

Don HENLEY (see also The EAGLES) *US, male vocalist / instrumentalist – drums (Singles: 30 Weeks, Albums: 30 Weeks)* pos/wks

12 Feb 83	**DIRTY LAUNDRY** *Asylum E 9894*	......	**59**	3
9 Feb 85	**THE BOYS OF SUMMER** *Geffen A 4945*	......	**12**	10
29 Jul 89	**THE END OF THE INNOCENCE** *Geffen GEF 57*	......	**48**	5

JAMELIA TOP 10

The gospel according to Jamelia, who chooses her favourite albums

Jamelia recently became the UK's most successful female R&B artist of this century. Here's her response to our request to name the 10 albums that have made the biggest impact on her personally.

album – act – (peak position)

DIARY OF A MAD BAND * Jodeci	STRIPPED Christina Aguilera (2)
THE NOTORIOUS K.I.M. Lil' Kim (67)	SUPA DUPA FLY * Missy 'Misdemeanor' Elliott
SCISSOR SISTERS Scissor Sisters (1)	TIL SHILOH * Buju Banton
SHOWTIME Dizzee Rascal (8)	THE ULTIMATE COLLECTION Nat 'King' Cole (26)
STREET'S DISCIPLE Nas (45)	WHAT'S THE 411? Mary J Blige (53)

* Did not chart

3 Oct 92	SOMETIMES LOVE JUST AIN'T ENOUGH *MCA MCS 1692* [1]	22	6
18 Jul 98	BOYS OF SUMMER (re-issue) *Geffen GFSTD 22350*	12	6
9 Mar 85	BUILDING THE PERFECT BEAST *Geffen GEF 25939*	14	11
8 Jul 89	THE END OF THE INNOCENCE *Geffen WX 253*	17	16
3 Jun 00	INSIDE JOB *Warner Bros. 9362470832*	25	3

[1] Patty Smyth with Don Henley

Cassius HENRY UK, male vocalist (Singles: 3 Weeks) pos/wks

30 Mar 02	BROKE *Blacklist 0130265 ERE*	31	2
3 Jul 04	THE ONE *Universal MCSTD 40334* [1]	56	1

[1] Cassius Henry featuring Freeway

Clarence 'Frogman' HENRY
US, male vocalist / instrumentalist – keyboards (Singles: 35 Weeks) pos/wks

4 May 61	● BUT I DO *Pye International 7N 25078*	3	19
13 Jul 61	● YOU ALWAYS HURT THE ONE YOU LOVE *Pye International 7N 25089*	6	12
21 Sep 61	LONELY STREET / WHY CAN'T YOU *Pye International 7N 25108*	42	2
17 Jul 93	(I DON'T KNOW WHY) BUT I DO (re-issue) *MCA MCSTD 1797*	65	2

Kevin HENRY See L.A. MIX

Pauline HENRY (see also The CHIMES)
UK, female vocalist (Singles: 21 Weeks, Albums: 1 Week) pos/wks

18 Sep 93	TOO MANY PEOPLE *Sony S2 6595942*	38	2
6 Nov 93	FEEL LIKE MAKING LOVE *Sony S2 6597972*	12	7
29 Jan 94	CAN'T TAKE YOUR LOVE *Sony S2 6599902*	30	3
21 May 94	WATCH THE MIRACLE START *Sony S2 6602772*	54	1
30 Sep 95	SUGAR FREE *Sony S2 6624362*	57	2
23 Dec 95	LOVE HANGOVER *Sony S2 6626132*	37	3
24 Feb 96	NEVER KNEW LOVE LIKE THIS *Sony S2 6629382* [1]	40	2
1 Jun 96	HAPPY *Sony S2 6630692*	46	1
19 Feb 94	PAULINE *Sony S2 4747442*	45	1

[1] Pauline Henry featuring Wayne Marshall

Pierre HENRY *France, male instrumentalist (Singles: 1 Week)* pos/wks

4 Oct 97	PSYCHE ROCK *Hi-Life 4620312*	58	1

Paul HENRY and the Mayson GLEN ORCHESTRA
UK, male actor / vocalist and orchestra (Singles: 2 Weeks) pos/wks

14 Jan 78	BENNY'S THEME *Pye 7N 46027*	39	2

HEPBURN UK, female vocal / instrumental
group (Singles: 15 Weeks, Albums: 2 Weeks) pos/wks

29 May 99	● I QUIT *Columbia 6674012*	8	7
28 Aug 99	BUGS *Columbia 6677382*	14	5
19 Feb 00	DEEP DEEP DOWN *Columbia 6683382*	16	3
11 Sep 99	HEPBURN *Columbia 4948352*	28	2

Band and Chorus of HER MAJESTY'S GUARDS DIVISION
UK, military band (Albums: 4 Weeks) pos/wks

22 Nov 75	30 SMASH HITS OF THE WAR YEARS *Warwick WW 5006*	38	4

HERBALISER UK, male DJ / production duo –
Jake Wherry and Ollie 'Teeba' Trattles (Albums: 1 Week) pos/wks

30 Mar 02	SOMETHING WICKED THIS WAY COMES *Ninja Tune ZENCD 64*	71	1

The HERD UK, male vocal / instrumental group –
includes Peter Frampton (Singles: 35 Weeks, Albums: 1 Week) pos/wks

13 Sep 67	● FROM THE UNDERWORLD *Fontana TF 856*	6	13
20 Dec 67	PARADISE LOST *Fontana TF 887*	15	9
10 Apr 68	● I DON'T WANT OUR LOVING TO DIE *Fontana TF 925*	5	13
24 Feb 68	PARADISE LOST *Fontana STL 5458*	38	1

HERMAN'S HERMITS (296 Top 500)

Manchester quintet fronted by teenage vocalist Peter Noone, b. 5 Nov 1947, whose US popularity in the mid-1960s rivalled The Beatles. This band sold more than 40 million records and at times had three singles simultaneously in the US Top 20 (Singles: 211 Weeks, Albums: 11 Weeks) pos/wks

20 Aug 64	★ I'M INTO SOMETHING GOOD *Columbia DB 7338*	1	15
19 Nov 64	SHOW ME GIRL *Columbia DB 7408*	19	9
18 Feb 65	● SILHOUETTES *Columbia DB 7475*	3	12
29 Apr 65	● WONDERFUL WORLD *Columbia DB 7546*	7	9
2 Sep 65	JUST A LITTLE BIT BETTER *Columbia DB 7670*	15	9
23 Dec 65	● A MUST TO AVOID *Columbia DB 7791*	6	11
24 Mar 66	YOU WON'T BE LEAVING *Columbia DB 7861*	20	7
23 Jun 66	THIS DOOR SWINGS BOTH WAYS *Columbia DB 7947*	18	7

6 Oct 66 ●	NO MILK TODAY *Columbia DB 8012*	7	11
1 Dec 66	EAST WEST *Columbia DB 8076*	37	7
9 Feb 67 ●	THERE'S A KIND OF HUSH *Columbia DB 8123*	7	11
17 Jan 68	I CAN TAKE OR LEAVE YOUR LOVING *Columbia DB 8327*	11	9
1 May 68	SLEEPY JOE *Columbia DB 8404*	12	10
17 Jul 68 ●	SUNSHINE GIRL *Columbia DB 8446*	8	14
18 Dec 68 ●	SOMETHING'S HAPPENING *Columbia DB 8504*	6	15
23 Apr 69 ●	MY SENTIMENTAL FRIEND *Columbia DB 8563*	2	12
8 Nov 69	HERE COMES THE STAR *Columbia DB 8626*	33	9
7 Feb 70 ●	YEARS MAY COME, YEARS MAY GO (re) *Columbia DB 8656*	7	12
23 May 70	BET YER LIFE I DO *RAK 102*	22	10
14 Nov 70	LADY BARBARA *RAK 106* [1]	13	12
18 Sep 65	HERMAN'S HERMITS *Columbia 33SX 1727*	16	2
25 Sep 71	THE MOST OF HERMAN'S HERMITS *MFP 5216*	14	5
8 Oct 77	GREATEST HITS *K-Tel NE 1001*	37	4

[1] Peter Noone and Herman's Hermits

HERMES HOUSE BAND *Holland, male / female vocal / instrumental group (Singles: 14 Weeks)* pos/wks

15 Dec 01 ●	COUNTRY ROADS *EMI / Liberty CDHHB 001*	7	12
13 Apr 02	QUE SERA SERA *EMI / Liberty CDHHB 002*	53	1
28 Dec 02	LIVE IS LIFE *EMI / Liberty CDLIVE 001* [1]	50	1

[1] Hermes House Band and DJ Otzi

HERNANDEZ *UK, male vocalist (Singles: 3 Weeks)* pos/wks

15 Apr 89	ALL MY LOVE *Epic HER 1*	58	3

Patrick HERNANDEZ *Guadeloupe, male vocalist (Singles: 14 Weeks)* pos/wks

16 Jun 79 ●	BORN TO BE ALIVE *Gem GEM 4*	10	14

The HERREYS *Sweden, male vocal group (Singles: 3 Weeks)* pos/wks

26 May 84	DIGGI LOO-DIGGI LEY *Panther PAN 5*	46	3

Kristin HERSH (see also THROWING MUSES) *US, female vocalist (Singles: 3 Weeks, Albums: 5 Weeks)* pos/wks

22 Jan 94	YOUR GHOST *4AD BAD 4001CD*	45	2
16 Apr 94	STRINGS *4AD BAD 4006CD*	60	1
5 Feb 94 ●	HIPS AND MAKERS *4AD CAD 4002CD*	7	4
14 Feb 98	STRANGE ANGELS *4AD CAD 8003CD*	64	1

Nick HEYWARD (see also HAIRCUT 100) *UK, male vocalist (Singles: 65 Weeks, Albums: 13 Weeks)* pos/wks

19 Mar 83	WHISTLE DOWN THE WIND *Arista HEY 1*	13	8
4 Jun 83	TAKE THAT SITUATION *Arista HEY 2*	11	10
24 Sep 83	BLUE HAT FOR A BLUE DAY *Arista HEY 3*	14	8
3 Dec 83	ON A SUNDAY *Arista HEY 4*	52	5
2 Jun 84	LOVE ALL DAY *Arista HEY 5*	31	6
3 Nov 84	WARNING SIGN (re) *Arista HEY 6*	25	9
8 Jun 85	LAURA *Arista HEY 8*	45	4
10 May 86	OVER THE WEEKEND *Arista HEY 9*	43	5
10 Sep 88	YOU'RE MY WORLD *Warner Bros. W 7758*	67	2
21 Aug 93	KITE *Epic 6594882*	44	2
16 Oct 93	HE DOESN'T LOVE YOU LIKE I DO *Epic 6597282*	58	2
30 Sep 95	THE WORLD *Epic 6623845*	47	2
13 Jan 96	ROLLERBLADE *Epic 6627912*	37	2
29 Oct 83 ●	NORTH OF A MIRACLE *Arista NORTH 1*	10	13

HI-FIVE *US, male vocal group (Singles: 8 Weeks)* pos/wks

1 Jun 91	I LIKE THE WAY (THE KISSING GAME) *Jive JIVE 271* ▲	43	6
24 Oct 92	SHE'S PLAYING HARD TO GET *Jive JIVE 316*	55	2

HI-GATE (see also CANDY GIRLS; CLERGY; DOROTHY; Paul MASTERSON; SLEAZE SISTERS; YOMANDA) *UK, male production duo – Julius (Judge Jules) O'Riordan and Paul Masterson (Singles: 14 Weeks)* pos/wks

29 Jan 00 ●	PITCHIN' (IN EVERY DIRECTION) *Incentive CENT 3CD*	6	6
26 Aug 00	I CAN HEAR VOICES / CANED AND UNABLE *Incentive CENT 9CDS*	12	5
7 Apr 01	GONNA WORK IT OUT *Incentive CENT 20CDS*	25	3

HI GLOSS *US, disco aggregation (Singles: 13 Weeks)* pos/wks

8 Aug 81	YOU'LL NEVER KNOW *Epic EPC A 1387*	12	13

HI JACK *US, male vocal group (Albums: 1 Week)* pos/wks

19 Oct 91	THE HORNS OF JERICHO *Warner Bros. 7599263861*	54	1

HI-LUX *UK, male instrumental / production duo (Singles: 3 Weeks)* pos/wks

18 Feb 95	FEEL IT *Cheeky CHEKCD 006*	41	2
2 Sep 95	NEVER FELT THIS WAY / FEEL IT (re-issue) *Champion CHAMPCD 319*	58	1

HI POWER *Germany, male rap group (Singles: 1 Week)* pos/wks

1 Sep 90	CULT OF SNAP / SIMBA GROOVE *Rumour RUMAT 24*	73	1

HI-TEK featuring JONELL *US, male producer – Tony Cottrell (Singles: 1 Week)* pos/wks

20 Oct 01	ROUND & ROUND *Rawkus RWK 3432*	73	1

HI-TEK 3 featuring YA KID K (see also TECHNOTRONIC) *Belgium, male / female vocal / instrumental group (Singles: 10 Weeks)* pos/wks

3 Feb 90	SPIN THAT WHEEL *Brothers Organisation BORG 1*	69	3
29 Sep 90	SPIN THAT WHEEL (TURTLES GET REAL) (re-issue) *Brothers Organisation BORG 16*	15	7

HI TENSION (see also David JOSEPH) *UK, male vocal / instrumental group – includes David Joseph (Singles: 23 Weeks, Albums: 4 Weeks)* pos/wks

6 May 78	HI TENSION *Island WIP 6422*	13	12
12 Aug 78 ●	BRITISH HUSTLE / PEACE ON EARTH *Island WIP 6446*	8	11
6 Jan 79	HI TENSION *Island ILPS 9564*	74	4

'Peace on Earth' credited with 'British Hustle' from 2 Sep 1978 to the end of its chart run

John HIATT *US, male vocalist (Albums: 3 Weeks)* pos/wks

7 Jul 90	STOLEN MOMENTS *A&M 3953101*	72	1
11 Sep 93	PERFECTLY GOOD GUITAR *A&M 5401302*	67	1
11 Nov 95	WALK ON *Capitol CDP 8334162*	74	1

Al HIBBLER *US, male vocalist, b. 16 Aug 1915, d. 24 Apr 2001 (Singles: 17 Weeks)* pos/wks

13 May 55 ●	UNCHAINED MELODY *Brunswick 05420*	2	17

Hinda HICKS *UK, female vocalist (Singles: 15 Weeks, Albums: 4 Weeks)* pos/wks

7 Mar 98	IF YOU WANT ME *Island CID 689*	25	3
16 May 98	YOU THINK YOU OWN ME *Island CID 700*	19	4
15 Aug 98	I WANNA BE YOUR LADY *Island CID 709*	14	5
24 Oct 98	TRULY *Island CID 721*	31	2
14 Oct 00	MY REMEDY *Island CID 765*	61	1
29 Aug 98	HINDA *Island CID 8068*	20	4

The HIDDEN CAMERAS *Canada, male vocal collective (Singles: 1 Week)* pos/wks

14 Jun 03	A MIRACLE *Rough Trade RTRADSCD 105*	70	1

Bertie HIGGINS *US, male vocalist (Singles: 4 Weeks)* pos/wks

5 Jun 82	KEY LARGO *Epic EPC A 2168*	60	4

HIGH *UK, male vocal group (Singles: 11 Weeks, Albums: 2 Weeks)* pos/wks

25 Aug 90	UP AND DOWN *London LON 272*	53	4
27 Oct 90	TAKE YOUR TIME *London LON 280*	56	2
12 Jan 91	BOX SET GO *London LONG 286*	28	3
6 Apr 91	MORE ... *London LON 297*	67	2
17 Nov 90	SOMEWHERE SOON *London 8282241*	59	2

HIGH CONTRAST *UK, male producer – Lincoln Barrett (Singles: 4 Weeks)* pos/wks

1 Jun 02	GLOBAL LOVE *Hospital NHS 44CD*	68	1
9 Aug 03	BASEMENT TRACK *Hospital NHS 60*	65	1
26 Jun 04	TWILIGHTS LAST GLEAMING / MADE IT LAST *Hospital NHS 73*	74	1
18 Sep 04	RACING GREEN *Hospital CSSN 029*	73	1

HIGH FIDELITY *UK, male vocal / instrumental group (Singles: 1 Week)* pos/wks

25 Jul 98	LUV DUP *Plastique FAKE 03CDS*	70	1

Singles re-entries are listed as (re), (2re), (3re).... which signifies that the hit re-entered the chart once, twice or three times...

The HIGH LLAMAS
UK, male vocal / instrumental group (Albums: 1 Week)   pos/wks

| 6 Apr 96 | HAWAII *Alpaca CDWOOL 2* | 62 | 1 |

The HIGH NUMBERS
UK, male vocal / instrumental group (Singles: 4 Weeks)   pos/wks

| 5 Apr 80 | I'M THE FACE *Back Door DOOR 4* | 49 | 4 |

The High Numbers were an early version of The Who

HIGH SOCIETY
UK, male vocal / instrumental group (Singles: 4 Weeks)   pos/wks

| 15 Nov 80 | I NEVER GO OUT IN THE RAIN *Eagle ERS 002* | 53 | 4 |

HIGHLY LIKELY
UK, male vocal / instrumental group (Singles: 4 Weeks)   pos/wks

| 21 Apr 73 | WHATEVER HAPPENED TO YOU ('LIKELY LADS' THEME) *BBC RESL 10* | 35 | 4 |

The HIGHWAYMEN *US, male vocal group (Singles: 18 Weeks)*   pos/wks

| 7 Sep 61 | ★ MICHAEL *HMV POP 910* ▲ | 1 | 14 |
| 7 Dec 61 | THE GYPSY ROVER (re) *HMV POP 948* | 41 | 4 |

HIJACK *UK, male rap group (Singles: 3 Weeks)*   pos/wks

| 6 Jan 90 | THE BADMAN IS ROBBIN' *Rhyme Syndicate 655517 7* | 56 | 3 |

Benny HILL *UK, male comedian / vocalist – Alfred Hill, b. 21 Jan 1924, d. 20 Apr 1992 (Singles: 43 Weeks, Albums: 8 Weeks)*   pos/wks

16 Feb 61	GATHER IN THE MUSHROOMS *Pye 7N 15327*	12	8
1 Jun 61	TRANSISTOR RADIO *Pye 7N 15359*	24	6
16 May 63	HARVEST OF LOVE *Pye 7N 15520*	20	8
13 Nov 71	★ ERNIE (THE FASTEST MILKMAN IN THE WEST) *Columbia DB 8833*	1	17
30 May 92	ERNIE (THE FASTEST MILKMAN IN THE WEST) (re-issue) *EMI ERN 1*	29	4
11 Dec 71	● WORDS AND MUSIC *Columbia SCX 6479*	9	8

Chris HILL *UK, male vocalist / DJ / producer (Singles: 14 Weeks)* pos/wks

| 6 Dec 75 | ● RENTA SANTA *Philips 6006 491* | 10 | 7 |
| 4 Dec 76 | ● BIONIC SANTA *Philips 6006 551* | 10 | 7 |

Dan HILL *Canada, male vocalist (Singles: 13 Weeks)*   pos/wks

| 18 Feb 78 | SOMETIMES WHEN WE TOUCH (re) *20th Century BTC 2355* | 13 | 13 |

Faith HILL *US, female vocalist – Audrey Hill (Singles: 34 Weeks, Albums: 29 Weeks)*   pos/wks

14 Nov 98	THIS KISS *Warner Bros. W 463CD*	13	11
17 Apr 99	LET ME LET GO *Warner Bros. W 473CD*	72	1
20 May 00	BREATHE *WEA WEA 520CD*	33	2
21 Apr 01	THE WAY YOU LOVE ME *Warner Bros. W 51CD*	15	5
30 Jun 01	● THERE YOU'LL BE *Warner Bros. W 563CD*	3	11
13 Oct 01	BREATHE (re-mix) *Warner Bros. W 572CD*	36	2
26 Oct 02	CRY *Warner Bros. W 593CD*	25	2
3 Jun 00	BREATHE *Warner Bros. 9362473732* ▲	19	16
27 Oct 01	● THERE YOU'LL BE *Warner Bros. 9362482402*	6	11
9 Nov 02	CRY *Warner Bros. 9362483682* ▲	29	2

Lauryn HILL (see also FUGEES)
US, female vocalist (Singles: 35 Weeks, Albums: 74 Weeks)   pos/wks

6 Sep 97	THE SWEETEST THING *Columbia 6649785* [1]	18	4
27 Dec 97	ALL MY TIME *World Entertainment OWECD 2* [2]	57	1
3 Oct 98	● DOO WOP (THAT THING) *Ruffhouse 6665152* ▲	3	7
27 Feb 99	● EX-FACTOR (re) *Columbia / Ruffhouse 6669452*	4	10
10 Jul 99	EVERYTHING IS EVERYTHING *Columbia / Ruffhouse 6675742*	19	6
11 Dec 99	TURN YOUR LIGHTS DOWN LOW *Columbia 6684362* [3]	15	7
10 Oct 98	● THE MISEDUCATION OF LAURYN HILL *Columbia 4898432* ▲	2	72
18 May 02	MTV UNPLUGGED 2.0 *Columbia 5080032*	40	2

[1] Refugee Camp Allstars featuring Lauryn Hill [2] Paid & Live featuring Lauryn Hill [3] Bob Marley featuring Lauryn Hill

Lonnie HILL *US, male vocalist (Singles: 4 Weeks)*   pos/wks

| 22 Mar 86 | GALVESTON BAY *10 TEN 111* | 51 | 4 |

Roni HILL *US, female vocalist (Singles: 4 Weeks)*   pos/wks

| 7 May 77 | YOU KEEP ME HANGIN' ON – STOP IN THE NAME OF LOVE (MEDLEY) *Creole CR 138* | 36 | 4 |

Vince HILL
UK, male vocalist (Singles: 91 Weeks, Albums: 10 Weeks)   pos/wks

7 Jun 62	THE RIVER'S RUN DRY (re) *Piccadilly 7N 35043*	41	2
6 Jan 66	TAKE ME TO YOUR HEART AGAIN *Columbia DB 7781*	13	11
17 Mar 66	HEARTACHES *Columbia DB 7852*	28	5
2 Jun 66	MERCI CHERI *Columbia DB 7924*	36	6
9 Feb 67	● EDELWEISS *Columbia DB 8127*	2	17
11 May 67	ROSES OF PICARDY *Columbia DB 8185*	13	11
27 Sep 67	LOVE LETTERS IN THE SAND *Columbia DB 8268*	23	9
26 Jun 68	THE IMPORTANCE OF YOUR LOVE *Columbia DB 8414*	32	12
12 Feb 69	DOESN'T ANYBODY KNOW MY NAME? *Columbia DB 8515*	50	1
25 Oct 69	LITTLE BLUE BIRD *Columbia DB 8616*	42	1
25 Sep 71	LOOK AROUND (AND YOU'LL FIND ME THERE) *Columbia DB 8804*	12	16
20 May 67	EDELWEISS *Columbia SCX 6141*	23	9
29 Apr 78	THAT LOVING FEELING *K-Tel NE 1017*	51	1

Steve HILLAGE
UK, male vocalist / instrumentalist – guitar (Albums: 40 Weeks)   pos/wks

3 May 75	FISH RISING *Virgin V 2031*	33	3
16 Oct 76	● L *Virgin V 2066*	10	12
22 Oct 77	MOTIVATION RADIO *Virgin V 2777*	28	5
29 Apr 78	GREEN VIRGIN *Virgin V 2098*	30	8
17 Feb 79	LIVE HERALD *Virgin VGD 3502*	54	5
5 May 79	RAINBOW DOME MUSIC *Virgin VR 1*	48	4
27 Oct 79	OPEN *Virgin V 2135*	71	1
5 Mar 83	FOR TO NEXT *Virgin V 2244*	48	2

HILLMAN MINX *UK / France, male / female vocal / instrumental group (Singles: 1 Week)*   pos/wks

| 5 Sep 98 | I'VE HAD ENOUGH *Mercury MERCD 509* | 72 | 1 |

The HILLTOPPERS *US, male vocal group (Singles: 30 Weeks)*   pos/wks

27 Jan 56	● ONLY YOU (AND YOU ALONE) (re) *London HLD 8221*	3	23
14 Sep 56	TRYIN' *London HLD 8298*	30	1
5 Apr 57	MARIANNE (re) *London HLD 8381*	20	6

Ronnie HILTON *UK, male vocalist – Adrian Hill, b. 26 Jan 1926, d. 21 Feb 2001 (Singles: 136 Weeks)*   pos/wks

26 Nov 54	● I STILL BELIEVE *HMV B 10785*	3	14
10 Dec 54	VENI VIDI VICI *HMV B 10785*	12	8
11 Mar 55	● A BLOSSOM FELL *HMV B 10808*	10	5
26 Aug 55	STARS SHINE IN YOUR EYES *HMV B 10901*	13	7
11 Nov 55	THE YELLOW ROSE OF TEXAS *HMV B 10924*	15	2
10 Feb 56	YOUNG AND FOOLISH (2re) *HMV POP 154*	17	3
20 Apr 56	★ NO OTHER LOVE *HMV POP 198*	1	14
29 Jun 56	● WHO ARE WE *HMV POP 221*	6	12
21 Sep 56	A WOMAN IN LOVE *HMV POP 248*	30	1
9 Nov 56	TWO DIFFERENT WORLDS *HMV POP 274*	13	13
24 May 57	● AROUND THE WORLD *HMV POP 338*	4	18
2 Aug 57	WONDERFUL! WONDERFUL! *HMV POP 364*	27	2
21 Feb 58	MAGIC MOMENTS *HMV POP 446*	22	2
18 Apr 58	I MAY NEVER PASS THIS WAY AGAIN (2re) *HMV POP 468* [1]	27	3
9 Jan 59	THE WORLD OUTSIDE *HMV POP 559* [1]	18	6
21 Aug 59	THE WONDER OF YOU *HMV POP 638*	22	3
21 May 64	DON'T LET THE RAIN COME DOWN *HMV POP 1291*	21	10
11 Feb 65	A WINDMILL IN OLD AMSTERDAM *HMV POP 1378*	23	13

[1] Ronnie Hilton with The Michael Sammes Singers

HIM *Finland, male vocal / instrumental group (Singles: 12 Weeks, Albums: 5 Weeks)*   pos/wks

17 May 03	BURIED ALIVE BY LOVE *RCA 82876523162*	30	2
20 Sep 03	MY SACRAMENT *RCA 82876558892*	23	2
24 Jan 04	THE FUNERAL OF HEARTS *RCA 82876585792*	15	4
8 May 04	● SOLITARY MAN *RCA 82876610652*	9	4
26 Apr 03	LOVE METAL *RCA 82876505042*	55	3
27 Mar 04	AND LOVE SAID NO ... 1997-2004 *RCA 82876606102*	30	4

HINDSIGHT
UK, male vocal / instrumental group (Singles: 3 Weeks)   pos/wks

| 5 Sep 87 | LOWDOWN *Circa YR 5* | 62 | 3 |

Deni HINES
Australia, female vocalist (Singles: 6 Weeks)   pos/wks

14 Jun 97	**IT'S ALRIGHT** *Mushroom D 1593*	.35 2
20 Sep 97	**I LIKE THE WAY** *Mushroom MUSH 7CDX*	.37 2
28 Feb 98	**DELICIOUS** *Mushroom MUSH 20CD* [1]	.52 1
23 May 98	**JOY** *Mushroom MUSH 30CDS*	.47 1

[1] Deni Hines featuring Don-E

Gregory HINES See Luther VANDROSS

HIPSWAY
UK, male vocal / instrumental
group (Singles: 21 Weeks, Albums: 23 Weeks)   pos/wks

13 Jul 85	**THE BROKEN YEARS** *Mercury MER 193*	.72 3
14 Sep 85	**ASK THE LORD** *Mercury MER 195*	.72 1
22 Feb 86	**THE HONEYTHIEF** *Mercury MER 212*	.17 9
10 May 86	**ASK THE LORD (re-recording)** *Mercury LORD 1*	.50 5
20 Sep 86	**LONG WHITE CAR** *Mercury MER 230*	.55 2
1 Apr 89	**YOUR LOVE** *Mercury MER 279*	.66 1
19 Apr 86	**HIPSWAY** *Mercury MERH 85*	.42 23

David HIRSCHFELDER
Australia, male composer (Albums: 9 Weeks)   pos/wks

8 Feb 97	**SHINE (FILM SOUNDTRACK)** *Philips 4547102*	.46 9

The HISS
US, male vocal / instrumental group (Singles: 3 Weeks)   pos/wks

1 Mar 03	**TRIUMPH** *Loog / Polydor 0657782*	.53 1
9 Aug 03	**CLEVER KICKS** *Polydor 9809465*	.49 1
15 Nov 03	**BACK ON THE RADIO** *Polydor 9813415*	.65 1

HISTORY featuring Q-TEE
UK, male production duo and female rapper (Singles: 5 Weeks)   pos/wks

21 Apr 90	**AFRIKA** *SBK SBK 7008*	.42 5

Carol HITCHCOCK
Australia, female vocalist (Singles: 5 Weeks)   pos/wks

30 May 87	**GET READY** *A&M AM 391*	.56 5

HITHOUSE
Holland, male producer – Peter Slaghuis,
b. 21 Aug 1961, d. 5 Sep 1991 (Singles: 13 Weeks)   pos/wks

5 Nov 88	**JACK TO THE SOUND OF THE UNDERGROUND** *Supreme SUPE 137*	.14 12
19 Aug 89	**MOVE YOUR FEET TO THE RHYTHM OF THE BEAT** *Supreme SUPE 149*	.69 1

HITMAN HOWIE TEE See REAL ROXANNE

The HIVES
Sweden, male vocal / instrumental
group (Singles: 15 Weeks, Albums: 37 Weeks)   pos/wks

23 Feb 02	**HATE TO SAY I TOLD YOU SO** *Burning Heart BHR 1059*	.23 3
18 May 02	**MAIN OFFENDER** *Poptones MC 5076SCD*	.24 2
17 Jul 04	**WALK IDIOT WALK** *Polydor 9867038*	.13 9
30 Oct 04	**TWO-TIMING TOUCH AND BROKEN BONES** *Polydor 9868351*	.44 1
12 Jan 02	● **YOUR NEW FAVOURITE BAND** *Poptones MC 5055CD*	.7 30
31 Jul 04	● **TYRANNOSAURUS HIVES** *Polydor 9866991*	.7 7

Helen HOBSON See Cliff RICHARD

Edmund HOCKRIDGE
Canada, male vocalist (Singles: 18 Weeks)   pos/wks

17 Feb 56	● **YOUNG AND FOOLISH (2re)** *Nixa N 15039*	.10 9
11 May 56	**NO OTHER LOVE (2re)** *Nixa N 15048*	.24 4
31 Aug 56	**BY THE FOUNTAINS OF ROME** *Pye Nixa N 15063*	.17 5

Eddie HODGES
US, male vocalist (Singles: 10 Weeks)   pos/wks

28 Sep 61	**I'M GONNA KNOCK ON YOUR DOOR** *London HLA 9369*	.37 6
9 Aug 62	**(GIRLS GIRLS GIRLS) MADE TO LOVE** *London HLA 9576*	.37 4

Roger HODGSON
(see also SUPERTRAMP)
UK, male vocalist / instrumentalist – bass (Albums: 4 Weeks)   pos/wks

20 Oct 84	**IN THE EYE OF THE STORM** *A&M AMA 5004*	.70 4

Mani HOFFMAN See SUPERMEN LOVERS featuring Mani HOFFMAN

Gerard HOFFNUNG
UK (b. Germany), male comedian /
instrumentalist, b. 1925, d. 28 Sep 1959 (Albums: 20 Weeks)   pos/wks

3 Sep 60	● **AT THE OXFORD UNION** *Decca LF 1330*	.4 20

Susanna HOFFS (see also The BANGLES)
US, female vocalist (Singles: 8 Weeks, Albums: 2 Weeks)   pos/wks

2 Mar 91	**MY SIDE OF THE BED** *Columbia 6565547*	.44 4
11 May 91	**UNCONDITIONAL LOVE** *Columbia 6567827*	.65 2
19 Oct 96	**ALL I WANT** *London LONCD 387*	.32 2
6 Apr 91	**WHEN YOU'RE A BOY** *Columbia 4672021*	.56 2

Hulk HOGAN with GREEN JELLY
US, male wrestler / vocalist – Terry
Bollea and US, male vocal / instrumental group (Singles: 4 Weeks)   pos/wks

25 Dec 93	**I'M THE LEADER OF THE GANG** *Arista 74321174892*	.25 4

HOGGBOY
UK, male vocal / instrumental group (Singles: 1 Week)   pos/wks

27 Apr 02	**SHOULDN'T LET THE SIDE DOWN** *Sobriety SOB 4CDA*	.74 1

Christopher HOGWOOD – See 007; ACADEMY OF ST MARTIN IN THE FIELDS; ACADEMY OF ANCIENT MUSIC conducted by Christopher HOGWOOD

Demi HOLBORN
UK, female vocalist (Singles: 2 Weeks)   pos/wks

27 Jul 02	**I'D LIKE TO TEACH THE WORLD TO SING** *Universal Classics & Jazz 0190982*	.27 2

HOLDEN & THOMPSON
UK, male producer and female
vocalist – James Holden and Julie Thompson (Singles: 1 Week)   pos/wks

17 May 03	**NOTHING** *Loaded LOAD 98CD*	.51 1

HOLE
US, female / male vocal / instrumental group –
leader Courtney Love (Singles: 15 Weeks, Albums: 10 Weeks)   pos/wks

17 Apr 93	**BEAUTIFUL SON** *City Slang EFA 0491603*	.54 1
9 Apr 94	**MISS WORLD** *City Slang EFA 049362*	.64 1
15 Apr 95	**DOLL PARTS** *Geffen GFSTD 91*	.16 3
29 Jul 95	**VIOLET** *Geffen GFSTD 94*	.17 2
12 Sep 98	**CELEBRITY SKIN** *Geffen GFSTD 22345*	.19 4
30 Jan 99	**MALIBU** *Geffen GFSTD 22369*	.22 2
10 Jul 99	**AWFUL** *Geffen INTDE 97098*	.42 2
12 Oct 91	**PRETTY ON THE INSIDE** *City Slang E 04071*	.59 1
23 Apr 94	**LIVE THROUGH THIS** *City Slang EFA 049352*	.13 5
19 Sep 98	**CELEBRITY SKIN** *Geffen GED 25164*	.11 4

HOLE IN ONE
Holland, male DJ / producer – Marcel Hol (Singles: 2 Weeks)   pos/wks

15 Feb 97	**LIFE'S TOO SHORT** *Manifesto FESCD 21*	.36 2

Billie HOLIDAY
US, female vocalist – Eleanor Fagan
Gough, b. 7 Apr 1915, d. 17 Jul 1959 (Albums: 11 Weeks)   pos/wks

16 Nov 85	**THE LEGEND OF BILLIE HOLIDAY** *MCA BHTV 1*	.60 10
6 Sep 97	**LADY DAY – THE VERY BEST OF BILLIE HOLIDAY** *Sony TV / Universal MOODCD 52*	.63 1

HOLIDAY PLAN
UK, male vocal / instrumental group (Singles: 1 Week)   pos/wks

26 Jun 04	**STORIES / SUNSHINE** *Island CID 858*	.58 1

Jools HOLLAND and his RHYTHM & BLUES ORCHESTRA
(see also SQUEEZE) *UK, male vocalist / instrumentalist –*
piano and orchestra (Singles: 3 Weeks, Albums: 76 Weeks)   pos/wks

24 Feb 01	**I'M IN THE MOOD FOR LOVE** *Warner.esp WSMS 001CD* [1]	.29 3
5 May 90	**WORLD OF HIS OWN** *IRS EIRSA 1018* [1]	.71 1
26 Oct 96	**SEX & JAZZ & ROCK & ROLL** *Coliseum HF 51CD*	.38 2
25 Oct 97	**LIFT THE LID** *Coalition 3984205252*	.50 1
1 Dec 01	● **SMALL WORLD BIG BAND** *WSM 927426562* [2]	.8 37
30 Nov 02	**SMALL WORLD BIG BAND 2 – MORE FRIENDS** *WSM 0927494192*	.17 14
29 Nov 03	**SMALL WORLD BIG BAND FRIENDS 3 – JACK O THE GREEN** *Radar RADAR 001CD*	.39 9
9 Oct 04	● **TOM JONES & JOOLS HOLLAND** *Radar 004CD* [3]	.5 12+

[1] Jools Holland and Jamiroquai   [1] Jools Holland [2] Jools Holland and his Rhythm & Blues Orchestra and Friends [3] Tom Jones & Jools Holland

HOLLAND-DOZIER featuring Lamont DOZIER *US, male vocal duo – Brian Holland and Lamont Dozier (Singles: 5 Weeks)* pos/wks

28 Oct 72	WHY CAN'T WE BE LOVERS *Invictus INV 525*	**29**	5

Jennifer HOLLIDAY *US, female vocalist (Singles: 6 Weeks)* pos/wks

4 Sep 82	AND I'M TELLING YOU I'M NOT GOING *Geffen GEF A 2644*	**32**	6

Michael HOLLIDAY *UK, male vocalist – Norman Milne, b. 26 Nov 1925, d. 29 Oct 1963 (Singles: 66 Weeks)* pos/wks

30 Mar 56	NOTHIN' TO DO (re) *Columbia DB 3746*	**20**	3
15 Jun 56	HOT DIGGITY (DOG ZIGGITY BOOM) / THE GAL WITH THE YALLER SHOES (2re) *Columbia DB 3783*	**13**	11
5 Oct 56	TEN THOUSAND MILES *Columbia DB 3813*	**24**	3
17 Jan 58 ★	THE STORY OF MY LIFE *Columbia DB 4058*	**1**	15
14 Mar 58	IN LOVE *Columbia DB 4087*	**26**	3
16 May 58 ●	STAIRWAY OF LOVE *Columbia DB 4121*	**3**	13
11 Jul 58	I'LL ALWAYS BE IN LOVE WITH YOU *Columbia DB 4155*	**27**	1
1 Jan 60 ★	STARRY EYED *Columbia DB 4378* [1]	**1**	13
14 Apr 60	SKYLARK *Columbia DB 4437*	**39**	3
1 Sep 60	LITTLE BOY LOST *Columbia DB 4475*	**50**	1

[1] Michael Holliday with The Michael Sammes Singers

When 'Hot Diggity (Dog Ziggity Boom)' / 'The Gal with the Yaller Shoes' re-entered the chart on 3 Aug 1956, 'Hot Diggity (Dog Ziggity Boom)' was listed by itself on 3 Aug and 10 Aug. Both sides were listed on 17 Aug – 'The Gal with the Yaller Shoes' peaking at No.25

The HOLLIES (87) Top 500 (see also CROSBY, STILLS, NASH and YOUNG; Graham NASH) *Distinctive, influential and well-respected Manchester group: Allan Clarke (v), Graham Nash (g), Tony Hicks (g), Eric Haydock (b), Bobby Elliott (d). They were among the most regular chart visitors of the 1960s, and their No.1s span 23 years. Total single sales: 4,597,450 (Singles: 318 Weeks, Albums: 154 Weeks)* pos/wks

30 May 63	(AIN'T THAT) JUST LIKE ME *Parlophone R 5030*	**25**	10
29 Aug 63	SEARCHIN' *Parlophone R 5052*	**12**	14
21 Nov 63 ●	STAY *Parlophone R 5077*	**8**	16
27 Feb 64 ●	JUST ONE LOOK *Parlophone R 5104*	**2**	13
21 May 64 ●	HERE I GO AGAIN *Parlophone R 5137*	**4**	12
17 Sep 64 ●	WE'RE THROUGH *Parlophone R 5178*	**7**	11
28 Jan 65	YES I WILL *Parlophone R 5232*	**9**	13
27 May 65 ★	I'M ALIVE *Parlophone R 5287*	**1**	14
2 Sep 65 ●	LOOK THROUGH ANY WINDOW *Parlophone R 5322*	**4**	11
9 Dec 65	IF I NEEDED SOMEONE *Parlophone R 5392*	**20**	10
24 Feb 66 ●	I CAN'T LET GO *Parlophone R 5409*	**2**	10
23 Jun 66 ●	BUS STOP *Parlophone R 5469*	**5**	9
13 Oct 66 ●	STOP STOP STOP *Parlophone R 5508*	**2**	12
16 Feb 67 ●	ON A CAROUSEL *Parlophone R 5562*	**4**	11
1 Jun 67 ●	CARRIE-ANNE *Parlophone R 5602*	**3**	11
27 Sep 67	KING MIDAS IN REVERSE *Parlophone R 5637*	**18**	8
27 Mar 68 ●	JENNIFER ECCLES *Parlophone R 5680*	**7**	11
2 Oct 68	LISTEN TO ME *Parlophone R 5733*	**11**	11
5 Mar 69 ●	SORRY SUZANNE *Parlophone R 5765*	**3**	12
4 Oct 69 ●	HE AIN'T HEAVY, HE'S MY BROTHER *Parlophone R 5806*	**3**	15
18 Apr 70 ●	I CAN'T TELL THE BOTTOM FROM THE TOP *Parlophone R 5837*	**7**	10
3 Oct 70	GASOLINE ALLEY BRED *Parlophone R 5862*	**14**	7
22 May 71	HEY WILLY *Parlophone R 5905*	**22**	7
26 Feb 72	THE BABY *Polydor 2058 199*	**26**	6
2 Sep 72	LONG COOL WOMAN IN A BLACK DRESS *Parlophone R 5939*	**32**	8
13 Oct 73	THE DAY THAT CURLY BILLY SHOT DOWN CRAZY SAM McGHEE *Polydor 2058 403*	**24**	6
9 Feb 74 ●	THE AIR THAT I BREATHE *Polydor 2058 435*	**2**	13
14 Jun 80	SOLDIER'S SONG *Polydor 2059 246*	**58**	3
29 Aug 81	HOLLIEDAZE (A MEDLEY) *EMI 5229*	**28**	7
3 Sep 88 ★	HE AIN'T HEAVY, HE'S MY BROTHER (re-issue) *EMI EM 74*	**1**	11
3 Dec 88	THE AIR THAT I BREATHE (re-issue) *EMI EM 80*	**60**	5
20 Mar 93	THE WOMAN I LOVE *EMI CDEM 264*	**42**	2
15 Feb 64 ●	STAY WITH THE HOLLIES *Parlophone PMC 1220*	**2**	25
2 Oct 65 ●	HOLLIES *Parlophone PMC 1261*	**8**	14
16 Jul 66	WOULD YOU BELIEVE? *Parlophone PCS 7008*	**16**	8
17 Dec 66	FOR CERTAIN BECAUSE *Parlophone PCS 17011*	**12**	7
17 Jun 67	EVOLUTION *Parlophone PCS 7022*	**13**	10
17 Aug 68 ★	THE HOLLIES' GREATEST HITS *Parlophone PCS 7057*	**1**	27
17 May 69	HOLLIES SIGN DYLAN *Parlophone PCS 7078*	**3**	7
28 Nov 70	CONFESSIONS OF THE MIND *Parlophone PCS 7117*	**30**	5
16 Mar 74	HOLLIES *Polydor 2383 262*	**38**	3
19 Mar 77 ●	HOLLIES LIVE HITS *Polydor 2383 428*	**4**	12

22 Jul 78 ●	20 GOLDEN GREATS *EMI EMTV 11*	**2**	20
1 Oct 88	ALL THE HITS AND MORE *EMI EM 1301*	**51**	5
3 Apr 93	THE AIR THAT I BREATHE – THE BEST OF THE HOLLIES *EMI CDEMTV 74*	**15**	7
5 Apr 03	GREATEST HITS *EMI 5820122*	**21**	4

The 1972 hit 'The Baby' featured Swedish lead vocalist Mikael Rickfors. Holliedaze (A Medley) comprised: Just One Look / Here I Go Again / I'm Alive / I Can't Let Go / Long Cool Woman In A Black Dress / Bus Stop / Carrie-Anne The two 'Hollies' albums are different

Mark HOLLIS (see also TALK TALK) *UK, male vocalist / instrumentalist (Albums: 1 Week)* pos/wks

14 Feb 98	MARK HOLLIS *Polydor 5376882*	**53**	1

Laurie HOLLOWAY See SOUTH BANK ORCHESTRA

Loleatta HOLLOWAY *US, female vocalist (Singles: 21 Weeks)* pos/wks

31 Aug 91	GOOD VIBRATIONS *Interscope A 8764* [1] ▲	**14**	7
18 Jan 92	TAKE ME AWAY *PWL Continental PWL 210* [2]	**25**	5
26 Mar 94	STAND UP *Six6 SIXCD 111*	**68**	1
1 Apr 95	KEEP THE FIRE BURNIN' *Columbia 6611552* [3]	**49**	1
11 Apr 98	SHOUT TO THE TOP *JBO JNR 5001573* [4]	**23**	2
20 Feb 99	(YOU GOT ME) BURNING UP *Wonderboy WBOYD 013* [5]	**14**	4
25 Nov 00	DREAMIN' *Defected DFECT 22CDS*	**59**	1

[1] Marky Mark and the Funky Bunch featuring Loleatta Holloway [2] Cappella featuring Loleatta Holloway [3] Dan Hartman starring Loleatta Holloway [4] Fire Island featuring Loleatta Holloway [5] Cevin Fisher / Loleatta Holloway

HOLLOWAY & CO *UK, male producer – Nicky Holloway (Singles: 1 Week)* pos/wks

21 Aug 99	I'LL DO ANYTHING – TO MAKE YOU MINE *INCredible INCS 2CD*	**58**	1

Buddy HOLLY (71) Top 500 *Highly respected and exceptionally influential singer / songwriter, b. Charles Hardin Holley, 7 Sep 1936, Texas, US, d. 3 Feb 1959 (aka 'the day the music died'). Despite a relatively brief career, his records and songs are still frequently heard around the globe (Singles: 190 Weeks, Albums: 339 Weeks)* pos/wks

6 Dec 57 ●	PEGGY SUE *Coral Q 72293*	**6**	17
14 Mar 58	LISTEN TO ME *Coral Q 72288*	**16**	2
20 Jun 58 ●	RAVE ON *Coral Q 72325*	**5**	14
29 Aug 58	EARLY IN THE MORNING *Coral Q 72333*	**17**	4
16 Jan 59	HEARTBEAT *Coral Q 72346*	**30**	1
27 Feb 59 ★	IT DOESN'T MATTER ANYMORE *Coral Q 72360*	**1**	21
31 Jul 59	MIDNIGHT SHIFT *Brunswick 05800*	**26**	3
11 Sep 59	PEGGY SUE GOT MARRIED *Coral Q 72376*	**13**	10
28 Apr 60	HEARTBEAT (re-issue) *Coral Q 72392*	**30**	3
26 May 60	TRUE LOVE WAYS *Coral Q 72397*	**25**	7
20 Oct 60	LEARNING THE GAME *Coral Q 72411*	**36**	3
26 Jan 61	WHAT TO DO *Coral Q 72419*	**34**	6
6 Jul 61	BABY I DON'T CARE / VALLEY OF TEARS *Coral Q 72432*	**12**	14
15 Mar 62	LISTEN TO ME (re-issue) *Coral Q 72449*	**48**	1
13 Sep 62	REMINISCING *Coral Q 72455*	**17**	11
14 Mar 63 ●	BROWN-EYED HANDSOME MAN *Coral Q 72459*	**3**	17
6 Jun 63 ●	BO DIDDLEY *Coral Q 72463*	**4**	12
5 Sep 63 ●	WISHING *Coral Q 72466*	**10**	11
19 Dec 63	WHAT TO DO (re-recording) *Coral Q 72469*	**27**	8
14 May 64	YOU'VE GOT LOVE *Coral Q 72472*	**40**	6
10 Sep 64	LOVE'S MADE A FOOL OF YOU *Coral Q 72475*	**39**	6
3 Apr 68	PEGGY SUE / RAVE ON (re-issue) *MCA MU 1012*	**32**	9
10 Dec 88	TRUE LOVE WAYS (re-issue) *MCA MCA 1302*	**65**	4
2 May 59 ●	THE BUDDY HOLLY STORY *Coral LVA 9105*	**2**	156
15 Oct 60 ●	THE BUDDY HOLLY STORY VOLUME 2 *Coral LVA 9127*	**7**	14
21 Oct 61 ●	THAT'LL BE THE DAY *Ace of Hearts AH 3*	**5**	14
6 Apr 63 ●	REMINISCING *Coral LVA 9212*	**2**	31
13 Jun 64 ●	BUDDY HOLLY SHOWCASE *Coral LVA 9222*	**3**	16
26 Jun 65	HOLLY IN THE HILLS *Coral LVA 9227*	**13**	6
15 Jul 67 ●	BUDDY HOLLY'S GREATEST HITS *Ace of Hearts AH 148*	**9**	40
12 Apr 69	GIANT *MCA MUPS 371*	**13**	1
21 Aug 71	BUDDY HOLLY'S GREATEST HITS (re-issue) *Coral CP 8*	**32**	6
12 Jul 75	BUDDY HOLLY'S GREATEST HITS (2nd re-issue) *Coral CDLM 8007*	**42**	3
11 Mar 78 ★	20 GOLDEN GREATS *MCA EMTV 8* [1]	**1**	20
8 Sep 84	BUDDY HOLLY'S GREATEST HITS (3rd re-issue) *MCA MCL 1618*	**100**	1

		pos/wks
18 Feb 89 ●	TRUE LOVE WAYS *Telstar STAR 2339*	.8 11
20 Feb 93 ★	WORDS OF LOVE *PolyGram TV 5144872* [1] ■	.1 9
7 Dec 96	THE VERY BEST OF BUDDY HOLLY *Dino DINCD 133*	.24 8
28 Aug 99	THE VERY BEST OF BUDDY HOLLY AND THE CRICKETS	
	Universal Music TV 1120462 [1]	.25 3

[1] Buddy Holly and The Crickets [1] Buddy Holly and The Crickets

Buddy Holly's version of 'Love's Made a Fool of You' is not the same version as The Crickets' hit of 1959, on which Holly did not appear. 'Valley of Tears' was not listed together with 'Baby I Don't Care' until 13 Jul 1961

HOLLY and the IVYS
UK, male / female vocal / instrumental group (Singles: 4 Weeks)   pos/wks

19 Dec 81	CHRISTMAS ON 45 *Decca SANTA 1*	.40 4

The HOLLYWOOD ARGYLES
US, male vocal group (Singles: 10 Weeks)   pos/wks

21 Jul 60	ALLEY-OOP *London HLU 9146* ▲	.24 10

HOLLYWOOD BEYOND *UK, male group (Singles: 14 Weeks)*   pos/wks

12 Jul 86 ●	WHAT'S THE COLOUR OF MONEY? *WEA YZ 76*	.7 10
20 Sep 86	NO MORE TEARS *WEA YZ 81*	.47 4

Eddie HOLMAN *US, male vocalist (Singles: 13 Weeks)*   pos/wks

19 Oct 74 ●	(HEY THERE) LONELY GIRL *ABC 4012*	.4 13

Dave HOLMES *UK, male producer (Singles: 1 Week)*   pos/wks

26 May 01	DEVOTION *Tidy Trax TIDY 154CD*	.66 1

David HOLMES (see also The FREE ASSOCIATION)
UK, male producer (Singles: 8 Weeks, Albums: 5 Weeks)   pos/wks

6 Apr 96	GONE *Go Discs GODCD 140*	.75 1
23 Aug 97	GRITTY SHAKER *Go Beat GOBCD 2*	.53 1
10 Jan 98	DON'T DIE JUST YET *Go Beat GOLCD 6*	.33 3
4 Apr 98	MY MATE PAUL *Go Beat GOBCD 8*	.39 2
19 Aug 00	69 POLICE *Go Beat / Polydor GOBCD 30*	.53 1
22 Jul 95	THIS FILM'S CRAP LET'S SLASH THE SEATS	
	Go Discs 8286312	.51 1
13 Sep 97	LET'S GET KILLED *Go Beat 5391002*	.34 2
24 Jun 00	BOW DOWN TO THE EXIT SIGN *Go Beat 5438662*	.22 2

Rupert HOLMES *US (b. UK), male vocalist (Singles: 14 Weeks)*   pos/wks

12 Jan 80	ESCAPE (THE PINA COLADA SONG) *Infinity INF 120* ▲	.23 7
22 Mar 80	HIM *MCA 565*	.31 7

Adele HOLNESS See Ben SHAW featuring Adele HOLNESS

John HOLT
Jamaica, male vocalist (Singles: 14 Weeks, Albums: 2 Weeks)   pos/wks

14 Dec 74 ●	HELP ME MAKE IT THROUGH THE NIGHT *Trojan TR 7909*	.6 14
1 Feb 75	ONE THOUSAND VOLTS OF HOLT *Trojan TRLS 75*	.42 2

Nichola HOLT *UK, female vocalist (Singles: 1 Week)*   pos/wks

21 Oct 00	THE GAME *RCA 74321798992*	.72 1

Paul HOLT *UK, male vocalist (Singles: 2 Weeks)*   pos/wks

18 Dec 04	FIFTY GRAND FOR CHRISTMAS *Sanctuary SANXS 348*	.35 2+

HOME *UK, male vocal / instrumental group (Albums: 1 Week)*   pos/wks

11 Nov 72	HOME *CBS 67522*	.41 1

A HOMEBOY, a HIPPIE and a FUNKI DREDD
UK, male vocal / instrumental group (Singles: 9 Weeks)   pos/wks

13 Oct 90	TOTAL CONFUSION *Tam Tam 7TTT 031*	.56 3
29 Dec 90	FREEDOM *Tam Tam 7TTT 039*	.68 4
8 Jan 94	HERE WE GO AGAIN *Polydor PZCD 302*	.57 2

HONDY
Italy, male / female production / vocal group (Singles: 2 Weeks)   pos/wks

12 Apr 97	HONDY (NO ACCESS) *Manifesto FESCD 20*	.26 2

HONEYBUS
UK, male vocal / instrumental group (Singles: 12 Weeks)   pos/wks

20 Mar 68 ●	I CAN'T LET MAGGIE GO *Deram DM 182*	.8 12

The HONEYCOMBS *UK, male / female vocal / instrumental group – lead vocal Dennis D'Ell (Dalziel) (Singles: 39 Weeks)*   pos/wks

23 Jul 64 ★	HAVE I THE RIGHT *Pye 7N 15664*	.1 15
22 Oct 64	IS IT BECAUSE *Pye 7N 15705*	.38 6
29 Apr 65	SOMETHING BETTER BEGINNING *Pye 7N 15827*	.39 4
5 Aug 65	THAT'S THE WAY *Pye 7N 15890*	.12 14

HONEYCRACK *UK, male vocal / instrumental group (Singles: 9 Weeks, Albums: 1 Week)*   pos/wks

4 Nov 95	SITTING AT HOME *Epic 6625382*	.42 2
24 Feb 96	GO AWAY *Epic 6628642*	.41 2
11 May 96	KING OF MISERY *Epic 6631472*	.32 2
20 Jul 96	SITTING AT HOME (re-issue) *Epic 6635032*	.32 2
16 Nov 96	ANYWAY *EG EGO 52A*	.67 1
1 Jun 96	PROZAIC *Epic 4842302*	.34 1

The HONEYDRIPPERS (see also Robert PLANT) *UK / US, male vocal / instrumental group (Singles: 3 Weeks, Albums: 10 Weeks)*   pos/wks

2 Feb 85	SEA OF LOVE *Es Paranza YZ 33*	.56 3
1 Dec 84	THE HONEYDRIPPERS VOLUME ONE *Es Paranza 790220*	.56 10

HONEYZ (see also ANOTHERSIDE; ZENA) *UK / France, female vocal trio (Singles: 57 Weeks, Albums: 22 Weeks)*   pos/wks

5 Sep 98 ●	FINALLY FOUND *1st Avenue / Mercury HNZCD 1*	.4 12
19 Dec 98 ●	END OF THE LINE (re) *1st Avenue / Mercury HNZCD 2*	.5 14
24 Apr 99 ●	LOVE OF A LIFETIME *1st Avenue / Mercury HNZCD 3*	.9 9
23 Oct 99 ●	NEVER LET YOU DOWN *1st Avenue / Mercury HNZCD 4*	.7 6
11 Mar 00 ●	WON'T TAKE IT LYING DOWN (re)	
	1st Avenue / Mercury HNZCD 5	.7 8
28 Oct 00	NOT EVEN GONNA TRIP (2re) *1st Avenue / Mercury HNZCD 7*	24 5
18 Aug 01	I DON'T KNOW *1st Avenue / Mercury HNZCD 8*	.28 3
5 Dec 98	WONDER NO.8 *Mercury 5588142*	.33 22

HONKY *UK, male vocal / instrumental group (Singles: 5 Weeks)*   pos/wks

28 May 77	JOIN THE PARTY *Creole CR 137*	.28 5

HONKY *UK, male vocal / instrumental group (Singles: 5 Weeks)*   pos/wks

30 Oct 93	THE HONKY DOODLE DAY EP *ZTT ZANG 45CD*	.61 1
19 Feb 94	THE WHISTLER *ZTT ZANG 48CD*	.42 2
20 Apr 96	HIP HOP DON'T YA DROP *Higher Ground HIGHS 1CD*	.70 1
10 Aug 96	WHAT'S GOIN DOWN *Higher Ground HIGHS 2CD*	.49 1

Tracks on The Honky Doodle Day EP: KKK (Boom Boom Tra La La La) / Honky Doodle Dub / Chains

HOOBASTANK *US, male vocal / instrumental group (Singles: 9 Weeks, Albums: 5 Weeks)*   pos/wks

13 Apr 02	CRAWLING IN THE DARK *Mercury 5828622*	.47 2
12 Jun 04	THE REASON *Mercury 9862567*	.12 7
5 Jun 04	THE REASON *Mercury 9862261*	.41 5

Peter HOOK See HYBRID featuring Peter HOOK; MONACO; NEW ORDER; JOY DIVISION

Frank HOOKER and POSITIVE PEOPLE
US, male / female vocal / instrumental group (Singles: 4 Weeks)   pos/wks

5 Jul 80	THIS FEELIN' *DJM DJS 10947*	.48 4

John Lee HOOKER *US, male vocalist / instrumentalist – guitar, b. 22 Aug 1917, d. 21 Jun 2001 (Singles: 23 Weeks, Albums: 31 Weeks)*   pos/wks

11 Jun 64	DIMPLES *Stateside SS 297*	.23 10
24 Oct 92	BOOM BOOM *Pointblank POB 3*	.16 5
16 Jan 93	BOOGIE AT RUSSIAN HILL *Pointblank POBDX 4*	.53 2
15 May 93	GLORIA *Exile VANCD 11* [1]	.31 3
11 Feb 95	CHILL OUT (THINGS GONNA CHANGE) *Pointblank POBD 10*	.45 2
20 Apr 96	BABY LEE *Silvertone ORECD 81* [2]	.65 1
4 Feb 67	HOUSE OF THE BLUES *Marble Arch MAL 663*	.34 2
11 Nov 89	THE HEALER *Silvertone ORELP 508*	.63 8
21 Sep 91 ●	MR. LUCKY *Silvertone ORELP 519*	.3 10

			pos/wks
7 Nov 92	BOOM BOOM *Pointblank VPBCD 12*	.........**15**	4
4 Mar 95	CHILL OUT *Pointblank VPBCD 22*	.........**23**	5
22 Mar 97	DON'T LOOK BACK *Pointblank VPBCD 39*	.........**63**	2

1 Van Morrison and John Lee Hooker 2 John Lee Hooker with Robert Cray

The HOOTERS
US, male vocal / instrumental group (Singles: 9 Weeks)   pos/wks

21 Nov 87	SATELLITE *CBS 651168 7*	.........**22**	9

HOOTIE & THE BLOWFISH *US, male vocal /*
instrumental group (Singles: 6 Weeks, Albums: 30 Weeks)   pos/wks

25 Feb 95	HOLD MY HAND *Atlantic A 7230CD*	.........**50**	3
27 May 95	LET HER CRY *Atlantic A 7188CD*	.........**75**	1
4 May 96	OLD MAN AND ME (WHEN I GET TO HEAVEN)		
	Atlantic A 5513CD	.........**57**	1
7 Nov 98	I WILL WAIT *Atlantic AT 0048CD*	.........**57**	1
18 Mar 95	CRACKED REAR VIEW *Atlantic 7826132* ▲	.........**12**	11
4 May 96 ●	FAIRWEATHER JOHNSON *Atlantic 7567828862* ▲	..........**9**	16
26 Sep 98	MUSICAL CHAIRS *Atlantic 7567831362*	.........**15**	3

HOPE A.D. (see also MIND OF KANE)
UK, male producer – David Hope (Singles: 1 Week)   pos/wks

4 Jun 94	TREE FROG *Sun-Up SUN 003CD*	.........**73**	1

HOPE OF THE STATES *UK, male vocal /*
instrumental group (Singles: 7 Weeks, Albums: 2 Weeks)   pos/wks

11 Oct 03	ENEMIES / FRIENDS *Sony Music 6742572*	.........**25**	2
5 Jun 04	THE RED THE WHITE THE BLACK THE BLUE		
	Sony Music 6749922	.........**15**	3
28 Aug 04	NEHEMIAH *Sony Music 6752472*	.........**30**	2
19 Jun 04	THE LOST RIOTS *Sony Music 5172649*	.........**21**	2

Mary HOPKIN (see also OASIS) *UK, female vocalist /*
instrumentalist – guitar (Singles: 74 Weeks, Albums: 9 Weeks)   pos/wks

4 Sep 68 ★	THOSE WERE THE DAYS *Apple 2*	..........**1**	21
2 Apr 69 ●	GOODBYE *Apple 10*	..........**2**	14
31 Jan 70 ●	TEMMA HARBOUR *Apple 22*	..........**6**	11
28 Mar 70 ●	KNOCK KNOCK WHO'S THERE *Apple 26*	..........**2**	14
31 Oct 70	THINK ABOUT YOUR CHILDREN (re) *Apple 30*	.........**19**	9
31 Jul 71	LET MY NAME BE SORROW *Apple 34*	.........**46**	1
20 Mar 76	IF YOU LOVE ME (I WON'T CARE) *Good Earth GD 2*	.........**32**	4
1 Mar 69 ●	POSTCARD *Apple SAPCOR 5*	..........**3**	9

Anthony HOPKINS *UK, male actor / vocalist (Singles: 1 Week)*   pos/wks

27 Dec 86	DISTANT STAR *Juice AA 5*	.........**75**	1

Nick HORNBY *See The PRETENDERS*

James HORNER *US, male composer (Albums: 82 Weeks)*   pos/wks

23 Sep 95	BRAVEHEART (FILM SOUNDTRACK) *Decca 4482952* 1	.....**27**	9
31 Jan 98 ★	TITANIC (FILM SOUNDTRACK) *Sony Classical SK 63213*	........**1**	55
12 Sep 98 ●	BACK TO TITANIC *Sony Classical SK 60691*	.........**10**	18

1 London Symphony Orchestra, music composed and conducted by James Horner

Bruce HORNSBY and the RANGE *US, male vocal /*
instrumental group (Singles: 15 Weeks, Albums: 54 Weeks)   pos/wks

2 Aug 86	THE WAY IT IS *RCA PB 49805* ▲	.........**15**	10
25 Apr 87	MANDOLIN RAIN *RCA PB 49769*	.........**70**	1
28 May 88	THE VALLEY ROAD *RCA PB 49561*	.........**44**	4
13 Sep 86	THE WAY IT IS *RCA PL 89901*	.........**16**	26
14 May 88	SCENES FROM THE SOUTHSIDE *RCA PL 86686*	.........**18**	18
30 Jun 90	A NIGHT ON THE TOWN *RCA PL 82041*	.........**23**	7
8 May 93	HARBOR LIGHTS *RCA 07863661142*	.........**32**	3

HORNY UNITED *See BONEY M*

Jane HORROCKS *UK, female actor / vocalist (Albums: 1 Week)*   pos/wks

21 Oct 00	THE FURTHER ADVENTURES OF LITTLE VOICE		
	Liberty 5287542	.........**63**	1

HORSE *UK, female / male vocal / instrumental*
group (Singles: 10 Weeks, Albums: 4 Weeks)   pos/wks

24 Nov 90	CAREFUL *Capitol CL 587*	.........**52**	3
21 Aug 93	SHAKE THIS MOUNTAIN *Oxygen GASPD 7*	.........**52**	2

			pos/wks
23 Oct 93	GOD'S HOME MOVIE *Oxygen GASXD 10*	.........**56**	1
15 Jan 94	CELEBRATE *Oxygen GASPD 11*	.........**49**	2
5 Apr 97	CAREFUL (re-mix) *Stress CDSTRX 79*	.........**44**	2
23 Jun 90	THE SAME SKY *Echo Chamber EST 2123*	.........**44**	2
13 Nov 93	GOD'S HOME MOVIE *Oxygen MCD 10935*	.........**42**	2

HORSLIPS
Ireland, male vocal / instrumental group (Albums: 3 Weeks)   pos/wks

30 Apr 77	THE BOOK OF INVASIONS – A CELTIC SYMPHONY		
	DJM DJF 20498	.........**39**	3

Johnny HORTON
US, male vocalist, b. 30 Apr 1925, d. 5 Nov 1960 (Singles: 15 Weeks)   pos/wks

26 Jun 59	THE BATTLE OF NEW ORLEANS *Philips PB 932* ▲	.........**16**	4
19 Jan 61	NORTH TO ALASKA *Philips PB 1062*	.........**23**	11

HOT ACTION COP
US, male vocal / instrumental group (Singles: 1 Week)   pos/wks

14 Jun 03	FEVER FOR THE FLAVA *Lava AT 0152CD*	.........**41**	1

HOT BLOOD *France, male instrumental group (Singles: 5 Weeks)*   pos/wks

9 Oct 76	SOUL DRACULA *Creole CR 132*	.........**32**	5

HOT BUTTER *US, production duo – Bill and*
Steve Jerome featuring Stan Free (Singles: 19 Weeks)   pos/wks

22 Jul 72 ●	POPCORN (re) *Pye International 7N 25583*	..........**5**	19

HOT CHOCOLATE   99   Top 500   *London-based band who were chart*
regulars throughout the 1970s and 1980s. Group founders were West Indian-
born Errol Brown (v) and Tony Wilson (b/v). The act had at least one hit every
year between 1970 and 1984 and 'You Sexy Thing' made the Top 10 in three
decades: 70s, 80s and 90s (Singles: 283 Weeks, Albums: 153 Weeks)   pos/wks

15 Aug 70 ●	LOVE IS LIFE *RAK 103*	..........**6**	12
6 Mar 71	YOU COULD HAVE BEEN A LADY *RAK 110*	.........**22**	9
28 Aug 71 ●	I BELIEVE (IN LOVE) *RAK 118*	..........**8**	11
28 Oct 72	YOU'LL ALWAYS BE A FRIEND *RAK 139*	.........**23**	8
14 Apr 73 ●	BROTHER LOUIE *RAK 149*	..........**7**	10
18 Aug 73	RUMOURS *RAK 157*	.........**44**	9
16 Mar 74 ●	EMMA *RAK 168*	..........**3**	10
30 Nov 74	CHERI BABE *RAK 188*	.........**31**	9
24 May 75	DISCO QUEEN *RAK 270*	.........**11**	7
9 Aug 75 ●	A CHILD'S PRAYER *RAK 212*	..........**7**	10
8 Nov 75 ●	YOU SEXY THING *RAK 221*	..........**2**	12
20 Mar 76	DON'T STOP IT NOW *RAK 230*	.........**11**	8
26 Jun 76	MAN TO MAN *RAK 238*	.........**14**	8
21 Aug 76	HEAVEN IS IN THE BACK SEAT OF MY CADILLAC *RAK 240*	..**25**	7
18 Jun 77 ★	SO YOU WIN AGAIN *RAK 259*	..........**1**	11
26 Nov 77 ●	PUT YOUR LOVE IN ME *RAK 266*	.........**10**	9
4 Mar 78	EVERY 1'S A WINNER *RAK 270*	.........**12**	11
2 Dec 78	I'LL PUT YOU TOGETHER AGAIN (FROM DEAR ANYONE)		
	RAK 286	.........**13**	11
19 May 79	MINDLESS BOOGIE *RAK 292*	.........**46**	5
28 Jul 79	GOING THROUGH THE MOTIONS *RAK 296*	.........**53**	4
3 May 80 ●	NO DOUBT ABOUT IT *RAK 310*	..........**2**	11
19 Jul 80	ARE YOU GETTING ENOUGH OF WHAT MAKES YOU HAPPY		
	RAK 318	.........**17**	7
13 Dec 80	LOVE ME TO SLEEP *RAK 324*	.........**50**	5
30 May 81	YOU'LL NEVER BE SO WRONG *RAK 331*	.........**52**	4
17 Apr 82 ●	GIRL CRAZY *RAK 341*	..........**7**	11
10 Jul 82 ●	IT STARTED WITH A KISS *RAK 344*	..........**5**	12
25 Sep 82	CHANCES *RAK 350*	.........**32**	5
7 May 83 ●	WHAT KINDA BOY YOU LOOKING FOR (GIRL) *RAK 357*	.........**10**	7
17 Sep 83	TEARS ON THE TELEPHONE *RAK 363*	.........**37**	5
4 Feb 84	I GAVE YOU MY HEART (DIDN'T I) *RAK 369*	.........**13**	10
17 Jan 87 ●	YOU SEXY THING (re-mix) *EMI 5592*	.........**10**	10
4 Apr 87	EVERY 1'S A WINNER (re-mix) *EMI 5607*	.........**69**	2
7 Mar 87	IT STARTED WITH A KISS (re-issue) *EMI CDEMCTS 7*	.........**31**	5
22 Nov 97 ●	YOU SEXY THING (re-issue) *EMI CDHOT 100*	..........**6**	8
14 Feb 98	IT STARTED WITH A KISS (2nd re-issue) *EMI CDHOT 101* 1	..**18**	3
15 Nov 75	HOT CHOCOLATE *RAK SRAK 516*	.........**34**	7
7 Aug 76	MAN TO MAN *RAK SRAK 522*	.........**32**	7
20 Nov 76	GREATEST HITS *RAK SRAK 524*	..........**6**	35
8 Apr 78	EVERY 1'S A WINNER *RAK SRAK 531*	.........**30**	7
15 Dec 79 ●	20 HOTTEST HITS *RAK EMTV 22*	..........**3**	19
25 Sep 82	MYSTERY *RAK SRAK 549*	.........**24**	7

21 Feb 87	★ THE VERY BEST OF HOT CHOCOLATE *RAK EMTV 42*	1	28
20 Mar 93	★ THEIR GREATEST HITS *EMI CDEMTV 73*	1	42

[1] Hot Chocolate featuring Errol Brown

HOT GOSSIP *See Sarah BRIGHTMAN*

HOT HOT HEAT *Canada, male vocal /*
instrumental group (Singles: 4 Weeks, Albums: 2 Weeks)   pos/wks

5 Apr 03	BANDAGES *B Unique BUN 045CDS*	25	3
9 Aug 03	NO, NOT NOW *Sub Pop W 615CD*	38	1
12 Apr 03	MAKE UP THE BREAKDOWN *WEA 5046646202*	35	2

HOT HOUSE
UK, male / female vocal / instrumental group (Singles: 3 Weeks)   pos/wks

14 Feb 87	DON'T COME TO STAY *Deconstruction CHEZ 1*	74	1
24 Sep 88	DON'T COME TO STAY (re-issue) *Deconstruction PB 42233*	70	2

HOT 'N' JUICY *See MOUSSE T*

HOT PANTZ *UK, female vocal duo (Singles: 1 Week)*   pos/wks

25 Dec 04	GIVE U ONE 4 CHRISTMAS *Tug CDSNOG 13*	64	1+

HOT RODS *See EDDIE and the HOT RODS*

HOT STREAK
US, male vocal / instrumental group (Singles: 8 Weeks)   pos/wks

10 Sep 83	BODY WORK *Polydor POSP 642*	19	8

HOTHOUSE FLOWERS *Ireland, male vocal /*
instrumental group (Singles: 36 Weeks, Albums: 51 Weeks)   pos/wks

14 May 88	DON'T GO *London LON 174*	11	8
23 Jul 88	I'M SORRY *London LON 187*	53	3
12 May 90	GIVE IT UP *London LON 258*	30	5
28 Jul 90	I CAN SEE CLEARLY NOW *London LON 269*	23	7
20 Oct 90	MOVIES *London LON 276*	68	2
13 Feb 93	EMOTIONAL TIME *London LONCD 335*	38	4
8 May 93	ONE TONGUE *London LOCDP 340*	45	3
19 Jun 93	ISN'T IT AMAZING *London LOCDP 343*	46	2
27 Nov 93	THIS IS IT (YOUR SOUL) *London LONCD 346*	67	1
16 May 98	YOU CAN LOVE ME NOW *London LONCD 410*	65	1
18 Jun 88	● PEOPLE *London LONLP 58*	2	19
16 Jun 90	● HOME *London 8281971*	5	21
20 Mar 93	● SONGS FROM THE RAIN *London 8283502*	7	11

HOTLEGS (see also 10CC; GODLEY and CREME)
UK, male vocal / instrumental group (Singles: 14 Weeks)   pos/wks

4 Jul 70	● NEANDERTHAL MAN *Fontana 6007 019*	2	14

The HOTSHOTS *UK, male vocal group (Singles: 15 Weeks)*   pos/wks

2 Jun 73	● SNOOPY VS THE RED BARON *Mooncrest MOON 5*	4	15

Steven HOUGHTON
UK, male actor / vocalist (Singles: 22 Weeks, Albums: 7 Weeks)   pos/wks

29 Nov 97	● WIND BENEATH MY WINGS *RCA 74321529272*	3	15
7 Mar 98	TRULY (re) *RCA 74321558552*	23	7
29 Nov 97	STEVEN HOUGHTON *RCA 74321542592*	21	7

HOUSE *See A HOUSE*

HOUSE ENGINEERS
UK, male vocal / instrumental duo (Singles: 2 Weeks)   pos/wks

5 Dec 87	GHOST HOUSE *Syncopate SY 8*	69	2

HOUSE OF GLASS (see also ECLIPSE; BINI &
MARTINI; GOODFELLAS featuring Lisa MILLETT) *Italy, male*
production duo – Gianni Bini and Paolo Martini (Singles: 1 Week)   pos/wks

14 Apr 01	DISCO DOWN *Azuli AZNY 138*	72	1

HOUSE OF LOVE *UK, male vocal / instrumental*
group (Singles: 21 Weeks, Albums: 14 Weeks)   pos/wks

22 Apr 89	NEVER *Fontana HOL 1*	41	2
18 Nov 89	I DON'T KNOW WHY I LOVE YOU *Fontana HOL 2*	41	3
3 Feb 90	SHINE ON *Fontana HOL 3*	20	4
7 Apr 90	BEATLES AND THE STONES *Fontana HOL 4*	36	4
26 Oct 91	THE GIRL WITH THE LONELIEST EYES *Fontana HOL 5*	58	1
2 May 92	FEEL *Fontana HOL 6*	45	3
27 Jun 92	YOU DON'T UNDERSTAND *Fontana HOL 7*	46	3
5 Dec 92	CRUSH ME *Fontana HOL 810*	67	1
10 Mar 90	● THE HOUSE OF LOVE *Fontana 8422931*	8	10
10 Nov 90	THE HOUSE OF LOVE *Fontana 8469781*	49	1
18 Jul 92	BABE RAINBOW *Fontana 5125492*	34	2
3 Jul 93	AUDIENCE WITH THE MIND *Fontana 5148802*	38	1

Identically titled albums are different

HOUSE OF PAIN
US, male rap group (Singles: 28 Weeks, Albums: 7 Weeks)   pos/wks

10 Oct 92	JUMP AROUND *Ruffness XLS 32*	32	4
22 May 93	● JUMP AROUND / TOP O' THE MORNING TO YA (re-issue) *Ruffness XL 43CD*	8	7
23 Oct 93	SHAMROCKS AND SHENANIGANS / WHO'S THE MAN *Ruffness XLS 46CD*	23	4
16 Jul 94	ON POINT *Ruffness XLS 52CD*	19	3
12 Nov 94	IT AIN'T A CRIME *Ruffness XLS 55CD1*	37	2
1 Jul 95	OVER THERE (I DON'T CARE) *Ruffness XLS 61CD1*	20	3
5 Oct 96	FED UP *Tommy Boy TBCD 7744*	68	1
20 Nov 04	JUMP AROUND (re-mix) *Tommy Boy 5046960110*	61	4
21 Nov 92	HOUSE OF PAIN *XL XLCD 111*	73	1
30 Jul 94	● SAME AS IT EVER WAS *XL XLCD 115*	8	6

HOUSE OF VIRGINISM (see also APOLLO presents HOUSE OF VIRGINISM)
Sweden, male vocal / instrumental group (Singles: 6 Weeks)   pos/wks

20 Nov 93	I'LL BE THERE FOR YOU (DOYA DODODO DOYA) *ffrr FCD 221*	29	3
30 Jul 94	REACHIN *ffrr FCD 238*	35	2
17 Feb 96	EXCLUSIVE *Logic 74321324102*	67	1

HOUSE OF ZEKKARIYAS *See WOMACK and WOMACK*

HOUSE TRAFFIC *Italy / UK, male / female*
vocal / production group (Singles: 3 Weeks)   pos/wks

4 Oct 97	EVERY DAY OF MY LIFE *Logic 74321249442*	24	3

The HOUSEMARTINS (see also The BEAUTIFUL SOUTH; BISCUIT BOY)
UK, male vocal / instrumental group – leaders Norman
Cook and Paul Heaton (Singles: 60 Weeks, Albums: 74 Weeks)   pos/wks

8 Mar 86	SHEEP (re) *Go Discs GOD 9*	54	4
7 Jun 86	● HAPPY HOUR *Go Discs GOD 11*	3	13
4 Oct 86	THINK FOR A MINUTE *Go Discs GOD 13*	18	8
6 Dec 86	★ CARAVAN OF LOVE *Go Discs GOD 16*	1	11
23 May 87	FIVE GET OVER EXCITED *Go Discs GOD 18*	11	6
5 Sep 87	ME AND THE FARMER *Go Discs GOD 19*	15	5
21 Nov 87	BUILD *Go Discs GOD 21*	15	8
23 Apr 88	THERE IS ALWAYS SOMETHING THERE TO REMIND ME *Go Discs GOD 22*	35	4
10 May 03	CHANGE THE WORLD *Free 2 Air 0146685 F2A* [1]	51	1
5 Jul 86	● LONDON 0 HULL 4 *Go Discs AGOLP 7*	3	41
27 Dec 86	THE HOUSEMARTINS' CHRISTMAS SINGLES BOX *Go Discs GOD 816*	84	1
3 Oct 87	● THE PEOPLE WHO GRINNED THEMSELVES TO DEATH *Go Discs AGOLP 9*	9	18
21 May 88	● NOW THAT'S WHAT I CALL QUITE GOOD *Go Discs AGOLP 11*	8	11
10 Apr 04	THE BEST OF THE HOUSEMARTINS *Go Discs 9818214*	29	3

[1] Dino Lenny vs The Housemartins

HOUSEMASTER BOYZ and the RUDE BOY OF HOUSE
US, male vocal / instrumental group (Singles: 14 Weeks)   pos/wks

9 May 87	● HOUSE NATION (re) *Magnetic Dance MAGD 1*	8	14

HOUSETRAP *See DJ SANDY vs HOUSETRAP*

HOUSTON featuring CHINGY, NATE DOGG & I-20
US, male rappers – Houston Summers, Howard Bailey Jr,
Nathan Hale and Bobby Sandimanie (Singles: 6 Weeks)   pos/wks

18 Sep 04	I LIKE THAT *Capitol CDCL 861*	11	6

Marques HOUSTON
US, male vocalist (Singles: 12 Weeks, Albums: 1 Week)   pos/wks

20 Mar 04	CLUBBIN' *Elektra E 7544CD* [1]	15	6

31 Jul 04	POP THAT BOOTY *East West E 7609CD* [2]	23	5
27 Nov 04	BECAUSE OF YOU *Atlantic AT 0188CD*	51	1
14 Feb 04	MH *Elektra 7559629352*	73	1

[1] Marques Houston featuring Joe Budden and Pied Piper [2] Marques Houston featuring Jermaine "JD" Dupri

Thelma HOUSTON
US, female vocalist (Singles: 22 Weeks) — pos/wks

5 Feb 77	DON'T LEAVE ME THIS WAY *Motown TMG 1060* ▲	13	8
27 Jun 81	IF YOU FEEL IT *RCA 77*	48	4
1 Dec 84	YOU USED TO HOLD ME SO TIGHT *MCA MCA 932*	49	8
21 Jan 95	DON'T LEAVE ME THIS WAY (re-recording) *Dynamo DYND 001*	35	2

Whitney HOUSTON 40 Top 500
Multi-award-winning, record-shattering vocalist, b. 9 Aug 1963, New Jersey, US. She has scored a record seven successive No.1s in the US. In 2001 and with sales exceeding 140 million behind her, she signed a record-breaking $100m recording deal. Best-selling single: 'I Will Always Love You' 1,355,055 (Singles: 315 Weeks, Albums: 383 Weeks) — pos/wks

16 Nov 85	★ SAVING ALL MY LOVE FOR YOU *Arista ARIST 640* ▲	1	16
25 Jan 86	● HOW WILL I KNOW *Arista ARIST 656* ▲	5	12
25 Jan 86	HOLD ME *Asylum EKR 32* [1]	44	5
12 Apr 86	● GREATEST LOVE OF ALL *Arista ARIST 658* ▲	8	11
23 May 87	★ I WANNA DANCE WITH SOMEBODY (WHO LOVES ME) *Arista RIS 1* ▲	1	16
22 Aug 87	DIDN'T WE ALMOST HAVE IT ALL *Arista RIS 31* ▲	14	8
14 Nov 87	● SO EMOTIONAL *Arista RIS 43* ▲	5	11
12 Mar 88	WHERE DO BROKEN HEARTS GO *Arista 109793* ▲	14	8
28 May 88	● LOVE WILL SAVE THE DAY *Arista 111516*	10	7
24 Sep 88	★ ONE MOMENT IN TIME *Arista 111613*	1	12
9 Sep 89	IT ISN'T, IT WASN'T, IT AIN'T NEVER GONNA BE *Arista 112545* [2]	29	5
20 Oct 90	● I'M YOUR BABY TONIGHT (re) *Arista 113594* ▲	5	10
22 Dec 90	ALL THE MAN THAT I NEED *Arista 114000* ▲	13	10
6 Jul 91	MY NAME IS NOT SUSAN *Arista 114510*	29	5
28 Sep 91	I BELONG TO YOU *Arista 114727*	54	2
14 Nov 92	★ I WILL ALWAYS LOVE YOU (re) *Arista 74321120657* ◆ ▲	1	29
20 Feb 93	● I'M EVERY WOMAN *Arista 74321131502*	4	11
24 Apr 93	● I HAVE NOTHING *Arista 74321146142*	3	10
31 Jul 93	RUN TO YOU *Arista 74321153332*	15	6
6 Nov 93	QUEEN OF THE NIGHT *Arista 74321169302*	14	5
22 Jan 94	SOMETHING IN COMMON *MCA MCSTD 1957* [3]	16	5
18 Nov 95	● EXHALE (SHOOP SHOOP) *Arista 74321332472* ▲	11	9
24 Feb 96	COUNT ON ME *Arista 74321345842* [4]	12	6
21 Dec 96	STEP BY STEP *Arista 74321449332*	13	13
29 Mar 97	I BELIEVE IN YOU AND ME *Arista 74321468602*	16	5
19 Dec 98	● WHEN YOU BELIEVE (re) *Columbia 6667522* [5]	4	13
6 Mar 99	● IT'S NOT RIGHT (BUT IT'S OK) *Arista 74321652402*	3	15
3 Jul 99	● MY LOVE IS YOUR LOVE *Arista 74321672862*	2	12
11 Dec 99	I LEARNED FROM THE BEST *Arista 74321723992*	19	11
17 Jun 00	● IF I TOLD YOU THAT (re) *Arista 74321766282* [6]	9	11
14 Oct 00	● COULD I HAVE THIS KISS FOREVER *Arista 74321795992* [7]	7	8
30 Dec 00	HEARTBREAK HOTEL *Arista 74321820572* [8]	25	5
9 Nov 02	WHATCHULOOKINAT *Arista 74321973062*	13	3
14 Dec 85	● WHITNEY HOUSTON *Arista 206978* ▲	2	119
13 Jun 87	★ WHITNEY *Arista 208141* ■	1	101
17 Nov 90	● I'M YOUR BABY TONIGHT *Arista 211039*	4	29
4 Jan 97	THE PREACHER'S WIFE (FILM SOUNDTRACK) *Arista 74321441252*	35	7
28 Nov 98	● MY LOVE IS YOUR LOVE *Arista 7822190372*	4	68
27 May 00	★ THE GREATEST HITS *Arista 74321757392* ■	1	56
16 Feb 02	LOVE WHITNEY *Arista 74321910272*	22	3

[1] Teddy Pendergrass with Whitney Houston [2] Aretha Franklin and Whitney Houston [3] Bobby Brown and Whitney Houston [4] Whitney Houston and CeCe Winans [5] Mariah Carey & Whitney Houston [6] Whitney Houston / George Michael [7] Whitney Houston and Enrique Iglesias [8] Whitney Houston featuring Faith Evans and Kelly Price

'I Will Always Love You' re-entered the chart in Dec 1993 and peaked at No.25

Adina HOWARD
US, female vocalist (Singles: 16 Weeks) — pos/wks

| 4 Mar 95 | FREAK LIKE ME (re) *East West A 4473CD* | 33 | 4 |
| 23 Nov 96 | ● WHAT'S LOVE GOT TO DO WITH IT *Interscope IND 97008* [1] | 2 | 12 |

[1] Warren G featuring Adina Howard

Billy HOWARD
UK, male comedian / vocalist (Singles: 12 Weeks) — pos/wks

| 13 Dec 75 | ● KING OF THE COPS *Penny Farthing PEN 892* | 6 | 12 |

Miki HOWARD
US, female vocalist (Singles: 2 Weeks) — pos/wks

| 26 May 90 | UNTIL YOU COME BACK (THAT'S WHAT I'M GONNA DO) *East West 7935* | 67 | 2 |

Nick HOWARD
Australia, male vocalist (Singles: 1 Week) — pos/wks

| 21 Jan 95 | EVERYBODY NEEDS SOMEBODY *Bell 74321220942* | 64 | 1 |

Robert HOWARD See Kym MAZELLE

Steve HOWE
(see also YES; GTR; ASIA; ANDERSON BRUFORD WAKEMAN HOWE)
UK, male vocalist / instrumentalist – guitar (Albums: 6 Weeks) — pos/wks

| 15 Nov 75 | BEGINNINGS *Atlantic K 50151* | 22 | 4 |
| 24 Nov 79 | THE STEVE HOWE ALBUM *Atlantic K 50621* | 68 | 2 |

Danny HOWELLS & Dick TREVOR featuring ERIRE
(see also SCIENCE DEPARTMENT featuring ERIRE)
UK, male production duo and female vocalist (Singles: 2 Weeks) — pos/wks

| 9 Oct 04 | DUSK TIL DAWN *C2 CDC 2004* | 37 | 2 |

HOWLIN' WOLF
US, male vocalist – Chester Burnette, b. 10 Jun 1910, d. 10 Jan 1976 (Singles: 5 Weeks) — pos/wks

| 4 Jun 64 | SMOKESTACK LIGHTNIN' *Pye International 7N 25244* | 42 | 5 |

The HUDDERSFIELD CHORAL SOCIETY
UK, male / female choir (Albums: 14 Weeks) — pos/wks

| 15 Mar 86 | ● THE HYMNS ALBUM *EMI EMTV 40* | 8 | 10 |
| 13 Dec 86 | THE CAROLS ALBUM *EMI EMTV 43* | 29 | 4 |

Al HUDSON
US, male vocalist (Singles: 20 Weeks) — pos/wks

9 Sep 78	DANCE, GET DOWN (FEEL THE GROOVE) / HOW DO YOU DO *ABC 4229*	57	4
15 Sep 79	YOU CAN DO IT *MCA 511* [1]	15	10
8 Dec 79	MUSIC *MCA 542* [2]	56	6

[1] Al Hudson and The Partners [2] One Way featuring Al Hudson

Lavine HUDSON
UK, female vocalist (Singles: 3 Weeks) — pos/wks

| 21 May 88 | INTERVENTION *Virgin VS 1067* | 57 | 3 |

HUDSON-FORD (see also The STRAWBS; The MONKS)
UK, male vocal / instrumental duo – Richard Hudson and John Ford (Singles: 20 Weeks) — pos/wks

18 Aug 73	● PICK UP THE PIECES *A&M AMS 7078*	8	9
16 Feb 74	BURN BABY BURN *A&M AMS 7096*	15	9
29 Jun 74	FLOATING IN THE WIND *A&M AMS 7116*	35	2

HUE AND CRY
UK, male vocal / instrumental duo – Pat and Greg Kane (Singles: 59 Weeks, Albums: 74 Weeks) — pos/wks

13 Jun 87	● LABOUR OF LOVE *Circa YR 4*	6	16
19 Sep 87	STRENGTH TO STRENGTH *Circa YR 6*	46	5
30 Jan 88	I REFUSE *Circa YR 8*	47	3
22 Oct 88	ORDINARY ANGEL *Circa YR 18*	42	6
28 Jan 89	LOOKING FOR LINDA *Circa YR 24*	15	9
6 May 89	VIOLENTLY (EP) *Circa YR 29*	21	6
30 Sep 89	SWEET INVISIBILITY *Circa YR 37*	55	3
25 May 91	MY SALT HEART *Circa YR 47*	47	3
3 Aug 91	LONG TERM LOVERS OF PAIN (EP) *Circa YR 71*	48	3
11 Jul 92	PROFOUNDLY YOURS *Fidelity FIDEL 1*	74	1
13 Mar 93	LABOUR OF LOVE (re-mix) *Circa HUESCD 1*	25	4
7 Nov 87	SEDUCED AND ABANDONED *Circa CIRCA 2*	22	11
10 Dec 88	REMOTE / THE BITTER SUITE *Circa CIRCA 6*	10	48
29 Jun 91	STARS CRASH DOWN *Circa CIRCA 15*	10	9
29 Aug 92	TRUTH AND LOVE *Fidelity FIDELCD 1*	33	2
10 Apr 93	LABOURS OF LOVE – THE BEST OF HUE AND CRY *Circa HACCD 1*	27	4

Tracks on Violently (EP): Violently / The Man with the Child In His Eyes / Calamity John. Tracks on Long Term Lovers of Pain (EP): Long Term Lovers of Pain / Heart of Saturday Night / Remembrance and Gold / Stars Crash Down 'Remote' re-entered the chart on 16 Dec 89 when it was made available with the free album 'The Bitter Suite'

The HUES CORPORATION
US, male / female vocal group (Singles: 16 Weeks)   pos/wks

27 Jul 74 ●	ROCK THE BOAT *RCA APBO 0232* ▲	6	10
19 Oct 74	ROCKIN' SOUL *RCA PB 10066*	24	6

HUFF & HERB (see also HUFF & PUFF) *UK, male DJ / production duo – Ben Langmaid and Jeff Patterson (Singles: 4 Weeks)*   pos/wks

6 Dec 97	FEELING GOOD *Planet 3 GXY 2018CD*	31	3
7 Nov 98	FEELING GOOD '98 (re-mix) *Planet 3 GXY 2020CD*	69	1

HUFF & PUFF (see also FAITHLESS; HUFF & HERB; OUR TRIBE / ONE TRIBE; ROLLO; DUSTED) *UK, male instrumental / production duo – Ben Langmaid and Roland Armstrong (Singles: 4 Weeks)*   pos/wks

2 Nov 96	HELP ME MAKE IT *Skyway SKYWCD 4*	31	2
21 Jun 97	HELP ME MAKE IT (re-mix) *Skyway SKYWCD 8*	37	2

David HUGHES *UK, male vocalist – Geoffrey Paddison, b. 11 Oct 1929, d. 19 Oct 1972 (Singles: 1 Week)*   pos/wks

21 Sep 56	BY THE FOUNTAINS OF ROME *Philips PB 606*	27	1

HUGO and LUIGI *US, orchestra and chorus – leaders Hugo Peretti, b. 6 Dec 1916, d. 1 May 1986, and Luigi Creatore (Singles: 2 Weeks)*   pos/wks

24 Jul 59	LA PLUME DE MA TANTE *RCA 1127*	29	2

Alan HULL (see also LINDISFARNE)
UK, male vocalist, b. 20 Feb 1945, d. 17 Nov 1995 (Albums: 3 Weeks)   pos/wks

28 Jul 73	PIPEDREAM *Charisma CAS 1069*	29	3

HUMAN LEAGUE   108 Top 500
Early-1980s UK pop sensation. Fronted by Phil Oakey (b. 2 Oct 1955, Sheffield) (v/syn) and joined in 1980 by vocalists Joanne Catherall and Susanne Sulley. The group, which also topped the US chart, won Best Newcomers at the 1982 Brit Awards. Best-selling single: 'Don't You Want Me' 1,430,000 (Singles: 156 Weeks, Albums: 263 Weeks)   pos/wks

3 May 80	HOLIDAY 80 (DOUBLE SINGLE) (re) *Virgin VS 105*	46	10
21 Jun 80	EMPIRE STATE HUMAN *Virgin VS 351*	62	2
28 Feb 81	BOYS AND GIRLS *Virgin VS 395*	48	4
2 May 81	THE SOUND OF THE CROWD *Virgin VS 416*	12	10
8 Aug 81 ●	LOVE ACTION (I BELIEVE IN LOVE) *Virgin VS 435*	3	13
10 Oct 81 ●	OPEN YOUR HEART *Virgin VS 453*	6	9
5 Dec 81 ★	DON'T YOU WANT ME *Virgin VS 466* ◆ ▲	1	13
9 Jan 82 ●	BEING BOILED *EMI FAST 4*	6	9
20 Nov 82 ●	MIRROR MAN *Virgin VS 522*	2	10
23 Apr 83 ●	(KEEP FEELING) FASCINATION *Virgin VS 569*	2	9
5 May 84	THE LEBANON (re) *Virgin VS 672*	11	7
30 Jun 84	LIFE ON YOUR OWN *Virgin VS 688*	16	6
17 Nov 84	LOUISE *Virgin VS 723*	13	10
23 Aug 86 ●	HUMAN *Virgin VS 880* ▲	8	8
22 Nov 86	I NEED YOUR LOVING *Virgin VS 900*	72	1
15 Oct 88	LOVE IS ALL THAT MATTERS *Virgin VS 1025*	41	5
18 Aug 90	HEART LIKE A WHEEL *Virgin VS 1262*	29	5
7 Jan 95 ●	TELL ME WHEN *East West YZ 882CD1*	6	9
18 Mar 95	ONE MAN IN MY HEART *East West YZ 904CD1*	13	8
17 Jun 95	FILLING UP WITH HEAVEN *East West YZ 944CD1*	36	2
28 Oct 95	DON'T YOU WANT ME (re-mix) *Virgin VSCDT 1557*	16	3
20 Jan 96	STAY WITH ME TONIGHT *East West EW 020CD*	40	2
11 Aug 01	ALL I EVER WANTED *Papillon BTFLYS 0012*	47	1
31 May 80	TRAVELOGUE *Virgin V 2160*	16	42
22 Aug 81	REPRODUCTION *Virgin V 2133*	34	23
24 Oct 81 ★	DARE *Virgin V 2192*	1	72
17 Jul 82 ●	LOVE AND DANCING *Virgin OVED 6* [1]	3	52
19 May 84 ●	HYSTERIA *Virgin V 2315*	3	18
20 Sep 86	CRASH *Virgin V 2391*	7	6
12 Nov 88 ●	GREATEST HITS *Virgin HLTV 1*	3	24
22 Sep 90	ROMANTIC? *Virgin V 2624*	24	2
4 Feb 95 ●	OCTOPUS *East West 4509987502*	6	12
11 Nov 95	GREATEST HITS *Virgin CDV 2792*	28	8
18 Aug 01	SECRETS *Papillon BTFLYCD 0019*	44	1
27 Sep 03	THE VERY BEST OF THE HUMAN LEAGUE *Virgin HLCDX 2*	24	3

[1] League Unlimited Orchestra

'Holiday 80 (Double Single)' only reached its peak position on re-entry in 1982. Tracks on double single: Being Boiled / Marianne / Rock and Roll – Nightclubbing / Dancevision

HUMAN MOVEMENT featuring Sophie MOLETA *UK, male production duo and Australia, female vocalist (Singles: 1 Week)*   pos/wks

3 Feb 01	LOVE HAS COME AGAIN *Renaissance Recordings RENCDS 005*	53	1

HUMAN NATURE *Australia, male vocal group (Singles: 7 Weeks)*   pos/wks

10 May 97	WISHES *Epic 6644485*	44	1
30 Aug 97	WHISPER YOUR NAME *Epic 6649465*	53	1
10 Mar 01	HE DON'T LOVE YOU *Epic 6708922*	18	4
30 Jun 01	WHEN WE WERE YOUNG *Epic 6713792*	43	1

HUMAN RESOURCE
Holland, male instrumental / production group (Singles: 14 Weeks)   pos/wks

14 Sep 91	DOMINATOR *R&S RSUK 4*	36	7
21 Dec 91	THE COMPLETE DOMINATOR (re-mix) *R&S RSUK 4X*	18	7

HUMANOID
(see also FUTURE SOUND OF LONDON; AMORPHOUS ANDROGYNOUS)
UK, male producer – Brian Dougans (Singles: 14 Weeks)   pos/wks

26 Nov 88	STAKKER HUMANOID *Westside WSR 12*	17	8
22 Apr 89	SLAM *Westside WSR 14*	54	2
8 Aug 92	STAKKER HUMANOID (re-issue) *Jumpin' + Pumpin' TOT 27*	40	3
3 Mar 01	STAKKER HUMANOID (re-mix) *Jumpin' + Pumpin' CDSTOT 43*	65	1

HUMATE *Germany, male production trio (Singles: 4 Weeks)*   pos/wks

30 Jan 99	LOVE STIMULATION *Deviant DVNT 22CDS*	18	4

HUMBLE PIE *UK, male vocal / instrumental group – includes Steve Marriott and Peter Frampton (Singles: 10 Weeks, Albums: 10 Weeks)*   pos/wks

23 Aug 69 ●	NATURAL BORN BUGIE *Immediate IM 082*	4	10
6 Sep 69	AS SAFE AS YESTERDAY IS *Immediate IMSP 025*	32	1
22 Jan 72	ROCKING AT THE FILLMORE *A&M AMLH 63506*	32	2
15 Apr 72	SMOKIN' *A&M AMLS 64342*	28	5
7 Apr 73	EAT IT *A&M AMLS 6004*	34	2

Engelbert HUMPERDINCK   76 Top 500   *Internationally popular cabaret entertainer and easy-on-the-ear vocalist, b. Arnold Dorsey, 2 May 1936, Madras, India. After a slow career start, an unlikely name change helped him to become one of the biggest-earning performers of the 1960s. This Vegas veteran was the UK's biggest-selling artist of 1967 and has reportedly amassed a personal fortune of £100m. Best-selling single: 'Release Me' 1,365,000 (Singles: 240 Weeks, Albums: 267 Weeks)*   pos/wks

26 Jan 67 ★	RELEASE ME *Decca F 12541* ◆	1	56
25 May 67 ●	THERE GOES MY EVERYTHING *Decca F 12610*	2	29
23 Aug 67 ★	THE LAST WALTZ *Decca F 12655* ◆	1	27
10 Jan 68 ●	AM I THAT EASY TO FORGET *Decca F 12722*	3	13
24 Apr 68 ●	A MAN WITHOUT LOVE *Decca F 12770*	2	15
25 Sep 68 ●	LES BICYCLETTES DE BELSIZE *Decca F 12834*	5	15
5 Feb 69 ●	THE WAY IT USED TO BE *Decca F 12879*	3	14
9 Aug 69	I'M A BETTER MAN (FOR HAVING LOVED YOU) *Decca F 12957*	15	13
15 Nov 69 ●	WINTER WORLD OF LOVE *Decca F 12980*	7	13
30 May 70	MY MARIE *Decca F 13032*	31	7
12 Sep 70	SWEETHEART (re) *Decca F 13068*	22	7
11 Sep 71	ANOTHER TIME, ANOTHER PLACE *Decca F 13212*	13	12
4 Mar 72	TOO BEAUTIFUL TO LAST *Decca F 13281*	14	10
20 Oct 73	LOVE IS ALL (re) *Decca F 13443*	44	4
30 Jan 99	QUANDO QUANDO QUANDO *The Hit Label HLC 15*	40	1
6 May 00	HOW TO WIN YOUR LOVE *Universal TV 8822682*	59	1
12 Jun 04	RELEASE ME (re-issue) *Universal TV 9819567*	51	1
20 May 67 ●	RELEASE ME *Decca SKL 4868*	6	58
25 Nov 67 ●	THE LAST WALTZ *Decca SKL 4901*	3	33
3 Aug 68 ●	A MAN WITHOUT LOVE *Decca SKL 4939*	3	45
1 Mar 69 ●	ENGELBERT *Decca SKL 4985*	3	8
6 Dec 69 ●	ENGELBERT HUMPERDINCK *Decca SKL 5030*	5	23
11 Jul 70	WE MADE IT HAPPEN *Decca SKL 5054*	17	11
18 Sep 71	ANOTHER TIME ANOTHER PLACE *Decca SKL 5097*	48	1
26 Feb 72	LIVE AT THE RIVIERA LAS VEGAS *Decca TXS 105*	45	1
21 Dec 74 ★	ENGELBERT HUMPERDINCK – HIS GREATEST HITS *Decca SKL 5198*	1	34
4 May 85	GETTING SENTIMENTAL *Telstar STAR 2254*	35	10
4 Apr 87	THE ENGELBERT HUMPERDINCK COLLECTION *Telstar STAR 2294*	35	9
10 Jun 95	LOVE UNCHAINED *EMI CDEMTV 94*	16	6

Singles re-entries are listed as (re), (2re), (3re).... which signifies that the hit re-entered the chart once, twice or three times...

8 Apr 00 ●	AT HIS VERY BEST *Universal Music TV 8449742*	5	14
20 Oct 01	I WANT TO WAKE UP WITH YOU *Universal Music TV 149462*	42	2
20 Mar 04 ●	HIS GREATEST LOVE SONGS *Universal TV 9817857*	4	12

HUNDRED REASONS *UK, male vocal / instrumental group (Singles: 15 Weeks, Albums: 9 Weeks)*   pos/wks

18 Aug 01	EP TWO *Columbia 6713922*	47	1
15 Dec 01	EP THREE *Columbia 6720782*	37	2
16 Mar 02	IF I COULD *Columbia 6724402*	19	3
18 May 02	SILVER *Columbia 6726642*	15	3
28 Sep 02	FALTER *Columbia 6731452*	38	1
15 Nov 03	THE GREAT TEST *Columbia 6743762*	29	2
28 Feb 04	WHAT YOU GET *Columbia 6745492*	30	2
16 Oct 04	HOW SOON IS NOW? *Sore Point 029CDS*	47	1
1 Jun 02 ●	IDEAS ABOVE OUR STATION *Columbia 5081482*	6	7
13 Mar 04	SHATTERPROOF IS NOT A CHALLENGE *Columbia 5136932*	20	2

Tracks on EP Two: Remmus / Soapbox / Shine. Tracks on EP Three: I'll Find You / Sunny / Slow Motion

Peter HUNNIGALE *See ARSENAL FC*

Geraldine HUNT *Canada, female vocalist (Singles: 5 Weeks)*   pos/wks

| 25 Oct 80 | CAN'T FAKE THE FEELING *Champagne FIZZ 501* | 44 | 5 |

Lisa HUNT *See LOVESTATION*

Marsha HUNT *US, female vocalist (Singles: 3 Weeks)*   pos/wks

| 21 May 69 | WALK ON GILDED SPLINTERS *Track 604 030* | 46 | 2 |
| 2 May 70 | KEEP THE CUSTOMER SATISFIED *Track 604 037* | 41 | 1 |

Tommy HUNT *US, male vocalist – Charles Hunt (Singles: 17 Weeks)*   pos/wks

11 Oct 75	CRACKIN' UP *Spark SRL 1132*	39	5
21 Aug 76	LOVING ON THE LOSING SIDE *Spark SRL 1146*	28	9
4 Dec 76	ONE FINE MORNING *Spark SRL 1148*	44	3

Alfonzo HUNTER *US, male rapper / instrumentalist (Singles: 2 Weeks)*   pos/wks

| 22 Feb 97 | JUST THE WAY *Cooltempo CDCOOL 326* | 38 | 2 |

Ian HUNTER (see also MOTT THE HOOPLE) *UK, male vocalist (Singles: 10 Weeks, Albums: 26 Weeks)*   pos/wks

3 May 75	ONCE BITTEN TWICE SHY *CBS 3194*	14	10
12 Apr 75	IAN HUNTER *CBS 80710*	21	15
29 May 76	ALL AMERICAN ALIEN BOY *CBS 81310*	29	4
5 May 79	YOU'RE NEVER ALONE WITH A SCHIZOPHRENIC *Chrysalis CHR 1214*	49	3
26 Apr 80	WELCOME TO THE CLUB *Chrysalis CJT 6*	61	2
29 Aug 81	SHORT BACK 'N' SIDES *Chrysalis CHR 1326*	79	2

Tab HUNTER *US, male actor / vocalist – Andrew Arthur Kelm (Singles: 30 Weeks)*   pos/wks

| 8 Feb 57 ★ | YOUNG LOVE *London HLD 8380* ▲ | 1 | 18 |
| 12 Apr 57 ● | NINETY-NINE WAYS (re) *London HLD 8410* | 5 | 12 |

Terry HUNTER *US, male DJ / producer (Singles: 1 Week)*   pos/wks

| 26 Jul 97 | HARVEST FOR THE WORLD *Delirious DELICD 4* | 48 | 1 |

HUNTER featuring Ruby TURNER *UK, male TV gladiator / vocalist and female vocalist (Singles: 1 Week)*   pos/wks

| 9 Dec 95 | SHAKABOOM! *Telstar HUNTCD 1* [1] | 64 | 1 |

[1] Hunter featuring Ruby Turner

Steve 'Silk' HURLEY (see also VOICES OF LIFE; JM SILK) *US, male producer (Singles: 9 Weeks)*   pos/wks

| 10 Jan 87 ★ | JACK YOUR BODY *DJ International LON 117* | 1 | 9 |

HURLEY & TODD *UK / South Africa, male production duo – Ross Hurley and Drew Todd (Singles: 2 Weeks)*   pos/wks

| 29 Apr 00 | SUNSTORM *Multiply CDMULTY 58* | 38 | 2 |

HURRAH! *UK, male vocal / instrumental group (Albums: 1 Week)*   pos/wks

| 28 Feb 87 | TELL GOD I'M HERE *Kitchenware 208 201* | 71 | 1 |

HURRICANE *See P DIDDY*

HURRICANE #1 *UK, male vocal / instrumental group (Singles: 17 Weeks, Albums: 3 Weeks)*   pos/wks

10 May 97	STEP INTO MY WORLD *Creation CRESCD 253*	29	2
5 Jul 97	JUST ANOTHER ILLUSION *Creation CRESCD 264*	35	2
6 Sep 97	CHAIN REACTION *Creation CRESCD 271*	30	2
1 Nov 97	STEP INTO MY WORLD (re-mix) *Creation CRESCD 276*	19	3
21 Feb 98	ONLY THE STRONGEST WILL SURVIVE *Creation CRESCD 285*	19	6
24 Oct 98	RISING SIGN *Creation CRESCD 303*	47	1
3 Apr 99	THE GREATEST HIGH *Creation CRESCD 309*	43	1
27 Sep 97	HURRICANE #1 *Creation CRECD 206*	11	2
1 May 99	ONLY THE STRONG WILL SURVIVE *Creation CRECD 237*	55	1

HURRICANES *See JOHNNY and the HURRICANES*

Phil HURTT *US, male vocalist (Singles: 5 Weeks)*   pos/wks

| 11 Nov 78 | GIVING IT BACK *Fantasy FTC 161* | 36 | 5 |

HUSAN *See BHANGRA KNIGHTS vs HUSAN*

HÜSKER DÜ (see also BOB MOULD; SUGAR) *US, male vocal / instrumental group (Albums: 1 Week)*   pos/wks

| 14 Feb 87 | WAREHOUSE: SONGS AND STORIES *Warner Bros. 925 5441* | 72 | 1 |

HUSTLERS CONVENTION featuring Dave LAUDAT and Ondrea DUVERNEY (see also FULL INTENTION; DISCO TEX presents CLOUDBURST; Michael GRAY; SEX-O-SONIQUE) *UK, male production duo and male vocalist and US, female vocalist (Singles: 1 Week)*   pos/wks

| 20 May 95 | DANCE TO THE MUSIC *Stress CDSTR 53* | 71 | 1 |

Willie HUTCH *US, male vocalist – Willie Hutchinson (Singles: 8 Weeks)*   pos/wks

| 4 Dec 82 | IN AND OUT *Motown TMG 1285* | 51 | 7 |
| 6 Jul 85 | KEEP ON JAMMIN' *Motown ZB 40173* | 73 | 1 |

June HUTTON and Axel STORDAHL *US, female vocalist, b. 11 Aug 1921, d. 2 May 1973, and orchestra leader (Singles: 7 Weeks)*   pos/wks

| 7 Aug 53 ● | SAY YOU'RE MINE AGAIN (re) *Capitol CL 13918* | 6 | 7 |

Act were joined by 'The Boys Next Door' on this hit

HYBRID *UK, male production trio (Singles: 5 Weeks, Albums: 1 Week)*   pos/wks

10 Jul 99	FINISHED SYMPHONY *Distinctive DISNCD 52*	58	1
11 Sep 99	IF I SURVIVE *Distinctive DISNCD 55* [1]	52	1
3 Jun 00	KID 2000 *Virgin / EMI VTS CD2* [2]	32	2
20 Sep 03	TRUE TO FORM *Distinctive DISNCD 111* [3]	59	1
25 Sep 99	WIDE ANGLE *Distinctive DISNCD 54*	45	1

[1] Hybrid featuring Julee Cruise [2] Hybrid featuring Chrissie Hynde [3] Hybrid featuring Peter Cook

HYDRAULIC DOGS *See DJD presents HYDRAULIC DOGS*

Brian HYLAND *US, male vocalist (Singles: 72 Weeks)*   pos/wks

7 Jul 60 ●	ITSY BITSY TEENIE WEENIE YELLOW POLKADOT BIKINI *London HLR 9161* ▲	8	13
20 Oct 60	FOUR LITTLE HEELS *London HLR 9203*	29	6
10 May 62 ●	GINNY COME LATELY *HMV POP 1013*	5	15
2 Aug 62 ●	SEALED WITH A KISS *HMV POP 1051*	3	15
8 Nov 62	WARMED OVER KISSES *HMV POP 1079*	28	6
27 Mar 71	GYPSY WOMAN (re) *Uni UN 530*	42	6
28 Jun 75 ●	SEALED WITH A KISS (re-issue) *ABC 4059*	7	11

Sheila HYLTON *Jamaica, female vocalist (Singles: 12 Weeks)*   pos/wks

| 15 Sep 79 | BREAKFAST IN BED *United Artists BP 304* | 57 | 5 |
| 17 Jan 81 | THE BED'S TOO BIG WITHOUT YOU *Island WIP 6671* | 35 | 7 |

Phyllis HYMAN *US, female vocalist, b. 6 Jul 1950,*
d. 30 Jun 1995 (Singles: 9 Weeks, Albums: 1 Week) pos/wks

16 Feb 80	YOU KNOW HOW TO LOVE ME *Arista ARIST 323*	47	6
12 Sep 81	YOU SURE LOOK GOOD TO ME *Arista ARIST 424*	56	3
20 Sep 86	LIVING ALL ALONE *Philadelphia International PHIL 4001*	97	1

Dick HYMAN TRIO *US, male instrumental trio –*
leader Dick Hyman – keyboards (Singles: 10 Weeks) pos/wks

| 16 Mar 56 ● | THEME FROM 'THE THREEPENNY OPERA' *MGM 890* | 9 | 10 |

Chrissie HYNDE (see also The PRETENDERS)
US, female vocalist / instrumentalist (Singles: 41 Weeks) pos/wks

3 Aug 85 ★	I GOT YOU BABE *DEP International DEP 20* [1]	1	13
18 Jun 88 ●	BREAKFAST IN BED *DEP International DEP 29* [1]	6	11
12 Oct 91	SPIRITUAL HIGH (STATE OF INDEPENDENCE) *Arista 114528* [2]	66	2
23 Jan 93	SPIRITUAL HIGH (STATE OF INDEPENDENCE) (re-mix) *Arista 74321127712* [2]	47	2
18 Mar 95 ★	LOVE CAN BUILD A BRIDGE *London COCD 1* [3]	1	8
3 Jun 00	KID 2000 *Virgin / EMI VTS CD2* [4]	32	2
7 Feb 04	STRAIGHT AHEAD *Direction 6746222* [5]	29	3

[1] UB40 featuring Chrissie Hynde [2] Moodswings featuring Chrissie Hynde
[3] Cher, Chrissie Hynde and Neneh Cherry with Eric Clapton [4] Hybrid featuring
Chrissie Hynde [5] Tube and Berger featuring Chrissie Hynde

HYPER GO GO *UK, male instrumental / production duo –*
Jamie Diplock and Alex Bell (Singles: 15 Weeks) pos/wks

22 Aug 92	HIGH *Deconstruction 74321110497*	30	5
31 Jul 93	NEVER LET GO *Positiva CDTIV 3*	45	3
5 Feb 94	RAISE *Positiva CDTIV 9*	36	2
26 Nov 94	IT'S ALRIGHT *Positiva CDTIV 20*	49	1
6 Apr 96	DO WATCHA DO *Avex UK AVEXCD 24* [1]	54	1
12 Oct 96	HIGH (re-mix) *Distinctive DISNCD 24*	32	2
12 Apr 97	DO WATCHA DO (re-mix) *Distinctive DISNCD 28* [1]	60	1

[1] Hyper Go Go and Adeva

HYPERLOGIC
UK, male instrumental / production trio (Singles: 3 Weeks) pos/wks

| 29 Jul 95 | ONLY ME *Systematic SYSCD 15* | 35 | 2 |
| 9 May 98 | ONLY ME (re-mix) *Tidy Trax TIDY 113CD1* | 48 | 1 |

HYPERSTATE
UK, male / female vocal / instrumental duo (Singles: 1 Week) pos/wks

| 6 Feb 93 | TIME AFTER TIME *M&G MAGCD 34* | 71 | 1 |

HYPNOSIS (see also BLOWING FREE; HARMONIUM; IN TUNE; JAMES
BOYS; RAINDANCE; SCHOOL OF EXCELLENCE) *UK, male production /*
instrumental duo – Stewart and Bradley Palmer (Albums: 16 Weeks) pos/wks

| 17 Aug 96 | VOICES OF TRANQUILITY *Dino DINCD 123* | 16 | 12 |
| 15 Mar 97 | VOICES OF TRANQUILITY – VOLUME 2 *Dino DINCD 135* | 32 | 4 |

HYPNOTIST (see also R.H.C.)
UK, male producer – Caspar Pound (Singles: 5 Weeks) pos/wks

| 28 Sep 91 | THE HOUSE IS MINE *Rising High RSN 4* | 65 | 2 |
| 21 Dec 91 | THE HARDCORE EP *Rising High RSN 13* | 68 | 3 |

Tracks on The Hardcore EP: Hardcore U Know the Score / The Ride / Night of the
Livin' E Heads / God of the Universe

HYPO PSYCHO
UK / US, male vocal / instrumental group (Singles: 1 Week) pos/wks

| 24 Jul 04 | PUBLIC ENEMY NO. 1 *Believe / Snapper SMASCD 059* | 53 | 1 |

HYSTERIC EGO
UK, male producer – Rob White (Singles: 8 Weeks) pos/wks

31 Aug 96	WANT LOVE *WEA WEA 070CD*	28	4
21 Jun 97	MINISTRY OF LOVE *WEA WEA 094CD*	39	2
28 Feb 98	WANT LOVE – THE REMIXES *WEA WEA 150CD*	46	1
13 Feb 99	TIME TO GET BACK *WEA WEA 198CD*	50	1

The HYSTERICS
UK, male vocal / instrumental group (Singles: 5 Weeks) pos/wks

| 12 Dec 81 | JINGLE BELLS LAUGHING ALL THE WAY *Record Delivery KA 5* | 44 | 5 |

HYSTERIX
UK, male / female vocal / instrumental group (Singles: 4 Weeks) pos/wks

| 7 May 94 | MUST BE THE MUSIC *Deconstruction 74321207362* | 40 | 3 |
| 18 Feb 95 | EVERYTHING *Deconstruction 74321236882* | 65 | 1 |

I AM KLOOT *UK, male vocal / instrumental*
group (Singles: 2 Weeks, Albums: 1 Week) pos/wks

21 Jun 03	LIFE IN A DAY *Echo ECSCD 140*	43	1
20 Sep 03	3 FEET TALL *Echo ECDCD 143*	46	1
27 Sep 03	I AM KLOOT *Echo ECHCD 46*	68	1

I DREAM featuring FRANKIE & CALVIN (see also S CLUB JUNIORS)
UK, male / female actors / vocal group (Singles: 5 Weeks) pos/wks

| 27 Nov 04 | DREAMING *19 9868872* | 19 | 5+ |

I KAMANCHI *UK, male production duo (Singles: 1 Week)* pos/wks

| 14 Jun 03 | NEVER CAN TELL / SOUL BEAT CALLING *Full Cycle FCY 052* | 69 | 1 |

I-LEVEL *UK, male vocal / instrumental*
group (Singles: 9 Weeks, Albums: 4 Weeks) pos/wks

16 Apr 83	MINEFIELD *Virgin VS 563*	52	6
18 Jun 83	TEACHER *Virgin VS 595*	56	3
9 Jul 83	I-LEVEL *Virgin V 2270*	50	4

I MONSTER *UK, male production / vocal duo –*
Dean Honer and Jarrod Gosling (Singles: 6 Weeks) pos/wks

| 16 Jun 01 | DAYDREAM IN BLUE *Instant Karma KARMA 7CD* | 20 | 6 |

IQ *UK, male vocal / instrumental group (Albums: 1 Week)* pos/wks

| 22 Jun 85 | THE WAKE *Sahara SAH 136* | 72 | 1 |

I-20 *See* HOUSTON featuring CHINGY, NATE DOGG & I-20

Janis IAN *US, female vocalist – Janis Fink (Singles: 10 Weeks)* pos/wks

| 17 Nov 79 | FLY TOO HIGH *CBS 7936* | 44 | 7 |
| 28 Jun 80 | THE OTHER SIDE OF THE SUN *CBS 8611* | 44 | 3 |

IAN VAN DAHL (see also DEE DEE)
Belgium, male / female production / vocal group – leader
AnneMie Coenen (Singles: 49 Weeks, Albums: 7 Weeks) pos/wks

21 Jul 01 ●	CASTLES IN THE SKY *Nulife 74321867142*	3	16
22 Dec 01 ●	WILL I *Nulife 74321903402*	5	13
1 Jun 02 ●	REASON *Nulife 74321938722*	8	8
12 Oct 02	TRY *Nulife 74321967942*	15	5
1 Nov 03	I CAN'T LET YOU GO *Nulife 82876570712*	20	4
17 Jul 04	BELIEVE *Nulife 82876626532*	27	3
8 Jun 02 ●	ACE *Nulife 74321934812*	7	7

ICE CUBE *US, male rapper – O'Shea Jackson*
(Singles: 26 Weeks, Albums: 11 Weeks) pos/wks

27 Mar 93	IT WAS A GOOD DAY *Fourth & Broadway BRCD 270*	27	4
7 Aug 93	CHECK YO SELF *Fourth & Broadway BRCD 283* [1]	36	4
11 Sep 93	WICKED *Fourth & Broadway BRCD 282*	62	1

18 Dec 93	REALLY DOE Fourth & Broadway BRCD 302	66	1
26 Mar 94	YOU KNOW HOW WE DO IT (re) Fourth & Broadway BRCD 303	41	5
27 Aug 94	BOP GUN (ONE NATION) Fourth & Broadway BRCD 308 [2]	22	3
11 Mar 95	HAND OF THE DEAD BODY Virgin America VUSCD 88 [3]	41	2
15 Apr 95	NATURAL BORN KILLAZ Death Row A 8197CD [4]	45	2
22 Mar 97	THE WORLD IS MINE Jive JIVECD 419	60	1
11 Dec 04 ●	YOU CAN DO IT All Around the World CDGLOBE 396 [5]	2	3+
28 Jul 90	AMERIKKKA'S MOST WANTED Fourth & Broadway BRLP 551	48	5
9 Mar 91	KILL AT WILL Fourth & Broadway BRLM 572	66	3
5 Dec 92	THE PREDATOR Fourth & Broadway BRCD 592 ▲	73	1
18 Dec 93	LETHAL INJECTION Fourth & Broadway BRCD 609	52	1
1 Apr 00	WAR & PEACE – VOL. II (THE PEACE DISC) Priority CDPTY 183	56	1

[1] Ice Cube featuring Das EFX [2] Ice Cube featuring George Clinton [3] Scarface featuring Ice Cube [4] Dr Dre and Ice Cube [5] Ice Cube featuring Mack 10 + Ms Toi

ICE MC UK, male rapper – Ian Campbell (Singles: 5 Weeks) pos/wks

6 Aug 94	THINK ABOUT THE WAY (BOM DIGI DIGI BOM ...) WEA YZ 829CD	42	2
8 Apr 95	IT'S A RAINY DAY Eternal YZ 902CD	73	1
14 Sep 96	BOM DIGI BOM (THINK ABOUT THE WAY) (re-issue) Eternal WEA 073CD	38	2

ICE-T US, male rapper – Tracy Morrow (Singles: 29 Weeks, Albums: 15 Weeks) pos/wks

18 Mar 89	HIGH ROLLERS Sire W 7574	63	2
17 Feb 90	YOU PLAYED YOURSELF Sire W 9994	64	2
29 Sep 90	SUPERFLY 1990 Capitol CL 586 [1]	48	3
8 May 93	I AIN'T NEW TA THIS Rhyme Syndicate SYNDD 1	62	2
18 Dec 93	THAT'S HOW I'M LIVIN' Rhyme Syndicate SYNDD 2	21	6
9 Apr 94	GOTTA LOTTA LOVE Rhyme Syndicate SYNDD 3	24	4
10 Dec 94	BORN TO RAISE HELL Fox 74321230152 [2]	47	2
1 Jun 96	I MUST STAND Rhyme Syndicate SYNDD 5	23	3
7 Dec 96	THE LANE Rhyme Syndicate SYNDD 6	18	5
21 Oct 89	THE ICEBERG/FREEDOM OF SPEECH Warner Bros. WX 316	42	2
25 May 91	OG – ORIGINAL GANGSTER Sire WX 412	38	4
3 Apr 93	HOME INVASION Rhyme Syndicate RSYND 1	15	7
8 Jun 96	VI: RETURN OF THE REAL Virgin RSYND 3	26	2

[1] Curtis Mayfield and Ice-T [2] Motörhead / Ice-T / Whitfield Crane

ICEBERG SLIMM UK, male rapper – Duane Dyer (Singles: 3 Weeks) pos/wks

| 7 Oct 00 | NURSERY RHYMES Polydor 5877632 | 37 | 2 |
| 6 Nov 04 | STARSHIP V2 ARV 5029063 [1] | 73 | 1 |

[1] Iceberg Slimm featuring Coree

ICEHOUSE Australia, male vocal / instrumental group (Singles: 28 Weeks, Albums: 7 Weeks) pos/wks

5 Feb 83	HEY LITTLE GIRL Chrysalis CHS 2670	17	10
23 Apr 83	STREET CAFE Chrysalis COOL 1	62	4
3 May 86	NO PROMISES Chrysalis CHS 2978	72	1
29 Aug 87	CRAZY (re) Chrysalis CHS 3156	38	9
14 May 88	ELECTRIC BLUE Chrysalis CHS 3239	53	4
5 Mar 83	LOVE IN MOTION Chrysalis CHR 1390	64	6
2 Apr 88	MAN OF COLOURS Chrysalis CHR 1592	93	1

The ICICLE WORKS UK, male vocal / instrumental group – lead vocal Ian McNabb (Singles: 28 Weeks, Albums: 19 Weeks) pos/wks

24 Dec 83	LOVE IS A WONDERFUL COLOUR Beggars Banquet BEG 99	15	8
10 Mar 84	BIRDS FLY (WHISPER TO A SCREAM) / IN THE CAULDRON OF LOVE Beggars Banquet BEG 108	53	4
26 Jul 86	UNDERSTANDING JANE Beggars Banquet BEG 160	52	3
4 Oct 86	WHO DO YOU WANT FOR YOUR LOVE? Beggars Banquet BEG 172	54	4
14 Feb 87	EVANGELINE Beggars Banquet BEG 181	53	4
30 Apr 88	LITTLE GIRL LOST Beggars Banquet BEG 215	59	4
17 Mar 90	MOTORCYCLE RIDER Epic WORKS 100	73	1
31 Mar 84	THE ICICLE WORKS Beggars Banquet BEGA 50	24	4
28 Sep 85	THE SMALL PRICE OF A BICYCLE Beggars Banquet BEGA 61	55	4
1 Mar 86	SEVEN SINGLES DEEP Beggars Banquet BEGA 71	52	2
21 Mar 87	IF YOU WANT TO DEFEAT YOUR ENEMY SING HIS SONG Beggars Banquet BEGA 78	28	4
14 May 88	BLIND Beggars Banquet IWA 2	40	3
5 Sep 92	THE BEST OF THE ICICLE WORKS Beggars Banquet BEGA 124CD	60	1

ICON UK, male / female vocal / instrumental duo (Singles: 1 Week) pos/wks

| 15 Jun 96 | TAINTED LOVE Eternal WEA 057CD | 51 | 1 |

IDEAL UK, male producer – Jon da Silva (Singles: 2 Weeks) pos/wks

| 6 Aug 94 | HOT Cleveland City CLECD 13019 | 49 | 2 |

IDEAL U.S. featuring LIL' MO US, male vocal group and female vocalist (Singles: 3 Weeks) pos/wks

| 23 Sep 00 | WHATEVER Virgin VUSCD 172 | 31 | 3 |

The IDES OF MARCH US, male vocal / instrumental group (Singles: 9 Weeks) pos/wks

| 6 Jun 70 | VEHICLE Warner Bros. WB 7378 | 31 | 9 |

Eric IDLE featuring Richard WILSON (see also MONTY PYTHON) UK, male actors / vocalists (Singles: 3 Weeks) pos/wks

| 17 Dec 94 | ONE FOOT IN THE GRAVE Victa CDVICTA 1 | 50 | 3 |

IDLEWILD UK, male vocal / instrumental group (Singles: 30 Weeks, Albums: 13 Weeks) pos/wks

9 May 98	A FILM FOR THE FUTURE Food CDFOOD 111	53	1
25 Jul 98	EVERYONE SAYS YOU'RE SO FRAGILE Food CDFOOD 113	47	1
24 Oct 98	I'M A MESSAGE Food CDFOOD 114	41	1
13 Feb 99	WHEN I ARGUE I SEE SHAPES Food CDFOOD 116	19	2
2 Oct 99	LITTLE DISCOURAGE Food CDFOOD 124	24	2
8 Apr 00	ACTUALLY IT'S DARKNESS Food CDFOOD 127	23	3
24 Jun 00	THESE WOODEN IDEAS Food CDFOOD 132	32	3
28 Oct 00	ROSEABILITY Food CDFOODS 134	38	2
4 May 02 ●	YOU HELD THE WORLD IN YOUR ARMS Parlophone CDRS 6575	9	4
13 Jul 02	AMERICAN ENGLISH Parlophone CDRS 6582	15	7
2 Nov 02	LIVE IN A HIDING PLACE Parlophone CDRS 6587	26	2
22 Feb 03	A MODERN WAY OF LETTING GO Parlophone CDR 6598	28	2
7 Nov 98	HOPE IS IMPORTANT Food FOODCD 28	53	1
22 Apr 00	100 BROKEN WINDOWS Food FOODCD 32	15	4
27 Jul 02 ●	THE REMOTE PART Parlophone 5402430	3	8

Billy IDOL (324 Top 500)
Snarling rock 'n' roll rebel of the 1980s. Former vocalist of punk hitmakers Generation X, b. William Broad, 30 Nov 1955, Middlesex, UK. He had his greatest success in the US, where four singles reached the Top 10 and 'Mony Mony' reached No.1 (Singles: 106 Weeks, Albums: 100 Weeks) pos/wks

11 Sep 82	HOT IN THE CITY Chrysalis CHS 2625	58	4
24 Mar 84	REBEL YELL Chrysalis IDOL 2	62	4
30 Jun 84	EYES WITHOUT A FACE Chrysalis IDOL 3	18	11
29 Sep 84	FLESH FOR FANTASY Chrysalis IDOL 4	54	3
13 Jul 85 ●	WHITE WEDDING Chrysalis IDOL 5	6	15
14 Sep 85 ●	REBEL YELL (re-issue) Chrysalis IDOL 6	6	12
4 Oct 86	TO BE A LOVER Chrysalis IDOL 8	22	8
7 Mar 87	DON'T NEED A GUN Chrysalis IDOL 9	26	5
13 Jun 87	SWEET SIXTEEN Chrysalis IDOL 10	17	9
3 Oct 87 ●	MONY MONY Chrysalis IDOL 11 ▲	7	10
16 Jan 88	HOT IN THE CITY (re-mix) Chrysalis IDOL 12	13	9
13 Aug 88	CATCH MY FALL Chrysalis IDOL 13	63	3
28 Apr 90	CRADLE OF LOVE Chrysalis IDOL 14	34	4
11 Aug 90	L.A. WOMAN Chrysalis IDOL 15	70	2
22 Dec 90	PRODIGAL BLUES Chrysalis IDOL 16	47	4
26 Jun 93	SHOCK TO THE SYSTEM Chrysalis CDCHS 3994	30	3
10 Sep 94	SPEED Fox 74321223472	47	2
8 Jun 85 ●	VITAL IDOL Chrysalis CUX 1502	7	34
28 Sep 85	REBEL YELL Chrysalis CHR 1450	36	11
1 Nov 86	WHIPLASH SMILE Chrysalis CDL 1514	8	20
2 Jul 88	IDOL SONGS: 11 OF THE BEST Chrysalis BILTVD 1	2	25
12 May 90	CHARMED LIFE Chrysalis CHR 1735	15	8
10 Jul 93	CYBERPUNK Chrysalis CDCHR 6000	20	2

The IDOLS UK, male / female vocal group (Singles: 5 Weeks) pos/wks

| 27 Dec 03 ● | HAPPY XMAS (WAR IS OVER) S 82876583822 | 5 | 5 |

Frank IFIELD (261 Top 500)
Early 60s superstar, b. 30 Nov 1937, Coventry, UK, and raised in Australia. This pop vocalist / yodeller had four No.1s in 12 months with revivals of US standards. Unlike many of his early 1960s UK contemporaries, his records also did well internationally. Best-selling single: 'I Remember You' 1,096,000 (Singles: 163 Weeks, Albums: 83 Weeks) pos/wks

| 19 Feb 60 | LUCKY DEVIL (re) Columbia DB 4399 | 22 | 8 |
| 29 Sep 60 | GOTTA GET A DATE Columbia DB 4496 | 49 | 1 |

			pos/wks
5 Jul 62 ★	I REMEMBER YOU *Columbia DB 4856* ◆	1	28
25 Oct 62 ★	LOVESICK BLUES *Columbia DB 4913*	1	17
24 Jan 63 ★	THE WAYWARD WIND *Columbia DB 4960*	1	13
11 Apr 63 ●	NOBODY'S DARLIN' BUT MINE *Columbia DB 7007*	4	16
27 Jun 63 ★	CONFESSIN' (THAT I LOVE YOU) *Columbia DB 7062*	1	16
17 Oct 63	MULE TRAIN *Columbia DB 7131*	22	6
9 Jan 64 ●	DON'T BLAME ME *Columbia DB 7184*	8	13
23 Apr 64	ANGRY AT THE BIG OAK TREE *Columbia DB 7263*	25	8
23 Jul 64	I SHOULD CARE *Columbia DB 7319*	33	3
1 Oct 64	SUMMER IS OVER *Columbia DB 7355*	25	6
19 Aug 65	PARADISE *Columbia DB 7655*	26	9
23 Jun 66	NO ONE WILL EVER KNOW *Columbia DB 7940*	25	4
8 Dec 66	CALL HER YOUR SWEETHEART *Columbia DB 8078*	24	11
7 Dec 91	SHE TAUGHT ME HOW TO YODEL *EMI 7YODEL 1* [1]	40	4
16 Feb 63 ●	I'LL REMEMBER YOU *Columbia 33SX 1467*	3	36
21 Sep 63 ●	BORN FREE *Columbia 33SX 1462*	3	32
28 Mar 64 ●	BLUE SKIES *Columbia 55SX 1588*	10	12
19 Dec 64 ●	GREATEST HITS *Columbia 33SX 1633*	9	3

[1] Frank Ifield featuring The Backroom Boys

Enrique IGLESIAS (395) Top 500
Multi-award winning Latin superstar, b. 8 May 1975, Madrid, Spain – son of Julio Iglesias (together they are the only father / son to both top the UK singles chart). In the last three years of the 20th century, he sold 13 million albums and earned 132 platinum discs around the globe (Singles: 89 Weeks, Albums: 84 Weeks)

			pos/wks
11 Sep 99 ●	BAILAMOS *Interscope IND 97131* ▲	4	9
18 Dec 99	RHYTHM DIVINE *Interscope 4972242*	45	2
14 Oct 00 ●	COULD I HAVE THIS KISS FOREVER *Arista 74321795992* [1]	7	8
2 Feb 02 ★	HERO *Interscope IND 97671* [2] ■	1	19
27 Apr 02	ESCAPE (IMPORT) *Interscope 4976922* [2]	71	2
25 May 02 ●	ESCAPE *Interscope 4977062* [2]	3	14
7 Sep 02	LOVE TO SEE YOU CRY *Interscope IND 97760*	12	7
7 Dec 02	MAYBE *Interscope 4978222* [2]	12	9
26 Apr 03	TO LOVE A WOMAN *Mercury 0779082* [3]	19	4
29 Nov 03	ADDICTED *Interscope 9814327*	11	6
20 Mar 04 ●	NOT IN LOVE *Interscope 9862022* [4]	5	9
26 Jan 02 ★	ESCAPE *Interscope 4931822*	1	71
6 Dec 03	7 *Interscope / Polydor 9861477*	13	13

[1] Whitney Houston and Enrique Iglesias [2] Enrique [3] Lionel Richie featuring Enrique Iglesias [4] Enrique featuring Kelis

Julio IGLESIAS (255) Top 500
Spain's most successful vocalist of all time with reported world sales of more than 225 million albums; b. 23 Sep 1943, Madrid, Spain. Suave singer was still adding to his hits and awards in the 21st century, and his son Enrique is one of the world's top-selling Latin artists (Singles: 75 Weeks, Albums: 175 Weeks)

			pos/wks
24 Oct 81 ★	BEGIN THE BEGUINE (VOLVER A EMPEZAR) *CBS A 1612*	1	14
6 Mar 82 ●	QUIEREME MUCHO (YOURS) *CBS A 1939*	3	9
9 Oct 82	AMOR *CBS A 2801*	32	7
9 Apr 83	HEY! *CBS JULIO 1*	31	7
7 Apr 84	TO ALL THE GIRLS I'VE LOVED BEFORE *CBS A 4252* [1]	17	10
7 Jul 84	ALL OF YOU *CBS A 4522* [2]	43	8
6 Aug 88 ●	MY LOVE *CBS JULIO 2* [3]	5	11
4 Jun 94	CRAZY (re) *Columbia 6603695*	43	5
26 Nov 94	FRAGILE (re) *Columbia 6610192*	53	4
7 Nov 81	DE NINA A MUJER *CBS 85063*	43	5
28 Nov 81 ●	BEGIN THE BEGUINE *CBS 85462*	5	28
16 Oct 82	AMOR *CBS 25103*	14	14
2 Jul 83	JULIO *CBS 10038*	5	17
1 Sep 84	1100 BEL AIR PLACE *CBS 86308*	14	14
19 Oct 85	LIBRA *CBS 26623*	61	4
3 Sep 88	NON STOP *CBS 4609901*	33	14
1 Dec 90	STARRY NIGHT *CBS 4667841*	27	20
28 May 94	CRAZY *Columbia 4747382*	6	37
12 Aug 95 ●	LA CARRETERA *Columbia 4807042*	6	6
30 Nov 96	TANGO *Columbia 4866752*	56	3
7 Nov 98	MY LIFE – THE GREATEST HITS *Columbia 4910902*	18	9
22 Jul 00	NOCHE DE CUATRO LUNAS *Columbia 4974222*	32	3
19 Jul 03	LOVE SONGS *Columbia 5126042*	64	1

[1] Julio Iglesias and Willie Nelson [2] Julio Iglesias and Diana Ross [3] Julio Iglesias featuring Stevie Wonder

The IGNORANTS *UK, male vocal duo (Singles: 3 Weeks)*

			pos/wks
25 Dec 93	PHAT GIRLS *Spaghetti CIOCD 8*	59	3

IIO
US, male / female production duo – Marcus Moser and Nadia Li (Singles: 15 Weeks)

			pos/wks
10 Nov 01 ●	RAPTURE *Made / Data / MoS DATA 27CDS*	2	12
14 Jun 03	AT THE END *Free 2 Air 0148065 F2A*	20	3

IKARA COLT
UK, male / female vocal / instrumental group (Singles: 4 Weeks)

			pos/wks
2 Mar 02	RUDD *Fantastic Plastic FPS 029*	72	1
28 Feb 04	WANNA BE THAT WAY *Fantastic Plastic FPS 038*	49	1
5 Jun 04	WAKE IN THE CITY *Fantastic Plastic FPS 040*	55	1
23 Oct 04	MODERN FEELING *Fantastic Plastic FPS 042*	61	1

IL DIVO
France / Spain / Switzerland / US, male vocal group (Albums: 7 Weeks)

			pos/wks
13 Nov 04 ★	IL DIVO *Syco Music 82876961952* ■	1	7+

IL PADRINOS featuring Jocelyn BROWN
(see also AKABU featuring Linda CLIFFORD; HED BOYS; Li KWAN; JAKATTA; Joey NEGRO; PHASE II; RAVEN MAIZE; Z FACTOR)
UK, male production duo – Dave Lee and Danny Rampling and US, female vocalist (Singles: 1 Week)

			pos/wks
7 Sep 02	THAT'S HOW GOOD YOUR LOVE IS *Defected DFTD 057CDS*	54	1

ILLEGAL MOTION featuring Simone CHAPMAN
UK, male / female vocal / instrumental duo (Singles: 1 Week)

			pos/wks
9 Oct 93	SATURDAY LOVE *Arista 74321163032*	67	1

ILLICIT featuring GRAM'MA FUNK
UK, male production duo and US, female vocalist (Singles: 1 Week)

			pos/wks
2 Sep 00	CHEEKY ARMADA *Yola YOLACDX 01*	72	1

ILS *UK, male producer (Singles: 1 Week)*

			pos/wks
23 Feb 02	NEXT LEVEL *Marine Parade MAPA 012*	75	1

IMAANI *UK, female vocalist –*
Imaani Saleem (Melanie Crosdale) (Singles: 7 Weeks)

			pos/wks
9 May 98	WHERE ARE YOU *EMI CDEM 510*	15	7

IMAGINATION (291) Top 500
Distinctive London-based trio, which created a unique blend of soul and dance music: Leee John (v), Ashley Ingram (v/k), Errol Kennedy (d). One of the most original British acts of the early 1980s, they were fronted by a charismatic and flamboyant lead singer (Singles: 105 Weeks, Albums: 122 Weeks)

			pos/wks
16 May 81 ●	BODY TALK *R&B RBS 201*	4	18
5 Sep 81	IN AND OUT OF LOVE *R&B RBS 202*	16	9
14 Nov 81	FLASHBACK *R&B RBS 206*	16	13
6 Mar 82 ●	JUST AN ILLUSION *R&B RBS 208*	2	11
26 Jun 82 ●	MUSIC AND LIGHTS *R&B RBS 210*	5	9
25 Sep 82	IN THE HEAT OF THE NIGHT *R&B RBS 211*	22	8
11 Dec 82	CHANGES *R&B RBS 213*	31	8
4 Jun 83	LOOKING AT MIDNIGHT *R&B RBS 214*	29	7
5 Nov 83	NEW DIMENSIONS *R&B RBS 216*	56	3
26 May 84	STATE OF LOVE *R&B RBS 218*	67	2
24 Nov 84	THANK YOU MY LOVE *R&B RBS 219*	22	15
16 Jan 88	INSTINCTUAL *RCA PB 41697*	62	2
24 Oct 81	BODY TALK *R&B RBLP 1001*	20	53
11 Sep 82 ●	IN THE HEAT OF THE NIGHT *R&B RBLP 1002*	7	29
14 May 83 ●	NIGHT DUBBING *R&B RBDUB 1*	9	20
12 Nov 83	SCANDALOUS *R&B RBLP 1004*	25	8
12 Aug 89 ●	IMAGINATION – ALL THE HITS *Stylus SMR 985*	4	12

IMAJIN
US, male vocal group (Singles: 7 Weeks)

			pos/wks
27 Jun 98	SHORTY (YOU KEEP PLAYING WITH MY MIND) *Jive 0521212* [1]	22	3
20 Feb 99	NO DOUBT *Jive 0521772*	42	2
24 Apr 99	BOUNCE, ROCK, SKATE, ROLL *Jive 0522142* [2]	45	1
12 Feb 00	FLAVA *Jive 9250012*	64	1

[1] Imajin featuring Keith Murray [2] Baby DC featuring Imajin

Natalie IMBRUGLIA (460 Top 500) *Australian actor turned sultry pop singer. b. 4 Feb 1975, Sydney. The 'Neighbours' star (1991-94) won six ARIAs (Australian music awards) in 1998, and two Brits in 1999. Although only a No.2 hit, the Grammy-nominated 'Torn' is among the UK's all-time Top 100 best-sellers (Singles: 53 Weeks, Albums: 102 Weeks)* pos/wks

8 Nov 97 ●	TORN	RCA 74321527982	2	17
14 Mar 98 ●	BIG MISTAKE	RCA 74321566782	2	10
6 Jun 98	WISHING I WAS THERE	RCA 74321585062	19	5
17 Oct 98 ●	SMOKE	RCA 74321621942	5	7
10 Nov 01	THAT DAY (re)	RCA 74321896792	11	5
23 Mar 02	WRONG IMPRESSION	RCA 74321928352	10	7
3 Aug 02	BEAUTY ON THE FIRE	RCA 74321947022	26	2
6 Dec 97 ●	LEFT OF THE MIDDLE	RCA 74321544412	5	87
17 Nov 01	WHITE LILIES ISLAND	RCA 74321891212	15	15

IMMACULATE FOOLS *UK, male vocal / instrumental group (Singles: 4 Weeks, Albums: 2 Weeks)* pos/wks

26 Jan 85	IMMACULATE FOOLS	A&M AM 227	51	4
11 May 85	HEARTS OF FORTUNE	A&M AMA 5030	65	2

IMMATURE featuring SMOOTH *US, male vocal group and US, female vocalist (Singles: 2 Weeks)* pos/wks

16 Mar 96	WE GOT IT	MCA MCSTD 48009	26	2

The IMPALAS *US, male vocal group (Singles: 1 Week)* pos/wks

21 Aug 59	SORRY (I RAN ALL THE WAY HOME)	MGM 1015	28	1

IMPEDANCE *UK, male producer – Daniel Haydon (Singles: 4 Weeks)* pos/wks

11 Nov 89	TAINTED LOVE	Jumpin' & Pumpin' TOT 4	54	4

IMPERIAL DRAG *UK, male vocal / instrumental group (Singles: 1 Week)* pos/wks

12 Oct 96	BOY OR A GIRL	Columbia 6632992	54	1

IMPERIAL TEEN *US, male / female vocal / instrumental group (Singles: 1 Week)* pos/wks

7 Sep 96	YOU'RE ONE	Slash LASCD 57	69	1

The IMPERIALS *US, male vocal group (Singles: 9 Weeks)* pos/wks

24 Dec 77	WHO'S GONNA LOVE ME	Power Exchange PX 266	17	9

IMPERIALS QUARTET See Elvis PRESLEY

IMPOSTER See Elvis COSTELLO

The IMPRESSIONS *US, male vocal group (Singles: 10 Weeks)* pos/wks

22 Nov 75	FIRST IMPRESSIONS	Curtom K 16638	16	10

The IN CROWD *UK, male vocal / instrumental group (Singles: 1 Week)* pos/wks

20 May 65	THAT'S HOW STRONG MY LOVE IS	Parlophone R 5276	48	1

IN TUA NUA *Ireland, male / female vocal / instrumental group (Singles: 2 Weeks)* pos/wks

14 May 88	ALL I WANTED	Virgin VS 1072	69	2

IN TUNE (see also BLOWING FREE; HYPNOSIS; JAMES BOYS; RAINDANCE; SCHOOL OF EXCELLENCE) *UK, male instrumental duo – Bradley and Stewart Palmer (Albums: 3 Weeks)* pos/wks

17 Jun 95	ACOUSTIC MOODS	Global Television RADCD 13	21	3

INAURA *UK, male vocal / instrumental group (Singles: 1 Week)* pos/wks

18 May 96	COMA AROMA	EMI CDEM 421	57	1

INCANTATION *UK, male instrumental group (Singles: 12 Weeks, Albums: 52 Weeks)* pos/wks

4 Dec 82	CACHARPAYA (ANDES PUMPSA DAESI)	Beggars Banquet BEG 84	12	12
11 Dec 82 ●	CACHARPAYA (PANPIPES OF THE ANDES)	Beggars Banquet BEGA 39	9	26
17 Dec 83	DANCE OF THE FLAMES	Beggars Banquet BEGA 49	61	7
28 Dec 85	BEST OF INCANTATION – MUSIC FROM THE ANDES	West Five CODA 19	28	19

INCOGNITO *UK, male / female vocal / instrumental group (Singles: 38 Weeks, Albums: 19 Weeks)* pos/wks

15 Nov 80	PARISIENNE GIRL	Ensign ENY 44	73	2
29 Jun 91 ●	ALWAYS THERE	Talkin Loud TLK 10 [1]	6	9
14 Sep 91	CRAZY FOR YOU	Talkin Loud TLK 14 [2]	59	2
6 Jun 92	DON'T YOU WORRY 'BOUT A THING	Talkin Loud TLK 21	19	6
15 Aug 92	CHANGE	Talkin Loud TLK 26	52	2
21 Aug 93	STILL A FRIEND OF MINE	Talkin Loud TLK 42	47	2
20 Nov 93	GIVIN' IT UP	Talkin Loud TLKCD 44	43	2
12 Mar 94	PIECES OF A DREAM	Talkin Loud TLKCD 46	35	2
27 May 95	EVERYDAY	Talkin Loud TLKCD 55	23	3
5 Aug 95	I HEAR YOUR NAME	Talkin Loud TLK 56	42	2
11 May 96	JUMP TO MY LOVE / ALWAYS THERE (re-recording)	Talkin Loud TLCD 7	29	3
26 Oct 96	OUT OF THE STORM	Talkin Loud TLCD 14	57	1
10 Apr 99	NIGHTS OVER EGYPT	Talkin Loud TLCD 40	56	1
18 Apr 81	JAZZ FUNK	Ensign ENVY 504	28	8
27 Jul 91	INSIDE LIFE	Talkin Loud 8485461	44	2
4 Jul 92	TRIBES VIBES AND SCRIBES	Talkin Loud 5123632	41	2
6 Nov 93	POSITIVITY	Talkin Loud 5182602	55	2
17 Jun 95	100 DEGREES AND RISING	Talkin Loud 5280002	11	4
1 Jun 96	REMIXED	Talkin Loud 5323092	56	1

[1] Incognito featuring Jocelyn Brown [2] Incognito featuring Chyna

The INCREDIBLE STRING BAND *UK, male / female vocal / instrumental group (Albums: 37 Weeks)* pos/wks

21 Oct 67	5000 SPIRITS OR THE LAYERS OF THE ONION	Elektra EUKS 257	25	5
6 Apr 68 ●	HANGMAN'S BEAUTIFUL DAUGHTER	Elektra EVKS 7258	5	21
20 Jul 68	THE INCREDIBLE STRING BAND	Elektra EKL 254	34	3
24 Jan 70	CHANGING HORSES	Elektra EKS 74057	30	1
9 May 70	I LOOKED UP	Elektra 2469002	30	4
31 Oct 70	U	Elektra 2665001	34	2
30 Oct 71	LIQUID ACROBAT AS REGARDS THE AIR	Island ILPS 9172	46	1

INCUBUS *US, male vocal / instrumental group (Singles: 12 Weeks, Albums: 8 Weeks)* pos/wks

20 May 00	PARDON ME	Epic 6693462	61	1
23 Jun 01	DRIVE	Epic 6713782	40	2
2 Feb 02	WISH YOU WERE HERE	Epic 6722552	27	3
14 Sep 02	ARE YOU IN?	Epic 6728482	34	2
7 Feb 04	MEGALOMANIAC	Epic 6746462	23	3
19 Jun 04	TALK SHOWS ON MUTE	Epic 6749022	43	1
3 Nov 01	MORNING VIEW	Epic 5040612	15	4
14 Feb 04 ●	A CROW LEFT OF THE MURDER ...	Epic 5150473	6	4

INDEEP *US, male / female vocal / rap group (Singles: 11 Weeks)* pos/wks

22 Jan 83	LAST NIGHT A DJ SAVED MY LIFE	Sound of New York SNY 1	13	9
14 May 83	WHEN BOYS TALK	Sound of New York SNY 3	67	2

INDIA *US, female vocalist – Linda Caballero (Singles: 15 Weeks)* pos/wks

26 Feb 94	LOVE AND HAPPINESS (YEMAYA Y OCHUN)	Cooltempo CDCOOL 287 [1]	50	2
5 Aug 95	I CAN'T GET NO SLEEP	A&M 5811412 [2]	44	2
16 Mar 96	OYE COMO VA	Media MCSTD 40013 [3]	36	2
8 Feb 97	RUNAWAY	Talkin Loud TLCD20 [4]	24	4
19 Jul 97	OYE COMO VA (re-issue)	Nukleuz MCSTD 40120 [3]	56	1
31 Jul 99	TO BE IN LOVE	Defected DEFECT 5CDS [5]	23	3
6 Jul 02	BACKFIRED	SuSu CDSUSU 4 [6]	62	1

[1] River Ocean featuring India [2] Masters at Work presents India [3] Tito Puente Jr and the Latin Rhythm featuring Tito Puente, India and Cali Aleman [4] Nuyorican Soul featuring India [5] MAW presents India [6] Masters at Work featuring India

INDIAN VIBES *UK, male vocal / instrumental group (Singles: 2 Weeks)* pos/wks

24 Sep 94	MATHAR	Virgin International DINSD 136	68	1
2 May 98	MATHAR (re-mix)	VC Recordings VCRD 32	52	1

INDIEN (see also EMMIE) UK, male / female production / vocal
duo – Mark Hadfield and Emma Morton-Smith (Singles: 1 Week) pos/wks

9 Aug 03	SHOW ME LOVE Concept CDCON 40	.....69 1

INDIGO GIRLS US, female vocal / instrumental
duo – Amy Ray and Emily Saliers (Albums: 3 Weeks) pos/wks

11 Jun 94	SWAMP OPHELIA Epic 4759312	.....66 1
15 Jul 95	4.5 Epic 4804392	.....43 2

INDO US, female vocal duo (Singles: 3 Weeks) pos/wks

18 Apr 98	R U SLEEPING Satellite 74321568212	.....31 3

INDUSTRY STANDARD UK, male DJ / production
duo – Clayton Mitchell and Dave Dellar (Singles: 3 Weeks) pos/wks

10 Jan 98	VOLUME 1 (WHAT YOU WANT WHAT YOU NEED) Satellite 74321543742	.....34 3

INFA RIOT UK, male vocal / instrumental group (Albums: 4 Weeks) pos/wks

7 Aug 82	STILL OUT OF ORDER Secret SEC 7	.....42 4

INFEXTIOUS See Darren STYLES & Mark BREEZE present INFEXTIOUS

INFINITI See GRAND PUBA

INFRARED vs Gil FELIX UK / Switzerland, production
duo and Brazil, male vocalist / guitarist (Singles: 1 Week) pos/wks

4 Oct 03	CAPOEIRA Infrared INFRA 24CD	.....67 1

INGRAM US, male vocal / instrumental group (Singles: 2 Weeks) pos/wks

11 Jun 83	SMOOTHIN' GROOVIN' Streetwave WAVE 3	.....56 2

James INGRAM
US, male vocalist (Singles: 42 Weeks, Albums: 19 Weeks) pos/wks

12 Feb 83	BABY COME TO ME Qwest K 15005 [1] ▲	.....11 10
18 Feb 84	YAH MO B THERE (2re) Qwest 9394 [2]	.....12 16
11 Jul 87 ●	SOMEWHERE OUT THERE MCA MCA 1132 [3]	.....8 13
31 Mar 90	SECRET GARDEN Qwest W 9992 [4]	.....67 1
16 Apr 94	THE DAY I FALL IN LOVE Columbia 6600282 [5]	.....64 2
31 Mar 84	IT'S YOUR NIGHT Qwest 9239701	.....25 17
30 Aug 86	NEVER FELT SO GOOD Qwest WX 44	.....72 2

[1] Patti Austin and James Ingram [2] James Ingram with Michael McDonald
[3] Linda Ronstadt and James Ingram [4] Quincy Jones featuring Al B Sure!,
James Ingram, El DeBarge and Barry White [5] Dolly Parton and James Ingram

The INK SPOTS US, male vocal group (Singles: 4 Weeks) pos/wks

29 Apr 55 ●	MELODY OF LOVE Parlophone R 3977	.....10 4

John INMAN UK, male actor / vocalist (Singles: 6 Weeks) pos/wks

25 Oct 75	ARE YOU BEING SERVED SIR? DJM DJS 602	.....39 6

INMATES UK, male vocal / instrumental group (Singles: 9 Weeks) pos/wks

8 Dec 79	THE WALK Radar ADA 47	.....36 9

INME UK, male vocal / instrumental
group (Singles: 7 Weeks, Albums: 2 Weeks) pos/wks

27 Jul 02	UNDERDOSE Music for Nations CDKUT 195	.....66 1
28 Sep 02	FIREFLY Music for Nations CDKUT 197	.....43 1
18 Jan 03	CRUSHED LIKE FRUIT Music for Nations CDKUT 200	.....25 2
26 Apr 03	NEPTUNE Music for Nations CDKUT 201	.....46 1
5 Jun 04	FASTER THE CHASE Music for Nations CDKUT 210	.....31 2
8 Feb 03	OVERGROWN EDEN Music for Nations CDMFNX 275	.....15 2

INNER CIRCLE Jamaica, male vocal /
instrumental group (Singles: 35 Weeks, Albums: 2 Weeks) pos/wks

24 Feb 79	EVERYTHING IS GREAT Island WIP 6472	.....37 8
12 May 79	STOP BREAKING MY HEART Island WIP 6488	.....50 3
31 Oct 92 ●	SWEAT (A LA LA LA LA LONG) (re) Magnet 9031776802	.....3 19
31 Jul 93	BAD BOYS Magnet MAG 1017CD	.....52 3
10 Sep 94	GAMES PEOPLE PLAY Magnet MAG 1026CD	.....67 2
29 May 93	BAD TO THE BONE Magnet 9031776772	.....44 2

'Sweat (A La La La La Long)' peaked on re-entry in May 1993

INNER CITY US, male vocal / production
group (Singles: 81 Weeks, Albums: 39 Weeks) pos/wks

3 Sep 88 ●	BIG FUN 10 TEN 240 [1]	.....8 14
10 Dec 88 ●	GOOD LIFE 10 TEN 249	.....4 12
22 Apr 89 ●	AIN'T NOBODY BETTER 10 TEN 252	.....10 7
29 Jul 89	DO YOU LOVE WHAT YOU FEEL 10 TEN 273	.....16 7
18 Nov 89	WATCHA GONNA DO WITH MY LOVIN' 10 TEN 290	.....12 9
13 Oct 90	THAT MAN (HE'S ALL MINE) 10 TEN 334	.....42 4
23 Feb 91	TILL WE MEET AGAIN Ten TEN 337	.....47 2
7 Dec 91	LET IT REIGN Ten TEN 392	.....51 2
4 Apr 92	HALLELUJAH '92 Ten TEN 398	.....22 4
13 Jun 92	PENNIES FROM HEAVEN Ten TEN 405	.....24 4
12 Sep 92	PRAISE Ten TENX 408	.....59 2
27 Feb 93	TILL WE MEET AGAIN (re-mix) Ten TENCD 414	.....55 1
14 Aug 93	BACK TOGETHER AGAIN Six6 SIXCD 104	.....49 1
5 Feb 94	DO YA Six6 SIXCD 107	.....44 2
9 Jul 94	SHARE MY LIFE Six6 SIXCD 114	.....62 1
10 Feb 96	YOUR LOVE Six6 SIXCD 127	.....28 2
5 Oct 96	DO ME RIGHT Six6 SIXXCD 2	.....47 1
6 Feb 99 ●	GOOD LIFE (BUENA VIDA) (re-recording) Pias Recordings PIASX 002CD	.....10 6
20 May 89 ●	PARADISE 10 DIX 81	.....3 30
10 Feb 90	PARADISE REMIXED 10 XID 81	.....17 6
11 Jul 92	PRAISE Ten 4718862	.....52 1
15 May 93	TESTAMENT 93 Ten CDOVD 438	.....33 2

[1] Inner City featuring Kevin Saunderson

INNER SANCTUM
Canada, male producer – Steve Bolton (Singles: 1 Week) pos/wks

23 May 98	HOW SOON IS NOW Malarky MLKD 6	.....75 1

INNERZONE ORCHESTRA
US, male producer – Carl Craig (Singles: 1 Week) pos/wks

28 Sep 96	BUG IN THE BASSBIN Mo Wax MW 049CD	.....68 1

INNOCENCE UK, male / female vocal /
instrumental group (Singles: 33 Weeks, Albums: 20 Weeks) pos/wks

3 Mar 90	NATURAL THING Cooltempo COOL 201	.....16 7
21 Jul 90	SILENT VOICE Cooltempo COOL 212	.....37 5
13 Oct 90	LET'S PUSH IT Cooltempo COOL 220	.....25 6
8 Dec 90	A MATTER OF FACT Cooltempo COOL 223	.....37 7
30 Mar 91	REMEMBER THE DAY Cooltempo COOL 226	.....56 2
20 Jun 92	I'LL BE THERE Cooltempo COOL 255	.....26 3
3 Oct 92	ONE LOVE IN MY LIFETIME Cooltempo COOL 263	.....40 2
21 Nov 92	BUILD Cooltempo COOL 267	.....72 1
10 Nov 90	BELIEF Cooltempo CTLP 20	.....24 19
31 Oct 92	BUILD Cooltempo CTCD 26	.....66 1

INSANE CLOWN POSSE
US, male rap duo (Singles: 2 Weeks) pos/wks

17 Jan 98	HALLS OF ILLUSION Island CID 685	.....56 1
6 Jun 98	HOKUS POKUS Island CIDX 705	.....53 1

INSPIRAL CARPETS UK, male vocal /
instrumental group (Singles: 51 Weeks, Albums: 37 Weeks) pos/wks

18 Nov 89	MOVE Cow DUNG 6	.....49 2
17 Mar 90	THIS IS HOW IT FEELS Cow DUNG 7	.....14 8
30 Jun 90	SHE COMES IN THE FALL Cow DUNG 10	.....27 6
17 Nov 90	ISLAND HEAD (EP) Cow DUNG 11	.....21 4
30 Mar 91	CARAVAN Cow DUNG 13	.....30 5
22 Jun 91	PLEASE BE CRUEL Cow DUNG 15	.....50 2
29 Feb 92	DRAGGING ME DOWN Cow DUNG 16	.....12 5
30 May 92	TWO WORLDS COLLIDE Cow DUNG 17	.....32 2
19 Sep 92	GENERATIONS Cow DUNG 18T	.....28 3
14 Nov 92	BITCHES BREW Cow DUNG 20T	.....36 2
5 Jun 93	HOW IT SHOULD BE Cow DUNG 22CD	.....49 1
22 Jan 94	SATURN 5 Cow DUNG 23CD	.....20 4
5 Mar 94	I WANT YOU Cow DUNG 24CD [1]	.....18 3
7 May 94	UNIFORM Cow DUNG 26CD	.....51 1
16 Sep 95	JOE Cow DUNG 27CD	.....37 2
26 Jul 03	COME BACK TOMORROW Mute DUNG 31CD	.....43 1
5 May 90 ●	LIFE Cow DUNG 8	.....2 21
4 May 91 ●	THE BEAST INSIDE Cow DUNG 14	.....5 6
17 Oct 92	REVENGE OF THE GOLDFISH Cow DUNG 19	.....17 3
19 Mar 94 ●	DEVIL HOPPING Cow LDUNG 25CD	.....10 3

| 30 Sep 95 | THE SINGLES *Cow CDMOOTEL 3* | 17 | 3 |
| 31 May 03 | COOL AS *Mute DUNG 30CD* | 65 | 1 |

[1] Inspiral Carpets featuring Mark E Smith

Tracks on Island Head (EP): Biggest Mountain / Gold Top / Weakness / I'll Keep it in Mind

INSPIRATIONAL CHOIR
US, male / female choir (Singles: 11 Weeks, Albums: 4 Weeks) pos/wks

22 Dec 84	ABIDE WITH ME *Epic A 4997*	44	5
14 Dec 85	ABIDE WITH ME (re-issue) *Portrait A 4997*	36	6
18 Jan 86	SWEET INSPIRATION *Portrait PRT 10048*	59	4

Label credits the Royal Choral Society

INSPIRATIONS *UK, male instrumentalist –*
keyboards – Neil Palmer (Albums: 35 Weeks) pos/wks

29 Apr 95 ●	PAN PIPE INSPIRATIONS *Pure Music PMCD 7011*	10	10
23 Sep 95 ●	PAN PIPE DREAMS *Pure Music PMCD 7016*	10	8
11 Nov 95	PURE EMOTIONS *Pure Music PMCD 7023*	37	4
6 Apr 96	PAN PIPE IMAGES *Telstar TCD 2819*	23	6
12 Oct 96	THE VERY BEST OF THE PAN PIPES *Telstar TCD 2845*	37	7

INSTANT FUNK
US, male vocal / instrumental group (Singles: 5 Weeks) pos/wks

| 20 Jan 79 | GOT MY MIND MADE UP *Salsoul SSOL 114* | 46 | 5 |

INTASTELLA
UK, male / female vocal / instrumental group (Singles: 6 Weeks) pos/wks

25 May 91	DREAM SOME PARADISE *MCA MCS 1520*	69	1
24 Aug 91	PEOPLE *MCA MCS 1559*	74	2
16 Nov 91	CENTURY *MCA MCS 1585*	70	2
23 Sep 95	THE NIGHT *Planet 3 GXY 2005CD*	60	1

INTELLIGENT HOODLUM
US, male rapper – Percy Chapman (Singles: 3 Weeks) pos/wks

| 6 Oct 90 | BACK TO REALITY *A&M AM 598* | 55 | 3 |

INTENSO PROJECT
UK, male production / vocal group (Singles: 7 Weeks) pos/wks

17 Aug 02	LUV DA SUNSHINE *Inferno CDFERN 47*	22	2
26 Jul 03	YOUR MUSIC *Concept CDCON 43* [1]	32	2
4 Dec 04	GET IT ON *Inspired INSPMOS 1CDS* [2]	23	3

[1] Intenso Project featuring Laura Jaye [2] Intenso Project featuring Lisa Scott-Lee

INTERACTIVE
Germany, male instrumental / production group (Singles: 6 Weeks) pos/wks

| 13 Apr 96 | FOREVER YOUNG *Ffrreedom TABCD 235* | 28 | 4 |
| 8 Mar 03 | FOREVER YOUNG (re-mix) *All Around the World CDGLOBE 253* | 37 | 2 |

INTERNATIONAL AIRPORT / TEENAGE FANCLUB
UK, male vocal / instrumental groups (Singles: 1 Week) pos/wks

| 4 Sep 04 | ASSOCIATION *Geographic GEORG 29CD* | 75 | 1 |

INTERPOL *US, male vocal / instrumental*
group (Singles: 5 Weeks, Albums: 2 Weeks) pos/wks

23 Nov 02	OBSTACLE 1 *Matador OLE 5702*	72	1
26 Apr 03	SAY HELLO TO THE ANGELS / NYC *Matador OLE 5822*	65	1
27 Sep 03	OBSTACLE 1 (re-mix) *Matador OLE 5942*	41	1
25 Sep 04	SLOW HANDS *Matador OLE 6362*	36	2
9 Oct 04	ANTICS *Matador OLE 6162*	21	2

INTI ILLIMANI-GUAMARY *Chile, male vocal /*
instrumental group – panpipes (Albums: 7 Weeks) pos/wks

| 17 Dec 83 | THE FLIGHT OF THE CONDOR – ORIGINAL TV SOUNDTRACK *BBC REB 440* | 62 | 7 |

The INTRUDERS *US, male vocal group (Singles: 21 Weeks)* pos/wks

| 13 Apr 74 | I'LL ALWAYS LOVE MY MAMA *Philadelphia International PIR 2159* | 32 | 7 |
| 6 Jul 74 | WIN, PLACE OR SHOW (SHE'S A WINNER) *Philadelphia International PIR 2212* | 14 | 9 |

| 22 Dec 84 | WHO DO YOU LOVE? *Streetwave KHAN 34* | 65 | 5 |

INVADERS OF THE HEART *See Jah WOBBLE'S INVADERS of the HEART*

INVISIBLE GIRLS *See Pauline MURRAY and The INVISIBLE GIRLS*

INVISIBLE MAN
UK, male producer – Graham Mew (Singles: 1 Week) pos/wks

| 17 Apr 99 | GIVE A LITTLE LOVE *Serious SERR 006CD* | 48 | 1 |

INXS 〔134〕 Top 500 (see also MAX Q)
Stadium-packing rock sextet led by Australian Michael Hutchence, b. 22 Jan 1960, Sydney, d. 22 Nov 1997. Both Hutchence and group won Brit awards in 1991, and the video for their US chart-topper 'Need You Tonight' won five MTV awards in 1988 (Singles: 132 Weeks, Albums: 240 Weeks) pos/wks

19 Apr 86	WHAT YOU NEED *Mercury INXS 5*	51	6
28 Jun 86	LISTEN LIKE THIEVES *Mercury INXS 6*	46	7
30 Aug 86	KISS THE DIRT (FALLING DOWN THE MOUNTAIN) *Mercury INXS 7*	54	3
24 Oct 87	NEED YOU TONIGHT *Mercury INXS 8* ▲	58	3
9 Jan 88	NEW SENSATION *Mercury INXS 9*	25	6
12 Mar 88	DEVIL INSIDE *Mercury INXS 10*	47	5
25 Jun 88	NEVER TEAR US APART *Mecury INXS 11*	24	7
12 Nov 88 ●	NEED YOU TONIGHT (re-issue) *Mercury INXS 12*	2	11
8 Apr 89	MYSTIFY *Mercury INXS 13*	14	7
15 Sep 90	SUICIDE BLONDE *Mercury INXS 14*	11	6
8 Dec 90	DISAPPEAR *Mercury INXS 15*	21	8
26 Jan 91	GOOD TIMES *Atlantic A 7751* [1]	18	8
30 Mar 91	BY MY SIDE *Mercury INXS 16*	42	4
13 Jul 91	BITTER TEARS *Mercury INXS 17*	30	3
2 Nov 91	SHINING STAR (EP) *Mercury INXS 18*	27	3
18 Jul 92	HEAVEN SENT *Mercury INXS 19*	31	3
5 Sep 92	BABY DON'T CRY *Mercury INXS 20*	20	5
14 Nov 92	TASTE IT *Mercury INXS 23*	21	4
13 Feb 93	BEAUTIFUL GIRL *Mercury INXCD 24*	23	5
23 Oct 93	THE GIFT *Mercury INXCD 25*	11	4
11 Dec 93	PLEASE (YOU GOT THAT ...) *Mercury INXCD 26*	50	3
22 Oct 94	THE STRANGEST PARTY (THESE ARE THE TIMES) *Mercury INXCD 27*	15	5
22 Mar 97	ELEGANTLY WASTED *Mercury INXCD 28*	20	4
7 Jun 97	EVERYTHING *Mercury INXDD 29*	71	1
18 Aug 01	PRECIOUS HEART (re) *Duty Free / Decode DFTELCD 001* [2]	14	5
3 Nov 01	I'M SO CRAZY (re) *Credence CDCRED 016* [3]	19	6
8 Feb 86	LISTEN LIKE THIEVES *Mercury MERH 82*	48	15
28 Nov 87 ●	KICK *Mercury MERH 114*	9	103
6 Oct 90 ●	X *Mercury 8466681*	2	44
16 Nov 91 ●	LIVE BABY LIVE *Mercury 5105801*	8	9
15 Aug 92 ★	WELCOME TO WHEREVER YOU ARE *Mercury 5125072* ■	1	33
13 Nov 93 ●	FULL MOON DIRTY HEARTS *Mercury 5186372*	3	8
12 Nov 94 ●	THE GREATEST HITS *Mercury 5262302*	3	22
19 Apr 97	ELEGANTLY WASTED *Mercury 5346132*	16	3
26 Oct 02	DEFINITIVE INXS *Mercury 0633562*	15	3

[1] Jimmy Barnes and Inxs [2] Tall Paul vs Inxs [3] Par-T-One vs Inxs

Tracks on Shining Star (EP): Shining Star / Send a Message (Live) / Faith in Each Other (Live) / Bitter Tears (Live). Although uncredited, 'Please (You Got That ...)' is a duet with Ray Charles

Tony IOMMI *See BLACK SABBATH*

Sweetie IRIE *See ASWAD; SCRITTI POLITTI; Ed CASE*

Tippa IRIE *UK, male vocalist – Anthony Henry (Singles: 14 Weeks)* pos/wks

22 Mar 86	HELLO DARLING *Greensleeves / UK Bubblers TIPPA 4*	22	7
19 Jul 86	HEARTBEAT *Greensleeves / UK Bubblers TIPPA 5*	59	3
15 May 93	SHOUTING FOR THE GUNNERS *London LONCD 342* [1]	34	3
8 Jul 95	STAYING ALIVE 95 *Telstar CDSTAS 2776* [2]	48	1

[1] Arsenal FA Cup Squad featuring Tippa Irie and Peter Hunnigale [2] Fever featuring Tippa Irie

IRON MAIDEN 〔131〕 Top 500 *Legendary London-based group named after a medieval torture device. Lead vocalists have included Paul Di'Anno and Blaze Bayley, but it was with frontman Bruce Dickinson that they enjoyed a period as one of the world's top metal bands. 'Bring Your Daughter ... to the Slaughter' was the first record to sell less than 30,000 in the week it reached No.1 (Singles: 169 Weeks, Albums: 207 Weeks)* pos/wks

23 Feb 80	RUNNING FREE *EMI 5032*	34	5
7 Jun 80	SANCTUARY *EMI 5065*	29	5
8 Nov 80	WOMEN IN UNIFORM *EMI 5105*	35	4

14 Mar 81	TWILIGHT ZONE / WRATH CHILD *EMI 5145*	**31**	5
27 Jun 81	PURGATORY *EMI 5184*	**52**	3
26 Sep 81	MAIDEN JAPAN (EP) *EMI 5219*	**43**	4
20 Feb 82 ●	RUN TO THE HILLS *EMI 5263*	**7**	10
15 May 82	THE NUMBER OF THE BEAST *EMI 5287*	**18**	8
23 Apr 83	FLIGHT OF ICARUS *EMI 5378*	**11**	6
2 Jul 83	THE TROOPER *EMI 5397*	**12**	7
18 Aug 84	2 MINUTES TO MIDNIGHT *EMI 5849*	**11**	6
3 Nov 84	ACES HIGH *EMI 5502*	**20**	5
5 Oct 85	RUNNING FREE (LIVE) *EMI 5532*	**19**	5
14 Dec 85	RUN TO THE HILLS (LIVE) *EMI 5542*	**26**	4
6 Sep 86	WASTED YEARS *EMI 5583*	**18**	4
22 Nov 86	STRANGER IN A STRANGE LAND (re) *EMI 5589*	**22**	6
26 Mar 88 ●	CAN I PLAY WITH MADNESS *EMI EM 49*	**3**	6
13 Aug 88 ●	THE EVIL THAT MEN DO *EMI EM 64*	**5**	5
19 Nov 88 ●	THE CLAIRVOYANT *EMI EM 79*	**6**	8
18 Nov 89 ●	INFINITE DREAMS (re) *EMI EM 117*	**6**	6
22 Sep 90 ●	HOLY SMOKE *EMI EM 153*	**3**	4
5 Jan 91 ★	BRING YOUR DAUGHTER ... TO THE SLAUGHTER *EMI EMPD 171* ■	**1**	5
25 Apr 92 ●	BE QUICK OR BE DEAD *EMI EM 229*	**2**	4
11 Jul 92	FROM HERE TO ETERNITY *EMI EMS 240*	**21**	4
13 Mar 93 ●	FEAR OF THE DARK (LIVE) *EMI CDEMS 263*	**8**	3
16 Oct 93 ●	HALLOWED BE THY NAME (LIVE) *EMI CDEM 288*	**9**	3
7 Oct 95 ●	MAN ON THE EDGE *EMI CDEMS 398*	**10**	3
21 Sep 96	VIRUS *EMI CDEM 443*	**16**	3
21 Mar 98	THE ANGEL AND THE GAMBLER *EMI CDEM 507*	**18**	4
20 May 00 ●	THE WICKER MAN *EMI CDEMS 568*	**9**	4
4 Nov 00	OUT OF THE SILENT PLANET *EMI CDEM 576*	**20**	3
23 Mar 02 ●	RUN TO THE HILLS (re-recording) *EMI CDEM 612*	**9**	4
13 Sep 03 ●	WILDEST DREAMS *EMI CDEM 627*	**6**	6
6 Dec 03	RAINMAKER *EMI CDEM 633*	**13**	5
26 Apr 80 ●	IRON MAIDEN *EMI EMC 3330*	**4**	15
28 Feb 81	KILLERS *EMI EMC 3357*	**12**	8
10 Apr 82 ★	THE NUMBER OF THE BEAST *EMI EMC 3400* ■	**1**	31
28 May 83 ●	PIECE OF MIND *EMI EMA 800*	**3**	18
15 Sep 84 ●	POWERSLAVE *EMI POWER 1*	**2**	13
15 Jun 85	IRON MAIDEN (re-issue) *Fame FA 4131211*	**71**	2
26 Oct 85 ●	LIVE AFTER DEATH *EMI RIP 1*	**2**	14
11 Oct 86 ●	SOMEWHERE IN TIME *EMI EMC 3512*	**3**	11
20 Jun 87	THE NUMBER OF THE BEAST (re-issue) *Fame FA 3178*	**98**	1
23 Apr 88 ★	SEVENTH SON OF A SEVENTH SON *EMI EMD 1006* ■	**1**	18
24 Feb 90 ●	RUNNING FREE / SANCTUARY *EMI IRN 1*	**10**	4
3 Mar 90 ●	WOMEN IN UNIFORM / ZONE *EMI IRN 2*	**10**	3
10 Mar 90 ●	PURGATORY / MAIDEN JAPAN *EMI IRN 3*	**5**	3
17 Mar 90 ●	RUN TO THE HILLS / THE NUMBER OF THE BEAST *EMI IRN 4*	**3**	2
24 Mar 90 ●	FLIGHT OF ICARUS / THE TROOPER *EMI IRN 5*	**7**	2
31 Mar 90	2 MINUTES TO MIDNIGHT / ACES HIGH *EMI IRN 6*	**11**	2
7 Apr 90 ●	RUNNING FREE (LIVE) / RUN TO THE HILLS (LIVE) *EMI IRN 7*	**9**	2
14 Apr 90 ●	WASTED YEARS / STRANGER IN A STRANGE LAND *EMI IRN 8*	**9**	2
21 Apr 90 ●	CAN I PLAY WITH MADNESS / THE EVIL THAT MEN DO *EMI IRN 9*	**10**	3
28 Apr 90	THE CLAIRVOYANT / INFINITE DREAMS (LIVE) *EMI IRN 10*	**11**	3
13 Oct 90 ●	NO PRAYER FOR THE DYING *EMI EMD 1017*	**2**	14
23 May 92 ★	FEAR OF THE DARK *EMI CDEMD 1032* ■	**1**	5
3 Apr 93 ●	A REAL LIVE ONE *EMI CDEMD 1042*	**3**	4
30 Oct 93	A REAL DEAD ONE *EMI CDEMD 1048*	**12**	3
20 Nov 93	LIVE AT DONNINGTON *EMI CDDON 1*	**23**	1
14 Oct 95 ●	THE X FACTOR *EMI CDEMD 1087*	**8**	4
5 Oct 96	BEST OF THE BEAST *EMI CDEMD 1097*	**16**	5
4 Apr 98	VIRTUAL XI *EMI 4939152*	**16**	2
10 Jun 00 ●	BRAVE NEW WORLD *EMI 5266052*	**7**	4
6 Apr 02	ROCK IN RIO *EMI 5386430*	**15**	3
16 Nov 02	EDWARD THE GREAT – THE GREATEST HITS *EMI 05431032*	**57**	1
20 Sep 03 ●	DANCE OF DEATH *EMI 5923402*	**2**	5

Live tracks on Maiden Japan (EP): Remember Tomorrow / Killers / Running Free / Innocent Exile. 'Run to the Hills' (re-recording) is a live version. Entries from Feb to Apr 1990 are double 12-inch singles ineligible for the singles chart due to their retail price.

IRONHORSE (see also Randy BACHMAN)
Canada, male vocal / instrumental group (Singles: 3 Weeks) pos/wks

5 May 79	SWEET LUI-LOUISE *Scotti Brothers K 11271*	**60**	3

Big Dee IRWIN *US, male vocalist – Difosco Erwin, b. 4 Aug 1939, d. 27 Aug 1995 (Singles: 17 Weeks)* pos/wks

21 Nov 63 ●	SWINGING ON A STAR *Colpix PX 11010*	**7**	17

Single was a vocal duet by Big Dee Irwin and Little Eva (uncredited)

Gregory ISAACS
Jamaica, male vocalist (Albums: 6 Weeks) pos/wks

12 Sep 81	MORE GREGORY *Charisma PREX 9*	**93**	1
4 Sep 82	NIGHT NURSE *Island ILPS 9721*	**32**	5

Chris ISAAK
US, male vocalist (Singles: 22 Weeks, Albums: 38 Weeks) pos/wks

24 Nov 90 ●	WICKED GAME *London LON 279*	**10**	10
2 Feb 91	BLUE HOTEL *Reprise W 0005*	**17**	7
3 Apr 93	CAN'T DO A THING (TO STOP ME) *Reprise W 0161CD*	**36**	3
10 Jul 93	SAN FRANCISCO DAYS *Reprise W 0182CD*	**62**	1
2 Oct 99	BABY DID A BAD BAD THING *Reprise W 503CD*	**44**	1
26 Jan 91 ●	WICKED GAME *Reprise WX 406*	**3**	30
24 Apr 93	SAN FRANCISCO DAYS *Reprise 9362451162*	**12**	5
3 Jun 95	FOREVER BLUE *Reprise 9362458452*	**27**	3

ISHA-D *UK, male / female vocal / instrumental duo – Phil Coxon and Beverley Reppion (Singles: 4 Weeks)* pos/wks

22 Jul 95	STAY (TONIGHT) *Cleveland City Blues CCBCD 15005*	**28**	3
5 Jul 97	STAY (re-issue) *Satellite 74321498212*	**58**	1

ISHANI See PIRATES featuring ENYA, SHOLA AMA, NAILA BOSS & ISHANI

Ronald ISLEY See Warren G; ISLEY BROTHERS; R KELLY; Rod STEWART

The ISLEY BROTHERS
US, male vocal / instrumental group – Ronald, O'Kelly, b. 25 Dec 1937, d. 31 Mar 1986 and Rudolph Isley (Singles: 108 Weeks, Albums: 24 Weeks) pos/wks

25 Jul 63	TWIST AND SHOUT *Stateside SS 112*	**42**	1
28 Apr 66 ●	THIS OLD HEART OF MINE (IS WEAK FOR YOU) (re) *Tamla Motown TMG 555*	**3**	17
1 Sep 66	I GUESS I'LL ALWAYS LOVE YOU *Tamla Motown TMG 572*	**45**	2
15 Jan 69	I GUESS I'LL ALWAYS LOVE YOU (re-issue) *Tamla Motown TMG 683*	**11**	9
16 Apr 69 ●	BEHIND A PAINTED SMILE *Tamla Motown TMG 693*	**5**	12
25 Jun 69	IT'S YOUR THING *Major Minor MM 621*	**30**	5
30 Aug 69	PUT YOURSELF IN MY PLACE *Tamla Motown TMG 708*	**13**	11
22 Sep 73	THAT LADY *Epic EPC 1704*	**14**	9
19 Jan 74	HIGHWAYS OF MY LIFE *Epic EPC 1980*	**25**	8
25 May 74	SUMMER BREEZE *Epic EPC 2244*	**16**	8
10 Jul 76 ●	HARVEST FOR THE WORLD *Epic EPC 4369*	**10**	8
13 May 78	TAKE ME TO THE NEXT PHASE *Epic EPC 6292*	**50**	4
3 Nov 79	IT'S A DISCO NIGHT (ROCK DON'T STOP) *Epic EPC 7911*	**14**	11
16 Jul 83	BETWEEN THE SHEETS *Epic A 3513*	**52**	3
14 Dec 68	THIS OLD HEART OF MINE *Tamla Motown STML 11034*	**23**	6
14 Aug 76	HARVEST FOR THE WORLD *Epic EPC 81268*	**50**	5
14 May 77	GO FOR YOUR GUNS *Epic EPC 86027*	**46**	2
24 Jun 78	SHOWDOWN *Epic EPC 86039*	**50**	1
5 Mar 88	GREATEST HITS *Telstar STAR 2306*	**41**	10

'This Old Heart of Mine (Is Weak For You)' originally peaked at No.47 before making No.3 in Nov 1968

ISLEY JASPER ISLEY
US, male vocal / instrumental group (Singles: 5 Weeks) pos/wks

23 Nov 85	CARAVAN OF LOVE *Epic A 6612*	**52**	5

ISOTONIK
UK, male producer – Chris Paul (Singles: 9 Weeks) pos/wks

11 Jan 92	DIFFERENT STROKES *Ffrreedom TAB 101*	**12**	5
2 May 92	EVERYWHERE I GO / LET'S GET DOWN *Ffrreedom TAB 108*	**25**	4

'Let's Get Down' listed only from 9 May 1992

IT BITES *UK, male vocal / instrumental group (Singles: 21 Weeks, Albums: 12 Weeks)* pos/wks

12 Jul 86 ●	CALLING ALL THE HEROES *Virgin VS 872*	**6**	12
18 Oct 86	WHOLE NEW WORLD *Virgin VS 896*	**54**	3
23 May 87	THE OLD MAN AND THE ANGEL *Virgin VS 941*	**72**	1
13 May 89	STILL TOO YOUNG TO REMEMBER *Virgin VS 1184*	**66**	3
24 Feb 90	STILL TOO YOUNG TO REMEMBER (re-issue) *Virgin VS 1238*	**60**	2
6 Sep 86	THE BIG LAD IN THE WINDMILL *Virgin V 2378*	**35**	5
2 Apr 88	ONCE AROUND THE WORLD *Virgin V 2456*	**43**	3
24 Jun 89	EAT ME IN ST. LOUIS *Virgin V 2591*	**40**	3
31 Aug 91	THANK YOU AND GOODNIGHT *Virgin VGD 24233*	**59**	1

Singles re-entries are listed as (re), (2re). (3re).... which signifies that the hit re-entered the chart once, twice or three times...

IT'S A BEAUTIFUL DAY
US, male / female vocal / instrumental group (Albums: 3 Weeks) pos/wks

23 May 70	IT'S A BEAUTIFUL DAY *CBS 63722*	58	1
18 Jul 70	MARRYING MAIDEN *CBS 66236*	45	2

IT'S IMMATERIAL
UK, male vocal / instrumental group (Singles: 10 Weeks, Albums: 3 Weeks) pos/wks

12 Apr 86	DRIVING AWAY FROM HOME (JIM'S TUNE) *Siren SIREN 15*	18	7
2 Aug 86	ED'S FUNKY DINER (FRIDAY NIGHT, SATURDAY MORNING) *Siren SIREN 24*	65	3
27 Sep 86	LIFE'S HARD AND THEN YOU DIE *Siren SIRENLP 4*	62	3

ITTY BITTY BOOZY WOOZY
(see also DA TECHNO BOHEMIAN; KLUBHEADZ; DRUNKENMONKEY)
Holland, male instrumental / production duo – Addy Van Der Zwan and Koen Groeneveld (Singles: 2 Weeks) pos/wks

25 Nov 95	TEMPO FIESTA (PARTY TIME) *Systematic SYSCD 23*	34	2

Burl IVES
US, male vocalist, b. 14 Jun 1909, d. 14 Apr 1995 (Singles: 25 Weeks) pos/wks

25 Jan 62	● A LITTLE BITTY TEAR *Brunswick 05863*	9	15
17 May 62	FUNNY WAY OF LAUGHIN' *Brunswick 05868*	29	10

The IVY LEAGUE
UK, male vocal trio (Singles: 31 Weeks) pos/wks

4 Feb 65	● FUNNY HOW LOVE CAN BE *Piccadilly 7N 35222*	8	9
6 May 65	THAT'S WHY I'M CRYING *Piccadilly 7N 35228*	22	8
24 Jun 65	● TOSSING AND TURNING *Piccadilly 7N 35251*	3	13
14 Jul 66	WILLOW TREE *Piccadilly 7N 35326*	50	1

IZIT
UK, male / female vocal / instrumental group (Singles: 3 Weeks) pos/wks

2 Dec 89	STORIES *ffrr F 122*	52	3

IZZY See GLADIATOR featuring IZZY

Ray J
US, male vocalist – Willie Ray Norwood Jr (Singles: 12 Weeks) pos/wks

17 Oct 98	THAT'S WHY I LIE *Atlantic AT 0049CD*	71	1
16 Jun 01	● ANOTHER DAY IN PARADISE *WEA WEA 327CD1* [1]	5	10
11 Aug 01	WAIT A MINUTE *Atlantic AT 0106CD* [2]	54	1

[1] Brandy and Ray J [2] Ray J featuring Lil' Kim

J.A.L.N. BAND
UK / Jamaica, male vocal / instrumental group (Singles: 17 Weeks) pos/wks

11 Sep 76	DISCO MUSIC / I LIKE IT *Magnet MAG 73*	21	9
27 Aug 77	I GOT TO SING *Magnet MAG 97*	40	4
1 Jul 78	GET UP (AND LET YOURSELF GO) *Magnet MAG 118*	53	4

JB's ALL STARS
UK, male / female vocal / instrumental group (Singles: 4 Weeks) pos/wks

11 Feb 84	BACKFIELD IN MOTION *RCA Victor RCA 384*	48	4

JC
UK, male producer (Singles: 1 Week) pos/wks

7 Feb 98	SO HOT *East West EW 146CD*	74	1

JC-001
UK, male rapper – Jonathan Chandra (Singles: 4 Weeks) pos/wks

24 Apr 93	NEVER AGAIN *AnXious ANX 1012CD*	67	2
26 Jun 93	CUPID *AnXious ANX 1014CD*	56	2

JD See SNOOP DOGG

JD aka 'DREADY'
UK, male vocalist – Karl Jairzhino Daniel (Singles: 1 Week) pos/wks

2 Aug 03	SIGNAL *Independiente SSB 2MS*	64	1

JDS
Italy / UK, male DJ / production duo – Julian Napolitano and Darren Pearce (Singles: 3 Weeks) pos/wks

27 Sep 97	NINE WAYS *ffrr FCD 310*	61	1
23 May 98	LONDON TOWN *Jive 0530042*	49	1
3 Mar 01	NINE WAYS (re-mix) *ffrr FCD 391*	47	1

JFK
UK, male producer – J.F. Kinch (Singles: 3 Weeks) pos/wks

15 Sep 01	GOOD GOD *Y2K Y2K 025CD*	71	1
26 Jan 02	WHIPLASH *Y2K Y2K 027CD*	47	1
4 May 02	THE SOUND OF BLUE *Y2K Y2K 030CD*	55	1

Gemma J See ONYX featuring Gemma J

JJ
UK, male / female vocal / instrumental duo (Singles: 3 Weeks) pos/wks

9 Feb 91	IF THIS IS LOVE *Columbia 6566097*	55	3

JJ See DJ LUCK & MC NEAT

JJ72
Ireland, male / female vocal / instrumental group (Singles: 13 Weeks, Albums: 22 Weeks) pos/wks

3 Jun 00	LONG WAY SOUTH *Lakota LAK 0015CD*	68	1
26 Aug 00	OXYGEN *Lakota LAK 0016CD*	23	3
4 Nov 00	OCTOBER SWIMMER *Lakota LAK 0018CD*	29	3
10 Feb 01	SNOW *Lakota LAK 0019CD*	21	3
12 Oct 02	FORMULAE *Lakota / Columbia 6731592*	28	2
22 Feb 03	ALWAYS AND FOREVER *Columbia 6734322*	43	1
9 Sep 00	JJ72 *Lakota LAKCD 0017*	16	20
26 Oct 02	I TO SKY *Lakota 5095292*	20	2

JKD BAND
UK, male vocal / instrumental group (Singles: 4 Weeks) pos/wks

1 Jul 78	DRAGON POWER *Satril SAT 132*	58	4

JMD See TYREE

J MAGIK See Ian POOLEY

JM SILK
US, male vocal / instrumental duo – Steve 'Silk' Hurley and Keith Nunnally (Singles: 6 Weeks) pos/wks

25 Oct 86	I CAN'T TURN AROUND *RCA PB 49793*	62	3
7 Mar 87	LET THE MUSIC TAKE CONTROL *RCA PB 49767*	47	3

J PAC
UK, male vocal / instrumental duo (Singles: 2 Weeks) pos/wks

22 Jul 95	ROCK 'N' ROLL (DOLE) *East West YZ 953CD*	51	2

JT and the BIG FAMILY
Italy, male / female vocal / instrumental group (Singles: 8 Weeks) pos/wks

3 Mar 90	● MOMENTS IN SOUL *Champion CHAMP 237*	7	8

JT PLAYAZ
UK, male production trio (Singles: 4 Weeks) pos/wks

5 Apr 97	JUST PLAYIN' *Pukka CDJTP 1*	30	3
2 May 98	LET'S GET DOWN *MCA MCSTD 40161*	64	1

JTQ
UK, male vocal / instrumental group (Singles: 6 Weeks, Albums: 5 Weeks) pos/wks

3 Apr 93	LOVE THE LIFE *Big Life BLRD 93* [1]	34	3
3 Jul 93	SEE A BRIGHTER DAY *Big Life BLRDA 97* [1]	49	2

		pos/wks
25 Feb 95	LOVE WILL KEEP US TOGETHER *Acid Jazz JAZID 112CD* [2]	63 1
1 May 93	SUPERNATURAL FEELING *Big Life BLRCD 21* [1]	36 3
29 Oct 94	EXTENDED PLAY *Acid Jazz JAZID 110CD* [2]	70 1
11 Mar 95	IN THE HAND OF THE INEVITABLE	
	Acid Jazz JAZID CD 115 [2]	63 1

[1] JTQ with Noel McKoy [2] JTQ featuring Alison Limerick [1] JTQ with Noel McKoy [2] James Taylor Quartet

J WEAV See CHINGY

JX UK, male producer – Jake Williams (Singles: 36 Weeks)
		pos/wks
2 Apr 94	SON OF A GUN *Internal Dance IDC 5*	13 6
1 Apr 95	YOU BELONG TO ME *Ffrreedom TABCD 227*	17 5
19 Aug 95 ●	SON OF A GUN (re-mix) *Ffrreedom TABCD 233*	6 6
18 May 96 ●	THERE'S NOTHING I WON'T DO *Ffrreedom TABCD 241*	4 13
8 Mar 97	CLOSE TO YOUR HEART *Ffrreedom TABCD 245*	18 3
6 Mar 04	RESTLESS *Tidy Two TIDYTWOJX 1C*	22 3

J-KWON US, male rapper – Jerrell Jones (Singles: 11 Weeks)
		pos/wks
24 Jul 04 ●	TIPSY *LaFace 82876624362*	4 11

JA RULE (391) Top 500
Mobo winner Jeffrey Atkins (hence JA), b. New York, US, 29 Feb 1976. One of this millennium's most regular transatlantic chart entrants, and one of just six acts to replace themselves at the top of the US chart (Singles: 107 Weeks, Albums: 67 Weeks)
		pos/wks
13 Mar 99	CAN I GET A ... *Def Jam 5668472* [1]	24 3
3 Mar 01	BETWEEN ME AND YOU *Def Jam 5727402* [2]	26 3
10 Nov 01	LIVIN' IT UP *Def Jam 5888142* [3]	27 4
10 Nov 01 ●	I'M REAL *Epic 6720322* ▲	4 15
2 Feb 02	ALWAYS ON TIME *Def Jam 5889462* [4] ▲	6 13
23 Mar 02 ●	AIN'T IT FUNNY *Epic 6724922* [5] ▲	4 13
3 Aug 02	LIVIN' IT UP (re-issue) *Def Jam 0639782* [3]	5 8
24 Aug 02	RAINY DAYZ *MCA MCSTD 40288* [6]	17 5
12 Oct 02 ●	DOWN 4 U (2re) *Murder Inc 0639002* [7]	4 10
21 Dec 02	THUG LOVIN' *Def Jam 0637872* [8]	15 8
29 Mar 03	MESMERIZE *Murder Inc / Mercury 0779582* [4]	12 8
6 Dec 03 ●	CLAP BACK / REIGNS *Def Jam / Mercury 9814618*	9 9
6 Nov 04 ★	WONDERFUL *Def Jam 9864605* [9] ■	1 8+
27 Oct 01 ●	PAIN IS LOVE *Def Jam 5864372* ▲	3 50
30 Nov 02	THE LAST TEMPTATION *Def Jam / Mercury 0635432*	14 13
15 Nov 03	BLOOD IN MY EYE *Def Jam / Mercury 9861329*	51 2
20 Nov 04	R.U.L.E. *Def Jam 9862918*	33 2

[1] Jay-Z featuring Amil & Ja Rule [2] Ja Rule featuring Christina Milian [3] Ja Rule featuring Case [4] Ja Rule featuring R Kelly and Ashanti

JABBA See NINA SKY

JACK 'N' CHILL
UK, male instrumental group (Singles: 21 Weeks)
		pos/wks
6 Jun 87 ●	THE JACK THAT HOUSE BUILT (re)	
	Oval / 10 / Virgin TEN 174	6 16
9 Jul 88	BEATIN' THE HEAT *10 TEN 234*	42 5

'The Jack that House Built' reached its peak postition only on re-entry in Jan 1988

Terry JACKS (see also The POPPY FAMILY)
Canada, male vocalist (Singles: 21 Weeks)
		pos/wks
23 Mar 74 ★	SEASONS IN THE SUN *Bell 1344* ▲	1 12
29 Jun 74 ●	IF YOU GO AWAY *Bell 1362*	8 9

Alan JACKSON
US, male vocalist / instrumentalist – guitar (Albums: 2 Weeks)
		pos/wks
3 Jul 04	THE VERY BEST OF ALAN JACKSON	
	Arista Nashville 82876601122	47 2

Chad JACKSON
UK, male DJ / producer – Mark Chadwick (Singles: 10 Weeks)
		pos/wks
2 Jun 90 ●	HEAR THE DRUMMER (GET WICKED) *Big Wave BWR 36*	3 10

Dee D JACKSON
UK, female vocalist – Deirdre Cozier (Singles: 14 Weeks)
		pos/wks
22 Apr 78 ●	AUTOMATIC LOVER *Mercury 6007 171*	4 9
2 Sep 78 ●	METEOR MAN *Mercury 6007 182*	48 5

Freddie JACKSON
US, male vocalist (Singles: 31 Weeks, Albums: 48 Weeks)
		pos/wks
23 Nov 85	YOU ARE MY LADY *Capitol CL 379*	49 4
22 Feb 86	ROCK ME TONIGHT (FOR OLD TIME'S SAKE) *Capitol CL 358*	18 9
11 Oct 86	TASTY LOVE *Capitol CL 428*	73 1
7 Feb 87	HAVE YOU EVER LOVED SOMEBODY *Capitol CL 437*	33 6
9 Jul 88	NICE 'N' SLOW *Capitol CL 502*	56 2
15 Oct 88	CRAZY (FOR ME) *Capitol CL 510*	41 3
5 Sep 92	ME AND MRS JONES *Capitol CL 668*	32 5
15 Jan 94	MAKE LOVE EASY *RCA 74321179162*	70 1
18 May 85	ROCK ME TONIGHT *Capitol EJ 24403161*	27 22
8 Nov 86	JUST LIKE THE FIRST TIME *Capitol EST 2023*	30 15
30 Jul 88	DON'T LET LOVE SLIP AWAY *Capitol EST 2067*	24 9
17 Nov 90	DO ME AGAIN *Capitol EST 2134E*	48 2

Gisele JACKSON US, female vocalist (Singles: 1 Week)
		pos/wks
30 Aug 97	LOVE COMMANDMENTS *Manifesto FESCD 28*	54 1

Janet JACKSON (63) Top 500 (see also Herb ALPERT)
Multi-award-winning, record-breaking vocalist / performer, b. 16 May 1966, Indiana, US. Although not an overnight sensation, the youngest of the talented Jackson family has amassed a staggering collection of gold albums and singles. A 'wardrobe malfunction' at the 2004 Super Bowl caught worldwide media attention. Best-selling single: 'Together Again' 747,238 (Singles: 297 Weeks, Albums: 270 Weeks)
		pos/wks
22 Mar 86 ●	WHAT HAVE YOU DONE FOR ME LATELY *A&M AM 308*	3 14
31 May 86	NASTY *A&M AM 316*	19 9
9 Aug 86 ●	WHEN I THINK OF YOU *A&M AM 337* ▲	10 10
1 Nov 86	CONTROL *A&M AM 359*	42 5
21 Mar 87 ●	LET'S WAIT AWHILE *Breakout USA 601*	3 10
13 Jun 87	PLEASURE PRINCIPLE *Breakout USA 604*	24 5
14 Nov 87	FUNNY HOW TIME FLIES (WHEN YOU'RE HAVING FUN)	
	A&M Breakout USA 613	59 2
2 Sep 89 ●	MISS YOU MUCH *Breakout USA 663* ▲	22 7
4 Nov 89	RHYTHM NATION *Breakout USA 673*	23 5
27 Jan 90	COME BACK TO ME *Breakout USA 681*	20 7
31 Mar 90	ESCAPADE *Breakout USA 684* ▲	17 7
7 Jul 90	ALRIGHT *A&M USA 693*	20 5
8 Sep 90	BLACK CAT *A&M AM 587* ▲	15 6
27 Oct 90	LOVE WILL NEVER DO (WITHOUT YOU) *A&M AM 700* ▲	34 4
15 Aug 92 ●	THE BEST THINGS IN LIFE ARE FREE	
	Perspective PERSS 7400 [1]	2 13
8 May 93 ●	THAT'S THE WAY LOVE GOES *Virgin VSCDG 1460* ▲	2 10
31 Jul 93	IF *Virgin VSCDT 1474*	14 7
20 Nov 93 ●	AGAIN *Virgin VSCDG 1481* ▲	6 11
12 Mar 94	BECAUSE OF LOVE *Virgin VSCDG 1488*	19 4
18 Jun 94	ANY TIME ANY PLACE *Virgin VSCDT 1501*	13 5
26 Nov 94	YOU WANT THIS *Virgin VSCDT 1519*	14 3
18 Mar 95 ●	WHOOPS NOW / WHAT'LL I DO *Virgin VSCDT 1533*	9 8
10 Jun 95 ●	SCREAM (re) *Epic 6620222* [2]	3 13
24 Jun 95	SCREAM (re-mix) *Epic 6621277* [2]	43 2
23 Sep 95 ●	RUNAWAY *A&M 5811972*	6 7
16 Dec 95 ●	THE BEST THINGS IN LIFE ARE FREE (re-mix)	
	A&M 5813092 [3]	7 7
6 Apr 96	TWENTY FOREPLAY *A&M 5815112*	22 4
4 Oct 97 ●	GOT 'TIL IT'S GONE *Virgin VSCDG 1666* [4]	6 9
13 Dec 97 ●	TOGETHER AGAIN *Virgin VSCDG 1670* [5] ▲	4 19
4 Apr 98 ●	I GET LONELY *Virgin VSCDT 1683* [6]	5 7
27 Jun 98	GO DEEP *Virgin VSCDT 1680* [5]	13 5
19 Dec 98	EVERY TIME *Virgin VSCDT 1720* [5]	46 1
17 Apr 99	GIRLFRIEND / BOYFRIEND *Interscope IND 95640* [7]	11 7
1 May 99 ●	WHAT'S IT GONNA BE?! *Elektra E 3762CD1* [8]	6 7
19 Aug 00 ●	DOESN'T REALLY MATTER *Def Soul 5629152* ▲	5 11
21 Apr 01 ●	ALL FOR YOU *Virgin VSCDT 1801* ▲	3 11
11 Aug 01	SOMEONE TO CALL MY LOVER *Virgin VSCDT 1813*	11 5
22 Dec 01	SON OF A GUN (I BETCHA THINK THIS SONG IS ABOUT YOU) (re) *Virgin VUSCD 232* [9]	13 9
28 Sep 02 ●	FEEL IT BOY (re) *Virgin VUSCD 258* [10]	9 7
24 Apr 04	JUST A LITTLE WHILE *Virgin VUSCD 285* [5]	15 5
19 Jun 04	ALL NITE (DON'T STOP) / I WANT YOU *Virgin VUSDX 292* [5]	19 4
5 Apr 86	CONTROL *A&M AMA 5016* ▲	8 72
14 Nov 87	CONTROL – THE REMIXES *Breakout MIXLP 1*	20 14
30 Sep 89 ●	JANET JACKSON'S RHYTHM NATION 1814	
	A&M AMA 3920 ▲	4 43
29 May 93 ★	JANET / JANET. REMIXED *Virgin CDV 2720* ■ ▲	1 57
14 Oct 95 ●	DESIGN OF A DECADE 1986-1996 *A&M 5404222*	2 21
18 Oct 97 ●	THE VELVET ROPE *Virgin CDV 2860* [1] ▲	6 43

5 May 01 ●	**ALL FOR YOU** *Virgin CDV 2950* [1] ▲	2	18
10 Apr 04	**DAMITA JO** *Virgin CDVUS 251* [1]	32	2

[1] Luther Vandross and Janet Jackson with special guests BBD and Ralph Tresvant
[2] Michael Jackson and Janet Jackson [3] Luther Vandross and Janet Jackson
[4] Janet featuring Q-Tip and Joni Mitchell [5] Janet [6] Janet featuring
BLACKstreet [7] BLACKstreet and Janet [8] Busta Rhymes featuring Janet [9] Janet
with Carly Simon featuring Missy Elliott [10] Beenie Man featuring Janet [1] Janet

From 25 Mar 95 'Janet' was listed with the re-mix album 'Janet. Remixed'

Jermaine JACKSON (see also The JACKSONS)
US, male vocalist (Singles: 43 Weeks, Albums: 12 Weeks)   pos/wks

10 May 80 ●	**LET'S GET SERIOUS** *Motown TMG 1183*	8	11
26 Jul 80	**BURNIN' HOT** *Motown TMG 1194*	32	6
30 May 81	**YOU LIKE ME DON'T YOU** *Motown TMG 1222*	41	5
12 May 84	**SWEETEST SWEETEST** *Arista JJK 1*	52	4
27 Oct 84	**WHEN THE RAIN BEGINS TO FALL** *Arista ARIST 584* [1]	68	2
16 Feb 85	**DO WHAT YOU DO** *Arista ARIST 609*	6	13
21 Oct 89	**DON'T TAKE IT PERSONAL** *Arista 112634*	69	2
31 May 80	**LET'S GET SERIOUS** *Motown STML 12127*	22	6
12 May 84	**DYNAMITE** *Arista 206 317*	57	6

[1] Jermaine Jackson and Pia Zadora

'Let's Get Serious' features uncredited vocalist Stevie Wonder

Joe JACKSON (462 Top 500) Many faceted singer / songwriter and
*pianist, b. 11 Aug 1955, Staffordshire, UK. Unique and critically acclaimed
recording artist whose five Grammy nominations span 1979 to 2001 (when
'Symphony No.1' became his first winner). His original 1980s band re-united
in 2003 (Singles: 49 Weeks, Albums: 106 Weeks)*   pos/wks

4 Aug 79	**IS SHE REALLY GOING OUT WITH HIM?** *A&M AMS 7459*	13	14
12 Jan 80 ●	**IT'S DIFFERENT FOR GIRLS** *A&M AMS 7493*	5	9
4 Jul 81	**JUMPIN' JIVE** *A&M AMS 8145* [1]	43	5
8 Jan 83 ●	**STEPPIN' OUT** *A&M AMS 8262*	6	8
12 Mar 83	**BREAKING US IN TWO** *A&M AM 101*	59	4
28 Apr 84	**HAPPY ENDING** *A&M AM 186*	58	3
7 Jul 84	**BE MY NUMBER TWO** *A&M AM 200*	70	2
7 Jun 86	**LEFT OF CENTER** *A&M AM 320* [2]	32	9
17 Mar 79	**LOOK SHARP!** *A&M AMLH 64743*	40	11
13 Oct 79	**I'M THE MAN** *A&M AMLH 64794*	12	16
18 Oct 80	**BEAT CRAZY** *A&M AMLH 64837*	42	3
4 Jul 81	**JUMPIN' LIVE** *A&M AMLH 68530* [1]	14	14
3 Jul 82 ●	**NIGHT AND DAY** *A&M AMLH 64906*	3	27
7 Apr 84	**BODY AND SOUL** *A&M AMLX 65000*	14	14
5 Apr 86	**BIG WORLD** *A&M JWA 3*	41	5
7 May 88	**LIVE 1980-86** *A&M AMA 6706*	66	2
29 Apr 89	**BLAZE OF GLORY** *A&M AMA 5249*	36	3
15 Sep 90 ●	**STEPPING OUT – THE VERY BEST OF JOE JACKSON** *A&M 3970521*	7	9
11 May 91	**LAUGHTER AND LUST** *Virgin America VUSLP 34*	41	2

[1] Joe Jackson's Jumpin' Jive [2] Suzanne Vega featuring Joe Jackson
[1] Joe Jackson's Jumpin' Jive

Michael JACKSON (8 Top 500) (see also The JACKSONS)
*The self-proclaimed 'King of Pop', b. 29 Aug 1958, Indiana, US, is arguably the
best-known living musical artist. The youngest vocalist (age 11, fronting
The Jackson Five) to top the US singles chart, he was also the first artist to
enter that chart at No.1 (with 'You Are Not Alone'). In 1991 he became the first
US act to enter the UK chart at No.1 since Elvis Presley in 1960 (whose daughter,
Lisa Marie, he married in 1994). This outstanding, innovative singer / songwriter and performer has broken countless other records for his singles,
albums, videos and tours. 'Thriller' is the world's biggest-selling record, with
global sales estimates varying between 47 and 51.2 million, including 26 million
in the US alone. It topped the US albums chart for an unprecedented 37 weeks
and had a record 12 Grammy nominations. Also on the album front, 'HIStory –
Past Present and Future Book 1' sold more copies in its first week than any
previous double album. 'Dangerous' sold a staggering 10 million worldwide
in its first month and 'Number Ones' returned him to the top in 2003. Both
'Thriller' and 'Bad' have sold more than three million copies in the UK.
Jackson, whose private life and physical appearance have attracted much
media attention, was the first entertainer to earn more than $100 million in a
year, and the first to receive an award for selling at least 100m albums outside
the US. Jacko was inducted into the UK Music Hall of Fame in 2004, representing
the 1980s. Total UK singles sales: 11,310,958. Best-selling single: 'Earth Song'
1,038,821 (Singles: 515 Weeks, Albums: 962 Weeks)*   pos/wks

12 Feb 72 ●	**GOT TO BE THERE** *Tamla Motown TMG 797*	5	11
20 May 72 ●	**ROCKIN' ROBIN** *Tamla Motown TMG 816*	3	14

19 Aug 72 ●	**AIN'T NO SUNSHINE** *Tamla Motown TMG 826*	8	11
25 Nov 72 ●	**BEN** *Tamla Motown TMG 834* ▲	7	14
18 Nov 78	**EASE ON DOWN THE ROAD** *MCA 396* [1]	45	4
15 Sep 79 ●	**DON'T STOP 'TIL YOU GET ENOUGH** *Epic EPC 7763* ▲	3	12
24 Nov 79	**OFF THE WALL** *Epic EPC 8045*	7	10
9 Feb 80 ●	**ROCK WITH YOU** *Epic EPC 8206* ▲	7	9
3 May 80 ●	**SHE'S OUT OF MY LIFE** *Epic EPC 8384*	3	9
26 Jul 80	**GIRLFRIEND** *Epic EPC 8782*	41	5
23 May 81 ★	**ONE DAY IN YOUR LIFE** *Motown TMG 976*	1	14
1 Aug 81	**WE'RE ALMOST THERE** *Motown TMG 977*	46	4
6 Nov 82 ●	**THE GIRL IS MINE** (re) *Epic EPC A 2729* [2]	8	10
29 Jan 83 ★	**BILLIE JEAN** *Epic EPC A 3084* ▲	1	15
9 Apr 83 ●	**BEAT IT** *Epic EPC A 3258* ▲	3	12
11 Jun 83 ●	**WANNA BE STARTIN' SOMETHIN'** *Epic A 3427*	8	9
23 Jul 83	**HAPPY (LOVE THEME FROM 'LADY SINGS THE BLUES')** *Tamla Motown TMG 986*	52	3
15 Oct 83 ●	**SAY SAY SAY** *Parlophone R 6062* [3] ▲	2	15
19 Nov 83 ●	**THRILLER** *Epic A 3643*	10	11
31 Mar 84 ●	**P.Y.T. (PRETTY YOUNG THING)** *Epic A 4136*	11	8
2 Jun 84 ●	**FAREWELL MY SUMMER LOVE** *Motown TMG 1342*	7	12
11 Aug 84	**GIRL YOU'RE SO TOGETHER** *Motown TMG 1355*	33	8
8 Aug 87 ★	**I JUST CAN'T STOP LOVING YOU** *Epic 650202 7* ▲	1	9
26 Sep 87 ●	**BAD** *Epic 651155 7* ▲	3	11
5 Dec 87 ●	**THE WAY YOU MAKE ME FEEL** *Epic 651275 7* ▲	3	10
20 Feb 88	**MAN IN THE MIRROR** *Epic 651388 7* ▲	21	5
16 Apr 88 ●	**I WANT YOU BACK** *Motown ZB 41919* [4]	8	9
28 May 88	**GET IT** *Motown ZB 41883* [5]	37	4
16 Jul 88 ●	**DIRTY DIANA** *Epic 651546 7* ▲	4	8
10 Sep 88	**ANOTHER PART OF ME** *Epic 652844 7*	15	6
26 Nov 88 ●	**SMOOTH CRIMINAL** *Epic 653026 7*	8	10
25 Feb 89 ●	**LEAVE ME ALONE** *Epic 654672 7*	2	9
15 Jul 89	**LIBERIAN GIRL** *Epic 654947 0*	13	6
23 Nov 91 ★	**BLACK OR WHITE** *Epic 6575987* ■	1	10
18 Jan 92	**BLACK OR WHITE** (re-mix) *Epic 6577316*	14	4
15 Feb 92 ●	**REMEMBER THE TIME / COME TOGETHER** *Epic 6577747*	3	8
2 May 92 ●	**IN THE CLOSET** *Epic 6580187*	8	6
25 Jul 92 ●	**WHO IS IT** *Epic 6581797*	10	7
12 Sep 92 ●	**JAM** *Epic 6583607*	13	5
5 Dec 92 ●	**HEAL THE WORLD** *Epic 6584887*	2	15
27 Feb 93 ●	**GIVE IN TO ME** *Epic 6590692*	2	9
10 Jul 93 ●	**WILL YOU BE THERE** *Epic 6592222*	9	8
18 Dec 93	**GONE TOO SOON** *Epic 6599762*	33	5
10 Jun 95 ●	**SCREAM** (re) *Epic 6620222* [6]	3	13
24 Jun 95	**SCREAM** (re-mix) *Epic 6621277* [6]	43	2
2 Sep 95 ★	**YOU ARE NOT ALONE** *Epic 6623102* ▲	1	15
9 Dec 95 ●	**EARTH SONG** *Epic 6626955* ◆ ■	1	17
20 Apr 96 ●	**THEY DON'T CARE ABOUT US** (2re) *Epic 6629502*	4	14
24 Aug 96 ●	**WHY** *Epic 6629502* [7]	2	9
16 Nov 96 ●	**STRANGER IN MOSCOW** (re) *Epic 6637872*	4	11
3 May 97 ●	**BLOOD ON THE DANCEFLOOR** *Epic 6644625* ■	1	9
19 Jul 97 ●	**HISTORY / GHOSTS** *Epic 6647962*	5	8
20 Oct 01 ●	**YOU ROCK MY WORLD** *Epic 6720292*	2	15
22 Dec 01	**CRY** *Epic 6721822*	25	4
6 Dec 03 ●	**ONE MORE CHANCE** *Epic 6744802*	5	9
3 Jun 72	**GOT TO BE THERE** *Tamla Motown STML 11205*	37	5
13 Jan 73	**BEN** *Tamla Motown STML 11220*	17	7
29 Sep 79 ●	**OFF THE WALL** *Epic EPC 83468*	5	189
4 Jul 81	**THE BEST OF MICHAEL JACKSON** *Motown STMR 9009*	11	18
18 Jul 81	**ONE DAY IN YOUR LIFE** *Motown STML 12158*	29	8
11 Dec 82 ★	**THRILLER** *Epic EPC 85930* ▲	1	201
12 Feb 83	**E.T. – THE EXTRA TERRESTRIAL** *MCA 7000*	82	2
9 Jul 83 ★	**18 GREATEST HITS** *Telstar STAR 2232*	1	58
3 Dec 83	**MICHAEL JACKSON 9 SINGLE PACK** *Epic MJ 1*	66	3
9 Jun 84 ●	**FAREWELL MY SUMMER LOVE** *Motown ZL 72227*	9	14
15 Nov 86	**DIANA ROSS. MICHAEL JACKSON. GLADYS KNIGHT. STEVIE WONDER. THEIR VERY BEST BACK TO BACK** *PrioriTyV PTVR 2* [2]	21	10
12 Sep 87 ★	**BAD** *Epic EPC 4502901* ■ ▲	1	125
31 Oct 87	**LOVE SONGS** *Telstar STAR 2298* [3]	12	24
26 Dec 87	**THE MICHAEL JACKSON MIX** *Stylus SMR 745*	27	25
30 Jul 88	**SOUVENIR SINGLES PACK** *Epic MJ 5*	91	1
30 Nov 91 ★	**DANGEROUS** *Epic 4658021* ■ ▲	1	96
29 Feb 92	**MOTOWN'S GREATEST HITS** *Motown 5300142*	53	2
15 Aug 92	**TOUR SOUVENIR PACK** *Epic MJ 4*	32	3
24 Jun 95 ★	**HISTORY – PAST PRESENT AND FUTURE BOOK 1** *Epic 4747092* ▲	1	78
24 May 97 ★	**BLOOD ON THE DANCE FLOOR – HISTORY IN THE MIX** *Epic 4875002* ■	1	16

		pos/wks
19 Jul 97 ●	THE BEST OF MICHAEL JACKSON AND THE JACKSON 5IVE – THE MOTOWN YEARS *PolyGram TV 5308042* [4]	5 12
10 Nov 01 ★	INVINCIBLE *Epic 4951742* ■ ▲	1 12
24 Nov 01	GREATEST HITS – HISTORY VOLUME 1 *Epic 5018692*	15 16
29 Nov 03 ★	NUMBER ONES *Epic 5138002* ■	1 36
4 Dec 04	THE ULTIMATE COLLECTION *Epic 5177433*	75 1

[1] Diana Ross and Michael Jackson [2] Michael Jackson and Paul McCartney
[3] Paul McCartney and Michael Jackson [4] Michael Jackson with The Jackson Five [5] Stevie Wonder and Michael Jackson [6] Michael Jackson and Janet Jackson
[7] 3T featuring Michael Jackson [1] Michael Jackson plus The Jackson Five
[2] Diana Ross / Michael Jackson / Gladys Knight / Stevie Wonder [3] Diana Ross and Michael Jackson [4] Michael Jackson and The Jackson Five

The sleeve of 'I Just Can't Stop Loving You' credits Siedah Garrett but the label does not. 'Come Together' was listed only from 7 Mar 1992. It peaked at No.10. Chart rules allow for a maximum of three formats; the additional three formats of 'Scream' – which each included re-mixed versions – were therefore listed separately (see 24 Jun 1995) 'Off the Wall' changed its catalogue number to 4500861 during its chart run. From 14 Jan 89, when multi-artist albums were excluded from the main chart, 'Love Songs' was listed in the compilation albums chart. 'The Ultimate Collection' is a career-spanning four-CD and DVD box set featuring singles, album tracks, demos, rarities and a previously unreleased live concert

Mick JACKSON *UK, male vocalist (Singles: 16 Weeks)*

		pos/wks
30 Sep 78	BLAME IT ON THE BOOGIE *Atlantic K 11102*	15 8
3 Feb 79	WEEKEND *Atlantic K 11224*	38 8

Millie JACKSON
US, female vocalist (Singles: 8 Weeks, Albums: 7 Weeks)

		pos/wks
18 Nov 72	MY MAN, A SWEET MAN *Mojo 2093 022*	50 1
10 Mar 84	I FEEL LIKE WALKIN' IN THE RAIN *Sire W 9348*	55 2
15 Jun 85	ACT OF WAR *Rocket EJS 8* [1]	32 5
18 Feb 84	E.S.P. *Sire 250382*	59 5
6 Apr 85	LIVE AND UNCENSORED *Important TADLP 001*	81 2

[1] Elton John and Millie Jackson

Paul JACKSON / Steve SMITH
UK, male producer and male vocalist (Singles: 2 Weeks)

		pos/wks
24 Jan 04	THE PUSH (FAR FROM HERE) *Underwater H20 041CD*	51 2

Stonewall JACKSON *US, male vocalist (Singles: 2 Weeks)*

		pos/wks
17 Jul 59	WATERLOO *Philips PB 941*	24 2

Tony JACKSON See Q

Tony JACKSON and The VIBRATIONS (see also The SEARCHERS)
*UK, male vocal / instrumental group – leader
b. 16 Jul 1940, d. 18 Aug 2003 (Singles: 3 Weeks)*

		pos/wks
8 Oct 64	BYE BYE BABY *Pye 7N 15685*	38 3

Wanda JACKSON *US, female vocalist (Singles: 11 Weeks)*

		pos/wks
1 Sep 60	LET'S HAVE A PARTY *Capitol CL 15147*	32 8
26 Jan 61	MEAN MEAN MAN (re) *Capitol CL 15176*	40 3

JACKSON SISTERS *US, female vocal group (Singles: 2 Weeks)*

		pos/wks
20 Jun 87	I BELIEVE IN MIRACLES *Urban URB 4*	72 2

The JACKSONS (117) Top 500 *One of the world's biggest-selling and most popular groups: brothers Jackie, Tito, Jermaine, Marlon and solo superstar Michael Jackson, with Randy joining in 1977. The Indiana quintet topped the US chart with their first four hits, and have reportedly sold more than 100 million records (Singles: 235 Weeks, Albums: 162 Weeks)* pos/wks

		pos/wks
31 Jan 70 ●	I WANT YOU BACK *Tamla Motown TMG 724* [1] ▲	2 13
16 May 70 ●	ABC *Tamla Motown TMG 738* [1] ▲	8 11
1 Aug 70 ●	THE LOVE YOU SAVE *Tamla Motown TMG 746* [1] ▲	7 9
21 Nov 70 ●	I'LL BE THERE *Tamla Motown TMG 758* [1] ▲	4 16
10 Apr 71	MAMA'S PEARL *Tamla Motown TMG 769* [1]	25 7
17 Jul 71	NEVER CAN SAY GOODBYE *Tamla Motown TMG 778* [1]	33 7
11 Nov 72 ●	LOOKIN' THROUGH THE WINDOWS *Tamla Motown TMG 833*	9 11
23 Dec 72	SANTA CLAUS IS COMING TO TOWN *Tamla Motown TMG 837* [1]	43 3
17 Feb 73 ●	DOCTOR MY EYES *Tamla Motown TMG 842* [1]	9 10

		pos/wks
9 Jun 73	HALLELUJAH DAY *Tamla Motown TMG 856* [1]	20 9
8 Sep 73	SKYWRITER *Tamla Motown TMG 865* [1]	25 8
9 Apr 77	ENJOY YOURSELF *Epic EPC 5063*	42 4
4 Jun 77 ★	SHOW YOU THE WAY TO GO *Epic EPC 5266*	1 10
13 Aug 77	DREAMER *Epic EPC 5458*	22 9
5 Nov 77	GOIN' PLACES *Epic EPC 5732*	26 7
11 Feb 78	EVEN THOUGH YOU'VE GONE *Epic EPC 5919*	31 4
23 Sep 78 ●	BLAME IT ON THE BOOGIE *Epic EPC 6683*	8 12
3 Feb 79	DESTINY *Epic EPC 6983*	39 6
24 Mar 79 ●	SHAKE YOUR BODY (DOWN TO THE GROUND) *Epic EPC 7181*	4 12
25 Oct 80	LOVELY ONE *Epic EPC 9302*	29 6
13 Dec 80	HEARTBREAK HOTEL *Epic EPC 9391*	44 6
28 Feb 81 ●	CAN YOU FEEL IT *Epic EPC 9554*	6 15
4 Jul 81 ●	WALK RIGHT NOW *Epic EPC A 1294*	7 11
7 Jul 84	STATE OF SHOCK *Epic A 4431* [2]	14 8
8 Sep 84	TORTURE *Epic A 4675*	26 6
16 Apr 88 ★	I WANT YOU BACK (re-mix) *Motown ZB 41913* [3]	8 9
13 May 89	NOTHIN' (THAT COMPARES 2 U) *Epic 654808 7*	33 6
21 Mar 70	DIANA ROSS PRESENTS THE JACKSON FIVE *Tamla Motown STML 11142* [1]	16 4
15 Aug 70	ABC *Tamla Motown STML 11153* [1]	22 6
7 Oct 72	GREATEST HITS *Tamla Motown STML 11212* [1]	26 14
18 Nov 72	LOOKIN' THROUGH THE WINDOWS *Tamla Motown STML 11214* [1]	16 8
16 Jul 77	THE JACKSONS *Epic EPC 86009*	54 1
3 Dec 77	GOIN' PLACES *Epic EPC 86035*	45 1
5 May 79	DESTINY *Epic EPC 83200*	33 7
11 Oct 80	TRIUMPH *Epic EPC 86112*	13 16
12 Dec 81	LIVE *Epic EPC 88562*	53 9
9 Jul 83 ★	18 GREATEST HITS *Telstar STAR 2232* [2]	1 58
21 Jul 84 ●	VICTORY *Epic EPC 86303*	3 13
1 Jul 89	2300 JACKSON ST *Epic 463352 1*	39 3
19 Jul 97 ●	THE BEST OF MICHAEL JACKSON AND THE JACKSON 5IVE – THE MOTOWN YEARS *PolyGram TV 5308042* [3]	5 12
10 Jul 04 ●	THE VERY BEST OF THE JACKSONS *Sony TV / Universal TV 5163669*	7 10

[1] The Jackson Five [2] The Jacksons, lead vocals Mick Jagger and Michael Jackson [3] Michael Jackson with The Jackson Five [1] The Jackson Five [2] Michael Jackson plus The Jackson Five [3] Michael Jackson and The Jackson Five

JACKY See Jackie LEE

JACQUELINE See MACK VIBE featuring JACQUELINE

JADA See SKIP RAIDERS featuring JADA

JADAKISS
US, male rapper – Jason Phillips (Albums: 1 Week) pos/wks

		pos/wks
3 Jul 04	KISS OF DEATH *Interscope 9862661* ▲	65 1

JADE
US, female vocal group (Singles: 28 Weeks, Albums: 3 Weeks) pos/wks

		pos/wks
20 Mar 93 ●	DON'T WALK AWAY *Giant W 0160CD*	7 8
3 Jul 93	I WANNA LOVE YOU *Giant 74321151662*	13 7
18 Sep 93	ONE WOMAN *Giant 74321165122*	22 5
5 Feb 94	ALL THRU THE NITE *Giant 74321187552* [1]	32 3
11 Feb 95	EVERY DAY OF THE WEEK *Giant 74321260242*	19 5
29 May 93	JADE TO THE MAX *Giant 74321148002*	43 3

[1] P.O.V. featuring Jade

Ashley JADE See SODA CLUB

JADE 4 U See Praga KHAN

JAEL See DELERIUM

JAGGED EDGE
UK, male vocal / instrumental group (Singles: 2 Weeks) pos/wks

		pos/wks
15 Sep 90	YOU DON'T LOVE ME *Polydor PO 97*	66 2

JAGGED EDGE (see also NIVEA)
US, male vocal group and male rapper (Singles: 8 Weeks) pos/wks

		pos/wks
27 Oct 01	WHERE THE PARTY AT? *Columbia 6719012* [1]	25 3
21 Feb 04	WALKED OUTTA HEAVEN *Columbia 6745452*	21 5

[1] Jagged Edge featuring Nelly

Mick JAGGER (see also The ROLLING STONES)
UK, male vocalist (Singles: 45 Weeks, Albums: 24 Weeks)   pos/wks

14 Nov 70	MEMO FROM TURNER *Decca F 13067*	32 5
7 Jul 84	STATE OF SHOCK *Epic A 4431* [1]	14 8
16 Feb 85	JUST ANOTHER NIGHT *CBS A 4722*	32 6
7 Sep 85 ★	DANCING IN THE STREET *EMI America EA 204* [2] ■	1 12
12 Sep 87	LET'S WORK *CBS 651028 7*	31 7
6 Feb 93	SWEET THING *Atlantic A 7410CD*	24 4
23 Mar 02	VISIONS OF PARADISE *Virgin VUSCD 240*	43 1
6 Nov 04	OLD HABITS DIE HARD *Virgin VSCDX 1887* [3]	45 2
16 Mar 85 ●	SHE'S THE BOSS *CBS 86310*	6 11
26 Sep 87	PRIMITIVE COOL *CBS 460 1231*	26 5
20 Feb 93	WANDERING SPIRIT *Atlantic 7567824362*	12 4
1 Dec 01	GODDESS IN THE DOORWAY *Virgin CDVUS 214*	44 4

[1] The Jacksons, lead vocals Mick Jagger and Michael Jackson [2] David Bowie and Mick Jagger [3] Mick Jagger and Dave Stewart

Bally JAGPAL *See GENERAL LEVY*

The JAGS
UK, male vocal / instrumental group (Singles: 11 Weeks)   pos/wks

8 Sep 79	BACK OF MY HAND *Island WIP 6501*	17 10
2 Feb 80	WOMAN'S WORLD *Island WIP 6531*	75 1

JAHAZIEL *See RAGHAV*

JAHEIM *US, male rapper – Jaheim*
Hoagland (Singles: 10 Weeks, Albums: 1 Week)   pos/wks

24 Mar 01	COULD IT BE *Warner Bros. W 551CD*	33 3
11 Aug 01	JUST IN CASE *Warner Bros. W 564CD*	34 2
29 Jun 02	JUST IN CASE (re-mix) *Warner Bros. WEA W 581CD*	38 3
8 Mar 03	FABULOUS *Warner Bros. WEA W 598CD*	41 2
7 Apr 01	GHETTO LOVE *Warner Bros. 9362474522*	50 1

JAHMALI *See BLAK TWANG*

JAIMESON *UK, male producer –*
Jamie Williams (Singles: 24 Weeks, Albums: 2 Weeks)   pos/wks

14 Sep 02	SELECTA (URBAN HEROES) *Universal Soundproof SPR 1CD* [1]	51 1
25 Jan 03 ●	TRUE *V2 / J-Did JAD 5021363* [2]	4 10
23 Aug 03 ●	COMPLETE *V2 / J-Did JAD 5021713*	4 8
7 Feb 04	TAKE CONTROL *V2 / J-Did JAD 5021738* [3]	16 5
21 Feb 04	THINK ON YOUR FEET *V2 / J-Did JAD 1021722*	42 2

[1] Jameson and Viper [2] Jameson featuring Angel Blu [3] Jaimeson featuring Angel Blu and CK

Jaimeson released 'Selecta (Urban Heroes)' under the name Jameson

JAKATTA (see also Li KWAN; Joey NEGRO; SEAL; PHASE II) *UK,*
male producer – Dave Lee (Singles: 30 Weeks, Albums: 4 Weeks)   pos/wks

24 Feb 01	AMERICAN DREAM (re) *Rulin RULIN 15CDS*	3 14
11 Aug 01	AMERICAN DREAM (re-mix) *Rulin RULIN 20CDS*	63 1
16 Feb 02 ●	SO LONELY *Rulin RULIN 25CDS*	8 5
12 Oct 02 ●	MY VISION *Rulin RULIN 26CDS* [1]	6 8
1 Mar 03	ONE FINE DAY *MoS / RULIN 29CDS*	39 2
26 Oct 02	VISIONS *Rulin RULINCD 01*	12 4

[1] Jakatta featuring Seal

The JAM 〔 114 〕 Top 500
Influential and extremely popular punk-based mod trio from Surrey: Paul Weller (v/g), Bruce Foxton (b), Rick Buckler (d). They hold the record for the most simultaneous Top 75 singles with 13 (all reactivated by their 1982 dissolution). Mass waves of re-entries dominated the charts on 26 Apr 1980 and 22 Jan 1983. Total UK single sales: 5,094,055 (Singles: 206 Weeks, Albums: 199 Weeks)   pos/wks

7 May 77	IN THE CITY (2re) *Polydor 2058 866*	40 14
23 Jul 77	ALL AROUND THE WORLD (2re) *Polydor 2058 903*	13 15
5 Nov 77	THE MODERN WORLD (2re) *Polydor 2058 945*	36 11
11 Mar 78	NEWS OF THE WORLD (2re) *Polydor 2058 995*	27 12
26 Aug 78	DAVID WATTS / 'A' BOMB IN WARDOUR STREET (2re) *Polydor 2059 054*	25 15
21 Oct 78	DOWN IN THE TUBE STATION AT MIDNIGHT (re) *Polydor POSP 8*	15 13
17 Mar 79	STRANGE TOWN (2re) *Polydor POSP 34*	15 18

25 Aug 79	WHEN YOU'RE YOUNG (re) *Polydor POSP 69*	17 11
3 Nov 79 ●	THE ETON RIFLES (re) *Polydor POSP 83*	3 15
22 Mar 80 ★	GOING UNDERGROUND / DREAMS OF CHILDREN (re) *Polydor POSP 113* ■	1 15
23 Aug 80 ★	START (re) *Polydor 2059 266*	1 10
7 Feb 81	THAT'S ENTERTAINMENT (IMPORT) *Metronome 0030 364*	21 7
6 Jun 81 ●	FUNERAL PYRE *Polydor POSP 257*	4 6
24 Oct 81 ●	ABSOLUTE BEGINNERS *Polydor POSP 350*	4 6
13 Feb 82 ★	TOWN CALLED MALICE / PRECIOUS (re) *Polydor POSP 400* ■	1 9
3 Jul 82 ●	JUST WHO IS THE FIVE O'CLOCK HERO *Polydor 2059 504*	8 5
18 Sep 82 ●	THE BITTEREST PILL (I EVER HAD TO SWALLOW) *Polydor POSP 505*	2 7
4 Dec 82 ★	BEAT SURRENDER *Polydor POSP 540* ■	1 9
29 Jan 83	THAT'S ENTERTAINMENT *Polydor POSP 482*	60 3
29 Jun 91	THAT'S ENTERTAINMENT (re-issue) *Polydor PO 155*	57 2
11 Oct 97	THE BITTEREST PILL (I EVER HAD TO SWALLOW) (re-issue) *Polydor 5715992*	30 2
11 May 02	IN THE CITY (re-issue) *Polydor 5876117*	36 1
28 May 77	IN THE CITY *Polydor 2383 447*	20 18
26 Nov 77	THIS IS THE MODERN WORLD *Polydor 2383 475*	22 5
11 Nov 78 ●	ALL MOD CONS *Polydor POLD 5008*	6 17
24 Nov 79 ●	SETTING SONS *Polydor POLD 5028*	4 19
6 Dec 80 ●	SOUND AFFECTS *Polydor POLD 5035*	2 19
20 Mar 82 ★	THE GIFT *Polydor POLD 5055* ■	1 24
18 Dec 82 ●	DIG THE NEW BREED *Polydor POLD 5075*	2 15
27 Aug 83	IN THE CITY (re-issue) *Polydor SPELP 27*	100 1
22 Oct 83 ●	SNAP! *Polydor SNAP 1*	2 30
13 Jul 91 ●	GREATEST HITS *Polydor 8495541*	2 21
18 Apr 92	EXTRAS *Polydor 5131772*	15 4
6 Nov 93	LIVE JAM *Polydor 5196672*	28 2
27 Jul 96	THE JAM COLLECTION *Polydor 5314932*	58 1
7 Jun 97 ●	DIRECTION REACTION CREATION *Polydor 5371432*	8 4
25 Oct 97 ●	THE VERY BEST OF THE JAM *Polydor / PolyGram TV 5374232*	9 10
18 May 02 ●	THE SOUND OF THE JAM *Polydor 5897812*	3 7
15 Jun 02	THE JAM AT THE BBC *Polydor 5896902*	33 2

JAM & SPOON featuring PLAVKA
(see also DANCE 2 TRANCE; STORM; TOKYO GHETTO PUSSY)
Germany, male production duo – Rolf Ellmer and Markus Loeffel and female vocalist – Plavka Lonich (Singles: 26 Weeks, Albums: 1 Week)   pos/wks

2 May 92	TALES FROM A DANCEOGRAPHIC OCEAN (EP) *R&S RSUK 14* [1]	49 1
6 Jun 92	THE COMPLETE STELLA (re-mix) *R&S RSUK 14X* [1]	66 2
26 Feb 94	RIGHT IN THE NIGHT (FALL IN LOVE WITH MUSIC) *Epic 6600822*	31 4
24 Sep 94	FIND ME (ODYSSEY TO ANYOONA) *Epic 6608082*	37 3
10 Jun 95 ●	RIGHT IN THE NIGHT (FALL IN LOVE WITH MUSIC) (re-issue) *Epic 6620182*	10 8
16 Sep 95	FIND ME (ODYSSEY TO ANYOONA) (re-issue) *Epic 6623242*	22 3
25 Nov 95	ANGEL (LADADI O-HEYO) *Epic 6626382*	26 2
30 Aug 97	KALEIDOSCOPE SKIES *Epic 6647614*	48 1
2 Mar 02	BE ANGELED *Nulife / Arista 74321878992* [2]	31 2
19 Feb 94	TRIPTOMATIC FAIRYTALES 2001 *Epic 4749282* [1]	71 1

[1] Jam and Spoon [2] Jam & Spoon featuring Rea [1] Jam & Spoon

Tracks on Tales From a Danceographic Ocean (EP): Stella / Keep on Movin' / My First Fantastic FF. 'The Complete Stella' is a re-mix of a track from the EP

JAM MACHINE
Italy / US, male vocal / instrumental group (Singles: 1 Week)   pos/wks

23 Dec 89	EVERYDAY *Deconstruction PB 43299*	68 1

JAM ON THE MUTHA
UK, male vocal / instrumental group (Singles: 2 Weeks)   pos/wks

11 Aug 90	HOTEL CALIFORNIA *M&G MAGS 3*	62 2

JAM TRONIK
Germany, male / female vocal / instrumental group (Singles: 7 Weeks)   pos/wks

24 Mar 90	ANOTHER DAY IN PARADISE *Debut DEBT 3093*	19 7

JAMAICA UNITED
Jamaica, male vocal ensemble (Singles: 1 Week)   pos/wks

4 Jul 98	RISE UP *Columbia 6660522*	54 1

JAMELIA *UK, female vocalist – Jamelia*
Davis (Singles: 72 Weeks, Albums: 38 Weeks) pos/wks

31 Jul 99	I DO *Parlophone Rhythm Series CDRHYTHM 21*	36 2
4 Mar 00 ●	MONEY *Parlophone Rhythm Series CDRHYTHM 27* [1]	5 9
24 Jun 00	CALL ME *Parlophone Rhythm Series CDRHYTHM 28*	11 5
21 Oct 00	BOY NEXT DOOR *Parlophone Rhythm Series CDRHYTHM 29*	42 2
21 Jun 03	BOUT *Parlophone CDRS 6597* [2]	37 2
27 Sep 03 ●	SUPERSTAR *Parlophone CDR 6615*	3 20
6 Mar 04 ●	THANK YOU *Parlophone CDR 6621*	2 14
24 Jul 04 ●	SEE IT IN A BOY'S EYES *Parlophone CDRS 6635*	5 11
13 Nov 04	DJ / STOP *Parlophone CDR 6646*	9 7+
8 Jul 00	DRAMA *Parlophone Rhythm 5272272*	39 2
11 Oct 03 ●	THANK YOU *Parlophone 5837772*	4 36+

[1] Jamelia featuring Beenie Man [2] Jamelia featuring Rah Digga

'Thank You' had a different catalogue number, Parlophone 5978132, for its 2004 chart run

JAMES (263 Top 500)
(see also BOOTH and the BAD ANGEL) *Anthemic indie pop band formed in 1982 in Manchester, UK, by mainstays Tim Booth (v) and Larry Gott (g). After several hitless years, critically acclaimed releases and record company changes, they became one of the most consistently successful acts of the 1990s (Singles: 89 Weeks, Albums: 155 Weeks)* pos/wks

12 May 90	HOW WAS IT FOR YOU? *Fontana JIM 5*	32 3
7 Jul 90	COME HOME *Fontana JIM 6*	32 4
8 Dec 90	LOSE CONTROL *Fontana JIM 7*	38 5
30 Mar 91 ●	SIT DOWN *Fontana JIM 8*	2 10
30 Nov 91 ●	SOUND *Fontana JIM 9*	9 7
1 Feb 92	BORN OF FRUSTRATION *Fontana JIM 10*	13 6
4 Apr 92	RING THE BELLS *Fontana JIM 11*	37 2
18 Jul 92	SEVEN (EP) *Fontana JIM 12*	46 2
11 Sep 93	SOMETIMES *Fontana JIMCD 13*	18 4
13 Nov 93	LAID *Fontana JIMCD 14*	25 4
2 Apr 94	JAM J / SAY SOMETHING *Fontana JIMCD 15*	24 4
22 Feb 97 ●	SHE'S A STAR *Fontana JIMCD 16*	9 5
3 May 97	TOMORROW *Fontana JIMCD 17*	12 3
5 Jul 97	WALTZING ALONG *Fontana JIMCD 18*	23 4
21 Mar 98	DESTINY CALLING *Fontana JIMCD 19*	17 4
6 Jun 98	RUNAGROUND *Fontana JIMCD 20*	29 2
21 Nov 98 ●	SIT DOWN (re-mix) *Fontana JIMCD 21*	7 7
31 Jul 99	I KNOW WHAT I'M HERE FOR *Mercury JIMCD 22*	22 5
16 Oct 99	JUST LIKE FRED ASTAIRE *Mercury JIMCD 23*	17 3
25 Dec 99	WE'RE GOING TO MISS YOU *Mercury JIMCD 24*	48 2
7 Jul 01	GETTING AWAY WITH IT (ALL MESSED UP) *Mercury JIMCD 25*	22 3
2 Aug 86	STUTTER *Blanco Y Negro JIMLP 1*	68 2
8 Oct 88	STRIP MINE *Sire JIMLP 2*	90 1
16 Jun 90 ●	GOLD MOTHER *Fontana 8485951*	2 34
29 Feb 92 ●	SEVEN *Fontana 5109322*	2 14
9 Oct 93 ●	LAID *Fontana 5149432*	3 16
24 Sep 94	WAH WAH *Fontana 5228272* [1]	11 2
8 Mar 97 ●	WHIPLASH *Fontana 5343542*	9 19
4 Apr 98 ★	THE BEST OF *Fontana 5368982* ■	1 53
23 Oct 99 ●	MILLIONAIRES *Mercury 5467892*	2 11
14 Jul 01	PLEASED TO MEET YOU *Mercury 5861462*	11 3

[1] James and Brian Eno

Tracks on Seven (EP): Seven / Goalie's Ball / William Burroughs / Still Alive. 'Say Something' listed with 'Jam J' only for first two weeks of record's run

David JAMES *UK, male DJ / producer (Singles: 1 Week)* pos/wks

11 Aug 01	ALWAYS A PERMANENT STATE *Hooj Choons HOOJ 108CD*	60 1

Dick JAMES *UK, male vocalist – Isaac Vapnic,*
b. 12 Dec 1920, d. 1 Feb 1986 (Singles: 13 Weeks) pos/wks

20 Jan 56	ROBIN HOOD / THE BALLAD OF DAVY CROCKETT (re) *Parlophone R 4117*	14 9
11 Jan 57	GARDEN OF EDEN *Parlophone R 4255*	18 4

'Robin Hood' is with Stephen James and his Chums. 'The Ballad of Davy Crockett' listed only from 18 May 1956

Duncan JAMES & KEEDIE (see also BLUE)
UK, male and female vocalists (Singles: 7 Weeks) pos/wks

23 Oct 04 ●	I BELIEVE MY HEART *Innocent 8677122*	2 7

Etta JAMES
US, female vocalist – Jamesetta Hawkins (Singles: 7 Weeks) pos/wks

10 Feb 96 ●	I JUST WANT TO MAKE LOVE TO YOU *MCA MCSTD 48003*	5 7

Freddie JAMES *Canada, male vocalist (Singles: 3 Weeks)* pos/wks

24 Nov 79	GET UP AND BOOGIE *Warner Bros. K 17478*	54 3

Holly JAMES *See Jason NEVINS*

Joni JAMES *US, female vocalist – Joan Babbo (Singles: 2 Weeks)* pos/wks

6 Mar 53	WHY DON'T YOU BELIEVE ME? *MGM 582* ▲	11 1
30 Jan 59	THERE MUST BE A WAY *MGM 1002*	24 1

Rick JAMES *US, male vocalist – James Johnson,*
b. 1 Jan 1948, d. 6 Aug 2004 (Singles: 30 Weeks, Albums: 2 Weeks) pos/wks

8 Jul 78	YOU AND I *Motown TMG 1110*	46 7
7 Jul 79	I'M A SUCKER FOR YOUR LOVE *Motown TMG 1146* [1]	43 8
6 Sep 80	BIG TIME *Motown TMG 1198*	41 6
4 Jul 81	GIVE IT TO ME BABY *Motown TMG 1229*	47 3
12 Jun 82	STANDING ON THE TOP (PART 1) *Motown TMG 1263* [2]	53 3
3 Jul 82	DANCE WIT' ME *Motown TMG 1266*	53 3
24 Jul 82	THROWIN' DOWN *Motown STML 12167*	93 2

[1] Teena Marie, co-lead vocals Rick James [2] The Temptations featuring Rick James

Sonny JAMES
US, male vocalist – James Loden (Singles: 8 Weeks) pos/wks

30 Nov 56	THE CAT CAME BACK *Capitol CL 14635*	30 1
8 Feb 57	YOUNG LOVE *Capitol CL 14683*	11 7

Tyler JAMES *UK, male vocalist (Singles: 4 Weeks)* pos/wks

13 Nov 04	WHY DO I DO? *Island CID 872*	25 4

Wendy JAMES (see also TRANSVISION VAMP)
UK, female vocalist (Singles: 4 Weeks, Albums: 1 Week) pos/wks

20 Feb 93	THE NAMELESS ONE *MCA MCSTD 1732*	34 3
17 Apr 93	LONDON'S BRILLIANT *MCA MCSTD 1763*	62 1
20 Mar 93	NOW AIN'T THE TIME FOR YOUR TEARS *MCA MCD 10800*	43 1

Jimmy JAMES and the VAGABONDS
UK, male vocal / instrumental group (Singles: 25 Weeks) pos/wks

11 Sep 68	RED RED WINE *Pye 7N 17579*	36 8
24 Apr 76	I'LL GO WHERE YOUR MUSIC TAKES ME *Pye 7N 45585*	23 8
17 Jul 76 ●	NOW IS THE TIME *Pye 7N 45606*	5 9

Tommy JAMES and the SHONDELLS *US, male vocal / instrumental group – leader Thomas Jackson (Singles: 25 Weeks)* pos/wks

21 Jul 66	HANKY PANKY *Roulette RK 7000* ▲	38 7
5 Jun 68 ★	MONY MONY *Major Minor MM 567*	1 18

The JAMES BOYS (see also BLOWING FREE; IN TUNE;
SCHOOL OF EXCELLENCE; RAINDANCE; HYPNOSIS)
UK, male vocal duo – Bradley and Stewart Palmer (Singles: 6 Weeks) pos/wks

19 May 73	OVER AND OVER *Penny Farthing PEN 806*	39 6

JAMESON *See JAIMESON*

JAMESTOWN featuring JOCELYN BROWN *US, male instrumentalist / producer – Kent Brainerd and US, female vocalist (Singles: 4 Weeks)* pos/wks

14 Sep 91	SHE GOT SOUL *A&M AM 819*	57 3
27 Mar 99	I BELIEVE *Playola 0091705 PLA*	62 1

JAMIROQUAI (147 Top 500)
One of the world's biggest-selling acts of the late 1990s features headdress-wearing vocalist Jay Kay, b. 30 Dec 1969, Manchester, UK. The group, whose videos have also earned numerous accolades, sold seven million copies of 1996 album 'Travelling Without Moving' and 1999 album 'Synkronized' topped many European charts (Singles: 141 Weeks, Albums: 215 Weeks) pos/wks

31 Oct 92	WHEN YOU GONNA LEARN (re) *Acid Jazz JAZID 46*	52 3
13 Mar 93 ●	TOO YOUNG TO DIE *Sony S2 6590112*	10 7
5 Jun 93	BLOW YOUR MIND *Sony S2 6592972*	12 6

Singles re-entries are listed as (re), (2re), (3re)…. which signifies that the hit re-entered the chart once, twice or three times…

14 Aug 93	EMERGENCY ON PLANET EARTH *Sony S2 6595782*	32	3
25 Sep 93	WHEN YOU GONNA LEARN (re-issue) *Sony S2 6596952*	28	3
8 Oct 94	SPACE COWBOY *Sony S2 6608512*	17	5
19 Nov 94	HALF THE MAN *Sony S2 6610032*	15	8
1 Jul 95 ●	STILLNESS IN TIME *Sony S2 6620255*	9	5
1 Jun 96	DO U KNOW WHERE YOU'RE COMING FROM *Renk CDRENK 63* [1]	12	5
31 Aug 96 ●	VIRTUAL INSANITY *Sony S2 6636132*	3	11
7 Dec 96 ●	COSMIC GIRL *Sony S2 6638292*	6	10
10 May 97 ●	ALRIGHT *Sony S2 6643252*	6	5
13 Dec 97	HIGH TIMES *Sony S2 6653702*	20	6
25 Jul 98 ★	DEEPER UNDERGROUND *Sony S2 6662182* ■	1	11
5 Jun 99	CANNED HEAT *Sony S2 6673022*	4	10
25 Sep 99	SUPERSONIC *Sony S2 6678392*	22	4
11 Dec 99	KING FOR A DAY *Sony S2 6679732*	20	7
24 Feb 01	I'M IN THE MOOD FOR LOVE *Warner.esp WSMS 001CD* [2]	29	3
25 Aug 01 ●	LITTLE L *Sony S2 6717182*	5	11
1 Dec 01	YOU GIVE ME SOMETHING *Sony S2 6720072*	16	9
9 Mar 02	LOVE FOOLOSOPHY (re) *Sony S2 6723252*	14	6
20 Jul 02	CORNER OF THE EARTH *Sony S2 6727882*	31	3
26 Jun 93 ★	EMERGENCY ON PLANET EARTH *Sony S2 4740692* ■	1	32
29 Oct 94 ★	THE RETURN OF THE SPACE COWBOY *Sony S2 4778132*	2	29
21 Sep 96 ●	TRAVELLING WITHOUT MOVING *Sony S2 4839999*	2	74
26 Jun 99 ★	SYNKRONIZED *Sony S2 4945172* ■	1	29
15 Sep 01 ★	A FUNK ODYSSEY *Sony S2 5040692* ■	1	51

[1] M-Beat featuring Jamiroquai [2] Jools Holland and Jamiroquai

The JAMMERS
US, male vocal / instrumental group (Singles: 2 Weeks)   pos/wks

29 Jan 83	BE MINE TONIGHT *Salsoul Sal 101*	65	2

JamX & DeLEON *Germany, male production duo –*
Jurgen Mutschall and Dominik DeLeon (Singles: 2 Weeks)   pos/wks

7 Sep 02	CAN U DIG IT? *Serious SERR 052CD*	40	2

JAN and DEAN *US, male vocal duo – Jan Berry, b. 3 Apr 1941, d. 27 Mar*
2004, and Dean Torrence (Singles: 18 Weeks, Albums: 2 Weeks)   pos/wks

24 Aug 61	HEART AND SOUL *London HLH 9395*	24	8
15 Aug 63	SURF CITY *Liberty LIB 55580* ▲	26	10
12 Jul 80	THE JAN AND DEAN STORY *K-Tel NE 1084*	67	2

JAN and KJELD
Denmark, male vocal duo – Jan and Kjeld Wennick (Singles: 4 Weeks)   pos/wks

21 Jul 60	BANJO BOY *Ember S 101*	36	4

JANE'S ADDICTION *US, male vocal /*
instrumental group (Singles: 8 Weeks, Albums: 5 Weeks)   pos/wks

23 Mar 91	BEEN CAUGHT STEALING *Warner Bros. W 0011*	34	3
1 Jun 91	CLASSIC GIRL *Warner Bros. W 0031*	60	1
26 Jul 03	JUST BECAUSE *Capitol CDCL 847*	14	4
8 Sep 90	RITUAL DE LO HABITUAL *Warner Bros. WX 306*	37	2
2 Aug 03	STRAYS *Parlophone 5921980*	14	3

Horst JANKOWSKI, his Orchestra and Chorus
Germany, male instrumentalist – piano (Singles: 18 Weeks)   pos/wks

29 Jul 65 ●	A WALK IN THE BLACK FOREST *Mercury MF 861*	3	18

Samantha JANUS *UK, female vocalist (Singles: 3 Weeks)*   pos/wks

11 May 91	A MESSAGE TO YOUR HEART *Hollywood HWD 104*	30	3

Philip JAP *UK, male vocalist (Singles: 8 Weeks)*   pos/wks

31 Jul 82	SAVE US *A&M AMS 8217*	53	4
25 Sep 82	TOTAL ERASURE *A&M JAP 1*	41	4

JAPAN (306) Top 500 *Rock quintet which subsequently became New*
Romantic figureheads fronted by David Sylvian (v), b. David Batt, 23 Feb 1958,
London, UK, who later recorded critically acclaimed solo work. Group folded
in 1982, but full line-up briefly reconvened as Rain Tree Crow in 1991
(Singles: 81 Weeks, Albums: 135 Weeks)   pos/wks

18 Oct 80	GENTLEMEN TAKE POLAROIDS *Virgin VS 379*	60	2
9 May 81	THE ART OF PARTIES *Virgin VS 409*	48	5
19 Sep 81	QUIET LIFE *Hansa HANSA 6*	19	9
7 Nov 81	VISIONS OF CHINA *Virgin VS 436*	32	12

23 Jan 82	EUROPEAN SON *Hansa HANSA 10*	31	6
20 Mar 82 ●	GHOSTS *Virgin VS 472*	5	8
22 May 82	CANTONESE BOY *Virgin VS 502*	24	6
3 Jul 82 ●	I SECOND THAT EMOTION *Hansa HANSA 12*	9	11
9 Oct 82	LIFE IN TOKYO *Hansa HANSA 17*	28	6
20 Nov 82	NIGHT PORTER *Virgin VS 554*	29	9
12 Mar 83	ALL TOMORROW'S PARTIES *Hansa HANSA 18*	38	4
21 May 83	CANTON (LIVE) *Virgin VS 581*	42	3
9 Feb 80	QUIET LIFE *Ariola Hansa AHAL 8011*	53	8
15 Nov 80	GENTLEMEN TAKE POLAROIDS *Virgin V 2180*	45	10
26 Sep 81	ASSEMBLAGE *Hansa HANLP 1*	26	46
28 Nov 81	TIN DRUM *Virgin V 2209*	12	50
18 Jun 83 ●	OIL ON CANVAS *Virgin VD 2513*	5	14
8 Dec 84	EXORCISING GHOSTS *Virgin VGD 3510*	45	7

JARK PRONGO
(see also GOODMEN; RHYTHMKILLAZ; CHOCOLATE PUMA;
TOMBA VIRA; RIVA featuring Dannii MINOGUE) *Holland, male production*
duo – Rene Ter Horst and Gaston Steenkist (Singles: 1 Week)   pos/wks

3 Apr 99	MOVIN' THRU YOUR SYSTEM *Hooj Choons HOOJ 72CD*	58	1

Jeff JARRATT and Don REEDMAN
(see also Pierre BELMONDE) *UK, male producers (Albums: 8 Weeks)* pos/wks

22 Nov 80	MASTERWORKS *K-Tel ONE 1093*	39	8

Jean-Michel JARRE (211) Top 500 *Distinctive synthesizer wizard,*
b. 24 Aug 1948, Lyon, France (son of composer / conductor Maurice) has
sold over 55 million albums worldwide. His spectacular, futuristic, live
sound and light extravaganzas have frequently broken attendance records
(Singles: 40 Weeks, Albums: 243 Weeks)   pos/wks

27 Aug 77 ●	OXYGENE PART IV *Polydor 2001 721*	4	9
20 Jan 79	EQUINOXE PART 5 *Polydor POSP 20*	45	5
23 Aug 86	FOURTH RENDEZ-VOUS *Polydor POSP 788*	65	4
5 Nov 88	REVOLUTIONS *Polydor PO 25*	52	2
7 Jan 89	LONDON KID *Polydor PO 32* [1]	52	3
7 Oct 89	OXYGENE PART IV (re-mix) *Polydor PO 55*	65	2
26 Jun 93	CHRONOLOGIE PART 4 *Polydor POCS 274*	55	2
30 Oct 93	CHRONOLOGIE PART 4 (re-mix) *Polydor POCS 274*	56	1
22 Mar 97	OXYGENE 8 *Epic 6643232*	17	3
5 Jul 97	OXYGENE 10 *Epic 6647152*	21	2
11 Jul 98	RENDEZ-VOUS '98 *Epic 6661102* [2]	12	6
26 Feb 00	C'EST LA VIE *Epic 6689302* [3]	40	1
20 Aug 77 ●	OXYGENE *Polydor 2310 555*	2	24
16 Dec 78	EQUINOXE *Polydor POLD 5007*	11	26
6 Jun 81 ●	MAGNETIC FIELDS *Polydor POLS 1033*	6	17
15 May 82 ●	THE CONCERTS IN CHINA *Polydor PODV 3*	6	17
12 Nov 83	THE ESSENTIAL JEAN-MICHEL JARRE *Polystar PROLP 3*	14	29
24 Nov 84	ZOOLOOK *Polydor POLH 15*	47	14
12 Apr 86 ●	RENDEZ-VOUS *Polydor POLH 27*	9	38
18 Jul 87	EN CONCERT HOUSTON/LYON *Polydor POLH 36*	18	15
8 Oct 88 ●	REVOLUTIONS *Polydor POLH 45*	2	13
14 Oct 89	JARRE LIVE *Polydor 841258 1*	16	4
23 Jun 90	WAITING FOR COUSTEAU *Dreyfus 8436141*	14	10
26 Oct 91	IMAGES – THE BEST OF JEAN-MICHEL JARRE *Dreyfus 5113061*	14	12
5 Jun 93	CHRONOLOGIE *Polydor 5193732*	11	8
28 May 94	CHRONOLOGIE PART 6 *Polydor 5195792*	60	1
1 Mar 97	OXYGENE 7-13 *Epic 4869849*	11	5
23 May 98	ODYSSEY THROUGH O2 *Epic 4897646*	50	2
12 Feb 00	METAMORPHOSES *Epic 4960222*	37	1
2 Oct 04	AERO *WSM 256461852*	14	7

[1] Jean-Michel Jarre featuring Hank Marvin [2] Jean-Michel Jarre and Apollo 440
[3] Jean-Michel Jarre featuring Natacha Atlas

Al JARREAU
US, male vocalist (Singles: 30 Weeks, Albums: 37 Weeks)   pos/wks

26 Sep 81	WE'RE IN THIS LOVE TOGETHER *Warner Bros. K 17849*	55	4
14 May 83	MORNIN' *WEA U9929*	28	6
16 Jul 83	TROUBLE IN PARADISE *WEA Int. U9871*	36	5
24 Sep 83	BOOGIE DOWN *WEA U9814*	63	3
16 Nov 85	DAY BY DAY *Polydor POSP 770* [1]	53	1
5 Apr 86	THE MUSIC OF GOODBYE (LOVE THEME FROM 'OUT OF AFRICA') *MCA MCA 1038* [2]	75	1
7 Mar 87 ●	'MOONLIGHTING' THEME *WEA U8407*	8	8
5 Sep 81	BREAKING AWAY *Warner Bros. K 56917*	60	8

		pos/wks
30 Apr 83	JARREAU *WEA International U 0070*	.39 18
17 Nov 84	HIGH CRIME *WEA 250807*	.81 1
13 Sep 86	L IS FOR LOVER *WEA International 2530801*	.45 10

1 Shakatak featuring Al Jarreau 2 Melissa Manchester and Al Jarreau

Kenny 'Jammin' JASON and 'Fast' Eddie SMITH
US, male DJ / production duo (Singles: 4 Weeks) pos/wks

11 Apr 87	CAN U DANCE (re) *Champion CHAMP 41*	.67 4

The JAVELLS featuring Nosmo KING (see also TRUTH)
UK, male vocalist – Stephen Gold (Singles: 8 Weeks) pos/wks

9 Nov 74	GOODBYE NOTHING TO SAY *Pye Disco Demand DDS 2003*	.26 8

JAVINE *UK, female vocalist – Javine*
Hylton (Singles: 22 Weeks, Albums: 1 Week) pos/wks

19 Jul 03 ●	REAL THINGS *Innocent SINCD 46*	.4 9
22 Nov 03	SURRENDER (YOUR LOVE) *Innocent SINCD 52*	.15 5
26 Jun 04	BEST OF MY LOVE *Innocent SINDX 63*	.18 4
21 Aug 04	DON'T WALK AWAY *Innocent SINDX 65*	.16 4
10 Jul 04	SURRENDER *Innocent CDSIN 15*	.73 1

Peter JAY and the JAYWALKERS *UK, male*
instrumental group – leader Peter Jay – drums (Singles: 11 Weeks) pos/wks

8 Nov 62	CAN CAN '62 *Decca F 11531*	.31 11

Candee JAY *Holland, female vocalist (Singles: 8 Weeks)* pos/wks

19 Jun 04	IF I WERE YOU *Incentive CENT 58CDX*	.14 6
13 Nov 04	BACK FOR ME *Incentive CENT 67CDS*	.23 2

Oris JAY presents DELSENA *Holland, male producer –*
Peran van Dijk and UK, female vocalist (Singles: 2 Weeks) pos/wks

23 Mar 02	TRIPPIN' *Gusto CDGUS 3*	.42 2

Simone JAY See DJ DADO

JAYDEE
Holland, male DJ / producer – Robin Albers (Singles: 7 Weeks) pos/wks

20 Sep 97	PLASTIC DREAMS *R&S RS 97117CD*	.18 3
10 Jan 04	PLASTIC DREAMS 2003 (re-mix) *Positiva CDTIVS 198*	.35 4

Laura JAYE See INTENSO PROJECT

Ollie JAYE See JON THE DENTIST vs Ollie JAYE

The JAYHAWKS *US, male / female vocal /*
instrumental group (Singles: 1 Week, Albums: 4 Weeks) pos/wks

15 Jul 95	BAD TIME *American 74321291632*	.70 1
25 Feb 95	TOMORROW THE GREEN GRASS *American 74321236802*	.41 1
3 May 97	SOUND OF LIES *American Recordings 74321464062*	.61 1
20 May 00	SMILE *Columbia 4979712*	.60 1
19 Apr 03	RAINY DAY MUSIC *American 0771362*	.70 1

JAY-Z 〈 430 Top 500 〉 *Foremost East Coast rapper, b. Shawn Carter,*
4 Dec 1969, New York, US, whose original rap name was "Jazzy". The owner of Rock-A-Fella Records has had 15 Top 20 singles and eight No.1 albums in the US. He took over as president of Def Jam Records in January 2005 (Singles: 138 Weeks, Albums: 25 Weeks) pos/wks

1 Mar 97	CAN'T KNOCK THE HUSTLE *Northwestside 74321447192* 1	.30 2
10 May 97	AIN'T NO PLAYA *Northwestside 74321474842* 2	.31 2
21 Jun 97 ●	I'LL BE *Def Jam 75710432* 3	.9 5
23 Aug 97	WHO YOU WIT *Qwest W 0411CD*	.65 1
25 Oct 97	SUNSHINE *Northwestside 74321528702* 4	.25 2
14 Feb 98	WISHING ON A STAR *Northwestside 74321554632* 5	.13 4
27 Jun 98	THE CITY IS MINE *Northwestside 74321588012* 6	.38 2
12 Dec 98 ●	HARD KNOCK LIFE (GHETTO ANTHEM) *Northwestside 74321635332*	.2 11
13 Mar 99	CAN I GET A ... *Def Jam 5668472* 7	.24 3
10 Apr 99	BE ALONE NO MORE *Northwestside 74321658472* 8	.11 9
19 Jun 99	LOBSTER & SCRIMP *Virgin DINSD 186* 9	.48 1
6 Nov 99 ●	HEARTBREAKER *Columbia 6683012* 10 ▲	.5 13
4 Dec 99	WHAT YOU THINK OF THAT *Def Jam 8708292*	.58 1
26 Feb 00	ANYTHING *Def Jam 5626502*	.18 4
24 Jun 00	BIG PIMPIN' *Def Jam 5627742*	.29 3

16 Dec 00	I JUST WANNA LOVE U (GIVE IT 2 ME) *Def Jam 5727462*	.17 8
23 Jun 01	FIESTA *Jive 9252142* 11	.23 3
27 Oct 01	IZZO (H.O.V.A.) *Roc-A-Fella / Def Jam 5888152*	.21 4
19 Jan 02	GIRLS, GIRLS, GIRLS (re) *Roc-A-Fella / Def Jam 5889062*	.11 7
25 May 02	HONEY *Jive 9253662* 12	.35 2
1 Feb 03 ●	'03 BONNIE & CLYDE *Roc-A-Fella 0770102* 13	.2 12
26 Apr 03	EXCUSE ME MISS *Roc-A-Fella 0779122*	.17 7
5 Jul 03	JOGI / BEWARE OF THE BOYS *Showbiz / Dharma DHARMA ICDS* 14	.25 3
16 Aug 03 ●	FRONTIN' *Arista 8267655332* 15	.6 10
20 Dec 03	CHANGE CLOTHES *Roc-A-Fella 9815225*	.32 7
22 May 04	99 PROBLEMS / DIRT OFF YOUR SHOULDER *Roc-A-Fella 9862391*	.12 8
4 Dec 04	NUMB (re-recording) / ENCORE *WEA W 660CD* 16	.14 4+
29 Sep 01	THE BLUEPRINT *Roc-A-Fella 5863962*	.30 4
30 Mar 02	CHAPTER ONE *Roc-A-Fella 74321920462*	.65 1
30 Mar 02	THE BEST OF BOTH WORLDS *Jive 9223512* 1	.37 2
30 Nov 02	THE BLUEPRINT 2 – THE GIFT & THE CURSE *Def Jam / Mercury 0633812* ▲	.23 7
29 Nov 03	THE BLACK ALBUM *Roc-A-fella / Mercury 9861121* ▲	.34 7
6 Nov 04	2004 UNFINISHED BUSINESS *Jive 82876658682* ▲ 1	.61 1
11 Dec 04	COLLISION COURSE *WEA 9362489662* ▲ 2	.38 3+

1 Jay-Z featuring Mary J Blige 2 Jay-Z featuring Foxy Brown 3 Foxy Brown featuring Jay-Z 4 Jay-Z featuring Babyface and Foxy Brown 5 Jay-Z featuring Gwen Dickey 6 Jay-Z featuring BLACKstreet 7 Jay-Z featuring Amil & Ja Rule 8 Another Level featuring Jay-Z 9 Timbaland featuring Jay-Z 10 Mariah Carey featuring Jay-Z 11 R Kelly featuring Jay-Z 12 R Kelly & Jay-Z 13 Jay-Z featuring Beyoncé Knowles 14 Panjabi MC featuring Jay-Z 15 Pharrell Williams featuring Jay-Z 16 Jay-Z / Linkin Park 1 R Kelly and Jay-Z 2 Jay-Z / Linkin Park

'Numb / Encore' is one song that combines Linkin Park's 'Numb' and Jay-Z's 'Encore'

JAZZ and the BROTHERS GRIMM
UK, male vocal / instrumental group (Singles: 2 Weeks) pos/wks

9 Jul 88	(LET'S ALL GO BACK) DISCO NIGHTS *Ensign ENY 616*	.57 2

JAZZY DEE
US, male rapper / instrumentalist – Darren Williams (Singles: 5 Weeks) pos/wks

5 Mar 83	GET ON UP *Laurie LRS 101*	.53 5

JAZZY JEFF See DJ JAZZY JEFF and FRESH PRINCE

JAZZY M
UK, male DJ / producer – Michael Connelly (Singles: 2 Weeks) pos/wks

21 Oct 00	JAZZIN' THE WAY YOU KNOW *Perfecto PERF 08CDS*	.47 2

Norma JEAN See Romina JOHNSON

Wyclef JEAN (see also FUGEES) *US, male rapper /*
vocalist / producer (Singles: 75 Weeks, Albums: 23 Weeks) pos/wks

28 Jun 97	WE TRYING TO STAY ALIVE *Columbia 6646815* 1	.13 5
27 Sep 97	GUANTANAMERA *Columbia 6650852* 1	.25 2
28 Mar 98 ●	NO, NO, NO *Columbia 6656592* 2	.5 8
16 May 98	GONE TILL NOVEMBER *Columbia 6658712*	.3 9
14 Nov 98 ●	ANOTHER ONE BITES THE DUST *Dreamworks DRMCD 22364* 3	.5 6
23 Oct 99	NEW DAY *Columbia 6682122* 4	.23 2
16 Sep 00 ●	IT DOESN'T MATTER *Columbia 6697782* 5	.3 8
16 Dec 00 ●	911 *Columbia 6706122* 6	.9 10
21 Jul 01 ●	PERFECT GENTLEMEN *Columbia 6710522*	.4 14
8 Dec 01	WISH YOU WERE HERE (re) *Columbia 6721562*	.28 5
6 Jul 02	TWO WRONGS *Columbia 6728902* 7	.14 6
5 Jul 97	THE CARNIVAL *Columbia 4874422* 1	.40 6
2 Sep 00 ●	THE ECLEFTIC – 2 SIDES II A BOOK *Columbia 4979792*	.5 15
20 Jul 02	MASQUERADE *Columbia 5078542*	.30 2

1 Wyclef Jean and The Refugee Allstars 2 Destiny's Child featuring Wyclef Jean 3 Queen with Wyclef Jean featuring Pras and Free 4 Wyclef Jean featuring Bono 5 Wyclef Jean featuring The Rock and Melky Sedeck 6 Wyclef Jean featuring Mary J Blige 7 Wyclef Jean featuring Claudette Ortiz 1 Wyclef Jean and The Refugee Allstars

The JEEVAS
UK, male vocal / instrumental group (Singles: 2 Weeks) pos/wks

22 Mar 03	ONCE UPON A TIME IN AMERICA *Cowboy Music COWCDA 005*	.61 1
28 Feb 04	HAVE YOU EVER SEEN THE RAIN *Cowboy Music COWCDB 008*	.70 1

JEFFERSON
UK, male vocalist – Geoff Turton (Singles: 8 Weeks)   pos/wks

9 Apr 69	**COLOUR OF MY LOVE** Pye 7N 17706	22	8

JEFFERSON AIRPLANE (see also Grace SLICK; Paul KANTNER) US / UK, female / male vocal / instrumental group (Albums: 34 Weeks)   pos/wks

28 Jun 69	**BLESS ITS POINTED LITTLE HEAD** RCA SF 8019	38	1
7 Mar 70	**VOLUNTEERS** RCA SF 8076	34	7
13 Feb 71	**BLOWS AGAINST THE EMPIRE** RCA SF 8163 [1]	12	6
2 Oct 71	**BARK** Grunt FTR 1001	42	1
2 Sep 72	**LONG JOHN SILVER** Grunt FTR 1007	30	1
31 Jul 76	**SPITFIRE** Grunt RFL 1557 [2]	30	2
9 Feb 80	**FREEDOM AT POINT ZERO** Grunt FL 13452 [2]	22	11
18 Jul 87	**NO PROTECTION** Grunt FL 86413 [3]	26	5

[1] Paul Kantner and Jefferson Airplane [2] Jefferson Starship [3] Starship

JEFFERSON STARSHIP See JEFFERSON AIRPLANE

Garland JEFFREYS
US, male vocalist (Singles: 1 Week)   pos/wks

8 Feb 92	**HAIL HAIL ROCK 'N' ROLL** RCA PB 49171	72	1

JELLYBEAN
US, male producer – John Benitez (Singles: 47 Weeks, Albums: 35 Weeks)   pos/wks

1 Feb 86	**SIDEWALK TALK** EMI America EA 210 [1]	47	4
26 Sep 87	**THE REAL THING** Chrysalis CHS 3167 [2]	13	10
28 Nov 87 ●	**WHO FOUND WHO** Chrysalis CHS JEL 1 [3]	10	10
12 Dec 87	**JINGO** Chrysalis JEL 2	12	10
12 Mar 88	**JUST A MIRAGE** Chrysalis JEL 3 [4]	13	10
20 Aug 88	**COMING BACK FOR MORE** Chrysalis JEL 4 [5]	41	3
31 Oct 87	**JUST VISITING THIS PLANET** Chrysalis CHR 1569	15	28
3 Sep 88	**ROCKS THE HOUSE!** Chrysalis CJB 1	16	7

[1] Jellybean featuring Catherine Buchanan [2] Jellybean featuring Steven Dante [3] Jellybean featuring Elisa Fiorillo [4] Jellybean featuring Adele Bertei [5] Jellybean featuring Richard Darbyshire

JELLYFISH
US, male vocal / instrumental group (Singles: 20 Weeks, Albums: 2 Weeks)   pos/wks

26 Jan 91	**THE KING IS HALF UNDRESSED** Charisma CUSS 1	39	6
27 Apr 91	**BABY'S COMING BACK** Charisma CUSS 2	51	4
3 Aug 91	**THE SCARY-GO-ROUND EP** Charisma CUSS 3	49	3
26 Oct 91	**I WANNA STAY HOME** Charisma CUSS 4	59	2
1 May 93	**THE GHOST AT NUMBER ONE** Charisma CUSDG 10	43	3
17 Jul 93	**NEW MISTAKE** Charisma CUSDG 11	55	2
22 May 93	**SPILT MILK** Charisma CDCUS 20	21	2

Tracks on The Scary-Go-Round EP: Now She Knows She's Wrong / Bedspring Kiss / She Still Loves Him (Live) / Baby's Coming Back (Live)

JEMINI
UK, male / female vocal duo – Jemma Abbey and Chris Crosby (Singles: 3 Weeks)   pos/wks

7 Jun 03	**CRY BABY** Integral INTEG 001CD	15	3

Katherine JENKINS
UK, female vocalist (Albums: 13 Weeks)   pos/wks

17 Apr 04	**PREMIERE** UCJ 9866064	31	4
30 Oct 04	**SECOND NATURE** UCJ 9868047	16	9+

JENTINA
UK, female vocalist (Singles: 6 Weeks)   pos/wks

3 Jul 04	**BAD ASS STRIPPA** Virgin VSCDX 1873	22	3
9 Oct 04	**FRENCH KISSES** Virgin VSCDX 1877	20	3

JERU THE DAMAJA
US, male rapper – Kendrick Davis (Singles: 1 Week)   pos/wks

7 Dec 96	**YA PLAYIN YASELF** ffrr FCD 289	67	1

JESSICA
Sweden, female vocalist – Jessica Folker (Singles: 1 Week)   pos/wks

20 Mar 99	**HOW WILL I KNOW (WHO YOU ARE)** Jive 0522412	47	1

JESSY
Belgium, female vocalist – Jessy de Smet (Singles: 3 Weeks)   pos/wks

12 Apr 03	**LOOK AT ME NOW** Data / Ministry of Sound DATA 46CDS	29	3

JESUS AND MARY CHAIN
UK, male vocal / instrumental group (Singles: 59 Weeks, Albums: 40 Weeks)   pos/wks

2 Mar 85	**NEVER UNDERSTAND** Blanco Y Negro NEG 8	47	4
8 Jun 85	**YOU TRIP ME UP** Blanco Y Negro NEG 13	55	3
12 Oct 85	**JUST LIKE HONEY** Blanco Y Negro NEG 17	45	3
26 Jul 86	**SOME CANDY TALKING** Blanco Y Negro NEG 19	13	5
2 May 87 ●	**APRIL SKIES** Blanco Y Negro NEG 24	8	6
15 Aug 87	**HAPPY WHEN IT RAINS** Blanco Y Negro NEG 25	25	5
7 Nov 87	**DARKLANDS** Blanco Y Negro NEG 29	33	4
9 Apr 88	**SIDEWALKING** Blanco Y Negro NEG 32	30	3
23 Sep 89	**BLUES FROM A GUN** Blanco Y Negro NEG 41	32	2
18 Nov 89	**HEAD ON** Blanco Y Negro NEG 42	57	2
8 Sep 90	**ROLLERCOASTER (EP)** Blanco Y Negro NEG 45	46	2
15 Feb 92 ●	**REVERENCE** Blanco Y Negro NEG 55	10	4
14 Mar 92	**FAR GONE AND OUT** Blanco Y Negro NEG 56	23	3
4 Jul 92	**ALMOST GOLD** Blanco Y Negro NEG 57	41	2
10 Jul 93	**SOUND OF SPEED (EP)** Blanco Y Negro NEG 66CD	30	2
30 Jul 94	**SOMETIMES ALWAYS** Blanco Y Negro NEG 70CD	22	3
22 Oct 94	**COME ON** Blanco Y Negro NEG 73CD1	52	2
17 Jun 95	**I HATE ROCK 'N' ROLL** Blanco Y Negro NEG 81CD	61	1
18 Apr 98	**CRACKING UP** Creation CRESCD 292	35	2
30 May 98	**ILOVEROCKNROLL** Creation CRESCD 296	38	1
30 Nov 85	**PSYCHOCANDY** Blanco Y Negro BYN 7	31	10
12 Sep 87 ●	**DARKLANDS** Blanco Y Negro BYN 11	5	7
30 Apr 88 ●	**BARBED WIRE KISSES** Blanco Y Negro BYN 15	9	7
21 Oct 89	**AUTOMATIC** Blanco Y Negro BYN 20	11	4
4 Apr 92	**HONEY'S DEAD** Blanco Y Negro 9031765542	14	5
24 Jul 93	**THE SOUND OF SPEED** Blanco Y Negro 4509931052	15	3
27 Aug 94	**STONED AND DETHRONED** Blanco Y Negro 4509967172	13	3
13 Jun 98	**MUNKI** Creation CRECD 232	47	1

Tracks on Rollercoaster (EP): Rollercoaster / Silverblade / Lowlife / Tower of Song. Tracks on Sound of Speed (EP): Snakedriver / Something I Can't Have / Write Record Release Blues / Little Red Rooster

JESUS JONES
UK, male vocal / instrumental group (Singles: 52 Weeks, Albums: 31 Weeks)   pos/wks

25 Feb 89	**INFO-FREAKO** Food FOOD 18	42	3
8 Jul 89	**NEVER ENOUGH** Food FOOD 21	42	3
23 Sep 89	**BRING IT ON DOWN** Food FOOD 22	46	3
7 Apr 90	**REAL REAL REAL** Food FOOD 24	19	8
6 Oct 90	**RIGHT HERE RIGHT NOW** Food FOOD 25	31	4
12 Jan 91 ●	**INTERNATIONAL BRIGHT YOUNG THING** Food FOOD 27	7	7
2 Mar 91	**WHO? WHERE? WHY?** Food FOOD 28	21	7
20 Jul 91	**RIGHT HERE RIGHT NOW (re-issue)** Food FOOD 30	31	4
9 Jan 93 ●	**THE DEVIL YOU KNOW** Food CDPERV 1	10	5
10 Apr 93	**THE RIGHT DECISION** Food CDPERV 2	36	3
10 Jul 93	**ZEROES & ONES** Food CDFOOD5 44	30	3
14 Jun 97	**THE NEXT BIG THING** Food CDFOOD 95	49	1
16 Aug 97	**CHEMICAL #1** Food CDFOOD 102	71	1
14 Oct 89	**LIQUIDIZER** Food FOODLP 3	32	3
9 Feb 91 ★	**DOUBT** Food FOODLP 5 ■	1	24
6 Feb 93 ●	**PERVERSE** Food FOODCD 8	6	4

JESUS LIZARD
US, male vocal / instrumental group (Singles: 2 Weeks, Albums: 1 Week)   pos/wks

6 Mar 93	**PUSS** Touch and Go TG 83CD	12	2
10 Sep 94	**DOWN** Touch and Go TG 131CD	64	1

The listed flip side of 'Puss' was 'Oh, the Guilt' by Nirvana

JESUS LOVES YOU
(see also CULTURE CLUB) UK, male vocalist – Boy George (Singles: 18 Weeks, Albums: 1 Week)   pos/wks

11 Nov 89	**AFTER THE LOVE** More Protein PROT 2	68	1
23 Feb 91	**BOW DOWN MISTER** More Protein PROT 8	27	8
8 Jun 91	**GENERATIONS OF LOVE** More Protein PROT 10	35	8
12 Dec 92	**SWEET TOXIC LOVE** Virgin VS 1449	65	1
13 Apr 91	**THE MARTYR MANTRAS** More Protein CUMLP 1	60	1

JET
Australia, male vocal / instrumental group (Singles: 14 Weeks, Albums: 36 Weeks)   pos/wks

6 Sep 03	**ARE YOU GONNA BE MY GIRL** Elektra E 7456CD1	23	2
15 Nov 03	**ROLLOVER DJ** Elektra E 748CCD1	34	2
20 Mar 04	**LOOK WHAT YOU'VE DONE** Elektra E 75257CD	28	3
5 Jun 04	**ARE YOU GONNA BE MY GIRL (re-issue)** Elektra E 7599CD	16	5
18 Sep 04	**COLD HARD BITCH** Elektra E 7607CD	34	2
27 Sep 03	**GET BORN** Elektra 7559628922	14	36

JETHRO TULL `188` Top 500

Unique folk / rock outfit, fronted by the unmistakable, eccentrically dressed Ian Anderson (fl/v), who ranked among the world's top album sellers of the progressive rock era. Surprisingly, picked up the first ever Grammy for hard rock / heavy metal in 1989 (Singles: 68 Weeks, Albums: 236 Weeks) pos/wks

1 Jan 69		LOVE STORY *Island WIP 6048*	**29**	8
14 May 69	●	LIVING IN THE PAST *Island WIP 6056*	**3**	14
1 Nov 69	●	SWEET DREAM *Chrysalis WIP 6070*	**7**	11
24 Jan 70	●	TEACHER / THE WITCH'S PROMISE *Chrysalis WIP 6077*	**4**	9
18 Sep 71		LIFE IS A LONG SONG / UP THE POOL *Chrysalis WIP 6106*	**11**	8
11 Dec 76		RING OUT SOLSTICE BELLS (EP) *Chrysalis CXP 2*	**28**	6
15 Sep 84		LAP OF LUXURY *Chrysalis TULL 1*	**70**	2
16 Jan 88		SAID SHE WAS A DANCER *Chrysalis TULL 4*	**55**	4
21 Mar 92		ROCKS ON THE ROAD *Chrysalis TULLX 7*	**47**	3
22 May 93		LIVING IN THE (SLIGHTLY MORE RECENT) PAST *Chrysalis CDCHSS 3970*	**32**	3
2 Nov 68	●	THIS WAS *Island ILPS 9085*	**10**	22
9 Aug 69	★	STAND UP *Island ILPS 9103* ■	**1**	29
9 May 70	●	BENEFIT *Island ILPS 9123*	**3**	13
3 Apr 71	●	AQUALUNG *Island ILPS 9145*	**4**	21
18 Mar 72	●	THICK AS A BRICK *Chrysalis CHR 1003* ▲	**5**	14
15 Jul 72	●	LIVING IN THE PAST *Chrysalis CJT 1*	**8**	11
28 Jul 73		A PASSION PLAY *Chrysalis CHR 1040* ▲	**13**	8
2 Nov 74		WAR CHILD *Chrysalis CHR 1067*	**14**	4
27 Sep 75		MINSTREL IN THE GALLERY *Chrysalis CHR 1082*	**20**	6
31 Jan 76		M.U. THE BEST OF JETHRO TULL *Chrysalis CHR 1078*	**44**	5
15 May 76		TOO OLD TO ROCK 'N' ROLL: TOO YOUNG TO DIE *Chrysalis CHR 1111*	**25**	10
19 Feb 77		SONGS FROM THE WOOD *Chrysalis CHR 1132*	**13**	12
29 Apr 78		HEAVY HORSES *Chrysalis CHR 1175*	**20**	10
14 Oct 78		LIVE BURSTING OUT *Chrysalis CJT 4*	**17**	8
6 Oct 79		STORM WATCH *Chrysalis CDL 1238*	**27**	4
6 Sep 80		A *Chrysalis CDL 1301*	**25**	5
17 Apr 82		BROADSWORD AND THE BEAST *Chrysalis CDL 1380*	**27**	19
15 Sep 84		UNDER WRAPS *Chrysalis CDL 1461*	**18**	5
2 Nov 85		ORIGINAL MASTERS *Chrysalis JTTV 1*	**63**	3
19 Sep 87		CREST OF A KNAVE *Chrysalis CDL 1590*	**19**	10
9 Jul 88		20 YEARS OF JETHRO TULL *Chrysalis TBOX 1*	**78**	1
2 Sep 89		ROCK ISLAND *Chrysalis CDL 1708*	**18**	6
14 Sep 91		CATFISH RISING *Chrysalis CHR 1886*	**27**	3
26 Sep 92		A LITTLE LIGHT MUSIC *Chrysalis CCD 1954*	**34**	2
16 Sep 95		ROOTS TO BRANCHES *Chrysalis CDCHR 6109*	**20**	3
29 Jun 96		AQUALUNG *Chrysalis CD25 AQUA 1*	**53**	1
4 Sep 99		J-TULL DOT COM *Papillon BTFLYCD 0001*	**44**	1

Tracks on Ring Out Solstice Bells (EP): Ring Out Solstice Bells / March the Mad Scientist / The Christmas Song / Pan Dance. 'Living in the (Slightly More Recent) Past' is a live version of 'Living in the Past'

The JETS *UK, male vocal / instrumental group (Singles: 38 Weeks, Albums: 6 Weeks)* pos/wks

22 Aug 81	SUGAR DOLL *EMI 5211*	**55**	3
31 Oct 81	YES TONIGHT JOSEPHINE *EMI 5247*	**25**	11
6 Feb 82	LOVE MAKES THE WORLD GO ROUND *EMI 5262*	**21**	9
24 Apr 82	THE HONEYDRIPPER *EMI 5289*	**58**	3
9 Oct 82	SOMEBODY TO LOVE *EMI 5342*	**56**	3
6 Aug 83	BLUE SKIES *EMI 5405*	**53**	3
17 Dec 83	ROCKIN' AROUND THE CHRISTMAS TREE *PRT 7P 297*	**62**	4
13 Oct 84	PARTY DOLL *PRT JETS 2*	**72**	2
10 Apr 82	100 PERCENT COTTON *EMI EMC 3399*	**30**	6

The JETS *US, male / female vocal / instrumental group (Singles: 19 Weeks, Albums: 4 Weeks)* pos/wks

31 Jan 87	●	CRUSH ON YOU *MCA MCA 1048*	**5**	13
25 Apr 87		CURIOSITY *MCA MCA 1119*	**41**	4
28 May 88		ROCKET 2 U *MCA MCA 1226*	**69**	2
11 Apr 87		CRUSH ON YOU *MCA MCF 3312*	**57**	4

Joan JETT and the BLACKHEARTS

US, female vocalist – leader Jean Larkin and male vocal / instrumental group (Singles: 21 Weeks, Albums: 7 Weeks) pos/wks

24 Apr 82	●	I LOVE ROCK 'N' ROLL *Epic EPC A 2152* ▲	**4**	10
10 Jul 82		CRIMSON AND CLOVER *Epic EPC A 2485*	**60**	3
20 Aug 88		I HATE MYSELF FOR LOVING YOU *London LON 195*	**46**	6
31 Mar 90		DIRTY DEEDS *Chrysalis CHS 3518* [1]	**69**	1
19 Feb 94		I LOVE ROCK & ROLL (re-issue) *Reprise W 0232CD*	**75**	1
8 May 82		I LOVE ROCK 'N' ROLL *Epic EPC 85686*	**25**	7

[1] Joan Jett

JEWEL *US, female vocalist / instrumentalist – guitar – Jewel Kilcher (Singles: 9 Weeks, Albums: 4 Weeks)* pos/wks

14 Jun 97	WHO WILL SAVE YOUR SOUL *Atlantic A 8514CD*	**52**	1
9 Aug 97	YOU WERE MEANT FOR ME (re) *Atlantic A 5463CD*	**32**	3
21 Nov 98	HANDS *Atlantic AT 0055CD*	**41**	2
26 Jun 99	DOWN SO LONG *Atlantic AT 0069CD*	**38**	2
30 Aug 03	INTUITION *Atlantic W 619CD*	**52**	1
28 Nov 98	SPIRIT *Atlantic 7567829502*	**54**	1
9 Mar 02	THIS WAY *Atlantic 7567835192*	**34**	3

JEZ & CHOOPIE *UK / Israel, male DJ / production duo – Jeremy Ansell and David Geyra (Singles: 2 Weeks)* pos/wks

21 Mar 98	YIM *Multiply CDMULTY 31*	**36**	2

JHELISA *US, female vocalist – Jhelisa Anderson (Singles: 1 Week)* pos/wks

1 Jul 95	FRIENDLY PRESSURE *Dorado DOR 040CD*	**75**	1

JIGSAW *UK, male vocal / instrumental group (Singles: 16 Weeks)* pos/wks

1 Nov 75	●	SKY HIGH *Splash CP1 1*	**9**	11
6 Aug 77		IF I HAVE TO GO AWAY *Splash CP 11*	**36**	5

JILTED JOHN

UK, male vocalist – Graham Fellows (Singles: 12 Weeks) pos/wks

12 Aug 78	●	JILTED JOHN *EMI International INT 567*	**4**	12

JIMMY EAT WORLD *US, male vocal / instrumental group (Singles: 8 Weeks, Albums: 6 Weeks)* pos/wks

17 Nov 01	SALT SWEAT SUGAR *Dreamworks 4508782*	**60**	1
9 Feb 02	THE MIDDLE *Dreamworks 4508482*	**26**	3
15 Jun 02	SWEETNESS *Dreamworks 4508342*	**38**	2
16 Oct 04	PAIN *Interscope 9864179*	**37**	2
9 Feb 02	JIMMY EAT WORLD *Dreamworks 4503482*	**62**	4
23 Oct 04	FUTURES *Interscope 9864241*	**22**	2

JIMMY THE HOOVER

UK, male / female vocal / instrumental group (Singles: 8 Weeks) pos/wks

25 Jun 83	TANTALISE (WO WO EE YEH YEH) *Innervision A 3406*	**18**	8

JINGLE BELLES *US / UK, female vocal group (Singles: 4 Weeks)* pos/wks

17 Dec 83	CHRISTMAS SPECTRE *Passion PASH 14*	**37**	4

JINNY *Italy, female vocalist – Janine Brown (Singles: 16 Weeks)* pos/wks

29 Jun 91	KEEP WARM *Virgin VS 1356*	**68**	3
22 May 93	FEEL THE RHYTHM *Logic 401633001022*	**74**	1
15 Jul 95	KEEP WARM (re-mix) *Multiply CDMULTY 5*	**11**	8
16 Dec 95	WANNA BE WITH YOU *Multiply CDMULTY 8*	**30**	4

JIVE BUNNY and the MASTERMIXERS

UK, male DJ / production duo – Andy Pickles and Les Hemstock (Singles: 70 Weeks, Albums: 29 Weeks) pos/wks

15 Jul 89	★	SWING THE MOOD *Music Factory Dance MFD 001*	**1**	19
14 Oct 89	★	THAT'S WHAT I LIKE *Music Factory Dance MFD 002*	**1**	12
2 Dec 89		IT TAKES TWO BABY *Spartan CIN 101* [1]	**53**	2
16 Dec 89	★	LET'S PARTY *Music Factory Dance MFD 003* ■	**1**	6
17 Mar 90	●	THAT SOUNDS GOOD TO ME *Music Factory Dance MFD 004*	**4**	6
25 Aug 90	●	CAN CAN YOU PARTY *Music Factory Dance MFD 007*	**8**	6
17 Nov 90		LET'S SWING AGAIN *Music Factory Dance MFD 009*	**19**	5
22 Dec 90		THE CRAZY PARTY MIXES *Music Factory Dance MFD 010*	**13**	5
23 Mar 91		OVER TO YOU JOHN (HERE WE GO AGAIN) *Music Factory Dance MFD 012*	**28**	5
20 Jul 91		HOT SUMMER SALSA *Music Factory Dance MFD 013*	**43**	2
23 Nov 91		ROCK 'N' ROLL DANCE PARTY *Music Factory Dance MFD 015*	**48**	2
9 Dec 89	●	JIVE BUNNY – THE ALBUM *Telstar STAR 2390*	**2**	22
8 Dec 90		IT'S PARTY TIME *Telstar STAR 2449*	**23**	7

[1] Liz Kershaw, Bruno Brookes, Jive Bunny and Londonbeat

JO JINGLES *UK, male / female vocal group (Singles: 3 Weeks)* pos/wks

13 Nov 04	WIND THE BOBBIN UP! *Jo Jingles JJ 21CD*	**21**	3

JO JO GUNNE

US, male vocal / instrumental group (Singles: 12 Weeks) pos/wks

25 Mar 72	●	RUN RUN RUN *Asylum AYM 501*	**6**	12

JOAN COLLINS FAN CLUB
UK, male comedian / vocalist – Julian Clary (Singles: 3 Weeks) pos/wks

18 Jun 88	LEADER OF THE PACK *10 TEN 227*	60	3

John Paul JOANS *UK, male vocalist (Singles: 7 Weeks)* pos/wks

19 Dec 70	THE MAN FROM NAZARETH (re) *RAK 107*	25	7

JOBABE See REAL & RICHARDSON featuring JOBABE

JOBOXERS
UK, male vocal / instrumental
group (Singles: 33 Weeks, Albums: 5 Weeks) pos/wks

19 Feb 83 ●	BOXERBEAT *RCA BOX 1*	3	15
21 May 83 ●	JUST GOT LUCKY *RCA BOXX 2*	7	9
13 Aug 83	JOHNNY FRIENDLY *RCA BOXX 3*	31	8
12 Nov 83	JEALOUS LOVE *RCA BOXX 4*	72	1
24 Sep 83	LIKE GANGBUSTERS *RCA BOXXLP 1*	18	5

JOCASTA *UK, male vocal / instrumental group (Singles: 2 Weeks)* pos/wks

15 Feb 97	GO *Epic 6641415*	50	1
3 May 97	CHANGE ME *Epic 6643902*	60	1

JOCKMASTER B.A. See MAD JOCKS featuring JOCKMASTER B.A.

JOCKO
US, male DJ / rapper – Doug "Jocko"
Henderson, b. 8 Mar 1918, d. 15 Jul 2000 (Singles: 3 Weeks) pos/wks

23 Feb 80	RHYTHM TALK *Philadelphia International PIR 8222*	56	3

JODE featuring YO-HANS
UK, male / female vocal duo (Singles: 2 Weeks) pos/wks

19 Dec 98	WALK ... (THE DOG) LIKE AN EGYPTIAN *Logic 74321640332*	48	2

JODECI (see also K-CI and JOJO)
US, male vocal group (Singles: 19 Weeks, Albums: 8 Weeks) pos/wks

16 Jan 93	CHERISH *Uptown MCSTD 1726*	56	2
11 Dec 93	CRY FOR YOU *Uptown MCSTD 1951*	56	1
16 Jul 94	FEENIN' *Uptown MCSTD 1984*	18	3
28 Jan 95	CRY FOR YOU (re-issue) *Uptown MCSTD 2039*	20	3
24 Jun 95	FREEK 'N YOU *Uptown MCSTD 2072*	17	5
9 Dec 95	LOVE U 4 LIFE *Uptown MCSTD 2105*	23	3
25 May 96	GET ON UP *MCA MCSTD 48010*	20	2
29 Jul 95 ●	THE SHOW THE AFTER PARTY THE HOTEL *Uptown MCD 11258*	4	8

JODIE *Australia, female vocalist – Jodie Wilson (Singles: 1 Week)* pos/wks

25 Feb 95	ANYTHING YOU WANT *Mercury MERCD 423*	47	1

JOE *US, male vocalist – Joseph Thomas*
(Singles: 52 Weeks, Albums: 12 Weeks) pos/wks

22 Jan 94	I'M IN LUV *Mercury JOECD 1*	22	4
25 Jun 94	THE ONE FOR ME *Mercury JOECD 2*	34	2
22 Oct 94	ALL OR NOTHING *Mercury JOECD 3*	56	1
27 Apr 96	ALL THE THINGS (YOUR MAN WON'T DO) *Island CID 634*	34	3
14 Jun 97	DON'T WANNA BE A PLAYER *Jive JIVECD 410*	16	3
27 Sep 97	THE LOVE SCENE *Jive JIVECD 430*	22	2
10 Jan 98	GOOD GIRLS *Jive JIVECD 442*	29	3
22 Aug 98	NO ONE ELSE COMES CLOSE *Jive 0521682*	41	2
31 Oct 98	ALL THAT I AM *Jive 0518532*	52	1
11 Mar 00 ●	THANK GOD I FOUND YOU (re) *Columbia 6690582* [1] ▲	10	10
15 Jul 00	TREAT HER LIKE A LADY *Jive 9250772*	60	1
17 Feb 01 ●	STUTTER *Jive 9251632* [2] ▲	7	8
5 May 01	I WANNA KNOW *Jive 9252102*	37	2
16 Feb 02	LET'S STAY HOME TONIGHT *Jive 9253222*	29	2
14 Sep 02	WHAT IF A WOMAN *Jive 9253962*	53	1
24 Apr 04	RIDE WIT U / MORE & MORE *Jive 82876609212* [3]	12	7
12 Feb 94	EVERYTHING *Vertigo 5188072*	53	1
9 Aug 97	ALL THAT I AM *Jive CHIP 183*	26	4
29 Apr 00	MY NAME IS JOE *Jive 9220352*	46	4
8 May 04	AND THEN ... *Jive 82876586402*	74	3

[1] Mariah Carey featuring Joe and 98 Degrees [2] Joe featuring Mystikal [3] Joe featuring G-Unit

JOE PUBLIC *US, male rap group (Singles: 5 Weeks)* pos/wks

11 Jul 92	LIVE AND LEARN *Columbia 6575267*	43	4
28 Nov 92	I'VE BEEN WATCHIN' *Columbia 6587657*	75	1

Billy JOEL ⟨ 78 ⟩ ⟨ Top 500 ⟩ *Platinum-plated singer / songwriter / pianist, b. 9 May 1949, Long Island, US. This relatively youthful Grammy Living Legend Award recipient was the first artist to have five albums pass the seven-million mark Stateside. Best-selling single: 'Uptown Girl' 974,000 (Singles: 146 Weeks, Albums: 354 Weeks)* pos/wks

11 Feb 78	JUST THE WAY YOU ARE *CBS 5872*	19	9
24 Jun 78	MOVIN' OUT (ANTHONY'S SONG) *CBS 6412*	35	6
2 Dec 78	MY LIFE *CBS 6821*	12	15
28 Apr 79	UNTIL THE NIGHT *CBS 7242*	50	3
12 Apr 80	ALL FOR LEYNA *CBS 8325*	40	4
9 Aug 80	IT'S STILL ROCK AND ROLL TO ME *CBS 8753* ▲	14	11
15 Oct 83 ★	UPTOWN GIRL *CBS A 3775*	1	17
10 Dec 83 ●	TELL HER ABOUT IT *CBS A 3655* ▲	4	10
18 Feb 84 ●	AN INNOCENT MAN *CBS A 4142*	8	10
28 Apr 84	THE LONGEST TIME *CBS A 4280*	25	8
23 Jun 84	LEAVE A TENDER MOMENT ALONE / GOODNIGHT SAIGON *CBS A 4521*	29	7
22 Feb 86	SHE'S ALWAYS A WOMAN / JUST THE WAY YOU ARE (re-issue) *CBS A 6862*	53	1
20 Sep 86	A MATTER OF TRUST *CBS 6500577*	52	4
30 Sep 89 ●	WE DIDN'T START THE FIRE *CBS JOEL 1* ▲	7	10
16 Dec 89	LENINGRAD *CBS JOEL 3*	53	4
10 Mar 90	I GO TO EXTREMES *CBS JOEL 2*	70	2
29 Aug 92	ALL SHOOK UP *Columbia 6583437*	27	4
31 Jul 93 ●	THE RIVER OF DREAMS *Columbia 6595432*	3	14
23 Oct 93	ALL ABOUT SOUL *Columbia 6597362*	32	4
26 Feb 94	NO MAN'S LAND *Columbia 6599202*	50	3
25 Mar 78	THE STRANGER *CBS 82311*	25	40
25 Nov 78 ●	52ND STREET *CBS 83181* ▲	10	43
22 Mar 80 ●	GLASS HOUSES *CBS 86108* ▲	9	24
10 Oct 81	SONGS IN THE ATTIC *CBS 85273*	57	3
2 Oct 82	THE NYLON CURTAIN *CBS 85959*	27	8
10 Sep 83 ●	AN INNOCENT MAN *CBS 25554*	2	95
4 Feb 84	COLD SPRING HARBOUR *CBS 32400*	95	1
23 Jun 84	PIANO MAN *CBS 32002*	98	1
20 Jul 85 ●	GREATEST HITS – VOLUME I & VOLUME II *CBS 88666*	7	39
16 Aug 86	THE BRIDGE *CBS 86323*	38	10
28 Nov 87	KOHYEPT – LIVE IN LENINGRAD *CBS 4604071*	92	1
4 Nov 89 ●	STORM FRONT *CBS 4656581* ▲	5	25
14 Aug 93 ●	RIVER OF DREAMS *Columbia 4738722* ▲	3	26
1 Nov 97	GREATEST HITS – VOLUME III *Columbia 4882362*	23	4
13 Jun 98	GREATEST HITS – VOLUMES I II & III *Columbia 4912742*	33	4
27 May 00	2000 YEARS – THE MILLENNIUM CONCERT *Columbia 4979812*	68	1
31 Mar 01	THE ULTIMATE COLLECTION *Columbia SONYTV 98CD*	4	24
27 Nov 04	PIANO MAN – THE VERY BEST OF BILLY JOEL *Columbia 5190182*	40	5+

'Goodnight Saigon' listed only from 30 Jun 1984

JOHANN
Germany, male producer – Johann Bley (Singles: 1 Week) pos/wks

16 Mar 96	NEW KICKS *Perfecto PERF 118CD*	54	1

Angela JOHN See José PADILLA featuring Angela JOHN

Elton JOHN ⟨ 6 ⟩ ⟨ Top 500 ⟩ *Flamboyant singer / songwriter / pianist, b. Reginald Dwight, 25 Mar 1947, Pinner, Middlesex, UK. Almost as famous for his outrageous wardrobe as his music, Elton was the biggest-selling pop act of the 1970s, and has sold more albums in the UK and US than any British male singer, with total worldwide sales exceeding 150 million. He is the only British act to enter the US singles chart at No.1 and he also recorded the first two albums to enter the US chart at No.1. He holds the record for headlining appearances at New York's Madison Square Garden. Elton, twice chairman of Watford Football Club, is the only act to chart every year from 1971 to 1999 in the UK and US. 'His Greatest Hits' album has sold more than 16 million in the US and he has topped the US adult contemporary chart a record 16 times. 'Candle in the Wind 1997' (which he performed at the funeral of Diana, Princess of Wales) topped the chart in almost every country. In the UK it sold nearly five million in six weeks and in the US had record advance orders of 8.7 million (and total sales in excess of 11 million). It also spent a staggering three years in the Canadian Top 20, which included 45 weeks at No.1. It is the world's best-selling single, with sales of 33 million (4,864,611 in the UK). His lyric-writing partners have included, most influentially, Bernie Taupin and, more recently, Sir Tim Rice. He became Sir Elton John in 1998. Total UK single sales: 13,475,063 (Singles: 628 Weeks, Albums: 987 Weeks)* pos/wks

23 Jan 71 ●	YOUR SONG *DJM DJS 233*	7	12
22 Apr 72 ●	ROCKET MAN (I THINK IT'S GOING TO BE A LONG LONG TIME) *DJM DJX 501*	2	13

9 Sep 72		**HONKY CAT** *DJM DJS 269*	31	6
4 Nov 72	●	**CROCODILE ROCK** *DJM DJS 271* ▲	5	14
20 Jan 73	●	**DANIEL** *DJM DJS 275*	4	10
7 Jul 73	●	**SATURDAY NIGHT'S ALRIGHT FOR FIGHTING** *DJM DJX 502*	7	9
29 Sep 73	●	**GOODBYE YELLOW BRICK ROAD** *DJM DJS 285*	6	16
8 Dec 73		**STEP INTO CHRISTMAS** *DJM DJS 290*	24	7
2 Mar 74		**CANDLE IN THE WIND** *DJM DJS 297*	11	9
1 Jun 74		**DON'T LET THE SUN GO DOWN ON ME** *DJM DJS 302*	16	8
14 Sep 74		**THE BITCH IS BACK** *DJM DJS 322*	15	7
23 Nov 74	●	**LUCY IN THE SKY WITH DIAMONDS** *DJM DJS 340* ▲	10	10
8 Mar 75		**PHILADELPHIA FREEDOM** *DJM DJS 354* [1] ▲	12	9
28 Jun 75		**SOMEONE SAVED MY LIFE TONIGHT** *DJM DJS 385*	22	5
4 Oct 75		**ISLAND GIRL** *DJM DJS 610* ▲	14	8
20 Mar 76	●	**PINBALL WIZARD** *DJM DJS 652*	7	7
3 Jul 76	★	**DON'T GO BREAKING MY HEART** *Rocket ROKN 512* [2] ▲	1	14
25 Sep 76		**BENNIE AND THE JETS** *DJM DJS 10705* ▲	37	5
13 Nov 76		**SORRY SEEMS TO BE THE HARDEST WORD** *Rocket ROKN 517*	11	10
26 Feb 77		**CRAZY WATER** *Rocket ROKN 521*	27	6
11 Jun 77		**BITE YOUR LIP (GET UP AND DANCE)** *Rocket ROKN 526*	28	4
15 Apr 78		**EGO** *Rocket ROKN 538*	34	6
21 Oct 78		**PART TIME LOVE** *Rocket XPRES 1*	15	13
16 Dec 78	●	**SONG FOR GUY** *Rocket XPRES 5*	4	10
12 May 79		**ARE YOU READY FOR LOVE** *Rocket XPRES 13*	42	6
24 May 80		**LITTLE JEANNIE** *Rocket XPRES 32*	33	7
23 Aug 80		**SARTORIAL ELOQUENCE** *Rocket XPRES 41*	44	5
21 Mar 81		**I SAW HER STANDING THERE** *DJM DJS 10965* [3]	40	4
23 May 81		**NOBODY WINS** *Rocket XPRES 54*	42	5
27 Mar 82	●	**BLUE EYES** *Rocket XPRES 71*	8	10
12 Jun 82		**EMPTY GARDEN** *Rocket XPRES 77*	51	4
30 Apr 83	●	**I GUESS THAT'S WHY THEY CALL IT THE BLUES** *Rocket XPRES 91*	5	15
30 Jul 83	●	**I'M STILL STANDING** *Rocket EJS 1*	4	11
15 Oct 83		**KISS THE BRIDE** *Rocket EJS 2*	20	7
10 Dec 83		**COLD AS CHRISTMAS (IN THE MIDDLE OF THE YEAR)** *Rocket EJS 3*	33	6
26 May 84	●	**SAD SONGS (SAY SO MUCH)** *Rocket PH 7*	7	12
11 Aug 84	●	**PASSENGERS** *Rocket EJS 5*	5	11
20 Oct 84		**WHO WEARS THESE SHOES** *Rocket EJS 6*	50	3
2 Mar 85		**BREAKING HEARTS (AIN'T WHAT IT USED TO BE)** *Rocket EJS 7*	59	3
15 Jun 85		**ACT OF WAR** *Rocket EJS 8* [4]	32	5
12 Oct 85	●	**NIKITA** *Rocket EJS 9*	3	13
9 Nov 85		**THAT'S WHAT FRIENDS ARE FOR** *Arista ARIST 638* [5] ▲	16	9
7 Dec 85		**WRAP HER UP** *Rocket EJS 10*	12	10
1 Mar 86		**CRY TO HEAVEN** *Rocket EJS 11*	47	4
4 Oct 86		**HEARTACHE ALL OVER THE WORLD** *Rocket EJS 12*	45	4
29 Nov 86		**SLOW RIVERS** *Rocket EJS 13* [6]	44	8
20 Jun 87		**FLAMES OF PARADISE** *CBS 6508657* [7]	59	3
16 Jan 88	●	**CANDLE IN THE WIND** *Rocket EJS 15*	5	11
4 Jun 88		**I DON'T WANNA GO ON WITH YOU LIKE THAT** *Rocket EJS 16*	30	8
3 Sep 88		**TOWN OF PLENTY** *Rocket EJS 17*	74	1
6 May 89		**THROUGH THE STORM** *Arista 112185* [8]	41	3
26 Aug 89		**HEALING HANDS** *Rocket EJS 19*	45	5
4 Nov 89		**SACRIFICE** *Rocket EJS 20*	55	3
9 Jun 90	★	**SACRIFICE / HEALING HANDS (re-issue)** *Rocket EJS 22*	1	15
18 Aug 90		**CLUB AT THE END OF THE STREET / WHISPERS** *Rocket EJS 23*	47	3
20 Oct 90		**YOU GOTTA LOVE SOMEONE** *Rocket EJS 24*	33	4
15 Dec 90		**EASIER TO WALK AWAY (re)** *Rocket EJS 25*	63	2
7 Dec 91	★	**DON'T LET THE SUN GO DOWN ON ME** *Epic 6576467* [9] ■ ▲	1	10
6 Jun 92	●	**THE ONE** *Rocket EJS 28*	10	8
1 Aug 92		**RUNAWAY TRAIN** *Rocket EJS 29* [10]	31	4
7 Nov 92		**THE LAST SONG** *Rocket EJS 30*	21	4
22 May 93		**SIMPLE LIFE** *Rocket EJSCD 31*	44	2
20 Nov 93	●	**TRUE LOVE** *Rocket EJSCX 32* [2]	2	10
26 Feb 94	●	**DON'T GO BREAKING MY HEART (re-recording)** *Rocket EJRCD 33* [11]	7	7
14 May 94		**AIN'T NOTHING LIKE THE REAL THING** *London LONCD 350* [12]	24	4
9 Jul 94		**CAN YOU FEEL THE LOVE TONIGHT** *Mercury EJCD 34*	14	9
8 Oct 94		**CIRCLE OF LIFE** *Rocket EJSCD 35*	11	12
4 Mar 95		**BELIEVE** *Rocket EJSCD 36*	15	7
20 May 95		**MADE IN ENGLAND** *Rocket EJSCD 37*	18	5
3 Feb 96		**PLEASE** *Rocket EJSCD 40*	33	3
14 Dec 96	●	**LIVE LIKE HORSES** *Rocket LLHDD 1* [13]	9	6
20 Sep 97	★	**CANDLE IN THE WIND 1997 / SOMETHING ABOUT THE WAY YOU LOOK TONIGHT** *Rocket PTCD 1* ◆ ■ ▲	1	24
14 Feb 98		**RECOVER YOUR SOUL** *Rocket EJSCD 42*	16	3
13 Jun 98		**IF THE RIVER CAN BEND** *Rocket EJSDD 43*	32	2
6 Mar 99	●	**WRITTEN IN THE STARS (re)** *Mercury EJSCD 45* [14]	10	8
6 Oct 01	●	**I WANT LOVE** *Rocket / Mercury 5887062*	9	10
26 Jan 02		**THIS TRAIN DON'T STOP THERE ANYMORE** *Rocket / Mercury 588962*	24	4
13 Apr 02		**ORIGINAL SIN** *Rocket / Mercury 5889992*	39	2
27 Jul 02	●	**YOUR SONG (re)** *Mercury 639972* [15]	4	10
21 Dec 02	★	**SORRY SEEMS TO BE THE HARDEST WORD (re-recording)** *Innocent SINDX 43* [16] ■	1	17
19 Jul 03		**ARE YOU READY FOR LOVE (12" RE-MIX)** *Southern Fried ECB 50LOVE*	66	1
6 Sep 03	★	**ARE YOU READY FOR LOVE (re-mix)** *Southern Fried ECB 50CDS*	1	13
13 Nov 04		**ALL THAT I'M ALLOWED (I'M THANKFUL)** *Rocket / Mercury 9868257*	20	5
23 May 70	●	**ELTON JOHN** *DJM DJLPS 406*	5	22
16 Jan 71	●	**TUMBLEWEED CONNECTION** *DJM DJLPS 410*	2	20
1 May 71		**THE ELTON JOHN LIVE ALBUM 17-11-70** *DJM DJLPS 414*	20	2
20 May 72		**MADMAN ACROSS THE WATER** *DJM DJLPH 420*	41	2
3 Jun 72	●	**HONKY CHÂTEAU** *DJM DJLPH 423* ▲	2	23
10 Feb 73	★	**DON'T SHOOT ME I'M ONLY THE PIANO PLAYER** *DJM DJLPH 427* ■ ▲	1	42
3 Nov 73	★	**GOODBYE YELLOW BRICK ROAD** *DJM DJLPO 1001* ▲	1	84
13 Jul 74	★	**CARIBOU** *DJM DJLPH 439* ■ ▲	1	18
23 Nov 74	★	**GREATEST HITS** *DJM DJLPH 442* ■ ▲	1	84
7 Jun 75	●	**CAPTAIN FANTASTIC AND THE BROWN DIRT COWBOY** *DJM DJLPX 1* ▲	2	24
8 Nov 75	●	**ROCK OF THE WESTIES** *DJM DJLPH 464* ▲	5	12
15 May 76	●	**HERE AND THERE** *DJM DJLPH 473*	6	9
6 Nov 76	●	**BLUE MOVES** *Rocket ROSP 1*	3	15
15 Oct 77	●	**ELTON JOHN'S GREATEST HITS VOLUME II** *DJM DJH 20520*	6	24
4 Nov 78	●	**A SINGLE MAN** *Rocket TRAIN 1*	8	26
20 Oct 79		**VICTIM OF LOVE** *Rocket HISPD 125*	41	3
8 Mar 80		**LADY SAMANTHA** *DJM 22085*	56	2
31 May 80		**21 AT 33** *Rocket HISPD 126*	12	13
25 Oct 80		**THE VERY BEST OF ELTON JOHN** *K-Tel NE 1094*	24	13
30 May 81		**THE FOX** *Rocket TRAIN 16*	12	12
17 Apr 82		**JUMP UP!** *Rocket HISPD 127*	13	12
6 Nov 82		**LOVE SONGS** *TV TVA 3*	39	13
11 Jun 83	●	**TOO LOW FOR ZERO** *Rocket HISPD 24*	7	73
30 Jun 84	●	**BREAKING HEARTS** *Rocket HISPD 25*	2	23
16 Nov 85	●	**ICE ON FIRE** *Rocket HISPD 26*	3	23
15 Nov 86		**LEATHER JACKETS** *Rocket EJLP 1*	24	9
12 Sep 87		**LIVE IN AUSTRALIA WITH THE MELBOURNE SYMPHONY ORCHESTRA** *Rocket EJBXL 1* [1]	43	7
16 Jul 88		**REG STRIKES BACK** *Rocket EJLP 3*	18	6
23 Sep 89	★	**SLEEPING WITH THE PAST** *Rocket 8388391*	1	42
10 Nov 90	★	**THE VERY BEST OF ELTON JOHN** *Rocket 8469471* ■	1	97
27 Jun 92	●	**THE ONE** *Rocket 5123602*	2	18
4 Dec 93	●	**DUETS** *Rocket 5184782*	5	18
1 Apr 95	●	**MADE IN ENGLAND** *Rocket 5261852*	3	14
18 Nov 95	●	**LOVE SONGS** *Rocket 5287882*	4	48
11 Oct 97	●	**THE BIG PICTURE** *Rocket 5362662*	3	23
3 Apr 99		**ELTON JOHN AND TIM RICE'S AIDA** *Mercury 5246512* [2]	29	2
25 Nov 00	●	**ONE NIGHT ONLY – THE GREATEST HITS** *Mercury 5483342*	7	13
13 Oct 01	●	**SONGS FROM THE WEST COAST** *Mercury 5863302*	2	34
20 Oct 01		**GOODBYE YELLOW BRICK ROAD (re-issue)** *Rocket 5281592*	41	4
23 Nov 02	●	**GREATEST HITS 1970-2002** *Mercury 634992*	3	52
20 Nov 04		**PEACHTREE ROAD** *Rocket 9868762*	21	6+

[1] Elton John Band [2] Elton John and Kiki Dee [3] Elton John Band featuring John Lennon and the Muscle Shoals Horns [4] Elton John and Millie Jackson [5] Dionne Warwick and Friends featuring Elton John, Stevie Wonder and Gladys Knight [6] Elton John and Cliff Richard [7] Jennifer Rush and Elton John [8] Aretha Franklin and Elton John [9] George Michael and Elton John [10] Elton John and Eric Clapton [11] Elton John with RuPaul [12] Marcella Detroit and Elton John [13] Elton John & Luciano Pavarotti [14] Elton John and LeAnn Rimes [15] Elton John and Alessandro Safina [16] Blue featuring Elton John [1] Elton John with the Melbourne Symphony Orchestra [2] Elton John and Friends

'Bite Your Lip (Get Up and Dance)' was one side of a double-sided chart entry, the other being 'Chicago' by Kiki Dee. 'Wrap Her Up' features George Michael as uncredited co-vocalist. 'Candle in the Wind' 1988 was a live recording 'Live In Australia...' reappeared in 1988 as EJLP 2; EJBXL 1 was the original 'de luxe' version. The two 'The Very Best of Elton John' and 'Love Songs' albums are different

Jennifer JOHN *See ONEHUNDREDPERCENT featuring Jennifer JOHN*

262

Singles re-entries are listed as (re), (2re), (3re).... which signifies that the hit re-entered the chart once, twice or three times...

Robert JOHN
US, male vocalist – Robert John Pedrick (Singles: 13 Weeks) pos/wks

			pos	wks
17 Jul 68		IF YOU DON'T WANT MY LOVE *CBS 3436*	42	5
20 Oct 79		SAD EYES *EMI American EA 101* ▲	31	8

JOHNNA
US, female vocalist – Johnna Cummings (Singles: 3 Weeks) pos/wks

			pos	wks
10 Feb 96		DO WHAT YOU FEEL *PWL International PWL 323CD*	43	2
11 May 96		IN MY DREAMS *PWL International PWL 325CD*	66	1

JOHNNY and CHARLEY
Spain, male vocal duo (Singles: 1 Week) pos/wks

			pos	wks
14 Oct 65		LA YENKA *Pye International 7N 25326*	49	1

JOHNNY and the HURRICANES
US, male instrumental quintet (Singles: 88 Weeks, Albums: 5 Weeks) pos/wks

			pos	wks
9 Oct 59	●	RED RIVER ROCK *London HL 8948*	3	16
25 Dec 59		REVEILLE ROCK *London HL 9017*	14	5
17 Mar 60	●	BEATNIK FLY *London HLI 9072*	8	19
16 Jun 60	●	DOWN YONDER *London HLX 9134*	8	11
29 Sep 60	●	ROCKING GOOSE *London HLX 9190*	3	20
2 Mar 61		JA-DA *London HLX 9289*	14	9
6 Jul 61		OLD SMOKIE / HIGH VOLTAGE *London HLX 9378*	24	8
3 Dec 60		STORMSVILLE *London HAI 2269*	18	1
1 Apr 61		BIG SOUND OF JOHNNY AND THE HURRICANES *London HAK 2322*	14	4

JOHNNY BOY
UK, male / female production / vocal duo (Singles: 2 Weeks) pos/wks

		pos	wks
14 Aug 04	YOU ARE THE GENERATION THAT BOUGHT MORE SHOES AND YOU GET WHAT YOU DESERVE *Mercury 9866935*	50	2

JOHNNY CORPORATE
US, male production duo (Singles: 2 Weeks) pos/wks

		pos	wks
28 Oct 00	SUNDAY SHOUTIN' *Defected DFECT 21CDS*	45	2

JOHNNY HATES JAZZ
UK, male vocal / instrumental group (Singles: 45 Weeks, Albums: 39 Weeks) pos/wks

			pos	wks
11 Apr 87	●	SHATTERED DREAMS *Virgin VS 948*	5	14
29 Aug 87		I DON'T WANT TO BE A HERO *Virgin VS 1000*	11	10
21 Nov 87		TURN BACK THE CLOCK *Virgin VS 1017*	12	11
27 Feb 88		HEART OF GOLD *Virgin VS 1045*	19	7
9 Jul 88		DON'T SAY IT'S LOVE *Virgin VS 1081*	48	3
23 Jan 88	★	TURN BACK THE CLOCK *Virgin V 2475* ■	1	39

JOHNNY PANIC
UK, male vocal / instrumental group (Singles: 1 Week) pos/wks

		pos	wks
18 Sep 04	BURN YOUR MOUTH *Concept CDCON 59*	69	1

JOHNSON
UK, male / female vocal / instrumental duo (Singles: 1 Week) pos/wks

		pos	wks
27 Mar 99	SAY YOU LOVE ME *Higher Ground HIGHS 18CD*	56	1

Andreas JOHNSON
Sweden, male vocalist (Singles: 12 Weeks, Albums: 2 Weeks) pos/wks

			pos	wks
5 Feb 00	●	GLORIOUS *WEA WEA 254CD*	4	11
27 May 00		THE GAMES WE PLAY *WEA WEA 264*	41	1
19 Feb 00		LIEBLING *WEA 3984269142*	46	2

Bryan JOHNSON
UK, male vocalist, b. 18 Jul 1926, d. 18 Oct 1995 (Singles: 11 Weeks) pos/wks

		pos	wks
10 Mar 60	LOOKING HIGH, HIGH, HIGH *Decca F 11213*	20	11

Carey JOHNSON
Australia, male vocalist – Reginald Johnson (Singles: 8 Weeks) pos/wks

		pos	wks
25 Apr 87	REAL FASHION REGGAE STYLE *Oval TEN 170*	19	8

Denise JOHNSON
UK, female vocalist (Singles: 4 Weeks) pos/wks

			pos	wks
24 Aug 91		DON'T FIGHT IT FEEL IT *Creation CRE 110* [1]	41	2
14 May 94		RAYS OF THE RISING SUN *Magnet MAG 1022CD*	45	2

[1] Primal Scream featuring Denise Johnson

Don JOHNSON
US, male vocalist / actor (Singles: 12 Weeks) pos/wks

		pos	wks
18 Oct 86	HEARTBEAT *Epic 650064 7*	46	5
5 Nov 88	TILL I LOVED YOU (LOVE THEME FROM 'GOYA') *CBS BARB 2* [1]	16	7

[1] Barbra Streisand and Don Johnson

General JOHNSON *See* CHAIRMEN OF THE BOARD

Holly JOHNSON
(see also FRANKIE GOES TO HOLLYWOOD) *UK, male vocalist – William Johnson (Singles: 38 Weeks, Albums: 17 Weeks)* pos/wks

			pos	wks
14 Jan 89	●	LOVE TRAIN *MCA MCA 1306*	4	11
1 Apr 89	●	AMERICANOS *MCA MCA 1323*	4	11
20 May 89	★	FERRY 'CROSS THE MERSEY *PWL PWL 41* [1] ■	1	7
24 Jun 89		ATOMIC CITY *MCA MCA 1342*	18	4
30 Sep 89		HEAVEN'S HERE *MCA MCA 1365*	62	2
1 Dec 90		WHERE HAS LOVE GONE? *MCA MCA 1460*	73	1
25 Dec 99		THE POWER OF LOVE *Pleasure Dome PLDCD 1005*	56	2
6 May 89	★	BLAST *MCA MCG 6042* ■	1	17

[1] The Christians, Holly Johnson, Paul McCartney, Gerry Marsden and Stock Aitken Waterman

Howard JOHNSON
US, male vocalist (Singles: 6 Weeks) pos/wks

		pos	wks
4 Sep 82	KEEPIN' LOVE NEW / SO FINE *A&M USA 1221*	45	6

'Keepin' Love New' listed on 4 Sep 1982 only

Johnny JOHNSON and the BANDWAGON
US, male vocal group (Singles: 50 Weeks) pos/wks

			pos	wks
16 Oct 68	●	BREAKIN' DOWN THE WALLS OF HEARTACHE *Direction 58-3670* [1]	4	15
5 Feb 69		YOU *Direction 58-3923*	34	4
28 May 69		LET'S HANG ON *Direction 58-4180*	36	6
25 Jul 70	●	SWEET INSPIRATION (re) *Bell 1111*	10	13
28 Nov 70	●	(BLAME IT) ON THE PONY EXPRESS *Bell 1128*	7	12

[1] Bandwagon

Kevin JOHNSON
Australia, male vocalist (Singles: 6 Weeks) pos/wks

		pos	wks
11 Jan 75	ROCK 'N ROLL (I GAVE YOU THE BEST YEARS OF MY LIFE) *UK UKR 84*	23	6

Laurie JOHNSON ORCHESTRA
UK, orchestra (Singles: 14 Weeks) pos/wks

			pos	wks
28 Sep 61	●	SUCU SUCU *Pye 7N 15383*	9	12
17 May 97		THEME FROM 'THE PROFESSIONALS' *Virgin VSCDT 1643* [1]	36	2

[1] Laurie Johnson's London Big Band

Linton Kwesi JOHNSON
Jamaica, male poet (Albums: 8 Weeks) pos/wks

		pos	wks
30 Jun 79	FORCES OF VICTORY *Island ILPS 9566*	66	1
31 Oct 80	BASS CULTURE *Island ILPS 9605*	46	5
10 Mar 84	MAKING HISTORY *Island ILPS 9770*	73	2

LJ JOHNSON
US, male vocalist – Louis Johnson (Singles: 6 Weeks) pos/wks

		pos	wks
7 Feb 76	YOUR MAGIC PUT A SPELL ON ME *Philips 6006 492*	27	6

Lou JOHNSON
US, male vocalist (Singles: 2 Weeks) pos/wks

		pos	wks
26 Nov 64	A MESSAGE TO MARTHA (KENTUCKY BLUEBIRD) *London HL 9929*	36	2

Marv JOHNSON
US, male vocalist, b. 15 Oct 1938, d. 16 May 1993 (Singles: 40 Weeks) pos/wks

			pos	wks
12 Feb 60	●	YOU GOT WHAT IT TAKES *London HLT 9013*	7	17
5 May 60		I LOVE THE WAY YOU LOVE *London HLT 9109*	35	3
11 Aug 60		AIN'T GONNA BE THAT WAY *London HLT 9165*	50	1
22 Jan 69	●	I'LL PICK A ROSE FOR MY ROSE *Tamla Motown TMG 680*	10	11
25 Oct 69		I MISS YOU BABY *Tamla Motown TMG 713*	25	8

Matt JOHNSON *See* The THE

Orlando JOHNSON *See* SECCHI featuring Orlando JOHNSON

BODY PART CHART

The human body has always been a source of fascination and inspiration for artists, from Michelangelo in the 1500s to the pop stars of this century and the last. Back in 1972, Chuck Berry delighted millions with his 'Ding-a-Ling' (wherever that is), and last year The Streets touched many hearts with his summer release 'Dry Your Eyes'. So, run your 'Goldfinger' down this list of singles name-checking parts of Beyoncé's body.

The figures in brackets indicate the peak position of each body part hit.

DRY YOUR EYES
The Streets (1)

SHE MAKES MY NOSE BLEED
Mansun (9)

WORLD SHUT YOUR MOUTH
Julian Cope (19)

TONGUE
R.E.M. (13)

JAWS
Lalo Schifrin (14)

MY HEART WILL GO ON
Celine Dion (1)

MY IRON LUNG
Radiohead (24)

INSANE IN THE BRAIN
Cypress Hill (19)

CAN'T GET YOU OUT OF MY HEAD
Kylie Minogue (1)

GOT SOME TEETH
Obie Trice (8)

LUCKY LIPS
Cliff Richard and The Shadows (4)

WEAR MY RING AROUND YOUR NECK
Elvis Presley (3)

PUT YOUR HEAD ON MY SHOULDER
Paul Anka (7)

MUSCLEBOUND
Spandau Ballet (10)

OPEN ARMS
Mariah Carey (4)

BACK STABBERS
The O'Jays (14)

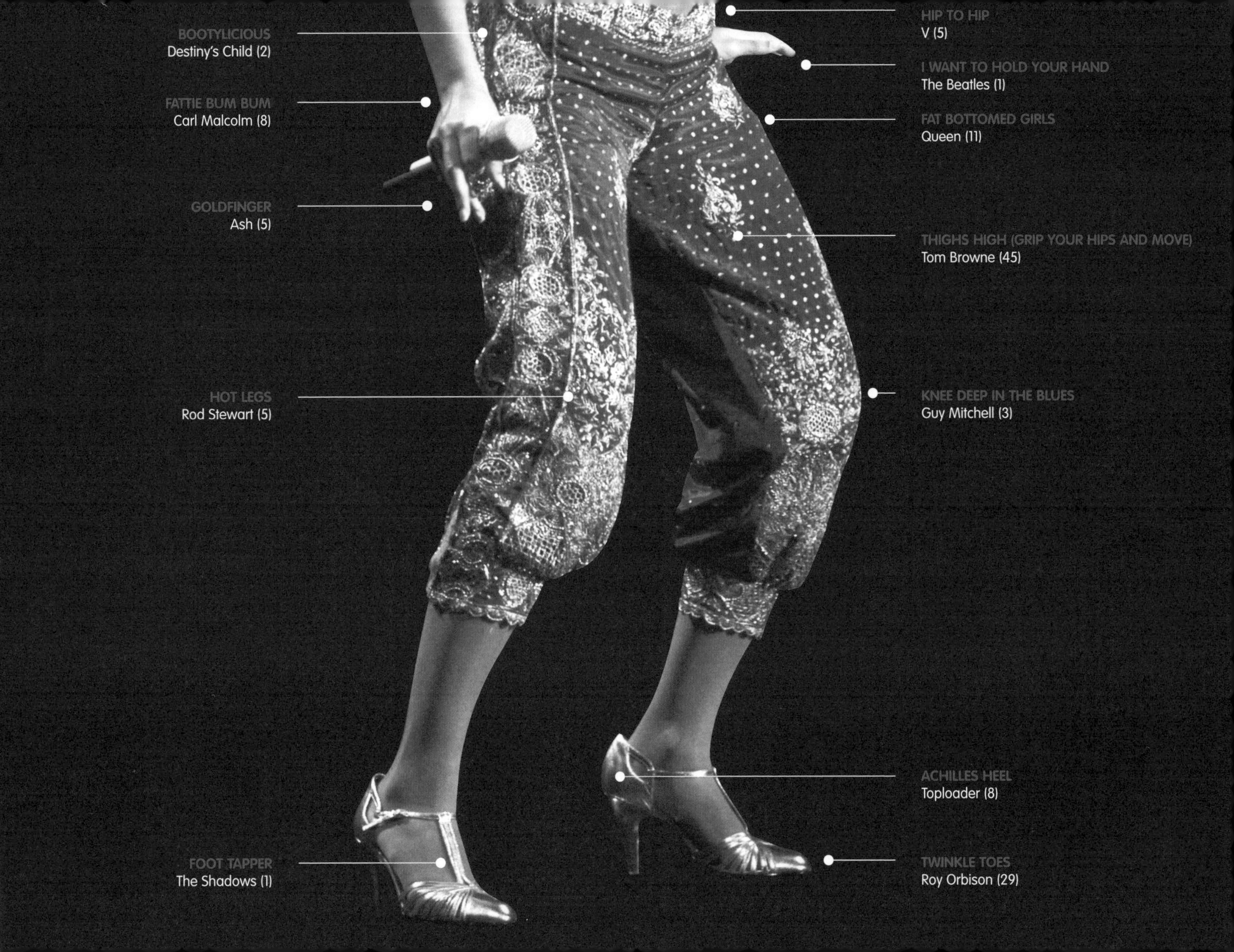

HIP TO HIP
V (5)

I WANT TO HOLD YOUR HAND
The Beatles (1)

FAT BOTTOMED GIRLS
Queen (11)

THIGHS HIGH (GRIP YOUR HIPS AND MOVE)
Tom Browne (45)

KNEE DEEP IN THE BLUES
Guy Mitchell (3)

ACHILLES HEEL
Toploader (8)

TWINKLE TOES
Roy Orbison (29)

BOOTYLICIOUS
Destiny's Child (2)

FATTIE BUM BUM
Carl Malcolm (8)

GOLDFINGER
Ash (5)

HOT LEGS
Rod Stewart (5)

FOOT TAPPER
The Shadows (1)

265

Paul JOHNSON
UK, male vocalist (Singles: 7 Weeks, Albums: 3 Weeks)   pos/wks

21 Feb 87	WHEN LOVE COMES CALLING *CBS PJOHN 1*	52	5
25 Feb 89	NO MORE TOMORROWS *CBS PJOHN 7*	67	2
4 Jul 87	PAUL JOHNSON *CBS 450640 1*	63	2
16 Sep 89	PERSONAL *CBS 463284 1*	70	1

Paul JOHNSON
US, male producer / instrumentalist (Singles: 8 Weeks)   pos/wks

25 Sep 99 ●	GET GET DOWN *Defected DEFECT 7CDS*	5	8

Puff JOHNSON *US, female vocalist (Singles: 6 Weeks)*
pos/wks

18 Jan 97	OVER AND OVER *Columbia 6640345*	20	4
12 Apr 97	FOREVER MORE *Work 644075*	29	2

Romina JOHNSON *UK, female vocalist (Singles: 13 Weeks)*
pos/wks

4 Mar 00 ●	MOVIN TOO FAST (re) *Locked On XL LOX 117CD* [1]	2	12
17 Jun 00	MY FORBIDDEN LOVER *51 Lexington CDLEX 1* [2]	59	1

[1] Artful Dodger and Romina Johnson [2] Romina Johnson featuring Luci Martin and Norma Jean

Syleena JOHNSON *US, female vocalist (Singles: 10 Weeks)*
pos/wks

26 Oct 02	TONIGHT I'M GONNA LET GO *Jive 9254252*	38	2
19 Jun 04 ●	ALL FALLS DOWN *Roc-A-Fella 9862670* [1]	10	8

[1] Kanye West featuring Syleena Johnson

Sleeve of 'Tonight I'm Gonna Let Go' credits Syleena Johnson featuring Busta Rhymes, Rampage, Sham & Spliff Star (of Flipmode Squad)

Teddy JOHNSON See Pearl CARR and Teddy JOHNSON

Ana JOHNSSON *Sweden, female vocalist (Singles: 6 Weeks)*
pos/wks

14 Aug 04 ●	WE ARE *Epic 6751622*	8	6

The JOHNSTON BROTHERS *UK, male vocal group – leader*
Johnny Johnston (Johnny Reine), d. Jun 1998 (Singles: 33 Weeks)   pos/wks

3 Apr 53 ●	OH, HAPPY DAY *Decca F 10071*	4	8
5 Nov 54	WAIT FOR ME, DARLING *Decca F 10362* [1]	18	1
21 Jan 55	HAPPY DAYS AND LONELY NIGHTS *Decca F 10389* [2]	14	2
7 Oct 55 ★	HERNANDO'S HIDEAWAY *Decca F 10608*	1	13
30 Dec 55 ●	JOIN IN AND SING AGAIN *Decca F 10636* [3]	9	1
13 Apr 56	NO OTHER LOVE *Decca F 10721*	22	1
30 Nov 56	IN THE MIDDLE OF THE HOUSE *Decca F 10781*	27	1
7 Dec 56	JOIN IN AND SING NO.3 (re) *Decca F 10814*	24	2
8 Feb 57	GIVE HER MY LOVE *Decca F 10828*	27	1
19 Apr 57	HEART *Decca F 10860*	23	3

[1] Joan Regan with The Johnston Brothers [2] Suzi Miller and The Johnston Brothers [3] The Johnston Brothers and The George Chisholm Sour-Note Six

The following two hits were medleys: Join In and Sing Again: Sheik of Araby / Yes Sir That's My Baby / California Here I Come / Some of These Days / Charleston / Margie. Join In and Sing No.3: Coal Black Morning / When You're Smiling / Alexander's Ragtime Band / Sweet Sue Just You / When You Wore a Tulip / If You Were the Only Girl in the World

Brian JOHNSTON
UK, male broadcaster, d. 5 Jan 1994 (Albums: 3 Weeks)   pos/wks

5 Mar 94	AN EVENING WITH JOHNNERS *Listen for Pleasure LFP 7742*	46	3

Bruce JOHNSTON (see also The BEACH BOYS)
US, male instrumentalist – keyboards (Singles: 4 Weeks)   pos/wks

27 Aug 77	PIPELINE *CBS 5514*	33	4

JAMES A JOHNSTON *US, male producer (Albums: 17 Weeks)*
pos/wks

13 Nov 99	WORLD WRESTLING FEDERATION – THE MUSIC – VOLUME 4 *Koch International 333612*	44	9
10 Mar 01	WORLD WRESTLING FEDERATION – THE MUSIC – VOLUME 5 *Koch KOCCD 8830*	11	8

Jan JOHNSTON *UK, female vocalist (Singles: 12 Weeks)*
pos/wks

8 Feb 97	TAKE ME BY THE HAND *AM:PM 5821012* [1]	28	2
28 Nov 98	SKYDIVE *Stress CDSTR 89* [2]	75	1
12 Feb 00	LOVE WILL COME *Xtravaganza XTRAV 6CDS* [3]	31	2
22 Jul 00	SKYDIVE (re-mix) *Renaissance Recordings RENCDS 002* [2]	43	2
21 Apr 01	FLESH *Perfecto PERF 05CDS*	36	2
28 Jul 01	SILENT WORDS *Perfecto PERF 16CDS*	57	1
8 Sep 01	SKYDIVE (I FEEL WONDERFUL) (2nd re-mix) *Incentive CENT 22CDS* [2]	35	2

[1] Submerge featuring Jan Johnston [2] Freefall featuring Jan Johnston [3] Tomski featuring Jan Johnston

Sabrina JOHNSTON *US, female vocalist (Singles: 19 Weeks)*
pos/wks

7 Sep 91 ●	PEACE *East West YZ 616*	8	10
7 Dec 91	FRIENDSHIP *East West YZ 637*	58	4
11 Jul 92	I WANNA SING *East West YZ 661*	46	2
3 Oct 92	PEACE (re-mix) *Epic 6584377*	35	2
13 Aug 94	SATISFY MY LOVE *Champion CHAMPCD 311*	62	1

The listed flipside of 'Peace' (re-mix) was 'Gypsy Woman' (re-mix) by Crystal Waters

JOJO *US, female vocalist – Joanne Levesque*
(Singles: 13 Weeks, Albums: 15 Weeks)   pos/wks

11 Sep 04 ●	LEAVE (GET OUT) *Mercury 9867841*	2	8
27 Nov 04 ●	BABY IT'S YOU *Mercury 9869056* [1]	8	5+
18 Sep 04	JOJO *Mercury 9867855*	22	15+

[1] JoJo featuring Bow Wow

JOJO See K-CI & JOJO; 2PAC

James JOLIS See Barry MANILOW

JOLLY BROTHERS
Jamaica, male vocal / instrumental group (Singles: 7 Weeks)   pos/wks

28 Jul 79	CONSCIOUS MAN *United Artists UP 36415*	46	7

JOLLY ROGER *UK, male instrumentalist /*
producer – Eddie Richards (Singles: 12 Weeks)   pos/wks

10 Sep 88	ACID MAN *10 TEN 236*	23	12

Al JOLSON *US, male vocalist – Asa Yoelson,*
b. 26 Mar 1886, d. 23 Oct 1950 (Albums: 11 Weeks)   pos/wks

14 Mar 81	20 GOLDEN GREATS *MCA MCTV 4*	18	7
17 Dec 83	THE AL JOLSON COLLECTION *Ronco RON LP 5*	67	4

JOMALSKI See WILDCHILD

JOMANDA *US, female vocal group (Singles: 10 Weeks)*
pos/wks

22 Apr 89	MAKE MY BODY ROCK *RCA PB 42749*	44	3
29 Jun 91	GOT A LOVE FOR YOU *Giant W 0040*	43	4
11 Sep 93	I LIKE IT *Big Beat A 8377CD*	67	1
13 Nov 93	NEVER *Big Beat A 8347CD*	40	2

JON and VANGELIS *UK, male vocalist and Greece,*
male multi-instrumentalist – Jon Anderson and Evangelos Papathanassiou (Singles: 28 Weeks, Albums: 53 Weeks)   pos/wks

5 Jan 80 ●	I HEAR YOU NOW *Polydor POSP 96*	8	11
12 Dec 81 ●	I'LL FIND MY WAY HOME *Polydor JV 1*	6	13
30 Jul 83	HE IS SAILING *Polydor JV 4*	61	2
18 Aug 84	STATE OF INDEPENDENCE *Polydor JV 5*	67	2
26 Jan 80 ●	SHORT STORIES *Polydor POLD 5030*	4	11
11 Jul 81	THE FRIENDS OF MR. CAIRO *Polydor POLD 5039*	17	8
23 Jan 82 ●	THE FRIENDS OF MR. CAIRO (re-issue) *Polydor POLD 5053*	6	15
2 Jul 83	PRIVATE COLLECTION *Polydor POLH 4*	22	10
11 Aug 84	THE BEST OF JON AND VANGELIS *Polydor POLH 6*	42	9

JON OF THE PLEASED WIMMIN
UK, male DJ / producer – Jonathan Cooper (Singles: 5 Weeks)   pos/wks

18 Feb 95	PASSION *Perfecto YZ 884CD*	27	3
6 Apr 96	GIVE ME STRENGTH *Perfecto PERF 119CD*	30	2

JON THE DENTIST vs Ollie JAYE *UK, male DJs /*
producers – John Vaughan and Ollie Jaye (Singles: 2 Weeks)   pos/wks

24 Jul 99	IMAGINATION *Tidy Trax TIDY 126CD*	72	1
10 Jun 00	FEEL SO GOOD *Tidy Trax TIDY 135CD*	72	1

JONAH Holland, male production group (Singles: 4 Weeks)

			pos/wks
22 Jul 00	SSSST (LISTEN) VC Recordings VCRD 69	....	**25** 4

JONELL See HI-TEK featuring JONELL

Aled JONES (366 Top 500)
Angelic choirboy famed for appearing on the soundtrack to 'The Snowman'. Welsh boy soprano, b. 29 Dec 1970, Llandegfan, Wales, who matured into a baritone has performed in classical, traditional, religious and pop styles. In July 1985, became the youngest soloist to feature on simultaneous Top 10 albums, and is now a broadcaster (Singles: 24 Weeks, Albums: 161 Weeks)

			pos/wks
20 Jul 85	MEMORY: THEME FROM THE MUSICAL 'CATS' BBC RESL 175	..	**42** 4
30 Nov 85 ●	WALKING IN THE AIR HMV ALED 1		**5** 11
14 Dec 85	PICTURES IN THE DARK Virgin VS 836 [1]		**50** 6
20 Dec 86	A WINTER STORY HMV ALED 2		**51** 3
27 Apr 85 ●	VOICES FROM THE HOLY LAND BBC REC 564 [1]		**6** 43
29 Jun 85 ●	ALL THROUGH THE NIGHT BBC REH 569 [1]		**2** 44
23 Nov 85	ALED JONES WITH THE BBC WELSH CHORUS 10 / BBC AJ 1 [1]		**11** 10
22 Feb 86	WHERE E'ER YOU WALK 10 DIX 21		**36** 6
12 Jul 86	PIE JESU 10 AJ 2		**25** 16
29 Nov 86	AN ALBUM OF HYMNS Telstar STAR 2272		**18** 11
14 Mar 87	ALED (MUSIC FROM THE TV SERIES) 10 AJ 3		**52** 6
5 Dec 87	THE BEST OF ALED JONES 10 AJ 5		**59** 5
26 Oct 02	ALED UCJ 0644792		**27** 9
11 Oct 03	HIGHER UCJ 9865579		**21** 7
4 Dec 04	THE CHRISTMAS ALBUM UCJ 9868649		**26** 4+

[1] Mike Oldfield featuring Aled Jones, Anita Hegerland and Barry Palmer
[1] Aled Jones with the BBC Welsh Chorus

Barbara JONES
Jamaica, female vocalist – Barbara Nation (Singles: 7 Weeks)

			pos/wks
31 Jan 81	JUST WHEN I NEEDED YOU MOST Sonet SON 2221	....	**31** 7

Catherine Zeta JONES
UK, female actor / vocalist (Singles: 9 Weeks)

			pos/wks
19 Sep 92	FOR ALL TIME Columbia 6583547	....	**36** 5
26 Nov 94	TRUE LOVE WAYS PolyGram TV TLWCD 2 [1]		**38** 3
1 Apr 95	IN THE ARMS OF LOVE Wow! WOWCD 7101		**72** 1

[1] David Essex and Catherine Zeta Jones

Donell JONES
US, male vocalist (Singles: 20 Weeks, Albums: 5 Weeks)

			pos/wks
15 Feb 97	KNOCKS ME OFF MY FEET LaFace 74321458502		**58** 1
22 Jan 00 ●	U KNOW WHAT'S UP LaFace 74321722752		**2** 11
20 May 00	SHORTY (GOT HER EYES ON ME) LaFace 74321748902		**19** 3
2 Dec 00	TRUE STEP TONIGHT Nulife 74321811312 [1]		**25** 3
24 Aug 02	YOU KNOW THAT I LOVE YOU Arista 74321956962		**41** 2
29 Jan 00	WHERE I WANNA BE LaFace 73008260602		**47** 3
22 Jun 02	LIFE GOES ON Arista 74321941552		**62** 2

[1] True Steppers featuring Brian Harvey and Donell Jones

Georgia JONES See DIVA SURPRISE featuring Georgia JONES; PLUX featuring Georgia JONES

Glenn JONES
US, male vocalist (Albums: 1 Week)

			pos/wks
31 Oct 87	GLENN JONES Jive HIP 51	....	**62** 1

Grace JONES Jamaica, female vocalist –
Grace Mendoza (Singles: 46 Weeks, Albums: 80 Weeks)

			pos/wks
26 Jul 80	PRIVATE LIFE Island WIP 6629		**17** 8
20 Jun 81	PULL UP TO THE BUMPER Island WIP 6696		**53** 4
30 Oct 82	THE APPLE STRETCHING / NIPPLE TO THE BOTTLE Island WIP 6779		**50** 4
9 Apr 83	MY JAMAICAN GUY Island IS 103		**56** 3
12 Oct 85	SLAVE TO THE RHYTHM ZTT IS 206		**12** 8
18 Jan 86	PULL UP TO THE BUMPER / LA VIE EN ROSE (re-issue) Island IS 240		**12** 9
1 Mar 86	LOVE IS THE DRUG Island IS 266		**35** 4
15 Nov 86	I'M NOT PERFECT (BUT I'M PERFECT FOR YOU) Manhattan MT 15		**56** 3

			pos/wks
7 May 94	SLAVE TO THE RHYTHM (re-mix) Zance ZANG 50CD1		**28** 2
25 Nov 00	PULL UP TO THE BUMPER Club Tools 0120375 CLU [1]		**60** 1
30 Aug 80	WARM LEATHERETTE Island ILPS 9592		**45** 2
23 May 81	NIGHTCLUBBING Island ILPS 9624		**35** 16
20 Nov 82	LIVING MY LIFE Island ILPS 9722		**15** 22
9 Nov 85	SLAVE TO THE RHYTHM ZTT GRACE 1		**12** 8
14 Dec 85 ●	ISLAND LIFE Island GJ 1		**4** 30
29 Nov 86	INSIDE STORY Manhattan MTL 1007		**61** 2

[1] Grace Jones vs Funkstar De Luxe
'La Vie En Rose' was listed only from 1 Feb 1986

Hannah JONES
US, female vocalist (Singles: 9 Weeks)

			pos/wks
14 Sep 91	BRIDGE OVER TROUBLED WATER Dance Pool 6565467		**21** 8
30 Jan 93	KEEP IT ON TMRC CDTMRC 7		**67** 1

Howard JONES (293 Top 500)
Accomplished singer / songwriter, b. John Howard Jones, 23 Feb 1955, Southampton, UK, who was a regular chart visitor in the mid-1980s with his brand of synth-based pop. Jones, who was equally popular in the US, appeared at Live Aid (Singles: 103 Weeks, Albums: 122 Weeks)

			pos/wks
17 Sep 83 ●	NEW SONG (re) WEA HOW 1		**3** 15
26 Nov 83 ●	WHAT IS LOVE WEA HOW 2		**2** 15
18 Feb 84	HIDE AND SEEK WEA HOW 3		**12** 9
26 May 84 ●	PEARL IN THE SHELL WEA HOW 4		**7** 10
11 Aug 84 ●	LIKE TO GET TO KNOW YOU WELL WEA HOW 5		**4** 12
9 Feb 85 ●	THINGS CAN ONLY GET BETTER WEA HOW 6		**6** 8
20 Apr 85 ●	LOOK MAMA WEA HOW 7		**10** 6
29 Jun 85	LIFE IN ONE DAY WEA HOW 8		**14** 7
15 Mar 86	NO ONE IS TO BLAME WEA HOW 9		**16** 7
4 Oct 86	ALL I WANT WEA HOW 10		**35** 4
29 Nov 86	YOU KNOW I LOVE YOU ... DON'T YOU? WEA HOW 11		**43** 3
21 Mar 87	LITTLE BIT OF SNOW WEA HOW 12		**70** 1
4 Mar 89	EVERLASTING LOVE WEA HOW 13		**62** 3
11 Apr 92	LIFT ME UP East West HOW 15		**52** 3
17 Mar 84 ★	HUMAN'S LIB WEA WX 1 ■		**1** 57
8 Dec 84	THE 12" ALBUM WEA WX 14		**15** 33
23 Mar 85 ●	DREAM INTO ACTION WEA WX 15		**2** 25
25 Oct 86 ●	ONE TO ONE WEA WX 68		**10** 4
1 Apr 89	CROSS THAT LINE WEA WX 225		**64** 1
5 Jun 93	THE BEST OF HOWARD JONES East West 4509927012		**36** 2

Jack JONES US, male vocalist (Albums: 70 Weeks)

			pos/wks
29 Apr 72 ●	A SONG FOR YOU RCA Victor SF 8228		**9** 6
3 Jun 72 ●	BREAD WINNERS RCA Victor SF 8280		**7** 36
7 Apr 73 ●	TOGETHER RCA Victor SF 8342		**8** 10
23 Feb 74 ●	HARBOUR RCA Victor APL1 0408		**10** 5
19 Feb 77	THE FULL LIFE RCA Victor PL 12067		**41** 5
21 May 77 ●	ALL TO YOURSELF RCA TVL 2		**10** 8

Janie JONES
UK, female vocalist – Marion Mitchell (Singles: 3 Weeks)

			pos/wks
27 Jan 66	WITCHES BREW HMV POP 1495		**46** 3

Jimmy JONES US, male vocalist (Singles: 47 Weeks)

			pos/wks
17 Mar 60 ●	HANDY MAN (re) MGM 1051		**3** 24
16 Jun 60 ★	GOOD TIMIN' MGM 1078		**1** 15
8 Sep 60	I JUST GO FOR YOU MGM 1091		**35** 4
17 Nov 60	READY FOR LOVE MGM 1103		**46** 1
30 Mar 61	I TOLD YOU SO MGM 1123		**33** 3

Juggy JONES
US, male multi-instrumentalist – Henry Murray (Singles: 4 Weeks)

			pos/wks
7 Feb 76	INSIDE AMERICA Contempo CS 2080		**39** 4

Kelly JONES See MANCHILD

Lavinia JONES
South Africa, female vocalist (Singles: 2 Weeks)

			pos/wks
18 Feb 95	SING IT TO YOU (DEE-DOOB-DEE-DOO) Virgin International DINDG 142		**45** 2

Mick JONES See AZTEC CAMERA; The CLASH

Norah JONES (412) Top 500

*The most successful new jazz artist in the rock era. b. 30 Mar 1979,
New York, US, is the daughter of Ravi Shankar. In 2003, the vocalist /
instrumentalist received a record-equalling five Grammy awards and the
International Breakthrough Artist award at the Brits and was a World Music
Award-winner in 2004 (Singles: 6 Weeks, Albums: 162 Weeks)*   pos/wks

25 May 02	DON'T KNOW WHY *Parlophone CDCL 836*	59 1
17 Aug 02	FEELIN' THE SAME WAY *Parlophone CDCL 838*	72 1
23 Aug 03	DON'T KNOW WHY (re-issue) / I'LL BE YOUR BABY TONIGHT	
	Parlophone CDCL 848	67 1
10 Apr 04	SUNRISE *Blue Note CDCL 853*	30 3
11 May 02 ★	COME AWAY WITH ME *Parlophone 5386092* ▲	1 126
21 Feb 04 ★	FEELS LIKE HOME *Blue Note 5983660* ■ ▲	1 36

Oran 'Juice' JONES

US, male vocalist (Singles: 14 Weeks)   pos/wks

15 Nov 86 ●	THE RAIN *Def Jam A 7303*	4 14

Paul JONES

(see also BLUES BAND; MANFRED MANN)
UK, male vocalist – Paul Pond (Singles: 34 Weeks)   pos/wks

6 Oct 66 ●	HIGH TIME *HMV POP 1554*	4 15
19 Jan 67 ●	I'VE BEEN A BAD, BAD BOY *HMV POP 1576*	5 9
23 Aug 67	THINKIN' AIN'T FOR ME (re) *HMV POP 1602*	32 8
5 Feb 69	AQUARIUS *Columbia DB 8514*	45 2

Quincy JONES

*US, male producer / instrumentalist –
keyboards (Singles: 42 Weeks, Albums: 41 Weeks)*   pos/wks

29 Jul 78	STUFF LIKE THAT *A&M AMS 7367*	34 9
11 Apr 81	AI NO CORRIDA (I-NO-KO-REE-DA)	
	A&M AMS 8109 [1]	14 10
20 Jun 81	RAZZAMATAZZ *A&M AMS 8140*	11 9
5 Sep 81	BETCHA' WOULDN'T HURT ME *A&M AMS 8157*	52 3
13 Jan 90	I'LL BE GOOD TO YOU *Qwest W 2697* [2]	21 7
31 Mar 90	SECRET GARDEN *Qwest W 9992* [3]	67 1
14 Sep 96	STOMP *Qwest W 0372CD* [4]	28 2
1 Aug 98	SOUL BOSSA NOVA *Manifesto FESCD 48* [5]	47 1
18 Apr 81	THE DUDE *A&M AMLK 63721*	19 25
20 Mar 82	THE BEST *A&M AMLH 68542*	41 4
20 Jan 90	BACK ON THE BLOCK *Qwest WX 313*	26 12

[1] Quincy Jones featuring Dune [2] Quincy Jones featuring Ray Charles and
Chaka Khan [3] Quincy Jones featuring Al B Sure!, James Ingram, El DeBarge and
Barry White [4] Quincy Jones featuring Melle Mel, Coolio, Yo-Yo, Shaquille O'Neal,
The Luniz [5] Cool, the Fab and the Groovy present Quincy Jones

*Uncredited vocals on 'Stuff Like That' were by Ashford and Simpson and
Chaka Khan. Uncredited vocals on 'Razzamatazz' and 'Betcha' Wouldn't
Hurt Me' were by Patti Austin*

Rickie Lee JONES

*US, female vocalist / instrumentalist – guitar
(Singles: 9 Weeks, Albums: 39 Weeks)*   pos/wks

23 Jun 79	CHUCK E'S IN LOVE *Warner Bros. K 17390*	18 9
16 Jun 79	RICKIE LEE JONES *Warner Bros. K 56628*	18 19
8 Aug 81	PIRATES *Warner Bros. K 56816*	37 11
2 Jul 83	GIRL AT HER VOLCANO *Warner Bros. 9238051*	51 3
13 Oct 84	THE MAGAZINE *Warner Bros. 925117*	40 4
7 Oct 89	FLYING COWBOYS *Geffen WX 309*	50 2

Shirley JONES *See The PARTRIDGE FAMILY*

Sonny JONES featuring Tara CHASE *Germany,*

male vocalist and Canada, female rapper (Singles: 2 Weeks)   pos/wks

7 Oct 00	FOLLOW YOU FOLLOW ME	
	Logic 74321772892	42 2

Tammy JONES

UK, female vocalist (Singles: 10 Weeks, Albums: 5 Weeks)   pos/wks

26 Apr 75 ●	LET ME TRY AGAIN *Epic EPC 3211*	5 10
12 Jul 75	LET ME TRY AGAIN *Epic EPC 80853*	38 5

Tom JONES (24) Top 500

*Unmistakable entertainer, who was re-named after the popular 1963 film and
has been an international headliner for five decades. b Thomas Woodward,
7 Jun, 1940, South Wales. Despite failure of his first two Joe Meek-produced
singles, the Welsh wonder became one of world's most popular singers, with
hits in the pop, country, R&B and easy listening fields. The Vegas veteran,
who hosted his own very successful late-1960s TV series, has had hits on 10
labels. This 60-something sex symbol, who was the top British solo singer of
the 1960s on both sides of Atlantic, had his best-selling album in 1999 with
'Reload' and received an Outstanding Contribution to British Music Brit Award
in 2003. Best-selling single: 'Green, Green Grass of Home' 1,205,000 (Singles:
394 Weeks, Albums: 521 Weeks)*   pos/wks

11 Feb 65 ★	IT'S NOT UNUSUAL *Decca F 12062*	1 14
6 May 65	ONCE UPON A TIME *Decca F 12121*	32 4
8 Jul 65	WITH THESE HANDS *Decca F 12191*	13 11
12 Aug 65	WHAT'S NEW PUSSYCAT? *Decca F 12203*	11 10
13 Jan 66	THUNDERBALL *Decca F 12292*	35 4
19 May 66	ONCE THERE WAS A TIME / NOT RESPONSIBLE	
	Decca F 12390	18 9
18 Aug 66	THIS AND THAT *Decca F 12461*	44 3
10 Nov 66 ★	GREEN, GREEN GRASS OF HOME *Decca F 22511* ◆	1 22
16 Feb 67	DETROIT CITY *Decca F 22555*	8 10
13 Apr 67 ●	FUNNY FAMILIAR FORGOTTEN FEELINGS *Decca F 12599*	7 15
26 Jul 67	I'LL NEVER FALL IN LOVE AGAIN *Decca F 12639*	2 25
22 Nov 67	I'M COMING HOME *Decca F 12693*	2 16
28 Feb 68 ●	DELILAH *Decca F 12747*	2 17
17 Jul 68 ●	HELP YOURSELF *Decca F 12812*	5 26
27 Nov 68	A MINUTE OF YOUR TIME *Decca F 12854*	14 15
14 May 69 ●	LOVE ME TONIGHT *Decca F 12924*	9 12
13 Dec 69 ●	WITHOUT LOVE (re) *Decca F 12990*	10 12
18 Apr 70 ●	DAUGHTER OF DARKNESS *Decca F 13013*	5 15
15 Aug 70	I (WHO HAVE NOTHING) (re) *Decca F 13061*	16 11
16 Jan 71	SHE'S A LADY (re) *Decca F 13113*	13 10
5 Jun 71	PUPPET MAN *Decca F 13183*	49 2
23 Oct 71 ●	TILL *Decca F 13236*	2 15
1 Apr 72 ●	THE YOUNG NEW MEXICAN PUPPETEER *Decca F 13298*	6 12
14 Apr 73	LETTER TO LUCILLE *Decca F 13393*	31 8
7 Sep 74	SOMETHING 'BOUT YOU BABY I LIKE *Decca F 13550*	36 5
16 Apr 77	SAY YOU'LL STAY UNTIL TOMORROW *EMI 2583*	40 7
18 Apr 87 ●	A BOY FROM NOWHERE *Epic OLE 1*	2 12
30 May 87	IT'S NOT UNUSUAL (re-issue) *Decca F 103*	17 8
2 Jan 88	I WAS BORN TO BE ME *Epic OLE 4*	61 1
29 Oct 88 ●	KISS *China CHINA 11* [1]	5 7
29 Apr 89	MOVE CLOSER *Jive JIVE 203*	49 3
26 Jan 91	COULDN'T SAY GOODBYE *Dover ROJ 10*	51 2
16 Mar 91	CARRYING A TORCH *Dover ROJ 12*	57 2
4 Jul 92	DELILAH (re-issue) *The Hit Label TOM 10*	68 2
6 Feb 93	ALL YOU NEED IS LOVE *Childline CHILDCD 93*	19 4
5 Nov 94	IF I ONLY KNEW *ZTT ZANG 59CD*	11 9
25 Sep 99 ●	BURNING DOWN THE HOUSE *Gut CDGUT 26* [2]	7 7
18 Dec 99	BABY, IT'S COLD OUTSIDE *Gut CDGUT 29* [3]	17 7
18 Mar 00 ●	MAMA TOLD ME NOT TO COME *Gut CDGUT 031* [4]	4 7
20 May 00 ●	SEX BOMB *Gut CDGUT 33* [5]	3 10
18 Nov 00	YOU NEED LOVE LIKE I DO *GUT CDGUT 36* [6]	24 3
9 Nov 02	TOM JONES INTERNATIONAL *V2 VVR 5021083*	31 2
8 Mar 03	BLACK BETTY / I WHO HAVE NOTHING *V2 VVR 5021763*	50 2
5 Jun 65	ALONG CAME JONES *Decca LK 6693*	11 5
8 Oct 66	FROM THE HEART *Decca LK 4814*	23 8
8 Apr 67 ●	GREEN GREEN GRASS OF HOME *Decca SKL 4855*	3 49
24 Jun 67 ●	LIVE AT THE TALK OF THE TOWN *Decca SKL 4874*	6 90
30 Dec 67 ●	13 SMASH HITS *Decca SKL 4909*	5 49
27 Jul 68 ★	DELILAH *Decca SKL 4946*	1 29
21 Dec 68 ●	HELP YOURSELF *Decca SKL 4982*	4 9
28 Jun 69 ●	THIS IS TOM JONES *Decca SKL 5007*	2 20
15 Nov 69 ●	TOM JONES LIVE IN LAS VEGAS *Decca SKL 5032*	2 45
25 Apr 70 ●	TOM *Decca SKL 5045*	4 18
14 Nov 70 ●	I WHO HAVE NOTHING *Decca SKL 5072*	10 10
29 May 71 ●	SHE'S A LADY *Decca SKL 5089*	9 7
27 Nov 71	LIVE AT CAESAR'S PALACE *Decca 1/11/2*	27 5
24 Jun 72	CLOSE UP *Decca SKL 5132*	17 4
23 Jun 73	THE BODY AND SOUL OF TOM JONES *Decca SKL 5162*	31 1
5 Jan 74	GREATEST HITS *Decca SKL 5176*	15 13
22 Mar 75 ★	20 GREATEST HITS *Decca TJD 1/11/2* ■	1 21
7 Oct 78	I'M COMING HOME *Lotus WH 5001*	12 9
16 May 87	THE GREATEST HITS *Telstar STAR 2296*	16 12
13 May 89	AT THIS MOMENT *Jive TOMTV 1*	34 3
8 Jul 89	AFTER DARK *Stylus SMR 978*	46 4

6 Apr 91	CARRYING A TORCH *Dover ADD 20*	44	4
27 Jun 92 ●	THE COMPLETE TOM JONES *The Hit Label 8442862*	8	6
26 Nov 94	THE LEAD AND HOW TO SWING IT *ZTT 6544924982*	55	1
14 Nov 98	THE ULTIMATE HITS COLLECTION *PolyGram TV 8449012*	26	6
9 Oct 99 ★	RELOAD *Gut GUTCD 009* ■	1	65
16 Nov 02	MR. JONES *V2 VVR 1021072*	36	2
1 Mar 03 ●	GREATEST HITS *Universal TV 8828632*	2	14
9 Oct 04 ●	TOM JONES & JOOLS HOLLAND *Radar 004CD* [1]	5	12+

[1] Art of Noise featuring Tom Jones [2] Tom Jones and The Cardigans [3] Tom Jones and Cerys Matthews [4] Tom Jones and Stereophonics [5] Tom Jones and Mousse T [6] Tom Jones and Heather Small [1] Tom Jones & Jools Holland

'I Who Have Nothing' (08 Mar 2003) is a re-recording The two 'Greatest Hits' albums, and the album entitled 'The Greatest Hits', are all different

Sue JONES-DAVIES See Julie COVINGTON, Rula LENSKA, Charlotte CORNWELL and Sue JONES-DAVIES

JONESTOWN *US, male vocal duo (Singles: 1 Week)*

			pos/wks
13 Jun 98	SWEET THANG *Universal UMD 70376*	49	1

Janis JOPLIN
US, female vocalist, b. 19 Jan 1943, d. 4 Oct 1970 (Albums: 14 Weeks) pos/wks

13 Mar 71	PEARL *CBS 64188* ▲	20	4
22 Jul 72	JANIS JOPLIN IN CONCERT *CBS 67241*	30	6
29 Aug 98	THE ULTIMATE COLLECTION *Columbia SONYTV 52CD*	26	4

Alison JORDAN *UK, female vocalist (Singles: 4 Weeks)*

			pos/wks
9 May 92	BOY FROM NEW YORK CITY *Arista 74431100427*	23	4

Dick JORDAN *UK, male vocalist (Singles: 4 Weeks)*

			pos/wks
17 Mar 60	HALLELUJAH, I LOVE HER SO *Oriole CB 1534*	47	1
9 Jun 60	LITTLE CHRISTINE *Oriole CB 1548*	39	3

Jack JORDAN See Frank CHACKSFIELD and his ORCHESTRA

Montell JORDAN
US, male vocalist (Singles: 21 Weeks, Albums: 3 Weeks) pos/wks

13 May 95	THIS IS HOW WE DO IT *Def Jam DEFCD 07* ▲	11	8
2 Sep 95	SOMETHIN' 4 DA HONEYZ *Def Jam DEFCD 10*	15	4
19 Oct 96	I LIKE *Def Jam DEFCD 19* [1]	24	3
23 May 98	LET'S RIDE *Def Jam 5686912* [2]	25	2
8 Apr 00	GET IT ON TONITE *Def Soul 5627222*	15	4
24 Jun 95	THIS IS HOW WE DO IT *RAL 5271792*	53	1
14 Sep 96	MORE ... *Def Jam 5331912*	66	1

[1] Montell Jordan featuring Slick Rick [2] Montell Jordan featuring Master P and Silkk the Shocker

Ronny JORDAN *UK, male instrumentalist – guitar –*
Ronnie Simpson (Singles: 7 Weeks, Albums: 7 Weeks) pos/wks

1 Feb 92	SO WHAT! *Antilles ANN 14*	32	4
25 Sep 93	UNDER YOUR SPELL *Island CID 565*	72	1
15 Jan 94	TINSEL TOWN *Island CID 566*	64	1
28 May 94	COME WITH ME *Island CID 584*	63	1
7 Mar 92	THE ANTIDOTE *Island CID 9988*	52	4
9 Oct 93	THE QUIET REVOLUTION *Island CID 8009*	49	2
3 Sep 94	BAD BROTHERS *Island IMCD 8024* [1]	58	1

[1] Ronny Jordan meets DJ Krush

JORDANAIRES See Elvis PRESLEY

JORIO *US, male producer – Fred Jorio (Singles: 1 Week)*

			pos/wks
24 Feb 01	REMEMBER ME *Wonderboy WBOYD 021*	54	1

David JOSEPH (see also HI TENSION)
UK, male vocalist (Singles: 21 Weeks) pos/wks

26 Feb 83	YOU CAN'T HIDE (YOUR LOVE FROM ME) *Island IS 101*	13	9
28 May 83	LET'S LIVE IT UP (NITE PEOPLE) *Island IS 116*	26	5
18 Feb 84	JOYS OF LIFE *Island IS 153*	61	2
31 May 86	EXPANSIONS '86 (EXPAND YOUR MIND) *Fourth & Broadway BRW 48* [1]	58	5

[1] Chris Paul featuring David Joseph

Dawn JOSEPH See LOGO featuring Dawn JOSEPH

Mark JOSEPH
UK, male vocalist – Mark Joseph Muzsnyai (Singles: 3 Weeks) pos/wks

1 Mar 03	GET THROUGH *Mark Joseph MJR 003*	38	1
30 Aug 03	FLY *14th Floor MJM 010*	28	1
27 Mar 04	BRINGING BACK THOSE MEMORIES *14th Floor MJM 02CD*	34	1

Martyn JOSEPH *UK, male vocalist (Singles: 10 Weeks)* pos/wks

20 Jun 92	DOLPHINS MAKE ME CRY *Epic 6581347*	34	4
12 Sep 92	WORKING MOTHER *Epic 6582937*	65	1
9 Jan 93	PLEASE SIR *Epic 6588552*	45	3
3 Jun 95	TALK ABOUT IT IN THE MORNING *Epic 6613342*	43	2

JOURNEY (see also Steve PERRY) *US, male vocal /*
instrumental group (Singles: 9 Weeks, Albums: 30 Weeks) pos/wks

27 Feb 82	DON'T STOP BELIEVIN' *CBS A 1728*	62	4
11 Sep 82	WHO'S CRYING NOW *CBS A 2725*	46	5
20 Mar 82	ESCAPE *CBS 85138* ▲	32	16
19 Feb 83 ●	FRONTIERS *CBS 25261*	6	8
6 Aug 83	EVOLUTION *CBS 32342*	100	1
24 May 86	RAISED ON RADIO *CBS 26902*	22	5

Ruth JOY *UK, female vocalist – Ann Saunderson (Singles: 4 Weeks)* pos/wks

26 Aug 89	DON'T PUSH IT *MCA RJOY 1*	66	2
22 Feb 92	FEEL *MCA MCS 1574*	67	1
14 Nov 92	WALKING ON SUNSHINE *Network NWK 55* [1]	71	1

[1] Krush featuring Ruth Joy

JOY DIVISION
(see also NEW ORDER) *UK, male vocal /*
instrumental group (Singles: 24 Weeks, Albums: 33 Weeks) pos/wks

28 Jun 80	LOVE WILL TEAR US APART (re) *Factory FAC 23*	13	16
18 Jun 88	ATMOSPHERE *Factory FAC 2137*	34	5
17 Jun 95	LOVE WILL TEAR US APART (re-mix) *London YOJCD 1*	19	3
26 Jul 80 ●	CLOSER *Factory FACT 25*	6	8
30 Aug 80	UNKNOWN PLEASURES *Factory FACT 10*	71	1
17 Oct 81 ●	STILL *Factory FACT 40*	5	12
23 Jul 88 ●	1977-1980 SUBSTANCE *Factory FAC 250*	7	8
1 Jul 95	PERMANENT – 1995 *London 8286242*	16	3
7 Feb 98	HEART AND SOUL *London 8289682*	70	1

'Love Will Tear Us Apart' re-entered and peaked at No.19 in Oct 1983

The JOY STRINGS *UK, male / female*
vocal / instrumental group (Singles: 11 Weeks) pos/wks

27 Feb 64	IT'S AN OPEN SECRET *Regal-Zonophone RZ 501*	32	7
17 Dec 64	A STARRY NIGHT *Regal-Zonophone RZ 504*	34	4

JOY ZIPPER
US, male / female vocal / instrumental duo (Singles: 1 Week) pos/wks

24 Apr 04	BABY YOU SHOULD KNOW *13 Amp / Vertigo 9866235*	59	1

JOYRIDER
UK, male vocal / instrumental group (Singles: 4 Weeks) pos/wks

27 Jul 96	RUSH HOUR *Paradox PDOXD 012*	22	3
28 Sep 96	ALL GONE AWAY *A&M 5819552*	54	1

JUCXI D See 2PLAY

JUDAS PRIEST *UK, male vocal / instrumental*
group (Singles: 51 Weeks, Albums: 78 Weeks) pos/wks

20 Jan 79	TAKE ON THE WORLD *CBS 6915*	14	10
12 May 79	EVENING STAR *CBS 7312*	53	4
29 Mar 80	LIVING AFTER MIDNIGHT *CBS 8379*	12	7
7 Jun 80	BREAKING THE LAW *CBS 8644*	12	6
23 Aug 80	UNITED *CBS 8897*	26	8
21 Feb 81	DON'T GO *CBS 9520*	51	3
25 Apr 81	HOT ROCKIN' *CBS A 1153*	60	3
21 Aug 82	YOU'VE GOT ANOTHER THING COMIN' *CBS A 2611*	66	2
21 Jan 84	FREEWHEEL BURNIN' *CBS A 4054*	42	3
23 Apr 88	JOHNNY B GOODE *Atlantic A 9114*	64	2
15 Sep 90	PAINKILLER *CBS 656273 7*	74	1
23 Mar 91	A TOUCH OF EVIL *Columbia 6565897*	58	1
24 Apr 93	NIGHT CRAWLER *Columbia 6590972*	63	1

		pos/wks
14 May 77	SIN AFTER SIN *CBS 82008*	23 6
25 Feb 78	STAINED CLASS *CBS 82430*	27 5
11 Nov 78	KILLING MACHINE *CBS 83135*	32 9
6 Oct 79 ●	UNLEASHED IN THE EAST *CBS 83852*	10 8
19 Apr 80 ●	BRITISH STEEL *CBS 84160*	4 17
7 Mar 81	POINT OF ENTRY *CBS 84834*	14 5
17 Jul 82	SCREAMING FOR VENGEANCE *CBS 85941*	11 9
28 Jan 84	DEFENDERS OF THE FAITH *CBS 25713*	19 5
19 Apr 86	TURBO *CBS 26641*	33 4
13 Jun 87	PRIEST LIVE *CBS 4506391*	47 2
28 May 88	RAM IT DOWN *CBS 4611081*	24 5
22 Sep 90	PAINKILLER *CBS 4672901*	26 2
8 May 93	METAL WORKS 73-93 *Columbia 4730502*	37 1

JUDGE DREAD UK, male vocalist – Alex Hughes,
b. 1945, d. 13 Mar 1998 (Singles: 95 Weeks, Albums: 14 Weeks)

		pos/wks
26 Aug 72	BIG SIX *Big Shot BI 608*	11 27
9 Dec 72 ●	BIG SEVEN *Big Shot BI 613*	8 18
21 Apr 73	BIG EIGHT *Big Shot BI 619*	14 10
5 Jul 75 ●	JE T'AIME (MOI NON PLUS) *Cactus CT 65*	9 9
27 Sep 75	BIG TEN *Cactus CT 77*	14 7
6 Dec 75	CHRISTMAS IN DREADLAND / COME OUTSIDE *Cactus CT 80*	14 7
8 May 76	THE WINKLE MAN *Cactus CT 90*	35 4
28 Aug 76	Y VIVA SUSPENDERS *Cactus CT 99*	27 4
2 Apr 77	5TH ANNIVERSARY (EP) *Cactus CT 98*	31 4
14 Jan 78	UP WITH THE COCK / BIG PUNK *Cactus CT 110*	49 1
16 Dec 78	HOKEY COKEY / JINGLE BELLS *EMI 2881*	59 4
6 Dec 75	BEDTIME STORIES *Cactus CTLP 113*	26 12
7 Mar 81	40 BIG ONES *Creole BIG 1*	51 2

Tracks on 5th Anniversary (EP): Jamaica Jerk (Off) / Bring Back the Skins / End of the World / Big Everything. 'Y Viva Suspenders' was listed, additionally, with 'Confessions of a Bouncer' in its second week on the chart

JUICE Denmark, female vocal trio (Singles: 3 Weeks)

		pos/wks
18 Apr 98	BEST DAYS *Chrysalis CDCHS 5081*	28 2
22 Aug 98	I'LL COME RUNNIN' *Chrysalis CDCHS 5090*	48 1

JUICY US, male / female vocal duo (Singles: 5 Weeks)

		pos/wks
22 Feb 86	SUGAR FREE *Epic A 6917*	45 5

JUICY LUCY UK, male vocal / instrumental
group (Singles: 17 Weeks, Albums: 5 Weeks)

		pos/wks
7 Mar 70	WHO DO YOU LOVE *Vertigo V 1*	14 12
10 Oct 70	PRETTY WOMAN (re) *Vertigo 6059 015*	44 5
18 Apr 70	JUICY LUCY *Vertigo VO 2*	41 4
21 Nov 70	LIE BACK AND ENJOY IT *Vertigo 6360 014*	53 1

Gary JULES
US, male producer (Singles: 15 Weeks, Albums: 3 Weeks)

		pos/wks
27 Dec 03 ★	MAD WORLD	
	Adventures in Music / Sanctuary SANXD 250 ■ [1]	1 15
31 Jan 04	TRADING SNAKEOIL FOR WOLFTICKETS	
	Adventure / Sanctuary SANDP 252	12 3

[1] Michael Andrews featuring Gary Jules

Thomas JULES-STOCK UK, male vocalist (Singles: 4 Weeks)

		pos/wks
15 Aug 98	DIDN'T I TELL YOU TRUE *Mercury MERCD 501*	59 1
4 Dec 04	CARELESS WHISPER *Inferno 2PSLCD 06* [1]	29 3

[1] 2Play featuring Thomas Jules & Jucxi D

JULIA and COMPANY US, male / female vocal
group – leader Julia McGirt (Singles: 10 Weeks)

		pos/wks
3 Mar 84	BREAKIN' DOWN (SUGAR SAMBA) *London LON 46*	15 8
23 Feb 85	I'M SO HAPPY *Next Plateau LON 61*	56 2

JULUKA (see also Johnny CLEGG and SAVUKA)
UK / South Africa, male / female vocal / instrumental
group (Singles: 4 Weeks, Albums: 3 Weeks)

		pos/wks
12 Feb 83	SCATTERLINGS OF AFRICA *Safari ZULU 1*	44 4
23 Jul 83	SCATTERLINGS *Safari SHAKA 1*	50 3

JUMP UK, male instrumental group (Singles: 1 Week)

		pos/wks
1 Mar 97	FUNKATARIUM *Heat Recordings HEATCD 005*	56 1

Wally JUMP Jr and the CRIMINAL ELEMENT
(see also Jack E. MAKOSSA) US, male producer /
multi-instrumentalist – Arthur Baker (Singles: 19 Weeks)

		pos/wks
28 Feb 87	TURN ME LOOSE *London LON 126*	60 2
5 Sep 87	PUT THE NEEDLE TO THE RECORD *Cooltempo COOL 150* [1]	63 3
12 Dec 87	TIGHTEN UP / I JUST CAN'T STOP DANCIN'	
	Breakout USA 621	24 7
19 Mar 88	PRIVATE PARTY *Breakout USA 624*	57 3
6 Oct 90	EVERYBODY (RAP) *Deconstruction PB 44701* [2]	30 4

[1] Criminal Element Orchestra [2] Criminal Element Orchestra and Wendell Williams

JUMPING JACKS See Danny PEPPERMINT and The JUMPING JACKS

Rosemary JUNE US, female vocalist (Singles: 9 Weeks)

		pos/wks
23 Jan 59	(I'LL BE WITH YOU) IN APPLE BLOSSOM TIME	
	Pye International 7N 25005	14 9

JUNGLE BOOK US, male / female vocal group (Singles: 8 Weeks)

		pos/wks
8 May 93	THE JUNGLE BOOK GROOVE *Hollywood HWCD 128*	14 8

JUNGLE BOYS UK, male celebrity vocal trio (Singles: 6 Weeks)

		pos/wks
20 Mar 04	JUNGLE ROCK *Bushtucker JUNGLE 001CD*	30 5
31 Jul 04	IN THE SUMMERTIME *MCS JUNGLE 002CD*	72 1

The JUNGLE BROTHERS US, male rap duo – Nathaniel Hall
and Michael Small (Singles: 40 Weeks, Albums: 3 Weeks)

		pos/wks
22 Oct 88	I'LL HOUSE YOU *Gee Street GEE 003* [1]	22 5
18 Mar 89	BLACK IS BLACK / STRAIGHT OUT OF THE JUNGLE	
	Gee Street GEE 15	72 1
31 Mar 90	WHAT 'U' WAITIN' '4' *Eternal W 9865*	35 5
21 Jul 90	DOIN' OUR OWN DANG *Eternal W 9754*	33 6
19 Jul 97	BRAIN *Gee Street GEE 5000388*	52 1
29 Nov 97	JUNGLE BROTHER (re) *Gee Street GEE 5000493*	18 5
11 Jul 98	I'LL HOUSE YOU '98 (re-mix) *Gee Street FCD 338*	26 5
28 Nov 98	BECAUSE I GOT IT LIKE THAT *Gee Street GEE 5003593*	32 2
10 Jul 99	V.I.P. *Gee Street / V2 GEE 5007953*	33 3
6 Nov 99	GET DOWN *Gee Street / V2 GEE 5010153*	52 1
25 Mar 00	FREAKIN' YOU *Gee Street GEE 5008808*	70 1
7 Feb 04	BREATHE, DON'T STOP *Positiva / Incentive CDTIVS 201* [2]	21 5
3 Feb 90	DONE BY THE FORCES OF NATURE *Eternal WX 332*	41 3

[1] Richie Rich meets The Jungle Brothers [2] Mr On vs The Jungle Brothers

'Doin' Our Own Dang' features the uncredited De La Soul and Monie Love. 'Jungle Brother' reached its peak position on re-entering the chart in May 1998

JUNGLE HIGH with BLUE PEARL
UK / Germany, male production / instrumental duo and UK /
US, male / female vocal / instrumental group (Singles: 1 Week)

		pos/wks
27 Nov 93	FIRE OF LOVE *Logic 74321170292*	71 1

JUNIOR UK, male vocalist – Norman
Giscombe (Singles: 57 Weeks, Albums: 14 Weeks)

		pos/wks
24 Apr 82 ●	MAMA USED TO SAY *Mercury MER 98*	7 13
10 Jul 82	TOO LATE *Mercury MER 112*	20 9
25 Sep 82	LET ME KNOW / I CAN'T HELP IT *Mercury MER 116*	53 3
23 Apr 83	COMMUNICATION BREAKDOWN *Mercury MER 134*	57 3
8 Sep 84	SOMEBODY *London LON 50*	64 2
9 Feb 85	DO YOU REALLY (WANT MY LOVE) *London LON 60*	47 4
30 Nov 85	OH LOUISE *London LON 75*	74 3
4 Apr 87 ●	ANOTHER STEP (CLOSER TO YOU) *MCA KIM 5* [1]	6 11
25 Aug 90	STEP OFF *MCA MCA 1432* [2]	63 3
15 Aug 92	THEN CAME YOU *MCA MCS 1676* [2]	32 5
31 Oct 92	ALL OVER THE WORLD *MCA MCS 1691* [2]	74 1
5 Jun 82	JI *Mercury MERS 3*	28 14

[1] Kim Wilde and Junior [2] Junior Giscombe

JUNIOR JACK
Italy, male producer – Vito Lucente (Singles: 20 Weeks)

		pos/wks
16 Dec 00	MY FEELING *Defected DFECT 24CDS*	31 4
2 Mar 02	THRILL ME *VC Recordings VCRD 102*	29 3
27 Sep 03	E SAMBA *Defected DFTDO 76CDS*	34 3
14 Feb 04	DA HYPE *Defected DFTD 083CDS* [1]	25 4
3 Jul 04	STUPIDISCO *Defected DFTD 089CDS*	26 6

[1] Junior Jack featuring Robert Smith

Singles re-entries are listed as (re), (2re), (3re).... which signifies that the hit re-entered the chart once, twice or three times…

JUNIOR M.A.F.I.A.
US, male / female rap ensemble (Singles: 2 Weeks) pos/wks

3 Feb 96	**I NEED YOU TONIGHT** *Big Beat A 8130CD* [1]	**66**	1
19 Oct 96	**GETTIN' MONEY** *Big Beat A 5674CD*	**63**	1

[1] Junior M.A.F.I.A. featuring Aaliyah

JUNIOR SENIOR
Denmark, male vocal / instrumental duo – Jesper Mortensen and Jeppe Laursen (Singles: 20 Weeks, Albums: 3 Weeks) pos/wks

8 Mar 03 ●	**MOVE YOU FEET** *Mercury 0198192*	**3**	17
9 Aug 03	**RHYTHM BANDITS** *Mercury 9810210*	**22**	3
22 Mar 03	**D D DON'T STOP THE BEAT** *Mercury FROG 0262CD*	**29**	3

JUNIORS *See DANNY and the JUNIORS*

JUNKIE XL
Holland, male producer – Tom Holkenborg (Singles: 15 Weeks) pos/wks

22 Jul 00	**ZEROTONINE** *Manifesto FESCD 71*	**63**	1
22 Jun 02 ★	**A LITTLE LESS CONVERSATION** *RCA 74321943572* [1]■	**1**	12
30 Nov 02	**OBSESSION** *Nebula NEBCD 029* [2]	**56**	1
7 Jun 03	**CATCH UP TO MY STEP** *Roadrunner RR 20209* [3]	**63**	1

[1] Elvis vs JXL [2] Tiësto and Junkie XL [3] Junkie XL featuring Solomon Burke

JUNO REACTOR
UK / Germany, male production duo (Singles: 1 Week) pos/wks

8 Feb 97	**JUNGLE HIGH** *Perfecto PERF 133CD*	**45**	1

JURASSIC 5
US, male rap group (Singles: 4 Weeks, Albums: 6 Weeks) pos/wks

25 Jul 98	**JAYOU** *Pan PAN 018CD*	**56**	1
24 Oct 98	**CONCRETE SCHOOLYARD** *Pan PAN 020CD*	**35**	3
13 Jun 98	**JURASSIC 5** *Pan PAN 015CD*	**70**	1
1 Jul 00	**QUALITY CONTROL** *Interscope 4907102*	**23**	3
19 Oct 02	**POWER IN NUMBERS** *Interscope 4934372*	**46**	2

Christopher JUST *Austria, male producer (Singles: 2 Weeks)* pos/wks

13 Dec 97	**I'M A DISCO DANCER** *Slut Trax SLUT 001CD*	**72**	1
6 Feb 99	**I'M A DISCO DANCER (re-mix)** *XL Recordings XLS 105CD*	**69**	1

JUST 4 JOKES featuring MC RB
UK, male production duo and male rapper (Singles: 1 Week) pos/wks

28 Sep 02	**JUMP UP** *Serious SERR 050CD*	**67**	1

JUST LUIS
Spain, male vocalist – Luis Sierra Pizarro (Singles: 3 Weeks) pos/wks

14 Oct 95	**AMERICAN PIE (re)** *Pro-Activ CDPTV 1*	**31**	3

Jimmy JUSTICE
UK, male vocalist – James Little (Singles: 35 Weeks) pos/wks

29 Mar 62 ●	**WHEN MY LITTLE GIRL IS SMILING** *Pye 7N 15421*	**9**	13
14 Jun 62 ●	**AIN'T THAT FUNNY** *Pye 7N 15443*	**8**	11
23 Aug 62	**SPANISH HARLEM** *Pye 7N 15457*	**20**	11

JUSTIFIED ANCIENTS OF MU MU (see also The TIMELORDS;
The KLF; 2K) *UK, male production duo (Singles: 6 Weeks)* pos/wks

9 Nov 91 ●	**IT'S GRIM UP NORTH (re)** *KLF Communications JAMS 028*	**10**	6

JUSTIN *UK, male vocalist – Justin Osuji (Singles: 13 Weeks)* pos/wks

22 Aug 98	**THIS BOY** *Virgin STCDT 1*	**34**	2
16 Jan 99	**OVER YOU** *Virgin STCDT 2*	**11**	4
17 Jul 99	**IT'S ALL ABOUT YOU** *Innocent STCDT 3*	**34**	3
22 Jan 00	**LET IT BE ME** *Innocent STCDTX 4*	**15**	4

Bill JUSTIS *US, male instrumentalist – alto sax,*
b. 14 Oct 1926, d. 15 Jul 1982 (Singles: 8 Weeks) pos/wks

10 Jan 58	**RAUNCHY (re)** *London HLS 8517*	**11**	8

Patrick JUVET *Switzerland, male vocalist (Singles: 19 Weeks)* pos/wks

2 Sep 78	**GOT A FEELING** *Casablanca CAN 127*	**34**	7
4 Nov 78	**I LOVE AMERICA** *Casablanca CAN 132*	**12**	12

JXL *See JUNKIE XL*

Frank K featuring Wiston OFFICE
Italy / US, male vocal / instrumental duo (Singles: 1 Week) pos/wks

26 Jan 91	**EVERYBODY LET'S SOMEBODY LOVE** *Urban URB 66*	**61**	1

Leila K
Sweden, female rapper – Leila El Khalifi (Singles: 22 Weeks) pos/wks

25 Nov 89 ●	**GOT TO GET** *Arista 112696* [1]	**8**	14
17 Mar 90	**ROK THE NATION** *Arista 112971* [1]	**41**	3
23 Jan 93	**OPEN SESAME** *Polydor PQCD 1*	**23**	4
3 Jul 93	**CA PLANE POUR MOI** *Polydor PQCD 3*	**69**	1

[1] Rob 'n' Raz featuring Leila K

KC & THE SUNSHINE BAND
US, male vocal / instrumental group – leader Harry Wayne Casey
(Singles: 104 Weeks, Albums: 17 Weeks) pos/wks

17 Aug 74 ●	**QUEEN OF CLUBS** *Jayboy BOY 88*	**7**	12
23 Nov 74	**SOUND YOUR FUNKY HORN** *Jayboy BOY 83*	**17**	9
29 Mar 75	**GET DOWN TONIGHT** *Jayboy BOY 93* ▲	**21**	9
2 Aug 75 ●	**THAT'S THE WAY (I LIKE IT)** *Jayboy BOY 99* ▲	**4**	10
22 Nov 75	**I'M SO CRAZY ('BOUT YOU)** *Jayboy BOY 101*	**34**	3
17 Jul 76	**(SHAKE, SHAKE, SHAKE) SHAKE YOUR BOOTY** *Jayboy BOY 110* ▲	**22**	8
11 Dec 76	**KEEP IT COMIN' LOVE** *Jayboy BOY 112*	**31**	8
30 Apr 77	**I'M YOUR BOOGIE MAN** *TK XB 2167* ▲	**41**	4
6 May 78	**BOOGIE SHOES** *TK TKR 6025*	**34**	5
22 Jul 78	**IT'S THE SAME OLD SONG** *TK TKR 6037*	**47**	5
8 Dec 79 ●	**PLEASE DON'T GO** *TK TKR 7558* ▲	**3**	12
16 Jul 83 ★	**GIVE IT UP** *Epic EPC A 3017*	**1**	14
24 Sep 83	**(YOU SAID) YOU'D GIMME SOME MORE** *Epic A 2760*	**41**	3
11 May 91	**THAT'S THE WAY I LIKE IT (re-mix)** *Music Factory Dance M7FAC 2*	**59**	2
30 Aug 75	**KC AND THE SUNSHINE BAND** *Jayboy JSL 9*	**26**	7
1 Mar 80 ●	**GREATEST HITS** *TK TKR 83385*	**10**	6
27 Aug 83	**ALL IN A NIGHT'S WORK** *Epic EPC 85847*	**46**	4

K-CI & JOJO
(see also JODECI) US, male vocal duo – Cedric and
Joel Hailey (Singles: 29 Weeks, Albums: 3 Weeks) pos/wks

27 Jul 96	**HOW DO YOU WANT IT** *Death Row DRWCD 4* [1] ▲	**17**	4
23 Aug 97	**YOU BRING ME UP** *MCA MCSTD 48057*	**21**	2
18 Apr 98 ●	**ALL MY LIFE** *MCA MCSTD 48076* ▲	**8**	11
19 Sep 98	**DON'T RUSH (TAKE LOVE SLOWLY)** *MCA MCSTD 48090*	**16**	3
2 Oct 99	**TELL ME IT'S REAL** *MCA MCSTD 40211*	**40**	2
23 Sep 00	**TELL ME IT'S REAL (re-mix)** *AM:PM CDAMPM 135*	**16**	5
12 May 01	**CRAZY** *MCA MCSTD 40253*	**35**	2
28 Jun 97	**LOVE ALWAYS** *MCA MCD 11613*	**51**	2
3 Jul 99	**IT'S REAL** *MCA MCD 11975*	**56**	1

[1] 2Pac featuring K-Ci and JoJo

K CREATIVE
UK, male vocal / instrumental group (Singles: 2 Weeks) pos/wks

7 Mar 92	**THREE TIMES A MAYBE** *Talkin Loud TLK 17*	**58**	2

The listed flipside of 'Three Times a Maybe' was 'Feed the Feeling' by Perception

Ernie K-DOE
US, male vocalist – Ernest Kador,
b. 22 Feb 1936, d. 5 Jul 2001 (Singles: 7 Weeks) pos/wks

11 May 61	MOTHER-IN-LAW *London HLU 9330* ▲	**29**	7

K-GEE
UK, male producer – Karl Gordon (Singles: 3 Weeks) pos/wks

4 Nov 00	I DON'T REALLY CARE *Instant Karma KARMA 3CD*	**22**	3

K.I.D.
Antilles, male / female vocal /
instrumental group (Singles: 4 Weeks) pos/wks

28 Feb 81	DON'T STOP *EMI 5143*	**49**	4

K-KLASS
UK, male / female vocal / instrumental
group (Singles: 31 Weeks, Albums: 1 Week) pos/wks

4 May 91	RHYTHM IS A MYSTERY *Deconstruction CREED 11* [1]	**61**	2
9 Nov 91 ●	RHYTHM IS A MYSTERY (re-issue) *Deconstruction R 6302* [2]	**3**	10
25 Apr 92	SO RIGHT *Deconstruction R 6309*	**20**	5
7 Nov 92	DON'T STOP *Deconstruction R 6325*	**32**	3
27 Nov 93	LET ME SHOW YOU *Deconstruction CDR 6367*	**13**	7
28 May 94	WHAT YOU'RE MISSING *Deconstruction CDRS 6380*	**24**	3
1 Aug 98	BURNIN' *Parlophone CDK 2001*	**45**	1
4 Jun 94	UNIVERSAL *Deconstruction CDPCSDX 149*	**73**	1

[1] K-Klass featuring Bobbie Depasois [2] K-Klass with vocals by Bobbie Depasois

The KLF (see also JUSTIFIED ANCIENTS OF MU MU; The TIMELORDS; 2K)
UK, male vocal / instrumental duo – Bill Drummond and
Jimmy Cauty (Singles: 51 Weeks, Albums: 46 Weeks) pos/wks

11 Aug 90 ●	WHAT TIME IS LOVE? (LIVE AT TRANCENTRAL) *KLF Communications KLF 004* [1]	**5**	12
19 Jan 91 ★	3:A.M. ETERNAL *KLF Communications KLF 005* [1]	**1**	11
4 May 91 ●	LAST TRAIN TO TRANCENTRAL *KLF Communications KLF 008*	**2**	9
7 Dec 91 ●	JUSTIFIED AND ANCIENT *KLF Communications KLF 099* [2]	**2**	12
7 Mar 92 ●	AMERICA: WHAT TIME IS LOVE? (re-mix) *KLF Communications KLFUSA 004*	**4**	7
16 Mar 91 ●	THE WHITE ROOM *KLF Communications JAMSLP 6*	**3**	46

[1] The KLF featuring the Children of the Revolution [2] The KLF – guest vocals: Tammy Wynette

KMC featuring DHANY
Italy, male production duo and female vocalist (Singles: 2 Weeks) pos/wks

25 May 02	I FEEL SO FINE *Incentive CENT 39CDS*	**33**	2

KP & ENVYI
US, female vocal / rap duo –
Kia Philips and Susan Hedgepath (Singles: 4 Weeks) pos/wks

13 Jun 98	SWING MY WAY *East West E 3849CD*	**14**	4

KRS ONE
US, male rapper – Lawrence
Parker (Singles: 8 Weeks, Albums: 1 Week) pos/wks

18 May 96	RAPPAZ R N DAINJA *Jive JIVECD 396*	**47**	1
8 Feb 97	WORD PERFECT *Jive JIVECD 418*	**70**	1
26 Apr 97	STEP INTO A WORLD (RAPTURE'S DELIGHT) *Jive JIVECD 411*	**24**	2
20 Sep 97	HEARTBEAT / A FRIEND *Jive JIVECD 431*	**66**	1
1 Nov 97	DIGITAL *ffrr FCD 316* [1]	**13**	3
31 May 97	I GOT NEXT *Jive CHIP 179*	**58**	1

[1] Goldie featuring KRS One

K7
US, male vocal / rap group (Singles: 22 Weeks, Albums: 3 Weeks) pos/wks

11 Dec 93 ●	COME BABY COME *Big Life BLRD 105*	**3**	16
2 Apr 94	HI DE HO *Big Life BLRD 108* [1]	**17**	5
25 Jun 94	ZUNGA ZENG *Big Life BLRD 111* [1]	**63**	1
5 Feb 94	SWING BATTA SWING *Big Life BLRCD 27*	**27**	3

[1] K7 and The Swing Kids

K3M
Italy, male / female vocal / instrumental duo (Singles: 1 Week) pos/wks

21 Mar 92	LISTEN TO THE RHYTHM *PWL Continental PWL 214*	**71**	1

K2 FAMILY
UK, male production / rap / vocal group (Singles: 3 Weeks) pos/wks

27 Oct 01	BOUNCING FLOW *Relentless RELENT 22CD*	**27**	3

K-WARREN featuring LEE-O
UK, male producer – Kevin Warren
Williams and UK, male vocalist – Leo Ihenacho (Singles: 2 Weeks) pos/wks

5 May 01	COMING HOME *Go Beat GOBCD 41*	**32**	2

KWS
UK, male vocal / instrumental group (Singles: 36 Weeks) pos/wks

25 Apr 92 ★	PLEASE DON'T GO / GAME BOY *Network NWK 46*	**1**	16
22 Aug 92 ●	ROCK YOUR BABY *Network NWK 54*	**8**	7
12 Dec 92	HOLD BACK THE NIGHT *Network NWK 65* [1]	**30**	5
5 Jun 93	CAN'T GET ENOUGH OF YOUR LOVE *Network NWKCD 72*	**71**	1
9 Apr 94	IT SEEMS TO HANG ON *X-clusive XCLU 006CD*	**58**	1
2 Jul 94	AIN'T NOBODY (LOVES ME BETTER) *X-clusive XCLU 010CD* [2]	**21**	4
19 Nov 94	THE MORE I GET THE MORE I WANT *X-clusive XCLU 011CD* [3]	**35**	2

[1] KWS features guest vocal from The Trammps [2] KWS and Gwen Dickey
[3] KWS featuring Teddy Pendergrass

'Game Boy' was listed only from 9 May 1992

KYO *See BEDROCK*

KACI
US, female vocalist – Kaci Battaglia
(Singles: 23 Weeks, Albums: 2 Weeks) pos/wks

10 Mar 01	PARADISE *Curb / London CUBC 61*	**11**	9
28 Jul 01	TU AMOR *Curb / London CUBC 71*	**24**	3
2 Feb 02 ●	I THINK I LOVE YOU *Curb / London CUBC 076*	**10**	10
9 Aug 03	I'M NOT ANYBODY'S GIRL *Curb / London CUBC 091*	**55**	1
16 Feb 02	PARADISE *Curb / London 927402192*	**47**	1

Joshua KADISON
US, male vocalist (Singles: 19 Weeks, Albums: 4 Weeks) pos/wks

26 Feb 94	JESSIE (re) *SBK CDSBK 43*	**48**	5
12 Nov 94	BEAUTIFUL IN MY EYES *SBK CDSBK 50*	**65**	1
29 Apr 95	JESSIE (re-issue) *SBK CDSBK 53*	**15**	10
12 Aug 95	BEAUTIFUL IN MY EYES (re-issue) *SBK CDSBK 55*	**37**	3
27 May 95	PAINTED DESERT SERENADE *SBK SBKCD 22*	**45**	4

KADOC
UK / Spain, male vocal / instrumental group (Singles: 11 Weeks) pos/wks

6 Apr 96	THE NIGHTTRAIN *Positiva CDTIV 26*	**14**	8
17 Aug 96	YOU GOT TO BE THERE *Positiva CDTIV 58*	**45**	1
23 Aug 97	ROCK THE BELLS *Manifesto FESCD 30*	**34**	2

Bert KAEMPFERT and his Orchestra
Germany, orchestra – leader b.
16 Oct 1923, d. 21 Jun 1980 (Singles: 10 Weeks, Albums: 104 Weeks) pos/wks

23 Dec 65	BYE BYE BLUES *Polydor BM 56 504*	**24**	10
5 Mar 66 ●	BYE BYE BLUES *Polydor BM 84086*	**4**	22
16 Apr 66	BEST OF BERT KAEMPFERT *Polydor 84012*	**27**	1
28 May 66	SWINGING SAFARI *Polydor LPHM 46384*	**20**	15
30 Jul 66	STRANGERS IN THE NIGHT *Polydor LPHM 84053*	**13**	26
4 Feb 67	RELAXING SOUND OF BERT KAEMPFERT *Polydor 583501*	**33**	3
18 Feb 67	BERT KAEMPFERT – BEST SELLER *Polydor 583551*	**25**	18
29 Apr 67	HOLD ME *Polydor 184072*	**36**	5
26 Aug 67	KAEMPFERT SPECIAL *Polydor 236207*	**24**	5
19 Jul 71	ORANGE COLOURED SKY *Polydor 2310091*	**49**	1
5 Jul 80	SOUNDS SENSATIONAL *Polydor POLTB 10*	**17**	8

KAISER CHIEFS
UK, male vocal / instrumental group (Singles: 3 Weeks) pos/wks

29 May 04	OH MY GOD *Drowned in Sound DIS 03*	**66**	1
13 Nov 04	I PREDICT A RIOT *B Unique BUN 088CD*	**22**	2

KAJAGOOGOO
UK, male vocal / instrumental group –
lead vocal Limahl (Singles: 50 Weeks, Albums: 23 Weeks) pos/wks

22 Jan 83 ★	TOO SHY *EMI 5359*	**1**	13
2 Apr 83 ●	OOH TO BE AH *EMI 5383*	**7**	8
4 Jun 83	HANG ON NOW *EMI 5394*	**13**	7
17 Sep 83 ●	BIG APPLE *EMI 5423*	**8**	8
3 Mar 84	THE LION'S MOUTH *EMI 5449*	**25**	7
5 May 84	TURN YOUR BACK ON ME *EMI 5646*	**47**	4
21 Sep 85	SHOULDN'T DO THAT *Parlophone R 6106* [1]	**63**	1
30 Apr 83 ●	WHITE FEATHERS *EMI EMC 3433*	**5**	20
26 May 84	ISLANDS *EMI KAJA 1*	**35**	3

[1] Kaja

KALEEF UK, male rap / vocal group (Singles: 12 Weeks) pos/wks

30 Mar 96	WALK LIKE A CHAMPION Payday KACD 5 [1]	23	3
7 Dec 96	GOLDEN BROWN Unity UNITY 010CD	22	4
14 Jun 97	TRIALS OF LIFE Unity UNITY 012CD	75	1
11 Oct 97	I LIKE THE WAY (THE KISSING GAME) Unity UNITY 015CD1	58	1
24 Jan 98	SANDS OF TIME Unity UNITY 016CD	26	3

[1] Kaliphz featuring Prince Naseem

Preeya KALIDAS UK, female vocalist (Singles: 2 Weeks) pos/wks

13 Jul 02	SHAKALAKA BABY Sony Classical 6726322	38	2

The KALIN TWINS US, male vocal duo – Herb and Hal Kalin (Singles: 18 Weeks) pos/wks

18 Jul 58	★ WHEN Brunswick 05751	1	18

KALLAGHAN See N'n'G featuring KALLAGHAN

Kitty KALLEN US, female vocalist (Singles: 23 Weeks) pos/wks

2 Jul 54	★ LITTLE THINGS MEAN A LOT Brunswick 05287 ▲	1	23

Gunter KALLMAN CHOIR Germany, male / female vocal group (Singles: 3 Weeks) pos/wks

24 Dec 64	ELISABETH SERENADE Polydor NH 24678	39	3

KAMASUTRA featuring Jocelyn BROWN Italy, male DJ / production duo and US, female vocalist (Singles: 1 Week) pos/wks

22 Nov 97	HAPPINESS Sony S2 KAMCD 2	45	1

Nick KAMEN UK, male vocalist (Singles: 33 Weeks, Albums: 7 Weeks) pos/wks

8 Nov 86	● EACH TIME YOU BREAK MY HEART WEA YZ 90	5	12
28 Feb 87	LOVING YOU IS SWEETER THAN EVER WEA YZ 106	16	9
16 May 87	NOBODY ELSE WEA YZ 122	47	3
28 May 88	TELL ME WEA YZ 184	40	5
28 Apr 90	I PROMISED MYSELF WEA YZ 454	50	4
18 Apr 87	NICK KAMEN WEA WX 84	34	7

Ini KAMOZE Jamaica, male vocalist (Singles: 15 Weeks) pos/wks

7 Jan 95	● HERE COMES THE HOTSTEPPER Columbia 6610472 ▲	4	15

KANDI US, female vocalist – Kandi Burruss (Singles: 10 Weeks) pos/wks

11 Nov 00	● DON'T THINK I'M NOT Columbia 6705102	9	10

KANDIDATE UK, male vocal / instrumental group (Singles: 28 Weeks) pos/wks

19 Aug 78	DON'T WANNA SAY GOODNIGHT RAK 280	47	6
17 Mar 79	I DON'T WANNA LOSE YOU RAK 289	11	12
4 Aug 79	GIRLS GIRLS GIRLS RAK 295	34	7
22 Mar 80	LET ME ROCK YOU RAK 306	58	3

KANE Holland, male vocal / instrumental group (Singles: 2 Weeks) pos/wks

4 Sep 04	RAIN DOWN ON ME BMG 82876627232	38	2

Big Daddy KANE See BIG DADDY KANE

Eden KANE UK (b. India), male vocalist – Richard Sarstedt (Singles: 73 Weeks) pos/wks

1 Jun 61	★ WELL I ASK YOU Decca F 11353	1	21
14 Sep 61	● GET LOST Decca F 11381	10	11
18 Jan 62	● FORGET ME NOT Decca F 11418	3	14
10 May 62	● I DON'T KNOW WHY Decca F 11460	7	13
30 Jan 64	● BOYS CRY Fontana TF 438	8	14

KANE GANG UK, male vocal / instrumental group (Singles: 37 Weeks, Albums: 12 Weeks) pos/wks

19 May 84	SMALLTOWN CREED Kitchenware SK 11	60	2
7 Jul 84	CLOSEST THING TO HEAVEN Kitchenware SK 15	12	11
10 Nov 84	RESPECT YOURSELF (re) Kitchenware SK 16	21	11
9 Mar 85	GUN LAW Kitchenware SK 20	53	4
27 Jun 87	MOTORTOWN Kitchenware SK 30	45	5

16 Apr 88	DON'T LOOK ANY FURTHER Kitchenware SK 33	52	4
23 Feb 85	THE BAD AND LOWDOWN WORLD OF THE KANE GANG Kitchenware KWLP 2	21	8
8 Aug 87	MIRACLE Kitchenware KWLP 7	41	4

KANSAS US, male vocal / instrumental group (Singles: 7 Weeks) pos/wks

1 Jul 78	CARRY ON WAYWARD SON Kirshner KIR 4932	51	7

Mory KANTE Guinea, male vocalist (Singles: 14 Weeks) pos/wks

23 Jul 88	YEKE YEKE London LON 171	29	9
11 Mar 95	YEKE YEKE (re-issue) Ffrreedom TABCD 226	25	3
30 Nov 96	YEKE YEKE (re-mix) ffrr FCD 288	28	2

Paul KANTNER and JEFFERSON AIRPLANE US, male vocalist / instrumentalist (Albums: 6 Weeks) pos/wks

13 Feb 71	BLOWS AGAINST THE EMPIRE RCA SF 8163	12	6

KAOMA France, male / female vocal / instrumental group (Singles: 20 Weeks) pos/wks

21 Oct 89	● LAMBADA CBS 655011 7	4	18
27 Jan 90	DANCANDO LAMBADA CBS 655235 7	62	2

KAOTIC CHEMISTRY UK, male instrumental / production group (Singles: 1 Week) pos/wks

31 Oct 92	LSD (EP) Moving Shadow SHADOW 20	68	1

Tracks on LSD (EP): Space Cakes / LSD / Illegal Substances / Drumtrip II

KARAJA Germany, female vocalist (Singles: 1 Week) pos/wks

19 Oct 02	SHE MOVES (LA LA LA) Ministry of Sound / Substance SUBS 14CDS	42	1

KARIN See UNIQUE 3

KARIYA US, female vocalist (Singles: 9 Weeks) pos/wks

8 Jul 89	LET ME LOVE YOU FOR TONIGHT (re) Sleeping Bag SBUK 4	44	9

Mick KARN (see also JAPAN) UK, male instrumentalist – bass – Anthony Michaelides (Singles: 6 Weeks, Albums: 4 Weeks) pos/wks

9 Jul 83	AFTER A FASHION Musicfest FEST 1 [1]	39	4
17 Jan 87	BUOY Virgin VS 910 [2]	63	2
20 Nov 82	TITLES Virgin V 2249	74	3
28 Feb 87	DREAMS OF REASON PRODUCE MONSTERS Virgin V 2389	89	1

[1] Midge Ure and Mick Karn [2] Mick Karn featuring David Sylvian

Vybz KARTEL See ZENA

KARTOON KREW US, rap / instrumental group (Singles: 6 Weeks) pos/wks

7 Dec 85	INSPECTOR GADGET Champion CHAMP 6	58	6

KASABIAN UK, male vocal / instrumental group (Singles: 12 Weeks, Albums: 14 Weeks) pos/wks

22 May 04	CLUB FOOT BMG PARADISE 08	19	3
21 Aug 04	● L.S.F. RCA PARADISE 14	10	7
23 Oct 04	PROCESSED BEATS RCA PARADISE 21	17	2
18 Sep 04	● KASABIAN RCA PARADISE 16	4	14+

The KASENETZ-KATZ SINGING ORCHESTRAL CIRCUS US, male vocal / instrumental group (Singles: 15 Weeks) pos/wks

20 Nov 68	QUICK JOEY SMALL (RUN JOEY RUN) Buddah 201 022	19	15

KATCHA UK, male DJ / producer – Jerry Dickens (Singles: 1 Week) pos/wks

21 Aug 99	TOUCHED BY GOD Hooj Choons HOOJ 77CD	57	1

KATOI Thailand, female DJ / producer – Katoi Henderson (Singles: 1 Week) pos/wks

29 Mar 03	TOUCH YOU Arista Dance 743219644	70	1

KATRINA and the WAVES US / UK, female / male
vocal / instrumental group (Singles: 34 Weeks, Albums: 7 Weeks) pos/wks

4 May 85 ●	WALKING ON SUNSHINE Capitol CL 354	8	12
5 Jul 86	SUN STREET Capitol CL 407	22	9
8 Jun 96	WALKING ON SUNSHINE (re-issue) EMI Premier PRESCD 2	53	1
10 May 97 ●	LOVE SHINE A LIGHT Eternal WEA 106CD1	3	12
8 Jun 85	KATRINA AND THE WAVES Capitol KTW 1	28	6
10 May 86	WAVES Capitol EST 2010	70	1

Bubbley KAUR See CORNERSHOP

KAVANA UK, male vocalist – Anthony
Kavanagh (Singles: 26 Weeks, Albums: 2 Weeks) pos/wks

11 May 96	CRAZY CHANCE Nemesis NMSD 1	35	3
24 Aug 96	WHERE ARE YOU Nemesis NMSD 2	26	2
11 Jan 97 ●	I CAN MAKE YOU FEEL GOOD Nemesis NMSDX 3	8	5
19 Apr 97 ●	MFEO Nemesis NMSD 4	8	4
13 Sep 97	CRAZY CHANCE 97 (re-recording) Nemesis NMSD 5	16	4
29 Aug 98	SPECIAL KIND OF SOMETHING Virgin VSCDT 1704	13	4
12 Dec 98	FUNKY LOVE (re) Virgin VSCDT 1711	32	3
20 Mar 99	WILL YOU WAIT FOR ME Virgin VSCDT 1726	29	2
10 May 97	KAVANA Nemesis CDNMS 1	29	2

Niamh KAVANAGH
Ireland, female vocalist (Singles: 5 Weeks) pos/wks

12 Jun 93	IN YOUR EYES Arista 74321154152	24	5

KAWALA
UK, male vocal / instrumental / production group (Singles: 1 Week) pos/wks

26 Feb 00	HUMANISTIC Pepper 9230022	68	1

Janet KAY
UK, female vocalist – Janet Bogle (Singles: 24 Weeks) pos/wks

9 Jun 79 ●	SILLY GAMES Scope SC 2	2	14
11 Aug 90	SILLY GAMES (re-recording) Arista 113452 [1]	22	7
11 Aug 90	SILLY GAMES (re-mix) Music Factory Dance MFD 006	62	3

[1] Lindy Layton featuring Janet Kay

Danny KAYE US, male actor / vocalist – David
Kaminsky, b. 18 Jan 1913, d. 3 Mar 1987 (Singles: 10 Weeks) pos/wks

27 Feb 53 ●	WONDERFUL COPENHAGEN Brunswick 05023	5	10

With Gordon Jenkins and his Orchestra and Chorus

The KAYE SISTERS
UK, female vocal group (Singles: 45 Weeks) pos/wks

25 May 56	IVORY TOWER HMV POP 209 [1]	20	5
1 Nov 57 ●	GOT-TA HAVE SOMETHING IN THE BANK, FRANK Philips PB 751 [2]	8	11
3 Jan 58	SHAKE ME I RATTLE / ALONE Philips PB 752	27	1
1 May 59 ●	COME SOFTLY TO ME Philips PB 913 [2]	9	9
7 Jul 60 ●	PAPER ROSES Philips PB 1024	7	19

[1] The Three Kayes [2] Frankie Vaughan and The Kaye Sisters

KAYESTONE
UK, male DJ / production duo (Singles: 1 Week) pos/wks

29 Jul 00	ATMOSPHERE Distinctive DISNCD 62	55	1

KÉ US, male vocalist – Kevin Griudis (Singles: 1 Week) pos/wks

13 Apr 96	STRANGE WORLD Venture 74321349412	73	1

KEANE UK, male vocal / instrumental
group (Singles: 32 Weeks, Albums: 32 Weeks) pos/wks

28 Feb 04 ●	SOMEWHERE ONLY WE KNOW Island CID 849	3	12
15 May 04 ●	EVERYBODY'S CHANGING (re) Island CID 855	4	9
28 Aug 04 ●	BEDSHAPED Island CID 870	10	7
4 Dec 04	THIS IS THE LAST TIME Island CID 880	18	4+
22 May 04 ★	HOPES AND FEARS Island CID 8145 ■	1	32+

Johnny KEATING UK, orchestra (Singles: 14 Weeks) pos/wks

1 Mar 62 ●	THEME FROM 'Z CARS' (JOHNNY TODD) Piccadilly 7N 35032	8	14

Ronan KEATING (239) *Top 500*
Record-setting Irish vocalist, b. 3 Mar 1977, Dublin, Ireland, who is still adding to his unprecedented chart start of 29 Top 10 singles (27 of them making the Top 5) including those as a member of Boyzone. In addition, seven of his nine albums (including three solo) entered at No.1. He formerly co-managed Westlife. Best-selling single: 'When You Say Nothing At All' 528.600 (Singles: 134 Weeks, Albums: 123 Weeks) pos/wks

7 Aug 99 ★	WHEN YOU SAY NOTHING AT ALL (2re) Polydor 5612902 ■	1	17
22 Jul 00 ★	LIFE IS A ROLLERCOASTER Polydor 5619362 ■	1	14
2 Dec 00 ●	THE WAY YOU MAKE ME FEEL (re) Polydor 5878852	6	12
28 Apr 01 ●	LOVIN' EACH DAY Polydor 5876872	2	14
18 May 02 ★	IF TOMORROW NEVER COMES Polydor 5707182 ■	1	15
21 Sep 02 ●	I LOVE IT WHEN WE DO (2re) Polydor 5709032	5	11
7 Dec 02 ●	WE'VE GOT TONIGHT Polydor 0658612 [1]	4	13
10 May 03 ●	THE LONG GOODBYE Polydor 0657372	3	10
22 Nov 03 ●	LOST FOR WORDS Polydor 9813304	9	4
21 Feb 04 ●	SHE BELIEVES (IN ME) Polydor 9816652	2	7
15 May 04 ●	LAST THING ON MY MIND Polydor / Curb 9866595 [2]	5	9
9 Oct 04 ●	I HOPE YOU DANCE Polydor / Curb 9868261	2	7
25 Dec 04 ●	FATHER AND SON Polydor 9869406 [3]	2	1+
12 Aug 00 ★	RONAN Polydor 5491032 ■	1	56
1 Jun 02 ★	DESTINATION Polydor 5897892 ■	1	40
29 Nov 03	TURN IT ON Polydor 9865882	21	17
23 Oct 04 ★	10 YEARS OF HITS Polydor 9868455 ■	1	10+

[1] Ronan Keating featuring Lulu [2] Ronan Keating & LeAnn Rimes [3] Ronan Keating featuring Yusuf

KEE See BM DUBS present MR RUMBLE featuring BRASSTOOTH and KEE

KEEDIE See Duncan JAMES & KEEDIE

Kevin KEEGAN UK, male footballer / vocalist (Singles: 6 Weeks) pos/wks

9 Jun 79	HEAD OVER HEELS IN LOVE EMI 2965	31	6

KEEL US, male vocal / instrumental group (Albums: 2 Weeks) pos/wks

17 May 86	THE FINAL FRONTIER Vertigo VERH 33	83	2

Howard KEEL
US, male vocalist – Harold Leek (Albums: 36 Weeks) pos/wks

14 Apr 84 ●	AND I LOVE YOU SO Warwick WW 5137	6	19
9 Nov 85	REMINISCING – THE HOWARD KEEL COLLECTION Telstar STAR 2259	20	12
28 Mar 88	JUST FOR YOU Telstar STAR 2318	51	5

Yvonne KEELEY See Scott FITZGERALD

Nelson KEENE
UK, male vocalist – Malcolm Holland (Singles: 5 Weeks) pos/wks

25 Aug 60	IMAGE OF A GIRL (re) HMV POP 771	37	5

KEITH US, male vocalist – James Keefer (Singles: 8 Weeks) pos/wks

26 Jan 67	98.6 Mercury MF 955	24	7
16 Mar 67	TELL ME TO MY FACE Mercury MF 968	50	1

KEITH 'N' SHANE (see also BOYZONE) Ireland, male
vocal duo – Keith Duffy and Shane Lynch (Singles: 3 Weeks) pos/wks

23 Dec 00	GIRL YOU KNOW IT'S TRUE Polydor 5879462	36	3

Lisa KEKAULA See BASEMENT JAXX

KELIS US, female vocalist – Kelis Rogers
(Singles: 85 Weeks, Albums: 49 Weeks) pos/wks

26 Feb 00	CAUGHT OUT THERE (Import) Virgin 8965102CD	52	1
4 Mar 00 ●	CAUGHT OUT THERE (re) Virgin VUSCD 158	4	12
17 Jun 00	GOOD STUFF Virgin VUSCD 164	19	5
8 Jul 00	GOT YOUR MONEY Elektra E 7077CD [1]	11	8
21 Oct 00	GET ALONG WITH YOU Virgin VUSCD 174	51	1
3 Nov 01	YOUNG FRESH N' NEW Virgin VUSCD 212	32	2
5 Oct 02	HELP ME Perfecto PERF 42CDS [2]	65	1
23 Aug 03 ●	FINEST DREAMS Virgin RXCD 2 [3]	8	5
23 Aug 03	LET'S GET ILL Bad Boy / Meanwhile MCSTD 40331 [4]	25	3
17 Jan 04 ●	MILKSHAKE Virgin VSCDX 1863	2	15

Singles re-entries are listed as (re), (2re), (3re).... which signifies that the hit re-entered the chart once, twice or three times...

20 Mar 04	●	NOT IN LOVE *Interscope 9862022* [5]	5 9
5 Jun 04	●	TRICK ME *Virgin VSCDX 1872*	2 14
30 Oct 04	●	MILLIONAIRE *Virgin VSCDX 1885* [6]	3 9+
11 Mar 00		KALEIDOSCOPE *Virgin CDVUS 167*	43 13
17 Jan 04		TASTY *Virgin CDV 2978*	11 36

[1] Ol' Dirty Bastard featuring Kelis [2] Timo Maas featuring Kelis [3] Richard X featuring Kelis [4] P Diddy featuring Kelis [5] Enrique featuring Kelis [6] Kelis featuring André 3000

Jerry KELLER *US, male vocalist (Singles: 14 Weeks)*

		pos/wks
28 Aug 59	★ HERE COMES SUMMER *London HLR 8890*	1 14

Frank KELLY
Ireland, male actor / vocalist – Francis O'Kelly (Singles: 5 Weeks) pos/wks

24 Dec 83	CHRISTMAS COUNTDOWN (re) *Ritz RITZ 062*	26 5

Re-entry peaked at No.54 in Dec 1984

Frankie KELLY
US, male vocalist / instrumentalist (Singles: 2 Weeks) pos/wks

2 Nov 85	AIN'T THAT THE TRUTH *10 TEN 87*	65 2

Grace KELLY *See Bing CROSBY*

Keith KELLY
UK, male vocalist – Michael Pailthorpe (Singles: 5 Weeks) pos/wks

5 May 60	TEASE ME (MUST YOU ALWAYS) (re) *Parlophone R 4640*	27 4
18 Aug 60	LISTEN LITTLE GIRL *Parlophone R 4676*	47 1

R KELLY `127` `Top 500` (see also PUBLIC ANNOUNCEMENT)
Phenomenally successful R&B vocalist, b. Robert Kelly, 8 Jan 1971, Chicago, US, whose writing and production skills are constantly in demand by other top artists. Amazingly, 1998 album 'R' yielded seven Top 20 hits but never reached the Top 20 itself. Best-selling single: 'I Believe I Can Fly' 677,060 (Singles: 236 Weeks, Albums: 147 Weeks) pos/wks

9 May 92		SHE'S GOT THAT VIBE *Jive JIVET 292* [1]	57 2
20 Nov 93		SEX ME *Jive JIVECD 346* [1]	75 1
14 May 94		YOUR BODY'S CALLIN' *Jive JIVECD 353*	19 4
3 Sep 94		SUMMER BUNNIES *Jive JIVECD 358*	23 3
22 Oct 94	●	SHE'S GOT THAT VIBE (re-issue) *Jive JIVECD 364*	3 13
21 Jan 95	●	BUMP 'N' GRIND *Jive JIVECD 368* ▲	8 9
6 May 95		THE 4 PLAY EPS *Jive JIVECD 376*	23 3
11 Nov 95		YOU REMIND ME OF SOMETHING *Jive JIVECD 388*	24 3
2 Mar 96		DOWN LOW (NOBODY HAS TO KNOW) *Jive JIVECD 392* [2]	23 3
22 Jun 96		THANK GOD IT'S FRIDAY *Jive JIVECD 395*	14 4
29 Mar 97	★	I BELIEVE I CAN FLY *Jive JIVECD 415*	1 17
19 Jul 97	●	GOTHAM CITY *Jive JIVECD 428*	9 8
18 Jul 98	●	BE CAREFUL (re) *Jive 0521452* [3]	7 7
26 Sep 98		HALF ON A BABY *Jive 0521802*	16 4
14 Nov 98		HOME ALONE *Jive 0522392* [4]	17 5
28 Nov 98	●	I'M YOUR ANGEL *Epic 6666282* [5] ▲	3 13
31 Jul 99		DID YOU EVER THINK *Jive 0523612*	20 5
16 Oct 99	●	IF I COULD TURN BACK THE HANDS OF TIME (Import) *Jive 0523182*	57 2
30 Oct 99	●	IF I COULD TURN BACK THE HANDS OF TIME *Jive 0523182*	2 19
19 Feb 00		SATISFY YOU (IMPORT) (re) *Bad Boy / Arista 792832* [6]	73 2
11 Mar 00	●	SATISFY YOU *Bad Boy / Arista 74321745592* [6]	8 8
22 Apr 00		ONLY THE LOOT CAN MAKE ME HAPPY / WHEN A WOMAN'S FED UP / I CAN'T SLEEP BABY (IF I) *Jive 9250282*	24 3
21 Oct 00		I WISH *Jive 9251262*	12 6
31 Mar 01		THE STORM IS OVER NOW *Jive 9251782*	18 6
23 Jun 01		FIESTA *Jive 9252142* [7]	23 3
2 Mar 02	●	THE WORLD'S GREATEST *Jive 9253242*	4 12
25 May 02		HONEY *Jive 9253662* [8]	35 2
17 May 03	★	IGNITION *Jive 9254972* ■	1 20
23 Aug 03	●	SNAKE *Jive 82876547232* [9]	10 5
15 Nov 03		STEP IN THE NAME OF LOVE / THOIA THOING *Jive 82876573912*	14 4
20 Mar 04		CLUBBIN' *Elektra E 7544CD* [10]	15 6
29 May 04		HOTEL *Jive 82876618532* [11]	14 8
30 Oct 04	●	HAPPY PEOPLE / U SAVED ME *Jive 82876656182*	6 9+
6 Nov 04	★	WONDERFUL *Def Jam 9864605* [12] ■	1 8+
20 Nov 04		SO SEXY *Atlantic AT 0187CD* [13]	28 3
29 Feb 92		BORN INTO THE 90'S *Jive CHIP 123* [1]	67 1

27 Nov 93		12 PLAY *Jive CHIP 144*	20 44
25 Nov 95		R KELLY *Jive CHIP 166* ▲	18 10
21 Nov 98		R *Jive 517932*	27 26
18 Nov 00		TP-2.COM *Jive 9220262* ▲	21 3
30 Mar 02		THE BEST OF BOTH WORLDS *Jive 9223512* [2]	37 2
1 Mar 03	●	CHOCOLATE FACTORY *Jive 9225082* ▲	10 22
4 Oct 03	●	THE R IN R & B – GREATEST HITS COLLECTION – VOL.1 *Jive 82876561792*	4 30
4 Sep 04		HAPPY PEOPLE / U SAVED ME *BMG 82876615082*	11 8
6 Nov 04		2004 UNFINISHED BUSINESS *Jive 82876658682* ▲ [2]	61 1

[1] R Kelly and Public Announcement [2] R Kelly featuring Ronald Isley [3] Sparkle featuring R Kelly [4] R Kelly featuring Keith Murray [5] Celine Dion and R Kelly [6] Puff Daddy featuring R Kelly [7] R Kelly featuring Jay-Z [8] R Kelly & Jay-Z [9] R Kelly featuring Big Tigger [10] Marques Houston featuring Joe Budden and Pied Piper [11] Cassidy featuring R Kelly [12] Ja Rule featuring R Kelly & Ashanti [13] Twista featuring R Kelly [1] R Kelly and Public Announcement [2] R Kelly and Jay-Z

The 4 Play EP was available on two CDs, each featuring 'Your Body's Callin" and three further tracks. R Kelly appeared on 'Clubbin" under the name Pied Piper

Ramona KELLY *See Cevin FISHER*

Roberta KELLY *US, female vocalist (Singles: 3 Weeks)* pos/wks

21 Jan 78	ZODIACS (re) *Oasis / Hansa 3*	44 3

The KELLY FAMILY *Ireland, male / female vocal / instrumental group (Singles: 1 Week)* pos/wks

21 Oct 95	AN ANGEL *EMI CDEM 390*	69 1

Tricia Lee KELSHALL *See WAY OUT WEST*

Johnny KEMP *Barbados, male vocalist (Singles: 1 Week)* pos/wks

27 Aug 88	JUST GOT PAID *CBS 651470 7*	68 1

Tara KEMP *US, female vocalist (Singles: 2 Weeks)* pos/wks

20 Apr 91	HOLD YOU TIGHT *Giant W 0020*	69 2

Felicity KENDAL
UK, female exercise instructor / actor (Albums: 47 Weeks) pos/wks

19 Jun 82	SHAPE UP AND DANCE (VOLUME 1) *Lifestyle LEG 1*	29 47

Graham KENDRICK *UK, male vocalist (Singles: 4 Weeks)* pos/wks

9 Sep 89	LET THE FLAME BURN BRIGHTER *Power P 30*	55 4

Eddie KENDRICKS (see also The TEMPTATIONS)
US, male vocalist, b. 17 Dec 1939, d. 5 Oct 1992 (Singles: 20 Weeks) pos/wks

3 Nov 73	KEEP ON TRUCKIN' *Tamla Motown TMG 873* ▲	18 14
16 Mar 74	BOOGIE DOWN *Tamla Motown TMG 888*	39 4
21 Sep 85	A NIGHT AT THE APOLLO LIVE! *RCA PB 49935* [1]	58 2

[1] Daryl Hall and John Oates featuring David Ruffin and Eddie Kendrick

A Night at the Apollo Live! is a medley of 'The Way You Do the Things You Do' and 'My Girl'. Kendricks dropped the 's' from his name for last hit

KENICKIE *UK, female / male vocal / instrumental group (Singles: 13 Weeks, Albums: 5 Weeks)* pos/wks

14 Sep 96		PUNKA *Emidisc CDDISC 001*	43 2
16 Nov 96		MILLIONAIRE SWEEPER *Emidisc CDDISC 002*	60 1
11 Jan 97		IN YOUR CAR *Emidisc CDDISC 005*	24 2
3 May 97		NIGHTLIFE *Emidisc CDDISC 006*	27 2
5 Jul 97		PUNKA (re-issue) *Emidisc CDDISC 007*	38 2
6 Jun 98		I WOULD FIX YOU *EMI CDEM 513*	36 2
22 Aug 98		STAY IN THE SUN *EMI CDEMS 520*	43 1
24 May 97	●	AT THE CLUB *Emidisc ADISCCD 002*	9 3
12 Sep 98		GET IN *EMI 4958512*	32 2

Jane KENNAWAY and STRANGE BEHAVIOUR
UK, female vocalist and male instrumental group (Singles: 3 Weeks) pos/wks

24 Jan 81	I.O.U. *Deram DM 436*	65 3

Brian KENNEDY
Ireland, male vocalist (Singles: 8 Weeks, Albums: 4 Weeks) pos/wks

22 Jun 96	A BETTER MAN *RCA 7432138264 2*	28 3
21 Sep 96	LIFE, LOVE AND HAPPINESS *RCA 74321409921*	27 3

		pos/wks
5 Apr 97	PUT THE MESSAGE IN THE BOX RCA 74321462272	37 2
31 Mar 90	THE GREAT WAR OF WORDS RCA PL 74475	64 1
19 Oct 96	A BETTER MAN RCA 74321409132	19 3

Kevin KENNEDY
UK, male actor / vocalist – Kevin Williams (Singles: 1 Week) pos/wks

24 Jun 00	BULLDOG NATION D2m 74321759742	70 1

Nigel KENNEDY
UK, male instrumentalist – violin (Albums: 124 Weeks) pos/wks

1 Mar 86	ELGAR: VIOLIN CONCERTO EMI EMX 4120581 [1]	97 1
7 Oct 89 ●	VIVALDI: THE FOUR SEASONS EMI NIGE 2 [2]	3 81
5 May 90	MENDELSSOHN / BRUCH / SCHUBERT HMV 7496631 [3]	28 15
6 Apr 91	BRAHMS: VIOLIN CONCERTO EMI NIGE 3	16 12
22 Feb 92	JUST LISTEN ... EMI Classics CDNIGE 4	56 1
21 Nov 92	BEETHOVEN: VIOLIN CONCERTO EMI Classics CDC 7545742 [4]	40 6
29 Jun 96	KAFKA EMI CDEMD 1095	67 1
6 Nov 99	CLASSIC KENNEDY EMI Classics CDC 5568902 [2]	51 6
2 Nov 02	NIGEL KENNEDY'S GREATEST HITS EMI Classics 5574112	71 1

[1] Nigel Kennedy with the London Philharmonic Orchestra conducted by Vernon Handley [2] Nigel Kennedy with the English Chamber Orchestra [3] Nigel Kennedy with Jeffrey Tate and the English Chamber Orchestra [4] Nigel Kennedy with Klaus Tennstedt and the North German Radio Symphony Orchestra

KENNY
Ireland, male vocalist – Tony Kenny (Singles: 16 Weeks) pos/wks

3 Mar 73	HEART OF STONE RAK 144	11 13
30 Jun 73	GIVE IT TO ME NOW RAK 153	38 3

KENNY
UK, male vocal / instrumental group (Singles: 39 Weeks, Albums: 1 Week) pos/wks

7 Dec 74 ●	THE BUMP RAK 186	3 15
8 Mar 75 ●	FANCY PANTS RAK 196	4 9
7 Jun 75	BABY I LOVE YOU, OK! RAK 207	12 7
16 Aug 75 ●	JULIE ANNE RAK 214	10 8
17 Jan 76	THE SOUND OF SUPER K RAK SRAK 518	56 1

Although uncredited, all lead and background vocals on 'The Bump' were performed by Barry Palmer

Gerard KENNY
US, male vocalist (Singles: 21 Weeks, Albums: 4 Weeks) pos/wks

9 Dec 78	NEW YORK, NEW YORK RCA PB 5117	43 8
21 Jun 80	FANTASY (re) RCA PB 5256	34 6
18 Feb 84	THE OTHER WOMAN, THE OTHER MAN Impression IMS 3	69 4
4 May 85	NO MAN'S LAND WEA YZ 38	56 4
21 Jul 79	MADE IT THROUGH THE RAIN RCA Victor PL 25218	19 4

Patsy KENSIT See MERRION, McCALL & KENSIT; EIGHTH WONDER

KENT
Sweden, male vocal / instrumental group (Singles: 1 Week) pos/wks

13 Mar 99	747 RCA 74321645912	61 1

Klark KENT (see also The POLICE)
US, male vocalist / multi-instrumentalist – Stewart Copeland (Singles: 4 Weeks) pos/wks

26 Aug 78	DON'T CARE A&M AMS 7376	48 4

Carol KENYON See Paul HARDCASTLE; HEAVEN 17; RAPINATION

KERBDOG
Ireland, male vocal / instrumental group (Singles: 5 Weeks, Albums: 1 Week) pos/wks

12 Mar 94	DRY RISER Vertigo VERCC 83	60 1
6 Aug 94	DUMMY CRUSHER Vertigo VERCD 86	37 2
12 Oct 96	SALLY Fontana KERCD 2	69 1
29 Mar 97	MEXICAN WAVE Fontana KERCD 3	49 1
12 Apr 97	ON THE TURN Fontana 5329992	64 1

Dick KERR See Slim DUSTY

Anita KERR SINGERS See Bobby HELMS

KERRI and MICK
Australia, female / male vocal duo (Singles: 3 Weeks) pos/wks

28 Apr 84	'SONS AND DAUGHTERS' THEME A1 A1 286	68 3

KERRI-ANN
Ireland, female vocalist (Singles: 1 Week) pos/wks

8 Aug 98	DO YOU LOVE ME BOY? Raglan Road 5671012	58 1

Liz KERSHAW and Bruno BROOKES
UK, male / female DJ / vocal duo (Singles: 3 Weeks) pos/wks

2 Dec 89	IT TAKES TWO BABY Spartan CIN 101 [1]	53 2
1 Dec 90	LET'S DANCE Jive BRUNO 1 [2]	54 1

[1] Liz Kershaw, Bruno Brookes, Jive Bunny and Londonbeat [2] Bruno and Liz and the Radio 1 DJ Posse

Nik KERSHAW (357) Top 500
One time jazz-funk guitarist whose melodic pop repertoire made him a mid-1980s teen idol, b. 1 Mar 1958, Bristol, UK. His 50 weeks on the singles chart in 1984 beat all other soloists. He appeared at Live Aid, and penned hits for Let Loose, The Hollies and a No.1 for Chesney Hawkes (Singles: 89 Weeks, Albums: 100 Weeks) pos/wks

19 Nov 83	I WON'T LET THE SUN GO DOWN ON ME MCA MCA 816	47 5
28 Jan 84 ●	WOULDN'T IT BE GOOD MCA NIK 2	4 14
14 Apr 84	DANCING GIRLS MCA NIK 3	13 9
16 Jun 84 ●	I WON'T LET THE SUN GO DOWN ON ME (re-issue) MCA NIK 4	2 13
15 Sep 84	HUMAN RACING MCA NIK 5	19 7
17 Nov 84 ●	THE RIDDLE MCA NIK 6	3 11
16 Mar 85 ●	WIDE BOY MCA NIK 7	9 8
3 Aug 85 ●	DON QUIXOTE MCA NIK 8	10 7
30 Nov 85	WHEN A HEART BEATS MCA NIK 9	27 7
11 Oct 86	NOBODY KNOWS MCA NIK 10	44 3
13 Dec 86	RADIO MUSICOLA MCA NIK 11	43 2
4 Feb 89	ONE STEP AHEAD MCA NIK 12	55 1
27 Feb 99	SOMEBODY LOVES YOU Eagle EAGXA 023	70 1
7 Aug 99	SOMETIMES Wall of Sound WALLD 054 [1]	56 1
10 Mar 84 ●	HUMAN RACING MCA MCF 3197	5 61
1 Dec 84 ●	THE RIDDLE MCA MCF 3245	8 36
8 Nov 86	RADIO MUSICOLA MCA MCG 6016	47 3

[1] Les Rythmes Digitales featuring Nik Kershaw

KEVIN and PERRY See PRECOCIOUS BRATS featuring KEVIN and PERRY

KEVIN THE GERBIL
UK, male gerbil vocalist (Singles: 6 Weeks) pos/wks

4 Aug 84	SUMMER HOLIDAY Magnet RAT 3	50 6

KEY SESSIONS QUARTET
UK, male instrumental group (Albums: 2 Weeks) pos/wks

20 Mar 04	THE PIANO SESSIONS T2 / Telstar TCD 3387	54 2

KEY WEST featuring ERIK (see also The RAH BAND)
UK, female vocalist (Singles: 2 Weeks) pos/wks

10 Apr 03	LOOKS LIKE I'M IN LOVE AGAIN PWL Sanctuary PWCD 252	46 2

KEYNOTES See Dave KING

Alicia KEYS (400) Top 500
Multi-award-winning R&B singer / songwriter and pianist, b. Alicia Cook, 25 Jan 1981, New York, US. Both her albums entered at No.1 in the US and the first sold over 10 million copies worldwide. She picked up a record-equalling five Grammy awards in 2002 (Singles: 57 Weeks, Albums: 115 Weeks) pos/wks

10 Nov 01 ●	FALLIN' J 74321903692 ▲	3 10
9 Mar 02	BROTHA PART II J 74321922142 [1]	37 2
30 Mar 02	A WOMAN'S WORTH J 74321928692	18 5
20 Jul 02	HOW COME YOU DON'T CALL ME J 74321943122	26 3
5 Oct 02 ●	GANGSTA LOVIN' Ruff Ryders / Interscope 4978042 [2]	6 8
7 Dec 02	GIRLFRIEND J 74321974972	24 5
20 Dec 03	YOU DON'T KNOW MY NAME J 82876581612	19 5
10 Apr 04	IF I AIN'T GOT YOU J 82876608172	18 5
13 Nov 04 ●	MY BOO LaFace / Arista 82876655292 [3] ▲	5 7+
22 Sep 01 ●	SONGS IN A MINOR J 80813200022 ▲	6 79
13 Dec 03	THE DIARY OF ALICIA KEYS J 82876586202 ▲	13 36

[1] Angie Stone featuring Alicia Keys and Eve [2] Eve featuring Alicia Keys
[3] Usher featuring Alicia Keys

Chaka KHAN (see also RUFUS)
US, female vocalist – Yvette Stevens (Singles: 97 Weeks, Albums: 45 Weeks) pos/wks

2 Dec 78	I'M EVERY WOMAN Warner Bros. K 17269	11 13
31 Mar 84 ●	AIN'T NOBODY Warner Bros. RCK 1 [1]	8 12

			pos/wks
20 Oct 84 ★	I FEEL FOR YOU *Warner Bros. W 9209*	1	16
19 Jan 85	THIS IS MY NIGHT *Warner Bros. W 9097*	14	6
20 Apr 85	EYE TO EYE *Warner Bros. W 9009*	16	7
12 Jul 86	LOVE OF A LIFETIME *Warner Bros. W 8671*	52	4
21 Jan 89	IT'S MY PARTY *Warner Bros. W 7678*	71	2
6 May 89 ●	I'M EVERY WOMAN (re-mix) *Warner Bros. W 2963*	8	8
8 Jul 89 ●	AIN'T NOBODY (re-mix) *Warner Bros. W 2880* [1]	6	9
7 Oct 89	I FEEL FOR YOU (re-mix) *Warner Bros. W 2764*	45	5
13 Jan 90	I'LL BE GOOD TO YOU *Qwest W 2697* [2]	21	7
28 Mar 92	LOVE YOU ALL MY LIFETIME *Warner Bros. W 0087*	49	3
17 Jul 93	DON'T LOOK AT ME THAT WAY *Warner Bros. W 0192CD*	73	1
19 Aug 95	WATCH WHAT YOU SAY *Cooltempo CDCOOL 308* [3]	28	3
1 Mar 97	NEVER MISS THE WATER *Reprise W 1393CD* [4]	59	1
11 Nov 00	ALL GOOD *Tommy Boy TBCD 2154B* [5]	33	3
21 Apr 84	STOMPIN' AT THE SAVOY *Warner Bros. 923679* [1]	64	5
20 Oct 84	I FEEL FOR YOU *Warner Bros. 925 162*	15	22
9 Aug 86	DESTINY *Warner Bros. WX 45*	77	2
3 Jun 89	LIFE IS A DANCE – THE REMIX PROJECT *Warner Bros. WX 268*	14	15
4 Sep 99	BEST OF CHAKA KHAN – I'M EVERY WOMAN *Warner.esp 9362475072*	62	1

[1] Rufus and Chaka Khan [2] Quincy Jones featuring Ray Charles and Chaka Khan [3] Guru featuring Chaka Khan [4] Chaka Khan featuring Me'Shell Ndegeocello [5] De La Soul featuring Chaka Khan [1] Rufus and Chaka Khan

Nusrat Fateh Ali KHAN / Michael BROOK *Pakistan, male*
vocalist and Canada, male instrumentalist – guitar (Albums: 1 Week) pos/wks

6 Apr 96	NIGHT SONG *Realworld CDRW 50*	65	1

Praga KHAN
Belgium, male producer – Maurice Engelen (Singles: 9 Weeks) pos/wks

4 Apr 92	FREE YOUR BODY / INJECTED WITH A POISON *Profile PROFT 347* [1]	16	6
11 Jul 92	RAVE ALERT *Profile PROF 369*	39	2
24 Nov 01	INJECTED WITH A POISON (re-mix) *Nukleuz NUKC 0238*	52	1

[1] Praga Khan featuring Jade 4 U

Aram KHATCHATURIAN / VIENNA PHILHARMONIC ORCHESTRA
Russia, male conductor and Austria, orchestra (Albums: 15 Weeks) pos/wks

22 Jan 72	SPARTACUS *Decca SXL 6000*	16	15

KHIA *US, female vocalist – Khia Finch (Singles: 11 Weeks)* pos/wks

16 Oct 04 ●	MY NECK, MY BACK (LICK IT) *Direction 6753802*	4	11+

Mary KIANI *UK, female vocalist (Singles: 15 Weeks)* pos/wks

12 Aug 95	WHEN I CALL YOUR NAME *Mercury MERCD 440*	18	4
23 Dec 95	I GIVE IT ALL TO YOU / I IMAGINE *Mercury MERCD 449*	35	4
27 Apr 96	LET THE MUSIC PLAY *Mercury MERCD 456*	19	3
18 Jan 97	100% *Mercury MERCD 469*	23	3
21 Jun 97	WITH OR WITHOUT YOU *Mercury MERCD 487*	46	1

KICK HORNS *See DODGY*

KICK SQUAD
UK / Germany, male vocal / instrumental group (Singles: 2 Weeks) pos/wks

10 Nov 90	SOUND CLASH (CHAMPION SOUND) *Kickin KICK 2*	59	2

KICKING BACK with TAXMAN *UK, male / female*
vocal / instrumental duo and male rapper (Singles: 8 Weeks) pos/wks

17 Mar 90	DEVOTION *10 TEN 297*	47	4
7 Jul 90	EVERYTHING *10 TEN 307*	54	4

KICKS LIKE A MULE *UK, male instrumental / production*
duo – Nick Halkes and Richard Russell (Singles: 6 Weeks) pos/wks

1 Feb 92 ●	THE BOUNCER *Tribal Bass TRIBE 3S*	7	6

KID CREME
Belgium, male producer – Nicolas Skaravilli (Singles: 3 Weeks) pos/wks

22 Mar 03	DOWN AND UNDER (TOGETHER) *Ink NIBNE 13CD* [1]	55	1
10 May 03	HYPNOTISING *Positiva CDTIV 189* [2]	31	2

[1] Kid Creme featuring Shurakano [2] Kid Creme featuring Charlise

KID 'N' PLAY *US, male rap duo (Singles: 7 Weeks)* pos/wks

18 Jul 87	LAST NIGHT *Cooltempo COOL 148*	71	1
26 Mar 88	DO THIS MY WAY *Cooltempo COOL 164*	48	3
17 Sep 88	GITTIN' FUNKY *Cooltempo COOL 168*	55	3

KID ROCK *US, male vocalist / rapper –*
Robert Ritchie (Singles: 8 Weeks, Albums: 1 Week) pos/wks

23 Oct 99	COWBOY *Atlantic AT 0076CD*	36	2
9 Sep 00	AMERICAN BAD ASS *Atlantic AT 0085CD*	25	4
12 May 01	BAWITDABA *Atlantic AT 0098CD*	41	2
10 Jun 00	THE HISTORY OF ROCK *Atlantic 7567833142*	73	1

KID UNKNOWN
UK, male producer – Paul Fitzpatrick (Singles: 1 Week) pos/wks

2 May 92	NIGHTMARE *Warp WAP 20CD*	64	1

Carol KIDD featuring Terry WAITE
UK, female / male vocal duo (Singles: 3 Weeks) pos/wks

17 Oct 92	WHEN I DREAM *The Hit Label HLS 1*	58	3

Johnny KIDD and the PIRATES
UK, male vocal / instrumental group – leader b. Frederick
Heath, 23 Dec 1939, d. 7 Oct 1966 (Singles: 62 Weeks) pos/wks

12 Jun 59	PLEASE DON'T TOUCH (re) *HMV POP 615*	25	5
12 Feb 60	YOU GOT WHAT IT TAKES *HMV POP 698*	25	3
16 Jun 60 ★	SHAKIN' ALL OVER *HMV POP 753*	1	19
6 Oct 60	RESTLESS *HMV POP 790*	22	7
13 Apr 61	LINDA LU *HMV POP 853*	47	1
10 Jan 63	A SHOT OF RHYTHM AND BLUES *HMV POP 1088*	48	1
25 Jul 63 ●	I'LL NEVER GET OVER YOU *HMV POP 1173*	4	15
28 Nov 63	HUNGRY FOR LOVE *HMV POP 1228*	20	10
30 Apr 64	ALWAYS AND EVER *HMV POP 1269*	46	1

Nicole KIDMAN
Australia, female actor / vocalist (Singles: 17 Weeks) pos/wks

6 Oct 01	COME WHAT MAY *Interscope / Polydor 4976302* [1]	27	5
22 Dec 01 ★	SOMETHIN' STUPID *Chrysalis CDCHS 5132* [2] ■	1	12

[1] Nicole Kidman and Ewan McGregor [2] Robbie Williams and Nicole Kidman

The KIDS FROM 'FAME' 472 Top 500
TV's original 'Fame' academy students along with singing dance teacher
Debbie Allen. These US actor / singers (backed by session musicians), who
spent 12 weeks at No.1 with their debut album, oddly failed to crack the Top
40 in their homeland (Singles: 36 Weeks, Albums: 117 Weeks) pos/wks

14 Aug 82 ●	HI-FIDELITY *RCA 254* [1]	5	10
2 Oct 82 ●	STARMAKER *RCA 280*	3	10
11 Dec 82	MANNEQUIN *RCA 299* [2]	50	6
9 Apr 83	FRIDAY NIGHT (LIVE VERSION) *RCA 320*	13	10
24 Jul 82 ★	THE KIDS FROM 'FAME' *BBC REP 447*	1	45
16 Oct 82 ●	THE KIDS FROM 'FAME' AGAIN *RCA RCALP 6057*	2	21
26 Feb 83 ●	THE KIDS FROM 'FAME' LIVE *BBC KIDLP 003*	8	28
14 May 83	THE KIDS FROM 'FAME' SONGS *BBC KIDLP 004*	14	16
20 Aug 83	THE KIDS FROM 'FAME' SING FOR YOU *BBC KIDLP 005*	28	7

[1] The Kids from 'Fame' featuring Valerie Landsberg [2] The Kids from 'Fame' featuring Gene Anthony Ray

Greg KIHN BAND
US, male vocal / instrumental group (Singles: 2 Weeks) pos/wks

23 Apr 83	JEOPARDY *Beserkley E 9847*	63	2

KILL CITY
UK, female / male vocal / instrumental group (Singles: 1 Week) pos/wks

14 Aug 04	JUST LIKE BRUCE LEE *Poptones MC 5091SCD*	63	1

KILLAH PRIEST *US, male rapper – Walter Reed (Singles: 1 Week)* pos/wks

7 Feb 98	ONE STEP *Geffen GFSTD 22318*	45	1

KILLER MIKE (see also OUTKAST)
US, male rapper – Michael Render (Singles: 3 Weeks) pos/wks

10 May 03	A.D.I.D.A.S. *Columbia 6738652*	22	3

The KILLERS
US, male vocal / instrumental group (Singles: 10 Weeks, Albums: 28 Weeks) pos/wks

27 Mar 04	SOMEBODY TOLD ME *Lizard King LIZARD 009*	28	2
5 Jun 04 ●	MR BRIGHTSIDE *Lizard King LIZARD 010CD2*	10	4
11 Sep 04	ALL THESE THINGS THAT I'VE DONE *Lizard King LIZARD 012*	18	4
19 Jun 04 ●	HOT FUSS *Lizard King LIZARD 011*	6	28+

KILLING JOKE
UK, male vocal / instrumental group (Singles: 50 Weeks, Albums: 35 Weeks) pos/wks

23 May 81	FOLLOW THE LEADERS *Malicious Damage EGMDS 101*	55	5
20 Mar 82	EMPIRE SONG *Malicious Damage EGO 4*	43	4
30 Oct 82	BIRDS OF A FEATHER *EG EGO 10*	64	2
25 Jun 83	LET'S ALL (GO TO THE FIRE DANCES) *EG EGO 11*	51	3
15 Oct 83	ME OR YOU? *EG EGO 14*	57	1
7 Apr 84	EIGHTIES *EG EGO 16*	60	5
21 Jul 84	A NEW DAY *EG EGO 17*	56	2
2 Feb 85	LOVE LIKE BLOOD *EG EGO 20*	16	9
30 Mar 85	KINGS AND QUEENS *EG EGO 21*	58	3
16 Aug 86	ADORATIONS *EG EGO 27*	42	6
18 Oct 86	SANITY *EG EGO 30*	70	1
7 May 94	MILLENNIUM *Butterfly BFLD 12*	34	2
16 Jul 94	THE PANDEMONIUM SINGLE *Butterfly BFLD 17*	28	3
4 Feb 95	JANA *Butterfly BFLDA 21*	54	1
23 Mar 96	DEMOCRACY *Butterfly BFLDA 33*	39	1
26 Jul 03	KILLING JOKE *Zuma ZUMAD 004*	25	2
25 Oct 80	KILLING JOKE *Polydor EGMD 545*	39	4
20 Jun 81	WHAT'S THIS FOR *Malicious Damage EGMD 550*	42	4
8 May 82	REVELATIONS *Malicious Damage EGMD 3*	12	6
27 Nov 82	'HA' – KILLING JOKE LIVE *EG EGMD1 4*	66	2
23 Jul 83	FIRE DANCES *EG EGMD 5*	29	1
9 Mar 85	NIGHT TIME *EG EGLP 61*	11	9
22 Nov 86	BRIGHTER THAN A THOUSAND SUNS *EG EGLP 66*	54	1
9 Jul 88	OUTSIDE THE GATE *EG EGLP 73*	92	1
6 Aug 94	PANDEMONIUM *Butterfly BFLCD 9*	16	3
13 Apr 96	DEMOCRACY *Butterfly BFLCD 17*	71	1
9 Aug 03	KILLING JOKE *Zuma ZUMACD 002*	43	1

The KILLS
UK, male / female vocal / instrumental group (Singles: 1 Week, Albums: 1 Week) pos/wks

26 Apr 03	FRIED MY LITTLE BRAINS *Domino RUG 154CD*	55	1
22 Mar 03	KEEP ON YOUR MEAN SIDE *Domino WIGCD 124*	47	1

KILLSWITCH ENGAGE
US, male vocal / instrumental group (Albums: 1 Week) pos/wks

22 May 04	THE END OF HEARTACHE *Roadrunner RR 83732*	40	1

Andy KIM
Canada, male vocalist – Andrew Joachim (Singles: 12 Weeks) pos/wks

24 Aug 74 ●	ROCK ME GENTLY *Capitol CL 15787* ▲	2	12

KIMERA with the LONDON SYMPHONY ORCHESTRA
Korea, female vocalist and UK, orchestra (Albums: 4 Weeks) pos/wks

26 Oct 85	HITS ON OPERA *Stylus SMR 8505*	38	4

KINANE
Ireland, female vocalist – Bianca Kinane (Singles: 4 Weeks) pos/wks

18 May 96	ALL THE LOVER I NEED *Coliseum TOGA 003CD* [1]	59	1
21 Sep 96	THE WOMAN IN ME *Coliseum TOGA 007CD* [1]	73	1
16 May 98	HEAVEN *Coalition COLA 047CD*	49	1
22 Aug 98	SO FINE *Coalition COLA 055CD1*	63	1

[1] Bianca Kinane

KINESIS
UK, male vocal / instrumental group (Singles: 3 Weeks) pos/wks

22 Mar 03	... AND THEY OBEY *Independiente ISOM 68MS*	63	1
28 Jun 03	FOREVER REELING *Independiente ISOM 74MS*	65	1
27 Sep 03	ONE WAY MIRROR *Independiente ISOM 77MS*	71	1

KING
UK / Ireland, male vocal / instrumental group – leader Paul King (Singles: 44 Weeks, Albums: 32 Weeks) pos/wks

12 Jan 85 ●	LOVE AND PRIDE *CBS A 4988*	2	14
23 Mar 85	WON'T YOU HOLD MY HAND NOW *CBS A 6094*	24	8
17 Aug 85 ●	ALONE WITHOUT YOU *CBS A 6308*	8	9

19 Oct 85	THE TASTE OF YOUR TEARS *CBS A 6618*	11	9
11 Jan 86	TORTURE *CBS A 6761*	23	4
9 Feb 85 ●	STEPS IN TIME *CBS 26095*	6	21
23 Nov 85	BITTER SWEET *CBS 86320*	16	11

Albert KING See Gary MOORE

B.B. KING
US, male vocalist / instrumentalist – guitar – Riley King (Singles: 10 Weeks, Albums: 24 Weeks) pos/wks

15 Apr 89 ●	WHEN LOVE COMES TO TOWN *Island IS 411* [1]	6	7
18 Jul 92	SINCE I MET YOU BABY *Virgin VS 1423* [2]	59	3
25 Aug 79	TAKE IT HOME *MCA MCF 3010*	60	5
1 May 99	HIS DEFINITIVE GREATEST HITS *Universal Music TV 5473402*	24	4
24 Jun 00	RIDING WITH THE KING *Reprise 9362476122* [1]	15	15

[1] U2 with B.B. King [2] Gary Moore and B.B. King [1] B.B. King and Eric Clapton

Ben E KING
(see also The DRIFTERS) US, male vocalist – Benjamin Nelson (Singles: 35 Weeks, Albums: 30 Weeks) pos/wks

2 Feb 61	FIRST TASTE OF LOVE *London HLK 9258*	27	11
22 Jun 61	STAND BY ME (re) *London HLK 9358*	27	7
5 Oct 61	AMOR, AMOR *London HLK 9416*	38	4
14 Feb 87 ★	STAND BY ME (re-issue) *Atlantic A 9361*	1	11
4 Jul 87	SAVE THE LAST DANCE FOR ME *Manhattan MT 25*	69	2
1 Jul 67	SPANISH HARLEM *Atlantic 590001*	30	3
14 Mar 87	STAND BY ME (THE ULTIMATE COLLECTION) *Atlantic WX 90* [1]	14	8
20 Oct 90	THE VERY BEST OF BEN E. KING & THE DRIFTERS *Telstar STAR 2373* [1]	15	16
7 Nov 98	THE VERY BEST OF BEN E. KING & THE DRIFTERS *Warner.esp / Global TV RADCD 108* [1]	41	3

[1] Ben E. King & The Drifters

Carole KING
US, female vocalist / instrumentalist – piano – Carole Klein (Singles: 29 Weeks, Albums: 108 Weeks) pos/wks

20 Sep 62 ●	IT MIGHT AS WELL RAIN UNTIL SEPTEMBER *London HLU 9591*	3	13
7 Aug 71 ●	IT'S TOO LATE *A&M AMS 849* ▲	6	12
28 Oct 72	IT MIGHT AS WELL RAIN UNTIL SEPTEMBER (re-issue) *London HL 10391*	43	4
24 Jul 71 ●	TAPESTRY *A&M AMLS 2025* ▲	4	90
15 Jan 72	MUSIC *A&M AMLH 67013* ▲	18	10
2 Dec 72	RHYMES AND REASONS *Ode 77016*	40	2
7 Feb 98	TAPESTRY (re-issue) *Epic CD 32110*	24	3
30 Sep 00	NATURAL WOMAN – THE VERY BEST OF CAROLE KING *Columbia SONYTV 93CD*	31	3

Dave KING
UK, male vocalist, b. 23 Jun 1929, d. 17 Apr 2002 (Singles: 29 Weeks) pos/wks

17 Feb 56 ●	MEMORIES ARE MADE OF THIS *Decca F 10684* [1]	5	15
13 Apr 56	YOU CAN'T BE TRUE TO TWO *Decca F 10720* [1]	11	9
21 Dec 56	CHRISTMAS AND YOU *Decca F 10791*	23	2
24 Jan 58	THE STORY OF MY LIFE *Decca F 10973*	20	3

[1] Dave King featuring The Keynotes

Denis KING See KING BROTHERS; STUTZ BEARCATS and The Denis KING ORCHESTRA

Diana KING
Jamaica, female vocalist (Singles: 22 Weeks, Albums: 2 Weeks) pos/wks

8 Jul 95 ●	SHY GUY *Columbia 6621682*	2	13
28 Oct 95	AIN'T NOBODY *Columbia 6625495*	13	5
1 Nov 97	I SAY A LITTLE PRAYER *Columbia 6651472*	17	4
12 Aug 95	TOUGHER THAN LOVE *Columbia 4777562*	50	2

Evelyn 'Champagne' KING
US, female vocalist (Singles: 76 Weeks, Albums: 9 Weeks) pos/wks

13 May 78	SHAME *RCA PC 1122*	39	23
3 Feb 79	I DON'T KNOW IF IT'S RIGHT *RCA PB 1386*	67	2
27 Jun 81	I'M IN LOVE *RCA 95* [1]	27	11
26 Sep 81	IF YOU WANT MY LOVIN' *RCA 131* [1]	43	6
28 Aug 82 ●	LOVE COME DOWN *RCA 249* [1]	7	13
20 Nov 82	BACK TO LOVE *RCA 287* [1]	40	4
19 Feb 83	GET LOOSE *RCA 315* [1]	45	5

Singles re-entries are listed as (re), (2re), (3re)…. which signifies that the hit re-entered the chart once, twice or three times…

		pos	wks
9 Nov 85	YOUR PERSONAL TOUCH *RCA PB 49915*	37	5
29 Mar 86	HIGH HORSE *RCA PB 49891*	55	3
23 Jul 88	HOLD ON TO WHAT YOU'VE GOT *Manhattan MT 49*	47	3
10 Oct 92	SHAME (re-mix) *Network NWKTEN 56* [2]	74	1
11 Sep 82	GET LOOSE *RCA RCALP 3093*	35	9

[1] Evelyn King [2] Altern 8 vs Evelyn King

Jonathan KING
UK, male producer / vocalist – Kenneth King (Singles: 128 Weeks) pos/wks

		pos	wks
29 Jul 65 ●	EVERYONE'S GONE TO THE MOON *Decca F 12187*	4	11
10 Jan 70	LET IT ALL HANG OUT *Decca F 12988*	26	7
16 Jan 71	IT'S THE SAME OLD SONG *B&C CB 139* [1]	19	9
3 Apr 71	SUGAR SUGAR *RCA 2064* [2]	12	14
29 May 71	LAZY BONES *Decca F 13177*	23	8
20 Nov 71	HOOKED ON A FEELING *Decca F 13241*	23	10
5 Feb 72	FLIRT! *Decca F 13276*	22	9
14 Oct 72 ●	LOOP DI LOVE *UK 7* [3]	4	13
26 Jan 74	(I CAN'T GET NO) SATISFACTION *UK 53* [4]	29	5
6 Sep 75	UNA PALOMA BLANCA (WHITE DOVE) *UK 105*	5	11
20 Sep 75	CHICK-A-BOOM (DON'T YA JES LOVE IT) *UK 2012 002* [5]	36	4
7 Feb 76	IN THE MOOD *UK 121* [6]	46	3
26 Jun 76 ●	IT ONLY TAKES A MINUTE *UK 135* [7]	9	9
7 Oct 78	ONE FOR YOU, ONE FOR ME *GTO GT 237*	29	6
16 Dec 78	LICK A SMURP FOR CHRISTMAS (ALL FALL DOWN) *Petrol GAS 1 / Magnet MAG 139* [8]	58	4
16 Jun 79	YOU'RE THE GREATEST LOVER *UK International INT 586*	67	2
3 Nov 79	GLORIA *Ariola ARO 198*	65	3

[1] Weathermen [2] Sakkarin [3] Shag [4] Bubblerock [5] 53rd and 3rd featuring the Sound of Shag [6] Sound 9418 [7] One Hundred Ton and a Feather [8] Father Abraphart and The Smurps

Mark KING (see also LEVEL 42)
UK, male vocalist / instrumentalist – bass (Albums: 2 Weeks) pos/wks

		pos	wks
21 Jul 84	INFLUENCES *Polydor MKLP 1*	77	2

Nosmo KING See The JAVELLS featuring Nosmo KING

Paul KING
(see also KING) *UK, male vocalist (Singles: 3 Weeks)* pos/wks

		pos	wks
2 May 87	I KNOW *CBS PKING 1*	59	3

Solomon KING
US, male vocalist (Singles: 28 Weeks, Albums: 1 Week) pos/wks

		pos	wks
3 Jan 68 ●	SHE WEARS MY RING *Columbia DB 8325*	3	18
1 May 68	WHEN WE WERE YOUNG *Columbia DB 8402*	21	10
22 Jun 68	SHE WEARS MY RING *Columbia SCX 6250*	40	1

Tony KING See Kylie MINOGUE

KING ADORA
UK, male vocal / instrumental group (Singles: 6 Weeks, Albums: 1 Week) pos/wks

		pos	wks
4 Nov 00	SMOULDER *Superior Quality / A&M RQSD 010CD*	62	1
3 Mar 01	SUFFOCATE *Superior Quality / A&M RQS 11DD*	39	2
26 May 01	BIONIC *Superior Quality / A&M RQS 012CD*	30	2
31 May 03	BORN TO LOSE / KAMIKAZE *MHR MHRCD 001*	68	1
2 Jun 01	VIBRATE YOU *Superior Quality RQS 13CD*	30	1

KING BEE
Holland, male rapper (Singles: 6 Weeks) pos/wks

		pos	wks
26 Jan 91	MUST BEE THE MUSIC *Columbia 6565827* [1]	44	4
23 Mar 91	BACK BY DOPE DEMAND *First Bass 7RUFF 6X*	61	2

[1] King Bee featuring Michele

The KING BROTHERS
UK, male vocal / instrumental trio – Dennis, Michael and Tony King (Singles: 74 Weeks) pos/wks

		pos	wks
31 May 57 ●	A WHITE SPORT COAT (AND A PINK CARNATION) *Parlophone R 4310*	6	14
9 Aug 57	IN THE MIDDLE OF AN ISLAND *Parlophone R 4338*	19	13
6 Dec 57	WAKE UP LITTLE SUSIE *Parlophone R 4367*	22	3
31 Jan 58	PUT A LIGHT IN THE WINDOW (2re) *Parlophone R 4389*	25	4
14 Apr 60 ●	STANDING ON THE CORNER *Parlophone R 4639*	4	11
28 Jul 60	MAIS OUI *Parlophone R 4672*	16	10
12 Jan 61	DOLL HOUSE *Parlophone R 4715*	21	8
2 Mar 61	76 TROMBONES *Parlophone R 4737*	19	11

KING CRIMSON (see also Bill BRUFORD; Greg LAKE; Robert FRIPP)
UK / US, male vocal / instrumental group (Albums: 55 Weeks) pos/wks

		pos	wks
1 Nov 69 ●	IN THE COURT OF THE CRIMSON KING *Island ILPS 9111*	5	18
30 May 70 ●	IN THE WAKE OF POSEIDON *Island ILPS 9127*	4	13
16 Jan 71	LIZARD *Island ILPS 9141*	29	2
8 Jan 72	ISLANDS *Island ILPS 9175*	30	1
7 Apr 73	LARKS' TONGUES IN ASPIC *Island ILPS 9230*	20	4
13 Apr 74	STARLESS AND BIBLE BLACK *Island ILPS 9275*	28	2
26 Oct 74	RED *Island ILPS 9308*	45	1
10 Oct 81	DISCIPLINE *EG EGLP 49*	41	4
26 Jun 82	BEAT *EG EGLP 51*	39	5
31 Mar 84	THREE OF A PERFECT PAIR *EG EGLP 55*	30	4
15 Apr 95	THRAK *Virgin KCCDY 1*	58	1

KING KURT
UK, male vocal / instrumental group (Singles: 16 Weeks, Albums: 5 Weeks) pos/wks

		pos	wks
15 Oct 83	DESTINATION ZULULAND *Stiff BUY 189*	36	6
28 Apr 84	MACK THE KNIFE *Stiff BUY 199*	55	4
4 Aug 84	BANANA BANANA *Stiff BUY 206*	54	4
15 Nov 86	AMERICA *Polydor KURT 1*	73	1
2 May 87	THE LAND OF RING DANG DO *Polydor KURT 2*	67	1
10 Dec 83	OOH WALLAH WALLAH *Stiff SEEZ 52*	99	1
8 Mar 86	BIG COCK *Stiff SEEZ 62*	50	4

KING SUN-D'MOET
US, male rap / DJ duo (Singles: 3 Weeks) pos/wks

		pos	wks
11 Jul 87	HEY LOVE *Flame MELT 5*	66	3

KING TRIGGER
UK, male / female vocal / instrumental group (Singles: 4 Weeks) pos/wks

		pos	wks
14 Aug 82	THE RIVER *Chrysalis CHS 2623*	57	4

KINGDOM COME
US, male vocal / instrumental group (Singles: 2 Weeks, Albums: 10 Weeks) pos/wks

		pos	wks
16 Apr 88	GET IT ON *Polydor KCS 1*	75	1
6 May 89	DO YOU LIKE IT *Polydor KCS 3*	73	1
28 Mar 88	KINGDOM COME *Polydor KCLP 1*	43	6
13 May 89	IN YOUR FACE *Polydor 839192 1*	25	4

KINGMAKER
UK, male vocal / instrumental group (Singles: 22 Weeks, Albums: 10 Weeks) pos/wks

		pos	wks
18 Jan 92	IDIOTS AT THE WHEEL (EP) *Scorch SCORCH 3*	30	3
23 May 92	EAT YOURSELF WHOLE *Scorch SCORCHG 5*	15	3
31 Oct 92	ARMCHAIR ANARCHIST *Scorch SCORCH 6*	47	2
8 May 93	10 YEARS ASLEEP *Scorch CDSCORCHS 8*	15	4
19 Jun 93	QUEEN JANE *Scorch CDSCORS 9*	29	4
30 Oct 93	SATURDAY'S NOT WHAT IT USED TO BE *Scorch CDSCORCH 10*	63	1
15 Apr 95	YOU AND I WILL NEVER SEE THINGS EYE TO EYE *Scorch CDSCORCHS 11*	33	3
3 Jun 95	IN THE BEST POSSIBLE TASTE (PART 2) *Scorch CDSCORCHS 12*	41	2
19 Oct 91	EAT YOURSELF WHOLE *Scorch CHR 1878*	29	3
29 May 93	SLEEPWALKING *Scorch CDCHR 6014*	15	7

Tracks on Idiots at the Wheel (EP): Really Scrape the Sky / Revelation / Every Teenage Suicide / Strip Away

The Choir of KING'S COLLEGE CAMBRIDGE
UK, choir (Albums: 3 Weeks) pos/wks

		pos	wks
11 Dec 71	THE WORLD OF CHRISTMAS *Argo SPAA 104*	38	3

KING'S X
US, male vocal / instrumental group (Albums: 4 Weeks) pos/wks

		pos	wks
1 Jul 89	GRETCHEN GOES TO NEBRASKA *Atlantic WX 279*	52	1
10 Nov 90	FAITH HOPE LOVE *Megaforce 756821451*	70	1
28 Mar 92	KING'S X *Atlantic 7567805062*	46	1
12 Feb 94	DOGMAN *Atlantic 7567825582*	49	1

KINGS OF CONVENIENCE
Norway, male vocal / instrumental duo (Singles: 3 Weeks, Albums: 2 Weeks) pos/wks

		pos	wks
21 Apr 01	TOXIC GIRL *Source SOURCDSE 1025*	44	1
14 Jul 01	FAILURE *Source SOURCD 036*	63	1
4 Sep 04	I'D RATHER DANCE WITH YOU *Source SOURCDX 102*	60	1
10 Feb 01	QUIET IS THE NEW LOUD *Source SOURCD 019*	72	1
3 Jul 04	RIOT ON AN EMPTY STREET *Source CDSOUR 099*	49	1

KINGS OF LEON US, male vocal / instrumental
group (Singles: 13 Weeks, Albums: 31 Weeks)   pos/wks

8 Mar 03	HOLY ROLLER NOVOCAINE *Hand Me Down / RCA HMD 21*	53	1
14 Jun 03	WHAT I SAW *Hand Me Down HMD 23*	22	3
23 Aug 03	MOLLY'S CHAMBERS *Hand Me Down HMD 29*	23	3
1 Nov 03	WASTED TIME *Hand Me Down HMD 32*	51	2
28 Feb 04	CALIFORNIA WAITING *Hand Me Down HMD 36*	61	1
6 Nov 04	THE BUCKET *Hand Me Down HMD 41*	16	3
19 Jul 03 ●	YOUTH & YOUNG MANHOOD *Hand Me Down HMD 27*	3	24
13 Nov 04 ●	AHA SHAKE HEARTBREAK *Hand Me Down HMD 39*	3	7+

KINGS OF SWING ORCHESTRA
Australia, orchestra (Singles: 5 Weeks, Albums: 11 Weeks)   pos/wks

1 May 82	SWITCHED ON SWING *Philips Swing 1*	48	5
29 May 82	SWITCHED ON SWING *K-Tel ONE 1166*	28	11

KINGS OF TOMORROW (see also LAYO & BUSHWACKA!)
*US, male production / instrumental duo –
Sandy Rivera and Jason Sealee (Singles: 8 Weeks)*   pos/wks

14 Apr 01	FINALLY *Distance DI 2029* [1]	54	1
29 Sep 01	FINALLY (re-mix) *Defected DFECT 37CDS* [1]	24	3
13 Apr 02	YOUNG HEARTS *Defected DFECT 46CDS*	45	2
25 Oct 03	DREAMS / THROUGH *Defected DFTD 079*	74	1
31 Jul 04	DREAMS (re-mix) *Defected DFTD 090CDS* [2]	69	1

[1] Kings of Tomorrow featuring Julie McKnight [2] Kings of Tomorrow featuring Haze

The KINGSMEN
US, male vocal / instrumental group (Singles: 7 Weeks)   pos/wks

30 Jan 64	LOUIE, LOUIE *Pye International 7N 25231*	26	7

The KINGSTON TRIO
US, male vocal / instrumental group (Singles: 15 Weeks)   pos/wks

21 Nov 58 ●	TOM DOOLEY *Capitol CL 14951* ▲	5	14
4 Dec 59	SAN MIGUEL *Capitol CL 15073*	29	1

The KINKS (146 Top 500) *Well-respected and innovative London band
who had few equals in the 1960s: Ray Davies (v/g), Dave Davies (g), Pete
Quaife (b), Mick Avory (d). Ray Davies, regarded as one of rock's premier
songwriters, remains active over 40 years after the group's first hit (Singles:
217 Weeks, Albums: 140 Weeks)*   pos/wks

13 Aug 64 ★	YOU REALLY GOT ME *Pye 7N 15673*	1	12
29 Oct 64 ●	ALL DAY AND ALL OF THE NIGHT *Pye 7N 15714*	2	14
21 Jan 65 ★	TIRED OF WAITING FOR YOU *Pye 7N 15759*	1	10
25 Mar 65	EVERYBODY'S GONNA BE HAPPY *Pye 7N 15813*	17	8
27 May 65 ●	SET ME FREE *Pye 7N 15854*	9	11
5 Aug 65 ●	SEE MY FRIEND *Pye 7N 15919*	10	9
2 Dec 65 ●	TILL THE END OF THE DAY *Pye 7N 15981*	8	12
3 Mar 66 ●	DEDICATED FOLLOWER OF FASHION *Pye 7N 17064*	4	11
9 Jun 66 ★	SUNNY AFTERNOON *Pye 7N 17125*	1	13
24 Nov 66 ●	DEAD END STREET *Pye 7N 17222*	5	11
11 May 67 ●	WATERLOO SUNSET *Pye 7N 17321*	2	11
18 Oct 67 ●	AUTUMN ALMANAC *Pye 7N 17400*	3	11
17 Apr 68	WONDERBOY *Pye 7N 17468*	36	5
17 Jul 68	DAYS *Pye 7N 17573*	12	10
16 Apr 69	PLASTIC MAN *Pye 7N 17724*	31	4
10 Jan 70	VICTORIA *Pye 7N 17865*	33	4
4 Jul 70 ●	LOLA *Pye 7N 17961*	2	14
12 Dec 70 ●	APEMAN *Pye 7N 45016*	5	14
27 May 72	SUPERSONIC ROCKET SHIP *RCA 2211*	16	8
27 Jun 81	BETTER THINGS *Arista ARIST 415*	46	5
6 Aug 83	COME DANCING *Arista ARIST 502*	12	9
15 Oct 83	DON'T FORGET TO DANCE *Arista ARIST 524*	58	3
15 Oct 83	YOU REALLY GOT ME (re-issue) *PRT KD1*	47	4
18 Jan 97	THE DAYS EP *When! WENX 1016*	35	2
18 Sep 04	YOU REALLY GOT ME (2nd re-issue) *Sanctuary SANXD 317*	42	2
17 Oct 64 ●	KINKS *Pye NPL 18096*	3	25
13 Mar 65 ●	KINDA KINKS *Pye NPL 18112*	3	15
4 Dec 65 ●	THE KINK KONTROVERSY *Pye NPL 18131*	9	12
11 Sep 66 ●	WELL RESPECTED KINKS *Marble Arch MAL 612*	5	31
5 Nov 66	FACE TO FACE *Pye NPL 18149*	12	11
14 Oct 67	SOMETHING ELSE *Pye NSPL 18193*	35	2
2 Dec 67 ●	SUNNY AFTERNOON *Marble Arch MAL 716*	9	11
23 Oct 71	GOLDEN HOUR OF THE KINKS *Golden Hour GH 501*	21	4

14 Oct 78	20 GOLDEN GREATS *Ronco RPL 2031*	19	6
5 Nov 83	KINKS GREATEST HITS – DEAD END STREET *PRT KINK 1*	96	1
16 Sep 89	THE ULTIMATE COLLECTION *Castle Communications CTVLP 001*	35	7
18 Sep 93	THE DEFINITIVE COLLECTION *PolyGram TV 5164652*	18	7
12 Apr 97	THE VERY BEST OF THE KINKS *PolyGram TV 5375542*	42	3
8 Jun 02	THE ULTIMATE COLLECTION *Sanctuary SANDD 109*	32	5

*Tracks on The Days EP: Days / You Really Got Me / Dead End Street / Lola
'The Ultimate Collection' in 2002 is an expanded version of the 1989 release*

KINKY (see also ERASURE)
UK, female rapper – Caron Geary (Singles: 1 Week)   pos/wks

24 Aug 96	EVERYBODY *Feverpitch CDFVR 1009*	71	1

KINKY MACHINE
UK, male vocal / instrumental group (Singles: 4 Weeks)   pos/wks

6 Mar 93	SUPERNATURAL GIVER *Lemon LEMON 006CD*	70	1
29 May 93	SHOCKAHOLIC *Oxygen GASPD 5*	70	1
14 Aug 93	GOING OUT WITH GOD *Oxygen GASPD 9*	74	1
2 Jul 94	10 SECOND BIONIC MAN *Oxygen GASPD 14*	66	1

Fern KINNEY
US, female vocalist – Fern Kinney-Lewis (Singles: 11 Weeks)   pos/wks

16 Feb 80 ★	TOGETHER WE ARE BEAUTIFUL *WEA K 79111*	1	11

KINSHASA BAND *See Johnny WAKELIN*

KIOKI *Japan, male vocalist (Singles: 1 Week)*   pos/wks

17 Aug 02	DO & DON'T FOR LOVE *V2 VVR 5020803*	66	1

KIRA
Belgium, female vocalist – Natasja De Witte (Singles: 5 Weeks) pos/wks

1 Mar 03 ●	I'LL BE YOUR ANGEL *Nulife 74321970362*	9	5

Kathy KIRBY *UK, female vocalist – Kathleen
O'Rourke (Singles: 54 Weeks, Albums: 8 Weeks)*   pos/wks

15 Aug 63	DANCE ON *Decca F 11682*	11	13
7 Nov 63 ●	SECRET LOVE *Decca F 11759*	4	18
20 Feb 64	LET ME GO LOVER! *Decca F 11832*	10	11
7 May 64	YOU'RE THE ONE *Decca F 11892*	17	9
4 Mar 65	I BELONG *Decca F 12087*	36	3
4 Jan 64	16 HITS FROM STARS AND GARTERS *Decca LK 5475*	11	8

Bo KIRKLAND and Ruth DAVIS
US, male / female vocal duo (Singles: 9 Weeks)   pos/wks

4 Jun 77	YOU'RE GONNA GET NEXT TO ME *EMI International INT 532*	12	9

Dominic KIRWAN *Ireland, male vocalist (Albums: 1 Week)*   pos/wks

1 Nov 97	THE MUSIC'S BACK *Ritz RITZCD 0084*	54	1

KISS (see also Vinnie VINCENT; FREHLEY'S COMET; Gene SIMMONS)
*US / Israel, male vocal / instrumental group
(Singles: 57 Weeks, Albums: 71 Weeks)*   pos/wks

30 Jun 79	I WAS MADE FOR LOVIN' YOU *Casablanca CAN 152*	50	7
20 Feb 82	A WORLD WITHOUT HEROES *Casablanca KISS 002*	55	3
30 Apr 83	CREATURES OF THE NIGHT *Casablanca KISS 4*	34	4
29 Oct 83	LICK IT UP *Vertigo KISS 5*	31	5
8 Sep 84	HEAVEN'S ON FIRE *Vertigo VER 12*	43	3
9 Nov 85	TEARS ARE FALLING *Vertigo KISS 6*	57	2
3 Oct 87 ●	CRAZY CRAZY NIGHTS *Vertigo KISS 7*	4	9
5 Dec 87	REASON TO LIVE *Vertigo KISS 8*	33	7
10 Sep 88	TURN ON THE NIGHT *Vertigo KISS 9*	41	3
18 Nov 89	HIDE YOUR HEART *Vertigo KISS 10*	59	2
31 Mar 90	FOREVER *Vertigo KISS 11*	65	2
11 Jan 92 ●	GOD GAVE ROCK AND ROLL TO YOU II *Interscope A 8696*	4	8
9 May 92	UNHOLY *Mercury KISS 12*	26	2
29 May 76	DESTROYER *Casablanca CBSP 4008*	22	5
25 Jun 76	ALIVE! *Casablanca CBSP 401*	49	2
17 Dec 77	ALIVE *Casablanca CALD 5004*	60	1
7 Jul 79	DYNASTY *Casablanca CALH 2051*	50	6
28 Jun 80	UNMASKED *Mercury 6302 032*	48	3
5 Dec 81	THE ELDER *Casablanca 6302 163*	51	3
26 Jun 82	KILLERS *Casablanca CANL 1*	42	6

		pos/wks
6 Nov 82	CREATURES OF THE NIGHT *Casablanca CANL 4*	22 4
8 Oct 83 ●	LICK IT UP *Vertigo VERL 9*	7 7
6 Oct 84	ANIMALIZE *Vertigo VERL 18*	11 4
5 Oct 85	ASYLUM *Vertigo VERH 32*	12 3
7 Nov 87 ●	CRAZY NIGHTS *Vertigo VERH 49*	4 14
10 Dec 88	SMASHES THRASHES AND HITS *Vertigo 836759 1*	62 2
4 Nov 89	HOT IN THE SHADE *Fontana 838913 1*	35 2
23 May 92 ●	REVENGE *Mercury 8480372*	10 3
29 May 93	ALIVE III *Mercury 5148272*	24 2
23 Mar 96	MTV UNPLUGGED *Mercury 5289502*	74 1
12 Jul 97	GREATEST HITS *PolyGram TV 5361592*	58 2
3 Oct 98	PSYCHO-CIRCUS *Mercury 5589922*	47 1

KISS AMC *UK, female rap duo (Singles: 5 Weeks)*

		pos/wks
1 Jul 89	A BIT OF U2 (re) *Syncopate SY 29*	58 4
3 Feb 90	MY DOCS *Syncopate XAMC 1*	66 1

Before its re-entry in Aug '89, due to copyright problems, 'A Bit of U2' was unable to be given its full title

KISSING THE PINK *UK, male / female vocal / instrumental group (Singles: 14 Weeks, Albums: 5 Weeks)*

		pos/wks
5 Mar 83	LAST FILM *Magnet KTP 3*	19 14
4 Jun 83	NAKED *Magnet KTPL 1001*	54 5

Mac and Katie KISSOON

Trinidad / UK, male / female vocal duo (Singles: 33 Weeks)

		pos/wks
19 Jun 71	CHIRPY CHIRPY CHEEP CHEEP *Young Blood YB 1026*	41 1
18 Jan 75 ●	SUGAR CANDY KISSES *Polydor 2058 531*	3 10
3 May 75 ●	DON'T DO IT BABY *State STAT 4*	9 8
30 Aug 75	LIKE A BUTTERFLY *State STAT 9*	18 9
15 May 76	THE TWO OF US *State STAT 21*	46 5

Kevin KITCHEN *UK, male vocalist (Singles: 3 Weeks)*

		pos/wks
20 Apr 85	PUT MY ARMS AROUND YOU *China WOK 1*	64 3

KITCHENS OF DISTINCTION

UK, male vocal / instrumental group (Albums: 2 Weeks)

		pos/wks
30 Mar 91	STRANGE FREE WORLD *One Little Indian TPLP 19*	45 1
15 Aug 92	THE DEATH OF COOL *One Little Indian TPLP 39CD*	72 1

Joy KITIKONTI

Italy, male producer – Massimo Chiticonti (Singles: 2 Weeks)

		pos/wks
17 Nov 01	JOYENERGIZER *BXR BXRC 0347*	57 2

Eartha KITT

US, female vocalist (Singles: 34 Weeks, Albums: 1 Week)

		pos/wks
1 Apr 55 ●	UNDER THE BRIDGES OF PARIS (re) *HMV B 10647*	7 10
3 Dec 83	WHERE IS MY MAN *Record Shack SOHO 11*	36 11
7 Jul 84	I LOVE MEN *Record Shack SOHO 21*	50 3
12 Apr 86	THIS IS MY LIFE *Record Shack SOHO 61*	73 1
1 Jul 89	CHA CHA HEELS *Arista 112331* [1]	32 7
5 Mar 94	IF I LOVE YA THEN I NEED YA IF I NEED YA THEN I WANT YOU AROUND *RCA 74321190342*	43 2
11 Feb 61	REVISITED *London HA 2296*	17 1

[1] Eartha Kitt and Bronski Beat

KITTIE

Canada, female vocal / instrumental group (Singles: 2 Weeks)

		pos/wks
25 Mar 00	BRACKISH *Epic 6691292*	46 1
22 Jul 00	CHARLOTTE *Epic 6696222*	60 1

Myleene KLASS (see also HEAR'SAY)

UK, female vocalist / instrumentalist – piano (Albums: 3 Weeks)

		pos/wks
1 Nov 03	MOVING ON *UCJ 9865632*	32 3

The KLAXONS

Belgium, male vocal / instrumental group (Singles: 6 Weeks)

		pos/wks
10 Dec 83	THE CLAP CLAP SOUND *PRT 7P 290*	45 6

KLEA

UK, male / female production / vocal / rap trio (Singles: 1 Week)

		pos/wks
7 Sep 02	TIC TOC *Incentive CENT 41CDS*	61 1

KLEEER *US, male / female vocal / instrumental group (Singles: 10 Weeks, Albums: 1 Week)*

		pos/wks
17 Mar 79	KEEEP YOUR BODY WORKIN' *Atlantic LV 21*	51 6
14 Mar 81	GET TOUGH *Atlantic 11560*	49 4
6 Jul 85	SEEEKRET *Atlantic 7812541*	96 1

D.D. KLEIN See ALIVE featuring D.D. KLEIN

KLESHAY *UK, female vocal trio (Singles: 5 Weeks)*

		pos/wks
19 Sep 98	REASONS *Epic KLE 1CD*	33 2
20 Feb 99	RUSH *Epic KLE 2CD*	19 3

KLUBBHEADS (see also DA TECHNO BOHEMIAN; DRUNKENMONKEY; ITTY BITTY BOOZY WOOZY) *Holland, male instrumental / production group (Singles: 10 Weeks)*

		pos/wks
11 May 96 ●	KLUBBHOPPING *AM:PM 5815572*	10 6
16 Aug 97	DISCOHOPPING *AM:PM 5823032*	35 2
15 Aug 98	KICKIN' HARD *Wonderboy WBOYD 011*	36 2

Earl KLUGH See George BENSON

KLUSTER featuring Ron CARROLL

France, male DJ / production duo (Singles: 1 Week)

		pos/wks
28 Apr 01	MY LOVE *Scorpio Music 1928112*	73 1

The KNACK *US, male vocal / instrumental group (Singles: 12 Weeks, Albums: 2 Weeks)*

		pos/wks
30 Jun 79 ●	MY SHARONA *Capitol CL 16087* ▲	6 10
13 Oct 79	GOOD GIRLS DON'T *Capitol CL 16097*	66 2
4 Aug 79	GET THE KNACK *Capitol EST 11948* ▲	65 2

KNACK See MOUNT RUSHMORE presents The KNACK

Beverley KNIGHT *UK, female vocalist – Beverley Smith (Singles: 52 Weeks, Albums: 44 Weeks)*

		pos/wks
8 Apr 95	FLAVOUR OF THE OLD SCHOOL *Dome CDDOME 101*	50 2
2 Sep 95	DOWN FOR THE ONE *Dome CDDOME 102*	55 1
21 Oct 95	FLAVOUR OF THE OLD SCHOOL (re-mix) *Dome CDDOME 105*	33 2
23 Mar 96	MOVING ON UP (ON THE RIGHT SIDE) *Dome CDDOME 107*	42 1
30 May 98	MADE IT BACK *Parlophone Rhythm CDRHYTHM 11* [1]	21 3
22 Aug 98	REWIND (FIND A WAY) *Parlophone Rhythm CDRHYTHS 13*	40 1
10 Apr 99	MADE IT BACK 99 (re-mix) *Parlophone Rhythm CDRHYTHM 18*	19 5
17 Jul 99	GREATEST DAY *Parlophone Rhythm CDRHYTHS 22*	14 5
4 Dec 99	SISTA SISTA *Parlophone Rhythm CDRHYTHM 26*	31 2
17 Nov 01	GET UP *Parlophone CDRS 6564*	17 4
9 Mar 02 ●	SHOULDA WOULDA COULDA *Parlophone CDRS 6570*	10 9
6 Jul 02	GOLD *Parlophone CDRS 6580*	27 4
3 Jul 04 ●	COME AS YOU ARE *Parlophone CDRS 6636*	9 10
9 Oct 04	NOT TOO LATE FOR LOVE *Parlophone CDRS 6645*	31 2
5 Sep 98	PRODIGAL SISTA *Parlophone Rhythm 4962962*	42 14
23 Mar 02 ●	WHO I AM *Parlophone 5360320*	7 24
10 Jul 04	AFFIRMATION *Parlophone 4733102*	11 6

[1] Beverley Knight featuring Redman

Curtis KNIGHT See The Jimi HENDRIX EXPERIENCE

Frederick KNIGHT *US, male vocalist (Singles: 10 Weeks)*

		pos/wks
10 Jun 72	I'VE BEEN LONELY SO LONG *Stax 2025 098*	22 10

Gladys KNIGHT and the PIPS `190` `Top 500` *One of soul music's foremost female singers for almost 40 years, b. 28 May 1944, Georgia, US. The celebrated vocalist (who first appeared on US TV aged eight) and her family quartet The Pips (they split in 1989) were inducted into the Rock and Roll Hall of Fame in 1996 (Singles: 187 Weeks, Albums: 117 Weeks)*

		pos/wks
8 Jun 67	TAKE ME IN YOUR ARMS AND LOVE ME *Tamla Motown TMG 604*	13 15
27 Dec 67	I HEARD IT THROUGH THE GRAPEVINE *Tamla Motown TMG 629*	47 1
17 Jun 72	JUST WALK IN MY SHOES *Tamla Motown TMG 813*	35 8
25 Nov 72	HELP ME MAKE IT THROUGH THE NIGHT *Tamla Motown TMG 830*	11 17
3 Mar 73	THE LOOK OF LOVE *Tamla Motown TMG 844*	21 9
26 May 73	NEITHER ONE OF US (WANTS TO BE THE FIRST TO SAY GOODBYE) *Tamla Motown TMG 855*	31 7

		pos/wks
5 Apr 75 ●	THE WAY WE WERE – TRY TO REMEMBER *Buddah BDS 428* ..4	15
2 Aug 75 ●	BEST THING THAT EVER HAPPENED TO ME	
	Buddah BDS 432 7	10
15 Nov 75	PART TIME LOVE *Buddah BDS 438* 30	5
8 May 76 ●	MIDNIGHT TRAIN TO GEORGIA *Buddah BDS 444* ▲ 10	9
21 Aug 76	MAKE YOURS A HAPPY HOME *Buddah BDS 447* 35	4
6 Nov 76	SO SAD THE SONG *Buddah BDS 448* 20	9
15 Jan 77	NOBODY BUT YOU *Buddah BDS 451* 34	2
28 May 77 ●	BABY DON'T CHANGE YOUR MIND *Buddah BDS 458* 4	12
24 Sep 77	HOME IS WHERE THE HEART IS *Buddah BDS 460* 35	4
8 Apr 78	THE ONE AND ONLY (re) *Buddah BDS 470* 32	5
24 Jun 78	COME BACK AND FINISH WHAT YOU STARTED	
	Buddah BDS 473 15	13
30 Sep 78	IT'S A BETTER THAN GOOD TIME *Buddah BDS 478* 59	4
30 Aug 80	TASTE OF BITTER LOVE *CBS 8890* 35	6
8 Nov 80	BOURGIE, BOURGIE *CBS 9081* 32	6
26 Dec 81	WHEN A CHILD IS BORN *CBS S 1758* [1] 74	2
9 Nov 85	THAT'S WHAT FRIENDS ARE FOR *Arista ARIST 638* [2] ▲ 16	9
16 Jan 88	LOVE OVERBOARD *MCA MCA 1223* 42	4
10 Jun 89 ●	LICENCE TO KILL *MCA MCA 1339* [3] 6	11
31 May 75	I FEEL A SONG *Buddah BDLP 4030* 20	15
28 Feb 76 ●	THE BEST OF GLADYS KNIGHT & THE PIPS	
	Buddah BDLH 5013 6	43
16 Jul 77	STILL TOGETHER *Buddah BDLH 5014* 42	3
12 Nov 77 ●	30 GREATEST *K-Tel NE 1004* 3	22
4 Oct 80	A TOUCH OF LOVE *K-Tel NE 1090* 16	6
4 Feb 84	THE COLLECTION – 20 GREATEST HITS *Starblend NITE 1* 43	5
15 Nov 86	DIANA ROSS. MICHAEL JACKSON. GLADYS KNIGHT.	
	STEVIE WONDER. THEIR VERY BEST BACK TO BACK	
	Priority TV PTVR 2 [1] 21	10
27 Feb 88	ALL OUR LOVE *MCA MCF 3409* 80	1
28 Oct 89	THE SINGLES ALBUM *PolyGram GKTV 1* 13	10
29 Mar 97	THE SINGLES ALBUM (re-issue) *PolyGram TV 8420032* 69	2

[1] Johnny Mathis and Gladys Knight [2] Dionne Warwick and Friends featuring
Elton John, Stevie Wonder and Gladys Knight [3] Gladys Knight [1] Diana Ross /
Michael Jackson / Gladys Knight / Stevie Wonder

Jordan KNIGHT (see also NEW KIDS ON THE BLOCK)
US, male vocalist (Singles: 9 Weeks)   pos/wks

16 Oct 99 ●	GIVE IT TO YOU (re) *Interscope 4971672* 5	9

Robert KNIGHT *US, male vocalist (Singles: 26 Weeks)*   pos/wks

17 Jan 68	EVERLASTING LOVE *Monument MON 1008* 40	2
24 Nov 73 ●	LOVE ON A MOUNTAIN TOP *Monument MNT 1875* 10	16
9 Mar 74	EVERLASTING LOVE (re-issue) *Monument MNT 2106* 19	8

The KNIGHTSBRIDGE STRINGS
UK, male orchestra (Albums: 1 Week)   pos/wks

25 Jun 60	STRING SWAY *Top Rank BUY 017* 20	1

KNOC-TURN'AL See DR DRE

David KNOPFLER (see also DIRE STRAITS)
UK, male vocalist / instrumentalist – guitar (Albums: 1 Week)   pos/wks

19 Nov 83	RELEASE *Peach River DAVID 1* 82	1

Mark KNOPFLER (see also DIRE STRAITS; The NOTTING HILLBILLIES)
UK, male vocalist / instrumentalist – guitar
(Singles: 9 Weeks, Albums: 64 Weeks)   pos/wks

12 Mar 83	GOING HOME (THEME OF 'LOCAL HERO') *Vertigo DSTR 4* ...56	3
16 Mar 96	DARLING PRETTY *Vertigo VERCD 88* 33	2
25 May 96	CANNIBALS *Vertigo VERCD 89* 42	2
2 Oct 04	BOOM, LIKE THAT *Mercury 9867839* 34	2
16 Apr 83	LOCAL HERO (FILM SOUNDTRACK) *Vertigo VERL 4* 14	11
20 Oct 84	CAL (FILM SOUNDTRACK) *Vertigo VERH 17* 65	3
24 Nov 90	NECK AND NECK *CBS 4674351* [1] 41	11
6 Apr 96 ●	GOLDEN HEART *Vertigo 5147322* 9	17
7 Oct 00 ●	SAILING TO PHILADELPHIA *Mercury 5429812* 4	13
12 Oct 02 ●	THE RAGPICKER'S DREAM *Mercury 0632932* 7	5
9 Oct 04	SHANGRI-LA *Mercury 9867715* 11	4

[1] Chet Atkins and Mark Knopfler

KNOWLEDGE *Italy, male production duo (Singles: 1 Week)*   pos/wks

8 Nov 97	AS (UNTIL THE DAY) *ffrr FCD 312* 70	1

Buddy KNOX
US, male vocalist, b. 20 Jul 1933, d. 14 Feb 1999 (Singles: 5 Weeks)   pos/wks

10 May 57	PARTY DOLL *Columbia DB 3914* ▲ 29	3
16 Aug 62	SHE'S GONE *Liberty LIB 55473* 45	2

Frankie KNUCKLES
US, male producer (Singles: 19 Weeks, Albums: 2 Weeks)   pos/wks

17 Jun 89	TEARS *ffrr F 108* [1] 50	3
21 Oct 89	YOUR LOVE *Trax TRAXT 3* 59	4
27 Jul 91	THE WHISTLE SONG *Virgin America VUS 47* 17	5
23 Nov 91	IT'S HARD SOMETIMES *Virgin America VUS 52* 67	1
6 Jun 92	RAIN FALLS *Virgin America VUST 60* [2] 48	2
27 May 95	TOO MANY FISH *Virgin America VUSCD 89* [3] 34	2
18 Nov 95	WHADDA U WANT (FROM ME) *Virgin America VUSCD 98* [3] ..36	2
17 Aug 91	BEYOND THE MIX *Virgin America VUSLP 6* 59	2

[1] Frankie Knuckles presents Satoshi Tomiie [2] Frankie Knuckles featuring Lisa
Michaelis [3] Frankie Knuckles featuring Adeva

Moe KOFFMAN QUARTETTE
Canada, male instrumental group – leader Moe Koffman –
flute, b. 28 Dec 1928, d. 28 Mar 2001 (Singles: 2 Weeks)   pos/wks

28 Mar 58	SWINGIN' SHEPHERD BLUES *London HLJ 8549* 23	2

Mike KOGLIN *Germany, male producer (Singles: 4 Weeks)*   pos/wks

28 Nov 98	THE SILENCE *Multiply CDMULTY 44* 20	2
29 May 99	ON MY WAY *Multiply CDMULTY 51* [1] 28	2

[1] Mike Koglin featuring Beatrice

KOKOMO
US, male instrumentalist – piano – Jimmy Wisner (Singles: 7 Weeks) pos/wks

13 Apr 61	ASIA MINOR *London HLU 9305* 35	7

KOKOMO
UK, male / female vocal / instrumental group (Singles: 3 Weeks)   pos/wks

29 May 82	A LITTLE BIT FURTHER AWAY *CBS A 2064* 45	3

KON KAN *Canada, male vocal / instrumental duo –*
Barry Harris and Kevin Wynne (Singles: 13 Weeks)   pos/wks

4 Mar 89 ●	I BEG YOUR PARDON *Atlantic A 8969* 5	13

John KONGOS *South Africa, male vocalist /*
multi-instrumentalist (Singles: 25 Weeks, Albums: 2 Weeks)   pos/wks

22 May 71 ●	HE'S GONNA STEP ON YOU AGAIN *Fly BUG 8* 4	14
20 Nov 71 ●	TOKOLOSHE MAN *Fly BUG 14* 4	11
15 Jan 72	KONGOS *Fly HIFLY 7* 29	2

KONKRETE *UK, female production duo (Singles: 1 Week)*   pos/wks

22 Sep 01	LAW UNTO MYSELF *Perfecto PERF 23CDS* 60	1

Laurent KONRAD See FIGHT CLUB featuring Laurent KONRAD

KONTAKT *UK, male production duo – Scott*
Attrill and Jim Sullivan (Singles: 4 Weeks)   pos/wks

20 Sep 03	SHOW ME A SIGN *Nulife 82876557432* 19	4

KOOL and the GANG   `164` `Top 500`
One of the most consistently successful R&B acts, hailing from New Jersey
and including Robert 'Kool' Bell (b) and James 'JT' Taylor (v). The band
spent 10 years as top US R&B stars before starting an impressive run
of international hits (Singles: 218 Weeks, Albums: 116 Weeks)   pos/wks

27 Oct 79 ●	LADIES NIGHT *Mercury KOOL 7* 9	12
19 Jan 80	TOO HOT *Mercury KOOL 8* 23	8
12 Jul 80	HANGIN' OUT *De-Lite KOOL 9* 52	4
1 Nov 80 ●	CELEBRATION *De-Lite KOOL 10* ▲ 7	13
21 Feb 81	JONES VS JONES / SUMMER MADNESS *De-Lite KOOL 11* ...17	11
30 May 81	TAKE IT TO THE TOP *De-Lite DE 2* 15	9
31 Oct 81	STEPPIN' OUT *De-Lite DE 4* 12	13
19 Dec 81 ●	GET DOWN ON IT *De-Lite DE 5* 3	12
6 Mar 82	TAKE MY HEART (YOU CAN HAVE IT IF YOU WANT IT)	
	De-Lite DE 6 29	7

7 Aug 82		BIG FUN *De-Lite DE 7*	14 8
16 Oct 82	●	OOH LA LA LA (LET'S GO DANCIN') *De-Lite DE 9*	6 9
4 Dec 82		HI DE HI, HI DE HO *De-Lite DE 14*	29 8
10 Dec 83		STRAIGHT AHEAD *De-Lite DE 15*	15 10
11 Feb 84	●	JOANNA / TONIGHT *De-Lite DE 16*	2 11
14 Apr 84	●	(WHEN YOU SAY YOU LOVE SOMEBODY) IN THE HEART *De-Lite DE 17*	7 8
24 Nov 84		FRESH *De-Lite DE 18*	11 12
9 Feb 85		MISLED *De-Lite DE 19*	28 5
11 May 85	●	CHERISH *De-Lite DE 20*	4 22
2 Nov 85		EMERGENCY *De-Lite DE 21*	50 3
22 Nov 86		VICTORY (re) *Club JAB 44*	30 12
21 Mar 87		STONE LOVE *Club JAB 47*	45 4
31 Dec 88		CELEBRATION (re-mix) *Club JAB 78*	56 5
6 Jul 91		GET DOWN ON IT (re-mix) *Mercury MER 346*	69 1
27 Dec 03	●	LADIES NIGHT *Innocent SINCD 53* [1]	8 11
21 Nov 81	●	SOMETHING SPECIAL *De-Lite DSR 001*	10 20
2 Oct 82		AS ONE *De-Lite DSR 3*	49 10
7 May 83	●	TWICE AS KOOL *De-Lite PROLP 2*	4 23
14 Jan 84		IN THE HEART *De-Lite DSR 4*	18 23
15 Dec 84		EMERGENCY *De-Lite DSR 6*	47 25
12 Nov 88		THE SINGLES COLLECTION *De-Lite KGTV 1*	28 13
27 Oct 90		KOOL LOVE *Telstar STAR 2435*	50 1
26 Jun 04		THE HITS: RELOADED *Unique Corp / Virgin / EMI VTDCD 618*	56 1

[1] Atomic Kitten featuring Kool and the Gang

'Jones vs Jones' and 'Summer Madness' were labelled as A and B sides with 'Funky Stuff' and 'Hollywood Swinging' as the C and D sides of a two-disc release

KOOL ROCK STEADY *See TYREE*

KOON + STEPHENSON *See WESTBAM*

The KORGIS *UK, male vocal / instrumental duo (Singles: 27 Weeks, Albums: 4 Weeks)* pos/wks

23 Jun 79		IF I HAD YOU *Rialto TREB 103*	13 12
24 May 80	●	EVERYBODY'S GOT TO LEARN SOMETIME *Rialto TREB 115*	5 12
30 Aug 80		IF IT'S ALRIGHT WITH YOU BABY *Rialto TREB 118*	56 3
26 Jul 80		DUMB WAITERS *Rialto TENOR 104*	40 4

KORN *US, male vocal / instrumental group (Singles: 25 Weeks, Albums: 20 Weeks)* pos/wks

19 Oct 96		NO PLACE TO HIDE *Epic 6638452*	26 2
15 Feb 97		A.D.I.D.A.S. *Epic 6642042*	22 2
7 Jun 97		GOOD GOD *Epic 6646585*	25 2
22 Aug 98		GOT THE LIFE *Epic 6663912*	23 2
8 May 99		FREAK ON A LEASH *Epic 6672522*	24 2
12 Feb 00		FALLING AWAY FROM ME *Epic 6688692*	24 2
3 Jun 00		MAKE ME BAD *Epic 6694332*	25 2
1 Jun 02		HERE TO STAY *Epic 6727425*	12 5
21 Sep 02		THOUGHTLESS *Epic 6731572*	37 2
23 Aug 03		DID MY TIME *Epic 6741422*	15 4
26 Oct 96		LIFE IS PEACHY *Epic 4853692*	32 2
29 Aug 98	●	FOLLOW THE LEADER *Epic 4912212* ▲	5 4
27 Nov 99		ISSUES *Epic 4963592* ▲	37 1
22 Jun 02	●	UNTOUCHABLES *Epic 5017700*	4 9
6 Dec 03		TAKE A LOOK IN THE MIRROR *Epic 05133253*	53 1
16 Oct 04		GREATEST HITS VOL.1 *Epic 5187923*	22 3

KOSHEEN *UK, male / female production / vocal trio (Singles: 31 Weeks, Albums: 29 Weeks)* pos/wks

17 Jun 00		EMPTY SKIES / HIDE U *Moksha Recordings MOKSHA 05CD*	73 1
14 Apr 01		(SLIP & SLIDE) SUICIDE *Moksha Recordings MOKSHA 07CD*	50 2
1 Sep 01		HIDE U (re) (re-mix) *Arista 74321879412*	6 7
22 Dec 01		CATCH *Moksha / Arista 74321913722*	15 8
4 May 02		HUNGRY *Moksha / Arista 74321934382*	13 4
31 Aug 02		HARDER *Moksha / Arista 74321954452*	53 1
9 Aug 03	●	ALL IN MY HEAD (re) *Moksha / Arista 82876527242*	7 7
1 Nov 03		WASTING MY TIME *Moksha / Arista 82876570022*	49 1
29 Sep 01	●	RESIST *Arista 74321880812*	8 23
23 Aug 03	●	KOKOPELLI *Moksha / Arista 82876527232*	7 6

KOWDEAN *See OXIDE & NEUTRINO*

KRAFTWERK 475 Top 500 *German electronic robot 'n' roll pioneers: Ralf Hutter (k/v), Florian Schneider (prc/v), Karl Bartos (prc), Wolfgang Flur (prc). The first German act to top the UK singles chart, they influenced disco and synth pop movements and helped to lay the foundation stones for hip hop (Singles: 79 Weeks, Albums: 73 Weeks)* pos/wks

10 May 75		AUTOBAHN *Vertigo 6147 012*	11 9
28 Oct 78		NEON LIGHTS *Capitol CL 15998*	53 3
9 May 81		POCKET CALCULATOR *EMI 5175*	39 6
11 Jul 81	★	COMPUTER LOVE / THE MODEL (re) *EMI 5207*	1 21
20 Feb 82		SHOWROOM DUMMIES *EMI 5272*	25 5
6 Aug 83		TOUR DE FRANCE (re) *EMI 5413*	22 19
1 Jun 91		THE ROBOTS *EMI EM 192*	20 4
2 Nov 91		RADIOACTIVITY (re-mix) *EMI EM 201*	43 2
23 Oct 99		TOUR DE FRANCE (re-issue) *EMI 8874210*	61 1
18 Mar 00		EXPO 2000 *EMI CDEM 562*	27 2
19 Jul 03		TOUR DE FRANCE 2003 *EMI CDEM 626*	20 4
27 Mar 04		AERODYNAMIK *EMI CDEM 637*	33 3
17 May 75	●	AUTOBAHN *Vertigo 6360 620*	4 18
20 May 78	▲	THE MAN-MACHINE *Capitol EST 11728*	9 13
23 May 81		COMPUTER WORLD *EMI EMC 3370*	15 22
6 Feb 82		TRANS-EUROPE EXPRESS *Capitol EST 11603*	49 7
22 Jun 85		AUTOBAHN (re-issue) *Parlophone AUTO 1*	61 3
15 Nov 86		ELECTRIC CAFÉ *EMI EMD 1001*	58 2
22 Jun 91		THE MIX *EMI EM 1408*	15 6
16 Aug 03		TOUR DE FRANCE SOUNDTRACKS *EMI 5917082*	21 2

'Computer Love / The Model' did not make No.1 until re-entry in Dec 1981. 'Tour de France' peaked at No.24 after re-entry in Aug 1984

DIANA KRALL *Canada, female vocalist / instrumentalist – piano (Albums: 22 Weeks)* pos/wks

12 Jun 99		WHEN I LOOK IN YOUR EYES *Verve 503042*	72 1
29 Sep 01		THE LOOK OF LOVE *Verve 5498462*	23 7
23 Nov 02		LIVE IN PARIS *Verve 0653692*	30 6
24 Apr 04	●	THE GIRL IN THE OTHER ROOM *Verve 9862063*	4 8

Billy J KRAMER and the DAKOTAS *UK, male vocal / instrumental group (Singles: 71 Weeks, Albums: 17 Weeks)* pos/wks

2 May 63	●	DO YOU WANT TO KNOW A SECRET? *Parlophone R 5023*	2 15
1 Aug 63	★	BAD TO ME *Parlophone R 5049*	1 14
7 Nov 63	●	I'LL KEEP YOU SATISFIED *Parlophone R 5073*	4 13
27 Feb 64	★	LITTLE CHILDREN *Parlophone R 5105*	1 13
23 Jul 64		FROM A WINDOW *Parlophone R 5156*	10 8
20 May 65		TRAINS AND BOATS AND PLANES *Parlophone R 5285*	12 8
16 Nov 63		LISTEN TO BILLY J. KRAMER *Parlophone PMC 1209*	11 17

The KRANKIES *UK, male / female vocal duo (Singles: 6 Weeks)* pos/wks

7 Feb 81		FAN'DABI'DOZI (re) *Monarch MON 21*	46 6

Alison KRAUSS and UNION STATION *US, female vocalist instrumentalist – fiddle and instrumental group (Albums: 1 Week)* pos/wks

25 Aug 01		NEW FAVORITE *Rounder RRCD 0495*	72 1

Lenny KRAVITZ 361 Top 500 *Grammy and Brit-winning, soulful rock vocalist and multi-instrumentalist who has worked with Madonna, Mick Jagger, David Bowie and Stevie Wonder, b. 26 May 1964, New York City, US. His Greatest Hits album reached the Top 10 in 25 countries and sold more than eight million copies worldwide (Singles: 72 Weeks, Albums: 114 Weeks)* pos/wks

2 Jun 90		MR CABDRIVER *Virgin America VUS 20*	58 2
4 Aug 90		LET LOVE RULE *Virgin America VUS 26*	39 4
30 Mar 91		ALWAYS ON THE RUN *Virgin America VUS 34*	41 3
15 Jun 91		IT AIN'T OVER TIL IT'S OVER *Virgin America VUS 43*	11 8
14 Sep 91		STAND BY MY WOMAN *Virgin America VUS 45*	55 3
20 Feb 93	●	ARE YOU GONNA GO MY WAY *Virgin America VUSDG 65*	4 11
22 May 93		BELIEVE *Virgin America VUSDG 72*	30 5
28 Aug 93		HEAVEN HELP *Virgin America VUSDG 73*	20 7
4 Dec 93		IS THERE ANY LOVE IN YOUR HEART *Virgin America VUSDG 76*	52 2
4 Dec 93		BUDDHA OF SUBURBIA *Arista 74321177052* [1]	35 3
9 Sep 95		ROCK AND ROLL IS DEAD *Virgin America VUSCD 93*	22 3
23 Dec 95		CIRCUS *Virgin America VUSCD 96*	54 2
2 Mar 96		CAN'T GET YOU OFF MY MIND *Virgin America VUSCD 100*	54 2
16 May 98		IF YOU CAN'T SAY NO *Virgin VUSCD 130*	48 2
10 Oct 98		I BELONG TO YOU *Virgin VUSCD 138*	75 1

Jonny L
UK, male vocalist / instrumentalist / producer – Johny Listners (Singles: 2 Weeks)   pos/wks

28 Aug 93	OOH I LIKE IT *XL Recordings XLS 44CD*	**73**	1
31 Oct 98	20 DEGREES *XL Recordings XLS 103CD* [1]	**66**	1

[1] Jonny L featuring Silvah Bullet

LA GANZ
US, male vocal / instrumental group (Singles: 1 Week)   pos/wks

9 Nov 96	LIKE A PLAYA *Jive JIVECD 405*	**75**	1

L.A. GUNS
US, male / female vocal / instrumental group (Singles: 4 Weeks, Albums: 4 Weeks)   pos/wks

30 Nov 91	SOME LIE 4 LOVE *Mercury MER 358*	**61**	1
21 Dec 91	THE BALLAD OF JAYNE *Mercury MER 361*	**53**	3
5 Mar 88	L.A. GUNS *Vertigo VERH 55*	**73**	1
30 Sep 89	COCKED AND LOADED *Vertigo 8385921*	**45**	2
13 Jul 91	HOLLYWOOD VAMPIRES *Mercury 8496041*	**44**	1

L.A. MIX
UK, male / female vocal / instrumental duo (Singles: 25 Weeks)   pos/wks

10 Oct 87	DON'T STOP (JAMMIN') *Breakout USA 615*	**47**	4
21 May 88 ●	CHECK THIS OUT *Breakout USA 629*	**6**	7
8 Jul 89	GET LOOSE *Breakout USA 659* [1]	**25**	6
16 Sep 89	LOVE TOGETHER *Breakout USA 662* [2]	**66**	2
15 Sep 90	COMING BACK FOR MORE *A&M AM 579*	**50**	3
19 Jan 91	MYSTERIES OF LOVE *A&M AM 707*	**46**	2
23 Mar 91	WE SHOULDN'T HOLD HANDS IN THE DARK *A&M AM 755*	**69**	1

[1] LA Mix featuring Jazzi P [2] LA Mix featuring Kevin Henry

LCD
UK, male production group (Singles: 9 Weeks)   pos/wks

27 Jun 98	ZORBA'S DANCE *Virgin VSCDT 1693*	**20**	5
9 Oct 99	ZORBA'S DANCE (re-issue) *Virgin VSCDT 1757*	**22**	4

LCD SOUNDSYSTEM
US, male production duo – James Murphy and Tim Goldsworthy (Singles: 1 Week)   pos/wks

20 Nov 04	MOVEMENT *EMI DFAEM 12141CD*	**52**	1

LFO
UK, male instrumental group (Singles: 15 Weeks, Albums: 3 Weeks)   pos/wks

14 Jul 90	LFO *Warp WAP 5*	**12**	10
6 Jul 91	WE ARE BACK / NURTURE *Warp 7WAP 14*	**47**	3
1 Feb 92	WHAT IS HOUSE (EP) *Warp WAP 17*	**62**	2
3 Aug 91	FREQUENCIES *Warp WARPLP 3*	**42**	2
10 Feb 96	ADVANCE *Warp WARPCD 39*	**44**	1

Tracks on What Is House (EP): Tan Ta Ra / Mashed Potato / What Is House / Syndrome

LL COOL J   486 Top 500
With a moniker abbreviated from Ladies Love Cool James, the most durable rap star was born James Todd Smith, 18 Jun 1968, New York, US. The first solo rap act to score a UK Top 10 hit with 'I Need Love', which was also the first successful rap 'ballad', he has amassed a record eight US No.1 rap hits (Singles: 105 Weeks, Albums: 44 Weeks)   pos/wks

4 Jul 87	I'M BAD *Def Jam 650856 7*	**71**	1
12 Sep 87 ●	I NEED LOVE *Def Jam 651101 7*	**8**	10
21 Nov 87	GO CUT CREATOR GO *Def Jam LLCJ 1*	**66**	2
13 Feb 88	GOING BACK TO CALI / JACK THE RIPPER *Def Jam LLCJ 2*	**37**	4
10 Jun 89	I'M THAT TYPE OF GUY *Def Jam LLCJ 3*	**43**	5
1 Dec 90	AROUND THE WAY GIRL / MAMA SAID KNOCK YOU OUT *Def Jam 6564470*	**41**	4
9 Mar 91	AROUND THE WAY GIRL (re-mix) *Columbia 6564470*	**36**	4
10 Apr 93	HOW I'M COMIN' *Def Jam 6591692*	**37**	2
20 Jan 96	HEY LOVER *Def Jam DEFCD 14* [1]	**17**	4
1 Jun 96	DOIN' IT *Def Jam DEFCD 15* [2]	**15**	3
5 Oct 96 ●	LOUNGIN' *Def Jam DEFCD 30*	**7**	8
8 Feb 97 ★	AIN'T NOBODY *Geffen GFSTD 22195* ■	**1**	9
5 Apr 97 ●	HIT EM HIGH (THE MONSTARS' ANTHEM) *Atlantic A 5449CD* [3]	**8**	6
1 Nov 97 ●	PHENOMENON *Def Jam 5681172*	**9**	5
28 Mar 98 ●	FATHER *Def Jam 5685292*	**10**	5
11 Jul 98	ZOOM *Interscope IND 95594* [4]	**15**	3
5 Dec 98	INCREDIBLE *Jive 0522102* [5]	**52**	1
26 Oct 02 ●	LUV U BETTER *Def Jam 0638722*	**7**	7
22 Feb 03	PARADISE *Def Jam 0637032* [6]	**18**	5
22 Mar 03 ●	ALL I HAVE *Epic 6736782* [7] ▲	**2**	13
28 Aug 04	HEADSPRUNG *Def Jam 9863759*	**25**	4
15 Feb 86	RADIO *Def Jam DEF 26745*	**71**	1
13 Jun 87	BIGGER AND DEFFER *Def Jam 450 5151*	**54**	19
8 Jul 89	WALKING WITH A PANTHER *Def Jam 465112 1*	**43**	3
13 Oct 90	MAMA SAID KNOCK YOU OUT *Def Jam 4673151*	**49**	2
17 Apr 93	14 SHOTS TO THE DOME *Def Jam 4736782*	**74**	1
16 Nov 96	ALL WORLD *Def Jam 5341252*	**23**	8
25 Oct 97	PHENOMENON *Def Jam 5391862*	**37**	4
23 Sep 00	G.O.A.T. FEATURING JAMES T. SMITH – THE GREATEST OF ALL TIME *Def Jam 5429972* ▲	**29**	2
2 Nov 02	10 *Def Jam 0632192*	**26**	3
11 Sep 04	THE DEFINITION *Def Jam 9863650*	**66**	1

[1] LL Cool J featuring Boyz II Men [2] LL Cool J, guest vocals by LeShaun [3] B Real / Busta Rhymes / Coolio / LL Cool J / Method Man [4] Dr Dre and LL Cool J [5] Keith Murray featuring LL Cool J [6] LL Cool J featuring Amerie [7] Jennifer Lopez featuring LL Cool J

'Jack the Ripper' listed only from 20 Feb 1988

LMC vs U2
UK, male production trio and Ireland, male vocal / instrumental group (Singles: 12 Weeks)   pos/wks

7 Feb 04 ★	TAKE ME TO THE CLOUDS ABOVE *All Around the World CDGLOBE 313* ■	**1**	12

LNR
US, male vocal / instrumental duo (Singles: 2 Weeks)   pos/wks

3 Jun 89	WORK IT TO THE BONE *Kool Kat KOOL 501*	**64**	2

LRS
See D MOB

LSG
Germany, male DJ / producer – Oliver Lieb (Singles: 1 Week)   pos/wks

10 May 97	NETHERWORLD *Hooj Choons HOOJCD 52*	**63**	1

L7
US, female vocal / instrumental group (Singles: 18 Weeks, Albums: 8 Weeks)   pos/wks

4 Apr 92	PRETEND WE'RE DEAD *Slash LASH 34*	**21**	7
30 May 92	EVERGLADE *Slash LASH 36*	**27**	3
12 Sep 92	MONSTER *Slash LASH 38*	**33**	3
28 Nov 92	PRETEND WE'RE DEAD (re-issue) *Slash LASH 42*	**50**	3
9 Jul 94	ANDRES *Slash LASCD 48*	**34**	2
2 May 92	BRICKS ARE HEAVY *Slash 8283072*	**24**	6
23 Jul 94	HUNGRY FOR STINK *Slash 8285312*	**26**	2

L.T.D.
US, male vocal / instrumental group (Singles: 3 Weeks)   pos/wks

9 Sep 78	HOLDING ON (WHEN LOVE IS GONE) *A&M AMS 7378*	**70**	3

LV
US, male vocalist – Larry Sanders (Singles: 25 Weeks)   pos/wks

28 Oct 95 ★	GANGSTA'S PARADISE *Tommy Boy MCSTD 2104* [1] ◆ ■ ▲	**1**	20
23 Dec 95	THROW YOUR HANDS UP / GANGSTA'S PARADISE (re-recording) *Tommy Boy TBCD 699*	**24**	4
4 May 96	I AM LV *Tommy Boy TBCD 7724*	**64**	1

[1] Coolio featuring LV

The version of 'Gangsta's Paradise' coupled with 'Throw Your Hands Up' is a re-recorded version without Coolio's vocals

LWS
Italy, male instrumental group (Singles: 1 Week)   pos/wks

29 Oct 94	GOSP *Transworld TRANNY 4CD*	**65**	1

LA BELLE EPOQUE
France, female vocal trio (Singles: 14 Weeks) pos/wks

27 Aug 77 ●	BLACK IS BLACK (re) *Harvest HAR 5133*	.....2 14

LA BOUCHE
US, male / female rap / vocal duo –
Lane McCray and Melanie Thornton (Singles: 12 Weeks) pos/wks

24 Sep 94	SWEET DREAMS *Bell 74321223912*	.....63 1
15 Jul 95	BE MY LOVER *Arista 74321265402*	.....27 4
30 Sep 95	FALLING IN LOVE *Arista 74321305102*	.....43 2
2 Mar 96	BE MY LOVER (re-mix) *Arista 74321339822*	.....25 4
7 Sep 96	SWEET DREAMS (re-issue) *Arista 74321398542*	.....44 1

LA FLEUR
Holland, male / female vocal / instrumental group (Singles: 4 Weeks) pos/wks

30 Jul 83	BOOGIE NIGHTS *Proto ENA 111*	.....51 4

Sam LA MORE
Australia, male producer – Sam Littlemore (Singles: 1 Week) pos/wks

5 Apr 03	TAKIN' HOLD *Underwater H20 023X*	.....70 1

LA NA NEE NEE NOO NOO *See BANANARAMA*

Danny LA RUE
UK, male vocalist – Daniel Carroll (Singles: 9 Weeks) pos/wks

18 Dec 68	ON MOTHER KELLY'S DOORSTEP *Page One POF 108*	.....33 9

LA TREC *See SASH!*

LaBELLE (see also Nona HENDRYX)
US, female vocal group – lead vocal Patti LaBelle (Singles: 9 Weeks) pos/wks

22 Mar 75	LADY MARMALADE (VOULEZ-VOUS COUCHER AVEC MOI CE SOIR?) *Epic EPC 2852* ▲	.....17 9

Patti LaBELLE (see also LaBELLE)
US, female vocalist – Patricia Holt (Singles: 21 Weeks, Albums: 17 Weeks) pos/wks

3 May 86 ●	ON MY OWN *MCA MCA 1045* [1] ▲	.....2 13
2 Aug 86	OH, PEOPLE *MCA MCA 1075*	.....26 6
3 Sep 94	THE RIGHT KINDA LOVER *MCA MCSTD 1995*	.....50 2
24 May 86	WINNER IN YOU *MCA MCF 3319* ▲	.....30 17

[1] Patti LaBelle and Michael McDonald

Tiff LACEY *See REDD SQUARE featuring Tiff LACEY*

LADIES CHOICE
UK, male vocal / instrumental group (Singles: 4 Weeks) pos/wks

25 Jan 86	FUNKY SENSATION *Sure Delight SD 01*	.....41 4

LADIES FIRST
UK, female vocal trio (Singles: 8 Weeks) pos/wks

24 Nov 01	MESSIN' *Polydor 5873422*	.....30 2
13 Apr 02	I CAN'T WAIT *Polydor 5706912*	.....19 6

LADY G *See B-15 PROJECT featuring Crissy D and Lady G*

LADY J *See RAZE*

LADY OF RAGE
US, female rapper – Robin Allen (Singles: 1 Week) pos/wks

8 Oct 94	AFRO PUFFS *Interscope A 8288CD*	.....72 1

LADY SAW
Jamaica, female vocalist – Marion Hall (Singles: 3 Weeks) pos/wks

16 Dec 00	BUMP N GRIND (I AM FEELING HOT TONIGHT) *Telstar CDSTAS 3129* [1]	.....59 1
20 Oct 01	SINCE I MET YOU LADY / SPARKLE OF MY EYES *DEP International DEPD 55* [2]	.....40 2

[1] M Dubs featuring Lady Saw [2] UB40 featuring Lady Saw

LADYSMITH BLACK MAMBAZO
South Africa, male vocal group (Singles: 26 Weeks, Albums: 69 Weeks) pos/wks

3 Jun 95	SWING LOW SWEET CHARIOT *PolyGram TV SWLOW 2* [1]	.....15 6
3 Jun 95	WORLD IN UNION '95 *PolyGram TV RUGBY 2* [2]	.....47 5
15 Nov 97	INKANYEZI NEZAZI (THE STAR AND THE WISEMAN) *A&M 5823892*	.....33 3
11 Jul 98	THE STAR AND THE WISEMAN (re-issue) *AM:PM 5825692*	.....63 1
16 Oct 99	AIN'T NO SUNSHINE *Universal Music TV 1564332* [3]	.....42 2
18 Dec 99	I SHALL BE THERE *Glow Worm / Epic 6683332* [4]	.....13 9
11 Apr 87	SHAKA ZULU *Warner Bros. WX 94*	.....34 11
22 Nov 97	HEAVENLY *A&M 5407902*	.....53 16
3 Oct 98 ●	THE BEST OF LADYSMITH BLACK MAMBAZO – THE STAR AND THE WISEMAN *PolyGram TV 5652982*	.....2 34
16 Oct 99	IN HARMONY *Universal Music TV 1537392*	.....15 5
12 May 01	THE ULTIMATE COLLECTION *Universal Music TV 5566822*	.....37 3

[1] Ladysmith Black Mambazo featuring China Black [2] Ladysmith Black Mambazo featuring PJ Powers [3] Ladysmith Black Mambazo featuring Des'ree [4] B*Witched featuring Ladysmith Black Mambazo

'The Best of Ladysmith Black Mambazo – The Star and the Wiseman' changed label to Universal Music TV from 13 Mar 99

LADYTRON
UK / Bulgaria, male / female vocal production group (Singles: 3 Weeks) pos/wks

7 Dec 02	SEVENTEEN *Telstar / Invicta Hi-Fi CDSTAS 3284*	.....68 1
22 Mar 03	BLUE JEANS *Invicta Hi-Fi / Telstar CDSTAS 3311*	.....43 1
12 Jul 03	EVIL *Invicta Hi-Fi / Telstar CDSTAS 3331*	.....44 1

LAGUNA (see also SPILLER)
Italy, male DJ / production duo – Cristiano Spiller and Tommy Vee (Singles: 2 Weeks) pos/wks

1 Nov 97	SPILLER FROM RIO (DO IT EASY) *Positiva CDTIV 83*	.....40 2

LAID BACK
Denmark, male vocal / instrumental duo (Singles: 4 Weeks) pos/wks

5 May 90	BAKERMAN *Arista 112356*	.....44 4

LAIN *See WOOKIE*

Cleo LAINE
UK, female vocalist – Clementina Campbell (Singles: 14 Weeks, Albums: 37 Weeks) pos/wks

29 Dec 60	LET'S SLIP AWAY *Fontana H 269*	.....42 1
14 Sep 61	YOU'LL ANSWER TO ME *Fontana H 326*	.....5 13
7 Jan 78	BEST OF FRIENDS *RCA RS 1094* [1]	.....18 22
2 Dec 78	CLEO *Arcade ADEP 37*	.....68 1
31 May 80	SOMETIMES WHEN WE TOUCH *RCA PL 25296* [2]	.....15 14

[1] Cleo Laine and John Williams [2] Cleo Laine and James Galway

Frankie LAINE 〔181 Top 500〕
Powerfully-voiced No.1 hitmaker of the pre-rock years, b. Frank Lovecchio, 30 Mar 1913, Chicago, US. He spent an unequalled 27 weeks at the top of the UK chart in 1953, including a record 18 with 'I Believe'. At one time he had three singles in the Top 5 (Singles: 282 Weeks, Albums: 29 Weeks) pos/wks

14 Nov 52 ●	HIGH NOON (DO NOT FORSAKE ME) *Columbia DB 3113*	.....7 7
14 Nov 52 ●	SUGARBUSH (re) *Columbia DB 3123* [1]	.....8 8
20 Mar 53	THE GIRL IN THE WOOD *Columbia DB 2907*	.....11 1
3 Apr 53 ★	I BELIEVE *Philips PB 117*	.....1 36
8 May 53 ●	TELL ME A STORY (re) *Philips PB 126* [2]	.....5 16
4 Sep 53 ●	WHERE THE WINDS BLOW *Philips PB 167*	.....2 12
16 Oct 53 ★	HEY JOE! *Philips PB 172*	.....1 8
30 Oct 53 ★	ANSWER ME *Philips PB 196*	.....1 17
8 Jan 54 ●	BLOWING WILD *Philips PB 207*	.....2 12
26 Mar 54 ●	GRANADA (re) *Philips PB 242*	.....9 2
16 Apr 54 ●	THE KID'S LAST FIGHT *Philips PB 258*	.....3 10
13 Aug 54 ●	MY FRIEND *Philips PB 316*	.....3 15
8 Oct 54 ●	THERE MUST BE A REASON *Philips PB 306*	.....9 9
22 Oct 54 ●	RAIN, RAIN, RAIN *Philips PB 311* [3]	.....8 16
11 Mar 55	IN THE BEGINNING *Philips PB 404*	.....20 1
24 Jun 55 ●	COOL WATER *Philips PB 465* [4]	.....2 22
15 Jul 55 ●	STRANGE LADY IN TOWN *Philips PB 478*	.....6 13
11 Nov 55	HUMMING BIRD *Philips PB 498*	.....16 1
25 Nov 55 ●	HAWK-EYE *Philips PB 519*	.....7 8
20 Jan 56 ●	SIXTEEN TONS *Philips PB 539* [4]	.....10 3
4 May 56	HELL HATH NO FURY *Philips PB 585*	.....28 1
7 Sep 56 ★	A WOMAN IN LOVE *Philips PB 617*	.....1 21
28 Dec 56	MOONLIGHT GAMBLER (re) *Philips PB 638*	.....13 13
26 Apr 57	LOVE IS A GOLDEN RING *Philips PB 676* [5]	.....19 2
4 Oct 57	GOOD EVENING FRIENDS / UP ABOVE MY HEAD, I HEAR MUSIC IN THE AIR *Philips PB 708* [6]	.....25 4
13 Nov 59 ●	RAWHIDE (re) *Philips PB 965*	.....6 20

			pos/wks
11 May 61		GUNSLINGER *Philips PB 1135*	**50** 1
24 Jun 61	●	HELL BENT FOR LEATHER *Philips BBL 7468*	**7** 23
24 Sep 77	●	THE VERY BEST OF FRANKIE LAINE *Warwick PR 5032*	**7** 6

1 Doris Day and Frankie Laine 2 Jimmy Boyd – Frankie Laine 3 Frankie Laine and The Four Lads 4 Frankie Laine with The Mellomen 5 Frankie Laine and The Easy Riders 6 Frankie Laine and Johnnie Ray

Greg LAKE (see also EMERSON, LAKE and PALMER; EMERSON, LAKE and POWELL; KING CRIMSON)
UK, male vocalist (Singles: 12 Weeks, Albums: 3 Weeks)

			pos/wks
6 Dec 75	●	I BELIEVE IN FATHER CHRISTMAS (2re) *Manticore K 13511* **2** 12
17 Oct 81		GREG LAKE *Chrysalis CHR 1357*	**62** 3

Re-entries occurred in Dec '82 and Dec '83

LAMB *UK, male / female vocal / production duo – Andy Barlow and Louise Rhodes (Singles: 4 Weeks, Albums: 2 Weeks)*

		pos/wks
29 Mar 97	GORECKI *Fontana LAMCD 4*	**30** 2
3 Apr 99	B LINE *Fontana LAMCD 5*	**52** 1
22 May 99	ALL IN YOUR HANDS *Fontana LAMCD 6*	**71** 1
29 May 99	FEAR OF FOURS *Fontana 5588212*	**37** 1
20 Oct 01	WHAT SOUND *Mercury 5865382*	**54** 1

Annabel LAMB
UK, female vocalist (Singles: 7 Weeks, Albums: 1 Week)

		pos/wks
27 Aug 83	RIDERS ON THE STORM *A&M AM 131*	**27** 7
28 Apr 84	THE FLAME *A&M AMLX 68564*	**84** 1

LAMBCHOP *US, male / female vocal / instrumental group (Singles: 1 Week, Albums: 5 Weeks)*

		pos/wks
20 May 00	UP WITH PEOPLE *City Slang 201592*	**66** 1
19 Feb 00	NIXON *City Slang 201522*	**60** 1
2 Mar 02	IS A WOMAN *City Slang 201902*	**38** 2
21 Feb 04	AW CMON / NO YOU CMON *City Slang 5958900*	**45** 2

The LAMBRETTAS *UK, male vocal / instrumental group (Singles: 24 Weeks, Albums: 8 Weeks)*

			pos/wks
1 Mar 80	●	POISON IVY *Rocket XPRESS 25*	**7** 12
24 May 80		D-A-A-ANCE *Rocket XPRESS 33*	**12** 8
23 Aug 80		ANOTHER DAY (ANOTHER GIRL) *Rocket XPRESS 36*	**49** 4
5 Jul 80		BEAT BOYS IN THE JET AGE *Rocket TRAIN 10*	**28** 8

The LAMPIES
US, male / female / canine cartoon vocal group (Singles: 3 Weeks)

		pos/wks
22 Dec 01	LIGHT UP THE WORLD FOR CHRISTMAS *Bluecrest LAMPCD 001*	**48** 3

The LANCASTRIANS
UK, male vocal / instrumental group (Singles: 2 Weeks)

		pos/wks
24 Dec 64	WE'LL SING IN THE SUNSHINE *Pye 7N 15732*	**44** 2

Major LANCE
US, male vocalist, b. 4 Apr 1942, d. 3 Sep 1994 (Singles: 2 Weeks)

		pos/wks
13 Feb 64	UM, UM, UM, UM, UM, UM *Columbia DB 7205*	**40** 2

LANCERS See Teresa BREWER

Valerie LANDSBERG See KIDS FROM 'FAME'

Charlie LANDSBOROUGH
UK, male vocalist / instrumentalist – guitar (Albums: 19 Weeks)

		pos/wks
12 Oct 96	WITH YOU IN MIND *Ritz RITZCD 0078*	**49** 6
8 Nov 97	FURTHER DOWN THE ROAD *Ritz RITZCD 0085*	**42** 3
10 Oct 98	THE VERY BEST OF CHARLIE LANDSBOROUGH *Ritz RZCD 0087*	**41** 2
2 Oct 99	STILL CAN'T SAY GOODBYE *Ritz RZCD 0092*	**39** 2
16 Aug 03	SMILE *Telstar Premiere TPECD 5516*	**37** 6

LANDSCAPE *UK, male vocal / instrumental group (Singles: 20 Weeks, Albums: 12 Weeks)*

			pos/wks
28 Feb 81	●	EINSTEIN A GO-GO *RCA 22*	**5** 13
23 May 81		NORMAN BATES *RCA 60*	**40** 7
21 Mar 81		FROM THE TEAROOMS OF MARS TO THE HELLHOLES OF URANUS *RCA RCALP 5003*	**13** 12

Desmond LANE See Alma COGAN; Cyril STAPLETON and his ORCHESTRA

Ronnie LANE (see also The SMALL FACES) *UK, male vocalist, b. 1 Apr 1946, d. 4 Jun 1997 (Singles: 12 Weeks, Albums: 4 Weeks)*

			pos/wks
12 Jan 74		HOW COME? *GM GMS 011* 1	**11** 8
15 Jun 74		THE POACHER *GM GMS 024* 1	**36** 4
17 Aug 74		ANYMORE FOR ANYMORE ... *GM GML 1013* 1	**48** 1
15 Oct 77		ROUGH MIX *Polydor 2442147* 2	**44** 3

1 Ronnie Lane accompanied by the band Slim Chance 1 Ronnie Lane with the band Slim Chance 2 Pete Townshend and Ronnie Lane

Mark LANEGAN BAND
UK, male vocalist / instrumentalist (Albums: 1 Week)

		pos/wks
14 Aug 04	BUBBLEGUM *Beggars Banquet BBQCD 237*	**43** 1

Emma LANFORD See MOUSSE T

Don LANG *UK, male vocalist / instrumentalist – trombone – Gordon Langhorn, b. 19 Jan 1925, d. 3 Aug 1992 (Singles: 18 Weeks)*

		pos/wks
4 Nov 55	CLOUDBURST (2re) *HMV POP 115*	**16** 4
5 Jul 57	SCHOOL DAY (RING! RING! GOES THE BELL) *HMV POP 350* 1	**26** 2
23 May 58	● WITCH DOCTOR *HMV POP 488* 1	**5** 11
10 Mar 60	SINK THE BISMARCK *HMV POP 714*	**43** 1

1 Don Lang and his Frantic Five

kd lang *Canada, female vocalist – Katherine Dawn Lang (Singles: 25 Weeks, Albums: 71 Weeks)*

			pos/wks
16 May 92		CONSTANT CRAVING *Sire W 0100*	**52** 4
22 Aug 92		CRYING *Virgin America VUS 63* 1	**13** 6
27 Feb 93		CONSTANT CRAVING (re-issue) *Sire W 0157CD*	**15** 8
1 May 93		THE MIND OF LOVE (WHERE IS YOUR HEAD, KATHRYN?) *Sire W 0170CD1*	**72** 1
26 Jun 93		MISS CHATELAINE *Sire W 0181CDX*	**68** 2
11 Dec 93		JUST KEEP ME MOVING *Sire W 0227CD*	**59** 1
30 Sep 95		IF I WERE YOU *Sire W 0319CD*	**53** 1
18 May 96		YOU'RE OK *Warner Bros. W 0332CD*	**44** 2
28 Mar 92	●	INGENUE *Sire 7599268402*	**3** 52
13 Nov 93		EVEN COWGIRLS GET THE BLUES *Sire 9362454332*	**36** 2
14 Oct 95	●	ALL YOU CAN EAT *Warner Bros. 9362460342*	**7** 5
12 Jul 97		DRAG *Warner Bros. 9362466232*	**19** 3
15 Jul 00		INVINCIBLE SUMMER *Warner Bros. 9362476052*	**17** 6
5 Jul 03		A WONDERFUL WORLD *Columbia 5098702* 1	**33** 3

1 Roy Orbison (duet with kd lang) 1 Tony Bennett & kd lang

Thomas LANG
UK, male vocalist (Singles: 3 Weeks, Albums: 1 Week)

		pos/wks
30 Jan 88	THE HAPPY MAN *Epic VOW 4*	**67** 3
20 Feb 88	SCALLYWAG JAZ *Epic 450996 1*	**92** 1

LANGE *UK, male producer – Stuart Langelaan (Singles: 8 Weeks)*

			pos/wks
19 Jun 99		I BELIEVE *Additive 12AD 039* 1	**68** 1
19 Jan 02	●	DRIFTING AWAY *VC Recordings VCRD 101* 2	**9** 6
22 Mar 03		DON'T THINK IT (FEEL IT) *Nebula NEBCD 037* 3	**59** 1

1 Lange featuring Sarah Dwyer 2 Lange featuring Skye 3 Lange featuring Leah

The LANTERNS
UK, male / female vocal / instrumental trio (Singles: 1 Week)

		pos/wks
6 Feb 99	HIGHRISE TOWN *Columbia 6665712*	**50** 1

Mario LANZA *US, male vocalist – Alfredo Cocozza, b. 31 Jan 1921, d. 7 Oct 1959 (Singles: 32 Weeks, Albums: 68 Weeks)*

			pos/wks
14 Nov 52	●	BECAUSE YOU'RE MINE *HMV DA 2017*	**3** 24
4 Feb 55		DRINKING SONG *HMV DA 2065*	**13** 1
18 Feb 55		I'LL WALK WITH GOD (re) *HMV DA 2062*	**18** 2
22 Apr 55		SERENADE (re) *HMV DA 2065*	**15** 3
14 Sep 56		SERENADE (re) *HMV DA 2085*	**25** 2
11 Aug 56	●	THE STUDENT PRINCE *HMV ALP 1186* ▲	**1**
6 Dec 58	●	THE STUDENT PRINCE / THE GREAT CARUSO *RCA RB 16113* ..**4** 21
23 Jul 60	●	THE GREAT CARUSO *RCA RB 16112*	**3** 15
9 Jan 71		HIS GREATEST HITS VOLUME 1 *RCA LSB 4000*	**39** 1
5 Sep 81		THE LEGEND OF MARIO LANZA *K-Tel NE 1110*	**29** 11

14 Nov 87	A PORTRAIT OF MARIO LANZA *Stylus SMR 741*	49	8
12 Mar 94	MARIO LANZA – THE ULTIMATE COLLECTION *RCA Victor 74321185742*	13	7
12 Jun 04	THE DEFINITIVE COLLECTION *BMG 82876614032*	41	4

DA 2065 and DA 2085 are two different songs 'Great Caruso' in 1958 is a film soundtrack

LAPTOP
US, male vocalist / instrumentalist – Jesse Hartman (Singles: 1 Week) pos/wks

12 Jun 99	NOTHING TO DECLARE *Island CID 744*	74	1

LARD *UK, male vocal / instrumental group (Albums: 1 Week)* pos/wks

6 Oct 90	THE LAST TEMPTATION OF REID *Alternative Tentacles VIRUS 84*	69	1

Julius LAROSA *US, male vocalist (Singles: 9 Weeks)* pos/wks

4 Jul 58	TORERO *RCA 1063*	15	9

The LA's *UK, male vocal / instrumental group (Singles: 20 Weeks, Albums: 20 Weeks)* pos/wks

14 Jan 89	THERE SHE GOES *Go Discs GOLASEP 2*	59	4
15 Sep 90	TIMELESS MELODY *Go Discs GOLAS 4*	57	2
3 Nov 90	THERE SHE GOES (re-issue) *Go Discs GOLAS 5*	13	9
16 Feb 91	FEELIN' *Go Discs GOLAS 6*	43	3
10 May 97	FEVER PITCH THE EP *Blanco Y Negro NEG 104CD* [1]	65	1
2 Oct 99	THERE SHE GOES (2nd re-issue) *Polydor 5614032*	65	1
13 Oct 90	THE LA'S *Go Discs 8282021*	30	20

[1] The Pretenders, The La's, Orlando, Neil MacColl, Nick Hornby

Tracks on Fever Pitch the EP: Goin' Back – The Pretenders / There She Goes – The La's / How Can We Hang on to a Dream – Orlando / Football – Neil MacColl, Boo Hewerdine and Nick Hornby

LAS KETCHUP *Spain, female vocal trio (Singles: 26 Weeks)* pos/wks

2 Sep 02	THE KETCHUP SONG (ASEREJE) (IMPORT) *Columbia 6729602CD*	49	4
19 Oct 02	★ THE KETCHUP SONG (ASEREJE) *Columbia 6731932* ■	1	22

Denise LASALLE
US, female vocalist – Denise Craig (Singles: 13 Weeks) pos/wks

15 Jun 85	● MY TOOT TOOT *Epic A 6334*	6	13

LASGO *Belgium, male / female production / vocal / instrumental trio (Singles: 34 Weeks, Albums: 3 Weeks)* pos/wks

9 Mar 02	● SOMETHING *Positiva CDTIV 169*	4	15
24 Aug 02	● ALONE *Positiva CDTIVS 176*	7	8
30 Nov 02	PRAY *Positiva CDTIVS 182*	17	7
1 May 04	SURRENDER *Positiva CDTIVS 205*	24	4
7 Sep 02	SOME THINGS *Positiva 5419362*	30	3

Lisa LASHES
UK, female DJ / producer – Lisa Rose-Wyatt (Singles: 3 Weeks) pos/wks

8 Jul 00	UNBELIEVABLE *Tidy Trax TIDY 138CD*	63	1
25 Oct 03	WHAT CAN YOU DO 4 ME? *Tidy Trax TIDY 194CD*	52	2

James LAST (95) Top 500
The most charted big band formed in 1964 and fronted by German producer / arranger / conductor and composer, b. Hans Last, 17 Apr 1929. Known for his non-stop dance party records, he has reportedly sold in excess of 70 million albums worldwide (Singles: 4 Weeks, Albums: 446 Weeks) pos/wks

3 May 80	THE SEDUCTION (LOVE THEME) *Polydor PD 2071* [1]	48	4
15 Apr 67	● THIS IS JAMES LAST *Polydor 104678* [1]	6	48
22 Jul 67	HAMMOND A-GO-GO *Polydor 249043*	27	10
26 Aug 67	LOVE THIS IS MY SONG *Polydor 583553*	32	2
26 Aug 67	NON-STOP DANCING *Polydor 236203*	35	1
22 Jun 68	JAMES LAST GOES POP *Polydor 249160*	32	3
8 Feb 69	DANCING '68 VOLUME 1 *Polydor 249216*	40	1
31 May 69	TRUMPET A-GO-GO *Polydor 249239*	13	1
9 Aug 69	NON-STOP DANCING '69 *Polydor 249294*	26	1
24 Jan 70	NON-STOP DANCING '69/2 *Polydor 249354*	27	3
23 May 70	NON-STOP EVERGREENS *Polydor 249370*	26	1
11 Jul 70	NON-STOP DANCING '70 *Polydor 237104*	44	1
11 Jul 70	CLASSICS UP TO DATE *Polydor 249371*	67	1

24 Oct 70	VERY BEST OF JAMES LAST *Polydor 2371054*	45	4
8 May 71	NON-STOP DANCING '71 *Polydor 2371111*	21	4
26 Jun 71	SUMMER HAPPENING *Polydor 2371133*	38	1
18 Sep 71	BEACH PARTY 2 *Polydor 2371121*	47	1
2 Oct 71	YESTERDAY'S MEMORIES *Contour 2870117*	17	14
16 Oct 71	NON-STOP DANCING 12 *Polydor 2371141*	30	3
19 Feb 72	NON-STOP DANCING 13 *Polydor 2371189*	32	2
4 Mar 72	POLKA PARTY *Polydor 2371190*	22	3
29 Apr 72	JAMES LAST IN CONCERT *Polydor 2371191*	13	6
24 Jun 72	VOODOO PARTY *Polydor 2371235*	45	1
16 Sep 72	CLASSICS UP TO DATE VOLUME 2 *Polydor 184061*	49	1
30 Sep 72	LOVE MUST BE THE REASON *Polydor 2371281*	32	2
27 Jan 73	THE MUSIC OF JAMES LAST *Polydor 2683010*	19	12
24 Feb 73	NON-STOP DANCING VOLUME 14 *Polydor 2371319*	27	3
24 Feb 73	JAMES LAST IN RUSSIA *Polydor 2371293*	12	9
28 Jul 73	OLE *Polydor 2371384*	24	5
1 Sep 73	NON-STOP DANCING VOLUME 15 *Polydor 2371376*	34	2
20 Apr 74	NON-STOP DANCING VOLUME 16 *Polydor 2371444*	43	2
29 Jun 74	IN CONCERT VOLUME 2 *Polydor 2371320*	49	1
23 Nov 74	GOLDEN MEMORIES *Polydor 2371472*	39	2
26 Jul 75	● TEN YEARS NON-STOP JUBILEE *Polydor 2660111*	5	16
2 Aug 75	VIOLINS IN LOVE *K-Tel 1*	60	1
22 Nov 75	● MAKE THE PARTY LAST *Polydor 2371612*	3	19
8 May 76	CLASSICS UP TO DATE VOLUME 3 *Polydor 2371538*	54	1
6 May 78	EAST TO WEST *Polydor 2630092*	49	4
14 Apr 79	● LAST THE WHOLE NIGHT LONG *Polydor PTD 001*	2	45
23 Aug 80	THE BEST FROM 150 GOLD RECORDS *Polydor 2681 211*	56	3
1 Nov 80	CLASSICS FOR DREAMING *Polydor POLTV 11*	12	18
14 Feb 81	ROSES FROM THE SOUTH *Polydor 2372 051*	41	5
21 Nov 81	HANSIMANIA *Polydor POLTV 14*	18	13
28 Nov 81	LAST FOREVER *Polydor 2630 135*	88	2
5 Mar 83	BLUEBIRD *Polydor POLD 5072*	57	3
30 Apr 83	NON-STOP DANCING '83 – PARTY POWER *Polydor POLD 5094*	56	2
30 Apr 83	THE BEST OF MY GOLD RECORDS *Polydor PODV 7*	42	5
3 Dec 83	THE GREATEST SONGS OF THE BEATLES *Polydor POLD 5119*	52	8
24 Mar 84	THE ROSE OF TRALEE AND OTHER IRISH FAVOURITES *Polydor POLD 5131*	21	11
13 Oct 84	PARADISE *Polydor POLD 5163*	74	2
8 Dec 84	JAMES LAST IN SCOTLAND *Polydor POLD 5166*	68	9
14 Sep 85	LEAVE THE BEST TO LAST *Polydor PROLP 7*	11	27
18 Apr 87	BY REQUEST *Polydor POLH 34*	22	11
26 Nov 88	DANCE DANCE DANCE *Polydor JLTV 1*	38	8
14 Apr 90	CLASSICS BY MOONLIGHT *Polydor 8432181*	12	12
15 Jun 91	● POP SYMPHONIES *Polydor 8494291*	10	11
9 Nov 91	TOGETHER AT LAST *Delphine / Polydor 5115251* [2]	14	15
12 Sep 92	VIVA ESPANA *PolyGram TV 5172202*	23	5
20 Nov 93	JAMES LAST PLAYS ANDREW LLOYD WEBBER *Polydor 5199102*	12	10
19 Nov 94	IN HARMONY *Polydor 5238242* [2]	28	7
18 Nov 95	THE VERY BEST OF JAMES LAST & HIS ORCHESTRA *Polydor 5295562*	36	7
28 Mar 98	POP SYMPHONIES 2 *Polydor 5396242* [3]	32	3
24 Apr 99	COUNTRY ROADS *Polydor / Universal TV 5474022*	18	5
3 Nov 01	JAMES LAST AND HIS ORCHESTRA PLAYS ABBA *Polydor 5891982* [3]	29	4
6 Sep 03	THE CLASSICAL COLLECTION *UCJ 9810457*	44	3

[1] James Last Band [1] James Last Band [2] Richard Clayderman and James Last [3] James Last and his Orchestra

LAST RHYTHM
Italy, male instrumental / production group (Singles: 1 Week) pos/wks

14 Sep 96	LAST RHYTHM *Stress CDSTR 76*	62	1

LATANZA WATERS See E-SMOOVE featuring Latanza WATERS

The LATE SHOW
UK, male vocal / instrumental group (Singles: 6 Weeks) pos/wks

3 Mar 79	BRISTOL STOMP *Decca F 13822*	40	6

LATIN QUARTER *UK, male / female vocal / instrumental group (Singles: 10 Weeks, Albums: 3 Weeks)* pos/wks

18 Jan 86	RADIO AFRICA *Rockin' Horse RH 102*	19	9
18 Apr 87	NOMZAMO (ONE PEOPLE ONE CAUSE) *Rockin' Horse RH 113*	73	1
1 Mar 86	MODERN TIMES *Rockin' Horse RHLP 1*	91	2
6 Jun 87	MICK AND CAROLINE *Rockin' Horse 208 142*	96	1

°LATIN RHYTHM See Tito PUENTE Jr and The LATIN RHYTHM featuring Tito PUENTE, INDIA and Cali ALEMAN

LATIN THING Canada / Spain, male / female vocal / instrumental group (Singles: 1 Week)   pos/wks

13 Jul 96	LATIN THING Faze 2 CDFAZE 33	41 1

Gino LATINO Italy, male producer – Giacomo Maiolini (aka Lorenzo Cherubini) (Singles: 7 Weeks)   pos/wks

20 Jan 90	WELCOME ffrr F 126	17 7

LATINO RAVE See VARIOUS ARTISTS (MONTAGES)

LATOUR US, male vocalist / producer – William LaTour (Singles: 7 Weeks)   pos/wks

8 Jun 91	PEOPLE ARE STILL HAVING SEX Polydor PO 147	15 7

Stacy LATTISAW US, female vocalist (Singles: 14 Weeks)   pos/wks

14 Jun 80 ●	JUMP TO THE BEAT Atlantic / Cotillion K 11496	3 11
30 Aug 80	DYNAMITE Atlantic K 11554	51 3

Dave LAUDAT See HUSTLERS CONVENTION featuring Dave LAUDAT and Ondrea DUVERNEY

LAUNCHERS See Ezz RECO and The LAUNCHERS with Boysie GRANT

Cyndi LAUPER 349 Top 500 Flamboyant and versatile singer / songwriter, b. 20 Jun 1953, New York, US. Her debut album, 'She's So Unusual' (1983), spawned four Top 5 US singles, and she won a Grammy for Best New Artist of 1984 (easily outpacing her major female rival, Madonna) (Singles: 103 Weeks, Albums: 92 Weeks)   pos/wks

14 Jan 84 ●	GIRLS JUST WANT TO HAVE FUN Portrait A 3943	2 12
24 Mar 84 ●	TIME AFTER TIME (re) Portrait A 4290 ▲	3 17
1 Sep 84	SHE BOP Portrait A 4620	46 5
17 Nov 84	ALL THROUGH THE NIGHT Portrait A 4849	64 4
20 Sep 86	TRUE COLOURS Portrait 650026 7 ▲	12 11
27 Dec 86	CHANGE OF HEART (re) Portrait CYNDI 1	67 2
28 Mar 87	WHAT'S GOING ON Portrait CYN 1	57 3
20 May 89 ●	I DROVE ALL NIGHT Epic CYN 4	7 12
5 Aug 89	MY FIRST NIGHT WITHOUT YOU Epic CYN 5	53 4
30 Dec 89	HEADING WEST Epic CYN 6	68 1
6 Jun 92	THE WORLD IS STONE Epic 6579707	15 7
13 Nov 93	THAT'S WHAT I THINK Epic 6598782	31 4
8 Jan 94	WHO LET IN THE RAIN Epic 6590392	32 4
17 Sep 94 ●	HEY NOW (GIRLS JUST WANT TO HAVE FUN) (re-recording) Epic 6608072	4 13
11 Feb 95	I'M GONNA BE STRONG Epic 6611962	37 2
26 Aug 95	COME ON HOME Epic 6614255	39 2
1 Feb 97	YOU DON'T KNOW Epic 6641845	27 2
18 Feb 84	SHE'S SO UNUSUAL Portrait PRT 25792	16 32
11 Oct 86	TRUE COLORS Portrait PRT 26948	25 12
1 Jul 89 ●	A NIGHT TO REMEMBER Epic 462499 1	9 12
27 Nov 93	HAT FULL OF STARS Epic 4730542	56 1
3 Sep 94 ●	TWELVE DEADLY CYNS ... AND THEN SOME Epic 4773632	2 34
22 Feb 97	SISTERS OF AVALON Epic 4853702	59 1

LAUREL and HARDY UK / US, male comedians / actors / vocal / instrumental duo – Stan Laurel, b. Arthur Jefferson, 16 Jun 1890, d. 23 Feb 1965, and Oliver Hardy, b. 18 Jan 1892, d. 7 Aug 1957 (Singles: 10 Weeks, Albums: 4 Weeks)   pos/wks

22 Nov 75 ●	THE TRAIL OF THE LONESOME PINE United Artists UP 36026 [1]	2 10
6 Dec 75	THE GOLDEN AGE OF HOLLYWOOD COMEDY United Artists UAG 29676	55 4

[1] Laurel and Hardy with the Avalon Boys featuring Chill Wills

LAUREL and HARDY UK, male vocal / instrumental reggae duo (Singles: 2 Weeks)   pos/wks

2 Apr 83	CLUNK CLINK CBS A 3213	65 2

LAURNEA US, female vocalist – Laurnea Wilkinson (Singles: 2 Weeks)   pos/wks

12 Jul 97	DAYS OF YOUTH Epic 6646932	36 2

Lauren LAVERNE See KENICKIE; MINT ROYALE

Avril LAVIGNE 465 Top 500 Internationally successful pop punk princess who was the first female soloist under the age of 20 to top the albums chart, b. 30 Sep 1984, Ontario, Canada. 'Let Go' sold over 14 million worldwide and she won Best Female Pop / Rock Artist at the 2004 World Music Awards (Singles: 58 Weeks, Albums: 96 Weeks)   pos/wks

7 Sep 02	COMPLICATED (import) (re) RCA 74321955782	64 2
5 Oct 02 ●	COMPLICATED Arista 74321965962	3 9
28 Dec 02 ●	SK8ER BOI Arista 74321979782	8 9
12 Apr 03 ●	I'M WITH YOU Arista 82876506712	7 10
19 Jul 03	LOSING GRIP (re) Arista 82876534542	22 6
22 May 04 ●	DON'T TELL ME Arista 82876617422	5 9
14 Aug 04 ●	MY HAPPY ENDING Arista 82876636492	5 9
27 Nov 04	NOBODY'S HOME Arista 82876663652	24 4
14 Sep 02 ★	LET GO Arista 74321949312	1 66
5 Jun 04 ★	UNDER MY SKIN Arista 82876617872 ■ ▲	1 30+

The LAW UK, male vocal / instrumental duo – Paul Rodgers and Kenny Jones (Albums: 1 Week)   pos/wks

6 Apr 91	THE LAW Atlantic 7567821951	61 1

Joanna LAW UK, female vocalist (Singles: 8 Weeks)   pos/wks

7 Jul 90	FIRST TIME EVER Citybeat CBE 752	67 3
14 Sep 96	THE GIFT Deconstruction 74321401912 [1]	15 5

[1] Way Out West featuring Miss Joanna Law

Law's contribution to 'The Gift' is a sample from 'First Time Ever'

Steve LAWLER UK, male DJ / producer (Singles: 1 Week)   pos/wks

11 Nov 00	RISE 'IN Bedrock BEDRCDS 008	50 1

Belle LAWRENCE UK, female vocalist (Singles: 1 Week)   pos/wks

30 Mar 02	EVERGREEN Euphoric CDUPH 024	73 1

Billy LAWRENCE See RAMPAGE featuring Billy LAWRENCE

Joey LAWRENCE US, male vocalist (Singles: 15 Weeks, Albums: 3 Weeks)   pos/wks

26 Jun 93	NOTHIN' MY LOVE CAN'T FIX EMI CDEM 271	13 7
28 Aug 93	I CAN'T HELP MYSELF EMI CDEM 277	27 4
30 Oct 93	STAY FOREVER EMI CDEM 289	41 3
19 Sep 98	NEVER GONNA CHANGE MY MIND Curb CUBC 34	49 1
31 Jul 93	JOEY LAWRENCE EMI CDEMC 3657	39 3

Lee LAWRENCE UK, male vocalist – Leon Siroto, b. 1921, d. Feb 1961 (Singles: 10 Weeks)   pos/wks

20 Nov 53 ●	CRYING IN THE CHAPEL (re) Decca F 10177	7 6
2 Dec 55	SUDDENLY THERE'S A VALLEY (re) Columbia DB 3681	14 4

With Ray Martin and his Orchestra

Sophie LAWRENCE UK, female vocalist (Singles: 7 Weeks)   pos/wks

3 Aug 91	LOVE'S UNKIND IQ ZB 44821	21 7

Steve LAWRENCE US, male vocalist – Sidney Leibowitz (Singles: 27 Weeks)   pos/wks

21 Apr 60 ●	FOOTSTEPS HMV POP 726	4 13
18 Aug 60	GIRLS, GIRLS, GIRLS London HLT 9166	49 1
22 Aug 63 ●	I WANT TO STAY HERE CBS AAG 163 [1]	3 13

[1] Steve and Eydie

Syd LAWRENCE UK, orchestra – leader b. 26 Jun 1924, d. 5 May 1998 (Albums: 9 Weeks)   pos/wks

8 Aug 70	MORE MILLER AND OTHER BIG BAND MAGIC Philips 6642001	14 4
25 Dec 71	MUSIC OF GLENN MILLER IN SUPER STEREO Philips 6641017	43 2
25 Dec 71	SYD LAWRENCE WITH THE GLENN MILLER SOUND Fontana SFL 13178	31 2
26 Feb 72	SOMETHING OLD SOMETHING NEW Philips 6308090	34 1

Lisa LAWS See CM2 featuring Lisa LAWS

Ronnie LAWS
US, male vocalist / instrumentalist – saxophone (Albums: 1 Week) pos/wks

| 17 Oct 81 | SOLID GROUND *Liberty LBG 30336* | 100 | 1 |

LAYO & BUSHWACKA! *UK, male DJ / production duo – Layo*
Paskin and Matthew Benjamin (Singles: 12 Weeks, Albums: 1 Week) pos/wks

22 Jun 02	LOVE STORY *XL Recordings XLS 144CD*	30	2
25 Jan 03	● LOVE STORY (VS FINALLY) *XL Recordings XLS 154CD*	8	7
16 Aug 03	IT'S UP TO YOU (SHINING THROUGH) *XL Recordings XLS 163CD*	25	3
13 Jul 02	NIGHT WORKS *XL Recordings XLCD 154*	61	1

Lindy LAYTON
UK, female vocalist – Belinda Layton (Singles: 28 Weeks) pos/wks

10 Feb 90	★ DUB BE GOOD TO ME *Go Beat GOD 39* [1]	1	13
11 Aug 90	SILLY GAMES *Arista 113452* [2]	22	7
26 Jan 91	ECHO MY HEART *Arista 113845*	42	2
31 Aug 91	WITHOUT YOU (ONE AND ONE) *Arista 114636*	71	2
24 Apr 93	WE GOT THE LOVE *PWL International PWCD 250*	38	3
30 Oct 93	SHOW ME *PWL International PWCD 275*	47	1

[1] Beats International featuring Lindy Layton [2] Lindy Layton featuring Janet Kay

Peter LAZONBY
UK, male DJ / producer (Singles: 1 Week) pos/wks

| 10 Jun 00 | SACRED CYCLES *Hooj Choons HOOJ 93CD* | 49 | 1 |

Doug LAZY
US, male rapper – Gene Finley
(Singles: 9 Weeks, Albums: 1 Week) pos/wks

15 Jul 89	LET IT ROLL *Atlantic A 8866* [1]	27	5
4 Nov 89	LET THE RHYTHM PUMP *Atlantic A 8784*	45	3
26 May 90	LET THE RHYTHM PUMP (re-mix) *East West A 7919*	63	1
10 Mar 90	DOUG LAZY GETTIN' CRAZY *Atlantic 7567820661*	65	1

[1] Raze presents Doug Lazy

Keith LE BLANC *See Malcolm X*

LE CLICK *Sweden / US, male / female vocal duo –*
Kayo Shekoni and Robert Haynes (Singles: 2 Weeks) pos/wks

| 30 Aug 97 | CALL ME *Logic 74321509672* | 38 | 2 |

Kele LE ROC *UK, female vocalist – Kelly*
Biggs (Singles: 17 Weeks, Albums: 2 Weeks) pos/wks

31 Oct 98	● LITTLE BIT OF LOVIN' *1st Avenue / Wild Card / Polydor 5672812*	8	7
27 Mar 99	● MY LOVE *1st Avenue / Wild Card / Polydor 5636112*	8	7
30 Sep 00	THINKING OF YOU *Telstar CDSTAS 3136* [1]	70	1
7 Jun 03	FEELIN' U *London FCD 409* [2]	34	2
10 Apr 99	EVERYBODY'S SOMEBODY *Wild Card 5596662*	44	2

[1] Curtis Lynch Jr featuring Kele Le Roc and Red Rat [2] Shy FX and T-Power featuring Kele Le Roc

LEAGUE UNLIMITED ORCHESTRA *See HUMAN LEAGUE*

LEAH *See LANGE*

Vicky LEANDROS *Greece, female vocalist –*
Vassiliki Papathanassiou (Singles: 29 Weeks) pos/wks

8 Apr 72	● COME WHAT MAY *Philips 6000 049*	2	16
23 Dec 72	THE LOVE IN YOUR EYES (2re) *Philips 6000 081*	40	8
7 Jul 73	WHEN BOUZOUKIS PLAYED (re) *Philips 6000 111*	44	5

Denis LEARY
US, male vocalist / comedian (Singles: 2 Weeks) pos/wks

| 13 Jan 96 | ASSHOLE *A&M 5813352* | 58 | 2 |

The LEAVES *Iceland, male vocal /*
instrumental group (Singles: 1 Week, Albums: 1 Week) pos/wks

| 18 May 02 | RACE *B Unique BUN 020CDS* | 66 | 1 |
| 31 Aug 02 | BREATHE *B Unique 0927487392* | 71 | 1 |

LED ZEPPELIN [79] Top 500
(see also COVERDALE / PAGE) *Hard rock's most successful album act: Robert Plant (v), Jimmy Page (g), John Paul Jones (b/k), John Bonham (d), d. 1980. Innovative, pioneering quartet have sold an estimated 200 million albums, including over 100 million in the US, where they scored seven No.1s from 1969-2003 (Singles: 2 Weeks, Albums: 495 Weeks)* pos/wks

13 Sep 97	WHOLE LOTTA LOVE *Atlantic ATT 0013CD*	21	2
12 Apr 69	● LED ZEPPELIN *Atlantic 588171*	6	71
8 Nov 69	★ LED ZEPPELIN II *Atlantic 588198* ▲	1	136
7 Nov 70	★ LED ZEPPELIN III *Atlantic 2401002* ■ ▲	1	40
27 Nov 71	★ FOUR SYMBOLS (LED ZEPPELIN IV) *Atlantic K 2401012*	1	69
14 Apr 73	★ HOUSES OF THE HOLY *Atlantic K 50014* ■ ▲	1	13
15 Mar 75	★ PHYSICAL GRAFFITI *Swan Song SSK 89400* ■ ▲	1	27
24 Apr 76	★ PRESENCE *Swan Song SSK 59402* ■ ▲	1	14
6 Nov 76	★ THE SONG REMAINS THE SAME *Swan Song SSK 89402*	1	15
8 Sep 79	★ IN THROUGH THE OUT DOOR *Swan Song SSK 59410* ■ ▲	1	16
4 Dec 82	● CODA *Swan Song A 0051*	4	7
27 Oct 90	● REMASTERS *Atlantic ZEP 1*	10	45
10 Nov 90	LED ZEPPELIN *Atlantic 7567821441*	48	2
9 Oct 93	LED ZEPPELIN BOXED SET II *Atlantic 7567824772*	56	1
29 Nov 97	BBC SESSIONS *Atlantic 7567830612*	23	7
1 Apr 00	LATTER DAYS – THE BEST OF LED ZEPPELIN VOLUME TWO *Atlantic 7567832782*	40	1
1 Apr 00	EARLY DAYS – THE BEST OF LED ZEPPELIN VOLUME ONE *Atlantic 7567832682*	55	1
8 Mar 03	VERY BEST OF – EARLY DAYS & LATTER DAYS *Atlantic 7567836195*	11	23
7 Jun 03	● HOW THE WEST WAS WON *Atlantic 7567835872* ▲	5	7

'Led Zeppelin II' changed label / number to Atlantic K 40037 and 'Four Symbols (Led Zeppelin IV)' changed to Atlantic K 50008 during their chart runs. The fourth Led Zeppelin album appeared in the chart under various guises: 'The Fourth Led Zeppelin Album', 'Runes', 'The New Led Zeppelin Album', 'Led Zeppelin IV' and 'Four Symbols'. The two albums titled Led Zeppelin are different. (The 1990 entry was a boxed CD set of old and previously unreleased material).

Angel LEE
UK, female vocalist – Angelique Beckford (Singles: 1 Week) pos/wks

| 3 Jun 00 | WHAT'S YOUR NAME? *WEA WEA 258CD* | 39 | 1 |

Ann LEE
UK, female vocalist – Annerley Gordon (Singles: 21 Weeks) pos/wks

11 Sep 99	2 TIMES (import) *ZYX ZYX 90188*	57	2
16 Oct 99	● 2 TIMES *Systematic SYSCD 31*	2	16
4 Mar 00	VOICES *Systematic SYSCD 32*	27	3

Brenda LEE [223] Top 500
Biggest-selling teenage female vocalist of the early rock years, b. Brenda Tarpley, 11 Dec 1944, Georgia, US. She first recorded aged 11, had back-to-back UK / US hits in the early 1960s, was inducted into the Country Music Hall of Fame in 1997 and the Rock and Roll Hall of Fame in 2002 (Singles: 210 Weeks, Albums: 64 Weeks) pos/wks

17 Mar 60	● SWEET NUTHIN'S (re) *Brunswick 05819*	4	19
30 Jun 60	I'M SORRY *Brunswick 05833* ▲	12	16
20 Oct 60	I WANT TO BE WANTED *Brunswick 05839* ▲	31	6
19 Jan 61	LET'S JUMP THE BROOMSTICK *Brunswick 05823*	12	15
6 Apr 61	EMOTIONS *Brunswick 05847*	45	1
20 Jul 61	DUM DUM *Brunswick 05854*	22	8
16 Nov 61	FOOL NUMBER ONE *Brunswick 05860*	38	3
8 Feb 62	BREAK IT TO ME GENTLY *Brunswick 05864*	46	2
5 Apr 62	● SPEAK TO ME PRETTY *Brunswick 05867*	3	12
21 Jun 62	HERE COMES THAT FEELING *Brunswick 05871*	5	12
13 Sep 62	IT STARTED ALL OVER AGAIN *Brunswick 05876*	15	11
29 Nov 62	● ROCKIN' AROUND THE CHRISTMAS TREE *Brunswick 05880*	6	7
17 Jan 63	ALL ALONE AM I *Brunswick 05882*	7	17
28 Mar 63	● LOSING YOU *Brunswick 05886*	10	16
18 Jul 63	I WONDER *Brunswick 05891*	14	9
31 Oct 63	SWEET IMPOSSIBLE YOU *Brunswick 05896*	28	6
9 Jan 64	● AS USUAL *Brunswick 05899*	5	15
9 Apr 64	THINK *Brunswick 05903*	26	8
10 Sep 64	IS IT TRUE *Brunswick 05915*	17	8
10 Dec 64	CHRISTMAS WILL BE JUST ANOTHER LONELY DAY *Brunswick 05921*	25	1
4 Feb 65	THANKS A LOT *Brunswick 05927*	41	2
29 Jul 65	TOO MANY RIVERS *Brunswick 05936*	22	12
24 Nov 62	ALL THE WAY *Brunswick LAT 8383*	20	2
16 Feb 63	BRENDA – THAT'S ALL *Brunswick LAT 8516*	13	9

13 Apr 63 ●	ALL ALONE AM I *Brunswick LAT 8530*	8	20
16 Jul 66	BYE BYE BLUES *Brunswick LAT 8649*	21	2
1 Nov 80	LITTLE MISS DYNAMITE *Warwick WW 5083*	15	11
7 Jan 84	25TH ANNIVERSARY *MCA MCLD 609*	65	4
30 Mar 85	THE VERY BEST OF BRENDA LEE *MCA LETV 1*	16	9
15 Oct 94	THE VERY BEST OF BRENDA LEE ... WITH LOVE		
	Telstar TCD 2738	20	7

Byron LEE *See Boris GARDINER*

Curtis LEE *US, male vocalist (Singles: 2 Weeks)*   pos/wks

31 Aug 61	PRETTY LITTLE ANGEL EYES (re) *London HLX 9397*	47	2

Dave LEE *See HED BOYS; Li KWAN; RAVEN MAIZE; Joey NEGRO; Z FACTOR; JAKATTA; AKABU featuring Linda CLIFFORD; IL PADRINOS featuring Jocelyn BROWN*

Dee C LEE (see also The STYLE COUNCIL)
UK, female vocalist – Diane Sealey (Singles: 20 Weeks)   pos/wks

9 Nov 85 ●	SEE THE DAY *CBS A 6570*	3	12
8 Mar 86	COME HELL OR WATERS HIGH *CBS A 6869*	46	5
13 Nov 93	NO TIME TO PLAY *Cooltempo CDCOOL 282* [1]	25	3

[1] Guru featuring Dee C Lee

Garry LEE and SHOWDOWN
Canada, male vocal / instrumental group (Singles: 3 Weeks)   pos/wks

31 Jul 93	THE RODEO SONG *Party Dish VCD 101*	44	3

Jackie LEE
UK, female vocalist – Jackie Flood (Singles: 31 Weeks)   pos/wks

10 Apr 68 ●	WHITE HORSES *Philips BF 1647* [1]	10	14
2 Jan 71	RUPERT *Pye 7N 45003*	14	17

[1] Jacky

Jacknife LEE *See RUN-DMC*

Leapy LEE
UK, male vocalist – Lee Graham (Singles: 28 Weeks)   pos/wks

21 Aug 68 ●	LITTLE ARROWS *MCA MU 1028*	2	21
20 Dec 69	GOOD MORNING (re) *MCA MK 5021*	29	7

Murphy LEE *See NELLY*

LEE-O *See K-WARREN featuring LEE-O*

Peggy LEE *US, female vocalist – Norma Jean Egstrom, b. 26 May 1920, d. 22 Jan 2002 (Singles: 29 Weeks, Albums: 23 Weeks)*   pos/wks

24 May 57 ●	MR WONDERFUL *Brunswick 05671*	5	13
15 Aug 58 ●	FEVER *Capitol CL 14902*	5	11
23 Mar 61	TILL THERE WAS YOU (re) *Capitol CL 15184*	30	4
22 Aug 92	FEVER (re-issue) *Capitol PEG 1*	75	1
4 Jun 60 ●	LATIN A LA LEE *Capitol T 1290*	8	15
11 Jun 60	BEAUTY AND THE BEAT *Capitol T 1219* [1]	16	6
20 May 61	BEST OF PEGGY LEE VOLUME 2 *Brunswick LAT 8355*	18	1
21 Oct 61	BLACK COFFEE *Ace of Hearts AH 5*	20	1

[1] Peggy Lee and George Shearing

Toney LEE *US, male vocalist (Singles: 4 Weeks)*   pos/wks

29 Jan 83	REACH UP *TMT TMT 2*	64	4

Tracey LEE *US, male vocalist (Singles: 1 Week)*   pos/wks

19 Jul 97	THE THEME *Universal UND 56133*	51	1

LEE-CABRERA *US, male production duo – Steve Lee and Albert Cabrera (Singles: 10 Weeks)*   pos/wks

12 Apr 03	SHAKE IT (NO TE MUEVAS TANTO) *Credence 12CDRED 035*	..58	1
6 Sep 03	SHAKE IT (MOVE A LITTLE CLOSER)		
	Credence CDCRED 039 [1]	16	6
15 Nov 03	SPECIAL 2003 *Credence CDCRED 040*	45	2
10 Jul 04	VOODOO LOVE *C2 CDC 2001* [2]	58	1

[1] Lee-Cabrera featuring Alex Cartaña [2] Lee-Cabrera presents Phase 2

'Shake it (Move a Little Closer)' is an English language version of the first hit

LEEDS UNITED FC
UK, male football team vocalists (Singles: 13 Weeks)   pos/wks

29 Apr 72 ●	LEEDS UNITED *Chapter One SCH 168*	10	10
25 Apr 92	LEEDS, LEEDS, LEEDS (re) *Q Music LUFC 2*	54	3

Carol LEEMING *See STAXX*

Raymond LEFEVRE
France, orchestra (Singles: 2 Weeks, Albums: 9 Weeks)   pos/wks

15 May 68	SOUL COAXING *Major Minor MM 559*	46	2
7 Oct 67 ●	RAYMOND LEFEVRE *Major Minor MMLP 4*	10	7
17 Feb 68	RAYMOND LEFEVRE VOLUME 2 *Major Minor SMLP 13*	37	2

LEFTFIELD *UK, male instrumental / production duo – Neil Barnes and Paul Daley (Singles: 23 Weeks, Albums: 114 Weeks)*   pos/wks

12 Dec 92	SONG OF LIFE *Hard Hands HAND 002T*	59	1
13 Nov 93	OPEN UP *Hard Hands HAND 009CD* [1]	13	5
25 Mar 95	ORIGINAL *Hard Hands HAND 18CD* [2]	18	3
5 Aug 95	THE AFRO-LEFT EP *Hard Hands HAND 23CD* [3]	22	3
20 Jan 96	RELEASE THE PRESSURE *Hard Hands HAND 29CD*	13	3
18 Sep 99 ●	AFRIKA SHOX *Hard Hands HAND 057CD1* [4]	7	5
11 Dec 99	DUSTED (re) *Hard Hands HAND 058CD1* [5]	28	3
11 Feb 95 ●	LEFTISM *Hard Hands HANDCD 2*	3	94
2 Oct 99 ★	RHYTHM AND STEALTH		
	Higher Ground / Hard Hands HANDCD 4 ■	1	20

[1] Leftfield Lydon [2] Leftfield Halliday [3] Leftfield featuring Djum Djum [4] Leftfield / Bambaataa [5] Leftfield / Roots Manuva

Tracks on The Afro-Left EP: Afro-Left / Afro Ride / Afro Central / Afro Sol

LEGEND B
Germany, male production duo (Singles: 1 Week)   pos/wks

22 Feb 97	LOST IN LOVE *Perfecto PERF 132CD*	45	1

Tom LEHRER *US, male comedian / vocalist (Albums: 26 Weeks)*   pos/wks

8 Nov 58 ●	SONGS BY TOM LEHRER *Decca LF 1311*	7	19
25 Jun 60 ●	AN EVENING WASTED WITH TOM LEHRER *Decca LK 4332*	7	7

Jody LEI *South Africa, female vocalist (Singles: 2 Weeks)*   pos/wks

22 Feb 03	SHOWDOWN *Independiente ISOM 66MS*	34	2

Denise LEIGH & Jane GILCHRIST
UK, female vocalists (Albums: 2 Weeks)   pos/wks

8 Nov 03	OPERATUNITY WINNERS *EMI Classics 05575942*	60	2

LEILANI
UK, female vocalist – Leilani Sen (Singles: 7 Weeks)   pos/wks

6 Feb 99	MADNESS THING *ZTT ZTT 124CD*	19	4
12 Jun 99	DO YOU WANT ME? *ZTT ZTT 134CD*	40	2
3 Jun 00	FLYING ELVIS *ZTT ZTT 145CD*	73	1

Paul LEKAKIS *US, male vocalist (Singles: 4 Weeks)*   pos/wks

30 May 87	BOOM BOOM (LET'S GO BACK TO MY ROOM)		
	Champion CHAMP 43	60	4

LEMAR *UK, male vocalist – Lamar Obika*
(Singles: 33 Weeks, Albums: 22 Weeks)   pos/wks

30 Aug 03 ●	DANCE (WITH U) *Sony Music 6741325*	2	11
29 Nov 03 ●	50/50 / LULLABY *Sony Music 6744182*	5	11
6 Mar 04 ●	ANOTHER DAY *Sony Music 6746592*	9	6
27 Nov 04 ●	IF THERE'S ANY JUSTICE *Sony Music 6756072*	3	5+
6 Dec 03	DEDICATED *Sony Music 5137912*	16	19
11 Dec 04 ●	TIME TO GROW *Sony Music 5190822*	8	3+

LEMON JELLY *UK, male production duo – Fred Deakin and Nick Franglan (Singles: 8 Weeks, Albums: 6 Weeks)*   pos/wks

19 Oct 02	SPACE WALK *Impotent Fury / XL Recordings IFXLS 150CD*	..36	2
1 Feb 03	NICE WEATHER FOR DUCKS		
	Impotent Fury / XL Recordings IFXLS 156CD	16	3
4 Dec 04	STAY WITH YOU *Impotent Fury / XL Recordings IFXL 201CD*	..31	3
2 Nov 02	LOST HORIZONS *Impotent Fury / XL IFXLCD 160*	20	6

The LEMON PIPERS
US, male vocal / instrumental group (Singles: 16 Weeks)   pos/wks

| 7 Feb 68 | ● | GREEN TAMBOURINE *Pye International 7N 25444* ▲ | 7 | 11 |
| 1 May 68 | | RICE IS NICE *Pye International 7N 25454* | 41 | 5 |

The LEMON TREES
UK, male vocal / instrumental group – included Guy Chambers (Singles: 9 Weeks)   pos/wks

26 Sep 92	LOVE IS IN YOUR EYES *Oxygen GASP 1*	75	1
7 Nov 92	THE WAY I FEEL *Oxygen GASP 2*	62	2
13 Feb 93	LET IT LOOSE *Oxygen GASPD 3*	55	2
17 Apr 93	CHILD OF LOVE *Oxygen GASPD 4*	55	3
3 Jul 93	I CAN'T FACE THE WORLD *Oxygen GASPD 6*	52	1

LEMONESCENT
UK, female vocal group (Singles: 5 Weeks)   pos/wks

29 Jun 02	BEAUTIFUL *Supertone SUPTCD 1*	70	1
9 Nov 02	SWING MY HIPS (SEX DANCE) *Supertone SUPTCD 2*	48	1
5 Apr 03	HELP ME MAMA *Supertone SUPTCD 4*	36	1
21 Jun 03	CINDERELLA *Supertone SUPTCD 8*	31	1
3 Jul 04	ALL RIGHT NOW *Supertone SUPTCD 11*	37	1

LEMONHEADS
US / Australia, male vocal / instrumental group – leader Evan Dando (Singles: 26 Weeks, Albums: 32 Weeks)   pos/wks

17 Oct 92	IT'S A SHAME ABOUT RAY *Atlantic A 7423*	70	1
5 Dec 92	MRS ROBINSON / BEIN' AROUND *Atlantic A 7401*	19	9
6 Feb 93	CONFETTI / MY DRUG BUDDY *Atlantic A 7430CD*	44	2
10 Apr 93	IT'S A SHAME ABOUT RAY (re-issue) *Atlantic A 5764CD*	31	3
16 Oct 93	INTO YOUR ARMS *Atlantic A 7302CD*	14	4
27 Nov 93	IT'S ABOUT TIME *Atlantic A 7296CD*	57	2
14 May 94	BIG GAY HEART *Atlantic A 7259CD*	55	2
28 Sep 96	IF I COULD TALK I'D TELL YOU *Atlantic A 5561CD*	39	2
14 Dec 96	IT'S ALL TRUE *Atlantic A 5635CD*	61	1
1 Aug 92	IT'S A SHAME ABOUT RAY *Atlantic 7567824602*	33	16
23 Oct 93	● COME ON FEEL THE LEMONHEADS *Atlantic 7567825372*	5	14
12 Oct 96	CAR BUTTON CLOTH *Atlantic 7567927262*	28	2

Group was male / female for first album

LEN
Canada, male / female DJ / vocal group (Singles: 15 Weeks)   pos/wks

| 18 Dec 99 | ● STEAL MY SUNSHINE *Columbia 6685062* | 8 | 13 |
| 10 Jun 00 | CRYPTIK SOULS CREW *Columbia 6693832* | 28 | 2 |

John LENNON (66 Top 500)
One of the century's greatest musical talents, b. 9 Oct 1940, Liverpool, UK, d. 8 Dec 1980. World-famous singer / songwriter who, together with Paul McCartney, fronted The Beatles and penned their hits. Three of his singles topped the UK chart in the two months after his murder in New York. He was recently included in the BBC's Top 10 Great Britons of all time. Best-selling single: 'Imagine' 1,486,581 (Singles: 200 Weeks, Albums: 344 Weeks)   pos/wks

9 Jul 69	● GIVE PEACE A CHANCE (re) *Apple 13* [1]	2	18
1 Nov 69	COLD TURKEY *Apple APPLES 1001*	14	8
21 Feb 70	● INSTANT KARMA *Apple APPLES 1003* [2]	5	9
20 Mar 71	● POWER TO THE PEOPLE *Apple R 5892* [3]	7	9
9 Dec 72	● HAPPY XMAS (WAR IS OVER) (4re) *Apple R 5970* [4]	2	26
24 Nov 73	MIND GAMES *Apple R 5994*	26	9
19 Oct 74	WHATEVER GETS YOU THRU' THE NIGHT *Apple R 5998* [5] ▲	36	4
8 Feb 75	#9 DREAM *Apple R 6003*	23	8
3 May 75	STAND BY ME *Apple R 6005*	30	7
1 Nov 75	IMAGINE (re) *Apple R 6009* ◆	1	24
8 Nov 80	★ (JUST LIKE) STARTING OVER *Geffen K 79186* ▲	1	15
24 Jan 81	★ WOMAN *Geffen K 79195*	1	11
21 Mar 81	I SAW HER STANDING THERE *DJM DJS 10965* [6]	40	4
4 Apr 81	WATCHING THE WHEELS *Geffen K 79207*	30	4
20 Nov 82	LOVE *Parlophone R 6059*	41	7
21 Jan 84	● NOBODY TOLD ME *Ono Music / Polydor POSP 700*	6	6
17 Mar 84	BORROWED TIME *Polydor POSP 701*	32	6
30 Nov 85	JEALOUS GUY *Parlophone R 6117*	65	2
10 Dec 88	IMAGINE / JEALOUS GUY / HAPPY XMAS (WAR IS OVER) (re-issue) *Parlophone R 6199*	45	5
25 Dec 99	● IMAGINE (re) (re-issue) *Parlophone CDR 6534*	3	13
20 Dec 03	HAPPY XMAS (WAR IS OVER) (re-issue) *Parlophone CDR 6627* [7]	33	3
16 Jan 71	● JOHN LENNON / PLASTIC ONO BAND *Apple PCS 7124* [1]	8	11
30 Oct 71	★ IMAGINE *Apple PAS 10004* [2] ■ ▲	1	101
14 Oct 72	SOMETIME IN NEW YORK CITY *Apple PCSP 716* [3]	11	6

8 Dec 73	MIND GAMES *Apple PCS 7165*	13	12
19 Oct 74	● WALLS AND BRIDGES *Apple PCTC 253* ▲	6	10
8 Mar 75	● ROCK 'N' ROLL *Apple PCS 7169*	6	28
8 Nov 75	● SHAVED FISH *Apple PCS 7173*	8	29
22 Nov 80	★ DOUBLE FANTASY *Geffen K 99131* [4] ▲	1	36
20 Nov 82	★ THE JOHN LENNON COLLECTION *Parlophone EMTV 37*	1	43
4 Feb 84	● MILK AND HONEY *Polydor POLH 5* [4]	3	13
8 Mar 86	LIVE IN NEW YORK CITY *Parlophone PCS 7031*	55	3
22 Oct 88	IMAGINE (FILM SOUNDTRACK) *Parlophone PCSP 722*	64	6
8 Nov 97	● LENNON LEGEND – THE VERY BEST OF JOHN LENNON *Parlophone 8219542*	4	44
14 Nov 98	ANTHOLOGY *Capitol 8306142*	62	1
26 Feb 00	IMAGINE (re-issue) *Parlophone 5248582*	51	1

[1] Plastic Ono Band [2] Lennon, Ono and the Plastic Ono Band [3] John Lennon / Plastic Ono Band [4] John and Yoko with the Plastic Ono Band with the Harlem Community Choir [5] John Lennon with the Plastic Ono Nuclear Band [6] Elton John Band featuring John Lennon and the Muscle Shoals Horns [7] John and Yoko and the Plastic Ono Band [1] John Lennon and the Plastic Ono Band [2] John Lennon and the Plastic Ono Band with the Flux Fiddlers [3] John and Yoko Lennon with the Plastic Ono Band and Elephant's Memory [4] John Lennon and Yoko Ono

'Give Peace a Chance' re-entry made No.33 in Jan 1981. 'Happy Xmas (War Is Over)' peaked at No.4 in Dec 1972, No.48 in Jan 1975, and No.2 in Dec 1980, and the re-entry made No.28 in Dec 1981 and peaked at No.56 in Dec 1982. 'Imagine' peaked at No.6 in 1975, and topped the chart on re-entry in Dec 1980 'Imagine' changed its label credit to Parlophone PAS 10004 between its initial chart run and later runs. 'Imagine' (Film Soundtrack) includes tracks by The Beatles

Julian LENNON
UK, male vocalist – John Lennon (Singles: 47 Weeks, Albums: 20 Weeks)   pos/wks

6 Oct 84	● TOO LATE FOR GOODBYES *Charisma JL 1*	6	11
15 Dec 84	VALOTTE *Charisma JL 2*	55	6
9 Mar 85	SAY YOU'RE WRONG *Charisma JL 3*	75	1
7 Dec 85	BECAUSE *EMI 5538*	40	7
11 Mar 89	NOW YOU'RE IN HEAVEN *Virgin VS 1154*	59	3
24 Aug 91	● SALTWATER *Virgin VS 1361*	6	13
30 Nov 91	HELP YOURSELF *Virgin VS 1379*	53	2
25 Apr 92	GET A LIFE *Virgin VS 1398*	56	3
23 May 98	DAY AFTER DAY *Music from Another JULIAN 4CD*	66	1
3 Nov 84	VALOTTE *Charisma JLLP 1*	20	15
5 Apr 86	THE SECRET VALUE OF DAYDREAMING *Charisma CAS 1171*	93	1
5 Oct 91	HELP YOURSELF *Virgin V 2668*	42	4

Annie LENNOX (314 Top 500)
Innovative, groundbreaking singer / songwriter who has remained consistently successful around the globe, b. 25 Dec, 1954, Aberdeen, Scotland. Former focal point of The Tourists and Eurythmics has won more Brit awards than any other female performer and won an Oscar for best song in 2004 for 'Into the West' from The Lord of the Rings: The Return of the King (Singles: 68 Weeks, Albums: 143 Weeks)   pos/wks

3 Dec 88	PUT A LITTLE LOVE IN YOUR HEART *A&M AM 484* [1]	28	8
28 Mar 92	● WHY *RCA PB 45317*	5	8
6 Jun 92	PRECIOUS *RCA 74321100257*	23	5
22 Aug 92	● WALKING ON BROKEN GLASS *RCA 74321107227*	8	8
31 Oct 92	COLD *RCA 74321116902*	26	4
13 Feb 93	● LITTLE BIRD / LOVE SONG FOR A VAMPIRE *RCA 74321133832*	3	12
18 Feb 95	● NO MORE 'I LOVE YOU'S *RCA 74321257162*	2	12
10 Jun 95	A WHITER SHADE OF PALE *RCA 74321284822*	16	6
30 Sep 95	WAITING IN VAIN *RCA 74321316132*	31	3
9 Dec 95	SOMETHING SO RIGHT *RCA 74321332392* [2]	44	2
18 Apr 92	★ DIVA *RCA PD 75326* ■	1	80
18 Mar 95	★ MEDUSA *RCA 74321257172* ■	1	49
21 Jun 03	● BARE *RCA 82876524052*	3	14

[1] Annie Lennox and Al Green [2] Annie Lennox featuring Paul Simon

Dino LENNY
Italy, male producer (Singles: 2 Weeks)   pos/wks

| 4 May 02 | I FEEL STEREO *Incentive CENT 40CDS* | 60 | 1 |
| 10 May 03 | CHANGE THE WORLD *Free 2 Air 0146685 F2A* [1] | 51 | 1 |

[1] Dino Lenny vs The Housemartins

Rula LENSKA See Julie COVINGTON, Rula LENSKA, Charlotte CORNWELL and Sue JONES-DAVIES

Phillip LEO
UK, male vocalist (Singles: 3 Weeks)   pos/wks

| 23 Jul 94 | SECOND CHANCE *EMI CDEM 327* | 57 | 2 |
| 25 Mar 95 | THINKING ABOUT YOUR LOVE *EMI CDEM 358* | 64 | 1 |

Deke LEONARD
UK, male vocalist / instrumentalist – guitar (Albums: 1 Week)   pos/wks

13 Apr 74		KAMIKAZE *United Artists UAG 29544*	50	1

Paul LEONI
UK, male instrumentalist – pan flute (Albums: 19 Weeks)   pos/wks

24 Sep 83		FLIGHTS OF FANCY *Nouveau Music NML 1002*	17	19

Kristian LEONTIOU
UK, male vocalist (Singles: 14 Weeks, Albums: 11 Weeks)   pos/wks

5 Jun 04	●	STORY OF MY LIFE *Polydor 9866632*	9	7
28 Aug 04		SHINING *Polydor 9867640*	13	6
4 Dec 04		SOME SAY *Polydor 9868820*	54	1
12 Jun 04		SOME DAY SOON *Polydor 9866206*	14	11

LES RYTHMES DIGITALES *UK, male DJ / producer –*
Jacques Lu Cont (Stuart Price) (Singles: 3 Weeks, Albums: 1 Week) pos/wks

25 Apr 98		MUSIC MAKES YOU LOSE CONTROL		
		Wall of Sound WALLD 037	69	1
7 Aug 99		SOMETIMES *Wall of Sound WALLD 054* [1]	56	1
30 Oct 99		JACQUES YOUR BODY (MAKE ME SWEAT)		
		Wall of Sound WALLD 060	60	1
5 Jun 99		DARKDANCER *Wall of Sound WALLCD 021*	53	1

[1] Les Rythmes Digitales featuring Nik Kershaw

LeSHAUN See LL COOL J

LESS THAN JAKE *US, male vocal / instrumental*
group (Singles: 3 Weeks, Albums: 2 Weeks)   pos/wks

5 Aug 00		ALL MY BEST FRIENDS ARE METALHEADS		
		Golf CDSHOLE 027	51	1
8 Sep 01		GAINESVILLE ROCK CITY *Golf CDSHOLE 48*	57	1
24 May 03		SHE'S GONNA BREAK SOON *Sire W 606CD*	39	1
31 May 03		ANTHEM *Sire 9362484852*	37	2

LESTER See Norman COOK

Ketty LESTER
US, female vocalist – Revoyda Frierson (Singles: 16 Weeks)   pos/wks

19 Apr 62	●	LOVE LETTERS *London HLN 9527*	4	12
19 Jul 62		BUT NOT FOR ME *London HLN 9574*	45	4

LET LOOSE *UK, male vocal / instrumental*
group (Singles: 62 Weeks, Albums: 15 Weeks)   pos/wks

24 Apr 93		CRAZY FOR YOU *Vertigo VERCD 74*	44	3
9 Apr 94		SEVENTEEN *Mercury MERCD 400*	44	2
25 Jun 94	●	CRAZY FOR YOU (re) (re-issue) *Mercury MERCD 402*	2	24
22 Oct 94		SEVENTEEN (re) (re-mix) *Mercury MERCD 406*	11	9
28 Jan 95		ONE NIGHT STAND *Mercury MERCD 419*	12	6
29 Apr 95	●	BEST IN ME *Mercury MERCD 428*	8	5
4 Nov 95		EVERYBODY SAY EVERYBODY DO (re) *Mercury MERCD 446*	29	4
22 Jun 96	●	MAKE IT WITH YOU *Mercury MERCD 464*	7	6
7 Sep 96		TAKE IT EASY *Mercury MERCD 472*	25	2
16 Nov 96		DARLING BE HOME SOON *Mercury MERCD 475*	65	1
19 Nov 94		LET LOOSE *Mercury 5260182*	20	14
5 Oct 96		ROLLERCOASTER *Mercury 5329552*	42	1

Gerald LETHAN See WALL OF SOUND featuring Gerald LETHAN

The LETTERMEN *US, male vocal group (Singles: 3 Weeks)*   pos/wks

23 Nov 61		THE WAY YOU LOOK TONIGHT *Capitol CL 15222*	36	3

LEVEL 42 (115) Top 500
*Critically acclaimed Isle of Wight / Hong Kong /
London band: Mark King (v/b), Boon Gould (g), Mike Lindup (k/v), Phil Gould (d).
Boasting a world-class bass player in King, they went from Brit-funk cult heroes
to international stardom (Singles: 177 Weeks, Albums: 228 Weeks)*   pos/wks

30 Aug 80		LOVE MEETING LOVE *Polydor POSP 170*	61	4
18 Apr 81		LOVE GAMES *Polydor POSP 234*	38	6
8 Aug 81		TURN IT ON *Polydor POSP 286*	57	6
14 Nov 81		STARCHILD *Polydor POSP 343*	47	4
8 May 82		ARE YOU HEARING (WHAT I HEAR?) *Polydor POSP 396*	49	5
2 Oct 82		WEAVE YOUR SPELL *Polydor POSP 500*	43	4

15 Jan 83		THE CHINESE WAY *Polydor POSP 538*	24	8
16 Apr 83		OUT OF SIGHT, OUT OF MIND *Polydor POSP 570*	41	4
30 Jul 83	●	THE SUN GOES DOWN (LIVING IT UP) *Polydor POSP 622*	10	12
22 Oct 83		MICRO KID *Polydor POSP 643*	37	5
1 Sep 84		HOT WATER *Polydor POSP 697*	18	9
3 Nov 84		THE CHANT HAS BEGUN *Polydor POSP 710*	41	5
21 Sep 85	●	SOMETHING ABOUT YOU *Polydor POSP 759*	6	17
7 Dec 85		LEAVING ME NOW *Polydor POSP 776*	15	11
26 Apr 86	●	LESSONS IN LOVE *Polydor POSP 790*	3	13
14 Feb 87	●	RUNNING IN THE FAMILY *Polydor POSP 842*	6	10
25 Apr 87	●	TO BE WITH YOU AGAIN *Polydor POSP 855*	10	7
12 Sep 87	●	IT'S OVER *Polydor POSP 900*	10	8
12 Dec 87		CHILDREN SAY *Polydor POSP 911*	22	6
3 Sep 88		HEAVEN IN MY HANDS *Polydor PO 14*	12	5
29 Oct 88		TAKE A LOOK *Polydor PO 24*	32	4
21 Jan 89		TRACIE *Polydor PO 34*	25	5
28 Oct 89		TAKE CARE OF YOURSELF *Polydor PO 58*	39	3
17 Aug 91		GUARANTEED *RCA PB 44745*	17	4
19 Oct 91		OVERTIME *RCA PB 44997*	62	2
18 Apr 92		MY FATHER'S SHOES *RCA PB 45271*	55	1
26 Feb 94		FOREVER NOW *RCA 74321190272*	19	4
30 Apr 94		ALL OVER YOU *RCA 74321205662*	26	2
6 Aug 94		LOVE IN A PEACEFUL WORLD *RCA 74321220332*	31	3
29 Aug 81		LEVEL 42 *Polydor POLS 1036*	20	18
10 Apr 82		THE EARLY TAPES JULY-AUGUST 1980 *Polydor POLS 1064*	46	6
18 Sep 82		THE PURSUIT OF ACCIDENTS *Polydor POLD 5067*	17	16
3 Sep 83	●	STANDING IN THE LIGHT *Polydor POLD 5110*	9	13
13 Oct 84		TRUE COLOURS *Polydor POLH 10*	14	8
6 Jul 85		A PHYSICAL PRESENCE *Polydor POLH 23*	28	5
26 Oct 85	●	WORLD MACHINE *Polydor POLH 25*	3	72
28 Mar 87	●	RUNNING IN THE FAMILY *Polydor POLH 42*	2	54
1 Oct 88	●	STARING AT THE SUN *Polydor POLH 50*	2	11
18 Nov 89	●	LEVEL BEST *Polydor LEVTV 1*	5	15
14 Sep 91	●	GUARANTEED *RCA PL 75005*	3	5
26 Mar 94	●	FOREVER NOW *RCA 74321189962*	8	3
7 Nov 98		THE VERY BEST OF LEVEL 42 *Polydor 5593732*	41	2

LEVELLERS *UK, male vocal / instrumental*
group (Singles: 59 Weeks, Albums: 81 Weeks)   pos/wks

21 Sep 91		ONE WAY *China WOK 2008*	51	2
7 Dec 91		FAR FROM HOME *China WOK 2010*	71	1
23 May 92		15 YEARS (EP) *China WOKX 2020*	11	5
10 Jul 93		BELARUSE *China WOKCD 2034*	12	5
30 Oct 93		THIS GARDEN *China WOKCD 2039*	12	4
14 May 94		JULIE (EP) *China WOKCD 2042*	17	3
12 Aug 95		HOPE ST *China WOKCD 2059*	12	5
14 Oct 95		FANTASY *China WOKCD 2067*	16	3
23 Dec 95		JUST THE ONE *China WOKCD 2076* [1]	12	8
20 Jul 96		EXODUS – LIVE *China WOKCD 2082*	24	2
9 Aug 97		WHAT A BEAUTIFUL DAY *China WOKCD 2088*	13	5
18 Oct 97		CELEBRATE *China WOKCD 2089*	28	2
20 Dec 97		DOG TRAIN *China WOKCD 2090*	24	5
14 Mar 98		TOO REAL *China WOKCD 2091*	46	1
24 Oct 98		BOZOS *China WOKCD 2096*	44	2
6 Feb 99		ONE WAY (re-recording) *China WOKCD 2102*	33	2
9 Sep 00		HAPPY BIRTHDAY REVOLUTION *China EW 218CD*	57	1
21 Sep 02		COME ON *Eagle / Hag EHAGXS 001*	44	1
18 Jan 03		WILD AS ANGELS EP *Eagle / Hag EHAGXS 003*	34	2
19 Oct 91		LEVELLING THE LAND *China WOL 1022*	14	30
4 Sep 93	●	LEVELLERS *China WOLCD 1034*	2	14
9 Sep 95	★	ZEITGEIST *China WOLCD 1064*	1	14
31 Aug 96		BEST LIVE – HEADLIGHTS WHITE LINES BLACK TAR		
		RIVERS *China WOLCDX 1074*	13	4
6 Sep 97	●	MOUTH TO MOUTH *China WOLCD 1084*	5	6
7 Nov 98		ONE WAY OF LIFE – BEST OF THE LEVELLERS		
		China / Jive 521732	15	11
16 Sep 00		HELLO PIG *China 8573843392*	28	2

[1] Levellers, special guest Joe Strummer

*Tracks on 15 Years (EP): 15 Years / Dance Before the Storm / The River Flow (Live) /
Plastic Jeezus. Tracks on Julie (EP): Julie / English Civil War / Lowlands of Holland /
100 Years of Solitude*

LEVERT
US, male vocal group (Singles: 10 Weeks, Albums: 1 Week)   pos/wks

22 Aug 87	●	CASANOVA *Atlantic A 9217*	9	10
29 Aug 87		THE BIG THROWDOWN *Atlantic 7817731*	86	1

↗ BILL HALEY MAY HAVE ENCOURAGED THE METEORIC RISE OF ROCK 'N' ROLL IN 1955 BUT HE WAS HARDLY A REBELLIOUS TEENAGER HIMSELF

↓ IN 1955 BELFAST-BORN RUBY MURRAY WAS AS HOT AS THE CURRY WITH WHICH HER NAME BECAME SYNONYMOUS

50 YEARS AGO

1955 – Rock 'n' roll was on the rise but Ruby Murray ruled

On the first chart of 1955, not only did Bill Haley and his Comets' 'Shake Rattle and Roll' become the first rock 'n' roll single to enter the Top 10, but the group's follow-up, 'Rock Around the Clock', also made its chart debut – albeit only for a brief two-week stay at the tail end of the Top 20. Other rock 'n' roll-related UK Top 20 entries that year were The Crew Cuts' cover of The Penguins' doo-wop million seller 'Earth Angel', The McGuire Sisters' rendition of The Moonglows' 'Sincerely', Pat Boone's version of Fats Domino's 'Ain't That a Shame' and Frankie Vaughan and Georgia Gibbs' interpretations of Lavern Baker's R&B novelty hit 'Tweedle Dee'.

Commercial TV launches; a single costs £7.50 and the words "rock 'n' roll" gets a first mention in NME

Don't be misled into thinking that from then on rock ruled, or indeed that all British teenagers instantly took to rock 'n' roll music. The majority were still quite content to listen to less revolutionary sounds. The phrase "rock 'n' roll" had been coined by US DJ Alan Freed only in November 1954, and was still not established in the UK at the time of those early Haley hits. Freed's "rock 'n' roll" stage shows may have been breaking box-office records stateside but the words "rock 'n' roll" were not even mentioned in the New Musical Express until September 1955. No rock 'n' roll acts fared well in the November 1955 NME Readers' Poll. The main winners were Frank Sinatra (Outstanding Popular Singer and American Male Singer), Dickie Valentine (British Male Solo), Doris Day (American Female Singer), Ruby Murray (British Female Singer) and The Stargazers (British Group). Significantly, in the same month, commercial TV was launched in Britain. However, there was still only one UK-based radio station that played popular music, the BBC's Light Programme, although the number of records that it could play was quite limited. At a time when the average wage was £8 a week, singles cost five shillings. As a percentage of today's average wage of £240, that would take the equivalent cost to about £7.50. Albums were priced at £1.12s 4d (around £48.60 in today's money). There was no shortage of novelty hits for your money in 1955. Among the most popular were 'Mister Sandman' (The Chordettes, Dickie Valentine, Max Bygraves, The Four Aces), 'The Yellow Rose of Texas' (Mitch Miller, Gary Miller, Ronnie Hilton), 'Twenty Tiny Fingers' (The Stargazers, Alma Cogan, The Coronets) and the year's last No.1, 'Christmas Alphabet' (Dickie Valentine).

Ruby Murray rules and 'Rose Marie' stays top for 11 weeks

The year's biggest singing sensation was 19-year-old Irish girl Ruby Murray, whose sentimental ballads were light years away from Haley's hard-hitting rockers. Interestingly, teen hero Haley was no teenager himself; he was 10 years older than Miss Murray and older than most of the "square" heart-throbs that rock music replaced, including Johnnie Ray, Guy Mitchell, Dickie Valentine and Eddie Fisher. Within just three months of making her chart debut, Ruby became the youngest artist to top the chart and the first ever to have five tracks simultaneously in the Top 20, a record that no female has yet equalled. Another record-setting achievement in 1955 came from US country singer / yodeller Slim Whitman, whose 11 consecutive weeks at the top with 'Rose Marie' were unsurpassed until Bryan Adams beat him in 1991.

Britain goes mambo and Kismet crazy

The big 1955 dance craze was the mambo, with 'Mambo Italiano' by Rosemary Clooney and Dean Martin, Perry Como's 'Papa Loves Mambo' and Bill Haley's hybrid 'Mambo Rock' all gracing the charts. The biggest mambo hit of the year was the instrumental 'Cherry Pink and Apple Blossom White', which topped the charts by both the "king of the mambo" Perez Prado and Britain's own Eddie Calvert. Top musicals of 1955 were 'The Pajama Game' and 'Kismet'. The former spawned the hits 'Hey There' (Rosemary Clooney, Johnnie Ray, Lita Roza, Sammy Davis Jr) and 'Hernando's Hideaway'. Sadly, that show's co-composer Jerry Ross died on the day The Johnston Brothers' recording of 'Hernando's Hideaway' reached No.1. 'Kismet' provided one of the year's most recorded songs, 'Stranger in Paradise', which charted by six different acts including Tony Bennett, whose version went all the way to the top.

Teddy boys rip it up at the cinema

Movie chart-toppers included 'Unchained Melody' (from the film 'Unchained') and the title song from 'The Man from Laramie', while the theme music from the British war film 'The Dam Busters' also flew high. The last of the year's movie theme chart-toppers came from the juvenile delinquent film 'The Blackboard Jungle', and it was Bill Haley's minor hit from the first month of the year, 'Rock Around the Clock', that inspired teddy boys to riot in cinemas, rip up seats and jive in the aisles.

News travels slowly from the US as Elvis emerges into the spotlight

Disneyland and McDonald's first opened their doors in 1955 and Alan Freed's rock 'n' roll package shows were packing them in. Rock 'n' roll was already off and running on the pop charts, with ground-breaking acts such as Chuck Berry, Fats Domino and The Platters scoring Top 20 hits. Ray Charles and Bo Diddley broke big in the R&B market and Little Richard's musical milestone 'Tutti Frutti' was released. In addition, Eddie Cochran, Connie Francis and Johnny Cash released their debut discs and Buddy Holly recorded for the first time.

In the last month of 1955, 'Rock Around the Clock' topped the UK chart and filming started on the movie of that name. Also, the similar-sounding Boyd Bennett and his Rockets' original version of 'Seventeen' charted alongside a cover by Frankie Vaughan. To help to put things in perspective, no British record companies were even considering looking for local rock 'n' roll acts and very few column inches that year were taken up on the subject or what was happening across the Atlantic. A small number of UK teens did have their fingers on the pulse and managed to keep in touch with the US music scene via Radio Luxembourg and AFN (American Forces Network), but otherwise new music travelled slowly to post-war Britain. If you lived in the UK you probably would not have known that in December 1955, Sun Records in Memphis recorded Carl Perkins singing 'Blue Suede Shoes' and sold the emerging Elvis Presley's contract to RCA for a record fee, as his final Sun single 'I Forgot to Remember to Forget' topped the C&W chart. Billboard could not contain its excitement over this event and its front-page headline on 3 December read: "Double deals hurl Presley into stardom", while inside RCA raved about "the most talked about new personality in the last 10 years of recorded music".

The author of this trip back in time is British Hits Singles & Albums chart consultant Dave McAleer. For those who would like to know much more about the UK and US music scene and the rise of rock in the 1950s, check out Dave's regular updates on our website: www.bibleofpop.com

LEVERT SWEAT GILL (see also Johnny GILL; Keith SWEAT)
US, male vocal group (Singles: 7 Weeks)   pos/wks

14 Mar 98	**MY BODY** *East West E 3857CD*	.21	3
6 Jun 98	**CURIOUS** *East West E 3842CD*	.23	2
12 Sep 98	**DOOR #1** *East West E 3817CD*	.45	2

Hank LEVINE *US, orchestra (Singles: 4 Weeks)*   pos/wks

21 Dec 61	**IMAGE** *HMV POP 947*	.45	4

LEVITATION
UK, male vocal / instrumental group (Albums: 1 Week)   pos/wks

16 May 92	**NEED FOR NOT** *Rough Trade R 2862*	.45	1

LEVITICUS *UK, male producer – J.J. Frost (Singles: 1 Week)*   pos/wks

25 Mar 95	**BURIAL** *ffrr FCD 255*	.66	1

Barrington LEVY *Jamaica, male vocalist (Singles: 13 Weeks)* pos/wks

2 Feb 85	**HERE I COME** *London LON 62*	.41	4
15 Jun 91	**TRIBAL BASE** *Desire WANT 44* [1]	.20	6
24 Sep 94	**WORK** *MCA MCSTD 2003*	.65	1
13 Oct 01	**HERE I COME (SING DJ) (re-recording)** *Nulife / Arista 74321895622* [2]	.37	2

[1] Rebel MC featuring Tenor Fly and Barrington Levy [2] Talisman P featuring Barrington Levy

General LEVY See GENERAL LEVY

Jona LEWIE (see also Terry DACTYL and the DINOSAURS)
UK, male vocalist – John Lewis (Singles: 20 Weeks)   pos/wks

10 May 80	**YOU'LL ALWAYS FIND ME IN THE KITCHEN AT PARTIES** *Stiff BUY 73*	.16	9
29 Nov 80	● **STOP THE CAVALRY** *Stiff BUY 104*	.3	11

On some copies first title was simply 'Kitchen at Parties'

CJ LEWIS *UK, male vocalist – Steven James*
Lewis (Singles: 32 Weeks, Albums: 2 Weeks)   pos/wks

23 Apr 94	● **SWEETS FOR MY SWEET** *Black Market BMITD 017*	.3	13
23 Jul 94	● **EVERYTHING IS ALRIGHT (UPTIGHT)** *Black Market BMITD 019*	.10	7
8 Oct 94	**BEST OF MY LOVE** *Black Market BMITD 021*	.13	6
17 Dec 94	**DOLLARS** *Black Market BMITD 023*	.34	4
9 Sep 95	**R TO THE A** *Black Market BMITD 030*	.34	2
3 Sep 94	**DOLLARS** *Black Market MCD 11131*	.44	2

Danny J LEWIS *UK, male producer (Singles: 2 Weeks)*   pos/wks

20 Jun 98	**SPEND THE NIGHT** *Locked On LOX 98CD*	.29	2

Darlene LEWIS *US, female vocalist (Singles: 4 Weeks)*   pos/wks

16 Apr 94	**LET THE MUSIC (LIFT YOU UP)** *KMS / Eastern Bloc KMSCD 10*	.16	4

All formats of 'Let the Music Lift You Up' featured versions by Loveland featuring Rachel McFarlane and also by Darlene Lewis

Dee LEWIS *UK, female vocalist (Singles: 5 Weeks)*   pos/wks

18 Jun 88	**BEST OF MY LOVE** *Mercury DEE 3*	.47	5

Donna LEWIS
UK, female vocalist (Singles: 16 Weeks, Albums: 1 Week)   pos/wks

7 Sep 96	● **I LOVE YOU ALWAYS FOREVER** *Atlantic A 5495CD*	.5	14
8 Feb 97	**WITHOUT LOVE** *Atlantic A 5468CD*	.39	2
12 Oct 96	**NOW IN A MINUTE** *Atlantic 7567827622*	.52	1

Gary LEWIS and the PLAYBOYS *US, male vocal /*
instrumental group – leader Gary Levitch (Singles: 7 Weeks) pos/wks

8 Feb 75	**MY HEART'S SYMPHONY** *United Artists UP 35780*	.36	7

Huey LEWIS and the NEWS (439 Top 500)
One of the most popular 1980s US acts, formed San Francisco, US, in 1980. Leader b. Hugh Cregg III, 5 Jul 1950, New York. The Grammy and Brit-winning band took 'The Power of Love' into the Top 20 twice within six months (Singles: 66 Weeks, Albums: 94 Weeks)   pos/wks

27 Oct 84	**IF THIS IS IT** *Chrysalis CHS 2803*	.39	6
31 Aug 85	**THE POWER OF LOVE** *Chrysalis HUEY 1* ▲	.11	10
23 Nov 85	**HEART AND SOUL (EP)** *Chrysalis HUEY 2*	.61	4

8 Feb 86	● **THE POWER OF LOVE (re-issue) / DO YOU BELIEVE IN LOVE** *Chrysalis HUEY 3*	.9	12
10 May 86	**THE HEART OF ROCK AND ROLL** *Chrysalis HUEY 4*	.49	3
23 Aug 86	**STUCK WITH YOU** *Chrysalis HUEY 5* ▲	.12	12
6 Dec 86	**HIP TO BE SQUARE** *Chrysalis HUEY 6*	.41	8
21 Mar 87	**SIMPLE AS THAT** *Chrysalis HUEY 7*	.47	5
16 Jul 88	**PERFECT WORLD** *Chrysalis HUEY 10*	.48	6
14 Sep 85	**SPORTS** *Chrysalis CHR 1412* ▲	.23	24
20 Sep 86	**FORE!** *Chrysalis CDL 1534* ▲	.8	52
6 Aug 88	**SMALL WORLD** *Chrysalis CDL 1622*	.12	8
18 May 91	**HARD AT PLAY** *Chrysalis CHR 1847*	.39	2
21 Nov 92	**THE HEART OF ROCK & ROLL – THE BEST OF HUEY LEWIS AND THE NEWS** *Chrysalis CDCHR 1934*	.23	8

Tracks on Heart and Soul (EP): Heart and Soul / Hope You Love Me Like You Say You Do / Heart of Rock and Roll / Buzz Buzz Buzz. 'Do You Believe in Love' listed only from 15 Feb 1986

Jerry LEWIS
US, male actor / vocalist – Joseph Levitch (Singles: 8 Weeks)   pos/wks

8 Feb 57	**ROCK-A-BYE YOUR BABY WITH A DIXIE MELODY (re)** *Brunswick 05636*	.12	8

Jerry Lee LEWIS *US, male vocalist / instrumentalist – piano (Singles: 68 Weeks, Albums: 6 Weeks)*   pos/wks

27 Sep 57	● **WHOLE LOTTA SHAKIN' GOIN' ON (re)** *London HLS 8457*	.8	11
20 Dec 57	★ **GREAT BALLS OF FIRE** *London HLS 8529*	.1	12
11 Apr 58	● **BREATHLESS** *London HLS 8592*	.8	7
23 Jan 59	**HIGH SCHOOL CONFIDENTIAL** *London HLS 8780*	.12	6
1 May 59	**LOVIN' UP A STORM** *London HLS 8840*	.28	1
9 Jun 60	**BABY, BABY, BYE BYE** *London HLS 9131*	.47	1
4 May 61	● **WHAT'D I SAY (re)** *London HLS 9335*	.10	14
6 Sep 62	**SWEET LITTLE SIXTEEN** *London HLS 9584*	.38	5
14 Mar 63	**GOOD GOLLY MISS MOLLY** *London HLS 9688*	.31	6
6 May 72	**CHANTILLY LACE** *Mercury 6052 141*	.33	5
2 Jun 62	**JERRY LEE LEWIS VOLUME 2** *London HA 2440*	.14	6

Linda LEWIS
UK, female vocalist (Singles: 31 Weeks, Albums: 4 Weeks)   pos/wks

2 Jun 73	**ROCK-A-DOODLE-DOO** *Raft RA 18502*	.15	11
12 Jul 75	● **IT'S IN HIS KISS** *Arista 17*	.6	8
17 Apr 76	**BABY I'M YOURS** *Arista 43*	.33	6
2 Jun 79	**I'D BE SURPRISINGLY GOOD FOR YOU** *Ariola ARO 166*	.40	5
19 Aug 00	**REACH OUT** *Skint SKINT 54CD* [1]	.61	1
9 Aug 75	**NOT A LITTLE GIRL ANYMORE** *Arista ARTY 109*	.40	4

[1] Midfield General featuring Linda Lewis

Linda Gail LEWIS See Van MORRISON

Ramsey LEWIS
US, male instrumentalist – piano (Singles: 8 Weeks)   pos/wks

15 Apr 72	**WADE IN THE WATER** *Chess 6145 004*	.31	8

Shaznay LEWIS (see also ALL SAINTS)
UK, female vocalist (Singles: 11 Weeks, Albums: 3 Weeks)   pos/wks

17 Jul 04	● **NEVER FELT LIKE THIS BEFORE** *London LONCD 484*	.8	10
30 Oct 04	**YOU** *London LONCD 486*	.56	1
31 Jul 04	**OPEN** *London 2564617602*	.22	3

Shirley LEWIS See Arthur BAKER

Ramsey LEWIS TRIO
US, male instrumental trio (Albums: 4 Weeks)   pos/wks

21 May 66	**HANG ON RAMSEY** *Chess CRL 4520*	.20	4

John LEYTON *UK, male vocalist / actor (Singles: 70 Weeks)* pos/wks

3 Aug 61	★ **JOHNNY REMEMBER ME** *Top Rank JAR 577*	.1	15
5 Oct 61	● **WILD WIND** *Top Rank JAR 585*	.2	10
28 Dec 61	**SON THIS IS SHE** *HMV POP 956*	.15	10
15 Mar 62	**LONE RIDER** *HMV POP 992*	.40	5
3 May 62	**LONELY CITY** *HMV POP 1014*	.14	11
23 Aug 62	**DOWN THE RIVER NILE** *HMV POP 1054*	.42	3
21 Feb 63	**CUPBOARD LOVE** *HMV POP 1122*	.22	12
18 Jul 63	**I'LL CUT YOUR TAIL OFF (re)** *HMV POP 1175*	.36	3
20 Feb 64	**MAKE LOVE TO ME** *HMV POP 1264* [1]	.49	1

[1] John Leyton and The LeRoys

The LEYTON BUZZARDS
UK, male vocal / instrumental group (Singles: 5 Weeks)   pos/wks

3 Mar 79	**SATURDAY NIGHT (BENEATH THE PLASTIC PALM TREES)**	
	Chrysalis CHS 2288	**53** 5

The LIARS
US, male vocal / instrumental group (Singles: 1 Week)   pos/wks

21 Feb 04	**THERE'S ALWAYS ROOM ON THE BROOM** *Mute CDMUTE 317* ..**74** 1	

LIBERACE *US, male instrumentalist – piano / vocalist, b. Wladziu*
Valentino Liberace, 16 May 1919, d. 4 Feb 1987 (Singles: 2 Weeks)   pos/wks

17 Jun 55	**UNCHAINED MELODY** *Philips PB 430* **20** 1	
19 Oct 56	**I DON'T CARE (AS LONG AS YOU CARE FOR ME)**	
	Columbia DB 3834 ....**28** 1	

LIBERATION *UK, male instrumental / production*
duo – William Linch and David Cooper (Singles: 3 Weeks)   pos/wks

24 Oct 92	**LIBERATION** *ZYX ZYX 68657* **28** 3	

The LIBERTINES (see also PETER DOHERTY) *UK, male vocal /*
instrumental group (Singles: 20 Weeks, Albums: 20 Weeks)   pos/wks

15 Jun 02	**WHAT A WASTER** *Rough Trade RTRADSCD 054* **37** 2	
12 Oct 02	**UP THE BRACKET** *Rough Trade RTRADSCD 064* **29** 2	
25 Jan 03	**TIME FOR HEROES** *Rough Trade RTRADSCD 074* **20** 2	
30 Aug 03	**DON'T LOOK BACK INTO THE SUN**	
	Rough Trade RTRADSCD 199 ....**11** 4	
21 Aug 04 ●	**CAN'T STAND ME NOW** *Rough Trade RTRADSCD 163* **2** 6	
6 Nov 04 ●	**WHAT BECAME OF THE LIKELY LADS**	
	Rough Trade RTRADSCD 215 ....**9** 4	
2 Nov 02	**UP THE BRACKET** *Rough Trade RTRADSCD 065* **35** 7	
11 Sep 04 ★	**THE LIBERTINES** *Rough Trade RTRADSCD 166* ■ **1** 13	

LIBERTY X
UK, male / female vocal group (Singles: 76 Weeks, Albums: 62 Weeks) pos/wks

6 Oct 01 ●	**THINKING IT OVER** *V2 VVR 5017773* [1] **5** 8	
15 Dec 01 ●	**DOIN' IT** *V2 VVR 5017793* [1] **14** 6	
25 May 02 ★	**JUST A LITTLE** *V2 VVR 5018963* ■ **1** 16	
21 Sep 02 ●	**GOT TO HAVE YOUR LOVE** *V2 VVR 5020503* **2** 12	
14 Dec 02 ●	**HOLDING ON FOR YOU** *V2 VVR 5020763* **5** 11	
29 Mar 03 ●	**BEING NOBODY** *Virgin RXCD 1* [2] **3** 11	
1 Nov 03 ●	**JUMPIN' (re)** *V2 VVR 5023543* **6** 7	
24 Jan 04	**EVERYBODY CRIES** *V2 VVR 5023558* **13** 5	
8 Jun 02 ●	**THINKING IT OVER** *V2 VVR 1017782* **3** 58	
15 Nov 03	**BEING SOMEBODY** *V2 VVR 1023562* **12** 4	

[1] Liberty [2] Richard X vs Liberty X

LIBIDO *Norway, male vocal / instrumental group (Singles: 1 Week)* pos/wks

31 Jan 98	**OVERTHROWN** *Fire BLAZE 119CD* **53** 1	

LIBRA *US, male / female production / vocal trio (Singles: 3 Weeks)* pos/wks

26 Oct 96	**ANOMALY – CALLING YOUR NAME** *Platipus PLATCD 24* ..**71** 1	
18 Mar 00	**ANOMALY – CALLING YOUR NAME (re-mix)**	
	Platipus PLATCD 56 [1] **43** 2	

[1] Libra Presents Taylor

LICK THE TINS
UK, male / female vocal / instrumental group (Singles: 8 Weeks)   pos/wks

29 Mar 86	**CAN'T HELP FALLING IN LOVE** *Sedition EDIT 3308* **42** 8	

Oliver LIEB presents SMOKED (see also LSG)
Germany, male producer (Singles: 1 Week)   pos/wks

30 Sep 00	**METROPOLIS** *Duty Free DF 019CD* **72** 1	

Ben LIEBRAND *Holland, male DJ / producer (Singles: 2 Weeks)* pos/wks

9 Jun 90	**PULS(T)AR** *Epic LIEB 1* **68** 2	

LIEUTENANT PIGEON
UK, male / female instrumental group (Singles: 29 Weeks)   pos/wks

16 Sep 72 ★	**MOULDY OLD DOUGH** *Decca F 13278* **1** 19	
16 Dec 72	**DESPERATE DAN** *Decca F 13365* **17** 10	

LIFEHOUSE
US, male vocal / instrumental group (Singles: 4 Weeks)   pos/wks

8 Sep 01	**HANGING BY A MOMENT** *Dreamworks / Polydor 4975612* **25** 4	

LIFFORD *See ARTFUL DODGER*

LIGHT OF THE WORLD *UK, male vocal /*
instrumental group (Singles: 25 Weeks, Albums: 1 Week)   pos/wks

14 Apr 79	**SWINGIN'** *Ensign ENY 22* **45** 5	
14 Jul 79	**MIDNIGHT GROOVIN'** *Ensign ENY 29* **72** 1	
18 Oct 80	**LONDON TOWN** *Ensign ENY 43* **41** 5	
17 Jan 81	**I SHOT THE SHERIFF** *Ensign ENY 46* **40** 5	
28 Mar 81	**I'M SO HAPPY / TIME** *Ensign MER 64* **35** 6	
21 Nov 81	**RIDE THE LOVE TRAIN** *EMI 5242* **49** 3	
24 Jan 81	**ROUND TRIP** *Ensign ENVY 14* **73** 1	

LIGHTER SHADE OF BROWN
US, male vocal duo (Singles: 3 Weeks)   pos/wks

9 Jul 94	**HEY DJ** *Mercury MERCD 401* **33** 3	

Gordon LIGHTFOOT *Canada, male vocalist /*
instrumentalist – guitar (Singles: 26 Weeks, Albums: 2 Weeks)   pos/wks

19 Jun 71	**IF YOU COULD READ MY MIND** *Reprise RS 20974* **30** 9	
3 Aug 74	**SUNDOWN** *Reprise K 14327* ▲ **33** 7	
15 Jan 77	**THE WRECK OF THE EDMUND FITZGERALD** *Reprise K 14451* 40 4	
16 Sep 78	**DAYLIGHT KATY** *Warner Bros. K 17214* **41** 6	
20 May 72	**DON QUIXOTE** *Reprise K 44166* **44** 1	
17 Aug 74	**SUNDOWN** *Reprise K 54020* ▲ **45** 1	

Terry LIGHTFOOT'S NEW ORLEANS JAZZMEN *UK, vocalist /*
instrumentalist – clarinet and male band (Singles: 17 Weeks)   pos/wks

7 Sep 61	**TRUE LOVE** *Columbia DB 4696* **33** 4	
23 Nov 61	**KING KONG** *Columbia SCD 2165* **29** 12	
3 May 62	**TAVERN IN THE TOWN** *Columbia DB 4822* **49** 1	

LIGHTFORCE *Germany, male production duo (Singles: 1 Week)* pos/wks

28 Oct 00	**JOIN ME** *Slinky Music SLINKY 004CD* **53** 1	

LIGHTHOUSE FAMILY (151 Top 500) *Smooth, easy-on-the-ear pop /*
soul duo formed in Newcastle-upon-Tyne, UK; Nigerian-born Tunde Baiyewu
(v) and Londoner Paul Tucker (k). After slow start, debut album 'Ocean Drive'
(1995) sold more than 1.6 million in the UK and made a name for them in the
rest of Europe (Singles: 89 Weeks, Albums: 263 Weeks)   pos/wks

27 May 95	**LIFTED** *Wild Card CARDW 17* **61** 2	
14 Oct 95	**OCEAN DRIVE** *Wild Card 5797072* **34** 3	
10 Feb 96 ●	**LIFTED (re-issue)** *Wild Card 5779432* **4** 10	
1 Jun 96	**OCEAN DRIVE (re-issue)** *Wild Card 5766192* **11** 8	
21 Sep 96	**GOODBYE HEARTBREAK** *Wild Card 5753492* **14** 6	
21 Dec 96	**LOVING EVERY MINUTE** *Wild Card 5731012* **20** 7	
11 Oct 97	**RAINCLOUD** *Wild Card 5717932* **6** 7	
10 Jan 98 ●	**HIGH** *Polydor 5691492* **4** 14	
27 Jun 98 ●	**LOST IN SPACE** *Polydor 5670592* **6** 8	
10 Oct 98	**QUESTION OF FAITH** *Wild Card 5673932* **21** 5	
9 Jan 99	**POSTCARD FROM HEAVEN** *Wild Card 5633952* **24** 6	
24 Nov 01 ●	**(I WISH I KNEW HOW IT WOULD FEEL TO BE) FREE / ONE**	
	Wild Card / Polydor 5873812 ....**6** 9	
9 Mar 02	**RUN** *Wild Card / Polydor 5705702* **30** 3	
6 Jul 02	**HAPPY** *Wild Card / Polydor 5707902* **51** 1	
18 Nov 95 ●	**OCEAN DRIVE** *Wild Card 5237872* **3** 154	
1 Nov 97 ●	**POSTCARDS FROM HEAVEN** *Wild Card 5395162* **2** 73	
1 Dec 01 ●	**WHATEVER GETS YOU THROUGH THE DAY** *Wild Card 5894122...***7** 18	
30 Nov 02 ●	**GREATEST HITS** *Wild Card / Polydor 0654482* **23** 6	
19 Apr 03 ●	**THE VERY BEST OF LIGHTHOUSE FAMILY**	
	Wild Card / Polydor 0761662 ....**9** 12	

The LIGHTNING SEEDS (266 Top 500)
Conceived as a 'perfect pop' studio project by producer and group veteran
Ian Broudie (v/g), b. 4 Aug 1958, Liverpool, UK. England's most popular
footballing anthem, 'Three Lions', became the first song to top the charts
twice with different lyrics (Singles: 104 Weeks, Albums: 139 Weeks) pos/wks

22 Jul 89	**PURE** *Ghetto GTG 4* **16** 8	
14 Mar 92	**THE LIFE OF RILEY** *Virgin VS 1402* **28** 6	
30 May 92	**SENSE** *Virgin VS 1414* **31** 5	

20 Aug 94	LUCKY YOU Epic 6606282	43	2
14 Jan 95	CHANGE Epic 6609865	13	6
15 Apr 95	MARVELLOUS Epic 6614265	24	5
22 Jul 95	PERFECT Epic 6621792	18	5
21 Oct 95	LUCKY YOU (re-issue) Epic 6625182	15	6
9 Mar 96	READY OR NOT Epic 6629672	20	4
1 Jun 96 ★	THREE LIONS (THE OFFICIAL SONG OF THE ENGLAND FOOTBALL TEAM) Epic 6632732 [1] ■	1	15
2 Nov 96	WHAT IF ... (re) Epic 6638635	14	4
18 Jan 97	SUGAR COATED ICEBERG Epic 6640432	12	4
26 Apr 97 ●	YOU SHOWED ME Epic 6643282	8	5
13 Dec 97	WHAT YOU SAY Epic 6653572	41	5
20 Jun 98 ★	THREE LIONS '98 Epic 6660982 [1] ■	1	13
27 Nov 99	LIFE'S TOO SHORT (re) Epic 6681502	27	4
18 Mar 00	SWEETEST SOUL SENSATIONS Epic 6689422	67	1
15 Jun 02	THREE LIONS '98 (re) (re-issue) Epic 6728152 [2]	16	6
10 Feb 00	CLOUDCUCKOOLAND Ghetto GHETT 3	50	2
18 Apr 92	SENSE Virgin CDV 2690	53	1
17 Sep 94	JOLLIFICATION Epic 4772379	12	58
18 May 96	PURE LIGHTNING SEEDS Virgin CDV 2805	27	9
23 Nov 96	DIZZY HEIGHTS Epic 4866402	11	26
22 Nov 97 ●	LIKE YOU DO ... BEST OF THE LIGHTNING SEEDS Epic 4890342	5	41
4 Dec 99	TILT Epic 4962632	46	2

[1] Baddiel and Skinner and The Lightning Seeds [2] Baddiel, Skinner and The Lightning Seeds

LIL BOW WOW See BOW WOW

LIL' DEVIOUS (see also PERCY FILTH) *UK, male production duo – Mark Baker and Gary Little (Singles: 1 Week)* pos/wks

15 Sep 01	COME HOME Rulin RULIN 16CDS	55	1

LIL' FLIP (see also Mario WINANS)
US, male rapper (Singles: 6 Weeks) pos/wks

11 Sep 04	NEVER REALLY WAS Bad Boy MCSTD 40372 [1]	44	2
30 Oct 04	SUNSHINE Columbia 6751842	14	4

[1] Mario Winans featuring Lil' Flip

LIL' JON See USHER

LIL' KIM *US, female vocalist – Kimberly Jones (Singles: 56 Weeks, Albums: 1 Week)* pos/wks

26 Apr 97	NO TIME Atlantic A 5594CD [1]	45	1
5 Jul 97	CRUSH ON YOU (re) Atlantic AT 0002CD	23	5
16 Aug 97	NOT TONIGHT Atlantic AT 0007CD	11	5
22 Aug 98	HIT 'EM WIT DA HEE East West E 3824 CD1 [2]	25	3
5 Feb 00	NOTORIOUS B.I.G. Puff Daddy / Arista 74732173731 [3]	16	5
2 Sep 00	NO MATTER WHAT THEY SAY Atlantic 7567846972	35	2
30 Jun 01 ★	LADY MARMALADE Interscope / Polydor 4975612 [4] ■ ▲	1	16
11 Aug 01	WAIT A MINUTE Atlantic AT 0106CD [5]	54	1
22 Sep 01	IN THE AIR TONITE WEA WEA 331CD [6]	26	2
10 May 03	THE JUMP OFF Atlantic AT 0151CD [7]	16	7
20 Sep 03 ●	CAN'T HOLD US DOWN RCA 87876556332 [8]	6	9
8 Jul 00	THE NOTORIOUS K.I.M. Atlantic 7567928402	67	1

[1] Lil' Kim featuring Puff Daddy [2] Missy 'Misdemeanor' Elliott featuring Lil' Kim [3] Notorious B.I.G. featuring Puff Daddy and Lil' Kim [4] Christina Aguilera, Lil' Kim, Mya and Pink [5] Ray J featuring Lil' Kim [6] Lil' Kim featuring Phil Collins [7] Lil' Kim featuring Mr Cheeks [8] Christina Aguilera featuring Lil' Kim

'Crush on You' peaked at No.23 when it re-entered in Oct '97

LIL' LOUIS (see also BLACK MAGIC) *US, male producer – Marvin Burns (Singles: 21 Weeks, Albums: 5 Weeks)* pos/wks

29 Jul 89 ●	FRENCH KISS ffrr FX 115	2	11
13 Jan 90	I CALLED U ffrr F 123	16	6
26 Sep 92	SAVED MY LIFE ffrr FX 197 [1]	74	1
12 Aug 00	HOW'S YOUR EVENING SO FAR ffrr FCD 384 [2]	23	3
26 Aug 89	FRENCH KISSES ffrr 828170 1	35	5

[1] Lil' Louis and the World [2] Josh Wink and Lil' Louis

LIL' MISS MAX See BLUE ADONIS featuring LIL' MISS MAX

LIL' MO
US, female vocalist – Cynthia Long (Singles: 12 Weeks) pos/wks

21 Nov 98	5 MINUTES Elektra E 3803CD [1]	72	1

23 Sep 00	WHATEVER Virgin VUSCD 172 [2]	31	3
6 Apr 02	WHERE'S MY ...? EMI CDEMS 598 [3]	37	2
15 Feb 03	IF I COULD GO! Elektra E 7331CD [4]	61	1
16 Aug 03	CAN'T LET YOU GO Elektra E 7408CD [5]	14	5

[1] Lil' Mo featuring Missy 'Misdemeanor' Elliott [2] Ideal U.S. featuring Lil' Mo [3] Adam F featuring Lil' Mo [4] Angie Martinez featuring Lil' Mo and Sacario [5] Fabolous featuring Mike Shorey and Lil' Mo

LIL MO' YIN YANG (see also REEL 2 REAL featuring The MAD STUNTMAN) *US, male instrumental / production duo – Erick 'More' Morillo and 'Lil' Louis Vega (Singles: 2 Weeks)* pos/wks

9 Mar 96	REACH Multiply CDMULTY 9	28	2

LIL' ROMEO *US, male rapper – Percy Miller (Singles: 1 Week)* pos/wks

22 Sep 01	MY BABY Priority PTYCD 136	67	1

L'IL T See MANIJAMA featuring MUKUPA & L'IL T

LILY See MAXIMA featuring LILY

LILYS
US, male vocal / instrumental group (Singles: 4 Weeks) pos/wks

21 Feb 98	A NANNY IN MANHATTAN Che CHE 77CD	16	4

LIMA See Tom NOVY

LIMAHL (see also KAJAGOOGOO) *UK, male vocalist – Chris Hamill (Singles: 25 Weeks, Albums: 3 Weeks)* pos/wks

5 Nov 83	ONLY FOR LOVE (re) EMI LML 1	16	8
2 Jun 84	TOO MUCH TROUBLE EMI LML 2	64	3
13 Oct 84 ●	NEVER ENDING STORY EMI LML 3	4	14
1 Dec 84	DON'T SUPPOSE EMI PLML 1	63	3

Alison LIMERICK
UK, female vocalist (Singles: 41 Weeks, Albums: 2 Weeks) pos/wks

30 Mar 91	WHERE LOVE LIVES Arista 144208	27	8
12 Oct 91	COME BACK (FOR REAL LOVE) Arista 114530	53	2
21 Dec 91	MAGIC'S BACK (THEME FROM 'THE GHOSTS OF OXFORD STREET') RCA PB 45223 [1]	42	4
29 Feb 92	MAKE IT ON MY OWN Arista 114996	16	6
18 Jul 92	GETTIN' IT RIGHT Arista 74321102867	57	2
28 Nov 92	HEAR MY CALL Arista 115337	73	1
8 Jan 94	TIME OF OUR LIVES Arista 74321180332	36	4
19 Mar 94	LOVE COME DOWN Arista 74321191952	36	2
25 Feb 95	LOVE WILL KEEP US TOGETHER Acid Jazz JAZID 112CD [2]	63	1
6 Jul 96 ●	WHERE LOVE LIVES (re-mix) Arista 74321381592	9	6
14 Sep 96	MAKE IT ON MY OWN (re-mix) Arista 74321407812	30	2
23 Aug 97	PUT YOUR FAITH IN ME MBA XES 9001	42	1
15 Mar 03	WHERE LOVE LIVES (re-mix) Arista Dance 74321981442	44	2
4 Apr 92	AND STILL I RISE Arista 262365	53	2

[1] Malcolm McLaren featuring Alison Limerick [2] JTQ featuring Alison Limerick

The LIMIT *Holland, male vocal / instrumental duo – Bernard Oates and Rob van Schaik (Singles: 8 Weeks)* pos/wks

5 Jan 85	SAY YEAH Portrait A 4808	17	8

Gwen Guthrie is the uncredited vocalist on 'Say Yeah'

LIMMIE and the FAMILY COOKIN'
US, male / female vocal group (Singles: 28 Weeks) pos/wks

21 Jul 73 ●	YOU CAN DO MAGIC Avco 6105 019	3	13
20 Oct 73	DREAMBOAT Avco 6105 025	31	5
6 Apr 74 ●	A WALKIN' MIRACLE Avco 6105 027	6	10

LIMP BIZKIT `449` `Top 500`
Masters of the metal, punk and hip hop mixing 'rapcore' genre, formed 1995, Florida, US, include Fred Durst (v) and Wes Borland (g), who was replaced in 2003 by Mike Smith (ex-Snot). Award-winning quintet have sold 30 million albums worldwide (Singles: 62 Weeks, Albums: 95 Weeks) pos/wks

15 Jul 00 ●	TAKE A LOOK AROUND (THEME FROM 'MI:2') Interscope 4973682	3	13
11 Nov 00	MY GENERATION (re) Interscope IND 97448	15	8

Singles re-entries are listed as (re), (2re), (3re).... which signifies that the hit re-entered the chart once, twice or three times...

27 Jan 01	★	ROLLIN' *Interscope IND 97474* ■	**1** 13
23 Jun 01	●	MY WAY *Interscope 4975732*	**6** 10
10 Nov 01		BOILER *Interscope 4976362*	**18** 5
27 Sep 03	●	EAT YOU ALIVE *Interscope 9811757*	**10** 7
6 Dec 03		BEHIND BLUE EYES *Interscope 9814744*	**18** 6
3 Jul 99	●	SIGNIFICANT OTHER *Interscope IND 90335* ▲	**10** 37
9 Sep 00		THREE DOLLAR BILL Y'ALL$ *Interscope IND 90124*	**50** 5
28 Oct 00	★	CHOCOLATE STARFISH AND THE HOT DOG FLAVORED WATER *Interscope 4907932* ▲	**1** 48
4 Oct 03	●	RESULTS MAY VARY *Interscope 9860971*	**7** 5

LINA *US, female vocalist (Singles: 1 Week)*   pos/wks
3 Mar 01	PLAYA NO MO' *Atlantic AT 0094CD*	**46** 1

LINCOLN CITY FC featuring Michael COURTNEY
UK, male football team and male vocalist (Singles: 1 Week)   pos/wks
4 May 02	CHIRPY CHIRPY CHEEP CHEEP / JAGGED END *Nap Music SLCPD 0001*	**64** 1

Bob LIND *US, male vocalist (Singles: 10 Weeks)*   pos/wks
10 Mar 66	●	ELUSIVE BUTTERFLY *Fontana TF 670*	**5** 9
26 May 66		REMEMBER THE RAIN *Fontana TF 702*	**46** 1

LINDA and the FUNKY BOYS See Linda CARR

LINDISFARNE ⟨397 Top 500⟩ *Perennial folk-rock hybrid, who blend wistful sensitivity, social sentiments and boozy revelry, formed 1969 Newcastle-upon-Tyne; included Alan Hull, b. 1945, d. 1996 (v/g/p), and Ray Jackson (g). 'Fog on the Tyne' was the top selling album by a UK act in 1971 (Singles: 55 Weeks, Albums: 118 Weeks)*   pos/wks
26 Feb 72	●	MEET ME ON THE CORNER *Charisma CB 173*	**5** 11
13 May 72	●	LADY ELEANOR *Charisma CB 153*	**3** 11
23 Sep 72		ALL FALL DOWN *Charisma CB 191*	**34** 5
3 Jun 78	●	RUN FOR HOME *Mercury 6007 177*	**10** 15
7 Oct 78		JUKE BOX GYPSY *Mercury 6007 187*	**56** 4
10 Nov 90	●	FOG ON THE TYNE (REVISITED) *Best ZB 44083* ⟨1⟩	**2** 9
30 Oct 71	★	FOG ON THE TYNE *Charisma CAS 1050*	**1** 56
15 Jan 72	●	NICELY OUT OF TUNE *Charisma CAS 1025*	**8** 30
30 Sep 72	●	DINGLY DELL *Charisma CAS 1057*	**5** 10
11 Aug 73		LINDISFARNE LIVE *Charisma CLASS 2*	**25** 6
18 Oct 75		FINEST HOUR *Charisma CAS 1108*	**55** 1
24 Jun 78		BACK AND FOURTH *Mercury 9109 609*	**22** 11
9 Dec 78		MAGIC IN THE AIR *Mercury 6641 877*	**71** 1
23 Oct 82		SLEEPLESS NIGHTS *LMP GET 1*	**59** 3

⟨1⟩ Gazza and Lindisfarne

LINDSAY *UK, female vocalist – Lindsay Dracas (Singles: 4 Weeks)*   pos/wks
12 May 01	NO DREAM IMPOSSIBLE *Universal TV 1589562*	**32** 4

LINER *UK, male vocal / instrumental group (Singles: 6 Weeks)*   pos/wks
10 Mar 79	KEEP REACHING OUT FOR LOVE *Atlantic K 11235*	**49** 3
26 May 79	YOU AND ME *Atlantic K 11285*	**44** 3

Andy LING *UK, male producer (Singles: 1 Week)*   pos/wks
13 May 00	FIXATION *Hooj Choons HOOJ 094CD*	**55** 1

Laurie LINGO and the DIPSTICKS *UK, male DJ / vocal duo – Dave Lee Travis and Paul Burnett (Singles: 7 Weeks)*   pos/wks
17 Apr 76	● CONVOY GB *State STAT 23*	**4** 7

LINK *US, male rapper – Lincoln Browder (Singles: 1 Week)*   pos/wks
7 Nov 98	WHATCHA GONE DO? *Relativity 6666055*	**48** 1

LINKIN PARK ⟨365 Top 500⟩ (see also X-ECUTIONERS featuring Mike SHINODA and Mr HAHN of LINKIN PARK) *Pioneering alternative metal / rap-rock sextet formed Los Angeles, US. Members include Chester Bennington (v), Mike Shinoda (rap/v) and Joseph Hahn (DJ). Grammy-winning 'Hybrid Theory' was top selling US album of 2001 with 4.8 million (world total now more than 17 million) (Singles: 61 Weeks, Albums: 124 Weeks)*   pos/wks
27 Jan 01	ONE STEP CLOSER *Warner Bros. W 550CD*	**24** 4
21 Apr 01	CRAWLING *Warner Bros. W 556CD*	**16** 8
30 Jun 01	PAPERCUT *Warner Bros. W 562CD*	**14** 6

20 Oct 01	●	IN THE END *Warner Bros. W 569CD*	**8** 9
3 Aug 02	●	H! VLTG3 / PTS.OF.ATHRTY *Warner Bros. W 588CD*	**9** 6
29 Mar 03	●	SOMEWHERE I BELONG *Warner Bros. W 602CD*	**10** 8
21 Jun 03		FAINT *Warner Bros. W 610CD1*	**15** 8
20 Sep 03		NUMB *Warner Bros. W 622CD1*	**14** 6
19 Jun 04		BREAKING THE HABIT *Warner Bros. W 645CD*	**39** 2
4 Dec 04		NUMB (re-recording) / ENCORE *WEA W 660CD* ⟨1⟩	**14** 4+
20 Jan 01	●	(HYBRID THEORY) *Warner Bros. 9362477552*	**4** 77
10 Aug 02	●	REANIMATION *Warner Bros. 9362483542*	**3** 8
5 Apr 03	★	METEORA *Warner Bros. 9362484612* ■ ▲	**1** 33
6 Dec 03		LIVE IN TEXAS *Warner Bros. WB485632*	**47** 3
11 Dec 04		COLLISION COURSE *WEA 9362489662* ▲ ⟨1⟩	**38** 3+

⟨1⟩ Jay-Z / Linkin Park ⟨1⟩ Jay-Z / Linkin Park

'Numb / Encore' is one song that combines Linkin Park's 'Numb' and Jay-Z's 'Encore' 'Reanimation' is a re-mix album of songs from '(Hybrid Theory)'

LINOLEUM
UK, male / female vocal / instrumental group (Singles: 1 Week)   pos/wks
12 Jul 97	MARQUIS *Lino Vinyl LINO 004CD1*	**73** 1

LINUS LOVES featuring Sam OBERNIK *UK, male producer – Linus O'Brien and female vocalist (Singles: 3 Weeks)*   pos/wks
22 Nov 03	STAND BACK *Data / MoS DATA 62CD*	**31** 3

LINX *UK, male vocal / instrumental duo – David Grant and Peter Martin (Singles: 45 Weeks, Albums: 23 Weeks)*   pos/wks
20 Sep 80		YOU'RE LYING *Chrysalis CHS 2461*	**15** 10
7 Mar 81	●	INTUITION *Chrysalis CHS 2500*	**7** 11
13 Jun 81		THROW AWAY THE KEY *Chrysalis CHS 2519*	**21** 9
5 Sep 81		SO THIS IS ROMANCE *Chrysalis CHS 2546*	**15** 9
21 Nov 81		CAN'T HELP MYSELF *Chrysalis CHS 2565*	**55** 3
10 Jul 82		PLAYTHING *Chrysalis CHS 2621*	**48** 3
28 Mar 81	●	INTUITION *Chrysalis CHR 1332*	**8** 19
31 Oct 81		GO AHEAD *Chrysalis CHR 1358*	**35** 4

LIONROCK *UK, male producer – Justin Robertson (Singles: 14 Weeks, Albums: 3 Weeks)*   pos/wks
5 Dec 92	LIONROCK *Deconstruction 74321124381*	**63** 1
8 May 93	PACKET OF PEACE *Deconstruction 74321144372*	**32** 3
23 Oct 93	CARNIVAL *Deconstruction 74321164862*	**34** 2
27 Aug 94	TRIPWIRE *Deconstruction 74321204702*	**44** 1
6 Apr 96	STRAIGHT AT YER HEAD *Deconstruction 74321342972*	**33** 2
27 Jul 96	FIRE UP THE SHOESAW *Deconstruction 74321382652*	**43** 1
14 Mar 98	RUDE BOY ROCK *Concrete HARD 31CD*	**20** 3
30 May 98	SCATTER & SWING *Concrete HARD 35CD*	**54** 1
20 Apr 96	AN INSTINCT FOR DETECTION *Deconstruction 74321342812*	**30** 2
28 Mar 98	CITY DELIRIOUS *Concrete HARD 32LPCD*	**73** 1

LIPPS INC
US, male / female vocal / instrumental group (Singles: 13 Weeks)   pos/wks
17 May 80	●	FUNKYTOWN *Casablanca CAN 194* ▲	**2** 13

LIQUID *UK, male producer – Eamon Downes (Singles: 20 Weeks)* pos/wks
21 Mar 92	SWEET HARMONY *XL Recordings XLS 28*	**15** 6
5 Sep 92	THE FUTURE MUSIC (EP) *XL Recordings XLT 33*	**59** 2
20 Mar 93	TIME TO GET UP *XL Recordings XLS 40CD*	**46** 2
8 Jul 95	SWEET HARMONY (RE-MIX) / ONE LOVE FAMILY *XL Recordings XLS 65CD*	**14** 6
21 Oct 95	CLOSER *XL Recordings XLS 66CD*	**47** 2
25 Jul 98	STRONG *Higher Ground HIGHS 7CD*	**59** 1
21 Oct 00	ORLANDO DAWN *Xtravaganza XTRAV 16CDS*	**53** 1

Tracks on The Future Music (EP): Liquid Is Liquid / Music / House (Is a Feeling) / The Year 3000. On the first two hits act also included Shane Heneghan

LIQUID CHILD *Germany, male production duo – Tobias Menguser and Jurgen Herbarth (Singles: 2 Weeks)*   pos/wks
23 Oct 99	DIVING FACES *Essential Recordings ESCD 9*	**25** 2

LIQUID GOLD *UK, male / female vocal / instrumental group (Singles: 46 Weeks, Albums: 3 Weeks)*   pos/wks
2 Dec 78		ANYWAY YOU DO IT *Creole CR 159*	**41** 7
23 Feb 80	●	DANCE YOURSELF DIZZY *Polo POLO 1*	**2** 14

31 May 80	● SUBSTITUTE *Polo POLO 4*	8	9
1 Nov 80	THE NIGHT THE WINE AND THE ROSES *POLO 6*	32	7
28 Mar 81	DON'T PANIC *Polo POLO 8*	42	5
21 Aug 82	WHERE DID WE GO WRONG *Polo POLO 23*	56	4
16 Aug 80	LIQUID GOLD *Polo POLP 101*	34	3

LIQUID OXYGEN
US, male producer – Frankie Bones (Singles: 2 Weeks)   pos/wks

28 Apr 90	THE PLANET DANCE (MOVE YA BODY) *Champion CHAMP 242*	56	2

LIQUID PEOPLE *UK, male production duo and*
UK, male vocal / instrumental group (Singles: 2 Weeks)   pos/wks

20 Jul 02	MONSTER *Defected DFECT 49* [1]	67	1
21 Jun 03	IT'S MY LIFE (re-mix) *Nebula NEBCD 045* [2]	64	1

[1] Liquid People vs Simple Minds [2] Liquid People vs Talk Talk

LIQUID STATE featuring Marcella WOODS
UK, male production duo and female vocalist (Singles: 1 Week)   pos/wks

30 Mar 02	FALLING *Perfecto PERF 29CDS*	60	1

LISA LISA
US, female vocalist – Lisa Velez (Singles: 32 Weeks, Albums: 1 Week) pos/wks

4 May 85	I WONDER IF I TAKE YOU HOME (re) *CBS A 6057* [1]	12	17
31 Oct 87	LOST IN EMOTION *CBS 651036 7* [2] ▲	58	4
13 Jul 91	LET THE BEAT HIT 'EM *Columbia 6572867* [2]	17	6
24 Aug 91	LET THE BEAT HIT 'EM PART 2 *Columbia 6573747* [2]	49	2
26 Mar 94	SKIP TO MY LU *Chrysalis CDCHS 5006*	34	3
21 Sep 85	LISA LISA AND CULT JAM WITH FULL FORCE *CBS 26593* [1]	96	1

[1] Lisa Lisa and Cult Jam with Full Force [2] Lisa Lisa and Cult Jam [1] Lisa Lisa and Cult Jam with Full Force

LISA MARIE See Malcolm McLAREN

LISA MARIE EXPERIENCE *UK, male instrumental /*
production duo – Dean Marriot and Neil Hynde (Singles: 15 Weeks) pos/wks

27 Apr 96	● KEEP ON JUMPIN' (re) *ffrr FCD 271*	7	13
10 Aug 96	DO THAT TO ME *Positiva CDTIV 57*	33	2

LISBON LIONS featuring Martin O'NEILL & CELTIC CHORUS
UK, male football supporters vocal group (Singles: 4 Weeks)   pos/wks

11 May 02	THE BEST DAY OF OUR LIVES *Concept CDCON 32*	17	4

LIT *US, male vocal / instrumental group*
(Singles: 7 Weeks, Albums: 1 Week)   pos/wks

26 Jun 99	MY OWN WORST ENEMY *RCA 74321669992*	16	4
25 Sep 99	ZIP – LOCK *RCA 74321701852*	60	1
19 Aug 00	OVER MY HEAD *Capitol 8889532*	37	2
10 Jul 99	A PLACE IN THE SUN *RCA 7863677752*	55	1

LITHIUM and Sonya MADAN (see also ECHOBELLY) *US, male producer*
– Victor Imbres and UK, female vocalist (Singles: 2 Weeks)   pos/wks

1 Mar 97	RIDE A ROCKET *ffrr FCD 293*	40	2

De Etta LITTLE and Nelson PIGFORD
US, female / male vocal duo (Singles: 5 Weeks)   pos/wks

13 Aug 77	YOU TAKE MY HEART AWAY *United Artists UP 36257*	35	5

LITTLE ANGELS *UK, male vocal / instrumental*
group (Singles: 41 Weeks, Albums: 15 Weeks)   pos/wks

4 Mar 89	BIG BAD EP *Polydor LTLEP 2*	74	1
24 Feb 90	KICKING UP DUST *Polydor LTL 5*	46	4
12 May 90	RADICAL YOUR LOVER *Polydor LTL 6* [1]	34	4
4 Aug 90	SHE'S A LITTLE ANGEL *Polydor LTL 7*	21	3
2 Feb 91	BONEYARD *Polydor LTL 8*	33	4
30 Mar 91	PRODUCT OF THE WORKING CLASS *Polydor LTL 9*	40	2
1 Jun 91	YOUNG GODS *Polydor LTL 10*	34	2
20 Jul 91	I AIN'T GONNA CRY *Polydor LTL 11*	26	3
7 Nov 92	TOO MUCH TOO YOUNG *Polydor LTL 12*	22	3
9 Jan 93	WOMANKIND *Polydor LTLCD 13*	12	5
24 Apr 93	SOAPBOX *Polydor LTLCD 14*	33	4
25 Sep 93	SAIL AWAY *Polydor LTLCD 15*	45	3

9 Apr 94	TEN MILES HIGH *Polydor LTLCD 16*	18	3
2 Mar 91	YOUNG GODS *Polydor 8478461*	17	6
6 Feb 93	★ JAM *Polydor 5176422* ■	1	5
23 Apr 94	LITTLE OF THE PAST *Polydor 5219362*	20	2
2 Jul 94	TOO POSH TO MOSH TOO GOOD TO LAST! *Essential ESSCD 213*	18	2

[1] Little Angels featuring the Big Bad Horns

Tracks on Big Bad EP: She's a Little Angel / Don't Waste My Time / Better Than the Rest / Sex in Cars

LITTLE ANTHONY and the IMPERIALS
US, male vocal group – leader Anthony Gourdine (Singles: 4 Weeks) pos/wks

31 Jul 76	BETTER USE YOUR HEAD *United Artists UP 36141*	42	4

LITTLE BENNY and the MASTERS
US, male rapper / instrumentalist – trumpet – Benjamin
Harris and male instrumental group (Singles: 7 Weeks)   pos/wks

2 Feb 85	WHO COMES TO BOOGIE *Bluebird 10 BR 13*	33	7

LITTLE CAESAR *UK, male vocalist (Singles: 3 Weeks)*   pos/wks

9 Jun 90	THE WHOLE OF THE MOON *A1 EAU 1*	68	3

LITTLE EVA (see also Big Dee IRWIN) *US, female vocalist –*
Eva Boyd, b. 29 Jun 1945, d. 10 Apr 2003 (Singles: 45 Weeks) pos/wks

6 Sep 62	● THE LOCO-MOTION (re) *London HL 9581* ▲	2	28
3 Jan 63	KEEP YOUR HANDS OFF MY BABY *London HLU 9633*	30	5
7 Mar 63	LET'S TURKEY TROT *London HLU 9687*	13	12

'The Loco-motion' re-entry peaked at No.11 in Jul 1972

LITTLE FEAT (see also Lowell GEORGE)
US, male vocal / instrumental group (Albums: 19 Weeks)   pos/wks

6 Dec 75	THE LAST RECORD ALBUM *Warner Bros. K 56156*	36	3
21 May 77	● TIME LOVES A HERO *Warner Bros. K 56349*	8	11
11 Mar 78	WAITING FOR COLUMBUS *Warner Bros. K 66075*	43	1
1 Dec 79	DOWN ON THE FARM *Warner Bros. K 56667*	46	3
8 Aug 81	HOY-HOY! *Warner Bros. K 666100*	76	1

LITTLE LOUIE See Louie VEGA

LITTLE MS MARCIE See MELT featuring LITTLE MS MARCIE

LITTLE RICHARD *US, male vocalist / instrumentalist –*
piano – Richard Penniman (Singles: 116 Weeks)   pos/wks

14 Dec 56	RIP IT UP *London HLO 8336*	30	1
8 Feb 57	● LONG TALL SALLY *London HLO 8366*	3	16
22 Feb 57	TUTTI FRUTTI *London HLO 8366*	29	1
8 Mar 57	SHE'S GOT IT (re) *London HLO 8382*	15	9
15 Mar 57	● THE GIRL CAN'T HELP IT *London HLO 8382*	9	11
28 Jun 57	● LUCILLE *London HLO 8446*	10	9
13 Sep 57	JENNY JENNY *London HLO 8470*	11	5
29 Nov 57	KEEP A KNOCKIN' *London HLO 8509*	21	7
28 Feb 58	● GOOD GOLLY MISS MOLLY *London HLU 8560*	8	9
11 Jul 58	OOH! MY SOUL (re) *London HLU 8647*	22	4
2 Jan 59	● BABY FACE *London HLU 8770*	2	15
3 Apr 59	BY THE LIGHT OF THE SILVERY MOON *London HLU 8831*	17	5
5 Jun 59	KANSAS CITY *London HLU 8868*	26	5
11 Oct 62	HE GOT WHAT HE WANTED (BUT HE LOST WHAT HE HAD) *Mercury AMT 1189*	38	4
4 Jun 64	BAMA LAMA BAMA LOO *London HL 9896*	20	7
2 Jul 77	GOOD GOLLY MISS MOLLY (re-recording) / RIP IT UP (re-recording) *Creole CR 140*	37	4
14 Jun 86	GREAT GOSH A'MIGHTY! (IT'S A MATTER OF TIME) *MCA MCA 1049*	62	2
25 Oct 86	OPERATOR *WEA YZ 89*	67	2

LITTLE STEVEN *US, male vocalist / instrumentalist –*
guitar – Steve Van Zandt (Singles: 3 Weeks, Albums: 4 Weeks) pos/wks

23 May 87	BITTER FRUIT *Manhattan MT 21*	66	3
6 Nov 82	MEN WITHOUT WOMEN *EMI America 3027* [1]	73	1
6 Jun 87	FREEDOM NO COMPROMISE *Manhattan MTL 1010*	52	2

[1] Little Steven and The Disciples of Soul

LITTLE T See REBEL MC

LITTLE TONY and his BROTHERS
Italy, male vocal group – leader Anthony Ciacci (Singles: 3 Weeks)   pos/wks
15 Jan 60   **TOO GOOD** *Decca F 11190* **19** 3

LITTLE TREES *Denmark, female vocal group (Singles: 7 Weeks)*   pos/wks
1 Sep 01   **HELP! I'M A FISH** *RCA 74321874652* **11** 7

LITTLE VILLAGE
UK / US, male vocal / instrumental group (Albums: 4 Weeks)   pos/wks
29 Feb 92   **LITTLE VILLAGE** *Reprise 7599267132* **23** 4

LIVE *US, male vocal / instrumental*
group (Singles: 13 Weeks, Albums: 9 Weeks)   pos/wks

18 Feb 95	**I ALONE** *Radioactive RAXTD 13*	**48** 4
1 Jul 95	**SELLING THE DRAMA** *Radioactive RAXTD 17*	**30** 2
7 Oct 95	**ALL OVER YOU** *Radioactive RAXTD 20*	**48** 1
13 Jan 96	**LIGHTNING CRASHES** *Radioactive RAXTD 23*	**33** 2
15 Mar 97	**LAKINI'S JUICE** *Radioactive RAD 49023*	**29** 2
12 Jul 97	**FREAKS** *Radioactive RAXTD 29*	**60** 1
5 Feb 00	**THE DOLPHIN'S CRY** *Radioactive RAXTD 39*	**62** 1
15 Jul 95	**THROWING COPPER** *Radioactive RAD 10997* ▲	**37** 6
29 Mar 97	**SECRET SAMADHI** *Radioactive RAD 11590* ▲	**31** 2
16 Oct 99	**THE DISTANCE TO HERE** *Radioactive RAD 11966*	**56** 1

LIVE ELEMENT *US, male production duo –*
Greg Bahary and Chris Malinchak (Singles: 2 Weeks)   pos/wks
26 Jan 02   **BE FREE** *Strictly Rhythm SRUKCD 11* **26** 2

LIVE REPORT
UK, male vocal / instrumental group (Singles: 1 Week)   pos/wks
20 May 89   **WHY DO I ALWAYS GET IT WRONG** *Brouhaha CUE 7* **73** 1

LIVERPOOL EXPRESS
UK, male vocal / instrumental group (Singles: 26 Weeks)   pos/wks

26 Jun 76	**YOU ARE MY LOVE** *Warner Bros. K 16743*	**11** 9
16 Oct 76	**HOLD TIGHT** *Warner Bros. K 16799*	**46** 2
18 Dec 76	**EVERY MAN MUST HAVE A DREAM** *Warner Bros. K 16854*	**17** 11
4 Jun 77	**DREAMIN'** *Warner Bros. K 16933*	**40** 4

LIVERPOOL FC
UK, male football team vocalists (Singles: 21 Weeks)   pos/wks

28 May 77	**WE CAN DO IT (EP)** *State STAT 50*	**15** 4
23 Apr 83	**LIVERPOOL (WE'RE NEVER GONNA ...)** / **LIVERPOOL (ANTHEM)** *Mean MEAN 102*	**54** 4
17 May 86	**SITTING ON THE TOP OF THE WORLD** *Columbia DB 9116*	**50** 2
14 May 88 ●	**ANFIELD RAP (RED MACHINE IN FULL EFFECT)** *Virgin LFC 1*	**3** 6
18 May 96 ●	**PASS AND MOVE (IT'S THE LIVERPOOL GROOVE)** *Telstar LFCCD 96* 1	**4** 5

1 Liverpool FC and The Boot Room Boyz

Tracks on We Can Do It (EP): We Can Do It / Liverpool Lou / We Shall Not Be Moved / You'll Never Walk Alone

LIVIN' JOY (see also ALEX PARTY)
US / Italy, male / female vocal / instrumental group –
leader Paolo Visnadi (Singles: 44 Weeks, Albums: 2 Weeks)   pos/wks

3 Sep 94	**DREAMER** *Undiscovered MCSTD 1993*	**18** 6
13 May 95 ★	**DREAMER (re-mix)** *Undiscovered MCSTD 2056* ■	**1** 11
15 Jun 96 ●	**DON'T STOP MOVIN'** *Undiscovered MCSTD 40041*	**5** 14
2 Nov 96 ●	**FOLLOW THE RULES** *Undiscovered MCSTD 40081*	**9** 5
5 Apr 97	**WHERE CAN I FIND LOVE** *Undiscovered MCSTD 40108*	**12** 4
23 Aug 97	**DEEP IN YOU** *Universal MCSTD 40136*	**17** 4
16 Nov 96	**DON'T STOP MOVIN'** *Undiscovered MCD 60023*	**41** 2

LIVING COLOUR *US, male vocal / instrumental*
group (Singles: 22 Weeks, Albums: 22 Weeks)   pos/wks

27 Oct 90	**TYPE** *Epic LCL 7*	**75** 1
2 Feb 91	**LOVE REARS ITS UGLY HEAD** *Epic 6565937*	**12** 11
1 Jun 91	**SOLACE OF YOU** *Epic 6569087*	**33** 5
26 Oct 91	**CULT OF PERSONALITY** *Epic 6575357*	**67** 2
20 Feb 93	**LEAVE IT ALONE** *Epic 6589762*	**34** 2
17 Apr 93	**AUSLANDER** *Epic 6591732*	**53** 1
15 Sep 90	**TIME'S UP** *Epic 4669201*	**20** 19
6 Mar 93	**STAIN** *Epic 4728562*	**19** 3

LIVING IN A BOX *UK, male vocal / instrumental group – including*
Richard Darbyshire (Singles: 62 Weeks, Albums: 35 Weeks)   pos/wks

4 Apr 87 ●	**LIVING IN A BOX** *Chrysalis LIB 1*	**5** 13
13 Jun 87	**SCALES OF JUSTICE** *Chrysalis LIB 2*	**30** 6
26 Sep 87	**SO THE STORY GOES** *Chrysalis LIB 3* 1	**34** 8
30 Jan 88	**LOVE IS THE ART** *Chrysalis LIB 4*	**45** 4
18 Feb 89 ●	**BLOW THE HOUSE DOWN** *Chrysalis LIB 5*	**10** 9
10 Jun 89	**GATECRASHING** *Chrysalis LIB 6*	**36** 6
23 Sep 89 ●	**ROOM IN YOUR HEART** *Chrysalis LIB 7*	**5** 13
30 Dec 89	**DIFFERENT AIR (re)** *Chrysalis LIB 8*	**57** 3
9 May 87	**LIVING IN A BOX** *Chrysalis CDL 1547*	**25** 19
8 Jul 89	**GATECRASHING** *Chrysalis CDI 1676*	**21** 16

1 Living in a Box featuring Bobby Womack

Dandy LIVINGSTONE *Jamaica, male vocalist –*
Robert Livingstone Thompson (Singles: 19 Weeks)   pos/wks
2 Sep 72   **SUZANNE BEWARE OF THE DEVIL** *Horse HOSS 16* **14** 11
13 Jan 73   **BIG CITY / THINK ABOUT THAT** *Horse HOSS 25* **26** 8

LLAMA FARMERS
UK, male / female vocal / instrumental group (Singles: 2 Weeks)   pos/wks
6 Feb 99   **BIG WHEELS** *Beggars Banquet BBQ 333CD* **67** 1
15 May 99   **GET THE KEYS AND GO** *Beggars Banquet BBQ 335CD* **74** 1

Kelly LLORENNA (see also N-TRANCE)
UK, female vocalist (Singles: 36 Weeks, Albums: 2 Weeks)   pos/wks

7 May 94	**SET YOU FREE** *All Around the World CDGLOBE 124* 1	**39** 4
24 Feb 96	**BRIGHTER DAY** *Pukka CDPUKKA 5*	**43** 2
25 Jul 98	**HEART OF GOLD** *Diverse VERSE 2CD* 2	**55** 1
24 Mar 01	**TRUE LOVE NEVER DIES** *All Around the World CDGLOBE 240* 3	**34** 3
2 Feb 02 ●	**TRUE LOVE NEVER DIES (re-mix)** *All Around the World CDGLOBE 248* 3	**7** 10
6 Jul 02 ●	**TELL IT TO MY HEART** *All Around the World CDGLOBE 256*	**9** 8
30 Nov 02	**HEART OF GOLD** *All Around the World CDGLOBE 271*	**19** 4
6 Mar 04	**THIS TIME I KNOW IT'S FOR REAL** *All Around the World CXGLOBE 295*	**14** 4
7 Dec 02	**ALL CLUBBED UP – THE BEST OF KELLY LLORENNA** *Universal TV 0666082*	**62** 2

1 N-Trance featuring Kelly Llorenna 2 Force and Styles featuring Kelly Llorenna
3 Flip & Fill featuring Kelly Llorenna

Andrew LLOYD WEBBER
UK, male composer / producer (Albums: 38 Weeks)   pos/wks
11 Feb 78 ● **VARIATIONS** *MCA MCF 2824* **2** 19
23 Mar 85 ● **REQUIEM** *HMV ALW 1* **4** 18
25 Dec 04   **ANDREW LLOYD WEBBER'S THE PHANTOM OF THE OPERA (FILM SOUNDTRACK) – SPECIAL EDITION** *Sony Classical SK 93521* ....**48** 1+

'Variations' features cellist Julian Lloyd Webber. 'Requiem' credits Placido Domingo, Sarah Brightman, Paul Miles-Kingston, the Winchester Cathedral Choir and the English Chamber Orchestra conducted by Lorin Maazel. 'Andrew Lloyd Webber's The Phantom of the Opera' features the London Boys Choir

Julian LLOYD WEBBER
(see also ANDREW LLOYD WEBBER)
UK, male instrumentalist – cello (Albums: 19 Weeks)   pos/wks
14 Sep 85   **PIECES** *Polydor PROLP 6* **59** 5
21 Feb 87   **ELGAR CELLO CONCERTO** *Philips 416 3541* **94** 1
27 Oct 90   **LLOYD WEBBER PLAYS LLOYD WEBBER** *Philips 4322911* **15** 13

First two albums credit the London Symphony Orchestra, the third credits the Royal Philharmonic Orchestra

Don LLOYDIE See **SOUNDMAN** and **Don LLOYDIE** with **Elisabeth TROY**

LO FIDELITY ALLSTARS *UK, male vocal /*
instrumental group (Singles: 5 Weeks, Albums: 4 Weeks)   pos/wks
11 Oct 97   **DISCO MACHINE GUN** *Skint SKINT 30CD* **50** 1
2 May 98   **VISION INCISION** *Skint SKINT 33CD* **30** 2
28 Nov 98   **BATTLEFLAG** *Skint SKINT 38CD* 1 ....**36** 2
6 Jun 98   **HOW TO OPERATE WITH A BLOWN MIND** *Skint BRASSIC 8CD* ..**15** 4

1 Lo Fidelity Allstars featuring Pigeonhed

LOBO *US, male vocalist – Kent LaVoie (Singles: 25 Weeks)* pos/wks
19 Jun 71 ● ME AND YOU AND A DOG NAMED BOO *Philips 6073 801* **4** 14
8 Jun 74 ● I'D LOVE YOU TO WANT ME *UK 68* **5** 11

LOBO *Holland, male vocalist – Imrich Lobo (Singles: 11 Weeks)* pos/wks
25 Jul 81 ● THE CARIBBEAN DISCO SHOW *Polydor POSP 302* **8** 11

LOCK 'N' LOAD *Holland, male DJ / production duo – Francis Rooijen and Nilz Pijpers (Singles: 13 Weeks)* pos/wks
15 Apr 00 ● BLOW YA MIND (re) *Pepper 9230162* **6** 11
3 Mar 01 HOUSE SOME MORE *Pepper 9230422* **45** 2

Josef LOCKE *Ireland, male vocalist – Joseph McLaughlin, b. 23 Mar 1917, d. 15 Oct 1999 (Albums: 20 Weeks)* pos/wks
28 Jun 69 THE WORLD OF JOSEF LOCKE TODAY *Decca SPA 21* **29** 1
21 Mar 92 ● HEAR MY SONG (THE BEST OF JOSEF LOCKE) *EMI CDGO 2034* ..**7** 17
27 Jun 92 TAKE A PAIR OF SPARKLING EYES *EMI CDGO 2038* **41** 2

Kimberley LOCKE *US, female vocalist (Singles: 2 Weeks)* pos/wks
31 Jul 04 8TH WORLD WONDER *Curb / London CUBC 097* **49** 2

Hank LOCKLIN *US, male vocalist – Lawrence Locklin (Singles: 41 Weeks)* pos/wks
11 Aug 60 ● PLEASE HELP ME, I'M FALLING *RCA 1188* **9** 19
15 Feb 62 FROM HERE TO THERE TO YOU *RCA 1273* **44** 3
15 Nov 62 WE'RE GONNA GO FISHIN' *RCA 1305* **18** 11
5 May 66 I FEEL A CRY COMING ON *RCA 1510* **29** 8

LOCKSMITH *US, male vocal / instrumental group (Singles: 6 Weeks)* pos/wks
23 Aug 80 UNLOCK THE FUNK *Arista ARIST 364* **42** 6

LOCOMOTIVE *UK, male vocal / instrumental group (Singles: 8 Weeks)* pos/wks
16 Oct 68 RUDI'S IN LOVE *Parlophone R 5718* **25** 8

John LODGE (see also The MOODY BLUES) *UK, male vocalist / instrumentalist – guitar (Albums: 20 Weeks)* pos/wks
29 Mar 75 ● BLUE JAYS *Threshold THS 12* [1] **4** 18
19 Feb 77 NATURAL AVENUE *Decca TXS 120* **38** 2

[1] Justin Hayward and John Lodge

LODGER *UK, male / female vocal / instrumental group (Singles: 2 Weeks)* pos/wks
2 May 98 I'M LEAVING *Island CID 693* **40** 2

Lisa LOEB and NINE STORIES *US, female / male vocal / instrumental group (Singles: 17 Weeks, Albums: 2 Weeks)* pos/wks
3 Sep 94 ● STAY (I MISSED YOU) *RCA 74321212522* ▲ **6** 15
16 Sep 95 DO YOU SLEEP? *Geffen GFSTD 96* **45** 2
7 Oct 95 TAILS *Geffen GED 24734* **39** 2

Nils LOFGREN *US, male vocalist / instrumentalist – guitar (Singles: 3 Weeks, Albums: 30 Weeks)* pos/wks
8 Jun 85 SECRETS IN THE STREET *Towerbell TOW 68* **53** 3
17 Apr 76 ● CRY TOUGH *A&M AMLH 64573* **8** 11
26 Mar 77 I CAME TO DANCE *A&M AMLH 64628* **30** 4
5 Nov 77 NIGHT AFTER NIGHT *A&M AMLH 68439* **38** 2
26 Sep 81 NIGHT FADES AWAY *Backstreet MCF 3121* **50** 3
1 May 82 A RHYTHM ROMANCE *A&M AMLH 68543* **100** 1
6 Jul 85 FLIP *Towerbell TOWLP 11* **36** 7
5 Apr 86 CODE OF THE ROAD *Towerbell TOWDLP 17* **86** 1
27 Apr 91 SILVER LINING *Essential ESSLP 145* **61** 1

Johnny LOGAN *Ireland, male vocalist – Sean Sherrard (Singles: 24 Weeks, Albums: 1 Week)* pos/wks
3 May 80 ★ WHAT'S ANOTHER YEAR *Epic EPC 8572* **1** 8
23 May 87 ● HOLD ME NOW *Epic LOG 1* **2** 11
22 Aug 87 I'M NOT IN LOVE *Epic LOG 2* **51** 5
22 Aug 87 HOLD ME NOW *CBS 451 073 1* **83** 1

Kenny LOGGINS *US, male vocalist / instrumentalist (Singles: 21 Weeks)* pos/wks
28 Apr 84 ● FOOTLOOSE *CBS A 4101* ▲ **6** 10
1 Nov 86 DANGER ZONE *CBS A 7188* **45** 11

LOGO featuring Dawn JOSEPH *UK, male production duo and female vocalist (Singles: 1 Week)* pos/wks
8 Dec 01 DON'T PANIC *Manifesto FESCD 89* **42** 1

LOLA *US, female vocalist – Lola Blank (Singles: 1 Week)* pos/wks
28 Mar 87 WAX THE VAN *Syncopate SY 1* **65** 1

LOLLY *UK, female vocalist – Anna Klumby (Singles: 44 Weeks, Albums: 12 Weeks)* pos/wks
10 Jul 99 ● VIVA LA RADIO *Polydor 5639492* **6** 9
18 Sep 99 ● MICKEY *Polydor 5613682* **4** 10
4 Dec 99 ● BIG BOYS DON'T CRY / ROCKIN' ROBIN *Polydor 5615552* **10** 9
6 May 00 PER SEMPRE AMORE (FOREVER IN LOVE) (re) *Polydor 5617882* **11** 10
9 Sep 00 GIRLS JUST WANNA HAVE FUN *Polydor 5619762* **14** 6
2 Oct 99 MY FIRST ALBUM *Polydor 5479622* **21** 12

Alain LOMBARD See Mady MESPLE and Danielle MILLET with the PARIS OPERA-COMIQUE ORCHESTRA conducted by Alain LOMBARD

Julie LONDON *US, female vocalist – b. Julie Peck, 26 Sep 1926, d. 18 Oct 2000 (Singles: 3 Weeks)* pos/wks
5 Apr 57 CRY ME A RIVER *London HLU 8240* **22** 3

Laurie LONDON *UK, male vocalist (Singles: 12 Weeks)* pos/wks
8 Nov 57 HE'S GOT THE WHOLE WORLD IN HIS HANDS *Parlophone R 4359* **12** 12

With Geoff Love, his Orchestra and Chorus

LONDON BOYS *UK, male vocal duo – Edem Ephraim, b. 1959, and Dennis Fuller, b. 1960, both d. 21 Sep 1996 (Singles: 46 Weeks, Albums: 29 Weeks)* pos/wks
10 Dec 88 ● REQUIEM (re) *WEA YZ 345* **4** 21
1 Jul 89 ● LONDON NIGHTS *WEA YZ 393* **2** 9
16 Sep 89 HARLEM DESIRE *WEA YZ 415* **17** 7
2 Dec 89 MY LOVE *WEA YZ 433* **46** 6
16 Jun 90 CHAPEL OF LOVE *East West YZ 458* **75** 1
19 Jan 91 FREEDOM *East West YZ 554* **54** 2
29 Jul 89 ● THE TWELVE COMMANDMENTS OF DANCE *WEA WX 278* **2** 29

'Requiem' peaked at No.4 after re-entering in April 1989

LONDON COMMUNITY CHOIR See Ana ANN

LONDON COMMUNITY GOSPEL CHOIR See Sal SOLO

LONDON PHILHARMONIC CHOIR (see also ADIEMUS) *UK, male / female choir (Albums: 20 Weeks)* pos/wks
3 Dec 60 ● THE MESSIAH *Pye Golden Guinea GGL 0062* [1] **10** 7
13 Nov 76 ● SOUND OF GLORY *Arcade ADEP 25* [2] **10** 10
13 Apr 91 PRAISE – 18 CHORAL MASTERPIECES *Pop & Arts PATLP 301* [3] **54** 3

[1] London Philharmonic Choir with the London Orchestra conducted by Peter Susskind [2] London Philharmonic Choir with the National Philharmonic Orchestra conducted by John Aldiss [3] London Philharmonic Choir with the National Philharmonic Orchestra

LONDON PHILHARMONIC ORCHESTRA (see also Nigel KENNEDY; Ennio MORRICONE; Justin HAYWARD) *UK, male / female orchestra (Albums: 22 Weeks)* pos/wks
23 Apr 60 RAVEL'S BOLERO *London HAV 2189* **15** 4
8 Apr 61 VICTORY AT SEA *Pye GGL 0073* **12** 4
21 May 83 ● DRESSED FOR THE OCCASION *EMI EMC 3432* [1] **7** 17

[1] Cliff Richard and the London Philharmonic Orchestra

LONDON STRING CHORALE
UK, orchestra / choir (Singles: 13 Weeks)   pos/wks

15 Dec 73	**GALLOPING HOME (re)** *Polydor 2058 280*	31	13

LONDON SYMPHONY ORCHESTRA `286` `Top 500`
(see also Andrea BOCELLI) *Formed in 1904, one of the chart's largest acts. Principal conductors have included Andre Previn, Sir Colin Davis and John Williams. Famous for global tours and soundtrack recordings, they achieved greatest chart success with symphonic arrangements of rock classics (Singles: 7 Weeks, Albums: 221 Weeks)*   pos/wks

6 Jan 79	**THEME FROM 'SUPERMAN' (MAIN TITLE)** *Warner Bros. K 17292*	32	5
6 Dec 97	**JUST SHOW ME HOW TO LOVE YOU** *Coalition COLA 035CD* 1	54	2
18 Mar 72	**TOP TV THEMES** *Studio Two STWO 372*	13	7
16 Dec 72 ●	**THE STRAUSS FAMILY** *Polydor 2659 014* 1	2	21
5 Jul 75	**MUSIC FROM 'EDWARD VII'** *Polydor 2659 041*	52	1
18 Dec 76	**THE SNOW GOOSE** *RCA RS 1088* 2	49	1
21 Jan 78	**STAR WARS (FILM SOUNDTRACK)** *20th Century BTD 541*	21	12
8 Jul 78 ●	**CLASSIC ROCK** *K-Tel ONE 1009*	3	39
10 Feb 79	**CLASSIC ROCK – THE SECOND MOVEMENT** *K-Tel NE 1039*	26	8
5 Jan 80	**RHAPSODY IN BLACK** *K-Tel ONE 1063*	34	5
1 Aug 81 ●	**CLASSIC ROCK – ROCK CLASSICS** *K-Tel ONE 1123*	5	23
27 Nov 82	**THE BEST OF CLASSIC ROCK** *K-Tel ONE 1080*	35	11
27 Aug 83	**CLASSIC ROCK – ROCK SYMPHONIES** *K-Tel ONE 1243*	40	9
26 Oct 85	**HITS ON OPERA** *Stylus SMR 8505* 3	38	4
16 Nov 85	**THE POWER OF CLASSIC ROCK** *Portrait PRT 10049*	13	15
14 Nov 87	**CLASSIC ROCK COUNTDOWN** *CBS MOOD 3*	32	16
18 Nov 89	**CLASSIC ROCK – THE LIVING YEARS** *CBS MOOD 9*	51	6
18 Jan 92	**WIND OF CHANGE – CLASSIC ROCK** *Columbia MOODCD 19* 4	24	8
19 Nov 94	**THE WORKS OF RICE AND LLOYD WEBBER** *Vision VISCD 4*	55	2
23 Sep 95	**BRAVEHEART (FILM SOUNDTRACK)** *Decca 4482952* 5	27	9
25 Oct 97	**PAUL McCARTNEY'S STANDING STONE** *EMI Classics CDC 5564842* 6	34	2
15 May 99 ●	**STAR WARS – THE PHANTOM MENACE (FILM SOUNDTRACK)** *Sony Classical SK 61816*	8	17
11 May 02	**STAR WARS EPISODE II – ATTACK OF THE CLONES (FILM SOUNDTRACK)** *Sony Classical SK 89932*	15	5

1 Sarah Brightman and the LSO featuring José Cura 1 London Symphony Orchestra conducted by Cyril Ornadel 2 Spike Milligan with the London Symphony Orchestra 3 Kimera with the London Symphony Orchestra 4 London Symphony Orchestra and the Royal Choral Society 5 London Symphony Orchestra, music composed and conducted by James Horner 6 London Symphony Orchestra conducted by Lawrence Foster

'Star Wars – The Phantom Menace' and 'Star Wars Episode II – Attack of the Clones' are conducted by John Williams

LONDON WELSH MALE VOICE CHOIR
UK, male choir (Albums: 10 Weeks)   pos/wks

5 Sep 81	**SONGS OF THE VALLEYS** *K-Tel NE 1117*	61	10

LONDONBEAT *UK / US, male vocal group – includes*
Jimmy Helms (Singles: 47 Weeks, Albums: 6 Weeks)   pos/wks

26 Nov 88	**9 AM (THE COMFORT ZONE)** *AnXious ANX 008*	19	10
18 Feb 89	**FAILING IN LOVE AGAIN** *AnXious ANX 007*	60	2
2 Dec 89	**IT TAKES TWO BABY** *Spartan CIN 101* 1	53	2
1 Sep 90 ●	**I'VE BEEN THINKING ABOUT YOU** *AnXious ANX 14* ▲	2	13
24 Nov 90	**A BETTER LOVE** *AnXious ANX 21*	52	1
2 Mar 91	**NO WOMAN NO CRY** *AnXious ANX 25*	64	2
20 Jul 91	**A BETTER LOVE (re-issue)** *AnXious ANX 32*	23	6
27 Jun 92	**YOU BRING ON THE SUN** *AnXious ANX 37*	32	4
24 Oct 92	**THAT'S HOW I FEEL ABOUT YOU** *AnXious ANX 40*	69	1
8 Apr 95	**I'M JUST YOUR PUPPET ON A ... (STRING)** *AnXious 74321270982*	55	1
20 May 95	**COME BACK** *AnXious 74321226682*	69	1
13 Oct 90	**IN THE BLOOD** *AnXious ZL 74810*	34	6

1 Liz Kershaw, Bruno Brookes, Jive Bunny and Londonbeat

LONE JUSTICE *US, female / male vocal /*
instrumental group (Singles: 4 Weeks, Albums: 5 Weeks)   pos/wks

7 Mar 87	**I FOUND LOVE** *Geffen GEF 18*	45	4
6 Jul 85	**LONE JUSTICE** *Geffen GEF 26288*	49	2
8 Nov 86	**SHELTER** *Geffen WX 73*	84	3

LONE STAR *UK, male vocal / instrumental group (Albums: 7 Weeks)* pos/wks

2 Oct 76	**LONE STAR** *Epic EPC 81545*	47	1
17 Sep 77	**FIRING ON ALL SIX** *CBS 82213*	36	6

LONESTAR
US, male vocal / instrumental group (Singles: 24 Weeks)   pos/wks

15 Apr 00	**AMAZED** *BMG / Grapevine 74321742582* ▲	21	22
7 Sep 00	**SMILE** *BMG / Grapevine 74321786132*	55	2

Shorty LONG *US, male vocalist – Frederick Long,*
b. 20 May 1940, d. 29 Jun 1969 (Singles: 7 Weeks)   pos/wks

17 Jul 68	**HERE COMES THE JUDGE** *Tamla Motown TMG 663*	30	7

The LONG AND THE SHORT
UK, male vocal / instrumental group (Singles: 8 Weeks)   pos/wks

10 Sep 64	**THE LETTER** *Decca F 11964*	35	5
24 Dec 64	**CHOC ICE** *Decca F 12043*	40	3

LONG RYDERS *US, male vocal / instrumental*
group (Singles: 4 Weeks, Albums: 1 Week)   pos/wks

5 Oct 85	**LOOKING FOR LEWIS AND CLARKE** *Island IS 237*	59	4
16 Nov 85	**STATE OF OUR UNION** *Island ILPS 9802*	66	1

LONGPIGS *UK, male vocal / instrumental*
group (Singles: 17 Weeks, Albums: 10 Weeks)   pos/wks

22 Jul 95	**SHE SAID** *Mother MUMCD 66*	67	1
28 Oct 95	**JESUS CHRIST** *Mother MUMCD 68*	61	1
17 Feb 96	**FAR** *Mother MUMCD 71*	37	2
13 Apr 96	**ON AND ON** *Mother MUMCD 74*	16	3
22 Jun 96	**SHE SAID (re-issue)** *Mother MUMCD 77*	16	4
5 Oct 96	**LOST MYSELF** *Mother MUMCD 82*	22	3
9 Oct 99	**BLUE SKIES** *Mother MUMCD 113*	21	2
18 Dec 99	**THE FRANK SONATA** *Mother MUMCD 114*	57	1
11 May 96	**THE SUN IS OFTEN OUT** *Mother MUMCD 9602*	26	9
23 Oct 99	**MOBILE HOME** *Mother MUMCD 9901*	33	1

Joe LONGTHORNE
UK, male vocalist (Singles: 6 Weeks, Albums: 32 Weeks)   pos/wks

30 Apr 94	**YOUNG GIRL** *EMI CDEM 310*	61	2
10 Dec 94	**PASSING STRANGERS** *EMI CDEM 362* 1	34	4
3 Dec 88	**THE JOE LONGTHORNE SONGBOOK** *Telstar STAR 2353*	16	12
29 Jul 89	**ESPECIALLY FOR YOU** *Telstar STAR 2365*	22	10
9 Dec 89	**THE JOE LONGTHORNE CHRISTMAS ALBUM** *Telstar STAR 2385*	44	4
13 Nov 93	**I WISH YOU LOVE** *EMI CDEMC 3662*	47	4
8 Oct 94	**LIVE AT THE ROYAL ALBERT HALL** *Premier CDDPR 126*	57	2

1 Joe Longthorne and Liz Dawn

LONGVIEW *UK, male vocal / instrumental*
group (Singles: 6 Weeks, Albums: 2 Weeks)   pos/wks

26 Oct 02	**WHEN YOU SLEEP** *4:45 Recordings LVIEW 02CD*	74	1
8 Feb 03	**NOWHERE** *4:45 Recordings LVIEW 03CD*	72	1
19 Jul 03	**FURTHER** *14th Floor 14FLR 01CD1*	27	2
11 Oct 03	**CAN'T EXPLAIN** *14th Floor 14FLR 02CD1*	51	1
10 Jul 04	**IN A DREAM** *14th Floor 14FLR 06CD*	38	1
2 Aug 03	**MERCURY** *14th Floor 5046668862*	45	2

LONYO
UK, male vocalist / producer – Lonyo Engele (Singles: 9 Weeks)   pos/wks

8 Jul 00 ●	**SUMMER OF LOVE** *Riverhorse RIVHCD 3* 1	8	7
7 Apr 01	**GARAGE GIRLS** *Riverhorse RIVHCD 12* 2	39	2

1 Lonyo – Comme Ci Comme Ca 2 Lonyo featuring MC Onyx Stone

The LOOK
UK, male vocal / instrumental group (Singles: 15 Weeks)   pos/wks

20 Dec 80 ●	**I AM THE BEAT** *MCA 647*	6	12
29 Aug 81	**FEEDING TIME** *MCA 736*	50	3

LOON *See Lenny KRAVITZ*

LOOP *UK, male vocal / instrumental group (Albums: 2 Weeks)* pos/wks

4 Feb 89	**FADE OUT** *Chapter 22 CHAPLP 34*	51	1
3 Feb 90	**A GILDED ETERNITY** *Situation Two SITU 27*	39	1

LOOP DA LOOP
UK, male producer – Nick Dresti (Singles: 4 Weeks)   pos/wks

| 7 Jun 97 | GO WITH THE FLOW *Manifesto FESCD 24* .... | **47** | 1 |
| 20 Feb 99 | HAZEL *Manifesto FESCD 53* .... | **20** | 3 |

LOOSE ENDS *UK, male vocal / instrumental trio – Carl McIntosh, Jane*
Eugene and Steve Nichol (Singles: 76 Weeks, Albums: 41 Weeks)   pos/wks

25 Feb 84	TELL ME WHAT YOU WANT *Virgin VS 658*	**74**	1
28 Apr 84	EMERGENCY (DIAL 999) *Virgin VS 677*	**41**	6
21 Jul 84	CHOOSE ME (RESCUE ME) *Virgin VS 697*	**59**	3
23 Feb 85	HANGIN' ON A STRING (CONTEMPLATING) *Virgin VS 748* 13		13
11 May 85	MAGIC TOUCH *Virgin VS 761*	**16**	7
27 Jul 85	GOLDEN YEARS *Virgin VS 795*	**59**	4
14 Jun 86	STAY A LITTLE WHILE, CHILD *Virgin VS 819*	**52**	5
20 Sep 86	SLOW DOWN *Virgin VS 884*	**27**	7
29 Nov 86	NIGHTS OF PLEASURE *Virgin VS 919*	**42**	7
4 Jun 88	MR BACHELOR *Virgin VS 1080*	**50**	4
25 Aug 90	DON'T BE A FOOL *10 TEN 312*	**13**	9
17 Nov 90	LOVE'S GOT ME *10 TEN 330*	**40**	4
20 Jun 92	HANGIN' ON A STRING (re-mix) *Ten TEN 406*	**25**	5
5 Sep 92	MAGIC TOUCH (re-mix) *Ten TEN 409*	**75**	1
21 Apr 84	A LITTLE SPICE *Virgin V 2301*	**46**	9
20 Apr 85	SO WHERE ARE YOU? *Virgin V 2340*	**13**	13
18 Oct 86	ZAGORA *Virgin V 2384*	**15**	8
2 Jul 88	THE REAL CHUCKEEBOO *Virgin V 2528*	**52**	4
22 Sep 90	LOOK HOW LONG *Ten DIX 94*	**19**	5
19 Sep 92	TIGHTEN UP VOLUME 1 *Ten DIXCD 112*	**40**	2

Lisa 'Left Eye' LOPES (see also TLC) *US, female*
rapper, b. 27 May 1971, d. 25 Apr 2002 (Singles: 20 Weeks)   pos/wks

| 1 Apr 00 | ★ NEVER BE THE SAME AGAIN (re) *Virgin VSCDT 1762* [1] ■ ...1 | | 16 |
| 27 Oct 01 | THE BLOCK PARTY *LaFace / Arista 74321895912* .... | **16** | 4 |

[1] Melanie C / Lisa 'Left Eye' Lopes

Jennifer LOPEZ (208 Top 500) *Globally successful, photogenic singer*
/ actress. J.Lo, b. 24 Jul 1970, Bronx, New York, US, starred in such movies
as 'The Wedding Planner', 'The Cell' and 'Selena' (life story of the late Latin
superstar) (Singles: 146 Weeks, Albums: 139 Weeks)   pos/wks

3 Jul 99	● IF YOU HAD MY LOVE *Columbia 6675772* ▲	**4**	13
13 Nov 99	● WAITING FOR TONIGHT *Columbia 6683072*	**5**	12
1 Apr 00	● FEELIN' SO GOOD *Columbia 6691972* [1]	**15**	6
20 Jan 01	★ LOVE DON'T COST A THING (re) *Epic 6707282* ■	**1**	11
12 May 01	● PLAY (re) *Epic 6712272*	**3**	12
18 Aug 01	● AIN'T IT FUNNY (re) *Epic 6717592*	**3**	9
10 Nov 01	● I'M REAL *Epic 6720322* ▲	**4**	15
23 Mar 02	● AIN'T IT FUNNY *Epic 6724922* [2] ▲	**4**	13
13 Jul 02	● I'M GONNA BE ALRIGHT *Epic 6728442* [3]	**3**	10
30 Nov 02	● JENNY FROM THE BLOCK *Epic 6733572*	**3**	13
22 Mar 03	● ALL I HAVE *Epic 6736782* [4] ▲	**2**	13
21 Jun 03	I'M GLAD *Epic 6740152*	**11**	9
20 Mar 04	● BABY I LOVE U *Epic 6747902*	**3**	10
17 Jul 99	ON THE 6 *Columbia 4949302*	**14**	30
3 Feb 01	● J.LO *Epic 5005502* ▲	**2**	48
30 Mar 02	● J TO THA L–O – THE REMIXES *Epic 5060242* ▲	**4**	27
7 Dec 02	THIS IS ME ... THEN *Epic 5101282*	**13**	34

[1] Jennifer Lopez featuring Big Pun and Fat Joe [2] Jennifer Lopez featuring
Ja Rule & Caddillac Tah [3] Jennifer Lopez featuring Nas [4] Jennifer Lopez
featuring LL Cool J

The two singles titled 'Ain't it Funny' are different songs

Trini LOPEZ *US, male vocalist – Trinidad*
Lopez (Singles: 37 Weeks, Albums: 42 Weeks)   pos/wks

12 Sep 63	● IF I HAD A HAMMER *Reprise R 20198*	**4**	17
12 Dec 63	KANSAS CITY *Reprise R 20236*	**35**	5
12 May 66	I'M COMING HOME CINDY *Reprise R 20455*	**28**	5
6 Apr 67	GONNA GET ALONG WITHOUT YA NOW *Reprise R 20547* ...	**41**	5
19 Dec 81	TRINI TRAX *RCA 154*	**59**	5
26 Oct 63	● TRINI LOPEZ AT P.J.'S *Reprise R 6093*	**7**	25
25 Mar 67	● TRINI LOPEZ IN LONDON *Reprise RSLP 6238*	**6**	17

LO-PRO *See X-PRESS 2*

Jeff LORBER
US, male vocalist / instrumentalist – keyboards (Albums: 2 Weeks) pos/wks

| 18 May 85 | STEP BY STEP *Club JABH 9* .... | **97** | 2 |

L'ORCHESTRE ELECTRONIQUE
UK, male synthesized orchestra (Albums: 1 Week)   pos/wks

| 29 Oct 83 | SOUND WAVES *Nouveau Musique NML 1005* .... | **75** | 1 |

LORD ROCKINGHAM'S XI *UK, male / female*
instrumental group – leader Harry Robinson (Singles: 21 Weeks)   pos/wks

24 Oct 58	★ HOOTS MON *Decca F 11059* [1]	**1**	17
6 Feb 59	WEE TOM *Decca F 11104* [1]	**16**	3
25 Sep 93	HOOTS MON (re-issue) *Decca 8820982*	**60**	1

[1] Jack Good presents Lord Rockingham's XI

LORD TANAMO *Trinidad and Tobago,*
male vocalist – Joseph Gordon (Singles: 2 Weeks)   pos/wks

| 1 Dec 90 | I'M IN THE MOOD FOR LOVE *Mooncrest MOON 1009* ..... | **58** | 2 |

LORD TARIQ and Peter GUNZ *US, male vocal / rap*
duo – Sean Hamilton and Peter Panky (Singles: 3 Weeks)   pos/wks

| 2 May 98 | DEJA VU (UPTOWN BABY) *Columbia 6658722* .... | **21** | 3 |

Erin LORDAN *See ASCENSION; BBG; SHUT UP AND DANCE*

Jerry LORDAN
UK, male vocalist, b. 30 Apr 1934, d. 24 Jul 1995 (Singles: 16 Weeks) pos/wks

8 Jan 60	I'LL STAY SINGLE (re) *Parlophone R 4588*	**26**	3
26 Feb 60	WHO COULD BE BLUER (re) *Parlophone R 4627*	**16**	11
2 Jun 60	SING LIKE AN ANGEL *Parlophone R 4653*	**36**	2

LORDS OF THE UNDERGROUND
US, male rap group (Albums: 1 Week)   pos/wks

| 12 Nov 94 | KEEPERS OF THE FUNK *Pendulum CDCHR 6088* .... | **68** | 1 |

Traci LORDS *US, female vocalist – Nora Kuzma (Singles: 1 Week)* pos/wks

| 7 Oct 95 | FALLEN ANGEL *Radioactive RAXTD 18* .... | **72** | 1 |

Sophia LOREN *See Peter SELLERS*

Trey LORENZ (see also Mariah CAREY)
US, male vocalist – Lloyd Lorenz Smith (Singles: 5 Weeks)   pos/wks

| 21 Nov 92 | SOMEONE TO HOLD *Epic 6587857* .... | **65** | 2 |
| 30 Jan 93 | PHOTOGRAPH OF MARY *Epic 6589542* .... | **38** | 3 |

LORI and the CHAMELEONS
UK, female / male vocal / instrumental group (Singles: 1 Week) pos/wks

| 8 Dec 79 | TOUCH *Sire SIR 4025* .... | **70** | 1 |

Lea LORIEN *See David MORALES*

LORRAINE *See BOMB THE BASS*

LOS BRAVOS *Spain / Germany, male vocal /*
instrumental group (Singles: 24 Weeks, Albums: 1 Week)   pos/wks

30 Jun 66	● BLACK IS BLACK *Decca F 22419*	**2**	13
8 Sep 66	I DON'T CARE *Decca F 22484*	**16**	11
8 Oct 64	BLACK IS BLACK *Decca LK 4822*	**29**	4

LOS DEL CHIPMUNKS *See The CHIPMUNKS*

LOS DEL MAR featuring Wil VELOZ
Cuba / Canada, male vocal / instrumental
group (Singles: 7 Weeks)   pos/wks

| 8 Jun 96 | MACARENA (re) *Pulse 8 CDLOSE 101* .... | **43** | 7 |

LOS DEL RIO *Spain, male vocal / instrumental duo –*
Antonio Monge and Rafael Perdigones (Singles: 19 Weeks)   pos/wks

| 1 Jun 96 | ● MACARENA (re) *RCA 74321345372* ▲ .... | **2** | 19 |

LOS INDIOS TABAJARAS *Brazil, male instrumental duo –*
Natalicio and Antenor Lima – guitars (Singles: 17 Weeks)   pos/wks

| 31 Oct 63 | ● MARIA ELENA *RCA 1365* .... | **5** | 17 |

LOS LOBOS *US, male vocal / instrumental group – lead vocal David Hildago (Singles: 24 Weeks, Albums: 9 Weeks)* pos/wks

6 Apr 85	**DON'T WORRY BABY / WILL THE WOLF SURVIVE** *London LASH 4*	**57**	4
18 Jul 87 ★	**LA BAMBA** *Slash LASH 13* ▲	**1**	11
26 Sep 87	**COME ON LET'S GO** *Slash LASH 14*	**18**	9
6 Apr 85	**HOW WILL THE WOLF SURVIVE?** *Slash SLMP 3*	**77**	6
7 Feb 87	**BY THE LIGHT OF THE MOON** *Slash SLAP 13*	**77**	3

LOS NINOS *UK, male instrumental group (Albums: 1 Week)* pos/wks

22 Jul 95	**FRAGILE – MYSTICAL SOUNDS OF THE PANPIPE** *Pearls DPWKF 4253*	**74**	1

LOS POP TOPS *Spain, male vocal group (Singles: 6 Weeks)* pos/wks

9 Oct 71	**MAMY BLUE** *A&M AMS 859*	**35**	6

LOS UMBRELLOS
Denmark, male / female vocal trio (Singles: 2 Weeks) pos/wks

3 Oct 98	**NO TENGO DINERO** *Virgin VUSCD 139*	**33**	2

Joe LOSS and his ORCHESTRA (see also The George MITCHELL MINSTRELS) *UK, orchestra, leader b. 22 Jun 1909, d. 6 Jun 1990 (Singles: 52 Weeks, Albums: 10 Weeks)* pos/wks

29 Jun 61	**WHEELS CHA CHA** *HMV POP 880*	**21**	21
19 Oct 61	**SUCU SUCU** *HMV POP 937*	**48**	1
29 Mar 62	**THE MAIGRET THEME** *HMV POP 995*	**20**	10
1 Nov 62	**MUST BE MADISON** *HMV POP 1075*	**20**	13
5 Nov 64	**MARCH OF THE MODS (2re)** *HMV POP 1351*	**31**	7
30 Oct 71	**ALL-TIME PARTY HITS** *MFP 5227*	**24**	10

[1] Joe Loss

LOST *UK, male / instrumental / production duo (Singles: 1 Week)* pos/wks

22 Jun 91	**TECHNO FUNK** *Perfecto PT 44560*	**75**	1

LOST BOYZ
US, male rap group (Singles: 2 Weeks, Albums: 1 Week) pos/wks

2 Nov 96	**MUSIC MAKES ME HIGH** *Universal MCSTD 48015*	**42**	1
12 Jul 97	**LOVE, PEACE & NAPPINESS** *Universal UND 56131*	**57**	1
6 Jul 96	**LEGAL DRUG MONEY** *Universal UND 53010*	**64**	1

LOST BROTHERS featuring G Tom MAC
UK, male production group and male vocalist (Singles: 9 Weeks) pos/wks

20 Dec 03	**CRY LITTLE SISTER (I NEED U NOW)** *Incentive CENT 60CDS*	**21**	9

LOST IT.COM *UK, male vocal / production duo (Singles: 1 Week)* pos/wks

7 Apr 01	**ANIMAL** *Perfecto PERF 13CDS*	**70**	1

LOST TRIBE
(see also MELT featuring LITTLE MS MARCIE; SUNBURST; MDM) *UK, male production duo – Matt Darey and Red Jerry (Singles: 4 Weeks)* pos/wks

11 Sep 99	**GAMEMASTER** *Hooj Choons HOOJ 81CD*	**24**	3
6 Dec 03	**GAMEMASTER (re-mix)** *Liquid Asset ASSETCD 12015*	**61**	1

LOST WITNESS
UK, male production duo and female vocalist (Singles: 13 Weeks) pos/wks

29 May 99	**HAPPINESS HAPPENING** *Ministry of Sound MOSCDS 129*	**18**	4
18 Sep 99	**RED SUN RISING** *Ministry of Sound MOSCDS 133*	**22**	3
16 Dec 00	**7 COLOURS** *Data DATA 15CDS*	**28**	3
18 May 02	**DID I DREAM (SONG TO THE SIREN)** *Ministry of Sound / Data DATA 28CDS*	**28**	3

LOSTPROPHETS *UK, male vocal / instrumental group (Singles: 26 Weeks, Albums: 36 Weeks)* pos/wks

8 Dec 01	**SHINOBI VS DRAGON NINJA** *Visible Noise TORMENT 16*	**41**	2
23 Mar 02	**THE FAKE SOUND OF PROGRESS** *Visible Noise TORMENT 19*	**21**	3
15 Nov 03	**BURN BURN** *Visible Noise TORMENT 29CD*	**17**	3
7 Feb 04 ●	**LAST TRAIN HOME** *Visible Noise TORMENT 36CD*	**8**	7
15 May 04	**WAKE UP (MAKE A MOVE)** *Visible Noise TORMENT 40CD*	**18**	4
4 Sep 04	**LAST SUMMER** *Visible Noise TORMENT 43CD*	**13**	5
4 Dec 04	**GOODBYE TONIGHT** *Visible Noise TORMENT 47CD*	**42**	2
2 Mar 02	**THEFAKESOUNDOFPROGRESS** *Visible Noise TORMENT 10CD*	**44**	8
14 Feb 04 ●	**START SOMETHING** *Visible Noise TORMENT 32*	**4**	28

The LOTUS EATERS *UK, male vocal / instrumental duo – Peter Coyle and Jerry Kelley (Singles: 16 Weeks, Albums: 1 Week)* pos/wks

2 Jul 83	**FIRST PICTURE OF YOU** *Sylvan SYL 1*	**15**	12
8 Oct 83	**YOU DON'T NEED SOMEONE NEW** *Sylvan SYL 2*	**53**	4
16 Jun 84	**NO SENSE OF SIN** *Sylvan 206 263*	**96**	1

Bonnie LOU
US, female vocalist – Bonnie Lou Kath (Singles: 10 Weeks) pos/wks

5 Feb 54 ●	**TENNESSEE WIG WALK** *Parlophone R 3730*	**4**	10

Lippy LOU *UK, female rapper (Singles: 2 Weeks)* pos/wks

22 Apr 95	**LIBERATION** *More Protein PROCD 105*	**57**	2

Louchie LOU and Michie ONE *UK, female rap duo – Louise Gold and Michelle Charles (Singles: 36 Weeks)* pos/wks

29 May 93 ●	**SHOUT** *ffrr FCD 211*	**7**	8
14 Aug 93	**SOMEBODY ELSE'S GUY** *ffrr FCD 216*	**54**	2
26 Aug 95	**GET DOWN ON IT** *China WOKCD 2054*	**58**	1
13 Apr 96 ●	**CECILIA (2re)** *WEA WEA 042CD1* [1]	**4**	19
15 Jun 96	**GOOD SWEET LOVIN'** *Indochina ID 050CD*	**34**	2
21 Sep 96	**NO MORE ALCOHOL** *WEA WEA 065CD1* [1]	**24**	4

[1] Suggs featuring Louchie Lou and Michie One

LOUD *UK, male vocal / instrumental group (Singles: 2 Weeks)* pos/wks

28 Mar 92	**EASY** *China WOK 2016*	**67**	2

John D LOUDERMILK *US, male vocalist (Singles: 10 Weeks)* pos/wks

4 Jan 62	**THE LANGUAGE OF LOVE** *RCA 1269*	**13**	10

James LOUGHRAN *See BBC SYMPHONY ORCHESTRA SINGERS and CHORUS*

Louie LOUIE *US, male vocalist – Louie Cordero (Singles: 5 Weeks)* pos/wks

19 Dec 92	**THE THOUGHT OF IT** *Hardback YZ 724*	**34**	5

LOUISE (see also ETERNAL) *UK, female vocalist – Louise Redknapp (Singles: 83 Weeks, Albums: 59 Weeks)* pos/wks

7 Oct 95 ●	**LIGHT OF MY LIFE** *EMI CDEMS 397*	**8**	8
16 Mar 96	**IN WALKED LOVE** *EMI CDEMS 413*	**17**	6
8 Jun 96 ●	**NAKED** *EMI CDEM 431*	**5**	8
31 Aug 96 ●	**UNDIVIDED LOVE** *EMI CDEM 441*	**5**	6
30 Nov 96	**ONE KISS FROM HEAVEN** *EMI CDEM 454*	**9**	7
4 Oct 97 ●	**ARMS AROUND THE WORLD** *EMI CDEM 490*	**4**	7
29 Nov 97	**LET'S GO ROUND AGAIN** *EMI CDEM 500*	**10**	9
4 Apr 98	**ALL THAT MATTERS (re)** *1st Avenue CDEM 506*	**11**	6
29 Jul 00 ●	**2 FACED** *1st Avenue / EMI CDEMS 570*	**3**	8
11 Nov 00	**BEAUTIFUL INSIDE** *1st Avenue / EMI CDEMS 575*	**13**	4
8 Sep 01 ●	**STUCK IN THE MIDDLE WITH YOU** *1st Avenue / EMI CDEM 600*	**4**	9
27 Sep 03	**PANDORA'S KISS** *Positive POSCDS 001*	**5**	5
6 Jul 96 ●	**NAKED** *EMI CDEMC 3748*	**7**	31
18 Oct 97 ●	**WOMAN IN ME** *EMI 8219032*	**5**	19
12 Aug 00	**ELBOW BEACH** *EMI 5276142*	**12**	4
22 Sep 01 ●	**CHANGING FACES – THE BEST OF LOUISE** *EMI 5349672*	**9**	5

Jacques LOUSSIER
France, male instrumentalist – piano (Albums: 3 Weeks) pos/wks

30 Mar 85	**THE BEST OF PLAY BACH** *Start STL 1*	**58**	3

LOVE *US, male vocal / instrumental group (Albums: 9 Weeks)* pos/wks

24 Feb 68	**FOREVER CHANGES** *Elektra EKS 74013*	**24**	7
16 May 70	**OUT HERE** *Harvest Show 3/4*	**29**	2

Courtney LOVE (see also HOLE) *US, female vocalist / instrumentalist – guitar – Love Michelle Harrison (Singles: 2 Weeks, Albums: 1 Week)* pos/wks

27 Mar 04	**MONO** *Virgin VUSDX 283*	**41**	2
21 Feb 04	**AMERICA'S SWEETHEART** *Virgin CDVUS 249*	**56**	1

Darlene LOVE (see also The CRYSTALS)
US, female vocalist – Darlene Wright (Singles: 5 Weeks) pos/wks

19 Dec 92	**ALL ALONE ON CHRISTMAS (re)** *Arista 74321124767*	**31**	5

Re-entry made No.72 in Jan 1994

Geoff LOVE (see also Laurie LONDON;
MANUEL and his MUSIC of the MOUNTAINS) *UK, male orchestra leader, b. 4 Sep 1917, d. 8 Jul 1991 (Albums: 28 Weeks)* pos/wks

7 Aug 71	**BIG WAR MOVIE THEMES** *MFP 5171*	**11**	20
21 Aug 71	**BIG WESTERN MOVIE THEMES** *MFP 5204*	**38**	3
30 Oct 71	**BIG LOVE MOVIE THEMES** *MFP 5221*	**28**	5

Helen LOVE
UK, male / female vocal / instrumental group (Singles: 2 Weeks) pos/wks

20 Sep 97	**DOES YOUR HEART GO BOOM** *Che CHE 72CD*	**71**	1
19 Sep 98	**LONG LIVE THE UK MUSIC SCENE** *Che CHE 82CD*	**65**	1

Monie LOVE *UK, female rapper – Simone
Johnson (Singles: 51 Weeks, Albums: 3 Weeks)* pos/wks

4 Feb 89	**I CAN DO THIS** *Cooltempo COOL 177*	**37**	4
24 Jun 89	**GRANDPA'S PARTY** *Cooltempo COOL 184*	**16**	9
14 Jul 90	**MONIE IN THE MIDDLE** *Cooltempo COOL 210*	**46**	3
22 Sep 90	**IT'S A SHAME (MY SISTER)** *Cooltempo COOL 219* 1	**12**	8
1 Dec 90	**DOWN TO EARTH** *Cooltempo COOL 222*	**31**	6
6 Apr 91	**RING MY BELL** *Cooltempo COOL 224* 2	**20**	5
25 Jul 92	**FULL TERM LOVE** *Cooltempo COOL 258*	**34**	4
13 Mar 93	**BORN 2 B.R.E.E.D.** *Cooltempo CDCOOL 269*	**18**	5
12 Jun 93	**IN A WORD OR 2 / THE POWER** *Cooltempo CDCOOL 273*	**33**	3
21 Aug 93	**NEVER GIVE UP** *Cooltempo CDCOOL 276*	**41**	2
22 Apr 00	**SLICE OF DA PIE** *Relentless RELENT 2CDS*	**29**	2
20 Oct 90	**DOWN TO EARTH** *Cooltempo CTLP 14*	**30**	3

1 Monie Love featuring True Image 2 Monie Love vs Adeva

Vikki LOVE See The JUNGLE BROTHERS; NUANCE featuring Vikki LOVE

LOVE AFFAIR *UK, male vocal / instrumental
group – lead vocal Steve Ellis (Singles: 56 Weeks)* pos/wks

3 Jan 68	★ **EVERLASTING LOVE** *CBS 3125*	**1**	12
17 Apr 68	● **RAINBOW VALLEY** *CBS 3366*	**5**	13
11 Sep 68	● **A DAY WITHOUT LOVE** *CBS 3674*	**6**	12
19 Feb 69	**ONE ROAD** *CBS 3994*	**16**	9
16 Jul 69	● **BRINGING ON BACK THE GOOD TIMES** *CBS 4300*	**9**	10

LOVE AND MONEY *UK, male vocal /
instrumental group (Singles: 23 Weeks, Albums: 2 Weeks)* pos/wks

24 May 86	**CANDYBAR EXPRESS** *Mercury MONEY 1*	**56**	4
25 Apr 87	**LOVE AND MONEY** *Mercury MONEY 4*	**68**	4
17 Sep 88	**HALLELUIAH MAN** *Fontana MONEY 5*	**63**	4
14 Jan 89	**STRANGE KIND OF LOVE** *Fontana MONEY 6*	**45**	5
25 Mar 89	**JOCELYN SQUARE** *Fontana MONEY 7*	**51**	4
16 Nov 91	**WINTER** *Fontana MONEY 9*	**52**	2
29 Oct 88	**STRANGE KIND OF LOVE** *Fontana SFLP 7*	**71**	1
3 Aug 91	**DOGS IN THE TRAFFIC** *Fontana 8489931*	**41**	1

LOVE BITE
Italy, male / female production / vocal group (Singles: 1 Week) pos/wks

7 Oct 00	**TAKE YOUR TIME** *AM:PM CDAMPM 134*	**56**	1

LOVE CITY GROOVE *UK, male / female
vocal / rap / instrumental group (Singles: 11 Weeks)* pos/wks

8 Apr 95	● **LOVE CITY GROOVE** *Planet 3 GXY 2003CD*	**7**	11

LOVE CONNECTION *Italy / Germany, male /
female vocal / production group (Singles: 1 Week)* pos/wks

2 Dec 00	**THE BOMB** *Multiply CDMULTY 63*	**53**	1

LOVE DECADE
UK, male / female vocal / instrumental group (Singles: 14 Weeks) pos/wks

6 Jul 91	**DREAM ON (IS THIS A DREAM)** *All Around the World GLOBE 100*	**52**	2
23 Nov 91	**SO REAL** *All Around the World GLOBE 106*	**14**	7
11 Apr 92	**I FEEL YOU** *All Around the World GLOBE 107*	**34**	3
6 Feb 93	**WHEN THE MORNING COMES** *All Around the World CDGLOBE 114*	**69**	1
17 Feb 96	**IS THIS A DREAM (re-recording)** *All Around the World CDGLOBE 132*	**39**	1

LOVE DECREE
UK, male vocal / instrumental group (Singles: 4 Weeks) pos/wks

16 Sep 89	**SOMETHING SO REAL (CHINHEADS THEME)** *Ariola 112642*	**61**	4

LOVE / HATE *US, male vocal /
instrumental group (Singles: 4 Weeks, Albums: 5 Weeks)* pos/wks

30 Nov 91	**EVIL TWIN** *Columbia 6575967*	**59**	1
4 Apr 92	**WASTED IN AMERICA** *Columbia 6578897*	**38**	3
7 Mar 92	**WASTED IN AMERICA** *Columbia 4694532*	**20**	4
24 Jul 93	**LET'S RUMBLE** *RCA 74321153112*	**24**	1

LOVE INC.
*Jamaica / Canada, male / female production / vocal duo –
Chris Sheppard and Simone Denny (Singles: 22 Weeks)* pos/wks

28 Dec 02	● **YOU'RE A SUPERSTAR** *Nulife / Arista 74321973842*	**7**	13
31 May 03	● **BROKEN BONES** *Nulife / Arista 82876523172*	**8**	7
6 Mar 04	**INTO THE NIGHT** *Nulife 82876585782*	**39**	2

LOVE INCORPORATED featuring MC NOISE
UK, male vocal / production duo (Singles: 3 Weeks) pos/wks

9 Feb 91	**LOVE IS THE MESSAGE** *Love EVOL 1*	**59**	3

LOVE NELSON See FIRE ISLAND

LOVE REACTION See ZODIAC MINDWARP and the LOVE REACTION

LOVE SCULPTURE (see also Dave EDMUNDS)
UK, instrumental group (Singles: 14 Weeks) pos/wks

27 Nov 68	● **SABRE DANCE** *Parlophone R 5744*	**5**	14

LOVE SQUAD See Linda CARR

A LOVE SUPREME
UK, male vocal / instrumental group (Singles: 2 Weeks) pos/wks

17 Apr 99	**NIALL QUINN'S DISCO PANTS** *A Love Supreme / Cherry Red CDVINNIE 3*	**59**	2

[LOVE] TATTOO
Australia, male producer – Stephen Allkins (Singles: 1 Week) pos/wks

6 Oct 01	**DROP SOME DRUMS** *Positiva CDTIV 162*	**58**	1

LOVE TO INFINITY
UK, male / female vocal / instrumental group (Singles: 4 Weeks) pos/wks

24 Jun 95	**KEEP LOVE TOGETHER** *Mushroom D 00467*	**38**	2
18 Nov 95	**SOMEDAY** *Mushroom D 1143*	**75**	1
3 Aug 96	**PRAY FOR LOVE** *Mushroom D 1213*	**69**	1

LOVE TRIBE
*US, male / female vocal / instrumental duo –
Tanya Walters and Dewey Bullock (Singles: 3 Weeks)* pos/wks

29 Jun 96	**STAND UP** *AM:PM 5816272*	**23**	3

LOVE UNLIMITED
US, female vocal group (Singles: 19 Weeks) pos/wks

17 Jun 72	**WALKIN' IN THE RAIN WITH THE ONE I LOVE** *Uni UN 539*	**14**	10
25 Jan 75	**IT MAY BE WINTER OUTSIDE (BUT IN MY HEART IT'S SPRING)** *20th Century BTC 2149*	**11**	9

LOVE UNLIMITED ORCHESTRA
*US, male / female orchestra – leader Barry White
b. 12 Sep 1944, d. 5 Jul 2003 (Singles: 10 Weeks)* pos/wks

2 Feb 74	● **LOVE'S THEME** *Pye International 7N 25635* ▲	**10**	10

LOVEBUG
UK, male / female production / vocal trio (Singles: 2 Weeks) pos/wks

18 Oct 03	**WHO'S THE DADDY** *Sony Music 6742702*	**35**	2

LOVEBUG STARSKI
US, male rapper – Kevin Smith (Singles: 9 Weeks) pos/wks

31 May 86	**AMITYVILLE (THE HOUSE ON THE HILL)** *Epic A 7182*	**12**	9

LOVEDEEJAY AKEMI See YOSH presents LOVEDEEJAY AKEMI

LOVEHAPPY
US / UK, male / female vocal / instrumental group (Singles: 3 Weeks)   pos/wks

| 18 Feb 95 | MESSAGE OF LOVE MCA MCSTD 2040 | 37 | 2 |
| 20 Jul 96 | MESSAGE OF LOVE (re-mix) MCA MCSTD 40052 | 70 | 1 |

Bill LOVELADY UK, male vocalist (Singles: 10 Weeks)   pos/wks

| 18 Aug 79 | REGGAE FOR IT NOW Charisma CB 337 | 12 | 10 |

LOVELAND featuring the voice of Rachel McFARLANE
UK, male / female vocal / instrumental group (Singles: 17 Weeks)   pos/wks

16 Apr 94	LET THE MUSIC (LIFT YOU UP)		
	KMS / Eastern Bloc KMSCD 10	16	4
5 Nov 94	(KEEP ON) SHINING / HOPE (NEVER GIVE UP)		
	Eastern Bloc BLOCCD 016	37	2
14 Jan 95	I NEED SOMEBODY Eastern Bloc BLOCCD 019	21	3
10 Jun 95	DON'T MAKE ME WAIT Eastern Bloc BLOC 20CD	22	3
2 Sep 95	THE WONDER OF LOVE Eastern Bloc BLOC 22CD	53	1
11 Nov 95	I NEED SOMEBODY (re-mix) Eastern Bloc BLOC 23CD	38	2
1 Aug 98	LOVER Multiply CDMULTY 37 [1]	38	2

[1] Rachel McFarlane

All formats of 'Let the Music (Lift You Up)' feature versions by Loveland featuring Rachel McFarlane and also by Darlene Lewis

The LOVER SPEAKS
UK, male vocal / instrumental duo (Singles: 5 Weeks)   pos/wks

| 16 Aug 86 | NO MORE 'I LOVE YOU'S' A&M AM 326 | 58 | 5 |

Michael LOVESMITH US, male vocalist (Singles: 1 Week)   pos/wks

| 5 Oct 85 | AIN'T NOTHIN' LIKE IT Motown ZB 40369 | 75 | 1 |

LOVESTATION
UK, male / female vocal / instrumental group (Singles: 21 Weeks)   pos/wks

13 Mar 93	SHINE ON ME RCA 743211337912 [1]	71	1
13 Nov 93	BEST OF MY LOVE Fresh FRSHD 1	73	1
18 Mar 95	LOVE COME RESCUE ME Fresh FRSHD 22	42	2
1 Aug 98	TEARDROPS Fresh FRSHD 65	14	6
5 Dec 98	SENSUALITY Fresh FRSHD 71	16	7
5 Feb 00	TEARDROPS (re-mix) Fresh FRSHD 79	24	4

[1] Lovestation featuring Lisa Hunt

Lyle LOVETT US, male vocalist (Albums: 2 Weeks)   pos/wks

| 8 Oct 94 | I LOVE EVERYBODY MCA MCD 10808 | 54 | 1 |
| 29 Jun 96 | THE ROAD TO ENSENADA MCA MCD 11409 | 62 | 1 |

Lene LOVICH US, female vocalist – Lili
Premilovich (Singles: 38 Weeks, Albums: 17 Weeks)   pos/wks

17 Feb 79 ●	LUCKY NUMBER Stiff BUY 42	3	11
12 May 79	SAY WHEN Stiff BUY 46	19	10
20 Oct 79	BIRD SONG Stiff BUY 53	39	7
29 Mar 80	WHAT WILL I DO WITHOUT YOU Stiff BUY 69	58	3
14 Mar 81	NEW TOY Stiff BUY 97	53	5
27 Nov 82	IT'S YOU ONLY YOU (MEIN SCHMERZ) Stiff BUY 164	68	2
17 Mar 79	STATELESS Stiff SEEZ 7	35	11
2 Feb 80	FLEX Stiff SEEZ 19	19	6

The LOVIN' SPOONFUL US / Canada, male vocal /
instrumental group (Singles: 33 Weeks, Albums: 11 Weeks)   pos/wks

14 Apr 66 ●	DAYDREAM Pye International 7N 25361	2	13
14 Jul 66 ●	SUMMER IN THE CITY Kama Sutra KAS 200 ▲	8	11
5 Jan 67	NASHVILLE CATS Kama Sutra KAS 204	26	7
9 Mar 67	DARLING BE HOME SOON Kama Sutra KAS 207	44	2
7 May 66 ●	DAYDREAM Pye NPL 28078	8	11

LOVINDEER Jamaica, male vocalist (Singles: 3 Weeks)   pos/wks

| 27 Sep 86 | MAN SHORTAGE TSOJ TS 1 | 69 | 3 |

Gary LOW Italy, male vocalist (Singles: 3 Weeks)   pos/wks

| 8 Oct 83 | I WANT YOU Savoir Faire FAIS 004 | 52 | 3 |

Patti LOW See BUG KANN and the PLASTIC JAM

Jim LOWE and the HIGH FIVES
US, male vocalist (Singles: 9 Weeks)   pos/wks

| 26 Oct 56 ● | THE GREEN DOOR London HLD 8317 | 8 | 9 |

Nick LOWE (see also ROCKPILE)
UK, male vocalist (Singles: 27 Weeks, Albums: 17 Weeks)   pos/wks

11 Mar 78 ●	I LOVE THE SOUND OF BREAKING GLASS Radar ADA 1	7	8
9 Jun 79	CRACKING UP Radar ADA 34	34	5
25 Aug 79	CRUEL TO BE KIND Radar ADA 43	12	11
26 May 84	HALF A BOY AND HALF A MAN F Beat XX 34	53	3
11 Mar 78	THE JESUS OF COOL Radar RAD 1	22	9
23 Jun 79	LABOUR OF LUST Radar RAD 21	43	6
20 Feb 82	NICK THE KNIFE F Beat XXLP 14	99	2

LOWGOLD UK, male vocal / instrumental
group (Singles: 4 Weeks, Albums: 2 Weeks)   pos/wks

30 Sep 00	BEAUTY DIES YOUNG Nude NUD 52CD	67	1
10 Feb 01	MERCURY Nude NUD 53CD	48	1
12 May 01	COUNTERFEIT Nude NUD 55CD	52	1
8 Sep 01	BEAUTY DIES YOUNG (re-mix) Nude NUD 59CD	40	1
24 Feb 01	JUST BACKWARD OF SQUARE Nude NUDE 17CD	33	2

LOWRELL US, male vocalist – Lowrell Simon (Singles: 9 Weeks)   pos/wks

| 24 Nov 79 | MELLOW MELLOW RIGHT ON AVI AVIS 108 | 37 | 9 |

LUCAS Denmark, male vocalist – Lucas Secon (Singles: 4 Weeks)   pos/wks

| 6 Aug 94 | LUCAS WITH THE LID OFF WEA YZ 832CD | 37 | 4 |

Carrie LUCAS US, female vocalist (Singles: 6 Weeks)   pos/wks

| 16 Jun 79 | DANCE WITH YOU Solar FB 1482 | 40 | 6 |

Tammy LUCAS See Teddy RILEY

LUCIANA
UK, female vocalist – Luciana Caporaso (Singles: 5 Weeks)   pos/wks

23 Apr 94	GET IT UP FOR LOVE Chrysalis CDCHS 5008	55	2
6 Aug 94	IF YOU WANT Chrysalis CDCHS 5009	47	2
5 Nov 94	WHAT GOES AROUND / ONE MORE RIVER		
	Chrysalis CDCHS 5015	67	1

LUCID
UK, male / female vocal / instrumental group (Singles: 15 Weeks)   pos/wks

8 Aug 98 ●	I CAN'T HELP MYSELF ffrr FCD 339	7	8
27 Feb 99	CRAZY ffrr / Delirious / Indirect FCD 355	14	5
16 Oct 99	STAY WITH ME TILL DAWN ffrr FCD 368	25	2

LUCKY MONKEYS (see also FLUKE)
UK, male instrumental group (Singles: 1 Week)   pos/wks

| 9 Nov 96 | BJANGO Hi-Life 5757132 | 50 | 1 |

LUCY PEARL US, male / female vocal / rap /
instrumental / production trio (Singles: 7 Weeks)   pos/wks

29 Jul 00	DANCE TONIGHT Virgin VSCDT 1775	36	2
25 Nov 00	DON'T MESS WITH MY MAN Virgin VSCDT 1778	20	4
28 Jul 01	WITHOUT YOU Virgin VSCDT 1805	51	1

LUDACRIS US, male rapper – Christopher
Bridges (Singles: 60 Weeks, Albums: 6 Weeks)   pos/wks

9 Jun 01	WHAT'S YOUR FANTASY Def Jam 5729842	19	5
18 Aug 01 ●	ONE MINUTE MAN Elektra E 7245CD [1]	10	8
29 Sep 01	AREA CODES Def Jam 5887722 [2]	25	3
22 Jun 02	ROLLOUT (MY BUSINESS) Def Jam 5829632	20	7
5 Oct 02	SATURDAY (OOOH OOOH) Def Jam 0639142	31	2
9 Nov 02	WHY DON'T WE FALL IN LOVE Columbia 6732212 [3]	40	2
22 Mar 03 ●	GOSSIP FOLKS Elektra E 7389CD [4]	9	9
22 Nov 03	STAND UP Def Jam / Mercury 9814001 [5] ▲	14	7
21 Feb 04	HOLIDAE IN Capitol CDCL 852 [6]	35	3
27 Mar 04 ★	YEAH! Arista 82876606002 [7] ■ ▲	1	14
29 Jun 02	WORD OF MOUF Def Jam 5864462	57	2
18 Oct 03	CHICKEN 'N' BEER Def Jam / Mercury 9861137 ▲	44	4

[1] Missy 'Misdemeanor' Elliott feat. Ludacris [2] Ludacris feat. Nate Dogg
[3] Amerie feat. Ludacris [4] Missy Elliott feat. Ludacris [5] Ludacris feat. Shawnna
[6] Chingy feat. Ludacris & Snoop Dogg [7] Usher feat. Lil' Jon & Ludacris

The LUDES
Canada, male vocal / instrumental group (Singles: 1 Week) pos/wks

| 18 Dec 04 | RADIO *Double Dragon DD 2018CD* ....**68** 1 |

Baz LUHRMANN
Australia, male producer – Bazmark Luhrman (Singles: 16 Weeks) pos/wks

| 12 Jun 99 | ★ EVERYBODY'S FREE (TO WEAR SUNSCREEN) – THE SUNSCREEN SONG (CLASS OF '99) *EMI CDBAZ 001* ■ ..**1** 16 |

Uncredited vocals by actor Lee Perry

Robin LUKE *US, male vocalist (Singles: 6 Weeks)* pos/wks

| 17 Oct 58 | SUSIE DARLIN' (2re) *London HLD 8676* ....**23** 6 |

LUKK featuring Felicia COLLINS
US, male / female vocal / instrumental group (Singles: 1 Week) pos/wks

| 28 Sep 85 | ON THE ONE *Important TAN 6* ....**72** 1 |

LULU (320) Top 500
One of Scotland's best-known female vocalists, b. Marie Lawrie, 3 Nov 1948, Strathclyde. She scored her first hit aged 15, had a US chart-topper ('To Sir with Love') aged 18, won the Eurovision Song Contest aged 20, and finally reached No.1 aged 44 (Singles: 188 Weeks, Albums: 19 Weeks) pos/wks

14 May 64	● SHOUT *Decca F 11884* [1] **7** 13
12 Nov 64	HERE COMES THE NIGHT *Decca F 12017* **50** 1
17 Jun 65	● LEAVE A LITTLE LOVE *Decca F 12169* **8** 11
2 Sep 65	TRY TO UNDERSTAND *Decca F 12214* **25** 8
13 Apr 67	● THE BOAT THAT I ROW *Columbia DB 8169* **6** 11
29 Jun 67	LET'S PRETEND *Columbia DB 8221* **11** 11
8 Nov 67	LOVE LOVES TO LOVE LOVE *Columbia DB 8295* **32** 6
28 Feb 68	● ME, THE PEACEFUL HEART *Columbia DB 8358* **9** 9
5 Jun 68	BOY *Columbia DB 8425* **15** 7
6 Nov 68	● I'M A TIGER *Columbia DB 8500* **9** 13
12 Mar 69	● BOOM BANG-A-BANG *Columbia DB 8550* **2** 13
22 Nov 69	OH ME OH MY (I'M A FOOL FOR YOU BABY) *Atco 226008* **47** 2
26 Jan 74	● THE MAN WHO SOLD THE WORLD *Polydor 2001 490* **3** 9
19 Apr 75	TAKE YOUR MAMA FOR A RIDE *Chelsea 2005 022* **37** 4
12 Dec 81	I COULD NEVER MISS YOU (MORE THAN I DO) (re) *Alfa ALFA 1700* **62** 5
19 Jul 86	● SHOUT *Jive LULU1 / Decca SHOUT 1* **8** 11
30 Jan 93	INDEPENDENCE *Dome CDDOME 1001* **11** 5
3 Apr 93	I'M BACK FOR MORE *Dome CDDOME 1002* [2] **27** 5
4 Sep 93	LET ME WAKE UP IN YOUR ARMS *Dome CDDOME 1005* **51** 2
9 Oct 93	★ RELIGHT MY FIRE *RCA 74321167722* [3] ■ **1** 14
27 Nov 93	HOW 'BOUT US *Dome CDDOME 1007* **46** 3
27 Aug 94	GOODBYE BABY AND AMEN *Dome CDDOME 1011* **40** 2
26 Nov 94	EVERY WOMAN KNOWS *Dome CDDOME 1013* **44** 2
29 May 99	HURT ME SO BAD *Rocket / Mercury 5726132* **42** 2
8 Jan 00	BETTER GET READY *Mercury 5625852* **59** 1
18 Mar 00	WHERE THE POOR BOYS DANCE *Mercury 1568452* **24** 5
7 Dec 02	● WE'VE GOT TONIGHT *Polydor 0658612* [4] **4** 13
25 Sep 71	THE MOST OF LULU *MFP 5215* **15** 6
6 Mar 93	INDEPENDENCE *Dome DOMECD 1* **67** 1
1 Jun 02	◉ TOGETHER *Mercury 630212* **4** 9
22 Nov 03	THE GREATEST HITS *Mercury / Universal TV 9865879* **35** 2
27 Mar 04	BACK ON TRACK *Mercury 9866136* **68** 1

[1] Lulu and The Luvvers [2] Lulu and Bobby Womack [3] Take That featuring Lulu [4] Ronan Keating featuring Lulu

The newly recorded 'Shout' entered the chart on 19 Jul 1986, and the next week the original Decca version by Lulu and The Luvvers also charted. For all subsequent weeks Gallup amalgamated both versions under one entry and we have added an extra week on chart for the 'double week' to take account of this

Bob LUMAN *US, male vocalist, b. 15 Apr 1937, d. 27 Dec 1978 (Singles: 21 Weeks, Albums: 1 Week)* pos/wks

8 Sep 60	● LET'S THINK ABOUT LIVING *Warner Bros. WB 18* **6** 18
15 Dec 60	WHY, WHY, BYE, BYE *Warner Bros. WB 28* **46** 1
4 May 61	THE GREAT SNOWMAN *Warner Bros. WB 37* **49** 2
14 Jan 61	LET'S THINK ABOUT LIVING *Warner Bros. WM 4025* **18** 1

LUMIDEE *US, female vocalist – Lumidee Cadino (Singles: 14 Weeks, Albums: 3 Weeks)* pos/wks

| 9 Aug 03 | ● NEVER LEAVE YOU – UH OOH, UH OOOH! *Universal MCSTD 40328* ....**2** 13 |

| 29 Nov 03 | CRASHIN' A PARTY *Universal MCSTD 40341* [1] ....**55** 1 |
| 16 Aug 03 | ALMOST FAMOUS *Universal 9860622* ....**73** 3 |

[1] Lumidee featuring N.O.R.E.

LUMINAIRE See Jonathan PETERS presents LUMINAIRE

LUNIZ *US, male rap duo – Jerrold 'Yukmouth' Ellis Jr and Garrick 'Knumbskull' Husbands (Singles: 18 Weeks, Albums: 3 Weeks)* pos/wks

17 Feb 96	● I GOT 5 ON IT *Virgin America VUSCD 101* **3** 13
11 May 96	PLAYA HATA *Virgin America VUSCD 103* **20** 3
31 Oct 98	I GOT 5 ON IT (re-mix) *Virgin VCRD 41* **28** 2
16 Mar 96	OPERATION STACKOLA *Virgin VUSMC 94* **41** 3

LUPINE HOWL
UK, male vocal / instrumental group (Singles: 1 Week) pos/wks

| 22 Jan 00 | VAPORIZER *Vinyl Hiss VHISSCD 001* ....**68** 1 |

The LURKERS *UK, male vocal / instrumental group (Singles: 11 Weeks, Albums: 1 Week)* pos/wks

3 Jun 78	AIN'T GOT A CLUE *Beggars Banquet BEG 6* **45** 3
5 Aug 78	I DON'T NEED TO TELL HER *Beggars Banquet BEG 9* **49** 4
3 Feb 79	JUST THIRTEEN *Beggars Banquet BEG 14* **66** 2
9 Jun 79	OUT IN THE DARK / CYANIDE *Beggars Banquet BEG 19* **72** 1
17 Nov 79	NEW GUITAR IN TOWN *Beggars Banquet BEG 28* **72** 1
1 Jul 78	FULHAM FALLOUT *Beggars Banquet BEGA 2* **57** 1

LUSCIOUS JACKSON *US, female vocal / instrumental group (Singles: 5 Weeks, Albums: 1 Week)* pos/wks

18 Mar 95	DEEP SHAG / CITYSONG *Capitol CDCL 739* **69** 1
21 Oct 95	HERE *Capitol CDCL 758* **59** 1
12 Apr 97	NAKED EYE *Capitol CDCL 786* **25** 2
3 Jul 99	LADYFINGERS *Grand Royal / Parlophone CDCL 813* **43** 1
26 Apr 97	FEVER IN FEVER OUT *Capitol CDEST 2290* **55** 1

LUSH *UK, female / male vocal / instrumental group (Singles: 19 Weeks, Albums: 10 Weeks)* pos/wks

10 Mar 90	MAD LOVE (EP) *4AD BAD 003* **55** 1
27 Oct 90	SWEETNESS AND LIGHT *4AD BAD 0013* **47** 2
19 Oct 91	NOTHING NATURAL *4AD AD 1016* **43** 2
11 Jan 92	FOR LOVE (EP) *4AD BAD 2001* **35** 2
11 Jun 94	HYPOCRITE *4AD BAD 4008CD* **52** 2
11 Jun 94	DESIRE LINES *4AD BAD 4010CD* **60** 1
20 Jan 96	SINGLE GIRL *4AD BAD 6001CD* **21** 3
9 Mar 96	LADYKILLERS *4AD BAD 6002CD* **22** 3
27 Jul 96	500 (SHAKE BABY SHAKE) *4AD BAD 6009CD* **21** 3
8 Feb 92	● SPOOKY *4AD CAD 2002CD* **7** 3
25 Jun 94	SPLIT *4AD CAD 4011CD* **19** 2
30 Mar 96	● LOVELIFE *4AD CAD 6004CD* **8** 5

Tracks on Mad Love (EP): De-Luxe / Leaves Me Cold / Downer / Thoughtforms. Tracks on For Love (EP): For Love / Starlust / Outdoor Miner / Astronaut

LUSTRAL (see also ASCENCION; CHAKRA; OXYGEN featuring Andrea BRITTON; SPACE BROTHERS) *UK, male DJ / production duo – Ricky Simmons and Steve Jones (Singles: 3 Weeks)* pos/wks

| 18 Oct 97 | EVERYTIME *Hooj Choons HOOJCD 55* ....**60** 1 |
| 4 Dec 99 | EVERYTIME (re-mix) *Hooj Choons HOOJ 83CD* ....**30** 2 |

LUVVERS See LULU

LUZON *US, male producer – Stacy Burket (Singles: 1 Week)* pos/wks

| 14 Jul 01 | THE BAGUIO TRACK *Renaissance RENCDS 006* ....**67** 1 |

Annabella LWIN
Burma, female vocalist – Myant Myant Aye (Singles: 1 Week) pos/wks

| 28 Jan 95 | DO WHAT YOU DO *Sony S2 6611235* ....**61** 1 |

John LYDON (see also PUBLIC IMAGE LTD; SEX PISTOLS)
UK, male vocalist (Singles: 6 Weeks) pos/wks

| 13 Nov 93 | OPEN UP *Hard Hands HAND 009CD* [1] ....**13** 5 |
| 2 Aug 97 | SUN *Virgin VUSCD 122* ....**42** 1 |

[1] Leftfield Lydon

Frankie LYMON and the TEENAGERS US, male vocal
group – leader b. 30 Sep 1942, d. 28 Feb 1968 (Singles: 38 Weeks) pos/wks

29 Jun 56	★ WHY DO FOOLS FALL IN LOVE Columbia DB 3772 [1]	1	16
29 Mar 57	I'M NOT A JUVENILE DELINQUENT Columbia 33 DB 3878	12	7
12 Apr 57	● BABY, BABY Columbia DB 3878	4	12
20 Sep 57	GOODY GOODY Columbia DB 3983	24	3

[1] The Teenagers featuring Frankie Lymon

Des LYNAM featuring WIMBLEDON CHORAL SOCIETY
UK, male vocalist / TV presenter and choir (Singles: 3 Weeks) pos/wks

12 Dec 98	IF – READ TO FAURE'S 'PAVANE' BBC Worldwide WMSS 60062	45	3

Curtis LYNCH Jr featuring Kele LE ROC and RED RAT
UK, male producer and female vocalist and
Jamaica, male vocalist (Singles: 1 Week) pos/wks

30 Sep 00	THINKING OF YOU Telstar CDSTAS 3136	70	1

Kenny LYNCH UK, male vocalist (Singles: 59 Weeks) pos/wks

30 Jun 60	MOUNTAIN OF LOVE HMV POP 751	33	3
13 Sep 62	PUFF (re) HMV POP 1057	33	6
6 Dec 62	● UP ON THE ROOF HMV POP 1090	10	12
20 Jun 63	● YOU CAN NEVER STOP ME LOVING YOU HMV POP 1165	10	14
16 Apr 64	STAND BY ME HMV POP 1280	39	7
27 Aug 64	WHAT AM I TO YOU (re) HMV POP 1321	37	6
17 Jun 65	I'LL STAY BY YOU HMV POP 1430	29	7
20 Aug 83	HALF THE DAY'S GONE AND WE HAVEN'T EARNED A PENNY Satril SAT 510	50	4

Liam LYNCH US, male vocalist (Singles: 9 Weeks) pos/wks

7 Dec 02	● UNITED STATES OF WHATEVER Global Warming WARMCD 17	10	9

Cheryl LYNN US, female vocalist (Singles: 2 Weeks) pos/wks

8 Sep 84	ENCORE Streetwave KHAN 23	68	2

Patti LYNN UK, female vocalist (Singles: 5 Weeks) pos/wks

10 May 62	JOHNNY ANGEL Fontana H 391	37	5

Tami LYNN US, female vocalist (Singles: 20 Weeks) pos/wks

22 May 71	● I'M GONNA RUN AWAY FROM YOU Mojo 2092 001	4	14
3 May 75	I'M GONNA RUN AWAY FROM YOU (re-issue) Contempo Raries CS 9026	36	6

Vera LYNN UK, female vocalist – Vera
Welch (Singles: 46 Weeks, Albums: 15 Weeks) pos/wks

14 Nov 52	● AUF WIEDERSEH'N SWEETHEART Decca F 9927 ▲	10	1
14 Nov 52	● FORGET-ME-NOT (re) Decca F 9985	5	6
14 Nov 52	THE HOMING WALTZ Decca F 9959	9	3
5 Jun 53	THE WINDSOR WALTZ Decca F 10092	11	1
15 Oct 54	★ MY SON, MY SON Decca F 10372 [1]	1	14
8 Jun 56	WHO ARE WE Decca F 10715	30	1
26 Oct 56	A HOUSE WITH LOVE IN IT Decca F 10799	17	13
15 Mar 57	THE FAITHFUL HUSSAR (DON'T CRY MY LOVE) Decca F 10846	29	2
21 Jun 57	TRAVELLIN' HOME Decca F 10903	20	5
21 Nov 81	20 FAMILY FAVOURITES EMI EMTV 28	25	12
9 Sep 89	WE'LL MEET AGAIN Telstar STAR 2369	44	3

[1] Vera Lynn with Frank Weir, his Saxophone, his Orchestra and Chorus

Jeff LYNNE (see also ELECTRIC LIGHT ORCHESTRA; TRAVELING
WILBURYS) UK, male vocalist (Singles: 4 Weeks, Albums: 4 Weeks) pos/wks

30 Jun 90	EVERY LITTLE THING Reprise W 9799	59	4
4 Aug 90	ARMCHAIR THEATRE Reprise WX 347	24	4

Shelby LYNNE US, female vocalist (Singles: 1 Week) pos/wks

29 Apr 00	LEAVIN' Mercury 5627372	73	1

Philip LYNOTT (see also THIN LIZZY; MIDGE URE; GARY MOORE)
Ireland, male vocalist / instrumentalist, b. 20 Aug 1957,
d. 4 Jan 1986 (Singles: 36 Weeks, Albums: 16 Weeks) pos/wks

5 Apr 80	DEAR MISS LONELY HEARTS Vertigo SOLO 1	32	6
21 Jun 80	KING'S CALL Vertigo SOLO 2	35	6
21 Mar 81	YELLOW PEARL (re) Vertigo SOLO 3	14	12
18 May 85	● OUT IN THE FIELDS 10 TEN 49 [1]	5	10

24 Jan 87	KING'S CALL (re-mix) Vertigo LYN 1	68	2
26 Apr 80	SOLO IN SOHO Vertigo 9102 038	28	6
14 Nov 87	SOLDIER OF FORTUNE – THE BEST OF PHIL LYNOTT AND THIN LIZZY Telstar STAR 2300 [1]	55	10

[1] Gary Moore and Phil Lynott [1] Phil Lynott and Thin Lizzy

'Yellow Pearl' made its peak position on re-entry in Dec 1981

LYNYRD SKYNYRD US, male vocal / instrumental
group (Singles: 21 Weeks, Albums: 19 Weeks) pos/wks

11 Sep 76	SWEET HOME ALABAMA / DOUBLE TROUBLE (2re) MCA 251	21	21
3 May 75	NUTHIN' FANCY MCA MCF 2700	43	1
28 Feb 76	GIMME BACK MY BULLETS MCA MCF 2744	34	5
6 Nov 76	ONE MORE FOR THE ROAD MCA MCPS 279	17	4
12 Nov 77	STREET SURVIVORS MCA MCG 3525	13	4
4 Nov 78	SKYNYRD'S FIRST AND LAST MCA MCG 3529	50	1
9 Feb 80	THE VERY BEST OF LYNYRD SKYNYRD – GOLD & PLATINUM MCA MCSP 308	49	4

'Sweet Home Alabama / Double Trouble' was the chart listing for what was also
alternatively listed as the 'Freebird EP' for the two re-entries, which peaked at
No.43 in Dec 1979 and No.21 in 1982. 1976 chart peak was No.31

Barbara LYON
US, female vocalist, b. 9 Sep 1931, d. 10 Jul 1985 (Singles: 12 Weeks) pos/wks

24 Jun 55	STOWAWAY Columbia DB 3619	12	8
21 Dec 56	LETTER TO A SOLDIER Columbia DB 3865	27	4

LYTE FUNKIE ONES
US, male vocal / rap group (Singles: 20 Weeks, Albums: 1 Week) pos/wks

22 May 99	CAN'T HAVE YOU Logic 74321649152	54	1
18 Sep 99	SUMMER GIRLS Logic 74321701152	16	7
5 Feb 00	● GIRL ON TV Logic 74321717582	6	9
27 Apr 02	EVERY OTHER TIME Logic 74321925502	24	3
26 Feb 00	LYTE FUNKIE ONES Logic 74321706832	62	1

Humphrey LYTTELTON BAND UK, male jazz
band – Humphrey Lyttelton – trumpet (Singles: 6 Weeks) pos/wks

13 Jul 56	BAD PENNY BLUES Parlophone R 4184	19	6

Kevin LYTTLE St Vincent, male vocalist (Singles: 23 Weeks) pos/wks

25 Oct 03	● TURN ME ON Atlantic AT 0167CD	2	19
29 May 04	LAST DROP Atlantic AT 0176CD	22	4

M UK, male vocalist / multi-instrumentalist –
Robin Scott (Singles: 39 Weeks) pos/wks

7 Apr 79	● POP MUZIK MCA 413 ▲	2	14
8 Dec 79	MOONLIGHT AND MUZAK MCA 541	33	9
15 Mar 80	THAT'S THE WAY THE MONEY GOES MCA 570	45	5
22 Nov 80	OFFICIAL SECRETS MCA 650	64	2
10 Jun 89	POP MUZIK (re-mix) Freestyle FRS 1	15	9

Bobby M featuring Jean CARN
US, male / female vocal / instrumental duo (Singles: 3 Weeks) pos/wks

29 Jan 83	LET'S STAY TOGETHER Gordy TMG 1288	53	3

M and O BAND *UK, male vocal / instrumental*
duo – Muff Murfin and Colin Owen (Singles: 6 Weeks)   pos/wks
28 Feb 76		LET'S DO THE LATIN HUSTLE *Creole CR 120*	...........**16**	6

M&S presents GIRL NEXT DOOR
UK, male production duo and female vocalist (Singles: 13 Weeks)   pos/wks
7 Apr 01	●	SALSOUL NUGGET (IF U WANNA) *ffrr FCD 393*	.........**6**	13

MBD *See SO SOLID CREW*

M-BEAT *UK, male producer – Marlon Hart (Singles: 24 Weeks)*   pos/wks
18 Jun 94	INCREDIBLE *Renk RENK 42CD* [1]	..........**39**	3
10 Sep 94	INCREDIBLE (re-mix) *Renk CDRENK 44* [1]	..........**8**	9
17 Dec 94	SWEET LOVE *Renk CDRENK 49* [2]	..........**18**	7
1 Jun 96	DO U KNOW WHERE YOU'RE COMING FROM		
	Renk CDRENK 63 [3]	..........**12**	5

[1] M-Beat featuring General Levy [2] M-Beat featuring Nazlyn
[3] M-Beat featuring Jamiroquai

M-D-EMM *UK, male producer – Mark Ryder (Singles: 3 Weeks)*   pos/wks
22 Feb 92	GET DOWN *Strictly Underground 7STUR 13*	..........**55**	2
30 May 92	MOVE YOUR FEET *Strictly Underground STUR 15*	..........**67**	1

MDM (see also LOST TRIBE; MELT featuring LITTLE MS MARCIE; SUNBURST)
UK, male producer – Matt Darey (Singles: 1 Week)   pos/wks
27 Oct 01	MASH IT UP *Nulife / Arista 74321870472*	..........**66**	1

M DUBS featuring LADY SAW
UK / Jamaica, male producer and female vocalist (Singles: 1 Week) pos/wks
16 Dec 00	BUMP N GRIND (I AM FEELING HOT TONIGHT)		
	Telstar CDSTAS 3129	..........**59**	1

MFSB *US, orchestra (Singles: 18 Weeks)*   pos/wks
27 Apr 74	TSOP (THE SOUND OF PHILADELPHIA)		
	Philadelphia International PIR 2289 [1] ▲	..........**22**	9
26 Jul 75	SEXY *Philadelphia International PIR 3381*	..........**37**	5
31 Jan 81	MYSTERIES OF THE WORLD *Sound of Philadelphia PIR 9501*	..**41**	4

[1] MFSB featuring The Three Degrees

M FACTOR *UK, male DJ / production duo –*
Danny Harrison and Julian Jonah (Singles: 4 Weeks)   pos/wks
6 Jul 02	MOTHER *Serious SERR 042CD*	..........**18**	3
26 Jul 03	COME TOGETHER *Credence CDCRED 037*	..........**46**	1

MG's *See BOOKER T and the MG's*

MK *US, male producer – Mark Kinchen (Singles: 3 Weeks)*   pos/wks
4 Feb 95	ALWAYS *Activ CDTV 3* [1]	..........**69**	1
27 May 95	BURNING '95 *Activ CDTVR 6*	..........**44**	2

[1] MK featuring Alana

Alana appears on both hits, although she is credited only on the first

M + M (see also MARTHA and the MUFFINS)
Canada, male / female vocal duo (Singles: 4 Weeks)   pos/wks
28 Jul 84	BLACK STATIONS WHITE STATIONS *RCA 426*	..........**46**	4

M + M are Martha and a Muffin

MN8 *UK / Trinidad, male vocal group*
(Singles: 38 Weeks, Albums: 4 Weeks)   pos/wks
4 Feb 95	●	I'VE GOT A LITTLE SOMETHING FOR YOU *Columbia 6608802*	..**2**	13
29 Apr 95	●	IF YOU ONLY LET ME IN *Columbia 6613252*	..........**6**	7
15 Jul 95	●	HAPPY *Columbia 6622192*	..........**8**	7
4 Nov 95		BABY IT'S YOU (re) *Columbia 6624522*	..........**22**	3
24 Feb 96		PATHWAY TO THE MOON *Columbia 6629212*	..........**25**	2
31 Aug 96		TUFF ACT TO FOLLOW *Columbia 6635345*	..........**15**	3
26 Oct 96		DREAMING *Columbia 6638302*	..........**21**	3
27 May 95		TO THE NEXT LEVEL *Columbia 4802802*	..........**13**	4

MNO
Belgium, male instrumental / production group (Singles: 2 Weeks) pos/wks
28 Sep 91	GOD OF ABRAHAM *A&M AM 820*	..........**66**	2

M.O.P. *US, male rap duo – Jamal Grinnage*
and Eric Murry (Singles: 20 Weeks, Albums: 3 Weeks)   pos/wks
12 May 01	●	COLD AS ICE *Epic 6711762*	..........**4**	10
18 Aug 01	●	ANTE UP (re) *Epic 6717882* [1]	..........**7**	8
1 Dec 01		STAND CLEAR *Chrysalis CDEM 597* [2]	..........**43**	1
8 Jun 02		STAND CLEAR (re-mix) *Kaos KAOSCD 002* [2]	..........**50**	1
25 Aug 01		WARRIORZ *Epic 4982779*	..........**40**	3

[1] M.O.P. featuring Busta Rhymes [2] Adam F featuring M.O.P.

M1 *UK, male producer – Michael Woods (Singles: 1 Week)*   pos/wks
22 Feb 03	HEAVEN SENT *Inferno CDFERN 51*	..........**72**	1

M PEOPLE   (111   Top 500)
Clubland favourites turned pop soul sophisticates: Heather Small (v),
backed by Paul Heard and Mike Pickering (both k/prog). In 1994 this
Manchester act was voted Best British Dance Act at the Brits and won
the 1993 Mercury Music Prize for their LP 'Elegant Slumming'
(Singles: 137 Weeks, Albums: 278 Weeks)   pos/wks
26 Oct 91		HOW CAN I LOVE YOU MORE? *Deconstruction PB 44855*	..**29**	9
7 Mar 92		COLOUR MY LIFE *Deconstruction PB 45241*	..........**35**	4
18 Apr 92		SOMEDAY *Deconstruction PB 45369* [1]	..........**38**	3
10 Oct 92		EXCITED *Deconstruction 74321116337*	..........**29**	5
6 Feb 93	●	HOW CAN I LOVE YOU MORE? (re-mix)		
		Deconstruction 74321130232	..........**8**	8
26 Jun 93	●	ONE NIGHT IN HEAVEN *Deconstruction 74321151852*	..**6**	11
25 Sep 93	●	MOVING ON UP *Deconstruction 74321166162*	..........**2**	11
4 Dec 93	●	DON'T LOOK ANY FURTHER *Deconstruction 74321177112*	..**9**	10
12 Mar 94	●	RENAISSANCE *Deconstruction 74321194132*	..........**5**	7
17 Sep 94		ELEGANTLY AMERICAN: ONE NIGHT IN HEAVEN / MOVING		
		ON UP (EP) (re-mix) *Deconstruction 74321231882*	..........**31**	2
19 Nov 94	●	SIGHT FOR SORE EYES *Deconstruction 74321245472*	..**6**	9
4 Feb 95	●	OPEN YOUR HEART *Deconstruction 74321261532*	..........**9**	7
24 Jun 95	●	SEARCH FOR THE HERO *Deconstruction 74321287962*	..**9**	7
14 Oct 95		LOVE RENDEZVOUS *Deconstruction 74321319282*	..........**32**	4
25 Nov 95		ITCHYCOO PARK *Deconstruction 74321330732*	..........**11**	6
4 Oct 97	●	JUST FOR YOU *BMG 74321523002*	..........**8**	7
6 Dec 97		FANTASY ISLAND (re) *BMG 74321542932*	..........**33**	9
28 Mar 98	●	ANGEL STREET *M People 74321564182*	..........**8**	6
7 Nov 98		TESTIFY *M People 74321621742*	..........**12**	6
13 Feb 99		DREAMING *M People 74321645352*	..........**13**	4
6 Mar 93		NORTHERN SOUL *Deconstruction 74321117772*	..........**53**	2
16 Oct 93	●	ELEGANT SLUMMING *Deconstruction 74321166782*	..**2**	87
26 Nov 94	●	BIZARRE FRUIT / BIZARRE FRUIT II		
		Deconstruction 74321240812	..........**3**	115
16 Sep 95		NORTHERN SOUL (re-issue) *RCA PD 75157*	..........**26**	3
25 Oct 97	●	FRESCO *M People 74321524902*	..........**2**	40
14 Nov 98	●	THE BEST OF M PEOPLE *M People 74321613872*	..**2**	31

[1] M People with Heather Small

From 9 Dec 95 'Bizarre Fruit' was listed with the re-mix album 'Bizarre Fruit II'

MSG *See Michael SCHENKER GROUP*

M3 *UK, male / female production / vocal trio (Singles: 2 Weeks)* pos/wks
30 Oct 99	BAILAMOS *Inferno CDFERN 21*	..........**40**	2

M2M *Norway, female vocal / instrumental duo –*
Marit Larsen and Marion Raven (Singles: 6 Weeks)   pos/wks
1 Apr 00	DON'T SAY YOU LOVE ME *Atlantic AT 0081CD*	..........**16**	6

MXM
Italy, male / female vocal / instrumental group (Singles: 1 Week) pos/wks
2 Jun 90	NOTHING COMPARES 2 U *London LON 267*	..........**68**	1

Timo MAAS
Germany, male DJ / producer (Singles: 10 Weeks, Albums: 3 Weeks) pos/wks
1 Apr 00	DER SCHIEBER *48k / Perfecto SPECT 07CDS*	..........**50**	1
30 Sep 00	UBIK *Perfecto PERF 10CDS* [1]	..........**33**	2
23 Feb 02	TO GET DOWN *Perfecto PERF 30CDS*	..........**14**	4
11 May 02	SHIFTER *Perfecto PERF 31CDS* [2]	..........**38**	2
5 Oct 02	HELP ME *Perfecto PERF 42CDS* [3]	..........**65**	1
16 Mar 02	LOUD *Perfecto PERFALB 08CD*	..........**41**	3

[1] Timo Mass featuring Martin Bettinghaus [2] Timo Maas featuring MC
Chickaboo [3] Timo Maas featuring Kelis

Lorin MAAZEL *See Andrea BOCELLI*

Pete MAC Jr (see also GODIEGO)
US, male vocalist (Singles: 4 Weeks) pos/wks

15 Oct 77	**THE WATER MARGIN** *BBC RESL 50*	**37**	4

This is the Japanese version of the song which shared chart credit with the English language version by Godiego

Scott MAC *See SIGNUM*

MAC BAND featuring the McCAMPBELL BROTHERS
US, male vocal group (Singles: 17 Weeks, Albums: 3 Weeks) pos/wks

18 Jun 88 ●	**ROSES ARE RED** *MCA MCA 1264*	**8**	13
10 Sep 88	**STALEMATE** *MCA MCA 1271*	**40**	4
20 Aug 88	**THE MAC BAND** *MCA MCC 6032*	**61**	3

'Stalemate' credits the McCampbell Brothers on the sleeve only, not on the label

Keith MAC PROJECT
UK, male / female vocal / instrumental group (Singles: 1 Week) pos/wks

25 Jun 94	**DE DAH DAH (SPICE OF LIFE)** *Public Demand PPDCD 3*	**66**	1

Lara McALLEN *See ANGEL CITY*

David McALMONT (see also McALMONT & BUTLER)
UK, male vocalist (Singles: 5 Weeks) pos/wks

27 Apr 96	**HYMN** *Blanco Y Negro NEG 87CD* [1]	**65**	1
9 Aug 97	**LOOK AT YOURSELF** *Hut HUTCD 87*	**40**	2
22 Nov 97	**DIAMONDS ARE FOREVER** *East West EW 141CD* [2]	**39**	2

[1] Ultramarine featuring David McAlmont [2] David McAlmont / David Arnold

McALMONT and BUTLER
UK, male vocal / instrumental duo – David McAlmont and Bernard Butler (Singles: 17 Weeks, Albums: 10 Weeks) pos/wks

27 May 95 ●	**YES** *Hut HUTCD 53*	**8**	8
4 Nov 95	**YOU DO** *Hut HUTCD 57*	**17**	4
10 Aug 02	**FALLING** *Chrysalis CDCHS 5141*	**23**	3
9 Nov 02	**BRING IT BACK** *Chrysalis CDCHSS 5145*	**36**	2
9 Dec 95	**THE SOUND OF McALMONT AND BUTLER** *Hut CDHUT 32*	**33**	8
24 Aug 02	**BRING IT BACK** *Chrysalis 5399772*	**18**	2

Neil MacARTHUR (see also The ZOMBIES)
UK, male vocalist – Colin Blunstone (Singles: 5 Weeks) pos/wks

5 Feb 69	**SHE'S NOT THERE** *Deram DM 225*	**34**	5

David MacBETH *UK, male vocalist (Singles: 4 Weeks)* pos/wks

30 Oct 59	**MR BLUE** *Pye 7N 15231*	**18**	4

Nicko McBRAIN (see also IRON MAIDEN)
UK, male vocalist / instrumentalist – drums (Singles: 1 Week) pos/wks

13 Jul 91	**RHYTHM OF THE BEAST** *EMI NICK 01*	**72**	1

Frankie McBRIDE
Ireland, male vocalist (Singles: 15 Weeks, Albums: 3 Weeks) pos/wks

9 Aug 67	**FIVE LITTLE FINGERS** *Emerald MD 1081*	**19**	15
17 Feb 68	**FRANKIE McBRIDE** *Emerald SLD 28*	**29**	3

The MACC LADS
UK, male vocal / instrumental group (Albums: 1 Week) pos/wks

7 Oct 89	**FROM BEER TO ETERNITY** *Hectic House HHLP 12*	**72**	1

Dan McCAFFERTY
(see also NAZARETH) UK, male vocalist (Singles: 3 Weeks) pos/wks

13 Sep 75	**OUT OF TIME** *Mountain TOP 1*	**41**	3

CW McCALL *US, male vocalist – William Fries (Singles: 10 Weeks)* pos/wks

14 Feb 76 ●	**CONVOY** *MGM 2006 560* ▲	**2**	10

Davina McCALL *See MERRION, McCALL & KENSIT*

Noel McCALLA *See BIGFELLA featuring Noel McCALLA*

David McCALLUM *UK, male actor / vocalist (Singles: 4 Weeks)* pos/wks

14 Apr 66	**COMMUNICATION** *Capitol CL 15439*	**32**	4

McCAMPBELL BROTHERS *See MAC BAND featuring the McCAMPBELL BROTHERS*

Linda McCARTNEY *US, female vocalist – Linda Eastman, b. 24 Sep 1942, d. 17 Apr 1998 (Singles: 7 Weeks, Albums: 3 Weeks)* pos/wks

28 Aug 71	**BACK SEAT OF MY CAR** *Apple R 5914* [1]	**39**	5
21 Nov 98	**WIDE PRAIRIE** *Parlophone CDR 6510*	**74**	1
6 Feb 99	**THE LIGHT COMES FROM WITHIN** *Parlophone CDR 6513*	**56**	1
5 Jun 71 ★	**RAM** *Apple PAS 10003* [1] ■	**1**	24

[1] Paul and Linda McCartney [1] Paul and Linda McCartney

Paul McCARTNEY ⟨20⟩ [Top 500]
Pop's most successful singer / songwriter, b. 18 Jun 1942, Liverpool, UK. His composition 'Yesterday' is the world's most recorded song and has had more than eight million plays on US radio alone. The Ex-Beatle, known for his charitable work, has broken attendance records around the world, his 50-date 2002 US tour grossed a record $100m and a 1999 internet show attracted at least 50 million hits. Winner of a record number of Ivor Novello Awards, he was awarded the only Rhodium record (from Guinness) to honour outstanding sales and received a Lifetime Achievement Grammy (1990) and a knighthood (1997). He has reportedly amassed a personal fortune of £500m. Sir Paul is the only artist to have No.1s as a solo artist, part of a duo, trio, quartet, quintet and charity group. Total UK single sales: 9,781,603. Best-selling single: 'Mull of Kintyre / Girls' School' 2,050,000 (Singles: 413 Weeks, Albums: 570 Weeks) pos/wks

27 Feb 71 ●	**ANOTHER DAY** *Apple R 5889*	**2**	12
28 Aug 71	**BACK SEAT OF MY CAR** *Apple R 5914* [1]	**39**	5
26 Feb 72	**GIVE IRELAND BACK TO THE IRISH** *Apple R 5936* [2]	**16**	8
27 May 72 ●	**MARY HAD A LITTLE LAMB** *Apple R 5949* [2]	**9**	11
9 Dec 72 ●	**HI, HI, HI / C MOON** *Apple R 5973* [2]	**5**	13
7 Apr 73 ●	**MY LOVE** *Apple R 5985* [3] ▲	**9**	11
9 Jun 73 ●	**LIVE AND LET DIE (re)** *Apple R 5987* [2]	**9**	14
3 Nov 73	**HELEN WHEELS** *Apple R 5993* [3]	**12**	12
2 Mar 74	**JET** *Apple R 5996* [3]	**7**	9
6 Jul 74 ●	**BAND ON THE RUN** *Apple R 5997* [3] ▲	**3**	11
9 Nov 74	**JUNIOR'S FARM** *Apple R 5999* [3]	**16**	10
31 May 75 ●	**LISTEN TO WHAT THE MAN SAID** *Capitol R 6006* [2] ▲	**6**	8
18 Oct 75	**LETTING GO** *Capitol R 6008* [2]	**41**	3
15 May 76 ●	**SILLY LOVE SONGS** *Parlophone R 6014* [2] ▲	**2**	11
7 Aug 76 ●	**LET 'EM IN** *Parlophone R 6015* [2]	**2**	10
19 Feb 77	**MAYBE I'M AMAZED** *Parlophone R 6017* [2]	**28**	5
19 Nov 77 ★	**MULL OF KINTYRE / GIRLS' SCHOOL** *Capitol R 6018* [2] ◆	**1**	17
1 Apr 78 ●	**WITH A LITTLE LUCK** *Parlophone R 6019* [2] ▲	**5**	9
1 Jul 78	**I'VE HAD ENOUGH** *Parlophone R 6020* [2]	**42**	7
9 Sep 78	**LONDON TOWN** *Parlophone R 6021* [2]	**60**	4
7 Apr 79 ●	**GOODNIGHT TONIGHT** *Parlophone R 6023* [2]	**5**	10
16 Jun 79	**OLD SIAM SIR** *Parlophone R 6026* [2]	**35**	6
1 Sep 79	**GETTING CLOSER / BABY'S REQUEST** *R 6027* [2]	**60**	3
1 Dec 79 ●	**WONDERFUL CHRISTMASTIME** *Parlophone R 6029*	**6**	8
19 Apr 80 ●	**COMING UP** *Parlophone R 6035* ▲	**2**	9
21 Jun 80 ●	**WATERFALLS** *Parlophone R 6037*	**9**	8
10 Apr 82 ★	**EBONY AND IVORY** *Parlophone 6054* [4] ▲	**1**	10
3 Jul 82	**TAKE IT AWAY** *Parlophone R 6056*	**15**	10
9 Oct 82	**TUG OF WAR** *Parlophone R 6057*	**53**	3
6 Nov 82 ●	**THE GIRL IS MINE (re)** *Epic EPC A 2729* [5]	**8**	10
15 Oct 83 ●	**SAY SAY SAY** *Parlophone R 6062* [6] ▲	**2**	15
17 Dec 83 ★	**PIPES OF PEACE** *Parlophone R 6064*	**1**	12
6 Oct 84 ●	**NO MORE LONELY NIGHTS (BALLAD)** *Parlophone R 6080*	**2**	10
24 Nov 84	**WE ALL STAND TOGETHER (re)** *Parlophone R 6086* [7]	**3**	18
30 Nov 85	**SPIES LIKE US** *Parlophone R 6118*	**13**	10
26 Jul 86	**PRESS** *Parlophone R 6133*	**25**	8
13 Dec 86	**ONLY LOVE REMAINS** *Parlophone R 6148*	**34**	5
28 Nov 87 ●	**ONCE UPON A LONG AGO** *Parlophone R 6170*	**10**	7
20 May 89	**MY BRAVE FACE** *Parlophone R 6213*	**18**	5
20 May 89 ★	**FERRY 'CROSS THE MERSEY** *PWL PWL 41* [8] ■	**1**	7
29 Jul 89	**THIS ONE** *Parlophone R 6223*	**18**	6
25 Nov 89	**FIGURE OF EIGHT** *Parlophone R 6235*	**42**	3
17 Feb 90	**PUT IT THERE** *Parlophone R 6246*	**32**	2
20 Oct 90	**BIRTHDAY** *Parlophone R 6271*	**29**	3
8 Dec 90	**ALL MY TRIALS** *Parlophone CDR 6278*	**35**	5
9 Jan 93	**HOPE OF DELIVERANCE** *Parlophone CDR 6330*	**18**	6
6 Mar 93	**C'MON PEOPLE** *Parlophone CDRS 6338*	**41**	3
10 May 97	**YOUNG BOY** *Parlophone CDRS 6462*	**19**	3
19 Jul 97	**THE WORLD TONIGHT** *Parlophone CDR 6472*	**23**	2
27 Dec 97	**BEAUTIFUL NIGHT** *Parlophone CDR 6489*	**25**	4

6 Nov 99	NO OTHER BABY / BROWN EYED HANDSOME MAN		
	Parlophone CDR 6527	.42	2
10 Nov 01	FROM A LOVER TO A FRIEND *Parlophone CDR 6567*	.45	2
2 Oct 04	TROPIC ISLAND HUM / WE ALL STAND TOGETHER (re-issue)		
	Parlophone CDR 6649	.21	3
2 May 70 ●	McCARTNEY *Apple PCS 7102* ▲	.2	32
5 Jun 71 ★	RAM *Apple PAS 10003* [1] ■	.1	24
18 Dec 71	WILD LIFE *Apple PCS 7142* [2]	.11	9
19 May 73 ●	RED ROSE SPEEDWAY *Apple PCTC 251* [3] ▲	.5	16
15 Dec 73 ★	BAND ON THE RUN *Apple PAS 10007* [3] ▲	.1	124
21 Jun 75 ★	VENUS AND MARS *Apple PCTC 254* [2] ▲	.1	29
17 Apr 76 ●	WINGS AT THE SPEED OF SOUND *Apple PAS 10010* [2] ▲	.2	35
15 Jan 77 ●	WINGS OVER AMERICA *Parlophone PAS 720* [2] ▲	.8	22
15 Apr 78 ●	LONDON TOWN *Parlophone PAS 10012* [2]	.4	23
16 Dec 78 ●	WINGS GREATEST HITS *Parlophone PCTC 256* [2]	.5	32
23 Jun 79 ●	BACK TO THE EGG *Parlophone PCTC 257* [2]	.6	15
31 May 80 ★	McCARTNEY II *Parlophone PCTC 258* ■	.1	18
7 Mar 81	THE McCARTNEY INTERVIEW *EMI CHAT 1*	.34	4
8 May 82 ★	TUG OF WAR *Parlophone PCTC 259* ■ ▲	.1	27
12 Nov 83 ●	PIPES OF PEACE *Parlophone PCTC 1652301*	.4	23
3 Nov 84 ★	GIVE MY REGARDS TO BROAD STREET *Parlophone PCTC 2* ■ [1]	.1	21
13 Sep 86 ●	PRESS TO PLAY *Parlophone PCSD 103*	.8	6
14 Nov 87 ●	ALL THE BEST! *Parlophone PMTV 1*	.2	21
17 Jun 89 ★	FLOWERS IN THE DIRT *Parlophone PCSD 106*	.1	20
17 Nov 90	TRIPPING THE LIVE FANTASTIC – HIGHLIGHTS!		
	Parlophone PCST 7346	.17	11
1 Jun 91 ●	UNPLUGGED – THE OFFICIAL BOOTLEG		
	Parlophone PCSD 116	.7	3
12 Oct 91	CHOBA B CCCP (THE RUSSIAN ALBUM)		
	Parlophone CDPCSD 117	.63	1
13 Feb 93 ●	OFF THE GROUND *Parlophone CDPCSD 125*	.5	4
20 Nov 93	PAUL IS LIVE *Parlophone PDPCSD 147*	.34	2
17 May 97 ●	FLAMING PIE *Parlophone CDPCSD 171*	.2	15
27 Mar 99	BAND ON THE RUN (re-issue) *Parlophone 4991762* [3]	.69	1
16 Oct 99	RUN DEVIL RUN *Parlophone 5223512*	.12	11
19 May 01	WINGSPAN – HITS AND HISTORY *Parlophone 5328502*	.5	7
24 Nov 01	DRIVING RAIN *Parlophone 5355102*	.46	1
29 Mar 03 ●	BACK IN THE WORLD *Parlophone 5830052*	.5	13

[1] Paul and Linda McCartney [2] Wings [3] Paul McCartney and Wings [4] Paul McCartney with Stevie Wonder [5] Michael Jackson and Paul McCartney [6] Paul McCartney and Michael Jackson [7] Paul McCartney and the Frog Chorus [8] The Christians, Holly Johnson, Paul McCartney, Gerry Marsden and Stock Aitken Waterman [1] Paul and Linda McCartney [2] Wings [3] Paul McCartney and Wings

R 6027 credits no label at all, although the number is a Parlophone one

Kirsty MacCOLL *UK, female vocalist, b. 10 Oct 1959,*
d. 18 Dec 2000 (Singles: 65 Weeks, Albums: 58 Weeks) pos/wks

13 Jun 81	THERE'S A GUY WORKS DOWN THE CHIPSHOP SWEARS		
	HE'S ELVIS *Polydor POSP 250*	.14	9
19 Jan 85 ●	A NEW ENGLAND *Stiff BUY 216*	.7	10
15 Nov 86	GREETINGS TO THE NEW BRUNETTE *Go Discs GOD 15* [1]	.58	2
5 Dec 87 ●	FAIRYTALE OF NEW YORK *Pogue Mahone NY 7* [2]	.2	9
8 Apr 89	FREE WORLD *Virgin KMA 1*	.43	6
1 Jul 89	DAYS *Virgin KMA 2*	.12	9
25 May 91	WALKING DOWN MADISON *Virgin VS 1348*	.23	7
17 Aug 91	MY AFFAIR *Virgin VS 1354*	.56	2
14 Dec 91	FAIRYTALE OF NEW YORK (re-issue) *PM YZ 628* [2]	.36	5
4 Mar 95	CAROLINE *Virgin VSCDX 1517*	.58	1
24 Jun 95	PERFECT DAY *Virgin VSCDT 1552* [3]	.75	1
29 Jul 95	DAYS (re-issue) *Virgin VSCDT 1558*	.42	3
20 May 89	KITE *Virgin KMLP 1*	.34	12
6 Jul 91	ELECTRIC LANDLADY *Virgin V 2663*	.17	8
12 Mar 94	TITANIC DAYS *ZTT 4509947112*	.46	2
18 Mar 95 ●	GALORE – THE BEST OF KIRSTY MacCOLL *Virgin CDV 2763*	.6	27
1 Apr 00	TROPICAL BRAINSTORM *V2 VVR 1009872*	.39	9

[1] Billy Bragg with Johnny Marr and Kirsty MacColl [2] The Pogues featuring Kirsty MacColl [3] Kirsty MacColl and Evan Dando

Neil MacCOLL *See The LA's; The PRETENDERS*

Marilyn McCOO and Billy DAVIS Jr (see also 5TH DIMENSION)
US, female / male vocal duo (Singles: 9 Weeks) pos/wks

| 19 Mar 77 ● | YOU DON'T HAVE TO BE A STAR (TO BE IN MY SHOW) | | |
| | *ABC 4147* ▲ | .7 | 9 |

Del McCOURY BAND *See Steve EARLE*

Paul McCOY *See EVANESCENCE*

Van McCOY *US, orchestra – leader b. 6 Jan 1940,*
d. 6 Jul 1979 (Singles: 36 Weeks, Albums: 11 Weeks) pos/wks

31 May 75 ●	THE HUSTLE *Avco 6105 038* [1] ▲	.3	12
1 Nov 75	CHANGE WITH THE TIMES *Avco 6105 042*	.36	4
12 Feb 77	SOUL CHA CHA *H&L 6105 065*	.34	6
9 Apr 77 ●	THE SHUFFLE *H&L 6105 076*	.4	14
5 Jul 75	DISCO BABY *Avco 9109 004* [1]	.32	11

[1] Van McCoy with the Soul City Symphony [1] Van McCoy with the Soul City Symphony

The McCOYS
US, male vocal / instrumental group (Singles: 18 Weeks) pos/wks

| 2 Sep 65 ● | HANG ON SLOOPY *Immediate IM 001* ▲ ■ | .5 | 14 |
| 16 Dec 65 | FEVER *Immediate IM 021* | .44 | 4 |

George McCRAE
US, male vocalist (Singles: 62 Weeks, Albums: 29 Weeks) pos/wks

29 Jun 74 ★	ROCK YOUR BABY *Jayboy BOY 85* ▲	.1	14
5 Oct 74 ●	I CAN'T LEAVE YOU ALONE *Jayboy BOY 90*	.9	9
14 Dec 74	YOU CAN HAVE IT ALL *Jayboy BOY 92*	.23	9
22 Mar 75	SING A HAPPY SONG *Jayboy BOY 95*	.38	4
19 Jul 75 ●	IT'S BEEN SO LONG *Jayboy BOY 100*	.4	11
18 Oct 75	I AIN'T LYIN' *Jayboy BOY 105*	.12	7
24 Jan 76	HONEY I *Jayboy BOY 107*	.33	4
25 Feb 84	ONE STEP CLOSER (TO LOVE) *President PT 522*	.57	4
3 Aug 74	ROCK YOUR BABY *Jayboy JSL 3*	.13	28
13 Sep 75	GEORGE McCRAE *Jayboy JSL 10*	.54	1

Gwen McCRAE *US, female vocalist (Singles: 5 Weeks)* pos/wks

30 Apr 88	ALL THIS LOVE THAT I'M GIVING *Flame MELT 7*	.63	2
13 Feb 93	ALL THIS LOVE I'M GIVING (re-recording)		
	KTDA CDKTDA 2 [1]	.36	3

[1] Music and Mystery featuring Gwen McCrae

The McCRARYS *US, male / female vocal group (Singles: 4 Weeks)* pos/wks

| 31 Jul 82 | LOVE ON A SUMMER NIGHT *Capitol CL 251* | .52 | 4 |

Mindy McCREADY *US, female vocalist (Singles: 3 Weeks)* pos/wks

| 1 Aug 98 | OH ROMEO *BNA 74321597242* | .41 | 3 |

Ian McCULLOCH (see also ECHO and the BUNNYMEN)
UK, male vocalist (Singles: 15 Weeks, Albums: 4 Weeks) pos/wks

15 Dec 84	SEPTEMBER SONG *Korova KOW 40*	.51	5
2 Sep 89	PROUD TO FALL *WEA YZ 417*	.51	4
12 May 90	CANDLELAND (THE SECOND COMING) *East West YZ 452* [1]	.75	1
22 Feb 92	LOVER LOVER LOVER *East West YZ 643*	.47	4
26 Apr 03	SLIDING *Cooking Vinyl FRYCD 146*	.61	1
7 Oct 89	CANDLELAND *WEA WX 303*	.18	3
21 Mar 92	MYSTERIO *East West 9031762642*	.46	1

[1] Ian McCulloch featuring Elizabeth Fraser

Martine McCUTCHEON
UK, female actor / vocalist (Singles: 65 Weeks, Albums: 36 Weeks) pos/wks

18 Nov 95	ARE YOU MAN ENOUGH *Avex UK AVEX CD 14* [1]	.62	1
17 Apr 99 ★	PERFECT MOMENT (re) *Innocent SINCD 7* ■	.1	20
11 Sep 99 ●	I'VE GOT YOU *Innocent SINCD 12*	.6	10
4 Dec 99 ●	TALKING IN YOUR SLEEP / LOVE ME *Innocent SINCD 14*	.6	10
4 Nov 00 ●	I'M OVER YOU *Innocent SINCD 20*	.2	10
3 Feb 01 ●	ON THE RADIO *Innocent SINCD 21*	.7	8
18 Sep 99 ●	YOU ME & US *Innocent CDSIN 4*	.2	20
25 Nov 00	WISHING *Innocent CDSIN 7*	.25	14
14 Dec 02	MUSICALITY *EMI / Liberty 5805492*	.55	2

[1] Uno Clio featuring Martine McCutcheon

Gene McDANIELS *US, male vocalist (Singles: 2 Weeks)* pos/wks

| 16 Nov 61 | TOWER OF STRENGTH (re) *London HLG 9448* | .49 | 2 |

Julie McDERMOTT *See AWESOME 3; THIRD DIMENSION featuring Julie McDERMOTT*

Charles McDEVITT SKIFFLE GROUP featuring Nancy WHISKEY
UK, male / female vocal / instrumental group – Nancy Whiskey, b. 4 Mar 1935, d. 1 Feb 2003 (Singles: 20 Weeks) pos/wks

12 Apr 57	●	FREIGHT TRAIN (re) *Oriole CB 1352*	5 18
14 Jun 57		GREENBACK DOLLAR (re) *Oriole CB 1371*	28 2

Jane McDONALD
UK, female vocalist (Singles: 7 Weeks, Albums: 39 Weeks) pos/wks

26 Dec 98	●	CRUISE INTO CHRISTMAS MEDLEY *Focus Music Int CDFM 2*	10 7
25 Jul 98	★	JANE McDONALD *Focus Music International FMCD 1* ■	1 27
17 Jun 00	●	INSPIRATION *Universal Music TV 1578612*	6 9
27 Oct 01		LOVE AT THE MOVIES *Universal Music TV 149472*	24 3

Michael McDONALD (see also The DOOBIE BROTHERS) *US, male vocalist / instrumentalist (Singles: 49 Weeks, Albums: 49 Weeks)* pos/wks

18 Feb 84		YAH MO B THERE (2re) *Qwest 9394* [1]	12 16
3 May 86	●	ON MY OWN *MCA MCA 1045* [2] ▲	2 13
26 Jul 86		I KEEP FORGETTIN' *Warner Bros. K 17992*	43 6
6 Sep 86		SWEET FREEDOM *MCA MCA 1073*	12 10
24 Jan 87		WHAT A FOOL BELIEVES (re-issue) *Warner Bros. W 8451* [3]	57 3
5 Oct 02		SWEET FREEDOM *Serious SERR 55CD* [4]	54 1
22 Nov 86	●	SWEET FREEDOM: BEST OF MICHAEL McDONALD *Warner Bros. WX 67*	6 35
26 May 90		TAKE IT TO HEART *Reprise WX 285*	35 4
17 Mar 01		THE VERY BEST OF MICHAEL McDONALD *Rhino 8122735302*	21 6
17 May 03		MOTOWN *Universal TV 9800233*	29 4

[1] James Ingram with Michael McDonald [2] Patti LaBelle and Michael McDonald [3] The Doobie Brothers featuring Michael McDonald [4] Safri Duo featuring Michael McDonald

'Yah Mo B There' had its first chart listing in Feb 1984, peaking at No.44, and the first re-entry in Apr 1984, peaking at No.69. The 1985 second re-entry was a re-mix of the original hit with the same catalogue number

Carrie McDOWELL *US, female vocalist (Singles: 3 Weeks)* pos/wks

26 Sep 87		UH UH NO NO CASUAL SEX *Motown ZV 41501*	68 3

John McENROE and Pat CASH with the FULL METAL RACKETS *US / Australia, male vocal / instrumental duo and UK, backing group (Singles: 1 Week)* pos/wks

13 Jul 91		ROCK 'N' ROLL *Music for Nations KUT 141*	66 1

Reba McENTIRE *US, female vocalist (Singles: 1 Week)* pos/wks

19 Jun 99		DOES HE LOVE YOU *MCA Nashville MCSTD 55569*	62 1

MACEO & THE MACKS
US, male vocal / instrumental group (Singles: 5 Weeks) pos/wks

16 May 87		CROSS THE TRACK (WE BETTER GO BACK) *Urban URBX 1*	54 5

Brian McFADDEN (see also WESTLIFE)
Ireland, male vocalist (Singles: 16 Weeks, Albums: 3 Weeks) pos/wks

18 Sep 04	★	REAL TO ME *Modest! / Sony Music 6753032* ■	1 12
4 Dec 04	●	IRISH SON *Modest! / Sony Music 6745871*	6 4+
11 Dec 04		IRISH SON *Modest! / Sony Music 5190022*	24 3+

McFADDEN and WHITEHEAD
US, male vocal duo – Gene McFadden and John Whitehead, b. 2 Jul 1948, d. 11 May 2004 (Singles: 10 Weeks) pos/wks

19 May 79	●	AIN'T NO STOPPIN' US NOW *Philadelphia International PIR 7365*	5 10

Rachel McFARLANE *See LOVELAND featuring the voice of Rachel McFARLANE*

Bobby McFERRIN
US, male vocalist (Singles: 15 Weeks, Albums: 1 Week) pos/wks

24 Sep 88	●	DON'T WORRY BE HAPPY *Manhattan MT 56* ▲	2 11
17 Dec 88		THINKIN' ABOUT YOUR BODY *Manhattan BLUE 6*	46 4
29 Oct 88		SIMPLE PLEASURES *Manhattan MTL 1018*	92 1

McFLY *UK, male vocal / instrumental group (Singles: 37 Weeks, Albums: 24 Weeks)* pos/wks

10 Apr 04	★	5 COLOURS IN HER HAIR *Universal MCSTD 40357* ■	1 12
3 Jul 04	★	OBVIOUSLY *Universal MCSTD 40364* ■	1 13

18 Sep 04	●	THAT GIRL *Universal MCSXD 40378*	3 7
27 Nov 04	●	ROOM ON THE 3RD FLOOR *Island MCSXD 40389*	5 5+
17 Jul 04	★	ROOM ON THE 3RD FLOOR *Universal MCD 60094* ■	1 24+

The McGANNS *UK, male actors / vocal trio (Singles: 4 Weeks)* pos/wks

14 Nov 98		JUST MY IMAGINATION *Coalition COLA 062CD*	59 1
6 Feb 99		A HEARTBEAT AWAY *Coalition COLA 069CD*	42 3

Kate and Anna McGARRIGLE
Canada, female vocal duo (Albums: 4 Weeks) pos/wks

26 Feb 77		DANCER WITH BRUISED KNEES *Warner Bros. K 56356*	35 4

Mike McGEAR (see also The SCAFFOLD)
UK, male vocalist – Peter McCartney (Singles: 4 Weeks) pos/wks

5 Oct 74		LEAVE IT *Warner Bros. K 16446*	36 4

Maureen McGOVERN *US, female vocalist (Singles: 8 Weeks)* pos/wks

5 Jun 76		THE CONTINENTAL *20th Century BTC 2222*	16 8

Shane MacGOWAN and the POPES *UK, male vocal / instrumental group (Singles: 9 Weeks, Albums: 3 Weeks)* pos/wks

12 Dec 92		WHAT A WONDERFUL WORLD *Mute MUTE 151* [1]	72 1
3 Sep 94		THE CHURCH OF THE HOLY SPOOK *ZTT ZANG 57CD*	74 1
15 Oct 94		THAT WOMAN'S GOT ME DRINKING *ZTT ZANG 56CD*	34 3
29 Apr 95		HAUNTED *ZTT ZANG 65CD* [2]	30 2
20 Apr 96		MY WAY *ZTT ZANG 79CD* [3]	29 2
29 Oct 94		THE SNAKE *ZTT 4509981042*	37 2
8 Nov 97		THE CROCK OF GOLD *ZTT MACG 002CD*	59 1

[1] Nick Cave and Shane MacGowan [2] Shane MacGowan and Sinead O'Connor [3] Shane McGowan

Mark McGRATH *See Shania TWAIN*

Ewan McGREGOR *See PF PROJECT featuring Ewan McGREGOR; Nicole KIDMAN*

Freddie McGREGOR
Jamaica, male vocalist (Singles: 16 Weeks) pos/wks

27 Jun 87	●	JUST DON'T WANT TO BE LONELY *Germain DG 24*	9 11
19 Sep 87		THAT GIRL (GROOVY SITUATION) *Polydor POSP 884*	47 5

Mary MacGREGOR
US, female vocalist (Singles: 10 Weeks, Albums: 1 Week) pos/wks

19 Feb 77	●	TORN BETWEEN TWO LOVERS *Ariola America AA 111* ▲	4 10
23 Apr 77		TORN BETWEEN TWO LOVERS *Ariola America AAS 1504*	59 1

McGUINNESS FLINT (see also MANFRED MANN) *UK, male vocal / instrumental group (Singles: 26 Weeks, Albums: 2 Weeks)* pos/wks

21 Nov 70	●	WHEN I'M DEAD AND GONE *Capitol CL 15662*	2 14
1 May 71	●	MALT AND BARLEY BLUES *Capitol CL 15682*	5 12
23 Jan 71	●	McGUINNESS FLINT *Capitol EAST 22625*	9 2

Barry McGUIRE *US, male vocalist (Singles: 13 Weeks)* pos/wks

9 Sep 65	●	EVE OF DESTRUCTION *RCA 1469* ▲	3 13

The McGUIRE SISTERS
US, female vocal group (Singles: 24 Weeks) pos/wks

1 Apr 55		NO MORE *Vogue Coral Q 72050*	20 1
15 Jul 55		SINCERELY *Vogue Coral Q 72050* ▲	14 4
1 Jun 56		DELILAH JONES *Vogue Coral Q 72161*	24 2
14 Feb 58		SUGARTIME *Coral Q 72305*	14 6
1 May 59		MAY YOU ALWAYS (re) *Coral Q 72356*	15 11

MACHEL
Trinidad, male vocalist – Machel Montano (Singles: 2 Weeks) pos/wks

14 Sep 96		COME DIG IT *London LONCD 386*	56 2

MACHINE HEAD *UK, male vocal / instrumental group (Singles: 4 Weeks, Albums: 9 Weeks)* pos/wks

27 May 95		OLD *Roadrunner RR 23403*	43 2
6 Dec 97		TAKE MY SCARS *Roadrunner RR 22573*	73 1
18 Dec 99		FROM THIS DAY *Roadrunner RR 21383*	74 1

20 Aug 94	BURN MY EYES *Roadrunner RR 90169*	25	3
5 Apr 97	THE MORE THINGS CHANGE ... *Roadrunner RR 88602*	16	3
21 Aug 99	THE BURNING RED *Roadrunner RR 86512*	13	2
13 Oct 01	SUPERCHARGER *Roadrunner 12085002*	34	1

MACK 10 *See ICE CUBE*

Billy MACK
UK, male actor / vocalist – Bill Nighy (Singles: 3 Weeks)   pos/wks

| 27 Dec 03 | CHRISTMAS IS ALL AROUND *Island CID 841* | 26 | 3 |

Craig MACK
US, male rapper (Singles: 5 Weeks)   pos/wks

12 Nov 94	FLAVA IN YA EAR *Bad Boy 74321242582*	57	2
1 Apr 95	GET DOWN *Puff Daddy 74321263402*	54	1
7 Jun 97	SPIRIT *Perspective 5822312* [1]	35	2

[1] Sound of Blackness featuring Craig Mack

Lizzy MACK
UK, female vocalist (Singles: 3 Weeks)   pos/wks

| 5 Nov 94 | THE POWER OF LOVE *Media MCSTD 2016* [1] | 49 | 2 |
| 4 Nov 95 | DON'T GO *Power Station MCSTD 40004* | 52 | 1 |

[1] Fits of Gloom featuring Lizzy Mack

Lonnie MACK
US, male instrumentalist –
guitar – Lonnie McIntosh (Singles: 3 Weeks)   pos/wks

| 14 Apr 79 | MEMPHIS *Lightning LIG 9011* | 47 | 3 |

'Memphis' was coupled with 'Let's Dance' by Chris Montez as a double A-side

MACK VIBE featuring JACQUELINE
US, male / female vocal / instrumental duo (Singles: 1 Week)   pos/wks

| 4 Feb 95 | I CAN'T LET YOU GO *MCA MCSTD 20020* | 53 | 1 |

Duff McKAGAN (see also GUNS N' ROSES)
US, male vocalist / instrumentalist – bass (Albums: 2 Weeks)   pos/wks

| 9 Oct 93 | BELIEVE IN ME *Geffen GED 24605* | 27 | 2 |

McKAY *US, female vocalist – Stepanie McKay (Singles: 1 Week)*
pos/wks

| 23 Aug 03 | TAKE ME OVER *Go Beat GOBCD 57* | 65 | 1 |

Maria McKEE
US, female vocalist (Singles: 23 Weeks, Albums: 6 Weeks)   pos/wks

15 Sep 90 ★	SHOW ME HEAVEN *Epic 656303 7*	1	14
26 Jan 91	BREATHE *Geffen GFS 1*	59	1
1 Aug 92	SWEETEST CHILD *Geffen GFS 23*	45	4
22 May 93	I'M GONNA SOOTHE YOU *Geffen GFSTD 39*	35	3
18 Sep 93	I CAN'T MAKE IT ALONE *Geffen GFSTD 53*	74	1
24 Jun 89	MARIA McKEE *Geffen WX 270*	49	3
12 Jun 93	YOU GOTTA SIN TO GET SAVED *Geffen GED 24508*	26	3

Kenneth McKELLAR
UK, male vocalist (Singles: 4 Weeks, Albums: 10 Weeks)   pos/wks

10 Mar 66	A MAN WITHOUT LOVE *Decca F 12341*	30	4
28 Jun 69	THE WORLD OF KENNETH McKELLAR *Decca SPA 11*	27	7
31 Jan 70	ECCO DI NAPOLI *Decca SKL 5018*	45	3

Terence McKENNA *See The SHAMEN*

Billy MacKENZIE (see also ASSOCIATES)
UK, male vocalist, b. 27 Mar 1957, d. 22 Jan 1997 (Albums: 1 Week) pos/wks

| 18 Oct 97 | BEYOND THE SUN *Nude NUDE 8CD* | 64 | 1 |

Gisele MacKENZIE *Canada, female vocalist –*
Gisele LeFleche, b. 10 Jan 1927, d. 5 Sep 2003 (Singles: 6 Weeks)   pos/wks

| 17 Jul 53 ● | SEVEN LONELY DAYS (2re) *Capitol CL 13920* | 6 | 6 |

Scott McKENZIE
US, male vocalist – Philip Blondheim (Singles: 18 Weeks)   pos/wks

| 12 Jul 67 ★ | SAN FRANCISCO (BE SURE TO WEAR SOME FLOWERS IN YOUR HAIR) *CBS 2816* | 1 | 17 |
| 1 Nov 67 | LIKE AN OLD TIME MOVIE *CBS 3009* [1] | 50 | 1 |

[1] The Voice of Scott McKenzie

Ken MACKINTOSH, his Saxophone and his Orchestra
UK, orchestra (Singles: 9 Weeks)   pos/wks

15 Jan 54 ●	THE CREEP (re) *HMV BD 1295*	10	2
7 Feb 58	RAUNCHY *HMV POP 426*	19	6
10 Mar 60	NO HIDING PLACE *HMV POP 713*	45	1

Brian McKNIGHT *US, male vocalist (Singles: 4 Weeks)*   pos/wks

| 6 Jun 98 | ANYTIME *Motown 8607752* | 48 | 2 |
| 3 Oct 98 | YOU SHOULD BE MINE *Motown 8608412* | 36 | 2 |

Julie McKNIGHT (see also LAYO and BUSHWACKA!)
US, female vocalist (Singles: 6 Weeks)   pos/wks

14 Apr 01	FINALLY *Distance DI 2029* [1]	54	1
29 Sep 01	FINALLY (re-mix) *Defected DFECT 37CDS* [1]	24	3
15 Jun 02	HOME *Defected DFECT 51CDS*	61	1
23 Nov 02	DIAMOND LIFE *Distance DI 2409* [2]	52	1

[1] Kings of Tomorrow featuring Julie McKnight [2] Louie Vega and Jay 'Sinister' Sealee starring Julie McKnight

Vivienne McKONE *UK, female vocalist (Singles: 5 Weeks)*   pos/wks

| 25 Jul 92 | SING (OOH-EE-OOH) *ffrr F 183* | 47 | 4 |
| 31 Oct 92 | BEWARE *ffrr F 202* | 69 | 1 |

Noel McKOY *See JTQ; McKOY*

McKOY *UK, male / female vocal group (Singles: 2 Weeks)*   pos/wks

| 6 Mar 93 | FIGHT *Rightrack CDTUM 1* | 54 | 2 |

Craig McLACHLAN *Australia, male actor /*
vocalist (Singles: 40 Weeks, Albums: 11 Weeks)   pos/wks

16 Jun 90 ●	MONA *Epic 6557847* [1]	2	11
4 Aug 90	AMANDA *Epic 6561707* [1]	19	6
10 Nov 90	I ALMOST FELT LIKE CRYING *Epic 656310* [1]	50	3
23 May 92	ONE REASON WHY *Epic 6580677*	29	6
14 Nov 92	ON MY OWN *Epic 6584677*	59	2
24 Jul 93	YOU'RE THE ONE THAT I WANT *Epic 6595222* [2]	13	6
25 Dec 93	GREASE *Epic 6600242*	44	4
8 Jul 95	EVERYDAY *MDMC DEVCS 6* [3]	65	2
21 Jul 90 ●	CRAIG McLACHLAN AND CHECK 1-2 *Epic 4663471*	10	11

[1] Craig McLachlan and Check 1-2 [2] Craig McLachlan and Debbie Gibson [3] Craig McLachlan and The Culprits [1] Craig McLachlan and Check 1-2

Sarah McLACHLAN *Canada, female vocalist /*
instrumentalist – guitar (Singles: 14 Weeks, Albums: 15 Weeks)   pos/wks

3 Oct 98	ADIA *Arista 74321613902*	18	5
2 Feb 02	ANGEL *Nettwerk 331482*	36	3
20 Mar 04	FALLEN *Arista 82876590652*	50	1
26 Jun 04	WORLD ON FIRE *Arista 8287662832*	72	1
27 Nov 04	SILENCE 2004 *Nettwerk 332422* [1]	38	4
17 Oct 98	SURFACING *Arista 189702*	47	2
14 Feb 04	AFTERGLOW *Arista 82876596712*	33	13

[1] Delerium featuring Sarah McLachlan

Tommy McLAIN *US, male vocalist (Singles: 1 Week)*   pos/wks

| 8 Sep 66 | SWEET DREAMS *London HL 10065* | 49 | 1 |

Malcolm McLAREN
UK, male vocalist (Singles: 65 Weeks, Albums: 41 Weeks)   pos/wks

4 Dec 82 ●	BUFFALO GALS *Charisma MALC 1* [1]	9	12
26 Feb 83	SOWETO *Charisma MALC 2* [2]	32	5
2 Jul 83 ●	DOUBLE DUTCH *Charisma MALC 3*	3	13
17 Dec 83	DUCK FOR THE OYSTER *Charisma MALC 4*	54	5
1 Sep 84	MADAM BUTTERFLY (UN BEL DI VEDREMO) *Charisma MALC 5*	13	9
27 May 89	WALTZ DARLING *Epic WALTZ 2* [3]	31	8
19 Aug 89	SOMETHING'S JUMPIN' IN YOUR SHIRT *Epic WALTZ 3* [4]	29	7
25 Nov 89	HOUSE OF THE BLUE DANUBE *Epic WALTZ 4* [3]	73	1
21 Dec 91	MAGIC'S BACK (THEME FROM 'THE GHOSTS OF OXFORD STREET') *RCA PB 45223* [5]	42	4
3 Oct 98	BUFFALO GALS STAMPEDE (re-mix) *Virgin VSCDT 1717* [6]	65	1
4 Jun 83	DUCK ROCK *Charisma MMLP 1*	18	17
26 May 84	WOULD YA LIKE MORE SCRATCHIN' *Charisma CLAM 1* [1]	44	4

29 Dec 84	**FANS** *Charisma MMDL 2*	**47**	8
15 Jul 89	**WALTZ DARLING** *Epic 460736 1* [2]	**30**	11
20 Aug 94	**PARIS** *No! NOCD 101*	**44**	1

[1] Malcolm McLaren and the World's Famous Supreme Team [2] Malcolm McLaren and The McLarenettes [3] Malcolm McLaren and the Bootzilla Orchestra [4] Malcolm McLaren and the Bootzilla Orchestra featuring Lisa Marie [5] Malcolm McLaren featuring Alison Limerick [6] Malcolm McLaren and the World's Famous Supreme Team plus Rakim and Roger Sanchez [1] Malcolm McLaren and the World's Famous Supreme Team [2] Malcolm McLaren and the Bootzilla Orchestra

Mahavishnu John McLAUGHLIN See MAHAVISHNU ORCHESTRA

Bitty McLEAN
UK, male vocalist (Singles: 50 Weeks, Albums: 11 Weeks) pos/wks

31 Jul 93 ●	**IT KEEP RAININ' (TEARS FROM MY EYES)** *Brilliant CDBRIL 1*	**2**	15
30 Oct 93	**PASS IT ON** *Brilliant CDBRIL 2*	**35**	3
15 Jan 94 ●	**HERE I STAND** *Brilliant CDBRIL 3*	**10**	6
9 Apr 94 ●	**DEDICATED TO THE ONE I LOVE** *Brilliant CDBRIL 4*	**6**	10
6 Aug 94	**WHAT GOES AROUND** *Brilliant CDBRIL 5*	**36**	3
8 Apr 95	**OVER THE RIVER** *Brilliant CDBRIL 9*	**27**	4
17 Jun 95	**WE'VE ONLY JUST BEGUN** *Brilliant CDBRIL 10*	**23**	5
30 Sep 95	**NOTHING CAN CHANGE THIS LOVE** *Brilliant CDBRIL 11* ...	**55**	2
27 Jan 96	**NATURAL HIGH** *Brilliant CDBRIL 12*	**63**	1
5 Oct 96	**SHE'S ALRIGHT** *Kuff KUFFD 9*	**53**	1
19 Feb 94	**JUST TO LET YOU KNOW** *Brilliant BRILCD 1* ...	**19**	11

Don McLEAN (435) Top 500
Celebrated singer / songwriter / instrumentalist – guitar, b. 2 Oct, 1945, New York, US. The 8.5 minute 'American Pie', which was America's top single of 1972, is regarded as one of the all time great rock era records. No.1 song 'Killing Me Softly' was written about him (Singles: 68 Weeks, Albums: 92 Weeks) pos/wks

22 Jan 72 ●	**AMERICAN PIE** *United Artists UP 35325* ▲	**2**	16
13 May 72 ★	**VINCENT** *United Artists UP 35359*	**1**	15
14 Apr 73	**EVERYDAY** *United Artists UP 35519*	**38**	5
10 May 80 ★	**CRYING** *EMI 5051*	**1**	14
17 Apr 82	**CASTLES IN THE AIR** *EMI 5258*	**47**	8
5 Oct 91	**AMERICAN PIE (re-issue)** *Liberty EMCT 3*	**12**	10
11 Mar 72 ●	**AMERICAN PIE** *United Artists UAS 29285* ▲ ...	**3**	54
17 Jun 72	**TAPESTRY** *United Artists UAS 29350*	**16**	12
24 Nov 73	**PLAYIN' FAVOURITES** *United Artists UAG 29528* ...	**42**	2
14 Jun 80	**CHAIN LIGHTNING** *EMI International INS 3025* ...	**19**	9
27 Sep 80 ●	**THE VERY BEST OF DON McLEAN** *United Artists UAG 30314* ...	**4**	12
15 Apr 00	**AMERICAN PIE – THE GREATEST HITS** *Capitol 5258472* ...	**30**	3

Jackie McLEAN
US, male instrumentalist – alto sax (Singles: 4 Weeks) pos/wks

7 Jul 79	**DOCTOR JACKYLL AND MISTER FUNK** *RCA PB 1575* ...	**53**	4

Phil McLEAN
US, male vocalist (Singles: 4 Weeks) pos/wks

18 Jan 62	**SMALL SAD SAM** *Top Rank JAR 597*	**34**	4

McLUSKEY
UK, male vocal / instrumental group (Singles: 1 Week) pos/wks

8 May 04	**THAT MAN WILL NOT HANG** *Too Pure PURE 153CDS* ...	**71**	1

Andy McNAB
UK, male soldier (Albums: 2 Weeks) pos/wks

21 May 94	**BRAVO TWO ZERO** *PolyGram TV 5222002*	**45**	2

Ian McNABB (see also The ICICLE WORKS)
UK, male vocalist (Singles: 6 Weeks, Albums: 5 Weeks) pos/wks

23 Jan 93	**IF LOVE WAS LIKE GUITARS** *This Way Up WAY 233* ...	**67**	1
2 Jul 94	**YOU MUST BE PREPARED TO DREAM** *This Way Up WAY 3199* [1] ...	**54**	1
17 Sep 94	**GO INTO THE LIGHT** *This Way Up WAY 3699* ...	**66**	2
27 Apr 96	**DON'T PUT YOUR SPELL ON ME** *This Way Up WAY 5033* ...	**72**	1
6 Jul 96	**MERSEYBEAST** *This Way Up WAY 5266*	**74**	1
30 Jan 93	**TRUTH AND BEAUTY** *This Way Up 5143782* ...	**51**	1
16 Jul 94	**HEAD LIKE A ROCK** *This Way Up 5222982* ...	**29**	2
18 May 96	**MERSEYBEAST** *This Way Up 5242152*	**30**	2

[1] Ian McNabb featuring Ralph Molina and Billy Talbot

Lutricia McNEAL
US, female vocalist (Singles: 43 Weeks, Albums: 16 Weeks) pos/wks

29 Nov 97 ●	**AIN'T THAT JUST THE WAY** *Wildstar CXSTAS 2907* ...	**6**	18
23 May 98 ●	**STRANDED** *Wildstar CXSTAS 2973*	**3**	12
26 Sep 98 ●	**SOMEONE LOVES YOU HONEY** *Wildstar CDWILD 9* ...	**9**	7
19 Dec 98	**THE GREATEST LOVE YOU'LL NEVER KNOW** *Wildstar CDWILD 11* ...	**17**	6
25 Jul 98	**LUTRICIA McNEAL** *Wildstar CDWILD 5*	**16**	16

Patrick MacNEE and Honor BLACKMAN
UK, male / female actors / vocal duo (Singles: 7 Weeks) pos/wks

1 Dec 90 ●	**KINKY BOOTS** *Deram KINKY 1*	**5**	7

Rita MacNEIL
Canada, female vocalist (Singles: 10 Weeks, Albums: 4 Weeks) pos/wks

6 Oct 90	**WORKING MAN** *Polydor PO 98*	**11**	10
24 Nov 90	**REASON TO BELIEVE** *Polydor 8471061*	**32**	4

Clyde McPHATTER
US, male vocalist, b. 15 Nov 1932, d. 13 Jun 1972 (Singles: 1 Week) pos/wks

24 Aug 56	**TREASURE OF LOVE** *London HLE 8293*	**27**	1

Carmen McRAE See Sammy DAVIS Jr

Tom McRAE
UK, male vocalist (Singles: 1 Week, Albums: 2 Weeks) pos/wks

24 May 03	**KARAOKE SOUL** *DB DB 016CD*	**48**	1
15 Feb 03	**JUST LIKE BLOOD** *DB DB 006CDLP*	**26**	2

Ian McSHANE *UK, male vocalist (Albums: 7 Weeks)* pos/wks

21 Nov 92	**FROM BOTH SIDES NOW** *PolyGram TV 5176192* ...	**40**	7

Ralph McTELL
UK, male vocalist / instrumentalist – guitar – Ralph May (Singles: 18 Weeks, Albums: 17 Weeks) pos/wks

7 Dec 74 ●	**STREETS OF LONDON** *Reprise K 14380*	**2**	12
20 Dec 75	**DREAMS OF YOU** *Warner Bros. K 16648*	**36**	6
18 Nov 72	**NOT TILL TOMORROW** *Reprise K 44210*	**36**	1
2 Mar 74	**EASY** *Reprise K 54013*	**31**	4
15 Feb 75	**STREETS** *Warner Bros. K 56105*	**13**	12

Christine McVIE (see also CHICKEN SHACK; FLEETWOOD MAC)
UK, female vocalist – Christine Perfect (Albums: 4 Weeks) pos/wks

11 Feb 84	**CHRISTINE McVIE** *Warner Bros. 925059*	**58**	4

David McWILLIAMS
UK, male vocalist, b. 4 Jul 1945, d. 9 Jan 2002 (Albums: 9 Weeks) pos/wks

10 Jun 67	**DAVID McWILLIAMS SINGS** *Major Minor MMLP 2* ...	**38**	2
4 Nov 67	**DAVID McWILLIAMS VOLUME 2** *Major Minor MMLP 10* ...	**23**	6
9 Mar 68	**DAVID McWILLIAMS VOLUME 3** *Major Minor MMLP 11* ...	**39**	1

MAD COBRA featuring Richie STEPHENS
Jamaica / UK, male vocal duo (Singles: 2 Weeks) pos/wks

15 May 93	**LEGACY** *Columbia 6592852*	**64**	2

MAD DONNA *US, female vocalist (Singles: 4 Weeks)* pos/wks

4 May 02	**THE WHEELS ON THE BUS** *Star Harbour / All Around the World DISCO 0202R* ...	**17**	4

MAD JOCKS featuring JOCKMASTER B.A.
UK, male vocal / instrumental group (Singles: 9 Weeks) pos/wks

19 Dec 87	**JOCK MIX 1** *Debut DEBT 3037*	**46**	5
18 Dec 93	**PARTY FOUR (EP)** *SMP CDSSKM 24*	**57**	4

Tracks on Party Four (EP): No Lager / Here We Go Again / Jock Party Mix / Jock Jak Mix

MAD MOSES
US, male DJ / producer – 'Mad' Mitch Moses (Singles: 1 Week) pos/wks

16 Aug 97	**PANTHER PARTY** *Hi-Life 5744932*	**50**	1

MAD SEASON
UK, male vocal / instrumental group (Albums: 1 Week) pos/wks

25 Mar 95	**ABOVE** *Columbia 4785072*	**41**	1

MAD STUNTMAN See REEL 2 REAL featuring The MAD STUNTMAN

MADAM FRICTION See CORTINA

Sonya MADAN See LITHIUM and Sonya MADAN

MADASUN UK, female vocal group (Singles: 13 Weeks)
pos/wks

11 Mar 00	DON'T YOU WORRY V2 VVR 5011523	14	6
27 May 00	WALKING ON WATER V2 VVR 5012418	14	4
2 Sep 00	FEEL GOOD V2 VVR 5012983	29	3

Danny MADDEN US, male vocalist (Singles: 2 Weeks)
pos/wks

14 Jul 90	THE FACTS OF LIFE Eternal YZ 473	72	2

MADDER ROSE US, male / female vocal / instrumental group (Singles: 2 Weeks, Albums: 2 Weeks)
pos/wks

26 Mar 94	PANIC ON Atlantic A 8301CD	65	1
16 Jul 94	CAR SONG Seed A 7256CD	68	1
9 Apr 94	PANIC ON Atlantic 7567825812	52	2

MADDOG See STRETCH 'N' VERN present "MADDOG"

MADE IN LONDON
UK / Norway, female vocal group (Singles: 6 Weeks)
pos/wks

13 May 00	DIRTY WATER RCA 74321746192	15	5
9 Sep 00	SHUT YOUR MOUTH RCA 74321772602	74	1

MADELYNE (see also 4 STRINGS)
Holland, male producer – Carlo Resoort (Singles: 1 Week)
pos/wks

7 Sep 02	BEAUTIFUL CHILD (A DEEPER LOVE) Xtravaganza XTRAV 36CDS	63	1

MADEMOISELLE
France, male production / instrumental duo (Singles: 1 Week)
pos/wks

8 Sep 01	DO YOU LOVE ME RCA 74321878952	56	1

MAD'HOUSE France / Holland, male / female production / vocal group (Singles: 14 Weeks, Albums: 1 Week)
pos/wks

17 Aug 02 ●	LIKE A PRAYER Serious SERR 046CD	3	11
9 Nov 02	HOLIDAY Serious SER 058CD	24	3
31 Aug 02	ABSOLUTELY MAD Serious / Mercury SERRCD 001	57	1

MADISON AVENUE
Australia, male producer – Andy Van Dorsselaer and female vocalist – Cheyne Coates (Singles: 25 Weeks, Albums: 1 Week)
pos/wks

13 Nov 99	DON'T CALL ME BABY (2re) VC Recordings VCRD 56	30	6
20 May 00 ★	DON'T CALL ME BABY (re-issue) VC Recordings VCRD 64 ■	1	12
21 Oct 00 ●	WHO THE HELL ARE YOU VC Recordings VCRD 70	10	5
27 Jan 01	EVERYTHING YOU NEED VC Recordings VCRD 82	33	2
4 Nov 00	THE POLYESTER EMBASSY VC Recordings CDVCR 7	74	1

MADNESS 44 Top 500
London-based band whose ska-rooted 'nutty' sound earned them a huge haul of hits. The 2002 Madness-based production, 'Our House', won an Olivier Award for 'Best New Musical'. This good-time septet fronted by Graham 'Suggs' McPherson spent more weeks on the chart in the 1980s than any other group (Singles: 268 Weeks, Albums: 414 Weeks)
pos/wks

1 Sep 79	THE PRINCE 2 Tone TT 3	16	11
10 Nov 79 ●	ONE STEP BEYOND ... Stiff BUY 56	7	14
5 Jan 80 ●	MY GIRL Stiff BUY 62	3	10
5 Apr 80 ●	WORK REST AND PLAY (EP) Stiff BUY 71	6	8
13 Sep 80 ●	BAGGY TROUSERS Stiff BUY 84	3	20
22 Nov 80 ●	EMBARRASSMENT Stiff BUY 102	4	12
24 Jan 81 ●	THE RETURN OF THE LOS PALMAS SEVEN Stiff BUY 108	7	11
25 Apr 81 ●	GREY DAY Stiff BUY 112	4	10
26 Sep 81 ●	SHUT UP Stiff BUY 126	7	9
5 Dec 81 ●	IT MUST BE LOVE Stiff BUY 134	4	12
20 Feb 82	CARDIAC ARREST Stiff BUY 140	14	10
22 May 82 ★	HOUSE OF FUN Stiff BUY 146	1	9
24 Jul 82 ●	DRIVING IN MY CAR Stiff BUY 153	4	8
27 Nov 82 ●	OUR HOUSE Stiff BUY 163	5	13
19 Feb 83 ●	TOMORROW'S (JUST ANOTHER DAY) / MADNESS (IS ALL IN THE MIND) Stiff BUY 169	8	9

20 Aug 83 ●	WINGS OF A DOVE Stiff BUY 181	2	10
5 Nov 83 ●	THE SUN AND THE RAIN Stiff BUY 192	5	10
11 Feb 84	MICHAEL CAINE Stiff BUY 196	11	8
2 Jun 84	ONE BETTER DAY Stiff BUY 201	17	7
31 Aug 85	YESTERDAY'S MEN Zarjazz JAZZ 5	18	7
26 Oct 85	UNCLE SAM Zarjazz JAZZ 7	21	11
1 Feb 86	SWEETEST GIRL Zarjazz JAZZ 8	35	6
8 Nov 86	(WAITING FOR) THE GHOST TRAIN (re) Zarjazz JAZZ 9	18	8
19 Mar 88	I PRONOUNCE YOU Virgin VS 1054 1	44	4
15 Feb 92	IT MUST BE LOVE (re-issue) Virgin VS 1405	6	9
25 Apr 92	HOUSE OF FUN (re-issue) Virgin VS 1413	40	3
8 Aug 92	MY GIRL (re-issue) Virgin VS 1425	27	4
28 Nov 92	THE HARDER THEY COME Go Discs GOD 93	44	3
27 Feb 93	NIGHT BOAT TO CAIRO Virgin VSCDT 1447	56	1
31 Jul 99 ●	LOVESTRUCK Virgin VSCDT 1737	10	7
6 Nov 99	JOHNNY THE HORSE Virgin VSCDT 1740	44	2
11 Mar 00	DRIP FED FRED Virgin VSCDT 1768 2	55	1
3 Nov 79 ●	ONE STEP BEYOND ... Stiff SEEZ 17	2	78
4 Oct 80 ●	ABSOLUTELY Stiff SEEZ 29	2	46
10 Oct 81 ●	MADNESS 7 Stiff SEEZ 39	5	29
1 May 82 ★	COMPLETE MADNESS Stiff HIT-TV 1	1	88
13 Nov 82 ●	MADNESS PRESENTS THE RISE AND FALL Stiff SEEZ 46	10	22
3 Mar 84 ●	KEEP MOVING Stiff SEEZ 53	6	19
12 Oct 85	MAD NOT MAD Zarjazz JZLP 1	16	9
6 Dec 86	UTTER MADNESS Zarjazz JZLP 2	29	8
7 May 88	THE MADNESS Virgin V 2507	65	1
7 Mar 92 ★	DIVINE MADNESS Virgin CDV 2692	1	96
14 Nov 92	MADSTOCK Go Discs 8283672	22	9
13 Jun 98	THE HEAVY HEAVY HITS Virgin CDV 2862	19	5
13 Nov 99	WONDERFUL Virgin CDV 2889	17	2
2 Nov 02	OUR HOUSE – THE ORIGINAL SONGS Virgin CDV 2965	45	2

1 The Madness 2 Madness featuring Ian Dury

Tracks on Work Rest and Play (EP): Night Boat to Cairo / Deceives the Eye / The Young and the Old / Don't Quote Me on That. 'Night Boat to Cairo' in 1993 is a re-issue of a track from the Work Rest and Play EP

MADONNA 5 Top 500
The most successful female chart act of all time in the UK and US, with world sales in excess of 145 million records, b. Madonna Ciccone, 16 Aug 1958, Michigan, US. Continually ground-breaking and trend-setting, this often controversial artist has amassed an unequalled 35 consecutive UK Top 10 singles (includes two re-entries, a re-mix and a re-issue) and an unbeatable tally of Top 5 entries. She has also had more UK No.1 singles and albums than any other female soloist, and at one time held the top two slots on the singles chart (1985). Her accumulated UK Top 10 entries are more than The Beatles and The Rolling Stones combined, and her album 'The Immaculate Collection' has sold more than 3.6 million copies in the UK alone. In the US, the multi-award-winning singer holds the female record for 27 consecutive Top 20 entries and 16 successive Top 5s plus a dozen No.1s – 10 of which she wrote. Madonna has produced more No.1s than any female, played to packed stadiums around the globe and starred in several successful films. Her 2000 album 'Music' topped the chart in 26 countries and shipped five million albums. She was again voted Best International Female Singer at the 2001 Brits and grossed £40m for the 28 US dates of her Drowned World Tour – the highest figure for a female performer in that year. She is also the most impersonated performer on the TV show 'Stars In Their Eyes'. Madonna became a founder member of the UK Music Hall of Fame, representing the 1980s. Total UK singles sales: 14,562,856 (Singles: 621 Weeks, Albums: 1032 Weeks)
pos/wks

14 Jan 84 ●	HOLIDAY (re) Sire W 9405	2	21
17 Mar 84	LUCKY STAR Sire W 9522	14	9
2 Jun 84 ●	BORDERLINE (re) Sire W 9260	2	13
17 Nov 84 ●	LIKE A VIRGIN Sire W 9210 ▲	3	18
2 Mar 85 ●	MATERIAL GIRL Sire W 9083	3	10
8 Jun 85 ●	CRAZY FOR YOU Geffen A 6323 ▲	2	15
27 Jul 85 ★	INTO THE GROOVE Sire W 8934	1	14
21 Sep 85 ●	ANGEL Sire W 8881	5	9
12 Oct 85 ●	GAMBLER (re) Geffen A 6585	4	12
7 Dec 85 ●	DRESS YOU UP Sire W 8848	5	11
26 Apr 86 ●	LIVE TO TELL Sire W 8717 ▲	2	12
28 Jun 86 ★	PAPA DON'T PREACH Sire W 8636 ▲	1	14
4 Oct 86 ★	TRUE BLUE Sire W 8550	1	15
13 Dec 86 ●	OPEN YOUR HEART Sire W 8480 ▲	4	9
4 Apr 87 ★	LA ISLA BONITA Sire W 8378	1	11
18 Jul 87 ★	WHO'S THAT GIRL Sire W 8341 ▲	1	10
19 Sep 87 ●	CAUSING A COMMOTION Sire W 8224	4	9

12 Dec 87 ●	THE LOOK OF LOVE *Sire W 8115*	9	7
18 Mar 89 ★	LIKE A PRAYER *Sire W 7539* ▲	1	12
3 Jun 89 ●	EXPRESS YOURSELF *Sire W 2948*	5	10
16 Sep 89 ●	CHERISH *Sire W 2883*	3	8
16 Dec 89 ●	DEAR JESSIE *Sire W 2668*	5	9
7 Apr 90 ★	VOGUE *Sire W 9851* ▲	1	14
21 Jul 90 ●	HANKY PANKY *Sire W 9789*	2	9
8 Dec 90 ●	JUSTIFY MY LOVE *Sire W 9000* ▲	2	10
2 Mar 91 ●	CRAZY FOR YOU (re-mix) *Sire W 0008*	2	8
13 Apr 91 ●	RESCUE ME *Sire W 0024*	3	7
8 Jun 91 ●	HOLIDAY (re-issue) *Sire W 0037*	5	8
25 Jul 92 ●	THIS USED TO BE MY PLAYGROUND *Sire W 0122* ▲	3	9
17 Oct 92 ●	EROTICA (re) *Maverick W 0138*	3	9
12 Dec 92 ●	DEEPER AND DEEPER *Maverick W 0146*	6	9
6 Mar 93 ●	BAD GIRL *Maverick W 0154CD*	10	7
3 Apr 93 ●	FEVER *Maverick W 0168CD*	6	6
31 Jul 93 ●	RAIN *Maverick W 0190CD*	7	8
2 Apr 94 ●	I'LL REMEMBER *Maverick W 0240CD*	7	8
8 Oct 94 ●	SECRET *Maverick W 0268CD*	5	9
17 Dec 94	TAKE A BOW *Maverick W 0278CD* ▲	16	9
25 Feb 95 ●	BEDTIME STORY (re) *Maverick W 0285CD*	4	9
26 Aug 95 ●	HUMAN NATURE *Maverick W 0300CD*	8	5
4 Nov 95 ●	YOU'LL SEE *Maverick W 0324CD*	5	13
6 Jan 96	OH FATHER *Maverick W 0326CD*	16	6
23 Mar 96	ONE MORE CHANCE *Maverick W 0337CD*	11	4
2 Nov 96 ●	YOU MUST LOVE ME (re) *Maverick W 0378CD*	10	6
28 Dec 96 ●	DON'T CRY FOR ME ARGENTINA *Warner Bros. W 0384CD*	3	12
29 Mar 97 ●	ANOTHER SUITCASE IN ANOTHER HALL *Warner Bros. W 0388CD*	7	5
7 Mar 98 ★	FROZEN *Maverick W 0433CD* ■	1	13
9 May 98 ●	RAY OF LIGHT (re) *Maverick W 0444CD*	2	10
5 Sep 98 ●	DROWNED WORLD (SUBSTITUTE FOR LOVE) *Maverick W 0453CD1*	10	5
5 Dec 98 ●	THE POWER OF GOODBYE / LITTLE STAR *Maverick W 459CD*	6	9
13 Mar 99 ●	NOTHING REALLY MATTERS (re) *Maverick W 471CD*	7	9
19 Jun 99 ●	BEAUTIFUL STRANGER *Maverick W 495CD*	2	16
11 Mar 00 ★	AMERICAN PIE (re) *Maverick W 519CD* ■	1	14
2 Sep 00 ●	MUSIC *Maverick W 537CD1* ▲	1	23
9 Dec 00 ●	DON'T TELL ME *Maverick W 547CD1*	4	10
28 Apr 01 ●	WHAT IT FEELS LIKE FOR A GIRL (re) *Maverick W 533CD*	7	11
9 Nov 02 ●	DIE ANOTHER DAY *Warner W 595CD*	3	16
19 Apr 03	AMERICAN LIFE (import) *Maverick 166582*	57	1
26 Apr 03 ●	AMERICAN LIFE *Maverick W 603CD1*	2	11
19 Jul 03 ●	HOLLYWOOD *Maverick W 614CD1*	2	7
22 Nov 03 ●	ME AGAINST THE MUSIC *Jive 82876576432* [1]	2	12
20 Dec 03	LOVE PROFUSION *Maverick W 634CD1*	11	6
11 Feb 84 ●	MADONNA / THE FIRST ALBUM *Sire 923867*	6	123
24 Nov 84 ★	LIKE A VIRGIN *Sire 925157* ▲	1	152
12 Jul 86 ★	TRUE BLUE *Sire WX 54* ■ ▲	1	85
28 Nov 87 ●	YOU CAN DANCE *Sire WX 76* ■	5	16
1 Apr 89 ★	LIKE A PRAYER *Sire WX 239* ■ ▲	1	70
2 Jun 90 ●	I'M BREATHLESS *Sire WX 351*	2	9
24 Nov 90 ★	THE IMMACULATE COLLECTION *Sire WX 370* ■	1	213
24 Oct 92 ●	EROTICA *Maverick 9362450312*	2	38
5 Nov 94 ●	BEDTIME STORIES *Maverick 9362457672*	2	27
18 Nov 95 ●	SOMETHING TO REMEMBER *Maverick 9362461002*	3	29
9 Nov 96 ★	EVITA (FILM SOUNDTRACK) *Warner Bros. 9362464322* [1]	1	36
14 Mar 98 ★	RAY OF LIGHT *Maverick 9362468472* ■	1	116
30 Sep 00 ★	MUSIC *Maverick 9362478632* ■	1	64
24 Nov 01 ●	GHV2: GREATEST HITS VOLUME 2 *Maverick 9362480002*	2	24
3 May 03 ★	AMERICAN LIFE *Maverick / Warner Bros. 9362484542* ■ ▲	1	19

[1] Britney Spears featuring Madonna [1] Madonna / Various

Re-entries: 'Holiday' originally peaked at No.6 in 1984, making No.2 only on re-entry in Aug 1985. 'Borderline' peaked at No.56 on its first chart visit before making No.2 on re-entry in Jan 1986 From 22 Aug 85 'Madonna' was repacked as 'The First Album' (Sire WX 22). 'Like A Virgin' changed catalogue number to Sire WX 20 during its chart run. 'The Immaculate Collection' changed catalogue number to Sire 7599264402 for its 2004 chart run

Lisa MAFFIA (see also SO SOLID CREW)
UK, female vocalist (Singles: 15 Weeks, Albums: 1 Week) pos/wks

3 May 03 ●	ALL OVER *Independiente ISOM 69MS*	2	11
9 Aug 03	IN LOVE *Independiente ISOM 75MS*	13	4
23 Aug 03	FIRST LADY *Independiente ISOM 39CD*	44	1

MAGAZINE *UK, male vocal / instrumental group – lead vocal Howard Devoto (Singles: 7 Weeks, Albums: 24 Weeks)* pos/wks

11 Feb 78	SHOT BY BOTH SIDES *Virgin VS 200*	41	4

26 Jul 80	SWEET HEART CONTRACT *Virgin VS 368*	54	3
24 Jun 78	REAL LIFE *Virgin V 2100*	29	8
14 Apr 79	SECONDHAND DAYLIGHT *Virgin V 2121*	38	8
10 May 80	CORRECT USE OF SOAP *Virgin V 2156*	28	4
13 Dec 80	PLAY *Virgin V 2184*	69	1
27 Jun 81	MAGIC MURDER AND THE WEATHER *Virgin V 2200*	39	3

MAGIC AFFAIR *US / Germany, male / female vocal / instrumental group (Singles: 8 Weeks)* pos/wks

4 Jun 94	OMEN III *EMI CDEM 317*	17	4
27 Aug 94	GIVE ME ALL YOUR LOVE *EMI CDEM 340*	30	2
5 Nov 94	IN THE MIDDLE OF THE NIGHT *EMI CDEM 349*	38	2

MAGIC BAND *See CAPTAIN BEEFHEART and his MAGIC BAND*

MAGIC LADY *US, female vocal duo (Singles: 3 Weeks)* pos/wks

14 May 88	BETCHA CAN'T LOSE (WITH MY LOVE) *Motown ZB 42003*	58	3

The MAGIC LANTERNS
UK, male vocal / instrumental group (Singles: 3 Weeks) pos/wks

7 Jul 66	EXCUSE ME BABY (2re) *CBS 202094*	44	3

MAGNA CARTA
UK, male vocal / instrumental group (Albums: 2 Weeks) pos/wks

8 Aug 70	SEASONS *Vertigo 6360 003*	55	2

MAGNOLIA
Italy, male producer and UK, female vocalist (Singles: 1 Week) pos/wks

24 Jul 04	IT'S ALL VAIN *Data DATA 69CDS*	55	1

MAGNUM *UK, male vocal / instrumental group (Singles: 26 Weeks, Albums: 47 Weeks)* pos/wks

22 Mar 80	MAGNUM (DOUBLE SINGLE) *Jet 175*	47	6
12 Jul 86	LONELY NIGHT *Polydor POSP 798*	70	2
19 Mar 88	DAYS OF NO TRUST *Polydor POSP 910*	32	4
7 May 88	START TALKING LOVE *Polydor POSP 920*	22	4
2 Jul 88	IT MUST HAVE BEEN LOVE *Polydor POSP 930*	33	4
23 Jun 90	ROCKIN' CHAIR *Polydor PO 88*	27	4
25 Aug 90	HEARTBROKE AND BUSTED *Polydor PO 94*	49	2
16 Sep 78	KINGDOM OF MADNESS *Jet JETLP 210*	58	1
19 Apr 80	MARAUDER *Jet JETLP 230*	34	5
6 Mar 82	CHASE THE DRAGON *Jet JETLP 235*	17	7
21 May 83	THE ELEVENTH HOUR *Jet JETLP 240*	38	4
25 May 85	ON A STORYTELLER'S NIGHT *FM WKFMLP 34*	24	5
4 Oct 86	VIGILANTE *Polydor POLD 5198*	24	5
9 Apr 88 ●	WINGS OF HEAVEN *Polydor POLD 5221*	5	9
21 Jul 90 ●	GOODNIGHT L.A. *Polydor 8435681*	9	5
14 Sep 91	THE SPIRIT *Polydor 5111691*	50	1
24 Oct 92	SLEEPWALKING *Music For Nations CDMFN 143*	27	2
18 Jun 94	ROCK ART *EMI CDEMD 1066*	57	1

Tracks on Magnum (double single): Invasion / Kingdom of Madness / All of My Life / Great Adventure

MAGOO *US, male rapper – Melvin Barcliff (Singles: 4 Weeks)* pos/wks

13 Mar 99	HERE WE COME *Virgin DINSD 179* [1]	43	1
13 Mar 04	COP THAT SH*T *Unique Corp TIMBACD 001* [2]	22	3

[1] Timbaland / Missy Elliott and Magoo [2] Timbaland & Magoo featuring Missy Elliott

MAGOO:MOGWAI
UK, male vocal / instrumental groups (Singles: 1 Week) pos/wks

4 Apr 98	BLACK SABBATH / SWEET LEAF *Fierce Panda NING 47CD*	60	1

Sean MAGUIRE
UK, male vocalist / actor (Singles: 34 Weeks, Albums: 3 Weeks) pos/wks

20 Aug 94	SOMEONE TO LOVE *Parlophone CDR 6390*	14	7
5 Nov 94	TAKE THIS TIME (re) *Parlophone CDR 6395*	27	5
25 Mar 95	SUDDENLY *Parlophone CDR 6403*	18	5
24 Jun 95	NOW I'VE FOUND YOU *Parlophone CDLEEPYS 1*	22	3
18 Nov 95	YOU TO ME ARE EVERYTHING *Parlophone CDR 6420*	16	3
25 May 96	GOOD DAY *Parlophone CDR 6432*	12	4
3 Aug 96	DON'T PULL YOUR LOVE *Parlophone CDR 6440*	14	4

29 Mar 97	TODAY'S THE DAY *Parlophone CDR 6459*	27	3
26 Nov 94	SEAN MAGUIRE *Parlophone CDPCSDX 164*	75	1
15 Jun 96	SPIRIT *Parlophone CDPCSD 169*	43	2

MAHAVISHNU ORCHESTRA
UK / US, male instrumental group (Albums: 14 Weeks)　pos/wks

31 Mar 73	BIRDS OF FIRE *CBS 65321*	20	5
28 Jul 73 ●	LOVE DEVOTION SURRENDER *CBS 69037* [1]	7	9

[1] Carlos Santana and Mahavishnu John McLaughlin

Siobhan MAHER See OCEANIC

MAHLATHINI and the MAHOTELLA QUEENS See ART OF NOISE

MAI TAI
Guyana, female vocal group (Singles: 30 Weeks, Albums: 1 Week)　pos/wks

25 May 85 ●	HISTORY *Virgin VS 773*	8	13
3 Aug 85 ●	BODY AND SOUL *Virgin VS 801*	9	13
15 Feb 86	FEMALE INTUITION *Virgin VS 844*	54	4
6 Jul 85	HISTORY *Virgin V 2359*	91	1

The MAIN INGREDIENT
US, male vocal group – includes Cuba Gooding (Singles: 7 Weeks)　pos/wks

29 Jun 74	JUST DON'T WANT TO BE LONELY *RCA APBO 0205*	27	7

The MAISONETTES
UK, male / female vocal group (Singles: 12 Weeks)　pos/wks

11 Dec 82 ●	HEARTACHE AVENUE *Ready Steady Go! RSG 1*	7	12

The MAJESTICS *UK, male/female vocal group (Albums: 4 Weeks)* pos/wks

4 Apr 87	TUTTI FRUTTI *BBC REN 629*	64	4

J MAJIK *UK, male producer – Jamie Spratling (Singles: 4 Weeks)* pos/wks

5 May 01	LOVE IS NOT A GAME *Defected DFECT 31CDS* [1]	34	2
27 Apr 02	METROSOUND *Kaos KAOS 001P* [2]	54	1
22 May 04	SCOOBY DOO / SPYCATCHER *Infrared INFRA 28* [3]	67	1

[1] J Majik featuring Kathy Brown [2] Adam F and J Majik [3] J Majik and Wickaman

Niki MAK See Tony DE VIT

MAKADOPOULOS and his GREEK SERENADERS
Greece, male vocal / instrumental group (Singles: 14 Weeks)　pos/wks

20 Oct 60	NEVER ON SUNDAY *Palette PG 9005*	36	14

MAKAVELI (see also 2PAC)
US, male rapper – Tupac Shakur (Albums: 1 Week)　pos/wks

16 Nov 96	THE DON KILLUMINATI – THE 7 DAY THEORY *Death Row IND 90039*	53	1

Tommy MAKEM See CLANCY BROTHERS and Tommy MAKEM

Jack E. MAKOSSA
(see also Wally JUMP Jr and the CRIMINAL ELEMENT) *US, male producer / multi-instrumentalist – Arthur Baker (Singles: 5 Weeks)*　pos/wks

12 Sep 87	THE OPERA HOUSE *Champion CHAMP 50*	48	5

MALA See BOWA featuring MALA

MALACHI
UK, male vocalist – Malachi Cush (Singles: 1 Week, Albums: 4 Weeks) pos/wks

19 Apr 03	JUST SAY YOU LOVE ME *Mercury / Universal TV 0779072*	49	1
5 Apr 03	MALACHI *Mercury / Universal TV 0772802*	17	4

MALAIKA *US, female vocalist (Singles: 1 Week)* pos/wks

31 Jul 93	GOTTA KNOW (YOUR NAME) *A&M 5802732*	68	1

Carl MALCOLM *Jamaica, male vocalist (Singles: 8 Weeks)* pos/wks

13 Sep 75 ●	FATTIE BUM BUM *UK 108*	8	8

Valerie MALCOLM See The CANDY GIRLS

Stephen MALKMUS
US, male vocalist (Singles: 1 Week, Albums: 2 Weeks)　pos/wks

28 Apr 01	DISCRETION GROVE *Domino RUG 123CD*	60	1
24 Feb 01	STEPHEN MALKMUS *Domino Recordings WIGCD 90*	49	1
29 Mar 03	PIG LIB *Domino Recordings WIGCD 122X*	63	1

Timmy MALLETT See BOMBALURINA featuring Timmy MALLETT

Yngwie J. MALMSTEEN
Sweden, male instrumentalist – guitar (Albums: 11 Weeks)　pos/wks

21 May 88	ODYSSEY *Polydor POLD 5224*	27	7
4 Nov 89	TRIAL BY FIRE – LIVE IN LENINGRAD *Polydor 8397261*	65	1
28 Apr 90	ECLIPSE *Polydor 8434611*	43	2
29 Feb 92	FIRE AND ICE *Elektra 7559611372*	57	1

Raul MALO (see also The MAVERICKS)
US, male vocalist (Singles: 1 Week)　pos/wks

18 May 02	I SAID I LOVE YOU *Gravity 74321923082*	57	1

MAMA CASS (see also The MAMAS and the PAPAS) *US, female vocalist –*
Ellen Cohen, b. 19 Sep 1941, d. 29 Jul 1974 (Singles: 27 Weeks)　pos/wks

14 Aug 68	DREAM A LITTLE DREAM OF ME *RCA 1726*	11	12
16 Aug 69 ●	IT'S GETTING BETTER *Stateside SS 8021*	8	15

MAMA'S BOYS
Ireland, male vocal / instrumental group (Albums: 4 Weeks)　pos/wks

6 Apr 85	POWER AND PASSION *Jive HIP 24*	55	4

The MAMAS and the PAPAS (see also MAMA CASS) *US, male / female*
vocal / instrumental group (Singles: 71 Weeks, Albums: 71 Weeks)　pos/wks

28 Apr 66	CALIFORNIA DREAMIN' *RCA 1503*	23	9
12 May 66 ●	MONDAY MONDAY *RCA 1516* ▲	3	13
28 Jul 66	I SAW HER AGAIN *RCA 1533*	11	11
9 Feb 67	WORDS OF LOVE *RCA 1564*	47	3
6 Apr 67 ●	DEDICATED TO THE ONE I LOVE *RCA 1576*	2	17
26 Jul 67	CREEQUE ALLEY *RCA 1613*	9	11
2 Aug 97 ●	CALIFORNIA DREAMIN' (re-issue) *MCA MCSTD 48058*	9	7
25 Jun 66	THE MAMAS AND PAPAS *RCA Victor RD 7803* ▲	3	18
28 Jan 67	CASS JOHN MICHELLE DENNY *RCA Victor SF 7639*	24	6
24 Jun 67 ●	MAMAS AND PAPAS DELIVER *RCA Victor SF 7880*	4	22
26 Apr 69 ●	HITS OF GOLD *Stateside S 5007*	7	2
18 Jun 77 ●	THE BEST OF THE MAMAS AND PAPAS *Arcade ADEP 30*	6	13
28 Jan 95	CALIFORNIA DREAMIN' – THE VERY BEST OF THE MAMAS AND THE PAPAS *PolyGram TV 5239732*	14	6
6 Sep 97	CALIFORNIA DREAMIN' – GREATEST HITS OF THE MAMAS AND THE PAPAS *Telstar TV TTVCD 2931*	30	4

MAMBAS See Marc ALMOND

Cheb MAMI See STING

MAN *UK, male vocal / instrumental group (Albums: 11 Weeks)* pos/wks

20 Oct 73	BACK INTO THE FUTURE *United Artists UAD 60053/4*	23	3
25 May 74	RHINOS WINOS AND LUNATICS *United Artists UAG 29631*	24	4
11 Oct 75	MAXIMUM DARKNESS *United Artists UAG 29872*	25	2
17 Apr 76	WELSH CONNECTION *MCA MCF 2753*	40	2

A MAN CALLED ADAM
UK, male / female vocal / instrumental group (Singles: 4 Weeks)　pos/wks

29 Sep 90	BAREFOOT IN THE HEAD (re) *Big Life BLR 28*	60	4

MAN TO MAN
US, male vocal / instrumental group (Singles: 19 Weeks)　pos/wks

13 Sep 86 ●	MALE STRIPPER (2re) *Bolts BOLTS 4* [1]	4	16
4 Jul 87	I NEED A MAN / ENERGY'S EUROBEAT *Bolts BOLTS 5*	43	3

[1] Man 2 Man meet Man Parrish

'Male Stripper' reached its peak position on its second re-entry in Feb 1987

MAN WITH NO NAME
UK, male producer – Martin Freeland (Singles: 6 Weeks)　pos/wks

30 Sep 95	FLOOR-ESSENCE *Perfecto PERF 108CD*	68	1

20 Jan 96	PAINT A PICTURE *Perfecto PERF 114CD* [1]	42	2
12 Oct 96	TELEPORT / SUGAR RUSH *Perfecto PERF 126CD*	55	1
2 May 98	VAVOOM! *Perfecto PERF 159CD1*	43	1
18 Jul 98	THE FIRST DAY (HORIZON) *Perfecto PERF 164CD*	72	1

[1] Man with No Name featuring Hannah

MANASSAS *See Stephen STILLS*

Melissa MANCHESTER *See Al JARREAU*

MANCHESTER BOYS CHOIR *UK, male choir (Albums: 2 Weeks)* pos/wks

21 Dec 85	THE NEW SOUND OF CHRISTMAS *K-Tel ONE 1314*	80	2

MANCHESTER UNITED FOOTBALL CLUB
UK, male football team vocalists (Singles: 56 Weeks) pos/wks

8 May 76	MANCHESTER UNITED *Decca F 13633*	50	1
21 May 83	GLORY GLORY MAN UNITED *EMI 5390*	13	5
18 May 85 ●	WE ALL FOLLOW MAN UNITED *Columbia DB 9107*	10	5
19 Jun 93	UNITED (WE LOVE YOU) *Living Beat LBECD 026* [1]	37	2
30 Apr 94 ★	COME ON YOU REDS *PolyGram TV MANU 2*	1	15
13 May 95 ●	WE'RE GONNA DO IT AGAIN *PolyGram TV MANU 952* [2]	6	6
4 May 96 ●	MOVE MOVE MOVE (THE RED TRIBE) (re) *Music Collection MANUCD 1* [3]	6	15
29 May 99	LIFT IT HIGH (ALL ABOUT BELIEF) (re) *Music Collection MANUCD 4* [4]	11	7

[1] Manchester United and the Champions [2] Manchester United Football Squad featuring Stryker [3] 1996 Manchester United FA Cup Squad [4] 1999 Manchester United Squad

MANCHILD (see also STEREOPHONICS) *UK, male production duo – Max Odell and Brett Parker (Singles: 2 Weeks)* pos/wks

16 Sep 00	THE CLICHES ARE TRUE *One Little Indian 176TP 7CD* [1]	60	1
25 Aug 01	NOTHING WITHOUT ME *One Little Indian 183TP 7CD*	40	1

[1] Manchild featuring Kelly Jones

Henry MANCINI and his ORCHESTRA *US, orchestra / chorus – leader b. 14 Jun 1924, d. 14 Jun 1994 (Singles: 23 Weeks, Albums: 23 Weeks)* pos/wks

7 Dec 61	MOON RIVER (re) *RCA 1256*	44	3
24 Sep 64 ●	HOW SOON *RCA 1414*	10	12
25 Mar 72	THEME FROM 'CADE'S COUNTY' *RCA 2182*	42	1
11 Feb 84	MAIN THEME FROM 'THE THORN BIRDS' *Warner Bros. 9677* [1]	23	7
16 Oct 76	HENRY MANCINI *Arcade ADEP 24*	26	8
30 Jun 84	MAMMA *Decca 411959* [1]	96	1
8 Dec 84	IN THE PINK *RCA Red Seal RL 85315* [2]	62	6
13 Dec 86	THE HOLLYWOOD MUSICALS *CBS 4502581* [3]	46	8

[1] Luciano Pavarotti with the Henry Mancini Orchestra [2] James Galway and Henry Mancini and the National Philharmonic Orchestra [3] Johnny Mathis and Henry Mancini

Steve MANDELL *See 'DELIVERANCE' SOUNDTRACK*

MANFRED MANN (172 Top 500) (see also McGUINNESS FLINT)
One of the most regular chart entrants of the 1960s: Manfred Mann, b. S. Africa (k), Mike Vickers (g), Tom McGuinness (b), Mike Hugg (d), Paul Jones (v – replaced by Mike D'Abo in 1966). They were the first group from the south of England to top the US charts during 1964's so-called 'British Invasion' (Singles: 217 Weeks, Albums: 100 Weeks) pos/wks

23 Jan 64 ●	5-4-3-2-1 *HMV POP 1252*	5	13
16 Apr 64	HUBBLE BUBBLE (TOIL AND TROUBLE) *HMV POP 1282*	11	8
16 Jul 64 ★	DO WAH DIDDY DIDDY *HMV POP 1320* ▲	1	14
15 Oct 64 ●	SHA LA LA *HMV POP 1346*	3	12
14 Jan 65 ●	COME TOMORROW *HMV POP 1381*	4	9
15 Apr 65	OH NO, NOT MY BABY *HMV POP 1413*	11	10
16 Sep 65 ●	IF YOU GOTTA GO, GO NOW *HMV POP 1466*	2	12
21 Apr 66 ★	PRETTY FLAMINGO *HMV POP 1523*	1	12
7 Jul 66	YOU GAVE ME SOMEBODY TO LOVE *HMV POP 1541*	36	4
4 Aug 66 ●	JUST LIKE A WOMAN *Fontana TF 730*	10	10
27 Oct 66 ●	SEMI-DETACHED SUBURBAN MR JAMES *Fontana TF 757*	2	12
30 Mar 67 ●	HA! HA! SAID THE CLOWN *Fontana TF 812*	4	11
25 May 67	SWEET PEA *Fontana TF 828*	36	4
24 Jan 68 ★	MIGHTY QUINN *Fontana TF 897*	1	11
12 Jun 68 ●	MY NAME IS JACK *Fontana TF 943*	8	11
18 Dec 68 ●	FOX ON THE RUN *Fontana TF 985*	5	12

30 Apr 69 ●	RAGAMUFFIN MAN *Fontana TF 1013*	8	11
8 Sep 73 ●	JOYBRINGER *Vertigo 6059 083* [1]	9	10
28 Aug 76 ●	BLINDED BY THE LIGHT *Bronze BRO 29* [1] ▲	6	10
20 May 78 ●	DAVY'S ON THE ROAD AGAIN *Bronze BRO 52* [1]	6	12
17 Mar 79	YOU ANGEL YOU *Bronze BRO 68* [1]	54	5
7 Jul 79	DON'T KILL IT CAROL *Bronze BRO 77* [1]	45	4
19 Sep 64 ●	FIVE FACES OF MANFRED MANN *HMV CLP 1731*	3	24
23 Oct 65 ●	MANN MADE *HMV CLP 1911*	7	11
17 Sep 66	MANN MADE HITS *HMV CLP 3559*	11	17
29 Oct 66	AS IS *Fontana TL 5377*	22	4
21 Jan 67	SOUL OF MANN *HMV CSD 3594*	40	1
17 Jun 78	WATCH *Bronze BRON 507* [1]	33	6
24 Mar 79	ANGEL STATION *Bronze BRON 516* [1]	30	8
15 Sep 79 ●	SEMI-DETACHED SUBURBAN *EMI EMTV 19*	9	14
26 Feb 83	SOMEWHERE IN AFRIKA *Bronze BRON 543* [1]	87	1
18 Sep 86 ●	THE ROARING SILENCE *Bronze ILPS 9357* [1]	10	9
23 Jan 93	AGES OF MANN *PolyGram TV 5143622*	23	4
10 Sep 94	THE VERY BEST OF MANFRED MANN'S EARTH BAND *Arcade ARC 3100162*	69	1

[1] Manfred Mann's Earth Band [1] Manfred Mann's Earth Band

MANHATTAN TRANSFER (450 Top 500)
Multi-faceted four-part harmony vocal group formed New York, US, 1969, whose recordings include songs from the 1930s-80s. Their nostalgic sound earned them ten Grammy awards, although, oddly, their No.1 single did not chart in the US (Singles: 72 Weeks, Albums: 85 Weeks) pos/wks

7 Feb 76	TUXEDO JUNCTION *Atlantic K 10670*	24	6
5 Feb 77 ★	CHANSON D'AMOUR *Atlantic K 10886*	1	13
28 May 77	DON'T LET GO *Atlantic K 10930*	32	6
18 Feb 78	WALK IN LOVE (re) *Atlantic K 11075*	12	12
20 May 78	ON A LITTLE STREET IN SINGAPORE *Atlantic K 11136*	20	9
16 Sep 78	WHERE DID OUR LOVE GO / JE VOULAIS (TE DIRE QUE JE T'ATTENDS) *Atlantic K 11182*	40	4
23 Dec 78	WHO, WHAT, WHEN, WHERE, WHY *Atlantic K 11233*	49	6
17 May 80	TWILIGHT ZONE – TWILIGHT TONE (MEDLEY) *Atlantic K 11476*	25	8
21 Jan 84	SPICE OF LIFE *Atlantic A 9728*	19	8
12 Mar 77	COMING OUT *Atlantic K 50291*	12	20
19 Mar 77	MANHATTAN TRANSFER *Atlantic K 50138*	49	7
25 Feb 78 ●	PASTICHE *Atlantic K 50444*	10	34
11 Nov 78 ●	LIVE *Atlantic K 50540*	4	17
17 Nov 79	EXTENSIONS *Atlantic K 50674*	63	3
18 Feb 84	BODIES AND SOULS *Atlantic 780104*	53	4

The MANHATTANS
US, male vocal group (Singles: 31 Weeks, Albums: 3 Weeks) pos/wks

19 Jun 76 ●	KISS AND SAY GOODBYE *CBS 4317* ▲	4	11
2 Oct 76 ●	HURT *CBS 4562*	4	11
23 Apr 77	IT'S YOU *CBS 5093*	43	3
26 Jul 80	SHINING STAR *CBS 8624*	45	4
6 Aug 83	CRAZY *CBS A 3578*	63	2
14 Aug 76	MANHATTANS *CBS 81513*	37	3

MANIA *UK, female vocal duo – Niara Scarlett and Giselle Sommerville (Singles: 2 Weeks)* pos/wks

7 Aug 04	LOOKING FOR A PLACE *RCA 82876617852*	29	2

M.A.N.I.C. *UK, male vocal / production duo (Singles: 1 Week)* pos/wks

18 Apr 92	I'M COMIN' HARDCORE *Union City UCRT 2*	60	1

MANIC MCs featuring Sara CARLSON
UK, male production duo and female vocalist (Singles: 5 Weeks) pos/wks

12 Aug 89	MENTAL *RCA PB 43037*	30	5

MANIC STREET PREACHERS (144 Top 500) *Best-selling Welsh act of the 1990s; James Dean Bradfield (v/g), Nicky Wire (b), Sean Moore (d) and Richey Edwards (v/g – missing since 1995 and officially declared dead in 2002). Won trophies for the Best British Group and Best Album at the 1997 and 1999 Brit Awards (Singles: 154 Weeks, Albums: 205 Weeks)* pos/wks

25 May 91	YOU LOVE US *Heavenly HVN 10*	62	2
10 Aug 91	STAY BEAUTIFUL *Columbia 6573377*	40	3
9 Nov 91	LOVE'S SWEET EXILE / REPEAT *Columbia 6575827*	26	3
1 Feb 92	YOU LOVE US (re-issue) *Columbia 6577247*	16	4
28 Mar 92	SLASH 'N' BURN *Columbia 6578737*	20	4

13 Jun 92	MOTORCYCLE EMPTINESS *Columbia 6580837*	17	6
19 Sep 92 ●	THEME FROM M.A.S.H. (SUICIDE IS PAINLESS) *Columbia 6583827*	7	6
21 Nov 92	LITTLE BABY NOTHING *Columbia 6587967*	29	3
12 Jun 93	FROM DESPAIR TO WHERE *Columbia 6593372*	25	4
31 Jul 93	LA TRISTESSE DURERA (SCREAM TO A SIGH) *Columbia 6594772*	22	5
2 Oct 93	ROSES IN THE HOSPITAL *Columbia 6597272*	15	3
12 Feb 94	LIFE BECOMING A LANDSLIDE *Columbia 6600702*	36	2
11 Jun 94	FASTER / PCP *Epic 6604472*	16	3
13 Aug 94	REVOL *Epic 6606862*	22	3
15 Oct 94	SHE IS SUFFERING *Epic 6608952*	25	3
27 Apr 96 ●	A DESIGN FOR LIFE (re) *Epic 6630705*	2	11
3 Aug 96 ●	EVERYTHING MUST GO *Epic 6634685*	5	6
12 Oct 96 ●	KEVIN CARTER *Epic 6637752*	9	4
14 Dec 96 ●	AUSTRALIA *Epic 6640442*	7	7
13 Sep 97	MOTORCYCLE EMPTINESS (re-issue) *Epic MANIC 5CD*	41	2
13 Sep 97	YOU LOVE US (2nd re-issue) *Epic MANIC 3CD*	49	1
13 Sep 97	LITTLE BABY NOTHING (re-issue) *Epic MANIC 6CD*	50	1
13 Sep 97	STAY BEAUTIFUL (re-issue) *Epic MANIC 1CD*	52	1
13 Sep 97	SLASH 'N' BURN (re-issue) *Epic MANIC 4CD*	54	1
13 Sep 97	LOVE'S SWEET EXILE (re-issue) *Epic MANIC 2CD*	55	1
5 Sep 98 ★	IF YOU TOLERATE THIS YOUR CHILDREN WILL BE NEXT (re) *Epic 6663452* ■	1	11
12 Dec 98	THE EVERLASTING *Epic 6666862*	11	8
20 Mar 99 ●	YOU STOLE THE SUN FROM MY HEART *Epic 6669532*	5	8
17 Jul 99	TSUNAMI *Epic 6674112*	11	5
22 Jan 00 ★	THE MASSES AGAINST THE CLASSES (re) *Epic 6685302* ■	1	7
10 Mar 01 ●	FOUND THAT SOUL (re) *Epic 6708332*	9	4
10 Mar 01 ●	SO WHY SO SAD *Epic 6708322*	8	7
16 Jun 01	OCEAN SPRAY *Epic 6712532*	15	4
22 Sep 01	LET ROBESON SING *Epic 6717732*	19	2
26 Oct 02 ●	THERE BY THE GRACE OF GOD (re) *Epic 6731662*	6	5
30 Oct 04 ●	THE LOVE OF RICHARD NIXON *Sony Music 6753422*	2	4
22 Feb 92	GENERATION TERRORISTS *Columbia 4710602*	13	17
3 Jul 93 ●	GOLD AGAINST THE SOUL *Columbia 4640642*	8	11
10 Sep 94 ●	THE HOLY BIBLE *Epic 4774219*	6	4
1 Jun 96 ●	EVERYTHING MUST GO *Epic 4839302*	2	82
26 Sep 98 ★	THIS IS MY TRUTH TELL ME YOURS *Epic 4917039* ■	1	60
31 Mar 01 ●	KNOW YOUR ENEMY *Epic 5018802*	2	14
9 Nov 02 ●	FOREVER DELAYED – THE GREATEST HITS *Epic 5095519*	4	12
26 Jul 03	LIPSTICK TRACES – A SECRET HISTORY OF MANIC STREET PREACHERS *Sony Music 5123862*	11	3
13 Nov 04	LIFEBLOOD *Sony Music 5188852*	13	2

The listed flipside of 'Theme From M.A.S.H. (Suicide Is Painless)' was '(Everything I Do) I Do It for You' by Fatima Mansions

MANIJAMA featuring MUKUPA & L'IL T
UK, male / female production / vocal group (Singles: 1 Week) pos/wks

| 8 Feb 03 | NO NO NO *Defected DFTD 058CDS* | 66 | 1 |

Barry MANILOW 82 Top 500
Middle-of-the-road superstar, b. Barry Pincus, 17 Jun 1946, Brooklyn, US. This crowd-pulling singer / songwriter / pianist with a vast and loyal following on both sides of the Atlantic has sold in excess of 60 million albums (Singles: 136 Weeks, Albums: 355 Weeks) pos/wks

22 Feb 75	MANDY *Arista 1* ▲	11	9
6 May 78	CAN'T SMILE WITHOUT YOU *Arista 176*	43	7
29 Jul 78	SOMEWHERE IN THE NIGHT / COPACABANA (AT THE COPA) *Arista 196*	42	10
23 Dec 78	COULD IT BE MAGIC *Arista ARIST 229*	25	10
8 Nov 80	LONELY TOGETHER *Arista ARIST 373*	21	13
7 Feb 81	I MADE IT THROUGH THE RAIN *Arista ARIST 384*	37	6
11 Apr 81	BERMUDA TRIANGLE *Arista ARIST 406*	15	9
26 Sep 81	LET'S HANG ON *Arista ARIST 429*	12	11
12 Dec 81	THE OLD SONGS *Arista ARIST 443*	48	8
20 Feb 82	IF I SHOULD LOVE AGAIN *Arista ARIST 453*	66	2
17 Apr 82	STAY *Arista ARIST 464* [1]	23	8
16 Oct 82 ●	I WANNA DO IT WITH YOU *Arista ARIST 495*	8	8
4 Dec 82	I'M GONNA SIT RIGHT DOWN AND WRITE MYSELF A LETTER *Arista ARIST 503*	36	7
25 Jun 83	SOME KIND OF FRIEND *Arista ARIST 516*	48	2
27 Aug 83	YOU'RE LOOKING HOT TONIGHT *Arista ARIST 542*	47	6
10 Dec 83	READ 'EM AND WEEP *Arista ARIST 551*	17	7
8 Apr 89	PLEASE DON'T BE SCARED *Arista 112186*	35	5
10 Apr 93	COPACABANA (AT THE COPA) (re-mix) *Arista 74321136912*	22	4
20 Nov 93	COULD IT BE MAGIC 1993 *Arista 74321174882*	36	3

6 Aug 94	LET ME BE YOUR WINGS *EMI CDEM 336* [2]	73	1
23 Sep 78	EVEN NOW *Arista SPART 1047*	12	28
3 Mar 79 ●	MANILOW MAGIC – THE BEST OF BARRY MANILOW *Arista ARTV 2*	3	151
20 Oct 79	ONE VOICE *Arista SPART 1106*	18	7
29 Nov 80 ●	BARRY *Arista DLART 2*	5	34
25 Apr 81	GIFT SET *Arista BOX 1*	62	1
3 Oct 81 ●	IF I SHOULD LOVE AGAIN *Arista BMAN 1*	5	26
1 May 82 ★	BARRY LIVE IN BRITAIN *Arista ARTV 4* ■	1	23
27 Nov 82 ●	I WANNA DO IT WITH YOU *Arista BMAN 2*	7	9
8 Oct 83 ●	A TOUCH MORE MAGIC *Arista BMAN 3*	10	12
1 Dec 84	2:00 AM PARADISE CAFÉ *Arista 206496*	28	6
16 Nov 85	MANILOW *RCA PL 87044*	40	6
20 Feb 88	SWING STREET *Arista 208860*	81	1
20 May 89	SONGS TO MAKE THE WHOLE WORLD SING *Arista 209927*	20	4
17 Mar 90	LIVE ON BROADWAY *Arista 303785*	19	3
30 Jun 90	THE SONGS 1975–1990 *Arista 303868*	13	7
2 Nov 91	SHOWSTOPPERS *Arista 212091*	53	3
3 Apr 93	HIDDEN TREASURES *Arista 74321135682*	36	7
27 Nov 93	GREATEST HITS – THE PLATINUM COLLECTION *Arista 74321175452*	37	6
5 Nov 94	SINGIN' WITH THE BIG BANDS *Arista 07822187712*	54	2
30 Nov 96	SUMMER OF '78 *Arista 7822188092*	66	2
21 Nov 98	MANILOW SINGS SINATRA *Arista 7822190332*	72	2
25 May 02	HERE AT THE MAYFLOWER *Columbia 5077342*	18	3
20 Mar 04 ●	ULTIMATE MANILOW *Arista 82876604552*	8	12

[1] Barry Manilow featuring Kevin Desimone and James Jolis [2] Barry Manilow and Debra Byrd

'Stay' was available as both a live and studio recording

MANIX
UK, male / female vocal / instrumental group (Singles: 6 Weeks) pos/wks

23 Nov 91	MANIC MINDS *Reinforced RIVET 1209*	63	2
7 Mar 92	OBLIVION (HEAD IN THE CLOUDS) (EP) *Reinforced RIVET 1212*	43	3
8 Aug 92	RAINBOW PEOPLE *Reinforced RIVET 1221*	57	1

Tracks on Oblivion (Head in the Clouds) (EP): Oblivion (Head in the Clouds) / Never Been to Belgium (Gotta Rush) / I Can't Stand It / You Held My Hand

MANKEY *UK, male producer – Andy Manston (Singles: 1 Week)* pos/wks

| 16 Nov 96 | BELIEVE IN ME *Frisky DISKY 3* | 74 | 1 |

MANKIND *UK, male instrumental group (Singles: 12 Weeks)* pos/wks

| 25 Nov 78 | DR WHO *Pinnacle PIN 71* | 25 | 12 |

Aimee MANN
US, female vocalist (Singles: 9 Weeks, Albums: 3 Weeks) pos/wks

31 Oct 87	TIME STAND STILL *Vertigo RUSH 13* [1]	42	3
28 Aug 93	I SHOULD'VE KNOWN *Imago 72787250437*	55	2
20 Nov 93	STUPID THING *Imago 72787250527*	47	2
5 Mar 94	I SHOULD'VE KNOWN (re-issue) *Imago 72787250602*	45	2
18 Sep 93	WHATEVER *Imago 72787210172*	39	1
11 Nov 95	I'M WITH STUPID *Geffen GED 24951*	51	1
14 Sep 02	LOST IN SPACE *V2 VVR 1020882*	72	1

[1] Rush with Aimee Mann

Roberto MANN *UK, male orchestra leader (Albums: 9 Weeks)* pos/wks

| 9 Dec 67 | GREAT WALTZES *Deram SML 1010* | 19 | 9 |

Shelly MANNE *US, male instrumentalist – drums, b. 11 Jun 1920, d. 29 Sep 1984 (Albums: 1 Week)* pos/wks

| 18 Jun 60 | MY FAIR LADY *Vogue LAC 12100* | 20 | 1 |

Johnny MANN SINGERS
US, male / female vocal group (Singles: 13 Weeks) pos/wks

| 12 Jul 67 ● | UP-UP AND AWAY *Liberty LIB 55972* | 6 | 13 |

MANOWAR
US, male vocal / instrumental group (Albums: 3 Weeks) pos/wks

| 18 Feb 84 | HAIL TO ENGLAND *Music for Nations MFN 19* | 83 | 2 |
| 6 Oct 84 | SIGN OF THE HAMMER *10 DIX 10* | 73 | 1 |

MANSUN
UK, male vocal / instrumental
group (Singles: 45 Weeks, Albums: 27 Weeks) pos/wks

6 Apr 96	ONE (EP) *Parlophone CDR 6430*	**37** 2
15 Jun 96	TWO (EP) *Parlophone CDR 6437*	**32** 2
21 Sep 96	THREE (EP) *Parlophone CDR 6447*	**19** 3
17 Dec 96	WIDE OPEN SPACE *Parlophone CDR 6453*	**15** 4
15 Feb 97 ●	SHE MAKES MY NOSE BLEED *Parlophone CDR 6453*	**9** 5
10 May 97	TAXLOSS *Parlophone CDRS 6465*	**15** 3
18 Oct 97 ●	CLOSED FOR BUSINESS *Parlophone CDRS 6482*	**10** 3
11 Jul 98 ●	LEGACY (EP) *Parlophone CDRS 6497*	**7** 4
5 Sep 98	BEING A GIRL (PART ONE) (EP) *Parlophone CDR 6503*	**13** 3
7 Nov 98	NEGATIVE *Parlophone CDR 6508*	**27** 2
13 Feb 99	SIX *Parlophone CDR 6511*	**16** 3
12 Aug 00 ●	I CAN ONLY DISAPPOINT U *Parlophone CDR 6544*	**8** 6
18 Nov 00	ELECTRIC MAN *Parlophone CDR 6550*	**23** 2
10 Feb 01	FOOL *Parlophone CDRS 6553*	**28** 2
2 Oct 04	SLIPPING AWAY *Parlophone R 6650*	**55** 1
1 Mar 97 ★	ATTACK OF THE GREY LANTERN *Parlophone CDPCS 7387* ■..1 19
19 Sep 98	SIX *Parlophone 4967232*	**6** 4
26 Aug 00	LITTLE KIX *Parlophone 5277822*	**12** 4

Tracks on One (EP): Egg Shaped Fred / Ski Jump Nose / Lemonade Secret Drinker /
Thief. Tracks on Two (EP): Take It Easy Chicken / Drastic Sturgeon / The Greatest
Pain / Moronica. Tracks on Three (EP): Stripper Vicar / An Open Letter to the Lyrical
Trainspotter / No One Knows Us / Things Keep Falling Off Buildings. Tracks on
Legacy (EP) CD1: Legacy (Extended version) / Can't Afford to Die / Spasm of
Identity / Check Under the Bed. CD2: Legacy / Wide Open Space (The Perfecto
Remix) / GSOH / Face in the Crowd. Tracks on Being a Girl (Part One) (EP): Being
a Girl / I Care / Been Here Before / Hideout / Railings

MANTOVANI (348 **Top 500**) (see also David WHITFIELD) Britain's
most successful album act before The Beatles – leader b. Annunzio Paulo
Mantovani, 15 Nov 1905, Venice, Italy, d. 29 Mar 1980. UK orchestra were the
first act to sell a million stereo albums, and had six albums simultaneously
in US Top 30 in 1959 (Singles: 52 Weeks, Albums: 143 Weeks) pos/wks

19 Dec 52 ●	WHITE CHRISTMAS *Decca F 10017*	**6** 3
29 May 53 ★	THE SONG FROM THE MOULIN ROUGE (2re) *Decca F 10094* 1 23
23 Oct 53 ●	SWEDISH RHAPSODY (re) *Decca F 10168*	**2** 18
11 Feb 55	LONELY BALLERINA (re) *Decca F 10395*	**16** 4
31 May 57	AROUND THE WORLD *Decca F 10888*	**20** 4
21 Feb 59 ●	CONTINENTAL ENCORES *Decca LK 4298*	**4** 12
18 Feb 61	CONCERT SPECTACULAR *Decca LK 4377*	**16** 2
16 Apr 66 ●	MANTOVANI MAGIC *Decca LK 7949*	**3** 15
15 Oct 66	MR MUSIC – MANTOVANI *Decca LK 4809*	**24** 3
14 Jan 67 ●	MANTOVANI'S GOLDEN HITS *Decca SKL 4818*	**10** 35
30 Sep 67	HOLLYWOOD *Decca SKL 4887*	**37** 1
14 Jun 69 ●	THE WORLD OF MANTOVANI *Decca SPA 1*	**6** 31
4 Oct 69 ●	THE WORLD OF MANTOVANI VOLUME 2 *Decca SPA 36*	**4** 19
16 May 70	MANTOVANI TODAY *Decca SKL 5003*	**16** 8
26 Feb 72	TO LOVERS EVERYWHERE *Decca SKL 5112*	**44** 1
3 Nov 79 ●	20 GOLDEN GREATS *Warwick WW 5067*	**9** 13
16 Mar 85	MANTOVANI MAGIC *Telstar STAR 2237* [1]	**52** 3

[1] Mantovani Orchestra conducted by Roland Shaw

Kurtis MANTRONIK US, male vocalist /
instrumentalist / producer – Kurtis Khaleel (Singles: 6 Weeks) pos/wks

15 Aug 98	STRICTLY BUSINESS *Parlophone CDR 6502* [1]	**43** 1
9 Nov 02	77 STRINGS *Southern Fried ECB 35* [2]	**71** 1
28 Jun 03	HOW DID YOU KNOW *Southern Fried ECB 43CDS* [2]	**16** 4

[1] Kurtis Mantronik vs EPMD [2] Kurtis Mantronik presents Chamonix

MANTRONIX US / Jamaica, male vocal / instrumental
duo – Kurtis Kahleel and MC Tee (Toure Embden – replaced
Bryce Wilson 1989) (Singles: 48 Weeks, Albums: 17 Weeks) pos/wks

22 Feb 86	LADIES *10 TEN 116*	**55** 4
17 May 86	BASSLINE *10 TEN 118*	**34** 6
7 Feb 87	WHO IS IT? *10 TEN 137*	**40** 6
4 Jul 87	SCREAM (PRIMAL SCREAM) *10 TEN 169*	**46** 4
30 Jan 88	SING A SONG (BREAK IT DOWN) *10 TEN 206*	**61** 2
12 Mar 88	SIMPLE SIMON (YOU GOTTA REGARD) *10 TEN 217*	**72** 2
6 Jan 90 ●	GOT TO HAVE YOUR LOVE *Capitol CL 559* [1]	**4** 11
12 May 90 ●	TAKE YOUR TIME *Capitol CL 573* [1]	**10** 7
2 Mar 91	DON'T GO MESSIN' WITH MY HEART *Capitol CL 608*	**22** 5
22 Jun 91	STEP TO ME (DO ME) *Capitol CL 613*	**59** 1
29 Mar 86	THE ALBUM *10 DIX 37*	**45** 3
13 Dec 86	MUSICAL MADNESS *10 DIX 50*	**66** 3

2 Apr 88	IN FULL EFFECT *10 DIX 74*	**39** 3
17 Feb 90	THIS SHOULD MOVE YA *Capitol EST 2117*	**18** 6
30 Mar 91	THE INCREDIBLE SOUND MACHINE *Capitol EST 2139*	**36** 2

[1] Mantronix featuring Wondress

MANUEL and the MUSIC OF THE MOUNTAINS
UK, orchestra – leader Geoff Love, b. 4 Sep 1917,
d. 8 Jul 1991 (Singles: 31 Weeks, Albums: 38 Weeks) pos/wks

28 Aug 59	THE HONEYMOON SONG (2re) *Columbia DB 4323*	**22** 9
13 Oct 60	NEVER ON SUNDAY *Columbia DB 4515*	**29** 10
13 Oct 66	SOMEWHERE MY LOVE *Columbia DB 7969*	**42** 2
31 Jan 76 ●	RODRIGO'S GUITAR CONCERTO DE ARANJUEZ (THEME FROM 2ND MOVEMENT) *EMI 2383*	**3** 10
10 Sep 60	MUSIC OF THE MOUNTAINS *Columbia 33SX 1212*	**17** 1
7 Aug 71	THIS IS MANUEL *Studio Two STWO 5*	**18** 19
31 Jan 76 ●	CARNIVAL *Studio Two TWO 337*	**3** 18

Roots MANUVA UK, male rapper – Rodney
Hylton Smith (Singles: 7 Weeks, Albums: 4 Weeks) pos/wks

11 Dec 99	DUSTED (re) *Hard Hands HAND 058CD1* [1]	**28** 3
4 Aug 01	WITNESS (1 HOPE) *Big Dada BDCDS 022*	**45** 2
20 Oct 01	DREAMY DAYS *Big Dada BDCDS 033*	**53** 1
8 May 04	OH U WANT MORE? *Big Dada BDCDS 066* [2]	**65** 1
25 Aug 01	RUN COME SAVE ME *Big Dada BDCD 032*	**33** 3
20 Jul 02	DUB COME SAVE ME *Big Dada BDCD 040*	**75** 1

[1] Leftfield / Roots Manuva [2] Ty featuring Roots Manuva

Phil MANZANERA (see also ROXY MUSIC) UK, male vocalist /
instrumentalist – guitar – Philip Targett-Adams (Albums: 1 Week) pos/wks

24 May 75	DIAMOND HEAD *Island ILPS 9315*	**40** 1

MARATHON
Germany / UK, male vocal / instrumental group (Singles: 3 Weeks) pos/wks

25 Jan 92	MOVIN' *Ten TEN 395*	**36** 3

The MARAUDERS
UK, male vocal / instrumental group (Singles: 4 Weeks) pos/wks

8 Aug 63	THAT'S WHAT I WANT (re) *Decca F 11695*	**43** 4

The MARBLES UK, male vocal duo – Graham
Bonnet and Trevor Gordon (Singles: 18 Weeks) pos/wks

25 Sep 68 ●	ONLY ONE WOMAN *Polydor 56 272*	**5** 12
26 Mar 69	THE WALLS FELL DOWN *Polydor 56 310*	**28** 6

MARC and the MAMBAS See Marc ALMOND

MARC et CLAUDE Germany, male DJ / production
duo – Marc Romboy and Klaus Derichs (Singles: 15 Weeks) pos/wks

21 Nov 98	LA *Positiva CDTIV 104*	**28** 3
22 Jul 00	I NEED YOUR LOVIN' (LIKE THE SUNSHINE) *Positiva CDTIV 136*	**12** 7
6 Apr 02	TREMBLE *Positiva CDTIVS 170*	**29** 3
19 Apr 03	LOVING YOU '03 *Positive CDTIV 190*	**37** 2

The MARCELS US, male vocal group –
lead vocal Cornelius Harp (Singles: 17 Weeks) pos/wks

13 Apr 61 ★	BLUE MOON *Pye International 7N 25073* ▲	**1** 13
8 Jun 61	SUMMERTIME *Pye International 7N 25083*	**46** 4

Little Peggy MARCH
US, female vocalist – Margaret Battavio (Singles: 7 Weeks) pos/wks

12 Sep 63	HELLO HEARTACHE, GOODBYE LOVE *RCA 1362*	**29** 7

MARCO POLO
Italy, male instrumental / production duo (Singles: 1 Week) pos/wks

8 Apr 95	A PRAYER TO THE MUSIC *Hi-Life HICD 7*	**65** 1

MARCY PLAYGROUND US, male vocal /
instrumental trio (Singles: 3 Weeks, Albums: 1 Week) pos/wks

18 Apr 98	SEX AND CANDY *EMI CDEM 508*	**29** 3
9 May 98	MARCY PLAYGROUND *EMI 8535692*	**61** 1

MARDI GRAS
UK, male vocal / instrumental group (Singles: 9 Weeks) pos/wks

| 5 Aug 72 | TOO BUSY THINKING ABOUT MY BABY *Bell 1226* | 19 | 9 |

MARIA See Maria NAYLER

Kelly MARIE
UK, female vocalist – Jacqueline McKinnon (Singles: 36 Weeks) pos/wks

2 Aug 80 ★	FEELS LIKE I'M IN LOVE *Calibre PLUS 1*	1	16
18 Oct 80	LOVING JUST FOR FUN *Calibre PLUS 4*	21	7
7 Feb 81	HOT LOVE *Calibre PLUS 5*	22	10
30 May 81	LOVE TRIAL *Calibre PLUS 7*	51	3

Rose MARIE
Ireland, female vocalist (Singles: 5 Weeks, Albums: 35 Weeks) pos/wks

19 Nov 83	WHEN I LEAVE THE WORLD BEHIND (2re) *A1 284*	63	5
13 Apr 85	ROSE MARIE SINGS JUST FOR YOU *A1 RMTV 1*	30	13
24 May 86	SO LUCKY *A1-Spartan RMLP 2*	62	3
14 Nov 87	SENTIMENTALLY YOURS *Telstar STAR 2302*	22	11
19 Nov 88	TOGETHER AGAIN *Telstar STAR 2333*	52	7
23 Mar 96	MEMORIES OF HOME *Telstar TCD 2788*	51	1

Teena MARIE
US, female vocalist – Mary Brockert (Singles: 28 Weeks) pos/wks

7 Jul 79	I'M A SUCKER FOR YOUR LOVE *Motown TMG 1146* [1]	43	8
31 May 80 ●	BEHIND THE GROOVE *Motown TMG 1185*	6	10
11 Oct 80	I NEED YOUR LOVIN' *Motown TMG 1203*	28	6
26 Mar 88	OOO LA LA LA *Epic 651423 7*	74	2
10 Nov 90	SINCE DAY ONE *Epic 656429 7*	69	2

[1] Teena Marie, co-lead vocals Rick James

MARILLION `224` `Top 500`
Progressive rock group formed in Buckinghamshire and originally named after Tolkien's novel Silmarillion. They reached their peak of popularity in the 80s, when fronted by Scottish vocalist / songwriter Fish. When Fish left in 1989, the band continued to make regular visits to the charts with Steve Hogarth in the role of vocalist / songwriter (Singles: 108 Weeks, Albums: 165 Weeks) pos/wks

20 Nov 82	MARKET SQUARE HEROES (re) *EMI 5351*	53	8
12 Feb 83	HE KNOWS YOU KNOW *EMI 5362*	35	4
18 Jun 83	GARDEN PARTY *EMI 5393*	16	5
11 Feb 84	PUNCH AND JUDY *EMI MARIL 1*	29	4
12 May 84	ASSASSING *EMI MARIL 2*	22	5
18 May 85 ●	KAYLEIGH *EMI MARIL 3*	2	14
7 Sep 85 ●	LAVENDER *EMI MARIL 4*	5	9
30 Nov 85	HEART OF LOTHIAN *EMI MARIL 5*	29	5
23 May 87 ●	INCOMMUNICADO *EMI MARIL 6*	6	5
25 Jul 87	SUGAR MICE *EMI MARIL 7*	22	5
7 Nov 87	WARM WET CIRCLES *EMI MARIL 8*	22	4
26 Nov 88	FREAKS (LIVE) *EMI MARIL 9*	24	3
9 Sep 89	HOOKS IN YOU *Capitol MARIL 10*	30	3
9 Dec 89	UNINVITED GUEST *EMI MARIL 11*	53	2
14 Apr 90	EASTER *EMI MARIL 12*	34	2
8 Jun 91	COVER MY EYES (PAIN AND HEAVEN) *EMI MARIL 13*	34	4
3 Aug 91	NO ONE CAN *EMI MARIL 14*	33	4
5 Oct 91	DRY LAND *EMI MARIL 15*	34	2
23 May 92	SYMPATHY *EMI MARIL 16*	17	3
1 Aug 92	NO ONE CAN (re-issue) *EMI MARIL 17*	26	4
26 Mar 94	THE HOLLOW MAN *EMI CDEMS 307*	30	2
7 May 94	ALONE AGAIN IN THE LAP OF LUXURY *EMI CDEMS 318*	53	3
10 Jun 95	BEAUTIFUL *EMI CDMARILS 18*	29	2
1 May 04 ●	YOU'RE GONE *Intact CDINTACT 1*	7	3
24 Jul 04	DON'T HURT YOURSELF *Intact CDINTACT 2*	16	2
26 Mar 83 ●	SCRIPT FOR A JESTER'S TEAR *EMI EMC 3429*	7	31
24 Mar 84 ●	FUGAZI *EMI EMC 2400851*	5	20
17 Nov 84 ●	REAL TO REEL *EMI JEST 1*	8	22
29 Jun 85 ★	MISPLACED CHILDHOOD *EMI MRL 2* ■	1	41
4 Jul 87 ●	CLUTCHING AT STRAWS *EMI EMD 1002*	2	15
23 Jul 88	B SIDES THEMSELVES *EMI EMS 1295*	64	6
10 Dec 88	THE THIEVING MAGPIE *EMI MARIL 1*	25	6
7 Oct 89 ●	SEASON'S END *EMI EMD 1011 22*	7	4
6 Jul 91 ●	HOLIDAYS IN EDEN *EMI EMD 1022*	7	7
20 Jun 92	A SINGLES COLLECTION 1982-1992 *EMI CDEMD 1033*	27	2
19 Feb 94 ●	BRAVE *EMI CDEMC 1054*	10	4
8 Jul 95	AFRAID OF SUNLIGHT *EMI CDEMD 1079*	16	2
6 Apr 96	MADE AGAIN *EMI CDEMD 1094*	37	1

3 May 97	THIS STRANGE ENGINE *Raw Power RAWCD 121*	27	2
3 Oct 98	RADIATION *Raw Power RAWCD 126*	35	1
30 Oct 99	MARILLION.COM *Intact / Raw Power RAWCD 144*	53	1

MARILYN
UK, male vocalist – Peter Robinson (Singles: 26 Weeks) pos/wks

5 Nov 83 ●	CALLING YOUR NAME *Mercury MAZ 1*	4	12
11 Feb 84	CRY AND BE FREE *Mercury MAZ 2*	31	6
21 Apr 84	YOU DON'T LOVE ME *Mercury MAZ 3*	40	7
13 Apr 85	BABY U LEFT ME (IN THE COLD) *Mercury MAZ 4*	70	1

MARILYN MANSON
US, male vocal / instrumental group – leader Brian Warner (Singles: 42 Weeks, Albums: 21 Weeks) pos/wks

7 Jun 97	THE BEAUTIFUL PEOPLE *Nothing 95541*	18	3
20 Sep 97	TOURNIQUET *Nothing 95552*	28	2
21 Nov 98	THE DOPE SHOW *Nothing 95610*	12	3
26 Jun 99	ROCK IS DEAD *Maverick W 486CD*	23	2
18 Nov 00	DISPOSABLE TEENS *Nothing 4974372*	12	3
3 Mar 01	THE FIGHT SONG *Nothing / Interscope 4974902*	24	3
15 Sep 01	THE NOBODIES *Nothing IND 97604*	34	2
30 Mar 02 ●	TAINTED LOVE *Maverick / Warner Bros. W 579CD*	5	11
14 Jun 03	MOBSCENE *Interscope / Polydor 9807726*	13	6
13 Sep 03	THIS IS THE NEW *HIT *Interscope / Polydor 9810793*	29	2
16 Oct 04	PERSONAL JESUS *Interscope 9864166*	13	5
26 Oct 96	ANTICHRIST SUPERSTAR *Interscope IND 90086*	73	1
26 Sep 98 ●	MECHANICAL ANIMALS *Interscope IND 90273* ▲	8	4
27 Nov 99	THE LAST TOUR ON EARTH *Interscope 4905242*	61	1
25 Nov 00	HOLY WOOD *Nothing 4908292*	23	2
24 May 03 ●	THE GOLDEN AGE OF THE GROTESQUE *Interscope / Polydor 9800093* ▲	4	3
9 Oct 04 ●	LEST WE FORGET – THE BEST OF *Interscope 9863975*	4	6

Marino MARINI and his QUARTET
Italy, male vocalist and instrumental group (Singles: 23 Weeks) pos/wks

3 Oct 58	VOLARE (NEL BLU DIPINTO DI BLU) *Durium DC 16632*	13	7
10 Oct 58 ●	COME PRIMA *Durium DC 16632*	2	14
20 Mar 59	CIAO CIAO BAMBINA (PIOVE) (re) *Durium DC 16636*	24	2

MARIO
US, male vocalist – Mario Barrett (Singles: 6 Weeks) pos/wks

| 12 Apr 03 | JUST A FRIEND *J 82876508082* | 18 | 4 |
| 12 Jul 03 | C'MON *J 82876528282* | 28 | 2 |

MARION
UK, male vocal / instrumental group (Singles: 9 Weeks, Albums: 2 Weeks) pos/wks

25 Feb 95	SLEEP *London LONCD 360*	53	1
13 May 95	TOYS FOR BOYS *London LONCD 366*	57	1
21 Oct 95	LET'S ALL GO TOGETHER *London LONCD 371*	37	2
3 Feb 96	TIME *London LONCD 377*	29	2
30 Mar 96	SLEEP (re-mix) *London LONCD 381*	17	2
7 Mar 98	MIYAKO HIDEAWAY *London LONCD 403*	45	1
17 Feb 96 ●	THIS WORLD AND BODY *London 8286952*	10	2

MARK 'OH
Germany, male producer – Marko Albrecht (Singles: 3 Weeks) pos/wks

| 6 May 95 | TEARS DON'T LIE *Systematic SYSCD 9* | 24 | 3 |

Pigmeat MARKHAM
US, male vocalist / comedian, b. 18 Apr 1904, d. 13 Dec 1981 (Singles: 8 Weeks) pos/wks

| 17 Jul 68 | HERE COMES THE JUDGE *Chess CRS 8077* | 19 | 8 |

Biz MARKIE
US, male rapper – Marcel Hall (Singles: 2 Weeks) pos/wks

| 26 May 90 | JUST A FRIEND *Cold Chillin' W 9823* | 55 | 2 |

Yannis MARKOPOULOS
Greece, orchestra (Singles: 8 Weeks, Albums: 8 Weeks) pos/wks

| 17 Dec 77 | WHO PAYS THE FERRYMAN? *BBC RESL 51* | 11 | 8 |
| 26 Aug 78 | WHO PAYS THE FERRYMAN *BBC REB 315* | 22 | 8 |

Guy MARKS
US, male vocalist – Mario Scarpo, b. 1923 d. 28 Nov 1987 (Singles: 8 Weeks) pos/wks

| 13 May 78 | LOVING YOU HAS MADE ME BANANAS *ABC 4211* | 25 | 8 |

MARKSMEN See Houston WELLS and The MARKSMEN

MARKY MARK and the FUNKY BUNCH
US, male / female vocal / rap / instrumental group
(Singles: 14 Weeks, Albums: 1 Week) pos/wks

31 Aug 91	**GOOD VIBRATIONS** *Interscope A 8764* [1] ▲	**14**	7
2 Nov 91	**WILDSIDE** *Interscope A 8674*	**42**	3
12 Dec 92	**YOU GOTTA BELIEVE** *Interscope A 8480*	**54**	4
5 Oct 91	**MUSIC FOR THE PEOPLE** *Interscope 7567917371*	**61**	1

[1] Marky Mark and the Funky Bunch featuring Loleatta Holloway

Bob MARLEY & the WAILERS ⬤38 [Top 500] *Legendary, globally successful Jamaican group fronted by Bob Marley (v/g), nicknamed 'Tuff Gong', b. 6 Feb 1945, Jamaica, d. 11 May 1981, Miami. Varying line-up included Peter Tosh (v/g), b. 19 Oct 1944, Jamaica, d. 11 Sep 1987, Jamaica, and Bunny Wailer (v/prc). Their compilation 'Legend' is the biggest-selling reggae album in the world with sales of more than 17 million (10m in the US alone). Marley became a founder member of the UK Hall of Fame in 2004, representing the 1970s (Singles: 167 Weeks, Albums: 546 Weeks)* pos/wks

27 Sep 75	⬤ **NO WOMAN NO CRY (re)** *Island WIP 6244*	**8**	18
25 Jun 77	**EXODUS** *Island WIP 6390*	**14**	9
10 Sep 77	**WAITING IN VAIN** *Island WIP 6402*	**27**	6
10 Dec 77	⬤ **JAMMING / PUNKY REGGAE PARTY** *Island WIP 6410*	**9**	12
25 Feb 78	⬤ **IS THIS LOVE** *Island WIP 6420*	**9**	9
10 Jun 78	**SATISFY MY SOUL** *Island WIP 6440*	**21**	10
20 Oct 79	**SO MUCH TROUBLE IN THE WORLD** *Island WIP 6510*	**56**	4
21 Jun 80	⬤ **COULD YOU BE LOVED** *Island WIP 6610*	**5**	12
13 Sep 80	**THREE LITTLE BIRDS** *Island WIP 6641*	**17**	9
7 May 83	⬤ **BUFFALO SOLDIER** *Island / Tuff Gong IS 108*	**4**	12
21 Apr 84	⬤ **ONE LOVE – PEOPLE GET READY** *Island IS 169*	**5**	11
23 Jun 84	**WAITING IN VAIN (re-issue)** *Island IS 180*	**31**	7
8 Dec 84	**COULD YOU BE LOVED (re-issue)** *Island IS 210*	**71**	2
18 May 91	**ONE LOVE – PEOPLE GET READY (re)** *Tuff Gong TGX 1*	**42**	3
19 Sep 92	⬤ **IRON LION ZION** *Tuff Gong TGX 2*	**5**	9
28 Nov 92	**WHY SHOULD I / EXODUS (re)** *Tuff Gong TGX 3*	**42**	4
20 May 95	**KEEP ON MOVING** *Tuff Gong TGXCD 4*	**17**	4
8 Jun 96	**WHAT GOES AROUND COMES AROUND** *Anansi ANACS 002*	**42**	1
25 Sep 99	⬤ **SUN IS SHINING** *Club Tools / Edel 0066895 CLU* [1]	**3**	10
11 Dec 99	**TURN YOUR LIGHTS DOWN LOW** *Columbia 6684362* [2]	**15**	7
22 Jan 00	**RAINBOW COUNTRY** *Club Tools 0067225 CLU* [1]	**11**	6
24 Oct 00	**JAMMIN'** *Tuff Gong TGXCD 9* [3]	**42**	2
4 Oct 75	**NATTY DREAD** *Island ILPS 9281*	**43**	5
20 Dec 75	**LIVE!** *Island ILPS 9376*	**38**	11
8 May 76	**RASTAMAN VIBRATION** *Island ILPS 9383*	**15**	13
11 Jun 77	⬤ **EXODUS** *Island ILPS 9498*	**8**	56
1 Apr 78	**KAYA** *Island ILPS 9517*	**4**	24
16 Dec 78	**BABYLON BY BUS** *Island ISLD 11*	**40**	11
13 Oct 79	**SURVIVAL** *Island ILPS 9542*	**20**	6
28 Jun 80	⬤ **UPRISING** *Island ILPS 9596*	**6**	17
28 May 83	⬤ **CONFRONTATION** *Island ILPS 9760*	**5**	19
19 May 84	★ **LEGEND – THE BEST OF BOB MARLEY AND THE WAILERS** *Tuff Gong BMWX 1* ■	**1**	339
28 Jul 86	**REBEL MUSIC** *Island ILPS 9843*	**54**	3
3 Oct 92	**SONGS OF FREEDOM** *Tuff Gong TGCBX 1* [1]	**10**	5
3 Jun 95	⬤ **NATURAL MYSTIC** *Tuff Gong BMWCD 2*	**5**	8
4 Sep 99	**THE SUN IS SHINING** *Club Tools CLU 66730* [2]	**40**	3
2 Jun 01	⬤ **ONE LOVE – THE VERY BEST OF BOB MARLEY & THE WAILERS** *Tuff Gong BMWCD 3*	**5**	15
7 Jul 01	**LIVELY UP YOURSELF** *Music Collection 12691* [1]	**75**	1
10 Nov 01	**ONE LOVE – THE VERY BEST OF BOB MARLEY & THE WAILERS** *Tuff Gong 5865512*	**24**	8
5 Jun 04	**ROOTS OF A LEGEND** *Trojan TJODX 176*	**51**	2

[1] Bob Marley vs Funkstar De Luxe [2] Bob Marley featuring Lauryn Hill [3] Bob Marley featuring MC Lyte [1] Bob Marley [2] Bob Marley vs Funkstar De Luxe

'No Woman No Cry' on first chart visit made No.22 before making its peak position on re-entry in Jun 1981. 'Exodus' on Tuff Gong TGX 3 listed with 'Why Should I' only from 5 Dec 1992, and is a different version from the Island hit. It peaked at No.53. 'The Sun is Shining' is an import single that was too long to be eligible for the singles chart. 'Live!' returned to the chart in 1981 under the title 'Live at the Lyceum'. 'One Love – The Very Best of Bob Marley and the Wailers' (10 Nov 2001) is a repackaged version of the 2 Jun 2001 album and includes a bonus CD of rare tracks

Ziggy MARLEY and the MELODY MAKERS *Jamaica, male / female vocal / instrumental group (Singles: 11 Weeks)* pos/wks

11 Jun 88	**TOMORROW PEOPLE** *Virgin VS 1049*	**22**	10
23 Sep 89	**LOOK WHO'S DANCING** *Virgin America VUS 5*	**65**	1

Lene MARLIN *Norway, female vocalist – Lene Marlin Pederson (Singles: 20 Weeks, Albums: 34 Weeks)* pos/wks

11 Mar 00	⬤ **SITTING DOWN HERE** *Virgin DINSD 183*	**5**	11
16 Sep 00	**UNFORGIVABLE SINNER** *Virgin DINSD 202*	**13**	6
13 Jan 01	**WHERE I'M HEADED** *Virgin DINSD 196*	**31**	2
4 Oct 03	**YOU WEREN'T THERE** *Virgin DINSD 262*	**59**	1
25 Mar 00	**PLAYING MY GAME** *Virgin CDVIR 83*	**18**	34

MARLO
UK, male vocal / instrumental group (Singles: 1 Week) pos/wks

24 Jul 99	**HOW DO I KNOW?** *Polydor 5611362*	**56**	1

MARLY *Denmark, female vocalist (Singles: 2 Weeks)* pos/wks

28 Aug 04	**YOU NEVER KNOW** *All Around the World CDGLOBE 363*	**23**	2

MARMALADE *UK, male vocal / instrumental group – includes Junior Campbell (Singles: 130 Weeks)* pos/wks

22 May 68	⬤ **LOVIN' THINGS** *CBS 3412*	**6**	13
23 Oct 68	**WAIT FOR ME MARY-ANNE** *CBS 3708*	**30**	5
4 Dec 68	★ **OB-LA-DI, OB-LA-DA** *CBS 3892*	**1**	20
11 Jun 69	⬤ **BABY MAKE IT SOON** *CBS 4287*	**9**	13
20 Dec 69	⬤ **REFLECTIONS OF MY LIFE** *Decca F 12982*	**3**	12
18 Jul 70	⬤ **RAINBOW** *Decca F 13035*	**3**	14
27 Mar 71	⬤ **MY LITTLE ONE** *Decca F 13135*	**15**	11
4 Sep 71	⬤ **COUSIN NORMAN** *Decca F 13214*	**6**	11
27 Nov 71	**BACK ON THE ROAD (re)** *Decca F 13251*	**35**	8
1 Apr 72	⬤ **RADANCER** *Decca F 13297*	**6**	12
21 Feb 76	⬤ **FALLING APART AT THE SEAMS** *Target TGT 105*	**9**	11

MARMION *Spain / Holland, male instrumental / production duo (Singles: 2 Weeks)* pos/wks

18 May 96	**SCHONEBERG** *Hooj Choons HOOJCD 43*	**53**	1
14 Feb 98	**SCHONEBERG (re-mix)** *ffrr FCD 324*	**56**	1

MAROON5 *US, male vocal / instrumental group (Singles: 33 Weeks, Albums: 45 Weeks)* pos/wks

31 Jan 04	**HARDER TO BREATHE** *J 82876566922*	**13**	7
1 May 04	⬤ **THIS LOVE** *J 82876608452*	**3**	14
4 Sep 04	⬤ **SHE WILL BE LOVED** *J 82876643632*	**4**	10
18 Dec 04	**SUNDAY MORNING** *J 82876668042*	**27**	2+
31 Jan 04	★ **SONGS ABOUT JANE** *J 82876584302*	**1**	45+

Johnny MARR See Billy BRAGG; ELECTRONIC; Kirsty MacCOLL; The SMITHS

MARRADONA
UK, male DJ / production group (Singles: 5 Weeks) pos/wks

26 Feb 94	**OUT OF MY HEAD** *Peach PWCD 282*	**38**	3
26 Jul 97	**OUT OF MY HEAD 97 (re-mix)** *Soopa SPCD 1*	**39**	2

Neville MARRINER and the ACADEMY OF ST MARTIN IN THE FIELDS
UK, male conductor and chamber orchestra (Albums: 6 Weeks) pos/wks

6 Apr 85	**AMADEUS (FILM SOUNDTRACK)** *London LONDP 6*	**64**	6

M/A/R/R/S
UK, male instrumental / production group (Singles: 14 Weeks) pos/wks

5 Sep 87	★ **PUMP UP THE VOLUME / ANITINA (THE FIRST TIME I SEE SHE DANCE)** *4AD AD 70*	**1**	14

The MARS VOLTA *US, male vocal / instrumental group (Singles: 3 Weeks, Albums: 1 Week)* pos/wks

11 Oct 03	**INERTIATIC ESP** *Universal MCSTD 40332*	**42**	2
13 Mar 04	**TELEVATORS** *Universal MCSTD 40352*	**41**	1
5 Jul 03	**DE-LOUSED IN THE COMATORIUM** *Universal 9860460*	**43**	1

Bernie MARSDEN (see also WHITESNAKE)
UK, male vocalist / instrumentalist – guitar (Albums: 2 Weeks) pos/wks

5 Sep 81	**LOOK AT ME NOW** *Parlophone PCF 7217*	**71**	2

Gerry MARSDEN See The CHRISTIANS; GERRY and the PACEMAKERS; Holly JOHNSON; Paul McCARTNEY; STOCK AITKEN WATERMAN

Matthew MARSDEN
UK, male actor / vocalist (Singles: 10 Weeks)   pos/wks

| 11 Jul 98 | THE HEART'S LONE DESIRE *Columbia 6661152* | **13** 7 |
| 7 Nov 98 | SHE'S GONE *Columbia 6664915* [1] | **24** 3 |

[1] Matthew Marsden featuring Destiny's Child

Kym MARSH (see also HEAR'SAY)
UK, female vocalist (Singles: 21 Weeks, Albums: 3 Weeks)   pos/wks

19 Apr 03 ●	CRY *Island MCSTD 40314*	**2** 12
19 Jul 03 ●	COME ON OVER *Universal MCSTD 40323*	**10** 7
8 Nov 03	SENTIMENTAL *Universal MCSTD 40340*	**35** 2
2 Aug 03 ●	STANDING TALL *Universal 9800035*	**9** 3

Stevie MARSH *UK, female vocalist (Singles: 4 Weeks)*   pos/wks

| 4 Dec 59 | IF YOU WERE THE ONLY BOY IN THE WORLD (re) *Decca F 11181* | **24** 4 |

MARSHA See SHAGGY

Amanda MARSHALL *Canada, female vocalist (Albums: 2 Weeks)*   pos/wks

| 3 Aug 96 | AMANDA MARSHALL *Epic 4837912* | **47** 2 |

Joy MARSHALL *UK, female vocalist (Singles: 2 Weeks)*   pos/wks

| 23 Jun 66 | THE MORE I SEE YOU *Decca F 12422* | **34** 2 |

Keith MARSHALL *UK, male vocalist (Singles: 10 Weeks)*   pos/wks

| 4 Apr 81 | ONLY CRYING *Arrival PIK 2* | **12** 10 |

Louise Clare MARSHALL See SILICONE SOUL featuring Louise Clare MARSHALL

Wayne MARSHALL *UK, male vocalist (Singles: 7 Weeks)*   pos/wks

1 Oct 94	OOH AAH (G-SPOT) *Soultown SOULCDS 322*	**29** 3
3 Jun 95	SPIRIT *Soultown SOULCDS 00352*	**58** 1
24 Feb 96	NEVER KNEW LOVE LIKE THIS *Sony S2 6629382* [1]	**40** 2
7 Dec 96	G SPOT (re-mix) *MBA INTER 9006*	**50** 1

[1] Pauline Henry featuring Wayne Marshall

MARSHALL HAIN *UK, male / female vocal / instrumental*
duo – Julian Marshall and Kit Hain (Singles: 19 Weeks)   pos/wks

| 3 Jun 78 ● | DANCING IN THE CITY *Harvest HAR 5157* | **3** 15 |
| 14 Oct 78 | COMING HOME *Harvest HAR 5168* | **39** 4 |

MARTAY featuring ZZ TOP *UK, female rapper – Melone*
McKenzy and US, male vocal / instrumental trio (Singles: 2 Weeks) pos/wks

| 16 Oct 99 | GIMME ALL YOUR LOVIN' 2000 *Riverhorse RIVHCD 2* | **28** 2 |

Lena MARTELL *UK, female vocalist – Helen*
Thomson (Singles: 18 Weeks, Albums: 71 Weeks)   pos/wks

29 Sep 79 ★	ONE DAY AT A TIME *Pye 7N 46021*	**1** 18
25 May 74	THAT WONDERFUL SOUND OF LENA MARTELL *Pye SPL 18427*	**35** 2
8 Jan 77	THE BEST OF LENA MARTELL *Pye NSPL 18506*	**13** 16
27 May 78	THE LENA MARTELL COLLECTION *Ronco RTL 2028*	**12** 19
20 Oct 79 ●	LENA'S MUSIC ALBUM *Pye N 123*	**4** 18
19 Apr 80 ●	BY REQUEST *Ronco RTL 2046*	**9** 9
29 Nov 80	BEAUTIFUL SUNDAY *Ronco RTL 2052*	**23** 7

MARTHA and the MUFFINS (see also M + M) *Canada, female /*
male vocal / instrumental group (Singles: 10 Weeks, Albums: 6 Weeks) pos/wks

| 1 Mar 80 ● | ECHO BEACH *DinDisc DIN 9* | **10** 10 |
| 15 Mar 80 | METRO MUSIC *DinDisc DID 1* | **34** 6 |

MARTHA and the VANDELLAS See Martha REEVES and the VANDELLAS

MARTIKA *US, female vocalist – Marta*
Marrera (Singles: 57 Weeks, Albums: 52 Weeks)   pos/wks

29 Jul 89 ●	TOY SOLDIERS *CBS 655049 7* ▲	**5** 11
14 Oct 89 ●	I FEEL THE EARTH MOVE *CBS 655294 7*	**7** 14
13 Jan 90	MORE THAN YOU KNOW *CBS 655526 7*	**15** 7
17 Mar 90	WATER *CBS 655731 7*	**59** 3

17 Aug 91 ●	LOVE ... THY WILL BE DONE *Columbia 6573137*	**9** 9
30 Nov 91	MARTIKA'S KITCHEN *Columbia 6575687*	**17** 10
22 Feb 92	COLOURED KISSES *Columbia 6577097*	**41** 3
16 Sep 89	MARTIKA *CBS 463355 1*	**11** 37
7 Sep 91	MARTIKA'S KITCHEN *Columbia 4671891*	**15** 15

Billie Ray MARTIN *Germany, female vocalist –*
Birgit Dieckmann (Singles: 20 Weeks, Albums: 2 Weeks)   pos/wks

19 Nov 94	YOUR LOVING ARMS *Magnet MAG 1028CD*	**38** 3
20 May 95 ●	YOUR LOVING ARMS (re-mix) *Magnet MAG 1031CD*	**6** 10
2 Sep 95	RUNNING AROUND TOWN *Magnet MAG 1035CD*	**29** 2
6 Jan 96	IMITATION OF LIFE *Magnet MAG 1040CD*	**29** 3
6 Apr 96	SPACE OASIS *Magnet MAG 1042CD*	**66** 1
21 Aug 99	HONEY *React CDREACT 129*	**54** 1
3 Feb 96	DEADLINE FOR MY MEMORIES *Magnet 630121802*	**47** 2

Dean MARTIN (290 Top 500) (see also The RATPACK)
Acclaimed vocalist / entertainer / film actor and cabaret performer. b. Dino Crocetti, 7 Jun 1917, Ohio, US, d. 25 Dec 1995. He first found fame partnering Jerry Lewis (1946-56), and had a long and successful solo career. He was a member of Frank Sinatra's 'Rat Pack' and has an impressive 51-year chart span (Singles: 163 Weeks, Albums: 64 Weeks)   pos/wks

18 Sep 53 ●	KISS (re) *Capitol CL 13893*	**5** 8
22 Jan 54 ●	THAT'S AMORE *Capitol CL 14008*	**2** 11
1 Oct 54 ●	SWAY *Capitol CL 14138*	**6** 7
22 Oct 54	HOW DO YOU SPEAK TO AN ANGEL (re) *Capitol CL 14150*	**15** 6
28 Jan 55 ●	THE NAUGHTY LADY OF SHADY LANE *Capitol CL 14226.*	**5** 10
4 Feb 55	MAMBO ITALIANO *Capitol CL 14227*	**14** 2
25 Feb 55 ●	LET ME GO, LOVER *Capitol CL 14226*	**3** 9
1 Apr 55	UNDER THE BRIDGES OF PARIS *Capitol CL 14255*	**6** 8
10 Feb 56 ★	MEMORIES ARE MADE OF THIS *Capitol CL 14523* ▲	**1** 16
2 Mar 56	YOUNG AND FOOLISH *Capitol CL 14519*	**20** 1
27 Apr 56	INNAMORATA *Capitol CL 14507*	**21** 3
22 Mar 57	THE MAN WHO PLAYS THE MANDOLINO *Capitol CL 14690*	**21** 2
13 Jun 58 ●	RETURN TO ME *Capitol CL 14844*	**2** 22
29 Aug 58 ●	VOLARE (NEL BLU DIPINTO DI BLU) *Capitol CL 14910*	**2** 14
27 Aug 64	EVERYBODY LOVES SOMEBODY *Reprise R 20281* ▲	**11** 13
12 Nov 64	THE DOOR IS STILL OPEN TO MY HEART *Reprise R 20307*	**42** 4
5 Feb 69 ●	GENTLE ON MY MIND (re) *Reprise RS 23343*	**2** 24
22 Jun 96	THAT'S AMORE (re-issue) *EMI Premier PRESCD 3*	**43** 2
21 Aug 99	SWAY (re-issue) *Capitol CDSWAY 001*	**66** 1
13 May 61	THIS TIME I'M SWINGIN'I *Capitol T 1442*	**18** 1
25 Feb 67	AT EASE WITH DEAN *Reprise RSLP 6322*	**35** 1
4 Nov 67	WELCOME TO MY WORLD *Philips DBL 001*	**39** 1
12 Oct 68	DEAN MARTIN'S GREATEST HITS VOLUME 1 *Reprise RSLP 6301*	**40** 1
22 Feb 69 ●	GENTLE ON MY MIND *Reprise RSLP 6330*	**9** 8
22 Feb 69 ●	THE BEST OF DEAN MARTIN *Capitol ST 21194*	**9** 1
27 Nov 71	WHITE CHRISTMAS *MFP 524* [1]	**45** 1
13 Nov 76 ●	20 ORIGINAL DEAN MARTIN HITS *Reprise K 54066*	**7** 11
5 Jun 99 ●	THE VERY BEST OF DEAN MARTIN – THE CAPITOL & REPRISE YEARS *EMI 4967212*	**5** 29
26 Aug 00	THE VERY BEST OF DEAN MARTIN VOLUME 2 – THE CAPITOL & REPRISE YEARS *Capitol 5277712*	**40** 2
16 Feb 02	LOVE SONGS *Capitol 5377482*	**24** 3
10 Jan 04	VERY BEST OF DEAN MARTIN *EMI 5920802*	**59** 2
18 Sep 04	DINO – THE ESSENTIAL DEAN MARTIN *EMI 8665272*	**25** 3

[1] Nat 'King' Cole and Dean Martin

George MARTIN
(see also The BEATLES) *UK, male producer (Albums: 13 Weeks)*   pos/wks

| 4 Apr 98 ● | IN MY LIFE *Echo ECHCD 20* | **5** 13 |

Juan MARTIN *Spain, male instrumentalist –*
guitar (Singles: 7 Weeks, Albums: 9 Weeks)   pos/wks

| 28 Jan 84 ● | LOVE THEME FROM 'THE THORN BIRDS' *WEA X 9518* | **10** 7 |
| 11 Feb 84 | SERENADE *K-Tel NE 1267* [1] | **21** 9 |

[1] Juan Martin and the Royal Philharmonic Orchestra

Linda MARTIN *Ireland, female vocalist (Singles: 2 Weeks)*   pos/wks

| 30 May 92 | WHY ME *Columbia 6581317* | **59** 2 |

Luci MARTIN See Romina JOHNSON

Marilyn MARTIN See Phil COLLINS

Ray MARTIN and his CHORUS and ORCHESTRA
(see also Lee LAWRENCE) *UK, orchestra – leader*
b. 11 Oct 1918, d. 7 Feb 1988 (Singles: 11 Weeks) pos/wks

14 Nov 52 ●	BLUE TANGO (re) *Columbia DB 3051* 8	4
4 Dec 53 ●	SWEDISH RHAPSODY (re) *Columbia DB 3346* 4	4
15 Jun 56	THE CAROUSEL WALTZ (re) *Columbia DB 3771* 24	3

Ricky MARTIN 483 Top 500
Bon-bon shaking, ex-boy band singer and soap star, b. Enrique Martin Morales, 24 Dec 1971, Puerto Rico. The performer who put the Latin into platinum sold 15 million copies of his eponymous album, recorded the world's biggest-selling football single ('The Cup of Life') and has the world's biggest-selling Spanish language album ('Vuelve'). Biggest-selling UK single: 'Livin' La Vida Loca' 775,700 (Singles: 75 Weeks, Albums: 75 Weeks) pos/wks

20 Sep 97 ●	(UN, DOS, TRES) MARIA *Columbia 6649595* 6	6
11 Jul 98	THE CUP OF LIFE *Columbia 6661502* 29	3
17 Jul 99 ★	LIVIN' LA VIDA LOCA *Columbia 6676402* ■ ▲ 1	17
20 Nov 99	SHAKE YOUR BON-BON *Columbia 6683412* 12	9
29 Apr 00 ●	PRIVATE EMOTION *Columbia 6692692* [1] 9	9
4 Nov 00 ●	SHE BANGS *Columbia 6705422* 3	15
10 Mar 01 ●	NOBODY WANTS TO BE LONELY *Columbia 6709462* [2] 4	12
28 Jul 01	LOADED *Columbia 6714642* 19	4
12 Jun 99 ●	RICKY MARTIN *Columbia 4944060* ▲ 2	48
18 Nov 00	SOUND LOADED *Columbia 4977692* 14	21
1 Dec 01	THE BEST OF RICKY MARTIN *Columbia 5050192* 42	6

[1] Ricky Martin featuring Meja [2] Ricky Martin and Christina Aguilera

Tony MARTIN
US, male vocalist – Alvin Morris Jr. (Singles: 28 Weeks) pos/wks

22 Apr 55 ●	STRANGER IN PARADISE *HMV B 10849* 6	13
13 Jul 56 ●	WALK HAND IN HAND *HMV POP 222* 2	15

Both with Hugo Winterhalter's Orchestra and Chorus

Vince MARTIN *See The TARRIERS*

Wink MARTINDALE
US, male vocalist – Winston Conrad Martindale (Singles: 41 Weeks) pos/wks

4 Dec 59 ●	DECK OF CARDS (3re) *London HLD 8962* 5	29
20 Oct 73	DECK OF CARDS (re-issue) *Dot DOT 109* 22	12

'Deck of Cards' on the London label made No.18 in 1959, re-entering at No.28 in Jan 1960, again at No.45 in Mar 1960 before making No.5 with the third re-entry in Apr 1963

Alice MARTINEAU
UK, female vocalist, b. 8 Jun 1972, d. 6 Mar 2003 (Singles: 1 Week) pos/wks

23 Nov 02	IF I FALL *Epic 6732332* 45	1

Angie MARTINEZ featuring LIL' MO & SACARIO
US, female vocal / rap trio (Singles: 1 Week) pos/wks

15 Feb 03	IF I COULD GO! *Elektra E 7331CD* 61	1

Al MARTINO *US, male vocalist – Alfred Cini (Singles: 87 Weeks)* pos/wks

14 Nov 52 ★	HERE IN MY HEART *Capitol CL 13779* ▲ 1	18
21 Nov 52 ●	TAKE MY HEART *Capitol CL 13769* 9	1
30 Jan 53 ●	NOW *Capitol CL 13835* 3	12
10 Jul 53 ●	RACHEL (re) *Capitol CL 13879* 10	5
4 Jun 54 ●	WANTED (2re) *Capitol CL 14128* 4	16
1 Oct 54 ●	THE STORY OF TINA *Capitol CL 14163* 10	8
23 Sep 55	THE MAN FROM LARAMIE (re) *Capitol CL 14343* 19	3
31 Mar 60	SUMMERTIME *Top Rank JAR 312* 49	1
29 Aug 63	I LOVE YOU BECAUSE *Capitol CL 15300* 48	1
22 Aug 70 ●	SPANISH EYES (re) *Capitol CL 15430* 5	22

'Spanish Eyes' peaked only at No.49 in 1970 before re-entering in Jul 1973 to make No.5

John MARTYN
UK, male vocalist / instrumentalist – guitar (Albums: 30 Weeks) pos/wks

4 Feb 78	ONE WORLD *Island ILPS 9492* 54	1
1 Nov 80	GRACE AND DANGER *Island ILPS 9560* 54	2
26 Sep 81	GLORIOUS FOOL *Geffen K 99178* 25	7
4 Sep 82	WELL KEPT SECRET *WEA K 99255* 20	7

17 Nov 84	SAPPHIRE *Island ILPS 9779* 57	2
8 Mar 86	PIECE BY PIECE *Island ILPS 9807* 28	4
10 Oct 92	COULDN'T LOVE YOU MORE *Permanent PERMCD 9* 65	2
10 Aug 96	AND *Go Discs 8287982* 32	3
4 Apr 98	THE CHURCH WITH ONE BELL *Independiente ISOM 3CD* 51	1
3 Jun 00	GLASGOW WALKER *Independiente ISOM 15CD* 66	1

The MARVELETTES *US, female vocal group (Singles: 10 Weeks)* pos/wks

15 Jun 67	WHEN YOU'RE YOUNG AND IN LOVE *Tamla Motown TMG 609* ..13	10

MARVIN and TAMARA *UK, male / female vocal duo –*
Marvin Simmonds and Tamara Nicole (Singles: 9 Weeks) pos/wks

7 Aug 99	GROOVE MACHINE *Epic 6675582* 11	5
25 Dec 99	NORTH, SOUTH, EAST, WEST *Epic 6684902* 38	4

Hank MARVIN (see also MARVIN, WELCH and FARRAR; The SHADOWS)
UK, male vocalist / instrumentalist – guitar –
Brian Rankin (Singles: 36 Weeks, Albums: 72 Weeks) pos/wks

13 Sep 69 ●	THROW DOWN A LINE *Columbia DB 8615* [1] 7	9
21 Feb 70	THE JOY OF LIVING *Columbia DB 8657* [1] 25	8
6 Mar 82	DON'T TALK *Polydor POSP 420* 49	4
22 Mar 86 ★	LIVING DOLL *WEA YZ 65* [2] 1	11
7 Jan 89	LONDON KID *Polydor PO 32* [3] 52	3
17 Oct 92	WE ARE THE CHAMPIONS *PolyGram TV PO 229* [4] 66	1
22 Nov 69	HANK MARVIN *Columbia SCX 6352* 14	2
20 Mar 82	WORDS AND MUSIC *Polydor POLD 5054* 66	3
31 Oct 92	INTO THE LIGHT *Polydor 5171482* 18	10
20 Nov 93	HEARTBEAT *PolyGram TV 52132222* 17	9
22 Oct 94	THE BEST OF HANK MARVIN AND THE SHADOWS *PolyGram TV 5238212* [1] 19	11
18 Nov 95	HANK PLAYS CLIFF *PolyGram TV 5294262* 33	7
23 Nov 96	HANK PLAYS HOLLY *PolyGram TV 5337132* 34	7
5 Apr 97	HANK PLAYS LIVE *PolyGram TV 5374282* 71	1
22 Nov 97	PLAY ANDREW LLOYD WEBBER AND TIM RICE *PolyGram TV 5394792* [1] 41	6
14 Nov 98	VERY BEST OF HANK MARVIN AND THE SHADOWS – THE FIRST 40 YEARS *PolyGram TV 5592112* [1] 56	5
15 Apr 00	MARVIN AT THE MOVIES *Universal Music TV 1570572* 17	5
20 Apr 02 ●	GUITAR PLAYER *UMTV 171242* 10	6

[1] Cliff and Hank [2] Cliff Richard and the Young Ones featuring Hank B Marvin
[3] Jean-Michel Jarre featuring Hank Marvin [4] Hank Marvin featuring Brian May
[1] Hank Marvin and The Shadows

Lee MARVIN *US, male actor / vocalist,*
b. 19 Feb 1924, d. 28 Aug 1987 (Singles: 23 Weeks) pos/wks

7 Feb 70 ★	WAND'RIN' STAR (2re) *Paramount PARA 3004* 1	23

'I Talk to the Trees' by Clint Eastwood, the flip side of 'Wand'rin' Star', was listed for 7 Feb and 14 Feb 1970 only

MARVIN THE PARANOID ANDROID
UK, male robot (Singles: 4 Weeks) pos/wks

16 May 81	MARVIN *Polydor POSP 261* 53	4

MARVIN, WELCH and FARRAR (see also Hank MARVIN; The SHADOWS)
UK, male vocal / instrumental group (Albums: 4 Weeks) pos/wks

3 Apr 71	MARVIN, WELCH AND FARRAR *Regal Zonophone SRZA 8502* ..30	4

Richard MARX
US, male vocalist (Singles: 75 Weeks, Albums: 42 Weeks) pos/wks

27 Feb 88	SHOULD'VE KNOWN BETTER *Manhattan MT 32* 50	5
14 May 88	ENDLESS SUMMER NIGHTS *Manhattan MT 39* 50	3
17 Jun 89	SATISFIED *EMI-USA MT 64* ▲ 52	4
2 Sep 89 ●	RIGHT HERE WAITING *EMI-USA MT 72* ▲ 2	10
11 Nov 89	ANGELIA *EMI-USA MT 74* 45	4
24 Mar 90	TOO LATE TO SAY GOODBYE *EMI-USA MT 80* 38	3
7 Jul 90	CHILDREN OF THE NIGHT *EMI-USA MT 84* 54	2
1 Sep 90	ENDLESS SUMMER NIGHTS / HOLD ON TO THE NIGHTS (re-issue) *EMI-USA MT 89* 60	2
19 Oct 91	KEEP COMING BACK *Capitol CL 634* 55	2
9 May 92 ●	HAZARD *Capitol CL 654* 3	15
29 Aug 92	TAKE THIS HEART *Capitol CL 667* 13	6
28 Nov 92	CHAINS AROUND MY HEART *Capitol CL 676* 29	6
29 Jan 94	NOW AND FOREVER *Capitol CDCLS 703* 13	6

MICK HUCKNALL TOP 10

The gospel according to Mick Hucknall, who chooses his favourite singles and albums

Simply Red's Mick Hucknall, whose Stars album was the biggest seller in 1991 and 1992, plumps for the 10 least disposable singles and albums from his collection, including the 2005 Simply Dread compilation for which he has put the track listing together.

SINGLES	ALBUMS
single – act – (peak position)	album – act – (peak position)
BROWN SUGAR The Rolling Stones (2)	**ASTRAL WEEKS *** Van Morrison
CROSSTOWN TRAFFIC The Jimi Hendrix Experience (37)	**A HARD DAY'S NIGHT** The Beatles (1)
DRIVE-IN SATURDAY David Bowie (3)	**INNERVISIONS** Stevie Wonder (8)
HIGHER GROUND Stevie Wonder (29)	**KIND OF BLUE** Miles Davis (63)
I SAY A LITTLE PRAYER Aretha Franklin (4)	**LED ZEPPELIN II** Led Zeppelin (1)
MAGGIE MAY Rod Stewart (1)	**REVOLVER** The Beatles (1)
METAL GURU T. Rex (1)	**SGT. PEPPER'S LONELY HEARTS CLUB BAND** The Beatles (1)
RAINY NIGHT IN GEORGIA * Brook Benton	**BLOOD AND FIRE COMPILATION **** Simply Dread
STRAWBERRY FIELDS FOREVER The Beatles (2)	**STICKY FINGERS** The Rolling Stones (1)
WHAT'S GOING ON ** Marvin Gaye	**WHAT'S GOING ON** Marvin Gaye (56)

* Did not chart

** Failed to chart as a single. See 'The Hits That Never Were' on page 481

* Did not chart

** For release in 2005

---

30 Apr 94	**SILENT SCREAM** Capitol CDCLS 714	**32**	4
13 Aug 94	**THE WAY SHE LOVES ME** Capitol CDCL 721	**38**	3
9 Apr 88	**RICHARD MARX** Manhattan MTL 1017	**68**	2
20 May 89 ●	**REPEAT OFFENDER** EMI-USA MTL 1043 ▲	**8**	12
16 Nov 91 ●	**RUSH STREET** Capitol ESTU 2158	**7**	20
19 Feb 94	**PAID VACATION** Capitol CDESTU 2208	**11**	5
21 Feb 98	**GREATEST HITS** Capitol 8219142	**34**	3

MARXMAN UK / Ireland, rap / instrumental group (Singles: 5 Weeks, Albums: 1 Week)

		pos/wks	
6 Mar 93	**ALL ABOUT EVE** Talkin Loud TLKCD 35	**28**	4
1 May 93	**SHIP AHOY** Talkin Loud TLKCD 39	**64**	1
3 Apr 93	**33 REVOLUTIONS PER MINUTE** Talkin Loud 5145382	**69**	1

Sinead O'Connor provides uncredited vocals on 'Ship Ahoy'

MARY JANE GIRLS

US, female vocal group (Singles: 15 Weeks, Albums: 9 Weeks)

		pos/wks	
21 May 83	**CANDY MAN** Motown TMG 1301	**60**	4
25 Jun 83	**ALL NIGHT LONG** Gordy TMG 1309	**13**	9
8 Oct 83	**BOYS** Gordy TMG 1315	**74**	1
18 Feb 95	**ALL NIGHT LONG (re-mix)** Motown TMGCD 1436	**51**	1
28 May 83	**MARY JANE GIRLS** Gordy STML 12189	**51**	9

MARY MARY

US, female vocal duo – Erica and Tina Atkins (Singles: 14 Weeks)

		pos/wks	
10 Jun 00 ●	**SHACKLES (PRAISE YOU)** Columbia 6694202	**5**	12
18 Nov 00	**I SINGS** Columbia 6699742	**32**	2

Carolyne MAS US, female vocalist (Singles: 2 Weeks)

		pos/wks	
2 Feb 80	**QUOTE GOODBYE QUOTE** Mercury 6167 873	**71**	2

MASAI UK, female vocal duo – Sharon Amos and Anna Crane (Singles: 1 Week)

		pos/wks	
1 Mar 03	**DO THAT THING** Concept CDCON 36	**42**	1

MA$E US, male rapper – Mason Betha
(Singles: 55 Weeks, Albums: 10 Weeks)

		pos/wks	
29 Mar 97	**CAN'T NOBODY HOLD ME DOWN** Arista 74321464552 [1] ▲	**19**	4
9 Aug 97 ●	**MO MONEY MO PROBLEMS** Puff Daddy 74321492492 [2] ▲	**6**	10
27 Dec 97 ●	**FEEL SO GOOD** Puff Daddy 74321526442	**10**	8
18 Apr 98	**WHAT YOU WANT** Puff Daddy 74321578772 [3]	**15**	5
19 Sep 98	**HORSE AND CARRIAGE** Epic 6662612 [4]	**12**	4
10 Oct 98 ●	**TOP OF THE WORLD (re)** Atlantic AT 0046CD [5]	**2**	9
12 Dec 98 ●	**TAKE ME THERE** Interscope IND 95620 [6]	**7**	9

Singles re-entries are listed as (re), (2re), (3re).... which signifies that the hit re-entered the chart once, twice or three times...

					pos/wks
10 Jul 99		GET READY *Puff Daddy / Arista 74321682602* [7]		....	**32** 4
20 Nov 04		WELCOME BACK / BREATHE, STRETCH, SHAKE			
		Bad Boy MCSTD 40392			**29** 2
24 Jan 98		HARLEM WORLD *Puff Daddy 78612730172* ▲			**53** 7
24 Jul 99		DOUBLE UP *Puff Daddy 74321674332*			**47** 2
4 Sep 04		WELCOME BACK *Bad Boy 9863122*			**68** 1

[1] Puff Daddy featuring Ma$e [2] Notorious B.I.G. featuring Puff Daddy and Ma$e [3] Ma$e featuring Total [4] Cam'ron featuring Ma$e [5] Brandy featuring Ma$e [6] BLACKstreet and Mya featuring Ma$e and Blinky Blink [7] Ma$e featuring BLACKstreet

MASH
US, male vocal / instrumental group (Singles: 12 Weeks)   pos/wks

10 May 80	★ THEME FROM M*A*S*H (SUICIDE IS PAINLESS) *CBS 8536*	......**1** 12

MASH!
UK / US, male / female vocal group (Singles: 3 Weeks)   pos/wks

21 May 94	U DON'T HAVE TO SAY U LOVE ME *React CDREACT 37*	.........**37** 2
4 Feb 95	LET'S SPEND THE NIGHT TOGETHER *Playa CDXPLAYA 2*	...**66** 1

MASH UP See Matt DAREY

MASHONDA See CASSIDY

MASON See CHICANE

Barbara MASON *US, female vocalist (Singles: 5 Weeks)*   pos/wks

21 Jan 84	ANOTHER MAN *Streetwave KHAN 3*	....**45** 5

Glen MASON
UK, male vocalist – Tommy Lennon (Singles: 7 Weeks)   pos/wks

28 Sep 56	GLENDORA *Parlophone R 4203*	....................................**28** 2
16 Nov 56	THE GREEN DOOR *Parlophone R 4244*	.............................**24** 5

John MASON *UK, male instrumentalist (Albums: 1 Week)*   pos/wks

27 Dec 75	STRINGS OF SCOTLAND *Philips 6382 108*	..................**50** 1

Mary MASON *UK, female vocalist (Singles: 6 Weeks)*   pos/wks

8 Oct 77	ANGEL OF THE MORNING – ANY WAY THAT YOU	
	WANT ME (MEDLEY) *Epic EPC 5552*	...........................**27** 6

MASQUERADE
UK, male / female vocal group (Singles: 10 Weeks)   pos/wks

11 Jan 86	ONE NATION *Streetwave KHAN 59*	....**54** 6
5 Jul 86	(SOLUTION TO) THE PROBLEM (re) *Streetwave KHAN 67*	......**64** 4

MASS ORDER *US, male vocal / instrumental duo –*
Eugene Hanes and Marc Valentine (Singles: 5 Weeks)   pos/wks

14 Mar 92	LIFT EVERY VOICE (TAKE ME AWAY) *Columbia 6577487*	.........**35** 3
23 May 92	LET'S GET HAPPY *Columbia 6580737*	......................................**45** 2

MASS PRODUCTION
US, male vocal / instrumental group (Singles: 7 Weeks)   pos/wks

12 Mar 77	WELCOME TO OUR WORLD (OF MERRY MUSIC)	
	Atlantic K 10898	....**44** 3
17 May 80	SHANTE *Atlantic K 11475*	....**59** 4

MASS SYNDICATE featuring Su Su BOBIEN
US, male producer and US, female vocalist (Singles: 1 Week)   pos/wks

24 Oct 98	YOU DON'T KNOW *ffrr FCD 347*	....**71** 1

MASSED WELSH CHOIRS
UK, male voice choir (Albums: 7 Weeks)   pos/wks

9 Aug 69	● CYMANSA GANN *BBC REC 53M*	....**5** 7

Zeitia MASSIAH *UK, female vocalist (Singles: 2 Weeks)*   pos/wks

12 Mar 94	I SPECIALIZE IN LOVE *Union City UCRCD 27* [1]	....................**74** 1
24 Sep 94	THIS IS THE PLACE *Virgin VSCDT 1511*	...............................**62** 1

[1] Arizona featuring Zeitia

MASSIEL
Spain, female vocalist – Maria Espinosa (Singles: 4 Weeks)   pos/wks

24 Apr 68	LA LA LA *Philips BF 1667*	....**35** 4

MASSIVE ATTACK (233) Top 500
(see also Shara NELSON; NICOLETTE) *Trip hop titans who emerged from Bristol's legendary Wild Bunch: mainstays Robert '3D' Del Naja (v), Grant 'Daddy-G' Marshall (v) and Andrew 'Mushroom' Vowles (k). Brit-nominated band entered the European chart at No.1 in 2003 with '100th Window' (which featured Del Naja only) (Singles: 44 Weeks, Albums: 223 Weeks)*   pos/wks

23 Feb 91		UNFINISHED SYMPATHY *Wild Bunch WBRS 2* [1]		...............**13** 9
8 Jun 91		SAFE FROM HARM *Wild Bunch WBRS 3*		...........................**25** 4
22 Feb 92		MASSIVE ATTACK (EP) *Wild Bunch WBRS 4*		....................**27** 4
29 Oct 94		SLY *Wild Bunch WBRDX 5*		....**24** 4
21 Jan 95		PROTECTION *Wild Bunch WBRX 6* [2]		...........................**14** 4
1 Apr 95		KARMACOMA *Wild Bunch WBRX 7*		...............................**28** 4
19 Jul 97		RISINGSON *Circa WBRX 8*		....**11** 3
9 May 98	●	TEARDROP *Virgin WBRX 9*		....**10** 6
25 Jul 98		ANGEL *Virgin WBRX 10*		....**30** 2
8 Mar 03		SPECIAL CASES *Virgin VSCDT 1839*		...............................**15** 2
20 Apr 91		BLUE LINES *Wild Bunch WBRLP 1*		..................................**13** 84
8 Oct 94	●	PROTECTION / NO PROTECTION *Wild Bunch WBRCD 2*		.........**4** 78
2 May 98	★	MEZZANINE *Virgin WBRCD 4* ■		...................................**1** 54
22 Feb 03	★	100TH WINDOW *Virgin CDV 2967* ■		..............................**1** 6
23 Oct 04		DANNY THE DOG – ORIGINAL MOTION PICTURE		
		SOUNDTRACK *Virgin CDV 2988*		...........................**70** 1

[1] Massive [2] Massive Attack featuring Tracey Thorn

Vocals on first three releases by Shara Nelson. Tracks on Massive Attack (EP): Hymn of the Big Wheel / Home of the Whale / Be Thankful / Any Love. Teardrop features an uncredited vocal by Elizabeth Fraser from Cocteau Twins From 4 Mar 95 'Protection' was listed with the re-mix album 'No Protection'

MASSIVO featuring TRACY
UK, male / female vocal / instrumental group (Singles: 11 Weeks)   pos/wks

26 May 90	LOVING YOU *Debut DEBT 3097*	....**25** 11

MASTER BLASTER
Germany, male production trio (Singles: 1 Week)   pos/wks

7 Aug 04	HYPNOTIC TANGO *Mondo Pop 9867100*	..................................**64** 1

MASTER P See Montell JORDAN

The MASTER SINGERS *UK, male vocal group (Singles: 8 Weeks)*   pos/wks

14 Apr 66	HIGHWAY CODE *Parlophone R 5428*	.....................................**25** 6
17 Nov 66	WEATHER FORECAST (re) *Parlophone R 5523*	................**45** 2

MASTERMIXERS See JIVE BUNNY and the MASTERMIXERS

Sammy MASTERS
US, male vocalist – Samuel Lawmaster (Singles: 5 Weeks)   pos/wks

9 Jun 60	ROCKIN' RED WING *Warner Bros. WB 10*	...........................**36** 5

MASTERS AT WORK (see also NUYORICAN SOUL)
US, male production / instrumental duo – 'Lil' Louis Vega and Kenny 'Dope' Gonzales (Singles: 6 Weeks)   pos/wks

5 Aug 95	I CAN'T GET NO SLEEP *A&M 5811412* [1]	...............................**44** 2
31 Jul 99	TO BE IN LOVE *Defected DEFECT 5CDS* [2]	.........................**23** 3
6 Jul 02	BACKFIRED *SuSu CDSUSU 4* [3]	....**62** 1

[1] Masters at Work presents India [2] MAW presents India [3] Masters at Work featuring India

MASTERS of CEREMONIES See DJ PIED PIPER and the MASTERS OF CEREMONIES

Paul MASTERSON presents SUSHI
(see also CANDY GIRLS; CLERGY; DOROTHY; HI-GATE; SLEAZESISTERS; YOMANDA) *UK, male producer (Singles: 2 Weeks)*   pos/wks

2 Nov 02	THE EARTHSHAKER *Nulife 74321970372*	..............................**35** 2

MATCH *UK, male vocal / instrumental group (Singles: 3 Weeks)*   pos/wks

16 Jun 79	BOOGIE MAN *Flamingo FM 2*	....**48** 3

MATCHBOX *UK, male vocal / instrumental*
group (Singles: 66 Weeks, Albums: 14 Weeks)   pos/wks

3 Nov 79	ROCKABILLY REBEL *Magnet MAG 155*	................................**18** 12
19 Jan 80	BUZZ BUZZ A DIDDLE IT *Magnet MAG 157*	........................**22** 8

			pos/wks
10 May 80	MIDNITE DYNAMOS *Magnet MAG 169*	......**14**	12
27 Sep 80 ●	WHEN YOU ASK ABOUT LOVE *Magnet MAG 191*	......**4**	12
29 Nov 80	OVER THE RAINBOW – YOU BELONG TO ME (MEDLEY) *Magnet MAG 192*	......**15**	11
4 Apr 81	BABES IN THE WOOD *Magnet MAG 193*	......**46**	6
1 Aug 81	LOVE'S MADE A FOOL OF YOU *Magnet MAG 194*	......**63**	3
29 May 82	ONE MORE SATURDAY NIGHT *Magnet MAG 223*	......**63**	2
2 Feb 80	MATCHBOX *Magnet MAG 5031*	......**44**	5
11 Oct 80	MIDNITE DYNAMOS *Magnet MAG 5036*	......**23**	9

MATCHBOX TWENTY
US, male vocal / instrumental group – leader Rob
Thomas (Singles: 5 Weeks, Albums: 5 Weeks)   pos/wks

11 Apr 98	PUSH *Atlantic AT 0021CD* [1]	......**38**	2
4 Jul 98	3 AM *Atlantic AT 0034CD* [1]	......**64**	1
17 Feb 01	IF YOU'RE GONE *Atlantic AT 0090CD*	......**50**	1
22 Feb 03	DISEASE *Atlantic AT 0145CD*	......**50**	1
25 Apr 98	YOURSELF OR SOMEONE LIKE YOU *Atlantic 7567927212* [1]....**50**		1
3 Jun 00	MAD SEASON BY MATCHBOX TWENTY *Atlantic 7567833392* ..**31**		2
8 Mar 03	MORE THAN YOU THINK YOU ARE *Atlantic ATL 836122* **31**		2

[1] Matchbox 20 [1] Matchbox 20

MATCHROOM MOB *See CHAS and DAVE*

Mireille MATHIEU
France, female vocalist (Singles: 7 Weeks, Albums: 1 Week)   pos/wks

13 Dec 67	LA DERNIERE VALSE *Columbia DB 8323*	......**26**	7
2 Mar 68	MIREILLE MATHIEU *Columbia SCX 6210*	......**39**	1

Johnny MATHIS   138   Top 500
Legendary MOR vocal superstar, b. 30 Sep 1935, San Francisco, US. Frank
Sinatra and Elvis Presley are the only males with more hit albums in the US,
where his greatest hits album charted for almost 10 years – a record for a
solo performer (Singles: 138 Weeks, Albums: 228 Weeks)   pos/wks

23 May 58	TEACHER, TEACHER *Fontana H 130*	......**27**	5
26 Sep 58 ●	A CERTAIN SMILE *Fontana H 142*	......**4**	16
19 Dec 58	WINTER WONDERLAND *Fontana H 165*	......**17**	3
7 Aug 59 ●	SOMEONE *Fontana H 199*	......**6**	15
27 Nov 59	THE BEST OF EVERYTHING *Fontana H 218*	......**30**	1
29 Jan 60	MISTY (re) *Fontana H 219*	......**12**	12
24 Mar 60	YOU ARE BEAUTIFUL (re) *Fontana H 234*	......**38**	9
28 Jul 60	STARBRIGHT *Fontana H 254*	......**47**	2
6 Oct 60 ●	MY LOVE FOR YOU *Fontana H 267*	......**9**	18
4 Apr 63	WHAT WILL MARY SAY *CBS AAG 135*	......**49**	1
25 Jan 75 ●	I'M STONE IN LOVE WITH YOU *CBS 2653*	......**10**	12
13 Nov 76 ★	WHEN A CHILD IS BORN (SOLEADO) *CBS 4599*	......**1**	12
25 Mar 78 ●	TOO MUCH, TOO LITTLE, TOO LATE *CBS 6164* [1] ▲	......**3**	14
29 Jul 78	YOU'RE ALL I NEED TO GET BY *CBS 6483* [1]	......**45**	6
11 Aug 79	GONE, GONE, GONE *CBS 7730*	......**15**	10
26 Dec 81	WHEN A CHILD IS BORN *CBS S 1758* [2]	......**74**	2
8 Nov 58 ●	WARM *Fontana TBA TFL 5015*	......**6**	2
24 Jan 59 ●	SWING SOFTLY *Fontana TBA TFL 5039*	......**10**	1
13 Feb 60 ●	RIDE ON A RAINBOW *Fontana TFL 5061*	......**10**	2
10 Dec 60 ●	RHYTHMS AND BALLADS OF BROADWAY *Fontana SET 101* **6**		10
17 Jun 61	I'LL BUY YOU A STAR *Fontana TFL 5143*	......**18**	1
16 May 70	RAINDROPS KEEP FALLING ON MY HEAD *CBS 63587* **23**		10
3 Apr 71	LOVE STORY *CBS 64334*	......**27**	5
9 Sep 72	FIRST TIME EVER I SAW YOUR FACE *CBS 64930*	......**40**	3
16 Dec 72	MAKE IT EASY ON YOURSELF *CBS 65161*	......**49**	1
8 Mar 75	I'M COMING HOME *CBS 65690*	......**18**	11
5 Apr 75	THE HEART OF A WOMAN *CBS 80533*	......**39**	2
26 Jul 75	WHEN WILL I SEE YOU AGAIN *CBS 80738* **13**		10
3 Jul 76	I ONLY HAVE EYES FOR YOU *CBS 81329*	......**14**	12
19 Feb 77	GREATEST HITS VOLUME IV *CBS 86022*	......**31**	5
18 Jun 77 ★	THE JOHNNY MATHIS COLLECTION *CBS 10003*	......**1**	40
17 Dec 77	SWEET SURRENDER *CBS 86036*	......**55**	1
29 Apr 78 ●	YOU LIGHT UP MY LIFE *CBS 86055*	......**3**	19
26 Aug 78	THAT'S WHAT FRIENDS ARE FOR *CBS 86068* [1]	......**16**	11
7 Apr 79	THE BEST DAYS OF MY LIFE *CBS 86080*	......**38**	5
3 Nov 79	MATHIS MAGIC *CBS 86103*	......**59**	4
8 Mar 80 ★	TEARS AND LAUGHTER *CBS 10019*	......**1**	15
12 Jul 80	ALL FOR YOU *CBS 86115*	......**20**	8
19 Sep 81 ●	CELEBRATION *CBS 10028*	......**9**	16
15 May 82	FRIENDS IN LOVE *CBS 85652*	......**34**	7
17 Sep 83 ●	UNFORGETTABLE: A MUSICAL TRIBUTE TO NAT 'KING' COLE *CBS 10042* [2]	......**5**	16

			pos/wks
15 Sep 84	A SPECIAL PART OF ME *CBS 25475*	......**45**	3
13 Dec 86	THE HOLLYWOOD MUSICALS *CBS 4502581* [3]	......**46**	8

[1] Johnny Mathis and Deniece Williams [2] Johnny Mathis and Gladys Knight
[1] Johnny Mathis and Deniece Williams [2] Johnny Mathis and Natalie Cole
[3] Johnny Mathis and Henry Mancini

Ivan MATIAS *US, male vocalist (Singles: 1 Week)*   pos/wks

6 Apr 96	SO GOOD (TO COME HOME TO) / I'VE HAD ENOUGH *Arista 74321345072*	......**69**	1

MATT BIANCO
UK, male / female vocal /
instrumental duo (Singles: 65 Weeks, Albums: 67 Weeks)   pos/wks

11 Feb 84	GET OUT OF YOUR LAZY BED *WEA BIANCO 1*	......**15**	8
14 Apr 84	SNEAKING OUT THE BACK DOOR / MATT'S MOOD *WEA YZ 3* ..**44**		7
10 Nov 84	HALF A MINUTE *WEA YZ 26*	......**23**	10
2 Mar 85	MORE THAN I CAN BEAR *WEA YZ 34*	......**50**	7
5 Oct 85	YEH YEH *WEA YZ 46*	......**13**	10
1 Mar 86	JUST CAN'T STAND IT *WEA YZ 62*	......**66**	2
14 Jun 86	DANCING IN THE STREET *WEA YZ 72*	......**64**	3
4 Jun 88	DON'T BLAME IT ON THAT GIRL / WAP-BAM-BOOGIE *WEA YZ 188*	......**11**	13
27 Aug 88	GOOD TIMES *WEA YZ 302*	......**55**	3
4 Feb 89	NERVOUS / WAP-BAM-BOOGIE (re-mix) *WEA YZ 328* **59**		2
8 Sep 84	WHOSE SIDE ARE YOU ON *WEA WX 7* **35**		39
22 Mar 86	MATT BIANCO *WEA WX 35*	......**26**	13
9 Jul 88	INDIGO *WEA WX 181*	......**23**	13
2 Nov 90	THE BEST OF MATT BIANCO *East West WX 376*	......**49**	2

'Matt's Mood' credited only from 5 May 1984. Act was a UK / Poland, male /
female vocal / instrumental group on first five hits and first album

Kathy MATTEA *US, female vocalist (Albums: 2 Weeks)*   pos/wks

15 Apr 95	READY FOR THE STORM (FAVOURITE CUTS) *Mercury 5280062* ..**61**		1
8 Feb 97	LOVE TRAVELS *Mercury 5328992*	......**65**	1

Al MATTHEWS *US, male vocalist (Singles: 8 Weeks)*   pos/wks

23 Aug 75	FOOL *CBS 3429*	......**16**	8

Cerys MATTHEWS
(see also CATATONIA; Tom JONES)
UK, female vocalist (Singles: 16 Weeks, Albums: 5 Weeks)   pos/wks

7 Mar 98 ●	THE BALLAD OF TOM JONES *Gut CDGUT 018* [1]	......**4**	8
18 Dec 99	BABY, IT'S COLD OUTSIDE *Gut CDGUT 29*	......**17**	7
2 Aug 03	CAUGHT IN THE MIDDLE *Blano Y Negro NEG 147CD1* **47**		1
31 May 03	COCKAHOOP *Blanco Y Negro 2564603062*	......**30**	5

[1] Space with Cerys of Catatonia

John MATTHEWS *See UNDERCOVER*

Summer MATTHEWS
UK, female actor / vocalist – Holly Wilkinson (Singles: 2 Weeks)   pos/wks

28 Feb 04	LITTLE MISS PERFECT *Sony Music 6744732*	......**32**	2

Dave MATTHEWS BAND
US, male vocal / instrumental group (Singles: 2 Weeks)   pos/wks

1 Dec 01	THE SPACE BETWEEN *RCA 74321883192*	......**35**	2

MATTHEWS' SOUTHERN COMFORT
UK, male vocal / instrumental group – lead vocalist
Ian Matthews (Singles: 18 Weeks, Albums: 4 Weeks)   pos/wks

26 Sep 70 ★	WOODSTOCK *Uni UNS 526*	......**1**	18
25 Jul 70	SECOND SPRING *Uni UNLS 112*	......**52**	4

MATUMBI
UK, male vocal / instrumental group (Singles: 7 Weeks)   pos/wks

29 Sep 79	POINT OF VIEW (SQUEEZE A LITTLE LOVIN) *Matumbi RIC 101* ..**35**		7

Susan MAUGHAN
UK, female vocalist (Singles: 25 Weeks)   pos/wks

11 Oct 62 ●	BOBBY'S GIRL *Philips 326544 BF*	......**3**	19
14 Feb 63	HAND A HANDKERCHIEF TO HELEN *Philips 326562 BF* **41**		3
9 May 63	SHE'S NEW TO YOU *Philips 326586 BF*	......**45**	3

MAUREEN
UK, female vocalist – Maureen Walsh (Singles: 22 Weeks)   pos/wks
26 Nov 88 ●	SAY A LITTLE PRAYER *Rhythm King DOOD 3* [1]	10	10
16 Jun 90	THINKING OF YOU *Urban URB 55* [2]	11	9
12 Jan 91	WHERE HAS ALL THE LOVE GONE *Urban URB 65*	51	3

[1] Bomb the Bass featuring Maureen [2] Maureen Walsh

Some copies of 'Thinking of You' are credited to the fuller name of Maureen Walsh

Paul MAURIAT and his ORCHESTRA
France, orchestra (Singles: 14 Weeks)   pos/wks
| 21 Feb 68 | LOVE IS BLUE (L'AMOUR EST BLEU) *Philips BF 1637* ▲ | ....12 | 14 |

The MAVERICKS
US, male vocal / instrumental group – leader Raul Malo (Singles: 23 Weeks, Albums: 60 Weeks)   pos/wks
2 May 98 ●	DANCE THE NIGHT AWAY *MCA Nashville MCSTD 48081*	4	18
26 Sep 98	I'VE GOT THIS FEELING *MCA Nashville MCSTD 48095*	27	4
5 Jun 99	SOMEONE SHOULD TELL HER *MCA Nashville MCSTD 55567*	..45	1
11 May 96	MUSIC FOR ALL OCCASIONS *MCA MCD 11344*	56	1
14 Mar 98 ●	TRAMPOLINE *MCA Nashville UMD 80456*	10	48
4 Dec 99	THE BEST OF THE MAVERICKS *Mercury / Universal TV 1701202*	40	9
4 Oct 03	MAVERICKS *Sanctuary SANCD 192*	65	2

MAW *See MASTERS AT WORK*

MAX LINEN *UK, male production duo (Singles: 1 Week)*   pos/wks
| 17 Nov 01 | THE SOULSHAKER *Global Cuts GC 73CD* | ....55 | 1 |

MAX Q (see also INXS) *Australia, male vocal / instrumental duo (Singles: 3 Weeks, Albums: 1 Week)*   pos/wks
| 17 Feb 90 | SOMETIMES *Mercury MXQ 2* | ....53 | 3 |
| 4 Nov 89 | MAX Q *Mercury 838942 1* | ....69 | 1 |

MAX WEBSTER
Canada, male vocal / instrumental group (Singles: 3 Weeks)   pos/wks
| 19 May 79 | PARADISE SKIES *Capitol CL 16079* | ....43 | 3 |

MAXEE *US, female vocalist (Singles: 1 Week)*   pos/wks
| 17 Mar 01 | WHEN I LOOK INTO YOUR EYES *Mercury 5628702* | ....55 | 1 |

MAXIM (see also The PRODIGY)
UK, male producer / vocalist – Keith Palmer (Singles: 3 Weeks)   pos/wks
| 10 Jun 00 | CARMEN QUEASY *XL Recordings XLS 119CD* | ....33 | 2 |
| 23 Sep 00 | SCHEMING *XL Recordings XLS 121CD* | ....53 | 1 |

Skin from Skunk Anansie is the vocalist on 'Carmen Queasy'

MAXIMA featuring LILY *UK / Spain, male / female vocal / instrumental duo (Singles: 2 Weeks)*   pos/wks
| 14 Aug 93 | IBIZA *Yo! Yo! CDLILY 1* | ....55 | 2 |

MAXTREME *Holland, male production group (Singles: 1 Week)*   pos/wks
| 9 Mar 02 | MY HOUSE IS YOUR HOUSE *Y2K Y2K 028CD* | ....66 | 1 |

MAXWELL *US, male vocalist – Maxwell Menard (Singles: 10 Weeks, Albums: 20 Weeks)*   pos/wks
11 May 96	... TIL THE COPS COME KNOCKIN' *Columbia 6631792*	63	1
24 Aug 96	ASCENSION NO ONE'S GONNA LOVE YOU SO DON'T EVER WONDER *Columbia 6636265*	39	3
1 Mar 97	SUMTHIN' SUMTHIN' THE MANTRA *Columbia 6638642*	27	3
24 May 97	ASCENSION DON'T EVER WONDER (re-issue) *Columbia 6645952*	28	3
13 Apr 96	URBAN HANG SUITE *Columbia 4836992*	39	10
26 Jul 97	MTV UNPLUGGED (EP) *Columbia 4882922*	45	2
4 Jul 98	EMBRYA *Columbia 4894202*	11	6
22 Sep 01	NOW *Columbia 4974542* ▲	46	2

MAXX *UK / Sweden / Germany, male / female vocal / instrumental group (Singles: 24 Weeks, Albums: 1 Week)*   pos/wks
| 21 May 94 ● | GET-A-WAY *Pulse 8 CDLOSE 59* | ....4 | 12 |

6 Aug 94 ●	NO MORE (I CAN'T STAND IT) *Pulse 8 CDLOSE 66*	8	8
29 Oct 94	YOU CAN GET IT *Pulse 8 CDLOSE 75*	21	3
22 Jul 95	I CAN MAKE YOU FEEL LIKE *Pulse 8 CDLOSE 88*	56	1
23 Jul 94	TO THE MAXXIMUM *Pulse 8 PULSE 15CD*	66	1

Terry MAXX *See FUNKSTAR DE LUXE*

Billy MAY and his Orchestra *US, orchestra – leader b. 10 Nov 1916, d. 22 Jan 2004 (Singles: 10 Weeks)*   pos/wks
| 27 Apr 56 ● | MAIN TITLE THEME FROM 'MAN WITH THE GOLDEN ARM' *Capitol CL 14551* | ....9 | 10 |

Brian MAY (see also QUEEN) *UK, male vocalist / instrumentalist – guitar (Singles: 33 Weeks, Albums: 23 Weeks)*   pos/wks
5 Nov 83	STAR FLEET *EMI 5436* [1]	65	3
7 Dec 91 ●	DRIVEN BY YOU *Parlophone R 6304*	6	9
5 Sep 92 ●	TOO MUCH LOVE WILL KILL YOU *Parlophone R 6320*	5	9
17 Oct 92	WE ARE THE CHAMPIONS *PolyGram TV PO 229* [2]	66	1
21 Nov 92	BACK TO THE LIGHT *Parlophone R 6329*	19	4
19 Jun 93	RESURRECTION *Parlophone CDRS 6351* [3]	23	3
18 Dec 93	LAST HORIZON *Parlophone CDR 6371*	51	2
6 Jun 98	THE BUSINESS *Parlophone CDR 6498*	51	1
12 Sep 98	WHY DON'T WE TRY AGAIN *Parlophone CDR 6504*	44	1
12 Nov 83	STAR FLEET PROJECT *EMI SFLT 1078061* [1]	35	4
10 Oct 92 ●	BACK TO THE LIGHT *Parlophone CDPCSD 123*	6	14
19 Feb 94	LIVE AT THE BRIXTON ACADEMY *Parlophone CDPCSD 150* [2]	..20	3
13 Jun 98	ANOTHER WORLD *Parlophone 4949732*	23	2

[1] Brian May and Friends [2] Hank Marvin featuring Brian May [3] Brian May with Cozy Powell [1] Brian May and Friends [2] Brian May Band

Lisa MAY *UK, female vocalist (Singles: 2 Weeks)*   pos/wks
| 15 Jul 95 | WISHING ON A STAR *Urban Gorilla UG 3CD* [1] | ....61 | 1 |
| 14 Sep 96 | THE CURSE OF VOODOO RAY *Fontana VOOCD 1* | ....64 | 1 |

[1] 88.3 featuring Lisa May

Mary MAY *UK, female vocalist (Singles: 1 Week)*   pos/wks
| 27 Feb 64 | ANYONE WHO HAD A HEART *Fontana TF 440* | ....49 | 1 |

Shernette MAY *UK, female vocalist (Singles: 1 Week)*   pos/wks
| 6 Jun 98 | ALL THE MAN THAT I NEED *Virgin VSCDT 1691* | ....50 | 1 |

Simon MAY ORCHESTRA
UK, male / female orchestra (Singles: 42 Weeks, Albums: 7 Weeks) pos/wks
9 Oct 76 ●	THE SUMMER OF MY LIFE *Pye 7N 45627*	7	8
21 May 77	WE'LL GATHER LILACS – ALL MY LOVING (MEDLEY) (re) *Pye 7N 45688*	49	2
26 Oct 85	HOWARD'S WAY *BBC RESL 174*	21	11
9 Aug 86	ANYONE CAN FALL IN LOVE *BBC RESL 191* [1]	4	9
20 Sep 86	ALWAYS THERE *BBC RESL 190* [2]	13	12
27 Sep 86	SIMON'S WAY *BBC REB 594*	59	7

[1] Anita Dobson featuring the Simon May Orchestra
[2] Marti Webb and the Simon May Orchestra

MAYA *See The TAMPERER featuring MAYA*

John MAYALL
UK, male vocalist (Albums: 115 Weeks)   pos/wks
30 Jul 66 ●	BLUES BREAKERS *Decca LK 4804* [1]	6	17
4 Mar 67 ●	A HARD ROAD *Decca SKL 4853*	10	19
23 Sep 67 ●	CRUSADE *Decca SKL 4890*	8	14
25 Nov 67	THE BLUES ALONE *Ace of Clubs SCL 1243*	24	5
16 Mar 68	DIARY OF A BAND VOLUME 1 *Decca SKL 4918*	27	9
16 Mar 68	DIARY OF A BAND VOLUME 2 *Decca SKL 4919*	28	5
20 Jul 68 ●	BARE WIRES *Decca SKL 4945*	3	17
18 Jan 69	BLUES FROM LAUREL CANYON *Decca SKL 4972*	33	3
23 Aug 69	LOOKING BACK *Decca SKL 5010*	14	7
15 Nov 69	THE TURNING POINT *Polydor 583571*	11	7
11 Apr 70 ●	EMPTY ROOMS *Polydor 583580*	9	8
12 Dec 70	U.S.A. UNION *Polydor 2425020*	50	1
26 Jun 71	BACK TO THE ROOTS *Polydor 2657005*	31	2
17 Apr 93	WAKE UP CALL *Silvertone ORECD 527*	61	1

[1] John Mayall and Eric Clapton

John MAYER
US, male vocalist (Singles: 2 Weeks, Albums: 1 Week) pos/wks

23 Aug 03	NO SUCH THING *Columbia 6732322*	42	1
28 Feb 04	BIGGER THAN MY BODY *Columbia 6744392*	72	1
25 Oct 03	HEAVIER THINGS *Columbia 5134722* ▲	74	1

Curtis MAYFIELD *US, male vocalist / instrumentalist – guitar,*
b. 6 Jun 1942, d. 26 Dec 1999 (Singles: 20 Weeks, Albums: 5 Weeks) pos/wks

31 Jul 71	MOVE ON UP *Buddah 2011 080*	12	10
2 Dec 78	NO GOODBYES *Atlantic LV 1*	65	3
30 May 87	(CELEBRATE) THE DAY AFTER YOU *RCA MONK 6* [1]	52	2
29 Sep 90	SUPERFLY 1990 *Capitol CL 586* [2]	48	3
16 Jun 01	ASTOUNDED *Virgin VUSCD 194* [3]	40	2
20 Mar 71	CURTIS *Buddah 2318 015*	30	1
31 Mar 73	SUPERFLY *Buddah 2318 065* ▲	26	2
15 Feb 97	NEW WORLD ORDER *Warner Bros. 9362463482*	44	2

[1] The Blow Monkeys with Curtis Mayfield [2] Curtis Mayfield and Ice-T
[3] Bran Van 3000 featuring Curtis Mayfield

The MAYTALS
Jamaica, male vocal / instrumental group (Singles: 4 Weeks) pos/wks

| 25 Apr 70 | MONKEY MAN (re) *Trojan TR 7711* | 47 | 4 |

MAYTE *US, female vocalist – Mayte Garcia (Singles: 1 Week)* pos/wks

| 18 Nov 95 | IF EYE LOVE U 2 NIGHT *NPG 0061635* | 67 | 1 |

MAZE featuring Frankie BEVERLY *US, male vocal /*
instrumental group (Singles: 14 Weeks, Albums: 25 Weeks) pos/wks

20 Jul 85	TOO MANY GAMES *Capitol CL 363*	36	7
23 Aug 86	I WANNA BE WITH YOU *Capitol CL 421*	55	3
27 May 89	JOY AND PAIN *Capitol CL 531* [1]	57	4
7 May 83	WE ARE ONE *Capitol CL 12262*	38	6
9 Mar 85	CAN'T STOP THE LOVE *Capitol MAZE 1*	41	12
27 Sep 86	LIVE IN LOS ANGELES *Capitol ESTSP 24*	70	2
16 Sep 89	SILKY SOUL *Warner Bros. WX 301*	43	5

[1] Maze

Kym MAZELLE
US, female vocalist – Kimberley Grigsby (Singles: 66 Weeks) pos/wks

12 Nov 88	USELESS (I DON'T NEED YOU NOW) *Syncopate SY 18*	53	3
14 Jan 89 ●	WAIT *RCA PB 42595* [1]	7	10
25 Mar 89	GOT TO GET YOU BACK *Syncopate SY 25*	29	4
7 Oct 89	LOVE STRAIN *Syncopate SY 30*	53	3
20 Jan 90	WAS THAT ALL IT WAS *Syncopate SY 32*	33	6
26 May 90	USELESS (I DON'T NEED YOU NOW) (re-mix) *Syncopate SY 36*	48	2
24 Nov 90	MISSING YOU *Ten TEN 345* [2]	22	7
25 May 91	NO ONE CAN LOVE YOU MORE THAN ME *Parlophone R 6287*	62	2
26 Dec 92	LOVE ME THE RIGHT WAY *Arista 74321128097* [3]	22	10
11 Jun 94	NO MORE TEARS (ENOUGH IS ENOUGH) *Bell 74321209032* [4]	13	7
8 Oct 94	GIMME ALL YOUR LOVIN' *Bell 74321231322* [5]	55	3
23 Dec 95	SEARCHING FOR THE GOLDEN EYE *Eternal WEA 027CD* [6]	40	3
28 Sep 96	LOVE ME THE RIGHT WAY (re-mix) *Logic 74321404442* [3]	55	1
16 Aug 97	YOUNG HEARTS RUN FREE *EMI CDEM 488*	20	4
19 Feb 00	TRULY *Island Blue PFACD 4* [7]	55	1

[1] Robert Howard and Kym Mazelle [2] Soul II Soul featuring Kym Mazelle
[3] Rapination and Kym Mazelle [4] Kym Mazelle and Jocelyn Brown [5] Jocelyn
Brown and Kym Mazelle [6] Motiv 8 and Kym Mazelle [7] Peshay featuring
Kym Mazelle

MAZZY STAR *US, male / female vocal /*
instrumental group (Singles: 3 Weeks, Albums: 2 Weeks) pos/wks

27 Aug 94	FADE INTO YOU *Capitol CDCL 720*	48	1
2 Nov 96	FLOWERS IN DECEMBER *Capitol CDCL 781*	40	2
9 Oct 93	SO TONIGHT THAT I MIGHT SEE *Capitol CDEST 2206*	68	1
16 Nov 96	AMONG MY SWAN *Capitol CDEST 2288*	57	1

MC ALISTAIR See DREEM TEEM

MC CHICKABOO See Timo MAAS

MC DUKE *UK, male rapper – Anthony Hilaire (Singles: 1 Week)* pos/wks

| 11 Mar 89 | I'M RIFFIN (ENGLISH RASTA) *Music of Life 7NOTE 25* | 75 | 1 |

MC ERIC See TECHNOTRONIC

MC FIXX IT See ANTICAPPELLA

MC HAMMER *US, male rapper – Stanley Burrell*
(Singles: 68 Weeks, Albums: 67 Weeks) pos/wks

9 Jun 90 ●	U CAN'T TOUCH THIS *Capitol CL 578*	3	16
6 Oct 90 ●	HAVE YOU SEEN HER *Capitol CL 590*	8	7
8 Dec 90 ●	PRAY *Capitol CL 599*	8	10
23 Feb 91	HERE COMES THE HAMMER *Capitol CL 610*	15	5
1 Jun 91	YO!! SWEETNESS *Capitol CL 616*	16	5
20 Jul 91	(HAMMER HAMMER) THEY PUT ME IN THE MIX *Capitol CL 607*	20	4
26 Oct 91	2 LEGIT 2 QUIT *Capitol CL 636* [1]	60	2
21 Dec 91 ●	ADDAMS GROOVE *Capitol CL 642* [1]	4	9
21 Mar 92	DO NOT PASS ME BY *Capitol CL 650* [1]	14	6
12 Mar 94	IT'S ALL GOOD *RCA 74321188612* [1]	52	2
13 Aug 94	DON'T STOP *RCA 74321220012* [1]	72	1
3 Jun 95	STRAIGHT TO MY FEET *Priority PTYCD 102* [2]	57	1
28 Jul 90 ●	PLEASE HAMMER DON'T HURT 'EM *Capitol EST 2120* ▲	8	59
6 Apr 91	LET'S GET IT STARTED *Capitol EST 2140*	46	2
2 Nov 91	TOO LEGIT TO QUIT *Capitol ESTP 26* [1]	41	6

[1] Hammer [2] Hammer featuring Deion Saunders [1] Hammer

MC IMAGE See Jhay PALMER featuring MC IMAGE

MC JIG *Germany, male DJ / producer (Singles: 3 Weeks)* pos/wks

| 21 Feb 04 | CHA-CHA SLIDE (import) *ZYX ZYX 95838* | 37 | 3 |
| 13 Mar 04 | CHA-CHA SLIDE *NM Music SLIDE 001* | 33 | 4 |

MC KIE See TEEBONE featuring MC KIE and MC SPARKS

MC LETHAL *UK, male producer – Lee Whitney (Singles: 1 Week)* pos/wks

| 14 Nov 92 | THE RAVE DIGGER *Network NWKT 60* | 66 | 1 |

MC LYTE *US, female rapper – Lana Moorer (Singles: 19 Weeks)* pos/wks

15 Jan 94	RUFFNECK *Atlantic A 8336CD*	67	1
29 Jun 96	KEEP ON KEEPIN' ON *East West A 4287CD* [1]	39	2
18 Jan 97	COLD ROCK A PARTY *East West A 3975CD*	15	4
19 Apr 97	KEEP ON KEEPIN' ON (re-issue) *East West A 3950CD1* [1]	27	2
5 Sep 98	I CAN'T MAKE A MISTAKE *Elektra E 3813CD*	46	1
19 Dec 98	IT'S ALL YOURS *East West E 3789CD* [2]	36	4
24 Jun 00	JAMMIN' *Tuff Gong TGXCD 9* [3]	42	2
8 May 04	GIRLFRIEND'S STORY *Polydor 9866362* [4]	38	3

[1] MC Lyte featuring Xscape [2] MC Lyte featuring Gina Thompson
[3] Bob Marley featuring MC Lyte [4] Gemma Fox featuring MC Lyte

MC MALIBU See ROUND SOUND presents ONYX STONE & MC MALIBU

MC MARIO See AMBASSADORS OF FUNK featuring MC MARIO

MC MIKEE FREEDOM See NOMAD

MC MIKER 'G' and Deejay SVEN *Holland, male rap / instrumental*
duo – Lucien Witteveen and Sven Van Veen (Singles: 7 Weeks) pos/wks

| 6 Sep 86 ● | HOLIDAY RAP *Debut DEBT 3008* | 6 | 7 |

MC NEAT See DJ LUCK & MC NEAT; CORRUPTED CRU featuring MC NEAT

MC NOISE See LOVE INCORPORATED featuring MC NOISE

MC NUMBER 6 See FAB

MC ONYX STONE See LONYO

MC PARKER See FAB

MC RB See SUNSHIP featuring MCRB; JUST 4 JOKES featuring MC RB

MC SAR See The REAL McCOY

MC SHURAKANO See KID CREME

MC SKAT KAT and the STRAY MOB
US, male cartoon feline rap / vocal group (Singles: 2 Weeks) pos/wks

| 9 Nov 91 | SKAT STRUT *Virgin America VUS 51* | 64 | 2 |

Singles re-entries are listed as (re), (2re), (3re)…. which signifies that the hit re-entered the chart once, twice or three times…

MC SOLAAR *See Missy 'Misdemeanor' ELLIOTT; URBAN SPECIES*

MC SPARKS *See TEEBONE featuring MC KIE and MC SPARKS*

MC SPY-D + FRIENDS
UK, male / female vocal / instrumental group (Singles: 2 Weeks) pos/wks

11 Mar 95	THE AMAZING SPIDER-MAN *Parlophone CDR 6404*		.37	2

MC STYLES *See Scott GARCIA featuring MC STYLES*

MC TUNES *UK, male rapper – Nicholas*
Lockett (Singles: 19 Weeks, Albums: 3 Weeks) pos/wks

2 Jun 90 ●	THE ONLY RHYME THAT BITES *ZTT ZANG 3* [1]		.10	10
15 Sep 90	TUNES SPLITS THE ATOM *ZTT ZANG 6* [1]		.18	5
1 Dec 90	PRIMARY RHYMING *ZTT ZANG 10*		.67	1
6 Mar 99	THE ONLY RHYME THAT BITES 99 *ZTT ZTT 125CD* [1]		.53	1
13 Oct 90	THE NORTH AT ITS HEIGHTS *ZTT ZTT 3*		.26	3

[1] MC Tunes versus 808 State

MC VIPER *See REFLEX featuring MC VIPER*

MC WILDSKI *UK, male rapper (Singles: 10 Weeks)* pos/wks

8 Jul 89	BLAME IT ON THE BASSLINE *Go Beat GOD 33* [1]		.29	6
3 Mar 90	WARRIOR *Arista 112956*		.49	4

[1] Norman Cook featuring MC Wildski

'Blame It on the Bassline' was listed with 'Won't Talk About It' by Norman Cook featuring Billy Bragg

ME AND YOU featuring WE THE PEOPLE BAND *Jamaica /*
UK, male / female vocal / instrumental group (Singles: 9 Weeks) pos/wks

28 Jul 79	YOU NEVER KNOW WHAT YOU'VE GOT *Laser LAS 8*		.31	9

ME ME ME (see also FAT LES)
UK, male vocal / instrumental group (Singles: 4 Weeks) pos/wks

17 Aug 96	HANGING AROUND *Indolent DUFF 005CD*		.19	4

Abigail MEAD and Nigel GOULDING *UK / US, female / male*
producers – Vivian Kubrick and Nigel Goulding (Singles: 10 Weeks) pos/wks

26 Sep 87 ●	FULL METAL JACKET (I WANNA BE YOUR DRILL INSTRUCTOR) *Warner Bros. W 8187*		.2	10

Vaughn MEADER *US, male comedian,*
b. 20 Mar 1936, d. 29 Oct 2004 (Albums: 8 Weeks) pos/wks

29 Dec 62	THE FIRST FAMILY *London HAA 8048* ▲		.12	8

MEAT BEAT MANIFESTO
UK, male production duo (Singles: 1 Week) pos/wks

20 Feb 93	MINDSTREAM *Play It Again Sam BIAS 232CD*		.55	1

MEAT LOAF (23 | Top 500) *Larger-than-life vocalist / actor, b. Marvin*
Lee Aday, 27 Sep 1948, Dallas, US. His collaborations with producer / song-writer Jim Steinman resulted in some of rock's finest recordings. His album 'Bat Out of Hell' sold more than 30 million copies and spent more than almost 10 years in total in the UK chart. Best-selling single: 'I'd Do Anything For Love (But I Won't Do That)' 761,200 (Singles: 152 Weeks, Albums: 789 Weeks) pos/wks

20 May 78	YOU TOOK THE WORDS RIGHT OUT OF MY MOUTH *Epic EPC 5980*		.33	8
19 Aug 78	TWO OUT OF THREE AIN'T BAD *Epic EPC 6281*		.32	8
10 Feb 79	BAT OUT OF HELL *Epic EPC 7018*		.15	7
26 Sep 81	I'M GONNA LOVE HER FOR BOTH OF US *Epic EPCA 1580*		.62	3
28 Nov 81 ●	DEAD RINGER FOR LOVE *Epic EPCA 1697*		.5	17
28 May 83	IF YOU REALLY WANT TO *Epic A 3357*		.59	2
24 Sep 83	MIDNIGHT AT THE LOST AND FOUND *Epic A 3748*		.17	8
14 Jan 84	RAZOR'S EDGE *Epic A 4080*		.41	3
6 Oct 84	MODERN GIRL *Arista ARIST 585*		.17	9
22 Dec 84	NOWHERE FAST *Arista ARIST 600*		.67	4
23 Mar 85	PIECE OF THE ACTION *Arista ARIST 603*		.47	5
30 Aug 86	ROCK 'N' ROLL MERCENARIES *Arista ARIST 666* [1]		.31	6
22 Jun 91	DEAD RINGER FOR LOVE (re-issue) *Epic 6569827*		.53	2
27 Jun 92	TWO OUT OF THREE AIN'T BAD (re-issue) *Epic 6574917*		.69	1
9 Oct 93 ★	I'D DO ANYTHING FOR LOVE (BUT I WON'T DO THAT) *Virgin VSCDT 1443* ▲		.1	19
18 Dec 93 ●	BAT OUT OF HELL (re-issue) *Epic 6600062*		.8	9
19 Feb 94	ROCK AND ROLL DREAMS COME THROUGH *Virgin VSCDT 1479*		.11	7
7 May 94	OBJECTS IN THE REAR VIEW MIRROR MAY COME CLOSER THAN THEY ARE *Virgin VSCDT 1492*		.26	4
28 Oct 95 ●	I'D LIE FOR YOU (AND THAT'S THE TRUTH) *Virgin VSCDT 1563*		.2	11
27 Jan 96 ●	NOT A DRY EYE IN THE HOUSE *Virgin VSCDT 1567*		.7	6
27 Apr 96	RUNNIN' FOR THE RED LIGHT (I GOTTA LIFE) *Virgin VSCDX 1582*		.21	3
17 Apr 99	IS NOTHING SACRED *Virgin VSCDT 1734* [2]		.15	4
26 Apr 03	COULDN'T HAVE SAID IT BETTER *Mercury 0656842*		.31	2
6 Dec 03	MAN OF STEEL *Mercury 9815114*		.21	4
11 Mar 78 ●	BAT OUT OF HELL *Cleveland International EPC 82419*		.9	474
12 Sep 81 ★	DEAD RINGER *Epic EPC 83645* ■		.1	46
7 May 83 ●	MIDNIGHT AT THE LOST AND FOUND *Epic EPC 25243*		.7	23
10 Nov 84 ●	BAD ATTITUDE *Arista 206 619*		.8	16
26 Jan 85 ●	HITS OUT OF HELL *Epic EPC 26156*		.2	80
11 Oct 86	BLIND BEFORE I STOP *Arista 207 741*		.28	6
7 Nov 87	LIVE AT WEMBLEY *RCA 208599*		.60	2
18 Sep 93 ★	BAT OUT OF HELL II – BACK INTO HELL *Virgin CDV 2710* ■ ▲		.1	59
22 Oct 94	ALIVE IN HELL *Pure Music PMCD 7002*		.33	4
11 Nov 95 ●	WELCOME TO THE NEIGHBOURHOOD *Virgin CDV 2799*		.3	27
14 Nov 98	THE VERY BEST OF MEAT LOAF *Virgin / Sony TV CDV 2868*		.14	34
3 May 02 ●	COULDN'T HAVE SAID IT BETTER *Mercury 0761192*		.4	14
30 Oct 04	BAT OUT OF HELL LIVE WITH THE MELBOURNE SYMPHONY ORCHESTRA *Mercury 9868074*		.14	4

[1] Meat Loaf featuring John Parr [2] Meat Loaf featuring Patti Russo

'Dead Ringer for Love' features Cher as uncredited co-vocalist. 'I'd Do Anything For Love (But I Won't Do That)' features uncredited vocals by Lorraine Crosby (aka Mrs Loud) 'Hits Out of Hell' changed catalogue number to 4504471 during its chart run

MECHANICS *See MIKE and the MECHANICS*

MECO *US, orchestra – leader Meco Monardo (Singles: 9 Weeks)* pos/wks

1 Oct 77 ●	STAR WARS THEME – CANTINA BAND *RCA XB 1028* ▲		.7	9

Glenn MEDEIROS
US, male vocalist (Singles: 26 Weeks, Albums: 2 Weeks) pos/wks

18 Jun 88 ★	NOTHING'S GONNA CHANGE MY LOVE FOR YOU *London LON 184*		.1	13
3 Sep 88	LONG AND LASTING LOVE (ONCE IN A LIFETIME) *London LON 202*		.42	4
30 Jun 90	SHE AIN'T WORTH IT *London LON 265* [1] ▲		.12	9
8 Oct 88	NOT ME *London LONLP 68*		.63	2

[1] Glenn Medeiros featuring Bobby Brown

Paul MEDFORD *See Letitia DEAN and Paul MEDFORD*

MEDIAEVAL BAEBES *UK, female vocal group (Albums: 7 Weeks)* pos/wks

29 Nov 97	SALVA NOS *Venture CDVE 935*		.62	6
31 Oct 98	WORLDES BLYSSE *Venture CDVE 941*		.73	1

MEDICINE HEAD *UK, male vocal / instrumental duo –*
John Fiddler and Peter Hope Evans (Singles: 37 Weeks) pos/wks

26 Jun 71	(AND THE) PICTURES IN THE SKY *Dandelion DAN 7003*		.22	8
5 May 73 ●	ONE AND ONE IS ONE *Polydor 2001 432*		.3	13
4 Aug 73	RISING SUN *Polydor 2058 389*		.11	9
9 Feb 74	SLIP AND SLIDE *Polydor 2058 436*		.22	7

MEDICINE SHOW *See DR HOOK*

MEDICS *See DOCTOR and the MEDICS*

Bill MEDLEY (see also The RIGHTEOUS BROTHERS)
US, male vocalist (Singles: 29 Weeks) pos/wks

31 Oct 87 ●	(I'VE HAD) THE TIME OF MY LIFE (re) *RCA PB 49625* [1] ▲		.6	23
27 Aug 88	HE AIN'T HEAVY, HE'S MY BROTHER *Scotti Brothers PO 10*		.25	6

[1] Bill Medley and Jennifer Warnes

'(I've Had) The Time of My Life' re-entered in Dec 1990, peaking at No.8

MEDWAY *US, male producer – Jesse Skeens (Singles: 2 Weeks)* pos/wks

29 Apr 00	FAT BASTARD (EP) *Hooj Choons HOOJ 92CD*		.69	1
10 Mar 01	RELEASE *Hooj Choons HOOJ 105*		.67	1

Tracks on Fat Bastard (EP): Release / Flanker / Faith

Michael MEDWIN, Bernard BRESSLAW, Alfie BASS and Leslie FYSON *UK, male actors / vocalists (Singles: 9 Weeks)* pos/wks

30 May 58 ●	THE SIGNATURE TUNE OF 'THE ARMY GAME' *HMV POP 490* ..**5**	9

MEECHIE *US, female vocalist (Singles: 1 Week)* pos/wks

2 Sep 95	YOU BRING ME JOY *Vibe MCSTD 2069* **74**	1

Tony MEEHAN
(see also Jet HARRIS and Tony MEEHAN; The SHADOWS) *UK, male instrumentalist – drums – Daniel Meehan (Singles: 4 Weeks)* pos/wks

16 Jan 64	SONG OF MEXICO *Decca F 11801* **39**	4

MEEKER *UK, female vocal / production duo (Singles: 1 Week)* pos/wks

26 Feb 00	SAVE ME *Underwater H20 009CD* **60**	1

MEGA CITY FOUR *UK, male vocal / instrumental group (Singles: 7 Weeks, Albums: 3 Weeks)* pos/wks

19 Oct 91	WORDS THAT SAY *Big Life MEGA 2* **66**	1
8 Feb 92	STOP (EP) *Big Life MEGA 3* **36**	2
16 May 92	SHIVERING SAND *Big Life MEGA 4* **35**	2
1 May 93	IRON SKY *Big Life MEGAD 5* **48**	1
17 Jul 93	WALLFLOWER *Big Life MEGAD 6* **69**	1
17 Jun 89	TRANZOPHOBIA *Decoy DYL 3* **67**	1
7 Mar 92	SEBASTOPOL ROAD *Big Life MEGCD 1* **41**	1
22 May 93	MAGIC BULLETS *Big Life MEGCD 3* **57**	1

Tracks on Stop (EP): Stop / Desert Song / Back to Zero / Overlap

MEGABASS See VARIOUS ARTISTS (MONTAGES)

MEGADETH *US, male vocal / instrumental group (Singles: 32 Weeks, Albums: 27 Weeks)* pos/wks

19 Dec 87	WAKE UP DEAD *Capitol CL 476* **65**	2
27 Feb 88	ANARCHY IN THE UK *Capitol CL 480* **45**	3
21 May 88	MARY JANE *Capitol CL 489* **46**	2
13 Jan 90	NO MORE MR NICE GUY *SBK SBK 4* **13**	6
29 Sep 90	HOLY WARS ... THE PUNISHMENT DUE *Capitol CLP 588* **24**	3
16 Mar 91	HANGAR 18 *Capitol CLS 604* **26**	4
27 Jun 92	SYMPHONY OF DESTRUCTION *Capitol CLS 662* **15**	3
24 Oct 92	SKIN O' MY TEETH *Capitol CLP 669* **13**	3
29 May 93	SWEATING BULLETS *Capitol CDCL 682* **26**	3
7 Jan 95	TRAIN OF CONSEQUENCES *Capitol CDCL 730* **22**	3
26 Mar 88	SO FAR, SO GOOD ... SO WHAT *Capitol EST 2053* **18**	5
6 Oct 90 ●	RUST IN PEACE *Capitol EST 2132* **8**	4
18 Jul 92 ●	COUNTDOWN TO EXTINCTION *Capitol CDESTU 2175* **5**	8
5 Nov 94 ●	YOUTHANASIA / HIDDEN TREASURE *Capitol CDEST 2244*........**6**	5
19 Jul 97	CRYPTIC WRITINGS *Capitol CDEST 2297* **38**	1
18 Sep 99	RISK *Capitol 4991340* **29**	2
26 May 01	THE WORLD NEEDS A HERO *Metal Is MISCD 006* **45**	1
25 Sep 04	THE SYSTEM HAS FAILED *Sanctuary SANCD 297* **60**	1

From 25 Mar 95 'Youthanasia' was listed with bonus album 'Hidden Treasure'

MEGAMAN See OXIDE & NEUTRINO

MEHTA See José CARRERAS

Dieter MEIER See X-PRESS 2; YELLO

MEJA *Sweden, female vocalist – Meja Beckman (Singles: 14 Weeks)* pos/wks

24 Oct 98	ALL 'BOUT THE MONEY *Columbia 6665662* **12**	5
29 Apr 00 ●	PRIVATE EMOTION *Columbia 6692692* [1] **9**	9

[1] Ricky Martin featuring Meja

MEKKA *UK, male producer – Jake Williams (Singles: 1 Week)* pos/wks

24 Mar 01	DIAMOND BACK *Perfecto PERF 12CDS* **67**	1

MEKON *UK, male producer – John Gosling (Singles: 2 Weeks)* pos/wks

23 Sep 00	WHAT'S GOING ON *Wall of Sound WALD 064* [1] **43**	1
13 Mar 04	D-FUNKTIONAL *Wall of Sound WALLD 092* [2] **72**	1

[1] Mekon featuring Roxanne Shante [2] Mekon featuring Afrika Bambaataa

Melle MEL See GRANDMASTER FLASH

MEL and KIM *UK, female vocal duo – Mel, b. 11 Jul 1966, d. 18 Jan 1990, and Kim Appleby (Singles: 51 Weeks, Albums: 25 Weeks)* pos/wks

20 Sep 86 ●	SHOWING OUT (GET FRESH AT THE WEEKEND) *Supreme SUPE 107* **3**	19
7 Mar 87 ★	RESPECTABLE *Supreme SUPE 111* **1**	15
11 Jul 87 ●	F.L.M. *Supreme SUPE 113* **7**	10
27 Feb 88 ●	THAT'S THE WAY IT IS *Supreme SUPE 117* **10**	7
25 Apr 87 ●	F.L.M. *Supreme SU 2* **3**	25

MEL and KIM See Mel SMITH; Kim WILDE

George MELACHRINO ORCHESTRA *UK, orchestra – leader b. 1 May 1909, d. 18 Jun 1965 (Singles: 9 Weeks)* pos/wks

12 Oct 56	AUTUMN CONCERTO *HMV B 10958* **18**	9

MELANIE *US, female vocalist / instrumentalist – guitar – Melanie Safka (Singles: 35 Weeks, Albums: 66 Weeks)* pos/wks

26 Sep 70 ●	RUBY TUESDAY (re) *Buddah 2011 038* **9**	15
16 Jan 71	WHAT HAVE THEY DONE TO MY SONG MA *Buddah 2011 038* ...**39**	1
1 Jan 72 ●	BRAND NEW KEY *Buddah 2011 105* ▲ **4**	12
16 Feb 74	WILL YOU LOVE ME TOMORROW *Neighbourhood NBH 9* **37**	5
24 Sep 83	EVERY BREATH OF THE WAY *Neighbourhood HOOD NB1* **70**	2
19 Sep 70 ●	CANDLES IN THE RAIN *Buddah 23180 09* **5**	31
16 Jan 71	LEFTOVER WINE *Buddah 2318 011* **22**	4
29 May 71 ●	THE GOOD BOOK *Buddah 2322 001* **9**	9
8 Jan 72	GATHER ME *Buddah 2322 002* **14**	14
1 Apr 72	GARDEN IN THE CITY *Buddah 2318 054* **19**	6
7 Oct 72	THE FOUR SIDES OF MELANIE *Buddah 2659 013* **23**	2

MELBOURNE SYMPHONY ORCHESTRA See Elton JOHN

MELKY SEDECK *US, male / female vocal / instrumental duo – Melky and Sedeck Jean (Singles: 9 Weeks)* pos/wks

8 May 99	RAW *MCA MCSTD 48107* **50**	1
16 Sep 00 ●	IT DOESN'T MATTER *Columbia 6697782* [1] **3**	8

[1] Wyclef Jean featuring The Rock and Melky Sedeck

John Cougar MELLENCAMP *US, male vocalist / instrumentalist – guitar (Singles: 18 Weeks, Albums: 31 Weeks)* pos/wks

23 Oct 82	JACK AND DIANE *Riva RIVA 37* [1] ▲ **25**	8
1 Feb 86	SMALL TOWN *Riva JCM 5* **53**	4
10 May 86	R.O.C.K. IN THE USA *Riva JCM 6* **67**	3
3 Sep 94	WILD NIGHT *Mercury MERCD 409* [2] **34**	3
6 Nov 82	AMERICAN FOOL *Riva RVLP 16* [1] ▲ **37**	6
3 Mar 84	UH-HUH *Riva RIVL 1* **92**	1
3 Oct 87	THE LONESOME JUBILEE *Mercury MERH 109* **31**	12
27 May 89	BIG DADDY *Mercury MERH 838220 1* **25**	4
19 Oct 91	WHENEVER WE WANTED *Mercury 5101511* **39**	2
18 Sep 93	HUMAN WHEELS *Mercury 5180882* **37**	2
17 Jan 98	THE BEST THAT I COULD DO *PolyGram TV 5367382* [2] **25**	4

[1] John Cougar [2] John Mellencamp featuring Me'Shell Ndegeocello [1] John Cougar [2] John Mellencamp

MELLOMEN See Rosemary CLOONEY; Doris DAY; Frankie LAINE; Elvis PRESLEY

Will MELLOR *UK, male actor / vocalist (Singles: 9 Weeks)* pos/wks

28 Feb 98 ●	WHEN I NEED YOU *Unity UNITY 017RCD* **5**	6
27 Jun 98	NO MATTER WHAT I DO *Jive 0540012* **23**	3

MELLOW TRAX *Germany, male producer – Christian Schwarnweber (Singles: 2 Weeks)* pos/wks

14 Oct 00	OUTTA SPACE *Substance SUBS 3CDS* **41**	2

The MELODIANS *Jamaica, male vocal / instrumental group (Singles: 1 Week)* pos/wks

10 Jan 70	SWEET SENSATION *Trojan TR 695* **41**	1

MELODY MAKERS See Ziggy MARLEY and The MELODY MAKERS

MELT featuring LITTLE MS MARCIE
(see also LOST TRIBE; SUNBURST; MDM)
UK, male producer – Matt Darey and female vocalist (Singles: 1 Week) pos/wks

8 Apr 00	HARD HOUSE MUSIC *WEA WEA 257CD* **59**	1

MELTDOWN
UK / US, male instrumental / production duo (Singles: 1 Week) pos/wks

27 Apr 96	MY LIFE IS IN YOUR HANDS *Sony S3 DANU 7CD*	**44** 1

Katie MELUA
Georgia, female vocalist / instrumentalist – guitar (Singles: 26 Weeks, Albums: 59 Weeks) pos/wks

13 Dec 03 ●	THE CLOSEST THING TO CRAZY *Dramatico DRAMCDS 0003* ..**10** 20
27 Mar 04	CALL OFF THE SEARCH *Dramatico DRAMCDS 0004* **19** 4
31 Jul 04	CRAWLING UP A HILL *Dramatico DRAMCDS 0007* **46** 2
15 Nov 03 ★	CALL OFF THE SEARCH *Dramatico DRAMCD 0002* ....**1** 59+

A "special bonus edition" of 'Call Off the Search' was released in Oct 2004, featuring a free 70-minute DVD entitled 'On Stage & Backstage', which took the album back into the Top 20

Harold MELVIN and the BLUENOTES
US, male vocal group – leader b. 25 Jun 1939, d. 24 Mar 1997 (Singles: 52 Weeks) pos/wks

13 Jan 73 ●	IF YOU DON'T KNOW ME BY NOW *CBS 8496* **9** 9
12 Jan 74	THE LOVE I LOST (PART 1)	
	Philadelphia International PIR 1879 ....**21** 8
13 Apr 74	SATISFACTION GUARANTEED (OR TAKE YOUR LOVE BACK)	
	Philadelphia International PIR 2187 ....**32** 6
31 May 75	GET OUT (AND LET ME CRY) *Route RT 06* 1 ....**35** 5
28 Feb 76	WAKE UP EVERYBODY (PART 1)	
	Philadelphia International PIR 3866 ....**23** 7
22 Jan 77 ●	DON'T LEAVE ME THIS WAY	
	Philadelphia International PIR 4909 2 ....**5** 10
2 Apr 77	REACHING FOR THE WORLD *ABC 4161* 1 ....**48** 1
28 Apr 84	DON'T GIVE ME UP *London LON 47* 1 ....**59** 4
4 Aug 84	TODAY'S YOUR LUCKY DAY *London LON 52* 3 ....**66** 2

1 Harold Melvin and the Blue Notes 2 Harold Melvin and the Bluenotes featuring Theodore Pendergrass 3 Harold Melvin and the Blue Notes featuring Nikko

The MEMBERS
UK, male vocal / instrumental group (Singles: 14 Weeks, Albums: 5 Weeks) pos/wks

3 Feb 79	THE SOUND OF THE SUBURBS *Virgin VS 242* **12** 9
7 Apr 79	OFFSHORE BANKING BUSINESS *Virgin VS 248* **31** 5
28 Apr 79	AT THE CHELSEA NIGHTCLUB *Virgin V 2120* **45** 5

MEMBERS OF MAYDAY
Germany, male production duo – Klaus Jankuhn and Maximilian Lenz (Singles: 4 Weeks) pos/wks

23 Jun 01	10 IN 01 *Deviant DVNT 42CDS* **31** 3
13 Apr 02	SONIC EMPIRE *Low Spirit DVNT 49CDS* **59** 1

MEMPHIS BLEEK featuring JAY-Z
US, male rappers – Malik Cox and Shawn Carter (Singles: 1 Week) pos/wks

4 Dec 99	WHAT YOU THINK OF THAT *Def Jam 8708292* **58** 1

MEN AT WORK
Australia / UK, male vocal / instrumental group – lead vocal Colin James Hay (Singles: 39 Weeks, Albums: 71 Weeks) pos/wks

30 Oct 82	WHO CAN IT BE NOW? *Epic EPC A 2392* ▲ **45** 5
8 Jan 83 ★	DOWN UNDER *Epic EPC A 1980* ▲ **1** 12
9 Apr 83	OVERKILL *Epic EPC A 3220* **21** 10
2 Jul 83	IT'S A MISTAKE *Epic EPC A 3475* **33** 6
10 Sep 83	DR HECKYLL AND MR JIVE *Epic EPC A 3668* **31** 6
15 Jan 83 ★	BUSINESS AS USUAL *Epic EPC 85669* ▲ **1** 44
30 Apr 83 ●	CARGO *Epic EPC 25372* **8** 27

MEN OF VIZION
US, male vocal group (Singles: 2 Weeks) pos/wks

27 Mar 99	DO YOU FEEL ME? (... FREAK YOU) *MJJ / Epic 6670912* **36** 2

The MEN THEY COULDN'T HANG
UK, male vocal / instrumental group (Singles: 4 Weeks, Albums: 9 Weeks) pos/wks

2 Apr 88	THE COLOURS *Magnet SELL 6* **61** 4
27 Jul 85	NIGHT OF A THOUSAND CANDLES *Imp FIEND 50* **91** 2
8 Nov 86	HOW GREEN IS THE VALLEY *MCA MCF 3337* **68** 2
23 Apr 88	WAITING FOR BONAPARTE *Magnet MAGL 5075* **41** 2
6 May 89	SILVER TOWN *Silvertone ORELP 503* **39** 2
1 Sep 90	THE DOMINO CLUB *Silvertone ORELP 512* **53** 1

MEN WITHOUT HATS
Canada, male vocal / instrumental group (Singles: 11 Weeks, Albums: 1 Week) pos/wks

8 Oct 83 ●	THE SAFETY DANCE *Statik TAK 1* **6** 11
12 Nov 83	RHYTHM OF YOUTH *Statik STATLP 10* **96** 1

Sergio MENDES
Brazil, male conductor (Singles: 5 Weeks) pos/wks

9 Jul 83	NEVER GONNA LET YOU GO *A&M AM 118* **45** 5

Uncredited vocals by Joe Pizzulo and Leza Miller

Andrea MENDEZ
UK, female vocalist (Singles: 1 Week) pos/wks

3 Aug 96	BRING ME LOVE *AM:PM 5817872* **44** 1

MENSWEAR
UK, male vocal / instrumental group (Singles: 18 Weeks, Albums: 6 Weeks) pos/wks

15 Apr 95	I'LL MANAGE SOMEHOW *Laurel LAUCD 4* **49** 1
1 Jul 95	DAYDREAMER *Laurel LAUCD 5* **14** 4
30 Sep 95	STARDUST *Laurel LAUCD 6* **16** 3
16 Dec 95	SLEEPING IN *Laurel LAUCD 7* **24** 3
23 Mar 96 ●	BEING BRAVE *Laurel LAUCD 8* **10** 4
7 Sep 96	WE LOVE YOU *Laurel LAUCD 11* **22** 3
21 Oct 95	NUISANCE *Laurel 8286792* **11** 6

MENTAL AS ANYTHING
Australia, male vocal / instrumental group (Singles: 13 Weeks) pos/wks

7 Feb 87 ●	LIVE IT UP *Epic ANY 1* **3** 13

Natalie MERCHANT
(see also 10,000 MANIACS) US, female vocalist (Albums: 3 Weeks) pos/wks

1 Jul 95	TIGERLILY *Elektra 7559617452* **39** 2
13 Jun 98	OPHELIA *Elektra 7559621962* **52** 1

Freddie MERCURY 497 Top 500
Gregarious, versatile lead singer of Queen, b. Faroukh Bulsara, 5 Sep 1946, Zanzibar, Africa, d. 24 Nov 1991. UK-based performer was one of rock music's all-time great showmen, whose music has raised millions of pounds for Aids charities (Singles: 79 Weeks, Albums: 65 Weeks) pos/wks

22 Sep 84 ●	LOVE KILLS *CBS A 4735* **10** 8
20 Apr 85	I WAS BORN TO LOVE YOU *CBS A 6019* **11** 10
13 Jul 85	MADE IN HEAVEN *CBS A 6413* **57** 4
21 Sep 85	LIVING ON MY OWN *CBS A 6555* **50** 5
24 May 86	TIME *EMI EMI 5559* **32** 5
7 Mar 87 ●	THE GREAT PRETENDER *Parlophone R 6151* **4** 9
7 Nov 87 ●	BARCELONA *Polydor POSP 887* 1 ....**8** 9
8 Aug 92 ●	BARCELONA (re-issue) *Polydor PO 221* 1 ....**2** 8
12 Dec 92 ●	IN MY DEFENCE *Parlophone R 6331* **8** 7
6 Feb 93	THE GREAT PRETENDER (re-issue) *Parlophone CDR 6336* **29** 3
31 Jul 93 ★	LIVING ON MY OWN (re-mix) *Parlophone CDR 6355* **1** 13
11 May 85 ●	MR BAD GUY *CBS 86312.* **6** 23
22 Oct 88	BARCELONA *Polydor POLH 44* 1 ....**15** 8
28 Nov 92 ●	THE FREDDIE MERCURY ALBUM *Parlophone CDPCSD 124* **4** 25
4 Nov 00	SOLO *Parlophone 5280472* **13** 9

1 Freddie Mercury and Montserrat Caballé 1 Freddie Mercury and Montserrat Caballé

'Solo' is a 3-CD greatest hits boxed set

MERCURY REV
US, male vocal / instrumental group (Singles: 12 Weeks, Albums: 17 Weeks) pos/wks

14 Nov 98	GODDESS ON A HIWAY *V2 VVR 5003323* **51** 1
6 Feb 99	DELTA SUN BOTTLENECK STOMP *V2 VVR 5005413* **26** 2
22 May 99	OPUS 40 *V2 VVR 5006963* **31** 2
28 Aug 99	GODDESS ON A HIWAY (re-issue) *V2 VVR 5008493* **26** 2
6 Oct 01	NITE AND FOG *V2 VVR 5017723* **47** 1
26 Jan 02	THE DARK IS RISING *V2 VVR 5018713* **16** 3
27 Jul 02	LITTLE RHYMES *V2 VVR 5019783* **51** 1
12 Jun 93	BOCES *Beggars Banquet BBQCD 140.* **43** 1
17 Oct 98	DESERTER'S SONGS *V2 VVR 1002772* **27** 12
8 Sep 01	ALL IS DREAM *V2 VVR 1017528* **11** 4

MERCY MERCY
UK, male vocal / instrumental group (Singles: 2 Weeks) pos/wks

21 Sep 85	WHAT ARE WE GONNA DO ABOUT IT? *Ensign ENY 522* **59** 2

MERLE and ROY
UK, female / male vocal / instrumental duo (Albums: 5 Weeks) pos/wks

26 Sep 87	REQUESTS *Mynod Mawr RMBR 8713* **74** 5

MERLIN See The BEATMASTERS; BOMB THE BASS

MERO UK, male vocal duo – Tommy Clark
and Derek McDonald (Singles: 2 Weeks)   pos/wks

| 25 Mar 00 | **IT MUST BE LOVE** RCA 74321664772 | 33 | 2 |

Tony MERRICK UK, male vocalist (Singles: 1 Week)   pos/wks

| 2 Jun 66 | **LADY JANE** Columbia DB 7913 | 49 | 1 |

MERRION, McCALL & KENSIT
(see also EIGHTH WONDER; BO SELECTA) UK, male comedian / vocalist –
Leigh Francis and female TV celebrities / vocalists – Davina McCall
and Patsy Kensit (Singles: 1 Week)   pos/wks

| 25 Dec 04 ● | **I GOT YOU BABE / SODA POP** BMG 82876669872 | 5 | 1+ |

The MERSEYBEATS UK, male vocal /
instrumental group (Singles: 64 Weeks, Albums: 9 Weeks)   pos/wks

12 Sep 63	**IT'S LOVE THAT REALLY COUNTS** Fontana TF 412	24	12
16 Jan 64 ●	**I THINK OF YOU** Fontana TF 431	5	17
16 Apr 64	**DON'T TURN AROUND** Fontana TF 459	13	11
9 Jul 64	**WISHIN' AND HOPIN'** Fontana TF 482	13	10
5 Nov 64	**LAST NIGHT** Fontana TF 504	40	3
14 Oct 65	**I LOVE YOU, YES I DO** Fontana TF 607	22	8
20 Jan 66	**I STAND ACCUSED** Fontana TF 645	38	3
20 Jun 64	**THE MERSEYBEATS** Fontana TL 5210	12	9

The MERSEYS UK, male vocal duo (Singles: 13 Weeks)   pos/wks

| 28 Apr 66 ● | **SORROW** Fontana TF 694 | 4 | 13 |

The MERTON PARKAS
UK, male vocal / instrumental group (Singles: 6 Weeks)   pos/wks

| 4 Aug 79 | **YOU NEED WHEELS** Beggars Banquet BEG 22 | 40 | 6 |

MERZ UK, male vocalist /
instrumentalist – Conrad Lambert (Singles: 2 Weeks)   pos/wks

| 17 Jul 99 | **MANY WEATHERS APART** Epic 6674972 | 48 | 1 |
| 16 Oct 99 | **LOVELY DAUGHTER** Epic 6679132 | 60 | 1 |

MESCALEROS See Joe STRUMMER

**Mady MESPLE and Danielle MILLET with the PARIS OPERA-
COMIQUE ORCHESTRA conducted by Alain LOMBARD**
France, female vocal duo and orchestra (Singles: 4 Weeks)   pos/wks

| 6 Apr 85 | **FLOWER DUET (FROM 'LAKME')** EMI 5481 | 47 | 4 |

MESSIAH
UK, male instrumental / production group (Singles: 13 Weeks) pos/wks

20 Jun 92	**TEMPLE OF DREAMS** Kickin KICK 12S	20	5
26 Sep 92	**I FEEL LOVE** Kickin KICK 22S [1]	19	5
27 Nov 93	**THUNDERDOME** WEA YZ 790CD1	29	3

[1] Messiah featuring Precious Wilson

METAL GURUS
UK, male vocal / instrumental group (Singles: 2 Weeks)   pos/wks

| 8 Dec 90 | **MERRY XMAS EVERYBODY** Mercury GURU 1 | 55 | 2 |

METALHEADZ See GOLDIE

METALLICA ⟨334⟩ Top 500 Perennially popular hard rock group
formed in 1981 in Los Angeles by Denmark-born Lars Ulrich (d) and fronted
by James Hetfield (v/g). Festival favourites and multi-award winners have
sold more than 60 million albums in the US alone and 'St Anger' topped
charts in 13 countries (Singles: 72 Weeks, Albums: 129 Weeks) pos/wks

22 Aug 87	**THE $5.98 EP – GARAGE DAYS RE-VISITED** Vertigo METAL 112	27	4
3 Sep 88	**HARVESTER OF SORROW** Vertigo METAL 212	20	3
22 Apr 89	**ONE** Vertigo METAL 5	13	7
10 Aug 91 ●	**ENTER SANDMAN** Vertigo METAL 7	5	4
9 Nov 91	**THE UNFORGIVEN** Vertigo METAL 8	15	4
2 May 92 ●	**NOTHING ELSE MATTERS** Vertigo METAL 10	6	6
31 Oct 92	**WHEREVER I MAY ROAM** Vertigo METAL 9	25	4
20 Feb 93	**SAD BUT TRUE** Vertigo METCD 11	20	3

1 Jun 96 ●	**UNTIL IT SLEEPS** Vertigo METCD 12	5	4
28 Sep 96	**HERO OF THE DAY** Vertigo METCD 13	17	4
7 Dec 96	**MAMA SAID** Vertigo METCD 14	19	2
22 Nov 97	**THE MEMORY REMAINS** Vertigo METCD 15	13	3
7 Mar 98	**THE UNFORGIVEN II** Vertigo METDD 17	15	4
4 Jul 98	**FUEL** Vertigo METCD 16	31	2
27 Feb 99	**WHISKEY IN THE JAR** Vertigo METCD 19	29	2
12 Aug 00	**I DISAPPEAR** Hollywood 0113875 HWR	35	3
5 Jul 03 ●	**ST ANGER** Vertigo 9865412	9	8
4 Oct 03	**FRANTIC** Vertigo 9811513	16	3
24 Jan 04	**THE UNNAMED FEELING** Vertigo 9815661	42	2
11 Aug 84	**RIDE THE LIGHTNING** Music for Nations MFN 27	87	2
15 Mar 86	**MASTER OF PUPPETS** Music for Nations MFN 60	41	4
17 Sep 88 ●	**... AND JUSTICE FOR ALL** Vertigo VERH 61	4	6
19 May 90	**THE GOOD THE BAD AND THE LIVE** Vertigo 8754871	56	1
24 Aug 91 ★	**METALLICA** Vertigo 5100221 ■ ▲	1	72
11 Dec 93	**LIVE SHIT – BINGE AND PURGE** Vertigo 5187250	54	1
15 Jun 96 ★	**LOAD** Vertigo 5326182 ■ ▲	1	18
5 Oct 96	**HERO OF THE DAY** Vertigo METCY 13	47	1
29 Nov 97 ●	**RELOAD** Vertigo 5364092 ▲	4	9
5 Dec 98	**GARAGE INC.** Vertigo 5383512	29	2
4 Dec 99	**S&M** Vertigo 5467972	33	2
14 Jun 03 ●	**ST ANGER** Vertigo 9865338 ▲	3	11

Tracks on The $5.98 EP: Garage Days Re-Revisited / Helpless / Crash Course in Brain
Surgery / The Small Hours / Last Caress / Green Hell 'Live Shit – Binge and Purge'
is a boxed set containing two CDs, three video cassettes and a book

METEOR SEVEN
Germany, male producer – Jans Ebert (Singles: 1 Week)   pos/wks

| 18 May 02 | **UNIVERSAL MUSIC** Bulletproof PROOF 16CD | 71 | 1 |

METEORS UK, male vocal / instrumental
group (Singles: 2 Weeks, Albums: 3 Weeks)   pos/wks

| 26 Feb 83 | **JOHNNY REMEMBER ME** LD EYE 1 | 66 | 2 |
| 26 Feb 83 | **WRECKIN' CREW** LD NOSE 1 | 53 | 3 |

Pat METHENY GROUP See David BOWIE

METHOD MAN (see also WU-TANG CLAN) US, male
rapper – Clifford Smith (Singles: 24 Weeks, Albums: 7 Weeks) pos/wks

29 Apr 95	**RELEASE YO' SELF** Def Jam DEFCD 6	46	1
29 Jul 95 ●	**I'LL BE THERE FOR YOU – YOU'RE ALL I NEED TO GET BY** Def Jam DEFCD 11 [1]	10	5
5 Apr 97 ●	**HIT EM HIGH (THE MONSTARS' ANTHEM)** Atlantic A 5449CD [2]	8	6
22 May 99	**BREAK UPS 2 MAKE UPS** Def Jam 8709272 [3]	33	2
27 Sep 03	**LOVE @ 1ST SIGHT** MCA MCSTD 40338 [4]	18	5
22 May 04	**WHAT'S HAPPENIN'** Def Jam 98628517 [5]	17	5
28 Nov 98	**TICAL 2000: JUDGEMENT DAY** Def Jam 5589202	49	1
9 Oct 99	**BLACKOUT!** Def Jam 5466092 [1]	45	3
29 May 04	**TICAL O: THE PREQUEL** Def Jam / Mercury 9862641	29	3

[1] Method Man featuring Mary J Blige [2] B Real / Busta Rhymes / Coolio /
LL Cool J / Method Man [3] Method Man featuring D'Angelo [4] Mary J Blige
featuring Method Man [5] Method Man featuring Busta Rhymes [1] Method
Man and Redman

MEW Denmark, male vocal / instrumental group (Singles: 3 Weeks) pos/wks

5 Mar 03	**COMFORTING SOUNDS** Epic 6736432	48	1
28 Jun 03	**AM I WRY? NO** Epic 6739395	47	1
27 Dec 03	**SHE CAME HOME FOR CHRISTMAS** Epic 6744942	55	1

MEZZOFORTE Iceland, male instrumental
group (Singles: 10 Weeks, Albums: 10 Weeks)   pos/wks

5 Mar 83	**GARDEN PARTY** Steinar STE 705	17	9
11 Jun 83	**ROCKALL** Steinar STE 710	75	1
5 Mar 83	**SURPRISE SURPRISE** Steinar STELP 02	23	9
2 Jul 83	**CATCHING UP WITH MEZZOFORTE** Steinar STELP 03	95	1

MIAMI SOUND MACHINE (see also Gloria ESTEFAN)
Cuba, male / female vocal / instrumental group (Singles: 72 Weeks) pos/wks

11 Aug 84 ●	**DR BEAT** Epic A 4614	6	14
17 May 86	**BAD BOY** Epic A 6537	16	11
16 Jul 88 ●	**ANYTHING FOR YOU** Epic 651673 7 [1] ▲	10	16
22 Oct 88 ●	**1-2-3 (re)** Epic 652958 7 [1]	9	10

		pos/wks
17 Dec 88	RHYTHM IS GONNA GET YOU *Epic 654514 7* [1]	16 9
11 Feb 89 ●	CAN'T STAY AWAY FROM YOU *Epic 651 444 7* [1]	7 12

[1] Gloria Estefan and Miami Sound Machine

George MICHAEL (56) Top 500

(see also Elton JOHN; Lisa MOORISH) *Previously half of internationally celebrated duo Wham!, b. Georgios Panayiotou, 25 Jun 1963, London, UK. This multi-talented, award-winning singer / songwriter / producer / arranger and instrumentalist has successfully made the difficult transition from teeny-bopper hero to world-renowned solo star. Best-selling single: 'Careless Whisper' 1,365,995 (Singles: 287 Weeks, Albums: 340 Weeks)* pos/wks

		pos/wks
4 Aug 84 ★	CARELESS WHISPER *Epic A 4603* ◆ ▲	1 17
5 Apr 86 ★	A DIFFERENT CORNER *Epic A 7033*	1 9
31 Jan 87 ★	I KNEW YOU WERE WAITING (FOR ME) *Epic DUET 2* [1] ▲	1 9
13 Jun 87 ●	I WANT YOUR SEX *Epic LUST 1*	3 10
24 Oct 87 ●	FAITH *Epic EMU 3* ▲	2 12
9 Jan 88	FATHER FIGURE *Epic EMU 4* ▲	11 6
23 Apr 88 ●	ONE MORE TRY *Epic EMU 5* ▲	8 7
16 Jul 88	MONKEY *Epic EMU 6* ▲	13 6
3 Dec 88	KISSING A FOOL *Epic EMU 7*	18 6
25 Aug 90 ●	PRAYING FOR TIME *Epic GEO 1* ◆	6 7
27 Oct 90	WAITING FOR THAT DAY *Epic GEO 2*	23 5
15 Dec 90	FREEDOM! *Epic GEO 3*	28 6
16 Feb 91	HEAL THE PAIN *Epic 6566477*	31 4
30 Mar 91	COWBOYS AND ANGELS *Epic 6567747*	45 3
7 Dec 91 ●	DON'T LET THE SUN GO DOWN ON ME *Epic 6576467* [2] ■ ▲	1 10
13 Jun 92 ●	TOO FUNKY *Epic 6580587*	4 9
1 May 93 ★	FIVE LIVE (EP) (re) *Parlophone CDRS 6340* [3] ■	1 12
20 Jan 96 ★	JESUS TO A CHILD (2re) *Virgin VSCDG 1571* ■	1 13
4 May 96 ●	FASTLOVE *Virgin VSCDG 1579* ■	1 14
31 Aug 96 ●	SPINNING THE WHEEL *Virgin VSCDG 1595*	2 12
1 Feb 97 ●	OLDER / I CAN'T MAKE YOU LOVE ME (re) *Virgin VSCDG 1626*	3 9
10 May 97 ●	STAR PEOPLE '97 (re) *Virgin VSCDG 1641*	2 13
7 Jun 97 ●	WALTZ AWAY DREAMING *Aegean AECD 01* [4]	10 4
20 Sep 97 ●	YOU HAVE BEEN LOVED / THE STRANGEST THING '97 *Virgin VSCD 1663*	2 8
31 Oct 98 ●	OUTSIDE (re) *Epic 6665625*	2 16
13 Mar 99 ●	AS *Epic 6670122* [5]	4 10
17 Jun 00 ●	IF I TOLD YOU THAT (re) *Arista 74321766282* [6]	9 11
30 Mar 02 ●	FREEEK! *Polydor 5706812*	7 10
10 Aug 02	SHOOT THE DOG (re) *Polydor 5709242*	12 5
13 Mar 04 ●	AMAZING *Aegean / Sony 6747262*	4 11
10 Jul 04 ●	FLAWLESS (GO TO THE CITY) *Aegean / Sony 6750682*	8 10
13 Nov 04	ROUND HERE *Aegean / Sony 6754702*	32 2
14 Nov 87 ★	FAITH *Epic 4600001* ■ ▲	1 77
15 Sep 90 ★	LISTEN WITHOUT PREJUDICE VOLUME 1 *Epic 4672951* ■	1 57
25 May 96 ★	OLDER *Virgin CDV 2802* ■	1 99
21 Nov 98 ★	LADIES & GENTLEMEN – THE BEST OF GEORGE MICHAEL *Epic 4917052* ■	1 67
18 Dec 99 ●	SONGS FROM THE LAST CENTURY *Virgin CDVX 2920*	2 17
27 Mar 04 ★	PATIENCE *Aegean / Sony 5154022* ■	1 23

[1] Aretha Franklin and George Michael [2] George Michael and Elton John [3] George Michael and Queen with Lisa Stansfield [4] Toby Bourke with George Michael [5] George Michael and Mary J Blige [6] Whitney Houston / George Michael

Tracks on Five Live (EP): Somebody to Love / These Are the Days of Our Lives / Calling You / Papa Was a Rolling Stone – Killer (medley) / Dear Friends. Track one features Queen, the second Queen and Lisa Stansfield and the last track, Queen

MICHAELA
UK, female vocalist – Michaela Strachan (Singles: 6 Weeks) pos/wks

		pos/wks
2 Sep 89	H-A-P-P-Y RADIO *London H 1*	62 4
28 Apr 90	TAKE GOOD CARE OF MY HEART *London WAC 90*	66 2

Lisa MICHAELIS See Frankie KNUCKLES

Pras MICHEL
(see also FUGEES) *US, male rapper / producer – Prakazrel Michael (Singles: 36 Weeks, Albums: 3 Weeks)* pos/wks

		pos/wks
27 Jun 98 ●	GHETTO SUPASTAR (THAT IS WHAT YOU ARE) *Interscope IND 95593* [1]	2 17
7 Nov 98 ●	BLUE ANGELS *Ruffhouse 6666215* [2]	6 10
14 Nov 98 ●	ANOTHER ONE BITES THE DUST *Dreamworks DRMCD 22364* [3]	5 6

		pos/wks
1 Sep 01	MISS CALIFORNIA *Elektra E 7192CD* [4]	25 3
14 Nov 98	GHETTO SUPASTAR *Columbia 4914892* [1]	44 3

[1] Pras Michel featuring ODB & introducing Mya [2] Pras [3] Queen with Wyclef Jean featuring Pras and Free [4] Dante Thomas featuring Pras [1] Pras

MICHELE See KING BEE

Keith MICHELL
Australia, male actor / vocalist (Singles: 25 Weeks, Albums: 12 Weeks) pos/wks

		pos/wks
27 Mar 71	I'LL GIVE YOU THE EARTH (TOUS LES BATEAUX, TOUS LES OISEAUX) (re) *Spark SRL 1046*	30 11
26 Jan 80 ●	CAPTAIN BEAKY / WILFRED THE WEASEL *Polydor POSP 106*	5 10
29 Mar 80	THE TRIAL OF HISSING SID *Polydor HISS 1* [1]	53 4
9 Feb 80	CAPTAIN BEAKY AND HIS BAND *Polydor 238 3462*	28 12

[1] Keith Michell, Captain Beaky and his Band

MICHELLE
Trinidad, female vocalist (Singles: 1 Week) pos/wks

		pos/wks
8 Jun 96	STANDING HERE ALL ALONE *Positiva CDTIV 54*	69 1

MICHELLE
UK, female vocalist – Michelle McManus (Singles: 15 Weeks, Albums: 7 Weeks) pos/wks

		pos/wks
17 Jan 04 ★	ALL THIS TIME *S 82876590652* ■	1 11
17 Apr 04	THE MEANING OF LOVE *S 82876604032*	16 4
28 Feb 04 ●	THE MEANING OF LOVE *S 82876590662*	3 7

Yvette MICHELLE
US, female vocalist – Michele Bryant (Singles: 3 Weeks) pos/wks

		pos/wks
5 Apr 97	I'M NOT FEELING YOU *Loud 74321465222*	36 3

Lloyd MICHELS See MISTURA featuring Lloyd MICHELS

MICROBE
UK, male vocalist – Ian Doody, the youngest solo male chart entrant, aged 3 (Singles: 7 Weeks) pos/wks

		pos/wks
14 May 69	GROOVY BABY *CBS 4158*	29 7

MICRODISNEY
Ireland, male vocal / instrumental group (Singles: 3 Weeks) pos/wks

		pos/wks
21 Feb 87	TOWN TO TOWN *Virgin VS 927*	55 3

MIDDLE OF THE ROAD
UK, male / female vocal / instrumental group (Singles: 76 Weeks) pos/wks

		pos/wks
5 Jun 71 ★	CHIRPY CHIRPY CHEEP CHEEP *RCA 2047*	1 34
4 Sep 71 ●	TWEEDLE DEE, TWEEDLE DUM *RCA 2110*	2 17
11 Dec 71 ●	SOLEY SOLEY *RCA 2151*	5 12
25 Mar 72	SACRAMENTO (A WONDERFUL TOWN) (re) *RCA 2184*	23 7
29 Jul 72	SAMSON AND DELILAH *RCA 2237*	26 6

MIDDLESBROUGH FC featuring Bob MORTIMER and Chris REA
UK, male football team / vocal group, comedian / vocalist and vocalist / instrumentalist – guitar (Singles: 1 Week) pos/wks

		pos/wks
24 May 97	LET'S DANCE *Magnet EW 112CD*	44 1

MIDFIELD GENERAL featuring LINDA LEWIS *UK, male producer – Damian Harris and female vocalist (Singles: 1 Week)* pos/wks

		pos/wks
19 Aug 00	REACH OUT *Skint / SKINT 54CD*	61 1

MIDGET *UK, male vocal / instrumental group (Singles: 2 Weeks)* pos/wks

		pos/wks
31 Jan 98	ALL FALL DOWN *Radarscope TINYCDS 6X*	57 1
18 Apr 98	INVISIBLE BALLOON *Radarscope TINYCDS 7*	66 1

MIDI XPRESS
UK, male vocal / instrumental duo (Singles: 1 Week) pos/wks

		pos/wks
11 May 96	CHASE *Labello Dance LAD 26CD*	73 1

Bette MIDLER
US, female vocalist (Singles: 27 Weeks, Albums: 40 Weeks) pos/wks

		pos/wks
17 Jun 89 ●	WIND BENEATH MY WINGS *Atlantic A 8972* ▲	5 12
13 Oct 90 ●	FROM A DISTANCE (re) *Atlantic A 7820*	6 14
5 Dec 98	MY ONE TRUE FRIEND *Warner Bros. W 460CD*	58 1
15 Jul 89	BEACHES (FILM SOUNDTRACK) *Atlantic 7819931*	21 9

13 Jul 91	●	SOME PEOPLE'S LIVES *Atlantic 7567821291*	**5**	11
15 Feb 92		FOR THE BOYS (FILM SOUNDTRACK) *Atlantic 7567823292*	**75**	1
30 Oct 93	●	EXPERIENCE THE DIVINE – GREATEST HITS *Atlantic 7567824972*	**3**	15
25 Nov 95		BETTE OF ROSES *Atlantic 7567828232*	**55**	4

'From A Distance' peaked at No.6 in Jun 1991

MIDNIGHT COWBOY SOUNDTRACK
US, orchestra (Singles: 4 Weeks) pos/wks

8 Nov 80		MIDNIGHT COWBOY *United Artists UP 634*	**47**	4

MIDNIGHT OIL *Australia, male vocal /*
instrumental group (Singles: 32 Weeks, Albums: 21 Weeks) pos/wks

23 Apr 88		BEDS ARE BURNING *Sprint OIL 1*	**48**	5
2 Jul 88		THE DEAD HEART *Sprint OIL 2*	**68**	2
25 Mar 89	●	BEDS ARE BURNING (re-issue) *Sprint OIL 3*	**6**	13
1 Jul 89		THE DEAD HEART (re-issue) *Sprint OIL 4*	**62**	4
10 Feb 90		BLUE SKY MINE *CBS OIL 5*	**66**	2
17 Apr 93		TRUGANINI *Columbia 6590492*	**29**	4
3 Jul 93		MY COUNTRY *Columbia 6593702*	**66**	1
6 Nov 93		IN THE VALLEY *Columbia 6598492*	**60**	1
25 Jun 88		DIESEL AND DUST *CBS 4600051*	**19**	16
10 Mar 90		BLUE SKY MINING *CBS 4656531*	**28**	3
1 May 93		EARTH AND SUN AND MOON *Columbia 4736052*	**27**	2

MIDNIGHT STAR *US, male / female vocal /*
instrumental group (Singles: 26 Weeks, Albums: 6 Weeks) pos/wks

23 Feb 85		OPERATOR *Solar MCA 942*	**66**	2
28 Jun 86		HEADLINES *Solar MCA 1065*	**16**	8
4 Oct 86	●	MIDAS TOUCH *Solar MCA 1096*	**8**	10
7 Feb 87		ENGINE NO.9 *Solar MCA 1117*	**64**	3
2 May 87		WET MY WHISTLE *Solar MCA 1127*	**60**	3
2 Feb 85		PLANETARY INVASION *Solar MCF 3251*	**85**	2
5 Jul 86		HEADLINES *Solar MCF 3322*	**42**	4

MIDNITE BAND See Tony RALLO and The MIDNITE BAND

The MIGHTY AVENGERS
UK, male vocal / instrumental group (Singles: 2 Weeks) pos/wks

26 Nov 64		SO MUCH IN LOVE *Decca F 11962*	**46**	2

MIGHTY AVONS See Larry CUNNINGHAM and The MIGHTY AVONS

MIGHTY DUB KATZ (see also BEATS INTERNATIONAL; Norman COOK;
FATBOY SLIM; FREAKPOWER; The HOUSEMARTINS; PIZZAMAN)
UK, male producer – Norman Cook (Singles: 6 Weeks) pos/wks

7 Dec 96		JUST ANOTHER GROOVE *ffrr FCD 287*	**43**	1
2 Aug 97		MAGIC CARPET RIDE *ffrr FCD 306*	**24**	4
7 Dec 02		LET THE DRUMS SPEAK *Southern Fried ECB 31X*	**73**	1

MIGHTY LEMON DROPS *UK, male vocal /*
instrumental group (Singles: 6 Weeks, Albums: 5 Weeks) pos/wks

13 Sep 86		THE OTHER SIDE OF YOU *Blue Guitar AZUR 1*	**67**	1
18 Apr 87		OUT OF HAND *Blue Guitar AZUR 4*	**66**	3
23 Jan 88		INSIDE OUT *Blue Guitar AZUR 6*	**74**	2
4 Oct 86		HAPPY HEAD *Blue Guitar AZLP 1*	**58**	2
27 Feb 88		THE WORLD WITHOUT END *Blue Guitar AZLP 4*	**34**	3

The MIGHTY MIGHTY BOSSTONES *US, male vocal /*
instrumental group (Singles: 6 Weeks, Albums: 2 Weeks) pos/wks

25 Apr 98		THE IMPRESSION THAT I GET *Mercury 5748432*	**12**	5
27 Jun 98		THE RASCAL KING *Mercury 5661092*	**63**	1
16 May 98		LET'S FACE IT *Mercury 5344722*	**40**	2

MIGHTY MORPH'N POWER RANGERS *US, male /*
female vocal group (Singles: 13 Weeks, Albums: 3 Weeks) pos/wks

17 Dec 94	●	POWER RANGERS (3re) *RCA 74321253022*	**3**	13
24 Dec 94		POWER RANGERS – THE ALBUM *RCA 74321252982*	**50**	3

MIGHTY WAH See WAH!

The MIGIL FIVE
UK, male vocal / instrumental group (Singles: 20 Weeks) pos/wks

19 Mar 64	●	MOCKINGBIRD HILL *Pye 7N 15597*	**10**	13
4 Jun 64		NEAR YOU *Pye 7N 15645*	**31**	7

MIG29
Italy, male instrumental / production group (Singles: 2 Weeks) pos/wks

22 Feb 92		MIG29 *Champion CHAMP 292*	**62**	2

MIKAELA See SUPERCAR

MIKE *UK, male producer – Mark Jolley (Singles: 2 Weeks)* pos/wks

19 Nov 94		TWANGLING THREE FINGERS IN A BOX *Pukka CDMIKE 100*	**40**	2

MIKE and the MECHANICS 〈 414 | Top 500 〉
*Adult-orientated, radio-friendly pop act formed by Genesis guitarist
Mike Rutherford, Surrey. Vocalists included former Ace front man Paul
Carrack and ex-Sad Cafe singer Paul Young (d. 2000). 'The Living Years'
has been heard more than four million times on US radio (Singles: 67
Weeks, Albums: 101 Weeks)* pos/wks

15 Feb 86		SILENT RUNNING (ON DANGEROUS GROUND) *WEA U 8908*	**21**	9
31 May 86		ALL I NEED IS A MIRACLE *WEA U 8765*	**53**	4
14 Jan 89	●	THE LIVING YEARS *WEA U 7717* ▲	**2**	11
16 Mar 91		WORD OF MOUTH *Virgin VS 1345*	**13**	10
15 Jun 91		A TIME AND PLACE *Virgin VS 1351*	**58**	3
8 Feb 92		EVERYBODY GETS A SECOND CHANCE *Virgin VS 1396*	**56**	4
25 Feb 95		OVER MY SHOULDER *Virgin VSCDT 1526*	**12**	9
17 Jun 95		A BEGGAR ON A BEACH OF GOLD *Virgin VSCDT 1535*	**33**	5
2 Sep 95		ANOTHER CUP OF COFFEE *Virgin VSCDT 1554*	**51**	4
17 Feb 96		ALL I NEED IS A MIRACLE (re-mix) *Virgin VSCDT 1576*	**27**	4
1 Jun 96		SILENT RUNNING (re-issue) *Virgin VSCDT 1585*	**61**	1
5 Jun 99		NOW THAT YOU'VE GONE *Virgin VSCDT 1732*	**35**	2
28 Aug 99		WHENEVER I STOP *Virgin VSCDT 1743*	**73**	1
15 Mar 86		MIKE AND THE MECHANICS *WEA WX 49*	**78**	3
26 Nov 88	●	THE LIVING YEARS *WEA WX 203*	**2**	19
27 Apr 91		WORD OF MOUTH *Virgin V 2662*	**11**	7
18 Mar 95	●	BEGGAR ON A BEACH OF GOLD *Virgin CDV 2772*	**9**	33
2 Mar 96		THE LIVING YEARS (re-issue) *Atlantic K 2560042*	**67**	2
16 Mar 96	●	HITS *Virgin CDV 2797*	**3**	31
12 Jun 99		MIKE AND THE MECHANICS *Virgin CDV 2885*	**14**	4
19 Jun 04		REWIRED *Virgin CDVX 2984* [1]	**61**	1
18 Sep 04		REWIRED + THE HITS – THE LATEST + GREATEST *Virgin CDVX 2990*	**42**	1

[1] Mike and the Mechanics & Paul Carrack

The two 'Mike and the Mechanics' albums are different

MIKI and GRIFF *UK, female / male vocal duo –*
*Barbara Salisbury, b. 20 Jun 1920, d. 20 Apr 1989, and
Emyr Griffith, b. 9 May 1923, d. 24 Sep 1995 (Singles: 25 Weeks)* pos/wks

2 Oct 59		HOLD BACK TOMORROW *Pye 7N 15213* [1]	**26**	2
13 Oct 60		ROCKIN' ALONE *Pye 7N 15296* [2]	**44**	3
1 Feb 62		A LITTLE BITTY TEAR *Pye 7N 15412*	**16**	13
22 Aug 63		I WANT TO STAY HERE *Pye 7N 15555*	**23**	7

[1] Lonnie Donegan presents Miki and Griff with the Lonnie Donegan Group
[2] Miki and Griff with the Lonnie Donegan Group

Buddy MILES See SANTANA

John MILES *UK, male vocalist /*
multi-instrumentalist (Singles: 30 Weeks, Albums: 25 Weeks) pos/wks

18 Oct 75		HIGHFLY *Decca F 13595*	**17**	6
20 Mar 76	●	MUSIC *Decca F 13627*	**3**	9
16 Oct 76		REMEMBER YESTERDAY *Decca F 13667*	**32**	5
18 Jun 77	●	SLOW DOWN *Decca F 13709*	**10**	10
27 Mar 76	●	REBEL *Decca SKL 5231*	**9**	10
26 Feb 77		STRANGER IN THE CITY *Decca TXS 118*	**37**	3
1 Apr 78		ZARAGON *Decca TXS 126*	**43**	5
21 Apr 79		MORE MILES PER HOUR *Decca TXS 135*	**46**	5
29 Aug 81		MILES HIGH *EMI EMC 3374*	**96**	2

Robert MILES
*Italy, male instrumentalist – keyboards –
Roberto Concina (Singles: 49 Weeks, Albums: 51 Weeks)* pos/wks

24 Feb 96	●	CHILDREN *Deconstruction 74321348322*	**2**	18
8 Jun 96	●	FABLE (2re) *Deconstruction 74321382622*	**7**	9
16 Nov 96	●	ONE & ONE *Deconstruction 74321427692* [1]	**3**	17
29 Nov 97	●	FREEDOM *Deconstruction 74321536952* [2]	**15**	4
28 Jul 01		PATHS *Salt SALT 002CD* [3]	**74**	1

			pos/wks
22 Jun 96 ●	**DREAMLAND** *Deconstruction 74321391262*		.7 48
6 Dec 97	**23AM** *Deconstruction 74321541132*		.42 3

1 Robert Miles featuring Maria Nayler 2 Robert Miles featuring Kathy Sledge 3 Robert Miles featuring Nina Miranda

June MILES-KINGSTON *See Jimmy SOMERVILLE*

Paul MILES-KINGSTON *See Sarah BRIGHTMAN*

Christina MILIAN (see also JA RULE)
US, female vocalist (Singles: 47 Weeks, Albums: 15 Weeks)   pos/wks

			pos/wks
26 Jan 02 ●	**AM TO PM** *Def Soul 5889332*		.3 11
29 Jun 02 ●	**WHEN YOU LOOK AT ME** *Def Soul 5829802*		.3 10
9 Nov 02 ●	**IT'S ALL GRAVY** *Relentless RELENT 32CD* 1		.9 6
15 May 04 ●	**DIP IT LOW** *Def Jam 9862395*		.2 13
16 Oct 04 ●	**WHATEVER U WANT** *Def Jam 9864266* 2		.9 7
2 Feb 02	**CHRISTINA MILIAN** *Def Soul 5867392*		.23 11
12 Jun 04	**IT'S ABOUT TIME** *Def Jam UK / Mercury 9862835*		.21 4

1 Romeo featuring Christina Milian 2 Christina Milian featuring Joe Budden

MILK *See Jason DOWNS featuring MILK*

MILK AND HONEY featuring Gali ATARI
Israel, male / female vocal / instrumental group (Singles: 8 Weeks) pos/wks

			pos/wks
14 Apr 79 ●	**HALLELUJAH** *Polydor 2001 870*		.5 8

MILK & SUGAR *Germany, male production duo – Michael Kronenberger*
and Steffan Harning and Australia, male vocalist (Singles: 7 Weeks) pos/wks

			pos/wks
12 Jan 02	**LOVE IS IN THE AIR** *Positiva CDTIV 166* 1		.25 3
11 Oct 03	**LET THE SUNSHINE IN** *Data / MoS DATA 64CDS* 2		.18 4

1 Milk and Sugar vs John Paul Young 2 Milk and Sugar featuring Lizzy Pattinson

MILK INC. *Belgium, male / female production / vocal duo –*
Regi Penxten and An Vervoort (Singles: 21 Weeks, Albums: 1 Week) pos/wks

			pos/wks
28 Feb 98	**GOOD ENOUGH (LA VACHE)** *Malarky MLKD 5* 1		.23 3
25 May 02 ●	**IN MY EYES** *All Around the World CDGLOBE 252*		.9 8
21 Sep 02 ●	**WALK ON WATER** *Positiva CDTIV 179*		.10 6
11 Jan 03	**LAND OF THE LIVING** *Positiva CDTIVS 184*		.18 4
5 Oct 02	**MILK INC.** *Positiva 5419532*		.47 1

1 Milk Incorporated

MILKY *Italy, male production duo and Egypt,*
female vocalist – Sabrina Kassel (Singles: 7 Weeks) pos/wks

			pos/wks
31 Aug 02 ●	**JUST THE WAY YOU ARE** *Multiply CDMULTY 87*		.8 6
7 Dec 02	**IN MY MIND** *Multiply CDMULTY 92*		.48 1

MILL GIRLS *See Billy COTTON and his BAND*

MILLA *US, female vocalist / actor – Milla Jovovich (Singles: 1 Week)* pos/wks

			pos/wks
18 Jun 94	**GENTLEMAN WHO FELL** *SBK CDSBK 49*		.65 1

Dominic MILLER
Argentina, male instrumentalist (Albums: 3 Weeks) pos/wks

			pos/wks
14 Jun 03	**SHAPES** *BBC Music WMSF 60702*		.38 3

Frankie MILLER
UK, male vocalist (Singles: 32 Weeks, Albums: 1 Week) pos/wks

			pos/wks
4 Jun 77	**BE GOOD TO YOURSELF** *Chrysalis CHS 2147*		.27 6
14 Oct 78 ●	**DARLIN'** *Chrysalis CHS 2255*		.6 15
20 Jan 79	**WHEN I'M AWAY FROM YOU** *Chrysalis CHS 2276*		.42 5
21 Mar 92	**CALEDONIA** *MCS MCS 2001*		.45 6
14 Apr 79	**FALLING IN LOVE** *Chrysalis CHR 1220*		.54 1

Gary MILLER *UK, male vocalist –*
Neville Williams, b. 1924, d. 15 Jun 1968 (Singles: 35 Weeks) pos/wks

			pos/wks
21 Oct 55	**THE YELLOW ROSE OF TEXAS** *Nixa N 15004*		.13 5
13 Jan 56 ●	**ROBIN HOOD** *Nixa N 15020*		.10 6
11 Jan 57	**GARDEN OF EDEN (re)** *Pye Nixa N 15070*		.14 7
19 Jul 57	**WONDERFUL, WONDERFUL** *Pye Nixa N 15094*		.29 1
17 Jan 58	**THE STORY OF MY LIFE** *Pye Nixa N 15120*		.14 6

			pos/wks
21 Dec 61	**THERE GOES THAT SONG AGAIN / THE NIGHT IS YOUNG (AND YOU'RE SO BEAUTIFUL) (re)** *Pye 7N 15404*		.29 10

'The Night Is Young' listed with 'There Goes That Song Again' only for 21 and 28 Dec 1961 and 4 Jan 1962. It peaked at No.32

Glenn MILLER
US, orchestra leader – Glenn Miller – trombone, b. 1 Mar 1904,
d. 15 Dec 1944 (Singles: 9 Weeks, Albums: 82 Weeks) pos/wks

			pos/wks
12 Mar 54	**MOONLIGHT SERENADE** *HMV BD 5942*		.12 1
24 Jan 76	**MOONLIGHT SERENADE / LITTLE BROWN JUG / IN THE MOOD** *RCA 2644* ▲		.13 8
28 Jan 61 ●	**GLENN MILLER PLAYS SELECTIONS FROM 'THE GLENN MILLER STORY' AND OTHER HITS** *RCA 27068 0023*		.10 18
5 Jul 69 ●	**THE BEST OF GLENN MILLER** *RCA International 1002*		.5 14
6 Sep 69	**NEARNESS OF YOU** *RCA International INTS 1019*		.30 2
25 Apr 70	**A MEMORIAL 1944-1969** *RCA GM 1.*		.18 17
25 Dec 71	**THE REAL GLENN MILLER AND HIS ORCHESTRA PLAY THE ORIGINAL MUSIC OF THE FILM 'THE GLENN MILLER STORY' AND OTHER HITS (re-issue)** *RCA International NTS 1157*		.28 2
14 Feb 76	**A LEGENDARY PERFORMER** *RCA Victor DPM 2065*		.41 5
14 Feb 76	**A LEGENDARY PERFORMER VOLUME 2** *RCA Victor CPL 11349*		.53 2
9 Apr 77 ●	**THE UNFORGETTABLE GLENN MILLER** *RCA Victor TVL 1*		.4 8
20 Mar 93	**THE ULTIMATE GLENN MILLER** *Bluebird 74321131372*		.11 4
25 Jun 95	**THE LOST RECORDINGS** *Happy Days CDHD 4012*		.22 6
18 Oct 03	**IN THE MOOD – THE DEFINITIVE GLENN MILLER** *BMG 82876560302*		.43 2

US No.1 symbol refers only to 'In the Mood', which hit the top spot in 1939 'The Real Glenn Miller and his Orchestra Play ...' is a re-titled re-issue of the first album

Jody MILLER
US, female vocalist (Singles: 1 Week) pos/wks

			pos/wks
21 Oct 65	**HOME OF THE BRAVE** *Capitol CL 15415*		.49 1

Leza MILLER *See Sergio MENDES*

Mitch MILLER, his Orchestra and Chorus
US, orchestra and chorus (Singles: 13 Weeks) pos/wks

			pos/wks
7 Oct 55 ●	**THE YELLOW ROSE OF TEXAS** *Philips PB 505* ▲		.2 13

Ned MILLER *US, male vocalist (Singles: 22 Weeks)* pos/wks

			pos/wks
14 Feb 63 ●	**FROM A JACK TO A KING** *London HL 9658*		.2 21
18 Feb 65	**DO WHAT YOU DO DO WELL** *London HL 9937*		.48 1

Roger MILLER
US, male vocalist / instrumentalist – guitar, b. 2 Jan 1936, d.
25 Oct 1992 (Singles: 42 Weeks) pos/wks

			pos/wks
18 Mar 65 ★	**KING OF THE ROAD** *Philips BF 1397*		.1 15
3 Jun 65	**ENGINE ENGINE NO.9** *Philips BF 1416*		.33 5
21 Oct 65	**KANSAS CITY STAR** *Philips BF 1437*		.48 1
16 Dec 65	**ENGLAND SWINGS (re)** *Philips BF 1456*		.13 8
27 Mar 68	**LITTLE GREEN APPLES (2re)** *Mercury MF 1021*		.19 13

Steve MILLER BAND *US, male vocal / instrumental*
group (Singles: 36 Weeks, Albums: 51 Weeks) pos/wks

			pos/wks
23 Oct 76	**ROCK 'N ME** *Mercury 6078 804* ▲		.11 9
19 Jun 82 ●	**ABRACADABRA** *Mercury STEVE 3* ▲		.2 11
4 Sep 82	**KEEPS ME WONDERING WHY** *Mercury STEVE 4*		.52 3
11 Aug 90 ★	**THE JOKER** *Capitol CL 583* ▲		.1 13
12 Jun 76	**FLY LIKE AN EAGLE** *Mercury 9286 177*		.11 17
4 Jun 77	**BOOK OF DREAMS** *Mercury 9286 456.*		.12 12
19 Jun 82 ●	**ABRACADABRA** *Mercury 6302 204*		.10 16
7 May 83	**STEVE MILLER BAND LIVE!** *Mercury MERL 18.*		.79 2
6 Oct 90	**THE BEST OF 1968-1973** *Capitol EST 2133*		.34 3
10 Oct 98	**GREATEST HITS** *PolyGram TV 5592402*		.58 1

Suzi MILLER and The JOHNSTON BROTHERS
UK, female vocalist – Renee Lester and
male vocal group (Singles: 2 Weeks) pos/wks

			pos/wks
21 Jan 55	**HAPPY DAYS AND LONELY NIGHTS** *Decca F 10389*		.14 2

Lisa MILLETT *See BABY BUMPS; SHEER BRONZE featuring Lisa MILLETT; A.T.F.C.; GOODFELLAS featuring Lisa MILLETT*

MILLI VANILLI
France / Germany, male vocal (?) duo – Rob Pilatus, b. 8 Jun 1965, d. 2 Apr 1998, and Fabrice Morvan (Singles: 50 Weeks, Albums: 25 Weeks) pos/wks

1 Oct 88 ●	GIRL YOU KNOW IT'S TRUE *Cooltempo COOL 170*	3	13
17 Dec 88	BABY DON'T FORGET MY NUMBER *Cooltempo COOL 178* ▲	16	11
22 Jul 89	BLAME IT ON THE RAIN (re) *Cooltempo COOL 180* ▲	52	10
30 Sep 89 ●	GIRL I'M GONNA MISS YOU *Cooltempo COOL 191* ▲	2	15
10 Mar 90	ALL OR NOTHING *Cooltempo COOL 199*	74	1
21 Jan 89 ●	ALL OR NOTHING / 2X2 *Cooltempo CTLP 11*	6	25

'All or Nothing' was repackaged and available with a free re-mix album 2X2 from 16 Oct 89 onwards

MILLICAN and NESBIT
UK, male vocal duo – Alan Millican and Tim Nesbit (Singles: 14 Weeks, Albums: 24 Weeks) pos/wks

1 Dec 73	VAYA CON DIOS (MAY GOD BE WITH YOU) *Pye 7N 45310*	20	11
18 May 74	FOR OLD TIME'S SAKE *Pye 7N 45357*	38	3
23 Mar 74 ●	MILLICAN AND NESBIT *Pye NSPL 18428*	3	21
4 Jan 75	EVERYBODY KNOWS MILLICAN AND NESBIT *Pye NSPL 18446*	23	3

MILLIE
Jamaica, female vocalist – Millie Small (Singles: 33 Weeks) pos/wks

12 Mar 64 ●	MY BOY LOLLIPOP *Fontana TF 449*	2	18
25 Jun 64	SWEET WILLIAM *Fontana TF 479*	30	9
11 Nov 65	BLOODSHOT EYES *Fontana TF 617*	48	1
25 Jul 87	MY BOY LOLLIPOP (re-issue) *Island WIP 6574*	46	5

Spike MILLIGAN (see also The GOONS)
UK, male comedian, b. 16 Apr 1918, d. 27 Feb 2002 (Albums: 6 Weeks) pos/wks

25 Nov 61	MILLIGAN PRESERVED *Parlophone PMC 1152*	11	4
18 Apr 64	HOW TO WIN AN ELECTION *Philips AL 3464* [1]	20	1
18 Dec 76	THE SNOW GOOSE *RCA RS 1088* [2]	49	1

[1] Harry Secombe, Peter Sellers and Spike Milligan [2] Spike Milligan with the London Symphony Orchestra

MILLION DAN
UK, male rapper – Michael Dunn (Singles: 1 Week) pos/wks

27 Sep 03	DOGZ N SLEDGEZ *Gut CDGUT 52*	66	1

MILLION DEAD
UK, male vocal / instrumental group (Singles: 1 Week) pos/wks

29 May 04	I GAVE MY EYES TO STEVIE WONDER *Xtra Mile XMR 101*	72	1

MILLIONAIRE HIPPIES
UK, male producer – Danny Rampling (Singles: 4 Weeks) pos/wks

18 Dec 93	I AM THE MUSIC HEAR ME! *Deconstruction 74321175432*	52	3
10 Sep 94	C'MON *Deconstruction 74321229372*	59	1

MILLS BROTHERS
US, male vocal group (Singles: 1 Week) pos/wks

9 Jan 53 ●	THE GLOW WORM *Brunswick 05007*	10	1

With Hal McIntyre and his Orchestra

Garry MILLS
UK, male vocalist (Singles: 31 Weeks) pos/wks

7 Jul 60 ●	LOOK FOR A STAR *Top Rank JAR 336*	7	14
20 Oct 60	TOP TEEN BABY *Top Rank JAR 500*	24	12
22 Jun 61	I'LL STEP DOWN *Decca F 11358*	39	5

Hayley MILLS
UK, female actor / vocalist (Singles: 11 Weeks) pos/wks

19 Oct 61	LET'S GET TOGETHER *Decca F 21396*	17	11

Stephanie MILLS
US, female vocalist (Singles: 33 Weeks) pos/wks

18 Oct 80 ●	NEVER KNEW LOVE LIKE THIS BEFORE *20th Century TC 2460*	4	14
23 May 81	TWO HEARTS *20th Century TC 2492* [1]	49	5
15 Sep 84	THE MEDICINE SONG *Club JAB 8*	29	9
5 Sep 87	(YOU'RE PUTTIN') A RUSH ON ME *MCA MCA 1187*	62	2
1 May 93	NEVER DO YOU WRONG *MCA MCSTD 1767*	57	2
10 Jul 93	ALL DAY ALL NIGHT *MCA MCSTD 1778*	68	1

[1] Stephanie Mills featuring Teddy Pendergrass

Warren MILLS
Zambia, male vocalist (Singles: 1 Week) pos/wks

28 Sep 85	SUNSHINE *Jive JIVE 99*	74	1

MILLTOWN BROTHERS
UK, male vocal / instrumental group (Singles: 16 Weeks, Albums: 5 Weeks) pos/wks

2 Feb 91	WHICH WAY SHOULD I JUMP? *A&M AM 711*	38	5
13 Apr 91	HERE I STAND *A&M AM 758*	41	4
6 Jul 91	APPLE GREEN *A&M AM 787*	43	4
22 May 93	TURN OFF *A&M 5802692*	55	1
17 Jul 93	IT'S ALL OVER NOW BABY BLUE *A&M 5803332*	48	2
23 Mar 91	SLINKY *A&M 3953461*	27	5

MILLWALL FC
UK, male football team vocal group (Singles: 1 Week) pos/wks

29 May 04	OH MILLWALL *Absolute CDAME 4*	41	1

CB MILTON
Holland, male vocalist (Singles: 5 Weeks) pos/wks

21 May 94	IT'S A LOVING THING *Logic 74321208062*	49	2
25 Mar 95	IT'S A LOVING THING (re-mix) *Logic 74321267212*	34	2
19 Aug 95	HOLD ON *Logic 74321292112*	62	1

Garnet MIMMS and TRUCKIN' CO
US, male vocalist and male instrumental group (Singles: 1 Week) pos/wks

25 Jun 77	WHAT IT IS *Arista 109*	44	1

MIND OF KANE (see also HOPE A.D.)
UK, male producer – David Hope (Singles: 1 Week) pos/wks

27 Jul 91	STABBED IN THE BACK *Deja Vu DJV 007*	64	1

The MINDBENDERS
UK, male vocal / instrumental group (Singles: 79 Weeks, Albums: 5 Weeks) pos/wks

11 Jul 63	HELLO JOSEPHINE *Fontana TF 404* [1]	46	2
28 May 64	STOP LOOK AND LISTEN *Fontana TF 451* [1]	37	4
8 Oct 64 ●	UM, UM, UM, UM, UM, UM *Fontana TF 497* [1]	5	15
4 Feb 65	GAME OF LOVE *Fontana TF 535* [1] ▲	2	11
17 Jun 65	JUST A LITTLE BIT TOO LATE *Fontana TF 579* [1]	20	7
30 Sep 65	SHE NEEDS LOVE *Fontana TF 611* [1]	32	6
13 Jan 66 ●	A GROOVY KIND OF LOVE *Fontana TF 644*	2	14
5 May 66	CAN'T LIVE WITH YOU CAN'T LIVE WITHOUT YOU *Fontana TF 697*	28	7
25 Aug 66	ASHES TO ASHES *Fontana TF 731*	14	9
20 Sep 67	THE LETTER *Fontana TF 869*	42	4
20 Feb 65	WAYNE FONTANA AND THE MINDBENDERS *Fontana TL 5230*	18	1
25 Jun 66	THE MINDBENDERS *Fontana TL 5324*	28	4

[1] Wayne Fontana and The Mindbenders

MINDFUNK
US, male vocal / instrumental group (Albums: 1 Week) pos/wks

15 May 93	DROPPED *Megaforce CDZAZ 3*	60	1

MINDS OF MEN
UK, male / female vocal / instrumental group (Singles: 1 Week) pos/wks

22 Jun 96	BRAND NEW DAY *Perfecto PERF 121CD*	41	1

Sal MINEO
US, male vocalist / actor, b. 10 Jan 1939, d. 12 Feb 1976 (Singles: 11 Weeks) pos/wks

12 Jul 57	START MOVIN' (IN MY DIRECTION) *Philips PB 707*	16	11

Marcello MINERBI
Italy, orchestra (Singles: 16 Weeks) pos/wks

22 Jul 65 ●	ZORBA'S DANCE *Durium DRS 54001*	6	16

MINIMAL CHIC featuring Matt GOSS (see also BROS)
Italy, male production duo and UK, male vocalist (Singles: 1 Week) pos/wks

2 Oct 04	I NEED THE KEY *Inferno CDFERN 63*	54	1

MINIMAL FUNK 2
Italy, male production duo (Singles: 2 Weeks) pos/wks

18 Jul 98	THE GROOVY THANG *Cleveland City CLECD 13046*	65	1
18 May 02	DEFINITION OF HOUSE *Junior BRG 033* [1]	63	1

[1] Minimal Funk

MINIMALISTIX
Belgium, male production duo – Andy Vandierendonck and Peter Bellaert (Singles: 7 Weeks) pos/wks

16 Mar 02	CLOSE COVER *Data DATA 32CDS*	12	5
19 Jul 03	MAGIC FLY *Data / MoS DATA 48CDS*	36	2

MINI*POPS
UK, male / female vocal group
(Singles: 2 Weeks, Albums: 12 Weeks)   pos/wks

26 Dec 87	**SONGS FOR CHRISTMAS '87 (EP)** *Bright BULB 9*	39	2
26 Dec 81	**MINIPOPS** *K-Tel NE 1102*	63	7
19 Feb 83	**WE'RE THE MINIPOPS** *K-Tel ONE 1187*	54	5

Tracks on Songs for Christmas '87 (EP): Thanks for Giving Us Christmas / The Man in Red / Christmas Time Around the World / Shine On

MINISTERS DE LA FUNK
US, male production trio (Singles: 4 Weeks)   pos/wks

11 Mar 00	**BELIEVE** *Defected DFECT 14CDS*	45	2
27 Jan 01	**BELIEVE (re-mix)** *Defected DFECT 26CDS* [1]	42	2

[1] Ministers De La Funk featuring Jocelyn Brown

MINISTRY
(see also REVOLTING COCKS) US, male vocal /
instrumental group (Singles: 3 Weeks, Albums: 6 Weeks)   pos/wks

8 Aug 92	**NWO** *Sire W 0125TE*	49	1
6 Jan 96	**THE FALL** *Warner Bros. W 0328CD*	53	2
25 Jul 92	**PSALM 69** *Sire 7599267272*	33	5
10 Feb 96	**FILTH PIG** *Warner Bros. 9362458382*	43	1

MINK DeVILLE
US, male vocal / instrumental group (Singles: 9 Weeks)   pos/wks

6 Aug 77	**SPANISH STROLL** *Capitol CLX 103*	20	9

MINKY
UK, male producer – Gary Dedman (Singles: 1 Week)   pos/wks

30 Oct 99	**THE WEEKEND HAS LANDED** *Offbeat OFFCD 1001*	70	1

Liza MINNELLI
US, female vocalist (Singles: 15 Weeks, Albums: 27 Weeks) pos/wks

12 Aug 89	● **LOSING MY MIND** *Epic ZEE 1*	6	7
7 Oct 89	**DON'T DROP BOMBS** *Epic ZEE 2*	46	3
25 Nov 89	**SO SORRY I SAID** *Epic ZEE 3*	62	2
3 Mar 90	**LOVE PAINS** *Epic ZEE 4*	41	3
7 Apr 73	**LIZA WITH A 'Z'** *CBS 65212*	9	15
16 Jun 73	**THE SINGER** *CBS 65555*	45	1
21 Oct 89	● **RESULTS** *Epic 465511 1*	6	10
6 Jul 96	**GENTLY** *Angel CDQ 8354702*	58	1

Dannii MINOGUE   489   Top 500
Australian singer / actor, b. 20 Oct 1971, Melbourne, who like older sister Kylie made a chart comeback in 2001. The Minogues have had more singles success than any other sisters (Singles: 118 Weeks, Albums: 29 Weeks)   pos/wks

30 Mar 91	● **LOVE AND KISSES** *MCA MCS 1529*	8	8
18 May 91	**$UCCE$$** *MCA MCS 1538*	11	7
27 Jul 91	● **JUMP TO THE BEAT** *MCA MCS 1556*	8	6
19 Oct 91	**BABY LOVE** *MCA MCS 1580*	14	6
14 Dec 91	**I DON'T WANNA TAKE THIS PAIN** *MCA MCS 1600*	40	5
1 Aug 92	**SHOW YOU THE WAY TO GO** *MCA MCS 1671*	30	3
12 Dec 92	**LOVE'S ON EVERY CORNER** *MCA MCSR 1723*	44	4
17 Jul 93	● **THIS IS IT** *MCA MCSTD 1790*	10	8
2 Oct 93	**THIS IS THE WAY** *MCA MCSTD 1935*	27	3
11 Jun 94	**GET INTO YOU** *Mushroom D 11751*	36	2
23 Aug 97	● **ALL I WANNA DO** *Eternal WEA 119CD* [1]	4	8
1 Nov 97	**EVERYTHING I WANTED** *Eternal WEA 137CD* [1]	15	4
28 Mar 98	**DISREMEMBRANCE** *Eternal WEA 153CD* [1]	21	3
1 Dec 01	● **WHO DO YOU LOVE NOW (STRINGER)** *ffrr DFCD 002* [2]	3	15
16 Nov 02	● **PUT THE NEEDLE ON IT** *London LONCD 470*	7	11
15 Mar 03	● **I BEGIN TO WONDER** *London LONCD 473*	2	11
21 Jun 03	● **DON'T WANNA LOSE THIS FEELING (re)** *London LONCD 478*	5	9
6 Nov 04	● **YOU WON'T FORGET ABOUT ME** *All Around the World CXGLOBE 379* [3]	7	5
15 Jun 91	● **LOVE AND KISSES** *MCA MCA 10340*	8	20
16 Oct 93	**GET INTO YOU** *MCA MCD 10909*	52	1
20 Sep 97	**GIRL** *Eternal 3984205482* [1]	57	1
29 Mar 03	● **NEON NIGHTS** *London 2564600032*	8	7

[1] Dannii [2] Riva featuring Dannii Minogue [3] Dannii Minogue vs Flower Power [1] Dannii

Kylie MINOGUE   55   Top 500
Aussie soap teen star turned sex siren and the mistress of reinvention, b. 28 May 1968, Melbourne. She had the best ever chart start for a female soloist with 13 successive Top 10 entries and has the longest span of UK No.1 singles of any female solo artist – 15 years and 9 months. 'Come Into My World' won a Grammy in 2004. Best-selling single: 'Can't Get You Out of My Head' 1,037,235 (Singles: 354 Weeks, Albums: 292 Weeks)   pos/wks

23 Jan 88	★ **I SHOULD BE SO LUCKY** *PWL PWL 8*	1	16
14 May 88	● **GOT TO BE CERTAIN** *PWL PWL 12*	2	12
6 Aug 88	● **THE LOCO-MOTION** *PWL PWL 14*	2	11
22 Oct 88	● **JE NE SAIS PAS POURQUOI** *PWL PWL 21*	2	13
10 Dec 88	★ **ESPECIALLY FOR YOU** *PWL PWL 24* [1]	1	14
6 May 89	● **HAND ON YOUR HEART** *PWL PWL 35*	1	11
5 Aug 89	● **WOULDN'T CHANGE A THING** *PWL PWL 42*	2	9
4 Nov 89	● **NEVER TOO LATE** *PWL PWL 45*	4	10
20 Jan 90	★ **TEARS ON MY PILLOW** *PWL PWL 47*	1	8
12 May 90	● **BETTER THE DEVIL YOU KNOW** *PWL PWL 56*	2	10
3 Nov 90	● **STEP BACK IN TIME** *PWL PWL 64*	4	8
2 Feb 91	● **WHAT DO I HAVE TO DO** *PWL PWL 72*	6	8
1 Jun 91	● **SHOCKED** *PWL PWL 81* [2]	6	7
7 Sep 91	**WORD IS OUT** *PWL PWL 204*	16	5
2 Nov 91	● **IF YOU WERE WITH ME NOW** *PWL PWL 208* [3]	4	7
30 Nov 91	**KEEP ON PUMPIN' IT** *PWL PWL 207* [4]	49	1
25 Jan 92	● **GIVE ME JUST A LITTLE MORE TIME** *PWL PWL 212*	2	8
25 Apr 92	**FINER FEELINGS** *PWL International PWL 227* [5]	11	6
22 Aug 92	**WHAT KIND OF FOOL (HEARD ALL THAT BEFORE)** *PWL International PWL 241*	14	5
28 Nov 92	**CELEBRATION** *PWL International PWL 257*	20	7
10 Sep 94	● **CONFIDE IN ME** *Deconstruction 74321227482*	2	9
26 Nov 94	**PUT YOURSELF IN MY PLACE** *Deconstruction 74321246572*	11	9
22 Jul 95	**WHERE IS THE FEELING** *Deconstruction 74321293612*	16	3
14 Oct 95	**WHERE THE WILD ROSES GROW** *Mute CDMUTE 185* [6]	11	4
20 Sep 97	**SOME KIND OF BLISS** *Deconstruction 74321517252*	22	5
6 Dec 97	**DID IT AGAIN** *Deconstruction 74321535702*	14	6
21 Mar 98	**BREATHE** *Deconstruction 74321570132*	14	4
31 Oct 98	**GBI** *Arthrob ART 021CD* [7]	63	1
1 Jul 00	★ **SPINNING AROUND** *Parlophone CDRS 6542* ■	1	11
23 Sep 00	● **ON A NIGHT LIKE THIS** *Parlophone CDRS 6546* [5]	2	8
21 Oct 00	● **KIDS (2re)** *Chrysalis CDCHS 5119* [8]	2	19
23 Dec 00	● **PLEASE STAY** *Parlophone CDRS 6551* [5]	10	7
29 Sep 01	★ **CAN'T GET YOU OUT OF MY HEAD** *Parlophone CDRS 6562* ◆ ■	1	25
2 Mar 02	● **IN YOUR EYES** *Parlophone CDRS 6569*	3	17
22 Jun 02	● **LOVE AT FIRST SIGHT** *Parlophone CDRS 6577*	2	12
23 Nov 02	● **COME INTO MY WORLD** *Parlophone CDR 6590* [5]	8	10
15 Nov 03	★ **SLOW** *Parlophone CDR 6625* [5] ■	1	10
13 Mar 04	● **RED BLOODED WOMAN** *Parlophone CDRS 6633*	5	9
10 Jul 04	● **CHOCOLATE** *Parlophone CDRS 6639* [5]	6	7
18 Dec 04	● **I BELIEVE IN YOU** *Parlophone CDRS 6656* [5]	2	2+
16 Jul 88	★ **KYLIE** *PWL HF 3*	1	67
21 Oct 89	★ **ENJOY YOURSELF** *PWL HF 9* ■	1	33
24 Nov 90	● **RHYTHM OF LOVE** *PWL HF 18* [1]	9	22
26 Oct 91	**LET'S GET TO IT** *PWL HF 21* [1]	15	12
5 Sep 92	★ **GREATEST HITS** *PWL International HFCD 25* [1] ■	1	10
1 Oct 94	● **KYLIE MINOGUE** *Deconstruction 74321227492*	4	15
4 Apr 98	● **KYLIE MINOGUE** *Deconstruction 74321517272*	10	4
15 Aug 98	**MIXES** *Deconstruction 74321587152*	63	1
7 Oct 00	● **LIGHT YEARS** *Parlophone 5284002* [1]	2	28
28 Oct 00	**HITS +** *Deconstruction 74321785342*	41	1
13 Oct 01	★ **FEVER** *Parlophone 5358042* [1] ■	1	?
30 Nov 02	● **GREATEST HITS 87-92** *PWL 9224682* [1]	20	11
29 Nov 03	● **BODY LANGUAGE** *Parlophone 5957582*	6	14
4 Dec 04	● **ULTIMATE KYLIE** *Parlophone 8753652* [1]	4	4+

[1] Kylie Minogue and Jason Donovan [2] Kylie Minogue / rap by Jazzie P [3] Kylie Minogue and Keith Washington [4] Visionmasters with Tony King and Kylie Minogue [5] Kylie [6] Nick Cave and the Bad Seeds + Kylie Minogue [7] Towa Tei featuring Kylie Minogue [8] Robbie Williams / Kylie Minogue [1] Kylie

The single 'GBI' is an abbreviation of German Bold Italic Both eponymously titled albums are different. The second 'Kylie Minogue' was changed from its original title, 'Impossible Princess', following the death of Diana, Princess of Wales. The 2002 'Greatest Hits' album has a slightly different track listing to the 1992 album of the same name and includes an additional CD of re-mixes

Morris MINOR and the MAJORS
UK, male vocal / rap group (Singles: 11 Weeks)   pos/wks

19 Dec 87	● **STUTTER RAP (NO SLEEP 'TIL BEDTIME)** *10 TEN 203*	4	11

Sugar MINOTT *Jamaica, male vocalist (Singles: 16 Weeks)* pos/wks

		pos	wks
28 Mar 81 ●	GOOD THING GOING (WE'VE GOT A GOOD THING GOING) *RCA 58*	4	12
17 Oct 81	NEVER MY LOVE *RCA 138*	52	4

MINT CONDITION *US, male vocal group (Singles: 3 Weeks)* pos/wks

		pos	wks
21 Jun 97	WHAT KIND OF MAN WOULD I BE *Wild Card 5710492*	38	2
4 Oct 97	LET ME BE THE ONE *Wild Card 5717132*	63	1

The MINT JULEPS *UK, female vocal group (Singles: 7 Weeks)* pos/wks

		pos	wks
22 Mar 86	ONLY LOVE CAN BREAK YOUR HEART *Stiff BUY 241*	62	2
30 May 87	EVERY KINDA PEOPLE *Stiff BUY 257*	58	5

MINT ROYALE *UK, male production duo – Neil Claxton and Chris Baker (Singles: 10 Weeks)* pos/wks

		pos	wks
5 Feb 00	DON'T FALTER *Faith & Hope FHCD 014* [1]	15	4
6 May 00	TAKE IT EASY *Faith & Hope FHCD 016*	66	1
7 Sep 02	SEXIEST MAN IN JAMAICA *Faith & Hope FHCD 025*	20	3
8 Feb 03	BLUE SONG *Faith & Hope FHCD 030*	35	2

[1] Mint Royale featuring Lauren Laverne

MINTY *Australia, female vocalist – Angela Kelly (Singles: 1 Week)* pos/wks

		pos	wks
23 Jan 99	I WANNA BE FREE *Virgin VSCDT 1728*	67	1

MINUTEMAN *UK, male vocal / instrumental group (Singles: 3 Weeks)* pos/wks

		pos	wks
20 Jul 02	BIG BOY *Ignition IGNSCD 225*	69	1
21 Sep 02	5000 MINUTES OF PAIN *Ignition IGNSCD 27*	75	1
15 Feb 03	BIG BOY (re-issue) / MOTHER FIXATION *Ignition IGNSCD 28*	45	1

The MIRACLES *(see also Smokey ROBINSON)* *US, vocal / instrumental group (Singles: 81 Weeks)* pos/wks

		pos	wks
24 Feb 66	GOING TO A GO-GO *Tamla Motown TMG 547*	44	5
22 Dec 66	(COME 'ROUND HERE) I'M THE ONE YOU NEED *Tamla Motown TMG 584*	45	2
27 Dec 67	I SECOND THAT EMOTION *Tamla Motown TMG 631* [1]	27	11
3 Apr 68	IF YOU CAN WAIT *Tamla Motown TMG 648* [1]	50	1
7 May 69 ●	TRACKS OF MY TEARS *Tamla Motown TMG 696* [1]	9	13
1 Aug 70 ★	THE TEARS OF A CLOWN *Tamla Motown TMG 745* [1] ▲	1	14
30 Jan 71	(COME 'ROUND HERE) I'M THE ONE YOU NEED (re-issue) *Tamla Motown TMG 761* [1]	13	9
5 Jun 71	I DON'T BLAME YOU AT ALL *Tamla Motown TMG 774* [1]	11	10
10 Jan 76 ●	LOVE MACHINE *Tamla Motown TMG 1015* ▲	3	10
2 Oct 76	THE TEARS OF A CLOWN (re-issue) *Tamla Motown TMG 1048* [1]	34	6

[1] Smokey Robinson and The Miracles

MIRAGE *UK, male vocal / instrumental group (Singles: 35 Weeks, Albums: 33 Weeks)* pos/wks

		pos	wks
14 Jan 84	GIVE ME THE NIGHT (MEDLEY) *Passion PASH 15* [1]	49	4
9 May 87 ●	JACK MIX II / III *Debut DEBT 3022*	4	11
25 Jul 87	SERIOUS MIX *Debut DEBT 3028*	42	4
7 Nov 87 ●	JACK MIX IV *Debut DEBT 3035*	8	10
27 Feb 88	JACK MIX VII *Debut DEBT 3042*	50	3
2 Jul 88	PUSH THE BEAT *Debut DEBT 3050*	67	2
11 Nov 89	LATINO HOUSE *Debut DEBT 3085*	70	1
26 Dec 87 ●	THE BEST OF MIRAGE – JACK MIX '88 *Stylus SMR 746*	7	15
25 Jun 88	JACK MIX IN FULL EFFECT *Stylus SMR 856*	7	12
7 Jan 89	ROYAL MIX '89 *Stylus SMR 871*	34	6

[1] Mirage featuring Roy Gayle

'Jack Mix III' listed with 'Jack Mix II' only from 6 Jun 1987

MIRAGE *UK, male instrumental trio (Albums: 3 Weeks)* pos/wks

		pos	wks
23 Sep 95	CLASSIC GUITAR MOODS *PolyGram TV 5290562*	25	3

Nina MIRANDA See Robert MILES

Danny MIRROR *Holland, male vocalist – Eddy Ouwens (Singles: 9 Weeks)* pos/wks

		pos	wks
17 Sep 77 ●	I REMEMBER ELVIS PRESLEY (THE KING IS DEAD) *Sonet SON 2121*	4	9

MIRRORBALL *(see also PF PROJECT featuring Ewan McGREGOR; TZANT)* *UK, male production duo – Jamie White and Jamie Ford and female vocalist (Singles: 5 Weeks)* pos/wks

		pos	wks
13 Feb 99	GIVEN UP *Multiply CDMULTY 46*	12	4
24 Jun 00	BURNIN' *Multiply CDMULTY 56*	47	1

MIRWAIS *France, male producer – Mirwais Ahmadzai (Singles: 3 Weeks)* pos/wks

		pos	wks
20 May 00	DISCO SCIENCE *Epic 6693102*	68	1
23 Dec 00	NAIVE SONG *Epic 6706922*	50	2

MISHKA *Bermuda, male vocalist – Alexander Mishka Frith (Singles: 2 Weeks)* pos/wks

		pos	wks
15 May 99	GIVE YOU ALL THE LOVE *Creation CRESCD 311*	34	2

MISS BEHAVIN' *UK, female DJ / producer – Nichola Potterton (Singles: 1 Week)* pos/wks

		pos	wks
18 Jan 03	SUCH A GOOD FEELIN' *Tidy Two TIDYTWO 115CD*	62	1

MISS BUNTY See SATURATED SOUL featuring MISS BUNTY

MS DYNAMITE *UK, female rapper / vocalist – Niomi McLean Daley (Singles: 32 Weeks, Albums: 42 Weeks)* pos/wks

		pos	wks
23 Jun 01	BOOO! *ffrr / Public Demand / Social Circles FCD 399* [1]	12	6
1 Jun 02 ●	IT TAKES MORE *Polydor 5707982*	7	10
7 Sep 02 ●	DY-NA-MI-TEE *Polydor 5709782*	5	10
14 Dec 02	PUT HIM OUT *Polydor 0658942*	19	6
22 Jun 02 ●	A LITTLE DEEPER *Polydor 5899552*	10	42

[1] Sticky featuring Ms Dynamite

MISS JANE *Italy, production duo and UK, female vocalist (Singles: 1 Week)* pos/wks

		pos	wks
30 Oct 99	IT'S A FINE DAY *G1 Recordings G 1001CD*	62	1

MISS KITTIN See GOLDEN BOY with MISS KITTIN

MISS SHIVA *Germany, female DJ / producer – Khadra Bungardt (Singles: 2 Weeks)* pos/wks

		pos	wks
10 Nov 01	DREAMS *VC Recordings VCRD 99*	30	2

MS THING See BEENIE MAN

MS TOI See ICE CUBE

MISS X *UK, female vocalist – Joyce Blair (Singles: 6 Weeks)* pos/wks

		pos	wks
1 Aug 63	CHRISTINE *Ember S 175*	37	6

The MISSION *UK, male vocal / instrumental group (Singles: 58 Weeks, Albums: 48 Weeks)* pos/wks

		pos	wks
14 Jun 86	SERPENTS KISS *Chapter 22 CHAP 6*	70	3
26 Jul 86	GARDEN OF DELIGHT / LIKE A HURRICANE *Chapter 22 CHAP 7*	49	4
18 Oct 86	STAY WITH ME *Mercury MYTH 1*	30	4
17 Jan 87	WASTELAND *Mercury MYTH 2*	11	6
14 Mar 87	SEVERINA *Mercury MYTH 3*	25	5
13 Feb 88	TOWER OF STRENGTH *Mercury MYTH 4*	12	7
23 Apr 88	BEYOND THE PALE *Mercury MYTH 6*	32	4
13 Jan 90	BUTTERFLY ON A WHEEL *Mercury MYTH 8*	12	4
10 Mar 90	DELIVERANCE *Mercury MYTH 9*	27	4
2 Jun 90	INTO THE BLUE *Mercury MYTH 10*	32	3
17 Nov 90	HANDS ACROSS THE OCEAN *Mercury MYTH 11*	28	2
25 Apr 92	NEVER AGAIN *Mercury MYTH 12*	34	3
20 Jun 92	LIKE A CHILD AGAIN *Mercury MYTH 13*	30	2
17 Oct 92	SHADES OF GREEN *Vertigo MYTH 14*	49	2
8 Jan 94	TOWER OF STRENGTH (re-mix) *Vertigo MYTCD 15*	33	3
26 Mar 94	AFTERGLOW *Vertigo MYTCD 16*	53	1
4 Feb 95	SWOON *Neverland HOOKCD 002*	73	1
22 Nov 86	GOD'S OWN MEDICINE *Mercury MERH 102*	14	20
4 Jul 87	THE FIRST CHAPTER *Mercury MISH 1*	35	4
12 Mar 88 ●	CHILDREN *Mercury MISH 2*	2	9
17 Feb 90 ●	CARVED IN SAND *Mercury 8422511*	7	8
2 Nov 90	GRAINS OF SAND *Mercury 8469371*	28	2

4 Jul 92	MASQUE *Vertigo 5121212*	23	2
19 Feb 94	SUM AND SUBSTANCE *Vertigo 5184472*	49	1
25 Feb 95	NEVERLAND *Neverland SMEECD 001*	58	1
15 Jun 96	BLUE *Equator SMEECD 002*	73	1

MISS JONES
US, female vocalist – Tarsha Jones (Singles: 1 Week)   pos/wks

10 Oct 98	2 WAY STREET *Motown 8608572*	49	1

MISTA E (see also NOMAD)
UK, male producer – Damon Rochefort (Singles: 5 Weeks)   pos/wks

10 Dec 88	DON'T BELIEVE THE HYPE *Urban URB 28*	41	5

MIS-TEEQ
UK, female vocal group (Singles: 70 Weeks, Albums: 52 Weeks)   pos/wks

20 Jan 01 ●	WHY *Inferno / Telstar CDFERN 35*	8	7
23 Jun 01 ●	ALL I WANT *Inferno / Telstar CDSTAS 3184*	2	11
27 Oct 01 ●	ONE NIGHT STAND *Inferno / Telstar CDSTAS 3208*	5	12
2 Mar 02 ●	B WITH ME *Inferno / Telstar CDSTAS 3243*	5	8
29 Jun 02 ●	ROLL ON / THIS IS HOW WE DO IT *Inferno / Telstar CDSTAS 3255*	7	7
29 Mar 03 ●	SCANDALOUS *Telstar CDSTAS 3319*	2	11
12 Jul 03 ●	CAN'T GET IT BACK *Telstar CDSTAS 3337*	8	9
29 Nov 03	STYLE (re) *Telstar CDSTAS 3369*	13	5
10 Nov 01 ●	LICKIN' ON BOTH SIDES *Inferno / Telstar TCD 3212*	3	31
12 Apr 03 ●	EYE CANDY *Telstar TCD 3304*	6	21

●

MR and MRS SMITH
UK, male / female instrumental / production group (Singles: 1 Week)   pos/wks

12 Oct 96	GOTTA GET LOOSE *Hooj Choons HOOJCD 46*	70	1

MR BEAN and SMEAR CAMPAIGN featuring Bruce DICKINSON
UK, male comedian – Rowan Atkinson
and male vocalist (Singles: 5 Weeks)   pos/wks

4 Apr 92 ●	(I WANT TO BE) ELECTED *London LON 319*	9	5

MR BIG
UK, male vocal / instrumental group (Singles: 14 Weeks)   pos/wks

12 Feb 77 ●	ROMEO *EMI 2567*	4	10
21 May 77	FEEL LIKE CALLING HOME *EMI 2610*	35	4

MR BIG
US, male vocal / instrumental
group (Singles: 17 Weeks, Albums: 14 Weeks)   pos/wks

7 Mar 92 ●	TO BE WITH YOU *Atlantic A 7514* ▲	3	11
23 May 92	JUST TAKE MY HEART *Atlantic A 7490*	26	4
8 Aug 92	GREEN TINTED SIXTIES MIND *Atlantic A 7468*	72	1
20 Nov 93	WILD WORLD *Atlantic A 7310CD*	59	1
22 Jul 89	MR. BIG *Atlantic 781990 1*	60	1
13 Apr 91	LEAN INTO IT *Atlantic 7567822091*	28	12
2 Oct 93	BUMP AHEAD *Atlantic 7567824952*	61	1

MR BLOBBY
UK, male pink and yellow spotted blob vocalist (Singles: 16 Weeks)   pos/wks

4 Dec 93 ★	MR BLOBBY *Destiny Music CDDMUS 104*	1	12
16 Dec 95	CHRISTMAS IN BLOBBYLAND *Destiny DMUSCD 108*	36	4

MR BLOE UK, male instrumental group (Singles: 18 Weeks)   pos/wks

9 May 70 ●	GROOVIN' WITH MR BLOE *DJM DJS 216*	2	18

MR BUNGLE
US, male vocal / instrumental group (Albums: 1 Week)   pos/wks

21 Sep 91	MR BUNGLE *London 8282671*	57	1

Mr CHEEKS See LIL' KIM

MR FINGERS
US, male producer – Larry Heard (Singles: 5 Weeks)   pos/wks

17 Mar 90	WHAT ABOUT THIS LOVE *ffrr F 131*	74	1
7 Mar 92	CLOSER *MCA MCS 1601*	50	3
23 May 92	ON MY WAY *MCA MCS 1630*	71	1

MR FOOD UK, male vocalist (Singles: 3 Weeks)   pos/wks

9 Jun 90	... AND THAT'S BEFORE ME TEA! *Tangible TGB 005*	62	3

Mr HAHN See LINKIN PARK; X-ECUTIONERS featuring Mike SHINODA and Mr HAHN of LINKIN PARK

MR HANKEY
US, male Xmas excrement vocalist (Singles: 6 Weeks)   pos/wks

25 Dec 99 ●	MR HANKEY THE CHRISTMAS POO *Columbia 6685582*	4	6

MR JACK
Belgium, male producer – Lucente Vito (Singles: 2 Weeks)   pos/wks

25 Jan 97	WIGGLY WORLD *Extravaganza 0090965*	32	2

MR LEE
US, male producer – Leroy Haggard (Singles: 6 Weeks)   pos/wks

6 Aug 88	PUMP UP LONDON *Breakout USA 639*	64	2
11 Nov 89	GET BUSY (re) *Jive JIVE 231*	41	4

MR MISTER US, male vocal / instrumental
group (Singles: 22 Weeks, Albums: 24 Weeks)   pos/wks

21 Dec 85 ●	BROKEN WINGS *RCA PB 49945* ▲	4	13
1 Mar 86	KYRIE *RCA PB 49927* ▲	11	9
15 Feb 86 ●	WELCOME TO THE REAL WORLD *RCA PL 89647* ▲	6	24

MR OIZO
France, male producer – Quentin Dupieux (Singles: 15 Weeks)   pos/wks

3 Apr 99 ★	FLAT BEAT (re) *F Communications / Pias Recordings F 104CDUK* ■	1	15

MR ON vs The JUNGLE BROTHERS
UK, male producer and US, male rap duo (Singles: 5 Weeks)   pos/wks

7 Feb 04	BREATHE, DON'T STOP *Positiva / incentive CDTIVS 201*	21	5

MR PINK presents The PROGRAM
UK, male producer – Leiam Sullivan (Singles: 4 Weeks)   pos/wks

19 Jan 02	LOVE AND AFFECTION *Manifesto FESCD 90*	22	4

MR PRESIDENT
Germany, male / female vocal group (Singles: 13 Weeks)   pos/wks

14 Jun 97 ●	COCO JAMBOO *WEA WEA 110CD*	8	11
20 Sep 97	I GIVE YOU MY HEART *WEA WEA 126CD*	52	1
25 Apr 98	JOJO ACTION *WEA WEA 156CD*	73	1

MR REDS vs DJ SKRIBBLE UK, male producers –
Reduan Nabbach and Scott Ialachi (Singles: 6 Weeks)   pos/wks

24 May 03	EVERYBODY COME ON (CAN U FEEL IT) *ffrr FCD 410*	13	6

MR ROY
UK, male instrumental / production group (Singles: 6 Weeks)   pos/wks

7 May 94	SOMETHING ABOUT YOU *Fresh FRSHD 11*	74	1
21 Jan 95	SAVED *Fresh FRSHD 21*	24	4
16 Dec 95	SOMETHING ABOUT U (CAN'T BE BEAT) (re-mix) *Fresh FRSHCD 33*	49	1

MR RUMBLE See BM DUBS present MR RUMBLE featuring BRASSTOOTH and KEE

MR SCRUFF UK, male DJ / producer –
Andy Carthy (Singles: 1 Week, Albums: 2 Weeks)   pos/wks

14 Dec 02	SWEETSMOKE *Ninja Tune ZENCDS 12124*	75	1
21 Sep 02	TROUSER JAZZ *Ninja Tune ZENCD 65*	29	2

MR SHABZ See SO SOLID CREW

MR SMASH & FRIENDS featuring the
ENGLAND SUPPORTER'S BAND (see also MADNESS)
UK, male vocal football supporters group (Singles: 1 Week)   pos/wks

8 Jun 02	WE'RE COMING OVER *RGR RGRCD 2*	67	1

MR V
UK, male producer – Rob Villiers (Singles: 2 Weeks)   pos/wks

6 Aug 94	GIVE ME LIFE *Cheeky CHEKCD 005*	40	2

MR VEGAS
Jamaica, male vocalist – Clifford Smith (Singles: 7 Weeks)   pos/wks

22 Aug 98	**HEADS HIGH** *Greensleeves GRECD 650*	**71**	1
13 Nov 99	**HEADS HIGH (re-issue)** *Greensleeves GRECD 785*	**16**	6

MRS MILLS
UK, female instrumentalist – piano –
Gladys Mills, d. Feb 1978 (Singles: 6 Weeks, Albums: 13 Weeks)   pos/wks

14 Dec 61	**MRS MILLS MEDLEY** *Parlophone R 4856*	**18**	1
31 Dec 64	**MRS MILLS PARTY MEDLEY** *Parlophone R 5214*	**50**	1
10 Dec 66	**COME TO MY PARTY** *Parlophone PMC 7010*	**17**	7
28 Dec 68	**MRS. MILLS' PARTY PIECES** *Parlophone PCS 7066*	**32**	3
13 Dec 69	**LET'S HAVE ANOTHER PARTY** *Parlophone PCS 7035*	**23**	2
6 Nov 71	**I'M MIGHTY GLAD** *MFP 5225*	**49**	1

Mrs Mills Medley: I Want to Be Happy / Sheik of Araby / Baby Face / Somebody Stole My Gal / Ma (He's Making Eyes at Me) / Swanee / Ain't She Sweet / California Here I Come. Mrs Mills Party Medley: You Made Me Love You (I Didn't Want to Do It) / Shine on Harvest Moon / I Don't Want to Set the World on Fire / Around the World / Ramona / Charmaine

MRS WOOD
UK, female producer – Jane Wood (Singles: 6 Weeks)   pos/wks

16 Sep 95	**JOANNA** *React CDREACT 066*	**40**	2
6 Jul 96	**HEARTBREAK** *React CDREACT 78* [1]	**44**	1
4 Oct 97	**JOANNA (re-mix)** *React CDREACT 107*	**34**	2
15 Aug 98	**1234** *React CDREACT 121*	**54**	1

[1] Mrs Wood featuring Eve Gallagher

MISTURA featuring Lloyd MICHELS
US, male instrumental
group – Lloyd Michels – trumpet (Singles: 10 Weeks)   pos/wks

15 May 76	**THE FLASHER** *Route RT 30*	**23**	10

Des MITCHELL
UK / Belgium, male DJ / production trio (Singles: 5 Weeks)   pos/wks

29 Jan 00 ●	**(WELCOME) TO THE DANCE** *Code Blue BLUE 0087CD1*	**5**	5

Guy MITCHELL ⟨ 419 ⟩ Top 500
Extremely popular pre-rock vocalist,
b. Al Cernik, 27 Feb 1927, Detroit, US, d. 1 Jul 1999. He appeared on the first and last charts of the 1950s, and was one of most consistently successful singers and performers of that decade (Singles: 165 Weeks)   pos/wks

14 Nov 52 ●	**FEET UP!** *Columbia DB 3151*	**2**	10
13 Feb 53 ★	**SHE WEARS RED FEATHERS (re)** *Columbia DB 3238*	**1**	16
24 Apr 53 ●	**PRETTY LITTLE BLACK-EYED SUSIE** *Columbia DB 3255*	**2**	11
28 Aug 53 ●	**LOOK AT THAT GIRL** *Philips PB 162*	**1**	14
6 Nov 53 ●	**CHICKA BOOM (re)** *Philips PB 178*	**4**	15
18 Dec 53 ●	**CLOUD LUCKY SEVEN** *Philips PB 210A*	**2**	16
19 Feb 54 ●	**THE CUFF OF MY SHIRT (2re)** *Philips PB 225*	**9**	3
26 Feb 54	**SIPPIN' SODA** *Philips PB 210B*	**11**	1
30 Apr 54 ●	**A DIME AND A DOLLAR (re)** *Philips PB 248*	**8**	5
7 Dec 56 ★	**SINGING THE BLUES** *Philips PB 650* ▲	**1**	22
15 Feb 57 ●	**KNEE DEEP IN THE BLUES** *Philips PB 669*	**3**	12
26 Apr 57 ★	**ROCK-A-BILLY** *Philips PB 685*	**1**	14
26 Jul 57	**IN THE MIDDLE OF A DARK, DARK NIGHT / SWEET STUFF (re)** *Philips PB 712*	**25**	4
11 Oct 57	**CALL ROSIE ON THE PHONE** *Philips PB 743*	**17**	6
27 Nov 59 ●	**HEARTACHES BY THE NUMBER (re)** *Philips PB 964* ▲	**5**	16

Joni MITCHELL ⟨ 500 ⟩ Top 500
Canada's first lady of bohemian folk rock, b. Roberta Anderson, 7 Nov 1943, Fort Macleod, Alberta. The highly respected and influential singer / songwriter and guitarist, whose compositions include UK No.1 hit 'Woodstock', has four decades of album hits (five in the US) (Singles: 24 Weeks, Albums: 120 Weeks)   pos/wks

13 Jun 70	**BIG YELLOW TAXI** *Reprise RS 20906*	**11**	15
4 Oct 97 ●	**GOT 'TIL IT'S GONE** *Virgin VSCDG 1666* [1]	**6**	9
6 Jun 70	**LADIES OF THE CANYON** *Reprise RSLP 6376*	**8**	25
24 Jul 71 ●	**BLUE** *Reprise K 44128*	**3**	18
16 Mar 74	**COURT AND SPARK** *Asylum SYLA 8756*	**14**	11
1 Feb 75	**MILES OF AILES** *Asylum SYSP 902*	**34**	4
27 Dec 75	**THE HISSING OF SUMMER LAWNS** *Asylum SYLA 8763*	**14**	10
11 Dec 76	**HEJIRA** *Asylum K 53053*	**11**	5
21 Jan 78	**DON JUAN'S RECKLESS DAUGHTER** *Asylum K 63003*	**20**	7
14 Jul 79	**MINGUS** *Asylum K 53091*	**24**	7
4 Oct 80	**SHADOWS AND LIGHT** *Elektra K 62030*	**63**	3
4 Dec 82	**WILD THINGS RUN FAST** *Geffen GEF 25102*	**32**	8
30 Nov 85	**DOG EAT DOG** *Geffen GEF 26455*	**57**	3

2 Apr 88	**CHALK MARK IN A RAIN STORM** *Geffen WX 141*	**26**	7
9 Mar 91	**NIGHT RIDE HOME** *Geffen GEF 24302*	**25**	5
5 Nov 94	**TURBULENT INDIGO** *Reprise 9362457862*	**53**	2
10 Oct 98	**TAMING THE TIGER** *Reprise 9362464512*	**57**	1
11 Mar 00	**BOTH SIDES NOW** *Reprise 9362476202*	**50**	2
25 Sep 04	**DREAMLAND** *WSM 8122765202*	**43**	2

[1] Janet featuring Q-Tip and Joni Mitchell

VSCDG 1666 uses samples from RS 20906

George MITCHELL MINSTRELS ⟨ 201 ⟩ Top 500
Last and biggest-selling British minstrel band – leader b. 27 Feb 1917, d. 27 Aug 2002, Falkirk, Scotland. Although definitely non-PC now, this ensemble, which featured Tony Mercer and Dai Francis, had an extremely popular TV series and amassed record-breaking sales (Albums: 292 Weeks)   pos/wks

26 Nov 60 ★	**THE BLACK AND WHITE MINSTREL SHOW** *HMV CLP 1399*	**1**	142
21 Oct 61 ★	**ANOTHER BLACK AND WHITE MINSTREL SHOW** *HMV CLP 1460*	**1**	64
20 Oct 62 ★	**ON STAGE WITH THE GEORGE MITCHELL MINSTRELS** *HMV CLP 1599*	**1**	26
2 Nov 63 ●	**ON TOUR WITH THE GEORGE MITCHELL MINSTRELS** *HMV CLP 1667*	**6**	18
12 Dec 64 ●	**SPOTLIGHT ON THE GEORGE MITCHELL MINSTRELS** *HMV CLP 1803*	**6**	7
4 Dec 65 ●	**MAGIC OF THE MINSTRELS** *HMV CLP 1917*	**9**	7
26 Nov 66 ●	**HERE COME THE MINSTRELS** *HMV CLP 3579*	**11**	11
16 Dec 67 ●	**SHOWTIME** *HMV CSD 3642*	**26**	2
14 Dec 68	**SING THE IRVING BERLIN SONGBOOK** *Columbia SCX 6267*	**33**	4
19 Dec 70 ●	**THE MAGIC OF CHRISTMAS** *Columbia SCX 6431*	**32**	4
19 Nov 77 ●	**30 GOLDEN GREATS** *EMI EMTV 7* [1]	**10**	10

[1] George Mitchell Minstrels with the Joe Loss Orchestra

Willie MITCHELL
US, male instrumentalist – guitar (Singles: 3 Weeks)   pos/wks

24 Apr 68	**SOUL SERENADE** *London HLU 10186*	**43**	1
11 Dec 76	**THE CHAMPION** *London HL 10545*	**47**	2

MIX FACTORY
UK, male / female vocal / instrumental group (Singles: 2 Weeks)   pos/wks

30 Jan 93	**TAKE ME AWAY (PARADISE)** *All Around the World CDGLOBE 120*	**51**	2

MIXMASTER (see also BLACK BOX)
Italy, male producer – Daniele Davoli (Singles: 10 Weeks)   pos/wks

4 Nov 89 ●	**GRAND PIANO** *BCM BCM 344*	**9**	10

MIXMASTERS See UK MIXMASTERS

The MIXTURES
Australia, male vocal / instrumental group (Singles: 21 Weeks)   pos/wks

16 Jan 71 ●	**THE PUSHBIKE SONG** *Polydor 2058 083*	**2**	21

Hank MIZELL
US, male vocalist, b. 1924, d. Dec 1992 (Singles: 13 Weeks)   pos/wks

20 Mar 76 ●	**JUNGLE ROCK** *Charly CS 1005*	**3**	13

MOBB DEEP
US, male rap group (Albums: 2 Weeks)   pos/wks

23 Nov 96	**HELL ON EARTH** *Loud 74321425582*	**67**	1
21 Aug 04	**AMERIKAZ NIGHTMARE** *Jive 82876571312*	**68**	1

The MOBILES
UK, male / female vocal / instrumental group (Singles: 14 Weeks)   pos/wks

9 Jan 82 ●	**DROWNING IN BERLIN** *Rialto RIA 3*	**9**	10
27 Mar 82	**AMOUR AMOUR** *Rialto RIA 5*	**45**	4

MOBO ALLSTARS
UK / US, male / female vocal / instrumental group (Singles: 3 Weeks)   pos/wks

26 Dec 98	**AIN'T NO STOPPING US NOW** *PolyGram TV 5632302*	**47**	3

Artists featured include: Another Level, Shola Ama, Kéllé Bryan, Celetia, Cleopatra, Damage, Des'ree, D'Influence, E17, Michelle Gayle, Glamma Kid, Lynden David Hall, Hinda Hicks, Honeyz, Kle'Shay, Kele Le Roc, Beverley Knight, Tony Momrelle, Nine Yards, Mica Paris, Karen Ramirez, Connor Reeves, Roachford, 7th Son, Byron Stingily, Truce, Soundproof, Ultimate Kaos

MOBY ⟨340⟩ ⟨Top 500⟩ *Genre-bending, maverick producer / vocalist, b. Richard Hall, 11 Sep 1965, New York, US. Descendant of 'Moby Dick' author, Herman Melville. The Brit and Grammy-nominated 'Play' was the UK's biggest-selling independent album of 2000 and went platinum in more than 20 countries (Singles: 70 Weeks, Albums: 128 Weeks)* pos/wks

27 Jul 91	● GO (re) *Outer Rhythm FOOT 15*	.10	10
3 Jul 93	I FEEL IT *Equinox AXISCD 001*	.38	3
11 Sep 93	MOVE *Mute CDMUTE 158*	.21	5
28 May 94	HYMN *Mute CDMUTE 161*	.31	2
29 Oct 94	FEELING SO REAL *Mute CDMUTE 173*	.30	2
25 Feb 95	EVERY TIME YOU TOUCH ME *Mute CDMUTE 176*	.28	3
1 Jul 95	INTO THE BLUE *Mute CDMUTE 179A*	.34	2
7 Sep 96	THAT'S WHEN I REACH FOR MY REVOLVER *Mute CDMUTE 184*	.50	1
15 Nov 97	● JAMES BOND THEME (re) *Mute CDMUTE 210*	..8	8
5 Sep 98	HONEY *Mute CDMUTE 218*	.33	2
8 May 99	RUN ON *Mute CDMUTE 221*	.33	2
24 Jul 99	BODYROCK *Mute CDMUTE 225*	.38	2
23 Oct 99	WHY DOES MY HEART FEEL SO BAD *Mute CDMUTE 230*	.16	4
18 Mar 00	NATURAL BLUES *Mute CDMUTE 251*	.11	4
24 Jun 00	● PORCELAIN *Mute CDMUTE 252*	..5	6
28 Oct 00	WHY DOES MY HEART FEEL SO BAD (re-issue) *Mute CDMUTE 255*	.17	5
11 May 02	WE ARE ALL MADE OF STARS *Mute CDMUTE 268*	.11	4
31 Aug 02	EXTREME WAYS *Mute CDMUTE 270*	.39	1
16 Nov 02	IN THIS WORLD *Mute CDMUTE 276*	.35	2
25 Mar 95	EVERYTHING IS WRONG / MIXED & REMIXED *Mute LCDSTUMM 130*	.21	7
5 Oct 96	ANIMAL RIGHTS *Mute LCDSTUMM 150*	.38	1
29 May 99	★ PLAY *Mute CDSTUMM 172*	..1	81
1 Jul 00	I LIKE TO SCORE *Mute CDSTUMM 168*	.54	2
4 Nov 00	PLAY / THE B SIDES *Mute LCDSTUMM 172*	.24	3
25 May 02	★ 18 *Mute CDSTUMM 202* ■	..1	34

MOCA *See David MORALES*

MOCHA *See Missy 'Misdemeanor' ELLIOTT; Nicole RAY*

The MOCK TURTLES *UK, male / female vocal / instrumental group (Singles: 18 Weeks, Albums: 4 Weeks)* pos/wks

9 Mar 91	CAN YOU DIG IT? *Siren SRN 136*	.18	11
29 Jun 91	AND THEN SHE SMILES *Siren SRN 139*	.44	4
15 Mar 03	CAN YOU DIG IT? (re-mix) *Virgin CDMOCK 001*	.19	3
25 May 91	TURTLE SOUP *Imaginary ILLUSION 012*	.54	1
27 Jul 91	TWO SIDES *Siren SRNLP 31*	.33	3

MODERN EON *UK, male vocal / instrumental group (Albums: 1 Week)* pos/wks

13 Jun 81	FICTION TALES *DinDisc DID 11*	.65	1

MODERN LOVERS *See Jonathan RICHMAN and The MODERN LOVERS*

MODERN ROMANCE *UK, male vocal / instrumental group (Singles: 77 Weeks, Albums: 13 Weeks)* pos/wks

15 Aug 81	EVERYBODY SALSA *WEA K 18815*	.12	10
7 Nov 81	● AY AY AY AY MOOSEY *WEA K 18883*	.10	12
30 Jan 82	QUEEN OF THE RAPPING SCENE (NOTHING EVER GOES THE WAY YOU PLAN) *WEA K 18928*	.37	8
14 Aug 82	CHERRY PINK AND APPLE BLOSSOM WHITE *WEA K 19245* ⟨1⟩	.15	8
13 Nov 82	● BEST YEARS OF OUR LIVES *WEA ROM 1*	..4	13
26 Feb 83	● HIGH LIFE *WEA ROM 2*	..8	8
7 May 83	DON'T STOP THAT CRAZY RHYTHM *WEA ROM 3*	.14	6
6 Aug 83	● WALKING IN THE RAIN *WEA X 9733*	..7	12
16 Apr 83	TRICK OF THE LIGHT *WEA X 0127*	.53	7
3 Dec 83	PARTY TONIGHT *Ronco RONLP 3*	.45	6

⟨1⟩ Modern Romance featuring John du Prez

MODERN TALKING *Germany, male vocal / instrumental duo – Thomas Anders and Dieter Bohlen (Singles: 22 Weeks, Albums: 3 Weeks)* pos/wks

15 Jun 85	YOU'RE MY HEART, YOU'RE MY SOUL (re) *Magnet MAG 277*	.56	7
12 Oct 85	YOU CAN WIN IF YOU WANT *Magnet MAG 282*	.70	2
16 Aug 86	● BROTHER LOUIE *RCA PB 40875*	..4	10
4 Oct 86	ATLANTIS IS CALLING (S.O.S. FOR LOVE) *RCA PB 40969*	.55	3
11 Oct 86	READY FOR ROMANCE *RCA PL 71133*	.76	3

MODEST MOUSE *US, male vocal / instrumental group (Singles: 1 Week, Albums: 2 Weeks)* pos/wks

24 Jul 04	FLOAT ON *Epic 6750692*	.46	1
31 Jul 04	GOOD NEWS FOR PEOPLE WHO LOVE BAD NEWS *Epic 5162722*	.40	2

The MODETTES *UK, female vocal / instrumental group (Singles: 6 Weeks)* pos/wks

12 Jul 80	PAINT IT BLACK *Deram DET-R 1*	.42	5
18 Jul 81	TONIGHT *Deram DET 3*	.68	1

MODEY LEMON *US, male vocal / instrumental group (Singles: 1 Week)* pos/wks

22 May 04	CROWS *Mute CDMUTE 328*	.75	1

MODJO *France, male production / vocal duo – Yann Destangol and Romain Tranchart (Singles: 29 Weeks)* pos/wks

16 Sep 00	★ LADY (HEAR ME TONIGHT) *Polydor 5877582* ■	..1	20
14 Apr 01	CHILLIN' *Polydor 5870092*	.12	8
6 Oct 01	WHAT I MEAN *Polydor 5873462*	.59	1

Domenico MODUGNO *Italy, male vocalist, b. 9 Jan 1928, d. 6 Aug 1994 (Singles: 13 Weeks)* pos/wks

5 Sep 58	● VOLARE (NEL BLU DIPINTO DI BLU) *Oriole ICB 5000* ▲	.10	12
27 Mar 59	CIAO CIAO BAMBINA (PIOVE) *Oriole CB 1489*	.29	1

The MOFFATTS *Canada, male vocal / instrumental group (Singles: 6 Weeks, Albums: 1 Week)* pos/wks

20 Feb 99	CRAZY *Chrysalis CDEM 533*	.16	3
26 Jun 99	UNTIL YOU LOVED ME *Chrysalis CDEM 541*	.36	2
23 Oct 99	MISERY *EMI CDEM 551*	.47	1
6 Mar 99	CHAPTER 1: A NEW BEGINNING *Chrysalis 4992072*	.62	1

MOGUAI *Germany, male producer – Andre Tegeler (Singles: 1 Week)* pos/wks

8 Feb 03	U KNOW Y *Hope HOPECDS 038*	.62	1

MOGWAI *UK, male instrumental group (Singles: 3 Weeks, Albums: 7 Weeks)* pos/wks

4 Apr 98	SWEET LEAF / BLACK SABBATH *Fierce Panda NING 47CD* ⟨1⟩	.60	1
11 Apr 98	FEAR SATAN (re-mix) *Eye-Q EYEUK 032CD*	.57	1
11 Jul 98	NO EDUCATION NO FUTURE (F**K THE CURFEW) *Chemikal CHEM 026CD*	.68	1
8 Nov 97	YOUNG TEAM *Chemikal Underground CHEM 018CD*	.75	1
10 Apr 99	COME ON DIE YOUNG *Chemikal Underground CHEM 033CD*	.29	2
12 May 01	ROCK ACTION *Southpaw PAWCD 1*	.23	2
21 Jun 03	HAPPY SONGS FOR HAPPY PEOPLE *PIAS PIASX 035CD*	.47	2

⟨1⟩ Mogwai: Magoo

The MOHAWKS *Jamaica, male vocal / instrumental group (Singles: 2 Weeks)* pos/wks

24 Jan 87	THE CHAMP *Pama PM 1*	.58	2

Frank'o MOIRAGHI featuring AMNESIA *Italy, male / female vocal / instrumental duo (Singles: 4 Weeks)* pos/wks

1 Jun 96	FEEL MY BODY *Multiply CDMULTY 10*	.39	2
26 Oct 96	FEEL MY BODY (re-mix) *Multiply CDMULTY 15*	.40	2

MOIST *Canada, male vocal / instrumental group (Singles: 10 Weeks, Albums: 3 Weeks)* pos/wks

12 Nov 94	PUSH *Chrysalis CDCHS 5016*	.35	3
25 Feb 95	SILVER *Chrysalis CDCHS 5019*	.50	2
29 Apr 95	FREAKY BE BEAUTIFUL *Chrysalis CDCHS 5022*	.47	2
19 Aug 95	PUSH (re-issue) *Chrysalis CDCHS 5024*	.20	3
26 Aug 95	SILVER *Chrysalis CDCHR 6080*	.49	3

MOJO *UK, male instrumental group (Singles: 3 Weeks)* pos/wks

22 Aug 81	DANCE ON *Creole CR 17*	.70	3

MOJOLATORS featuring CAMILLA *US, male production duo and female vocalist (Singles: 1 Week)* pos/wks

6 Oct 01	DRIFTING *Multiply CDMULTY 81*	.52	1

The MOJOS
UK, male vocal / instrumental group (Singles: 26 Weeks) pos/wks

26 Mar 64 ●	EVERYTHING'S ALRIGHT *Decca F 11853*	9	11
11 Jun 64	WHY NOT TONIGHT *Decca F 11918*	25	10
10 Sep 64	SEVEN DAFFODILS *Decca F 11959*	30	5

MOKENSTEF
US, female vocal group (Singles: 1 Week) pos/wks

23 Sep 95	HE'S MINE *Def Jam DEFCD 13*	70	1

MOLELLA featuring the OUTHERE BROTHERS
Italy, male producer – Maurizio Molella and US, male rap / vocal duo – Lamar Mahone and Craig Simpkins (Singles: 10 Weeks) pos/wks

16 Dec 95 ●	IF YOU WANNA PARTY *Eternal WEA 030CD*	9	10

Sophie MOLETA See HUMAN MOVEMENT featuring Sophie MOLETA

Ralph MOLINA See Ian McNABB

Brian MOLKO See ALPINESTARS featuring Brian MOLKO

Sam MOLLISON See SASHA

MOLLY HALF HEAD
UK, male vocal / instrumental group (Singles: 1 Week) pos/wks

3 Jun 95	SHINE *Columbia 6620732*	73	1

MOLLY HATCHET
US, male vocal / instrumental group (Albums: 1 Week) pos/wks

25 Jan 86	DOUBLE TROUBLE – LIVE *Epic EPC 88670*	94	1

MOLOKO (see also PSYCHEDELIC WALTONS)
Ireland / UK, male / female vocal / instrumental duo – Roisin Murphy and Mark Brydon (Singles: 39 Weeks, Albums: 30 Weeks) pos/wks

24 Feb 96	DOMINOID *Echo ECSCD 016*	65	1
25 May 96	FUN FOR ME *Echo ECSCD 20*	36	2
20 Jun 98	THE FLIPSIDE *Echo ECSCD 54*	53	1
27 Mar 99	SING IT BACK *Echo ECSCD 71*	45	2
4 Sep 99 ●	SING IT BACK (re-mix) *Echo ECSCD 82*	4	9
1 Apr 00 ●	THE TIME IS NOW *Echo ECSCD 88*	2	10
5 Aug 00	PURE PLEASURE SEEKER *Echo ECSCD 99*	21	5
25 Nov 00	INDIGO *Echo ECSCD 104*	51	1
1 Mar 03 ●	FAMILIAR FEELING *Echo ECSCD 131*	10	4
5 Jul 03	FOREVER MORE *Echo ECSCD 136*	17	4
5 Sep 98	I AM NOT A DOCTOR *Echo ECHCD 21*	64	1
22 Apr 00 ●	THINGS TO MAKE AND DO *Echo ECHCD 31*	3	26
15 Mar 03	STATUES *Echo ECHCD 44*	18	3

MOMBASSA
UK, male production duo (Singles: 1 Week) pos/wks

8 Mar 97	CRY FREEDOM *Soundproof SPCD 021*	63	1

The MOMENTS
US, male vocal group (Singles: 32 Weeks) pos/wks

8 Mar 75 ●	GIRLS *All Platinum 6146 302* [1]	3	10
19 Jul 75 ●	DOLLY MY LOVE *All Platinum 6146 306*	10	9
25 Oct 75	LOOK AT ME (I'M IN LOVE) *All Platinum 6146 309*	42	4
22 Jan 77 ●	JACK IN THE BOX *All Platinum 6146 318*	7	9

[1] The Moments and The Whatnauts

Tony MOMRELLE
UK, male vocalist (Singles: 1 Week) pos/wks

15 Aug 98	LET ME SHOW YOU *Art & Soul ART 1CDS*	67	1

MONACO (see also NEW ORDER; JOY DIVISION)
UK, male vocal / instrumental duo – Peter Hook and David Potts (Singles: 11 Weeks, Albums: 3 Weeks) pos/wks

15 Mar 97	WHAT DO YOU WANT FROM ME? *Polydor 5731912*	11	6
31 May 97	SWEET LIPS *Polydor 5710552*	18	4
20 Sep 97	SHINE (SOMEONE WHO NEEDS ME) *Polydor 5714182*	55	1
21 Jun 97	MUSIC FOR PLEASURE *Polydor 5372422*	11	3

Pharoahe MONCH
US, male rapper – Troy Jamerson (Singles: 11 Weeks) pos/wks

19 Feb 00	SIMON SAYS *Rawkus RWK 205CD*	24	2
19 Aug 00	LIGHT *Rawkus RWK 259CD*	72	1

3 Feb 01	OH NO *Rawkus RWK 302* [1]	24	4
1 Dec 01	GOT YOU *Priority PTYCD 145*	27	3
14 Sep 02	THE LIFE *MCA MCSTD 402292* [2]	50	1

[1] Mos Def and Nate Dogg featuring Pharoahe Monch [2] Styles and Pharoahe Monch

Jay MONDI and the LIVING BASS
US, male / female vocal / instrumental group (Singles: 3 Weeks) pos/wks

24 Mar 90	ALL NIGHT LONG *10 TEN 304*	63	3

MONDO KANE
UK, male vocal / instrumental group (Singles: 3 Weeks) pos/wks

16 Aug 86	NEW YORK AFTERNOON *Lisson DOLE 2*	70	3

MONE
US, female vocalist (Singles: 2 Weeks) pos/wks

12 Aug 95	WE CAN MAKE IT *A&M 5811592*	64	1
16 Mar 96	MOVIN' *AM:PM 5814392*	48	1

MONEY MARK
US, male vocalist / instrumentalist / producer – Mark Ramos-Nishita (Singles: 3 Weeks, Albums: 6 Weeks) pos/wks

28 Feb 98	HAND IN YOUR HEAD *Mo Wax MW 066CD*	40	2
6 Jun 98	MAYBE I'M DEAD *Mo Wax MW 089CD1*	45	1
9 Sep 95	MARK'S KEYBOARD REPAIR *Mo Wax MW 034CD*	35	2
16 May 98	PUSH THE BUTTON *Mo Wax MW 090CD*	17	4

Zoot MONEY and the BIG ROLL BAND
UK, male vocal / instrumental group – leader George Bruno Money (Singles: 8 Weeks, Albums: 3 Weeks) pos/wks

18 Aug 66	BIG TIME OPERATOR *Columbia DB 7975*	25	8
15 Oct 66	ZOOT *Columbia SX 6075*	23	3

MONICA
US, female vocalist – Monica Arnold (Singles: 37 Weeks, Albums: 10 Weeks) pos/wks

29 Jul 95	DON'T TAKE IT PERSONAL (JUST ONE OF DEM DAYS) *Arista 74321301452*	32	3
17 Feb 96	LIKE THIS AND LIKE THAT *Rowdy 74321344222*	33	2
8 Jun 96	BEFORE YOU WALK OUT OF MY LIFE *Rowdy 74321374042*	22	3
24 May 97	FOR YOU I WILL *Atlantic A 5437CD*	27	2
6 Jun 98 ●	THE BOY IS MINE *Atlantic AT 0036CD* [1] ▲	2	20
17 Oct 98 ●	THE FIRST NIGHT *Rowdy 74321619342* ▲	6	6
4 Sep 99	ANGEL OF MINE *Arista 74321692892* ▲	55	1
25 Jul 98	THE BOY IS MINE *Arista 7822190112*	52	10

[1] Brandy and Monica

MONIFAH
US, female vocalist – Monifah Carter (Singles: 2 Weeks) pos/wks

30 Jan 99	TOUCH IT *Universal UND 56218*	29	2

TS MONK
US, male / female vocal / instrumental group (Singles: 6 Weeks) pos/wks

7 Mar 81	BON BON VIE *Mirage K 11653*	63	2
25 Apr 81	CANDIDATE FOR LOVE *Mirage K 11648*	58	4

The MONKEES (301 Top 500)
The world's top act of 1967: Davy Jones (v/g), Mike Nesmith (v/g), Peter Tork (v/k), Mickey Dolenz (v/d). This Anglo-American quartet was hand-picked for a Beatles-style TV series, which helped to rocket them, albeit briefly, to the very top (Singles: 101 Weeks, Albums: 118 Weeks) pos/wks

5 Jan 67 ★	I'M A BELIEVER *RCA 1560* ▲	1	17
26 Jan 67	LAST TRAIN TO CLARKSVILLE *RCA 1547* ▲	23	7
6 Apr 67 ●	A LITTLE BIT ME, A LITTLE BIT YOU *RCA 1580*	3	12
22 Jun 67 ●	ALTERNATE TITLE *RCA 1604*	2	12
16 Aug 67	PLEASANT VALLEY SUNDAY *RC 1620*	11	8
15 Nov 67 ●	DAYDREAM BELIEVER *RCA 1645* ▲	5	17
27 Mar 68	VALLERI *RCA 1673*	12	8
26 Jun 68	DW WASHBURN *RCA 1706*	17	6
26 Mar 69	TEAR DROP CITY *RCA 1802*	46	1
25 Jun 69	SOMEDAY MAN *RCA 1824*	47	1
15 Mar 80	THE MONKEES EP *Arista ARIST 326*	33	9
18 Oct 86	THAT WAS THEN, THIS IS NOW *Arista ARIST 673*	68	1
1 Apr 89	THE MONKEES EP *Arista 112157*	62	2
28 Jan 67 ★	THE MONKEES *RCA Victor SF 7844* ▲	1	36
15 Apr 67 ★	MORE OF THE MONKEES *RCA Victor SF 7868* ▲	1	25

Singles re-entries are listed as (re), (2re), (3re).... which signifies that the hit re-entered the chart once, twice or three times...

8 Jul 67 ●	HEADQUARTERS *RCA Victor SF 7886* ▲		.2	19
13 Jan 68 ●	PISCES AQUARIUS CAPRICORN & JONES LTD.			
	RCA Victor SF 7912 ▲		.5	11
28 Nov 81	THE MONKEES *Arista DARTY 12*		.99	1
15 Apr 89	HEY HEY IT'S THE MONKEES – GREATEST HITS *K-Tel NE 1432*	.12	9	
22 Mar 97	HERE THEY COME … THE GREATEST HITS OF THE MONKEES			
	Warner.esp / Telstar 9548352182		.15	10
10 Mar 01	THE DEFINITIVE MONKEES *WSM 8573866922*		.15	7

Tracks on Arista 326 EP: I'm a Believer / Daydream Believer / Last Train to Clarksville / A Little Bit Me a Little Bit You. Tracks on Arista 112157 EP: Daydream Believer / Monkees Theme / Last Train to Clarksville The two albums entitled 'The Monkees' are different

MONKEY BARS featuring Gabrielle WIDMAN *UK, male production / instrumental duo and female vocalist (Singles: 1 Week)* pos/wks

8 May 04	SHUGGIE LOVE *Subliminal SUB 117CD*		.61	1

MONKEY MAFIA *UK, male vocal / instrumental / DJ / production group (Singles: 3 Weeks, Albums: 1 Week)* pos/wks

10 Aug 96	WORK MI BODY *Heavenly HVN 53CD* [1]		.75	1
7 Jun 97	15 STEPS (EP) *Heavenly HVN 67CD*		.67	1
2 May 98	LONG AS I CAN SEE THE LIGHT *Heavenly HVN 84CD*	.51	1	
16 May 98	SHOOT THE BOSS *Heavenly HVNLP 21CD*		.69	1

[1] Monkey Mafia featuring Patra

Tracks on 15 Steps (EP): Lion in the Hall / Krash the Decks: Slaughter the Vinyl / Metro Love / Beats in the Hall

The MONKS (see also HUDSON-FORD; The STRAWBS) *UK, male vocal / instrumental duo – Richard Hudson and John Ford (Singles: 9 Weeks)* pos/wks

21 Apr 79	NICE LEGS SHAME ABOUT HER FACE *Carrere CAR 104*	.19	9	

MONKS AND CHOIRBOYS OF DOWNSIDE ABBEY
UK, male monastic choir (Albums: 6 Weeks) pos/wks

2 Nov 96	THE ABBEY *Virgin VTCD 99*		.54	5
3 Jan 98	GREGORIAN MOODS *Virgin / EMI VTCD 171*		.59	1

MONKS CHORUS SILOS See *CORO DE MUNJES DEL MONASTERIO BENEDICTINO DE SANTO DOMINGO DE SILOS*

MONKS OF AMPLEFORTH ABBEY
UK, male monastic choir (Albums: 2 Weeks) pos/wks

17 Jun 95	VISION OF PEACE *Classic FM CFMCD 1783*		.73	2

MONO *UK, male / female vocal / instrumental duo (Singles: 1 Week, Albums: 1 Week)* pos/wks

2 May 98	LIFE IN MONO *Echo ECSCD 64*		.60	1
8 Aug 98	FORMICA BLUES *Echo ECHCD 17*		.71	1

MONOBOY featuring DELORES *Ireland, male producer – Ian Masterson and female vocalist (Singles: 1 Week)* pos/wks

7 Jul 01	THE MUSIC IN YOU *Perfecto PERF 18CDS*		.50	1

The MONOCHROME SET
UK, male vocal / instrumental group (Albums: 4 Weeks) pos/wks

3 May 80	STRANGE BOUTIQUE *DinDisc DID 4*		.62	4

Tony MONOPOLY *Australia, male vocalist (Albums: 4 Weeks)* pos/wks

12 Jun 76	TONY MONOPOLY *BUK BULP 2000*		.25	4

Matt MONRO *UK, male vocalist – Terence Parsons, b. 1 Dec 1932, d. 7 Feb 1985 (Singles: 127 Weeks, Albums: 15 Weeks)* pos/wks

15 Dec 60 ●	PORTRAIT OF MY LOVE *Parlophone R 4714*		.3	16
9 Mar 61 ●	MY KIND OF GIRL *Parlophone R 4755*		.5	12
18 May 61	WHY NOT NOW / CAN THIS BE LOVE *Parlophone R 4775*	.24	9	
28 Sep 61	GONNA BUILD A MOUNTAIN *Parlophone R 4819*		.44	3
8 Feb 62 ●	SOFTLY AS I LEAVE YOU *Parlophone R 4868*		.10	18
14 Jun 62	WHEN LOVE COMES ALONG *Parlophone R 4911*		.46	3
8 Nov 62	MY LOVE AND DEVOTION *Parlophone R 4954*		.29	5
14 Nov 63	FROM RUSSIA WITH LOVE *Parlophone R 5068*		.20	13
17 Sep 64 ●	WALK AWAY *Parlophone R 5171*		.4	20
24 Dec 64	FOR MAMA *Parlophone R 5215*		.23	4

25 Mar 65	WITHOUT YOU *Parlophone R 5251*		.37	4
21 Oct 65 ●	YESTERDAY *Parlophone R 5348*		.8	12
24 Nov 73	AND YOU SMILED *EMI 2091*		.28	8
7 Aug 65	I HAVE DREAMED *Parlophone PMC 1250*		.20	1
17 Sep 66	THIS IS THE LIFE *Capitol T 2540*		.25	2
26 Aug 67	INVITATION TO THE MOVIES *Capitol ST 2730*		.30	1
15 Mar 80 ●	HEARTBREAKERS *EMI EMTV 23*		.5	11

MONROE *UK / Jamaica / Nigeria / Sri Lanka / Morocco, female vocal group (Singles: 1 Week)* pos/wks

31 Jul 04	SMILE *Zu ZUDB 001*		.60	1

Gerry MONROE *UK, male vocalist (Singles: 57 Weeks)* pos/wks

23 May 70 ●	SALLY *Chapter One CH 122*		.4	20
19 Sep 70	CRY *Chapter One CH 128*		.38	5
14 Nov 70 ●	MY PRAYER *Chapter One CH 132*		.9	12
17 Apr 71	IT'S A SIN TO TELL A LIE *Chapter One CH 144*	.13	12	
21 Aug 71	LITTLE DROPS OF SILVER *Chapter One CH 152*	.37	6	
12 Feb 72	GIRL OF MY DREAMS *Chapter One CH 159*		.43	2

Hollis P MONROE
Canada, male producer (Singles: 1 Week) pos/wks

24 Apr 99	I'M LONELY *City Beat CBE 778CD*		.51	1

MONSOON
UK, male / female vocal / instrumental group (Singles: 12 Weeks) pos/wks

3 Apr 82	EVER SO LONELY *Mobile Suit Corp CORP 2*	.12	9	
5 Jun 82	SHAKTI (THE MEANING OF WITHIN)			
	Mobile Suit Corp CORP 4		.41	3

MONSTA BOY featuring DENZIE
UK, male production / vocal instrumental duo (Singles: 3 Weeks) pos/wks

7 Oct 00	SORRY (I DIDN'T KNOW) *Locked On LOX 125CD*	.25	3	

MONSTER MAGNET *US, male vocal / instrumental group (Singles: 6 Weeks, Albums: 2 Weeks)* pos/wks

29 May 93	TWIN EARTH *A&M 5802812*		.67	1
18 Mar 95	NEGASONIC TEENAGE WARHEAD *A&M 5809812*	.49	1	
6 May 95	DOPES TO INFINITY *A&M 5810332*		.58	1
23 Jan 99	POWERTRIP *A&M 5828232*		.39	2
6 Mar 99	SPACE LORD *A&M 5632752*		.45	1
1 Apr 95	DOPES TO INFINITY *A&M 5403152*		.51	1
13 Jun 98	POWERTRIP *A&M 5409082*		.65	1

MONTAGE *UK, female vocal trio (Singles: 1 Week)* pos/wks

15 Feb 97	THERE AIN'T NOTHIN' LIKE THE LOVE *Wildcard 5733172*	.64	1	

MONTANA SEXTET
US, male instrumental group (Singles: 1 Week) pos/wks

15 Jan 83	HEAVY VIBES *Virgin VS 560*		.59	1

MONTANO vs The TRUMPET MAN
UK, male production / instrumental duo (Singles: 1 Week) pos/wks

18 Sep 99	ITZA TRUMPET THING *Serious SERR 010CD*		.46	1

Hugo MONTENEGRO, his Orchestra and Chorus *US, orchestra – leader b. 1 Jan 1925, d. 6 Feb 1981 (Singles: 26 Weeks)* pos/wks

11 Sep 68 ★	THE GOOD, THE BAD AND THE UGLY (re) *RCA 1727*	.1	25	
8 Jan 69	HANG 'EM HIGH *RCA 1771*		.50	1

Chris MONTEZ *US, male vocalist – Ezekiel Montanez (Singles: 61 Weeks)* pos/wks

4 Oct 62 ●	LET'S DANCE *London HLU 9596*		.2	18
17 Jan 63 ●	SOME KINDA FUN *London HLU 9650*		.10	9
30 Jun 66 ●	THE MORE I SEE YOU *Pye International 7N 25369*	.3	13	
22 Sep 66	THERE WILL NEVER BE ANOTHER YOU			
	Pye International 7N 25381		.37	4
14 Oct 72 ●	LET'S DANCE (re-issue) *London HLU 10205*	.9	14	
14 Apr 79	LET'S DANCE (2nd re-issue) *Lightning LIG 9011*	.47	3	

The second re-issue of 'Let's Dance' on Lightning was coupled with 'Memphis' by Lonnie Mack as a double A-side

MONTROSE
US, male vocal / instrumental
group (Singles: 2 Weeks, Albums: 1 Week)   pos/wks

28 Jun 80	**SPACE STATION NUMBER 5 / GOOD ROCKIN' TONIGHT**		
	Warner Bros. WB HM 9 ....**71** 2		
15 Jun 74	**MONTROSE** *Warner Bros. K 46276* **43** 1		

MONTROSE AVENUE
UK, male vocal / instrumental group (Singles: 4 Weeks)   pos/wks

28 Mar 98	**WHERE DO I STAND?** *Columbia 6656072* **38** 2		
20 Jun 98	**SHINE** *Columbia 6660012* **58** 1		
17 Oct 98	**START AGAIN** *Columbia 6664255* **59** 1		

MONTY PYTHON'S FLYING CIRCUS (see also Eric IDLE)
UK, male vocal comedy group (Singles: 9 Weeks, Albums: 33 Weeks) pos/wks

5 Oct 91	● **ALWAYS LOOK ON THE BRIGHT SIDE OF LIFE**		
	Virgin PYTH 1 [1] **3** 9		
30 Oct 71	**ANOTHER MONTY PYTHON RECORD** *Charisma CAS 1049* **26** 3		
27 Jan 73	**MONTY PYTHON'S PREVIOUS ALBUM** *Charisma CAS 1063* ...**39** 3		
23 Feb 74	**MATCHING TIE & HANDKERCHIEF** *Charisma CAS 1080* **49** 2		
27 Jul 74	**MONTY PYTHON LIVE AT DRURY LANE** *Charisma CLASS 4*....**19** 8		
9 Aug 75	**THE ALBUM OF THE SOUNDTRACK OF THE TRAILER**		
	OF THE FILM OF MONTY PYTHON AND THE HOLY GRAIL		
	Charisma CAS 1003 ....**45** 4		
24 Nov 79	**LIFE OF BRIAN** *Warner Bros. K 56751* **63** 3		
18 Oct 80	**MONTY PYTHON'S CONTRACTUAL OBLIGATION ALBUM**		
	Charisma CAS 1152 ....**13** 8		
16 Nov 91	**MONTY PYTHON SINGS** *Virgin MONT 1* **62** 2		

[1] Monty Python

MONYAKA
US / Jamaica, male vocal / instrumental group (Singles: 8 Weeks)   pos/wks

| 10 Sep 83 | **GO DEH YAKA (GO TO THE TOP)** *Polydor POSP 641* ....**14** 8 | | |

MOOD *UK, male vocal / instrumental group (Singles: 10 Weeks)*   pos/wks

6 Feb 82	**DON'T STOP** *RCA 171* **59** 4		
22 May 82	**PARIS IS ONE DAY AWAY** *RCA 211* **42** 5		
30 Oct 82	**PASSION IN DARK ROOMS** *RCA 276* **74** 1		

MOOD II SWING *US, male production / vocal duo –*
Jon Ciafone and Lem Springsteen (Singles: 2 Weeks)   pos/wks

| 31 Jan 04 | **CAN'T GET AWAY** *Defected DFTD 078CDS* ....**45** 2 | | |

MOODSWINGS / CHRISSIE HYNDE (see also The PRETENDERS)
UK, male instrumental group and US, female
vocalist / instrumentalist (Singles: 4 Weeks)   pos/wks

12 Oct 91	**SPIRITUAL HIGH (STATE OF INDEPENDENCE)** *Arista 114528* ..**66** 2		
23 Jan 93	**SPIRITUAL HIGH (STATE OF INDEPENDENCE) (re-mix)**		
	Arista 74321127712 ....**47** 2		

The MOODY BLUES ⟨ 97 ⟩ [Top 500]
Long-lived and internationally popular cosmic rock quintet from Birmingham,
UK. Line-up has included Denny Laine (v/g), Ray Thomas (fl/v), Mike Pinder
(k/v), Graeme Edge (d), Justin Hayward (v/g) and John Lodge (b/v). This
album-orientated act has sold more than 55 million records worldwide
(Singles: 114 Weeks, Albums: 335 Weeks)   pos/wks

10 Dec 64	★ **GO NOW** *Decca F 12022* **1** 14		
4 Mar 65	**I DON'T WANT TO GO ON WITHOUT YOU** *Decca F 12095* **33** 9		
10 Jun 65	**FROM THE BOTTOM OF MY HEART** *Decca F 12166* **22** 9		
18 Nov 65	**EVERYDAY** *Decca F 12266* **44** 2		
27 Dec 67	● **NIGHTS IN WHITE SATIN (2re)** *Deram DM 161* **9** 34		
7 Aug 68	**VOICES IN THE SKY** *Deram DM 196* **27** 10		
4 Dec 68	**RIDE MY SEE-SAW** *Deram DM 213* **42** 1		
2 May 70	● **QUESTION** *Threshold TH 4* **2** 12		
6 May 72	**ISN'T LIFE STRANGE** *Threshold TH 9* **13** 10		
10 Feb 73	**I'M JUST A SINGER (IN A ROCK & ROLL BAND)**		
	Threshold TH 13 ....**36** 4		
20 Aug 83	**BLUE WORLD** *Threshold TH 30* **35** 5		
25 Jun 88	**I KNOW YOU'RE OUT THERE SOMEWHERE** *Polydor POSP 921*..**52** 4		
27 Jan 68	**DAYS OF FUTURE PASSED** *Deram SML 707*....................**27** 16		
3 Aug 68	● **IN SEARCH OF THE LOST CHORD** *Deram SML 711* **5** 32		
3 May 69	★ **ON THE THRESHOLD OF A DREAM** *Deram SML 1035*................**1** 73		
6 Dec 69	● **TO OUR CHILDREN'S CHILDREN'S CHILDREN** *Threshold THS 1* ..**2** 44		
15 Aug 70	★ **A QUESTION OF BALANCE** *Threshold THS 3*....................**1** 19		

7 Aug 71	★ **EVERY GOOD BOY DESERVES FAVOUR** *Threshold THS 5* **1** 21		
2 Dec 72	● **SEVENTH SOJOURN** *Threshold THS 7* ▲ **5** 18		
16 Nov 74	**THIS IS THE MOODY BLUES** *Threshold MB 1/2*.........**14** 18		
24 Jun 78	● **OCTAVE** *Decca TXS 129* **6** 18		
10 Nov 79	**OUT OF THIS WORLD** *K-Tel NE 1051* **15** 10		
23 May 81	● **LONG DISTANCE VOYAGER** *Threshold TXS 139* ▲ **7** 19		
10 Sep 83	**THE PRESENT** *Threshold TXS 140* **15** 8		
10 May 86	**THE OTHER SIDE OF LIFE** *Threshold POLD 5190* **24** 6		
25 Jun 88	**SUR LA MER** *Polydor POLH 43* **21** 5		
20 Jan 90	**GREATEST HITS** *Threshold 8406591* **71** 1		
13 Jul 91	**KEYS OF THE KINGDOM** *Threshold 8494331* **54** 2		
5 Oct 96	**THE VERY BEST OF THE MOODY BLUES** *PolyGram TV 5358002*..**13** 15		
22 Apr 00	**THE VERY BEST OF THE MOODY BLUES (re-issue) /**		
	STRANGE TIMES *Universal Music TV 5414242* **19** 6		
11 May 02	**THE VERY BEST OF THE MOODY BLUES** *UMTV 5833442* **27** 4		

'Nights in White Satin' peaked at No.19 on its original chart visit then peaked at
No.9 in Dec 1972 and No.14 on re-entry in Nov 1979. The Very Best of The Moody
Blues (2002), is an expanded version of the 1996 album of the same name

Michael MOOG
US, male producer – Shivaun Gaines (Singles: 3 Weeks)   pos/wks

| 11 Dec 99 | **THAT SOUND** *ffrr FCD 374* ....**32** 2 | | |
| 25 Aug 01 | **YOU BELONG TO ME** *Strictly Rhythm SRUKECD 04* ....**62** 1 | | |

MOOGWAI *Switzerland / Holland, production duo (Singles: 2 Weeks)* pos/wks

| 6 May 00 | **VIOLA** *Platipus PLATCD 71* ....**55** 1 | | |
| 26 May 01 | **THE LABYRINTH** *Platipus PLATCD 83* ....**68** 1 | | |

MOONMAN
(see also ALBION; GOURYELLA; STARPARTY; SYSTEM F; VERACOCHA)
Holland, male DJ / producer – Ferry Corsten (Singles: 4 Weeks)   pos/wks

9 Aug 97	**DON'T BE AFRAID** *Heat Recordings HEATCD 009* **60** 1		
27 Nov 99	**DON'T BE AFRAID '99 (re-mix)**		
	Heat Recordings HEATCD 022 ....**41** 2		
7 Oct 00	**GALAXIA** *Heat Recordings HEATCD 025* [1] **50** 1		

[1] Moonman featuring Chantal

The MOONTREKKERS
UK, male instrumental group (Singles: 1 Week)   pos/wks

| 2 Nov 61 | **NIGHT OF THE VAMPIRE** *Parlophone R 4814* ....**50** 1 | | |

MOONY *Italy, female vocalist – Monica Bragato (Singles: 9 Weeks)* pos/wks

| 15 Jun 02 | ● **DOVE (I'LL BE LOVING YOU)** *Positiva / Cream CDMNY 1* ....**9** 8 | | |
| 1 Mar 03 | **ACROBATS (LOOKING FOR BALANCE)** *WEA WEA 363CD* .....**64** 1 | | |

Ian MOOR *US, male vocalist / instrumentalist (Albums: 2 Weeks)* pos/wks

| 7 Oct 00 | **NATURALLY** *BMG TV Projects 74321783862* ....**38** 2 | | |

Chanté MOORE *US, female vocalist (Singles: 11 Weeks)*   pos/wks

20 Mar 93	**LOVE'S TAKEN OVER** *MCA MCSTD 1744* **54** 3		
4 Mar 95	**FREE / SAIL ON** *MCA MCSTD 2042* **69** 1		
7 Apr 01	**STRAIGHT UP (re)** *MCA MCSTD 40250* **11** 7		

Christy MOORE *Ireland, male vocalist (Albums: 8 Weeks)*   pos/wks

4 May 91	**SMOKE AND STRONG WHISKEY** *Newberry CM 21* **49** 3		
21 Sep 91	**THE CHRISTY MOORE COLLECTION** *East West WX 434* **69** 1		
6 Nov 93	**KING PUCK** *Equator ATLASCD 003* **66** 2		
14 Sep 96	**GRAFFITI TONGUE** *Grapevine GRACD 215* **35** 2		

Dorothy MOORE *US, female vocalist (Singles: 24 Weeks)*   pos/wks

19 Jun 76	● **MISTY BLUE** *Contempo CS 2087* **5** 12		
16 Oct 76	**FUNNY HOW TIME SLIPS AWAY** *Contempo CS 2092* **38** 3		
15 Oct 77	**I BELIEVE YOU** *Epic EPC 5573* **20** 9		

Dudley MOORE (see also Peter COOK and Dudley MOORE)
UK, male comedian / vocalist / instrumentalist – piano,
b. 19 Apr 1935, d. 27 Mar 2002 (Albums: 24 Weeks)   pos/wks

4 Dec 65	**THE OTHER SIDE OF DUDLEY MOORE** *Decca LK 4732* **11** 9		
11 Jun 66	**GENUINE DUD** *Decca LK 4788* **13** 10		
26 Jan 91	**ORCHESTRA!** *Decca 4308361* [1] **38** 5		

[1] Sir George Solti and Dudley Moore

Gary MOORE `322` `Top 500` (see also BBM)

Noted blues guitarist, b. 4 Apr 1952, Belfast, Northern Ireland. Played in early 1970s Irish band Skid Row (with Phil Lynott), as well as Thin Lizzy and Colosseum II, before successfully launching his solo career (Singles: 103 Weeks, Albums: 104 Weeks) pos/wks

21 Apr 79 ●	PARISIENNE WALKWAYS *MCA 419*	8	11
21 Jan 84	HOLD ON TO LOVE *10 TEN 13*	65	3
11 Aug 84	EMPTY ROOMS *10 TEN 25*	51	5
18 May 85 ●	OUT IN THE FIELDS *10 TEN 49* [1]	5	10
27 Jul 85	EMPTY ROOMS (re-issue) *10 TEN 58*	23	8
20 Dec 86	OVER THE HILLS AND FAR AWAY *10 TEN 134*	20	8
28 Feb 87	WILD FRONTIER *10 TEN 159*	35	5
9 May 87	FRIDAY ON MY MIND *10 TEN 164*	26	6
29 Aug 87	THE LONER *10 TEN 178*	53	5
5 Dec 87	TAKE A LITTLE TIME (DOUBLE SINGLE) *10 TEN 190*	75	1
14 Jan 89	AFTER THE WAR *Virgin GMS 1*	37	4
18 Mar 89	READY FOR LOVE *Virgin GMS 2*	56	2
24 Mar 90	OH PRETTY WOMAN *Virgin VS 1233* [2]	48	3
12 May 90	STILL GOT THE BLUES (FOR YOU) *Virgin VS 1267*	31	7
18 Aug 90	WALKING BY MYSELF *Virgin VS 1281*	48	5
15 Dec 90	TOO TIRED *Virgin VS 1306*	71	1
22 Feb 92	COLD DAY IN HELL *Virgin VS 1393*	24	5
9 May 92	STORY OF THE BLUES *Virgin VS 1412*	40	4
18 Jul 92	SINCE I MET YOU BABY *Virgin VS 1423* [3]	59	1
24 Oct 92	SEPARATE WAYS *Virgin VS 1437*	59	1
8 May 93	PARISIENNE WALKWAYS (re-recording) *Virgin VSCDX 1456*	32	4
17 Jun 95	NEED YOUR LOVE SO BAD *Virgin VSCDG 1546*	48	2
3 Feb 79	BACK ON THE STREETS *MCA MCF 2853*	70	1
16 Oct 82	CORRIDORS OF POWER *Virgin V 2245*	30	6
18 Feb 84	VICTIMS OF THE FUTURE *10 DIX 2*	12	7
13 Oct 84	WE WANT MOORE! *10 GMDL 1*	32	3
14 Sep 85	RUN FOR COVER *10 DIX 16*	12	8
12 Jul 86	ROCKIN' EVERY NIGHT *10 XID 1*	99	1
14 Mar 87 ●	WILD FRONTIER *10 DIX 56*	8	14
11 Feb 89	AFTER THE WAR *Virgin V 2575*	23	5
7 Apr 90	STILL GOT THE BLUES *Virgin V 2612*	13	26
21 Mar 92 ●	AFTER HOURS *Virgin CDV 2684*	4	13
22 May 93 ●	BLUES ALIVE *Virgin CDVX 2716*	8	5
26 Nov 94	BALLADS AND BLUES 1982-1994 *Virgin CDV 2768*	33	6
10 Jun 95	BLUES FOR GREENEY *Virgin CDV 2784*	14	5
7 Jun 97	DARK DAYS IN PARADISE *Virgin CDV 2826*	43	2
31 Oct 98	OUT IN THE FIELDS – THE VERY BEST OF GARY MOORE *Virgin CDVX 2871*	54	1
24 Mar 01	BACK TO THE BLUES *Sanctuary SANCD 072*	53	1

[1] Gary Moore and Phil Lynott [2] Gary Moore featuring Albert King [3] Gary Moore and B.B. King

'Parisienne Walkways' features uncredited vocals by Phil Lynott. Tracks on Take a Little Time (double single): Take a Little Time / Out in the Fields / All Messed Up / Thunder Rising

Jackie MOORE *US, female vocalist (Singles: 5 Weeks)* pos/wks

15 Sep 79	THIS TIME BABY *CBS 7722*	49	5

Lynsey MOORE See RAMSEY and FEN featuring Lynsey MOORE

Mandy MOORE
US, female vocalist (Singles: 18 Weeks, Albums: 1 Week) pos/wks

6 May 00 ●	CANDY *Epic 6693452*	6	13
19 Aug 00	I WANNA BE WITH YOU *Epic 6695922*	21	5
20 May 00	I WANNA BE WITH YOU *Epic 4982769*	52	1

Mark MOORE See S EXPRESS

Melba MOORE
US, female vocalist – Melba Hill (Singles: 29 Weeks) pos/wks

15 May 76 ●	THIS IS IT *Buddah BDS 443*	9	8
26 May 79	PICK ME UP, I'LL DANCE *Epic EPC 7234*	48	5
9 Oct 82	LOVE'S COMIN' AT YA *EMI America EA 146*	15	8
15 Jan 83	MIND UP TONIGHT *Capitol CL 272*	22	6
5 Mar 83	UNDERLOVE *Capitol CL 281*	60	1

Ray MOORE
UK, male radio DJ / vocalist, b. 1942, d. Jan 1989 (Singles: 9 Weeks) pos/wks

29 Nov 86	O' MY FATHER HAD A RABBIT *Play PLAY 213*	24	7
5 Dec 87	BOG EYED JOG *Play PLAY 224*	61	2

Sam MOORE and LOU REED
(see also SAM and DAVE) *US, male duo (Singles: 10 Weeks)* pos/wks

17 Jan 87	SOUL MAN *A&M AM 364*	30	10

Tina MOORE *US, female vocalist (Singles: 18 Weeks)* pos/wks

30 Aug 97 ●	NEVER GONNA LET YOU GO *Delirious 74321511052*	7	15
25 Apr 98	NOBODY BETTER *RCA 74321571612*	20	3

Lisa MOORISH
UK, female vocalist – Lisa Morrish (Singles: 11 Weeks) pos/wks

7 Jan 95	JUST THE WAY IT IS *Go Beat GODCD 123*	42	3
19 Aug 95	I'M YOUR MAN *Go Beat GODCD 128*	24	3
3 Feb 96	MR FRIDAY NIGHT *Go Beat GODCD 137*	24	3
18 May 96	LOVE FOR LIFE *Go Beat GODCD 145*	37	2

'I'm Your Man' features the uncredited vocals of George Michael

Angel MORAES *US, male producer (Singles: 2 Weeks)* pos/wks

16 Nov 96	HEAVEN KNOWS – DEEP DEEP DOWN *ffrr FCD 282*	72	1
17 May 97	I LIKE IT *AM:PM 5871792*	70	1

David MORALES (see also BOSS; PULSE featuring Antoinette ROBERSON)
US, male DJ / producer (Singles: 22 Weeks) pos/wks

10 Jul 93	GIMME LUV (EENIE MEENIE MINY MO) *Mercury MERCD 390*	37	3
20 Nov 93	THE PROGRAM *Mercury MERCD 396*	66	1
24 Aug 96	IN DE GHETTO *Manifesto FESCD 12* [1]	35	2
15 Aug 98 ●	NEEDIN' U *Manifesto FESCD 46* [2]	8	8
24 Jun 00	HIGHER *Azuli AZNYCDX 120* [3]	41	2
20 Jan 01	NEEDIN' U II (re-mix) *Manifesto FESCD 78* [4]	11	5
2 Oct 04	HOW WOULD U FEEL *DMI DMI 01* [5]	71	1

[1] David Morales and the Bad Yard Club featuring Crystal Waters and Delta [2] David Morales presents The Face [3] David Morales and Albert Cabrera present Moca featuring Deanna [4] David Morales presents The Face featuring Juliet Roberts [5] David Morales featuring Lea Lorien

Mike MORAN See Lynsey DE PAUL

Patrick MORAZ (see also YES)
Switzerland, male instrumentalist – keyboards (Albums: 8 Weeks) pos/wks

10 Apr 76	PATRICK MORAZ *Charisma CDS 4002*	28	7
23 Jul 77	OUT IN THE SUN *Charisma CDS 4007*	44	1

MORCHEEBA *UK, male / female vocal / instrumental group (Singles: 14 Weeks, Albums: 108 Weeks)* pos/wks

13 Jul 96	TAPE LOOP *Indochina ID 045CD*	42	1
5 Oct 96	TRIGGER HIPPIE *Indochina ID 052CD*	40	2
15 Feb 97	THE MUSIC THAT WE HEAR (MOOG ISLAND) *Indochina ID 054CD*	47	1
11 Oct 97	SHOULDER HOLSTER *Indochina ID 064CD*	53	1
11 Apr 98	BLINDFOLD *Indochina ID 070CD*	56	1
20 Jun 98	LET ME SEE *Indochina ID 076CD*	46	1
29 Aug 98	PART OF THE PROCESS *China WOKCD 2097*	38	2
5 Aug 00	ROME WASN'T BUILT IN A DAY *East West EW 214CD*	34	3
31 Mar 01	WORLD LOOKING IN *East West EW 225CD*	48	1
6 Jul 02	OTHERWISE *East West EW 247CD*	64	1
12 Apr 97	WHO CAN YOU TRUST? *Indochina ZEN 009CD*	57	3
28 Mar 98	BIG CALM *Indochina ZEN 017CD*	18	71
22 Jul 00 ●	FRAGMENTS OF FREEDOM *East West 8573836022*	6	14
13 Jul 02 ●	CHARANGO *East West 927469632*	7	8
12 Jul 03 ●	PARTS OF THE PROCESS *East West 5046658702*	6	12

MORDRED *UK, male vocal / instrumental group (Albums: 1 Week)* pos/wks

16 Feb 91	IN THIS LIFE *Noise International NO 1591*	70	1

MORE *UK, male vocal / instrumental group (Singles: 2 Weeks)* pos/wks

14 Mar 81	WE ARE THE BAND *Atlantic K 11561*	59	2

MORE FIRE CREW
UK, vocal / rap / production group (Singles: 10 Weeks) pos/wks

16 Mar 02 ●	OI! *Go Beat GOBCD 48* [1]	8	8
25 Jan 03	BACK THEN *Go Beat GOBCD 54*	45	2

[1] Platinum 45 featuring More Fire Crew

MOREL
US, male vocalist / producer – Richard Morel (Singles: 1 Week) pos/wks

| 12 Aug 00 | **TRUE (THE FAGGOT IS YOU)** *Hooj Choons HOOJ 097CD* | ....64 | 1 |

George MOREL featuring Heather WILDMAN
US, male / female vocal / instrumental duo (Singles: 2 Weeks) pos/wks

| 26 Oct 96 | **LET'S GROOVE** *Positiva CDTIV 62* | ....42 | 2 |

MORGAN *UK, male vocal / instrumental duo (Singles: 1 Week)* pos/wks

| 27 Nov 99 | **MISS PARKER** *Source CDSOUR 002* | ....74 | 1 |

Debelah MORGAN *US, female vocalist (Singles: 9 Weeks)* pos/wks

| 24 Feb 01 | ● **DANCE WITH ME** *Atlantic AT 0087CD* | ....10 | 9 |

Derrick MORGAN *Jamaica, male vocalist (Singles: 1 Week)* pos/wks

| 17 Jan 70 | **MOON HOP** *Crab 32* | ....49 | 1 |

Jamie J MORGAN *US, male vocalist (Singles: 6 Weeks)* pos/wks

| 10 Feb 90 | **WALK ON THE WILD SIDE** *Tabu 655596 7* | ....27 | 6 |

Jane MORGAN
US, female vocalist – Jane Currier (Singles: 22 Weeks) pos/wks

5 Dec 58	★ **THE DAY THE RAINS CAME** *London HLR 8751*	1	16
22 May 59	**IF ONLY I COULD LIVE MY LIFE AGAIN** *London HLR 8810*	..27	1
21 Jul 60	**ROMANTICA** *London HLR 9120*	39	5

Meli'sa MORGAN *US, female vocalist (Singles: 7 Weeks)* pos/wks

| 9 Aug 86 | **FOOL'S PARADISE** *Capitol CL 415* | ....41 | 5 |
| 25 Jun 88 | **GOOD LOVE** *Capitol CL 483* | ....59 | 2 |

Ray MORGAN *UK, male vocalist (Singles: 6 Weeks)* pos/wks

| 25 Jul 70 | **THE LONG AND WINDING ROAD** *B&C CB 128* | ....32 | 6 |

Erick MORILLO (see also LIL MO' YIN YANG; REAL TO REEL; PIANOHEADZ)
US, male DJ / producer / instrumentalist (Singles: 3 Weeks) pos/wks

| 4 Feb 95 | **HIGHER (FEEL IT)** *A&M 5809412* [1] | ....74 | 1 |
| 26 Jun 04 | **BREAK DOWN THE DOORS** *Subliminal SUB 124CD* [2] | ....44 | 2 |

[1] Erick 'More' Morillo presents RAW [2] Morillo featuring Audio Bullys

Alanis MORISSETTE (230 Top 500) *Internationally successful, frank and rebellious, Canadian singer / songwriter, b. 1 Jun 1974, Ottawa. The child prodigy's Brit and Grammy-winning, 30 million-selling 'Jagged Little Pill' became the first album by a female to simultaneously top the US and UK charts (Singles: 57 Weeks, Albums: 212 Weeks)* pos/wks

5 Aug 95	**YOU OUGHTA KNOW** *Maverick W 0307CD*	22	7
28 Oct 95	**HAND IN MY POCKET** *Maverick W 0312CD*	26	3
24 Feb 96	**YOU LEARN** *Maverick W 0334CD*	24	4
20 Apr 96	**IRONIC** *Maverick W 0343CD*	11	9
3 Aug 96	● **HEAD OVER FEET** *Maverick W 0355CD*	7	7
7 Dec 96	**ALL I REALLY WANT** *Maverick W 0382CD*	59	1
31 Oct 98	● **THANK U** *Maverick W 0458CD*	5	10
13 Mar 99	**JOINING YOU** *Maverick W 472CD1*	28	2
31 Jul 99	**SO PURE** *Maverick W 492CD1*	38	2
2 Mar 02	**HANDS CLEAN** *Maverick W 574CD*	12	7
17 Aug 02	**PRECIOUS ILLUSIONS** *Maverick W 582CD*	53	1
22 May 04	**EVERYTHING** *Maverick W 641CD1*	22	3
31 Jul 04	**OUT IS THROUGH** *Maverick W 647CD1*	56	1
26 Aug 95	★ **JAGGED LITTLE PILL** *Maverick 9362459012* ▲	1	172
14 Nov 98	● **SUPPOSED FORMER INFATUATION JUNKIE** *Maverick 9362470942* ▲	3	21
4 Dec 99	**MTV UNPLUGGED** *Maverick 9362475892*	56	5
16 Mar 02	● **UNDER RUG SWEPT** *Maverick 9362482722* ▲	2	10
29 May 04	● **SO-CALLED CHAOS** *Maverick / Warner Bros. 9362487732*	8	4

MORJAC featuring Raz CONWAY
Denmark, male production duo and male vocalist (Singles: 2 Weeks) pos/wks

| 11 Oct 03 | **STARS** *Credence CDCRED 036* | ....38 | 2 |

Giorgio MORODER *Italy, male instrumentalist – synthesizer (Singles: 36 Weeks, Albums: 276 Weeks)* pos/wks

24 Sep 77	**FROM HERE TO ETERNITY** *Oasis 1* [1]	16	10
17 Mar 79	**CHASE** *Casablanca CAN 144*	48	6
22 Sep 84	● **TOGETHER IN ELECTRIC DREAMS** *Virgin VS 713* [2]	3	13
29 Jun 85	**GOOD-BYE BAD TIMES** *Virgin VS 772* [3]	44	5
11 Jul 98	**CARRY ON** *Almighty CDALMY 120* [4]	65	1
12 Feb 00	**THE CHASE (re-recording)** *Logic 74321732112* [5]	46	1
10 Aug 85	**PHILIP OAKEY AND GIORGIO MORODER** *Virgin V 2351* [1]	52	5

[1] Giorgio [2] Giorgio Moroder and Phil Oakey [3] Philip Oakey and Giorgio Moroder [4] Donna Summer and Giorgio Moroder [5] DJ Empire presents Giorgio Moroder [1] Philip Oakey & Giorgio Moroder

Joseph MOROVITZ *See SOUTH BANK ORCHESTRA*

Ennio MORRICONE (see also LONDON PHILHARMONIC ORCHESTRA)
Italy, orchestra (Singles: 12 Weeks, Albums: 17 Weeks) pos/wks

11 Apr 81	● **CHI MAI (THEME FROM THE TV SERIES 'THE LIFE AND TIMES OF DAVID LLOYD GEORGE')** *BBC RESL 92*	2	12
2 May 81	**THIS IS ENNIO MORRICONE** *EMI THIS 33*	23	5
9 May 81	**CHI MAI** *BBC REH 414*	29	6
7 Mar 87	**THE MISSION (FILM SOUNDTRACK)** *Virgin V 2402* [1]	73	4
30 Sep 00	**THE VERY BEST OF ENNIO MORRICONE** *Virgin CDV 2929*	48	1
10 Apr 04	**MOVIE MASTERPIECES** *BMG 82876596932*	69	1

[1] Ennio Morricone and the London Philharmonic Orchestra

Sarah Jane MORRIS *See The COMMUNARDS*

Diana MORRISON *See Michael BALL*

Dorothy Combs MORRISON *See Edwin HAWKINS SINGERS*

Mark MORRISON
UK, male vocalist / rapper (Singles: 69 Weeks, Albums: 39 Weeks) pos/wks

22 Apr 95	**CRAZY** *WEA YZ 907CD*	19	4
16 Sep 95	**LET'S GET DOWN** *WEA WEA 001CD*	39	2
16 Mar 96	★ **RETURN OF THE MACK (re)** *WEA WEA 040CD*	1	24
27 Jul 96	● **CRAZY (re) (re-mix)** *WEA WEA 054CD1*	6	9
19 Oct 96	● **TRIPPIN'** *WEA WEA 079CD1*	8	6
21 Dec 96	● **HORNY** *WEA WEA 090CD1*	5	9
15 Mar 97	● **MOAN & GROAN** *WEA WEA 096CD1*	7	7
20 Sep 97	**WHO'S THE MACK!** *WEA WEA 128CD1*	13	5
4 Sep 99	**BEST FRIEND** *WEA WEA 221CD1* [1]	23	3
14 Aug 04	**JUST A MAN / BACKSTABBERS** *2 Wikid WKDCD 007*	48	1
4 May 96	● **RETURN OF THE MACK** *WEA 630145862*	4	38
27 Sep 97	**ONLY GOD CAN JUDGE ME** *WEA 630195392*	50	1

[1] Mark Morrison and Conner Reeves

Van MORRISON (196 Top 500)
(see also THEM; Linda Gail LEWIS) Critically acclaimed singer / songwriter has amassed many international hits over five decades, b. 31 Aug 1945, Belfast, Northern Ireland. Received Outstanding Contribution Brit award (1994) and OBE (1996) and 'Brown Eyed Girl' achieved more than 6 million radio plays Stateside but never charted in the UK. Similarly, the 'Astral Weeks' album is regarded as one the greatest-ever long players by critics, but failed to chart here (Singles: 21 Weeks, Albums: 276 Weeks) pos/wks

20 Oct 79	**BRIGHT SIDE OF THE ROAD** *Mercury 6001 121*	63	3
1 Jul 89	**HAVE I TOLD YOU LATELY** *Polydor VANS 1*	74	1
9 Dec 89	**WHENEVER GOD SHINES HIS LIGHT** *Polydor VANS 2* [1]	20	6
15 May 93	**GLORIA** *Exile VANCD 11* [2]	31	3
18 Mar 95	**HAVE I TOLD YOU LATELY THAT I LOVE YOU (re-recording)** *RCA 74321271702* [3]	71	1
10 Jun 95	**DAYS LIKE THIS** *Exile VANCD 12*	65	1
2 Dec 95	**NO RELIGION** *Exile 5775792*	54	1
1 Mar 97	**THE HEALING GAME** *Exile 5733912*	46	1
6 Mar 99	**PRECIOUS TIME** *Pointblank / Virgin POBD 14*	36	2
22 May 99	**BACK ON TOP** *Exile / Pointblank / Virgin POBD 15*	69	1
18 May 02	**HEY MR DJ** *Polydor / Exile 5705962*	58	1
18 Apr 70	**MOONDANCE** *Warner Bros. WS 1835*	32	2
13 Feb 71	**VAN MORRISON, HIS BAND AND THE STREET CHOIR** *Warner Bros. WS 1884*	18	6
11 Aug 73	**HARD NOSE THE HIGHWAY** *Warner Bros. K 46242*	22	3
16 Nov 74	**VEEDON FLEECE** *Warner Bros. K 56068*	41	1
7 May 77	**A PERIOD OF TRANSITION** *Warner Bros. K 56322*	23	5
21 Oct 78	**WAVELENGTH** *Warner Bros. K 56526*	27	7
8 Sep 79	**INTO THE MUSIC** *Vertigo 9120 852*	21	9
20 Sep 80	**THE COMMON ONE** *Mercury 6302 021*	53	3
27 Feb 82	**BEAUTIFUL VISION** *Mercury 6302 122*	31	14
26 Mar 83	**INARTICULATE SPEECH OF THE HEART** *Mercury MERL 16*	14	8

3 Mar 84	**LIVE AT THE GRAND OPERA HOUSE BELFAST** *Mercury MERL 36*	47	4
9 Feb 85	**A SENSE OF WONDER** *Mercury MERH 54*	25	5
2 Aug 86	**NO GURU NO METHOD NO TEACHER** *Mercury MERH 94*	27	5
19 Sep 87	**POETIC CHAMPIONS COMPOSE** *Mercury MERH 110*	26	6
2 Jul 88	**IRISH HEARTBEAT** *Mercury MERH 124* [1]	18	7
10 Jun 89	**AVALON SUNSET** *Mercury 839262 1*	13	14
7 Apr 90 ●	**THE BEST OF VAN MORRISON** *Polydor 8419701*	4	87
20 Oct 90 ●	**ENLIGHTENMENT** *Polydor 8471001*	5	14
21 Sep 91 ●	**HYMNS TO THE SILENCE** *Polydor 8490261*	5	6
27 Feb 93	**THE BEST OF VAN MORRISON VOLUME 2** *Polydor 5177602*	31	3
12 Jun 93 ●	**TOO LONG IN EXILE** *Exile 5192192*	4	9
30 Apr 94 ●	**A NIGHT IN SAN FRANCISCO** *Polydor 5212902*	8	4
24 Jun 95 ●	**DAYS LIKE THIS** *Exile 5273072*	5	15
15 Mar 97 ●	**THE HEALING GAME** *Exile 5371012*	10	7
27 Jun 98	**THE PHILOSOPHER'S STONE** *Exile 5317892*	20	3
20 Mar 99	**BACK ON TOP** *Pointblank VPBCD 50*	11	16
29 Jan 00	**THE SKIFFLE SESSIONS – LIVE IN BELFAST** *Venture CDVE 945* [2]	14	3
7 Oct 00	**YOU WIN AGAIN** *Pointblank VPBCD 54* [3]	34	2
25 May 02 ●	**DOWN THE ROAD** *Exile 5891772*	6	6
1 Nov 03	**WHAT'S WRONG WITH THIS PICTURE** *Blue Note 5901672*	43	1

[1] Van Morrison with Cliff Richard [2] Van Morrison and John Lee Hooker
[3] The Chieftains with Van Morrison [1] Van Morrison and The Chieftains
[2] Van Morrison / Lonnie Donegan / Chris Barber [3] Van Morrison and Linda Gail Lewis

MORRISSEY `420` *Top 500*

Witty, often provocative vocalist / lyricist, b. Stephen Morrissey, 22 May 1959, Manchester, UK, who has now had more Top 20 singles and albums as a solo artist than as leader of the legendary Smiths. He was awarded the prestigious Nordoff-Robbins Silver Clef Award in 2004 for "his amazing contribution to music". (Singles: 90 Weeks, Albums: 75 Weeks) pos/wks

27 Feb 88 ●	**SUEDEHEAD** *HMV POP 1618*	5	6
11 Jun 88 ●	**EVERYDAY IS LIKE SUNDAY** *HMV POP 1619*	9	6
11 Feb 89 ●	**LAST OF THE FAMOUS INTERNATIONAL PLAYBOYS** *HMV POP 1620*	6	5
29 Apr 89 ●	**INTERESTING DRUG** *HMV POP 1621*	9	4
25 Nov 89	**OUIJA BOARD OUIJA BOARD** *HMV POP 1622*	18	4
5 May 90	**NOVEMBER SPAWNED A MONSTER** *HMV POP 1623*	12	4
20 Oct 90	**PICCADILLY PALARE** *HMV POP 1624*	18	2
23 Feb 91	**OUR FRANK** *HMV POP 1625*	26	3
13 Apr 91	**SING YOUR LIFE** *HMV POP 1626*	33	2
27 Jul 91	**PREGNANT FOR THE LAST TIME** *HMV POP 1627*	25	4
12 Oct 91	**MY LOVE LIFE** *HMV POP 1628*	29	2
9 May 92	**WE HATE IT WHEN OUR FRIENDS BECOME SUCCESSFUL** *HMV POP 1629*	17	3
18 Jul 92	**YOU'RE THE ONE FOR ME, FATTY** *HMV POP 1630*	19	3
19 Dec 92	**CERTAIN PEOPLE I KNOW** *HMV POP 1631*	35	4
12 Mar 94 ●	**THE MORE YOU IGNORE ME THE CLOSER I GET** *Parlophone CDR 6372*	8	3
11 Jun 94	**HOLD ON TO YOUR FRIENDS** *Parlophone CDR 6383*	47	2
20 Aug 94	**INTERLUDE** *Parlophone CDR 6365* [1]	25	2
28 Jan 95	**BOXERS** *Parlophone CDR 6400*	23	2
2 Sep 95	**DAGENHAM DAVE** *RCA Victor 74321299802*	26	2
9 Dec 95	**THE BOY RACER** *RCA Victor 74321332952*	36	2
23 Dec 95	**SUNNY** *Parlophone CDR 6243*	42	2
2 Aug 97	**ALMA MATTERS** *Island CID 667*	16	3
18 Oct 97	**ROY'S KEEN** *Island CID 671*	42	1
10 Jan 98	**SATAN REJECTED MY SOUL** *Island CID 686*	39	2
22 May 04 ●	**IRISH BLOOD, ENGLISH HEART** *Attack ATKXS 002*	3	5
24 Jul 04 ●	**FIRST OF THE GANG TO DIE** *Attack ATKXS 003*	6	7
23 Oct 04 ●	**LET ME KISS YOU** *Attack ATKXD 008*	8	3
25 Dec 04 ●	**I HAVE FORGIVEN JESUS** *Attack ATKXD 011*	10	1+
26 Mar 88 ★	**VIVA HATE** *HMV CSD 3787* ■	1	20
27 Oct 90 ●	**BONA DRAG** *HMV CLP 3788*	9	4
16 Mar 91 ●	**KILL UNCLE** *HMV CSD 3789*	8	4
8 Aug 92 ●	**YOUR ARSENAL** *HMV CDCSD 3790*	4	5
22 May 93	**BEETHOVEN WAS DEAF** *HMV CDSCD 3791*	13	2
26 Mar 94 ★	**VAUXHALL AND I** *Parlophone CDPCSD 148* ■	1	5
18 Feb 95	**WORLD OF MORRISSEY** *Parlophone CDPCSD 163*	15	2
9 Sep 95 ●	**SOUTHPAW GRAMMAR** *RCA Victor 74321299532*	4	3
23 Aug 97 ●	**MALADJUSTED** *Island CID 8059*	8	3
20 Sep 97	**THE BEST OF MORRISSEY – 'SUEDEHEAD'** *EMI CDEMC 3771*	25	9
29 May 04 ●	**YOU ARE THE QUARRY** *Attack ATKDX 001*	2	18

[1] Morrissey and Siouxsie

'The Best of Morrissey – 'Suedehead' reached its peak position in 2004

MORRISSEY MULLEN

UK, male vocal / instrumental duo (Albums: 11 Weeks) pos/wks

18 Jul 81	**BADNESS** *Beggars Banquet BEGA 27*	43	5
3 Apr 82	**LIFE ON THE WIRE** *Beggars Banquet BEGA 33*	47	5
23 Apr 83	**IT'S ABOUT TIME** *Beggars Banquet BEGA 44*	95	1

MORRISTON ORPHEUS MALE VOICE CHOIR See The ALARM

MORRISTOWN ORPHEUS CHOIR See G.U.S. (FOOTWEAR) BAND and the MORRISTOWN ORPHEUS CHOIR

Buddy MORROW

US, orchestra – leader Muni Zudecoff (Singles: 1 Week) pos/wks

20 Mar 53	**NIGHT TRAIN** *HMV B 10347*	12	1

MORTIIS

Norway, male vocal / instrumental group (Singles: 1 Week) pos/wks

28 Aug 04	**THE GRUDGE** *Earache MOSH 284CD*	51	1

Bob MORTIMER See EMF; MIDDLESBOROUGH FC featuring Bob MORTIMER and Chris REA

MOS DEF

US, male rapper – Dante Smith (Singles: 6 Weeks, Albums: 1 Week) pos/wks

24 Jun 00	**UMI SAYS** *Rawkus RWK 232CD*	60	1
4 Nov 00	**MISS FAT BOOTY – PART II** *Rawkus RWK 282CD* [1]	64	1
3 Feb 01	**OH NO** *Rawkus RWK 302* [2]	24	4
30 Oct 04	**THE NEW DANGER** *Geffen 9864634*	56	1

[1] Mos Def featuring Ghostface Killah [2] Mos Def and Nate Dogg featuring Pharoahe Monch

Kate MOSS See PRIMAL SCREAM

Mickie MOST

UK, male vocalist, b. 20 Jun 1938, d. 30 May 2003 (Singles: 1 Week) pos/wks

25 Jul 63	**MR PORTER** *Decca F 11664*	45	1

The MOTELS

US / UK, male / female vocal / instrumental group (Singles: 7 Weeks) pos/wks

11 Oct 80	**WHOSE PROBLEM?** *Capitol CL 16162*	42	4
10 Jan 81	**DAYS ARE O.K.** *Capitol CL 16149*	41	3

Wendy MOTEN

US, female vocalist (Singles: 13 Weeks, Albums: 2 Weeks) pos/wks

5 Feb 94 ●	**COME IN OUT OF THE RAIN** *EMI-USA CDMT 105*	8	9
14 May 94	**SO CLOSE TO LOVE** *EMI-USA CDMTS 106*	35	4
19 Mar 94	**WENDY MOTEN** *EMI CDMTL 1073*	42	2

MOTHER

UK, male instrumental / production duo – Jools Brettle and Lee Fisher (Singles: 4 Weeks) pos/wks

12 Jun 93	**ALL FUNKED UP** *Bosting BYSNCD 101*	34	2
1 Oct 94	**GET BACK** *Six6 SIXT 119*	73	1
31 Aug 96	**ALL FUNKED UP (re-mix)** *Six6 SIXXCD 1*	66	1

MOTHER EARTH

UK, male vocal / instrumental group (Albums: 2 Weeks) pos/wks

5 Mar 94	**THE PEOPLE TREE** *Acid Jazz JAZIDCD 083*	45	2

The MOTHERS OF INVENTION (see also Frank ZAPPA)

US, male vocal / instrumental group (Albums: 12 Weeks) pos/wks

29 Jun 68	**WE'RE ONLY IN IT FOR THE MONEY** *Verve SVLP 9199*	32	5
28 Mar 70	**BURNT WEENY SANDWICH** *Reprise RSLP 6370*	17	3
3 Oct 70	**WEASELS RIPPED MY FLESH** *Reprise RSLP 2028*	28	4

MOTHER'S PRIDE

UK, male DJ / production duo (Singles: 2 Weeks) pos/wks

21 Mar 98	**FLORIBUNDA** *Heat Recordings HEATCD 013*	42	1
6 Nov 99	**LEARNING TO FLY** *Devolution DEVR 001CDS*	54	1

MOTIV 8
UK, male producer – Steve Rodway (Singles: 10 Weeks) pos/wks

17 Jul 93	ROCKIN' FOR MYSELF *Nuff Respect NUFF 002CD* [1]	67	1
7 May 94	ROCKIN' FOR MYSELF (re-mix) *WEA YZ 814CD*	18	4
21 Oct 95	BREAK THE CHAIN *Eternal WEA 010CD*	31	2
23 Dec 95	SEARCHING FOR THE GOLDEN EYE *Eternal WEA 027CD* [2]	40	3

[1] Motiv 8 featuring Angie Brown [2] Motiv 8 and Kym Mazelle

MOTIVATION
Holland, male producer – Francis Louwers (Singles: 1 Week) pos/wks

17 Nov 01	PARA MI *Definitive CDDEF 1*	71	1

MOTIVO See SNAP!; SPANKOX

MÖTLEY CRÜE (see also Vince NEIL) *US, male vocal / instrumental group (Singles: 28 Weeks, Albums: 26 Weeks)* pos/wks

24 Aug 85	SMOKIN' IN THE BOYS ROOM *Elektra EKR 16*	71	2
8 Feb 86	HOME SWEET HOME / SMOKIN' IN THE BOYS ROOM (re-issue) *Elektra EKR 33*	51	3
1 Aug 87	GIRLS, GIRLS, GIRLS *Elektra EKR 59*	26	6
16 Jan 88	YOU'RE ALL I NEED / WILD SIDE *Elektra EKR 65*	23	4
4 Nov 89	DR FEELGOOD *Elektra EKR 97*	50	3
12 May 90	WITHOUT YOU *Elektra EKR 109*	39	3
7 Sep 91	PRIMAL SCREAM *Elektra EKR 133*	32	2
11 Jan 92	HOME SWEET HOME (re-mix) *Elektra EKR 136*	37	2
5 Mar 94	HOOLIGAN'S HOLIDAY *Elektra EKR 180CDX*	36	2
19 Jul 97	AFRAID *Elektra E 3936CD1*	58	1
13 Jul 85	THEATRE OF PAIN *Elektra EKT 8*	36	3
30 May 87	GIRLS GIRLS GIRLS *Elektra EKT 39*	14	11
16 Sep 89	● DR. FEELGOOD *Elektra EKT 59* ▲	4	7
19 Oct 91	DECADE OF DECADENCE '81-'91 *Elektra EKT 95*	20	3
26 Mar 94	MÖTLEY CRÜE *Elektra 7559615342*	17	2

'Wild Side' listed with 'You're All I Need' only from 30 Jan 1988. It peaked at No.26

Mikki MOTO See Bobby BLANCO & Mikki MOTO

MOTORCYCLE
UK, male / female production / vocal trio (Singles: 9 Weeks) pos/wks

17 Jan 04	AS THE RUSH COMES *Positiva CDTIVS 203*	11	9

MOTÖRHEAD 369 Top 500
Unashamedly loud mainstays of UK heavy rock formed in 1975 after Lemmy (v/b) (b. Ian Kilmister, 24 Dec 1945, Stoke-on-Trent, UK) left Hawkwind. Much admired in punk circles, they helped to show the way to 1980s heavy metal bands such as Metallica (Singles: 81 Weeks, Albums: 103 Weeks) pos/wks

16 Sep 78	LOUIE LOUIE (re) *Bronze BRO 60*	68	2
10 Mar 79	OVERKILL (re) *Bronze BRO 67*	39	7
30 Jun 79	NO CLASS *Bronze BRO 78*	61	7
1 Dec 79	BOMBER *Bronze BRO 85*	34	7
3 May 80	● THE GOLDEN YEARS (EP) *Bronze BRO 92*	8	7
1 Nov 80	ACE OF SPADES *Bronze BRO 106*	15	12
22 Nov 80	BEER DRINKERS AND HELL RAISERS *Big Beat SWT 61*	43	4
21 Feb 81	● ST VALENTINE'S DAY MASSACRE (EP) *Bronze BRO 116* [1]	5	8
11 Jul 81	● MOTÖRHEAD (LIVE) *Bronze BRO 124*	6	7
3 Apr 82	IRON FIST *Bronze BRO 146*	29	5
21 May 83	I GOT MINE *Bronze BRO 165*	46	2
30 Jul 83	SHINE *Bronze BRO 167*	59	2
1 Sep 84	KILLED BY DEATH *Bronze BRO 185*	51	2
5 Jul 86	DEAF FOREVER *GWR GWR 2*	67	1
5 Jan 91	THE ONE TO SING THE BLUES *Epic 6565787*	45	3
14 Nov 92	'92 TOUR (EP) *Epic 6588096*	63	1
11 Sep 93	ACE OF SPADES (re-mix) *WGAF CDWGAF 101*	23	5
10 Dec 94	BORN TO RAISE HELL *Fox 74321230152* [2]	47	2
24 Sep 77	MOTÖRHEAD *Chiswick WIK 2*	43	5
24 Mar 79	OVERKILL *Bronze BRON 515*	24	11
27 Oct 79	BOMBER *Bronze BRON 523*	12	13
8 Dec 79	ON PAROLE *United Artists LBR 1004*	65	2
8 Nov 80	● ACE OF SPADES *Bronze BRON 531*	4	16
27 Jun 81	★ NO SLEEP 'TIL HAMMERSMITH *Bronze BRON 535* ■	1	21
17 Apr 82	● IRON FIST *Bronze BRNA 539*	6	9
26 Feb 83	WHAT'S WORDS WORTH *Big Beat NED 2*	71	2
4 Jun 83	ANOTHER PERFECT DAY *Bronze BRON 546*	20	4
15 Sep 84	NO REMORSE *Bronze PROTV MOTOR 1*	14	6
9 Aug 86	ORGASMATRON *GWR GWLP 1*	21	4
5 Sep 87	ROCK 'N' ROLL *GWR GWLP 14*	34	3
15 Oct 88	NO SLEEP AT ALL *GWR GWR 31*	79	1

2 Feb 91	1916 *Epic 4674811*	24	4
8 Aug 92	MARCH OR DIE *Epic 4717232*	60	1
9 Sep 00	THE BEST OF MOTORHEAD *Metal Is MISDD 002*	52	1

[1] Motörhead and Girlschool (also known as Headgirl) [2] Motörhead / Ice-T / Whitfield Crane

Tracks on The Golden Years (EP): Dead Men Tell No Tales / Too Late Too Late / Leaving Here / Stone Dead Forever. Tracks on St Valentine's Day Massacre (EP): Please Don't Touch / Emergency / Bomber. Tracks on '92 Tour (EP): Hellraiser / You Better Run / Going to Brazil / Ramones

The MOTORS *UK, male vocal / instrumental group (Singles: 29 Weeks, Albums: 6 Weeks)* pos/wks

24 Sep 77	DANCING THE NIGHT AWAY *Virgin VS 186*	42	4
10 Jun 78	● AIRPORT *Virgin VS 219*	4	13
19 Aug 78	FORGET ABOUT YOU *Virgin VS 222*	13	9
12 Apr 80	LOVE AND LONELINESS *Virgin VS 263*	58	3
15 Oct 77	THE MOTORS *Virgin V 2089*	46	5
3 Jun 78	APPROVED BY THE MOTORS *Virgin V 2101*	60	1

MOTOWN SPINNERS See DETROIT SPINNERS

MOTT THE HOOPLE *UK, male vocal / instrumental group – includes Ian Hunter (Singles: 55 Weeks, Albums: 32 Weeks)* pos/wks

12 Aug 72	● ALL THE YOUNG DUDES *CBS 8271*	3	11
16 Jun 73	HONALOOCHIE BOOGIE *CBS 1530*	12	9
8 Sep 73	● ALL THE WAY FROM MEMPHIS *CBS 1764*	10	8
24 Nov 73	● ROLL AWAY THE STONE *CBS 1895*	8	12
30 Mar 74	THE GOLDEN AGE OF ROCK 'N' ROLL *CBS 2177*	16	7
22 Jun 74	FOXY, FOXY *CBS 2439*	33	5
2 Nov 74	SATURDAY GIG *CBS 2754*	41	3
2 May 70	MOTT THE HOOPLE *Island ILPS 9108*	66	1
17 Oct 70	MAD SHADOWS *Island ILPS 9119*	48	2
17 Apr 71	WILD LIFE *Island ILPS 9144*	44	2
23 Sep 72	ALL THE YOUNG DUDES *CBS 65184*	21	4
11 Aug 73	● MOTT *CBS 69038*	7	15
13 Apr 74	THE HOOPLE *CBS 69062*	11	5
23 Nov 74	LIVE *CBS 69093*	32	2
4 Oct 75	DRIVE ON *CBS 69154*	45	1

Bob MOULD (see also HÜSKER DÜ; SUGAR) *US, male vocalist / instrumentalist (Albums: 2 Weeks)* pos/wks

11 May 96	BOB MOULD *Creation CRECD 188*	52	1
5 Sep 98	THE LAST DOG AND PONY SHOW *Creation CRECD 215*	58	1

MOUNT RUSHMORE presents The KNACK
UK, male production duo / female vocalist (Singles: 1 Week) pos/wks

3 Apr 99	YOU BETTER *Universal MCSTD 40192*	53	1

MOUNTAIN
US / Canada, male vocal / instrumental group (Albums: 4 Weeks) pos/wks

5 Jun 71	NANTUCKET SLEIGHRIDE *Island ILPS 9148*	43	1
8 Jul 72	THE ROAD GOES EVER ON *Island ILPS 9199*	21	3

Nana MOUSKOURI 305 Top 500
Greece's No.1 musical export, b. 15 Oct 1934, Athens. Distinctive, bespectacled, folk based singer / guitarist, who collected the first of her numerous worldwide gold and platinum records in 1961, became a Member of the European Parliament in 1994 (Singles: 11 Weeks, Albums: 205 Weeks) pos/wks

11 Jan 86	● ONLY LOVE *Philips PH 38*	2	11
7 Jun 69	● OVER AND OVER *Fontana S 5511*	10	97
4 Apr 70	● THE EXQUISITE NANA MOUSKOURI *Fontana STL 5536*	10	25
10 Oct 70	RECITAL '70 *Fontana 6312 010*	68	1
3 Apr 71	TURN ON THE SUN *Fontana 6312 008*	16	15
29 Jul 72	BRITISH CONCERT *Fontana 6651 003*	29	11
28 Apr 73	SONGS FROM HER TV SERIES *Fontana 6312 036*	29	11
28 Sep 74	SPOTLIGHT ON NANA MOUSKOURI *Fontana 6641 197*	38	6
10 Jul 76	● PASSPORT *Philips 9101 061*	3	16
22 Feb 86	ALONE *Philips PHH 3*	19	10
8 Oct 88	THE MAGIC OF NANA MOUSKOURI *Philips NMTV 1*	44	8
3 Mar 01	AT HER VERY BEST *Philips 5485492*	39	5

MOUSSE T
Germany, male producer – Mustafa Gundogdu (Singles: 39 Weeks) pos/wks

6 Jun 98	● HORNY *AM:PM 5826712* [1]	2	17
20 May 00	● SEX BOMB *Gut CDGUT 33* [2]	3	10
10 Aug 02	FIRE *Serious SERR 44CD* [3]	58	1

			pos/wks
4 Sep 04	●	**IS IT COS I'M COOL?** *Fre2air F2A 1CDX* 3	9 9
18 Dec 04		**RIGHT ABOUT NOW** *Fre2air F2A CDX* 3	28 2+

1 Mousse T vs Hot 'N' Juicy 2 Tom Jones and Mousse T 3 Mousse T featuring Emma Lanford

MOUTH and MACNEAL
Holland, male / female vocal duo –
Willem Duyn and Sjoukje Van't Spijker (Singles: 10 Weeks)   pos/wks

			pos/wks
4 May 74	●	**I SEE A STAR** *Decca F 13504*	8 10

The MOVE
UK, male vocal / instrumental group – included Carl Wayne, b. 18 Aug 1943,
d. 31 Aug 2004, and Roy Wood (Singles: 110 Weeks, Albums: 9 Weeks) pos/wks

			pos/wks
5 Jan 67	●	**NIGHT OF FEAR** *Deram DM 109*	2 10
6 Apr 67	●	**I CAN HEAR THE GRASS GROW** *Deram DM 117*	5 10
6 Sep 67	●	**FLOWERS IN THE RAIN** *Regal Zonophone RZ3001*	2 13
7 Feb 68	●	**FIRE BRIGADE** *Regal Zonophone RZ3005*	3 11
25 Dec 68	★	**BLACKBERRY WAY** *Regal Zonophone RZ3015*	1 12
23 Jul 69		**CURLY** *Regal Zonophone RZ3021*	12 12
25 Apr 70	●	**BRONTOSAURUS** *Regal Zonophone RZ3026*	7 10
3 Jul 71		**TONIGHT** *Harvest HAR 5038*	11 10
23 Oct 71		**CHINATOWN** *Harvest HAR 5043*	23 8
13 May 72	●	**CALIFORNIA MAN** *Harvest HAR 5050*	7 14
13 Apr 68		**MOVE** *Regal Zonophone SLPZ 1002*	15 9

MOVEMENT
US, male vocal / instrumental group (Singles: 2 Weeks)   pos/wks

			pos/wks
24 Oct 92		**JUMP!** *Arista 74321116677*	57 2

MOVEMENT 98 featuring Carroll THOMPSON
UK, male / female vocal / instrumental group (Singles: 8 Weeks)   pos/wks

			pos/wks
19 May 90		**JOY AND HEARTBREAK** *Circa YR 45*	27 5
15 Sep 90		**SUNRISE** *Circa YR 51*	58 3

MOVIN' MELODIES (see also ARTEMESIA; ETHICS; SUBLIMINAL CUTS)
Holland, male producer – Patrick Prinz (Singles: 3 Weeks)   pos/wks

			pos/wks
22 Oct 94		**LA LUNA** *Effective EFFS 017CD* 1	64 1
29 Jun 96		**INDICA** *Hooj Choons HOOJCD 44*	62 1
26 Jul 97		**ROLLERBLADE** *Movin' Melodies 5822352*	71 1

1 Movin' Melodies Production

Alison MOYET 182 Top 500
After five Top 20 hits with Yazoo, the distinctive, bluesy-voiced vocalist, b.
Essex, UK, nicknamed Alf, enjoyed a string of solo successes. Her biggest
hits included revivals of songs made popular by Billie Holiday and Ketty
Lester (Singles: 107 Weeks, Albums: 202 Weeks)   pos/wks

			pos/wks
23 Jun 84	●	**LOVE RESURRECTION** *CBS A 4497*	10 11
13 Oct 84	●	**ALL CRIED OUT** *CBS A 4757*	8 11
1 Dec 84		**INVISIBLE** *CBS A 4930*	21 10
16 Mar 85	●	**THAT OLE DEVIL CALLED LOVE** *CBS A 6044*	2 10
29 Nov 86	●	**IS THIS LOVE?** *CBS MOYET 1*	3 16
7 Mar 87	●	**WEAK IN THE PRESENCE OF BEAUTY** *CBS MOYET 2*	6 10
30 May 87		**ORDINARY GIRL** *CBS MOYET 3*	43 4
28 Nov 87	●	**LOVE LETTERS** *CBS MOYET 5*	4 10
6 Apr 91		**IT WON'T BE LONG** *Columbia 6567577*	50 4
1 Jun 91		**WISHING YOU WERE HERE** *Columbia 6569397*	72 1
12 Oct 91		**THIS HOUSE** *Columbia 6575157*	40 5
16 Oct 93		**FALLING** *Columbia 6595962*	42 3
12 Mar 94		**WHISPERING YOUR NAME** *Columbia 6601622*	18 7
28 May 94		**GETTING INTO SOMETHING** *Columbia 6603565*	51 2
22 Oct 94		**ODE TO BOY** *Columbia 6607952*	59 1
26 Aug 95		**SOLID WOOD** *Columbia 6623265*	44 2
17 Nov 84	★	**ALF** *CBS 26229*	1 84
18 Apr 87	●	**RAINDANCING** *CBS 450 1521*	2 52
4 May 91		**HOODOO** *Columbia 4682721*	11 6
2 Apr 94		**ESSEX** *Columbia 4759552*	24 4
3 Jun 95	★	**SINGLES** *Columbia 4806632* ■	1 35
22 Sep 01		**THE ESSENTIAL ALISON MOYET** *Columbia STVCD 123*	16 4
31 Aug 02		**HOMETIME** *Sanctuary SANCD 128*	18 9
18 Sep 04	●	**VOICE** *Sanctuary SANCD 270*	7 8

MOZAIC
UK, female vocal group (Singles: 7 Weeks)   pos/wks

			pos/wks
5 Aug 95		**SING IT (THE HALLELUJAH SONG)** *Perfecto PERF 106CD*	14 4
10 Aug 96		**RAYS OF THE RISING SUN** *Perfecto PERF 123CD*	32 2
30 Nov 96		**MOVING UP MOVING ON** *Perfecto PERF 131CD*	62 1

MTUME
US, male / female vocal / instrumental
group (Singles: 12 Weeks, Albums: 1 Week)   pos/wks

			pos/wks
14 May 83		**JUICY FRUIT** *Epic A 3424*	34 9
22 Sep 84		**PRIME TIME** *Epic A 4720*	57 3
6 Oct 84		**YOU ME AND HE** *Epic EPC 26077*	85 1

MUD 342 Top 500
Rock 'n' roll-influenced Seventies stars: Les Gray
(v), b. 7 Apr 1946, d. 21 Feb 2004, Rob Davis (g/v), Ray Stiles (b/v), Dave Mount
(d/v). After joining RAK Records and teaming with writers / producers Nicky
Chinn and Mike Chapman, this good-time British band had a noteworthy run
of hits, including three No.1s. Davis is now one of the UK's most successful
songwriters, writing No.1 hits for Kylie Minogue and Spiller (Singles: 139
Weeks, Albums: 58 Weeks)   pos/wks

			pos/wks
10 Mar 73		**CRAZY** *RAK 146*	12 12
23 Jun 73		**HYPNOSIS** *RAK 152*	16 13
27 Oct 73	●	**DYNA-MITE** *RAK 159*	4 12
19 Jan 74	★	**TIGER FEET** *RAK 166*	1 11
13 Apr 74	●	**THE CAT CREPT IN** *RAK 170*	2 9
27 Jul 74	●	**ROCKET** *RAK 178*	6 9
30 Nov 74	★	**LONELY THIS CHRISTMAS (re)** *RAK 187*	1 13
15 Feb 75	●	**THE SECRETS THAT YOU KEEP** *RAK 194*	3 9
26 Apr 75	★	**OH BOY** *RAK 201*	1 9
21 Jun 75	●	**MOONSHINE SALLY** *RAK 208*	10 7
2 Aug 75		**ONE NIGHT** *RAK 213*	32 4
4 Oct 75	●	**L'L'LUCY** *Private Stock PVT 41*	10 6
29 Nov 75	●	**SHOW ME YOU'RE A WOMAN** *Private Stock PVT 45*	8 8
15 May 76		**SHAKE IT DOWN** *Private Stock PVT 65*	12 8
27 Nov 76	●	**LEAN ON ME** *Private Stock PVT 85*	7 9
28 Sep 74	●	**MUD ROCK** *RAK SRAK 508*	8 35
26 Jul 75	●	**MUD ROCK VOLUME 2** *RAK SRAK 513*	6 12
1 Nov 75		**MUD'S GREATEST HITS** *RAK SRAK 6755*	25 6
27 Dec 75		**USE YOUR IMAGINATION** *Private Stock PVLP 1003*	33 5

'Lonely This Christmas' re-entered the chart and peaked at No.61 in Dec 1985

MUDHONEY
US, male vocal / instrumental
group (Singles: 2 Weeks, Albums: 5 Weeks)   pos/wks

			pos/wks
17 Aug 91		**LET IT SLIDE** *Subpop SP 15154*	60 1
24 Oct 92		**SUCK YOU DRY** *Reprise W 0137*	65 1
31 Aug 91		**EVERY GOOD BOY DESERVES FUDGE** *Subpop SP 18160*	34 2
17 Oct 92		**PIECE OF CAKE** *Reprise 9362450902*	39 2
8 Apr 95		**MY BROTHER THE COW** *Reprise 9362458402*	70 1

The MUDLARKS
UK, male / female vocal group (Singles: 19 Weeks)   pos/wks

			pos/wks
2 May 58	●	**LOLLIPOP** *Columbia DB 4099*	2 9
6 Jun 58	●	**BOOK OF LOVE** *Columbia DB 4133*	8 9
27 Feb 59		**THE LOVE GAME** *Columbia DB 4250*	30 1

MUFFINS See MARTHA and the MUFFINS

Idris MUHAMMAD
US, male instrumentalist – drums (Singles: 3 Weeks)   pos/wks

			pos/wks
17 Sep 77		**COULD HEAVEN EVER BE LIKE THIS** *Kudu 935*	42 3

Vocal by Frank Floyd

MUKKAA (see also EYE TO EYE featuring Taka BOOM; UMBOZA)
UK, male instrumental / production duo –
Stuart Crichton and Billy Kiltie (Singles: 1 Week)   pos/wks

			pos/wks
27 Feb 93		**BURUCHACCA** *Limbo LIMBO 008*	74 1

MUKUPA See MANIJAMA featuring MUKUPA and L'IL T

Maria MULDAUR
US, female vocalist – Maria D'Amato (Singles: 8 Weeks)   pos/wks

			pos/wks
29 Jun 74		**MIDNIGHT AT THE OASIS** *Reprise K 14331*	21 8

MULL HISTORICAL SOCIETY
UK, male vocal /
instrumental group (Singles: 7 Weeks, Albums: 5 Weeks)   pos/wks

			pos/wks
21 Jul 01		**ANIMAL CANNABUS** *Rough Trade RTRADSCD 021*	53 1
9 Feb 02		**WATCHING XANADU** *Blanco Y Negro NEG 138CD*	36 2
1 Mar 03		**THE FINAL ARREARS** *Blanco Y Negro NEG 144CD*	32 2
14 Jun 03		**AM I WRONG** *Blanco Y Negro NEG 146CD*	51 1

		pos/wks
24 Jul 04	HOW 'BOUT I LOVE YOU MORE *B Unique BUN 080CDS*	**37** 1
27 Oct 01	LOSS *Blanco Y Negro 927413072*	**43** 1
15 Mar 03	US *Blanco Y Negro 09276499562*	**19** 3
31 Jul 04	THIS IS HOPE *B Unique BUN 082*	**58** 1

Arthur MULLARD See Hylda BAKER and Arthur MULLARD

Larry MULLEN See Adam CLAYTON and Larry MULLEN

Gerry MULLIGAN and Ben WEBSTER *US, male instrumental*
duo – baritone and tenor sax – Gerry Mulligan, b. 6 Apr 1927, d. 20 Jan 1996,
and Ben Webster, b. 27 Mar 1909, d. 20 Sep 1973 (Albums: 1 Week) pos/wks

		pos/wks
24 Sep 60	GERRY MULLIGAN MEETS BEN WEBSTER *HMV CLP 1373*	**15** 1

Shawn MULLINS
US, male vocalist (Singles: 11 Weeks, Albums: 1 Week) pos/wks

		pos/wks
6 Mar 99 ●	LULLABY *Columbia 6669592*	**9** 10
2 Oct 99	WHAT IS LIFE *Columbia 6678212*	**62** 1
20 Mar 99	SOUL'S CORE *Columbia 4930372*	**60** 1

MULU *UK, male / female vocal / instrumental duo (Singles: 1 Week)* pos/wks

		pos/wks
2 Aug 97	PUSSYCAT *Dedicated MULU 003CD1*	**50** 1

Omero MUMBA *Ireland, male vocalist (Singles: 2 Weeks)* pos/wks

		pos/wks
20 Jul 02	LIL' BIG MAN *Polydor 5708852*	**42** 2

Samantha MUMBA
Ireland, female vocalist (Singles: 69 Weeks, Albums: 16 Weeks) pos/wks

		pos/wks
8 Jul 00 ●	GOTTA TELL YOU *Wild Card / Polydor 5618832*	**2** 12
28 Oct 00 ●	BODY II BODY *Wild Card / Polydor 5877742*	**5** 12
3 Mar 01 ●	ALWAYS COME BACK TO YOUR LOVE *Wild Card / Polydor 5879252*	**3** 15
22 Sep 01 ●	BABY COME ON OVER *Wild Card / Polydor 5872352*	**5** 10
22 Dec 01 ●	LATELY *Wild Card / Polydor 5705232*	**6** 12
26 Oct 02 ●	I'M RIGHT HERE (re) *Wild Card / Polydor 0659372*	**5** 8
11 Nov 00 ●	GOTTA TELL YOU *Wild Card 5492262*	**9** 16

Coati MUNDI See Kid CREOLE and the COCONUTS

MUNDY
Ireland, male vocalist – Edmund Enright (Singles: 2 Weeks) pos/wks

		pos/wks
3 Aug 96	TO YOU I BESTOW *Epic MUNDY 1CD*	**60** 1
5 Oct 96	LIFE'S A CINCH *Epic MUNDY 2CD*	**75** 1

MUNGO JERRY *UK, male vocal / instrumental group –*
leader Ray Dorset (Singles: 88 Weeks, Albums: 14 Weeks) pos/wks

		pos/wks
6 Jun 70 ★	IN THE SUMMERTIME *Dawn DNX 2502*	**1** 20
6 Feb 71 ★	BABY JUMP (re) *Dawn DNX 2505*	**1** 13
29 May 71 ●	LADY ROSE *Dawn DNX 2510*	**5** 12
18 Sep 71	YOU DON'T HAVE TO BE IN THE ARMY TO FIGHT IN THE WAR *Dawn DNX 2513*	**13** 8
22 Apr 72	OPEN UP *Dawn DNX 2514*	**21** 8
7 Jul 73 ●	ALRIGHT, ALRIGHT, ALRIGHT *Dawn DNS 1037*	**3** 12
10 Nov 73	WILD LOVE *Dawn DNS 1051*	**32** 5
6 Apr 74	LONG LEGGED WOMAN DRESSED IN BLACK *Dawn DNS 1061*	**13** 9
29 May 99	SUPPORT THE TOON – IT'S YOUR DUTY (EP) *Saraja TOONCD 001* [1]	**57** 1
8 Aug 70	MUNGO JERRY *Dawn DNLS 3008*	**13** 6
10 Apr 71	ELECTRONICALLY TESTED *Dawn DNLS 3020*	**14** 8

[1] Mungo Jerry and Toon Travellers

Tracks on Support the Toon – It's Your Duty (EP): Blaydon Races / Going to Wembley / Bottle of Beer

MUNICH MACHINE
Germany, male instrumental group (Singles: 8 Weeks) pos/wks

		pos/wks
10 Dec 77	GET ON THE FUNK TRAIN *Oasis OASIS 2*	**41** 4
4 Nov 78	A WHITER SHADE OF PALE *Oasis OASIS 5* [1]	**42** 4

[1] Munich Machine introducing Chris Bennett

The MUNROS featuring David METHREN
UK, male pipe band (Albums: 3 Weeks) pos/wks

		pos/wks
27 Jun 98	THE LONE PIPER *Virgin VTCD 185*	**46** 3

David MUNROW See EARLY MUSIC CONSORT directed by David MUNROW

The MUPPETS *US, frog-fronted puppet*
ensemble (Singles: 15 Weeks, Albums: 45 Weeks) pos/wks

		pos/wks
28 May 77 ●	HALFWAY DOWN THE STAIRS *Pye 7N 45698*	**7** 8
17 Dec 77	THE MUPPET SHOW MUSIC HALL EP *Pye 7NX 8004*	**19** 7
11 Jun 77 ★	THE MUPPET SHOW *Pye NSPH 19*	**1** 35
25 Feb 78	THE MUPPET SHOW VOLUME 2 *Pye NSPH 21*	**16** 10

'Halfway Down the Stairs' is sung by Jerry Nelson as Kermit the Frog's nephew, Robin. Tracks on The Muppet Show Music Hall EP: Don't Dilly Dally on the Way / Waiting at the Church / The Boy in the Gallery / Wotcher (Knocked 'Em in the Old Kent Road)

The MURDERDOLLS *US, male vocal / instrumental*
group (Singles: 4 Weeks, Albums: 1 Week) pos/wks

		pos/wks
16 Nov 02	DEAD IN HOLLYWOOD *Roadrunner RR 20223*	**54** 1
26 Jul 03	WHITE WEDDING *Roadrunner RR 20155*	**24** 3
31 Aug 02	BEYOND THE VALLEY OF THE MURDERDOLLS *Roadrunner RR 84262*	**40** 1

Lydia MURDOCK *US, female vocalist (Singles: 9 Weeks)* pos/wks

		pos/wks
24 Sep 83	SUPERSTAR *Korova KOW 30*	**14** 9

Shirley MURDOCK *US, female vocalist (Singles: 2 Weeks)* pos/wks

		pos/wks
12 Apr 86	TRUTH OR DARE *Elektra EKR 36*	**60** 2

Eddie MURPHY See Shabba RANKS

Noel MURPHY *Ireland, male vocalist (Singles: 4 Weeks)* pos/wks

		pos/wks
27 Jun 87	MURPHY AND THE BRICKS *Murphy's STACK 1*	**57** 4

Peter MURPHY (see also BAUHAUS)
UK, male vocalist (Albums: 1 Week) pos/wks

		pos/wks
26 Jul 86	SHOULD THE WORLD FAIL TO FALL APART *Beggars Banquet BEGA 69*	**82** 1

Roisin MURPHY See MOLOKO; PSYCHEDELIC WALTONS

Walter MURPHY and the BIG APPLE BAND
US, orchestra (Singles: 9 Weeks) pos/wks

		pos/wks
10 Jul 76	A FIFTH OF BEETHOVEN *Private Stock PVT 59* ▲	**28** 9

Anne MURRAY
Canada, female vocalist (Singles: 40 Weeks, Albums: 10 Weeks) pos/wks

		pos/wks
24 Oct 70	SNOWBIRD *Capitol CL 15654*	**23** 17
21 Oct 72	DESTINY *Capitol CL 15734*	**41** 4
9 Dec 78	YOU NEEDED ME *Capitol CL 16011* ▲	**22** 14
21 Apr 79	I JUST FALL IN LOVE AGAIN *Capitol CL 16069*	**58** 2
19 Apr 80	DAYDREAM BELIEVER *Capitol CL 16123*	**61** 3
3 Oct 81	THE VERY BEST OF ANNE MURRAY *Capitol EMTV 31*	**14** 10

Keith MURRAY *US, male rapper (Singles: 10 Weeks)* pos/wks

		pos/wks
2 Nov 96	THE RHYME *Jive JIVECD 407*	**59** 1
27 Jun 98	SHORTY (YOU KEEP PLAYING WITH MY MIND) *Jive 0521212* [1]	**22** 3
14 Nov 98	HOME ALONE *Jive 0522392* [2]	**17** 5
5 Dec 98	INCREDIBLE *Jive 0522102* [3]	**52** 1

[1] Imajin featuring Keith Murray [2] R Kelly featuring Keith Murray [3] Keith Murray featuring LL Cool J

Pauline MURRAY and The INVISIBLE GIRLS
(see also PENETRATION) *UK, female vocalist and male (really) vocal / instrumental group (Singles: 2 Weeks, Albums: 4 Weeks)* pos/wks

		pos/wks
2 Aug 80	DREAM SEQUENCE (ONE) *Illusive IVE 1*	**67** 2
11 Oct 80	PAULINE MURRAY AND THE INVISIBLE GIRLS *Illusive 2394 227*	**25** 4

Ruby MURRAY *UK, female vocalist,*
b. 29 Mar 1935, d. 17 Dec 1996 (Singles: 114 Weeks) pos/wks

		pos/wks
3 Dec 54 ●	HEARTBEAT *Columbia DB 3542*	**3** 16
28 Jan 55 ★	SOFTLY, SOFTLY (re) *Columbia DB 3558*	**1** 23
4 Feb 55 ●	HAPPY DAYS AND LONELY NIGHTS *Columbia DB 3577*	**6** 8
4 Mar 55 ●	LET ME GO LOVER *Columbia DB 3577*	**5** 7

Singles re-entries are listed as (re), (2re), (3re).... which signifies that the hit re-entered the chart once, twice or three times...

		pos/wks
18 Mar 55 ●	IF ANYONE FINDS THIS, I LOVE YOU	
	Columbia DB 3580 [1] 4 11	
1 Jul 55 ●	EVERMORE Columbia DB 3617 ....3 17	
14 Oct 55 ●	I'LL COME WHEN YOU CALL Columbia DB 3643 ....6 7	
31 Aug 56	YOU ARE MY FIRST LOVE (re) Columbia DB 3770 ....16 5	
12 Dec 58	REAL LOVE Columbia DB 4192 ....18 6	
5 Jun 59 ●	GOODBYE JIMMY, GOODBYE (re) Columbia DB 4305 ....10 14	

[1] Ruby Murray with Anne Warren

Junior MURVIN
Jamaica, male vocalist – Mervin Smith (Singles: 9 Weeks) pos/wks

3 May 80	POLICE AND THIEVES Island WIP 6539 ....23 9

MUSE UK, male vocal / instrumental
group (Singles: 51 Weeks, Albums: 87 Weeks) pos/wks

26 Jun 99	UNO Mushroom / Taste Media MUSH 50CDS 73 1
18 Sep 99	CAVE Mushroom / Taste Media MUSH 58CDS 52 1
4 Dec 99	MUSCLE MUSEUM Mushroom / Taste Media MUSH 66CDS ..43 2
4 Mar 00	SUNBURN Mushroom / Taste Media MUSH 68CDS 22 2
17 Jun 00	UNINTENDED Mushroom / Taste Media MUSH 72CDS 20 4
21 Oct 00	MUSCLE MUSEUM (re-issue)
	Mushroom / Taste Media MUSH 84CDS 25 3
24 Mar 01	PLUG IN BABY Mushroom / Taste Media MUSH 89CDS 11 5
16 Jun 01	NEW BORN Mushroom / Taste Media MUSH 92CDS 12 4
1 Sep 01	BLISS Mushroom / Taste Media MUSH 96CDS 22 2
1 Dec 01	HYPER MUSIC / FEELING GOOD Mushroom MUSH 97CDS ...24 3
29 Jun 02	DEAD STAR / IN YOUR WORLD Mushroom MUSH 104CDS ...13 3
20 Sep 03 ●	TIME IS RUNNING OUT East West EW 272CD 8 8
13 Dec 03	HYSTERIA East West EW 278CD 17 6
29 May 04	SING FOR ABSOLUTION East West EW 285CD 16 4
2 Oct 04	BUTTERFLIES & HURRICANES Atlantic ATUK 003CD 14 3
16 Oct 99	SHOWBIZ Mushroom MUSH 59CD 29 16
30 Jun 01 ●	ORIGIN OF SYMMETRY Mushroom MUSH 93CDX..............3 24
13 Jul 02 ●	HULLABALOO SOUNDTRACK Mushroom MUSH 105CD 10 4
4 Oct 03 ★	ABSOLUTION East West 5046685872 ■ 1 43

The MUSIC UK, male vocal / instrumental
group (Singles: 11 Weeks, Albums: 9 Weeks) pos/wks

31 Aug 02	TAKE THE LONG ROAD AND WALK IT Hut / Virgin HUTCD 158 ..14 3
30 Nov 02	GETAWAY Hut / Virgin HUTCD 162 ....26 2
1 Mar 03	THE TRUTH IS NO WORDS Hut / Virgin VSCDT 1845 ....18 2
18 Sep 04	FREEDOM FIGHTERS Virgin VSCDX 1883 ....15 4
14 Sep 02 ●	THE MUSIC Hut / Virgin CDHUTX 76 ....4 5
2 Oct 04 ●	WELCOME TO THE NORTH Virgin CDV 2989 ....8 4

MUSIC and MYSTERY featuring Gwen McCRAE
UK, male production group and US, female vocalist (Singles: 3 Weeks) pos/wks

13 Feb 93	ALL THIS LOVE I'M GIVING KTDA CDKTDA 2 ....36 3

MUSIC OF THE MOUNTAINS See MANUEL and the MUSIC OF THE MOUNTAINS

MUSIC RELIEF '94
UK, male / female vocal / instrumental group (Singles: 1 Week) pos/wks

5 Nov 94	WHAT'S GOING ON Jive RWANDACD 1 ....70 1

MUSIC STUDENTS See Ian DURY and the BLOCKHEADS

MUSICAL YOUTH (see also Donna SUMMER)
UK, male vocal / instrumental group – lead vocal
Dennis Seaton (Singles: 55 Weeks, Albums: 22 Weeks) pos/wks

25 Sep 82 ★	PASS THE DUTCHIE (re) MCA YOU 1 ....1 13
20 Nov 82	YOUTH OF TODAY MCA YOU 2 ....13 9
12 Feb 83	NEVER GONNA GIVE YOU UP MCA YOU 3 ....6 10
16 Apr 83	HEARTBREAKER MCA YOU 4 ....44 3
9 Jul 83	TELL ME WHY MCA YOU 5 ....33 6
22 Oct 83	007 MCA YOU 6 ....26 6
14 Jan 84	SIXTEEN MCA YOU 7 ....23 8
4 Dec 82	THE YOUTH OF TODAY MCA YOULP 1.....................24 22

MUSIQ See ROOTS

MUSIQUE US, female vocal group (Singles: 12 Weeks) pos/wks

18 Nov 78	IN THE BUSH CBS 6791 ....16 12

MUSIQUE vs U2 (see also PF PROJECT featuring Ewan McGREGOR)
UK, male production duo – Nick Hanson and Moussa Clarke
and Ireland, male vocal / instrumental group (Singles: 5 Weeks) pos/wks

2 Jun 01	NEW YEAR'S DUB (re) Serious SERR 030CD 15 5

MUSTAFAS See STAIFFI and his MUSTAFAS

MUTINY UK (see also HELICOPTER) UK, male production
duo – Dylan Barnes and Rob Davy (Singles: 3 Weeks) pos/wks

19 May 01	SECRETS Sunflower VCRD 86 [1] 47 1
25 Aug 01	VIRUS VC Recordings VCRD 91 ....42 2

[1] Vocals by Lorraine Cato

The MUTTON BIRDS
New Zealand, male vocal / instrumental group (Albums: 1 Week) pos/wks

12 Jul 97	ENVY OF ANGELS Virgin CDVIR 55 ....64 1

MY BLOODY VALENTINE UK, male / female vocal /
instrumental group (Singles: 5 Weeks, Albums: 2 Weeks) pos/wks

5 May 90	SOON Creation CRE 073 ....41 3
16 Feb 91	TO HERE KNOWS WHEN Creation CRE 085 ....29 2
23 Nov 91	LOVELESS Creation CRELP 060 ....24 2

MY CHEMICAL ROMANCE
US, male vocal / instrumental group (Singles: 1 Week) pos/wks

25 Dec 04	THANK YOU FOR THE VENOM Reprise W 661 ....71 1+

MY LIFE STORY UK, male / female vocal /
instrumental group (Singles: 12 Weeks, Albums: 1 Week) pos/wks

17 Aug 96	12 REASONS WHY I LOVE HER Parlophone CDR 6442 ....32 2
9 Nov 96	SPARKLE Parlophone CDR 6450 ....34 2
1 Mar 97	THE KING OF KISSINGDOM Parlophone CDRS 6457 ....35 1
17 May 97	STRUMPET Parlophone CDR 6464 ....27 2
23 Aug 97	DUCHESS Parlophone CDR 6474 ....39 1
19 Jun 99	IT'S A GIRL THING IT ITR 001 ....37 2
30 Oct 99	EMPIRE LINE IT ITR 003 ....58 1
19 Feb 00	WALK / DON'T WALK IT ITR 007 ....48 1
22 Mar 97	THE GOLDEN MILE Parlophone CDPCS 7386 ....36 1

MY MORNING JACKET
US, male vocal / instrumental group (Albums: 1 Week) pos/wks

20 Sep 03	IT STILL MOVES RCA 82876559252 ....62 1

MY RED CELL
UK, male vocal / instrumental group (Singles: 1 Week) pos/wks

12 Jun 04	IN A CAGE (ON PROZAC) V2 VVR 5027133 ....61 1

MY VITRIOL UK, male / female vocal /
instrumental group (Singles: 7 Weeks, Albums: 2 Weeks) pos/wks

22 Jul 00	CEMENTED SHOES Infectious INFECT 89CDS 65 1
11 Nov 00	PIECES Infectious INFECT 94CDS 56 1
24 Feb 01	ALWAYS: YOUR WAY Infectious INFECT 95CDS 31 2
19 May 01	GROUNDED Infectious INFECT 97CD 29 2
27 Jul 02	MOODSWINGS / THE GENTLE ART OF CHOKING
	Infectious INFECT 107CDSX 39 1
17 Mar 01	FINELINES Infectious INFECT 96CD 24 2

MYA US, female vocalist – Mya Harrison (Singles: 66 Weeks) pos/wks

27 Jun 98 ●	GHETTO SUPASTAR (THAT IS WHAT YOU ARE)
	Interscope IND 95593 [1] 2 17
12 Dec 98 ●	TAKE ME THERE Interscope IND 95620 [2] 7 9
10 Feb 01 ●	CASE OF THE EX Interscope 4974772 ....3 11
24 Mar 01	GIRLS DEM SUGAR Virgin VUSCD 173 [3] 13 5
9 Jun 01	FREE Interscope 4975002 ....52 1
30 Jun 01 ★	LADY MARMALADE Interscope / Polydor 4975612 [4] ■ ▲ ...1 16
20 Sep 03	MY LOVE IS LIKE ... WO Interscope / Polydor 9810305 ......33 2

[1] Pras Michel featuring ODB & introducing Mya [2] BLACKstreet and Mya
featuring Ma$e and Blinky Blink [3] Beenie Man featuring Mya [4] Christina
Aguilera, Lil' Kim, Mya and Pink

Tim MYCROFT See SOUNDS NICE featuring Tim MYCROFT

Alicia MYERS
US, female vocalist (Singles: 3 Weeks) pos/wks

1 Sep 84	**YOU GET THE BEST FROM ME (SAY, SAY, SAY)** *MCA MCA 914*	.58	3

Billie MYERS
UK, female vocalist (Singles: 12 Weeks, Albums: 9 Weeks) pos/wks

11 Apr 98 ●	**KISS THE RAIN** *Universal UND 56182*	.4	9
25 Jul 98	**TELL ME** *Universal UND 56201*	28	3
2 May 98	**GROWING PAINS** *Universal UND 53100*	19	9

Richard MYHILL
UK, male vocalist (Singles: 9 Weeks) pos/wks

1 Apr 78	**IT TAKES TWO TO TANGO** *Mercury 6007 167*	17	9

Alannah MYLES
Canada, female vocalist (Singles: 17 Weeks, Albums: 21 Weeks) pos/wks

17 Mar 90 ●	**BLACK VELVET** *East West A 8742* ▲	.2	15
16 Jun 90	**LOVE IS** *East West A 8918*	61	2
28 Apr 90 ●	**ALANNAH MYLES** *Atlantic 7819561*	.3	21

MYLO
UK, male producer – Miles MacInnes (Singles: 6 Weeks) pos/wks

30 Oct 04	**DROP THE PRESSURE** *Breastfed BFD 009CD*	19	6

Marie MYRIAM *France, female vocalist (Singles: 4 Weeks)* pos/wks

28 May 77	**L'OISEAU ET L'ENFANT** *Polydor 2056 634*	42	4

MYRON *US, male vocalist – Myron Davis (Singles: 1 Week)* pos/wks

22 Nov 97	**WE CAN GET DOWN** *Island Black Music CID 677*	74	1

MYSTERIANS *See ? (QUESTION MARK) and the MYSTERIANS*

MYSTERY (see also Ron VAN DEN BEUKEN)
Holland, male production duo (Singles: 2 Weeks) pos/wks

6 Oct 01	**MYSTERY** *Inferno CDFERN 42*	56	1
10 Aug 02	**ALL I EVER WANTED (DEVOTION)** *Xtravaganza XTRAV 33CDS*	57	1

MYSTI *See CAMOUFLAGE featuring MYSTI*

MYSTIC MERLIN
US, male vocal / instrumental group (Singles: 9 Weeks) pos/wks

26 Apr 80	**JUST CAN'T GIVE YOU UP** *Capitol CL 16133*	20	9

MYSTIC 3
UK / Italy, male production group (aka Blockster) (Singles: 1 Week) pos/wks

24 Jun 00	**SOMETHING'S GOIN' ON** *Rulin RULIN 2CDS*	63	1

MYSTICA *Israel, male production trio (Singles: 2 Weeks)* pos/wks

24 Jan 98	**EVER REST** *Perfecto PERF 152CD*	62	1
9 May 98	**AFRICAN HORIZON** *Perfecto PERF 161CD*	59	1

MYSTIKAL (see also Mariah CAREY)
US, male rapper – Michael Tyler (Singles: 23 Weeks) pos/wks

9 Dec 00	**SHAKE YA ASS** *Jive 9251552*	30	5
17 Feb 01 ●	**STUTTER** *Jive 9251632* [1] ▲	.7	8
3 Mar 01	**DANGER (BEEN SO LONG)** *Jive 9251722* [2]	28	3
29 Dec 01	**DON'T STOP (FUNKIN' 4 JAMAICA)** *Virgin VUSCD 228* [3]	32	4
23 Feb 02	**BOUNCIN' BACK (BUMPIN' ME AGAINST THE WALL)** *Jive 9253272*	45	1
10 May 03	**LAUNDROMAT / DON'T MESS WITH MY MAN (re-mix)** *Jive 9254822* [3]	33	2

[1] Joe featuring Mystikal [2] Mystikal featuring Nivea [3] Mariah Carey featuring Mystikal [4] Nivea featuring Brian and Brandon Casey of Jagged Edge and Mystikal

MYTOWN
Ireland, male vocal group (Singles: 2 Weeks) pos/wks

13 Mar 99	**PARTY ALL NIGHT** *Universal UND 56231*	22	2

MZ MAY *See DREEM TEEM*

N-JOI
UK, male instrumental / production group (Singles: 28 Weeks) pos/wks

27 Oct 90	**ANTHEM** *Deconstruction PB 44041*	45	5
2 Mar 91	**ADRENALIN (EP)** *Deconstruction PT 44344*	23	5
6 Apr 91 ●	**ANTHEM (re-issue)** *Deconstruction PB 44445*	.8	8
22 Feb 92	**LIVE IN MANCHESTER (PARTS 1 + 2)** *Deconstruction PT 45252*	12	5
24 Jul 93	**THE DRUMSTRUCK EP** *Deconstruction 74321154832*	33	3
17 Dec 94	**PAPILLON** *Deconstruction 74321252132*	70	1
8 Jul 95	**BAD THINGS** *Deconstruction 74321277292* [1]	57	1

[1] NJoi

Tracks on Adrenalin (EP): Adrenalin / The Kraken / Rhythm Zone / Phoenix.
Tracks on The Drumstruck EP: The Void / Boom Bass / Drumstruck

NKOTB *See NEW KIDS ON THE BLOCK*

N'n'G featuring KALLAGHAN
UK, male / female production / vocal group (Singles: 6 Weeks) pos/wks

1 Apr 00	**RIGHT BEFORE MY EYES** *Urban Heat UHTCD 003*	12	6

N.O.R.E.
US, male rapper – Victor Santiago (Singles: 9 Weeks, Albums: 1 Week) pos/wks

21 Sep 02	**NOTHIN' (re)** *Def Jam 639262*	11	8
29 Nov 03	**CRASHIN' A PARTY** *Def Jam MCSTD 40341* [1]	55	1
25 Jul 98	**N.O.R.E.** *Penalty Recordings PENCD 3077* [1]	72	1

[1] Lumidee featuring N.O.R.E. [1] Noreaga

NPG *See NEW POWER GENERATION*

NRG *UK, male DJ / production duo (Singles: 3 Weeks)* pos/wks

29 Mar 97	**NEVER LOST HIS HARDCORE** *Top Banana TOPCD 04*	71	1
12 Dec 98	**NEVER LOST HIS HARDCORE '98 (re-mix)** *Top Banana TOPCD 010*	61	1
20 Mar 04	**NEVER LEFT HIS HARDCORE (2nd re-mix)** *Tidy Trax TIDY 200T*	59	1

'N SYNC (see also JC CHASEZ; Justin TIMBERLAKE)
US, male vocal group (Singles: 79 Weeks, Albums: 32 Weeks) pos/wks

13 Sep 97	**TEARIN' UP MY HEART** *Arista 74321505152*	40	2
22 Nov 97	**I WANT YOU BACK** *Arista 74321541122*	62	1
27 Feb 99 ●	**I WANT YOU BACK (re) (re-issue)** *Transcontinental / Northwestside 74321646972*	.5	10
26 Jun 99 ●	**TEARIN' UP MY HEART (re) (re-issue)** *Northwestside / Arista 74321675832*	.9	10
8 Jan 00	**MUSIC OF MY HEART** *Epic 6685272* [1]	34	3
11 Mar 00 ●	**BYE BYE BYE** *Jive 9250202*	.3	8
22 Jul 00	**I'LL NEVER STOP** *Jive 9250762*	13	6
16 Sep 00 ●	**IT'S GONNA BE ME** *Jive 9251082* ▲	.9	8
2 Dec 00	**THIS I PROMISE YOU** *Jive 9251302*	21	7
21 Jul 01 ●	**POP** *Jive 9252422*	.9	8
8 Dec 01	**GONE (re)** *Jive 9252772*	24	4
27 Apr 02 ●	**GIRLFRIEND** *Jive 9253312* [2]	.2	12
17 Jul 99	***N SYNC** *Northwestside 74321681902*	30	2
1 Apr 00	**NO STRINGS ATTACHED** *Jive 9220272* ▲	14	22
4 Aug 01	**CELEBRITY** *Jive 9222032* ▲	12	8

[1] 'N Sync / Gloria Estefan [2] 'N Sync featuring Nelly

NT GANG
Germany, male vocal / instrumental group (Singles: 1 Week)   pos/wks

2 Apr 88	WAM BAM *Cooltempo COOL 163*	......	71	1

N-TRANCE
UK, male production duo –
Dale Longworth and Kevin O'Toole (Singles: 85 Weeks)   pos/wks

7 May 94	SET YOU FREE *All Around the World CDGLOBE 124* [1]	......	39	4
22 Oct 94	TURN UP THE POWER *All Around the World CDGLOBE 125*	......	23	3
14 Jan 95 ●	SET YOU FREE (re-mix) *All Around the World CDGLOBE 126*	..2	15	
16 Sep 95 ●	STAYIN' ALIVE *All Around the World CDGLOBE 131* [2]	....	2	11
24 Feb 96	ELECTRONIC PLEASURE *All Around the World CDGLOBE 135*	..11	4	
5 Apr 97	D.I.S.C.O. *All Around the World CDGLOBE 153*	......	11	6
23 Aug 97	THE MIND OF THE MACHINE			
	All Around the World CDGLOBE 159	....	15	4
1 Nov 97 ●	DA YA THINK I'M SEXY			
	All Around the World CDGLOBE 150 [3]	....	7	10
12 Sep 98	PARADISE CITY *All Around the World CDGLOBE 140*	....	28	3
19 Dec 98	TEARS IN THE RAIN *All Around the Globe CDGLOBE 185*	53	1	
20 May 00	SHAKE YA BODY *All Around the World CDGLOBE 204*	....	37	1
22 Sep 01 ●	SET YOU FREE (2nd re-mix)			
	All Around the World CDGLOBE 242	....	4	11
14 Sep 02 ●	FOREVER (re) *All Around the World CDGLOBE 257*	....	6	8
19 Jul 03	DESTINY *All Around the World CDGLOBE 282*	....	37	2
4 Dec 04	I'M IN HEAVEN *All Around the World CDGLOBE 343*	....	46	2

[1] N-Trance featuring Kelly Llorenna [2] N-Trance featuring Ricardo Da Force
[3] N-Trance featuring Rod Stewart

Although she is vocalist on all versions of 'Set You Free', Kelly Llorenna is given label credit only on the first entry. Similarly, Ricardo Da Force appears on several tracks but receives label credit only for 'Stayin' Alive'

N-TYCE
UK, female vocal group (Singles: 15 Weeks, Albums: 1 Week)   pos/wks

5 Jul 97	HEY DJ! (PLAY THAT SONG) *Telstar CDSTAS 2885*	......	20	2
13 Sep 97	WE COME TO PARTY *Telstar CDSTAS 2915*	......	14	4
28 Feb 98	TELEFUNKIN' *Telstar CDSTAS 2944*	......	16	5
6 Jun 98	BOOM BOOM *Telstar CDSTAS 2971*	......	18	4
20 Jun 98	ALL DAY EVERY DAY *Telstar TCD 2945*	......	44	1

N.W.A. (see also DR DRE; EAZY-E; ICE CUBE)
US, male rap group (Singles: 15 Weeks, Albums: 14 Weeks)   pos/wks

9 Sep 89	EXPRESS YOURSELF (re) *Fourth & Broadway BRW 144*	......	26	9
1 Sep 90	GANGSTA, GANGSTA *Fourth & Broadway BRW 191*	......	70	1
10 Nov 90	100 MILES AND RUNNIN' *Fourth & Broadway BRW 200*	......	38	3
23 Nov 91	ALWAYZ INTO SOMETHIN' *Fourth & Broadway BRW 238*	......	60	2
30 Sep 89	STRAIGHT OUTTA COMPTON *Fourth & Broadway BRLP 534*	..41	6	
15 Jun 91	EFIL4ZAGGIN *Fourth & Broadway BRLP 562* ▲	......	25	2
31 Aug 96	GREATEST HITS *Priority CDPTY 126*	......	56	1
4 Oct 03	STRAIGHT OUTTA COMPTON (re-issue) *Priority 5379362*	......	35	5

'Express Yourself' made No.50 on its first visit and peaked at No.26 on re-entry in May 1990

NYCC *Germany, male rap trio (Singles: 6 Weeks)*   pos/wks

30 May 98	FIGHT FOR YOUR RIGHT (TO PARTY) *Control 0042645 CON*	14	5	
19 Sep 98	CAN YOU FEEL IT (ROCK DA HOUSE) *Control 0042785 CON*	..68	1	

NADA SURF
US, male vocal / instrumental group (Singles: 1 Week)   pos/wks

24 May 03	INSIDE OF LOVE *Heavenly HVN 133CD*	......	73	1

NADIA *Portugal, female vocalist – Nadia Almada (Singles: 3 Weeks)*   pos/wks

11 Dec 04	A LITTLE BIT OF ACTION *Virgin / EMI VISCDX 6*	......	27	3+

Jimmy NAIL   (444   Top 500)   *Singer / songwriter, b. James Michael Aloysius Bradford, 1954, Newcastle, UK, whose R&B mixed with a Geordie take on country provided a flip side to an acting career which included key characters in both 'Auf Wiedersehen Pet' and 'Spender'. His longest stay on the charts was courtesy of another TV series, 'Crocodile Shoes', in which he combined acting and singing (Singles: 73 Weeks, Albums: 85 Weeks)*   pos/wks

27 Apr 85 ●	LOVE DON'T LIVE HERE ANYMORE *Virgin VS 764*	......	3	11
11 Jul 92 ★	AIN'T NO DOUBT *East West YZ 686*	......	1	12
3 Oct 92	LAURA *East West YZ 702*	......	58	2
26 Nov 94 ●	CROCODILE SHOES (2re) *East West YZ 867CD*	......	4	20
11 Feb 95	COWBOY DREAMS *East West YZ 878CD*	......	13	7
6 May 95	CALLING OUT YOUR NAME *East West YZ 935CD*	......	65	1
28 Oct 95	BIG RIVER *East West EW 008CD*	......	18	5
23 Dec 95	LOVE *East West EW 018CD*	......	33	4
3 Feb 96	BIG RIVER (re-mix) *East West EW 024CD*	......	72	2
16 Nov 96	COUNTRY BOY *East West EW 070CD*	......	25	8
21 Nov 98	THE FLAME STILL BURNS *London LONCD 420* [1]	......	47	1
8 Aug 92 ●	GROWING UP IN PUBLIC *East West 4509901442*	......	2	12
3 Dec 94 ●	CROCODILE SHOES *East West 4509985562*	......	2	31
18 Nov 95 ●	BIG RIVER *East West 0630128232*	......	8	15
30 Nov 96 ●	CROCODILE SHOES II *East West 630169352*	......	10	13
18 Oct 97 ●	THE NAIL FILE – THE BEST OF JIMMY NAIL			
	East West 3984207392	......	8	14

[1] Jimmy Nail with Strange Fruit

NAILBOMB
Brazil / UK, male vocal / instrumental duo (Albums: 1 Week)   pos/wks

2 Apr 94	POINT BLANK *Roadrunner RR 90552*	......	62	1

NAKATOMI
UK, male / female production group (Singles: 4 Weeks)   pos/wks

7 Feb 98	CHILDREN OF THE NIGHT *Peach PCHCD 006*	......	47	2
26 Oct 02	CHILDREN OF THE NIGHT (re-mix) *Jive 9254212*	......	31	2

NAKED EYES (see also CLIMIE FISHER)
UK, male vocal / instrumental duo – Pete Byrne and Rob Fisher, b. 5 Nov 1959, d. 25 Aug 1999 (Singles: 3 Weeks)   pos/wks

23 Jul 83	ALWAYS SOMETHING THERE TO REMIND ME *RCA 348*	....	59	3

NALIN & KANE *Germany, male DJ / production*
duo – Andry Nalin and Harry Cane (Singles: 6 Weeks)   pos/wks

1 Nov 97	BEACHBALL *ffrr FCD 318*	......	48	1
28 Mar 98	PLANET VIOLET *Logic 74321565702* [1]	......	51	1
3 Oct 98	BEACHBALL (re-mix) *LONDON FCD 349*	......	17	5

[1] Nalin I.N.C.

NANA See ARCHITECHS

NAPALM DEATH
UK, male vocal / instrumental group (Albums: 3 Weeks)   pos/wks

15 Sep 90	HARMONY OF CORRUPTION *Earache MOSH 19*	......	67	1
30 May 92	UTOPIA BANISHED *Earache MOSH 53CD*	......	58	1
3 Feb 96	DIATRIBES *Earache MOSH 141CDD*	......	74	1

NAPOLEON XIV
US, male vocalist – Jerry Samuels (Singles: 10 Weeks)   pos/wks

4 Aug 66 ●	THEY'RE COMING TO TAKE ME AWAY, HA-HAAA!			
	Warner Bros. WB 5831	......	4	10

Narada See Narada Michael WALDEN

NARCOTIC THRUST *UK, male / female*
production duo and female vocalist (Singles: 9 Weeks)   pos/wks

10 Aug 02	SAFE FROM HARM *ffrr FCD 406*	......	24	3
17 Apr 04 ●	I LIKE IT *Fre2Air 0153656 F2A*	......	9	6

Michelle NARINE See BIG BASS vs Michelle NARINE

NAS (see also QB FINEST featuring NAS & BRAVEHEARTS) *US, male rapper – Nasir Jones (Singles: 59 Weeks, Albums: 18 Weeks)*   pos/wks

28 May 94	IT AIN'T HARD TO TELL *Columbia 6604702*	......	64	1
17 Aug 96	IF I RULED THE WORLD *Columbia 6634022*	......	12	7
25 Jan 97	STREET DREAMS *Columbia 6641302*	......	12	4
14 Jun 97	HEAD OVER HEELS *Epic 6645942* [1]	......	18	3
29 May 99	HATE ME NOW *Columbia 6672562* [2]	......	14	6
15 Jan 00	NASTRADAMUS *Columbia 6685572*	......	24	3
22 Jan 00	HOT BOYZ *Elektra E 7002CD* [3]	......	18	3
21 Apr 01	OOCHIE WALLY *Columbia 67010852* [4]	......	30	3
2 Feb 02	GOT UR SELF A ... (re) *Columbia 6723022*	......	30	5
13 Jul 02 ●	I'M GONNA BE ALRIGHT *Epic 6728442* [5]	......	3	10
25 Jan 03	MADE YOU LOOK *Columbia 6734792*	......	27	3
5 Apr 03	I CAN *Columbia 6737382*	......	19	7

THE POP PREMIER LEAGUE

BRITISH **HIT** SINGLES & ALBUMS

Cups, championships and goals scored count for nothing in this run-down of the most successful football club chart hits. In the time-honoured tradition of football success being measured as a marathon and not a sprint, positions in this chart are determined by most weeks on the UK singles chart. If your team isn't represented, why not do something about it? Several of the hits included in the totals below are the work of fans extolling the virtues of their favourite teams.

Pos / CLUB and highest placed hit – number of hits – total weeks on chart

1. MANCHESTER UNITED – 'Come On You Reds' (No.1) – 11 – 73
United's best result, from a number of sources, came in 1994 when Status Quo adapted their 1988 hit 'Burning Bridges' and joined forces with Giggsy, Robbo, Sparky and the rest of the lads for the only club song ever to top the charts.

2. TOTTENHAM HOTSPUR – 'Ossie's Dream' (No.5) – 5 – 35
'Tottingham's' top tune was the story of the little Argentine's knee-trembling trip to Wembley, which featured support from chart regulars Chas and Dave. For the full Spurs chart listings, also check out Cockerel Chorus.

3. CHELSEA – 'Blue Is the Colour' (No.5) – 5 – 23
Five chart hits included contributions from the act calling itself Stamford Bridge and from Suggs, who collaborated with the team on 'Blue Day'.

4. LIVERPOOL – 'Anfield Rap' (No.3) – 5 – 21
Liverpool's best of five chart hits was written by midfield dynamo Craig Johnston and featured, among others, John Barnes, whose rap two years later for England helped 'World in Motion ...' to reach the top spot.

5. ARSENAL – 'Hot Stuff' (No.9) – 4 – 16
The double-winning team of 1998 was responsible for the Gunners' highest chart placing with this Donna Summer cover, which surpassed the previous double-winning rousing anthem 'Good Old Arsenal' from 1971.

6. LEEDS UNITED – 'Leeds United' (No.10) – 2 – 13
Not the most imaginative when it came to song titles. The lads from Elland Road followed up their 1972 smash hit 'Leeds United' with 'Leeds, Leeds, Leeds' 20 years later.

7. CELTIC – 'The Best Day of Our Lives' (No.17) – 4 – 9
Celtic's nine chart weeks came courtesy of Scoobie, the Celtic supporters group, the Bhoys from Paradise, Dance to Tipperary and the Lisbon Lions.

8. EVERTON – 'Here We Go' (No.14) – 2 – 8
The blue half of Merseyside's first hit was the very repetitive 'Here We Go'. The second time round, The Farm's 'All Together Now' propelled them to No.24 before being whisked away, Rooney style, to a bigger audience as England's Euro 2004 anthem.

9. NOTTINGHAM FOREST – 'We Got the Whole World in Our Hands' (No.24) – 1 – 6
Lace-making was once big business in the city by the Trent. Thus Nottingham-based Paper Lace were born and gave birth to one UK No.1, a US No.1 and this rather less successful release with Brian Clough's young men. Bizarrely, this old Laurie London hit made No.3 in the Dutch chart and No.5 in Belgium.

10. SUNDERLAND – 'Daydream Believer (Cheer Up Peter Reid)' (No.41) – 1 – 4
This Monkees classic was revisited by Simply Red and White. The Black Cats supporters group single was recorded in 1996 before the fans' love affair with manager Peter Reid ended. Also contributing to the points total is the catchy 'Niall Quinn's Disco Pants' by A Love Supreme.

11. NEWCASTLE UNITED – 'Black & White Army' (No.26) – 2 – 8
A brace of hits attributed to the Magpies. Their best effort was released by 250 Geordie fans (with assistance from Mungo Jerry) calling themselves 'Black & White Army'. Mungo Jerry and Toon Travellers were responsible for the second offering.

**12. WEST HAM UNITED –
'I'm Forever Blowing Bubbles' (No.31) – 1 – 2**
Sung at Upton Park since Mooreo was a lad, 'Bubbles' made the chart when Trevor and Co made the 1975 Cup Final, beating Bobby Moore's Fulham in the process.

**13. STOKE CITY –
'We'll Be with You' (No.34) – 1 – 2**
The act name might have been The Potters but there was no hiding the fact that these Stoke City fans were anxious to let the team have their backing in 1972. The response was the Football League Cup in the trophy cabinet and pop-star status for two weeks.

**14. CRYSTAL PALACE – 'Glad All Over' /
'Where Eagles Fly' (No.50) – 1 – 2**
The Dave Clark Five's 1960s classic was reborn as a foot-stomping rallying cry for the Selhurst Park fans. The record credits Crystal Palace with the Fab Four, who were footballers Alan Pardew, Andy Gray, Gary O'Reilly and Mark Bright.

**15. RANGERS – 'Glasgow Rangers
(Nine in a Row)' (No.54) – 1 – 2**
'Nine in a Row' refers to the nine consecutive Scottish League Championships secured by the Ibrox club, and was sung by the players in 1997 on the Gers label.

**16. COVENTRY CITY – 'Go For It!'
(No.61) – 1 –**
Go for it they certainly did. Spurred on by this Cup Final release, they defeated Tottenham 3-2 at Wembley in 1987. Spurs had two pop stars in their line-up, Glenn [Hoddle] and Chris [Waddle], who charted a month before this Sky Blues offering.

**17. BRIGHTON AND HOVE ALBION –
'The Boys in the Old Brighton Blue'
(No.65) – 1 –**
Another Cup Final song from the heady days when the Sussex club took on the might of Manchester United in 1983.

**18. SOUTHAMPTON – 'Southampton Boys'
(No.16) – 1 –**
Southampton supporters, in the guise of the Red 'n' White Machines, celebrated their appearance at the Millennium Stadium in 2003.

**19. YEOVIL TOWN –
'Yeovil True' (No.36) – 1 – 1**
The first ever Third Division (now League Two) club to enter the Top 40.

20. MILLWALL – 'Oh Millwall' (No.41) – 1 – 1
To the tune of 'Volare', Dennis Wise and the boys exercised their vocal cords in celebration of their FA Cup Final appearance.

**21. MIDDLESBROUGH – 'Let's Dance'
(No.44) - 1 – 1**
"Let's sing of the joy that Boro bring", says the song. The team down by the Riverside brought in two new signings, Bob Mortimer and Chris Rea, for this reworking of Chris Rea's 1987 hit.

**22. FULHAM – 'Viva El Fulham'
(No.46) – 1 – 1**
Tony Rees and the Cottagers were the vocal group of Fulham fans responsible for this reworded cover of Sylvia's 1975 summer sing-a-long 'Y Viva España'.

**23. QUEENS PARK RANGERS – 'Soopa Hoopz'
(No.54) – 1 – 1**
Released in Oct 2004 when manager Ian Holloway's boys couldn't stop winning, the full act title is recorded as Soopa Hoopz featuring QPR Massive.

**24. LINCOLN CITY –
'Chirpy Chirpy Cheep Cheep' / 'Jagged End'
(No.64) – 1 – 1**
A chart entry for Lincoln City might, on the face of it, be surprising, but their 2002 hit, recorded with professional singer and Imps fan Michael Courtney, was an attempt to raise money to keep the club afloat.

20 Nov 04	**BRIDGING THE GAP** *Columbia 6754682* [6]	**18**	4
13 Jul 96	**IT WAS WRITTEN** *Columbia 4841962* ▲	**38**	6
17 Apr 99	**I AM ...** *Columbia 4894192* ▲	**31**	4
25 Jan 03	**GOD'S SON** *Columbia 5098115*	**57**	6
11 Dec 04	**STREET'S DISCIPLE** *Columbia 5177249*	**45**	2

[1] Allure featuring Nas [2] Nas featuring Puff Daddy [3] Missy 'Misdemeanor' Elliott featuring Nas, Eve and Q Tip [4] QB Finest featuring Nas & Bravehearts [5] Jennifer Lopez featuring Nas [6] Nas / Olu Dara

Nas' full name, Nasir Jones, appears on the sleeve of 'God's Son' and 'Street's Disciple'

Graham NASH (see also CROSBY STILLS NASH and YOUNG; The HOLLIES) *UK, male vocalist (Albums: 13 Weeks)* pos/wks

26 Jun 71	**SONGS FOR BEGINNERS** *Atlantic 2401011*	**13**	8
13 May 72	**GRAHAM NASH DAVID CROSBY** *Atlantic K 50011* [1]	**13**	5

[1] Graham Nash David Crosby

Johnny NASH
US, male singer / actor (Singles: 106 Weeks, Albums: 17 Weeks) pos/wks

7 Aug 68 ●	**HOLD ME TIGHT** *Regal Zonophone RZ 3010*	**5**	16
8 Jan 69 ●	**YOU GOT SOUL** *Major Minor MM 586*	**6**	12
2 Apr 69 ●	**CUPID** (re) *Major Minor MM 603*	**6**	12
1 Apr 72	**STIR IT UP** *CBS 7800*	**13**	12
24 Jun 72 ●	**I CAN SEE CLEARLY NOW** *CBS 8113* ▲	**5**	15
7 Oct 72 ●	**THERE ARE MORE QUESTIONS THAN ANSWERS** *CBS 8351*	**9**	9
14 Jun 75 ★	**TEARS ON MY PILLOW** *CBS 3220*	**1**	11
11 Oct 75	**LET'S BE FRIENDS** *CBS 3597*	**42**	3
12 Jun 76	**(WHAT A) WONDERFUL WORLD** *Epic EPC 4294*	**25**	7
9 Nov 85	**ROCK ME BABY** *2000 ADFED 19*	**47**	4
15 Apr 89	**I CAN SEE CLEARLY NOW** (re-mix) *Epic JN 1*	**54**	5
5 Aug 72	**I CAN SEE CLEARLY NOW** *CBS 64860*	**39**	6
10 Dec 77	**JOHNNY NASH COLLECTION** *Epic EPC 10008*	**18**	11

Leigh NASH See DELERIUM

NASH THE SLASH *Canada, male vocalist / multi-instrumentalist – Jeff Plewman (Albums: 1 Week)* pos/wks

21 Feb 81	**CHILDREN OF THE NIGHT** *DinDisc DID 9*	**61**	1

The NASHVILLE TEENS
UK, male vocal / instrumental group (Singles: 36 Weeks) pos/wks

9 Jul 64 ●	**TOBACCO ROAD** *Decca F 11930*	**6**	13
22 Oct 64 ●	**GOOGLE EYE** *Decca F 12000*	**10**	10
4 Mar 65	**FIND MY WAY BACK HOME** *Decca F 12089*	**34**	6
20 May 65	**THIS LITTLE BIRD** *Decca F 12143*	**38**	4
3 Feb 66	**THE HARD WAY** (re) *Decca F 12316*	**45**	3

NATASHA *UK, female vocalist – Natasha England (Singles: 16 Weeks, Albums: 3 Weeks)* pos/wks

5 Jun 82 ●	**IKO IKO** *Towerbell TOW 22*	**10**	11
4 Sep 82	**THE BOOM BOOM ROOM** *Towerbell TOW 25*	**44**	5
9 Oct 82	**CAPTURED** *Towerbell TOWLP 2*	**53**	3

Ultra NATÉ *US, female vocalist – Ultra Naté Wyche (Singles: 39 Weeks, Albums: 4 Weeks)* pos/wks

9 Dec 89	**IT'S OVER NOW** *Eternal YZ 440*	**62**	3
23 Feb 91	**IS IT LOVE?** *Eternal YZ 509* [1]	**71**	1
29 Jan 94	**SHOW ME** *Warner Bros. W 0219CD*	**62**	1
14 Jun 97 ●	**FREE** *AM:PM 5822432*	**4**	17
24 Jan 98	**FREE** (re-mix) *AM:PM 5825012*	**33**	2
18 Apr 98 ●	**FOUND A CURE** *AM:PM 5826452*	**6**	7
25 Jul 98	**NEW KIND OF MEDICINE** *AM:PM 5827492*	**14**	5
22 Jul 00	**DESIRE** *AM:PM CDAMPM 133*	**40**	2
9 Jun 01	**GET IT UP (THE FEELING)** *AM:PM CDAMPM 140*	**51**	1
9 May 98	**SITUATION: CRITICAL** *AM:PM 5408242*	**17**	4

[1] Basement Boys present Ultra Naté

NATIONAL BRASS BAND *UK, orchestra (Albums: 10 Weeks)* pos/wks

10 May 80	**GOLDEN MELODIES** *K-Tel ONE 1075*	**15**	10

NATIONAL PHILHARMONIC ORCHESTRA See James GALWAY

NATIVE (see also BEAT RENEGADES; DREAM FREQUENCY; QUAKE featuring Marcia RAE; RED) *UK, male production duo (Singles: 2 Weeks)* pos/wks

10 Feb 01	**FEEL THE DRUMS** *Slinky Music SLINKY 009 CD*	**46**	2

NATURAL *US, male vocal group (Singles: 2 Weeks)* pos/wks

10 Aug 02	**PUT YOUR ARMS AROUND ME** *Ariola 74321947892*	**32**	2

NATURAL BORN CHILLERS *UK, male production duo – Arif Salih and Lee Parker (Singles: 3 Weeks)* pos/wks

1 Nov 97	**ROCK THE FUNKY BEAT** *East West EW 138CD1*	**30**	3

NATURAL BORN GROOVES *Belgium, male DJ / production duo – Burn Boon and Jaco van Rijsvijck (Singles: 3 Weeks)* pos/wks

2 Nov 96	**FORERUNNER** *XL XLS 76CD*	**64**	1
19 Apr 97	**GROOVEBIRD** *Positiva CDTIV 75*	**21**	2

NATURAL LIFE *UK, male / female vocal / instrumental group (Singles: 3 Weeks)* pos/wks

7 Mar 92	**NATURAL LIFE** *Tribe NLIFE 3*	**47**	3

NATURAL SELECTION *US, male vocal / instrumental duo (Singles: 2 Weeks)* pos/wks

9 Nov 91	**DO ANYTHING** *East West A 8724*	**69**	2

The NATURALS *UK, male vocal / instrumental group (Singles: 9 Weeks)* pos/wks

20 Aug 64	**I SHOULD HAVE KNOWN BETTER** *Parlophone R 5165*	**24**	9

David NAUGHTON *US, male actor / vocalist (Singles: 6 Weeks)* pos/wks

25 Aug 79	**MAKIN' IT** *RSO 32*	**44**	6

NAUGHTY BY NATURE
US, male rap group (Singles: 18 Weeks, Albums: 5 Weeks) pos/wks

9 Nov 91	**O.P.P.** *Big Life BLR 62*	**73**	1
20 Jun 92	**O.P.P.** (re-issue) *Big Life BLR 74*	**35**	3
30 Jan 93	**HIP HOP HOORAY** *Big Life BLRD 89*	**22**	3
19 Jun 93	**IT'S ON** *Big Life BLRD 99*	**48**	2
27 Nov 93	**HIP HOP HOORAY** (re-mix) *Big Life BLRDA 104*	**20**	4
29 Apr 95	**FEEL ME FLOW** *Big Life BLRD 115*	**23**	3
11 Sep 99	**JAMBOREE** *Arista 74321692882* [1]	**51**	1
19 Oct 02	**FEELS GOOD (DON'T WORRY BOUT A THING)** *Island CID 806* [2]	**44**	1
6 Mar 93	**19 NAUGHTY III** *Big Life BLRCD 23*	**40**	2
27 May 95	**POVERTY'S PARADISE** *Big Life BLRCD 28*	**20**	1

[1] Naughty By Nature featuring Zhané [2] Naughty By Nature featuring 3LW

NAVIGATOR See FREESTYLERS

Maria NAYLER *UK, female vocalist (Singles: 26 Weeks)* pos/wks

9 Mar 96	**BE AS ONE** *Deconstruction 74321342962* [1]	**17**	4
16 Nov 96 ●	**ONE & ONE** *Deconstruction 74321427692* [2]	**3**	17
7 Mar 98	**NAKED AND SACRED** *Deconstruction 74321534242*	**32**	3
5 Sep 98	**WILL YOU BE WITH ME / LOVE IS THE GOD** *Deconstruction 74321591772*	**65**	1
27 May 00	**ANGRY SKIES** *Deconstruction 74321759492*	**42**	1

[1] Sasha and Maria [2] Robert Miles featuring Maria Nayler

NAZARETH (see also DAN McCAFFERTY) *UK, male vocal / instrumental group (Singles: 75 Weeks, Albums: 51 Weeks)* pos/wks

5 May 73 ●	**BROKEN DOWN ANGEL** *Mooncrest MOON 1*	**9**	11
21 Jul 73 ●	**BAD BAD BOY** *Mooncrest MOON 9*	**10**	9
13 Oct 73	**THIS FLIGHT TONIGHT** *Mooncrest MOON 14*	**11**	13
23 Mar 74	**SHANGHAI'D IN SHANGHAI** *Mooncrest MOON 22*	**41**	4
14 Jun 75	**MY WHITE BICYCLE** *Mooncrest MOON 47*	**14**	8
15 Nov 75	**HOLY ROLLER** *Mountain TOP 3*	**36**	4
24 Sep 77	**HOT TRACKS (EP)** *Mountain NAZ 1*	**15**	11
18 Feb 78	**GONE DEAD TRAIN** *Mountain NAZ 002*	**49**	2
13 May 78	**PLACE IN YOUR HEART** (re) *Mountain TOP 37*	**70**	2
27 Jan 79	**MAY THE SUNSHINE** *Mountain NAZ 003*	**22**	8
28 Jul 79	**STAR** *Mountain TOP 45*	**54**	3
26 May 73	**RAZAMANAZ** *Mooncrest CREST 1*	**11**	25
24 Nov 73 ●	**LOUD 'N' PROUD** *Mooncrest CREST 4*	**10**	7
18 May 74	**RAMPANT** *Mooncrest CREST 15*	**13**	3
13 Dec 75	**GREATEST HITS** *Mountain TOPS 108*	**54**	1
3 Feb 79	**NO MEAN CITY** *Mountain TOPS 123*	**34**	9
28 Feb 81	**THE FOOL CIRCLE** *NEMS NEL 6019*	**60**	1
3 Oct 81	**NAZARETH LIVE** *NEMS NELD 102*	**78**	3

Tracks on Hot Tracks (EP): Love Hurts / This Flight Tonight / Broken Down Angel / Hair of the Dog

NAZLYN *See M-BEAT*

Me'Shell NDEGEOCELLO

US, female vocalist / instrumentalist – bass (Singles: 5 Weeks) pos/wks

12 Feb 94	IF THAT'S YOUR BOYFRIEND (HE WASN'T LAST NIGHT) *Maverick W 0223CD1*	**74**	1
3 Sep 94	WILD NIGHT *Mercury MERCD 409* [1]	**34**	3
1 Mar 97	NEVER MISS THE WATER *Reprise W 0393CD* [2]	**59**	1

[1] John Mellencamp featuring Me'Shell Ndegeocello [2] Chaka Khan featuring Me'Shell Ndegeocello

Youssou N'DOUR *Senegal, male vocalist (Singles: 35 Weeks)* pos/wks

3 Jun 89	SHAKIN' THE TREE *Virgin VS 1167* [1]	**61**	3
22 Dec 90	SHAKIN' THE TREE (re-issue) *Virgin VS 1322* [1]	**57**	4
25 Jun 94 ●	7 SECONDS (re) *Columbia 6605082* [2]	**3**	25
14 Jan 95	UNDECIDED *Columbia 6609712*	**53**	2
10 Oct 98	HOW COME *Interscope IND 95598* [3]	**52**	1

[1] Youssou N'Dour and Peter Gabriel [2] Youssou N'Dour (featuring Neneh Cherry) [3] Youssou N'Dour and Canibus

The re-issue of 'Shaking the Tree' was listed with its flip side, 'Solsbury Hill' by Peter Gabriel

NEARLY GOD *(see also TRICKY) UK, male / female vocal / instrumental group (Singles: 2 Weeks, Albums: 4 Weeks)* pos/wks

20 Apr 96	POEMS *Durban Poison DPCD 3*	**28**	2
4 May 96 ●	NEARLY GOD *Fourth & Broadway DPCD 1001*	**10**	4

Terry NEASON *UK, female vocalist (Singles: 1 Week)* pos/wks

25 Jun 94	LIFEBOAT *WEA YZ 830*	**72**	1

NEBULA II *UK, male instrumental / production group (Singles: 3 Weeks)* pos/wks

1 Feb 92	SEANCE / ATHEAMA *Reinforced RIVET 1211*	**55**	2
16 May 92	FLATLINERS *J4M 12NEBULA 2*	**54**	1

NED'S ATOMIC DUSTBIN *UK, male vocal / instrumental group (Singles: 24 Weeks, Albums: 8 Weeks)* pos/wks

14 Jul 90	KILL YOUR TELEVISION *Chapter 22 CHAP 48*	**53**	2
27 Oct 90	UNTIL YOU FIND OUT *Chapter 22 CHAP 52*	**51**	2
9 Mar 91	HAPPY *Columbia 6566807*	**16**	4
21 Sep 91	TRUST *Furtive 6574627*	**21**	4
10 Oct 92	NOT SLEEPING AROUND *Furtive 6583866*	**19**	3
5 Dec 92	INTACT *Furtive 6588166*	**36**	6
25 Mar 95	ALL I ASK OF MYSELF IS THAT I HOLD TOGETHER *Furtive 6613565*	**33**	2
15 Jul 95	STUCK *Furtive 6620562*	**64**	1
9 Feb 91	BITE (IMPORT) *Rough Trade Germany RTD 14011831*	**72**	1
13 Apr 91 ●	GOD FODDER *Furtive 4681121*	**4**	5
31 Oct 92	ARE YOU NORMAL? *Furtive 4726332*	**13**	2

Raja NEE *US, female vocalist (Singles: 2 Weeks)* pos/wks

4 Mar 95	TURN IT UP *Perspective 5874872*	**42**	2

NEEDLE DAMAGE *See DJ DAN presents NEEDLE DAMAGE*

Joey NEGRO *(see also AKABU featuring Linda CLIFFORD; HED BOYS; JAKATTA; Li KWAN; IL PADRINOS featuring Jocelyn BROWN; PHASE II; RAVEN MAIZE; Z FACTOR) UK, male producer – Dave Lee (Singles: 15 Weeks)* pos/wks

16 Nov 91	DO WHAT YOU FEEL *Ten TEN 391* [1]	**36**	3
21 Dec 91	REACHIN' *Republic LIC 160* [1]	**70**	1
18 Jul 92	ENTER YOUR FANTASY (EP) *Ten TEN 397*	**35**	3
25 Sep 93	WHAT HAPPENED TO THE MUSIC *Virgin VSCD 1466*	**51**	2
19 Feb 00 ●	MUST BE THE MUSIC *Incentive CENT 4CDS* [2]	**8**	5
16 Sep 00	SATURDAY *Yola YOLACDX 03* [2]	**41**	1

[1] Joey Negro presents Phase II [2] Joey Negro featuring Taka Boom

Tracks on Enter Your Fantasy (EP): Love Fantasy / Get Up / Enter Your Mind / Everybody

neil

UK, male actor / vocalist – Nigel Planer (Singles: 10 Weeks) pos/wks

14 Jul 84 ●	HOLE IN MY SHOE *WEA YZ 10*	**2**	10

Vince NEIL *(see also MÖTLEY CRÜE) US, male vocalist – Vince Wharton (Singles: 1 Week, Albums: 1 Week)* pos/wks

3 Oct 92	YOU'RE INVITED (BUT YOUR FRIEND CAN'T COME) *Hollywood HWD 123*	**63**	1
8 May 93	EXPOSED *Warner Bros. 9362452602*	**44**	1

NEJA *Italy, female vocalist – Agnese Cacciola (Singles: 1 Week)* pos/wks

26 Sep 98	RESTLESS (I KNOW YOU KNOW) *Panorama CDPAN 1*	**47**	1

NEK *Italy, male vocalist (Singles: 1 Week)* pos/wks

29 Aug 98	LAURA *Coalition COLA 054CD*	**59**	1

NELLY ⟨ 344 ⟩ Top 500

Southern rap superstar, b. Cornell Hayes, 2 Nov 1974, Travis, Texas, US. Leader of the St Louis rap pack, the St Lunatics, he was the first act since The Beatles to have initial two US No.1 hits replace each other at the top (Singles: 117 Weeks, Albums: 80 Weeks) pos/wks

11 Nov 00 ●	(HOT S**T) COUNTRY GRAMMAR *Universal MCSTD 40242*	**7**	9
24 Feb 01	EI *Universal MCSTD 40249*	**11**	5
19 May 01 ●	RIDE WIT ME *Universal MCSTD 40252* [1]	**3**	12
15 Sep 01	BATTER UP *Universal MCSTD 40261* [2]	**28**	3
27 Oct 01	WHERE THE PARTY AT? *Columbia MCSTD 6719012* [3]	**25**	3
27 Apr 02	GIRLFRIEND *Jive 9253312* [4]	**2**	12
29 Jun 02 ●	HOT IN HERRE *Universal MCSTD 40289* ▲	**4**	15
26 Oct 02 ★	DILEMMA *Universal MCSTD 40299* [5] ■ ▲	**1**	21
15 Mar 03	WORK IT *Universal MCSCD 40312* [6]	**7**	11
20 Sep 03	SHAKE YA TAILFEATHER *Bad Boy MCSTD 40337* [7] ▲	**10**	7
13 Dec 03	IZ U *Universal MCSTD 40346*	**36**	4
11 Sep 04 ★	MY PLACE / FLAP YOUR WINGS *Universal MCSTD 40379* ■	**1**	11
4 Dec 04 ●	TILT YA HEAD BACK *Universal MCSTD 40396* [8]	**5**	4+
3 Feb 01	COUNTRY GRAMMAR *Universal 1577432* ▲	**14**	31
13 Jul 02 ●	NELLYVILLE *Universal 186902* ▲	**2**	38
25 Sep 04 ●	SUIT *Universal 9863936* ▲	**8**	7
25 Sep 04	SWEAT *Universal 9863935*	**11**	4

[1] Nelly featuring City Spud [2] Nelly and St Lunatics [3] Jagged Edge featuring Nelly [4] 'N Sync featuring Nelly [5] Nelly featuring Kelly Rowland [6] Nelly featuring Justin Timberlake [7] Nelly, P Diddy and Murphy Lee [8] Nelly & Christina Aguilera

'My Place' features uncredited vocalist Jaheim

NELSON

US, male vocal duo (Singles: 3 Weeks) pos/wks

27 Oct 90	(CAN'T LIVE WITHOUT YOUR) LOVE AND AFFECTION *DGC GEF 82* ▲	**54**	3

Bill NELSON

(see also BE BOP DELUXE; RED NOISE)
UK, male vocalist / instrumentalist – guitar and synthesizer (Singles: 12 Weeks, Albums: 21 Weeks) pos/wks

24 Feb 79	FURNITURE MUSIC *Harvest HAR 5176* [1]	**59**	3
5 May 79	REVOLT INTO STYLE *Harvest HAR 5183* [1]	**69**	2
5 Jul 80	DO YOU DREAM IN COLOUR? *Cocteau COQ 1*	**52**	4
13 Jun 81	YOUTH OF NATION ON FIRE *Mercury WILL 2*	**73**	3
24 Feb 79	SOUND ON SOUND *Harvest SHSP 4095* [1]	**33**	5
23 May 81 ●	QUIT DREAMING AND GET ON THE BEAM *Mercury 6359 055*	**7**	6
3 Jul 82	THE LOVE THAT WHIRLS (DIARY OF A THINKING HEART) *Mercury WHIRL 3*	**28**	4
14 May 83	CHIMERA *Mercury MERB 19*	**30**	5
3 May 86	GETTING THE HOLY GHOST ACROSS *Portrait PRT 26602*	**91**	1

[1] Bill Nelson's Red Noise [1] Bill Nelson's Red Noise

Phyllis NELSON

US, female vocalist (Singles: 24 Weeks, Albums: 10 Weeks) pos/wks

23 Feb 85 ★	MOVE CLOSER *Carrere CAR 337*	**1**	21
21 May 94	MOVE CLOSER (re-issue) *EMI CDEMCT 9*	**34**	3
20 Apr 85	MOVE CLOSER *Carrere CAL 203*	**29**	10

Ricky NELSON ⟨ 484 ⟩ Top 500

TV star turned teen idol and later singer / songwriter, b. 8 May 1940, New Jersey, US, d. 31 Dec 1985. He was virtually raised on a US radio / TV family show. In the 1950s, he enjoyed sales on a par with Elvis Presley and Pat Boone. Both his father and his two sons also topped the US chart (1935 and 1990) (Singles: 150 Weeks) pos/wks

21 Feb 58	STOOD UP (re) *London HLP 8542*	**27**	2
22 Aug 58 ●	POOR LITTLE FOOL (re) *London HLP 8670* ▲	**4**	14

7 Nov 58 ●	SOMEDAY *London HLP 8732*	9	13
21 Nov 58	I GOT A FEELING *London HLP 8732*	27	1
17 Apr 59	IT'S LATE *London HLP 8817*	3	20
15 May 59	NEVER BE ANYONE ELSE BUT YOU (re) *London HLP 8817*	14	10
4 Sep 59	SWEETER THAN YOU *London HLP 8927*	19	3
11 Sep 59	JUST A LITTLE TOO MUCH *London HLP 8927*	11	8
15 Jan 60	I WANNA BE LOVED *London HLP 9021*	30	1
7 Jul 60	YOUNG EMOTIONS *London HLP 9121*	48	1
1 Jun 61 ●	HELLO MARY LOU / TRAVELLIN' MAN *London HLP 9347* ▲	2	18
16 Nov 61	EVERLOVIN' *London HLP 9440* [1]	23	5
29 Mar 62	YOUNG WORLD *London HLP 9524*	19	13
30 Aug 62	TEENAGE IDOL *London HLP 9583* [1]	39	4
17 Jan 63	IT'S UP TO YOU *London HLP 9648* [1]	22	9
17 Oct 63	FOOLS RUSH IN *Brunswick 05895* [1]	12	9
30 Jan 64	FOR YOU *Brunswick 05900* [1]	14	10
21 Oct 72	GARDEN PARTY *MCA MU 1165* [1]	41	4
24 Aug 91	HELLO MARY LOU (GOODBYE HEART) (re-issue) *Liberty EMCT 2*	45	5

[1] Rick Nelson

Sandy NELSON *US, male instrumentalist – drums – Sander Nelson (Singles: 42 Weeks)*   pos/wks

6 Nov 59 ●	TEEN BEAT (re) *Top Rank JAR 197*	9	12
14 Dec 61 ●	LET THERE BE DRUMS *London HLP 9466*	3	16
22 Mar 62	DRUMS ARE MY BEAT *London HLP 9521*	30	6
7 Jun 62	DRUMMIN' UP A STORM *London HLP 9558*	39	8

Shara NELSON (see also MASSIVE ATTACK)
UK, female vocalist (Singles: 23 Weeks, Albums: 11 Weeks)   pos/wks

24 Jul 93	DOWN THAT ROAD *Cooltempo CDCOOL 275*	19	6
18 Sep 93	ONE GOODBYE IN TEN *Cooltempo CDCOOL 279*	21	5
12 Feb 94	UPTIGHT *Cooltempo CDCOOL 286*	19	5
4 Jun 94	NOBODY *Cooltempo CDCOOL 290*	49	1
10 Sep 94	INSIDE OUT / DOWN THAT ROAD (re-mix) *Cooltempo CDCOOLX 295*	34	3
16 Sep 95	ROUGH WITH THE SMOOTH *Cooltempo CDCOOL 311*	30	2
5 Dec 98	SENSE OF DANGER *Pagan PAGAN 024CDS* [1]	61	1
2 Oct 93	WHAT SILENCE KNOWS *Cooltempo CTCD 35*	22	9
7 Oct 95	FRIENDLY FIRE *Cooltempo CTCD 48*	44	2

[1] Presence featuring Shara Nelson

Shelley NELSON See TIN TIN OUT

Willie NELSON
US, male vocalist / instrumentalist – guitar (Singles: 13 Weeks)   pos/wks

31 Jul 82	ALWAYS ON MY MIND *CBS A 2511*	49	3
7 Apr 84	TO ALL THE GIRLS I'VE LOVED BEFORE *CBS A 4252* [1]	17	10

[1] Julio Iglesias and Willie Nelson

NENA *Germany, female / male vocal / instrumental group – lead vocal Gabriele (Nena) Kerner (Singles: 14 Weeks, Albums: 5 Weeks)*   pos/wks

4 Feb 84 ★	99 RED BALLOONS *Epic A 4074*	1	12
5 May 84	JUST A DREAM *Epic H 3249*	70	2
24 Mar 84	NENA *Epic EPC 25925*	31	5

NEO CORTEX *Italy, male production trio (Singles: 1 Week)*   pos/wks

23 Oct 04	ELEMENTS *All Around the World CDGLOBE 332*	67	1

The NEPTUNES (see also P DIDDY; N*E*R*D) *US, male production / vocal / rap duo – Pharrell Williams and Chad Hugo, (Albums: 8 Weeks)*   pos/wks

30 Aug 03 ●	THE NEPTUNES PRESENT ... CLONES *Arista 82876533852* ▲	2	8

'The Neptunes Present ... Clones' appeared on the Compilations Chart only

N*E*R*D (see also The NEPTUNES)
US, male vocal / production trio (Singles: 27 Weeks, Albums: 34 Weeks) pos/wks

9 Jun 01	LAPDANCE *Virgin VUSCD 196* [1]	33	2
10 Aug 02	ROCK STAR *Virgin VUSCD 253*	15	4
29 Mar 03	PROVIDER / LAPDANCE (re-mix) *Virgin VUSCD 262* [1]	20	4
27 Mar 04 ●	SHE WANTS TO MOVE *Virgin VUSCD 284*	5	12
26 Jun 04	MAYBE *Virgin VUSDX 291*	25	5
17 Aug 02	IN SEARCH OF ... *Virgin CDVUSX 216*	28	18
3 Apr 04	FLY OR DIE *Virgin CDVUS250*	4	16

[1] N*E*R*D featuring Lee Harvey and Vita

NERIO'S DUBWORK See Darryl PANDY

Frances NERO *US, female vocalist (Singles: 9 Weeks)*   pos/wks

13 Apr 91	FOOTSTEPS FOLLOWING ME *Debut DEBT 3109*	17	9

NERO and the GLADIATORS
UK, male instrumental group (Singles: 6 Weeks)   pos/wks

23 Mar 61	ENTRY OF THE GLADIATORS (re) *Decca F 11329*	37	5
27 Jul 61	IN THE HALL OF THE MOUNTAIN KING *Decca F 11367*	48	1

Ann NESBY *US, female vocalist (Singles: 3 Weeks)*   pos/wks

21 Dec 96	WITNESS (EP) *AM:PM 5875612*	42	2
17 May 97	HOLD ON (EP) *AM:PM 5822332*	75	1

Tracks on Witness (EP): Can I Get a Witness / (mix) / In the Spirit / I'm Still Wearing Your Name. Tracks on Hold On (EP): Hold On (Mousse T's Uplifting Garage Edit) / Hold On (Mousse T's Hard Soul Remix) / Hold On (Klub Head Mix) / This Weekend (Laidback Mix)

Michael NESMITH (see also The MONKEES) *US, male vocalist / instrumentalist – guitar – Robert Nesmith (Singles: 6 Weeks)*   pos/wks

26 Mar 77	RIO *Island WIP 6373*	28	6

NETWORK
UK, male vocal / instrumental group (Singles: 4 Weeks)   pos/wks

12 Dec 92	BROKEN WINGS *Chrysalis CHS 3923*	46	4

NEVADA
UK, male / female vocal / instrumental group (Singles: 1 Week)   pos/wks

8 Jan 83	IN THE BLEAK MID WINTER *Polydor POSP 203*	71	1

NEVADA See STEREOPOL featuring NEVADA

NEVE See Y-TRAXX

Robbie NEVIL
US, male vocalist (Singles: 24 Weeks, Albums: 1 Week)   pos/wks

20 Dec 86 ●	C'EST LA VIE *Manhattan MT 14*	3	11
2 May 87	DOMINOES *Manhattan MT 19*	26	6
11 Jul 87	WOT'S IT TO YA *Manhattan MT 24*	43	7
13 Jun 87	C'EST LA VIE *Manhattan MTL 1006*	93	1

Aaron NEVILLE See NEVILLE BROTHERS; Linda RONSTADT

Tom NEVILLE *UK, male DJ / producer (Singles: 1 Week)*   pos/wks

6 Mar 04	JUST FUCK *Nukleuz 0555PNUK*	60	1

NEVILLE BROTHERS *US, male vocal / instrumental group (Singles: 7 Weeks, Albums: 3 Weeks)*   pos/wks

25 Nov 89	WITH GOD ON OUR SIDE *A&M AM 545*	47	6
7 Jul 90	BIRD ON A WIRE *A&M AM 568*	72	1
18 Aug 90	BROTHER'S KEEPER *A&M 3953121*	35	3

Jason NEVINS *US, male DJ / producer (Singles: 29 Weeks)*   pos/wks

21 Feb 98	IT'S LIKE THAT (GERMAN IMPORT) *Columbia 6652932* [1]	63	3
14 Mar 98	IT'S LIKE THAT (US IMPORT) *Columbia 6652932* [1]	65	1
21 Mar 98 ★	IT'S LIKE THAT *Sm:)e Communications SM 90652* [1] ◆ ■	1	16
18 Apr 98	IT'S TRICKY (IMPORT) *Epidrome EPD 6656982* [1]	74	1
26 Jun 99	INSANE IN THE BRAIN (re-mix) *INCredible INCRL 17CD* [2]	19	3
16 Aug 03 ●	I'M IN HEAVEN *Free2Air / Incentive 0148665 F2A* [3]	9	5

[1] Run-DMC vs Jason Nevins [2] Jason Nevins vs Cypress Hill [3] Jason Nevins featuring UKNY / Holly James

NEW ATLANTIC *UK, male instrumental / production duo – Richard Lloyd and Cameron Saunders (Singles: 15 Weeks)*   pos/wks

29 Feb 92	I KNOW *3 Beat 3BT 1*	12	7
3 Oct 92	INTO THE FUTURE *3 Beat 3BT 2* [1]	70	1
13 Feb 93	TAKE OFF SOME TIME *3 Beat 3BTCD 14*	64	1
26 Nov 94	THE SUNSHINE AFTER THE RAIN *Ffrreedom TABCD 223* [2]	26	6

[1] New Atlantic featuring Linda Wright [2] New Atlantic / U4EA featuring Berri

'The Sunshine After the Rain' was re-issued in 1995, credited simply to the vocalist Berri

NEW BOHEMIANS *See Edie BRICKELL and the NEW BOHEMIANS*

Choir of NEW COLLEGE OXFORD / Edward HIGGINBOTTOM
UK, male / female choir and male conductor (Albums: 7 Weeks) pos/wks

12 Oct 96	AGNUS DEI *Erato 630146342*	.49 5
18 Apr 98	AGNUS DEI II *Erato 3984216592*	.57 2

NEW EDITION (see also BELL BIV DEVOE)
US, male vocal trio – Bobby Brown, Johnny Gill and Ralph Tresvant (Singles: 36 Weeks, Albums: 3 Weeks) pos/wks

16 Apr 83 ★	CANDY GIRL *London LON 21*	.1 13
13 Aug 83	POPCORN LOVE *London LON 31*	.43 5
23 Feb 85	MR TELEPHONE MAN *MCA MCA 938*	.19 9
15 Apr 89	CRUCIAL *MCA MCA 23934*	.70 1
10 Aug 96	HIT ME OFF *MCA MCSTD 48014*	.20 4
7 Jun 97	SOMETHING ABOUT YOU *MCA MCSTD 48032*	.16 4
14 Sep 96	HOME AGAIN *MCA MCD 11480* ▲	.22 3

NEW FAST AUTOMATIC DAFFODILS
UK, male vocal / instrumental group (Albums: 2 Weeks) pos/wks

17 Nov 90	PIGEON HOLE *Play It Again Sam BIAS 185*	.49 1
24 Oct 92	BODY EXIT MIND *Play It Again Sam BIAS 205CD*	.57 1

NEW FOUND GLORY
US, male vocal / instrumental group (Singles: 7 Weeks, Albums: 10 Weeks) pos/wks

16 Jun 01	HIT OR MISS (WAITED TOO LONG) *MCA 1558232*	.58 1
3 Aug 02	MY FRIENDS OVER YOU *MCA MCSTD 40286*	.30 3
19 Oct 02	HEAD ON COLLISION *MCA MCSTD 40298*	.64 1
12 Jun 04	ALL DOWNHILL FROM HERE *Geffen 9862523*	.58 1
11 Sep 04	FAILURE'S NOT FLATTERING *Geffen MCSTD 40380*	.67 1
29 Jun 02 ●	STICKS AND STONES *MCA 1129452*	.10 8
29 May 04	CATALYST *Geffen / Polydor 9862440*	.27 2

NEW GENERATION
UK, male vocal / instrumental group (Singles: 5 Weeks) pos/wks

26 Jun 68	SMOKEY BLUES AWAY *Spark SRL 1007*	.38 5

NEW INSPIRATIONAL CHOIR *See Sharlene HECTOR*

NEW KIDS ON THE BLOCK `346` `Top 500`
Highest earning boy band of all time; Jordan and Jon Knight, Donnie Wahlberg, Danny Wood, Joey McIntyre. Formed Boston, US, by producer / manager Maurice Starr as a pop version of his act New Edition. In 1990, they grossed a reported $861 million and became the first group to score eight UK Top 10 entries in a year (Singles: 90 Weeks, Albums: 106 Weeks) pos/wks

16 Sep 89	HANGIN' TOUGH *CBS BLOCK 1*	.52 4
11 Nov 89 ★	YOU GOT IT (THE RIGHT STUFF) *CBS BLOCK 2*	.1 13
6 Jan 90 ★	HANGIN' TOUGH (re-issue) *CBS BLOCK 3* ▲	.1 9
17 Mar 90 ●	I'LL BE LOVING YOU (FOREVER) *CBS BLOCK 4* ▲	.5 8
12 May 90 ●	COVER GIRL *CBS BLOCK 5*	.4 8
16 Jun 90 ●	STEP BY STEP *CBS BLOCK 6* ▲	.2 7
4 Aug 90 ●	TONIGHT *CBS BLOCK 7*	.3 10
13 Oct 90 ●	LET'S TRY AGAIN / DIDN'T I BLOW YOUR MIND *CBS BLOCK 8*	.8 5
8 Dec 90 ●	THIS ONE'S FOR THE CHILDREN *CBS BLOCK 9*	.9 7
9 Feb 91	GAMES *CBS 6566267*	.14 4
18 May 91	CALL IT WHAT YOU WANT *Columbia 6567857*	.12 5
14 Dec 91 ●	IF YOU GO AWAY *Columbia 6576667*	.9 5
19 Feb 94	DIRTY DAWG *Columbia 6600362* [1]	.27 3
26 Mar 94	NEVER LET YOU GO *Columbia 6602072* [1]	.42 2
9 Dec 89 ●	HANGIN' TOUGH *CBS 4608741* ▲	.2 41
30 Jun 90 ★	STEP BY STEP *CBS 4666861* ■ ▲	.1 31
2 Nov 90 ●	NEW KIDS ON THE BLOCK *CBS 4675041*	.6 13
15 Dec 90	MERRY MERRY CHRISTMAS *CBS 4659071*	.13 5
2 Mar 91	NO MORE GAMES – THE REMIX ALBUM *Columbia 4674941*	.15 11
21 Dec 91	H.I.T.S. *Columbia 4694381*	.50 4
12 Mar 94	FACE THE MUSIC *Columbia 4743592* [1]	.36 1

[1] NKOTB [1] NKOTB

NEW MODEL ARMY
UK, male vocal / instrumental group (Singles: 33 Weeks, Albums: 21 Weeks) pos/wks

27 Apr 85	NO REST *EMI NMA 1*	.28 5
3 Aug 85	BETTER THAN THEM / NO SENSE *EMI NMA 2*	.49 2
30 Nov 85	BRAVE NEW WORLD *EMI NMA 3*	.57 1
8 Nov 86	51ST STATE *EMI NMA 4*	.71 2
28 Feb 87	POISON STREET *EMI NMA 5*	.64 1
26 Sep 87	WHITE COATS (EP) *EMI NMA 6*	.50 2
21 Jan 89	STUPID QUESTIONS *EMI NMA 7*	.31 3

11 Mar 89	VAGABONDS *EMI NMA 8*	.37 3
10 Jun 89	GREEN AND GREY *EMI NMA 9*	.37 3
8 Sep 90	GET ME OUT *EMI NMA 10*	.34 2
3 Nov 90	PURITY *EMI NMA 11*	.61 2
8 Jun 91	SPACE *EMI NMA 12*	.39 2
20 Feb 93	HERE COMES THE WAR *Epic 6589352*	.25 2
24 Jul 93	LIVING IN THE ROSE (THE BALLADS EP) *Epic 6592492*	.51 1
12 May 84	VENGEANCE *Abstract ABT 008*	.73 5
25 May 85	NO REST FOR THE WICKED *EMI NMAL 1*	.22 3
11 Oct 86	THE GHOST OF CAIN *EMI EMC 3516*	.45 3
18 Feb 89	THUNDER AND CONSOLATION *EMI EMC 3552*	.20 3
6 Oct 90	IMPURITY *EMI EMC 3581*	.23 2
22 Jun 91	RAW MELODY MEN *EMI EMC 3595*	.43 2
10 Apr 93	THE LOVE OF HOPELESS CAUSES *Epic 4735622*	.22 2
25 Apr 98	STRANGE BROTHERHOOD *Eagle EAGCD 021*	.72 1

Better Than Them / No Sense are the lead tracks from 'The Acoustic EP', which included the following tracks: Better Than Them / No Sense / Adrenalin / Trust. Tracks on White Coats (EP): White Coats / The Charge / Chinese Whispers / My Country. Tracks on Living in the Rose (The Ballads EP): Living in the Rose / Drummy B / Marry the Sea / Sleepwalking

NEW MUSIK
UK, male vocal / instrumental group (Singles: 27 Weeks, Albums: 11 Weeks) pos/wks

6 Oct 79	STRAIGHT LINES *GTO GT 255*	.53 5
19 Jan 80	LIVING BY NUMBERS *GTO GT 261*	.13 8
26 Apr 80	THIS WORLD OF WATER *GTO GT 268*	.31 7
12 Jul 80	SANCTUARY *GTO GT 275*	.31 7
17 May 80	FROM A TO B *GTO GTLP 041*	.35 9
14 Mar 81	ANYWHERE *GTO GTLP 044*	.68 2

NEW ORDER `160` `Top 500`
(see also ELECTRONIC; MONACO; The OTHER TWO) Innovative Mancunian group featuring three former members of critically acclaimed Joy Division: Bernard Sumner (v/g), Peter Hook (b), Stephen Morris (d), and augmented by Gillian Gilbert (k). 'Blue Monday' remains the UK's biggest-selling 12-inch single of all time and is their best-selling single (all formats totalling 1,001,400) (Singles: 191 Weeks, Albums: 149 Weeks) pos/wks

14 Mar 81	CEREMONY *Factory FAC 33*	.34 5
3 Oct 81	PROCESSION / EVERYTHING'S GONE GREEN *Factory FAC 53*	.38 5
22 May 82	TEMPTATION *Factory FAC 63*	.29 7
19 Mar 83 ●	BLUE MONDAY (2re) *Factory FAC 73* ◆	.9 38
3 Sep 83	CONFUSION *Factory FAC 93*	.12 7
28 Apr 84	THIEVES LIKE US *Factory FAC 103*	.18 5
25 May 85	THE PERFECT KISS *Factory FAC 123*	.46 4
9 Nov 85	SUB-CULTURE *Factory FAC 133*	.63 4
29 Mar 86	SHELLSHOCK *Factory FAC 143*	.28 5
27 Sep 86	STATE OF THE NATION *Factory FAC 153*	.30 3
27 Sep 86	THE PEEL SESSIONS (1ST JUNE 1982) EP *Strange Fruit SFPS 001*	.54 1
15 Nov 86	BIZARRE LOVE TRIANGLE *Factory FAC 163*	.56 2
1 Aug 87	TRUE FAITH *Factory FAC 183*	.4 10
19 Dec 87	TOUCHED BY THE HAND OF GOD *Factory FAC 1937*	.20 7
7 May 88 ●	BLUE MONDAY (re-mix) *Factory FAC 737*	.3 11
10 Dec 88	FINE TIME *Factory FAC 2237*	.11 8
11 Mar 89	ROUND AND ROUND *Factory FAC 2637*	.21 7
9 Sep 89	RUN 2 *Factory FAC 273*	.49 2
2 Jun 90 ★	WORLD IN MOTION ... *Factory / MCA FAC 2937* [1]	.1 12
17 Apr 93 ●	REGRET *Centredate Co. NUOCD 1*	.4 7
3 Jul 93	RUINED IN A DAY *Centredate Co. NUOCD 2*	.22 4
4 Sep 93	WORLD (THE PRICE OF LOVE) *Centredate Co. NUOCD 3*	.13 5
18 Dec 93	SPOOKY *Centredate Co. NUOCD 4*	.22 4
19 Nov 94 ●	TRUE FAITH (re-mix) *Centredate Co. NUOCD 5*	.9 8
21 Jan 95	NINETEEN63 *London NUOCD 6*	.21 4
5 Aug 95	BLUE MONDAY (2nd re-mix) *London NUOCD 7*	.17 4
25 Aug 01 ●	CRYSTAL *London NUOCD 8*	.8 4
1 Dec 01	60 MILES AN HOUR *London NUOCD 9*	.29 2
27 Apr 02	HERE TO STAY *London NUOCD 11*	.15 3
15 Jun 02	WORLD IN MOTION (re-issue) *London / MCA NUDOCD 12* [1]	.43 2
30 Nov 02	CONFUSION (re-mix) *Whacked WACKT 002CD* [2]	.64 1
28 Nov 81	MOVEMENT *Factory FACT 50*	.30 10
14 May 83 ●	POWER CORRUPTION AND LIES *Factory FACT 75*	.4 29
25 May 85 ●	LOW-LIFE *Factory FACT 100*	.7 10
11 Oct 86 ●	BROTHERHOOD *Factory FACT 150*	.9 5
29 Aug 87 ●	SUBSTANCE 1987 *Factory FACT 200*	.3 37
11 Feb 89 ★	TECHNIQUE *Factory FACT 275* ■	.1 14
22 Feb 92	BBC RADIO 1 LIVE IN CONCERT *Windsong International WINCD 011*	.33 2

15 May 93 ★	REPUBLIC *London 8284132* ■	...1 19
17 Jul 93	SUBSTANCE 1987 (re-issue) *London 5200082*	...32 2
3 Dec 94 ●	? (THE BEST OF NEW ORDER) / ? (THE REST OF NEW ORDER)	...4 17
	Centredate Co. 8285802	
8 Sep 01 ●	GET READY *London 8573896212*	...6 4

[1] Englandneworder (New Order, Keith Allen, England footballer / rapper John Barnes and the rest of the England World Cup squad)
[2] Arthur Baker vs New Order

Group was male only on first hit. 'Blue Monday's first visit to the chart peaked at No.12, with the first re-entry making No.9 in Oct 1983 and the second peaking at No.52 after re-entry in Jan 1984. 'Blue Monday' in 1988 is a re-mixed version of the original 1983 hit which was made available on seven-inch for the first time, hence the slight difference in catalogue number. Sales for the re-mix and the original were combined from 7 May 1988 onwards when calculating its chart position. Tracks on The Peel Sessions (1st June 1982) EP: Turn the Heater On / We All Stand / Too Late / 5-8-6. From 2 Sep 95 '? (The Best of New Order)' was listed with the re-mix album '? (The Rest of New Order)'

NEW ORLEANS JAZZMEN See Terry LIGHTFOOT'S NEW ORLEANS JAZZMEN

NEW POWER GENERATION (see also PRINCE) *US, male / female vocal / instrumental group (Singles: 64 Weeks, Albums: 3 Weeks)* pos/wks

31 Aug 91 ●	GETT OFF *Paisley Park W 0056* [1]	...4 8
21 Sep 91	CREAM *Paisley Park W 0061* [1] ▲	...15 7
7 Dec 91	DIAMONDS AND PEARLS *Paisley Park W 0075* [1]	...25 6
28 Mar 92	MONEY DON'T MATTER 2 NIGHT *Paisley Park W 0091* [1]	...19 5
27 Jun 92	THUNDER *Paisley Park W 0113* [1]	...28 3
18 Jul 92 ●	SEXY MF / STROLLIN' *Paisley Park W 0123* [1]	...4 7
10 Oct 92 ●	MY NAME IS PRINCE *Paisley Park W 0132* [1]	...7 5
14 Nov 92	MY NAME IS PRINCE (re-mix) *Paisley Park W 0142T* [1]	...51 1
5 Dec 92	7 *Paisley Park W 0147* [1]	...27 6
13 Mar 93	THE MORNING PAPERS *Paisley Park W 0162CD* [1]	...52 3
1 Apr 95	GET WILD *NPG 0061045*	...19 4
19 Aug 95	THE GOOD LIFE (re) *NPG 0061515*	...15 8
21 Nov 98	COME ON *RCA 74321634722*	...65 1
8 Apr 95	EXODUS *NPG 0061032*	...11 3

[1] Prince and the New Power Generation

'The Good Life' peaked at No.29 on its first visit before re-entering at its peak position in Jul 1997

NEW RADICALS *US, male vocalist – Gregg Alexander (Singles: 18 Weeks, Albums: 14 Weeks)* pos/wks

3 Apr 99 ●	YOU GET WHAT YOU GIVE *MCA MCSTD 48111*	...5 17
25 Sep 99	SOMEDAY WE'LL KNOW *MCA MCSTD 40217*	...48 1
17 Apr 99 ●	MAYBE YOU'VE BEEN BRAINWASHED TOO *MCA MCD 11858*	...10 14

NEW RHODES *UK, male vocal / instrumental group (Singles: 1 Week)* pos/wks

7 Aug 04	I WISH I WAS YOU *Moshi Moshi MOSH 11CD*	...63 1

The NEW SEEKERS `352` `Top 500`

UK / Australia, male / female vocal / instrumental group: Keith Potger, Eve Graham, Lyn Paul, Peter Doyle, Paul Layton and Marty Kristian. Hits included a Coca-Cola advertisement and a Eurovision entry. The group sold more than 25 million records worldwide and equalled the eight Top 20 entries by The Seekers. Biggest-selling single: 'I'd Like to Teach the World to Sing' 990,000 (Singles: 143 Weeks, Albums: 49 Weeks) pos/wks

17 Oct 70	WHAT HAVE THEY DONE TO MY SONG MA (re) *Philips 6006 027*	...44 2
10 Jul 71 ●	NEVER ENDING SONG OF LOVE *Philips 6006 125*	...2 19
18 Dec 71 ★	I'D LIKE TO TEACH THE WORLD TO SING (IN PERFECT HARMONY) *Polydor 2058 184*	...1 21
4 Mar 72 ●	BEG, STEAL OR BORROW *Polydor 2058 201*	...2 13
10 Jun 72 ●	CIRCLES *Polydor 2058 242*	...4 16
2 Dec 72	COME SOFTLY TO ME *Polydor 2058 315* [1]	...20 11
24 Feb 73	PINBALL WIZARD – SEE ME, FEEL ME (MEDLEY) *Polydor 2058 338*	...16 8
7 Apr 73	NEVERTHELESS (I'M IN LOVE WITH YOU) *Polydor 2068 340* [2]	...34 5
16 Jun 73	GOODBYE IS JUST ANOTHER WORD *Polydor 2058 368*	...36 5
24 Nov 73 ★	YOU WON'T FIND ANOTHER FOOL LIKE ME *Polydor 2058 421* [3]	...1 16
9 Mar 74 ●	I GET A LITTLE SENTIMENTAL OVER YOU *Polydor 2058 439* [3]	...5 9
14 Aug 76	IT'S SO NICE (TO HAVE YOU HOME) *CBS 4391*	...44 4
29 Jan 77	I WANNA GO BACK *CBS 4786*	...25 4

15 Jul 78	ANTHEM (ONE DAY IN EVERY WEEK) *CBS 6413*	...21 10
5 Feb 72	NEW COLOURS *Polydor 2383 066*	...40 4
1 Apr 72 ●	WE'D LIKE TO TEACH THE WORLD TO SING *Polydor 2883 103*	...2 25
12 Aug 72	NEVER ENDING SONG OF LOVE *Polydor 2383 126*	...35 4
14 Oct 72	CIRCLES *Polydor 2442 102*	...23 5
21 Apr 73	NOW *Polydor 2383 195*	...47 2
30 Mar 74	TOGETHER *Polydor 2383 264*	...12 9

[1] The New Seekers featuring Marty Kristian [2] Eve Graham and The New Seekers [3] The New Seekers featuring Lyn Paul

NEW TONE AGE FAMILY See Dread FLIMSTONE and the MODERN TONE AGE FAMILY

The NEW VAUDEVILLE BAND *UK, male vocal / instrumental group (Singles: 43 Weeks)* pos/wks

8 Sep 66 ●	WINCHESTER CATHEDRAL *Fontana TF 741* ▲	...4 19
26 Jan 67 ●	PEEK-A-BOO *Fontana TF 784* [1]	...7 11
11 May 67	FINCHLEY CENTRAL *Fontana TF 824*	...11 9
2 Aug 67	GREEN STREET GREEN *Fontana TF 853*	...37 4

[1] The New Vaudeville Band featuring Tristram

NEW VISION (see also David MORALES; LEE-CABRERA) *US, male vocal / instrumental duo – Samuel Morales and Albert Cabrerra (Singles: 2 Weeks)* pos/wks

29 Jan 00	(JUST) YOU AND ME *AM:PM CDAMPM 128*	...23 2

NEW WORLD *Australia, male vocal / instrumental group (Singles: 53 Weeks)* pos/wks

27 Feb 71	ROSE GARDEN *RAK 111*	...15 11
3 Jul 71 ●	TOM-TOM TURNAROUND *RAK 117*	...6 15
4 Dec 71	KARA, KARA *RAK 123*	...17 13
13 May 72 ●	SISTER JANE *RAK 130*	...9 13
12 May 73	ROOFTOP SINGING *RAK 148*	...50 1

NEW WORLD THEATRE ORCHESTRA *UK, orchestra (Albums: 1 Week)* pos/wks

24 Dec 60	LET'S DANCE TO THE HITS OF THE 30'S AND 40'S *Pye Golden Guinea GGL 0026*	...20 1

NEW YORK CITY *US, male vocal group (Singles: 11 Weeks)* pos/wks

21 Jul 73	I'M DOIN' FINE NOW *RCA 2351*	...20 11

NEW YORK SKYY *US, male / female vocal / instrumental group (Singles: 2 Weeks)* pos/wks

16 Jan 82	LET'S CELEBRATE (re) *Epic EPC A 1898*	...67 2

The NEWBEATS *US, male vocal group (Singles: 22 Weeks)* pos/wks

10 Sep 64	BREAD AND BUTTER *Hickory 1269*	...15 9
23 Oct 71 ●	RUN, BABY, RUN *London HLE 10341*	...10 13

Booker NEWBERRY III *US, male vocalist (Singles: 11 Weeks)* pos/wks

28 May 83 ●	LOVE TOWN *Polydor POSP 613*	...6 8
8 Oct 83	TEDDY BEAR *Polydor POSP 637*	...44 3

Mickey NEWBURY *US, male vocalist / instrumentalist – guitar – Milton Newbury, b. 19 May 1940, d. 29 Sep 2002 (Singles: 5 Weeks)* pos/wks

1 Jul 72	AMERICAN TRILOGY *Elektra K 12047*	...42 5

NEWCLEUS *US, male rap / instrumental group (Singles: 6 Weeks, Albums: 2 Weeks)* pos/wks

3 Sep 83	JAM ON REVENGE (THE WIKKI WIKKI SONG) *Beckett BKS 8*	44 6
25 Aug 84	JAM ON REVENGE *Sunnyview SVLP 6600*	...84 1

Bob NEWHART *US, male comedian (Albums: 37 Weeks)* pos/wks

1 Oct 60 ●	BUTTON-DOWN MIND OF BOB NEWHART *Warner Bros. WM 4010* ▲	...2 37

Anthony NEWLEY `464` `Top 500` *Acclaimed actor / vocalist and composer, b. 24 Sep 1931, London, UK, d. 14 Apr 1999. He appeared in more than 20 films before his singing career started. He was among the most innovative UK acts of the early rock years before moving into musicals and cabaret (Singles: 130 Weeks, Albums: 24 Weeks)* pos/wks

1 May 59 ●	I'VE WAITED SO LONG *Decca F 11127*	...3 15
8 May 59	IDLE ON PARADE (EP) *Decca DFE 6566*	...13 4

Singles re-entries are listed as (re), (2re), (3re).... which signifies that the hit re-entered the chart once, twice or three times...

12 Jun 59 ●	PERSONALITY *Decca F 11142*	**6**	12
15 Jan 60 ★	WHY *Decca F 11194*	**1**	18
24 Mar 60 ★	DO YOU MIND *Decca F 11220*	**1**	15
14 Jul 60 ●	IF SHE SHOULD COME TO YOU *Decca F 11254* ...	**4**	15
24 Nov 60 ●	STRAWBERRY FAIR *Decca F 11295*	**3**	11
16 Mar 61 ●	AND THE HEAVENS CRIED *Decca F 11331*	**6**	12
15 Jun 61	POP GOES THE WEASEL / BEE BOM *Decca F 11362*	**12**	9
3 Aug 61	WHAT KIND OF FOOL AM I? *Decca F 11376*	**36**	8
25 Jan 62	D-DARLING *Decca F 11419*	**25**	6
26 Jul 62	THAT NOISE *Decca F 11486*	**34**	5
14 May 60	LOVE IS A NOW AND THEN THING *Decca LK 4343*	**19**	2
8 Jul 61	TONY *Decca LK 4406*	**5**	12
28 Sep 63 ●	FOOL BRITANNIA *Ember CEL 902* [1]	**10**	10

[1] Anthony Newley, Peter Sellers, Joan Collins

'Bee Bom' listed together with 'Pop Goes the Weasel' only for weeks of 15 and 22 Jun 1961. It peaked at No.15. Tracks on Idle on Parade (EP): I've Waited So Long / Idle Rock-a-Boogie / Idle on Parade / Saturday Night Rock-a-Boogie

Tara NEWLEY *See E-ZEE POSSEE*

Brad NEWMAN *UK, male vocalist – Charles Thomas, b. 1938, d. 18 Jan 1999 (Singles: 1 Week)* pos/wks

22 Feb 62	SOMEBODY TO LOVE *Fontana H 357*	**47**	1

Dave NEWMAN *UK, male vocalist (Singles: 6 Weeks)* pos/wks

15 Apr 72	THE LION SLEEPS TONIGHT (WIMOWEH) (re) *Pye 7N 45134*	**34**	6

Paul NEWMAN *See CAMISRA; ESCRIMA; PARTIZAN; The GRIFTERS*

The NEWS *UK, male vocal / instrumental group (Singles: 3 Weeks)* pos/wks

29 Aug 81	AUDIO VIDEO *George GEORGE 1*	**52**	3

NEWS *See Huey LEWIS and the NEWS*

NEWTON *UK, male vocalist – William Myers (Singles: 6 Weeks)* pos/wks

15 Jul 95	SKY HIGH *Bags of Fun BAGSCD 6*	**56**	2
15 Feb 97	SOMETIMES WHEN WE TOUCH *Dominion CDDMIN 202*	**32**	3
16 Aug 97	DON'T WORRY *Dominion CDDMIN 206*	**61**	1

Juice NEWTON
US, female vocalist – Judy Newton (Singles: 6 Weeks) pos/wks

2 May 81	ANGEL OF THE MORNING *Capitol CL 16189* ...	**43**	6

Andy NEWTON-LEE *See The CHEEKY GIRLS*

Olivia NEWTON-JOHN `156` `Top 500`
Top female vocalist in the US in the 1970s, b. 26 Sep 1948, Cambridge, UK. This photogenic Australian-raised singer / actress has won numerous pop and country awards and was the first solo female to score a dozen US Top 5 singles (Singles: 234 Weeks, Albums: 112 Weeks) pos/wks

20 Mar 71 ●	IF NOT FOR YOU *Pye International 7N 25543*	**7**	11
23 Oct 71 ●	BANKS OF THE OHIO *Pye International 7N 25568*	**6**	17
11 Mar 72	WHAT IS LIFE *Pye International 7N 25575*	**16**	8
13 Jan 73	TAKE ME HOME COUNTRY ROADS *Pye International 7N 25599*	**15**	13
16 Mar 74	LONG LIVE LOVE *Pye International 7N 25638* ...	**11**	8
12 Oct 74	I HONESTLY LOVE YOU *EMI 2216* ▲	**22**	6
11 Jun 77 ●	SAM *EMI 2616*	**6**	11
20 May 78 ★	YOU'RE THE ONE THAT I WANT *RSO 006* [1] ◆ ▲	**1**	26
16 Sep 78 ★	SUMMER NIGHTS *RSO 18* [2] ◆	**1**	19
4 Nov 78 ●	HOPELESSLY DEVOTED TO YOU *RSO 17*	**2**	11
16 Dec 78 ●	A LITTLE MORE LOVE *EMI 2879*	**4**	12
30 Jun 79	DEEPER THAN THE NIGHT *EMI 2954*	**64**	3
21 Jun 80 ★	XANADU *Jet 185* [3]	**1**	11
23 Aug 80	MAGIC *Jet 196* ▲	**32**	7
25 Oct 80	SUDDENLY *Jet 7002* [4]	**15**	7
10 Oct 81 ●	PHYSICAL *EMI 5234* ▲	**7**	16
16 Jan 82	LANDSLIDE *EMI 5257*	**18**	9
17 Apr 82	MAKE A MOVE ON ME *EMI 5291*	**43**	3
23 Oct 82	HEART ATTACK *EMI 5347*	**46**	4
15 Jan 83	I HONESTLY LOVE YOU (re-issue) *EMI 5360* ...	**52**	4
12 Nov 83	TWIST OF FATE *EMI 5438*	**57**	2
22 Dec 90 ●	THE GREASE MEGAMIX *Polydor PO 114* [1]	**3**	10
23 Mar 91	GREASE – THE DREAM MIX *PWL / Polydor PO 136* [5]	**47**	2
4 Jul 92	I NEED LOVE *Mercury MER 370*	**75**	1

9 Dec 95	HAD TO BE *EMI CDEMS 410* [6]	**22**	4
25 Jul 98 ●	YOU'RE THE ONE THAT I WANT (re-issue) *Polydor 0441332* [1]	**.4**	9
2 Mar 74	MUSIC MAKES MY DAY *Pye NSPL 28186*	**37**	3
29 Jun 74	LONG LIVE LOVE *EMI EMC 3028*	**40**	2
26 Apr 75	HAVE YOU NEVER BEEN MELLOW *EMI EMC 3069* ▲	**37**	2
29 May 76	COME ON OVER *EMI EMC 3124*	**49**	4
27 Aug 77	MAKING A GOOD THING BETTER *EMI EMC 3192*	**60**	1
21 Jan 78	GREATEST HITS *EMI EMA 785*	**19**	9
9 Dec 78	TOTALLY HOT *EMI EMA 789*	**30**	9
31 Oct 81	PHYSICAL *EMI EMC 3386*	**11**	22
23 Oct 82 ●	GREATEST HITS *EMI EMTV 36*	**8**	38
8 Mar 86	SOUL KISS *Mercury MERH 77*	**66**	3
25 Jul 92	BACK TO BASICS – THE ESSENTIAL COLLECTION 1971–1992 *Mercury 5126412*	**12**	6
4 Feb 95	GAIA (ONE WOMAN'S JOURNEY) *D-Sharp DSHLCD 7017*	**33**	4
30 Oct 04	THE DEFINITIVE COLLECTION *Universal TV 05842792*	**11**	9+

[1] John Travolta and Olivia Newton-John [2] John Travolta, Olivia Newton-John and Cast [3] Olivia Newton-John and Electric Light Orchestra [4] Olivia Newton-John and Cliff Richard [5] Frankie Valli, John Travolta and Olivia Newton-John [6] Cliff Richard and Olivia Newton-John

NEXT *US, male vocal trio (Singles: 8 Weeks)* pos/wks

6 Jun 98	TOO CLOSE *Arista 74321580672* ▲	**24**	3
16 Sep 00	WIFEY *Arista 74321790912*	**19**	5

NEXT OF KIN
UK, male vocal / instrumental group (Singles: 6 Weeks) pos/wks

20 Feb 99	24 HOURS FROM YOU *Universal MCSTD 40201*	**13**	4
19 Jun 99	MORE LOVE *Universal MCSTD 40207*	**33**	2

NIAGRA
UK, male / female vocal / DJ / production duo (Singles: 1 Week) pos/wks

27 Sep 97	CLOUDBURST *Freeflow FLOWCD 2*	**65**	1

The NICE *UK, male instrumental group*
(Singles: 15 Weeks, Albums: 38 Weeks) pos/wks

10 Jul 68	AMERICA *Immediate IM 068*	**21**	15
13 Sep 69 ●	NICE *Immediate IMSP 026*	**3**	6
27 Jun 70 ●	FIVE BRIDGES *Charisma CAS 1014*	**2**	21
17 Apr 71 ●	ELEGY *Charisma CAS 1030*	**5**	11

Hector NICHOL *UK, male comedian (Albums: 1 Week)* pos/wks

28 Apr 84	BRAVO JULIET! *Klub KLP 42*	**92**	1

Paul NICHOLAS *UK, male actor / vocalist –*
Paul Beuselinck (Singles: 31 Weeks, Albums: 8 Weeks) pos/wks

17 Apr 76	REGGAE LIKE IT USED TO BE *RSO 2090 185* ...	**17**	8
9 Oct 76 ●	DANCING WITH THE CAPTAIN *RSO 2090 206* ..	**8**	9
4 Dec 76 ●	GRANDMA'S PARTY *RSO 2090 216*	**9**	11
9 Jul 77	HEAVEN ON THE 7TH FLOOR *RSO 2090 249* ...	**40**	3
29 Nov 86	JUST GOOD FRIENDS *K-Tel ONE 1334*	**30**	8

Grandma's Party was an EP featuring Grandma's Party / Flat Foot Floozy / Mr Sax and the Girl / Shufflin' Shoes

Sue NICHOLLS *UK, female actor / vocalist (Singles: 8 Weeks)* pos/wks

3 Jul 68	WHERE WILL YOU BE *Pye 7N 17565*	**17**	8

NICKELBACK *Canada, male vocal / instrumental group –*
leader Chad Kroeger (Singles: 45 Weeks, Albums: 79 Weeks) pos/wks

23 Feb 02	HOW YOU REMIND ME (IMPORT) *Roadrunner 23203323CD*	**65**	2
9 Mar 02 ●	HOW YOU REMIND ME *Roadrunner 23203320* ▲	**4**	21
7 Sep 02 ●	TOO BAD (re) *Roadrunner 20373*	**9**	9
7 Dec 02	NEVER AGAIN *Roadrunner RR 20253*	**30**	2
27 Sep 03 ●	SOMEDAY *Roadrunner RR 20088*	**6**	9
27 Mar 04	FEELIN' WAY TOO DAMN GOOD *Roadrunner RR 39983*	**39**	2
19 Jan 02 ★	SILVER SIDE UP *Roadrunner 12084852*	**1**	67
4 Oct 03 ●	THE LONG ROAD *Roadrunner RR 84002*	**5**	12

Stevie NICKS (see also FLEETWOOD MAC)
US, female vocalist (Singles: 30 Weeks, Albums: 82 Weeks) pos/wks

15 Aug 81	STOP DRAGGIN' MY HEART AROUND *WEA K 79231* [1]	**50**	4
25 Jan 86	I CAN'T WAIT *Parlophone R 6110*	**54**	4
29 Mar 86	TALK TO ME *Parlophone R 6124*	**68**	2
6 May 89	ROOMS ON FIRE *EMI EM 90*	**16**	7
12 Aug 89	LONG WAY TO GO *EMI EM 97*	**60**	2

11 Nov 89	WHOLE LOTTA TROUBLE *EMI EM 114*	.62	2
24 Aug 91	SOMETIMES IT'S A BITCH *EMI EM 203*	.40	4
9 Nov 91	I CAN'T WAIT (re-issue) *EMI EM 214*	.47	2
2 Jul 94	MAYBE LOVE *EMI CDEMS 328*	.42	3
8 Aug 81	BELLA DONNA *WEA K 99169* ▲	.11	16
2 Jul 83	THE WILD HEART *WEA 2500711*	.28	19
14 Dec 85	ROCK A LITTLE *Modern PCS 7300*	.30	22
10 Jun 89 ●	THE OTHER SIDE OF THE MIRROR *EMI EMD 1008*	..3	14
14 Sep 91	TIMESPACE – THE BEST OF STEVIE NICKS *EMI EMD 3595*	.15	6
4 Jun 94	STREET ANGEL *EMI CDEMC 3671*	.16	3
12 May 01	TROUBLE IN SHANGRI-LA *Reprise 9362473722*	.43	2

[1] Stevie Nicks with Tom Petty and the Heartbreakers

NICO *See* VELVET UNDERGROUND

NICOLE *Germany, female vocalist –*
Nicole Hohloch (Singles: 10 Weeks, Albums: 2 Weeks)   pos/wks

8 May 82 ★	A LITTLE PEACE *CBS A 2365*	..1	9
21 Aug 82	GIVE ME MORE TIME *CBS A 2467*	.75	1
2 Oct 82	A LITTLE PEACE *CBS 85011*	.85	2

NICOLE *US, female vocalist – Nicole McLeod (Singles: 9 Weeks)*   pos/wks

28 Dec 85	NEW YORK EYES *Portrait A 6805* [1]	.41	7
26 Dec 92	ROCK THE HOUSE *React 12REACT 12* [2]	.63	1
6 Jul 96	RUNNIN' AWAY *Ore AG 18CD*	.69	1

[1] Nicole with Timmy Thomas [2] Source featuring Nicole

NICOLETTE (see also MASSIVE ATTACK) *UK, female*
vocalist – Nicolette Suwoton (Singles: 1 Week, Albums: 2 Weeks)   pos/wks

23 Dec 95	NO GOVERNMENT *Talkin Loud TLCD 1*	.67	1
10 Aug 96	LET NO-ONE LIVE RENT FREE IN YOUR HEAD *Talkin Loud 5328142*	.36	2

NIGEL & MARVIN *Trinidad, male vocal duo –*
Nigel and Marvin Lewis (Singles: 10 Weeks)   pos/wks

18 May 02 ●	FOLLOW DA LEADER *Relentless RELENT 19CD*	..5	10

NIGHTBREED (see also ANGEL CITY) *Holland, male production*
duo – Aldwin Oomen and Hugo Zentveld (Singles: 1 Week)   pos/wks

9 Oct 04	PACK OF WOLVES *Ram RAMM 52CD*	.45	1

NIGHTCRAWLERS featuring John REID *UK, male / female*
vocal / production group (Singles: 36 Weeks, Albums: 5 Weeks)   pos/wks

15 Oct 94	PUSH THE FEELING ON *ffrr FCD 245* [1]	.22	5
4 Mar 95 ●	PUSH THE FEELING ON (re-mix) *ffrr FCD 257*	..3	11
27 May 95 ●	SURRENDER YOUR LOVE *Final Vinyl 74321283982*	..7	7
9 Sep 95	DON'T LET THE FEELING GO *Final Vinyl 7432129882*	.13	4
20 Jan 96	LET'S PUSH IT *Final Vinyl 74321328142*	.23	4
20 Apr 96	SHOULD I EVER (FALL IN LOVE) *Arista 74321358072*	.34	2
27 Jul 96	KEEP ON PUSHING OUR LOVE *Arista 74321390422* [2]	.30	2
3 Jul 99	NEVER KNEW LOVE *Riverhorse RIVHCD 1* [1]	.59	1
30 Sep 95	LET'S PUSH IT *Final Vinyl 74321309702*	.14	5

[1] Nightcrawlers [2] Nightcrawlers featuring John Reid and Alysha Warren

Maxine NIGHTINGALE *UK, female vocalist (Singles: 16 Weeks)*   pos/wks

1 Nov 75 ●	RIGHT BACK WHERE WE STARTED FROM *United Artists UP 36015*	..8	8
12 Mar 77	LOVE HIT ME *United Artists UP 36215*	.11	8

NIGHTMARES ON WAX *UK, male producer / vocalist / instrumentalist –*
George Evelyn (Singles: 6 Weeks, Albums: 4 Weeks)   pos/wks

27 Oct 90	AFTERMATH / I'M FOR REAL *Warp WAP 6*	.38	5
26 Jun 99	FINER *Warp WAP 123CD*	.63	1
24 Apr 99	CAR BOOT SOUL *Warp WARPCD 61*	.71	2
14 Sep 02	MIND ELEVATION *Warp WARPCD 95*	.47	2

NIGHTWISH
Finland, male / female vocal / instrumental group (Singles: 1 Week) pos/wks

9 Oct 04	WISH I HAD AN ANGEL *Nuclear Blast NB 1336CD*	.60	1

NIGHTWRITERS
US, male vocal / instrumental duo (Singles: 2 Weeks)   pos/wks

23 May 92	LET THE MUSIC USE YOU *Ffrreedom TABX 112*	.51	2

NIKKE? NICOLE!
US, female rapper – Nicole Miller (Singles: 1 Week)   pos/wks

1 Jun 91	NIKKE DOES IT BETTER *Love EVOL 5*	.73	1

Markus NIKOLAI *Germany, male producer (Singles: 1 Week)*   pos/wks

6 Oct 01	BUSHES *Southern Fried ECB 24CD*	.74	1

Kurt NILSEN *Norway, male vocalist (Singles: 3 Weeks)*   pos/wks

29 May 04	SHE'S SO HIGH *RCA 82876610882*	.25	3

NILSSON *US, male vocalist – Harry Nilsson, b. 15 Jun 1941,*
d. 15 Jan 1994 (Singles: 55 Weeks, Albums: 43 Weeks)   pos/wks

27 Sep 69	EVERYBODY'S TALKIN' (2re) *RCA 1876*	.23	15
5 Feb 72 ★	WITHOUT YOU *RCA 2165* ▲	..1	20
3 Jun 72	COCONUT *RCA 2214*	.42	5
16 Oct 76	WITHOUT YOU (re-issue) *RCA 2733*	.22	8
20 Aug 77	ALL I THINK ABOUT IS YOU *RCA PB 9104*	.43	3
19 Feb 94	WITHOUT YOU (2nd re-issue) *RCA 74321193092*	.47	4
29 Jan 72	THE POINT *RCA Victor SF 8166*	.46	1
5 Feb 72 ●	NILSSON SCHMILSSON *RCA Victor SF 8242*	..4	22
19 Aug 72	SON OF SCHMILSSON *RCA Victor SF 8297*	.41	1
28 Jul 73	A LITTLE TOUCH OF SCHMILSSON IN THE NIGHT *RCA Victor SF 8371*	.20	19

'Everybody's Talkin'' made No.50 on its first chart visit, followed by No.23 on first re-entry in Oct 1969 and No.39 on second re-entry in Mar 1970

Charlotte NILSSON *Sweden, female vocalist (Singles: 4 Weeks)* pos/wks

3 Jul 99	TAKE ME TO YOUR HEAVEN *Arista 74321686952*	.20	4

NINA and FREDERIK *Denmark, female / male vocal duo –*
Baroness Nina and Baron Frederik von Pallandt, b. 14 May 1934,
d. 15 May 1994 (Singles: 29 Weeks, Albums: 6 Weeks)   pos/wks

18 Dec 59	MARY'S BOY CHILD *Columbia DB 4375*	.26	1
10 Mar 60	LISTEN TO THE OCEAN (re) *Columbia DB 4332*	.46	2
17 Nov 60 ●	LITTLE DONKEY *Columbia DB 4536*	..3	10
28 Sep 61	LONGTIME BOY *Columbia DB 4703*	.43	3
5 Oct 61	SUCU-SUCU *Columbia DB 4632*	.23	13
13 Feb 60	NINA AND FREDERIK *Pye NPT 19023*	..9	2
29 Apr 61	NINA AND FREDERIK *Columbia COL 1314*	.11	4

The two eponymous albums are different

NINA SKY
US, female vocal duo – Natalie and Nicole Albino (Singles: 11 Weeks) pos/wks

17 Jul 04 ●	MOVE YA BODY *Universal MCSTD 40373*	..6	11

'Move Ya Body' features the uncredited vocals of Jabba

9 BELOW ZERO
UK, male vocal / instrumental group (Albums: 12 Weeks)   pos/wks

14 Mar 81	DON'T POINT YOUR FINGER *A&M AMLH 68521*	.56	6
20 Mar 82	THIRD DEGREE *A&M AMLH 68537*	.38	6

NINE INCH NAILS *US, male vocal / instrumental group –*
leader Trent Reznor (Singles: 15 Weeks, Albums: 13 Weeks)   pos/wks

14 Sep 91	HEAD LIKE A HOLE *TVT IS 484*	.45	4
16 Nov 91	SIN *TVT IS 508*	.35	2
9 Apr 94	MARCH OF THE PIGS *TVT CID 592*	.45	3
18 Jun 94	CLOSER *TVT CIDX 596*	.25	3
13 Sep 97	THE PERFECT DRUG *Interscope IND 95542*	.43	1
18 Dec 99	WE'RE IN THIS TOGETHER *Island 4971402*	.39	2
12 Oct 91	PRETTY HATE MACHINE *TVT ILPS 9973*	.67	1
17 Oct 92	BROKEN *Island IMCD 8004*	.18	3
19 Mar 94 ●	THE DOWNWARD SPIRAL *Island CID 8012*	..9	4
9 Oct 99 ●	THE FRAGILE *Island CIDD 8091* ▲	.10	4
16 Mar 02	AND ALL THAT COULD HAVE BEEN – LIVE *Nothing CID 8113*	.54	1

999 *UK, male vocal / instrumental*
group (Singles: 13 Weeks, Albums: 1 Week)   pos/wks

25 Nov 78	HOMICIDE *United Artists UP 36467*	.40	3
27 Oct 79	FOUND OUT TOO LATE *Radar ADA 46*	.69	2
16 May 81	OBSESSED *Albion ION 1011*	.71	1
18 Jul 81	LIL RED RIDING HOOD *Albion ION 1017*	.59	3
14 Nov 81	INDIAN RESERVATION *Albion ION 1023*	.51	4
25 Mar 78	999 *United Artists UAG 30199*	.53	1

911
UK, male vocal trio – Lee Brennan, Jimmy Constable and Simon 'Spike' Dawbarn (Singles: 94 Weeks, Albums: 26 Weeks)

		pos/wks
11 May 96	NIGHT TO REMEMBER Ginga CDGINGA 1	38 2
10 Aug 96	LOVE SENSATION Ginga CDGINGA 2	21 4
9 Nov 96 ●	DON'T MAKE ME WAIT (re) Ginga VSCDT 1618	10 8
22 Feb 97 ●	THE DAY WE FIND LOVE Virgin VSCDT 1619	4 8
3 May 97 ●	BODYSHAKIN' Virgin VSCDT 1634	3 7
12 Jul 97 ●	THE JOURNEY Virgin VSCDT 1645	3 7
1 Nov 97 ●	PARTY PEOPLE … FRIDAY NIGHT (re) Ginga VSCDT 1658	5 10
4 Apr 98 ●	ALL I WANT IS YOU (re) Virgin VSCDT 1681	4 7
4 Jul 98 ●	HOW DO YOU WANT ME TO LOVE YOU? (re) Ginga VSCDT 1686	10 9
24 Oct 98 ●	MORE THAN A WOMAN (re) Virgin VSCDT 1707	2 13
23 Jan 99 ★	A LITTLE BIT MORE Virgin VSCDT 1719 ■	1 9
15 May 99 ●	PRIVATE NUMBER Virgin VSCDT 1730	3 7
23 Oct 99	WONDERLAND Virgin VSCDT 1755	13 3
8 Mar 97	THE JOURNEY Virgin CDV 2820	13 17
18 Jul 98 ●	MOVING ON Virgin CDV 2852	10 4
6 Feb 99 ●	THERE IT IS Virgin CDV 2873	8 4
6 Nov 99	THE GREATEST HITS AND A LITTLE BIT MORE … Virgin CDV 2899	40 1

9.9
US, female vocal group (Singles: 3 Weeks)

		pos/wks
6 Jul 85	ALL OF ME FOR ALL OF YOU RCA PB 49951	53 3

NINE STORIES See Lisa LOEB and NINE STORIES

NINE YARDS
UK, male vocal group (Singles: 3 Weeks)

		pos/wks
21 Nov 98	LONELINESS IS GONE Virgin VSCDT 1696	70 1
10 Apr 99	MATTER OF TIME Virgin VSCDT 1723	59 1
28 Aug 99	ALWAYS FIND A WAY Virgin VSCDT 1746	50 1

1910 FRUITGUM CO.
US, male vocal / instrumental group (Singles: 16 Weeks)

		pos/wks
20 Mar 68 ●	SIMON SAYS Pye International 7N 25447	2 16

1927
Australia, male vocal / instrumental group (Singles: 6 Weeks)

		pos/wks
22 Apr 89	THAT'S WHEN I THINK OF YOU WEA YZ 351	46 6

98°
US, male vocal group (Singles: 17 Weeks)

		pos/wks
29 Nov 97	INVISIBLE MAN Motown 8607092	66 1
31 Oct 98	TRUE TO YOUR HEART Motown 8608832 [1]	51 1
13 Mar 99	BECAUSE OF YOU Motown 8609012	36 2
11 Mar 00 ●	THANK GOD I FOUND YOU (re) Columbia 6690582 [2] ▲	10 10
11 Mar 00	THE HARDEST THING Universal MCSTD 40228	29 2
2 Dec 00	GIVE ME JUST ONE MORE NIGHT (UNA NOCHE) Universal MCSTD 40243	61 1

[1] 98° featuring Stevie Wonder [2] Mariah Carey featuring Joe and 98°

99TH FLOOR ELEVATORS
UK, male DJ / production duo – Adrian Fusiarski and Clive Latham (Singles: 5 Weeks)

		pos/wks
12 Aug 95	HOOKED Labello Dance LAD 18CD [1]	28 2
30 May 96	I'LL BE THERE Labello Dance LAD 25CD1 [1]	37 2
8 Apr 00	HOOKED (re-mix) Tripoli Trax TTRAX 061CD	66 1

[1] 99th Floor Elevators featuring Tony De Vit

NIO
UK, male vocalist / rapper / producer – Robert Medcalf (Singles: 1 Week)

		pos/wks
23 Aug 03	DO YOU THINK YOU'RE SPECIAL Echo ECSD 132	52 1

NIRVANA
UK, / Ireland, male vocal / instrumental duo (Singles: 6 Weeks)

		pos/wks
15 May 68	RAINBOW CHASER Island WIP 6029	34 6

NIRVANA 148 Top 500
Legendary grunge pioneers: Kurt Cobain (g/v, d. 1994), Krist Novoselic (b), Dave Grohl (d) (founder of Foo Fighters). Notorious Seattle superstars topped US album chart twice before and twice after Cobain's suicide. XFM listeners voted 'Smells Like Teen Spirit' the Greatest Record of All Time (Singles: 36 Weeks, Albums: 318 Weeks)

		pos/wks
30 Nov 91 ●	SMELLS LIKE TEEN SPIRIT DGC DGCS 5	7 6
14 Mar 92 ●	COME AS YOU ARE DGC DGCS 7	9 5
25 Jul 92	LITHIUM DGC DGCS 9	11 6
12 Dec 92	IN BLOOM Geffen GFS 34	28 7
6 Mar 93	OH THE GUILT Touch and Go TG 83CD	12 2
11 Sep 93 ●	HEART-SHAPED BOX Geffen GFSTD 54	5 5
18 Dec 93	ALL APOLOGIES / RAPE ME Geffen GFSTD 66	32 5
5 Oct 91 ●	NEVERMIND DGC DGC 24425 ▲	7 187
7 Mar 92	BLEACH Tupelo TUPCD 6	33 7
26 Dec 92	INCESTICIDE Geffen GED 24504	14 11
25 Sep 93 ★	IN UTERO Geffen GED 24536 ■ ▲	1 43
12 Nov 94 ★	MTV UNPLUGGED IN NEW YORK Geffen GED 24727 ■ ▲	1 40
12 Oct 96 ●	FROM THE MUDDY BANKS OF THE WISHKAH Geffen GED 25105 ▲	4 6
9 Nov 02 ●	NIRVANA Geffen / Polydor 4935232	3 23
4 Dec 04	WITH THE LIGHTS OUT Geffen 9864838	56 1

The listed flip side of 'Oh the Guilt' was 'Puss' by Jesus Lizard 'Nevermind' re-entered the chart in 2004 with the catalogue number Geffen / Polydor DGCD 24425. 'With the Lights Out' is a three-CD and DVD box set of previously unreleased material

NITRO DELUXE
US, male multi-instrumentalist – Lee Junior (Singles: 16 Weeks)

		pos/wks
14 Feb 87	THIS BRUTAL HOUSE (re) Cooltempo COOL 142	47 11
6 Feb 88	LET'S GET BRUTAL (re-mix) Cooltempo COOLX 142	24 5

'Let's Get Brutal' is a re-mixed version of 'This Brutal House'

NITZER EBB
UK, male vocal / instrumental group (Singles: 3 Weeks)

		pos/wks
11 Jan 92	GODHEAD Mute 1MUTE 135T	56 1
11 Apr 92	ASCEND Mute 110MUTE 145	52 1
4 Mar 95	KICK IT Mute LCDMUTE 155	75 1

NIVEA
US, female vocalist – Nivea Hamilton (Singles: 8 Weeks)

		pos/wks
3 Mar 01	DANGER (BEEN SO LONG) Jive 9251722 [1]	28 3
4 May 02	RUN AWAY (I WANNA BE WITH U) / DON'T MESS WITH THE RADIO Jive 9253362	48 1
21 Sep 02	DON'T MESS WITH MY MAN Jive 9254082 [2]	41 2
10 May 03	LAUNDROMAT / DON'T MESS WITH MY MAN (re-mix) Jive 9254822 [3]	33 2

[1] Mystikal featuring Nivea [2] Nivea featuring Brian and Brandon Casey
[3] Nivea featuring Brian and Brandon Casey of Jagged Edge and Mystikal

NO AUTHORITY
US, male vocal group (Singles: 1 Week)

		pos/wks
14 Mar 98	DON'T STOP Epic 6655592	54 1

NO DICE
UK, male vocal / instrumental group (Singles: 2 Weeks)

		pos/wks
5 May 79	COME DANCING EMI 2927	65 2

NO DOUBT 459 Top 500
Critically acclaimed Grammy and World Music Award-winning Californian new wave rock band formed in 1986 and fronted by Gwen Stefani, b. 3 Oct 1969. They won Grammys for 'Hey Baby' and 'Underneath It All', and 'Tragic Kingdom' sold over 15 million worldwide. Stefani, who is married to Gavin Rossdale of Bush, also had solo success in 2004. Best-selling single: 'Don't Speak' 834,000 (Singles: 74 Weeks, Albums: 81 Weeks)

		pos/wks
26 Oct 96	JUST A GIRL Interscope IND 80034	38 2
22 Feb 97 ★	DON'T SPEAK Interscope IND 95515 ■	1 18
5 Jul 97 ●	JUST A GIRL (re-issue) Interscope IND 95539	3 7
4 Oct 97	SPIDERWEBS Interscope IND 95551	16 3
20 Dec 97	SUNDAY MORNING Interscope IND 95566	50 3
12 Jun 99	NEW Higher Ground HIGHS 22CD	30 2
25 Mar 00	EX-GIRLFRIEND Interscope 4972992	23 3
7 Oct 00	SIMPLE KIND OF LIFE Interscope 4974162	69 1
16 Feb 02 ●	HEY BABY Interscope 4976682	2 9
15 Jun 02	HELLA GOOD Interscope 4977362	12 7
12 Oct 02	UNDERNEATH IT ALL Interscope 4977792	18 5
6 Dec 03	IT'S MY LIFE Interscope 9813724	20 7
13 Mar 04	IT'S MY LIFE (re-release) / BATHWATER Interscope 9861993	17 7
18 Jan 97 ●	TRAGIC KINGDOM Interscope IND 90003 ▲	3 44
22 Apr 00	RETURN OF SATURN Interscope 4906382	31 2
16 Feb 02	ROCK STEADY Interscope 4931582	43 6
13 Dec 03 ●	THE SINGLES 1992-2003 Interscope / Polydor 9861382	5 29

Bounty Killer supplied uncredited vocals on 'Hey Baby'

NO MERCY
US, male vocal / instrumental group (Singles: 26 Weeks, Albums: 4 Weeks)

		pos/wks
18 Jan 97 ●	WHERE DO YOU GO Arista 74321401502	2 15
24 May 97 ●	PLEASE DON'T GO Arista 74321481372	4 7

			pos/wks
6 Sep 97	KISS YOU ALL OVER *Arista 7432151452*	16	4
7 Jun 97	MY PROMISE *Arista 74321466902*	17	4

NO ONE DRIVING See NOVACANE vs NO ONE DRIVING

NO REASON *UK, male vocal group (Singles: 1 Week)*

			pos/wks
11 Sep 04	MAN LIKE ME *Mad as Toast TOAST 002*	53	1

NO SWEAT
Ireland, male vocal / instrumental group (Singles: 5 Weeks)

			pos/wks
13 Oct 90	HEART AND SOUL *London LON 274*	64	4
2 Feb 91	TEAR DOWN THE WALLS *London LON 257*	61	1

NO WAY JOSÉ *US, male instrumental group (Singles: 6 Weeks)*

			pos/wks
3 Aug 85	TEQUILA *Fourth & Broadway BRW 28*	47	6

NO WAY SIS
UK, male vocal / instrumental group (Singles: 4 Weeks)

			pos/wks
21 Dec 96	I'D LIKE TO TEACH THE WORLD TO SING *EMI CDEM 461*	27	4

NODDY
Toytown, male animated character / vocalist (Singles: 4 Weeks)

			pos/wks
20 Dec 03	MAKE WAY FOR NODDY *BMG 82876582142*	29	4

NODESHA *US, female vocalist (Singles: 8 Weeks)*

			pos/wks
6 Sep 03	MISS PERFECT *BMG 82876556742* [1]	5	7
1 Nov 03	GET IT WHILE IT'S HOT *Arista 82876559592*	55	1

[1] Abs featuring Nodesha

NOFX *US, male vocal / instrumental group (Albums: 4 Weeks)*

			pos/wks
10 Feb 96	HEAVY PETTING ZOO *Epitaph 864572*	60	1
10 Jun 00	PUMP UP THE VALUUM *Epitaph 65842*	50	1
23 Mar 02	SPLIT SERIES – VOL.3 *BYO BYO 079CD* [1]	75	1
17 May 03	WAR ON ERRORISM *Fat Wreck FAT 657CD*	48	1

[1] Rancid / NOFX

The NOISE NEXT DOOR
UK, male vocal / instrumental trio (Singles: 4 Weeks)

			pos/wks
6 Nov 04	LOCK UP YA DAUGHTERS / MINISTRY OF MAYHEM *Us & Them USTHEMS 10*	12	4

Bernie NOLAN (see also The NOLANS) *Ireland, female actor / vocalist – Bernadette Nolan (Singles: 3 Weeks)*

			pos/wks
6 Mar 04	MACUSHLA *Laurel Bank 4KATECD 1*	38	3

The NOLANS (393 Top 500) *Dublin-born singing sisters, with considerable MOR / pop appeal: Anne, Maureen, Bernadette, Linda and Coleen Nolan. First European act to win the Grand Prize at the prestigious Tokyo Music Festival (1981) (Singles: 90 Weeks, Albums: 84 Weeks)* pos/wks

6 Oct 79	SPIRIT BODY AND SOUL *Epic EPC 7796* [1]	34	6
22 Dec 79 ●	I'M IN THE MOOD FOR DANCING *Epic EPC 8068*	3	15
12 Apr 80	DON'T MAKE WAVES *Epic EPC 8349*	12	11
13 Sep 80 ●	GOTTA PULL MYSELF TOGETHER *Epic EPC 8878*	9	13
6 Dec 80	WHO'S GONNA ROCK YOU *Epic EPC 9325*	12	11
14 Mar 81 ●	ATTENTION TO ME *Epic EPC 9571*	9	13
15 Aug 81	CHEMISTRY *Epic EPC A 1485*	15	8
20 Feb 82	DON'T LOVE ME TOO HARD *Epic EPC A 1927*	14	12
1 Apr 95	I'M IN THE MOOD FOR DANCING (re-recording) *Living Beat LBECD 31*	51	1
20 Jul 78 ●	20 GIANT HITS *Target TGS 502* [1]	3	12
19 Jan 80	NOLANS *Epic EPC 83892*	15	13
25 Oct 80	MAKING WAVES *Epic EPC 10023*	11	33
27 Mar 82 ●	PORTRAIT *Epic EPC 10033*	7	10
20 Nov 82	ALTOGETHER *Epic EPC 10037*	52	8
17 Nov 84	GIRLS JUST WANNA HAVE FUN *Towerbell TOWLP 10*	39	8

[1] The Nolan Sisters [1] The Nolan Sisters

NOMAD *UK, male / female vocal / instrumental duo – Damon Rochefort and Sharon Dee Clarke (Singles: 22 Weeks, Albums: 2 Weeks)* pos/wks

2 Feb 91 ●	(I WANNA GIVE YOU) DEVOTION *Rumour RUMA 25* [1]	2	10
4 May 91	JUST A GROOVE *Rumour RUMA 33*	16	6
28 Sep 91	SOMETHING SPECIAL *Rumour RUMA 35*	73	1
25 Apr 92	YOUR LOVE IS LIFTING ME *Rumour RUMA 48*	60	2
7 Nov 92	24 HOURS A DAY *Rumour RUMA 60*	61	1

25 Nov 95	(I WANNA GIVE YOU) DEVOTION (re-mix) *Rumour RUMACD 75*	42	2
22 Jun 91	CHANGING CABINS *Rumour RULP 100*	48	2

[1] Nomad featuring MC Mikee Freedom

NONCHALANT
US, female vocalist – Tanya Pointer (Singles: 1 Week)

			pos/wks
29 Jun 96	5 O'CLOCK *MCA MCSTD 48011*	44	1

Peter NOONE (see also HERMAN'S HERMITS)
UK, male vocalist (Singles: 9 Weeks)

			pos/wks
22 May 71	OH YOU PRETTY THING *RAK 114*	12	9

NOOTROPIC
UK, male instrumental / production duo (Singles: 1 Week)

			pos/wks
16 Mar 96	I SEE ONLY YOU *Hi-Life 5779832*	42	1

Ken NORDENE See Billy VAUGHN and his Orchestra

NOREAGA See N.O.R.E.

Chris NORMAN See Suzi QUATRO; SMOKIE

NORTH AND SOUTH
UK, male vocal / instrumental group (Singles: 16 Weeks)

			pos/wks
17 May 97 ●	I'M A MAN NOT A BOY *RCA 74321461142*	7	5
9 Aug 97	TARANTINO'S NEW STAR *RCA 74321501242*	18	5
8 Nov 97	BREATHING *RCA 74321528422*	27	2
4 Apr 98	NO SWEAT '98 *RCA 74321562212*	29	4

NORTHERN HEIGHTZ
UK, male / female DJ / production / vocal group (Singles: 3 Weeks) pos/wks

20 Mar 04	LOOK AT US *Iconic CDXIC 002*	29	3

NORTHERN LINE
UK, / South Africa, male vocal group (Singles: 12 Weeks)

			pos/wks
9 Oct 99	RUN FOR YOUR LIFE *Global Talent GTR 002CDS1*	18	4
11 Mar 00	LOVE ON THE NORTHERN LINE *Global Talent GTR 003CDS1*	15	5
17 Jun 00	ALL AROUND THE WORLD *Global Talent GTR 004CDS1*	27	3

NORTHERN UPROAR *UK, male vocal / instrumental group (Singles: 11 Weeks, Albums: 2 Weeks)* pos/wks

21 Oct 95	ROLLERCOASTER / ROUGH BOYS *Heavenly HVN 047CD*	41	2
3 Feb 96	FROM A WINDOW / THIS MORNING *Heavenly HVN 051CD*	17	3
20 Apr 96	LIVIN' IT UP *Heavenly HVN 52CD*	24	2
22 Jun 96	TOWN *Heavenly HVN 54CD*	48	1
7 Jun 97	ANY WAY YOU LOOK *Heavenly HVN 70CD*	36	2
23 Aug 97	A GIRL I ONCE KNEW *Heavenly HVN 73CD*	63	1
11 May 96	NORTHERN UPROAR *Heavenly HVNLP 12CD*	22	2

NORTHSIDE *UK, male vocal / instrumental group (Singles: 12 Weeks, Albums: 3 Weeks)* pos/wks

9 Jun 90	SHALL WE TAKE A TRIP / MOODY PLACES *Factory FAC 268*	50	5
3 Nov 90	MY RISING STAR *Factory FAC 2987*	32	3
1 Jun 91	TAKE 5 *Factory FAC 3087*	40	4
29 Jun 91	CHICKEN RHYTHMS *Factory FACT 310*	19	3

NOT THE 9 O'CLOCK NEWS CAST
(see also Mel SMITH; MR BEAN; SMITH and JONES)
UK / New Zealand, male / female comedians (Albums: 51 Weeks) pos/wks

8 Nov 80 ●	NOT THE 9 O'CLOCK NEWS *BBC REB 400*	5	23
17 Oct 81 ●	HEDGEHOG SANDWICH *BBC REB 421*	5	24
23 Oct 82	THE MEMORY KINDA LINGERS *BBC REF 453*	63	4

Freddie NOTES and the RUDIES
Jamaica, male vocal / instrumental group (Singles: 2 Weeks)

			pos/wks
10 Oct 70	MONTEGO BAY *Trojan TR 7791*	45	2

NOTORIOUS B.I.G. *US, male rapper – Christopher Wallace, b. 21 May 1972, d. 9 Mar 1997 (Singles: 36 Weeks, Albums: 17 Weeks)* pos/wks

29 Oct 94	JUICY *Bad Boy 74321240102*	72	1
1 Apr 95	BIG POPPA *Puff Daddy 74321263412*	63	1
15 Jul 95	CAN'T YOU SEE *Tommy Boy TBCD 700* [1]	43	2
19 Aug 95	ONE MORE CHANCE / STAY WITH ME *Puff Daddy 7432130O782*	34	2

Singles re-entries are listed as (re), (2re), (3re).... which signifies that the hit re-entered the chart once, twice or three times...

3 May 97 ●	HYPNOTIZE *Arista 74321466412* ▲	10	4
9 Aug 97 ●	MO MONEY MO PROBLEMS *Puff Daddy 74321492492* [2] ▲	6	10
14 Feb 98	SKY'S THE LIMIT *Puff Daddy 74321561992* [3]	35	2
18 Jul 98	RUNNIN' *Black Jam BJAM 9005* [4]	15	3
5 Feb 00	NOTORIOUS B.I.G *Puff Daddy / Arista 74321737312* [5]	16	5
31 Jan 04	RUNNIN' (DYING TO LIVE) *Interscope / Polydor 9815329* [6]	17	6
5 Apr 97	LIFE AFTER DEATH *Puff Daddy 78612730112* ▲	23	16
18 Dec 99	BORN AGAIN *Puff Daddy 74321717182* ▲	70	1

[1] Total featuring The Notorious B.I.G. [2] Notorious B.I.G. featuring Puff Daddy and Ma$e [3] Notorious B.I.G. featuring 112 [4] 2Pac and Notorious B.I.G. [5] Notorious B.I.G. featuring Puff Daddy and Lil' Kim [6] Tupac featuring Notorious B.I.G.

The NOTTING HILLBILLIES
(see also DIRE STRAITS) *UK, male vocal / instrumental group – leader Mark Knopfler (Albums: 14 Weeks)* pos/wks

17 Mar 90 ●	MISSING ... PRESUMED HAVING A GOOD TIME *Vertigo 8426711*	2	14

NOTTINGHAM FOREST with PAPER LACE *UK, football team and male vocal / instrumental group (Singles: 6 Weeks)* pos/wks

4 Mar 78	WE GOT THE WHOLE WORLD IN OUR HANDS *Warner Bros. K 17110*	24	6

Heather NOVA
Bermuda, female vocalist (Singles: 1 Week, Albums: 2 Weeks) pos/wks

25 Feb 95	WALK THIS WORLD *Butterfly BFLD 19*	69	1
8 Apr 95	OYSTER *Butterfly BFLCD 12*	72	1
20 Jun 98	SIREN *V2 VVR 1001872*	55	1

Nancy NOVA *UK, female vocalist (Singles: 2 Weeks)* pos/wks

4 Sep 82	NO, NO, NO *EMI 5328*	63	2

NOVACANE vs NO ONE DRIVING
UK, male production group (Singles: 1 Week) pos/wks

15 Jun 02	LOVE BE MY LOVER (PLAYA SOL) *Direction 6727792*	69	1

NOVASPACE *Germany, male production / vocal duo – Felix Gauder and Jessi (Singles: 3 Weeks)* pos/wks

22 Feb 03	TIME AFTER TIME *MoS / Substance SUBS 15CDS*	29	3

Tom NOVY
Germany, male producer – Thomas Reichold (Singles: 8 Weeks) pos/wks

2 May 98	SUPERSTAR *D:disco 74321569352* [1]	32	3
3 Jun 00	PUMPIN *Positiva CDTIV 132* [1]	19	3
2 Sep 00	I ROCK *Rulin RULIN 3CDS* [2]	55	1
4 Aug 01	NOW OR NEVER *Rulin RULIN 14CDS* [3]	64	1

[1] Novy vs Eniac [2] Tom Novy featuring Virginia [3] Tom Novy featuring Lima

NU–BIRTH *UK, male production duo (Singles: 2 Weeks)* pos/wks

6 Sep 97	ANYTIME *XL XLS 85CD*	48	1
6 Jun 98	ANYTIME (re-issue) *Locked On LOX 97CD*	41	1

NU CIRCLES featuring Emma B
UK, male producer – Andy Lysandrou and female vocalist – Emma Blocksage (Singles: 1 Week) pos/wks

8 Feb 03	WHAT YOU NEED (TONIGHT) *East West EW 258CD*	46	1

NU COLOURS
UK, male / female vocal / instrumental group (Singles: 11 Weeks) pos/wks

6 Jun 92	TEARS *Wild Card CARD 1*	55	2
10 Oct 92	POWER *Wild Card CARD 3*	64	1
5 Jun 93	WHAT IN THE WORLD *Wild Card CARDD 4*	57	2
27 Nov 93	POWER (re-mix) *Wild Card CARDD 5*	40	2
25 May 96	DESIRE *Wild Card 5763652*	31	2
24 Aug 96	SPECIAL KIND OF LOVER *Wild Card 5752012*	38	2

NU GENERATION
UK, male producer – Aston Harvey (Singles: 9 Weeks) pos/wks

29 Jan 00 ●	IN YOUR ARMS (RESCUE ME) *Concept CDCON 7*	8	8
21 Oct 00	NOWHERE TO RUN 2000 *Concept CDCON 16*	66	1

NU-MATIC
UK, male instrumental / production duo (Singles: 1 Week) pos/wks

8 Aug 92	SPRING IN MY STEP *XL Recordings XLS 31*	58	1

NU SHOOZ *US, male / female vocal duo – John Smith and Valerie Day (Singles: 17 Weeks, Albums: 8 Weeks)* pos/wks

24 May 86 ●	I CAN'T WAIT *Atlantic A 9446*	2	14
26 Jul 86	POINT OF NO RETURN *Atlantic A 9392*	48	3
14 Jun 86	POOLSIDE *Atlantic WX 60*	32	8

NU SOUL featuring Kelli RICH *US, male / female vocal / instrumental duo – Carnell Newbill and Kelli Richardson (Singles: 2 Weeks)* pos/wks

13 Jan 96	HIDE-A-WAY *ffrr FCD 269*	27	2

NUANCE featuring Vikki LOVE
US, male / female vocal / instrumental group (Singles: 3 Weeks) pos/wks

19 Jan 85	LOVERIDE *Fourth & Broadway BRW 20*	59	3

NUBIAN PRINZ See POWERCUT featuring NUBIAN PRINZ

NUCLEAR ASSAULT
US, male vocal / instrumental group (Albums: 1 Week) pos/wks

7 Oct 89	HANDLE WITH CARE *Under One Flag FLAG 35*	60	1

NUCLEUS *UK, male instrumental group (Albums: 1 Week)* pos/wks

11 Jul 70	ELASTIC ROCK *Vertigo 6360 006*	46	1

NUFF JUICE See D MOB

Ted NUGENT
US, male vocalist / instrumentalist – guitar (Albums: 14 Weeks) pos/wks

4 Sep 76	TED NUGENT *Epic EPC 81268*	56	1
30 Oct 76	FREE FOR ALL *Epic EPC 81397*	33	2
2 Jul 77	CAT SCRATCH FEVER *Epic EPC 82010*	28	5
11 Mar 78	DOUBLE LIVE GONZO! *Epic EPC 88282*	47	2
14 Jun 80	SCREAM DREAM *Epic EPC 86111*	37	4
25 Apr 81	IN 10 CITIES *Epic EPC 84917*	75	1

NUKLEUZ DJ'S (see also DJ NATION)
UK, collection of DJs / producers (Singles: 9 Weeks) pos/wks

24 Aug 02	DJ NATION *Nukleuz NUKF 0440*	40	2
8 Feb 03	DJ NATION – BOOTLEG EDITION (re) *Nukleuz 0468 FNUK*	33	4
15 Nov 03	DJ NATION – HARDER EDITION *Nukleuz 0572 FNUK* [1]	48	3

[1] Various

All releases in this series contain tracks by various combinations of DJ / producers spread across three chart-eligible singles

Gary NUMAN 176 Top 500 (see also Paul GARDINER)
The moody, synthesized sound of London-born Gary Webb first hit the charts in 1979 under the group name Tubeway Army. Four-times chart hit 'Cars' was also the basis of Armand Van Helden's Top 20 hit 'Koochy' in 2000 (Singles: 169 Weeks, Albums: 145 Weeks) pos/wks

19 May 79 ★	ARE 'FRIENDS' ELECTRIC? *Beggars Banquet BEG 18* [1]	1	16
1 Sep 79 ★	CARS *Beggars Banquet BEG 23*	1	11
24 Nov 79 ●	COMPLEX *Beggars Banquet BEG 29*	6	9
24 May 80 ●	WE ARE GLASS *Beggars Banquet BEG 35*	5	7
30 Aug 80 ●	I DIE: YOU DIE *Beggars Banquet BEG 46*	6	7
20 Dec 80	THIS WRECKAGE *Beggars Banquet BEG 50*	20	7
29 Aug 81 ●	SHE'S GOT CLAWS *Beggars Banquet BEG 62*	6	6
5 Dec 81	LOVE NEEDS NO DISGUISE *Beggars Banquet BEG 68* [2]	33	7
6 Mar 82	MUSIC FOR CHAMELEONS *Beggars Banquet BEG 70*	19	7
19 Jun 82 ●	WE TAKE MYSTERY (TO BED) *Beggars Banquet BEG 77*	9	4
28 Aug 82	WHITE BOYS AND HEROES *Beggars Banquet BEG 81*	20	4
3 Sep 83	WARRIORS *Beggars Banquet BEG 95*	20	5
22 Oct 83	SISTER SURPRISE *Beggars Banquet BEG 101*	32	3
3 Nov 84	BERSERKER *Numa NU 4*	32	3
22 Dec 84	MY DYING MACHINE *Numa NU 6*	66	1
9 Feb 85	CHANGE YOUR MIND *Polydor POSP 722* [3]	17	8
25 May 85	THE LIVE EP *Numa NUM 7*	27	4
10 Aug 85	YOUR FASCINATION *Numa NU 9*	46	5
21 Sep 85	CALL OUT THE DOGS *Numa NU 11*	49	2
16 Nov 85	MIRACLES *Numa NU 13*	49	3

		pos/wks
19 Apr 86	THIS IS LOVE *Numa NU 16*	**28** 3
28 Jun 86	I CAN'T STOP *Numa NU 17*	**27** 4
4 Oct 86	NEW THING FROM LONDON TOWN *Numa NU 19* [3]	**52** 3
6 Dec 86	I STILL REMEMBER *Numa NU 21*	**74** 1
28 Mar 87	RADIO HEART *GFM GFM 109* [4]	**35** 6
13 Jun 87	LONDON TIMES *GFM GFM 112* [4]	**48** 2
19 Sep 87	CARS (E REG MODEL) / ARE 'FRIENDS' ELECTRIC? (re-mix)	
	Beggars Banquet BEG 199	**16** 7
30 Jan 88	NO MORE LIES *Polydor POSP 894* [3]	**34** 3
1 Oct 88	NEW ANGER *Illegal ILS 1003*	**46** 2
3 Dec 88	AMERICA *Illegal ILS 1004*	**49** 1
3 Jun 89	I'M ON AUTOMATIC *Polydor PO 43* [3]	**44** 2
16 Mar 91	HEART *IRS NUMAN 1*	**43** 2
21 Mar 92	THE SKIN GAME *Numa NU 23*	**68** 1
1 Aug 92	MACHINE + SOUL *Numa NUM 124*	**72** 1
4 Sep 93	CARS (2nd re-mix) *Beggars Banquet BEG 264CD*	**53** 1
16 Mar 96	CARS (re-issue) (re-mix) *PolyGram TV PRMCD 1*	**17** 3
13 Jul 02	RIP *Jagged Halo JHCD 5*	**29** 2
5 Jul 03	CRAZIER *Jagged Halo JHCDV 6* [5]	**13** 3
9 Jun 79 ★	REPLICAS *Beggars Banquet BEGA 7* [1]	**1** 31
25 Aug 79	TUBEWAY ARMY *Beggars Banquet BEGA 4* [1]	**14** 10
22 Sep 79	THE PLEASURE PRINCIPLE *Beggars Banquet BEGA 10* ■	**1** 21
13 Sep 80 ★	TELEKON *Beggars Banquet BEGA 19* ■	**1** 11
2 May 81	LIVING ORNAMENTS 1979 *Beggars Banquet BEGA 24*	**47** 3
2 May 81 ●	LIVING ORNAMENTS 1979-1980 *Beggars Banquet BOX 1*	**2** 4
2 May 81	LIVING ORNAMENTS 1980 *Beggars Banquet BEGA 25*	**39** 3
12 Sep 81 ●	DANCE *Beggars Banquet BEGA 28*	**3** 8
18 Sep 82 ●	I ASSASSIN *Beggars Banquet BEGA 40*	**8** 6
27 Nov 82	NEW MAN NUMAN – THE BEST OF GARY NUMAN *TV TVA 7*	**45** 7
24 Sep 83	WARRIORS *Beggars Banquet BEGA 47*	**12** 6
6 Oct 84	THE PLAN 1978 *Beggars Banquet BEGA 55*	**29** 4
24 Nov 84	BERSERKER *Numa NUMA 1001*	**45** 2
13 Apr 85	WHITE NOISE – LIVE *Numa NUMAD 1002*	**29** 5
28 Sep 85	THE FURY *Numa NUMA 1003*	**24** 5
8 Nov 86	STRANGE CHARM *Numa NUMA 1005*	**59** 2
3 Oct 87	EXHIBITION *Beggars Banquet BEGA 88*	**43** 3
8 Oct 88	METAL RHYTHM *Illegal ILP 035*	**48** 2
8 Jul 89	AUTOMATIC *Polydor 8395201* [2]	**59** 1
28 Oct 89	SKIN MECHANIC *IRS EIRSA 1019*	**55** 1
30 Mar 91	OUTLAND *IRS EIRSA 1039*	**39** 1
22 Aug 92	MACHINE AND SOUL *Numa NUMACD 1009*	**42** 1
2 Oct 93	BEST OF GARY NUMAN 1978–83	
	Beggars Banquet BEGA 150CD	**70** 1
30 Mar 96	THE PREMIER HITS *PolyGram TV 5311492* [3]	**21** 3
1 Nov 97	EXILE *Eagle EAGCD 008*	**48** 1
21 Oct 00	PURE *Eagle EAGCD 078*	**58** 1
1 Jun 02	EXPOSURE – THE BEST OF GARY NUMAN 1977-2002	
	Jagged Halo JHCD 2	**44** 1

[1] Tubeway Army [2] Gary Numan and Dramatis [3] Sharpe and Numan [4] Radio Heart featuring Gary Numan [5] Gary Numan vs Rico [1] Tubeway Army [2] Sharpe and Numan [3] Gary Numan / Tubeway Army

Tracks on The Live EP: Are 'Friends' Electric? / Berserker / Cars / We Are Glass. 'Living Ornaments 1979-1980' is a boxed set of 'Living Ornaments 1979' and 'Living Ornaments 1980'

NUMBER ONE CUP
US, male vocal / instrumental group (Singles: 1 Week)

		pos/wks
2 Mar 96	DIVEBOMB *Blue Rose BRRC 10032*	**61** 1

José NUÑEZ featuring OCTAHVIA (see also CHOO CHOO PROJECT)
US, male DJ / producer (Singles: 2 Weeks)

		pos/wks
5 Sep 98	IN MY LIFE *Ministry of Sound MOSCDS 126*	**56** 1
5 Jun 99	HOLD ON *Ministry of Sound MOSCDS 130*	**44** 1

Bobby NUNN
US, male vocalist / multi-instrumentalist –
Ulysses Nunn, b. 20 Sep 1925, d. 5 Nov 1986 (Singles: 3 Weeks)

		pos/wks
4 Feb 84	DON'T KNOCK IT (UNTIL YOU TRY IT) *Motown TMG 1323*	**65** 3

NUSH
UK, male instrumental / production duo –
Danny Matlock and Danny Harrison (Singles: 7 Weeks)

		pos/wks
23 Jul 94	U GIRLS *Blunted Vinyl BLNCDX 006*	**58** 1
22 Apr 95	MOVE THAT BODY *Blunted Vinyl BLNCD 012*	**46** 2
16 Sep 95	U GIRLS (LOOK SO SEXY) (re-mix) *Blunted Vinyl BLNCD 13*	**15** 4

NUT
UK, female vocalist (Singles: 4 Weeks)

		pos/wks
8 Jun 96	BRAINS *Epic NUTCD 2*	**64** 1
21 Sep 96	CRAZY *Epic NUTCD 5*	**56** 1
11 Jan 97	SCREAM *Epic NUTCD 6*	**43** 2

NUTTIN' NYCE
US, female vocal group (Singles: 2 Weeks)

		pos/wks
10 Jun 95	DOWN 4 WHATEVA *Jive JIVECD 365*	**62** 1
12 Aug 95	FROGGY STYLE *Jive JIVECD 381*	**68** 1

NUYORICAN SOUL (see also MASTERS AT WORK) US, male
DJ / production group (Singles: 8 Weeks, Albums: 2 Weeks)

		pos/wks
8 Feb 97	RUNAWAY *Talkin Loud TLCD 20* [1]	**24** 4
10 May 97	IT'S ALRIGHT, I FEEL IT! *Talkin Loud TLCD 22* [2]	**26** 2
25 Oct 97	I AM THE BLACK GOLD OF THE SUN *Talkin Loud TLCD 26* [2]	**31** 2
1 Mar 97	NUYORICAN SOUL *Talkin Loud 5344602*	**25** 2

[1] Nuyorican Soul featuring India [2] Nuyorican Soul featuring Jocelyn Brown

Joe NYE *See DNA*

NYLON MOON
Italy, male instrumental duo (Singles: 2 Weeks)

		pos/wks
13 Apr 96	SKY PLUS *Positiva CDTIV 50*	**43** 2

Michael NYMAN
UK, male instrumentalist –
piano (Singles: 2 Weeks, Albums: 15 Weeks)

		pos/wks
19 Mar 94	THE HEART ASKS PLEASURE FIRST / THE PROMISE	
	Virgin VEND 3	**60** 2
12 Feb 94	THE PIANO (FILM SOUNDTRACK) *Venture CDVE 919*	**31** 15

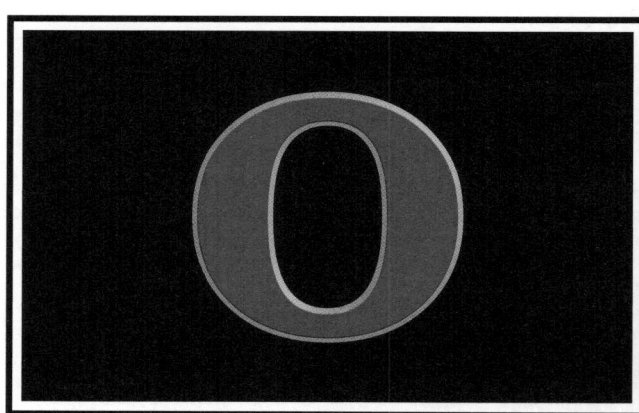

OMC
New Zealand, male vocalist –
Paul Fuemana Lawrence (Singles: 17 Weeks)

		pos/wks
20 Jul 96 ●	HOW BIZARRE *Polydor 5776202*	**5** 16
18 Jan 97	ON THE RUN *Polydor 5732452*	**56** 1

OMD *See ORCHESTRAL MANOEUVRES IN THE DARK*

OPM
US, male vocal / instrumental
group (Singles: 18 Weeks, Albums: 8 Weeks)

		pos/wks
14 Jul 01 ●	HEAVEN IS A HALFPIPE *Atlantic AT 0107CD*	**4** 14
12 Jan 02	EL CAPITAN (re) *Atlantic AT 0118CD*	**20** 4
21 Jul 01	MENACE TO SOBRIETY *Atlantic 7567929772*	**31** 8

O.R.G.A.N.
Spain, male DJ / producer – Vidana Crespo (Singles: 2 Weeks)

		pos/wks
16 May 98	TO THE WORLD *Multiply CDMULTY 34*	**33** 2

O.T. QUARTET *See OUR TRIBE / ONE TRIBE*

O-TOWN
US, male vocal group (Singles: 27 Weeks, Albums: 5 Weeks)

		pos/wks
28 Apr 01 ●	LIQUID DREAMS *J 74321853202*	**3** 10
4 Aug 01 ●	ALL OR NOTHING *J 74321875822*	**4** 10

		pos/wks
3 Nov 01	WE FIT TOGETHER (re) J 74321893692	20 4
23 Feb 02	LOVE SHOULD BE A CRIME J 74321920232	38 2
15 Feb 03	THESE ARE THE DAYS J 82876503052	36 1
18 Aug 01 ●	O-TOWN RCA / J Records 74321882992	7 5

OTT *Ireland, male vocal group (Singles: 18 Weeks)*

		pos/wks
15 Feb 97	LET ME IN Epic 6642052	12 5
17 May 97	FOREVER GIRL Epic 6645082	24 3
23 Aug 97	ALL OUT OF LOVE Epic 6649152	11 4
24 Jan 98	THE STORY OF LOVE Epic OTT 1CD	11 6

O-ZONE
Romania, male vocal trio (Singles: 17 Weeks)

		pos/wks
19 Jun 04 ●	DRAGOSTEA DIN TEI Jive 82876618412	3 17

OAKENFOLD (see also VIRUS) UK, male DJ / producer –
Paul Oakenfold (Singles: 16 Weeks, Albums: 12 Weeks)

		pos/wks
25 Aug 01	PLANET ROCK Tommy Boy TBCD2266 [1]	47 1
22 Jun 02	SOUTHERN SUN / READY STEADY GO Perfecto PERF 17CDS	16 4
31 Aug 02	STARRY EYED SURPRISE Perfecto PERF 27CDS	6 8
22 Feb 03	THE HARDER THEY COME Perfecto PERF 49CDS [2]	38 2
27 Sep 03	HYPNOTISED East West EW 271CD	57 1
6 Jul 02	BUNKKA Perfecto PERFALB 09CD	25 12

[1] Paul Oakenfold presents Afrika Bambaataa and the Soulsonic Force [2] Vocals by Keisha White and Tricky

Philip OAKEY (see also HUMAN LEAGUE) UK, male vocal / instrumentalist – keyboards (Singles: 1 Week, Albums: 5 Weeks)

		pos/wks
22 Sep 84 ●	TOGETHER IN ELECTRIC DREAMS Virgin VS 713 [1]	3 13
26 Apr 03	L.A. TODAY Xtravaganza XTRAV 37CDS [2]	68 1
10 Aug 85	PHILIP OAKEY AND GIORGIO MORODER Virgin V 2351 [1]	52 5

[1] Giorgio Moroder and Phil Oakey [2] Alex Gold featuring Philip Oakey
[1] Philip Oakey & Giorgio Moroder

OASIS (see also Mary HOPKIN and Peter SKELLERN)
UK, male / female vocal / instrumental group – includes Mary Hopkin and Peter Skellern (Albums: 15 Weeks)

		pos/wks
28 Apr 84	OASIS WEA WX 3	23 15

OASIS 28 Top 500

Peerless Manchester-based, Beatles-influenced band: original line-up Liam (v) and Noel (g/v) Gallagher, Gem Archer (g), Andy Bell (b), Alan White (d). The often controversial Britpop group smashed the record for most weeks on the chart in one year (134 in 1996), and in the UK sold 356,000 copies of 'Be Here Now' in one day and a million in a record 17 days. Best-selling single: 'Wonderwall' 966,940 (Singles: 348 Weeks, Albums: 488 Weeks) pos/wks

		pos/wks
23 Apr 94	SUPERSONIC (5re) Creation CRESCD 176	31 14
2 Jul 94	SHAKERMAKER (5re) Creation CRESCD 181	11 15
20 Aug 94 ●	LIVE FOREVER (6re) Creation CRESCD 185	10 18
22 Oct 94 ●	CIGARETTES & ALCOHOL (9re) Creation CRESCD 190	7 35
31 Dec 94 ●	WHATEVER (8re) Creation CRESCD 195	3 50
6 May 95 ★	SOME MIGHT SAY (6re) Creation CRESCD 204 ■	1 27
13 May 95	SOME MIGHT SAY Creation CRE 204T	71 1
26 Aug 95 ●	ROLL WITH IT (3re) Creation CRESCD 212	2 18
11 Nov 95 ●	WONDERWALL (2re) Creation CRESCD 215	2 34
25 Nov 95	WIBBLING RIVALRY (INTERVIEWS WITH NOEL AND LIAM GALLAGHER) Fierce Panda NING 12CD [1]	52 2
2 Mar 96 ★	DON'T LOOK BACK IN ANGER (2re) Creation CRESCD 221 ■	1 24
19 Jul 97 ●	D'YOU KNOW WHAT I MEAN? Creation CRESCD 256 ■	1 18
4 Oct 97 ●	STAND BY ME Creation CRESCD 278	2 18
24 Jan 98 ●	ALL AROUND THE WORLD Creation CRESCD 282 ■	1 9
19 Feb 00 ★	GO LET IT OUT (re) Big Brother RKIDSCD 001 ■	1 12
29 Apr 00 ●	WHO FEELS LOVE? (re) Big Brother RKIDSCD 003	4 8
15 Jul 00 ●	SUNDAY MORNING CALL Big Brother RKIDSCD 004	4 6
27 Apr 02 ★	THE HINDU TIMES Big Brother RKIDSCD 23 ■	1 11
29 Jun 02 ●	STOP CRYING YOUR HEART OUT Big Brother RKIDSCD 24	2 10
5 Oct 02 ●	LITTLE BY LITTLE / SHE IS LOVE Big Brother RKIDSCD 26	2 8
15 Feb 03 ●	SONGBIRD Big Brother RKIDSCD 27	3 10
10 Sep 94 ★	DEFINITELY MAYBE Creation CRECD 169 ■	1 182
14 Oct 95 ★	(WHAT'S THE STORY) MORNING GLORY? Creation CRECD 189 ■	1 145
16 Nov 96	(WHAT'S THE STORY) MORNING GLORY? SINGLES BOX – GOLD Creation CREMG 002	24 3
16 Nov 96	DEFINITELY MAYBE SINGLES BOX – SILVER Creation CREDM 002	23 3
30 Aug 97 ★	BE HERE NOW Creation CRECD 219 ■	1 36
14 Nov 98 ●	THE MASTERPLAN Creation CRECD 241	2 28
11 Mar 00 ★	STANDING ON THE SHOULDER OF GIANTS Big Brother RKIDCD 002 ■	1 29
17 Jun 00	(WHAT'S THE STORY) MORNING GLORY? (re-issue) Big Brother RKIDCD 008	63 9
25 Nov 00 ●	FAMILIAR TO MILLIONS Big Brother RKIDCD 005	5 10
13 Jul 02 ★	HEATHEN CHEMISTRY Big Brother RKIDCD 25 ■	1 43

[1] Oas*s

Chart rules allow for a maximum of three formats; the 12-inch of 'Some Might Say' – already available on CD, 7-inch and cassette – was therefore listed separately. Oasis had a record number of re-entries between 1995 and 1997 as new releases were accompanied by the regular return of singles from their back catalogue

John OATES See Daryl HALL and John OATES

Sam OBERNIK See Tim DELUXE; LINUS LOVES featuring Sam OBERNIK

OBERNKIRCHEN CHILDREN'S CHOIR
Germany, children's choir (Singles: 26 Weeks)

		pos/wks
22 Jan 54 ●	THE HAPPY WANDERER (re) Parlophone R 3799	2 26

OBI PROJECT featuring HARRY, ASHER D and DJ WHAT?
UK, male vocal / rap / production group (Singles: 1 Week) pos/wks

		pos/wks
4 Aug 01	BABY, CAN I GET YOUR NUMBER East West EW 235CD	75 1

OBITUARY
US, male vocal / instrumental group (Albums: 2 Weeks) pos/wks

		pos/wks
18 Apr 92	THE END COMPLETE Roadrunner RC 92012	52 1
17 Sep 94	WORLD DEMISE Roadrunner RR 89955	65 1

Dermot O'BRIEN and his CLUBMEN
Ireland, male vocal / instrumental group (Singles: 2 Weeks) pos/wks

		pos/wks
20 Oct 66	THE MERRY PLOUGHBOY (re) Envoy ENV 016	46 2

Billy OCEAN 194 Top 500 *Top British-based R&B singer / songwriter of the 1980s, b. Leslie Charles, 21 Jan 1950, Trinidad. He waited seven years after scoring his first four UK Top 20 hits before accumulating an impressive run of transatlantic successes, which included three US No.1s. His only UK No.1 was featured in the Michael Douglas movie 'Romancing the Stone' (Singles: 153 Weeks, Albums: 145 Weeks)* pos/wks

		pos/wks
21 Feb 76 ●	LOVE REALLY HURTS WITHOUT YOU GTO GT 52	2 10
10 Jul 76	L.O.D. (LOVE ON DELIVERY) GTO GT 62	19 8
13 Nov 76	STOP ME (IF YOU'VE HEARD IT ALL BEFORE) GTO GT 72	12 11
19 Mar 77 ●	RED LIGHT SPELLS DANGER GTO GT 85	2 10
1 Sep 79	AMERICAN HEARTS GTO GT 244	54 5
19 Jan 80	ARE YOU READY GTO GT 259	42 7
13 Oct 84 ●	CARIBBEAN QUEEN (NO MORE LOVE ON THE RUN) Jive JIVE 77 ▲	6 14
19 Jan 85	LOVERBOY Jive JIVE 80	15 10
11 May 85 ●	SUDDENLY Jive JIVE 90	4 14
17 Aug 85	MYSTERY LADY Jive JIVE 98	49 4
25 Jan 86 ★	WHEN THE GOING GETS TOUGH, THE TOUGH GET GOING Jive JIVE 114	1 13
12 Apr 86	THERE'LL BE SAD SONGS (TO MAKE YOU CRY) Jive JIVE 117 ▲	12 13
9 Aug 86	LOVE ZONE Jive JIVE 124	49 3
11 Oct 86	BITTERSWEET Jive JIVE 133	44 4
10 Jan 87	LOVE IS FOREVER Jive JIVE 134	34 7
6 Feb 88 ●	GET OUTTA MY DREAMS GET INTO MY CAR Jive BOS 1 ▲	3 11
7 May 88	CALYPSO CRAZY Jive BOS 2	35 4
6 Aug 88	THE COLOUR OF LOVE Jive BOS 3	65 3
6 Feb 93	PRESSURE Jive BOSCD 6	55 2
24 Nov 84 ●	SUDDENLY Jive JIP 12	9 59
17 May 86 ●	LOVE ZONE Jive HIP 35	2 32
19 Mar 88 ●	TEAR DOWN THESE WALLS Jive HIP 57	3 13
28 Oct 89 ●	GREATEST HITS Jive BOTV 1	4 15
16 Aug 97 ●	LOVE IS FOR EVER Jive BOCD 2	7 21
15 Feb 03	LET'S GET BACK TOGETHER Jive 9225232	69 1
19 Jun 04	THE ULTIMATE COLLECTION Jive 82876614022	28 4

OCEAN COLOUR SCENE 303 Top 500

Birmingham-based retro-rockers, formed in 1990, include Simon Fowler (v) and Steve Cradock (g). Publicly championed by Paul Weller and Noel Gallagher, whose brother Liam partnered Cradock on a Top 10 hit. They ended the 1990s with nine successive Top 20 singles (Singles: 70 Weeks, Albums: 149 Weeks)

		pos/wks	
23 Mar 91	YESTERDAY TODAY *!Phfft FIT 2*	49	1
17 Feb 96	THE RIVERBOAT SONG *MCA MCSTD 40021*	15	5
6 Apr 96 ●	YOU'VE GOT IT BAD *MCA MCSTD 40036*	7	4
15 Jun 96 ●	THE DAY WE CAUGHT THE TRAIN *MCA MCSTD 40046*	4	11
28 Sep 96 ●	THE CIRCLE *MCA MCSTD 40077*	6	6
28 Jun 97 ●	HUNDRED MILE HIGH CITY *MCA MCSTD 40133*	4	7
6 Sep 97 ●	TRAVELLERS TUNE *MCA MCSTD 40144*	5	5
22 Nov 97 ●	BETTER DAY *MCA MCSTD 40151*	9	5
28 Feb 98	IT'S A BEAUTIFUL THING *MCA MCSTD 40157*	12	4
4 Sep 99	PROFIT IN PEACE *Island CID 757*	13	5
27 Nov 99	SO LOW *Island CID 759*	34	2
8 Jul 00	JULY / I AM THE NEWS *Island CID 763*	31	2
7 Apr 01	UP ON THE DOWN SIDE *Island CID 774*	19	3
14 Jul 01	MECHANICAL WONDER *Island CID 779*	49	1
22 Dec 01	CRAZY LOWDOWN WAYS *Island CID 787*	64	1
21 Jul 03	I JUST NEED MYSELF *Sanctuary SANXD 159*	13	3
6 Sep 03	MAKE THE DEAL *Sanctuary SANXD 219*	35	2
10 Jan 04	GOLDEN GATE BRIDGE *Sanctuary SANXD 244*	40	3
20 Apr 96 ●	MOSELEY SHOALS *MCA MCD 60008*	2	73
21 Sep 96	OCEAN COLOUR SCENE *Fontana 5122692*	54	2
15 Mar 97 ●	B-SIDES SEASIDES & FREERIDES *MCA MCD 60034*	4	14
27 Sep 97 ★	MARCHIN' ALREADY *MCA MCD 60048* ■	1	37
25 Sep 99 ●	ONE FROM THE MODERN *Island CID 8090*	4	11
21 Apr 01 ●	MECHANICAL WONDER *Island CID 8104*	7	4
17 Nov 01	SONGS FOR THE FRONT ROW – THE BEST OF OCEAN COLOUR SCENE *Island CID 8111*	16	4
19 Jul 03	NORTH ATLANTIC DRIFT *Sanctuary SANDP 160*	14	3
13 Sep 03	ANTHOLOGY *Island 9807210*	75	1

OCEANIA *New Zealand / UK, male / female vocal / instrumental group (Albums: 1 Week)*

		pos/wks	
23 Oct 99	OCEANIA *Universal TV / Point Music 5367752*	70	1

OCEANIC *UK, male / female vocal / instrumental group (Singles: 26 Weeks, Albums: 2 Weeks)*

		pos/wks	
24 Aug 91 ●	INSANITY *Dead Dead Good GOOD 4*	3	15
30 Nov 91	WICKED LOVE (re) *Dead Dead Good GOOD 5*	25	5
13 Jun 92	CONTROLLING ME *Dead Dead Good GOOD 14*	14	5
14 Nov 92	IGNORANCE *Dead Dead Good GOOD 22* [1]	72	1
4 Jul 92	THAT ALBUM BY OCEANIC *Dead Dead Good 4509900832*	49	2

[1] Oceanic featuring Siobhan Maher

OCEANLAB *UK, male production trio (Singles: 5 Weeks)*

		pos/wks	
27 Apr 02	CLEAR BLUE WATER *Code Blue BLU 024CD* [1]	48	1
1 May 04	SATELLITE *Nulife 82876614002*	19	4

[1] Oceanlab featuring Justine Suissa

OCEANSIZE
UK, male vocal / instrumental group (Singles: 1 Week)

		pos/wks	
14 Feb 04	CATALYST *Beggars Banquet BBQ 375CD*	73	1

Des O'CONNOR 428 Top 500

Entertainer, comedian and MOR vocalist, b. 12 Jan 1932. This London-based all-rounder toured with Buddy Holly and Lonnie Donegan in the 1950s, had a series of hits in the 1960s and has been a top-rated TV star for over 40 years (Singles: 117 Weeks, Albums: 47 Weeks)

		pos/wks	
1 Nov 67 ●	CARELESS HANDS *Columbia DB 8275* [1]	6	17
8 May 68 ★	I PRETEND *Columbia DB 8397*	1	36
20 Nov 68 ●	ONE, TWO THREE O'LEARY *Columbia DB 8492*	4	11
7 May 69	DICK-A-DUM-DUM (KING'S ROAD) *Columbia DB 8566*	14	10
29 Nov 69	LONELINESS *Columbia DB 8632*	18	11
14 Mar 70	I'LL GO ON HOPING *Columbia DB 8661*	30	7
26 Sep 70	THE TIP OF MY FINGERS *Columbia DB 8713*	15	15
8 Nov 86 ●	THE SKYE BOAT SONG *Tembo TML 119* [2]	10	10
7 Dec 68 ●	I PRETEND *Columbia SCX 6295*	8	10
5 Dec 70	WITH LOVE *Columbia SCX 6417*	40	4
2 Dec 72	SING A FAVOURITE SONG *Pye NSPL 18390*	25	6
2 Feb 80	JUST FOR YOU *Warwick WW 5071*	17	7
13 Oct 84	DES O'CONNOR NOW *Telstar STAR 2245*	24	14
5 Dec 92	PORTRAIT *Columbia 4727302*	63	4
17 Nov 01	A TRIBUTE TO THE CROONERS *UMTV / Decca 4704702*	51	2

[1] Des O'Connor with the Michael Sammes Singers [2] Roger Whittaker and Des O'Connor

Hazel O'CONNOR
UK, female vocalist (Singles: 46 Weeks, Albums: 45 Weeks)

		pos/wks	
16 Aug 80 ●	EIGHTH DAY *A&M AMS 7553*	5	11
25 Oct 80	GIVE ME AN INCH *A&M AMS 7569*	41	4
21 Mar 81 ●	D-DAYS *Albion ION 1009*	10	9
23 May 81 ●	WILL YOU *A&M AMS 8131*	8	10
1 Aug 81	(COVER PLUS) WE'RE ALL GROWN UP *Albion ION 1018*	41	6
3 Oct 81	HANGING AROUND *Albion ION 1022*	45	3
23 Jan 82	CALLS THE TUNE *A&M AMS 8203*	60	3
9 Aug 80 ●	BREAKING GLASS (FILM SOUNDTRACK) *A&M AMLH 64820*	5	38
12 Sep 81	COVER PLUS *Albion ALB 108*	32	7

Sinead O'CONNOR 458 Top 500

(see also MARXMAN; Jah WOBBLE'S INVADERS of the HEART) Distinctive singer / songwriter who never ducked controversy, b. 12 Dec 1966, Glenageary, Ireland. The one time In Tua Nua vocalist was the first Irish woman to top either the UK or US album chart and the first person to refuse to collect Brit or Grammy awards (1991) (Singles: 65 Weeks, Albums: 90 Weeks)

		pos/wks	
16 Jan 88	MANDINKA *Ensign ENY 611*	17	9
20 Jan 90 ★	NOTHING COMPARES 2 U *Ensign ENY 630* ▲	1	14
21 Jul 90	THE EMPEROR'S NEW CLOTHES *Ensign ENY 633*	31	5
20 Oct 90	THREE BABIES *Ensign ENY 635*	42	4
8 Jun 91	MY SPECIAL CHILD *Ensign ENY 646*	42	3
14 Dec 91	SILENT NIGHT *Ensign ENY 652*	60	4
12 Sep 92	SUCCESS HAS MADE A FAILURE OF OUR HOME *Ensign ENY 656*	18	4
12 Dec 92	DON'T CRY FOR ME ARGENTINA *Ensign ENY 657*	53	4
19 Feb 94	YOU MADE ME THE THIEF OF YOUR HEART *Island CID 588*	42	3
26 Nov 94	THANK YOU FOR HEARING ME *Ensign CDENYS 662*	13	7
29 Apr 95	HAUNTED *ZTT ZANG 65CD* [1]	30	2
26 Aug 95	FAMINE *Ensign CDENY 663*	51	1
17 May 97	GOSPEL OAK (EP) *Chrysalis CDCHS 5051*	28	3
6 Dec 97	THIS IS A REBEL SONG *Columbia 6652992*	60	1
24 Aug 02	TROY (THE PHOENIX FROM THE FLAME) *Devolution DEVR 003CDS*	48	1
23 Jan 88	THE LION AND THE COBRA *Ensign CHEN 7*	27	20
24 Mar 90 ★	I DO NOT WANT WHAT I HAVEN'T GOT *Ensign CHEN 14* ■ ▲	1	51
26 Sep 92 ●	AM I NOT YOUR GIRL? *Ensign CCD 1952*	6	6
24 Sep 94	UNIVERSAL MOTHER *Ensign CDCHEN 34*	19	8
22 Nov 97	SO FAR ... THE BEST OF SINEAD O'CONNOR *Chrysalis 8215812*	28	3
24 Jun 00	FAITH AND COURAGE *Atlantic 7567833372*	61	1
19 Oct 02	SEAN NOS NUA *R&M Entertainment RAMCD 001*	52	1

[1] Shane MacGowan and Sinead O'Connor

Tracks on Gospel Oak (EP): This Is to Mother You / I Am Enough for Myself / Petit Poulet / 4 My Love

OCTAHVIA *See Jose NUNEZ featuring OCTAHVIA; CHOO CHOO PROJECT*

OCTAVE ONE featuring Ann SAUNDERSON
US, male production trio and US, female vocalist (Singles: 2 Weeks)

		pos/wks	
16 Feb 02	BLACKWATER *Concept / 430 West CDCON 26*	47	1
28 Sep 02	BLACKWATER (re-mix) *Concept / 430 CDCON 34*	69	1

OCTOPUS
UK / France, male vocal / instrumental group (Singles: 5 Weeks)

		pos/wks	
22 Jun 96	YOUR SMILE *Food CDFOOD 78*	42	2
14 Sep 96	SAVED *Food CDFOODS 84*	40	2
23 Nov 96	JEALOUSY *Food CDFOODS 87*	59	1

Alan O'DAY *US, male vocalist (Singles: 3 Weeks)*

		pos/wks	
2 Jul 77	UNDERCOVER ANGEL *Atlantic K 10926* ▲	43	3

ODETTA *See Harry BELAFONTE*

Daniel O'DONNELL `235` `Top 500`

Britain's top country vocalist who received an MBE in 2002, b. 12 Dec 1961,
County Donegal, Ireland. A popular live performer, who held six of the Top
7 places on the UK country chart (1991), he is only act with at least one hit
album every year since 1988 (Singles: 68 Weeks, Albums: 195 Weeks) pos/wks

12 Sep 92		I JUST WANT TO DANCE WITH YOU *Ritz RITZ 250P*	**20** 7
2 Jan 93		THE THREE BELLS *Ritz RITZCD 239*	**71** 1
8 May 93		THE LOVE IN YOUR EYES *Ritz RITZCD 257*	**47** 3
7 Aug 93		WHAT EVER HAPPENED TO OLD FASHIONED LOVE	
		Ritz RITZCD 262	**21** 5
16 Apr 94		SINGING THE BLUES *Ritz RITZCD 270*	**23** 3
26 Nov 94		THE GIFT *Ritz RITZCD 275*	**46** 3
10 Jun 95		SECRET LOVE *Ritz RITZCD 285* 1	**28** 3
9 Mar 96		TIMELESS *Ritz RITZCD 293* 1	**32** 3
28 Sep 96		FOOTSTEPS *Ritz RITZCD 300*	**25** 5
7 Jun 97		THE LOVE SONGS EP *Ritz RITZCD 306*	**27** 4
11 Apr 98	●	GIVE A LITTLE LOVE *Ritz RITZCD 315*	**7** 5
17 Oct 98		THE MAGIC IS THERE *Ritz RZCD 320*	**16** 4
20 Mar 99		THE WAY DREAMS ARE *Ritz RZCD 325*	**18** 3
24 Jul 99		UNO MAS *Ritz RZCD 326*	**25** 3
18 Dec 99		A CHRISTMAS KISS *Ritz RZCD 330*	**20** 4
15 Apr 00		LIGHT A CANDLE *Ritz RZCD 335*	**23** 4
16 Dec 00		MORNING HAS BROKEN *Ritz RZCD 341*	**32** 4
13 Dec 03		YOU RAISE ME UP *Rosette ROSCD 310*	**22** 4
15 Oct 88		FROM THE HEART *Telstar STAR 2327*	**56** 12
28 Oct 89		THOUGHTS OF HOME *Telstar STAR 2372*	**43** 10
21 Apr 90		FAVOURITES *Ritz RITZLP 052*	**61** 3
17 Nov 90		THE LAST WALTZ *Ritz RITZALP 058*	**46** 7
9 Nov 91		THE VERY BEST OF DANIEL O'DONNELL *Ritz RITZBLD 700*	**34** 14
21 Nov 92		FOLLOW YOUR DREAM *Ritz RITZBLD 701*	**17** 9
6 Nov 93		A DATE WITH DANIEL O'DONNELL LIVE *Ritz RITZBCD 702*	**21** 10
22 Oct 94		ESPECIALLY FOR YOU *Ritz RITZBCD 703*	**14** 11
3 Dec 94		CHRISTMAS WITH DANIEL *Ritz RITZBCD 704*	**34** 5
11 Nov 95		THE CLASSIC COLLECTION *Ritz RITZBCD 705*	**34** 9
6 Apr 96		TIMELESS *Ritz RITZBCD 707* 1	**13** 5
20 Jul 96		IRISH COLLECTION *Ritz RITZCD 0080*	**35** 3
26 Oct 96		SONGS OF INSPIRATION *Ritz RITZBCD 709*	**11** 16
8 Nov 97		I BELIEVE *Ritz RITZBCD 710*	**11** 11
31 Oct 98	●	LOVE SONGS *Ritz RZBCD 715*	**9** 10
2 Oct 99	●	GREATEST HITS *Ritz RZBCD 716*	**10** 8
28 Oct 00	●	FAITH & INSPIRATION *Ritz RZBCD 717*	**4** 10
1 Dec 01		LIVE, LAUGH, LOVE *Rosette ROSCD 2002*	**27** 5
2 Nov 02		YESTERDAY'S MEMORIES *Rosette ROSCD 2020*	**19** 3
22 Mar 03	●	DANIEL IN BLUE JEANS – 20 GREAT ROCK 'N' ROLL	
		LOVE SONGS *DMG DMGTV 001*	**3** 10
25 Oct 03		AT THE END OF THE DAY *Rosette ROSCD 2040*	**11** 6
20 Mar 04	●	THE JUKEBOX YEARS – 20 MORE BLUE JEANS CLASSICS	
		DMG TV DMGTV 005	**3** 8
23 Oct 04	●	WELCOME TO MY WORLD – 20 CLASSICS FROM THE	
		JIM REEVES SONGBOOK *Rosette ROSCD 2050*	**6** 10+

1 Daniel O'Donnell and Mary Duff 1 Daniel O'Donnell and Mary Duff

Tracks on The Love Songs EP: Save the Last Dance for Me / I Can't Stop Loving
You / You're the Only Good Thing / Limerick You're a Lady

Ryan & Rachel O'DONNELL *Ireland, male / female vocal /*
instrumental duo (Albums: 13 Weeks) pos/wks

16 Mar 02	THE CELTIC CHILLOUT ALBUM *Decadance DECTV 001*	**17** 10
22 Mar 03	THE CELTIC CHILLOUT ALBUM 2 *Decadance DECTV 009*	**37** 3

ODYSSEY *US, male / female vocal trio*
(Singles: 82 Weeks, Albums: 32 Weeks) pos/wks

24 Dec 77	●	NATIVE NEW YORKER *RCA PC 1129*	**5** 11
21 Jun 80	★	USE IT UP AND WEAR IT OUT *RCA PB 1962*	**1** 12
13 Sep 80	●	IF YOU'RE LOOKIN' FOR A WAY OUT *RCA 5*	**6** 15
17 Jan 81		HANG TOGETHER *RCA 23*	**36** 7
30 May 81	●	GOING BACK TO MY ROOTS *RCA 85*	**4** 12
19 Sep 81		IT WILL BE ALRIGHT *RCA 128*	**43** 5
12 Jun 82	●	INSIDE OUT *RCA 226*	**3** 11
11 Sep 82		MAGIC TOUCH *RCA 275*	**41** 5
17 Aug 85		(JOY) I KNOW IT *Mirror BUTCH 12*	**51** 4
16 Aug 80		HANG TOGETHER *RCA PL 13526*	**38** 3
4 Jul 81		I'VE GOT THE MELODY *RCA RCALP 5028*	**29** 7
3 Jul 82		HAPPY TOGETHER *RCA RCALP 6036*	**21** 9
20 Nov 82		THE MAGIC TOUCH OF ODYSSEY *Telstar STAR 2223*	**69** 5
26 Sep 87		THE GREATEST HITS *Stylus SMR 735*	**26** 8

Esther and Abi OFARIM
Israel, female / male vocal duo – Esther Zaled and Abraham
Reichstadt (Singles: 22 Weeks, Albums: 24 Weeks) pos/wks

14 Feb 68	★	CINDERELLA ROCKEFELLA *Philips BF 1640*	**1** 13
19 Jun 68		ONE MORE DANCE *Philips BF 1678*	**13** 9
24 Feb 68	●	2 IN 3 *Philips SBL 7825*	**6** 20
12 Jul 69		OFARIM CONCERT – LIVE '69 *Philips XL 4*	**29** 4

Wiston OFFICE *See Frank K featuring Wiston OFFICE*

Kardinal OFFISHALL *See TEXAS*

OFF-SHORE *Germany, male instrumental / production*
duo – Jens Lissat and Peter Harder (Singles: 12 Weeks) pos/wks

22 Dec 90	●	I CAN'T TAKE THE POWER *CBS 6565707*	**7** 11
17 Aug 91		I GOT A LITTLE SONG *Dance Pool 6568257*	**64** 1

The OFFSPRING `407` `Top 500`

Celebrated California based punk pop band formed 1984, fronted by 'Dexter'
Holland (v), b. 29 Dec 1966. 'Smash' sold more than 11 million worldwide and
their No.1 single reportedly had a record 22 million downloads – pretty fly for
a white group (Singles: 64 Weeks, Albums: 106 Weeks) pos/wks

25 Feb 95		SELF ESTEEM *Golf CDSHOLE 001*	**37** 3
19 Aug 95		GOTTA GET AWAY *Out of Step WOOS 2CDS*	**43** 2
1 Feb 97		ALL I WANT *Epitaph 64912*	**31** 2
26 Apr 97		GONE AWAY *Epitaph 64982*	**42** 1
30 Jan 99	★	PRETTY FLY (FOR A WHITE GUY) *Columbia 666802* ■	**1** 11
8 May 99	●	WHY DON'T YOU GET A JOB? *Columbia 6673542*	**2** 8
11 Sep 99		THE KIDS AREN'T ALRIGHT *Columbia 6677632*	**11** 6
4 Dec 99		SHE'S GOT ISSUES *Columbia 6683772*	**41** 2
18 Nov 00	●	ORIGINAL PRANKSTER *Columbia 6699972*	**6** 8
31 Mar 01		WANT YOU BAD (re) *Columbia 6709292*	**15** 9
7 Jul 01		MILLION MILES AWAY *Columbia 6714082*	**21** 4
31 Jan 04		HIT THAT *Columbia 6745475*	**11** 7
5 Jun 04		(CAN'T GET MY) HEAD AROUND YOU *Columbia 6748262*	**48** 1
4 Mar 95		SMASH *Epitaph E 864322*	**21** 34
15 Feb 97		IXNAY ON THE HOMBRE *Epitaph 64872*	**17** 3
28 Nov 98	●	AMERICANA *Columbia 4916562*	**10** 44
25 Nov 00		CONSPIRACY OF ONE *Columbia 4984819*	**12** 18
13 Dec 03		SPLINTER *Columbia 5122013*	**35** 7

OH WELL
Germany, male producer – Ackim Faulker (Singles: 7 Weeks) pos/wks

14 Oct 89	OH WELL *Parlophone R 6236*	**28** 6
3 Mar 90	RADAR LOVE *Parlophone R 6244*	**65** 1

Mary O'HARA
UK, female vocalist / instrumentalist – harp (Albums: 12 Weeks) pos/wks

8 Apr 78	MARY O'HARA AT THE ROYAL FESTIVAL HALL	
	Chrysalis CHR 1159	**37** 3
1 Dec 79	TRANQUILLITY *Warwick WW 5072*	**12** 9

The OHIO EXPRESS
US, male vocal / instrumental group (Singles: 15 Weeks) pos/wks

5 Jun 68	●	YUMMY YUMMY YUMMY *Pye International 7N 25459*	**5** 15

The OHIO PLAYERS
US, male vocal / instrumental group (Singles: 4 Weeks) pos/wks

10 Jul 76	WHO'D SHE COO? *Mercury PLAY 001*	**43** 4

The O'JAYS *US, male vocal group (Singles: 72 Weeks)* pos/wks

23 Sep 72		BACK STABBERS *CBS 8270*	**14** 9
3 Mar 73	●	LOVE TRAIN *CBS 1181* ▲	**9** 13
31 Jan 76		I LOVE MUSIC *Philadelphia International PIR 3879*	**13** 9
12 Feb 77		DARLIN' DARLIN' BABY (SWEET, TENDER, LOVE)	
		Philadelphia International PIR 4834	**24** 6
8 Apr 78		I LOVE MUSIC (re-issue)	
		Philadelphia International PIR 6093	**36** 3
17 Jun 78		USED TA BE MY GIRL *Philadelphia International PIR 6332*	**12** 12
30 Sep 78		BRANDY *Philadelphia International PIR 6658*	**21** 9
29 Sep 79		SING A HAPPY SONG *Philadelphia International PIR 7825*	**39** 6
30 Jul 83		PUT OUR HEADS TOGETHER	
		Philadelphia International A 3642	**45** 5

OK GO *US, male vocal / instrumental group (Singles: 3 Weeks)* pos/wks

22 Mar 03	**GET OVER IT** *Capitol CDR 6603*	**21**	3

John O'KANE *UK, male vocalist (Singles: 4 Weeks)* pos/wks

9 May 92	**STAY WITH ME** *Circa YR 88*	**41**	4

OL' DIRTY BASTARD (see also WU-TANG CLAN) *US, male rapper – Russell Jones, b. 15 Nov 1968, d. 13 Nov 2004 (Singles: 25 Weeks)* pos/wks

27 Jun 98	● **GHETTO SUPASTAR (THAT IS WHAT YOU ARE)** *Interscope IND 95593* [1]	**2**	17
8 Jul 00	**GOT YOUR MONEY** *Elektra E 7077CD* [2]	**11**	8

[1] Pras Michel featuring ODB & introducing Mya
[2] Ol' Dirty Bastard featuring Kelis

OLD SKOOL ORCHESTRA (see also STRETCH 'N' VERN present "MADDOG") *UK, male DJ / production duo (Singles: 1 Week)* pos/wks

23 Jan 99	**B-BOY HUMP** *East West EW 186CD1*	**55**	1

Mike OLDFIELD ⟨48⟩ *Top 500* *Composer / producer / multi-instrumentalist, b. 15 May 1953, Reading, UK. His chart-topping 1973 debut album, 'Tubular Bells', spent five years on the chart, and the belated 'Tubular Bells II' also reached No.1 (1992) (Singles: 113 Weeks, Albums: 551 Weeks)* pos/wks

13 Jul 74	**MIKE OLDFIELD'S SINGLE (THEME FROM TUBULAR BELLS)** *Virgin VS 101*	**31**	6
20 Dec 75	● **IN DULCE JUBILO / ON HORSEBACK** *Virgin VS 131*	**4**	10
27 Nov 76	● **PORTSMOUTH** *Virgin VS 163*	**3**	12
23 Dec 78	**TAKE 4 (EP)** *Virgin VS 238*	**72**	3
21 Apr 79	**GUILTY** *Virgin VS 245*	**22**	8
8 Dec 79	**BLUE PETER** *Virgin VS 317*	**19**	9
20 Mar 82	**FIVE MILES OUT** *Virgin VS 464* [1]	**43**	5
12 Jun 82	**FAMILY MAN** *Virgin VS 489* [1]	**45**	6
28 May 83	● **MOONLIGHT SHADOW** *Virgin VS 586* [2]	**4**	17
14 Jan 84	**CRIME OF PASSION** *Virgin VS 648* [3]	**61**	3
30 Jun 84	**TO FRANCE** *Virgin VS 686* [1]	**48**	7
14 Dec 85	**PICTURES IN THE DARK** *Virgin VS 836* [4]	**50**	6
3 Oct 92	● **SENTINEL** *WEA YZ 698*	**10**	6
19 Dec 92	**TATTOO** *WEA YZ 708*	**33**	5
17 Apr 93	**THE BELL** *WEA YZ 737CD*	**50**	2
9 Oct 93	**MOONLIGHT SHADOW (re-issue)** *Virgin VSCDT 1477*	**52**	2
17 Dec 94	**HIBERNACULUM** *WEA YZ 871CD*	**47**	3
2 Sep 95	**LET THERE BE LIGHT** *WEA YZ 880CD*	**51**	1
22 Nov 97	**WOMEN OF IRELAND** *WEA WEA 093CD*	**70**	1
24 Apr 99	**FAR ABOVE THE CLOUDS** *WEA WEA 206CD1*	**53**	1
14 Jul 73	★ **TUBULAR BELLS** *Virgin V 2001*	**1**	279
14 Sep 74	★ **HERGEST RIDGE** *Virgin V 2013* ■	**1**	17
8 Feb 75	**THE ORCHESTRAL TUBULAR BELLS** *Virgin V 2026* [1]	**17**	7
15 Nov 75	● **OMMADAWN** *Virgin V 2043*	**4**	23
20 Nov 76	**BOXED** *Virgin V BOX 1*	**22**	13
9 Dec 78	**INCANTATIONS** *Virgin VDT 101*	**14**	17
11 Aug 79	**EXPOSED** *Virgin VD 2511*	**16**	9
8 Dec 79	**PLATINUM** *Virgin V 2141*	**24**	9
8 Nov 80	**QE 2** *Virgin V 2181*	**27**	12
27 Mar 82	● **FIVE MILES OUT** *Virgin V 2222*	**7**	27
4 Jun 83	● **CRISES** *Virgin V 2262*	**6**	29
7 Jul 84	**DISCOVERY** *Virgin V 2308*	**15**	16
15 Dec 84	**THE KILLING FIELDS** *Virgin V 2328*	**97**	1
2 Nov 85	**THE COMPLETE MIKE OLDFIELD** *Virgin MOC 1*	**36**	17
10 Oct 87	**ISLANDS** *Virgin V 2466*	**29**	5
22 Jul 89	**EARTH MOVING** *Virgin V 2610*	**30**	5
9 Jun 90	**AMAROK** *Virgin V 2640*	**49**	2
12 Sep 92	★ **TUBULAR BELLS II** *WEA 4509906182* ■	**1**	30
25 Sep 93	● **ELEMENTS – THE BEST OF MIKE OLDFIELD** *Virgin VTCD 18...*	**5**	10
3 Dec 94	**THE SONGS OF DISTANT EARTH** *WEA 4509985812*	**24**	6
7 Sep 96	**VOYAGER** *WEA 630158962*	**12**	5
12 Sep 98	● **TUBULAR BELLS III** *WEA 3984243492*	**4**	7
5 Jun 99	**GUITARS** *WEA 3984274012*	**40**	2
16 Jun 01	**THE BEST OF TUBULAR BELLS** *Virgin CDV 2936*	**60**	2
7 Jun 03	**TUBULAR BELLS 2003** *WEA 2564602042*	**51**	1

[1] Mike Oldfield featuring Maggie Reilly [2] Mike Oldfield with vocals by Maggie Reilly [3] Mike Oldfield featuring Barry Palmer [4] Mike Oldfield featuring Aled Jones, Anita Hegerland and Barry Palmer [1] Mike Oldfield with the Royal Philharmonic Orchestra

Tracks on Take 4 (EP): Portsmouth / In Dulce Jubilo / Wrekorder Wrondo / Sailors Hornpipe. Barry Palmer supplied uncredited vocals on 'Crime of Passion'. 'The Bell' credits Vivian Stanshall

Sally OLDFIELD *UK, female vocalist (Singles: 13 Weeks)* pos/wks

9 Dec 78	**MIRRORS** *Bronze BRO 66*	**19**	13

Misty OLDLAND *UK, female vocalist (Singles: 7 Weeks)* pos/wks

16 Oct 93	**GOT ME A FEELING** *Columbia 6597872*	**59**	2
12 Mar 94	**A FAIR AFFAIR (JE T'AIME)** *Columbia 6601612*	**49**	4
9 Jul 94	**I WROTE YOU A SONG** *Columbia 6603732*	**73**	1

OLGA *Italy, female vocalist (Singles: 1 Week)* pos/wks

1 Oct 94	**I'M A BITCH** *UMM UMM 144UKCD*	**68**	1

OLIVE *UK, male / female vocal / instrumental group – lead vocal Ruth Ann Boyle (Singles: 24 Weeks, Albums: 3 Weeks)* pos/wks

7 Sep 96	**YOU'RE NOT ALONE** *RCA 74321406272*	**42**	4
15 Mar 97	**MIRACLE** *RCA 74321461242*	**41**	2
17 May 97	★ **YOU'RE NOT ALONE (re-issue)** *RCA 74321473232* ■	**1**	13
16 Aug 97	**OUTLAW** *RCA 74321508372*	**14**	4
8 Nov 97	**MIRACLE (re-mix)** *RCA 74321530842*	**41**	1
31 May 97	**EXTRA VIRGIN** *RCA 74321392302*	**15**	3

OLIVER *US, male vocalist – William Swofford, b. 22 Feb 1945, d. 12 Feb 2000 (Singles: 18 Weeks)* pos/wks

9 Aug 69	● **GOOD MORNING STARSHINE (re)** *CBS 4435*	**6**	18

Frankie OLIVER *UK, male vocalist (Singles: 1 Week)* pos/wks

7 Jun 97	**GIVE HER WHAT SHE WANTS** *Island Jamaica IJCD 2011*	**58**	1

OLLIE and JERRY *US, male vocal duo – Ollie Brown and Jerry Knight (Singles: 14 Weeks)* pos/wks

23 Jun 84	● **BREAKIN' ... THERE'S NO STOPPING US** *Polydor POSP 690*	**5**	11
9 Mar 85	**ELECTRIC BOOGALOO** *Polydor POSP 730*	**57**	3

OLYMPIC ORCHESTRA *UK, orchestra (Singles: 15 Weeks)* pos/wks

1 Oct 83	**REILLY** *Red Bus RBUS 82*	**26**	15

The OLYMPIC RUNNERS
UK, male vocal / instrumental group (Singles: 21 Weeks) pos/wks

13 May 78	**WHATEVER IT TAKES** *RCA PC 5078*	**61**	2
14 Oct 78	**GET IT WHILE YOU CAN** *Polydor RUN 7*	**35**	6
20 Jan 79	**SIR DANCEALOT** *Polydor POSP 17*	**35**	6
28 Jul 79	**THE BITCH** *Polydor POSP 63*	**37**	7

The OLYMPICS *US, male vocal group (Singles: 9 Weeks)* pos/wks

3 Oct 58	**WESTERN MOVIES** *HMV POP 528*	**12**	8
19 Jan 61	**I WISH I COULD SHIMMY LIKE MY SISTER KATE** *Vogue V 9174*	**40**	1

OMAR *UK, male vocalist – Omar Hammer (Singles: 18 Weeks, Albums: 14 Weeks)* pos/wks

22 Jun 91	**THERE'S NOTHING LIKE THIS** *Talkin Loud TLK 9*	**14**	7
23 May 92	**YOUR LOSS MY GAIN** *Talkin Loud TLK 22*	**47**	2
26 Sep 92	**MUSIC** *Talkin Loud TLK 28*	**53**	2
23 Jul 94	**OUTSIDE / SATURDAY** *RCA 74321213982*	**43**	2
15 Oct 94	**KEEP STEPPIN'** *RCA 74321233682*	**57**	1
2 Aug 97	**SAY NOTHIN'** *RCA 74321502872*	**29**	2
18 Oct 97	**GOLDEN BROWN** *RCA 74321525422*	**37**	2
14 Jul 90	**THERE'S NOTHING LIKE THIS** *Kongo Dance KDLP 2*	**54**	4
27 Jul 91	**THERE'S NOTHING LIKE THIS (re-issue)** *Talkin Loud 5100211*	**19**	6
24 Oct 92	**MUSIC** *Talkin Loud 5124012*	**37**	2
2 Jul 94	**FOR PLEASURE** *RCA 74321208532*	**50**	1
16 Aug 97	**THIS IS NOT A LOVE SONG** *RCA 74321496262*	**50**	1

OMNI TRIO
UK, male producer – Rob Haigh (Singles: 4 Weeks, Albums: 2 Weeks) pos/wks

7 Jul 01	**THE ANGELS & SHADOWS PROJECT** *Moving Shadow SHADOW 150CD*	**44**	3
26 Jul 03	**RENEGADE SNARES** *Moving Shadow SHADOW 166*	**61**	2
11 Feb 95	**THE DEEPEST CUT VOL.1** *Moving Shadow ASHADOW 1CD*	**60**	1
24 Aug 96	**THE HAUNTED SCIENCE** *Moving Shadow ASHADOW 6CD*	**43**	1

The ONE *UK, male vocal group (Singles: 2 Weeks)* pos/wks

11 Jan 97	**ONE MORE CHANCE** *Mercury MERDD 478*	**31**	2

Michie ONE *See Louchie LOU and Michie ONE*

ONE DOVE (see also Dot ALLISON) *UK, male / female vocal / instrumental group (Singles: 9 Weeks, Albums: 2 Weeks)*

		pos/wks
7 Aug 93	WHITE LOVE *Boy's Own BOICD 14* 43 3	
16 Oct 93	BREAKDOWN *Boy's Own BOICD 15* 24 3	
15 Jan 94	WHY DON'T YOU TAKE ME *Boy's Own BOICD 16* ...30 3	
25 Sep 93	MORNING DOVE WHITE *London 8283522* 30 2	

187 LOCKDOWN (see also REFLEX featuring MC VIPER) *UK, male production duo – Danny Harrison and Julian Jonah (Singles: 16 Weeks)* pos/wks

15 Nov 97	GUNMAN *East West EW 140CD* 16 4	
25 Apr 98 ●	KUNG-FU *East West EW 155CD* 9 5	
25 Jul 98	GUNMAN (re-mix) *East West EW 176CD* 17 4	
3 Oct 98	THE DON *East West EW 180CD* 29 2	
13 Feb 99	ALL 'N' ALL *East West EW 194CD* [1] 43 1	

[1] 187 Lockdown (featuring D'Empress)

1 GIANT LEAP *UK, male production duo – Jamie Catto and Duncan Bridgeman (Singles: 6 Weeks, Albums: 3 Weeks)* pos/wks

20 Apr 02 ●	MY CULTURE *Palm Pictures PPCD 70732* 9 6	
27 Apr 02	ONE GIANT LEAP *Palm Pictures PALMCD 2077* 51 3	

'My Culture' features vocals by Robbie Williams and Maxi Jazz (Faithless)

101 STRINGS *Germany, orchestra (Albums: 35 Weeks)* pos/wks

26 Sep 59 ●	GYPSY CAMPFIRES *Pye GGL 0009* 9 7	
26 Mar 60	THE SOUL OF SPAIN *Pye GGL 0017* 17 1	
16 Apr 60 ●	GRAND CANYON SUITE *Pye GGL 0048* 10 1	
27 Aug 60 ★	DOWN DRURY LANE TO MEMORY LANE *Pye GGL 0061* ...1 21	
15 Oct 83	MORNING NOON AND NIGHT *Ronco RTL 2094* 32 5	

The orchestra was American based for last album

ONE HUNDRED TON AND A FEATHER *See Jonathan KING*

ONE MINUTE SILENCE *UK, male vocal / rap / instrumental group (Singles: 2 Weeks, Albums: 1 Week)* pos/wks

20 Jan 01	FISH OUT OF WATER *V2 VVR 5013213* 56 1	
5 Jul 03	I WEAR MY SKIN *Taste Media TMCDS 5005* 44 1	
22 Apr 00	BUY NOW ... SAVED LATER *V2 VVR 1012362* 61 1	

112 *US, male vocal / instrumental group (Singles: 34 Weeks)* pos/wks

28 Jun 97 ★	I'LL BE MISSING YOU *Puff Daddy 74321499102* [1] ◆ ■ ▲ ...1 21	
10 Jan 98	ALL CRIED OUT *Epic 6652715* [2] 12 5	
14 Feb 98	SKY'S THE LIMIT *Puff Daddy 74321561992* [3] 35 2	
30 Jun 01	IT'S OVER NOW *Puff Daddy / Arista 74321849912* ...22 3	
8 Sep 01	PEACHES & CREAM *Arista 74321882632* 32 3	

[1] Puff Daddy and Faith Evans featuring 112 [2] Allure featuring 112
[3] Notorious B.I.G. featuring 112

ONE THE JUGGLER
UK, male vocal / instrumental group (Singles: 1 Week) pos/wks

19 Feb 83	PASSION KILLER *Regard RG 107* 71 1	

1000 CLOWNS
US, male / female vocal / rap group (Singles: 4 Weeks) pos/wks

22 May 99	(NOT THE) GREATEST RAPPER *Elektra E 3759CD* 23 4	

ONE TRIBE *See OUR TRIBE / ONE TRIBE*

ONE TRUE VOICE
UK, male vocal group (Singles: 14 Weeks) pos/wks

28 Dec 02 ●	SACRED TRUST / AFTER YOU'RE GONE (I'LL STILL BE LOVING YOU) *Ebul / Jive 9201532* 2 9	
14 Jul 03 ●	SHAKESPEARE'S (WAY WITH) WORDS (re) *Ebul / Jive 9201572* 10 5	

ONE 2 MANY *Norway, male / female vocal / instrumental group (Singles: 11 Weeks)* pos/wks

12 Nov 88	DOWNTOWN *A&M AM 476* 65 4	
3 Jun 89	DOWNTOWN (re-issue) *A&M AM 456* 43 7	

ONE WAY *US, male vocal / instrumental group (Singles: 8 Weeks)* pos/wks

8 Dec 79	MUSIC *MCA 542* [1] 56 6	
29 Jun 85	LET'S TALK ABOUT SHHH *MCA 972* 64 2	

[1] One Way featuring Al Hudson

ONE WORLD
UK, male vocal / instrumental group (Albums: 3 Weeks) pos/wks

9 Jun 90	ONE WORLD ONE VOICE *Virgin V 2632* 27 3	

Alexander O'NEAL 〔 221 〕 Top 500

Soulful ex-vocalist with Minneapolis-based Flyte Time (line-up featured star producers Jimmy Jam and Terry Lewis, who worked on most of his hits), b. 15 Nov 1953, Mississippi, US. Co-wrote his biggest hit and clocked up an impressive five Top 20 albums between 1985 and 1993 (Singles: 107 Weeks, Albums: 168 Weeks) pos/wks

28 Dec 85 ●	SATURDAY LOVE *Tabu A 6829* [1] 6 11	
15 Feb 86	IF YOU WERE HERE TONIGHT *Tabu A 6391* 13 10	
5 Apr 86	A BROKEN HEART CAN MEND *Tabu A 6244* 53 4	
6 Jun 87	FAKE *Tabu A 6891* 33 6	
31 Oct 87 ●	CRITICIZE *Tabu 651211 7* 4 14	
6 Feb 88	NEVER KNEW LOVE LIKE THIS *Tabu 651382 7* [2] ...26 7	
28 May 88	THE LOVERS *Tabu 651595 7* 28 4	
23 Jul 88	(WHAT CAN I SAY) TO MAKE YOU LOVE ME *Tabu 652852 7* ...27 5	
24 Sep 88	FAKE '88 (re-mix) *Tabu 652949 7* 16 7	
10 Dec 88	CHRISTMAS SONG (CHESTNUTS ROASTING ON AN OPEN FIRE) /THANK YOU FOR A GOOD YEAR *Tabu 653182 7* ...30 5	
25 Feb 89	HEARSAY '89 *Tabu 654667 7* 56 2	
2 Sep 89	SUNSHINE *Tabu 655191 7* 72 1	
9 Dec 89	HITMIX (OFFICIAL BOOTLEG MEGA-MIX) *Tabu 655504 7* ...19 7	
24 Mar 90	SATURDAY LOVE (re-mix) *Tabu 655680 7* [1] 55 2	
12 Jan 91	ALL TRUE MAN *Tabu 6565717* 18 6	
23 Mar 91	WHAT IS THIS THING CALLED LOVE? *Tabu 6567317* ...53 2	
11 May 91	SHAME ON ME *Tabu 6568737* 71 1	
9 May 92	SENTIMENTAL *Tabu 6580147* 53 2	
30 Jan 93	LOVE MAKES NO SENSE *Tabu AMCD 7708* 26 3	
3 Jul 93	IN THE MIDDLE *Tabu 5877152* 32 3	
25 Sep 93	ALL THAT MATTERS TO ME *Tabu 6577232* 67 1	
2 Nov 96	LET'S GET TOGETHER *EMI Premier PRESCD 11* 38 2	
2 Aug 97	BABY COME TO ME *One World OWECD 1* [2] 56 1	
12 Dec 98	CRITICIZE '98 MIX (re-recording) *One World OWECD 3* ...51 1	
1 Jun 85	ALEXANDER O'NEAL *Tabu TBU 26485* 19 18	
8 Aug 87 ●	HEARSAY / ALL MIXED UP *Tabu 4509361* 4 103	
17 Dec 88	MY GIFT TO YOU *Tabu 463152 1* 53 3	
2 Feb 91 ●	ALL TRUE MAN *Tabu 4658821* 2 16	
30 May 92 ●	THIS THING CALLED LOVE – THE GREATEST HITS OF ALEXANDER O'NEAL *Tabu 4717142* 4 18	
20 Feb 93	LOVE MAKES NO SENSE *Tabu 5495022* 14 4	
4 Sep 04	GREATEST HITS *EMI 5785022* 12 6	

[1] Cherrelle with Alexander O'Neal [2] Alexander O'Neal featuring Cherrelle

'All Mixed Up', a re-mixed album of 'Hearsay' was listed with 'Hearsay' from 15 Jul 89

Shaquille O'NEAL *US, male rapper (Singles: 4 Weeks)* pos/wks

26 Mar 94	I'M OUTSTANDING *Jive JIVECD 349* 70 1	
1 Feb 97	YOU CAN'T STOP THE REIGN *Interscope IND 95522* ...40 2	
17 Oct 98	THE WAY IT'S GOIN' DOWN (T.W.I.S.M. FOR LIFE) *A&M 5827932* 62 1	

ONEHUNDREDPERCENT featuring Jennifer JOHN
UK, male production duo and female vocalist (Singles: 1 Week) pos/wks

25 Dec 04	JUST CAN'T WAIT (SATURDAY) *CR2 CDC2X 005* .....28 1+	

Martin O'NEILL *See LISBON LIONS featuring Martin O'NEILL & CELTIC CHORUS*

ONEPHATDEEVA *See A.T.F.C.*

The ONES *US, male production trio (Singles: 13 Weeks)* pos/wks

20 Oct 01 ●	FLAWLESS (re) *Positiva CDTIV 164* 7 12	
1 Mar 03	SUPERSTAR *Positiva CDTIVS 186* 45 1	

The ONLY ONES *UK, male vocal / instrumental group (Singles: 2 Weeks, Albums: 8 Weeks)* pos/wks

1 Feb 92	ANOTHER GIRL – ANOTHER PLANET *Columbia 6577507* ...57 2	
3 Jun 78	THE ONLY ONES *CBS 82830* 56 1	

		pos/wks
31 Mar 79	EVEN SERPENTS SHINE *CBS 83451*	42 2
3 May 80	BABY'S GOT A GUN *CBS 84089*	37 5

Yoko ONO
Japan, female vocalist (Singles: 45 Weeks, Albums: 57 Weeks) pos/wks

21 Feb 70 ●	INSTANT KARMA *Apple APPLES 1003* [1]	5 9
9 Dec 72 ●	HAPPY XMAS (WAR IS OVER) (4re) *Apple R 5970* [2]	2 26
28 Feb 81	WALKING ON THIN ICE *Geffen K 79202*	35 5
14 Jun 03	WALKING ON THIN ICE (re-mix) *Parlophone CDMINDS 002* [3]	35 2
20 Dec 03 ●	HAPPY XMAS (WAR IS OVER) (re-issue) *Parlophone CDR 6627* [4]	33 3
14 Oct 72	SOMETIME IN NEW YORK CITY *Apple PCSP 716* [1]	11 6
22 Nov 80 ★	DOUBLE FANTASY *Geffen K 99131* [2] ▲	1 36
20 Jun 81	SEASON OF GLASS *Geffen K 99164*	47 2
4 Feb 84 ●	MILK AND HONEY *Polydor POLH 5* [2]	3 13

[1] Lennon, Ono and the Plastic Ono Band [2] John and Yoko and the Plastic Ono Band with the Harlem Community Choir [3] Ono [4] John and Yoko and the Plastic Ono Band [1] John and Yoko Lennon with the Plastic Ono Band and Elephant's Memor [2] John Lennon and Yoko Ono

Ben ONONO See FUTURESHOCK; Saffron HILL featuring Ben ONONO

ONSLAUGHT *UK, male vocal / instrumental group (Singles: 3 Weeks, Albums: 2 Weeks)* pos/wks

6 May 89	LET THERE BE ROCK *London LON 224*	50 3
20 May 89	IN SEARCH OF SANITY *London 828142 1*	46 2

ONYX *US, male rap group (Singles: 8 Weeks, Albums: 3 Weeks)* pos/wks

28 Aug 93	SLAM *Columbia 6596302*	31 4
27 Nov 93	THROW YA GUNZ *Columbia 6598312*	34 3
20 Feb 99	ROC-IN-IT *Independiente ISOM 21MS* [1]	59 1
4 Sep 93	BACDAFUCUP *Columbia 4729802*	59 3

[1] Deejay Punk-Roc vs Onyx

ONYX featuring Gemma J
UK, male production duo and female vocalist (Singles: 1 Week) pos/wks

11 Dec 04	EVERY LITTLE TIME *Data DATA 78CDS*	66 1

ONYX STONE See ROUND SOUND presents ONYX STONE & MC MALIBU

OO LA LA
UK, male vocal / instrumental group (Singles: 2 Weeks) pos/wks

5 Sep 92	OO ... AH ... CANTONA *North Speed OOAH 1*	64 2

OOBERMAN
UK, male / female vocal / instrumental group (Singles: 5 Weeks) pos/wks

8 May 99	BLOSSOMS FALLING *Independiente ISOM 26MS*	39 2
17 Jul 99	MILLION SUNS *Independiente ISOM 30MS*	43 1
23 Oct 99	TEARS FROM A WILLOW *Independiente ISOM 37MS*	63 1
8 Apr 00	SHORLEY WALL *Independiente ISOM 41MS*	47 1

OOE See COLUMBO featuring OOE

The OPEN *UK, male vocal / instrumental group (Singles: 3 Weeks, Albums: 1 Week)* pos/wks

13 Mar 04	CLOSE MY EYES *Logic / Polydor 9817294*	46 1
3 Jul 04	JUST WANT TO LIVE *Loog / Polydor 9866489*	52 1
11 Sep 04	ELEVATION *Loog / Polydor 9867495*	54 1
13 Nov 04	NEVER ENOUGH *Loog / Polydor 9868779*	53 1
17 Jul 04	THE SILENT HOURS *Loog / Polydor 9866160*	72 1

OPEN ARMS featuring ROWETTA
UK, male / female vocal / instrumental group (Singles: 1 Week) pos/wks

15 Jun 96	HEY MR DJ *All Around the World CDGLOBE 136*	62 1

OPERABABES *UK, female vocal duo – Karen England and Rebecca Knight (Singles: 1 Week, Albums: 6 Weeks)* pos/wks

6 Jul 02	ONE FINE DAY *Sony Classical 6727062*	54 1
8 Jun 02	BEYOND IMAGINATION *Sony Classical SK 89916*	24 6

OPTICAL See Ed RUSH & OPTICAL / UNIVERSAL PROJECT

OPTIMYSTIC
UK, male / female vocal group (Singles: 6 Weeks) pos/wks

17 Sep 94	CAUGHT UP IN MY HEART *WEA YZ 841CD*	49 3
10 Dec 94	NOTHING BUT LOVE *WEA 864CD1*	37 2
13 May 95	BEST THING IN THE WORLD *WEA YZ 920CD*	70 1

OPUS
Austria, male vocal / instrumental group (Singles: 15 Weeks) pos/wks

15 Jun 85 ●	LIVE IS LIFE *Polydor POSP 743*	6 15

OPUS III
UK, male / female vocal / instrumental group (Singles: 10 Weeks) pos/wks

22 Feb 92 ●	IT'S A FINE DAY *PWL International PWL 215*	5 8
27 Jun 92	I TALK TO THE WIND *PWL International PWL 235*	52 1
11 Jun 94	WHEN YOU MADE THE MOUNTAIN *PWL International PWCD 302*	71 1

ORANGE *UK, male vocal / instrumental group (Singles: 1 Week)* pos/wks

8 Oct 94	JUDY OVER THE RAINBOW *Chrysalis CDCHS 5012*	73 1

ORANGE JUICE (see also Edwyn COLLINS) *UK, male vocal / instrumental group (Singles: 34 Weeks, Albums: 18 Weeks)* pos/wks

7 Nov 81	L.O.V.E. ... LOVE *Polydor POSP 357*	65 2
30 Jan 82	FELICITY *Polydor POSP 386*	63 3
21 Aug 82	TWO HEARTS TOGETHER / HOKOYO *Polydor POSP 470*	60 2
23 Oct 82	I CAN'T HELP MYSELF *Polydor POSP 522*	42 3
19 Feb 83 ●	RIP IT UP *Polydor POSP 547*	8 11
4 Jun 83	FLESH OF MY FLESH *Polydor OJ 4*	41 6
25 Feb 84	BRIDGE *Polydor OJ 5*	67 2
12 May 84	WHAT PRESENCE? *Polydor OJ 6*	47 4
27 Oct 84	LEAN PERIOD *Polydor OJ 7*	74 1
6 Mar 82	YOU CAN'T HIDE YOUR LOVE FOREVER *Polydor POLS 1057*	21 6
20 Nov 82	RIP IT UP *Holden Caulfield Universal POLS 1076*	39 8
10 Mar 84	TEXAS FEVER *Polydor OJMLP 1*	34 4

The ORB *UK, male instrumental / production duo – Dr Alex Paterson and Kris Weston (Singles: 32 Weeks, Albums: 28 Weeks)* pos/wks

15 Jun 91	PERPETUAL DAWN (re) *Big Life BLRD 46*	18 6
20 Jun 92 ●	BLUE ROOM *Big Life BLRT 75*	8 6
17 Oct 92	ASSASSIN *Big Life BLRT 81*	12 5
13 Nov 93	LITTLE FLUFFY CLOUDS *Big Life BLRD 98*	10 5
27 May 95	OXBOW LAKES *Island CID 609*	38 2
8 Feb 97 ●	TOXYGENE *Island CID 652*	4 4
24 May 97	ASYLUM *Island CID 657*	20 2
24 Feb 01	ONCE MORE *Island CID 767*	38 2
27 Apr 91	ORB'S ADVENTURES BEYOND THE ULTRAWORLD *Big Life BLRDLP 5*	29 5
18 Jul 92 ★	U.F. ORB *Big Life BLRCD 18* ■	1 9
4 Dec 93	LIVE 93 *Island CIDD 8022*	23 2
25 Jun 94 ●	POMME FRITZ *Inter-Modo ORBCD 1*	6 4
1 Apr 95	ORBVS TERRARVM *Island CIDX 8037*	20 3
8 Mar 97	ORBLIVION *Island CID 8055*	19 3
17 Oct 98	U.F.OFF – THE BEST OF THE ORB *Island CID 8078*	38 2

'Perpetual Dawn' made No.61 on its original visit to the chart before re-entering in Feb 1994 and making its peak position

Roy ORBISON `59` `Top 500` Unmistakable vocalist, b. 23 Apr 1936, Texas, US, d. 6 Dec 1988. The "Big O" recorded for the legendary Sun label in the mid-1950s, and was the most popular US singer in Britain during the Beat Boom era (1963-65), when The Beatles supported him on tour. The performer, whose trademark was his dark glasses, had a hit span of 44 years and was enjoying a successful comeback, both as a soloist and member of the Traveling Wilburys, when he died. This multi-award-winner is in the Grammy Hall of Fame as well as the Songwriters' and Rock and Roll Halls of Fame
(Singles: 345 Weeks, Albums: 248 Weeks) pos/wks

28 Jul 60 ★	ONLY THE LONELY (KNOW HOW I FEEL) (re) *London HLU 9149*	1 24
27 Oct 60	BLUE ANGEL *London HLU 9207*	11 16
25 May 61 ●	RUNNING SCARED *London HLU 9342* ▲	9 15
21 Sep 61	CRYIN' *London HLU 9405*	25 9
8 Mar 62 ●	DREAM BABY *London HLU 9511*	2 14
28 Jun 62	THE CROWD *London HLU 9561*	40 4
8 Nov 62	WORKIN' FOR THE MAN *London HLU 9607*	50 1

Singles re-entries are listed as (re), (2re), (3re).... which signifies that the hit re-entered the chart once, twice or three times...

28 Feb 63 ●	IN DREAMS *London HLU 9676*	6	23
30 May 63 ●	FALLING *London HLU 9727*	9	11
19 Sep 63 ●	BLUE BAYOU / MEAN WOMAN BLUES *London HLU 9777*	3	19
20 Feb 64	BORNE ON THE WIND *London HLU 9845*	15	10
30 Apr 64 ★	IT'S OVER *London HLU 9882*	1	18
10 Sep 64 ★	OH, PRETTY WOMAN *London HLU 9919* ▲	1	18
19 Nov 64 ●	PRETTY PAPER *London HLU 9930*	6	11
11 Feb 65	GOODNIGHT *London HLU 9951*	14	9
22 Jul 65	(SAY) YOU'RE MY GIRL *London HLU 9978*	23	8
9 Sep 65	RIDE AWAY *London HLU 9986*	34	6
4 Nov 65	CRAWLING BACK *London HLU 10000*	19	9
27 Jan 66	BREAKIN' UP IS BREAKIN' MY HEART *London HLU 10015*	22	6
7 Apr 66	TWINKLE TOES *London HLU 10034*	29	5
16 Jun 66	LANA *London HLU 10051*	15	9
18 Aug 66 ●	TOO SOON TO KNOW *London HLU 10067*	3	17
1 Dec 66	THERE WON'T BE MANY COMING HOME *London HLU 10096*	12	9
23 Feb 67	SO GOOD *London HLU 10113*	32	6
24 Jul 68	WALK ON *London HLU 10206*	39	10
25 Sep 68	HEARTACHE *London HLU 10222*	44	4
30 Apr 69	MY FRIEND *London HLU 10261*	35	4
13 Sep 69	PENNY ARCADE (re) *London HLU 10285*	27	14
14 Jan 89 ●	YOU GOT IT *Virgin VS 1166*	3	10
1 Apr 89	SHE'S A MYSTERY TO ME *Virgin VS 1173*	27	5
4 Jul 92 ●	I DROVE ALL NIGHT *MCA MCS 1652*	7	10
22 Aug 92	CRYING *Virgin America VUS 63* [1]	13	6
7 Nov 92	HEARTBREAK RADIO *Virgin America VUS 68*	36	3
13 Nov 93	I DROVE ALL NIGHT (re-issue) *Virgin America VUSCD 79*	47	1
8 Jun 63	LONELY AND BLUE *London HAU 2342*	15	8
29 Jun 63	CRYING *London HAU 2437*	17	3
30 Nov 63 ●	IN DREAMS *London HAU 8108*	6	57
25 Jul 64	THE EXCITING SOUNDS OF ROY ORBISON *Ember NR 5013*	17	2
5 Dec 64 ●	OH PRETTY WOMAN *London HAU 8207*	4	16
25 Sep 65 ●	THERE IS ONLY ONE ROY ORBISON *London HAU 8252*	10	11
26 Feb 66	THE ORBISON WAY *London HAU 8279*	11	10
24 Sep 66	THE CLASSIC ROY ORBISON *London HAU 8297*	12	8
22 Jul 67	ORBISONGS *Monument SMO 5004*	40	1
30 Sep 67	ROY ORBISON'S GREATEST HITS *Monument SMO 5007*	40	1
27 Jan 73	ALL-TIME GREATEST HITS *Monument MNT 67290*	39	3
29 Nov 75 ★	THE BEST OF ROY ORBISON *Arcade ADEP 19*	1	20
18 Jul 81	GOLDEN DAYS *CBS 10026*	63	1
4 Jul 87	IN DREAMS: THE GREATEST HITS *Virgin VGD 3514*	86	2
29 Oct 88 ★	THE LEGENDARY ROY ORBISON *Telstar STAR 2330*	1	38
11 Feb 89 ●	MYSTERY GIRL *Virgin V 2576*	2	23
25 Nov 89	A BLACK AND WHITE NIGHT *Virgin V 2601*	51	3
2 Nov 90	BALLADS – 22 CLASSIC LOVE SONGS *Telstar STAR 2441*	38	10
28 Nov 92	KING OF HEARTS *Virgin America CDVUS 58*	23	4
16 Nov 96	THE VERY BEST OF ROY ORBISON *Virgin CDV 2804*	18	11
10 Feb 01 ●	LOVE SONGS *Virgin VTDCD 360*	4	10
14 Aug 04	THE PLATINUM COLLECTION *Virgin / EMI VTDCDX 632*	16	5

[1] Roy Orbison (duet with kd lang)

William ORBIT (see also BASS-O-MATIC) UK, male producer – William Wainwright (Singles: 29 Weeks, Albums: 14 Weeks)

		pos/wks	
26 Jun 93	WATER FROM A VINE LEAF *Guerilla VSCDT 1465*	59	1
18 Dec 99 ●	BARBER'S ADAGIO FOR STRINGS (re) *WEA WEA 247CD*	4	15
6 May 00	RAVEL'S PAVANE POUR UNE INFANTE DEFUNTE *WEA WEA 269CD*	31	2
19 Jul 03 ●	FEEL GOOD TIME *Columbia 6741062* [1]	3	11
29 Jan 00 ●	PIECES IN A MODERN STYLE *WEA 3984289572*	2	14

[1] Pink featuring William Orbit

ORBITAL UK, male instrumental duo – Paul and Phil Hartnoll (Singles: 58 Weeks, Albums: 37 Weeks)

		pos/wks	
24 Mar 90	CHIME *ffrr F B5*	17	7
22 Sep 90	OMEN *ffrr F 145*	46	3
19 Jan 91	SATAN *ffrr FX 149*	31	4
15 Feb 92	MUTATIONS (EP) *ffrr FCD 181*	24	3
26 Sep 92	RADICCIO (EP) *Internal LIARX 1*	37	2
21 Aug 93	LUSH *Internal LIECD 7*	43	2
24 Sep 94	ARE WE HERE *Internal LIECD 15*	33	2
27 May 95	BELFAST *Volume VOLCD 1*	53	1
27 Apr 96	THE BOX *Internal LIECD 30*	11	4
11 Jan 97 ●	SATAN (re-recording) *Internal LIECD 37*	3	6
19 Apr 97	THE SAINT *ffrr FCD 296*	3	7
20 Mar 99	STYLE *ffrr FCD 358*	13	4
17 Jul 99	NOTHING LEFT *ffrr FCD 365*	32	2
11 Mar 00	BEACHED *ffrr FCD 377* [1]	36	3

28 Apr 01	FUNNY BREAK (ONE IS ENOUGH) *ffrr FCD 395*	21	3
8 Jun 02	REST & PLAY (EP) *ffrr FCD 407*	33	3
17 Jul 04	ONE PERFECT SUNRISE *Orbital Music ORBITALCD 03X*	29	2
12 Oct 91	ORBITAL *ffrr 8282481*	71	1
5 Jun 93	ORBITAL *Internal TRUCD 2*	28	2
19 Mar 94	PEEL SESSIONS *Internal LIECD 12*	32	2
20 Aug 94 ●	SNIVILISATION *Internal TRUCD 5*	4	4
11 May 96 ●	IN SIDES *Internal TRUCD 10*	5	12
25 Jan 97	SATAN LIVE *Internal LIARX 37*	48	1
17 Apr 99 ●	THE MIDDLE OF NOWHERE *ffrr 5560762*	4	7
12 May 01	THE ALTOGETHER *ffrr 8573877822*	11	4
15 Jun 02	WORK 1989–2002 *London 927461902*	36	3
3 Jul 04	BLUE ALBUM *Orbital Music ORBITALCD 001*	44	1

[1] Orbital and Angelo Badalamenti

Tracks on Mutations (EP): Chime Crime / Oolaa / Farenheit 3D 3 / Speed Freak. Tracks on Radiccio (EP): Halcyon / The Naked and the Dead / Sunday. Tracks on Rest & Play (EP): Frenetic / Illuminate (featuring David Gray) / Chime. The listed flip side of 'Belfast' was 'Innocent X' by Therapy? The first two albums are different and are often referred to as the Green and Brown albums due to the colour of the sleeves

ORCHESTRA ON THE HALF SHELL
US, male vocal / instrumental group (Singles: 6 Weeks) pos/wks

15 Dec 90	TURTLE RHAPSODY *SBK SBK 17*	36	6

ORCHESTRAL MANOEUVRES IN THE DARK (104 Top 500)
One of the most regular chart visitors of the 1980s had a nucleus of Andy McCluskey (v/syn/b) and Paul Humphries (syn), who left in 1989. This Liverpool-based synthesizer band had numerous international hits including 'Maid of Orleans (The Waltz Joan of Arc)', which was Germany's biggest seller in 1982 (Singles: 201 Weeks, Albums: 226 Weeks) pos/wks

9 Feb 80	RED FRAME WHITE LIGHT *DinDisc DIN 6*	67	2
10 May 80	MESSAGES *DinDisc DIN 15*	13	11
4 Oct 80 ●	ENOLA GAY *DinDisc DIN 22*	8	15
29 Aug 81 ●	SOUVENIR *DinDisc DIN 24*	3	12
24 Oct 81	JOAN OF ARC *DinDisc DIN 36*	5	14
23 Jan 82 ●	MAID OF ORLEANS (THE WALTZ JOAN OF ARC) *DinDisc DIN 40*	4	10
19 Feb 83	GENETIC ENGINEERING *Virgin VS 527*	20	8
9 Apr 83	TELEGRAPH *Virgin VS 580*	42	4
14 Apr 84 ●	LOCOMOTION *Virgin VS 660*	5	11
16 Jun 84	TALKING LOUD AND CLEAR *Virgin VS 685*	11	10
8 Sep 84	TESLA GIRLS *Virgin VS 705*	21	8
10 Nov 84	NEVER TURN AWAY *Virgin VS 727*	70	2
25 May 85	SO IN LOVE *Virgin VS 766*	27	7
20 Jul 85	SECRET *Virgin VS 796*	34	7
26 Oct 85	LA FEMME ACCIDENT *Virgin VS 811*	42	4
3 May 86	IF YOU LEAVE *Virgin VS 843*	48	4
6 Sep 86	(FOREVER) LIVE AND DIE *Virgin VS 888*	11	10
15 Nov 86	WE LOVE YOU *Virgin VS 911*	54	5
2 May 87	SHAME *Virgin VS 938*	52	3
6 Feb 88	DREAMING (re) *Virgin VS 987*	50	6
30 Mar 91 ●	SAILING ON THE SEVEN SEAS *Virgin VS 1310*	3	13
6 Jul 91 ●	PANDORA'S BOX *Virgin VS 1331*	7	10
14 Sep 91	THEN YOU TURN AWAY *Virgin VS 1368*	50	4
7 Dec 91	CALL MY NAME *Virgin VS 1380*	50	4
15 May 93	STAND ABOVE ME *Virgin VSCDG 1444*	21	4
17 Jul 93	DREAM OF ME (BASED ON LOVE'S THEME) *Virgin VSCDT 1461*	24	5
18 Sep 93	EVERYDAY *Virgin VSCDT 1471*	59	2
17 Aug 96	WALKING ON THE MILKY WAY *Virgin VSCDT 1599*	17	5
2 Nov 96	UNIVERSAL *Virgin VSCDT 1606*	55	1
26 Sep 98	THE OMD REMIXES (EP) *Virgin VSCDT 1694*	35	2
1 Mar 80	ORCHESTRAL MANOEUVRES IN THE DARK *DinDisc DID 2*	27	29
1 Nov 80 ●	ORGANISATION *DinDisc DID 6*	6	25
14 Nov 81 ●	ARCHITECTURE & MORALITY *DinDisc DID 12*	3	39
12 Mar 83 ●	DAZZLE SHIPS *Telegraph V 2261*	5	13
12 May 84 ●	JUNK CULTURE *Virgin V 2310*	9	27
29 Jun 85	CRUSH *Virgin V 2349*	13	12
11 Oct 86	THE PACIFIC AGE *Virgin V 2398*	15	7
12 Mar 88 ●	THE BEST OF O.M.D. *Virgin OMD 1*	2	33
18 May 91 ●	SUGAR TAX *Virgin V 2648*	3	29
26 Jun 93	LIBERATOR *Virgin CDV 2715*	14	6
14 Sep 96	UNIVERSAL *Virgin CDV 2807*	24	2
10 Oct 98	THE O.M.D. SINGLES *Virgin CDV 2859*	16	4

Group often known as OMD. Tracks on The OMD Remixes (EP): Enola Gay / Souvenir / Electricity

ORCHESTRE NATIONALE DE LA RADIO DIFFUSION FRANÇAISE See Sir Thomas BEECHAM

The ORDINARY BOYS
UK, male vocal / instrumental group (Singles: 8 Weeks, Albums: 4 Weeks) pos/wks

17 Apr 04	WEEK IN WEEK OUT *B Unique WEA 372CD*	36	3
10 Jul 04	TALK TALK TALK *B Unique WEA 377CD2*	17	3
2 Oct 04	SEASIDE *B Unique WEA 3979CD2*	27	2
17 Jul 04	OVER THE COUNTER CULTURE *B Unique 5046745432*	19	4

Raul ORELLANA
Spain, male producer (Singles: 8 Weeks) pos/wks

30 Sep 89	THE REAL WILD HOUSE *RCA BCM 322*	29	8

ORIGIN
UK, male production duo (Singles: 1 Week) pos/wks

12 Aug 00	WIDE EYED ANGEL *Lost Language LOST 001CD*	73	1

ORIGIN UNKNOWN
UK, male instrumental / production duo (Singles: 2 Weeks) pos/wks

13 Jul 96	VALLEY OF THE SHADOWS *Ram RAMM 16CD*	60	1
11 May 02	TRULY ONE *Ram RAMM 38CD*	53	1

ORIGINAL
(see also DIVA SUPREME featuring GEORGIA JONES) *US, male vocal / instrumental duo – Everett Bradley and Walter Taieb (Singles: 14 Weeks)* pos/wks

14 Jan 95	I LUV U BABY *Ore AG 8CD*	31	3
19 Aug 95 ●	I LUV U BABY (re-mix) *Ore AGR 8CD*	2	9
11 Nov 95	B 2 GETHER *Ore AG 12CD*	29	2

ORIGINOO GUNN CLAPPAZ *See HELTAH SKELTAH and ORIGINOO GUNN CLAPPAZ as the FABULOUS FIVE*

ORION
(see also ANGELIC; CITIZEN CANED; Jurgen VRIES; DT8 PROJECT) *UK, male / female production / vocal / instrumental duo – Darren Tate and Sarah J (Singles: 2 Weeks)* pos/wks

7 Oct 00	ETERNITY *Incentive CENT 11CDS*	38	2

ORION TOO
Belgium, male producer and female vocalist (Singles: 1 Week) pos/wks

9 Nov 02	HOPE AND WAIT *Data DATA 40CDS*	46	1

ORLANDO *See The LA's; The PRETENDERS*

Tony ORLANDO
(see also DAWN) *US, male vocalist – Michael Anthony Orlando Cassavitis (Singles: 82 Weeks)* pos/wks

5 Oct 61 ●	BLESS YOU *Fontana H 330*	5	11
31 Jul 71 ●	WHAT ARE YOU DOING SUNDAY *Bell 1169* [1]	3	12
10 Mar 73 ★	TIE A YELLOW RIBBON ROUND THE OLE OAK TREE (re) *Bell 1287* [1] ▲	1	40
4 Aug 73	SAY, HAS ANYBODY SEEN MY SWEET GYPSY ROSE *Bell 1322* [1]	12	15
9 Mar 74	WHO'S IN THE STRAWBERRY PATCH WITH SALLY *Bell 1343* [2]	37	4

[1] Dawn featuring Tony Orlando [2] Tony Orlando and Dawn

The ORLONS
US, female / male vocal group (Singles: 3 Weeks) pos/wks

27 Dec 62	DON'T HANG UP (re) *Cameo Parkway C 231*	39	3

ORN
UK, male DJ / producer – Omio Nourizadeh (Singles: 1 Week) pos/wks

1 Mar 97	SNOW *Deconstruction 74321447612*	61	1

Cyril ORNADEL *See LONDON SYMPHONY ORCHESTRA*

Stacie ORRICO
US, female vocalist (Singles: 22 Weeks, Albums: 19 Weeks) pos/wks

23 Aug 03 ●	STUCK *Virgin VUSCD 269*	9	8
1 Nov 03	(THERE'S GOTTA BE) MORE TO LIFE *Virgin VUSCD 275*	12	8
24 Jan 04	I PROMISE *Virgin VUSCD 280*	22	4
12 Jun 04	I COULD BE THE ONE *Virgin VUSDX 289*	34	2
4 Oct 03	STACIE ORRICO *Virgin CDVUS 238*	37	19

Claudette ORTIZ *See Wyclef JEAN*

Beth ORTON
UK, female vocalist (Singles: 13 Weeks, Albums: 18 Weeks) pos/wks

1 Feb 97	TOUCH ME WITH YOUR LOVE *Heavenly HVN 64CD*	60	1
5 Apr 97	SOMEONE'S DAUGHTER *Heavenly HVN 65CD*	49	1
14 Jun 97	SHE CRIES YOUR NAME *Heavenly HVN 68CD*	40	2
13 Dec 97	BEST BIT (EP) *Heavenly HVN 72CD* [1]	36	3
13 Mar 99	STOLEN CAR *Heavenly HVN 89CD*	34	2
25 Sep 99	CENTRAL RESERVATION *Heavenly HVN 92CD*	37	2
16 Nov 02	ANYWHERE *Heavenly HVN 125CDS*	55	1
12 Apr 03	THINKING ABOUT TOMORROW *Heavenly HVN 129CD*	57	1
26 Oct 96	TRAILER PARK *Heavenly HVNLP 17CD*	68	3
27 Mar 99	CENTRAL RESERVATION *Heavenly HVNLP 22CD*	17	8
10 Aug 02 ●	DAYBREAKER *Heavenly HVNLP 37CD*	8	5
4 Oct 03	PASS IN TIME – THE DEFINITIVE COLLECTION *Heavenly HVNLP 45CD*	45	2

[1] Beth Orton featuring Terry Callier

Tracks on Best Bit (EP): Best Bit / Skimming Stone / Dolphins / Lean on Me

Jeffrey OSBORNE
(see also LTD) *US, male vocalist (Singles: 38 Weeks, Albums: 10 Weeks)* pos/wks

17 Sep 83	DON'T YOU GET SO MAD *A&M AM 140*	54	2
14 Apr 84	STAY WITH ME TONIGHT *A&M AM 188*	18	11
23 Jun 84	ON THE WINGS OF LOVE *A&M AM 198*	11	14
20 Oct 84	DON'T STOP *A&M AM 222*	61	2
26 Jul 86	SOWETO (re) *A&M AM 334*	44	6
15 Aug 87	LOVE POWER *Arista RIS 27* [1]	63	3
5 May 84	STAY WITH ME TONIGHT *A&M AMLX 64940*	56	7
13 Oct 84	DON'T STOP *A&M AMA 5017*	59	3

[1] Dionne Warwick and Jeffrey Osborne

Joan OSBORNE
US, female vocalist (Singles: 13 Weeks, Albums: 18 Weeks) pos/wks

10 Feb 96 ●	ONE OF US *Blue Gorilla JOACD 1*	6	10
8 Jun 96	ST TERESA *Blue Gorilla JOACD 3*	33	3
9 Mar 96 ●	RELISH *Blue Gorilla 5266992*	5	18

Tony OSBORNE SOUND
UK, orchestra (Singles: 3 Weeks) pos/wks

23 Feb 61	THE MAN FROM MADRID *HMV POP 827* [1]	50	1
3 Feb 73	THE SHEPHERD'S SONG *Philips 6006 266*	46	2

[1] Tony Osborne Sound featuring Joanne Brown

Kelly OSBOURNE
UK, female vocalist (Singles: 35 Weeks, Albums: 2 Weeks) pos/wks

24 Aug 02	PAPA DON'T PREACH (IMPORT) *Epic 6729152*	65	3
21 Sep 02 ●	PAPA DON'T PREACH (re) *Epic 6731602*	3	10
8 Feb 03	SHUT UP *Epic 6735552*	12	6
20 Dec 03 ★	CHANGES *Sanctuary SANXD 234* [1] ■	1	16
22 Feb 03	SHUT UP *Epic 5094782*	31	2

[1] Kelly and Ozzy Osbourne

Ozzy OSBOURNE
(see also BLACK SABBATH; BLIZZARD OF OZZ) *UK, male vocalist – John Osbourne (Singles: 64 Weeks, Albums: 67 Weeks)* pos/wks

13 Sep 80	CRAZY TRAIN *Jet 197* [1]	49	4
15 Nov 80	MR CROWLEY *Jet 7003* [1]	46	3
26 Nov 83	BARK AT THE MOON *Epic A 3915*	21	8
2 Jun 84	SO TIRED *Epic A 4452*	20	9
1 Feb 86	SHOT IN THE DARK *Epic A 6859*	20	6
9 Aug 86	THE ULTIMATE SIN / LIGHTNING STRIKES *Epic A 7311*	72	1
20 May 89	CLOSE MY EYES FOREVER *Dreamland PB 49409* [2]	47	3
28 Sep 91	NO MORE TEARS *Epic 6574407*	32	3
30 Nov 91	MAMA I'M COMING HOME *Epic 6576177*	46	2
25 Nov 95	PERRY MASON *Epic 6626395*	23	2
31 Aug 96	I JUST WANT YOU *Epic 6635702*	43	1
8 Jun 02	DREAMER / GETS ME THROUGH *Epic 6724122*	18	6
20 Dec 03 ★	CHANGES *Sanctuary SANXD 234* [3] ■	1	16
20 Sep 80 ●	BLIZZARD OF OZZ *Jet JETLP 234* [1]	7	8
7 Nov 81	DIARY OF A MADMAN *Jet JETLP 237*	14	12
27 Nov 82	TALK OF THE DEVIL *Jet JETDP 401*	21	6
10 Dec 83	BARK AT THE MOON *Epic EPC 25739*	24	7
22 Feb 86 ●	THE ULTIMATE SIN *Epic EPC 26404*	8	10
23 May 87	TRIBUTE *Epic 4504751*	13	6
22 Oct 88	NO REST FOR THE WICKED *Epic 4625811*	23	4
17 Mar 90	JUST SAY OZZY *Epic 4659401*	69	1

19 Oct 91	NO MORE TEARS *Epic 4678591*	17	3
4 Nov 95	OZZMOSIS *Epic 4810222*	22	3
15 Nov 97	THE OZZMAN COMETH – THE BEST OF OZZY OSBOURNE *Epic 4872602*	68	1
27 Oct 01	DOWN TO EARTH *Epic 4984742*	19	3
15 Mar 03	THE ESSENTIAL OZZY OSBOURNE *Epic 5108402*	21	3

1 Ozzy Osbourne's Blizzard of Ozz 2 Lita Ford duet with Ozzy Osbourne
3 Kelly and Ozzy Osbourne 1 Ozzy Osbourne's Blizzard of Ozz

OSIBISA

Ghana / Nigeria, male vocal / instrumental group (Singles: 12 Weeks, Albums: 17 Weeks) pos/wks

17 Jan 76	SUNSHINE DAY *Bronze BRO 20*	17	6
5 Jun 76	DANCE THE BODY MUSIC *Bronze BRO 26*	31	6
22 May 71	OSIBISA *MCA MDKS 8001*	11	10
5 Feb 72	WOYAYA *MCA MDKS 8005*	11	7

Donny OSMOND 265 Top 500

(see also Donny and Marie OSMOND) *Teenage teen-idol vocalist, b. 9 Dec 1957, Utah, US. The main focal point of the hitmaking family act The Osmonds, he was one of the most popular pin-ups of the 1970s. He had three solo No.1s before his 16th birthday and returned to the album Top 30 in 2004 (Singles: 123 Weeks, Albums: 120 Weeks)* pos/wks

17 Jun 72	★ PUPPY LOVE (3re) *MGM 2006 104*	1	23
16 Sep 72	● TOO YOUNG (re) *MGM 2006 113*	5	15
11 Nov 72	● WHY *MGM 2006 119*	3	20
10 Mar 73	★ THE TWELFTH OF NEVER *MGM 2006 199*	1	14
18 Aug 73	★ YOUNG LOVE *MGM 2006 300*	1	10
10 Nov 73	● WHEN I FALL IN LOVE *MGM 2006 365*	4	13
9 Nov 74	WHERE DID ALL THE GOOD TIMES GO *MGM 2006 468*	18	10
26 Sep 87	I'M IN IT FOR LOVE *Virgin VS 994*	70	1
6 Aug 88	SOLDIER OF LOVE *Virgin VS 1094*	29	8
12 Nov 88	IF IT'S LOVE THAT YOU WANT *Virgin VS 1140*	70	2
9 Feb 91	MY LOVE IS A FIRE *Capitol CL 600*	64	2
2 Oct 04	● BREEZE ON BY *Decca 9863140*	8	5
23 Sep 72	● PORTRAIT OF DONNY *MGM 2315 108*	5	43
16 Dec 72	● TOO YOUNG *MGM 2315 113*	7	24
26 May 73	● ALONE TOGETHER *MGM 2315 210*	6	19
15 Dec 73	● A TIME FOR US *MGM 2315 273*	4	13
8 Feb 75	● DONNY *MGM 2315 314*	16	4
2 Oct 76	DISCOTRAIN *Polydor 2391 226*	59	1
21 Apr 01	● THIS IS THE MOMENT *Decca 1587772*	10	3
7 Dec 02	SOMEWHERE IN TIME *Decca 0665302*	12	10
27 Nov 04	WHAT I MEANT TO SAY *Decca 9863139*	26	3

Donny and Marie OSMOND

US, male / female vocal duo (Singles: 37 Weeks, Albums: 19 Weeks) pos/wks

3 Aug 74	● I'M LEAVING IT (ALL) UP TO YOU *MGM 2006 446*	2	12
14 Dec 74	● MORNING SIDE OF THE MOUNTAIN *MGM 2006 474*	5	12
21 Jun 75	MAKE THE WORLD GO AWAY *MGM 2006 523*	18	6
17 Jan 76	DEEP PURPLE *MGM 2006 561*	25	7
2 Nov 74	I'M LEAVING IT ALL UP TO YOU *MGM 2315 307*	13	15
26 Jul 75	MAKE THE WORLD GO AWAY *MGM 2315 343*	30	3
5 Jun 76	DEEP PURPLE *Polydor 2391 220*	48	1

Little Jimmy OSMOND

US, male vocalist (Singles: 50 Weeks, Albums: 12 Weeks) pos/wks

25 Nov 72	★ LONG HAIRED LOVER FROM LIVERPOOL (re) *MGM 2006 109* 1	1	27
31 Mar 73	● TWEEDLEE DEE *MGM 2006 175*	4	13
23 Mar 74	I'M GONNA KNOCK ON YOUR DOOR *MGM 2006 389* 2	11	10
17 Feb 73	KILLER JOE *MGM 2315 157*	20	12

1 Little Jimmy Osmond with The Mike Curb Congregation 2 Jimmy Osmond

Marie OSMOND

(see also Donny and Marie OSMOND) *US, female vocalist – Olive Osmond (Singles: 15 Weeks, Albums: 1 Week)* pos/wks

17 Nov 73	● PAPER ROSES *MGM 2006 315*	2	15
9 Feb 74	PAPER ROSES *MGM 2315 262*	46	1

The OSMOND BOYS *US, male vocal group (Singles: 6 Weeks)* pos/wks

9 Nov 91	BOYS WILL BE BOYS *Curb 6573847*	65	2
11 Jan 92	SHOW ME THE WAY *Curb 6577227*	60	4

The OSMONDS 310 Top 500

Top teeny-bop act: brothers Donny, Alan, Wayne, Merrill and Jay Osmond from Utah, US. Polished pop quintet created hysteria wherever they appeared. The Osmond family (including Marie and Little Jimmy) had a record 13 UK hits in 1973 (Singles: 94 Weeks, Albums: 119 Weeks) pos/wks

25 Mar 72	DOWN BY THE LAZY RIVER *MGM 2006 096*	40	5
11 Nov 72	● CRAZY HORSES *MGM 2006 142*	2	18
14 Jul 73	● GOIN' HOME *MGM 2006 288*	4	10
27 Oct 73	● LET ME IN *MGM 2006 321*	2	14
20 Apr 74	I CAN'T STOP *MCA 129*	12	10
24 Aug 74	★ LOVE ME FOR A REASON *MGM 2006 458*	1	9
1 Mar 75	HAVING A PARTY *MGM 2006 492*	28	8
24 May 75	● THE PROUD ONE *MGM 2006 520*	5	8
15 Nov 75	I'M STILL GONNA NEED YOU *MGM 2006 551*	32	4
30 Oct 76	I CAN'T LIVE A DREAM *Polydor 2066 726*	37	5
23 Sep 95	CRAZY HORSES (re-mix) *Polydor 5793212*	50	1
12 Jun 99	CRAZY HORSES (re-issue) (re-mix) *Polydor 5611372*	34	2
18 Nov 72	● OSMONDS LIVE *MGM 2315 117*	13	22
16 Dec 72	● CRAZY HORSES *MGM 2315 123*	9	19
25 Aug 73	● THE PLAN *MGM 2315 251*	6	25
17 Aug 74	● OUR BEST TO YOU *MGM 2315 300*	5	20
7 Dec 74	LOVE ME FOR A REASON *MGM 2315 312*	13	9
14 Jun 75	I'M STILL GONNA NEED YOU *MGM 2315 342*	19	7
10 Jan 76	AROUND THE WORLD – LIVE IN CONCERT *MGM 2659 044*	41	1
20 Apr 96	THE VERY BEST OF THE OSMONDS *Polydor 5270722*	17	5
12 Jul 03	● ULTIMATE COLLECTION *Polydor / Universal TV 9808355*	4	11

Gilbert O'SULLIVAN 157 Top 500

Distinctive Irish singer / songwriter / pianist, b. Raymond O'Sullivan, 1 Dec 1946, Waterford. His unusual image – short trousers, flat cap and pudding-basin haircut – helped to launch the successful international career of the performer voted No.1 UK Male Singer of 1972 (Singles: 145 Weeks, Albums: 201 Weeks) pos/wks

28 Nov 70	● NOTHING RHYMED *MAM 3*	8	11
3 Apr 71	UNDERNEATH THE BLANKET GO (re) *MAM 13*	40	4
24 Jul 71	WE WILL *MAM 30*	16	11
27 Nov 71	● NO MATTER HOW I TRY *MAM 53*	5	15
4 Mar 72	● ALONE AGAIN (NATURALLY) *MAM 66* ▲	3	12
17 Jun 72	● OOH-WAKKA-DOO-WAKKA-DAY *MAM 78*	8	11
21 Oct 72	★ CLAIR *MAM 84*	1	14
17 Mar 73	★ GET DOWN *MAM 96*	1	13
15 Sep 73	OOH BABY *MAM 107*	18	7
10 Nov 73	● WHY, OH WHY, OH WHY *MAM 111*	6	14
9 Feb 74	HAPPINESS IS ME AND YOU *MAM 114*	19	7
24 Aug 74	A WOMAN'S PLACE *MAM 122*	42	3
14 Dec 74	CHRISTMAS SONG *MAM 124*	12	6
14 Jun 75	I DON'T LOVE YOU BUT I THINK I LIKE YOU *MAM 130*	14	6
27 Sep 80	WHAT'S IN A KISS *CBS 8929*	19	9
24 Feb 90	SO WHAT *Dover ROJ 3*	70	2
25 Sep 71	● HIMSELF *MAM 501*	5	82
18 Nov 72	★ BACK TO FRONT *MAM 502*	1	65
6 Oct 73	● I'M A WRITER, NOT A FIGHTER *MAMS 505*	2	25
26 Oct 74	● A STRANGER IN MY OWN BACK YARD *MAM MAMS 506*	9	8
18 Dec 76	GREATEST HITS *MAM MAMA 2003*	13	11
12 Sep 81	20 GOLDEN GREATS *K-Tel NE 1133*	98	1
11 May 91	NOTHING BUT THE BEST *Castle Communications CTVLP 107*	50	4
27 Mar 04	THE BERRY VEST OF *EMI 5986722*	20	5

The OTHER TWO (see also NEW ORDER) *UK, male / female vocal / instrumental duo – Stephen Morris and Gillian Gilbert (Singles: 5 Weeks)* pos/wks

9 Nov 91	TASTY FISH *Factory FAC 3297*	41	3
6 Nov 93	SELFISH *London TWOCD 1*	46	2

The OTHERS

UK, male vocal / instrumental group (Singles: 3 Weeks) pos/wks

29 May 04	THIS IS FOR THE POOR *Poptones MC 5090SCD*	42	1
6 Nov 04	STAN BOWLES *Vertigo 9868521*	36	2

Johnny OTIS SHOW

US, male band – leader John Veliotes (Singles: 22 Weeks) pos/wks

22 Nov 57	● MA (HE'S MAKING EYES AT ME) *Capitol CL 14794* 1	2	15
10 Jan 58	BYE BYE BABY *Capitol CL 14817* 2	20	7

1 Johnny Otis and his Orchestra with Marie Adams and the Three Tons of Joy
2 Johnny Otis Show, vocals by Marie Adams and Johnny Otis

OTTAWAN
France, male / female vocal duo –
Jean Patrick and Annette (Singles: 45 Weeks)   pos/wks

13 Sep 80 ●	D.I.S.C.O. *Carrere CAR 161*	2	18
13 Dec 80	YOU'RE OK *Carrere CAR 168*	56	6
29 Aug 81 ●	HANDS UP (GIVE ME YOUR HEART) *Carrere CAR 183*	3	15
5 Dec 81	HELP, GET ME SOME HELP! *Carrere CAR 215*	49	6

John OTWAY and Wild Willy BARRETT *UK, male vocal /*
instrumental duo (Singles: 15 Weeks, Albums: 1 Week)   pos/wks

3 Dec 77	REALLY FREE *Polydor 2058 951*	27	8
5 Jul 80	DK 50–80 *Polydor 2059 250* [1]	45	4
12 Oct 02 ●	BUNSEN BURNER *U-Vibe OTWAY 02X* [2]	9	3
1 Jul 78	DEEP AND MEANINGLESS *Polydor 2382 501*	44	1

[1] Otway and Barrett [2] John Otway

OUI 3 *UK / US / Switzerland, male / female rap /*
instrumental group (Singles: 21 Weeks, Albums: 3 Weeks)   pos/wks

20 Feb 93	FOR WHAT IT'S WORTH *MCA MCSTD 1736*	28	6
24 Apr 93	ARMS OF SOLITUDE *MCA MCSTD 1759*	54	2
17 Jul 93	BREAK FROM THE OLD ROUTINE *MCA MCSTD 1793*	17	6
23 Oct 93	FOR WHAT IT'S WORTH (re-mix) *MCA MCSTD 1941*	26	3
29 Jan 94	FACT OF LIFE *MCA MCSTD 1939*	38	2
27 May 95	JOY OF LIVING *MCA MCSTD 2057*	55	2
7 Aug 93	OUI LOVE YOU *MCA MCD 10833*	39	3

OUR DAUGHTER'S WEDDING
US, male vocal / instrumental group (Singles: 6 Weeks)   pos/wks

1 Aug 81	LAWNCHAIRS *EMI America EA 124*	49	6

OUR HOUSE
Australia, male instrumental production duo (Singles: 1 Week) pos/wks

31 Aug 96	FLOOR SPACE *Perfecto PERF 125CD*	52	1

OUR KID *UK, male vocal group (Singles: 11 Weeks)*   pos/wks

29 May 76 ●	YOU JUST MIGHT SEE ME CRY *Polydor 2058 729*	2	11

OUR LADY PEACE
Canada, male vocal / instrumental group (Singles: 1 Week)   pos/wks

15 Jan 00	ONE MAN ARMY *Epic 6688662*	70	1

OUR TRIBE / ONE TRIBE
(see also FAITHLESS; ROLLO; SPHINX; DUSTED) *UK / US,*
male / female vocal / instrumental group (Singles: 13 Weeks) pos/wks

20 Jun 92	WHAT HAVE YOU DONE (IS THIS ALL) *Inner Rhythm HEART 03* [1]	52	2
27 Mar 93	I BELIEVE IN YOU *Ffrreedom TABCD 117* [2]	42	2
30 Apr 94	HOLD THAT SUCKER DOWN *Cheeky CHEKCD 004* [3]	24	3
21 May 94	LOVE COME HOME *Triangle BLUESCD 001* [4]	73	1
13 May 95	HIGH AS A KITE *ffrr FCD 259* [5]	55	1
30 Sep 95	HOLD THAT SUCKER DOWN (re-mix) *Cheeky CHEKCD 009* [3]	26	3
9 Dec 00	HOLD THAT SUCKER DOWN (re-issue) *Champion CHAMPCD 786* [3]	45	1

[1] One Tribe featuring Gem [2] Our Tribe [3] OT Quartet [4] Our Tribe with
Franke Pharoah and Kristine W [5] One Tribe featuring Roger

OUT OF MY HAIR
UK, male vocal / instrumental group (Singles: 1 Week)   pos/wks

1 Jul 95	MISTER JONES *RCA 74321267812*	73	1

OUTHERE BROTHERS
US, male rap / vocal duo – Lamar Mahone and
Craig Simpkins (Singles: 50 Weeks, Albums: 9 Weeks)   pos/wks

18 Mar 95 ★	DON'T STOP (WIGGLE WIGGLE) *Eternal YZ 917CD*	1	15
17 Jun 95 ★	BOOM BOOM BOOM *Eternal YZ 938CD*	1	15
23 Sep 95 ●	LA LA LA HEY HEY *Eternal YZ 974CD*	7	7
16 Dec 95 ●	IF YOU WANNA PARTY *Eternal WEA 030CD*	9	10
25 Jan 97	LET ME HEAR YOU SAY 'OLE OLE' *WEA 089CD*	18	3
27 May 95	1 POLISH 2 BISCUITS AND A FISH SANDWICH *Eternal 0630105852*	56	5
30 Dec 95	THE PARTY ALBUM *Eternal 0630127812*	41	4

'The Party Album' is a sanitized version of '1 Polish 2 Biscuits and a Fish Sandwich'

OUTKAST
US, male rap / vocal duo – André '3000' Benjamin and Antwan
'Big Boi' Patton (Singles: 68 Weeks, Albums: 66 Weeks)   pos/wks

23 Dec 00	B.O.B (BOMBS OVER BAGHDAD) *LaFace / Arista 74321822942*	61	1
3 Feb 01	MS JACKSON (IMPORT) *LaFace 73008245252*	48	4
3 Mar 01 ●	MS JACKSON *LaFace / Arista 74321836822* ▲	2	10
9 Jun 01	SO FRESH, SO CLEAN *LaFace / Arista 74321863402*	16	8
6 Apr 02	THE WHOLE WORLD *LaFace / Arista 74321917592* [1]	19	5
27 Jul 02	LAND OF A MILLION DRUMS *Atlantic AT 0134CD* [2]	46	1
4 Oct 03	GHETTO MUSIK *Arista 82876567232*	55	1
22 Nov 03 ●	HEY YA! *Arista 82876579532* ▲	3	21
3 Apr 04 ●	THE WAY YOU MOVE *Arista 82876605602* [3] ▲	7	10
3 Jul 04 ●	ROSES *Arista 82876624392*	4	7
20 Jan 01 ●	STANKONIA *LaFace 73008260722*	10	15
11 Oct 03 ●	SPEAKERBOXXX / THE LOVE BELOW *Arista 82876529052* ▲	8	51

[1] Outkast featuring Killer Mike [2] Outkast featuring Killer Mike and Sleepy
Brown [3] Outkast featuring Sleepy Brown

OUTLANDER
Belgium, male producer – Marcos Salon (Singles: 3 Weeks)   pos/wks

31 Aug 91	VAMP *R&S RSUK 1*	51	2
7 Feb 98	THE VAMP (REVAMPED) *R&S RS 97113CDX*	62	1

OUTLANDISH
Morocco / Pakistan / Honduras, male rap /
production trio (Singles: 2 Weeks)   pos/wks

31 May 03	GUANTANAMO *RCA 82876517702*	31	2

The OUTLAWS
UK, male instrumental group (Singles: 29 Weeks)   pos/wks

13 Apr 61	SWINGIN' LOW *HMV POP 844*	46	2
8 Jun 61	AMBUSH *HMV POP 877*	43	2
12 Oct 61	TRIBUTE TO BUDDY HOLLY *HMV POP 912* [1]	24	6
3 Jan 63 ●	DON'T YOU THINK IT'S TIME *HMV POP 1105* [1]	6	12
11 Apr 63	MY LITTLE BABY *HMV POP 1142* [1]	34	7

[1] Mike Berry and The Outlaws

2PAC and OUTLAWZ
US, male rapper and rap group (Albums: 1 Week)   pos/wks

8 Jan 00	STILL I RISE *Interscope 4904172*	75	1

OUTRAGE
US, male vocalist (Singles: 2 Weeks)   pos/wks

11 Mar 95	TALL 'N' HANDSOME *Effective ECFL 001CD*	57	1
23 Nov 96	TALL 'N' HANDSOME (re-mix) *Positiva CDTIV 64*	51	1

OUTSIDAZ featuring
Rah DIGGA and Melanie BLATT
US, male rap group and female rapper
and UK female vocalist (Singles: 2 Weeks)   pos/wks

2 Mar 02	I'M LEAVIN' *Rufflife RLCDM 03*	41	2

The OVERLANDERS
UK, male vocal / instrumental group –
lead vocal Laurie Mason (Singles: 10 Weeks)   pos/wks

13 Jan 66 ★	MICHELLE *Pye 7N 17034*	1	10

OVERLORD X
UK, male rapper – Benjamin Balogun (Albums: 1 Week)   pos/wks

4 Feb 89	WEAPON IS MY LYRIC *Mango Street ILPS 9924*	68	1

OVERWEIGHT POOCH featuring Ce Ce PENISTON
US, female rapper and female vocalist (Singles: 2 Weeks)   pos/wks

18 Jan 92	I LIKE IT *A&M AM 847*	58	2

Mark OWEN
(see also TAKE THAT) *UK, male vocalist*
(Singles: 36 Weeks, Albums: 12 Weeks)   pos/wks

30 Nov 96 ●	CHILD (re) *RCA 74321424422*	3 15
15 Feb 97 ●	CLEMENTINE *RCA 74321454982*	3 6
23 Aug 97	I AM WHAT I AM *RCA 74321501222*	29 3
16 Aug 03 ●	FOUR MINUTE WARNING *Universal MCSTD 40329* ...	4 9
8 Nov 03	ALONE WITHOUT YOU *Universal MCSTD 40342*	26 2
19 Jun 04	MAKIN' OUT *Cedna CDSEDNA 1*	30 1
14 Dec 96	GREEN MAN *RCA 74321435142*	33 11
15 Nov 03	IN YOUR OWN TIME *Universal MCD 60092*........	59 1

Reg OWEN and his ORCHESTRA
UK, orchestra – leader b. 3 Feb 1921, d. 1978 (Singles: 10 Weeks)   pos/wks

27 Feb 59	MANHATTAN SPIRITUAL *Pye International 7N 25009*	20 8
27 Oct 60	OBSESSION *Palette PG 9004*	43 2

Sid OWEN
UK, male actor / vocalist – David Sutton (Singles: 6 Weeks)   pos/wks

16 Dec 95	BETTER BELIEVE IT (CHILDREN IN NEED)	
	Trinity TDM 001CD [1]	60 1
8 Jul 00	GOOD THING GOING *Mushroom MUSH 74CDS*	14 5

[1] Sid Owen and Patsy Palmer

Robert OWENS
US, male vocalist (Singles: 6 Weeks)   pos/wks

7 Dec 91	I'LL BE YOUR FRIEND *Perfecto PB 45161*	75 2
26 Apr 97	I'LL BE YOUR FRIEND (re-mix) *Perfecto PERF 137CD1*	25 2
24 Feb 01	MINE TO GIVE *Science QEDCD 10* [1]	44 1
15 Feb 03	LAST NIGHT A DJ BLEW MY MIND *Illustrious CDILL 013*	34 1

[1] Photek featuring Robert Owens

OXIDE & NEUTRINO
(see also SO SOLID CREW) *UK, male production / rap duo – Alex Rivers and Mark Oseitutu (Singles: 45 Weeks, Albums: 22 Weeks)*   pos/wks

6 May 00 ★	BOUND 4 DA RELOAD (CASUALTY)	
	East West OXIDE 01CD1 ■	1 11
30 Dec 00 ●	NO GOOD 4 ME *East West OXIDE 02CD* [1]	6 8
26 May 01 ●	UP MIDDLE FINGER *East West OXIDE 03CD*	7 7
28 Jul 01	DEVIL'S NIGHTMARE *East West OXIDE 07CD1*	16 5
8 Dec 01	RAP DIS (U CAN'T STOP DIS S**T) / ONLY WANNA KNOW	
	U COS URE FAMOUS *East West OXIDE 08CD*	12 8
28 Sep 02 ●	DEM GIRLZ (I DON'T KNOW WHY) (re)	
	East West OXIDE 09CD1 [2]	10 6
6 May 00	BOUND 4 DA RELOAD (CASUALTY) *East West OXIDE 01T*....	71 1
9 Jun 01	EXECUTE *East West 8573885592*	11 19
12 Oct 02	2 STEPZ AHEAD *East West 5046607562*..............	28 2

[1] Oxide & Neutrino featuring Megaman, Romeo and Lisa Maffia [2] Oxide & Neutrino featuring Kowdean

The double 12-inch vinyl format of the act's No.1 single was ineligible for the singles chart but sales were sufficient to qualify for a place on the albums chart

OXYGEN featuring Andrea BRITTON (see also ASCENSION;
CHAKRA; ESSENCE; LUSTRAL; SPACE BROTHERS)
UK, male production duo and female vocalist (Singles: 3 Weeks)   pos/wks

11 Jan 03	AM I ON YOUR MIND *Innocent SINCD 40*	30 3

OZOMATLI
US, male vocal / instrumental group (Singles: 2 Weeks)   pos/wks

20 Mar 99	CUT CHEMIST SUITE *Almo Sounds CDALM 62*	58 1
22 May 99	SUPER BOWL SUNDAE *Almo Sounds CDALM 63*	68 1

OZRIC TENTACLES
UK, male instrumental / vocal group (Albums: 7 Weeks)   pos/wks

31 Aug 91	STRANGEITUDE *Dovetail DOVELP 3*	70 1
1 May 93	JURASSIC SHIFT *Dovetail DOVECD 6*	11 4
9 Jul 94	ARBORESCENCE *Dovetail DOVECD 7*	18 2

Jazzi P
UK, female rapper – Pauline Bennett (Singles: 12 Weeks)   pos/wks

8 Jul 89	GET LOOSE *Breakout USA 659* [1]	25 6
9 Jun 90	FEEL THE RHYTHM *A&M USA 691*	51 2
3 Aug 91	REBEL WOMAN *DNA 7DNA 001* [2]	42 4

[1] LA Mix featuring Jazzi P [2] DNA featuring Jazzi P

P DIDDY (364   Top 500)
World Music Award-winning rapper / songwriter / producer and record label owner, formerly known as Puff Daddy, b. Sean Combs 1970, New York, US. Only producer to score three successive US No.1 singles in the 1990s. 'I'll Be Missing You', a tribute to (his discovery) Notorious B.I.G., is the most successful rap single of all time and sold 1,409,688 copies in the UK (Singles: 154 Weeks, Albums: 31 Weeks)   pos/wks

29 Mar 97	CAN'T NOBODY HOLD ME DOWN *Arista 74321464552* [1] ▲	19 4
26 Apr 97	NO TIME *Atlantic A 5594CD* [2]	45 1
28 Jun 97 ★	I'LL BE MISSING YOU *Puff Daddy 74321499102* [3] ◆ ■ ▲	1 21
9 Aug 97 ●	MO MONEY MO PROBLEMS *Puff Daddy 74321492492* [4] ▲	6 10
13 Sep 97	SOMEONE *RCA 74321513942* [5]	34 2
1 Nov 97	BEEN AROUND THE WORLD (re) *Puff Daddy 74321539442* [6]	20 6
7 Feb 98	IT'S ALL ABOUT THE BENJAMINS *Puff Daddy 74321561972* [6]	18 3
1 Aug 98	COME WITH ME (IMPORT) *Epic 34K 78954* [7]	75 1
8 Aug 98 ●	COME WITH ME *Epic 6662842* [7]	2 10
1 May 99	ALL NIGHT LONG *Puff Daddy / Arista 74321665692* [8]	23 3
29 May 99	HATE ME NOW *Columbia 6672562* [9]	14 6
21 Aug 99	P.E. 2000 *Puff Daddy / Arista 74321694972* [10]	13 4
20 Nov 99	BEST FRIEND *Puff Daddy / Arista 74321712312* [11]	24 4
5 Feb 00	NOTORIOUS B.I.G. *Puff Daddy / Arista 74321737312* [12]	16 5
19 Feb 00	SATISFY YOU (IMPORT) (re) *Bad Boy / Arista 7928322* [13]	73 2
11 Mar 00 ●	SATISFY YOU (IMPORT) *Puff Daddy / Arista 74321745592* [13] ..8	8
6 Oct 01	BAD BOY FOR LIFE *Bad Boy / Arista 74321889982* [14]	13 6
26 Jan 02	DIDDY *Puff Daddy / Arista 74321911652* [15]	19 4
8 Jun 02	PASS THE COURVOISIER – PART II (re) *J 74321937902* [16]	16 8
10 Aug 02 ●	I NEED A GIRL (PART ONE)	
	Puff Daddy / Arista 74321947242 [17]	4 11
29 Mar 03	BUMP, BUMP, BUMP *Epic 6736452*	11 8
23 Aug 03	LET'S GET ILL *Bad Boy / Meanwhile MCSTD 40331* [19]	25 3
20 Sep 03 ●	SHAKE YA TAILFEATHER *Bad Boy MCSTD 40337* [20]	10 7
7 Feb 04	SHOW ME YOUR SOUL *Puff Daddy / Island MCSTD 40350* [21] ...	35 2
5 Jun 04	I DON'T WANNA KNOW (IMPORT) *Universal 9862372PMI* [22] ..	71 1
12 Jun 04 ★	I DON'T WANNA KNOW *Bad Boy MCSTD 40369* [22] ■	1 14
2 Aug 97 ●	NO WAY OUT *Puff Daddy 78612730122* [1] ▲	8 13
4 Sep 99 ●	FOREVER *Puff Daddy 74321689052*.....................	9 6
8 Jun 02	WE INVENTED THE REMIX *Puff Daddy 74321945402* [2].........	17 12

[1] Puff Daddy featuring Ma$e [2] Lil' Kim featuring Puff Daddy [3] Puff Daddy and Faith Evans featuring 112 [4] Notorious B.I.G. featuring Puff Daddy and Ma$e [5] SWV featuring Puff Daddy [6] Puff Daddy and the Family [7] Puff Daddy featuring Jimmy Page [8] Faith Evans featuring Puff Daddy [9] Nas featuring Puff Daddy [10] Puff Daddy featuring Hurricane G [11] Puff Daddy featuring Mario Winans [12] Notorious B.I.G. featuring Puff Daddy and Lil' Kim [13] Puff Daddy featuring R Kelly [14] P Diddy, Black Rob and Mark Curry [15] P Diddy featuring The Neptunes [16] Busta Rhymes featuring P Diddy and Pharrell [17] P Diddy featuring Usher and Loon [18] B2K featuring P Diddy [19] P Diddy featuring Kelis [20] Nelly, P Diddy and Murphy Lee [21] Lenny Kravitz / P Diddy / Loon / Pharrell Williams [22] Mario Winans featuring Enya & P Diddy [1] Puff Daddy and the Family [2] P Diddy & the Bad Boy Family

PF PROJECT featuring Ewan McGREGOR
(see also TZANT; MUSIQUE vs U2) *UK, male production duo –*
Jamie White and Moussa Clarke and actor (Singles: 11 Weeks)   pos/wks

| 15 Nov 97 | ● | CHOOSE LIFE *Positiva CDTIV 84* | ...... | **6** 11 |

PhD *UK, male vocal / instrumental trio – leader*
Jim Diamond (Singles: 14 Weeks, Albums: 8 Weeks)   pos/wks

| 3 Apr 82 | ● | I WON'T LET YOU DOWN *WEA K 79209* | ...... | **3** 14 |
| 1 May 82 | | PHD *WEA K 99150* | ...... | **33** 8 |

P.I.L. See PUBLIC IMAGE LTD

PJ *Canada, male producer – Paul Jacobs (Singles: 2 Weeks)*   pos/wks

| 20 Sep 97 | HAPPY DAYS *Deconstruction 74321511822* | ...... | **72** 1 |
| 4 Sep 99 | HAPPY DAYS (re-mix) *Defected DEFECT 6CDS* | ...... | **57** 1 |

PJ and DUNCAN See ANT & DEC

PJB featuring HANNAH and her SISTERS
(see also Hannah JONES) *Germany, male production*
group and US, female vocalists (Singles: 8 Weeks)   pos/wks

| 14 Sep 91 | BRIDGE OVER TROUBLED WATER *Dance Pool 6565467* | ...... | **21** 8 |

P J POWERS See LADYSMITH BLACK MAMBAZO

PKA *UK, male producer – Phil Kelsey (Singles: 2 Weeks)*   pos/wks

| 20 Apr 91 | TEMPERATURE RISING *Stress SS 4* | ...... | **68** 1 |
| 7 Mar 92 | POWERGEN (ONLY YOUR LOVE) *Stress PKA 1* | ...... | **70** 1 |

PM DAWN *US, male vocal / instrumental / rap duo – Attrell*
and Jarrett Cordes (Singles: 39 Weeks, Albums: 17 Weeks)   pos/wks

8 Jun 91		A WATCHER'S POINT OF VIEW (DON'T CHA THINK)		
		Gee Street GEE 32	......	**36** 5
17 Aug 91	●	SET ADRIFT ON MEMORY BLISS *Gee Street GEE 33* ▲	......	**3** 8
19 Oct 91		PAPER DOLL *Gee Street GEE 35*	......	**49** 3
22 Feb 92		REALITY USED TO BE A FRIEND OF MINE *Gee Street GEE 37*	..	**29** 4
7 Nov 92		I'D DIE WITHOUT YOU *Gee Street GEE 39*	......	**30** 5
13 Mar 93		LOOKING THROUGH PATIENT EYES *Gee Street GESCD 47*	..	**11** 7
12 Jun 93		MORE THAN LIKELY *Gee Street GESCD 49* [1]	......	**40** 3
30 Sep 95		DOWNTOWN VENUS *Gee Street GESCD 63*	......	**58** 2
6 Apr 96		SOMETIMES I MISS YOU SO MUCH *Gee Street GESCD 65*	..	**58** 1
31 Oct 98		GOTTA BE ... MOVIN' ON UP *Gee Street GEE 5003933* [2]	..	**68** 1
14 Sep 91	●	OF THE HEART OF THE SOUL AND OF THE CROSS		
		Gee Street GEEA 7	......	**8** 12
3 Apr 93	●	THE BLISS ALBUM ... ? *Gee Street GEED 9*	......	**9** 5

[1] PM Dawn featuring Boy George [2] PM Dawn featuring Ky-Mani

POB featuring DJ Patrick REID
UK, male producer – Paul Brogden and DJ (Singles: 1 Week)   pos/wks

| 11 Dec 99 | BLUEBOTTLE / FLY *Platipus PLAT 63CD* | ...... | **74** 1 |

P.O.D. *US, male vocal / instrumental*
group (Singles: 10 Weeks, Albums: 6 Weeks)   pos/wks

2 Feb 02	ALIVE *Atlantic AT 0119CD*	......	**19** 6
18 May 02	YOUTH OF THE NATION *Atlantic AT 0127CD*	......	**36** 2
7 Jun 03	SLEEPING AWAKE *Maverick W 608CD*	......	**42** 1
24 Jun 04	WILL YOU *Atlantic AT 0169CD*	......	**68** 1
19 Jan 02	SATELLITE *Atlantic 7567834752*	......	**16** 6

P.O.V. featuring JADE
US, male vocal group and female vocal group (Singles: 3 Weeks)   pos/wks

| 5 Feb 94 | ALL THRU THE NITE *Giant 74321187552* | ...... | **32** 3 |

PPK *Russia, male production / instrumental duo –*
Sergey Pimenov and Alexander Polyakov (Singles: 17 Weeks)   pos/wks

| 8 Dec 01 | ● | RESURECTION *Perfecto PERF 32CDS* | ...... | **3** 15 |
| 26 Oct 02 | | RELOAD *Perfecto PERF 41CDS* | ...... | **39** 2 |

PQM featuring CICA
US, male producer and female vocalist (Singles: 1 Week)   pos/wks

| 9 Dec 00 | THE FLYING SONG *Renaissance / Yoshitoshi RENCDS 004* | .... | **68** 1 |

PSG See COLOUR GIRL

Petey PABLO *US, male rapper – Moses Barrett (Singles: 1 Week)* pos/wks

| 9 Feb 02 | I *Jive 9253092* | ...... | **51** 1 |

Thom PACE *US, male vocalist (Singles: 15 Weeks)*   pos/wks

| 19 May 79 | MAYBE *RSO 34* | ...... | **14** 15 |

PACEMAKERS See GERRY and the PACEMAKERS

PACIFICA *UK, male production duo (Singles: 1 Week)*   pos/wks

| 31 Jul 99 | LOST IN THE TRANSLATION *Wildstar CDWILD 25* | ...... | **54** 1 |

PACK featuring Nigel BENN *UK, male vocal /*
instrumental group and UK boxer / rapper (Singles: 2 Weeks)   pos/wks

| 8 Dec 90 | STAND AND FIGHT *IQ ZB 44237* | ...... | **61** 2 |

The PACKABEATS
UK, male instrumental group (Singles: 1 Week)   pos/wks

| 23 Feb 61 | GYPSY BEAT *Parlophone R 4729* | ...... | **49** 1 |

The PADDINGTONS
UK, male vocal / instrumental group (Singles: 1 Week)   pos/wks

| 23 Oct 04 | 21 / SOME OLD GIRL *Poptones MC 5093SCD* | ...... | **47** 1 |

José PADILLA featuring Angela JOHN
Spain, male DJ and UK female vocalist (Singles: 1 Week)   pos/wks

| 8 Aug 98 | WHO DO YOU LOVE *Manifesto FESCD 45* | ...... | **59** 1 |

PAFFENDORF *Germany, male production duo –*
Gottfried Engels and Ramon Zenker (Singles: 8 Weeks)   pos/wks

| 15 Jun 02 | ● | BE COOL *Data DATA 29CDS* | ...... | **7** 7 |
| 26 Apr 03 | | CRAZY SEXY MARVELLOUS *Data / MoS DATA 51CDS* | .... | **52** 1 |

PAGANINI TRAXX
Italy, male DJ / producer – Sam Paganini (Singles: 1 Week)   pos/wks

| 1 Feb 97 | ZOE *Sony S3 DANUCD 18X* | ...... | **47** 1 |

Jimmy PAGE (see also LED ZEPPELIN; COVERDALE PAGE) *UK, male*
instrumentalist – guitar (Singles: 16 Weeks, Albums: 37 Weeks)   pos/wks

17 Dec 94		GALLOWS POLE *Fontana PPCD 2* [1]	......	**35** 3
11 Apr 98		MOST HIGH *Mercury 5687512* [2]	......	**26** 2
1 Aug 98		COME WITH ME (IMPORT) *Epic 34K 78954* [3]	......	**75** 1
8 Aug 98	●	COME WITH ME *Epic 6662842* [3]	......	**2** 10
27 Feb 82		DEATHWISH II (FILM SOUNDTRACK) *Swansong SSK 59415*	....	**40** 4
16 Mar 85		WHATEVER HAPPENED TO JUGULA?		
		Beggars Banquet BEGA 60 [1]	......	**44** 4
2 Jul 88		OUTRIDER *Geffen WX 155*	......	**27** 6
19 Nov 94	●	NO QUARTER *Fontana 5263622* [2]	......	**7** 13
2 May 98	●	WALKING INTO CLARKSDALE *Mercury 5580252* [2]	......	**3** 6
22 Jul 00		LIVE AT THE GREEK *SPV Recordings SPV 09172022* [3]	....	**39** 4

[1] Jimmy Page and Robert Plant [2] Page and Plant [3] Puff Daddy featuring
Jimmy Page [1] Roy Harper with Jimmy Page [2] Jimmy Page and Robert Plant
[3] Jimmy Page and The Black Crowes

Patti PAGE
US, female vocalist – Clara Ann Fowler (Singles: 5 Weeks)   pos/wks

| 27 Mar 53 | ● | (HOW MUCH IS) THAT DOGGIE IN THE WINDOW | | |
| | | *Oriole CB 1156* ▲ | ...... | **9** 5 |

Tommy PAGE *US, male vocalist (Singles: 3 Weeks)*   pos/wks

| 26 May 90 | I'LL BE YOUR EVERYTHING *Sire W 9959* ▲ | ...... | **53** 3 |

Wendy PAGE See TIN TIN OUT

PAGLIARO
Canada, male vocalist – Michel Pagliaro (Singles: 6 Weeks)   pos/wks

| 19 Feb 72 | LOVING YOU AIN'T EASY *Pye 7N 45111* | ...... | **31** 6 |

PAID & LIVE featuring Lauryn HILL *US, male*
production duo and female rapper / vocalist (Singles: 1 Week)   pos/wks

| 27 Dec 97 | ALL MY TIME *World Entertainment OWECD 2* | ...... | **57** 1 |

Elaine PAIGE ⟨ 338 ⟩ *Top 500* Revered actor / vocalist who has been
a West End stage regular for 40 years, b. Elaine Bickerstaff, 5 Mar 1948,
London, UK. An entertainer who will be forever associated with Lloyd Webber /
Rice musicals. Of the 600 recordings of 'Memory', hers was the biggest hit
(Singles: 41 Weeks, Albums: 159 Weeks)   pos/wks

Date	Title	pos	wks
21 Oct 78	DON'T WALK AWAY TILL I TOUCH YOU *EMI 2862*	46	5
6 Jun 81 ●	MEMORY (re) *Polydor POSP 279*	6	15
14 Apr 84	SOMETIMES (THEME FROM 'CHAMPIONS') *Island IS 174*	72	1
5 Jan 85 ★	I KNOW HIM SO WELL *RCA CHESS 3* [1]	1	16
21 Nov 87	THE SECOND TIME (THEME FROM 'BILITIS') *WEA YZ 163*	69	1
21 Jan 95	HYMNE A L'AMOUR (IF YOU LOVE ME) *WEA YZ 899CD*	68	1
24 Oct 98	MEMORY (re-recording) *WEA WEA 197CD*	36	2
1 May 82	ELAINE PAIGE *WEA K 58385*	56	6
5 Nov 83 ●	STAGES *K-Tel NE 1262*	2	48
20 Oct 84 ●	CINEMA *K-Tel NE 1282*	12	25
16 Nov 85 ●	LOVE HURTS *WEA WX 28*	8	20
29 Nov 86	CHRISTMAS *WEA WX 80*	27	6
5 Dec 87	MEMORIES – THE BEST OF ELAINE PAIGE *Telstar STAR 2313*	14	15
19 Nov 88	THE QUEEN ALBUM *Siren SRNLP 22*	51	8
27 Apr 91	LOVE CAN DO THAT *RCA PL 74932*	36	4
28 Nov 92	THE BEST OF ELAINE PAIGE AND BARBARA DICKSON *Telstar TCD 2632* [1]	22	9
10 Apr 93	ROMANCE AND THE STAGE *RCA 74321136152*	71	1
19 Nov 94	PIAF *WEA 4509946412*	46	3
1 Jul 95	ENCORE *WEA 0630104762*	20	6
28 Nov 98	ON REFLECTION – THE VERY BEST OF ELAINE PAIGE *Telstar TV / WEA TTVCD 2999*	60	4
5 Jun 04	CENTRE STAGE – THE VERY BEST OF ELAINE PAIGE *WSM WSMCD 171*	35	4

[1] Elaine Paige and Barbara Dickson [1] Elaine Paige and Barbara Dickson

Hal PAIGE and the WHALERS
US, male vocal / instrumental group (Singles: 1 Week)   pos/wks

Date	Title	pos	wks
25 Aug 60	GOING BACK TO MY HOME TOWN *Melodisc MEL 1553*	50	1

Jennifer PAIGE
US, female vocalist (Singles: 13 Weeks, Albums: 1 Week)   pos/wks

Date	Title	pos	wks
12 Sep 98 ●	CRUSH *EAR 0039425*	4	12
20 Mar 99	SOBER *EAR / Edel 0044185 ERE*	68	1
31 Oct 98	JENNIFER PAIGE *EAR 0039842 ERE*	67	1

Orchestre de Chambre Jean-Francois PAILLARD
France, male conductor and orchestra (Singles: 3 Weeks)   pos/wks

Date	Title	pos	wks
20 Aug 88	THEME FROM 'VIETNAM' (CANON IN D) *Debut DEBT 3053*	61	3

PALE *Ireland, male vocal / instrumental group (Singles: 2 Weeks)* pos/wks

Date	Title	pos	wks
13 Jun 92	DOGS WITH NO TAILS *A&M AM 866*	51	2

PALE FOUNTAINS *UK, male vocal /*
instrumental group (Singles: 6 Weeks, Albums: 3 Weeks)   pos/wks

Date	Title	pos	wks
27 Nov 82	THANK YOU *Virgin VS 557*	48	6
10 Mar 84	PACIFIC STREET *Virgin V 2274*	85	2
16 Feb 85	FROM ACROSS THE KITCHEN TABLE *Virgin V 2333*	94	1

PALE SAINTS *UK, male / female vocal /*
instrumental group (Singles: 1 Week, Albums: 3 Weeks)   pos/wks

Date	Title	pos	wks
6 Jul 91	KINKY LOVE *4AD AD 1009*	72	1
24 Feb 90	THE COMFORTS OF MADNESS *4AD CAD 0002*	40	2
4 Apr 92	IN RIBBONS *4AD CAD 2004CD*	61	1

PALE X *Holland, male producer – Michael Pollen (Singles: 1 Week)* pos/wks

Date	Title	pos	wks
3 Feb 01	NITRO *Nukleuz NUKP 0280*	74	1

PALLAS *UK, male vocal / instrumental group (Albums: 4 Weeks)* pos/wks

Date	Title	pos	wks
25 Feb 84	SENTINEL *Harvest SHSP 2400121*	41	3
22 Feb 86	THE WEDGE *Harvest SHVL 850*	70	1

Nerina PALLOT *UK, female vocalist (Singles: 3 Weeks)* pos/wks

Date	Title	pos	wks
18 Aug 01	PATIENCE *Polydor 5872122*	61	1
28 Feb 04	TRULY *Nettwerk 332202* [1]	54	2

[1] Delerium featuring Nerina Pallot

Barry PALMER See Mike OLDFIELD

Jhay PALMER featuring MC IMAGE
UK, male producer / vocalist and rapper (Singles: 1 Week)   pos/wks

Date	Title	pos	wks
27 Apr 02	HELLO *Bagatrix CDBTX 002*	69	1

Patsy PALMER See Sid OWEN

Robert PALMER ⟨ 198 ⟩ *Top 500* Grammy-winning UK rock-group
veteran and former member of Vinegar Joe, b. Alan Palmer, 19 Jan 1949,
Yorkshire, d. 26 Sep 2003. This vocalist's hottest run of transatlantic hits
came after he fronted short-lived Anglo-American supergroup Power Station
in 1985. He benefited from some striking award-winning videos featuring an
all-female backing band (parodied in a 1999 Shania Twain video) (Singles:
129 Weeks, Albums: 166 Weeks)   pos/wks

Date	Title	pos	wks
20 May 78	EVERY KINDA PEOPLE *Island WIP 6425*	53	4
7 Jul 79	BAD CASE OF LOVIN' YOU (DOCTOR DOCTOR) *Island WIP 6481*	61	2
6 Sep 80	JOHNNY AND MARY *Island WIP 6638*	44	8
22 Nov 80	LOOKING FOR CLUES *Island WIP 6651*	33	9
13 Feb 82	SOME GUYS HAVE ALL THE LUCK *Island WIP 6754*	16	8
2 Apr 83	YOU ARE IN MY SYSTEM *Island IS 104*	53	4
18 Jun 83	YOU CAN HAVE IT (TAKE MY HEART) *Island IS 121*	66	2
10 May 86 ●	ADDICTED TO LOVE *Island IS 270* ▲	5	15
19 Jul 86 ●	I DIDN'T MEAN TO TURN YOU ON *Island IS 283*	9	9
1 Nov 86	DISCIPLINE OF LOVE *Island IS 242*	68	1
26 Mar 88	SWEET LIES *Island IS 352*	58	3
11 Jun 88	SIMPLY IRRESISTIBLE *EMI EM 61*	44	4
15 Oct 88 ●	SHE MAKES MY DAY *EMI EM 65*	6	12
13 May 89	CHANGE HIS WAYS *EMI EM 85*	28	7
26 Aug 89	IT COULD HAPPEN TO YOU *EMI EM 99*	71	1
3 Nov 90 ●	I'LL BE YOUR BABY TONIGHT *EMI EM 167* [1]	6	10
5 Jan 91 ●	MERCY MERCY ME – I WANT YOU *EMI EM 173*	9	9
15 Jun 91	DREAMS TO REMEMBER *EMI EM 193*	68	1
7 Mar 92	EVERY KINDA PEOPLE (re-mix) *Island IS 498*	43	3
17 Oct 92	WITCHCRAFT *EMI EM 251*	50	3
9 Jul 94	GIRL U WANT *EMI CDEMS 331*	57	2
3 Sep 94	KNOW BY NOW *EMI CDEMS 343*	25	5
24 Dec 94	YOU BLOW ME AWAY *EMI CDEMS 350*	38	4
14 Oct 95	RESPECT YOURSELF *EMI CDEMS 399*	45	2
18 Jan 03	ADDICTED TO LOVE *Serious SER 060CD* [2]	42	1
6 Nov 76	SOME PEOPLE CAN DO WHAT THEY LIKE *Island ILPS 9420*	46	1
14 Jul 79	SECRETS *Island ILPS 9544*	54	4
6 Sep 80	CLUES *Island ILPS 9595*	31	8
3 Apr 82	MAYBE IT'S LIVE *Island ILPS 9665*	32	6
23 Apr 83	PRIDE *Island ILPS 9720*	37	9
16 Nov 85 ●	RIPTIDE *Island ILPS 9801*	5	37
9 Jul 88	HEAVY NOVA *EMI EMD 1007*	17	25
11 Nov 89 ●	ADDICTIONS VOLUME 1 *Island ILPS 9944*	7	17
17 Nov 90 ●	DON'T EXPLAIN *EMI EMDX 1018*	9	20
4 Apr 92	ADDICTIONS VOLUME 2 *Island CIDTV 4*	12	7
31 Oct 92	RIDIN' HIGH *EMI CDEMD 1038*	32	3
24 Sep 94	HONEY *EMI CDEMD 1069*	25	4
28 Oct 95 ●	THE VERY BEST OF ROBERT PALMER *EMI CDEMD 1088*	4	21
16 Nov 02	AT HIS VERY BEST *Universal TV 697812*	38	4

[1] Robert Palmer and UB40 [2] Shake B4 Use vs Robert Palmer

Suzanne PALMER See ABSOLUTE; CLUB 69; DJ TIESTO

Tyrone 'Visionary' PALMER See SLAM

PAN POSITION *Italy / Venezuela, male*
instrumental / production group (Singles: 1 Week)   pos/wks

Date	Title	pos	wks
18 Jun 94	ELEPHANT PAW (GET DOWN TO THE FUNK) *Positiva CDTIV 13*	55	1

PANDORA'S BOX
US, male / female vocal / instrumental group (Singles: 3 Weeks)   pos/wks

Date	Title	pos	wks
21 Oct 89	IT'S ALL COMING BACK TO ME NOW *Virgin VS 1216*	51	3

Darryl PANDY *US, male vocalist (Singles: 5 Weeks)* pos/wks

Date	Title	pos	wks
14 Dec 96	LOVE CAN'T TURN AROUND *4 Liberty LIBTCD 27* [1]	40	2
20 Feb 99	RAISE YOUR HANDS *VC Recordings VCRD 44* [2]	40	2
2 Oct 99	SUNSHINE & HAPPINESS *Azuli AZNYCD 103* [3]	68	1

[1] Farley 'Jackmaster' Funk with Darryl Pandy [2] Big Room Girl featuring Darryl Pandy [3] Darryl Pandy / Nerio's Dubwork

Johnny PANIC and the BIBLE OF DREAMS
(see also TEARS FOR FEARS) *UK, male / female vocal / instrumental group (Singles: 2 Weeks)* pos/wks

| 2 Feb 91 | JOHNNY PANIC AND THE BIBLE OF DREAMS *Fontana PANIC 1* | **70** | 2 |

PANJABI MC
UK, male DJ / producer – Rajinder Singh (Singles: 19 Weeks) pos/wks

4 Jan 03	MUNDIAN TO BACH KE (IMPORT) *Big Star BIGCDMO 76*	**59**	3
25 Jan 03 ●	MUNDIAN TO BACK KE *Showbiz / Instant Karma KARMA 28CD*	**5**	13
5 Jul 03	JOGI / BEWARE OF THE BOYS *Showbiz / Dharma DHARMA ICDS* [1]	**25**	3

[1] Panjabi MC featuring Jay-Z

PANTERA
US, male vocal / instrumental group (Singles: 8 Weeks, Albums: 10 Weeks) pos/wks

10 Oct 92	MOUTH FOR WAR *Atco A 5845T*	**73**	1
27 Feb 93	WALK *Atco B 6076CD*	**35**	2
19 Mar 94	I'M BROKEN *Atco B 5932CD1*	**19**	2
22 Oct 94	PLANET CARAVAN *East West A 5836CD1*	**26**	3
7 Mar 92	VULGAR DISPLAY OF POWER *Atco 7567917582*	**64**	1
2 Apr 94 ●	FAR BEYOND DRIVEN *Atco 7567923752* ▲	**3**	4
18 May 96	THE GREAT SOUTHERN TRENDKILL *East West 7559619082*	**17**	3
30 Aug 97	OFFICIAL LIVE – 101 PROOF *East West 7559620682*	**54**	1
8 Apr 00	REINVENTING THE STEEL *Elektra 7559624512*	**33**	1

PAPA ROACH
US, male vocal / instrumental group (Singles: 27 Weeks, Albums: 45 Weeks) pos/wks

17 Feb 01 ●	LAST RESORT *Dreamworks / Polydor 4509212*	**3**	10
5 May 01	BETWEEN ANGELS & INSECTS *Dreamworks / Polydor 4509082*	**17**	6
22 Jun 02	SHE LOVES ME NOT *Dreamworks / Polydor 4508182*	**14**	8
2 Nov 02	TIME AND TIME AGAIN *Dreamworks / Polydor 4508052*	**54**	1
18 Sep 04	GETTING AWAY WITH MURDER *Geffen 9863647*	**45**	2
13 Jan 01 ●	INFEST *Dreamworks 4502232*	**9**	36
29 Jun 02 ●	LOVEHATETRAGEDY *Dreamworks 4503672*	**4**	7
11 Sep 04	GETTING AWAY WITH MURDER *Geffen 9863643*	**30**	2

The PAPER DOLLS
UK, female vocal group (Singles: 13 Weeks) pos/wks

| 13 Mar 68 | SOMETHING HERE IN MY HEART (KEEPS A-TELLIN' ME NO) *Pye 7N 17456* | **11** | 13 |

PAPER LACE
UK, male vocal / instrumental group – lead vocal Phil Wright (Singles: 41 Weeks) pos/wks

23 Feb 74 ★	BILLY DON'T BE A HERO *Bus Stop BUS 1014*	**1**	14
4 May 74 ●	THE NIGHT CHICAGO DIED *Bus Stop BUS 1016* ▲	**3**	11
24 Aug 74	THE BLACK EYED BOYS *Bus Stop BUS 1019*	**11**	10
4 Mar 78	WE GOT THE WHOLE WORLD IN OUR HANDS *Warner Bros. K 17110* [1]	**24**	6

[1] Nottingham Forest with Paper Lace

PAPERDOLLS
UK, female vocal group (Singles: 1 Week) pos/wks

| 12 Sep 98 | GONNA MAKE YOU BLUSH *MCA MCSTD 40175* | **65** | 1 |

PAPPA BEAR featuring VAN DER TOORN
US, male rapper – June Rollocks and Holland, male vocalist – Jan Van Der Toorn (Singles: 1 Week) pos/wks

| 16 May 98 | CHERISH *Universal UMD 70316* | **47** | 1 |

PAR-T-ONE vs INXS
Italy, male production trio and Australia, male vocal / instrumental group (Singles: 6 Weeks) pos/wks

| 3 Nov 01 | I'M SO CRAZY (re) *Credence CDCRED 016* | **19** | 6 |

Vanessa PARADIS
France, female vocalist (Singles: 30 Weeks, Albums: 2 Weeks) pos/wks

13 Feb 88 ●	JOE LE TAXI *FA Productions POSP 902*	**3**	10
10 Oct 92 ●	BE MY BABY *Remark PO 235*	**6**	15
27 Feb 93	SUNDAY MONDAYS *Remark PZCD 251*	**49**	4

| 24 Jul 93 | JUST AS LONG AS YOU ARE THERE *Remark PZCD 272* | **57** | 1 |
| 7 Nov 92 | VANESSA PARADIS *Remark 5139542* | **45** | 2 |

PARADISE
UK, male vocal / instrumental group (Singles: 4 Weeks) pos/wks

| 10 Sep 83 | ONE MIND, TWO HEARTS *Priority P 1* | **42** | 4 |

PARADISE LOST
UK, male vocal / instrumental group (Singles: 3 Weeks, Albums: 6 Weeks) pos/wks

20 May 95	THE LAST TIME *Music for Nations CDKUT 165*	**60**	1
7 Oct 95	FOREVER FAILURE *Music for Nations CDKUT 169*	**66**	1
28 Jun 97	SAY JUST WORDS *Music for Nations CDKUT 174*	**53**	1
24 Jun 95	DRACONIAN TIMES *Music for Nations CDMFNX 184*	**16**	3
26 Jul 97	ONE SECOND *Music for Nations CDMFNX 222*	**31**	2
19 Jun 99	HOST *EMI 5205672*	**61**	1

PARADISE ORGANISATION
UK, male instrumental / production group (Singles: 1 Week) pos/wks

| 23 Jan 93 | PRAYER TOWER *Cowboy RODEO 13* | **70** | 1 |

PARADOX
UK, male instrumental duo (Singles: 2 Weeks) pos/wks

| 24 Feb 90 | JAILBREAK *Ronin 7R2* | **66** | 2 |

Norrie PARAMOR
(see also BIG BEN BANJO BAND) *UK, orchestra – leader b. 1913, d. 9 Sep 1979 (Singles: 25 Weeks, Albums: 16 Weeks)* pos/wks

17 Mar 60	THEME FROM 'A SUMMER PLACE' *Columbia DB 4419*	**36**	2
22 Mar 62	THEME FROM 'Z CARS' *Columbia DB 4789*	**33**	6
10 May 62 ●	I'M LOOKING OUT THE WINDOW *Columbia DB 4828* [1]	**2**	17
21 Oct 61 ★	21 TODAY *Columbia 33SX 1368* [1]	**1**	16

[1] Cliff Richard with the Norrie Paramor Orchestra [1] Cliff Richard, The Shadows and Norrie Paramor and his Orchestra

PARAMOUNT JAZZ BAND See Acker BILK

The PARAMOUNTS
UK, male vocal / instrumental group (Singles: 7 Weeks) pos/wks

| 16 Jan 64 | POISON IVY *Parlophone R 5093* | **35** | 7 |

PARCHMENT
UK, male / female vocal / instrumental group (Singles: 5 Weeks) pos/wks

| 16 Sep 72 | LIGHT UP THE FIRE *Pye 7N 45178* | **31** | 5 |

PARIS
UK, male / female vocal group (Singles: 4 Weeks) pos/wks

| 19 Jun 82 | NO GETTING OVER YOU *RCA 222* | **49** | 4 |

PARIS
US, male vocalist – Oscar Jackson (Singles: 2 Weeks) pos/wks

| 21 Jan 95 | GUERRILLA FUNK *Priority PTYCD 100* | **38** | 2 |

Mica PARIS
UK, female vocalist – Michelle Wallen (Singles: 63 Weeks, Albums: 40 Weeks) pos/wks

7 May 88 ●	MY ONE TEMPTATION *Fourth & Broadway BRW 85*	**7**	11
30 Jul 88	LIKE DREAMERS DO *Fourth & Broadway BRW 108* [1]	**26**	5
22 Oct 88	BREATHE LIFE INTO ME *Fourth & Broadway BRW 115*	**26**	10
21 Jan 89	WHERE IS THE LOVE *Fourth & Broadway BRW 122* [2]	**19**	7
6 Oct 90	CONTRIBUTION *Fourth & Broadway BRW 188*	**33**	4
1 Dec 90	SOUTH OF THE RIVER *Fourth & Broadway BRW 199*	**50**	2
23 Feb 91	IF I LOVE U 2 NITE *Fourth & Broadway BRW 207*	**43**	3
31 Aug 91	YOUNG SOUL REBELS *Big Life BLR 57*	**61**	3
3 Apr 93	I NEVER FELT LIKE THIS BEFORE *Fourth & Broadway BRCD 263*	**15**	5
5 Jun 93	I WANNA HOLD ON TO YOU *Fourth & Broadway BRCD 275*	**27**	3
7 Aug 93	TWO IN A MILLION *Fourth & Broadway BRCD 285*	**51**	2
4 Dec 93	WHISPER A PRAYER *Fourth & Broadway BRCD 287*	**65**	1
8 Apr 95	ONE *Cooltempo CDCOOL 304*	**29**	4
16 May 98	STAY *Cooltempo CDCOOL 334*	**40**	2
14 Nov 98	BLACK ANGEL *Cooltempo CDCOOL 341*	**72**	1
3 Sep 88 ●	SO GOOD *Fourth & Broadway BRLP 525*	**6**	32
27 Oct 90	CONTRIBUTION *Fourth & Broadway BRLP 558*	**26**	3
26 Jun 93	WHISPER A PRAYER *Fourth & Broadway BRCD 591*	**20**	4
22 Aug 98	BLACK ANGEL *Cooltempo 4958132*	**59**	1

[1] Mica Paris featuring Courtney Pine
[2] Mica Paris and Will Downing

Ryan PARIS
France, male vocalist – Fabio Roscioli (Singles: 10 Weeks)   pos/wks

| 3 Sep 83 ● | DOLCE VITA *Carrere CAR 289* .... | 5 | 10 |

PARIS & SHARP
UK, male production duo (Singles: 1 Week)   pos/wks

| 1 Dec 01 | APHRODITE *Cream / Parlophone CREAM 16CD* .... | 61 | 1 |

PARIS ANGELS
UK, male / female vocal / instrumental group (Singles: 5 Weeks, Albums: 2 Weeks)   pos/wks

3 Nov 90	SCOPE *Sheer Joy SHEER 0047*	75	1
20 Jul 91	PERFUME *Virgin VS 1360*	55	3
21 Sep 91	FADE *Virgin VS 1365*	70	1
17 Aug 91	SUNDEW *Virgin V 2667*	37	2

PARIS RED
US / Germany, male / female vocal / instrumental duo (Singles: 2 Weeks)   pos/wks

| 29 Feb 92 | GOOD FRIEND *Columbia 6569417* .... | 61 | 1 |
| 15 May 93 | PROMISES *Columbia 6592342* .... | 59 | 1 |

John PARISH and Polly Jean HARVEY
(see also PJ HARVEY) *US, male producer / instrumentalist and UK female vocalist (Singles: 1 Week)*   pos/wks

| 23 Nov 96 | THAT WAS MY VEIL *Island CID 648* .... | 75 | 1 |

Simon PARK ORCHESTRA
UK, orchestra (Singles: 24 Weeks) pos/wks

| 25 Nov 72 ★ | EYE LEVEL (THEME FROM THE TV SERIES 'VAN DER VALK') (re) *Columbia DB 8946* ◆ .... | 1 | 24 |

'Eye Level' made No.41 on its original visit to the chart before re-entering and peaking at No.1 in Sep 1973

Graham PARKER and the RUMOUR
UK, male vocal / instrumental group (Singles: 16 Weeks, Albums: 35 Weeks)   pos/wks

19 Mar 77	THE PINK PARKER EP *Vertigo PARK 001*	24	5
22 Apr 78	HEY LORD, DON'T ASK ME QUESTIONS *Vertigo PARK 002*	32	7
20 Mar 82	TEMPORARY BEAUTY *RCA PARK 100* [1]	50	4
27 Nov 76	HEAT TREATMENT *Vertigo 6360 137*	52	2
12 Nov 77	STICK TO ME *Vertigo 9102 017*	19	4
27 May 78	PARKERILLA *Vertigo 6641 797*	14	5
7 Apr 79	SQUEEZING OUT SPARKS *Vertigo 9102 030*	18	8
7 Jun 80	THE UP ESCALATOR *Stiff SEEZ 23*	11	10
27 Mar 82	ANOTHER GREY AREA *RCA RCALP 6029* [1]	40	6

[1] Graham Parker [1] Graham Parker

Tracks on The Pink Parker EP: Hold Back the Night / (Let Me Get) Sweet on You / White Honey / Soul Shoes

Ray PARKER Jr (see also RAYDIO)
US, male vocalist / instrumentalist – guitar (Singles: 47 Weeks, Albums: 7 Weeks)   pos/wks

25 Aug 84 ●	GHOSTBUSTERS *Arista ARIST 580* ▲	2	31
18 Jan 86	GIRLS ARE MORE FUN *Arista ARIST 641*	46	4
3 Oct 87	I DON'T THINK THAT MAN SHOULD SLEEP ALONE *Geffen GEF 27*	13	10
30 Jan 88	OVER YOU *Geffen GEF 33*	65	2
10 Oct 87	AFTER DARK *WEA WX 122*	40	7

Robert PARKER
US, male vocalist / instrumentalist – saxophone (Singles: 8 Weeks) pos/wks

| 4 Aug 66 | BAREFOOTIN' *Island WI 286* .... | 24 | 8 |

Sara PARKER
US, female vocalist (Singles: 2 Weeks)   pos/wks

| 12 Apr 97 | MY LOVE IS DEEP *Manifesto FESCD 22* .... | 22 | 2 |

Jimmy PARKINSON
Australia, male vocalist (Singles: 19 Weeks) pos/wks

2 Mar 56 ●	THE GREAT PRETENDER *Columbia DB 3729*	9	13
17 Aug 56	WALK HAND IN HAND (re) *Columbia DB 3775*	26	2
9 Nov 56	IN THE MIDDLE OF THE HOUSE (re) *Columbia DB 3833*	20	4

Alex PARKS
UK, female vocalist (Singles: 13 Weeks, Albums: 15 Weeks)   pos/wks

29 Nov 03 ●	MAYBE THAT'S WHAT IT TAKES *Polydor 9814581*	3	9
28 Feb 04	CRY *Polydor 9816985*	13	4
6 Dec 03 ●	INTRODUCTION *Polydor 9866005*	5	15

PARKS & WILSON
UK, male production duo – Michael Parks and Michael Wilson (Singles: 1 Week)   pos/wks

| 9 Sep 00 | FEEL THE DRUM (EP) *Hooj Choons HOOJ 099* .... | 71 | 1 |

Tracks on Feel the Drum (EP): My Orbit / The Dragon / My Orbit (re-mix) / Drum Parade (No UFOs)

PARLIAMENT *See Scott GROOVES*

John PARR
UK, male vocalist (Singles: 22 Weeks, Albums: 2 Weeks)   pos/wks

14 Sep 85 ●	ST ELMO'S FIRE (MAN IN MOTION) *London LON 73* ▲	6	13
18 Jan 86	NAUGHTY NAUGHTY *London LON 80*	58	3
30 Aug 86	ROCK 'N' ROLL MERCENARIES *Arista ARIST 666* [1]	31	6
2 Nov 85	JOHN PARR *London LONLP 12*	60	2

[1] Meat Loaf featuring John Parr

Dean PARRISH
US, male vocalist – Phil Anastasi (Singles: 5 Weeks)   pos/wks

| 8 Feb 75 | I'M ON MY WAY *UK USA 2* .... | 38 | 5 |

Man PARRISH
US, male DJ / producer – Manny Parrish (Singles: 26 Weeks)   pos/wks

26 Mar 83	HIP HOP, BE BOP (DON'T STOP) *Polydor POSP 575*	41	6
23 Mar 85	BOOGIE DOWN (BRONX) *Boiling Point POSP 731*	56	4
13 Sep 86 ●	MALE STRIPPER (2re) *Bolts BOLTS 4* [1]	4	16

[1] Man 2 Man meet Man Parrish

'Male Stripper' made No.64 on its first chart visit followed by No.63 in Jan 1987 and No.4 on its second re-entry in Feb 1987

Karen PARRY *See FLIP & FILL; PASCAL featuring Karen PARRY*

Bill PARSONS
US, male vocalist (Singles: 2 Weeks)   pos/wks

| 10 Apr 59 | THE ALL AMERICAN BOY *London HL 8798* .... | 22 | 2 |

Record erroneously credited to Bill Parsons; actual vocalist is Bobby Bare

The Alan PARSONS PROJECT
UK, male vocal / instrumental group (Singles: 4 Weeks, Albums: 38 Weeks)   pos/wks

15 Jan 83	OLD AND WISE *Arista ARIST 494* [1]	74	1
10 Mar 84	DON'T ANSWER ME *Arista ARIST 553*	58	3
28 Aug 76	TALES OF MYSTERY AND IMAGINATION *Charisma CDS 4003*	56	1
13 Aug 77	I ROBOT *Arista SPARTY 1016*	30	1
10 Jun 78	PYRAMID *Arista SPART 1054*	49	4
29 Sep 79	EVE *Arista SPARTY 1100*	74	1
15 Nov 80	THE TURN OF A FRIENDLY CARD *Arista DLART 1*	38	4
29 May 82	EYE IN THE SKY *Arista 204 666*	27	11
26 Nov 83	THE BEST OF THE ALAN PARSONS PROJECT *Arista APP 1*	99	1
3 Mar 84	AMMONIA AVENUE *Arista 206 100*	24	8
23 Feb 85	VULTURE CULTURE *Arista 206 577*	40	5
14 Feb 87	GAUDI *Arista 208 084*	66	2

[1] The Alan Parsons Project: lead vocals by Colin Blunstone

The PARTISANS
UK, male vocal / instrumental group (Albums: 1 Week)   pos/wks

| 19 Feb 83 | THE PARTISANS *No Future PUNK 4* .... | 94 | 1 |

PARTIZAN (see also CAMISRA; ESCRIMA; The GRIFTERS)
UK, male DJ / production duo – 'Tall Paul' Newman and Craig Daniel-Yefet (Singles: 3 Weeks)   pos/wks

| 8 Feb 97 | DRIVE ME CRAZY *Multiply CDMULTY 17* .... | 36 | 2 |
| 6 Dec 97 | KEEP YOUR LOVE *Multiply CDMULTY 29* [1] .... | 53 | 1 |

[1] Partizan featuring Natalie Robb

PARTNERS *See Al HUDSON*

PARTNERS IN KRYME
US, male rap duo – James Alpem and Richard Usher (Singles: 10 Weeks)   pos/wks

| 21 Jul 90 ★ | TURTLE POWER *SBK TURTLE 1* .... | 1 | 10 |

David PARTON
UK, male vocalist (Singles: 9 Weeks)   pos/wks

| 15 Jan 77 ● | ISN'T SHE LOVELY *Pye 7N 45663* .... | 4 | 9 |

Dolly PARTON
US, female vocalist / instrumentalist – guitar (Singles: 34 Weeks, Albums: 46 Weeks) pos/wks

15 May 76 ●	JOLENE *RCA 2675*	**7**	10
21 Feb 81	9 TO 5 *RCA 25* ▲	**47**	5
12 Nov 83 ●	ISLANDS IN THE STREAM *RCA 378* [1] ▲	**7**	15
7 Apr 84	HERE YOU COME AGAIN *RCA 395*	**75**	1
16 Apr 94	THE DAY I FALL IN LOVE *Columbia 6600282* [2]	**64**	2
19 Oct 02	IF *Sanctuary SANX 139*	**73**	1
25 Nov 78	BOTH SIDES *Lotus WH 5006*	**45**	12
7 Sep 85	GREATEST HITS *RCA PL 84422*	**74**	1
14 Mar 87	TRIO *Warner Bros. 9254911* [1]	**60**	4
22 Oct 94	THE GREATEST HITS *Telstar TCD 2739*	**65**	2
8 Nov 97	A LIFE IN MUSIC – ULTIMATE COLLECTION *RCA 74321443632*	**38**	3
26 Sep 98	HUNGRY AGAIN *MCA Nashville UMD 80522*	**41**	1
24 Feb 01	LITTLE SPARROW *Sanctuary SANCD 074*	**30**	6
3 Mar 01	GOLD – GREATEST HITS *RCA 74321840202*	**23**	5
20 Jul 02	HALOS & HORNS *Sanctuary SANCD 126*	**37**	4
2 Aug 03	ULTIMATE DOLLY PARTON *RCA 82876542012*	**17**	6

[1] Kenny Rogers and Dolly Parton [2] Dolly Parton and James Ingram [1] Dolly Parton / Emmylou Harris / Linda Ronstadt

Stella PARTON
US, female vocalist (Singles: 4 Weeks) pos/wks

22 Oct 77	THE DANGER OF A STRANGER *Elektra K 12272*	**35**	4

Alan PARTRIDGE
UK, male comedian – Steve Coogan (Albums: 3 Weeks) pos/wks

18 Mar 95	KNOWING ME KNOWING YOU 3 *BBC Canned Laughter ZBBC 1671CD*	**41**	3

Don PARTRIDGE
UK, male vocalist / instrumentalist – one-man band (Singles: 32 Weeks) pos/wks

7 Feb 68 ●	ROSIE *Columbia DB 8330*	**4**	12
29 May 68 ●	BLUE EYES *Columbia DB 8416*	**3**	13
19 Feb 69	BREAKFAST ON PLUTO *Columbia DB 8538*	**26**	7

The PARTRIDGE FAMILY (see also David CASSIDY)
US, male / female actor / vocal group (Singles: 53 Weeks, Albums: 13 Weeks) pos/wks

13 Feb 71	I THINK I LOVE YOU *Bell 1130* [1] ▲	**18**	9
26 Feb 72	IT'S ONE OF THOSE NIGHTS (YES LOVE) *Bell 1203* [1]	**11**	11
8 Jul 72 ●	BREAKING UP IS HARD TO DO *Bell MABEL 1* [1]	**3**	13
3 Feb 73 ●	LOOKING THRU THE EYES OF LOVE *Bell 1278* [2]	**9**	9
19 May 73 ●	WALKING IN THE RAIN *Bell 1293* [2]	**10**	11
8 Jan 72	UP TO DATE *Bell SBLL 143*	**46**	2
22 Apr 72	THE PARTRIDGE FAMILY SOUND MAGAZINE *Bell BELLS 206*	**14**	7
30 Sep 72	SHOPPING BAG *Bell BELLS 212*	**28**	3
9 Dec 72	CHRISTMAS CARD *Bell BELLS 214*	**45**	1

[1] The Partridge Family starring Shirley Jones featuring David Cassidy
[2] The Partridge Family starring David Cassidy

PARTY ANIMALS
Holland, male instrumental / production duo (Singles: 3 Weeks) pos/wks

1 Jun 96	HAVE YOU EVER BEEN MELLOW *Mokum DB 17553*	**56**	1
19 Oct 96	HAVE YOU EVER BEEN MELLOW (EP) *Mokum DB 17413*	**43**	2

Tracks on Have You Ever Been Mellow (EP): Have You Ever Been Mellow / Hava Naquilla / Aquarius

PARTY BOYS
Holland, male production group (Singles: 2 Weeks) pos/wks

10 Jan 04	BUILD ME UP BUTTERCUP 2003 *Liberty CDUP 001*	**44**	2

PARTY FAITHFUL
UK, male / female vocal / instrumental group (Singles: 1 Week) pos/wks

22 Jul 95	BRASS: LET THERE BE HOUSE *Ore AG 10CD*	**54**	1

The PASADENAS
UK, male vocal group (Singles: 57 Weeks, Albums: 32 Weeks) pos/wks

28 May 88 ●	TRIBUTE (RIGHT ON) *CBS PASA 1*	**5**	14
17 Sep 88	RIDING ON A TRAIN *CBS PASA 2*	**13**	9
26 Nov 88	ENCHANTED LADY *CBS PASA 3*	**31**	6
12 May 90	LOVE THING *CBS PASA 4*	**22**	5
14 Jul 90	REELING *CBS PASA 5*	**75**	1
1 Feb 92 ●	I'M DOING FINE NOW *Columbia 6577187*	**4**	10

4 Apr 92	MAKE IT WITH YOU *Columbia 6579257*	**20**	4
6 Jun 92	I BELIEVE IN MIRACLES *Columbia 6580567*	**34**	3
29 Aug 92	MOVING IN THE RIGHT DIRECTION *Columbia 6583417*	**49**	2
21 Nov 92	LET'S STAY TOGETHER *Columbia 6587747*	**22**	3
22 Oct 88 ●	TO WHOM IT MAY CONCERN *CBS 462877 1*	**3**	21
7 Mar 92 ●	YOURS SINCERELY *Columbia 4712642*	**6**	11

PASCAL featuring Karen PARRY (see also FLIP & FILL)
UK, male producer and female vocalist (Singles: 5 Weeks) pos/wks

28 Dec 02	I THINK WE'RE ALONE NOW *All Around the World CDGLOBE 267*	**23**	5

PASSENGERS
Ireland / UK / Italy, male vocal / instrumental group (Singles: 9 Weeks, Albums: 5 Weeks) pos/wks

2 Dec 95 ●	MISS SARAJEVO *Island CID 625*	**6**	9
18 Nov 95	ORIGINAL SOUNDTRACKS 1 *Island CID 8043*	**12**	5

PASSION
UK, male vocal / rap group (Singles: 1 Week) pos/wks

25 Jan 97	SHARE YOUR LOVE (NO DIGGITY) *Charm CRTCDS 269*	**62**	1

The PASSIONS
UK, male / female vocal / instrumental group (Singles: 8 Weeks, Albums: 1 Week) pos/wks

31 Jan 81	I'M IN LOVE WITH A GERMAN FILM STAR *Polydor POSP 222*	**25**	8
3 Oct 81	THIRTY THOUSAND FEET OVER CHINA *Polydor POLS 1041*	**92**	1

PAT and MICK
UK, male DJ / vocal duo – Pat Sharp and Mick Brown (Singles: 27 Weeks) pos/wks

9 Apr 88	LET'S ALL CHANT / ON THE NIGHT *PWL PWL 10* [1]	**11**	9
25 Mar 89 ●	I HAVEN'T STOPPED DANCING YET *PWL PWL 33*	**9**	8
14 Apr 90	USE IT UP AND WEAR IT OUT *PWL PWL 55*	**22**	6
23 Mar 91	GIMME SOME *PWL PWL 75*	**53**	2
15 May 93	HOT HOT HOT *PWL International PARKCD 1*	**47**	2

[1] Mick and Pat

'On the Night' listed only from 4 Jun 1988. It peaked at No.70

PATIENCE and PRUDENCE
US, female vocal duo – Patience and Prudence McIntyre (Singles: 8 Weeks) pos/wks

2 Nov 56	TONIGHT YOU BELONG TO ME *London HLU 8321*	**28**	3
1 Mar 57	GONNA GET ALONG WITHOUT YA NOW (re) *London HLU 8369*	**22**	5

PATRA
Jamaica, female vocalist (Singles: 11 Weeks) pos/wks

25 Dec 93	FAMILY AFFAIR *Polydor PZCD 304* [1]	**18**	8
30 Sep 95	PULL UP TO THE BUMPER *Epic 6623942*	**50**	2
10 Aug 96	WORK MI BODY *Heavenly HVN 53CD* [2]	**75**	1

[1] Shabba Ranks featuring Patra and Terri & Monica [2] Monkey Mafia featuring Patra

PATRIC (see also WORLDS APART)
UK, male vocalist – Patric Osborne (Singles: 2 Weeks) pos/wks

9 Jul 94	LOVE ME *Bell 7432125352*	**54**	2

Dee PATTEN
UK, male DJ / producer (Singles: 1 Week) pos/wks

30 Jan 99	WHO'S THE BAD MAN? *Higher Ground HIGHS 15CD*	**42**	1

Kellee PATTERSON
US, female vocalist (Singles: 7 Weeks) pos/wks

18 Feb 78	IF IT DON'T FIT DON'T FORCE IT *EMI International INT 544*	**44**	7

Rahsaan PATTERSON
US, male vocalist (Singles: 2 Weeks) pos/wks

26 Jul 97	STOP BY *MCA MCSTD 48055*	**50**	1
21 Mar 98	WHERE YOU ARE *MCA MCSTD 48073*	**55**	1

Lizzy PATTINSON See MILK & SUGAR

Billy PAUL
US, male vocalist – Paul Williams (Singles: 44 Weeks) pos/wks

13 Jan 73	ME AND MRS JONES *Epic EPC 1055* ▲	**12**	9
12 Jan 74	THANKS FOR SAVING MY LIFE *Philadelphia International PIR 1928*	**33**	6
22 May 76	LET'S MAKE A BABY *Philadelphia International PIR 4144*	**30**	5
30 Apr 77	LET 'EM IN *Philadelphia International PIR 5143*	**26**	5

16 Jul 77	YOUR SONG *Philadelphia International PIR 5391*	...........**37**	7
19 Nov 77	ONLY THE STRONG SURVIVE		
	Philadelphia International PIR 5699	.........**33**	7
14 Jul 79	BRING THE FAMILY BACK		
	Philadelphia International PIR 7456	..........**51**	5

Chris PAUL (see also ISOTONIK)
UK, male producer / instrumentalist – guitar (Singles: 8 Weeks)   pos/wks

31 May 86	EXPANSIONS '86 (EXPAND YOUR MIND)		
	Fourth & Broadway BRW 48 [1]	...........**58**	5
21 Nov 87	BACK IN MY ARMS *Syncopate SY 5*	..........**74**	2
13 Aug 88	TURN THE MUSIC UP *Syncopate SY 13*	..........**73**	1

[1] Chris Paul featuring David Joseph

Frankie PAUL See APACHE INDIAN

Les PAUL and Mary FORD
US, male instrumentalist – guitar – Les Polsfuss and female vocalist – Colleen Summers, b. 7 Jul 1924, d. 30 Sep 1977 (Singles: 4 Weeks)   pos/wks

| 20 Nov 53 | ● VAYA CON DIOS (MAY GOD BE WITH YOU) *Capitol CL 13943* ▲ | **7** | 4 |

Lyn PAUL (see also The NEW SEEKERS)
UK, female vocalist – Lynda Belcher (Singles: 6 Weeks)   pos/wks

| 28 Jun 75 | IT OUGHTA SELL A MILLION *Polydor 2058 602* | ....**37** | 6 |

Owen PAUL *UK, male vocalist – Owen McGee (Singles: 14 Weeks)*   pos/wks

| 31 May 86 | ● MY FAVOURITE WASTE OF TIME *Epic A 7125* | ....**3** | 14 |

Sean PAUL *Jamaica, male vocalist – Sean
Paul Henriques (Singles: 80 Weeks, Albums: 45 Weeks)*   pos/wks

21 Sep 02	GIMME THE LIGHT (re) *VP VPCD 6400*	..........**32**	7
15 Feb 03	● GIMME THE LIGHT (re-issue) *VP / Atlantic AT 0146CD*	....**5**	10
24 May 03	● GET BUSY *VP / Atlantic ATO 155CD* ▲	.............**4**	7
19 Jul 03	BREATHE (IMPORT) *Arista 8786509842* [1]	.........**59**	3
9 Aug 03	★ BREATHE *Arista 82876545722* [1] ■	.............**1**	18
6 Sep 03	● LIKE GLUE *VP / Atlantic 0162*	.............**3**	10
18 Oct 03	● BABY BOY (re) *Columbia 6744082* [2] ▲	.............**2**	11
17 Jan 04	● I'M STILL IN LOVE WITH YOU *VP / Atlantic AT 0170CD* [3]	......**6**	14
10 May 03	● DUTTY ROCK *Atlantic 7567836202*	.............**2**	45

[1] Blu Cantrell featuring Sean Paul [2] Beyoncé featuring Sean Paul [3] Sean Paul featuring Sasha

PAUL and PAULA *US, male / female vocal duo –
Ray Hildebrand and Jill Jackson (Singles: 31 Weeks)*   pos/wks

| 14 Feb 63 | ● HEY PAULA (re) *Philips 304012 BF* ▲ | ....**8** | 17 |
| 18 Apr 63 | ● YOUNG LOVERS *Philips 304016 BF* | ....**9** | 14 |

Luciano PAVAROTTI ⬭169 Top 500 *The world's best known opera
singer, b. 12 Oct 1935, Modena, Italy. The tenor who first took opera to the top of
the pop charts and onto the world's football terraces was also the first Italian to
score a No.1 album (Singles: 30 Weeks, Albums: 298 Weeks)*   pos/wks

16 Jun 90	● NESSUN DORMA *Decca PAV 03*	.............**2**	11
24 Oct 92	MISERERE *London LON 329* [1]	..........**15**	5
30 Jul 94	LIBIAMO / LA DONNA E MOBILE *Teldec YZ 843CD* [2]	..........**21**	4
14 Dec 96	● LIVE LIKE HORSES *Rocket LLHDD 1* [3]	.............**9**	6
25 Jul 98	YOU'LL NEVER WALK ALONE *Decca 4607982* [4]	..........**35**	4
15 May 82	PAVAROTTI'S GREATEST HITS *Decca D 2362*	..........**95**	1
30 Jun 84	MAMMA *Decca 411959* [1]	..........**96**	1
9 Aug 86	THE PAVAROTTI COLLECTION *Stylus SMR 8617*	..........**12**	34
16 Jul 88	THE NEW PAVAROTTI COLLECTION LIVE! *Stylus SMR 857*	..........**63**	8
17 Mar 90	★ THE ESSENTIAL PAVAROTTI *Decca 4302101*	.............**1**	72
1 Sep 90	★ IN CONCERT *Decca 4304331* [2]	.............**1**	78
20 Jul 91	★ ESSENTIAL PAVAROTTI II *Decca 4304701*	.............**1**	28
15 Feb 92	PAVAROTTI IN HYDE PARK *Decca 4363202*	..........**19**	7
4 Sep 93	TI AMO – PUCCINI'S GREATEST LOVE SONGS *Decca 4250992*	..........**23**	4
12 Feb 94	MY HEART'S DELIGHT *Decca 4432602*	..........**44**	4
10 Sep 94	★ THE THREE TENORS IN CONCERT 1994 *Teldec 4509962002* [3]	..**1**	26
30 Mar 96	TOGETHER FOR THE CHILDREN OF BOSNIA *Decca 4521002* [4]	..**11**	6
14 Dec 96	FOR WAR CHILD *Decca 4529002*	..........**45**	4
25 Oct 97	THE ULTIMATE COLLECTION *Decca 4580002*	..........**39**	5
29 Aug 98	THE THREE TENORS IN PARIS 1998 *Decca 4605002* [2]	..........**14**	6
19 Jun 99	LOVE SONGS *Decca 4664002*	..........**26**	6
23 Dec 00	THE THREE TENORS CHRISTMAS *Sony Classical SK 89131* [5]	..**57**	2

| 21 Jul 01 | AMORE – THE LOVE ALBUM *Decca 4701302* | ....**41** | 2 |
| 15 Nov 03 | TI ADORO *Decca 4754602* | ....**21** | 4 |

[1] Zucchero with Luciano Pavarotti [2] José Carreras featuring Placido Domingo and Luciano Pavarotti with Mehta [3] Elton John & Luciano Pavarotti [4] José Carreras, Placido Domingo and Luciano Pavarotti with Mehta [1] Luciano Pavarotti with the Henry Mancini Orchestra [2] José Carreras, Placido Domingo and Luciano Pavarotti [3] José Carreras, Placido Domingo and Luciano Pavarotti conducted by Zubin Mehta [4] Pavarotti and Friends [5] José Carreras, Placido Domingo and Luciano Pavarotti featuring Zubin Mehta

PAVEMENT *US, male vocal / instrumental
group (Singles: 6 Weeks, Albums: 13 Weeks)*   pos/wks

28 Nov 92	WATERY, DOMESTIC (EP) *Big Cat ABB 38T*	..........**58**	1
12 Feb 94	CUT YOUR HAIR *Big Cat ABB 55SCD*	..........**52**	1
8 Feb 97	STEREO *Domino RUG 51CD*	..........**48**	1
3 May 97	SHADY LANE *Domino RUG 53CD*	..........**40**	1
22 May 99	CARROT ROPE *Domino RUG 90CD1*	..........**27**	2
25 Apr 92	SLANTED AND ENCHANTED *Big Cat ABB 34CD*	..........**72**	1
3 Apr 93	WESTING (BY MUSKET AND SEXTANT) *Big Cat ABBCD 40*	..........**30**	2
26 Feb 94	CROOKED RAIN CROOKED RAIN *Big Cat ABB 56CD*	..........**15**	3
22 Apr 95	WOWEE ZOWEE *Big Cat ABB 84CD*	..........**18**	2
22 Feb 97	BRIGHTEN THE CORNERS *Domino Recordings WIGCD 31*	..........**27**	2
19 Jun 99	TERROR TWILIGHT *Domino Recordings WIGCD 66*	..........**19**	3

Tracks on Watery, Domestic (EP): Texas Never Whispers / Frontwards / Feed 'Em / The Linden Lions / Shoot the Singer (1 Sick Verse)

Rita PAVONE *Italy, female vocalist (Singles: 19 Weeks)*   pos/wks

| 1 Dec 66 | HEART *RCA 1553* | ....**27** | 12 |
| 19 Jan 67 | YOU ONLY YOU *RCA 1561* | ....**21** | 7 |

Tom PAXTON *US, male vocalist (Albums: 11 Weeks)*   pos/wks

13 Jun 70	NO.6 *Elektra 2469003*	..........**23**	5
27 Mar 71	THE COMPLEAT TOM PAXTON *Elektra EKD 2003*	..........**18**	5
1 Jul 72	PEACE WILL COME *Reprise K 44182*	..........**47**	1

PAY AS U GO *UK, male rap / production group (Singles: 4 Weeks)*   pos/wks

| 27 Apr 02 | CHAMPAGNE DANCE *So Urban 6721362* | ....**13** | 4 |

Freda PAYNE *US, female vocalist (Singles: 30 Weeks)*   pos/wks

5 Sep 70	★ BAND OF GOLD *Invictus INV 502*	.............**1**	19
21 Nov 70	DEEPER AND DEEPER *Invictus INV 505*	..........**33**	9
27 Mar 71	CHERISH WHAT IS DEAR TO YOU (WHILE IT'S NEAR TO YOU)		
	Invictus INV 509	..........**46**	2

Tammy PAYNE *UK, female vocalist (Singles: 2 Weeks)*   pos/wks

| 20 Jul 91 | TAKE ME NOW *Talkin Loud TLK 12* | ....**55** | 2 |

Heather PEACE *UK, female vocalist (Singles: 1 Week)*   pos/wks

| 13 May 00 | THE ROSE *RCA 74321742892* | ....**56** | 1 |

PEACE BY PIECE *UK, male vocal group (Singles: 2 Weeks)*   pos/wks

| 21 Sep 96 | SWEET SISTER *Blanco Y Negro NEG 94CD* | ....**46** | 1 |
| 25 Apr 98 | NOBODY'S BUSINESS *Blanco Y Negro NEG 110CD1* | ....**50** | 1 |

PEACH *UK / Belgium, female / male
vocal / production group (Singles: 1 Week)*   pos/wks

| 17 Jan 98 | ON MY OWN *Mute CDMUTE 215* | ....**69** | 1 |

PEACHES *Canada, female producer /
vocalist – Merrill Nisker (Singles: 5 Weeks)*   pos/wks

| 15 Jun 02 | SET IT OFF *Epic 6726862* | ....**36** | 2 |
| 17 Jan 04 | KICK IT *XL Recordings XLS 176CD* [1] | ....**39** | 3 |

[1] Peaches featuring Iggy Pop

PEACHES and HERB *US, female / male vocal duo –
Linda Green and Herbert Feemster (Singles: 23 Weeks)*   pos/wks

| 20 Jan 79 | SHAKE YOUR GROOVE THING *Polydor 2066 992* | ....**26** | 10 |
| 21 Apr 79 | ● REUNITED *Polydor POSP 43* ▲ | ....**4** | 13 |

Mary PEARCE See UP YER RONSON featuring Mary PEARCE

Natasha PEARL *See TASTE XPERIENCE featuring Natasha PEARL*

PEARL JAM ⟨ 431 ⟩ Top 500
Stadium-packing Seattle rock band fronted by Eddie Vedder, b. Edward Mueller, 23 Dec 1966, Illinois, US. Quintet that evolved from revered pioneers Mother Love Bone, have released over 50 live albums, with a record 18 of them charting Stateside (Singles: 43 Weeks, Albums: 120 Weeks) pos/wks

		pos	wks
15 Feb 92	ALIVE *Epic 6575727*	16	6
18 Apr 92	EVEN FLOW *Epic 6578577*	27	3
26 Sep 92	JEREMY *Epic 6582587*	15	4
1 Jan 94	DAUGHTER *Epic 6600202*	18	5
28 May 94	DISSIDENT *Epic 6604415*	14	4
26 Nov 94 ●	SPIN THE BLACK CIRCLE *Epic 6610362*	10	3
25 Feb 95	NOT FOR YOU *Epic 6612032*	34	2
16 Dec 95	MERKINBALL *Epic 6627162*	25	3
17 Aug 96	WHO YOU ARE *Epic 6635392*	18	2
31 Jan 98	GIVEN TO FLY *Epic 6653942*	12	3
23 May 98	WISHLIST *Epic 6657902*	30	2
14 Aug 99	LAST KISS *Epic 6674791*	42	1
13 May 00	NOTHING AS IT SEEMS *Epic 6693742*	22	2
22 Jul 00	LIGHT YEARS *Epic 6696282*	52	1
9 Nov 02	I AM MINE *Epic 6733082*	26	2
7 Mar 92	TEN *Epic 4688842*	18	65
23 Oct 93 ●	VS *Epic 4745492* ▲	2	24
3 Dec 94 ●	VITALOGY *Epic 4778611* ▲	4	11
7 Sep 96 ●	NO CODE *Epic 4844482* ▲	3	5
14 Feb 98 ●	YIELD *Epic 4893652*	7	7
5 Dec 98	LIVE – ON TWO LEGS *Epic 4928592*	68	1
27 May 00 ●	BINAURAL *Epic 4945902*	5	4
23 Nov 02	RIOT ACT *Epic 5100002*	34	2
11 Dec 04	REARVIEWMIRROR (GREATEST HITS '91-'03) *Epic 5191132*	58	1

'Merkinball' is the title of the single featuring 'I Got Id' and 'Long Road'

The PEARLS *UK, female vocal duo –*
Lyn Cornell and Ann Simmons (Singles: 24 Weeks) pos/wks

		pos	wks
27 May 72	THIRD FINGER, LEFT HAND *Bell 1217*	31	6
23 Sep 72	YOU CAME, YOU SAW, YOU CONQUERED *Bell 1254*	32	5
24 Mar 73	YOU ARE EVERYTHING *Bell 1284*	41	3
1 Jun 74 ●	GUILTY *Bell 1352*	10	10

Johnny PEARSON Orchestra
UK, orchestra – Johnny Pearson – piano (Singles: 15 Weeks) pos/wks

		pos	wks
18 Dec 71 ●	SLEEPY SHORES *Penny Farthing PEN 778*	8	15

David PEASTON *UK, male vocalist (Albums: 1 Week)* pos/wks

		pos	wks
26 Aug 89	INTRODUCING ... DAVID PEASTON *Geffen 924228 1*	66	1

PEBBLES *US, female vocalist – Perri*
McKissack (Singles: 17 Weeks, Albums: 4 Weeks) pos/wks

		pos	wks
19 Mar 88 ●	GIRLFRIEND *MCA MCA 1233*	8	11
28 May 88	MERCEDES BOY *MCA MCA 1248*	42	4
27 Oct 90	GIVING YOU THE BENEFIT *MCA MCA 1448*	73	2
14 May 88	PEBBLES *MCA MCF 3418*	56	4

The PEDDLERS *UK, male vocal / instrumental*
group (Singles: 14 Weeks, Albums: 16 Weeks) pos/wks

		pos	wks
7 Jan 65	LET THE SUNSHINE IN *Philips BF 1375*	50	1
23 Aug 69	BIRTH *CBS 4449*	17	9
31 Jan 70	GIRLIE *CBS 4720*	34	4
16 Mar 68	FREE WHEELERS *CBS SBPG 63183*	27	13
7 Feb 70	BIRTHDAY *CBS 63682*	16	3

PEE BEE SQUAD
UK, male vocalist – Paul Burnett (Singles: 3 Weeks) pos/wks

		pos	wks
5 Oct 85	RUGGED AND MEAN, BUTCH AND ON SCREEN *Project PRO 3*	52	3

Ann PEEBLES *US, female vocalist (Singles: 3 Weeks)* pos/wks

		pos	wks
20 Apr 74	I CAN'T STAND THE RAIN (re) *London HLU 10428*	41	3

The PEECH BOYS
US, male vocal / instrumental group (Singles: 3 Weeks) pos/wks

		pos	wks
30 Oct 82	DON'T MAKE ME WAIT *TMT TMT 7001*	49	3

Kevin PEEK *(see also SKY)*
UK, male instrumentalist – guitar (Albums: 8 Weeks) pos/wks

		pos	wks
21 Mar 81	AWAKENING *Ariola ARL 5065*	52	2
13 Oct 84	BEYOND THE PLANETS *Telstar STAR 2244* [1]	64	6

[1] Kevin Peek and Rick Wakeman

'Beyond the Planets' also features Jeff Wayne, with narration by Patrick Allen

Donald PEERS
UK, male vocalist, b. 10 Jul 1908, d. 9 Aug 1973 (Singles: 28 Weeks) pos/wks

		pos	wks
29 Dec 66	GAMES THAT LOVERS PLAY *Columbia DB 8079*	46	1
18 Dec 68 ●	PLEASE DON'T GO (re) *Columbia DB 8502*	3	21
24 Jun 72	GIVE ME ONE MORE CHANCE *Decca F 13302*	36	6

PELE
UK, male / female vocal / instrumental group (Singles: 3 Weeks) pos/wks

		pos	wks
15 Feb 92	MEGALOMANIA *M&G MAGS 20*	73	1
13 Jun 92	FAIR BLOWS THE WIND FOR FRANCE *M&G MAGS 24*	62	1
31 Jul 93	FAT BLACK HEART *M&G MAGCD 43*	75	1

Marti PELLOW *(see also WET WET WET) UK, male vocalist –*
Mark McLoughlin (Singles: 9 Weeks, Albums: 16 Weeks) pos/wks

		pos	wks
16 Jun 01 ●	CLOSE TO YOU *Mercury MERCD 532*	9	6
1 Dec 01	I'VE BEEN AROUND THE WORLD *Mercury 5887772*	28	2
22 Nov 03	A LOT OF LOVE *Universal TV 9813763*	59	1
7 Jul 01 ●	SMILE *Mercury 5860032*	7	7
30 Nov 02	MARTI PELLOW SINGS THE HITS OF WET WET WET & SMILE *UMTV TV 0632902*	36	8
29 Nov 03	BETWEEN THE COVERS *Universal TV 9812067*	66	1

Debbie PENDER
US, female vocalist (Singles: 1 Week) pos/wks

		pos	wks
30 May 98	MOVIN' ON *AM:PM 5826492*	41	1

Teddy PENDERGRASS
(see also Harold MELVIN and the BLUENOTES) US, male vocalist –
Theodore Pendergrass (Singles: 24 Weeks, Albums: 11 Weeks) pos/wks

		pos	wks
21 May 77	THE WHOLE TOWN'S LAUGHING AT ME *Philadelphia International PIR 5116*	44	3
28 Oct 78	ONLY YOU / CLOSE THE DOOR *Philadelphia International PIR 6713*	41	6
23 May 81	TWO HEARTS *20th Century TC 2492* [1]	49	5
25 Jan 86	HOLD ME *Asylum EKR 32* [2]	44	5
28 May 88	JOY *Elektra EKR 75*	58	3
19 Nov 94	THE MORE I GET THE MORE I WANT *X-clusive XCLU 011CD* [3]	35	2
21 May 88	JOY *Elektra 960775 1*	45	8
20 Mar 04	SATISFACTION GUARANTEED – THE VERY BEST OF TEDDY PENDERGRASS *WSM WSMCD 166*	26	3

[1] Stephanie Mills featuring Teddy Pendergrass [2] Teddy Pendergrass with Whitney Houston [3] KWS featuring Teddy Pendergrass

PENDULUM
Australia, male DJ / production trio (Singles: 2 Weeks) pos/wks

		pos	wks
6 Mar 04	ANOTHER PLANET / VOYAGER *Breakbeat Kaos BBK 003*	46	2

PENETRATION
(see also Pauline MURRAY and the INVISIBLE GIRLS)
UK, male / female vocal / instrumental group (Albums: 8 Weeks) pos/wks

		pos	wks
28 Oct 78	MOVING TARGETS *Virgin V 2109*	22	4
6 Oct 79	COMING UP FOR AIR *Virgin V 2131*	36	4

PENGUIN CAFE ORCHESTRA
UK, male instrumental group (Albums: 5 Weeks) pos/wks

		pos	wks
4 Apr 87	SIGNS OF LIFE *Edition EG EGED 50*	49	5

Ce Ce PENISTON *US, female vocalist – Cecelia*
Peniston (Singles: 53 Weeks, Albums: 21 Weeks) pos/wks

		pos	wks
12 Oct 91	FINALLY *A&M AM 822*	29	7
11 Jan 92 ●	WE GOT A LOVE THANG *A&M AM 846*	6	8
18 Jan 92	I LIKE IT *A&M AM 847* [1]	58	2
21 Mar 92 ●	FINALLY (re-issue) *A&M AM 858*	2	8

KATIE MELUA TOP 10

The gospel according to Katie Melua, who chooses her favourite albums

Katie, whose acclaimed debut album Call off the Search spent 59 consecutive weeks on the chart since first appearing in November 2003, couldn't stick to the rules when nominating 10 albums. So, with the stipulation that we can't print them in 1-10 order as they are all worthy of the No.1 spot in her opinion and that there are actually 11, as she just couldn't whittle them down to 10, here's what Katie did …

album – act – (peak position)

BRYTER LAYTER * Nick Drake	A NIGHT AT THE OPERA Queen (1)
CHICKASAW COUNTRY CHILD: THE ARTISTRY OF BOBBIE GENTRY * Bobbie Gentry	O Damien Rice (8)
DESIRE Bob Dylan (3)	ON AND ON * Jack Johnson
SONG TO A SEAGULL * Joni Mitchell	TEA FOR THE TILLERMAN Cat Stevens (20)
FOUR SYMBOLS (LED ZEPPELIN IV) Led Zeppelin (1)	TIME AFTER TIME Eva Cassidy (25)
	VARIOUS POSITIONS Leonard Cohen (52)

* Did not chart

		pos/wks
23 May 92 ●	KEEP ON WALKIN' *A&M AM 878*	**10** 6
5 Sep 92	CRAZY LOVE *A&M AM 0060*	**44** 3
12 Dec 92	INSIDE THAT I CRIED *A&M AM 0121*	**42** 2
15 Jan 94	I'M IN THE MOOD *A&M 5804552*	**16** 4
2 Apr 94	KEEP GIVIN' ME YOUR LOVE *A&M 5805492*	**36** 2
6 Aug 94	HIT BY LOVE *A&M 5806932*	**33** 2
13 Sep 97	FINALLY (re-mix) *AM:PM 5823432*	**26** 5
7 Feb 98	SOMEBODY ELSE'S GUY *AM:PM 5825112*	**13** 4
8 Feb 92 ●	FINALLY *A&M 3971822*	**10** 19
5 Feb 94	THOUGHT 'YA KNEW *A&M 5402012*	**31** 2

1 Overweight Pooch featuring Ce Ce Peniston

Dawn PENN *Jamaica, female vocalist –*
Dawn Pickering (Singles: 12 Weeks, Albums: 2 Weeks)   pos/wks

11 Jun 94 ●	YOU DON'T LOVE ME (NO, NO, NO) *Big Beat A 8295CD*	**3**	12
9 Jul 94	NO NO NO *Big Beat 7567923652*	**51**	2

Barbara PENNINGTON
US, female vocalist (Singles: 8 Weeks)   pos/wks

27 Apr 85	FAN THE FLAME *Record Shack SOHO 37*	**62**	3
27 Jul 85	ON A CROWDED STREET *Record Shack SOHO 49*	**57**	5

Tricia PENROSE *UK, female actor / vocalist (Singles: 2 Weeks)*   pos/wks

7 Dec 96	WHERE DID OUR LOVE GO *RCA 74321428152*	**71**	1
4 Mar 00	DON'T WANNA BE ALONE *Doop DP 2001CD*	**44**	1

PENTANGLE *UK, male / female vocal /*
instrumental group (Singles: 4 Weeks, Albums: 39 Weeks)   pos/wks

28 May 69	ONCE I HAD A SWEETHEART *Big T BIG 124*	**46**	1
14 Feb 70	LIGHT FLIGHT (re) *Big T BIG 128*	**43**	3
15 Jun 68	THE PENTANGLE *Transatlantic TRA 162*	**21**	9
1 Nov 69 ●	BASKET OF LIGHT *Transatlantic TRA 205*	**5**	28
12 Dec 70	CRUEL SISTER *Transatlantic TRA 228*	**51**	2

PENTHOUSE 4
UK, male vocal / instrumental duo (Singles: 3 Weeks)   pos/wks

23 Apr 88	BUST THIS HOUSE DOWN *Syncopate SY 10*	**56**	3

PEOPLES CHOICE
US, male vocal / instrumental group (Singles: 9 Weeks)   pos/wks

20 Sep 75	DO IT ANY WAY YOU WANNA *Philadelphia International PIR 3500*	**36**	5
21 Jan 78	JAM, JAM, JAM (ALL NIGHT LONG) *Philadelphia International PIR 5891* 1	**40**	4

1 People's Choice

PEPE DELUXE
Finland, male DJ / production group (Singles: 3 Weeks)   pos/wks

26 May 01	BEFORE YOU LEAVE *Catskills / INCredible 6712392*	**20**	3

Danny PEPPERMINT and The JUMPING JACKS
US, male vocal / instrumental group – leader Danny Lamego
(Singles: 8 Weeks)   pos/wks

18 Jan 62	THE PEPPERMINT TWIST *London HLL 9478*	**26**	8

The PEPPERS
France, male instrumental group (Singles: 12 Weeks)   pos/wks

26 Oct 74 ●	PEPPER BOX *Spark SRL 1100*	**6**	12

PEPSI and SHIRLIE *UK, female vocal duo – Helen DeMacque*
and Shirley Holliman (Singles: 24 Weeks, Albums: 2 Weeks)   pos/wks

17 Jan 87 ●	HEARTACHE *Polydor POSP 837*	**2**	12
30 May 87 ●	GOODBYE STRANGER *Polydor POSP 865*	**9**	7
26 Sep 87	CAN'T GIVE ME LOVE *Polydor POSP 885*	**58**	3
12 Dec 87	ALL RIGHT NOW *Polydor POSP 896*	**50**	2
7 Nov 87	ALL RIGHT NOW *Polydor POLH 38*	**69**	2

PERAN *Holland, male producer – Peran van Dijk (Singles: 2 Weeks)* pos/wks

23 Mar 02	**GOOD TIME** *Incentive CENT 37CDS*	**37** 2

PERCEPTION *UK, male vocal group (Singles: 2 Weeks)* pos/wks

7 Mar 92	**FEED THE FEELING** *Talkin Loud TLK 17*	**58** 2

The listed flip side of 'Feed the Feeling' was 'Three Times a Maybe' by K-Creative

Lance PERCIVAL
UK, male vocalist / comedian (Singles: 3 Weeks) pos/wks

28 Oct 65	**SHAME AND SCANDAL IN THE FAMILY** *Parlophone R 5335*	**37** 3

PERCY FILTH (see also LIL' DEVIOUS) *UK, male*
production duo – Mark Baker and Gary Little (Singles: 1 Week) pos/wks

9 Aug 03	**SHOW ME YOUR MONKEY** *Southern Fried ECB 53CDS*	**72** 1

PERFECT CIRCLE See A PERFECT CIRCLE

PERFECT DAY
UK, male vocal / instrumental group (Singles: 4 Weeks) pos/wks

21 Jan 89	**LIBERTY TOWN** *London LON 214*	**58** 3
1 Apr 89	**JANE** *London LON 188*	**68** 1

PERFECT PHASE *Holland, male production duo –*
Freek Fontein and Willem Faber (Singles: 8 Weeks) pos/wks

25 Dec 99	**HORNY HORNS** *Positiva CDTIV 123*	**21** 7
12 Jun 04	**BLOW YOUR HORNY HORNS** *Feverpitch 12FEV 3*	**75** 1

PERFECTLY ORDINARY PEOPLE
UK, male vocal / instrumental group (Singles: 3 Weeks) pos/wks

22 Oct 88	**THEME FROM P.O.P.** *Urban URB 25*	**61** 3

PERFECTO ALLSTARZ
(see also VIRUS; OAKENFOLD; RISE) *UK, male instrumental / production*
duo – Paul Oakenfold and Steve Osborne (Singles: 11 Weeks) pos/wks

4 Feb 95 ●	**REACH UP (PAPA'S GOT A BRAND NEW PIG BAG)** *Perfecto YZ 892CD*	**6** 11

PERFUME *UK, male vocal / instrumental group (Singles: 1 Week)* pos/wks

10 Feb 96	**HAVEN'T SEEN YOU** *Aromasound AROMA 005CDS*	**71** 1

Emilio PERICOLI *Italy, male vocalist (Singles: 14 Weeks)* pos/wks

28 Jun 62	**AL DI LA** *Warner Bros. WB 69*	**30** 14

Carl PERKINS *US, male vocalist, b. 9 Apr 1932,*
d. 19 Jan 1998 (Singles: 8 Weeks, Albums: 3 Weeks) pos/wks

18 May 56 ●	**BLUE SUEDE SHOES** *London HLU 8271*	**10** 8
15 Apr 78	**OL' BLUE SUEDES IS BACK** *Jet UATV 30146*	**38** 3

PERPETUAL MOTION
UK, male instrumental / production group (Singles: 5 Weeks) pos/wks

2 May 98	**KEEP ON DANCIN' (LET'S GO)** *Positiva CDTIV 90*	**12** 5

Lee PERRY See Baz LUHRMANN

Lee 'Scratch' PERRY (see also The UPSETTERS)
Jamaica, male producer / vocalist (Albums: 1 Week) pos/wks

26 Jul 97	**ARKOLOGY** *Island Jamaica CRNCD 6*	**49** 1

Steve PERRY *UK, male vocalist (Singles: 1 Week)* pos/wks

4 Aug 60	**STEP BY STEP** *HMV POP 745*	**41** 1

Steve PERRY (see also JOURNEY)
US, male vocalist (Albums: 3 Weeks) pos/wks

14 Jul 84	**STREET TALK** *CBS 25967*	**59** 2
27 Aug 94	**FOR THE LOVE OF STRANGE MEDICINE** *Columbia 4771962*	**64** 1

Nina PERSSON and David ARNOLD
(see also The CARDIGANS) *Sweden, female vocalist*
and UK, male instrumentalist / producer (Singles: 1 Week) pos/wks

29 Apr 00	**THEME FROM 'RANDALL & HOPKIRK (DECEASED)'** *Island CID 762*	**49** 1

Jon PERTWEE *UK, male actor / vocalist,*
b. 7 Jul 1919, d. 20 May 1996 (Singles: 7 Weeks) pos/wks

1 Mar 80	**WORZEL'S SONG** *Decca F 13885*	**33** 7

PESHAY *UK, male DJ / producer –*
Paul Pesce (Singles: 6 Weeks, Albums: 1 Week) pos/wks

9 May 98	**MILES FROM HOME** *Mo Wax MW 092*	**75** 1
17 Jul 99	**SWITCH** *Island Blue PFACD 1*	**59** 1
19 Feb 00	**TRULY** *Island Blue PFACD 4* [1]	**55** 1
4 May 02	**YOU GOT ME BURNING / FUZION** *Cubik Music CUBIKSAMPCD 001CD* [2]	**41** 2
24 Aug 02	**SATISFY MY LOVE** *Cubik Music CUBIK 002CD* [3]	**67** 1
31 Jul 99	**MILES FROM HOME** *Island Blue PFA 1CD*	**63** 1

[1] Peshay featuring Kym Mazelle [2] Peshay featuring Co-ordinate [3] Peshay vs Flytronix

PESTALOZZI CHILDREN'S CHOIR
International, male / female vocal group (Albums: 2 Weeks) pos/wks

26 Dec 81	**SONGS OF JOY** *K-Tel NE 1140*	**65** 2

PET SHOP BOYS 58 Top 500
Critically acclaimed and quintessentially English duo: former assistant editor
of Smash Hits, Neil Tennant (v), and Chris Lowe (k). No duo has amassed
more chart entries than this act, whose first hit was voted Best British Single
at the 1987 Brit Awards (Singles: 244 Weeks, Albums: 352 Weeks) pos/wks

23 Nov 85 ★	**WEST END GIRLS** *Parlophone R 6115* ▲	**1** 15
8 Mar 86	**LOVE COMES QUICKLY** *Parlophone R 6116*	**19** 9
31 May 86	**OPPORTUNITIES (LET'S MAKE LOTS OF MONEY)** *Parlophone R 6129*	**11** 8
4 Oct 86 ●	**SUBURBIA** *Parlophone R 6140*	**8** 9
27 Jun 87 ★	**IT'S A SIN** *Parlophone R 6158*	**1** 11
22 Aug 87 ●	**WHAT HAVE I DONE TO DESERVE THIS?** *Parlophone R 6163* [1]	**2** 9
24 Oct 87 ●	**RENT** *Parlophone R 6168*	**8** 7
12 Dec 87 ★	**ALWAYS ON MY MIND** *Parlophone R 6171*	**1** 11
2 Apr 88 ★	**HEART** *Parlophone R 6177*	**1** 10
24 Sep 88 ●	**DOMINO DANCING** *Parlophone R 6190*	**7** 8
26 Nov 88 ●	**LEFT TO MY OWN DEVICES** *Parlophone R 6198*	**4** 8
8 Jul 89 ●	**IT'S ALRIGHT** *Parlophone R 6220*	**5** 8
6 Oct 90 ●	**SO HARD** *Parlophone R 6269*	**4** 6
24 Nov 90	**BEING BORING** *Parlophone R 6275*	**20** 8
23 Mar 91	**WHERE THE STREETS HAVE NO NAME – CAN'T TAKE MY EYES OFF YOU / HOW CAN YOU EXPECT TO BE TAKEN SERIOUSLY** *Parlophone R 6285*	**4** 8
8 Jun 91	**JEALOUSY** *Parlophone R 6283*	**12** 5
26 Oct 91	**DJ CULTURE** *Parlophone R 6301*	**13** 3
23 Nov 91	**DJ CULTURE (re-mix)** *Parlophone 12RX 6301*	**40** 2
21 Dec 91	**WAS IT WORTH IT?** *Parlophone R 6306*	**24** 4
12 Jun 93 ●	**CAN YOU FORGIVE HER** *Parlophone CDR 6348*	**7** 7
18 Sep 93	**GO WEST** *Parlophone CDR 6356*	**2** 7
11 Dec 93	**I WOULDN'T NORMALLY DO THIS KIND OF THING** *Parlophone CDR 6370*	**13** 7
16 Apr 94	**LIBERATION** *Parlophone CDR 6377*	**14** 5
11 Jun 94	**ABSOLUTELY FABULOUS** *Spaghetti CDR 6382* [2]	**6** 7
10 Sep 94	**YESTERDAY WHEN I WAS MAD** *Parlophone CDR 6386*	**13** 4
5 Aug 95	**PANINARO** *Parlophone CDR 6414*	**15** 4
4 May 96 ●	**BEFORE** *Parlophone CDR 6431*	**7** 5
24 Aug 96 ●	**SE A VIDA É (THAT'S THE WAY LIFE IS)** *Parlophone CDR 6443*	**8** 8
23 Nov 96	**SINGLE** *Parlophone CDR 6452*	**14** 3
29 Mar 97 ●	**A RED LETTER DAY** *Parlophone CDR 6460*	**9** 3
5 Jul 97 ●	**SOMEWHERE** *Parlophone CDR 6470*	**9** 5
31 Jul 99	**I DON'T KNOW WHAT YOU WANT BUT I CAN'T GIVE IT ANYMORE** *Parlophone CDR 6523*	**15** 3
9 Oct 99	**NEW YORK CITY BOY** *Parlophone CDR 6525*	**14** 4
15 Jan 00 ●	**YOU ONLY TELL ME YOU LOVE ME WHEN YOU'RE DRUNK** *Parlophone CDR 6533*	**8** 4
30 Mar 02	**HOME AND DRY** *Parlophone CDRS 6572*	**14** 6
27 Jul 02	**I GET ALONG** *Parlophone CDRS 6581*	**18** 3
29 Nov 03 ●	**MIRACLES** *Parlophone CDR 6620*	**10** 4
10 Apr 04	**FLAMBOYANT** *Parlophone CDRS 6629*	**12** 4
5 Apr 86 ●	**PLEASE** *Parlophone PSB 1*	**3** 82
29 Nov 86	**DISCO** *EMI PRG 1001*	**15** 72
19 Sep 87 ●	**ACTUALLY** *Parlophone PCSD 104*	**2** 59
22 Oct 88 ●	**INTROSPECTIVE** *Parlophone PCS 7325*	**2** 39
3 Nov 90 ●	**BEHAVIOUR** *Parlophone PCSD 113*	**2** 14

16 Nov 91 ●	DISCOGRAPHY – THE COMPLETE SINGLES COLLECTION	
	Parlophone PMTV 3 ....3 30	
9 Oct 93 ★	VERY *Parlophone CDPCSD 143* ■ 1 22	
24 Sep 94 ●	DISCO 2 *Parlophone CDPCSD 159* 6 4	
19 Aug 95 ●	ALTERNATIVE *Parlophone CDPCSD 166* 2 5	
14 Sep 96 ●	BILINGUAL *Parlophone CDPCSD 170* 4 8	
23 Oct 99 ●	NIGHTLIFE *Parlophone 5218572* 7 3	
13 Apr 02 ●	RELEASE *Parlophone 5381502* 7 4	
15 Feb 03	DISCO 3 *Parlophone 5821402* 36 1	
6 Dec 03	THE HITS – POPART *Parlophone 5950932* 30 9	

[1] Pet Shop Boys and Dusty Springfield [2] Absolutely Fabulous

PETER and GORDON *UK, male vocal duo – Peter Asher and Gordon Waller (Singles: 77 Weeks, Albums: 1 Week)*

		pos/wks
12 Mar 64 ★	A WORLD WITHOUT LOVE *Columbia DB 7225* ▲ 1 14	
4 Jun 64 ●	NOBODY I KNOW *Columbia DB 7292* 10 11	
8 Apr 65 ●	TRUE LOVE WAYS *Columbia DB 7524* 2 15	
24 Jun 65 ●	TO KNOW YOU IS TO LOVE YOU *Columbia DB 7617* 5 10	
21 Oct 65	BABY I'M YOURS *Columbia DB 7729* 19 9	
24 Feb 66	WOMAN *Columbia DB 7834* 28 11	
22 Sep 66	LADY GODIVA *Columbia DB 8003* 16 11	
20 Jun 64	PETER AND GORDON *Columbia 33SX 1630* 18 1	

PETER, PAUL and MARY *US, male / female vocal / instrumental group (Singles: 38 Weeks, Albums: 26 Weeks)*

		pos/wks
10 Oct 63	BLOWING IN THE WIND *Warner Bros. WB 104* 13 16	
16 Apr 64	TELL IT ON THE MOUNTAIN *Warner Bros. WB 127* 33 4	
15 Oct 64	THE TIMES THEY ARE A-CHANGIN' *Warner Bros. WB 142* 44 2	
17 Jan 70 ●	LEAVING ON A JET PLANE *Warner Bros. WB 7340* ▲ 2 16	
4 Jan 64	PETER PAUL AND MARY *Warner Bros. WM 4064* ▲ 18 1	
21 Mar 64	IN THE WIND *Warner Bros. WM 8142* ▲ 11 19	
13 Feb 65	IN CONCERT VOLUME 1 *Warner Bros. WM 8158* 20 1	
5 Sep 70	TEN YEARS TOGETHER *Warner Bros. WS 2552* 60 4	

PETERS and LEE `295` `Top 500` *London based Opportunity Knocks-winning MOR duo: Lennie Peters (p/v), b. 1939, d. 10 Oct 1992, and Diane Lee (v). Peters, Rolling Stone Charlie Watts' uncle and blind since 16, first recorded in 1962 backed by The Migil Five. Lee married Wizzard's Rick Price (Singles: 57 Weeks, Albums: 166 Weeks)*

		pos/wks
26 May 73 ★	WELCOME HOME *Philips 6006 307* 1 24	
3 Nov 73	BY YOUR SIDE *Philips 6006 339* 39 4	
20 Apr 74 ●	DON'T STAY AWAY TOO LONG *Philips 6006 388* 3 15	
17 Aug 74	RAINBOW *Philips 6006 406* 17 7	
6 Mar 76	HEY MR MUSIC MAN *Philips 6006 502* 16 7	
30 Jun 73 ★	WE CAN MAKE IT *Philips 6308 165* 1 55	
22 Dec 73	BY YOUR SIDE *Philips 6308 192* 9 48	
21 Sep 74 ●	RAINBOW *Philips 6308 208* 6 27	
4 Oct 75 ●	FAVOURITES *Philips 9109 205* 2 32	
18 Dec 76	INVITATION *Philips 9101 027* 44 4	

Jonathan PETERS presents LUMINAIRE
US, male DJ / producer (Singles: 1 Week)

		pos/wks
24 Jul 99	FLOWER DUET *Pelican PELID 001* 75 1	

Ray PETERSON
US, male vocalist, b. 23 Apr 1939, d. 25 Jan 2005 (Singles: 9 Weeks) pos/wks

4 Sep 59	THE WONDER OF YOU *RCA 1131* 23 1	
24 Mar 60	ANSWER ME *RCA 1175* 47 1	
19 Jan 61	CORINNA, CORINNA (re) *London HLX 9246* 41 7	

Tom PETTY and the HEARTBREAKERS `491` `Top 500`
One of America's most popular rock groups of the last 30 years, formed in Los Angeles in 1975. Petty, b. Florida, was also a Traveling Wilbury. The Grammy-winning group signed a $20 million deal with Warner Brothers in 1993 (Singles: 43 Weeks, Albums: 104 Weeks)

		pos/wks
25 Jun 77	ANYTHING THAT'S ROCK 'N' ROLL *Shelter WIP 6396* 36 3	
13 Aug 77	AMERICAN GIRL *Shelter WIP 6403* 40 5	
15 Aug 81	STOP DRAGGIN' MY HEART AROUND *WEA K 79231* [1] 50 4	
13 Apr 85	DON'T COME AROUND HERE NO MORE *MCA MCA 926* 50 4	
13 May 89	I WON'T BACK DOWN *MCA MCA 1334* [2] 28 10	
12 Aug 89	RUNNIN' DOWN A DREAM *MCA MCA 1359* [2] 55 4	
25 Nov 89	FREE FALLIN' *MCA MCA 1381* [2] 64 2	
29 Jun 91	LEARNING TO FLY *MCA MCS 1555* 46 4	
4 Apr 92	TOO GOOD TO BE TRUE *MCA MCS 1616* 34 3	

30 Oct 93	SOMETHING IN THE AIR *MCA MCSTD 1945* [2] 53 2	
12 Mar 94	MARY JANE'S LAST DANCE *MCA MCSTD 1966* 52 2	
4 Jun 77	TOM PETTY AND THE HEARTBREAKERS *Shelter ISA 5014* 24 12	
1 Jul 78	YOU'RE GONNA GET IT *Island ISA 5017* 34 5	
17 Nov 79	DAMN THE TORPEDOES *MCA MCF 3044* 57 4	
23 May 81	HARD PROMISES *MCA MCF 3098* 32 5	
20 Nov 82	LONG AFTER DARK *MCA MCF 3155* 45 4	
20 Apr 85	SOUTHERN ACCENTS *MCA MCF 3260* 23 6	
2 May 87	LET ME UP (I'VE HAD ENOUGH) *MCA MCG 6014* 59 2	
8 Jul 89 ●	FULL MOON FEVER *MCA MCG 6034* [1] 8 16	
20 Jul 91 ●	INTO THE GREAT WIDE OPEN *MCA MCA 10317* 3 18	
13 Nov 93 ●	GREATEST HITS *MCA MCD 10964* 10 20	
12 Nov 94	WILDFLOWERS *Warner Bros. 9362457592* [1] 36 2	
24 Aug 96	SHE'S THE ONE (FILM SOUNDTRACK)	
	Warner Bros. 9362462852 ....37 2	
1 May 99	ECHO *Warner Bros. 9362472942* 43 2	
16 Jun 01	ANTHOLOGY – THROUGH THE YEARS *MCA 1701772* 14 6	

[1] Stevie Nicks with Tom Petty and the Heartbreakers [2] Tom Petty [1] Tom Petty

PEYTON *UK, production group (Singles: 1 Week)* pos/wks

22 May 04	A HIGHER PLACE *Hed Kandi HEDK 12006* 68 1	

PHANTOMS *See Johnny BRANDON with The PHANTOMS*

PHARAO *Germany, male / female vocal / instrumental group (Singles: 2 Weeks)* pos/wks

4 Mar 95	THERE IS A STAR *Epic 6611832* 43 2	

PHARAOHS *See SAM THE SHAM and The PHARAOHS*

The PHARCYDE
US, male rap group (Singles: 6 Weeks, Albums: 2 Weeks) pos/wks

31 Jul 93	PASSIN' ME BY *Atlantic A 8360CD* 55 3	
6 Apr 96	RUNNIN' *Go Beat GODCD 142* 36 2	
10 Aug 96	SHE SAID *Go Beat GODCD 144* 51 1	
21 Aug 93	BIZARRE RIDE II THE PHARCYDE *Atlantic 756792222* 58 1	
13 Apr 96	LABCABINCALIFORNIA *Go Beat 8287332* 46 1	

Franke PHAROAH *See FRANKE*

PHARRELL (see also N*E*R*D; The NEPTUNES) *US, male producer / vocalist – Pharrell Williams (Singles: 52 Weeks)* pos/wks

8 Jun 02	PASS THE COURVOISIER – PART II (re) *J 74321897902* [1] 16 8	
10 Aug 02 ●	BOYS *Jive 9253912* [2] 7 8	
5 Apr 03	BEAUTIFUL *Priority CDCL 842* [3] 23 20	
16 Aug 03 ●	FRONTIN' *Arista 8267655332* [4] 6 10	
29 Nov 03	LIGHT YOUR ASS ON FIRE *Arista 82876572512* [5] 62 1	
28 Feb 04	SHOW ME YOUR SOUL *Puff Daddy / Island MCSTD 40350* [6] 35 2	
11 Dec 04 ●	DROP IT LIKE IT'S HOT *Geffen 2103461* [7] ▲ ....10 3+	

[1] Busta Rhymes featuring P Diddy and Pharrell [2] Britney Spears featuring Pharrell Williams [3] Snoop Dogg featuring Pharrell, Uncle Charlie Wilson [4] Pharrell Williams featuring Jay-Z [5] Busta Rhymes featuring Pharrell [6] Lenny Kravitz / P Diddy / Loon / Pharrell Williams [7] Snoop Dogg featuring Pharrell

PHASE 2 *See LEE-CABRERA*

PHASE II (see also Li KWAN; Joey NEGRO)
UK, male producer – Dave Lee (Singles: 2 Weeks) pos/wks

18 Mar 89	REACHIN' *Republic 006* 70 1	
21 Dec 91	REACHIN' *Republic LIC 160* [1] 70 1	

[1] Joey Negro presents Phase II

PHAT 'N' PHUNKY
UK, male production duo (Singles: 1 Week) pos/wks

14 Jun 97	LET'S GROOVE *Chase CDCHASE 8* 61 1	

PHATS & SMALL *UK, male DJ / production duo – Jason Hayward and Russell Small (Singles: 36 Weeks)* pos/wks

10 Apr 99 ●	TURN AROUND *Multiply CDMULTY 49* 2 16	
14 Aug 99 ●	FEEL GOOD *Multiply CDMULTY 54* 7 8	
4 Dec 99	TONITE *Multiply CDMULTY 57* 11 6	
30 Jun 01	THIS TIME AROUND *Multiply CDMULTY 75* 15 5	
24 Nov 01	CHANGE *Multiply CDMULTY 80* 45 1	

PHATT B *Holland, male DJ / producer –*
Bernsquil Verndoom (Singles: 1 Week) pos/wks

| 11 Nov 00 | **AND DA DRUM MACHINE** *Nulife / Arista 74321801902* ....**58** 1 |

Barrington PHELOUNG *Australia, male*
conductor (Singles: 2 Weeks, Albums: 55 Weeks) pos/wks

13 Mar 93	'INSPECTOR MORSE' THEME *Virgin VSCDT 1458* **61** 2
2 Mar 91 ●	INSPECTOR MORSE MUSIC FROM THE TV SERIES *Virgin Television VTLP 2* **4** 30
7 Mar 92	INSPECTOR MORSE VOLUME 2 *Virgin Television VTCD 14*......**18** 12
16 Jan 93	INSPECTOR MORSE VOLUME 3 *Virgin Television VTCD 16*......**20** 11
25 Nov 00	THE MAGIC OF INSPECTOR MORSE *Virgin VTDCD 353* **62** 2

PHENOMENA
UK, male vocal / instrumental group (Albums: 2 Weeks) pos/wks

| 6 Jul 85 | PHENOMENA *Bronze PM 1* ....**63** 2 |

PHILADELPHIA INTERNATIONAL ALL-STARS
US, male / female vocal / instrumental group (Singles: 8 Weeks) pos/wks

| 13 Aug 77 | **LET'S CLEAN UP THE GHETTO** *Philadelphia International PIR 5451* ....**34** 8 |

PHILHARMONIA ORCHESTRA, conductor Lorin MAAZEL
UK, orchestra and US, male conductor (Singles: 7 Weeks) pos/wks

| 30 Jul 69 | **THUS SPAKE ZARATHUSTRA** *Columbia DB 8607* ....**33** 7 |

Arlene PHILLIPS
UK, female exercise instructor (Albums: 24 Weeks) pos/wks

| 28 Aug 82 | KEEP IN SHAPE SYSTEM *Supershape SUP 01* ....**41** 23 |
| 18 Feb 84 | KEEP IN SHAPE SYSTEM VOLUME 2 *Supershape SUP 2* ......**100** 1 |

'Keep in Shape System' features music by Funk Federation

Chynna PHILLIPS (see also WILSON PHILLIPS)
US, female vocalist (Singles: 1 Week) pos/wks

| 3 Feb 96 | **NAKED AND SACRED** *EMI CDEM 409* ....**62** 1 |

Esther PHILLIPS *US, female vocalist – Esther Mae*
Jones, b. 23 Dec 1935, d. 7 Aug 1984 (Singles: 8 Weeks) pos/wks

| 4 Oct 75 ● | **WHAT A DIFFERENCE A DAY MADE** *Kudu 925* ....**6** 8 |

PHIXX *UK, male vocal group (Singles: 12 Weeks)* pos/wks

8 Nov 03 ●	**HOLD ME ON** *Concept CDCON 51* **10** 4
20 Mar 04	**LOVE REVOLUTION** *Concept CDCON 55* **13** 5
3 Jul 04	**WILD BOYS** *Concept CON 56X* **12** 3

PHOEBE ONE
UK, female rapper – Phoebe Espirit (Singles: 3 Weeks) pos/wks

| 12 Dec 98 | **DOIN' OUR THING / ONE MAN'S BITCH** *Mecca Recordings MECX 1020* ....**59** 1 |
| 15 May 99 | **GET ON IT** *Mecca Recordings MECX 1026* ....**38** 2 |

Paul PHOENIX *UK, male vocalist (Singles: 4 Weeks)* pos/wks

| 3 Nov 79 | **NUNC DIMITTIS** *Different HAVE 20* ....**56** 4 |

Full artist credit on hit as follows: Paul Phoenix (treble) with Instrumental Ensemble – James Watson (trumpet), John Scott (organ), conducted by Barry Rose

PHOENIX
France, male vocal / instrumental group (Singles: 3 Weeks) pos/wks

3 Feb 01	IF I EVER FEEL BETTER *Source DINSD 210* **65** 1
1 May 04	RUN RUN RUN *Source SOURCD 094* **66** 1
24 Jul 04	EVERYTHING IS EVERYTHING *Source SOURCDX 097* **74** 1

PHOTEK *UK, male producer – Rupert*
Parkes (Singles: 4 Weeks, Albums: 4 Weeks) pos/wks

22 Mar 97	NI-TEN-ICHI-RYU (TWO SWORDS TECHNIQUE) *Science QEDCD 2* **37** 2
28 Feb 98	MODUS OPERANDI *Virgin QEDCD 6* **66** 1
24 Feb 01	MINE TO GIVE *Science QEDCD 10* [1] **44** 1
15 Jun 96	THE HIDDEN CAMERA *Science QEDCD 1*...................**39** 1

| 27 Sep 97 | MODUS OPERANDI *Science CDQED 1* ....**30** 2 |
| 26 Sep 98 | FORM & FUNCTION *Science CDQED 2* ....**61** 1 |

[1] Photek featuring Robert Owens

The PHOTOS *UK, male / female vocal / instrumental*
group (Singles: 4 Weeks, Albums: 9 Weeks) pos/wks

| 17 May 80 | IRENE *Epic EPC 8517* ....**56** 4 |
| 21 Jun 80 ● | THE PHOTOS *CBS PHOTO 5* ....**4** 9 |

PHUNKY PHANTOM (see also GAT DECOR; REST ASSURED)
UK, male producer – Lawrence Nelson (Singles: 3 Weeks) pos/wks

| 16 May 98 | **GET UP STAND UP** *Club for Life DISNCD 44* ....**27** 3 |

PHUTURE ASSASSINS
UK, male instrumental / production group (Singles: 1 Week) pos/wks

| 6 Jun 92 | **FUTURE SOUND (EP)** *Suburban Base SUBBASE 010* ....**64** 1 |

Tracks on Future Sound (EP): Future Sound / African Sanctus / Rydim Come Forward / Freedom Sound

PIA *See Pia ZADORA*

Edith PIAF *France, female vocalist – Edith Gassion,*
b. 19 Dec 1915, d. 11 Oct 1963 (Singles: 15 Weeks, Albums: 5 Weeks) pos/wks

| 12 May 60 | MILORD (re) *Columbia DC 754* ....**24** 15 |
| 26 Sep 87 | HEART AND SOUL *Stylus SMR 736*...................**58** 5 |

PIANOHEADZ
(see also LIL MO' YIN YANG; REAL TO REEL) *US, male DJ /*
production duo – Erick Morillo and Jose Nunez (Singles: 2 Weeks) pos/wks

| 11 Jul 98 | IT'S OVER (DISTORTION) *INCredible Music INCRL 3CD* ....**39** 2 |

PIANOMAN (see also BASS BOYZ)
UK, male producer – James Sammon (Singles: 8 Weeks) pos/wks

| 15 Jun 96 ● | BLURRED *Ffrreedom TABCD 243* ....**6** 7 |
| 26 Apr 97 | PARTY PEOPLE (LIVE YOUR LIFE BE FREE) *3 Beat 3BTCD 1* ..**43** 1 |

Mark PICCHIOTTI presents BASSTOY featuring DANA
(see also SANDSTORM)
US, male / female production / vocal duo (Singles: 5 Weeks) pos/wks

| 19 Jan 02 | RUNNIN' *Black & White NEOCD 073*...................**13** 5 |

Wilson PICKETT *US, male vocalist (Singles: 61 Weeks)* pos/wks

23 Sep 65	IN THE MIDNIGHT HOUR *Atlantic AT 4036* **12** 11
25 Nov 65	DON'T FIGHT IT *Atlantic AT 4052* **29** 8
10 Mar 66	634-5789 *Atlantic AT 4072* **36** 5
1 Sep 66	LAND OF 1000 DANCES *Atlantic 584 039* **22** 9
15 Dec 66	MUSTANG SALLY *Atlantic 584 066* **28** 7
27 Sep 67	FUNKY BROADWAY *Atlantic 584 130* **43** 3
11 Sep 68	I'M A MIDNIGHT MOVER *Atlantic 584 203* **38** 6
8 Jan 69	HEY JUDE *Atlantic 584 236* **16** 9
21 Nov 87	IN THE MIDNIGHT HOUR (re-recording) *Motown ZB 41583* **62** 3

Bobby 'Boris' PICKETT and The CRYPT-KICKERS
US, male vocal / instrumental group (Singles: 13 Weeks) pos/wks

| 1 Sep 73 ● | MONSTER MASH *London HLU 10320* ▲ ....**3** 13 |

PICKETTYWITCH *UK, male / female vocal /*
instrumental group – includes Polly Brown (Singles: 34 Weeks) pos/wks

28 Feb 70 ●	THAT SAME OLD FEELING *Pye 7N 17887* **5** 14
4 Jul 70	(IT'S LIKE A) SAD OLD KINDA MOVIE *Pye 7N 17951* **16** 10
7 Nov 70	BABY I WON'T LET YOU DOWN *Pye 7N 45002* **27** 10

Mauro PICOTTO (see also R.A.F.; CRW)
Italy, male producer (Singles: 23 Weeks) pos/wks

12 Jun 99	LIZARD (GONNA GET YOU) *VC Recordings VCRD 50* **27** 3
20 Nov 99	LIZARD (GONNA GET YA) (re-mix) *VC Recordings VCRD 57* ..**33** 2
15 Jul 00	IGUANA *VC Recordings VCRD 68* **33** 3
13 Jan 01	KOMODO (SAVE A SOUL) *VC Recordings VCRD 85* **13** 5
11 Aug 01	LIKE THIS LIKE THAT *VC Recordings VCRD 92* **21** 4
25 Aug 01	VERDI *BXR BXRP 0318* **74** 1
16 Mar 02	PULSAR 2002 *BXR BXRC 0162* **35** 3
3 Aug 02	BACK TO CALI *BXR BXRC 0433* **42** 1

PIGBAG
UK, male instrumental group
(Singles: 20 Weeks, Albums: 14 Weeks) pos/wks

7 Nov 81	SUNNY DAY *Y Records Y 12*	53	3
27 Feb 82	GETTING UP *Y Records Y 16*	61	3
3 Apr 82 ●	PAPA'S GOT A BRAND NEW PIGBAG *Y Records Y 10*	3	11
10 Jul 82	THE BIG BEAN *Y Records Y 24*	40	3
13 Mar 82	DR HECKLE AND MR JIVE *Y Y 17*	18	14

PIGEON HED See LO FIDELITY ALLSTARS

Nelson PIGFORD See De Etta LITTLE and Nelson PIGFORD

The PIGLETS
UK, female vocal group *(Singles: 12 Weeks)* pos/wks

6 Nov 71 ●	JOHNNY REGGAE *Bell 1180*	3	12

Dick PIKE See Ruby WRIGHT

PILOT
UK, male vocal / instrumental
group *(Singles: 29 Weeks, Albums: 1 Week)* pos/wks

2 Nov 74	MAGIC *EMI 2217*	11	11
18 Jan 75 ★	JANUARY *EMI 2255*	1	10
19 Apr 75	CALL ME ROUND *EMI 2287*	34	4
27 Sep 75	JUST A SMILE *EMI 2338*	31	4
31 May 75	SECOND FLIGHT *EMI EMC 3075*	48	1

The PILTDOWN MEN
US, male instrumental group *(Singles: 36 Weeks)* pos/wks

8 Sep 60	MCDONALD'S CAVE *Capitol CL 15149*	14	18
12 Jan 61	PILTDOWN RIDES AGAIN *Capitol CL 15175*	14	10
9 Mar 61	GOODNIGHT MRS. FLINTSTONE *Capitol CL 15186*	18	8

Courtney PINE
UK, male instrumentalist –
saxophone *(Singles: 6 Weeks, Albums: 13 Weeks)* pos/wks

30 Jul 88	LIKE DREAMERS DO *Fourth & Broadway BRW 108* [1]	26	5
7 Jul 90	I'M STILL WAITING *Mango MNG 749* [2]	66	1
25 Oct 86	JOURNEY TO THE URGE WITHIN *Island ILPS 9846*	39	11
6 Feb 88	DESTINY'S SONGS *Antilles AN 8275*	54	1

[1] Mica Paris featuring Courtney Pine [2] Courtney Pine featuring Carroll Thompson

'PING PING' and AL VERLAINE
Belgium, male vocal duo *(Singles: 4 Weeks)* pos/wks

28 Sep 61	SUCU SUCU *Oriole CB 1589*	41	4

PINK (241) Top 500
Brit-winning diva whose hair colour often matches her name. b. Alecia Moore, 8 Sep 1979, Pennsylvania, US. Rock-influenced UK million-selling 'M!ssundaztood' was 2002's top-selling album by a female artist in both the US and UK. She won a Best Female Rock Performance Grammy in 2004 for 'Trouble' *(Singles: 119 Weeks, Albums: 138 Weeks)* pos/wks

10 Jun 00 ●	THERE YOU GO *LaFace / Arista 74321757602*	6	9
30 Jun 00 ●	MOST GIRLS *LaFace / Arista 74321792012*	5	8
27 Jan 01 ●	YOU MAKE ME SICK *LaFace / Arista 74321828702*	9	6
30 Jun 01 ★	LADY MARMALADE *Interscope / Polydor 4975612* [1] ■ ▲	1	16
26 Jan 02 ●	GET THE PARTY STARTED *LaFace / Arista 74321913372*	2	15
25 May 02 ●	DON'T LET ME GET ME *Arista 74321939212*	6	11
28 Sep 02 ★	JUST LIKE A PILL *Arista 74321959652* ■	1	11
14 Dec 02	FAMILY PORTRAIT (IMPORT) *Arista 74321982102*	66	1
21 Dec 02	FAMILY PORTRAIT *Arista 74321982052*	11	9
19 Jul 03 ●	FEEL GOOD TIME *Columbia 6741062 XXX* [2]	3	11
8 Nov 03 ●	TROUBLE *Arista 82876572172*	7	12
7 Feb 04	GOD IS A DJ *Arista 829876589352*	11	6
1 May 04	LAST TO KNOW *Arista 82876611732*	21	4
27 May 00	CAN'T TAKE ME HOME *Arista 73008260622*	13	41
9 Feb 02 ●	M!SSUNDAZTOOD *Arista 7822147182*	3	73
22 Nov 03 ●	TRY THIS *Arista 82876571852* [1]	3	24

[1] Christina Aguilera, Lil' Kim, Mya and Pink [2] Pink featuring William Orbit
[1] P!nk

The PINK FAIRIES
UK, male vocal / instrumental group *(Albums: 1 Week)* pos/wks

29 Jul 72	WHAT A BUNCH OF SWEETIES *Polydor 2383 132*	48	1

PINK FLOYD (21) Top 500
(see also Syd BARRETT) *One of the world's most respected rock groups formed in London in 1965: David Gilmour (g), Roger Waters (b), Rick Wright (k) and Nick Mason (d). In the US, 'Dark Side of the Moon' has spent a record 28 years on the chart and 'The Wall' sold over 23 million (Singles: 55 Weeks, Albums: 911 Weeks)* pos/wks

30 Mar 67	ARNOLD LAYNE *Columbia DB 8156*	20	8
22 Jun 67 ●	SEE EMILY PLAY *Columbia DB 8214*	6	12
1 Dec 79 ★	ANOTHER BRICK IN THE WALL (PART 2) *Harvest HAR 5194* ▲	1	12
7 Aug 82	WHEN THE TIGERS BROKE FREE *Harvest HAR 5222*	39	5
7 May 83	NOT NOW JOHN *Harvest HAR 5224*	30	4
19 Dec 87	ON THE TURNING AWAY *EMI EM 34*	55	4
25 Jun 88	ONE SLIP *EMI EM 52*	50	3
4 Jun 94	TAKE IT BACK *EMI CDEMS 309*	23	4
29 Oct 94	HIGH HOPES / KEEP TALKING *EMI CDEMS 342*	26	3
19 Aug 67 ●	THE PIPER AT THE GATES OF DAWN *Columbia SCX 6157*	6	14
13 Jul 68 ●	A SAUCERFUL OF SECRETS *Columbia SCX 6258*	9	11
28 Jun 69 ●	MORE (FILM SOUNDTRACK) *Columbia SCX 6346*	9	5
15 Nov 69 ●	UMMAGUMMA *Harvest SHDW 1/2*	5	21
24 Oct 70 ★	ATOM HEART MOTHER *Harvest SHVL 781* ■	1	18
7 Aug 71	RELICS *Starline SRS 5071*	32	6
20 Nov 71 ●	MEDDLE *Harvest SHVL 795*	3	82
17 Jun 72 ●	OBSCURED BY CLOUDS (FILM SOUNDTRACK) *Harvest SHSP 4020*	6	14
31 Mar 73 ●	THE DARK SIDE OF THE MOON *Harvest SHVL 804* ▲	2	364
19 Jan 74	A NICE PAIR (DOUBLE re-issue) *Harvest SHDW 403*	21	20
27 Sep 75 ★	WISH YOU WERE HERE *Harvest SHVL 814* ▲	1	89
19 Feb 77 ●	ANIMALS *Harvest SHVL 815*	2	33
8 Dec 79 ●	THE WALL *Harvest SHDW 411* ▲	3	56
5 Dec 81	A COLLECTION OF GREAT DANCE SONGS *Harvest SHVL 822*	37	10
2 Apr 83 ★	THE FINAL CUT *Harvest SHPF 1983* ■	1	25
19 Sep 87 ●	A MOMENTARY LAPSE OF REASON *EMI EMD 1003*	3	34
3 Dec 88	DELICATE SOUND OF THUNDER *EMI EQ 5009*	11	12
9 Apr 94 ★	THE DIVISION BELL *EMI CDEMD 1055* ■ ▲	1	51
10 Jun 95 ★	PULSE *EMI CDEMD 1078* ■ ▲	1	21
9 Mar 96	RELICS (re-issue) *EMI CDEMD 1082*	48	2
16 Aug 97	THE PIPER AT THE GATES OF DAWN (re-issue) *EMI CDEMD 1110*	44	2
8 Apr 00	IS THERE ANYBODY OUT THERE? – THE WALL LIVE 1980-81 *EMI 5235622*	15	5
17 Nov 01 ●	ECHOES – THE BEST OF PINK FLOYD *EMI 5361112*	2	16

'A Nice Pair' is a double re-issue of the first two albums

PINK GREASE
UK, male vocal / instrumental group *(Singles: 1 Week)* pos/wks

26 Jun 04	THE PINK G.R.EASE *Mute CDMUTE 316*	75	1

The PINKEES
UK, male vocal / instrumental group *(Singles: 9 Weeks)* pos/wks

18 Sep 82 ●	DANGER GAMES *Creole CR 39*	8	9

PINKERTON'S ASSORTED COLOURS
UK, male vocal / instrumental group *(Singles: 12 Weeks)* pos/wks

13 Jan 66 ●	MIRROR MIRROR *Decca F 12307*	9	11
21 Apr 66	DON'T STOP LOVING ME BABY *Decca F 12377*	50	1

PINKY and PERKY
UK, piglet puppet duo *(Singles: 3 Weeks)* pos/wks

29 May 93	REET PETITE *Telstar CDPIGGY 1*	47	3

Lisa PIN-UP
UK, female DJ / producer – Lisa Chilcott *(Singles: 4 Weeks)* pos/wks

25 May 02	TURN UP THE SOUND *Nukleuz NUKC 0406*	60	1
21 Dec 02	BLOW YOUR MIND (I AM THE WOMAN) *Nukleuz 0450 FNUK*	60	3

The PIONEERS
Jamaica, male vocal / instrumental group *(Singles: 34 Weeks)* pos/wks

18 Oct 69	LONG SHOT KICK DE BUCKET (re) *Trojan TR 672*	21	11
31 Jul 71 ●	LET YOUR YEAH BE YEAH *Trojan TR 7825*	5	12
15 Jan 72	GIVE AND TAKE *Trojan TR 7846*	35	6
29 Mar 80	LONG SHOT KICK DE BUCKET (re-issue) *Trojan TRO 9063*	42	5

Re-issue of 'Long Shot Kick De Bucket' coupled with re-issue of Liquidator by Harry J All Stars

Billie PIPER
UK, female vocalist (Singles: 87 Weeks, Albums: 27 Weeks) pos/wks

11 Jul 98 ★	BECAUSE WE WANT TO *Innocent SINCD 2* [1] ■	1	12
17 Oct 98 ★	GIRLFRIEND (re) *Innocent SINCD 3* [1] ■	1	12
19 Dec 98 ●	SHE WANTS YOU (re) *Innocent SINDXX 6* [1]	3	13
3 Apr 99 ●	HONEY TO THE BEE (re) *Innocent SINCD 8* [1]	3	11
10 Apr 99	THANK ABBA FOR THE MUSIC *Epic ABCD 1* [2]	4	13
27 May 00 ★	DAY & NIGHT (re) *Innocent SINCD 11* ■	1	12
30 Sep 00 ●	SOMETHING DEEP INSIDE (re) *Innocent SINCD 19*	4	9
23 Dec 00	WALK OF LIFE *Innocent SINCD 23*	25	5
31 Oct 98	HONEY TO THE B *Innocent CDSIN 1* [1]	14	23
14 Oct 00	WALK OF LIFE *Innocent CDSINX 3*	14	4

[1] Billie [2] Steps, Tina Cousins, Cleopatra, B*Witched, Billie [1] Billie

The PIPKINS (see also BLUE MINK; DAVID and JONATHAN; EDISON LIGHTHOUSE; WHITE PLAINS; BROTHERHOOD OF MAN) *UK, male vocal duo – Roger Greenaway and Tony Burrows (Singles: 10 Weeks)* pos/wks

28 Mar 70 ●	GIMME DAT DING *Columbia DB 8662*	6	10

PIPS See Gladys KNIGHT and the PIPS

The PIRANHAS *UK, male vocal / instrumental group (Singles: 21 Weeks, Albums: 3 Weeks)* pos/wks

2 Aug 80 ●	TOM HARK *Sire SIR 4044*	6	12
16 Oct 82	ZAMBESI *Dakota DAK 6* [1]	17	9
20 Sep 80	PIRANHAS *Sire SRK 6098*	69	3

[1] Piranhas featuring Boring Bob Grover

The PIRATES *UK, male vocal / instrumental group (Singles: 57 Weeks, Albums: 3 Weeks)* pos/wks

12 Feb 60	YOU GOT WHAT IT TAKES *HMV POP 698* [1]	25	3
16 Jun 60 ★	SHAKIN' ALL OVER *HMV POP 753* [1]	1	19
6 Oct 60	RESTLESS *HMV POP 790* [1]	22	7
13 Apr 61	LINDA LU *HMV POP 853* [1]	47	1
10 Jan 63	A SHOT OF RHYTHM AND BLUES *HMV POP 1088* [1]	48	1
25 Jul 63 ●	I'LL NEVER GET OVER YOU *HMV POP 1173* [1]	4	15
28 Nov 63	HUNGRY FOR LOVE *HMV POP 1228* [1]	20	10
30 Apr 64	ALWAYS AND EVER *HMV POP 1269* [1]	46	1
19 Nov 77	OUT OF THEIR SKULLS *Warner Bros. K 56411*	57	3

[1] Johnny Kidd and The Pirates

PIRATES featuring ENYA, SHOLA AMA, NAILA BOSS & ISHANI
UK, male production duo – Mohammed Nabulsi and Ryan Perera and Ireland, UK, female vocalists (Singles: 8 Weeks) pos/wks

11 Sep 04 ●	YOU SHOULD REALLY KNOW *Relentless RELCD 9*	8	8

'You Should Really Know' was a response to 'I Don't Wanna Know' by Mario Winans featuring Enya & P Diddy. Both tracks are based on a sample of Enya's 'Boadicea'.

PITCHSHIFTER *UK, male vocal / instrumental group (Singles: 4 Weeks, Albums: 2 Weeks)* pos/wks

28 Feb 98	GENIUS *Geffen GFSTD 22324*	71	1
26 Sep 98	MICROWAVED *Geffen GFSTD 22348*	54	1
21 Oct 00	DEAD BATTERY *MCA MCSTD 40241*	71	1
29 Jun 02	SHUTDOWN *Mayan MYNX 008*	66	1
3 Jun 00	DEVIANT *MCA 1122542*	35	1
11 May 02	P.SI *Mayan MYNCD 004*	54	1

Gene PITNEY | 206 | Top 500 |
Leading US performer in the 1960s, b. 17 Feb 1941, Connecticut. This unmistakable vocalist and songwriter had a longer and more impressive track record in the UK than in his homeland. Nonetheless, it took him 28 years to reach No.1 (Singles: 212 Weeks, Albums: 75 Weeks) pos/wks

23 Mar 61	(I WANNA) LOVE MY LIFE AWAY *London HL 9270*	26	11
8 Mar 62	TOWN WITHOUT PITY *HMV POP 952*	32	6
5 Dec 63 ●	TWENTY FOUR HOURS FROM TULSA *United Artists UP 1035*	5	19
5 Mar 64 ●	THAT GIRL BELONGS TO YESTERDAY *United Artists UP 1045*	7	14
15 Oct 64	IT HURTS TO BE IN LOVE *United Artists UP 1063*	36	4
12 Nov 64 ●	I'M GONNA BE STRONG *Stateside SS 358*	2	14
18 Feb 65 ●	I MUST BE SEEING THINGS *Stateside SS 390*	6	10
10 Jun 65 ●	LOOKING THRU THE EYES OF LOVE *Stateside SS 420*	3	12
4 Nov 65 ●	PRINCESS IN RAGS *Stateside SS 471*	9	12

17 Feb 66 ●	BACKSTAGE *Stateside SS 490*	4	10
9 Jun 66 ●	NOBODY NEEDS YOUR LOVE *Stateside SS 518*	2	13
10 Nov 66 ●	JUST ONE SMILE *Stateside SS 558*	8	12
23 Feb 67	(IN THE) COLD LIGHT OF DAY *Stateside SS 597*	38	6
15 Nov 67 ●	SOMETHING'S GOTTEN HOLD OF MY HEART *Stateside SS 2060*	5	13
3 Apr 68	SOMEWHERE IN THE COUNTRY *Stateside SS 2103*	19	9
27 Nov 68	YOURS UNTIL TOMORROW *Stateside SS 2131*	34	7
5 Mar 69	MARIA ELENA *Stateside SS 2142*	25	6
14 Mar 70	A STREET CALLED HOPE *Stateside SS 2164*	37	5
3 Oct 70	SHADY LADY *Stateside SS 2177*	29	8
28 Apr 73	24 SYCAMORE *Pye International 7N 25606*	34	7
2 Nov 74	BLUE ANGEL (re) *Bronze BRO 11*	39	4
14 Jan 89 ★	SOMETHING'S GOTTEN HOLD OF MY HEART *Parlophone R 6201* [1]	1	12
11 Apr 64 ●	BLUE GENE *United Artists ULP 1061*	7	11
6 Feb 65	GENE PITNEY'S BIG 16 *Stateside SL 10118*	12	6
20 Mar 65	I'M GONNA BE STRONG *Stateside SL 10120*	15	2
20 Nov 65	LOOKIN' THRU THE EYES OF LOVE *Stateside SL 10148*	15	5
17 Sep 66	NOBODY NEEDS YOUR LOVE *Stateside SL 10183*	13	17
4 Mar 67	YOUNG WARM AND WONDERFUL *Stateside SL 10194*	39	1
22 Apr 67	GENE PITNEY'S BIG SIXTEEN *Stateside SSL 10199*	40	1
20 Sep 69 ●	BEST OF GENE PITNEY *Stateside SSL 10286*	8	9
2 Oct 76 ●	HIS 20 GREATEST HITS *Arcade ADEP 22*	6	14
20 Oct 90	BACKSTAGE – THE GREATEST HITS AND MORE *Polydor 8471191*	17	7
22 Sep 01	LOOKING THROUGH – THE ULTIMATE COLLECTION *Sequel NEECD 380*	40	2

[1] Marc Almond featuring special guest star Gene Pitney

Mario PIU *Italy, male DJ / producer (Singles: 14 Weeks)* pos/wks

11 Dec 99 ●	COMMUNICATION (SOMEBODY ANSWER THE PHONE) *Incentive CENT 2CDS*	5	9
10 Mar 01	THE VISION (re) *BXR BXRC 0253* [1]	16	5

[1] Mario Piu presents DJ Arabesque

PIXIES *US, male / female vocal / instrumental group (Singles: 13 Weeks, Albums: 34 Weeks)* pos/wks

1 Apr 89	MONKEY GONE TO HEAVEN *4AD AD 904*	60	3
1 Jul 89	HERE COMES YOUR MAN *4AD AD 909*	54	1
28 Jul 90	VELOURIA *4AD AD 0009*	28	3
10 Nov 90	DIG FOR FIRE *4AD AD 0014*	62	1
8 Jun 91	PLANET OF SOUND *4AD AD 1008*	27	3
4 Oct 97	DEBASER *4AD BAD 7010CD*	23	2
29 Apr 89 ●	DOOLITTLE *4AD CAD 905*	8	9
25 Aug 90 ●	BOSSANOVA *4AD CAD 0010*	3	8
5 Oct 91 ●	TROMPE LE MONDE *4AD CAD 1014*	7	5
18 Oct 97	DEATH TO THE PIXIES *4AD DAD 7011CD*	28	3
18 Oct 97	DEATH TO THE PIXIES – DELUXE EDITION *4AD DADD 7011CD*	20	2
18 Jul 98	AT THE BBC *4AD GAD 8013CD*	45	1
17 Mar 01	COMPLETE 'B' SIDES *4AD GAD 2103CD*	53	1
15 May 04	BEST OF PIXIES – WAVE OF MUTILATION *4AD CAD 2406CD*	16	5

PIZZAMAN (see also BEATS INTERNATIONAL; MIGHTY DUB KATZ; FREAKPOWER; The HOUSEMARTINS)
UK, male producer – Norman Cook (Singles: 18 Weeks) pos/wks

27 Aug 94	TRIPPIN' ON SUNSHINE *Cowboy Records CDLOAD 16*	33	2
10 Jun 95	SEX ON THE STREETS (re) *Cowboy Records CDLOAD 24*	23	8
18 Nov 95	HAPPINESS *Cowboy Records CDLOAD 29*	19	4
1 Jun 96	TRIPPIN' ON SUNSHINE (re-issue) *Cowboy Records CDLOAD 32*	18	3
14 Sep 96	HELLO HONKY TONKS (ROCK YOUR BODY) *Cowboy Records CDLOAD 39*	41	1

PIZZICATO FIVE
Japan, male / female vocal / instrumental group (Singles: 1 Week) pos/wks

1 Nov 97	MON AMOUR TOKYO *Matador OLE 2902*	72	1

Joe PIZZULO See Sergio MENDES

PLACEBO *US / Sweden / UK, male vocal / instrumental group (Singles: 51 Weeks, Albums: 51 Weeks)* pos/wks

28 Sep 96	TEENAGE ANGST *Elevator Music FLOORCD 3*	30	3
1 Feb 97 ●	NANCY BOY *Elevator Music FLOORCD 4*	4	6
24 May 97	BRUISE PRISTINE *Elevator Music FLOORCD 5*	14	3

Singles re-entries are listed as (re), (2re), (3re)… which signifies that the hit re-entered the chart once, twice or three times…

PLAYN JAYN
UK, male vocal / instrumental group (Albums: 1 Week) pos/wks

1 Sep 84	FRIDAY THE 13TH (AT THE MARQUEE CLUB) *A&M JAYN 13*	..93	1

PLAYTHING (see also TRIPLE X) *Italy, male production*
duo – Luca Moretti and Riccardo Romanini (Singles: 6 Weeks) pos/wks

5 May 01	INTO SPACE *Manifesto FESCD 81*	..48	1
24 Aug 02	DO YOU SEE THE LIGHT? *Data MoS DATA 33CDS* [1]	..14	5

[1] Snap! vs Plaything

PLUMB
US, female vocalist – Tiffany Arbuckle-Lee (Singles: 2 Weeks) pos/wks

14 Feb 04	REAL *Curb / London CUBC 095*	..41	2

PLUMMET
US, male DJ / producer – Eric B Muniz (Singles: 12 Weeks) pos/wks

26 Apr 03	DAMAGED *Serious SER 68CD*	..12	10
8 May 04	CHERISH THE DAY *Manifesto 9866389*	..35	2

PLUS ONE featuring SIRRON
UK, male / female vocal / instrumental group (Singles: 4 Weeks) pos/wks

19 May 90	IT'S HAPPENIN' *MCA MCA 1405*	..40	4

PLUTO See Pluto SHERVINGTON

PLUX featuring Georgia JONES
US, male / female vocal / instrumental group (Singles: 2 Weeks) pos/wks

4 May 96	OVER AND OVER *ffrr FCD 277*	..33	2

The POETS *UK, male vocal / instrumental group (Singles: 5 Weeks)* pos/wks

29 Oct 64	NOW WE'RE THRU *Decca F 11995*	..31	5

The POGUES ⟨473⟩ *Top 500*
Irish band who presented an aggressive, compelling collision of folk, punk and rock, led by Shane McGowan (v/g) and originally named Pogue Mahone (Kiss My Ass). 'The Irish Rover' was the final Top 20 hit released by the legendary Stiff label (Singles: 70 Weeks, Albums: 83 Weeks) pos/wks

6 Apr 85	A PAIR OF BROWN EYES *Stiff BUY 220*	..72	2
22 Jun 85	SALLY MACLENNANE *Stiff BUY 224*	..51	4
14 Sep 85	DIRTY OLD TOWN *Stiff BUY 229*	..62	3
8 Mar 86	POGUETRY IN MOTION (EP) *Stiff BUY 243*	..29	6
30 Aug 86	HAUNTED *MCA MCA 1084*	..42	4
28 Mar 87 ●	THE IRISH ROVER *Stiff BUY 258* [1]	..8	8
5 Dec 87 ●	FAIRYTALE OF NEW YORK *Pogue Mahone NY 7* [2]	..2	9
5 Mar 88	IF I SHOULD FALL FROM GRACE WITH GOD *Pogue Mahone PG 1*	..58	3
16 Jul 88	FIESTA *Pogue Mahone PG 2*	..24	5
17 Dec 88	YEAH, YEAH, YEAH, YEAH, YEAH *Pogue Mahone YZ 355*	..43	4
8 Jul 89	MISTY MORNING, ALBERT BRIDGE *PM YZ 407*	..41	3
16 Jun 90	JACK'S HEROES / WHISKEY IN THE JAR *PM YZ 500* [1]	..63	2
15 Sep 90	SUMMER IN SIAM *PM YZ 519*	..64	2
21 Sep 91	A RAINY NIGHT IN SOHO *PM YZ 603*	..67	1
14 Dec 91	FAIRYTALE OF NEW YORK (re-issue) *PM YZ 628* [2]	..36	5
30 May 92	HONKY TONK WOMEN *PM YZ 673*	..56	2
21 Aug 93	TUESDAY MORNING *PM YZ 758 CD*	..18	5
22 Jan 94	ONCE UPON A TIME *PM YZ 771CD*	..66	2
3 Nov 84	RED ROSES FOR ME *Stiff SEEZ 55*	..89	1
17 Aug 85	RUM SODOMY & THE LASH *Stiff SEEZ 58*	..13	14
30 Jan 88 ●	IF I SHOULD FALL FROM GRACE WITH GOD *Stiff NYR 1*	..3	16
29 Jul 89 ●	PEACE AND LOVE *WEA WX 247*	..5	8
13 Oct 90	HELL'S DITCH *Pogue Mahone WX 366*	..12	5
12 Oct 91	THE BEST OF THE POGUES *PM WX 430*	..11	17
11 Sep 93	WAITING FOR HERB *PM 4509934632*	..20	3
17 Mar 01	THE VERY BEST OF THE POGUES *WSM 8573874592*	..18	19

[1] The Pogues and The Dubliners [2] The Pogues featuring Kirsty MacColl

Tracks on Poguetry in Motion (EP): London Girl / The Body of an American / A Rainy Night in Soho / Planxty Noel Hill The group was male / female for the first two albums

POINT BREAK
UK, male vocal group (Singles: 21 Weeks, Albums: 3 Weeks) pos/wks

9 Oct 99	DO WE ROCK *Eternal WEA 216CD1*	..29	2
22 Jan 00 ●	STAND TOUGH *Eternal WEA 248CD1*	..7	5
22 Apr 00	FREAKYTIME *Eternal WEA 265CD1*	..13	6

5 Aug 00	YOU *Eternal WEA 290CD1*	..14	5
2 Dec 00	WHAT ABOUT US *Eternal WEA 314CD1*	..24	3
19 Aug 00	APOCADELIC *Eternal 8573828882*	..21	3

The POINTER SISTERS ⟨390⟩ *Top 500* *Talented sibling vocal quartet formed 1971, Oakland, California, US, whose recordings touched many musical bases. Reduced to trio – June, Anita and Ruth – when Bonnie left in 1978. Soulful sisters surprisingly won a country music Grammy for 'Fairytale' in 1974 (Singles: 87 Weeks, Albums: 88 Weeks)* pos/wks

3 Feb 79	EVERYBODY IS A STAR *Planet K 12324*	..61	3
17 Mar 79	FIRE *Planet K 12339*	..34	8
22 Aug 81 ●	SLOWHAND *Planet K 12530*	..10	11
5 Dec 81	SHOULD I DO IT? *Planet K 12578*	..50	5
14 Apr 84 ●	AUTOMATIC *Planet RPS 105*	..2	15
23 Jun 84 ●	JUMP (FOR MY LOVE) *Planet RPS 106*	..6	10
11 Aug 84	I NEED YOU *Planet RPS 107*	..25	9
27 Oct 84	I'M SO EXCITED *Planet RPS 108*	..11	11
12 Jan 85	NEUTRON DANCE *Planet RPS 109*	..31	7
20 Jul 85	DARE ME *RCA PB 49957*	..17	8
29 Aug 81	BLACK AND WHITE *Planet K 52300*	..21	13
5 May 84 ●	BREAK OUT *Planet PL 84705*	..9	58
27 Jul 85	CONTACT *Planet PL 85457*	..34	7
29 Jul 89	JUMP – THE BEST OF THE POINTER SISTERS *RCA PL 90319*	..11	10

POISON *US, male vocal / instrumental group (Singles: 43 Weeks, Albums: 37 Weeks)* pos/wks

23 May 87	TALK DIRTY TO ME *Music for Nations KUT 125*	..67	1
7 May 88	NOTHIN' BUT A GOOD TIME *Capitol CL 486*	..35	3
5 Nov 88	FALLEN ANGEL *Capitol CL 500*	..59	1
11 Feb 89	EVERY ROSE HAS ITS THORN *Capitol CL 520* ▲	..13	9
29 Apr 89	YOUR MAMA DON'T DANCE *Capitol CL 523*	..13	7
23 Sep 89	NOTHIN' BUT A GOOD TIME (re-issue) *Capitol CL 539*	..48	3
30 Jun 90	UNSKINNY BOP *Capitol CL 582*	..15	7
27 Oct 90	SOMETHING TO BELIEVE IN *Capitol CL 594*	..35	4
23 Nov 91	SO TELL ME WHY *Capitol CL 640*	..25	2
13 Feb 93	STAND *Capitol CDCL 679*	..25	3
24 Apr 93	UNTIL YOU SUFFER SOME (FIRE AND ICE) *Capitol CDCL 685*	..32	3
21 May 88	OPEN UP AND SAY ... AAH! *Capitol EST 2059*	..18	21
21 Jul 90 ●	FLESH AND BLOOD *Enigma EST 2126*	..3	11
14 Dec 91	SWALLOW THIS LIVE *Capitol ESTU 2159*	..52	2
6 Mar 93	NATIVE TONGUE *Capitol CDSETU 2190*	..20	3

POKEMON ALLSTARS See 50 GRIND featuring POKEMON ALLSTARS

POLECATS *UK, male vocal / instrumental group (Singles: 18 Weeks, Albums: 2 Weeks)* pos/wks

7 Mar 81	JOHN I'M ONLY DANCING / BIG GREEN CAR *Mercury POLE 1*	..35	8
16 May 81	ROCKABILLY GUY *Mercury POLE 2*	..35	6
22 Aug 81	JEEPSTER / MARIE CELESTE *Mercury POLE 3*	..53	4
4 Jul 81	POLECATS *Vertigo 6359 057*	..28	2

The POLICE ⟨64⟩ *Top 500* (see also Klark KENT) *World-famous Anglo-American rock trio: Sting (b. Gordon Sumner) (v/b), Andy Summers (g/v), Stewart Copeland (d/v). These Brit and Grammy award winners were one of the 1980s' most popular acts. The Rock and Roll Hall of Fame members had five successive albums entering the UK chart at No.1. Total UK singles sales: 5,617,175 (Singles: 153 Weeks, Albums: 405 Weeks)* pos/wks

7 Oct 78 ●	CAN'T STAND LOSING YOU (re) *A&M AMS 7381*	..2	16
28 Apr 79	ROXANNE *A&M AMS 7348*	..12	9
22 Sep 79 ★	MESSAGE IN A BOTTLE *A&M AMS 7474*	..1	11
17 Nov 79	FALL OUT *Illegal IL 001*	..47	4
1 Dec 79 ★	WALKING ON THE MOON *A&M AMS 7494*	..1	10
16 Feb 80 ●	SO LONELY *A&M AMS 7402*	..6	10
14 Jun 80	SIX PACK *A&M AMPP 6001*	..17	4
27 Sep 80 ★	DON'T STAND SO CLOSE TO ME *A&M AMS 7564* ■	..1	10
13 Dec 80 ●	DE DO DO DO, DE DA DA DA *A&M AMS 7578*	..5	8
26 Sep 81 ●	INVISIBLE SUN *A&M AMS 8164*	..2	8
24 Oct 81 ★	EVERY LITTLE THING SHE DOES IS MAGIC *A&M AMS 8174*	..1	13
12 Dec 81	SPIRITS IN THE MATERIAL WORLD *A&M AMS 8194*	..12	8
28 May 83 ★	EVERY BREATH YOU TAKE *A&M AM 117* ▲	..1	11
23 Jul 83 ●	WRAPPED AROUND YOUR FINGER *A&M AM 127*	..7	7
5 Nov 83	SYNCHRONICITY II *A&M AM 153*	..17	5
14 Jan 84	KING OF PAIN *A&M AM 176*	..17	4
11 Oct 86	DON'T STAND SO CLOSE TO ME '86 (re-mix) *A&M AM 354*	..24	4
13 May 95	CAN'T STAND LOSING YOU (LIVE) *A&M 5810372*	..27	2
20 Dec 97	ROXANNE '97 (re-mix) *A&M 5824552* [1]	..17	6

			pos/wks
5 Aug 00	**WHEN THE WORLD IS RUNNING DOWN**		
	Pagan PAGAN 039CDS [2]	28	3
21 Apr 79 ●	**OUTLANDOS D'AMOUR** *A&M AMLH 68502*	6	96
13 Oct 79	**REGGATTA DE BLANC** *A&M AMLH 64792* ■	1	74
11 Oct 80 ★	**ZENYATTA MONDATTA** *A&M AMLH 64831* ■	1	31
10 Oct 81 ★	**GHOST IN THE MACHINE** *A&M AMLK 63730* ■	1	27
25 Jun 83 ★	**SYNCHRONICITY** *A&M AMLX 63735* ■ ▲	1	48
8 Nov 86 ★	**EVERY BREATH YOU TAKE – THE SINGLES** *A&M EVERY 1* ■	..1	55
10 Oct 92 ●	**GREATEST HITS** *A&M 5400302*	10	21
10 Jun 95	**LIVE!** *A&M 540222*	25	3
22 Nov 97 ★	**THE VERY BEST OF STING AND THE POLICE**		
	A&M 5404282 [1] ■	1	50

[1] Sting and The Police [2] Different Gear vs The Police [1] Sting and The Police

'Can't Stand Losing You' made No.42 on its first visit and peaked at No.2 only on re-entry in Jul 1979. Six Pack consists of six separate Police singles as follows: The Bed's Too Big Without You / Roxanne / Message in a Bottle / Walking on the Moon / So Lonely / Can't Stand Losing You 'The Very Best of Sting and The Police' originally peaked at No.11. On 2 Mar 2002, an updated version containing three new tracks re-entered the chart and sales were combined with the original album

Su POLLARD
UK, female actor / vocalist (Singles: 11 Weeks, Albums: 3 Weeks) pos/wks

5 Oct 85	**COME TO ME (I AM WOMAN)** *Rainbow RBR 1*	71	1
1 Feb 86 ●	**STARTING TOGETHER** *Rainbow RBR 4*	2	10
22 Nov 86	**SU** *K-Tel NE 1327*	86	3

Jimi POLO *US, male vocalist (Singles: 5 Weeks)* pos/wks

9 Nov 91	**NEVER GOIN' DOWN** *MCA MCS 1578* [1]	51	2
1 Aug 92	**EXPRESS YOURSELF** *Perfecto 74321101827*	59	2
9 Aug 97	**EXPRESS YOURSELF (re-mix)** *Perfecto PERF 146CD1*	62	1

[1] Adamski featuring Jimi Polo

The listed flip side of 'Never Goin' Down' was 'Born to Be Alive' by Adamski featuring Soho

POLOROID
UK, male / female production / vocal trio (Singles: 2 Weeks) pos/wks

11 Oct 03	**SO DAMN BEAUTIFUL** *Decode / Telstar CDSTAS 3351*	28	2

POLTERGEIST (see also VICIOUS CIRCLES)
UK, male producer – Simon Berry (Singles: 2 Weeks) pos/wks

6 Jul 96	**VICIOUS CIRCLES** *Manifesto FESCD 8*	32	2

Peter POLYCARPOU *UK, male actor / vocalist (Singles: 4 Weeks)* pos/wks

20 Feb 93	**LOVE HURTS** *Soundtrack Music CDEM 259*	26	4

POLYGON WINDOW (see also APHEX TWIN; AFX)
UK, male producer – Richard James (Singles: 1 Week) pos/wks

3 Apr 93	**QUOTH** *Warp WAP 33CD*	49	1

The POLYPHONIC SPREE (see also TRIPPING DAISY)
US, male / female vocal / instrumental ensemble – leader Tim DeLaughter (Singles: 5 Weeks, Albums: 2 Weeks) pos/wks

2 Nov 02	**HANGING AROUND** *679 Recordings 679L 012CD*	39	1
22 Feb 03	**LIGHT AND DAY** *679 Recordings 679L 015CD1*	40	1
26 Jul 03	**SOLDIER GIRL** *679 Recordings 679L 014CD*	26	2
7 Aug 04	**HOLD ME NOW** *Good CDPOLY 1*	72	1
12 Jul 03	**THE BEGINNING STAGES OF ... THE POLYPHONIC SPREE**		
	679 Recordings 5046609182	70	1
24 Jul 04	**TOGETHER WE'RE HEAVY** *Good POLYCD 1*	61	1

The PONI-TAILS *US, female vocal group (Singles: 14 Weeks)* pos/wks

19 Sep 58 ●	**BORN TOO LATE** *HMV POP 516*	5	11
10 Apr 59	**EARLY TO BED** *HMV POP 596*	26	3

Brian POOLE and the TREMELOES *See The TREMELOES*

Glyn POOLE *UK, male vocalist (Singles: 8 Weeks)* pos/wks

20 Oct 73	**MILLY MOLLY MANDY** *York SYK 565*	35	8

Ian POOLEY *Germany, male DJ / producer (Singles: 3 Weeks)* pos/wks

10 Mar 01	**900 DEGREES** *V2 VVR 5015143*	57	1
11 Aug 01	**BALMES** *V2 VVR 5016613* [1]	65	1
23 Nov 02	**PIHA** *Honchos Music HONMO 019CD* [2]	53	1

[1] Ian Pooley featuring Esthero [2] Ian Pooley and Magik J

POP! *UK, male vocal group (Singles: 5 Weeks)* pos/wks

12 Jun 04	**HEAVEN AND EARTH** *Jive 82876619582*	14	2
11 Sep 04	**CAN'T SAY GOODBYE** *Jive 82876639492*	26	3

'Heaven and Earth' was withdrawn from sale after one week because the CD single contained a combined track length longer than that permitted for the format

Iggy POP (see also The STOOGES) *US, male vocalist – James Jewel Osterburg (Singles: 31 Weeks, Albums: 27 Weeks)* pos/wks

13 Dec 86 ●	**REAL WILD CHILD (WILD ONE)** *A&M AM 368*	10	11
10 Feb 90	**LIVIN' ON THE EDGE OF THE NIGHT** *Virgin America VUS 18*	51	4
13 Oct 90	**CANDY** *Virgin America VUS 29*	67	1
5 Jan 91	**WELL DID YOU EVAH!** *Chrysalis CHS 3646* [1]	42	4
4 Sep 93	**WILD AMERICA (EP)** *Virgin America VUSCD 74*	63	1
21 May 94	**BESIDE YOU** *Virgin America VUSCD 77*	47	2
23 Nov 96	**LUST FOR LIFE** *Virgin America VUSCD 116*	26	2
7 Mar 98	**THE PASSENGER** *Virgin VSCDT 1689*	22	3
17 Jan 04	**KICK IT** *XL Recordings XLS 176CD* [2]	39	3
9 Apr 77	**THE IDIOT** *RCA Victor PL 12275*	30	3
4 Jun 77	**RAW POWER** *Embassy 31464* [1]	44	2
1 Oct 77	**LUST FOR LIFE** *RCA PL 12488*	28	5
19 May 79	**NEW VALUES** *Arista SPART 1092*	60	4
16 Feb 80	**SOLDIER** *Arista SPART 1117*	62	2
11 Oct 86	**BLAH-BLAH-BLAH** *A&M AMA 5145*	43	7
2 Jul 88	**INSTINCT** *A&M AMA 5198*	61	1
21 Jul 90	**BRICK BY BRICK** *Virgin America VUSLP 19*	50	2
25 Sep 93	**AMERICAN CAESAR** *Virgin CDVUS 64*	43	1

[1] Deborah Harry and Iggy Pop [2] Peaches featuring Iggy Pop [1] Iggy and The Stooges

Tracks on Wild America (EP): Wild America / Credit Card / Come Back Tomorrow / My Angel

POP WILL EAT ITSELF *UK, male vocal / instrumental group (Singles: 43 Weeks, Albums: 14 Weeks)* pos/wks

30 Jan 88	**THERE IS NO LOVE BETWEEN US ANYMORE**		
	Chapter 22 CHAP 20	66	1
23 Jul 88	**DEF CON ONE** *Chapter 22 PWEI 001*	63	4
11 Feb 89	**CAN U DIG IT?** *RCA PB 42621*	38	4
22 Apr 89	**WISE UP! SUCKER** *RCA PB 42761*	41	3
2 Sep 89	**VERY METAL NOISE POLLUTION (EP)** *RCA PB 42883*	45	3
9 Jun 90	**TOUCHED BY THE HAND OF CICCIOLINA** *RCA PB 43735*	28	4
13 Oct 90	**DANCE OF THE MAD** *RCA PB 44023*	32	2
12 Jan 91	**X Y & ZEE** *RCA PB 44243*	15	2
1 Jun 91	**92°F** *RCA PB 44555*	23	3
6 Jun 92	**KARMADROME / EAT ME DRINK ME LOVE ME** *RCA PB 45467*	17	2
29 Aug 92	**BULLETPROOF!** *RCA 74321110137*	24	3
16 Jan 93 ●	**GET THE GIRL! KILL THE BADDIES!** *RCA 74321128802*	9	4
16 Oct 93	**RSVP / FAMILIUS HORRIBILUS** *Infectious INFECT 1CD*	27	2
12 Mar 94	**ICH BIN EIN AUSLANDER** *Infectious INFECT 4CD*	28	2
10 Sep 94	**EVERYTHING'S COOL** *Infectious INFECT 9CD*	23	2
13 May 89	**THIS IS THE DAY ... THIS IS THE HOUR ... THIS IS THIS!**		
	RCA PL 74141	24	2
2 Nov 90	**CURE FOR SANITY** *RCA PL 74828*	33	2
19 Sep 92	**THE LOOKS OR THE LIFESTYLE** *RCA 74321102652*	15	3
6 Mar 93	**WEIRD'S BAR AND GRILL** *RCA 74321133432*	44	1
6 Nov 93	**16 DIFFERENT FLAVOURS OF HELL** *RCA 74321153172*	73	1
1 Oct 94	**DOS DEDOS MIS AMIGOS** *Infectious INFECT 10CDX*	11	2
18 Mar 95	**TWO FINGERS MY FRIENDS** *Infectious INFECT 10CDRX*	25	2

Tracks on Very Metal Noise Pollution (EP): Def Con 1989 AD including the Twilight Zone / Preaching to the Perverted / PWEI-zation / 92°F 'Two Fingers My Friends' is a re-mixed version of 'Dos Dedos Mis Amigos'

POPE JOHN PAUL II
Poland, male pontiff – Karol J Wojtyla (Albums: 8 Weeks) pos/wks

3 Jul 82	**JOHN PAUL II – THE PILGRIM POPE** *BBC REB 445*	71	4
10 Dec 94	**THE ROSARY** *Pure Music PMCD 7009*	50	4

'The Rosary' is a double CD / cassette, one with the Rosary in Latin by the Pope, the other featuring its English reading by Father Kilcoyne

POPES *See Shane MacGOWAN*

POPPERS presents AURA
UK, male production trio and female vocalist (Singles: 1 Week) pos/wks

25 Oct 97	**EVERY LITTLE TIME** *VC VCRD 26*	44	1

FRANZ FERDINAND TOP 10

The gospel according to Franz Ferdinand, who choose their favourite albums

The 2004 Mercury Music Prize winners deliberate over and select their essential listening from five decades of music.

album – act – (peak position)

DRAGNET * The Fall	HATFUL OF HOLLOW The Smiths (7)
FEAR OF MUSIC Talking Heads (33)	LOVE THE CUP * Sons & Daughters
FOR YOUR PLEASURE Roxy Music (4)	PROPAGANDA Sparks (9)
GALLOWSBIRD'S BARK * The Fiery Furnaces	RIO Duran Duran (2)
THE GREATEST HITS Queen (1)	STRANGE BOUTIQUE The Monochrome Set (62)

* Did not chart

The POPPY FAMILY
(see also Terry JACKS) *Canada, male / female vocal / instrumental duo – Terry Jacks and Susan Peklevits (Singles: 14 Weeks)*   pos/wks
15 Aug 70 ● **WHICH WAY YOU GOIN' BILLY?** *Decca F 22976* 7 14

The POPPY FIELDS
(see also The ALARM) *UK, male vocal / instrumental group (Singles: 2 Weeks)*   pos/wks
21 Feb 04   **45 R.P.M.** *Snapper Music SMASCD 054* 28 2

The Poppy Fields are The Alarm under a different name

PORN KINGS
UK, male instrumental / production group (Singles: 12 Weeks)   pos/wks
28 Sep 96   **UP TO NO GOOD** *All Around the World CDGLOBE 145* 28 2
21 Jun 97   **AMOUR (C'MON)** *All Around the World CDGLOBE 152* 17 3
16 Jan 99 ● **UP TO THE WILDSTYLE**
             All Around the World CDGLOBE 170 [1] 10 4
10 Feb 01   **SLEDGER** *All Around the World CDGLOBE 229* 71 1
22 Mar 03   **SHAKE YA SHIMMY** *All Around the World CDGLOBE 213* [2] ..28 2

[1] Porn Kings vs DJ Supreme [2] Porn Kings vs Flip & Fill featuring 740 Boyz

PORNO FOR PYROS
US, male vocal / instrumental group (Singles: 2 Weeks, Albums: 5 Weeks)   pos/wks
5 Jun 93   **PETS** *Warner Bros. W 0177CD* 53 2
8 May 93   **PORNO FOR PYROS** *Warner Bros. 9362452282*..........13 3
8 Jun 96   **GOOD GOD'S URGE** *Warner Bros. 9362461262* 40 2

PORTISHEAD
(see also Beth GIBBONS & RUSTIN' MAN) *UK, male / female vocal / instrumental group (Singles: 20 Weeks, Albums: 95 Weeks)*   pos/wks
13 Aug 94   **SOUR TIMES (re)** *Go Beat GODCD 116* 13 5
14 Jan 95   **GLORY BOX** *Go Beat GODCD 120* 13 7
20 Sep 97 ● **ALL MINE** *Go Beat 5715972* 8 4
22 Nov 97   **OVER** *Go Beat 5719932* 25 2
14 Mar 98   **ONLY YOU** *Go Beat 5694752* 35 2
3 Sep 94 ●   **DUMMY** *Go Beat 8285222* 2 71
11 Oct 97 ● **PORTISHEAD** *Go Beat 5391892* 2 22
14 Nov 98   **PNYC** *Go Beat 5594242* 40 2

'Sour Times' made No.57 on its first visit and peaked at No.13 in Apr 1995

Nick PORTLOCK See ROYAL PHILHARMONIC ORCHESTRA

Gary PORTNOY
US, male vocalist (Singles: 3 Weeks)   pos/wks
25 Feb 84   **THEME FROM 'CHEERS'** *Starblend CHEER 1* 58 3

PORTOBELLA
UK, male / female vocal / instrumental group (Singles: 1 Week)   pos/wks
26 Jun 04   **COVERED IN PUNK** *Island CID 962* 54 1

PORTRAIT
US, male vocal group (Singles: 6 Weeks)   pos/wks
27 Mar 93   **HERE WE GO AGAIN** *Capitol CDCL 683* 37 3
8 Apr 95   **I CAN CALL YOU** *Capitol CDCL 740* 61 1
8 Jul 95   **HOW DEEP IS YOUR LOVE** *Capitol CDCL 751* 41 2

PORTSMOUTH SINFONIA
UK, orchestra (Singles: 4 Weeks)   pos/wks
12 Sep 81   **CLASSICAL MUDDLY** *Island WIP 6736* 38 4

Sandy POSEY
US, female vocalist (Singles: 32 Weeks, Albums: 1 Week)   pos/wks
15 Sep 66   **BORN A WOMAN** *MGM 1321* 24 11
5 Jan 67   **SINGLE GIRL** *MGM 1330* 15 13
13 Apr 67   **WHAT A WOMAN IN LOVE WON'T DO** *MGM 1335* 48 3
6 Sep 75   **SINGLE GIRL (re-issue)** *MGM 2006 533* 35 5
11 Mar 67   **BORN A WOMAN** *MGM MGMCS 8035* 39 1

The POSIES
US, male vocal / instrumental group (Singles: 1 Week) pos/wks
19 Mar 94   **DEFINITE DOOR** *Geffen GFSTD 68* 67 1

POSITIVE FORCE
US, female vocal duo – Brenda Reynolds and Vicki Drayton (Singles: 9 Weeks)   pos/wks
22 Dec 79   **WE GOT THE FUNK** *Sugarhill SHL 102* 18 9

POSITIVE GANG
UK, male / female instrumental / vocal group (Singles: 5 Weeks)   pos/wks
17 Apr 93   **SWEET FREEDOM** *PWL Continental PWCD 261* 34 4
31 Jul 93   **SWEET FREEDOM PART 2** *PWL Continental PWCD 264* 67 1

POSITIVE K
US, male rapper – Darryl Gibson (Singles: 2 Weeks)   pos/wks
15 May 93   **I GOT A MAN** *Fourth & Broadway BRCD 280* 43 2

Mike POST US, orchestra (Singles: 18 Weeks)
pos/wks
9 Aug 75	**AFTERNOON OF THE RHINO (re)** Warner Bros. K 16588 [1]	..47	2
16 Jan 82	**THEME FROM 'HILL STREET BLUES'** Elektra K 12576 [2]	25	11
29 Sep 84	**THE A TEAM** RCA 443	.45	5

[1] Mike Post Coalition [2] Mike Post featuring Larry Carlton

The POTTERS UK, male Stoke City football
supporters vocal group (Singles: 2 Weeks)
pos/wks
1 Apr 72	**WE'LL BE WITH YOU** Pye JT 100	.34	2

Frank POURCEL France, male orchestra leader,
b. 1 Jan 1915, d. 12 Dec 2000 (Albums: 7 Weeks)
pos/wks
20 Nov 71 ●	**THIS IS POURCEL** Studio Two STWO 7	.8	7

POWDER
UK, male / female vocal / instrumental group (Singles: 1 Week)
pos/wks
24 Jun 95	**AFRODISIAC** Parkway PARK 002CD	.72	1

Bryan POWELL UK, male vocalist (Singles: 3 Weeks)
pos/wks
13 Mar 93	**IT'S ALRIGHT** Talkin Loud TLKCD 34	.73	1
15 May 93	**I THINK OF YOU** Talkin Loud TLKCD 38	.61	1
7 Aug 93	**NATURAL** Talkin Loud TLKCD 41	.73	1

Cozy POWELL (see also EMERSON, LAKE and POWELL; Graham BONNET;
BLACK SABBATH; Gary MOORE; RAINBOW; Michael SCHENKER GROUP;
WHITESNAKE; Bernie MARSDEN) UK, male instrumentalist – Colin Flooks,
b. 29 Dec 1947, d. 5 Apr 1998 (Singles: 38 Weeks, Albums: 8 Weeks)
pos/wks
8 Dec 73 ●	**DANCE WITH THE DEVIL** RAK 164	.3	15
25 May 74	**THE MAN IN BLACK** RAK 173	.18	8
10 Aug 74 ●	**NA NA NA** RAK 180	.10	10
10 Nov 79	**THEME ONE** Ariola ARO 189	.62	2
19 Jun 93	**RESURRECTION** Parlophone CDRS 6351 [1]	.23	3
26 Jan 80	**OVER THE TOP** Ariola ARL 5038	.34	3
19 Sep 81	**TILT** Polydor POLD 5047	.58	4
28 May 83	**OCTOPUSS** Polydor POLD 5093	.86	1

[1] Brian May with Cozy Powell

Kobie POWELL See Us3

Peter POWELL UK, male exercise instructor (Albums: 13 Weeks)
pos/wks
20 Mar 82 ●	**KEEP FIT AND DANCE** K-Tel NE 1167	.9	13

POWER CIRCLE See CHICANE

POWER OF DREAMS
Ireland, male vocal / instrumental group (Singles: 2 Weeks)
pos/wks
19 Jan 91	**AMERICAN DREAM** Polydor PO 117	.74	1
11 Apr 92	**THERE I GO AGAIN** Polydor PO 200	.65	1

POWER STATION (see also CHIC; DURAN DURAN; Robert PALMER)
UK / US, male vocal / instrumental group
(Singles: 17 Weeks, Albums: 23 Weeks)
pos/wks
16 Mar 85	**SOME LIKE IT HOT** Parlophone R 6091	.14	8
11 May 85	**GET IT ON** Parlophone R 6096	.22	7
9 Nov 85	**COMMUNICATION** Parlophone R 6114	.75	1
12 Oct 96	**SHE CAN ROCK IT** Chrysalis CDCHS 5039	.63	1
6 Apr 85	**THE POWER STATION** Parlophone POST 1	.12	23

POWERCUT featuring NUBIAN PRINZ
US, male vocal / instrumental group (Singles: 4 Weeks)
pos/wks
22 Jun 91	**GIRLS** Eternal YZ 570	.50	4

POWERHOUSE UK, male production duo –
Hamilton Dean and Julian Slatter (Singles: 4 Weeks)
pos/wks
20 Dec 97	**RHYTHM OF THE NIGHT** Satellite 74321522592	.38	4

POWERHOUSE featuring Duane HARDEN
(see also Armand VAN HELDEN) US, male producer –
Lenny Fontana and male vocalist (Singles: 5 Weeks)
pos/wks
22 May 99	**WHAT YOU NEED** Defected DEFECT 3CDS	.13	5

POWERPILL
UK, male instrumental / production group (Singles: 3 Weeks)
pos/wks
6 Jun 92	**PAC-MAN** Ffrreedom TABX 110	.43	3

POWERS THAT BE UK / Sweden, male production duo –
Giles Goodman and Pierre Jerksten (Singles: 1 Week)
pos/wks
26 Jul 03	**PLANET ROCK / FUNKY PLANET** Defected DFTD 074	.63	1

Will POWERS
US, female vocalist – Lyn Goldsmith (Singles: 9 Weeks)
pos/wks
1 Oct 83	**KISSING WITH CONFIDENCE** Island IS 134	.17	9

Hit features uncredited vocals by Carly Simon

Perez PRADO and his Orchestra Cuba, orchestra leader –
Damas Prado, b. 11 Dec 1916, d. 14 Sep 1989 (Singles: 57 Weeks)
pos/wks
25 Mar 55 ★	**CHERRY PINK AND APPLE BLOSSOM WHITE** HMV B 10833 [1] ▲	.1	17
25 Jul 58 ●	**PATRICIA** RCA 1067	.8	16
10 Dec 94 ●	**GUAGLIONE (2re)** RCA 74321250192 [2]	.2	24

[1] Perez 'Prez' Prado and his Orchestra, the King of the Mambo [2] Perez 'Prez' Prado and his Orchestra

'Guaglione' did not made its peak position until its second re-entry in May 1995 after first making No.41 in 1994 and No.58 on its first re-entry

PRAISE
UK, male / female vocal / instrumental group (Singles: 7 Weeks)
pos/wks
2 Feb 91 ●	**ONLY YOU** Epic 6566117	.4	7

Uncredited vocals by Miriam Stockley

PRAISE CATS (see also E-SMOOVE featuring Latanza WATERS; THICK D)
US, male producer – Eric 'E-Smoove' Miller (Singles: 1 Week)
pos/wks
26 Oct 02	**SHINED ON ME** Pias PIAS 028CD	.56	1

Pras See Pras MICHEL

PRATT and McCLAIN with BROTHERLOVE
US, male vocal duo – Truett Pratt and Jerry McClain
with male instrumental group (Singles: 6 Weeks)
pos/wks
1 Oct 77	**HAPPY DAYS** Reprise K 14435	.31	6

PRAXIS featuring KATHY BROWN UK, male producer –
David Shaw and US, female vocalist (Singles: 5 Weeks)
pos/wks
25 Nov 95	**TURN ME OUT** Stress CDSTR 40	.44	2
20 Sep 97	**TURN ME OUT (TURN TO SUGAR) (re-mix)** ffrr FCD 314 [1]	.35	3

[1] Praxis featuring Kathy Brown

PRAYING MANTIS UK, male vocal /
instrumental group (Singles: 2 Weeks, Albums: 2 Weeks)
pos/wks
31 Jan 81	**CHEATED** Arista ARIST 378	.69	2
11 Apr 81	**TIME TELLS NO LIES** Arista SPART 1153	.60	2

PRECIOUS UK, female vocal group (Singles: 20 Weeks)
pos/wks
29 May 99 ●	**SAY IT AGAIN (re)** EMI CDEM 544	.6	11
1 Apr 00	**REWIND** EMI CDEM 557	.11	5
15 Jul 00	**IT'S GONNA BE MY WAY** EMI CDEM 569	.27	3
25 Nov 00	**NEW BEGINNING** EMI CDEM 573	.50	1

PRECOCIOUS BRATS featuring KEVIN and PERRY
UK, male production duo – Julius O'Riordan (Judge Jules)
and Matt Smith and UK, male / female comedy / vocal duo –
Harry Enfield and Kathy Burke (Singles: 4 Weeks)
pos/wks
6 May 00	**BIG GIRL** Virgin / EMI VTSCD 1	.16	4

PREFAB SPROUT `418` `Top 500` Critically-acclaimed, intelligent,
fragile pop band, formed 1978 in Newcastle, England. Named after a phrase
from the Sinatra / Hazlewood hit 'Jackson' misheard by leader / songwriter
Paddy McAloon (v/g). Stevie Wonder and Pete Townshend guested on 'From
Langley Park to Memphis' (Singles: 60 Weeks, Albums: 106 Weeks) pos/wks
28 Jan 84	**DON'T SING** Kitchenware SK 9	.62	2
20 Jul 85	**FARON YOUNG** Kitchenware SK 22	.74	1
9 Nov 85	**WHEN LOVE BREAKS DOWN** Kitchenware SK 21	.25	10
8 Feb 86	**JOHNNY JOHNNY** Kitchenware SK 24	.64	2
13 Feb 88	**CARS AND GIRLS** Kitchenware SK 35	.44	5
30 Apr 88 ●	**THE KING OF ROCK 'N' ROLL** Kitchenware SK 37	.7	10
23 Jul 88	**HEY MANHATTAN!** Kitchenware SK 38	.72	2
18 Aug 90	**LOOKING FOR ATLANTIS** Kitchenware SK 47	.51	3

20 Oct 90	WE LET THE STARS GO *Kitchenware SK 48*	**50**	3
5 Jan 91	JORDAN: THE EP *Kitchenware SK 49*	**35**	4
13 Jun 92	THE SOUND OF CRYING *Kitchenware SK 58*	**23**	5
8 Aug 92	IF YOU DON'T LOVE ME *Kitchenware SK 60*	**33**	4
3 Oct 92	ALL THE WORLD LOVES LOVERS *Kitchenware SK 62*	**61**	2
9 Jan 93	LIFE OF SURPRISES *Kitchenware SKCD 63*	**24**	4
10 May 97	A PRISONER OF THE PAST *Columbia SKZD 70*	**30**	2
2 Aug 97	ELECTRIC GUITARS *Columbia SKZD 71*	**53**	1
17 Mar 84	SWOON *Kitchenware KWLP 1*	**22**	7
22 Jun 85	STEVE MCQUEEN *Kitchenware KWLP 3*	**21**	35
26 Mar 88 ●	FROM LANGLEY PARK TO MEMPHIS *Kitchenware KWLP 9*	**5**	24
1 Jul 89	PROTEST SONGS *Kitchenware KWLP 4*	**18**	4
8 Sep 90 ●	JORDAN: THE COMEBACK *Kitchenware KWLP 14*	**7**	17
11 Jul 92 ●	A LIFE OF SURPRISES – THE BEST OF PREFAB SPROUT *Kitchenware 4718862*	**3**	13
17 May 97 ●	ANDROMEDA HEIGHTS *Columbia KWCD 30*	**7**	5
30 Jun 01	THE GUNMAN AND OTHER STORIES *Liberty 5326132*	**60**	1

Tracks on Jordan: The EP: Carnival 2000 / The Ice Maiden / One of the Broken / Jordan: The Comeback

PRELUDE *UK, male / female vocal group (Singles: 26 Weeks)*   pos/wks

26 Jan 74	AFTER THE GOLDRUSH *Dawn DNS 1052*	**21**	9
26 Apr 80	PLATINUM BLONDE *EMI 5046*	**45**	7
22 May 82	AFTER THE GOLDRUSH (re-recording) *After Hours AFT 02*	**28**	7
31 Jul 82	ONLY THE LONELY *After Hours AFT 06*	**55**	3

PRESENCE
UK, male / female vocal / production group (Singles: 2 Weeks)   pos/wks

5 Dec 98	SENSE OF DANGER *Pagan PAGAN 024CDS* [1]	**61**	1
19 Jun 99	FUTURE LOVE *Pagan PAGAN 028CDS*	**66**	1

[1] Presence featuring Shara Nelson

PRESIDENT BROWN *See SABRE featuring PRESIDENT BROWN*

The PRESIDENTS OF THE UNITED STATES OF AMERICA *US, male vocal / instrumental trio (Singles: 21 Weeks, Albums: 31 Weeks)*   pos/wks

6 Jan 96	LUMP *Columbia 6624962*	**15**	7
20 Apr 96 ●	PEACHES *Columbia 6631072*	**8**	7
20 Jul 96	DUNE BUGGY *Columbia 6634892*	**15**	4
2 Nov 96	MACH 5 *Columbia 6638812*	**29**	2
1 Aug 98	VIDEO KILLED THE RADIO STAR *Maverick W 0450CD*	**52**	1
13 Jan 96	THE PRESIDENTS OF THE UNITED STATES OF AMERICA *Columbia 4810392*	**14**	29
16 Nov 96	II *Columbia 4850922*	**36**	2

Elvis PRESLEY   [1]   *Top 500*

The most important, most influential and most impersonated artist of the 20th century, b. 8 Jan 1935, Mississippi, US, d. 16 Aug 1977. The singer, whose first five US singles failed to reach the pop charts, went from rock 'n' roll rebel to Las Vegas veteran and on the way sold more records than any other performer in history. He holds, or has held, almost every chart-related record, including perhaps the most important: more No.1s than any act in chart history. No other solo artist of the rock era can match his number of singles (if you include re-issues) and album chart entries in the UK or US, nor his collection of platinum and gold records. The "King of Rock 'n' Roll" was the first artist to enter the UK chart at No.1 and the first to amass US advance orders in excess of one million copies for a single. He now has a 46-year span of UK No.1 albums, holds the record for most simultaneous UK album chart entries (27 in the Top 100) and held the record for the most entries on the UK singles chart (nine). The most documented entertainer ever has won hundreds of awards, starred in dozens of successful films, broken numerous box office records in North America (the only continent he ever performed in), made Memphis a major tourist attraction and was the first artist credited with sales of one billion records (20 million of which were reportedly sold the day after his death). In 2002, after a 25-year gap, he returned to top the UK singles chart and his album 'ELVIS' entered at No.1 in 17 countries. In 2004, representing the 1950s, he became a founder member of the UK Music Hall of Fame. Scotland, home of his Aberdeenshire ancestors, was the only piece of British soil Elvis ever stepped on when, on 3 March 1960, he made a two hour stop-over at Prestwick airport on the way back from serving in the US army in Germany. UK single sales: 19,293,118. Best-selling single (UK): 'It's Now or Never' 1,210,000 (Singles: 1198 Weeks, Albums: 1265 Weeks)   pos/wks

11 May 56 ●	HEARTBREAK HOTEL (re) *HMV POP 182* ▲	**2**	22
25 May 56 ●	BLUE SUEDE SHOES (re) *HMV POP 213*	**9**	10

13 Jul 56	I WANT YOU, I NEED YOU, I LOVE YOU (re) *HMV POP 235* ▲	**14**	11
21 Sep 56 ●	HOUND DOG *HMV POP 249* ▲	**2**	23
16 Nov 56 ●	BLUE MOON *HMV POP 272*	**9**	11
23 Nov 56	I DON'T CARE IF THE SUN DON'T SHINE (re) *HMV POP 272*	**23**	4
7 Dec 56	LOVE ME TENDER *HMV POP 253* ▲	**11**	9
15 Feb 57	MYSTERY TRAIN *HMV POP 295*	**25**	5
8 Mar 57	RIP IT UP *HMV POP 305*	**27**	1
10 May 57 ●	TOO MUCH (re) *HMV POP 330* [1]	**6**	10
14 Jun 57 ★	ALL SHOOK UP (re) *HMV POP 359* [1] ▲	**1**	21
12 Jul 57 ●	(LET ME BE YOUR) TEDDY BEAR *RCA 1013* [1] ▲	**3**	19
30 Aug 57 ●	PARALYZED *HMV POP 378*	**8**	10
4 Oct 57 ●	PARTY *RCA 1020* [1]	**2**	15
18 Oct 57	GOT A LOT O' LIVIN' TO DO *RCA 1020* [1]	**17**	4
1 Nov 57	LOVING YOU *RCA 1013* [1]	**24**	2
1 Nov 57	TRYING TO GET TO YOU *HMV POP 408*	**16**	4
8 Nov 57	LAWDY MISS CLAWDY *RCA 1025*	**15**	5
15 Nov 57 ●	SANTA BRING MY BABY BACK (TO ME) *RCA 1025*	**7**	8
17 Jan 58	I'M LEFT, YOU'RE RIGHT, SHE'S GONE (re) *HMV POP 428*	**21**	3
24 Jan 58 ★	JAILHOUSE ROCK (re) *RCA 1028* ■ ▲	**1**	20
31 Jan 58	JAILHOUSE ROCK (EP) *RCA RCX 106* [1]	**18**	5
28 Feb 58 ●	DON'T *RCA 1043* [1] ▲	**2**	11
2 May 58 ●	WEAR MY RING AROUND YOUR NECK *RCA 1058* [1]	**3**	10
25 Jul 58 ●	HARD HEADED WOMAN *RCA 1070* [1] ▲	**2**	11
3 Oct 58 ●	KING CREOLE *RCA 1081* [1]	**2**	15
23 Jan 59 ●	ONE NIGHT / I GOT STUNG *RCA 1100*	**1**	12
24 Apr 59 ★	A FOOL SUCH AS I / I NEED YOUR LOVE TONIGHT *RCA 1113* [1]	**1**	15
24 Jul 59 ●	A BIG HUNK O' LOVE *RCA 1136* [1] ▲	**4**	9
12 Feb 60	STRICTLY ELVIS (EP) *RCA RCX 175*	**26**	1
7 Apr 60 ●	STUCK ON YOU *RCA 1187* ▲	**3**	14
28 Jul 60 ●	A MESS OF BLUES *RCA 1194* [1]	**2**	18
3 Nov 60 ★	IT'S NOW OR NEVER *RCA 1207* [1] ◆ ■ ▲	**1**	19
19 Jan 61 ★	ARE YOU LONESOME TO-NIGHT? *RCA 1216* [1] ▲	**1**	15
9 Mar 61 ●	WOODEN HEART *RCA 1226*	**1**	27
25 May 61 ★	SURRENDER *RCA 1227* [1] ▲	**1**	15
7 Sep 61 ●	WILD IN THE COUNTRY / I FEEL SO BAD *RCA 1244* [1]	**4**	12
2 Nov 61 ★	(MARIE'S THE NAME) HIS LATEST FLAME / LITTLE SISTER *RCA 1258*	**1**	13
1 Feb 62 ★	ROCK-A-HULA BABY / CAN'T HELP FALLING IN LOVE *RCA 1270* [1]	**1**	20
10 May 62 ★	GOOD LUCK CHARM *RCA 1280* [1] ▲	**1**	17
21 Jun 62	FOLLOW THAT DREAM (EP) *RCA RCX 211*	**34**	2
30 Aug 62 ★	SHE'S NOT YOU *RCA 1303* [1]	**1**	14
29 Nov 62 ★	RETURN TO SENDER *RCA 1320* [1]	**1**	14
28 Feb 63	ONE BROKEN HEART FOR SALE *RCA 1337* [2]	**12**	9
4 Jul 63 ★	(YOU'RE THE) DEVIL IN DISGUISE *RCA 1355* [1]	**1**	12
24 Oct 63	BOSSA NOVA BABY *RCA 1374* [1]	**13**	8
19 Dec 63	KISS ME QUICK *RCA 1375* [1]	**14**	10
12 Mar 64	VIVA LAS VEGAS *RCA 1390* [1]	**17**	12
25 Jun 64 ●	KISSIN' COUSINS *RCA 1404* [1]	**10**	11
20 Aug 64	SUCH A NIGHT *RCA 1411* [1]	**13**	10
29 Oct 64	AIN'T THAT LOVING YOU BABY *RCA 1422* [1]	**15**	8
3 Dec 64	BLUE CHRISTMAS *RCA 1430* [1]	**11**	7
11 Mar 65	DO THE CLAM *RCA 1443* [3]	**19**	8
27 May 65 ★	CRYING IN THE CHAPEL *RCA 1455* [1]	**1**	15
11 Nov 65	TELL ME WHY *RCA 1489* [1]	**15**	10
24 Feb 66	BLUE RIVER *RCA 1504*	**22**	7
7 Apr 66	FRANKIE AND JOHNNY *RCA 1509*	**21**	9
7 Jul 66 ●	LOVE LETTERS *RCA 1526*	**6**	10
13 Oct 66	ALL THAT I AM *RCA 1545* [1]	**18**	8
1 Dec 66 ●	IF EVERY DAY WAS LIKE CHRISTMAS *RCA 1557* [4]	**9**	7
9 Feb 67	INDESCRIBABLY BLUE *RCA 1565* [4]	**21**	5
11 May 67	YOU GOTTA STOP / THE LOVE MACHINE *RCA 1593*	**38**	5
16 Aug 67	LONG LEGGED GIRL (WITH THE SHORT DRESS ON) *RCA RCA 1616* [1]	**49**	2
21 Feb 68	GUITAR MAN *RCA 1663*	**19**	9
15 May 68	U.S. MALE *RCA 1688* [1]	**15**	8
17 Jul 68	YOUR TIME HASN'T COME YET BABY *RCA 1714* [1]	**22**	11
16 Oct 68	YOU'LL NEVER WALK ALONE *RCA 1747* [1]	**44**	3
26 Feb 69	IF I CAN DREAM *RCA 1795*	**11**	10
11 Jun 69 ●	IN THE GHETTO (re) *RCA 1831*	**2**	17
6 Sep 69	CLEAN UP YOUR OWN BACK YARD *RCA 1869*	**21**	7
29 Nov 69 ●	SUSPICIOUS MINDS *RCA 1900* ▲	**2**	14
28 Feb 70 ●	DON'T CRY DADDY *RCA 1916*	**8**	11
16 May 70	KENTUCKY RAIN *RCA 1949*	**21**	12
11 Jul 70 ●	THE WONDER OF YOU (re) *RCA 1974*	**1**	21
14 Nov 70 ●	I'VE LOST YOU *RCA 1999*	**9**	12
9 Jan 71 ●	YOU DON'T HAVE TO SAY YOU LOVE ME (re) *RCA 2046*	**9**	10
20 Mar 71 ●	THERE GOES MY EVERYTHING *RCA 2060* [5]	**6**	11

Singles re-entries are listed as (re), (2re), (3re)…. which signifies that the hit re-entered the chart once, twice or three times…

15 May 71 ●	RAGS TO RICHES *RCA 2084* [5]	9 11
17 Jul 71 ●	HEARTBREAK HOTEL / HOUND DOG (re-issue)	
	RCA Maximillion 2104	10 12
2 Oct 71 ●	I'M LEAVIN' *RCA 2125* [5]	23 9
4 Dec 71 ●	I JUST CAN'T HELP BELIEVING *RCA 2158* [6]	6 16
11 Dec 71	JAILHOUSE ROCK (re-issue) *RCA Maximillion 2153*	42 5
1 Apr 72 ●	UNTIL IT'S TIME FOR YOU TO GO *RCA 2188* [5]	5 9
17 Jun 72 ●	AN AMERICAN TRILOGY *RCA 2229*	8 11
30 Sep 72 ●	BURNING LOVE *RCA 2267* [7]	7 9
16 Dec 72 ●	ALWAYS ON MY MIND *RCA 2304* [7]	9 13
26 May 73	POLK SALAD ANNIE *RCA 2359*	23 7
11 Aug 73	FOOL *RCA 2393* [7]	15 10
24 Nov 73	RAISED ON ROCK *RCA 2435*	36 5
16 Mar 74	I'VE GOT A THING ABOUT YOU BABY *RCA APBO 0196* [7]	33 5
13 Jul 74	IF YOU TALK IN YOUR SLEEP *RCA APBO 0280*	40 3
16 Nov 74 ●	MY BOY *RCA 2458*	5 13
18 Jan 75 ●	PROMISED LAND *RCA PB 10074*	9 8
24 May 75	T.R.O.U.B.L.E. *RCA 2562*	31 4
29 Nov 75	GREEN GREEN GRASS OF HOME *RCA 2635*	29 7
1 May 76	HURT *RCA 2674*	37 5
4 Sep 76 ●	THE GIRL OF MY BEST FRIEND *RCA 2729*	9 12
25 Dec 76 ●	SUSPICION *RCA 2768*	9 12
5 Mar 77 ●	MOODY BLUE *RCA PB 0857* [8]	6 9
13 Aug 77 ★	WAY DOWN *RCA PB 0998* [9]	1 13
3 Sep 77 ●	ALL SHOOK UP (re-issue) *RCA PB 2694* [1]	41 2
3 Sep 77 ●	ARE YOU LONESOME TO-NIGHT? (re-issue) *RCA PB 2699* [1]	46 1
3 Sep 77 ●	CRYING IN THE CHAPEL (re-issue) *RCA PB 2708* [1]	43 2
3 Sep 77 ●	IT'S NOW OR NEVER (re-issue) *RCA PB 2698* [1]	39 2
3 Sep 77 ●	JAILHOUSE ROCK (2nd re-issue) *RCA PB 2695* [1]	44 2
3 Sep 77 ●	RETURN TO SENDER (re-issue) *RCA PB 2706* [1]	42 3
3 Sep 77 ●	THE WONDER OF YOU (re-issue) *RCA PB 2709* [1]	48 1
3 Sep 77 ●	WOODEN HEART (re-issue) *RCA PB 2700*	49 1
10 Dec 77 ●	MY WAY *RCA PB 1165* [10]	9 8
24 Jun 78	DON'T BE CRUEL *RCA PB 9265*	24 12
15 Dec 79	IT WON'T SEEM LIKE CHRISTMAS (WITHOUT YOU)	
	RCA PB 9464	13 6
30 Aug 80 ●	IT'S ONLY LOVE / BEYOND THE REEF *RCA 4*	3 10
6 Dec 80	SANTA CLAUS IS BACK IN TOWN *RCA 16*	41 6
14 Feb 81	GUITAR MAN (re-recording) *RCA 43*	43 4
18 Apr 81	LOVING ARMS *RCA 48*	47 6
13 Mar 82	ARE YOU LONESOME TO-NIGHT? (LIVE) *RCA 196* [10]	25 7
26 Jun 82	THE SOUND OF YOUR CRY *RCA 232* [5]	59 2
7 May 83	BABY I DON'T CARE *RCA 332*	61 3
3 Dec 83	I CAN HELP *RCA 369* [11]	30 9
10 Nov 84	THE LAST FAREWELL *RCA 459* [8]	48 6
19 Jan 85	THE ELVIS MEDLEY *RCA 476* [1]	51 3
10 Aug 85	ALWAYS ON MY MIND (re-mix) *RCA PB 49943*	59 4
11 Apr 87	AIN'T THAT LOVIN' YOU BABY / BOSSA NOVA BABY	
	(re-recording) *RCA ARON 1*	47 5
22 Aug 87	LOVE ME TENDER / IF I CAN DREAM (re-issue) *RCA ARON 2*	56 3
16 Jan 88	STUCK ON YOU (re-issue) *RCA PB 49595* [1]	58 2
17 Aug 91	ARE YOU LONESOME TO-NIGHT? (LIVE) (re-issue)	
	RCA PB 49177	68 2
29 Aug 92	DON'T BE CRUEL (re-issue) *RCA 74321110777* [1]	42 2
11 Nov 95	THE TWELFTH OF NEVER *RCA 74321320122* [11]	21 3
18 May 96	HEARTBREAK HOTEL / I WAS THE ONE (2nd re-issue)	
	RCA 74321336862	45 1
24 May 97	ALWAYS ON MY MIND (re-issue) (re-mix) *RCA 74321485412*	13 6
14 Apr 01	SUSPICIOUS MINDS (LIVE) *RCA 74321855822*	15 4
10 Nov 01	AMERICA THE BEAUTIFUL *RCA 74321904022*	69 1
22 Jun 02 ★	A LITTLE LESS CONVERSATION *RCA 74321943572* [12] ■	1 12
4 Oct 03 ●	RUBBERNECKIN' (re) *RCA 82876543412*	5 8
17 Jul 04	THAT'S ALL RIGHT *RCA 82876619212*	3 5
3 Nov 56 ★	ROCK 'N ROLL *HMV CLP 1093*	1 16
4 May 57 ●	ROCK 'N ROLL (NO.2) *HMV CLP 1105*	3 3
31 Aug 57 ★	LOVING YOU (SOUNDTRACK) *RCA RC 24001* ▲	1 25
26 Oct 57 ●	THE BEST OF ELVIS *RCA DLP 1159*	3 7
30 Nov 57 ●	ELVIS' CHRISTMAS ALBUM *RCA RD 27052* ▲	2 6
13 Sep 58 ★	KING CREOLE (FILM SOUNDTRACK) *RCA RD 27086*	1 22
11 Oct 58 ●	ELVIS' GOLDEN RECORDS *RCA RB 16069*	4 48
8 Aug 59 ●	A DATE WITH ELVIS *RCA RD 27128*	4 15
18 Jun 60 ●	ELVIS' GOLDEN RECORDS VOLUME 2 *RCA RD 27159*	4 20
18 Jun 60 ★	ELVIS IS BACK! *RCA RD 27171*	1 27
10 Dec 60 ●	G.I. BLUES (FILM SOUNDTRACK) *RCA RD 27192* ▲	1 55
20 May 61 ●	HIS HAND IN MINE *RCA RD 27211*	3 25
4 Nov 61 ●	SOMETHING FOR EVERYBODY *RCA RD 27224* ▲	2 18
9 Dec 61 ★	BLUE HAWAII (FILM SOUNDTRACK) *RCA RD 27238* ▲	1 65
7 Jul 62 ★	POT LUCK *RCA RD 27265*	1 25
8 Dec 62 ●	ROCK 'N' ROLL NO.2 *RCA RD 7528*	3 17

26 Jan 63 ●	GIRLS! GIRLS! GIRLS! (FILM SOUNDTRACK) *RCA RD 7534*	2 21
11 May 63 ●	IT HAPPENED AT THE WORLD'S FAIR (FILM SOUNDTRACK)	
	RCA RD 7565	4 21
28 Dec 63 ●	FUN IN ACAPULCO (FILM SOUNDTRACK) *RCA RD 7609*	9 14
11 Apr 64 ●	ELVIS' GOLDEN RECORDS VOLUME 3 *RCA RD 7630*	6 13
4 Jul 64 ●	KISSIN' COUSINS (FILM SOUNDTRACK) *RCA RD 7645*	5 17
9 Jan 65 ●	ROUSTABOUT *RCA RD 7678* ▲	12 4
1 May 65 ●	GIRL HAPPY (FILM SOUNDTRACK) *RCA RD 7714*	8 18
25 Sep 65 ●	FLAMING STAR AND SUMMER KISSES *RCA RD 7723*	11 4
4 Dec 65 ●	ELVIS FOR EVERYONE *RCA RD 7782*	8 8
15 Jan 66 ●	HAREM HOLIDAY (FILM SOUNDTRACK) *RCA RD 7767*	11 5
30 Apr 66 ●	FRANKIE AND JOHNNY (FILM SOUNDTRACK) *RCA RD 7793*	11 5
6 Aug 66 ●	PARADISE HAWAIIAN STYLE (FILM SOUNDTRACK)	
	RCA Victor RD 7810	7 9
26 Nov 66	CALIFORNIA HOLIDAY (FILM SOUNDTRACK)	
	RCA Victor RD 7820	17 5
8 Apr 67 ●	HOW GREAT THOU ART *RCA Victor SF 7867*	11 14
2 Sep 67	DOUBLE TROUBLE (FILM SOUNDTRACK) *RCA Victor SF 7892*	34 1
20 Apr 68	CLAMBAKE (FILM SOUNDTRACK) *RCA Victor SD 7917*	39 1
3 May 69 ●	ELVIS – NBC TV SPECIAL *RCA RD 8011*	2 26
5 Jul 69 ●	ELVIS SINGS FLAMING STAR *RCA International INTS 1012*	2 14
23 Aug 69 ★	FROM ELVIS IN MEMPHIS *RCA SF 8029*	1 13
28 Feb 70	PORTRAIT IN MUSIC (IMPORT) *RCA 558*	36 1
14 Mar 70 ●	FROM MEMPHIS TO VEGAS – FROM VEGAS TO MEMPHIS	
	RCA SF 8080/1	3 16
1 Aug 70 ●	ON STAGE – FEBRUARY 1970 *RCA SF 8128*	2 18
5 Dec 70 ●	ELVIS' GOLDEN RECORDS VOLUME 1 (re-issue) *RCA SF 8129*	21 11
12 Dec 70	WORLDWIDE 50 GOLD AWARD HITS VOLUME 1 *RCA LPM 6401*	49 2
30 Jan 71	THAT'S THE WAY IT IS *RCA SF 8162*	12 35
10 Apr 71 ●	I'M 10000 YEARS OLD – ELVIS COUNTRY *RCA SF 8172*	6 9
24 Jul 71 ●	LOVE LETTERS FROM ELVIS *RCA SF 8202*	7 5
7 Aug 71 ●	C'MON EVERYBODY *RCA International INTS 1286*	5 21
7 Aug 71	YOU'LL NEVER WALK ALONE *RCA Camden CDM 1088*	20 4
25 Sep 71	ALMOST IN LOVE *RCA International INTS 1206*	38 2
4 Dec 71 ●	ELVIS' CHRISTMAS ALBUM (re-issue)	
	RCA International INTS 1126	7 5
18 Dec 71	I GOT LUCKY *RCA International INTS 1322*	26 3
27 May 72	ELVIS NOW *RCA Victor SF 8266*	12 8
3 Jun 72	ELVIS FOR EVERYONE *RCA Victor SF 8232*	48 1
3 Jun 72	ROCK AND ROLL (re-issue of ROCK 'N' ROLL)	
	RCA Victor SF 8233	34 4
15 Jul 72 ●	ELVIS AS RECORDED AT MADISON SQUARE GARDEN	
	RCA Victor SF 8296	3 20
12 Aug 72 ●	HE TOUCHED ME *RCA Victor SF 8275*	38 3
24 Feb 73	ALOHA FROM HAWAII VIA SATELLITE	
	RCA Victor DPS 2040 ▲	11 10
15 Sep 73	ELVIS *RCA Victor SF 8378*	16 4
2 Mar 74	ELVIS – A LEGENDARY PERFORMER VOL.1	
	RCA Victor CPL1 0341	20 3
25 May 74	GOOD TIMES *RCA Victor APL1 0475*	42 1
7 Sep 74	ELVIS RECORDED LIVE ON STAGE IN MEMPHIS	
	RCA Victor APL1 0606	44 1
22 Feb 75	PROMISED LAND *RCA Victor APL1 0873*	21 4
14 Jun 75	TODAY *RCA Victor RS 1011*	48 3
5 Jul 75 ★	40 GREATEST HITS *Arcade ADEP 12*	1 38
6 Sep 75	THE ELVIS PRESLEY SUN COLLECTION *RCA Starcall HY 1001*	16 13
19 Jun 76	FROM ELVIS PRESLEY BOULEVARD MEMPHIS TENNESSEE	
	RCA Victor RS 1060	29 5
19 Feb 77	ELVIS IN DEMAND *RCA Victor PL 42003*	12 11
27 Aug 77 ●	MOODY BLUE *RCA PL 12428*	3 15
3 Sep 77 ●	WELCOME TO MY WORLD *RCA PL 12274*	7 9
3 Sep 77	G.I. BLUES (re-issue) *RCA SF 5078*	14 10
10 Sep 77	BLUE HAWAII (re-issue) *RCA SF 8145*	49 2
10 Sep 77	ELVIS' GOLDEN RECORDS VOLUME 3 (re-issue)	
	RCA SF 7630	26 6
10 Sep 77	ELVIS' GOLDEN RECORDS VOLUME 2 (re-issue)	
	RCA SF 8151	27 4
10 Sep 77	HITS OF THE 70'S *RCA LPL1 7527*	30 4
10 Sep 77	PICTURES OF ELVIS *RCA Starcall HY 1023*	52 1
8 Oct 77	THE SUN YEARS *Charly SUN 1001*	31 2
15 Oct 77	LOVING YOU (re-issue) *RCA PL 42358*	24 3
19 Nov 77	ELVIS IN CONCERT *RCA PL 02578*	13 11
22 Apr 78	HE WALKS BESIDE ME *RCA PL 12772*	37 1
3 Jun 78	THE '56 SESSIONS VOLUME 1 *RCA PL 42101*	47 4
2 Sep 78	TV SPECIAL *RCA PL 42370*	50 2
11 Nov 78	40 GREATEST HITS (re-issue) *RCA PL 42691*	40 14
3 Feb 79	A LEGENDARY PERFORMER VOLUME 3 *RCA PL 13082*	43 3
5 May 79	OUR MEMORIES OF ELVIS *RCA PL 13279*	72 1
24 Nov 79 ●	LOVE SONGS *K-Tel NE 1062*	4 13

		pos/wks
21 Jun 80	ELVIS PRESLEY SINGS LEIBER AND STOLLER	
	RCA International INTS 5031 32	5
23 Aug 80	ELVIS ARON PRESLEY *RCA ELVIS 25* 21	4
23 Aug 80	PARADISE HAWAIIAN STYLE (re-issue)	
	RCA International INTS 5037 53	2
29 Nov 80 ●	INSPIRATION *K-Tel NE 1101* 6	8
14 Mar 81	GUITAR MAN *RCA RCALP 5010* 33	5
9 May 81	THIS IS ELVIS PRESLEY *RCA RCALP 5029* ...47	4
28 Nov 81	THE ULTIMATE PERFORMANCE *K-Tel NE 1141* ...45	6
13 Feb 82	THE SOUND OF YOUR CRY *RCA RCALP 3060* ...31	12
6 Mar 82	ELVIS PRESLEY EP PACK *RCA EP1* 97	1
21 Aug 82	ROMANTIC ELVIS / ROCKIN' ELVIS *RCA RCALP 1000/1* ...62	5
18 Dec 82	IT WON'T SEEM LIKE CHRISTMAS WITHOUT YOU	
	RCA INTS 5235 80	1
30 Apr 83	JAILHOUSE ROCK / LOVE IN LAS VEGAS *RCA RCALP 9020* ...40	2
20 Aug 83	I WAS THE ONE *RCA PL 3105* 83	1
3 Dec 83	A LEGENDARY PERFORMER VOLUME 4 *RCA PL 84848* ...91	1
7 Apr 84	I CAN HELP *RCA PL 89287* 71	3
21 Jul 84	THE FIRST LIVE RECORDINGS *RCA International PG 89387* ...69	2
26 Jan 85	20 GREATEST HITS VOLUME 2 *RCA International NL 89168* ...98	1
25 May 85	RECONSIDER BABY *RCA PL 85418* 92	1
12 Oct 85	BALLADS *Telstar STAR 2264* 23	17
29 Aug 87 ●	PRESLEY – THE ALL TIME GREATEST HITS *RCA PL 90100* ...4	34
28 Jan 89	STEREO '57 (ESSENTIAL ELVIS VOLUME 2) *RCA PL 90250* ...60	2
21 Jul 90	HITS LIKE NEVER BEFORE (VOL.3) *RCA PL 90486* ...71	1
1 Sep 90	THE GREAT PERFORMANCES *RCA PL 82227* ...62	1
24 Aug 91	COLLECTORS GOLD *RCA PL 90574* 57	1
22 Feb 92 ●	FROM THE HEART – HIS GREATEST LOVE SONGS	
	RCA PD 90642 4	18
10 Sep 94 ●	THE ESSENTIAL COLLECTION *RCA 74321228712* ...6	25
11 May 96	ELVIS 56 *RCA 7863668562* 42	3
7 Jun 97 ●	ALWAYS ON MY MIND – ULTIMATE LOVE SONGS	
	RCA 74321489842 3	33
28 Feb 98	BLUE SUEDE SHOES *RCA 74321556282* ...39	4
2 Dec 00 ●	THE 50 GREATEST HITS *RCA 74321811022* ...8	25
31 Mar 01	THE LIVE GREATEST HITS *RCA 74321847082* ...50	3
24 Nov 01	THE 50 GREATEST LOVE SONGS *RCA 74321900752* ...21	9
5 Oct 02 ★	ELV1S – 30 #1 HITS *RCA 07863680792* ■ ▲ ...1	32
18 Oct 03 ●	2ND TO NONE *RCA 82876570852* 4	12
6 Dec 03	CHRISTMAS PEACE *RCA 82876574892* 41	8+

[1] With the Jordanaires [2] With the Mellomen [3] With the Jordanaires Jubilee Four & Carol Lombard Trio [4] With the Jordanaires and Imperials Quartet [5] Vocal Accompaniment: The Imperial Quartet [6] Vocal acc. the Imperials Quartet & the Sweet Inspirations [7] Vocal acc. J.D. Sumner & the Stamps [8] Vocal acc. J.D. Sumner & the Stamps Qt. Kathy Westmoreland, Myrna Smith [9] Vocal acc. J.D. Sumner & the Stamps Qt. K. Westmoreland, S. Neilson & M. Smith [10] Vocal acc. J.D. Sumner & the Stamps, the Sweet Inspirations and Kathy Westmoreland [11] Vocal accompaniment the Voice [12] Elvis vs JXL

'Jailhouse Rock' re-entry was in Feb 1983, peaking at No.27. Tracks on Jailhouse Rock (EP): Jailhouse Rock / Young and Beautiful / I Want to Be Free / Don't Leave Me Now / Baby I Don't Care. Tracks on Strictly Elvis (EP): Old Shep / Any Place Is Paradise / Paralyzed / Is It So Strange. Tracks on Follow That Dream (EP): Follow That Dream / Angel / What a Wonderful Life / I'm Not the Marrying Kind. On 5 Jul 1962, a note on the Top 50 for that week stated: "Due to difficulties in assessing returns of Follow That Dream EP, it has been decided not to include it in Britain's Top 50. It is of course No.1 in the EP charts." Therefore this EP had only a two-week run on the chart when its sales would certainly have justified a much longer one. 'Beyond the Reef' listed only from 30 Aug to 13 Sep 1980. It peaked at No.7. RCA PB 49177 is a re-issue of RCA 196. 'Can't Help Falling in Love' credited from 1 Mar 1962. Tracks on the Elvis Medley: Jailhouse Rock / Teddy Bear / Hound Dog / Don't Be Cruel / Burning Love / Suspicious Minds. 'Guitar Man' on 14 Feb 1981 is an overdubbed release

Sharp-eyed readers will have counted 17 US No.1 hits listed for 'The King'. However, he actually scored 18 chart-toppers - 'Don't Be Cruel' gets an individual top placing in the US in addition to a joint listing with 'Hound Dog'

Lisa Marie PRESLEY
US, female vocalist (Singles: 5 Weeks, Albums: 1 Week)   pos/wks

12 Jul 03	LIGHTS OUT (re) *Capitol CDCL 844* 16	5
26 Jul 03	TO WHOM IT MAY CONCERN *Capitol 5905220* ...52	1

PRESSURE DROP
UK, male vocal / instrumental duo (Singles: 2 Weeks)   pos/wks

21 Mar 98	SILENTLY BAD MINDED *Higher Ground HIGHS 6CD* ...53	1
17 Mar 01	WARRIOR SOUND *Higher Ground 6697192* ...72	1

Billy PRESTON *US, male vocalist / instrumentalist*
– keyboards (Singles: 51 Weeks)   pos/wks

23 Apr 69 ★	GET BACK (2re) *Apple R 5777* [1] ■ ▲ ...1	23
2 Jul 69	THAT'S THE WAY GOD PLANNED IT *Apple 12* ...11	10
16 Sep 72	OUTA SPACE *A&M AMS 7007* 44	3
15 Dec 79 ●	WITH YOU I'M BORN AGAIN *Motown TMG 1159* [2] ...2	11
8 Mar 80	IT WILL COME IN TIME *Motown TMG 1175* [2] ...47	4

[1] The Beatles with Billy Preston [2] Billy Preston and Syreeta

Johnny PRESTON
US, male vocalist – Johnny Courville (Singles: 46 Weeks)   pos/wks

12 Feb 60 ★	RUNNING BEAR (re) *Mercury AMT 1079* ▲ ...1	16
21 Apr 60 ●	CRADLE OF LOVE *Mercury AMT 1092* 2	16
28 Jul 60	I'M STARTING TO GO STEADY *Mercury AMT 1104* ...49	1
11 Aug 60	FEEL SO FINE *Mercury AMT 1104* 18	10
8 Dec 60	CHARMING BILLY (re) *Mercury AMT 1114* ...34	3

Mike PRESTON
UK, male vocalist – Jack Davis (Singles: 33 Weeks)   pos/wks

30 Oct 59	MR BLUE *Decca F 11167* 12	8
25 Aug 60	I'D DO ANYTHING *Decca F 11255* 23	10
22 Dec 60	TOGETHERNESS *Decca F 11287* 41	5
9 Mar 61	MARRY ME *Decca F 11335* 14	10

The PRETENDERS   191   Top 500
Internationally successful, British-based post-punk group with an ever-changing line-up, but with ex-NME journalist Chrissie Hynde, b. 7 Sep 1951, Ohio, US (v/g), as a common factor. Hynde was briefly married to the lead singer of Simple Minds, Jim Kerr, and had a child with Ray Davies of The Kinks (Singles: 132 Weeks, Albums: 171 Weeks)   pos/wks

10 Feb 79	STOP YOUR SOBBING *Real ARE 6* 34	9
14 Jul 79	KID *Real ARE 9* 33	7
17 Nov 79 ★	BRASS IN POCKET *Real ARE 11* 1	17
5 Apr 80 ●	TALK OF THE TOWN *Real ARE 12* 8	8
14 Feb 81	MESSAGE OF LOVE *Real ARE 15* 11	7
5 Sep 81	DAY AFTER DAY *Real ARE 17* 45	4
14 Nov 81	I GO TO SLEEP *Real ARE 18* 7	10
2 Oct 82	BACK ON THE CHAIN GANG *Real ARE 19* ...17	9
26 Nov 83	2000 MILES *Real ARE 20* 15	9
9 Jun 84	THIN LINE BETWEEN LOVE AND HATE *Real ARE 22* ...49	3
11 Oct 86	DON'T GET ME WRONG *Real YZ 85* 10	9
13 Dec 86	HYMN TO HER *Real YZ 93* 8	12
15 Aug 87	IF THERE WAS A MAN *Real YZ 149* [1] 49	6
23 Apr 94 ●	I'LL STAND BY YOU *WEA YZ 815CD* 10	10
2 Jul 94	NIGHT IN MY VEINS *WEA YZ 825CD* 25	5
15 Oct 94	977 *WEA YZ 848CD1* 66	2
14 Oct 95	KID (re-recording) *WEA 014CD* 73	1
10 May 97	FEVER PITCH THE EP *Blanco Y Negro NEG 104CD* [2] ...65	1
15 May 99	HUMAN *WEA WEA 207CD* 33	3
19 Jan 80 ★	PRETENDERS *Real RAL 3* ■ 1	35
15 Aug 81 ●	PRETENDERS II *Real SRK 3572* 7	27
21 Jan 84	LEARNING TO CRAWL *Real WX 2* 11	16
1 Nov 86 ●	GET CLOSE *WEA WX 64* 6	28
7 Nov 87 ●	THE SINGLES *WEA WX 135* 6	32
26 May 90	PACKED! *WEA WX 346* 19	5
21 May 94 ●	LAST OF THE INDEPENDENTS *WEA 4509958222* ...8	13
28 Oct 95	THE ISLE OF VIEW *WEA 0630102592* 23	4
29 May 99	VIVA EL AMOR *WEA 3984271522* 32	2
30 Sep 00	GREATEST HITS *Warner.esp 8573846072* ...21	8
31 May 03	LOOSE SCREW *Eagle EAGCD 256* 55	1

[1] The Pretenders for 007 [2] The Pretenders, The La's, Orlando, Neil MacColl, Nick Hornby

Tracks on Fever Pitch the EP: Goin' Back – The Pretenders; There She Goes – The La's; How Can We Hang on to a Dream – Orlando; Football – Neil MacColl; Boo Hewerdine – Nick Hornby

PRETTY BOY FLOYD
US, male vocal / instrumental group (Singles: 1 Week)   pos/wks

10 Mar 90	ROCK AND ROLL (IS GONNA SET THE NIGHT ON FIRE)	
	MCA MCA 1393 75	1

The PRETTY THINGS *UK, male vocal / instrumental*
group (Singles: 41 Weeks, Albums: 13 Weeks)   pos/wks

18 Jun 64	ROSALYN *Fontana TF 469* 41	5
22 Oct 64 ●	DON'T BRING ME DOWN *Fontana TF 503* ...10	11

		pos/wks
25 Feb 65	HONEY I NEED *Fontana TF 537*	13 10
15 Jul 65	CRY TO ME *Fontana TF 585*	28 7
20 Jan 66	MIDNIGHT TO SIX MAN *Fontana TF 647*	46 1
5 May 66	COME SEE ME *Fontana TF 688*	43 5
21 Jul 66	A HOUSE IN THE COUNTRY (re) *Fontana TF 722*	50 2
27 Mar 65 ●	PRETTY THINGS *Fontana TL 5239*	6 10
27 Jun 70	PARACHUTE *Harvest SHVL 774*	43 3

Alan PRICE (see also The ANIMALS) UK, male vocalist / instrumentalist (Singles: 87 Weeks, Albums: 10 Weeks)

		pos/wks
31 Mar 66 ●	I PUT A SPELL ON YOU *Decca F 12367* [1]	9 10
14 Jul 66	HI LILI, HI LO *Decca F 12442* [1]	11 12
2 Mar 67 ●	SIMON SMITH AND HIS AMAZING DANCING BEAR *Decca F 12570* [1]	4 12
2 Aug 67 ●	THE HOUSE THAT JACK BUILT *Decca F 12641* [1]	4 10
15 Nov 67	SHAME *Decca F 12691* [1]	45 2
31 Jan 68	DON'T STOP THE CARNIVAL *Decca F 12731* [1]	13 8
10 Apr 71	ROSETTA *CBS 7108* [2]	11 10
25 May 74 ●	JARROW SONG *Warner Bros. K 16372*	6 9
29 Apr 78	JUST FOR YOU *Jet 36358*	43 7
17 Feb 79	BABY OF MINE / JUST FOR YOU (re-issue) *Jet 135*	32 3
30 Apr 88	CHANGES *Ariola 109911*	54 4
8 Jun 74 ●	BETWEEN TODAY AND YESTERDAY *Warner Bros. K 56032*	9 10

[1] Alan Price Set [2] Fame and Price Together

Kelly PRICE US, female vocalist (Singles: 10 Weeks)

		pos/wks
7 Nov 98	FRIEND OF MINE *Island Black Music CID 723*	25 3
8 May 99	SECRET LOVE *Island Black Music CID 739*	26 2
30 Dec 00	HEARTBREAK HOTEL *Arista 74321820572* [1]	25 5

[1] Whitney Houston featuring Faith Evans and Kelly Price

Lloyd PRICE US, male vocalist (Singles: 36 Weeks)

		pos/wks
13 Feb 59 ●	STAGGER LEE *HMV POP 580* ▲	7 14
15 May 59	WHERE WERE YOU (ON OUR WEDDING DAY)? *HMV POP 598*	15 6
12 Jun 59 ●	PERSONALITY (re) *HMV POP 626*	9 10
11 Sep 59	I'M GONNA GET MARRIED *HMV POP 650*	23 5
21 Apr 60	LADY LUCK *HMV POP 712*	45 1

PRICKLY HEAT UK, male producer (Singles: 1 Week)

		pos/wks
26 Dec 98	OOOIE, OOOIE, OOOIE *Virgin VSCDT 1727*	57 1

Charley PRIDE US, male vocalist (Albums: 17 Weeks)

		pos/wks
10 Apr 71	CHARLEY PRIDE SPECIAL *RCA SF 8171*	29 1
28 May 77	SHE'S JUST AN OLD LOVE TURNED MEMORY *RCA Victor PL 12261*	34 2
3 Jun 78	SOMEONE LOVES YOU HONEY *RCA PL 12478*	48 2
26 Jan 80 ●	GOLDEN COLLECTION *K-Tel NE 1056*	6 12

Dickie PRIDE UK, male vocalist – Richard Knellar, b. 21 Oct 1941, d. May 1969 (Singles: 1 Week)

		pos/wks
30 Oct 59	PRIMROSE LANE *Columbia DB 4340*	28 1

Maxi PRIEST UK, male vocalist – Max Elliott (Singles: 106 Weeks, Albums: 35 Weeks)

		pos/wks
29 Mar 86	STROLLIN' ON *10 TEN 84*	32 9
12 Jul 86	IN THE SPRINGTIME *10 TEN 127*	54 3
8 Nov 86	CRAZY LOVE *10 TEN 135*	67 5
4 Apr 87	LET ME KNOW *10 TEN 156*	49 4
24 Oct 87	SOME GUYS HAVE ALL THE LUCK *10 TEN 198*	12 12
20 Feb 88	HOW CAN WE EASE THE PAIN *10 TEN 207*	41 4
4 Jun 88 ●	WILD WORLD *10 TEN 221*	5 9
27 Aug 88	GOODBYE TO LOVE AGAIN *10 TEN 238*	57 3
9 Jun 90 ●	CLOSE TO YOU *10 TEN 294* ▲	7 10
1 Sep 90	PEACE THROUGHOUT THE WORLD *10 TEN 317* [1]	41 4
1 Dec 90	HUMAN WORK OF ART (re) *10 TEN 328*	71 4
24 Aug 91	HOUSECALL *Epic 6573477* [2]	31 7
5 Oct 91	JUST A LITTLE BIT LONGER (EP) *Ten TEN 343*	62 3
26 Sep 92	GROOVIN' IN THE MIDNIGHT *Ten TEN 412*	50 2
28 Nov 92	JUST WANNA KNOW / FE' REAL *Ten TEN 416* [3]	33 3
20 Mar 93	ONE MORE CHANCE *Ten TENCD 420*	40 3
8 May 93 ●	HOUSECALL (re-mix) *Epic 6592842* [2]	8 8
31 Jul 93	WAITING IN VAIN *GRP MCSTD 1921* [4]	65 2
22 Jun 96	THAT GIRL *Virgin America VUSCD 106* [5]	15 7

		pos/wks
21 Sep 96	WATCHING THE WORLD GO BY *Virgin America VUSCD 108*	36 2
6 Dec 87	INTENTIONS *10 DIX 32*	96 1
5 Dec 87	MAXI *10 DIX 64*	25 15
15 Jul 90	BONAFIDE *10 DIX 92*	11 13
9 Nov 91	BEST OF ME *10 DIX 111*	23 5
14 Nov 92	FE REAL *10 DIXCD 113*	60 1

[1] Maxi Priest featuring Jazzie B [2] Shabba Ranks featuring Maxi Priest [3] Maxi Priest / Maxi Priest featuring Apache Indian [4] Lee Ritenour and Maxi Priest [5] Maxi Priest featuring Shaggy

Tracks on Just a Little Bit Longer (EP): Just a Little Bit Longer / Best of Me / Searching / Fever

Louis PRIMA US, male vocalist, b. 7 Dec 1911, d. 24 Aug 1978 (Singles: 1 Week)

		pos/wks
21 Feb 58	BUONA SERA *Capitol CL 14821*	25 1

PRIMA DONNA UK, male / female vocal group (Singles: 4 Weeks)

		pos/wks
26 Apr 80	LOVE ENOUGH FOR TWO *Ariola ARO 221*	48 4

PRIMAL SCREAM UK, male vocal / instrumental group (Singles: 54 Weeks, Albums: 76 Weeks)

		pos/wks
3 Mar 90	LOADED *Creation CRE 070*	16 9
18 Aug 90	COME TOGETHER *Creation CRE 078*	26 6
22 Jun 91	HIGHER THAN THE SUN *Creation CRE 096*	40 2
24 Aug 91	DON'T FIGHT IT FEEL IT *Creation CRE 110* [1]	41 2
8 Feb 92	DIXIE-NARCO (EP) *Creation CRE 117*	11 6
12 Mar 94 ●	ROCKS / FUNKY JAM *Creation CRESCD 129*	7 5
18 Jun 94	JAILBIRD *Creation CRESCD 145*	29 2
10 Dec 94	(I'M GONNA) CRY MYSELF BLIND *Creation CRESCD 183*	49 2
15 Jun 96	THE BIG MAN AND THE SCREAM TEAM MEET THE BARMY ARMY UPTOWN *Creation CRESCD 194* [2]	17 2
17 May 97 ●	KOWALSKI *Creation CRESCD 245* ▲	8 3
28 Jun 97	STAR *Creation CRESCD 263*	16 3
25 Oct 97	BURNING WHEEL *Creation CRESCD 272*	17 2
20 Nov 99	SWASTIKA EYES *Creation CRESCD 326*	22 2
1 Apr 00	KILL ALL HIPPIES *Creation CRESCD 332*	24 2
23 Sep 00	ACCELERATOR *Creation CRESCD 333*	34 1
3 Aug 02	MISS LUCIFER *Columbia 6728252*	25 2
9 Nov 02	AUTOBAHN 66 *Columbia 6733122*	44 1
29 Nov 03	SOME VELVET MORNING *Columbia 6744022* [3]	44 2
17 Oct 87	SONIC FLOWER GROOVE *Elevation ELV 2*	62 1
5 Oct 91 ●	SCREAMADELICA *Creation CRELP 076*	8 30
9 Apr 94 ●	GIVE OUT BUT DON'T GIVE UP *Creation CRECD 146*	2 18
19 Jul 97 ●	VANISHING POINT *Creation CRECD 178*	2 10
8 Nov 97	ECHO DEK *Creation CRECD 224*	43 1
12 Feb 00	EXTERMINATOR *Creation CRECD 239*	3 10
17 Aug 02 ●	EVIL HEAT *Columbia 5089232*	9 3
15 Nov 03	DIRTY HITS *Columbia 5136039*	25 3

[1] Primal Scream featuring Denise Johnson [2] Primal Scream, Irvine Welsh and On-U Sound [3] Primal Scream featuring Kate Moss

Tracks on Dixie-Narco (EP): Movin' On Up / Stone My Soul / Carry Me Home / Screamadelica

PRIME MOVERS US, male vocal / instrumental group (Singles: 1 Week)

		pos/wks
8 Feb 86	ON THE TRAIL *Island IS 263*	74 1

PRIMITIVE RADIO GODS US, male vocalist – Chris O'Connor (Singles: 1 Week)

		pos/wks
30 Mar 96	STANDING OUTSIDE A BROKEN PHONE BOOTH WITH MONEY IN MY HAND *Columbia 6627692*	74 1

The PRIMITIVES UK, male / female vocal / instrumental group (Singles: 27 Weeks, Albums: 13 Weeks)

		pos/wks
27 Feb 88 ●	CRASH *Lazy PB 41761*	5 10
30 Apr 88	OUT OF REACH *Lazy PB 42011*	25 4
3 Sep 88	WAY BEHIND ME *Lazy PB 42209*	36 4
29 Jul 89	SICK OF IT *Lazy PB 42947*	24 4
30 Sep 89	SECRETS *Lazy PB 43173*	49 3
3 Aug 91	YOU ARE THE WAY *RCA PB 44481*	58 2
9 Apr 88 ●	LOVELY *RCA PL 71688*	6 10
2 Sep 89	LAZY 86-88 *Lazy 15*	73 1
28 Oct 89	PURE *RCA PL 74252*	33 2

PRIMUS *US, male vocal / instrumental group (Albums: 1 Week)*   pos/wks

| 8 May 93 | PORK SODA *Interscope 75679922572* | 56 | 1 |

PRINCE 35 *Top 500*

(see also NEW POWER GENERATION) *Prolific singer / songwriter / producer / multi-instrumentalist / actor / label and studio owner, b. Prince Rogers Nelson, 7 Jun 1958, Minneapolis, US. This often controversial entertainer has packed stadiums and collected awards worldwide. The entertainer, who has recorded under a variety of monikers, including a symbol and 'The Artist Formerly Known As Prince' (T.A.F.K.A.P.), was seen by over 1.4 million people on his 2004 tour (Singles: 306 Weeks, Albums: 442 Weeks)*   pos/wks

19 Jan 80	I WANNA BE YOUR LOVER *Warner Bros. K 17537*	41	3
29 Jan 83	1999 *Warner Bros. W 9896*	25	7
30 Apr 83	LITTLE RED CORVETTE *Warner Bros. W 9688*	54	6
26 Nov 83	LITTLE RED CORVETTE (re-issue) *Warner Bros. W 9436*	66	2
30 Jun 84 ●	WHEN DOVES CRY *Warner Bros. W 9286* ▲	4	15
22 Sep 84 ●	PURPLE RAIN *Warner Bros. W 9174*	8	9
8 Dec 84 ●	I WOULD DIE 4 U *Warner Bros. W 9121* 1	58	6
19 Jan 85 ●	1999 / LITTLE RED CORVETTE (re-issue) *Warner Bros. W 1999*	2	10
23 Feb 85 ●	LET'S GO CRAZY / TAKE ME WITH U *Warner Bros. W 2000* 1	7	9
25 May 85	PAISLEY PARK *WEA W 9052* 1	18	10
27 Jul 85	RASPBERRY BERET *WEA W 8929* 1	25	8
26 Oct 85	POP LIFE *Paisley Park W 8858* 1	60	2
8 Mar 86 ●	KISS *Paisley Park W 8751* 1 ▲	6	9
14 Jun 86	MOUNTAINS *Paisley Park W 8711* 1	45	4
16 Aug 86	GIRLS AND BOYS *Paisley Park W 8586* 1	11	8
1 Nov 86	ANOTHERLOVERHOLENYOHEAD *Paisley Park W 8521* 1	36	3
14 Mar 87	SIGN 'O' THE TIMES *Paisley Park W 8399*	10	7
20 Jun 87	IF I WAS YOUR GIRLFRIEND *Paisley Park W 8334*	20	6
15 Aug 87	U GOT THE LOOK *Paisley Park W 8289*	11	9
28 Nov 87	I COULD NEVER TAKE THE PLACE OF YOUR MAN *Paisley Park W 8288*	29	6
7 May 88 ●	ALPHABET STREET *Paisley Park W 7900*	9	6
23 Jul 88	GLAM SLAM *Paisley Park W 7806*	29	4
5 Nov 88	I WISH U HEAVEN *Paisley Park W 7745*	24	5
24 Jun 89 ●	BATDANCE *Warner Bros. W 2924* ▲	2	12
9 Sep 89	PARTYMAN *Warner Bros. W 2814*	14	6
18 Nov 89	THE ARMS OF ORION *Warner Bros. W 2757* 2	27	5
4 Aug 90 ●	THIEVES IN THE TEMPLE *Paisley Park W 9751*	7	6
10 Nov 90	NEW POWER GENERATION *Paisley Park W 9525*	26	4
31 Aug 91 ●	GETT OFF *Paisley Park W 0056* 3	4	8
21 Sep 91	CREAM *Paisley Park W 0061* 3 ▲	15	7
7 Dec 91	DIAMONDS AND PEARLS *Paisley Park W 0075* 3	25	6
28 Mar 92	MONEY DON'T MATTER 2 NIGHT *Paisley Park W 0091* 3	19	5
27 Jun 92	THUNDER *Paisley Park W 0113* 3	28	3
18 Jul 92 ●	SEXY MF / STROLLIN' *Paisley Park W 0123* 3	4	7
10 Oct 92 ●	MY NAME IS PRINCE *Paisley Park W 0132* 3	7	5
14 Nov 92	MY NAME IS PRINCE (re-mix) *Paisley Park W 0142T* 3	51	1
5 Dec 92	7 *Paisley Park W 0147* 3	27	6
13 Mar 93	THE MORNING PAPERS *Paisley Park W 0162CD* 3	52	3
16 Oct 93	PEACH *Paisley Park W 0210CD*	14	5
11 Dec 93 ●	CONTROVERSY *Paisley Park W 0215CD1*	5	5
9 Apr 94 ★	THE MOST BEAUTIFUL GIRL IN THE WORLD *NPG NPG 60155* 4	1	12
4 Jun 94	THE BEAUTIFUL EXPERIENCE (re-mix) *NPG NPG 60212*	18	3
10 Sep 94	LETITGO *Warner Bros. W 0260CD*	30	4
18 Mar 95	PURPLE MEDLEY *Warner Bros. W 0289CD*	33	2
23 Sep 95	EYE HATE U *Warner Bros. W 0315CD*	20	3
9 Dec 95 ●	GOLD *Warner Bros. W 0325CD*	10	9
3 Aug 96	DINNER WITH DELORES *Warner Bros. 9362437422*	36	2
14 Dec 96	BETCHA BY GOLLY WOW *NPG CDEM 463* 5	11	7
8 Mar 97	THE HOLY RIVER *EMI CDEM 467* 5	19	3
9 Jan 99 ●	1999 (re) (re-issue) *Warner Bros. W 467CD*	10	9
26 Feb 00	THE GREATEST ROMANCE EVER SOLD *NPG / Arista 74321745002* 5	65	1
20 Nov 04	CINNAMON GIRL *Columbia 6751422*	43	1
21 Jul 84 ●	PURPLE RAIN (FILM SOUNDTRACK) *Warner Bros. 9251101* 1 ▲	7	91
8 Sep 84	1999 *Warner Bros. 923720*	30	21
4 May 85 ●	AROUND THE WORLD IN A DAY *Warner Bros. 92-5286-1* 1 ▲	5	20
12 Apr 86 ●	PARADE – MUSIC FROM 'UNDER THE CHERRY MOON' (FILM SOUNDTRACK) *Warner Bros. WX 39* 1	4	26
11 Apr 87 ●	SIGN 'O' THE TIMES *Paisley Park WX 88*	4	32
21 May 88 ★	LOVESEXY *Paisley Park WX 164* ■	1	32

1 Jul 89 ★	BATMAN (FILM SOUNDTRACK) *Warner Bros. WX 281* ■ ▲	1	20
1 Sep 90 ★	GRAFFITI BRIDGE *Paisley Park WX 361* ■	1	8
24 Aug 91	GETT OFF (IMPORT) *Paisley Park WX 432*	33	3
12 Oct 91 ●	DIAMONDS AND PEARLS *Paisley Park WX 432* 2	2	57
17 Oct 92 ★	SYMBOL *Paisley Park 9362450372* 2 ■	1	21
25 Sep 93	THE HITS 1 *Paisley Park 9362454312*	5	27
25 Sep 93	THE HITS 2 *Paisley Park 9362454322*	5	20
25 Sep 93	THE HITS / THE B-SIDES *Paisley Park 9362454402*	4	7
27 Aug 94 ★	COME *Warner Bros. 9362457002* ■	1	8
3 Dec 94	THE BLACK ALBUM *Warner Bros. 9362457932*	36	3
7 Oct 95 ●	THE GOLD EXPERIENCE *Warner Bros. 9362459992* 3	4	5
20 Jul 96	CHAOS AND DISORDER *Warner Bros. 9362463172* 4	14	4
30 Nov 96	EMANCIPATION *NPG CDEMD 1102* 5	18	6
11 Jul 98	NEWPOWER SOUL *RCA 74321605982* 5	38	2
4 Sep 99	THE VAULT ... OLD FRIENDS 4 SALE *Warner Bros. 9362475222*	47	1
11 Aug 01 ●	THE VERY BEST OF PRINCE *Warner Bros. 8122742722*	2	14
1 May 04 ●	MUSICOLOGY *Columbia / NPG 5171659*	3	6

1 Prince and the Revolution 2 Prince with Sheena Easton 3 Prince and the New Power Generation 4 (Symbol) 5 The Artist 1 Prince and the Revolution 2 Prince and the New Power Generation 3 (Symbol) 4 T.A.F.K.A.P. 5 Artist

Although uncredited, Sheena Easton also sings on 'U Got the Look'. 'Let's Go Crazy' was the track from the double A-side single that topped the US chart. 'The Beautiful Experience' was a seven-track CD featuring 'The Most Beautiful Girl in the World' and six further mixes of the track. 'Purple Medley' comprised re-recordings of Batdance / When Doves Cry / Kiss / Erotic City / Darling Nikki / 1999 / Baby I'm a Star / Diamonds and Pearls / Purple Rain / Let's Go Crazy

PRINCE BUSTER *Jamaica, male vocalist – Cecil Campbell (Singles: 16 Weeks)*   pos/wks

| 23 Feb 67 | AL CAPONE *Blue Beat BB 324* | 18 | 13 |
| 4 Apr 98 | WHINE AND GRINE *Island CID 691* | 21 | 3 |

PRINCE CHARLES and the CITY BEAT BAND *US, male vocal / instrumental group (Singles: 2 Weeks, Albums: 1 Week)*   pos/wks

| 22 Feb 86 | WE CAN MAKE IT HAPPEN *PRT 7P 348* | 56 | 2 |
| 30 Apr 83 | STONE KILLERS *Virgin V 2271* | 84 | 1 |

PRINCE NASEEM See KALEEF

PRINCESS *UK, female vocalist – Desiree Heslop (Singles: 44 Weeks, Albums: 14 Weeks)*   pos/wks

3 Aug 85 ●	SAY I'M YOUR NUMBER ONE *Supreme SUPE 101*	7	12
9 Nov 85	AFTER THE LOVE HAS GONE *Supreme SUPE 103*	28	13
19 Apr 86	I'LL KEEP ON LOVING YOU *Supreme SUPE 105*	16	8
5 Jul 86	TELL ME TOMORROW *Supreme SUPE 106*	34	5
25 Oct 86	IN THE HEAT OF A PASSIONATE MOMENT *Supreme SUPE 109*	74	1
13 Jun 87	RED HOT *Polydor POSP 868*	58	5
17 May 86	PRINCESS *Supreme SU 1*	15	14

PRINCESS IVORI *US, female rapper (Singles: 2 Weeks)*   pos/wks

| 17 Mar 90 | WANTED *Supreme SUPE 163* | 69 | 2 |

PRINCESS SUPERSTAR *US, female vocalist – Concetta Kirschner (Singles: 7 Weeks)*   pos/wks

| 2 Mar 02 | BAD BABYSITTER *Rapster RR 007CDM* | 11 | 7 |

Patrick PRINZ See ARTEMESIA; ETHICS; MOVIN' MELODIES; SUBLIMINAL CUTS

Maddy PRIOR See STATUS QUO; STEELEYE SPAN

PRIORY OF THE RESURRECTION *UK, male / female choir (Albums: 1 Week)*   pos/wks

| 31 Mar 01 | ETERNAL LIGHT – MUSIC OF INNER PEACE *Deutsche Grammophon 4710902* | 68 | 1 |

PRIVATE LIVES *UK, male vocal / instrumental duo (Singles: 4 Weeks)*   pos/wks

| 11 Feb 84 | LIVING IN A WORLD (TURNED UPSIDE DOWN) *EMI PRIV 2* | 53 | 4 |

PRIZNA featuring DEMOLITION MAN *UK, male vocal / instrumental group (Singles: 2 Weeks)*   pos/wks

| 29 Apr 95 | FIRE *Labello Blanco NLBCDX 18* | 33 | 2 |

PROBOT US, male vocal / instrumental group (Albums: 2 Weeks) pos/wks

28 Feb 04	PROBOT Southern Lord STHL 302	34	2

PJ PROBY US, male vocalist – James Marcus
Smith (Singles: 91 Weeks, Albums: 3 Weeks) pos/wks

28 May 64	●	HOLD ME Decca F 11904	3	15
3 Sep 64	●	TOGETHER Decca F 11967	8	11
10 Dec 64	●	SOMEWHERE Liberty LIB 10182	6	12
25 Feb 65		I APOLOGISE Liberty LIB 10188	11	8
8 Jul 65		LET THE WATER RUN DOWN Liberty LIB 10206	19	8
30 Sep 65		THAT MEANS A LOT Liberty LIB 10215	30	6
25 Nov 65	●	MARIA Liberty LIB 10218	8	9
10 Feb 66		YOU'VE COME BACK Liberty LIB 10223	25	7
16 Jun 66		TO MAKE A BIG MAN CRY Liberty LIB 10236	34	3
27 Oct 66		I CAN'T MAKE IT ALONE Liberty LIB 10250	37	5
6 Mar 68		IT'S YOUR DAY TODAY Liberty LBF 15046	32	5
28 Dec 96		YESTERDAY HAS GONE (re) EMI Premier CDPRESX 13 [1]	58	2
27 Feb 65		I'M PJ PROBY Liberty LBY 1235	16	3

[1] PJ Proby and Marc Almond featuring the My Life Story Orchestra

The PROCLAIMERS UK, male vocal / instrumental duo –
Charlie and Craig Reid (Singles: 50 Weeks, Albums: 62 Weeks) pos/wks

14 Nov 87	●	LETTER FROM AMERICA Chrysalis CHS 3178	3	10
5 Mar 88		MAKE MY HEART FLY Chrysalis CLAIM 1	63	3
27 Aug 88		I'M GONNA BE (500 MILES) Chrysalis CLAIM 2	11	11
12 Nov 88		SUNSHINE ON LEITH Chrysalis CLAIM 3	41	5
11 Feb 89		I'M ON MY WAY Chrysalis CLAIM 4	43	4
24 Nov 90	●	KING OF THE ROAD (EP) Chrysalis CLAIM 5	9	8
19 Feb 94		LET'S GET MARRIED Chrysalis CDCLAIMS 6	21	4
16 Apr 94		WHAT MAKES YOU CRY Chrysalis CDCLAIMS 7	38	3
22 Oct 94		THESE ARMS OF MINE Chrysalis CDCLAIM 8	51	2
9 May 87		THIS IS THE STORY Chrysalis CHR 1602	43	21
24 Sep 88	●	SUNSHINE ON LEITH Chrysalis CHR 1668	6	27
19 Mar 94	●	HIT THE HIGHWAY Chrysalis CDCHR 6066	8	6
9 Jun 01		PERSEVERE Persevere PERSRECCD 04	61	1
25 May 02		THE BEST OF THE PROCLAIMERS Chrysalis 5386822	30	6
27 Sep 03		BORN INNOCENT Persevere PERSRECCD 09	70	1

Tracks on King of the Road (EP): King of the Road / Long Black Veil / Lulu Selling Tea / Not Ever

PROCOL HARUM UK, male vocal / instrumental group –
lead vocal Gary Brooker (Singles: 56 Weeks, Albums: 11 Weeks) pos/wks

25 May 67	★	A WHITER SHADE OF PALE Deram DM 126	1	15
4 Oct 67	●	HOMBURG Regal Zonophone RZ 3003	6	10
24 Apr 68		QUITE RIGHTLY SO Regal Zonophone RZ 3007	50	1
18 Jun 69		A SALTY DOG (2re) Regal Zonophone RZ 3019	44	3
22 Apr 72		A WHITER SHADE OF PALE (re-issue) Fly Magnify ECHO 101	13	13
5 Aug 72		CONQUISTADOR Chrysalis CHS 2003	22	7
23 Aug 75		PANDORA'S BOX Chrysalis CHS 2073	16	7
19 Jul 69		A SALTY DOG Regal Zonophone SLRZ 1009	27	2
27 Jun 70		HOME Regal Zonophone SLRZ 1014	49	1
3 Jul 71		BROKEN BARRICADES Island ILPS 9158	42	1
6 May 72		PROCOL HARUM IN CONCERT WITH THE EDMONTON SYMPHONY ORCHESTRA Chrysalis CHR 1004	48	1
6 May 72		A WHITER SHADE OF PALE / A SALTY DOG (re-issue) Fly Double Back TOOFA 7/8	26	4
30 Aug 75		PROCOL'S NINTH Chrysalis CHR 1080	41	2

'A Whiter Shade of Pale / A Salty Dog' is a double re-issue, although 'A Whiter Shade of Pale' was not previously a hit

Michael PROCTOR See URBAN BLUES PROJECT presents Michael PROCTER

The PRODIGY [158] [Top 500]

Confrontational dance-rock collision masterminded by Liam Howlett (k/prog) and featuring charismatic Keith Flint (v). This act has achieved a run of 12 successive Top 20 singles, while their 1997 album, 'Fat of the Land', debuted at No.1 in more than 20 countries, including the UK and the US. MC / dancer Maxim went solo in 2000. Best-selling single: 'Breathe' 722,554 (Singles: 150 Weeks, Albums: 195 Weeks) pos/wks

24 Aug 91	●	CHARLY (re) XL XL Recordings 21CD	3	11
4 Jan 92	●	EVERYBODY IN THE PLACE (EP) (re) XL XL Recordings 26CD1	2	10
26 Sep 92		FIRE / JERICHO (re) XL XL Recordings 30CD	11	5
21 Nov 92	●	OUT OF SPACE / RUFF IN THE JUNGLE BIZNESS (re) XL XL Recordings 35CD	5	14
17 Apr 93		WIND IT UP (REWOUND) (re) XL XL Recordings 39CD	11	8
16 Oct 93	●	ONE LOVE XL XL Recordings 47CD	8	6
28 May 94	●	NO GOOD (START THE DANCE) (re) XL XL Recordings 51CD	4	14
24 Sep 94		VOODOO PEOPLE (re) XL XL Recordings 54CD	13	6
18 Mar 95		POISON (re) XL XL Recordings 58CD	15	7
30 Mar 96	★	FIRESTARTER (2re) XL XL Recordings 70CD ■	1	30
23 Nov 96	★	BREATHE (re) XL XL Recordings 80CD ■	1	18
29 Nov 97	●	SMACK MY BITCH UP XL XL Recordings 90CD	8	10
13 Jul 02	●	BABY'S GOT A TEMPER XL XL Recordings XLS 145CD	5	6
11 Sep 04		GIRLS XL XL Recordings XLS 195CD	19	4
4 Dec 04		CHARLY (re-mix) XL XL Recordings XLXV 1506	73	1
10 Oct 92		EXPERIENCE XL Recordings XLCD 110	12	31
16 Jul 94	★	MUSIC FOR THE JILTED GENERATION XL Recordings XLCD 114	1	98
12 Jul 97	★	THE FAT OF THE LAND XL Recordings XLCD 121 ■ ▲	1	60
4 Sep 04	★	ALWAYS OUTNUMBERED, NEVER OUTGUNNED XL Recordings XLCD 183 ■	1	6

Tracks on Everybody in the Place (EP): Everybody in the Place / Crazy Man / G-Force (Energy Flow) / Rip Up the Sound System. Eight of their singles re-entered the chart in Apr 1996

PRODUCT G&B See SANTANA

The PROFESSIONALS
UK, male vocal / instrumental group (Singles: 4 Weeks) pos/wks

11 Oct 80	1-2-3 Virgin VS 376	43	4

PROFESSOR See DJ PROFESSOR

PROFESSOR T See SHUT UP AND DANCE

PROGRAM See MR PINK presents The PROGRAM

PROGRAM 2 BELTRAM See BELTRAM

PROGRESS FUNK Italy, male production trio (Singles: 1 Week) pos/wks

11 Oct 97	AROUND MY BRAIN Deconstruction 74321518182	73	1

PROGRESS presents the BOY WUNDA
UK, male DJ / producer – Robert Webster (Singles: 10 Weeks) pos/wks

18 Dec 99	●	EVERYBODY Manifesto FESCD 65	7	10

PROJECT D (see also SYMPHONIQUE) UK, male instrumental
duo – Chris Cozens and Nick Magnus (Albums: 18 Weeks) pos/wks

17 Feb 90	THE SYNTHESIZER ALBUM Telstar STAR 2371	13	11
29 Sep 90	SYNTHESIZED VOL.2 Telstar STAR 2428	25	7

PROJECT featuring GERIDEAU US, male vocal / instrumental /
production duo – Jose Burgos and Theo Gerideau (Singles: 1 Week) pos/wks

27 Aug 94	BRING IT BACK 2 LUV Fruittree FTREE 10CD	65	1

PROJECT ONE
UK, male producer – Mark Williams (Singles: 3 Weeks) pos/wks

16 May 92	ROUGHNECK (EP) Rising High RSN 22	49	2
29 Aug 92	DON GARGON COMIN' Rising High RSN 35	64	1

Tracks on Roughneck (EP): Come My Selector / Can't Take the Heartbreak / Live Vibe 4 (Summer Vibes)

PRONG US, male vocal / instrumental
group (Singles: 1 Week, Albums: 1 Week) pos/wks

25 Apr 92	WHOSE FIST IS THIS ANYWAY (EP) Epic 6580026	58	1
12 Feb 94	CLEANSING Epic 4747962	71	1

Tracks on Whose Fist Is This Anyway (EP): Prove You Wrong / Hell If I Could / (Get a) Grip (On Yourself) / Prove You Wrong (re-mix)

PROPAGANDA Germany, male / female vocal /
instrumental group (Singles: 35 Weeks, Albums: 16 Weeks) pos/wks

17 Mar 84	DR MABUSE ZTT ZTAS 2	27	9
4 May 85	DUEL ZTT ZTAS 8	21	12
10 Aug 85	P MACHINERY ZTT ZTAS 12	50	5

		pos/wks	
28 Apr 90	HEAVEN GIVE ME WORDS *Virgin VS 1245*	...........**36**	5
8 Sep 90	ONLY ONE WORD *Virgin VS 1271*	...........**71**	4
13 Jul 85	A SECRET WISH *ZTT ZTTIQ 3*	...........**16**	12
23 Nov 85	WISHFUL THINKING *ZTT ZTTIQ 20*	...........**82**	1
9 Jun 90	1234 *Virgin V 2625*	...........**46**	2

PROPELLERHEADS *UK, male instrumental / production duo –*
Alex Gifford and Will White (Singles: 15 Weeks, Albums: 13 Weeks)   pos/wks

7 Dec 96	TAKE CALIFORNIA *Wall of Sound WALLD 024*	...........**69**	1
17 May 97	SPYBREAK! *Wall of Sound WALLD 029X*	...........**40**	1
18 Oct 97 ●	ON HER MAJESTY'S SECRET SERVICE		
	East West EW 136CD [1]	...........**7**	5
20 Dec 97	HISTORY REPEATING *Wall of Sound WALLD 036* [2]	...........**19**	7
27 Jun 98	BANG ON! *Wall of Sound WALLD 039*	...........**53**	1
7 Feb 98 ●	DECKSANDRUMSANDROCKANDROLL		
	Wall of Sound WALLCD 015	...........**6**	13

[1] Propellerheads / David Arnold [2] Propellerheads featuring Miss Shirley Bassey

PROPHETS OF SOUND
UK, male instrumental / production duo (Singles: 2 Weeks)   pos/wks

14 Nov 98	HIGH *Distinctive DISNCD 47*	...........**73**	1
23 Feb 02	NEW DAWN *Ink NIBNE 10CD*	...........**51**	1

PROSPECT PARK / Carolyn HARDING
UK, male / female vocal / production duo (Singles: 1 Week)   pos/wks

8 Aug 98	MOVIN' ON *AM:PM 5827312*	...........**55**	1

Shaila PROSPERE *See RIMES featuring Shaila PROSPERE*

Brian PROTHEROE
UK, male vocalist (Singles: 6 Weeks)   pos/wks

7 Sep 74	PINBALL *Chrysalis CHS 2043*	...........**22**	6

PROUD MARY
UK, male vocal / instrumental group (Singles: 1 Week)   pos/wks

25 Aug 01	VERY BEST FRIEND *Sour Mash JDNCSCD 004*	...........**75**	1

Dorothy PROVINE
US, female actor / vocalist (Singles: 15 Weeks, Albums: 49 Weeks)   pos/wks

7 Dec 61	DON'T BRING LULU *Warner Bros. WB 53*	...........**17**	12
28 Jun 62	CRAZY WORDS, CRAZY TUNE *Warner Bros. WB 70*	...........**45**	3
2 Dec 61 ●	THE ROARING TWENTIES – SONGS FROM THE TV SERIES		
	Warner Bros. WM 4035	...........**3**	42
10 Feb 62 ●	VAMP OF THE ROARING TWENTIES *Warner Bros. WM 4053*	...........**9**	7

Eric PRYDZ
Sweden, male producer (Singles: 15 Weeks)   pos/wks

21 Aug 04	WOZ NOT WOZ *C2 CDC 2002* [1]	...........**55**	1
25 Sep 04 ★	CALL ON ME *Data DATA 68CDS* ■	...........**1**	14+

[1] Eric Prydz & Steve Angello

PSEUDO ECHO
Australia, male vocal / instrumental group (Singles: 12 Weeks)   pos/wks

18 Jul 87 ●	FUNKY TOWN *RCA PB 49705*	...........**8**	12

The PSYCHEDELIC FURS *UK, male vocal /*
instrumental group (Singles: 31 Weeks, Albums: 39 Weeks)   pos/wks

2 May 81	DUMB WAITERS *CBS A 1166*	...........**59**	2
27 Jun 81	PRETTY IN PINK *CBS A 1327*	...........**43**	5
31 Jul 82	LOVE MY WAY *CBS A 2549*	...........**42**	6
31 Mar 84	HEAVEN *CBS A 4300*	...........**29**	6
16 Jun 84	GHOST IN YOU *CBS A 4470*	...........**68**	2
23 Aug 86	PRETTY IN PINK (re-recording) *CBS A 7242*	...........**18**	9
9 Jul 88	ALL THAT MONEY WANTS *CBS FURS 4*	...........**75**	1
15 Mar 80	PSYCHEDELIC FURS *CBS 84084*	...........**18**	6
23 May 81	TALK TALK TALK *CBS 84892*	...........**30**	9
2 Oct 82	FOREVER NOW *CBS 85909*	...........**20**	6
19 May 84	MIRROR MOVES *CBS 25950*	...........**15**	9
14 Feb 87	MIDNIGHT TO MIDNIGHT *CBS 4502561*	...........**12**	6
13 Aug 88	ALL OF THIS AND NOTHING *CBS 461101*	...........**67**	1
18 Nov 89	BOOK OF DAYS *CBS 4659821*	...........**74**	1
13 Jul 91	WORLD OUTSIDE *East West WX 422*	...........**68**	1

PSYCHEDELIC WALTONS (see also MOLOKO; SOUL II SOUL)
UK, male production duo – Nellee Hooper
and Fabien Waltmann (Singles: 3 Weeks)   pos/wks

19 Jan 02	WONDERLAND *Echo ECSCD 120* [1]	...........**37**	2
12 Apr 03	PAYBACK TIME *Sony Music 6737622* [2]	...........**48**	1

[1] Psychedelic Waltons featuring Roisin Murphy [2] Dysfunctional Psychedelic Waltons

PSYCHIC TV
UK, male / female vocal / instrumental group (Singles: 4 Weeks)   pos/wks

26 Apr 86	GODSTAR *Temple TOPY 009* [1]	...........**67**	2
20 Sep 86	GOOD VIBRATIONS / ROMAN P *Temple TOPY 23*	...........**65**	2

[1] Psychic TV and the Angels of Light

PSYCHO RADIO *See LC ANDERSON vs PSYCHO RADIO*

PSYCHOTROPIC *See FREEFALL featuring PSYCHOTROPIC; SALT-N-PEPA*

PUBLIC ANNOUNCEMENT (see also R KELLY)
US, male vocal / instrumental group (Singles: 5 Weeks)   pos/wks

9 May 92	SHE'S GOT THAT VIBE *Jive JIVET 292* [1]	...........**57**	2
20 Nov 93	SEX ME *Jive JIVECD 346* [1]	...........**75**	1
4 Jul 98	BODY BUMPIN' (YIPPEE-YI-YO) *A&M 5826972*	...........**38**	2

[1] R Kelly and Public Announcement

PUBLIC DEMAND *UK, male vocal group (Singles: 2 Weeks)*   pos/wks

15 Feb 97	INVISIBLE *ZTT ZANG 85CD*	...........**41**	2

PUBLIC DOMAIN
UK, male production / vocal group (Singles: 18 Weeks)   pos/wks

2 Dec 00 ●	OPERATION BLADE (BASS IN THE PLACE)		
	Xtrahard / Xtravaganza X2H 1CDS	...........**5**	13
23 Jun 01	ROCK DA FUNKY BEATS		
	Xtrahard / Xtravaganza X2H 3CDS [1]	...........**19**	3
12 Jan 02	TOO MANY MC'S / LET ME CLEAR MY THROAT		
	Xtrahard/Xtravaganza X2H 8CDS	...........**34**	2

[1] Public Domain featuring Chuck D

PUBLIC ENEMY *US, male rap group – leader*
Chuck D (Singles: 53 Weeks, Albums: 37 Weeks)   pos/wks

21 Nov 87	REBEL WITHOUT A PAUSE (re) *Def Jam 6512457*	...........**37**	7
9 Jan 88	BRING THE NOISE *Def Jam 6513357*	...........**32**	5
2 Jul 88	DON'T BELIEVE THE HYPE *Def Jam 6528337*	...........**18**	5
15 Oct 88	NIGHT OF THE LIVING BASEHEADS *Def Jam 6530460*	...........**63**	2
24 Jun 89	FIGHT THE POWER *Motown ZB 42877*	...........**29**	5
20 Jan 90	WELCOME TO THE TERRORDOME *Def Jam 6554760*	...........**18**	4
7 Apr 90	911 IS A JOKE *Def Jam 6558307*	...........**41**	3
23 Jun 90	BROTHERS GONNA WORK IT OUT *Def Jam 6560181*	...........**46**	2
3 Nov 90	CAN'T DO NUTTIN' FOR YA MAN *Def Jam 6563857*	...........**53**	2
12 Oct 91	CAN'T TRUSS IT *Def Jam 6575307*	...........**22**	4
25 Jan 92	SHUT 'EM DOWN *Def Jam 6577617*	...........**21**	3
11 Apr 92	NIGHTTRAIN *Def Jam 6578647*	...........**55**	2
13 Aug 94	GIVE IT UP *Def Jam DEFCD 1*	...........**18**	3
29 Jul 95	SO WATCHA GONNA DO NOW *Def Jam DEFCD 5*	...........**50**	1
6 Jun 98	HE GOT GAME *Def Jam 5689852* [1]	...........**16**	4
25 Sep 99	DO YOU WANNA GO OUR WAY???		
	Pias Recordings PIASX 005CDX	...........**66**	1
30 Jul 88 ●	IT TAKES A NATION OF MILLIONS TO HOLD US BACK		
	Def Jam 4624151	...........**8**	9
28 Apr 90 ●	FEAR OF A BLACK PLANET *Def Jam 4662811*	...........**4**	10
19 Oct 91 ●	APOCALYPSE 91 – THE ENEMY STRIKES BLACK		
	Def Jam 4687511	...........**8**	7
3 Oct 92	GREATEST MISSES *Def Jam 4720312*	...........**14**	3
3 Sep 94	MUSE SICK-N-HOUR MESS AGE *Def Jam 5233622*	...........**12**	3
16 May 98	HE GOT GAME (FILM SOUNDTRACK) *Def Jam 5581302*	...........**50**	4
31 Jul 99	THERE'S A POISON GOIN ON ...		
	Pias Recordings PIASXCD 004	...........**55**	1

[1] Public Enemy featuring Stephen Stills

PUBLIC IMAGE LTD (PIL) (see also John LYDON) *UK, male vocal /*
instrumental group (Singles: 61 Weeks, Albums: 51 Weeks)   pos/wks

21 Oct 78 ●	PUBLIC IMAGE *Virgin VS 228*	...........**9**	8
7 Jul 79	DEATH DISCO *Virgin VS 274*	...........**20**	7

20 Oct 79	MEMORIES *Virgin VS 299*	.60	2
4 Apr 81	FLOWERS OF ROMANCE *Virgin VS 397*	.24	7
17 Sep 83 ●	THIS IS NOT A LOVE SONG *Virgin VS 529*	.5	10
19 May 84	BAD LIFE *Virgin VS 675*	.71	2
1 Feb 86	RISE *Virgin VS 841*	.11	8
3 May 86	HOME *Virgin VS 855*	.75	1
22 Aug 87	SEATTLE *Virgin VS 988*	.47	4
6 May 89	DISAPPOINTED *Virgin VS 1181*	.38	5
20 Oct 90	DON'T ASK ME *Virgin VS 1231*	.22	5
22 Feb 92	CRUEL *Virgin VS 1390*	.49	2
23 Dec 78	PUBLIC IMAGE *Virgin V 2114*	.22	11
8 Dec 79	METAL BOX *Virgin METAL 1*	.18	8
8 Mar 80	SECOND EDITION OF PIL *Virgin VD 2512*	.46	2
22 Nov 80	PARIS AU PRINTEMPS (PARIS IN THE SPRING) *Virgin V 2183*	.61	2
18 Apr 81	FLOWERS OF ROMANCE *Virgin V 2189*	.11	5
8 Oct 83	LIVE IN TOKYO *Virgin VGD 3508*	.28	6
21 Jul 84	THIS IS WHAT YOU WANT ... THIS IS WHAT YOU GET *Virgin V 2309*	.56	2
15 Feb 86	ALBUM / CASSETTE / COMPACT DISC *Virgin V 2366*	.14	6
26 Sep 87	HAPPY? *Virgin V 2455*	.40	2
10 Jun 89	9 *Virgin V 2588*	.36	2
10 Nov 90	THE GREATEST HITS, SO FAR *Virgin V 2644*	.20	3
7 Mar 92	THAT WHAT IS NOT *Virgin CDV 2681*	.46	2

Gary PUCKETT and the UNION GAP *US, male vocal / instrumental group (Singles: 47 Weeks, Albums: 4 Weeks)* pos/wks

17 Apr 68 ★	YOUNG GIRL *CBS 3365* [1]	.1	17
7 Aug 68 ●	LADY WILLPOWER *CBS 3551* [1]	.5	16
28 Aug 68	WOMAN, WOMAN *CBS 3110*	.48	1
15 Jun 74 ●	YOUNG GIRL (re-issue) *CBS 8202*	.6	13
29 Jun 68	UNION GAP *CBS 63342*	.24	4

[1] Union Gap featuring Gary Puckett

PUDDLE OF MUDD
US, male vocal / instrumental group (Singles: 22 Weeks, Albums: 36 Weeks) pos/wks

23 Feb 02	CONTROL (re) *Flawless / Geffen 4976822*	.15	5
15 Jun 02 ●	BLURRY *Flawless / Geffen 4977342*	.8	9
28 Sep 02	SHE HATES ME *Flawless / Geffen 4977982*	.14	7
13 Dec 03	AWAY FROM ME *Flawless / Geffen 9814810*	.55	1
2 Feb 02	COME CLEAN *Interscope 4930742*	.12	36

Tito PUENTE Jr and the LATIN RHYTHM featuring Tito PUENTE, INDIA and Cali ALEMAN
US, male / female vocal / instrumental group (Singles: 3 Weeks) pos/wks

16 Mar 96	OYE COMO VA *Media MCSTD 40013*	.36	2
19 Jul 97	OYE COMA VA (re-mix) *Nukleuz MCSTD 40120*	.56	1

Puff DADDY *See P DIDDY*

PULP ⬤316 ▮Top 500
Jarvis Cocker, b. 19 Sep 1963, Sheffield, UK, is frontman of Pulp, or Arabacus Pulp as his band was called in 1978. After countless line-up changes and modest commercial success, 17 years passed before No.1 album 'Different Class' and a string of Top 10 singles troubled the charts. Cocker's unique brand of wit and wisdom was then exposed to the wider world, culminating in the legendary bottom-wiggling "protest" at Michael Jackson's 1996 Brit Awards performance (Singles: 74 Weeks, Albums: 136 Weeks) pos/wks

27 Nov 93	LIP GLOSS *Island CID 567*	.50	2
2 Apr 94	DO YOU REMEMBER THE FIRST TIME (re) *Island CID 574*	.33	5
4 Jun 94	THE SISTERS (EP) *Island CID 595*	.19	4
3 Jun 95 ●	COMMON PEOPLE *Island CID 613*	.2	13
7 Oct 95 ●	MIS-SHAPES / SORTED FOR E'S AND WIZZ (re) *Island CID 620*	.2	11
9 Dec 95 ●	DISCO 2000 *Island CID 623*	.7	11
6 Apr 96 ●	SOMETHING CHANGED (2re) *Island CID 632*	.10	7
22 Nov 97 ●	HELP THE AGED (re) *Island CID 679*	.8	9
28 Mar 98	THIS IS HARDCORE *Island CID 695*	.12	4
20 Jun 98	A LITTLE SOUL *Island CID 708*	.22	2
19 Sep 98	PARTY HARD *Island CID 719*	.29	2
20 Oct 01	SUNRISE / THE TREES *Island CID 786*	.23	2
27 Apr 02	BAD COVER VERSION *Island CID 794*	.27	2
30 Apr 94 ●	HIS 'N' HERS *Island CID 8025*	.9	43
11 Nov 95 ★	DIFFERENT CLASS *Island CID 8041* ▮	.1	62

23 Mar 96 ●	COUNTDOWN 1992-1983 *Nectar Masters NTMCDD 521*	.10	6
11 Apr 98 ★	THIS IS HARDCORE *Island 8066* ▮	.1	21
3 Nov 01	WE LOVE LIFE *Island CID 8110*	.6	3
30 Nov 02	HITS *Island / Uni-Island CID 8126*	.71	1

Tracks on The Sisters (EP): Babies / Your Sister's Clothes / Seconds / His 'n' Hers

PULSE featuring Antoinette ROBERSON
(see also BOSS) US, male / female vocal / production duo – David Morales and Antoinette Roberson (Singles: 3 Weeks) pos/wks

25 May 96	THE LOVER THAT YOU ARE *ffrr FCD 278*	.22	3

PUNK CHIC
Sweden, male producer – Johan Strandkvist (Singles: 1 Week) pos/wks

6 Oct 01	DJ SPINNIN' *WEA WEA 333CD*	.69	1

PUNX *Germany, male production trio (Singles: 1 Week)* pos/wks

16 Nov 02	THE ROCK *Data / Ministry of Sound DATA 38CDS*	.59	1

PURE REASON REVOLUTION
UK, male vocal / instrumental group (Singles: 1 Week) pos/wks

1 May 04	APPRENTICE OF THE UNIVERSE *Poptones MC 5089SCD*	.74	1

PURE SUGAR
UK, male / female vocal / instrumental trio (Singles: 1 Week) pos/wks

24 Oct 98	DELICIOUS *Geffen GFSTD 22355*	.70	1

PURESSENCE *UK, male vocal / instrumental group (Singles: 6 Weeks, Albums: 2 Weeks)* pos/wks

23 May 98	THIS FEELING *Island CID 688*	.33	2
8 Aug 98	IT DOESN'T MATTER ANYMORE *Island CID 703*	.47	1
21 Nov 98	ALL I WANT *Island CID 722*	.39	2
5 Oct 02	WALKING DEAD *Island CID 803*	.40	1
29 Aug 98	ONLY FOREVER *Island CID 8064*	.36	2

PURETONE
Australia, male producer – Josh Abrahams (Singles: 17 Weeks) pos/wks

12 Jan 02 ●	ADDICTED TO BASS *Gusto CDGUS 6*	.2	15
10 May 03	STUCK IN A GROOVE *Illustrious CDILL 014*	.26	2

James and Bobby PURIFY *US, male vocal duo – James Purify and Robert Dickey (Singles: 16 Weeks)* pos/wks

24 Apr 76	I'M YOUR PUPPET *Mercury 6167 324*	.12	10
7 Aug 76	MORNING GLORY *Mercury 6167 380*	.27	6

The PURPLE HEARTS
UK, male vocal / instrumental group (Singles: 5 Weeks) pos/wks

22 Sep 79	MILLIONS LIKE US *Fiction FICS 003*	.57	3
8 Mar 80	JIMMY *Fiction FICS 9*	.60	2

PURPLE KINGS *UK, male vocal / instrumental duo – Rob Tillen and Glen Williamson (Singles: 3 Weeks)* pos/wks

15 Oct 94	THAT'S THE WAY YOU DO IT *Positiva CDTIV 21*	.26	3

PUSH
Belgium, male producer – Dirk Dierickx (Singles: 19 Weeks) pos/wks

15 May 99	UNIVERSAL NATION *Bonzai / Inferno CDFERN 16*	.36	2
9 Oct 99	UNIVERSAL NATION '99 (re-mix) *Inferno CDFERN 20*	.35	2
23 Sep 00	TILL WE MEET AGAIN *Inferno CDFERN 29*	.46	1
12 May 01	STRANGE WORLD *Inferno CDFERN 38*	.21	4
20 Oct 01	PLEASE SAVE ME *Inferno / Five AM FAMFERN 1CD* [1]	.36	2
3 Nov 01	THE LEGACY *Inferno CDFERN 43*	.22	4
4 May 02	TRANZY STATE OF MIND *Inferno CDFERN 45*	.31	2
5 Oct 02	STRANGE WORLD (re-issue) / THE LEGACY (re-mix) *Inferno CDFERN 49*	.55	1
15 Mar 03	UNIVERSAL NATION (re-mix) *Inferno CDFERN 53*	.54	1

[1] Sunscreem vs Push

PUSSY 2000 *UK, male production duo (Singles: 1 Week)* pos/wks

3 Nov 01	IT'S GONNA BE ALRIGHT *Ink NIBNE 9CD*	.70	1

PUSSYCAT
Holland, male / female vocal / instrumental group (Singles: 30 Weeks) pos/wks

| 28 Aug 76 | ★ MISSISSIPPI *Sonet SON 2077* | 1 | 22 |
| 25 Dec 76 | SMILE *Sonet SON 2096* | 24 | 8 |

The PYRAMIDS
Jamaica, male vocal / instrumental group (Singles: 4 Weeks) pos/wks

| 22 Nov 67 | TRAIN TOUR TO RAINBOW CITY *President PT 161* | 35 | 4 |

PYTHON LEE JACKSON
Australia, male vocal / instrumental group (Singles: 12 Weeks) pos/wks

| 30 Sep 72 | ● IN A BROKEN DREAM *Youngblood YB 1002* | 3 | 12 |

Uncredited lead vocals by Rod Stewart

Q
UK, male instrumental / production duo –
Mark Taylor and Terry Adams (Singles: 6 Weeks) pos/wks

| 5 Jun 93 | GET HERE *Arista 74321145972* [1] | 37 | 4 |
| 12 Mar 94 | (EVERYTHING I DO) I DO IT FOR YOU *Bell 74321193062* [2] | 47 | 2 |

[1] Q featuring Tracy Ackerman [2] Q featuring Tony Jackson

QB FINEST featuring NAS & BRAVEHEARTS
US, male rappers (Singles: 3 Weeks) pos/wks

| 21 Apr 01 | OOCHIE WALLY *Columbia 6710852* | 30 | 3 |

Q-BASS
UK, male production / instrumental group (Singles: 1 Week) pos/wks

| 8 Feb 92 | HARDCORE WILL NEVER DIE *Suburban Base SUBBASE 007* | 64 | 1 |

Q-CLUB
Italy, male / female vocal / instrumental group (Singles: 3 Weeks) pos/wks

| 6 Jan 96 | TELL IT TO MY HEART *Manifesto FESCD 5* | 28 | 3 |

QFX
UK, male vocal / instrumental
group (Singles: 18 Weeks, Albums: 1 Week) pos/wks

6 May 95	FREEDOM (EP) *Epidemic EPICD 004*	41	3
3 Feb 96	EVERYTIME YOU TOUCH ME *Epidemic EPICD 006*	22	4
3 Aug 96	YOU GOT THE POWER *Epidemic EPICD 007*	33	3
18 Jan 97	FREEDOM 2 (re-mix) *Epidemic EPICD 008*	21	4
20 Mar 99	SAY YOU'LL BE MINE *Quality Recordings QUAL 005CD*	34	2
23 Aug 03	FREEDOM *Data / MoS DATA 57CDS*	36	2
8 Mar 97	ALIEN CHILD *Epidemic EPICD 009*	62	1

Tracks on Freedom (EP): Freedom / Metropolis / Sianora Baby / The Machine

Q-TEE
UK, female rapper – Tatiana Mais (Singles: 7 Weeks) pos/wks

| 21 Apr 90 | AFRIKA *SBK SBK 7008* [1] | 42 | 5 |
| 10 Feb 96 | GIMME THAT BODY *Heavenly HVN 48CD* | 40 | 2 |

[1] History featuring Q-Tee

Q-TEX
UK, male / female vocal / instrumental group (Singles: 7 Weeks) pos/wks

| 9 Apr 94 | THE POWER OF LOVE *Stoatin' STOAT 002CD* | 65 | 1 |
| 26 Nov 94 | BELIEVE *23rd Precinct THIRD 2CD* | 41 | 2 |

15 Jun 96	LET THE LOVE *23rd Precinct THIRD 4CD*	30	2
30 Nov 96	DO YOU WANT ME *23rd Precinct THIRD 5CD*	48	1
28 Jun 97	POWER OF LOVE '97 (re-mix) *23rd Precinct THIRD 7CD*	49	1

Q-TIP (see also DEEE-LITE; A TRIBE CALLED QUEST)
US, male rapper – John Davis (Singles: 23 Weeks) pos/wks

4 Oct 97	● GOT 'TIL IT'S GONE *Virgin VSCDG 1666* [1]	6	9
19 Jun 99	GET INVOLVED *Hollywood 0101185 HWR* [2]	36	2
22 Jan 00	HOT BOYZ *Elektra E 7002CD* [3]	18	3
12 Feb 00	BREATHE AND STOP *Arista 74321727062*	12	7
6 May 00	VIVRANT THING *Arista 74321751302*	39	2

[1] Janet featuring Q-Tip and Joni Mitchell [2] Raphael Saadiq and Q-Tip
[3] Missy 'Misdemeanor' Elliott featuring Nas, Eve and Q-Tip

Q-TIPS (see also Paul YOUNG)
UK, male vocal / instrumental group (Albums: 1 Week) pos/wks

| 30 Aug 80 | Q-TIPS *Chrysalis CHR 1255* | 50 | 1 |

Q UNIQUE See C & C MUSIC FACTORY

QATTARA (see also Alex WHITCOMBE & BIG C)
UK, male
production duo – Andy Cato and Alex Whitcombe (Singles: 2 Weeks) pos/wks

| 15 Mar 97 | COME WITH ME *Positiva CDTIV 71* | 31 | 2 |

QPR MASSIVE See SOOPA HOOPZ featuring QPR MASSIVE

QUAD CITY DJs
US, male rap duo (Singles: 1 Week) pos/wks

| 15 Nov 97 | SPACE JAM *Atlantic EW 773* | 57 | 1 |

QUADROPHONIA
Belgium, male
instrumental / production group (Singles: 15 Weeks) pos/wks

13 Apr 91	QUADROPHONIA *ARS 6567687*	14	9
6 Jul 91	THE WAVE OF THE FUTURE *ARS 6569937*	40	3
21 Dec 91	FIND THE TIME (PART ONE) *ARS 6576260*	41	3

The QUADS
UK, male vocal / instrumental group (Singles: 2 Weeks) pos/wks

| 22 Sep 79 | THERE MUST BE THOUSANDS *Big Bear BB 23* | 66 | 2 |

QUAKE featuring Marcia RAE (see also DREAM FREQUENCY;
NATIVE; RED; BEAT RENEGADES) *UK, male producers – Rob*
Tissera and Ian Bland and UK, female vocalist (Singles: 1 Week) pos/wks

| 29 Aug 98 | THE DAY WILL COME *ffrr FCD 344* | 53 | 1 |

QUANTUM JUMP
UK, male vocal / instrumental group (Singles: 10 Weeks) pos/wks

| 2 Jun 79 | ● THE LONE RANGER *Electric WOT 33* | 5 | 10 |

QUARTERFLASH
US, male / female vocal / instrumental group (Singles: 5 Weeks) pos/wks

| 27 Feb 82 | HARDEN MY HEART *Geffen GEF A 1838* | 49 | 5 |

Jakie QUARTZ
France, female vocalist (Singles: 3 Weeks) pos/wks

| 11 Mar 89 | A LA VIE, A L'AMOUR *PWL PWL 30* | 55 | 3 |

QUARTZ
UK, male instrumental group (Singles: 19 Weeks) pos/wks

17 Mar 90	WE'RE COMIN' AT YA *Mercury ITMR 2* [1]	65	2
2 Feb 91	● IT'S TOO LATE *Mercury ITM 3* [2]	8	14
15 Jun 91	NAKED LOVE (JUST SAY YOU WANT ME) *Mercury ITM 4* [3]	39	3

[1] Quartz featuring Stepz [2] Quartz introducing Dina Carroll [3] Quartz and
Dina Carroll

QUARTZ LOCK featuring Lonnie GORDON
UK, male production / instrumental duo – Mark Andrews
and Donald Lynch and US, female vocalist (Singles: 2 Weeks) pos/wks

| 7 Oct 95 | LOVE EVICTION *X:Plode BANG 2CD* | 32 | 2 |

Suzi QUATRO
US, female vocalist / instrumentalist – guitar –
Suzi Quatrocchio (Singles: 122 Weeks, Albums: 13 Weeks) pos/wks

| 19 May 73 | ★ CAN THE CAN *RAK 150* | 1 | 14 |

28 Jul 73 ●	48 CRASH *RAK 158*	3	9
27 Oct 73	DAYTONA DEMON *RAK 161*	14	13
9 Feb 74 ★	DEVIL GATE DRIVE *RAK 167*	1	11
29 Jun 74	TOO BIG *RAK 175*	14	6
9 Nov 74 ●	THE WILD ONE *RAK 185*	7	10
8 Feb 75	YOUR MAMMA WON'T LIKE ME *RAK 191*	31	5
5 Mar 77	TEAR ME APART *RAK 248*	27	6
18 Mar 78 ●	IF YOU CAN'T GIVE ME LOVE *RAK 271*	4	13
22 Jul 78	THE RACE IS ON *RAK 278*	43	5
11 Nov 78	STUMBLIN' IN *RAK 285* [1]	41	8
20 Oct 79	SHE'S IN LOVE WITH YOU *RAK 299*	11	9
19 Jan 80	MAMA'S BOY *RAK 303*	34	5
5 Apr 80	I'VE NEVER BEEN IN LOVE *RAK 307*	56	3
25 Oct 80	ROCK HARD *Dreamland DLSP 6*	68	2
13 Nov 82	HEART OF STONE *Polydor POSP 477*	60	3
13 Oct 73	SUZI QUATRO *RAK SRAK 505*	32	4
26 Apr 80 ●	SUZI QUATRO'S GREATEST HITS *RAK EMTV 24*	4	9

[1] Suzi Quatro and Chris Norman

Finley QUAYE *UK, male vocalist / instrumentalist – guitar (Singles: 23 Weeks, Albums: 59 Weeks)*

		pos/wks	
21 Jun 97	SUNDAY SHINING *Epic 6644552*	16	6
13 Sep 97	EVEN AFTER ALL *Epic 6649712*	10	5
29 Nov 97	IT'S GREAT WHEN WE'RE TOGETHER *Epic 6653382*	29	3
7 Mar 98	YOUR LOVE GETS SWEETER *Epic 6656065*	16	5
15 Aug 98	ULTRA STIMULATION *Epic 6660792*	51	1
23 Sep 00	SPIRITUALIZED *Epic 6698032*	26	3
4 Oct 97 ●	MAVERICK A STRIKE *Epic 4887582*	3	56
14 Oct 00	VANGUARD *Epic 4997102*	35	2
11 Oct 03	MUCH MORE THAN LOVE *Sony Music 5125492*	56	1

QUEDO BRASS *See CHAQUITO ORCHESTRA*

QUEEN 4 Top 500

World-renowned British quartet, who rank second only to The Beatles in chart success when it comes to UK groups: Freddie Mercury (v), b. 5 Sep 1946, d. 24 Nov 1991, Brian May (g/v), John Deacon (b/v), Roger Taylor (d/v). 'Bohemian Rhapsody' (which in places has 180 vocal overdubs) was voted 'No.1 Single of All-Time' by the readers of this book. It was the first recording to top the UK singles chart on two separate occasions (selling over a million each time) and was No.1 in a record four calendar years. They were also the first act to have chart-topping singles in the 1970s, 1980s, 1990s and 21st century. Front man Mercury is rightfully regarded as one of the greatest entertainers in rock, and the group, who stole the show at Live Aid, have attracted millions to their concerts around the globe. Queen have sold over 25 million Greatest Hits albums and are the only act to sell in excess of two million copies of two Greatest Hits albums in the UK. Additionally, they have held the top four places on the UK video chart (1992) and 'We are the Champions' has become the most sung song by the world's sporting crowds. The group, which has contributed enormously to AIDS awareness, won the Brit Award for Outstanding Contribution to British Music (1992) and were inducted into the Rock and Roll Hall of Fame (2000). The Queen musical 'We Will Rock You', penned by Ben Elton and backed by Robert De Niro, has been running successfully since 2002. The band were inducted into the UK Music Hall of Fame in 2004, representing the 1970s. Total UK singles sales: 10,334,713. Best-selling single: 'Bohemian Rhapsody' 2,130,000 (Singles: 423 Weeks, Albums: 1302 Weeks).

		pos/wks	
9 Mar 74 ●	SEVEN SEAS OF RHYE *EMI 2121*	10	10
26 Oct 74 ●	KILLER QUEEN *EMI 2229*	2	12
25 Jan 75	NOW I'M HERE *EMI 2256*	11	7
8 Nov 75 ★	BOHEMIAN RHAPSODY *EMI 2375* ◆	1	17
3 Jul 76 ●	YOU'RE MY BEST FRIEND *EMI 2494*	7	8
27 Nov 76 ●	SOMEBODY TO LOVE *EMI 2565*	2	9
19 Mar 77	TIE YOUR MOTHER DOWN *EMI 2593*	31	4
4 Jun 77	QUEEN'S FIRST EP *EMI 2623*	17	10
22 Oct 77 ●	WE ARE THE CHAMPIONS *EMI 2708*	2	11
25 Feb 78	SPREAD YOUR WINGS *EMI 2757*	34	4
28 Oct 78 ●	BICYCLE RACE / FAT BOTTOMED GIRLS *EMI 2870*	11	12
10 Feb 79 ●	DON'T STOP ME NOW *EMI 2910*	9	12
14 Jul 79	LOVE OF MY LIFE *EMI 2959*	63	2
20 Oct 79 ●	CRAZY LITTLE THING CALLED LOVE *EMI 5001* ▲	2	14
2 Feb 80	SAVE ME *EMI 5022*	11	6
14 Jun 80	PLAY THE GAME *EMI 5076*	14	8
6 Sep 80 ●	ANOTHER ONE BITES THE DUST *EMI 5102* ▲	7	9
6 Dec 80 ●	FLASH *EMI 5126*	10	13
14 Nov 81 ★	UNDER PRESSURE *EMI 5250* [1]	1	11

1 May 82	BODY LANGUAGE *EMI 5293*	25	6
12 Jun 82	LAS PALABRAS DE AMOR *EMI 5316*	17	8
21 Aug 82	BACKCHAT *EMI 5325*	40	4
4 Feb 84 ●	RADIO GAGA *EMI QUEEN 1*	2	9
14 Apr 84 ●	I WANT TO BREAK FREE *EMI QUEEN 2*	3	15
28 Jul 84 ●	IT'S A HARD LIFE *EMI QUEEN 3*	6	9
22 Sep 84	HAMMER TO FALL *EMI QUEEN 4*	13	7
8 Dec 84	THANK GOD IT'S CHRISTMAS *EMI QUEEN 5*	21	6
16 Nov 85 ●	ONE VISION *EMI QUEEN 6*	7	10
29 Mar 86 ●	A KIND OF MAGIC *EMI QUEEN 7*	3	11
21 Jun 86	FRIENDS WILL BE FRIENDS *EMI QUEEN 8*	14	8
27 Sep 86	WHO WANTS TO LIVE FOREVER *EMI QUEEN 9*	24	5
13 May 89 ●	I WANT IT ALL *Parlophone QUEEN 10*	3	7
1 Jul 89 ●	BREAKTHRU' *Parlophone QUEEN 11*	7	7
19 Aug 89	THE INVISIBLE MAN *Parlophone QUEEN 12*	12	6
21 Oct 89	SCANDAL *Parlophone QUEEN 14*	25	4
9 Dec 89	THE MIRACLE *Parlophone QUEEN 15*	21	5
26 Jan 91 ★	INNUENDO *Parlophone QUEEN 16* ■	1	6
25 May 91	I'M GOING SLIGHTLY MAD *Parlophone QUEEN 17*	22	5
25 May 91	HEADLONG *Parlophone QUEEN 18*	14	4
26 Oct 91	THE SHOW MUST GO ON (re) *Parlophone QUEEN 19*	16	10
21 Dec 91 ★	BOHEMIAN RHAPSODY / THESE ARE THE DAYS OF OUR LIVES (re-issue) *Parlophone QUEEN 20* ◆ ■	1	14
1 May 93 ★	FIVE LIVE (EP) (re) *Parlophone CDRS 6340* [2] ■	1	12
4 Nov 95 ●	HEAVEN FOR EVERYONE *Parlophone CDQUEEN 21*	2	12
23 Dec 95 ●	A WINTER'S TALE *Parlophone CDQUEEN 22*	6	6
9 Mar 96	TOO MUCH LOVE WILL KILL YOU *Parlophone CDQUEEN 23*	15	6
29 Jun 96 ●	LET ME LIVE *Parlophone CDQUEEN 24*	9	4
30 Nov 96	YOU DON'T FOOL ME *Parlophone CDQUEEN 25*	17	4
17 Jan 98	NO-ONE BUT YOU / TIE YOUR MOTHER DOWN *Parlophone CDQUEEN 27*	13	4
14 Nov 98 ●	ANOTHER ONE BITES THE DUST *Dreamworks DRMCD 22364* [3]	5	6
18 Dec 99	UNDER PRESSURE (re-mix) *Parlophone CDQUEEN 28* [1]	14	7
29 Jul 00 ●	WE WILL ROCK YOU (re) *RCA 74321774022* [4] ■	1	13
29 Mar 03	FLASH *Nebula NEBCD 041* [5]	15	4
23 Mar 74 ●	QUEEN 2 *EMI EMA 767*	5	29
30 Mar 74	QUEEN *EMI EMC 3006*	24	18
23 Nov 74 ●	SHEER HEART ATTACK *EMI EMC 3061*	2	42
13 Dec 75 ★	A NIGHT AT THE OPERA *EMI EMTC 103*	1	50
25 Dec 76 ★	A DAY AT THE RACES *EMI EMTC 104*	1	24
12 Nov 77 ●	NEWS OF THE WORLD *EMI EMA 784*	4	20
25 Nov 78 ●	JAZZ *EMI EMA 788*	2	27
7 Jul 79 ●	LIVE KILLERS *EMI EMSP 330*	3	29
12 Jul 80 ★	THE GAME *EMI EMA 795* ▲	1	18
20 Dec 80 ●	FLASH GORDON (FILM SOUNDTRACK) *EMI EMC 3351*	10	15
7 Nov 81 ★	GREATEST HITS *EMI EMTV 30*	1	450
15 May 82 ●	HOT SPACE *EMI EMA 797*	4	19
10 Mar 84 ●	THE WORKS *EMI EMC 240014*	2	93
14 Jun 86 ★	A KIND OF MAGIC *EMI EU 3509* ■	1	63
13 Dec 86 ●	LIVE MAGIC *EMI EMC 3519*	3	43
3 Jun 89 ★	THE MIRACLE *Parlophone PCSD 107* ■	1	32
16 Dec 89	QUEEN AT THE BEEB *Band of Joy BOJLP 001*	67	1
16 Feb 91 ★	INNUENDO *Parlophone PCSD 115* ■	1	37
9 Nov 91 ★	GREATEST HITS II *Parlophone PMTV 2*	1	106
6 Jun 92 ●	LIVE AT WEMBLEY '86 *Parlophone CDPCSP 725*	2	15
19 Nov 94	GREATEST HITS I AND II *Parlophone CDPCSD 161*	37	7
18 Nov 95 ★	MADE IN HEAVEN *Parlophone CDPCSD 167* ■	1	28
15 Nov 97 ●	QUEEN ROCKS *Parlophone 8230912*	7	12
20 Nov 99 ●	GREATEST HITS III *Parlophone 5238942*	5	19
25 Nov 00 ●	GREATEST HITS I II & III – THE PLATINUM COLLECTION *Parlophone 5298832*	2	99+
21 Jun 03	LIVE AT WEMBLEY '86 (re-issue) *Parlophone 5904402*	38	2
6 Nov 04	QUEEN ON FIRE – LIVE AT THE BOWL *Parlophone 8632112*	20	4

[1] Queen and David Bowie [2] George Michael and Queen with Lisa Stansfield [3] Queen with Wyclef Jean featuring Pras and Free [4] Five and Queen [5] Queen & Vanguard

Tracks on Queen's First EP: Good Old Fashioned Lover Boy / Death on Two Legs (Dedicated to ...) / Tenement Funster / White Queen (As it Began). Tracks on Five Live (EP): Somebody to Love / These Are the Days of Our Lives / Calling You / Papa Was a Rolling Stone – Killer (medley). Queen appear only on the first two tracks. The first credits George Michael and Queen and the second Queen and George Michael with Lisa Stansfield 'The Works' changed label number to EMI WORK 1 during its chart run. 'Greatest Hits III' is credited to Queen+ and features solo tracks and collaborations as well as the hits of Queen

QUEEN LATIFAH
US, female rapper – Dana Owens (Singles: 17 Weeks)   pos/wks

24 Mar 90	**MAMA GAVE BIRTH TO THE SOUL CHILDREN** *Gee Street GEE 26* [1]	...14 7
26 May 90	**FIND A WAY** *Ahead of Our Time CCUT 8* [2]	.52 2
31 Aug 91	**FLY GIRL** *Gee Street GEE 34*	.67 1
26 Jun 93	**WHAT'CHA GONNA DO** *Epic 6593072* [3]	.21 4
26 Mar 94	**U.N.I.T.Y.** *Motown TMGCD 1422*	.74 1
12 Apr 97	**MR BIG STUFF** *Motown 5736572* [4]	.31 2

[1] Queen Latifah + De La Soul [2] Coldcut featuring Queen Latifah [3] Shabba Ranks featuring Queen Latifah [4] Queen Latifah, Shades and Free

QUEEN PEN
US, female rapper – Lynise Walters (Singles: 10 Weeks)   pos/wks

7 Mar 98	**MAN BEHIND THE MUSIC** *Interscope IND 95562*	.38 2
9 May 98	**ALL MY LOVE** *Interscope IND 95584* [1]	.11 5
5 Sep 98	**IT'S TRUE** *Interscope IND 95597*	.24 3

[1] Queen Pen featuring Eric Williams

QUEENS OF THE STONE AGE *US, male vocal / instrumental group (Singles: 14 Weeks, Albums: 25 Weeks)*   pos/wks

26 Aug 00	**THE LOST ART OF KEEPING A SECRET** *Interscope 4973912*	..31 2
16 Nov 02	**NO ONE KNOWS** *Interscope / Polydor 4978122*	.15 7
19 Apr 03	**GO WITH THE FLOW** *Interscope / Polydor 4978702*	.21 3
30 Aug 03	**FIRST IT GIVETH** *Interscope / Polydor 9810505*	.33 2
2 Sep 00	● **R** *Interscope 4906832*	.54 3
7 Sep 02	● **SONGS FOR THE DEAF** *Interscope / Polydor 4934440*	...4 22

QUEENSRŸCHE *US, male vocal / instrumental group (Singles: 21 Weeks, Albums: 12 Weeks)*   pos/wks

13 May 89	**EYES OF A STRANGER** *EMI USA MT 65*	.59 1
10 Nov 90	**EMPIRE** *EMI USA MT 90*	.61 1
20 Apr 91	**SILENT LUCIDITY** *EMI USA MT 94*	.34 5
6 Jul 91	**BEST I CAN** *EMI USA MT 97*	.36 3
7 Sep 91	**JET CITY WOMAN** *EMI USA MT 98*	.39 2
8 Aug 92	**SILENT LUCIDITY (re-issue)** *EMI USA MT 104*	.18 4
28 Jan 95	**I AM I** *EMI CDMT 109*	.40 2
25 Mar 95	**BRIDGE** *EMI CDMT 111*	.40 3
29 Sep 84	**THE WARNING** *EMI America EJ 2402201*	.100 1
26 Jul 86	**RAGE FOR ORDER** *EMI America AML 3105*	.66 1
4 Jun 88	**OPERATION MINDCRIME** *Manhattan MTL 1023*	.58 3
22 Sep 90	**EMPIRE** *EMI-USA MTL 1058*	.13 3
22 Oct 94	**PROMISED LAND** *EMI CDMTL 1081*	.13 3
29 Mar 97	**HEAR IN THE NOW FRONTIER** *EMI CDEMC 3764*	.46 1

QUENCH
Australia, male instrumental / production duo (Singles: 1 Week)   pos/wks

17 Feb 96	**DREAMS** *Infectious INFECT 3CD*	.75 1

QUENTIN and ASH *UK, female actor / vocal duo –*
Caroline Quentin and Leslie Ash (Singles: 3 Weeks)   pos/wks

6 Jul 96	**TELL HIM** *East West EW 049CD*	.25 3

? (QUESTION MARK) and the MYSTERIANS
US, male vocal / instrumental group (Singles: 4 Weeks)   pos/wks

17 Nov 66	**96 TEARS** *Cameo Parkway C 428* ▲	.37 4

The QUESTIONS
UK, male vocal / instrumental group (Singles: 8 Weeks)   pos/wks

23 Apr 83	**PRICE YOU PAY** *Respond KOB 702*	.56 3
17 Sep 83	**TEAR SOUP** *Respond KOB 705*	.66 1
10 Mar 84	**TUESDAY SUNSHINE** *Respond KOB 707*	.46 4

QUICK *UK, male vocal / instrumental group (Singles: 7 Weeks)*   pos/wks

15 May 82	**RHYTHM OF THE JUNGLE** *Epic EPC A 2013*	.41 7

Tommy QUICKLY and the REMO FOUR *UK, male*
vocalist and male vocal / instrumental group (Singles: 8 Weeks)   pos/wks

22 Oct 64	**WILD SIDE OF LIFE** *Pye 7N 15708*	.33 8

The QUIET FIVE
UK, male vocal / instrumental group (Singles: 3 Weeks)   pos/wks

13 May 65	**WHEN THE MORNING SUN DRIES THE DEW** *Parlophone R 5273*	.45 1
21 Apr 66	**HOMEWARD BOUND** *Parlophone R 5421*	.44 2

QUIET RIOT *US, male vocal / instrumental*
group (Singles: 5 Weeks, Albums: 1 Week)   pos/wks

3 Dec 83	**METAL HEALTH / CUM ON FEEL THE NOIZE** *Epic A 3968*	......45 5
4 Aug 84	**CONDITION CRITICAL** *Epic EPC 26075*	.71 1

'Cum on Feel the Noize' credited only from 10 Dec 1983

Eimear QUINN *Ireland, female vocalist (Singles: 2 Weeks)*   pos/wks

15 Jun 96	**THE VOICE** *Polydor 5768842*	.40 2

Paul QUINN and EDWYN COLLINS
UK, male vocalists / instrumentalists (Singles: 2 Weeks)   pos/wks

11 Aug 84	**PALE BLUE EYES** *Swamplands SWP 1*	.72 2

Sinead QUINN
UK, female vocalist (Singles: 15 Weeks, Albums: 2 Weeks)   pos/wks

22 Mar 03	● **I CAN'T BREAK DOWN** *Mercury 0637282*	.2 12
12 Jul 03	**WHAT YOU NEED IS ... (re)** *Fontana 980971*	.19 3
26 Jul 03	**READY TO RUN** *Fontana 9865367*	.48 2

QUINTESSENCE
UK / Australia, male vocal / instrumental group (Albums: 6 Weeks)   pos/wks

27 Jun 70	**QUINTESSENCE** *Island ILPS 9128*	.22 4
3 Apr 71	**DIVE DEEP** *Island ILPS 9143*	.43 1
27 May 72	**SELF** *RCA Victor SF 8273*	.50 1

The QUIREBOYS *UK, male vocal / instrumental*
group (Singles: 27 Weeks, Albums: 17 Weeks)   pos/wks

4 Nov 89	**7 O'CLOCK** *Parlophone R 6230*	.36 4
6 Jan 90	**HEY YOU** *Parlophone R 6241*	.14 7
7 Apr 90	**I DON'T LOVE YOU ANYMORE** *Parlophone R 6248*	.24 6
8 Sep 90	**THERE SHE GOES AGAIN / MISLED** *Parlophone R 6267*	.37 4
10 Oct 92	**TRAMPS AND THIEVES** *Parlophone RS 6323*	.41 3
20 Feb 93	**BROTHER LOUIE** *Parlophone CDR 6335*	.31 3
10 Feb 90	● **A BIT OF WHAT YOU FANCY** *Parlophone PCS 7335*	.2 15
27 Mar 93	**BITTER SWEET AND TWISTED** *Parlophone CDPCSD 120*	.31 2

QUIVER *See The SUTHERLAND BROTHERS and QUIVER*

QUIVVER
UK, male instrumental / production duo (Singles: 3 Weeks)   pos/wks

5 Mar 94	**SAXY LADY** *A&M 5805152*	.56 2
18 Nov 95	**BELIEVE IN ME** *Perfecto PERF 111CD*	.56 1

QUO VADIS
UK, male production trio (Singles: 1 Week)   pos/wks

16 Dec 00	**SONIC BOOM (LIFE'S TOO SHORT)** *Serious SERR 028CD*	.49 1

QWILO *See FELIX DA HOUSECAT*

R.A.F. (see also CRW)
Italy, male producer – Mauro Picotto (Singles: 6 Weeks)   pos/wks

14 Mar 92	**WE'VE GOT TO LIVE TOGETHER** *PWL Continental PWL 218*	....34 3
5 Mar 94	**TAKE ME HIGHER** *Media MRLCD 0012*	.71 1

| 23 Mar 96 | TAKE ME HIGHER (re-mix) *Media MCSTD 40026* ....**59** | 1 |
| 27 Jul 96 | ANGEL'S SYMPHONY *Media MCSTD 40051* ....**73** | 1 |

R.E.M. `32` Top 500

"America's Best Rock Band", according to Rolling Stone: Michael Stipe (v), Peter Buck (g), Mike Mills (b), Bill Berry (d). This Georgia group went from the US college circuit to packing stadiums worldwide. In 1996, the award-winning, platinum-album-earning quartet signed an $80 million record deal (Singles: 180 Weeks, Albums: 581 Weeks) pos/wks

28 Nov 87	THE ONE I LOVE *IRS IRM 46* **51**	8
30 Apr 88	FINEST WORKSONG *IRS IRM 161* **50**	2
4 Feb 89	STAND *Warner Bros. W 7577* **51**	3
3 Jun 89	ORANGE CRUSH *Warner Bros. W 2960* **28**	5
12 Aug 89	STAND (re-issue) *Warner Bros. W 2833* **48**	2
9 Mar 91	LOSING MY RELIGION *Warner Bros. W 0015* **19**	9
18 May 91	● SHINY HAPPY PEOPLE *Warner Bros. W 0027* **6**	11
17 Aug 91	NEAR WILD HEAVEN *Warner Bros. W 0055* **27**	4
21 Sep 91	THE ONE I LOVE (re-issue) *IRS IRM 178* **16**	6
16 Nov 91	RADIO SONG *Warner Bros. W 0072* **28**	3
14 Dec 91	IT'S THE END OF THE WORLD AS WE KNOW IT *IRS IRM 180* ..**39**	4
3 Oct 92	DRIVE *Warner Bros. W 0136* **11**	9
28 Nov 92	MAN ON THE MOON *Warner Bros. W 0143* **18**	8
20 Feb 93	THE SIDEWINDER SLEEPS TONITE *Warner Bros. W 0152CD1* **17**	6
17 Apr 93	● EVERYBODY HURTS *Warner Bros. W 0169CD1* **7**	12
24 Jul 93	NIGHTSWIMMING *Warner Bros. W 0184CD* **27**	4
11 Dec 93	FIND THE RIVER *Warner Bros. W 0211CD* **54**	1
17 Sep 94	● WHAT'S THE FREQUENCY, KENNETH *Warner Bros. W 0265CD* ..**9**	7
12 Nov 94	BANG AND BLAME *Warner Bros. W 0275CD* **15**	4
4 Feb 95	CRUSH WITH EYELINER *Warner Bros. W 0281CD* **23**	3
15 Apr 95	● STRANGE CURRENCIES *Warner Bros. W 0290CD* **9**	4
29 Jul 95	TONGUE *Warner Bros. W 0308CD* **13**	5
31 Aug 96	● E-BOW THE LETTER *Warner Bros. W 0369CD* **4**	5
2 Nov 96	BITTERSWEET ME *Warner Bros. W 0377CD* **19**	2
14 Dec 96	ELECTROLITE *Warner Bros. W 0383CD* **29**	2
24 Oct 98	● DAYSLEEPER *Warner Bros. W 0455CD* **6**	6
19 Dec 98	LOTUS *Warner Bros. W 466CD* **26**	5
20 Mar 99	● AT MY MOST BEAUTIFUL *Warner Bros. W 477CD* **10**	4
5 Feb 00	● THE GREAT BEYOND *Warner Bros. W 516CD* **3**	10
12 May 01	● IMITATION OF LIFE *Warner Bros. W 559CD* **6**	9
4 Aug 01	ALL THE WAY TO RENO *Warner Bros. W 568CD* **24**	3
1 Dec 01	I'LL TAKE THE RAIN *Warner Bros. W 573CD* **44**	1
25 Oct 03	● BAD DAY *Warner Bros. W 624CD1* **8**	7
17 Jan 04	ANIMAL *Warner Bros. W 633CD* **33**	2
9 Oct 04	● LEAVING NEW YORK *Warner Bros. W 654CD1* **5**	5
11 Dec 04	AFTERMATH *Warner Bros. W 658CD* **41**	2
28 Apr 84	RECKONING *IRS A 7045* **91**	2
29 Jun 85	FABLES OF THE RECONSTRUCTION *IRS MIRF 1003* **35**	4
6 Sep 86	LIFE'S RICH PAGEANT *IRS MIRG 1014* **43**	4
16 May 87	DEAD LETTER OFFICE *IRS SP 70054* **60**	2
26 Sep 87	DOCUMENT *IRS MIRG 1025* **28**	5
29 Oct 88	EPONYMOUS *IRS MIRG 1038* **69**	3
19 Nov 88	GREEN *Warner Bros. WX 234* **27**	22
23 Mar 91	★ OUT OF TIME *Warner Bros. WX 404* ■ ▲ **1**	183
12 Oct 91	● THE BEST OF R.E.M. *IRS MIRH 1* **7**	28
10 Oct 92	★ AUTOMATIC FOR THE PEOPLE *Warner Bros. 9362450552* ■ ...**1**	179
8 Oct 94	★ MONSTER *Warner Bros. 9362457632* ■ ▲ **1**	56
21 Sep 96	★ NEW ADVENTURES IN HI-FI *Warner Bros. 9362463202* ■ **1**	20
7 Nov 98	● UP *Warner Bros. 9362471122* **2**	9
26 May 01	★ REVEAL *Warner Bros. 9362479462* ■ **1**	15
8 Nov 03	★ THE BEST OF R.E.M. – IN TIME – 1988–2003 *Warner Bros. 9362483812* ■ **1**	21
8 Nov 03	THE BEST OF R.E.M. – IN TIME – 1988–2003 – LTD *Warner Bros. 9362486022* **36**	1
16 Oct 04	★ AROUND THE SUN *Warner Bros. 9362489112* ■ **1**	7+

REO SPEEDWAGON *US, male vocal / instrumental group (Singles: 38 Weeks, Albums: 36 Weeks)* pos/wks

11 Apr 81	● KEEP ON LOVING YOU *Epic EPC 9544* ▲ **7**	14
27 Jun 81	TAKE IT ON THE RUN *Epic EPC A 1207* **19**	14
16 Mar 85	CAN'T FIGHT THIS FEELING *Epic A 4880* ▲ **16**	10
25 Apr 81	● HI INFIDELITY *Epic EPC 84700* ▲ **6**	29
17 Jul 82	GOOD TROUBLE *Epic EPC 85789* **29**	7

R.H.C. (see also HYPNOTIST) *UK / US, male / female vocal / instrumental / production trio (Singles: 1 Week)* pos/wks

| 11 Jan 92 | FEVER CALLED LOVE *R&S RSUK 9* ....**65** | 1 |

RIP PRODUCTIONS
(see also CARNIVAL featuring RIP vs RED RAT; DOUBLE 99)
UK, male production duo (Singles: 1 Week) pos/wks

| 29 Nov 97 | THE CHANT (WE R) / RIP PRODUCTIONS *Satellite 74321534022* ....**58** | 1 |

RM PROJECT *UK, production group (Singles: 1 Week)* pos/wks

| 3 Jul 99 | GET IT UP *Inferno CDFERN 15* ....**49** | 1 |

RMXCRW featuring EBON-E plus AMBUSH
Holland, male production group (Singles: 2 Weeks) pos/wks

| 17 Jan 04 | TURN ME ON *Digi Dance 871486697203* ....**52** | 2 |

RTE CONCERT ORCHESTRA See Bill WHELAN

Eddie RABBITT
US, male vocalist, b. 27 Nov 1941, d. 7 May 1998 (Singles: 14 Weeks) pos/wks

| 27 Jan 79 | EVERY WHICH WAY BUT LOOSE *Elektra K 12331* ....**41** | 9 |
| 28 Feb 81 | I LOVE A RAINY NIGHT *Elektra K 12498* ▲ ....**53** | 5 |

Harry RABINOWITZ See ROYAL PHILHARMONIC ORCHESTRA

Steve RACE *UK, male instrumentalist – piano (Singles: 9 Weeks)* pos/wks

| 28 Feb 63 | PIED PIPER (THE BEEJE) *Parlophone R 4981* ....**29** | 9 |

RACEY *UK, male vocal / instrumental group (Singles: 44 Weeks)* pos/wks

25 Nov 78	● LAY YOUR LOVE ON ME *RAK 284* **3**	14
31 Mar 79	● SOME GIRLS *RAK 291* **2**	11
18 Aug 79	BOY OH BOY *RAK 297* **22**	9
20 Dec 80	RUNAROUND SUE *RAK 325* **13**	10

The RACING CARS *UK, male vocal / instrumental group (Singles: 7 Weeks, Albums: 6 Weeks)* pos/wks

| 12 Feb 77 | THEY SHOOT HORSES DON'T THEY? *Chrysalis CHS 2129* .....**14** | 7 |
| 19 Feb 77 | DOWNTOWN TONIGHT *Chrysalis CHR 1099* ....**39** | 6 |

RACKETEERS See Elbow BONES and the RACKETEERS

Jimmy RADCLIFFE
US, male vocalist, b. 18 Nov 1936, d. 27 Jul 1973 (Singles: 2 Weeks) pos/wks

| 4 Feb 65 | LONG AFTER TONIGHT IS ALL OVER *Stateside SS 374* ....**40** | 2 |

RADHA KRISHNA TEMPLE
UK, male / female vocal / instrumental group (Singles: 17 Weeks) pos/wks

| 13 Sep 69 | HARE KRISHNA MANTRA *Apple 15* ....**12** | 9 |
| 28 Mar 70 | GOVINDA *Apple 25* ....**23** | 8 |

RADICAL ROB
UK, male producer – Rob McLuan (Singles: 1 Week) pos/wks

| 11 Jan 92 | MONKEY WAH *R&S RSUK 8* ....**67** | 1 |

Jack RADICS See Chaka DEMUS and PLIERS; SUPERCAT

RADIO 4
US, male vocal / instrumental group (Singles: 2 Weeks) pos/wks

| 24 Jul 04 | PARTY CRASHERS *City Slang 5494920* ....**75** | 1 |
| 18 Sep 04 | ABSOLUTE AFFIRMATION *Labels 5498030* ....**61** | 1 |

RADIO HEART featuring Gary NUMAN *UK, male instrumental group and male vocalist / instrumentalist (Singles: 8 Weeks)* pos/wks

| 28 Mar 87 | RADIO HEART *GFM GFM 109* ....**35** | 6 |
| 13 Jun 87 | LONDON TIMES *GFM GFM 112* ....**48** | 2 |

RADIO 1 DJ POSSE See Liz KERSHAW and Bruno BROOKES

RADIO REVELLERS See Anthony STEEL and the RADIO REVELLERS

The RADIO STARS
UK, male vocal / instrumental group (Singles: 3 Weeks) pos/wks

| 4 Feb 78 | NERVOUS WRECK *Chiswick NS 23* ....**39** | 3 |

RADIOHEAD (105) Top 500

Innovative boundary-bending group is a regular Top 10 album fixture around the globe. This Grammy-winning band, formed in Oxford in 1991, is fronted by Thom Yorke (g/v/k) and is the only contemporary UK act to top US chart in the 21st century (Singles: 63 Weeks, Albums: 361 Weeks) pos/wks

13 Feb 93		ANYONE CAN PLAY GUITAR *Parlophone CDR 6333*	32	2
22 May 93		POP IS DEAD *Parlophone CDR 6345*	42	2
18 Sep 93	●	CREEP *Parlophone CDR 6359*	7	6
8 Oct 94		MY IRON LUNG *Parlophone CDR 6394*	24	2
11 Mar 95		HIGH AND DRY / PLANET TELEX *Parlophone CDR 6405*	17	4
27 May 95		FAKE PLASTIC TREES *Parlophone CDR 6411*	20	4
2 Sep 95		JUST *Parlophone CDR 6415*	19	3
3 Feb 96	●	STREET SPIRIT (FADE OUT) *Parlophone CDR 6419*	5	4
7 Jun 97	●	PARANOID ANDROID *Parlophone CDODATAS 01*	3	5
6 Sep 97	●	KARMA POLICE *Parlophone CDODATAS 03*	8	4
24 Jan 98	●	NO SURPRISES (re) *Parlophone CDODATAS 04*	4	7
2 Jun 01	●	PYRAMID SONG *Parlophone CDSFHEIT 45102*	5	5
18 Aug 01		KNIVES OUT *Parlophone CDFHEIT 45103*	13	4
7 Jun 03	●	THERE THERE *Parlophone CDR 6608*	4	4
30 Aug 03		GO TO SLEEP *Parlophone CDR 6613*	12	4
29 Nov 03		2 + 2 = 5 *Parlophone CDR 6623*	15	3
6 Mar 93		PABLO HONEY *Parlophone CDPCS 7360*	22	82
25 Mar 95	●	THE BENDS *Parlophone CDPCS 7372*	4	160
28 Jun 97	★	OK COMPUTER *Parlophone CDNODATA 02* ■	1	75
14 Oct 00	★	KID A *Parlophone CDKIDA 1* ■ ▲	1	15
16 Jun 01	★	AMNESIAC *Parlophone CDFHEIT 45101* ■	1	12
24 Nov 01		I MIGHT BE WRONG – LIVE RECORDINGS *Parlophone CDFHEIT 45104*	23	2
21 Jun 03	★	HAIL TO THE THIEF *Palophone 5848082* ■	1	14
22 May 04		COM LAG – 2 + 2 = 5 *Parlophone TOCP 66280*	37	1

RADISH *US, male vocal / instrumental group (Singles: 3 Weeks)* pos/wks

30 Aug 97	LITTLE PINK STARS *Mercury MERCD 494*	32	2
15 Nov 97	SIMPLE SINCERITY *Mercury MERCD 498*	50	1

Fonda RAE *US, female vocalist (Singles: 4 Weeks)* pos/wks

6 Oct 84	TUCH ME *Streetwave KHAN 28*	49	4

Jesse RAE *UK, male vocalist (Singles: 2 Weeks)* pos/wks

11 May 85	OVER THE SEA *Scotland-Video YZ 36*	65	2

Marcia RAE *See QUAKE featuring Marcia RAE*

RAE & CHRISTIAN *UK, male production duo and UK, female vocalist (Singles: 1 Week, Albums: 1 Week)* pos/wks

6 Mar 99	ALL I ASK *Grand Central GCCD 120* [1]	67	1
10 Mar 01	SLEEPWALKING *K7 K 7096CD*	57	1

[1] Rae and Christian featuring Veba

Gerry RAFFERTY (493) Top 500

Mellow, folk-rocker and former Humblebum (with Billy Connolly) and Stealers Wheel vocalist / guitarist. b. 16 Apr 1947, Paisley, Scotland. Won an Ivor Novello award for the classic 'Baker Street' (composed in that street), which has been heard on US radio more than four million times (Singles: 47 Weeks, Albums: 99 Weeks) pos/wks

18 Feb 78	●	BAKER STREET *United Artists UP 36346*	3	15
26 May 79	●	NIGHT OWL *United Artists UP 36512*	5	13
18 Aug 79		GET IT RIGHT NEXT TIME *United Artists BP 301*	30	9
22 Mar 80		BRING IT ALL HOME *United Artists BP 340*	54	4
21 Jun 80		ROYAL MILE *United Artists BP 354*	67	2
10 Mar 90		BAKER STREET (re-mix) *EMI EM 132*	53	4
25 Feb 78	●	CITY TO CITY *United Artists UAS 30104* ▲	6	37
2 Jun 79	●	NIGHT OWL *United Artists UAK 30238*	9	24
26 Apr 80		SNAKES AND LADDERS *United Artists UAK 30298*	15	9
25 Sep 82		SLEEPWALKING *Liberty LBG 30352*	39	4
21 May 88		NORTH AND SOUTH *London LONLP 55*	43	4
13 Feb 93		ON A WING & A PRAYER *A&M 5174952*	73	1
28 Oct 95		ONE MORE DREAM – THE VERY BEST OF GERRY RAFFERTY *PolyGram TV 5292792*	17	20

RAGE *UK, male vocal / instrumental group (Singles: 15 Weeks)* pos/wks

31 Oct 92	●	RUN TO YOU *Pulse 8 LOSE 33*	3	11
27 Feb 93		WHY DON'T YOU *Pulse 8 CDLOSE 39*	44	2
15 May 93		HOUSE OF THE RISING SUN *Pulse 8 CDLOSE 43*	41	2

RAGE AGAINST THE MACHINE *US, male vocal / instrumental group (Singles: 19 Weeks, Albums: 53 Weeks)* pos/wks

27 Feb 93		KILLING IN THE NAME *Epic 6584922*	25	4
8 May 93		BULLET IN THE HEAD *Epic 6592582*	16	4
4 Sep 93		BOMBTRACK *Epic 6594712*	37	2
13 Apr 96	●	BULLS ON PARADE *Epic 6631522*	8	3
7 Sep 96		PEOPLE OF THE SUN *Epic 6636282*	26	2
6 Nov 99		GUERRILLA RADIO *Epic 6683142*	32	2
15 Apr 00		SLEEP NOW IN THE FIRE *Epic 6691362*	43	2
13 Feb 93		RAGE AGAINST THE MACHINE *Epic 4722242*	17	43
27 Apr 96	●	EVIL EMPIRE *Epic 4810262* ▲	4	7
13 Nov 99		THE BATTLE OF LOS ANGELES *Epic 4919932* ▲	23	2
9 Dec 00		RENEGADES *Epic 4999210*	71	1

RAGGA TWINS *UK, male vocal duo – Flinty Badman and Deman Rocker (Singles: 10 Weeks, Albums: 5 Weeks)* pos/wks

10 Nov 90		ILLEGAL GUNSHOT / SPLIFFHEAD *Shut Up and Dance SUAD 7*	51	2
6 Apr 91		WIPE THE NEEDLE / JUGGLING *Shut Up and Dance SUAD 12S*	71	2
6 Jul 91		HOOLIGAN 69 *Shut Up and Dance SUAD 16S*	56	2
7 Mar 92		MIXED TRUTH / BRING UP THE MIC SOME MORE *Shut Up and Dance SUAD 27S*	65	2
11 Jul 92		SHINE EYE *Shut Up and Dance SUAD 32S* [1]	63	2
1 Jun 91		REGGAE OWES ME MONEY *Shut Up and Dance SUADLP 2*	26	5

[1] Ragga Twins featuring Junior Reid

RAGHAV *Canada, male vocalist – Raghav Mathur (Singles: 18 Weeks, Albums: 2 Weeks)* pos/wks

28 Feb 04	●	CAN'T GET ENOUGH *A&R ANR 1CDS*	10	8
22 May 04	●	IT CAN'T BE RIGHT *2PSL / Inferno 2PSLCD 04* [1]	8	7
4 Sep 04		LET'S WORK IT OUT *V2 ARV 5028628* [2]	15	3
18 Sep 04		STORYTELLER *V2 ARV 1028642*	36	2

[1] 2Play featuring Raghav & Naila Boss [2] Raghav featuring Jahaziel

RAGING SPEEDHORN *UK, male vocal / instrumental group (Singles: 2 Weeks, Albums: 1 Week)* pos/wks

16 Jun 01		THE GUSH *ZTT GIR 004CD*	47	1
6 Jul 02		THE HATE SONG *ZTT RSH 001CD*	69	1
17 Aug 02		WE WILL BE DEAD TOMORROW *ZTT RSH 002CD*	63	1

The RAGTIMERS *UK, male instrumental group (Singles: 8 Weeks)* pos/wks

16 Mar 74	THE STING (re) *Pye 7N 45323*	31	8

The RAH BAND (see also KEY WEST)

UK, male / female vocal / instrumental group – leaders Richard A and Liz Hewson (Singles: 50 Weeks, Albums: 6 Weeks) pos/wks

9 Jul 77	●	THE CRUNCH *Good Earth GD 7*	6	12
1 Nov 80		FALCON *DJM DJS 10954*	35	7
7 Feb 81		SLIDE *DJM DJS 10964*	50	7
1 May 82		PERFUMED GARDEN *KR KR 5*	45	7
9 Jul 83		MESSAGES FROM THE STARS *TMT TMT 5*	42	7
19 Jan 85		ARE YOU SATISFIED? (FUNKA NOVA) *RCA RCA 470*	70	1
30 Mar 85	●	CLOUDS ACROSS THE MOON *RCA PB 40025*	6	10
6 Apr 85		MYSTERY *RCA PL 70640*	60	6

RAHZEL *See Roni SIZE / REPRAZENT*

The RAILWAY CHILDREN *UK, male vocal / instrumental group (Singles: 13 Weeks, Albums: 3 Weeks)* pos/wks

24 Mar 90	EVERY BEAT OF THE HEART (re) *Virgin VS 1237*	24	8
2 Jun 90	MUSIC STOP *Virgin VS 1255*	66	1
20 Oct 90	SO RIGHT *Virgin VS 1289*	68	1
20 Apr 91	SOMETHING SO GOOD *Virgin VS 1318*	57	2
21 May 88	RECURRENCE *Virgin V 2525*	96	1
16 Mar 91	NATIVE PLACE *Virgin V 2627*	59	2

'Every Beat of the Heart' debuted on the chart at No.68 before making its peak position after re-entry in Feb 1991

RAIN *See Stephanie DE SYKES*

The RAIN BAND

UK, male vocal / instrumental group (Singles: 2 Weeks) pos/wks

1 Mar 03	EASY RIDER *Temptation TEMPCD 003*	63	1
19 Jul 03	KNEE DEEP AND DOWN *Temptation TEMPTCD 007*	56	1

RAIN PARADE
US, male vocal / instrumental group (Albums: 1 Week)   pos/wks

29 Jun 85	BEYOND THE SUNSET *Island IMA 17*	78	1

RAIN TREE CROW (see also JAPAN) *UK, male vocal / instrumental group (Singles: 1 Week, Albums: 3 Weeks)*   pos/wks

30 Mar 91	BLACKWATER *Virgin VS 1340*	62	1
20 Apr 91	RAIN TREE CROW *Virgin V 2659*	24	3

Group is Japan under an assumed name

RAINBOW   `294`   `Top 500`
Melodic Anglo-American hard rock band with ever changing personnel, formed UK, 1975, by ex-Deep Purple guitarist Ritchie Blackmore. Original vocalist Ronnie James Dio replaced by Graham Bonnet (1979), then Joe Lynn Turner (1980). After band split in 1984, Blackmore rejoined Deep Purple (Singles: 62 Weeks, Albums: 163 Weeks)   pos/wks

17 Sep 77	KILL THE KING *Polydor 2066 845*	44	3
8 Apr 78	LONG LIVE ROCK 'N' ROLL *Polydor 2066 913*	33	3
30 Sep 78	L.A. CONNECTION *Polydor 2066 968*	40	4
15 Sep 79	● SINCE YOU'VE BEEN GONE *Polydor POSP 70*	6	10
16 Feb 80	● ALL NIGHT LONG *Polydor POSP 104*	5	11
31 Jan 81	● I SURRENDER *Polydor POSP 221*	3	10
20 Jun 81	CAN'T HAPPEN HERE *Polydor POSP 251*	20	8
11 Jul 81	KILL THE KING (re-issue) *Polydor POSP 274*	41	4
3 Apr 82	STONE COLD *Polydor POSP 421*	34	4
27 Aug 83	STREET OF DREAMS *Polydor POSP 631*	52	4
5 Nov 83	CAN'T LET YOU GO *Polydor POSP 654*	43	2
13 Sep 75	RITCHIE BLACKMORE'S RAINBOW *Oyster OYA 2001* `1`	11	6
5 Jun 76	RAINBOW RISING *Polydor 2490 137* `1`	11	33
30 Jul 77	● ON STAGE *Polydor 2657 016*	7	10
6 May 78	● LONG LIVE ROCK 'N' ROLL *Polydor POLD 5002*	7	12
18 Aug 79	● DOWN TO EARTH *Polydor POLD 5023*	6	37
21 Feb 81	● DIFFICULT TO CURE *Polydor POLD 5036*	3	22
8 Aug 81	RITCHIE BLACKMORE'S RAINBOW (re-issue) *Polydor 2940141* `1`	91	2
21 Nov 81	THE BEST OF RAINBOW *Polydor POLDV 2*	14	17
24 Apr 82	● STRAIGHT BETWEEN THE EYES *Polydor POLD 5056*	5	14
17 Sep 83	BENT OUT OF SHAPE *Polydor POLD 5116*	11	6
8 Mar 86	FINYL VINYL *Polydor PODV 8*	31	4

`1` Ritchie Blackmore's Rainbow

RAINBOW *UK, male puppet rappers – DJ George and MC Zippy (Roy Skelton) (Singles: 6 Weeks)*   pos/wks

14 Dec 02	IT'S A RAINBOW *BBC Music ZIPPCD 1*	15	6

RAINBOW COTTAGE
UK, male vocal / instrumental group (Singles: 4 Weeks)   pos/wks

6 Mar 76	SEAGULL *Penny Farthing PEN 906*	33	4

RAINDANCE (see also BLOWING FREE; HARMONIUM; HYPNOSIS; IN TUNE; JAMES BOYS; SCHOOL OF EXCELLENCE) *UK, male production / instrumental duo – Stewart and Bradley Palmer (Albums: 7 Weeks)*   pos/wks

27 Apr 96	RAINDANCE *PolyGram TV 5298622*	15	7

RAINMAKERS
US, male vocal / instrumental group (Singles: 11 Weeks)   pos/wks

7 Mar 87	LET MY PEOPLE GO-GO *Mercury MER 238*	18	11

Marvin RAINWATER
US, male vocalist – Marvin Percy (Singles: 22 Weeks)   pos/wks

7 Mar 58	★ WHOLE LOTTA WOMAN *MGM 974*	1	15
6 Jun 58	I DIG YOU BABY *MGM 980*	19	7

RAISSA *UK, female vocalist – Raissa Khan-Panni (Singles: 1 Week)*   pos/wks

12 Feb 00	HOW LONG DO I GET *Polydor 5616282*	47	1

Bonnie RAITT *US, female vocalist / instrumentalist – guitar (Singles: 9 Weeks, Albums: 17 Weeks)*   pos/wks

14 Dec 91	I CAN'T MAKE YOU LOVE ME *Capitol CL 639*	50	4
9 Apr 94	LOVE SNEAKIN' UP ON YOU *Capitol CDCL 713*	69	1
18 Jun 94	YOU *Capitol CDCLS 718*	31	2
11 Nov 95	ROCK STEADY *Capitol CDCL 763* `1`	50	2
28 Apr 90	NICK OF TIME *Capitol EST 2095* ▲	51	5
6 Jul 91	LUCK OF THE DRAW *Capitol EST 2145*	38	3
16 Apr 94	LONGING IN THEIR HEARTS *Capitol CDEST 2227* ▲	26	5
25 Nov 95	ROAD TESTED *Capitol CDEST 2274*	69	1
18 Apr 98	FUNDAMENTAL *Capitol 8563972*	52	1
24 May 03	BEST OF *Capitol 5821132*	37	2

`1` Bonnie Raitt and Bryan Adams

Dionne RAKEEM *UK, female vocalist (Singles: 2 Weeks)*   pos/wks

4 Aug 01	SWEETER THAN WINE *Virgin VSCDT 1809*	46	2

The RAKES *UK, male vocal / instrumental group (Singles: 1 Week)*   pos/wks

9 Oct 04	STRASBOURG *City Rockers ROCKERS 28CD*	57	1

RAKIM (see also Eric B and RAKIM) *US, male rapper – William Griffin (Singles: 17 Weeks, Albums: 1 Week)*   pos/wks

27 Dec 97	GUESS WHO'S BACK *Universal UND 56151*	32	3
22 Aug 98	STAY A WHILE *Universal UND 56203*	53	1
3 Oct 98	BUFFALO GIRLS STAMPEDE (re-mix) *Virgin VSCDT 1717* `1`	65	1
31 Aug 02	● ADDICTIVE *Aftermath / Interscope 4977782* `2`	3	12
22 Nov 97	18TH LETTER *Universal U 253113*	72	1

`1` Malcolm McLaren and the World's Famous Supreme Team plus Rakim and Roger Sanchez `2` Truth Hurts featuring Rakim

Tony RALLO and the MIDNITE BAND
France / US, male vocal / instrumental group (Singles: 8 Weeks)   pos/wks

23 Feb 80	HOLDIN' ON *Calibre CAB 150*	34	8

Sheryl Lee RALPH *US, female vocalist (Singles: 2 Weeks)*   pos/wks

26 Jan 85	IN THE EVENING *Arista ARIST 595*	64	2

RAM JAM *US, male vocal / instrumental group (Singles: 20 Weeks)*   pos/wks

10 Sep 77	● BLACK BETTY *Epic EPC 5492*	7	12
17 Feb 90	BLACK BETTY (re-mix) *Epic 655430 7*	13	8

RAM JAM BAND See Geno WASHINGTON & The RAM JAM BAND

RAM TRILOGY *UK, male production trio (Singles: 3 Weeks)*   pos/wks

6 Jul 02	CHAPTER FOUR *Ram RAMM 39*	71	1
20 Jul 02	CHAPTER 5 *Ram RAMM 40*	62	1
3 Aug 02	CHAPTER 6 *Ram RAMM 41*	60	1

RAMBLERS See Perry COMO

The RAMBLERS (from the Abbey Hey Junior School)
UK, children's choir (Singles: 15 Weeks)   pos/wks

13 Oct 79	THE SPARROW *Decca F 13860*	11	15

Karen RAMIREZ *UK, female vocalist – Karen Ramelize (Singles: 15 Weeks, Albums: 2 Weeks)*   pos/wks

28 Mar 98	TROUBLED GIRL *Manifesto FESCD 31*	50	1
27 Jun 98	● LOOKING FOR LOVE *Manifesto FESCD 44*	8	11
21 Nov 98	IF WE TRY *Manifesto FESCD 50*	23	3
1 Aug 98	DISTANT DREAMS *Manifesto 5586742*	45	2

RAMMSTEIN *Germany, male vocal / instrumental group (Singles: 8 Weeks, Albums: 1 Week)*   pos/wks

25 May 02	ICH WILL *Motor / Universal MCSTD 40280*	30	2
23 Nov 02	FEUER FREI *Universal MCSTD 40302*	35	2
14 Aug 04	MEIN TEIL (Import) *Universal 9866978*	61	2
30 Oct 04	AMERIKA *Universal MCSTD 40394*	38	2
9 Oct 04	REISE, REISE *Universal 9868150*	37	1

The RAMONES *US, male vocal / instrumental group (Singles: 32 Weeks, Albums: 30 Weeks)*   pos/wks

21 May 77	SHEENA IS A PUNK ROCKER *Sire RAM 001*	22	7
6 Aug 77	SWALLOW MY PRIDE *Sire 6078 607*	36	6
30 Sep 78	DON'T COME CLOSE *Sire SRE 1031*	39	5
8 Sep 79	ROCK 'N' ROLL HIGH SCHOOL *Sire SIR 4021*	67	2
26 Jan 80	● BABY, I LOVE YOU *Sire SIR 4031*	8	9

19 Apr 80	DO YOU REMEMBER ROCK 'N' ROLL RADIO? *Sire SIR 4037*	..54	3
10 May 86	SOMEBODY PUT SOMETHING IN MY DRINK / SOMETHING		
	TO BELIEVE IN *Beggars Banquet BEG 157*	69	1
19 Dec 92	POISON HEART *Chrysalis CHS 3917*	69	1
23 Apr 77	LEAVE HOME *Philips 9103 254*	45	1
24 Dec 77	ROCKET TO RUSSIA *Sire 9103 255*	60	2
7 Oct 78	ROAD TO RUIN *Sire SRK 6063*	32	2
16 Jun 79	IT'S ALIVE *Sire SRK 26074*	27	8
19 Jan 80	END OF THE CENTURY *Sire SRK 6077*	14	8
26 Jan 85	TOO TOUGH TO DIE *Beggars Banquet BEGA 59*	63	3
31 May 86	ANIMAL BOY *Beggars Banquet BEGA 70*	38	2
10 Oct 87	HALFWAY TO SANITY *Beggars Banquet BEGA 89*	78	1
19 Aug 89	BRAIN DRAIN *Chrysalis CHR 1725*	75	1
8 Jul 95	!ADIOS AMIGOS! *Chrysalis CDCHR 6104*	62	1
9 Jun 01	ANTHOLOGY – HEY HO LET'S GO! *Warner Bros. 8122735572*	..74	1

RAMP (see also SLACKER) *UK, male instrumental / production*
duo – Shem McCauley and Simon Rogers (Singles: 1 Week)   pos/wks

8 Jun 96	ROCK THE DISCOTEK *Loaded LOADCD 30*	49	1

RAMPAGE *UK, male DJ / production group (Singles: 1 Week)*   pos/wks

25 Nov 95	THE MONKEES *Almo Sounds CDALMOS 017*	51	1

RAMPAGE featuring Billy LAWRENCE *US, male*
rapper – Roger McNair and US, male vocalist (Singles: 1 Week)   pos/wks

18 Oct 97	TAKE IT TO THE STREETS *Elektra E 3914CD*	58	1

The RAMRODS
US, male / female instrumental group (Singles: 12 Weeks)   pos/wks

23 Feb 61 ●	RIDERS IN THE SKY *London HLU 9282*	8	12

RAMSEY and FEN featuring Lynsey MOORE
UK, male production duo and female vocalist (Singles: 1 Week)   pos/wks

10 Jun 00	LOVE BUG *Nebula VCNEBD 4*	75	1

RANCID *US, male vocal / instrumental*
group (Singles: 3 Weeks, Albums: 7 Weeks)   pos/wks

7 Oct 95	TIME BOMB *Out of Step WOOS 8CDS*	56	1
27 Sep 03	FALL BACK DOWN *Hellcat / WEA W 618CD*	42	2
2 Sep 95	... AND OUT COME THE WOLVES *Epitaph 864442*	55	1
4 Jul 98	LIFE WON'T WAIT *Epitaph 864972*	32	2
5 Aug 00	RANCID *Hellcat 4272*	68	1
23 Mar 02	SPLIT SERIES – VOL.3 *BYO BYO 079CD* [1]	75	1
6 Sep 03	INDESTRUCTIBLE *WEA 9362485392*	29	2

[1] Rancid / NOFX

RANGE See Bruce HORNSBY and the RANGE

RANGERS FC *UK, male football team vocalists (Singles: 2 Weeks)* pos/wks

4 Oct 97	GLASGOW RANGERS (NINE IN A ROW) *Gers GERSCD 1*	54	2

RANI See DELERIUM

RANK 1 *Holland, male production duo –*
Piet Bervoets and Benno de Goeij (Singles: 5 Weeks)   pos/wks

15 Apr 00 ●	AIRWAVE *Manifesto FESCD 69*	10	5

RANKING ANN See SCRITTI POLITTI

RANKING ROGER See Pato BANTON

Shabba RANKS *Jamaica, male vocalist – Rexton Rawlston*
Fernando Gordon (Singles: 67 Weeks, Albums: 10 Weeks)   pos/wks

16 Mar 91	SHE'S A WOMAN *Virgin VS 1333* [1]	20	7
18 May 91	TRAILER LOAD A GIRLS *Epic 6568747*	63	2
24 Aug 91	HOUSECALL *Epic 6573477* [2]	31	7
8 Aug 92	MR LOVERMAN *Epic 6582517*	23	7
28 Nov 92	SLOW AND SEXY *Epic 6587727* [3]	17	7
6 Mar 93	I WAS A KING *Motown TMGCD 1414* [4]	64	1
13 Mar 93 ●	MR LOVERMAN (re-issue) *Epic 6590782*	3	11
8 May 93 ●	HOUSECALL (re-mix) *Epic 6592842* [2]	8	8
26 Jun 93	WHAT'CHA GONNA DO *Epic 6593072* [5]	21	4
25 Dec 93	FAMILY AFFAIR *Polydor PZCD 304* [6]	18	8
29 Apr 95	LET'S GET IT ON *Epic 6614122*	22	3
5 Aug 95	SHINE EYE GAL *Epic 6622332* [7]	46	2
22 Jun 91	AS RAW AS EVER *Epic 4681021*	51	2
22 Aug 92	ROUGH AND READY VOLUME 1 *Epic 4714422*	71	2
24 Apr 93	X-TRA NAKED *Epic 4723332*	38	6

[1] Scritti Politti featuring Shabba Ranks [2] Shabba Ranks featuring Maxi Priest [3] Shabba Ranks featuring Johnny Gill [4] Eddie Murphy featuring Shabba Ranks [5] Shabba Ranks featuring Queen Latifah [6] Shabba Ranks featuring Patra and Terri & Monica [7] Shabba Ranks (featuring Mykal Rose)

Bubbler RANX See Peter ANDRE

RAPINATION *Italy, male instrumental / production*
duo – Marco Sabiu and Charlie Mallozzi (Singles: 12 Weeks)   pos/wks

26 Dec 92	LOVE ME THE RIGHT WAY *Logic 74321128097* [1]	22	10
10 Jul 93	HERE'S MY A *Logic 74321153092* [2]	69	1
28 Sep 96	LOVE ME THE RIGHT WAY (re-mix) *Logic 7432140442* [1]	55	1

[1] Rapination featuring Kym Mazelle [2] Rapination featuring Carol Kenyon

RAPPIN' 4-TAY
US, male rapper – Anthony Forte (Singles: 5 Weeks)   pos/wks

24 Jun 95	I'LL BE AROUND *Cooltempo CDCOOL 306* [1]	30	4
30 Sep 95	PLAYAZ CLUB *Cooltempo CDCOOL 310*	63	1

[1] Rappin' 4-Tay featuring The Spinners

The Spinners on 'I'll Be Around' are The Detroit Spinners

The RAPTURE *US, male vocal / instrumental*
group (Singles: 4 Weeks, Albums: 2 Weeks)   pos/wks

6 Sep 03	HOUSE OF JEALOUS LOVERS *Vertigo 9810767*	27	2
13 Dec 03	SISTER SAVIOUR *DFA / Output / Vertigo 9814181*	51	1
21 Feb 04	LOVE IS ALL *DFA / Output / Vertigo 9816808*	38	1
20 Sep 03	ECHOES *DFA / Output / Vertigo 9865447*	32	2

RARE
UK, male / female vocal / instrumental group (Singles: 1 Week)   pos/wks

17 Feb 96	SOMETHING WILD *Equator AXISCD 011*	57	1

RARE BIRD
UK, male vocal / instrumental group (Singles: 8 Weeks)   pos/wks

14 Feb 70	SYMPATHY *Charisma CB 120*	27	8

O RASBURY See Rahni HARRIS and F.L.O.

RASCALS See YOUNG RASCALS

RASHAAN See US3

The RASMUS *Finland, male vocal /*
instrumental group (Singles: 23 Weeks, Albums: 23 Weeks)   pos/wks

17 Apr 04 ●	IN THE SHADOWS *Universal MCSXD 40351*	3	16
21 Aug 04	GUILTY *Universal MCSTD 40376*	15	6
13 Nov 04	FIRST DAY OF MY LIFE *Universal MCSTD 40391*	50	1
3 Apr 04 ●	DEAD LETTERS *Motor 9806934*	10	23

Roland RAT SUPERSTAR *UK, male rodent*
vocalist / rapper (Singles: 20 Weeks, Albums: 3 Weeks)   pos/wks

19 Nov 83	RAT RAPPING *Rodent RAT 1*	14	12
28 Apr 84	LOVE ME TENDER *Rodent RAT 2*	32	7
2 Mar 85	NO.1 RAT FAN *Rodent RAT 4*	72	1
15 Dec 84	THE CASSETTE OF THE ALBUM *Rodent RATL 1001*	67	3

RATPACK
UK, male instrumental / production duo (Singles: 3 Weeks)   pos/wks

6 Jun 92	SEARCHIN' FOR MY RIZLA *Big Giant BIGT 02*	58	3

The RATPACK *US, male vocalists – Sammy Davis Jr, b. 6 Dec 1925,*
d. 16 May 1990, Dean Martin, b. 7 Jun 1917, d. 25 Dec 1995, and
Frank Sinatra, b. 12 Dec 1915, d. 14 May 1998 (Albums: 1 Week)   pos/wks

27 Nov 04	BOYS NIGHT OUT *Capitol 5708902*	70	1

Singles re-entries are listed as (re), (2re), (3re).... which signifies that the hit re-entered the chart once, twice or three times...

RATT US, male vocal / instrumental group (Albums: 5 Weeks)

pos/wks

13 Jul 85	INVASION OF YOUR PRIVACY Atlantic 7812571	50	2
25 Oct 86	DANCING UNDERCOVER Atlantic 7816831	51	1
12 Nov 88	REACH FOR THE SKY Atlantic 781929	82	1
8 Sep 90	DETONATOR Atlantic 7567821271	55	1

The RATTLES
Germany, male vocal / instrumental group (Singles: 15 Weeks)   pos/wks

| 3 Oct 70 ● | THE WITCH Decca F 23058 | 8 | 15 |

Mark RATTRAY UK, male vocalist (Albums: 8 Weeks)

pos/wks

| 8 Dec 90 | SONGS OF THE MUSICALS Telstar STAR 2458 | 46 | 7 |
| 10 Oct 92 | THE MAGIC OF THE MUSICALS Quality Television QTV 013 [1] | 55 | 1 |

[1] Marti Webb and Mark Rattray

RATTY Germany, male production group (Singles: 1 Week)

pos/wks

| 24 Mar 01 | SUNRISE (HERE I AM) Neo NEOCD 051 | 51 | 1 |

RAVEN UK, male vocal / instrumental group (Albums: 3 Weeks)

pos/wks

| 17 Oct 81 | ROCK UNTIL YOU DROP Neat NEAT 1001 | 63 | 3 |

RAVEN MAIZE (see also AKABU featuring Linda CLIFFORD; HED BOYS; Li KWAN; Joey NEGRO; Z FACTOR; JAKATTA; PHASE II; IL PADRINOS featuring Jocelyn BROWN) UK, male producer – Dave Lee (Singles: 9 Weeks)   pos/wks

5 Aug 89	FOREVER TOGETHER Republic LIC 014	67	1
18 Aug 01	THE REAL LIFE (re) Rulin / MoS / Credence RULIN 18CDS	12	6
17 Aug 02	FASCINATED Ministry of Sound / Rulin RULIN 27CDS	37	2

The RAVEONETTES Denmark, male / female vocal / instrumental group (Singles: 5 Weeks, Albums: 1 Week)   pos/wks

21 Dec 02	ATTACK OF THE GHOSTRIDERS Columbia 6733892	73	1
30 Aug 03	THAT GREAT LOVE SOUND Columbia RAVEON 005	34	2
20 Dec 03	HEARTBREAK STROLL Columbia RAVEON 008	49	1
22 May 04	THAT GREAT LOVE SOUND (re-mix) Columbia RAVEON 010	52	1
6 Sep 03	CHAIN GANG OF LOVE Columbia 5123782	43	1

RAVESIGNAL III (see also CJ BOLLAND)
Belgium, male producer – Christian Bolland (Singles: 2 Weeks)   pos/wks

| 14 Dec 91 | HORSEPOWER R&S RSUK 6 | 61 | 2 |

RAW See Erick MORILLO

RAW SILK US, female vocal group (Singles: 12 Weeks)

pos/wks

| 16 Oct 82 | DO IT TO THE MUSIC KR KR 14 | 18 | 9 |
| 10 Sep 83 | JUST IN TIME West End WEND 2 | 49 | 3 |

RAW STYLUS
UK, male / female vocal / instrumental duo (Singles: 1 Week)   pos/wks

| 26 Oct 96 | BELIEVE IN ME Wired WIRED 234 | 66 | 1 |

Lou RAWLS US, male vocalist (Singles: 10 Weeks)

pos/wks

| 31 Jul 76 ● | YOU'LL NEVER FIND ANOTHER LOVE LIKE MINE Philadelphia International PIR 4372 | 10 | 10 |

Gene Anthony RAY See KIDS FROM 'FAME'

Jimmy RAY
UK, male vocalist – James Edwards (Singles: 6 Weeks)   pos/wks

| 25 Oct 97 | ARE YOU JIMMY RAY? Sony S2 6650125 | 13 | 5 |
| 14 Feb 98 | GOIN' TO VEGAS Sony S2 6654652 | 49 | 1 |

Johnnie RAY `411` `Top 500` A sensation in the 1950s, the heart-wrenching vocal delivery of the 'Cry Guy' (b. 10 Jan 1927, Oregon, US, d. 25 Feb 1990) influenced many acts, including Elvis, and was the prime target for teen hysteria in the pre-Presley days (Singles: 168 Weeks)   pos/wks

14 Nov 52	WALKIN' MY BABY BACK HOME Columbia DB 3060	12	1
19 Dec 52 ●	FAITH CAN MOVE MOUNTAINS (re) Columbia DB 3154 [1]	7	3
3 Apr 53	MA SAYS, PA SAYS Columbia DB3242 [2]	12	1
10 Apr 53 ●	SOMEBODY STOLE MY GAL (3re) Philips PB 123	6	7
17 Apr 53	FULL TIME JOB Columbia DB 3242 [2]	11	1

24 Jul 53 ●	LET'S WALK THAT-A-WAY Philips PB 157 [2]	4	14
9 Apr 54 ★	SUCH A NIGHT Philips PB 244	1	18
8 Apr 55 ●	IF YOU BELIEVE (re) Philips PB 379	7	11
20 May 55	PATHS OF PARADISE Philips PB 441	20	1
7 Oct 55	HERNANDO'S HIDEAWAY Philips PB 495	11	5
14 Oct 55 ●	HEY THERE Philips PB 495	5	9
28 Oct 55 ●	SONG OF THE DREAMER Philips PB 516	10	5
17 Feb 56	WHO'S SORRY NOW Philips PB 546	17	2
20 Apr 56	AIN'T MISBEHAVIN' (re) Philips PB 580	17	7
12 Oct 56 ★	JUST WALKING IN THE RAIN Philips PB 624	1	19
18 Jan 57	YOU DON'T OWE ME A THING Philips PB 655	12	15
8 Feb 57	LOOK HOMEWARD ANGEL Philips PB 655	7	16
10 May 57 ★	YES TONIGHT JOSEPHINE Philips PB 686	1	16
6 Sep 57	BUILD YOUR LOVE (ON A STRONG FOUNDATION) Philips PB 721	17	7
4 Oct 57	GOOD EVENING FRIENDS / UP ABOVE MY HEAD, I HEAR MUSIC IN THE AIR Philips PB 708 [3]	25	4
4 Dec 59	I'LL NEVER FALL IN LOVE AGAIN (2re) Philips PB 952	26	6

[1] Johnnie Ray and The Four Lads [2] Doris Day and Johnnie Ray [3] Frankie Laine and Johnnie Ray

The chart history of 'You Don't Owe Me a Thing' and 'Look Homeward Angel' is complicated and is as follows: 'You Don't Owe Me a Thing' entered the chart by itself on 18 Jan 1957. On 8 and 15 Feb 1957, 'Look Homeward Angel' was coupled with 'You Don't Owe Me a Thing', but from 22 Feb 1957 the two sides went their individual ways on the chart and were listed separately: 'You Don't Owe Me a Thing' for a further 10 weeks and 'Look Homeward Angel' for a further 14 weeks

Nicole RAY US, female vocalist – Nicole Wray (Singles: 5 Weeks) pos/wks

| 22 Aug 98 | MAKE IT HOT East West E 3821CD [1] | 22 | 4 |
| 5 Dec 98 | I CAN'T SEE East West E 3801CD | 55 | 1 |

[1] Nicole featuring Missy 'Misdemeanor' Elliott and Mocha

RAYDIO (see also Ray PARKER Jr)
US, male vocal / instrumental group (Singles: 21 Weeks)   pos/wks

| 8 Apr 78 | JACK AND JILL Arista 161 | 11 | 12 |
| 8 Jul 78 | IS THIS A LOVE THING Arista 193 | 27 | 9 |

RAYVON Barbados, male rapper /
vocalist – Bruce Brewster (Singles: 26 Weeks)   pos/wks

8 Jul 95 ●	IN THE SUMMERTIME Virgin VSCDT 1542 [1]	5	9
9 Jun 01 ★	ANGEL MCA MCSTD 40257 [1] ■ ▲	1	16
3 Aug 02	2-WAY MCA MCSTD 40287	67	1

[1] Shaggy featuring Rayvon

RAZE
US, male / female vocal / instrumental group (Singles: 48 Weeks)   pos/wks

1 Nov 86	JACK THE GROOVE (re) Champion CHAMP 23	20	15
28 Feb 87	LET THE MUSIC MOVE U Champion CHAMP 27	57	3
31 Dec 88	BREAK 4 LOVE (re) Champion CHAMP 67	28	16
15 Jul 89	LET IT ROLL Atlantic A 8866 [1]	27	6
27 Jan 90	ALL 4 LOVE (BREAK 4 LOVE 1990) Champion CHAMP 228 [2]	30	5
10 Feb 90	CAN YOU FEEL IT / CAN YOU FEEL IT Champion CHAMP 227 [3]	62	1
24 Sep 94	BREAK 4 LOVE (re-mix) Champion CHAMPCD 314	44	2
29 Mar 03	BREAK 4 LOVE (2nd re-mix) Champion CHAMPCD 784	64	1

[1] Raze presents Doug Lazy [2] Raze featuring Lady J and Secretary of Entertainment [3] Raze / Championship Legend

'Can You Feel It' by Championship Legend is a montage of six Raze tracks

RAZORLIGHT UK, male vocal / instrumental
group (Singles: 19 Weeks, Albums: 25 Weeks)   pos/wks

30 Aug 03	ROCK 'N' ROLL LIES Vertigo 9800413	56	1
22 Nov 03	RIP IT UP Vertigo 9814045	42	1
7 Feb 04	STUMBLE & FALL Vertigo 9816396	27	3
26 Jun 04 ●	GOLDEN TOUCH Vertigo 9866836	9	7
25 Sep 04	VICE Vertigo 9867759	18	4
11 Dec 04	RIP IT UP (re-recording) Vertigo 9869076	20	3+
10 Jul 04 ●	UP ALL NIGHT Vertigo 9866944	3	25+

RE-FLEX
UK, male vocal / instrumental group (Singles: 9 Weeks)   pos/wks

| 28 Jan 84 | THE POLITICS OF DANCING EMI FLEX 2 | 28 | 9 |

REA See JAM & SPOON featuring PLAVKA

Chris REA `85` `Top 500`

One of the most popular UK singer / songwriters of the late 1980s, b. 4 Mar 1951, Middlesbrough. He was already a major European star by the time he finally cracked the UK Top 10 with his 18th chart entry, 'The Road to Hell (Part 2)' (Singles: 120 Weeks, Albums: 357 Weeks) pos/wks

7 Oct 78	FOOL (IF YOU THINK IT'S OVER) *Magnet MAG 111*	**30** 7
21 Apr 79	DIAMONDS *Magnet MAG 144*	**44** 3
27 Mar 82	LOVING YOU *Magnet MAG 215*	**65** 3
1 Oct 83	I CAN HEAR YOUR HEARTBEAT *Magnet MAG 244*	**60** 2
17 Mar 84	I DON'T KNOW WHAT IT IS BUT I LOVE IT *Magnet MAG 255*	**65** 4
30 Mar 85	STAINSBY GIRLS *Magnet MAG 276*	**26** 10
29 Jun 85	JOSEPHINE *Magnet MAG 280*	**67** 2
29 Mar 86	IT'S ALL GONE *Magnet MAG 283*	**69** 1
31 May 86	ON THE BEACH (2re) *Magnet MAG 294*	**57** 8
6 Jun 87	LET'S DANCE *Magnet MAG 299*	**12** 10
29 Aug 87	LOVING YOU AGAIN *Magnet MAG 300*	**47** 4
5 Dec 87	JOYS OF CHRISTMAS *Magnet MAG 314*	**67** 1
13 Feb 88	QUE SERA *Magnet MAG 318*	**73** 2
13 Aug 88	ON THE BEACH SUMMER '88 (re-recording) *WEA YZ 195* ...	**12** 6
22 Oct 88	I CAN HEAR YOUR HEARTBEAT (re-recording) *WEA YZ 320* ..	**74** 2
17 Dec 88	THE CHRISTMAS EP *WEA YZ 325*	**53** 3
18 Feb 89	WORKING ON IT *WEA YZ 350*	**53** 3
14 Oct 89 ●	THE ROAD TO HELL (PART 2) *WEA YZ 431*	**10** 9
10 Feb 90	TELL ME THERE'S A HEAVEN *East West YZ 455*	**24** 6
5 May 90	TEXAS *East West YZ 468*	**69** 1
16 Feb 91	AUBERGE *East West YZ 555*	**16** 6
6 Apr 91	HEAVEN *East West YZ 566*	**57** 2
29 Jun 91	LOOKING FOR THE SUMMER *East West YZ 584*	**49** 3
9 Nov 91	WINTER SONG *East West YZ 629*	**27** 4
24 Oct 92	NOTHING TO FEAR *East West YZ 699*	**16** 4
28 Nov 92	GOD'S GREAT BANANA SKIN *East West YZ 706*	**31** 3
30 Jan 93	SOFT TOP HARD SHOULDER *East West YZ 710CD*	**53** 2
23 Oct 93	JULIA *East West YZ 772CD*	**18** 5
12 Nov 94	YOU CAN GO YOUR OWN WAY *East West YZ 835CD*	**28** 3
24 Dec 94	TELL ME THERE'S A HEAVEN (re-issue) *East West YZ 885CD*	**70** 1
16 Nov 96	'DISCO' LA PASSIONE *East West EW 072CD* [1]	**41** 1
24 May 97	LET'S DANCE *Magnet EW 112CD* [2]	**44** 1
28 Apr 79	DELTICS *Magnet MAG 5028*	**54** 3
12 Apr 80	TENNIS *Magnet MAG 5032*	**60** 1
3 Apr 82	CHRIS REA *Magnet MAGL 5040*	**52** 4
18 Jun 83	WATER SIGN *Magnet MAGL 5048*	**64** 2
21 Apr 84	WIRED TO THE MOON *Magnet MAGL 5057*	**35** 7
25 May 85	SHAMROCK DIARIES *Magnet MAGL 5062*	**15** 14
26 Apr 86	ON THE BEACH *Magnet MAGL 5069*	**11** 37
26 Sep 87 ●	DANCING WITH STRANGERS *Magnet MAGL 5071*	**2** 46
13 Aug 88	ON THE BEACH (re-issue) *WEA WX 191*	**37** 10
29 Oct 88 ●	NEW LIGHT THROUGH OLD WINDOWS *WEA WX 200*	**5** 51
11 Nov 89 ★	THE ROAD TO HELL *WEA WX 317* ■	**1** 76
9 Mar 91 ★	AUBERGE *East West 9031735801* ■	**1** 37
14 Nov 92 ●	GOD'S GREAT BANANA SKIN *East West 4509909952*	**4** 15
13 Nov 93 ●	ESPRESSO LOGIC *East West 4509943112*	**8** 9
5 Nov 94 ●	THE BEST OF CHRIS REA *East West 4509980402*	**3** 18
23 Nov 96	LA PASSIONE (FILM SOUNDTRACK) *East West 630166952* ...	**43** 4
31 Jan 98 ●	THE BLUE CAFÉ *East West 3984216882*	**10** 7
20 Nov 99	THE ROAD TO HELL – PART 2 *East West 8573803992*	**54** 1
14 Oct 00	KING OF THE BEACH *East West 8573850172*	**26** 3
1 Dec 01	THE VERY BEST OF CHRIS REA *East West 927421282*	**69** 1
28 Sep 02	DANCING DOWN THE STONY ROAD *Jazzee Blue JBLUECD 01X*	**14** 7
3 Apr 04	THE BLUE JUKEBOX *Jazzee Blue JBLUECD 08X*	**27** 3

[1] Chris Rea and Shirley Bassey [2] Middlesbrough FC featuring Bob Mortimer and Chris Rea

Tracks on The Christmas EP: Driving Home for Christmas / Footsteps in the Snow / Joys of Christmas / Smile

REACT 2 RHYTHM
UK, male production group (Singles: 1 Week) pos/wks

28 Jun 97	INTOXICATION *Jackpot WIN 014CD*	**73** 1

REACTOR
UK, male vocal / instrumental group (Singles: 1 Week) pos/wks

10 Apr 04	FEELING THE LOVE *Liberty CDREACT 001*	**56** 1

Eddi READER (see also FAIRGROUND ATTRACTION)
UK, female vocalist (Singles: 14 Weeks, Albums: 21 Weeks) pos/wks

4 Jun 94	PATIENCE OF ANGELS *Blanco Y Negro NEG 68CD*	**33** 5
13 Aug 94	JOKE (I'M LAUGHING) *Blanco Y Negro NEG 72CD*	**42** 3
5 Nov 94	DEAR JOHN *Blanco Y Negro NEG 75CD1*	**48** 2
22 Jun 96	TOWN WITHOUT PITY *Blanco Y Negro NEG 90CD1*	**26** 3
21 Aug 99	FRAGILE THING *Track TRACK 0004A* [1]	**69** 1
7 Mar 92	MIRMAMA *RCA PD 75156*	**34** 2
2 Jul 94 ●	EDDI READER *Blanco Y Negro 4509461772*	**4** 12
20 Jul 96	CANDYFLOSS AND MEDICINE *Blanco Y Negro 630151202* ...	**24** 5
23 May 98	ANGELS & ELECTRICITY *Blanco Y Negro 3984228162*	**49** 2

[1] Big Country featuring Eddi Reader

READY FOR THE WORLD
US, male vocal / instrumental group (Singles: 8 Weeks) pos/wks

26 Oct 85	OH SHEILA *MCA MCA 1005* ▲	**50** 5
14 Mar 87	LOVE YOU DOWN *MCA MCA 1110*	**60** 3

REAL & RICHARDSON featuring JOBABE
UK, male production duo and female vocalist (Singles: 1 Week) pos/wks

10 May 03	SUNSHINE ON A RAINY DAY *Nukleuz 0489 CNUK*	**69** 1

REAL EMOTION
UK, male / female vocal / instrumental group (Singles: 1 Week) pos/wks

1 Jul 95	BACK FOR GOOD *Living Beat LBECD 34*	**67** 1

The REAL McCOY *Germany / US, male / female vocal / instrumental duo (Singles: 36 Weeks, Albums: 5 Weeks)* pos/wks

6 Nov 93	ANOTHER NIGHT *Logic 74321173732* [1]	**61** 1
5 Nov 94 ●	ANOTHER NIGHT (re-issue) *Logic 74321236992* [1]	**2** 12
28 Jan 95	RUN AWAY *Logic 74321258822* [1]	**6** 10
22 Apr 95	LOVE AND DEVOTION *Logic 74321272702* [1]	**11** 8
26 Aug 95	COME AND GET YOUR LOVE *Logic 74321301272*	**19** 4
11 Nov 95	AUTOMATIC LOVER (CALL FOR LOVE) *Logic 74321325042* ...	**58** 1
20 May 95 ●	ANOTHER NIGHT – U.S. ALBUM *Logic 74321280972*	**6** 5

[1] (MC Sar &) The Real McCoy

REAL PEOPLE *UK, male vocal / instrumental group (Singles: 8 Weeks, Albums: 1 Week)* pos/wks

16 Feb 91	OPEN UP YOUR MIND (LET ME IN) *CBS 6566127*	**70** 1
20 Apr 91	THE TRUTH *Columbia 6567877*	**73** 1
6 Jul 91	WINDOW PANE (EP) *Columbia 6569327*	**60** 1
11 Jan 92	THE TRUTH (re-issue) *Columbia 6576987*	**41** 3
23 May 92	BELIEVER *Columbia 658006*	**38** 2
18 May 91	THE REAL PEOPLE *Columbia 4680841*	**59** 1

Tracks on Window Pane (EP): Window Pane / See Through You / Everything Must Change

REAL ROXANNE
US, female rapper – Joanne Martinez (Singles: 10 Weeks) pos/wks

28 Jun 86	(BANG ZOOM) LET'S GO-GO *Cooltempo COOL 124* [1]	**11** 9
12 Nov 88	RESPECT *Cooltempo COOL 176*	**71** 1

[1] Real Roxanne with Hitman Howie Tee

The REAL THING
UK, male vocal quartet (Singles: 114 Weeks, Albums: 17 Weeks) pos/wks

5 Jun 76 ★	YOU TO ME ARE EVERYTHING *Pye International 7N 25709*	**1** 11
4 Sep 76 ●	CAN'T GET BY WITHOUT YOU *Pye 7N 45618*	**2** 10
12 Feb 77	YOU'LL NEVER KNOW WHAT YOU'RE MISSING *Pye 7N 45662*	**16** 9
30 Jul 77	LOVE'S SUCH A WONDERFUL THING *Pye 7N 45701*	**33** 5
4 Mar 78	WHENEVER YOU WANT MY LOVE *Pye 7N 46045*	**18** 9
3 Jun 78	LET'S GO DISCO *Pye 7N 46078*	**39** 7
12 Aug 78	RAININ' THROUGH MY SUNSHINE *Pye 7N 46113*	**40** 8
17 Feb 79 ●	CAN YOU FEEL THE FORCE? *Pye 7N 46147*	**5** 11
21 Jul 79	BOOGIE DOWN (GET FUNKY NOW) *Pye 7P 109*	**33** 6
22 Nov 80	SHE'S A GROOVY FREAK *Calibre CAB 105*	**52** 4
8 Mar 86 ●	YOU TO ME ARE EVERYTHING (THE DECADE REMIX 76-86) (re) *PRT 7P 349*	**5** 13
24 May 86 ●	CAN'T GET BY WITHOUT YOU (THE SECOND DECADE REMIX) *PRT 7P 352*	**6** 13
2 Aug 86	CAN YOU FEEL THE FORCE? ('86 REMIX) *PRT 7P 358*	**24** 6
25 Oct 86	STRAIGHT TO THE HEART *Jive JIVE 129*	**71** 2

6 Nov 76	REAL THING *Pye NSPL 18507*	34	3
7 Apr 79	CAN YOU FEEL THE FORCE *Pye NSPH 18601*	73	1
10 May 80	20 GREATEST HITS *K-Tel NE 1073*	56	2
12 Jul 86	BEST OF THE REAL THING *West Five NRT 1*	24	11

REAL TO REEL (see also LIL MO' YIN YANG; Erick MORILLO)
US, male vocal / instrumental group (Singles: 2 Weeks)   pos/wks

21 Apr 84	LOVE ME LIKE THIS *Arista ARIST 565*	68	2

REBEL MC
UK, male rapper – Mike West (Singles: 52 Weeks, Albums: 11 Weeks) pos/wks

27 May 89	JUST KEEP ROCKIN' *Desire WANT 9* [1]	11	12
7 Oct 89 ●	STREET TUFF *Desire WANT 18* [2]	3	14
31 Mar 90	BETTER WORLD *Desire WANT 25*	20	6
2 Jun 90	REBEL MUSIC *Desire WANT 31*	53	2
6 Apr 91	WICKEDEST SOUND *Desire WANT 40* [3]	43	6
15 Jun 91	TRIBAL BASE *Desire WANT 44* [4]	20	6
31 Aug 91	BLACK MEANING GOOD *Desire WANT 47*	73	1
21 Mar 92	RICH AH GETTING RICHER *Big Life BLR 70* [5]	48	4
8 Aug 92	HUMANITY *Big Life BLR 78* [6]	62	1
28 Apr 90	REBEL MUSIC *Desire LUVLP 5*	18	7
13 Jul 91	BLACK MEANING GOOD *Desire LUVLP 12*	23	1

[1] Double Trouble and the Rebel MC [2] Rebel MC and Double Trouble [3] Rebel MC featuring Tenor Fly [4] Rebel MC featuring Tenor Fly and Barrington Levy [5] Rebel MC introducing Little T [6] Rebel MC featuring Lincoln Thompson

REBEL ROUSERS See Cliff BENNETT and the REBEL ROUSERS

REBELETTES See Duane EDDY

REBELS See Duane EDDY

Ivan REBROFF
Germany, male vocalist – Hans Rippert (Albums: 4 Weeks)   pos/wks

16 Jun 90	THE VERY BEST OF IVAN REBROFF *BBC REB 778*	57	4

Ezz RECO and the LAUNCHERS with Boysie GRANT
Jamaica, male vocal / instrumental group (Singles: 4 Weeks)   pos/wks

5 Mar 64	KING OF KINGS *Columbia DB 7217*	44	4

RECOIL *UK, male vocal / instrumental group (Singles: 1 Week)*   pos/wks

21 Mar 92	FAITH HEALER *Mute MUTE 110*	60	1

RED (see also DREAM FREQUENCY;
QUAKE featuring Marcia RAE; BEAT RENEGADES) *UK, male production duo – Ian Bland and Paul Fitzpatrick (Singles: 1 Week)* pos/wks

20 Jan 01	HEAVEN & EARTH *Slinky Music SLINKY 008CD*	41	1

RED 'N' WHITE MACHINES
UK, Southampton football supporters vocal group (Singles: 1 Week) pos/wks

24 May 03	SOUTHAMPTON BOYS *Centric CEN 008*	16	1

RED BOX *UK, male vocal / instrumental duo – Julian
Close and Simon Toulson (Singles: 28 Weeks, Albums: 4 Weeks)* pos/wks

24 Aug 85 ●	LEAN ON ME (AH-LI-AYO) *Sire W 8926*	3	14
25 Oct 86 ●	FOR AMERICA *Sire YZ 84*	10	12
31 Jan 87	HEART OF THE SUN *Sire YZ 100*	71	2
6 Dec 86	THE CIRCLE AND THE SQUARE *Sire WX 79*	73	4

RED CAR AND THE BLUE CAR
UK, male vocal / instrumental group (Singles: 4 Weeks)   pos/wks

14 Dec 91	HOME FOR CHRISTMAS DAY *Virgin VS 1394*	44	4

RED CARPET *Belgium, male production
duo and female vocalist (Singles: 2 Weeks)*   pos/wks

11 Dec 04	ALRIGHT *Positiva CDTIVS 212*	58	2

RED DRAGON with Brian and Tony GOLD
Jamaica, male vocal group (Singles: 15 Weeks)   pos/wks

30 Jul 94 ●	COMPLIMENTS ON YOUR KISS (re) *Mango CIDM 820*	2	15

RED EYE
UK, male instrumental / production duo (Singles: 1 Week)   pos/wks

3 Dec 94	KUT IT *Champion CHAMPCD 315*	62	1

RED 5
Germany, male producer – Thomas Kukula (Singles: 10 Weeks)   pos/wks

10 May 97	I LOVE YOU … STOP! *Multiply CDMULTY 20*	11	5
20 Dec 97	LIFT ME UP *Multiply CDMULTY 30*	26	5

RED HED See VINYLGROOVER and The RED HED; Rob TISSERA

RED HILL CHILDREN
UK, male / female children's choir (Singles: 2 Weeks)   pos/wks

30 Nov 96	WHEN CHILDREN RULE THE WORLD *Really Useful 5797262*	40	2

RED HOT CHILI PEPPERS ⟨91⟩ [Top 500]
Los Angeles-based funk / punk rock quartet formed by high school pals Anthony Kiedis (v) and Michael "Flea" Balzary (b) (currently featuring John Frusciante (g) and Chad Smith (d)). Their 'By the Way' album sold more than a million copies in both the US and UK in 2002, taking their worldwide album sales tally to more than 30 million. Their three Hyde Park concerts were seen by over 250,000 people and grossed $17 million – a 2004 record (Singles: 91 Weeks, Albums: 364 Weeks)   pos/wks

10 Feb 90	HIGHER GROUND *EMI-USA MT 75*	55	3
23 Jun 90	TASTE THE PAIN *EMI-USA MT 85*	29	3
8 Sep 90	HIGHER GROUND (re-issue) *EMI-USA MT 88*	54	3
14 Mar 92	UNDER THE BRIDGE *Warner Bros. W 0084*	26	4
15 Aug 92	BREAKING THE GIRL *Warner Bros. W 0126*	41	3
5 Feb 94 ●	GIVE IT AWAY *Warner Bros. W 0225CD1*	9	4
30 Apr 94	UNDER THE BRIDGE (re-issue) *Warner Bros. W 0237CD*	13	5
2 Sep 95	WARPED *Warner Bros. W 0316CD*	31	2
21 Oct 95	MY FRIENDS *Warner Bros. W 0317CD*	29	2
17 Feb 96	AEROPLANE *Warner Bros. W 0331CD*	11	3
14 Jun 97	LOVE ROLLERCOASTER *Geffen GFSTD 22188*	7	8
12 Jun 99	SCAR TISSUE *Warner Bros. W 490CD*	15	6
4 Sep 99	AROUND THE WORLD *Warner Bros. W 500CD1*	35	2
12 Feb 00	OTHERSIDE *Warner Bros. W 510CD1*	33	2
19 Aug 00	CALIFORNICATION *Warner Bros. W 534CD*	16	5
13 Jan 01	ROAD TRIPPIN' *Warner Bros. W 546CD1*	30	2
13 Jul 02 ●	BY THE WAY *Warner Bros. W 580CD*	2	10
2 Nov 02	THE ZEPHYR SONG *Warner Bros. W 592CD*	11	10
22 Feb 03	CAN'T STOP *Warner Bros. W 599CD*	22	6
28 Jun 03	UNIVERSALLY SPEAKING *Warner Bros. W 609CD1*	27	2
22 Nov 03	FORTUNE FADED *Warner Bros. W 630CD1*	11	5
12 Oct 91	BLOOD SUGAR SEX MAGIK *Warner Bros. WX 441*	25	86
17 Oct 92	WHAT HITS!? *EMI-USA CDMTL 1071*	23	6
19 Nov 94	OUT IN L.A. *EMI CDMTL 1082*	61	1
23 Sep 95 ●	ONE HOT MINUTE *Warner Bros. 9362457332*	2	11
19 Jun 99 ●	CALIFORNICATION *Warner Bros. 9362473862*	5	130
20 Jul 02 ★	BY THE WAY *Warner Bros. 9362481402* ■	1	77
5 Apr 03	WHAT HITS!? (re-issue) *EMI CDP 7947622*	44	5
29 Nov 03 ●	GREATEST HITS *Warner Bros. 9362485962*	4	39
7 Aug 04 ★	LIVE IN HYDE PARK *Warner Bros. 9362488632* ■	1	9

'Blood Sugar Sex Magik' had a new catalogue number, Warner Bros. 7599266812, when it returned to the chart in 2004

RED HOUSE PAINTERS
US, male vocal / instrumental group (Albums: 2 Weeks)   pos/wks

5 Jun 93	RED HOUSE PAINTERS *4AD DAD 3008CD*	63	1
30 Oct 93	RED HOUSE PAINTERS *4AD CAD 3016CD*	68	1

The identically titled albums are different

RED JERRY See WESTBAM; LOST TRIBE

RED NOISE See Bill NELSON

RED RAT See CARNIVAL featuring RIP vs RED RAT; Curtis LYNCH Jr featuring Kele LE ROC and RED RAT

RED RAW featuring 007
(see also CLOCK) *UK, male vocal / instrumental duo –
Stuart Allen and Peter Pritchard (Singles: 1 Week)*   pos/wks

28 Oct 95	OOH LA LA LA *Media MCSTD 2065*	59	1

RED SNAPPER
UK, male vocal / instrumental / production group (Singles: 1 Week, Albums: 2 Weeks) pos/wks

21 Nov 98	IMAGE OF YOU *Warp WAP 111CD*	60	1
21 Sep 96	PRINCE BLIMEY *Warp WARPCD 45*	60	1
10 Oct 98	MAKING BONES *Warp WARPCD 56*	59	1

RED VENOM See BIG BOSS STYLUS presents RED VENOM

REDBONE
US, male vocal / instrumental group (Singles: 12 Weeks) pos/wks

25 Sep 71 ●	THE WITCH QUEEN OF NEW ORLEANS *Epic EPC 7351*	2	12

Sharon REDD
US, female vocalist, b. 19 Oct 1945, d. 1 May 1992 (Singles: 32 Weeks, Albums: 5 Weeks) pos/wks

28 Feb 81	CAN YOU HANDLE IT *Epic EPC 9572*	31	8
2 Oct 82	NEVER GIVE YOU UP *Prelude PRL A2 755*	20	9
15 Jan 83	IN THE NAME OF LOVE *Prelude PRL A 2905*	31	5
22 Oct 83	LOVE HOW YOU FEEL *Prelude A 3868*	39	5
1 Feb 92	CAN YOU HANDLE IT (re-recording) *EMI EM 219* [1]	17	5
23 Oct 82	REDD HOTT *Prelude PRL 25056*	59	5

[1] DNA featuring Sharon Redd

REDD KROSS
US, male vocal / instrumental group (Singles: 4 Weeks) pos/wks

5 Feb 94	VISIONARY *This Way Up WAY 2733*	75	1
10 Sep 94	YESTERDAY ONCE MORE *A&M 5807932*	45	2
1 Feb 97	GET OUT OF MYSELF *This Way Up WAY 5466*	63	1

The listed flip side of 'Yesterday Once More' was 'Superstar' by Sonic Youth

REDD SQUARE featuring Tiff LACEY
UK, male production group and UK, female vocalist (Singles: 1 Week) pos/wks

26 Oct 02	IN YOUR HANDS *Inferno CDFERN 50*	64	1

Otis REDDING (145 Top 500)
Peerless singer / songwriter, b. 9 Sep 1941, Georgia, US, d. 10 Dec 1967. He was one of the first and most influential Sixties soul stars. He replaced Elvis as the World's Top Male Singer in a Melody Maker poll shortly before his death in a plane crash (Singles: 124 Weeks, Albums: 235 Weeks) pos/wks

25 Nov 65	MY GIRL *Atlantic AT 4050*	11	16
7 Apr 66	(I CAN'T GET NO) SATISFACTION *Atlantic AT 4080*	33	4
14 Jul 66	MY LOVER'S PRAYER *Atlantic 584 019*	37	6
25 Aug 66	I CAN'T TURN YOU LOOSE *Atlantic 584 030*	29	8
24 Nov 66	FA FA FA FA FA (SAD SONG) *Atlantic 584 049*	23	9
26 Jan 67	TRY A LITTLE TENDERNESS *Atlantic 584 070*	46	4
23 Mar 67	DAY TRIPPER *Stax 601 005*	43	6
4 May 67	LET ME COME ON HOME *Stax 601 007*	48	1
15 Jun 67	SHAKE *Stax 601 011*	28	10
19 Jul 67	TRAMP *Stax 601 012* [1]	18	11
11 Oct 67	KNOCK ON WOOD *Stax 601 021* [1]	35	5
14 Feb 68	MY GIRL (re-issue) *Atlantic 584 092*	36	9
21 Feb 68	(SITTIN' ON) THE DOCK OF THE BAY *Stax 601 031* ▲	3	15
29 May 68	THE HAPPY SONG (DUM-DUM) *Stax 601 040*	24	5
31 Jul 68	HARD TO HANDLE *Atlantic 584 199*	15	12
9 Jul 69	LOVE MAN *Atco 226 001*	43	3
19 Jun 66 ●	OTIS BLUE / OTIS REDDING SINGS SOUL *Atlantic ATL 5041*	6	21
23 Apr 66	SOUL BALLADS *Atlantic ATL 5029*	30	1
23 Jul 66	THE SOUL ALBUM *Atlantic 587011*	22	9
21 Jan 67	OTIS BLUE (re-issue) *Atlantic 587036*	23	16
21 Jan 67 ●	COMPLETE & UNBELIEVABLE – THE OTIS REDDING DICTIONARY OF SOUL *Atlantic 588050*	7	54
29 Apr 67	PAIN IN MY HEART *Atlantic 587042*	28	9
1 Jul 67	KING & QUEEN *Atlantic 589007* [1]	18	17
10 Feb 68 ●	HISTORY OF OTIS REDDING *Volt S 418*	2	43
30 Mar 68	OTIS REDDING IN EUROPE *Stax 589016*	14	16
1 Jun 68 ★	DOCK OF THE BAY *Stax 231001*	1	15
12 Oct 68	THE IMMORTAL OTIS REDDING *Atlantic 588113*	19	8
11 Sep 93	DOCK OF THE BAY – THE DEFINITIVE COLLECTION (re-issue) *Atlantic 954817092*	44	18
11 Nov 00	THE VERY BEST OF OTIS REDDING *Atco 9548380872*	26	8

[1] Otis Redding and Carla Thomas [1] Otis Redding and Carla Thomas

Helen REDDY
Australia, female vocalist (Singles: 18 Weeks, Albums: 27 Weeks) pos/wks

18 Jan 75 ●	ANGIE BABY *Capitol CL 15799* ▲	5	10
28 Nov 81	I CAN'T SAY GOODBYE TO YOU *MCA 744*	43	8

8 Feb 75	FREE AND EASY *Capitol EST 11348*	17	9
14 Feb 76 ●	THE BEST OF HELEN REDDY *Capitol EST 11467*	5	18

REDHEAD KINGPIN and the FBI
US, male rapper – David Guppy and rap group (Singles: 11 Weeks, Albums: 3 Weeks) pos/wks

22 Jul 89	DO THE RIGHT THING *10 TEN 271*	13	10
2 Dec 89	SUPERBAD SUPERSLICK *10 TEN 286*	68	1
9 Sep 89	A SHADE OF RED *10 DIX 85*	35	3

REDMAN
US, male rapper – Reggie Noble (Singles: 38 Weeks, Albums: 7 Weeks) pos/wks

25 Apr 98	RAP SCHOLAR *East West E 3853CD* [1]	42	1
30 May 98	MADE IT BACK *Parlophone Rhythm CDRHYTHM 11* [2]	21	3
24 Oct 98 ●	HOW DEEP IS YOUR LOVE (re) *Island Black Music CID 725* [3]	9	8
12 Jun 99	DA GOODNESS *Def Jam 8709232*	52	1
22 Jul 00	OOOH *Tommy Boy TBCD 2102* [4]	29	2
15 Sep 01	SMASH SUMTHIN' *Def Jam 5886932* [5]	11	7
31 Aug 02	SMASH SUMTHIN' (re-mix) *Kaos KAOSCD 003* [6]	47	2
23 Nov 02 ★	DIRRTY *RCA 74321962722* [7] ■	1	9
11 Jan 03	REACT *J 74321988492* [8]	14	5
9 Oct 99	BLACKOUT! *Def Jam 5466092* [1]	45	3
9 Jun 01	MALPRACTICE *Def Jam 5483812*	57	4

[1] Das EFX featuring Redman [2] Beverley Knight featuring Redman [3] Dru Hill featuring Redman [4] De La Soul featuring Redman [5] Redman featuring Adam F [6] Adam F featuring Redman [7] Christina Aguilera featuring Redman [8] Erick Sermon featuring Redman [1] Method Man and Redman

REDNEX
Sweden, male / female vocal / instrumental group (Singles: 23 Weeks) pos/wks

17 Dec 94 ★	COTTON EYE JOE *Internal Affairs KGBCD 016*	1	16
25 Mar 95	OLD POP IN AN OAK *Internal Affairs KGBD 019*	12	6
21 Oct 95	WILD 'N FREE *Internal Affairs KGBD 024*	55	1

REDS UNITED
UK, male vocal group – 40 Manchester United FC fans (Singles: 13 Weeks) pos/wks

6 Dec 97	SING UP FOR THE CHAMPIONS *Music Collection MANUCDP 2*	12	9
9 May 98	UNITED CALYPSO '98 *Music Collection MANUCDP 3*	33	4

REDSKINS
UK, male vocal / instrumental trio (Singles: 12 Weeks, Albums: 4 Weeks) pos/wks

10 Nov 84	KEEP ON KEEPIN' ON *Decca F 1*	43	5
22 Jun 85	BRING IT DOWN (THIS INSANE THING) *Decca F 2*	33	5
22 Feb 86	THE POWER IS YOURS *Decca F 3*	59	2
22 Mar 86	NEITHER WASHINGTON NOR MOSCOW ... *Decca FLP 1*	31	4

Alex REECE
UK, male producer (Singles: 7 Weeks, Albums: 5 Weeks) pos/wks

16 Dec 95	FEEL THE SUNSHINE *Blunted Vinyl BLNCD 016*	69	1
11 May 96	FEEL THE SUNSHINE (re-mix) *Fourth & Broadway BRCD 332*	26	3
27 Jul 96	CANDLES *Fourth & Broadway BRCD 333*	33	2
18 Nov 96	ACID LAB *Fourth & Broadway BRCD 344*	64	1
17 Aug 96	SO FAR *Fourth & Broadway BRCD 621*	19	5

Jimmy REED
US, male vocalist / instrumentalist – guitar / harmonica – Mathis Reed, b. 6 Sep 1925, d. 29 Aug 1976 (Singles: 2 Weeks) pos/wks

10 Sep 64	SHAME, SHAME, SHAME *Stateside SS 330*	45	2

Les REED See Donald PEERS

Lou REED (see also VELVET UNDERGROUND)
US, male vocalist – Lou Firbank (Singles: 26 Weeks, Albums: 98 Weeks) pos/wks

12 May 73 ●	WALK ON THE WILD SIDE *RCA 2303*	10	9
17 Jan 87	SOUL MAN *A&M AM 364* [1]	30	10
31 Jul 04	SATELLITE OF LOVE *Nulife 82876636472*	10	7
21 Apr 73	TRANSFORMER *RCA Victor LSP 4807*	13	26
20 Oct 73 ●	BERLIN *RCA Victor RS 1002*	7	5
16 Mar 74	ROCK 'N' ROLL ANIMAL *RCA Victor APLI 0472*	26	1
14 Feb 76	CONEY ISLAND BABY *RCA Victor RS 1035*	52	1
3 Jul 82	TRANSFORMER (re-issue) *RCA INTS 5061*	91	2
9 Jun 84	NEW SENSATIONS *RCA PL 84998*	92	1
24 May 86	MISTRIAL *RCA PL 87190*	69	1
28 Jan 89	NEW YORK *Sire WX 246*	14	22
7 Oct 89	RETRO *RCA PL 90389*	29	5

Singles re-entries are listed as (re), (2re), (3re)…. which signifies that the hit re-entered the chart once, twice or three times…

		pos/wks
5 May 90	SONGS FOR DRELLA *Sire WX 345* [1]	22 5
25 Jan 92 ●	MAGIC AND LOSS *Sire 7599266622*	6 6
28 Oct 95	THE BEST OF LOU REED & THE VELVET UNDERGROUND	
	Global Television RADCD 21 [2]	56 4
2 Mar 96	SET THE TWILIGHT REELING *Warner Bros. 9362461592*	26 2
7 Feb 98	TRANSFORMER (2nd re-issue) *RCA ND 83806*	16 10
15 Apr 00	ECSTASY *Reprise 9362474252*	54 1
24 May 03	NYC MAN *BMG 74321984012*	31 3
7 Aug 04	NYC MAN – GREATEST HITS *BMG 82876631122*	43 2
9 Oct 04	TRANSFORMER (3rd re-issue) *RCA 74321601812*	45 1

[1] Sam Moore and Lou Reed [1] Lou Reed and John Cale [2] Lou Reed and The Velvet Underground

'NYC Man – Greatest Hits' is a slimmed-down version of the double-disc retrospective 'NYC Man' but contains additional re-mixes

Dan REED NETWORK *US, male vocal / instrumental group (Singles: 16 Weeks, Albums: 6 Weeks)*

		pos/wks
20 Jan 90	COME BACK BABY *Mercury DRN 2*	51 3
17 Mar 90	RAINBOW CHILD *Mercury DRN 3*	60 3
21 Jul 90	STARDATE 1990 / RAINBOW CHILD (re-issue) *Mercury DRN 4*	39 4
8 Sep 90	LOVER / MONEY *Mercury DRN 5*	45 3
13 Jul 91	MIX IT UP *Mercury MER 345*	49 2
21 Sep 91	BABY NOW I *Mercury MER 352*	65 1
4 Nov 89	SLAM *Mercury 8388681*	66 2
27 Jul 91	THE HEAT *Mercury 8488551*	15 4

Michael REED ORCHESTRA See Richard HARTLEY / Michael REED ORCHESTRA

Don REEDMAN See Jeff JARRATT and Don REEDMAN

REEF *UK, male vocal / instrumental group (Singles: 48 Weeks, Albums: 55 Weeks)*

		pos/wks
15 Apr 95	GOOD FEELING *Sony S2 6613602*	24 4
3 Jun 95	NAKED *Sony S2 6620622*	11 5
5 Aug 95	WEIRD *Sony S2 6622772*	19 3
2 Nov 96 ●	PLACE YOUR HANDS *Sony S2 6635712*	6 7
25 Jan 97 ●	COME BACK BRIGHTER *Sony S2 6640972*	8 5
5 Apr 97	CONSIDERATION *Sony S2 6643125*	13 4
2 Aug 97	YER DARK *Sony S2 6647032*	21 3
10 Apr 99	I'VE GOT SOMETHING TO SAY *Sony S2 6669542*	15 6
5 Jun 99	SWEETY *Sony S2 6673732*	46 1
11 Sep 99	NEW BIRD *Sony S2 6678512*	73 1
12 Aug 00	SET THE RECORD STRAIGHT *Sony S2 6695952*	19 5
16 Dec 00	SUPERHERO *Sony S2 66999382*	55 1
19 May 01	ALL I WANT *Sony S2 6708222*	51 1
25 Jan 03	GIVE ME YOUR LOVE *Sony S2 6731645*	44 1
28 Jun 03	WASTER *Snapper / Reef SMASCD 051*	56 1
1 Jul 95 ●	REPLENISH *Sony S2 4806982*	9 11
8 Feb 97 ★	GLOW *Sony S2 4869402* ■	1 32
1 May 99 ●	RIDES *Sony S2 4928822*	3 7
2 Sep 00	GETAWAY *Sony S2 4988912*	15 4
8 Feb 03	TOGETHER – THE BEST OF *Sony S2 5094352*	52 1

REEL *Ireland, male vocal group (Singles: 3 Weeks)*

		pos/wks
24 Nov 01	LIFT ME UP *Universal TV 0154632*	39 1
8 Jun 02	YOU TAKE ME AWAY *Universal TV 0190172*	31 2

REEL BIG FISH *US, male vocal / instrumental group (Singles: 1 Week)*

		pos/wks
6 Apr 02	SOLD OUT (EP) *Jive 9270002*	62 1

Tracks on Sold Out (EP): Sell Out / Take on Me / Hungry Like the Wolf

REEL 2 REAL featuring The MAD STUNTMAN
(see also LIL MO' YIN YANG; PIANOHEADS)
US, male vocal / production duo – Erick Morillo and Mark 'The Mad Stuntman' Quashie (Singles: 53 Weeks, Albums: 8 Weeks)

		pos/wks
12 Feb 94 ●	I LIKE TO MOVE IT *Positiva CDTIV 10*	5 20
2 Jul 94 ●	GO ON MOVE *Positiva CDTIV 15*	7 9
1 Oct 94	CAN YOU FEEL IT *Positiva CDTIV 22*	13 5
3 Dec 94	RAISE YOUR HANDS *Positiva CDTIV 27*	14 6
1 Apr 95	CONWAY *Positiva CDTIVS 30*	27 4
6 Jul 96 ●	JAZZ IT UP *Positiva CDTIV 59* [1]	7 7
5 Oct 96	ARE YOU READY FOR SOME MORE *Positiva CDTIV 56* [1]	24 2
22 Oct 94 ●	MOVE IT! *Positiva CDTIVA 1003*	8 8

[1] Reel 2 Real

The REELISTS *UK, male vocal / production duo – Kaywan Qazzaz and Saif Naqvi (Singles: 13 Weeks)*

		pos/wks
19 Jan 02 ●	HATERS *Relentless RELENT 23CD* [1]	8 7
25 May 02	FREAK MODE (re) *Go Beat GOBCD 45*	16 6

[1] So Solid Crew presents Mr Shabz featuring MBD and The Reelists

Maureen REES *UK, female TV learner driver / vocalist (Singles: 4 Weeks)*

		pos/wks
20 Dec 97	DRIVING IN MY CAR *Eagle EAGXS 014*	49 4

Tony REES and the COTTAGERS *UK, male Fulham FC supporters vocal group (Singles: 1 Week)*

		pos/wks
10 May 75	VIVA EL FULHAM *Sonet SON 2059*	46 1

REESE PROJECT *US, male producer – Kevin Saunderson (Singles: 7 Weeks)*

		pos/wks
8 Aug 92	THE COLOUR OF LOVE *Network NWK 51*	52 2
12 Dec 92	I BELIEVE *Network NWKT 63*	74 1
13 Mar 93	SO DEEP *Network NWKCD 68*	54 2
24 Sep 94	THE COLOUR OF LOVE (re-mix) *Network NWKCD 81*	55 1
6 May 95	DIRECT-ME *Network NWKCD 87*	44 1

Conner REEVES *UK, male vocalist (Singles: 18 Weeks, Albums: 8 Weeks)*

		pos/wks
30 Aug 97	MY FATHER'S SON *Wildstar CDWILD 1*	12 5
22 Nov 97	EARTHBOUND *Wildstar CDWILD 2*	14 4
11 Apr 98	READ MY MIND *Wildstar CXWILD 4*	19 4
3 Oct 98	SEARCHING FOR A SOUL *Wildstar CDWILD 6*	28 2
4 Sep 99	BEST FRIEND *WEA WEA 221CD1* [1]	23 3
6 Dec 97	EARTHBOUND *Wildstar CDWILD 3*	25 8

[1] Mark Morrison and Conner Reeves

Jim REEVES ⟨36⟩ ⟨Top 500⟩ *Internationally acclaimed velvet-voiced vocalist, b. 20 Aug 1924, Texas, US, d. 31 Jul 1964. 'Gentleman Jim', who only managed two hit LPs in his lifetime then 27 posthumously, had a record-breaking eight albums simultaneously on the UK chart three months after his death (Singles: 322 Weeks, Albums: 408 Weeks)*

		pos/wks
24 Mar 60	HE'LL HAVE TO GO (re) *RCA 1168*	12 31
16 Mar 61	WHISPERING HOPE *RCA 1223*	50 1
23 Nov 61	YOU'RE THE ONLY GOOD THING (THAT HAPPENED TO ME) *RCA 1261*	17 19
28 Jun 62	ADIOS AMIGO *RCA 1293*	23 21
22 Nov 62	I'M GONNA CHANGE EVERYTHING *RCA 1317*	42 2
13 Jun 63 ●	WELCOME TO MY WORLD *RCA 1342*	6 15
17 Oct 63	GUILTY *RCA 1364*	29 7
20 Feb 64 ●	I LOVE YOU BECAUSE *RCA 1385*	5 39
18 Jun 64 ●	I WON'T FORGET YOU (re) *RCA 1400*	3 26
5 Nov 64 ●	THERE'S A HEARTACHE FOLLOWING ME *RCA 1423*	6 13
4 Feb 65 ●	IT HURTS SO MUCH (TO SEE YOU GO) *RCA 1437*	8 10
15 Apr 65	NOT UNTIL THE NEXT TIME *RCA 1446*	13 12
6 May 65	HOW LONG HAS IT BEEN *RCA 1445*	45 5
15 Jul 65	THIS WORLD IS NOT MY HOME *RCA 1412*	22 9
11 Nov 65	IS IT REALLY OVER *RCA 1488*	17 9
18 Aug 66 ★	DISTANT DRUMS *RCA 1537*	1 25
2 Feb 67	I WON'T COME IN WHILE HE'S THERE *RCA 1563*	12 11
26 Jul 67	TRYING TO FORGET *RCA 1611*	33 5
22 Nov 67	I HEARD A HEART BREAK LAST NIGHT *RCA 1643*	38 6
27 Mar 68	PRETTY BROWN EYES *RCA 1672*	33 5
25 Jun 69	WHEN TWO WORLDS COLLIDE *RCA 1830*	17 17
6 Dec 69	BUT YOU LOVE ME DADDY *RCA 1899*	15 16
21 Mar 70	NOBODY'S FOOL *RCA 1915*	32 5
12 Sep 70	ANGELS DON'T LIE (re) *RCA 1997*	32 3
26 Jun 71	I LOVE YOU BECAUSE (re-issue) / HE'LL HAVE TO GO (re-issue) / MOONLIGHT & ROSES *RCA Maximillion 2092*	34 8
19 Feb 72	YOU'RE FREE TO GO *RCA 2174*	48 2
28 Mar 64 ●	GOOD 'N' COUNTRY *RCA Camden CDN 5114*	10 34
9 May 64 ●	GENTLEMAN JIM *RCA RD 7541*	3 23
15 Aug 64	INTERNATIONAL JIM REEVES *RCA RD 7577*	11 15
15 Aug 64 ●	A TOUCH OF VELVET *RCA RD 7521*	8 9
22 Aug 64	HE'LL HAVE TO GO *RCA RD 27176*	16 4
29 Aug 64	THE INTIMATE JIM REEVES *RCA RD 27193*	12 4
29 Aug 64 ●	GOD BE WITH YOU *RCA RD 7636*	10 10
5 Sep 64 ●	MOONLIGHT AND ROSES *RCA RD 7639*	2 51
19 Sep 64	COUNTRY SIDE OF JIM REEVES *RCA Camden CDN 5100*	12 5

EP CHART RECORDS

On 10 March 1960 Record Retailer began printing a separate extended play (EP) chart for the first time. With more tracks than a single, but not enough material for an album, this format was a good conveyor belt for the prodigious output of 1960s acts trying to keep their fickle fans happy. The very first No.1 in this category was Cliff Richard's EP 'Expresso Bongo'. This separate run-down of 45rpm discs in shiny, high-quality sleeves typically contained two and sometimes three tracks on each side. Although not exactly an overnight fad, the EP chart lasted just over seven years, with the last printed run-down appearing on 30 November 1967. During this period, four acts had the distinction of topping the singles, albums and EP charts in the same week: The Beatles (21 times), The Rolling Stones (twice), The Shadows (once), and Elvis Presley (once). Although the actual Record Retailer EP chart was relatively short-lived, EPs have always been around and, chart rules permitting, still appear in the singles chart to this day.

Most weeks on the EP chart by act

THE SHADOWS 461 weeks

Most weeks on the EP chart by title

SHADOWS TO THE FORE (The Shadows) 116 weeks

Most weeks on the EP chart by title consecutively

NINA AND FREDERICK (Nina and Frederick) 115 weeks

Most EPs by artist

CLIFF RICHARD (23)

Most EPs by label

Columbia (111)

THE BEATLES' 'LONG TALL SALLY' WAS JUST ONE OF THEIR EIGHT RECORD-BREAKING no.1 EPS THAT SPENT A TOTAL OF 63 WEEKS IN THE TOP SPOT. THE DISC INCLUDES RINGO STARR'S RENDITION OF THE OLD CARL PERKINS NUMBER 'MATCHBOX'

THE CHART-TOPPING WHO EP 'READY STEADY WHO' COMPRISED TWO PETE TOWNSHEND COMPOSITIONS ('DISGUISES' AND 'CIRCLES'), BACKED BY COVER VERSIONS OF 'BATMAN', 'BUCKET "T"' AND 'BARBARA ANN'. THESE LIVE RECORDINGS, FEATURING SMOKE BOMBS AND SMASHED GUITARS, WERE ALL FROM A SPECIAL EDITION OF THE REDIFFUSION TV SHOW READY STEADY GO!, WHICH THE BAND TOOK OVER FROM START TO FINISH

		pos/wks
26 Sep 64	WE THANK THEE *RCA RD 7637*	17 3
28 Nov 64 ●	TWELVE SONGS OF CHRISTMAS *RCA RD 7663*	3 17
30 Jan 65 ●	THE BEST OF JIM REEVES *RCA RD 7666*	3 47
10 Apr 65	HAVE I TOLD YOU LATELY THAT I LOVE YOU *RCA Camden CDN 5122*	12 5
22 May 65	THE JIM REEVES WAY *RCA RD 7694*	16 4
5 Nov 66 ●	DISTANT DRUMS *RCA Victor RD 7814*	2 34
18 Jan 69	A TOUCH OF SADNESS *RCA SF 7978*	15 5
5 Jul 69 ★	ACCORDING TO MY HEART *RCA International INTS 1013*	1 14
23 Aug 69	JIM REEVES AND SOME FRIENDS *RCA SF 8022*	24 4
29 Nov 69	ON STAGE *RCA SF 8047*	13 4
26 Dec 70	MY CATHEDRAL *RCA SF 8146*	48 2
3 Jul 71	JIM REEVES WRITES YOU A RECORD *RCA SF 8176*	47 2
7 Aug 71 ●	JIM REEVES' GOLDEN RECORDS *RCA International INTS 1070*	9 21
14 Aug 71 ●	THE INTIMATE JIM REEVES (re-issue) *RCA International INTS 1256*	8 15
21 Aug 71	GIRLS I HAVE KNOWN *RCA International INTS 1140*	35 5
27 Nov 71	A TOUCH OF VELVET (re-issue) *RCA International INTS 1089*	49 2
27 Nov 71 ●	TWELVE SONGS OF CHRISTMAS (re-issue) *RCA International INTS 1188*	3 6
15 Apr 72	MY FRIEND *RCA SF 8258*	32 5
20 Sep 75 ★	40 GOLDEN GREATS *Arcade ADEP 16*	1 25
6 Sep 80	COUNTRY GENTLEMAN *K-Tel NE 1088*	53 4
8 Aug 92 ●	THE DEFINITIVE JIM REEVES *Arcade ARC 94982*	9 10
28 Sep 96	THE ULTIMATE COLLECTION *RCA Victor 74321410872*	17 6
5 Jul 03	GENTLEMAN JIM – DEFINITIVE COLLECTION *RCA 82876530372*	21 10
3 Jul 04	GENTLEMAN JIM – MEMORIES ARE MADE OF THIS *RCA 82876627842*	35 3

Martha REEVES and the VANDELLAS
US, female vocal trio (Singles: 85 Weeks) pos/wks

		pos/wks
29 Oct 64	DANCING IN THE STREET *Stateside SS 345* [1]	28 8
1 Apr 65 ●	NOWHERE TO RUN *Tamla Motown TMG 502* [1]	26 8
1 Dec 66 ●	I'M READY FOR LOVE *Tamla Motown TMG 582* [1]	22 8
30 Mar 67	JIMMY MACK (re) *Tamla Motown TMG 599* [1]	21 21
17 Jan 68	HONEY CHILE *Tamla Motown TMG 636*	30 9
15 Jan 69 ●	DANCING IN THE STREET (re-issue) *Tamla Motown TMG 684*	4 12
16 Apr 69	NOWHERE TO RUN (re-issue) *Tamla Motown TMG 694*	42 1
13 Feb 71	FORGET ME NOT *Tamla Motown TMG 762*	11 8
8 Jan 72	BLESS YOU *Tamla Motown TMG 794*	33 5
23 Jul 88	NOWHERE TO RUN (2nd re-issue) *A&M AM 444*	52 3

[1] Martha and the Vandellas

The listed flip side of 'Nowhere to Run' in 1988 was 'I Got You (I Feel Good)' by James Brown. 'Jimmy Mack' re-entry peaked at No.21 in 1970

Vic REEVES *UK, male comedian / vocalist –*
Jim Moir (Singles: 29 Weeks, Albums: 9 Weeks) pos/wks

		pos/wks
27 Apr 91 ●	BORN FREE *Sense SIGH 710* [1]	6 6
26 Oct 91 ★	DIZZY *Sense SIGH 712* [2]	1 12
14 Dec 91	ABIDE WITH ME *Sense SIGH 713*	47 3
8 Jul 95	I'M A BELIEVER *Parlophone CDR 6412* [3]	3 8
16 Nov 91	I WILL CURE YOU *Sense SIGH 111*	16 9

[1] Vic Reeves and The Roman Numerals [2] Vic Reeves and The Wonder Stuff [3] EMF and Reeves and Mortimer

REFLEX featuring MC VIPER (see also 187 LOCKDOWN)
UK, male production duo – Danny Harrison and Julian Jonah and male rapper (Singles: 1 Week) pos/wks

		pos/wks
19 May 01	PUT YOUR HANDS UP *Gusto CDGUS 2*	72 1

REFUGEE ALLSTARS See FUGEES; Wyclef JEAN

REFUGEE CAMP ALLSTARS See Lauryn HILL

Joan REGAN *UK, female vocalist (Singles: 62 Weeks)* pos/wks

		pos/wks
11 Dec 53 ●	RICOCHET (re) *Decca F 10193* [1]	8 5
14 May 54 ●	SOMEONE ELSE'S ROSES *Decca F 10257*	5 8
1 Oct 54 ●	IF I GIVE MY HEART TO YOU (re) *Decca F 10373*	3 11
5 Nov 54	WAIT FOR ME, DARLING *Decca F 10362* [2]	18 1
25 Mar 55	PRIZE OF GOLD *Decca F 10432*	6 8
6 May 55	OPEN UP YOUR HEART *Decca F 10474* [3]	19 1
1 May 59 ●	MAY YOU ALWAYS *HMV POP 593*	9 16
5 Feb 60	HAPPY ANNIVERSARY (re) *Pye 7N 15238*	29 2
28 Jul 60	PAPA LOVES MAMA *Pye 7N 15278*	29 8

		pos/wks
24 Nov 60	ONE OF THE LUCKY ONES *Pye 7N 15310*	47 1
5 Jan 61	IT MUST BE SANTA *Pye 7N 15303*	42 1

[1] Joan Regan with The Squadronaires [2] Joan Regan with The Johnston Brothers [3] Joan and Rusty Regan

The REGENTS
UK, male / female vocal / instrumental group (Singles: 14 Weeks) pos/wks

		pos/wks
22 Dec 79	7 TEEN *Rialto TREB 111*	11 12
7 Jun 80	SEE YOU LATER *Arista ARIST 350*	55 2

REGGAE BOYZ
Jamaica, male vocal / instrumental group (Singles: 1 Week) pos/wks

		pos/wks
27 Jun 98	KICK IT *Universal MCSTD 40167*	59 1

REGGAE PHILHARMONIC ORCHESTRA
UK, male / female vocal / instrumental group (Singles: 11 Weeks) pos/wks

		pos/wks
19 Nov 88	MINNIE THE MOOCHER *Mango IS 378*	35 9
28 Jul 90	LOVELY THING *Mango MNG 742* [1]	71 2

[1] Featuring Jazzy Joyce

REGGAE REVOLUTION See Pato BANTON

REGGIE See TECHNOTRONIC

REGINA
US, female vocalist – Regina Richards (Singles: 3 Weeks) pos/wks

		pos/wks
1 Feb 86	BABY LOVE *Funkin' Marvellous MARV 01*	50 3

REID *UK, male vocal group (Singles: 12 Weeks)* pos/wks

		pos/wks
8 Oct 88	ONE WAY OUT *Syncopate SY 16*	66 2
11 Feb 89	REAL EMOTION *Syncopate SY 24*	65 2
15 Apr 89	GOOD TIMES *Syncopate SY 27*	55 6
21 Oct 89	LOVIN' ON THE SIDE *Syncopate REID 1*	71 2

Eileen REID See CADETS with Eileen REID

Ellen REID See CRASH TEST DUMMIES

John REID See NIGHTCRAWLERS featuring John REID

Junior REID See COLDCUT; RAGGA TWINS; The SOUP DRAGONS

Mike REID *UK, male actor / comedian (Singles: 10 Weeks)* pos/wks

		pos/wks
22 Mar 75 ●	THE UGLY DUCKLING *Pye 7N 45434*	10 8
24 Apr 99	THE MORE I SEE YOU *Telstar TV CDSTAS 3049* [1]	46 2

[1] Barbara Windsor and Mike Reid

Neil REID
UK, male vocalist (Singles: 26 Weeks, Albums: 18 Weeks) pos/wks

		pos/wks
1 Jan 72 ●	MOTHER OF MINE *Decca F 13264*	2 20
8 Apr 72	THAT'S WHAT I WANT TO BE (re) *Decca F 13300*	45 6
5 Feb 72 ★	NEIL REID *Decca SKL 5122*	1 16
2 Sep 72	SMILE *Decca SKL 5136*	47 2

Patrick REID See POB featuring DJ Patrick REID

Maggie REILLY See Mike OLDFIELD

Keith RELF (see also The YARDBIRDS)
UK, male vocalist, b. 22 Mar 1943, d. 14 May 1976 (Singles: 1 Week) pos/wks

		pos/wks
26 May 66	MR ZERO *Columbia DB 7920*	50 1

The REMBRANDTS *US, male vocal / instrumental*
group (Singles: 28 Weeks, Albums: 5 Weeks) pos/wks

		pos/wks
2 Sep 95 ●	I'LL BE THERE FOR YOU (THEME FROM 'FRIENDS') (re) *East West A 4390CD*	3 27
20 Jan 96	THIS HOUSE IS NOT A HOME *East West A 4336CD*	58 1
23 Sep 95	LP *East West 7559617522*	14 5

The re-entry of 'I'll Be There For You' made No.5 in May 1997

REMO FOUR See Tommy QUICKLY and The REMO FOUR

REMY See TERROR SQUAD featuring FAT JOE & REMY

REMY ZERO
US, male vocal / instrumental group (Singles: 1 Week) pos/wks

27 Apr 02	**SAVE ME** *Elektra E 7297CD*	**55** 1

RENAISSANCE
UK, male / female vocal / instrumental group (Singles: 11 Weeks, Albums: 10 Weeks) pos/wks

15 Jul 78 ●	**NORTHERN LIGHTS** *Warner Bros. K 17177*	**10** 11
21 Feb 70	**RENAISSANCE** *Island ILPS 9114*	**60** 1
19 Aug 78	**A SONG FOR ALL SEASONS** *Warner Bros. K 56460*	**35** 8
2 Jun 79	**AZUR D'OR** *Warner Bros. K 56633*	**73** 1

RENÉ and ANGELA
US, male / female vocal duo – René Moore and Angela Winbush (Singles: 15 Weeks) pos/wks

15 Jun 85	**SAVE YOUR LOVE (FOR NUMBER 1)** *Club JAB 14* [1]	**66** 2
7 Sep 85	**I'LL BE GOOD** *Club JAB 18*	**22** 10
2 Nov 85	**SECRET RENDEZVOUS** *Champion CHAMP 5*	**54** 3

[1] René and Angela featuring Kurtis Blow

RENÉ and YVETTE
UK, male / female vocal duo (Singles: 4 Weeks) pos/wks

22 Nov 86	**JE T'AIME ('ALLO 'ALLO) / RENÉ DMC (DEVASTATING MACHO CHARISMA)** *Sedition EDIT 3319*	**57** 4

Nicole RENÉE
US, female vocalist (Singles: 1 Week) pos/wks

12 Dec 98	**STRAWBERRY** *Atlantic AT 0050CD*	**55** 1

RENÉE and RENATO
UK / Italy, female / male vocal duo – Hilary Lester and Renato Pagliari (Singles: 22 Weeks, Albums: 14 Weeks) pos/wks

30 Oct 82 ★	**SAVE YOUR LOVE** *Hollywood HWD 003*	**1** 16
12 Feb 83	**JUST ONE MORE KISS** *Hollywood HWD 006*	**48** 6
25 Dec 82	**SAVE YOUR LOVE** *Lifestyle LEG 9* [1]	**26** 14

[1] Renato

RENEGADE SOUNDWAVE
UK, male vocal / instrumental group (Singles: 7 Weeks, Albums: 1 Week) pos/wks

3 Feb 90	**PROBABLY A ROBBERY** *Mute MUTE 102*	**38** 6
5 Feb 94	**RENEGADE SOUNDWAVE** *Mute CDMUTE 146*	**64** 1
24 Mar 90	**SOUNDCLASH** *Mute STUMM 63*	**74** 1

REPARATA and The DELRONS
US, female vocal group (Singles: 12 Weeks) pos/wks

20 Mar 68	**CAPTAIN OF YOUR SHIP** *Bell 1002*	**13** 10
18 Oct 75	**SHOES** *Dart 2066 562* [1]	**43** 2

[1] Reparata

REPRAZENT See Roni SIZE / REPRAZENT

REPUBLICA
(see also SAFFRON) *UK, male / female vocal / instrumental group (Singles: 18 Weeks, Albums: 38 Weeks)* pos/wks

27 Apr 96	**READY TO GO** *Deconstruction 74321326132*	**43** 2
1 Mar 97	**READY TO GO (re-issue)** *Deconstruction 74321421332*	**13** 6
3 May 97 ●	**DROP DEAD GORGEOUS** *Deconstruction 74321408442*	**7** 7
3 Oct 98	**FROM RUSH HOUR WITH LOVE** *Deconstruction 74321610472* ...**20** 3
15 Mar 97 ●	**REPUBLICA** *Deconstruction 74321410522*	**4** 36
17 Oct 98	**SPEED BALLADS** *Deconstruction 74321610462*	**37** 2

The RESEARCH
UK, male vocal / instrumental group (Singles: 1 Week) pos/wks

27 Nov 04	**SHE'S NOT LEAVING** *At Large FUGCD 005*	**73** 1

RESONANCE featuring The BURRELLS
US, male producer and male vocal duo (Singles: 1 Week) pos/wks

26 May 01	**DJ** *Strictly Rhythm SRUKCD 02*	**67** 1

RESOURCE
Germany, male production / vocal group (Singles: 2 Weeks) pos/wks

31 May 03	**(I JUST) DIED IN YOUR ARMS** *Substance SUBS 17CDS* ...**42** 2

REST ASSURED
(see also GAT DECOR; PHUNKY PHANTOM) *UK, male production trio (Singles: 7 Weeks)* pos/wks

28 Feb 98	**TREAT INFAMY** *ffrr FCD 333*	**14** 7

REUBEN
UK, male vocal / instrumental trio (Singles: 2 Weeks) pos/wks

19 Jun 04	**FREDDY KREUGER** *Xtra Mile XMR 102*	**53** 1
28 Aug 04	**MOVING TO BLACKWATER** *Xtra Mile XMR 104*	**59** 1

REUNION
US, male vocal group (Singles: 4 Weeks) pos/wks

21 Sep 74	**LIFE IS A ROCK (BUT THE RADIO ROLLED ME)** *RCA PB 10056* ..**33** 4

REVELATION
UK, male / female production / vocal group (Singles: 2 Weeks) pos/wks

10 May 03	**JUST BE DUB TO ME** *Multiply CDMULTY 99*	**36** 2

REVILLOS See The REZILLOS

REVIVAL 3000
UK, male DJ / production trio (Singles: 1 Week) pos/wks

1 Nov 97	**THE MIGHTY HIGH** *Hi-Life 5718092*	**47** 1

REVOLTING COCKS
(see also MINISTRY) *US, male vocal / instrumental group (Singles: 1 Week, Albums: 1 Week)* pos/wks

18 Sep 93	**DA YA THINK I'M SEXY** *Devotion CDDVN 111*	**61** 1
2 Oct 93	**LINGER FICKEN' GOOD** *Devotion CDDVN 22*	**39** 1

REVOLUTION See PRINCE

Debbie REYNOLDS
US, female actor / vocalist – Mary Reynolds (Singles: 17 Weeks) pos/wks

30 Aug 57 ●	**TAMMY** *Vogue-Coral Q 72274* ▲	**2** 17

Jody REYNOLDS
US, male vocalist (Singles: 1 Week) pos/wks

14 Apr 79	**ENDLESS SLEEP** *Lightning LIG 9015*	**66** 1

'Endless Sleep' was coupled with 'To Know Him Is to Love Him' by The Teddy Bears as a double A-side

LJ REYNOLDS
US, male vocalist – Larry Reynolds (Singles: 3 Weeks) pos/wks

30 Jun 84	**DON'T LET NOBODY HOLD YOU DOWN** *Club JAB 5*	**53** 3

REYNOLDS GIRLS
UK, female vocal duo – Linda and Aisling Reynolds (Singles: 12 Weeks) pos/wks

25 Feb 89 ●	**I'D RATHER JACK** *PWL PWL 25*	**8** 12

The REZILLOS
UK, male / female vocal / instrumental group (Singles: 21 Weeks, Albums: 15 Weeks) pos/wks

12 Aug 78	**TOP OF THE POPS** *Sire SIR 4001*	**17** 9
25 Nov 78	**DESTINATION VENUS** *Sire SIR 4008*	**43** 4
18 Aug 79	**I WANNA BE YOUR MAN / I CAN'T STAND MY BABY (re)** *Sensible SAB 1*	**71** 2
26 Jan 80	**MOTORBIKE BEAT** *DinDisc DIN 5* [1]	**45** 6
5 Aug 78	**CAN'T STAND THE REZILLOS** *Sire WEA K 56530*	**16** 10
28 Apr 79	**MISSION ACCOMPLISHED BUT THE BEAT GOES ON** *Sire SRK 6069*	**30** 5

[1] The Revillos

REZONANCE Q
UK, male / female production / vocal duo – Mike Di Scala and Nanzene (Singles: 2 Weeks) pos/wks

1 May 03	**SOMEDAY** *All Around the World CDGLOBE 266*	**29** 2

RHIANNA
UK, female vocalist – Rhianna Kelly (Singles: 6 Weeks) pos/wks

1 Jun 02	**OH BABY** *S2 6726232*	**18** 5
14 Sep 02	**WORD LOVE** *S2 6730112*	**41** 1

RHODA with the SPECIAL AKA
(see also The SPECIALS) *UK, female vocalist and male vocal / instrumental group (Singles: 5 Weeks)* pos/wks

23 Jan 82	**THE BOILER** *2 Tone CHSTT 18*	**35** 5

Busta RHYMES
(see also Syleena JOHNSON) *US, male rapper – Trevor Smith (Singles: 96 Weeks, Albums: 21 Weeks)* pos/wks

11 May 96 ●	**WOO-HAH!! GOT YOU ALL IN CHECK** *Elektra EKR 220CD*	**8** 7
21 Sep 96	**IT'S A PARTY** *Elektra EKR 226CD* [1]	**23** 2
5 Apr 97 ●	**HIT EM HIGH (THE MONSTARS' ANTHEM)** *Atlantic A 5449CD* [2]	**8** 6

3 May 97	DO MY THING *Elektra EKR 235CD*	**39**	1
18 Oct 97	PUT YOUR HANDS WHERE MY EYES COULD SEE *Elektra E 3900CD*	**16**	3
20 Dec 97	DANGEROUS *Elektra E 3877CD*	**32**	4
18 Apr 98 ●	TURN IT UP / FIRE IT UP *Elektra E 3847CD*	**2**	10
11 Jul 98	ONE *Elektra E 3833CD1* 3	**23**	3
30 Jan 99 ●	GIMME SOME MORE *Elektra E 3782CD*	**5**	6
1 May 99 ●	WHAT'S IT GONNA BE?! *Elektra E 3762CD1* 4	**6**	6
22 Jul 00	GET OUT *Elektra E 7075CD*	**57**	1
16 Dec 00	FIRE *East West E 7136*	**60**	1
18 Aug 01 ●	ANTE UP (re) *Epic 6717882* 5	**7**	8
16 Mar 02	BREAK YA NECK *J 74321922332*	**11**	6
8 Jun 02	PASS THE COURVOISIER – PART II (re) *J 74321937902* 6	**16**	8
8 Feb 03	MAKE IT CLAP *J 82876502062* 7	**16**	4
7 Jun 03	I KNOW WHAT YOU WANT *J 82876528292* 8	**3**	13
29 Nov 03	LIGHT YOUR ASS ON FIRE *Arista 82876572512* 9	**62**	1
22 May 04	WHAT'S HAPPENIN' *Def Jam 9862517* 10	**17**	5
30 Mar 96	THE COMING *Elektra 7559617422*	**48**	4
4 Oct 97	WHEN DISASTER STRIKES ... *Elektra 7559621542*	**34**	5
16 Jan 99	EXTINCTION LEVEL EVENT/FINAL WORLD FRONT *Elektra 7559622112*	**54**	7
1 Jul 00	ANARCHY *Elektra 7559625172*	**38**	1
29 Sep 01	TURN IT UP! – THE VERY BEST *Elektra 8122735802*	**44**	3
23 Mar 02	GENESIS *J 80813200092*	**58**	1

1 Busta Rhymes featuring Zhané 2 B Real / Busta Rhymes / Coolio / LL Cool J / Method Man 3 Busta Rhymes featuring Erykah Badu 4 Busta Rhymes featuring Janet 5 M.O.P. featuring Busta Rhymes 6 Busta Rhymes featuring P Diddy and Pharrell 7 Busta Rhymes featuring Spliff Star 8 Busta Rhymes and Mariah Carey featuring The Flipmode Squad 9 Busta Rhymes featuring Pharrell 10 Method Man featuring Busta Rhymes

RHYTHIM IS RHYTHIM
US, male production group (Singles: 1 Week) pos/wks

11 Nov 89	STRINGS OF LIFE *Kool Kat KOOL 509*	**74**	1

RHYTHM BANGERS *See Robbie RIVERA*

RHYTHM ETERNITY
UK, male / female vocal / instrumental group (Singles: 1 Week) pos/wks

23 May 92	PINK CHAMPAGNE *Dead Dead Good GOOD 15T*	**72**	1

RHYTHM FACTOR
US, male / female vocal / instrumental group (Singles: 2 Weeks) pos/wks

29 Apr 95	YOU BRING ME JOY *Multiply CDMULTY 4*	**53**	2

RHYTHM MASTERS (see also BIG ROOM GIRL
featuring Darryl PANDY; RHYTHMATIC JUNKIES)
UK / Malta, male DJ / production duo (Singles: 4 Weeks) pos/wks

16 Aug 97	COME ON Y'ALL *Faze 2 CDFAZE 37*	**49**	1
6 Dec 97	ENTER THE SCENE *Distinctive DISNCD 40* 1	**49**	1
18 Aug 01	UNDERGROUND *Black & Blue NEOCD 056*	**50**	1
30 Mar 02	GHETTO *Black & Blue NEOCD 074* 2	**71**	1

1 DJ Supreme vs Rhythm Masters 2 Rhythm Masters featuring Joe Watson

RHYTHM-N-BASS
UK, male vocal group (Singles: 4 Weeks) pos/wks

19 Sep 92	ROSES *Epic 6582907*	**56**	2
3 Jul 93	CAN'T STOP THIS FEELING *Epic 6592002*	**59**	2

RHYTHM OF LIFE
UK, male DJ / producer – Steve Burgess (Singles: 2 Weeks) pos/wks

13 May 00	YOU PUT ME IN HEAVEN WITH YOUR TOUCH *Xtravaganza XTRAV 4CDS*	**24**	2

RHYTHM ON THE LOOSE
UK, male producer – Geoff Hibbert (Singles: 2 Weeks) pos/wks

19 Aug 95	BREAK OF DAWN *Six6 SIXCD 126*	**36**	2

RHYTHM QUEST
UK, male producer – Mark Hadfield (Singles: 2 Weeks) pos/wks

20 Jun 92	CLOSER TO ALL YOUR DREAMS *Network NWK 40*	**45**	2

RHYTHM SECTION
UK, male vocal / instrumental group (Singles: 1 Week) pos/wks

18 Jul 92	MIDSUMMER MADNESS (EP) *Rhythm Section RSEC 006*	**66**	1

Tracks on Midsummer Madness (EP): Dreamworld / Burnin' Up / Perfect Love 2am / Perfect Love 8am

RHYTHM SOURCE
UK, male / female vocal / instrumental group (Singles: 1 Week) pos/wks

17 Jun 95	LOVE SHINE *A&M 5810672*	**74**	1

RHYTHM SPINNERS *See Rolf HARRIS*

RHYTHMATIC
UK, male instrumental / production duo (Singles: 3 Weeks) pos/wks

12 May 90	TAKE ME BACK (re) *Network NWK 8*	**71**	2
3 Nov 90	FREQUENCY *Network NWK 13*	**62**	1

RHYTHMATIC JUNKIES
UK, male vocal / production group (Singles: 1 Week) pos/wks

15 May 99	THE FEELIN (CLAP YOUR HANDS) *Sound of Ministry RIDE 2CDS*	**67**	1

RHYTHMKILLAZ (see also GOODMEN; CHOCOLATE PUMA; JARK
PRONGO; RIVA featuring Dannii MINOGUE; TOMBA VIRA) *Holland, male production duo – Rene ter Horst and Gaston Steenkist (Singles: 2 Weeks)* pos/wks

31 Mar 01	WACK ASS MF *Incentive CENT18 CDS*	**32**	2

RIALTO *UK, male vocal / instrumental
group (Singles: 8 Weeks, Albums: 3 Weeks)* pos/wks

8 Nov 97	MONDAY MORNING 5:19 *East West EW 116CD*	**37**	2
17 Jan 98	UNTOUCHABLE *East West EW 107CD1*	**20**	3
28 Mar 98	DREAM ANOTHER DREAM *East West EW 156CD1*	**39**	2
17 Oct 98	SUMMER'S OVER *China WOKCDR 2099*	**60**	1
25 Jul 98	RIALTO *China WOLCD 1086*	**21**	3

Rosie RIBBONS *UK, female vocalist (Singles: 7 Weeks)* pos/wks

2 Nov 02	BLINK *T2 / Telstar CDSTAS 3288*	**12**	4
25 Jan 03	A LITTLE BIT *T2 / Telstar CDSTAS 3312*	**19**	3

Reva RICE and Greg ELLIS
UK, male / female vocal duo (Singles: 2 Weeks) pos/wks

27 Mar 93	NEXT TIME YOU FALL IN LOVE *Really Useful RURCD 12*	**59**	2

Damien RICE *Ireland, male vocalist / instrumentalist –
guitar (Singles: 10 Weeks, Albums: 60 Weeks)* pos/wks

1 Nov 03	CANNONBALL *DRM / 14th Floor DR 03CD1*	**32**	2
17 Jul 04	CANNONBALL (re) (re-mix) *DRM / 14th Floor DR 03CD2*	**19**	7
25 Dec 04	THE BLOWERS DAUGHTER *14th Floor DR 06CD*	**27**	1+
2 Aug 03 ●	O *DRM / 14th Floor DRM 002CD*	**8**	60+

The re-mix of 'Cannonball' was released on two CDs, the first featuring a 'radio mix' and the second a live version

Charlie RICH *US, male vocalist / instrumentalist – keyboards, b. 14 Dec
1932, d. 25 July 1995 (Singles: 29 Weeks, Albums: 28 Weeks)* pos/wks

16 Feb 74 ●	THE MOST BEAUTIFUL GIRL *Epic EPC 1897* ▲	**2**	14
13 Apr 74	BEHIND CLOSED DOORS *Epic EPC 1539*	**16**	10
1 Feb 75	WE LOVE EACH OTHER *Epic EPC 2868*	**37**	5
23 Mar 74 ●	BEHIND CLOSED DOORS *Epic 65716*	**4**	26
13 Jul 74	VERY SPECIAL LOVE SONGS *Epic 80031*	**34**	2

Kelli RICH *See NU SOUL featuring Kelli RICH*

The RICH KIDS *UK, male vocal / instrumental
group (Singles: 5 Weeks, Albums: 1 Week)* pos/wks

28 Jan 78	RICH KIDS *EMI 2738*	**24**	5
7 Oct 78	GHOSTS OF PRINCES IN TOWERS *EMI EMC 3263*	**51**	1

Richie RICH *UK, male DJ / producer –
Richard Morgan (Singles: 16 Weeks, Albums: 1 Week)* pos/wks

16 Jul 88	TURN IT UP *Club JAB 68*	**48**	3

22 Oct 88	I'LL HOUSE YOU *Gee Street GEE 003* 1	**22**	5
10 Dec 88	MY DJ (PUMP IT UP SOME) *Gee Street GEE 7*	**74**	1
2 Sep 89	SALSA HOUSE *ffrr F 113*	**50**	3
9 Mar 91	YOU USED TO SALSA *ffrr F 156* 2	**52**	3
29 Mar 97	STAY WITH ME *Castle CATX 1001* 3	**58**	1
22 Jul 89	I CAN MAKE YOU DANCE *Gee Street GEEA 3*	**65**	1

1 Richie Rich meets The Jungle Brothers 2 Richie Rich featuring Ralphi Rosario
3 Richie Rich and Esera Tuaolo

'You Used to Salsa' is a re-mix of 'Salsa House'

Tony RICH PROJECT *US, male vocalist –*
Antonio Jeffries (Singles: 22 Weeks, Albums: 10 Weeks) pos/wks

4 May 96 ●	NOBODY KNOWS *LaFace 74321356422*	**4**	17
31 Aug 96 ●	LIKE A WOMAN *LaFace 74321401612*	**27**	4
14 Dec 96	LEAVIN' *LaFace 74321438382*	**52**	1
25 May 96 ●	WORDS *LaFace 73008260222*	**27**	10

Cliff RICHARD (2 Top 500) *'The Peter Pan of Pop' – Britain's most successful solo vocalist, b. Harry Webb, 14 Oct 1940, Lucknow, India. Ex-member of The Dick Teague Skiffle Group was instantly successful and almost overnight became the UK's No.1 rock 'n' roll star, despite bad press due to his "too sexy" live performances. He has had more different chart singles than any other artist, had hits in every major market around the globe and was the first UK act named World's No.1 Artist by Billboard (1963 – Elvis was second and The Shadows third). Between 1959 and 2004, Cliff had a staggering 36 Top 10 albums, including seven No.1s, and had more Top 10 albums in the 1980s than any other artist. He was brought to a wider audience by a successful series of films, including 'Summer Holiday', was seen on the first 'Top of the Pops' and has appeared on the TV show more than any other solo artist. He is one of the few performers to top the chart with two different recordings of the same song (Living Doll). This seemingly ageless entertainer's record number of 66 Top 10 entries now spans 46 years, and at times he held the record for being the youngest (1959) and oldest (1999) British singer to top the singles chart. Cliff, who has sold more than 260 million records (singles, albums, EPs) worldwide, was awarded the Outstanding Contribution to British Music trophy at the 1989 Brits, was made an OBE in 1980, was knighted in 1995, and holds the unique achievement of a UK No.1 single in five different decades. Cliff was inducted into the UK Music Hall of Fame in 2004, representing the 1950s. Best-selling single: 'The Young Ones' 1,052,000 (Singles: 1160 Weeks, Albums: 812 Weeks)* pos/wks

12 Sep 58 ●	MOVE IT! *Columbia DB 4178* 1	**2**	17
21 Nov 58 ●	HIGH CLASS BABY *Columbia DB 4203* 1	**7**	10
30 Jan 59	LIVIN' LOVIN' DOLL *Columbia DB 4249* 1	**20**	6
8 May 59 ●	MEAN STREAK *Columbia DB 4290 (A)* 1	**10**	9
15 May 59	NEVER MIND *Columbia DB 4290 (B)* 1	**21**	2
10 Jul 59 ★	LIVING DOLL (2re) *Columbia DB 4306* 1	**1**	23
9 Oct 59 ★	TRAVELLIN' LIGHT *Columbia DB 4351 (B)* 2	**1**	17
9 Oct 59	DYNAMITE (re) *Columbia DB 4351 (A)* 2	**16**	4
15 Jan 60	EXPRESSO BONGO (EP) *Columbia SEG 7971* 2	**14**	7
22 Jan 60 ●	A VOICE IN THE WILDERNESS (re) *Columbia DB 4398* 2	**2**	16
24 Mar 60 ●	FALL IN LOVE WITH YOU *Columbia DB 4431* 2	**2**	15
30 Jun 60 ★	PLEASE DON'T TEASE *Columbia DB 4479* 2	**1**	18
22 Sep 60 ●	NINE TIMES OUT OF TEN *Columbia DB 4506* 2	**3**	12
1 Dec 60 ★	I LOVE YOU *Columbia DB 4547* 2	**1**	16
2 Mar 61 ●	THEME FOR A DREAM *Columbia DB 4593* 2	**3**	10
30 Mar 61 ●	GEE WHIZ IT'S YOU *Columbia DC 756* 2	**4**	14
22 Jun 61 ●	A GIRL LIKE YOU *Columbia DB 4667* 2	**3**	14
19 Oct 61 ●	WHEN THE GIRL IN YOUR ARMS IS THE GIRL IN YOUR HEART *Columbia DB 4716*	**3**	15
11 Jan 62 ★	THE YOUNG ONES *Columbia DB 4761* 2 ◆ ■	**1**	21
10 May 62 ●	I'M LOOKING OUT THE WINDOW / DO YOU WANT TO DANCE *Columbia DB 4828* 3	**2**	17
6 Sep 62 ●	IT'LL BE ME *Columbia DB 4886* 2	**2**	12
6 Dec 62 ★	THE NEXT TIME / BACHELOR BOY *Columbia DB 4950* 2	**1**	18
21 Feb 63 ★	SUMMER HOLIDAY *Columbia DB 4977* 2	**1**	18
9 May 63 ●	LUCKY LIPS *Columbia DB 7034* 2	**4**	15
22 Aug 63 ●	IT'S ALL IN THE GAME *Columbia DB 7089*	**2**	13
7 Nov 63 ●	DON'T TALK TO HIM (re) *Columbia DB 7150* 2	**2**	14
6 Feb 64 ●	I'M THE LONELY ONE *Columbia DB 7203* 2	**8**	10
30 Apr 64 ●	CONSTANTLY *Columbia DB 7272*	**4**	13
2 Jul 64 ●	ON THE BEACH *Columbia DB 7305* 2	**7**	13
8 Oct 64 ●	THE TWELFTH OF NEVER *Columbia DB 7372*	**8**	11
10 Dec 64 ●	I COULD EASILY FALL *Columbia DB 7420* 2	**6**	11
11 Mar 65 ★	THE MINUTE YOU'RE GONE *Columbia DB 7496*	**1**	14
10 Jun 65	ON MY WORD *Columbia DB 7596*	**12**	10

19 Aug 65	THE TIME IN BETWEEN *Columbia DB 7660* 2	**22**	8
4 Nov 65 ●	WIND ME UP (LET ME GO) *Columbia DB 7745*	**2**	16
24 Mar 66	BLUE TURNS TO GREY *Columbia DB 7866* 2	**15**	9
21 Jul 66 ●	VISIONS *Columbia DB 7968*	**7**	12
13 Oct 66 ●	TIME DRAGS BY *Columbia DB 8017* 2	**10**	11
15 Dec 66 ●	IN THE COUNTRY *Columbia DB 8094* 2	**6**	10
16 Mar 67 ●	IT'S ALL OVER *Columbia DB 8150*	**9**	10
8 Jun 67 ●	I'LL COME RUNNIN' *Columbia DB 8210*	**26**	8
16 Aug 67 ●	THE DAY I MET MARIE *Columbia DB 8245*	**10**	14
15 Nov 67 ●	ALL MY LOVE *Columbia DB 8293*	**6**	12
20 Mar 68 ★	CONGRATULATIONS *Columbia DB 8376*	**1**	13
26 Jun 68	I'LL LOVE YOU FOREVER TODAY *Columbia DB 8437*	**27**	6
25 Sep 68	MARIANNE *Columbia DB 8476*	**22**	8
27 Nov 68	DON'T FORGET TO CATCH ME *Columbia DB 8503* 2	**21**	10
26 Feb 69	GOOD TIMES (BETTER TIMES) *Columbia DB 8548*	**12**	11
28 May 69 ●	BIG SHIP *Columbia DB 8581*	**8**	10
13 Sep 69 ●	THROW DOWN A LINE *Columbia DB 8615* 4	**7**	9
6 Dec 69	WITH THE EYES OF A CHILD *Columbia DB 8641*	**20**	11
21 Feb 70	THE JOY OF LIVING *Columbia DB 8657* 4	**25**	8
6 Jun 70 ●	GOODBYE SAM, HELLO SAMANTHA *Columbia DB 8685*	**6**	15
5 Sep 70	I AIN'T GOT TIME ANYMORE *Columbia DB 8708*	**21**	7
23 Jan 71	SUNNY HONEY GIRL *Columbia DB 8747*	**19**	8
10 Apr 71	SILVERY RAIN *Columbia DB 8774*	**27**	6
17 Jul 71	FLYING MACHINE *Columbia DB 8797*	**37**	7
13 Nov 71	SING A SONG OF FREEDOM *Columbia DB 8836*	**13**	12
11 Mar 72	JESUS *Columbia DB 8864*	**35**	3
26 Aug 72	LIVING IN HARMONY *Columbia DB 8917*	**12**	10
17 Mar 73 ●	POWER TO ALL OUR FRIENDS *EMI 2012*	**4**	12
12 May 73	HELP IT ALONG / TOMORROW RISING *EMI 2022*	**29**	6
1 Dec 73	TAKE ME HIGH *EMI 2088*	**27**	12
18 May 74	(YOU KEEP ME) HANGIN' ON *EMI 2150*	**13**	8
7 Feb 76	MISS YOU NIGHTS *EMI 2376*	**15**	10
8 May 76 ●	DEVIL WOMAN *EMI 2458*	**9**	8
21 Aug 76	I CAN'T ASK FOR ANYTHING MORE THAN YOU *EMI 2499*	**17**	8
4 Dec 76	HEY MR DREAM MAKER *EMI 2559*	**31**	5
5 Mar 77	MY KINDA LIFE *EMI 2584*	**15**	8
16 Jul 77	WHEN TWO WORLDS DRIFT APART *EMI 2633*	**46**	3
31 Mar 79	GREEN LIGHT *EMI 2920*	**57**	3
21 Jul 79 ★	WE DON'T TALK ANYMORE *EMI 2975*	**1**	14
3 Nov 79	HOT SHOT *EMI 5003*	**46**	5
2 Feb 80 ●	CARRIE *EMI 5006*	**4**	10
16 Aug 80 ●	DREAMIN' *EMI 5095*	**8**	10
25 Oct 80	SUDDENLY *Jet 7002* 5	**15**	7
24 Jan 81	A LITTLE IN LOVE *EMI 5123*	**15**	8
29 Aug 81 ●	WIRED FOR SOUND *EMI 5221*	**4**	9
21 Nov 81 ●	DADDY'S HOME *EMI 5251*	**2**	12
17 Jul 82 ●	THE ONLY WAY OUT *EMI 5318*	**10**	9
25 Sep 82	WHERE DO WE GO FROM HERE *EMI 5341*	**60**	3
4 Dec 82	LITTLE TOWN *EMI 5348*	**11**	7
19 Feb 83 ●	SHE MEANS NOTHING TO ME *Capitol CL 276* 6	**9**	9
16 Apr 83 ●	TRUE LOVE WAYS *EMI 5385* 7	**8**	8
4 Jun 83	DRIFTING *DJM SHEIL 1* 8	**64**	2
3 Sep 83	NEVER SAY DIE (GIVE A LITTLE BIT MORE) *EMI 5415*	**15**	7
26 Nov 83 ●	PLEASE DON'T FALL IN LOVE *EMI 5437*	**7**	9
31 Mar 84	BABY YOU'RE DYNAMITE / OCEAN DEEP (re) *EMI 5457*	**27**	7
3 Nov 84	SHOOTING FROM THE HEART *EMI RICH 1*	**51**	4
9 Feb 85	HEART USER *EMI RICH 2*	**46**	3
14 Sep 85	SHE'S SO BEAUTIFUL *EMI 5531*	**17**	7
7 Dec 85	IT'S IN EVERY ONE OF US *EMI 5537*	**45**	6
22 Mar 86 ★	LIVING DOLL *WEA YZ 65* 9	**1**	11
4 Oct 86 ●	ALL I ASK OF YOU *Polydor POSP 802* 10	**3**	16
29 Nov 86	SLOW RIVERS *Rocket EJS 13* 11	**44**	8
20 Jun 87 ●	MY PRETTY ONE *EMI EM 4*	**6**	10
29 Aug 87 ●	SOME PEOPLE *EMI EM 18*	**3**	10
31 Oct 87	REMEMBER ME *EMI EM 31*	**35**	4
13 Feb 88	TWO HEARTS *EMI EM 42*	**34**	3
3 Dec 88 ★	MISTLETOE AND WINE *EMI EM 78*	**1**	8
10 Jun 89 ●	THE BEST OF ME *EMI EM 92*	**2**	7
26 Aug 89 ●	I JUST DON'T HAVE THE HEART *EMI EM 101*	**3**	8
14 Oct 89	LEAN ON YOU *EMI EM 105*	**17**	6
9 Dec 89	WHENEVER GOD SHINES HIS LIGHT *Polydor VANS 2* 12	**20**	6
24 Feb 90	STRONGER THAN THAT *EMI EM 129*	**14**	5
25 Aug 90 ●	SILHOUETTES *EMI EM 152*	**10**	7
13 Oct 90	FROM A DISTANCE *EMI EM 155*	**11**	6
8 Dec 90 ★	SAVIOUR'S DAY *EMI XMAS 90*	**1**	7
14 Sep 91	MORE TO LIFE *EMI EM 205*	**23**	5
7 Dec 91 ●	WE SHOULD BE TOGETHER *EMI XMAS 91*	**10**	6
11 Jan 92	THIS NEW YEAR *EMI EMS 218*	**30**	2
5 Dec 92 ●	I STILL BELIEVE IN YOU *EMI EM 255*	**7**	6

			pos/wks
27 Mar 93	●	PEACE IN OUR TIME *EMI CDEM 265* 8	5
12 Jun 93		HUMAN WORK OF ART *EMI CDEM 267* **24**	4
2 Oct 93		NEVER LET GO *EMI CDEM 281* **32**	3
18 Dec 93		HEALING LOVE *EMI CDEM 294* 19	5
10 Dec 94		ALL I HAVE TO DO IS DREAM / MISS YOU NIGHTS (re)	
		(re-issue) *EMI CDEM 359* [13] 14	9
2 Oct 95		MISUNDERSTOOD MAN *EMI CDEM 394* 19	3
9 Dec 95		HAD TO BE *EMI CDEM 410* [14] **22**	4
30 Mar 96		THE WEDDING *EMI CDEM 422* [15] **40**	1
25 Jan 97		BE WITH ME ALWAYS *EMI CDEM 453* 52	1
24 Oct 98	●	CAN'T KEEP THIS FEELING IN *EMI CDEM 526* 10	4
7 Aug 99		THE MIRACLE *EMI / Blacknight CDEM 546* **23**	2
27 Nov 99	★	THE MILLENNIUM PRAYER *Papillon PROMISECD 01* ...1 16
15 Dec 01		SOMEWHERE OVER THE RAINBOW / WHAT A WONDERFUL	
		WORLD *Papillon CLIFF CD1* 11	6
13 Apr 02		LET ME BE THE ONE *Papillon CLIFF CD2* **29**	3
20 Dec 03	●	SANTA'S LIST *EMI SANTA 01* 5	5
23 Oct 04	●	SOMETHIN' IS GOIN' ON *Decca / UCJ 4756419* 9	3
25 Dec 04		I CANNOT GIVE YOU MY LOVE *Decca / UCJ 4756611* 13	1+
18 Apr 59	●	CLIFF *Columbia 33SX 1147* [1] 4 31
14 Nov 59	●	CLIFF SINGS *Columbia 33SX 1192* [2] 2 36
15 Oct 60	●	ME AND MY SHADOWS *Columbia 33SX 1261* [2] 2 33
22 Apr 61	●	LISTEN TO CLIFF *Columbia 33SX 1320* 2 28
21 Oct 61	★	21 TODAY *Columbia 33SX 1368* [3] 1 16
23 Dec 61	★	THE YOUNG ONES (FILM SOUNDTRACK)	
		Columbia 33SX 1384 [4] 1 42
29 Sep 62	●	32 MINUTES AND 17 SECONDS *Columbia 33SX 1431* [2] ...3 21
26 Jan 63	★	SUMMER HOLIDAY (FILM SOUNDTRACK)	
		Columbia 33SX 1472 [2] 1 36
13 Jul 63	●	CLIFF'S HIT ALBUM *Columbia 33SX 1512* [2] 2 19
28 Sep 63	●	WHEN IN SPAIN *Columbia 33SX 1541* [2] 8 10
11 Jul 64		WONDERFUL LIFE (FILM SOUNDTRACK)	
		Columbia 33SX 1628 [2] 2 23
9 Jan 65		HITS FROM ALADDIN AND HIS WONDERFUL LAMP	
		(PANTOMIME) *Columbia 33SX 1676* [2] 13	5
17 Apr 65	●	CLIFF RICHARD *Columbia 33SX 1709* [5] 9	5
14 Aug 65		MORE HITS BY CLIFF *Columbia 33SX 1737* 20	1
8 Jan 66		LOVE IS FOREVER *Columbia 33SX 1769* 19	1
21 May 66	●	KINDA LATIN *Columbia SX 6039* 9 12
17 Dec 66		FINDERS KEEPERS (FILM SOUNDTRACK)	
		Columbia SX 6079 [2] 6 18
7 Jan 67		CINDERELLA (PANTOMIME) *Columbia 33SX 6103* [2] ...30	6
15 Apr 67		DON'T STOP ME NOW! *Columbia SCX 6133* 23	9
11 Nov 67		GOOD NEWS *Columbia SCX 6167* 37	1
1 Jun 68		CLIFF IN JAPAN *Columbia SCX 6244* 29	2
16 Nov 68		ESTABLISHED 1958 *Columbia SCX 6282* [2] 30	4
12 Jul 69	●	THE BEST OF CLIFF *Columbia SCX 6343* 5 17
27 Sep 69		SINCERELY *Columbia SCX 6357* 24	3
12 Dec 70		TRACKS 'N' GROOVES *Columbia SCX 6435* 37	2
23 Dec 72		THE BEST OF CLIFF VOLUME 2 *Columbia SCX 6519* ...49	2
19 Jan 74		TAKE ME HIGH (FILM SOUNDTRACK) *EMI EMC 3016* ...41	4
29 May 76	●	I'M NEARLY FAMOUS *EMI EMC 3122* 5 21
26 Mar 77	●	EVERY FACE TELLS A STORY *EMI EMC 3172* 8 10
22 Oct 77	★	40 GOLDEN GREATS *EMI EMTV 6* 1 19
4 Mar 78		SMALL CORNERS *EMI EMC 3219* 33	5
21 Oct 78	●	GREEN LIGHT *EMI EMC 3231* 25	3
17 Feb 79		THANK YOU VERY MUCH – REUNION CONCERT AT THE	
		LONDON PALLADIUM *EMI EMTV 15* [2] 5 12
15 Sep 79	●	ROCK 'N' ROLL JUVENILE *EMI EMC 3307* 3 22
13 Sep 80	●	I'M NO HERO *EMI EMA 796* 4 12
4 Jul 81	★	LOVE SONGS *EMI EMTV 27* 1 43
26 Sep 81	●	WIRED FOR SOUND *EMI EMC 3377* 4 25
4 Sep 82	●	NOW YOU SEE ME ... NOW YOU DON'T *EMI EMC 3415* ...4 14
21 May 83	●	DRESSED FOR THE OCCASION *EMI EMC 3432* [6] ...7 17
15 Oct 83	●	SILVER *EMI EMC 1077871* 7 24
14 Jul 84		20 ORIGINAL GREATS *EMI CRS 1* [2] 43	6
1 Dec 84		THE ROCK CONNECTION *EMI CLF 2* 43	5
26 Sep 87	●	ALWAYS GUARANTEED *EMI EMD 1004* 5 25
19 Nov 88	★	PRIVATE COLLECTION 1979–1988 *EMI CRTV 30* 1 26
11 Nov 89	●	STRONGER *EMI EMD 1012* 7 21
17 Nov 90		FROM A DISTANCE ... THE EVENT *EMI CRTV 31* 3 15
30 Nov 91		TOGETHER WITH CLIFF RICHARD *EMI EMD 1028* ...10	7
1 May 93	★	THE ALBUM *EMI CDEMD 1043* ■ 1 15
15 Oct 94		THE HIT LIST *EMI CDEMTV 84* 3 21
11 Nov 95		SONGS FROM 'HEATHCLIFF' *EMI CDEMD 1091* 15	9
24 Aug 96		AT THE MOVIES – 1959–1974 *EMI CDEMD 1096* 17	3
2 Aug 97		THE ROCK 'N' ROLL YEARS *EMI CDEMD 1109* 32	3
31 Oct 98	●	REAL AS I WANNA BE *EMI 4974062* 10	9
21 Oct 00	●	THE WHOLE STORY – HIS GREATEST HITS *EMI 5293222* ...6 13

			pos/wks
17 Nov 01		WANTED *Papillon WANTED 1* 11	8
29 Nov 03	●	CLIFF AT CHRISTMAS *EMI 5934982* 9	8
6 Nov 04	●	SOMETHING'S GOIN' ON *Decca / UCJ 4756408* 7	4

[1] Cliff Richard and The Drifters [2] Cliff Richard and The Shadows [3] Cliff Richard with the Norrie Paramor Orchestra / Cliff Richard / The Shadows [4] Cliff and Hank [5] Olivia Newton-John and Cliff Richard [6] Phil Everly and Cliff Richard [7] Cliff Richard with the London Philharmonic Orchestra [8] Sheila Walsh and Cliff Richard [9] Cliff Richard and The Young Ones featuring Hank B Marvin [10] Cliff Richard and Sarah Brightman [11] Elton John and Cliff Richard [12] Van Morrison with Cliff Richard [13] Cliff Richard with Phil Everly / Cliff Richard [14] Cliff Richard and Olivia Newton-John [15] Cliff Richard featuring Helen Hobson
[1] Cliff Richard and The Drifters [2] Cliff Richard and The Shadows [3] Cliff Richard, The Shadows and Norrie Paramor and his Orchestra [4] Cliff Richard – The Shadows with Grazina Frame [5] Cliff Richard with The Shadows [6] Cliff Richard and the London Philharmonic Orchestra

Tracks on Expresso Bongo (EP): Love / A Voice in the Wilderness / The Shrine on the Second Floor / Bongo Blues. 'Bongo Blues' features only The Shadows. 'Gee Whiz It's You' was an 'export' single. 'Bachelor Boy' was listed with 'The Next Time' from 10 Jan 1963. 'Ocean Deep' listed from 28 Apr 1984 onwards. It peaked at No.41. 'I Cannot Give You My Love' features the uncredited vocals of Barry Gibb.

Wendy RICHARD See Mike SARNE

Keith RICHARDS (see also The ROLLING STONES)
UK, male vocalist / instrumentalist – guitar (Albums: 4 Weeks) pos/wks
| 15 Oct 88 | | TALK IS CHEAP *Virgin V 2554* ....37 | 3 |
| 31 Oct 92 | | MAIN OFFENDER *Virgin America CDVUS 59* ......45 | 1 |

Calvin RICHARDSON *US, male vocalist (Singles: 1 Week)* pos/wks
| 27 Mar 04 | | I'VE GOT TO MOVE *Hollywood HOL 004CD* ......74 | 1 |

Lionel RICHIE 〈 51 〉 **Top 500** *Singer / composer / producer, b. 20 Jun 1949, Alabama, US. Launched a solo career in 1982 after 12 years fronting The Commodores. Arguably the most successful US songwriter of the 1980s, who composed at least one US chart-topper per year for a record nine successive years (Singles: 190 Weeks, Albums: 465 Weeks)* pos/wks

12 Sep 81	●	ENDLESS LOVE *Motown TMG 1240* [1] ▲ 7 12
20 Nov 82	●	TRULY *Motown TMG 1284* ▲ 6 11
29 Jan 83		YOU ARE *Motown TMG 1290* 43	7
7 May 83		MY LOVE *Motown TMG 1300* 70	3
1 Oct 83	●	ALL NIGHT LONG (ALL NIGHT) *Motown TMG 1319* ▲ ...2 16
3 Dec 83	●	RUNNING WITH THE NIGHT *Motown TMG 1324* 9 12
10 Mar 84	★	HELLO *Motown TMG 1330* ▲ 1 15
23 Jun 84		STUCK ON YOU *Motown TMG 1341* 12 12
20 Oct 84		PENNY LOVER *Motown TMG 1356* 18	7
16 Nov 85	●	SAY YOU, SAY ME *Motown ZB 40421* ▲ 8 11
26 Jul 86	●	DANCING ON THE CEILING *Motown LIO 1* 7 11
11 Oct 86		LOVE WILL CONQUER ALL *Motown LIO 2* 45	5
20 Dec 86		BALLERINA GIRL / DEEP RIVER WOMAN *Motown LIO 3* ...17	8
28 Mar 87		SELA *Motown LIO 4* 43	6
9 May 92		DO IT TO ME *Motown TMG 1407* 33	6
22 Aug 92	●	MY DESTINY *Motown TMG 1408* 7 13
28 Nov 92		LOVE OH LOVE (re) *Motown TMG 1413* 52	4
6 Apr 96		DON'T WANNA LOSE YOU *Mercury MERCD 461* 17	5
23 Nov 96		STILL IN LOVE *Mercury MERCD 477* 66	1
27 Jun 98		CLOSEST THING TO HEAVEN *Mercury 5661312* 26	2
21 Oct 00		ANGEL *Mercury 5726702* 18	5
23 Dec 00		DON'T WANNA LOSE YOU *Mercury 5688992* 34	5
17 Mar 01		TENDER HEART *Mercury 5728462* 29	3
23 Jun 01		I FORGOT *Mercury 5729922* 34	2
26 Apr 03		TO LOVE A WOMAN *Mercury 0779082* [2] 19	4
20 Mar 04		JUST FOR YOU *Mercury 9862071* 20	4
27 Nov 82		LIONEL RICHIE *Motown STMA 8037* 9 86
29 Oct 83	★	CAN'T SLOW DOWN *Motown STMA 8041* ▲ 1 154
23 Aug 86	●	DANCING ON THE CEILING *Motown ZL 72412* ▲ 2 53
6 Jun 92	★	BACK TO FRONT *Motown 5300182* ■ 1 81
20 Apr 96		LOUDER THAN WORDS *Mercury 5322412* 11	5
31 Jan 98	●	TRULY – THE LOVE SONGS *Motown / PolyGram TV 5308432* ...5 21
11 Jul 98		TIME *Mercury 5585182* 31	3
28 Oct 00		RENAISSANCE *Island 5482202* 6 24
7 Dec 02		ENCORE *Mercury 0633482* 8 10
22 Nov 03	●	THE DEFINITIVE COLLECTION *Universal TV 9861394* [1] ...10 20
20 Mar 04	●	JUST FOR YOU *Mercury 9861710* 5	8

[1] Diana Ross and Lionel Richie [2] Lionel Richie featuring Enrique Iglesias
[1] Lionel Richie / The Commodores

'Deep River Woman' was listed only from 17 Jan 1987. It has the following credit: background vocal Alabama

Shane RICHIE UK, male actor / vocalist (Singles: 14 Weeks)
pos/wks
6 Dec 03 ●	I'M YOUR MAN BMG 82876578582	2 14

Jonathan RICHMAN and The MODERN LOVERS US, male
vocal / instrumental group (Singles: 27 Weeks, Albums: 3 Weeks) pos/wks
16 Jul 77	ROADRUNNER Beserkley BZZ 1	11 9
29 Oct 77 ●	EGYPTIAN REGGAE Beserkley BZZ 2	5 14
21 Jan 78	THE MORNING OF OUR LIVES Beserkley BZZ 7 [1]	29 4
27 Aug 77	ROCK 'N' ROLL WITH THE MODERN LOVERS Beserkley BSERK 9	50 3

[1] The Modern Lovers

RICHMOND STRINGS / MIKE SAMMES SINGERS
UK, orchestra and male / female vocal group (Albums: 7 Weeks) pos/wks
19 Jan 76	MUSIC OF AMERICA Ronco TRD 2016	18 7

Adam RICKITT
UK, male actor / vocalist (Singles: 19 Weeks, Albums: 1 Week) pos/wks
26 Jun 99 ●	I BREATHE AGAIN Polydor 5611862	5 10
16 Oct 99	EVERYTHING MY HEART DESIRES Polydor 5614392	15 6
5 Feb 00	BEST THING Polydor 5616132	25 3
30 Oct 99	GOOD TIMES Polydor 5431422	41 1

RICKY UK, male vocal / instrumental group (Singles: 1 Week)
pos/wks
18 Sep 04	THAT EXTRA MILE Garcia GARCIA 004CD	50 1

RICO See Gary NUMAN; The SPECIALS

Frank RICOTTI ALL STARS
UK, male instrumental group (Albums: 1 Week) pos/wks
26 Jun 93	THE BEIDERBECKE COLLECTION Dormouse DM 20CD	73 1

Album first entered the chart on 24 Dec 88 as a compilation

Nelson RIDDLE ORCHESTRA See Shirley BASSEY; Linda RONSTADT; Kiri
TE KANAWA

RIDE UK, male vocal / instrumental
group (Singles: 22 Weeks, Albums: 16 Weeks) pos/wks
27 Jan 90	RIDE (EP) Creation CRE 072T	71 2
14 Apr 90	PLAY (EP) Creation CRE 075T	32 3
29 Sep 90	FALL (EP) Creation CRE 087T	34 3
16 Mar 91	TODAY FOREVER (EP) Creation CRE 100T	14 4
15 Feb 92 ●	LEAVE THEM ALL BEHIND Creation CRE 123T	9 3
25 Apr 92	TWISTERELLA Creation CRE 150T	36 2
30 Apr 94	BIRDMAN Creation CRESCD 155	38 2
25 Jun 94	HOW DOES IT FEEL TO FEEL Creation CRESCD 184	58 1
8 Oct 94	I DON'T KNOW WHERE IT COMES FROM Creation CRESCD 189R	46 1
24 Feb 96	BLACK NITE CRASH Creation CRESCD 199	67 1
27 Oct 90	NOWHERE Creation CRELP 074	11 5
21 Mar 92 ●	GOING BLANK AGAIN Creation CRECD 124	5 5
2 Jul 94 ●	CARNIVAL OF LIGHT Creation CRECD 147	5 4
23 Mar 96	TARANTULA Creation CRECD 180	21 2

Tracks on Ride (EP): Chelsea Girl / Drive Blind / All I Can See / Close My Eyes. Tracks
on Play (EP): Like a Daydream / Silver / Furthest Sense / Perfect Time. Tracks on Fall
(EP): Dreams Burn Down / Taste / Hear and Now / Nowhere. Tracks on Today
Forever (EP): Unfamiliar / Sennen / Beneath / Today

RIDER & Terry VENABLES UK, male vocal / instrumental
group and football pundit / vocalist (Singles: 2 Weeks) pos/wks
1 Jun 02	ENGLAND CRAZY East West EW 248CD	46 2

Andrew RIDGELEY (see also WHAM!)
UK, male vocalist (Singles: 3 Weeks) pos/wks
31 Mar 90	SHAKE Epic AJR 1	58 3

Stan RIDGWAY US, male vocalist (Singles: 12 Weeks)
pos/wks
5 Jul 86 ●	CAMOUFLAGE IRS IRM 114	4 12

André RIEU
Holland, male orchestra leader and producer (Albums: 2 Weeks) pos/wks
22 Apr 00	CELEBRATION! Philips 5430692	51 2

RIGHEIRA Italy, male vocal duo (Singles: 3 Weeks)
pos/wks
24 Sep 83	VAMOS A LA PLAYA A&M AM 137	53 3

RIGHT SAID FRED UK, male vocal / instrumental group – lead
vocal Richard Fairbrass (Singles: 66 Weeks, Albums: 53 Weeks) pos/wks
27 Jul 91 ●	I'M TOO SEXY Tug SNOG 1 ▲	2 16
7 Dec 91 ●	DON'T TALK JUST KISS Tug SNOG 2 [1]	3 11
21 Mar 92 ★	DEEPLY DIPPY Tug SNOG 3	1 14
1 Aug 92	THOSE SIMPLE THINGS / DAYDREAM Tug SNOG 4	29 5
27 Feb 93 ●	STICK IT OUT Tug CDCOMIC 1 [2]	4 7
23 Oct 93	BUMPED Tug CDSNOG 7	32 4
18 Dec 93	HANDS UP (4 LOVERS) Tug CDSNOG 8	60 3
19 Mar 94	WONDERMAN Tug CDSNOG 9	55 1
13 Oct 01	YOU'RE MY MATE Kingsize 74321895632	18 5
28 Mar 92 ★	UP Tug SNOGCD 1	1 49
13 Nov 93	SEX AND TRAVEL Tug SNOGCD 2	35 4

[1] Right Said Fred. Guest vocals: Jocelyn Brown [2] Right Said Fred and Friends

The RIGHTEOUS BROTHERS
US, male vocal duo – Bill Medley and Bobby Hatfield, b. 10 Aug
1940, d. 5 Nov 2003 (Singles: 86 Weeks, Albums: 17 Weeks) pos/wks
14 Jan 65 ★	YOU'VE LOST THAT LOVIN' FEELIN' London HLU 9943 ▲	1 10
12 Aug 65	UNCHAINED MELODY London HL 9975	14 12
13 Jan 66	EBB TIDE London HL 10011	48 2
14 Apr 66	(YOU'RE MY) SOUL AND INSPIRATION Verve VS 535 ▲	15 10
10 Nov 66	THE WHITE CLIFFS OF DOVER London HL 10086	21 9
22 Dec 66	ISLAND IN THE SUN Verve VS 547	24 5
12 Feb 69 ●	YOU'VE LOST THAT LOVIN' FEELIN' (re-issue) London HL 10241	10 11
19 Nov 77	YOU'VE LOST THAT LOVIN' FEELIN' (2nd re-issue) Phil Spector International 2010 022	42 4
27 Oct 90 ★	UNCHAINED MELODY (re-issue) Verve / Polydor PO 101	1 14
15 Dec 90 ●	YOU'VE LOST THAT LOVIN' FEELIN' / EBB TIDE (3rd re-issue) Verve / Polydor PO 116	3 9
1 Dec 90	THE VERY BEST OF THE RIGHTEOUS BROTHERS Verve 8472481	11 17

RIKKI and DAZ featuring Glen CAMPBELL
UK, male production duo – John Matthews and Darren
Sampson and US, male vocalist (Singles: 8 Weeks) pos/wks
30 Nov 02	RHINESTONE COWBOY (GIDDY UP GIDDY UP) Serious SER 059CD	12 8

RIKROK See Ricardo 'Rikrok' DUCENT; SHAGGY

Cheryl Pepsii RILEY US, female vocalist (Singles: 1 Week)
pos/wks
28 Jan 89	THANKS FOR MY CHILD CBS 653153 7	75 1

Jeannie C RILEY
US, female vocalist – Jeanne C Stephenson (Singles: 15 Weeks) pos/wks
16 Oct 68	HARPER VALLEY P.T.A. Polydor 56748 ▲	12 15

Teddy RILEY (see also BLACKSTREET)
US, male producer (Singles: 5 Weeks) pos/wks
21 Mar 92	IS IT GOOD TO YOU MCA MCS 1611 [1]	53 2
19 Jun 93	BABY BE MINE MCA MCSTD 1772 [2]	37 3

[1] Teddy Riley featuring Tammy Lucas [2] BLACKstreet featuring Teddy Riley

RIMES featuring Shaila PROSPERE
UK, male rapper – Julian Johnson (Singles: 1 Week) pos/wks
22 May 99	IT'S OVER Universal MCSTD 40199	51 1

LeAnn RIMES (434) Top 500
Song stylist, b. 28 Aug 1982, Mississippi, US, who first recorded at 11, was the
youngest artist (at 13) to top the US country chart. She won a Grammy at 14
and twice topped the US pop album chart by 15. Her best-selling single, 'How
Do I Live' (713,900), spent a record four years on the US country singles sales
Top 20 (Singles: 102 Weeks, Albums: 60 Weeks) pos/wks
7 Mar 98 ●	HOW DO I LIVE (re) Curb CUBCX 30	7 34
12 Sep 98	LOOKING THROUGH YOUR EYES / COMMITMENT Curb CUBC 32	38 2
12 Dec 98	BLUE Curb CUBC 39	23 6

		pos/wks	
6 Mar 99 ●	WRITTEN IN THE STARS (re) *Mercury EJSCD 45* [1]	**10**	8
18 Dec 99	CRAZY *Curb CUBC 52*	**36**	3
25 Nov 00 ★	CAN'T FIGHT THE MOONLIGHT *Curb CUBC 58* ■	**1**	17
31 Mar 01	I NEED YOU (re) *Curb CUBC 60*	**13**	7
23 Feb 02	BUT I DO LOVE YOU *London / Curb CUBC 075*	**20**	4
12 Oct 02	LIFE GOES ON *Curb / London CUBC 085*	**11**	8
8 May 03	SUDDENLY *Curb / London CUBC 088*	**47**	1
23 Aug 03	WE CAN *Curb / London CUBC 092*	**27**	2
14 Feb 04	THIS LOVE *Curb / London CUBC 096*	**54**	1
15 May 04 ●	LAST THING ON MY MIND *Polydor / Curb 9866595* [2]	**5**	9
6 Jun 98	SITTIN' ON TOP OF THE WORLD *Curb / The Hit Label 5560202*	**11**	22
14 Apr 01 ●	I NEED YOU *Curb / London 8573876382*	**7**	15
26 Oct 02	TWISTED ANGEL *Curb / London 5046611562*	**14**	3
14 Feb 04 ●	THE BEST OF *Curb / London 5046714812*	**2**	20

[1] Elton John and LeAnn Rimes [2] Ronan Keating & LeAnn Rimes

The RIMSHOTS
US, male / female instrumental / vocal group (Singles: 5 Weeks) pos/wks

19 Jul 75	7-6-5-4-3-2-1 (BLOW YOUR WHISTLE) *All Platinum 6146 304*	**26**	5

RIO and MARS
France / UK, male / female vocal / instrumental duo (Singles: 3 Weeks) pos/wks

28 Jan 95	BOY I GOTTA HAVE YOU *Dome CDDOME 1014*	**43**	2
13 Apr 96	BOY I GOTTA HAVE YOU (re-issue) *Feverpitch CDFVR 1007*	**46**	1

Miguel RIOS
Spain, male vocalist (Singles: 12 Weeks) pos/wks

11 Jul 70	SONG OF JOY *A&M AMS 790*	**16**	12

Waldo de los RIOS
Argentina, orchestra – leader Osvaldo Ferraro Guiterrez (Singles: 16 Weeks, Albums: 26 Weeks) pos/wks

10 Apr 71 ●	MOZART SYMPHONY NO.40 IN G MINOR K550 1ST MOVEMENT (ALLEGRO MOLTO) *A&M AMS 836*	**5**	16
1 May 71 ●	SYMPHONIES FOR THE SEVENTIES *A&M AMLS 2014*	**6**	26

RIP RIG AND PANIC (see also Neneh CHERRY)
UK / US, male / female vocal / instrumental group (Albums: 3 Weeks) pos/wks

26 Jun 82	I AM COLD *Virgin V 2228*	**67**	3

Minnie RIPERTON
US, female vocalist, b. 8 Nov 1947, d. 12 Jul 1979 (Singles: 10 Weeks, Albums: 3 Weeks) pos/wks

12 Apr 75 ●	LOVIN' YOU *Epic EPC 3121* ▲	**2**	10
17 May 75	PERFECT ANGEL *Epic EPC 80426*	**33**	3

Angela RIPPON
UK, female broadcaster / exercise instructor (Albums: 26 Weeks) pos/wks

17 Apr 82 ●	SHAPE UP AND DANCE (VOLUME II) *Lifestyle LEG 2*	**8**	26

RISE (see also OAKENFOLD; PERFECTO ALL STARZ; VIRUS)
UK, male production duo – Paul Oakenfold and Steve Osborne (Singles: 1 Week) pos/wks

3 Sep 94	THE SINGLE *East West YZ 839CD*	**70**	1

The RISHI RICH PROJECT
UK, male production / vocal / rap group – leader Rishpal Rekhi (Singles: 15 Weeks) pos/wks

20 Sep 03	DANCE WITH YOU (NACHNA TERE NAAL) *Relentless RELCD 1* [1]	**12**	5
3 Jul 04 ●	EYES ON YOU *Relentless RELCD 5* [2]	**6**	10

[1] The Rishi Rich Project featuring Jay Sean & Juggy D [2] Jay Sean featuring The Rishi Rich Project

RITCHIE FAMILY
US, female vocal group (Singles: 19 Weeks) pos/wks

23 Aug 75	BRAZIL *Polydor 2058 625*	**41**	4
18 Sep 76 ●	THE BEST DISCO IN TOWN *Polydor 2058 777*	**10**	9
17 Feb 79	AMERICAN GENERATION *Mercury 6007 199*	**49**	6

Lee RITENOUR and Maxi PRIEST
US, male instrumentalist – guitar and UK, male vocalist (Singles: 2 Weeks) pos/wks

31 Jul 93	WAITING IN VAIN *GRP MCSTD 1921*	**65**	2

RITMO-DYNAMIC
France, male producer – Laurent Debuire (Singles: 1 Week) pos/wks

15 Nov 03	CALINDA *Xtravaganza XTRAV 42CDS*	**68**	1

Tex RITTER
US, male vocalist – Maurice Ritter, b. 12 Jan 1905, d. 3 Jan 1974 (Singles: 14 Weeks) pos/wks

22 Jun 56 ●	THE WAYWARD WIND *Capitol CL 14581*	**8**	14

RIVA featuring Dannii MINOGUE (see also GOODMEN; JARK PRONGO; RHYTHMKILLAZ; CHOCOLATE PUMA; TOMBA VIRA)
Holland, male production duo – Rene ter Horst and Gaston Steenkist and Australia, female vocalist (Singles: 15 Weeks) pos/wks

1 Dec 01 ●	WHO DO YOU LOVE NOW (STRINGER) *ffrr DFCD 002*	**3**	15

RIVAL SCHOOLS
US, male vocal / instrumental group (Singles: 2 Weeks) pos/wks

30 Mar 02	USED FOR GLUE *Mercury 5889652*	**42**	1
20 Jul 02	GOOD THINGS *Mercury 5829662*	**74**	1

Paco RIVAZ See GAMBAFREAKS

RIVER CITY PEOPLE
UK, male / female vocal / instrumental group (Singles: 27 Weeks, Albums: 10 Weeks) pos/wks

12 Aug 89	(WHAT'S WRONG WITH) DREAMING? *EMI EM 95*	**70**	3
3 Mar 90	WALKING ON ICE *EMI EM 130*	**62**	2
30 Jun 90	CARRY THE BLAME / CALIFORNIA DREAMIN' *EMI EM 145*	**13**	10
22 Sep 90	(WHAT'S WRONG WITH) DREAMING? (re-issue) *EMI EM 156*	**40**	3
2 Mar 91	WHEN I WAS YOUNG *EMI EM 176*	**62**	2
28 Sep 91	SPECIAL WAY *EMI EM 207*	**44**	3
22 Feb 92	STANDING IN THE NEED OF LOVE *EMI EM 216*	**36**	4
25 Aug 90	SAY SOMETHING GOOD *EMI EMCX 3561*	**23**	9
2 Nov 91	THIS IS THE WORLD *EMI EMC 3611*	**56**	1

RIVER DETECTIVES
UK, male vocal / instrumental duo (Singles: 4 Weeks, Albums: 1 Week) pos/wks

29 Jul 89	CHAINS *WEA YZ 383*	**51**	4
23 Sep 89	SATURDAY NIGHT SUNDAY MORNING *WEA WX 295*	**51**	1

RIVER OCEAN featuring INDIA
US, male producer – Louie Vega and female vocalist (Singles: 2 Weeks) pos/wks

26 Feb 94	LOVE AND HAPPINESS (YEMAYA Y OCHUN) *Cooltempo CDCOOL 287*	**50**	2

Robbie RIVERA
Puerto Rico, male producer (Singles: 8 Weeks) pos/wks

2 Sep 00	BANG *Multiply CDMULTY 64* [1]	**13**	7
12 Oct 02	SEX *352 Recordings 352CD 001* [2]	**55**	1

[1] Robbie Rivera presents Rhythm Bangers [2] Robbie Rivera vs Billy Paul W

Sandy RIVERA (see also KINGS OF TOMORROW)
US, male producer (Singles: 3 Weeks) pos/wks

18 Jan 03	CHANGES *Defected DFTD 059* [1]	**48**	2
5 Apr 03	I CAN'T STOP *Defected DFTD 063*	**58**	1

[1] Sandy Rivera featuring Haze

Danny RIVERS
UK, male vocalist – David Baker (Singles: 3 Weeks) pos/wks

12 Jan 61	CAN'T YOU HEAR MY HEART *Decca F 11294*	**36**	3

David ROACH
UK, male vocalist / instrumentalist – saxophone (Albums: 1 Week) pos/wks

14 Apr 84	I LOVE SAX *Nouveau Music NML 1006*	**73**	1

ROACH MOTEL
UK, male instrumental / production group (Singles: 2 Weeks) pos/wks

21 Aug 93	AFRO SLEEZE / TRANSATLANTIC *Junior Boy's Own JBO 1412*	**73**	1
10 Dec 94	HAPPY BIZZNESS / WILD LUV *Junior Boy's Own JBO 24*	**75**	1

ROACHFORD
UK, male / female / instrumental group – leader Andrew Roachford (Singles: 61 Weeks, Albums: 56 Weeks) pos/wks

18 Jun 88	CUDDLY TOY *CBS ROA 2*	**61**	4
14 Jan 89 ●	CUDDLY TOY (re-issue) *CBS ROA 4*	**4**	9
18 Mar 89	FAMILY MAN *CBS ROA 5*	**25**	6
1 Jul 89	KATHLEEN *CBS ROA 6*	**43**	5
13 Apr 91	GET READY! *Columbia 6567057*	**22**	8
19 Mar 94	ONLY TO BE WITH YOU *Columbia 6601562*	**21**	7

18 Jun 94	LAY YOUR LOVE ON ME *Columbia 6603722*	36	5
20 Aug 94	THIS GENERATION *Columbia 6607452*	38	4
3 Dec 94	CRY FOR ME *Columbia 6610742*	46	2
1 Apr 95	I KNOW YOU DON'T LOVE ME *Columbia 6612525*	42	2
11 Oct 97	THE WAY I FEEL *Columbia 6651042*	20	4
14 Feb 98	HOW COULD I? (INSECURITY) *Columbia 6653462*	34	3
11 Jul 98	NAKED WITHOUT YOU *Columbia 6659362*	53	2
23 Jul 88	ROACHFORD *CBS 460630 1*	11	27
18 May 91	GET READY! *Columbia 4681361*	20	5
16 Apr 94	PERMANENT SHADE OF BLUE *Columbia 4758429*	25	21
25 Oct 97	FEEL *Columbia 4885262*	19	3

ROB 'N' RAZ featuring Leila K *Sweden, male production duo and female rapper (Singles: 17 Weeks)* pos/wks

25 Nov 89 ●	GOT TO GET *Arista 112696* [1]	8	14
17 Mar 90	ROK THE NATION *Arista 112971* [1]	41	3

[1] Rob 'n' Raz featuring Leila K

Kate ROBBINS and BEYOND
UK, female / male vocal / instrumental group (Singles: 10 Weeks) pos/wks

30 May 81 ●	MORE THAN IN LOVE *RCA 69*	2	10

Marty ROBBINS
US, male vocalist / instrumentalist – guitar – Marty Robinson, b. 26 Sep 1925, d. 8 Dec 1982 (Singles: 33 Weeks, Albums: 15 Weeks) pos/wks

29 Jan 60	EL PASO (re) *Fontana H 233* ▲	19	9
26 May 60	BIG IRON *Fontana H 229*	48	1
27 Sep 62 ●	DEVIL WOMAN *CBS AAG 114*	5	17
17 Jan 63	RUBY ANN *CBS AAG 128*	24	6
13 Aug 60	GUNFIGHTER BALLADS AND TRAIL SONGS *Fontana TFL 5063*	20	1
10 Feb 79 ●	MARTY ROBBINS COLLECTION *Lotus WH 5009*	5	14

Antoinette ROBERSON See PULSE featuring Antoinette ROBERSON

Austin ROBERTS *US, male vocalist (Singles: 7 Weeks)* pos/wks

25 Oct 75	ROCKY *Private Stock PVT 33*	22	7

Joe ROBERTS *UK, male vocalist (Singles: 17 Weeks)* pos/wks

28 Aug 93	BACK IN MY LIFE *ffrr FCD 215*	59	1
29 Jan 94	LOVER *ffrr FCD 220*	22	5
14 May 94	BACK IN MY LIFE (re-issue) *ffrr FCD 230*	39	3
6 Aug 94	ADORE *ffrr FCD 240*	45	3
18 Feb 95	YOU ARE EVERYTHING *Columbia 6611755* [1]	28	4
24 Feb 96	HAPPY DAYS *Grass Green GRASS 10CD* [2]	63	1

[1] Melanie Williams and Joe Roberts [2] Sweet Mercy featuring Joe Roberts

Juliet ROBERTS
UK, female vocalist (Singles: 34 Weeks, Albums: 1 Week) pos/wks

31 Jul 93	CAUGHT IN THE MIDDLE *Cooltempo CDCOOL 272*	24	6
6 Nov 93	FREE LOVE *Cooltempo CDCOOL 281*	25	3
19 Mar 94	AGAIN / I WANT YOU *Cooltempo CDCOOL 285*	33	3
2 Jul 94	CAUGHT IN THE MIDDLE (re-mix) *Cooltempo CDCOOL 291*	14	5
15 Oct 94	I WANT YOU (re-issue) *Cooltempo CDCOOL 297*	28	3
31 Jan 98	SO GOOD / FREE LOVE 98 (re-mix) *Delirious 74321554002*	15	4
23 Jan 99	BAD GIRLS / I LIKE *Delirious DELICD 11*	17	5
20 Jan 01	NEEDIN' YOU II (re-mix) *Manifesto FESCD 78* [1]	11	5
2 Apr 94	NATURAL THING *Cooltempo CTCD 39*	65	1

[1] David Morales presents The Face featuring Juliet Roberts

Malcolm ROBERTS
UK, male vocalist, b. 31 Mar 1944, d. 7 Feb 2003 (Singles: 29 Weeks) pos/wks

11 May 67	TIME ALONE WILL TELL *RCA 1578*	45	2
30 Oct 68 ●	MAY I HAVE THE NEXT DREAM WITH YOU (re) *Major Minor MM 581*	8	15
22 Nov 69	LOVE IS ALL *Major Minor MM 637*	12	12

Paddy ROBERTS
South Africa, male vocalist, b. 1910, d. Sep 1975 (Albums: 6 Weeks) pos/wks

26 Sep 59 ●	STRICTLY FOR GROWN-UPS *Decca LF 1322*	8	5
17 Sep 60	PADDY ROBERTS TRIES AGAIN *Decca LK 4358*	16	1

B A ROBERTSON *UK, male vocalist – Brian Alexander Robertson (Singles: 60 Weeks, Albums: 10 Weeks)* pos/wks

28 Jul 79 ●	BANG BANG *Asylum K 13152*	2	12
27 Oct 79 ●	KNOCKED IT OFF *Asylum K 12396*	8	12
1 Mar 80	KOOL IN THE KAFTAN *Asylum K 12427*	17	12
31 May 80 ●	TO BE OR NOT TO BE *Asylum K 12449*	9	11
17 Oct 81	HOLD ME *Swansong BAM 1* [1]	11	8
17 Dec 83	TIME *Epic A 3983* [2]	45	5
29 Mar 80	INITIAL SUCCESS *Asylum K 52216*	32	8
4 Apr 81	BULLY FOR YOU *Asylum K 52275*	61	2

[1] B A Robertson and Maggie Bell [2] Frida and B A Robertson

Don ROBERTSON
US, male instrumentalist – piano and whistle (Singles: 9 Weeks) pos/wks

11 May 56 ●	THE HAPPY WHISTLER *Capitol CL 14575*	8	9

Robbie ROBERTSON (see also The BAND) *Canada, male vocalist / instrumentalist (Singles: 11 Weeks, Albums: 16 Weeks)* pos/wks

23 Jul 88	SOMEWHERE DOWN THE CRAZY RIVER *Geffen GEF 40*	15	10
11 Apr 98	TAKE YOUR PARTNER BY THE HAND *Polydor 5693272* [1]	74	1
14 Nov 87	ROBBIE ROBERTSON *Geffen WX 133*	23	14
12 Oct 91	STORYVILLE *Geffen GEF 24303*	30	2

[1] Howie B featuring Robbie Robertson

Ivo ROBIC *Croatia, male vocalist (Singles: 1 Week)* pos/wks

6 Nov 59	MORGEN *Polydor 23923*	23	1

Dawn ROBINSON See The FIRM

Floyd ROBINSON *US, male vocalist (Singles: 9 Weeks)* pos/wks

16 Oct 59 ●	MAKIN' LOVE *RCA 1146*	9	9

Smokey ROBINSON (see also The MIRACLES) *US, male vocalist – William Robinson (Singles: 109 Weeks, Albums: 21 Weeks)* pos/wks

27 Dec 67	I SECOND THAT EMOTION *Tamla Motown TMG 631* [1]	27	11
3 Apr 68	IF YOU CAN WANT *Tamla Motown TMG 648* [1]	50	1
7 May 69 ●	TRACKS OF MY TEARS *Tamla Motown TMG 696* [1]	9	13
1 Aug 70 ★	THE TEARS OF A CLOWN *Tamla Motown TMG 745* [1]	1	14
30 Jan 71	(COME 'ROUND HERE) I'M THE ONE YOU NEED (re-issue) *Tamla Motown TMG 761* [1]	13	9
5 Jun 71	I DON'T BLAME YOU AT ALL *Tamla Motown TMG 774* [1]	11	10
23 Feb 74	JUST MY SOUL RESPONDING *Tamla Motown TMG 883*	35	6
2 Oct 76	THE TEARS OF A CLOWN (re-issue) *Tamla Motown TMG 1048*	34	6
24 Feb 79	POPS, WE LOVE YOU *Motown TMG 1136* [2]	66	5
9 May 81 ★	BEING WITH YOU *Motown TMG 1223*	1	13
13 Mar 82	TELL ME TOMORROW *Motown TMG 1255*	51	4
28 Mar 87	JUST TO SEE HER *Motown ZB 41147*	52	6
17 Sep 88	INDESTRUCTIBLE *Arista 111717* [3]	55	4
25 Feb 89	INDESTRUCTIBLE *Arista 112074* [3]	30	7
20 Jun 81	BEING WITH YOU *Motown STML 12151*	17	10
12 Nov 88	LOVE SONGS *Telstar STAR 2331* [1]	69	9
14 Nov 92	THE GREATEST HITS *PolyGram TV 5301212* [2]	65	2

[1] Smokey Robinson and The Miracles [2] Diana Ross, Marvin Gaye, Smokey Robinson and Stevie Wonder [3] The Four Tops featuring Smokey Robinson
[1] Marvin Gaye and Smokey Robinson [2] Smokey Robinson and The Miracles

The original US recording of 'Indestructible' was not issued until after the chart run of the UK-only mix

Tom ROBINSON BAND *UK, male vocalist / instrumentalist (Singles: 41 Weeks, Albums: 23 Weeks)* pos/wks

22 Oct 77 ●	2-4-6-8 MOTORWAY *EMI 2715*	5	9
18 Feb 78	RISING FREE (EP) *EMI 2749*	18	6
13 May 78	UP AGAINST THE WALL *EMI 2787*	33	6
17 Mar 79	BULLY FOR YOU *EMI 2916*	68	2
25 Jun 83 ●	WAR BABY *Panic NIC 2* [1]	6	9
12 Nov 83	LISTEN TO THE RADIO: ATMOSPHERICS *Panic NIC 3* [1]	39	6
15 Sep 84	RIKKI DON'T LOSE THAT NUMBER *Castaway TR 2* [1]	58	3
3 Jun 78 ●	POWER IN THE DARKNESS *EMI EMC 3226*	4	12
24 Mar 79	TRB TWO *EMI EMC 3296*	18	6
29 Sep 84	HOPE AND GLORY *Castaway ZL 70483* [1]	21	5

[1] Tom Robinson [1] Tom Robinson

Tracks on Rising Free (EP): Don't Take No For an Answer / Sing If You're Glad to Be Gay / Martin / Right On Sister

Vicki Sue ROBINSON
US, female vocalist, b. 31 May 1954, d. 27 Apr 2000 (Singles: 1 Week)   pos/wks

27 Sep 97	HOUSE OF JOY *Logic 74321511492*	**48** 1

ROBO BABE *See SIR KILLALOT vs ROBO BABE*

ROBSON and JEROME
UK, male actors / vocal duo – Robson
Green and Jerome Flynn (Singles: 45 Weeks, Albums: 53 Weeks)   pos/wks

20 May 95	★ UNCHAINED MELODY / (THERE'LL BE BLUEBIRDS OVER) THE WHITE CLIFFS OF DOVER (re) *RCA 74321284362* 1 ◆ ■	**1** 17
11 Nov 95	★ I BELIEVE / UP ON THE ROOF *RCA 74321326882* ◆ ■	**1** 14
9 Nov 96	★ WHAT BECOMES OF THE BROKENHEARTED / SATURDAY NIGHT AT THE MOVIES / YOU'LL NEVER WALK ALONE *RCA 74321424732* ■	**1** 14
25 Nov 95	★ ROBSON & JEROME *RCA 74321323902* ■	**1** 31
23 Nov 96	★ TAKE TWO *RCA 74321426252* ■	**1** 16
29 Nov 97	HAPPY DAYS – THE BEST OF ROBSON & JEROME *RCA 74321542602*	**20** 6

1 Robson Green and Jerome Flynn

ROBYN
Sweden, female vocalist – Robyn Carlsson (Singles: 14 Weeks)   pos/wks

20 Jul 96	YOU'VE GOT THAT SOMETHIN' *RCA 74321393462*	**54** 1
16 Aug 97	DO YOU KNOW (WHAT IT TAKES) *RCA 74321509932*	**26** 3
7 Mar 98	● SHOW ME LOVE *RCA 74321555032*	**8** 6
30 May 98	DO YOU REALLY WANT ME *RCA 74321582982*	**20** 4

ROC PROJECT featuring Tina ARENA
US, male producer – Ray Checo and Australia, female vocalist (Singles: 1 Week)   pos/wks

12 Apr 03	NEVER (PAST TENSE) *Illustrious CDILL 010*	**42** 1

John ROCCA *See FREEEZ*

Erin ROCHA
UK, female vocalist (Singles: 5 Weeks)   pos/wks

27 Dec 03	CAN'T DO RIGHT FOR DOING WRONG *Flying Sparks TBDCDS 76*	**36** 5

ROCHELLE
US, female vocalist (Singles: 6 Weeks)   pos/wks

1 Feb 86	MY MAGIC MAN *Warner Bros. W 8838*	**27** 6

Chubb ROCK
US, male rapper – Richard Simpson (Singles: 1 Week)   pos/wks

19 Jan 91	TREAT 'EM RIGHT *Champion CHAMP 272*	**67** 1

Sir Monti ROCK III *See DISCO TEX & the SEX-O-LETTES*

ROCK *See Wyclef JEAN*

Pete ROCK and CL SMOOTH
US, male DJ / rap duo – Peter Philips and Corey Penn (Albums: 1 Week)   pos/wks

19 Nov 94	THE MAIN INGREDIENT *Elektra 7559616612*	**69** 1

ROCK AID ARMENIA
UK, male vocal / instrumental charity ensemble (Singles: 5 Weeks)   pos/wks

16 Dec 89	SMOKE ON THE WATER *Life Aid Armenia ARMEN 001*	**39** 5

ROCK CANDY
UK, male vocal / instrumental group (Singles: 6 Weeks)   pos/wks

11 Sep 71	REMEMBER *MCA MK 5069*	**32** 6

ROCK GODDESS
UK, female vocal / instrumental group (Singles: 5 Weeks, Albums: 3 Weeks)   pos/wks

5 Mar 83	MY ANGEL *A&M AMS 8311*	**64** 2
24 Mar 84	I DIDN'T KNOW I LOVED YOU (TILL I SAW YOU ROCK 'N' ROLL) *A&M AMS 185*	**57** 3
12 Mar 83	ROCK GODDESS *A&M AMLH 68554*	**65** 2
29 Oct 83	HELL HATH NO FURY *A&M AMLX 68560*	**84** 1

ROCKER'S REVENGE featuring Donnie CALVIN
US, male / female vocal / instrumental group (Singles: 20 Weeks)   pos/wks

14 Aug 82	● WALKING ON SUNSHINE *London LON 11*	**4** 13
29 Jan 83	THE HARDER THEY COME *London LON 18*	**30** 7

ROCKET FROM THE CRYPT
US, male vocal / instrumental group (Singles: 7 Weeks, Albums: 4 Weeks)   pos/wks

27 Jan 96	BORN IN 69 *Elemental ELM 32CD*	**68** 1
13 Apr 96	YOUNG LIVERS *Elemental ELM 33CDS*	**67** 1
14 Sep 96	ON A ROPE *Elemental ELM 38CDS 1*	**12** 4
29 Aug 98	LIPSTICK *Elemental ELM 48CDS 1*	**64** 1
3 Feb 96	SCREAM DRACULA SCREAM! *Elemental ELM 34CD*	**41** 3
18 Jul 98	RFTC *Elemental ELM 50CD*	**63** 1

ROCKETS *See Tony CROMBIE and his ROCKETS*

ROCKFORD FILES
UK, male instrumental / production duo – Ben McColl and Matthew Brooks (Singles: 4 Weeks)   pos/wks

11 Mar 95	YOU SEXY DANCER *Escapade CDJAPE 7*	**34** 3
6 Apr 96	YOU SEXY DANCER (re-issue) *Escapade CDJAPE 14*	**59** 1

The ROCKIN' BERRIES
UK, male vocal / instrumental group – includes Geoff 'Jefferson' Turton (Singles: 41 Weeks, Albums: 1 Week)   pos/wks

1 Oct 64	I DIDN'T MEAN TO HURT YOU *Piccadilly 7N 35197*	**43** 1
15 Oct 64	● HE'S IN TOWN *Piccadilly 7N 35203*	**3** 13
21 Jan 65	WHAT IN THE WORLD'S COME OVER YOU *Piccadilly 7N 35217*	**23** 7
13 May 65	● POOR MAN'S SON *Piccadilly 7N 35236*	**5** 11
26 Aug 65	YOU'RE MY GIRL *Piccadilly 7N 35254*	**40** 7
6 Jan 66	THE WATER IS OVER MY HEAD (re) *Piccadilly 7N 35270*	**43** 2
19 Jun 65	THEY'RE IN TOWN *Pye NPL 38013*	**15** 1

ROCKNEY *See CHAS and DAVE*

ROCKPILE (see also Dave EDMUNDS; Nick LOWE)
UK, male vocal / instrumental group (Albums: 5 Weeks)   pos/wks

18 Oct 80	SECONDS OF PLEASURE *F-Beat XXLP 7*	**34** 5

The ROCKSTEADY CREW
US, male / female vocal group (Singles: 16 Weeks, Albums: 1 Week)   pos/wks

1 Oct 83	● (HEY YOU) THE ROCKSTEADY CREW *Charisma / Virgin RSC 1*	**6** 12
5 May 84	UPROCK *Charisma / Virgin RSC 2*	**64** 4
16 Jun 84	READY FOR BATTLE *Charisma RSC LP1*	**73** 1

ROCKWELL
US, male vocalist – Kennedy Gordy (Singles: 11 Weeks, Albums: 5 Weeks)   pos/wks

4 Feb 84	● SOMEBODY'S WATCHING ME *Motown TMG 1331*	**6** 11
25 Feb 84	SOMEBODY'S WATCHING ME *Motown ZL 72147*	**52** 5

'Somebody's Watching Me' features uncredited vocal by Michael Jackson

Spalding ROCKWELL *See Armand VAN HELDEN*

ROCKY V *See Joey B ELLIS*

ROCOCO
UK / Italy, male / female vocal / instrumental group (Singles: 5 Weeks)   pos/wks

16 Dec 89	ITALO HOUSE MIX *Mercury MER 314*	**54** 5

RODEO JONES
UK / Grenada, male / female vocal / instrumental group (Singles: 2 Weeks)   pos/wks

30 Jan 93	NATURAL WORLD *A&M AMCD 0165*	**75** 1
3 Apr 93	SHADES OF SUMMER *A&M AMCD 212*	**59** 1

Clodagh RODGERS
Ireland, female vocalist (Singles: 59 Weeks, Albums: 1 Week)   pos/wks

26 Mar 69	● COME BACK AND SHAKE ME *RCA 1792*	**3** 14
9 Jul 69	● GOODNIGHT MIDNIGHT (re) *RCA 1852*	**4** 12
8 Nov 69	BILJO *RCA 1891*	**22** 9
4 Apr 70	EVERYBODY GO HOME THE PARTY'S OVER *RCA 1930*	**47** 2
20 Mar 71	● JACK IN THE BOX *RCA 2066*	**4** 10
9 Oct 71	LADY LOVE BUG *RCA 2117*	**28** 12
13 Sep 69	CLODAGH RODGERS *RCA SF 8033*	**27** 1

Jimmie RODGERS
US, male vocalist (Singles: 37 Weeks)   pos/wks

1 Nov 57	HONEYCOMB *Columbia DB 3986* ▲	**30** 1
20 Dec 57	● KISSES SWEETER THAN WINE *Columbia DB 4052*	**7** 11
28 Mar 58	OH-OH, I'M FALLING IN LOVE AGAIN *Columbia DB 4078*	**18** 6
19 Dec 58	WOMAN FROM LIBERIA *Columbia DB 4206*	**18** 6
14 Jun 62	● ENGLISH COUNTRY GARDEN *Columbia DB 4847*	**5** 13

Paul RODGERS
(see also BAD COMPANY; FREE; The FIRM; The LAW)
UK, male vocalist (Singles: 2 Weeks, Albums: 11 Weeks) pos/wks

12 Feb 94	**MUDDY WATER BLUES** *Victory ROGCD 1*	45 2
3 Jul 93 ●	**MUDDY WATER BLUES** *London 8284242*	9 7
15 Feb 97	**NOW** *SPV Recordings SPV 08544662*	30 4

RODRIGUEZ See SASH!

The Rods See EDDIE and the HOT RODS

Tommy ROE
US, male vocalist (Singles: 74 Weeks) pos/wks

6 Sep 62 ●	**SHEILA** *HMV POP 1060* ▲	3 14
6 Dec 62	**SUSIE DARLIN'** *HMV POP 1092*	37 5
21 Mar 63 ●	**THE FOLK SINGER** *HMV POP 1138*	4 13
26 Sep 63 ●	**EVERYBODY (re)** *HMV POP 1207*	9 14
16 Apr 69 ★	**DIZZY** *Stateside SS 2143* ▲	1 19
23 Jul 69	**HEATHER HONEY** *Stateside SS 2152*	24 9

ROFO
UK, male instrumental / production duo (Singles: 3 Weeks) pos/wks

1 Aug 92	**ROFO'S THEME** *PWL Continental PWLT 236*	44 3

ROGER (see also ZAPP)
US, male vocalist – Roger Troutman, b. 29 Nov 1951, d. 24 Apr 1999 (Singles: 8 Weeks) pos/wks

17 Oct 87	**I WANT TO BE YOUR MAN** *Reprise W 8229*	61 4
12 Nov 88	**BOOM! THERE SHE WAS** *Virgin VS 1143*	55 3
13 May 95	**HIGH AS A KITE** *ffrr FCD 259* [1]	55 1

[1] One Tribe featuring Roger

Julie ROGERS
UK, female vocalist – Julie Rolls (Singles: 38 Weeks) pos/wks

13 Aug 64 ●	**THE WEDDING** *Mercury MF 820* [1]	3 23
10 Dec 64	**LIKE A CHILD** *Mercury MF 838*	20 9
25 Mar 65	**HAWAIIAN WEDDING SONG** *Mercury MF 849*	31 6

[1] Julie Rogers with Johnny Arthey and his Orchestra and Chorus

Kenny ROGERS `299` `Top 500`
Celebrated crossover country vocalist / actor, who was one of the US's top-selling artists of the past 35 years, b. 21 Aug 1938, Houston. This Grammy-winning ex-New Christy Minstrel has collected more than 20 US gold albums and is a household name in many countries (Singles: 109 Weeks, Albums: 111 Weeks) pos/wks

18 Oct 69 ●	**RUBY, DON'T TAKE YOUR LOVE TO TOWN** *Reprise RS 20829* [1]	2 23
7 Feb 70 ●	**SOMETHING'S BURNING** *Reprise RS 20888* [1]	8 14
30 Apr 77 ★	**LUCILLE** *United Artists UP 36242*	1 14
17 Sep 77	**DAYTIME FRIENDS** *United Artists UP 36289*	39 4
2 Jun 79	**SHE BELIEVES IN ME** *United Artists UP 36533*	42 7
26 Jan 80 ★	**COWARD OF THE COUNTY** *United Artists UP 614*	1 12
15 Nov 80	**LADY** *United Artists UP 635* ▲	12 12
12 Feb 83	**WE'VE GOT TONIGHT** *Liberty UP 658* [2]	28 7
22 Oct 83	**EYES THAT SEE IN THE DARK** *RCA 358*	61 1
12 Nov 83 ●	**ISLANDS IN THE STREAM** *RCA 378* [3] ▲	7 15
18 Jun 77	**KENNY ROGERS** *United Artists UAS 30046*	14 7
6 Oct 79	**THE KENNY ROGERS SINGLES ALBUM** *United Artists UAK 30263*	12 22
9 Feb 80 ●	**KENNY ROGERS** *United Artists UAG 30273*	7 10
31 Jan 81	**LADY** *Liberty LBG 30334*	40 5
1 Oct 83	**EYES THAT SEE IN THE DARK** *RCA RCALP 6088*	53 19
27 Oct 84	**WHAT ABOUT ME?** *RCA PL 85043*	97 1
27 Jul 85 ●	**THE KENNY ROGERS STORY** *Liberty EMTV 39*	4 29
25 Sep 93	**DAYTIME FRIENDS – THE VERY BEST OF KENNY ROGERS** *EMI CDEMTV 79*	16 5
22 Nov 97	**LOVE SONGS** *Virgin KENNYCD 1*	27 7
29 May 99	**ALL THE HITS & ALL NEW LOVE SONGS** *EMI 5207782*	14 6

[1] Kenny Rogers and the First Edition [2] Kenny Rogers and Sheena Easton
[3] Kenny Rogers and Dolly Parton

ROKOTTO
UK, male vocal / instrumental group (Singles: 10 Weeks) pos/wks

22 Oct 77	**BOOGIE ON UP** *State STAT 62*	40 4
10 Jun 78	**FUNK THEORY** *State STAT 80*	49 6

ROLLERGIRL
Germany, female vocalist – Nicci Juice (Singles: 3 Weeks) pos/wks

16 Sep 00	**DEAR JESSIE** *Neo NEOCD 038*	22 3

The ROLLING STONES `16` `Top 500`
'World's No.1 rock group': Sir Mick Jagger (v), Keith Richards (g), Brian Jones (g) (d. 1969), Bill Wyman (b) (left 1991), Charlie Watts (d) – Ron Wood (g) joined in 1975, replacing Mick Taylor. No group has accumulated more UK or US Top 10 albums, more gold and platinum albums and grossed more income from touring than this legendary British band, which has broken box office records on every continent and is still the world's highest earning live band. Transportation of the 300 person entourage and 350 tons of stage set during the 2003 40 Licks tour required 10 buses, 53 trucks and a tour jet. Played in front of a world record paying crowd of 489,176 when they topped the bill at a 2003 Toronto gig. Jagger and Richards, nicknamed The Glimmer Twins, were inducted into the Songwriters' Hall of Fame and the group, who were early members of the Rock and Roll Hall of Fame, received a Grammy Lifetime Achievement award (1986). Jagger was awarded a knighthood in 2002 and the band were inducted into the UK Music Hall of Fame in 2004, representing the 1960s (Singles: 374 Weeks, Albums: 799 Weeks) pos/wks

25 Jul 63	**COME ON** *Decca F 11675*	21 14
14 Nov 63	**I WANNA BE YOUR MAN** *Decca F 11764*	12 14
27 Feb 64 ●	**NOT FADE AWAY** *Decca F 11845*	3 15
2 Jul 64 ★	**IT'S ALL OVER NOW** *Decca F 11934*	1 15
19 Nov 64 ★	**LITTLE RED ROOSTER** *Decca F 12014*	1 12
4 Mar 65 ★	**THE LAST TIME** *Decca F 12104*	1 13
26 Aug 65 ★	**(I CAN'T GET NO) SATISFACTION** *Decca F 12220* ▲	1 12
28 Oct 65 ●	**GET OFF OF MY CLOUD** *Decca F 12263* ▲	1 12
10 Feb 66 ●	**NINETEENTH NERVOUS BREAKDOWN** *Decca F 12331*	2 8
19 May 66 ★	**PAINT IT BLACK** *Decca F 12395* ▲	1 10
29 Sep 66 ●	**HAVE YOU SEEN YOUR MOTHER BABY STANDING IN THE SHADOW** *Decca F 12497*	5 8
19 Jan 67 ●	**LET'S SPEND THE NIGHT TOGETHER / RUBY TUESDAY** *Decca F 12546* ▲	3 10
23 Aug 67 ●	**WE LOVE YOU / DANDELION** *Decca F 12654*	8 8
29 May 68 ★	**JUMPIN' JACK FLASH** *Decca F 12782*	1 11
9 Jul 69 ★	**HONKY TONK WOMEN** *Decca F 12952* ▲	1 17
24 Apr 71 ●	**BROWN SUGAR / BITCH / LET IT ROCK** *Rolling Stones RS 19100* ▲	2 13
3 Jul 71	**STREET FIGHTING MAN** *Decca F 13195*	21 8
29 Apr 72 ●	**TUMBLING DICE** *Rolling Stones RS 19103*	5 8
1 Sep 73 ●	**ANGIE** *Rolling Stones RS 19105* ▲	5 10
3 Aug 74 ●	**IT'S ONLY ROCK AND ROLL** *Rolling Stones RS 19114*	10 7
20 Sep 75	**OUT OF TIME** *Decca F 13597*	45 2
1 May 76 ●	**FOOL TO CRY** *Rolling Stones RS 19121*	6 10
3 Jun 78 ●	**MISS YOU / FARAWAY EYES** *Rolling Stones EMI 2802* ▲	3 13
30 Sep 78	**RESPECTABLE** *Rolling Stones EMI 2861*	23 9
5 Jul 80 ●	**EMOTIONAL RESCUE** *Rolling Stones RSR 105*	9 8
4 Oct 80	**SHE'S SO COLD** *Rolling Stones RSR 106*	33 6
29 Aug 81 ●	**START ME UP** *Rolling Stones RSR 108*	7 9
12 Dec 81	**WAITING ON A FRIEND** *Rolling Stones RSR 109*	50 6
12 Jun 82	**GOING TO A GO GO** *Rolling Stones RSR 110*	26 6
2 Oct 82	**TIME IS ON MY SIDE** *Rolling Stones RSR 111*	62 2
12 Nov 83	**UNDERCOVER OF THE NIGHT** *Rolling Stones RSR 113*	11 9
11 Feb 84	**SHE WAS HOT** *Rolling Stones RSR 114*	42 4
21 Jul 84	**BROWN SUGAR (re-issue)** *Rolling Stones SUGAR 1*	58 2
15 Mar 86	**HARLEM SHUFFLE** *Rolling Stones A 6864*	13 7
2 Sep 89	**MIXED EMOTIONS** *Rolling Stones 655193 7*	36 5
2 Dec 89	**ROCK AND A HARD PLACE** *Rolling Stones 655422 7*	63 1
23 Jun 90	**PAINT IT BLACK (re-issue)** *London LON 264*	61 3
30 Jun 90	**ALMOST HEAR YOU SIGH** *Rolling Stones 656065 7*	31 5
30 Mar 91	**HIGHWIRE** *Rolling Stones 6567567*	29 4
1 Jun 91	**RUBY TUESDAY (LIVE)** *Rolling Stones 6568927*	59 2
16 Jul 94	**LOVE IS STRONG** *Virgin VSCDT 1503*	14 5
8 Oct 94	**YOU GOT ME ROCKING** *Virgin VSCDG 1518*	23 3
10 Dec 94	**OUT OF TEARS** *Virgin VSCDT 1524*	36 4
15 Jul 95	**I GO WILD** *Virgin VSCDX 1539*	29 3
11 Nov 95	**LIKE A ROLLING STONE** *Virgin VSCDT 1562*	12 5
4 Oct 97	**ANYBODY SEEN MY BABY?** *Virgin VSCDT 1653*	22 3
7 Feb 98	**SAINT OF ME** *Virgin VSCDT 1667*	26 2
22 Aug 98	**OUT OF CONTROL** *Virgin VSCDT 1700*	51 1
28 Dec 02	**DON'T STOP** *Virgin VCSDT 1838*	36 2
13 Sep 03	**SYMPATHY FOR THE DEVIL** *Mercury 9810612*	14 6
25 Apr 64 ★	**THE ROLLING STONES** *Decca LK 4605*	1 51
23 Jan 65 ★	**THE ROLLING STONES NO.2** *Decca LK 4661*	1 37
2 Oct 65 ●	**OUT OF OUR HEADS** *Decca LK 4733* ▲	2 24
23 Apr 66 ★	**AFTERMATH** *Decca LK 4786*	1 28

		pos/wks
12 Nov 66 ●	BIG HITS (HIGH TIDE AND GREEN GRASS) *Decca TXS 101*	3 43
28 Jan 67 ●	BETWEEN THE BUTTONS *Decca SKL 4852*	3 22
23 Dec 67 ●	THEIR SATANIC MAJESTIES REQUEST *Decca TXS 103*	3 13
21 Dec 68 ●	BEGGARS BANQUET *Decca SKL 4955*	3 12
27 Sep 69 ●	THROUGH THE PAST DARKLY (BIG HITS VOL.2) *Decca SKL 5019*	2 37
20 Dec 69 ★	LET IT BLEED *Decca SKL 5025* ■	1 29
19 Sep 70 ★	GET YER YA-YA'S OUT! *Decca SKL 5065* ■	1 15
27 Mar 71 ●	STONE AGE *Decca SKL 5084*	4 8
8 May 71 ★	STICKY FINGERS *Rolling Stones COC 59100* ■ ▲	1 25
18 Sep 71	GIMME SHELTER *Decca SKL 5101*	19 5
11 Mar 72	MILESTONES *Decca SKL 5098*	14 8
10 Jun 72 ★	EXILE ON MAIN ST *Rolling Stones COC 69100* ■ ▲	1 16
11 Nov 72	ROCK 'N' ROLLING STONES *Decca SKL 5149*	41 1
22 Sep 73 ★	GOAT'S HEAD SOUP *Rolling Stones COC 59101* ■ ▲	1 14
2 Nov 74 ●	IT'S ONLY ROCK 'N' ROLL *Rolling Stones COC 59103* ▲	2 9
28 Jun 75	MADE IN THE SHADE *Rolling Stones COC 59104*	14 12
28 Jun 75	METAMORPHOSIS *Decca SKL 5212*	45 1
29 Nov 75 ●	ROLLED GOLD – THE VERY BEST OF THE ROLLING STONES *Decca ROST 1/2*	7 50
8 May 76 ●	BLACK AND BLUE *Rolling Stones COC 59106* ▲	2 14
8 Oct 77 ●	LOVE YOU LIVE *Rolling Stones COC 89101*	3 8
5 Nov 77 ●	GET STONED *Arcade ADEP 32*	8 15
24 Jun 78 ●	SOME GIRLS *Rolling Stones CUN 39108* ▲	2 25
5 Jul 80 ★	EMOTIONAL RESCUE *Rolling Stones CUN 39111* ■ ▲	1 18
12 Sep 81 ●	TATTOO YOU *Rolling Stones CUNS 39114* ▲	2 29
12 Jun 82 ●	STILL LIFE (AMERICAN CONCERTS 1981) *Rolling Stones CUN 39115*	4 18
31 Jul 82	IN CONCERT (IMPORT) *Decca (Holland) 6640 037*	94 3
11 Dec 82	STORY OF THE STONES *K-Tel NE 1201*	24 12
19 Nov 83 ●	UNDERCOVER *Rolling Stones CUN 1654361*	3 18
7 Jul 84	REWIND 1971-1984 (THE BEST OF THE ROLLING STONES) *Rolling Stones 4501991*	23 18
5 Apr 86 ●	DIRTY WORK *Rolling Stones CUN 86321*	4 10
23 Sep 89 ●	STEEL WHEELS *CBS 4657521*	2 18
7 Jul 90 ●	HOT ROCKS 1964-1971 *London 8201401*	3 24
20 Apr 91 ●	FLASHPOINT *Rolling Stones 4681351*	6 7
4 Dec 93	THE BEST OF THE ROLLING STONES – JUMP BACK – '71-'93 *Virgin CDV 2726*	16 28
2 Jul 94	STICKY FINGERS (re-issue) *Virgin CDVX 2730*	74 1
23 Jul 94 ★	VOODOO LOUNGE *Virgin CDV 2750* ■	1 24
25 Nov 95 ●	STRIPPED *Virgin CDV 2801*	9 11
11 Oct 97 ●	BRIDGES TO BABYLON *Virgin CDV 2840*	6 6
14 Nov 98	NO SECURITY *Virgin CDV 2880*	67 1
12 Oct 02 ●	FORTY LICKS *Virgin / Decca CDVDX 2964*	2 29
13 Nov 04	LIVE LICKS *Virgin CDVDX 3000*	38 2

US No.1 symbol referring to 'Let's Spend The Night Together / Ruby Tuesday' applies to Ruby Tuesday, which hit the top spot in 1967

'Faraway Eyes' was listed from 15 July 1978, with a peak position of No.10

ROLLINS BAND
US, male vocal / instrumental group
(Singles: 4 Weeks, Albums: 2 Weeks)   pos/wks

12 Sep 92	TEARING *Imago 72787250187*	54 2
10 Sep 94	LIAR / DISCONNECTED *Imago 74321213052*	27 2
23 Apr 94	WEIGHT *Imago 72787210342*	22 2

ROLLO (see also FAITHLESS; OUR TRIBE / ONE TRIBE; SPHINX; DUSTED)
UK, male producer – Roland Armstrong (Singles: 8 Weeks)   pos/wks

29 Jan 94	GET OFF YOUR HIGH HORSE (re) *Cheeky CHEKCD 003* [1]	43 4
10 Jun 95	LOVE LOVE LOVE – HERE I COME *Cheeky CHEKCD 007* [2]	32 2
8 Jun 96	LET THIS BE A PRAYER *Cheeky CHEKCD 013* [3]	26 2

[1] Rollo Goes Camping [2] Rollo Goes Mystic [3] Rollo Goes Spiritual with Pauline Taylor

ROMAN HOLLIDAY
UK, male vocal / instrumental group (Singles: 19 Weeks, Albums: 3 Weeks)   pos/wks

2 Apr 83	STAND BY *Jive JIVE 31*	61 3
2 Jul 83	DON'T TRY TO STOP IT *Jive JIVE 39*	14 9
24 Sep 83	MOTORMANIA *Jive JIVE 49*	40 7
22 Oct 83	COOKIN' ON THE ROOF *Jive HIP 9*	31 3

ROMAN NUMERALS See Vic REEVES

ROMANTICS See RUBY and The ROMANTICS

ROMEO (see also SO SOLID CREW) UK, male rapper –
Marvin Dawkins (Singles: 24 Weeks, Albums: 2 Weeks)   pos/wks

30 Dec 00 ●	NO GOOD 4 ME *East West OXIDE 02CD* [1]	6 8
24 Aug 02 ●	ROMEO DUNN *Relentless RELENT 29CD*	3 9
9 Nov 02 ●	IT'S ALL GRAVY *Relentless RELENT 32CD* [2]	9 6
6 Dec 03	I SEE GIRLS (CRAZY) *Multiply CDMULTY 109* [3]	52 1
23 Nov 02	SOLID LOVE *Relentless RELEN 006CD*	46 2

[1] Oxide & Neutrino featuring Megaman, Romeo and Lisa Maffia [2] Romeo featuring Christina Milian [3] Studio B / Romeo and Harry Brooks

Max ROMEO
Jamaica, male vocalist – Maxie Smith (Singles: 25 Weeks)   pos/wks

28 May 69 ●	WET DREAM (re) *Unity UN 503*	10 25

Harry 'Choo-Choo' ROMERO (see also CHOO CHOO PROJECT)
US, male producer (Singles: 3 Weeks)   pos/wks

22 May 99	JUST CAN'T GET ENOUGH *AM:PM CDAMPM 121* [1]	39 2
1 Sep 01	I WANT OUT (I CAN'T BELIEVE) *Perfecto PERF 22CDS*	51 1

[1] Harry 'Choo Choo' Romero presents Inaya Day

RONALDO'S REVENGE (see also DISCO TEX presents CLOUDBURST;
FULL INTENTION; HUSTLERS CONVENTION featuring Dave LAUDAT and Ondrea DUVERNEY; SEX-O-SONIQUE; SHENA) UK, male production duo – Mike Gray and Jean Pearn (Singles: 2 Weeks)   pos/wks

1 Aug 98	MAS QUE MANCADA *AM:PM 5827532*	37 2

RONDO VENEZIANO
Italy, orchestra (Singles: 3 Weeks, Albums: 33 Weeks)   pos/wks

22 Oct 83	LA SERENISSIMA (THEME FROM 'VENICE IN PERIL') *Ferroway 7 RON 1*	58 3
5 Nov 83	VENICE IN PERIL *Ferroway RON 1*	39 13
10 Nov 84	THE GENIUS OF VENICE *Ferroway RON 2*	60 13
9 Jul 88	VENICE IN PERIL (re-issue) *Fanfare RON 1*	34 7

The RONETTES
US, female vocal group (Singles: 34 Weeks)   pos/wks

17 Oct 63 ●	BE MY BABY *London HLU 9793*	4 13
9 Jan 64	BABY, I LOVE YOU *London HLU 9826*	11 14
27 Aug 64	(THE BEST PART OF) BREAKIN' UP *London HLU 9905*	43 3
8 Oct 64	DO I LOVE YOU *London HLU 9922*	35 4

RONNETTE See FIDELFATTI featuring RONNETTE

Mark RONSON featuring GHOSTFACE KILLAH & Nate DOGG
UK, male DJ / producer and US,
male rapper and vocalist (Singles: 7 Weeks)   pos/wks

1 Nov 03	OOH WEE *Elektra E 7490CD*	15 7

Mick RONSON
(see also MOTT THE HOOPLE) UK, male vocalist / instrumentalist – guitar,
b. 26 May 1946, d. 29 Apr 1993 (Singles: 1 Week, Albums: 10 Weeks) pos/wks

7 May 94	DON'T LOOK DOWN *Epic 6603582* [1]	55 1
16 Mar 74 ●	SLAUGHTER ON TENTH AVENUE *RCA Victor APL1 0353*	9 7
8 Mar 75	PLAY DON'T WORRY *RCA Victor APL1 0681*	29 3

[1] Mick Ronson with Joe Elliott

Linda RONSTADT
US, female vocalist (Singles: 34 Weeks, Albums: 46 Weeks)   pos/wks

8 May 76	TRACKS OF MY TEARS *Asylum K 13034*	42 3
28 Jan 78	BLUE BAYOU *Asylum K 13106*	35 4
26 May 79	ALISON *Asylum K 13149*	66 2
11 Jul 87 ●	SOMEWHERE OUT THERE *MCA MCA 1132* [1]	8 13
11 Nov 89	DON'T KNOW MUCH *Elektra EKR 101* [2]	2 12
4 Sep 76	HASTEN DOWN THE WIND *Asylum K 53045*	32 8
25 Dec 76	GREATEST HITS *Asylum K 53055*	37 9
1 Oct 77	SIMPLE DREAMS *Asylum K 53065* ▲	15 5
14 Oct 78	LIVING IN THE USA *Asylum K 53085* ▲	39 2
8 Mar 80	MAD LOVE *Asylum K 52210*	65 1
28 Jan 84	WHAT'S NEW *Asylum 96 0260* [1]	31 5
19 Jan 85	LUSH LIFE *Asylum 9603871* [1]	100 1
14 Mar 87	TRIO *Warner Bros. 9254911* [2]	60 4

11 Nov 89	CRY LIKE A RAINSTORM – HOWL LIKE THE WIND		
	Elektra EKT 76	43	8
11 Oct 03	THE VERY BEST OF LINDA RONSTADT Elektra 8122736052	46	3

[1] Linda Ronstadt and James Ingram [2] Linda Ronstadt featuring Aaron Neville
[1] Linda Ronstadt with the Nelson Riddle Orchestra [2] Dolly Parton / Emmylou Harris / Linda Ronstadt

The ROOFTOP SINGERS
US, male / female vocal group (Singles: 12 Weeks) pos/wks

| 31 Jan 63 | ● WALK RIGHT IN Fontana 271700 TF ▲ | 10 | 12 |

ROOM 5 featuring Oliver CHEATHAM (see also JUNIOR JACK) *Italy, male producer – Vito Lucente and US, male vocalist (Singles: 17 Weeks)* pos/wks

| 5 Apr 03 | ★ MAKE LUV Positiva CDTIV 187 [1] ■ | 1 | 15 |
| 6 Dec 03 | MUSIC & YOU Positiva CDTIV 197 [1] | 38 | 2 |

[1] Room 5 featuring Oliver Cheatham

ROONEY *US, male vocal / instrumental group (Singles: 1 Week)* pos/wks

| 26 Jun 04 | I'M SHAKIN' Geffen 9862557 | 73 | 1 |

ROOSTER
UK, male vocal / instrumental group (Singles: 6 Weeks) pos/wks

| 23 Oct 04 | ● COME GET SOME Brightside 82876652382 | 7 | 6 |

ROOTJOOSE *UK, male vocal / instrumental group (Singles: 3 Weeks, Albums: 1 Week)* pos/wks

17 May 97	CAN'T KEEP LIVING THIS WAY Rage RAGECD 2	73	1
2 Aug 97	MR FIXIT Rage RAGECDX 3	54	1
4 Oct 97	LONG WAY Rage RAGECD 5	68	1
18 Oct 97	RHUBARB Rage RAGECD 6	58	1

ROOTS
US, male rap / production group (Singles: 6 Weeks, Albums: 1 Week) pos/wks

3 May 97	WHAT THEY DO Geffen GFSTD 22240	49	1
6 Mar 99	YOU GOT ME MCA MCSTD 48110 [1]	31	2
12 Apr 03	THE SEED (2.0) MCA MCSTD 40316 [2]	33	2
16 Aug 03	BREAK YOU OFF MCA MCSTD 40330 [3]	59	1
24 Jul 04	THE TIPPING POINT Geffen 9863067	71	1

[1] Roots featuring Erykah Badu [2] Roots featuring Cody Chesnutt [3] Roots featuring Musiq

Ralphi ROSARIO See Richie RICH

Mykal ROSE See Shabba RANKS

ROSE OF ROMANCE ORCHESTRA
UK, orchestra (Singles: 1 Week) pos/wks

| 9 Jan 82 | TARA'S THEME FROM 'GONE WITH THE WIND' BBC RESL 108 | 71 | 1 |

ROSE ROYCE [388] [Top 500]
The best-selling nine-piece soul / dance combo from Los Angeles, US, whose biggest hits featured vocalist Gwen Dickey, started as a backing band for Motown acts and topped the UK album chart with their Greatest Hits collection in 1980 (Singles: 113 Weeks, Albums: 62 Weeks) pos/wks

25 Dec 76	● CAR WASH MCA 267 ▲	9	12
22 Jan 77	PUT YOUR MONEY WHERE YOUR MOUTH IS MCA 259	44	5
2 Apr 77	I WANNA GET NEXT TO YOU MCA 278	14	8
24 Sep 77	DO YOUR DANCE Whitfield K 17006	30	6
14 Jan 78	● WISHING ON A STAR Warner Bros. K 17060	3	14
6 May 78	IT MAKES YOU FEEL LIKE DANCIN' Warner Bros. K 17148	16	10
16 Sep 78	● LOVE DON'T LIVE HERE ANYMORE Whitfield K 17236	2	10
3 Feb 79	I'M IN LOVE (AND I LOVE THE FEELING) Whitfield K 17291	51	4
17 Nov 79	IS IT LOVE YOU'RE AFTER Whitfield K 17456	13	13
8 Mar 80	OOH BOY Whitfield K 17575	46	7
21 Nov 81	R.R. EXPRESS Whitfield K 17875	52	3
1 Sep 84	MAGIC TOUCH Streetwave KHAN 21	43	8
6 Apr 85	LOVE ME RIGHT NOW Streetwave KHAN 39	60	3
11 Jun 88	CAR WASH / IS IT LOVE YOU'RE AFTER (re-issue)		
	MCA MCA 1253	20	7
31 Oct 98	CAR WASH (re-recording) MCA MCSTD 48096 [1]	18	3
22 Oct 77	IN FULL BLOOM Warner Bros. K 56394	18	13
30 Sep 78	● STRIKES AGAIN Whitfield 56257	7	11

22 Sep 79	RAINBOW CONNECTION IV Atlantic K 56714	72	2
1 Mar 80	★ GREATEST HITS Whitfield K RRTV 1	1	34
13 Oct 84	MUSIC MAGIC Streetwave MKL 2	69	2

[1] Rose Royce featuring Gwen Dickey

ROSE TATTOO *Australia, male vocal / instrumental group (Singles: 4 Weeks, Albums: 4 Weeks)* pos/wks

| 11 Jul 81 | ROCK 'N' ROLL OUTLAW Carrere CAR 200 | 60 | 4 |
| 26 Sep 81 | ASSAULT AND BATTERY Carrere CAL 127 | 40 | 4 |

Jimmy ROSELLI *US, male vocalist (Singles: 8 Weeks)* pos/wks

5 Mar 83	WHEN YOUR OLD WEDDING RING WAS NEW A1 282	51	5
20 Jun 87	WHEN YOUR OLD WEDDING RING WAS NEW (re-issue)		
	First Night SCORE 9	52	3

ROSIE See G NATION featuring ROSIE

Diana ROSS [13] [Top 500]
Perennially popular ex-leader of The Supremes, the most successful girl group of all time, b. Diane Earle, 26 Mar 1944, Detroit, US. Ross continued to clock up worldwide hits after leaving the trio in 1970 and sang lead on at least one hit every year for a record 33 years (1964-1996). The classy vocalist has also had more albums on the UK chart than any other American female artist. Diana, who starred in the movies 'Lady Sings the Blues' (1972), 'Mahogany' (1976) and 'The Wiz' (1978), moved from Motown to RCA in 1981 for a (female) record $20 million. In 1994, she was the star of the opening ceremony of football's World Cup, and in 1998 was sampled on US chart-topping singles by Puff Daddy and Monica. In her homeland this supreme song stylist has collected a staggering 22 Top 5 entries during her career, even though she has not had a major hit there since 1984. She has been inducted into the Soul Train and Songwriters' Hall of Fame and was the recipient of a Lifetime Achievement trophy at the World Music Awards in 1996 (Singles: 560 Weeks, Albums: 743 Weeks) pos/wks

30 Aug 67	● REFLECTIONS Tamla Motown TMG 616 [1]	5	14
29 Nov 67	IN AND OUT OF LOVE Tamla Motown TMG 632 [1]	13	13
10 Apr 68	FOREVER CAME TODAY Tamla Motown TMG 650 [1]	28	8
3 Jul 68	SOME THINGS YOU NEVER GET USED TO		
	Tamla Motown TMG 662 [1]	34	6
20 Nov 68	LOVE CHILD Tamla Motown TMG 677 [1] ▲	15	14
29 Jan 69	● I'M GONNA MAKE YOU LOVE ME (re)		
	Tamla Motown TMG 685 [2]	3	12
23 Apr 69	I'M LIVIN' IN SHAME (re) Tamla Motown TMG 695 [1]	14	10
16 Jul 69	NO MATTER WHAT SIGN YOU ARE		
	Tamla Motown TMG 704 [1]	37	7
20 Sep 69	I SECOND THAT EMOTION Tamla Motown TMG 709 [2]	18	8
13 Dec 69	SOMEDAY WE'LL BE TOGETHER		
	Tamla Motown TMG 721 [1] ▲	13	13
21 Mar 70	WHY (MUST WE FALL IN LOVE) Tamla Motown TMG 730 [2]	31	7
18 Jul 70	REACH OUT AND TOUCH Tamla Motown TMG 743	33	5
12 Sep 70	● AIN'T NO MOUNTAIN HIGH ENOUGH		
	Tamla Motown TMG 751 ▲	6	12
3 Apr 71	● REMEMBER ME Tamla Motown TMG 768	7	12
31 Jul 71	★ I'M STILL WAITING Tamla Motown TMG 781	1	14
30 Oct 71	● SURRENDER Tamla Motown TMG 792	10	11
13 May 72	DOOBEDOOD'NDOOBE DOOBEDOOD'NDOOBE		
	Tamla Motown TMG 812	12	9
14 Jul 73	● TOUCH ME IN THE MORNING (re) Tamla Motown TMG 861 ▲	9	13
5 Jan 74	● ALL OF MY LIFE Tamla Motown TMG 880	9	13
23 Mar 74	● YOU ARE EVERYTHING Tamla Motown TMG 890 [3]	5	12
4 May 74	LAST TIME I SAW HIM Tamla Motown TMG 893	35	4
20 Jul 74	STOP LOOK LISTEN (TO YOUR HEART)		
	Tamla Motown TMG 906 [3]	25	8
24 Aug 74	BABY LOVE (re-issue) Tamla Motown TMG 915 [1]	12	10
28 Sep 74	LOVE ME Tamla Motown TMG 917	38	5
29 Mar 75	SORRY DOESN'T ALWAYS MAKE IT RIGHT		
	Tamla Motown TMG 941	23	9
3 Apr 76	● THEME FROM 'MAHOGANY' (DO YOU KNOW		
	WHERE YOU'RE GOING TO) Tamla Motown TMG 1010 ▲	5	8
24 Apr 76	● LOVE HANGOVER Tamla Motown TMG 1024 ▲	10	10
10 Jul 76	I THOUGHT IT TOOK A LITTLE TIME (BUT TODAY I FELL		
	IN LOVE) Tamla Motown TMG 1032	32	5
16 Oct 76	I'M STILL WAITING (re-issue) Tamla Motown TMG 1041	41	4
19 Nov 77	GETTIN' READY FOR LOVE Tamla Motown TMG 1090	23	7
22 Jul 78	LOVIN' LIVIN' AND GIVIN' Motown TMG 1112	54	6
18 Nov 78	EASE ON DOWN THE ROAD MCA 396 [4]	45	4

24 Feb 79	POPS, WE LOVE YOU *Motown TMG 1136* [5]	66	5
21 Jul 79	THE BOSS *Motown TMG 1150*	40	7
6 Oct 79	NO ONE GETS THE PRIZE *Motown TMG 1160*	59	3
24 Nov 79	IT'S MY HOUSE *Motown TMG 1169*	32	10
19 Jul 80 ●	UPSIDE DOWN *Motown TMG 1195* ▲	2	12
20 Sep 80 ●	MY OLD PIANO *Motown TMG 1202*	5	9
15 Nov 80	I'M COMING OUT *Motown TMG 1210*	13	10
17 Jan 81	IT'S MY TURN *Motown TMG 1217*	16	8
28 Mar 81	ONE MORE CHANCE *Motown TMG 1227*	49	5
13 Jun 81	CRYIN' MY HEART OUT FOR YOU *Motown TMG 1233*	58	3
12 Sep 81 ●	ENDLESS LOVE *Motown TMG 1240* [6] ▲	7	12
7 Nov 81 ●	WHY DO FOOLS FALL IN LOVE *Capitol CL 226*	4	12
23 Jan 82	TENDERNESS (re) *Motown TMG 1248*	73	2
30 Jan 82	MIRROR MIRROR *Capitol CL 234*	36	5
29 May 82 ●	WORK THAT BODY *Capitol CL 241*	7	11
7 Aug 82	IT'S NEVER TOO LATE *Capitol CL 256*	41	4
23 Oct 82	MUSCLES *Capitol CL 268*	15	4
15 Jan 83	SO CLOSE *Capitol CL 277*	43	4
23 Jul 83	PIECES OF ICE *Capitol CL 298*	46	3
7 Jul 84	ALL OF YOU *CBS A 4522* [7]	43	8
15 Sep 84	TOUCH BY TOUCH *Capitol CL 337*	47	6
28 Sep 85	EATEN ALIVE *Capitol CL 372*	71	1
25 Jan 86 ★	CHAIN REACTION *Capitol CL 386*	1	17
3 May 86	EXPERIENCE *Capitol CL 400*	47	3
13 Jun 87	DIRTY LOOKS *EMI EM 2*	49	3
8 Oct 88	MR LEE *EMI EM 73*	58	2
26 Nov 88	LOVE HANGOVER (re-mix) *Motown ZB 42307*	75	1
18 Feb 89	STOP! IN THE NAME OF LOVE (re-issue) *Motown ZB 41963*	62	1
6 May 89	WORKIN' OVERTIME *EMI EM 91*	32	5
29 Jul 89	PARADISE *EMI EM 94*	61	2
7 Jul 90	I'M STILL WAITING (re-mix) *Motown ZB 43781*	21	6
30 Nov 91 ●	WHEN YOU TELL ME THAT YOU LOVE ME *EMI EM 217*	2	11
15 Feb 92	THE FORCE BEHIND THE POWER *EMI EM 221*	27	3
20 Jun 92 ●	ONE SHINING MOMENT *EMI EM 239*	10	8
28 Nov 92	IF WE HOLD ON TOGETHER *EMI EM 257*	11	10
13 Mar 93	HEART (DON'T CHANGE MY MIND) *EMI CDEM 261*	31	4
9 Oct 93	CHAIN REACTION (re-issue) *EMI CDEM 290*	20	5
11 Dec 93	YOUR LOVE *EMI CDEM 299*	14	8
2 Apr 94	THE BEST YEARS OF MY LIFE *EMI CDEM 305*	28	4
9 Jul 94	WHY DO FOOLS FALL IN LOVE / I'M COMING OUT (re-issue) (re-mix) *EMI CDEM 332*	36	4
2 Sep 95	TAKE ME HIGHER *EMI CDEM 388*	32	4
25 Nov 95	I'M GONE *EMI CDEM 402*	36	3
17 Feb 96	I WILL SURVIVE *EMI CDEM 415* [8]	14	4
21 Dec 96	IN THE ONES YOU LOVE *EMI CDEM 457*	34	4
6 Nov 99 ●	NOT OVER YOU YET (re) *EMI CDEMS 553*	9	7
20 Jan 68 ★	GREATEST HITS *Tamla Motown STML 11063* [1] ▲	1	60
30 Mar 68 ●	LIVE AT THE TALK OF THE TOWN *Tamla Motown STML 11070* [1]	6	18
20 Jul 68	REFLECTIONS *Tamla Motown STML 11073* [1]	30	2
25 Jan 69 ★	DIANA ROSS AND THE SUPREMES JOIN THE TEMPTATIONS *Tamla Motown STML 11096* [2] ▲	1	15
1 Feb 69 ●	LOVE CHILD *Tamla Motown STML 11095* [1]	8	6
28 Jun 69 ●	TCB *Tamla Motown STML 11110* [2]	11	12
14 Feb 70	TOGETHER *Tamla Motown STML 11122* [2]	28	4
24 Oct 70	DIANA ROSS *Tamla Motown SFTML 11159*	14	5
19 Jun 71	EVERYTHING IS EVERYTHING *Tamla Motown STML 11178*	31	3
9 Oct 71	I'M STILL WAITING *Tamla Motown STML 11193*	43	1
9 Oct 71 ●	DIANA *Tamla Motown STMA 8001*	10	11
11 Nov 72	GREATEST HITS *Tamla Motown STMA 8006*	34	10
1 Sep 73 ●	TOUCH ME IN THE MORNING *Tamla Motown STML 11239*	7	35
27 Oct 73	LADY SINGS THE BLUES *Tamla Motown TMSP 1131* ▲	50	1
19 Jan 74 ●	DIANA&MARVIN *Tamla Motown STMA 8015* [3]	6	43
2 Mar 74	LAST TIME I SAW HIM *Tamla Motown STML 11255*	41	1
8 Jun 74	LIVE *Tamla Motown STML 11248*	21	8
27 Mar 76 ●	DIANA ROSS *Tamla Motown STML 12022*	4	26
7 Aug 76 ●	GREATEST HITS 2 *Tamla Motown STML 12036*	2	29
19 Mar 77	AN EVENING WITH DIANA ROSS *Motown TMSP 6005*	52	1
17 Sep 77 ★	20 GOLDEN GREATS *Motown EMTV 5* [1] ■	1	34
4 Aug 79	THE BOSS *Motown STML 12118*	52	2
17 Nov 79 ●	20 GOLDEN GREATS *Motown EMTV 21*	2	29
21 Jun 80	DIANA *Motown STMA 8033*	12	32
28 Mar 81	TO LOVE AGAIN *Motown STML 12152*	26	10
29 Aug 81	DIANA AND MARVIN (re-issue) *Motown STMS 5001* [3]	78	2
7 Nov 81	WHY DO FOOLS FALL IN LOVE *Capitol EST 26733*	17	24
21 Nov 81	ALL THE GREAT HITS *Motown STMA 8036*	21	31
13 Feb 82	DIANA'S DUETS *Motown STML 12163*	43	6
23 Oct 82	SILK ELECTRIC *Capitol EAST 27313*	33	12

4 Dec 82 ●	LOVE SONGS *K-Tel NE 1200*	5	17
19 Jul 83	ROSS *Capitol EST 1867051*	44	5
24 Dec 83 ●	PORTRAIT *Telstar STAR 2238*	8	31
6 Oct 84	SWEPT AWAY *Capitol ROSS 1*	40	5
28 Sep 85	EATEN ALIVE *Capitol ROSS 2*	11	19
15 Nov 86	DIANA ROSS. MICHAEL JACKSON. GLADYS KNIGHT. STEVIE WONDER. THEIR VERY BEST BACK TO BACK *Priorty TV PTVR 2* [4]	21	10
30 May 87	RED HOT RHYTHM 'N' BLUES *EMI EMC 3532*	47	4
31 Oct 87	LOVE SONGS *Telstar STAR 2298* [5]	12	24
27 May 89	WORKIN' OVERTIME *EMI EMD 1009*	23	4
25 Nov 89	GREATEST HITS LIVE *EMI EMD 1001*	34	6
14 Dec 91	THE FORCE BEHIND THE POWER *EMI EMD 1023*	11	31
29 Feb 92	MOTOWN'S GREATEST HITS *Motown 5300132*	20	11
24 Apr 93	LIVE STOLEN MOMENTS *EMI CDEMD 1044*	45	2
30 Oct 93 ★	ONE WOMAN – THE ULTIMATE COLLECTION *EMI CDONE 1*	1	67
25 Dec 93	CHRISTMAS IN VIENNA *Sony Classical SK 53358* [6]	71	2
23 Apr 94	DIANA EXTENDED – THE REMIXES *EMI CDDREX 1*	58	2
26 Nov 94	A VERY SPECIAL SEASON *EMI CDEMD 1075*	37	6
16 Sep 95 ●	TAKE ME HIGHER *EMI CDEMD 1085*	10	3
23 Nov 96	VOICE OF LOVE *EMI CDEMD 1100*	42	7
31 Oct 98	40 GOLDEN MOTOWN GREATS *Motown / PolyGram TV 5309612* [1]	35	4
20 Nov 99	EVERY DAY IS A NEW DAY *EMI 5214762*	71	1
17 Nov 01	LOVE & LIFE – THE VERY BEST OF DIANA ROSS *EMI / Universal TV 5358622*	28	7
29 May 04	THE NO.1'S *Motown 9818019* [1]	26	3

[1] Diana Ross and The Supremes [2] Diana Ross and The Supremes and The Temptations [3] Diana Ross and Marvin Gaye [4] Diana Ross and Michael Jackson [5] Diana Ross, Marvin Gaye, Smokey Robinson and Stevie Wonder [6] Diana Ross and Lionel Richie [7] Julio Iglesias and Diana Ross [8] Diana [1] Diana Ross and The Supremes [2] Diana Ross and The Supremes with The Temptations [3] Diana Ross and Marvin Gaye [4] Diana Ross / Michael Jackson / Gladys Knight / Stevie Wonder [5] Diana Ross and Michael Jackson [6] Placido Domingo, Diana Ross and José Carreras

The two 'Diana' albums and the three 'Diana Ross' titles are all different. From 14 Jan 89, when multi-artist albums were excluded from the main chart, 'Love Songs' by Diana Ross and Michael Jackson was listed in the compilation albums chart

Ricky ROSS (see also DEACON BLUE)
UK, male vocalist (Singles: 3 Weeks, Albums: 1 Week)   pos/wks

18 May 96	RADIO ON *Epic 6631352*	35	2
10 Aug 96	GOOD EVENING PHILADELPHIA *Epic 6635352*	58	1
15 Jun 96	WHAT YOU ARE *Epic 4839982*	36	1

Francis ROSSI (see also STATUS QUO)
UK, male vocalist (Singles: 6 Weeks)   pos/wks

11 May 85	MODERN ROMANCE (I WANT TO FALL IN LOVE AGAIN) *Vertigo FROS 1* [1]	54	4
3 Aug 96	GIVE MYSELF TO LOVE *Virgin VSCDT 1594* [2]	42	2

[1] Francis Rossi and Bernard Frost [2] Francis Rossi of Status Quo

Natalie ROSSI *See The FOUNDATION featuring Natalie ROSSI*

Nini ROSSO *Italy, male instrumentalist –*
trumpet – Celeste Rosso (Singles: 14 Weeks)   pos/wks

26 Aug 65 ●	IL SILENZIO *Durium DRS 54000*	8	14

ROSTAL and SCHAEFER
UK, male instrumental duo (Albums: 2 Weeks)   pos/wks

14 Jul 79	BEATLES CONCERTO *Parlophone PAS 10014*	61	2

David Lee ROTH (see also VAN HALEN)
US, male vocalist (Singles: 15 Weeks, Albums: 32 Weeks)   pos/wks

23 Feb 85	CALIFORNIA GIRLS *Warner Bros. W 9102*	68	2
5 Mar 88	JUST LIKE PARADISE *Warner Bros. W 8119*	27	7
3 Sep 88	DAMN GOOD / STAND UP *Warner Bros. W 7753*	72	1
12 Jan 91	A LIL' AIN'T ENOUGH *Warner Bros. W 0002*	32	3
19 Feb 94	SHE'S MY MACHINE *Reprise W 0229CD*	64	1
28 May 94	NIGHT LIFE *Reprise W 0249CD*	72	1
2 Mar 85	CRAZY FROM THE HEAT *Warner Bros. 9252221*	91	2
19 Jul 86	EAT 'EM AND SMILE *Warner Bros. WX 56*	28	9
6 Feb 88	SKYSCRAPER *Warner Bros. 925671 1*	11	12
26 Jan 91 ●	A LITTLE AIN'T ENOUGH *Warner Bros. WX 403*	4	7
19 Mar 94	YOUR FILTHY LITTLE MOUTH *Reprise 9362453912*	28	2

Uli Jon ROTH and ELECTRIC SUN
Germany, male vocal / instrumental group (Albums: 2 Weeks)   pos/wks

23 Feb 85	**BEYOND THE ASTRAL SKIES** *EMI ROTH 1*	64	2

ROTTERDAM TERMINATION SOURCE
Holland, male instrumental / production duo –
Maurice Steenbergen and Danny Scholte (Singles: 6 Weeks)   pos/wks

7 Nov 92	**POING** *SEP EDGE 74*	27	4
25 Dec 93	**MERRY X-MESS** *React CDREACT 33*	73	2

ROULA See 20 FINGERS

ROULETTES See Adam FAITH

Thomas ROUND See June BRONHILL and Thomas ROUND

ROUND SOUND presents ONYX STONE & MC MALIBU
UK, male production trio and UK, male rappers (Singles: 1 Week)   pos/wks

16 Mar 02	**WHADDA WE LIKE?** *Cooltempo CDCOOL 358*	69	1

Demis ROUSSOS 354 Top 500
Unmistakable Greek MOR vocalist / multi-instrumentalist and entertainer, b. 15 Jun 1947, Egypt. He was in Aphrodites Child (with Vangelis) before starting a successful solo career. 'The Roussos Phenomenon' was the first four track EP to top the singles chart (Singles: 44 Weeks, Albums: 147 Weeks)   pos/wks

22 Nov 75	● **HAPPY TO BE ON AN ISLAND IN THE SUN** *Philips 6042 033*	5	10
28 Feb 76	**CAN'T SAY HOW MUCH I LOVE YOU** *Philips 6042 114*	35	5
26 Jun 76	★ **THE ROUSSOS PHENOMENON (EP)** *Philips Demis 001*	1	12
2 Oct 76	● **WHEN FOREVER HAS GONE** *Philips 6042 186*	2	10
19 Mar 77	**BECAUSE** *Philips 6042 245*	39	4
18 Jun 77	**KYRILA (EP)** *Philips Demis 002*	33	3
22 Jun 74	● **FOREVER AND EVER** *Philips 6325 021*	2	68
19 Apr 75	**SOUVENIRS** *Philips 6325 201*	25	18
24 Apr 76	● **HAPPY TO BE** *Philips 9101 027*	4	34
3 Jul 76	**MY ONLY FASCINATION** *Philips 6325 094*	39	6
16 Apr 77	**THE MAGIC OF DEMIS ROUSSOS** *Philips 9101 131*	29	6
28 Oct 78	**LIFE AND LOVE** *Philips 9199 873*	29	11
16 Mar 02	**FOREVER AND EVER – THE DEFINITIVE COLLECTION** *Philips 5867702*	17	4

Tracks on The Roussos Phenomenon (EP): Forever and Ever / Sing an Ode to Love / So Dreamy / My Friend the Wind. Tracks on Kyrila (EP): Kyrila / I'm Gonna Fall in Love / I Dig You / Sister Emilyne

The ROUTERS
US, male instrumental group (Singles: 7 Weeks)   pos/wks

27 Dec 62	**LET'S GO** *Warner Bros. WB 77*	32	7

Maria ROWE
UK, female vocalist (Singles: 2 Weeks)   pos/wks

20 May 95	**SEXUAL** *ffrr FCD 248*	67	2

ROWETTA See OPEN ARMS featuring ROWETTA

Kelly ROWLAND
(see also DESTINY'S CHILD) US, female vocalist –
Kelendria Rowland (Singles: 54 Weeks, Albums: 26 Weeks)   pos/wks

26 Oct 02	★ **DILEMMA** *Universal MCSTD 40299* 1 ■ ▲	1	21
28 Dec 02	**STOLE (IMPORT)** *Columbia 6732122*	57	5
8 Feb 03	● **STOLE (re)** *Columbia 6735182*	2	14
10 May 03	● **CAN'T NOBODY** *Columbia 6738142*	5	10
16 Aug 03	**TRAIN ON A TRACK** *Columbia 6742155*	20	4
15 Feb 03	★ **SIMPLY DEEP** *Columbia 5096042* ■	1	26

1 Nelly featuring Kelly Rowland

Kevin ROWLAND See DEXY'S MIDNIGHT RUNNERS

John ROWLES
New Zealand, male vocalist (Singles: 28 Weeks)   pos/wks

13 Mar 68	● **IF I ONLY HAD TIME** *MCA MU 1000*	3	18
19 Jun 68	**HUSH ... NOT A WORD TO MARY** *MCA MU 1023*	12	10

Lisa ROXANNE
UK, female vocalist – Lisa Roxanne Naraine (Singles: 2 Weeks)   pos/wks

9 Jun 01	**NO FLOW** *Palm Pictures PPCD 70542*	18	2

ROXETTE 189 Top 500
The most successful Scandinavian act in the US singles chart: Marie Fredriksson (v), Per Gessle (v/g). The duo, who have even appeared on postage stamps in their homeland, can claim total worldwide sales in excess of 40 million. In Sweden, Gessle scored a solo No.1 album in 2003 and Fredriksson followed suit in 2004 (Singles: 143 Weeks, Albums: 161 Weeks)   pos/wks

22 Apr 89	● **THE LOOK** *EMI EM 87* ▲	7	10
15 Jul 89	**DRESSED FOR SUCCESS** *EMI EM 96*	48	5
28 Oct 89	**LISTEN TO YOUR HEART** *EMI EM 108* ▲	62	3
2 Jun 90	● **IT MUST HAVE BEEN LOVE** *EMI EM 141* ▲	3	14
11 Aug 90	● **LISTEN TO YOUR HEART / DANGEROUS (re-issue)** *EMI EM 149*	6	9
27 Oct 90	**DRESSED FOR SUCCESS (re-issue)** *EMI EM 162*	18	7
9 Mar 91	● **JOYRIDE** *EMI EM 177* ▲	4	10
11 May 91	**FADING LIKE A FLOWER (EVERY TIME YOU LEAVE)** *EMI EM 190*	12	6
7 Sep 91	**THE BIG L** *EMI EM 204*	21	6
23 Nov 91	**SPENDING MY TIME** *EMI EM 215*	22	4
28 Mar 92	**CHURCH OF YOUR HEART** *EMI EM 227*	21	4
1 Aug 92	**HOW DO YOU DO!** *EMI EM 241*	13	7
7 Nov 92	**QUEEN OF RAIN** *EMI EM 253*	28	4
24 Jul 93	● **ALMOST UNREAL** *EMI CDEM 268*	7	9
18 Sep 93	● **IT MUST HAVE BEEN LOVE (re-issue)** *EMI CDEM 285*	10	8
26 Mar 94	**SLEEPING IN MY CAR** *EMI CDEM 314*	14	6
4 Jun 94	**CRASH! BOOM! BANG!** *EMI CDEM 324*	26	5
17 Sep 94	**FIREWORKS** *EMI CDEM 345*	30	4
3 Dec 94	**RUN TO YOU** *EMI CDEM 360*	27	6
8 Apr 95	**VULNERABLE** *EMI CDEM 369*	44	2
25 Nov 95	**THE LOOK (re-mix)** *EMI CDEM 406*	28	3
30 Mar 96	**YOU DON'T UNDERSTAND ME** *EMI CDEM 418*	42	2
20 Jul 96	**JUNE AFTERNOON** *EMI CDEM 437*	52	1
20 May 99	**WISH I COULD FLY** *EMI CDEM 537*	11	7
9 Oct 99	**STARS** *EMI CDEM 550*	56	1
17 Jun 89	● **LOOK SHARP!** *EMI EMC 3557*	4	53
13 Apr 91	● **JOYRIDE** *EMI EMD 1019*	2	48
12 Sep 92	● **TOURISM** *EMI CDEMD 1036*	2	17
23 Apr 94	● **CRASH BOOM BANG** *EMI CDEMD 1056*	3	16
4 Nov 95	● **DON'T BORE US – GET TO THE CHORUS! – ROXETTE'S GREATEST HITS** *EMI CDXEMTV 98*	5	20
10 Apr 99	**HAVE A NICE DAY** *EMI 4994612*	28	3
15 Feb 03	**THE BALLAD HITS** *Capitol 5427982*	11	4

ROXY MUSIC 61 Top 500
Stylish art-rock group regarded as highly influential pioneers. Nucleus of oft-changing group line-up: Bryan Ferry (v), Andy Mackay (sax), Phil Manzanera (g). A major act of its time, this group amassed 11 Top 10 albums (Singles: 155 Weeks, Albums: 430 Weeks)   pos/wks

19 Aug 72	● **VIRGINIA PLAIN** *Island WIP 6144*	4	12
10 Mar 73	● **PYJAMARAMA** *Island WIP 6159*	10	12
17 Nov 73	● **STREET LIFE** *Island WIP 6173*	9	12
12 Oct 74	**ALL I WANT IS YOU** *Island WIP 6208*	12	8
11 Oct 75	● **LOVE IS THE DRUG** *Island WIP 6248*	2	10
27 Dec 75	**BOTH ENDS BURNING** *Island WIP 6262*	25	5
22 Oct 77	**VIRGINIA PLAIN (re-issue)** *Polydor 2001 739*	11	6
3 Mar 79	**TRASH** *Polydor POSP 32*	40	6
28 Apr 79	● **DANCE AWAY** *Polydor POSP 44*	2	14
11 Aug 79	● **ANGEL EYES** *Polydor POSP 67*	4	11
17 May 80	● **OVER YOU** *Polydor POSP 93*	5	9
2 Aug 80	● **OH YEAH (ON THE RADIO)** *Polydor 2001 972*	5	8
8 Nov 80	**THE SAME OLD SCENE** *Polydor ROXY 1*	12	7
21 Feb 81	★ **JEALOUS GUY** *EG ROXY 2*	1	11
3 Apr 82	● **MORE THAN THIS** *EG ROXY 3*	6	8
19 Jun 82	**AVALON** *EG ROXY 4*	13	6
25 Sep 82	**TAKE A CHANCE WITH ME** *EG ROXY 5*	26	6
27 Apr 96	**LOVE IS THE DRUG (re-mix)** *EG VSCDT 1580*	33	2
29 Jul 72	● **ROXY MUSIC** *Island ILPS 9200*	10	14
7 Apr 73	● **FOR YOUR PLEASURE** *Island ILPS 9232*	4	27
1 Dec 73	★ **STRANDED** *Island ILPS 9252*	1	17
30 Nov 74	● **COUNTRY LIFE** *Island ILPS 9303*	3	10
8 Nov 75	● **SIREN** *Island ILPS 9344*	4	17
31 Jul 76	● **VIVA! ROXY MUSIC** *Island ILPS 9400*	6	12
19 Nov 77	● **GREATEST HITS** *Polydor 2302 073*	20	11
24 Mar 79	● **MANIFESTO** *Polydor POLH 001*	7	34
31 May 80	★ **FLESH AND BLOOD** *Polydor POLH 002*	1	60
5 Jun 82	★ **AVALON** *EG EGLP 50* ■	1	57
19 Mar 83	**THE HIGH ROAD (IMPORT)** *EG EGMLP 1*	26	7
12 Nov 83	**ATLANTIC YEARS 1973-1980** *EG EGLP 54*	23	25
26 Apr 86	★ **STREET LIFE – 20 GREAT HITS** *EG EGTV 1* 1 ■	1	77

		pos/wks
19 Nov 88 ●	THE ULTIMATE COLLECTION *EG EGTV 2* [1]	6 35
4 Nov 95	MORE THAN THIS – THE BEST OF BRYAN FERRY AND ROXY MUSIC *Virgin CDV 2791* [1]	15 15
23 Jun 01	THE BEST OF ROXY MUSIC *Virgin CDV 2939*	12 6
19 Jun 04	THE PLATINUM COLLECTION *Virgin BFRM 1* [1]	17 4

[1] Bryan Ferry and Roxy Music

Central Band of the ROYAL AIR FORCE, Conductor W/Cdr AE SIMS OBE *UK, military band (Singles: 1 Week)*

		pos/wks
21 Oct 55	THE DAM BUSTERS MARCH *HMV B 10877*	18 1

Billy Joe ROYAL *US, male vocalist (Singles: 4 Weeks)*

		pos/wks
7 Oct 65	DOWN IN THE BOONDOCKS *CBS 201802*	38 4

ROYAL CHORAL SOCIETY See LONDON SYMPHONY ORCHESTRA

ROYAL GIGOLOS
Germany / UK, male production / vocal group (Singles: 3 Weeks)

		pos/wks
31 Jul 04	CALIFORNIA DREAMIN' *Manifesto 9866931*	44 3

The ROYAL GUARDSMEN
US, male vocal / instrumental group (Singles: 17 Weeks)

		pos/wks
19 Jan 67 ●	SNOOPY VS THE RED BARON *Stateside SS 574*	8 13
6 Apr 67	RETURN OF THE RED BARON *Stateside SS 2010*	37 4

ROYAL HOUSE
(see also BLACK RIOT; The GYPSYMEN; SWAN LAKE)
US, male DJ / producer – Todd Terry (Singles: 18 Weeks)

		pos/wks
10 Sep 88	CAN YOU PARTY *Champion CHAMP 79*	14 14
7 Jan 89	YEAH! BUDDY *Champion CHAMP 91*	35 4

ROYAL LIVERPOOL PHILHARMONIC ORCHESTRA See Carl DAVIS and the ROYAL LIVERPOOL PHILHARMONIC ORCHESTRA

ROYAL PHILHARMONIC ORCHESTRA (437 Top 500)
(see also Elkie BROOKS; Richard CLAYDERMAN; Elvis COSTELLO; Julian LLOYD WEBBER; Andy WILLIAMS) *Formed in 1946 by Sir Thomas Beecham, who wanted a first rate ensemble that would attract the countries top musicians. Since his death (1961), it has come under various maestros including Andre Previn and Louis Clark (who was behind its biggest sellers) (Singles: 19 Weeks, Albums: 141 Weeks)*

		pos/wks
25 Jul 81 ●	HOOKED ON CLASSICS *RCA 109* [1]	2 11
24 Oct 81	HOOKED ON CAN-CAN *RCA 151* [1]	47 3
10 Jul 82	BBC WORLD CUP GRANDSTAND *BBC RESL 116*	61 3
7 Aug 82	IF YOU KNEW SOUSA (AND FRIENDS) *RCA 256* [1]	71 2
8 Jan 77	CLASSICAL GOLD *Ronco RTD 42020*	24 13
23 Dec 78	CLASSIC GOLD VOLUME 2 *Ronco RTD 42032*	31 4
19 Sep 81 ●	HOOKED ON CLASSICS *K-Tel ONE 1146*	4 43
31 Jul 82	CAN'T STOP THE CLASSICS – HOOKED ON CLASSICS 2 *K-Tel ONE 1173*	13 26
9 Apr 83	JOURNEY THROUGH THE CLASSICS – HOOKED ON CLASSICS 3 *K-Tel ONE 1266*	19 15
8 Oct 83	LOVE CLASSICS *Nouveau Music NML 1003* [1]	30 9
10 Dec 83	THE BEST OF HOOKED ON CLASSICS *K-Tel ONE 1266*	51 6
11 Feb 84	SERENADE *K-Tel ONE 1267* [2]	21 9
26 May 84	AS TIME GOES BY *Telstar STAR 2240* [3]	95 2
26 Nov 84	RHYTHM AND CLASSICS *Telstar STAR 2344*	96 1
22 Sep 90	MUSIC FOR THE LAST NIGHT OF THE PROMS *Cirrus TVLP 501* [4]	39 4
5 Oct 91	SERIOUSLY ORCHESTRAL *Virgin RPOLP 1*	31 6
30 Jul 94	BIG SCREEN CLASSICS *Quality Television GIGSCD 1*	49 2
26 Jun 04	SYMPHONIC ROCK *Virgin / EMI VTDCD 620*	42 1

[1] arranged and conducted by Louis Clark [1] Royal Philharmonic Orchestra conducted by Nick Portlock [2] Juan Martin and the Royal Philharmonic Orchestra [3] Royal Philharmonic Orchestra conducted by Harry Rabinowitz [4] Sir Charles Groves Royal Philharmonic Orchestra and Chorus with Sarah Walker

Pipes and Drums and Military Band of the ROYAL SCOTS DRAGOON GUARDS *UK, military band (Singles: 43 Weeks)*

		pos/wks
1 Apr 72 ★	AMAZING GRACE (re) *RCA 2191*	1 27
19 Aug 72	HEYKENS SERENADE (STANDCHEN) / THE DAY IS ENDED (THE DAY THOU GAVE US LORD, IS ENDED) *RCA 2251*	30 7
2 Dec 72	LITTLE DRUMMER BOY *RCA 2301*	13 9

ROYALLE DELITE
US, female vocal group (Singles: 6 Weeks)

		pos/wks
14 Sep 85	(I'LL BE A) FREAK FOR YOU *Streetwave KHAN 51*	45 6

ROYCE DA 5'9" See BAD MEETS EVIL featuring EMINEM & ROYCE DA 5'9"

RÖYKSOPP *Norway, male production duo – Svein Berge and Torbjorn Brundtland (Singles: 10 Weeks, Albums: 41 Weeks)*

		pos/wks
15 Dec 01	POOR LENO *Wall of Sound WALLD 073*	59 1
17 Aug 02	REMIND ME / SO EASY *Wall of Sound WALLD 074X*	21 3
30 Nov 02	POOR LENO (re-issue) *Wall of Sound WALLD 079CD*	38 2
8 Mar 03	EPLE *Wall of Sound WALLD 080*	16 3
28 Jun 03	SPARKS *Wall of Sound WALLD 084*	41 1
24 Aug 02 ●	MELODY AM *Wall of Sound WALLCD 027*	9 41

Lita ROZA *UK, female vocalist (Singles: 18 Weeks)*

		pos/wks
13 Mar 53 ★	(HOW MUCH IS) THAT DOGGIE IN THE WINDOW *Decca F 10070*	1 11
7 Oct 55	HEY THERE *Decca F 10611*	17 2
23 Mar 56	JIMMY UNKNOWN *Decca F 10679*	15 5

ROZALLA *Zimbabwe, female vocalist – Rozalla Miller (Singles: 49 Weeks, Albums: 4 Weeks)*

		pos/wks
27 Apr 91	FAITH (IN THE POWER OF LOVE) *Pulse 8 LOSE 7*	65 2
7 Sep 91 ●	EVERYBODY'S FREE (TO FEEL GOOD) *Pulse 8 LOSE 13*	6 11
16 Nov 91	FAITH (IN THE POWER OF LOVE) (re-issue) *Pulse 8 LOSE 15*	11 6
22 Feb 92	ARE YOU READY TO FLY *Pulse 8 LOSE 21*	14 6
9 May 92	LOVE BREAKDOWN *Pulse 8 LOSE 25*	65 2
15 Aug 92	IN 4 CHOONS LATER *Pulse 8 LOSE 29*	50 2
30 Oct 93	DON'T PLAY WITH ME *Pulse 8 CDLOSE 52*	50 1
5 Feb 94	I LOVE MUSIC *Epic 6598932*	18 5
6 Aug 94	THIS TIME I FOUND LOVE *Epic 6603742*	33 3
29 Oct 94	YOU NEVER LOVE THE SAME WAY TWICE *Epic 6609052*	16 5
4 Mar 95	BABY *Epic 6611955*	26 3
31 Aug 96	EVERYBODY'S FREE (re-mix) *Pulse 8 CDLOSE 110*	30 2
22 Nov 03	LIVE ANOTHER LIFE *Inferno CDFERN 59* [1]	55 1
4 Apr 92	EVERYBODY'S FREE *Pulse 8 PULSECD 3*	20 4

[1] Plastic Boy featuring Rozalla

RUBBADUBB
UK, male / female vocal / instrumental group (Singles: 1 Week)

		pos/wks
18 Jul 98	TRIBUTE TO OUR ANCESTORS *Perfecto PERF 165CD*	56 1

The RUBETTES *UK, male vocal / instrumental group – leader Alan Williams (Singles: 68 Weeks, Albums: 1 Week)*

		pos/wks
4 May 74 ★	SUGAR BABY LOVE *Polydor 2058 442*	1 10
13 Jul 74	TONIGHT *Polydor 2058 499*	12 9
16 Nov 74 ●	JUKE BOX JIVE *Polydor 2058 529*	3 12
8 Mar 75 ●	I CAN DO IT *State STAT 1*	7 9
21 Jun 75	FOE-DEE-O-DEE *State STAT 7*	15 6
22 Nov 75	LITTLE DARLING *State STAT 13*	30 5
1 May 76	YOU'RE THE REASON WHY *State STAT 20*	28 4
25 Sep 76	UNDER ONE ROOF *State STAT 27*	40 3
12 Feb 77 ●	BABY I KNOW *State STAT 37*	10 10
10 May 75	WE CAN DO IT *State ETAT 001*	41 1

Maria RUBIA (see also FRAGMA)
UK, female vocalist (Singles: 2 Weeks)

		pos/wks
19 May 01	SAY IT *Neo NEOCD 055*	40 2

Paulina RUBIO
Mexico, female vocalist – Paulina Dosamantes (Singles: 1 Weeks)

		pos/wks
28 Sep 02	DON'T SAY GOODBYE *Universal MCSTD 40291* ▲	68 1

RUBY and the ROMANTICS
US, female / male vocal group (Singles: 6 Weeks)

		pos/wks
28 Mar 63	OUR DAY WILL COME *London HLR 9679* ▲	38 6

RUDE BOY OF HOUSE See HOUSEMASTER BOYZ and The RUDE BOY OF HOUSE

RUDIES See Freddie NOTES and The RUDIES

RUFF DRIVERZ (see also Brad CARTER)
UK, male / female vocal / production trio (Singles: 21 Weeks) pos/wks

7 Feb 98	**DON'T STOP** *Inferno CDFERN 003* **30**	2
23 May 98	**DEEPER LOVE** *Inferno CDFERN 006* **19**	3
24 Oct 98	**SHAME** *Inferno CXFERN 9* **51**	2
28 Nov 98 ●	**DREAMING** *Inferno CXFERN 11* [1] **10**	8
24 Apr 99	**LA MUSICA** *Inferno CDFERN 14* [1] **14**	4
2 Oct 99	**WAITING FOR THE SUN** *Inferno CDFERN 19* **37**	2

[1] Ruff Driverz presents Arrola

RUFF ENDZ *US, male vocal duo –*
David Chance and Dante Jordan (Singles: 5 Weeks) pos/wks

19 Aug 00	**NO MORE** *Epic 6696202* **11**	5

Frances RUFFELLE *UK, female vocalist (Singles: 6 Weeks)* pos/wks

16 Apr 94	**LONELY SYMPHONY** *Virgin VSCDT 1499* **25**	6

Bruce RUFFIN
Jamaica, male vocalist – Bernardo Balderamus (Singles: 23 Weeks) pos/wks

1 May 71	**RAIN** *Trojan TR 7814* **19**	11
24 Jun 72 ●	**MAD ABOUT YOU** *Rhino RNO 101* **9**	12

David RUFFIN (see also The TEMPTATIONS)
US, male vocalist, b. 18 Jan 1941, d. 1 Jun 1991 (Singles: 10 Weeks) pos/wks

17 Jan 76 ●	**WALK AWAY FROM LOVE** *Tamla Motown TMG 1017* **10**	8
21 Sep 85	**A NIGHT AT THE APOLLO LIVE!** *RCA PB 49935* [1] **58**	2

[1] Daryl Hall and John Oates featuring David Ruffin and Eddie Kendrick

Jimmy RUFFIN
US, male vocalist (Singles: 106 Weeks, Albums: 10 Weeks) pos/wks

27 Oct 66 ●	**WHAT BECOMES OF THE BROKENHEARTED**	
	Tamla Motown TMG 577 ....**8**	15
9 Feb 67	**I'VE PASSED THIS WAY BEFORE** *Tamla Motown TMG 593* ...**29**	7
20 Apr 67	**GONNA GIVE HER ALL THE LOVE I'VE GOT**	
	Tamla Motown TMG 603 ....**26**	6
9 Aug 69	**I'VE PASSED THIS WAY BEFORE** (re-issue)	
	Tamla Motown TMG 703 ....**33**	6
28 Feb 70 ●	**FAREWELL IS A LONELY SOUND** *Tamla Motown TMG 726* **8**	16
4 Jul 70 ●	**I'LL SAY FOREVER MY LOVE** *Tamla Motown TMG 740* ...**7**	12
17 Oct 70 ●	**IT'S WONDERFUL (TO BE LOVED BY YOU)**	
	Tamla Motown TMG 753 ....**6**	14
27 Jul 74 ●	**WHAT BECOMES OF THE BROKENHEARTED** (re-issue)	
	Tamla Motown TMG 911 ....**4**	12
2 Nov 74	**FAREWELL IS A LONELY SOUND** (re-issue)	
	Tamla Motown TMG 922 ....**30**	5
16 Nov 74	**TELL ME WHAT YOU WANT** *Polydor 2058 433* **39**	4
3 May 80 ●	**HOLD ON TO MY LOVE** *RSO 57* **7**	8
26 Jan 85	**THERE WILL NEVER BE ANOTHER YOU** *EMI 5541* **68**	1
13 May 67	**THE JIMMY RUFFIN WAY** *Tamla Motown STML 11048*...........**32**	6
1 Jun 74	**GREATEST HITS** *Tamla Motown STML 11259* **41**	4

Kim RUFFIN *See Chubby CHUNKS*

RUFFNECK featuring YAVAHN *US, male*
production group and US, female vocalist (Singles: 6 Weeks) pos/wks

11 Nov 95	**EVERYBODY BE SOMEBODY** *Positiva CDTIV 46* **13**	4
7 Sep 96	**MOVE YOUR BODY** *Positiva CDTIV 61* **60**	1
1 Dec 01	**EVERYBODY BE SOMEBODY** (re-mix)	
	Strictly Rhythm SRUKCD 08 ....**66**	1

RUFUS *US, male / female vocal / instrumental group –*
includes Chaka Khan (Singles: 12 Weeks, Albums: 7 Weeks) pos/wks

31 Mar 84 ●	**AIN'T NOBODY** *Warner Bros. RCK 1* [1] **8**	12
12 Apr 75	**RUFUSIZED** *ABC ABCL 5063* **48**	2
21 Apr 84	**STOMPIN' AT THE SAVOY** *Warner Bros. 923679* [1] **64**	5

[1] Rufus and Chaka Khan [1] Rufus and Chaka Khan

RUKMANI *See SNAP!*

Dick RULES *See SCOOTER*

RUMOUR *See Graham PARKER and the RUMOUR*

RUMPLE-STILTS-SKIN
US, male / female vocal / instrumental group (Singles: 4 Weeks) pos/wks

24 Sep 83	**I THINK I WANT TO DANCE WITH YOU** *Polydor POSP 649* **51**	4

RUN-DMC
US, male rap group (Singles: 62 Weeks, Albums: 44 Weeks) pos/wks

19 Jul 86	**MY ADIDAS / PETER PIPER** *London LON 101* **62**	2
6 Sep 86 ●	**WALK THIS WAY** *London LON 104* **8**	10
7 Feb 87	**YOU BE ILLIN'** *Profile LON 118* **42**	4
30 May 87	**IT'S TRICKY** *Profile LON 130* **16**	7
12 Dec 87	**CHRISTMAS IN HOLLIS** *Profile LON 163* **56**	4
21 May 88	**RUN'S HOUSE** *London LON 177* **37**	4
2 Sep 89	**GHOSTBUSTERS** *MCA 1360* **65**	2
1 Dec 90	**WHAT'S IT ALL ABOUT** *Profile PROF 315* **48**	3
27 Mar 93	**DOWN WITH THE KING** *Profile PROFCD 39* **69**	2
21 Feb 98	**IT'S LIKE THAT (GERMAN IMPORT)** *Columbia 6652932* [1] **63**	1
14 Mar 98	**IT'S LIKE THAT (US IMPORT)** *Columbia 6652932* [1] **65**	1
21 Mar 98 ★	**IT'S LIKE THAT** *Sm:)e Communications SM 90652* [1] ◆ ■ **1**	16
18 Apr 98	**IT'S TRICKY (IMPORT)** *Epidrome EPD 6656982* [1] **74**	1
19 Apr 03	**IT'S TRICKY 2003** (re-mix) *Arista 82876513712* [2] **20**	3
26 Jul 86	**RAISING HELL** *Profile LONLP 21* **41**	26
4 Jun 88	**TOUGHER THAN LEATHER** *Profile LONLP 38* **13**	5
15 May 93	**DOWN WITH THE KING** *Profile FILECD 440*...........**44**	2
6 Jun 98	**TOGETHER FOREVER – GREATEST HITS 1983-1998**	
	Profile FILECD 474 ....**31**	3
26 Apr 03	**GREATEST HITS** *Arista 74321980602* **15**	8

[1] Run-DMC vs Jason Nevins [2] Run-DMC featuring Jacknife Lee
'Walk This Way' features Steve Tyler and Joe Perry of Aerosmith

RUN TINGS
UK, male instrumental / production duo (Singles: 1 Week) pos/wks

16 May 92	**FIRES BURNING** *Suburban Base SUBBASE 009* **58**	1

Todd RUNDGREN (see also UTOPIA) *US, male vocalist /*
instrumentalist (Singles: 8 Weeks, Albums: 9 Weeks) pos/wks

30 Jun 73	**I SAW THE LIGHT** *Bearsville K 15506* **36**	6
14 Dec 85	**LOVING YOU'S A DIRTY JOB BUT SOMEBODY'S GOTTA DO IT**	
	CBS A 6662 [1] **73**	2
29 Jan 77	**RA** *Bearsville K 55514*...............................**27**	6
6 May 78	**HERMIT OF MINK HOLLOW** *Bearsville K 55521* **42**	3

[1] Bonnie Tyler, guest vocals Todd Rundgren

Bic RUNGA *New Zealand, female vocalist (Albums: 2 Weeks)* pos/wks

3 Apr 04	**BEAUTIFUL COLLISION** *Epic 5127279* **55**	2

RUNRIG *UK, male vocal / instrumental*
group (Singles: 28 Weeks, Albums: 50 Weeks) pos/wks

29 Sep 90	**CAPTURE THE HEART (EP)** *Chrysalis CHS 3594* **49**	2
7 Sep 91	**HEARTHAMMER (EP)** *Chrysalis CHS 3754* **25**	4
9 Nov 91	**FLOWER OF THE WEST** *Chrysalis CHS 3805* **43**	2
6 Mar 93	**WONDERFUL** *Chrysalis CDCHS 3952* **29**	3
15 May 93	**THE GREATEST FLAME** *Chrysalis CDCHS 3975* **36**	3
7 Jan 95	**THIS TIME OF YEAR** *Chrysalis CDCHS 5018* **38**	2
6 May 95	**AN UBHAL AS AIRDE (THE HIGHEST APPLE)**	
	Chrysalis CDCHS 5021 ....**18**	5
4 Nov 95	**THINGS THAT ARE** *Chrysalis CDCHS 5029* **40**	2
12 Oct 96	**RHYTHM OF MY HEART** *Chrysalis CDCHS 5035* **24**	2
11 Jan 97	**THE GREATEST FLAME** (re-issue) *Chrysalis CDCHSS 5045* **30**	3
26 Nov 88	**ONCE IN A LIFETIME** *Chrysalis CHR 1695* **61**	2
7 Oct 89	**SEARCHLIGHT** *Chrysalis CHR 1713* **11**	4
22 Jun 91 ●	**THE BIG WHEEL** *Chrysalis CHR 1858*...........**4**	15
27 Mar 93 ●	**AMAZING THINGS** *Chrysalis CDCHR 2000* **2**	6
26 Nov 94	**TRANSMITTING LIVE** *Chrysalis CDCHR 6090*...........**41**	3
20 May 95	**THE CUTTER AND THE CLAN** *Chrysalis CCD 1669* **45**	2
18 Nov 95	**MARA** *Chrysalis CDCHR 6111*...........**24**	4
19 Oct 96	**LONG DISTANCE – THE BEST OF RUNRIG**	
	Chrysalis CDCHRS 6116 ....**13**	10
23 May 98	**THE GAELIC COLLECTION 1973-1995** *Ridge RR 009*...........**71**	1
13 Mar 99	**IN SEARCH OF ANGELS** *Ridge RR 010*...........**29**	1
26 May 01	**THE STAMPING GROUND** *Ridge RR 016*...........**64**	1

Tracks on Capture the Heart (EP): Stepping Down the Glory Road / Satellite Flood /
Harvest Moon / The Apple Came Down. Tracks on Hearthammer (EP):
Hearthammer / Pride of the Summer (Live) / Loch Lomond (Live) / Solus Na Madain

Singles re-entries are listed as (re), (2re), (3re)…. which signifies that the hit re-entered the chart once, twice or three times…

RuPAUL
US, male, female impersonator / vocalist – Rupaul Charles (Singles: 19 Weeks)   pos/wks

26 Jun 93	SUPERMODEL (YOU BETTER WORK) *Union City UCRD 21*	**39**	4
18 Sep 93	HOUSE OF LOVE / BACK TO MY ROOTS *Union City UCRD 23*	**40**	2
22 Jan 94	SUPERMODEL / LITTLE DRUMMER BOY (re-mix) *Union City UCRD 25*	**61**	2
26 Feb 94 ●	DON'T GO BREAKING MY HEART *Rocket EJCD 33* [1]	**7**	7
21 May 94	HOUSE OF LOVE *Union City UCRDG 29*	**68**	1
28 Feb 98	IT'S RAINING MEN …THE SEQUEL *Logic 74321555412* [2]	**21**	3

[1] Elton John with RuPaul [2] Martha Wash featuring RuPaul

RUPEE
Barbados (b. Germany), male vocalist (Singles: 2 Weeks)   pos/wks

| 23 Oct 04 | TEMPTED TO TOUCH *Atlantic AT 0185CD* | **44** | 2 |

Kate RUSBY
UK, female vocalist / instrumentalist – guitar (Albums: 1 Week)   pos/wks

| 9 Jun 01 | LITTLE LIGHTS *Pure PRCD 07* | **75** | 1 |

RUSH (499) (Top 500)
Enduring Canadian pomp rockers Geddy Lee (v/b), Alex Lifeson (g) and Neil Peart (d), who were hailed Ambassadors of Music by the Canadian government in the late 70s and honoured as officers of the Order of Canada in 1997 (Singles: 43 Weeks, Albums: 101 Weeks)   pos/wks

11 Feb 78	CLOSER TO THE HEART *Mercury RUSH 7*	**36**	3
15 Mar 80	THE SPIRIT OF RADIO *Mercury RADIO 7*	**13**	7
28 Mar 81	VITAL SIGNS / A PASSAGE TO BANGKOK *Mercury VITAL 7*	**41**	4
31 Oct 81	TOM SAWYER *Mercury EXIT 7*	**25**	6
4 Sep 82	NEW WORLD MAN *Mercury RUSH 8*	**42**	4
30 Oct 82	SUBDIVISIONS *Mercury RUSH 9*	**53**	2
7 May 83	COUNTDOWN / NEW WORLD MAN (LIVE) *Mercury RUSH 10*	**36**	5
26 May 84	THE BODY ELECTRIC *Vertigo RUSH 11*	**56**	3
12 Oct 85	THE BIG MONEY *Vertigo RUSH 12*	**46**	3
31 Oct 87	TIME STAND STILL *Vertigo RUSH 13* [1]	**42**	3
23 Apr 88	PRIME MOVER *Vertigo RUSH 14*	**43**	3
7 Mar 92	ROLL THE BONES *Atlantic A 7524*	**49**	1
8 Oct 77	FAREWELL TO KINGS *Mercury 9100 042*	**22**	4
25 Nov 78	HEMISPHERES *Mercury 9100 059*	**14**	6
26 Jan 80 ●	PERMANENT WAVES *Mercury 9100 071*	**3**	16
21 Feb 81 ●	MOVING PICTURES *Mercury 6337 160*	**3**	11
7 Nov 81 ●	EXIT … STAGE LEFT *Mercury 6619 053*	**6**	14
18 Sep 82 ●	SIGNALS *Mercury 6337 243*	**3**	9
28 Apr 84 ●	GRACE UNDER PRESSURE *Vertigo VERH 12*	**5**	12
9 Nov 85 ●	POWER WINDOWS *Vertigo VERH 31*	**9**	4
21 Nov 87 ●	HOLD YOUR FIRE *Vertigo VERH 47*	**10**	4
28 Jan 89	A SHOW OF HANDS *Vertigo 836346*	**12**	4
9 Dec 89	PRESTO *Atlantic WX 327*	**27**	2
13 Oct 90	CHRONICLES *Vertigo CBTV 1*	**42**	2
14 Sep 91 ●	ROLL THE BONES *Vertigo WX 436*	**10**	4
30 Oct 93	COUNTERPARTS *Atlantic 7567825282*	**14**	3
21 Sep 96	TEST FOR ECHO *Atlantic 7567829252*	**25**	3
25 May 02	VAPOR TRAILS *Atlantic 7567835312*	**38**	2
17 Jul 04	FEEDBACK (EP) *Atlantic 7567837282*	**68**	1

[1] Rush with Aimee Mann

Tracks on Feedback (EP): Summertime Blues / Heart Full of Soul / The Seeker / For What It's Worth / Shapes of Things / Mr Soul / Crossroads / Seven and Seven Is

Donell RUSH
US, male vocalist (Singles: 1 Week)   pos/wks

| 5 Dec 92 | SYMPHONY *ID 6587977* | **66** | 1 |

Ed RUSH & OPTICAL
UK, male production duo (Singles: 2 Weeks)   pos/wks

| 1 Jun 02 | PACMAN *Virus VRS 010* | **61** | 1 |
| 20 Nov 04 | REMIXES – VOL.2 *Virus VRS 0146* | **69** | 1 |

'Pacman' shared chart billing with 'Vessel' by Universal Project. 'Remixes – Vol.2' contains re-mixes of the tracks 'Bacteria' and 'Gas Mask'

Jennifer RUSH
US, female vocalist – Heidi Stein (Singles: 58 Weeks, Albums: 43 Weeks)   pos/wks

29 Jun 85 ★	THE POWER OF LOVE (re) *CBS A 5003* ◆	**1**	36
14 Dec 85	RING OF ICE *CBS A 4745*	**14**	10
20 Jun 87	FLAMES OF PARADISE *CBS 650865 7* [1]	**59**	3
27 May 89	TILL I LOVED YOU *CBS 654843 7* [2]	**24**	9

16 Nov 85 ●	JENNIFER RUSH *CBS 26488*	**7**	35
3 May 86	MOVIN' *CBS 26710*	**32**	5
18 Apr 87	HEART OVER MIND *CBS 450 4701*	**48**	3

[1] Jennifer Rush and Elton John [2] Placido Domingo and Jennifer Rush

'The Power of Love' peaked at No.55, when it re-entered the chart in Dec 1986

Patrice RUSHEN
US, female vocalist (Singles: 25 Weeks, Albums: 17 Weeks)   pos/wks

1 Mar 80	HAVEN'T YOU HEARD *Elektra K 12414*	**62**	3
24 Jan 81	NEVER GONNA GIVE YOU UP (WON'T LET YOU BE) *Elektra K 12494*	**66**	3
24 Apr 82 ●	FORGET ME NOTS *Elektra K 13173*	**8**	11
10 Jul 82	I WAS TIRED OF BEING ALONE *Elektra K 13184*	**39**	5
9 Jun 84	FEELS SO REAL (WON'T LET GO) *Elektra E 9742*	**51**	3
1 May 82	STRAIGHT FROM THE HEART *Elektra K 52352*	**24**	14
16 Jun 84	NOW *Elektra 960360*	**73**	3

RUSLANA
Ukraine, female vocalist (Singles: 1 Week)   pos/wks

| 19 Jun 04 | WILD DANCES *Liberty 5490542* | **47** | 1 |

RUSSELL
US, male vocalist – Russell Taylor (Singles: 1 Week)   pos/wks

| 27 May 00 | FOOL FOR LOVE *Rulin RULIN 1CDS* | **52** | 1 |

Brenda RUSSELL
US, female vocalist / instrumentalist – keyboards – Brenda Gordon (Singles: 17 Weeks, Albums: 4 Weeks)   pos/wks

19 Apr 80	SO GOOD SO RIGHT / IN THE THICK OF IT *A&M AM 7515*	**51**	5
12 Mar 88	PIANO IN THE DARK *Breakout USA 623*	**23**	12
23 Apr 88	GET HERE *A&M AMA 5178*	**77**	4

Leon RUSSELL
US, male vocalist (Albums: 1 Week)   pos/wks

| 3 Jul 71 | LEON RUSSELL AND THE SHELTER PEOPLE *A&M AMLS 65003* | **29** | 1 |

Nicole RUSSO *See The BRAND NEW HEAVIES*

Patti RUSSO *See MEAT LOAF*

RUSTIN' MAN *See Beth GIBBONS & RUSTIN' MAN*

RUTH
UK, male vocal / instrumental group (Singles: 1 Week)   pos/wks

| 12 Apr 97 | I DON'T KNOW *Arc 5737812* | **66** | 1 |

Mike RUTHERFORD (see also MIKE and the MECHANICS; GENESIS)
UK, male vocalist / instrumentalist – guitar (Albums: 11 Weeks)   pos/wks

| 23 Feb 80 | SMALLCREEP'S DAY *Charisma CAS 1149* | **13** | 7 |
| 18 Sep 82 | ACTING VERY STRANGE *WEA K 99249* | **23** | 4 |

Paul RUTHERFORD (see also FRANKIE GOES TO HOLLYWOOD)
UK, male vocalist (Singles: 6 Weeks)   pos/wks

| 8 Oct 88 | GET REAL *Fourth & Broadway BRW 113* | **47** | 3 |
| 19 Aug 89 | OH WORLD *Fourth & Broadway BRW 136* | **61** | 3 |

RUTHLESS RAP ASSASSINS
UK, male rap group (Singles: 2 Weeks)   pos/wks

| 9 Jun 90 | JUST MELLOW *Syncopate SY 35* | **75** | 1 |
| 1 Sep 90 | AND IT WASN'T A DREAM *Syncopate SY 38* [1] | **75** | 1 |

[1] Ruthless Rap Assassins featuring Tracey Carmen

The RUTLES
UK, male vocal group (Singles: 5 Weeks, Albums: 11 Weeks)   pos/wks

15 Apr 78	I MUST BE IN LOVE (re) *Warner Bros. K 17125*	**39**	4
16 Nov 96	SHANGRI-LA *Virgin America VUSCD 117*	**68**	1
15 Apr 78	THE RUTLES *Warner Bros. K 56459*	**12**	11

The RUTS
UK, male vocal / instrumental group (Singles: 28 Weeks, Albums: 10 Weeks)   pos/wks

16 Jun 79 ●	BABYLON'S BURNING *Virgin VS 271*	**7**	11
8 Sep 79	SOMETHING THAT I SAID *Virgin VS 285*	**29**	5
19 Apr 80	STARING AT THE RUDE BOYS *Virgin VS 327*	**22**	8
30 Aug 80	WEST ONE (SHINE ON ME) *Virgin VS 370*	**43**	4
13 Oct 79	THE CRACK *Virgin V 2132*	**16**	6
18 Oct 80	GRIN AND BEAR IT *Virgin V 2188* [1]	**28**	4

[1] Ruts D.C.

John RUTTER *UK, male composer (Albums: 1 Week)*

pos/wks

| 2 Nov 02 | THE JOHN RUTTER COLLECTION *UCJ 4726222* .... | 75 | 1 |

'The John Rutter Collection' features the Cambridge Singers and the City of London Sinfonia

Barry RYAN (see also Paul and Barry RYAN)
UK, male vocalist – Barry Sapherson (Singles: 33 Weeks)

pos/wks

23 Oct 68 ●	ELOISE *MGM 1442*	2	12
19 Feb 69	LOVE IS LOVE *MGM 1464*	25	4
4 Oct 69	THE HUNT *Polydor 56 348*	34	5
21 Feb 70	MAGICAL SPIEL *Polydor 56 370*	49	1
16 May 70	KITSCH *Polydor 2001 035* [1]	37	6
15 Jan 72	CAN'T LET YOU GO *Polydor 2001 256*	32	5

[1] Barry Ryan with the Paul Ryan Orchestra

Joshua RYAN *US, male producer (Singles: 3 Weeks)*

pos/wks

| 27 Jan 01 | PISTOL WHIP *Nulife / Arista 74321825482* .... | 29 | 3 |

Marion RYAN *UK, female vocalist – Marion Sapherson, b. 4 Feb 1931, d. 15 Jan 1999 (Singles: 11 Weeks)*

pos/wks

| 24 Jan 58 ● | LOVE ME FOREVER *Pye Nixa N 15121* .... | 5 | 11 |

With the Peter Knight Orchestra and the Beryl Stott Chorus

Paul and Barry RYAN *UK, male vocal duo – Paul, b. 24 Oct 1948, d. 28 Nov 1992 and Barry Sapherson (Singles: 43 Weeks)*

pos/wks

11 Nov 65	DON'T BRING ME YOUR HEARTACHES *Decca F 12260*	13	9
3 Feb 66	HAVE PITY ON THE BOY *Decca F 12319*	18	6
12 May 66	I LOVE HER *Decca F 12391*	17	8
14 Jul 66	I LOVE HOW YOU LOVE ME *Decca F 12445*	21	7
29 Sep 66	HAVE YOU EVER LOVED SOMEBODY *Decca F 12494*	49	1
8 Dec 66	MISSY MISSY *Decca F 12520*	43	4
2 Mar 67	KEEP IT OUT OF SIGHT *Decca F 12567*	30	6
29 Jun 67	CLAIRE *Decca F 12633*	47	2

Rebekah RYAN *UK, female vocalist (Singles: 5 Weeks)*

pos/wks

18 May 96	YOU LIFT ME UP *MCA MCSTD 40022*	26	3
7 Sep 96	JUST A LITTLE BIT OF LOVE *MCA MCSTD 40063*	51	1
17 May 97	WOMAN IN LOVE *MCA MCSTD 40109*	64	1

Bobby RYDELL
US, male vocalist – Robert Ridarelli (Singles: 60 Weeks)

pos/wks

10 Mar 60 ●	WILD ONE (re) *Columbia DB 4429*	7	15
30 Jun 60	SWINGIN' SCHOOL *Columbia DB 4471*	44	1
1 Sep 60	VOLARE (re) *Columbia DB 4495*	22	6
15 Dec 60	SWAY *Columbia DB 4545*	12	13
23 Mar 61	GOOD TIME BABY *Columbia DB 4600*	42	7
19 Apr 62	TEACH ME TO TWIST *Columbia DB 4802* [1] ...	45	1
20 Dec 62	JINGLE BELL ROCK *Cameo Parkway C 205* [1] ...	40	3
23 May 63	FORGET HIM *Cameo Parkway C 108*	13	14

[1] Chubby Checker and Bobby Rydell

Mitch RYDER and the DETROIT WHEELS
US, male vocal / instrumental group (Singles: 5 Weeks)

pos/wks

| 10 Feb 66 | JENNY TAKE A RIDE (re) *Stateside SS 481* .... | 33 | 5 |

Mark RYDER (see also M-D-EMM)
UK, male producer – Mark Rydquist (Singles: 2 Weeks)

pos/wks

| 31 Mar 01 | JOY *Relentless Public Demand RELENT 9CDS* .... | 34 | 2 |

Shaun RYDER *See BLACK GRAPE; HAPPY MONDAYS; HEADS with Shaun RYDER; Russell WATSON*

RYTHM SYNDICATE
US, male vocal / instrumental group (Singles: 5 Weeks)

pos/wks

| 27 Jul 91 | P.A.S.S.I.O.N. *Impact American EM 197* .... | 58 | 5 |

RYZE *UK, male vocal trio (Singles: 1 Week)*

pos/wks

| 2 Nov 02 | IN MY LIFE *Inferno Cool CDFERN 48* .... | 46 | 1 |

RZA (see also WU-TANG CLAN; GRAVEDIGGAZ)
US, male producer / rapper – Robert Diggs (Albums: 1 Week)

pos/wks

| 28 Nov 98 | BOBBY DIGITAL IN STEREO *Gee Street GEE 1003802* [1] ...... | 70 | 1 |

Robin S *US, female vocalist – Robin Stone (Singles: 38 Weeks, Albums: 3 Weeks)*

pos/wks

16 Jan 93 ●	SHOW ME LOVE (re) *Champion CHAMPCD 300*	6	17
31 Jul 93	LUV 4 LUV *Champion CHAMPCD 301*	11	7
4 Dec 93	WHAT I DO BEST *Champion CHAMPCD 307*	43	2
19 Mar 94	I WANT TO THANK YOU *Champion CHAMPCD 310*	48	1
5 Nov 94	BACK IT UP *Champion CHAMPCD 312*	43	2
8 Mar 97 ●	SHOW ME LOVE (re-mix) *Champion CHAMPCD 326*	9	5
12 Jul 97	IT MUST BE LOVE *Atlantic A 5596CD*	37	2
4 Oct 97	YOU GOT THE LOVE *Champion CHAMPCD 330*	62	1
7 Dec 02	SHOW ME LOVE (2ND REMIX) (2nd re-mix) *Champion CHAMPCD 796*	61	1
4 Sep 93	SHOW ME LOVE *Champion CHAMPCD 1028*	34	3

S CLUB JUNIORS (see also I DREAM featuring FRANKIE & CALVIN) *UK, male / female vocal group (Singles: 78 Weeks, Albums: 17 Weeks)*

pos/wks

4 May 02 ●	ONE STEP CLOSER *Polydor 5707322*	2	16
3 Aug 02 ●	AUTOMATIC HIGH *Polydor 5708922*	2	13
19 Oct 02 ●	NEW DIRECTION *Polydor 0659692*	2	13
21 Dec 02 ●	PUPPY LOVE / SLEIGH RIDE (re) *Polydor 0658442*	6	10
12 Jul 03 ●	FOOL NO MORE *Polydor 9808753* [1]	4	8
25 Oct 03 ●	SUNDOWN *Polydor 9865703* [1]	4	10
10 Jan 04	DON'T TELL ME YOU'RE SORRY *Polydor 9815342* [1]	11	8
2 Nov 02 ●	TOGETHER *Polydor 0652502*	5	13
25 Oct 03	SUNDOWN *Polydor 9865703* [1]	13	4

[1] S Club 8 [1] S Club 8

S CLUB 7 173 Top 500

Made-for-TV act (series seen in more than 100 countries) had the best start to its career of any mixed vocal group, with nine Top 3 hits from first nine releases including four No.1s. Award-winning septet is the largest vocal group ever to top the chart, comprising Jo O'Meara, Tina Barrett, Hannah Spearritt, Rachel Stevens, Paul Cattermole, Bradley McIntosh and Jon Lee. When Cattermole left in 2002 the sextet became S Club and they then disbanded in 2003. Best-selling single: 'Don't Stop Movin' – 709,198 (Singles: 166 Weeks, Albums: 149 Weeks)

pos/wks

19 Jun 99 ★	BRING IT ALL BACK *Polydor 5610852* ■	1	15
2 Oct 99 ●	S CLUB PARTY (re) *Polydor 5614172*	2	14
25 Dec 99 ●	TWO IN A MILLION / YOU'RE MY NUMBER ONE *Polydor 5615962*	2	14
3 Jun 00 ●	REACH *Polydor 5618302*	2	17
23 Sep 00 ●	NATURAL (re) *Polydor 5877602*	3	16
9 Dec 00 ★	NEVER HAD A DREAM COME TRUE (re) *Polydor 5879032* ■ ...	1	18
5 May 01 ★	DON'T STOP MOVIN' *Polydor 5870832* ■	1	19
1 Dec 01 ★	HAVE YOU EVER *Polydor 5705002* ■	1	14
23 Feb 02 ●	YOU *Polydor 5705812*	2	14
30 Nov 02 ●	ALIVE (2re) *Polydor 0658912* [1]	5	16
7 Jun 03 ●	SAY GOODBYE / LOVE AIN'T GONNA WAIT FOR YOU *Polydor 9807139* [1]	2	12
16 Oct 99 ●	S CLUB *Polydor 5431032*	2	46
24 Jun 00 ★	7 *Polydor 5438572* ■	1	61
8 Dec 01 ●	SUNSHINE *Polydor 5894092*	3	24
7 Dec 02	SEEING DOUBLE *Polydor 0654962* [1]	17	5
14 Jun 03 ●	BEST – THE GREATEST HITS OF S CLUB 7 *Polydor 9807374*	2	13

[1] S Club [1] S Club

S EXPRESS
UK, male / female vocal / instrumental group –
leader Mark Moore (Singles: 50 Weeks, Albums: 9 Weeks)   pos/wks

16 Apr 88 ★	**THEME FROM S-EXPRESS** *Rhythm King LEFT 21*	...1 13
23 Jul 88 ●	**SUPERFLY GUY** *Rhythm King LEFT 28*	...5 9
18 Feb 89 ●	**HEY MUSIC LOVER** *Rhythm King LEFT 30*	...6 10
16 Sep 89	**MANTRA FOR A STATE OF MIND** *Rhythm King LEFT 35*	...21 8
15 Sep 90	**NOTHING TO LOSE** *Rhythm King SEXY 01*	...32 4
30 May 92	**FIND 'EM, FOOL 'EM, FORGET 'EM** *Rhythm King 6580137*	...43 2
11 May 96	**THEME FROM S-EXPRESS (re-mix)** *Rhythm King SEXY 9CD* [1]	...14 4
1 Apr 89 ●	**ORIGINAL SOUNDTRACK** *Rhythm King LEFTLP 8*	...5 9

[1] Mark Moore presents S Express

SFX
UK, male instrumental / production duo (Singles: 3 Weeks)   pos/wks

15 May 93	**LEMMINGS** *Parlophone CDR 6343*	...51 3

S.F.X. BOYS' CHOIR, LIVERPOOL See The FARM

S-J
UK, female vocalist – Sarah James Jiminez-Heany (Singles: 4 Weeks)   pos/wks

11 Jan 97	**FEVER** *React CDREACT 93*	...46 1
24 Jan 98	**I FEEL DIVINE** *React CDREACT 113*	...30 2
7 Nov 98	**SHIVER** *React CDREACT 138*	...59 1

SL2 (see also SLIPMATT)
UK, male DJ / production duo – Matt
'Slipmatt' Nelson and John 'Lime' Fernandez (Singles: 25 Weeks)   pos/wks

2 Nov 91	**DJS TAKE CONTROL / WAY IN MY BRAIN (re)** *XL Recordings XLS 24*	...11 6
18 Apr 92 ●	**ON A RAGGA TIP** *XL Recordings XLS 29*	...2 11
19 Dec 92	**WAY IN MY BRAIN (re-mix) / DRUMBEATS** *XL Recordings XLS 36*	...26 6
15 Feb 97	**ON A RAGGA TIP '97 (re-mix)** *XL Recordings XLSR 29CD*	...31 2

The S.O.S. BAND
US, male / female vocal / instrumental group (Singles: 46 Weeks, Albums: 19 Weeks)   pos/wks

19 Jul 80	**TAKE YOUR TIME (DO IT RIGHT) PART 1** *Tabu TBU 8564*	...51 4
26 Feb 83	**GROOVIN' (THAT'S WHAT WE'RE DOIN')** *Tabu TBU A 3120*	...72 1
7 Apr 84	**JUST BE GOOD TO ME** *Tabu A 3626*	...13 11
4 Aug 84	**JUST THE WAY YOU LIKE IT** *Tabu A 4621*	...32 7
13 Oct 84	**WEEKEND GIRL** *Tabu A 4785*	...51 5
29 Mar 86	**THE FINEST** *Tabu A 6997*	...17 10
5 Jul 86	**BORROWED LOVE** *Tabu A 7241*	...50 5
2 May 87	**NO LIES** *Tabu 650444 7*	...64 3
1 Sep 84	**JUST THE WAY YOU LIKE IT** *Tabu TBU 26058*	...29 10
17 May 86	**SANDS OF TIME** *Tabu TBU 26863*	...15 9

SWV
US, female vocal group (Singles: 43 Weeks, Albums: 27 Weeks)   pos/wks

1 May 93	**I'M SO INTO YOU** *RCA 74321144972*	...17 6
26 Jun 93	**WEAK** *RCA 74321153352* ▲	...33 3
28 Aug 93 ●	**RIGHT HERE** *RCA 74321160482*	...3 12
26 Feb 94	**DOWNTOWN** *RCA 74321189012*	...19 5
11 Jun 94	**ANYTHING** *RCA 74321212212*	...24 3
25 May 96	**YOU'RE THE ONE** *RCA 74321383312*	...13 3
21 Dec 96	**IT'S ALL ABOUT U** *RCA 74321442152*	...36 5
12 Apr 97	**CAN WE** *Jive JIVECD 423*	...18 4
13 Sep 97	**SOMEONE** *RCA 74321513942* [1]	...34 2
17 Jul 93	**IT'S ABOUT TIME** *RCA 7863660742*	...17 17
4 May 96	**NEW BEGINNING** *RCA 7863664872*	...26 5
16 Aug 97	**RELEASE SOME TENSION** *RCA 74321493162*	...19 5

[1] SWV featuring Puff Daddy

Raphael SAADIQ (see also TONY TONI TONÉ; LUCY PEARL)
US, male vocalist – Raphael Wiggins (Singles: 4 Weeks)   pos/wks

23 Nov 96	**STRESSED OUT** *Jive JIVECD 404* [1]	...33 2
19 Jun 99	**GET INVOLVED** *Hollywood 0101185 HWR* [2]	...36 2

[1] A Tribe Called Quest featuring Faith Evans and Raphael Saadiq [2] Raphael Saadiq and Q-Tip

SABRE featuring PRESIDENT BROWN
Jamaica, male vocal duo (Singles: 1 Week)   pos/wks

19 Aug 95	**WRONG OR RIGHT** *Greensleeves GRECD 485*	...71 1

SABRES See Denny SEYTON and the SABRES

SABRES OF PARADISE
UK, male production group (Singles: 8 Weeks, Albums: 3 Weeks)   pos/wks

2 Oct 93	**SMOKEBELCH II** *Sabres of Paradise PT 009CD*	...55 3
9 Apr 94	**THEME** *Sabres of Paradise PT 014CD*	...56 3
17 Sep 94	**WILMOT** *Warp WAP 50CD*	...36 2
23 Oct 93	**SABRESONIC** *Warp WARPCD 16*	...29 2
10 Dec 94	**HAUNTED DANCEHALL** *Warp WARPCD 26*	...57 1

SABRINA
Italy, female vocalist – Sabrina Salerno (Singles: 22 Weeks)   pos/wks

6 Feb 88 ●	**BOYS (SUMMERTIME LOVE) (re)** *IBIZA IBIZ 1*	...3 14
1 Oct 88	**ALL OF ME** *PWL PWL 19*	...25 7
1 Jul 89	**LIKE A YO-YO** *Videogram DCUP 1*	...72 1

'Boys' peaked during re-entry in Jun 1988

SACARIO See Angie MARTINEZ featuring LIL' MO & SACARIO

SACRED SPIRIT (see also DIVINE WORKS)
Germany, male production trio utilising Native
American chants (Singles: 5 Weeks, Albums: 30 Weeks)   pos/wks

15 Apr 95	**YEHA-NOHA (WISHES OF HAPPINESS AND PROSPERITY)** *Virgin VSCDT 1514*	...71 1
18 Nov 95	**WISHES OF HAPPINESS AND PROSPERITY (YEHA-NOHA) (re-issue)** *Virgin VSC 1568*	...37 2
16 Mar 96	**WINTER CEREMONY (TOR-CHENEY-NAHANA)** *Virgin VSCDT 1574*	...45 2
1 Apr 95 ●	**CHANTS AND DANCES OF THE NATIVE AMERICANS** *Virgin CDV 2753*	...9 27
26 Apr 97	**SACRED SPIRIT VOLUME 2 – CULTURE CLASH** *Virgin CDV 2827*	...24 3

SAD CAFÉ
UK, male vocal / instrumental group (Singles: 44 Weeks, Albums: 36 Weeks)   pos/wks

22 Sep 79 ●	**EVERY DAY HURTS** *RCA PB 5180*	...3 12
19 Jan 80	**STRANGE LITTLE GIRL** *RCA PB 5202*	...32 5
15 Mar 80	**MY OH MY** *RCA SAD 3*	...14 11
21 Jun 80	**NOTHING LEFT TOULOUSE** *RCA SAD 4*	...62 4
27 Sep 80	**LA-DI-DA** *RCA SAD 5*	...41 6
20 Dec 80	**I'M IN LOVE AGAIN** *RCA SAD 6*	...40 6
1 Oct 77	**FANX TA RA** *RCA PL 25101*	...56 1
29 Apr 78	**MISPLACED IDEALS** *RCA PL 25133*	...50 1
29 Sep 79 ●	**FACADES** *RCA PL 25249*	...8 23
25 Oct 80	**SAD CAFÉ** *RCA SADLP 4*	...46 5
21 Mar 81	**LIVE** *RCA SAD LP 5*	...37 4
24 Oct 81	**OLE** *Polydor POLD 5045*	...72 2

SADE 〔214 Top 500〕
Ever popular jazz-styled vocalist, b. Helen Folasade Adu, 16 Jan 1959, Nigeria. UK-based Brit and Grammy winner, who received an OBE in 2002, is the only African artist to top the albums chart in the UK or US (where all her albums have reached the Top 10) (Singles: 69 Weeks, Albums: 213 Weeks)   pos/wks

25 Feb 84 ●	**YOUR LOVE IS KING (re)** *Epic A 4137*	...6 12
26 May 84	**WHEN AM I GONNA MAKE A LIVING** *Epic A 4437*	...36 5
15 Sep 84	**SMOOTH OPERATOR** *Epic A 4655*	...19 10
12 Oct 85	**THE SWEETEST TABOO** *Epic A 6609*	...31 5
11 Jan 86	**IS IT A CRIME** *Epic A 6742*	...49 3
2 Apr 88	**LOVE IS STRONGER THAN PRIDE** *Epic SADE 1*	...44 3
4 Jun 88	**PARADISE** *Epic SADE 2*	...29 7
10 Oct 92	**NO ORDINARY LOVE (re)** *Epic 6583562*	...14 11
28 Nov 92	**FEEL NO PAIN** *Epic 6588297*	...56 2
8 May 93	**KISS OF LIFE** *Epic 6591162*	...44 3
31 Jul 93	**CHERISH THE DAY** *Epic 6594812*	...53 2
18 Nov 00	**BY YOUR SIDE** *Epic 6699992*	...17 5
24 Mar 01	**KING OF SORROW** *Epic 6708672*	...59 1
28 Jul 84 ●	**DIAMOND LIFE** *Epic EPC 26044*	...2 99
16 Nov 85 ★	**PROMISE** *Epic EPC 86318* ■ ▲	...1 31
14 May 88 ●	**STRONGER THAN PRIDE** *Epic 4604971*	...3 17
7 Nov 92 ●	**LOVE DELUXE** *Epic 4726262*	...10 27
12 Nov 94 ●	**THE BEST OF SADE** *Epic 4777932*	...6 16
25 Nov 00	**LOVERS ROCK** *Epic 5007662*	...18 21
2 Mar 02	**LOVERS LIVE** *Epic 5061252*	...51 2

'No Ordinary Love' first peaked at No.26 and did not reach its peak position until re-entering in Jun 1993

Staff Sergeant Barry SADLER
US, male vocalist, b. 1 Nov 1940, d. 5 Nov 1989 (Singles: 8 Weeks)   pos/wks

| 24 Mar 66 | THE BALLAD OF THE GREEN BERETS *RCA 1506* ▲ | 24 | 8 |

SAFFRON (see also REPUBLICA)
UK, female vocalist – Samantha Sprackling (Singles: 2 Weeks)   pos/wks

| 16 Jan 93 | CIRCLES *WEA SAFF 9CD* | 60 | 2 |

SAFFRON HILL featuring Ben ONONO *UK, male DJ /*
producer – Tim 'Deluxe' Liken and male vocalist (Singles: 3 Weeks) pos/wks

| 17 May 03 | MY LOVE IS ALWAYS *Illustrious CDILL 016* | 28 | 3 |

SAFFRONS See CINDY and the SAFFRONS

Alessandro SAFINA *Italy, male vocalist (Albums: 2 Weeks)*   pos/wks

| 30 Mar 02 | SAFINA *Mercury 167432* | 27 | 2 |

SAFRI DUO *Denmark, male instrumental / production*
duo – Uffe Savery and Morten Friis (Singles: 10 Weeks)   pos/wks

| 3 Feb 01 | ● PLAYED-A-LIVE (THE BONGO SONG) *AM:PM CDAMPM 141* | 6 | 9 |
| 5 Oct 02 | SWEET FREEDOM *Serious SERR 55CD* [1] | 54 | 1 |

[1] Safri Duo featuring Michael McDonald

Mike SAGAR and the CRESTERS
UK, male vocalist (Singles: 5 Weeks)   pos/wks

| 8 Dec 60 | DEEP FEELING *HMV POP 819* | 44 | 5 |

SAGAT *US, male rapper – Faustin Lenon (Singles: 6 Weeks)*   pos/wks

| 4 Dec 93 | FUNK DAT *ffrr FCD 224* | 25 | 5 |
| 3 Dec 94 | LUVSTUFF *ffrr FCD 250* | 71 | 1 |

Carole Bayer SAGER *US, female vocalist (Singles: 9 Weeks)*   pos/wks

| 28 May 77 | ● YOU'RE MOVING OUT TODAY *Elektra K 12257* | 6 | 9 |

Bally SAGOO *UK, male producer /*
instrumentalist (Singles: 8 Weeks, Albums: 1 Week)   pos/wks

3 Sep 94	CHURA LIYA *Columbia 6607092*	64	1
22 Apr 95	CHOLI KE PEECHE *Columbia 6613352*	45	1
19 Oct 96	DIL CHEEZ (MY HEART ...) *Higher Ground 6634882*	12	3
1 Feb 97	TUM BIN JIYA *Higher Ground 6641372*	21	3
9 Nov 96	RISING FROM THE EAST *Higher Ground 4850162*	63	1

SAILOR *UK, male vocal / instrumental*
group (Singles: 24 Weeks, Albums: 8 Weeks)   pos/wks

6 Dec 75	● GLASS OF CHAMPAGNE *Epic EPC 3770*	2	12
27 Mar 76	● GIRLS GIRLS GIRLS *Epic EPC 3858*	7	8
19 Feb 77	ONE DRINK TOO MANY *Epic EPC 4804*	35	4
7 Feb 76	TROUBLE *Epic EPC 69192*	45	8

SAINT featuring Suzanna DEE *UK, male production duo – Mark*
Smith and Dave Pickard and female vocalist (Singles: 2 Weeks) pos/wks

| 12 Apr 03 | SHOW ME HEAVEN *Inferno CDFERN 52* | 36 | 2 |

ST ANDREWS CHORALE *UK, church choir (Singles: 5 Weeks)* pos/wks

| 14 Feb 76 | CLOUD 99 *Decca F 13617* | 31 | 5 |

ST CECILIA
UK, male vocal / instrumental group (Singles: 17 Weeks)   pos/wks

| 19 Jun 71 | LEAP UP AND DOWN (WAVE YOUR KNICKERS IN THE AIR) *Polydor 2058 104* | 12 | 17 |

SAINT ETIENNE *UK, male / female vocal / instrumental group –*
lead vocal Sarah Cracknell (Singles: 54 Weeks, Albums: 31 Weeks) pos/wks

18 May 91	NOTHING CAN STOP US / SPEEDWELL *Heavenly HVN 009*	54	3
7 Sep 91	ONLY LOVE CAN BREAK YOUR HEART / FILTHY *Heavenly HVN 12*	39	4
16 May 92	JOIN OUR CLUB / PEOPLE GET REAL *Heavenly HVN 15*	21	3
17 Oct 92	AVENUE *Heavenly HVN 2312*	40	2
13 Feb 93	YOU'RE IN A BAD WAY *Heavenly HVN 25CD*	12	5

22 May 93	HOBART PAVING / WHO DO YOU THINK YOU ARE *Heavenly HVN 29CD*	23	5
18 Dec 93	I WAS BORN ON CHRISTMAS DAY *Heavenly HVN 36CD* [1]	37	5
19 Feb 94	PALE MOVIE *Heavenly HVN 37CD*	28	3
28 May 94	LIKE A MOTORWAY *Heavenly HVN 40CD*	47	2
1 Oct 94	HUG MY SOUL *Heavenly HVN 42CD*	32	2
11 Nov 95	HE'S ON THE PHONE *Heavenly HVN 50CDR* [2]	11	5
7 Feb 98	SYLVIE *Creation CRESCD 279*	12	3
2 May 98	THE BAD PHOTOGRAPHER *Creation CRESCD 290*	27	2
20 May 00	● TELL ME WHY (THE RIDDLE) *Deviant DVNT 36CDS* [3]	7	5
24 Jun 00	HEART FAILED (IN THE BACK OF A TAXI) *Mantra / Beggars Banquet MNT 54CD*	50	1
20 Jan 01	BOY IS CRYING *Mantra / Beggars Banquet MNT 60CD*	34	2
7 Sep 02	ACTION *Mantra / Beggars Banquet MNT 73CD*	41	1
29 Mar 03	SOFT LIKE ME *Mantra MNT 78CD*	40	1
26 Oct 91	FOXBASE ALPHA *Heavenly HVNLP 1*	34	3
6 Mar 93	● SO TOUGH *Heavenly HVNLP 6CD*	7	7
12 Mar 94	● TIGER BAY *Heavenly HVNLP 8CD*	8	4
25 Nov 95	TOO YOUNG TO DIE – THE SINGLES *Heavenly HVNLP 10CD*	17	9
27 Jan 96	RESERECTION *Virgin DINSD 150* [1]	50	1
19 Oct 96	CASINO CLASSICS *Heavenly HVNLP 16CD*	34	2
16 May 98	GOOD HUMOR *Creation CRECD 225*	18	3
3 Jun 00	SOUND OF WATER *Mantra MNTCD 1018*	33	1
19 Oct 02	FINISTERRE *Mantra / Beggars Banquet MNTCD 1033*	55	1

[1] Saint Etienne co-starring Tim Burgess [2] Saint Etienne featuring Etienne Daho
[3] Paul Van Dyk featuring Saint Etienne [1] Saint Etienne Daho

ST GERMAIN *France, male producer –*
Ludovic Navarre (Singles: 3 Weeks, Albums: 1 Week)   pos/wks

31 Aug 96	ALABAMA BLUES (REVISITED) *F Communications F 050CD*	50	1
10 Mar 01	ROSE ROUGE *Blue Note CDROSE 001*	54	2
20 May 00	TOURIST *Blue Note 5262012*	73	1

Barry ST JOHN *UK, female vocalist (Singles: 1 Week)*   pos/wks

| 9 Dec 65 | COME AWAY MELINDA *Columbia DB 7783* | 47 | 1 |

ST JOHN'S COLLEGE SCHOOL CHOIR
and the Band of the GRENADIER GUARDS
UK, school choir and military band (Singles: 3 Weeks)   pos/wks

| 3 May 86 | THE QUEEN'S BIRTHDAY SONG *Columbia Q 1* | 40 | 3 |

ST LOUIS UNION
UK, male vocal / instrumental group (Singles: 10 Weeks)   pos/wks

| 13 Jan 66 | GIRL *Decca F 12318* | 11 | 10 |

ST LUNATICS See NELLY

ST PAUL'S BOYS' CHOIR *UK, male choir (Albums: 8 Weeks)*   pos/wks

| 29 Nov 80 | REJOICE *K-Tel NE 1064* | 36 | 8 |

Crispian ST PETERS
UK, male vocalist – Robin Smith (Singles: 31 Weeks)   pos/wks

6 Jan 66	● YOU WERE ON MY MIND *Decca F 12287*	2	14
31 Mar 66	● THE PIED PIPER *Decca F 12359*	5	13
15 Sep 66	CHANGES (re) *Decca F 12480*	47	4

ST PHILIPS CHOIR *UK, choir (Singles: 4 Weeks)*   pos/wks

| 12 Dec 87 | SING FOR EVER *BBC RESL 222* | 49 | 4 |

ST THOMAS MORE SCHOOL CHOIR See Scott FITZGERALD

ST WINIFRED'S SCHOOL CHOIR
(see also Bill TARMY; BRIAN AND MICHAEL)
UK, school choir – lead vocal Dawn Ralph (Singles: 11 Weeks)   pos/wks

| 22 Nov 80 | ★ THERE'S NO ONE QUITE LIKE GRANDMA *MFP FP 900* | 1 | 11 |

Buffy SAINTE-MARIE
Canada, female vocalist (Singles: 29 Weeks, Albums: 2 Weeks) pos/wks

17 Jul 71	● SOLDIER BLUE *RCA 2081*	7	18
18 Mar 72	I'M GONNA BE A COUNTRY GIRL AGAIN *Vanguard VRS 35143*	34	5
8 Feb 92	THE BIG ONES GET AWAY *Ensign ENY 650*	39	5
4 Jul 92	FALLEN ANGELS *Ensign ENY 655*	57	1
21 Mar 92	COINCIDENCE (AND LIKELY STORIES) *Ensign CCD 1920*	39	2

The SAINTS
Australia, male vocal / instrumental group (Singles: 4 Weeks)   pos/wks

16 Jul 77	**THIS PERFECT DAY** *Harvest HAR 5130* **34** 4

Kyu SAKAMOTO
Japan, male vocalist,
b. 10 Nov 1941, d. 12 Aug 1985 (Singles: 13 Weeks)   pos/wks

27 Jun 63	● **SUKIYAKI** *HMV POP 1171* ▲ **6** 13

Ryuichi SAKAMOTO
Japan, male instrumentalist – keyboards (Albums: 9 Weeks)   pos/wks

3 Sep 83	**MERRY CHRISTMAS MR LAWRENCE (FILM SOUNDTRACK)** *Virgin V 2276* **36** 9

SAKKARIN *See Jonathan KING*

SALAD
UK / Holland, male / female vocal /
instrumental group (Singles: 5 Weeks, Albums: 2 Weeks)   pos/wks

11 Mar 95	**DRINK THE ELIXIR** *Island Red CIRD 104* **66** 1
13 May 95	**MOTORBIKE TO HEAVEN** *Island Red CIRD 106* **42** 1
16 Sep 95	**GRANITE STATUE** *Island Red CIRD 108* **50** 1
26 Oct 96	**I WANT YOU** *Island CID 646* **60** 1
17 May 97	**CARDBOY KING** *Island CID 654* **65** 1
27 May 95	**DRINK ME** *Island Red CIRDX 1002* **16** 2

The SALFORD JETS
UK, male vocal / instrumental group (Singles: 2 Weeks)   pos/wks

31 May 80	**WHO YOU LOOKING AT?** *RCA PB 5239* **72** 2

SALIVA
US, male vocal / instrumental group (Singles: 1 Week)   pos/wks

15 Mar 03	**ALWAYS** *Mercury 0637082* **47** 1

SALSOUL ORCHESTRA *See CHARO and the SALSOUL ORCHESTRA*

SALT TANK
UK, male production duo –
Malcolm Stanners and David Gates (Singles: 4 Weeks)   pos/wks

11 May 96	**EUGINA** *Internal LIECD 29* **40** 2
3 Jul 99	**DIMENSION** *Hooj Choons HOOJ 74CD* **52** 1
9 Dec 00	**EUGINA (re-mix)** *Lost Language LOST 004CD* **58** 1

SALT-N-PEPA ⌐380⌐ Top 500
Rappers Cheryl "Salt" James (b. 28 Mar 1969, Brooklyn, US) and Sandra "Pepa" Denton (b. 9 Nov 1969, Kingston, Jamaica), backed up by DJ Dee Dee "Spinderella" Roper, are the most commercially successful female rap troupe of all time (Singles: 123 Weeks, Albums: 57 Weeks)   pos/wks

26 Mar 88	**PUSH IT / I AM DOWN** *ffrr FFR 2* **41** 6
25 Jun 88	● **PUSH IT (re-issue) / TRAMP** *Champion CHAMP 51 & ffrr FFR 2* ..2 13
3 Sep 88	**SHAKE YOUR THANG (IT'S YOUR THING)** *ffrr FFR 11* ⌐1⌐ **22** 8
12 Nov 88	● **TWIST AND SHOUT** *ffrr FFR 16* **4** 9
14 Apr 90	**EXPRESSION** *ffrr F 127* **40** 6
25 May 91	● **DO YOU WANT ME** *ffrr F 151* **5** 12
31 Aug 91	● **LET'S TALK ABOUT SEX** *ffrr F 162* **2** 13
30 Nov 91	**YOU SHOWED ME** *ffrr F 174* ⌐2⌐ **15** 9
28 Mar 92	**EXPRESSION (re-mix)** *ffrr F 182* **23** 6
3 Oct 92	**START ME UP** *ffrr F 196* **39** 3
9 Oct 93	**SHOOP** *ffrr FCD 219* **29** 3
19 Mar 94	● **WHATTA MAN** *ffrr FCD 222* ⌐3⌐ **7** 10
28 May 94	**SHOOP (re-mix)** *ffrr FCD 234* **13** 8
12 Nov 94	**NONE OF YOUR BUSINESS** *ffrr FCD 244* **19** 5
21 Dec 96	**CHAMPAGNE** *MCA MCSTD 48025* **23** 6
29 Nov 97	**R U READY** *ffrr FCDP 322* **24** 2
11 Dec 99	**THE BRICK TRACK VERSUS GITTY UP** *ffrr FCD 373* ⌐4⌐ **22** 4
6 Aug 88	**A SALT WITH A DEADLY PEPA** *ffrr FFRLP 3* **19** 27
12 May 90	**BLACKS' MAGIC** *ffrr 8281641* **70** 1
6 Jul 91	**A BLITZ OF SALT-N-PEPA HITS – THE HITS REMIXED** *ffrr 8282491* **70** 2
19 Oct 91	● **GREATEST HITS** *ffrr 8282911* **6** 20
25 Apr 92	**RAPPED IN REMIXES** *ffrr 8282972* **37** 2
23 Apr 94	**VERY NECESSARY** *ffrr 8284542* **36** 5

⌐1⌐ Salt-N-Pepa featuring EU ⌐2⌐ Additional vocals Joyce Martin & Cari Linger
⌐3⌐ Salt-N-Pepa with En Vogue ⌐4⌐ Saltnpepa

'I Am Down' listed only from 2 Apr 1988. The disc re-entered on 25 Jun when it was made available on Champion with a different flip side. Sales for both discs were amalgamated

SALVATION ARMY
UK, brass band (Albums: 5 Weeks)   pos/wks

24 Dec 77	**BY REQUEST** *Warwick WW 5038* **16** 5

SAM and DAVE (see also Lou REED)
US, male vocal duo – Sam Moore and Dave Prater, b. 9 May 1937,
d. 9 Apr 1998 (Singles: 39 Weeks, Albums: 20 Weeks)   pos/wks

16 Mar 67	**SOOTHE ME (re)** *Stax 601 004* **35** 8
1 Nov 67	**SOUL MAN** *Stax 601 023* **24** 14
13 Mar 68	**I THANK YOU** *Stax 601 030* **34** 9
29 Jan 69	**SOUL SISTER, BROWN SUGAR** *Atlantic 584 237* **15** 8
21 Jan 67	**HOLD ON I'M COMIN'** *Atlantic 588045.* **35** 7
22 Apr 67	**DOUBLE DYNAMITE** *Stax 589003* **28** 5
23 Mar 68	**SOUL MEN** *Stax 589015* **32** 2

SAM & MARK *UK, male vocal duo –*
Sam Nixon and Mark Rhodes (Singles: 13 Weeks)   pos/wks

21 Feb 04	★ **WITH A LITTLE HELP FROM MY FRIENDS / MEASURE OF A MAN** *19 19RECS 9* ■ **1** 10
5 Jun 04	**THE SUN HAS COME YOUR WAY** *19 / UMTV 9866906* **19** 3

SAM THE SHAM and the PHARAOHS
US, male vocal / instrumental group (Singles: 18 Weeks)   pos/wks

24 Jun 65	**WOOLY BULLY** *MGM 1269* **11** 15
4 Aug 66	**LIL' RED RIDING HOOD (re)** *MGM 1315* **46** 3

Richie SAMBORA (see also BON JOVI) *US, male vocalist /*
instrumentalist – guitar (Singles: 4 Weeks, Albums: 5 Weeks)   pos/wks

7 Sep 91	**BALLAD OF YOUTH** *Mercury MER 350* **59** 1
7 Mar 98	**HARD TIMES COME EASY** *Mercury 5686972* **37** 2
1 Aug 98	**IN IT FOR LOVE** *Mercury 5660632* **58** 1
14 Sep 91	**STRANGER IN THIS TOWN** *Mercury 8488951* **20** 3
14 Mar 98	**UNDISCOVERED SOUL** *Mercury 5369722* **24** 2

Mike SAMMES SINGERS (see also Michael FLANDERS;
Michael HOLLIDAY; Des O'CONNOR; Andy STEWART; Malcolm VAUGHAN;
Jimmy YOUNG) *UK, male / female vocal group – leader b.19 Feb 1928,*
d. 19 May 2001 (Singles: 38 Weeks, Albums: 7 Weeks)   pos/wks

15 Sep 66	**SOMEWHERE MY LOVE (re)** *HMV POP 1546* **14** 38
19 Jan 76	**MUSIC OF AMERICA** *Ronco TRD 2016* ⌐1⌐ **18** 7

'Somewhere My Love' first peaked at No.22 and reached No.14 after re-entry in 1967

⌐1⌐ Richmond Strings / Mike Sammes Singers

Dave SAMPSON
UK, male vocalist (Singles: 6 Weeks)   pos/wks

19 May 60	**SWEET DREAMS (re)** *Columbia DB 4449* **29** 6

SAMSON *UK, male vocal / instrumental*
group (Singles: 6 Weeks, Albums: 6 Weeks)   pos/wks

4 Jul 81	**RIDING WITH THE ANGELS** *RCA 67* **55** 3
24 Jul 82	**LOSING MY GRIP** *Polydor POSP 471* **63** 2
5 Mar 83	**RED SKIES** *Polydor POSP 554* **65** 1
26 Jul 80	**HEAD ON** *Gem GEMLP 108* **34** 6

SAN JOSE featuring Rodriguez ARGENTINA (see also ARGENT;
SILSOE) *UK, male instrumental group (Singles: 8 Weeks)*   pos/wks

17 Jun 78	**ARGENTINE MELODY (CANCION DE ARGENTINA)** *MCA 369* ..**14** 8

Rodriguez Argentina is Rod Argent

SAN REMO STRINGS
US, orchestra (Singles: 8 Weeks)   pos/wks

18 Dec 71	**FESTIVAL TIME** *Tamla Motown TMG 795* **39** 8

David SANBORN
UK, male instrumentalist – saxophone (Albums: 1 Week)   pos/wks

14 Mar 87	**A CHANGE OF HEART** *Warner Bros. 925 4791* **86** 1

Junior SANCHEZ featuring DAJAE *US, male DJ / producer*
and US, female vocalist – Karen Gordon (Singles: 2 Weeks)   pos/wks

16 Oct 99	**B WITH U** *Manifesto FESCD 62* **31** 2

Roger SANCHEZ
(see also EL MARIACHI; TRANSATLANTIC SOUL; FUNK JUNKEEZ)
US, male producer (Singles: 21 Weeks, Albums: 2 Weeks) pos/wks

3 Oct 98	BUFFALO GALS STAMPEDE (re-mix) *Virgin VSCDT 1717* [1]	65 1
20 Feb 99	I WANT YOUR LOVE *Perpetual PERPCDS 001* [2]	31 2
29 Jan 00	I NEVER KNEW *INCredible INCS 4CDS* [3]	24 2
14 Jul 01	★ ANOTHER CHANCE *Defected DFECT 35CDS* ■	1 12
15 Dec 01	YOU CAN'T CHANGE ME *Defected DFECT 41CDS* [4]	25 4
11 Aug 01	FIRST CONTACT *Defected SMAN 01CD*	34 2

[1] Malcolm McLaren and the World's Famous Supreme Team plus Rakim and Roger Sanchez [2] Roger Sanchez presents Twilight [3] Roger Sanchez featuring Cooly's Hot Box [4] Roger Sanchez featuring Armand Van Helden and N'Dea Davenport

Chris SANDFORD *UK, male actor / vocalist (Singles: 9 Weeks)* pos/wks

12 Dec 63	NOT TOO LITTLE NOT TOO MUCH *Decca F 11778*	17 9

The SANDPIPERS *US, male vocal group (Singles: 33 Weeks)* pos/wks

15 Sep 66	● GUANTANAMERA *Pye International 7N 25380*	7 17
5 Jun 68	QUANDO M'INNAMORO (A MAN WITHOUT LOVE) *A&M AMS 723*	33 6
26 Mar 69	KUMBAYA (re) *A&M AMS 744*	38 2
27 Nov 76	HANG ON SLOOPY *Satril SAT 114*	32 8

SANDRA
Germany, female vocalist – Sandra Lauer (Singles: 8 Weeks) pos/wks

17 Dec 88	EVERLASTING LOVE *Siren SRN 85*	45 8

Jodie SANDS *US, female vocalist (Singles: 10 Weeks)* pos/wks

17 Oct 58	SOMEDAY (YOU'LL WANT ME TO WANT YOU) *HMV POP 533*	14 10

Tommy SANDS *US, male vocalist (Singles: 7 Weeks)* pos/wks

4 Aug 60	THE OLD OAKEN BUCKET *Capitol CL 15143*	25 7

SANDSTORM (see also Mark PICCHIOTTI presents BASSTOY featuring DANA) *US, male producer – Mark Picchiotti (Singles: 1 Week)* pos/wks

13 May 00	THE RETURN OF NOTHING *Renaissance Recordings RENCDS 001*	54 1

Samantha SANG
Australia, female vocalist – Cheryl Gray (Singles: 13 Weeks) pos/wks

4 Feb 78	EMOTION *Private Stock PVT 128*	11 13

SANTA CLAUS and the CHRISTMAS TREES
UK, male vocal / instrumental group (Singles: 10 Weeks) pos/wks

11 Dec 82	SINGALONG-A-SANTA *Polydor IVY 1*	19 5
10 Dec 83	SINGALONG-A-SANTA AGAIN *Polydor IVY 2*	39 5

SANTA ESMERALDA and Leroy GOMEZ *US / France, male / female vocal / instrumental group (Singles: 5 Weeks)* pos/wks

12 Nov 77	DON'T LET ME BE MISUNDERSTOOD *Philips 6042 325*	41 5

SANTANA 152 Top 500 *1960s Latin rock band who peaked in the 21st Century, formed in San Francisco in 1966 by Carlos Santana, b. 20 Jul 1947, Mexico. Their first US No.1 for 28 years, 'Supernatural', won a record eight Grammy awards (2000) and sold in excess 21 million worldwide (Singles: 53 Weeks, Albums: 298 Weeks)* pos/wks

28 Sep 74	SAMBA PA TI *CBS 2561*	27 7
15 Oct 77	SHE'S NOT THERE *CBS 5671*	11 12
25 Nov 78	WELL ALL RIGHT *CBS 6755*	53 3
22 Mar 80	ALL I EVER WANTED *CBS 8160*	57 3
23 Oct 99	SMOOTH *Arista 74321709492* [1]	75 1
1 Apr 00	SMOOTH (re-issue) *Arista 74321748762* [1]	3 10
5 Aug 00	● MARIA MARIA *Arista 74321769372* [2] ▲	6 9
23 Nov 02	THE GAME OF LOVE *Arista 74321959442* [3]	16 8
2 May 70	SANTANA *CBS 63815*	26 11
28 Nov 70	● ABRAXAS *CBS 64807* ▲	7 52
13 Nov 71	● SANTANA III *CBS 69015* ▲	6 14
26 Aug 72	CARLOS SANTANA AND BUDDY MILES LIVE *CBS 65142* [1]	29 4
25 Nov 72	● CARAVANSERAI *CBS 65299*	6 11
28 Jul 73	● LOVE DEVOTION AND SURRENDER *CBS 69037* [2]	7 9

8 Dec 73	● WELCOME *CBS 69040*	8 6
21 Sep 74	GREATEST HITS *CBS 69081*	14 15
2 Nov 74	ILLUMINATIONS *CBS 69063* [3]	40 1
30 Nov 74	BARBOLETTA *CBS 69084*	18 5
10 Apr 76	AMIGOS *CBS 86005*	21 9
8 Jan 77	FESTIVAL *CBS 86020*	27 3
5 Nov 77	● MOONFLOWER *CBS 88272*	7 27
11 Nov 78	INNER SECRETS *CBS 86075*	17 16
24 Mar 79	ONENESS – SILVER DREAMS GOLDEN REALITY *CBS 86037* [4]	55 4
27 Oct 79	MARATHON *CBS 86098*	28 5
20 Sep 80	THE SWING OF DELIGHT *CBS 22075* [4]	65 2
18 Apr 81	ZEBOP! *CBS 84946*	33 4
14 Aug 82	SHANGO *CBS 85914*	35 7
30 Apr 83	HAVANA MOON *CBS 25350* [4]	84 1
23 Mar 85	BEYOND APPEARANCES *CBS 86307*	58 3
15 Nov 86	VIVA! SANTANA – THE VERY BEST *K-Tel NE 1338.*	50 3
14 Jul 90	SPIRITS DANCING IN THE FLESH *CBS 4669131*	68 1
15 Aug 98	THE ULTIMATE COLLECTION *Columbia SONYTV 47CD*	12 26
4 Sep 99	★ SUPERNATURAL *Arista 7822190802* ▲	1 47
2 Nov 02	SHAMAN *RCA 74321959382* ▲	15 5

[1] Santana featuring Rob Thomas [2] Santana featuring the Product G&B [3] Santana featuring Michelle Branch [1] Carlos Santana and Buddy Miles [2] Carlos Santana and Mahavishnu John McLaughlin [3] Carlos Santana and Alice Coltrane [4] Carlos Santana

Juelz SANTANA See CAM'RON

SANTO and JOHNNY *US, male instrumental duo – steel and electric guitars – Santo and Johnny Farina (Singles: 5 Weeks)* pos/wks

16 Oct 59	SLEEP WALK *Pye International 7N 25037* ▲	22 4
31 Mar 60	TEARDROP *Parlophone R 4619*	50 1

SANTOS *Italy, male producer – Sante Pucello (Singles: 6 Weeks)* pos/wks

20 Jan 01	● CAMELS *Incentive CENT 15CDS*	9 6

Mike SARNE
UK, male vocalist – Mike Scheuer (Singles: 43 Weeks) pos/wks

10 May 62	★ COME OUTSIDE *Parlophone R 4902* [1]	1 19
30 Aug 62	WILL I WHAT *Parlophone R 4932* [2]	18 10
10 Jan 63	JUST FOR KICKS *Parlophone R 4974*	22 7
28 Mar 63	CODE OF LOVE *Parlophone R 5010*	29 7

[1] Mike Sarne with Wendy Richard [2] Mike Sarne with Billie Davis

Joy SARNEY *UK, female vocalist (Singles: 6 Weeks)* pos/wks

7 May 77	NAUGHTY NAUGHTY NAUGHTY *Alaska ALA 2005*	26 6

The SARR BAND *Italy / UK / France, male / female vocal / instrumental group (Singles: 1 Week)* pos/wks

16 Sep 78	MAGIC MANDRAKE *Calendar DAY 111*	68 1

Peter SARSTEDT
UK, male vocalist (Singles: 25 Weeks, Albums: 4 Weeks) pos/wks

5 Feb 69	★ WHERE DO YOU GO TO (MY LOVELY) *United Artists UP 2262*	1 16
4 Jun 69	● FROZEN ORANGE JUICE *United Artists UP 35021*	10 9
8 Mar 69	● PETER SARSTEDT *United Artists SULP 1219*	8 4

Robin SARSTEDT
UK, male vocalist – Clive Sarstedt (Singles: 9 Weeks) pos/wks

8 May 76	● MY RESISTANCE IS LOW *Decca F 13624*	3 9

SARTORELLO
Italy, male / female vocal / instrumental duo (Singles: 1 Week) pos/wks

10 Aug 96	MOVE BABY MOVE *Multiply CDMULTY 12*	56 1

SASH! 413 Top 500 *German pop / dance act named after instrumentalist / producer Sascha (aka Sasha) Lappessen, featuring programmers Thomas Alisson and Ralf Kappmeier. First four hits uniquely featured vocals in different languages (French, Spanish, English, Italian) (Singles: 103 Weeks, Albums: 65 Weeks)* pos/wks

1 Mar 97	● ENCORE UNE FOIS *Multiply CDMULTY 18*	2 15
5 Jul 97	● ECUADOR *Multiply CDMULTY 23* [1]	2 12

			pos/wks
18 Oct 97 ●	STAY *Multiply CDMULTY 26* [2]	2	14
4 Apr 98 ●	LA PRIMAVERA *Multiply CXMULTY 32*	3	12
15 Aug 98 ●	MYSTERIOUS TIMES *Multiply CXMULTY 40* [3]	2	12
28 Nov 98 ●	MOVE MANIA *Multiply CDMULTY 45* [4]	8	10
3 Apr 99	COLOUR THE WORLD *Multiply CDMULTY 48*	15	6
12 Feb 00 ●	ADELANTE *Multiply CDMULTY 60*	2	10
22 Apr 00 ●	JUST AROUND THE HILL *Multiply CDMULTY 62* [3]	8	7
23 Sep 00 ●	WITH MY OWN EYES *Multiply CDMULTY 67*	10	5
19 Jul 97 ●	IT'S MY LIFE – THE ALBUM *Multiply MULTYCD 1*	6	38
5 Sep 98 ●	LIFE GOES ON *Multiply MULTYCD 2*	5	19
29 Apr 00	TRILENIUM *Multiply MULTYCD 7*	13	5
11 Nov 00	ENCORE UNE FOIS – THE GREATEST HITS *Multiply MULTYCD 10*	33	3

[1] Sash! featuring Rodriguez [2] Sash! featuring La Trec [3] Sash! featuring Tina Cousins [4] Sash! featuring Shannon

SASHA
UK, male producer – Alexander Coe (Singles: 18 Weeks, Albums: 9 Weeks)   pos/wks

31 Jul 93	TOGETHER *ffrr FCD 212* [1]	57	1
19 Feb 94	HIGHER GROUND *Deconstruction 74321189002* [2]	19	3
27 Aug 94	MAGIC *Deconstruction 74321221862* [2]	32	4
9 Mar 96	BE AS ONE *Deconstruction 74321342962* [3]	17	4
23 Sep 00	SCORCHIO *Arista 74321788222* [4]	23	3
31 Aug 02	WAVY GRAVY *Arista 74321960602*	64	1
27 Nov 04	WATCHING CARS GO BY *Emperor Norton ENR 532* [5]	49	2
12 Mar 94	THE QAT COLLECTION *Deconstruction 74321191962*	55	2
17 Jul 99	EXPANDER (EP) *Deconstruction 74321681992*	18	3
17 Aug 02	AIRDRAWNDAGGER *Arista 74321947862*	18	3
26 Jun 04	INVOLVER *Global Underground GUSA 001CDX*	61	1

[1] Danny Campbell and Sasha [2] Sasha with Sam Mollison [3] Sasha and Maria [4] Sasha / Emerson [5] Felix Da Housecat vs Sasha and Armand Van Helden

SASHA See Sean PAUL

Joe SATRIANI
US, male instrumentalist – guitar (Singles: 1 Week, Albums: 13 Weeks) pos/wks

13 Feb 93	THE SATCH EP *Relativity 6589532*	53	1
15 Aug 92	THE EXTREMIST *Epic 4716722*	13	6
6 Nov 93	TIME MACHINE *Relativity 4745152*	32	2
14 Oct 95	JOE SATRIANI *Relativity 4811022*	21	3
14 Mar 98	CRYSTAL PLANET *Epic 4894732*	32	2

Tracks on The Satch EP: The Extremist / Cryin / Banana Bongo / Crazy

SATURATED SOUL featuring MISS BUNTY
US / UK, male production duo and Holland, female vocalist (Singles: 1 Week)   pos/wks

14 Aug 04	GOT TO RELEASE *Defected DFTD 093*	56	1

SATURDAY NIGHT BAND
US, male vocal / instrumental group (Singles: 9 Weeks)   pos/wks

1 Jul 78	COME ON, DANCE DANCE *CBS 6367*	16	9

Deion SAUNDERS See MC HAMMER

Ann SAUNDERSON See OCTAVE ONE featuring Ann SAUNDERSON

Kevin SAUNDERSON See INNER CITY

Anne SAVAGE
UK, female DJ / producer (Singles: 1 Week)   pos/wks

19 Apr 03	HELLRAISER *Tidy Trax TIDY 186T*	74	1

Chantay SAVAGE
US, female vocalist (Singles: 9 Weeks, Albums: 1 Week)   pos/wks

4 May 96	I WILL SURVIVE *RCA 74321377682*	12	8
8 Nov 97	REMINDING ME (OF SEF) *Relativity 6560762* [1]	59	1
25 May 96	I WILL SURVIVE (DOIN' IT MY WAY) *RCA 74321381622*	66	1

[1] Common featuring Chantay Savage

Edna SAVAGE
UK, female vocalist, b. 21 Apr 1936, d. 31 Dec 2000 (Singles: 1 Week) pos/wks

13 Jan 56	ARRIVEDERCI DARLING *Parlophone R 4097*	19	1

SAVAGE GARDEN   277   Top 500
Australian pop vocal / instrumental duo: Daniel Jones and Darren Hayes. Eponymous debut album sold more than 11 million copies worldwide and huge critical acclaim followed with a record-breaking 10 Arias at the 1997 Australian music industry awards. The duo went their separate ways in 2001 and Hayes had solo success. Best-selling single: 'Truly, Madly, Deeply' 657,500 (Singles: 101 Weeks, Albums: 132 Weeks)   pos/wks

21 Jun 97	I WANT YOU *Columbia 6645452*	11	7
27 Sep 97	TO THE MOON AND BACK *Columbia 6648932*	55	1
28 Feb 98 ●	TRULY MADLY DEEPLY *Columbia 6656022* ▲	4	23
22 Aug 98 ●	TO THE MOON AND BACK (re-issue) *Columbia 6662882*	3	16
12 Dec 98	I WANT YOU '98 (re-mix) *Columbia 6667332*	12	10
10 Jul 99	THE ANIMAL SONG *Columbia 6675882*	16	9
13 Nov 99 ●	I KNEW I LOVED YOU *Columbia 6683102* ▲	10	12
1 Apr 00	CRASH AND BURN *Columbia 6690442*	14	6
29 Jul 00 ●	AFFIRMATION *Columbia 6696882*	8	10
25 Nov 00	HOLD ME (re) *Columbia 6706032*	16	7
31 Mar 01	THE BEST THING (re) *Columbia 6709852*	35	3
14 Mar 98 ●	SAVAGE GARDEN *Columbia 4871612*	2	68
20 Nov 99 ●	AFFIRMATION *Columbia 4949352*	7	64

Telly SAVALAS
US, male actor / vocalist – Aristotle Savalas, b. 21 Jan 1924, d. 22 Jan 1994 (Singles: 12 Weeks, Albums: 10 Weeks)   pos/wks

22 Feb 75 ★	IF *MCA 174*	1	9
31 May 75	YOU'VE LOST THAT LOVIN' FEELIN' *MCA 189*	47	3
22 Mar 75	TELLY *MCA MCF 2699*	12	10

SAVANA
UK, male rapper (Singles: 1 Week)   pos/wks

24 Jul 04	PRETTY LADY *Jetstar JECDS 1805*	48	1

SAVANNA
UK, male vocal group (Singles: 4 Weeks)   pos/wks

10 Oct 81	I CAN'T TURN AWAY *R&B RBS 203*	61	4

SAVOY BROWN
UK, male vocal / instrumental group (Albums: 1 Week)   pos/wks

28 Nov 70	LOOKIN' IN *Decca SKL 5066*	50	1

SAVUKA See Johnny CLEGG and SAVUKA

The SAW DOCTORS
Ireland, male vocal / instrumental group (Singles: 10 Weeks, Albums: 12 Weeks)   pos/wks

12 Nov 94	SMALL BIT OF LOVE *Shamtown SAW 001CD*	24	3
27 Jan 96	WORLD OF GOOD *Shamtown SAW 002CD*	15	3
13 Jul 96	TO WIN JUST ONCE *Shamtown SAW 004CD*	14	2
6 Dec 97	SIMPLE THINGS *Shamtown SAW 006CD*	56	1
1 Jun 02	THIS IS ME *Shamtown SAW 012CD*	31	1
8 Jun 91	IF THIS IS ROCK AND ROLL I WANT MY OLD JOB BACK *Solid ROCK 7*	69	2
31 Oct 92	ALL THE WAY FROM TUAM *Solid 4509911462*	33	2
24 Feb 96 ●	SAME OUL' TOWN *Shamtown SAWDOC 004CD*	6	5
24 Oct 98	SONGS FROM SUN STREET *Shamtown SAWDOC 006CD*	24	2
13 Oct 01	VILLAINS? *Shamtown SAWDOC 008CD*	58	1

Nitin SAWHNEY
UK, male instrumentalist / producer (Singles: 1 Week, Albums: 4 Weeks)   pos/wks

28 Jul 01	SUNSET *V2 VVR 5016763* [1]	65	1
25 Sep 99	BEYOND SKIN *Outcaste CASTE 9CD*	44	2
30 Jun 01	PROPHESY *V2 VVR 1015912*	40	1
26 Jul 03	HUMAN *V2 VVR 1021852*	54	1

[1] Nitin Sawhney featuring Eska

SAXON   446   Top 500
Key band on the early 1980s British New Wave of Heavy Metal scene, formed in Barnsley (originally as Son of a Bitch) in 1977, and fronted by Peter 'Biff' Byford. In the 1980s, the group's 15 hit singles all missed the Top 10 (Singles: 61 Weeks, Albums: 97 Weeks)   pos/wks

22 Mar 80	WHEELS OF STEEL *Carrere CAR 143*	20	11
21 Jun 80	747 (STRANGERS IN THE NIGHT) *Carrere CAR 151*	13	9
28 Jun 80	BACKS TO THE WALL *Carrere HM 6*	64	2
28 Jun 80	BIG TEASER / RAINBOW THEME – FROZEN RAINBOW *Carrere HM 5*	66	2
29 Nov 80	STRONG ARM OF THE LAW *Carrere CAR 170*	63	3
11 Apr 81	AND THE BANDS PLAYED ON *Carrere CAR 180*	12	8

			pos/wks
18 Jul 81	NEVER SURRENDER *Carrere CAR 204*	....................**18**	6
31 Oct 81	PRINCESS OF THE NIGHT *Carrere CAR 208*	....................**57**	3
23 Apr 83	POWER AND THE GLORY *Carrere SAXON 1*	....................**32**	5
30 Jul 83	NIGHTMARE *Carrere CAR 284*	....................**50**	3
31 Aug 85	BACK ON THE STREETS *Parlophone R 6103*	....................**75**	1
29 Mar 86	ROCK 'N' ROLL GYPSY *Parlophone R 6112*	....................**71**	1
30 Aug 86	WAITING FOR THE NIGHT *EMI EMI 5575*	....................**66**	2
5 Mar 88	RIDE LIKE THE WIND *EMI EM 43*	....................**52**	4
30 Apr 88	I CAN'T WAIT ANYMORE *EMI EM 54*	....................**71**	1
12 Apr 80 ●	WHEELS OF STEEL *Carrere CAL 115*	....................**5**	29
15 Nov 80	STRONG ARM OF THE LAW *Carrere CAL 120*	....................**11**	13
3 Oct 81 ●	DENIM AND LEATHER *Carrere CAL 128*	....................**9**	11
22 May 82 ●	THE EAGLE HAS LANDED *Carrere CAL 157*	....................**5**	19
26 Mar 83	POWER AND THE GLORY *Carrere CAL 147*	....................**15**	9
11 Feb 84	CRUSADER *Carrere CAL 200*	....................**18**	7
14 Sep 85	INNOCENCE IS NO EXCUSE *Parlophone SAXON 2*	....................**36**	4
27 Sep 86	ROCK THE NATIONS *EMI EMC 3515*	....................**34**	3
9 Apr 88	DESTINY *EMI EMC 3543*	....................**49**	2

Al SAXON
UK, male vocalist – Allan Fowler (Singles: 10 Weeks) pos/wks

16 Jan 59	YOU'RE THE TOP CHA *Fontana H 164*	....................**17**	4
28 Aug 59	ONLY SIXTEEN *Fontana H 205*	....................**24**	3
22 Dec 60	BLUE-EYED BOY *Fontana H 278*	....................**39**	2
7 Sep 61	THERE I'VE SAID IT AGAIN *Piccadilly 7N 35011*	....................**48**	1

Leo SAYER [124] *Top 500*
Distinctive singer / songwriter (b. 21 May 1948, Sussex, UK) who was a top singles and album act on both sides of the Atlantic in the late 1970s. His first seven hits all reached the Top 10 – a feat first achieved by his manager, Adam Faith (Singles: 151 Weeks, Albums: 238 Weeks) pos/wks

15 Dec 73 ●	THE SHOW MUST GO ON *Chrysalis CHS 2023*	....................**2**	13
15 Jun 74 ●	ONE MAN BAND *Chrysalis CHS 2045*	....................**6**	9
14 Sep 74 ●	LONG TALL GLASSES *Chrysalis CHS 2052*	....................**4**	9
30 Aug 75 ●	MOONLIGHTING *Chrysalis CHS 2076*	....................**2**	8
30 Oct 76 ●	YOU MAKE ME FEEL LIKE DANCING *Chrysalis CHS 2119* ▲	....................**2**	12
29 Jan 77 ★	WHEN I NEED YOU *Chrysalis CHS 2127* ▲	....................**1**	13
9 Apr 77 ●	HOW MUCH LOVE *Chrysalis CHS 2140*	....................**10**	8
10 Sep 77	THUNDER IN MY HEART *Chrysalis CHS 2163*	....................**22**	8
16 Sep 78 ●	I CAN'T STOP LOVING YOU (THOUGH I TRY) *Chrysalis CHS 2240*	....................**6**	11
25 Nov 78	RAINING IN MY HEART *Chrysalis CHS 2277*	....................**21**	10
5 Jul 80 ●	MORE THAN I CAN SAY *Chrysalis CHS 2442*	....................**2**	11
13 Mar 82 ●	HAVE YOU EVER BEEN IN LOVE *Chrysalis CHS 2596*	....................**10**	9
19 Jun 82	HEART (STOP BEATING IN TIME) *Chrysalis CHS 2616*	....................**22**	10
12 Mar 83	ORCHARD ROAD *Chrysalis CHS 2677*	....................**16**	8
15 Oct 83	TILL YOU COME BACK TO ME *Chrysalis LEO 01*	....................**51**	3
8 Feb 86	UNCHAINED MELODY *Chrysalis LEO 3*	....................**54**	4
13 Feb 93	WHEN I NEED YOU (re-issue) *Chrysalis CDCHS 3926*	....................**65**	2
8 Aug 98	YOU MAKE ME FEEL LIKE DANCING *Brothers Org. CDBRUV 8* [1]	....................**32**	3
5 Jan 74 ●	SILVER BIRD *Chrysalis CHR 1050*	....................**2**	22
26 Oct 74 ●	JUST A BOY *Chrysalis CHR 1068*	....................**4**	14
20 Sep 75 ●	ANOTHER YEAR *Chrysalis CHR 1087*	....................**8**	9
27 Nov 76 ●	ENDLESS FLIGHT *Chrysalis CHR 1125*	....................**4**	66
22 Oct 77 ●	THUNDER IN MY HEART *Chrysalis CDL 1154*	....................**8**	16
2 Sep 78	LEO SAYER *Chrysalis CDL 1198*	....................**15**	25
31 Mar 79 ★	THE VERY BEST OF LEO SAYER *Chrysalis CDL 1222*	....................**1**	37
13 Oct 79	HERE *Chrysalis CDL 1240*	....................**44**	4
23 Aug 80	LIVING IN A FANTASY *Chrysalis CDL 1297*	....................**15**	9
8 May 82	WORLD RADIO *Chrysalis CDL 1345*	....................**30**	12
12 Nov 83	HAVE YOU EVER BEEN IN LOVE *Chrysalis LEOTV 1*	....................**15**	18
6 Mar 93	ALL THE BEST *Chrysalis CDCHR 1980*	....................**26**	4
20 Feb 99	THE DEFINITIVE HITS COLLECTION *PolyGram TV 5471152*	....................**35**	2

[1] Groove Generation featuring Leo Sayer

Alexei SAYLE
UK, male comedian / vocalist (Singles: 8 Weeks, Albums: 5 Weeks) pos/wks

25 Feb 84	'ULLO JOHN GOT A NEW MOTOR? *Island IS 162*	....................**15**	8
17 Mar 84	THE FISH PEOPLE TAPES *Island IMA 9*	....................**62**	5

The SCAFFOLD (see also Mike McGEAR)
UK, male vocal group (Singles: 62 Weeks) pos/wks

22 Nov 67 ●	THANK U VERY MUCH *Parlophone R 5643*	....................**4**	12
27 Mar 68	DO YOU REMEMBER *Parlophone R 5679*	....................**34**	5
6 Nov 68 ★	LILY THE PINK *Parlophone R 5734*	....................**1**	24

1 Nov 69	GIN GAN GOOLIE (re) *Parlophone R 5812*	....................**38**	12
1 Jun 74 ●	LIVERPOOL LOU *Warner Bros. K 16400*	....................**7**	9

Boz SCAGGS
US, male vocalist – William Royce Scaggs (Singles: 31 Weeks, Albums: 29 Weeks) pos/wks

30 Oct 76	LOWDOWN *CBS 4563*	....................**28**	4
22 Jan 77 ●	WHAT CAN I SAY *CBS 4869*	....................**10**	10
14 May 77	LIDO SHUFFLE *CBS 5136*	....................**13**	9
10 Dec 77	HOLLYWOOD *CBS 5836*	....................**33**	8
12 Mar 77	SILK DEGREES *CBS 81296*	....................**37**	24
17 Dec 77	DOWN TWO THEN LEFT *CBS 86036*	....................**55**	1
3 May 80	MIDDLE MAN *CBS 86094*	....................**52**	4

SCANTY SANDWICH
UK, male DJ / producer – Richard Marshall (Singles: 8 Weeks) pos/wks

29 Jan 00 ●	BECAUSE OF YOU *Southern Fried ECB 18CDS*	....................**3**	8

SCARFACE
US, male rapper – Brad Jordan (Singles: 6 Weeks) pos/wks

11 Mar 95	HAND OF THE DEAD BODY *Virgin America VUSCD 88* [1]	....................**41**	2
5 Aug 95	I SEEN A MAN DIE *Virgin America VUSCD 94*	....................**55**	1
5 Jul 97	GAME OVER *Virgin VUSCD 121*	....................**34**	2

[1] Scarface featuring Ice Cube

SCARFO
UK, male vocal / instrumental group (Singles: 2 Weeks) pos/wks

19 Jul 97	ALKALINE *Deceptive BLUFF 044CD*	....................**61**	1
18 Oct 97	COSMONAUT NO.7 *Deceptive BLUFF 053CD*	....................**67**	1

SCARLET
UK, female vocal / instrumental duo – Cheryl Parker and Joe Youle (Singles: 18 Weeks, Albums: 2 Weeks) pos/wks

21 Jan 95	INDEPENDENT LOVE SONG *WEA YZ 820CD*	....................**12**	12
29 Apr 95	I WANNA BE FREE (TO BE WITH HIM) *WEA YZ 913CD*	....................**21**	4
5 Aug 95	LOVE HANGOVER *WEA YZ 969CD*	....................**54**	1
6 Jul 96	BAD GIRL *WEA WEA 046CD*	....................**54**	1
11 Mar 95	NAKED *WEA 4509976432*	....................**59**	2

SCARLET FANTASTIC
UK, male / female vocal / instrumental group (Singles: 12 Weeks) pos/wks

3 Oct 87	NO MEMORY *Arista RIS 36*	....................**24**	10
23 Jan 88	PLUG ME IN (TO THE CENTRAL LOVE LINE) *Arista 109693*	....................**67**	2

SCARLET PARTY
UK, male vocal / instrumental group (Singles: 5 Weeks) pos/wks

16 Oct 82	101 DAM-NATIONS *Parlophone R 6058*	....................**44**	5

SCARS
UK, male vocal / instrumental group (Albums: 3 Weeks) pos/wks

18 Apr 81	AUTHOR! AUTHOR! *Pre PREX 5*	....................**67**	3

SCATMAN JOHN
US, male vocalist – John Larkin, b. 13 Mar 1942, d. 3 Dec 1999 (Singles: 19 Weeks) pos/wks

13 May 95 ●	SCATMAN (SKI-BA-BOP-BA-DOP-BOP) *RCA 74321281712*	....................**3**	12
2 Sep 95 ●	SCATMAN'S WORLD *RCA 74321289952*	....................**10**	7

SCENT
Italy / Ireland, male / female production / vocal trio (Singles: 3 Weeks) pos/wks

21 Aug 04	UP & DOWN *Positiva CDTIVS 209*	....................**23**	3

SCHAEFER See ROSTAL and SCHAEFER

Michael SCHENKER GROUP (see also MSG; UFO)
Germany / UK, male vocal / instrumental group (Singles: 9 Weeks, Albums: 44 Weeks) pos/wks

13 Sep 80	ARMED AND READY *Chrysalis CHS 2455*	....................**53**	3
8 Nov 80	CRY FOR THE NATIONS *Chrysalis CHS 2471*	....................**56**	3
11 Sep 82	DANCER *Chrysalis CHS 2636*	....................**52**	3
6 Sep 80 ●	MICHAEL SCHENKER GROUP *Chrysalis CHR 1302*	....................**8**	8
19 Sep 81	MICHAEL SCHENKER GROUP (re-issue) *Chrysalis CHR 1336*	....................**14**	8
13 Mar 82 ●	ONE NIGHT AT BUDOKAN *Chrysalis CTY 1375*	....................**5**	11
23 Oct 82	ASSAULT ATTACK *Chrysalis CHR 1393*	....................**19**	5
10 Sep 83	BUILT TO DESTROY *Chrysalis CHR 1441*	....................**23**	5
23 Jun 84	ROCK WILL NEVER DIE *Chrysalis CUX 1470*	....................**24**	5
24 Oct 87	PERFECT TIMING *EMI EMC 3539* [1]	....................**65**	2

[1] MSG

Lalo SCHIFRIN Argentina, male conductor –
Boris Schifrin and US, orchestra (Singles: 11 Weeks)   pos/wks

9 Oct 76	**JAWS** CTI CTSP 005	**14**	9
25 Oct 97	**BULLITT** Warner.esp WESP 002CD	**36**	2

SCHILLER Germany, male production duo –
Christopher von Deylen and Mirko von Schlieffen (Singles: 3 Weeks) pos/wks

28 Apr 01	**DAS GLOCKENSPIEL** Data DATA 22CDS	**17**	3

Peter SCHILLING Germany, male vocalist (Singles: 6 Weeks)   pos/wks

5 May 84	**MAJOR TOM (COMING HOME) (re)** PSP / WEA X 9438	**42**	6

Phillip SCHOFIELD
UK, male TV presenter / actor / vocalist (Singles: 6 Weeks)   pos/wks

5 Dec 92	**CLOSE EVERY DOOR** Really Useful RUR 11	**27**	6

SCHON See HAGAR SCHON AARONSON SHRIEVE

SCHOOL OF EXCELLENCE
(see also HARMONIUM; HYPNOSIS; IN TUNE; JAMES BOYS; RAINDANCE)
UK, male instrumental duo (Albums: 2 Weeks)   pos/wks

28 Oct 95	**PIANO MOODS** Dino DINCD 114	**47**	2

SCHOOL OF ROCK
US, male / female actors / vocalists (Singles: 2 Weeks)   pos/wks

21 Feb 04	**SCHOOL OF ROCK** Atlantic AT 0172CD	**51**	2

SCIENCE DEPARTMENT featuring ERIRE
UK, male production duo and female vocalist (Singles: 1 Week)   pos/wks

10 Nov 01	**BREATHE** Renaissance Recordings RENCDS 010	**64**	1

SCIENTIST
UK, male producer – Phil Sebastiane (Singles: 13 Weeks)   pos/wks

6 Oct 90	**THE EXORCIST** Kickin KICK 1	**62**	3
1 Dec 90	**THE EXORCIST (re-mix)** Kickin KICK 1TR	**46**	3
15 Dec 90	**THE BEE (re)** Kickin KICK 3S	**47**	6
11 May 91	**SPIRAL SYMPHONY** Kickin KICK 5	**74**	1

SCISSOR SISTERS US, male / female vocal /
instrumental group (Singles: 31 Weeks, Albums: 46 Weeks)   pos/wks

8 Nov 03	**LAURA** Polydor 9812788	**54**	2
31 Jan 04 ●	**COMFORTABLY NUMB** Polydor 9815883	**10**	7
10 Apr 04	**TAKE YOUR MAMA** Polydor 9866277	**17**	6
19 Jun 04	**LAURA (re-issue)** Polydor 9866833	**12**	10
23 Oct 04	**MARY** Polydor 9868282	**14**	6
14 Feb 04 ★	**SCISSOR SISTERS** Polydor 9866058	**1**	46+

SCOOBIE UK, male / female vocal /
production / Celtic FC supporters group (Singles: 3 Weeks)   pos/wks

22 Dec 01	**THE MAGNIFICENT 7** Big Tongue BTR 001CDS	**58**	2
1 Jun 02	**THE MAGNIFICENT 7 (re-mix)** Big Tongue BTR 001CDSX	**71**	1

SCOOCH
UK, male / female vocal group (Singles: 20 Weeks, Albums: 2 Weeks) pos/wks

6 Nov 99	**WHEN MY BABY** Accolade CDAC 002	**29**	4
22 Jan 00 ●	**MORE THAN I NEEDED TO KNOW** Accolade CDAC 003	**5**	5
6 May 00	**THE BEST IS YET TO COME (re)** Accolade CDAC 004	**12**	5
5 Aug 00	**FOR SURE** Accolade CDAS 005	**15**	6
19 Aug 00	**FOUR SURE** Accolade 5278190	**41**	2

SCOOTER UK / Germany, male vocal /
instrumental group (Singles: 65 Weeks, Albums: 23 Weeks)   pos/wks

21 Oct 95	**THE MOVE YOUR ASS EP** Club Tools 0061675 CLU	**23**	4
17 Feb 96	**BACK IN THE UK** Club Tools 0061955 CLU	**18**	3
25 May 96	**REBEL YELL** Club Tools 0062575 CLU	**30**	2
19 Oct 96	**I'M RAVING** Club Tools 0063015 CLU	**33**	3
17 May 97	**FIRE** Club Tools 006005 CLU	**45**	2
22 Jun 02 ●	**THE LOGICAL SONG** Sheffield Tunes 0139295 STU	**2**	15
21 Sep 02	**NESSAJA** Sheffield Tunes 0142165 STU	**4**	9
7 Dec 02	**POSSE (I NEED YOU ON THE FLOOR)** Sheffield Tunes 0143775 STU	**15**	7
5 Apr 03	**WEEKEND!** Sheffield Tunes 0147315 STU	**12**	10

5 Jul 03	**THE NIGHT** Sheffield Tunes 0149005 STU	**16**	5
18 Oct 03	**MARIA (I LIKE IT LOUD)** Sheffield Tunes 051135 STU [1]	**16**	4
10 Jul 04	**JIGGA JIGGA!** All Around the World CDGLOBE 348	**48**	1
13 Apr 96	**OUR HAPPY HARDCORE** Club Tools 0062282 CLU	**24**	5
10 Aug 02 ●	**PUSH THE BEAT FOR THIS JAM (THE SINGLES '94–'02)** Sheffield Tunes 0141172 STU	**6**	14
26 Apr 03	**THE STADIUM TECHNO EXPERIENCE** Sheffield Tunes / Edel UK STU 00147112CD	**20**	4

[1] Scooter vs Marc Acardipane and Dick Rules

Tracks on The Move Your Ass EP: Move Your Ass / Friends / Endless Summer / Move Your Ass (remix)

SCORPIONS Germany, male vocal /
instrumental group (Singles: 35 Weeks, Albums: 56 Weeks)   pos/wks

26 May 79	**IS THERE ANYBODY THERE? / ANOTHER PIECE OF MEAT** Harvest HAR 5185	**39**	4
25 Aug 79	**LOVEDRIVE** Harvest HAR 5188	**69**	2
31 May 80	**MAKE IT REAL** Harvest HAR 5206	**72**	2
20 Sep 80	**THE ZOO** Harvest HAR 5212	**75**	1
3 Apr 82	**NO ONE LIKE YOU (re)** Harvest HAR 5219	**64**	4
17 Jul 82	**CAN'T LIVE WITHOUT YOU** Harvest HAR 5221	**63**	2
4 Jun 88	**RHYTHM OF LOVE** Harvest HAR 5240	**59**	2
18 Feb 89	**PASSION RULES THE GAME** Harvest 5242	**74**	1
1 Jun 91	**WIND OF CHANGE** Vertigo VER 54	**53**	3
28 Sep 91 ●	**WIND OF CHANGE (re-issue)** Vertigo VER 58	**2**	9
30 Nov 91	**SEND ME AN ANGEL (re)** Vertigo VER 60	**27**	5
21 Apr 79	**LOVE DRIVE** Harvest SHSP 4097	**36**	11
3 May 80	**ANIMAL MAGNETISM** Harvest SHSP 4113	**23**	6
10 Apr 82	**BLACKOUT** Harvest SHVL 823	**11**	11
24 Mar 84	**LOVE AT FIRST STING** Harvest SHSP 2400071	**17**	6
29 Jun 85	**WORLD WIDE LIVE** Harvest SCORP 1	**18**	8
14 May 88	**SAVAGE AMUSEMENT** Harvest SHSP 4125	**18**	6
17 Nov 90	**CRAZY WORLD** Vertigo 8469081	**27**	7
25 Sep 93	**FACE THE HEAT** Mercury 5182802	**51**	1

SCOTLAND WORLD CUP SQUAD UK, male football
team vocalists (Singles: 27 Weeks, Albums: 9 Weeks)   pos/wks

22 Jun 74	**EASY EASY** Polydor 2058 452	**20**	4
27 May 78 ●	**OLE OLA (MULHER BRASILEIRA)** Riva 15 [1]	**4**	6
1 May 82 ●	**WE HAVE A DREAM** WEA K 19145 [2]	**5**	9
9 Jun 90	**SAY IT WITH PRIDE** RCA PB 43791 [2]	**45**	3
15 Jun 96	**PURPLE HEATHER** Warner Bros. W 0354CD [3]	**16**	5
25 May 74 ●	**EASY EASY** Polydor 2383 282	**3**	9

[1] Rod Stewart featuring the Scottish World Cup Squad '78 [2] Scottish World Cup Squad [3] Rod Stewart with the Scottish Euro '96 Squad

Band of the SCOTS GUARDS
UK, military band (Albums: 2 Weeks)   pos/wks

28 Jun 69	**BAND OF THE SCOTS GUARDS** Fontana SFXL 54	**25**	2

Jack SCOTT Canada, male vocalist –
Jack Scafone Jr (Singles: 28 Weeks, Albums: 12 Weeks)   pos/wks

10 Oct 58 ●	**MY TRUE LOVE** London HLU 8626	**9**	10
25 Sep 59	**THE WAY I WALK** London HLL 8912	**30**	1
10 Mar 60	**WHAT IN THE WORLD'S COME OVER YOU** Top Rank JAR 280	**11**	15
2 Jun 60	**BURNING BRIDGES** Top Rank JAR 375	**32**	2
7 May 60 ●	**I REMEMBER HANK WILLIAMS** Top Rank BUY 034	**7**	11
3 Sep 60	**WHAT IN THE WORLD'S COME OVER YOU** Top Rank 25/024	**11**	1

Jamie SCOTT UK, male vocalist (Singles: 2 Weeks)   pos/wks

4 Sep 04	**JUST** Sony Music 6752282	**29**	2

Jill SCOTT
US, female vocalist (Singles: 5 Weeks, Albums: 6 Weeks)   pos/wks

4 Nov 00	**GETTIN' IN THE WAY** Epic 6705272	**30**	3
7 Apr 01	**A LONG WALK** Epic 6710382	**54**	1
6 Nov 04	**GOLDEN** Epic 6751772	**59**	1
29 Jul 00	**WHO IS JILL SCOTT? – WORDS AND SOUNDS VOL.1** Epic 4986252	**69**	3
11 Sep 04	**BEAUTIFULLY HUMAN – WORDS AND SOUNDS VOL.2** Epic 5176522	**27**	3

Josey SCOTT See Chad KROEGER featuring Josey SCOTT

Linda SCOTT
US, female vocalist – Linda Sampson (Singles: 14 Weeks) pos/wks

18 May 61 ●	I'VE TOLD EVERY LITTLE STAR *Columbia DB 4638*	..7	13
14 Sep 61	DON'T BET MONEY HONEY *Columbia DB 4692*	..50	1

Mike SCOTT
UK, male vocalist / instrumentalist (Singles: 4 Weeks, Albums: 4 Weeks) pos/wks

16 Sep 95	BRING 'EM ALL IN *Chrysalis CDCHS 5025*	..56	1
11 Nov 95	BUILDING THE CITY OF LIGHT *Chrysalis CDCHS 5026*	..60	1
27 Sep 97	LOVE ANYWAY *Chrysalis CDCHS 5064*	..50	1
14 Feb 98	RARE, PRECIOUS AND GONE *Chrysalis CDCHSS 5073*	..74	1
30 Sep 95	BRING 'EM ALL IN *Chrysalis CDCHR 6108*	..23	2
11 Oct 97	STILL BURNING *Chrysalis CDCHR 6122*	..34	2

Millie SCOTT
US, female vocalist (Singles: 11 Weeks) pos/wks

12 Apr 86	PRISONER OF LOVE *Fourth & Broadway BRW 45*	..52	4
23 Aug 86	AUTOMATIC *Fourth & Broadway BRW 51*	..56	3
21 Feb 87	EV'RY LITTLE BIT *Fourth & Broadway BRW 58*	..63	4

Simon SCOTT
UK (b. India), male vocalist (Singles: 8 Weeks) pos/wks

13 Aug 64	MOVE IT BABY *Parlophone R 5164*	..37	8

Tony SCOTT
Holland, male rapper (Singles: 6 Weeks) pos/wks

15 Apr 89	THAT'S HOW I'M LIVING / THE CHIEF *Champion CHAMP 97* [1]	..48	4
10 Feb 90	GET INTO IT / THAT'S HOW I'M LIVING (re-issue) *Champion CHAMP 232*	..63	2

[1] Toni Scott

'The Chief' listed only from 22 Apr 1989

SCOTT & LEON
UK, male production duo – Scott Anderson and Leon McCormack (Singles: 6 Weeks) pos/wks

30 Sep 00	YOU USED TO HOLD ME *AM:PM CDAMPM 137*	..19	4
19 May 01	SHINE ON *AM:PM CDAMPM 143*	..34	2

Lisa SCOTT-LEE (see also STEPS)
UK, female vocalist (Singles: 15 Weeks) pos/wks

24 May 03 ●	LATELY *Fontana 9800295*	..6	8
20 Sep 03	TOO FAR GONE *Fontana 981642*	..11	4
4 Dec 04	GET IT ON *Inspired INSPMOS 1CDS* [1]	..23	3

[1] Intenso Project featuring Lisa Scott-Lee

SCOTTISH RUGBY TEAM with Ronnie BROWNE
UK, male rugby team vocalists (Singles: 1 Week) pos/wks

2 Jun 90	FLOWER OF SCOTLAND *Greentrax STRAX 1001*	..73	1

SCREAMING BLUE MESSIAHS
US / UK, male vocal / instrumental group (Singles: 6 Weeks, Albums: 1 Week) pos/wks

16 Jan 88	I WANNA BE A FLINTSTONE *WEA YZ 166*	..28	6
17 May 86	GUN-SHY *WEA WX 41*	..90	1

SCREAMING TREES
US, male vocal / instrumental group (Singles: 2 Weeks, Albums: 4 Weeks) pos/wks

6 Mar 93	NEARLY LOST YOU (EP) *Epic 6582372*	..50	1
1 May 93	DOLLAR BILL *Epic 6591792*	..52	1
20 Jul 96	DUST *Epic 4839802*	..32	4

Tracks on Nearly Lost You (EP): E.S.K. / Song of a Baker / Winter Song (acoustic)

SCREEN II
UK, male vocal / instrumental group (Albums: 1 Week) pos/wks

9 Apr 94	LET THE RECORD SPIN *Cleveland City CLE 13015*	..36	1

SCRITTI POLITTI
UK, male vocal / instrumental group – leader Green Gartside (Singles: 78 Weeks, Albums: 39 Weeks) pos/wks

21 Nov 81	THE SWEETEST GIRL *Rough Trade RT 091*	..64	3
22 May 82	FAITHLESS *Rough Trade RT 101*	..56	4
7 Aug 82	ASYLUMS IN JERUSALEM / JACQUES DERRIDA *Rough Trade RT 111*	..43	5
10 Mar 84 ●	WOOD BEEZ (PRAY LIKE ARETHA FRANKLIN) *Virgin VS 657*	..10	12
9 Jun 84	ABSOLUTE *Virgin VS 680*	..17	9
17 Nov 84	HYPNOTIZE *Virgin VS 725*	..68	2

11 May 85 ●	THE WORD GIRL *Virgin VS 747*	..6	12
7 Sep 85	PERFECT WAY *Virgin VS 780*	..48	5
7 May 88	OH PATTI (DON'T FEEL SORRY FOR LOVERBOY) *Virgin VS 1006*	..13	9
27 Aug 88	FIRST BOY IN THIS TOWN (LOVE SICK) *Virgin VS 1082*	..63	3
12 Nov 88	BOOM! THERE SHE WAS *Virgin VS 1143*	..55	3
16 Mar 91	SHE'S A WOMAN *Virgin VS 1333* [1]	..20	7
3 Aug 91	TAKE ME IN YOUR ARMS AND LOVE ME *Virgin VS 1346* [2]	..47	3
31 Jul 99	TINSELTOWN TO THE BOOGIEDOWN *Virgin VSCDT 1731*	..46	1
11 Sep 82	SONGS TO REMEMBER *Rough Trade ROUGH 20*	..12	7
22 Jun 85 ●	CUPID & PSYCHE 85 *Virgin V 2350*	..5	19
18 Jun 88 ●	PROVISION *Virgin V 2515*	..8	11
7 Aug 99	ANOMIE & BONHOMIE *Virgin CDV 2884*	..33	2

[1] Scritti Politti featuring Shabba Ranks [2] Scritti Politti and Sweetie Irie

Earl SCRUGGS See Lester FLATT and Earl SCRUGGS

SCUMFROG
Holland, male producer – Jesse Houk (Singles: 3 Weeks) pos/wks

11 May 02	LOVING THE ALIEN *Positiva CDTIV 172* [1]	..41	1
31 May 03	MUSIC REVOLUTION *Positiva CDTIV 191*	..46	2

[1] Scumfrog vs Bowie

SEA FRUIT
UK, male vocal / instrumental group (Singles: 1 Week) pos/wks

24 Jul 99	HELLO WORLD *Electric Canyon ECCD 3055*	..59	1

SEA LEVEL
US, male instrumental group (Singles: 4 Weeks) pos/wks

17 Feb 79	FIFTY-FOUR *Capricorn POSP 28*	..63	4

SEAFOOD
UK, male / female vocal / instrumental group (Singles: 2 Weeks) pos/wks

28 Jul 01	CLOAKING *Infectious INFEC 103CDS*	..71	1
1 May 04	GOOD REASON *Cooking Vinyl FRYCD 189*	..65	1

The SEAHORSES (see also John SQUIRE)
UK, male vocal / instrumental group (Singles: 26 Weeks, Albums: 38 Weeks) pos/wks

10 May 97 ●	LOVE IS THE LAW *Geffen GFSTD 22243*	..3	7
26 Jul 97 ●	BLINDED BY THE SUN *Geffen GFSTD 22266*	..7	7
11 Oct 97	LOVE ME AND LEAVE ME *Geffen GFSTD 22282*	..16	4
13 Dec 97	YOU CAN TALK TO ME *Geffen GFSTD 22297*	..15	8
7 Jun 97 ●	DO IT YOURSELF *Geffen GED 25134*	..2	38

SEAL [292] [Top 500] (see also ADAMSKI) *Golden-voiced soul artist, b. Sealhenry Samuel, 19 Feb 1963, London, UK. Found fame in 1990 thanks to his Adamski collaboration 'Killer'. Seal proceeded to record and perform with an impressive array of artists: Queen, Joni Mitchell, Jeff Beck and The Rolling Stones (Singles: 82 Weeks, Albums: 144 Weeks)* pos/wks

8 Dec 90 ●	CRAZY *ZTT ZANG 8*	..2	15
4 May 91	FUTURE LOVE (EP) *ZTT ZANG 11*	..12	6
20 Jul 91	THE BEGINNING *ZTT ZANG 21*	..24	6
16 Nov 91 ●	KILLER (EP) *ZTT ZANG 23*	..8	8
29 Feb 92	VIOLET *ZTT ZANG 27*	..39	2
21 May 94	PRAYER FOR THE DYING *ZTT ZANG 51CD*	..14	5
30 Jul 94	KISS FROM A ROSE *ZTT ZANG 52CD1*	..20	5
5 Nov 94	NEWBORN FRIEND *ZTT ZANG 58CD*	..45	2
15 Jul 95 ●	KISS FROM A ROSE / I'M ALIVE (re-issue) *ZTT ZANG 70CD* ▲	..4	13
9 Dec 95	DON'T CRY / PRAYER FOR THE DYING (re-issue) *ZTT ZANG 75CD*	..51	2
29 Mar 97	FLY LIKE AN EAGLE *ZTT ZEAL 1CD*	..13	5
14 Nov 98	HUMAN BEINGS *Warner Bros. W 464CD*	..50	1
12 Oct 02 ●	MY VISION *Rulin RULIN 26CDS* [1]	..6	8
20 Sep 03	GET IT TOGETHER *Warner W 620CD1*	..25	3
22 Nov 03	LOVE'S DIVINE *Warner W 629CD*	..68	1
1 Jun 91 ★	SEAL *ZTT ZTT 9* ■	..1	65
4 Jun 94 ★	SEAL *ZTT 4509962562* ■	..1	65
28 Nov 98	HUMAN BEING *Warner Bros. 9362468282*	..44	2
27 Sep 03 ●	IV *Warner Bros. 9362485412*	..4	6
20 Nov 04	BEST – 1991-2004 *Warner Bros. 9362489582*	..27	6+

[1] Jakatta featuring Seal

Tracks on Future Love (EP): Future Love Paradise / A Minor Groove / Violet. Tracks on Killer (EP): Killer / Hey Joe / Come See What Love Has Done. The US No.1 symbol applies to 'Kiss from a Rose', but not 'I'm Alive' The two eponymous albums are different

Jay 'Sinister' SEALEE *See Louie VEGA*

Jay SEAN *UK, male vocalist (Singles: 16 Weeks, Albums: 2 Weeks)* pos/wks

3 Jul 04	●	EYES ON YOU *Relentless RELCD 5* [1]	6 10
6 Nov 04	●	STOLEN *Relentless RELDX 11*	4 6
20 Nov 04		ME AGAINST MYSELF *Relentless CDREL 05*	29 2

[1] Jay Sean featuring The Rishi Rich Project

The SEARCHERS (308) Top 500 *This Merseybeat combo, formed in 1960 and named after the 1956 movie starring John Wayne, were initially tipped to be as big as The Beatles: Mike Pender (v/g), John McNally (g/v), Tony Jackson, b. 1940, d. 2003 (v/b) (left 1964 – replaced by Frank Allen), Chris Curtis (Christopher Crummey) (d), b. 26 Aug 1941, d. 28 Feb 2005. Unlike The Beatles, however, most of this influential act's early hits were cover versions of US originals (Singles: 128 Weeks, Albums: 87 Weeks)* pos/wks

27 Jun 63	★	SWEETS FOR MY SWEET *Pye 7N 15533*	1 16
10 Oct 63		SWEET NOTHINS *Philips BF 1274*	48 1
24 Oct 63	●	SUGAR AND SPICE *Pye 7N 15566*	2 13
16 Jan 64	★	NEEDLES AND PINS *Pye 7N 15594*	1 15
16 Apr 64	★	DON'T THROW YOUR LOVE AWAY *Pye 7N 15630*	1 11
16 Jul 64		SOMEDAY WE'RE GONNA LOVE AGAIN *Pye 7N 15670*	11 8
17 Sep 64	●	WHEN YOU WALK IN THE ROOM *Pye 7N 15694*	3 12
3 Dec 64		WHAT HAVE THEY DONE TO THE RAIN *Pye 7N 15739*	13 11
4 Mar 65	●	GOODBYE MY LOVE *Pye 7N 15794*	4 11
8 Jul 65		HE'S GOT NO LOVE *Pye 7N 15878*	12 10
14 Oct 65		WHEN I GET HOME *Pye 7N 15950*	35 3
16 Dec 65		TAKE ME FOR WHAT I'M WORTH *Pye 7N 15992*	20 8
21 Apr 66		TAKE IT OR LEAVE IT *Pye 7N 17094*	31 6
13 Oct 66		HAVE YOU EVER LOVED SOMEBODY *Pye 7N 17170*	48 2
10 Aug 63	●	MEET THE SEARCHERS *Pye NPL 18086*	2 44
16 Nov 63	●	SUGAR AND SPICE *Pye NPL 18089*	5 21
30 May 64	●	IT'S THE SEARCHERS *Pye NPL 18092*	4 17
27 Mar 65	●	SOUNDS LIKE THE SEARCHERS *Pye NPL 18111*	8 5

The SEASHELLS *UK, female vocal group (Singles: 5 Weeks)* pos/wks

9 Sep 72	MAYBE I KNOW *CBS 8218*	32 5

SEB *UK, male instrumentalist – keyboards – Sebastian Wronski (Singles: 1 Week)* pos/wks

18 Feb 95	SUGAR SHACK *React CDREACT 50*	61 1

SEBADOH *US, male vocal / instrumental group (Singles: 4 Weeks, Albums: 5 Weeks)* pos/wks

27 Jul 96	BEAUTY OF THE RIDE *Domino RUG 47CD*	74 1
30 Jan 99	FLAME *Domino RUG 80CD1*	30 3
8 May 93	BUBBLE AND SCRAPE *Domino WIGCD 4*	63 1
3 Sep 94	BAKESALE *Domino WIGCD 11*	40 2
31 Aug 96	HARMACY *Domino Recordings WIGCD 26*	38 1
6 Mar 99	THE SEBADOH *Domino Recordings WIGCD 57*	45 1

Jon SECADA *Cuba, male vocalist – Juan Secada (Singles: 42 Weeks, Albums: 16 Weeks)* pos/wks

18 Jul 92	●	JUST ANOTHER DAY *SBK SBK 35*	5 15
31 Oct 92		DO YOU BELIEVE IN US *SBK SBK 37*	30 4
6 Feb 93		ANGEL *SBK CDSBK 39*	23 5
17 Jul 93		DO YOU REALLY WANT ME *SBK CDSBK 41*	30 4
16 Oct 93		I'M FREE *SBK CDSBK 44*	50 2
14 May 94		IF YOU GO (re) *SBK CDSBK 51*	39 5
4 Feb 95		MENTAL PICTURE *SBK CDSBK 54*	44 2
16 Dec 95		IF I NEVER KNEW YOU (LOVE THEME FROM 'POCAHONTAS') *Walt Disney WD 7023C* [1]	51 4
14 Jun 97		TOO LATE, TOO SOON *SBK CDSBK 57*	43 1
5 Sep 92		JON SECADA *SBK SBKCD 19*	20 11
4 Jun 94		HEART SOUL AND A VOICE *SBK SBKCD 29*	17 5

[1] Jon Secada and Shanice

SECCHI featuring Orlando JOHNSON
Italy / US, male vocal / instrumental duo (Singles: 3 Weeks) pos/wks

4 May 91	I SAY YEAH *Epic 6568467*	46 3

Harry SECOMBE (see also The GOONS) *UK, male vocalist / comedian, b. 8 Sep 1921, d. 12 Apr 2001 (Singles: 35 Weeks, Albums: 62 Weeks)* pos/wks

9 Dec 55	ON WITH THE MOTLEY (VESTA LA GIUBBA) *Philips PB 523*	16 3
3 Oct 63	IF I RULED THE WORLD (re) *Philips BF 1261*	18 17

23 Feb 67	●	THIS IS MY SONG *Philips BF 1539*	2 15
31 Mar 62		SACRED SONGS *Philips RBL 7501*	16 1
18 Apr 64		HOW TO WIN AN ELECTION *Philips AL 3464* [1]	20 1
22 Apr 67	●	SECOMBE'S PERSONAL CHOICE *Philips BETS 707*	6 13
7 Aug 71		IF I RULED THE WORLD *Contour 6870 501*	17 20
16 Dec 78	●	20 SONGS OF JOY *Warwick WW 5052*	8 12
5 Dec 81		GOLDEN MEMORIES *Warwick WW 5107* [2]	46 5
13 Dec 86		HIGHWAY OF LIFE *Telstar STAR 2289*	45 5
30 Nov 91		YOURS SINCERELY *Philips 5107321*	46 5

[1] Harry Secombe, Peter Sellers and Spike Milligan [2] Harry Secombe and Moira Anderson

SECOND CITY SOUND
UK, male instrumental group (Singles: 8 Weeks) pos/wks

20 Jan 66	TCHAIKOVSKY ONE *Decca F 12310*	22 7
2 Apr 69	DREAM OF OLWEN *Major Minor MM 600*	43 1

SECOND IMAGE *UK, male vocal / instrumental group (Singles: 11 Weeks, Albums: 1 Week)* pos/wks

24 Jul 82	STAR *Polydor POSP 457*	60 2
2 Apr 83	BETTER TAKE TIME *Polydor POSP 565*	67 2
26 Nov 83	DON'T YOU *MCA 848*	68 2
11 Aug 84	SING AND SHOUT *MCA 882*	53 3
2 Feb 85	STARTING AGAIN *MCA 936*	65 2
30 Mar 85	STRANGE REFLECTIONS *MCA MCF 3255*	100 1

SECOND PHASE
US, male producer – Joey Beltram (Singles: 2 Weeks) pos/wks

21 Sep 91	MENTASM *R&S RSUK 2*	48 2

SECOND PROTOCOL
UK, male production duo (Singles: 2 Weeks) pos/wks

23 Sep 00	BASSLICK *East West EW 216CD*	58 2

SECOND SUN *See Paul VAN DYK*

SECRET AFFAIR *UK, male vocal / instrumental group (Singles: 34 Weeks, Albums: 15 Weeks)* pos/wks

1 Sep 79	TIME FOR ACTION *I-Spy SEE 1*	13 10
10 Nov 79	LET YOUR HEART DANCE *I-Spy SEE 3*	32 6
8 Mar 80	MY WORLD *I-Spy SEE 5*	16 9
23 Aug 80	SOUND OF CONFUSION *I-Spy SEE 8*	45 5
17 Oct 81	DO YOU KNOW *I-Spy SEE 10*	57 4
1 Dec 79	GLORY BOYS *I-Spy 1*	41 8
20 Sep 80	BEHIND CLOSED DOORS *I-Spy 2*	48 4
13 Mar 82	BUSINESS AS USUAL *I-Spy 3*	84 3

SECRET KNOWLEDGE
UK / US, male / female vocal / instrumental duo (Singles: 2 Weeks) pos/wks

27 Apr 96	LOVE ME NOW *Deconstruction 74321342432*	66 1
24 Aug 96	SUGAR DADDY *Deconstruction 74321400242*	75 1

SECRET LIFE
UK, male vocal / production group (Singles: 10 Weeks) pos/wks

12 Dec 92	AS ALWAYS *Cowboy 7RODEO 9*	45 4
7 Aug 93	LOVE SO STRONG *Cowboy RODEO 18CD*	38 2
7 May 94	SHE HOLDS THE KEY *Pulse 8 CDLOSE 58*	63 1
29 Oct 94	I WANT YOU *Pulse 8 CDLOSE 71*	70 1
28 Jan 95	LOVE SO STRONG (re-mix) *Pulse 8 CDLOSE 79*	37 2

SECRET MACHINES
US, male vocal / instrumental trio (Singles: 1 Week) pos/wks

7 Aug 04	NOWHERE AGAIN *Reprise W 648CD*	49 1

SECRETARY OF ENTERTAINMENT *See RAZE*

SECTION-X
France, male instrumental duo (Singles: 1 Week) pos/wks

8 Mar 97	ATLANTIS *Perfecto PERF 136*	42 1

Neil SEDAKA `229` `Top 500`

The man who put the 'Tra-La-La' into 1960s pop, b. 13 Mar 1939, New York, US. Ultra-commercial singer / songwriter / pianist who enjoyed two separate chart runs as an artist and wrote many hits for numerous other acts (Singles: 190 Weeks, Albums: 80 Weeks)

pos/wks

24 Apr 59 ●	I GO APE *RCA 1115*	9 13
13 Nov 59 ●	OH! CAROL *RCA 1152*	3 17
14 Apr 60 ●	STAIRWAY TO HEAVEN *RCA 1178*	8 15
1 Sep 60	YOU MEAN EVERYTHING TO ME *RCA 1198*	45 3
2 Feb 61 ●	CALENDAR GIRL *RCA 1220*	8 14
18 May 61 ●	LITTLE DEVIL *RCA 1236*	9 12
21 Dec 61 ●	HAPPY BIRTHDAY, SWEET SIXTEEN *RCA 1266*	3 18
19 Apr 62	KING OF CLOWNS *RCA 1282*	23 11
19 Jul 62 ●	BREAKING UP IS HARD TO DO *RCA 1298* ▲	7 16
22 Nov 62	NEXT DOOR TO AN ANGEL *RCA 1319*	29 4
30 May 63	LET'S GO STEADY AGAIN (re) *RCA 1343*	42 3
7 Oct 72	OH CAROL / BREAKING UP IS HARD TO DO / LITTLE DEVIL (re-issue) *RCA Maximillion 2259*	19 14
4 Nov 72	BEAUTIFUL YOU *RCA 2269*	43 3
24 Feb 73	THAT'S WHEN THE MUSIC TAKES ME *RCA 2310*	18 10
2 Jun 73	STANDING ON THE INSIDE *MGM 2006 267*	26 9
25 Aug 73	OUR LAST SONG TOGETHER *MGM 2006 307*	31 8
9 Feb 74	A LITTLE LOVIN' *Polydor 2058 434*	34 4
22 Jun 74	LAUGHTER IN THE RAIN *Polydor 2058 494* ▲	15 9
22 Mar 75	THE QUEEN OF 1964 *Polydor 2058 546*	35 5
1 Sep 73	THE TRA-LA DAYS ARE OVER *MGM 2315 248*	13 10
22 Jun 74	LAUGHTER IN THE RAIN *Polydor 2383 265*	17 10
23 Nov 74	LIVE AT THE ROYAL FESTIVAL HALL *Polydor 2383 299*	48 1
1 Mar 75	OVERNIGHT SUCCESS *Polydor 2442 131*	31 6
10 Jul 76 ●	LAUGHTER AND TEARS – THE BEST OF NEIL SEDAKA TODAY *Polydor 2383 399*	2 25
2 Nov 91 ●	TIMELESS – THE VERY BEST OF NEIL SEDAKA *Polydor 5114421*	10 16
4 Nov 95	CLASSICALLY SEDAKA *Vision VISCD 5*	23 9
19 Jun 99	THE VERY BEST OF NEIL SEDAKA *Universal Music TV 5646452*	33 3

Max SEDGLEY *UK, male producer (Singles: 3 Weeks)*

pos/wks

17 Jul 04	HAPPY *Sunday Best SBEST C14*	30 3

SEDUCTION *US, female vocal group (Singles: 1 Week)*

pos/wks

21 Apr 90	HEARTBEAT *Breakout USA 685*	75 1

The SEEKERS `120` `Top 500`

First Australian act to top the UK singles or albums charts: Judith Durham (v), Keith Potger (g), Bruce Woodley (g), Athol Guy (b). Their unique harmony vocals were displayed on many of their hits, which were penned and produced by Tom Springfield. Durham went solo in 1967, and Potger later went on to form The New Seekers. Best-selling single: 'The Carnival Is Over' 1,400,000 (Singles: 120 Weeks, Albums: 275 Weeks)

pos/wks

7 Jan 65 ★	I'LL NEVER FIND ANOTHER YOU *Columbia DB 7431*	1 23
15 Apr 65 ●	A WORLD OF OUR OWN *Columbia DB 7532*	3 18
28 Oct 65 ★	THE CARNIVAL IS OVER *Columbia DB 7711* ◆	1 17
24 Mar 66	SOMEDAY ONE DAY *Columbia DB 7867*	11 11
8 Sep 66 ●	WALK WITH ME *Columbia DB 8000*	10 12
24 Nov 66 ●	MORNINGTOWN RIDE *Columbia DB 8060*	2 15
23 Feb 67 ●	GEORGY GIRL *Columbia DB 8134*	3 11
20 Sep 67	WHEN WILL THE GOOD APPLES FALL *Columbia DB 8273*	11 12
13 Dec 67	EMERALD CITY *Columbia DB 8313*	50 1
3 Jul 65	A WORLD OF OUR OWN *Columbia 33SX 1722*	5 37
3 Jul 65	THE SEEKERS *Decca LK 4694*	16 1
19 Nov 66 ●	COME THE DAY *Columbia SX 6093*	2 67
25 Nov 67	SEEKERS – SEEN IN GREEN *Columbia SCX 6193*	15 10
14 Sep 68	LIVE AT THE TALK OF THE TOWN *Columbia SCX 6278*	2 29
16 Nov 68 ★	THE BEST OF THE SEEKERS *Columbia SCX 6268*	1 117
23 Apr 94 ●	A CARNIVAL OF HITS *EMI CDEMTV 83* `1`	7 14

`1` Judith Durham and The Seekers

SEELENLUFT featuring Michael SMITH *Switzerland, male producer (Beat Soler) and US, male rapper (Singles: 1 Week)*

pos/wks

4 Oct 03	MANILA *Back Yard BACK 10CSC 1*	70 1

Bob SEGER and the SILVER BULLET BAND *US, male vocal / instrumental group (Singles: 30 Weeks, Albums: 52 Weeks)*

pos/wks

30 Sep 78	HOLLYWOOD NIGHTS *Capitol CL 16004*	42 6
3 Feb 79	WE'VE GOT TONITE *Capitol CL 16028*	41 6

24 Oct 81	HOLLYWOOD NIGHTS *Capitol CL 223*	49 3
6 Feb 82	WE'VE GOT TONITE *Capitol CL 235*	60 4
9 Apr 83	EVEN NOW *Capitol CL 284*	73 2
28 Jan 95	WE'VE GOT TONIGHT (re-issue) *Capitol CDCL 734*	22 5
29 Apr 95	NIGHT MOVES *Capitol CDCL 741*	45 2
29 Jul 95	HOLLYWOOD NIGHTS (re-issue) *Capitol CDCL 749*	52 1
10 Feb 96	LOCK AND LOAD *Parlophone CDCL 765*	57 1
3 Jun 78	STRANGER IN TOWN *Capitol EAST 11698*	31 6
15 Mar 80	AGAINST THE WIND *Capitol EAST 12041* ▲	26 6
26 Sep 81	NINE TONIGHT *Capitol ESTSP 23*	24 10
8 Jan 83	THE DISTANCE *Capitol EST 12254*	45 10
26 Apr 86	LIKE A ROCK *Capitol EST 2011*	35 6
21 Sep 91	THE FIRE INSIDE *Capitol EST 2149*	54 2
18 Feb 95 ●	GREATEST HITS *Capitol CDEST 2241*	6 12

Capitol CL 223 and CL 235 were live versions of earlier studio hits

Shea SEGER *US, female vocalist (Singles: 1 Week)*

pos/wks

5 May 01	CLUTCH *RCA 74321828142*	47 1

SEIKO and Donnie WAHLBERG (see also NEW KIDS ON THE BLOCK) *Japan / US, female / male vocal duo (Singles: 5 Weeks)*

pos/wks

18 Aug 90	THE RIGHT COMBINATION *Epic 656203 7*	44 5

SELECTER *UK, male / female vocal / instrumental group (Singles: 28 Weeks, Albums: 17 Weeks)*

pos/wks

13 Oct 79 ●	ON MY RADIO *2 Tone CHSTT 4*	8 9
2 Feb 80	THREE MINUTE HERO *2 Tone CHSTT 8*	16 6
29 Mar 80	MISSING WORDS *2 Tone CHSTT 10*	23 8
23 Aug 80	THE WHISPER *Chrysalis CHSS 1*	36 5
23 Feb 80 ●	TOO MUCH PRESSURE *2 Tone CDLTT 5002*	5 13
7 Mar 81	CELEBRATE THE BULLET *Chrysalis CHR 1306*	41 4

SELENA vs X MEN *UK, female vocalist and male production duo (Singles: 1 Week)*

pos/wks

14 Jul 01	GIVE IT UP *Go Beat BOBCD 40*	61 1

SELFISH CUNT *UK, male vocal / instrumental duo (1 Week)*

pos/wks

17 Jul 04	AUTHORITY CONFRONTATION *Horseglue UHU 008*	66 1

Peter SELLERS `477` `Top 500` *Comedian, character actor and movie star who first came to prominence through the Goons radio shows, b. Richard Sellers, 8 Sep 1925, Southsea, Hampshire, d. 24 Jul 1980 (Singles: 39 Weeks, Albums: 113 Weeks)*

pos/wks

2 Aug 57	ANY OLD IRON (re) *Parlophone R 4337* `1`	17 11
10 Nov 60 ●	GOODNESS GRACIOUS ME *Parlophone R 4702* `2`	4 14
12 Jan 61	BANGERS AND MASH *Parlophone R 4724* `2`	22 5
23 Dec 65	A HARD DAY'S NIGHT *Parlophone R 5393*	14 7
27 Nov 93	A HARD DAY'S NIGHT (re-issue) *EMI CDEMS 293*	52 2
14 Feb 59 ●	THE BEST OF SELLERS *Parlophone PMD 1069*	3 47
12 Dec 59 ●	SONGS FOR SWINGING SELLERS *Parlophone PMC 1111*	3 37
3 Dec 60 ●	PETER AND SOPHIA *Parlophone PMC 1131* `1`	5 18
28 Sep 63	FOOL BRITANNIA *Ember CEL 902* `2`	10 10
18 Apr 64	HOW TO WIN AN ELECTION *Philips AL 3464* `3`	20 1

`1` Peter Sellers presents Mate's Skiffle Group featuring Fred Spoons E.P.N.S. `2` Peter Sellers and Sophia Loren `1` Peter Sellers and Sophia Loren `2` Anthony Newley, Peter Sellers, Joan Collins `3` Harry Secombe, Peter Sellers, Spike Milligan

Michael SEMBELLO *US, male vocalist (Singles: 6 Weeks)*

pos/wks

20 Aug 83	MANIAC *Casablanca CAN 1017* ▲	43 6

SEMISONIC *US, male vocal / instrumental group (Singles: 20 Weeks, Albums: 41 Weeks)*

pos/wks

10 Jul 99	SECRET SMILE *MCA MCSTD 40210*	13 11
6 Nov 99	CLOSING TIME *MCA MCSTD 40221*	25 5
1 Apr 00	SINGING IN MY SLEEP *MCA MCSTD 40227*	39 2
3 Mar 01	CHEMISTRY *MCA MCSTD 40248*	35 2
24 Jul 99	FEELING STRANGELY FINE *MCA MCD 11733*	16 37
17 Mar 01	ALL ABOUT CHEMISTRY *MCA 1125012*	13 4

SEMPRINI *UK, male pianist – Fernando Riccardo Alberto Semprini, b. 1908, d. 19 Jan 1990, and orchestra (Singles: 8 Weeks)*

pos/wks

16 Mar 61	MAIN THEME FROM 'EXODUS' *HMV POP 842*	25 8

The SENSATIONAL ALEX HARVEY BAND
UK, male vocal / instrumental group – leader b. 5 Feb 1935,
d. 4 Feb 1982 (Singles: 25 Weeks, Albums: 42 Weeks) pos/wks

26 Jul 75 ●	DELILAH *Vertigo ALEX 001*	**7** 7
22 Nov 75	GAMBLIN' BAR ROOM BLUES *Vertigo ALEX 002*	**38** 8
19 Jun 76	THE BOSTON TEA PARTY *Mountain TOP 12*	**13** 10
26 Oct 74	THE IMPOSSIBLE DREAM *Vertigo 6360 112*	**16** 4
10 May 75 ●	TOMORROW BELONGS TO ME *Vertigo 9102 003*	**9** 10
23 Aug 75	NEXT *Vertigo 6360 103*	**37** 5
27 Sep 75	LIVE *Vertigo 6360 122*	**14** 7
10 Apr 76	PENTHOUSE TAPES *Vertigo 9102 007*	**14** 7
31 Jul 76	SAHB STORIES *Mountain TOPS 112*	**11** 9

SENSELESS THINGS *UK, male vocal /*
instrumental group (Singles: 19 Weeks, Albums: 2 Weeks) pos/wks

22 Jun 91	EVERYBODY'S GONE *Epic 6569807*	**73** 1
28 Sep 91	GOT IT AT THE DELMAR *Epic 6574497*	**50** 3
11 Jan 92	EASY TO SMILE *Epic 6576957*	**18** 4
11 Apr 92	HOLD IT DOWN *Epic 6579267*	**19** 4
5 Dec 92	HOMOPHOBIC ASSHOLE *Epic 6588337*	**52** 2
13 Feb 93	PRIMARY INSTINCT *Epic 6589402*	**41** 2
12 Jun 93	TOO MUCH KISSING *Epic 6592502*	**69** 1
5 Nov 94	CHRISTINE KEELER *Epic 6609572*	**56** 1
28 Jan 95	SOMETHING TO MISS *Epic 6611162*	**57** 1
26 Oct 91	THE FIRST OF TOO MANY *Epic 4691571*	**66** 1
13 Mar 93	EMPIRE OF THE SENSELESS *Epic 4735252*	**37** 1

SENSER *UK, male / female vocal /*
instrumental group (Singles: 5 Weeks, Albums: 6 Weeks) pos/wks

25 Sep 93	THE KEY *Ultimate TOPP 019CD*	**47** 1
19 Mar 94	SWITCH *Ultimate TOPP 022CD*	**39** 2
23 Jul 94	AGE OF PANIC *Ultimate TOPP 027CD*	**52** 1
17 Aug 96	CHARMING DEMONS *Ultimate TOPP 045CD*	**42** 1
7 May 94 ●	STACKED UP *Ultimate TOPPCD 008*	**4** 5
2 May 98	ASYLUM *Ultimate TOPPCD 064*	**73** 1

Nick SENTIENCE See BK

SEPULTURA *Brazil, male vocal /*
instrumental group (Singles: 12 Weeks, Albums: 12 Weeks) pos/wks

2 Oct 93	TERRITORY *Roadrunner RR 23823*	**66** 2
26 Feb 94	REFUSE-RESIST *Roadrunner RR 23773*	**51** 2
4 Jun 94	SLAVE NEW WORLD *Roadrunner RR 23745*	**46** 2
24 Feb 96	ROOTS BLOODY ROOTS *Roadrunner RR 23205*	**19** 2
17 Aug 96	RATAMAHATTA *Roadrunner RR 23145*	**23** 2
14 Dec 96	ATTITUDE *Roadrunner RR 22995*	**46** 2
6 Apr 91	ARISE *Roadracer RO 93281*	**40** 2
23 Oct 93	CHAOS A.D. *Roadrunner RR 90002*	**11** 4
9 Mar 96 ●	ROOTS *Roadrunner RR 89002*	**4** 5
17 Oct 98	AGAINST *Roadrunner RR 87002*	**40** 1

SERAFIN *UK, male vocal / instrumental group (Singles: 2 Weeks)* pos/wks

15 Mar 03	THINGS FALL APART *Taste Media TMCDS 5003*	**49** 1
16 Aug 03	DAY BY DAY *Taste Media TMCDS 5006*	**49** 1

SERAPHIM SUITE (see also Jeremy HEALY and AMOS; Mica PARIS)
UK, male / female production / vocal trio (Singles: 2 Weeks) pos/wks

27 Mar 04	HEART *Inferno CDFERN 61*	**45** 2

SERIAL DIVA
UK, male / female production group (Singles: 3 Weeks) pos/wks

18 Jan 97	KEEP HOPE ALIVE *Sound of Ministry SOMCD 26*	**57** 1
15 May 99	PEARL RIVER *Low Sense SENSECD 24* [1]	**32** 2

[1] Three 'N One presents Johnny Shaker featuring Serial Diva

SERIOUS DANGER
UK, male producer – Richard Phillips (Singles: 4 Weeks) pos/wks

20 Dec 97	DEEPER *Fresh FRSHD 68*	**40** 3
2 May 98	HIGH NOON *Fresh FRSHD 69*	**54** 1

SERIOUS INTENTION
US, male vocal / instrumental group (Singles: 6 Weeks) pos/wks

16 Nov 85	YOU DON'T KNOW (OH-OH-OH) *Important TAN 8*	**75** 1
5 Apr 86	SERIOUS *Pow Wow LON 93*	**51** 5

SERIOUS ROPE
UK, male / female vocal / production group (Singles: 3 Weeks) pos/wks

22 May 93	HAPPINESS *Rumour RUMACD 64* [1]	**54** 2
1 Oct 94	HAPPINESS – YOU MAKE ME HAPPY (re-mix)	
	Mercury MERCD 407	**70** 1

[1] Serious Rope presents Sharon Dee Clarke

Erick SERMON (see also EPMD)
US, male rapper (Singles: 8 Weeks) pos/wks

6 Oct 01	MUSIC *Polydor 4976222* [1]	**36** 2
11 Jan 03	REACT *J 74321988492* [2]	**14** 5
19 Apr 03	LOVE IZ *J 82876510971*	**72** 1

[1] Erick Sermon featuring Marvin Gaye [2] Erick Sermon featuring Redman

Eric SERRA *France, male composer (Albums: 2 Weeks)* pos/wks

28 Jun 97	THE FIFTH ELEMENT (FILM SOUNDTRACK) *Virgin CDVIRX 63*	**58** 2

SERTAB
Turkey, female vocalist – Sertab Erener (Singles: 1 Week) pos/wks

21 Jun 03	EVERY WAY THAT I CAN *Columbia 6739621*	**72** 1

SET THE TONE
UK, male vocal / instrumental group (Singles: 4 Weeks) pos/wks

22 Jan 83	DANCE SUCKER *Island WIP 6836*	**62** 2
26 Mar 83	RAP YOUR LOVE *Island IS 110*	**67** 2

The SETTLERS
UK, male / female vocal / instrumental group (Singles: 5 Weeks) pos/wks

16 Oct 71	THE LIGHTNING TREE *York SYK 505*	**36** 5

Brian SETZER ORCHESTRA (see also The STRAY CATS)
US, male vocal / instrumental group (Singles: 3 Weeks) pos/wks

3 Apr 99	JUMP JIVE AN' WAIL *Interscope IND 95601*	**34** 3

Taja SEVELLE
US, female vocalist (Singles: 13 Weeks, Albums: 4 Weeks) pos/wks

20 Feb 88 ●	LOVE IS CONTAGIOUS *Paisley Park W 8257*	**7** 9
14 May 88	WOULDN'T YOU LOVE TO LOVE ME? *Paisley Park W 8127*	**59** 4
26 Mar 88	TAJA SEVELLE *Paisley Park WX 165*	**48** 4

702 *US, female vocal group (Singles: 10 Weeks)* pos/wks

14 Dec 96	STEELO *Motown 8606072*	**41** 2
29 Nov 97	NO DOUBT *Motown 8607052*	**59** 1
7 Aug 99	WHERE MY GIRLS AT? *Motown TMGCD 1500*	**22** 4
27 Nov 99	YOU DON'T KNOW *Motown TMGCD 1502*	**36** 3

740 BOYZ *US, male vocal / instrumental*
duo – Winston and Eddie Rosa (Singles: 1 Week) pos/wks

4 Nov 95	SHIMMY SHAKE *MCA MCSTD 40002*	**54** 1

SEVEN GRAND HOUSING AUTHORITY
UK, male producer – Terence Parker (Singles: 1 Week) pos/wks

23 Oct 93	THE QUESTION *Olympic ELYCD 010*	**70** 1

7669 *US, female rap group (Singles: 1 Week)* pos/wks

18 Jun 94	JOY *Motown TMGCD 1429*	**60** 1

7TH HEAVEN
UK, male vocal group (Singles: 5 Weeks) pos/wks

14 Sep 85	HOT FUN *Mercury MER 199*	**47** 5

SÉVERINE
France, female vocalist – Josiane Grizeau (Singles: 11 Weeks) pos/wks

24 Apr 71 ●	UN BANC, UN ARBRE, UNE RUE *Philips 6009 135*	**9** 11

David SEVILLE (see also The CHIPMUNKS; ALFI and HARRY)
US, male vocalist – Ross Bagdasarian,
b. 27 Jan 1919, d. 16 Jan 1972 (Singles: 6 Weeks) pos/wks

23 May 58	WITCH DOCTOR *London HLU 8619* ▲	**11** 6

Janette SEWELL *See* DOUBLE TROUBLE

SEX CLUB featuring BROWN SUGAR
US, male / female vocal / instrumental duo (Singles: 1 Week) pos/wks

28 Jan 95	**BIG DICK MAN** *Club Tools CLU 60775*	67	1

SEX-O-LETTES *See* DISCO TEX & the SEX-O-LETTES

SEX-O-SONIQUE (see also FULL INTENTION;
HUSTLERS CONVENTION featuring Dave LAUDAT and Ondrea
DUVERNEY; Michael GRAY; RONALDO'S REVENGE) *UK, male production /
instrumental duo – Mike Gray and Jon Pearn (Singles: 3 Weeks)* pos/wks

6 Dec 97	**I THOUGHT IT WAS YOU** *ffrr FCD 321*	32	3

SEX PISTOLS ⟨ 319 | Top 500 ⟩ (see also PUBLIC IMAGE LIMITED)
*Provocative and influential quartet who popularised punk. Formed 1975
in London, UK, split 1978: Johnny Rotten (v), Steve Jones (g), Paul Cook (d)
and Glen Matlock (b) – replaced 1977 by Sid Vicious, b. John Ritchie, 10 May
1957, d. 2 Feb 1979). Notorious group reunited for brief and profitable tours
in 1996 and 2003. Rotten (John Lydon) is now a popular TV personality
(Singles: 91 Weeks, Albums: 116 Weeks)* pos/wks

18 Dec 76	**ANARCHY IN THE UK** *EMI 2566*	38	4
4 Jun 77 ●	**GOD SAVE THE QUEEN** *Virgin VS 181*	2	9
9 Jul 77 ●	**PRETTY VACANT** *Virgin VS 184*	6	8
22 Oct 77 ●	**HOLIDAYS IN THE SUN** *Virgin VS 191*	8	6
8 Jul 78 ●	**NO ONE IS INNOCENT (A PUNK PRAYER BY RONALD** **BIGGS) / MY WAY** *Virgin VS 220* [1]	7	10
3 Mar 79 ●	**SOMETHING ELSE / FRIGGIN' IN THE RIGGIN'** *Virgin VS 240* [2]	3	12
7 Apr 79 ●	**SILLY THING** *Virgin VS 256*	6	8
30 Jun 79 ●	**C'MON EVERYBODY** *Virgin VS 272* [3]	3	9
13 Oct 79	**THE GREAT ROCK 'N' ROLL SWINDLE** *Virgin VS 290*	21	6
14 Jun 80	**(I'M NOT YOUR) STEPPING STONE** *Virgin VS 339*	21	8
3 Oct 92	**ANARCHY IN THE UK (re-issue)** *Virgin VS 1431*	33	3
5 Dec 92	**PRETTY VACANT (re-issue)** *Virgin VS 1448*	56	2
27 Jul 96	**PRETTY VACANT (LIVE)** *Virgin America VUSCD 113*	18	3
8 Jun 02	**GOD SAVE THE QUEEN (re-issue)** *Virgin VSCDT 1832*	15	3
12 Nov 77 ★	**NEVER MIND THE BOLLOCKS HERE'S THE SEX PISTOLS** *Virgin V 2086* ■	1	58
10 Mar 79 ●	**THE GREAT ROCK 'N' ROLL SWINDLE (FILM SOUNDTRACK)** *Virgin VD 2410*	7	33
11 Aug 79 ●	**SOME PRODUCT – CARRI ON SEX PISTOLS** *Virgin VR 2*	6	10
16 Feb 80	**FLOGGING A DEAD HORSE** *Virgin V 2142*	23	6
17 Oct 92 ●	**KISS THIS** *Virgin CDV 2702*	10	4
10 Aug 96	**FILTHY LUCRE LIVE** *Virgin CDVUS 116*	26	2
15 Jun 02	**JUBILEE** *Virgin CDV 2961*	29	3

[1] Uncredited vocal by Ronald Biggs [2] Sex Pistols: vocals, Sid Vicious /
Sex Pistols: vocals, Steve Jones [3] Sex Pistols: vocals, Sid Vicious

*The listed flip side of 'Silly Thing' was 'Who Killed Bambi' by Ten Pole Tudor. The
listed flip side of 'The Great Rock 'n' Roll Swindle' was 'Rock Around the Clock',
also by Ten Pole Tudor*

Ron SEXSMITH *See* Alex CUBA BAND featuring Ron SEXSMITH

Denny SEYTON and the SABRES
UK, male vocal / instrumental group (Singles: 1 Week) pos/wks

17 Sep 64	**THE WAY YOU LOOK TONIGHT** *Mercury MF 824*	48	1

SHABOOM
UK, male instrumental / production group (Singles: 1 Week) pos/wks

31 Jul 99	**SWEET SENSATION** *WEA WEA 218CD1*	64	1

SHACK *UK, male vocal / instrumental*
group (Singles: 4 Weeks, Albums: 3 Weeks) pos/wks

26 Jun 99	**COMEDY** *London LONCD 427*	44	1
14 Aug 99	**NATALIE'S PARTY** *London LONCD 436*	63	1
11 Mar 00	**OSCAR** *London LONCD 445*	67	1
4 Oct 03	**BYRDS TURN TO STONE** *North Country NCCDA 002*	63	1
3 Jul 99	**H.M.S. FABLE** *London 5561132*	25	2
23 Aug 03	**... HERE'S TOM WITH THE WEATHER** *North Country NCCD 002*	.55	1

SHADES *US, female vocal group (Singles: 3 Weeks)* pos/wks

12 Apr 97	**MR BIG STUFF** *Motown 5736572* [1]	31	2
20 Sep 97	**SERENADE** *Motown 8606892*	75	1

[1] Queen Latifah, Shades and Free

SHADES OF LOVE
US, male instrumental / production duo (Singles: 1 Week) pos/wks

22 Apr 95	**KEEP IN TOUCH (BODY TO BODY)** *Vicious Muzik MUZCD 102* **64**	1

SHADES OF RHYTHM *UK, male instrumental /
production group (Singles: 25 Weeks, Albums: 3 Weeks)* pos/wks

2 Feb 91	**HOMICIDE / EXORCIST** *ZTT ZANG 13*	53	3
13 Apr 91	**SWEET SENSATION** *ZTT ZANG 18*	54	4
20 Jul 91	**THE SOUND OF EDEN** *ZTT ZANG 22*	35	5
30 Nov 91	**EXTACY** *ZTT ZANG 24*	16	7
20 Feb 93	**SWEET REVIVAL (KEEP IT COMIN')** *ZTT ZANG 40CD*	61	1
11 Sep 93	**SOUND OF EDEN (re-issue)** *ZTT ZANG 44CD*	37	3
5 Nov 94	**THE WANDERING DRAGON** *Public Demand PPDCD 5*	55	1
21 Jun 97	**PSYCHO BASE** *Coalition CRUM 002CD*	57	1
17 Aug 91	**SHADES** *ZTT ZTT 8*	51	3

The SHADOWS ⟨ 7 | Top 500 ⟩
(see also Jet HARRIS and Tony MEEHAN; MARVIN, WELCH and FARRAR)
*Headliners for five decades until their final gig in June 2004 and Britain's
most successful instrumental group: Hank Marvin (g), b. Brian Rankin, 28 Oct
1941, Newcastle-upon-Tyne, Bruce Welch OBE (g), b. Bruce Cripps, 2 Nov
1941, Bognor Regis, Terence 'Jet' Harris (b), b. Terence Hawkins, 6 Jul 1939,
London and Tony Meehan (d), b. Daniel Meehan, 2 Mar 1943, London.
Bespectacled Marvin and Welch, who started together in The Railroaders
skiffle group, first recorded with The Five Chesternuts (1958) before joining
Cliff Richard's backing band, The Drifters. The group (with the above line-up)
released its first single, 'Feelin' Fine', in early 1959 and later replaced
Meehan with drummer Brian Bennett OBE. After another couple of
unsuccessful releases and a name change, they started a staggering run of
successive hit singles and albums and clocked up more weeks on the 60s EP
chart than any other act. They were Britain's most influential and imitated act
before The Beatles and the 'Shadows walk' (which they say they borrowed
from R&B band The Treniers) was aped by hundreds of UK groups. They won
countless awards during the 1960s and were named the world's third most
successful recording act of 1963 (behind Cliff and Elvis) by Billboard. In
addition, they were the first group to top the UK albums chart, a feat they
managed before Cliff, and were the first to have a 40 year span of hit albums
(Singles: 770 Weeks, Albums: 808 Weeks)* pos/wks

12 Sep 58 ●	**MOVE IT!** *Columbia DB 4178* [1]	2	17
21 Nov 58 ●	**HIGH CLASS BABY** *Columbia DB 4203* [1]	7	10
30 Jan 59	**LIVIN' LOVIN' DOLL** *Columbia DB 4249* [1]	20	6
8 May 59 ●	**MEAN STREAK** *Columbia DB 4290 (A)* [1]	10	9
15 May 59	**NEVER MIND** *Columbia DB 4290 (B)* [1]	21	2
10 Jul 59 ★	**LIVING DOLL (2re)** *Columbia DB 4306* [1]	1	23
9 Oct 59 ★	**TRAVELLIN' LIGHT** *Columbia DB 4351 (B)* [2]	1	17
9 Oct 59	**DYNAMITE (re)** *Columbia DB 4351* [2]	16	4
15 Jan 60	**EXPRESSO BONGO (EP)** *Columbia SEG 7971* [2]	14	7
22 Jan 60 ●	**A VOICE IN THE WILDERNESS (re)** *Columbia DB 4398* [2]	2	16
24 Mar 60 ●	**FALL IN LOVE WITH YOU** *Columbia DB 4431* [2]	2	15
30 Jun 60 ●	**PLEASE DON'T TEASE** *Columbia 4479* [2]	1	18
21 Jul 60 ★	**APACHE** *Columbia DB 4484*	1	21
22 Sep 60 ●	**NINE TIMES OUT OF TEN** *Columbia DB 4506* [2]	3	14
10 Nov 60 ●	**MAN OF MYSTERY / THE STRANGER** *Columbia DB 4530*	5	15
1 Dec 60 ★	**I LOVE YOU** *Columbia DB 4547* [2]	1	16
9 Feb 61 ●	**F.B.I.** *Columbia DB 4580*	6	19
2 Mar 61 ●	**THEME FOR A DREAM** *Columbia DB 4593* [2]	3	14
30 Mar 61 ●	**GEE WHIZ IT'S YOU** *Columbia DC 756* [2]	4	14
11 May 61 ●	**THE FRIGHTENED CITY** *Columbia DB 4637* [2]	3	20
22 Jun 61 ●	**A GIRL LIKE YOU** *Columbia DB 4667* [2]	3	14
7 Sep 61 ★	**KON-TIKI (re)** *Columbia DB 4698* [2]	1	12
16 Nov 61 ●	**THE SAVAGE** *Columbia DB 4726*	10	8
11 Jan 62 ★	**THE YOUNG ONES** *Columbia DB 4761* [2] ◆ ■	1	21
1 Mar 62 ★	**WONDERFUL LAND** *Columbia DB 4790*	1	19
10 May 62 ●	**I'M LOOKING OUT THE WINDOW / DO YOU WANT TO DANCE** *Columbia DB 4828* [3]	2	17
2 Aug 62 ●	**GUITAR TANGO** *Columbia DB 4870*	4	15
6 Sep 62 ●	**IT'LL BE ME** *Columbia DB 4886* [2]	2	12
6 Dec 62 ★	**THE NEXT TIME / BACHELOR BOY** *Columbia DB 4950* [2]	1	18
13 Dec 62 ★	**DANCE ON!** *Columbia DB 4948*	1	15
21 Feb 63 ★	**SUMMER HOLIDAY** *Columbia DB 4977* [2]	1	18
7 Mar 63 ★	**FOOT TAPPER** *Columbia DB 4984*	1	16
9 May 63 ●	**LUCKY LIPS** *Columbia DB 7034* [2]	4	15
6 Jun 63 ●	**ATLANTIS** *Columbia DB 7047*	2	17
19 Sep 63 ●	**SHINDIG** *Columbia DB 7106*	6	12
7 Nov 63 ●	**DON'T TALK TO HIM (re)** *Columbia DB 7150* [2]	2	14
5 Dec 63	**GERONIMO** *Columbia DB 7163*	11	12

Date	Title	pos	wks
6 Feb 64 ●	I'M THE LONELY ONE *Columbia DB 7203* [2]	8	10
5 Mar 64	THEME FOR YOUNG LOVERS *Columbia DB 7231*	12	10
7 May 64 ●	THE RISE AND FALL OF FLINGEL BUNT *Columbia DB 7261*	5	14
2 Jul 64 ●	ON THE BEACH *Columbia DB 7305*	7	13
3 Sep 64	RHYTHM AND GREENS *Columbia DB 7342*	22	7
3 Dec 64	GENIE WITH THE LIGHT BROWN LAMP *Columbia DB 7416*	17	10
10 Dec 64 ●	I COULD EASILY FALL *Columbia DB 7420* [2]	6	11
11 Feb 65	MARY ANNE *Columbia DB 7476*	17	10
10 Jun 65	STINGRAY *Columbia DB 7588*	19	7
5 Aug 65 ●	DON'T MAKE MY BABY BLUE *Columbia DB 7650*	10	10
19 Aug 65	THE TIME IN BETWEEN *Columbia DB 7660* [2]	22	8
25 Nov 65	THE WAR LORD *Columbia DB 7769*	18	9
17 Mar 66	I MET A GIRL *Columbia DB 7853*	22	5
24 Mar 66	BLUE TURNS TO GREY *Columbia DB 7866* [2]	15	9
7 Jul 66	A PLACE IN THE SUN *Columbia DB 7952*	24	6
13 Oct 66 ●	TIME DRAGS BY *Columbia DB 8017* [2]	10	11
3 Nov 66	THE DREAMS I DREAM *Columbia DB 8034*	42	6
15 Dec 66 ●	IN THE COUNTRY *Columbia DB 8094* [2]	6	10
13 Apr 67	MAROC 7 *Columbia DB 8170*	24	8
27 Nov 68	DON'T FORGET TO CATCH ME *Columbia DB 8503* [2]	21	10
8 Mar 75	LET ME BE THE ONE *EMI 2269*	12	9
16 Dec 78 ●	DON'T CRY FOR ME ARGENTINA *EMI 2890*	5	14
28 Apr 79 ●	THEME FROM 'THE DEER HUNTER' (CAVATINA) *EMI 2939*	9	14
26 Jan 80	RIDERS IN THE SKY *EMI 5027*	12	12
23 Aug 80	EQUINOXE (PART V) *EMI 5072*	50	3
2 May 81	THE THIRD MAN *Polydor POSP 255*	44	4
18 Apr 59 ●	CLIFF *Columbia 33SX 1147* [1]	4	31
14 Nov 59 ●	CLIFF SINGS *Columbia 33SX 1192* [2]	2	36
15 Oct 60 ●	ME AND MY SHADOWS *Columbia 33SX 1261* [2]	2	23
16 Sep 61 ★	THE SHADOWS *Columbia 33SX 1374*	1	57
21 Oct 61 ★	21 TODAY *Columbia 33SX 1368* [3]	1	16
23 Dec 61 ★	THE YOUNG ONES (FILM SOUNDTRACK) *Columbia 33SX 1384* [4]	1	42
29 Sep 62 ●	32 MINUTES AND 17 SECONDS *Columbia 33SX 1431* [2]	3	21
13 Oct 62 ★	OUT OF THE SHADOWS *Columbia 33SX 1458*	1	38
26 Jan 63 ★	SUMMER HOLIDAY (FILM SOUNDTRACK) *Columbia 33SX 1472* [2]	1	36
22 Jun 63 ●	GREATEST HITS *Columbia 33SX 1522*	2	49
13 Jul 63 ●	CLIFF'S HIT ALBUM *Columbia 33SX 1512* [2]	2	19
28 Sep 63 ●	WHEN IN SPAIN *Columbia 33SX 1541* [2]	8	10
9 May 64 ●	DANCE WITH THE SHADOWS *Columbia 33SX 1619*	2	27
11 Jul 64 ●	WONDERFUL LIFE (FILM SOUNDTRACK) *Columbia 33SX 1628* [2]	2	23
9 Jan 65	HITS FROM ALADDIN AND HIS WONDERFUL LAMP (PANTOMIME) *Columbia 33SX 1676* [2]	13	5
17 Apr 65 ●	CLIFF RICHARD *Columbia 33SX 1709* [5]	9	5
17 Jul 65 ●	THE SOUND OF THE SHADOWS *Columbia 33SX 1736*	4	17
21 May 66 ●	SHADOW MUSIC *Columbia SX 6041*	5	17
17 Dec 66 ●	FINDERS KEEPERS (FILM SOUNDTRACK) *Columbia SX 6079*	6	18
7 Jan 67	CINDERELLA (PANTOMIME) *Columbia 33SX 6103* [2]	30	6
15 Jul 67 ●	JIGSAW *Columbia SCX 6148*	8	16
16 Nov 68	ESTABLISHED 1958 *Columbia SCX 6282* [2]	30	4
24 Oct 70	SHADES OF ROCK *Columbia SCX 6420*	30	4
13 Apr 74	ROCKIN' WITH CURLY LEADS *EMI EMA 762*	45	1
11 May 74	GREATEST HITS (re-issue) *Columbia SCX 1522*	48	6
29 Mar 75	SPECS APPEAL *EMI EMC 3066*	30	5
12 Feb 77 ★	20 GOLDEN GREATS *EMI EMTV 3*	1	43
17 Feb 79 ●	THANK YOU VERY MUCH – REUNION CONCERT AT THE LONDON PALLADIUM *EMI EMTV 15* [2]	5	12
15 Sep 79 ★	STRING OF HITS *EMI EMC 3310*	1	43
26 Jul 80	ANOTHER STRING OF HITS *EMI EMC 3339*	16	8
13 Sep 80	CHANGE OF ADDRESS *Polydor 2442 179*	17	6
19 Sep 81	HITS RIGHT UP YOUR STREET *Polydor POLD 5046*	15	16
25 Sep 82	LIFE IN THE JUNGLE / LIVE AT ABBEY ROAD *Polydor SHADS 1*	24	6
22 Oct 83	XXV *Polydor POLD 5120*	34	6
14 Jul 84	20 ORIGINAL GREATS *EMI CRS 1* [2]	43	6
17 Nov 84	GUARDIAN ANGEL *Polydor POLD 5169*	98	1
24 May 86 ●	MOONLIGHT SHADOWS *Polydor PROLP 8*	6	19
24 Oct 87	SIMPLY SHADOWS *Polydor SHAD 1*	11	17
20 May 89	STEPPIN' TO THE SHADOWS *Polydor SHAD 30*	11	9
16 Dec 89	AT THEIR VERY BEST *Polydor 8415201*	12	9
13 Oct 90 ●	REFLECTION *Roll Over 8471201*	5	15
16 Nov 91	THEMES AND DREAMS *Polydor 5113741*	21	11
15 May 93	SHADOWS IN THE NIGHT – 16 CLASSIC TRACKS *PolyGram TV 8437982*	22	4
22 Oct 94	THE BEST OF HANK MARVIN AND THE SHADOWS *PolyGram TV 5238212* [6]	19	11

Date	Title	pos	wks
22 Nov 97	HANK MARVIN AND THE SHADOWS PLAY THE MUSIC OF ANDREW LLOYD WEBBER AND TIM RICE *PolyGram TV 5394792* [6]	41	6
14 Nov 98	THE VERY BEST OF HANK MARVIN & THE SHADOWS – THE FIRST 40 YEARS *PolyGram TV 5592112* [6]	56	5
12 Aug 00	50 GOLDEN GREATS *EMI 5275862*	35	3
8 May 04 ●	LIFE STORY – THE VERY BEST OF THE SHADOWS *Universal TV 9817819*	7	10

[1] Cliff Richard and The Drifters [2] Cliff Richard and The Shadows [3] Cliff Richard with the Norrie Paramor Orchestra / Cliff Richard / The Shadows [1] Cliff Richard and The Drifters [2] Cliff Richard and The Shadows [3] Cliff Richard, The Shadows and Norrie Paramor and his Orchestra [4] Cliff Richard – The Shadows with Grazina Frame [5] Cliff Richard with The Shadows [6] Hank Marvin and The Shadows

All The Shadows' hits without Cliff Richard were instrumentals except for 'Mary Anne', 'Don't Make My Baby Blue', 'I Met a Girl', 'The Dreams I Dream' and 'Let Me Be the One'. Tracks on Expresso Bongo (EP): Love / A Voice in the Wilderness / The Shrine on the Second Floor / Bongo Blues. Last track featured The Shadows only. Only albums where The Shadows are credited in full alongside Cliff Richard, as the named act, on the record sleeve are included where associations with Cliff Richard are concerned. They did collaborate on a number of other albums but without this kind of billing.

SHAFT
UK, male producer – Mark Pritchard (Singles: 9 Weeks)   pos/wks

Date	Title	pos	wks
21 Dec 91 ●	ROOBARB AND CUSTARD *Ffrreedom TAB 100*	7	8
25 Jul 92	MONKEY *Ffrreedom TAB 114*	61	1

SHAFT (see also DA MUTTZ) *UK, male production duo – Elliot Ireland and Alex Rizzo (Singles: 19 Weeks)*   pos/wks

Date	Title	pos	wks
4 Sep 99 ●	(MUCHO MAMBO) SWAY *Wonderboy WBOYD 015*	2	12
20 May 00	MAMBO ITALIANO *Wonderboy WBDD 017*	12	6
21 Jul 01	KIKI RIRI BOOM *Wonderboy WBOYD 026*	62	1

SHAG *See Jonathan KING*

SHAGGY   326   **Top 500**

World's top selling Jamaican artist. b. Orville Burrell, 22 Oct 1968, Kingston, Jamaica, who has more UK and US No.1s than any other West Indian-born act. US-based artist sold 345,000 copies of 'It Wasn't Me' in first week in UK (then 1,180,700 in total), and album 'Hot Shot' sold more than 12 million globally (Singles: 144 Weeks, Albums: 61 Weeks)   pos/wks

Date	Title	pos	wks
6 Feb 93 ★	OH CAROLINA *Greensleeves GRECD 361*	1	19
10 Jul 93	SOON BE DONE *Greensleeves GRECD 380*	46	3
8 Jul 95 ●	IN THE SUMMERTIME *Virgin VSCDT 1542* [1]	5	9
23 Sep 95 ★	BOOMBASTIC *Virgin VSCDT 1536* ■	1	12
13 Jan 96	WHY YOU TREAT ME SO BAD *Virgin VSCDT 1566* [2]	11	5
23 Mar 96	SOMETHING DIFFERENT / THE TRAIN IS COMING *Virgin VSCDT 1581* [3]	21	5
22 Jun 96	THAT GIRL *Virgin America VUSCDX 106* [4]	15	7
19 Jul 97 ●	PIECE OF MY HEART *Virgin VSCDT 1647* [5]	7	6
17 Feb 01	IT WASN'T ME (IMPORT) *MCA 1558032* [6]	31	3
10 Mar 01 ★	IT WASN'T ME *MCA 1558022* [6] ◆ ■ ▲	1	20
9 Jun 01 ★	ANGEL *MCA MCSTD 40257* [1] ■ ▲	1	16
29 Sep 01 ●	LUV ME LUV ME *MCA MCSTD 40263*	5	10
1 Dec 01	DANCE AND SHOUT / HOPE *MCA MCSTD 40272*	19	7
23 Mar 02 ●	ME JULIE *Island CID 793* [7]	2	14
9 Nov 02	HEY SEXY LADY (re) *MCA MCSTD 40304* [8]	10	7
3 Jul 04	YOUR EYES *VP VPCD 6415* [9]	57	1
24 Jul 93	PURE PLEASURE *Greensleeves GRELCD 184*	67	1
14 Oct 95	BOOMBASTIC *Virgin CDV 2782*	37	6
17 Feb 01 ★	HOT SHOT *MCA 1122932* ▲	1	47
16 Feb 02	MR. LOVER LOVER – THE BEST OF SHAGGY – PART 1 *Virgin VTCD 429*	20	5
16 Nov 02	LUCKY DAY *MCA / Uni-Island 1131192*	54	2

[1] Shaggy featuring Rayvon [2] Shaggy featuring Grand Puba [3] Shaggy featuring Wayne Wonder / Shaggy [4] Maxi Priest featuring Shaggy [5] Shaggy featuring Marsha [6] Shaggy featuring Ricardo "Rikrok" Ducent [7] Ali G and Shaggy [8] Shaggy featuring Brian and Tony Gold [9] Rik Rok featuring Shaggy

SHAH
UK, female vocalist – Sarah Morriss (Singles: 1 Week)   pos/wks

Date	Title	pos	wks
6 Jun 98	SECRET LOVE *Evocative EVOKE 5CDS*	69	1

SHAI
US, male vocal group (Singles: 6 Weeks)   pos/wks

Date	Title	pos	wks
19 Dec 92	IF I EVER FALL IN LOVE *MCA MCS 1727*	36	6

SHAKATAK `445` `Top 500` *London-based pop / jazz / funk ensemble which was big in Japan. Their sound was typified by the tinkling piano of Bill Sharpe and Jill Saward's soothing vocals. Sharpe later worked with Gary Numan, while Nigel Wright (k) produced hits for Madonna, Take That, Robson and Jerome, Barbra Streisand, Cliff Richard and Boyzone (Singles: 85 Weeks, Albums: 73 Weeks)*

		pos/wks
8 Nov 80	FEELS LIKE THE RIGHT TIME *Polydor POSP 188*	41 5
7 Mar 81	LIVING IN THE UK *Polydor POSP 230*	52 4
25 Jul 81	BRAZILIAN DAWN *Polydor POSP 282*	48 3
21 Nov 81	EASIER SAID THAN DONE *Polydor POSP 375*	12 17
3 Apr 82 ●	NIGHT BIRDS *Polydor POSP 407*	9 8
19 Jun 82	STREETWALKIN' *Polydor POSP 452*	38 6
4 Sep 82	INVITATIONS *Polydor POSP 502*	24 7
6 Nov 82	STRANGER *Polydor POSP 530*	43 3
4 Jun 83	DARK IS THE NIGHT *Polydor POSP 595*	15 8
27 Aug 83	IF YOU COULD SEE ME NOW *Polydor POSP 635*	49 4
7 Jul 84 ●	DOWN ON THE STREET *Polydor POSP 688*	9 11
15 Sep 84	DON'T BLAME IT ON LOVE *Polydor POSP 699*	55 3
16 Nov 85	DAY BY DAY *Polydor POSP 770* [1]	53 3
24 Oct 87	MR MANIC AND SISTER COOL *Polydor MANIC 1*	56 3
30 Jan 82	DRIVIN' HARD *Polydor POLS 1030*	35 17
15 May 82 ●	NIGHT BIRDS *Polydor POLS 1059*	4 28
27 Nov 82	INVITATIONS *Polydor POLD 5068*	30 11
22 Oct 83	OUT OF THIS WORLD *Polydor POLD 5115*	30 4
25 Aug 84	DOWN ON THE STREET *Polydor POLD 5148*	17 9
23 Feb 85	LIVE! *Polydor POLH 21*	82 3
22 Oct 88	THE COOLEST CUTS *K-Tel NE 1422*	73 1

[1] Shakatak featuring Al Jarreau

SHAKE B4 USE vs Robert PALMER
UK, male production trio and male vocalist (Singles: 1 Week)

		pos/wks
18 Jan 03	ADDICTED TO LOVE *Serious SER 060CD*	42 1

SHAKEDOWN *Switzerland, male DJ / production duo – Stephan and Sebastien Kohler (Singles: 10 Weeks)*

		pos/wks
11 May 02 ●	AT NIGHT *Defected DFECT 50CDS*	6 8
28 Jun 03	DROWSY WITH HOPE *Defected DFTD 071CDS*	46 2

Johnny SHAKER *See THREE 'N ONE*

SHAKESPEAR'S SISTER (see also BANANARAMA)
UK / US, female vocal / instrumental duo – Siobhan Fahey and Marcella (Detroit) Levy (Singles: 52 Weeks, Albums: 63 Weeks)

		pos/wks
29 Jul 89 ●	YOU'RE HISTORY *ffrr F 112*	7 9
14 Oct 89	RUN SILENT *ffrr F 119*	54 3
10 Mar 90	DIRTY MIND *ffrr F 128*	71 1
12 Oct 91	GOODBYE CRUEL WORLD *London LON 309*	59 2
25 Jan 92 ★	STAY *London LON 314*	1 16
16 May 92	I DON'T CARE *London LON 318*	7 7
18 Jul 92	GOODBYE CRUEL WORLD (re-issue) *London LON 322*	32 4
7 Nov 92	HELLO (TURN YOUR RADIO ON) *London LON 330*	14 6
27 Feb 93	MY 16TH APOLOGY (EP) *London LONCD 337*	61 1
22 Jun 96	I CAN DRIVE *London LONCD 383*	30 3
2 Sep 89 ●	SACRED HEART *London 828131 1*	9 8
29 Feb 92 ●	HORMONALLY YOURS *London 8282262*	3 55

Tracks on My 16th Apology (EP): My 16th Apology / Catwoman / Dirty Mind (live re-recording) / Hot Love. From 1996 Shakespear's Sister was essentially just vocalist Siobhan Fahey

The SHAKIN' PYRAMIDS
UK, male vocal / instrumental group (Albums: 4 Weeks)

		pos/wks
4 Apr 81	SKIN 'EM UP *Cuba Libra V 2199*	48 4

SHAKIRA *Colombia, female vocalist – Shakira Isabel Mebarek Ripoll, b. 2 Feb 1977 (Singles: 42 Weeks, Albums: 47 Weeks)*

		pos/wks
9 Mar 02 ●	WHENEVER, WHEREVER *Epic 6724262*	2 19
3 Aug 02 ●	UNDERNEATH YOUR CLOTHES *Epic 6729532*	3 15
23 Nov 02	OBJECTION (TANGO) *Epic 6733402*	17 8
23 Mar 02 ●	LAUNDRY SERVICE *Epic 4987202*	2 47

SHAKY *See Shakin' STEVENS*

SHAKY and BONNIE *See Shakin' STEVENS; Bonnie TYLER*

SHALAMAR `244` `Top 500` (see also BABYFACE)
Influential US dance music vocal trio masterminded by 'Soul Train' TV producer Don Cornelius. Line-up 1979-1983: Jeffrey Daniel, Jody Watley, Howard Hewett. Regarded as fashion icons and trendsetters, they helped to introduce "body-popping" to Britain (Singles: 134 Weeks, Albums: 121 Weeks)

		pos/wks
14 May 77	UPTOWN FESTIVAL *Soul Train FB 0885*	30 5
9 Dec 78	TAKE THAT TO THE BANK *RCA FB 1379*	20 12
24 Nov 79	THE SECOND TIME AROUND *Solar FB 1709*	45 9
9 Feb 80	RIGHT IN THE SOCKET *Solar SO 2*	44 6
30 Aug 80	I OWE YOU ONE *Solar SO 11*	13 10
28 Mar 81	MAKE THAT MOVE *Solar SO 17*	30 10
27 Mar 82 ●	I CAN MAKE YOU FEEL GOOD *Solar K 12599*	7 11
12 Jun 82 ●	A NIGHT TO REMEMBER *Solar K 13162*	5 12
4 Sep 82 ●	THERE IT IS *Solar K 13194*	5 10
27 Nov 82	FRIENDS *Solar CHUM 1*	12 10
11 Jun 83 ●	DEAD GIVEAWAY *Solar E 9819*	8 10
13 Aug 83	DISAPPEARING ACT *Solar E 9807*	18 8
15 Oct 83	OVER AND OVER *Solar E 9792*	23 6
24 Mar 84	DANCING IN THE SHEETS *CBS A 4171*	41 3
31 Mar 84	DEADLINE USA *MCA MCA 866*	52 3
24 Nov 84	AMNESIA *Solar / MCA SHAL 1*	61 2
2 Feb 85	MY GIRL LOVES ME *MCA SHAL 2*	45 3
26 Apr 86	A NIGHT TO REMEMBER (re-mix) *MCA SHAL 3*	52 4
27 Mar 82 ●	FRIENDS *Solar K 52345*	6 72
11 Sep 82	GREATEST HITS *Solar SOLA 3001*	71 5
30 Jul 83 ●	THE LOOK *Solar 960239*	7 20
12 Apr 86 ●	THE GREATEST HITS *Stylus SMR 8615*	5 24

SHAM ROCK
Ireland, male / female vocal / instrumental group (Singles: 11 Weeks)

		pos/wks
7 Nov 98	TELL ME MA *Jive 0522352*	13 11

SHAM 69 *UK, male vocal / instrumental group (Singles: 53 Weeks, Albums: 27 Weeks)*

		pos/wks
13 May 78	ANGELS WITH DIRTY FACES *Polydor 2059 023*	19 10
29 Jul 78 ●	IF THE KIDS ARE UNITED *Polydor 2059 050*	9 9
14 Oct 78	HURRY UP HARRY *Polydor POSP 7*	10 8
24 Mar 79	QUESTIONS AND ANSWERS *Polydor POSP 27*	18 9
4 Aug 79 ●	HERSHAM BOYS *Polydor POSP 64*	6 9
27 Oct 79	YOU'RE A BETTER MAN THAN I *Polydor POSP 82*	49 5
12 Apr 80	TELL THE CHILDREN *Polydor POSP 136*	45 3
11 Mar 78	TELL US THE TRUTH *Polydor 2383 491*	25 8
2 Dec 78	THAT'S LIFE *Polydor POLD 5010*	27 11
29 Sep 79 ●	THE ADVENTURES OF THE HERSHAM BOYS *Polydor POLD 5025*	8 8

The SHAMEN *UK, male vocal / instrumental duo – Richard West and Colin Angus (Singles: 77 Weeks, Albums: 54 Weeks)*

		pos/wks
7 Apr 90	PRO-GEN *One Little Indian 36TP 7*	55 4
22 Sep 90	MAKE IT MINE *One Little Indian 46TP 7*	42 5
6 Apr 91	HYPERREAL *One Little Indian 48TP 7*	29 5
27 Jul 91 ●	MOVE ANY MOUNTAIN (re-mix) *One Little Indian 52TP 7*	4 10
18 Jul 92	L.S.I. *One Little Indian 68TP 7*	6 8
5 Sep 92 ★	EBENEEZER GOODE *One Little Indian 78TP 7*	1 10
7 Nov 92 ●	BOSS DRUM *One Little Indian 88TP 7*	4 7
7 Nov 92	BOSS DRUM (re-mix) *One Little Indian 88TP 12*	58 1
19 Dec 92 ●	PHOREVER PEOPLE *One Little Indian 98TP 7*	5 10
6 Mar 93	RE: EVOLUTION *One Little Indian 118TP 7CD* [1]	18 2
6 Nov 93	THE SOS (EP) *One Little Indian 108TP 7CD*	14 4
19 Aug 95	DESTINATION ESCHATON *One Little Indian 128TP 7CDL*	15 4
21 Oct 95	TRANSAMAZONIA *One Little Indian 138TP 7CD*	28 2
10 Feb 96	HEAL (THE SEPARATION) *One Little Indian 158TP 7CDL*	31 2
21 Dec 96	MOVE ANY MOUNTAIN '96 (2ND (2nd re-mix) *One Little Indian 169TP 7CD*	35 3
2 Nov 90	EN-TACT *One Little Indian TPLP 22*	31 10
28 Sep 91	PROGENY *One Little Indian TPLP 32*	23 2
26 Sep 92 ●	BOSS DRUM / DIFFERENT DRUM *One Little Indian TPLP 42CD*	3 35
20 Nov 93	ON AIR *Band of Joy BOJCD 006*	61 1
4 Nov 95	AXIS MUTATIS *One Little Indian TPLP 52CDL*	27 2
2 May 98	THE SHAMEN COLLECTION *One Little Indian TPLP 72CDE*	26 4

[1] The Shamen with Terence McKenna

'Move Any Mountain' is a re-mix of 'Pro-Gen'. Tracks on The SOS (EP): Comin' On / Make It Mine / Possible Worlds (re-mix) From 18 Dec 93 sales of 'Boss Drum' and the re-mix album 'Different Drum' were amalgamated

KIM WILDE TOP 10

The gospel according to Kim Wilde, who chooses her favourite albums

Kim's selection is influenced by a whole heap of memories: head-banging sessions on long car journeys (Queen's Sheer Heart Attack), hired convertibles, Angelina posters and the Hollywood Hills (Todd Rundgren's A Capella). Then, more recently, she admits to grooving to Mary J Blige – "A funky lady that gets me through the school run" – and Rufus Wainwright, a new acquisition. "I heard him sing on Frank Skinner and was sold."

album – act – (peak position)

A CAPELLA *
Todd Rundgren

THE HISSING OF SUMMER LAWNS
Joni Mitchell (14)

NEW BOOTS AND PANTIES!!
Ian Dury (5)

ONE FROM THE HEART (OST) *
Tom Waits and Crystal Gayle

ON AND ON *
Jack Johnson

PET SOUNDS
The Beach Boys (2)

POSES *
Rufus Wainwright

RAM
Paul and Linda McCartney (1)

SHEER HEART ATTACK
Queen (2)

WHAT'S THE 411?
Mary J Blige (53)

* Did not chart

SHAMPOO *UK, female vocal duo – Jacqui Blake and Carrie Askew (Singles: 28 Weeks, Albums: 2 Weeks)* pos/wks

30 Jul 94	TROUBLE *Food CDFOOD 51*	11	12
15 Oct 94	VIVA LA MEGABABES *Food CDFOOD 54*	27	4
18 Feb 95	DELICIOUS *Food CDFOOD 58*	21	4
5 Aug 95	TROUBLE (re-issue) *Food CDFOOD 66*	36	3
13 Jul 96	GIRL POWER *Food CDFOOD 76*	25	4
21 Sep 96	I KNOW WHAT BOYS LIKE *Food CDFOOD 83*	42	1
5 Nov 94	WE ARE SHAMPOO *Food FOODCD 12*	45	2

Jimmy SHAND BAND
UK, male instrumentalist – accordion – leader – b. 29 Jan 1908, d. 23 Dec 2000 (Singles: 2 Weeks, Albums: 2 Weeks) pos/wks

23 Dec 55	BLUEBELL POLKA *Parlophone F 3436*	20	2
24 Dec 83	FIFTY YEARS ON WITH JIMMY SHAND *Ross WGR 062* [1]	97	2

[1] Jimmy Shand, his Band and Guests

Paul SHANE and the YELLOWCOATS *UK, male actor / vocalist and male / female vocal group (Singles: 5 Weeks)* pos/wks

16 May 81	HI-DE-HI (HOLIDAY ROCK) *EMI 5180*	36	5

The SHANGRI-LAS *US, female vocal group (Singles: 47 Weeks)* pos/wks

8 Oct 64	REMEMBER (WALKIN' IN THE SAND) *Red Bird RB 10008*	14	12
14 Jan 65	LEADER OF THE PACK *Red Bird RB 10014* ▲	11	9
14 Oct 72 ●	LEADER OF THE PACK (re-issue) *Kama Sutra 2013 024*	3	14
5 Jun 76 ●	LEADER OF THE PACK (2nd re-issue) *Charly CS 1009*	7	12

From 19 Jun 1976 until 14 Aug 1976, the last week of the disc's chart run, the Charly and another Contempo release of 'Leader of the Pack' were bracketed together on the chart

SHANICE *US, female vocalist – Shanice Wilson (Singles: 24 Weeks, Albums: 4 Weeks)* pos/wks

23 Nov 91	I LOVE YOUR SMILE *Motown ZB 44907*	55	4
22 Feb 92 ●	I LOVE YOUR SMILE (re-mix) *Motown TMG 1401*	2	10
14 Nov 92	LOVIN' YOU *Motown TMG 1409*	54	1
16 Jan 93	SAVING FOREVER FOR YOU *Giant W 0148CD*	42	3
13 Aug 94	I LIKE *Motown TMGCD 1427*	49	2

16 Dec 95	IF I NEVER KNEW YOU (LOVE THEME FROM 'POCAHONTAS') *Walt Disney WD 7023CD* [1]	51	4
21 Mar 92	INNER CHILD *Motown 5300082*	21	4

[1] Jon Secada and Shanice

SHANKS & BIGFOOT (see also DOOLALLY) *UK, male production duo – Stephen Meade and Daniel Langsman (Singles: 24 Weeks)* pos/wks

29 May 99 ★	SWEET LIKE CHOCOLATE (re) *Pepper / Jive / Chocolate Boy 0530352* ■	1	16
29 Jul 00	SING-A-LONG (re) *Pepper 9230232*	12	8

SHANNON *US, female vocalist – Brenda Shannon Greene (Singles: 54 Weeks, Albums: 12 Weeks)* pos/wks

19 Nov 83	LET THE MUSIC PLAY (re) *Club LET 1*	14	15
7 Apr 84	GIVE ME TONIGHT *Club JAB 1*	24	7
30 Jun 84	SWEET SOMEBODY *Club JAB 3*	25	8
20 Jul 85	STRONGER TOGETHER *Club JAB 15*	46	6
6 Dec 97	IT'S OVER LOVE *Manifesto FESCD 37* [1]	16	8
28 Nov 98 ●	MOVE MANIA *Multiply CDMULTY 45* [2]	8	10
10 Mar 84	LET THE MUSIC PLAY *Club JABL 1*	52	12

[1] Todd Terry presents Shannon [2] Sash! featuring Shannon

Del SHANNON `406` `Top 500`

Early 1960s chart regular, b. Charles Westover, 30 Dec 1934, Michigan, US, d. 8 Feb 1990. This unmistakable singer / songwriter who used a falsetto vocal on most hits topped both the UK and US charts with the first of his many hits (Singles: 147 Weeks, Albums: 23 Weeks) pos/wks

27 Apr 61 ★	RUNAWAY *London HLX 9317* ▲	1	22
14 Sep 61 ●	HATS OFF TO LARRY *London HLX 9402*	6	12
7 Dec 61 ●	SO LONG BABY *London HLX 9462*	10	11
15 Mar 62 ●	HEY! LITTLE GIRL *London HLX 9515*	2	15
6 Sep 62	CRY MYSELF TO SLEEP *London HLX 9587*	29	6
11 Oct 62 ●	THE SWISS MAID *London HLX 9609*	2	17
17 Jan 63 ●	LITTLE TOWN FLIRT *London HLX 9653*	4	13
25 Apr 63 ●	TWO KINDS OF TEARDROPS *London HLX 9710*	5	13
22 Aug 63	TWO SILHOUETTES *London HLX 9761*	23	8

24 Oct 63		SUE'S GOTTA BE MINE *London HLU 9800*	..............**21**	8
12 Mar 64		MARY JANE *Stateside SS 269*	..............**35**	5
30 Jul 64		HANDY MAN *Stateside SS 317*	..............**36**	4
14 Jan 65	●	KEEP SEARCHIN' (WE'LL FOLLOW THE SUN)	..............**3**	11
		Stateside SS 368		
18 Mar 65		STRANGER IN TOWN *Stateside SS 395*	..............**40**	2
11 May 63	●	HATS OFF TO DEL SHANNON *London HAX 8071*	..............**9**	17
2 Nov 63		LITTLE TOWN FLIRT *London HAX 8091*	..............**15**	6

The Oct 1963 hit 'Sue's Gotta Be Mine' is the correct title, although a label printing error shows 'Sue's Gonna Be Mine' on copies of the record

Roxanne SHANTE
US, female rapper – Lolita Gooden (Singles: 11 Weeks)   pos/wks

1 Aug 87	HAVE A NICE DAY *Breakout USA 612*	..............**58**	3
4 Jun 88	GO ON GIRL *Breakout USA 633*	..............**55**	3
29 Oct 88	SHARP AS A KNIFE *Club JAB 73* [1]	..............**45**	3
14 Apr 90	GO ON GIRL (re-mix) *Breakout USA 689*	..............**74**	1
23 Sep 00	WHAT'S GOING ON *Wall of Sound WALLD 064* [2]	..............**43**	1

[1] Brandon Cooke featuring Roxanne Shante [2] Mekon featuring Roxanne Shante

SHAPESHIFTERS *UK / Sweden, male production*
duo – Simon Marlin and Max Reich (Singles: 15 Weeks)   pos/wks

24 Jul 04	★	LOLA'S THEME *Positiva CDTIVS 207* ■	..............**1** 15

Helen SHAPIRO `496` `Top 500`
Youngest female chart-topper, b. 28 Sep 1946, London, UK. Before she was 16 years old, she amassed four Top 5 hits (including two No.1s) and had been voted Britain's Top Female Singer. She headlined the first UK tour on which The Beatles appeared (as her support act) (Singles: 119 Weeks, Albums: 25 Weeks)   pos/wks

23 Mar 61	●	DON'T TREAT ME LIKE A CHILD *Columbia DB 4589*	..............**3**	20
29 Jun 61		YOU DON'T KNOW *Columbia DB 4670*	..............**1**	23
28 Sep 61	★	WALKIN' BACK TO HAPPINESS *Columbia DB 4715*	..............**1**	19
15 Feb 62	●	TELL ME WHAT HE SAID *Columbia DB 4782*	..............**2**	15
3 May 62		LET'S TALK ABOUT LOVE *Columbia DB 4824*	..............**23**	7
12 Jul 62	●	LITTLE MISS LONELY *Columbia DB 4869*	..............**8**	11
18 Oct 62		KEEP AWAY FROM OTHER GIRLS *Columbia DB 4908*	..............**40**	6
7 Feb 63		QUEEN FOR TONIGHT *Columbia DB 4966*	..............**33**	5
25 Apr 63		WOE IS ME *Columbia DB 7026*	..............**35**	6
24 Oct 63		LOOK WHO IT IS *Columbia DB 7130*	..............**47**	3
23 Jan 64		FEVER *Columbia DB 7190*	..............**38**	4
10 Mar 62	●	'TOPS' WITH ME *Columbia 33SX 1397*	..............**2**	25

SHARADA HOUSE GANG
Italy, male / female vocal / instrumental group (Singles: 4 Weeks)   pos/wks

12 Aug 95	KEEP IT UP *Media MCSTD 2071*	..............**36**	2
11 May 96	LET THE RHYTHM MOVE YOU *Media MCSTD 40035*	..............**50**	1
18 Oct 97	GYPSY BOY, GYPSY GIRL *Gut CXGUT 12*	..............**52**	1

SHARKEY *UK, male DJ / producer / instrumentalist – Jonathan Sharkey (Singles: 1 Week)*   pos/wks

8 Mar 97	REVOLUTIONS (EP) *React CDREACT 95*	..............**53**	1

Tracks on Revolutions (EP): Revolution Part One / Revolution Part Two / Revolution Part Two (re-mix)

Feargal SHARKEY *(see also ASSEMBLY; The UNDERTONES)*
UK, male vocalist (Singles: 58 Weeks, Albums: 24 Weeks)   pos/wks

13 Oct 84		LISTEN TO YOUR FATHER *Zarjazz JAZZ 1*	..............**23**	7
29 Jun 85		LOVING YOU *Virgin VS 770*	..............**26**	10
12 Oct 85	★	A GOOD HEART *Virgin VS 808*	..............**1**	16
4 Jan 86	●	YOU LITTLE THIEF *Virgin VS 840*	..............**5**	9
5 Apr 86		SOMEONE TO SOMEBODY *Virgin VS 828*	..............**64**	3
16 Jan 88		MORE LOVE *Virgin VS 992*	..............**44**	5
16 Mar 91		I'VE GOT NEWS FOR YOU *Virgin VS 1294*	..............**12**	8
23 Nov 85		FEARGAL SHARKEY *Virgin V 2360*	..............**12**	20
20 Apr 91		SONGS FROM THE MARDI GRAS *Virgin V 2642*	..............**27**	4

The SHARONETTES *US, female vocal group (Singles: 8 Weeks)*   pos/wks

26 Apr 75	PAPA OOM MOW MOW *Black Magic BM 102*	..............**26**	5
12 Jul 75	GOING TO A GO-GO *Black Magic BM 104*	..............**46**	3

Barrie K SHARPE *See Diana BROWN and Barrie K SHARPE*

Debbie SHARP *See DREAM FREQUENCY*

Dee Dee SHARP
US, female vocalist – Dione LaRue (Singles: 2 Weeks)   pos/wks

25 Apr 63	DO THE BIRD *Cameo Parkway C 244*	..............**46**	2

SHARPE and NUMAN *See Gary NUMAN*

Rocky SHARPE and the REPLAYS
UK, male / female vocal group (Singles: 41 Weeks)   pos/wks

16 Dec 78		RAMA LAMA DING DONG *Chiswick CHIS 104*	..............**17**	10
24 Mar 79		IMAGINATION *Chiswick CHIS 110*	..............**39**	6
25 Aug 79		LOVE WILL MAKE YOU FAIL IN SCHOOL		
		Chiswick CHIS 114 [1]	..............**60**	4
9 Feb 80		MARTIAN HOP *Chiswick CHIS 121* [1]	..............**55**	4
17 Apr 82		SHOUT SHOUT (KNOCK YOURSELF OUT) *Chiswick DICE 3*	..............**19**	9
7 Aug 82		CLAP YOUR HANDS *RAK 345*	..............**54**	3
26 Feb 83		IF YOU WANNA BE HAPPY *Polydor POSP 560*	..............**46**	5

[1] Rocky Sharpe and the Replays featuring the Top Liners

Ben SHAW featuring Adele HOLNESS
UK, male producer and female vocalist (Singles: 1 Week)   pos/wks

14 Jul 01	SO STRONG *Fire Recordings ERIF 009CDS*	..............**72**	1

Mark SHAW
(see also THEN JERICO) UK, male vocalist (Singles: 1 Week)   pos/wks

17 Nov 90	LOVE SO BRIGHT *EMI EM 161*	..............**54**	1

Roland SHAW ORCHESTRA *See MANTOVANI; David WHITFIELD*

Sandie SHAW `381` `Top 500`
Barefoot pop princess of the Sixties, b. Sandra Goodrich, 26 Feb 1947, Essex, UK. This distinctive vocalist, who has a 30-year chart span, was the first UK act to win the Eurovision Song Contest (with 'Puppet on a String' in 1967) (Singles: 165 Weeks, Albums: 14 Weeks)   pos/wks

8 Oct 64	★	(THERE'S) ALWAYS SOMETHING THERE TO REMIND ME		
		Pye 7N 15704	..............**1**	11
10 Dec 64	●	GIRL DON'T COME *Pye 7N 15743*	..............**3**	12
18 Feb 65	●	I'LL STOP AT NOTHING *Pye 7N 15783*	..............**4**	11
13 May 65	★	LONG LIVE LOVE *Pye 7N 15841*	..............**1**	14
23 Sep 65	●	MESSAGE UNDERSTOOD *Pye 7N 15940*	..............**6**	10
18 Nov 65		HOW CAN YOU TELL *Pye 7N 15987*	..............**21**	9
27 Jan 66	●	TOMORROW *Pye 7N 17036*	..............**9**	9
19 May 66		NOTHING COMES EASY *Pye 7N 17086*	..............**14**	9
8 Sep 66		RUN *Pye 7N 17163*	..............**32**	5
24 Nov 66		THINK SOMETIMES ABOUT ME *Pye 7N 17212*	..............**32**	4
19 Jan 67		I DON'T NEED ANYTHING *Pye 7N 17239*	..............**50**	1
16 Mar 67	★	PUPPET ON A STRING *Pye 7N 17272*	..............**1**	18
12 Jul 67		TONIGHT IN TOKYO *Pye 7N 17346*	..............**21**	6
4 Oct 67		YOU'VE NOT CHANGED *Pye 7N 17378*	..............**18**	12
7 Feb 68		TODAY *Pye 7N 17441*	..............**27**	7
12 Feb 69	●	MONSIEUR DUPONT *Pye 7N 17675*	..............**6**	15
14 May 69		THINK IT ALL OVER *Pye 7N 17726*	..............**42**	4
21 Apr 84		HAND IN GLOVE *Rough Trade RT 130*	..............**27**	5
14 Jun 86		ARE YOU READY TO BE HEARTBROKEN? *Polydor POSP 793*	..............**68**	1
12 Nov 94		NOTHING LESS THAN BRILLIANT *Virgin VSCDT 1521*	..............**66**	2
6 Mar 65	●	SANDIE *Pye NPL 18110*	..............**3**	13
19 Nov 94		NOTHING LESS THAN BRILLIANT *Virgin VTCD 34*	..............**64**	1

Tracy SHAW *UK, female actor / vocalist (Singles: 1 Week)*   pos/wks

4 Jul 98	HAPPENIN' ALL OVER AGAIN *Recognition CDREC 2*	..............**46**	1

Winifred SHAW
US, female vocalist, b. 25 Feb 1899, d. 2 May 1982 (Singles: 4 Weeks)   pos/wks

14 Aug 76	LULLABY OF BROADWAY *United Artists UP 36131*	..............**42**	4

SHE *See URBAN DISCHARGE featuring SHE*

SHE ROCKERS *UK, female rap duo (Singles: 2 Weeks)*   pos/wks

13 Jan 90	JAM IT JAM *Jive JIVE 233*	..............**58**	2

George SHEARING *US (b. UK), male instrumentalist – piano (Singles: 15 Weeks, Albums: 13 Weeks)*   pos/wks

19 Jul 62	LET THERE BE LOVE *Capitol CL 15257* [1]	..............**11**	14
4 Oct 62	BAUBLES, BANGLES AND BEADS *Capitol CL 15269* [2]	..............**49**	1

		pos/wks	
11 Jun 60	BEAUTY AND THE BEAT *Capitol T 1219* [1]	16	6
20 Oct 62 ●	NAT 'KING' COLE SINGS/GEORGE SHEARING PLAYS WITH THE QUINTET AND STRING CHOIR *Capitol W 1675* [2]	8	7

[1] Nat 'King' Cole with George Shearing [2] George Shearing Quintet [1] Peggy Lee and George Shearing [2] Nat 'King' Cole and the George Shearing Quintet

Gary SHEARSTON *Australia, male vocalist (Singles: 8 Weeks)* pos/wks

		pos/wks	
5 Oct 74 ●	I GET A KICK OUT OF YOU *Charisma CB 234*	7	8

SHED SEVEN *UK, male vocal / instrumental group (Singles: 50 Weeks, Albums: 46 Weeks)* pos/wks

		pos/wks	
25 Jun 94	DOLPHIN *Polydor YORCD 2*	28	4
27 Aug 94	SPEAKEASY *Polydor YORCD 3*	24	3
12 Nov 94	OCEAN PIE *Polydor YORCD 4*	33	2
13 May 95	WHERE HAVE YOU BEEN TONIGHT *Polydor YORCD 5*	23	2
27 Jan 96	GETTING BETTER *Polydor 5778912*	14	3
23 Mar 96 ●	GOING FOR GOLD *Polydor 5762152*	8	5
18 May 96	BULLY BOY *Polydor 5765972*	22	3
31 Aug 96	ON STANDBY *Polydor 5752732*	12	4
23 Nov 96	CHASING RAINBOWS *Polydor 5759292*	17	5
14 Mar 98	SHE LEFT ME ON FRIDAY *Polydor 5695412*	11	4
23 May 98	THE HEROES *Polydor 5699172*	18	3
22 Aug 98	DEVIL IN YOUR SHOES (WALKING ALL OVER) *Polydor 5672072*	37	2
5 Jun 99	DISCO DOWN *Polydor 5638752*	13	6
5 May 01	CRY FOR HELP *Artful CD 35ARTFUL*	30	2
24 May 03	WHY CAN'T I BE YOU? *Taste Media TMCDS 5004*	23	2
17 Sep 94	CHANGE GIVER *Polydor 5236152*	16	2
13 Apr 96 ●	A MAXIMUM HIGH *Polydor 5310392*	8	26
13 Jun 98 ●	LET IT RIDE *Polydor 5573592*	9	7
12 Jun 99 ●	GOING FOR GOLD – THE GREATEST HITS *Polydor 5474422*	7	10
19 May 01	TRUTH BE TOLD *Artful ARTFULCD 38*	42	1

SHEEP ON DRUGS *UK, male vocal / instrumental duo – Duncan Gil-Rodriguez and Lee Fraser (Singles: 5 Weeks, Albums: 1 Week)* pos/wks

		pos/wks	
27 Mar 93	15 MINUTES OF FAME *Transglobal CID 564*	44	2
30 Oct 93	FROM A TO H AND BACK AGAIN *Transglobal CID 575*	40	2
14 May 94	LET THE GOOD TIMES ROLL *Transglobal CID 576*	56	1
10 Apr 93	GREATEST HITS *Transglobal CID 8006*	55	1

SHEER BRONZE featuring Lisa MILLETT
UK, male / female vocal / instrumental duo (Singles: 1 Week) pos/wks

		pos/wks	
3 Sep 94	WALKIN' ON *Go Beat GODCD 115*	63	1

SHEER ELEGANCE *UK, male vocal group (Singles: 23 Weeks)* pos/wks

		pos/wks	
20 Dec 75	MILKY WAY *Pye International 7N 25697*	18	10
3 Apr 76 ●	LIFE IS TOO SHORT GIRL *Pye International 7N 25703*	9	9
24 Jul 76	IT'S TEMPTATION *Pye International 7N 25715*	41	4

SHEILA B DEVOTION *France, female vocalist – Anny Chancel and male vocal trio (Singles: 33 Weeks)* pos/wks

		pos/wks	
11 Mar 78	SINGIN' IN THE RAIN PART 1 *Carrere EMI 2751*	11	13
22 Jul 78	YOU LIGHT MY FIRE *Carrere EMI 2828*	44	6
24 Nov 79	SPACER *Carrere CAR 128* [1]	18	14

[1] Sheila & B Devotion (Some pressings credited Sheila B Devotion)

Shade SHEIST featuring Nate DOGG and KURUPT
US, male rappers – leader Tremayne Thompson (Singles: 7 Weeks) pos/wks

		pos/wks	
25 Aug 01	WHERE I WANNA BE (re) *London LONCD 461*	14	7

Doug SHELDON *UK, male vocalist (Singles: 15 Weeks)* pos/wks

		pos/wks	
9 Nov 61	RUNAROUND SUE *Decca F 11398*	36	3
4 Jan 62	YOUR MA SAID YOU CRIED IN YOUR SLEEP LAST NIGHT *Decca F 11416*	29	6
7 Feb 63	I SAW LINDA YESTERDAY *Decca F 11564*	36	6

Michelle SHELLERS See SOUL PROVIDERS featuring Michelle SHELLERS

Pete SHELLEY (see also The BUZZCOCKS) *UK, male vocalist – Peter McNeish (Singles: 1 Week, Albums: 4 Weeks)* pos/wks

		pos/wks	
12 Mar 83	TELEPHONE OPERATOR *Genetic XX 1*	66	1
2 Jul 83	XL-1 *Genetic XL 1*	42	4

Peter SHELLEY *UK, male vocalist (Singles: 20 Weeks)* pos/wks

		pos/wks	
14 Sep 74 ●	GEE BABY *Magnet MAG 12*	4	10
22 Mar 75 ●	LOVE ME LOVE MY DOG *Magnet MAG 22*	3	10

Anne SHELTON *UK, female vocalist – Patricia Sibley, b. 10 Nov 1928, d. 31 Jul 1994 (Singles: 31 Weeks)* pos/wks

		pos/wks	
16 Dec 55	ARRIVEDERCI DARLING *HMV POP 146*	17	4
13 Apr 56	SEVEN DAYS *Philips PB 567*	20	4
24 Aug 56 ★	LAY DOWN YOUR ARMS *Philips PB 616*	1	14
20 Nov 59	THE VILLAGE OF ST BERNADETTE *Philips PB 969*	27	1
26 Jan 61 ●	SAILOR *Philips PB 1096*	10	8

SHENA
UK, female vocalist – Shena McSween (Singles: 6 Weeks) pos/wks

		pos/wks	
2 Aug 97	LET THE BEAT HIT 'EM *VC VCRD 24*	28	2
1 Sep 01	I'LL BE WAITING *Rulin RULIN 17CDS* [1]	44	1
4 Oct 03	WILDERNESS *Direction 6742692* [2]	20	3

[1] Full Intention presents Shena [2] Jurgen Vries featuring Shena

Vikki SHEPARD See SLEAZESISTERS

Vonda SHEPARD
US, female vocalist (Singles: 9 Weeks, Albums: 49 Weeks) pos/wks

		pos/wks	
5 Dec 98 ●	SEARCHIN' MY SOUL *Epic 6666332*	10	9
17 Oct 98 ●	SONGS FROM ALLY McBEAL *Epic 4911242*	3	34
12 Jun 99	BY 7:30 *Epic 4945792*	39	2
20 Nov 99 ●	HEART & SOUL – NEW SONGS FROM ALLY McBEAL *Epic 4950912*	9	13

SHEPHERD SISTERS *US, female vocal group (Singles: 6 Weeks)* pos/wks

		pos/wks	
15 Nov 57	ALONE (WHY MUST I BE) (re) *HMV POP 411*	14	6

SHERBET
Australia, male vocal / instrumental group (Singles: 10 Weeks) pos/wks

		pos/wks	
25 Sep 76 ●	HOWZAT *Epic EPC 4574*	4	10

Tony SHERIDAN and The BEATLES
UK, male vocalist and vocal / instrumental group (Singles: 1 Week) pos/wks

		pos/wks	
6 Jun 63	MY BONNIE *Polydor NH 66833*	48	1

Allan SHERMAN *US, male vocalist / comedian – Allan Copelon, b. 30 Nov 1924, d. 21 Nov 1973 (Singles: 10 Weeks)* pos/wks

		pos/wks	
12 Sep 63	HELLO MUDDAH! HELLO FADDAH! *Warner Bros. WB 106*	14	10

Bobby SHERMAN *US, male vocalist (Singles: 4 Weeks)* pos/wks

		pos/wks	
31 Oct 70	JULIE DO YA LOVE ME *CBS 5144*	28	4

SHERRICK *US, male vocalist – F Lamonte-Smith, b. 6 Jul 1957, d. 22 Jan 1999 (Singles: 10 Weeks, Albums: 6 Weeks)* pos/wks

		pos/wks	
1 Aug 87	JUST CALL *Warner Bros. W 8380*	23	8
21 Nov 87	LET'S BE LOVERS TONIGHT *Warner Bros. W 8146*	63	2
29 Aug 87	SHERRICK *Warner Bros. WX 118*	27	6

Pluto SHERVINGTON
Jamaica, male vocalist (Singles: 20 Weeks) pos/wks

		pos/wks	
7 Feb 76 ●	DAT *Opal Pal 5*	6	8
10 Apr 76	RAM GOAT LIVER *Trojan TR 7978*	43	4
6 Mar 82	YOUR HONOUR *KR KR 4* [1]	19	8

[1] Pluto

Holly SHERWOOD *US, female vocalist (Singles: 7 Weeks)* pos/wks

		pos/wks	
5 Feb 72	DAY BY DAY *Bell 1182*	29	7

Tony SHEVETON *UK, male vocalist (Singles: 1 Week)* pos/wks

		pos/wks	
13 Feb 64	A MILLION DRUMS *Oriole CB 1895*	49	1

SHIFTY (see also CRAZY TOWN) *US, male rapper – Shifty Shellshock (aka Steve Brooks) (Singles: 3 Weeks)* pos/wks

		pos/wks	
11 Sep 04	SLIDE ALONG SIDE *Maverick W 649*	29	3

SHIMMON & WOOLFSON (see also SUNDANCE)
UK, male DJ / production duo (Singles: 1 Week) pos/wks

| 10 Jan 98 | WELCOME TO THE FUTURE *React CDREACT 119* | 69 | 1 |

SHIMON & Andy C *UK, male production duo –*
Shimon Alcoby and Andy Clarke (Singles: 5 Weeks) pos/wks

| 15 Sep 01 | BODY ROCK (re) *Ram RAMM 34CD* | 28 | 5 |

Brendan SHINE *Ireland, male vocalist (Albums: 29 Weeks)* pos/wks

12 Nov 83	THE BRENDON SHINE COLLECTION *Play PLAYTV 1*	51	12
3 Nov 84	WITH LOVE *Play PLAYTV 2*	74	4
16 Nov 85	MEMORIES *Play PLAYTV 3*	81	7
18 Nov 89	MAGIC MOMENTS *Stylus SMR 991*	62	6

SHINEHEAD
Jamaica, male vocalist – Edmund Aiken (Singles: 6 Weeks) pos/wks

| 3 Apr 93 | JAMAICAN IN NEW YORK *Elektra EKR 161CD* | 30 | 5 |
| 26 Jun 93 | LET 'EM IN *Elektra EKR 168CD* | 70 | 1 |

The SHINING *UK, male vocal / instrumental*
group (Singles: 2 Weeks, Albums: 1 Week) pos/wks

6 Jul 02	I WONDER HOW *Zuma ZUMAD 002*	58	1
14 Sep 02	YOUNG AGAIN *Zuma ZUMASCD 003*	52	1
28 Sep 02	TRUE SKIES *Zuma ZUMACD 001*	73	1

Mike SHINODA *See X-ECUTIONERS featuring Mike SHINODA and Mr HAHN*
of LINKIN PARK

The SHINS *US, male vocal / instrumental group (Singles: 1 Week)* pos/wks

| 13 Mar 04 | SO SAYS I *Sub Pop SPCD 621* | 73 | 1 |

The SHIREHORSES *UK, male vocal instrumental group –*
includes Mark Radcliffe and Marc 'Lard' Riley (Albums: 8 Weeks) pos/wks

| 15 Nov 97 | THE WORST ALBUM IN THE WORLD EVER ... EVER! *East West 3984208512* | 22 | 4 |
| 26 May 01 | OUR KID EH *Columbia 5030492* | 20 | 4 |

The SHIRELLES *US, female vocal group (Singles: 29 Weeks)* pos/wks

9 Feb 61	● WILL YOU LOVE ME TOMORROW *Top Rank JAR 540* ▲	4	15
31 May 62	SOLDIER BOY *HMV POP 1019* ▲	23	9
23 May 63	FOOLISH LITTLE GIRL *Stateside SS 181*	38	5

SHIRLEY and COMPANY *US, female vocalist and*
male vocal / instrumental backing group (Singles: 9 Weeks) pos/wks

| 8 Feb 75 | ● SHAME SHAME SHAME *All Platinum 6146 301* | 6 | 9 |

SHIVA
UK, male / female vocal / instrumental group (Singles: 5 Weeks) pos/wks

| 13 May 95 | WORK IT OUT *ffrr FCD 261* | 36 | 2 |
| 19 Aug 95 | FREEDOM *ffrr FCD 263* | 18 | 3 |

SHIVAREE
US, female / male vocal / instrumental group (Singles: 1 Week) pos/wks

| 17 Feb 01 | GOODNIGHT MOON *Capitol CDCL 825* | 63 | 1 |

SHO NUFF *US, male vocal / instrumental group (Singles: 4 Weeks)* pos/wks

| 24 May 80 | IT'S ALRIGHT *Ensign ENY 37* | 53 | 4 |

Michelle SHOCKED *US, female vocalist –*
Michelle Johnston (Singles: 10 Weeks, Albums: 24 Weeks) pos/wks

8 Oct 88	ANCHORAGE *Cooking Vinyl LON 193*	60	4
14 Jan 89	IF LOVE WAS A TRAIN *Cooking Vinyl LON 212*	63	3
11 Mar 89	WHEN I GROW UP *Cooking Vinyl LON 219*	67	3
10 Sep 88	SHORT SHARP SHOCKED *Cooking Vinyl CVLP 1*	33	19
18 Nov 89	CAPTAIN SWING *Cooking Vinyl 838878 1*	31	3
11 Apr 92	ARKANSAS TRAVELER *London 5121892*	46	2

SHOCKING BLUE *Holland, male /*
female vocal / instrumental group (Singles: 14 Weeks) pos/wks

| 17 Jan 70 | ● VENUS *Penny Farthing PEN 702* ▲ | 8 | 11 |
| 25 Apr 70 | MIGHTY JOE *Penny Farthing PEN 713* | 43 | 3 |

SHOLAN
Germany, male / female production / vocal trio (Singles: 1 Week) pos/wks

| 5 Apr 03 | CAN YOU FEEL (WHAT I'M GOING THRU) *Data / Ministry of Sound DATA 39CDS* | 47 | 1 |

Troy SHONDELL
US, male vocalist – Gary Schelton (Singles: 11 Weeks) pos/wks

| 2 Nov 61 | THIS TIME *London HLG 9432* | 22 | 11 |

SHONDELLS *See Tommy JAMES and the SHONDELLS*

SHOOTING PARTY *UK, male vocal duo (Singles: 2 Weeks)* pos/wks

| 31 Mar 90 | LET'S HANG ON *Lisson DOLE 15* | 66 | 2 |

The SHOP ASSISTANTS
UK, male / female vocal / instrumental group (Albums: 1 Week) pos/wks

| 29 Nov 86 | SHOP ASSISTANTS *Blue Guitar AZLP 2* | 100 | 1 |

Howard SHORE *US, male composer (Albums: 34 Weeks)* pos/wks

5 Jan 02	● THE LORD OF THE RINGS – THE FELLOWSHIP OF THE RING (FILM SOUNDTRACK) *Reprise 9362481102*	10	14
11 Jan 03	THE LORD OF THE RINGS – THE TWO TOWERS (FILM SOUNDTRACK) *Reprise 936248212*	28	9
27 Dec 03	THE LORD OF THE RINGS – THE RETURN OF THE KING (FILM SOUNDTRACK) *Reprise 9362486092*	34	11

Mike SHOREY *See FABOLOUS*

SHORTIE vs BLACK LEGEND
Italy, male production duo and male vocalist (Singles: 2 Weeks) pos/wks

| 4 Aug 01 | SOMEBODY *WEA WEA 328CD* | 37 | 2 |

SHOWADDYWADDY `161` `Top 500` *Rock 'n' roll revival octet from*
Leicester, UK, who have 30 year chart span, included vocalists Dave Bartram and
Buddy Gask. At the peak of their career, they had seven successive Top 5 entries
with rousing revivals of old US rock 'n' roll songs. Best-selling single: 'Under the
Moon of Love' 985,000 (Singles: 209 Weeks, Albums: 130 Weeks) pos/wks

18 May 74	● HEY ROCK AND ROLL *Bell 1357*	2	14
17 Aug 74	ROCK 'N' ROLL LADY *Bell 1374*	15	9
30 Nov 74	HEY MR CHRISTMAS *Bell 1387*	13	8
22 Feb 75	SWEET MUSIC *Bell 1403*	14	9
17 May 75	● THREE STEPS TO HEAVEN *Bell 1426*	2	11
6 Sep 75	● HEARTBEAT *Bell 1450*	7	7
15 Nov 75	HEAVENLY *Bell 1460*	34	6
29 May 76	TROCADERO *Bell 1476*	32	3
6 Nov 76	★ UNDER THE MOON OF LOVE *Bell 1495*	1	15
5 Mar 77	WHEN *Arista 91*	3	11
23 Jul 77	YOU GOT WHAT IT TAKES *Arista 126*	2	10
5 Nov 77	● DANCIN' PARTY *Arista 149*	4	11
25 Mar 78	● I WONDER WHY *Arista 174*	2	11
24 Jun 78	● A LITTLE BIT OF SOAP *Arista 191*	5	12
4 Nov 78	● PRETTY LITTLE ANGEL EYES *Arista ARIST 222*	5	12
31 Mar 79	REMEMBER THEN *Arista 247*	17	8
28 Jul 79	SWEET LITTLE ROCK 'N' ROLLER *Arista 278*	15	9
10 Nov 79	A NIGHT AT DADDY GEES *Arista 314*	39	5
27 Sep 80	WHY DO LOVERS BREAK EACH OTHERS' HEARTS *Arista ARIST 359*	22	10
29 Nov 80	BLUE MOON *Arista ARIST 379*	32	9
13 Jun 81	MULTIPLICATION *Arista ARIST 416*	39	4
28 Nov 81	FOOTSTEPS *Bell BELL 1499*	31	9
28 Aug 82	WHO PUT THE BOMP (IN THE BOMP-A-BOMP-A-BOMP) *RCA 236*	37	6
7 Dec 74	● SHOWADDYWADDY *Bell BELLS 248*	9	19
12 Jul 75	● STEP TWO *Bell BELLS 256*	7	17
29 May 76	TROCADERO *Bell SYBEL 8003*	41	3
25 Dec 76	● GREATEST HITS *Arista ARTY 145*	4	26
3 Dec 77	RED STAR *Arista SPARTY 1023*	20	10
9 Dec 78	★ GREATEST HITS (1976-1978) *Arista ARTV 1*	1	17
10 Nov 79	● CREPES AND DRAPES *Arista ARTV 3*	8	14
20 Dec 80	BRIGHT LIGHTS *Arista SPART 1142*	54	8
7 Nov 81	HEY ROCK 'N' ROLL – THE VERY BEST OF SHOWADDYWADDY *Arista SPART 1178*	33	11
5 Dec 87	THE BEST STEPS TO HEAVEN *Tiger SHTV 1*	90	1
27 Nov 04	HEY! ROCK 'N' ROLL – THE VERY BEST OF SHOWADDYWADDY *DMG TV DMGTV 011*	56	4+

'Hey! Rock 'n' Roll – The Very Best of Showaddywaddy' is a repackaged version
of the 1981 album of (almost) the same name, featuring the same tracks but in
a different order

SHOWDOWN
US, male vocal / instrumental group (Singles: 3 Weeks) pos/wks

17 Dec 77	KEEP DOIN' IT *State STAT 63* **41**	3

SHOWDOWN See Garry LEE and SHOWDOWN

The SHOWSTOPPERS *US, male vocal group (Singles: 25 Weeks)* pos/wks

13 Mar 68	AIN'T NOTHING BUT A HOUSEPARTY *Beacon 3-100* **11**	15
13 Nov 68	EENY MEENY *MGM 1436* **33**	7
30 Jan 71	AIN'T NOTHING BUT A HOUSEPARTY (2re) (re-issue)	
	Beacon BEA 100 ....**33**	3

SHRIEKBACK *UK, male vocal / instrumental group (Singles: 4 Weeks, Albums: 1 Week)* pos/wks

28 Jul 84	HAND ON MY HEART *Arista SHRK 1* **52**	4
11 Aug 84	JAM SCIENCE *Arista 206 416* **85**	1

SHRIEVE See HAGAR SCHON AARONSON SHRIEVE

SHRINK
Holland, male DJ / production trio (Singles: 4 Weeks) pos/wks

10 Oct 98	NERVOUS BREAKDOWN *VC Recordings VCRD 42* **42**	2
19 Aug 00	ARE YOU READY TO PARTY *Nulife 74321783772* **39**	2

SHUT UP AND DANCE *UK, male vocal / production group (Singles: 14 Weeks, Albums: 2 Weeks)* pos/wks

21 Apr 90	£20 TO GET IN *Shut Up and Dance SUAD 3* **56**	3
28 Jul 90	LAMBORGHINI *Shut Up and Dance SUAD 4* **55**	2
8 Feb 92	AUTOBIOGRAPHY OF A CRACKHEAD / THE GREEN MAN	
	Shut Up and Dance SUAD 21 ....**43**	2
30 May 92 ●	RAVING I'M RAVING *Shut Up and Dance SUAD 30S* [1] **2**	2
15 Aug 92	THE ART OF MOVING BUTTS	
	Shut Up and Dance SUAD 34S [2] **69**	1
1 Apr 95	SAVE IT 'TIL THE MOURNING AFTER *Pulse 8 PULS 84CD* **25**	3
8 Jul 95	I LOVE U *Pulse 8 PULS 90CD* [3] **68**	1
27 Jun 92	DEATH IS NOT THE END *Shut Up and Dance SUADCD 005*......**38**	2

[1] Shut Up and Dance featuring Peter Bouncer [2] Shut Up and Dance featuring Erin [3] Shut Up and Dance featuring Richie Davis and Professor T

SHY *UK, male vocal / instrumental group (Singles: 3 Weeks, Albums: 2 Weeks)* pos/wks

19 Apr 80	GIRL (IT'S ALL I HAVE) *Gallery GA 1* **60**	3
11 Apr 87	EXCESS ALL AREAS *RCA PL 71221* **74**	2

SHY FX (see also EBONY DUBSTERS) *UK, male instrumentalist / producer – Andre Williams (Singles: 22 Weeks)* pos/wks

1 Oct 94	ORIGINAL NUTTAH *Sound of Underground SOUR 008CD* [1] **39**	3
20 Mar 99	BAMBAATA 2012 *Ebony EBR 020CD* **60**	1
6 Apr 02 ●	SHAKE UR BODY *Positiva CDTIV 171* [2] **7**	11
23 Nov 02	DON'T WANNA KNOW *ffrr FCD 408* [3] **19**	4
28 Dec 02	WOLF *Ebony Dubs EBD 001* **60**	1
7 Jun 03	FEELIN' U *London FCD 409* [4] **34**	2

[1] UK Apachi with Shy FX [2] Shy FX and T-Power featuring Di [3] Shy FX and T-Power featuring Di and Skibadee [4] Shy FX and T-Power featuring Kele Le Roc

SHYHEIM
US, male rapper – Shyheim Franklin (Singles: 1 Week) pos/wks

8 Jun 96	THIS IZ REAL *Noo Trybe VUSCD 105* **61**	1

SHYSTIE
UK, female rapper – Chanelle Calica (Singles: 3 Weeks) pos/wks

17 Jul 04	ONE WISH *Polydor 9866875* **40**	2
2 Oct 04	MAKE IT EASY *Polydor 9867988* **59**	1

SIA *Australia, female vocalist – Sia Furler (Singles: 11 Weeks)* pos/wks

3 Jun 00 ●	TAKEN FOR GRANTED *Long Lost Brother S 002CD1* **10**	5
18 Aug 01	DESTINY *Ultimate Dilemma UDRCDS 043* [1] **30**	3
30 Mar 02	DISTRACTIONS *Ultimate Dilemma UDRCDS 046* [2] **45**	1
1 May 04	BREATHE ME *Go Beat 9866392* **71**	1
29 May 04	SOMERSAULT *Ultimate Dilemma EW 290CD* [2] **56**	1

[1] Zero 7 featuring Sia & Sophie [2] Zero 7 featuring Sia

Labi SIFFRE *UK, male vocalist / instrumentalist – guitar (Singles: 44 Weeks, Albums: 2 Weeks)* pos/wks

27 Nov 71	IT MUST BE LOVE *Pye International 7N 25572* **14**	12
25 Mar 72	CRYING LAUGHING LOVING LYING	
	Pye International 7N 25576 ....**11**	9
29 Jul 72	WATCH ME *Pye International 7N 25586* **29**	6
4 Apr 87 ●	(SOMETHING INSIDE) SO STRONG *China WOK 12* **4**	13
21 Nov 87	NOTHIN'S GONNA CHANGE *China WOK 16* **52**	4
24 Jul 71	SINGER AND THE SONG *Pye NSPL 28147* **47**	1
14 Oct 72	CRYING LAUGHING LOVING LYING *Pye NSPL 28163*...........**46**	1

SIGNUM *Holland, male production duo – Ronald Hagen and Pascal Minnard (Singles: 6 Weeks)* pos/wks

28 Nov 98	WHAT YA GOT 4 ME *Tidy Trax TIDY 118CD* **70**	1
31 Jul 99	COMING ON STRONG *Tidy Trax TIDY 128T* [1] **66**	1
9 Feb 02	WHAT YA GOT 4 ME (re-mix) *Tidy Trax TIDY 163CD* **35**	3
29 Jun 02	COMING ON STRONG (re-mix) *Tidy Two TIDYTWO 104CD* [1] **50**	1

[1] Signum featuring Scott Mac

SIGUE SIGUE SPUTNIK *UK, male vocal / instrumental group (Singles: 20 Weeks, Albums: 7 Weeks)* pos/wks

1 Mar 86 ●	LOVE MISSILE F1-11 *Parlophone SSS 1* **3**	9
7 Jun 86	21ST CENTURY BOY *Parlophone SSS 2* **20**	5
19 Nov 88	SUCCESS *Parlophone SSS 3* **31**	3
1 Apr 89	DANCERAMA *Parlophone SSS 5* **50**	2
20 May 89	ALBINONI VS STAR WARS *Parlophone SSS 4* **75**	1
9 Aug 86 ●	FLAUNT IT *Parlophone PCS 7305* **10**	6
15 Apr 89	DRESS FOR EXCESS *Parlophone PCS 7328* **53**	1

SIGUR ROS *Iceland, male vocal / instrumental group (Singles: 1 Week, Albums: 2 Weeks)* pos/wks

24 May 03	( ) *Pias CD 10FAT 02* **72**	1
26 Aug 00	AGAETIS BYRJUN *Fat Cat / Pias FATCD 11* **52**	1
9 Nov 02	( ) *Fat Cat FATCD 22* **49**	1

SIL *Holland, male DJ / production duo (Singles: 1 Week)* pos/wks

11 Apr 98	WINDOWS '98 *Hooj Choons HOOJCD 60* **58**	1

The SILENCERS *UK, male vocal / instrumental group (Singles: 7 Weeks, Albums: 3 Weeks)* pos/wks

25 Jun 88	PAINTED MOON *RCA HUSH 1* **57**	4
27 May 89	SCOTTISH RAIN *RCA PB 42701* **71**	2
15 May 93	I CAN FEEL IT *RCA 74321147112* **62**	1
23 Mar 91	DANCE TO THE HOLY MAN *RCA PL 74924* **39**	2
5 Jun 93	SECONDS OF PLEASURE *RCA 74321141132* **52**	1

SILENT UNDERDOG
UK, male instrumentalist – Paul Hardcastle (Singles: 1 Week) pos/wks

16 Feb 85	PAPA'S GOT A BRAND NEW PIGBAG *Kaz KAZ 50* **73**	1

SILICONE SOUL featuring Louise Clare MARSHALL
UK, male production duo and female vocalist (Singles: 5 Weeks) pos/wks

6 Oct 01	RIGHT ON! (re) *VC Recordings / Soma VCRD 96* **15**	5

SILJE *Norway, female vocalist – Silje Nergaard (Singles: 6 Weeks)* pos/wks

15 Dec 90	TELL ME WHERE YOU'RE GOING *EMI EM 159* **55**	6

SILK *US, male vocal group (Singles: 10 Weeks)* pos/wks

24 Apr 93	FREAK ME (re) *Elektra EKR 165CD* ▲ **46**	6
5 Jun 93	GIRL U FOR ME *Elektra EKR 167CD* **67**	2
9 Oct 93	BABY IT'S YOU *Elektra EKR 173CD* **44**	2

The SILKIE *UK, male / female vocal / instrumental group (Singles: 6 Weeks)* pos/wks

23 Sep 65	YOU'VE GOT TO HIDE YOUR LOVE AWAY *Fontana TF 603* **28**	6

SILKK THE SHOCKER See Montell JORDAN

SILSOE (see also ARGENT; SAN JOSÉ featuring Rodriguez ARGENTINA) *UK, male instrumentalist – Rod Argent (Singles: 4 Weeks)* pos/wks

21 Jun 86	AZTEC GOLD *CBS A 7231* **48**	4

'Aztec Gold' was the ITV theme to the 1986 World Cup

Lucie SILVAS *UK, female vocalist /*
instrumentalist – piano (Singles: 7 Weeks, Albums: 4 Weeks) pos/wks

17 Jun 00	IT'S TOO LATE *EMI CDEM 565*	.62 1
16 Oct 04 ●	WHAT YOU'RE MADE OF ... *Mercury 9867463*	.7 7
23 Oct 04	BREATHE IN *Mercury 9867025*	.11 4

John SILVER *Switzerland / Italy, male production / vocal*
duo – Dimitri Derisiotis and Gabriel Rizzo (Singles: 2 Weeks) pos/wks

25 Jan 01	COME ON OVER *Cream CREAM 20CD*	.35 2

SILVER BULLET *UK, male rapper –*
Richard Brown (Singles: 20 Weeks, Albums: 2 Weeks) pos/wks

2 Sep 89	BRING FORTH THE GUILLOTINE (re) *Tam Tam TTT 013*	.45 6
9 Dec 89	20 SECONDS TO COMPLY *Tam Tam 7TTT 019*	.11 10
13 Apr 91	UNDERCOVER ANARCHIST *Parlophone R 6284*	.33 4
4 May 91	BRING DOWN THE WALLS NO LIMIT SQUAD *Parlophone PCS 7350*	.38 2

'Bring Forth the Guillotine' reached its peak position on re-entry during Mar 1990

SILVER BULLET BAND *See Bob SEGER and the SILVER BULLET BAND*

SILVER CITY
UK, male / female vocal / instrumental duo (Singles: 1 Week) pos/wks

30 Oct 93	LOVE INFINITY *Silver City GFJMCD 1*	.62 1

SILVER CONVENTION *Germany / US, female*
vocal group (Singles: 35 Weeks, Albums: 3 Weeks) pos/wks

5 Apr 75	SAVE ME *Magnet MAG 26*	.30 7
15 Nov 75	FLY ROBIN FLY *Magnet MAG 43* ▲	.28 8
3 Apr 76 ●	GET UP AND BOOGIE *Magnet MAG 55*	.7 11
19 Jun 76	TIGER BABY / NO NO JOE *Magnet MAG 69*	.41 4
29 Jan 77	EVERYBODY'S TALKIN' 'BOUT LOVE *Magnet MAG 81*	.25 5
25 Jun 77	SILVER CONVENTION: GREATEST HITS *Magnet MAG 6001*	.34 3

SILVER SUN *UK, male vocal / instrumental*
group (Singles: 13 Weeks, Albums: 2 Weeks) pos/wks

2 Nov 96	LAVA *Polydor 5756872*	.54 1
22 Feb 97	LAST DAY *Polydor 5732432*	.48 1
3 May 97	GOLDEN SKIN *Polydor 5738272*	.32 2
5 Jul 97	JULIA *Polydor 5711752*	.51 1
18 Oct 97	LAVA (re-issue) *Polydor 5714242*	.35 2
20 Jun 98	TOO MUCH, TOO LITTLE, TOO LATE *Polydor 5699152*	.20 4
26 Sep 98	I'LL SEE YOU AROUND *Polydor 5674532*	.26 1
24 May 97	SILVER SUN *Polydor 5372082*	.30 1
17 Oct 98	NEO WAVE *Polydor 5590852*	.74 1

SILVERCHAIR *Australia, male vocal /*
instrumental group (Singles: 8 Weeks, Albums: 5 Weeks) pos/wks

29 Jul 95	PURE MASSACRE *Murmur 6622642*	.71 1
9 Sep 95	TOMORROW *Murmur 6623952*	.59 2
5 Apr 97	FREAK *Murmur 6640765*	.34 2
19 Jul 97	ABUSE ME *Murmur 6647907*	.40 2
15 May 99	ANA'S SONG *Columbia 6673452*	.45 1
23 Sep 95	FROGSTOMP *Murmur 4803402*	.49 1
15 Feb 97	FREAK SHOW *Columbia 4871032*	.38 2
27 Mar 99	NEON BALLROOM *Columbia 4933092*	.29 2

SILVERFISH
US, male vocal / instrumental group (Albums: 1 Week) pos/wks

27 Jun 92	ORGAN FAN *Creation CRECD 118*	.65 1

Dooley SILVERSPOON *US, male vocalist (Singles: 3 Weeks)* pos/wks

31 Jan 76	LET ME BE THE NUMBER 1 (LOVE OF YOUR LIFE) *Seville SEV 1020*	.44 3

Harry SIMEONE CHORALE *US, choir (Singles: 14 Weeks)* pos/wks

13 Feb 59	LITTLE DRUMMER BOY *Top Rank JAR 101*	.13 7
22 Dec 60	ONWARD CHRISTIAN SOLDIERS (2re) *Ember EMBS 118*	.35 5
20 Dec 62	ONWARD CHRISTIAN SOLDIERS (re-issue) *Ember EMBS 144*	38 2

SIMIAN *UK, male vocal / instrumental group (Singles: 1 Week)* pos/wks

14 Jun 03	LA BREEZE *Source SOURCD 069*	.55 1

Gene SIMMONS *(see also KISS)*
US, male vocalist – Chaim Witz (Singles: 4 Weeks) pos/wks

27 Jan 79	RADIOACTIVE *Casablanca CAN 134*	.41 4

SIMON *UK, male producer – Simon Pearson (Singles: 2 Weeks)* pos/wks

31 Mar 01	FREE AT LAST *Positiva CDTIV 152*	.36 2

Carly SIMON 442 Top 500 *(see also Will POWERS) First charted in*
the US in 1964 as half of folk duo Simon Sisters with sister Lucy, b. 25 Jun
1945, New York. Winner of 1971's Best New Artist Grammy was married to
fellow singer / songwriter James Taylor (1972-1983). Elected to Songwriters
Hall of Fame in 1994 (Singles: 85 Weeks, Albums: 74 Weeks) pos/wks

16 Dec 72 ●	YOU'RE SO VAIN *Elektra K 12077* ▲	.3 15
31 Mar 73	THE RIGHT THING TO DO *Elektra K 12095*	.17 9
16 Mar 74	MOCKINGBIRD *Electra K 12134* [1]	.34 5
6 Aug 77	NOBODY DOES IT BETTER *Elektra K 12261*	.7 12
21 Aug 82	WHY *WEA K 79300*	.10 13
24 Jan 87 ●	COMING AROUND AGAIN *Arista ARIST 687*	.10 12
10 Jun 89	WHY (re-issue) *WEA U 7501*	.56 5
20 Apr 91	YOU'RE SO VAIN (re-issue) *Elektra EKR 123*	.41 5
22 Dec 01	SON OF A GUN (I BETCHA THINK THIS SONG IS ABOUT YOU) (re) *Virgin VUSCD 232* [2]	.13 9
20 Jan 73 ●	NO SECRETS *Elektra K 42127* ▲	.3 26
16 Mar 74	HOTCAKES *Elektra K 52005*	.19 9
9 May 87	COMING AROUND AGAIN *Arista 208 140*	.25 20
3 Sep 88	GREATEST HITS LIVE *Arista 209196*	.49 6
20 Mar 99	NOBODY DOES IT BETTER – THE VERY BEST OF CARLY SIMON *Warner.esp / Global TV RADCD 103*	.22 6
12 Jun 04	REFLECTIONS – CARLY SIMON'S GREATEST HITS *Elektra / Rhino 8122789702*	.25 7

[1] Includes uncredited vocals by James Taylor [2] Janet with Carly Simon
featuring Missy Elliott

'Mockingbird' was a duet with uncredited vocals by James Taylor

Joe SIMON *US, male vocalist (Singles: 10 Weeks)* pos/wks

16 Jun 73	STEP BY STEP *Mojo 2093 030*	.14 10

Paul SIMON 132 Top 500 *Acclaimed award-winning singer / song-*
writer, b. 13 Oct 1941, New Jersey, US. Recorded under various names in the
early 1960s before forming top duo Simon and Garfunkel. Married to actress
Carrie Fisher (1983-85) and later Edie Brickell (1991-present). Also helped to
popularise world music (Singles: 85 Weeks, Albums: 291 Weeks) pos/wks

19 Feb 72 ●	MOTHER AND CHILD REUNION *CBS 7793*	.5 12
29 Apr 72	ME AND JULIO DOWN BY THE SCHOOLYARD *CBS 7964*	.15 9
16 Jun 73	TAKE ME TO THE MARDI GRAS *CBS 1578*	.7 11
22 Sep 73	LOVES ME LIKE A ROCK *CBS 1700*	.39 5
10 Jan 76	50 WAYS TO LEAVE YOUR LOVER *CBS 3887* ▲	.23 6
3 Dec 77	SLIP SLIDIN' AWAY *CBS 5770*	.36 5
6 Sep 80	LATE IN THE EVENING *Warner Bros. K 17666*	.58 4
13 Sep 86 ●	YOU CAN CALL ME AL *Warner Bros. W 8667*	.4 13
13 Dec 86	THE BOY IN THE BUBBLE *Warner Bros. W 8509*	.26 8
6 Oct 90	THE OBVIOUS CHILD *Warner Bros. W 9549*	.15 10
9 Dec 95	SOMETHING SO RIGHT *RCA 74321332392* [1]	.44 2
26 Feb 72 ★	PAUL SIMON *CBS 69007*	.1 26
2 Jun 73 ●	THERE GOES RHYMIN' SIMON *CBS 69035*	.4 22
1 Nov 75 ●	STILL CRAZY AFTER ALL THESE YEARS *CBS 86001* ▲	.6 31
3 Dec 77	GREATEST HITS ETC. *CBS 10007*	.6 15
30 Aug 80	ONE-TRICK PONY *Warner Bros. K 56846*	.17 12
12 Nov 83	HEARTS AND BONES *Warner Bros. 9239421*	.34 8
13 Sep 86 ★	GRACELAND *Warner Bros. WX 52*	.1 115
24 Jan 87	GREATEST HITS ETC. (re-issue) *CBS 450 1661*	.73 2
5 Nov 88	NEGOTIATIONS AND LOVE SONGS 1971–1986 *Warner Bros. WX 223*	.17 15
27 Oct 90 ★	THE RHYTHM OF THE SAINTS *Warner Bros. WX 340* ■	.1 28
23 Nov 91	PAUL SIMON'S CONCERT IN THE PARK – AUGUST 15TH 1991 *Warner Bros. WX 448*	.60 1
27 May 00 ●	GREATEST HITS – SHINING LIKE A NATIONAL GUITAR *Warner Bros. 9362477212*	.6 12
14 Oct 00	YOU'RE THE ONE *Warner Bros. 9362478442*	.20 4

[1] Annie Lennox featuring Paul Simon

Ronni SIMON *UK, male vocalist (Singles: 2 Weeks)* pos/wks

13 Aug 94	B GOOD 2 ME *Network NWKCD 80*	.73 1
10 Jun 95	TAKE YOU THERE *Network NWKCD 85*	.58 1

Tito SIMON
Jamaica, male vocalist (Singles: 4 Weeks) pos/wks

8 Feb 75	**THIS MONDAY MORNING FEELING** *Horse HOSS 57*	**45**	4

SIMON and GARFUNKEL `15` `Top 500`
The most successful recording duo ever: singer / songwriter / guitarist Paul Simon, b. 13 Oct 1941, New Jersey, US, and vocalist Art Garfunkel, b. 5 Nov 1941, New York, US. The pair met at High School and joined doo-wop group The Peptones. Their first US hit was as Tom and Jerry in 1957. They then both recorded solo, with Simon charting as both Jerry Landis and Tico and the Triumphs. The duo reunited and released 'Wednesday Morning, 3AM'. When this album flopped, Simon went on a solo UK folk club tour (when he penned 'Homeward Bound'). Producer Tom Wilson re-mixed the album track 'The Sound of Silence', transforming it into a folk rock track that quickly took off. Paul rushed home, re-united with Art and the rest is history. Before splitting in 1971, they won numerous Grammy awards, became the first duo to top either the UK and US albums chart, and at times had three of America's Top 5 albums (1968). 'Simon and Garfunkel's Greatest Hits' is the world's biggest seller by a duo (13 million copies in the US alone) and 'Bridge Over Troubled Water' (one of the most performed songs on reality TV pop shows) was voted Best Single of All Time at the Brits (1977), while it's parent LP – the UK's top seller in 1970 and 1971, was named Best Album. The duo, who reunited for a very successful tour in 2003 / 2004, were inducted into the Rock and Roll Hall of Fame (1990) and received a Lifetime Achievement Grammy (2003) (Singles: 87 Weeks, Albums: 1114 Weeks) pos/wks

24 Mar 66	● **HOMEWARD BOUND** *CBS 202045*	**9**	12
16 Jun 66	**I AM A ROCK** *CBS 202303*	**17**	10
10 Jul 68	● **MRS ROBINSON** *CBS 3443* ▲	**4**	12
8 Jan 69	● **MRS ROBINSON (EP)** *CBS EP 6400*	**9**	5
30 Apr 69	● **THE BOXER** *CBS 4162*	**6**	14
21 Feb 70	★ **BRIDGE OVER TROUBLED WATER (re)**		
	CBS 4790 [1] ▲	**1**	20
7 Oct 72	**AMERICA** *CBS 8336*	**25**	7
7 Dec 91	**A HAZY SHADE OF WINTER / SILENT NIGHT – SEVEN**		
	O'CLOCK NEWS *Columbia 6576537*	**30**	6
15 Feb 92	**THE BOXER (re-issue)** *Columbia 6578067*	**75**	1
16 Apr 66	**SOUNDS OF SILENCE** *CBS 62690*	**13**	104
3 Aug 68	★ **BOOKENDS** *CBS 63101* ▲	**1**	77
31 Aug 68	**PARSLEY, SAGE, ROSEMARY AND THYME** *CBS 62860*	**13**	58
26 Oct 68	● **THE GRADUATE (FILM SOUNDTRACK)** *CBS 70042* ▲	**3**	71
9 Nov 68	**WEDNESDAY MORNING, 3AM** *CBS 63370*	**24**	4
21 Feb 70	● **BRIDGE OVER TROUBLED WATER** *CBS 63699* ■ ▲	**1**	307
22 Jul 72	● **SIMON AND GARFUNKEL'S GREATEST HITS** *CBS 69003*	**2**	283
4 Apr 81	**SOUNDS OF SILENCE (re-issue)** *CBS 32020*	**68**	1
21 Nov 81	● **THE SIMON AND GARFUNKEL COLLECTION** *CBS 10029*	**4**	80
20 Mar 82	● **THE CONCERT IN CENTRAL PARK** *Geffen GEF 96008*	**6**	43
30 Nov 91	● **THE DEFINITIVE SIMON AND GARFUNKEL**		
	Columbia MOODCD 21	**8**	57
5 Feb 00	● **THE VERY BEST OF SIMON AND GARFUNKEL – TALES**		
	FROM NEW YORK *Columbia SONYTV 81CD*	**8**	12
6 Dec 03	**THE ESSENTIAL SIMON AND GARFUNKEL**		
	Columbia 5134702	**25**	13
11 Dec 04	**OLD FRIENDS – LIVE ON STAGE**		
	Columbia 5191732	**61**	2

[1] Keyboard: Larry Knechtel

Tracks on Mrs Robinson (EP): Mrs Robinson / Scarborough Fair – Canticle / The Sound of Silence / April Come She Will. This EP would have stayed more than five weeks on chart had a decision to exclude EPs from the chart in Feb 1969 not been taken

SIMONE *US, female vocalist (Singles: 1 Week)* pos/wks

23 Nov 91	**MY FAMILY DEPENDS ON ME** *Strictly Rhythm A 8678*	**75**	1

Nina SIMONE
US, female vocalist / instrumentalist – keyboards – Eunice Waymon, b. 21 Feb 1933, d. 21 Apr 2003 (Singles: 46 Weeks, Albums: 33 Weeks) pos/wks

5 Aug 65	**I PUT A SPELL ON YOU** *Philips BF 1415*	**49**	1
16 Oct 68	● **AIN'T GOT NO – I GOT LIFE / DO WHAT YOU GOTTA DO**		
	RCA 1743	**2**	18
15 Jan 69	● **TO LOVE SOMEBODY** *RCA 1779*	**5**	9
15 Jan 69	**I PUT A SPELL ON YOU (re-issue)** *Philips BF 1736*	**28**	4
31 Oct 87	● **MY BABY JUST CARES FOR ME** *Charly CYZ 7112*	**5**	11
9 Jul 94	**FEELING GOOD** *Mercury MERCD 403*	**40**	3
24 Jul 65	**I PUT A SPELL ON YOU** *Philips BL 7671*	**18**	3
15 Feb 69	**NUFF SAID** *RCS SF 7979*	**11**	1
14 Nov 87	**MY BABY JUST CARES FOR ME** *Charly CR 30217*	**56**	8
16 Jul 94	● **FEELING GOOD – THE VERY BEST OF NINA SIMONE**		
	PolyGram TV 5226692	**9**	8
7 Feb 98	**BLUE FOR YOU – THE VERY BEST OF NINA SIMONE**		
	Global Television RADCD 84	**12**	10
21 Jun 03	**GOLD** *UCJ 9808087*	**27**	3

'Do What You Gotta Do' was listed only for the first eight weeks of the record's chart run. It peaked at No.7

Victor SIMONELLI presents SOLUTION
US, male producer (Singles: 1 Week) pos/wks

2 Nov 96	**FEELS SO RIGHT** *Soundproof MCSTD 40068*	**63**	1

SIMPLE KID
UK, male vocalist – Phil Nicholls (Singles: 3 Weeks) pos/wks

13 Sep 03	**THE AVERAGE MAN** *2M 2M 005CD*	**72**	1
14 Feb 04	**TRUCK ON** *2M 2M 007CD1*	**38**	2

SIMPLE MINDS `67` `Top 500`
The most successful Scottish band of the 1980s, fronted by Jim Kerr (b. 9 Jul 1959, Glasgow), who married Chrissie Hynde, lead singer of The Pretenders. Five of the quintet's albums entered the UK chart at No.1, and world sales topped 30 million (Singles: 190 Weeks, Albums: 354 Weeks) pos/wks

12 May 79	**LIFE IN A DAY** *Zoom ZUM 10*	**62**	2
23 May 81	**THE AMERICAN** *Virgin VS 410*	**59**	3
15 Aug 81	**LOVE SONG** *Virgin VS 434*	**47**	4
7 Nov 81	**SWEAT IN BULLET** *Virgin VS 451*	**52**	3
10 Apr 82	**PROMISED YOU A MIRACLE** *Virgin VS 488*	**13**	11
28 Aug 82	**GLITTERING PRIZE** *Virgin VS 511*	**16**	11
13 Nov 82	**SOMEONE SOMEWHERE (IN SUMMERTIME)**		
	Virgin VS 538	**36**	5
26 Nov 83	**WATERFRONT** *Virgin VS 636*	**13**	10
28 Jan 84	**SPEED YOUR LOVE TO ME** *Virgin VS 649*	**20**	4
24 Mar 84	**UP ON THE CATWALK** *Virgin VS 661*	**27**	5
20 Apr 85	● **DON'T YOU (FORGET ABOUT ME) (4re)** *Virgin VS 749* ▲	**7**	24
12 Oct 85	● **ALIVE AND KICKING (re)** *Virgin VS 817*	**7**	11
1 Feb 86	● **SANCTIFY YOURSELF** *Virgin SM 1*	**10**	7
12 Apr 86	● **ALL THE THINGS SHE SAID (re)** *Virgin VS 860*	**9**	9
15 Nov 86	**GHOSTDANCING (re)** *Virgin VS 907*	**13**	8
20 Jun 87	**PROMISED YOU A MIRACLE (LIVE)** *Virgin SM 2*	**19**	7
18 Feb 89	★ **BELFAST CHILD** *Virgin SMX 3*	**1**	11
22 Apr 89	**THIS IS YOUR LAND** *Virgin SMX 4*	**13**	4
29 Jul 89	**KICK IT IN** *Virgin SM 5*	**15**	5
9 Dec 89	**THE AMSTERDAM EP** *Virgin SMX 6*	**18**	6
23 Mar 91	● **LET THERE BE LOVE** *Virgin VS 1332*	**6**	7
25 May 91	**SEE THE LIGHTS** *Virgin VS 1343*	**20**	4
31 Aug 91	**STAND BY LOVE** *Virgin VS 1358*	**13**	4
26 Oct 91	**REAL LIFE** *Virgin VS 1382*	**34**	3
10 Oct 92	● **LOVE SONG / ALIVE AND KICKING (re-issue)**		
	Virgin VS 1440	**6**	6
28 Jan 95	● **SHE'S A RIVER** *Virgin VSCDX 1509*	**9**	5
8 Apr 95	**HYPNOTISED** *Virgin VSCDX 1534*	**18**	5
14 Mar 98	**GLITTERBALL** *Chrysalis CDCHSS 5078*	**18**	2
30 May 98	**WAR BABIES** *Chrysalis CDCHS 5088*	**43**	1
2 Feb 02	**BELFAST TRANCE** *Nebula BELFCD 001* [1]	**74**	1
30 Mar 02	**CRY** *Eagle EAGXS 218*	**47**	1
20 Jul 02	**MONSTER** *Defected DFECT 49* [2]	**67**	1
5 May 79	**LIFE IN A DAY** *Zoom ZULP 1*	**30**	6
27 Sep 80	**EMPIRES AND DANCE** *Arista SPART 1140*	**41**	2
12 Sep 81	**SONS AND FASCINATIONS / SISTER FEELINGS CALL**		
	Virgin V 2207	**11**	7
27 Feb 82	**CELEBRATION** *Arista SPART 1183*	**45**	7
25 Sep 82	● **NEW GOLD DREAM (81 82 83 84)** *Virgin V 2230*	**3**	52
18 Feb 84	★ **SPARKLE IN THE RAIN** *Virgin V 2300* ■	**1**	57
2 Nov 85	★ **ONCE UPON A TIME** *Virgin V 2364* ■	**1**	83
6 Jun 87	★ **LIVE IN THE CITY OF LIGHT** *Virgin V SMDL 1* ■	**1**	26
13 May 89	★ **STREET FIGHTING YEARS** *Virgin MINDS 1* ■	**1**	28
20 Apr 91	● **REAL LIFE** *Virgin V 2660*	**2**	25
24 Oct 92	★ **GLITTERING PRIZE 81/92** *Virgin SMTVD 1* ■	**1**	39
11 Feb 95	● **GOOD NEWS FROM THE NEXT WORLD**		
	Virgin CDV 2760	**2**	14
28 Mar 98	**NEAPOLIS** *Chrysalis 4937122*	**19**	3
17 Nov 01	**THE BEST OF SIMPLE MINDS** *Virgin CDVD 2953*	**34**	4

[1] John "00" Fleming vs Simple Minds [2] Liquid People vs Simple Minds

Tracks on The Amsterdam EP: Let It All Come Down / Jerusalem / Sign of the Times

SIMPLE PLAN
US, male vocal / instrumental group (Singles: 1 Weeks) pos/wks

5 Jul 03	**ADDICTED** *Lava / Atlantic AT 0158CD*	**63**	1

SIMPLICIOUS
US, male vocal group (Singles: 9 Weeks) pos/wks

29 Sep 84	**LET HER FEEL IT** *Fourth & Broadway BRW 13*	**65**	3
2 Feb 85	**LET HER FEEL IT** (re-issue) *Fourth & Broadway BRW 18*	**34**	6

The re-issue of 'Let Her Feel It' was listed with 'Personality' by Eugene Wilde

SIMPLY RED 26 Top 500
The unmistakable Mick Hucknall, b. 8 Jun 1960, Manchester, UK, quickly became the representative face and voice of this internationally popular outfit. Their 'Stars' album sold more than two million in the UK and was the biggest British seller in 1991 and 1992. Best-selling single: 'Fairground' 783,000 (Singles: 240 Weeks, Albums: 609 Weeks) pos/wks

15 Jun 85	**MONEY'S TOO TIGHT (TO MENTION)** *Elektra EKR 9*	**13**	12
21 Sep 85	**COME TO MY AID** *Elektra EKR 19*	**66**	2
16 Nov 85	**HOLDING BACK THE YEARS** *Elektra EKR 29* ▲	**51**	4
8 Mar 86	**JERICHO** *WEA YZ 63*	**53**	3
17 May 86 ●	**HOLDING BACK THE YEARS** (re-issue) *WEA YZ 70*	**2**	13
9 Aug 86	**OPEN UP THE RED BOX** *WEA YZ 75*	**61**	4
14 Feb 87	**THE RIGHT THING** *WEA YZ 103*	**11**	10
23 May 87	**INFIDELITY** *Elektra YZ 114*	**31**	5
28 Nov 87	**EV'RY TIME WE SAY GOODBYE** *Elektra YZ 161*	**11**	9
12 Mar 88	**I WON'T FEEL BAD** *Elektra YZ 172*	**68**	3
28 Jan 89	**IT'S ONLY LOVE** *Elektra YZ 349*	**13**	8
8 Apr 89 ●	**IF YOU DON'T KNOW ME BY NOW** *Elektra YZ 377* ▲	**2**	10
8 Jul 89	**A NEW FLAME** *WEA YZ 404*	**17**	8
28 Oct 89	**YOU'VE GOT IT** *Elektra YZ 424*	**46**	3
21 Sep 91	**SOMETHING GOT ME STARTED** *East West YZ 614*	**11**	8
30 Nov 91 ●	**STARS** *East West YZ 626*	**8**	10
8 Feb 92 ●	**FOR YOUR BABIES** *East West YZ 642*	**9**	8
2 May 92	**THRILL ME** *East West YZ 671*	**33**	5
25 Jul 92	**YOUR MIRROR** *East West YZ 689*	**17**	4
21 Nov 92	**MONTREUX (EP)** *East West YZ 716*	**11**	10
30 Sep 95 ★	**FAIRGROUND** *East West EW 001CD1* ■	**1**	14
16 Dec 95	**REMEMBERING THE FIRST TIME** *East West EW 015CD1*	**22**	6
24 Feb 96	**NEVER NEVER LOVE** *East West EW 029CD1*	**18**	4
22 Jun 96	**WE'RE IN THIS TOGETHER** *East West EW 046CD1*	**11**	6
9 Nov 96 ●	**ANGEL** *East West EW 074CD1*	**4**	13
20 Sep 97	**NIGHT NURSE** *East West EW 129CD1* [1]	**13**	8
16 May 98 ●	**SAY YOU LOVE ME** *East West EW 164CD*	**7**	7
22 Aug 98 ●	**THE AIR THAT I BREATHE** *East West EW 3821CD*	**6**	7
12 Dec 98	**GHETTO GIRL** *East West EW 191CD1*	**34**	2
30 Oct 99	**AIN'T THAT A LOT OF LOVE** *East West EW 208CD1*	**14**	6
19 Feb 00	**YOUR EYES** *East West EW 212CD1*	**26**	2
29 Mar 03 ●	**SUNRISE** *Simplyred.com SRS 001CD1*	**7**	11
19 Jul 03	**FAKE** *Simplyred.com SRS 002CD1*	**21**	4
13 Dec 03 ●	**YOU MAKE ME FEEL BRAND NEW** *Simplyred.com SRS 003CD1*	**7**	9
10 Apr 04	**HOME** *Simplyred.com SRS 004CD*	**40**	2
26 Oct 85 ●	**PICTURE BOOK** *Elektra EKT 27*	**2**	130
21 Mar 87 ●	**MEN AND WOMEN** *WEA WX 85*	**2**	60
25 Feb 89 ★	**A NEW FLAME** *Elektra WX 242* ■	**1**	84
12 Oct 91 ★	**STARS** *East West WX 427* ■	**1**	134
4 Mar 95	**MEN AND WOMEN** (re-issue) *East West K 2420712*	**20**	7
21 Oct 95 ★	**LIFE** *East West YZ 1014* ■	**1**	47
24 Feb 96	**A NEW FLAME** (re-issue) *East West K 2446892*	**28**	6
24 Feb 96	**PICTURE BOOK** (re-issue) *East West 9031769932*	**33**	5
19 Oct 96 ★	**GREATEST HITS** *East West 630165522* ■	**1**	52
30 May 98 ●	**BLUE** *East West 3984230972* ■	**1**	26
13 Nov 99 ●	**LOVE AND THE RUSSIAN WINTER** *East West 3984299422*	**6**	17
25 Nov 00	**IT'S ONLY LOVE** *East West 8573855372*	**27**	6
5 Apr 03 ●	**HOME** *Simplyred.com SRA 001CD*	**2**	35

[1] Sly and Robbie featuring Simply Red

Tracks on Montreux (EP): Drowning In My Own Tears / Grandma's Hands / Lady Godiva's Room / Love for Sale

SIMPLY RED AND WHITE
UK, male Sunderland FC supporters vocal group (Singles: 4 Weeks) pos/wks

6 Apr 96	**DAYDREAM BELIEVER (CHEER UP PETER REID)** (re) *Ropery SHAYISGOD 1D*	**41**	4

SIMPLY SMOOTH
US, male / female vocal group (Singles: 1 Week) pos/wks

17 Oct 98	**LADY (YOU BRING ME UP)** *Big Bang CDBANG 07*	**70**	1

Ashlee SIMPSON
US, female vocalist (Singles: 10 Weeks, Albums: 4 Weeks) pos/wks

9 Oct 04 ●	**PIECES OF ME** *Geffen 9863811*	**4**	10
16 Oct 04	**AUTOBIOGRAPHY** *Geffen 9863256* ▲	**31**	4

Jessica SIMPSON
US, female vocalist (Singles: 32 Weeks, Albums: 7 Weeks) pos/wks

22 Apr 00 ●	**I WANNA LOVE YOU FOREVER** (re) *Columbia 6691272*	**7**	11
15 Jul 00	**I THINK I'M IN LOVE WITH YOU** *Columbia 6695942*	**15**	7
14 Jul 01	**IRRESISTIBLE** *Columbia 6714102*	**11**	6
26 Jun 04 ●	**WITH YOU** *Columbia 6748302*	**7**	8
6 May 00	**SWEET KISSES** *Columbia 4949332*	**36**	2
1 May 04	**IN THIS SKIN** *Columbia SNY865602*	**36**	5

Paul SIMPSON featuring ADEVA
US, male producer / instrumentalist and female vocalist (Singles: 8 Weeks) pos/wks

25 Mar 89	**MUSICAL FREEDOM (MOVING ON UP)** *Cooltempo CDCOOL 182*	**22**	8

Vida SIMPSON
US, female vocalist (Singles: 1 Week) pos/wks

18 Feb 95	**OOHHH BABY** *Hi-Life HICD 6*	**70**	1

The SIMPSONS
US, male / female cartoon group – lead vocal Bart Simpson (Nancy Cartwright) (Singles: 19 Weeks, Albums: 30 Weeks) pos/wks

26 Jan 91 ★	**DO THE BARTMAN** *Geffen GEF 87*	**1**	12
6 Apr 91 ●	**DEEP DEEP TROUBLE** *Geffen GEF 88* [1]	**7**	7
2 Feb 91 ●	**THE SIMPSONS SING THE BLUES** *Geffen 7599243081*	**6**	30

[1] The Simpsons featuring Bart and Homer

W/Cdr AE SIMS *See Central Band of the ROYAL AIR FORCE, Conductor W/Cdr AE SIMS OBE*

Joyce SIMS
US, female vocalist (Singles: 36 Weeks, Albums: 25 Weeks) pos/wks

19 Apr 86	**ALL AND ALL** *London LON 94*	**16**	10
13 Jun 87	**LIFETIME LOVE** *London LON 137*	**34**	6
9 Jan 88 ●	**COME INTO MY LIFE** *London LON 161*	**7**	9
23 Apr 88	**WALK AWAY** *London LON 176*	**24**	6
17 Jun 89	**LOOKING FOR A LOVE** *ffrr F 109*	**39**	4
27 May 95	**COME INTO MY LIFE** (re-mix) *Club Tools 0060435 CLU*	**72**	1
9 Jan 88 ●	**COME INTO MY LIFE** *London LONLP 47*	**5**	24
16 Sep 89	**ALL ABOUT LOVE** *London 828129 1*	**64**	1

Kym SIMS
US, female vocalist (Singles: 23 Weeks, Albums: 2 Weeks) pos/wks

7 Dec 91 ●	**TOO BLIND TO SEE IT** *Atco B 8667*	**5**	12
28 Mar 92	**TAKE MY ADVICE** *Atco B 8591*	**13**	7
27 Jun 92	**A LITTLE BIT MORE** *Atco B 8528*	**30**	3
8 Jun 96	**WE GOTTA LOVE** *Pulse 8 CDLOSE 104*	**58**	1
18 Apr 92	**TOO BLIND TO SEE IT** *Atco 7567921042*	**39**	2

SIN WITH SEBASTIAN
Germany, male vocalist – Sebastian Roth (Singles: 2 Weeks) pos/wks

16 Sep 95	**SHUT UP (AND SLEEP WITH ME)** *Sing Sing 74321253592*	**44**	1
27 Jan 96	**SHUT UP (AND SLEEP WITH ME)** (re-mix) *Sing Sing 74321337972*	**46**	1

Frank SINATRA 12 Top 500 (see also The RATPACK)
Legendary entertainer regarded by many as the greatest song stylist of the 20th century, b. 12 Dec 1915, New Jersey, US, d. 14 May 1998. The vocalist (with Tommy Dorsey Orchestra) on the first US No.1, 'I'll Never Smile Again', (1940) was the first teen idol. 'Songs for Swingin' Lovers' is the only album to reach the UK Top 20 singles chart and is one of 34 US gold albums amassed by the influential vocalist, who has scored more US Top 10 LPs than any other soloist. Sinatra, the first recipient of a Grammy Lifetime Achievement award (1965), holds the UK chart longevity record with 'My Way'. Total UK single sales: 4,597,630 (Singles: 440 Weeks, Albums: 892 Weeks) pos/wks

9 Jul 54	**YOUNG-AT-HEART** *Capitol CL 14064*	**12**	1
16 Jul 54 ★	**THREE COINS IN THE FOUNTAIN** *Capitol CL 14120*	**1**	19
10 Jun 55	**YOU MY LOVE** (2re) *Capitol CL 14240*	**13**	7
5 Aug 55 ●	**LEARNIN' THE BLUES** *Capitol CL 14296*	**2**	13
2 Sep 55	**NOT AS A STRANGER** *Capitol CL 14326*	**18**	1

13 Jan 56 ●	LOVE AND MARRIAGE *Capitol CL 14503*	3	8
20 Jan 56 ●	(LOVE IS) THE TENDER TRAP *Capitol CL 14511*	2	9
15 Jun 56	SONGS FOR SWINGIN' LOVERS (LP) *Capitol LCT 6106*	12	8
22 Nov 57 ●	ALL THE WAY / CHICAGO (3re) *Capitol CL 14800*	3	20
7 Feb 58	WITCHCRAFT *Capitol CL 14819*	12	8
14 Nov 58	MR SUCCESS (2re) *Capitol CL 14956*	25	4
10 Apr 59	FRENCH FOREIGN LEGION *Capitol CL 14997*	18	5
15 May 59	COME DANCE WITH ME! (LP) *Capitol LCT 6179* [1]	30	1
28 Aug 59 ●	HIGH HOPES (2re) *Capitol CL 15052* [2]	6	15
7 Apr 60	IT'S NICE TO GO TRAV'LING *Capitol CL 15116*	48	2
16 Jun 60	RIVER STAY 'WAY FROM MY DOOR *Capitol CL 15135*	18	9
8 Sep 60	NICE 'N' EASY *Capitol CL 15150*	15	12
24 Nov 60	OL' MACDONALD *Capitol CL 15168*	11	8
20 Apr 61	MY BLUE HEAVEN *Capitol CL 15193*	33	7
28 Sep 61	GRANADA *Reprise R 20010*	15	8
23 Nov 61	THE COFFEE SONG *Reprise R 20035*	39	3
5 Apr 62	EV'RYBODY'S TWISTING *Reprise R 20063*	22	12
13 Dec 62	ME AND MY SHADOW (re) *Reprise R 20128* [3]	20	9
7 Mar 63	MY KIND OF GIRL *Reprise R 20148* [4]	35	6
24 Sep 64	HELLO DOLLY *Reprise R 20351* [4]	47	1
12 May 66 ★	STRANGERS IN THE NIGHT *Reprise R 23052* ▲	1	20
29 Sep 66	SUMMER WIND *Reprise RS 20509*	36	5
15 Dec 66	THAT'S LIFE *Reprise RS 20531*	44	5
23 Mar 67 ★	SOMETHIN' STUPID *Reprise RS 23166* [5] ▲	1	18
23 Aug 67	THE WORLD WE KNEW (OVER AND OVER) *Reprise RS 20610*	33	11
2 Apr 69 ●	MY WAY (8re) *Reprise RS 20817*	5	122
4 Oct 69 ●	LOVE'S BEEN GOOD TO ME *Reprise RS 20852*	8	18
6 Mar 71	I WILL DRINK THE WINE *Reprise RS 23487*	16	12
20 Dec 75	I BELIEVE I'M GONNA LOVE YOU *Reprise K 14400*	34	7
9 Aug 80 ●	THEME FROM 'NEW YORK, NEW YORK' (re) *Reprise K 14502*	4	14
4 Dec 93 ●	I'VE GOT YOU UNDER MY SKIN *Island CID 578* [6]	4	9
16 Apr 94	MY WAY (re-issue) *Reprise W 0163CD*	45	2
30 Jan 99	THEY ALL LAUGHED *Reprise W 469CD*	41	1
28 Jul 56 ●	SONGS FOR SWINGIN' LOVERS *Capitol LCT 6106*	1	34
16 Feb 57 ★	THIS IS SINATRA! *Capitol LCT 6123*	1	13
25 May 57 ●	CLOSE TO YOU *Capitol LCT 6130*	2	9
20 Jul 57 ●	FRANKIE *Philips BBL 7168*	3	7
7 Sep 57 ★	A SWINGIN' AFFAIR! *Capitol LCT 6135*	1	19
1 Mar 58 ●	WHERE ARE YOU? *Capitol LCT 6152*	3	5
21 Jun 58 ●	THIS IS SINATRA (VOL.2) *Capitol LCT 6155*	3	12
13 Sep 58 ●	COME FLY WITH ME! *Capitol LCT 6154* [1]	2	18
29 Nov 58 ●	FRANK SINATRA STORY *Fontana TFL 5030*	8	1
13 Dec 58 ●	FRANK SINATRA SINGS FOR ONLY THE LONELY *Capitol LCT 6168*	5	13
16 May 59 ●	COME DANCE WITH ME! *Capitol LCT 6179*	2	30
22 Aug 59 ●	LOOK TO YOUR HEART *Capitol LCT 6181*	6	9
11 Jun 60 ●	COME BACK TO SORRENTO *Fontana TFL 5082*	6	9
29 Oct 60 ●	SWING EASY *Capitol W 587*	5	17
21 Jan 61 ●	NICE 'N EASY *Capitol W 1417* ▲	4	27
15 Jul 61	SINATRA SOUVENIR *Fontana TFL 5138*	18	1
19 Aug 61 ●	WHEN YOUR LOVER HAS GONE *Encore ENC 101*	6	10
23 Sep 61 ●	SINATRA'S SWINGIN' SESSION!!! AND MORE *Capitol W 1491*	6	8
28 Oct 61 ●	SINATRA SWINGS *Reprise R 1002*	8	8
25 Nov 61 ●	SINATRA PLUS *Fontana SET 303*	7	9
16 Dec 61 ●	RING-A-DING-DING *Reprise R 1001*	8	9
17 Feb 62 ●	COME SWING WITH ME *Capitol W 1594*	13	4
7 Apr 62 ●	I REMEMBER TOMMY ... *Reprise R 1003*	10	12
9 Jun 62 ●	SINATRA AND STRINGS *Reprise R 1004*	6	20
27 Oct 62 ●	GREAT SONGS FROM GREAT BRITAIN *Reprise R 1006*	12	9
29 Dec 62 ●	SINATRA WITH SWINGING BRASS *Reprise R 1005*	14	11
23 Feb 63 ●	SINATRA – BASIE *Reprise R 1008* [1]	2	23
27 Jul 63 ●	CONCERT SINATRA *Reprise R 1009*	8	18
5 Oct 63 ●	SINATRA'S SINATRA *Reprise R 1010*	9	24
19 Sep 64 ●	IT MIGHT AS WELL BE SWING *Reprise R 1012*	17	4
20 Mar 65	SOFTLY AS I LEAVE YOU *Reprise R 1013*	20	1
22 Jan 66 ●	A MAN AND HIS MUSIC *Reprise R 1016*	9	19
21 May 66 ●	MOONLIGHT SINATRA *Reprise R 1018*	18	8
2 Jul 66 ●	STRANGERS IN THE NIGHT *Reprise R 1017* ▲	4	18
1 Oct 66 ●	SINATRA AT 'THE SANDS' *Reprise RLP 1019*	7	18
3 Dec 66	FRANK SINATRA SINGS SONGS FOR PLEASURE *MFP 1120*	26	2
25 Feb 67	THAT'S LIFE *Reprise RSLP 1020*	22	12
7 Oct 67	FRANK SINATRA *Reprise RSLP 1022*	28	5
19 Oct 68 ●	GREATEST HITS *Reprise RSLP 1025*	8	38
7 Dec 68	BEST OF FRANK SINATRA *Capitol ST 21140*	17	10
7 Jun 69 ●	MY WAY *Reprise RSLP 1029*	2	51
4 Oct 69	A MAN ALONE – THE WORDS & MUSIC OF ROD McKUEN *Reprise RSLP 1030*	18	7
9 May 70	WATERTOWN *Reprise RSLP 1031*	14	9
12 Dec 70 ●	GREATEST HITS VOLUME 2 *Reprise RSLP 1032*	6	39

5 Jun 71 ●	SINATRA AND COMPANY *Reprise RSLP 1033*	9	9
27 Nov 71	FRANK SINATRA SINGS RODGERS AND HART *Starline SRS 5083*	35	1
8 Jan 72	GREATEST HITS VOLUME 2 (re-issue) *Reprise K 44018*	29	3
8 Jan 72	MY WAY (re-issue) *Reprise K 44015*	35	1
1 Dec 73 ●	OL' BLUE EYES IS BACK *Warner Bros. K 44249*	12	13
17 Aug 74	SOME NICE THINGS I'VE MISSED *Reprise K 54020*	35	3
15 Feb 75	THE MAIN EVENT (TV SOUNDTRACK) *Reprise K 54031*	30	2
14 Jun 75	THE BEST OF OL' BLUE EYES *Reprise K 54042*	30	3
19 Mar 77 ★	PORTRAIT OF SINATRA *Reprise K 64039*	1	18
13 May 78 ●	20 GOLDEN GREATS *Capitol EMTV 10*	4	11
18 Aug 84	L.A. IS MY LADY *Qwest 925145*	41	5
22 Mar 86	NEW YORK NEW YORK (GREATEST HITS) *Warner Bros. WX 32*	13	12
4 Oct 86	THE FRANK SINATRA COLLECTION *Capitol EMTV 41*	40	7
6 Nov 93 ●	DUETS *Capitol CDEST 2218*	5	14
26 Nov 94	DUETS II *Capitol CDEST 2245*	29	6
11 Mar 95	THIS IS FRANK SINATRA 1953–1957 *Music for Pleasure CDDL 1275*	56	1
2 Dec 95	SINATRA 80TH – ALL THE BEST *Capitol CDESTD 2*	49	5
16 Aug 97 ●	MY WAY – THE BEST OF FRANK SINATRA *Reprise 9362467122*	7	128
24 Jun 00 ●	CLASSIC SINATRA – HIS GREAT PERFORMANCES 1953–1960 *Capitol 5235022*	10	7
9 Feb 02 ●	A FINE ROMANCE – THE LOVE SONGS OF FRANK SINATRA *Reprise 8122735892*	6	9
28 Aug 04 ●	THE PLATINUM COLLECTION – THE BEST OF THE ORIGINAL CAPITOL RECORDINGS *Capitol 8647602*	11	4

[1] Frank Sinatra with Billy May and his Orchestra [2] Frank Sinatra with a bunch of kids [3] Frank Sinatra and Sammy Davis Jr [4] Frank Sinatra with Count Basie [5] Nancy Sinatra and Frank Sinatra [6] Frank Sinatra with Bono [1] Frank Sinatra and Count Basie

As a re-entry 'My Way' peaked at No.49, No.30, No.33, No.28 and No.18 in 1970, No.22 and No.39 in 1971 and No.50 in 1972. 'Theme From 'New York, New York' reached its peak position only on re-entry in Feb 1996. Tracks on Songs for Swinging Lovers (LP): You Make Me Feel So Young / It Happened In Monterey / You're Getting to be a Habit with Me / You Brought a New Kind of Love to Me / Too Marvellous for Words / Old Devil Moon / Pennies from Heaven / Love Is Here to Stay / I've Got You Under My Skin / I Thought About You / We'll Be Together Again / Makin' Whoopee / Swingin' Down the Lane / Anything Goes / How About You. Tracks on Come Dance With Me (LP): Come Dance With Me / Something's Gotta Give / Just in Time / Dancing in the Dark / Too Close for Comfort / I Could Have Danced All Night / Saturday Night Is the Loneliest Night of the Week / Day In Day Out / Cheek to Cheek / Baubles Bangles and Beads / The Song Is You / The Last Dance. 'All the Way' and 'Chicago', were at first billed separately, then together for one week, then 'All the Way' on its own. 'I've Got You Under My Skin' was the flip side of 'Stay (Faraway So Close)' by U2 'Songs for Swinging Lovers' was re-released in 1998 with a new catalogue number, Capitol CDP 7465702

Nancy SINATRA

US, female vocalist (b. 8 Jun 1940)
(Singles: 100 Weeks, Albums: 32 Weeks)** pos/wks

27 Jan 66 ★	THESE BOOTS ARE MADE FOR WALKIN' *Reprise R 20432* ▲	1	14
28 Apr 66	HOW DOES THAT GRAB YOU DARLIN' *Reprise R 20461*	19	8
19 Jan 67 ●	SUGAR TOWN *Reprise RS 20527*	8	10
23 Mar 67 ★	SOMETHIN' STUPID *Reprise RS 23166* [1] ▲	1	18
5 Jul 67	YOU ONLY LIVE TWICE / JACKSON *Reprise RS 20595* [2]	11	19
8 Nov 67	LADYBIRD *Reprise RS 20629* [3]	47	1
29 Nov 69	THE HIGHWAY SONG *Reprise RS 20869*	21	10
21 Aug 71 ●	DID YOU EVER *Reprise K 14093* [4]	2	19
23 Oct 04	LET ME KISS YOU *Attack ATKXS 005*	46	1
16 Apr 66	BOOTS *Reprise R 6202*	12	9
18 Jun 66	HOW DOES THAT GRAB YOU? *Reprise R 6207*	17	3
29 Jun 68	NANCY / LEE 3 *Reprise RSLP 6273* [1]	17	12
10 Oct 70	NANCY'S GREATEST HITS *Reprise RSLP 6409*	39	3
25 Sep 71	NANCY / LEE 3 (re-issue) *Reprise K 44126* [1]	42	1
29 Jan 72	DID YOU EVER *RCA Victor SF 8240* [1]	31	4

[1] Nancy Sinatra and Frank Sinatra [2] Nancy Sinatra / Nancy Sinatra and Lee Hazlewood [3] Nancy Sinatra and Lee Hazlewood [4] Nancy and Lee [1] Nancy Sinatra and Lee Hazlewood

'Jackson' listed with 'You Only Live Twice' from 12 Jul 1967

SINCLAIR

UK, male vocalist – Mike Sinclair (Singles: 8 Weeks) pos/wks

21 Aug 93	AIN'T NO CASANOVA *Dome CDDOME 1004*	28	5
26 Feb 94	(I WANNA KNOW) WHY *Dome CDDOME 1009*	58	2
6 Aug 94	DON'T LIE *Dome CDDOME 1010*	70	1

Bob SINCLAR
France, male DJ / producer (Singles: 10 Weeks) pos/wks

20 Mar 99	MY ONLY LOVE *East West EW 196CD* [1]	56	1
19 Aug 00 ●	I FEEL FOR YOU *Defected DEFECT 18CDS*	9	5
7 Apr 01	DARLIN' *Defected DFECT 30CDS*	46	1
25 Jan 03	THE BEAT GOES ON *Defected DFTD 062CDS*	33	2
2 Aug 03	KISS MY EYES *Defected DFTD 070CDS*	67	1

[1] Bob Sinclar featuring Lee A Genesis [2] Bob Sinclar featuring James Williams

SINDY
UK, female doll vocalist (Singles: 1 Week) pos/wks

5 Oct 96	SATURDAY NIGHT *Love This LUVTHISCD 13*	70	1

SINE
US, male / female vocal / instrumental group (Singles: 9 Weeks) pos/wks

10 Jun 78	JUST LET ME DO MY THING *CBS 6351*	33	9

SINFONIA OF LONDON *See Peter AUTY and the SINFONIA OF LONDON conducted by Howard BLAKE*

Talvin SINGH
UK, male instrumentalist / producer (Albums: 5 Weeks) pos/wks

18 Sep 99	OK *Island CID 8075*	41	4
7 Apr 01	HA *Island CID 8103*	57	1

SINGING CORNER meets DONOVAN
UK, male vocal duo and male vocalist (Singles: 1 Week) pos/wks

1 Dec 90	JENNIFER JUNIPER *Fontana SYP 1*	68	1

The SINGING DOGS – Don CARLOS presents The SINGING DOGS
Denmark, canine vocal group (Singles: 4 Weeks) pos/wks

25 Nov 55	THE SINGING DOGS (MEDLEY) *Nixa N 15009* [1]	13	4

Tracks on The Singing Dogs (Medley): Pat-a-Cake / Three Blind Mice / Jingle Bells / Oh Susanna

The SINGING NUN (Soeur Sourire)
Belgium, female vocalist – Jeanine Deckers, b. 17 Oct 1933, d. 31 Mar 1985 (Singles: 14 Weeks) pos/wks

5 Dec 63 ●	DOMINIQUE *Philips BF 1293* ▲	7	14

SINGING SHEEP
UK, computerised sheep noises (Singles: 5 Weeks) pos/wks

18 Dec 82	BAA BAA BLACK SHEEP *Sheep BAA 1*	42	5

Maxine SINGLETON
US, female vocalist (Singles: 3 Weeks) pos/wks

2 Apr 83	YOU CAN'T RUN FROM LOVE *Creole CR 50*	57	3

SINITTA
US, female vocalist – Sinitta Malone (Singles: 104 Weeks, Albums: 23 Weeks) pos/wks

8 Mar 86 ●	SO MACHO / CRUISING (re) *Fanfare FAN 7*	2	28
11 Oct 86	FEELS LIKE THE FIRST TIME *Fanfare FAN 8*	45	5
25 Jul 87 ●	TOY BOY *Fanfare FAN 12*	4	14
12 Dec 87	G.T.O. *Fanfare FAN 14*	15	9
19 Mar 88 ●	CROSS MY BROKEN HEART *Fanfare FAN 15*	6	9
24 Sep 88	I DON'T BELIEVE IN MIRACLES *Fanfare FAN 16*	22	8
3 Jun 89 ●	RIGHT BACK WHERE WE STARTED FROM *Fanfare FAN 18*	4	10
7 Oct 89	LOVE ON A MOUNTAIN TOP *Fanfare FAN 21*	20	6
21 Apr 90	HITCHIN' A RIDE *Fanfare FAN 24*	24	6
22 Sep 90	LOVE AND AFFECTION *Fanfare FAN 31*	62	3
4 Jul 92	SHAME SHAME SHAME *Arista 74321100327*	28	4
17 Apr 93	THE SUPREME EP *Arista 74321139592*	49	2
26 Dec 87	SINITTA! *Fanfare BOYLP 1*	34	19
9 Dec 89	WICKED! *Fanfare FARE 2*	52	4

Tracks on The Supreme EP: Where Did Our Love Go / Stop! In the Name of Love / You Can't Hurry Love / Remember Me

SINNAMON
US, male vocal / instrumental group (Singles: 1 Week) pos/wks

28 Sep 96	I NEED YOU NOW *Worx WORXCD 003*	70	1

SIOUXSIE and the BANSHEES `232` `Top 500` (see also GLOVE)
Long-running commercially successful UK punk band included Susan 'Siouxsie' Ballion (v), Steve Severin (b) (also recorded as The Glove), Siouxsie's husband, Peter 'Budgie' Clark (d) (who recorded with Siouxsie as The Creatures) and, at times, Cure front man Robert Smith (g) (Singles: 150 Weeks, Albums: 119 Weeks) pos/wks

26 Aug 78 ●	HONG KONG GARDEN *Polydor 2059 052*	7	10
31 Mar 79	THE STAIRCASE (MYSTERY) *Polydor POSP 9*	24	8
7 Jul 79	PLAYGROUND TWIST *Polydor POSP 59*	28	6
29 Sep 79	MITTAGEISEN (METAL POSTCARD) *Polydor 2059 151*	47	3
15 Mar 80	HAPPY HOUSE *Polydor POSP 117*	17	8
7 Jun 80	CHRISTINE *Polydor 2059 249*	22	8
6 Dec 80	ISRAEL *Polydor POSP 205*	41	8
30 May 81	SPELLBOUND *Polydor POSP 273*	22	8
1 Aug 81	ARABIAN KNIGHTS *Polydor POSP 309*	32	7
29 May 82	FIRE WORKS *Polydor POSPG 450*	22	8
9 Oct 82	SLOWDIVE *Polydor POSP 510*	41	4
4 Dec 82	MELT / IL EST NE LE DIVIN ENFANT *Polydor POSP 539*	49	5
1 Oct 83 ●	DEAR PRUDENCE *Wonderland SHE 4*	3	8
24 Mar 84	SWIMMING HORSES *Wonderland SHE 6*	28	4
2 Jun 84	DAZZLE *Wonderland SHE 7*	33	3
27 Oct 84	THE THORN EP *Wonderland SHEEP 8*	47	3
26 Oct 85	CITIES IN DUST *Wonderland SHE 9*	21	6
8 Mar 86	CANDYMAN *Wonderland SHE 10*	34	5
17 Jan 87	THIS WHEEL'S ON FIRE *Wonderland SHE 11*	14	6
28 Mar 87	THE PASSENGER *Wonderland SHE 12*	41	6
25 Jul 87	SONG FROM THE EDGE OF THE WORLD *Wonderland SHE 13*	59	3
30 Jul 88	PEEK-A-BOO *Wonderland SHE 14*	16	6
8 Oct 88	THE KILLING JAR *Wonderland SHE 15*	41	3
3 Dec 88	THE LAST BEAT OF MY HEART *Wonderland SHE 16*	44	1
25 May 91	KISS THEM FOR ME *Wonderland SHE 19*	32	4
13 Jul 91	SHADOWTIME *Wonderland SHE 20*	57	1
25 Jul 92	FACE TO FACE *Wonderland SHE 21*	21	4
20 Aug 94	INTERLUDE *Parlophone CDR 6365* [1]	25	2
7 Jan 95	O BABY *Wonderland SHECD 22*	34	3
18 Feb 95	STARGAZER *Wonderland SHECD 23*	64	1
2 Dec 78	THE SCREAM *Polydor POLD 5009*	12	11
22 Sep 79	JOIN HANDS *Polydor POLD 5024*	13	5
16 Aug 80 ●	KALEIDOSCOPE *Polydor 2442 177*	5	6
27 Jun 81	JU JU *Polydor POLS 1034*	7	17
12 Dec 81	ONCE UPON A TIME – THE SINGLES *Polydor POLS 1056*	21	26
13 Nov 82	A KISS IN THE DREAMHOUSE *Polydor POLD 5064*	11	11
3 Dec 83	NOCTURNE *Wonderland SHAH 1*	29	10
16 Jun 84	HYAENA *Wonderland SHELP 2*	15	6
26 Apr 86	TINDERBOX *Wonderland SHELP 3*	13	6
14 Mar 87	THROUGH THE LOOKING GLASS *Wonderland SHELP 4*	15	8
17 Sep 88	PEEPSHOW *Wonderland SHELP 5*	20	5
22 Jun 91	SUPERSTITION *Wonderland 8477311*	25	4
17 Oct 92	TWICE UPON A TIME – THE SINGLES *Wonderland 5171602*	26	2
28 Jan 95	THE RAPTURE *Wonderland 5237252*	33	2

[1] Morrissey and Siouxsie

Tracks on The Thorn EP: Overground / Voices / Placebo Effect / Red Over White

SIR DOUGLAS QUINTET
US, male vocal / instrumental group – leader Doug Sahm, b. 6 Nov 1941, d. 18 Nov 1999 (Singles: 10 Weeks) pos/wks

17 Jun 65	SHE'S ABOUT A MOVER *London HLU 9964*	15	10

SIR KILLALOT vs ROBO BABE
UK, male robot rapper and female vocalist (Singles: 3 Weeks) pos/wks

30 Dec 00	ROBOT WARS (ANDROID LOVE) *Polydor 5879362*	51	3

SIR MIX-A-LOT
US, male rapper – Anthony Ray (Singles: 2 Weeks) pos/wks

8 Aug 92	BABY GOT BACK *Def American DEFA 20* ▲	56	2

SIRENS
UK, female vocal group (Singles: 1 Week) pos/wks

28 Aug 04	BABY (OFF THE WALL) *Kitchenware SKCD 742*	49	1

SIRRON *See PLUS ONE featuring SIRRON*

SISQO (see also DRU HILL)
US, male vocalist – Mark Andrews (Singles: 43 Weeks, Albums: 41 Weeks) pos/wks

12 Feb 00	GOT TO GET IT *Def Soul 5626442*	14	4
22 Apr 00 ●	THONG SONG *Def Soul 5688902*	3	14

Singles re-entries are listed as (re), (2re), (3re)…. which signifies that the hit re-entered the chart once, twice or three times…

			pos/wks
30 Sep 00	●	**UNLEASH THE DRAGON** Def Soul 5726422	**6** 7
16 Dec 00	●	**INCOMPLETE** Def Soul 5727542 ▲	**13** 8
28 Jul 01	●	**DANCE FOR ME** Def Soul 5887002	**6** 10
26 Feb 00		**UNLEASH THE DRAGON** Def Soul 5449392	**15** 36
4 Aug 01		**RETURN OF DRAGON** Def Soul 5864182	**22** 5

SISSEL Norway, female vocalist –
Sissel Kyrkjebo (Singles: 7 Weeks, Albums: 56 Weeks) pos/wks

10 Jan 98	**PRINCE IGOR** Def Jam 5749652 [1]	**15** 7
20 May 95	**DEEP WITHIN MY SOUL** Mercury 5267752	**58** 1
30 Jan 98	★ **TITANIC (FILM SOUNDTRACK)** Sony Classical SK 63213 [1]	**1** 55

[1] Warren G featuring Sissel [1] James Horner – vocals by Sissel

SISTER BLISS (see also FAITHLESS) UK, female DJ /
producer / instrumentalist – Ayalah Ben-Tovim (Singles: 11 Weeks) pos/wks

15 Oct 94	**CANTGETAMAN CANTGETAJOB (LIFE'S A BITCH)** Go Beat GODCD 124 [1]	**31** 4
15 Jul 95	**OH! WHAT A WORLD** Go Beat GODCD 126 [1]	**40** 2
29 Jun 96	**BAD MAN** Junk Dog JDOGCD 1	**51** 1
7 Oct 00	**SISTER SISTER** Multiply CDMULTY 68	**34** 2
24 Mar 01	**DELIVER ME** Multiply CDMULTY 72 [2]	**31** 2

[1] Sister Bliss featuring Collette [2] Sister Bliss featuring John Martyn

SISTER SLEDGE (410 Top 500) Successful US family group from
Philadelphia: Kathy, Debra, Joni and Kim Sledge. They found more fame in
the UK than in the US, and recorded some of the best-known disco records
with noted producers / songwriters Nile Rodgers and Bernard Edwards
(Singles: 111 Weeks, Albums: 58 Weeks) pos/wks

21 Jun 75		**MAMA NEVER TOLD ME** Atlantic K 10619	**20** 6
17 Mar 79	●	**HE'S THE GREATEST DANCER** Atlantic / Cotillion K 11257	**6** 11
26 May 79	●	**WE ARE FAMILY** Atlantic / Cotillion K 11293	**8** 10
11 Aug 79		**LOST IN MUSIC** Atlantic / Cotillion K 11337	**17** 10
19 Jan 80		**GOT TO LOVE SOMEBODY** Atlantic / Cotillion K 11404	**34** 4
28 Feb 81		**ALL AMERICAN GIRLS** Atlantic K 11656	**41** 5
26 May 84		**THINKING OF YOU** Cotillion / Atlantic B 9744	**11** 13
8 Sep 84		**LOST IN MUSIC (re-mix)** Cotillion / Atlantic B 9718	**4** 12
17 Nov 84		**WE ARE FAMILY (re-mix)** Cotillion / Atlantic B 9692	**33** 4
1 Jun 85	★	**FRANKIE** Atlantic A 9547	**1** 16
31 Aug 85		**DANCING ON THE JAGGED EDGE** Atlantic A 9520	**50** 3
23 Jan 93		**WE ARE FAMILY (2nd re-mix)** Atlantic A 4508CD	**5** 8
13 Mar 93		**LOST IN MUSIC (2nd re-mix)** Atlantic A 4509CD	**14** 5
12 Jun 93		**THINKING OF YOU (re-mix)** Atlantic A 4515CD	**17** 4
12 May 79	●	**WE ARE FAMILY** Atlantic K 50587	**7** 39
22 Jun 85		**WHEN THE BOYS MEET THE GIRLS** Atlantic 7812551	**19** 11
5 Dec 87		**FREAK OUT** Telstar STAR 2319 [1]	**72** 3
20 Feb 93		**THE VERY BEST OF SISTER SLEDGE 1973-1993** Atlantic 9548318132	**19** 5

[1] Chic and Sister Sledge

SISTER 2 SISTER Australia, female vocal duo –
Christine and Sharon Muscat (Singles: 5 Weeks) pos/wks

22 Apr 00	**SISTER** Mushroom MUSH 70CDS	**18** 4
28 Oct 00	**WHAT'S A GIRL TO DO** Mushroom MUSH 76CDS	**61** 1

SISTERHOOD
UK, male vocal / instrumental group (Albums: 1 Week) pos/wks

26 Jul 86	**GIFT** Merciful Release SIS 020	**90** 1

The SISTERS OF MERCY UK, male / female vocal / instrumental group –
leader Andrew Eldritch (Singles: 40 Weeks, Albums: 42 Weeks) pos/wks

16 Jun 84		**BODY AND SOUL / TRAIN** Merciful Release MR 029	**46** 3
20 Oct 84		**WALK AWAY** Merciful Release MR 033	**45** 3
9 Mar 85		**NO TIME TO CRY** Merciful Release MR 035	**63** 2
3 Oct 87	●	**THIS CORROSION** Merciful Release MR 39	**7** 6
27 Feb 88		**DOMINION** Merciful Release MR 43	**13** 6
18 Jun 88		**LUCRETIA MY REFLECTION** Merciful Release MR 45	**20** 4
13 Oct 90		**MORE** Merciful Release MR 47	**14** 4
22 Dec 90		**DOCTOR JEEP** Merciful Release MR 51	**37** 4
2 May 92		**TEMPLE OF LOVE** Merciful Release MR 53	**3** 5
28 Aug 93		**UNDER THE GUN** Merciful Release MR 59CDX	**19** 3
23 Mar 85		**FIRST AND LAST AND ALWAYS** Merciful Release MR 337L	**14** 8
28 Nov 87	●	**FLOODLAND** Merciful Release MR 441L	**9** 20
2 Nov 90		**VISION THING** Merciful Release 9031726632	**11** 4

9 May 92	●	**SOME GIRLS WANDER BY MISTAKE** Merciful Release 9031764762 [1]	**5** 5
4 Sep 93		**GREATEST HITS VOLUME 1** Merciful Release 4509935792	**14** 5

[1] Sisters

Act was male-only group for first album

SIVUCA Brazil, male instrumentalist –
Severino Dias de Oliveira (Singles: 3 Weeks) pos/wks

28 Jul 84	**AIN'T NO SUNSHINE** London LON 51	**56** 3

SIX BY SEVEN UK, male vocal / instrumental
group (Singles: 2 Weeks, Albums: 1 Week) pos/wks

9 May 98	**CANDLELIGHT** Mantra MNT 34CD	**70** 1
2 Mar 02	**I.O.U. LOVE** Mantra MNT 68CD	**48** 1
23 Mar 02	**THE WAY I FEEL TODAY** Mantra MNTCD 1027	**69** 1

6 BY SIX UK, male instrumental / production duo (Singles: 1 Week) pos/wks

4 May 96	**INTO YOUR HEART** Six6 SIXCD 130	**51** 1

SIX CHIX UK, female vocal group (Singles: 1 Week) pos/wks

26 Feb 00	**ONLY THE WOMEN KNOW** EMI CDCHIX 001	**72** 1

666 Germany, male production duo –
Thomas Detert and Mike Griesheimer (Singles: 5 Week) pos/wks

3 Oct 98	**ALARMA** Danceteria CDDAN 001	**58** 1
25 Nov 00	**DEVIL** Echo ECSCD 102	**18** 4

SIXPENCE NONE THE RICHER US, male / female vocal /
instrumental group (Singles: 17 Weeks, Albums: 3 Weeks) pos/wks

29 May 99	●	**KISS ME** Elektra E 3750CD	**4** 12
18 Sep 99		**THERE SHE GOES** Elektra E 3728CD	**14** 5
26 Jun 99		**SIXPENCE NONE THE RICHER** Elektra 7559624202	**27** 3

60FT DOLLS UK, male vocal /
instrumental group (Singles: 4 Weeks, Albums: 2 Weeks) pos/wks

3 Feb 96	**STAY** Indolent DOLLS 002CD	**48** 1
11 May 96	**TALK TO ME** Indolent DOLLS 003CD	**37** 1
20 Jul 96	**HAPPY SHOPPER** Indolent DOLLS 005CD	**38** 1
9 May 98	**ALISON'S ROOM** Indolent DOLLS 007CD1	**61** 1
8 Jun 96	**THE BIG 3** Indolent DOLLSCD 004	**36** 2

SIZE 9 US, male producer – Josh Wink (Singles: 4 Weeks) pos/wks

17 Jun 95	**I'M READY** Virgin America VUSCD 92	**52** 1
11 Nov 95	**I'M READY (re-issue)** VC VCRD 2 [1]	**30** 3

[1] Josh Wink's Size 9

Roni SIZE / REPRAZENT
UK, male producer – Ryan Williams and male / female vocal /
instrumental group (Singles: 28 Weeks, Albums: 39 Weeks) pos/wks

14 Jun 97		**SHARE THE FALL** Talkin Loud TLCD 21	**37** 2
13 Sep 97		**HEROES** Talkin Loud TLCD 25	**31** 2
15 Nov 97		**BROWN PAPER BAG** Talkin Loud TLCD 28	**20** 3
14 Mar 98		**WATCHING WINDOWS** Talkin Loud TLCD 31	**28** 2
7 Oct 00		**WHO TOLD YOU** Talkin Loud TLCD 61	**17** 3
24 Mar 01		**DIRTY BEATS** Talkin Loud TLCDD 63	**32** 3
23 Jun 01		**LUCKY PRESSURE** Talkin Loud TLCD 64	**58** 1
19 Oct 02		**SOUND ADVICE** Full Cycle FCY 044 [1]	**69** 1
9 Nov 02		**PLAYTIME** Full Cycle FCY 045 [1]	**53** 2
7 Dec 02		**SCRAMBLED EGGS / SWINGS & ROUNDABOUTS** Full Cycle FCY 046 [1]	**57** 1
18 Jan 03		**FEEL THE HEAT** Full Cycle FCY 048 [1]	**55** 1
22 Feb 03		**SNAPSHOT 3 / SORRY FOR YOU** Full Cycle FCY 033 [1]	**61** 1
12 Jul 03		**SIREN SOUNDS / AT THE MOVIES** Full Cycle FCY 054 [1]	**67** 1
6 Sep 03		**SOUND ADVICE (re-mix) / FORGET ME NOTS** Full Cycle FCY 056 [1]	**61** 1
17 Apr 04		**STRICTLY SOCIAL / AUTUMN** Liquid V LQD 001 [2]	**70** 1
24 Apr 04		**BAMBAKITA / FASSY HOLE** V VO 45	**60** 1
9 Oct 04		**OUT OF BREATH** V VRECUK 002X [3]	**44** 2
5 Jul 97	●	**NEW FORMS** Talkin Loud 5349332	**8** 34
21 Oct 00		**IN THE MODE** Talkin Loud 5481762	**15** 4
2 Nov 02		**TOUCHING DOWN** Full Cycle FCYCDLP 010 [1]	**72** 1

[1] Roni Size [2] Roni Size and Die [3] Roni Size featuring Rahzel [1] Roni Size

SKY `312` `Top 500` *Anglo-Australian jazz-rock fusion quintet with a progressive element. Classical guitarist John Williams OBE was joined by similarly accomplished instrumentalists including Herbie Flowers (b) and Tristan Fry (d). In Feb 1981, Sky gave the only concert ever held in Westminster Abbey (Singles: 11 Weeks, Albums: 202 Weeks)* pos/wks

5 Apr 80	● TOCCATA *Ariola ARO 300*	.5 11
2 Jun 79	● SKY *Ariola ARLH 5022*	.9 56
26 Apr 80	★ SKY 2 *Ariola ADSKY 2*	.1 53
28 Mar 81	● SKY 3 *Ariola ASKY 3*	.3 23
3 Apr 82	● SKY 4 – FORTHCOMING *Ariola ASKY 4*	.7 22
22 Jan 83	SKY FIVE LIVE *Ariola 302 171*	.14 14
3 Dec 83	CADMIUM *Ariola 205 885*	.44 10
12 May 84	MASTERPIECES – THE VERY BEST OF SKY *Telstar STAR 2241*	.15 18
13 Apr 85	THE GREAT BALLOON RACE *Epic EPC 26419*	.63 6

SKYE *See LANGE*

The SKYHOOKS
Australia, male vocal / instrumental group (Singles: 1 Week) pos/wks

9 Jun 79	WOMEN IN UNIFORM *United Artists UP 36508*	.73 1

SKYLARK *UK / France, Male DJ / production group (Singles: 1 Week)* pos/wks

27 Mar 04	THAT'S MORE LIKE IT *Credence CDCRED 042*	.62 1

SKYY *US, male vocal / instrumental group (Albums: 1 Week)* pos/wks

21 Jun 86	FROM THE LEFT SIDE *Capitol EST 2014*	.85 1

SLACKER (see also RAMP) *UK, male production duo – Shem McCauley and Simon Rogers (Singles: 4 Weeks)* pos/wks

26 Apr 97	SCARED *XL XLS 84CD*	.36 2
30 Aug 97	YOUR FACE *XL XLS 87CD*	.33 2

SLADE `81` `Top 500` *Top UK group of the 1970s: Noddy Holder (v/g), Dave Hill (g), Jimmy Lea (b/p), Don Powell (d). They were the first act to have three singles enter at No.1. All six of the Wolverhampton band's chart-topping stompers were penned by Holder and Lea. Noddy, who is now a popular TV personality, was made an MBE in 2000. Total UK single sales: 6,520,171. Best-selling single: 'Merry Xmas Everybody' 1,006,500 (Singles: 279 Weeks, Albums: 212 Weeks)* pos/wks

19 Jun 71	GET DOWN AND GET WITH IT *Polydor 2058 112*	.16 14
30 Oct 71	★ COZ I LUV YOU *Polydor 2058 155*	.1 15
5 Feb 72	● LOOK WOT YOU DUN *Polydor 2058 195*	.4 10
3 Jun 72	★ TAKE ME BAK 'OME *Polydor 2058 231*	.1 13
2 Sep 72	● MAMA WEER ALL CRAZEE NOW *Polydor 2058 274*	.1 10
25 Nov 72	● GUDBUY T'JANE *Polydor 2058 312*	.2 13
3 Mar 73	★ CUM ON FEEL THE NOIZE *Polydor 2058 339* ■	.1 12
30 Jun 73	★ SKWEEZE ME PLEEZE ME *Polydor 2058 377* ■	.1 10
6 Oct 73	● MY FRIEND STAN *Polydor 2058 407*	.2 9
15 Dec 73	★ MERRY XMAS EVERYBODY (4re) *Polydor 2058 422* ◆ ■	.1 25
6 Apr 74	● EVERYDAY *Polydor 2058 453*	.3 7
6 Jul 74	● THE BANGIN' MAN *Polydor 2058 492*	.3 7
19 Oct 74	● FAR FAR AWAY *Polydor 2058 522*	.2 6
15 Feb 75	HOW DOES IT FEEL? *Polydor 2058 547*	.15 7
17 May 75	● THANKS FOR THE MEMORY (WHAM BAM THANK YOU MAM) *Polydor 2058 585*	.7 7
22 Nov 75	● IN FOR A PENNY *Polydor 2058 663*	.11 8
7 Feb 76	LET'S CALL IT QUITS *Polydor 2058 690*	.11 7
5 Feb 77	GYPSY ROADHOG *Barn 2014 105*	.48 2
29 Oct 77	MY BABY LEFT ME – THAT'S ALL RIGHT *Barn 2014 114*	.32 4
18 Oct 80	SLADE – ALIVE AT READING (EP) *Cheapskate CHEAP 5*	.44 5
27 Dec 80	MERRY XMAS EVERYBODY (re-recording) *Cheapskate CHEAP 11* `1`	.70 2
31 Jan 81	● WE'LL BRING THE HOUSE DOWN *Cheapskate CHEAP 16*	.10 9
4 Apr 81	WHEELS AIN'T COMING DOWN *Cheapskate CHEAP 21*	.60 3
19 Sep 81	LOCK UP YOUR DAUGHTERS *RCA 124*	.29 8
27 Mar 82	RUBY RED *RCA 191*	.51 3
27 Nov 82	(AND NOW – THE WALTZ) C'EST LA VIE *RCA 291*	.50 6
19 Nov 83	● MY OH MY *RCA 373*	.2 11
4 Feb 84	● RUN RUNAWAY *RCA 385*	.7 10
17 Nov 84	ALL JOIN HANDS *RCA 455*	.15 9
26 Jan 85	7 YEAR BITCH *RCA 475*	.60 3
23 Mar 85	MYZSTERIOUS MIZSTER JONES *RCA PB 40027*	.50 5
30 Nov 85	DO YOU BELIEVE IN MIRACLES *RCA PB 40449*	.54 6
21 Dec 85	MERRY XMAS EVERYBODY (re) (re-issue) *Polydor POSP 780*	.48 4

21 Feb 87	STILL THE SAME *RCA PB 41137*	.73 2
19 Oct 91	RADIO WALL OF SOUND *Polydor PO 180*	.21 5
26 Dec 98	MERRY XMAS EVERYBODY '98 (re-mix) *Polydor 5633532* `2`	.30 3
8 Apr 72	● SLADE ALIVE! *Polydor 2383 101*	.2 58
9 Dec 72	★ SLAYED? *Polydor 2383 163*	.1 34
6 Oct 73	★ SLADEST *Polydor 2442 119* ■	.1 24
23 Feb 74	● OLD NEW BORROWED AND BLUE *Polydor 2383 261*	.1 16
14 Dec 74	● SLADE IN FLAME *Polydor 2442 126*	.6 18
27 Mar 76	NOBODY'S FOOL *Polydor 2383 377*	.14 4
22 Nov 80	SLADE SMASHES *Polydor POLTV 13*	.21 15
21 Mar 81	WE'LL BRING THE HOUSE DOWN *Cheapskate SKATE 1*	.25 4
28 Nov 81	TILL DEAF US DO PART *RCA RCALP 6021*	.68 2
18 Dec 82	SLADE ON STAGE *RCA RCALP 3107*	.58 3
24 Dec 83	THE AMAZING KAMIKAZE SYNDROME *RCA PL 70116*	.49 13
9 Jun 84	SLADE'S GREATS *Polydor SLAD 1*	.89 1
6 Apr 85	ROGUES GALLERY *RCA PL 70604*	.60 2
30 Nov 85	CRACKERS – THE CHRISTMAS PARTY ALBUM *Telstar STAR 2271*	.34 7
9 May 87	YOU BOYZ MAKE BIG NOIZE *RCA PL 71260*	.98 1
23 Nov 91	WALL OF HITS *Polydor 5116121*	.34 5
25 Jan 97	GREATEST HITS – FEEL THE NOIZE *Polydor 5371052*	.19 5

`1` Slade and the Reading Choir `2` Slade vs Flush

'Merry Xmas Everybody' re-entries peaked at No.32 in 1981, No.67 in 1982, No.20 in 1983, No.47 in 1984 and the re-entry of the 1985 re-issue made No.71 in 1986. Tracks on Slade – Alive at Reading (EP): When I'm Dancin' / I Ain't Fightin' / Born to Be Wild / Somethin' Else / Pistol Packin' Mama / Keep a Rollin'

SLAM *UK, male production duo – Orde Meikle and Stuart McMillan (Singles: 4 Weeks)* pos/wks

17 Feb 01	POSITIVE EDUCATION *VC Recordings VCRD 84*	.44 2
17 Mar 01	NARCO TOURISTS *Soma SOMA 100CD* `1`	.66 1
7 Jul 01	LIFETIMES *Soma SOMA 107CDS* `2`	.61 1

`1` Slam vs Unkle `2` Slam featuring Tyrone 'Visionary' Palmer

SLAMM *UK, male vocal / instrumental group (Singles: 6 Weeks)* pos/wks

17 Jul 93	ENERGIZE *PWL International PWCD 266*	.57 2
23 Oct 93	VIRGINIA PLAIN *PWL International PWCD 274*	.60 1
22 Oct 94	THAT'S WHERE MY MIND GOES *PWL International PWCD 310*	.68 1
4 Feb 95	CAN'T GET BY *PWL International PWCD 316*	.47 2

SLARTA JOHN *See HATIRAS featuring SLARTA JOHN*

SLASH'S SNAKEPIT (see also GUNS N' ROSES)
US, male vocal / instrumental group (Albums: 4 Weeks) pos/wks

25 Feb 95	IT'S FIVE O'CLOCK SOMEWHERE *Geffen GED 24730*	.15 4

Luke SLATER *UK, male producer (Singles: 2 Weeks)* pos/wks

16 Sep 00	ALL EXHALE *Novamute CDNOMU 79*	.74 1
6 Apr 02	NOTHING AT ALL *Mute CDMUTE 261*	.70 1

SLAUGHTER *US, male vocal / instrumental group (Singles: 2 Weeks, Albums: 1 Week)* pos/wks

29 Sep 90	UP ALL NIGHT *Chrysalis CHS 3556*	.62 1
2 Feb 91	FLY TO THE ANGELS *Chrysalis CHS 3634*	.55 1
23 May 92	THE WILD LIFE *Chrysalis CCD 1911*	.64 1

SLAVE
US, male vocal / instrumental group (Singles: 3 Weeks) pos/wks

8 Mar 80	JUST A TOUCH OF LOVE *Atlantic / Cotillion K 11442*	.64 3

SLAYER *US, male vocal / instrumental group (Singles: 3 Weeks, Albums: 21 Weeks)* pos/wks

13 Jun 87	CRIMINALLY INSANE *Def Jam LON 133*	.64 1
26 Oct 91	SEASONS IN THE ABYSS *Def American DEFA 9*	.51 1
9 Sep 95	SERENITY IN MURDER *American 74321312482*	.50 1
2 May 87	REIGN IN BLOOD *Def Jam LONLP 34*	.47 3
23 Jul 88	SOUTH OF HEAVEN *London LONLP 63*	.25 4
6 Oct 90	SEASONS IN THE ABYSS *Def American 8468711*	.18 3
2 Nov 91	DECADE OF AGGRESSION – LIVE *Def American 5106051*	.29 2
15 Oct 94	DIVINE INTERVENTION *American 74321236772*	.15 4
1 Jun 96	UNDISPUTED ATTITUDE *American Recordings 74321357592*	.31 2
20 Jun 98	DIABOLUS IN MUSICA *Columbia 4913022*	.27 2
22 Sep 01	GOD HATES US ALL *Mercury 5863312*	.31 1

SLEAZESISTERS (see also The CANDY GIRLS; DOROTHY; YOMANDA; HI-GATE; CLERGY; Paul MASTERSON presents SUSHI)
UK, male producer – Paul Masterson (Singles: 3 Weeks) pos/wks

29 Jul 95	SEX *Pulse 8 CDLOSE 92* [1]	53 1
30 Mar 96	LET'S WHIP IT UP (YOU GO GIRL) *Pulse 8 CDLOSE 102* [1]	46 1
26 Sep 98	WORK IT UP *Logic 74321616622* [2]	74 1

[1] Sleazesisters with Vikki Shepard [2] Sleaze Sisters

Kathy SLEDGE (see also SISTER SLEDGE)
US, female vocalist (Singles: 7 Weeks) pos/wks

16 May 92	TAKE ME BACK TO LOVE AGAIN *Epic 6579837*	62 2
18 Feb 95	ANOTHER STAR *NRC DEACD 002*	54 1
29 Nov 97	FREEDOM *Deconstruction 74321536952* [1]	15 4

[1] Robert Miles featuring Kathy Sledge

Percy SLEDGE
US, male vocalist (Singles: 34 Weeks, Albums: 4 Weeks) pos/wks

12 May 66 ●	WHEN A MAN LOVES A WOMAN *Atlantic 584 001* ▲	4 17
4 Aug 66	WARM AND TENDER LOVE *Atlantic 584 034*	34 7
14 Feb 87 ●	WHEN A MAN LOVES A WOMAN (re-issue) *Atlantic YZ 96* ▲	2 10
14 Mar 87	WHEN A MAN LOVES A WOMAN (THE ULTIMATE COLLECTION) *Atlantic WX 89*	36 4

SLEEPER
UK, female / male vocal / instrumental group (Singles: 29 Weeks, Albums: 48 Weeks) pos/wks

21 May 94	DELICIOUS *Indolent SLEEP 003CD*	75 1
21 Jan 95	INBETWEENER *Indolent SLEEP 006CD*	16 4
8 Apr 95	VEGAS *Indolent SLEEP 008CD*	33 3
7 Oct 95	WHAT DO I DO NOW *Indolent SLEEP 009CD1*	14 4
4 May 96 ●	SALE OF THE CENTURY *Indolent SLEEP 011CD*	10 5
13 Jul 96 ●	NICE GUY EDDIE *Indolent SLEEP 013CD*	10 5
5 Oct 96	STATUESQUE *Indolent SLEEP 014CD1*	17 3
4 Oct 97	SHE'S A GOOD GIRL *Indolent SLEEP 015CD*	28 2
6 Dec 97	ROMEO ME *Indolent SLEEP 17CD1*	39 2
25 Feb 95 ●	SMART *Indolent SLEEPCD 007*	5 11
18 May 96 ●	THE IT GIRL *Indolent SLEEPCD 012*	5 34
25 Oct 97 ●	PLEASED TO MEET YOU *Indolent SLEEPCD 016*	7 3

SLEEPY JACKSON *Australia, male vocal / instrumental trio (Singles: 2 Weeks, Albums: 1 Week)*
pos/wks

19 Jul 03	VAMPIRE RACECOURSE *Virgin DINSD 261*	50 1
25 Jul 03	GOOD DANCERS *Virgin DINSD 265*	71 1
26 Jul 03	LOVERS *Virgin CDVIR 208*	69 1

SLEIGHRIDERS
UK, male vocal / instrumental group (Albums: 1 Week) pos/wks

17 Dec 83	A VERY MERRY DISCO *Warwick WW 5136*	100 1

SLICK
US, male / female vocal / instrumental group (Singles: 15 Weeks) pos/wks

16 Jun 79	SPACE BASS *Fantasy FTC 176*	16 10
15 Sep 79	SEXY CREAM *Fantasy FTC 182* [1]	47 5

[1] Slick featuring Doris James

Grace SLICK (see also JEFFERSON AIRPLANE)
US, female vocalist (Singles: 4 Weeks, Albums: 6 Weeks) pos/wks

24 May 80	DREAMS *RCA PB 9534*	50 4
31 May 80	DREAMS *RCA PL 13544*	28 6

SLICK RICK *See Montell JORDAN; Al B SURE!*

SLIK *UK, male vocal / instrumental group –*
lead vocal Midge Ure (Singles: 18 Weeks, Albums: 1 Week) pos/wks

17 Jan 76 ★	FOREVER AND EVER *Bell 1464*	1 9
8 May 76	REQUIEM *Bell 1478*	24 9
12 Jun 76	SLIK *Bell SYBEL 8004*	58 1

SLIM CHANCE *See Ronnie LANE*

SLIPKNOT *US, male vocal / instrumental*
group (Singles: 19 Weeks, Albums: 17 Weeks) pos/wks

11 Mar 00	WAIT AND BLEED *Roadrunner RR 21125*	27 3
16 Sep 00	SPIT IT OUT *Roadrunner RR 20903*	28 2

10 Nov 01	LEFT BEHIND *Roadrunner 23203355*	24 4
20 Jul 02	MY PLAGUE *Roadrunner RR 20453*	43 2
26 Jun 04	DUALITY (re) *Roadrunner RR 39880*	15 6
30 Oct 04	VERMILION *Roadrunner RR 39770*	31 2
10 Jul 99	SLIPKNOT *Roadrunner RR 86552*	37 5
8 Sep 01 ★	IOWA *Roadrunner 12085642* ■	1 7
5 Jun 04 ●	VOL.3: (THE SUBLIMINAL VERSES) *Roadrunner RR 83888*	5 5

SLIPMATT
(see also SL2) *UK, male producer – Matt Nelson (Singles: 2 Weeks)* pos/wks

19 Apr 03	SPACE *Concept CDCON 37*	41 2

SLIPSTREAM *UK, male vocal group (Singles: 7 Weeks)* pos/wks

19 Dec 92	WE ARE RAVING – THE ANTHEM *Boogie Food 7BF 1*	18 7

The SLITS *UK, female vocal /*
instrumental group (Singles: 3 Weeks, Albums: 5 Weeks) pos/wks

13 Oct 79	TYPICAL GIRLS / I HEARD IT THROUGH THE GRAPEVINE *Island WIP 6505*	60 3
22 Sep 79	CUT *Island ILPS 9573*	30 5

PF SLOAN
US, male vocalist – Philip 'Flip' Sloan (Singles: 3 Weeks) pos/wks

4 Nov 65	SINS OF THE FAMILY *RCA 1482*	38 3

SLO-MOSHUN
UK / US, male / female production / vocal trio (Singles: 4 Weeks) pos/wks

5 Feb 94	BELLS OF NY *Six6 SIXCD 108*	29 3
30 Jul 94	HELP MY FRIEND *Six6 SIXCD 117*	52 1

SLOWDIVE *UK, male / female vocal /*
instrumental group (Singles: 2 Weeks, Albums: 3 Weeks) pos/wks

15 Jun 91	CATCH THE BREEZE / SHINE *Creation CRE 112*	52 1
29 May 93	OUTSIDE YOUR ROOM (EP) *Creation CRESCD 119*	69 1
14 Sep 91	JUST FOR A DAY *Creation CRELP 094*	32 2
12 Jun 93	SOUVLAKI *Creation CRECD 139*	51 1

Tracks on Outside Your Room (EP): Outside Your Room / Alison / So Tired / Souvlaki Space Station

SLUSNIK LUNA
Finland, male producer – Niko Nyman (Singles: 2 Weeks) pos/wks

1 Sep 01	SUN *Incentive CENT 29CDS*	40 2

SLY and the FAMILY STONE
US, male / female vocal / instrumental / production group – includes Sly Stone and Larry Graham (Singles: 42 Weeks, Albums: 2 Weeks) pos/wks

10 Jul 68 ●	DANCE TO THE MUSIC *Direction 58 3568*	7 14
2 Oct 68	M'LADY *Direction 58 3707*	32 7
19 Mar 69	EVERYDAY PEOPLE (re) *Direction 58 3938* ▲	36 5
8 Jan 72	FAMILY AFFAIR *Epic EPC 7632* ▲	15 8
15 Apr 72	RUNNIN' AWAY *Epic EPC 7810*	17 8
5 Feb 72	THERE'S A RIOT GOIN' ON *Epic EPC 64613* ▲	31 2

SLY and ROBBIE
Jamaica, male vocal / instrumental duo – Sly Dunbar and Robbie Shakespeare (Singles: 23 Weeks, Albums: 5 Weeks) pos/wks

4 Apr 87	BOOPS (HERE TO GO) *Fourth & Broadway BRW 61*	12 11
25 Jul 87	FIRE *Fourth & Broadway BRW 71*	60 4
20 Sep 97	NIGHT NURSE *East West EW 129CD1* [1]	13 8
9 May 87	RHYTHM KILLERS *Fourth & Broadway BRLP 512*	35 5

[1] Sly and Robbie featuring Simply Red

SLY FOX *US, male vocal / instrumental duo –*
Gary Cooper and Michael Camacho (Singles: 16 Weeks) pos/wks

31 May 86 ●	LET'S GO ALL THE WAY *Capitol CL 403*	3 16

The SMALL ADS
UK, male vocal / instrumental group (Singles: 3 Weeks) pos/wks

18 Apr 81	SMALL ADS *Bronze BRO 115*	63 3

Singles re-entries are listed as (re), (2re), (3re).... which signifies that the hit re-entered the chart once, twice or three times...

The SMALL FACES `318` `Top 500`

Revered London-based mod quartet: Steve Marriott (v/g) (d. 1991), Ronnie Lane (b) (d. 1997), Ian McLagan (k), Kenney Jones (d). Marriott and Lane penned most of the act's UK hits. Further international fame came when Marriott formed Humble Pie and the other members formed The Faces (Singles: 137 Weeks, Albums: 71 Weeks) pos/wks

		pos	wks
2 Sep 65	WHATCHA GONNA DO ABOUT IT? *Decca F 12208*	14	12
10 Feb 66 ●	SHA-LA-LA-LA-LEE *Decca F 12317*	3	11
12 May 66 ●	HEY GIRL *Decca F 12393*	10	9
11 Aug 66 ★	ALL OR NOTHING *Decca F 12470*	1	12
17 Nov 66 ●	MY MIND'S EYE *Decca F 12500*	4	11
9 Mar 67	I CAN'T MAKE IT *Decca F 12565*	26	7
8 Jun 67	HERE COME THE NICE *Immediate IM 050*	12	10
9 Aug 67 ●	ITCHYCOO PARK *Immediate IM 057*	3	14
6 Dec 67 ●	TIN SOLDIER *Immediate IM 062*	9	12
17 Apr 68 ●	LAZY SUNDAY *Immediate IM 064*	2	11
10 Jul 68	UNIVERSAL *Immediate IM 069*	16	11
19 Mar 69	AFTERGLOW OF YOUR LOVE *Immediate IM 077*	36	1
13 Dec 75 ●	ITCHYCOO PARK (re-issue) *Immediate IMS 102*	9	11
20 Mar 76	LAZY SUNDAY (re-issue) *Immediate IMS 106*	39	5
14 May 66 ●	SMALL FACES *Decca LK 4790*	3	25
17 Jun 67	FROM THE BEGINNING *Decca LK 4879*	17	5
1 Jul 67	SMALL FACES *Immediate IMSP 008*	12	17
15 Jun 68 ★	OGDENS' NUT GONE FLAKE *Immediate IMLP 012*	1	19
11 May 96	THE DECCA ANTHOLOGY 1965-1967 *Deram 8445832*	66	1
7 Jun 03	ULTIMATE COLLECTION *Sanctuary TDSAN 004*	24	4

The two albums entitled 'Small Faces' are different

Heather SMALL (see also M PEOPLE)

UK, female vocalist (Singles: 12 Weeks, Albums: 4 Weeks) pos/wks

		pos	wks
18 Apr 92	SOMEDAY *Deconstruction PB 45369* [1]	38	3
20 May 00	PROUD *Arista 74321748902*	16	5
19 Aug 00	HOLDING ON *Arista 74321781332*	58	1
18 Nov 00	YOU NEED LOVE LIKE I DO *GUT CDGUT 36* [2]	24	3
10 Jun 00	PROUD *Arista 74321765482*	12	4

[1] M People with Heather Small [2] Tom Jones and Heather Small

SMALLER *UK, male vocal / instrumental group (Singles: 2 Weeks)* pos/wks

		pos	wks
28 Sep 96	WASTED *Better BETSCD 006*	72	1
29 Mar 97	IS *Better BETSCD 008*	55	1

SMART E'S

UK, male instrumental / production group (Singles: 9 Weeks) pos/wks

		pos	wks
11 Jul 92 ●	SESAME'S TREET *Suburban Base SUBBASE 12S*	2	9

S*M*A*S*H *UK, male vocal / instrumental group (Singles: 1 Week, Albums: 4 Weeks)* pos/wks

		pos	wks
6 Aug 94	(I WANT TO) KILL SOMEBODY *Hi-Rise FLATSCD 5*	26	1
2 Apr 94	S*M*A*S*H *Hi-Rise FLATMCD 2*	28	3
17 Sep 94	SELF ABUSED *Hi-Rise FLATCD 6*	59	1

SMASH MOUTH

US, male vocal / instrumental group (Singles: 9 Weeks) pos/wks

		pos	wks
25 Oct 97	WALKIN' ON THE SUN *Interscope IND 95555*	19	4
31 Jul 99	ALL STAR *Interscope 4971172*	24	5

The SMASHING PUMPKINS *US, male / female vocal / instrumental group (Singles: 36 Weeks, Albums: 71 Weeks)* pos/wks

		pos	wks
5 Sep 92	I AM ONE *Hut HUTT 18*	73	1
3 Jul 93	CHERUB ROCK *Hut HUTCD 31*	31	2
25 Sep 93	TODAY *Hut HUTCD 37*	44	2
5 Mar 94	DISARM *Hut HUTCD 43*	11	3
28 Oct 95	BULLET WITH BUTTERFLY WINGS *Hut HUTCD 63*	20	3
10 Feb 96	1979 *Hut HUTCD 67*	16	3
18 May 96 ●	TONIGHT TONIGHT *Hut HUTDX 69*	7	6
23 Nov 96	THIRTY THREE *Hut HUTCD 78*	21	2
14 Jun 97 ●	THE END IS THE BEGINNING IS THE END *Warner Bros. W 0404CD*	10	4
23 Aug 97	THE END IS THE BEGINNING IS THE END (re-mix) *Warner Bros. W 0410CD*	72	1
30 May 98	AVA ADORE *Hut HUTCD 101*	11	4
19 Sep 98	PERFECT *Hut HUTCD 106*	24	2
4 Mar 00	STAND INSIDE YOUR LOVE *Hut HUTCD 127*	23	2

		pos	wks
23 Sep 00	TRY TRY TRY *Hut HUTCD 140*	73	1
31 Jul 93 ●	SIAMESE DREAM *Hut CDHUT 11*	4	15
4 Nov 95 ●	MELLON COLLIE AND THE INFINITE SADNESS *Hut CDHUTD 30* ▲	4	37
13 Jun 98 ●	ADORE *Hut CDHUTX 51*	5	12
11 Mar 00 ●	MACHINA / THE MACHINES OF GOD *Hut CDHUT 59*	7	4
1 Dec 01	ROTTEN APPLES – THE SMASHING PUMPKINS GREATEST HITS *Hut CDHUTD 70*	28	3

SMEAR CAMPAIGN See MR BEAN and SMEAR CAMPAIGN featuring Bruce DICKINSON

SMELLS LIKE HEAVEN

Italy, male producer – Fabio Paras (Singles: 1 Week) pos/wks

		pos	wks
10 Jul 93	LONDRES STRUTT *Deconstruction 74321154312*	57	1

Steven SMITH and FATHER

UK, male instrumental duo (Albums: 3 Weeks) pos/wks

		pos	wks
13 May 72	STEVEN SMITH AND FATHER AND 16 GREAT SONGS *Decca SKL 5128*	17	3

Brian SMITH and his HAPPY PIANO

UK, male instrumentalist – piano (Albums: 1 Week) pos/wks

		pos	wks
19 Sep 81	PLAY IT AGAIN *Deram DS 047*	97	1

Ann-Marie SMITH

UK, female vocalist (Singles: 5 Weeks) pos/wks

		pos	wks
23 Jan 93	MUSIC *Synthetic CDR 6334* [1]	34	2
18 Mar 95	ROCKIN' MY BODY *Media MCSTD 2021* [2]	31	2
15 Jul 95	(YOU'RE MY ONE AND ONLY) TRUE LOVE *Media MCSTD 2060*	46	1

[1] Fargetta and Anne-Marie Smith [2] 49ers featuring Ann-Marie Smith

Elliott SMITH *US, male vocalist / instrumentalist – Steven Smith, b. 6 Aug 1969, d. 21 Oct 2003 (Singles: 3 Weeks, Albums: 3 Weeks)* pos/wks

		pos	wks
19 Dec 98	WALTZ #2 (XO) *Dreamworks DRMCD 22347*	52	1
1 May 99	BABY BRITAIN *Dreamworks DRMDM 50950*	55	1
8 Jul 00	SON OF SAM *Dreamworks DRMCD 4509492*	55	1
29 Apr 00	FIGURE 8 *Dreamworks 4502252*	37	2
30 Oct 04	FROM A BASEMENT ON THE HILL *Domino WIGCD 147*	41	1

'Fast' Eddie SMITH See DJ 'FAST' EDDIE

Hurricane SMITH

UK, male vocalist – Norman Smith (Singles: 35 Weeks) pos/wks

		pos	wks
12 Jun 71 ●	DON'T LET IT DIE *Columbia DB 8785*	2	12
29 Apr 72 ●	OH BABE, WHAT WOULD YOU SAY? *Columbia DB 8878*	4	16
2 Sep 72	WHO WAS IT *Columbia DB 8916*	23	7

Jimmy SMITH *US, male instrumentalist – organ (Singles: 3 Weeks, Albums: 3 Weeks)* pos/wks

		pos	wks
28 Apr 66	GOT MY MOJO WORKING (re) *Verve VS 536*	48	3
18 Jun 66	GOT MY MOJO WORKING *Verve VLP 912*	19	3

Keely SMITH *US, female vocalist – Dorothy Smith (Singles: 10 Weeks, Albums: 9 Weeks)* pos/wks

		pos	wks
18 Mar 65	YOU'RE BREAKIN' MY HEART *Reprise R 20346*	14	10
16 Jan 65	LENNON-McCARTNEY SONGBOOK *Reprise R 6142*	12	9

Mandy SMITH

UK, female vocalist (Singles: 2 Weeks) pos/wks

		pos	wks
20 May 89	DON'T YOU WANT ME BABY *PWL PWL 37*	59	2

Mark E SMITH See The FALL; INSPIRAL CARPETS

Mel SMITH (see also SMITH and JONES; NOT THE NINE O'CLOCK NEWS CAST) *UK, male vocalist / comedian (Singles: 10 Weeks)* pos/wks

		pos	wks
5 Dec 87 ●	ROCKIN' AROUND THE CHRISTMAS TREE *10 TEN 2* [1]	3	7
21 Dec 91	ANOTHER BLOOMING CHRISTMAS *Epic 6576877*	59	3

[1] Mel and Kim [Kim is Kim Wilde]

Michael SMITH See SEELENLUFT featuring Michael SMITH

Muriel SMITH
US, female vocalist, b. 23 Feb 1923, d. 13 Sep 1985 (Singles: 17 Weeks)

pos/wks

15 May 53 ●	HOLD ME, THRILL ME, KISS ME *Philips PB 122*	3	17

With Wally Stott and his Orchestra

OC SMITH
US, male vocalist – Ocie Smith, b. 21 Jun 1936, d. 23 Nov 2001 (Singles: 23 Weeks, Albums: 1 Week)

pos/wks

29 May 68 ●	THE SON OF HICKORY HOLLER'S TRAMP *CBS 3343*	2	15
26 Mar 77	TOGETHER *Caribou CRB 4910*	25	8
17 Aug 68	HICKORY HOLLER REVISITED *CBS 63362*	40	1

Patti SMITH GROUP
US, female / male vocal / instrumental group (Singles: 16 Weeks, Albums: 24 Weeks)

pos/wks

29 Apr 78 ●	BECAUSE THE NIGHT *Arista 181*	5	12
19 Aug 78	PRIVILEGE (SET ME FREE) *Arista 197*	72	1
2 Jun 79	FREDERICK *Arista 264*	63	3
1 Apr 78	EASTER *Arista SPART 1043*	16	14
19 May 79	WAVE *Arista SPART 1086*	41	6
16 Jul 88	DREAM OF LIFE *Arista 209172* [1]	70	1
13 Jul 96	GONE AGAIN *Arista 7822187472* [1]	44	2
8 May 04	TRAMPIN' *Columbia 5152159* [1]	70	1

[1] Patti Smith

Rex SMITH and Rachel SWEET
US, male / female vocalists (Singles: 7 Weeks)

pos/wks

22 Aug 81	EVERLASTING LOVE *CBS A 1405*	35	7

Richard Jon SMITH
South Africa, male vocalist (Singles: 2 Weeks)

pos/wks

16 Jul 83	SHE'S THE MASTER OF THE GAME *Jive JIVE 38*	63	2

Robert SMITH *See The CURE; JUNIOR JACK*

Rose SMITH *See DELAKOTA*

Sheila SMITH *See Cevin FISHER*

Simon 'BASSLINE' SMITH *See DRUMSOUND & Simon 'BASSLINE' SMITH*

Steve SMITH *See Paul JACKSON / Steve SMITH*

Whistling Jack SMITH
UK, male whistler – Billy Moeller (Singles: 12 Weeks)

pos/wks

2 Mar 67 ●	I WAS KAISER BILL'S BATMAN *Deram DM 112*	5	12

Will SMITH 345 Top 500
(see also DJ JAZZY JEFF and FRESH PRINCE) Artist formerly known as the Fresh Prince was not only one of the 1990s most successful rap stars, but also a top TV personality and Oscar-nominated movie actor, b. 25 Sep 1968, Philadelphia, US. The quadruple World Music Award winner (1999) helped to make rap accessible to all ages. Best-selling single: 'Men In Black' 883,000 (Singles: 110 Weeks, Albums: 87 Weeks)

pos/wks

16 Aug 97 ★	MEN IN BLACK *Columbia 6648682* ■	1	16
13 Dec 97	JUST CRUISIN' *Columbia 6653482*	23	6
7 Feb 98 ●	GETTIN' JIGGY WIT IT *Columbia 6655605* ▲	3	10
1 Aug 98 ●	JUST THE TWO OF US *Columbia 6662092*	2	10
5 Dec 98 ●	MIAMI *Columbia 6666782*	3	14
13 Feb 99 ●	BOY YOU KNOCK ME OUT (re) *MJJ / Epic 6669372* [1]	3	9
10 Jul 99 ●	WILD WILD WEST *Columbia 6675962* [2] ▲	2	16
20 Nov 99 ●	WILL 2K *Columbia 6684452*	2	11
25 Mar 00	FREAKIN' IT (re) *Columbia 6691052*	15	8
10 Aug 02 ●	BLACK SUITS COMIN' (NOD YA HEAD) *Columbia 6730132* [3]	3	10
6 Dec 97 ●	BIG WILLIE STYLE *Columbia 4886622*	9	70
27 Nov 99 ●	WILLENNIUM *Columbia 4949392*	10	15
24 Aug 02	BORN TO REIGN *Columbia 5079552*	24	2

[1] Tatyana Ali featuring Will Smith [2] Will Smith featuring Dru Hill – additional vocals Kool Moe Dee [3] Will Smith featuring Tra-Knox

SMITH and JONES
UK, male comedy duo – Mel Smith and Griff Rhys Jones (Albums: 8 Weeks)

pos/wks

15 Nov 86	SCRATCH AND SNIFF *10 DIX 51*	62	8

The SMITHS 174 Top 500
Mancunian quartet with loyal fan base: Morrissey (b. Stephen Morrissey) (v), Johnny Marr (g), Andy Rourke (b), Mike Joyce (d). Their achievements include monopolising the Top 3 indie chart placings (Feb 1984) and having seven albums simultaneously in the UK chart (Mar 1995) (Singles: 105 Weeks, Albums: 210 Weeks)

pos/wks

12 Nov 83	THIS CHARMING MAN *Rough Trade RT 136*	25	12
28 Jan 84	WHAT DIFFERENCE DOES IT MAKE *Rough Trade RT 146*	12	9
2 Jun 84 ●	HEAVEN KNOWS I'M MISERABLE NOW *Rough Trade RT 156*	10	8
1 Sep 84	WILLIAM, IT WAS REALLY NOTHING *Rough Trade RT 166*	17	6
9 Feb 85	HOW SOON IS NOW? *Rough Trade RT 176*	24	6
30 Mar 85	SHAKESPEARE'S SISTER *Rough Trade RT 181*	26	4
13 Jul 85	THAT JOKE ISN'T FUNNY ANYMORE *Rough Trade RT 186*	49	3
5 Oct 85	THE BOY WITH THE THORN IN HIS SIDE *Rough Trade RT 191*	23	5
31 May 86	BIG MOUTH STRIKES AGAIN *Rough Trade RT 192*	26	4
2 Aug 86	PANIC *Rough Trade RT 193*	11	8
1 Nov 86	ASK *Rough Trade RT 194*	14	5
7 Feb 87	SHOPLIFTERS OF THE WORLD UNITE *Rough Trade RT 195*	12	4
25 Apr 87 ●	SHEILA TAKE A BOW *Rough Trade RT 196*	10	5
22 Aug 87	GIRLFRIEND IN A COMA *Rough Trade RT 197*	13	5
14 Nov 87	I STARTED SOMETHING I COULDN'T FINISH *Rough Trade RT 198*	23	4
19 Dec 87	LAST NIGHT I DREAMT THAT SOMEBODY LOVED ME *Rough Trade RT 200*	30	4
15 Aug 92 ●	THIS CHARMING MAN (re-issue) *WEA YZ 0001*	8	5
12 Sep 92	HOW SOON IS NOW (re-issue) *WEA YZ 0002*	16	4
24 Oct 92	THERE IS A LIGHT THAT NEVER GOES OUT *WEA YZ 0003*	25	4
18 Feb 95	ASK (re-issue) *WEA YZ 0004CDX*	62	1
3 Mar 84 ●	THE SMITHS *Rough Trade ROUGH 61*	2	33
24 Nov 84 ●	HATFUL OF HOLLOW *Rough Trade ROUGH 76*	7	46
23 Feb 85 ★	MEAT IS MURDER *Rough Trade ROUGH 81* ■	1	13
28 Jun 86 ●	THE QUEEN IS DEAD *Rough Trade ROUGH 96*	2	22
7 Mar 87 ●	THE WORLD WON'T LISTEN *Rough Trade ROUGH 101*	2	15
30 May 87	LOUDER THAN BOMBS (IMPORT) *Rough Trade ROUGH 255*	38	5
10 Oct 87 ●	STRANGEWAYS HERE WE COME *Rough Trade ROUGH 106*	2	17
17 Sep 88 ●	RANK *Rough Trade ROUGH 126*	2	7
29 Aug 92 ★	BEST … I *WEA 4509903272* ■	1	9
14 Nov 92	BEST … II *WEA 4509904062*	29	5
4 Mar 95	HATFUL OF HOLLOW (re-issue) *WEA 4509918932*	26	3
4 Mar 95	MEAT IS MURDER (re-issue) *WEA 4509918952*	39	2
4 Mar 95 ●	SINGLES *WEA 4509990902*	5	13
4 Mar 95	STRANGEWAYS HERE WE COME (re-issue) *WEA 4509918992*	38	4
4 Mar 95	THE QUEEN IS DEAD (re-issue) *WEA 4509918962*	30	4
4 Mar 95	THE SMITHS (re-issue) *WEA 4509918922*	42	4
4 Mar 95	THE WORLD WON'T LISTEN (re-issue) *WEA 4509918982*	52	2
14 Oct 00	LOUDER THAN BOMBS (re-issue) *WEA 4509938332*	52	2
16 Jun 01	THE VERY BEST OF THE SMITHS *WEA 8573889482*	30	4

SMOKE
UK, male vocal / instrumental group (Singles: 3 Weeks)

pos/wks

9 Mar 67	MY FRIEND JACK *Columbia DB 8115*	45	3

SMOKE CITY
UK / Brazil, male / female vocal / instrumental group (Singles: 5 Weeks)

pos/wks

12 Apr 97 ●	UNDERWATER LOVE *Jive JIVECD 422*	4	5

SMOKE 2 SEVEN
UK, female vocal trio (Singles: 2 Weeks)

pos/wks

16 Mar 02	BEEN THERE DONE THAT *Curb / London CUBC 077*	26	2

SMOKED *See Oliver LIEB presents SMOKED*

SMOKIE 408 Top 500
British group who became European superstars, fronted by vocalist Chris Norman. Especially popular in Germany, many of their hits were penned by Mike Chapman and Nicky Chinn (Singles: 125 Weeks, Albums: 45 Weeks)

pos/wks

19 Jul 75 ●	IF YOU THINK YOU KNOW HOW TO LOVE ME *RAK 206* [1]	3	9
4 Oct 75 ●	DON'T PLAY YOUR ROCK 'N ROLL TO ME *RAK 217* [1]	8	7
31 Jan 76	SOMETHING'S BEEN MAKING ME BLUE *RAK 227*	17	8
25 Sep 76	I'LL MEET YOU AT MIDNIGHT *RAK 241*	11	9
4 Dec 76 ●	LIVING NEXT DOOR TO ALICE *RAK 244*	5	11
19 Mar 77	LAY BACK IN THE ARMS OF SOMEONE *RAK 251*	12	9
16 Jul 77 ●	IT'S YOUR LIFE *RAK 260*	5	9
15 Oct 77	NEEDLES AND PINS *RAK 263*	10	9
28 Jan 78	FOR A FEW DOLLARS MORE *RAK 267*	17	6
20 May 78 ●	OH CAROL *RAK 276*	5	13
23 Sep 78	MEXICAN GIRL *RAK 283*	19	9

19 Apr 80	TAKE GOOD CARE OF MY BABY *RAK 309*	34	7
13 May 95 ●	LIVING NEXT DOOR TO ALICE (WHO THE F**K IS ALICE) (re) *NOW CDWAG 245* [2]	3	19
1 Nov 75	SMOKIE / CHANGING ALL THE TIME *RAK SRAK 517*.........18	18	5
30 Apr 77 ●	GREATEST HITS *RAK SRAK 526*	6	22
4 Nov 78	THE MONTREUX ALBUM *RAK SRAK 6757*...................	52	2
11 Oct 80	SMOKIE'S HITS *RAK SRAK 540*.........................23	23	13
17 Mar 01	UNCOVERED – THE VERY BEST OF SMOKIE *Universal Music TV 138172*	63	3

[1] Smokey [2] Smokie featuring Roy 'Chubby' Brown

*'Living Next Door to Alice (Who The F**k Is Alice)' is a re-recorded version of 'Living Next Door to Alice' and peaked on re-entry in Aug 1995*

SMOKIN BEATS featuring Lyn EDEN
UK, male DJ / production duo – Neil Rumney and Paul Landon and female vocalist (Singles: 3 Weeks) pos/wks

17 Jan 98	DREAMS *AM:PM 5824711*	23	3

SMOKIN' MOJO FILTERS *UK / US, male /*
female vocal / instrumental charity group (Singles: 5 Weeks) pos/wks

23 Dec 95	COME TOGETHER (WAR CHILD) *Go Discs GODCD 136* 19	19	5

SMOOTH *US, female vocalist – Juanita Stokes (Singles: 7 Weeks)* pos/wks

22 Jul 95	MIND BLOWIN' *Jive JIVECD 379* 36	36	2
7 Oct 95	IT'S SUMMERTIME (LET IT GET INTO YOU) *Jive JIVECD 383* ..46	46	1
16 Mar 96	WE GOT IT *MCA MCSTD 48009* [1] 26	26	2
16 Mar 96	LOVE GROOVE (GROOVE WITH YOU) *Jive JIVECD 390* 46	46	1
6 Jul 96	UNDERCOVER LOVER *Jive JIVECD 397* 41	41	1

[1] Immature featuring Smooth

CL SMOOTH *See Pete ROCK and CL SMOOTH*

Joe SMOOTH *US, male producer (Singles: 4 Weeks)* pos/wks

4 Feb 89	PROMISED LAND *DJ International DJIN 6* 56	56	4

SMOOTH TOUCH
US, male instrumental / production duo (Singles: 1 Week) pos/wks

2 Apr 94	HOUSE OF LOVE (IN MY HOUSE) *Six6 SIXCD 112* 58	58	1

Jean Jacques SMOOTHIE
UK, male DJ / producer – Steve Robson (Singles: 7 Weeks) pos/wks

13 Oct 01	2 PEOPLE *Echo ECSCD 112* 12	12	7

SMUJJI *Jamaica, male vocalist (Singles: 9 Weeks)* pos/wks

13 Mar 04	MUST BE LOVE *Def Jam 9817508* [1] 13	13	7
31 Jul 04	K.O. *Def Jam 9867077* 43	43	2

[1] Fya featuring Smujji

The SMURFS *Holland, small blue creatures*
vocal group (Singles: 52 Weeks, Albums: 77 Weeks) pos/wks

3 Jun 78 ●	THE SMURF SONG *Decca F 13759* [1] 2	2	17
30 Sep 78	DIPPETY DAY *Decca F 13798* [1] 13	13	12
2 Dec 78	CHRISTMAS IN SMURFLAND *Decca F 13819* 19	19	7
7 Sep 96 ●	I'VE GOT A LITTLE PUPPY *EMI TV CDSMURF 100* 4	4	10
21 Dec 96 ●	YOUR CHRISTMAS WISH *EMI TV CDSMURF 100* 8	8	6
25 Nov 78	FATHER ABRAHAM IN SMURFLAND *Decca SMURF 1* [1] 19	19	11
6 Jul 96 ●	THE SMURFS GO POP! *EMI TV CDEMTV 121* 2	2	33
16 Nov 96 ●	SMURF'S CHRISTMAS PARTY *EMI TV CDEMTV 140* 8	8	9
22 Feb 97 ●	THE SMURFS HITS '97 – VOLUME 1 *EMI TV CDEMTV 150*.........2	2	11
6 Sep 97	GO POP! AGAIN *EMI CDEMTV 155* 15	15	7
18 Apr 98	GREATEST HITS *EMI 4941972* 28	28	6

[1] Father Abraham and The Smurfs [1] Father Abraham and The Smurfs

Patty SMYTH with Don HENLEY (see also The EAGLES)
US, female / male vocal duo (Singles: 6 Weeks) pos/wks

3 Oct 92	SOMETIMES LOVE JUST AIN'T ENOUGH *MCA MCS 1692* 22	22	6

SNAKEBITE
Italy, male production trio (Singles: 2 Weeks) pos/wks

9 Aug 97	THE BIT GOES ON *Multiply CDMULTY 22* 25	25	2

SNAP! (375) Top 500 *German-based producers Benito Benites*
(b. Michael Munzing) and John Garrett Virgo III (b. Luca Anzilotti) master-minded a string of worldwide dance hits for this act, which featured a host of mostly US vocalists and rappers including Turbo B, Jackie Harris, Penny Ford and Thea Austin. Best-selling single: 'Rhythm Is a Dancer' 582,700
(Singles: 126 Weeks, Albums: 56 Weeks) pos/wks

24 Mar 90 ★	THE POWER *Arista 113133* 1	1	15
16 Jun 90 ●	OOOPS UP *Arista 113296* 5	5	12
22 Sep 90 ●	CULT OF SNAP! *Arista 113596* 8	8	7
8 Dec 90 ●	MARY HAD A LITTLE BOY *Arista 113831* 8	8	10
30 Mar 91 ●	SNAP! MEGAMIX *Arista 114169* 10	10	6
21 Dec 91	THE COLOUR OF LOVE *Arista 114678* 54	54	3
4 Jul 92 ★	RHYTHM IS A DANCER *Arista 115309* 1	1	19
9 Jan 93 ●	EXTERMINATE! *Arista 74321106962* [1] 2	2	11
12 Jun 93 ●	DO YOU SEE THE LIGHT (LOOKING FOR) *Arista 74321147622* [1] 10	10	8
17 Sep 94 ●	WELCOME TO TOMORROW (re) *Arista 74321223852* [2] 6	6	14
1 Apr 95	THE FIRST THE LAST ETERNITY (TIL THE END) *Arista 74321234672* [2] 15	15	7
28 Oct 95	THE WORLD IN MY HANDS *Arista 74321314792* [2] 44	44	1
13 Apr 96	RAME *Arista 74321368902* [3] 50	50	1
24 Aug 96	THE POWER 96 *Arista 74321398672* [4] 42	42	1
24 Aug 02	DO YOU SEE THE LIGHT? *Data MOS DATA 33CDS* [5] 14	14	5
17 May 03	RHYTHM IS A DANCER *Data / Mos DATA 47CDS* 17	17	4
6 Sep 03	THE POWER (OF BHANGRA) (re-mix) *Data / MoS DATA 60CDS* [6] 34	34	2
26 May 90 ●	WORLD POWER *Arista 210682* 10	10	39
8 Aug 92 ●	THE MADMAN'S RETURN *Logic 262552* 8	8	15
15 Oct 94	WELCOME TO TOMORROW *Ariola 74321223842* 69	69	1
7 Sep 96	SNAP! ATTACK – THE BEST OF SNAP! / THE REMIXES *Ariola 74321395192* 47	47	1

[1] Snap! featuring Niki Haris [2] Snap! featuring Summer [3] Snap! featuring Rukmani [4] Snap! featuring Einstein [5] Snap! vs Plaything [6] Snap! vs Motivo

'The Madman's Return' changed catalogue number to Arista 74321128512 during its chart run

SNEAKER PIMPS *UK, male / female vocal /*
instrumental group (Singles: 19 Weeks, Albums: 7 Weeks) pos/wks

19 Oct 96	6 UNDERGROUND *Clean Up CUP 023CDS* 15	15	4
15 Mar 97	SPIN SPIN SUGAR *Clean Up CUP 033CDS* 21	21	3
7 Jun 97 ●	6 UNDERGROUND (re-mix) *Clean Up CUP 036CDM* 9	9	4
30 Aug 97	POST MODERN SLEAZE *Clean Up CUP 038CDM* 22	22	3
7 Feb 98	SPIN SPIN SUGAR (re-mix) *Clean Up CUP 037X* 46	46	2
21 Aug 99	LOW FIVE *Clean Up CUP 052CDM* 39	39	2
30 Oct 99	TEN TO TWENTY *Clean Up CUP 054CDS* 56	56	1
31 Aug 96	BECOMING X *Clean Up CUP 020CD* 27	27	4

David SNEDDON
UK, male vocalist (Singles: 33 Weeks, Albums: 5 Weeks) pos/wks

25 Jan 03 ★	STOP LIVING THE LIE *Mercury 0637292* 1	1	18
3 May 03	DON'T LET GO *Mercury 9800044* 3	3	10
23 Aug 03	BEST OF ORDER *Fontana 9810276* 19	19	3
8 Nov 03	BABY GET HIGHER *Fontana 9813421* 38	38	2
10 May 03 ●	SEVEN YEARS – TEN WEEKS *Mercury 9800063* 5	5	5

SNIFF 'N' THE TEARS
UK, male vocal / instrumental group (Singles: 5 Weeks) pos/wks

23 Jun 79	DRIVER'S SEAT *Chiswick CHIS 105* 42	42	5

SNOOP DOGG (455) Top 500
Groundbreaking g-funk rapper, b. Calvin Broadus, 20 Oct 1972, Long Beach, California, US. Discovered by Dr Dre, he was the first artist to enter the US album chart at No.1 with a debut album. The distinctive rapper coached his son's american football team to the Junior Superbowl. (Singles: 102 Weeks, Albums: 54 Weeks) pos/wks

4 Dec 93	WHAT'S MY NAME? *Death Row A 8337CD* [1] 20	20	8
12 Feb 94	GIN AND JUICE *Death Row A 8316CD* [1] 39	39	3
20 Aug 94	DOGGY DOGG WORLD *Death Row A 8289CD* [1] 32	32	3
14 Dec 96	SNOOP'S UPSIDE YA HEAD *Interscope IND 95520* [2] 12	12	7
26 Apr 97	WANTED DEAD OR ALIVE *Def Jam 5744052* [3] 16	16	3
3 May 97	VAPORS *Interscope IND 95530* [1] 18	18	2
20 Sep 97	WE JUST WANNA PARTY WITH YOU *Columbia 6649902* [4] ..21	21	2
24 Jan 98	THA DOGGFATHER *Interscope IND 95550* [1] 36	36	2
12 Dec 98	COME AND GET WITH ME *Elektra E 3787CD* [5] 58	58	2

25 Mar 00 ●	**STILL D.R.E.** *Interscope 4972742* [6] 6	10
3 Feb 01 ●	**THE NEXT EPISODE (re)** *Interscope 4974762* [6] 3	12
17 Mar 01	**X** *Epic 6709072* [7] 14	7
28 Apr 01	**SNOOP DOGG** *Priority PTYCD 134* 13	5
30 Nov 02	**FROM THA CHUUUCH TO DA PALACE**	
	Priority / Capitol 5516102 27	6
1 Mar 03	**THE STREETS** *Def Jam 0779852* [8] 48	2
5 Apr 03	**BEAUTIFUL** *Priority CDCL 842* [9] 23	20
21 Feb 04	**HOLIDAE IN** *Capitol CDCL 852* [10] 35	3
14 Aug 04	**I WANNA THANK YA** *J 82876624782* [10] 31	3
11 Dec 04 ●	**DROP IT LIKE IT'S HOT** *Geffen 2103461* [11] ▲ 10	3+
11 Dec 93	**DOGGYSTYLE** *Death Row 6544922792* [1] 38	27
23 Nov 96	**THA DOGGFATHER** *Interscope INTD 90038* [1] ▲ 15	11
15 Aug 98	**DA GAME IS TO BE SOLD NOT TO BE TOLD**	
	Priority CDPTY 153 ▲ 28	3
5 Jun 99	**TOP DOGG** *Priority CDPTY 171* 48	1
5 May 01	**THA LAST MEAL** *Priority CDPTY 199* 62	2
10 May 03	**PAID THA COST TO BE DA BO$$** *Priority 5391572* 64	6
4 Dec 04	**R & G – RHYTHM & GANGSTA – THE MASTERPIECE**	
	Geffen 9864841 33	4+

[1] Snoop Doggy Dogg [2] Snoop Doggy Dogg featuring Charlie Wilson [3] 2Pac and Snoop Doggy Dogg [4] Snoop Doggy Dogg featuring JD [5] Keith Sweat featuring Snoop Dogg [6] Dr Dre featuring Snoop Dogg [7] Xzibit featuring Snoop Dogg [8] WC featuring Snoop Dogg and Nate Dogg [9] Snoop Dogg featuring Pharrell, Uncle Charlie Wilson [10] Chingy featuring Ludacris & Snoop Dogg [11] Angie Stone featuring Snoop Dogg [12] Snoop Dogg featuring Pharrell [1] Snoop Doggy Dogg

SNOW *Canada, male rapper – Darrin O'Brien*
(Singles: 18 Weeks, Albums: 4 Weeks) pos/wks

13 Mar 93 ●	**INFORMER** *East West America A 8436CD* ▲ 2	15
5 Jun 93	**GIRL I'VE BEEN HURT** *East West America A 8417CD* 48	2
4 Sep 93	**UHH IN** *Atlantic A 8378CD* 67	1
17 Apr 93	**12 INCHES OF SNOW** *East West America 7567922072*......41	4

Mark SNOW *US, male instrumentalist –*
keyboards (Singles: 15 Weeks, Albums: 2 Weeks) pos/wks

30 Mar 96 ●	**THE X-FILES** *Warner Bros. W 0341CD* 2	15
12 Oct 96	**THE TRUTH AND THE LIGHT – MUSIC FROM THE X-FILES**	
	Warner Bros. 9362464482 42	2

Phoebe SNOW *US, female vocalist /*
instrumentalist – guitar – Phoebe Laub (Singles: 7 Weeks) pos/wks

6 Jan 79	**EVERY NIGHT** *CBS 6842* 37	7

SNOW PATROL *UK, male vocal /*
instrumental group (Singles: 25 Weeks, Albums: 46 Weeks) pos/wks

27 Sep 03	**SPITTING GAMES** *Polydor 9809350* 54	1
7 Feb 04 ●	**RUN** *Fiction / Polydor 9816353* 5	11
24 Apr 04	**CHOCOLATE** *Fiction / Polydor 9866355* 24	6
24 Jul 04	**SPITTING GAMES (re-issue)** *Fiction / Polydor 9867126* 23	5
6 Nov 04	**HOW TO BE DEAD** *Polydor 9868777* 39	2
14 Feb 04 ●	**FINAL STRAW** *Fiction / Polydor 9865408*....................3	46+

SNOWMAN See Peter AUTY and the SINFONIA OF LONDON conducted by Howard BLAKE

The SNOWMEN
UK, male vocal / instrumental group (Singles: 12 Weeks) pos/wks

12 Dec 81	**HOKEY COKEY** *Stiff ODB 1* 18	8
18 Dec 82	**XMAS PARTY** *Solid STOP 006* 44	4

SNUG *UK, male vocal / instrumental group (Singles: 1 Week)* pos/wks

18 Apr 98	**BEATNIK GIRL** *WEA WEA 151CDX* 55	1

SO *UK, male vocal / instrumental group (Singles: 3 Weeks)* pos/wks

13 Feb 88	**ARE YOU SURE** *Parlophone R 6173* 62	3

SO SOLID CREW (see also OXIDE & NEUTRINO; Asher D;
ROMEO; HARVEY; Lisa MAFFIA) *UK, male / female vocal /
rap / production collective (Singles: 43 Weeks, Albums: 25 Weeks)* pos/wks

18 Aug 01 ★	**21 SECONDS (re)** *Relentless RELENT 16CD* ■ 1	15
17 Nov 01 ●	**THEY DON'T KNOW** *Relentless RELENT 26CD* 3	9
19 Jan 02 ●	**HATERS** *Relentless RELENT 23CD* [1] 8	7
20 Apr 02	**RIDE WID US** *Relentless / Independiente ISOM 55MS* 19	6
27 Sep 03 ●	**BROKEN SILENCE** *Independiente ISOM 71MS* 9	5

3 Apr 04	**SO GRIMEY** *Independiente ISOM 82MS* 62	1
1 Dec 01 ●	**THEY DON'T KNOW** *Relentless / Independiente ISOM 27CD*......6	20
26 Jan 02 ●	**FUCK IT** *Relentless REL 004CD* 3	4
11 Oct 03	**2ND VERSE** *Independiente ISOM 35CD* 70	1

[1] So Solid Crew presents Mr Shabz featuring MBD and The Reelists

'Fuck It' appeared only on the UK Compilation Chart and not on the standard Top 75

S.O.A.P.
*Denmark, female vocal duo – Heidi and
Line Sorensen (Singles: 2 Weeks)* pos/wks

25 Jul 98	**THIS IS HOW WE PARTY** *Columbia 6661295* 36	2

SOAPY
*UK, male instrumental / production duo –
Jak Kaleniuk and Dan Bewick (Singles: 2 Weeks)* pos/wks

14 Sep 96	**HORNY AS FUNK** *WEA WEA 074CD* 35	2

Gino SOCCIO
Canada, male instrumentalist – keyboards (Singles: 5 Weeks) pos/wks

28 Apr 79	**DANCER** *Warner Bros. K 17357* 46	5

SODA CLUB
*UK, male production duo – Andy and
Pete Lee (Singles: 12 Weeks)* pos/wks

9 Nov 02	**TAKE MY BREATH AWAY** *Concept CDCON 33* [1] 16	4
8 Feb 03	**HEAVEN IS A PLACE ON EARTH** *Concept CDCON 39* [1] 13	4
23 Aug 03	**KEEP LOVE TOGETHER** *Concept CDCON 44* [2] 31	2
28 Aug 04	**AIN'T NO LOVE (AIN'T NO USE)** *Concept CDCON 58* [3] 40	2

[1] Soda Club featuring Hannah Alethea [2] Soda Club featuring Andrea Anatola [3] Soda Club featuring Ashley Jade

SOEUR SOURIRE See The SINGING NUN (Soeur Sourire)

SOFT CELL (311 | Top 500)
*Successful synth-driven duo from Leeds: Marc Almond (v), David Ball (k).
The visually striking pair's revival of northern soul classic 'Tainted Love' was
the top UK single of 1981, went on to sell 1,135,000 and broke the longevity
record in the US Top 100 (Singles: 110 Weeks, Albums: 103 Weeks)* pos/wks

1 Aug 81 ★	**TAINTED LOVE (3re)** *Some Bizzare BZS 2* ◆ 1	36
14 Nov 81 ●	**BEDSITTER** *Some Bizzare BZS 6* 4	12
6 Feb 82 ●	**SAY HELLO WAVE GOODBYE** *Some Bizzare BZS 7* 3	9
29 May 82 ●	**TORCH** *Some Bizzare BZS 9* 3	9
21 Aug 82 ●	**WHAT** *Some Bizzare BZS 11* 3	8
4 Dec 82	**WHERE THE HEART IS** *Some Bizzare BZS 16* 21	7
5 Mar 83	**NUMBERS / BARRIERS** *Some Bizzare BZS 17* 25	4
24 Sep 83	**SOUL INSIDE** *Some Bizzare BZS 20* 16	5
25 Feb 84	**DOWN IN THE SUBWAY** *Some Bizzare BZS 22* 24	6
23 Mar 91	**SAY HELLO WAVE GOODBYE '91 (re-recording)**	
	Mercury SOFT 1 [1] 38	3
18 May 91 ●	**TAINTED LOVE (re-issue)** *Mercury SOFT 2* [1] 5	8
28 Sep 02	**MONOCULTURE** *Cooking Vinyl FRYCD 132* 52	1
8 Feb 03	**THE NIGHT** *Cooking Vinyl FRYCD 135* 39	2
5 Dec 81 ●	**NON-STOP EROTIC CABARET** *Some Bizzare BZLP 2*......5	46
26 Jun 82	**NON-STOP ECSTATIC DANCING** *Some Bizzare BZS 1012*......6	18
22 Jan 83	**THE ART OF FALLING APART** *Some Bizzare BIZL 3* 5	10
31 Mar 84	**THIS LAST NIGHT IN SODOM** *Some Bizzare BIZL 6*......12	5
20 Dec 86	**THE SINGLES ALBUM** *Some Bizzare BZLP 3* 58	9
1 Jun 91 ●	**MEMORABILIA – THE SINGLES** *Mercury 8485121* 8	13
13 Apr 02	**THE VERY BEST OF SOFT CELL** *UMTV 5868342* 37	2

[1] Soft Cell / Marc Almond

*'Tainted Love' re-entries made No.43 in Jan 1982, No.50 in Jul 1982 and No.43
in Feb 1985*

SOFT MACHINE
*(see also Robert WYATT) UK, male vocal /
instrumental group (Albums: 8 Weeks)* pos/wks

4 Jul 70	**THIRD** *CBS 66246* 18	6
3 Apr 71	**FOURTH** *CBS 64280* 32	2

SOFT PARADE See ELECTRIC SOFT PARADE

SOHO
UK, male / female vocal / instrumental group (Singles: 11 Weeks) pos/wks

5 May 90 ●	HIPPY CHICK (re) *Savage 7SAV 106*	8	9
9 Nov 91	BORN TO BE ALIVE *MCA MCS 1578* [1]	51	2

[1] Adamski featuring Soho

'Hippy Chick' originally peaked at No.67 and made its peak position only on re-entry to the chart in Jan 1991. The listed flip side of 'Born to Be Alive' was 'Never Goin' Down' by Adamski featuring Jimi Polo •

SOHO DOLLS
UK, female / male vocal / instrumental group (Singles: 1 Week) pos/wks

27 Nov 04	PRINCE HARRY *Poptones MC 5096SCD*	57	1

SOIL *US, male vocal / instrumental group (Singles: 2 Weeks)* pos/wks

9 Nov 02	HALO *J 74321970132*	74	1
5 Jun 04	REDEFINE *J 82876618512*	68	1

SOLAR STONE *UK, male DJ / production trio (Singles: 5 Weeks)* pos/wks

21 Feb 98	THE IMPRESSIONS EP *Hooj Choons HOOJCD 57*	75	1
6 Nov 99	7 CITIES *Hooj Choons HOOJ 85CD*	39	2
28 Sep 02	7 CITIES (re-mix) *Lost Language LOST 018CD*	44	2

Tracks on The Impressions EP: The Calling / Day By Day / So Clear

SOLID GOLD CHARTBUSTERS
UK, male / female production / vocal group (Singles: 1 Week) pos/wks

25 Dec 99	I WANNA 1-2-1 WITH YOU *Virgin VSCDT 1765*	62	1

SOLID HARMONIE
UK / US, female vocal group (Singles: 11 Weeks) pos/wks

31 Jan 98	I'LL BE THERE FOR YOU *Jive JIVECD 437*	18	3
18 Apr 98	I WANT YOU TO WANT ME *Jive JIVECD 452*	16	3
15 Aug 98	I WANNA LOVE YOU *Jive 0521742*	20	4
21 Nov 98	TO LOVE ONCE AGAIN *Jive 0522472*	55	1

The SOLID SENDERS
UK, male vocal / instrumental group (Albums: 3 Weeks) pos/wks

23 Sep 78	SOLID SENDERS *Virgin V 2105*	42	3

SOLID SESSIONS
Holland, male production duo (Singles: 1 Week) pos/wks

14 Sep 02	JANEIRO *Posititva CDTIV 175*	47	1

SOLITAIRE *UK, male production duo (Singles: 2 Weeks)* pos/wks

29 Nov 03	I LIVE LOVE (I LOVE LOVE) *Susu CDSUSU 21*	57	2

SOLO *UK, male producer – Stuart Crichton (Singles: 4 Weeks)* pos/wks

20 Jul 91	RAINBOW (SAMPLE FREE) *Reverb RVBT 003*	59	2
18 Jan 92	COME ON! *Reverb RVBT 008*	75	1
11 Sep 93	COME ON! (re-mix) *Stoatin' STOAT 003CD*	63	1

Ed SOLO *See BROCKIE & ED SOLO*

Sal SOLO *(see also CLASSIX NOUVEAUX)*
UK, male vocalist (Singles: 13 Weeks) pos/wks

15 Dec 84	SAN DAMIANO (HEART AND SOUL) *MCA MCA 930*	15	10
6 Apr 85	MUSIC AND YOU *MCA MCA 946* [1]	52	3

[1] Sal Solo with the London Community Gospel Choir

SOLO (US) *US, male vocal group (Singles: 3 Weeks)* pos/wks

3 Feb 96	HEAVEN *Perspective 5875212*	35	2
30 Mar 96	WHERE DO U WANT ME TO PUT IT *Perspective 5875312*	45	1

Diane SOLOMON *UK, female vocalist (Albums: 6 Weeks)* pos/wks

9 Aug 75	TAKE TWO *Philips 6308 236*	26	6

Sir George SOLTI *See Peter COOK and Dudley MOORE; Dudley MOORE*

SOLUTION *See Victor SIMONELLI presents SOLUTION*

Martin SOLVEIG
France, male DJ / producer (Singles: 5 Weeks) pos/wks

24 Apr 04	ROCKING MUSIC *Defected DFTD 082CDS*	35	4
26 Jun 04	I'M A GOOD MAN *Defected DFTD 091CDS*	57	1

Belouis SOME
UK, male vocalist – Neville Keighley (Singles: 26 Weeks) pos/wks

27 Apr 85	IMAGINATION *Parlophone R 6097*	50	7
18 Jan 86	IMAGINATION (re-issue) *Parlophone R 1986*	17	10
12 Apr 86	SOME PEOPLE *Parlophone R 6130*	33	7
16 May 87	LET IT BE WITH YOU *Parlophone R 6154*	53	2

Jimmy SOMERVILLE *(see also BRONSKI BEAT; The COMMUNARDS)*
UK, male vocalist (Singles: 53 Weeks, Albums: 46 Weeks) pos/wks

11 Nov 89	COMMENT TE DIRE ADIEU *London LON 241* [1]	14	9
13 Jan 90 ●	YOU MAKE ME FEEL (MIGHTY REAL) *London LON 249*	5	8
17 Mar 90	READ MY LIPS (ENOUGH IS ENOUGH) *London LON 254*	26	6
3 Nov 90 ●	TO LOVE SOMEBODY *London LON 281*	8	11
2 Feb 91	SMALLTOWN BOY (re-mix) *London LON 287* [2]	32	4
10 Aug 91	RUN FROM LOVE *London LON 301*	52	2
28 Jan 95	HEARTBEAT *London LONCD 358*	24	4
27 May 95	HURT SO GOOD *London LONCD 364*	15	6
28 Oct 95	BY YOUR SIDE *London LONCD 372*	41	2
13 Sep 97	DARK SKY *Gut CXGUT 11*	66	1
9 Dec 89	READ MY LIPS *London 8281661*	29	14
24 Nov 90 ●	THE SINGLES COLLECTION 1984/1990 *London 8282261*	4	26
24 Jun 95	DARE TO LOVE *London 8285402*	38	2
22 Sep 01	THE VERY BEST OF JIMMY SOMERVILLE, BRONSKI BEAT AND THE COMMUNARDS *London 927412582* [1]	29	4

[1] Jimmy Somerville featuring June Miles-Kingston [2] Jimmy Somerville with Bronski Beat [1] Jimmy Somerville, Bronski Beat and The Communards

SOMETHIN' FOR THE PEOPLE featuring TRINA and TAMARA
US, male vocal / instrumental group and female vocal duo – Trina and Tamara Powell (Singles: 1 Week) pos/wks

7 Feb 98	MY LOVE IS THE SHHH! *Warner Bros. W 0427CD*	64	1

SOMETHING CORPORATE
US, male vocal / instrumental group (Singles: 3 Weeks) pos/wks

29 Mar 03	PUNK ROCK PRINCESS *MCA MCSTD 40315*	33	2
12 Jul 03	IF YOU C JORDAN *MCA MCSTD 40324*	68	1

SOMORE featuring Damon TRUEITT
US, male production group and male vocalist (Singles: 2 Weeks) pos/wks

24 Jan 98	I REFUSE (WHAT YOU WANT) *XL Recordings XLS 93CD*	21	2

SONGSTRESS
US, male production / vocal duo (Singles: 1 Week) pos/wks

27 Feb 99	SEE LINE WOMAN '99 *Locked On LOX 106CD*	64	1

SONIA *UK, female vocalist – Sonia Evans*
(Singles: 78 Weeks, Albums: 14 Weeks) pos/wks

24 Jun 89 ★	YOU'LL NEVER STOP ME LOVING YOU *Chrysalis CHS 3385*	1	13
7 Oct 89	CAN'T FORGET YOU *Chrysalis CHS 3419*	17	6
9 Dec 89 ●	LISTEN TO YOUR HEART *Chrysalis CHS 3465*	10	10
7 Apr 90	COUNTING EVERY MINUTE *Chrysalis CHS 3492*	16	7
23 Jun 90	YOU'VE GOT A FRIEND *Jive CHILD 90* [1]	14	6
25 Aug 90	END OF THE WORLD *Chrysalis / PWL CHS 3557*	18	7
1 Jun 91 ●	ONLY FOOLS (NEVER FALL IN LOVE) *IQ ZB 44613*	10	8
31 Aug 91	BE YOUNG BE FOOLISH BE HAPPY *IQ ZB 44935*	22	5
16 Nov 91	YOU TO ME ARE EVERYTHING *IQ ZB 45121*	13	5
12 Sep 92	BOOGIE NIGHTS *Arista 74321113467*	30	3
1 May 93	BETTER THE DEVIL YOU KNOW *Arista 74321146872*	15	7
30 Jul 94	HOPELESSLY DEVOTED TO YOU *Cockney COCCD 2*	61	1
5 May 90 ●	EVERYBODY KNOWS *Chrysalis CHR 1734*	7	10
19 Oct 91	SONIA *IQ ZL 751675*	33	2
29 May 93	BETTER THE DEVIL YOU KNOW *Arista 74321149802*	32	2

[1] Big Fun and Sonia featuring Gary Barnacle

SONIC BOOM
UK, male vocal / instrumental group (Albums: 1 Week) pos/wks

17 Mar 90	SPECTRUM *Silvertone ORELP 56*	65	1

SONIC SOLUTION *Belgium, male production*
duo – CJ Bolland and Steve Cop (Singles: 1 Week) pos/wks

4 Apr 92	**BEATSTIME** *R&S RSUK 11*	59 1

SONIC SURFERS
Holland, male instrumental / production duo (Singles: 2 Weeks) pos/wks

20 Mar 93	**TAKE ME UP** *A&M AMCD 210* [1]	61 1
30 Jul 94	**DON'T GIVE IT UP** *Brilliant CDBRIL 6*	54 1

[1] Sonic Surfers featuring Jocelyn Brown

SONIC THE HEDGEHOG See HWA featuring SONIC THE HEDGEHOG

SONIC YOUTH *US, male / female vocal /*
instrumental group (Singles: 14 Weeks, Albums: 14 Weeks) pos/wks

11 Jul 92	**100%** *DGC DGCS 11*	28 4
7 Nov 92	**YOUTH AGAINST FASCISM** *Geffen GFS 26*	52 2
3 Apr 93	**SUGAR KANE** *Geffen GFSTD 37*	26 3
7 May 94	**BULL IN THE HEATHER** *Geffen GFSTD 72*	24 2
10 Sep 94	**SUPERSTAR** *A&M 5807932*	45 2
11 Jul 98	**SUNDAY** *Geffen GFSTD 22332*	72 1
29 Oct 88	**DAYDREAM NATION** *Blast First BFFP 34*	99 1
4 Feb 89	**THE WHITEY ALBUM** *Blast First BFFP 28* [1]	63 1
7 Jul 90	**GOO** *DGC 7599242971*	32 2
4 May 91	**DIRTY BOOTS – PLUS 5 LIVE TRACKS** *DGC DGC 21634*	69 1
1 Aug 92 ●	**DIRTY** *DGC DGCD 24485*	6 5
21 May 94 ●	**EXPERIMENTAL JET SET TRASH AND NO STAR** *Geffen GED 24632*	10 2
14 Oct 95	**WASHING MACHINE** *Geffen GED 24825*	39 1
23 May 98	**A THOUSAND LEAVES** *Geffen GED 25203*	38 1

[1] Ciccone Youth

The listed flip side of 'Superstar' was 'Yesterday Once More' by Redd Kross

SONIQUE *UK, female vocalist / DJ –*
Sonia Clarke (Singles: 47 Weeks, Albums: 37 Weeks) pos/wks

13 Jun 98	**I PUT A SPELL ON YOU** *Serious SERR 001CD*	36 2
5 Dec 98	**IT FEELS SO GOOD** *Serious SERR 004CD*	24 3
3 Jun 00 ★	**IT FEELS SO GOOD** *(re-mix) Universal MCSTD 40233* ■	1 17
16 Sep 00	**SKY** *Universal MCSTD 40240*	2 10
9 Dec 00 ●	**I PUT A SPELL ON YOU** *(re-issue) Universal MCSTD 40245*	8 10
31 May 03	**CAN'T MAKE UP MY MIND** *Serious 9807217*	17 4
13 Sep 03	**ALIVE** *Serious 9811500*	70 1
24 Jun 00 ●	**HEAR MY CRY** *Universal 1592302*	6 37

SONNY (see also SONNY and CHER) *US, male vocalist –*
Salvatore Bono, b. 16 Feb 1935, d. 5 Jan 1998 (Singles: 11 Weeks) pos/wks

19 Aug 65 ●	**LAUGH AT ME** *Atlantic AT 4038*	9 11

SONNY and CHER *US, male / female vocal / instrumental*
duo – Salvatore Bono, b. 16 Feb 1935, d. 5 Jan 1998, and
Cherilyn LaPierre (Singles: 78 Weeks, Albums: 20 Weeks) pos/wks

12 Aug 65 ★	**I GOT YOU BABE** *Atlantic AT 4035* ▲	1 12
16 Sep 65	**BABY DON'T GO** *Reprise R 20309*	11 9
21 Oct 65	**BUT YOU'RE MINE** *Atlantic AT 4047*	17 8
17 Feb 66	**WHAT NOW MY LOVE** *Atlantic AT 4069*	13 11
30 Jun 66	**HAVE I STAYED TOO LONG** *Atlantic 584 018*	42 3
8 Sep 66 ●	**LITTLE MAN** *Atlantic 584 040*	4 10
17 Nov 66	**LIVING FOR YOU** *Atlantic 584 057*	44 4
2 Feb 67	**THE BEAT GOES ON** *Atlantic 584 078*	29 8
15 Jan 72 ●	**ALL I EVER NEED IS YOU** *(2re) MCA MU 1145*	8 12
22 May 93	**I GOT YOU BABE** *(re-issue) Epic 6592402*	66 1
16 Oct 65 ●	**LOOK AT US** *Atlantic ATL 5036*	7 13
14 May 66	**THE WONDROUS WORLD OF SONNY AND CHER** *Atlantic 587006*	15 7

SONO
Germany, male production duo (Singles: 1 Week) pos/wks

16 Jun 01	**KEEP CONTROL** *Code Blue BLU 020CD1*	66 1

SONS AND DAUGHTERS
UK, male / female vocal / instrumental group (Singles: 1 Week) pos/wks

16 Oct 04	**JOHNNY CASH** *Domino RUG 186CD*	68 1

SON'Z OF A LOOP DA LOOP ERA
UK, male producer – Danny Breaks (Singles: 4 Weeks) pos/wks

15 Feb 92	**FAR OUT** *Suburban Base SUBBASE 008*	36 3
17 Oct 92	**PEACE + LOVEISM** *Suburban Base SUBBASE 14*	60 1

SOOPA HOOPZ featuring QPR MASSIVE *UK, Queens*
Park Rangers supporters vocal group (Singles: 1 Week) pos/wks

16 Oct 04	**SOOPA HOOPZ** *Sniper Alley SNIPER 001*	54 1

SOOZY Q *See BIG TIME CHARLIE*

SOPHIE *See ZERO 7*

The SORROWS
UK, male vocal / instrumental group (Singles: 8 Weeks) pos/wks

16 Sep 65	**TAKE A HEART** *Piccadilly 7N 35260*	21 8

Aaron SOUL *UK, male vocalist – Aaron Anyia (Singles: 4 Weeks)* pos/wks

2 Jun 01	**RING RING RING** *Def Soul 5689042*	14 4

David SOUL *US, male actor / vocalist –*
David Solberg (Singles: 56 Weeks, Albums: 51 Weeks) pos/wks

18 Dec 76 ★	**DON'T GIVE UP ON US** *Private Stock PVT 84* ◆ ▲	1 16
26 Mar 77 ●	**GOING IN WITH MY EYES OPEN** *Private Stock PVT 99*	2 8
27 Aug 77 ★	**SILVER LADY** *Private Stock PVT 115*	1 14
17 Dec 77 ●	**LET'S HAVE A QUIET NIGHT IN** *Private Stock PVT 130*	8 9
27 May 78	**IT SURE BRINGS OUT THE LOVE IN YOUR EYES** *Private Stock PVT 137*	12 9
27 Nov 76 ●	**DAVID SOUL** *Private Stock PVLP 1012*	2 28
17 Sep 77 ●	**PLAYING TO AN AUDIENCE OF ONE** *Private Stock PVLP 1026*	8 23

Jimmy SOUL *US, male vocalist – James McCleese,*
b. 24 Aug 1942, d. 25 Jun 1988 (Singles: 5 Weeks) pos/wks

11 Jul 63	**IF YOU WANNA BE HAPPY** *Stateside SS 178* ▲	39 2
15 Jun 91	**IF YOU WANNA BE HAPPY** *(re-issue) Epic 6569647*	68 3

SOUL ASYLUM *US, male vocal /*
instrumental group (Singles: 33 Weeks, Albums: 29 Weeks) pos/wks

19 Jun 93 ●	**RUNAWAY TRAIN** *(re) Columbia 6593902*	7 19
4 Sep 93	**SOMEBODY TO SHOVE** *Columbia 6596492*	34 3
22 Jan 94	**BLACK GOLD** *Columbia 6598442*	26 4
26 Mar 94	**SOMEBODY TO SHOVE** *(re-issue) Columbia 6602245*	32 3
15 Jul 95	**MISERY** *Columbia 6621092*	30 3
2 Dec 95	**JUST LIKE ANYONE** *Columbia 6624785*	52 1
31 Jul 93	**GRAVE DANCERS UNION** *Columbia 4722532*	27 25
1 Jul 95	**LET YOUR DIM LIGHT SHINE** *Columbia 4803202*	22 4

'Runaway Train' peaked during re-entry in Nov 1993

SOUL BROTHERS
UK, male vocal / instrumental group (Singles: 3 Weeks) pos/wks

22 Apr 65	**I KEEP RINGING MY BABY** *Decca F 12116*	42 3

SOUL CITY ORCHESTRA
UK, male instrumental / production group (Singles: 1 Week) pos/wks

11 Dec 93	**IT'S JURASSIC** *London JURCD 1*	70 1

SOUL CITY SYMPHONY See Van McCOY

SOUL CONTROL *Germany, male vocal / rap duo –*
Thomas Quella and Leonard Buck (Singles: 3 Weeks) pos/wks

18 Sep 04	**CHOCOLATE (CHOCO CHOCO)** *Tug CDSNOG 12*	25 3

SOUL FAMILY SENSATION
UK / US, male / female vocal / instrumental group (Singles: 4 Weeks) pos/wks

11 May 91	**I DON'T EVEN KNOW IF I SHOULD CALL YOU BABY** *One Little Indian 47TP 7*	49 4

SOUL FOR REAL *US, male vocal group (Singles: 4 Weeks)* pos/wks

8 Jul 95	**CANDY RAIN** *Uptown MCSTD 2052*	23 2
23 Mar 96	**EVERY LITTLE THING I DO** *Uptown MCSTD 48005*	31 2

SOUL II SOUL (343) Top 500

(see also PSYCHEDELIC WALTONS) *Enormously influential UK dance music project led by entrepreneurial producer / DJ Jazzie B, b. Beresford Romeo, London. Act featured Nellee Hooper's innovative arrangements and was fronted by a succession of vocalists, most notably Caron Wheeler. Unlike UK contemporaries they were equally successful in the US (Singles: 89 Weeks, Albums: 108 Weeks)* pos/wks

			pos	wks
21 May 88	FAIRPLAY *10 TEN 228* [1]		63	3
17 Sep 88	FEEL FREE *10 TEN 236* [2]		64	2
18 Mar 89 ●	KEEP ON MOVING *10 TEN 263* [3]		5	12
10 Jun 89 ★	BACK TO LIFE (HOWEVER DO YOU WANT ME) *10 TEN 265* [3]		1	14
9 Dec 89 ●	GET A LIFE *10 TEN 284*		3	13
5 May 90 ●	A DREAM'S A DREAM *10 TEN 300*		6	6
24 Nov 90	MISSING YOU *10 TEN 345* [4]		22	7
4 Apr 92 ●	JOY *Ten TEN 350*		4	7
13 Jun 92	MOVE ME NO MOUNTAIN *Ten TEN 400* [5]		31	4
26 Sep 92	JUST RIGHT *Ten TEN 410*		38	2
6 Nov 93	WISH *Virgin VSCDG 1480*		24	4
22 Jul 95	LOVE ENUFF *Virgin VSCDT 1527*		12	6
21 Oct 95	I CARE (SOUL II SOUL) *Virgin VSCDT 1560*		17	4
19 Oct 96	KEEP ON MOVIN' (re-mix) *Virgin VSCDT 1612*		31	2
30 Aug 97	REPRESENT *Island CID 668*		39	2
8 Nov 97	PLEASURE DOME *Island CID 669*		51	1
22 Apr 89 ★	CLUB CLASSICS VOL. ONE *10 DIX 82*		1	60
2 Jun 90 ★	VOLUME II (1990 A NEW DECADE) *10 DIX 90* ■		1	20
25 Apr 92 ●	VOLUME III JUST RIGHT *Ten DIXCD 100*		3	11
27 Nov 93 ●	VOLUME IV THE CLASSIC SINGLES 88-93 *Virgin CDV 2724*		10	13
12 Aug 95	VOLUME V – BELIEVE *Virgin CDV 2739*		13	4

[1] Soul II Soul featuring Rose Windross [2] Soul II Soul featuring Do'reen
[3] Soul II Soul featuring Caron Wheeler [4] Soul II Soul featuring Kym Mazelle
[5] Soul II Soul: lead vocals Kofi

SOUL PROVIDERS featuring Michelle SHELLERS

UK, male production duo and US, female vocalist (Singles: 1 Week) pos/wks

14 Jul 01	RISE *AM:PM CDAMPM 147*		59	1

SOUL SONIC FORCE See Afrika BAMBAATAA; OAKENFOLD

S.O.U.L. S.Y.S.T.E.M. introducing Michelle VISAGE

(see also C & C MUSIC FACTORY) *US, male / female vocal / instrumental group (Singles: 5 Weeks)* pos/wks

16 Jan 93	IT'S GONNA BE A LOVELY DAY *Arista 74321125692*		17	5

SOUL U*NIQUE

UK, male / female vocal group (Singles: 2 Weeks) pos/wks

19 Feb 00	BE MY FRIEND *M&J MAJCD 2*		53	1
29 Jul 00	3IL (THRILL) *M&J MAJCD 3X*		66	1

SOUL VISION See EVERYTHING BUT THE GIRL

SOULED OUT

Italy / US / UK, male / female vocal / instrumental group (Singles: 1 Week) pos/wks

9 May 92	IN MY LIFE *Columbia 6578367*		75	1

SOULFLY

Brazil / US, male vocal / instrumental group (Albums: 4 Weeks) pos/wks

2 May 98	SOULFLY *Roadrunner RR 87482*		16	2
7 Oct 00	PRIMITIVE *Roadrunner RR 85652*		45	1
6 Jul 02	3 *Roadrunner RR 84552*		61	1

SOULSEARCHER

US, male / female production / vocal group (Singles: 9 Weeks) pos/wks

13 Feb 99 ●	CAN'T GET ENOUGH *Defected DEFECT 1CDS*		8	7
8 Apr 00	DO IT TO ME AGAIN *Defected DFECT 15CDS*		32	2

SOULSONIC FORCE See OAKENFOLD

SOULWAX

Belgium, male vocal / instrumental duo – Stephen and David Dewaele (Singles: 7 Weeks, Albums: 1 Week) pos/wks

25 Mar 00	CONVERSATION INTERCOM *Pias Recordings PIASB 018CD*		65	1
24 Jun 00	MUCH AGAINST EVERYONE'S ADVICE *Pias Recordings PIASB 026CD*		56	1
30 Sep 00	TOO MANY DJ'S *Pias Recordings PIASB 036CD*		40	2

3 Mar 01	CONVERSATION INTERCOM (re-mix) *Pias Recordings PIASB 046CD*		50	1
21 Aug 04	ANY MINUTE NOW *Pias Recordings PIASB 126CDM*		34	2
4 Sep 04	ANY MINUTE NOW *Pias PIASB 060CD*		53	1

SOUND BLUNTZ

Germany, male production / vocal group (Singles: 2 Weeks) pos/wks

30 Nov 02	BILLIE JEAN *Incentive CENT 51CDS*		32	2

SOUND-DE-ZIGN

Holland, male DJ / production duo – Adri Blok and Arjen Rietvink (Singles: 5 Weeks) pos/wks

14 Apr 01	HAPPINESS *Nulife / Arista 74321844002*		19	5

SOUND FACTORY

Sweden, male vocal / instrumental duo (Singles: 1 Week) pos/wks

5 Jun 93	2 THE RHYTHM *Logic 74321149422*		72	1

SOUND 5

UK, male vocal / instrumental group (Singles: 1 Week) pos/wks

24 Apr 99	ALA KABOO *Gut CDGUT 23*		69	1

SOUND 9418 See Jonathan KING

SOUND OF ONE featuring GLADEZZ

US, male / female vocal / instrumental duo (Singles: 1 Week) pos/wks

20 Nov 93	AS I AM *Cooltempo CDCOOL 280*		65	1

SOUNDGARDEN

US, male vocal / instrumental group (Singles: 24 Weeks, Albums: 32 Weeks) pos/wks

11 Apr 92	JESUS CHRIST POSE *A&M AM 862*		30	3
20 Jun 92	RUSTY CAGE *A&M AM 874*		41	1
21 Nov 92	OUTSHINED *A&M AM 0102*		50	1
26 Feb 94	SPOONMAN *A&M 5805392*		20	3
30 Apr 94	THE DAY I TRIED TO LIVE *A&M 5805952*		42	2
20 Aug 94	BLACK HOLE SUN *A&M 5807532*		12	5
28 Jan 95	FELL ON BLACK DAYS *A&M 5809472*		24	2
18 May 96	PRETTY NOOSE *A&M 5816202*		14	3
28 Sep 96	BURDEN IN MY HAND *A&M 5818552*		33	2
28 Dec 96	BLOW UP THE OUTSIDE WORLD *A&M 5819862*		40	2
25 Apr 92	BADMOTORFINGER *A&M 3953742*		39	2
19 Mar 94 ●	SUPERUNKNOWN *A&M 5402152* ▲		4	24
1 Jun 96 ●	DOWN ON THE UPSIDE *A&M 5405262*		7	6

SOUNDMAN and Don LLOYDIE with Elisabeth TROY

UK, male / female vocal / production group (Singles: 2 Weeks) pos/wks

25 Feb 95	GREATER LOVE *Sound of Underground SOURCD 016*		49	2

SOUNDS INCORPORATED (see also Gene VINCENT)

UK, male instrumental group (Singles: 11 Weeks) pos/wks

23 Apr 64	THE SPARTANS *Columbia DB 7239*		30	6
30 Jul 64	SPANISH HARLEM *Columbia DB 7321*		35	5

SOUNDS NICE featuring Tim MYCROFT

UK, male instrumental group (Singles: 11 Weeks) pos/wks

6 Sep 69	LOVE AT FIRST SIGHT (JE T'AIME ... MOI NON PLUS) *Parlophone R 5797*		18	11

SOUNDS OF BLACKNESS

US, male / female gospel choir (Singles: 32 Weeks, Albums: 6 Weeks) pos/wks

22 Jun 91	OPTIMISTIC *Perspective PERSS 786*		45	4
28 Sep 91	THE PRESSURE PART 1 *Perspective PERSS 816*		71	1
15 Feb 92	OPTIMISTIC (re-issue) *Perspective PERSS 849*		28	4
25 Apr 92	THE PRESSURE PART 1 (re-mix) *Perspective PERSS 867*		49	2
8 May 93	I'M GOING ALL THE WAY *Perspective 5874252*		27	3
26 Mar 94	I BELIEVE *A&M 5874512*		17	4
2 Jul 94	GLORYLAND *Mercury MERCD 404* [1]		36	4
20 Aug 94	EVERYTHING IS GONNA BE ALRIGHT *A&M 5874672*		29	3
14 Jan 95	I'M GOING ALL THE WAY (re-issue) *A&M 5874832*		14	4
7 Jun 97	SPIRIT *A&M 5822292* [2]		35	2
14 Feb 98	THE PRESSURE (2ND RE-MIX) (2nd re-mix) *AM:PM 5824872*	46	1
30 Apr 94	AFRICA TO AMERICA: THE JOURNEY OF THE DRUM *A&M 5490092*		28	6

[1] Daryl Hall and Sounds of Blackness [2] Sounds of Blackness / Craig Mack

SOUNDS ORCHESTRAL
UK, orchestra (Singles: 18 Weeks, Albums: 1 Week)   pos/wks

3 Dec 64 ●	CAST YOUR FATE TO THE WIND *Piccadilly 7N 35206*	5 16
8 Jul 65	MOONGLOW *Piccadilly 7N 35248*	43 2
12 Jun 65	CAST YOUR FATE TO THE WIND *Piccadilly NPL 38041*	17 1

SOUNDSATION *UK, male producer (Singles: 1 Week)*   pos/wks

14 Jan 95	PEACE AND JOY *Ffrreedom TABCD 224*	48 1

SOUNDSCAPE *UK, male DJ / production group (Singles: 1 Week)* pos/wks

14 Feb 98	DUBPLATE CULTURE *Satellite 74321552002*	61 1

SOUNDSOURCE
Sweden / UK, male instrumental / production group (Singles: 1 Week) pos/wks

11 Jan 92	TAKE ME UP *ffrr FX 177*	62 1

SOUNDTRACKS (films, TV etc) See VARIOUS ARTISTS (EPs and LPs)

The SOUP DRAGONS *UK, male vocal /*
instrumental group (Singles: 23 Weeks, Albums: 17 Weeks)   pos/wks

20 Jun 87	CAN'T TAKE NO MORE *Raw TV RTV 3*	65 1
5 Sep 87	SOFT AS YOUR FACE *Raw TV RTV 4*	66 2
14 Jul 90 ●	I'M FREE *Raw TV RTV 9* [1]	5 12
20 Oct 90	MOTHER UNIVERSE *Big Life BLR 30*	26 5
11 Apr 92	DIVINE THING *Big Life BLR 68*	53 3
7 May 88	THIS IS OUR ART *Sire WX 169*	60 1
5 May 90 ●	LOVEGOD *Raw TV SOUPLP 2*	7 15
16 May 92	HOTWIRED *Big Life BLRCD 15*	74 1

[1] The Soup Dragons featuring Junior Reid

SOURCE *UK, male producer – John Truelove (Singles: 22 Weeks)* pos/wks

2 Feb 91 ●	YOU GOT THE LOVE *Truelove TLOVE 7001* [1]	4 11
26 Dec 92	ROCK THE HOUSE *React 12REACT 12* [2]	63 1
1 Mar 97 ●	YOU GOT THE LOVE (re-mix) *React CDREACT 89* [1]	3 8
23 Aug 97	CLOUDS *XL Recordings XLS 83CD*	38 2

[1] Source featuring Candi Staton [2] Source featuring Nicole

SOURMASH *UK, male production trio (Singles: 1 Week)*   pos/wks

23 Dec 00	PILGRIMAGE / MESCALITO *Hooj Choons HOOJ 102*	73 1

SOUTH *UK, male vocal / instrumental group (Singles: 4 Weeks)*   pos/wks

17 Mar 01	PAINT THE SILENCE *Mo Wax MWR 134CD*	69 1
23 Aug 03	LOOSEN YOUR HOLD *Double Dragon DD 2010CD*	73 1
3 Apr 04	COLOURS IN WAVES *Sanctuary SANXD 249*	60 1
14 Aug 04	MOTIVELESS CRIME *Sanctuary SANXD 286*	72 1

Joe SOUTH *US, male vocalist – Joe Souter (Singles: 11 Weeks)*   pos/wks

5 Mar 69 ●	GAMES PEOPLE PLAY *Capitol CL 15579*	6 11

SOUTH BANK ORCHESTRA *UK, orchestra (Albums: 6 Weeks)* pos/wks

2 Dec 78	LILLIE *Sounds MOR 516*	47 6

Album was conducted by Joseph Morovitz and Laurie Holloway

SOUTH ST. PLAYER
US, male vocalist / producer – Roland Clark (Singles: 1 Week)   pos/wks

2 Sep 00	WHO KEEPS CHANGING YOUR MIND *Cream CREAM 4CD*	49 1

Jeri SOUTHERN *US, female vocalist –*
Genevieve Hering, b. 5 Aug 1926, d. 4 Aug 1991 (Singles: 3 Weeks)   pos/wks

21 Jun 57	FIRE DOWN BELOW *Brunswick 05665*	22 3

SOUTHERN DEATH CULT See The CULT

The SOUTHLANDERS
Jamaica / UK, male vocal group (Singles: 10 Weeks)   pos/wks

22 Nov 57	ALONE *Decca F 10946*	17 10

SOUTHSIDE SPINNERS *Holland, male production duo –*
Marco Verkuylen and Benjamin Kuyten (Singles: 7 Weeks)   pos/wks

27 May 00 ●	LUVSTRUCK *AM:PM CDAMPM 132*	9 7

SOUVERNANCE *Holland, male production duo (Singles: 1 Week)* pos/wks

31 Aug 02	HAVIN' A GOOD TIME *Positiva CDTIV 174*	63 1

SOUVLAKI *UK, male producer – Mark Summers (Singles: 4 Weeks)* pos/wks

15 Feb 97	INFERNO *Wonderboy WBOYD 003*	24 3
8 Aug 98	MY TIME *Wonderboy WBOYD 009*	63 1

The SOVEREIGN COLLECTION *UK, orchestra (Singles: 6 Weeks)* pos/wks

3 Apr 71	MOZART 40 *Capitol CL 15676*	27 6

Red SOVINE *US, male vocalist – Woodrow Wilson*
Sovine, b. 17 Jul 1918, d. 4 Apr 1980 (Singles: 8 Weeks)   pos/wks

13 Jun 81 ●	TEDDY BEAR *Starday SD 142*	4 8

SOX *UK, female vocal / instrumental group –*
lead vocal Samantha Fox (Singles: 1 Week)   pos/wks

15 Apr 95	GO FOR THE HEART *Living Beat LBECD 33*	47 1

Bob B SOXX and the BLUE JEANS
US, male / female vocal group (Singles: 2 Weeks)   pos/wks

31 Jan 63	ZIP-A-DEE-DOO-DAH *London HLU 9646*	45 2

SPACE *France, male instrumental*
group (Singles: 12 Weeks, Albums: 9 Weeks)   pos/wks

13 Aug 77 ●	MAGIC FLY *Pye International 7N 25746*	2 12
17 Sep 77	MAGIC FLY *Pye NSPL 28232*	11 9

SPACE *UK, male vocal / instrumental*
group (Singles: 52 Weeks, Albums: 67 Weeks)   pos/wks

6 Apr 96	NEIGHBOURHOOD *Gut CDGUT 1*	56 1
8 Jun 96	FEMALE OF THE SPECIES *Gut CDGUT 2*	14 10
7 Sep 96	ME AND YOU VERSUS THE WORLD *Gut CDGUT 4*	9 6
2 Nov 96	NEIGHBOURHOOD (re-issue) *Gut CDGUT 5*	11 6
22 Feb 97	DARK CLOUDS *Gut CDGUT 6*	14 4
10 Jan 98 ●	AVENGING ANGELS *Gut CDGUT 16*	6 8
7 Mar 98 ●	THE BALLAD OF TOM JONES *Gut CDGUT 018* [1]	4 8
4 Jul 98	BEGIN AGAIN *Gut CDGUT 19*	21 4
5 Dec 98	THE BAD DAYS (EP) *Gut CDGUT 22*	20 3
8 Jul 00	DIARY OF A WIMP *Gut CDGUT 34*	49 1
6 Mar 04	SUBURBAN ROCK 'N' ROLL *R&M Entertainment RAMCDS 001* 67	1
28 Sep 96 ●	SPIDERS *Gut GUTCD 1*	5 42
21 Mar 98 ●	TIN PLANET *Gut GUTCD 5*	3 25

[1] Space with Cerys of Catatonia

Tracks on The Bad Days (EP): Bad Days / We Gotta Get Out of This Place / The Unluckiest Man in the World

SPACE BABY
(see also LOST TRIBE; MELT featuring LITTLE MS MARCIE; SUNBURST; MDM) *UK, male producer – Matt Darey (Singles: 1 Week)*   pos/wks

8 Jul 95	FREE YOUR MIND *Hooj Choons HOOJ 34CD*	55 1

SPACE BROTHERS (see also ASCENCION; CHAKRA; ESSENCE; LUSTRAL; OXYGEN featuring Andrea BRITTON) *UK, male production duo – Ricky Simmonds and Stephen Jones (Singles: 19 Weeks)*   pos/wks

17 May 97	SHINE *Manifesto FESCD 23*	23 3
13 Dec 97	FORGIVEN (I FEEL YOUR LOVE) *Manifesto FESCD 36*	27 7
10 Jul 99	LEGACY (SHOW ME LOVE) *Manifesto FESCD 55*	31 3
9 Oct 99	HEAVEN WILL COME *Manifesto FESCD 61*	25 2
5 Feb 00	SHINE 2000 (re-mix) *Manifesto FESCD 67*	18 4

SPACE COWBOY
France, male producer – Nick Dresti (Singles: 3 Weeks)   pos/wks

6 Jul 02	I WOULD DIE 4 U *Southern Fried ECB 29CD*	55 2
2 Aug 03	JUST PUT YOUR HAND IN MINE *Southern Fried ECB 37CD*	71 1

SPACE FROG *Germany, male production duo (Singles: 1 Week)* pos/wks

16 Mar 02	(X RAY) FOLLOW ME *Tripoli Trax TTRAX 082CD*	70 1

SPACE KITTENS
UK, male instrumental / production group (Singles: 1 Week)   pos/wks

13 Apr 96	STORM *Hooj Choons HOOJCD 41*	58 1

SPACE MANOEUVRES
UK, male producer – John Graham (Singles: 2 Weeks)   pos/wks

29 Jan 00	STAGE ONE *Hooj Choons HOOJ 79CD*	25	2

SPACE MONKEY
UK, male producer – Paul Goodchild (Singles: 4 Weeks)   pos/wks

8 Oct 83	CAN'T STOP RUNNING *Innervision A 3742*	53	4

SPACE MONKEYZ vs GORILLAZ
UK, male production / instrumental duo (Singles: 1 Week)   pos/wks

3 Aug 02	LIL' DUB CHEFIN' *Parlophone CDR 6584*	73	1

SPACE RAIDERS *UK, male production trio (Singles: 1 Week)*   pos/wks

28 Mar 98	GLAM RAID *Skint SKINT 32CD*	68	1

SPACE 2000 *UK, male vocal / instrumental duo (Singles: 1 Week)*   pos/wks

12 Aug 95	DO U WANNA FUNK *Wired WIRED 218*	50	1

SPACECORN
Sweden, male DJ / producer – Daniel Ellenson (Singles: 1 Week)   pos/wks

28 Apr 01	AXEL F *69 SN 069CD*	74	1

SPACEDUST *UK, male production duo –*
Paul Glancey and Duncan Glasson (Singles: 12 Weeks)   pos/wks

24 Oct 98	★ GYM AND TONIC (re) *East West EW 188CD* ■	1	10
27 Mar 99	LET'S GET DOWN *East West EW 195CD*	20	2

SPACEHOG *UK, male vocal /*
instrumental group (Singles: 8 Weeks, Albums: 2 Weeks)   pos/wks

11 May 96	IN THE MEANTIME (re) *Sire 7559643162*	29	7
7 Feb 98	CARRY ON *Sire W 0428CD*	43	1
15 Feb 97	RESIDENT ALIEN *Sire 7559618342*	40	2

'In the Meantime' peaked during re-entry in Dec 1996

SPACEMAID
UK, male vocal / instrumental group (Singles: 1 Week)   pos/wks

5 Apr 97	BABY COME ON *Big Star STARC 105*	70	1

SPACEMEN 3 *UK, male instrumental group (Albums: 1 Week)*   pos/wks

9 Mar 91	RECURRING *Fire FIRELP 23*	46	1

SPAGHETTI SURFERS
UK, male instrumental / production duo (Singles: 1 Week)   pos/wks

22 Jul 95	MISIRLOU (THE THEME TO THE MOTION PICTURE 'PULP FICTION') *Tempo Toons CDTOON 4*	55	1

SPAGNA *Italy, female vocalist – Ivana Spagna (Singles: 23 Weeks)*   pos/wks

25 Jul 87	● CALL ME *CBS 650279 7*	2	12
17 Oct 87	EASY LADY *CBS 651169 7*	62	3
20 Aug 88	EVERY GIRL AND BOY *CBS SPAG 1*	23	8

SPAN *Norway, male vocal / instrumental group (Singles: 1 Week)*   pos/wks

21 Feb 04	DON'T THINK THE WAY THEY DO *Island CID 846*	52	1

SPANDAU BALLET (101) [Top 500] *Kilt-clad New Romantic revolutionaries. This London band went on to become smart-suited Top 10 regulars: Tony Hadley (v), Gary Kemp (g), Martin Kemp (b), Steve Norman (g/sax/prc), John Keeble (d). The Kemp brothers later went into the movies and TV, including lead roles in 'The Krays' (1990), and Martin, who starred in 'EastEnders' and other TV programmes, was voted Best Actor and Sexiest Male at the 2002 Soap Awards. Hadley won 2003 reality TV pop show 'Reborn in the USA' (Singles: 159 Weeks, Albums: 274 Weeks)*   pos/wks

15 Nov 80	● TO CUT A LONG STORY SHORT *Reformation CHS 2473*	5	11
24 Jan 81	THE FREEZE *Reformation CHS 2486*	17	8
4 Apr 81	MUSCLEBOUND / GLOW *Reformation CHS 2509*	10	10
18 Jul 81	● CHANT NO.1 (I DON'T NEED THIS PRESSURE ON) *Reformation CHS 2528*	3	10
14 Nov 81	PAINT ME DOWN *Chrysalis CHS 2560*	30	5
30 Jan 82	SHE LOVED LIKE DIAMOND *Chrysalis CHS 2585*	49	4

10 Apr 82	● INSTINCTION *Chrysalis CHS 2602*	10	11
2 Oct 82	● LIFELINE *Chrysalis CHS 2642*	7	9
12 Feb 83	COMMUNICATION *Reformation CHS 2662*	12	10
23 Apr 83	★ TRUE *Reformation SPAN 1*	1	12
13 Aug 83	● GOLD *Reformation SPAN 2*	2	9
9 Jun 84	● ONLY WHEN YOU LEAVE (re) *Reformation SPAN 3*	3	10
25 Aug 84	I'LL FLY FOR YOU *Reformation SPAN 4*	9	9
20 Oct 84	HIGHLY STRUNG *Reformation SPAN 5*	15	5
8 Dec 84	ROUND AND ROUND *Reformation SPAN 6*	18	8
26 Jul 86	FIGHT FOR OURSELVES *Reformation A 7264*	15	7
8 Nov 86	● THROUGH THE BARRICADES *Reformation SPANS 1*	6	10
14 Feb 87	HOW MANY LIES *Reformation SPANS 2*	34	4
3 Sep 88	RAW *CBS SPANS 3*	47	3
26 Aug 89	BE FREE WITH YOUR LOVE *CBS SPANS 4*	42	4
14 Mar 81	● JOURNEYS TO GLORY *Reformation CHR 1331*	5	29
20 Mar 82	DIAMOND *Reformation CDL 1353*	15	18
12 Mar 83	★ TRUE *Reformation CDL 1403*	1	90
7 Jul 84	● PARADE *Reformation CDL 1473*	2	39
16 Nov 85	● THE SINGLES COLLECTION *Chrysalis SBTV 1*	3	53
29 Nov 86	● THROUGH THE BARRICADES *Reformation CBS 450 2591*	7	19
30 Sep 89	HEART LIKE A SKY *CBS 463 3181*	31	3
28 Sep 91	THE BEST OF SPANDAU BALLET *Chrysalis CHR 1894*	44	3
16 Sep 00	● GOLD – THE BEST OF SPANDAU BALLET *Chrysalis 5267002*	7	20

SPANKOX (see also MOTIVO)
Italy, male producer – Agostino Carollo (Singles: 1 Week)   pos/wks

9 Oct 04	TO THE CLUB *Inferno CDFERN 62*	69	1

SPARKLE *US, female vocalist – Stephanie*
Edwards (Singles: 10 Weeks, Albums: 1 Week)   pos/wks

18 Jul 98	● BE CAREFUL (re) *Jive 0521452* [1]	7	7
7 Nov 98	TIME TO MOVE ON *Jive 0522032*	40	2
28 Aug 99	LOVIN' YOU *Jive 0523450*	65	1
1 Aug 98	SPARKLE *Jive 521462*	57	1

[1] Sparkle featuring R Kelly

SPARKLEHORSE *US, male vocal / instrumental*
group (Singles: 2 Weeks, Albums: 4 Weeks)   pos/wks

31 Aug 96	RAINMAKER *Capitol CDCL 777*	61	1
17 Oct 98	SICK OF GOODBYES *Parlophone CDCLS 808*	57	1
18 May 96	VIVADIXIESUBMARINETRANSMISSIONPLOT *Parlophone CDP 8328162*	58	1
1 Aug 98	GOOD MORNING SPIDER *Parlophone 4960142*	30	2
23 Jun 01	IT'S A WONDERFUL LIFE *Capitol 5256162*	49	1

SPARKS *US / UK, male vocal / instrumental duo –*
Russell and Ron Mael (Singles: 81 Weeks, Albums: 42 Weeks)   pos/wks

4 May 74	● THIS TOWN AIN'T BIG ENOUGH FOR BOTH OF US *Island WIP 6193*	2	10
20 Jul 74	● AMATEUR HOUR *Island WIP 6203*	7	9
19 Oct 74	NEVER TURN YOUR BACK ON MOTHER EARTH *Island WIP 6211*	13	7
18 Jan 75	SOMETHING FOR THE GIRL WITH EVERYTHING *Island WIP 6221*	17	7
19 Jul 75	GET IN THE SWING *Island WIP 6236*	27	7
4 Oct 75	LOOKS, LOOKS, LOOKS *Island WIP 6249*	26	4
21 Apr 79	THE NUMBER ONE SONG IN HEAVEN *Virgin VS 244*	14	12
21 Jul 79	● BEAT THE CLOCK *Virgin VS 270*	10	9
27 Oct 79	TRYOUTS FOR THE HUMAN RACE *Virgin VS 289*	45	5
29 Oct 94	WHEN DO I GET TO SING 'MY WAY' *Logic 74321234472*	38	3
11 Mar 95	WHEN I KISS YOU (I HEAR CHARLIE PARKER PLAYING) *Logic 74321264272*	36	2
20 May 95	WHEN DO I GET TO SING 'MY WAY' (re-issue) *Logic 74321274002*	32	2
9 Mar 96	NOW THAT I OWN THE BBC *Logic 74321348672*	60	1
25 Oct 97	THE NUMBER ONE SONG IN HEAVEN (re-recording) *Roadrunner RR 22692*	70	1
13 Dec 97	THIS TOWN AIN'T BIG ENOUGH FOR BOTH OF US (re-recording) *Roadrunner RR 22513* [1]	40	2
1 Jun 74	● KIMONO MY HOUSE *Island ILPS 9272*	4	24
23 Nov 74	● PROPAGANDA *Island ILPS 9312*	9	13
18 Oct 75	INDISCREET *Island ILPS 9345*	18	4
8 Sep 79	NUMBER ONE IN HEAVEN *Virgin V 2115*	73	1

[1] Sparks vs Faith No More

Group was a UK / US group for first six hits and first three albums

Bubba SPARXXX
US, male rapper – Warren Mathis (Singles: 13 Weeks)   pos/wks

24 Nov 01	●	UGLY *Interscope / Polydor 4976542*	**7** 10
9 Mar 02		LOVELY *Interscope 4976752*	**24** 2
20 Mar 04		DELIVERANCE *Interscope 9862013*	**55** 1

SPEAR OF DESTINY
UK, male vocal / instrumental group (Singles: 43 Weeks, Albums: 35 Weeks)   pos/wks

21 May 83	THE WHEEL *Epic A 3372*	**59** 5
21 Jan 84	PRISONER OF LOVE *Epic A 4068*	**59** 3
14 Apr 84	LIBERATOR *Epic A 4310*	**67** 2
15 Jun 85	ALL MY LOVE (ASK NOTHING) *Epic A 6333*	**61** 3
10 Aug 85	COME BACK *Epic A 6445*	**55** 3
7 Feb 87	STRANGERS IN OUR TOWN *10 TEN 148*	**49** 4
4 Apr 87	NEVER TAKE ME ALIVE *10 TEN 162*	**14** 11
25 Jul 87	WAS THAT YOU? *10 TEN 173*	**55** 4
3 Oct 87	THE TRAVELLER *10 TEN 189*	**44** 3
24 Sep 88	SO IN LOVE WITH YOU *Virgin VS 1123*	**36** 5
23 Apr 83	GRAPES OF WRATH *Epic EPC 25318*	**62** 2
28 Apr 84	ONE EYED JACKS *Burning Rome EPC 25836*	**22** 7
7 Sep 85	WORLD SERVICE *Burning Rome EPC 26514*	**11** 7
2 May 87	OUTLAND *10 DIX 59*	**16** 13
16 May 87	S.O.D. – THE EPIC YEARS *Epic 450 8721*	**53** 3
22 Oct 88	THE PRICE YOU PAY *Virgin V 2549*	**37** 3

SPEARHEAD
US, male vocal / instrumental group (Singles: 5 Weeks, Albums: 1 Week)   pos/wks

17 Dec 94	OF COURSE YOU CAN *Capitol CDCL 733*	**74** 1
22 Apr 95	HOLE IN THE BUCKET *Capitol CDCL 742*	**55** 1
15 Jul 95	PEOPLE IN THA MIDDLE *Capitol CDCLS 752*	**49** 2
15 Mar 97	WHY OH WHY *Capitol CDCL 785*	**45** 1
29 Mar 97	CHOCOLATE SUPA HIGHWAY *Capitol CDEST 2293*	**68** 1

Billie Jo SPEARS
US, female vocalist (Singles: 40 Weeks, Albums: 28 Weeks)   pos/wks

12 Jul 75	●	BLANKET ON THE GROUND *United Artists UP 35805*	**6** 13
17 Jul 76	●	WHAT I'VE GOT IN MIND *United Artists UP 36118*	**4** 13
11 Dec 76		SING ME AN OLD FASHIONED SONG *United Artists UP 36179*	**34** 9
21 Jul 79		I WILL SURVIVE *United Artists UP 601*	**47** 5
11 Sep 76		WHAT I'VE GOT IN MIND *United Artists UAS 29955*	**47** 2
19 May 79	●	THE BILLIE JO SPEARS SINGLES ALBUM *United Artists UAK 30231*	**7** 17
21 Nov 81		COUNTRY GIRL *Warwick WW 5109*	**17** 9

Britney SPEARS   `107`   *Top 500*
One time world's top-selling teenager, who has album sales exceeding 40 million, b. 2 Dec 1981, Louisiana, US. Broke debut act first-week UK sales record with 464,000 for '... Baby One More Time' (going on to 1,450,154 in total) and is the youngest million-selling female in the history of the UK singles chart (Singles: 203 Weeks, Albums: 216 Weeks)   pos/wks

27 Feb 99	★	... BABY ONE MORE TIME *Jive 0522152* ◆ ■ ▲	**1** 22
26 Jun 99	●	SOMETIMES *Jive 0523202*	**3** 16
2 Oct 99	●	(YOU DRIVE ME) CRAZY *Jive 0550582*	**5** 11
29 Jan 00	★	BORN TO MAKE YOU HAPPY *Jive 9250022* ■	**1** 12
13 May 00	★	OOPS!...I DID IT AGAIN *Jive 9250542* ■	**1** 14
26 Aug 00	●	LUCKY *Jive 9251022*	**5** 11
16 Dec 00	●	STRONGER *Jive 9251502*	**7** 10
7 Apr 01		DON'T LET ME BE THE LAST TO KNOW *Jive 9251982*	**12** 8
27 Oct 01	●	I'M A SLAVE 4 U *Jive 9252892*	**4** 14
2 Feb 02	●	OVERPROTECTED *Jive 9253072*	**4** 12
13 Apr 02	●	I'M NOT A GIRL, NOT YET A WOMAN *Jive 9253472*	**2** 10
10 Aug 02	●	BOYS *Jive 9253912* `1`	**7** 8
16 Nov 02		I LOVE ROCK 'N' ROLL (re) *Jive 9254202*	**13** 8
22 Nov 03	●	ME AGAINST THE MUSIC *Jive 82876576432* `2`	**2** 12
13 Mar 04	★	TOXIC *Jive 82876602092* ■	**1** 14
26 Jun 04	★	EVERYTIME *Jive 82876622062* ■	**1** 14
13 Nov 04	●	MY PREROGATIVE *Jive 82876652582*	**3** 7+
20 Mar 99		... BABY ONE MORE TIME *Jive 522172* ▲	**2** 86
27 May 00		OOPS! ... I DID IT AGAIN *Jive 9220392* ▲	**2** 45
17 Nov 01	●	BRITNEY *Jive 9222532* ▲	**4** 36
29 Nov 03		IN THE ZONE *Jive 82876576442* ▲	**13** 43
20 Nov 04	●	GREATEST HITS: MY PREROGATIVE *Jive 82876666162*	**2** 6+

`1` Britney Spears featuring Pharrell Williams `2` Britney Spears featuring Madonna

SPECIAL D
Denmark, male / female production / vocal duo – Dennis Horstmann and Laura Nori (Singles: 11 Weeks)   pos/wks

17 Apr 04	●	COME WITH ME *All Around the World CDGLOBE 340*	**6** 11

SPECIAL NEEDS
UK, male vocal / instrumental group (Singles: 1 Week)   pos/wks

16 Oct 04	FRANCESCA – THAT MADDENING GLARE / THE WINTER GARDENS *Poptones MC 5092SCD*	**69** 1

The SPECIALS   `372`   *Top 500*
Midlands-based septet which led the early 1980s ska revival and, under Jerry Dammers (k), founded the trailblazing indie label 2 Tone. In 1981, Terry Hall (v), Neville Staples (v) and Lynval Golding (g) broke away to form Fun Boy Three (Singles: 101 Weeks, Albums: 82 Weeks)   pos/wks

28 Jul 79	●	GANGSTERS *2 Tone CHSTT 1* `1`	**6** 12
27 Oct 79	●	A MESSAGE TO YOU RUDY / NITE KLUB *2 Tone CHSTT 5* `2`	**10** 14
26 Jan 80	★	THE SPECIAL A.K.A. LIVE! EP *2 Tone CHSTT 7*	**1** 10
24 May 80	●	RAT RACE / RUDE BUOYS OUTA JAIL *2 Tone CHSTT 11*	**5** 9
20 Sep 80	●	STEREOTYPE / INTERNATIONAL JET SET *2 Tone CHSTT 13*	**6** 8
13 Dec 80	●	DO NOTHING / MAGGIE'S FARM *2 Tone CHSTT 16*	**4** 11
20 Jun 81	★	GHOST TOWN *2 Tone CHSTT 17*	**1** 14
23 Jan 82		THE BOILER *2 Tone CHSTT 18*	**35** 5
3 Sep 83		RACIST FRIEND / BRIGHT LIGHTS *2 Tone CHSTT 25* `1`	**60** 3
17 Mar 84	●	NELSON MANDELA *2 Tone CHSTT 26* `1`	**9** 10
8 Sep 84		WHAT I LIKE MOST ABOUT YOU IS YOUR GIRLFRIEND *2 Tone CHSTT 27* `1`	**51** 4
10 Feb 96		HYPOCRITE *Kuff KUFFD 3*	**66** 1
3 Nov 79	●	SPECIALS *2 Tone CDL TT 5001*	**4** 45
4 Oct 80	●	MORE SPECIALS *2 Tone CHR TT 5003*	**5** 19
23 Jun 84		IN THE STUDIO *2 Tone CHR TT 5008* `1`	**34** 6
7 Sep 91	●	THE SPECIALS SINGLES *2 Tone CHR TT 5010*	**10** 9
7 Jul 01		SPECIALS (re-issue) *Chrysalis CCD 5001*	**22** 3

`1` The Special A.K.A. `2` The Specials featuring Rico `1` The Special A.K.A.

Tracks on The Special A.K.A. Live! EP: Too Much Too Young / Guns of Navarone / Longshot Kick De Bucket / The Liquidator / Skinhead Moonstomp. 'Maggie's Farm' listed with 'Do Nothing' only from 10 Jan 1981. Group was male / female for last four hits Group was male / female for the third and fourth albums

Phil SPECTOR
US, male producer (Albums: 29 Weeks)   pos/wks

23 Dec 72	PHIL SPECTOR'S CHRISTMAS ALBUM *Apple SAPCOR 24*	**21** 3
15 Oct 77	PHIL SPECTOR'S ECHOES OF THE 60'S *Phil Spector International 2307 013*	**21** 10
25 Dec 82	PHIL SPECTOR'S CHRISTMAS ALBUM (re-issue) *Phil Spector International 2307 005*	**96** 2
10 Dec 83	PHIL SPECTOR'S GREATEST HITS / PHIL SPECTOR'S CHRISTMAS ALBUM (2nd re-issue) *Impression PSLP 1/2*	**19** 8
12 Dec 87	PHIL SPECTOR'S CHRISTMAS ALBUM (3rd re-issue) *Chrysalis CDL 1625*	**69** 6

SPECTRUM
UK, male instrumental / production group (Singles: 1 Week)   pos/wks

26 Sep 92	TRUE LOVE WILL FIND YOU IN THE END *Silvertone ORE 44*	**70** 1

Chris SPEDDING   (see also SOUNDS NICE; NUCLEUS)
UK, male vocalist / instrumentalist – guitar (Singles: 8 Weeks)   pos/wks

23 Aug 75	MOTOR BIKIN' *RAK 210*	**14** 8

SPEECH
US, male vocalist – Todd Thomas (Singles: 2 Weeks)   pos/wks

17 Feb 96	LIKE MARVIN GAYE SAID (WHAT'S GOING ON) *Cooltempo CDCOOL 314*	**35** 2

SPEEDWAY
UK, male / female vocal / instrumental duo – Jill Jackson and Jim Duguid (Singles: 10 Weeks, Albums: 1 Week)   pos/wks

6 Sep 03	●	GENIE IN A BOTTLE / SAVE YOURSELF *Innocent SINCD 47*	**10** 4
21 Feb 04		CAN'T TURN BACK *Innocent SINCD 55*	**12** 4
19 Jun 04		IN & OUT *Innocent SINDX 61*	**31** 2
6 Mar 04		SAVE YOURSELF *Innocent CDSIN 12*	**42** 1

SPEEDY
UK, male / female vocal / instrumental group (Singles: 1 Week)   pos/wks

9 Nov 96	BOY WONDER *Boiler House! BOIL 2CD*	**56** 1

SPEEDY J
Holland, male producer – Jochem Paap (Albums: 1 Week)   pos/wks

| 10 Jul 93 | GINGER *Warp WARPCD 14* | 68 | 1 |

SPEKTRUM
UK, male / female vocal / instrumental group (Singles: 1 Week)   pos/wks

| 18 Sep 04 | KINDA NEW *Non Stop SPEKD 004* | 70 | 1 |

SPELLBOUND
India, female vocal duo (Singles: 1 Week)   pos/wks

| 31 May 97 | HEAVEN ON EARTH *East West EW 098CD* | 73 | 1 |

Johnnie SPENCE
UK, orchestra (Singles: 15 Weeks)   pos/wks

| 1 Mar 62 | THE 'DR KILDARE' THEME *Parlophone R 4872* | 15 | 15 |

Don SPENCER
Australia, male vocalist (Singles: 12 Weeks)   pos/wks

| 21 Mar 63 | FIREBALL (re) *HMV POP 1087* | 32 | 12 |

Jon SPENCER BLUES EXPLOSION
US, male vocal / instrumental group (Singles: 3 Weeks, Albums: 2 Weeks)   pos/wks

10 May 97	WAIL *Mute CDMUTE 204*	66	1
6 Apr 02	SHE SAID *Mute LCDMUTE 263*	58	1
6 Jul 02	SWEET N SOUR *Mute LCDMUTE 271*	66	1
12 Oct 96	NOW I GOT WORRY *Mute CDSTUMM 132*	50	1
31 Oct 98	ACME *Mute CDSTUMM 154*	72	1

Tracie SPENCER
US, female vocalist (Singles: 3 Weeks)   pos/wks

| 4 May 91 | THIS HOUSE *Capitol CL 612* | 65 | 2 |
| 6 Nov 99 | IT'S ALL ABOUT YOU (NOT ABOUT ME) *Parlophone Rhythm Series CDCL 815* | 65 | 1 |

SPHINX (see also FAITHLESS; OUR TRIBE / ONE TRIBE; ROLLO; DUSTED)
UK / US, male vocal / instrumental group (Singles: 2 Weeks)   pos/wks

| 25 Mar 95 | WHAT HOPE HAVE I *Champion CHAMPCD 318* | 43 | 2 |

SPICE GIRLS   `175` `Top 500`
Britain's most successful and influential female vocal group: Geri Halliwell (Ginger Spice – left 1998), Melanie Chisholm (Mel C / Sporty Spice), Emma Bunton (Baby Spice), Victoria Adams – then Beckham (Posh Spice), Melanie Brown (Mel B / Mel G / Scary Spice). The ground-breaking girl-power group who made it a 'Spiceworld' was the first act to put its first six singles at No.1 and the only group to spawn five solo hitmakers. Total UK single sales: 7,507,213. Best-selling single: 'Wannabe' 1,269,841 (Singles: 179 Weeks, Albums: 135 Weeks)   pos/wks

20 Jul 96	★ WANNABE *Virgin VSCDX 1588* ◆ ▲	1	26
26 Oct 96	★ SAY YOU'LL BE THERE *Virgin VSCDT 1601* ■	1	17
28 Dec 96	★ 2 BECOME 1 (re) *Virgin VSCDT 1607* ◆ ■	1	23
15 Mar 97	★ MAMA / WHO DO YOU THINK YOU ARE *Virgin VSCDT 1623* ■	1	15
25 Oct 97	★ SPICE UP YOUR LIFE *Virgin VSCDT 1660* ■	1	15
27 Dec 97	★ TOO MUCH *Virgin VSCDR 1669* ■	1	15
21 Mar 98	● STOP (re) *Virgin VSCDT 1679*	2	17
1 Aug 98	★ VIVA FOREVER *Virgin VSCDT 1692* ■	1	13
26 Dec 98	★ GOODBYE *Virgin VSCDT 1721* ■	1	21
4 Nov 00	★ HOLLER / LET LOVE LEAD THE WAY *Virgin VSCDT 1788* ■	1	17
16 Nov 96	★ SPICE *Virgin CDV 2812* ■ ▲	1	72
15 Nov 97	★ SPICEWORLD *Virgin CDV 2850* ■	1	55
18 Nov 00	● FOREVER *Virgin CDVX 2928*	2	8

SPIDER
UK, male vocal / instrumental group (Singles: 5 Weeks, Albums: 2 Weeks)   pos/wks

5 Mar 83	WHY D'YA LIE TO ME *RCA 313*	65	2
10 Mar 84	HERE WE GO ROCK 'N' ROLL *A&M AM 180*	57	3
23 Oct 82	ROCK 'N' ROLL GYPSIES *RCA RCALP 3101*	75	1
7 Apr 84	ROUGH JUSTICE *A&M AMLX 68563*	96	1

SPIKEY TEE *See BOMB THE BASS*

SPILLER (see also LAGUNA; THEAUDIENCE; Sophie ELLIS-BEXTOR)
Italy / UK, male producer – Cristiano Spiller (Singles: 26 Weeks)   pos/wks

| 26 Aug 00 | ★ GROOVEJET (IF THIS AIN'T LOVE) *Positiva CDTIV 137* ■ | 1 | 24 |
| 2 Feb 02 | CRY BABY *Positiva CDTIV 167* | 40 | 2 |

'Groovejet (If This Ain't Love)' featured lead vocals by Sophie Ellis-Bextor

SPIN CITY
UK / Ireland, male vocal group (Singles: 3 Weeks)   pos/wks

| 26 Aug 00 | LANDSLIDE *Epic 6696132* | 30 | 3 |

SPIN DOCTORS
US, male vocal / instrumental group (Singles: 28 Weeks, Albums: 57 Weeks)   pos/wks

15 May 93	● TWO PRINCES *Epic 6591452*	3	15
14 Aug 93	LITTLE MISS CAN'T BE WRONG *Epic 6584892*	23	5
9 Oct 93	JIMMY OLSEN'S BLUES *Epic 6597582*	40	2
4 Dec 93	WHAT TIME IS IT *Epic 6599552*	56	1
25 Jun 94	CLEOPATRA'S CAT *Epic 6604192*	29	2
30 Jul 94	YOU LET YOUR HEART GO TOO FAST *Epic 6606612*	66	1
29 Oct 94	MARY JANE *Epic 6609772*	55	1
8 Jun 96	SHE USED TO BE MINE *Epic 6632682*	55	1
20 Mar 93	● POCKET FULL OF KRYPTONITE *Epic 4682502*	2	48
9 Jul 94	● TURN IT UPSIDE DOWN *Epic 4768862*	3	9

SPINAL TAP
US / UK, male vocal / instrumental group (Singles: 3 Weeks, Albums: 2 Weeks)   pos/wks

28 Mar 92	BITCH SCHOOL *MCA MCS 1624*	35	2
2 May 92	THE MAJESTY OF ROCK *MCA MCS 1629*	61	1
11 Apr 92	BREAK LIKE THE WIND *MCA MCAD 10514*	51	2

The SPINNERS
UK, male vocal / instrumental group (Albums: 24 Weeks)   pos/wks

5 Sep 70	THE SPINNERS ARE IN TOWN *Fontana 6309 014*	40	5
7 Aug 71	SPINNERS LIVE PERFORMANCE *Contour 6870 502*	14	12
13 Nov 71	THE SWINGING CITY *Philips 6382 002*	20	3
8 Apr 72	LOVE IS TEASING *Columbia SCX 6493*	33	4

SPINNERS *See The DETROIT SPINNERS*

SPIRAL TRIBE
UK, male / female vocal / instrumental group (Singles: 2 Weeks)   pos/wks

| 29 Aug 92 | BREACH THE PEACE (EP) *Butterfly BLRT 79* | 66 | 1 |
| 21 Nov 92 | FORWARD THE REVOLUTION *Butterfly BLRT 85* | 70 | 1 |

Tracks on Breach the Peace (EP): Breach the Peace / Do It / Seven / 25 Minute Warning

SPIRIT
US, male vocal / instrumental group (Albums: 1 Week)   pos/wks

| 13 Mar 71 | TWELVE DREAMS OF DR SARDONICUS *Epic EPC 64191* | 29 | 1 |

SPIRIT
US, male vocal / instrumental duo (Albums: 2 Weeks)   pos/wks

| 18 Apr 81 | POTATO LAND *Beggars Banquet BEGA 23* | 40 | 2 |

The SPIRITS
UK, male / female vocal duo – Beverly Thomas and Osmond Wright (Singles: 5 Weeks)   pos/wks

| 19 Nov 94 | DON'T BRING ME DOWN *MCA MCSTD 2018* | 31 | 3 |
| 8 Apr 95 | SPIRIT INSIDE *MCA MCSTD 2045* | 39 | 2 |

SPIRITUAL COWBOYS *See David A. STEWART*

SPIRITUALIZED
UK, male / female vocal / instrumental group (Singles: 19 Weeks, Albums: 26 Weeks)   pos/wks

30 Jun 90	ANYWAY THAT YOU WANT ME / STEP INTO THE BREEZE *Dedicated ZB 43783*	75	1
17 Aug 91	RUN *Dedicated SPIRT 002*	59	1
25 Jul 92	MEDICATION *Dedicated SPIRT 005T*	55	1
23 Oct 93	ELECTRIC MAINLINE *Dedicated SPIRT 007CD*	49	1
4 Feb 95	LET IT FLOW *Dedicated SPIRT 009CD* [1]	30	2
9 Aug 97	ELECTRICITY *Dedicated SPIRT 012CD1*	32	2
14 Feb 98	I THINK I'M IN LOVE *Dedicated SPIRT 014CD*	27	2
6 Jun 98	THE ABBEY ROAD EP *Dedicated SPIRT 015CD*	39	2
15 Sep 01	STOP YOUR CRYING *Spaceman / Arista OPM 002*	18	3
8 Dec 01	OUT OF SIGHT *Spaceman / Arista OPM 005*	65	1
23 Feb 02	DO IT ALL OVER AGAIN *Spaceman / Arista OPM 004*	31	2
13 Sep 03	SHE KISSED ME (IT FELT LIKE A HIT) *Sanctuary SANXD 222*	38	1
11 Apr 92	LAZER GUIDED MELODIES *Dedicated DEDCD 004*	27	2
18 Feb 95	PURE PHASE *Dedicated DEDCD 0175* [1]	20	2

28 Jun 97 ●	LADIES & GENTLEMEN WE ARE FLOATING IN SPACE		
	Dedicated DEDCD 034	4	15
7 Nov 98	LIVE AT THE ROYAL ALBERT HALL Dedicated 74321622852	38	1
29 Sep 01 ●	LET IT COME DOWN Arista OPM 001CD	3	4
20 Sep 03	AMAZING GRACE Spaceman / Sanctuary SANDCD 214X	25	2

[1] Spiritualized Electric Mainline [1] Spiritualized Electric Mainline

Tracks on The Abbey Road EP: Come Together / Broken Heart / Broken Heart (instrumental)

SPIRO and WIX UK, male instrumental duo –
Steve Spiro and Paul Wickens (Singles: 2 Weeks)   pos/wks

10 Aug 96	TARA'S THEME EMI Premier PRESCD 4	29	2

SPITTING IMAGE UK, male / female
latex puppets (Singles: 18 Weeks, Albums: 3 Weeks)   pos/wks

10 May 86 ★	THE CHICKEN SONG (re) Virgin SPIT 1	1	11
6 Dec 86	SANTA CLAUS IS ON THE DOLE / FIRST ATHEIST TABERNACLE CHOIR Virgin VS 921	22	7
18 Oct 86	SPIT IN YOUR EAR Virgin V 2403	55	3

SPLIFF STAR See Busta RHYMES

SPLINTER UK, male vocal / instrumental duo –
Bill Elliott and Bob Purvis (Singles: 10 Weeks)   pos/wks

2 Nov 74	COSTAFINE TOWN Dark Horse AMS 7135	17	10

SPLINTER GROUP See Peter GREEN

SPLIT ENZ New Zealand / UK, male vocal / instrumental group (Singles: 15 Weeks, Albums: 9 Weeks)   pos/wks

16 Aug 80	I GOT YOU A&M AMS 7546	12	11
23 May 81	HISTORY NEVER REPEATS A&M AMS 8128	63	4
30 Aug 80	TRUE COLOURS A&M AMLH 64822	42	8
8 May 82	TIME AND TIDE A&M AMLH 64894	71	1

A SPLIT SECOND Belgium / Italy, male instrumental / production group (Singles: 1 Week)   pos/wks

14 Dec 91	FLESH ffrr FX 178	68	1

SPLODGENESSABOUNDS
UK, male vocal / instrumental group (Singles: 17 Weeks)   pos/wks

14 Jun 80 ●	SIMON TEMPLER / TWO PINTS OF LAGER AND A PACKET OF CRISPS PLEASE Deram BUM 1	7	8
6 Sep 80	TWO LITTLE BOYS / HORSE Deram ROLF 1	26	7
13 Jun 81	COWPUNK MEDLUM Deram BUM 3	69	2

SPOILED & ZIGO Israel, male DJ / production
duo – Elad Avnon and Ziv Goland (Singles: 3 Weeks)   pos/wks

12 Aug 00	MORE & MORE Manifesto FESCD 72	31	3

SPONGE US, male vocal / instrumental group (Singles: 1 Week)   pos/wks

19 Aug 95	PLOWED Work 6623162	74	1

SPOOKS US, male / female vocal /
rap group (Singles: 17 Weeks, Albums: 12 Weeks)   pos/wks

27 Jan 01 ●	THINGS I'VE SEEN Epic 6706722	6	10
5 May 01	KARMA HOTEL Epic 6709012	15	6
15 Sep 01	SWEET REVENGE Epic 6718072	67	1
17 Feb 01	S.I.O.S.O.S. – VOLUME ONE Epic 4982612	25	12

SPOOKY UK, male vocal / instrumental duo (Singles: 1 Week)   pos/wks

13 Mar 93	SCHMOO Guerilla GRRR 45CD	72	1

SPORTY THIEVZ US, male rap / vocal group (Singles: 6 Weeks)   pos/wks

10 Jul 99	NO PIGEONS Columbia / Roc-a-Blok / Ruffhouse 6676022	21	6

The SPOTNICKS Sweden, male instrumental
group (Singles: 37 Weeks, Albums: 1 Week)   pos/wks

14 Jun 62	ORANGE BLOSSOM SPECIAL Oriole CB 1724	29	10
6 Sep 62	ROCKET MAN Oriole CB 1755	38	9

31 Jan 63	HAVA NAGILA Oriole CB 1790	13	12
25 Apr 63	JUST LISTEN TO MY HEART Oriole CB 1818	36	6
9 Feb 63	OUT-A-SPACE Oriole PS 40036	20	1

Dusty SPRINGFIELD   (153   Top 500)   Blonde-haired with heavy make-
up, Dusty was a sixties style icon and a critically acclaimed female vocalist, b. Mary O'Brien, 16 Apr 1939, London, d. 2 Mar 1999. After leaving The Springfields (which also featured brother Tom) in 1963, she had numerous transatlantic solo hits, and during the sixties was regularly voted the UK's Top Female Singer (Singles: 211 Weeks, Albums: 138 Weeks)   pos/wks

21 Nov 63 ●	I ONLY WANT TO BE WITH YOU Philips BF 1292	4	18
20 Feb 64	STAY AWHILE Philips BF 1313	13	10
2 Jul 64 ●	I JUST DON'T KNOW WHAT TO DO WITH MYSELF Philips BF 1348	3	12
22 Oct 64 ●	LOSING YOU Philips BF 1369	9	13
18 Feb 65	YOUR HURTIN' KINDA LOVE Philips BF 1396	37	4
1 Jul 65 ●	IN THE MIDDLE OF NOWHERE Philips BF 1418	8	10
16 Sep 65 ●	SOME OF YOUR LOVIN' Philips BF 1430	8	12
27 Jan 66	LITTLE BY LITTLE Philips BF 1466	17	9
31 Mar 66 ★	YOU DON'T HAVE TO SAY YOU LOVE ME Philips BF 1482	1	13
7 Jul 66 ●	GOIN' BACK Philips BF 1502	10	10
15 Sep 66 ●	ALL I SEE IS YOU Philips BF 1510	9	12
23 Feb 67	I'LL TRY ANYTHING Philips BF 1553	13	9
25 May 67	GIVE ME TIME Philips BF 1577	24	6
10 Jul 68 ●	I CLOSE MY EYES AND COUNT TO TEN Philips BF 1682	4	12
4 Dec 68 ●	SON-OF-A PREACHER MAN Philips BF 1730	9	9
20 Sep 69	AM I THE SAME GIRL (re) Philips BF 1811	43	9
19 Sep 70	HOW CAN I BE SURE Philips 6006 045	36	4
20 Oct 79	BABY BLUE Mercury DUSTY 4	61	5
22 Aug 87 ●	WHAT HAVE I DONE TO DESERVE THIS? Parlophone R 6163 [1]	2	9
25 Feb 89	NOTHING HAS BEEN PROVED Parlophone R 6207	16	7
2 Dec 89	IN PRIVATE Parlophone R 6234	14	10
26 May 90	REPUTATION Parlophone R 6253	38	5
24 Nov 90	ARRESTED BY YOU Parlophone R 6266	70	2
30 Oct 93	HEART AND SOUL Columbia 6598562 [2]	75	1
10 Jun 95	WHEREVER WOULD I BE Columbia 6620592 [3]	44	3
4 Nov 95	ROLL AWAY Columbia 6623682	68	1
25 Apr 64 ●	A GIRL CALLED DUSTY Philips BL 7594	6	23
23 Oct 65 ●	EV'RYTHING'S COMING UP DUSTY Philips RBL 1002	6	12
22 Oct 66 ●	GOLDEN HITS Philips BL 7737	2	36
11 Nov 67	WHERE AM I GOING Philips SBL 7820	40	1
21 Dec 68	DUSTY ... DEFINITELY Philips SBL 7864	30	6
2 May 70	FROM DUSTY ... WITH LOVE Philips SBL 7927	35	2
4 Mar 78	IT BEGINS AGAIN Mercury 9109 607	41	2
30 Jan 88	DUSTY – THE SILVER COLLECTION Phonogram DUSTV 1	14	10
7 Jul 90	REPUTATION Parlophone PCSD 111	18	6
14 May 94 ●	GOIN' BACK – THE VERY BEST OF DUSTY SPRINGFIELD 1962-1994 Philips 8487892	5	11
8 Jul 95	A VERY FINE LOVE Columbia 4785082	43	1
7 Nov 98	THE BEST OF DUSTY SPRINGFIELD Mercury / PolyGram TV 5383452	19	24
13 Mar 04	THE LOOK OF LOVE Universal TV 9816495	25	4

[1] Pet Shop Boys and Dusty Springfield [2] Cilla Black with Dusty Springfield
[3] Dusty Springfield and Daryl Hall

From 27 Mar 99 'The Best of Dusty Springfield' changed label to Mercury / Universal Music TV

Rick SPRINGFIELD
Australia, male vocalist / actor – Richard Springthorpe
(Singles: 13 Weeks, Albums: 8 Weeks)   pos/wks

14 Jan 84	HUMAN TOUCH / SOULS RCA RICK 1	23	7
24 Mar 84	JESSIE'S GIRL RCA RICK 2 ▲	43	6
11 Feb 84	LIVING IN OZ RCA PL 84660	41	4
25 May 85	TAO RCA PL 85370	68	3
26 Mar 88	ROCK OF LIFE RCA PL 86620	80	1

'Souls' listed only from 11 Feb 1984. It peaked at No.24

The SPRINGFIELDS (see also Dusty SPRINGFIELD)
UK, male / female vocal / instrumental group (Singles: 66 Weeks)   pos/wks

31 Aug 61	BREAKAWAY Philips BF 1168	31	8
16 Nov 61	BAMBINO Philips BF 1178	16	11
13 Dec 62 ●	ISLAND OF DREAMS Philips 326557 BF	5	26
28 Mar 63 ●	SAY I WON'T BE THERE Philips 326577 BF	5	15
25 Jul 63	COME ON HOME Philips BF 1263	31	6

Singles re-entries are listed as (re), (2re), (3re).... which signifies that the hit re-entered the chart once, twice or three times...

Bruce SPRINGSTEEN 47 Top 500

The Boss', b. 23 Sep 1949, New Jersey, US. Singer / songwriter / guitarist / rock superstar, whose legendary three to four-hour stage performances have packed stadiums worldwide for over 25 years. An insurance valuation of $3 million was once placed on Springsteen's voice. He released the biggest-selling box set: 'Live 1975-85' (Singles: 146 Weeks, Albums: 524 Weeks) pos/wks

22 Nov 80		HUNGRY HEART *CBS 9309*	44	4
13 Jun 81		THE RIVER *CBS A 1179*	35	6
26 May 84	●	DANCING IN THE DARK (re) *CBS A 4436*	4	23
6 Oct 84		COVER ME (re) *CBS A 4662*	16	13
15 Jun 85	●	I'M ON FIRE / BORN IN THE USA *CBS A 6342*	5	12
3 Aug 85		GLORY DAYS *CBS A 6375*	17	6
14 Dec 85	●	SANTA CLAUS IS COMIN' TO TOWN / MY HOMETOWN *CBS A 6773*	9	5
29 Nov 86		WAR *CBS 650193 7* [1]	18	7
7 Feb 87		FIRE *CBS 650381 7* [1]	54	2
23 May 87		BORN TO RUN *CBS BRUCE 2*	16	4
3 Oct 87		BRILLIANT DISGUISE *CBS 651141 7*	20	5
12 Dec 87		TUNNEL OF LOVE *CBS 651295 7*	45	4
18 Jun 88		TOUGHER THAN THE REST *CBS BRUCE 3*	13	8
24 Sep 88		SPARE PARTS *CBS BRUCE 4*	32	3
21 Mar 92		HUMAN TOUCH *Columbia 6578727*	11	5
23 May 92		BETTER DAYS *Columbia 6578907*	34	3
25 Jul 92		57 CHANNELS (AND NOTHIN' ON) *Columbia 6581387*	32	4
24 Oct 92		LEAP OF FAITH *Columbia 6583697*	46	3
10 Apr 93		LUCKY TOWN (LIVE) *Columbia 6592282*	48	3
19 Mar 94	●	STREETS OF PHILADELPHIA *Columbia 6600652*	2	12
22 Apr 95		SECRET GARDEN *Columbia 6612955*	44	3
11 Nov 95		HUNGRY HEART (re-issue) *Columbia 6626252*	28	3
4 May 96		THE GHOST OF TOM JOAD *Columbia 6630315*	26	2
19 Apr 97		SECRET GARDEN (re-issue) *Columbia 6643245*	17	4
14 Dec 02		LONESOME DAY *Columbia 6734082*	39	2
1 Nov 75		BORN TO RUN *CBS 69170*	17	50
17 Jun 78		DARKNESS ON THE EDGE OF TOWN *CBS 86061*	16	40
25 Oct 80	●	THE RIVER *CBS 88510* ▲	2	88
2 Oct 82	●	NEBRASKA *CBS 25100*	3	19
16 Jun 84	★	BORN IN THE U.S.A. *CBS 86304* ▲	1	129
15 Jun 85		GREETINGS FROM ASBURY PARK N.J. *CBS 32210*	41	10
15 Jun 85		THE WILD, THE INNOCENT & THE E STREET SHUFFLE *CBS 32363*	33	12
22 Nov 86	●	LIVE 1975-85 *CBS 450 2271* [1]	4	9
17 Oct 87	★	TUNNEL OF LOVE *CBS 460 2701* ■ ▲	1	33
4 Apr 92	●	LUCKY TOWN *Columbia 4714242*	2	11
4 Apr 92	★	HUMAN TOUCH *Columbia 4714232* ■	1	17
24 Apr 93	●	IN CONCERT – MTV PLUGGED *Columbia 4738602*	4	7
11 Mar 95	★	GREATEST HITS *Columbia 4785552* ■ ▲	1	44
25 Nov 95		THE GHOST OF TOM JOAD *Columbia 4816502*	16	14
21 Nov 98		TRACKS *Columbia 4926052*	50	1
24 Apr 99		18 TRACKS *Columbia 4942002*	23	7
14 Apr 01		LIVE IN NEW YORK CITY *Columbia 5000002* [1]	12	6
10 Aug 02	★	THE RISING *Columbia 5080002* ■ ▲	1	16
22 Nov 03		THE ESSENTIAL *Columbia 5137009*	28	2
22 Nov 03		THE ESSENTIAL *Columbia 5137002*	32	9

[1] Bruce Springsteen and the E-Street Band [1] Bruce Springsteen and the E Street Band

'Dancing in the Dark' debuted at No.28 before making its peak position on re-entry in Jan 1985. 'Cover Me' debuted at No.38 before making its peak position on re-entry in Mar 1985 'The Essential' (Columbia 5137009) is a three CD set and 'The Essential' (Columbia 5137002) is a double CD

SPRINGWATER

UK, male instrumentalist – Phil Cordell (Singles: 12 Weeks) pos/wks

23 Oct 71	●	I WILL RETURN *Polydor 2058 141*	5	12

SPRINKLER

UK / US, male / female vocal / rap group (Singles: 2 Weeks) pos/wks

11 Jul 98	LEAVE 'EM SOMETHING TO DESIRE *Island CID 706*	45	2

[SPUNGE]

UK, male vocal / instrumental group (Singles: 3 Weeks, Albums: 1 Week) pos/wks

15 Jun 02	JUMP ON DEMAND *Rough Trade RTRADSCD 054*	39	2
24 Aug 02	ROOTS *B Unique BUN 030CDS*	52	1
7 Sep 02	THE STORY SO FAR ... *B Unique 0927487452*	48	1

SPYRO GYRA

US, male instrumental group (Singles: 10 Weeks, Albums: 23 Weeks) pos/wks

21 Jul 79	MORNING DANCE *Infinity INF 111*	17	10
14 Jul 79	MORNING DANCE *Infinity INS 2003*	11	16
23 Feb 80	CATCHING THE SUN *MCA MCG 4009*	31	7

SQUADRONAIRES *See Joan REGAN*

SQUEEZE 247 Top 500

(see also DIFFORD and TILBROOK) Critically acclaimed for their lyrical story lines this London based band featured noted singer / songwriters Glenn Tilbrook (g/v) and Chris Difford (v/g). Fluctuating line-up included Jools Holland (k) and Paul Carrack (v/k – also of Ace, and Mike and the Mechanics fame) (Singles: 123 Weeks, Albums: 130 Weeks) pos/wks

8 Apr 78		TAKE ME I'M YOURS *A&M AMS 7335*	19	9
10 Jun 78		BANG BANG *A&M AMS 7360*	49	5
18 Nov 78		GOODBYE GIRL *A&M AMS 7398*	63	2
24 Mar 79	●	COOL FOR CATS *A&M AMS 7426*	2	11
2 Jun 79	●	UP THE JUNCTION *A&M AMS 7444*	2	11
8 Sep 79		SLAP & TICKLE *A&M AMS 7466*	24	8
1 Mar 80		ANOTHER NAIL IN MY HEART *A&M AMS 7507*	17	9
10 May 80		PULLING MUSSELS (FROM THE SHELL) *A&M AMS 7523*	44	6
16 May 81		IS THAT LOVE *A&M AMS 8129*	35	8
25 Jul 81		TEMPTED *A&M AMS 8147*	41	5
10 Oct 81	●	LABELLED WITH LOVE *A&M AMS 8166*	4	10
24 Apr 82		BLACK COFFEE IN BED *A&M AMS 8219*	51	4
23 Oct 82		ANNIE GET YOUR GUN *A&M AMS 8259*	43	4
15 Jun 85		LAST TIME FOREVER *A&M AM 255*	45	5
8 Aug 87		HOURGLASS *A&M AM 400*	16	10
17 Oct 87		TRUST ME TO OPEN MY MOUTH *A&M AM 412*	72	1
25 Apr 92		COOL FOR CATS (re-issue) *A&M AM 860*	62	2
24 Jul 93		THIRD RAIL *A&M 5803372*	39	2
11 Sep 93		SOME FANTASTIC PLACE *A&M 5803792*	73	1
9 Sep 95		THIS SUMMER *A&M 5811912*	36	3
18 Nov 95		ELECTRIC TRAINS *A&M 5812692*	44	2
15 Jun 96		HEAVEN KNOWS *A&M 5816052*	27	2
24 Aug 96		THIS SUMMER (re-mix) *A&M 5818372*	32	2
28 Apr 79		COOL FOR CATS *A&M AMLH 68503*	45	11
16 Feb 80		ARGY BARGY *A&M AMLH 64802*	32	15
23 May 81		EAST SIDE STORY *A&M AMLH 64854*	19	26
15 May 82		SWEETS FROM A STRANGER *A&M AMLH 64899*	20	7
6 Nov 82	●	SINGLES – 45'S AND UNDER *A&M AMLH 68552*	3	29
7 Sep 85		COSI FAN TUTTI FRUTTI *A&M AMA 5085*	31	7
19 Sep 87		BABYLON AND ON *A&M AMA 5161*	14	8
23 Sep 89		FRANK *A&M AMA 5278*	58	1
7 Apr 90		A ROUND AND A BOUT *IRS DFCLP 1*	50	1
7 Sep 91		PLAY *Reprise WX 428*	41	1
23 May 92	●	GREATEST HITS *A&M 3971812*	6	13
25 Sep 93		SOME FANTASTIC PLACE *A&M 5401402*	26	4
25 Nov 95		RIDICULOUS *A&M 5404402*	50	1
22 Jun 02	●	BIG SQUEEZE – THE VERY BEST OF SQUEEZE *UMTV 4932532*	8	6

Billy SQUIER

US, male vocalist / instrumentalist – guitar (Singles: 3 Weeks) pos/wks

3 Oct 81	THE STROKE *Capitol CL 214*	52	3

Chris SQUIRE (see also YES)

UK, male vocalist / instrumentalist – bass (Albums: 7 Weeks) pos/wks

6 Dec 75	FISH OUT OF WATER *Atlantic K 50203*	25	7

John SQUIRE

(see also The STONE ROSES; The SEAHORSES) UK, male vocalist / instrumentalist – guitar (Singles: 2 Weeks, Albums: 2 Weeks) pos/wks

2 Nov 02	JOE LOUIS *North Country NCCDA 001*	43	1
14 Feb 04	ROOM IN BROOKLYN *North Country NCCDA 003*	44	1
28 Sep 02	TIME CHANGES EVERYTHING *North Country NCCDS 001*	17	2

Dorothy SQUIRES

UK, female vocalist – Edna Squires, b. 25 Mar 1915, d. 14 Apr 1998 (Singles: 56 Weeks) pos/wks

5 Jun 53	I'M WALKING BEHIND YOU *Polygon P 1068*	12	1
24 Aug 61	SAY IT WITH FLOWERS *Columbia DB 4665* [1]	23	10
20 Sep 69	FOR ONCE IN MY LIFE (re) *President PT 267*	24	11
21 Feb 70	TILL (re) *President PT 281*	25	11
8 Aug 70	MY WAY (2re) *President PT 305*	25	23

[1] Dorothy Squires and Russ Conway

STABBS *Finland / US / Cameroon,*
male instrumental / production group (Singles: 1 Week) pos/wks

24 Dec 94	JOY AND HAPPINESS *Hi-Life HICD 3*	**65** 1

STACCATO *UK / Holland, male /*
female vocal / instrumental duo (Singles: 1 Week) pos/wks

20 Jul 96	I WANNA KNOW *Multiply CDMULTY 11*	**65** 1

Warren STACEY *UK, male vocalist (Singles: 3 Weeks)* pos/wks

23 Mar 02	MY GIRL MY GIRL *Def Soul 5889932*	**26** 3

Jim STAFFORD *US, male vocalist (Singles: 16 Weeks)* pos/wks

27 Apr 74	SPIDERS & SNAKES *MGM 2006 374*	**14** 8
6 Jul 74	MY GIRL BILL *MGM 2006 423*	**20** 8

Jo STAFFORD *US, female vocalist (Singles: 28 Weeks)* pos/wks

14 Nov 52	★ YOU BELONG TO ME *Columbia DB 3152* ▲	**1** 19
19 Dec 52	JAMBALAYA *Columbia DB 3169*	**11** 2
7 May 54	● MAKE LOVE TO ME! *Philips PB 233* ▲	**8** 1
9 Dec 55	SUDDENLY THERE'S A VALLEY (re) *Philips PB 509*	**12** 6

Terry STAFFORD
US, male vocalist, b. 22 Nov 1941, d. 17 Mar 1996 (Singles: 9 Weeks) pos/wks

7 May 64	SUSPICION *London HLU 9871*	**31** 9

STAGECOACH featuring Penny FOSTER
UK, male / female vocal ensemble (Singles: 1 Week) pos/wks

18 Oct 03	ANGEL LOOKING THROUGH *Stagecoach Theatre SCR 001*	**59** 1

STAIFFI and his MUSTAFAS
France, male vocal / instrumental group (Singles: 1 Week) pos/wks

28 Jul 60	MUSTAFA CHA CHA CHA *Pye International 7N 25057*	**43** 1

STAIND *US, male vocal / instrumental*
group (Singles: 11 Weeks, Albums: 29 Weeks) pos/wks

15 Sep 01	IT'S BEEN AWHILE *Elektra E 7252CD*	**15** 6
1 Dec 01	OUTSIDE *Elektra E 7277CD*	**33** 2
23 Feb 02	FOR YOU *Elektra E 7281CD*	**55** 1
24 May 03	PRICE TO PLAY *Elektra E 7417CD*	**36** 2
1 Sep 01	★ BREAK THE CYCLE *Elektra 7559626642* ■ ▲	**1** 26
31 May 03	14 SHADES OF GREY *Elektra 7559628822* ▲	**16** 3

STAKKA BO *Sweden, male rap / DJ duo –*
Johan Renck and Oscar Franzen (Singles: 12 Weeks) pos/wks

25 Sep 93	HERE WE GO *Polydor PZCD 280*	**13** 8
18 Dec 93	DOWN THE DRAIN *Polydor PZCD 301*	**64** 4

Frank STALLONE *US, male vocalist (Singles: 2 Weeks)* pos/wks

22 Oct 83	FAR FROM OVER *RSO 95*	**68** 2

STAMFORD AMP
UK, male vocal / instrumental group (Singles: 2 Weeks) pos/wks

12 Oct 02	ANYTHING FOR YOU *Mercury 638972*	**33** 2

STAMFORD BRIDGE
UK, male Chelsea FC supporters vocal group (Singles: 1 Week) pos/wks

16 May 70	CHELSEA *Penny Farthing PEN 715*	**47** 1

STAMINA MC *See DJ MARKY & XRS; D KAY & EPSILON featuring STAMINA MC*

STAMPS QUARTET *See Elvis PRESLEY*

STAN *UK, male vocal / instrumental duo –*
Simon Andrew and Kevin Stagg (Singles: 3 Weeks) pos/wks

31 Jul 93	SUNTAN *Hug CDBUM 1*	**40** 3

The STANDS *UK, male vocal /*
instrumental group (Singles: 6 Weeks, Albums: 2 Weeks) pos/wks

16 Aug 03	WHEN THE RIVER ROLLS OVER YOU *Echo ECSCD 142*	**32** 1
25 Oct 03	I NEED YOU *Echo ECSCD 146*	**39** 2

21 Feb 04	HERE SHE COMES AGAIN *Echo ECSCD 148*	**25** 2
5 Jun 04	OUTSIDE YOUR DOOR *Echo ECSCX 151*	**49** 1
6 Mar 04	ALL YEARS LEAVING *Echo ECHCD 50*	**28** 2

Lisa STANSFIELD 246 Top 500 *Only UK act to have three US R&B*
No.1 hits, b. 11 Apr 1966, Rochdale, Lancashire. Like Yazz, she was featured
vocalist on a Coldcut single before achieving a No.1 in her own right. This
multi-Brit award winner has sold millions of records all around the world
(Singles: 127 Weeks, Albums: 126 Weeks) pos/wks

25 Mar 89	PEOPLE HOLD ON *Ahead of Our Time CCUT 5* [1]	**11** 9
12 Aug 89	THIS IS THE RIGHT TIME *Arista 112512*	**13** 8
28 Oct 89	★ ALL AROUND THE WORLD *Arista 112693*	**1** 14
10 Feb 90	● LIVE TOGETHER *Arista 112914*	**10** 6
12 May 90	WHAT DID I DO TO YOU (EP) *Arista 113168*	**25** 4
19 Oct 91	● CHANGE *Arista 114820*	**10** 7
21 Dec 91	ALL WOMAN *Arista 115000*	**20** 8
14 Mar 92	TIME TO MAKE YOU MINE *Arista 115113*	**14** 8
6 Jun 92	SET YOUR LOVING FREE *Arista 74321100587*	**28** 4
19 Dec 92	● SOMEDAY (I'M COMING BACK) *Arista 74321123567*	**10** 9
1 May 93	★ FIVE LIVE (EP) (re) *Parlophone CDRS 6340* [2] ■	**1** 12
5 Jun 93	● IN ALL THE RIGHT PLACES *MCA MCSTD 1780*	**8** 11
23 Oct 93	SO NATURAL *Arista 74321169132*	**15** 5
11 Dec 93	LITTLE BIT OF HEAVEN *Arista 74321178202*	**32** 4
18 Jan 97	● PEOPLE HOLD ON (THE BOOTLEG MIXES) *Arista 74321452012* [3]	**4** 6
22 Mar 97	● THE REAL THING *Arista 74321463222*	**9** 7
21 Jun 97	NEVER, NEVER GONNA GIVE YOU UP *Arista 74321490392*	**25** 3
4 Oct 97	THE LINE *RCA 74321511372*	**64** 1
23 Jun 01	LET'S JUST CALL IT LOVE *Arista 74321863422*	**48** 1
2 Dec 89	● AFFECTION *Arista 210379*	**2** 31
23 Nov 91	● REAL LOVE *Arista 212300*	**3** 51
20 Nov 93	● SO NATURAL *Arista 74321172312*	**6** 14
5 Apr 97	● LISA STANSFIELD *Arista 74321458512*	**2** 18
7 Jul 01	FACE UP *Arista 74321863462*	**38** 2
15 Feb 03	● BIOGRAPHY – THE GREATEST HITS *Arista 82876502222*	**3** 9
9 Oct 04	THE MOMENT *ZTT ZTT 192CD*	**57** 1

[1] Coldcut featuring Lisa Stansfield [2] George Michael and Queen with Lisa Stansfield [3] Lisa Stansfield vs the Dirty Rotten Scoundrels

Tracks on What Did I Do to You (EP): What Did I Do to You / My Apple Heart / Lay Me Down / Something's Happenin'. Tracks on Five Live (EP): Somebody to Love / These Are the Days of Our Lives / Calling You / Papa Was a Rolling Stone – Killer (medley). Lisa Stansfield appears only on the second track

Vivian STANSHALL *See BONZO DOG DOO-DAH BAND; Mike OLDFIELD*

STANTON WARRIORS
UK, male production duo (Singles: 1 Week) pos/wks

22 Sep 01	DA ANTIDOTE *Mob MOBCD 006*	**69** 1

The STAPLE SINGERS
US, male / female vocal group (Singles: 14 Weeks) pos/wks

10 Jun 72	I'LL TAKE YOU THERE *Stax 2025 110* ▲	**30** 8
8 Jun 74	IF YOU'RE READY (COME GO WITH ME) *Stax 2025 224*	**34** 6

Cyril STAPLETON and his ORCHESTRA *UK, orchestra –*
leader b. 31 Dec 1914, d. 25 Feb 1974 (Singles: 27 Weeks) pos/wks

27 May 55	ELEPHANT TANGO (2re) *Decca F 10488*	**19** 4
23 Sep 55	● BLUE STAR (THE MEDIC THEME) *Decca F 10559* [1]	**2** 12
6 Apr 56	THE ITALIAN THEME *Decca F 10703*	**18** 2
1 Jun 56	THE HAPPY WHISTLER *Decca F 10735* [2]	**22** 4
19 Jul 57	FORGOTTEN DREAMS *Decca F 10912*	**27** 5

[1] Cyril Stapleton Orchestra featuring Julie Dawn [2] Cyril Stapleton Orchestra featuring Desmond Lane, penny whistle

STAR INC *See Ed STARINK*

The STAR SPANGLES
UK, male vocal / instrumental group (Singles: 1 Week) pos/wks

19 Apr 03	STAY AWAY FROM ME *Parlophone CDR 6604*	**52** 1

STAR TURN ON 45 (PINTS)
UK, male vocalist – Steve O'Donnell, d. 4 Aug 1997 (Singles: 9 Weeks) pos/wks

24 Oct 81	STARTURN ON 45 (PINTS) *V Tone V TONE 003*	**45** 4
30 Apr 88	PUMP UP THE BITTER *Pacific DRINK 1*	**12** 5

STARCHASER
Italy, male DJ / production trio (Singles: 4 Weeks) pos/wks

22 Jun 02	LOVE WILL SET YOU FREE (JAMBE MYTH) *Rulin RULIN 23CDS*	24	4

STARDUST
France, male / female vocal / instrumental group (Singles: 3 Weeks) pos/wks

8 Oct 77	ARIANA *Satril SAT 120*	42	3

STARDUST
France, male vocal / production group (Singles: 26 Weeks) pos/wks

1 Aug 98	MUSIC SOUNDS BETTER WITH YOU (IMPORT) *Roule ROULE 305*	55	3
22 Aug 98 ●	MUSIC SOUNDS BETTER WITH YOU *Virgin DINSD 175*	2	23

Alvin STARDUST (see also Shane FENTON and the FENTONES)
UK, male vocalist – Bernard Jewry (b. 27 Sep 1942)
(Singles: 119 Weeks, Albums: 17 Weeks) pos/wks

3 Nov 73 ●	MY COO-CA-CHOO *Magnet MAG 1*	2	21
16 Feb 74 ★	JEALOUS MIND *Magnet MAG 5*	1	11
4 May 74 ●	RED DRESS *Magnet MAG 8*	7	8
31 Aug 74 ●	YOU YOU YOU *Magnet MAG 13*	6	10
30 Nov 74	TELL ME WHY *Magnet MAG 19*	16	8
1 Feb 75	GOOD LOVE CAN NEVER DIE *Magnet MAG 21*	11	9
12 Jul 75	SWEET CHEATIN' RITA *Magnet MAG 32*	37	4
5 Sep 81 ●	PRETEND *Stiff BUY 124*	4	10
21 Nov 81	A WONDERFUL TIME UP THERE *Stiff BUY 132*	56	8
5 May 84 ●	I FEEL LIKE BUDDY HOLLY *Chrysalis CHS 2784*	7	11
27 Oct 84 ●	I WON'T RUN AWAY *Chrysalis CHS 2829*	7	13
15 Dec 84	SO NEAR TO CHRISTMAS *Chrysalis CHS 2835*	29	4
23 Mar 85	GOT A LITTLE HEARTACHE *Chrysalis CHS 2856*	55	2
16 Mar 74 ●	THE UNTOUCHABLE *Magnet MAG 5001*	4	12
21 Dec 74	ALVIN STARDUST *Magnet MAG 5004*	37	3
4 Oct 75	ROCK WITH ALVIN *Magnet MAG 5007*	52	2

STARFIGHTER
Belgium, male producer – Philip Dirix (Singles: 3 Weeks) pos/wks

5 Feb 00	APACHE *Sound of Ministry MOSCDS 136*	31	3

STARGARD *US, female vocal group (Singles: 14 Weeks)* pos/wks

28 Jan 78	THEME SONG FROM 'WHICH WAY IS UP' *MCA 346*	19	7
15 Apr 78	LOVE IS SO EASY *MCA 354*	45	1
9 Sep 78	WHAT YOU WAITIN' FOR *MCA 382*	39	6

STARGATE *Norway / US, male /*
female production / vocal / rap group (Singles: 1 Week) pos/wks

7 Sep 02	EASIER SAID THAN DONE *Telstar CDSTAS 3269*	55	1

The STARGAZERS
UK / Australia, male / female vocal group (Singles: 68 Weeks) pos/wks

13 Feb 53 ★	BROKEN WINGS (re) *Decca F 10047*	1	12
19 Feb 54 ★	I SEE THE MOON *Decca F 10213*	1	15
9 Apr 54	THE HAPPY WANDERER *Decca F 10259*	12	1
17 Dec 54 ★	THE FINGER OF SUSPICION *Decca F 10394* [1]	1	15
4 Mar 55	SOMEBODY *Decca F 10437*	20	1
3 Jun 55	THE CRAZY OTTO RAG *Decca F 10523*	18	3
9 Sep 55 ●	CLOSE THE DOOR *Decca F 10594*	6	9
11 Nov 55 ●	TWENTY TINY FINGERS *Decca F 10626*	4	11
22 Jun 56	HOT DIGGITY (DOG ZIGGITY BOOM) *Decca F 10731*	28	1

[1] Dickie Valentine with The Stargazers

The STARGAZERS
UK, male vocal / instrumental group (Singles: 3 Weeks) pos/wks

6 Feb 82	GROOVE BABY GROOVE (EP) *Epic EPC A 1924*	56	3

Tracks on Groove Baby Groove (EP): Groove Baby Groove / Jump Around / La Rock
'n' Roll (Quelques Uns a la Lune) / Red Light Green Light

Ed STARINK *US, male instrumentalist (Albums: 11 Weeks)* pos/wks

27 Oct 90	SYNTHESIZER GREATEST *Arcade ARC 938101* [1]	22	5
9 Jan 93	SYNTHESIZER GOLD *Arcade ARC 3100012*	29	6

[1] Star Inc

The STARJETS
UK, male vocal / instrumental group (Singles: 5 Weeks) pos/wks

8 Sep 79	WAR STORIES *Epic EPC 7770*	51	5

The STARLAND VOCAL BAND
US, male / female vocal group (Singles: 10 Weeks) pos/wks

7 Aug 76	AFTERNOON DELIGHT *RCA 2716* ▲	18	10

STARLIGHT
Italy, male instrumental / production group (Singles: 11 Weeks) pos/wks

19 Aug 89 ●	NUMERO UNO *Citybeat CBE 742*	9	11

STARLITERS *See Joey DEE and the STARLITERS*

STARPARTY (see also ALBION; MOONMAN; SYSTEM F; GOURYELLA; VERACOCHA) *Holland, male production duo – Ferry Corsten and Robert Smit (Singles: 2 Weeks)* pos/wks

26 Feb 00	I'M IN LOVE *Incentive CENT 5CDS*	26	2

Edwin STARR (see also UTAH SAINTS)
US, male vocalist, b. 21 Jan 1942, d. 2 Apr 2003 (Singles: 70 Weeks) pos/wks

12 May 66	STOP HER ON SIGHT (SOS) *Polydor BM 56 702*	35	8
18 Aug 66	HEADLINE NEWS *Polydor 56 717*	39	3
11 Dec 68	STOP HER ON SIGHT (SOS) / HEADLINE NEWS (re-issue) *Polydor 56 753*	11	11
13 Sep 69	25 MILES *Tamla Motown TMG 672*	36	6
24 Oct 70 ●	WAR *Tamla Motown TMG 754* ▲	3	12
20 Feb 71	STOP THE WAR NOW *Tamla Motown TMG 764*	33	1
27 Jan 79 ●	CONTACT *20th Century BTC 2396*	6	12
26 May 79 ●	H.A.P.P.Y. RADIO *RCA TC 2408*	9	11
1 Jun 85	IT AIN'T FAIR *Hippodrome HIP 101*	56	4
30 Oct 93	WAR (re-recording) *Weekend CDWEEK 103* [1]	69	2

[1] Edwin Starr and Shadow

'Headline News' not listed with 'SOS' from 22 Jan 1969 to 19 Feb 1969. It there-fore peaked at No.16. 'War' in 1993 was listed with the flip-side 'Wild Thing' by The Troggs and Wolf

Freddie STARR *UK, male vocalist / comedian –*
Fred Smith (Singles: 14 Weeks, Albums: 16 Weeks) pos/wks

23 Feb 74 ●	IT'S YOU *Tiffany 6121 501*	9	10
20 Dec 75	WHITE CHRISTMAS *Thunderbird THE 102*	41	4
18 Nov 89 ●	AFTER THE LAUGHTER *Dover ADD 10*	10	9
17 Nov 90	THE WANDERER *Dover ADD 17*	33	7

Kay STARR *US, female vocalist –*
Katherine Starks (Singles: 58 Weeks, Albums: 1 Week) pos/wks

5 Dec 52 ★	COMES A-LONG A-LOVE *Capitol CL 13808*	1	16
24 Apr 53 ●	SIDE BY SIDE *Capitol CL 13871*	7	4
19 Mar 54 ●	CHANGING PARTNERS *Capitol CL 14050*	4	14
15 Oct 54	AM I A TOY OR TREASURE (re) *Capitol CL 14151*	17	4
17 Feb 56 ★	ROCK AND ROLL WALTZ *HMV POP 168* ▲	1	20
26 Mar 60	MOVIN' *Capitol 1254*	16	1

Ringo STARR (see also The BEATLES) *UK, male vocalist –*
Richard Starkey (Singles: 56 Weeks, Albums: 28 Weeks) pos/wks

17 Apr 71 ●	IT DON'T COME EASY *Apple R 5898*	4	11
1 Apr 72 ●	BACK OFF BOOGALOO *Apple R 5944*	2	10
27 Oct 73 ●	PHOTOGRAPH *Apple R 5992* ▲	8	13
23 Feb 74 ●	YOU'RE SIXTEEN *Apple R 5995* ▲	4	10
30 Nov 74	ONLY YOU *Apple R 6000*	28	11
6 Jun 92	WEIGHT OF THE WORLD *Private Music 115392*	74	1
18 Apr 70 ●	SENTIMENTAL JOURNEY *Apple PCS 7101*	7	6
8 Dec 73 ●	RINGO *Apple PCTC 252*	7	20
7 Dec 74	GOODNIGHT VIENNA *Apple PMC 7168*	30	2

STARS ON 54 *US, female vocal trio (Singles: 3 Weeks)* pos/wks

28 Nov 98	IF YOU COULD READ MY MIND *Tommy Boy TBCD 7497*	23	3

STARSAILOR *UK, male vocal /*
instrumental group (Singles: 36 Weeks, Albums: 54 Weeks) pos/wks

17 Feb 01	FEVER *Chrysalis CDCHSS 5123*	18	3

5 May 01	GOOD SOULS *Chrysalis CDCHS 5125*	.....12 6
29 Sep 01 ●	ALCOHOLIC *Chrysalis CDCHSS 5130*	.....10 6
22 Dec 01	LULLABY *Chrysalis CDCHS 5131*	.....36 4
30 Mar 02	POOR MISGUIDED FOOL *Chrysalis CDCHS 5136*	.....23 3
13 Sep 03 ●	SILENCE IS EASY *EMI CDEM 625*	.....9 8
29 Nov 03	BORN AGAIN *EMI CDEM 632*	.....40 2
13 Mar 04	FOUR TO THE FLOOR *EMI CDEMS 634*	.....24 4
20 Oct 01 ●	LOVE IS HERE *Chrysalis 5353502*	.....2 41
27 Sep 03 ●	SILENCE IS EASY *EMI 5900072*	.....2 13

STARSHIP (see also JEFFERSON AIRPLANE)
US, female / male vocal / instrumental group (Singles: 41 Weeks) pos/wks

26 Jan 80	JANE *Grunt FB 1750* [1]	.....21 9
16 Nov 85	WE BUILT THIS CITY *RCA PB 49929* ▲	.....12 12
8 Feb 86	SARA *RCA FB 49893* ▲	.....66 3
11 Apr 87 ★	NOTHING'S GONNA STOP US NOW *Grunt FB 49757* ▲	.....1 17

[1] Jefferson Starship

STARSOUND *Holland, male producer – Jaap Eggermont and male / female session singers (Singles: 37 Weeks, Albums: 28 Weeks)* pos/wks

18 Apr 81 ●	STARS ON 45 *CBS A 1102* ▲	.....2 14
4 Jul 81 ●	STARS ON 45 VOL 2 *CBS A 1407*	.....2 10
19 Sep 81	STARS ON 45 VOL 3 *CBS A 1521*	.....17 6
27 Feb 82	STARS ON STEVIE *CBS A 2041*	.....14 7
16 May 81 ★	STARS ON 45 *CBS 86132*	.....1 21
19 Sep 81	STARS ON 45 VOLUME 2 *CBS 85181*	.....18 6
3 Apr 82	STARS MEDLEY *CBS 85651*	.....94 1

STARTRAX
UK, male / female vocal group (Singles: 8 Weeks, Albums: 7 Weeks) pos/wks

1 Aug 81	STARTRAX CLUB DISCO *Picksy KSY 1001*	.....18 8
1 Aug 81	STARTRAX CLUB DISCO *Picksy KSYA 1001*	.....26 7

STARVATION *Multinational, male / female vocal / instrumental charity assembly (Singles: 6 Weeks)* pos/wks

9 Mar 85	STARVATION / TAM-TAM POUR L'ETHIOPIE *Zarjazz JAZZ 3*	.....33 6

STARVING SOULS *UK, male vocal / instrumental group – leader Tricky (Singles: 1 Week)* pos/wks

21 Oct 95	I BE THE PROPHET EP *Durban Poison DPCD 1*	.....66 1

Tracks on the I Be the Prophet EP (includes vocals by Terry Hall): I Be The Prophet, If You Want My Love, I Be The Prophet (re-mix)

STATE OF MIND
UK, male / female vocal / production group (Singles: 3 Weeks) pos/wks

18 Apr 98	THIS IS IT *Ministry of Sound MOSCDS 123*	.....30 2
25 Jul 98	TAKE CONTROL *Ministry of Sound MOSCDS 124*	.....46 1

STATE OF THE HEART *UK, male vocal / instrumental group – includes Dave Lewis – saxophone (Albums: 9 Weeks)* pos/wks

16 Mar 96	PURE SAX *Virgin VTCD 78*	.....18 7
12 Oct 96	SAX AT THE MOVIES *Virgin VTCD 98*	.....62 2

STATE ONE
UK / Germany, male production group (Singles: 1 Week) pos/wks

27 Sep 03	FOREVER AND A DAY *Incentive CENT 54CDS*	.....62 1

STATIC REVENGER
US, male producer – Dennis White (Singles: 3 Weeks) pos/wks

7 Jul 01	HAPPY PEOPLE *Incentive / Rulin CENRUL 1CDS*	.....23 3

STATIC-X *US, male vocal / instrumental group (Singles: 1 Week, Albums: 2 Weeks)* pos/wks

6 Oct 01	BLACK AND WHITE *Warner W 560CD*	.....65 1
23 Jun 01	MACHINE *Warner Bros. 9362479482*	.....56 2

STATLER BROTHERS *US, male vocal group (Singles: 4 Weeks)* pos/wks

24 Feb 66	FLOWERS ON THE WALL *CBS 201976*	.....38 4

Candi STATON *US, female vocalist – Canzata Staton (Singles: 71 Weeks, Albums: 3 Weeks)* pos/wks

29 May 76 ●	YOUNG HEARTS RUN FREE *Warner Bros. K 16730*	.....2 13
18 Sep 76	DESTINY *Warner Bros. K 16806*	.....41 3

23 Jul 77 ●	NIGHTS ON BROADWAY *Warner Bros. K 16972*	.....6 12
3 Jun 78	HONEST I DO LOVE YOU *Warner Bros. K 17164*	.....48 5
24 Apr 82	SUSPICIOUS MINDS *Sugarhill SH 112*	.....31 9
31 May 86	YOUNG HEARTS RUN FREE *Warner Bros. W 8680*	.....47 5
2 Feb 91 ●	YOU GOT THE LOVE *Truelove TLOVE 7001* [1]	.....4 11
1 Mar 97 ●	YOU GOT THE LOVE (re-mix) *React CDREACT 89* [1]	.....3 8
17 Apr 99	LOVE ON LOVE *React CDREACT 143*	.....27 3
7 Aug 99	YOUNG HEARTS RUN FREE (re-recording) *React CDREACT 158*	.....29 2
24 Jul 76	YOUNG HEARTS RUN FREE *Warner Bros. K 56259*	.....34 3

[1] Source featuring Candi Staton

STATUS IV *US, male vocal group (Singles: 3 Weeks)* pos/wks

9 Jul 83	YOU AIN'T REALLY DOWN *TMT TMT 4*	.....56 3

STATUS QUO (25 Top 500) *Ever popular London-based three-chord boogie band: Francis Rossi (g/v), Rick Parfitt (g/v), Alan Lancaster (b), John Coghlan (d). These long-time festival favourites recorded as The Spectres and Traffic Jam before their psychedelic-sounding debut hit introduced them to the UK and US Top 20 (their only major American hit). Quo hold the record for most appearances on Top of the Pops with 106 live perfomances and videos. No group has accumulated more UK hit singles or has a wider Top 20 chart span and only The Beatles and The Rolling Stones can better their tally of Top 20 albums. These heroes of the head-banging set were chosen to open Live Aid in 1985 (Singles: 423 Weeks, Albums: 467 Weeks)* pos/wks

24 Jan 68 ●	PICTURES OF MATCHSTICK MEN *Pye 7N 17449*	.....7 12
21 Aug 68 ●	ICE IN THE SUN *Pye 7N 17581*	.....8 12
28 May 69	ARE YOU GROWING TIRED OF MY LOVE (re) *Pye 7N 17728*	.....46 3
2 May 70	DOWN THE DUSTPIPE *Pye 7N 17907*	.....12 17
7 Nov 70	IN MY CHAIR *Pye 7N 17998*	.....21 14
13 Jan 73 ●	PAPER PLANE *Vertigo 6059 071*	.....8 11
14 Apr 73	MEAN GIRL *Pye 7N 45229*	.....20 11
8 Sep 73 ●	CAROLINE *Vertigo 6059 085*	.....5 13
4 May 74 ●	BREAK THE RULES *Vertigo 6059 101*	.....8 8
7 Dec 74 ★	DOWN DOWN *Vertigo 6059 114*	.....1 11
17 May 75 ●	LIVE! (EP) *Vertigo QUO 103*	.....3 8
14 Feb 76 ●	RAIN *Vertigo 6059 133*	.....7 7
10 Jul 76	MYSTERY SONG *Vertigo 6059 146*	.....11 9
11 Dec 76 ●	WILD SIDE OF LIFE *Vertigo 6059 163*	.....9 12
8 Oct 77 ●	ROCKIN' ALL OVER THE WORLD *Vertigo 6059 184*	.....3 16
2 Sep 78 ●	AGAIN AND AGAIN *Vertigo QUO 1*	.....13 9
25 Nov 78	ACCIDENT PRONE *Vertigo QUO 2*	.....36 8
22 Sep 79 ●	WHATEVER YOU WANT *Vertigo 6059 242*	.....4 9
24 Nov 79	LIVING ON AN ISLAND *Vertigo 6059 248*	.....16 10
11 Oct 80 ●	WHAT YOU'RE PROPOSING *Vertigo QUO 3*	.....2 11
6 Dec 80	LIES / DON'T DRIVE MY CAR *Vertigo QUO 4*	.....11 10
28 Feb 81 ●	SOMETHING 'BOUT YOU BABY I LIKE *Vertigo QUO 5*	.....9 7
28 Nov 81 ●	ROCK 'N' ROLL *Vertigo QUO 6*	.....8 11
27 Mar 82 ●	DEAR JOHN *Vertigo QUO 7*	.....10 8
12 Jun 82	SHE DON'T FOOL ME *Vertigo QUO 8*	.....36 5
30 Oct 82	CAROLINE (LIVE AT THE NEC) *Vertigo QUO 10*	.....13 7
10 Sep 83 ●	OL' RAG BLUES *Vertigo QUO 11*	.....9 8
5 Nov 83	A MESS OF BLUES *Vertigo QUO 12*	.....15 6
10 Dec 83 ●	MARGUERITA TIME *Vertigo QUO 14*	.....3 11
19 May 84	GOING DOWN TOWN TONIGHT *Vertigo QUO 15*	.....20 6
27 Oct 84 ●	THE WANDERER *Vertigo QUO 16*	.....7 11
17 May 86 ●	ROLLIN' HOME *Vertigo QUO 18*	.....9 6
26 Jul 86	RED SKY *Vertigo QUO 19*	.....19 8
4 Oct 86 ●	IN THE ARMY NOW *Vertigo QUO 20*	.....2 14
6 Dec 86	DREAMIN' *Vertigo QUO 21*	.....15 8
26 Mar 88	AIN'T COMPLAINING *Vertigo QUO 22*	.....19 6
21 May 88	WHO GETS THE LOVE? *Vertigo QUO 23*	.....34 4
20 Aug 88	RUNNING ALL OVER THE WORLD *Vertigo QUAID 1*	.....17 6
3 Dec 88 ●	BURNING BRIDGES (ON AND OFF AND ON AGAIN) *Vertigo QUO 25*	.....5 10
28 Oct 89	NOT AT ALL *Vertigo QUO 26*	.....50 2
29 Sep 90 ●	THE ANNIVERSARY WALTZ – PART ONE *Vertigo QUO 28*	.....2 9
15 Dec 90	THE ANNIVERSARY WALTZ – PART TWO *Vertigo QUO 29*	.....16 7
7 Sep 91	CAN'T GIVE YOU MORE *Vertigo QUO 30*	.....37 3
18 Jan 92	ROCK 'TIL YOU DROP *Vertigo QUO 32*	.....38 3
10 Oct 92	ROADHOUSE MEDLEY (ANNIVERSARY WALTZ PART 25) *Polydor QUO 33*	.....21 4
6 Aug 94	I DIDN'T MEAN IT *Polydor QUOCD 34*	.....21 4
22 Oct 94	SHERRI DON'T FAIL ME NOW *Polydor QUOCD 35*	.....38 2
3 Dec 94	RESTLESS *Polydor QUOCD 36*	.....39 2
4 Nov 95	WHEN YOU WALK IN THE ROOM *PolyGram TV 5775122*	.....34 2
2 Mar 96	FUN FUN FUN *PolyGram TV 5762632* [1]	.....24 4

Singles re-entries are listed as (re), (2re), (3re).... which signifies that the hit re-entered the chart once, twice or three times...

THE HITS THAT NEVER WERE (Part II)

In The Hits That Never Were (edition 14 of British Hit Singles) we drew attention to a number of well-known songs that, bizarrely, failed to chart. The article was included in direct response to our readers' letters pointing out that there were no entries in our book for the likes of Van Morrison's 'Brown Eyed Girl', The Singing Postman's 'Hev Yew Gotta Loight Boy' and Led Zeppelin's 'Stairway to Heaven'.

However, rather than putting an end to our correspondence on this subject, the article caused letters and emails to increase, pointing to many more classics that failed to find a place in our book. So, in an effort to explain some further absentees, here are The Hits That Never Were (Part II).

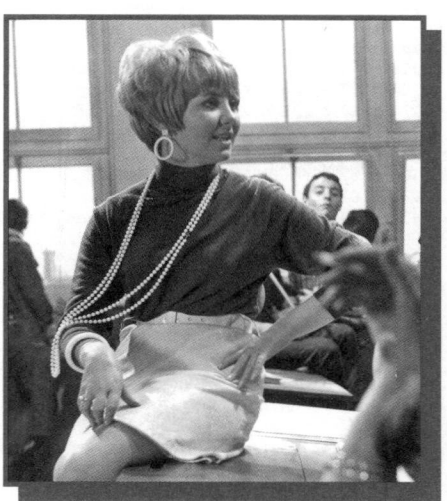

↗ IN A SCENE FROM THE MOVIE 'TO SIR, WITH LOVE', SCHOOLGIRL LULU PRE-DATES THE EARLY BRITNEY LOOK AND ENCOURAGES TWO MILLION AMERICANS TO BUY THE SINGLE OF THE SAME NAME

↘ UNLUCKY FOR SOME. EX LONDON BUS DRIVER MATT MONRO'S CHART CAREER INCLUDED 13 HIT SINGLES, EXCLUDING HIS MEMORABLE RENDITION OF 'BORN FREE'

BORN FREE Matt Monro
This Oscar-winning song, composed by John Barry (with lyrics by Don Black) for the film of the same name, became a hit only when revived by the comedian / singer Vic Reeves and The Roman Numerals in 1991. Matt's original version, rated alongside 'From Russia with Love' as some of his finest work, initially was removed from the film's soundtrack. However, when a cover version by American pianist Roger Williams made No.7 on the US Billboard chart in 1966, Monro's version was reinstated on the soundtrack album and played regularly on radio.

MATRIMONY Gilbert O'Sullivan
Considering visitors to Gilbert's official website voted this their third favourite song ahead of 'Clair', the bouncy 'Matrimony' is another mysterious omission from the pages of this book. Never originally released as a single, the track was included on his debut album 'Himself', which charted in 1971, and still managed thousands of plays on radio. His record label, MAM, eventually did put the track out as a single in 1976, but by then Gilbert's chart career was beginning to wane and no hit was forthcoming.

WHAT'S GOING ON Marvin Gaye
Although the single, from the album of the same name, made No.2 on the US Billboard Hot 100 in 1971, it nearly failed to get a release at all Stateside. Gaye was so incensed by Motown's reluctance to release his beautiful, movingly mournful masterpiece that he threatened to end his connections with the label. The song made three UK chart appearances with releases by Cyndi Lauper, Music Relief '94 and Artists Against Aids Worldwide.

TO SIR, WITH LOVE Lulu
This title song to the film starring Sidney Poitier was originally released on both sides of the Atlantic as a B-side to the single 'The Boat That I Row'. American disc jockeys preferred the flip side and, as a result, 'To Sir, With Love' was propelled to No.1 on the Billboard Hot 100, selling two million copies in the process. Despite three other UK hits in 1967, the track failed to make it as a hit over here. Check out Lulu's performance as a schoolgirl in the movie, alongside a cameo part by British group The Mindbenders.

DRIFT AWAY Dobie Gray
Few would argue that this track was Dobie Gray's finest hour, and yet there is no UK chart placing to prove it. It was certainly his biggest hit in the US, originally making No.5 in 1973 and No.9 in 2003 with Uncle Kracker. 'Drift Away"s only listing in our book comes courtesy of Michael Bolton's bold attempt to cover the song that resulted in a peak position of No.18 in 1992.

MRS BROWN YOU'VE GOT A LOVELY DAUGHTER Herman's Hermits
There is something of a theme developing here. Yet another massively successful British act Stateside was involved in the title song from a feature film that failed to make any impression on the UK chart. The song was composed by Vicar of Dibley actor Trevor Peacock and another actor, Tom Courtenay, who was first to record it in 1963. In 1965 this record was the first of two very British-sounding US chart-toppers for Peter Noone and his Manchester bandmates. Two years later the lads starred in the MGM movie 'Mrs Brown …' with Stanley Holloway. The song wasn't even given a single release in the UK.

13 Apr 96		DON'T STOP *PolyGram TV 5766352*	35 2
9 Nov 96		ALL AROUND MY HAT *PolyGram TV 5759452* [2]	47 1
20 Mar 99		THE WAY IT GOES *Eagle EAGXS 075*	39 2
12 Jun 99		LITTLE WHITE LIES *Eagle EAGXS 101*	47 1
2 Oct 99		TWENTY WILD HORSES *Eagle EAGXS 105*	53 1
13 May 00		MONY MONY *Universal TV 1580132*	48 1
17 Aug 02		JAM SIDE DOWN *Universal TV 192342*	17 3
9 Nov 02		ALL STAND UP (NEVER SAY NEVER) *Universal TV 0194872*	51 1
25 Sep 04		YOU'LL COME 'ROUND *Universal TV 9868038*	14 3
4 Dec 04		THINKING OF YOU *Universal TV 9825824*	21 3
20 Jan 73	●	PILEDRIVER *Vertigo 6360 082*	5 37
9 Jun 73		THE BEST OF STATUS QUO *Pye NSPL 18402*	32 7
6 Oct 73	★	HELLO *Vertigo 6360 098*	1 28
18 May 74	●	QUO *Vertigo 9102 001*	2 16
1 Mar 75	★	ON THE LEVEL *Vertigo 9102 002* ■	1 27
8 Mar 75		DOWN THE DUSTPIPE *Golden Hour CH 604*	20 6
20 Mar 76	★	BLUE FOR YOU *Vertigo 9102 006* ■	1 30
12 Mar 77	●	LIVE *Vertigo 6641 580*	3 14
26 Nov 77	●	ROCKIN' ALL OVER THE WORLD *Vertigo 9102 014*	5 15
11 Nov 78	●	IF YOU CAN'T STAND THE HEAT *Vertigo 9102 027*	3 14
20 Oct 79	●	WHATEVER YOU WANT *Vertigo 9102 037*	3 14
22 Mar 80	●	12 GOLD BARS *Vertigo QUO TV 1*	3 48
25 Oct 80	●	JUST SUPPOSIN' *Vertigo 6302 057*	4 18
28 Mar 81	●	NEVER TOO LATE *Vertigo 6302 104*	2 13
10 Oct 81		FRESH QUOTA *PRT DOW 2*	74 1
24 Apr 82	★	1982 *Vertigo 6302 169* ■	1 20
13 Nov 82	●	FROM THE MAKERS OF ... *Vertigo PROLP 1*	4 18
3 Dec 83	●	BACK TO BACK *Vertigo VERH 10*	9 22
4 Aug 84		LIVE AT THE N.E.C. *Vertigo (Holland) 8189 471*	83 3
1 Dec 84		12 GOLD BARS VOLUME 2 (AND 1) *Vertigo QUO TV 2*	12 18
6 Sep 86	●	IN THE ARMY NOW *Vertigo VERH 36*	7 23
18 Jun 88		AIN'T COMPLAINING *Vertigo VERH 58*	12 5
2 Dec 89		PERFECT REMEDY *Vertigo 842098 1*	49 2
20 Oct 90	●	ROCKING ALL OVER THE YEARS *Vertigo 8467971*	2 25
5 Oct 91	●	ROCK 'TIL YOU DROP *Vertigo 5103411*	10 7
14 Nov 92		LIVE ALIVE QUO *Polydor 5173672*	37 1
3 Sep 94		THIRSTY WORK *Polydor 5236072*	13 3
17 Feb 96		DON'T STOP – THE 30TH ANNIVERSARY ALBUM *PolyGram TV 5310352*	2 11
25 Oct 97		WHATEVER YOU WANT – THE VERY BEST OF STATUS QUO *Mercury / PolyGram TV 5535072*	13 6
10 Apr 99		UNDER THE INFLUENCE *Eagle EAGCD 076*	26 2
29 Apr 00		FAMOUS IN THE LAST CENTURY *Universal Music TV 1578142*	19 5
5 Oct 02		HEAVY TRAFFIC *Universal TV 0187902*	15 3
29 Nov 03		RIFFS *Universal TV 9813909*	44 2
2 Oct 04		XS ALL AREAS – THE GREATEST HITS *Universal TV 9824883*	16 3

[1] Status Quo with The Beach Boys [2] Status Quo with Maddy Prior from Steeleye Span

'Don't Drive My Car' listed from 20 Dec 1980 only. 'Running All Over the World' is a re-recorded version of 'Rockin' All Over the World' with a slightly changed lyric, released to promote the Race Against Time of 28 Aug 1988. The 'Live!' EP from 1975 featured three tracks: Roll Over Lay Down (Live) / Gerundula / Junior's Wailing (Live). 'The Anniversary Waltz – Part One' was a medley consisting of: Let's Dance / Red River Rock / No Particular Place to Go / The Wanderer / I Hear You Knocking / Lucille / Great Balls of Fire. 'The Anniversary Waltz – Part Two' consisted of Rock & Roll Music / Lover Please / That'll Be the Day / Singing the Blues / When Will I Be Loved / Let's Work Together / Keep a Knockin' / Long Tall Sally. 'Roadhouse Medley' consisted of: The Wanderer / Marguerita Time / Living on a Island / Break the Rules / Something 'Bout You Baby I Like

STAXX
UK, male / female vocal / instrumental group (Singles: 11 Weeks)   pos/wks

2 Oct 93	JOY *Champion CHAMPCD 303*	25 6
20 May 95	YOU *Champion CHAMPCD 316*	50 1
13 Sep 97	JOY (re-mix) *Champion CHAMPCD 328* [1]	14 4

[1] Staxx featuring Carol Leeming

Carol Leeming appears on the original version of 'Joy' but is only credited on the re-mix

STEALERS WHEEL
UK, male vocal / instrumental group (Singles: 22 Weeks)   pos/wks

26 May 73	●	STUCK IN THE MIDDLE WITH YOU *A&M AMS 7036*	8 10
1 Sep 73		EVERYTHING WILL TURN OUT FINE *A&M AMS 7079*	33 6
26 Jan 74		STAR *A&M AMS 7094*	25 6

STEAM
US, male vocal / instrumental group (Singles: 14 Weeks)   pos/wks

31 Jan 70	●	NA NA HEY HEY KISS HIM GOODBYE *Fontana TF 1058* ▲	9 14

STEEL See UNITONE ROCKERS featuring STEEL

Anthony STEEL and the RADIO REVELLERS with Jackie BROWN and his music
UK, male actor / vocalist, b. 21 May 1920, d. 21 Mar 2001, and male vocal group (Singles: 6 Weeks)   pos/wks

10 Sep 54	WEST OF ZANZIBAR *Polygon P 1114*	11 6

STEEL HORSES See TRUMAN & WOLFF featuring STEEL HORSES

STEEL PULSE
UK, male vocal / instrumental group (Singles: 12 Weeks, Albums: 18 Weeks)   pos/wks

1 Apr 78		KU KLUX KLAN *Island WIP 6428*	41 4
8 Jul 78		PRODIGAL SON *Island WIP 6449*	35 6
23 Jun 79		SOUND SYSTEM *Island WIP 6490*	71 2
5 Aug 78	●	HANDSWORTH REVOLUTION *Island EMI ILPS 9502*	9 12
14 Jul 79		TRIBUTE TO MARTYRS *Island ILPS 9568*	42 6

Tommy STEELE 377 Top 500
Britain's first home-grown rock 'n' roll star, b. Thomas Hicks, 17 Dec 1936, London. Just four months after his chart debut he was filming his life story. The singer / songwriter / guitarist, who was the first UK act to have a No.1 album and who topped the singles chart before Elvis, starred in many other movies and musicals (Singles: 147 Weeks, Albums: 34 Weeks)   pos/wks

26 Oct 56		ROCK WITH THE CAVEMAN (re) *Decca F 10795* [1]	13 5
14 Dec 56	★	SINGING THE BLUES (2re) *Decca F 10819* [1]	1 15
15 Feb 57		KNEE DEEP IN THE BLUES *Decca F 10849* [1]	15 9
3 May 57	●	BUTTERFINGERS (re) *Decca F 10877* [1]	8 18
16 Aug 57		WATER WATER / A HANDFUL OF SONGS (re) *Decca F 10923* [1]	5 17
30 Aug 57		SHIRALEE *Decca F 10896* [1]	11 4
22 Nov 57		HEY YOU! *Decca F 10941* [1]	28 1
7 Mar 58	●	NAIROBI *Decca F 10991*	3 11
25 Apr 58		HAPPY GUITAR *Decca F 10976*	20 5
18 Jul 58		THE ONLY MAN ON THE ISLAND *Decca F 11041* [1]	16 8
14 Nov 58	●	COME ON, LET'S GO *Decca F 11072*	10 13
14 Aug 59		TALLAHASSEE LASSIE (re) *Decca F 11152*	16 5
28 Aug 59		GIVE! GIVE! GIVE! *Decca F 11152*	28 2
4 Dec 59	●	LITTLE WHITE BULL (re) *Decca F 11177*	6 17
23 Jun 60	●	WHAT A MOUTH (WHAT A NORTH AND SOUTH) *Decca F 11245*	5 11
29 Dec 60		MUST BE SANTA *Decca F 11299*	40 1
17 Aug 61		THE WRITING ON THE WALL *Decca F 11372*	30 5
27 Apr 57	●	TOMMY STEELE STAGE SHOW *Decca LF 1287*	5 1
8 Jun 57	★	THE TOMMY STEELE STORY *Decca LF 1288*	1 21
12 Apr 58	★	THE DUKE WORE JEANS (SOUNDTRACK) *Decca LF 1308*	1 12

[1] Tommy Steele and the Steelmen

'Handful of Songs' listed together with 'Water Water' from 23 Aug 1957

STEELEYE SPAN
UK, male / female vocal / instrumental group (Singles: 18 Weeks, Albums: 48 Weeks)   pos/wks

8 Dec 73		GAUDETE *Chrysalis CHS 2007*	14 9
15 Nov 75	●	ALL AROUND MY HAT *Chrysalis CHS 2078*	5 9
10 Apr 71		PLEASE TO SEE THE KING *B&C CAS 1029*	45 2
14 Oct 72		BELOW THE SALT *Chrysalis CHR 1008*	43 1
28 Apr 73		PARCEL OF ROGUES *Chrysalis CHR 1046*	26 5
23 Mar 74		NOW WE ARE SIX *Chrysalis CHR 1053*	13 13
15 Feb 75		COMMONER'S CROWN *Chrysalis CHR 1071*	21 4
25 Oct 75	●	ALL AROUND MY HAT *Chrysalis CHR 1091*	7 20
16 Oct 76		ROCKET COTTAGE *Chrysalis CHR 1123*	41 3

STEELMEN See Tommy STEELE

STEELY DAN
US, male vocal / instrumental group – leaders Donald Fagen and Walter Becker (Singles: 21 Weeks, Albums: 91 Weeks)   pos/wks

30 Aug 75		DO IT AGAIN *ABC 4075*	39 4
11 Dec 76		HAITIAN DIVORCE *ABC 4152*	17 9
29 Jul 78		FM (NO STATIC AT ALL) (re) *MCA 374*	49 5
10 Mar 79		RIKKI DON'T LOSE THAT NUMBER *ABC 4241*	58 3
30 Mar 74		PRETZEL LOGIC *Probe SPBA 6282*	37 2
3 May 75		KATY LIED *ABC ABCL 5094*	13 6
20 Sep 75		CAN'T BUY A THRILL *ABC ABCL 5024*	38 5
22 May 76		THE ROYAL SCAM *ABC ABCL 5161*	11 13
8 Oct 77	●	AJA *ABC ABCL 5225*	5 10
2 Dec 78		GREATEST HITS *ABC BLD 616*	41 18

		pos/wks
29 Nov 80	GAUCHO *MCA MCF 3090*	27 12
3 Jul 82	GOLD *MCA MCF 3145*	44 6
26 Oct 85	REELIN' IN THE YEARS – THE VERY BEST OF STEELY DAN *MCA DANTV 1*	43 5
10 Oct 87	DO IT AGAIN – THE VERY BEST OF STEELY DAN *Telstar STAR 2297*	64 4
20 Nov 93	REMASTERED – THE BEST OF STEELY DAN *MCA MCD 10967*	42 5
28 Oct 95	ALIVE IN AMERICA *Giant 74321286912*	62 1
11 Mar 00	TWO AGAINST NATURE *Giant 74321621902*	11 5
21 Jun 03	EVERYTHING MUST GO *Reprise 9362484902*	21 3

Wout STEENHUIS *Holland, male instrumentalist – guitar, d. 12 Oct 1996 (Albums: 7 Weeks)* pos/wks

		pos/wks
21 Nov 81	HAWAIIAN PARADISE / CHRISTMAS *Warwick WW 510 6*	28 7

Gwen STEFANI (see also NO DOUBT)
US, female vocalist (Singles: 5 Weeks, Albums: 4 Weeks) pos/wks

		pos/wks
27 Nov 04 ●	WHAT YOU WAITING FOR? *Interscope 9864986*	4 5+
4 Dec 04	LOVE, ANGEL, MUSIC, BABY *Interscope 2103177*	14 4+

STEFY See DJH featuring STEFY

Jim STEINMAN
US, male producer (Singles: 9 Weeks, Albums: 25 Weeks) pos/wks

		pos/wks
4 Jul 81	ROCK AND ROLL DREAMS COME THROUGH *Epic EPC A 1236* [1]	52 7
23 Jun 84	TONIGHT IS WHAT IT MEANS TO BE YOUNG *MCA MCA 889* [2]	67 2
9 May 81 ●	BAD FOR GOOD *Epic EPC 84361*	7 25

[1] Jim Steinman, vocals by Rory Dodd [2] Jim Steinman and Fire Inc

STEINSKI and MASS MEDIA
US, male / female production group (Singles: 2 Weeks) pos/wks

		pos/wks
31 Jan 87	WE'LL BE RIGHT BACK *Fourth & Broadway BRW 59*	63 2

Mike STEIPHENSON See BURUNDI STEIPHENSON BLACK

STELLA BROWNE
UK, male production duo (Singles: 3 Weeks) pos/wks

		pos/wks
20 May 00	EVERY WOMAN NEEDS LOVE *Perfecto PERF 06*	55 1
9 Feb 02	NEVER KNEW LOVE *Perfecto PERF 26CDS*	42 1

STELLAR PROJECT featuring Brandi EMMA
Italy, male production trio and US, female vocalist (Singles: 4 Weeks) pos/wks

		pos/wks
14 Aug 04	GET UP STAND UP *Data DATA 74CDS*	14 4

STELLASTARR*
US, male / female vocal / instrumental group (Singles: 3 Weeks) pos/wks

		pos/wks
31 May 03	SOMEWHERE ACROSS FOREVER *Twenty-20 TWENTYCDS 001*	73 1
27 Sep 03	JENNY *Twenty-20 TWENTYCDS 002*	61 1
20 Mar 04	MY COCO *RCA 82876959082*	46 1

Doreen STEPHENS See Billy COTTON and his BAND

Richie STEPHENS
Jamaica, male vocalist (Singles: 3 Weeks) pos/wks

		pos/wks
15 May 93	LEGACY *Columbia 6592852* [1]	64 2
9 Aug 97	COME GIVE ME YOUR LOVE *Delirious 74321450442* [2]	61 1

[1] Mad Cobra featuring Richie Stephens [2] Richie Stephens and General Degree

Martin STEPHENSON and the DAINTEES *UK, male vocal / instrumental group (Singles: 7 Weeks, Albums: 11 Weeks)* pos/wks

		pos/wks
8 Nov 86	BOAT TO BOLIVIA *Kitchenware SL 27*	70 2
17 Jan 87	TROUBLE TOWN *Kitchenware SK 13* [1]	58 3
27 Jun 92	BIG SKY NEW LIGHT *Kitchenware SK 57*	71 2
17 May 86	BOAT TO BOLIVIA *Kitchenware KWLP 5*	85 3
16 Apr 88	GLADSOME HUMOUR AND BLUE *Kitchenware KWLP 8*	39 4
19 May 90	SALUTATION ROAD *Kitchenware 8281981*	35 3
25 Jul 92	THE BOY'S HEART *Kitchenware 8283242*	68 1

[1] Daintees

STEPPENWOLF *US / Canada, male vocal / instrumental group (Singles: 14 Weeks, Albums: 20 Weeks)* pos/wks

		pos/wks
11 Jun 69	BORN TO BE WILD (re) *Stateside SS 8017*	30 9
27 Feb 99	BORN TO BE WILD (re-issue) *MCA MCSTD 48104*	18 5
28 Feb 70	MONSTER *Stateside SSL 5021*	43 4
25 Apr 70	STEPPENWOLF *Stateside SSL 5020*	59 2
4 Jul 70	STEPPENWOLF LIVE *Stateside SSL 5029*	16 14

STEPS (123) *Top 500*

(see also H & CLAIRE; Russell WATSON; INTENSO PROJECT)

Steptacular pop vocal quintet; Lisa Scott-Lee, Claire Richards, Faye Tozer, Lee Latchford-Evans, Ian Watkins (aka H). The hard-working live act's 1999 tour was reportedly the biggest pop arena tour ever in the UK. They bagged 14 consecutive Top 5 singles, The Beatles being the only UK group to better this feat. Having sold more than 12 million records, they announced their split on Boxing Day 2001. Best-selling single: 'Heartbeat / Tragedy' 1,150,285 (Singles: 217 Weeks, Albums: 172 Weeks) pos/wks

		pos/wks
22 Nov 97	5, 6, 7, 8 *Jive JIVECD 438*	14 17
2 May 98 ●	LAST THING ON MY MIND *Jive 0518492*	6 14
5 Sep 98 ●	ONE FOR SORROW *Jive 0519092*	2 11
21 Nov 98 ★	HEARTBEAT / TRAGEDY *Jive 0519142* ◆	1 30
20 Mar 99 ●	BETTER BEST FORGOTTEN (re) *Ebul / Jive 0519242*	2 17
10 Apr 99 ●	THANK ABBA FOR THE MUSIC *Epic ABCD 1* [1]	4 13
24 Jul 99 ●	LOVE'S GOT A HOLD ON MY HEART (re) *Ebul / Jive 0519372*	2 12
23 Oct 99 ●	AFTER THE LOVE HAS GONE (re) *Ebul / Jive 0519462*	5 11
25 Dec 99 ●	SAY YOU'LL BE MINE / BETTER THE DEVIL YOU KNOW *Ebul 9201008*	4 17
15 Apr 00 ●	DEEPER SHADE OF BLUE *Ebul / Jive 9201022*	4 9
15 Jul 00 ●	WHEN I SAID GOODBYE / SUMMER OF LOVE *Ebul / Jive 9201162*	5 11
28 Oct 00 ★	STOMP *Ebul / Jive 9201212* ■	1 11
6 Jan 01 ●	IT'S THE WAY YOU MAKE ME FEEL / TOO BUSY THINKING 'BOUT MY BABY *Ebul / Jive 9201232*	2 11
16 Jun 01 ●	HERE AND NOW / YOU'LL BE SORRY *Ebul / Jive 9201322*	4 10
6 Oct 01 ●	CHAIN REACTION / ONE FOR SORROW (re-mix) *Ebul / Jive 9201422*	2 12
15 Dec 01 ●	WORDS ARE NOT ENOUGH / I KNOW HIM SO WELL *Ebul / Jive 9201452*	5 11
26 Sep 98 ●	STEP ONE *Jive 519112*	2 62
6 Nov 99 ★	STEPTACULAR *Jive 519442* ■	1 62
11 Nov 00 ●	BUZZ *Jive 9201172*	4 26
27 Oct 01 ★	GOLD – THE GREATEST HITS *Jive 9201412* ■	1 21
7 Dec 02	THE LAST DANCE *Jive 9201522*	57 1

[1] Steps, Tina Cousins, Cleopatra, B*Witched, Billie

STEREO MC's *UK, male / female vocal / rap group (Singles: 37 Weeks, Albums: 55 Weeks)* pos/wks

		pos/wks
29 Sep 90	ELEVATE MY MIND *Fourth & Broadway BRW 186*	74 1
9 Mar 91	LOST IN MUSIC *Fourth & Broadway BRW 198*	46 3
26 Sep 92	CONNECTED *Fourth & Broadway BRW 262*	18 6
5 Dec 92	STEP IT UP *Fourth & Broadway BRW 266*	12 12
20 Feb 93	GROUND LEVEL *Fourth & Broadway BRCD 268*	19 5
29 May 93	CREATION *Fourth & Broadway BRCD 276*	19 4
26 May 01	DEEP DOWN & DIRTY (re) *Island CID 777*	17 5
1 Sep 01	WE BELONG IN THIS WORLD TOGETHER *Island CID 782*	59 1
17 Oct 92 ●	CONNECTED *Fourth & Broadway BRCD 589*	2 52
9 Jun 01	DEEP DOWN & DIRTY *Island CID 8106*	17 3

STEREO NATION *UK, male vocal duo (Singles: 3 Weeks)* pos/wks

		pos/wks
17 Aug 96	I'VE BEEN WAITING *EMI Premier PRESCD 5*	53 1
27 Oct 01	LAILA *Wizard WIZ 015* [1]	44 2

[1] Taz / Stereo Nation

STEREOLAB *UK / France, male / female vocal / instrumental group (Singles: 6 Weeks, Albums: 11 Weeks)* pos/wks

		pos/wks
8 Jan 94	JENNY ONDIOLINE / FRENCH DISCO *Duophonic UHF DUHFCD 01*	75 1
30 Jul 94	PING PONG *Duophonic UHF DUHFCD 04*	45 2
12 Nov 94	WOW AND FLUTTER *Duophonic UHF DUHFCD 07*	70 1
2 Mar 96	CYBELE'S REVERIE *Duophonic UHF DUHFCD 10*	62 1
13 Sep 97	MISS MODULAR *Duophonic UHF DUHFCD 16*	60 1
18 Sep 93	TRANSIENT RANDOM NOISE BURSTS *Duophonic UHF DUHFCD 02*	62 1
20 Aug 94	MARS AUDIAC QUINTET *Duophonic UHF DUHFCD 05X*	16 3

		pos/wks
29 Apr 95	MUSIC FOR AMORPHOUS BODY STUDY CENTRE	
	Duophonic UHF DUHFCD 08	**59** 1
16 Sep 95	REFRIED ECTOPLASM (SWITCHED ON VOLUME 2)	
	Duophonic UHF DUHFCD 09	**30** 2
30 Mar 96	EMPEROR TOMATO KETCHUP *Duophonic UHF DUHFCD 11*	**27** 2
4 Oct 97	DOTS AND LOOPS *Duophonic UHF DUHFCD 17*	**19** 2

STEREOPHONICS (84) Top 500

1998 Best Newcomer Brit Award-winning rock trio – Kelly Jones (v/g), Richard Jones (b) and Stuart Cable (d) – from Cwmaman, Wales, UK. Their 14 hit singles and two chart-topping albums of new material between 1997 and 2001 cannot be bettered by any other group (Singles: 129 Weeks, Albums: 348 Weeks)　pos/wks

		pos/wks
29 Mar 97	LOCAL BOY IN THE PHOTOGRAPH *V2 SPHD 2*	**51** 1
31 May 97	MORE LIFE IN A TRAMP'S VEST *V2 SPHD 4*	**33** 2
23 Aug 97	A THOUSAND TREES *V2 VVR 5000443*	**22** 3
8 Nov 97	TRAFFIC *V2 VVR 5000948*	**20** 3
21 Feb 98	LOCAL BOY IN THE PHOTOGRAPH (re-issue) *V2 VVR 5001263*	**14** 4
21 Nov 98 ●	THE BARTENDER AND THE THIEF *V2 VVR 5004653*	**3** 12
6 Mar 99 ●	JUST LOOKING (re) *V2 VVR 5005303*	**4** 9
15 May 99 ●	PICK A PART THAT'S NEW *V2 VVR 5006778*	**4** 9
4 Sep 99	I WOULDN'T BELIEVE YOUR RADIO (re) *V2 VVR 5008823*	**11** 7
20 Nov 99	HURRY UP AND WAIT (re) *V2 VVR 5009323*	**11** 8
18 Mar 00 ●	MAMA TOLD ME NOT TO COME *Gut CDGUT 031* [1]	**4** 7
31 Mar 01 ●	MR WRITER *V2 VVR 5015933*	**5** 12
23 Jun 01 ●	HAVE A NICE DAY *V2 VVR 5016243*	**5** 9
6 Oct 01	STEP ON MY OLD SIZE NINES *V2 VVR 5016253*	**16** 5
15 Dec 01 ●	HANDBAGS AND GLADRAGS (re) *V2 VVR 5017753*	**4** 15
13 Apr 02	VEGAS TWO TIMES *V2 VVR 5019173*	**23** 2
31 May 03 ●	MADAME HELGA *V2 VVR 5021743*	**4** 4
2 Aug 03 ●	MAYBE TOMORROW *V2 VVR 5021893*	**3** 8
22 Nov 03	SINCE I TOLD YOU IT'S OVER *V2 VVR 5022623*	**16** 4
21 Feb 04 ●	MOVIESTAR *V2 VVR 5024658*	**5** 5
6 Sep 97 ●	WORD GETS AROUND *V2 VVR 1000438*	**6** 117
20 Mar 99 ★	PERFORMANCE AND COCKTAILS *V2 VVR 1004498* ■	**1** 101
21 Apr 01 ★	JUST ENOUGH EDUCATION TO PERFORM *V2 VVR 1015838* ■	**1** 87
14 Jun 03 ★	YOU GOTTA GO THERE TO COME BACK *V2 VVR 1021902* ■	**1** 43

[1] Tom Jones and Stereophonics

STEREOPOL featuring NEVADA
Sweden / UK, male production / vocal group and UK male vocalist – Nevado Cato (Singles: 2 Weeks)　pos/wks

		pos/wks
29 Mar 03	DANCIN' TONIGHT *Rulin' 28CDS*	**36** 2

STERIOGRAM
New Zealand, male vocal / instrumental group (Singles: 4 Weeks)　pos/wks

		pos/wks
20 Nov 04	WALKIE TALKIE MAN *EMI CDEMS 652*	**19** 4

STETSASONIC *US, male rap group (Singles: 3 Weeks)*　pos/wks

		pos/wks
24 Sep 88	TALKIN' ALL THAT JAZZ *Breakout USA 640*	**73** 2
7 Nov 98	TALKIN' ALL THAT JAZZ (re-mix) *Tommy Boy TBCD 7310A*	**54** 1

STEVE and EYDIE See Eydie GORME; Steve LAWRENCE

April STEVENS See Nino TEMPO and April STEVENS

Cat STEVENS (135) Top 500

Critically acclaimed folk-pop singer / songwriter, b. Steven Georgiou, 21 Jul 1947, London, UK, whose songs have been recorded by many top acts. One of the world's biggest album sellers in 1970s. Semi-retired in 1979, converted to Islam and changed his name to Yusuf Islam. Gave royalties for Boyzone's version of 'Father and Son' to charity (Singles: 97 Weeks, Albums: 274 Weeks)　pos/wks

		pos/wks
20 Oct 66	I LOVE MY DOG *Deram DM 102*	**28** 7
12 Jan 67 ●	MATTHEW AND SON *Deram DM 110*	**2** 10
30 Mar 67 ●	I'M GONNA GET ME A GUN *Deram DM 118*	**6** 10
2 Aug 67	A BAD NIGHT *Deram DM 140*	**20** 8
20 Dec 67	KITTY *Deram DM 156*	**47** 1
27 Jun 70 ●	LADY D'ARBANVILLE *Island WIP 6086*	**8** 13
28 Aug 71	MOON SHADOW *Island WIP 6092*	**22** 11
1 Jan 72 ●	MORNING HAS BROKEN *Island WIP 6121*	**9** 13
9 Dec 72	CAN'T KEEP IT IN *Island WIP 6152*	**13** 12
24 Aug 74	ANOTHER SATURDAY NIGHT *Island WIP 6206*	**19** 8
2 Jul 77	(REMEMBER THE DAYS OF THE) OLD SCHOOL YARD	
	Island WIP 6387	**44** 3
25 Dec 04 ●	FATHER AND SON *Polydor 9869406* [1]	**2** 1+
25 Mar 67 ●	MATTHEW AND SON *Deram SML 1004*	**7** 16
11 Jul 70	MONA BONE JAKON *Island ILPS 9118*	**63** 4

		pos/wks
28 Nov 70	TEA FOR THE TILLERMAN *Island ILPS 9135*	**20** 31
2 Oct 71 ●	TEASER AND THE FIRECAT *Island ILPS 9154*	**3** 93
7 Oct 72 ●	CATCH BULL AT FOUR *Island ILPS 9206* ▲	**2** 27
21 Jul 73	FOREIGNER *Island ILPS 9240*	**3** 10
6 Apr 74 ●	BUDDAH AND THE CHOCOLATE BOX *Island ILPS 9274*	**3** 15
19 Jul 75 ●	GREATEST HITS *Island ILPS 9310*	**2** 24
14 May 77	IZITSO *Island ILPS 9451*	**18** 15
3 Feb 90 ●	THE VERY BEST OF CAT STEVENS *Island CATV 1*	**4** 16
27 Nov 99	REMEMBER CAT STEVENS – THE ULTIMATE COLLECTION	
	Island CID 8079	**31** 6
25 Oct 03 ●	THE VERY BEST OF CAT STEVENS *Universal TV 9811208*	**6** 17+

[1] Ronan Keating featuring Yusuf

The two 'The Very Best of Cat Stevens' albums are different

Connie STEVENS
US, female vocalist / actor – Concetta Ingolia (Singles: 20 Weeks)　pos/wks

		pos/wks
5 May 60 ●	SIXTEEN REASONS (re) *Warner Bros. WB 3*	**9** 12
5 May 60	KOOKIE KOOKIE (LEND ME YOUR COMB)	
	Warner Bros. WB 5 [1]	**27** 8

[1] Edward Byrnes and Connie Stevens

Rachel STEVENS (see also S CLUB 7)
UK, female vocalist (Singles: 34 Weeks, Albums: 15 Weeks)　pos/wks

		pos/wks
27 Sep 03 ●	SWEET DREAMS MY L.A. EX *19 / Polydor 9811874*	**2** 10
20 Dec 03	FUNKY DORY *Polydor 9614984*	**26** 4
24 Jul 04 ●	SOME GIRLS *Polydor 9867433*	**2** 12
16 Oct 04 ●	MORE MORE MORE *Polydor 9868325*	**3** 8
11 Oct 03 ●	FUNKY DORY *19 / Polydor 9865702*	**9** 15

A new version of 'Funky Dory', with extra tracks, peaked at No.13 in Aug 2004

Ray STEVENS *US, male vocalist –*
Ray Ragsdale (Singles: 64 Weeks, Albums: 8 Weeks)　pos/wks

		pos/wks
16 May 70 ●	EVERYTHING IS BEAUTIFUL *CBS 4953* ▲	**6** 16
13 Mar 71 ●	BRIDGET THE MIDGET (THE QUEEN OF THE BLUES) *CBS 7070*	**2** 14
25 Mar 72	TURN YOUR RADIO ON *CBS 7634*	**33** 4
25 May 74 ★	THE STREAK *Janus 6146 201* ▲	**1** 12
21 Jun 75	MISTY *Janus 6146 204*	**2** 10
27 Sep 75	INDIAN LOVE CALL *Janus 6146 205*	**34** 4
5 Mar 77	IN THE MOOD *Warner Bros. K 16875*	**31** 4
26 Sep 70	EVERYTHING IS BEAUTIFUL *CBS 64074*	**62** 1
13 Sep 75	MISTY *Janus 9109 401*	**23** 7

'In the Mood' features Ray Stevens, not as a conventional vocalist but as a group of chickens

Ricky STEVENS *UK, male vocalist (Singles: 7 Weeks)*　pos/wks

		pos/wks
14 Dec 61	I CRIED FOR YOU *Columbia DB 4739*	**34** 7

Shakin' STEVENS (100) Top 500

With UK single sales totalling 7,108,330, Shaky, b. Michael Barratt, 4 Mar 1948, Glamorgan, Wales, performs and records under a broad umbrella of styles from rock and country blues to cajun. Shares with The Beatles (60s) and Elton John (70s) the distinction of being the most successful UK singles chart performer of a decade (80s) (Singles: 277 Weeks, Albums: 158 Weeks)　pos/wks

		pos/wks
16 Feb 80	HOT DOG *Epic EPC 8090*	**24** 9
16 Aug 80	MARIE MARIE *Epic EPC 8725*	**19** 10
28 Feb 81 ★	THIS OLE HOUSE *Epic EPC 9555*	**1** 17
2 May 81 ●	YOU DRIVE ME CRAZY *Epic A 1165*	**2** 12
25 Jul 81 ★	GREEN DOOR *Epic A 1354*	**1** 12
10 Oct 81 ●	IT'S RAINING *Epic A 1643*	**10** 9
16 Jan 82 ★	OH JULIE *Epic EPC A 1742*	**1** 10
24 Apr 82 ●	SHIRLEY *Epic EPC A 2087*	**6** 6
21 Aug 82	GIVE ME YOUR HEART TONIGHT *Epic EPC A 2656*	**11** 10
16 Oct 82 ●	I'LL BE SATISFIED *Epic EPC A 2846*	**10** 8
11 Dec 82 ●	THE SHAKIN' STEVENS EP *Epic SHAKY 1*	**2** 7
23 Jul 83	IT'S LATE *Epic EPC A 3565*	**11** 7
5 Nov 83 ●	CRY JUST A LITTLE BIT *Epic A 3774*	**3** 12
7 Jan 84 ●	A ROCKIN' GOOD WAY *Epic A 4071* [1]	**5** 9
24 Mar 84 ●	A LOVE WORTH WAITING FOR *Epic A 4291*	**2** 10
15 Sep 84 ●	A LETTER TO YOU *Epic A 4677*	**10** 8
24 Nov 84 ●	TEARDROPS *Epic A 4882*	**5** 9
2 Mar 85	BREAKING UP MY HEART *Epic A 6072*	**14** 7
12 Oct 85	LIPSTICK POWDER AND PAINT *Epic A 6610*	**11** 9
7 Dec 85 ★	MERRY CHRISTMAS EVERYONE (re) *Epic A 6769*	**1** 11

		pos/wks
8 Feb 86	TURNING AWAY *Epic A 6819*	**15** 7
1 Nov 86	BECAUSE I LOVE YOU *Epic SHAKY 2*	**14** 10
27 Jun 87	A LITTLE BOOGIE WOOGIE (IN THE BACK OF MY MIND)	
	Epic SHAKY 3	**12** 10
19 Sep 87	COME SEE ABOUT ME *Epic SHAKY 4*	**24** 6
28 Nov 87 ●	WHAT DO YOU WANT TO MAKE THOSE EYES AT ME FOR	
	Epic SHAKY 5	**5** 8
23 Jul 88	FEEL THE NEED IN ME *Epic SHAKY 6*	**26** 5
15 Oct 88	HOW MANY TEARS CAN YOU HIDE *Epic SHAKY 7*	**47** 4
10 Dec 88	TRUE LOVE *Epic SHAKY 8*	**23** 6
18 Feb 89	JEZEBEL *Epic SHAKY 9*	**58** 2
13 May 89	LOVE ATTACK *Epic SHAKY 10*	**28** 4
24 Feb 90	I MIGHT *Epic SHAKY 11*	**18** 6
12 May 90	YES I DO *Epic SHAKY 12*	**60** 2
18 Aug 90	PINK CHAMPAGNE *Epic SHAKY 13*	**59** 2
13 Oct 90	MY CUTIE CUTIE *Epic SHAKY 14*	**75** 1
15 Dec 90	THE BEST CHRISTMAS OF THEM ALL *Epic SHAKY 15*	**19** 4
7 Dec 91	I'LL BE HOME THIS CHRISTMAS *Epic 6576507*	**34** 5
10 Oct 92	RADIO *Epic 6584367* [2]	**37** 3
15 Mar 80	TAKE ONE! *Epic EPC 83978*	**62** 2
4 Apr 81 ●	THIS OLE HOUSE *Epic EPC 84985*	**2** 28
8 Aug 81	SHAKIN' STEVENS *Hallmark / Pickwick SHM 3065*	**34** 5
19 Sep 81 ★	SHAKY *Epic EPC 10027*	**1** 28
9 Oct 82 ●	GIVE ME YOUR HEART TONIGHT *Epic EPC 10035*	**3** 18
26 Nov 83	THE BOP WON'T STOP *Epic EPC 86301*	**21** 27
17 Nov 84 ●	GREATEST HITS *Epic EPC 10047*	**8** 22
16 Nov 85	LIPSTICK POWDER AND PAINT *Epic EPC 26646*	**37** 9
31 Oct 87	LET'S BOOGIE *Epic 460 1261*	**59** 7
19 Nov 88	A WHOLE LOTTA SHAKY *Epic MOOD 5*	**42** 8
20 Oct 90	THERE'S TWO KINDS OF MUSIC: ROCK 'N' ROLL	
	Telstar STAR 2454	**65** 2
31 Oct 92	THE EPIC YEARS *Epic 4724222* [1]	**57** 2

[1] Shaky and Bonnie [2] Shaky featuring Roger Taylor [1] Shaky

Tracks on The Shakin' Stevens EP: Blue Christmas / Que Sera Sera / Josephine / Lawdy Miss Clawdy. 'Merry Christmas Everyone' re-entered the chart and peaked at No.58 in Dec 1986

STEVENSON'S ROCKET
UK, male vocal / instrumental group (Singles: 5 Weeks) pos/wks

		pos/wks
29 Nov 75	ALRIGHT BABY (re) *Magnet MAG 47*	**37** 5

Al STEWART
UK, male vocalist (Singles: 6 Weeks, Albums: 20 Weeks) pos/wks

		pos/wks
29 Jan 77	YEAR OF THE CAT *RCA 2771*	**31** 6
11 Apr 70	ZERO SHE FLIES *CBS 63848*	**40** 4
5 Feb 77	YEAR OF THE CAT *RCA RS 1082*	**38** 7
21 Oct 78	TIME PASSAGES *RCA PL 25173*	**39** 1
6 Sep 80	24 CARAT *RCA PL 25306*	**55** 6
9 Jun 84	RUSSIANS AND AMERICANS *RCA PL 70307*	**83** 2

Amii STEWART
US, female vocalist (Singles: 61 Weeks) pos/wks

		pos/wks
7 Apr 79 ●	KNOCK ON WOOD *Atlantic / Hansa K 11214* ▲	**6** 12
16 Jun 79 ●	LIGHT MY FIRE / 137 DISCO HEAVEN (MEDLEY)	
	Atlantic / Hansa K 11278	**5** 11
3 Nov 79	JEALOUSY *Atlantic / Hansa K 11386*	**58** 3
19 Jan 80	THE LETTER / PARADISE BIRD *Atlantic / Hansa K 11424*	**39** 4
19 Jul 80	MY GUY – MY GIRL (MEDLEY) *Atlantic / Hansa K 11550* [1]	**39** 5
29 Dec 84	FRIENDS *RCA 471*	**12** 11
17 Aug 85 ●	KNOCK ON WOOD / LIGHT MY FIRE (re-mix)	
	Sedition EDIT 3303	**7** 12
25 Jan 86	MY GUY – MY GIRL (MEDLEY) *Sedition EDIT 3310* [2]	**63** 3

[1] Amii Stewart and Johnny Bristol [2] Amii Stewart and Deon Estus

Andy STEWART
UK, male vocalist, b. 20 Dec 1933, d. 11 Oct 1993 (Singles: 67 Weeks, Albums: 2 Weeks) pos/wks

		pos/wks
15 Dec 60	DONALD WHERE'S YOUR TROOSERS	
	Top Rank JAR 427 [1]	**37** 1
12 Jan 61	A SCOTTISH SOLDIER (re) *Top Rank JAR 512* [1]	**19** 40
1 Jun 61	THE BATTLE'S O'ER *Top Rank JAR 565* [1]	**28** 13
12 Aug 65	DR FINLAY (re) *HMV POP 1454*	**43** 5
9 Dec 89 ●	DONALD WHERE'S YOUR TROOSERS (re-issue)	
	Stone SON 2353 [1]	**4** 8
3 Feb 62	ANDY STEWART *Top Rank 35116*	**13** 2

[1] Andy Stewart with the Michael Sammes Singers

Billy STEWART
US, male vocalist, b. 24 Mar 1937, d. 17 Jan 1970 (Singles: 2 Weeks) pos/wks

		pos/wks
8 Sep 66	SUMMERTIME *Chess CRS 8040*	**39** 2

Dave STEWART
UK, male instrumentalist – keyboards (Singles: 30 Weeks) pos/wks

		pos/wks
14 Mar 81	WHAT BECOMES OF THE BROKEN HEARTED	
	Stiff BROKEN 1 [1]	**13** 10
19 Sep 81 ★	IT'S MY PARTY *Stiff BROKEN 2* [2]	**1** 13
13 Aug 83	BUSY DOING NOTHING *Broken BROKEN 5* [2]	**49** 4
14 Jun 86	THE LOCOMOTION *Broken BROKEN 8* [2]	**70** 3

[1] Dave Stewart: Guest vocals: Colin Blunstone [2] Dave Stewart with Barbara Gaskin

David A STEWART (see also EURYTHMICS; VEGAS; The TOURISTS) UK, male instrumentalist – guitar (Singles: 21 Weeks, Albums: 7 Weeks) pos/wks

		pos/wks
24 Feb 90 ●	LILY WAS HERE *RCA ZB 43045* [1]	**6** 12
18 Aug 90	JACK TALKING *RCA PB 43907* [2]	**69** 2
3 Sep 94	HEART OF STONE *East West YZ 845CD* [3]	**36** 5
6 Nov 04	OLD HABITS DIE HARD *Virgin VSCDX 1887* [4]	**45** 2
7 Apr 90	LILY WAS HERE (FILM SOUNDTRACK) *Anxious ZL 74233*	**35** 5
15 Sep 90	DAVE STEWART AND THE SPIRITUAL COWBOYS	
	RCA OB 74710 [1]	**38** 2

[1] David A Stewart featuring Candy Dulfer [2] Dave Stewart and the Spiritual Cowboys [3] Dave Stewart [4] Mick Jagger and Dave Stewart [1] Dave Stewart and the Spiritual Cowboys

Jermaine STEWART
US, male vocalist, b. 7 Sep 1957, d. 17 Mar 1997 (Singles: 42 Weeks, Albums: 12 Weeks) pos/wks

		pos/wks
9 Aug 86 ●	WE DON'T HAVE TO ... TAKE OUR CLOTHES OFF TO HAVE	
	A GOOD TIME *10 TEN 96*	**2** 14
1 Nov 86	JODY *10 TEN 143*	**50** 4
16 Jan 88	SAY IT AGAIN *10 TEN 188*	**7** 12
2 Apr 88	GET LUCKY *Siren SRN 82*	**13** 9
24 Sep 88	DON'T TALK DIRTY TO ME *Siren SRN 86*	**61** 3
4 Oct 86	FRANTIC ROMANTIC *10 DIX 26*	**49** 4
5 Mar 88	SAY IT AGAIN *Siren SRNLP 14*	**32** 8

John STEWART
US, male vocalist (Singles: 6 Weeks) pos/wks

		pos/wks
30 Jun 79	GOLD *RSO 35*	**43** 6

Rod STEWART 〔 11 〕 〔 Top 500 〕
(see also GLASS TIGER; PYTHON LEE JACKSON) *World-renowned rock superstar, b. 10 Jan 1945, London, UK, of Scottish parents. In the 1960s "Rod the Mod" recorded solo singles for Decca, EMI and Immediate but is best remembered in that period as a member of The Five Dimensions, Hoochie Coochie Men, Steampacket, Shotgun Express and The Jeff Beck Group. Between 1969 and 1975, the gravel-voiced vocalist fronted The Faces as well as having a successful solo career. Over the past 33 years, Stewart has played to packed stadiums worldwide and amassed a vast collection of platinum and gold albums. In the US, he is one of the top selling UK artists of all time with 11 Top 10 albums (and a No.1 span of 23 years) and 16 Top 10 singles. He is also the only UK solo artist to top the US singles or albums charts this century. In Britain, he has scored 27 Top 10 LPs, including seven solo No.1s. His songwriting skills have earned him a Lifetime Ivor Novello Award in the UK, while in the US he has recently been nominated for the prestigious Songwriters' Hall of Fame. Stewart, whose love life also attracts much media attention, earned a Grammy Living Legend Award in 1989 (Singles: 477 Weeks, Albums: 904 Weeks)* pos/wks

		pos/wks
4 Sep 71	REASON TO BELIEVE *Mercury 6052 097*	**19** 2
18 Sep 71 ★	MAGGIE MAY *Mercury 6052 097* ▲	**1** 19
12 Aug 72 ●	YOU WEAR IT WELL *Mercury 6052 171*	**1** 12
18 Nov 72 ●	ANGEL / WHAT MADE MILWAUKEE FAMOUS (HAS MADE	
	A LOSER OUT OF ME) *Mercury 6052 198*	**4** 11
5 May 73	I'VE BEEN DRINKING *RAK RR 4* [1]	**27** 6
8 Sep 73 ●	OH! NO NOT MY BABY *Mercury 6052 371*	**6** 9
5 Oct 74 ●	FAREWELL – BRING IT ON HOME TO ME / YOU SEND ME	
	Mercury 6167 033	**7** 7
7 Dec 74	YOU CAN MAKE ME DANCE SING OR ANYTHING (EVEN TAKE	
	THE DOG FOR A WALK, MEND A FUSE, FOLD AWAY THE	
	IRONING BOARD, OR ANY OTHER DOMESTIC SHORT	
	COMINGS) *Warner Bros. K 16494* [2]	**12** 9
16 Aug 75 ★	SAILING (2re) *Warner Bros. K 16600*	**1** 34
15 Nov 75 ●	THIS OLD HEART OF MINE *Riva 1*	**4** 9

5 Jun 76 ●	TONIGHT'S THE NIGHT *Riva 3* ▲	.5	9
21 Aug 76 ●	THE KILLING OF GEORGIE *Riva 4*	.2	10
20 Nov 76	GET BACK *Riva 6*	.11	9
4 Dec 76	MAGGIE MAY (re-issue) *Mercury 6160 006*	.31	7
23 Apr 77 ★	I DON'T WANT TO TALK ABOUT IT / FIRST CUT IS THE DEEPEST *Riva 7*	.1	13
15 Oct 77 ●	YOU'RE IN MY HEART *Riva 11*	.3	10
28 Jan 78 ●	HOT LEGS / I WAS ONLY JOKING *Riva 10*	.5	8
27 May 78 ●	OLE OLA (MULHER BRASILEIRA) *Riva 15* [3]	.4	5
18 Nov 78 ★	DA YA THINK I'M SEXY? *Riva 17* ▲	.1	13
3 Feb 79	AIN'T LOVE A BITCH *Riva 18*	.11	8
5 May 79	BLONDES (HAVE MORE FUN) *Riva 19*	.63	3
31 May 80	IF LOVING YOU IS WRONG (I DON'T WANT TO BE RIGHT) *Riva 23*	.23	9
8 Nov 80	PASSION *Riva 26*	.17	10
20 Dec 80	MY GIRL *Riva 28*	.32	7
17 Oct 81 ●	TONIGHT I'M YOURS (DON'T HURT ME) *Riva 33*	.8	13
12 Dec 81	YOUNG TURKS *Riva 34*	.11	9
27 Feb 82	HOW LONG *Riva 35*	.41	4
4 Jun 83 ★	BABY JANE *Warner Bros. W 9608*	.1	14
27 Aug 83 ●	WHAT AM I GONNA DO (I'M SO IN LOVE WITH YOU) *Warner Bros. W 9564*	.3	8
10 Dec 83	SWEET SURRENDER *Warner Bros. W 9440*	.23	9
26 May 84	INFATUATION *Warner Bros. W 9256*	.27	7
28 Jul 84	SOME GUYS HAVE ALL THE LUCK *Warner Bros. W 9204*	.15	10
24 May 86	LOVE TOUCH (re) *Warner Bros. W 8668*	.27	8
12 Jul 86 ●	EVERY BEAT OF MY HEART *Warner Bros. W 8625*	.2	9
20 Sep 86	ANOTHER HEARTACHE *Warner Bros. W 8631*	.54	2
28 May 88	LOST IN YOU *Warner Bros. W 7927*	.21	6
13 Aug 88	FOREVER YOUNG *Warner Bros. W 7796*	.57	3
6 May 89	MY HEART CAN'T TELL YOU NO *Warner Bros. W 7729*	.49	4
11 Nov 89	THIS OLD HEART OF MINE *Warner Bros. W 2686* [4]	.51	3
13 Jan 90 ●	DOWNTOWN TRAIN *Warner Bros. W 2647*	.10	12
24 Nov 90 ●	IT TAKES TWO *Warner Bros. ROD 1* [5]	.5	8
16 Mar 91 ●	RHYTHM OF MY HEART *Warner Bros. W 0017*	.3	11
15 Jun 91 ●	THE MOTOWN SONG *Warner Bros. W 0030* [6]	.10	8
7 Sep 91	BROKEN ARROW *Warner Bros. W 0059*	.54	3
7 Mar 92	PEOPLE GET READY *Epic 6577567* [1]	.49	3
18 Apr 92	YOUR SONG / BROKEN ARROW (re-issue) *Warner Bros. W 0104*	.41	4
5 Dec 92 ●	TOM TRAUBERT'S BLUES (WALTZING MATILDA) *Warner Bros. W 0144*	.6	9
20 Feb 93	RUBY TUESDAY *Warner Bros. W 0158CD*	.11	6
17 Apr 93	SHOTGUN WEDDING *Warner Bros. W 0171CD*	.21	4
26 Jun 93 ●	HAVE I TOLD YOU LATELY *Warner Bros. W 0185CD*	.5	9
21 Aug 93	REASON TO BELIEVE *Warner Bros. W 0198CD1*	.51	3
18 Dec 93	PEOPLE GET READY *Warner Bros. W 0226CD1*	.45	4
15 Jan 94 ●	ALL FOR LOVE *A&M 5804772* [7] ▲	.2	13
20 May 95	YOU'RE THE STAR *Warner Bros. W 0296CD*	.19	5
19 Aug 95	LADY LUCK *Warner Bros. W 0310CD*	.56	1
15 Jun 96	PURPLE HEATHER *Warner Bros. W 0354CD* [8]	.16	5
14 Dec 96	IF WE FALL IN LOVE TONIGHT *Warner Bros. W 0380CD*	.58	1
1 Nov 97 ●	DA YA THINK I'M SEXY? *All Around the World CDGLOBE 150* [9]	.7	10
30 May 98	OOH LA LA *Warner Brothers W 0446CD*	.16	5
5 Sep 98	ROCKS *Warner Brothers W 0452CD1*	.55	1
17 Apr 99	FAITH OF THE HEART *Universal UND 56235*	.60	1
24 Mar 01	I CAN'T DENY IT *Atlantic AT 0096CD*	.26	2
3 Oct 70	GASOLINE ALLEY *Vertigo 6360 500*	.62	7
24 Jul 71 ★	EVERY PICTURE TELLS A STORY *Mercury 6338 063* ▲	.1	81
5 Aug 72 ★	NEVER A DULL MOMENT *Philips 6499 153*	.1	36
25 Aug 73 ★	SING IT AGAIN ROD *Mercury 6499 484*	.1	30
26 Jan 74 ★	OVERTURE AND BEGINNERS *Mercury 9100 001* [1]	.3	7
19 Oct 74 ★	SMILER *Mercury 9104 011* ■	.1	20
30 Aug 75 ★	ATLANTIC CROSSING *Warner Bros. K 56151* ■	.1	88
3 Jul 76 ★	A NIGHT ON THE TOWN *Riva RVLP 1*	.1	47
16 Jul 77	THE BEST OF ROD STEWART *Mercury 6643 030*	.18	22
19 Nov 77 ●	FOOT LOOSE & FANCY FREE *Riva RVLP 5*	.3	26
21 Jan 78	ATLANTIC CROSSING (re-issue) *Riva RVLP 4*	.60	1
9 Dec 78 ●	BLONDES HAVE MORE FUN *Riva RVLP 8* ▲	.3	31
10 Nov 79 ★	GREATEST HITS *Riva ROD TV 1*	.1	74
22 Nov 80 ●	FOOLISH BEHAVIOUR *Riva RVLP 11*	.4	13
14 Nov 81 ●	TONIGHT I'M YOURS *Riva RVLP 14*	.8	21
13 Nov 82	ABSOLUTELY LIVE *Riva RVLP 17*	.35	5
18 Jun 83 ●	BODY WISHES *Warner Bros. K 923 8771*	.5	27
23 Jun 84	CAMOUFLAGE *Warner Bros. 925095*	.8	17
5 Jul 86 ●	EVERY BEAT OF MY HEART *Warner Bros. WX 53*	.5	17
4 Jun 88	OUT OF ORDER *Warner Bros. WX 152*	.11	8
25 Nov 89 ●	THE BEST OF ROD STEWART *Warner Bros. WX 314*	.3	127

6 Apr 91 ●	VAGABOND HEART *Warner Bros. WX 408*	.2	27
7 Nov 92	THE BEST OF ROD STEWART AND THE FACES 1971-1975 *Mercury 5141802* [1]	.58	1
6 Mar 93 ●	ROD STEWART LEAD VOCALIST *Warner Bros. 9362452582*	.3	9
5 Jun 93 ●	UNPLUGGED ... AND SEATED *Warner Bros. 9362452892*	.2	27
10 Jun 95 ●	A SPANNER IN THE WORKS *Warner Bros. 9362458672*	.4	12
16 Nov 96 ●	IF WE FALL IN LOVE TONIGHT *Warner Bros. 9362464672*	.8	19
13 Jun 98 ●	WHEN WE WERE THE NEW BOYS *Warner Bros. 9362467922*	.2	11
7 Apr 01 ●	HUMAN *Atlantic 7567929742*	.9	8
24 Nov 01 ●	THE STORY SO FAR – THE VERY BEST OF ROD STEWART *Warner Bros. 8122735812*	.7	36
9 Nov 02 ●	IT HAD TO BE YOU ... THE GREAT AMERICAN SONGBOOK *J 74321968672*	.8	18
1 Nov 03 ●	AS TIME GOES BY ... THE GREAT AMERICAN SONGBOOK VOLUME II *J 82876574842*	.4	17
1 Nov 03	CHANGING FACES – THE VERY BEST OF ROD STEWART & THE FACES – THE DEFINITIVE COLLECTION 1969-1974 *Universal TV 9812604* [1]	.13	5
30 Oct 04 ●	STARDUST ... THE GREAT AMERICAN SONGBOOK VOLUME III *J 82876659282* ▲	.3	9+

[1] Jeff Beck and Rod Stewart [2] The Faces / Rod Stewart [3] Rod Stewart featuring the Scottish World Cup Squad '78 [4] Rod Stewart featuring Ronald Isley [5] Rod Stewart and Tina Turner [6] Rod Stewart with backing vocals by The Temptations [7] Bryan Adams, Rod Stewart and Sting [8] Rod Stewart with the Scottish Euro '96 Squad [9] N-Trance featuring Rod Stewart [1] Rod Stewart & The Faces

'Reason to Believe' and 'People Get Ready' in 1993 are re-recordings. 'Reason to Believe' additionally credits Ronnie Wood on the sleeve. 'Sailing' re-entries peaked at No.3 in 1976 and No.41 in 1987. The two 'The Best of Rod Stewart' albums are different. 'Greatest Hits' changed label / number to Warner Bros. K 56744 during its chart run.

STEX
UK, male / female vocal / instrumental group (Singles: 2 Weeks) pos/wks

19 Jan 91	STILL FEEL THE RAIN *Some Bizzare SBZ 7002*	.63	2

STICKY featuring MS DYNAMITE *UK, male producer –*
Richard Forbes and female rapper (Singles: 6 Weeks) pos/wks

23 Jun 01	BOOO! *ffrr / Public Demand / Social Circles FCD 399*	.12	6

STIFF LITTLE FINGERS *UK, male vocal /*
instrumental group (Singles: 39 Weeks, Albums: 57 Weeks) pos/wks

29 Sep 79	STRAW DOGS *Chrysalis CHS 2368*	.44	4
16 Feb 80	AT THE EDGE *Chrysalis CHS 2406*	.15	9
24 May 80	NOBODY'S HERO / TIN SOLDIERS *Chrysalis CHS 2424*	.36	5
2 Aug 80	BACK TO FRONT *Chrysalis CHS 2447*	.49	4
28 Mar 81	JUST FADE AWAY *Chrysalis CHS 2510*	.47	6
30 May 81	SILVER LINING *Chrysalis CHS 2517*	.68	3
23 Jan 82	LISTEN (EP) *Chrysalis CHS 2580*	.33	6
18 Sep 82	BITS OF KIDS *Chrysalis CHS 2637*	.73	2
3 Mar 79	INFLAMMABLE MATERIAL *Rough Trade ROUGH 1*	.14	19
15 Mar 80 ●	NOBODY'S HEROES *Chrysalis CHR 1270*	.8	10
20 Sep 80	HANX! *Chrysalis CHR 1300*	.9	5
25 Apr 81	GO FOR IT *Chrysalis CHX 1339*	.14	8
2 Oct 82	NOW THEN *Chrysalis CHR 1400*	.24	6
12 Feb 83	ALL THE BEST *Chrysalis CTY 1414*	.19	9

Tracks on Listen (EP): That's When Your Blood Bumps / Two Guitars Clash / Listen / Sad-Eyed People

Curtis STIGERS
US, male vocalist (Singles: 34 Weeks, Albums: 52 Weeks) pos/wks

18 Jan 92 ●	I WONDER WHY *Arista 114716*	.5	10
28 Mar 92 ●	YOU'RE ALL THAT MATTERS TO ME *Arista 115273*	.6	12
11 Jul 92	SLEEPING WITH THE LIGHTS ON *Arista 74321102307*	.53	4
17 Oct 92	NEVER SAW A MIRACLE *Arista 74321117257*	.34	4
3 Jun 95	THIS TIME *Arista 74321286962*	.28	3
2 Dec 95	KEEP ME FROM THE COLD *Arista 74321319162*	.57	1
29 Feb 92 ●	CURTIS STIGERS *Arista 261953*	.7	50
1 Jul 95	TIME WAS *Arista 74321282792*	.34	2

The STILLS *Canada, male vocal /*
instrumental group (Singles: 5 Weeks, Albums: 1 Week) pos/wks

6 Sep 03	REMEMBERESE *679 Recordings 679L 026CD*	.75	1
28 Feb 04	LOLA STARS AND STRIPES *679 Recordings 679L 036CD*	.39	2
8 May 04	CHANGES ARE NO GOOD *679 Recordings / Vice 679L 072CD1*	.51	1

		pos/wks
28 Aug 04	STILL IN LOVE SONG *679 Recordings / Vice 679L 079CD2* **45**	1
6 Mar 04	LOGIC WILL BREAK YOUR HEART	
	679 Recordings / Vice 7567836742 ....**66**	1

Stephen STILLS (see also CROSBY, STILLS, NASH and YOUNG) *US, male vocalist / instrumentalist (Singles: 8 Weeks, Albums: 27 Weeks)*

		pos/wks
13 Mar 71	LOVE THE ONE YOU'RE WITH *Atlantic 2091 046* **37**	4
6 Jun 98	HE GOT GAME *Def Jam 5689852* [1] **16**	4
19 Dec 70 ●	STEPHEN STILLS *Atlantic 2401 004* **8**	9
14 Aug 71	STEPHEN STILLS 2 *Atlantic 2401 013*.................**22**	3
20 May 72	MANASSAS *Atlantic K 60021* [1] **30**	5
19 May 73	DOWN THE ROAD *Atlantic K 40440* [1] **33**	2
26 Jul 75	STILLS *CBS 69146*.................................**31**	1
29 May 76	ILLEGAL STILLS *CBS 81330* **54**	2
9 Oct 76	LONG MAY YOU RUN *Reprise K 54081* [2] **12**	5

[1] Public Enemy featuring Stephen Stills [1] Manassas [2] Stills-Young Band

For 1972 and 1973 albums act name was Manassas, a US, male vocal / instrumental group led by Stephen Stills

STILTSKIN (see also Armin VAN BUUREN featuring Ray WILSON) *UK, male vocal / instrumental group – lead vocal Ray Wilson (Singles: 15 Weeks, Albums: 4 Weeks)*

		pos/wks
7 May 94 ★	INSIDE *White Water LEV 1CD* **1**	13
24 Sep 94	FOOTSTEPS *White Water WWRD 2* **34**	2
29 Oct 94	THE MIND'S EYE *White Water WWD 1* **17**	4

STING ⟨65⟩ *Top 500*

World's best-known ex-Police-man, b. Gordon Sumner, 2 Oct 1951, Newcastle, UK. This singer / songwriter / bass player has amassed more solo hits than as front man of that top-selling trio. As a soloist, he has won both Brit and Grammy awards and reportedly earns £1 a second from touring and royalties (Singles: 166 Weeks, Albums: 387 Weeks)

		pos/wks
14 Aug 82	SPREAD A LITTLE HAPPINESS *A&M AMS 8242* **16**	8
8 Jun 85	IF YOU LOVE SOMEBODY SET THEM FREE *A&M AM 258* ..**26**	7
24 Aug 85	LOVE IS THE SEVENTH WAVE *A&M AM 272* **41**	5
19 Oct 85	FORTRESS AROUND YOUR HEART *A&M AM 286* **49**	3
7 Dec 85	RUSSIANS (re) *A&M AM 292* **12**	12
15 Feb 86	MOON OVER BOURBON STREET *A&M AM 305* **44**	4
7 Nov 87	WE'LL BE TOGETHER *A&M AM 410* **41**	4
20 Feb 88	ENGLISHMAN IN NEW YORK *A&M AM 431* **51**	3
9 Apr 88	FRAGILE *A&M AM 439* **70**	2
11 Aug 90	ENGLISHMAN IN NEW YORK (re-mix) *A&M AM 580* ...**15**	7
12 Jan 91	ALL THIS TIME *A&M AM 713* **22**	4
9 Mar 91	MAD ABOUT YOU *A&M AM 721* **56**	2
4 May 91	THE SOUL CAGES *A&M AM 759* **57**	1
29 Aug 92	IT'S PROBABLY ME *A&M AM 883* [1] **30**	5
13 Feb 93	IF I EVER LOSE MY FAITH IN YOU *A&M AMCD 0172* ..**14**	6
24 Apr 93	SEVEN DAYS *A&M 5802232* **25**	4
19 Jun 93	FIELDS OF GOLD *A&M 5803012* **16**	6
4 Sep 93	SHAPE OF MY HEART *A&M 5803532* **57**	1
20 Nov 93	DEMOLITION MAN *A&M 5804512* **21**	4
15 Jan 94 ●	ALL FOR LOVE *A&M 5804772* [2] ▲ **2**	13
26 Feb 94	NOTHING 'BOUT ME *A&M 5805292* **32**	3
29 Oct 94 ●	WHEN WE DANCE *A&M 5808612* **9**	7
11 Feb 95	THIS COWBOY SONG *A&M 5809652* [3] **15**	4
20 Jan 96	SPIRITS IN THE MATERIAL WORLD *MCA MCSTD 2113* [4] ...**36**	2
2 Mar 96	LET YOUR SOUL BE YOUR PILOT *A&M 5813312* **15**	4
11 May 96	YOU STILL TOUCH ME *A&M 5815472* **27**	3
22 Jun 96	LIVE AT TFI FRIDAY (EP) *A&M 5817652* **53**	2
14 Sep 96	I WAS BROUGHT TO MY SENSES *A&M 5818912* **31**	2
30 Nov 96	I'M SO HAPPY I CAN'T STOP CRYING *A&M 5820312* ..**54**	1
20 Dec 97	ROXANNE '97 (re-mix) *A&M 5824552* [5] **17**	6
25 Sep 99	BRAND NEW DAY *A&M / Polydor 4971522* **13**	5
29 Jan 00	DESERT ROSE *A&M / Mercury 4972402* [6] **15**	6
22 Apr 00	AFTER THE RAIN HAS FALLEN *A&M / Mercury 4973252* ...**31**	4
10 May 03 ●	RISE & FALL *Wildstar CDWILD 45* [7] **2**	10
27 Sep 03	SEND YOUR LOVE *A&M 9810103* **30**	2
20 Dec 03	WHENEVER I SAY YOUR NAME *A&M 9815394* [8] ...**60**	1
29 May 04	STOLEN CAR (TAKE ME DANCING) *A&M 9862266* ...**60**	1
29 Jun 85 ●	THE DREAM OF THE BLUE TURTLES *A&M DREAM 1* ...**3**	64
28 Jun 86	BRING ON THE NIGHT *A&M BRING 1* **16**	12
24 Oct 87 ★	... NOTHING LIKE THE SUN *A&M AMA 6402* ■ **1**	47
2 Feb 91 ★	THE SOUL CAGES *A&M 3964051* ■ **1**	16
13 Mar 93 ●	TEN SUMMONER'S TALES *A&M 5400752* **2**	60
19 Nov 94 ●	FIELDS OF GOLD – THE BEST OF STING 1984–1994 *A&M 5403072* **2**	41
16 Mar 96 ●	MERCURY FALLING *A&M 5404862* **4**	27

		pos/wks
22 Nov 97 ★	THE VERY BEST OF STING AND THE POLICE *A&M 5404282* [1] **1**	50
9 Oct 99 ●	BRAND NEW DAY *A&M 4904512* **5**	44
17 Nov 01 ●	ALL THIS TIME *A&M 4931802* **3**	15
4 Oct 03 ●	SACRED LOVE *A&M 9860619* **3**	11

[1] Sting with Eric Clapton [2] Bryan Adams, Rod Stewart and Sting [3] Sting featuring Pato Banton [4] Pato Banton with Sting [5] Sting and The Police [6] Sting featuring Cheb Mami [7] Craig David featuring Sting [8] Sting and Mary J Blige [1] Sting and The Police

Tracks on Live at TFI Friday (EP): You Still Touch Me / Lithium Sunset / Message in a Bottle 'The Very Best of Sting and The Police' originally peaked at No.11 but on 2 Mar 02 an updated version containing three new tracks re-entered the chart and sales were combined with the original album

STINGERS See B BUMBLE and the STINGERS

Byron STINGILY (see also TEN CITY) *US, male vocalist (Singles: 14 Weeks)*

		pos/wks
25 Jan 97	GET UP (EVERYBODY) *Manifesto FESCD 19* **14**	5
1 Nov 97	SING A SONG *Manifesto FESCD 35* **38**	2
31 Jan 98	YOU MAKE ME FEEL (MIGHTY REAL) *Manifesto FESCD 38* ...**13**	4
13 Jun 98	TESTIFY *Manifesto FESCD 42* **48**	1
12 Feb 00	THAT'S THE WAY LOVE IS *Manifesto FESCD 66* **32**	2

STINX *UK, female vocal duo (Singles: 3 Weeks)*

		pos/wks
24 Mar 01	WHY DO YOU KEEP ON RUNNING *HEBS HEBS 1* ...**49**	3

STIX 'N' STONED *UK, male instrumental / production duo – Julius O'Riordan and Jon Kelly (Singles: 2 Weeks)*

		pos/wks
20 Jul 96	OUTRAGEOUS *Positiva CDTIV 52* **39**	2

Catherine STOCK *UK, female vocalist (Singles: 6 Weeks)*

		pos/wks
18 Oct 86	TO HAVE AND TO HOLD *Sierra FED 29* **17**	6

STOCK AITKEN WATERMAN (see also 2 IN A TENT: 14-18) *UK, male producers – Mike Stock, Matt Aitken and Pete Waterman (Singles: 36 Weeks)*

		pos/wks
25 Jul 87	ROADBLOCK *Breakout USA 611* **13**	9
24 Oct 87 ●	MR SLEAZE *London NANA 14* **3**	10
12 Dec 87	PACKJAMMED (WITH THE PARTY POSSE) *Breakout USA 620* ..**41**	6
21 May 88	ALL THE WAY *MCA GOAL 1* [1] **64**	2
3 Dec 88	SS PAPARAZZI *PWL PWL 22* **68**	2
20 May 89 ★	FERRY 'CROSS THE MERSEY *PWL PWL 41* [2] ■ ...**1**	7

[1] England Football Team and the 'sound' of Stock, Aitken and Waterman [2] The Christians, Holly Johnson, Paul McCartney, Gerry Marsden and Stock Aitken Waterman

The listed flip side of 'Mr Sleaze' was 'Love in the First Degree' by Bananarama

Miriam STOCKLEY See PRAISE; ATLANTIS vs AVATAR

Rhet STOLLER
UK, male instrumentalist – guitar (Singles: 8 Weeks)

		pos/wks
12 Jan 61	CHARIOT *Decca F 11302* **26**	8

Morris STOLOFF *US, orchestra – leader b. 1 Aug 1898, d. 16 Apr 1980 (Singles: 11 Weeks)*

		pos/wks
1 Jun 56 ●	MOONGLOW AND THE THEME FROM 'PICNIC' *Brunswick 05553* **7**	11

Angie STONE *US, female vocalist (Singles: 24 Weeks, Albums: 4 Weeks)*

		pos/wks
15 Apr 00	LIFE STORY *Arista 74321748492* **22**	3
16 Dec 00	KEEP YOUR WORRIES *Virgin VUSCD 177* [1] **57**	1
9 Mar 02	BROTHA PART II *J 74321922142* [2] **37**	2
27 Jul 02	WISH I DIDN'T MISS YOU *J 74321939182* **30**	5
27 Dec 03	SIGNED, SEALED, DELIVERED, I'M YOURS *Innocent SINCD 50* [3] **11**	10
14 Aug 04	I WANNA THANK YA *J 82876624782* [4] **31**	3
11 Mar 00	BLACK DIAMOND *Arista 74321727752* **62**	3
10 Jul 04	STONE LOVE *J 82876597922* **56**	1

[1] Guru's Jazzmatazz featuring Angie Stone [2] Angie Stone featuring Alicia Keys and Eve [3] Blue featuring Stevie Wonder and Angie Stone [4] Angie Stone featuring Snoop Dogg

Joss STONE
UK, female vocalist – Jocelyn Stoker
(Singles: 20 Weeks, Albums: 57 Weeks) pos/wks

7 Feb 04	**FELL IN LOVE WITH A BOY** *Relentless / Virgin RELCD 3* 18 5
22 May 04	**SUPER DUPER LOVE (ARE YOU DIGGIN ON ME?)** *Relentless / Virgin RELCD 4* 18 4
25 Sep 04 ●	**YOU HAD ME** *Relentless / Virgin RELDX 10* 9 8
11 Dec 04	**RIGHT TO BE WRONG** *Relentless / Virgin RELDX 13* ....29 3+
17 Jan 04 ●	**THE SOUL SESSIONS** *Relentless CDREL 2* 4 45
9 Oct 04 ★	**MIND BODY & SOUL** *Relentless CDREL 04* ■ ....1 12+

R & J STONE *UK / US, male / female vocal*
duo – Russell and Joanne Stone (Singles: 9 Weeks) pos/wks

10 Jan 76 ●	**WE DO IT** *RCA 2616* 5 9

The STONE ROSES (275 Top 500)
(see also The SEAHORSES) 'Madchester', 'Baggy' pioneers who successfully combined rock guitar and acid house attitude, inspiring a massive return to guitar-based bands in northern Britain in the 90s: Ian Brown (v), John Squire (g), Mani (aka Gary Mountfield) (b), Reni (aka Alan Wren) (d/v), all from Manchester. Their eponymous debut album, which peaked no higher than No.19 in 1989, continues to register in the top five of best all-time album surveys *(Singles: 77 Weeks, Albums: 159 Weeks)* pos/wks

29 Jul 89	**SHE BANGS THE DRUMS (re)** *Silvertone ORE 6* 34 6
25 Nov 89 ●	**WHAT THE WORLD IS WAITING FOR / FOOL'S GOLD (re)** *Silvertone ORE 13* 8 19
6 Jan 90	**SALLY CINNAMON (re)** *Revolver REV 36* 46 5
3 Mar 90 ●	**ELEPHANT STONE** *Silvertone ORE 1* 8 6
17 Mar 90	**MADE OF STONE** *Silvertone ORE 2* 20 4
14 Jul 90 ●	**ONE LOVE** *Silvertone ORE 17* 4 7
14 Sep 91	**I WANNA BE ADORED** *Silvertone ORE 31* 20 3
11 Jan 92	**WATERFALL** *Silvertone ORE 35* 27 4
11 Apr 92	**I AM THE RESURRECTION** *Silvertone ORE 40* 33 2
30 May 92	**FOOL'S GOLD (re-issue)** *Silvertone ORET 13* 73 1
3 Dec 94 ●	**LOVE SPREADS** *Geffen GFSTD 84* 2 8
11 Mar 95	**TEN STOREY LOVE SONG** *Geffen GFSTD 87* 11 3
29 Apr 95	**FOOL'S GOLD (2nd re-issue)** *Silvertone ORECD 71* 25 3
11 Nov 95	**BEGGING YOU** *Geffen GFSTD 22060* 15 3
6 Mar 99	**FOOL'S GOLD (re-mix)** *Jive Electro 0523092* 25 3
13 May 89 ●	**THE STONE ROSES** *Silvertone ORELP 502* 9 88
1 Aug 92	**TURNS INTO STONE** *Silvertone ORECD 521* 32 3
17 Dec 94 ●	**SECOND COMING** *Geffen GED 24503* 4 28
27 May 95 ●	**THE COMPLETE STONE ROSES** *Silvertone ORECD 535* 4 25
7 Dec 96	**GARAGE FLOWER** *Silvertone GARAGECD 1* 58 1
16 Oct 99	**STONE ROSES – 10TH ANNIVERSARY EDITION** *Silvertone 591242* 26 3
11 Nov 00	**THE REMIXES** *Silvertone 9260152* 41 2
16 Nov 02	**THE VERY BEST OF THE STONE ROSES** *Silvertone 9260382* 19 9

'She Bangs the Drums' made No.36 on its chart debut and reached its peak position only on re-entry in Mar 1990. 'What the World Is Waiting For' / 'Fool's Gold' made No.22 on re-entry in Sep 1990 'The Stone Roses' reached its peak position in 2004 with a slighty different catalogue number, Silvertone OREZCD 502

STONE SOUR *US, male vocal / instrumental*
group (Singles: 3 Weeks, Albums: 1 Week) pos/wks

15 Mar 03	**BOTHER** *Roadrunner RR 20243* 28 2
19 Jul 03	**INHALE** *Roadrunner RR 20093* 63 1
7 Sep 02	**STONE SOUR** *Roadrunner RR 84252* 41 1

STONE TEMPLE PILOTS *US, male vocal /*
instrumental group (Singles: 11 Weeks, Albums: 19 Weeks) pos/wks

27 Mar 93	**SEX TYPE THING** *Atlantic A 5769CD* 60 2
4 Sep 93	**PLUSH** *Atlantic A 7349CD* 23 4
27 Nov 93	**SEX TYPE THING (re-issue)** *Atlantic A 7293CD* 55 2
20 Aug 94	**VASOLINE** *Atlantic A 5650CD* 48 2
10 Dec 94	**INTERSTATE LOVE SONG** *Atlantic A 7192CD* 53 1
4 Sep 93	**CORE** *Atlantic 7567824182* 27 4
18 Jun 94 ●	**PURPLE** *Atlantic 7567826072* ▲ 10 9
6 Apr 96	**TINY MUSIC ... SONGS FROM THE VATICAN GIFT SHOP** *Atlantic 7567828712* 31 2

STONE THE CROWS
UK, female / male vocal / instrumental group (Albums: 3 Weeks) pos/wks

7 Oct 72	**ONTINUOUS PERFORMANCE** *Polydor 2391 043* 33 3

STONEBRIDGE featuring THERESE
Sweden, male / female production / vocal group (Singles: 12 Weeks) pos/wks

13 Mar 04	**PUT 'EM HIGH (re)** *Hed Kandi HEDK 12004* 59 2
28 Aug 04 ●	**PUT 'EM HIGH (re-issue)** *Hed Kandi HEDKCDS 008* 6 10

STONEBRIDGE McGUINNESS
UK, male vocal / instrumental duo (Singles: 2 Weeks) pos/wks

14 Jul 79	**OO-EEH BABY** *RCA PB 5163* 54 2

STONEFREE *UK, male vocalist – Tony Stone (Singles: 1 Week)* pos/wks

23 May 87	**CAN'T SAY 'BYE** *Ensign ENY 607* 73 1

STONEPROOF
UK, male producer – John Graham (Singles: 1 Week) pos/wks

15 May 99	**EVERYTHING'S NOT YOU** *VC Recordings VCRD 47* 68 1

STONKERS See HALE and PACE and The STONKERS

STOOGES See Iggy POP

STOP THE VIOLENCE MOVEMENT
US, male / female rap charity ensemble (Singles: 1 Week) pos/wks

18 Feb 89	**SELF DESTRUCTION** *Jive BDPST 1* 75 1

Axel STORDAHL See June HUTTON and Axel STORDAHL

STORM
UK, male / female vocal / instrumental group (Singles: 10 Weeks) pos/wks

17 Nov 79	**IT'S MY HOUSE** *Scope SC 10* 36 10

STORM (see also DANCE 2 TRANCE; TOKYO GHETTO PUSSY)
Germany, male production duo – Rolf Ellmer and Markus Loffel (Singles: 19 Weeks) pos/wks

29 Aug 98	**STORM** *Positiva CDTIV 94* 32 2
12 Aug 00 ●	**TIME TO BURN** *Data DATA 16CDS* 3 10
23 Dec 00	**STORM ANIMAL** *Data DATA 20CDS* 21 5
26 May 01	**STORM (re-mix)** *Positiva CDTIV 154* 32 2

Danny STORM *UK, male vocalist (Singles: 4 Weeks)* pos/wks

12 Apr 62	**HONEST I DO** *Piccadilly 7N 35025* 42 4

Rebecca STORM *UK, female vocalist (Singles: 13 Weeks)* pos/wks

13 Jul 85	**THE SHOW (THEME FROM 'CONNIE')** *Towerbell TVP 3* 22 13

STORY OF THE YEAR
US, male vocal / instrumental group (Singles: 1 Week) pos/wks

12 Jun 04	**UNTIL THE DAY I DIE** *Maverick W 634CD* 62 1

STORYVILLE JAZZ BAND See Bob WALLIS and his STORYVILLE JAZZ BAND

Izzy STRADLIN and the JU JU HOUNDS (see also GUNS N' ROSES)
US, male vocalist / instrumentalist – guitar – Jeffrey Isbell and male vocal / instrumental group (Singles: 2 Weeks, Albums: 1 Week) pos/wks

26 Sep 92	**PRESSURE DROP** *Geffen GFS 25* 1 ....45 2
24 Oct 92	**IZZY STRADLIN AND THE JU JU HOUNDS** *Geffen GED 24490* 52 1

1 Izzy Stradlin

Nick STRAKER BAND
UK, male vocal / instrumental group (Singles: 15 Weeks) pos/wks

2 Aug 80	**A WALK IN THE PARK** *CBS 8525* 20 12
15 Nov 80	**LEAVING ON THE MIDNIGHT TRAIN** *CBS 9088* 61 3

Peter STRAKER and the HANDS OF DR TELENY *UK, male*
vocalist and male vocal / instrumental group (Singles: 4 Weeks) pos/wks

19 Feb 72	**THE SPIRIT IS WILLING** *RCA 2163* 40 4

STRANGE BEHAVIOUR See Jane KENNAWAY and STRANGE BEHAVIOUR

STRANGE FRUIT See Jimmy NAIL

STRANGELOVE UK, male vocal /
instrumental group (Singles: 8 Weeks, Albums: 3 Weeks)   pos/wks

20 Apr 96	LIVING WITH THE HUMAN MACHINES *Food CDFOOD 70*	53	1
15 Jun 96	BEAUTIFUL ALONE *Food CDFOOD 81*	35	2
19 Oct 96	SWAY *Food CDFOOD 82*	47	1
26 Jul 97	THE GREATEST SHOW ON EARTH *Food CDFOODS 97*	36	2
11 Oct 97	FREAK *Food CDFOOD 105*	43	1
21 Feb 98	ANOTHER NIGHT IN *Food CDFOOD 110*	46	1
13 Aug 94	TIME FOR THE REST OF YOUR LIFE *Food FOODCD 11*	69	1
29 Jun 96	LOVE AND OTHER DEMONS *Food FOODCD 15*	44	1
18 Oct 97	STRANGELOVE *Food FOODCD 24*	67	1

The STRANGLERS `106` `Top 500` *The most commercially successful and long-lasting group to emerge from the punk / new wave scene: Hugh Cornwell (v/g), Jean-Jacques Burnel (b/v), Dave Greenfield (k), Jet Black (d). This London-based band had at least one hit every year between 1977 and 1992 (Singles: 197 Weeks, Albums: 223 Weeks)*   pos/wks

19 Feb 77	(GET A) GRIP (ON YOURSELF) *United Artists UP 36211*	44	4
21 May 77 ●	PEACHES / GO BUDDY GO *United Artists UP 36248*	8	14
30 Jul 77 ●	SOMETHING BETTER CHANGE / STRAIGHTEN OUT *United Artists UP 36277*	9	8
24 Sep 77 ●	NO MORE HEROES *United Artists UP 36300*	8	9
4 Feb 78	5 MINUTES *United Artists UP 36350*	11	9
6 May 78	NICE 'N' SLEAZY *United Artists UP 36379*	18	8
12 Aug 78	WALK ON BY *United Artists UP 36429*	21	8
18 Aug 79	DUCHESS *United Artists BP 308*	14	9
20 Oct 79	NUCLEAR DEVICE (THE WIZARD OF AUS) *United Artists BP 318*	36	4
1 Dec 79	DON'T BRING HARRY (EP) *United Artists STR 1*	41	3
22 Mar 80	BEAR CAGE *United Artists BP 344*	36	5
7 Jun 80	WHO WANTS THE WORLD *United Artists BP 355*	39	4
31 Jan 81	THROWN AWAY *Liberty BP 383*	42	4
14 Nov 81	LET ME INTRODUCE YOU TO THE FAMILY *Liberty BP 405*	42	3
9 Jan 82 ●	GOLDEN BROWN *Liberty BP 407*	2	12
24 Apr 82	LA FOLIE *Liberty BP 410*	47	3
24 Jul 82 ●	STRANGE LITTLE GIRL *Liberty BP 412*	7	9
8 Jan 83 ●	EUROPEAN FEMALE *Epic EPC A 2893*	9	9
26 Feb 83	MIDNIGHT SUMMER DREAM *Epic EPC A 3167*	35	4
6 Aug 83	PARADISE *Epic A 3387*	48	3
6 Oct 84	SKIN DEEP *Epic A 4738*	15	7
1 Dec 84	NO MERCY *Epic A 4921*	37	7
16 Feb 85	LET ME DOWN EASY *Epic A 6045*	48	4
23 Aug 86	NICE IN NICE *Epic 6500557*	30	5
18 Oct 86	ALWAYS THE SUN *Epic SOLAR 1*	30	5
13 Dec 86	BIG IN AMERICA *Epic HUGE 1*	48	6
7 Mar 87	SHAKIN' LIKE A LEAF *Epic SHEIK 1*	58	4
9 Jan 88 ●	ALL DAY AND ALL OF THE NIGHT *Epic VICE 1*	7	7
28 Jan 89	GRIP '89 (GET A) GRIP (ON YOURSELF) (re-mix) *EMI EM 84*	33	3
17 Feb 90	96 TEARS *Epic TEARS 1*	17	6
21 Apr 90	SWEET SMELL OF SUCCESS *Epic TEARS 2*	65	2
5 Jan 91	ALWAYS THE SUN (re-mix) *Epic 6564307*	29	5
30 Mar 91	GOLDEN BROWN (re-mix) *Epic 6567617*	68	2
22 Aug 92	HEAVEN OR HELL *Psycho WOK 2025*	46	2
14 Feb 04	BIG THING COMING *Liberty 5480692*	31	2
24 Apr 04	LONG BLACK VEIL *Liberty 05489062*	51	1
30 Apr 77 ●	STRANGLERS IV (RATTUS NORVEGICUS) *United Artists UAG 30045*	4	34
8 Oct 77 ●	NO MORE HEROES *United Artists UAG 30200*	2	19
3 Jun 78 ●	BLACK AND WHITE *United Artists UAK 30222*	2	18
10 Mar 79 ●	LIVE (X CERT) *United Artists UAG 30224*	7	10
6 Oct 79 ●	THE RAVEN *United Artists UAG 30262*	4	8
21 Feb 81	THEMENINBLACK *Liberty LBG 30313*	8	5
21 Nov 81	LA FOLIE *Liberty LBG 30342*	11	18
25 Sep 82	THE COLLECTION 1977-1982 *Liberty LBS 30353*	12	16
22 Jan 83	FELINE *Epic EPC 25237*	4	11
17 Nov 84	AURAL SCULPTURE *Epic EPC 26220*	14	10
20 Sep 86	OFF THE BEATEN TRACK *Liberty LBG 5001*	80	2
8 Nov 86	DREAMTIME *Epic EPC 26648*	16	6
20 Feb 88	ALL LIVE AND ALL OF THE NIGHT *Epic 465259*	12	6
18 Feb 89	THE SINGLES *EMI EM 1314*	57	2
17 Mar 90	10 *Epic 4664831*	15	4
1 Dec 90 ●	GREATEST HITS 1977-1990 *Epic 4675411*	4	47
19 Sep 92	STRANGLERS IN THE NIGHT *Psycho WOLCD 1030*	33	1
27 May 95	ABOUT TIME *When! WENCD 001*	31	1
8 Feb 97	WRITTEN IN RED *When! WENCD 009*	52	1

22 Jun 02	PEACHES – THE VERY BEST OF THE STRANGLERS *EMI 5402022*	21	3
28 Feb 04	NORFOLK COAST *Liberty 5969512*	70	1

'Go Buddy Go' credited with 'Peaches' from 11 Jun 1977. 'Straighten Out' credited with 'Something Better Change' from 13 Aug 1977. Tracks on Don't Bring Harry (EP): Don't Bring Harry / Wired / Crabs (Live) / In the Shadows (Live)

STRAW UK, male vocal / instrumental group (Singles: 4 Weeks)   pos/wks

6 Feb 99	THE AEROPLANE SONG *WEA WEA 196CD*	37	2
24 Apr 99	MOVING TO CALIFORNIA *WEA WEA 205CD1*	50	1
3 Mar 01	SAILING OFF THE EDGE OF THE WORLD *Columbia 6708452*	52	1

STRAWBERRY SWITCHBLADE UK, female vocal duo – Rose McDowell and Jill Bryson (Singles: 26 Weeks, Albums: 4 Weeks)   pos/wks

17 Nov 84	SINCE YESTERDAY *Korova KOW 38*	5	17
23 Mar 85	LET HER GO *Korova KOW 39*	59	5
21 Sep 85	JOLENE *Korova KOW 42*	53	4
13 Apr 85	STRAWBERRY SWITCHBLADE *Korova KODE 11*	25	4

The STRAWBS (see also HUDSON FORD) UK, male vocal / instrumental group (Singles: 27 Weeks, Albums: 31 Weeks)   pos/wks

28 Oct 72	LAY DOWN *A&M AMS 7035*	12	13
27 Jan 73 ●	PART OF THE UNION *A&M AMS 7047*	2	11
6 Oct 73	SHINE ON SILVER SUN *A&M AMS 7082*	34	3
21 Nov 70	JUST A COLLECTION OF ANTIQUES AND CURIOS *A&M AMLS 994*	27	2
17 Jul 71	FROM THE WITCHWOOD *A&M AMLH 64304*	39	2
26 Feb 72	GRAVE NEW WORLD *A&M AMLH 68078*	11	12
24 Feb 73 ●	BURSTING AT THE SEAMS *A&M AMLH 68144*	2	12
27 Apr 74	HERO AND HEROINE *A&M AMLH 63607*	35	3

The STRAY CATS US, male vocal / instrumental group (Singles: 49 Weeks, Albums: 32 Weeks)   pos/wks

29 Nov 80 ●	RUNAWAY BOYS *Arista SCAT 1*	9	10
7 Feb 81 ●	ROCK THIS TOWN *Arista SCAT 2*	9	8
25 Apr 81	STRAY CAT STRUT *Arista SCAT 3*	11	10
20 Jun 81	THE RACE IS ON *Swansong SSK 19425* [1]	34	6
7 Nov 81	YOU DON'T BELIEVE ME *Arista SCAT 4*	57	3
6 Aug 83	(SHE'S) SEXY AND 17 *Arista SCAT 6*	29	9
4 Mar 89	BRING IT BACK AGAIN *EMI USA MT 62*	64	3
28 Feb 81 ●	STRAY CATS *Arista STRAY 1*	6	22
21 Nov 81	GONNA BALL *Arista STRAY 2*	48	4
3 Sep 83	RANT 'N' RAVE WITH THE STRAY CATS *Arista STRAY 3*	51	5
8 Apr 89	BLAST OFF *EMI MTL 1040*	58	1

[1] Dave Edmunds and The Stray Cats

STRAY MOB See MC SKAT KAT and The STRAY MOB

STREETBAND (see also Paul YOUNG) UK, male vocal / instrumental group (Singles: 6 Weeks)   pos/wks

4 Nov 78	TOAST / HOLD ON *Logo GO 325*	18	6

The STREETS (see also GRAFITI) UK, male producer – Mick Skinner (Singles: 47 Weeks, Albums: 88 Weeks)   pos/wks

20 Oct 01	HAS IT COME TO THIS (re) *WEA / 679L 001*	18	5
27 Apr 02	LET'S PUSH THINGS FORWARD *Locked On / 679 Recordings 679L 005CD*	30	3
3 Aug 02	WEAK BECOME HEROES *Locked On / 679 Recordings 679L 007CD*	27	3
2 Nov 02	DON'T MUG YOURSELF *Locked On / 679 Recordings 679L 008CDX*	21	3
8 May 04 ●	FIT BUT YOU KNOW IT *Locked On / 679 Recordings 679L 071CD2*	4	10
31 Jul 04 ★	DRY YOUR EYES *Locked On / 679 Recordings 679L 077CD1* ■	1	13
9 Oct 04 ●	BLINDED BY THE LIGHTS *Locked On / 679 Recordings 679L 085CD*	10	7
11 Dec 04	COULD WELL BE IN *Locked On / 679 Recordings 679L 092CD*	30	3+
6 Apr 02 ●	ORIGINAL PIRATE MATERIAL *Locked On / 679 Recordings 927435682*	10	56
22 May 04 ★	A GRAND DON'T COME FOR FREE *Locked On / 679 2564615342*	1	32+

'Original Pirate Material' reached its peak position in 2004

The STREETWALKERS UK, male vocal / instrumental group (Albums: 6 Weeks)   pos/wks

12 Jun 76	RED CARD *Vertigo 9102 010*	16	6

Barbra STREISAND 46 *Top 500*

Acclaimed song stylist who has more gold albums than any other female,
b. 24 Apr 1942, Brooklyn, US. This world-renowned MOR vocalist / actress
has collected countless awards for her recordings and her stage and film
work, and is a recipient of both Grammy Living Legend and Lifetime
Achievement awards (Singles: 155 Weeks, Albums: 523 Weeks) pos/wks

		pos	wks
20 Jan 66	SECOND HAND ROSE *CBS 202025*	14	13
30 Jan 71	STONEY END (re) *CBS 5321*	27	11
30 Mar 74	THE WAY WE WERE *CBS 1915* ▲	31	6
9 Apr 77 ●	LOVE THEME FROM 'A STAR IS BORN' (EVERGREEN)		
	CBS 4855 ▲	3	19
25 Nov 78 ●	YOU DON'T BRING ME FLOWERS *CBS 6803* ⊡ ▲	5	12
3 Nov 79 ●	NO MORE TEARS (ENOUGH IS ENOUGH)		
	Casablanca CAN 174 / CBS 8000 ⊡ ▲	3	13
4 Oct 80 ★	WOMAN IN LOVE *CBS 8966* ▲	1	16
6 Dec 80	GUILTY *CBS 9315* ⊡	34	10
30 Jan 82	COMIN' IN AND OUT OF YOUR LIFE *CBS A 1789*	66	3
20 Mar 82	MEMORY *CBS A 1903*	34	6
5 Nov 88	TILL I LOVED YOU (LOVE THEME FROM 'GOYA')		
	CBS BARB 2 ⊡	16	7
7 Mar 92	PLACES THAT BELONG TO YOU *Columbia 6577947*	17	5
5 Jun 93	WITH ONE LOOK *Columbia 6593422*	30	3
15 Jan 94	THE MUSIC OF THE NIGHT *Columbia 6597382* ⊡	54	3
30 Apr 94	AS IF WE NEVER SAID GOODBYE *Columbia 6603572*	20	3
8 Feb 97 ●	I FINALLY FOUND SOMEONE *A&M 5820832* ⊡	10	7
15 Nov 97 ●	TELL HIM *Epic 6653052* ⊡	3	15
30 Oct 99	IF YOU EVER LEAVE ME *Columbia 6681242* ⊡	26	3
22 Jan 66 ●	MY NAME IS BARBRA, TWO ... *CBS BPG 62603*	6	22
4 Apr 70	BARBRA STREISAND'S GREATEST HITS *CBS 63921*	44	2
17 Apr 71	STONEY END *CBS 64269*	28	2
15 Jun 74	THE WAY WE WERE *CBS 69057* ▲	49	1
9 Apr 77 ★	A STAR IS BORN *CBS 86021* ⊡ ▲	1	54
23 Jul 77	STREISAND SUPERMAN *CBS 86030*	32	9
15 Jul 78	SONGBIRD *CBS 86060*	48	2
17 Mar 79 ★	BARBRA STREISAND'S GREATEST HITS VOLUME 2		
	CBS 10012 ▲	1	30
17 Nov 79	WET *CBS 86104*	25	13
11 Oct 80 ★	GUILTY *CBS 86122* ▲	1	82
16 Jan 82 ★	LOVE SONGS *CBS 10031*	1	129
19 Nov 83	YENTL (FILM SOUNDTRACK) *CBS 86302*	21	35
27 Oct 84	EMOTION *CBS 86309*	15	12
18 Jan 86 ●	THE BROADWAY ALBUM *CBS 86322* ▲	3	16
30 May 87	ONE VOICE *CBS 450 8901*	27	7
3 Dec 88	TILL I LOVED YOU *CBS 462 9431*	29	13
25 Nov 89	A COLLECTION – GREATEST HITS ... AND MORE		
	CBS 465845 1	22	23
10 Jul 93 ●	BACK TO BROADWAY *Columbia 4738802* ▲	4	17
29 Oct 94	THE CONCERT *Columbia 4775992*	63	1
22 Nov 97	HIGHER GROUND *Columbia 4885322* ▲	12	12
2 Oct 99	A LOVE LIKE OURS *Columbia 4949342*	12	9
30 Sep 00	TIMELESS – LIVE IN CONCERT *Columbia 4974352*	54	1
9 Mar 02 ★	THE ESSENTIAL BARBRA STREISAND *Columbia 5062572*	1	22
30 Nov 02	DUETS *Columbia 5098129*	30	4
8 Nov 03	THE MOVIE ALBUM *Columbia 5134213*	25	3

⊡ Barbra and Neil [Neil was Neil Diamond] ⊡ Donna Summer and Barbra Streisand
⊡ Barbra Streisand and Barry Gibb ⊡ Barbra Streisand and Don Johnson ⊡ Barbra
Streisand (duet with Michael Crawford) ⊡ Barbra Streisand and Bryan Adams ⊡
Barbra Streisand and Celine Dion ⊡ Barbra Streisand / Vince Gill ⊡ Barbra Streisand
/ Kris Kristofferson

'No More Tears (Enough Is Enough)' was released simultaneously on two different
labels, a 7-inch single on Casablanca and a 12-inch on CBS

STRESS *UK, male vocal / instrumental group (Singles: 1 Week)* pos/wks

		pos	wks
13 Oct 90	BEAUTIFUL PEOPLE *Eternal YZ 495*	74	1

STRETCH *UK, male vocal / instrumental group (Singles: 9 Weeks)* pos/wks

		pos	wks
8 Nov 75	WHY DID YOU DO IT *Anchor ANC 1021*	16	9

STRETCH 'N' VERN present "MADDOG" *UK, male instrumental /*
production duo – Stuart Collins and Julian Peake (Singles: 14 Weeks) pos/wks

		pos	wks
14 Sep 96 ●	I'M ALIVE *ffrr FCD 284*	6	9
9 Aug 97	GET UP! GO INSANE! *ffrr FCD 304*	17	5

STRICT INSTRUCTOR *Russia, female vocalist (Singles: 1 Week)* pos/wks

		pos	wks
24 Oct 98	STEP-TWO-THREE-FOUR *All Around the World CDGLOBE 155*	49	1

STRIKE *UK / Australia, male /*
female vocal / instrumental group (Singles: 24 Weeks) pos/wks

		pos	wks
24 Dec 94 ●	U SURE DO (re) *Fresh FRSHD 19*	4	14
23 Sep 95	THE MORNING AFTER (FREE AT LAST) *Fresh FRSHD 37*	38	1
29 Jun 96	INSPIRATION *Fresh FRSHD 45*	27	2
16 Nov 96	MY LOVE IS FOR REAL *Fresh FRSHD 46*	35	2
31 May 97	I HAVE PEACE *Fresh FRSHCD 58*	17	4
25 Sep 99	U SURE DO (re-mix) *Fresh FRSHD 78*	53	1

'U Sure Do' debuted at No.31 and made its peak position only on re-entry in Apr 1995

The STRIKERS *US, male vocal / instrumental group (Singles: 5 Weeks)* pos/wks

		pos	wks
6 Jun 81	BODY MUSIC *Epic EPC A 1290*	45	5

The STRING-A-LONGS
US, male instrumental group (Singles: 16 Weeks) pos/wks

		pos	wks
23 Feb 61 ●	WHEELS *London HLU 9278*	8	16

STRINGS FOR PLEASURE *UK, orchestra (Albums: 1 Week)* pos/wks

		pos	wks
4 Dec 71	THE BEST OF BACHARACH *MFP 1334*	49	1

STRINGS OF LOVE
Italy, male / female vocal / instrumental group (Singles: 2 Weeks) pos/wks

		pos	wks
3 Mar 90	NOTHING HAS BEEN PROVED *Breakout USA 688*	59	2

The STROKES *US, male vocal / instrumental*
group (Singles: 26 Weeks, Albums: 60 Weeks) pos/wks

		pos	wks
7 Jul 01	HARD TO EXPLAIN / NEW YORK CITY COPS		
	Rough Trade RTRADCD 023	16	5
7 Jul 01	MODERN AGE (2re) *Rough Trade RTRADCD 010*	68	3
17 Nov 01	LAST NITE (re-recording) *Rough Trade RTRADCD 041*	14	5
5 Oct 02	SOMEDAY *Rough Trade RTRADCD 063*	27	2
18 Oct 03 ●	12:51 *Rough Trade RTRADCD 140*	7	4
21 Feb 04	REPTILIA *Rough Trade RTRADCD 155*	17	5
13 Nov 04	THE END HAS NO END *Rough Trade RTRADCD 205*	27	2
8 Sep 01 ●	IS THIS IT *Rough Trade RTRADCD 030*	2	40
1 Nov 03 ●	ROOM ON FIRE *Rough Trade RTRADCD 130*	2	20

'Modern Age' is a 3-track CD featuring Modern Age, Last Nite (later re-recorded
and released as the band's next single in 2001) Barely Legal

Joe STRUMMER (see also The CLASH)
UK, (b. Turkey, 21 Aug 1952), male vocalist – John Mellor
d. 23 Dec 2002 (Singles: 17 Weeks, Albums: 4 Weeks) pos/wks

		pos	wks
2 Aug 86	LOVE KILLS *CBS A 7244*	69	1
23 Dec 95	JUST THE ONE *China WOKCD 2076* ⊡	12	8
29 Jun 96 ●	ENGLAND'S IRIE *Radioactive RAXTD 25* ⊡	6	4
18 Oct 03	COMA GIRL *Hellcat 11352* ⊡	33	2
27 Dec 03	REDEMPTION SONG / ARMS ALOFT *Hellcat 11472* ⊡	46	2
14 Oct 89	EARTHQUAKE WEATHER *Epic 4653471*	58	1
30 Oct 99	ROCK ART AND THE X-RAY STYLE *Mercury 5466542* ⊡	71	1
28 Jul 01	GLOBAL A GO GO *Hellcat 4402* ⊡	68	1
1 Nov 03	STREETCORE *Hellcat 04542* ⊡	50	1

⊡ The Levellers, special guest Joe Strummer ⊡ Black Grape featuring
Joe Strummer and Keith Allen ⊡ Joe Strummer and The Mescaleros
⊡ Joe Strummer and The Mescaleros

STRYKER *See MANCHESTER UNITED FOOTBALL CLUB*

STUART
Holland, male producer – Sjoerd Wijdoogen (Singles: 2 Weeks) pos/wks

		pos	wks
5 Apr 03	FREE (LET IT BE) *Product / Incentive PDT 07CDS*	41	2

Chad STUART and Jeremy CLYDE
UK, male vocal duo (Singles: 7 Weeks) pos/wks

		pos	wks
28 Nov 63	YESTERDAY'S GONE *Ember EMB S 180*	37	7

STUDIO 2 *Jamaica, male vocalist – Errol Jones (Singles: 1 Week)* pos/wks

		pos	wks
27 Jun 98	TRAVELLING MAN *Multiply CDMULTY 35*	40	1

STUDIO B / ROMEO and Harry BROOKS (see also SO SOLID CREW)
UK, male production / vocal / rap trio (Singles: 1 Week) pos/wks

		pos	wks
6 Dec 03	I SEE GIRLS (CRAZY) *Multiply CDMULTY 109*	52	1

STUDIO 45 *Germany, male DJ / production duo –*
Tilo Cielsa and Jens Brachvogel (Singles: 2 Weeks)   pos/wks

20 Feb 99	FREAK IT! *Azuli AZNYCD 090*	**36**	2

Amy STUDT
UK, female vocalist (Singles: 26 Weeks, Albums: 11 Weeks)   pos/wks

13 Jul 02	JUST A LITTLE GIRL *Polydor 5708802*	**14**	6
21 Jun 03 ●	MISFIT *Polydor 9800107*	**6**	10
11 Oct 03 ●	UNDER THE THUMB *Polydor 9811793*	**10**	6
24 Jan 02 ●	ALL I WANNA DO *Polydor 9815012*	**21**	4
12 Jul 03	FALSE SMILES *Polydor 9801074*	**24**	11

STUMP *UK, male vocal / instrumental group (Singles: 1 Week)*   pos/wks

13 Aug 88	CHARLTON HESTON *Ensign ENY 614*	**72**	1

STUNTMASTERZ *UK, male production duo –*
Steve Harris and Pete Cook (Singles: 9 Weeks)   pos/wks

3 Mar 01 ●	THE LADYBOY IS MINE *East West EW 226CD*	**10**	9

STUTZ BEARCATS and the Denis KING ORCHESTRA
(see also The KING BROTHERS) *UK, male / female*
vocal group with orchestra (Singles: 6 Weeks)   pos/wks

24 Apr 82	THE SONG THAT I SING (THEME FROM 'WE'LL MEET AGAIN') *Multi-Media Tapes MMT 6*	**36**	6

The STYLE COUNCIL ⸢331⸥ Top 500
Eighties chart regulars: Paul Weller (v/g), Mick Talbot (k) and sometimes
Dee C Lee (v – former Wham! backing vocalist and Weller's wife). As with
Weller's previous band, The Jam, most of this London act's hits were in their
homeland (Singles: 103 Weeks, Albums: 100 Weeks)   pos/wks

19 Mar 83 ●	SPEAK LIKE A CHILD *Polydor TSC 1*	**4**	8
28 May 83	MONEY GO ROUND (PART 1) (re) *Polydor TSC 2*	**11**	7
13 Aug 83 ●	LONG HOT SUMMER / PARIS MATCH *Polydor TSC 3*	**3**	9
19 Nov 83	SOLID BOND IN YOUR HEART *Polydor TSC 4*	**11**	8
18 Feb 84 ●	MY EVER CHANGING MOODS *Polydor TSC 5*	**5**	7
26 May 84 ●	GROOVIN' (YOU'RE THE BEST THING / THE BIG BOSS GROOVE) *Polydor TSC 6*	**5**	8
13 Oct 84	SHOUT TO THE TOP *Polydor TSC 7*	**7**	8
11 May 85 ●	WALLS COME TUMBLING DOWN! *Polydor TSC 8*	**6**	7
6 Jul 85	COME TO MILTON KEYNES *Polydor TSC 9*	**23**	5
28 Sep 85	THE LODGERS *Polydor TSC 10*	**13**	6
5 Apr 86	HAVE YOU EVER HAD IT BLUE *Polydor CINE 1*	**14**	6
17 Jan 87 ●	IT DIDN'T MATTER *Polydor TSC 12*	**9**	6
14 Mar 87	WAITING *Polydor TSC 13*	**52**	3
31 Oct 87	WANTED *Polydor TSC 14*	**20**	4
28 May 88	LIFE AT A TOP PEOPLE'S HEALTH FARM *Polydor TSC 15*	**28**	3
23 Jul 88	HOW SHE THREW IT ALL AWAY (EP) *Polydor TSC 16*	**41**	2
18 Feb 89	PROMISED LAND *Polydor TSC 17*	**27**	5
27 May 89	LONG HOT SUMMER 89 (re-mix) *Polydor LHS 1*	**48**	2
24 Mar 84 ●	CAFE BLEU *Polydor TSCLP 1*	**2**	38
8 Jun 85 ★	OUR FAVOURITE SHOP *Polydor TSCLP 2* ■	**1**	22
17 May 86 ●	HOME AND ABROAD *Polydor TSCLP 3*	**8**	8
14 Feb 87 ●	THE COST OF LOVING *Polydor TSCLP 4*	**2**	7
2 Jul 88	CONFESSIONS OF A POP GROUP *Polydor TSCMC 5*	**15**	3
18 Mar 89 ●	THE SINGULAR ADVENTURES OF THE STYLE COUNCIL – GREATEST HITS VOL.1 *Polydor TSCTV 1*	**3**	15
10 Jul 93	HERE'S SOME THAT GOT AWAY *Polydor 5193722*	**39**	1
2 Mar 96	THE STYLE COUNCIL COLLECTION *Polydor 5294832*	**60**	1
2 Sep 00	GREATEST HITS *Polydor / Universal TV 5579002*	**28**	5

'Paris Match' was listed with 'Long Hot Summer' from 3 Sep 1983. It peaked at
No.7. Tracks on How She Threw It All Away (EP): How She Threw It All Away / Love
the First Time / Long Hot Summer / I Do Like to Be B-Side the A-Side. The version
of 'Long Hot Summer' on the EP is a re-recording of their third hit

Darren STYLES & Mark BREEZE present INFEXTIOUS
UK, male production duo (Singles: 5 Weeks)   pos/wks

5 Apr 03	LET ME FLY *Nukleuz 0432 CNUK*	**59**	1
31 Jul 04	YOU'RE SHINING *All Around the World CDGLOBE 333* ⸢1⸥	**19**	4

⸢1⸥ Styles & Breeze

STYLES & Pharoahe MONCH
US, male rappers (Singles: 1 Week)   pos/wks

14 Sep 02	THE LIFE *MCA MCSTD 40292*	**50**	1

STYLES P *See AKON featuring STYLES P*

The STYLISTICS ⸢207⸥ Top 500
Stylish and smooth vocal group from Philadelphia, US, fronted by falsetto-
voiced Russell Thompkins Jr, whose UK hits continued after success in their
homeland diminished. One of few US acts to have two chart-topping 'Greatest
Hits' albums (Singles: 143 Weeks, Albums: 142 Weeks)   pos/wks

24 Jun 72	BETCHA BY GOLLY WOW *Avco 6105 011*	**13**	12
4 Nov 72 ●	I'M STONE IN LOVE WITH YOU *Avco 6105 015*	**9**	10
17 Mar 73	BREAK UP TO MAKE UP *Avco 6105 020*	**34**	5
30 Jun 73	PEEK-A-BOO *Avco 6105 023*	**35**	6
19 Jan 74 ●	ROCKIN' ROLL BABY *Avco 6105 026*	**6**	9
13 Jul 74 ●	YOU MAKE ME FEEL BRAND NEW *Avco 6105 028*	**2**	14
19 Oct 74 ●	LET'S PUT IT ALL TOGETHER *Avco 6105 032*	**9**	9
25 Jan 75	STAR ON A TV SHOW *Avco 6105 035*	**12**	8
10 May 75 ●	SING BABY SING *Avco 6105 036*	**3**	10
26 Jul 75 ★	CAN'T GIVE YOU ANYTHING (BUT MY LOVE) *Avco 6105 039*	**1**	11
15 Nov 75 ●	NA-NA IS THE SADDEST WORD *Avco 6105 041*	**5**	10
14 Feb 76 ●	FUNKY WEEKEND *Avco 6105 044*	**10**	7
24 Apr 76 ●	CAN'T HELP FALLING IN LOVE *H&L 6105 050*	**4**	7
7 Aug 76 ●	SIXTEEN BARS *H&L 6105 059*	**7**	9
27 Nov 76	YOU'LL NEVER GET TO HEAVEN (EP) *H&L STYL 001*	**24**	9
26 Mar 77	$7000 AND YOU *H&L 6105 073*	**24**	7
24 Aug 74	ROCKIN' ROLL BABY *Avco 6466 012*	**42**	3
21 Sep 74	LET'S PUT IT ALL TOGETHER *Avco 6466 013*	**26**	14
1 Mar 75	FROM THE MOUNTAIN *Avco 9109 002*	**36**	1
5 Apr 75 ★	THE BEST OF THE STYLISTICS *Avco 9109 003*	**1**	63
5 Jul 75 ●	THANK YOU BABY *Avco 9109 005*	**5**	23
6 Dec 75	YOU ARE BEAUTIFUL *Avco 9109 006*	**26**	9
12 Jun 76	FABULOUS *Avco 9109 008*	**21**	5
18 Sep 76 ★	BEST OF THE STYLISTICS VOLUME 2 *H&L 9109 010*	**1**	21
17 Oct 92	THE GREATEST HITS OF THE STYLISTICS – LET'S PUT IT ALL TOGETHER *Mercury 5129852*	**34**	3

Tracks on You'll Never Get to Heaven (EP): You'll Never Get to Heaven / Country
Living / You Are Beautiful / The Miracle

STYLUS TROUBLE (see also FIRE ISLAND; HELLER & FARLEY
PROJECT) *UK, male producer – Pete Heller (Singles: 1 Week)*   pos/wks

23 Jun 01	SPUTNIK *Junior London BRG 014*	**63**	1

STYX *US, male vocal / instrumental group*
(Singles: 18 Weeks, Albums: 24 Weeks)   pos/wks

5 Jan 80 ●	BABE *A&M AMS 7489* ▲	**6**	10
24 Jan 81	THE BEST OF TIMES *A&M AMS 8102*	**42**	5
18 Jun 83	DON'T LET IT END *A&M AM 120*	**56**	3
3 Nov 79	CORNERSTONE *A&M AMLK 63711*	**36**	8
24 Jan 81 ●	PARADISE THEATER *A&M AMLH 63719* ▲	**8**	8
12 Mar 83	KILROY WAS HERE *A&M AMLX 63734*	**67**	6
5 May 84	CAUGHT IN THE ACT *A&M AMLM 66704*	**44**	2

SUB SUB
UK, male instrumental / production group (Singles: 12 Weeks)   pos/wks

10 Apr 93 ●	AIN'T NO LOVE (AIN'T NO USE) *Rob's CDROB 9* ⸢1⸥	**3**	11
19 Feb 94	RESPECT *Rob's CDROB 19*	**49**	1

⸢1⸥ Sub Sub featuring Melanie Williams

SUBCIRCUS
Denmark / UK, male vocal / instrumental group (Singles: 2 Weeks)   pos/wks

26 Apr 97	YOU LOVE YOU *Echo ECSCD 34*	**61**	1
12 Jul 97	86'D *Echo ECSCX 43*	**56**	1

SUBLIME *US, male vocal / instrumental group (Singles: 1 Week)*   pos/wks

5 Jul 97	WHAT I GOT *Gasoline Alley MCSTD 48045*	**71**	1

SUBLIMINAL CUTS (see also ARTEMESIA; ETHICS; MOVIN' MELODIES)
Holland, male producer – Patrick Prinz (Singles: 3 Weeks)   pos/wks

15 Oct 94	LE VOIE LE SOLEIL *XL XLS 53CD*	**69**	1
20 Jul 96	LE VOIE LE SOLEIL (re-mix) *XL XLSR 53CD*	**23**	2

SUBMERGE featuring Jan JOHNSTON
US, male producer / instrumentalist – Victor Imbres
and US, female vocalist (Singles: 2 Weeks)   pos/wks

8 Feb 97	TAKE ME BY THE HAND *AM:PM 5821012*	**28**	2

SUBSONIC 2 *UK, male rap duo (Singles: 3 Weeks)*

		pos/wks
13 Jul 91	**THE UNSUNG HEROES OF HIP HOP** *Unity 6577947* **63** 3	

SUBTERRANIA featuring Ann CONSUELO
Sweden, male / female vocal / instrumental duo (Singles: 1 Week) pos/wks

5 Jun 93	**DO IT FOR LOVE** *Champion CHAMPCD 297* **68** 1	

SUEDE `378` `Top 500` *London-based Britpop pioneers include photogenic front man Brett Anderson (v) and co-writer Bernard Butler (g), who left in 1994. Melody Maker's 'Best Band in Britain' won the Mercury Music Prize for their 1993 self-titled debut album, which sold more than 100,000 in the first week (Singles: 75 Weeks, Albums: 105 Weeks)* pos/wks

23 May 92	**THE DROWNERS / TO THE BIRDS** *Nude NUD 1S* **49** 2	
26 Sep 92	**METAL MICKEY** *Nude NUD 3S* **17** 3	
6 Mar 93 ●	**ANIMAL NITRATE** *Nude NUD 4CD* **7** 7	
29 May 93	**SO YOUNG** *Nude NUD 5CD* **22** 3	
26 Feb 94 ●	**STAY TOGETHER** *Nude NUD 9CD* **3** 6	
24 Sep 94	**WE ARE THE PIGS** *Nude NUD 10CD* **18** 3	
19 Nov 94	**THE WILD ONES** *Nude NUD 11CD* **18** 4	
11 Feb 95	**NEW GENERATION (re)** *Nude NUD 12CD1* **21** 4	
10 Aug 96 ●	**TRASH** *Nude NUD 21CD1* **3** 6	
26 Oct 96 ●	**BEAUTIFUL ONES** *Nude NUD 23CD1* **8** 5	
25 Jan 97 ●	**SATURDAY NIGHT** *Nude NUD 24CD1* **6** 4	
19 Apr 97	**LAZY** *Nude NUD 27CD1* **9** 3	
23 Aug 97 ●	**FILMSTAR** *Nude NUD 30CD1* **9** 4	
24 Apr 99 ●	**ELECTRICITY** *Nude NUD 43CD1* **5** 5	
3 Jul 99	**SHE'S IN FASHION** *Nude NUD 44CD1* **13** 5	
18 Sep 99	**EVERYTHING WILL FLOW** *Nude NUD 45CD1* **24** 2	
20 Nov 99	**CAN'T GET ENOUGH** *Nude NUD 47CD1* **23** 2	
28 Sep 02	**POSITIVITY** *Epic 6729492* **16** 2	
30 Nov 02	**OBSESSIONS** *Epic 6732942* **29** 2	
18 Oct 03	**ATTITUDE / GOLDEN GUN** *Sony Music 6743582* **14** 3	
10 Apr 93 ★	**SUEDE** *Nude NUDE 1CD* **1** 22	
22 Oct 94 ●	**DOG MAN STAR** *Nude 4778112* **3** 16	
14 Sep 96 ★	**COMING UP** *Nude NUDE 6CD* ■ **1** 44	
18 Oct 97	**SCI-FI LULLABIES** *Nude NUDE 9CD* **9** 3	
15 May 99 ★	**HEAD MUSIC** *Nude NUDE 14CD* ■ **1** 16	
12 Oct 02	**A NEW MORNING** *Epic 5089569* **24** 2	
1 Nov 03	**SINGLES** *Sony Music 5136042* **31** 2	

SUENO LATINO *Italy, male production duo (Singles: 6 Weeks)* pos/wks

23 Sep 89	**SUENO LATINO** *BCM BCM 323* [1] **47** 5	
11 Nov 00	**SUENO LATINO (re-mix)** *Distinctive DISNCD 64* **68** 1	

[1] Sueno Latino featuring Carolina Damas

SUGABABES `323` `Top 500` *Internationally successful soulful pop trio: Londoners Keisha Buchanan and Mutya Buena and Liverpudlian Heidi Range (replaced Siobhan Donaghy after act was dropped by London Records). At 18, these chart-toppers were the youngest all girl group to reach No.1 (Singles: 116 Weeks, Albums: 90 Weeks)* pos/wks

23 Sep 00 ●	**OVERLOAD** *London LONCD 449* **6** 8	
30 Dec 00	**NEW YEAR** *London LONCD 455* **12** 9	
21 Apr 01	**RUN FOR COVER** *London LONCD 459* **13** 7	
28 Jul 01	**SOUL SOUND** *London LONCD 460* **30** 2	
4 May 02 ★	**FREAK LIKE ME (re)** *Island CID 798* ■ **1** 14	
24 Aug 02 ★	**ROUND ROUND** *Island CID 804* ● **1** 13	
23 Nov 02	**STRONGER / ANGELS WITH DIRTY FACES** *Island CID 813* **7** 13	
22 Mar 03	**SHAPE** *Island CID 817* **11** 9	
25 Oct 03 ★	**HOLE IN THE HEAD** *Island CID 836* ■ **1** 13	
27 Dec 03	**TOO LOST IN YOU** *Island CID 844* **10** 13	
3 Apr 04 ●	**IN THE MIDDLE** *Island MCSXD 40360* **8** 8	
4 Sep 04 ●	**CAUGHT IN A MOMENT** *Universal MCSXD 40371* **8** 7	
23 Dec 00	**ONE TOUCH** *London 8573861072* **26** 15	
7 Sep 02 ●	**ANGELS WITH DIRTY FACES** *Island / Uni-Island CID 8122* **2** 40	
8 Nov 03 ●	**THREE** *Island / Uni-Island CID 8137* **3** 35	

SUGAR (see also BOB MOULD) *US, male vocal / instrumental group (Singles: 7 Weeks, Albums: 19 Weeks)* pos/wks

31 Oct 92	**A GOOD IDEA** *Creation CRE 143* **65** 1	
30 Jan 93	**IF I CAN'T CHANGE YOUR MIND** *Creation CRESCD 149* **30** 2	
21 Aug 93	**TILTED** *Creation CRECD 156* **48** 1	
3 Sep 94	**YOUR FAVORITE THING** *Creation CRESCD 186* **40** 2	
29 Oct 94	**BELIEVE WHAT YOU'RE SAYING** *Creation CRESCD 193* **73** 1	
19 Sep 92 ●	**COPPER BLUE** *Creation CRECD 129* **10** 11	

17 Apr 93 ●	**BEASTER** *Creation CRECD 153* **3** 5	
17 Sep 94 ●	**FILE UNDER EASY LISTENING** *Creation CRECD 172* **7** 3	

SUGAR CANE *US, male / female vocal group (Singles: 5 Weeks)* pos/wks

30 Sep 78	**MONTEGO BAY** *Ariola Hansa AHA 524* **54** 5	

SUGAR RAY *US, male vocal / instrumental group (Singles: 12 Weeks, Albums: 1 Week)* pos/wks

31 Jan 98	**FLY** *Atlantic AT 0008CD* **58** 1	
29 May 99	**EVERY MORNING** *Lava / Atlantic AT 0065CD* **10** 9	
20 Oct 01	**WHEN IT'S OVER** *Atlantic AT 0114CD* **32** 2	
19 Jun 99	**14:59** *Atlantic 7567831512* **60** 1	

SUGARCOMA
UK, male / female vocal / instrumental group (Singles: 1 Week) pos/wks

13 Apr 02	**YOU DRIVE ME CRAZY / WINDINGS** *Music for Nations CDKUT 190* **57** 1	

The SUGARCUBES
(see also BJÖRK) Iceland, female / male vocal / instrumental group – leader Björk (Singles: 22 Weeks, Albums: 14 Weeks) pos/wks

14 Nov 87	**BIRTHDAY** *One Little Indian 7TP 7* **65** 3	
30 Jan 88	**COLD SWEAT** *One Little Indian 7TP 9* **56** 4	
16 Apr 88	**DEUS** *One Little Indian 7TP 10* **51** 3	
3 Sep 88	**BIRTHDAY (re-recording)** *One Little Indian 7TP 11* **65** 3	
16 Sep 89	**REGINA** *One Little Indian 26TP 7* **55** 2	
11 Jan 92	**HIT** *One Little Indian 62TP 7* **17** 6	
3 Oct 92	**BIRTHDAY (re-mix)** *One Little Indian 104TP 12* **64** 1	
7 May 88	**LIFE'S TOO GOOD** *One Little Indian TPLP 5* **14** 6	
14 Oct 89	**HERE TODAY, TOMORROW NEXT WEEK!** *One Little Indian TPLP 15* **15** 3	
22 Feb 92	**STICK AROUND FOR JOY** *One Little Indian TPLP 30CD* **16** 4	
17 Oct 92	**IT'S-IT** *One Little Indian TPLP 40CD* **47** 1	

SUGARHILL GANG *US, male rap group (Singles: 16 Weeks)* pos/wks

1 Dec 79 ●	**RAPPER'S DELIGHT** *Sugarhill SHL 101* **3** 11	
11 Sep 82	**THE LOVER IN YOU** *Sugarhill SH 116* **54** 3	
25 Nov 89	**RAPPER'S DELIGHT (re-mix)** *Sugarhill SHRD 0007* **58** 2	

SUGGS (see also MADNESS) *UK, male vocalist – Graham McPherson (Singles: 46 Weeks, Albums: 5 Weeks)* pos/wks

12 Aug 95 ●	**I'M ONLY SLEEPING / OFF ON HOLIDAY** *WEA YZ 975CD* **7** 6	
14 Oct 95	**CAMDEN TOWN** *WEA WEA 019CD* **14** 6	
16 Dec 95	**THE TUNE** *WEA WEA 031CD* **33** 3	
13 Apr 96 ●	**CECILIA (2re)** *WEA WEA 042CD1* [1] **4** 19	
21 Sep 96	**NO MORE ALCOHOL** *WEA WEA 065CD1* [1] **24** 4	
17 May 97	**BLUE DAY** *WEA WEA 112CD* [2] **22** 5	
5 Sep 98	**I AM** *WEA WEA 174CD* **38** 3	
28 Oct 95	**THE LONE RANGER** *WEA 0630124782* **14** 5	

[1] Suggs featuring Louchie Lou and Michie One [2] Suggs & Co featuring Chelsea Team

SUICIDAL TENDENCIES
US, male vocal / instrumental group (Albums: 2 Weeks) pos/wks

9 May 87	**JOIN THE ARMY** *Virgin V 2424* **81** 1	
21 Jul 90	**LIGHTS ... CAMERA ... REVOLUTION** *Epic 4665691* **59** 1	

Justine SUISSA See Armin VAN BUUREN; OCEANLAB

SULTANA
Italy, male instrumental / production group (Singles: 1 Week) pos/wks

26 Mar 94	**TE AMO** *Union City UCRD 28* **57** 1	

SULTANS OF PING *Ireland, male vocal / instrumental group (Singles: 12 Weeks, Albums: 3 Weeks)* pos/wks

8 Feb 92	**WHERE'S ME JUMPER?** *Divine ATHY 01* [1] **67** 2	
9 May 92	**STUPID KID** *Divine ATHY 02* [1] **67** 1	
10 Oct 92	**VERONICA** *Divine ATHY 03* [1] **69** 1	
9 Jan 93	**YOU TALK TOO MUCH** *Rhythm King 6588872* [1] **26** 3	
11 Sep 93	**TEENAGE PUNKS** *Epic 6595792* **49** 2	
30 Oct 93	**MICHIKO** *Epic 6598222* **43** 2	
19 Feb 94	**WAKE UP AND SCRATCH ME** *Epic 6601122* **50** 1	
13 Feb 93	**CASUAL SEX IN THE CINEPLEX** *Rhythm King 4724952* [1] **26** 2	
5 Mar 94	**TEENAGE DRUG** *Epic 4747162* **57** 1	

[1] Sultans of Ping FC [1] Sultans of Ping FC

Singles re-entries are listed as (re), (2re), (3re).... which signifies that the hit re-entered the chart once, twice or three times...

SUM 41 *Canada, male vocal / instrumental*
group (Singles: 40 Weeks, Albums: 50 Weeks) pos/wks

13 Oct 01 ●	FAT LIP *Mercury 5888012*	**8** 9
15 Dec 01	IN TOO DEEP *Mercury 5888982*	**13** 11
6 Apr 02	MOTIVATION *Mercury 5889452*	**21** 7
29 Jun 02	IT'S WHAT WE'RE ALL ABOUT *Columbia 6728642*	**32** 3
30 Nov 02	STILL WAITING *Mercury 0638312*	**16** 7
22 Feb 03	THE HELL SONG *Mercury 0637202*	**35** 3
11 Aug 01 ●	ALL KILLER NO FILLER *Mercury 5486622*	**7** 43
7 Dec 02	DOES THIS LOOK INFECTED? *Mercury 0635590*	**39** 6
23 Oct 04	CHUCK *Mercury 9864426*	**59** 1

SUMMER *See SNAP!*

Donna SUMMER 〔 77 〕 Top 500 *"Queen of disco music", b. LaDonna*
Gaines, 31 Dec 1948, Massachusetts, US. Germany was the launching pad for this diva, who had eight successive US Top 5 singles in the late 1970s. She was also the first female to score three consecutive US No.1 albums (Singles: 299 Weeks, Albums: 204 Weeks) pos/wks

17 Jan 76 ●	LOVE TO LOVE YOU BABY *GTO GT 17*	**4** 9
29 May 76	COULD IT BE MAGIC *GTO GT 60*	**40** 7
25 Dec 76	WINTER MELODY *GTO GT 76*	**27** 6
9 Jul 77 ★	I FEEL LOVE *GTO GT 100*	**1** 11
20 Aug 77 ●	DOWN DEEP INSIDE (THEME FROM 'THE DEEP') *Casablanca CAN 111*	**5** 10
24 Sep 77	I REMEMBER YESTERDAY *GTO GT 107*	**14** 7
3 Dec 77 ●	LOVE'S UNKIND *GTO GT 113*	**3** 13
10 Dec 77 ●	I LOVE YOU *Casablanca CAN 114*	**10** 9
25 Feb 78	RUMOUR HAS IT *Casablanca CAN 122*	**19** 8
22 Apr 78	BACK IN LOVE AGAIN *GTO GT 117*	**29** 7
10 Jun 78	LAST DANCE (re) *Casablanca TGIF 2*	**51** 9
14 Oct 78 ●	MACARTHUR PARK *Casablanca CAN 131* ▲	**5** 10
17 Feb 79	HEAVEN KNOWS *Casablanca CAN 141*	**34** 8
12 May 79	HOT STUFF *Casablanca CAN 151* ▲	**11** 10
7 Jul 79	BAD GIRLS *Casablanca CAN 155* ▲	**14** 10
1 Sep 79	DIM ALL THE LIGHTS *Casablanca CAN 162*	**29** 9
3 Nov 79 ●	NO MORE TEARS (ENOUGH IS ENOUGH) *Casablanca CAN 174 / CBS 8000* 〔1〕▲	**3** 13
16 Feb 80	ON THE RADIO *Casablanca NB 2236*	**32** 6
21 Jun 80	SUNSET PEOPLE *Casablanca CAN 198*	**46** 5
27 Sep 80	THE WANDERER *Geffen K 79180*	**48** 6
17 Jan 81	COLD LOVE *Geffen K 79193*	**44** 3
10 Jul 82	LOVE IS IN CONTROL (FINGER ON THE TRIGGER) *Warner Bros. K 79302*	**18** 11
6 Nov 82	STATE OF INDEPENDENCE *Warner Bros. K 79344*	**14** 11
4 Dec 82	I FEEL LOVE (re-mix) *Casablanca FEEL 7*	**21** 10
5 Mar 83	THE WOMAN IN ME *Warner Bros. U 9983*	**62** 2
18 Jun 83	SHE WORKS HARD FOR THE MONEY *Mercury DONNA 1*	**25** 8
24 Sep 83	UNCONDITIONAL LOVE *Mercury DONNA 2*	**14** 12
21 Jan 84	STOP LOOK AND LISTEN *Mercury DONNA 3*	**57** 2
24 Oct 87	DINNER WITH GERSHWIN *Warner Bros. U 8237*	**13** 11
23 Jan 88	ALL SYSTEMS GO *WEA U 8122*	**54** 3
25 Feb 89 ●	THIS TIME I KNOW IT'S FOR REAL *Warner Bros. U 7780*	**3** 14
27 May 89 ●	I DON'T WANNA GET HURT *Warner Bros. U 7567*	**7** 9
26 Aug 89	LOVE'S ABOUT TO CHANGE MY HEART *Warner Bros. U 7494*	**20** 6
25 Nov 89	WHEN LOVE TAKES OVER YOU *WEA U 7361*	**72** 1
17 Nov 90	STATE OF INDEPENDENCE (re-issue) *Warner Bros. U 2857*	**45** 3
12 Jan 91	BREAKAWAY *Warner Bros. U 3308*	**49** 4
30 Nov 91	WORK THAT MAGIC *Warner Bros. U 5937*	**74** 1
12 Nov 94	MELODY OF LOVE (WANNA BE LOVED) *Mercury MERCD 418*	**21** 3
9 Sep 95 ●	I FEEL LOVE (re-recording) *Manifesto FESCD 1*	**8** 5
6 Apr 96	STATE OF INDEPENDENCE (re-mix) *Manifesto FESCD 7* 〔2〕	**13** 5
11 Jul 98	CARRY ON *Almighty CDALMY 120* 〔3〕	**65** 1
30 Oct 99	I WILL GO WITH YOU (CON TE PARTIRO) *Epic 6682092*	**44** 1
31 Jan 76	LOVE TO LOVE YOU BABY *GTO GTLP 008*	**16** 9
22 May 76	A LOVE TRILOGY *GTO GTLP 010*	**41** 10
25 Jun 77 ●	I REMEMBER YESTERDAY *GTO GTLP 025*	**3** 23
26 Nov 77	ONCE UPON A TIME *Casablanca CALD 5003*	**24** 13
7 Jan 78 ●	GREATEST HITS *GTO GTLP 028*	**4** 18
21 Oct 78	LIVE AND MORE *Casablanca CALD 5006* ▲	**16** 16
2 Jun 79	BAD GIRLS *Casablanca CALD 5007* ▲	**23** 23
10 Nov 79	ON THE RADIO – GREATEST HITS VOLUMES 1 & 2 *Casablanca CALD 5008* ▲	**24** 22
1 Nov 80	THE WANDERER *Geffen K 99124*	**55** 2
31 Jul 82	DONNA SUMMER *Warner Bros. K 99163*	**13** 16
16 Jul 83	SHE WORKS HARD FOR THE MONEY *Mercury MERL 21*	**28** 5
15 Sep 84	CATS WITHOUT CLAWS *Warner Bros. 250806*	**69** 2

25 Mar 89	ANOTHER PLACE AND TIME *Warner Bros. WX 219*	**17** 28
24 Nov 90	THE BEST OF DONNA SUMMER *Warner Bros. WX 397*	**24** 9
26 Nov 94	ENDLESS SUMMER – GREATEST HITS *Mercury 5262172*	**37** 2
26 Jun 04 ●	THE JOURNEY – THE VERY BEST OF DONNA SUMMER *Mercury 9862858*	**6** 6

〔1〕 Donna Summer and Barbra Streisand 〔2〕 Donna Summer featuring the All Star Choir 〔3〕 Donna Summer and Giorgio Moroder

'No More Tears (Enough Is Enough)' was released simultaneously on two different labels, a 7-inch single on Casablanca and a 12-inch on CBS. 'Unconditional Love' features the additional vocals of Musical Youth

SUMMER DAZE
UK, male instrumental / production duo (Singles: 1 Week) pos/wks

26 Oct 96	SAMBA MAGIC *VC VCRD 14*	**61** 1

Mark SUMMERS (see also SOUVLAKI)
UK, male producer (Singles: 6 Weeks) pos/wks

26 Jan 91	SUMMER'S MAGIC *Fourth & Broadway BRW 205*	**27** 6

J D SUMNER *See Elvis PRESLEY*

SUNBURST (see also LOST TRIBE;
Matt DAREY; MELT featuring LITTLE MS MARCIE; MDM)
UK, male producer – Matt Darey (Singles: 1 Week) pos/wks

8 Jul 00	EYEBALL (EYEBALL PAUL'S THEME) *Virgin / EMI VTSCD 4*	**48** 1

SUNCLUB *See UD Project vs SUNCLUB*

SUNDANCE (see also SHIMMON & WOOLFSON)
UK, male production duo – Nick Woolfson
and Mark Shimmon (Singles: 7 Weeks) pos/wks

8 Nov 97	SUNDANCE *React CDREACT 109*	**33** 2
3 Oct 98	SUNDANCE '98 (re-mix) *React CDREACTX 136*	**37** 2
27 Feb 99	THE LIVING DREAM *React CDREACT 134*	**56** 1
5 Feb 00	WON'T LET THIS FEELING GO *Inferno CDFERN 23*	**40** 2

SUNDANCE *See DJ 'FAST' EDDIE*

The SUNDAYS *UK, male / female vocal /*
instrumental group (Singles: 12 Weeks, Albums: 15 Weeks) pos/wks

11 Feb 89	CAN'T BE SURE *Rough Trade RT 218*	**45** 5
3 Oct 92	GOODBYE *Parlophone R 6319*	**27** 2
20 Sep 97	SUMMERTIME *Parlophone CDRS 6475*	**15** 4
22 Nov 97	CRY *Parlophone CDR 6487*	**43** 1
27 Jan 90 ●	READING WRITING AND ARITHMETIC *Rough Trade ROUGH 148*	**4** 8
31 Oct 92	BLIND *Parlophone CDPCSD 121*	**15** 3
4 Oct 97 ●	STATIC & SILENCE *Parlophone CDEST 2300*	**10** 4

SUNDRAGON
UK, male vocal / instrumental duo (Singles: 1 Week) pos/wks

21 Feb 68	GREEN TAMBOURINE *MGM 1380*	**50** 1

SUNFIRE *US, male vocal / instrumental group (Singles: 11 Weeks)* pos/wks

12 Mar 83	YOUNG, FREE AND SINGLE *Warner Bros. W 9897*	**20** 11

SUNKIDS featuring CHANCE
US, male production duo and US, female vocalist (Singles: 2 Weeks) pos/wks

13 Nov 99	RESCUE ME *AM:PM CDAMPM 126*	**50** 2

SUNNY *UK, female vocalist – Sunny Leslie (Singles: 10 Weeks)* pos/wks

30 Mar 74 ●	DOCTOR'S ORDERS *CBS 2068*	**7** 10

SUNSCREEM *UK, male / female vocal /*
instrumental group (Singles: 36 Weeks, Albums: 6 Weeks) pos/wks

29 Feb 92	PRESSURE *Sony S2 6578017*	**60** 2
18 Jul 92	LOVE U MORE *Sony S2 6581727*	**23** 6
17 Oct 92	PERFECT MOTION *Sony S2 6584057*	**18** 5
9 Jan 93	BROKEN ENGLISH *Sony S2 6589032*	**13** 5
27 Mar 93	PRESSURE US (re-mix) *Sony S2 6591102*	**19** 5
2 Sep 95	WHEN *Sony S2 6623222*	**47** 2
18 Nov 95	EXODUS *Sony S2 6625342*	**40** 2

20 Jan 96	**WHITE SKIES** *Sony S2 6627425* **25** 3	
23 Mar 96	**SECRETS** *Sony S2 6629342* **36** 2	
6 Sep 97	**CATCH** *Pulse-8 CDLOSE 117* **55** 1	
20 Oct 01	**PLEASE SAVE ME** *Inferno / Five AM FAMFERN 1CD* [1] **36** 2	
16 Nov 02	**PERFECT MOTION** (re-mix) *Five AM FAM 15CD* **71** 1	
13 Feb 93	**03** *Sony S2 4722182* **33** 5	
30 Mar 96	**CHANGE OR DIE** *Sony S2 4813132* **53** 1	

[1] Sunscreem vs Push

Monty SUNSHINE See Chris BARBER

SUNSHINE BAND See KC AND THE SUNSHINE BAND

SUNSHIP featuring MCRB *UK, male producer –*
Ceri Evans and male rapper – Ricky Benjamin (Singles: 1 Week) pos/wks

1 Apr 00	**CHEQUE ONE-TWO** *Filter FILT 044* **75** 1	

SUPATONIC
UK, male vocal / instrumental duo (Singles: 1 Week) pos/wks

6 Nov 04	**I WISH IT WASN'T TRUE** *Fluff Alley FLUFFA 001* **69** 1	

SUPER FURRY ANIMALS *UK, male vocal /*
instrumental group (Singles: 45 Weeks, Albums: 34 Weeks) pos/wks

9 Mar 96	**HOMETOWN UNICORN** *Creation CRESCD 222* **47** 1	
11 May 96	**GOD! SHOW ME MAGIC** *Creation CRESCD 231* **33** 2	
13 Jul 96	**SOMETHING 4 THE WEEKEND** *Creation CRESCD 235* **18** 3	
12 Oct 96	**IF YOU DON'T WANT ME TO DESTROY YOU**	
	Creation CRESCD 243 ....**18** 2	
14 Dec 96	**THE MAN DON'T GIVE A FUCK** *Creation CRESCD 247* **22** 2	
24 May 97	**HERMANN LOVES PAULINE** *Creation CRESCD 252* **26** 2	
26 Jul 97	**THE INTERNATIONAL LANGUAGE OF SCREAMING**	
	Creation CRESCD 269 ....**24** 2	
4 Oct 97	**PLAY IT COOL** *Creation CRESCD 275* **27** 2	
6 Dec 97	**DEMONS** *Creation CRESCD 283* **27** 2	
6 Jun 98	**ICE HOCKEY HAIR EP** *Creation CRESCD 288* **12** 3	
22 May 99	**NORTHERN LITES** *Creation CRESCD 314* **11** 4	
21 Aug 99	**FIRE IN MY HEART** *Creation CRESCD 323* **25** 3	
29 Jan 00	**DO OR DIE** *Creation CRESCD 329* **20** 2	
21 Jul 01	**JUXTAPOZED WITH U** *Epic 6712242* **14** 4	
20 Oct 01	**(DRAWING) RINGS AROUND THE WORLD** *Epic 6719082* **28** 2	
26 Jan 02	**IT'S NOT THE END OF THE WORLD?** *Epic 6721752* **30** 2	
26 Jul 03	**GOLDEN RETRIEVER** *Epic 6739062* **13** 3	
1 Nov 03	**HELLO SUNSHINE** *Epic 6743602* **31** 2	
9 Oct 04	**THE MAN DON'T GIVE A FUCK (LIVE)** *Epic 6753041* **16** 2	
1 Jun 96	**FUZZY LOGIC** *Creation CRECD 190* **23** 6	
6 Sep 97 ●	**RADIATOR** *Creation CRECD 214* **8** 3	
5 Dec 98	**OUT SPACED** *Creation CRECD 229* **44** 1	
26 Jun 99 ●	**GUERRILLA** *Creation CRECD 242* **10** 9	
27 May 00	**MWNG** *Placid Casual PLC 03CD* **11** 2	
4 Aug 01 ●	**RINGS AROUND THE WORLD** *Epic 5024132* **3** 7	
2 Aug 03 ●	**PHANTOM POWER** *Epic 5123759* **4** 4	
16 Oct 04 ●	**SONGBOOK – THE SINGLES – VOLUME ONE** *Epic 5176719*....**18** 2	

Tracks on Ice Hockey Hair EP: Smokin' / Ice Hockey Hair / Mu-Tron / Let's Quit Smoking The band's name is abbreviated to SFA on the album 'Guerrilla'

SUPERCAR *Italy, male DJ production duo –*
Alberto Pizarelli and Ricki Pagano (Singles: 6 Weeks) pos/wks

13 Feb 99	**TONITE** *Pepper 0530202* **15** 5	
21 Aug 99	**COMPUTER LOVE** *Pepper 0530392* [1] **67** 1	

[1] Supercar featuring Mikaela

SUPERCAT
Jamaica, male vocalist – William Maragh (Singles: 5 Weeks) pos/wks

1 Aug 92	**IT FE DONE** *Columbia 6582737* **66** 1	
6 May 95	**MY GIRL JOSEPHINE** *Columbia 6614702* [1] **22** 4	

[1] Supercat featuring Jack Radics

SUPERFUNK
France, male production trio (Singles: 2 Weeks) pos/wks

4 Mar 00	**LUCKY STAR** *Virgin DINSD 198* [1] **42** 1	
10 Jun 00	**THE YOUNG MC** *Virgin DINSD 206* **62** 1	

[1] Superfunk featuring Ron Carroll

SUPERGRASS (405) `Top 500`
(see also TWISTED X) Acclaimed power-pop group, formed in Oxford in 1994; Gaz Coombes (g/v). Danny Goffey (d/v), Mick Quinn (b/v) and in 1995 Gaz's brother Rob (k). Popular live band were voted Best British Newcomers at the 1996 Brit awards. Their first three albums achieved platinum status (Singles: 65 Weeks, Albums: 105 Weeks) pos/wks

29 Oct 94	**CAUGHT BY THE FUZZ** *Parlophone CDR 6396* **43** 2	
18 Feb 95	**MANSIZE ROOSTER** *Parlophone CDR 6402* **20** 3	
25 Mar 95	**LOSE IT** *Sub Pop SP 281* **75** 1	
13 May 95 ●	**LENNY** *Parlophone CDR 6410* **10** 3	
15 Jul 95 ●	**ALRIGHT / TIME** *Parlophone CDR 6413* **2** 10	
9 Mar 96 ●	**GOING OUT** *Parlophone CDR 6428* **5** 6	
12 Apr 97 ●	**RICHARD III** *Parlophone CDR 6461* **2** 5	
21 Jun 97	**SUN HITS THE SKY** *Parlophone CDR 6469* **10** 4	
18 Oct 97	**LATE IN THE DAY** *Parlophone CDR 6484* **18** 4	
5 Jun 99	**PUMPING ON YOUR STEREO** (re) *Parlophone CDR 6518* **11** 7	
18 Sep 99 ●	**MOVING** *Parlophone CDR 6524* **9** 5	
4 Dec 99	**MARY** (re) *Parlophone CDR 6531* **36** 4	
13 Jul 02	**NEVER DONE NOTHING LIKE THAT BEFORE**	
	Parlophone CDR 6563 ....**75** 1	
28 Sep 02	**GRACE** *Parlophone CDR 6586* **13** 4	
8 Feb 03	**SEEN THE LIGHT** *Parlophone CDR 6592* **22** 3	
5 Jun 04	**KISS OF LIFE** *Parlophone CDRS 6638* **23** 3	
27 May 95 ★	**I SHOULD COCO** *Parlophone CDPCS 7373* **1** 36	
3 May 97 ●	**IN IT FOR THE MONEY** *Parlophone CDPCS 7388* **2** 25	
2 Oct 99 ●	**SUPERGRASS** *Parlophone 5220562* **3** 25	
12 Oct 02 ●	**LIFE ON OTHER PLANETS** *Parlophone 5418002* **9** 6	
19 Jun 04 ●	**SUPERGRASS IS 10 – THE BEST OF 94-04**	
	Parlophone 5708602 ....**4** 13	

SUPERMEN LOVERS featuring Mani HOFFMAN *France, male*
producer – Guillaume Atlan and male vocalist (Singles: 16 Weeks) pos/wks

15 Sep 01 ●	**STARLIGHT** (re) *Independiente ISOM 53MS* **2** 16	

The SUPERNATURALS *UK, male vocal /*
instrumental group (Singles: 15 Weeks, Albums: 7 Weeks) pos/wks

26 Oct 96	**LAZY LOVER** *Food CDFOOD 85* **34** 2	
8 Feb 97	**THE DAY BEFORE YESTERDAY'S MAN** *Food CDFOODS 88* **25** 3	
26 Apr 97	**SMILE** *Food CDFOOD 92* **23** 2	
12 Jul 97	**LOVE HAS PASSED AWAY** *Food CDFOOD 99* **38** 2	
25 Oct 97	**PREPARE TO LAND** *Food CDFOODS 106* **48** 1	
1 Aug 98	**I WASN'T BUILT TO GET UP** *Food CDFOOD 112* **25** 3	
24 Oct 98	**SHEFFIELD SONG** *Food CDFOODS 115* **45** 1	
13 Mar 99	**EVEREST** *Food CDFOOD 119* **52** 1	
17 May 97 ●	**IT DOESN'T MATTER ANYMORE** *Food FOODCD 21* **9** 4	
22 Aug 98	**A TUNE A DAY** *Food 4960662* **21** 3	

SUPERNOVA
UK, male / female vocal / instrumental duo (Singles: 1 Week) pos/wks

11 May 96	**SOME MIGHT SAY** *Sing Sing 74321369442* **55** 1	

SUPERSISTER
UK, female vocal group (Singles: 8 Weeks) pos/wks

14 Oct 00	**COFFEE** *Gut CDGUT 35* **16** 5	
25 Aug 01	**SHOPPING** *Gut CDGUT 37* **36** 2	
17 Nov 01	**SUMMER GONNA COME AGAIN** *Gut CDGUT 38* **51** 1	

SUPERSTAR
UK, male vocal / instrumental group (Singles: 2 Weeks) pos/wks

7 Feb 98	**EVERY DAY I FALL APART** *Camp Fabulous CFAB 003CD* **66** 1	
25 Apr 98	**SUPERSTAR** *Camp Fabulous CFAB 007CD* **49** 1	

SUPERTRAMP (278) `Top 500` *Acclaimed Anglo-American group*
formed in 1969 by UK musicians Rick Davies (v/k) and Roger Hodgson (v/g). A change of sound from progressive rock to more focused pop in the mid-70s was internationally successful: 'Breakfast In America', their biggest seller, shifted 18 million albums (Singles: 52 Weeks, Albums: 181 Weeks) pos/wks

15 Feb 75	**DREAMER** *A&M AMS 7132* **13** 10	
25 Jun 77	**GIVE A LITTLE BIT** *A&M AMS 7293* **29** 7	
31 Mar 79 ●	**THE LOGICAL SONG** *A&M AMS 7427* **7** 11	
30 Jun 79 ●	**BREAKFAST IN AMERICA** *A&M AMS 7451* **9** 10	
27 Oct 79	**GOODBYE STRANGER** *A&M AMS 7481* **57** 3	
30 Oct 82	**IT'S RAINING AGAIN** *A&M AMS 8255* [1] **26** 11	

23 Nov 74 ●	CRIME OF THE CENTURY *A&M AMLS 68258*	4	22
6 Dec 75	CRISIS? WHAT CRISIS? *A&M AMLH 68347*	20	15
23 Apr 77	EVEN IN THE QUIETEST MOMENTS *A&M AMLK 64634*	12	22
31 Jan 79 ●	BREAKFAST IN AMERICA *A&M AMLK 63708* ▲	3	53
4 Oct 80 ●	PARIS *A&M AMLM 66702*	7	17
6 Nov 82 ●	FAMOUS LAST WORDS *A&M AMLK 63732*	6	16
25 May 85	BROTHER WHERE YOU BOUND *A&M AMA 5014*	20	5
18 Oct 86 ●	THE AUTOBIOGRAPHY OF SUPERTRAMP *A&M TRAMP 1*	9	19
31 Oct 87	FREE AS A BIRD *A&M AMA 5181*	93	1
15 Aug 92	THE VERY BEST OF SUPERTRAMP *A&M TRACD 1992*	24	4
3 May 97	SOME THINGS NEVER CHANGE *EMI CDCHR 6121*	74	1
27 Sep 97 ●	THE VERY BEST OF SUPERTRAMP (re-issue) *PolyGram TV 3970912*	8	6

[1] Supertramp featuring vocals by Roger Hodgson

The SUPREMES 70 Top 500

World's most successful female group: Diana Ross, Mary Wilson, Florence Ballard, b. 1944, d. 1976. Before Ross went solo in 1969, this Detroit-based trio had amassed a dozen US No.1s and became the first female trio to top the UK singles chart. They were inducted into the Rock and Roll Hall of Fame in 1988 (Singles: 306 Weeks, Albums: 229 Weeks)   pos/wks

3 Sep 64 ●	WHERE DID OUR LOVE GO *Stateside SS 327* ▲	3	14
22 Oct 64 ★	BABY LOVE *Stateside SS 350* ▲	1	15
21 Jan 65	COME SEE ABOUT ME *Stateside SS 376* ▲	27	6
25 Mar 65 ●	STOP! IN THE NAME OF LOVE *Tamla Motown TMG 501* ▲	7	12
10 Jun 65	BACK IN MY ARMS AGAIN *Tamla Motown TMG 516* ▲	40	5
9 Dec 65	I HEAR A SYMPHONY (re) *Tamla Motown TMG 543* ▲	39	5
8 Sep 66 ●	YOU CAN'T HURRY LOVE *Tamla Motown TMG 575* ▲	3	12
1 Dec 66 ●	YOU KEEP ME HANGIN' ON *Tamla Motown TMG 585* ▲	8	10
2 Mar 67	LOVE IS HERE AND NOW YOU'RE GONE *Tamla Motown TMG 597* ▲	17	10
11 May 67 ●	THE HAPPENING *Tamla Motown TMG 607* ▲	6	12
30 Aug 67 ●	REFLECTIONS *Tamla Motown TMG 616* [1]	5	14
29 Nov 67	IN AND OUT OF LOVE *Tamla Motown TMG 632* [1]	13	13
10 Apr 68	FOREVER CAME TODAY *Tamla Motown TMG 650* [1]	28	8
3 Jul 68	SOME THINGS YOU NEVER GET USED TO *Tamla Motown TMG 662* [1]	34	6
20 Nov 68 ●	LOVE CHILD *Tamla Motown TMG 677* [1] ▲	15	14
29 Jan 69 ●	I'M GONNA MAKE YOU LOVE ME (re) *Tamla Motown TMG 685* [2]	3	12
23 Apr 69	I'M LIVIN' IN SHAME (re) *Tamla Motown TMG 695* [1]	14	10
16 Jul 69	NO MATTER WHAT SIGN YOU ARE *Tamla Motown TMG 704*	37	7
20 Sep 69	I SECOND THAT EMOTION *Tamla Motown TMG 709* [2]	18	8
13 Dec 69	SOMEDAY WE'LL BE TOGETHER *Tamla Motown TMG 721* [1] ▲	13	13
21 Mar 70	WHY (MUST WE FALL IN LOVE) *Tamla Motown TMG 730* [2]	31	7
2 May 70 ●	UP THE LADDER TO THE ROOF *Tamla Motown TMG 735*	6	15
16 Jan 71 ●	STONED LOVE *Tamla Motown TMG 760*	3	13
26 Jun 71	RIVER DEEP MOUNTAIN HIGH *Tamla Motown TMG 777* [2]	11	10
21 Aug 71 ●	NATHAN JONES *Tamla Motown TMG 782*	5	11
20 Nov 71	YOU GOTTA HAVE LOVE IN YOUR HEART *Tamla Motown TMG 793* [3]	25	10
4 Mar 72 ●	FLOY JOY *Tamla Motown TMG 804*	9	10
15 Jul 72 ●	AUTOMATICALLY SUNSHINE *Tamla Motown TMG 821*	10	9
21 Apr 73	BAD WEATHER *Tamla Motown TMG 847*	37	4
24 Aug 74 ●	BABY LOVE (re-issue) *Tamla Motown TMG 915* [1]	12	10
18 Feb 89	STOP! IN THE NAME OF LOVE (re-issue) *Motown ZB 41963* [1]	62	1
5 Dec 64 ●	MEET THE SUPREMES *Stateside SL 10109*	8	6
17 Dec 66 ●	SUPREMES A GO-GO *Tamla Motown STML 11039* ▲	15	21
13 May 67	THE SUPREMES SING MOTOWN *Tamla Motown STML 11047*	15	16
30 Sep 67	THE SUPREMES SING RODGERS & HART *Tamla Motown STML 11054*	25	7
20 Jan 68 ★	GREATEST HITS *Tamla Motown STML 11063* ▲	1	60
30 Mar 68 ●	LIVE AT THE TALK OF THE TOWN *Tamla Motown STML 11070* [1]	6	18
20 Jul 68	REFLECTIONS *Tamla Motown STML 11073* [1]	30	2
25 Jan 69 ★	DIANA ROSS AND THE SUPREMES JOIN THE TEMPTATIONS *Tamla Motown STML 11096* [2] ▲	1	15
1 Feb 69 ●	LOVE CHILD *Tamla Motown STML 11095* [1]	8	6
28 Jun 69	TCB *Tamla Motown STML 11110* [2]	11	12
14 Feb 70	TOGETHER *Tamla Motown STML 11122* [2]	28	4
29 May 71 ●	MAGNIFICENT SEVEN *Tamla Motown STML 11179* [3]	6	11

25 Sep 71	TOUCH *Tamla Motown STML 11189*	40	1
17 Sep 77 ★	20 GOLDEN GREATS *Motown EMTV 5* [1]	1	34
21 Jan 89 ●	LOVE SUPREME *Motown ZL 72701* [1]	10	9
31 Oct 98	40 GOLDEN MOTOWN GREATS *Motown / PolyGram TV 5309612* [1]	35	4
29 May 04	THE NO 1'S *Motown 9818019* [1]	26	3

[1] Diana Ross and The Supremes [2] Diana Ross and The Supremes and The Temptations [3] The Supremes and The Four Tops [1] Diana Ross and The Supremes [2] Diana Ross and The Supremes with The Temptations [3] The Supremes and The Four Tops

Al B SURE!
US, male vocalist – Al Brown (Singles: 13 Weeks)   pos/wks

16 Apr 88	NITE AND DAY *Uptown W 8192*	44	5
30 Jul 88	OFF ON YOUR OWN (GIRL) *Uptown W 7870*	70	2
10 Jun 89	IF I'M NOT YOUR LOVER *Uptown W 2908* [1]	54	3
31 Mar 90	SECRET GARDEN *Qwest W 9992* [2]	67	1
12 Jun 93	BLACK TIE WHITE NOISE *Arista 74321148682* [3]	36	2

[1] Al B Sure! featuring Slick Rick [2] Quincy Jones featuring Al B Sure!, James Ingram, El DeBarge and Barry White [3] David Bowie featuring Al B Sure!

SUREAL
UK, male / female production / vocal group (Singles: 4 Weeks)   pos/wks

7 Oct 00	YOU TAKE MY BREATH AWAY *Cream CREAM 7CD*	15	4

SURFACE *US, male vocal / instrumental duo (Singles: 14 Weeks)* pos/wks

23 Jul 83	FALLING IN LOVE *Salsoul SAL 104*	67	3
23 Jun 84	WHEN YOUR 'EX' WANTS YOU BACK *Salsoul SAL 106*	52	4
28 Feb 87	HAPPY *CBS 650393 7*	56	5
12 Jan 91	THE FIRST TIME *Columbia 6564767* ▲	60	2

SURFACE NOISE
UK, male instrumental group (Singles: 11 Weeks)   pos/wks

31 May 80	THE SCRATCH *WEA K 18291*	26	8
30 Aug 80	DANCIN' ON A WIRE *Groove Production GP 102*	59	3

The SURFARIS *US, male instrumental group (Singles: 14 Weeks)* pos/wks

25 Jul 63 ●	WIPE OUT *London HLD 9751*	5	14

SURPRISE SISTERS
Australia, female vocal group (Singles: 3 Weeks)   pos/wks

13 Mar 76	LA BOOGA ROOGA *Good Earth GD 1*	38	3

SURVIVOR *US, male vocal / instrumental group – lead vocal Dave Bickler (Singles: 26 Weeks, Albums: 10 Weeks)*   pos/wks

31 Jul 82 ★	EYE OF THE TIGER *Scotti Bros. SCT A 2411* ▲	1	15
1 Feb 86 ●	BURNING HEART *Scotti Bros. A 6708*	5	11
21 Aug 82	EYE OF THE TIGER *Scotti Bros. SCT 85845*	12	10

SUSHI See Paul MASTERSON presents SUSHI

Walter SUSSKIND See LONDON PHILHARMONIC CHOIR

The SUTHERLAND BROTHERS and QUIVER *UK, male vocal / instrumental group (Singles: 20 Weeks, Albums: 11 Weeks)*   pos/wks

3 Apr 76 ●	ARMS OF MARY *CBS 4001*	5	12
20 Nov 76	SECRETS *CBS 4668*	35	4
2 Jun 79	EASY COME, EASY GO *CBS 7121* [1]	50	4
15 May 76	REACH FOR THE SKY *CBS 69191*	26	8
9 Oct 76	SLIPSTREAM *CBS 81593*	49	3

[1] The Sutherland Brothers

Pat SUZUKI
US, female vocalist – Chiyoko Suzuki (Singles: 1 Week)   pos/wks

14 Apr 60	I ENJOY BEING A GIRL *RCA 1171*	49	1

SVENSON and GIELEN (see also AIRSCAPE; BLUE BAMBOO; CUBIC 22; Johan GEILEN presents ABNEA; TRANSFORMER 2) *Belgium, male production duo – Sven Maes and Johan Gielen (Singles: 2 Weeks)*   pos/wks

22 Sep 01	THE BEAUTY OF SILENCE *Xtrahard / Xtravaganza X2H 5CDS*	41	2

Billy SWAN US, male vocalist (Singles: 13 Weeks)　　pos/wks
14 Dec 74 ●	I CAN HELP Monument MNT 2752 ▲	6 9
24 May 75	DON'T BE CRUEL Monument MNT 3244	42 4

SWAN LAKE (see also BLACK RIOT; ROYAL HOUSE; The GYPSYMEN; Todd TERRY PROJECT) US, male producer – Todd Terry (Singles: 4 Weeks)　pos/wks
17 Sep 88	IN THE NAME OF LOVE Champion CHAMP 86	53 4

SWANS WAY UK, male / female vocal / instrumental group (Singles: 12 Weeks, Albums: 1 Week)　pos/wks
4 Feb 84	SOUL TRAIN Exit EXT 3	20 7
26 May 84	ILLUMINATIONS Balgier PH 5	57 5
3 Nov 84	THE FUGITIVE KIND Balgier SWAN 1	88 1

Patrick SWAYZE featuring Wendy FRASER
US, male / female vocal / actor duo (Singles: 11 Weeks)　pos/wks
26 Mar 88	SHE'S LIKE THE WIND RCA PB 49565	17 11

Keith SWEAT
US, male vocalist (Singles: 23 Weeks, Albums: 32 Weeks)　pos/wks
20 Feb 88	I WANT HER Vintertainment EKR 68	26 10
14 May 88	SOMETHING JUST AIN'T RIGHT Vintertainment EKR 72	55 3
14 May 94	HOW DO YOU LIKE IT Elektra EKR 185CD	71 1
22 Jun 96	TWISTED Elektra EKR 223CD	39 2
23 Nov 96	JUST A TOUCH Elektra EKR 227CD	35 2
3 May 97	NOBODY Elektra EKR 233CD [1]	30 2
6 Dec 97	I WANT HER (re-mix) Elektra E 3887CD	44 1
12 Dec 98	COME AND GET WITH ME Elektra E 3787CD [2]	58 1
27 Mar 99	I'M NOT READY Elektra E 3767CD	53 1
16 Jan 88	MAKE IT LAST FOREVER Elektra 960763 1	41 21
23 Jun 90	I'LL GIVE ALL MY LOVE TO YOU Vintertainment EKT 60	47 4
9 Jul 94	GET UP ON IT Elektra 7559615502	20 4
29 Jun 96	KEITH SWEAT Elektra 7559617072	36 2
3 Oct 98	STILL IN THE GAME Elektra 7559622622	62 1

[1] Keith Sweat featuring Athena Cage [2] Keith Sweat featuring Snoop Dogg

Claire SWEENEY
UK, female actor / vocalist (Albums: 3 Weeks)　pos/wks
27 Jul 02	CLAIRE T2 TCD 3254	15 3

Michelle SWEENEY US, female vocalist (Singles: 1 Week)　pos/wks
29 Oct 94	THIS TIME Big Beat A 8229CD	57 1

The SWEET (396) [Top 500]
Glam-rock giants: Brian Connolly (v), b. 1944, d. 1997, Andy Scott (g), Steve Priest (b), Mick Tucker (d), b. 1948, d. 2002. The flamboyantly-attired UK quartet was very popular in Europe and the US. Despite topping the chart only once, they achieved five No.2 hits (Singles: 159 Weeks, Albums: 14 Weeks)　pos/wks
13 Mar 71	FUNNY FUNNY RCA 2051	13 14
12 Jun 71 ●	CO-CO RCA 2087	2 15
16 Oct 71	ALEXANDER GRAHAM BELL RCA 2121	33 5
5 Feb 72	POPPA JOE RCA 2164	11 12
10 Jun 72 ●	LITTLE WILLY RCA 2225	4 14
9 Sep 72 ●	WIG-WAM BAM RCA 2260	4 13
13 Jan 73 ★	BLOCKBUSTER! RCA 2305	1 15
5 May 73 ●	HELL RAISER RCA 2357	2 11
22 Sep 73 ●	THE BALLROOM BLITZ RCA 2403	2 9
19 Jan 74 ●	TEENAGE RAMPAGE RCA LPBO 5004	2 8
13 Jul 74 ●	THE SIX TEENS RCA LPBO 5037	9 7
9 Nov 74	TURN IT DOWN RCA 2480	41 2
15 Mar 75 ●	FOX ON THE RUN RCA 2524	2 10
12 Jul 75	ACTION RCA 2578	15 6
24 Jan 76	THE LIES IN YOUR EYES RCA 2641	35 4
28 Jan 78 ●	LOVE IS LIKE OXYGEN Polydor POSP 1	9 9
26 Jan 85	IT'S ... IT'S ... THE SWEET MIX Anagram ANA 28	45 5
18 May 74	SWEET FANNY ADAMS RCA LPI 5038	27 2
22 Sep 84	SWEET 16 IT'S ... IT'S ... SWEET'S HITS Anagram GRAM 16	49 6
20 Jan 96	BALLROOM HITZ – THE VERY BEST OF SWEET PolyGram TV 5350012	15 6

'It's ... It's ... the Sweet Mix' is a medley of the following songs: Blockbuster / Fox on the Run / Teenage Rampage / Hell Raiser / Ballroom Blitz

Rachel SWEET US, female vocalist (Singles: 15 Weeks)　pos/wks
9 Dec 78	B-A-B-Y Stiff BUY 39	35 8
22 Aug 81	EVERLASTING LOVE CBS A 1405	35 7

SWEET DREAMS UK, male / female vocal duo – Polly Brown and Tony Jackson (Singles: 12 Weeks)　pos/wks
20 Jul 74 ●	HONEY HONEY Bradley's BRAD 7408	10 12

SWEET DREAMS
UK, male / female vocal group (Singles: 7 Weeks)　pos/wks
9 Apr 83	I'M NEVER GIVING UP Ariola ARO 333	21 7

SWEET FEMALE ATTITUDE UK, female vocal duo – Leanne Brown and Catherine Cassidy (Singles: 14 Weeks)　pos/wks
15 Apr 00 ●	FLOWERS WEA WEA 267CD	2 12
7 Oct 00	8 DAYS A WEEK WEA WEA 296CD	43 2

SWEET MERCY featuring Joe ROBERTS UK, male production / instrumental duo and male vocalist (Singles: 1 Week)　pos/wks
24 Feb 96	HAPPY DAYS Grass Green GRASS 10CD	63 1

The SWEET PEOPLE
France, male vocal / instrumental group (Singles: 10 Weeks)　pos/wks
4 Oct 80 ●	ET LES OISEAUX CHANTAIENT (AND THE BIRDS WERE SINGING) (re) Polydor POSP 179	4 10

Re-entry made No.73 in Aug 1987

SWEET PUSSY PAULINE See The CANDY GIRLS

SWEET SENSATION UK, male vocal group – lead vocal Marcel King, b. 1958, d. 1995 (Singles: 17 Weeks)　pos/wks
14 Sep 74 ★	SAD SWEET DREAMER Pye 7N 45385	1 10
18 Jan 75	PURELY BY COINCIDENCE Pye 7N 45421	11 7

SWEET TEE US, female rapper – Toi Jackson (Singles: 8 Weeks)　pos/wks
16 Jan 88	IT'S LIKE THAT Y'ALL / I GOT DA FEELIN' Cooltempo COOL 160	31 6
13 Aug 94	THE FEELING Deep Distraxion OILYCD 029 [1]	32 2

[1] Tin Tin Out featuring Sweet Tee

SWEETBACK
UK, male vocal / instrumental group (Singles: 1 Week)　pos/wks
29 Mar 97	YOU WILL RISE Epic 6643155	64 1

SWEETBOX Germany / US, male / female vocal / production duo – Rosan Roberto and Tina Harris (Singles: 12 Weeks)　pos/wks
22 Aug 98 ●	EVERYTHING'S GONNA BE ALRIGHT RCA 74321606842	5 12

Sally SWEETLAND See Eddie FISHER

SWERVEDRIVER UK, male vocal / instrumental group (Singles: 3 Weeks, Albums: 2 Weeks)　pos/wks
10 Aug 91	SANDBLASTED (EP) Creation CRE 102	67 1
30 May 92	NEVER LOSE THAT FEELING Creation CRE 120	62 1
14 Aug 93	DUEL Creation CRESCD 136	60 1
12 Oct 91	RAISE Creation CRELP 093	44 1
9 Oct 93	MEZCAL HEAD Creation CCRE 143	55 1

Tracks on Sandblasted (EP): Sandblaster / Flawed / Out / Laze It Up

Mampi SWIFT UK, male producer – Philip Anim (Singles: 1 Week)　pos/wks
5 Jun 04	HI-TEK / DRUNKEN STARS Charge CHRG 024	72 1

SWIMMING WITH SHARKS
Germany, female vocal duo (Singles: 3 Weeks)　pos/wks
7 May 88	CARELESS LOVE WEA YZ 173	63 3

SWING featuring DR ALBAN US, male rapper and Nigeria, male vocalist – Alban Nwapa (Singles: 1 Week)　pos/wks
29 Apr 95	SWEET DREAMS Logic 74321251552	59 1

SWING 52
US, male vocal / instrumental group (Singles: 1 Week)　　pos/wks
25 Feb 95	COLOR OF MY SKIN *ffrr FCD 256*	60	1

SWING KIDS See K7

SWING OUT SISTER
UK, male / female vocal / instrumental trio (Singles: 55 Weeks, Albums: 36 Weeks)　　pos/wks
25 Oct 86 ●	BREAKOUT *Mercury SWING 2*	4	14
10 Jan 87 ●	SURRENDER *Mercury SWING 3*	7	8
18 Apr 87	TWILIGHT WORLD *Mercury SWING 4*	32	6
11 Jul 87	FOOLED BY A SMILE *Mercury SWING 5*	43	4
8 Apr 89	YOU ON MY MIND *Fontana SWING 6*	28	9
8 Jul 89	WHERE IN THE WORLD *Fontana SWING 7*	47	4
11 Apr 92	AM I THE SAME GIRL *Fontana SWING 9*	21	6
20 Jun 92	NOTGONNACHANGE *Fontana SWING 10*	49	2
27 Aug 94	LA LA (MEANS I LOVE YOU) *Fontana SWIDD 11*	37	2
23 May 87 ★	IT'S BETTER TO TRAVEL *Mercury OUTLP 1* ■	1	21
20 May 89 ●	KALEIDOSCOPE WORLD *Fontana 838293 1*	3	11
16 May 92	GET IN TOUCH WITH YOURSELF *Fontana 5122412*	27	4

Act became male / female duo in 1989

The SWINGING BLUE JEANS
UK, male vocal / instrumental group (Singles: 57 Weeks)　　pos/wks
20 Jun 63	IT'S TOO LATE NOW (re) *HMV POP 1170*	30	9
12 Dec 63 ●	HIPPY HIPPY SHAKE *HMV POP 1242*	2	17
19 Mar 64	GOOD GOLLY MISS MOLLY *HMV POP 1273*	11	10
4 Jun 64 ●	YOU'RE NO GOOD *HMV POP 1304*	3	13
20 Jan 66	DON'T MAKE ME OVER *HMV POP 1501*	31	8

SWINGLE SISTERS
US / France, male / female vocal group (Albums: 18 Weeks)　　pos/wks
1 Feb 64	JAZZ SEBASTIAN BACH *Philips BL 7572*	13	18

SWIRL 360
US, male vocal duo (Singles: 1 Week)　　pos/wks
14 Nov 98	HEY NOW NOW *Mercury 5665352*	61	1

SWITCH
US, male vocal / instrumental group (Singles: 3 Weeks)　　pos/wks
10 Nov 84	KEEPING SECRETS *Total Experience RCA XE 502*	61	3

SWITCHFOOT
US, male vocal / instrumental group (Singles: 2 Weeks)　　pos/wks
14 Aug 04	MEANT TO LIVE *Columbia 6750812*	29	2

SWIZZ BEATS See DMX

SYBIL
US, female vocalist – Sybil Lynch (Singles: 69 Weeks, Albums: 12 Weeks)　　pos/wks
1 Nov 86	FALLING IN LOVE *Champion CHAMP 22*	68	3
25 Apr 87	LET YOURSELF GO *Champion CHAMP 42*	32	6
29 Aug 87	MY LOVE IS GUARANTEED *Champion CHAMPX 55*	42	5
22 Jul 89	DON'T MAKE ME OVER (re) *Champion CHAMP 213*	19	11
27 Jan 90 ●	WALK ON BY *PWL PWL 48*	6	9
21 Apr 90	CRAZY FOR YOU *PWL PWL 53*	71	1
16 Jan 93 ●	THE LOVE I LOST *PWL Sanctuary PWCD 253* [1]	3	13
20 Mar 93 ●	WHEN I'M GOOD AND READY *PWL International PWCD 260*	5	13
26 Jun 93	BEYOND YOUR WILDEST DREAMS *PWL International PWCD 265*	41	2
11 Sep 93	STRONGER TOGETHER *PWL International PWCD 269*	41	2
11 Dec 93	MY LOVE IS GUARANTEED (re-mix) *PWL International PWCD 277*	48	1
9 Mar 96	SO TIRED OF BEING ALONE *PWL International PWL 324CD*	53	1
8 Mar 97	WHEN I'M GOOD AND READY (re-mix) *Next Plateau NP 14183*	66	1
26 Jul 97	STILL A THRILL *Coalition COLA 007CD*	55	1
5 Sep 87	LET YOURSELF GO *Champion CHAMP 1009*	92	1
24 Feb 90	WALK ON BY *PWL HF 10*	21	5
12 Jun 93	GOOD 'N' READY *PWL International HFCD 28*	13	6

[1] West End featuring Sybil

SYLK 130
US, male production duo – King Britt and John Wicks (Singles: 2 Weeks)　　pos/wks
25 Apr 98	LAST NIGHT A DJ SAVED MY LIFE *Sony S2 SYLK 1CD*	33	2

SYLVER
Belgium, male / female DJ / production / vocal duo (Singles: 1 Week)　　pos/wks
1 Jun 02	TURN THE TIDE *Pepper 9230562*	56	1

SYLVESTER
US, male vocalist – Sylvester James, b. 6 Sep 1947, d. 16 Dec 1988 (Singles: 45 Weeks, Albums: 3 Weeks)　　pos/wks
19 Aug 78 ●	YOU MAKE ME FEEL (MIGHTY REAL) *Fantasy FTC 160*	8	15
18 Nov 78	DANCE (DISCO HEAT) *Fantasy FTC 163*	29	12
31 Mar 79	I (WHO HAVE NOTHING) *Fantasy FTC 171*	46	5
7 Jul 79	STARS *Fantasy FTC 177*	47	3
11 Sep 82	DO YOU WANNA FUNK *London LON 13* [1]	32	8
3 Sep 83	BAND OF GOLD *London LON 33*	67	2
23 Jun 79	MIGHTY REAL *Fantasy FTA 3009*	62	3

[1] Sylvester with Patrick Cowley

SYLVIA
US, female vocalist – Sylvia Vanderpool (Singles: 11 Weeks)　　pos/wks
23 Jun 73	PILLOW TALK *London HL 10415*	14	11

SYLVIA
Sweden, female vocalist – Sylvia Vrethammar (Singles: 33 Weeks)　　pos/wks
10 Aug 74 ●	Y VIVA ESPANA (re) *Sonet SON 2037*	4	28
26 Apr 75	HASTA LA VISTA *Sonet SON 2055*	38	5

David SYLVIAN
(see also JAPAN) UK, male vocalist – David Batt (Singles: 36 Weeks, Albums: 27 Weeks)　　pos/wks
7 Aug 82	BAMBOO HOUSES / BAMBOO MUSIC *Virgin VS 510* [1]	30	4
2 Jul 83	FORBIDDEN COLOURS *Virgin VS 601* [2]	16	8
2 Jun 84	RED GUITAR *Virgin VS 633*	17	5
18 Aug 84	THE INK IN THE WELL *Virgin VS 700*	36	3
3 Nov 84	PULLING PUNCHES *Virgin VS 717*	56	2
14 Dec 85	WORDS WITH THE SHAMAN *Virgin VS 835*	72	1
9 Aug 86	TAKING THE VEIL *Virgin VS 815*	53	3
17 Jan 87	BUOY *Virgin VS 910* [3]	63	2
10 Oct 87	LET THE HAPPINESS IN *Virgin VS 1001*	66	1
13 Jun 92	HEARTBEAT (TAINAI KAIKI II) RETURNING TO THE WOMB *Virgin America VUS 57* [4]	58	3
28 Aug 93	JEAN THE BIRDMAN *Virgin VSCDG 1462* [5]	68	2
27 Mar 99	I SURRENDER *Virgin VSCDT 1722*	40	2
7 Jul 84 ●	BRILLIANT TREES *Virgin V 2290*	4	14
13 Sep 86	GONE TO EARTH *Virgin VDL 1*	24	5
7 Nov 87	SECRETS OF THE BEEHIVE *Virgin V 2471*	37	2
2 Apr 88	PLIGHT AND PREMONITION *Virgin VE 11* [1]	71	1
17 Jul 93	THE FIRST DAY *Virgin CDVX 2712* [2]	21	2
10 Apr 99	DEAD BEES ON A CAKE *Virgin CDV 2876*	31	2
21 Oct 00	EVERYTHING AND NOTHING *Virgin CDVD 2897*	57	1

[1] Sylvian Sakamoto [2] David Sylvian and Riuichi Sakamoto [3] Mick Karn featuring David Sylvian [4] David Sylvian / Riuichi Sakamoto featuring Ingrid Chavez [5] David Sylvian and Robert Fripp [1] David Sylvian and Holgar Czukay [2] David Sylvian and Robert Fripp

SYMARIP
UK, male vocal / instrumental group (Singles: 3 Weeks)　　pos/wks
2 Feb 80	SKINHEAD MOONSTOMP *Trojan TRO 9062*	54	3

The SYMBOLS
UK, male vocal / instrumental group (Singles: 15 Weeks)　　pos/wks
2 Aug 67	BYE BYE BABY *President PT 144*	44	3
3 Jan 68	(THE BEST PART OF) BREAKING UP *President PT 173*	25	12

Terri SYMON
UK, female vocalist (Singles: 1 Week)　　pos/wks
10 Jun 95	I WANT TO KNOW WHAT LOVE IS *A&M 5810592*	54	1

SYMPHONIQUE
UK, male instrumentalist – keyboards – Chris Cozens (Albums: 4 Weeks)　　pos/wks
1 Apr 95	MOODS SYMPHONIQUE 95 *Vision VISCD 10*	21	4

SYMPOSIUM
(see also HELL IS FOR HEROES) *UK, male*
vocal / instrumental group (Singles: 10 Weeks, Albums: 3 Weeks)   pos/wks

22 Mar 97	**FAREWELL TO TWILIGHT** *Infectious INFECT 34CD*	**25**	2
31 May 97	**THE ANSWER TO WHY I HATE YOU**		
	Infectious INFECT 37CD	**32**	2
30 Aug 97	**FAIRWEATHER FRIEND** *Infectious INFECT 44CD*	**25**	3
14 Mar 98	**AVERAGE MAN** *Infectious INFECT 52CD*	**45**	1
16 May 98	**BURY YOU** *Infectious INFECT 55CDS*	**41**	1
18 Jul 98	**BLUE** *Infectious INFECT 57CD*	**48**	1
8 Nov 97	**ONE DAY AT A TIME** *Infectious INFECT 49CD*	**29**	2
30 May 98	**ON THE OUTSIDE** *Infectious INFECT 56CD*	**32**	1

SYNTAX
UK, male producer – Mike Tournier (Singles: 4 Weeks)   pos/wks

| 8 Feb 03 | **PRAY** *Illustrious CDILL 012* | **28** | 3 |
| 28 Feb 04 | **BLISS** *Illustrious / Epic CDILLX 020* | **69** | 1 |

SYNTHPHONIC VARIATIONS
UK, session musicians (Albums: 1 Week)   pos/wks

| 1 Nov 86 | **SEASONS** *CBS 450 1491* | **84** | 1 |

SYREETA
US, female vocalist – Rita Wright, b. 3 Aug 1946,
d. 6 Jul 2004 (Singles: 30 Weeks)   pos/wks

21 Sep 74	**SPINNIN' AND SPINNIN'** *Tamla Motown TMG 912*	**49**	3
1 Feb 75	**YOUR KISS IS SWEET** *Tamla Motown TMG 933*	**12**	8
12 Jul 75	**HARMOUR LOVE** *Tamla Motown TMG 954*	**32**	4
15 Dec 79 ●	**WITH YOU I'M BORN AGAIN** *Motown TMG 1159* [1]	**2**	11
8 Mar 80	**IT WILL COME IN TIME** *Motown TMG 1175* [1]	**47**	4

[1] Billy Preston and Syreeta

Stanislas SYREWICZ See Anthony WAY

The SYSTEM
US, male vocal / instrumental duo (Singles: 2 Weeks)   pos/wks

| 9 Jun 84 | **I WANNA MAKE YOU FEEL GOOD** *Polydor POSP 685* | **73** | 2 |

SYSTEM F
(see also ALBION; Ferry CORSTEN; GOURYELLA; MOONMAN; STARPARTY)
Holland, male producer – Ferry Corsten (Singles: 10 Weeks)   pos/wks

| 3 Apr 99 | **OUT OF THE BLUE** *Essential Recordings ESCD 1* | **14** | 6 |
| 6 May 00 | **CRY** *Essential Recordings ESCD 14* | **19** | 4 |

SYSTEM OF A DOWN
US, male vocal / instrumental group
(Singles: 9 Weeks, Albums: 28 Weeks)   pos/wks

3 Nov 01	**CHOP SUEY!** *Columbia 6720342*	**17**	4
23 Mar 02	**TOXICITY** *Columbia 6725022*	**25**	3
27 Jul 02	**AERIALS** *Columbia 6728692*	**34**	2
8 Sep 01	**TOXICITY** *Columbia 5015346* ▲	**13**	27
7 Dec 02	**STEAL THIS ALBUM!** *American Recordings 5102489*	**56**	1

SYSTEM OF LIFE
UK, production group (Singles: 1 Week)   pos/wks

| 29 May 04 | **LUV IS COOL** *Freedream CDFDREAM 1* | **63** | 1 |

SYSTEM presents KERRI B
UK, male production group and
female vocalist (Singles: 1 Week)   pos/wks

| 8 Nov 03 | **IF YOU LEAVE ME NOW** | | |
| | *All Around the World CDGLOBE 288* | **55** | 1 |

SYSTEM 7
UK / France, male / female instrumental duo – Steve Hillage
and Miquette Giraudy (Singles: 2 Weeks, Albums: 3 Weeks)   pos/wks

13 Feb 93	**7:7 EXPANSION** *Butterfly BFLD 2*	**39**	1
17 Jul 93	**SINBAD / QUEST** *Butterfly BFLD 8*	**74**	1
20 Jun 92	**ALTITUDE** *Ten TENG 403*	**75**	1
20 Mar 93	**777** *Big Life BFLCD 1*	**30**	2

T-BOZ (see also TLC)
US, female vocalist – Tionne Watkins (Singles: 2 Weeks)   pos/wks

| 23 Nov 96 | **TOUCH MYSELF** *LaFace 74321422882* | **48** | 1 |
| 14 Apr 01 | **MY GETAWAY** *Maverick W 549CD* [1] | **44** | 1 |

[1] Tionne 'T-Boz' Watkins

TC
Italy, male instrumental / production group (Singles: 5 Weeks)   pos/wks

14 Mar 92	**BERRY** *Union City UCRT 1* [1]	**73**	1
21 Nov 92	**FUNKY GUITAR** *Union City UCRT 13* [2]	**40**	2
10 Jul 93	**HARMONY** *Union UCRD 20* [3]	**51**	2

[1] TC 1991 [2] TC 1992 [3] TC 1993

T-CONNECTION
US, male vocal / instrumental group (Singles: 27 Weeks)   pos/wks

18 Jun 77	**DO WHAT YOU WANNA DO** *TK XC 9109*	**11**	8
14 Jan 78	**ON FIRE** *TK TKR 6006*	**16**	5
10 Jun 78	**LET YOURSELF GO** *TK TKR 6024*	**52**	3
24 Feb 79	**AT MIDNIGHT** *TK TKR 7517*	**53**	5
5 May 79	**SATURDAY NIGHT** *TK TKR 7536*	**41**	6

T-COY See VARIOUS ARTISTS (EPs and LPs)

T-EMPO
UK, male / female vocal / instrumental group (Singles: 4 Weeks)   pos/wks

| 7 May 94 | **SATURDAY NIGHT SUNDAY MORNING** *ffrr FCD 232* | **19** | 3 |
| 9 Nov 96 | **THE LOOK OF LOVE / THE BLUE ROOM** *ffrr FCD 281* | **71** | 1 |

T-FACTORY *Italy, male production group (Singles: 2 Weeks)*   pos/wks

| 13 Apr 02 | **MESSAGE IN A BOTTLE** *Inferno CDFERN 44* | **51** | 2 |

THS – THE HORN SECTION
US, male / female vocal / instrumental group (Singles: 3 Weeks)   pos/wks

| 18 Aug 84 | **LADY SHINE (SHINE ON)** *Fourth & Broadway BRW 10* | **54** | 3 |

TJR featuring XAVIER
UK, male instrumental / production group (Singles: 2 Weeks)   pos/wks

| 27 Sep 97 | **JUST GETS BETTER** *Multiply CDMULTY 25* | **28** | 2 |

TLC 376 Top 500 *Multi-award-winning 1990s female trio; Tionne 'T-Boz' Watkins, Lisa 'Left Eye' Lopes (b. 27 May 1971, d. 25 Apr 2002) and Rozonda "Chilli" Thomas. They have nine US gold singles, and The Supremes are the only female group with more US No.1s. Best-selling single: 'No Scrubs' 553,200 (Singles: 85 Weeks, Albums: 97 Weeks)*   pos/wks

20 Jun 92	**AIN'T 2 PROUD 2 BEG** *Arista 115265*	**13**	5
22 Aug 92	**BABY-BABY-BABY** *LaFace 74321111297*	**55**	3
24 Oct 92	**WHAT ABOUT YOUR FRIENDS** *LaFace 74321118177*	**59**	2
21 Jan 95	**CREEP** *LaFace 74321254212* ▲	**22**	4
22 Apr 95	**RED LIGHT SPECIAL** *LaFace 74321273662*	**18**	4
5 Aug 95 ●	**WATERFALLS** *LaFace 74321298812* ▲	**4**	14
4 Nov 95	**DIGGIN' ON YOU** *LaFace 74321319252*	**18**	5
13 Jan 96 ●	**CREEP (re-issue)** *LaFace 74321340942*	**6**	7
3 Apr 99 ●	**NO SCRUBS** *LaFace 74321660952* ▲	**3**	19
28 Aug 99 ●	**UNPRETTY** *LaFace 74321695842* ▲	**6**	11

Singles re-entries are listed as (re), (2re), (3re).... which signifies that the hit re-entered the chart once, twice or three times...

		pos	wks
18 Dec 99	**DEAR LIE** *LaFace 74321724012*	**31**	9
14 Dec 02	**GIRL TALK** *Arista 74321983482*	**30**	2
20 May 95 ●	**CRAZYSEXYCOOL** *LaFace 73008260092*	**4**	39
6 Mar 99 ●	**FANMAIL** *LaFace 73008260552* ▲	**7**	57
23 Nov 02	**3D** *Arista 74321981502*	**45**	1

T99
Belgium, male instrumental / production group (Singles: 10 Weeks) pos/wks

		pos	wks
11 May 91	**ANASTHASIA** *XL XLS 19*	**14**	6
19 Oct 91	**NOCTURNE** *Emphasis 6574097*	**33**	4

T-POWER (see also EBONY DUBSTERS)
UK, male producer – Mark Royal (Singles: 18 Weeks) pos/wks

		pos	wks
13 Apr 96	**POLICE STATE** *Sound of Underground TPOWCD 001*	**63**	1
6 Apr 02 ●	**SHAKE UR BODY** *Positiva CDTIV 171* [1]	**7**	11
23 Nov 02	**DON'T WANNA KNOW** *ffrr FCD 408* [2]	**19**	4
7 Jun 03	**FEELIN' U** *London FCD 409* [3]	**34**	2

[1] Shy FX and T-Power featuring Di [2] Shy FX and T-Power featuring Di and Skibadee [3] Shy FX and T-Power featuring Kele Le Roc

TQ *US, male rapper – Terrance Quaites*
(Singles: 35 Weeks, Albums: 9 Weeks) pos/wks

		pos	wks
30 Jan 99 ●	**WESTSIDE** *Epic 6668102*	**4**	9
1 May 99 ●	**BYE BYE BABY** *Epic 6672372*	**7**	7
21 Aug 99	**BETTER DAYS** *Epic 6677532*	**32**	2
4 Sep 99 ●	**SUMMERTIME** *Northwestside 74321694672* [1]	**7**	7
29 Apr 00	**DAILY** *Epic 6692752*	**14**	5
13 Oct 01	**LET'S GET BACK TO BED … BOY** *Epic 6718662* [2]	**16**	5
8 May 99	**THEY NEVER SAW ME COMING** *Epic 4914032*	**27**	7
20 May 00	**THE SECOND COMING** *Epic 4977602*	**32**	2

[1] Another Level featuring TQ [2] Sarah Connor featuring TQ

T. REX ⟨88 Top 500⟩
Highly influential acoustic act turned superstar glam rock boogie duo; singer / songwriter / guitarist Marc Bolan (b. Mark Feld, 30 Sep 1947, London, UK, d. 16 Sep 1977) and percussionist Steve Peregrin Took (b. 28 Jul 1949, d. 27 Oct 1980) – replaced by Mickey Finn in 1969 (b. 3 Jun 1947, d. 12 Jan 2003)
(Singles: 236 Weeks, Albums: 232 Weeks) pos/wks

		pos	wks
8 May 68	**DEBORA** *Regal Zonophone RZ 3008* [1]	**34**	7
4 Sep 68	**ONE INCH ROCK** *Regal Zonophone RZ 3011* [1]	**28**	7
9 Aug 69	**KING OF THE RUMBLING SPIRES** *Regal Zonophone RZ 3022* [1]	**44**	1
24 Oct 70 ●	**RIDE A WHITE SWAN** *Fly BUG 1*	**2**	20
27 Feb 71 ★	**HOT LOVE** *Fly BUG 6*	**1**	17
10 Jul 71 ★	**GET IT ON** *Fly BUG 10*	**1**	13
13 Nov 71 ●	**JEEPSTER** *Fly BUG 16*	**2**	15
29 Jan 72 ★	**TELEGRAM SAM** (re) *T. Rex 101*	**1**	14
1 Apr 72 ●	**DEBORA / ONE INCH ROCK** (re-issue) *Magnifly ECHO 102* [1]	**7**	10
13 May 72 ★	**METAL GURU** *EMI MARC 1*	**1**	14
16 Sep 72 ●	**CHILDREN OF THE REVOLUTION** *EMI MARC 2*	**2**	10
9 Dec 72 ●	**SOLID GOLD EASY ACTION** *EMI MARC 3*	**2**	11
10 Mar 73 ●	**20TH CENTURY BOY** *EMI MARC 4*	**3**	9
16 Jun 73 ●	**THE GROOVER** *EMI MARC 5*	**4**	9
24 Nov 73	**TRUCK ON (TYKE)** *EMI MARC 6*	**12**	11
9 Feb 74	**TEENAGE DREAM** *EMI MARC 7* [2]	**13**	5
13 Jul 74	**LIGHT OF LOVE** *EMI MARC 8*	**22**	5
16 Nov 74	**ZIP GUN BOOGIE** *EMI MARC 9*	**41**	3
12 Jul 75	**NEW YORK CITY** *EMI MARC 10*	**15**	8
11 Oct 75	**DREAMY LADY** *EMI MARC 11* [3]	**30**	5
6 Mar 76	**LONDON BOYS** *EMI MARC 13*	**40**	3
19 Jun 76	**I LOVE TO BOOGIE** *EMI MARC 14*	**13**	9
2 Oct 76	**LASER LOVE** *EMI MARC 15*	**41**	4
2 Apr 77	**THE SOUL OF MY SUIT** *EMI MARC 16*	**42**	3
9 May 81	**RETURN OF THE ELECTRIC WARRIOR (EP)** *Rarn MBSF 001* [4]	**50**	4
19 Sep 81	**YOU SCARE ME TO DEATH** *Cherry Red CHERRY 29* [4]	**51**	4
18 May 85	**MEGAREX** *Marc on Wax TANX 1* [2]	**72**	2
9 May 87	**GET IT ON** (re-mix) *Marc on Wax MARC 10* [2]	**54**	4
24 Aug 91	**20TH CENTURY BOY** (re-issue) *Marc on Wax MARC 501* [2]	**13**	8
7 Oct 00	**GET IT ON** *All Around the World CDGLOBE 225* [5]	**59**	1
13 Jul 68	**MY PEOPLE WERE FAIR AND HAD SKY IN THEIR HAIR BUT NOW THEY'RE CONTENT TO WEAR STARS ON THEIR BROWS** *Regal Zonophone SLRZ 1003* [1]	**15**	9
7 Jun 69	**UNICORN** *Regal Zonophone S 1007* [1]	**12**	3
14 Mar 70	**A BEARD OF STARS** *Regal Zonophone SLRZ 1013* [1]	**21**	6
16 Jan 71 ●	**T. REX** *Fly HIFLY 2*	**7**	25

		pos	wks
27 Mar 71	**THE BEST OF T. REX** *Flyback TON 2*	**21**	8
9 Oct 71 ★	**ELECTRIC WARRIOR** *Fly HIFLY 6*	**1**	44
29 Mar 72 ★	**PROPHETS SEERS & SAGES THE ANGELS OF THE AGES / MY PEOPLE WERE FAIR AND HAD SKY IN THEIR HAIR BUT NOW THEY'RE CONTENT TO WEAR STARS ON THEIR BROWS** (re-issue) *Fly Double Back TOOFA 3/4* [1]	**1**	12
20 May 72 ★	**BOLAN BOOGIE** *Fly HIFLY 8* ■	**1**	19
5 Aug 72 ●	**THE SLIDER** *EMI BLN 5001*	**4**	18
9 Dec 72	**A BEARD OF STARS** (re-issue) / **UNICORN** *Cube TOOFA 9/10* [1]	**44**	2
31 Mar 73 ●	**TANX** *EMI BLN 5002*	**4**	12
10 Nov 73	**GREAT HITS** *EMI BLN 5003*	**32**	3
16 Mar 74	**ZINC ALLOY AND THE HIDDEN RIDERS OF TOMORROW** *EMI BLNA 7751* [2]	**12**	3
21 Feb 76	**FUTURISTIC DRAGON** *EMI BLN 5004*	**50**	1
9 Apr 77	**DANDY IN THE UNDERWORLD** *EMI BLN 5005*	**26**	3
30 Jun 79	**SOLID GOLD** *EMI NUT 5*	**51**	3
12 Sep 81	**T. REX IN CONCERT** *Marc ABOLAN 1*	**35**	6
7 Nov 81	**YOU SCARE ME TO DEATH** *Cherry Red ERED 20* [3]	**88**	1
24 Sep 83	**DANCE IN THE MIDNIGHT** *Marc on Wax MARCL 501* [3]	**83**	3
4 May 85 ●	**BEST OF THE 20TH CENTURY BOY** *K-Tel NE 1297* [2]	**5**	21
28 Sep 91 ●	**THE ULTIMATE COLLECTION** *Telstar TCD 2539* [2]	**4**	16
7 Oct 95	**THE ESSENTIAL COLLECTION** *PolyGram TV 5259612* [2]	**24**	6
28 Sep 02	**THE ESSENTIAL COLLECTION – 25TH ANNIVERSARY EDITION** *Universal TV 4934882* [2]	**18**	8

[1] Tyrannosaurus Rex [2] Marc Bolan and T. Rex [3] T. Rex Disco Party [4] Marc Bolan [5] Bus Stop featuring T. Rex [1] Tyrannosaurus Rex [2] Marc Bolan and T. Rex [3] Marc Bolan

'Telegram Sam' made No.69 on re-entry in Mar 1982. Tracks on Return of the Electric Warrior (EP): Sing Me a Song / Endless Sleep Extended / The Lilac Hand of Menthol Dan. Megarex is a medley of extracts from the following T. Rex hits: Truck On (Tyke) / The Groover / Telegram Sam / Shock Rock / Metal Guru / 20th Century Boy / Children of the Revolution / Hot Love   'The Essential Collection' (1995) returned to the chart in 2000 with a new label, Universal Music TV. The catalogue number was the same

TSD
UK, female vocal group (Singles: 2 Weeks) pos/wks

		pos	wks
17 Feb 96	**HEART AND SOUL** *Avex UK AVEXCD 21*	**69**	1
30 Mar 96	**BABY I LOVE YOU** *Avex UK AVEXCD 34*	**64**	1

T-SHIRT
UK, female vocal duo (Singles: 1 Week) pos/wks

		pos	wks
13 Sep 97	**YOU SEXY THING** *Eternal WEA 122CD*	**63**	1

T-SPOON *Holland, male / female*
vocal / instrumental group (Singles: 15 Weeks) pos/wks

		pos	wks
19 Sep 98 ●	**SEX ON THE BEACH** *Control 0042395 CON*	**2**	13
23 Jan 99	**TOM'S PARTY** *Control 0043505 CON*	**27**	2

T2 featuring Robin S
US, male production duo and female vocalist (Singles: 1 Week) pos/wks

		pos	wks
4 Oct 97	**YOU GOT THE LOVE** *Champion CHAMPCD 330*	**62**	1

TWA
UK, male instrumental / production group (Singles: 1 Week) pos/wks

		pos	wks
16 Sep 95	**NASTY GIRLS** *Mercury MERCD 441*	**51**	1

TABERNACLE
UK, male instrumental / production group (Singles: 2 Weeks) pos/wks

		pos	wks
4 Mar 95	**I KNOW THE LORD** *Good Groove CDGG 1*	**62**	1
3 Feb 96	**I KNOW THE LORD** (re-mix) *Good Groove CDGGX 1*	**55**	1

TACKHEAD
US / UK, male vocal / production / rap group (Singles: 3 Weeks) pos/wks

		pos	wks
30 Jun 90	**DANGEROUS SEX** *SBK SBK 7014*	**48**	3

TAFFY
UK, female vocalist – Catherine Quaye (Singles: 14 Weeks) pos/wks

		pos	wks
10 Jan 87 ●	**I LOVE MY RADIO (MY DEE JAY'S RADIO)** *Transglobal TYPE 1*	**6**	10
18 Jul 87	**STEP BY STEP** *Transglobal TYPE 5*	**59**	4

TAG TEAM
US, male rap duo – Cecil Glenn and
Steve Gibson (Singles: 8 Weeks) pos/wks

8 Jan 94	**WHOOMP! (THERE IT IS)** *Club Tools SHXCD 1*	**34**	5
29 Jan 94	**ADDAMS FAMILY (WHOOMP!)** *Atlas PZCD 305*	**53**	1
10 Sep 94	**WHOOMP! (THERE IT IS) (re-mix)** *Club Tools SHXR 1*	**48**	2

Caddillac TAH See JA RULE; Jennifer LOPEZ

TAIKO *Germany, male DJ / production duo –*
Oliver Huntemann and Stephan Bodzin (Singles: 1 Week) pos/wks

29 Jun 02	**SILENCE** *Nukleuz NUKC 0330*	**72**	1

TAK TIX
US, male / female vocal / production group (Singles: 2 Weeks) pos/wks

20 Jan 96	**FEEL LIKE SINGING** *A&M 5813212*	**33**	2

TAKE 5
US, male vocal group (Singles: 4 Weeks) pos/wks

7 Nov 98	**I GIVE** *Edel 0039635 ERE*	**70**	1
27 Mar 99	**NEVER HAD IT SO GOOD** *Edel 0039355 ERE*	**34**	3

TAKE THAT ⌈ 126 ⌉ Top 500
Record-breaking British boy band: Robbie Williams (v), Gary Barlow (v),
Jason Orange (v), Howard Donald (v), Mark Owen (v). They were the first
artists since The Beatles to score four consecutive chart-toppers, and the first
act to release eight singles entering at No.1. Robbie Williams departed in July
1995 and Gary Barlow dissolved the band in Feb 1996 having sold nine million
albums and 10 million singles. Best-selling single: 'Back For Good' 959,582
(Singles: 158 Weeks, Albums: 228 Weeks) pos/wks

23 Nov 91	**PROMISES** *RCA PB 45085*	**38**	2
8 Feb 92	**ONCE YOU'VE TASTED LOVE** *RCA PB 45257*	**47**	3
6 Jun 92 ●	**IT ONLY TAKES A MINUTE** *RCA 74321101007*	**7**	8
15 Aug 92	**I FOUND HEAVEN** *RCA 74321108137*	**15**	6
10 Oct 92 ●	**A MILLION LOVE SONGS** *RCA 74321116307*	**7**	9
12 Dec 92 ●	**COULD IT BE MAGIC** *RCA 74321123137*	**3**	12
20 Feb 93 ●	**WHY CAN'T I WAKE UP WITH YOU** *RCA 74321133102*	**2**	10
17 Jul 93 ★	**PRAY** *RCA 74321154502* ■	**1**	11
9 Oct 93 ★	**RELIGHT MY FIRE** *RCA 74321167722* ⌈1⌉ ■	**1**	14
18 Dec 93 ★	**BABE** *RCA 74321182122* ■	**1**	10
9 Apr 94 ●	**EVERYTHING CHANGES** *RCA 74321167732* ■	**1**	10
9 Jul 94 ●	**LOVE AIN'T HERE ANYMORE (re)** *RCA 74321214832*	**3**	12
15 Oct 94 ★	**SURE** *RCA 74321236622* ■	**1**	15
8 Apr 95 ●	**BACK FOR GOOD** *RCA 74321271462* ■	**1**	13
5 Aug 95 ★	**NEVER FORGET** *RCA 74321299572* ■	**1**	9
9 Mar 96 ★	**HOW DEEP IS YOUR LOVE (re)** *RCA 74321355592* ■	**1**	14
5 Sep 92 ●	**TAKE THAT & PARTY** *RCA 74321109232*	**2**	73
23 Oct 93 ★	**EVERYTHING CHANGES** *RCA 74321169262* ■	**1**	78
13 May 95 ★	**NOBODY ELSE** *RCA 74321279092* ■	**1**	33
26 Aug 95	**NOBODY ELSE (IMPORT)** *Arista 07822188002*	**26**	4
6 Apr 96 ★	**GREATEST HITS** *RCA 74321355582* ■	**1**	40

⌈1⌉ Take That featuring Lulu

TAKING BACK SUNDAY *US, male vocal /*
instrumental group (Singles: 1 Week, Albums: 1 Week) pos/wks

2 Oct 04	**A DECADE UNDER THE INFLUENCE** *Victory VR 236CD*	**70**	1
7 Aug 04	**WHERE YOU WANT TO BE** *Victory VR 228CD*	**71**	1

Billy TALBOT See Ian McNABB

TALI
New Zealand, female DJ / producer – Natalia Scott (Singles: 5 Weeks) pos/wks

10 Aug 02	**LYRIC ON MY LIP** *Full Cycle FCY 042*	**75**	1
7 Feb 04	**BLAZIN'** *Full Cycle FCYCDS 059*	**42**	2
15 May 04	**LYRIC ON MY LIP (re-issue)** *Full Cycle FYCD 065*	**39**	2

The first issue of 'Lyric on My Lip' was available on 12" only

TALISMAN P featuring Barrington LEVY
UK, male producer – Philip Larsen and Jamaica,
male vocalist (Singles: 2 Weeks) pos/wks

13 Oct 01	**HERE I COME (SING DJ)** *Nulife / Arista 74321895622*	**37**	2

TALK TALK ⌈ 438 ⌉ Top 500 (see also Beth GIBBONS & RUSTIN' MAN)
London-based synth-pop band which rapidly evolved into an organic,
reflective rock group; Mark Hollis (v/g/k), Paul Webb (b) and Lee Harris
(d). Act, who had several legal wrangles with EMI, also scored four Top 20
singles in Italy (Singles: 74 Weeks, Albums: 86 Weeks) pos/wks

24 Apr 82	**TALK TALK** *EMI 5284*	**52**	4
24 Jul 82	**TODAY** *EMI 5314*	**14**	13
13 Nov 82	**TALK TALK (re-mix)** *EMI 5352*	**23**	10
19 Mar 83	**MY FOOLISH FRIEND** *EMI 5373*	**57**	3
14 Jan 84	**IT'S MY LIFE** *EMI 5443*	**46**	5
7 Apr 84	**SUCH A SHAME** *EMI 5433*	**49**	6
11 Aug 84	**DUM DUM GIRL** *EMI 5480*	**74**	1
18 Jan 86	**LIFE'S WHAT YOU MAKE IT** *EMI EMI 5540*	**16**	9
15 Mar 86	**LIVING IN ANOTHER WORLD** *EMI EMI 5551*	**48**	4
17 May 86	**GIVE IT UP** *Parlophone R 6131*	**59**	3
19 May 90	**IT'S MY LIFE (re-issue)** *Parlophone R 6254*	**13**	9
1 Sep 90	**LIFE'S WHAT YOU MAKE IT (re-issue)** *Parlophone R 6264*	**23**	6
21 Jun 03	**IT'S MY LIFE (re-mix)** *Nebula NEBCD 045* ⌈1⌉	**64**	1
24 Jul 82	**THE PARTY'S OVER** *EMI EMC 3413*	**21**	25
25 Feb 84	**IT'S MY LIFE** *EMI EMC 2400021*	**35**	8
1 Mar 86 ●	**THE COLOUR OF SPRING** *EMI EMC 3506*	**8**	21
24 Sep 88	**SPIRIT OF EDEN** *Parlophone PCSD 105*	**19**	5
9 Jun 90 ●	**THE VERY BEST OF TALK TALK – NATURAL HISTORY** *Parlophone PCSD 109*	**3**	21
6 Apr 91	**HISTORY REVISITED – THE REMIXES** *Parlophone PCS 7349*	**35**	2
28 Sep 91	**LAUGHING STOCK** *Verve 8477171*	**26**	2
8 Feb 97	**THE VERY BEST OF TALK TALK** *EMI CDEMC 3763*	**54**	2

⌈1⌉ Liquid People vs Talk Talk

TALKING HEADS ⌈ 204 ⌉ Top 500 (see also HEADS with Shaun
RYDER; David BYRNE) *Unorthodox US 'punk funk' eccentrics, formed in 1974,*
New York. Tina Weymouth (b) and husband Chris Frantz (d) had successful
side project, Tom Tom Club, while Scottish-born frontman David Byrne (v/g)
went solo and won an Oscar for his soundtrack to The Last Emperor (Singles:
54 Weeks, Albums: 236 Weeks) pos/wks

7 Feb 81	**ONCE IN A LIFETIME** *Sire SIR 4048*	**14**	10
9 May 81	**HOUSES IN MOTION** *Sire SIR 4050*	**50**	3
21 Jan 84	**THIS MUST BE THE PLACE** *Sire W 9451*	**51**	3
3 Nov 84	**SLIPPERY PEOPLE** *EMI 5504*	**68**	2
12 Oct 85 ●	**ROAD TO NOWHERE** *EMI EMI 5530*	**6**	16
8 Feb 86	**AND SHE WAS** *EMI EMI 5543*	**17**	8
6 Sep 86	**WILD WILD LIFE** *EMI EMI 5567*	**43**	4
16 May 87	**RADIO HEAD** *EMI EM 1*	**52**	2
13 Aug 88	**BLIND** *EMI EM 68*	**59**	3
10 Oct 92	**LIFETIME PILING UP** *EMI EM 250*	**50**	3
25 Feb 78	**TALKING HEADS '77** *Sire 9103 328*	**60**	1
29 Jul 78	**MORE SONGS ABOUT BUILDINGS AND FOOD** *Sire K 56531*	**21**	3
15 Sep 79	**FEAR OF MUSIC** *Sire SRK 6076*	**33**	5
1 Nov 80	**REMAIN IN LIGHT** *Sire SRK 6095*	**21**	17
10 Apr 82	**THE NAME OF THIS BAND IS TALKING HEADS** *Sire SRK 23590*	**22**	5
18 Jun 83	**SPEAKING IN TONGUES** *Sire K 923 8831*	**21**	12
27 Oct 84	**STOP MAKING SENSE** *EMI TAH 1*	**24**	84
29 Jun 85 ●	**LITTLE CREATURES** *EMI TAH 2*	**10**	65
27 Sep 86 ●	**TRUE STORIES** *EMI EU 3511*	**7**	9
26 Mar 88 ●	**NAKED** *EMI EMD 1005*	**3**	15
24 Oct 92 ●	**ONCE IN A LIFETIME – THE BEST OF TALKING HEADS / SAND IN THE VASELINE** *EMI CDEQ 5010*	**7**	16
30 Oct 04	**THE BEST OF TALKING HEADS** *Rhino 8122764882*	**30**	4

TALL PAUL (see also CAMISRA; ESCRIMA; The GRIFTERS; Paul NEWMAN)
UK, male DJ / producer – Paul Newman (Singles: 15 Weeks) pos/wks

29 Mar 97	**ROCK DA HOUSE** *VC Recordings VCRD 18*	**12**	4
29 May 99	**BE THERE** *Duty Free DF 009CD*	**45**	1
8 Apr 00	**FREEBASE** *Duty Free DF 015CD*	**43**	2
2 Jun 01	**ROCK DA HOUSE (re-mix)** *VC Recordings VCRD 89*	**29**	2
18 Aug 01	**PRECIOUS HEART (re)** *Duty Free / Decode DFTELCD 001* ⌈1⌉	**14**	5
13 Apr 02	**EVERYBODY'S A ROCKSTAR** *Duty Free / Decode DFTELCD 003*	**60**	1

⌈1⌉ Tall Paul vs Inxs

TAMBA TRIO
Argentina, male vocal / instrumental group (Singles: 2 Weeks) pos/wks

18 Jul 98	**MAS QUE NADA** *Talkin Loud TLCD 34*	**34**	2

Singles re-entries are listed as (re), (2re), (3re)…. which signifies that the hit re-entered the chart once, twice or three times…

TAMIA See FABOLOUS

The TAMPERER featuring MAYA (see also FARGETTA)
Italy, male production duo – Alex Farolfi and
Mario Fargetta and female vocalist (Singles: 38 Weeks) pos/wks

25 Apr 98	★	FEEL IT *Pepper 0530032*	1 17
14 Nov 98	●	IF YOU BUY THIS RECORD YOUR LIFE WILL BE BETTER *Pepper 0530082*	3 14
12 Feb 00	●	HAMMER TO THE HEART (re) *Pepper 9230032*	6 7

The TAMS
US, male vocal group – lead vocal
Joseph Pope (Singles: 31 Weeks) pos/wks

14 Feb 70		BE YOUNG, BE FOOLISH, BE HAPPY *Stateside SS 2123*	32 7
31 Jul 71	★	HEY GIRL DON'T BOTHER ME *Probe PRO 532*	1 17
21 Nov 87		THERE AIN'T NOTHING LIKE SHAGGIN' *Virgin VS 1029*	21 7

Norma TANEGA *US, female vocalist (Singles: 8 Weeks)*
7 Apr 66		WALKIN' MY CAT NAMED DOG *Stateside SS 496*	22 8

TANGERINE DREAM
Germany, male instrumental group (Albums: 77 Weeks) pos/wks

20 Apr 74		PHAEDRA *Virgin V 2010*	15 15
5 Apr 75		RUBYCON *Virgin V 2025*	12 14
20 Dec 75		RICOCHET *Virgin V 2044*	40 2
13 Nov 76		STRATOSFEAR *Virgin V 2068*	39 4
23 Jul 77		SORCERER (FILM SOUNDTRACK) *MCA MCF 2806*	25 7
19 Nov 77		ENCORE *Virgin VD 2506*	55 1
1 Apr 78		CYCLONE *Virgin V 2097*	37 4
17 Feb 79		FORCE MAJEURE *Virgin V 2111*	26 7
7 Jun 80		TANGRAM *Virgin V 2147*	36 5
18 Apr 81		THIEF (FILM SOUNDTRACK) *Virgin V 2198*	43 3
19 Sep 81		EXIT *Virgin V 2212*	43 5
10 Apr 82		WHITE EAGLE *Virgin V 2226*	57 5
5 Nov 83		HYPERBOREA *Virgin V 2292*	45 2
10 Nov 84		POLAND *Jive Electro HIP 22*	90 1
26 Jul 86		UNDERWATER SUNLIGHT *Jive Electro HIP 40*	97 1
27 Jun 87		TYGER *Jive Electro HIP 47*	88 1

TANK
UK, male vocal / instrumental group (Albums: 5 Weeks) pos/wks

13 Mar 82		FILTH HOUNDS OF HADES *Kamaflage KAMLP 1*	33 5

Children of TANSLEY SCHOOL
UK, children's choir (Singles: 4 Weeks) pos/wks

28 Mar 81		MY MUM IS ONE IN A MILLION *EMI 5151*	27 4

Jimmy TARBUCK
UK, male comedian / vocalist (Singles: 2 Weeks) pos/wks

16 Nov 85		AGAIN (re) *Safari SAFE 68*	68 2

TARLISA See CO-RO featuring TARLISA

Bill TARMEY
UK, male actor / vocalist –
Bill Piddington (Singles: 9 Weeks, Albums: 25 Weeks) pos/wks

3 Apr 93		ONE VOICE *Arista 74321140852* [1]	16 4
19 Feb 94		WIND BENEATH MY WINGS *EMI CDEM 304*	40 3
19 Nov 94		IOU *EMI CDEM 361*	55 2
27 Nov 93		A GIFT OF LOVE *EMI CDEMC 3665*	15 14
5 Nov 94		TIME FOR LOVE *EMI CDEMTV 85*	28 9
18 May 96		AFTER HOURS *EMI Premier PRMTVCD 2*	61 2

[1] Bill Tarmey – backing vocals by St Winifred's School Choir

The TARRIERS
US, male vocal / instrumental group (Singles: 6 Weeks) pos/wks

14 Dec 56		CINDY, OH CINDY *London HLN 8340* [1]	26 1
1 Mar 57		THE BANANA BOAT SONG *Columbia DB 3891*	15 5

[1] Vince Martin and The Tarriers

TARTAN ARMY *UK, male vocal ensemble (Singles: 4 Weeks)* pos/wks
6 Jun 98		SCOTLAND BE GOOD *The Precious JWLCD 33*	54 4

TASTE
Ireland, male vocal / instrumental group (Albums: 16 Weeks) pos/wks

7 Feb 70		ON THE BOARDS *Polydor 583083*	18 11
6 Mar 71		LIVE TASTE *Polydor 2310 082*	14 4
9 Sep 72		LIVE AT THE ISLE OF WIGHT *Polydor 2383 120*	41 1

A TASTE OF HONEY *US, female vocal duo –*
Janice Marie Johnson and Hazel Payne (Singles: 19 Weeks) pos/wks

17 Jun 78	●	BOOGIE OOGIE OOGIE *Capitol CL 15988* ▲	3 16
18 May 85		BOOGIE OOGIE OOGIE (re-mix) *Capitol CL 357*	59 3

TASTE XPERIENCE featuring Natasha PEARL *UK, male instrumen-*
tal / production group and UK, female vocalist (Singles: 1 Week) pos/wks

6 Nov 99		SUMMERSAULT *Manifesto FESCD 64*	66 1

TATA BOX INHIBITORS
Holland, male production duo (Singles: 1 Week) pos/wks

3 Feb 01		FREET *Hooj Choons HOOJ 103CD*	67 1

Jeffrey TATE See Nigel KENNEDY

TATJANA
Croatia, female vocalist – Tatjana Simic (Singles: 2 Weeks) pos/wks

21 Sep 96		SANTA MARIA *Love This LUVTHISCDX 4*	40 2

t.A.T.u. *Russia, female vocal duo – Julia Volkova*
and Lena Katina (Singles: 25 Weeks, Albums: 15 Weeks) pos/wks

25 Jan 03		ALL THE THINGS SHE SAID (IMPORT) *Interscope 0193332*	44 2
8 Feb 03	★	ALL THE THINGS SHE SAID *Interscope 0196972* ■	1 15
31 May 03	●	NOT GONNA GET US *Interscope 9806961*	7 8
25 Jan 03		200 KMH IN THE WRONG LANE *Interscope / Polydor 0674562*	12 15

TAVARES
US, male vocal group (Singles: 77 Weeks, Albums: 15 Weeks) pos/wks

10 Jul 76	●	HEAVEN MUST BE MISSING AN ANGEL *Capitol CL 15876*	4 11
9 Oct 76	●	DON'T TAKE AWAY THE MUSIC *Capitol CL 15886*	4 10
5 Feb 77		THE MIGHTY POWER OF LOVE *Capitol CL 15905*	25 6
9 Apr 77	●	WHODUNIT *Capitol CL 15914*	5 10
2 Jul 77		ONE STEP AWAY *Capitol CL 15930*	16 7
18 Mar 78		THE GHOST OF LOVE *Capitol CL 15968*	29 6
6 May 78	●	MORE THAN A WOMAN *Capitol CL 15977*	7 11
12 Aug 78		SLOW TRAIN TO PARADISE *Capitol CL 15996*	62 3
22 Feb 86		HEAVEN MUST BE MISSING AN ANGEL (re-mix) *Capitol TAV 1*	12 9
3 May 86		IT ONLY TAKES A MINUTE *Capitol TAV 2*	46 4
21 Aug 76		SKY HIGH *Capitol EST 11533*	22 13
1 Apr 78		THE BEST OF TAVARES *Capitol EST 11701*	39 2

TAXMAN See KICKING BACK with TAXMAN

TAYLOR See LIBRA

Andy TAYLOR (see also DURAN DURAN) *UK, male vocalist /*
instrumentalist – guitar (Singles: 2 Weeks, Albums: 1 Week) pos/wks

20 Oct 90		LOLA *A&M AM 596*	60 2
30 May 87		THUNDER *MCA MCG 6018*	61 1

Becky TAYLOR
UK, female vocalist (Singles: 1 Week, Albums: 1 Week) pos/wks

16 Jun 01		SONG OF DREAMS *EMI Classics 8794880*	60 1
23 Jun 01		A DREAM COME TRUE *EMI Classics CDC 5571422*	67 1

Dina TAYLOR See BBG

Felice TAYLOR *US, female vocalist (Singles: 13 Weeks)* pos/wks
25 Oct 67		I FEEL LOVE COMIN' ON *President PT 155*	11 13

James TAYLOR (see also Carly SIMON) *US, male vocalist /*
instrumentalist – guitar (Singles: 18 Weeks, Albums: 122 Weeks) pos/wks

21 Nov 70		FIRE AND RAIN *Warner Bros. WB 6104*	42 3
28 Aug 71	●	YOU'VE GOT A FRIEND *Warner Bros. WB 16085* ▲	4 15
21 Nov 70	●	SWEET BABY JAMES *Warner Bros. ES 1843*	6 53

29 May 71 ●	MUD SLIDE SLIM AND THE BLUE HORIZON		
	Warner Bros. WS 2561 ....**4**	41
8 Jan 72	SWEET BABY JAMES (re-issue) *Warner Bros. K 46043* **34**	6
18 Mar 72 ●	MUD SLIDE SLIM AND THE BLUE HORIZON (re-issue)		
	Warner Bros. K 46085 ....**49**	1
9 Dec 72 ●	ONE MAN DOG *Warner Bros. K 46185* **27**	5
4 Apr 87	CLASSIC SONGS *CBS / WEA JTV 1* **53**	5
21 Jun 97	HOURGLASS *Columbia 4877482* **46**	1
24 Aug 02	OCTOBER ROAD *Columbia 5032922* **39**	3
13 Sep 03 ●	YOU'VE GOT A FRIEND – THE BEST OF JAMES TAYLOR		
	Warner Bros. 8122738372 ....**4**	7

James TAYLOR QUARTET *See JTQ*

John TAYLOR (see also DURAN DURAN)
UK, male vocalist – Nigel Taylor (Singles: 4 Weeks) pos/wks

15 Mar 86	I DO WHAT I DO ... THEME FOR '9 1/2 WEEKS'		
	Parlophone R 6125 ....**42**	4

Johnnie TAYLOR
US, male vocalist, b. 5 May 1938, d. 31 May 2000 (Singles: 7 Weeks) pos/wks

24 Apr 76	DISCO LADY *CBS 4044* ▲ **25**	7

JT TAYLOR (see also KOOL and the GANG)
US, male vocalist (Singles: 5 Weeks) pos/wks

24 Aug 91	LONG HOT SUMMER NIGHT *MCA MCS 1567* **63**	2
30 Nov 91	FEEL THE NEED *MCA MCS 1592* **57**	1
18 Apr 92	FOLLOW ME *MCA MCS 1617* **59**	2

Pauline TAYLOR *UK, female vocalist (Singles: 3 Weeks)* pos/wks

8 Jun 96	LET THIS BE A PRAYER *Cheeky CHEKCD 013* [1] **26**	2
9 Nov 96	CONSTANTLY WAITING *Cheeky CHEKCD 015* **51**	1

[1] Rollo Goes Spiritual with Pauline Taylor

R Dean TAYLOR *Canada, male vocalist (Singles: 48 Weeks)* pos/wks

19 Jun 68	GOTTA SEE JANE *Tamla Motown TMG 656* **17**	12
3 Apr 71 ●	INDIANA WANTS ME *Tamla Motown TMG 763* **2**	15
11 May 74 ●	THERE'S A GHOST IN MY HOUSE *Tamla Motown TMG 896* **3**	12
31 Aug 74	WINDOW SHOPPING *Polydor 2058 502* **36**	5
21 Sep 74	GOTTA SEE JANE (re-issue) *Tamla Motown TMG 918* **41**	4

Rob TAYLOR *See Mathias WARE featuring Rob TAYLOR*

Roger TAYLOR (see also QUEEN) *UK, male vocalist / instrumentalist – drums (Singles: 18 Weeks, Albums: 11 Weeks)* pos/wks

18 Apr 81	FUTURE MANAGEMENT *EMI 5157* **49**	4
16 Jun 84	MAN ON FIRE *EMI 5478* **66**	2
10 Oct 92	RADIO *Epic 6584367* [1] **37**	3
14 May 94	NAZIS *Parlophone CDR 6379* **22**	2
1 Oct 94	FOREIGN SAND *Parlophone CDR 6389* [2] **26**	2
26 Nov 94	HAPPINESS *Parlophone CDR 6399* **32**	2
10 Oct 98	PRESSURE ON *Parlophone CDR 6507* **45**	1
10 Apr 99	SURRENDER! *Parlophone CDR 6517* **38**	2
18 Apr 81	FUN IN SPACE *EMI EMC 3369* **18**	5
7 Jul 84	STRANGE FRONTIER *EMI RTA 1* **30**	4
17 Sep 94	HAPPINESS? *Parlophone CDPCSD 157* **22**	1
10 Oct 98	ELECTRIC FIRE *Parlophone 4967242* **53**	1

[1] Shaky featuring Roger Taylor [2] Roger Taylor and Yoshiki

TAZ *UK, male vocalist (Singles: 4 Weeks)* pos/wks

27 Oct 01	LAILA *Wizard WIZ 015* [1] **44**	2
26 Jun 04	CAN'T CONTAIN ME *Def Jam UK / Mercury 9866825* **46**	2

[1] Taz / Stereo Nation

Kiri TE KANAWA *New Zealand, female vocalist (Singles: 11 Weeks, Albums: 53 Weeks)* pos/wks

28 Sep 91 ●	WORLD IN UNION *Columbia 6574817* **4**	11
2 Apr 83	CHANTS D'AUVERGNE VOLUME 1 *Decca SXDL 7604* [1] **57**	1
26 Oct 85	BLUE SKIES *London KTKT 1* [2] **40**	29
13 Dec 86	CHRISTMAS WITH KIRI *Decca PROLP 12* **47**	4
17 Dec 88	KIRI *K-Tel NE 1424* **70**	3
29 Feb 92	THE ESSENTIAL KIRI *Decca 4362862* **23**	10

23 May 92	KIRI SIDETRACKS THE JAZZ ALBUM *Philips 4340922* **73**	1
9 Apr 94	KIRI! *PolyGram 4436002* **16**	4
10 Nov 01	KIRI – THE DEFINITIVE COLLECTION		
	EMI Classics CDC 5572312 ....**73**	1

[1] Kiri Te Kanawa with the English Chamber Orchestra [2] Kiri Te Kanawa with the Nelson Riddle Orchestra

TEACH-IN
Holland, male / female vocal / instrumental group (Singles: 7 Weeks) pos/wks

12 Apr 75	DING-A-DONG *Polydor 2058 570* **13**	7

Clare TEAL
UK, female vocalist (Albums: 3 Weeks) pos/wks

30 Oct 04	DON'T TALK *Columbia 5186702* **20**	3

TEAM
UK, male vocal / instrumental group (Singles: 5 Weeks) pos/wks

1 Jun 85	WICKI WACKY HOUSE PARTY *EMI 5519* **55**	5

TEAM DEEP
Belgium, male production duo (Singles: 1 Week) pos/wks

17 May 97	MORNINGLIGHT *Multiply CDMULTY 19* **42**	1

TEARDROP EXPLODES
(see also Julian COPE) *UK, male vocal / instrumental group (Singles: 50 Weeks, Albums: 45 Weeks)* pos/wks

27 Sep 80	WHEN I DREAM *Mercury TEAR 1* **47**	6
31 Jan 81 ●	REWARD *Vertigo TEAR 2* **6**	13
2 May 81	TREASON (IT'S JUST A STORY) *Mercury TEAR 3* **18**	8
29 Aug 81	PASSIONATE FRIEND *Zoo / Mercury TEAR 5* **25**	10
21 Nov 81	COLOURS FLY AWAY *Mercury TEAR 6* **54**	3
19 Jun 82	TINY CHILDREN *Mercury TEAR 7* **44**	7
19 Mar 83	YOU DISAPPEAR FROM VIEW *Mercury TEAR 8* **41**	3
18 Oct 80	KILIMANJARO *Mercury 6359 035* **24**	35
5 Dec 81	WILDER *Mercury 6359 056* **29**	6
14 Apr 90	EVERYBODY WANTS TO SHAG ... THE TEARDROP EXPLODES		
	Fontana 8424391 72 ....**72**	1
15 Aug 92	FLOORED GENIUS – THE BEST OF JULIAN COPE AND THE		
	TEARDROP EXPLODES *Island CID 8000* [1] **22**	3

[1] Julian Cope and The Teardrop Explodes

TEARS FOR FEARS `140` `Top 500`
Bath-based band at the forefront of the mid-1980s 'British Invasion' of the US: Roland Orzabal (v/g/k), Curt Smith (v/b; left in 1991 and returned in 2003). The first of their two US No.1s, 'Everybody Wants to Rule the World', also won the 1986 Brit award for Best Single. (Singles: 143 Weeks, Albums: 220 Weeks) pos/wks

2 Oct 82 ●	MAD WORLD *Mercury IDEA 3* **3**	16
5 Feb 83 ●	CHANGE *Mercury IDEA 4* **4**	9
30 Apr 83 ●	PALE SHELTER *Mercury IDEA 5* **5**	8
3 Dec 83	THE WAY YOU ARE *Mercury IDEA 6* **24**	8
18 Aug 84	MOTHER'S TALK *Mercury IDEA 7* **14**	8
1 Dec 84 ●	SHOUT *Mercury IDEA 8* ▲ **4**	16
30 Mar 85	EVERYBODY WANTS TO RULE THE WORLD (re)		
	Mercury IDEA 9 ▲ **2**	15
22 Jun 85	HEAD OVER HEELS *Mercury IDEA 10* **12**	9
31 Aug 85	SUFFER THE CHILDREN *Mercury IDEA 1* **52**	4
7 Sep 85	PALE SHELTER (re-issue) *Mercury IDEA 2* **73**	2
12 Oct 85	I BELIEVE (A SOULFUL RE-RECORDING) *Mercury IDEA 11* **23**	4
31 May 86 ●	EVERYBODY WANTS TO RUN THE WORLD (re)		
	Mercury RACE 1 ....**5**	7
2 Sep 89 ●	SOWING THE SEEDS OF LOVE *Fontana IDEA 12* **5**	9
18 Nov 89	WOMAN IN CHAINS *Fontana IDEA 13* **26**	8
3 Mar 90	ADVICE FOR THE YOUNG AT HEART *Fontana IDEA 14* **36**	4
22 Feb 92	LAID SO LOW (TEARS ROLL DOWN) *Fontana IDEA 17* **17**	5
25 Apr 92	WOMAN IN CHAINS (re-issue) *Fontana IDEA 16* [1] **57**	1
29 May 93	BREAK IT DOWN AGAIN *Mercury IDECD 18* **20**	5
31 Jul 93	COLD *Mercury IDECD 19* **72**	1
7 Oct 95	RAOUL AND THE KINGS OF SPAIN *Epic 6624765* **31**	3
29 Jun 96	GOD'S MISTAKE *Epic 6634185* **61**	1
19 Mar 83 ★	THE HURTING *Mercury MERS 17* **1**	65
9 Mar 85 ★	SONGS FROM THE BIG CHAIR *Mercury MERH 58* ▲ **2**	81
7 Oct 89 ★	THE SEEDS OF LOVE *Fontana 838730 1* ■ **1**	30
14 Mar 92 ●	TEARS ROLL DOWN (GREATEST HITS 1982-1992)		
	Fontana 5109392 ....**2**	26

		pos/wks
19 Jun 93 ●	ELEMENTAL *Mercury 5148752*	**5** 7
28 Oct 95	RAOUL AND THE KINGS OF SPAIN *Epic 4809822*	**41** 1
24 Jan 04 ●	TEARS ROLL DOWN – GREATEST HITS '82-'92 (re-issue) *Fontana 5109392*	**6** 10

1 Tears for Fears featuring Oleta Adams

Mercury RACE 1 was a slightly changed version of Mercury IDEA 9, released to promote the Race Against Time of 15 May 1986. Oleta Adams is given no label credit on the original release of 'Woman in Chains'.

TECHNATION
UK, male production duo (Singles: 1 Week) pos/wks

7 Apr 01	SEA OF BLUE *Slinky Music SLINKY 012CD*	**56** 1

TECHNICIAN 2
UK, male instrumental / production group (Singles: 1 Week) pos/wks

14 Nov 92	PLAYING WITH THE BOY *MCA MCS 1710*	**70** 1

TECHNIQUE
UK, female vocal / instrumental duo (Singles: 2 Weeks) pos/wks

10 Apr 99	SUN IS SHINING *Creation CRESCD 306*	**64** 1
28 Aug 99	YOU + ME *Creation CRESCD 315*	**56** 1

The TECHNO TWINS
UK, male / female vocal duo (Singles: 2 Weeks) pos/wks

16 Jan 82	FALLING IN LOVE AGAIN (re) *PRT 7P 224*	**70** 2

TECHNOCAT
UK, male producer – Tom Wilson (Singles: 3 Weeks) pos/wks

2 Dec 95	TECHNOCAT *Pukka CDPUKKA 4*	**33** 3

TECHNOHEAD (see also GTO; TRICKY DISCO)
UK, male / female vocal / instrumental duo –
Michael Wells and Lee Newman (Singles: 20 Weeks) pos/wks

3 Feb 96 ●	I WANNA BE A HIPPY *Mokum DB 17703*	**6** 14
27 Apr 96	HAPPY BIRTHDAY *Mokum DB 17593*	**18** 5
12 Oct 96	BANANA-NA-NA (DUMB DI DUMB) *Mokum DB 17473*	**64** 1

TECHNOTRONIC (see also HI-TEK 3 featuring YA KID K) *Belgium,*
male producer – Jo Bogaert (Singles: 66 Weeks, Albums: 62 Weeks) pos/wks

2 Sep 89 ●	PUMP UP THE JAM *Swanyard SYR 4* 1	**2** 15
3 Feb 90 ●	GET UP (BEFORE THE NIGHT IS OVER) *Swanyard SYR 8* 2	**2** 10
7 Apr 90	THIS BEAT IS TECHNOTRONIC *Swanyard SYR 9* 3	**14** 7
14 Jul 90 ●	ROCKIN' OVER THE BEAT *Swanyard SYR 14* 2	**9** 9
6 Oct 90 ●	MEGAMIX *Swanyard SYR 19*	**6** 8
15 Dec 90	TURN IT UP *Swanyard SYD 9* 4	**42** 4
25 May 91	MOVE THAT BODY *ARS 6568377* 5	**12** 7
3 Aug 91	WORK *ARS 6573317* 5	**40** 4
14 Dec 96	PUMP UP THE JAM (re-mix) *Worx WORXCD 004*	**36** 2
6 Jan 90 ●	PUMP UP THE JAM *Swanyard SYRLP 1*	**2** 14
2 Nov 90 ●	TRIP ON THIS – REMIXES *Telstar STAR 2461*	**7** 14
15 Jun 91	BODY TO BODY *ARS 4683421*	**27** 4

1 Technotronic featuring Felly 2 Technotronic featuring Ya Kid K 3
Technotronic featuring MC Eric 4 Technotronic featuring Melissa and Einstein 5
Technotronic featuring Reggie

The TEDDY BEARS *US, male / female vocal*
trio – includes Phil Spector (Singles: 17 Weeks) pos/wks

19 Dec 58 ●	TO KNOW HIM IS TO LOVE HIM *London HLN 8733* ▲	**2** 16
14 Apr 79	TO KNOW HIM IS TO LOVE HIM (re-issue) *Lightning LIG 9015*	**66** 1

'To Know Him Is to Love Him' re-issue was coupled with 'Endless Sleep' by Jody Reynolds as a double A-side

TEEBONE featuring MC KIE and MC SPARKS *UK, male producer –*
Leon Thompson and UK, male rap duo (Singles: 2 Weeks) pos/wks

5 Aug 00	FLY BI *East West EW 217CD*	**43** 2

TEENAGE FANCLUB *UK, male vocal /*
instrumental group (Singles: 23 Weeks, Albums: 24 Weeks) pos/wks

24 Aug 91	STAR SIGN *Creation CRE 105*	**44** 2
2 Nov 91	THE CONCEPT *Creation CRE 111*	**51** 1

		pos/wks
8 Feb 92	WHAT YOU DO TO ME (EP) *Creation CRE 115*	**31** 2
26 Jun 93	RADIO *Creation CRESCD 130*	**31** 2
2 Oct 93	NORMAN 3 *Creation CRESCD 142*	**50** 1
2 Apr 94	FALLIN' *Epic 6602622* 1	**59** 1
8 Apr 95	MELLOW DOUBT *Creation CRESCD 175*	**34** 2
27 May 95	SPARKY'S DREAM *Creation CRESCD 201*	**40** 2
2 Sep 95	NEIL JUNG *Creation CRESCD 210*	**62** 1
16 Dec 95	HAVE LOST IT (EP) *Creation CRESCD 216*	**53** 1
12 Jul 97	AIN'T THAT ENOUGH *Creation CRESCD 228*	**17** 3
30 Aug 97	I DON'T WANT CONTROL OF YOU *Creation CRESCD 238*	**43** 1
29 Nov 97	START AGAIN *Creation CRESCD 280*	**54** 1
28 Oct 00	I NEED DIRECTION *Columbia 6699512*	**48** 1
2 Mar 02	NEAR TO YOU *Geographic GEOG 013CD* 2	**68** 1
4 Sep 04	ASSOCIATION *Geographic GEOG 29CD* 3	**75** 1
7 Sep 91	THE KING *Creation CRELP 096*	**53** 2
16 Nov 91	BANDWAGONESQUE *Creation CRELP 106*	**22** 7
16 Oct 93	THIRTEEN *Creation CRECD 144*	**14** 3
10 Jun 95 ●	GRAND PRIX *Creation CRECD 173*	**7** 4
2 Aug 97 ●	SONGS FROM NORTHERN BRITAIN *Creation CRECD 196*	**3** 5
4 Nov 00	HOWDY! *Columbia 5006222*	**33** 2
8 Feb 03	FOUR THOUSAND SEVEN HUNDRED & SIXTY SIX *Poolside POOLS 3CDX*	**47** 1

1 Teenage Fanclub and De La Soul 2 Teenage Fanclub and Jad Fair 3
International Airport / Teenage Fanclub

Tracks on What You Do to Me (EP): What You Do to Me / B-Side / Life's a Gas / Filler. Tracks on Have Lost It (EP): Don't Look Back / Everything Flows / Star Sign (re-recorded version of the band's first hit) / 120 mins

TEENAGERS See Frankie LYMON and the TEENAGERS

Towa TEI featuring Kylie MINOGUE *Japan, male*
DJ / producer and Australia, female vocalist (Singles: 1 Week) pos/wks

31 Oct 98	GBI *Athrob ART 021CD*	**63** 1

TEKNO TOO
UK, male instrumental / production duo (Singles: 2 Weeks) pos/wks

13 Jul 91	JET-STAR *D-Zone DANCE 012*	**56** 2

TELEPOPMUSIK *France, male instrumental /*
production trio and UK, female vocalist (Singles: 1 Week) pos/wks

2 Mar 02	BREATHE *Chrysalis CDCHS 5133*	**42** 1

TELETUBBIES *UK, male / female cuddly*
alien vocal group (Singles: 32 Weeks, Albums: 4 Weeks) pos/wks

13 Dec 97 ★	TELETUBBIES SAY EH-OH! (2re) *BBC Worldwide WMXS 00092* ◆ ■	**1** 32
4 Apr 98	THE ALBUM *BBC Worldwide Music WMXU 00142*	**31** 4

TELEVISION (see also Tom VERLAINE) *US, male vocal / instrumental*
group (Singles: 10 Weeks, Albums: 17 Weeks) pos/wks

16 Apr 77	MARQUEE MOON *Elektra K 12252*	**30** 4
30 Jul 77	PROVE IT *Elektra K 12262*	**25** 4
22 Apr 78	FOXHOLE *Elektra K 12287*	**36** 2
26 Mar 77	MARQUEE MOON *Elektra K 52046*	**28** 13
29 Apr 78 ●	ADVENTURE *Elektra K 52072*	**7** 4

TELEX
Belgium, male vocal / instrumental trio (Singles: 7 Weeks) pos/wks

21 Jul 79	ROCK AROUND THE CLOCK *Sire SIR 4020*	**34** 7

Sylvia TELLA See The BLOW MONKEYS

The TEMPERANCE SEVEN *UK, male vocal / instrumental group –*
lead vocal Paul MacDowell (Singles: 45 Weeks, Albums: 10 Weeks) pos/wks

30 Mar 61 ★	YOU'RE DRIVING ME CRAZY *Parlophone R 4757*	**1** 16
15 Jun 61 ●	PASADENA *Parlophone R 4781*	**4** 17
28 Sep 61	HARD HEARTED HANNAH / CHILI BOM BOM *Parlophone R 4823*	**28** 4
7 Dec 61	THE CHARLESTON *Parlophone R 4851*	**22** 8
13 May 61	TEMPERANCE SEVEN PLUS ONE *Argo RG 11*	**19** 1
25 Nov 61 ●	TEMPERANCE SEVEN 1961 *Parlophone PMC 1152*	**8** 9

'Chili Bom Bom' listed with 'Hard Hearted Hannah' only for the weeks of 12 and 19 Oct 1961

TEMPLE CHURCH CHOIR
UK, male vocal / instrumental group (Albums: 3 Weeks)   pos/wks

16 Dec 61 ● CHRISTMAS CAROLS *HMV CLP 1309* 8 3

TEMPLE OF THE DOG
US, male vocal / instrumental group (Singles: 2 Weeks)   pos/wks

24 Oct 92   HUNGER STRIKE *A&M AM 0091* **51** 2

Nino TEMPO and April STEVENS US, male / female
vocal duo – Antonio and Carol Lo Tempio (Singles: 19 Weeks)   pos/wks

7 Nov 63   DEEP PURPLE *London HLK 9782* ▲ **17** 11
16 Jan 64   WHISPERING *London HLK 9829* **20** 8

The TEMPTATIONS (155 Top 500)
The world's most successful R&B vocal group: Eddie Kendricks (b. 1939 d. 1992), Otis Williams, Paul Williams (b. 1939, d. 1973), Melvin Franklin (b. 1942, d. 1995), David Ruffin (b. 1941, d. 1991). The Detroit quintet's biggest UK hit, 'My Girl', was a 27-year-old US No.1. The current line-up of the group is still active Stateside (Singles: 211 Weeks, Albums: 137 Weeks)   pos/wks

18 Mar 65   MY GIRL *Stateside SS 378* ▲ **43** 1
1 Apr 65   IT'S GROWING (re) *Tamla Motown TMG 504* **45** 2
14 Jul 66   AIN'T TOO PROUD TO BEG *Tamla Motown TMG 565* **21** 11
6 Oct 66   BEAUTY IS ONLY SKIN DEEP *Tamla Motown TMG 578* **18** 10
15 Dec 66   (I KNOW) I'M LOSING YOU *Tamla Motown TMG 587* **19** 9
6 Sep 67   YOU'RE MY EVERYTHING *Tamla Motown TMG 620* **26** 15
6 Mar 68   I WISH IT WOULD RAIN *Tamla Motown TMG 641* **45** 1
12 Jun 68   I COULD NEVER LOVE ANOTHER *Tamla Motown TMG 658* ...**47** 1
29 Jan 69 ● I'M GONNA MAKE YOU LOVE ME (re)
           Tamla Motown TMG 685 [1] **3** 12
5 Mar 69 ● GET READY *Tamla Motown TMG 688* **10** 9
23 Aug 69   CLOUD NINE *Tamla Motown TMG 707* **15** 10
20 Sep 69   I SECOND THAT EMOTION *Tamla Motown TMG 709* [1] ...**18** 8
17 Jan 70   I CAN'T GET NEXT TO YOU *Tamla Motown TMG 722* ▲ ...**13** 9
21 Mar 70   WHY (MUST WE FALL IN LOVE) *Tamla Motown TMG 730* [1] ...**31** 7
13 Jun 70   PSYCHEDELIC SHACK *Tamla Motown TMG 741* **33** 7
19 Sep 70 ● BALL OF CONFUSION (THAT'S WHAT THE WORLD
           IS TODAY) (re) *Tamla Motown TMG 749* **7** 15
22 May 71 ● JUST MY IMAGINATION (RUNNING AWAY WITH ME)
           Tamla Motown TMG 773 ▲ **8** 16
5 Feb 72   SUPERSTAR (REMEMBER HOW YOU GOT WHERE YOU ARE)
           Tamla Motown TMG 800 ....**32** 5
15 Apr 72   TAKE A LOOK AROUND *Tamla Motown TMG 808* **13** 10
13 Jan 73   PAPA WAS A ROLLIN' STONE *Tamla Motown TMG 839* ▲ ...**14** 8
29 Sep 73   LAW OF THE LAND *Tamla Motown TMG 866* **41** 4
12 Jun 82   STANDING ON THE TOP (PART 1) *Motown TMG 1263* [2] ...**53** 10
17 Nov 84   TREAT HER LIKE A LADY *Motown TMG 1365* **12** 10
15 Aug 87   PAPA WAS A ROLLIN' STONE (re-mix) *Motown ZB 41431* ...**31** 6
6 Feb 88   LOOK WHAT YOU STARTED *Motown ZB 41733* **63** 2
21 Oct 89   ALL I WANT FROM YOU *Motown ZB 43233* **71** 1
15 Jun 91 ● THE MOTOWN SONG *Warner Bros. W 0030* [3] **10** 8
15 Feb 92 ● MY GIRL (re-issue) *Epic 6576767* **2** 10
22 Feb 92   THE JONES' *Motown TMG 1403* **69** 1
24 Dec 66   GETTING READY *Tamla Motown STML 11035* **40** 1
11 Feb 67   TEMPTATIONS GREATEST HITS *Tamla Motown STML 11042*..**17** 40
22 Jul 67   TEMPTATIONS LIVE! *Tamla Motown STML 11053* **20** 4
18 Nov 67   TEMPTATIONS WITH A LOT OF SOUL
           Tamla Motown STML 11057 ....**19** 18
25 Jan 69 ★ DIANA ROSS AND THE SUPREMES JOIN THE TEMPTATIONS
           Tamla Motown STML 11096 [1] **1** 15
28 Jun 69   TCB *Tamla Motown STML 11110* [1] **11** 12
20 Sep 69   CLOUD NINE *Tamla Motown STML 11109* **32** 1
14 Feb 70   PUZZLE PEOPLE *Tamla Motown STML 11133* **20** 4
14 Feb 70   TOGETHER *Tamla Motown STML 11122* [1] **28** 4
11 Jul 70   PSYCHEDELIC SHACK *Tamla Motown STML 11147* **56** 1
26 Dec 70   GREATEST HITS VOLUME 2 *Tamla Motown STML 11170* ...**28** 5
29 Apr 72   SOLID ROCK *Tamla Motown STML 11202* **34** 2
20 Jan 73   ALL DIRECTIONS *Tamla Motown STML 11218* **19** 7
7 Jul 73   MASTERPIECE *Tamla Motown STML 11229* **28** 3
8 Dec 84   TRULY FOR YOU *Motown ZL 72342* **75** 1
11 Apr 92 ● MOTOWN'S GREATEST HITS *Motown 5300152* **8** 9
27 Jan 01   AT THEIR VERY BEST *Universal Music TV 135782* ...**28** 5
30 Mar 02   AT THEIR VERY BEST – TEMPTATIONS / FOUR TOPS
           Universal TV 5830142 ....**18** 1

[1] Diana Ross and The Supremes and The Temptations [2] The Temptations featuring Rick James [3] Rod Stewart with backing vocals by The Temptations
[1] Diana Ross and The Supremes with The Temptations

'At Their Very Best – Temptations / Four Tops' appeared only in the UK Compilation Chart and was not listed in the standard Top 75

10cc (150 Top 500) (see also WAX) Multi-talented Manchester
supergroup: Graham Gouldman (previously penned hits for The Hollies, The Yardbirds and Herman's Hermits), Eric Stewart (ex-Mindbenders, Hotlegs), and Lol Creme and Kevin Godley (both ex-Hotlegs). Godley and Creme went on to have hits as a duo and produced award-winning videos (Singles: 133 weeks, Albums: 219 weeks)   pos/wks

23 Sep 72 ● DONNA *UK 6* **2** 13
19 May 73 ★ RUBBER BULLETS *UK 36* **1** 13
25 Aug 73 ● THE DEAN AND I *UK 48* **10** 8
15 Jun 74 ● THE WALL STREET SHUFFLE *UK 69* **10** 10
14 Sep 74   SILLY LOVE *UK 77* **24** 7
5 Apr 75 ● LIFE IS A MINESTRONE *Mercury 6008 010* **7** 8
31 May 75 ★ I'M NOT IN LOVE *Mercury 6008 014* **1** 11
29 Nov 75 ● ART FOR ART'S SAKE *Mercury 6008 017* **5** 10
20 Mar 76 ● I'M MANDY FLY ME *Mercury 6008 019* **6** 9
11 Dec 76 ● THE THINGS WE DO FOR LOVE *Mercury 6008 022* ...**6** 11
16 Apr 77 ● GOOD MORNING JUDGE *Mercury 6008 025* **5** 12
12 Aug 78 ★ DREADLOCK HOLIDAY *Mercury 6008 035* **1** 13
7 Aug 82   RUN AWAY *Mercury MER 113* **50** 4
18 Mar 95   I'M NOT IN LOVE (re-recording) *Avex UK AVEXCD 2* ...**29** 2
1 Sep 73   10 C.C. *UK UKAL 1005* **36** 1
15 Jun 74 ● SHEET MUSIC *UK UKAL 1007* **9** 24
22 Mar 75 ● THE ORIGINAL SOUNDTRACK *Mercury 9102 500* ..**4** 40
7 Jun 75 ● GREATEST HITS OF 10cc *Decca UKAL 1012* **9** 18
31 Jan 76 ● HOW DARE YOU! *Mercury 9102 501* **5** 31
14 May 77 ● DECEPTIVE BENDS *Mercury 9102 502* **3** 21
10 Dec 77   LIVE AND LET LIVE *Mercury 6641 698* **14** 15
23 Sep 78 ● BLOODY TOURISTS *Mercury 9102 503* **3** 15
6 Oct 79 ● GREATEST HITS 1972-1978 *Mercury 9102 504* **5** 21
5 Apr 80   LOOK HERE *Mercury 9102 505* **35** 5
15 Oct 83   WINDOW IN THE JUNGLE *Mercury MERL 28* **70** 2
29 Aug 87 ● CHANGING FACES – THE VERY BEST OF 10cc AND
           GODLEY AND CREME *ProTV TGCLP 1* [1] **4** 18
5 Apr 97   THE VERY BEST OF 10cc *Mercury / PolyGram TV 5346122* ...**37** 4

[1] 10cc and Godley and Creme

From 'The Things We do for Love', 10cc were a male vocal / instrumental duo

TEN CITY US, male vocal / instrumental
group (Singles: 21 Weeks, Albums: 12 Weeks)   pos/wks

21 Jan 89 ● THAT'S THE WAY LOVE IS *Atlantic A 8963* **8** 10
8 Apr 89   DEVOTION *Atlantic A 8916* **29** 4
22 Jul 89   WHERE DO WE GO? *Atlantic A 8864* **60** 1
27 Oct 90   WHATEVER MAKES YOU HAPPY *Atlantic A 7819* ...**60** 2
15 Aug 92   ONLY TIME WILL TELL / MY PEACE OF HEAVEN
           East West America A 8516 ....**63** 2
11 Sep 93   FANTASY *Columbia 6595042* **45** 2
18 Feb 89   FOUNDATION *Atlantic WX 249* **22** 12

10 REVOLUTIONS
UK, male production group (Singles: 1 Week)   pos/wks

30 Aug 03   TIME FOR THE REVOLUTION *Incentive CENT 53CDS* ...**59** 1

TEN SHARP Holland, male vocal /
instrumental duo (Singles: 15 Weeks, Albums: 2 Weeks)   pos/wks

21 Mar 92 ● YOU *Columbia 6566647* **10** 13
20 Jun 92   AIN'T MY BEATING HEART *Columbia 6580947* **63** 2
9 May 92   UNDER THE WATER-LINE *Columbia 4690702* **46** 2

10,000 MANIACS US, female / male vocal / instrumental group –
leader Natalie Merchant (Singles: 7 Weeks, Albums: 12 Weeks)   pos/wks

12 Sep 92   THESE ARE DAYS *Elektra EKR 156* **58** 3
10 Apr 93   CANDY EVERYBODY WANTS *Elektra EKR 160CD1* ...**47** 3
23 Oct 93   BECAUSE THE NIGHT *Elektra EKR 175CD* **65** 1
27 May 89   BLIND MAN'S ZOO *Elektra EKT 57* **18** 8
10 Oct 92   OUR TIME IN EDEN *Elektra 7559613852* **33** 2
6 Nov 93   UNPLUGGED *Elektra 7559615692* **40** 2

TEN YEARS AFTER UK, male vocal / instrumental group,
leader – Alvin Lee (Singles: 18 Weeks, Albums: 70 Weeks)   pos/wks

6 Jun 70 ● LOVE LIKE A MAN *Deram DM 299* **10** 18
21 Sep 68   UNDEAD *Deram SML 1023* **26** 7
22 Feb 69 ● STONEDHENGE *Deram SML 1029* **6** 5
4 Oct 69 ● SSSSH *Deram SML 1052* **4** 18
2 May 70 ● CRICKLEWOOD GREEN *Deram SML 1065* **4** 27

9 Jan 71 ●	WATT Deram SML 1078	5	9
13 Nov 71	A SPACE IN TIME Chrysalis CHR 1001	36	1
7 Oct 72	ROCK & ROLL MUSIC TO THE WORLD Chrysalis CHR 1009	27	1
28 Jul 73	RECORDED LIVE Chrysalis CHR 1049	36	2

TENACIOUS D US, male vocal / instrumental duo –
Jack Black and Kyle Gass (Singles: 2 Weeks, Albums: 34 Weeks)   pos/wks

| 23 Nov 02 | WONDERBOY Epic 6733512 | 34 | 2 |
| 13 Jul 02 | TENACIOUS D Epic 5077352 | 38 | 34 |

Danny TENAGLIA US, male DJ / producer (Singles: 5 Weeks)   pos/wks

5 Sep 98	MUSIC IS THE ANSWER (DANCIN' AND PRANCIN') Twisted UK TWCD 10038 [1]	36	3
10 Apr 99	TURN ME ON Twisted UK TWCD 10045 [2]	53	1
23 Oct 99	MUSIC IS THE ANSWER (re-mix) Twisted UK TWCD 10052 [1]	50	1

[1] Danny Tenaglia and Celeda [2] Danny Tenaglia featuring Liz Torres

TENNESSEE THREE See Johnny CASH

TENOR FLY
UK, male vocalist – Jonathan Sutter (Singles: 17 Weeks)   pos/wks

6 Apr 91	WICKEDEST SOUND Desire WANT 40 [1]	43	6
15 Jun 91	TRIBAL BASE Desire WANT 44 [2]	20	6
7 Jan 95	BRIGHT SIDE OF LIFE Mango CIDM 825	51	2
7 Feb 98	B-BOY STANCE Freskanova FND 7 [3]	23	3

[1] Rebel MC featuring Tenor Fly [2] Rebel MC featuring Tenor Fly and Barrington Levy [3] Freestylers featuring Tenor Fly

TENPOLE TUDOR UK, male vocal / instrumental group (Singles: 40 Weeks, Albums: 8 Weeks)   pos/wks

7 Apr 79 ●	WHO KILLED BAMBI Virgin VS 256 [1]	6	8
13 Oct 79	ROCK AROUND THE CLOCK Virgin VS 290	21	6
25 Apr 81 ●	SWORDS OF A THOUSAND MEN Stiff BUY 109	6	12
1 Aug 81	WUNDERBAR Stiff BUY 120	16	9
14 Nov 81	THROWING MY BABY OUT WITH THE BATHWATER Stiff BUY 129	49	5
9 May 81	EDDIE OLD BOB DICK & GARRY Stiff SEEZ 31	44	8

[1] Ten Pole Tudor

The listed flip side of 'Who Killed Bambi' was 'Silly Thing' by Sex Pistols. The listed flip side of 'Rock Around the Clock' was 'The Great Rock 'n' Roll Swindle', also by Sex Pistols

The TENTH PLANET
UK, male / female vocal / production group (Singles: 1 Week)   pos/wks

| 14 Apr 01 | GHOSTS Nebula NEBCD 015 | 59 | 1 |

Bryn TERFEL UK, male vocalist (Albums: 24 Weeks)   pos/wks

16 Nov 96	SOMETHING WONDERFUL Deutsche Grammophon 4491632	72	1
28 Oct 00	WE'LL KEEP A WELCOME – THE WELSH ALBUM Deutsche Grammophon 4635932	33	10
3 Nov 01	SOME ENCHANTED EVENING Deutsche Grammophon 4714252	49	2
8 Nov 03 ●	BRYN Deutsche Grammophon 4747032	6	11

TERMINATERS See ARNEE and the TERMINATERS

TERRA FIRMA
Italy, male producer – Claudio Giussani (Singles: 1 Week)   pos/wks

| 18 May 96 | FLOATING Platipus PLAT 21CD | 64 | 1 |

TERRAPLANE
UK, male vocal / instrumental group (Albums: 1 Week)   pos/wks

| 25 Jan 86 | BLACK AND WHITE Epic EPC 26439 | 74 | 1 |

Tammi TERRELL See Marvin GAYE

TERRIS UK, male vocal / instrumental group (Singles: 1 Week)   pos/wks

| 17 Mar 01 | FABRICATED LUNACY Blanco Y Negro NEG 130CD | 62 | 1 |

TERROR SQUAD featuring FAT JOE & REMY
US, male / female rap group (Singles: 5 Weeks)   pos/wks

| 16 Oct 04 | LEAN BACK Universal MCSTD 40385 ▲ | 24 | 5 |

Sleeve credit: Terror Squad featuring Fat Joe (aka Joey Crack) & Remy

TERRORIZE
UK, male producer – Shaun Imrei (Singles: 6 Weeks)   pos/wks

2 May 92	IT'S JUST A FEELING Hamster STER 1	52	3
22 Aug 92	FEEL THE RHYTHM Hamster 12STER 2	69	1
14 Nov 92	IT'S JUST A FEELING (re-issue) Hamster STER 8	47	2

TERRORVISION UK, male vocal / instrumental group (Singles: 55 Weeks, Albums: 41 Weeks)   pos/wks

19 Jun 93	AMERICAN TV Total Vegas CDVEGAS 3	63	1
30 Oct 93	NEW POLICY ONE Total Vegas CDVEGAS 4	42	2
8 Jan 94	MY HOUSE Total Vegas CDVEGAS 5	29	4
9 Apr 94	OBLIVION Total Vegas CDVEGAS 6	21	5
25 Jun 94	MIDDLEMAN Total Vegas CDVEGAS 7	25	4
3 Sep 94	PRETEND BEST FRIEND Total Vegas CDVEGAS 8	25	3
29 Oct 94	ALICE WHAT'S THE MATTER Total Vegas CDVEGAS 9	24	4
18 Mar 95	SOME PEOPLE SAY Total Vegas CDVEGAS 10	22	3
2 Mar 96 ●	PERSEVERANCE Total Vegas CDVEGAS 11	5	4
4 May 96	CELEBRITY HIT LIST Total Vegas CDVEGAS 12	20	3
20 Jul 96 ●	BAD ACTRESS Total Vegas CDVEGAS 13	10	3
11 Jan 97	EASY Total Vegas CDVEGAS 14	12	4
3 Oct 98	JOSEPHINE EMI CDVEGAS 15	23	2
30 Jan 99 ●	TEQUILA Total Vegas CDVEGAS 16	2	10
15 May 99	III WISHES Total Vegas CDVEGAS 17	42	1
27 Jan 01	D'YA WANNA GO FASTER Papillon BTFLYS 0007	28	2
15 May 93	FORMALDEHYDE Total Vegas VEGASCD 1	75	1
30 Apr 94	HOW TO MAKE FRIENDS AND INFLUENCE PEOPLE Total Vegas VEGASCD 2	18	25
23 Mar 96 ●	REGULAR URBAN SURVIVORS Total Vegas VEGASCD 3	8	12
17 Oct 98	SHAVING PEACHES Total Vegas 4961322	34	2
17 Feb 01	GOOD TO GO Papillon BTFLYCD 0011	48	1

Helen TERRY
UK, female vocalist (Singles: 6 Weeks)   pos/wks

| 12 May 84 | LOVE LIES LOST Virgin VS 678 | 34 | 27 |

Todd TERRY (see also BLACK RIOT; ROYAL HOUSE; SWAN LAKE; The GYPSYMEN) US, male producer (Singles: 33 Weeks, Albums: 1 Week)   pos/wks

12 Nov 88	WEEKEND Sleeping Bag SBUK 1T [1]	56	3
14 Oct 95	WEEKEND (re-mix) Ore AG 13CD [1]	28	3
13 Jul 96 ●	KEEP ON JUMPIN' Manifesto FESCD 11 [2]	8	6
12 Jul 97 ●	SOMETHING GOIN' ON Manifesto FESCD 25 [2]	5	10
6 Dec 97	IT'S OVER LOVE Manifesto FESCD 37 [3]	16	8
11 Apr 98	READY FOR A NEW DAY Manifesto FESCD 40 [4]	20	2
3 Jul 99	LET IT RIDE Innocent RESTCD 1 [1]	58	1
5 Aug 95	A DAY IN THE LIFE OF TODD TERRY Sound of Ministry SOMCD 2	73	1

[1] Todd Terry Project [2] Todd Terry featuring Martha Wash and Jocelyn Brown [3] Todd Terry presents Shannon [4] Todd Terry featuring Martha Wash

Tony TERRY
US, male vocalist (Singles: 6 Weeks)   pos/wks

| 27 Feb 88 | LOVEY DOVEY Epic TONY 2 | 44 | 6 |

TESLA US, male vocal / instrumental group (Singles: 1 Week, Albums: 6 Weeks)   pos/wks

27 Apr 91	SIGNS Geffen GFS 3	70	1
11 Feb 89	THE GREAT RADIO CONTROVERSY Geffen WX 244	34	2
2 Mar 91	FIVE MAN ACOUSTICAL JAM Geffen 9243111	59	1
21 Sep 91	PSYCHOTIC SUPPER Geffen GEF 24424	44	2
3 Sep 94	BUST A NUT Geffen GED 24713	51	1

TESTAMENT
US, male vocal / instrumental group (Albums: 6 Weeks)   pos/wks

28 May 88	THE NEW ORDER Megaforce 781849 1	81	1
19 Aug 89	PRACTICE WHAT YOU PREACH Atlantic WX 297	40	2
6 Oct 90	SOULS OF BLACK Megaforce 7567821431	35	2
30 May 92	THE RITUAL Atlantic 7567823922	48	1

Joe TEX
US, male vocalist – Joe Arlington, b. 8 Aug 1933, d. 13 Aug 1982 (Singles: 11 Weeks)   pos/wks

| 23 Apr 77 ● | AIN'T GONNA BUMP NO MORE (WITH NO BIG FAT WOMAN) Epic EPC 5035 | 2 | 11 |

TEXAS `133` `Top 500`

Named after Wim Wenders' movie 'Paris, Texas' the Scots blues turned pop-chart mainstays are: Sharleen Spiteri (v), Ally McErlaine (g), Johnny McElhone (b), Eddie Campbell (k), all from Glasgow. Stuart Kerr, Richard Hynde and Mykey Wilson have all contributed on drums with Tony McGovern (g) the most recent recruit to a band now well established among the multi-million-selling album elite (Singles: 135 Weeks, Albums: 240 Weeks) pos/wks

4 Feb 89 ●	I DON'T WANT A LOVER *Mercury TEX 1*	....8 11
6 May 89	THRILL HAS GONE *Mercury TEX 2*	..60 3
5 Aug 89	EVERYDAY NOW *Mercury TEX 3*	..44 5
2 Dec 89	PRAYER FOR YOU *Mercury TEX 4*	..73 1
7 Sep 91	WHY BELIEVE IN YOU *Mercury TEX 5*	..66 1
26 Oct 91	IN MY HEART *Mercury TEX 6*	..74 1
8 Feb 92	ALONE WITH YOU *Mercury TEX 7*	..32 4
25 Apr 92	TIRED OF BEING ALONE *Mercury TEX 8*	..19 6
11 Sep 93	SO CALLED FRIEND *Vertigo TEXCD 9*	..30 3
30 Oct 93	YOU OWE IT ALL TO ME *Vertigo TEXCD 10*	..39 3
12 Feb 94	SO IN LOVE WITH YOU *Vertigo TEXCD 11*	..28 2
18 Jan 97 ●	SAY WHAT YOU WANT *Mercury MERCD 480*	....3 10
19 Apr 97 ●	HALO *Mercury MERCD 482*	..10 7
9 Aug 97 ●	BLACK EYED BOY *Mercury MERCD 490*	....5 6
15 Nov 97 ●	PUT YOUR ARMS AROUND ME (2re) *Mercury MERCD 497*	..10 8
21 Mar 98 ●	INSANE / SAY WHAT YOU WANT (ALL DAY EVERY DAY) (re-mix) *Mercury MERCD 499* `1`	....4 7
1 May 99 ●	IN OUR LIFETIME *Mercury MERCD 517*	....4 9
28 Aug 99 ●	SUMMER SON *Mercury MERCD 520*	....5 9
27 Nov 99	WHEN WE ARE TOGETHER *Mercury MERCD 525*	..12 9
14 Oct 00 ●	IN DEMAND (re) *Mercury MERCD 528*	....6 10
20 Jan 01	INNER SMILE *Mercury MERCD 531*	....6 8
21 Jul 01	I DON'T WANT A LOVER (re-mix) *Mercury MERCD 533*	..16 4
18 Oct 03 ●	CARNIVAL GIRL *Mercury 9812253* `2`	....9 5
20 Dec 03	I'LL SEE IT THROUGH *Mercury 9815221*	..40 3
25 Mar 89 ●	SOUTHSIDE *Mercury 8381711*	....3 30
5 Oct 91	MOTHERS HEAVEN *Mercury 8485781*	..32 4
13 Nov 93	RICKS ROAD *Vertigo 5182522*	..18 2
15 Feb 97 ★	WHITE ON BLONDE *Mercury 5343152* ■	....1 102
22 May 99 ★	THE HUSH *Mercury 5389722* ■	....1 47

`1` Texas featuring the Wu-Tang Clan `2` Texas featuring Kardinal Offishall

'Say What You Want (All Day Every Day)' is a new mix of the hit from 18 Jan 1997 with rap by Method Man and the RZA

THA DOGG POUND (see also SNOOP DOGG; KURUPT) *US, male rap duo – Ricardo Brown and Delmar Amaud (Albums: 2 Weeks)* pos/wks

11 Nov 95	DOGG FOOD *Death Row 5241772* ▲	..66 2

THAT KID CHRIS
US, male DJ / producer – Chris Staropoli (Singles: 1 Week) pos/wks

22 Feb 97	FEEL THA VIBE *Manifesto FESCD 16*	..52 1

THAT PETROL EMOTION *UK / US, male vocal / instrumental group (Singles: 24 Weeks, Albums: 8 Weeks)* pos/wks

11 Apr 87	BIG DECISION *Polydor TPE 1*	..43 7
11 Jul 87	DANCE *Polydor TPE 2*	..64 2
17 Oct 87	GENIUS MOVE *Virgin VS 1002*	..65 2
31 Mar 90	ABANDON *Virgin VS 1242*	..73 1
1 Sep 90	HEY VENUS *Virgin VS 1290*	..49 4
9 Feb 91	TINGLE *Virgin VS 1312*	..49 4
27 Apr 91	SENSITIZE *Virgin VS 1261*	..55 4
10 May 86	MANIC POP THRILL *Demon FIEND 70*	..84 2
23 May 87	BABBLE *Polydor TPE LP 1*	..30 3
24 Sep 88	END OF MILLENNIUM PSYCHOSIS BLUES *Virgin V 2550*	..53 2
21 Apr 90	CHEMICRAZY *Virgin V 2618*	..62 1

The THE *UK, male vocalist / multi-instrumentalist – Matt Johnson and backing musicians (Singles: 52 Weeks, Albums: 53 Weeks)* pos/wks

4 Dec 82	UNCERTAIN SMILE *Epic EPC A 2787*	..68 3
17 Sep 83	THIS IS THE DAY *Epic A 3710*	..71 3
9 Aug 86	HEARTLAND *Some Bizzare TRUTH 2*	..29 10
25 Oct 86	INFECTED *Some Bizzare TRUTH 3*	..48 5
24 Jan 87	SLOW TRAIN TO DAWN *Some Bizzare TENSE 1*	..64 2
23 May 87	SWEET BIRD OF TRUTH *Epic TENSE 2*	..55 2
1 Apr 89	THE BEAT(EN) GENERATION *Epic EMU 8*	..18 5
22 Jul 89	GRAVITATE TO ME *Epic EMU 9*	..63 3
7 Oct 89	ARMAGEDDON DAYS ARE HERE (AGAIN) *Epic EMU 10*	..70 2

2 Mar 91	SHADES OF BLUE (EP) *Epic 6557968*	..54 1
16 Jan 93	DOGS OF LUST *Epic 6584572*	..25 4
17 Apr 93	SLOW EMOTION REPLAY *Epic 6590772*	..35 3
19 Jun 93	LOVE IS STRONGER THAN DEATH *Epic 6593712*	..39 3
15 Jan 94	DIS-INFECTED (EP) *Epic 6598112*	..17 4
4 Feb 95	I SAW THE LIGHT *Epic 6610912*	..31 2
29 Oct 83	SOUL MINING *Some Bizzare EPC 25525*	..27 5
29 Nov 86	INFECTED *Some Bizzare EPC 26770*	..14 30
27 May 89 ●	MIND BOMB *Epic 4633191*	....4 9
6 Feb 93 ●	DUSK *Epic 4724682*	....2 4
19 Jun 93	BURNING BLUE SOUL *4AD HAD 113CD*	..65 1
25 Feb 95	HANKY PANKY *Epic 4781392*	..28 2
11 Mar 00	NAKED SELF *Nothing 4905102*	..45 1
1 Jun 02	45 RPM – THE SINGLES OF THE THE *Epic 5044699*	..60 1

Tracks on Shades of Blue (EP): Jealous of Youth / Another Boy Drowning (Live) / Solitude / Dolphins. Tracks on Dis-Infected (EP): This is The Day / Dis-Infected / Helpline Operator (sickboy remix) / Dogs of Lust (germicide remix). 'This Was the Day' and 'Dis-Infected' on the EP are re-recordings of earlier hits. 'Dogs of Lust' is a re-mix. Matt Johnson leads The The, which is an informal group of his studio guests and friends

THEATRE OF HATE *UK, male vocal / instrumental group (Singles: 9 Weeks, Albums: 9 Weeks)* pos/wks

23 Jan 82	DO YOU BELIEVE IN THE WESTWORLD *Burning Rome BRR 2*	..40 7
29 May 82	THE HOP *Burning Rome BRR 3*	..70 2
13 Mar 82	WESTWORLD *Burning Rome TOH 1*	..17 6
18 Aug 84	REVOLUTION *Burning Rome TOH 2*	..67 3

THEAUDIENCE *UK, male / female vocal / instrumental group – lead vocal Sophie Ellis-Bextor (Singles: 5 Weeks, Albums: 2 Weeks)* pos/wks

7 Mar 98	IF YOU CAN'T DO IT WHEN YOU'RE YOUNG, WHEN CAN YOU DO IT? *Mercury AUDCD 2*	..48 1
23 May 98	A PESSIMIST IS NEVER DISAPPOINTED *Mercury AUDCD 3*	..27 1
8 Aug 98	I KNOW ENOUGH (I DON'T GET ENOUGH) *Elleffe AUDC 4*	..25 2
29 Aug 98	THEAUDIENCE *Mercury 5587712*	..22 2

THEE UNSTRUNG
UK, male vocal / instrumental group (Singles: 1 Week) pos/wks

13 Nov 04	CONTRARY MARY / YOU *Poptones MC 5094SCD*	..59 1

THEM *UK, male vocal / instrumental group – leader Van Morrison (Singles: 23 Weeks)* pos/wks

7 Jan 65 ●	BABY PLEASE DON'T GO *Decca F 12018*	..10 9
25 Mar 65 ●	HERE COMES THE NIGHT *Decca F 12094*	....2 12
9 Feb 91	BABY PLEASE DON'T GO (re-issue) *London LON 292*	..65 2

THEN JERICO (see also Mark SHAW) *UK, male vocal / instrumental group (Singles: 36 Weeks, Albums: 24 Weeks)* pos/wks

31 Jan 87	LET HER FALL *London LON 97*	..65 3
25 Jul 87	THE MOTIVE (LIVING WITHOUT YOU) *London LON 145*	..18 12
24 Oct 87	MUSCLE DEEP *London LON 156*	..48 4
28 Jan 89	BIG AREA *London LON 204*	..13 7
8 Apr 89	WHAT DOES IT TAKE? *London LON 223*	..33 4
12 Aug 89	SUGAR BOX *London LON 235*	..22 6
3 Oct 87	FIRST (THE SOUND OF MUSIC) *London LONLP 26*	..35 7
4 Mar 89 ●	THE BIG AREA *London 828122 1*	....4 17

THERAPY? *UK, male vocal / instrumental group (Singles: 33 Weeks, Albums: 24 Weeks)* pos/wks

31 Oct 92	TEETHGRINDER *A&M AM 0097*	..30 2
20 Mar 93 ●	SHORTSHARPSHOCK (EP) *A&M AMCD 208*	....9 4
12 Jun 93	FACE THE STRANGE (EP) *A&M 5803052*	..18 3
28 Aug 93	OPAL MANTRA *A&M 5803612*	..13 3
29 Jan 94	NOWHERE *A&M 5805052*	..18 4
12 Mar 94	TRIGGER INSIDE *A&M 5805352*	..22 3
11 Jun 94	DIE LAUGHING *A&M 5805892*	..29 2
27 May 95	INNOCENT X *Volume VOLCD 1*	..53 1
3 Jun 95	STORIES *A&M 5811052*	..14 3
29 Jul 95	LOOSE *A&M 5811652*	..25 3
18 Nov 95	DIANE *A&M 5812912*	..26 2
14 Mar 98	CHURCH OF NOISE *A&M 5825392*	..29 2
30 May 98	LONELY, CRYIN' ONLY *A&M 0441212*	..32 1
8 Feb 92	PLEASURE DEATH *Wiiija WIJ 11*	..52 1
14 Nov 92	NURSE *A&M 5400442*	..38 3
19 Feb 94 ●	TROUBLEGUM *A&M 5401962*	....5 11

24 Jun 95	●	INFERNAL LOVE A&M 5403792	9	7
11 Apr 98		SEMI-DETACHED A&M 5408912	21	1
30 Oct 99		SUICIDE PACT – YOU FIRST Ark 21 1539722	61	1

Tracks on Shortsharpshock (EP): Screamager / Auto Surgery / Totally Random Man / Accelerator. Tracks on Face the Strange (EP): Turn / Speedball / Bloody Blue / Neckfreak. The listed flip side of 'Innocent X' was 'Belfast' by Orbital

THERESE See STONEBRIDGE featuring THERESE

THESE ANIMAL MEN
UK, male vocal / instrumental group (Singles: 3 Weeks, Albums: 4 Weeks) pos/wks

24 Sep 94		THIS IS THE SOUND OF YOUTH Hi-Rise FLATSCD 7	72	1
8 Feb 97		LIFE SUPPORT MACHINE Hut HUTCD 76	62	1
12 Apr 97		LIGHT EMITTING ELECTRICAL WAVE Hut HUTCD 81	72	1
2 Jul 94		TOO SUSSED Hi-Rise FLATMCD 4	39	2
8 Oct 94		(COME ON JOIN) THE HIGH SOCIETY Hi-Rise FLATCD 8	...62	1
25 Mar 95		TAXI FOR THESE ANIMAL MEN Hi-Rise FLATMCD 14	64	1

THEY MIGHT BE GIANTS
US, male vocal / instrumental duo – John Flansburgh and John Linnell (Singles: 18 Weeks, Albums: 12 Weeks) pos/wks

3 Mar 90	●	BIRDHOUSE IN YOUR SOUL Elektra EKR 104	6	11
2 Jun 90		ISTANBUL (NOT CONSTANTINOPLE) Elektra EKR 110	61	2
28 Jul 01		BOSS OF ME Pias / Restless PIASREST 001CD	21	5
7 Apr 90		FLOOD Elektra EKT 68	14	12

THICK D (see also PRAISE CATS; E-SMOOVE featuring Latanza WATERS)
US, male producer – Eric 'E-Smoove' Miller (Singles: 3 Weeks) pos/wks

| 12 Oct 02 | | INSATIABLE Multiply CDMULTY 88 | ....35 | 3 |

THIN LIZZY [125] *Top 500*
Accomplished Irish hard-rock group (which at times included noted guitarists Gary Moore, Snowy White and Midge Ure) was built around distinctive singer / bass guitarist Phil Lynott, b. West Bromwich, UK, 20 Aug 1949, d. 4 Jan 1986. After a slow start, they wrote their own chapter in British rock history (Singles: 128 Weeks, Albums: 261 Weeks) pos/wks

20 Jan 73	●	WHISKY IN THE JAR Decca F 13355	6	12
29 May 76	●	THE BOYS ARE BACK IN TOWN Vertigo 6059 139	8	10
14 Aug 76		JAILBREAK Vertigo 6059 150	31	4
15 Jan 77		DON'T BELIEVE A WORD Vertigo Lizzy 001	12	7
13 Aug 77		DANCIN' IN THE MOONLIGHT (IT'S CAUGHT ME IN ITS SPOTLIGHT) Vertigo 6059 177	14	8
13 May 78		ROSALIE – (COWGIRLS' SONG) (MEDLEY) Vertigo LIZZY 2	...20	13
3 Mar 79	●	WAITING FOR AN ALIBI Vertigo LIZZY 003	9	8
16 Jun 79		DO ANYTHING YOU WANT TO Vertigo LIZZY 004	14	9
20 Oct 79		SARAH Vertigo LIZZY 5	24	13
24 May 80		CHINATOWN Vertigo LIZZY 6	21	9
27 Sep 80	●	KILLER ON THE LOOSE Vertigo LIZZY 7	10	7
2 May 81		KILLERS LIVE (EP) Vertigo LIZZY 8	19	7
8 Aug 81		TROUBLE BOYS Vertigo LIZZY 9	53	4
6 Mar 82		HOLLYWOOD (DOWN ON YOUR LUCK) Vertigo LIZZY 10	53	3
12 Feb 83		COLD SWEAT Vertigo LIZZY 11	27	5
7 May 83		THUNDER AND LIGHTNING Vertigo LIZZY 12	39	2
6 Aug 83		THE SUN GOES DOWN Vertigo LIZZY 13	52	3
26 Jan 91		DEDICATION Vertigo LIZZY 14	35	3
23 Mar 91		THE BOYS ARE BACK IN TOWN (re-issue) Vertigo LIZZY 15	..63	1
27 Sep 75		FIGHTING Vertigo 6360 121	60	1
10 Apr 76	●	JAILBREAK Vertigo 9102 008	10	50
6 Nov 76		JOHNNY THE FOX Vertigo 9102 012	11	24
1 Oct 77	●	BAD REPUTATION Vertigo 9102 016	4	9
17 Jun 78	●	LIVE AND DANGEROUS Vertigo 6641 807	2	62
5 May 79	●	BLACK ROSE (A ROCK LEGEND) Vertigo 9102 032	2	21
18 Oct 80	●	CHINATOWN Vertigo 6359 030	7	7
11 Apr 81	●	THE ADVENTURES OF THIN LIZZY Vertigo LIZTV 1	6	13
5 Dec 81		RENEGADE Vertigo 6359 083	38	8
12 Mar 83	●	THUNDER AND LIGHTNING Vertigo VERL 3	4	11
26 Nov 83		LIFE – LIVE Vertigo VERD 6	29	6
14 Nov 87		SOLDIER OF FORTUNE – THE BEST OF PHIL LYNOTT AND THIN LIZZY Telstar STAR 2300 [1]	...55	10
16 Feb 91	●	DEDICATION – THE VERY BEST OF THIN LIZZY Vertigo 8481921	8	17
13 Jan 96		WILD ONE – THE VERY BEST OF THIN LIZZY Vertigo 5281132	..18	11
19 Jun 04	●	GREATEST HITS Universal TV 9821111	3	11

[1] Phil Lynott and Thin Lizzy

Tracks on Killers Live (EP): Bad Reputation / Are You Ready / Dear Miss Lonely Hearts

3RD BASS
US, male rap group (Singles: 5 Weeks, Albums: 1 Week) pos/wks

10 Feb 90		THE GAS FACE Def Jam 6556270	71	1
7 Apr 90		BROOKLYN-QUEENS Def Jam 6558307	61	2
22 Jun 91		POP GOES THE WEASEL Def Jam 6569547	64	2
20 Jul 91		DERELICTS OF DIALECT Def Jam 4683171	46	1

THIRD DIMENSION featuring Julie McDERMOTT
UK, male / female vocal / instrumental group (Singles: 2 Weeks) pos/wks

| 12 Oct 96 | | DON'T GO Soundproof MCSTD 40082 | ....34 | 2 |

THIRD EAR BAND
UK, male instrumental group (Albums: 2 Weeks) pos/wks

| 27 Jun 70 | | AIR EARTH FIRE WATER Harvest SHVL 773 | ....49 | 2 |

3RD EDGE
UK, male production / vocal group (Singles: 5 Weeks) pos/wks

| 31 Aug 02 | | IN AND OUT (re) Q Zone / Parlophone CDR 6568 | ....15 | 5 |

THIRD EYE BLIND
US, male vocal / instrumental group (Singles: 6 Weeks) pos/wks

| 27 Sep 97 | | SEMI-CHARMED LIFE Elektra E 3907CD | ....33 | 5 |
| 21 Mar 98 | | HOW'S IT GOING TO BE Elektra E 3863CD | ....51 | 1 |

3RD STOREE
US, male vocal group (Singles: 1 Week) pos/wks

| 5 Jun 99 | | IF EVER Yab Yum / Elektra E 3752CD | ....53 | 1 |

3RD WISH
US, male vocal trio (Singles: 2 Weeks) pos/wks

| 18 Dec 04 | | OBSESION (SI ES AMOR) Three8 CXTHREE 8004 | ....15 | 2+ |

THIRD WORLD
Jamaica, male vocal / instrumental group (Singles: 53 Weeks, Albums: 18 Weeks) pos/wks

23 Sep 78	●	NOW THAT WE'VE FOUND LOVE Island WIP 6457	10	9
6 Jan 79		COOL MEDITATION Island WIP 6469	17	10
16 Jun 79		TALK TO ME Island WIP 6496	56	5
6 Jun 81	●	DANCING ON THE FLOOR (HOOKED ON LOVE) CBS A 1214	..10	15
17 Apr 82		TRY JAH LOVE CBS A 2063	47	6
9 Mar 85		NOW THAT WE'VE FOUND LOVE (re-issue) Island IS 219	...22	8
21 Oct 78		JOURNEY TO ADDIS Island ILPS 9554	30	6
11 Jul 81		ROCKS THE WORLD CBS 85027	37	9
15 May 82		YOU'VE GOT THE POWER CBS 85563	87	3

THIRST
UK, male vocal / instrumental group (Singles: 2 Weeks) pos/wks

| 6 Jul 91 | | THE ENEMY WITHIN Ten TEN 379 | ....61 | 2 |

1300 DRUMS featuring the UNJUSTIFIED ANCIENTS OF MU
UK, male instrumental / production group (Singles: 4 Weeks) pos/wks

| 18 May 96 | | OOH! AAH! CANTONA Dynamo DYND 5 | ....11 | 4 |

THIRTEEN SENSES
UK, male vocal / instrumental group (Singles: 4 Weeks, Albums: 1 Week) pos/wks

12 Jun 04		DO NO WRONG Vertigo 9866745	38	2
25 Sep 04		INTO THE FIRE Vertigo 9867851	35	2
9 Oct 04		THE INVITATION Vertigo 9866910	60	1

THIS ISLAND EARTH
UK, male / female vocal / instrumental group (Singles: 5 Weeks) pos/wks

| 5 Jan 85 | | SEE THAT GLOW Magnet MAG 266 | ....47 | 5 |

THIS MORTAL COIL
UK, male / female vocal / instrumental group (Singles: 3 Weeks, Albums: 10 Weeks) pos/wks

22 Oct 83		SONG TO THE SIREN (re) 4AD AD 310	66	3
20 Oct 84		IT'LL END IN TEARS 4AD CAD 411	38	4
11 Oct 86		FILIGREE AND SHADOW 4AD DAD 609	53	3
4 May 91		BLOOD 4AD DAD 1005	65	3

THIS WAY UP
UK, male vocal / instrumental duo (Singles: 2 Weeks) pos/wks

| 22 Aug 87 | | TELL ME WHY Virgin VS 954 | ....72 | 2 |

THIS YEAR'S BLONDE
UK, male / female vocal / instrumental group (Singles: 8 Weeks) pos/wks

10 Oct 81	**PLATINUM POP** *Creole CR 19*	46	5
14 Nov 87	**WHO'S THAT MIX** *Debut DEBT 3034*	62	3

BJ THOMAS
US, male vocalist – Billy Joe Thomas (Singles: 4 Weeks) pos/wks

21 Feb 70	**RAINDROPS KEEP FALLIN' ON MY HEAD (re)** *Wand WN1* ▲ 38	4

Carla THOMAS See Otis REDDING

Dante THOMAS featuring PRAS *US, male vocalist –*
Darin Espinoza and US, male rapper (Singles: 3 Weeks) pos/wks

1 Sep 01	**MISS CALIFORNIA** *Elektra E 7192CD*	25	3

Evelyn THOMAS *US, female vocalist (Singles: 29 Weeks)* pos/wks

24 Jan 76	**WEAK SPOT** *20th Century BTC 1014*	26	7
17 Apr 76	**DOOMSDAY (re)** *20th Century BTC 1017*	41	2
21 Apr 84 ●	**HIGH ENERGY** *Record Shack SOHO 18*	5	17
25 Aug 84	**MASQUERADE** *Record Shack SOHO 25*	60	3

Jamo THOMAS and his PARTY BROTHERS ORCHESTRA
US, male vocalist (Singles: 2 Weeks) pos/wks

26 Feb 69	**I SPY (FOR THE FBI) (re)** *Polydor 56755*	44	2

Kenny THOMAS
UK, male vocalist (Singles: 54 Weeks, Albums: 28 Weeks) pos/wks

26 Jan 91	**OUTSTANDING** *Cooltempo COOL 227*	12	10
1 Jun 91 ●	**THINKING ABOUT YOUR LOVE** *Cooltempo COOL 235*	4	13
5 Oct 91	**BEST OF YOU** *Cooltempo COOL 243*	11	7
30 Nov 91	**TENDER LOVE** *Cooltempo COOL 247*	26	6
10 Jul 93	**STAY** *Cooltempo CDCOOL 271*	22	6
4 Sep 93	**TRIPPIN' ON YOUR LOVE** *Cooltempo CDCOOL 277*	17	5
6 Nov 93	**PIECE BY PIECE** *Cooltempo CDCOOL 283*	36	3
14 May 94	**DESTINY** *Cooltempo CDCOOL 289*	59	1
2 Sep 95	**WHEN I THINK OF YOU** *Cooltempo CDCOOL 309*	27	3
26 Oct 91 ●	**VOICES** *Cooltempo CTLP 24*	3	23
25 Sep 93 ●	**WAIT FOR ME** *Cooltempo CTCD 36*	10	5

Lillo THOMAS
US, male vocalist (Singles: 10 Weeks, Albums: 7 Weeks) pos/wks

27 Apr 85	**SETTLE DOWN** *Capitol CL 356*	66	2
21 Mar 87	**SEXY GIRL** *Capitol CL 445*	23	5
30 May 87	**I'M IN LOVE** *Capitol CL 450*	54	3
2 May 87	**LILLO** *Capitol EST 2031*	43	7

Mickey THOMAS See Elvin BISHOP

Millard THOMAS See Harry BELAFONTE

Nicky THOMAS
Jamaica, male vocalist – Cecil Thomas (Singles: 14 Weeks) pos/wks

13 Jun 70 ●	**LOVE OF THE COMMON PEOPLE** *Trojan TR 7750*	9	14

Ray THOMAS (see also The MOODY BLUES)
UK, male vocalist (Albums: 3 Weeks) pos/wks

26 Jul 75	**FROM MIGHTY OAKS** *Threshold THS 16*	23	3

Rob THOMAS See MATCHBOX TWENTY; SANTANA

Rufus THOMAS
US, male vocalist, b. 26 Mar 1917, d. 15 Dec 2001 (Singles: 12 Weeks) pos/wks

11 Apr 70	**DO THE FUNKY CHICKEN** *Stax 144*	18	12

Tasha THOMAS
US, female vocalist, b. 1950, d. 8 Nov 1984 (Singles: 3 Weeks) pos/wks

20 Jan 79	**SHOOT ME (WITH YOUR LOVE)** *Atlantic LV 4*	59	3

Timmy THOMAS *US, male vocalist (Singles: 20 Weeks)* pos/wks

24 Feb 73	**WHY CAN'T WE LIVE TOGETHER** *Mojo 2027 012*	12	11
28 Dec 85	**NEW YORK EYES** *Portrait A 6805* [1]	41	7
14 Jul 90	**WHY CAN'T WE LIVE TOGETHER (re-mix)** *TK TKR 1*	54	2

[1] Nicole with Timmy Thomas

THOMAS and TAYLOR
US, male / female vocal duo (Singles: 5 Weeks) pos/wks

17 May 86	**YOU CAN'T BLAME LOVE** *Cooltempo COOL 123*	53	5

Amanda THOMPSON See Lesley GARRETT

Carroll THOMPSON See MOVEMENT 98 featuring Carroll THOMPSON; Courtney PINE

Chris THOMPSON *UK, male vocalist (Singles: 5 Weeks)* pos/wks

27 Oct 79	**IF YOU REMEMBER ME** *Planet K 12389*	42	5

Gina THOMPSON See MC LYTE

Lincoln THOMPSON See REBEL MC

Richard THOMPSON (see also FAIRPORT CONVENTION)
UK, male vocalist / instrumentalist – guitar (Albums: 16 Weeks) pos/wks

27 Apr 85	**ACROSS A CROWDED ROOM** *Polydor POLD 5175*	80	2
18 Oct 86	**DARING ADVENTURES** *Polydor POLD 5202*	92	1
29 Oct 88	**AMNESIA** *Capitol EST 2075*	89	1
25 May 91	**RUMOR AND SIGH** *Capitol EST 2142*	32	3
29 Jan 94	**MIRROR BLUE** *Capitol CDEST 2207*	23	3
20 Apr 96	**YOU? ME? US?** *Capitol CDEST 2282*	32	2
24 May 97	**INDUSTRY** *Parlophone CDPCS 7383* [1]	69	1
4 Sep 99	**MOCK TUDOR** *Capitol 4988602*	28	2
15 Feb 03	**THE OLD KIT BAG** *Cooking Vinyl COOKCD 251*	52	1

[1] Richard and Danny Thompson

Sue THOMPSON
US, female vocalist – Eva Sue McKee (Singles: 9 Weeks) pos/wks

2 Nov 61	**SAD MOVIES (MAKE ME CRY) (re)** *Polydor NH 66967*	46	2
21 Jan 65	**PAPER TIGER (re)** *Hickory 1284*	30	7

THOMPSON TWINS 272 *Top 500* *British-based synth-rock trio: Tom Bailey (v/syn), New Zealand-born Alannah Currie (v/prc/s), Joe Leeway (prc). Named after characters in a Tin Tin cartoon, they were joined on stage at Live Aid by Madonna and were at the forefront of the second so-called 'British Invasion' (Singles: 110 Weeks, Albums: 128 Weeks)* pos/wks

6 Nov 82	**LIES** *Arista ARIST 486*	67	3
29 Jan 83 ●	**LOVE ON YOUR SIDE** *Arista ARIST 504*	9	12
16 Apr 83 ●	**WE ARE DETECTIVE** *Arista ARIST 526*	7	9
16 Jul 83	**WATCHING** *Arista TWINS 1*	33	6
19 Nov 83 ●	**HOLD ME NOW** *Arista TWINS 2*	4	15
4 Feb 84 ●	**DOCTOR DOCTOR** *Arista TWINS 3*	3	10
31 Mar 84 ●	**YOU TAKE ME UP** *Arista TWINS 4*	2	9
7 Jul 84	**SISTER OF MERCY (re)** *Arista TWINS 5*	11	9
8 Dec 84	**LAY YOUR HANDS ON ME** *Arista TWINS 6*	13	9
31 Aug 85	**DON'T MESS WITH DOCTOR DREAM** *Arista TWINS 9*	15	6
19 Oct 85	**KING FOR A DAY** *Arista TWINS 7*	22	6
7 Dec 85	**REVOLUTION (re)** *Arista TWINS 10*	56	4
21 Mar 87	**GET THAT LOVE (re)** *Arista TWINS 12*	66	3
15 Oct 88	**IN THE NAME OF LOVE '88** *Arista 111808*	46	3
28 Sep 91	**COME INSIDE** *Warner Bros. W 0058*	56	4
25 Jan 92	**THE SAINT** *Warner Bros. W 0080*	53	2
13 Mar 82	**SET** *Tee TELP 2*	48	3
26 Feb 83 ●	**QUICK STEP & SIDE KICK** *Arista 204 924*	2	56
25 Feb 84 ★	**INTO THE GAP** *Arista 205 971* ■	1	51
28 Sep 85 ●	**HERE'S TO FUTURE DAYS** *Arista 207 164*	5	9
2 May 87	**CLOSE TO THE BONE** *Arista 208 143*	90	1
10 Mar 90	**GREATEST HITS** *Stylus SMR 92*	23	8

Tracey THORN See EVERYTHING BUT THE GIRL; MASSIVE ATTACK

David THORNE *US, male vocalist (Singles: 8 Weeks)* pos/wks

24 Jan 63	**THE ALLEY CAT SONG** *Stateside SS 141*	21	8

Ken THORNE *UK, orchestra (Singles: 15 Weeks)* pos/wks

18 Jul 63 ●	**THEME FROM THE FILM 'THE LEGION'S LAST PATROL'** *HMV POP 1176*	4	15

Trumpet solo by Ray Davies

The THORNS *US, male vocal / instrumental trio (Albums: 1 Week)* pos/wks

14 Jun 03	**THE THORNS** *Columbia 5113732*	68	1

George THOROGOOD and the DESTROYERS
US, male vocal / instrumental group (Albums: 1 Week) pos/wks

2 Dec 78	GEORGE THOROGOOD AND THE DESTROYERS *Sonet SNTF 781*	67 1

THOSE 2 GIRLS (see also DENISE and JOHNNY; Andy WILLIAMS)
UK, female vocal duo – Denise Van Outen and Cathy Warwick (Singles: 4 Weeks) pos/wks

5 Nov 94	WANNA MAKE YOU GO ... UUH! *Final Vinyl 74321233782*	74 1
4 Mar 95	ALL I WANT *Final Vinyl 74321254202*	36 3

THOUSAND YARD STARE
UK, male vocal / instrumental group (Singles: 5 Weeks, Albums: 2 Weeks) pos/wks

26 Oct 91	SEASONSTREAM (EP) *Stifled Aardvark AARD 5T*	65 1
8 Feb 92	COMEUPPANCE *Stifled Aardvark AARD 007*	37 2
11 Jul 92	SPINDRIFT (EP) *Stifled Aardvark AARDT 010*	58 1
8 May 93	VERSION OF ME *Polydor AARDC 012*	57 1
7 Mar 93	HANDS ON *Polydor 5130012*	38 2

Tracks on Seasonstream (EP): O-O AET / Village End / Keepsake / Worse for Wear
Tracks on Spindrift (EP): Wideshire Two / Hand, Son / Happenstance / Mocca Pune

THRASHING DOVES
UK, male vocal / instrumental group (Singles: 3 Weeks) pos/wks

24 Jan 87	BEAUTIFUL IMBALANCE *A&M TDOVE 1*	50 3

The THREE AMIGOS
UK, male production trio (Singles: 8 Weeks) pos/wks

3 Jul 99	LOUIE LOUIE *Inferno CDFERN 17*	15 6
24 Mar 01	25 MILES 2001 *Wonderboy WBOYD 25*	30 2

3 COLOURS RED
UK, male vocal / instrumental group (Singles: 17 Weeks, Albums: 4 Weeks) pos/wks

18 Jan 97	NUCLEAR HOLIDAY *Creation CRESCD 250*	22 2
15 Mar 97	SIXTY MILE SMILE *Creation CRESCD 254*	20 3
10 May 97	PURE *Creation CRESCD 265*	28 1
12 Jul 97	COPPER GIRL *Creation CRESCD 270*	30 2
8 Nov 97	THIS IS MY HOLLYWOOD *Creation CRESCD 277*	48 1
23 Jan 99	BEAUTIFUL DAY *Creation CRESCD 308*	11 6
29 May 99	THIS IS MY TIME *Creation CRESCD 313*	36 2
24 May 97	PURE *Creation CRESCD 208*	16 2
20 Feb 99	REVOLT *Creation CRECD 227*	17 2

The THREE DEGREES 329 Top 500
US R&B vocal group who became top UK stars in the 1970s: Sheila Ferguson, Valerie Holiday, Fayette Pinkney. The trio, tagged by the media as 'Prince Charles' favourites', was the first girl group to top the UK chart since The Supremes in 1964 (Singles: 113 weeks, Albums: 91 weeks) pos/wks

13 Apr 74	YEAR OF DECISION *Philadelphia International PIR 2073*	13 10
27 Apr 74	TSOP (THE SOUND OF PHILADELPHIA) *Philadelphia International PIR 2289* [1] ▲	22 9
13 Jul 74 ★	WHEN WILL I SEE YOU AGAIN *Philadelphia International PIR 2155*	1 16
2 Nov 74	GET YOUR LOVE BACK *Philadelphia International PIR 2737*	34 4
12 Apr 75 ●	TAKE GOOD CARE OF YOURSELF *Philadelphia International PIR 3177*	9 9
5 Jul 75	LONG LOST LOVER *Philadelphia International PIR 3352*	40 4
1 May 76	TOAST OF LOVE *Epic EPC 4215*	36 4
7 Oct 78	GIVING UP, GIVING IN *Ariola ARO 130*	12 10
13 Jan 79 ●	WOMAN IN LOVE *Ariola ARO 141*	3 11
24 Mar 79 ●	THE RUNNER *Ariola ARO 154*	10 10
23 Jun 79	THE GOLDEN LADY *Ariola ARO 170*	56 3
29 Sep 79	JUMP THE GUN *Ariola ARO 183*	48 5
24 Nov 79 ●	MY SIMPLE HEART *Ariola ARO 202*	9 11
5 Oct 85	THE HEAVEN I NEED *Supreme SUPE 102*	42 5
26 Dec 98	LAST CHRISTMAS *Wildstar CDWILD 15*	54 2
10 Aug 74	THREE DEGREES *Philadelphia International 65858*	12 22
17 May 75 ●	TAKE GOOD CARE OF YOURSELF *Philadelphia International PIR 69137*	6 16
24 Feb 79	NEW DIMENSIONS *Ariola ARLH 5012*	34 13
3 Mar 79 ●	A COLLECTION OF THEIR 20 GREATEST HITS *Epic EPC 10013*	8 18
15 Dec 79	3D *Ariola 3D 1*	61 7
27 Sep 80 ●	GOLD *Ariola 3D 2*	9 15

[1] MFSB featuring The Three Degrees

THREE DOG NIGHT
US, male vocal / instrumental group (Singles: 23 Weeks) pos/wks

8 Aug 70 ●	MAMA TOLD ME NOT TO COME *Stateside SS 8052* ▲	3 14
29 May 71	JOY TO THE WORLD *Probe PRO 523* ▲	24 9

THREE DRIVES
Holland, male vocal / instrumental group (Singles: 9 Weeks) pos/wks

27 Jun 98	GREECE 2000 *Hooj Choons HOOJCD 63* [1]	44 1
30 Jan 99	GREECE 2000 (re-mix) *Hooj Choons HOOJ 70CD* [1]	12 4
17 Nov 01	SUNSET ON IBIZA *Xtravaganza XTRAV 27CDS* [2]	44 2
7 Jun 03	CARERRA 2 *Nebula NEBCD 043*	57 1
14 Aug 04	AIR TRAFFIC *Nebula NEBCD 056*	75 1

[1] Three Drives [2] Three Drives on a Vinyl

THREE GOOD REASONS
UK, male vocal / instrumental group (Singles: 3 Weeks) pos/wks

10 Mar 66	NOWHERE MAN *Mercury MF 899*	47 3

3 JAYS
UK, male production / vocal trio (Singles: 5 Weeks) pos/wks

31 Jul 99	FEELING IT TOO *Multiply CDMULTY 53*	17 5

THREE KAYES See The KAYE SISTERS

3LW
US, female vocal group (Singles: 13 Weeks, Albums: 1 Week) pos/wks

2 Jun 01 ●	NO MORE (BABY I'MA DO RIGHT) (re) *Epic 6712722*	6 9
8 Sep 01	PLAYAS GON' PLAY *Epic 6717932*	21 3
19 Oct 02	FEELS GOOD (DON'T WORRY BOUT A THING) *Island CID 806* [1]	44 1
16 Jun 01	3LW *Epic 4989142*	75 1

[1] Naughty By Nature featuring 3LW

THREE 'N ONE (see also Billy HENDRIX)
Germany, male production duo – Sharam Khososi and Andre Straesser (Singles: 3 Weeks) pos/wks

7 Jun 97	REFLECT *ffrr FCD 301*	66 1
15 May 99	PEARL RIVER *Low Sense SENSECD 24* [1]	32 2

[1] Three 'N One presents Johnny Shaker featuring Serial Diva

3 OF A KIND
UK, male / female vocal group (Singles: 14 Weeks) pos/wks

21 Aug 04 ★	BABY CAKES *Relentless RELDX 6* ■	1 14

3SL
UK, male vocal trio (Singles: 10 Weeks) pos/wks

20 Apr 02	TAKE IT EASY (re) *Epic 6724042*	11 6
7 Sep 02	TOUCH ME TEASE ME (re) *Epic 6727872*	16 4

3T
US, male vocal trio (Singles: 45 Weeks, Albums: 15 Weeks) pos/wks

27 Jan 96 ●	ANYTHING *MJJ 6627152*	2 14
4 May 96	24/7 *MJJ 6631995*	11 7
24 Aug 96 ●	WHY *MJJ 6636482* [1]	2 9
7 Dec 96 ●	I NEED YOU *Epic 6639912*	3 10
5 Apr 97 ●	GOTTA BE YOU *Epic 6643645* [2]	10 5
24 Feb 96	BROTHERHOOD *Epic 4816942*	11 15

[1] 3T featuring Michael Jackson [2] 3T: rap by Herbie

THREE TONS OF JOY See Johnny OTIS SHOW

THRICE
US, male vocal / instrumental group (Singles: 1 Week) pos/wks

18 Oct 03	ALL THAT'S LEFT *Island / Mercury 9811957*	69 1

The THRILLS
Ireland, male vocal / instrumental group (Singles: 14 Weeks, Albums: 29 Weeks) pos/wks

22 Mar 03	ONE HORSE TOWN *Virgin VSCDT 1845*	18 3
21 Jun 03	BIG SUR *Virgin VSCDT 1852*	17 4
6 Dec 03	DON'T STEAL OUR SUN *Virgin VSCDT 1864*	45 1
11 Sep 04	WHATEVER HAPPENED TO COREY HAIM? *Virgin VSCDX 1876*	22 4
27 Nov 04	NOT FOR ALL THE LOVE IN THE WORLD *Virgin VSCDX 1890*	39 2
12 Jul 03 ●	SO MUCH FOR THE CITY *Virgin CDV 2974*	3 25
25 Sep 04 ●	LET'S BOTTLE BOHEMIA *Virgin CDV 2986*	9 4

THRILLSEEKERS UK, male producer /
instrumentalist – Steve Helstrip (Singles: 3 Weeks) — pos/wks

17 Feb 01	**SYNAESTHESIA (FLY AWAY)** *Neo NEOCD 050* [1]	**28**	2
7 Sep 02	**DREAMING OF YOU** *Ministry of Sound / Data DATA 36CDS*	**48**	1

[1] Thrillseekers featuring Sheryl Deane

THROWING MUSES US, male / female vocal / instrumental group –
leader Kristin Hersh (Singles: 6 Weeks, Albums: 14 Weeks) — pos/wks

9 Feb 91	**COUNTING BACKWARDS** *4AD AD 1001*	**70**	2
1 Aug 92	**FIREPILE (EP)** *4AD BAD 2012*	**46**	1
24 Dec 94	**BRIGHT YELLOW GUN** *4AD BAD 4018CD*	**51**	2
10 Aug 96	**SHARK** *4AD BAD 6016CD*	**53**	1
4 Feb 89	**HUNKPAPA** *4AD CAD 901*	**59**	1
2 Mar 91	**THE REAL RAMONA** *4AD CAD 1002*	**26**	4
22 Aug 92	**RED HEAVEN** *4AD CAD 2013CD*	**13**	3
28 Nov 92	**THE CURSE** *4AD TAD 2019CD*	**74**	1
28 Jan 95 ●	**UNIVERSITY** *4AD CADD 5002CD*	**10**	3
31 Aug 96	**LIMBO** *4AD CAD 6014CD*	**36**	1
29 Mar 03	**THROWING MUSES** *4AD CAD 2301CD*	**75**	1

Tracks on Firepile (EP): Firepile / Manic Depression / Snailhead / City of the Dead

Harry THUMANN (see also WONDER DOG)
Germany, male instrumentalist – keyboards (Singles: 6 Weeks) — pos/wks

21 Feb 81	**UNDERWATER** *Decca F 13901*	**41**	6

THUNDER UK, male vocal / instrumental
group (Singles: 55 Weeks, Albums: 39 Weeks) — pos/wks

17 Feb 90	**DIRTY LOVE** *EMI EM 126*	**32**	4
12 May 90	**BACKSTREET SYMPHONY** *EMI EM 137*	**25**	4
14 Jul 90	**GIMME SOME LOVIN'** *EMI EM 148*	**36**	3
29 Sep 90	**SHE'S SO FINE** *EMI EM 158*	**34**	3
23 Feb 91	**LOVE WALKED IN** *EMI EM 175*	**21**	4
15 Aug 92	**LOW LIFE IN HIGH PLACES** *EMI EM 242*	**22**	5
10 Oct 92	**EVERYBODY WANTS HER** *EMI EM 249*	**36**	4
13 Feb 93	**A BETTER MAN** *EMI CDBETTER 1*	**18**	4
19 Jun 93	**LIKE A SATELLITE (EP)** *EMI CDEM 272*	**28**	2
7 Jan 95	**STAND UP** *EMI CDEM 365*	**23**	4
25 Feb 95	**RIVER OF PAIN** *EMI CDEM 367*	**31**	2
6 May 95	**CASTLES IN THE SAND** *EMI CDEM 372*	**30**	3
23 Sep 95	**IN A BROKEN DREAM** *EMI CDEM 384*	**26**	2
25 Jan 97	**DON'T WAIT UP** *Raw Power RAWX 1020*	**27**	2
5 Apr 97	**LOVE WORTH DYING FOR** *Raw Power RAWX 1043*	**60**	1
7 Feb 98	**THE ONLY ONE** *Eagle EAGXA 016*	**31**	2
27 Jun 98	**PLAY THAT FUNKY MUSIC** *Eagle EAGXS 030*	**39**	2
20 Mar 99	**YOU WANNA KNOW** *Eagle EAGXA 037*	**49**	1
31 May 03	**LOSER** *STC Recordings STC 20032*	**48**	1
4 Dec 04	**I LOVE YOU MORE THAN ROCK 'N ROLL** *STC Recordings STC 20044*	**27**	2
17 Mar 90	**BACK STREET SYMPHONY** *EMI EMC 3570*	**21**	16
5 Sep 92 ●	**LAUGHING ON JUDGEMENT DAY** *EMI CDEMD 1035*	**2**	10
4 Feb 95 ●	**BEHIND CLOSED DOORS** *EMI CDEMD 1076*	**5**	5
7 Oct 95	**BEST OF THUNDER – THEIR FINEST HOUR (AND A BIT)** *EMI CDEMD 1086*	**22**	3
15 Feb 97	**THE THRILL OF IT ALL** *Raw Power RAWCD 115*	**14**	3
28 Feb 98	**LIVE** *Eagle EDGCD 016*	**35**	1
27 Mar 99	**GIVING THE GAME AWAY** *Eagle EAGCD 046*	**49**	1

Tracks on Like a Satellite (EP): Like a Satellite / The Damage Is Done / Like a Satellite (Live) / Gimme Shelter

THUNDERBIRDS See Chris FARLOWE

THUNDERBUGS UK / France / Germany,
female vocal / instrumental group (Singles: 15 Weeks) — pos/wks

18 Sep 99 ●	**FRIENDS FOREVER (re)** *First Avenue / Epic 6676932*	**5**	10
18 Dec 99	**IT'S ABOUT TIME YOU WERE MINE** *First Avenue / Epic 6683972*	**43**	5

THUNDERCLAP NEWMAN UK, male vocal / instrumental
group – lead vocal John "Speedy" Keen (Singles: 13 Weeks) — pos/wks

11 Jun 69 ★	**SOMETHING IN THE AIR** *Track 604-031*	**1**	12
27 Jun 70	**ACCIDENTS** *Track 2094 001*	**46**	1

THUNDERTHIGHS UK, female vocal group (Singles: 5 Weeks) — pos/wks

22 Jun 74	**CENTRAL PARK ARREST** *Philips 6006 386*	**30**	5

THURSDAY US, male vocal /
instrumental group (Singles: 2 Weeks, Albums: 1 Week) — pos/wks

25 Oct 03	**BRAINWASHED (CALL YOU)** *Data DATA 63CDS*	**43**	2
27 Sep 03	**WAR ALL THE TIME** *Island US / Mercury 9860874*	**62**	1

Bobby THURSTON US, male vocalist (Singles: 10 Weeks) — pos/wks

29 Mar 80 ●	**CHECK OUT THE GROOVE** *Epic EPC 8348*	**10**	10

TIFFANY US, female vocalist –
Tiffany Darwish (Singles: 45 Weeks, Albums: 27 Weeks) — pos/wks

16 Jan 88 ★	**I THINK WE'RE ALONE NOW** *MCA MCA 1211* ▲	**1**	13
19 Mar 88 ●	**COULD'VE BEEN** *MCA TIFF 2* ▲	**4**	9
4 Jun 88 ●	**I SAW HIM STANDING THERE** *MCA TIFF 3*	**8**	7
6 Aug 88	**FEELINGS OF FOREVER** *MCA TIFF 4*	**52**	2
12 Nov 88	**RADIO ROMANCE** *MCA TIFF 5*	**13**	11
11 Feb 89	**ALL THIS TIME** *MCA TIFF 6*	**47**	3
27 Feb 88 ●	**TIFFANY** *MCA MCF 3415* ▲	**5**	21
17 Dec 88	**HOLD AN OLD FRIEND'S HAND** *MCA MCF 3437*	**56**	6

TIGA Canada / Finland, male DJ / production duo –
Tiga Sontag and Jori Hulkonen (Singles: 6 Weeks) — pos/wks

11 May 02	**SUNGLASSES AT NIGHT** *City Rockers ROCKERS 15CD* [1]	**25**	3
6 Sep 03	**HOT IN HERRE** *Skint SKINT 90CD*	**46**	2
19 Jun 04	**PLEASURE FROM THE BASS** *Different DIFB 1028CDM*	**57**	1

[1] Tiga and Zyntherius

TIGER UK / Ireland, male / female
vocal / instrumental group (Singles: 5 Weeks) — pos/wks

31 Aug 96	**RACE** *Trade 2 TRDCD 004*	**37**	2
16 Nov 96	**MY PUPPET PAL** *Trade 2 TRDCD 005*	**62**	1
22 Feb 97	**ON THE ROSE** *Trade 2 TRDCD 008*	**57**	1
22 Aug 98	**FRIENDS** *Trade 2 TRDCD 013*	**72**	1

TIGERTAILZ US, male vocal /
instrumental group (Singles: 2 Weeks, Albums: 2 Weeks) — pos/wks

24 Jun 89	**LOVE BOMB BABY** *Music for Nations KUT 132*	**75**	1
16 Feb 91	**HEAVEN** *Music for Nations KUT 137*	**71**	1
7 Apr 90	**BEZERK** *Music for Nations MFN 96*	**36**	2

TIGHT FIT
UK, male / female vocal group (Singles: 49 Weeks, Albums: 6 Weeks) — pos/wks

18 Jul 81 ●	**BACK TO THE SIXTIES** *Jive JIVE 002*	**4**	11
26 Sep 81	**BACK TO THE SIXTIES PART 2** *Jive JIVE 005*	**33**	5
23 Jan 82 ★	**THE LION SLEEPS TONIGHT** *Jive JIVE 9*	**1**	15
1 May 82 ●	**FANTASY ISLAND** *Jive JIVE 13*	**5**	12
31 Jul 82	**SECRET HEART** *Jive JIVE 20*	**41**	6
26 Sep 81	**BACK TO THE SIXTIES** *Jive HIP 1*	**38**	4
4 Sep 82	**TIGHT FIT** *Jive HIP 2*	**87**	2

TIJUANA BRASS See Herb ALPERT and the TIJUANA BRASS

TIK and TOK
UK, male vocal duo (Singles: 2 Weeks, Albums: 2 Weeks) — pos/wks

8 Oct 83	**COOL RUNNING** *Survival SUR 016*	**69**	2
4 Aug 84	**INTOLERANCE** *Survival SURLP 008*	**89**	1

Tanita TIKARAM
UK, female vocalist (Singles: 31 Weeks, Albums: 62 Weeks) — pos/wks

30 Jul 88 ●	**GOOD TRADITION** *WEA YZ 196*	**10**	10
22 Oct 88	**TWIST IN MY SOBRIETY** *WEA YZ 321*	**22**	8
14 Jan 89	**CATHEDRAL SONG** *WEA YZ 331*	**48**	3
18 Mar 89	**WORLD OUTSIDE YOUR WINDOW** *WEA YZ 363*	**58**	2
13 Jan 90	**WE ALMOST GOT IT TOGETHER** *WEA YZ 443*	**52**	3
9 Feb 91	**ONLY THE ONES WE LOVE** *East West YZ 558*	**69**	1
4 Feb 95	**I MIGHT BE CRYING** *East West YZ 879CD*	**64**	2
6 Jun 98	**STOP LISTENING** *Mother MUMCD 102*	**67**	1
29 Aug 98	**I DON'T WANNA LOSE AT LOVE** *Mother MUMCD 105*	**73**	1
24 Sep 88 ●	**ANCIENT HEART** *WEA WX 210*	**3**	49
10 Feb 90 ●	**THE SWEET KEEPER** *East West WX 330*	**3**	7
16 Feb 91	**EVERYBODY'S ANGEL** *East West WX 401*	**19**	4
25 Feb 95	**LOVERS IN THE CITY** *East West 4509988042*	**75**	1
19 Sep 98	**THE CAPPUCCINO SONGS** *Mother MUMCD 9801*	**69**	1

GUY CHAMBERS TOP 10

The gospel according to Guy Chambers, who chooses his favourite singles and albums

Brit and Ivor Novello award-winning composer Guy Chambers toured with Julian Cope, The Waterboys and World Party and formed his own band (The Lemon Trees) before making his name as Robbie Williams's songwriting partner on five No.1 albums. More recently, he has worked with Kylie, Busted, Natasha Bedingfield, Will Young, Texas and Delta Goodrem and co-wrote Brian McFadden's No.1 debut single, 'Real to Me'.

SINGLES
single – act – (peak position)

CRAZY IN LOVE
Beyoncé (1)

GIMME SHELTER *
The Rolling Stones

GOOD VIBRATIONS
The Beach Boys (1)

HEY JUDE
The Beatles (1)

HEY YA!
Outkast (3)

HOW SWEET IT IS
Marvin Gaye (49)

I CAN SEE FOR MILES
The Who (10)

I WANT TO TAKE YOU HIGHER *
Sly and the Family Stone

RIVER DEEP – MOUNTAIN HIGH
Ike and Tina Turner (3)

THERE SHE GOES
The La's (13)

ALBUMS
album – act – (peak position)

FRANCIS ALBERT SINATRA AND
ANTONIO CARLOS JOBIM *
Francis Albert Sinatra and Antonio Carlos Jobim

FRESH *
Sly and the Family Stone

HEJIRA
Joni Mitchell (11)

LADY IN SATIN *
Duke Ellington

LED ZEPPELIN
Led Zeppelin (6)

THE MAN-MACHINE
Kraftwerk (9)

OFF THE WALL
Michael Jackson (5)

REVOLVER
The Beatles (1)

SMILE
Brian Wilson (7)

WHO'S NEXT
The Who (1)

* Did not chart   * Did not chart

TINMAN
UK, male producer – Paul Dakeyne (Singles: 9 Weeks)   pos/wks
20 Aug 94 ● EIGHTEEN STRINGS ffrr FCD 242 ....9 8
3 Jun 95 GUDVIBE ffrr FCD 262 ....49 1

TINY TIM US, male vocalist / instrumentalist – banjo –
Herbert Khaury, b. 12 Apr 1930, d. 30 Nov 1996 (Singles: 1 Week) pos/wks
5 Feb 69 GREAT BALLS OF FIRE Reprise RS 20802 ....45 1

Rob TISSERA See VINYLGROOVER and the RED HED

TITANIC
Norway / UK, male instrumental group (Singles: 12 Weeks)   pos/wks
25 Sep 71 ● SULTANA CBS 5365 ....5 12

TITIYO Sweden, female vocalist – Titiyo Jah (Singles: 6 Weeks) pos/wks
3 Mar 90 AFTER THE RAIN Arista 112722 ....60 3
6 Oct 90 FLOWERS Arista 113212 ....71 1
5 Feb 94 TELL ME I'M NOT DREAMING Arista 74321185622 ....45 2

Cara TIVEY See Billy BRAGG

TOADS See Stan FREBERG

Art and Dotty TODD US, male / female vocal duo –
Dotty Todd, b. 22 Jun 1913, d. 12 Dec 2000 (Singles: 7 Weeks)   pos/wks
13 Feb 53 ● BROKEN WINGS HMV B 10399 ....6 7

TOGETHER
UK, male vocal / instrumental group (Singles: 8 Weeks)   pos/wks
4 Aug 90 HARDCORE UPROAR ffrr F 143 ....12 8

TOGETHER
(see also DAFT PUNK) France, male production duo –
Thomas Bangalter and DJ Falcon (Martial Weiss) (Singles: 1 Week) pos/wks
4 Jan 03 SO MUCH LOVE TO GIVE (IMPORT) Roule TOGETHER 2 ....71 1

TOI See Warren G

The TOKENS US, male vocal group (Singles: 12 Weeks)

		pos/wks
21 Dec 61	THE LION SLEEPS TONIGHT (WIMOWEH) RCA 1263 ▲ 11	12

TOKYO DRAGONS
UK, male vocal / instrumental group (Singles: 2 Weeks)

		pos/wks
26 Jun 04	TEENAGE SCREAMERS Island CID 864 61	1
23 Oct 04	GET 'EM OFF! Island CID 876 75	1

TOKYO GHETTO PUSSY (see also JAM and SPOON
featuring PLAVKA; STORM) *Germany, male instrumental /
production duo – Rolf Ellmer and Markus Loeffel (Singles: 4 Weeks)* pos/wks

		pos/wks
16 Sep 95	EVERYBODY ON THE FLOOR (PUMP IT) Epic 6611132 26	2
16 Mar 96	I KISS YOUR LIPS Epic 6623212 55	2

TOL and TOL
Holland, male vocal / instrumental duo (Singles: 2 Weeks)

		pos/wks
14 Apr 90	ELENI Dover ROJ 5 73	2

TOM TOM CLUB
(see also TALKING HEADS) *US, female / male vocal /
instrumental group (Singles: 20 Weeks, Albums: 1 Week)* pos/wks

		pos/wks
20 Jun 81 ●	WORDY RAPPINGHOOD Island WIP 6694 7	9
10 Oct 81	GENIUS OF LOVE Island WIP 6735 65	2
7 Aug 82	UNDER THE BOARDWALK Island WIP 6762 22	9
24 Oct 81	TOM TOM CLUB Island ILPS 9686 78	1

TOMBA VIRA
(see also CHOCOLATE PUMA; GOODMEN; JARK PRONGO; RHYTHMKILLAZ;
RIVA featuring Dannii MINOGUE) *Holland, male production duo – Rene ter
Horst and Gaston Steenkist (Singles: 1 Week)* pos/wks

		pos/wks
16 Jun 01	THE SOUND OF: OH YEAH VC Recordings VCRD 88 51	1

TOMCAT
UK, male vocal / instrumental group (Singles: 1 Week)

		pos/wks
14 Oct 00	CRAZY Virgin VSCDT 1785 48	1

TOMCRAFT
Germany, male producer – Thomas Bruckner (Singles: 13 Weeks) pos/wks

		pos/wks
10 May 03 ★	LONELINESS Data / Ministry of Sound DATA 52CDS ■ 1	13

Satoshi TOMIIE See Frankie KNUCKLES

TOMITA *Japan, male instrumentalist –
synthesizer – Isao Tomita (Albums: 33 Weeks)* pos/wks

		pos/wks
7 Jun 75	SNOWFLAKES ARE DANCING RCA Red Seal ARL 10488 17	20
16 Aug 75	PICTURES AT AN EXHIBITION RCA Red Seal ARL 10838 42	5
7 May 77	HOLST: THE PLANETS RCA Red Seal RL 11919 41	6
9 Feb 80	TOMITA'S GREATEST HITS RCA Red Seal RL 43076 66	2

Ricky TOMLINSON
UK, male actor / vocalist – Eric Tomlinson (Singles: 3 Weeks) pos/wks

		pos/wks
10 Nov 01	ARE YOU LOOKIN' AT ME? All Around the World CDRICKY 1 28	3

TOMMI *UK, female vocal group (Singles: 8 Weeks)*

		pos/wks
5 Jul 03	LIKE WHAT Sony Music 6739095 12	8

TOMSKI
UK, male producer – Tom Jankiewicz (Singles: 3 Weeks) pos/wks

		pos/wks
18 Apr 98	14 HOURS TO SAVE THE EARTH Xtravaganza 0091515 EXT 42	1
12 Feb 00	LOVE WILL COME Xtravaganza XTRAV 6CDS [1] 31	2

[1] Tomski featuring Jan Johnston

TONE LOC *US, male rapper –
Anthony Smith (Singles: 19 Weeks, Albums: 16 Weeks)* pos/wks

		pos/wks
11 Feb 89	WILD THING / LOC'ED AFTER DARK Fourth & Broadway BRW 121 21	8
20 May 89	FUNKY COLD MEDINA / ON FIRE Fourth & Broadway BRW 129 13	9
5 Aug 89	I GOT IT GOIN' ON Fourth & Broadway BRW 140 55	2
25 Mar 89	LOC'ED AFTER DARK Delicious BRLP 526 ▲ 22	16

TONGUE 'N' CHEEK *UK, male / female vocal /
instrumental group (Singles: 28 Weeks, Albums: 3 Weeks)* pos/wks

		pos/wks
27 Feb 88	NOBODY (CAN LOVE ME) Criminal BUS 6 [1] 59	6
25 Nov 89	ENCORE Syncopate SY 33 41	4
14 Apr 90	TOMORROW Syncopate SY 34 20	7
4 Aug 90	NOBODY (re-recording) Syncopate SY 37 37	5
19 Jan 91	FORGET ME NOTS Syncopate SY 39 26	6
22 Sep 90	THIS IS TONGUE 'N' CHEEK Syncopate SYLP 6006 45	3

[1] Tongue 'n Cheek

TONICS See Adrian BAKER and The TONICS

TONIGHT
UK, male vocal / instrumental group (Singles: 10 Weeks) pos/wks

		pos/wks
28 Jan 78	DRUMMER MAN Target TDS 1 14	8
20 May 78	MONEY THAT'S YOUR PROBLEM Target TDS 2 66	2

TONY TONI TONÉ (see also Raphael SAADIQ)
US, male vocal group (Singles: 12 Weeks, Albums: 1 Week) pos/wks

		pos/wks
30 Jun 90	OAKLAND STROKE Wing WING 7 [1] 50	5
9 Mar 91	IT NEVER RAINS (IN SOUTHERN CALIFORNIA) Wing WING 10 [1] 69	2
4 Sep 93	IF I HAD NO LOOT Polydor PZCD 292 44	3
3 May 97	LET'S GET DOWN Mercury MERCD 485 [2] 33	2
2 Oct 93	SONS OF SOUL Polydor 5149332 66	1

[1] Tony! Toni! Toné! [2] Tony Toni Toné featuring DJ Quick [1] Tony! Toni! Toné!

TOO TOUGH TEE See DYNAMIX II featuring TOO TOUGH TEE

TOOL *US, male vocal / instrumental group (Albums: 3 Weeks)* pos/wks

		pos/wks
26 May 01	LATERALUS Tool Dissectional 9210132 ▲ 16	3

TOON TRAVELLERS See MUNGO JERRY

TOP *UK, male vocal / instrumental group (Singles: 2 Weeks)* pos/wks

		pos/wks
20 Jul 91	NUMBER ONE DOMINATOR Island IS 496 67	2

TOP LINERS See Rocky SHARPE and The REPLAYS

Martina TOPLEY-BIRD *UK, female vocalist (Albums: 1 Week)* pos/wks

		pos/wks
26 Jul 03	QUIXOTIC Independiente ISOM 34CD 70	1

TOPLOADER *UK, male vocal / instrumental
group (Singles: 56 Weeks, Albums: 66 Weeks)* pos/wks

		pos/wks
22 May 99	ACHILLES HEEL Sony S2 6671612 64	1
7 Aug 99	LET THE PEOPLE KNOW Sony S2 6677132 52	1
4 Mar 00	DANCING IN THE MOONLIGHT Sony S2 6689412 19	7
13 May 00 ●	ACHILLES HEEL (re-issue) Sony S2 6691872 8	7
2 Sep 00	JUST HOLD ON Sony S2 6696242 20	4
25 Nov 00 ●	DANCING IN THE MOONLIGHT (re-issue) Sony S2 6699852 7	25
21 Apr 01	ONLY FOR A WHILE Sony S2 6708612 19	4
17 Aug 02	TIME OF MY LIFE Sony S2 6728862 18	7
3 Jun 00 ●	ONKA'S BIG MOKA Sony S2 4947802 4	61
31 Aug 02 ●	MAGIC HOTEL Sony S2 5084712 3	5

TOPOL *Israel, male vocalist / actor –
Chaim Topol (Singles: 20 Weeks, Albums: 1 Week)* pos/wks

		pos/wks
20 Apr 67 ●	IF I WERE A RICH MAN CBS 202651 9	20
11 May 85	TOPOL'S ISRAEL BBC REH 529 80	1

Bernie TORMÉ (see also GILLAN)
Ireland, male vocalist / instrumentalist – guitar (Albums: 3 Weeks) pos/wks

		pos/wks
3 Jul 82	TURN OUT THE LIGHTS Kamaflage KAMLP 2 50	3

Mel TORMÉ *US, male vocalist, b. 13 Sep 1925,
d. 5 Jun 1999 (Singles: 32 Weeks, Albums: 8 Weeks)* pos/wks

		pos/wks
27 Apr 56 ●	MOUNTAIN GREENERY (re) Vogue / Coral Q 72150 4	24
3 Jan 63	COMIN' HOME BABY London HLK 9643 13	8
28 Jul 56 ●	MEL TORMÉ AT THE CRESCENDO Vogue-Coral LVA 9004 3	4
18 Aug 56 ●	MEL TORMÉ WITH THE MARTY PAICH DEK-TETTE London Jazz LTZ N 15009 3	4

The TORNADOS
UK, male instrumental group – includes Heinz (Singles: 59 Weeks) pos/wks

30 Aug 62	★	TELSTAR *Decca F 11494* ▲	1 25
10 Jan 63	●	GLOBETROTTER *Decca F 11562*	5 11
21 Mar 63		ROBOT *Decca F 11606*	17 12
6 Jun 63		THE ICE CREAM MAN *Decca F 11662*	18 9
10 Oct 63		DRAGONFLY *Decca F 11745*	41 2

Mitchell TOROK
US, male vocalist (Singles: 19 Weeks) pos/wks

28 Sep 56	●	WHEN MEXICO GAVE UP THE RHUMBA (re) *Brunswick 05586*	6 18
11 Jan 57		RED LIGHT, GREEN LIGHT *Brunswick 05626*	29 1

Liz TORRES *See Danny TENAGLIA*

Emiliana TORRINI
Iceland, female vocalist (Singles: 3 Weeks) pos/wks

10 Jun 00	EASY *One Little Indian 274TP 7CD*	63 1
9 Sep 00	UNEMPLOYED IN SUMMERTIME *One Little Indian 275TP 7CDL*	63 1
3 Feb 01	TO BE FREE *One Little Indian 276TP 7CD*	44 1

Peter TOSH
Jamaica, male vocalist, b. Winston McIntosh, 9 Oct 1944, d. 11 Sep 1987 (Singles: 12 Weeks, Albums: 1 Week) pos/wks

21 Oct 78	(YOU GOTTA WALK) DON'T LOOK BACK *Rolling Stones 2859*	43 7
2 Apr 83	JOHNNY B GOODE *EMI RIC 115*	48 5
25 Sep 76	LEGALIZE IT *Virgin V 2061*	54 1

TOTAL
US, female vocal group (Singles: 11 Weeks) pos/wks

15 Jul 95	CAN'T YOU SEE *Tommy Boy TBCD 700* [1]	43 2
14 Sep 96	KISSIN' YOU *Arista 74321404172*	29 2
15 Feb 97	DO YOU THINK ABOUT US *Puff Daddy 74321458492*	49 1
18 Apr 98	WHAT YOU WANT *Puff Daddy 74321578772* [2]	15 5
30 Sep 00	I WONDER WHY HE'S THE GREATEST DJ *Tommy Boy TBCD 2100* [3]	68 1

[1] Total featuring Notorious B.I.G. [2] Ma$e featuring Total [3] Tony Touch featuring Total

TOTAL CONTRAST
UK, male vocal / instrumental duo – Robin Achampong and Delroy Murray (Singles: 22 Weeks, Albums: 3 Weeks) pos/wks

3 Aug 85	TAKES A LITTLE TIME *London LON 71*	17 10
19 Oct 85	HIT AND RUN *London LON 76*	41 5
1 Mar 86	THE RIVER *London LON 83*	44 3
10 May 86	WHAT YOU GONNA DO ABOUT IT *London LON 95*	63 4
8 Mar 86	TOTAL CONTRAST *London LONLP 15*	66 3

TOTO
US, male vocal / instrumental group (Singles: 35 Weeks, Albums: 39 Weeks) pos/wks

10 Feb 79		HOLD THE LINE *CBS 6784*	14 11
5 Feb 83	●	AFRICA *CBS A 2510* ▲	3 10
9 Apr 83		ROSANNA *CBS A 2079*	12 8
18 Jun 83		I WON'T HOLD YOU BACK *CBS A 3392*	37 5
18 Nov 95		I WILL REMEMBER *Columbia 6626552*	64 1
31 Mar 79		TOTO *CBS 83148*	37 5
26 Feb 83	●	TOTO IV *CBS 85529*	4 30
17 Nov 84		ISOLATION *CBS 86305*	67 2
20 Sep 86		FAHRENHEIT *CBS 57091*	99 1
9 Apr 88		THE SEVENTH ONE *CBS 460465 1*	73 1

TOTO COELO
UK, female vocal group (Singles: 14 Weeks) pos/wks

7 Aug 82	●	I EAT CANNIBALS PART 1 *Radialchoice TIC 10*	8 10
13 Nov 82		DRACULA'S TANGO / MUCHO MACHO *Radialchoice TIC 11*	54 4

TOTTENHAM HOTSPUR FA CUP FINAL SQUAD
(see also COCKEREL CHORUS) *UK, male football team vocalists (Singles: 23 Weeks)* pos/wks

9 May 81	●	OSSIE'S DREAM (SPURS ARE ON THEIR WAY TO WEMBLEY) *Shelf SHELF 1*	5 8
1 May 82		TOTTENHAM TOTTENHAM *Shelf SHELF 2*	19 7
9 May 87		HOT SHOT TOTTENHAM! *Rainbow RBR 16*	18 5
11 May 91		WHEN THE YEAR ENDS IN 1 *A1 A 1324*	44 3

All hits feature the vocal and instrumental talents of Chas and Dave

TOUCH & GO
UK, male / female vocal / production group (Singles: 12 Weeks) pos/wks

7 Nov 98	●	WOULD YOU ...? *Oval VVR 5003083*	3 12

TOUCH OF SOUL
UK, male / female vocal / instrumental group (Singles: 3 Weeks) pos/wks

19 May 90	WE GOT THE LOVE *Cooltempo COOL 204*	46 3

Tony TOUCH featuring TOTAL
US, male producer – Anthony Hernandez and US, female vocal group (Singles: 1 Week) pos/wks

30 Sep 00	I WONDER WHY HE'S THE GREATEST DJ *Tommy Boy TBCD 2100*	68 1

TOUR DE FORCE
UK, male production trio (Singles: 1 Week) pos/wks

16 May 98	CATALAN *East West EW 161CD*	71 1

Ali Farka TOURE *See Ry COODER*

The TOURISTS
(see also EURYTHMICS; VEGAS; David A STEWART; Annie LENNOX) *UK, male / female vocal / instrumental group (Singles: 40 Weeks, Albums: 18 Weeks)* pos/wks

9 Jun 79		BLIND AMONG THE FLOWERS *Logo GO 350*	52 5
8 Sep 79		THE LONELIEST MAN IN THE WORLD *Logo GO 360*	32 7
10 Nov 79		I ONLY WANT TO BE WITH YOU *Logo GO 370*	4 14
9 Feb 80	●	SO GOOD TO BE BACK HOME AGAIN *Logo TOUR 1*	8 9
18 Oct 80		DON'T SAY I TOLD YOU SO *RCA TOUR 2*	40 5
14 Jul 79		THE TOURISTS *Logo GO 1018*	72 1
3 Nov 79		REALITY EFFECT *Logo GO 1019*	23 16
22 Nov 80		LUMINOUS BASEMENT *RCA RCALP 5001*	75 1

TOUTES LES FILLES
UK, female vocal group (Singles: 1 Week) pos/wks

4 Sep 99	THAT'S WHAT LOVE CAN DO *London LONCD 434*	44 1

Carol Lynn TOWNES
US, female vocalist (Singles: 7 Weeks) pos/wks

4 Aug 84	99 1/2 *Polydor POSP 693*	47 4
19 Jan 85	BELIEVE IN THE BEAT *Polydor POSP 720*	56 3

Fuzz TOWNSHEND
UK, male producer (Singles: 1 Week) pos/wks

6 Sep 97	HELLO DARLIN *Echo ECSCD 46*	51 1

Pete TOWNSHEND
(see also The WHO) *UK, male vocalist / instrumentalist – guitar (Singles: 17 Weeks, Albums: 28 Weeks)* pos/wks

5 Apr 80	ROUGH BOYS *Atco K 11460*	39 6
21 Jun 80	LET MY LOVE OPEN YOUR DOOR *Atco K 11486*	46 6
21 Aug 82	UNIFORMS (CORPS D'ESPRIT) *Atco K 11751*	48 5
21 Oct 72	WHO CAME FIRST *Track 2408 201*	30 2
15 Oct 77	ROUGH MIX *Polydor 2442147* [1]	44 3
3 May 80	EMPTY GLASS *Atco K 50699*	11 14
3 Jul 82	ALL THE BEST COWBOYS HAVE CHINESE EYES *Atco K 50889*	32 8
30 Nov 85	WHITE CITY *Atco 2523921*	70 1

[1] Pete Townshend and Ronnie Lane

TOXIC TWO
US, male instrumental / production duo – Ray Love and Damon Wild (Singles: 6 Weeks) pos/wks

7 Mar 92	RAVE GENERATOR *PWL International PWL 223*	13 6

The TOY DOLLS
UK, male vocal / instrumental group (Singles: 12 Weeks, Albums: 1 Week) pos/wks

1 Dec 84	●	NELLIE THE ELEPHANT *Volume VOL 11*	4 12
25 May 85		A FAR OUT DISC *Volume VOLP 2*	71 1

TOYAH **371** **Top 500**
Visually striking punk / pop vocalist and actor, b. Toyah Willcox, 16 May 1958, Birmingham, UK. Came to prominence through acting – first major role in 1977 movie 'Jubilee'. Married King Crimson guitarist Robert Fripp in 1986 and featured in the ITV series I'm a Celebrity ... Get Me Out of Here! in 2004 (Singles: 87 Weeks, Albums: 97 Weeks) pos/wks

14 Feb 81	●	FOUR FROM TOYAH (EP) *Safari TOY 1*	4 14
16 May 81	●	I WANT TO BE FREE *Safari SAFE 34*	8 11
3 Oct 81	●	THUNDER IN THE MOUNTAINS *Safari SAFE 38*	4 9
28 Nov 81		FOUR MORE FROM TOYAH (EP) *Safari TOY 2*	14 9
22 May 82		BRAVE NEW WORLD *Safari SAFE 45*	21 8
17 Jul 82		IEYA *Safari SAFE 28*	48 5
9 Oct 82		BE LOUD BE PROUD (BE HEARD) *Safari SAFE 52*	30 7
24 Sep 83		REBEL RUN *Safari SAFE 56*	24 5

		pos/wks
19 Nov 83	THE VOW *Safari SAFE 58*	50 5
27 Apr 85	DON'T FALL IN LOVE (I SAID) *Portrait A 6160*	22 6
29 Jun 85	SOUL PASSING THROUGH SOUL *Portrait A 6359*	57 3
25 Apr 87	ECHO BEACH *EG EGO 31*	54 5
14 Jun 80	THE BLUE MEANING *Safari IEYA 666*	40 4
17 Jan 81	TOYAH! TOYAH! TOYAH! *Safari LIVE 2*	22 14
30 May 81	● ANTHEM *Safari VOOR 1*	2 46
19 Jun 82	● THE CHANGELING *Safari VOOR 9*	6 12
13 Nov 82	WARRIOR ROCK – TOYAH ON TOUR *Safari TNT 1*	20 6
5 Nov 83	LOVE IS THE LAW *Safari VOOR 10*	28 7
25 Feb 84	TOYAH! TOYAH! TOYAH! *K-Tel NE 1268*	43 4
3 Aug 85	MINX *Portrait PRT 26415*	24 4

Tracks on Four From Toyah (EP): It's a Mystery / Revelations / War Boys / Angels and Demons. Tracks on Four More From Toyah (EP): Good Morning Universe / Urban Tribesman / In the Fairground / The Furious Futures The two 'Toyah! Toyah! Toyah!' albums are different

TOY-BOX
Denmark, male / female vocal duo (Singles: 2 Weeks) pos/wks

18 Sep 99	BEST FRIEND *Edel 0058245 ERE*	41 2

The TOYS *US, female vocal group (Singles: 17 Weeks)* pos/wks

4 Nov 65	● A LOVER'S CONCERTO *Stateside SS 460*	5 13
27 Jan 66	ATTACK *Stateside SS 483*	36 4

Faye TOZER See STEPS; Russell WATSON

T'PAU 433 Top 500
Shropshire lads and a lass whose No.1 hit in 1987 had the distinction of being the 600th chart-topper. T'Pau (Mr Spock's Vulcan friend in 'Star Trek') comprised writers Carol Decker (v) and Ron Rogers (g), plus Michael Chetwood (k), Paul Jackson (b), Tim Burgess (d) and Taj Wyzgowski (g) (Singles: 77 Weeks, Albums: 85 Weeks) pos/wks

8 Aug 87	● HEART AND SOUL *Siren SRN 41*	4 13
24 Oct 87	★ CHINA IN YOUR HAND *Siren SRN 64*	1 15
30 Jan 88	● VALENTINE *Siren SRN 69*	9 8
2 Apr 88	SEX TALK (LIVE) *Siren SRN 80*	23 7
25 Jun 88	I WILL BE WITH YOU *Siren SRN 87*	14 6
1 Oct 88	SECRET GARDEN *Siren SRN 93*	18 7
3 Dec 88	ROAD TO OUR DREAM *Siren SRN 100*	42 6
25 Mar 89	ONLY THE LONELY *Siren SRN 107*	28 6
18 May 91	WHENEVER YOU NEED ME *Siren SRN 140*	16 6
27 Jul 91	WALK ON AIR *Siren SRN 142*	62 2
20 Feb 93	VALENTINE (re-issue) *Virgin VALEG 1*	53 1
26 Sep 87	★ BRIDGE OF SPIES *Siren SIRENLP 8*	1 59
5 Nov 88	● RAGE *Siren SRNLP 20*	4 17
22 Jun 91	● THE PROMISE *Siren SRNLP 32*	10 7
27 Feb 93	HEART AND SOUL – THE VERY BEST OF T'PAU *Virgin TPAUD 1*	35 2

Ian TRACEY / LIVERPOOL CATHEDRALS' CHOIRS
UK, conductor and male / female choirs (Albums: 3 Weeks) pos/wks

21 Mar 92	YOUR FAVOURITE HYMNS *Virgin Classics 7912092*	62 3

TRACIE *UK, female vocalist –*
Tracie Young (Singles: 24 Weeks, Albums: 2 Weeks) pos/wks

26 Mar 83	● THE HOUSE THAT JACK BUILT *Respond KOB 701*	9 8
16 Jul 83	GIVE IT SOME EMOTION *Respond KOB 704*	24 9
14 Apr 84	SOUL'S ON FIRE *Respond KOB 708*	73 2
9 Jun 84	(I LOVE YOU) WHEN YOU SLEEP *Respond KOB 710*	59 3
17 Aug 85	I CAN'T LEAVE YOU ALONE *Respond SBS 1* [1]	60 2
30 Jun 84	FAR FROM THE HURTING KIND *Respond RRL 502*	64 2

[1] Tracie Young

Gordon TRACKS See AIR

TRACY See MASSIVO featuring TRACY

Jeanie TRACY *US, female vocalist (Singles: 3 Weeks)* pos/wks

11 Jun 94	IF THIS IS LOVE *Pulse 8 CDLOSE 63*	73 1
5 Nov 94	DO YOU BELIEVE IN THE WONDER *Pulse 8 CDLOSE 74*	57 1
13 May 95	IT'S A MAN'S MAN'S MAN'S WORLD *Pulse 8 CDLOSE 89* [1]	73 1

[1] Jeanie Tracy and Bobby Womack

TRAFFIC (see also Steve WINWOOD; Jim CAPALDI) *UK, male vocal / instrumental group (Singles: 40 Weeks, Albums: 41 Weeks)* pos/wks

1 Jun 67	● PAPER SUN *Island WIP 6002*	5 10
6 Sep 67	● HOLE IN MY SHOE *Island WIP 6017*	2 14
29 Nov 67	● HERE WE GO ROUND THE MULBERRY BUSH *Island WIP 6025*	8 12
6 Mar 68	NO FACE, NO NAME, NO NUMBER *Island WIP 6030*	40 4
30 Dec 67	● MR. FANTASY *Island ILP 9061*	8 16
26 Oct 68	● TRAFFIC *Island ILPS 9081T*	9 8
8 Aug 70	JOHN BARLEYCORN MUST DIE *Island ILPS 9116*	11 9
24 Nov 73	ON THE ROAD *Island ISLD 2*	40 3
28 Sep 74	WHEN THE EAGLE FLIES *Island ILPS 9273*	31 1
21 May 94	FAR FROM HOME *Virgin CDV 2727*	29 4

TRAIN *US, male vocal / instrumental group (Singles: 10 Weeks, Albums: 9 Weeks)* pos/wks

11 Aug 01	● DROPS OF JUPITER (TELL ME) *Columbia 6714472*	10 8
2 Mar 02	SHE'S ON FIRE *Columbia 6722812*	49 2
18 Aug 01	● DROPS OF JUPITER *Columbia 5023069*	8 9

TRA-KNOX See Will SMITH

TRAMAINE
US, female vocalist – Tramaine Hawkins (Singles: 2 Weeks) pos/wks

5 Oct 85	FALL DOWN (SPIRIT OF LOVE) *A&M AM 281*	60 2

The TRAMMPS *US, male vocal group (Singles: 55 Weeks)* pos/wks

23 Nov 74	ZING WENT THE STRINGS OF MY HEART *Buddah BDS 405*	29 10
1 Feb 75	SIXTY MINUTE MAN *Buddah BDS 415*	40 4
11 Oct 75	● HOLD BACK THE NIGHT *Buddah BDS 437*	5 8
13 Mar 76	THAT'S WHERE THE HAPPY PEOPLE GO *Atlantic K 10703*	35 8
24 Jul 76	SOUL SEARCHIN' TIME *Atlantic K 10797*	42 3
14 May 77	DISCO INFERNO *Atlantic K 10914*	16 7
24 Jun 78	DISCO INFERNO (re-issue) *Atlantic K 11135*	47 10
12 Dec 92	HOLD BACK THE NIGHT *Network NWK 65* [1]	30 5

[1] KWS features guest vocal from The Trammps

TRANCESETTERS
Holland, male production duo (Singles: 2 Weeks) pos/wks

4 Mar 00	ROACHES *Hooj Choons HOOJ 89CD*	55 1
9 Jun 01	SYNERGY *Hooj Choons 107*	72 1

TRANSA *UK, male DJ / production duo (Singles: 2 Weeks)* pos/wks

30 Aug 97	PROPHASE *Perfecto PERF 147CD*	65 1
21 Feb 98	ENERVATE *Perfecto PERF 155CD*	42 1

TRANSATLANTIC SOUL
US, male producer – Roger Sanchez (Singles: 1 Week) pos/wks

22 Mar 97	RELEASE YO SELF *Deconstruction 74321459102*	43 1

TRANSFER
UK, male production duo and female vocalist (Singles: 1 Week) pos/wks

3 Nov 01	POSSESSION *Multiply CDMULTY 76*	54 1

TRANSFORMER 2 (see also CONVERT) *Belgium / Holland, male / female vocal / instrumental group (Singles: 1 Week)* pos/wks

24 Feb 96	JUST CAN'T GET ENOUGH *Positiva CDTIV 49*	45 1

TRANSGLOBAL UNDERGROUND
UK, male / female vocal / instrumental group (Albums: 3 Weeks) pos/wks

30 Oct 93	DREAM OF 100 NATIONS *Nation NR 021CD*	45 1
29 Oct 94	INTERNATIONAL TIMES *Nation NATCD 38*	40 1
25 May 96	PSYCHIC KARAOKE *Nation NRCD 1067*	62 1

TRANSISTER
UK / US, male / female vocal / instrumental group (Singles: 1 Week) pos/wks

28 Mar 98	LOOK WHO'S PERFECT NOW *Virgin VSCDT 1678*	56 1

TRANSPLANTS
US, male vocal / instrumental group (Singles: 3 Weeks) pos/wks

19 Apr 03	DIAMONDS AND GUNS *Hellcat 11082*	27 2
19 Jul 03	DJ DJ *Hellcat 11122*	49 1

TRANSVISION VAMP
UK, female / male vocal / instrumental group (Singles: 59 Weeks, Albums: 58 Weeks)   pos/wks

16 Apr 88	TELL THAT GIRL TO SHUT UP *MCA TVV 2*	**45** 3
25 Jun 88 ●	I WANT YOUR LOVE *MCA TVV 3*	**5** 13
17 Sep 88	REVOLUTION BABY *MCA TVV 4*	**30** 5
19 Nov 88	SISTER MOON *MCA TVV 5*	**41** 5
1 Apr 89 ●	BABY I DON'T CARE *MCA TVV 6*	**3** 11
10 Jun 89	THE ONLY ONE *MCA TVV 7*	**15** 6
5 Aug 89	LANDSLIDE OF LOVE *MCA TVV 8*	**14** 5
4 Aug 89	BORN TO BE SOLD *MCA TVV 9*	**22** 4
13 Apr 91	(I JUST WANNA) B WITH U *MCA TVV 10*	**30** 4
22 Jun 91	IF LOOKS COULD KILL *MCA TVV 11*	**41** 3
15 Oct 88 ●	POP ART *MCA MCF 3421*	**4** 32
8 Jul 89 ★	VELVETEEN *MCA MCG 6050* ■	**1** 26

TRANS-X
Canada, female / male vocal / instrumental group (Singles: 9 Weeks)   pos/wks

13 Jul 85 ●	LIVING ON VIDEO *Boiling Point POSP 650*	**9** 9

TRASH *UK, male vocal / instrumental group (Singles: 3 Weeks)*   pos/wks

25 Oct 69	GOLDEN SLUMBERS / CARRY THAT WEIGHT *Apple 17*	**35** 3

The TRASH CAN SINATRAS
UK, male vocal / instrumental group (Singles: 1 Week, Albums: 2 Weeks)   pos/wks

24 Apr 93	HAYFEVER *Go Discs GODCD 98*	**61** 1
7 Jul 90	CAKE *Go Discs 82820211*	**74** 1
15 May 93	I'VE SEEN EVERYTHING *Go Discs 8284082*	**50** 1

TRAVEL
France, male producer – Laurent Gutbier (Singles: 2 Weeks)   pos/wks

24 Apr 99	BULGARIAN *Tidy Trax TIDY 121CD*	**67** 2

TRAVELING WILBURYS *UK / US, male vocal /*
instrumental group (see also Jeff LYNNE; Roy ORBISON; Tom PETTY; George HARRISON) (Singles: 19 Weeks, Albums: 44 Weeks)   pos/wks

29 Oct 88	HANDLE WITH CARE *Wilbury W 7732*	**21** 13
11 Mar 89	END OF THE LINE *Wilbury W 7637*	**52** 4
30 Jun 90	NOBODY'S CHILD *Wilbury W 9773*	**44** 2
5 Nov 88	THE TRAVELING WILBURYS VOLUME 1 *Wilbury WX 224*	**16** 35
10 Nov 90	THE TRAVELING WILBURYS VOLUME 3 *Wilbury WX 384*	**14** 9

Pat TRAVERS
Canada, male instrumentalist – guitar (Albums: 3 Weeks)   pos/wks

2 Apr 77	MAKIN' MAGIC *Polydor 2383 436*	**40** 3

TRAVIS   (213   Top 500)
Scottish melodic rock merchants named after a character from the 1984 movie 'Paris, Texas', consisting of English-born Fran Healy (v/g) and native Glaswegians Andy Dunlop (g), Dougie Payne (b) and Neil Primrose (d). Their Brit Award-winning 'The Man Who' was the best-selling album by a British act in the UK in 1999 (Singles: 92 Weeks, Albums: 190 Weeks)   pos/wks

12 Apr 97	U16 GIRLS *Independiente ISOM 1MS*	**40** 2
28 Jun 97	ALL I WANT TO DO IS ROCK *Independiente ISOM 3MS*	**39** 2
23 Aug 97	TIED TO THE 90'S *Independiente ISOM 5MS*	**30** 2
25 Oct 97	HAPPY *Independiente ISOM 6MS*	**38** 2
11 Apr 98	MORE THAN US (EP) *Independiente ISOM 11MS*	**16** 3
20 Mar 99	WRITING TO REACH YOU *Independiente ISOM 22MS*	**14** 5
29 May 99	DRIFTWOOD *Independiente ISOM 27MS*	**13** 5
14 Aug 99 ●	WHY DOES IT ALWAYS RAIN ON ME? *Independiente ISOM 33MS*	**10** 8
20 Nov 99 ●	TURN *Independiente ISOM 39MS*	**8** 11
17 Jun 00 ●	COMING AROUND (2re) *Independiente ISOM 45MS*	**5** 10
9 Jun 01 ●	SING *Independiente ISOM 49MS*	**3** 14
29 Sep 01	SIDE *Independiente ISOM 54MS*	**14** 8
6 Apr 02	FLOWERS IN THE WINDOW *Independiente ISOM 56MS*	**18** 7
11 Oct 03 ●	RE-OFFENDER *Independiente ISOM 78SMS*	**7** 4
27 Dec 03	THE BEAUTIFUL OCCUPATION *Independiente ISOM 81MS*	**48** 3
3 Apr 04	LOVE WILL COME THROUGH *Independiente ISOM 84MS*	**28** 3
30 Oct 04	WALKING IN THE SUN *Independiente ISOM 88MS*	**20** 3
20 Sep 97 ●	GOOD FEELING *Independiente ISOM 1CD*	**9** 16
5 Jun 99 ★	THE MAN WHO *Independiente ISOM 9CD*	**1** 102
23 Jun 01 ★	THE INVISIBLE BAND *Independiente ISOM 25CD* ■	**1** 54

25 Oct 03 ●	12 MEMORIES *Independiente ISOM 40CD*	**3** 11
13 Nov 04 ●	SINGLES *Independiente ISOM 46CD*	**4** 7+

Tracks on More Than Us (EP): More Than Us / Give Me Some Truth / All I Want to Do is Rock / Funny Thing

Randy TRAVIS
US, male vocalist / instrumentalist – guitar (Singles: 6 Weeks, Albums: 2 Weeks)   pos/wks

21 May 88	FOREVER AND EVER, AMEN *Warner Bros. W 8384*	**55** 6
6 Aug 88	OLD 8X10 *Warner Bros. WX 162*	**64** 2

John TRAVOLTA
US, male actor / vocalist (Singles: 90 Weeks, Albums: 6 Weeks)   pos/wks

20 May 78 ★	YOU'RE THE ONE THAT I WANT *RSO 006* [1] ◆ ▲	**1** 26
16 Sep 78 ★	SUMMER NIGHTS *RSO 18* [2] ◆	**1** 19
7 Oct 78 ●	SANDY *Polydor POSP 6*	**2** 15
2 Dec 78	GREASED LIGHTNING *Polydor POSP 14*	**11** 9
22 Dec 90	THE GREASE MEGAMIX *Polydor PO 114* [1]	**3** 10
23 Mar 91	GREASE – THE DREAM MIX *PWL / Polydor PO 136* [3]	**47** 2
25 Jul 98 ●	YOU'RE THE ONE THAT I WANT (re-issue) *Polydor 0441332* [1]	**4** 9
23 Dec 78	SANDY *Polydor POLD 5014*	**40** 6

[1] John Travolta and Olivia Newton-John [2] John Travolta, Olivia Newton-John and Cast [3] Frankie Valli, John Travolta and Olivia Newton-John

The TREMELOES   (284   Top 500)
Brian Poole and The Tremeloes were formed in 1959 and signed by Decca in preference to The Beatles (they auditioned on the same day). The first south of England group to top the chart in the Beat Boom era. Poole, b. 2 Nov 1941, Essex, UK, went solo in 1966. Poole's daughters hit in the late 90s as Alisha's Attic. After supporting Poole on his many hits, The Tremeloes: Len "Chip" Hawkes (v/b), Rick West (g), Alan Blakely (g), b. 1 Apr 1942, d. 1 Jun 1996, Dave Munden (d), went on to score even more hits in their own right. Hawkes is the father of 1991 chart-topper Chesney Hawkes (Singles: 222 Weeks, Albums: 7 Weeks)   pos/wks

4 Jul 63 ●	TWIST AND SHOUT *Decca F 11694* [1]	**4** 14
12 Sep 63 ★	DO YOU LOVE ME *Decca F 11739* [1]	**1** 14
28 Nov 63	I CAN DANCE *Decca F 11771* [1]	**31** 8
30 Jan 64 ●	CANDY MAN *Decca F 11823* [1]	**6** 13
7 May 64 ●	SOMEONE, SOMEONE *Decca F 11893* [1]	**2** 17
20 Aug 64	TWELVE STEPS TO LOVE *Decca F 11951* [1]	**32** 7
31 Dec 64	THREE BELLS *Decca F 12037* [1]	**17** 10
22 Jul 65	I WANT CANDY *Decca F 12197* [1]	**25** 8
2 Feb 67 ●	HERE COMES MY BABY *CBS 202519*	**4** 11
27 Apr 67 ★	SILENCE IS GOLDEN *CBS 2723*	**1** 15
2 Aug 67 ●	EVEN THE BAD TIMES ARE GOOD *CBS 2930*	**4** 13
8 Nov 67	BE MINE *CBS 3043*	**39** 2
17 Jan 68 ●	SUDDENLY YOU LOVE ME *CBS 3234*	**6** 11
8 May 68	HELULE HELULE *CBS 2889*	**14** 9
18 Sep 68 ●	MY LITTLE LADY *CBS 3680*	**6** 12
11 Dec 68	I SHALL BE RELEASED *CBS 3873*	**29** 5
19 Mar 69	HELLO WORLD *CBS 4065*	**14** 8
1 Nov 69 ●	(CALL ME) NUMBER ONE *CBS 4582*	**2** 14
21 Mar 70	BY THE WAY *CBS 4815*	**35** 6
12 Sep 70 ●	ME AND MY LIFE *CBS 5139*	**4** 18
10 Jul 71	HELLO BUDDY *CBS 7294*	**32** 7
3 Jun 67	HERE COME THE TREMELOES – THE COMPLETE 1967 SESSIONS *CBS SBPG 63017*	**15** 7

[1] Brian Poole and The Tremeloes

Jackie TRENT
UK, female vocalist – Yvonne Burgess (Singles: 17 Weeks)   pos/wks

22 Apr 65 ★	WHERE ARE YOU NOW *Pye 7N 15776*	**1** 11
1 Jul 65	WHEN THE SUMMERTIME IS OVER *Pye 7N 15865*	**39** 2
2 Apr 69	I'LL BE THERE *Pye 7N 17693*	**38** 4

Ralph TRESVANT (see also NEW EDITION)
US, male vocalist (Singles: 21 Weeks, Albums: 3 Weeks)   pos/wks

12 Jan 91	SENSITIVITY *MCA MCS 1462*	**18** 8
15 Aug 92 ●	THE BEST THINGS IN LIFE ARE FREE *Perspective PERSS 7400* [1]	**2** 13
23 Feb 91	RALPH TRESVANT *MCA MCG 6120*	**37** 3

[1] Luther Vandross and Janet Jackson with special guests BBD and Ralph Tresvant

TREVOR & SIMON UK, male production duo –
Trevor Reilly and Simon Foy (Singles: 5 Weeks) pos/wks

10 Jun 00	HANDS UP *Substance SUBS 1CDS*	12	5

Dick TREVOR See Danny HOWELLS & Dick TREVOR featuring ERIRE; SCIENCE DEPARTMENT

TRI UK, male vocal / instrumental group (Singles: 1 Week)
pos/wks

2 Sep 95	WE GOT THE LOVE *Epic 6623642*	61	1

TRIBAL HOUSE
US, male vocal / instrumental group (Singles: 2 Weeks) pos/wks

3 Feb 90	MOTHERLAND-A-FRI-CA *Cooltempo COOL 198*	57	2

Tony TRIBE Jamaica, male vocalist (Singles: 2 Weeks)
pos/wks

16 Jul 69	RED RED WINE (re) *Downtown DT 419*	46	2

A TRIBE CALLED QUEST (see also Q-TIP; LUCY PEARL)
US, male rap group (Singles: 18 Weeks, Albums: 9 Weeks) pos/wks

18 Aug 90	BONITA APPLEBUM *Jive JIVE 256*	47	3
19 Jan 91	CAN I KICK IT? *Jive JIVE 265*	15	7
11 Jun 94	OH MY GOD *Jive JIVECD 355*	68	1
13 Jul 96	1NCE AGAIN *Jive JIVECD 399*	34	2
23 Nov 96	STRESSED OUT *Jive JIVECD 404* [1]	33	2
23 Aug 97	THE JAM EP *Jive JIVECD 427*	61	1
29 Aug 98	FIND A WAY *Jive 0518982*	41	2
19 May 90	PEOPLE'S INSTINCTIVE TRAVELS AND THE PATHS OF RHYTHM *Jive HIP 96*	54	2
12 Oct 91	THE LOW END THEORY *Jive HIP 117*	58	1
27 Nov 93	MIDNIGHT MARAUDERS *Jive CHIP 143*	70	1
10 Aug 96	BEATS RHYMES AND LIFE *Jive CHIP 170* ▲	28	4
10 Oct 98	THE LOVE MOVEMENT *Jive 521032*	38	1

[1] A Tribe Called Quest featuring Faith Evans and Raphael Saadiq

Tracks on The Jam EP: Jam / Get a Hold / Mardi Gras at Midnight / Same Ol' Thing

TRIBE OF TOFFS
UK, male vocal / instrumental group (Singles: 5 Weeks) pos/wks

24 Dec 88	JOHN KETTLEY (IS A WEATHERMAN) *Completely Different DAFT 1*	21	5

Obie TRICE
US, male rapper (Singles: 14 Weeks, Albums: 8 Weeks) pos/wks

1 Nov 03 ●	GOT SOME TEETH (re) *Interscope 9813061*	8	11
14 Feb 04	THE SET UP (YOU DON'T KNOW) *Interscope 9815333* [1]	32	3
11 Oct 03	CHEERS *Interscope / Polydor 9860986*	11	8

[1] Obie Trice featuring Nate Dogg

TRICKBABY
UK, female vocal / instrumental group (Singles: 2 Weeks) pos/wks

12 Oct 96	INDIE-YARN *Logic 74321423152*	47	2

TRICKSTER
UK, male producer – Liam Sullivan (Singles: 3 Weeks) pos/wks

4 Apr 98	MOVE ON UP *AM:PM 5825812*	19	3

TRICKY (see also NEARLY GOD; STARVING SOULS)
UK, male vocalist / multi-instrumentalist – Adrian Thaws (Singles: 29 Weeks, Albums: 43 Weeks) pos/wks

5 Feb 94	AFTERMATH *Fourth & Broadway BRCD 288*	69	1
28 Jan 95	OVERCOME *Fourth & Broadway BRCD 304*	34	3
15 Apr 95	BLACK STEEL *Fourth & Broadway BRCD 320*	28	3
5 Aug 95	THE HELL (EP) *Fourth & Broadway BRCD 326* [1]	12	3
11 Nov 95	PUMPKIN *Fourth & Broadway BRCD 330*	26	2
9 Nov 96	CHRISTIANSANDS *Fourth & Broadway BRCD 340*	36	2
23 Nov 96 ●	MILK (re) *Mushroom D 1494* [2]	10	8
11 Jan 97	TRICKY KID *Fourth & Broadway BRCD 341*	28	2
3 May 97	MAKES ME WANNA DIE *Fourth & Broadway BRCD 348*	29	2
30 May 98	MONEY GREEDY / BROKEN HOMES *Island CID 701*	25	2
21 Aug 99	FOR REAL *Island CID 753*	45	1
4 Mar 95 ●	MAXINQUAYE *Fourth & Broadway BRCD 610*	3	35
23 Nov 96	PRE-MILLENNIUM TENSION *Fourth & Broadway BRCDX 623*	30	2
6 Jun 98	ANGELS WITH DIRTY FACES *Island CID 8071*	23	2

28 Aug 99	JUXTAPOSE *Island CID 8087* [1]	22	2
14 Jul 01	BLOWBACK *Anti 65962*	34	2

[1] Tricky vs The Gravediggaz [2] Garbage featuring Tricky [1] Tricky with DJ Muggs and Grease

Tracks on The Hell (EP): Hell Is Round the Corner (original) / Hell Is Round the Corner (Hell and Water mix) / Psychosis / Tonite Is a Special Nite (Chaos mass confusion mix)

The TRICKY DISCO (see also GTO; TECHNOHEAD)
UK, male instrumental / production duo – Lee Newman and Michael Wells (Singles: 10 Weeks) pos/wks

28 Jul 90	TRICKY DISCO *Warp WAP 7*	14	8
20 Apr 91	HOUSE FLY *Warp 7WAP 11*	55	2

TRIFFIDS Australia, male vocal /
instrumental group (Singles: 1 Week, Albums: 1 Week) pos/wks

6 Feb 88	A TRICK OF THE LIGHT *Island IS 350*	73	1
22 Apr 89	THE BLACK SWAN *Island ILPS 9928*	63	1

TRINA US, female vocalist – Katrina Taylor (Singles: 1 Week)
pos/wks

19 Oct 02	NO PANTIES *Atlantic AT 0141CD*	45	1

TRINA and TAMARA
US, female vocal duo – Trina and Tamara Powell (Singles: 3 Weeks) pos/wks

7 Feb 98	MY LOVE IS THE SHHH! *Warner Bros. W 0427CD*	64	1
12 Jun 99	WHAT'D YOU COME HERE FOR? *Columbia 6673382*	46	2

TRINIDAD OIL COMPANY Trinidad, male /
female vocal / instrumental group (Singles: 5 Weeks) pos/wks

21 May 77	THE CALENDAR SONG (JANUARY, FEBRUARY, MARCH, APRIL, MAY) *Harvest HAR 5122*	34	5

TRINITY See Julie DRISCOLL, Brian AUGER and the TRINITY

TRINITY-X
UK, male / female production / vocal trio (Singles: 3 Weeks) pos/wks

19 Oct 02	FOREVER *All Around the World CDGLOBE 255*	19	3

TRIO Germany, male vocal / instrumental group (Singles: 10 Weeks)
pos/wks

3 Jul 82 ●	DA DA DA *Mobile Suit Corporation CORP 5*	2	10

TRIPLE EIGHT UK, male vocal group (Singles: 9 Weeks)
pos/wks

3 May 03 ●	KNOCK OUT *Polydor 9800048*	8	4
2 Aug 03 ●	GIVE ME A REASON (re) *Polydor 9809136*	9	5

TRIPLE X (see also PLAYTHING) Italy, male production
duo – Lucia Moretti and Ricky Romanini (Singles: 2 Weeks) pos/wks

30 Oct 99	FEEL THE SAME *Sound of Ministry MOSCDS 135*	32	2

TRIPPING DAISY (see also The POLYPHONIC SPREE) US, male vocal /
instrumental group – leader Tim DeLaughter (Singles: 1 Week) pos/wks

30 Mar 96	PIRANHA *Island CID 638*	72	1

TRISCO UK, male production duo –
Harvey Dawson and Rupert Edwards (Singles: 2 Weeks) pos/wks

30 Jun 01	MUSAK *Positiva CDTIV 155*	28	2

TRIUMPH Canada, male vocal /
instrumental group (Singles: 2 Weeks, Albums: 8 Weeks) pos/wks

22 Nov 80	I LIVE FOR THE WEEKEND *RCA 13*	59	2
10 May 80	PROGRESSIONS OF POWER *RCA PL 13524*	61	5
3 Oct 81	ALLIED FORCES *RCA RCALP 6002*	64	3

The TROGGS UK, male vocal / instrumental group –
leader Reg Presley (Singles: 86 Weeks, Albums: 35 Weeks) pos/wks

5 May 66 ●	WILD THING *Fontana TF 689* ▲	2	12
14 Jul 66 ★	WITH A GIRL LIKE YOU *Fontana TF 717*	1	12
29 Sep 66 ●	I CAN'T CONTROL MYSELF *Page One POF 001*	2	13
15 Dec 66 ●	ANY WAY THAT YOU WANT ME *Page One POF 010*	8	10
16 Feb 67	GIVE IT TO ME *Page One POF 015*	12	10
1 Jun 67	NIGHT OF THE LONG GRASS *Page One POF 022*	17	6

26 Jul 67	HI HI HAZEL *Page One POF 030*	............**42**	3
18 Oct 67 ●	LOVE IS ALL AROUND *Page One POF 040*	...........**5**	14
28 Feb 68	LITTLE GIRL *Page One POF 056*	...........**37**	4
30 Oct 93	WILD THING (re-recording) *Weekend CDWEEK 103* [1]	....**69**	2
30 Jul 66 ●	FROM NOWHERE ... THE TROGGS *Fontana TL 5355*.....	....**6**	16
25 Feb 67 ●	TROGGLODYNAMITE *Page One POL 001*	.....**10**	11
5 Aug 67	THE BEST OF THE TROGGS *Page One FOR 001*	....**24**	5
16 Jul 94	GREATEST HITS *PolyGram TV 5227392*	....**27**	3

[1] The Troggs and Wolf

'Wild Thing' in 1993 and was listed with the flip side, 'War', by Edwin Starr and Shadow

TRONIKHOUSE
US, male producer – Kevin Saunderson (Singles: 1 Week)   pos/wks

14 Mar 92	UP TEMPO *KMS UK KMSUK 1*	.......**68**	1

TROUBADOURS DU ROI BAUDOUIN *Zaire, male /*
female vocal group (Singles: 11 Weeks, Albums: 1 Week)   pos/wks

19 Mar 69	SANCTUS (MISSA LUBA) (re) *Philips BF 1732*	....**28**	11
22 May 76	MISSA LUBA *Philips SBL 7592*	....**59**	1

TROUBLE FUNK *US, male vocal /*
instrumental group (Singles: 3 Weeks, Albums: 4 Weeks)   pos/wks

27 Jun 87	WOMAN OF PRINCIPLE *Fourth & Broadway BRW 70*	....**65**	3
8 Nov 86	SAY WHAT! *Fourth & Broadway DCLP 101*	....**75**	2
5 Sep 87	TROUBLE OVER HERE TROUBLE OVER THERE *Fourth & Broadway BRLP 513*.	....**54**	2

Roger TROUTMAN See ZAPP; ROGER

Robin TROWER (see also PROCOL HARUM; The PARAMOUNTS)
UK, male instrumentalist – guitar (Albums: 16 Weeks)   pos/wks

1 Mar 75	FOR EARTH BELOW *Chrysalis CHR 1073*	....**26**	4
13 Mar 76	LIVE! *Chrysalis CHR 1089*	....**15**	6
30 Oct 76	LONG MISTY DAYS *Chrysalis CHR 1107*	....**31**	1
29 Oct 77	IN CITY DREAMS *Chrysalis CHR 1148*	....**58**	1
16 Feb 80	VICTIMS OF THE FURY *Chrysalis CHR 1215*	....**61**	4

Doris TROY *US, female vocalist, b. Doris*
Higginson, 6 Jan 1937, d. 16 Feb 2004 (Singles: 12 Weeks)   pos/wks

19 Nov 64	WHATCHA GONNA DO ABOUT IT (re) *Atlantic AT 4011*	....**37**	12

Elisabeth TROY See MJ COLE; SOUNDMAN and Don LLOYDIE with Elisabeth TROY; Y-TRIBE featuring Elisabeth TROY; 4 VINI featuring Elisabeth TROY

TRU FAITH & DUB CONSPIRACY
UK, male production groups (Singles: 5 Weeks)   pos/wks

9 Sep 00	FREAK LIKE ME *Public Demand / Positiva CDTIV 138*	....**12**	5

TRUBBLE
UK, male / female production / vocal trio (Singles: 5 Weeks)   pos/wks

26 Dec 98	DANCING BABY (OOGA-CHAKA) *Island YYCD 1*	....**21**	5

TRUCE *UK, female vocal group (Singles: 6 Weeks)*   pos/wks

2 Sep 95	THE FINEST *Big Life BLRD 118*	....**54**	1
30 Mar 96	CELEBRATION OF LIFE *Big Life BLRD 126*	....**51**	1
29 Nov 97	NOTHIN' BUT A PARTY *Big Life BLRD 138*	....**71**	1
5 Sep 98	EYES DON'T LIE *Big Life BLRD 146*	....**20**	3

TRUCKIN' CO See Garnet MIMMS and TRUCKIN' CO

TRUCKS
UK / Norway, male vocal / instrumental group (Singles: 2 Weeks)   pos/wks

5 Oct 02	IT'S JUST PORN MUM *Gut CDGUT 43*	....**35**	2

Andrea TRUE CONNECTION
US, female vocalist and male instrumental backing group
(Singles: 16 Weeks)   pos/wks

17 Apr 76 ●	MORE, MORE, MORE *Buddah BDS 442*	....**5**	10
4 Mar 78	WHAT'S YOUR NAME, WHAT'S YOUR NUMBER *Buddah BDS 467*	....**34**	6

TRUE FAITH and Bridgette GRACE with FINAL CUT
US, male / female vocal / instrumental group (Singles: 4 Weeks)   pos/wks

2 Mar 91	TAKE ME AWAY *Network NWK 20*	....**51**	4

TRUE IMAGE See Monie LOVE

TRUE PARTY
UK, male production / vocal group (Singles: 6 Weeks)   pos/wks

2 Dec 00	WHAZZUP *Positiva CDBUD 001*	....**13**	6

TRUE STEPPERS *UK, male production / instrumental*
duo – Jonny Linders and Andy Lysandrou (Singles: 31 Weeks)   pos/wks

29 Apr 00 ●	BUGGIN *Nulife 74321753342* [1]	....**6**	8
26 Aug 00	OUT OF YOUR MIND (re) *Nulife 74321782942* [2]	....**2**	20
2 Dec 00	TRUE STEP TONIGHT *Nulife 74321811312* [3]	....**25**	5

[1] True Steppers featuring Dane Bowers [2] True Steppers and Dane Bowers featuring Victoria Beckham [3] True Steppers featuring Brian Harvey and Donell Jones

Damon TRUEITT See SOMORE featuring Damon TRUEITT

TRUMAN & WOLFF featuring STEEL HORSES
UK, male production duo and UK, male rap group (Singles: 1 Week)   pos/wks

22 Aug 98	COME AGAIN *Multiply CDMULTY 38*	....**57**	1

TRUMPET MAN See MONTANO vs The TRUMPET MAN

TRUSSEL *US, male vocal / instrumental group (Singles: 4 Weeks)*   pos/wks

8 Mar 80	LOVE INJECTION *Elektra K 12412*	....**43**	4

The TRUTH
(see also The JAVELLS featuring Nosmo KING) UK, male vocal duo –
Stephen 'Nosmo King' Gold and Francis Aiello (Singles: 6 Weeks)   pos/wks

3 Feb 66	GIRL *Pye 7N 17035*	....**27**	6

TRUTH *UK, male vocal / instrumental group (Singles: 16 Weeks)*   pos/wks

11 Jun 83	CONFUSION (HITS US EVERY TIME) *Formation TRUTH 1*	....**22**	7
27 Aug 83	A STEP IN THE RIGHT DIRECTION *Formation TRUTH 2*	....**32**	7
4 Feb 84	NO STONE UNTURNED *Formation TRUTH 3*	....**66**	2

TRUTH HURTS *US, female vocalist –*
Shari Watson (Singles: 12 Weeks, Albums: 4 Weeks)   pos/wks

31 Aug 02 ●	ADDICTIVE *Aftermath / Interscope 4977782* [1]	....**3**	12
24 Aug 02	TRUTHFULLY SPEAKING *Interscope 4934592*	....**61**	4

[1] Truth Hurts featuring Rakim

Esera TUAOLO See Richie RICH

TUBBY T *UK, male vocalist – Anthony Robinson (Singles: 3 Weeks)*   pos/wks

21 Sep 02	TALES OF THE HOOD *Go Beat GOBCD 51*	....**47**	1
24 May 03	BIG N BASHY *Virgin VSCDT 1847* [1]	....**45**	2

[1] Fallacy featuring Tubby T

TUBE & BERGER featuring Chrissie HYNDE
(see also The PRETENDERS) UK, male production
duo and US, female vocalist (Singles: 3 Weeks)   pos/wks

7 Feb 04	STRAIGHT AHEAD *Direction 6746222*	....**29**	3

The TUBES *US, male vocal / instrumental*
group (Singles: 18 Weeks, Albums: 7 Weeks)   pos/wks

19 Nov 77	WHITE PUNKS ON DOPE *A&M AMS 7323*	....**28**	4
28 Apr 79	PRIME TIME *A&M AMS 7423*	....**34**	10
12 Sep 81	DON'T WANT TO WAIT ANYMORE *Capitol CL 208*	....**60**	4
4 Mar 78	WHAT DO YOU WANT FROM LIFE *A&M AMS 68460*	....**38**	1
2 Jun 79	REMOTE CONTROL *A&M AMLH 64751*	....**40**	5
4 Jun 83	OUTSIDE INSIDE *Capitol EST 12260*	....**77**	1

TUBEWAY ARMY See Gary NUMAN

Barbara TUCKER *US, female vocalist (Singles: 12 Weeks)*   pos/wks

5 Mar 94	BEAUTIFUL PEOPLE *Positiva CDTIV 11*	....**23**	3
26 Nov 94	I GET LIFTED *Positiva CDTIV 23*	....**33**	2

23 Sep 95	**STAY TOGETHER** *Positiva CDTIV 39*	.....**46**	1
8 Aug 98	**EVERYBODY DANCE (THE HORN SONG)** *Positiva CDTIV 96*	....**28**	2
18 Mar 00	**STOP PLAYING WITH MY MIND** *Positiva CDTIV 127* [1]	.........**17**	4

[1] Barbara Tucker featuring Darryl D'Bonneau

Junior TUCKER
UK, male vocalist (Singles: 2 Weeks) pos/wks

2 Jun 90	**DON'T TEST** *10 TEN 299*	.....**54**	2

Louise TUCKER
UK, female vocalist (Singles: 5 Weeks) pos/wks

9 Apr 83	**MIDNIGHT BLUE** *Ariola ARO 289*	.....**59**	5

Tommy TUCKER
US, male vocalist, b. Robert Higginbotham, 5 Mar 1939, d. 22 Jan 1982 (Singles: 10 Weeks) pos/wks

26 Mar 64	**HI-HEEL SNEAKERS** *Pye International 7N 25238*	.....**23**	10

TUFF JAM
UK, male production duo (Singles: 1 Week) pos/wks

10 Oct 98	**NEED GOOD LOVE** *Locked On LOX 99CD*	.....**44**	1

TUKAN
Denmark, male production duo – Soren Weile and Lars Fredriksen (Singles: 3 Weeks) pos/wks

15 Dec 01	**LIGHT A RAINBOW** *Incentive CENT 33CDS*	.....**38**	3

TUNDE (see also LIGHTHOUSE FAMILY)
Nigeria, male vocalist – Tunde Baiyewu (Albums: 2 Weeks) pos/wks

30 Oct 04	**TUNDE** *RCA 82876652262*	.....**32**	2

TURIN BRAKES
UK, male vocal / instrumental duo – Gale Paridjanian and Olly Knight (Singles: 15 Weeks, Albums: 29 Weeks) pos/wks

3 Mar 01	**THE DOOR** *Source SOURCDS 024*	.....**67**	1
12 May 01	**UNDERDOG (SAVE ME)** *Source SOURCDSE 101*	.....**39**	2
11 Aug 01	**MIND OVER MONEY** *Source SOURCD 038*	.....**31**	2
27 Oct 01	**72** *Source SOURCD 041*	.....**41**	1
2 Nov 02	**LONG DISTANCE** *Source SOURCD 064*	.....**22**	2
1 Mar 03 ●	**PAIN KILLER** *Source SOURCD 068*	.....**5**	3
7 Jun 03	**AVERAGE MAN** *Source SOURCD 85*	.....**35**	2
11 Oct 03	**5 MILE** *Source SOURCD 089*	.....**31**	2
17 Mar 01	**THE OPTIMIST LP** *Source SOURCD 023*	.....**27**	18
15 Mar 03 ●	**ETHER SONG** *Source CDSOURX 054*	.....**4**	11

Ike and Tina TURNER
US, male / female vocal instrumental duo (Singles: 44 Weeks, Albums: 1 Week) pos/wks

9 Jun 66 ●	**RIVER DEEP – MOUNTAIN HIGH** *London HLU 10046*	.....**3**	13
28 Jul 66	**TELL HER I'M NOT HOME** *Warner Bros. WB 5753*	.....**48**	1
27 Oct 66	**A LOVE LIKE YOURS (DON'T COME KNOCKING EVERY DAY)** *London HLU 10083*	.....**16**	10
12 Feb 69	**RIVER DEEP MOUNTAIN HIGH (re-issue)** *London HLU 10242*	.....**33**	7
8 Sep 73 ●	**NUTBUSH CITY LIMITS** *United Artists UP 35582*	.....**4**	13
1 Oct 66	**RIVER DEEP – MOUNTAIN HIGH** *London HAU 8298*	.....**27**	1

Ruby TURNER
UK, female vocalist (Singles: 31 Weeks, Albums: 19 Weeks) pos/wks

25 Jan 86	**IF YOU'RE READY (COME GO WITH ME)** *Jive JIVE 109* [1]	.....**30**	7
29 Mar 86	**I'M IN LOVE** *Jive JIVE 118*	.....**61**	4
13 Sep 86	**BYE BABY** *Jive JIVE 126*	.....**52**	3
14 Mar 87	**I'D RATHER GO BLIND** *Jive RTS 1*	.....**24**	8
16 May 87	**I'M IN LOVE (re-issue)** *Jive RTS 2*	.....**57**	2
13 Jan 90	**IT'S GONNA BE ALRIGHT** *Jive RTS 7*	.....**57**	3
5 Feb 94	**STAY WITH ME BABY** *M&G MAGCD 53*	.....**39**	3
9 Dec 95	**SHAKABOOM!** *Telstar HUNTCD 1* [2]	.....**64**	1
18 Oct 86	**WOMEN HOLD UP HALF THE SKY** *Jive HIP 36*	.....**47**	11
8 Oct 88	**THE MOTOWN SONGBOOK** *Jive HIP 58*	.....**22**	6
17 Feb 90	**PARADISE** *Jive HIP 89*	.....**74**	2

[1] Ruby Turner featuring Jonathan Butler [2] Hunter featuring Ruby Turner

Sammy TURNER
US, male vocalist – Samuel Black (Singles: 2 Weeks) pos/wks

13 Nov 59	**ALWAYS** *London HLX 8963*	.....**26**	2

Tina TURNER (34) Top 500 (see also Ike and Tina TURNER)
Supreme soul singer-cum-rock legend, b. Anna Mae Bullock, 26 Nov 1939, Tennessee, US. After a successful, if stormy, partnership with husband Ike, she reached greater heights as a Grammy-winning soloist and is one of the world's most popular live acts with a 40 year US chart span (Singles: 227 Weeks, Albums: 528 Weeks) pos/wks

19 Nov 83 ●	**LET'S STAY TOGETHER** *Capitol CL 316*	.....**6**	13
25 Feb 84	**HELP** *Capitol CL 325*	.....**40**	6

16 Jun 84 ●	**WHAT'S LOVE GOT TO DO WITH IT** *Capitol CL 334* ▲	.....**3**	16
15 Sep 84	**BETTER BE GOOD TO ME** *Capitol CL 338*	.....**45**	5
17 Nov 84	**PRIVATE DANCER** *Capitol CL 343*	.....**26**	9
2 Mar 85	**I CAN'T STAND THE RAIN** *Capitol CL 352*	.....**57**	3
20 Jul 85	**WE DON'T NEED ANOTHER HERO (THUNDERDOME)** *Capitol CL 364*	.....**3**	12
12 Oct 85	**ONE OF THE LIVING** *Capitol CL 376*	.....**55**	2
2 Nov 85	**IT'S ONLY LOVE** *A&M AM 285* [1]	.....**29**	6
23 Aug 86	**TYPICAL MALE** *Capitol CL 419*	.....**33**	6
8 Nov 86	**TWO PEOPLE** *Capitol CL 430*	.....**43**	4
14 Mar 87	**WHAT YOU GET IS WHAT YOU SEE** *Capitol CL 439*	.....**30**	7
13 Jun 87	**BREAK EVERY RULE** *Capitol CL 452*	.....**43**	3
20 Jun 87	**TEARING US APART** *Duck W 8299* [2]	.....**56**	3
19 Mar 88	**ADDICTED TO LOVE (LIVE)** *Capitol CL 484*	.....**71**	2
2 Sep 89 ●	**THE BEST** *Capitol CL 543*	.....**5**	12
18 Nov 89 ●	**I DON'T WANNA LOSE YOU** *Capitol CL 553*	.....**8**	11
17 Feb 90	**STEAMY WINDOWS** *Capitol CL 560*	.....**13**	6
11 Aug 90	**LOOK ME IN THE HEART** *Capitol CL 584*	.....**31**	6
13 Oct 90	**BE TENDER WITH ME BABY** *Capitol CL 593*	.....**28**	4
24 Nov 90 ●	**IT TAKES TWO** *Warner Bros. ROD 1* [3]	.....**5**	8
21 Sep 91	**NUTBUSH CITY LIMITS (re-recording)** *Capitol CL 630*	.....**23**	5
23 Nov 91	**WAY OF THE WORLD** *Capitol CL 637*	.....**13**	7
15 Feb 92	**LOVE THING** *Capitol CL 644*	.....**29**	4
6 Jun 92	**I WANT YOU NEAR ME** *Capitol CL 659*	.....**22**	4
22 May 93	**I DON'T WANNA FIGHT** *Parlophone CDRS 6346*	.....**7**	9
28 Aug 93	**DISCO INFERNO** *Parlophone CDR 6357*	.....**12**	6
30 Oct 93	**WHY MUST WE WAIT UNTIL TONIGHT** *Parlophone CDR 6366*	.....**16**	4
18 Nov 95 ●	**GOLDENEYE** *Parlophone CDR 0071001*	.....**10**	9
23 Mar 96	**WHATEVER YOU WANT** *Parlophone CDR 6429*	.....**23**	6
8 Jun 96	**ON SILENT WINGS** *Parlophone CDR 6434*	.....**13**	6
27 Jul 96	**MISSING YOU** *Parlophone CDR 6441* [4]	.....**12**	5
19 Oct 96	**SOMETHING BEAUTIFUL REMAINS** *Parlophone CDR 6448*	.....**27**	2
21 Dec 96	**IN YOUR WILDEST DREAMS** *Parlophone CDR 6451* [5]	.....**32**	3
30 Oct 99	**WHEN THE HEARTACHE IS OVER** *Parlophone CDR 6529* [4]	.....**10**	7
12 Feb 00	**WHATEVER YOU NEED** *Parlophone CDR 6532* [4]	.....**27**	3
6 Nov 04	**OPEN ARMS** *Parlophone CDCLS 862* [4]	.....**25**	3
30 Jun 84 ●	**PRIVATE DANCER** *Capitol TINA 1*	.....**2**	147
20 Sep 86	**BREAK EVERY RULE** *Capitol EST 2018*	.....**2**	49
2 Apr 88	**LIVE IN EUROPE** *Capitol ESTD 1*	.....**8**	13
30 Sep 89 ★	**FOREIGN AFFAIR** *Capitol ESTU 2103* ■	.....**1**	78
12 Oct 91 ●	**SIMPLY THE BEST** *Capitol ESTV 1*	.....**2**	141
19 Jun 93 ★	**WHAT'S LOVE GOT TO DO WITH IT (FILM SOUNDTRACK)** *Parlophone CDPCSD 128* ■	.....**1**	33
13 Apr 96 ●	**WILDEST DREAMS** *Parlophone CDEST 2279*	.....**4**	41
13 Nov 99 ●	**TWENTY FOUR SEVEN** *Parlophone 5231802*	.....**9**	19
13 Nov 04 ●	**ALL THE BEST** *Parlophone 8667172* [1]	.....**6**	7+

[1] Bryan Adams and Tina Turner [2] Eric Clapton and Tina Turner [3] Rod Stewart and Tina Turner [4] Tina [5] Tina Turner featuring Barry White [1] Tina

TURNTABLE ORCHESTRA
US, male vocal / instrumental duo (Singles: 4 Weeks) pos/wks

21 Jan 89	**YOU'RE GONNA MISS ME** *Republic LIC 012*	.....**52**	4

The TURTLES
US, male vocal / instrumental group (Singles: 39 Weeks, Albums: 9 Weeks) pos/wks

23 Mar 67	**HAPPY TOGETHER** *London HLU 10115* ▲	.....**12**	12
15 Jun 67	**SHE'D RATHER BE WITH ME** *London HLU 10135*	.....**4**	15
30 Oct 68	**ELENORE** *London HLU 10223*	.....**7**	12
22 Jul 67	**HAPPY TOGETHER** *London HAU 8330*	.....**18**	9

TUXEDOS See Bobby ANGELO and The TUXEDOS

Shania TWAIN (162) Top 500
Pop and country music queen whose first three albums have sold 50 million copies worldwide, b. Eileen Regina Edwards, 28 Aug 1965, Ontario, Canada. Self-penned 'Come On Over' album sold more than 36 million, including two million in the UK and a record-breaking 19 million in the US. She is the only act to have three successive 10 million-selling albums in the US, and at the 2004 World Music Awards was named World's Top Selling Female. Best-selling single: 'That Don't Impress Me Much' 763,000 (Singles: 121 Weeks, Albums: 216 Weeks) pos/wks

28 Feb 98	**YOU'RE STILL THE ONE** *Mercury 5684932*	.....**10**	10
13 Jun 98	**WHEN** *Mercury 5661192*	.....**18**	4
28 Nov 98 ●	**FROM THIS MOMENT ON** *Mercury 5665632*	.....**9**	8
22 May 99 ●	**THAT DON'T IMPRESS ME MUCH** *Mercury 8708032*	.....**3**	21
2 Oct 99 ●	**MAN! I FEEL LIKE A WOMAN!** *Mercury 5623242*	.....**3**	18

		pos/wks
26 Feb 00 ●	**DON'T BE STUPID (YOU KNOW I LOVE YOU) (re)**	
	Mercury 1721492 ....**5** 11	
16 Nov 02 ●	**I'M GONNA GETCHA GOOD!** Mercury 1722702 ....**4** 15	
22 Mar 03 ●	**KA-CHING!** Mercury 1722862 ....**8** 8	
14 Jun 03 ●	**FOREVER AND FOR ALWAYS** Mercury 9807733 ....**6** 10	
6 Sep 03	**THANK YOU BABY (FOR MAKIN' SOMEDAY COME SO SOON)**	
	Mercury 9810627 ....**11** 7	
29 Nov 03	**WHEN YOU KISS ME / UP! (re)** Mercury 9814003 .....**21** 5	
4 Dec 04 ●	**PARTY FOR TWO** Mercury 2103239 [1] ....**10** 4+	
21 Mar 98 ★	**COME ON OVER** Mercury 5580002 ....**1** 138	
18 Mar 00 ●	**THE WOMAN IN ME** Mercury 1701292 ....**7** 25	
15 Jul 00	**WILD & WICKED** RWP RWPCD 1123 ....**62** 2	
30 Nov 02	**UP!** Mercury 1703442 ▲ **4** 45	
20 Nov 04 ●	**GREATEST HITS** Mercury 9863604 ....**6** 6+	

[1] Shania Twain with Mark McGrath

TWEENIES UK, male / female kiddie
TV characters (Singles: 58 Weeks, Albums: 9 Weeks)   pos/wks

		pos/wks
11 Nov 00 ●	**NO.1 (2re)** BBC Music WMSS 60332 ....**5** 27	
31 Mar 01	**BEST FRIENDS FOREVER (re)** BBC Music WMSS 60382 ...**12** 10	
4 Aug 01	**DO THE LOLLIPOP** BBC Music WMSS 60452 ....**17** 8	
15 Dec 01 ●	**I BELIEVE IN CHRISTMAS** BBC Music WMSS 60502 ....**9** 6	
14 Sep 02	**HAVE FUN, GO MAD!** BBC Music WMSS 60572 ....**20** 7	
25 Nov 00	**FRIENDS FOREVER** BBC Music WMSF 60362 ....**56** 4	
1 Dec 01	**THE CHRISTMAS ALBUM** BBC Music WMSF 60482 ....**34** 5	

TWEET US, female vocalist –
Charlene Keys (Singles: 10 Weeks, Albums: 5 Weeks)   pos/wks

		pos/wks
11 May 02 ●	**OOPS (OH MY)** Elektra E 7306CD **5** 8	
7 Sep 02	**CALL ME** Elektra E 7326CD **35** 2	
25 May 02	**SOUTHERN HUMMINGBIRD** Elektra 7559627772 ......**15** 5	

The TWEETS
UK, male feathered vocal / instrumental group (Singles: 34 Weeks) pos/wks

		pos/wks
12 Sep 81 ●	**THE BIRDIE SONG (BIRDIE DANCE) (re)** PRT 7P 219 ...**2** 28	
5 Dec 81	**LET'S ALL SING LIKE THE BIRDIES SING** PRT 7P 226 ...**44** 6	

'The Birdie Song (Birdie Dance)' re-entered in Dec 1982, peaking at No.48

TWELFTH NIGHT
UK, male vocal / instrumental group (Albums: 2 Weeks)   pos/wks

		pos/wks
27 Oct 84	**ART AND ILLUSION** Music for Nations MFN 36 ....**83** 2	

20 FINGERS US, male instrumental / production duo –
Charles Babie and Manfred Mohr (Singles: 14 Weeks)   pos/wks

		pos/wks
26 Nov 94	**SHORT DICK MAN** Multiply CDMULT 12 [1] **21** 4	
30 Sep 95	**SHORT SHORT MAN (re-mix)** Multiply CXMULTY 7 [1] ...**11** 7	
30 Sep 95	**LICK IT** Zyx ZYX 75908 [2] **48** 3	

[1] 20 Fingers featuring Gillette [2] 20 Fingers featuring Roula

21ST CENTURY GIRLS
UK, female vocal / instrumental group (Singles: 4 Weeks)   pos/wks

		pos/wks
12 Jun 99	**21ST CENTURY GIRLS** EMI NTNCDS 001 ....**16** 4	

TWENTY 4 SEVEN US / Germany, male / female
vocal / instrumental group (Singles: 21 Weeks, Albums: 2 Weeks) pos/wks

		pos/wks
22 Sep 90 ●	**I CAN'T STAND IT** BCM BCMR 395 [1] **7** 10	
24 Nov 90	**ARE YOU DREAMING** BCM BCM 07504 [1] **17** 10	
12 Jun 04	**HIDE** Diablo MND 2 ....**42** 1	
19 Jan 91	**STREET MOVES** BCM BCM 3124 ....**69** 2	

[1] Twenty 4 Seven featuring Captain Hollywood

29 PALMS
UK, male producer – Pete Lorimar (Singles: 1 Week)   pos/wks

		pos/wks
25 May 02	**TOUCH THE SKY** Perfecto PERF 35CDS **51** 1	

22-20s UK, male vocal / instrumental
group (Singles: 6 Weeks, Albums: 1 Week)   pos/wks

		pos/wks
17 Apr 04	**WHY DON'T YOU DO IT FOR ME?** Heavenly HVN 138CD ...**41** 2	
10 Jul 04	**SHOOT YOUR GUN** Heavenly HVN 141CD **30** 2	
25 Sep 04	**22 DAYS** Heavenly HVN 144CD **34** 2	
2 Oct 04	**22-20S** Heavenly HVNLP 51CD **40** 1	

TWICE AS MUCH UK, male vocal duo –
David Skinner and Stephen Rose (Singles: 9 Weeks)   pos/wks

		pos/wks
16 Jun 66	**SITTIN' ON A FENCE** Immediate IM 033 ....**25** 9	

TWIGGY UK, female model / vocalist –
Lesley Hornby (Singles: 10 Weeks, Albums: 11 Weeks)   pos/wks

		pos/wks
14 Aug 76	**HERE I GO AGAIN** Mercury 6007 100 ....**17** 10	
21 Aug 76	**TWIGGY** Mercury 9102 600 ....**33** 8	
30 Apr 77	**PLEASE GET MY NAME RIGHT** Mercury 9102 601.......**35** 3	

TWILIGHT See Roger SANCHEZ

TWIN HYPE US, male rap duo (Singles: 2 Weeks)   pos/wks

		pos/wks
15 Jul 89	**DO IT TO THE CROWD** Profile PROF 255 ....**65** 2	

TWINKLE
UK, female vocalist – Lynn Ripley (Singles: 20 Weeks)   pos/wks

		pos/wks
26 Nov 64 ●	**TERRY** Decca F 12013 ....**4** 15	
25 Feb 65	**GOLDEN LIGHTS** Decca F 12076 ....**21** 5	

TWISTA US, male rapper – Carl Mitchell
(Singles: 33 Weeks, Albums: 22 Weeks)   pos/wks

		pos/wks
10 Apr 04 ●	**SLOW JAMZ** Atlantic AT 0174CD ▲ **3** 10	
3 Jul 04	**OVERNIGHT CELEBRITY** Atlantic AT 0180CD **16** 7	
14 Aug 04	**SUNSHINE (Import)** Atlantic 7567932652CD [1] **60** 3	
11 Sep 04 ●	**SUNSHINE** Atlantic ATO 181CD [1] **3** 10	
20 Nov 04	**SO SEXY** Atlantic AT 0187CD [2] **28** 3	
28 Feb 04	**KAMIKAZE** Atlantic 7567835982 ▲ **19** 22	

[1] Twista featuring Anthony Hamilton [2] Twista featuring R Kelly

'Slow Jamz' credits Kanye West & Jamie Foxx on the CD only

TWISTED INDIVIDUAL
UK, male producer – Lee Greenaway (Singles: 1 Week)   pos/wks

		pos/wks
9 Aug 03	**BANDWAGON BLUES** Formation FORM 12102 ....**51** 1	

TWISTED SISTER US, male vocal /
instrumental group (Singles: 28 Weeks, Albums: 20 Weeks)   pos/wks

		pos/wks
26 Mar 83	**I AM (I'M ME)** Atlantic A 9854 ....**18** 9	
28 May 83	**THE KIDS ARE BACK** Atlantic A 9827 ....**32** 6	
20 Aug 83	**YOU CAN'T STOP ROCK 'N' ROLL** Atlantic A 9792 ......**43** 4	
2 Jun 84	**WE'RE NOT GONNA TAKE IT** Atlantic A 9657 ....**58** 6	
18 Jan 86	**LEADER OF THE PACK** Atlantic A 9478 ....**47** 3	
25 Sep 82	**UNDER THE BLADE** Secret SECX 9 ....**70** 3	
7 May 83	**YOU CAN'T STOP ROCK 'N' ROLL** Atlantic A 0074 ......**14** 9	
16 Jun 84	**STAY HUNGRY** Atlantic 780156 ....**34** 5	
14 Dec 85	**COME OUT AND PLAY** Atlantic 7812751 ....**95** 1	
25 Jul 87	**LOVE IS FOR SUCKERS** Atlantic WX 120 ....**57** 2	

TWISTED X
UK, male vocal group – England football fans (Singles: 3 Weeks) pos/wks

		pos/wks
19 Jun 04 ●	**BORN IN ENGLAND** Universal TV 9867021 ....**9** 3	

Includes members of Supergrass, The Libertines, Delays, The Wheatleys, Bernard Butler, actor James Nesbitt and XFM DJ Christian O'Connell

Conway TWITTY US, male vocalist,
b. Harold Jenkins, 1 Sep 1933, d. 5 Jun 1993 (Singles: 36 Weeks) pos/wks

		pos/wks
14 Nov 58 ★	**IT'S ONLY MAKE BELIEVE** MGM 992 ▲ **1** 15	
27 Mar 59	**THE STORY OF MY LOVE** MGM 1003 ....**30** 1	
21 Aug 59 ●	**MONA LISA** MGM 1029 ....**5** 14	
21 Jul 60	**IS A BLUE BIRD BLUE** MGM 1082 ....**43** 3	
23 Feb 61	**C'EST SI BON** MGM 1118 ....**40** 3	

2 BAD MICE
UK, male instrumental / production group (Singles: 4 Weeks)   pos/wks

		pos/wks
15 Feb 92	**HOLD IT DOWN (re)** Moving Shadow SHADOW 14 ....**48** 3	
7 Sep 96	**BOMBSCARE** Arista 74321397662 ....**46** 1	

TWO COWBOYS Italy, male instrumental / production duo –
Roberto Sagotto and Maurizio Braccagni (Singles: 11 Weeks)   pos/wks

		pos/wks
9 Jul 94 ●	**EVERYBODY GONFI-GON** 3 Beat TABCD 221 ....**7** 11	

Singles re-entries are listed as (re), (2re), (3re)…. which signifies that the hit re-entered the chart once, twice or three times…

2 EIVISSA Germany, female vocal duo –
Pascale Jean Louis and Ellen Helbig (Singles: 6 Weeks)   pos/wks

4 Oct 97	OH LA LA LA Club Tools 0063475 CLU	13	6

2 FOR JOY
UK, male instrumental / production duo (Singles: 3 Weeks)   pos/wks

1 Dec 90	IN A STATE Mercury MER 333	61	1
9 Nov 91	LET THE BASS KICK All Around the World CDGLOBE 102	67	2

2-4 FAMILY
UK / US / Korea, male / female rap / vocal group (Singles: 1 Week)   pos/wks

29 May 99	LEAN ON ME (WITH THE FAMILY) Epic 6670132	69	1

2 FUNKY 2 starring Kathryn DION
UK, male / female vocal / instrumental group (Singles: 4 Weeks)   pos/wks

6 Nov 93	BROTHERS AND SISTERS Logic 74321170772	56	2
30 Nov 96	BROTHERS AND SISTERS (re-mix) All Around the World CDGLOBE 138	36	2

2 HOUSE US, male instrumental / production duo (Singles: 1 Week)   pos/wks

21 Mar 92	GO TECHNO Atlantic A 7519	65	1

2 IN A ROOM US, male vocal duo – Roger Pauletta
and Rafael Vargas (Singles: 15 Weeks, Albums: 1 Week)   pos/wks

18 Nov 89	SOMEBODY IN THE HOUSE SAY YEAH! Big Life BLR 12	66	1
26 Jan 91 ●	WIGGLE IT SBK SBK 19	3	8
6 Apr 91	SHE'S GOT ME GOING CRAZY SBK SBK 23	54	2
22 Oct 94	EL TRAGO (THE DRINK) Positiva CDTIV 18	34	2
8 Apr 95	AHORA ES (NOW IS THE TIME) Positiva CDTIV 32	43	1
17 Aug 96	GIDDY-UP Encore CDCOR 008	74	1
2 Mar 91	WIGGLE IT SBK SBKLP 11	73	1

2 IN A TENT (see also STOCK AITKEN WATERMAN) UK, male instrumental / production duo – Mike Stock and Matt Aitken (Singles: 7 Weeks)   pos/wks

17 Dec 94	WHEN I'M CLEANING WINDOWS (TURNED OUT NICE AGAIN) (re) Love This SPONCD 1	25	6
13 May 95	BOOGIE WOOGIE BUGLE BOY (DON'T STOP) Bald Cat BALDCD 1 [1]	48	1

[1] 2 In a Tank

First hit, which features the sampled vocals of George Formby, re-entered and peaked at No.62 in Jan 1996

2K (see also JUSTIFIED ANCIENTS OF MU MU; The KLF; The TIMELORDS) UK, male production duo – Bill Drummond and Jimmy Cauty (Singles: 2 Weeks)   pos/wks

25 Oct 97	***K THE MILLENNIUM Blast First BFFP 146CDK	28	2

2 MAD UK, male vocal / instrumental duo (Singles: 4 Weeks)   pos/wks

9 Feb 91	THINKIN' ABOUT YOUR BODY Big Life BLR 37	43	4

TWO MAN SOUND
Belgium, male vocal / instrumental group (Singles: 7 Weeks)   pos/wks

20 Jan 79	QUE TAL AMERICA Miracle M 1	46	7

TWO MEN, A DRUM MACHINE AND A TRUMPET
(see also FINE YOUNG CANNIBALS) UK, male instrumental duo – Andy Cox and David Steele (Singles: 17 Weeks)   pos/wks

9 Jan 88	TIRED OF GETTING PUSHED AROUND London LON 141	18	8
25 Jun 88	HEAT IT UP Jive JIVE 174 [1]	21	9

[1] Wee Papa Girl Rappers featuring Two Men and a Drum Machine

TWO NATIONS
UK, male vocal / instrumental group (Singles: 1 Week)   pos/wks

20 Jun 87	THAT'S THE WAY IT FEELS 10 TEN 168	74	1

2PAC 467 Top 500 Legendary rapper / actor, b. Tupac Amaru Shakur, New York City, US, 16 Jun 1971, d. 13 Sep 1998, who achieved more UK and US single and album hits after his death (in a Las Vegas shooting incident) than before. In his homeland, no artist has had more posthumous chart success (Singles: 87 Weeks, Albums: 67 Weeks)   pos/wks

13 Apr 96 ●	CALIFORNIA LOVE Death Row DRWCD 3 [1]	6	8
27 Jul 96	HOW DO YOU WANT IT Death Row DRWCD 4 [2] ▲	17	4
30 Nov 96	I AIN'T MAD AT CHA Death Row DRWCD 5	13	9
12 Apr 97 ●	TO LIVE & DIE IN LA Interscope IND 95529 [3]	10	4
26 Apr 97	WANTED DEAD OR ALIVE Def Jam 5744052 [4]	16	3
9 Aug 97	TOSS IT UP Interscope IND 95521 [3]	15	3
10 Jan 98	I WONDER IF HEAVEN GOT A GHETTO Jive JIVECD 446	21	4
14 Feb 98	HAIL MARY Interscope IND 95575 [3]	43	1
13 Jun 98	DO FOR LOVE Jive 0518512 [5]	12	4
18 Jul 98	RUNNIN' Black Jam BJAM 9005 [6]	15	3
28 Nov 98	HAPPY HOME Eagle EAGXS 058	17	2
20 Feb 99 ●	CHANGES Jive 0522832	3	12
3 Jul 99	DEAR MAMA Jive 0523702	27	3
23 Jun 01 ●	UNTIL THE END OF TIME Interscope / Polydor 4975812	4	11
10 Nov 01	LETTER 2 MY UNBORN Interscope / Polydor 4976142	21	5
22 Feb 03	THUGZ MANSION Interscope / Polydor 4978542	24	5
31 Jan 04	RUNNIN' (DYING TO LIVE) Interscope / Polydor 9815329 [7]	17	6
9 Mar 96	ALL EYEZ ON ME Death Row 5242042 ▲	32	7
16 Nov 96	THE DON KILLUMINATI - THE 7 DAY THEORY Death Row IND 90039	53	1
6 Dec 97	R U STILL DOWN? (REMEMBER ME) Jive CHIP 195	44	1
8 Aug 98	IN HIS OWN WORDS Eagle EAGCD 050	65	1
12 Dec 98	GREATEST HITS Jive 522662	17	35
8 Jan 00	STILL I RISE Interscope 4904172 [2]	75	1
21 Apr 01	UNTIL THE END OF TIME Interscope 4908402 ▲	31	17
14 Dec 02	BETTER DAYZ Interscope 4970702	68	1
22 Nov 03	RESURRECTION (OST) Interscope / Polydor 9861159 [3]	62	1
28 Aug 04	LIVE Koch 2357462	67	1
25 Dec 04	LOYAL TO THE GAME Interscope 2103291	64	1+

[1] 2Pac featuring Dr Dre [2] 2Pac featuring K-Ci and JoJo [3] Makaveli [4] 2Pac and Snoop Doggy Dogg [5] 2Pac featuring Eric Williams [6] 2Pac and Notorious B.I.G. [7] Tupac featuring Notorious B.I.G. [1] Makaveli [2] 2Pac and Outlawz [3] Tupac

TWO PEOPLE
UK, male vocal / instrumental group (Singles: 2 Weeks)   pos/wks

31 Jan 87	HEAVEN Polydor POSP 844	63	2

2PLAY UK, male producer – Wessley (Singles: 23 Weeks)   pos/wks

24 Jan 04	SO CONFUSED 2PSL 2PSLCD 02 [1]	63	2
22 May 04 ●	IT CAN'T BE RIGHT 2PSL / Inferno 2PSLCD 04 [2]	8	7
4 Dec 04	CARELESS WHISPER Inferno 2PSLCD 06 [3]	63	2

[1] 2Play featuring Raghav & Jucxi [2] 2Play featuring Raghav & Naila Boss [3] 2Play featuring Thomas Jules & Jucxi D

2WO THIRD3
UK, male vocal / instrumental group (Singles: 15 Weeks)   pos/wks

19 Feb 94	HEAR ME CALLING Epic 6600642	48	3
11 Jun 94	EASE THE PRESSURE Epic 6604782	45	2
8 Oct 94	I WANT THE WORLD Epic 6608542	20	5
17 Dec 94	I WANT TO BE ALONE Epic 6610852	29	5

2 UNLIMITED 481 Top 500
The brainchild of Jean-Paul de Coster and Phil Wilde, fronted by the minimalist vocals / chants / raps of Dutch duo Ray Slijngaard and Anita Dels. Their youth-aimed, infectious dance tracks sold millions around Europe and gave them 11 successive UK Top 20 hits. Best-selling UK single: 'No Limit' 531,900 (Singles: 112 Weeks, Albums: 38 Weeks)   pos/wks

5 Oct 91 ●	GET READY FOR THIS PWL Continental PWL 206	2	15
25 Jan 92 ●	TWILIGHT ZONE PWL Continental PWL 211	2	10
2 May 92 ●	WORKAHOLIC PWL Continental PWL 228	4	7
15 Aug 92	THE MAGIC FRIEND PWL Continental PWL 240	11	7
30 Jan 93 ★	NO LIMIT PWL Continental PWCD 256	1	16
8 May 93 ●	TRIBAL DANCE PWL Continental PWCD 262	4	11
4 Sep 93 ●	FACES PWL Continental PWCD 268	8	7
20 Nov 93	MAXIMUM OVERDRIVE PWL Continental PWCD 276	15	8
19 Feb 94 ●	LET THE BEAT CONTROL YOUR BODY PWL Continental PWCD 280	6	9
21 May 94 ●	THE REAL THING PWL Continental PWCD 306	6	7
1 Oct 94	NO ONE PWL Continental PWCD 314	17	6
25 Mar 95	HERE I GO PWL Continental PWCD 317	22	3
21 Oct 95	DO WHAT'S GOOD FOR ME PWL Continental PWL 322CD1	16	4
11 Jul 98	WANNA GET UP Big Life BLRD 143	38	2
7 Mar 92	GET READY PWL Continental HFCD 23	37	3
22 May 93 ★	NO LIMITS PWL Continental HFCD 27	1	21
18 Jun 94 ★	REAL THINGS PWL Continental HFCD 38 ■	1	9
11 Nov 95	HITS UNLIMITED PWL Continental HF 47CD	27	5

In 1995 both Ray Slijngaard and Anita Dels left the act, which was fronted by a Dutch female duo for 'Wanna Get Up'

TY featuring ROOTS MANUVA
UK, male rappers (Singles: 1 Week)   pos/wks

8 May 04	OH U WANT MORE? *Big Dada BDCDS 066*	65	1

Tommy TYCHO *See David GRAY and Tommy TYCHO*

TYGERS OF PAN TANG *UK, male vocal /*
instrumental group (Singles: 15 Weeks, Albums: 20 Weeks)   pos/wks

14 Feb 81	HELLBOUND *MCA 672*	48	3
27 Mar 82	LOVE POTION NO. 9 *MCA 769*	45	6
10 Jul 82	RENDEZVOUS *MCA 777*	49	4
11 Sep 82	PARIS BY AIR *MCA 790*	63	2
30 Aug 80	WILD CAT *MCA MCF 3075*	18	5
18 Apr 81	SPELLBOUND *MCA MCF 3104*	33	4
21 Nov 81	CRAZY NIGHTS *MCA MCF 3123*	51	3
28 Aug 82	THE CAGE *MCA MCF 3150*	13	8

Bonnie TYLER   436   Top 500
Raspy-voiced vocalist, b. Gaynor Hopkins, 8 Jun 1953, Swansea, Wales. Made the US country Top 10 with 'It's a Heartache', and 'Total Eclipse of the Heart' was the first record by a Welsh artist to top the US pop chart (Singles: 81 Weeks, Albums: 79 Weeks)   pos/wks

30 Oct 76	● LOST IN FRANCE *RCA 2734*	9	10
19 Mar 77	MORE THAN A LOVER *RCA PB 5008*	27	6
3 Dec 77	● IT'S A HEARTACHE *RCA PB 5057*	4	12
30 Jun 79	MARRIED MEN *RCA PB 5164*	35	6
19 Feb 83	★ TOTAL ECLIPSE OF THE HEART *CBS TYLER 1* ▲	1	12
7 May 83	FASTER THAN THE SPEED OF NIGHT *CBS A 3338*	43	4
25 Jun 83	HAVE YOU EVER SEEN THE RAIN *CBS A 3517*	47	3
7 Jan 84	● A ROCKIN' GOOD WAY *Epic A 4071* [1]	5	9
31 Aug 85	● HOLDING OUT FOR A HERO *CBS A 4251*	2	13
14 Dec 85	LOVING YOU'S A DIRTY JOB BUT SOMEBODY'S GOTTA DO IT *CBS A 6662* [2]	73	2
28 Dec 91	HOLDING OUT FOR A HERO (re-issue) *Total TYLER 10*	69	2
27 Jan 96	MAKING LOVE (OUT OF NOTHING AT ALL) *East West EW 010CD*	45	2
16 Apr 83	★ FASTER THAN THE SPEED OF NIGHT *CBS 25304* ■	1	45
17 May 86	SECRET DREAMS AND FORBIDDEN FIRE *CBS 86319*	24	12
29 Nov 86	THE GREATEST HITS *Telstar STAR 2291*	24	17
21 May 88	HIDE YOUR HEART *CBS 460125 1*	78	1
14 Jul 01	GREATEST HITS *Sanctuary / Sony TV SANCD 082*	18	4

[1] Shaky and Bonnie [2] Bonnie Tyler, guest vocals Todd Rundgren

'The Greatest Hits' and 'Greatest Hits' albums are different

The TYMES *US, male vocal group – lead vocal George*
Williams, b. 6 Dec 1935, d. 28 Jul 2004 (Singles: 41 Weeks)   pos/wks

25 Jul 63	SO MUCH IN LOVE *Cameo Parkway P 871* ▲	21	8
15 Jan 69	PEOPLE *Direction 58 3903*	16	10
21 Sep 74	YOU LITTLE TRUSTMAKER *RCA 2456*	18	9
21 Dec 74	★ MS GRACE *RCA 2493*	1	11
17 Jan 76	GOD'S GONNA PUNISH YOU *RCA 2626*	41	3

TYMES 4 *UK, female vocal group (Singles: 5 Weeks)*   pos/wks

25 Aug 01	BODYROCK *Edel 0118635 ERE*	23	3
15 Dec 01	SHE GOT GAME *Blacklist 0133135 ERE*	40	2

TYPE O NEGATIVE
US, male vocal / instrumental group (Albums: 2 Weeks)   pos/wks

14 Sep 96	OCTOBER RUST *Roadrunner RR 88742*	26	1
2 Oct 99	WORLD COMING DOWN *Roadrunner RR 86602*	49	1

TYPICALLY TROPICAL *UK, male vocal /*
instrumental duo – Jeff Calvert and Max West (Singles: 11 Weeks)   pos/wks

5 Jul 75	★ BARBADOS *Gull GULS 14*	1	11

TYREE *US, male producer – Tyree Cooper (Singles: 10 Weeks)*   pos/wks

25 Feb 89	TURN UP THE BASS *ffrr FFR 24* [1]	12	7
6 May 89	HARDCORE HIP HOUSE *DJ International DJIN 11*	70	2
2 Dec 89	MOVE YOUR BODY *CBS 655470 7* [2]	72	1

[1] Tyree featuring Kool Rock Steady [2] Tyree featuring JMD

TYRELL CORPORATION *UK, male vocal /*
instrumental duo – Joe Watson and Tony Barry (Singles: 9 Weeks)   pos/wks

14 Mar 92	THE BOTTLE *Volante TYR 1*	71	1

15 Aug 92	GOING HOME *Volante TYR 2*	58	2
10 Oct 92	WAKING WITH A STRANGER / ONE DAY *Volante TYRS 3*	59	1
24 Sep 94	YOU'RE NOT HERE *Cooltempo CDCOOL 292*	42	2
14 Jan 95	BETTER DAYS AHEAD *Cooltempo CDCOOL 303*	29	3

TYRESE
US, male vocalist – Tyrese Gibson (Singles: 6 Weeks)   pos/wks

31 Jul 99	NOBODY ELSE *RCA 74321688282*	59	1
25 Sep 99	SWEET LADY *RCA 74321700842*	55	1
26 Jul 03	HOW YOU GONNA ACT LIKE THAT *J 82876544892*	30	4

TZANT *UK, male rap / instrumental duo – Jamie White*
and Marcus Thomas (aka ODC MC) (Singles: 10 Weeks)   pos/wks

7 Sep 96	HOT AND WET (BELIEVE IT) *Logic 74321376832*	36	2
25 Apr 98	SOUNDS OF WICKEDNESS *Logic 74321568842*	11	6
22 Aug 98	BOUNCE WITH THE MASSIVE *Logic 74321602102*	39	2

Judie TZUKE
UK, female vocalist (Singles: 10 Weeks, Albums: 61 Weeks)   pos/wks

14 Jul 79	STAY WITH ME TILL DAWN *Rocket XPRES 17*	16	10
4 Aug 79	WELCOME TO THE CRUISE *Rocket TRAIN 7*	14	17
10 May 80	● SPORTS CAR *Rocket TRAIN 9*	7	11
16 May 81	I AM PHOENIX *Rocket TRAIN 15*	17	10
17 Apr 82	SHOOT THE MOON *Chrysalis CDL 1382*	19	10
30 Oct 82	ROAD NOISE – THE OFFICIAL BOOTLEG *Chrysalis CTY 1405*	39	4
1 Oct 83	RITMO *Chrysalis CDL 1442*	26	5
15 Jun 85	THE CAT IS OUT *Legacy LLP 102*	35	3
29 Apr 89	TURNING STONES *Polydor 839087 1*	57	1

UB40   22   Top 500
Reggae's most successful transatlantic group: includes brothers Ali (v/g) and Robin (v/g) Campbell and Earl Falconer (b). Only three groups can claim more chart hits than this Birmingham act, named after the number of the UK unemployment benefit form (Singles: 345 Weeks, Albums: 610 Weeks)   pos/wks

8 Mar 80	● KING / FOOD FOR THOUGHT *Graduate GRAD 6* [1]	4	13
14 Jun 80	● MY WAY OF THINKING / I THINK IT'S GOING TO RAIN *Graduate GRAD 8* [1]	6	10
1 Nov 80	● THE EARTH DIES SCREAMING / DREAM A LIE *Graduate GRAD 10*	10	12
23 May 81	DON'T LET IT PASS YOU BY / DON'T SLOW DOWN *DEP International DEP 1*	16	9
8 Aug 81	● ONE IN TEN *DEP International DEP 2*	7	10
13 Feb 82	I WON'T CLOSE MY EYES *DEP International DEP 3*	32	6
15 May 82	LOVE IS ALL IS ALRIGHT *DEP International DEP 4*	29	7
28 Aug 82	SO HERE I AM *DEP International DEP 5*	25	9
5 Feb 83	I'VE GOT MINE *DEP International 7 DEP 6*	45	4
20 Aug 83	★ RED RED WINE *DEP International 7 DEP 7* ▲	1	14
15 Oct 83	● PLEASE DON'T MAKE ME CRY *DEP International 7 DEP 8*	10	10
10 Dec 83	MANY RIVERS TO CROSS *DEP International 7 DEP 9*	16	8
17 Mar 84	CHERRY OH BABY *DEP International DEP 10*	12	8
22 Sep 84	● IF IT HAPPENS AGAIN *DEP International DEP 11*	9	8
1 Dec 84	RIDDLE ME *DEP International DEP 15*	59	2
3 Aug 85	★ I GOT YOU BABE *DEP International DEP 20* [2]	1	13

		pos	wks
26 Oct 85 ●	DON'T BREAK MY HEART *DEP International DEP 22*	3	13
12 Jul 86 ●	SING OUR OWN SONG *DEP International DEP 23*	5	9
27 Sep 86	ALL I WANT TO DO *DEP International DEP 24*	41	4
17 Jan 87	RAT IN MI KITCHEN *DEP International DEP 25*	12	7
9 May 87	WATCHDOGS *DEP International DEP 26*	39	4
10 Oct 87	MAYBE TOMORROW *DEP International DEP 27*	14	8
27 Feb 88	RECKLESS *EMI EM 41* [3]	17	8
18 Jun 88 ●	BREAKFAST IN BED *DEP International DEP 29* [2]	6	11
20 Aug 88	WHERE DID I GO WRONG *DEP International DEP 30*	26	6
17 Jun 89	I WOULD DO FOR YOU *DEP International DEP 32*	45	4
18 Nov 89 ●	HOMELY GIRL *DEP International DEP 33*	6	10
27 Jan 90	HERE I AM (COME AND TAKE ME) *DEP International DEP 34* 46		3
31 Mar 90 ●	KINGSTON TOWN *DEP International DEP 35*	4	12
28 Jul 90	WEAR YOU TO THE BALL *DEP International DEP 36*	35	6
3 Nov 90 ●	I'LL BE YOUR BABY TONIGHT *EMI EM 167* [4]	6	10
1 Dec 90	IMPOSSIBLE LOVE *DEP International DEP 37*	47	2
2 Feb 91	THE WAY YOU DO THE THINGS YOU DO		
	DEP International DEP 38	49	3
12 Dec 92	ONE IN TEN (re-mix) *ZTT ZANG 39* [5]	17	8
22 May 93 ★	(I CAN'T HELP) FALLING IN LOVE WITH YOU		
	DEP International DEPDG 40 ▲	1	16
21 Aug 93 ●	HIGHER GROUND *DEP International DEPD 41*	8	9
11 Dec 93	BRING ME YOUR CUP *DEP International DEPD 42*	24	6
2 Apr 94	C'EST LA VIE *DEP International DEPD 43*	37	3
27 Aug 94	REGGAE MUSIC *DEP International DEPDG 44*	28	2
4 Nov 95	UNTIL MY DYING DAY *DEP International DEPD 45*	15	4
30 Aug 97	TELL ME IT IS TRUE *DEP International DEP 48*	14	4
15 Nov 97	ALWAYS THERE *DEP International DEPD 49*	53	1
10 Oct 98 ●	COME BACK DARLING *DEP International DEPD 50*	10	6
19 Dec 98	HOLLY HOLY *DEP International DEPD 51*	31	3
1 May 99	THE TRAIN IS COMING *DEP International DEPD 52*	30	2
9 Dec 00	LIGHT MY FIRE *DEP International DEPD 53*	63	1
20 Oct 01	SINCE I MET YOU LADY / SPARKLE OF MY EYES		
	DEP International DEPD 55 [6]	40	2
2 Mar 02	COVER UP *DEP International DEPD 56*	54	1
8 Nov 03	SWING LOW *DEP International DEPD 58* [7]	17	14
6 Sep 80 ●	SIGNING OFF *Graduate GRADLP 2*	2	71
6 Jun 81 ●	PRESENT ARMS *DEP International LPDEP 1*	2	38
10 Oct 81	PRESENT ARMS IN DUB *DEP International LPDEP 2*	38	7
28 Aug 82	THE SINGLES ALBUM *Graduate GRADLSP 3*	17	8
9 Oct 82 ●	UB 44 *DEP International LPDEP 3*	4	8
26 Feb 83	UB40 LIVE *DEP International LPDEP 4*	44	5
24 Sep 83 ★	LABOUR OF LOVE *DEP International LPDEP 5* ■	1	76
20 Oct 84 ●	GEFFERY MORGAN *DEP International LPDEP 6*	3	14
14 Sep 85	BAGGARIDDIM *DEP International LPDEP 10*	14	23
9 Aug 86 ●	RAT IN THE KITCHEN *DEP International LPDEP 11*	8	20
7 Nov 87 ●	THE BEST OF UB40 VOLUME ONE *Virgin UBTV 1*	3	132
23 Jul 88	UB40 *DEP International LPDEP 13*	12	12
9 Dec 89 ●	LABOUR OF LOVE II *DEP International LPDEP 14*	3	69
24 Jul 93 ★	PROMISES AND LIES *DEP International DEPCD 15* ■	1	37
12 Nov 94 ●	LABOUR OF LOVE VOLUMES I AND II (re-issue)		
	DEP International DEPDD 1	5	15
11 Nov 95	THE BEST OF UB40 – VOLUME TWO		
	DEP International DUBTV 2	12	11
12 Jul 97 ●	GUNS IN THE GHETTO *DEP International DEPCD 16*	7	9
24 Oct 98 ●	LABOUR OF LOVE III *DEP International DEPCD 18*	8	12
4 Nov 00 ●	THE VERY BEST OF UB40 1980-2000 *Virgin DUBTVX 3*	7	23
3 Nov 01	COVER UP *Virgin DEPCD 19*	29	2
14 Jun 03 ●	LABOUR OF LOVE – VOL I II & III *Virgin 5847242*	7	16
15 Nov 03	HOME GROWN *DEP International DEPCD 22*	49	2

[1] U.B.40 [2] UB40 featuring Chrissie Hynde [3] Afrika Bambaataa and Family featuring UB40 [4] Robert Palmer and UB40 [5] 808 State vs UB40 [6] UB40 featuring Lady Saw [7] UB40 featuring United Colours of Sound

UBM
Germany, male / female vocal / instrumental group (Singles: 1 Week) pos/wks

		pos	wks
23 May 98	LOVIN' YOU *Logic 74321571692*	46	1

UCC See URBAN COOKIE COLLECTIVE

UD PROJECT
Germany, male producer – Vick Krishna (Singles: 10 Weeks) pos/wks

		pos	wks
4 Oct 03	SUMMER JAM *Free 2 Air / Kontor 0150345 KON* [1]	14	6
21 Feb 04	SATURDAY NIGHT *Free 2 Air / Kontor 0152955 KON*	19	4

[1] UD Project vs. Sunclub

UFO
UK / Germany, male vocal / instrumental group (Singles: 31 Weeks, Albums: 48 Weeks) pos/wks

		pos	wks
5 Aug 78	ONLY YOU CAN ROCK ME *Chrysalis CHS 2241*	50	4
27 Jan 79	DOCTOR DOCTOR *Chrysalis CHS 2287*	35	6
31 Mar 79	SHOOT, SHOOT *Chrysalis CHS 2318*	48	5
12 Jan 80	YOUNG BLOOD *Chrysalis CHS 2399*	36	5
17 Jan 81	LONELY HEART *Chrysalis CHS 2482*	41	5
30 Jan 82	LET IT RAIN *Chrysalis CHS 2576*	62	3
19 Mar 83	WHEN IT'S TIME TO ROCK *Chrysalis CHS 2672*	70	3
4 Jun 77	LIGHTS OUT *Chrysalis CHR 1127*	54	2
15 Jul 78	OBSESSION *Chrysalis CDL 1182*	26	7
10 Feb 79 ●	STRANGERS IN THE NIGHT *Chrysalis CJT 5*	7	11
19 Jan 80	NO PLACE TO RUN *Chrysalis CDL 1239*	11	7
24 Jan 81	THE WILD THE WILLING AND THE INNOCENT		
	Chrysalis CHR 1307	19	5
20 Feb 82 ●	MECHANIX *Chrysalis CHR 1360*	8	6
12 Feb 83	MAKING CONTACT *Chrysalis CHR 1402*	32	4
3 Sep 83	HEADSTONE – THE BEST OF UFO *Chrysalis CTY 1437*	39	4
16 Nov 85	MISDEMEANOUR *Chrysalis CHR 1518*	74	2

U4EA featuring BERRI See NEW ATLANTIC

UHF
US, male instrumental / production group (Singles: 4 Weeks) pos/wks

		pos	wks
14 Dec 91	UHF / EVERYTHING *XL Recordings XLS 25*	46	4

U.T.F.O. *US, male vocal group (Albums: 1 Week)* pos/wks

		pos	wks
16 Mar 85	ROXANNE ROXANNE (6 TRACK VERSION)		
	Streetwave 6 Track XKHAN 506	72	1

UGLY DUCKLING
US, male production / rap trio (Singles: 1 Week) pos/wks

		pos	wks
13 Oct 01	A LITTLE SAMBA *XL Recordings XLS 135CD*	70	1

UGLY KID JOE *US, male vocal / instrumental group (Singles: 28 Weeks, Albums: 42 Weeks)* pos/wks

		pos	wks
16 May 92 ●	EVERYTHING ABOUT YOU *Mercury MER 367*	3	9
22 Aug 92	NEIGHBOR *Mercury MER 374*	28	4
31 Oct 92	SO DAMN COOL *Mercury MER 383*	44	2
13 Mar 93 ●	CATS IN THE CRADLE *Mercury MERCD 385*	7	9
19 Jun 93	BUSY BEE *Mercury MERCD 389*	39	2
8 Jul 95	MILKMAN'S SON *Mercury MERCD 435*	39	2
13 Jun 92 ●	AS UGLY AS THEY WANNA BE *Mercury 8688232*	9	13
12 Sep 92	AMERICA'S LEAST WANTED *Vertigo 5125712*	11	24
17 Jun 95	MENACE TO SOBRIETY *Mercury 5282622*	25	5

Tillmann UHRMACHER (see also TILLMANN and REIS)
Germany, male producer (Singles: 3 Weeks) pos/wks

		pos	wks
23 Mar 02	ON THE RUN *Direction 6721352*	16	3

UK
UK, male vocal / instrumental group (Singles: 2 Weeks, Albums: 3 Weeks) pos/wks

		pos	wks
30 Jun 79	NOTHING TO LOSE *Polydor POSP 55*	67	2
27 May 78	U.K. *Polydor 2302 080*	43	3

UK *Canada / Spain, male vocal / instrumental group (Singles: 1 Week)* pos/wks

		pos	wks
3 Aug 96	SMALL TOWN BOY *Media MCSTD 400*	74	1

UK APACHI / APACHE *UK, male vocalist / rapper / instrumentalist – Lafta Wahab (Singles: 4 Weeks)* pos/wks

		pos	wks
1 Oct 94	ORIGINAL NUTTAH *Sound of Underground SOUR 008CD* [1]	39	3
28 Jul 01	SIGNS *Outcaste OUT 38CD1* [2]	63	1

[1] UK Apachi with Shy FX [2] DJ Badmarsh and Shri featuring UK Apache

UK MIXMASTERS
UK, male producer – Nigel Wright (Singles: 15 Weeks) pos/wks

		pos	wks
2 Feb 91	THE NIGHT FEVER MEGAMIX *IQ ZB 44339* [1]	23	5
27 Jul 91	LUCKY 7 MEGAMIX *IQ ZB 44731*	43	3
14 Dec 91	THE BARE NECESSITIES MEGAMIX *Connect ZB 35135*	14	7

[1] Mixmasters

The UK PLAYERS
UK, male vocal / instrumental group (Singles: 3 Weeks) pos/wks

14 May 83		LOVE'S GONNA GET YOU *RCA 326*	52	3

UK SUBS
UK, male vocal / instrumental group (Singles: 39 Weeks, Albums: 26 Weeks) pos/wks

23 Jun 79		STRANGLEHOLD *Gem GEMS 5*	26	8
8 Sep 79		TOMORROW'S GIRLS *Gem GEMS 10*	28	6
1 Dec 79		SHE'S NOT THERE / KICKS (EP) *Gem GEMS 14*	36	7
8 Mar 80		WARHEAD *Gem GEMS 23*	30	4
17 May 80		TEENAGE *Gem GEMS 30*	32	5
25 Oct 80		PARTY IN PARIS *Gem GEMS 42*	37	4
18 Apr 81		KEEP ON RUNNIN' (TILL YOU BURN) *Gem GEMS 45*	41	5
13 Oct 79		ANOTHER KIND OF BLUES *Gem GEMLP 100*	21	6
19 Apr 80		BRAND NEW AGE *Gem GEMLP 106*	18	9
27 Sep 80	●	CRASH COURSE *Gem GEMLP 111*	8	6
21 Feb 81		DIMINISHED RESPONSIBILITY *Gem GEMLP 112*	18	5

Tracks on She's Not There / Kicks (EP): She's Not There / Kicks / Victim / The Same Thing

UKNY See Jason NEVINS

Tracey ULLMAN
UK, female vocalist / actor (Singles: 49 Weeks, Albums: 22 Weeks) pos/wks

19 Mar 83	●	BREAKAWAY *Stiff BUY 168*	4	11
24 Sep 83	●	THEY DON'T KNOW *Stiff BUY 180*	2	11
3 Dec 83		MOVE OVER DARLING *Stiff BUY 195*	8	9
3 Mar 84		MY GUY *Stiff BUY 197*	23	6
28 Jul 84		SUNGLASSES *Stiff BUY 205*	18	9
27 Oct 84		HELPLESS *Stiff BUY 211*	61	3
3 Dec 83		YOU BROKE MY HEART IN 17 PLACES *Stiff SEEZ 51*	14	20
8 Dec 84		YOU CAUGHT ME OUT *Stiff SEEZ 56*	92	2

ULTIMATE KAOS
UK, male vocal group (Singles: 28 Weeks, Albums: 1 Week) pos/wks

22 Oct 94	●	SOME GIRLS (re) *Wild Card CARDD 12*	9	9
21 Jan 95		HOOCHIE BOOTY *Wild Card CARDW 14*	17	4
1 Apr 95		SHOW A LITTLE LOVE *Wild Card CARDW 18*	23	5
1 Jul 95		RIGHT HERE *Wild Card 5795832*	18	4
8 Mar 97		CASANOVA *Polydor 5759312*	24	3
18 Jul 98		CASANOVA (re-issue) *Mercury MERCD 505*	29	2
5 Jun 99		ANYTHING YOU WANT (I'VE GOT IT) *Mercury MERCD 510*	52	1
29 Apr 95		ULTIMATE KAOS *Polydor 5274442*	51	1

ULTRA
UK, male vocal / instrumental group (Singles: 22 Weeks, Albums: 2 Weeks) pos/wks

18 Apr 98		SAY YOU DO *East West EW 124CD*	11	7
4 Jul 98		SAY IT ONCE *East West EW 171CD1*	16	6
10 Oct 98		THE RIGHT TIME (re) *East West EW 182CD*	28	3
16 Jan 99	●	RESCUE ME *East West EW 193CD1*	8	6
6 Feb 99		ULTRA *East West 3984222452*	37	2

ULTRA HIGH
UK, male vocalist – Michael McCloud (Singles: 3 Weeks) pos/wks

2 Dec 95		STAY WITH ME *MCA MCSTD 40007*	36	2
20 Jul 96		ARE YOU READY FOR LOVE *MCA MCSTD 40039*	45	1

ULTRA VIVID SCENE
US, male vocalist – Kurt Ralske (Albums: 1 Week) pos/wks

19 May 90		JOY 1967-1990 *4AD CAD 005*	58	1

ULTRABEAT
UK, male DJ / production / vocal trio (Singles: 31 Weeks) pos/wks

16 Aug 03	●	PRETTY GREEN EYES *All Around the World CDGLOBE 281*	2	14
27 Dec 03		FEELIN' FINE *All Around the World CDGLOBE 320*	12	12
11 Sep 04		BETTER THAN LIFE *All Around the World CDGLOBE 360*	23	5

ULTRACYNIC
UK, male / female vocal / instrumental group (Singles: 3 Weeks) pos/wks

29 Aug 92		NOTHING IS FOREVER *380 PEW 2*	50	2
19 Apr 97		NOTHING IS FOREVER (re-mix) *All Around the World CDGLOBE 139*	47	1

ULTRAMARINE
UK, male instrumental duo (Singles: 4 Weeks, Albums: 1 Week) pos/wks

24 Jul 93		KINGDOM *Blanco Y Negro NEG 65CD*	46	2
29 Jan 94		BAREFOOT (EP) *Blanco Y Negro NEG 67CD*	61	1
27 Apr 96		HYMN *Blanco Y Negro NEG 87CD* [1]	65	1
4 Sep 93		UNITED KINGDOMS *Blanco Y Negro 4509934252*	49	1

[1] Ultramarine featuring David McAlmont

Tracks on Barefoot (EP): Hooter / The Badger / Urf / Happy Land

ULTRA-SONIC
UK, male instrumental / production duo (Singles: 2 Weeks, Albums: 1 Week) pos/wks

3 Sep 94		OBSESSION *Clubscene DCSRT 027*	75	1
21 Sep 96		DO YOU BELIEVE IN LOVE *Clubscene DCSRT 070*	47	1
11 Nov 95		GLOBAL TEKNO *Clubscene DCSR 007*	58	1

ULTRASOUND
UK, male / female vocal / instrumental group (Singles: 5 Weeks, Albums: 1 Week) pos/wks

7 Mar 98		BEST WISHES *Nude NUD 33CD*	68	1
13 Jun 98		STAY YOUNG *Nude NUD 35CD1*	30	2
10 Apr 99		FLOODLIT WORLD *Nude NUD 41CD1*	39	2
1 May 99		EVERYTHING PICTURE *Nude NUDE 12CD*	23	1

ULTRAVOX　136　Top 500
Ground-breaking British electro-rock quartet: Midge Ure (v/g) (replaced John Foxx in 1979), Billy Currie (k/syn), Chris Cross (b/syn), Warren Cann (d). Ex-Slik and Visage vocalist Ure was a driving force behind Band Aid hits, Live Aid and Nelson Mandela's birthday concerts (Singles: 142 Weeks, Albums: 227 Weeks) pos/wks

5 Jul 80		SLEEPWALK *Chrysalis CHS 2441*	29	11
18 Oct 80		PASSING STRANGERS *Chrysalis CHS 2457*	57	4
17 Jan 81		VIENNA *Chrysalis CHS 2481*	2	14
28 Mar 81		SLOW MOTION *Island WIP 6691*	33	4
6 Jun 81	●	ALL STOOD STILL *Chrysalis CHS 2522*	8	10
22 Aug 81		THE THIN WALL *Chrysalis CHS 2540*	14	8
7 Nov 81		THE VOICE *Chrysalis CHS 2559*	16	12
25 Sep 82		REAP THE WILD WIND *Chrysalis CHS 2639*	12	9
27 Nov 82		HYMN *Chrysalis CHS 2657*	11	11
19 Mar 83		VISIONS IN BLUE *Chrysalis CHS 2676*	15	6
4 Jun 83		WE CAME TO DANCE *Chrysalis VOX 1*	18	7
11 Feb 84		ONE SMALL DAY *Chrysalis VOX 2*	27	6
19 May 84	●	DANCING WITH TEARS IN MY EYES (re) *Chrysalis UV 1*	3	11
7 Jul 84		LAMENT (re) *Chrysalis UV 2*	22	7
20 Oct 84		LOVE'S GREAT ADVENTURE *Chrysalis UV 3*	12	9
27 Sep 86		SAME OLD STORY *Chrysalis UV 4*	31	4
22 Nov 86		ALL FALL DOWN *Chrysalis UV 5*	30	5
6 Feb 93		VIENNA (re-issue) *Chrysalis CDCHSS 3936*	13	4
19 Jul 80	●	VIENNA *Chrysalis CHR 1296*	3	72
19 Sep 81	●	RAGE IN EDEN *Chrysalis CDL 1338*	4	23
23 Oct 82	●	QUARTET *Chrysalis CDL 1394*	6	30
22 Oct 83	●	MONUMENT – THE SOUNDTRACK *Chrysalis CUX 1452*	9	15
14 Apr 84	●	LAMENT *Chrysalis CDL 1459*	8	26
10 Nov 84	●	THE COLLECTION *Chrysalis UTV 1*	2	53
25 Oct 86	●	U-VOX *Chrysalis CDL 1545*	9	6
10 Nov 01		THE VERY BEST OF MIDGE URE & ULTRAVOX *EMI 5358112*	45	2

UMBOZA (see also MUKKAA; EYE TO EYE featuring Taka BOOM)
UK, male instrumental / production duo – Bryan Chamberlyn and Stuart Crichton (Singles: 9 Weeks) pos/wks

23 Sep 95		CRY INDIA *Positiva CDTIV 43*	19	4
20 Jul 96		SUNSHINE *Positiva CDTIV 47*	14	5

Piero UMILIANI
Italy, orchestra and chorus – leader b. 1926, d. Feb 2001 (Singles: 8 Weeks) pos/wks

30 Apr 77	●	MAH-NA, MAH-NA *EMI International INT 530*	8	8

UNA MAS
UK, male production duo (Singles: 1 Week) pos/wks

6 Apr 02		I WILL FOLLOW *Defected DFECT 47CDS*	55	1

UNATION
UK, male / female vocal / instrumental group (Singles: 3 Weeks) pos/wks

5 Jun 93		HIGHER AND HIGHER *MCA MCSTD 1773*	42	2
7 Aug 93		DO YOU BELIEVE IN LOVE *MCA MCSTD 1796*	75	1

Singles re-entries are listed as (re), (2re), (3re)…. which signifies that the hit re-entered the chart once, twice or three times…

UNBELIEVABLE TRUTH
*UK, male vocal /
instrumental group (Singles: 5 Weeks, Albums: 2 Weeks)*   pos/wks

14 Feb 98	HIGHER THAN REASON *Virgin VSCDT 1676*	38	2
9 May 98	SOLVED *Virgin VSCDT 1684*	39	2
18 Jul 98	SETTLE DOWN / DUNE SEA *Virgin VSCDT 1697*	46	1
23 May 98	ALMOST HERE *Virgin CDV 2849*	21	2

UNCANNY ALLIANCE
*US, male / female vocal / instrumental
duo – Brinsley Evans and E.V. Mystique (Singles: 5 Weeks)*   pos/wks

| 19 Dec 92 | I GOT MY EDUCATION *A&M AM 0128* | 39 | 5 |

UNCLE KRACKER
*US, male vocalist –
Matt Shafer (Singles: 18 Weeks, Albums: 3 Weeks)*   pos/wks

| 8 Sep 01 ● | FOLLOW ME *Atlantic AT 0108CD* | 3 | 18 |
| 22 Sep 01 | DOUBLE WIDE *Atlantic 7567832792* | 40 | 3 |

UNCLE SAM
US, male vocalist – Sam Turner (Singles: 2 Weeks)   pos/wks

| 16 May 98 | I DON'T EVER WANT TO SEE YOU AGAIN *Epic 6656382* | 30 | 2 |

UN-CUT
UK, male production duo and female vocalist (Singles: 4 Weeks)   pos/wks

| 29 Mar 03 | MIDNIGHT *WEA WEA 364CD1* | 26 | 3 |
| 28 Jun 03 | FALLIN' *WEA WEA 368CD1* | 63 | 1 |

UNDERCOVER
*UK, male vocal /
instrumental group (Singles: 30 Weeks, Albums: 9 Weeks)*   pos/wks

15 Aug 92 ●	BAKER STREET *PWL International PWL 239*	2	14
14 Nov 92 ●	NEVER LET HER SLIP AWAY *PWL International PWL 255*	5	11
6 Feb 93	I WANNA STAY WITH YOU *PWL International PWCD 258*	28	3
14 Aug 93	LOVESICK *PWL International PWCD 271* [1]	62	1
3 Jul 04	VIVA ENGLAND *MCS MCSRECS 1*	49	1
5 Dec 92	CHECK OUT THE GROOVE *PWL International HFCD 26*	26	9

[1] Undercover featuring John Matthews

The UNDERTAKERS
UK, male vocal / instrumental group (Singles: 1 Week)   pos/wks

| 9 Apr 64 | JUST A LITTLE BIT *Pye 7N 15607* | 49 | 1 |

The UNDERTONES (see also Feargal SHARKEY) *UK, male
vocal / instrumental group (Singles: 67 Weeks, Albums: 52 Weeks)*   pos/wks

21 Oct 78	TEENAGE KICKS *Sire SIR 4007*	31	6
3 Feb 79	GET OVER YOU *Sire SIR 4010*	57	4
28 Apr 79	JIMMY JIMMY *Sire SIR 4015*	16	10
21 Jul 79	HERE COMES THE SUMMER *Sire SIR 4022*	34	6
20 Oct 79	YOU'VE GOT MY NUMBER (WHY DON'T YOU USE IT!) *Sire SIR 4024*	32	6
5 Apr 80 ●	MY PERFECT COUSIN *Sire SIR 4038*	9	10
5 Jul 80	WEDNESDAY WEEK *Sire SIR 4042*	11	9
2 May 81	IT'S GOING TO HAPPEN! *Ardeck ARDS 8*	18	9
25 Jul 81	JULIE OCEAN *Ardeck ARDS 9*	41	5
9 Jul 83	TEENAGE KICKS (re-issue) *Ardeck ARDS 1*	60	2
19 May 79	THE UNDERTONES *Sire SRK 6071*	13	21
26 Apr 80 ●	HYPNOTISED *Sire SRK 6088*	6	10
16 May 81	POSITIVE TOUCH *Ardeck ARD 103*	17	6
19 Mar 83	THE SIN OF PRIDE *Ardeck ARD 104*	43	5
10 Dec 83	ALL WRAPPED UP *Ardeck ARD 1654281/3*	67	4
14 Jun 86	CHER O'BOWLIES – PICK OF THE UNDERTONES *Ardeck EMS 1172*	96	1
25 Sep 93	THE BEST OF THE UNDERTONES – TEENAGE KICKS *Castle Communications CTVCD 121*	45	3
13 Sep 03	TEENAGE KICKS – THE BEST OF THE UNDERTONES *Sanctuary / Sony TV TVSAN 005*	35	2

UNDERWORLD
*UK, male instrumental /
vocal group (Singles: 49 Weeks, Albums: 54 Weeks)*   pos/wks

18 Dec 93	SPIKEE / DOGMAN GO *Junior Boy's Own JBO 17CD*	63	1
25 Jun 94	DARK AND LONG *Junior Boy's Own JBO 19CDS*	57	1
13 May 95	BORN SLIPPY *Junior Boy's Own JBO 29CDS*	52	2
18 May 96	PEARL'S GIRL *Junior Boy's Own JBO 38CDS 1*	24	2
13 Jul 96 ●	BORN SLIPPY (re) (re-mix) *Junior Boy's Own JBO 44CDS*	2	21
9 Nov 96	PEARL'S GIRL (re-issue) *Junior Boy's Own JBO 45CDS 1*	22	3
27 Mar 99	PUSH UPSTAIRS *Junior Boy's Own JBO 5005443*	12	4

5 Jun 99	JUMBO *Junior Boy's Own JBO 5007193*	21	2
28 Aug 99	KING OF SNAKE *Junior Boy's Own JBO 5008793*	17	3
2 Sep 00	COWGIRL *Junior Boy's Own JBO 5012513*	24	2
14 Sep 00	TWO MONTHS OFF *Junior Boy's Own JBO 5020093*	12	4
1 Feb 03	DINOSAUR ADVENTURE 3D *Junior Boy's Own JBO 5020523*	34	1
8 Nov 03	BORN SLIPPY NUXX (2nd re-mix) *Junior Boy's Own JBO 5024703*	27	3
5 Feb 94	DUBNOBASSWITHMYHEADMAN *Junior Boy's Own JBOCD 1*	12	6
23 Mar 96 ●	SECOND TOUGHEST IN THE INFANTS *Junior Boy's Own JBOCD 4*	9	28
13 Mar 99 ●	BEAUCOUP FISH *JBO JBO 1005438*	3	12
16 Sep 00	UNDERWORLD LIVE: EVERYTHING, EVERYTHING *JBO JBO 1012542*	22	3
28 Sep 02	A HUNDRED DAYS OFF *JBO JBO 1020102*	16	3
15 Nov 03	1992-2002 *JBO JBO 1024698*	43	2

The UNDISPUTED TRUTH
US, male / female vocal group (Singles: 4 Weeks)   pos/wks

| 22 Jan 77 | YOU + ME = LOVE *Warner Bros. K 16804* | 43 | 4 |

U96
Germany, male producer – Alex Christiansen (Singles: 7 Weeks)   pos/wks

29 Aug 92	DAS BOOT *M&G MAGS 28*	18	5
4 Jun 94	INSIDE YOUR DREAMS *Logic 74321209722*	44	1
29 Jun 96	CLUB BIZARRE *Urban 5750152*	70	1

UNION *UK, male instrumental group (Albums: 6 Weeks)*   pos/wks

| 26 Oct 91 | WORLD IN UNION *Columbia 4690471* | 17 | 6 |

UNION featuring the ENGLAND WORLD CUP SQUAD
*UK / Holland, male instrumental group
and UK, rugby team vocalists (Singles: 7 Weeks)*   pos/wks

| 12 Oct 91 | SWING LOW (RUN WITH THE BALL) *Columbia 6575317* | 16 | 7 |

UNION GAP *See Gary PUCKETT and the UNION GAP*

UNION STATION *See Alison KRAUSS and UNION STATION*

UNIQUE
US, male / female vocal / instrumental group (Singles: 7 Weeks)   pos/wks

| 10 Sep 83 | WHAT I GOT IS WHAT YOU NEED *Prelude A 3707* | 27 | 7 |

UNIQUE 3 *UK, male rap / DJ group (Singles: 12 Weeks)*   pos/wks

4 Nov 89	THE THEME *10 TEN 285*	61	3
14 Apr 90	MUSICAL MELODY / WEIGHT FOR THE BASS *10 TEN 298*	29	5
10 Nov 90	RHYTHM TAKES CONTROL *10 TEN 327* [1]	41	3
16 Nov 91	NO MORE *10 TEN 387*	74	1

[1] Unique 3 featuring Karin

UNIT FOUR PLUS TWO *UK, male vocal /
instrumental group – lead vocal Peter Moules (Singles: 29 Weeks)*   pos/wks

13 Feb 64	GREEN FIELDS *Decca F 11821*	48	2
25 Feb 65 ★	CONCRETE AND CLAY *Decca F 12071*	1	15
13 May 65	(YOU'VE) NEVER BEEN IN LOVE LIKE THIS BEFORE *Decca F 12144*	14	11
17 Mar 66	BABY NEVER SAY GOODBYE *Decca F 12333*	49	1

UNITED CITIZEN FEDERATION featuring Sarah BRIGHTMAN
UK, male production duo and UK, female vocalist (Singles: 1 Week)   pos/wks

| 14 Feb 98 | STARSHIP TROOPERS *Coalition COLA 040CD* | 58 | 1 |

UNITED COLOURS OF SOUND *See UB40*

UNITED KINGDOM SYMPHONY
UK, male / female orchestra (Singles: 4 Weeks)   pos/wks

| 27 Jul 85 | SHADES (THEME FROM THE CROWN PAINT TELEVISION COMMERCIAL) *Food for Thought YUM 108* | 68 | 4 |

UNITING NATIONS *UK, male production duo –
Paul Keenan and Daz Sampson (Singles: 4 Weeks)*   pos/wks

| 4 Dec 04 | OUT OF TOUCH *Gusto CDGUS 13* | 12 | 4+ |

UNITONE *See Laurel AITKEN and the UNITONE*

UNITONE ROCKERS featuring STEEL
UK, male vocal / instrumental group (Singles: 1 Week) pos/wks

26 Jun 93	CHILDREN OF THE REVOLUTION *The Hit Label HLC 4*	60	1

UNITY
UK, male / female vocal / instrumental group (Singles: 2 Weeks) pos/wks

31 Aug 91	UNITY *Cardiac CNY 6*	64	2

UNIVERSAL
Australia, male vocal group (Singles: 6 Weeks) pos/wks

2 Aug 97	ROCK ME GOOD *London LONCD 397*	19	4
18 Oct 97	MAKE IT WITH YOU *London LONCD 404*	33	2

UNIVERSAL PROJECT
UK, male production group (Singles: 1 Week) pos/wks

1 Jun 02	VESSEL *Virus VRS 010*	61	1

'Vessel' shared chart billing with 'Pacman' by Ed Rush & Optical

UNJUSTIFIED ANCIENTS OF MU See 1300 DRUMS featuring the UNJUSTIFIED ANCIENTS OF MU

UNKLE
US / UK, male DJ / production duo – Josh Davis and James Lavelle (Singles: 13 Weeks, Albums: 12 Weeks) pos/wks

20 Feb 99 ●	BE THERE *Mo Wax MW 108CD1* [1]	8	6
17 Mar 01	NARCO TOURISTS *Soma SOMA 100CD* [2]	66	1
6 Sep 03	EYE FOR AN EYE *Mo Wax CID 826*	31	2
15 Nov 03	IN A STATE *Mo Wax CID 839*	44	2
27 Nov 04	REIGN *Mo Wax GUSIN 007CDS* [1]	40	2
21 Jan 95	THE TIME HAS COME (EP) *Mo Wax MW 028P* [1]	73	1
5 Sep 98 ●	PSYENCE FICTION *Mo Wax MW 085CD*	4	9
4 Oct 03	NEVER NEVER LAND *Mo Wax MWU 001CD*	24	2

[1] Unkle featuring Ian Brown [2] Slam vs Unkle [1] U.N.K.L.E.

UNO CLIO featuring Martine McCUTCHEON
UK, male instrumental group and UK, female vocalist (Singles: 1 Week) pos/wks

18 Nov 95	ARE YOU MAN ENOUGH *Avex UK AVEXCD 14*	62	1

The UNTOUCHABLES
US, male vocal / instrumental group (Singles: 16 Weeks, Albums: 7 Weeks) pos/wks

6 Apr 85	FREE YOURSELF *Stiff BUY 221*	26	11
27 Jul 85	I SPY FOR THE FBI *Stiff BUY 227*	59	5
13 Jul 85	WILD CHILD *Stiff SEEZ 57*	51	7

UP YER RONSON featuring Mary PEARCE
UK, male / female vocal / instrumental group (Singles: 7 Weeks) pos/wks

5 Aug 95	LOST IN LOVE *Hi-Life 5795572*	27	3
30 Mar 96	ARE YOU GONNA BE THERE *Hi-Life 5763272*	27	2
19 Apr 97	I WILL BE RELEASED *Hi-Life 5737352*	32	2

Phil UPCHURCH COMBO
US, male instrumental group – leader Phil Upchurch – bass guitar (Singles: 2 Weeks) pos/wks

5 May 66	YOU CAN'T SIT DOWN *Sue WI 4005*	39	2

The UPSETTERS
Jamaica, male instrumental group (Singles: 15 Weeks) pos/wks

4 Oct 69 ●	RETURN OF DJANGO / DOLLAR IN THE TEETH *Upsetter US 301*	5	15

Dawn UPSHAW (soprano) / LONDON SINFONIETTA / David ZINMAN (conductor)
US, female vocalist, UK, orchestra and US, conductor (Albums: 18 Weeks) pos/wks

23 Jan 93 ●	GORECKI SYMPHONY NO.3 *Elektra Nonsuch 7559792822*	6	18

UPSIDE DOWN
UK, male vocal group (Singles: 16 Weeks) pos/wks

20 Jan 96	CHANGE YOUR MIND *World CDWORLD 1A*	11	7
13 Apr 96	EVERY TIME I FALL IN LOVE (re) *World CDWORLD 2A*	18	4
29 Jun 96	NEVER FOUND A LOVE LIKE THIS BEFORE *World CDWORLD 3A*	19	3
23 Nov 96	IF YOU LEAVE ME NOW *World CDWORLD 4A*	27	2

URBAN ALL STARS
UK, male producer – Norman Cook and US, male / female vocal / instrumental groups (Singles: 2 Weeks) pos/wks

27 Aug 88	IT BEGAN IN AFRICA *Urban URB 23*	64	2

URBAN BLUES PROJECT presents Michael PROCTER
US, male vocal / instrumental group (Singles: 1 Week) pos/wks

10 Aug 96	LOVE DON'T LIVE *AM:PM 5817932*	55	1

URBAN COOKIE COLLECTIVE
UK, male / female vocal / instrumental group (Singles: 37 Weeks, Albums: 2 Weeks) pos/wks

10 Jul 93 ●	THE KEY THE SECRET *Pulse 8 CDLOSE 48*	2	16
13 Nov 93 ●	FEELS LIKE HEAVEN *Pulse 8 CDLOSE 55*	5	9
19 Feb 94	SAIL AWAY *Pulse 8 CDLOSE 56*	18	4
23 Apr 94	HIGH ON A HAPPY VIBE *Pulse 8 CDLOSE 60*	31	3
15 Oct 94	BRING IT ON HOME *Pulse 8 CDLOSE 73*	56	1
27 May 95	SPEND THE DAY *Pulse 8 CDLOSE 85*	59	1
9 Sep 95	REST OF MY LOVE *Pulse 8 CDLOSE 93*	67	1
16 Dec 95	SO BEAUTIFUL *Pulse 8 CDLOSE 100*	68	1
24 Aug 96	THE KEY THE SECRET (re-mix) *Pulse 8 CDLOSE 109* [1]	52	1
26 Mar 94	HIGH ON A HAPPY VIBE *Pulse 8 PULSE 13CD*	28	2

[1] UCC

URBAN DISCHARGE featuring SHE
US, male / female vocal / instrumental group (Singles: 1 Week) pos/wks

27 Jan 96	WANNA DROP A HOUSE (ON THAT BITCH) *MCA MCSTD 40020*	51	1

URBAN HYPE
UK, male production / instrumental duo – Robert Dibden and Mark Chitty (Singles: 12 Weeks) pos/wks

11 Jul 92 ●	A TRIP TO TRUMPTON *Faze 2 FAZE 5*	6	8
17 Oct 92	THE FEELING *Faze 2 FAZE 10*	67	1
9 Jan 93	LIVING IN A FANTASY *Faze 2 CDFAZE 13*	57	3

URBAN SHAKEDOWN
UK / Italy, male DJ / production duo – Michael Hearn and Gavin King (Singles: 8 Weeks) pos/wks

27 Jun 92	SOME JUSTICE *Urban Shakedown URBST 1*	23	5
12 Sep 92	BASS SHAKE *Urban Shakedown URBST 2* [1]	59	2
10 Jun 95	SOME JUSTICE (re-recording) *Urban Shakedown URBCD 3* [2]	49	1

[1] Urban Shakedown featuring Mickey Finn [2] Urban Shakedown featuring DBO General

URBAN SOUL
UK / US, male / female vocal / production group (Singles: 11 Weeks) pos/wks

30 Mar 91	ALRIGHT *Cooltempo COOL 231*	60	4
21 Sep 91	ALRIGHT (re-mix) *Cooltempo COOL 244*	43	3
28 Mar 92	ALWAYS *Cooltempo COOL 251*	41	3
13 Jun 98	LOVE IS SO NICE *VC Recordings VCRD 33*	75	1

URBAN SPECIES
UK, male vocal / instrumental group (Singles: 10 Weeks, Albums: 2 Weeks) pos/wks

12 Feb 94	SPIRITUAL LOVE *Talkin Loud TLKCD 45*	35	4
16 Apr 94	BROTHER *Talkin Loud TLKCD 47*	40	3
20 Aug 94	LISTEN *Talkin Loud TLKCD 50* [1]	47	1
6 Mar 99	BLANKET *Talkin Loud TLDD 39* [2]	56	1
7 May 94	LISTEN *Talkin Loud 5186482*	43	2

[1] Urban Species featuring MC Solaar [2] Urban Species featuring Imogen Heap

Midge URE (see also RICH KIDS; SLIK; ULTRAVOX; VISAGE)
UK, male vocalist (Singles: 56 Weeks, Albums: 28 Weeks) pos/wks

12 Jun 82 ●	NO REGRETS *Chrysalis CHS 2618*	9	10
9 Jul 83	AFTER A FASHION *Musicfest FEST 1* [1]	39	4
14 Sep 85 ★	IF I WAS *Chrysalis URE 1*	1	11
16 Nov 85	THAT CERTAIN SMILE *Chrysalis URE 2*	28	4
8 Feb 86	WASTELANDS *Chrysalis URE 3*	46	3
7 Jun 86	CALL OF THE WILD *Chrysalis URE 4*	27	8
20 Aug 88	ANSWERS TO NOTHING *Chrysalis URE 5*	49	4
19 Nov 88	DEAR GOD *Chrysalis URE 6*	55	4
17 Aug 91	COLD COLD HEART *Arista 114555*	17	5
25 May 96	BREATHE *Arista 74321371172*	70	1
19 Oct 85 ●	THE GIFT *Chrysalis CHR 1508*	2	15

10 Sep 88	ANSWERS TO NOTHING *Chrysalis CHR 1649*	.30	3
28 Sep 91	PURE *Arista 211922*	.36	2
6 Mar 93 ●	IF I WAS: THE VERY BEST OF MIDGE URE & ULTRAVOX [1] *Chrysalis CDCHR 1987*	.10	6
10 Nov 01	THE VERY BEST OF MIDGE URE & ULTRAVOX *EMI 5358112* [1]	.45	2

[1] Midge Ure and Mick Karn   [1] Midge Ure and Ultravox

'If I Was: The Very Best of Midge Ure & Ultravox' includes tracks by Ultravox, Visage, Band Aid and Phil Lynott

URGE OVERKILL
US, male vocal / instrumental group (Singles: 6 Weeks)   pos/wks

21 Aug 93	SISTER HAVANA *Geffen GFSTD 51*	.67	1
16 Oct 93	POSITIVE BLEEDING *Geffen GFSTD 57*	.61	1
19 Nov 94	GIRL, YOU'LL BE A WOMAN SOON *MCA MCSTD 2024*	.37	4

URIAH HEEP
UK, male vocal / instrumental group (Albums: 51 Weeks)   pos/wks

13 Nov 71	LOOK AT YOURSELF *Island ILPS 9169*	.39	1
10 Jun 72	DEMONS AND WIZARDS *Bronze ILPS 9193*	.20	11
2 Dec 72	THE MAGICIAN'S BIRTHDAY *Bronze ILPS 9213*	.28	3
19 May 73	LIVE *Island ISLD 1*	.23	8
29 Sep 73	SWEET FREEDOM *Island ILPS 9245*	.18	3
29 Jun 74	WONDERWORLD *Bronze ILPS 9280*	.23	3
5 Jul 75 ●	RETURN TO FANTASY *Bronze ILPS 9335*	.7	6
12 Jun 76	HIGH AND MIGHTY *Island ILPS 9384*	.55	1
22 Mar 80	CONQUEST *Bronze BRON 524*	.37	3
17 Apr 82	ABOMINOG *Bronze BRON 538*	.34	6
18 Jun 83	HEAD FIRST *Bronze BRON 545*	.46	4
6 Apr 85	EQUATOR *Portrait PRT 261414*	.79	2

URUSEI YATSURA
UK, male / female vocal / instrumental group (Singles: 4 Weeks, Albums: 1 Week)   pos/wks

22 Feb 97	STRATEGIC HAMLETS *Che CHE 67CD*	.64	1
28 Jun 97	FAKE FUR *Che CHE 70CD*	.58	1
21 Feb 98	HELLO TIGER *Che CHE 75CD1*	.40	1
6 Jun 98	SLAIN BY ELF *Che CHE 80CD1*	.63	1
14 Mar 98	SLAIN BY *Che CHE 76CD*	.64	1

USA FOR AFRICA
US, male / female vocal charity ensemble (Singles: 9 Weeks, Albums: 5 Weeks)   pos/wks

13 Apr 85 ★	WE ARE THE WORLD *CBS USAID 1* ▲	.1	9
25 May 85	WE ARE THE WORLD *CBS USAID F1* ▲	.31	5

Soloists: Lionel Richie, Stevie Wonder, Paul Simon, Kenny Rogers, James Ingram, Tina Turner, Billy Joel, Michael Jackson, Diana Ross, Dionne Warwick, Willie Nelson, Al Jarreau, Bruce Springsteen, Kenny Loggins, Steve Perry, Daryl Hall, Huey Lewis, Cyndi Lauper, Kim Carnes, Bob Dylan, Ray Charles. Also credited: Dan Aykroyd, Harry Belafonte, Lindsey Buckingham, Sheila E, Bob Geldof, John Oates, Jackie Jackson, La Toya Jackson, Marlon Jackson, Randy Jackson, Tito Jackson, Waylon Jennings, The News, Bette Midler, Jeffrey Osborne, The Pointer Sisters, Smokey Robinson Album contains tracks by various artists in addition to the title track

The USED
US, male vocal / instrumental group (Singles: 1 Week)   pos/wks

22 Mar 03	THE TASTE OF INK *Reprise W 601CD*	.52	1

USHER   339   Top 500
Award-winning R&B vocalist / composer who first charted at the age of 15, b. Usher Raymond, 14 Oct 1978, Chattanooga, Tennessee, US. In the US in 2004, he had three singles simultaneously in the Top 10, replaced himself at No.1 twice and broke an all-time record by spending 28 weeks at No.1 in a calendar year (Singles: 95 Weeks, Albums: 104 Weeks)   pos/wks

18 Mar 95	THINK OF YOU *LaFace 74321269252*	.70	1
31 Jan 98 ★	YOU MAKE ME WANNA ... (re) *LaFace 74321560652* ■	.1	13
2 May 98	NICE & SLOW *LaFace 74321579102* ▲	.24	2
3 Feb 01 ●	POP YA COLLAR *LaFace 74321828692*	.2	9
7 Jul 01 ●	U REMIND ME *LaFace 74321863382* ▲	.3	9
20 Oct 01 ●	U GOT IT BAD *LaFace 74321898552* ▲	.5	8
20 Apr 02	U-TURN *LaFace 74321934072*	.16	9
10 Aug 02 ●	I NEED A GIRL (PART ONE) *Puff Daddy / Arista 74321947242* [1]	.4	11
27 Mar 04 ★	YEAH! *Arista 82876606002* [2] ■ ▲	.1	14
10 Jul 04 ★	BURN *Arista 82876624362* ■ ▲	.1	12

13 Nov 04 ●	CONFESSIONS PART II ▲ / MY BOO *LaFace / Arista 82876655292* [3] ▲	.5	7+
17 Jan 98	MY WAY *LaFace 73008260432*	.16	18
21 Jul 01 ★	8701 *Arista 74321874712* ■	.1	47
3 Apr 04 ★	CONFESSIONS *Arista 82876609902* ■ ▲	.1	39+

[1] P Diddy featuring Usher and Loon [2] Usher featuring Lil' Jon & Ludacris
[3] Usher / Usher featuring Alicia Keys

Both 'Confessions Part II' and 'My Boo' were US No.1s separately 'Confessions' was repackaged with four additional tracks, taking it back into the Top 10 in Oct 2004

US3
UK, male instrumental / production / vocal trio (Singles: 15 Weeks, Albums: 6 Weeks)   pos/wks

10 Jul 93	RIDDIM *Blue Note CDCL 686* [1]	.34	6
25 Sep 93	CANTALOOP *Blue Note CDCL 696* [2]	.23	5
28 May 94	I GOT IT GOIN' ON *Blue Note CDCL 708* [3]	.52	2
1 Mar 97	COME ON EVERYBODY (GET DOWN) *Blue Note CDCL 784*	.38	2
31 Jul 93	HAND ON THE TORCH *Capitol CDEST 2195*	.40	6

[1] Us3 featuring Tukka Yoot [2] Us3 featuring Rahsaan [3] Us3 featuring Kobie Powell and Rahsaan

USURA
Italy, male / female vocal / instrumental group (Singles: 15 Weeks)   pos/wks

23 Jan 93 ●	OPEN YOUR MIND *Deconstruction 74321128042*	.7	9
10 Jul 93	SWEAT *Deconstruction 74321154602*	.29	3
6 Dec 97	OPEN YOUR MIND 97 (re-mix) *Malarky MLKD 4* [1]	.21	3

[1] U.S.U.R.A.

UTAH SAINTS
UK, male instrumental / production duo – Jez Willis and Tim Garbutt (Singles: 39 Weeks, Albums: 15 Weeks)   pos/wks

24 Aug 91 ●	WHAT CAN YOU DO FOR ME *ffrr F 164*	.10	11
6 Jun 92 ●	SOMETHING GOOD *ffrr F 187*	.4	9
8 May 93 ●	BELIEVE IN ME *ffrr FCD 209*	.8	6
17 Jul 93	I WANT YOU *ffrr FCD 213*	.25	5
25 Jun 94	I STILL THINK OF YOU *ffrr FCD 225*	.32	2
2 Sep 95	OHIO *ffrr FCD 264*	.42	2
5 Feb 00	LOVE SONG *Echo ECSCD 83*	.37	2
20 May 00	FUNKY MUSIC (SHO NUFF TURNS ME ON) *Echo ECSCD 96*	.23	2
5 Jun 93	UTAH SAINTS *ffrr 8283792*	.10	15

'Funky Music (Sho Nuff Turns Me On) features uncredited vocals by Edwin Starr

UTOPIA
UK, male vocal / instrumental group (Albums: 3 Weeks)   pos/wks

1 Oct 77	OOPS! SORRY WRONG PLANET *Bearsville K 53517*	.59	1
16 Feb 80	ADVENTURES IN UTOPIA *Island ILPS 9602*	.57	2

U2   10   Top 500
The most successful group of the past 20 years: Paul (Bono) Hewson (v), b. 10 May 1960, Dublin, David (The Edge) Evans (g), b. 8 Aug 1961, Barking, Essex, Adam Clayton (b), b. 13 Mar 1960, Chinnor, Oxfordshire, and Larry Mullen Jr (d), b. 31 Oct 1961, Dublin. The Ireland-based act, named after an American spy plane, has come a long way since winning a Guinness-sponsored talent contest in 1978 in Limerick. Their first release, the EP 'U2.2', topped the Irish charts but success overseas came slower: their first London show drew nine people and their first few UK releases sold poorly. However, in 1981 they made their UK and US chart debuts and since then have broken countless attendance, sales and concert-grossing records. These arena and stadium-packing giants of rock, whose humanitarian work is legendary, have the ear of many top politicians. The first act to sell a million albums on CD ('The Joshua Tree'), U2 have had seven albums simultaneously on both the US and UK charts and scored five consecutive US No.1s. In total they have sold over 120 million albums and won 14 Grammy awards (including four in 2004). Winners of the Q magazine Icon award in 2004 and founder members of the UK Music Hall of Fame, representing the 1990s, in the same year, they are the only non-UK act to receive a Brits Outstanding Contribution to British Music award and the only musical act in 70 years to receive the Freedom of Dublin (Singles: 288 Weeks, Albums: 1114 Weeks)   pos/wks

8 Aug 81	FIRE *Island WIP 6679*	.35	6
17 Oct 81	GLORIA *Island WIP 6733*	.55	4
3 Apr 82	A CELEBRATION *Island WIP 6770*	.47	4
22 Jan 83 ●	NEW YEARS DAY *Island WIP 6848*	.10	8
2 Apr 83	TWO HEARTS BEAT AS ONE *Island IS 109*	.18	5
15 Sep 84 ●	PRIDE (IN THE NAME OF LOVE) *Island IS 202*	.3	11
4 May 85 ●	THE UNFORGETTABLE FIRE *Island IS 220*	.6	6
28 Mar 87 ●	WITH OR WITHOUT YOU *Island IS 319* ▲	.4	11
6 Jun 87 ●	I STILL HAVEN'T FOUND WHAT I'M LOOKING FOR *Island IS 328* ▲	.6	11

		pos/wks
12 Sep 87 ●	WHERE THE STREETS HAVE NO NAME *Island IS 340* 4	6
26 Dec 87	IN GOD'S COUNTRY (IMPORT) *Island 7-99385* 48	4
1 Oct 88 ★	DESIRE *Island IS 400* 1	8
17 Dec 88 ●	ANGEL OF HARLEM *Island IS 402* 9	6
15 Apr 89 ●	WHEN LOVE COMES TO TOWN *Island IS 411* ☐ 6	7
24 Jun 89 ●	ALL I WANT IS YOU *Island IS 422* 4	6
2 Nov 91 ★	THE FLY (re) *Island IS 500* ■ 1	6
14 Dec 91	MYSTERIOUS WAYS *Island IS 509* 13	7
7 Mar 92 ●	ONE *Island IS 515* 7	6
20 Jun 92 ●	EVEN BETTER THAN THE REAL THING *Island IS 525* 12	7
11 Jul 92 ●	EVEN BETTER THAN THE REAL THING (re-mix)	
	Island REALU 2 8	7
5 Dec 92	WHO'S GONNA RIDE YOUR WILD HORSES *Island IS 550* 14	8
4 Dec 93 ●	STAY (FARAWAY, SO CLOSE) *Island IS 578* 4	9
17 Jun 95 ●	HOLD ME THRILL ME KISS ME KILL ME *Atlantic A 7131CD* 2	14
15 Feb 97 ★	DISCOTHEQUE (re) *Island CID 649* ■ 1	11
26 Apr 97 ●	STARING AT THE SUN *Island CID 658* 3	6
2 Aug 97 ●	LAST NIGHT ON EARTH (re) *Island CID 664* 10	5
4 Oct 97 ●	PLEASE *Island CID 673* 7	4
20 Dec 97	IF GOD WILL SEND HIS ANGELS *Island CID 684* 12	3
31 Oct 98 ●	SWEETEST THING *Island CID 727* 3	13
21 Oct 00 ●	BEAUTIFUL DAY *Island CID 766* ■ 1	16
10 Feb 01 ●	STUCK IN A MOMENT YOU CAN'T GET OUT OF *Island CID 770* ..2	8
2 Jun 01	NEW YEAR'S DUB (re) *Serious SERR 030CD* ☐ 15	5
28 Jul 01 ●	ELEVATION *Island CID 780* 3	8
1 Dec 01 ●	WALK ON *Island CID 788* 5	8
2 Nov 02 ●	ELECTRICAL STORM *Island CID 808* 5	13
7 Feb 04 ★	TAKE ME TO THE CLOUDS ABOVE	
	All Around the World CDGLOBE 313 ☐ ■ 1	12
20 Nov 04 ★	VERTIGO *Island CIDX 878* ■ 1	6+
29 Aug 81	BOY *Island ILPS 9646* 52	31
24 Oct 81	OCTOBER *Island ILPS 9680* 11	42
12 Mar 83 ★	WAR *Island ILPS 9733* 1	147
3 Dec 83 ●	LIVE – UNDER A BLOOD RED SKY *Island IMA 3* 2	203
13 Oct 84 ★	THE UNFORGETTABLE FIRE *Island U 25* 1	130
27 Jul 85	WIDE AWAKE IN AMERICA (IMPORT) *Island 902791 A* 11	16
21 Mar 87 ★	THE JOSHUA TREE *Island U 26* ■ ▲ 1	156
20 Feb 88	THE JOSHUA TREE SINGLES *Island U2PK 1* 100	1
22 Oct 88 ★	RATTLE AND HUM *Island U 27* ■ ▲ 1	61
30 Nov 91 ●	ACHTUNG BABY *Island U 28* ▲ 2	87
17 Jul 93 ●	ZOOROPA *Island CIDU 29* ■ ▲ 1	31
15 Mar 97 ★	POP *Island CIDU 210* ■ ▲ 1	35
14 Nov 98 ★	THE BEST OF 1980-1990 & B-SIDES *Island CIDDU 211* ■....1	12
21 Nov 98 ●	THE BEST OF 1980-1990 *Island CIDU 211* 4	64
11 Nov 00 ●	ALL THAT YOU CAN'T LEAVE BEHIND *Island CIDU 212* ■ 1	62
16 Nov 02 ●	THE BEST OF 1990-2000 & B-SIDES	
	Island / Uni-Island CIDTU 213 2	21
23 Nov 02	THE BEST OF 1990-2000 *Island / Uni-Island CIDU 213* 37	11
4 Dec 04 ★	HOW TO DISMANTLE AN ATOMIC BOMB	
	Island CIDXU 214 ■ ▲ 1	4+

☐ U2 with B B King ☐ Musique vs U2 ☐ LMC vs U2

'Stay (Faraway, So Close)' was listed with 'I've Got You Under My Skin' by Frank Sinatra with Bono, which was featured on many but not all formats. 'Take Me to the Clouds Above' features uncredited vocalist Rachel McFarlane

V *UK, male vocal group (Singles: 15 Weeks)*   pos/wks

		pos/wks
5 Jun 04 ●	BLOOD SWEAT AND TEARS *Universal MCSXD 40362* 6	5
21 Aug 04 ●	HIP TO HIP / CAN YOU FEEL IT? *Universal MCSXD 40374* 5	6
20 Nov 04	YOU STOOD UP *Universal MCSXD 40388* 12	4

Verna V *See HELIOTROPIC featuring Verna V*

VDC *See BLAST featuring VDC*

V.I.M. *UK, male instrumental / production group (Singles: 1 Week)* pos/wks

		pos/wks
26 Jan 91	MAGGIE'S LAST PARTY *F2 BOZ 1* 68	1

The V.I.P.'s *UK, male vocal / instrumental group (Singles: 4 Weeks)* pos/wks

		pos/wks
6 Sep 80	THE QUARTER MOON *Gem GEMS 39* 55	4

VAGABONDS *See Jimmy JAMES and The VAGABONDS*

Steve VAI *US, male instrumentalist – guitar (Albums: 20 Weeks)* pos/wks

		pos/wks
2 Jun 90 ●	PASSION AND WARFARE *Food for Thought GRUB 17* 8	10
7 Aug 93	SEX AND RELIGION *Relativity 4729472* ☐ 17	6
15 Apr 95	ALIEN LOVE SECRETS *Relativity 4785862* 39	2
28 Sep 96	FIRE GARDEN *Epic 4850622* 41	2

☐ Vai

Holly VALANCE *Australia, female vocalist –*
Holly Vukadinovic (Singles: 49 Weeks, Albums: 12 Weeks) pos/wks

		pos/wks
11 May 02 ★	KISS KISS *London LONCD 464* ■ 1	16
12 Oct 02 ●	DOWN BOY *London LONCD 469* 2	11
21 Dec 02	NAUGHTY GIRL *London LONCD 472* 16	9
4 Jan 03	DOWN BOY *London LONCD 469* 66	3
8 Nov 03 ●	STATE OF MIND *London LONCD 482* 8	10
26 Oct 02 ●	FOOTPRINTS *London 0927493722* 9	11
22 Nov 03	STATE OF MIND *London 5046701625* 60	1

Ricky VALANCE
UK, male vocalist – David Spencer (Singles: 16 Weeks) pos/wks

		pos/wks
25 Aug 60 ★	TELL LAURA I LOVE HER *Columbia DB 4493* 1	16

Ritchie VALENS *US, male vocalist / instrumentalist – guitar –*
Ritchie Valenzuela, b. 13 May 1941, d. 3 Feb 1959 (Singles: 5 Weeks) pos/wks

		pos/wks
6 Mar 59	DONNA *London HL 8803* 29	1
1 Aug 87	LA BAMBA *RCA PB 41435* 49	4

Caterina VALENTE with Werner MULLER and the RIAS DANCE ORCHESTRA *France, female vocalist and Germany, orchestra – leader b. 2 Aug 1920, d. 28 Dec 1998 (Singles: 14 Weeks)* pos/wks

		pos/wks
19 Aug 55 ●	THE BREEZE AND I *Polydor BM 6002* 5	14

Dickie VALENTINE *UK, male vocalist – Richard Brice,*
b. 4 Nov 1929, d. 6 May 1971 (Singles: 92 Weeks) pos/wks

		pos/wks
20 Feb 53	BROKEN WINGS *Decca F 9954* 12	1
13 Mar 53 ●	ALL THE TIME AND EVERYWHERE *Decca F 10038* 9	3
5 Jun 53 ●	IN A GOLDEN COACH (THERE'S A HEART OF GOLD)	
	Decca F 10098 7	1
5 Nov 54	ENDLESS *Decca F 10346* 19	1
17 Dec 54 ●	MISTER SANDMAN *Decca F 10415* 5	12
17 Dec 54 ★	THE FINGER OF SUSPICION *Decca F 10394* ☐ 1	15
18 Feb 55 ●	A BLOSSOM FELL (re) *Decca F 10430* 9	10
3 Jun 55 ●	I WONDER *Decca F 10493* 4	15
25 Nov 55 ★	CHRISTMAS ALPHABET *Decca F 10628* 1	7
16 Dec 55	THE OLD PI-ANNA RAG *Decca F 10645* 15	5
7 Dec 56 ●	CHRISTMAS ISLAND *Decca F 10798* 8	5
27 Dec 57	SNOWBOUND FOR CHRISTMAS *Decca F 10950* 28	1
13 Mar 59	VENUS (4re) *Pye Nixa 7N 15192* 20	8
23 Oct 59	ONE MORE SUNRISE (MORGEN) *Pye 7N 15221* 14	8

☐ Dickie Valentine with The Stargazers

VALENTINE BROTHERS *US, male vocal duo (Singles: 1 Week)* pos/wks

		pos/wks
23 Apr 83	MONEY'S TOO TIGHT (TO MENTION) *Energy NRG 1* 73	1

Joe VALINO *US, male vocalist – Joseph Paolino,*
b. 9 Mar 1929, d. 26 Dec 1996 (Singles: 2 Weeks) pos/wks

		pos/wks
18 Jan 57	THE GARDEN OF EDEN *HMV POP 283* 23	2

Frankie VALLI *Unmistakable falsetto-styled vocalist, b. Francis Castelluccio, 3 May 1937, New Jersey, US. The lead singer of The Four Seasons, America's most successful singles group in the early 1960s, first recorded in 1953 as Frank Valley (Singles: 117 Weeks, Albums: 28 Weeks)* pos/wks

		pos/wks
27 Aug 64 ●	RAG DOLL *Philips BF 1347* ☐ ▲ 2	13
18 Nov 65 ●	LET'S HANG ON *Philips BF 1439* ☐ 4	16

Singles re-entries are listed as (re), (2re), (3re).... which signifies that the hit re-entered the chart once, twice or three times...

31 Mar 66	WORKIN' MY WAY BACK TO YOU *Philips BF 1474* [2]	**50**	3
2 Jun 66	OPUS 17 (DON'T YOU WORRY 'BOUT ME) *Philips BF 1493* [2]	**20**	9
29 Sep 66	I'VE GOT YOU UNDER MY SKIN *Philips BF 1511* [2]	**12**	11
12 Dec 70	YOU'RE READY NOW *Philips 320226 BF*	**11**	13
1 Feb 75 ●	MY EYES ADORED YOU *Private Stock PVT 1* ▲	**5**	11
19 Apr 75 ●	THE NIGHT *Mowest MW 3024* [3]	**7**	9
21 Jun 75	SWEARIN' TO GOD *Private Stock PVT 21*	**31**	5
17 Apr 76	FALLEN ANGEL *Private Stock PVT 51*	**11**	7
26 Aug 78 ●	GREASE *RSO 012* ▲	**3**	14
29 Oct 88	DECEMBER, 1963 (OH, WHAT A NIGHT) (re-mix) *BR 452772* [3]	**49**	4
23 Mar 91	GREASE – THE DREAM MIX *PWL / Polydor PO 136* [4]	**47**	2
21 May 88	THE COLLECTION *Telstar STAR 2320*	**38**	9
7 Mar 92 ●	THE VERY BEST OF FRANKIE VALLI AND THE FOUR SEASONS *PolyGram TV 5131192* [1]	**7**	15
13 Oct 01	THE DEFINITIVE FRANKIE VALLI AND THE FOUR SEASONS *WSM 8122735552* [1]	**26**	4

[1] The Four Seasons with the sounds of Frankie Valli [2] The Four Seasons with Frankie Valli [3] Frankie Valli and The Four Seasons [4] Frankie Valli, John Travolta and Olivia Newton-John [1] Frankie Valli and The Four Seasons

Armin VAN BUUREN
Holland, male DJ / producer (Singles: 9 Weeks) pos/wks

14 Feb 98	BLUE FEAR *Xtravaganza 0091485 EXT* [1]	**45**	1
12 Feb 00	COMMUNICATION *AM:PM CDAMPM 129* [1]	**18**	3
10 May 03	YET ANOTHER DAY *Nebula NEBCD 042* [2]	**70**	1
20 Mar 04	BURNED WITH DESIRE *Nebula NEBCD 055* [3]	**45**	2
28 Aug 04	BLUE FEAR 2004 (re-mix) *Nebula NEBCD 061*	**52**	2

[1] Armin [2] Armin Van Buuren featuring Ray Wilson [3] Armin Van Buuren featuring Justine Suissa

VAN DAHL *See IAN VAN DAHL*

Mark VAN DALE with ENRICO
Belgium, male production duo (Singles: 1 Week) pos/wks

3 Oct 98	WATER WAVE *Club Tools 0065815 CLU*	**71**	1

David VAN DAY (see also DOLLAR; GUYS 'N' DOLLS)
UK, male vocalist (Singles: 3 Weeks) pos/wks

14 May 83	YOUNG AMERICANS TALKING *WEA DAY 1*	**43**	3

Ron VAN DEN BEUKEN (see also MYSTERY)
Holland, male producer (Singles: 1 Week) pos/wks

19 Jun 04	TIMELESS (KEEP ON MOVIN') *Manifesto 9866717*	**65**	1

VAN DER GRAAF GENERATOR
UK, male vocal / instrumental group (Albums: 2 Weeks) pos/wks

25 Apr 70	THE LEAST WE CAN DO IS WAVE TO EACH OTHER *Charisma CAS 1007*	**47**	2

VAN DER TOORN *See PAPPA BEAR featuring VAN DER TOORN*

George VAN DUSEN UK, male vocalist –
George Harrington, b. 1905, d. 1992 (Singles: 4 Weeks) pos/wks

17 Dec 88	IT'S PARTY TIME AGAIN *Bri-Tone 7BT 001*	**43**	4

Paul VAN DYK
Germany, male DJ / producer (Singles: 34 Weeks, Albums: 3 Weeks) pos/wks

17 May 97	FORBIDDEN FRUIT *Deviant DVNT 18CDR*	**69**	1
15 Nov 97	WORDS *Deviant DVNT 26CDS* [1]	**54**	1
5 Sep 98	FOR AN ANGEL *Deviant DVT 24CDS*	**28**	4
20 Nov 99	ANOTHER WAY / AVENUE (re) *Deviant DVNT 35CDS*	**13**	7
20 May 00 ●	TELL ME WHY (THE RIDDLE) *Deviant DVNT 36CDS* [2]	**7**	5
2 Dec 00	WE ARE ALIVE *Deviant DVNT 38CDS*	**15**	4
12 Jul 03	NOTHING BUT YOU *Positiva CDTIVS 192* [3]	**14**	5
18 Oct 03	TIME OUT OF LIVES / CONNECTED *Positiva CDTIVS 196* [4]	**28**	2
17 Apr 04	CRUSH *Positiva CDTIVS 204* [5]	**42**	3
17 Jun 00	OUT THERE AND BACK *Deviant DVNT 37CD*	**12**	3

[1] Paul Van Dyk featuring Toni Halliday [2] Paul Van Dyk featuring Saint Etienne [3] Paul Van Dyk featuring Hemstock [4] Paul Van Dyk featuring Vega 4 [5] Paul Van Dyk featuring Second Sun

Leroy VAN DYKE US, male vocalist (Singles: 20 Weeks)
pos/wks

4 Jan 62 ●	WALK ON BY *Mercury AMT 1166*	**5**	17
26 Apr 62	BIG MAN IN A BIG HOUSE *Mercury AMT 1173*	**34**	3

Niels VAN GOGH
Germany, male producer (Singles: 1 Week) pos/wks

10 Apr 99	PULVERTURM *Logic 74321649192*	**75**	1

VAN HALEN (440) Top 500
Hard rock heroes formed in 1974, California, US, whose members included Dutch born Eddie (g) and Alex Van Halen (d), David Lee Roth (v), Sammy Hagar (v) and Gary Cherone (ex-Extreme) (v). Their first 12 albums each topped two million sales Stateside (with two passing 10 million) (Singles: 51 Weeks, Albums: 109 Weeks) pos/wks

28 Jun 80	RUNNIN' WITH THE DEVIL *Warner Bros. HM 10*	**52**	3
4 Feb 84 ●	JUMP *Warner Bros. W 9384* ▲	**7**	13
19 May 84	PANAMA *Warner Bros. W 9273*	**61**	2
5 Apr 86 ●	WHY CAN'T THIS BE LOVE *Warner Bros. W 8740*	**8**	14
12 Jul 86	DREAMS *Warner Bros. W 8642*	**62**	2
6 Aug 88	WHEN IT'S LOVE *Warner Bros. W 7816*	**28**	7
1 Apr 89	FEELS SO GOOD *Warner Bros. W 7565*	**63**	1
22 Jun 91	POUNDCAKE *Warner Bros. W 0045*	**74**	1
19 Oct 91	TOP OF THE WORLD *Warner Bros. W 0066*	**63**	1
27 Mar 93	JUMP (LIVE) *Warner Bros. W 0155CD*	**26**	3
21 Jan 95	DON'T TELL ME *Warner Bros. W 0280CD*	**27**	2
1 Apr 95	CAN'T STOP LOVIN' YOU *Warner Bros. W 0288CD*	**33**	2
27 May 78	VAN HALEN *Warner Bros. K 56470*	**34**	11
14 Apr 79	VAN HALEN II *Warner Bros. K 566116*	**23**	7
5 Apr 80	WOMEN AND CHILDREN FIRST *Warner Bros. K 56793*	**15**	7
23 May 81	FAIR WARNING *Warner Bros. K 56899*	**49**	4
1 May 82	DIVER DOWN *Warner Bros. K 57003*	**36**	5
4 Feb 84	MCMLXXXIV (1984) *Warner Bros. 923985*	**15**	24
5 Apr 86	5150 *Warner Bros. WS 5150* ▲	**16**	18
4 Jun 88	OU812 *Warner Bros. WX 177* ▲	**16**	12
29 Jun 91	FOR UNLAWFUL CARNAL KNOWLEDGE *Warner Bros. WX 420* ▲	**12**	5
6 Mar 93	LIVE: RIGHT HERE RIGHT NOW *Warner Bros. 9362451982*	**24**	3
4 Feb 95 ●	BALANCE *Warner Bros. 9362457602* ▲	**8**	3
9 Nov 96	THE BEST OF VAN HALEN – VOLUME 1 *Warner Bros. 9362464742* ▲	**45**	1
28 Mar 98	VAN HALEN 3 *Warner Bros. 9362466622*	**43**	1
31 Jul 04	THE BEST OF BOTH WORLDS *Warner Bros. 8122765152*	**15**	8

Armand VAN HELDEN (see also DEEP CREED '94)
US, male DJ / producer (Singles: 48 Weeks, Albums: 7 Weeks) pos/wks

8 Mar 97	THE FUNK PHENOMENA *ZYX ZYX 8523U8*	**38**	2
8 Nov 97	ULTRAFUNKULA *ffrr FCD 317*	**46**	1
6 Feb 99 ★	YOU DON'T KNOW ME (re) *ffrr FCD 357* [1] ■	**1**	12
1 May 99	FLOWERZ *ffrr FCD 361* [2]	**18**	5
20 May 00 ●	KOOCHY *ffrr FCD 379*	**4**	7
3 Nov 01	WHY CAN'T YOU FREE SOME TIME *ffrr FCD 402*	**34**	2
15 Dec 01	YOU CAN'T CHANGE ME *Defected DFECT 41CDS* [3]	**25**	4
1 May 04	HEAR MY NAME *Southern Fried ECB 64CDS* [4]	**34**	2
11 Sep 04	MY MY MY *Southern Fried ECB 67CDS*	**15**	11
27 Nov 04	WATCHING CARS GO BY *Emperor Norton ENR 532* [5]	**49**	2
10 Apr 99	2 FUTURE 4 U *ffrr 5560902*	**22**	6
10 Jun 00	KILLING PURITANS *ffrr 8573833192*	**38**	1

[1] Armand Van Helden featuring Duane Harden [2] Armand Van Helden featuring Roland Clark [3] Roger Sanchez featuring Armand Van Helden and N'Dea Davenport [4] Armand Van Helden featuring Spalding Rockwell [5] Felix Da Housecat vs Sasha and Armand Van Helden

Denise VAN OUTEN (see also DENISE and JOHNNY; THOSE 2 GIRLS)
UK, female actor / vocalist (Singles: 16 Weeks, Albums: 2 Weeks) pos/wks

26 Dec 98 ●	ESPECIALLY FOR YOU (re) *RCA 74321644722* [1]	**3**	12
29 Jun 02	CAN'T TAKE MY EYES OFF YOU *Columbia 6721052* [2]	**23**	4
26 Apr 03	TELL ME ON A SUNDAY *Really Useful / Polydor 4932922*	**34**	2

[1] Denise and Johnny [Johnny Vaughan] [2] Andy Williams and Denise Van Outen

VAN TWIST Zaire / Belgium, male / female
vocal / instrumental group (Singles: 2 Weeks) pos/wks

16 Feb 85	SHAFT *Polydor POSP 729*	**57**	2

VANDELLAS *See Martha REEVES and the VANDELLAS*

Despina VANDI
Greece, female vocalist (Singles: 1 Week) pos/wks

20 Mar 04	GIA *Positiva CDTIVS 199*	**63**	1

Luther VANDROSS `94` `Top 500` *Superior soul singer / songwriter and producer, b. 20 Apr 1951, New York, US. Former David Bowie backing vocalist fronted chart group Change before embarking on a solo career that earned him 10 successive US platinum albums and a stack of awards including four Grammys in 2004 (Singles: 152 Weeks, Albums: 298 Weeks)*

pos/wks

19 Feb 83	NEVER TOO MUCH *Epic EPC A 3101*	44	6
26 Jul 86	GIVE ME THE REASON *Epic A 7288*	60	3
21 Feb 87	GIVE ME THE REASON (re-issue) *Epic 650216 7*	71	2
28 Mar 87	SEE ME *Epic LUTH 1*	60	4
11 Jul 87	I REALLY DIDN'T MEAN IT *Epic LUTH 3*	16	10
5 Sep 87	STOP TO LOVE *Epic LUTH 2*	24	7
7 Nov 87	SO AMAZING *Epic LUTH 4*	33	6
23 Jan 88	GIVE ME THE REASON (2nd re-issue) *Epic LUTH 5*	26	6
16 Apr 88	I GAVE IT UP (WHEN I FELL IN LOVE) *Epic LUTH 6*	28	5
9 Jul 88	THERE'S NOTHING BETTER THAN LOVE *Epic LUTH 7* 1	72	1
8 Oct 88	ANY LOVE *Epic LUTH 8*	31	4
4 Feb 89	SHE WON'T TALK TO ME *Epic LUTH 9*	34	4
22 Apr 89	COME BACK *Epic LUTH 10*	53	3
28 Oct 89	NEVER TOO MUCH (re-mix) *Epic LUTH 12*	13	7
6 Jan 90	HERE AND NOW *Epic LUTH 13*	43	3
27 Apr 91	POWER OF LOVE – LOVE POWER *Epic 6568227*	46	5
18 Jan 92	THE RUSH *Epic 6577237*	53	3
15 Aug 92 ●	THE BEST THINGS IN LIFE ARE FREE *Perspective PERSS 7400* 2	2	13
22 May 93	LITTLE MIRACLES (HAPPEN EVERY DAY) *Epic 6590442*	28	3
18 Sep 93	HEAVEN KNOWS *Epic 6596522*	34	3
4 Dec 93	LOVE IS ON THE WAY *Epic 6599592*	38	2
17 Sep 94 ●	ENDLESS LOVE (2re) *Epic 6608062* 3	3	16
26 Nov 94	LOVE THE ONE YOU'RE WITH *Epic 6610612*	31	4
4 Feb 95	ALWAYS AND FOREVER *Epic 6611942*	20	5
15 Apr 95	AIN'T NO STOPPING US NOW *Epic 6614242*	22	3
11 Nov 95	POWER OF LOVE – LOVE POWER (re-mix) *Epic 6625902*	31	3
16 Dec 95 ●	THE BEST THINGS IN LIFE ARE FREE (re-mix) *A&M 5813092* 4	7	7
23 Dec 95	EVERY YEAR EVERY CHRISTMAS *Epic 6627762*	43	2
12 Oct 96	YOUR SECRET LOVE *Epic 6638385*	14	5
28 Dec 96	I CAN MAKE IT BETTER *Epic 6640632*	44	2
20 Oct 01	TAKE YOU OUT *J 74321899442*	59	1
28 Feb 04	DANCE WITH MY FATHER *J 82876569982*	21	4
21 Jan 84	BUSY BODY *Epic EPC 25608*	42	8
6 Apr 85	THE NIGHT I FELL IN LOVE *Epic EPC 26387*	19	10
1 Nov 86 ●	GIVE ME THE REASON *Epic EPC 4501341*	3	99
21 Feb 87	NEVER TOO MUCH *Epic EPC 32807*	41	30
4 Jul 87	FOREVER FOR ALWAYS FOR LOVE *Epic EPC 25013*	23	16
16 Apr 88	BUSY BODY (re-issue) *Epic 4601831*	78	4
29 Oct 88 ●	ANY LOVE *Epic 4629081*	3	22
11 Nov 89	BEST OF LUTHER VANDROSS – BEST OF LOVE *Epic 4658011*	14	23
25 May 91 ●	POWER OF LOVE *Epic 4680121*	9	9
12 Jun 93	NEVER LET ME GO *Epic 4735982*	11	5
1 Oct 94 ★	SONGS *Epic 4766562* ■	1	28
28 Oct 95	GREATEST HITS 1981-1995 *Epic 4811002*	12	14
19 Oct 96	YOUR SECRET LOVE *Epic 4843832*	14	4
11 Oct 97	ONE NIGHT WITH YOU – THE BEST OF LOVE *Epic 4888882*	56	2
22 Aug 98	I KNOW *EMI 8460892*	42	1
16 Feb 02	THE ESSENTIAL LUTHER VANDROSS *Epic 5050252*	18	8
5 Jul 03	DANCE WITH MY FATHER *J 82876540732* ▲	41	15

1 Luther Vandross, duet with Gregory Hines 2 Luther Vandross and Janet Jackson with special guests BBD and Ralph Tresvant 3 Luther Vandross and Mariah Carey 4 Luther Vandross and Janet Jackson

'The Essential Luther Vandross' peaked at No.72 in 2002. A repackaged version, with the catalogue number Epic 5133532 and the same track listing, peaked at No.18 in 2003

VANESSA-MAE
Singapore, female vocalist / instrumentalist – violin – Vanessa-Mae Vanakorn Nicholson (Singles: 21 Weeks, Albums: 34 Weeks)

pos/wks

28 Jan 95	TOCCATA AND FUGUE *EMI Classics MAE 8816812*	16	10
20 May 95	RED HOT *EMI CDMAE 2*	37	2
18 Nov 95	CLASSICAL GAS *EMI CDEM 404*	41	2
26 Oct 96	I'M A DOUN FOR LACK O' JOHNNIE (A LITTLE SCOTTISH FANTASY) *EMI CDMAE 3*	28	2
25 Oct 97	STORM *EMI CDEM 497*	54	1
20 Dec 97	I FEEL LOVE *EMI CDEM 553*	41	2
5 Dec 98	DEVIL'S TRILL / REFLECTION *EMI CDEM 530*	53	1
28 Jul 01	WHITE BIRD *EMI CDVAN 002*	66	1
25 Feb 95	THE VIOLIN PLAYER *EMI Classics CDC 5550892*	11	21

2 Nov 96	THE CLASSICAL ALBUM 1 *EMI Classics CDC 5553952*	47	2
8 Nov 97	STORM *EMI 8218002*	27	5
7 Feb 98	CHINA GIRL – THE CLASSICAL ALBUM 2 *EMI Classics CDC 5564832*	56	3
26 May 01	SUBJECT TO CHANGE *EMI 5331002*	58	2
30 Oct 04	CHOREOGRAPHY *Sony Classical SK 90895*	66	1

VANGELIS `356` `Top 500`
Synthesiser soundtrack whizzkid, b. Evangelos Papathanassiou, 29 Mar 1943, Volos, Greece. Grammy nominated artist, whose 'Conquest of Paradise' is one of Germany's biggest-selling singles, also had hits in Aphrodite's Child and Jon and Vangelis (Singles: 25 Weeks, Albums: 165 Weeks)

pos/wks

9 May 81	CHARIOTS OF FIRE – TITLES (re) *Polydor POSP 246* ▲	12	17
11 Jul 81	HEAVEN AND HELL, THIRD MOVEMENT (THEME FROM THE BBC-TV SERIES 'THE COSMOS') *BBC 1*	48	6
31 Oct 92	CONQUEST OF PARADISE *East West YZ 704*	60	2
10 Jan 76	HEAVEN AND HELL *RCA Victor RS 1025*	31	7
9 Oct 76	ALBEDO 0.39 *RCA Victor RS 1080*	18	6
18 Apr 81 ●	CHARIOTS OF FIRE (FILM SOUNDTRACK) *Polydor POLS 1026*	5	97
5 May 84	CHARIOTS OF FIRE (FILM SOUNDTRACK) (re-issue) *Polydor POLD 5160*	39	10
13 Oct 84	SOIL FESTIVITIES *Polydor POLH 11*	55	4
30 Mar 85	MASK *Polydor POLH 19*	69	2
22 Jul 89	THEMES *Polydor VGTV 1*	11	13
24 Oct 92	1492 – THE CONQUEST OF PARADISE (FILM SOUNDTRACK) *East West 4509910142*	33	6
18 Jun 94	BLADERUNNER (FILM SOUNDTRACK) *East West 4509965742*	20	6
2 Mar 96	VOICES *East West 630127862*	58	1
20 Apr 96	PORTRAIT (SO LONG AGO SO CLEAR) *Polydor 5311512*	14	6
8 Nov 03	ODYSSEY – THE DEFINITIVE COLLECTION *Universal TV 9813149*	20	7

'Chariots of Fire – Titles' re-entered in Apr 1982, peaking at No.41

VANGUARD *See QUEEN*

VANILLA *UK, female vocal group (Singles: 10 Weeks)*

pos/wks

22 Nov 97	NO WAY NO WAY (re) *EMI CDEM 487*	14	8
23 May 98	TRUE TO US *EMI CDEM 509*	36	2

VANILLA FUDGE *US, male vocal / instrumental group (Singles: 11 Weeks, Albums: 3 Weeks)*

pos/wks

9 Aug 67	YOU KEEP ME HANGIN' ON *Atlantic 584123*	18	11
4 Nov 67	VANILLA FUDGE *Atlantic 588086*	31	3

VANILLA ICE *US, male rapper – Robert Van Winkle (Singles: 32 Weeks, Albums: 23 Weeks)*

pos/wks

24 Nov 90 ★	ICE ICE BABY *SBK SBK 18* ▲	1	13
2 Feb 91 ●	PLAY THAT FUNKY MUSIC *SBK SBK 20*	10	6
30 Mar 91	I LOVE YOU *SBK SBK 22*	45	5
29 Jun 91	ROLLIN' IN MY 5.0 *SBK SBK 27*	27	4
10 Aug 91	SATISFACTION *SBK SBK 29*	22	4
15 Dec 90 ●	TO THE EXTREME *SBK SBKLP 9* ▲	4	20
6 Jul 91	EXTREMELY LIVE *SBK SBKLP 12*	35	3

VANITY FARE
UK, male vocal / instrumental group (Singles: 34 Weeks)

pos/wks

28 Aug 68	I LIVE FOR THE SUN *Page One POF 075*	20	9
23 Jul 69 ●	EARLY IN THE MORNING *Page One POF 142*	8	12
27 Dec 69	HITCHIN' A RIDE *Page One POF 158*	16	13

Joe T VANNELLI PROJECT
Italy, male producer (Singles: 2 Weeks)

pos/wks

17 Jun 95	SWEETEST DAY OF MAY *Positiva CDTIV 36*	45	2

Randy VANWARMER *US, male vocalist – Randall Van Wormer, b. 30 Mar 1955, d. 12 Jan 2004 (Singles: 11 Weeks)*

pos/wks

4 Aug 79 ●	JUST WHEN I NEEDED YOU MOST *Bearsville WIP 6516*	8	11

The VAPORS *UK, male vocal / instrumental group (Singles: 23 Weeks, Albums: 6 Weeks)*

pos/wks

9 Feb 80 ●	TURNING JAPANESE *United Artists BP 334*	3	13
5 Jul 80	NEWS AT TEN *United Artists BP 345*	44	4
11 Jul 81	JIMMIE JONES *Liberty BP 401*	44	6
7 Jun 80	NEW CLEAR DAYS *United Artists UAG 30300*	44	6

Singles re-entries are listed as (re), (2re), (3re).... which signifies that the hit re-entered the chart once, twice or three times...

VARDIS *UK, male vocal / instrumental group (Singles: 4 Weeks, Albums: 1 Week)*

		pos/wks	
27 Sep 80	**LET'S GO** *Logo VAR 1*	59	4
1 Nov 80	**100 MPH** *Logo MOGO 4012*	52	1

Halo VARGA *US, male producer (Singles: 1 Week)*

		pos/wks	
9 Dec 00	**FUTURE** *Hooj Choons HOOJ 101CD*	67	1

VARIOUS ARTISTS (Singles and EPs) *(Singles: 74 Weeks)*

		pos/wks	
15 Jun 56	**CAROUSEL – ORIGINAL SOUNDTRACK (LP)** (re) *Capitol LCT 6105*	26	2
29 Jun 56 ●	**ALL STAR HIT PARADE** *Decca F 10752*	2	9
26 Jul 57	**ALL STAR HIT PARADE NO.2** *Decca F 10915*	15	7
9 Dec 89	**THE FOOD CHRISTMAS EP** *Food FOOD 23*	63	1
20 Jan 90	**THE FURTHER ADVENTURES OF NORTH (EP)** *Deconstruction PT 43372*	64	2
2 Nov 91	**THE APPLE EP** *Apple APP 1*	60	1
11 Jul 92	**FOURPLAY (EP)** *XL XLFP 1*	45	2
7 Nov 92	**THE FRED EP** *Heavenly HVN 19*	26	3
24 Apr 93	**GIMME SHELTER (EP)** *Food CDORDERA 1*	23	4
5 Jun 93	**SUBPLATES VOLUME 1 (EP)** *Suburban Base SUBBASE 24CD*	69	1
9 Oct 93	**THE TWO TONE EP** *2 Tone CHSTT 31*	30	3
4 Nov 95	**HELP (EP)** *Go Discs GODCD 135*	51	1
16 Mar 96	**NEW YORK UNDERCOVER (EP)** *Uptown MCSTD 48002*	39	1
30 Mar 96	**DANGEROUS MINDS (EP)** *MCA MCSTD 48007*	35	1
29 Nov 97 ★	**PERFECT DAY** (re) *Chrysalis CDNEED 01* ◆ ■	1	21
12 Sep 98	**THE FULL MONTY - MONSTER MIX** *RCA Victor 74321602582*	62	1
26 Sep 98	**TRADE (EP) (DISC 2)** *Tidy Trax TREP 2*	75	1
25 Dec 99	**IT'S ONLY ROCK 'N' ROLL** (re) *Universal TV 1566012*	19	10
17 Jun 00	**PERFECT DAY** (re-recording) *Chrysalis 8887840*	69	1
10 Nov 01	**HARD BEAT EP 19** *Nukleuz NUKP 0369*	71	1

Tracks and artists on Carousel are as follows: Carousel Waltz – Orchestra conducted by Alfred Newman; You're a Queer One Julie Jordan – Barbara Ruick and Shirley Jones; Mister Snow – Barbara Ruick; If I Loved You – Shirley Jones and Gordon MacRae; June Is Busting Out All Over – Claramae Turner; Soliloquy – Gordon MacRae; Blow High Blow Low – Cameron Mitchell; When the Children Are Asleep – Robert Rounseville and Barbara Ruick; This Was a Real Nice Clambake – Barbara Ruick, Claramae Turner, Robert Rounseville and Cameron Mitchell; Stonecutters Cut it on Stone (There's Nothing So Bad for a Woman) – Cameron Mitchell; What's the Use of Wonderin' – Shirley Jones; You'll Never Walk Alone – Claramae Turner; If I Loved You – Gordon MacRae; You'll Never Walk Alone – Shirley Jones; Tracks on All Star Hit Parade: Theme from The Threepenny Opera – Winifred Atwell; No Other Love – Dave King; My September Love – Joan Regan; A Tear Fell – Lita Roza; Out of Town – Dickie Valentine; It's Almost Tomorrow – David Whitfield. Tracks on All Star Hit Parade No.2: Around the World – Johnston Brothers; Puttin' On the Style – Billy Cotton; When I Fall In Love – Jimmy Young; A White Sport Coat – Max Bygraves; Freight Train – Beverley Sisters; Butterfly – Tommy Steele. Tracks on The Food Christmas EP: Like Princes Do – Crazyhead; I Don't Want That Kind of Love – Jesus Jones; Info Freako – Diesel Park West. Tracks on The Further Adventures of North (EP): Dream 17 – Annette; Carino 90 – T-Coy; The Way I Feel – Frequency 9; Stop This Thing – Dynasty of Two featuring Rowetta. Tracks on The Apple EP: Those Were the Days – Mary Hopkin; That's the Way God Planned It – Billy Preston; Sour Milk Sea – Jackie Lomax; Come and Get It – Badfinger. Tracks on Fourplay (EP): DJs Unite; Alright – Glide; Be Free – Noisy Factory; True Devotion – EQ. Tracks on The Fred EP: Deeply Dippy – Rockingbirds; Don't Talk Just Kiss - Flowered Up; I'm Too Sexy – Saint Etienne. Gimme Shelter EP was available on all four formats, each featuring an interview with the featured artist plus the following artists performing versions of Gimme Shelter: (cassette) Jimmy Somerville and Voice of the Beehive; Heaven 17; (12") Blue Pearl, 808 State and Robert Owens; Pop Will Eat Itself vs Gary Clail; Ranking Roger and the Mighty Diamonds; (CD) Thunder; Little Angels; Hawkwind and Sam Fox; (2nd CD) Cud with Sandie Shaw; Kingmaker; New Model Army and Tom Jones. Tracks on Subplates Volume 1 (EP): Style Warz – Son'z of a Loop Da Loop Era; Funky Dope Track – Q-Bass; The Chopper – DJ Hype; Look No Further – Run Tings – Selecter; Tears of a Clown – The Beat. Tracks on Help (EP): Lucky – Radiohead; 50ft Queenie (Live) – PJ Harvey; Momentum – Guru featuring Big Shug; an untitled piece of incidental music. Tracks on New York Undercover (EP): Tell Me What You Like – Guy; Dom Perignon – Little Shawn; I Miss You – Monifah; Jeeps, Lex Coups, Bimax & Menz – Lost Boys. Tracks on Dangerous Minds (EP): Curiosity – Aaron Hall; Gin & Dance – De Vante; It's Alright – Sista featuring Craig Mack. Artists on Perfect Day are as follows: BBC Symphony Orchestra and Andrew Davis; Bono (U2); Boyzone; Brett Anderson (Suede), Brodsky Quartet, Burning Spear, Courtney Pine, David Bowie, Dr John, Elton John, Emmylou Harris, Evan Dando (Lemonheads), Gabrielle, Heather Small (M People), Huey (Fun Lovin' Criminals), Ian Broudie (The Lightning Seeds), Joan Armatrading, Laurie Anderson, Lesley Garrett, Lou Reed, Robert Cray, Shane MacGowan, Sheona White, Skye (Morcheeba), Suzanne Vega, Tammy Wynette, Thomas Allen, Tom Jones, Visual Ministry Orchestra. Tracks on The

Full Monty – Monster Mix (medley): You Sexy Thing – Hot Chocolate; Hot Stuff – Donna Summer; You Can Leave Your Hat On – Tom Jones. CD also has a full version of 'You Can Leave Your Hat On' by Tom Jones and 'The Stripper' by David Rose. Tracks on Trade (EP) (disc 2): Put Your House in Order – Steve Thomas; The Dawn – Tony De Vit. Artists on 'It's Only Rock 'n' Roll': Keith Richards, Kid Rock, Mary J Blige, Kelly Jones (Stereophonics), Jon Bon Jovi, Kéllé Bryan (Eternal), Jay Kay (Jamiroquai), Ozzy Osbourne, Womack and Womack, Lionel Richie, Bonnie Raitt, Dolores O'Riordan (The Cranberries), James Brown, Spice Girls (minus Geri), Mick Jagger, Robin Williams, Jackson Browne, Iggy Pop, Chrissie Hynde, Skin (Skunk Anansie), Annie Lennox, Mark Owen, Natalie Imbruglia, Huey (Fun Lovin' Criminals), Dina Carroll, Gavin Rossdale (Bush), BB King, Joe Cocker, The Corrs, Steve Cradock and Simon Fowler (Ocean Colour Scene), Ronan Keating, Ray Barretto, Herbie Hancock, Francis Rossi and Rick Parfitt (Status Quo), S Club 7 and Eric Idle. Tracks on 'Hard Beat EP 19': 'Eternal '99' – Eternal Rhythm and 'Tragic', 'F**k Me' and 'Don't Give Up', all by BK

VARIOUS ARTISTS (MONTAGES) *(Singles: 31 Weeks)*

		pos/wks	
17 May 80	**CALIBRE CUTS** *Calibre CAB 502*	75	2
25 Nov 89	**DEEP HEAT '89** *Deep Heat DEEP 10*	12	11
3 Mar 90 ●	**THE BRITS 1990** *RCA PB 43565*	2	7
28 Apr 90	**THE SIXTH SENSE** *Deep Heat DEEP 12*	49	2
10 Nov 90	**TIME TO MAKE THE FLOOR BURN** *Megabass MEGAX 1*	16	9

The following tracks are sampled: Calibre Cuts: Big Apples Rock – Black Ivory; Don't Hold Back – Chanson; The River Drive – Jupiter Beyond; Dancing in the Disco – LAX; Mellow Mellow Right On – Lowrell; Pata Pata – Osibisa; I Like It – The Players Association; We Got the Funk – Positive Force; Holdin' On – Tony Rallo and The Midnite Band; Can You Feel the Force – The Real Thing; Miami Heatwave – Seventh Avenue; Rapper's Delight – Sugarhill Gang; Que Tal America – Two Man Sound; Remakes by session musicians: Ain't No Stoppin' Us Now, Bad Girls, We Are Family. Deep Heat '89 (credited to Latino Rave): Pump Up the Jam – Technotronics; Stakker Humanoid – Humanoid; A Day in the Life – Black Riot; Work it to the Bone – LNR; I Can Make U Dance – DJ 'Fast' Eddie; Voodoo Ray – A Guy Called Gerald; Numero Uno – Starlight; Bango (to the Batmobile) – Todd Terry; Break 4 Love – Raze; Don't Scandalize Mine – Sugar Bear. The Brits 1990: Street Tuff – Double Trouble and the Rebel MC; Voodoo Ray – A Guy Called Gerald; Theme From S Express – S Express; Hey DJ I Can't Dance to That Music You're Playing – The Beatmasters; Eve of the War – Jeff Wayne; Pacific State – 808 State; We Call It Acieed – D Mob; Got to Keep On – The Cookie Crew. The Sixth Sense (credited to Latino Rave): Get Up – Technotronic; The Magic Number – De La Soul; G'Ding G'Ding (Do Wanna Wanna) – Anna G; Show 'M the Bass – MC Miker G; Turn It Out (Go Base) – Rob Base; Eve of the War (War of the Worlds) – Project D; Moments In Love – 2 to the Power. Time to Make the Floor Burn (credited to Megabass): Do This My Way – Kid 'N' Play; Street Tuff – Double Trouble and the Rebel MC; Sex 4 Daze – Lake Eerie; Ride on Time – Black Box; Make My Body Rock – Jomanda; Don't Miss the Partyline – Bizz Nizz; Pump Pump It Up – Hypnotek; Big Fun – Inner City; Pump That Body – Mr Lee; Pump Up the Jam – Technotronic; This Beat Is Technotronic – Technotronic; Get Busy – Mr Lee; Touch Me – 49ers; Thunderbirds Are Go – FAB

Junior VASQUEZ *US, male DJ / producer – Donald Martin (Singles: 5 Weeks)*

		pos/wks	
15 Jul 95	**GET YOUR HANDS OFF MY MAN!** *Positiva CDTIV 37*	22	3
31 Aug 96	**IF MADONNA CALLS** *Multiply CDMULTY 13*	24	2

Elaine VASSELL See The BEATMASTERS

VAST *Australia, male vocal / instrumental group (Singles: 1 Week)*

		pos/wks	
16 Sep 00	**FREE** *Mushroom MUSH 79CDS*	55	1

Sven VATH *Germany, male DJ / producer (Singles: 5 Weeks)*

		pos/wks	
24 Jul 93	**L'ESPERANZA** *Eye Q YZ 757*	63	2
6 Nov 93	**AN ACCIDENT IN PARADISE** *Eye Q YZ 778CD*	57	2
22 Oct 94	**HARLEQUIN – THE BEAUTY AND THE BEAST** *Eye Q YZ 857*	72	1

Frankie VAUGHAN 248 *Top 500*

High-kicking 50s heart-throb vocalist, b. Frank Abelson, 3 Feb 1928, Liverpool, UK, d. 17 Sep 1999. This variety-show veteran was made an OBE in 1965 for his charity work and was one of the most popular performers of the 1950s *(Singles: 232 Weeks, Albums: 20 Weeks)*

		pos/wks	
29 Jan 54	**ISTANBUL (NOT CONSTANTINOPLE)** *HMV B 10599* [1]	11	1
28 Jan 55	**HAPPY DAYS AND LONELY NIGHTS** *HMV B 10783*	12	3
22 Apr 55	**TWEEDLE DEE** *Philips PB 423*	17	1
2 Dec 55	**SEVENTEEN** *Philips PB 511*	18	3
3 Feb 56	**MY BOY FLAT TOP** *Philips PB 544*	20	2
9 Nov 56 ●	**THE GREEN DOOR** *Philips PB 640*	2	15
11 Jan 57 ★	**THE GARDEN OF EDEN** *Philips PB 660*	1	13
4 Oct 57 ●	**MAN ON FIRE / WANDERIN' EYES** *Philips PB 729*	6	12
1 Nov 57 ●	**GOT-TA HAVE SOMETHING IN THE BANK, FRANK** *Philips PB 751* [2]	8	11

		pos/wks
20 Dec 57 ●	KISSES SWEETER THAN WINE *Philips PB 775*	.........**8** 11
7 Mar 58	CAN'T GET ALONG WITHOUT YOU / WE ARE NOT ALONE	
	Philips PB 793	...........**11** 6
9 May 58 ●	KEWPIE DOLL *Philips PB 825*	........**10** 12
1 Aug 58	WONDERFUL THINGS (re) *Philips PB 834*	..........**22** 6
10 Oct 58	AM I WASTING MY TIME ON YOU (re) *Philips PB 865*	....**25** 4
30 Jan 59	THAT'S MY DOLL *Philips PB 895*	..........**28** 2
1 May 59 ●	COME SOFTLY TO ME *Philips PB 913* [2]	........**9** 9
24 Jul 59 ●	THE HEART OF A MAN *Philips PB 930*	......**5** 14
18 Sep 59	WALKIN' TALL (re) *Philips PB 931*	..........**28** 2
29 Jan 60	WHAT MORE DO YOU WANT *Philips PB 985*	.......**25** 2
22 Sep 60	KOOKIE LITTLE PARADISE *Philips PB 1054*	.....**31** 5
27 Oct 60	MILORD *Philips PB 1066*	........**34** 6
9 Nov 61 ★	TOWER OF STRENGTH *Philips PB 1195*	......**1** 13
1 Feb 62	DON'T STOP – TWIST! *Philips BF 1219*	......**22** 7
27 Sep 62	HERCULES *Philips 326542 BF*	........**42** 2
24 Jan 63 ●	LOOP DE LOOP *Philips 326566 BF*	........**5** 12
20 Jun 63	HEY MAMA *Philips BF 1254*	........**21** 9
4 Jun 64	HELLO, DOLLY! *Philips BF 1339*	......**18** 11
11 Mar 65	SOMEONE MUST HAVE HURT YOU A LOT *Philips BF 1394*	...**46** 1
23 Aug 67 ●	THERE MUST BE A WAY *Columbia DB 8248*	......**7** 21
15 Nov 67	SO TIRED *Columbia DB 8298*	........**21** 9
28 Sep 68	NEVERTHELESS *Columbia DB 8354*	.......**29** 5
5 Sep 59 ●	FRANKIE VAUGHAN AT THE LONDON PALLADIUM	
	Philips BDL 7330	........**6** 2
4 Nov 67	FRANKIE VAUGHAN SONGBOOK *Philips DBL 001*	.....**40** 1
25 Nov 67	THERE MUST BE A WAY *Columbia SCX 6200*	.......**22** 8
12 Nov 77	100 GOLDEN GREATS *Ronco RTDX 2021*	.......**24** 9

[1] Frankie Vaughan with the Peter Knight Singers [2] Frankie Vaughan and The Kaye Sisters

Malcolm VAUGHAN
UK, male vocalist – Malcolm Thomas (Singles: 106 Weeks) pos/wks

		pos/wks
1 Jul 55 ●	EV'RY DAY OF MY LIFE *HMV B 10874*	........**5** 16
27 Jan 56	WITH YOUR LOVE (2re) *HMV POP 130*	........**18** 3
26 Oct 56	ST THERESE OF THE ROSES (re) *HMV POP 250*	.....**3** 20
12 Apr 57	THE WORLD IS MINE (2re) *HMV POP 303*	........**26** 4
10 May 57	CHAPEL OF THE ROSES *HMV POP 325*	........**13** 8
29 Nov 57 ●	MY SPECIAL ANGEL *HMV POP 419*	........**3** 14
21 Mar 58	TO BE LOVED *HMV POP 459*	........**14** 12
17 Oct 58 ●	MORE THAN EVER (COME PRIMA) *HMV POP 538*	....**5** 14
27 Feb 59	WAIT FOR ME / WILLINGLY (re) *HMV POP 590*	....**13** 15

'With Your Love' is with the Peter Knight Singers. 'To Be Loved' and 'More Ever (Come Prima)' are with the Michael Sammes Singers

Norman VAUGHAN
UK, male vocalist / comedian (Singles: 5 Weeks) pos/wks

		pos/wks
17 May 62	SWINGING IN THE RAIN *Pye 7N 15438*	........**34** 5

Sarah VAUGHAN
US, female vocalist, b. 27 Mar 1924, d. 3 Apr 1990 (Singles: 34 Weeks, Albums: 1 Week) pos/wks

		pos/wks
27 Sep 57	PASSING STRANGERS *Mercury MT 164* [1]	.....**22** 2
11 Sep 59 ●	BROKEN HEARTED MELODY *Mercury AMT 1057*	......**7** 13
29 Dec 60	LET'S / SERENATA (re) *Columbia DB 4542*	.....**37** 4
12 Mar 69	PASSING STRANGERS (re-issue) *Mercury MF 1082* [1]	....**20** 15
26 Mar 60	NO COUNT – SARAH *Mercury MMC 14021*	.......**19** 1

[1] Billy Eckstine and Sarah Vaughan

Stevie Ray VAUGHAN and DOUBLE TROUBLE
US, male vocalist and instrumental group – leader b. 3 Oct 1954, d. 27 Aug 1990 (Albums: 1 Week) pos/wks

		pos/wks
15 Jul 89	IN STEP *Epic 463395 1*	........**63** 1

VAUGHAN BROTHERS
US, male vocal / instrumental group (Albums: 1 Week) pos/wks

		pos/wks
20 Oct 90	FAMILY STYLE *Epic 4670141*	........**63** 1

Billy VAUGHN and his Orchestra
US, orchestra and chorus – leader b. Richard Vaughn, 12 Apr 1919, d. 26 Sep 1991 (Singles: 8 Weeks) pos/wks

		pos/wks
27 Jan 56	THE SHIFTING WHISPERING SANDS PART 1	
	London HLD 8205 [1]	........**20** 1
23 Mar 56	THEME FROM "THE THREEPENNY OPERA" *London HLD 8238*	..**12** 7

[1] Billy Vaughn Orchestra and Chorus, narration by Ken Nordene

The VAULTS
UK, male vocal / instrumental group (Singles: 1 Week) pos/wks

		pos/wks
20 Mar 04	NO SLEEP NO NEED (EP) *Red Flag RF 09CDS*	........**70** 1

Tracks on the No Sleep No Need (EP): 'Lady Hell', 'No Sleep No Need', 'Leaving Here'

VBIRDS
UK, female cartoon vocal group (Singles: 3 Weeks) pos/wks

		pos/wks
3 May 03	VIRTUALITY *EMI / Liberty CDSVIRT 001*	........**21** 3

VEBA See RAE & CHRISTIAN

Bobby VEE (321 Top 500)
Early 1960s teen idol, b. Robert Velline, 30 Apr 1943, North Dakota, US. This photogenic, Buddy Holly-influenced teenaged vocalist (whose backing band once included Bob Dylan) was rarely away from the UK or US charts in the pre-Beat Boom years (Singles: 134 Weeks, Albums: 73 Weeks) pos/wks

		pos/wks
19 Jan 61 ●	RUBBER BALL *London HLG 9255*	........**4** 11
13 Apr 61 ●	MORE THAN I CAN SAY / STAYIN' IN *London HLG 9316*	....**4** 16
3 Aug 61 ●	HOW MANY TEARS *London HLG 9389*	......**10** 13
26 Oct 61 ●	TAKE GOOD CARE OF MY BABY *London HLG 9438* ▲	....**3** 16
21 Dec 61 ●	RUN TO HIM *London HLG 9470*	........**6** 15
8 Mar 62	PLEASE DON'T ASK ABOUT BARBARA *Liberty LIB 55419*	....**29** 9
7 Jun 62	SHARING YOU *Liberty LIB 55451*	........**10** 13
27 Sep 62	A FOREVER KIND OF LOVE *Liberty LIB 10046*	....**13** 19
7 Feb 63 ●	THE NIGHT HAS A THOUSAND EYES *Liberty LIB 10069*	....**3** 12
20 Jun 63	BOBBY TOMORROW *Liberty LIB 55530*	........**21** 10
24 Feb 62 ●	TAKE GOOD CARE OF MY BABY *London HAG 2428*	......**7** 8
31 Mar 62	HITS OF THE ROCKIN' 50'S *London HAG 2406*	........**20** 1
27 Oct 62 ●	BOBBY VEE MEETS THE CRICKETS *Liberty LBY 1086* [1]	....**2** 27
12 Jan 63 ●	A BOBBY VEE RECORDING SESSION *Liberty LBY 1084*	....**10** 11
20 Apr 63 ●	BOBBY VEE'S GOLDEN GREATS *Liberty LBY 1112*	....**10** 14
5 Oct 63	THE NIGHT HAS A THOUSAND EYES *Liberty LIB 1139*	....**15** 2
19 Apr 80 ●	THE BOBBY VEE SINGLES ALBUM *United Artists UAG 30253*	..**5** 10

[1] Bobby Vee and the Crickets

'Stayin' In' listed with 'More Than I Can Say' from 13 Apr to 4 May 1961. It peaked at No.13

Louie VEGA (see also LIL MO' YIN YANG; MASTERS AT WORK)
US, male producer (Singles: 5 Weeks) pos/wks

		pos/wks
5 Oct 91	RIDE ON THE RHYTHM *Atlantic A 7602* [1]	........**71** 1
23 May 92	RIDE ON THE RHYTHM *Atlantic A 7486* [1]	........**70** 1
31 Jan 98	RIDE ON THE RHYTHM (re-mix) *Perfecto PERF 151CD1* [2]	..**36** 2
23 Nov 02	DIAMOND LIFE *Distance DI 2409* [3]	........**52** 1

[1] Little Louie Vega and Marc Anthony [2] Little Louie and Marc Anthony [3] Louie Vega and Jay 'Sinister' Sealee starring Julie McKnight

Suzanne VEGA (370 Top 500)
Award-winning singer / songwriter / guitarist, who started as a fragile folk-pop performer, was educated at New York's High School for Performing Arts, b. 11 Jul 1959, Santa Monica, California, US. First artist to chart with accompanied and unaccompanied version of the same song ('Tom's Diner' – inspired by her brother's restaurant) (Singles: 52 Weeks, Albums: 132 Weeks) pos/wks

		pos/wks
18 Jan 86	SMALL BLUE THING *A&M AM 294*	........**65** 3
22 Mar 86	MARLENE ON THE WALL *A&M AM 309*	........**21** 9
7 Jun 86	LEFT OF CENTER *A&M AM 320* [1]	........**32** 9
23 May 87	LUKA *A&M VEGA 1*	........**23** 8
18 Jul 87	TOM'S DINER *A&M VEGA 2*	........**58** 3
19 May 90	BOOK OF DREAMS *A&M AM 559*	........**66** 1
28 Jul 90 ●	TOM'S DINER (re-mix) *A&M AM 592* [2]	........**2** 10
22 Aug 92	IN LIVERPOOL *A&M AM 0029*	........**52** 2
24 Oct 92	99.9 F *A&M AM 0085*	........**46** 2
19 Dec 92	BLOOD MAKES NOISE *A&M AM 0112*	........**60** 3
6 Mar 93	WHEN HEROES GO DOWN *A&M AM AMCD 0158*	........**58** 1
22 Feb 97	NO CHEAP THRILL *A&M AM 5818692*	........**40** 2
19 Oct 85	SUZANNE VEGA *A&M AMA 5072*	........**11** 71
9 May 87 ●	SOLITUDE STANDING *A&M SUZLP 2*	........**2** 39
28 Apr 90 ●	DAYS OF OPEN HAND *A&M 3952931*	........**7** 7
19 Sep 92	99.9 F *A&M 5400122*	........**20** 4
8 Mar 97	NINE OBJECTS OF DESIRE *A&M 5405832*	........**43** 2
31 Oct 98	TRIED AND TRUE – THE BEST OF SUZANNE VEGA	
	A&M 5409502	........**46** 3
19 Jul 03	RETROSPECTIVE – THE BEST OF SUZANNE VEGA	
	Universal TV 9808884	........**27** 5

[1] Suzanne Vega featuring Joe Jackson [2] DNA featuring Suzanne Vega

Singles re-entries are listed as (re), (2re), (3re).... which signifies that the hit re-entered the chart once, twice or three times...

Tata VEGA
US, female vocalist – Carmen Rosa Vega (Singles: 4 Weeks) — pos/wks

26 May 79	GET IT UP FOR LOVE / I JUST KEEP THINKING ABOUT YOU BABY *Motown TMG 1140*	52	4

VEGA 4 *See Paul VAN DYK*

VEGAS
(see also EURYTHMICS; FUN BOY THREE; The SPECIALS; The TOURISTS) *UK, male vocal / instrumental duo – David A Stewart and Terry Hall (Singles: 10 Weeks)* — pos/wks

19 Sep 92	POSSESSED *RCA 74321110437*	32	4
28 Nov 92	SHE *RCA 74321124657*	43	4
3 Apr 93	WALK INTO THE WIND *RCA 74321122462*	65	2

The VEILS
UK, male vocal / instrumental group (Singles: 2 Weeks) — pos/wks

7 Feb 04	THE WILD SON *Rough Trade RTRADESCD 154*	74	1
19 Jun 04	THE TIDE THAT LEFT AND NEVER CAME BACK *Rough Trade RTRADESCD 164*	63	1

Rosie VELA
US, female vocalist (Singles: 7 Weeks, Albums: 11 Weeks) — pos/wks

17 Jan 87	MAGIC SMILE *A&M AM 369*	27	7
31 Jan 87	ZAZU *A&M AMA 5016*	20	11

Wil VELOZ *See LOS DEL MAR featuring Wil VELOZ*

The VELVELETTES
US, female vocal group (Singles: 7 Weeks) — pos/wks

31 Jul 71	THESE THINGS WILL KEEP ME LOVING YOU *Tamla Motown TMG 780*	34	7

VELVET REVOLVER
US, male vocal / instrumental group (Singles: 5 Weeks, Albums: 15 Weeks) — pos/wks

24 Jul 04	SLITHER *RCA 8287663312*	35	3
23 Oct 04	FALL TO PIECES *RCA 82876647692*	32	2
19 Jun 04	CONTRABAND *RCA 82876628352* ▲	11	15

VELVET UNDERGROUND
(see also NICO; Lou REED; John CALE) *UK / US, male / female vocal / instrumental group (Singles: 1 Week, Albums: 10 Weeks)* — pos/wks

12 Mar 94	VENUS IN FURS *Sire W 0224CD*	71	1
23 Feb 85	V.U. *Polydor POLD 5167*	47	4
13 Nov 93	LIVE MCMXCIII *Sire 9362454642*	70	1
28 Oct 95	THE BEST OF LOU REED & THE VELVET UNDERGROUND *Global Television RADCD 21* [1]	56	4
6 Jul 02	THE VELVET UNDERGROUND & NICO *Polydor 8232902* [2]	59	1

[1] Lou Reed and The Velvet Underground [2] The Velvet Underground & Nico

The VELVETS
US, male vocal group (Singles: 2 Weeks) — pos/wks

11 May 61	THAT LUCKY OLD SUN *London HLU 9328*	46	1
17 Aug 61	TONIGHT (COULD BE THE NIGHT) *London HLU 9372*	50	1

Terry VENABLES *See RIDER & Terry VENABLES*

The VENGABOYS 386 Top 500
Hungary / Trinidad / Brazil / Holland, male / female vocal / production dance-pop troupe formed in 1992 by Spanish DJs Danski and Delmundo. In 1996 they added singers / dancers Kim, Robin (replaced by Yorick in 1999), Roy and Denice to front group. First Netherlands-based act to score six successive Top 5 singles. Best-selling single: 'Boom, Boom, Boom!!' 578,900 (Singles: 99 Weeks, Albums: 77 Weeks) — pos/wks

28 Nov 98	● UP AND DOWN *Positiva CDTIV 105*	4	15
13 Mar 99	● WE LIKE TO PARTY! (THE VENGABUS) *Positiva CDTIV 108*	3	14
26 Jun 99	★ BOOM, BOOM, BOOM, BOOM!! *Positiva CDTIV 114* ■	1	15
11 Sep 99	WE'RE GOING TO IBIZA (IMPORT) *Jive 550422*	69	1
18 Sep 99	★ WE'RE GOING TO IBIZA! *Positiva CDTIV 119* ■	1	12
18 Dec 99	● KISS (WHEN THE SUN DON'T SHINE) *Positiva CDTIV 122*	3	18
11 Mar 00	● SHALALA LALA *Positiva CDTIV 126*	5	10
8 Jul 00	● UNCLE JOHN FROM JAMAICA *Positiva CDTIV 135*	6	7
14 Oct 00	CHEEKAH BOW BOW (THAT COMPUTER SONG) *Positiva CDTIV 142*	19	5
24 Feb 01	FOREVER AS ONE *Positiva CDTIV 148*	28	2
3 Apr 99	● UP & DOWN – THE PARTY ALBUM! *Positiva 4993472*	6	49
25 Mar 00	● THE PLATINUM ALBUM *Positiva 5259530*	9	28

VENOM
UK, male vocal / instrumental group (Albums: 2 Weeks) — pos/wks

21 Apr 84	AT WAR WITH SATAN *Neat NEAT 1015*	64	1
13 Apr 85	POSSESSED *Neat NEAT 1024*	99	1

VENT 414
UK, male vocal / instrumental group (Singles: 1 Week) — pos/wks

28 Sep 96	FIXER *Polydor 5753292*	71	1

Anthony VENTURA ORCHESTRA
Switzerland, orchestra (Albums: 4 Weeks) — pos/wks

20 Jan 79	DREAM LOVER *Lotus WH 5007*	44	4

The VENTURES
US, male instrumental group (Singles: 31 Weeks) — pos/wks

8 Sep 60	● WALK DON'T RUN *Top Rank JAR 417*	8	13
1 Dec 60	● PERFIDIA *London HLG 9232*	4	13
9 Mar 61	RAM-BUNK-SHUSH *London HLG 9292*	45	1
11 May 61	LULLABY OF THE LEAVES *London HLG 9344*	43	4

VERACOCHA
(see also MOONMAN; SYSTEM F; GOURYELLA; STARPARTY) *Holland, male production duo – Vincent de Moor and Ferry Corsten (Singles: 4 Weeks)* — pos/wks

15 May 99	CARTE BLANCHE *Positiva CDTIV 110*	22	4

Al VERLAINE *See 'PING PING' and AL VERLAINE*

Tom VERLAINE
(see also TELEVISION) *US, male vocalist (Albums: 1 Week)* — pos/wks

14 Mar 87	FLASH LIGHT *Fontana SFLP 1*	99	1

The VERNONS GIRLS
UK, female vocal group (Singles: 31 Weeks) — pos/wks

17 May 62	LOVER PLEASE / YOU KNOW WHAT I MEAN (3re) *Decca F 11450*	16	20
6 Sep 62	LOCO-MOTION *Decca F 11495*	47	1
3 Jan 63	FUNNY ALL OVER *Decca F 11549*	31	8
18 Apr 63	DO THE BIRD (re) *Decca F 11629*	44	2

'You Know What I Mean' was not coupled with 'Lover Please' on the chart of 23 Aug 1962, but both sides of this record were listed for the following six weeks

VERNON'S WONDERLAND
Germany, male producer – Matthias Hoffmann (Singles: 1 Week) — pos/wks

25 May 96	VERNON'S WONDERLAND *Eye-Q Classics EYECL 004CD*	59	1

VERONIKA *See CRW*

VERTICAL HORIZON
US, male vocal / instrumental group (Singles: 2 Weeks) — pos/wks

26 Aug 00	EVERYTHING YOU WANT *RCA 74321748692* ▲	42	2

VERUCA SALT
US, male / female vocal / instrumental group (Singles: 5 Weeks, Albums: 2 Weeks) — pos/wks

2 Jul 94	SEETHER *Scared Hitless FRET 003CD*	61	1
3 Dec 94	SEETHER (re-issue) *Hi-Rise FLATSDG 12*	73	1
4 Feb 95	NUMBER ONE BLIND *Hi-Rise FLATSCD 16*	68	1
22 Feb 97	VOLCANO GIRLS *Outpost OPRCD 22197*	56	1
30 Aug 97	BENJAMIN *Outpost OPRCD 22261*	75	1
15 Oct 94	AMERICAN THIGHS *Hi-Rise FLATCD 9*	47	2

The VERVE 402 Top 500
Anthemic UK indie-rock band, formed 1991, Wigan, fronted by Richard Ashcroft (v/g). Double Brit-winners' swansong, 'Urban Hymns', went gold in 17 countries and sold a million in the UK in two successive years (1997/98). Ashcroft went solo when group split in 1999 (Singles: 50 Weeks, Albums: 121 Weeks) — pos/wks

4 Jul 92	SHE'S A SUPERSTAR *Hut HUT 16*	66	1
22 May 93	BLUE *Hut HUTCD 29*	69	1
13 May 95	THIS IS MUSIC *Hut HUTCD 54*	35	3
24 Jun 95	ON YOUR OWN *Hut HUTCD 55*	28	2
30 Sep 95	HISTORY *Hut HUTCD 59*	24	3
28 Jun 97	● BITTER SWEET SYMPHONY (re) *Hut HUTDG 82*	2	13
13 Sep 97	★ THE DRUGS DON'T WORK (re) *Hut HUTDG 88* ■	1	13
6 Dec 97	● LUCKY MAN *Hut HUTDG 92*	7	13
30 May 98	SONNET (IMPORT) *Hut 8950752*	74	1
3 Jul 93	A STORM IN HEAVEN *Hut CDHUT 10* [1]	27	2
15 Jul 95	A NORTHERN SOUL *Hut DGHUT 27*	13	11
11 Oct 97	★ URBAN HYMNS *Hut CDHUT 45* ■	1	102
13 Nov 04	THIS IS MUSIC – THE SINGLES 92-98 *Virgin CDV 2991*	15	6

[1] Verve

A VERY GOOD FRIEND OF MINE *Italy, male / female*
vocal / production / instrumental group (Singles: 1 Week)   pos/wks

3 Jul 99	JUST ROUND *Positiva CDTIV 109*	55	1

VEX RED *UK, male vocal / instrumental*
group (Singles: 1 Week, Albums: 1 Week)   pos/wks

2 Mar 02	CAN'T SMILE *Virgin VUSCD 237*	45	1
16 Mar 02	START WITH A STRONG AND PERSISTENT DESIRE *Virgin CDVUS 215*	48	1

VIBRATIONS *See Tony JACKSON and The VIBRATIONS*

The VIBRATORS *UK, male vocal /*
instrumental group (Singles: 8 Weeks, Albums: 7 Weeks)   pos/wks

18 Mar 78	AUTOMATIC LOVER *Epic EPC 6137*	35	5
17 Jun 78	JUDY SAYS (KNOCK YOU IN THE HEAD) *Epic EPC 6393*	70	3
25 Jun 77	THE VIBRATORS *Epic EPC 82907*	49	5
29 Apr 78	V2 *Epic EPC 82495*	33	2

The VICE SQUAD *UK, male / female vocal /*
instrumental group (Singles: 1 Week, Albums: 10 Weeks)   pos/wks

13 Feb 82	OUT OF REACH *Zonophone Z 26*	68	1
24 Oct 81	NO CAUSE FOR CONCERN *Zonophone ZEM 103*	32	5
22 May 82	STAND STRONG STAND PROUD *Zonophone ZEM 104*	47	5

Sid VICIOUS (see also SEX PISTOLS) *UK, male vocalist,*
b. John Beverley, 10 May 1957, d. 25 May 1965 (Albums: 8 Weeks)   pos/wks

15 Dec 79	SID SINGS *Virgin V 2144*	30	8

VICIOUS CIRCLES (see also POLTERGEIST)
UK, male producer – Simon Berry (Singles: 1 Week)   pos/wks

16 Dec 00	VICIOUS CIRCLES *Platipus PLATCD 82*	68	1

VICIOUS PINK
UK, male / female vocal / instrumental duo (Singles: 4 Weeks)   pos/wks

15 Sep 84	CCCAN'T YOU SEE *Parlophone R 6074*	67	4

Mike VICKERS *See Kenny EVERETT*

Maria VIDAL *US, female vocalist (Singles: 13 Weeks)*   pos/wks

24 Aug 85	BODY ROCK *EMI America EA 189*	11	13

The VIDEO KIDS
Holland, male / female vocal duo (Singles: 1 Week)   pos/wks

5 Oct 85	WOODPECKERS FROM SPACE *Epic A 6504*	72	1

VIDEO SYMPHONIC *UK, orchestra (Singles: 3 Weeks)*   pos/wks

24 Oct 81	THE FLAME TREES OF THIKA *EMI EMI 5222*	42	3

VIENNA PHILHARMONIC ORCHESTRA
Austria, male / female orchestra – conducted by
Aram Khatchaturian (Singles: 14 Weeks, Albums: 15 Weeks)   pos/wks

18 Dec 71	THEME FROM 'THE ONEDIN LINE' *Decca F 13259*	15	14
22 Jan 72	SPARTACUS *Decca SXL 6000* [1]	16	15

[1] Aram Khatchaturian / Vienna Philharmonic Orchestra

VIENNA SYMPHONY ORCHESTRA
Austria, male / female orchestra (Albums: 4 Weeks)   pos/wks

4 Apr 87	SYMPHONIC ROCK WITH THE VIENNA SYMPHONY ORCHESTRA *Stylus SMR 730*	43	4

VIEW FROM THE HILL
UK, male / female vocal / instrumental group (Singles: 6 Weeks)   pos/wks

19 Jul 86	NO CONVERSATION *EMI EMI 5565*	58	3
21 Feb 87	I'M NO REBEL *EMI EM 5580*	59	3

VIKKI
UK, female vocalist – Vikki Watson (Singles: 3 Weeks)   pos/wks

4 May 85	LOVE IS ... *PRT 7P 326*	49	3

The VILLAGE PEOPLE
US, male vocal group (Singles: 66 Weeks, Albums: 29 Weeks)   pos/wks

3 Dec 77	SAN FRANCISCO (YOU'VE GOT ME) *DJM DJS 10817*	45	5
25 Nov 78	★ Y.M.C.A. *Mercury 6007 192* ◆	1	16
17 Mar 79	● IN THE NAVY *Mercury 6007 209*	2	9
16 Jun 79	GO WEST *Mercury 6007 221*	15	8
9 Aug 80	CAN'T STOP THE MUSIC *Mercury MER 16*	11	11
9 Feb 85	SEX OVER THE PHONE *Record Shack SOHO 34*	59	5
4 Dec 93	Y.M.C.A. (re-mix) *Bell 74321177182*	12	7
28 May 94	IN THE NAVY (re-mix) *Bell 74321198192*	36	2
27 Nov 99	Y.M.C.A. (re-mix) *Wrasse WRASX 002*	35	3
27 Jan 79	CRUISIN' *Mercury 9109 614*	24	9
12 May 79	GO WEST *Mercury 9109 621*	14	19
18 Dec 93	THE BEST OF THE VILLAGE PEOPLE *Bell 4321178312*	72	1

Gene VINCENT
US, male vocalist, b. Eugene Craddock, 11 Feb 1935,
d. 12 Oct 1971 (Singles: 51 Weeks, Albums: 2 Weeks)   pos/wks

13 Jul 56	BE-BOP-A-LULA (2re) *Capitol CL 14599* [1]	16	7
12 Oct 56	RACE WITH THE DEVIL *Capitol CL 14628* [1]	28	1
19 Oct 56	BLUEJEAN BOP *Capitol CL 14637* [1]	16	5
8 Jan 60	WILD CAT (re) *Capitol CL 15099*	21	6
10 Mar 60	MY HEART (2re) *Capitol CL 15115* [1]	16	8
16 Jun 60	PISTOL PACKIN' MAMA *Capitol CL 15136* [2]	15	9
1 Jun 61	SHE SHE LITTLE SHEILA (re) *Capitol CL 15202*	22	11
31 Aug 61	I'M GOING HOME (TO SEE MY BABY) *Capitol CL 15215* [3]	36	4
16 Jul 60	CRAZY TIMES *Capitol T 1342*	12	2

[1] Gene Vincent and The Blue Caps [2] Gene Vincent with The Beat Boys
[3] Gene Vincent with Sounds Incorporated

Vinnie VINCENT (see also KISS)
US, male vocalist / instrumentalist – guitar (Albums: 2 Weeks)   pos/wks

28 May 88	ALL SYSTEMS GO *Chrysalis CHR 1626*	51	2

VINDALOO SUMMER SPECIAL
UK, male / female vocal / instrumental group (Singles: 3 Weeks)   pos/wks

19 Jul 86	ROCKIN' WITH RITA (HEAD TO TOE) *Vindaloo UGH 13*	56	3

The VINES *Australia, male vocal /*
instrumental group (Singles: 12 Weeks, Albums: 9 Weeks)   pos/wks

20 Apr 02	HIGHLY EVOLVED *Heavenly HVN 112CD*	32	2
29 Jun 02	GET FREE *Heavenly HVN 113CD*	24	3
19 Oct 02	OUTTATHAWAY *Heavenly HVN 120CDS*	20	2
20 Mar 04	RIDE *Heavenly HVN 137CD*	25	3
5 Jun 04	WINNING DAYS *Heavenly HVN 139CDS*	42	2
20 Jul 02	● HIGHLY EVOLVED *Heavenly HVNLP 36CD*	3	7
3 Apr 04	WINNING DAYS *Heavenly HVNLP 48CD*	29	2

Bobby VINTON
US, male vocalist – Stanley Vinton
(Singles: 29 Weeks, Albums: 2 Weeks)   pos/wks

2 Aug 62	ROSES ARE RED (MY LOVE) *Columbia DB 4878* ▲	15	8
19 Dec 63	THERE! I'VE SAID IT AGAIN *Columbia DB 7179* ▲	34	10
29 Sep 90	● BLUE VELVET *Epic 6505240* ▲	2	10
17 Nov 90	ROSES ARE RED (MY LOVE) (re-issue) *Epic 6564677*	71	1
17 Nov 90	BLUE VELVET *Epic 4675701*	67	2

VINYLGROOVER and The RED HED
UK, male production duo (Singles: 2 Weeks)   pos/wks

27 Jan 01	ROK DA HOUSE *Nukleuz NUKP 0285*	72	1
10 Jul 04	STAY *Tidy Trax TIDYTWO 133C* [1]	61	1

[1] Rob Tisseria, Vinylgroover & The Red Hed

VIOLENT DELIGHT
UK, male vocal / instrumental group (Singles: 4 Weeks)   pos/wks

1 Mar 03	I WISH I WAS A GIRL *WEA WEA 362CD*	25	2
21 Jun 03	ALL YOU EVER DO *WEA WEA 367CD1*	38	1
13 Sep 03	TRANSMISSION *WEA WEA 370CD1*	64	1

VIOLENT FEMMES
US, male / female vocal / instrumental group (Albums: 1 Week)   pos/wks

1 Mar 86	THE BLIND LEADING THE NAKED *Slash SLAP 10*	81	1

Singles re-entries are listed as (re). (2re). (3re).... which signifies that the hit re-entered the chart once, twice or three times...

VIOLINSKI
UK, male instrumental group (Singles: 9 Weeks, Albums: 1 Week) pos/wks

17 Feb 79	CLOG DANCE *Jet 136*	**17**	9
26 May 79	NO CAUSE FOR ALARM *Jet JETLU 219*	**49**	1

VIPER
Belgium, male production group (Singles: 1 Week) pos/wks

7 Feb 98	THE TWISTER *Hooj Choons HOOJCD 59*	**55**	1

The VIPERS SKIFFLE GROUP
UK, male vocal / instrumental group (Singles: 18 Weeks) pos/wks

25 Jan 57 ●	DON'T YOU ROCK ME DADDY-O *Parlophone R 4261*	**10**	9
22 Mar 57 ●	THE CUMBERLAND GAP *Parlophone R 4289*	**10**	6
31 May 57	STREAMLINE TRAIN *Parlophone R 4308*	**23**	3

VIRGINIA *See Tom NOVY*

VIRUS (see also OAKENFOLD; PERFECTO ALL STARZ)
UK, male instrumental / production duo – Paul Oakenfold and Steve Osborne (Singles: 3 Weeks) pos/wks

26 Aug 95	SUN *Perfecto PERF 107CD*	**62**	1
25 Jan 97	MOON *Perfecto PERF 134CD*	**36**	2

VISAGE (see also Midge URE)
UK, male vocal / instrumental group (Singles: 56 Weeks, Albums: 58 Weeks) pos/wks

20 Dec 80 ●	FADE TO GREY *Polydor POSP 194*	**8**	15
14 Mar 81	MIND OF A TOY *Polydor POSP 236*	**13**	8
11 Jul 81	VISAGE *Polydor POSP 293*	**21**	7
13 Mar 82	DAMNED DON'T CRY *Polydor POSP 390*	**11**	8
26 Jun 82	NIGHT TRAIN *Polydor POSP 441*	**12**	10
13 Nov 82	PLEASURE BOYS *Polydor POSP 523*	**44**	3
1 Sep 84	LOVE GLOVE *Polydor POSP 691*	**54**	3
28 Aug 93	FADE TO GREY (re-mix) *Polydor PZCD 282*	**39**	2
24 Jan 81	VISAGE *Polydor 2490 157*	**13**	29
3 Apr 82 ●	THE ANVIL *Polydor POLD 5050*	**6**	16
19 Nov 83	FADE TO GREY – THE SINGLES COLLECTION *Polydor POLD 5117*	**38**	11
3 Nov 84	BEAT BOY *Polydor POLH 12*	**79**	2

Michelle VISAGE *See S.O.U.L. S.Y.S.T.E.M. introducing Michelle VISAGE*

The VISCOUNTS
UK, male vocal group (Singles: 18 Weeks) pos/wks

13 Oct 60	SHORT'NIN' BREAD *Pye 7N 15287*	**16**	8
14 Sep 61	WHO PUT THE BOMP (IN THE BOMP, BOMP, BOMP) *Pye 7N 15379*	**21**	10

VISION
UK, male vocal / instrumental group (Singles: 1 Week) pos/wks

9 Jul 83	LOVE DANCE *MVM MVM 2886*	**74**	1

VISIONMASTERS with Tony KING and Kylie MINOGUE
UK, male DJ / production duo, UK, male DJ / producer and Australia, female vocalist (Singles: 1 Week) pos/wks

30 Nov 91	KEEP ON PUMPIN' IT *PWL PWL 207*	**49**	1

VITA *See N*E*R*D; Irv GOTTI*

VITAMIN C
US, female vocalist – Colleen Fitzpatrick (Singles: 1 Week) pos/wks

19 Jul 03	LAST NITE *V2 VVR 5023283*	**70**	1

Soraya VIVIAN
UK, female vocalist (Singles: 1 Week) pos/wks

16 Mar 02	WHEN YOU'RE GONE *Activ 8 ACT 501*	**59**	1

VIXEN
US, female vocal / instrumental group (Singles: 21 Weeks, Albums: 5 Weeks) pos/wks

3 Sep 88	EDGE OF A BROKEN HEART *Manhattan MT 48*	**51**	4
4 Mar 89	CRYIN' *EMI Manhattan MT 60*	**27**	4
3 Jun 89	LOVE MADE ME *EMI-USA MT 66*	**36**	4
2 Sep 89	EDGE OF A BROKEN HEART (re-issue) *EMI-USA MT 48*	**59**	2
28 Jul 90	HOW MUCH LOVE *EMI-USA MT 87*	**35**	3
20 Oct 90	LOVE IS A KILLER *EMI-USA MT 91*	**41**	2
16 Mar 91	NOT A MINUTE TOO SOON *EMI-USA MT 93*	**37**	2
8 Oct 88	VIXEN *Manhattan MTL 1028*	**66**	1
18 Aug 90	REV IT UP *EMI-USA MTL 1054*	**20**	4

VOGGUE
Canada, male / female production / vocal group (Singles: 6 Weeks) pos/wks

18 Jul 81	DANCIN' THE NIGHT AWAY *Mercury MER 76*	**39**	6

VOICE OF THE BEEHIVE
US / UK, male / female vocal / instrumental group (Singles: 51 Weeks, Albums: 26 Weeks) pos/wks

14 Nov 87	I SAY NOTHING *London LON 151*	**45**	5
5 Mar 88	I WALK THE EARTH *London LON 169*	**42**	4
14 May 88	DON'T CALL ME BABY *London LON 175*	**15**	10
23 Jul 88	I SAY NOTHING (re-issue) *London LON 190*	**22**	6
22 Oct 88	I WALK THE EARTH (re-issue) *London LON 206*	**46**	4
13 Jul 91	MONSTERS AND ANGELS *London LON 302*	**17**	10
28 Sep 91	I THINK I LOVE YOU *London LON 308*	**25**	5
11 Jan 92	PERFECT PLACE *London LON 312*	**37**	6
2 Jul 88	LET IT BEE *London LONLP 57*	**13**	13
24 Aug 91	HONEY LINGERS *London 8282591*	**17**	13

VOICES OF LIFE
US, male / female vocal / production duo – Sharon Pass and Steve 'Silk' Hurley (Singles: 2 Weeks) pos/wks

21 Mar 98	THE WORD IS LOVE (SAY THE WORD) *AM:PM 5825272*	**26**	2

Sterling VOID
UK, male instrumentalist / vocalist (Singles: 3 Weeks) pos/wks

4 Feb 89	RUNAWAY GIRL / IT'S ALL RIGHT *ffrr FFR 21*	**53**	3

VOLATILE AGENTS featuring Simone BENN
UK, male production duo and UK, female vocalist (Singles: 3 Weeks) pos/wks

15 Dec 01	HOOKED ON YOU *Melting Pot MPRCD 10*	**54**	3 •

VOLCANO
Norway / UK, male / female vocal / instrumental group (Singles: 4 Weeks) pos/wks

23 Jul 94	MORE TO LOVE *Deconstruction 74321221832*	**32**	3
18 Nov 95	THAT'S THE WAY LOVE IS *EXP EXPCD 002* [1]	**72**	1

[1] Volcano with Sam Cartwright

The VON BONDIES
US, male vocal / instrumental group (Singles: 3 Weeks, Albums: 2 Weeks) pos/wks

14 Feb 04	C'MON C'MON *Sire W 635CD*	**21**	2
15 May 04	TELL ME WHAT YOU SEE *Sire W 639CD1*	**43**	1
21 Feb 04	PAWN SHOPPE HEART *Sire 9362485352*	**36**	2

Herbert VON KARAJAN
Austria, male conductor, b. 5 Apr 1908, d. 16 Jul 1989 (Albums: 18 Weeks) pos/wks

26 Sep 70	BEETHOVEN TRIPLE CONCERTO *HMV ASD 2582*	**51**	2
16 Apr 88	THE ESSENTIAL KARAJAN *Deutsche Grammophon HVKTV 1*	**51**	5
3 Aug 91	HOLST: THE PLANETS *Deutsche Grammophon 4352891*	**52**	2
7 Oct 95	KARAJAN: ADAGIO *Deutsche Grammophon 4452822*	**30**	8
13 Apr 96	ADAGIO 2 *Deutsche Grammophon 4495152* [1]	**63**	1

[1] Berlin Philharmonic Orchestra / Herbert Von Karajan

On 'Beethoven Triple Concerto' the soloists are David Oistrakh (violin), Mstislav Rostropovich (cello) and Sviatoslav Richter (piano). Von Karajan also conducted the Berlin Philharmonic Orchestra

Anne Sofie VON OTTER meets Elvis COSTELLO
Sweden, female vocalist and UK male vocalist (Albums: 1 Week) pos/wks

31 Mar 01	FOR THE STARS *Deutsche Grammophon 4695302*	**67**	1

VOODOO & SERANO
Germany, male production duo – Reinhard Raith and Tommy Serano (Singles: 6 Weeks) pos/wks

3 Feb 01	BLOOD IS PUMPIN' *Xtrahard / Xtravaganza X2H 2CDS*	**19**	4
16 Aug 03	OVERLOAD *All Around the World CDGLOBE 284*	**30**	2

VOW WOW
Japan / US, male vocal / instrumental group (Albums: 1 Week) pos/wks

18 Mar 89	HELTER SKELTER *Arista 209691*	**75**	1

VOYAGE
UK / France, disco aggregation (Singles: 27 Weeks, Albums: 1 Week) pos/wks

17 Jun 78	FROM EAST TO WEST / SCOTS MACHINE *GTO GT 224*	**13**	13
25 Nov 78	SOUVENIRS *GTO GT 241*	**56**	7

		pos/wks
24 Mar 79	LET'S FLY AWAY *GTO GT 245*	**38** 7
9 Sep 78	VOYAGE *GTO GTLP 030*	**59** 1

'Scots Machine' credited from 24 Jun 1978 until end of record's chart run

VOYAGER *UK, male vocal / instrumental group (Singles: 8 Weeks)* pos/wks

26 May 79	HALFWAY HOTEL *Mountain VOY 001*	**33** 8

Jurgen VRIES (see also ANGELIC; ORION; DT8 PROJECT; CITIZEN CANED)
UK, male DJ / producer – Darren Tate (Singles: 20 Weeks) pos/wks

14 Sep 02	THE THEME *Direction 6730952*	**13** 4
1 Feb 03 ●	THE OPERA SONG (BRAVE NEW WORLD) (re) *Direction 6734642* [1]	**3** 10
4 Oct 03	WILDERNESS *Direction 6742692* [2]	**20** 3
19 Jun 04	TAKE MY HAND *Direction 6749932* [3]	**23** 3

[1] Jurgen Vries featuring CMC (Charlotte Church) [2] Jurgen Vries featuring Shena [3] Jurgen Vries featuring Andrea Britton

VS *UK, male / female vocal / rap group (Singles: 15 Weeks)* pos/wks

6 Mar 04 ●	LOVE YOU LIKE MAD *Innocent SINCD 59*	**7** 7
19 Jun 04	CALL U SEXY *Innocent SINDX 62*	**11** 6
23 Oct 04	MAKE IT HOT *Innocent SINDX 66*	**29** 2

VYBE *US, female vocal group (Singles: 1 Week)* pos/wks

7 Oct 95	WARM SUMMER DAZE *Fourth & Broadway BRCD 315*	**60** 1

Billy Paul W *See Robbie RIVERA*

Kristine W *US, female vocalist – Kristine Weitz (Singles: 8 Weeks)* pos/wks

21 May 94	LOVE COME HOME *Triangle BLUESCD 001* [1]	**73** 1
25 Jun 94	FEEL WHAT YOU WANT *Champion CHAMPCD 304*	**33** 3
25 May 96	ONE MORE TRY *Champion CHAMPCD 317*	**41** 1
21 Dec 96	LAND OF THE LIVING *Champion CHAMPCD 324*	**57** 1
5 Jul 97	FEEL WHAT YOU WANT (re-issue) *Champion CHAMPCD 329*	**40** 2

[1] Our Tribe with Franke Pharoah and Kristine W

WC featuring SNOOP DOGG & Nate DOGG
US, male rappers (WC is William Calhoun) (Singles: 2 Weeks) pos/wks

1 Mar 03	THE STREETS *Def Jam 0779852*	**48** 2

W.I.P. featuring EMMIE
UK, male production duo and UK, female vocalist (Singles: 1 Week) pos/wks

16 Feb 02	I WON'T LET YOU DOWN *Decode / Telstar CDSTAS 3210*	**53** 1

Andrew W.K. *US, male vocalist / producer –*
Andrew Wilkes-Krier (Singles: 5 Weeks, Albums: 1 Week) pos/wks

10 Nov 01	PARTY HARD *Mercury 5888132*	**19** 4
9 Mar 02	SHE IS BEAUTIFUL *Mercury 5889522*	**55** 1
24 Nov 01	I GET WET *Mercury 5865882*	**71** 1

W.O.S.P.
UK, male / female production / vocal duo (Singles: 1 Week) pos/wks

17 Nov 01	GETTIN' INTO U *Data DATA 26CDS*	**48** 1

WWF SUPERSTARS *US / UK, male wrestling*
vocalists (Singles: 15 Weeks, Albums: 5 Weeks) pos/wks

12 Dec 92 ●	SLAM JAM (re) *Arista 74321124887*	**4** 9
3 Apr 93	WRESTLEMANIA *Arista 74321136832*	**14** 5
10 Jul 93	USA *Arista 74321153092* [1]	**71** 1
17 Apr 93 ●	WRESTLEMANIA – THE ALBUM *Arista 74321138062*	**10** 5

[1] WWF Superstars featuring Hacksaw Jim Duggan

Bill WADDINGTON *See CORONATION STREET CAST featuring Bill WADDINGTON*

Adam WADE *US, male vocalist (Singles: 6 Weeks)* pos/wks

8 Jun 61	TAKE GOOD CARE OF HER (re) *HMV POP 843*	**38** 6

With the George Paxton Orchestra and Chorus

WAG YA TAIL
UK, male vocal / instrumental group (Singles: 1 Week) pos/wks

3 Oct 92	XPAND YA MIND (EXPANSIONS) *PWL International PWL 238*	**49** 1

WAH! *UK, male vocal / instrumental group – leader Pete Wylie*
(Singles: 26 Weeks, Albums: 11 Weeks) pos/wks

25 Dec 82 ●	THE STORY OF THE BLUES *Eternal JF 1*	**3** 12
19 Mar 83	HOPE (I WISH YOU'D BELIEVE ME) *WEA X 9880*	**37** 5
30 Jun 84	COME BACK *Beggars Banquet BEG 111* [1]	**20** 9
18 Jul 81	NAH-POO = THE ART OF BLUFF *Eternal CLASSIC 1*	**33** 5
4 Aug 84	A WORD TO THE WISE GUY *Beggars Banquet BEGA 54* [1]	**28** 6

[1] Mighty Wah! [1] Mighty Wah!

Donnie WAHLBERG *See NEW KIDS ON THE BLOCK; SEIKO and Donnie WAHLBERG*

The WAIKIKIS
Belgium, male instrumental group (Singles: 2 Weeks) pos/wks

11 Mar 65	HAWAII TATTOO *Pye International 7N 25286*	**41** 2

WAILERS *See Bob MARLEY & The WAILERS*

Rufus WAINWRIGHT *US, male vocalist (Singles: 1 Week)* pos/wks

7 Aug 04	I DON'T KNOW WHAT IT IS *Dreamworks 9863229*	**74** 1

John WAITE (see also The BABYS: BROKEN ENGLISH)
UK, male vocalist (Singles: 13 Weeks, Albums: 3 Weeks) pos/wks

29 Sep 84 ●	MISSING YOU *EMI America EA 182* ▲	**9** 11
13 Feb 93	MISSING YOU (re-issue) *Chrysalis CDCHS 3938*	**56** 2
10 Nov 84	NO BRAKES *EMI America WAIT 1*	**64** 3

The WAITRESSES
US, male / female vocal / instrumental group (Singles: 4 Weeks) pos/wks

18 Dec 82	CHRISTMAS WRAPPING *Ze / Island WIP 6821*	**45** 4

Tom WAITS *US, male vocalist (Albums: 31 Weeks)* pos/wks

8 Oct 83	SWORDFISHTROMBONES *Island ILPS 9762*	**62** 3
19 Oct 85	RAIN DOGS *Island ILPS 9803*	**29** 5
5 Sep 87	FRANKS WILD YEARS *Island ITW 3*	**20** 5
8 Oct 88	BIG TIME *Island ITW 4*	**84** 1
19 Sep 92	BONE MACHINE *Island CID 9993*	**26** 3
20 Nov 93	THE BLACK RIDER *Island CID 8021*	**47** 2
27 Jun 98	BEAUTIFUL MALADIES – THE ISLAND YEARS *Island 5245192*	**63** 1
1 May 99 ●	MULE VARIATIONS *Epitaph 65472*	**9** 5
18 May 02	ALICE *Anti 66322*	**20** 2
18 May 02	BLOOD MONEY *Anti 66292*	**21** 2
16 Oct 04	REAL GONE *Anti 66782*	**16** 2

Johnny WAKELIN *UK, male vocalist (Singles: 20 Weeks)* pos/wks

18 Jan 75 ●	BLACK SUPERMAN (MUHAMMAD ALI) *Pye 7N 45420* [1]	**7** 10
24 Jul 76	IN ZAIRE *Pye 7N 45595*	**4** 10

[1] Johnny Wakelin and The Kinshasa Band

Rick WAKEMAN
(see also ANDERSON BRUFORD WAKEMAN HOWE; The STRAWBS; YES)
UK, male instrumentalist – keyboards (Albums: 131 Weeks) pos/wks

24 Feb 73 ●	THE SIX WIVES OF HENRY VIII *A&M AMLH 64361*	**7** 22
18 May 74 ★	JOURNEY TO THE CENTRE OF THE EARTH *A&M AMLH 63621*	**1** 30
12 Apr 75 ●	THE MYTHS AND LEGENDS OF KING ARTHUR & THE KNIGHTS OF THE ROUND TABLE *A&M AMLH 645150022*	**2** 28

24 Apr 76 ●	NO EARTHLY CONNECTION *A&M AMLK 64583* **9**	9
12 Feb 77	WHITE ROCK *A&M AMLH 64614* **14**	9
3 Dec 77	RICK WAKEMAN'S CRIMINAL RECORD *A&M AMLK 64660* **25**	5
2 Jun 79	RHAPSODIES *A&M AMLX 68508* **25**	10
27 Jun 81	1984 *Charisma CDS 4022* **24**	9
13 Oct 84	BEYOND THE PLANETS *Telstar STAR 2244* [1] **64**	6
16 May 87	THE GOSPELS *Stylus SMR 729* **94**	1
27 Mar 99	RETURN TO THE CENTRE OF THE EARTH	
	EMI Classics CDC 5567632 ....**34**	2

[1] Kevin Peek and Rick Wakeman

Narada Michael WALDEN
US, male vocalist / producer (Singles: 28 Weeks, Albums: 1 Week) pos/wks

23 Feb 80	TONIGHT I'M ALRIGHT *Atlantic K 11437* **34**	9
26 Apr 80 ●	I SHOULDA LOVED YA *Atlantic K 11413* **8**	9
23 Apr 88 ●	DIVINE EMOTIONS *Reprise W 7967* [1] **8**	10
14 May 88	DIVINE EMOTION *Reprise WX 172* [1] **60**	5

[1] Narada [1] Narada

Gary WALKER (see also The WALKER BROTHERS) *US, male vocalist / instrumentalist – drums – Gary Leeds (Singles: 12 Weeks)* pos/wks

24 Feb 66	YOU DON'T LOVE ME *CBS 202036* **26**	6
26 May 66	TWINKIE-LEE *CBS 202081* **26**	6

John WALKER (see also The WALKER BROTHERS) *US, male vocalist / instrumentalist – guitar – John Maus (Singles: 6 Weeks)* pos/wks

5 Jul 67	ANNABELLA (re) *Philips BF 1593* **24**	6

Scott WALKER (see also The WALKER BROTHERS) *US, male vocalist – Scott Engel (Singles: 30 Weeks, Albums: 58 Weeks)* pos/wks

6 Dec 67	JACKIE *Philips BF 1628* **22**	9
1 May 68 ●	JOANNA *Philips BF 1662* **7**	11
11 Jun 69	LIGHTS OF CINCINNATI *Philips BF 1793* **13**	10
16 Sep 67 ●	SCOTT *Philips SBL 7816* **3**	17
20 Apr 68 ★	SCOTT 2 *Philips SBL 7840* **1**	18
5 Apr 69 ●	SCOTT 3 *Philips S 7882* **3**	4
5 Jul 69 ●	SONGS FROM HIS TV SERIES *Philips SBL 7900* **7**	3
31 Mar 84	CLIMATE OF HUNTER *Virgin V 2303* **60**	2
25 Jan 92 ●	NO REGRETS – THE BEST OF SCOTT WALKER AND THE	
	WALKER BROTHERS 1965-1976 *Fontana 5108312* [1] **4**	13
20 May 95	TILT *Fontana 5268592* **27**	1

[1] Scott Walker and The Walker Brothers

Terri WALKER *UK, female vocalist (Singles: 3 Weeks)* pos/wks

1 Mar 03	GUESS YOU DIDN'T LOVE ME *Def Soul 779962* **60**	1
17 May 03	CHING CHING (LOVIN' YOU STILL) *Def Soul 9800075* **38**	2

Jr WALKER & The ALL-STARS *US, male instrumental / vocal group – leader b. 14 Jun 1931, d. 23 Nov 1995 (Singles: 59 Weeks)* pos/wks

18 Aug 66	HOW SWEET IT IS (TO BE LOVED BY YOU)	
	Tamla Motown TMG 571 ....**22**	10
2 Apr 69	ROAD RUNNER *Tamla Motown TMG 691* **12**	12
18 Oct 69	WHAT DOES IT TAKE (TO WIN YOUR LOVE)	
	Tamla Motown TMG 712 ....**13**	12
26 Aug 72	WALK IN THE NIGHT *Tamla Motown TMG 824* **16**	11
27 Jan 73	TAKE ME GIRL, I'M READY *Tamla Motown TMG 840* **16**	9
30 Jun 73	WAY BACK HOME *Tamla Motown TMG 857* **35**	5

The WALKER BROTHERS `333` `Top 500`
Unrelated US trio who were top UK teen idols in the mid-60s. Members Scott Walker (Engel) (v/b/k), John Walker (Maus) (v/g), and Gary Walker (Leeds) (d) all had solo hits after the trio split in 1967, with Scott (who first recorded solo in 1957) creating a large cult following (Singles: 93 Weeks, Albums: 109 Weeks) pos/wks

29 Apr 65	LOVE HER *Philips BF 1409* **20**	13
19 Aug 65 ★	MAKE IT EASY ON YOURSELF *Philips BF 1428* **1**	14
2 Dec 65 ●	MY SHIP IS COMING IN *Philips BF 1454* **3**	12
3 Mar 66 ★	THE SUN AIN'T GONNA SHINE ANYMORE *Philips BF 1473* **1**	11
14 Jul 66	(BABY) YOU DON'T HAVE TO TELL ME *Philips BF 1497* **13**	8
22 Sep 66	ANOTHER TEAR FALLS *Philips BF 1514* **12**	8
15 Dec 66	DEADLIER THAN THE MALE *Philips BF 1537* **34**	6
9 Feb 67	STAY WITH ME BABY *Philips BF 1548* **26**	6
18 May 67	WALKING IN THE RAIN *Philips BF 1576* **26**	6

17 Jan 76 ●	NO REGRETS *GTO GT 42* **7**	9
18 Dec 65 ●	TAKE IT EASY WITH THE WALKER BROTHERS	
	Philips BL 7691 ....**3**	36
3 Sep 66 ●	PORTRAIT *Philips BL 7691* **3**	23
18 Mar 67 ●	IMAGES *Philips SBL 7770* **6**	15
16 Sep 67 ●	THE WALKER BROTHERS' STORY *Philips DBL 002* **9**	19
21 Feb 76	NO REGRETS *GTO GTLP 007* **49**	3
25 Jan 92 ●	NO REGRETS – THE BEST OF SCOTT WALKER AND THE	
	WALKER BROTHERS 1965-1976 *Fontana 5108312* [1] **4**	13

[1] Scott Walker and The Walker Brothers

The WALKMEN *US, male vocal / instrumental group (Singles: 2 Weeks, Albums: 1 Week)* pos/wks

1 May 04	THE RAT *WEA W 640CD* **45**	1
10 Jul 04	LITTLE HOUSE OF SAVAGES *Record Collection W 646CD 2* ...**72**	1
8 May 04	BOWS + ARROWS *WEA 9362486802* **62**	1

WALL OF SOUND featuring Gerald LETHAN *US, male vocal / instrumental group (Singles: 1 Week)* pos/wks

31 Jul 93	CRITICAL (IF YOU ONLY KNEW) *Positiva CDTIV 4* **73**	1

WALL OF VOODOO *US, male vocal / instrumental group (Singles: 3 Weeks)* pos/wks

19 Mar 83	MEXICAN RADIO *Illegal ILS 36* **64**	3

Jerry WALLACE *US, male vocalist (Singles: 1 Week)* pos/wks

23 Jun 60	YOU'RE SINGING OUR LOVE SONG TO SOMEBODY ELSE	
	London HLH 9110 ....**46**	1

Rik WALLER *UK, male vocalist (Singles: 12 Weeks)* pos/wks

16 Mar 02 ●	I WILL ALWAYS LOVE YOU (re) *EMI / Liberty CDRIK 001* **6**	8
6 Jul 02	(SOMETHING INSIDE) SO STRONG *EMI / Liberty CDRIK 002* ..**25**	4

The WALLFLOWERS *US, male vocal / instrumental group (Singles: 1 Week, Albums: 2 Weeks)* pos/wks

12 Jul 97	ONE HEADLIGHT *Interscope IND 95532* **54**	1
21 Jun 97	BRINGING DOWN THE HORSE *Interscope IND 90055* **58**	2

Bob WALLIS and his STORYVILLE JAZZ BAND *UK, male vocalist / instrumentalist – trumpet, b. 3 Jun 1934, d. 10 Jan 1991, and male jazz band (Singles: 7 Weeks, Albums: 1 Week)* pos/wks

6 Jul 61	I'M SHY MARY ELLEN, I'M SHY *Pye Jazz 7NJ 2043* **44**	2
4 Jan 62	COME ALONG PLEASE *Pye Jazz 7NJ 2048* **33**	5
11 Jun 60	EVERYBODY LOVES SATURDAY NIGHT *Top Rank BUY 023* **20**	1

Joe WALSH (see also The EAGLES) *US, male vocalist / instrumentalist – guitar (Singles: 15 Weeks, Albums: 20 Weeks)* pos/wks

16 Jul 77	ROCKY MOUNTAIN WAY (EP) *ABC ABE 12002* **39**	4
8 Jul 78	LIFE'S BEEN GOOD *Asylum K 13129* **14**	11
17 Apr 76	YOU CAN'T ARGUE WITH A SICK MIND *Anchor ABCL 5156* **28**	3
10 Jun 78	BUT SERIOUSLY FOLKS *Asylum K 53081* **16**	17

Tracks on Rocky Mountain Way (EP): Rocky Mountain Way / Turn to Stone / Meadows / Walk Away

Maureen WALSH See MAUREEN

Sheila WALSH and Cliff RICHARD *UK, female / male vocal duo (Singles: 2 Weeks)* pos/wks

4 Jun 83	DRIFTING *DJM SHEIL 1* **64**	2

Steve WALSH *UK, male DJ / vocalist, b. 1959, d. 3 July 1988 (Singles: 18 Weeks)* pos/wks

18 Jul 87 ●	I FOUND LOVIN' (re) *A1 A1 299* **9**	13
12 Dec 87	LET'S GET TOGETHER TONITE *A1 A1 303* **74**	1
30 Jul 88	AIN'T NO STOPPING US NOW (PARTY FOR THE WORLD)	
	A1 A1 304 ....**44**	4

Trevor WALTERS *UK, male vocalist (Singles: 22 Weeks)* pos/wks

24 Oct 81	LOVE ME TONIGHT *Magnet MAG 198* **27**	8
21 Jul 84 ●	STUCK ON YOU *Sanity IS 002* **9**	12
1 Dec 84	NEVER LET HER SLIP AWAY *Polydor POSP 716* **73**	2

WAMDUE PROJECT
US, male producer – Chris Brann (Singles: 19 Weeks)   pos/wks
20 Nov 99	KING OF MY CASTLE (IMPORT) *Orange ORCDM 53584CD*	61	1
27 Nov 99 ★	KING OF MY CASTLE (re) *AM:PM CDAMPM 127*■	1	16
15 Apr 00	YOU'RE THE REASON *AM:PM CDAMPM 130*	39	2

WANG CHUNG
UK, male vocal / instrumental group (Singles: 12 Weeks, Albums: 5 Weeks)   pos/wks
| 28 Jan 84 | DANCE HALL DAYS *Geffen A 3837* | 21 | 12 |
| 21 Apr 84 | POINTS ON THE CURVE *Geffen GEF 25589* | 34 | 5 |

The WANNADIES
Sweden, male / female vocal / instrumental group (Singles: 12 Weeks, Albums: 4 Weeks)   pos/wks
18 Nov 95	MIGHT BE STARS *Indolent DIE 003CD1*	51	2
24 Feb 96	HOW DOES IT FEEL *Indolent DIE 004CD1*	53	1
20 Apr 96	YOU AND ME SONG *Indolent DIE 005CD*	18	3
7 Sep 96	SOMEONE SOMEWHERE *Indolent DIE 006CD*	38	1
26 Apr 97	HIT *Indolent DIE 009CD1*	20	2
5 Jul 97	SHORTY *Indolent DIE 010CD1*	41	2
4 Mar 00	YEAH *RCA 74321745552*	56	1
17 May 97	BAGSY ME *Indolent DIECD 008*	37	3
18 Mar 00	YEAH *RCA 74321687022*	73	1

Dexter WANSELL
US, male instrumentalist – keyboards (Singles: 3 Weeks)   pos/wks
| 20 May 78 | ALL NIGHT LONG *Philadelphia International PIR 6255* | 59 | 3 |

WAR
(see also Eric BURDON and WAR) *US / Canada / Denmark, male vocal / instrumental group (Singles: 32 Weeks)*   pos/wks
24 Jan 76	LOW RIDER *Island WIP 6267*	12	7
26 Jun 76	ME AND BABY BROTHER *Island WIP 6303*	21	7
14 Jan 78	GALAXY *MCA 339*	14	7
15 Apr 78	HEY SENORITA *MCA 359*	40	2
10 Apr 82	YOU GOT THE POWER *RCA 201*	58	4
6 Apr 85	GROOVIN' *Bluebird BR 16*	43	5

Stephen WARBECK
UK, male composer (Albums: 5 Weeks)   pos/wks
| 19 May 01 | CAPTAIN CORELLI'S MANDOLIN (FILM SOUNDTRACK) *Decca 4676782* | 30 | 5 |

Anita WARD
US, female vocalist (Singles: 11 Weeks)   pos/wks
| 2 Jun 79 ★ | RING MY BELL *TK TKR 7543* ▲ | 1 | 11 |

Chrissy WARD
US, female vocalist (Singles: 2 Weeks)   pos/wks
| 24 Jun 95 | RIGHT AND EXACT *Ore AG 6CD* | 62 | 1 |
| 8 Feb 97 | RIGHT AND EXACT (re-mix) *Ore AG 21CD* | 59 | 1 |

Clifford T WARD
UK, male vocalist / instrumentalist – keyboards, b. 10 Feb 1944, d. 18 Dec 2001 (Singles: 16 Weeks, Albums: 5 Weeks)   pos/wks
30 Jun 73 ●	GAYE *Charisma CB 205*	8	11
26 Jan 74	SCULLERY *Charisma CB 221*	37	5
21 Jul 73	HOME THOUGHTS *Charisma CAS 1066*	40	3
16 Feb 74	MANTLE PIECES *Charisma CAS 1077*	42	2

Michael WARD
UK, male vocalist (Singles: 13 Weeks, Albums: 3 Weeks)   pos/wks
| 29 Sep 73 | LET THERE BE PEACE ON EARTH (LET IT BEGIN WITH ME) (re) *Philips 6006 340* | 15 | 13 |
| 5 Jan 74 | INTRODUCING MICHAEL WARD *Philips 6308 189* | 26 | 3 |

Billy WARD and his DOMINOES
US, male vocal group – leader b. 19 Sep 1921, d. 15 Feb 2002 (Singles: 13 Weeks)   pos/wks
| 13 Sep 57 | STARDUST (re) *London HLU 8465* | 13 | 12 |
| 29 Nov 57 | DEEP PURPLE *London HLU 8502* | 30 | 1 |

WARD BROTHERS
UK, male vocal / instrumental group (Singles: 8 Weeks)   pos/wks
| 10 Jan 87 | CROSS THAT BRIDGE *Siren SIREN 37* | 32 | 8 |

Mathias WARE featuring Rob TAYLOR
Germany, male producer and male vocalist (Singles: 1 Week)   pos/wks
| 9 Mar 02 | HEY LITTLE GIRL *Manifesto FESCD 91* | 42 | 1 |

Justin WARFIELD *See BOMB THE BASS*

WARLOCK
Germany, male / female vocal / instrumental group (Albums: 2 Weeks)   pos/wks
| 14 Nov 87 | TRIUMPH AND AGONY *Vertigo VERH 50* | 54 | 2 |

WARM JETS
UK / Canada, male vocal / instrumental group (Singles: 4 Weeks, Albums: 1 Week)   pos/wks
14 Feb 98	NEVER NEVER *Island WAY 6766*	37	2
25 Apr 98	HURRICANE *Island CID 697*	34	2
7 Mar 98	FUTURE SIGNS *Island 5243542*	40	1

WARM SOUNDS
UK, male vocal duo – Barry Husband and Denver Gerrard (Singles: 6 Weeks)   pos/wks
| 4 May 67 | BIRDS AND BEES *Deram DM 120* | 27 | 6 |

Toni WARNE
UK, female vocalist (Singles: 4 Weeks)   pos/wks
| 25 Apr 87 | BEN *Mint CHEW 110* | 50 | 4 |

Jennifer WARNES
US, female vocalist (Singles: 37 Weeks, Albums: 12 Weeks)   pos/wks
15 Jan 83 ●	UP WHERE WE BELONG *Island WIP 6830* [1] ▲	7	13
25 Jul 87	FIRST WE TAKE MANHATTAN *Cypress PB 49709*	74	1
31 Oct 87 ●	(I'VE HAD) THE TIME OF MY LIFE (re) *RCA PB 49625* [2] ▲	6	23
18 Jul 87	FAMOUS BLUE RAINCOAT *RCA PL 90048*	33	12

[1] Joe Cocker and Jennifer Warnes [2] Bill Medley and Jennifer Warnes
'(I've Had) the Time of My Life' re-entered in Dec 1990, peaking at No.8

WARP BROTHERS
Germany, male DJ / production group (Singles: 18 Weeks)   pos/wks
11 Nov 00	PHATT BASS (IMPORT) *Dos or Die BMSCDM 40009*	58	3
9 Dec 00 ●	PHATT BASS *Nulife / Arista 74321817102* [1]	9	8
17 Feb 01	WE WILL SURVIVE *Nulife / Arista 74321832722*	19	4
29 Dec 01	BLAST THE SPEAKERS *Nulife 74321899162*	40	3

[1] Warp Brothers vs Aquagen

WARRANT
US, male vocal / instrumental group (Singles: 7 Weeks, Albums: 1 Week)   pos/wks
17 Nov 90	CHERRY PIE *CBS 6562587*	59	2
9 Mar 91	CHERRY PIE (re-issue) *Columbia 6566867*	35	5
19 Sep 92	DOG EAT DOG *Columbia 4720332*	74	1

Alysha WARREN
UK, female vocalist (Singles: 4 Weeks)   pos/wks
24 Sep 94	I'M SO IN LOVE *Wild Card CARDD 10*	61	1
25 Mar 95	I THOUGHT I MEANT THE WORLD TO YOU *Wild Card CARDD 16*	40	1
27 Jul 96	KEEP ON PUSHING OUR LOVE *Arista 74321390422* [1]	30	2

[1] Nightcrawlers featuring John Reid and Alysha Warren

Ann WARREN *See Ruby MURRAY*

Nikita WARREN
Italy, female vocalist (Singles: 1 Week)   pos/wks
| 13 Jul 96 | I NEED YOU *VC VCRD 12* | 48 | 1 |

WARRIOR
UK, male vocal / production / instrumental duo – Stacey Charles and Michael Woods (Singles: 7 Weeks)   pos/wks
21 Oct 00	WARRIOR *Incentive CENT 12CDS*	19	4
30 Jun 01	VOODOO *Incentive CENT 26CDS*	37	2
4 Oct 03	X *Incentive CENT 56CDS*	64	1

Dionne WARWICK 243 Top 500
Super-stylish soul diva, b. 12 Dec 1940, New Jersey, US, whose classy and unmistakable vocals on songs written by Burt Bacharach and Hal David produced more than 30 US hits for her between 1962 and 1972. She is a cousin of Whitney Houston (Singles: 101 Weeks, Albums: 154 Weeks) pos/wks
13 Feb 64	ANYONE WHO HAD A HEART *Pye International 7N 25234*	42	3
16 Apr 64 ●	WALK ON BY *Pye International 7N 25241*	9	14
30 Jul 64	YOU'LL NEVER GET TO HEAVEN (IF YOU BREAK MY HEART) *Pye International 7N 25256*	20	8
8 Oct 64	REACH OUT FOR ME *Pye International 7N 25265*	23	7
1 Apr 65	YOU CAN HAVE HIM *Pye International 7N 25290*	37	5
13 Mar 68	(THEME FROM) VALLEY OF THE DOLLS *Pye International 7N 25445*	28	8

			pos/wks
15 May 68 ●	DO YOU KNOW THE WAY TO SAN JOSE		
	Pye International 7N 25457		8 10
19 Oct 74	THEN CAME YOU Atlantic K 10495 [1] ▲		29 6
23 Oct 82 ●	HEARTBREAKER Arista ARIST 496		2 13
11 Dec 82 ●	ALL THE LOVE IN THE WORLD Arista ARIST 507		10 10
26 Feb 83	YOURS Arista ARIST 518		66 2
28 May 83	I'LL NEVER LOVE THIS WAY AGAIN Arista ARIST 530		62 3
9 Nov 85	THAT'S WHAT FRIENDS ARE FOR Arista ARIST 638 [2] ▲		16 9
15 Aug 87	LOVE POWER Arista RIS 27 [3]		63 3
23 May 64	PRESENTING DIONNE WARWICK Pye NPL 28037		14 10
7 May 66 ●	BEST OF DIONNE WARWICK Pye NPL 28078		8 11
4 Feb 67	HERE WHERE THERE IS LOVE Pye NPL 28096		39 2
18 May 68 ●	VALLEY OF THE DOLLS Pye NSPL 28114		10 13
23 May 70	GREATEST HITS VOLUME 1 Wand WNS 1		31 26
6 Jun 70	GREATEST HITS VOLUME 2 Wand WNS 2		28 14
30 Oct 82 ●	HEARTBREAKER Arista 204 974		3 33
21 May 83	THE COLLECTION – HER ALL-TIME GREATEST HITS		
	Arista DIONE 1		11 17
29 Oct 83	SO AMAZING Arista 205 755		60 3
23 Feb 85	WITHOUT YOUR LOVE Arista 206 571		86 2
6 Jan 90 ●	LOVE SONGS Arista 410441		6 13
10 Dec 94	CHRISTMAS IN VIENNA II Sony Classical SK 64304 [1]		60 2
14 Dec 96	THE ESSENTIAL COLLECTION Global Television RADCD 48		58 4
3 Aug 02	HEARTBREAKER – THE VERY BEST OF DIONNE WARWICK		
	BMG TV / WSM WSMCD 101		32 4

[1] Dionne Warwicke and The Detroit Spinners [2] Dionne Warwick and Friends featuring Elton John, Stevie Wonder and Gladys Knight [3] Dionne Warwick and Jeffrey Osborne [1] Dionne Warwick and Placido Domingo

WAS (NOT WAS)
US, male vocal / instrumental duo – Don Fagenson and David Weiss (Singles: 58 Weeks, Albums: 15 Weeks)   pos/wks

			pos/wks
3 Mar 84	OUT COME THE FREAKS Ze / Geffen A 4178		41 5
18 Jul 87	SPY IN THE HOUSE OF LOVE (re) Fontana WAS 2		21 15
3 Oct 87 ●	WALK THE DINOSAUR Fontana WAS 3		10 10
7 May 88	OUT COME THE FREAKS (AGAIN) Fontana WAS 4		44 3
16 Jul 88	ANYTHING CAN HAPPEN Fontana WAS 5		67 3
26 May 90	PAPA WAS A ROLLING STONE Fontana WAS 7		12 7
11 Aug 90	HOW THE HEART BEHAVES Fontana WAS 8		53 2
23 May 92	LISTEN LIKE THIEVES Fontana WAS 10		58 2
11 Jul 92 ●	SHAKE YOUR HEAD Fontana WAS 11		4 9
26 Sep 92	SOMEWHERE IN AMERICA (THERE'S A STREET NAMED		
	AFTER MY DAD) Fontana WAS 12		57 1
9 Apr 88	WHAT UP DOG? Fontana SFLP 4		47 6
21 Jul 90	ARE YOU OKAY? Fontana 8463511		35 6
13 Jun 92	HELLO DAD … I'M IN JAIL Fontana 5124642		61 3

'Spy In the House of Love' first peaked at No.51 and only made its peak position on re-entry in Feb 1988. Fontana WAS 4 was a re-recorded version of their first hit. 'Shake Your Head' features uncredited vocals by Ozzy Osbourne and Kim Basinger. The group dropped the brackets from their name during the chart run of 'Papa Was a Rolling Stone'

Martha WASH *(see also The WEATHER GIRLS)*
US, female vocalist (Singles: 34 Weeks)   pos/wks

			pos/wks
28 Nov 92	CARRY ON RCA 74321125457		74 1
6 Mar 93	GIVE IT TO YOU RCA 74321136562		37 4
10 Jul 93	RUNAROUND / CARRY ON RCA 74321153702		49 2
18 Feb 95	I FOUND LOVE Columbia 6612112 [1]		26 2
13 Jul 96 ●	KEEP ON JUMPIN' Manifesto FESCD 11 [2]		8 6
12 Jul 97 ●	SOMETHING GOIN' ON Manifesto FESCD 25 [2]		5 10
25 Oct 97	CARRY ON (2nd re-mix) Delirious DELICD 6		49 1
28 Feb 98	IT'S RAINING MEN … THE SEQUEL Logic 74321555412 [3]		21 3
11 Apr 98	READY FOR A NEW DAY Manifesto FESCD 40 [4]		20 2
15 Aug 98	CATCH THE LIGHT Logic 74321587912		45 1
3 Jul 99	COME Logic 74321653942		64 1
5 Feb 00	IT'S RAINING MEN (re-recording) Logic 74321726282		56 1

[1] C & C Music Factory featuring Martha Wash [2] Todd Terry featuring Martha Wash and Jocelyn Brown [3] Martha Wash featuring RuPaul [4] Todd Terry featuring Martha Wash

The listed flip side of 'I Found Love' was 'Take a Toke' by C & C Music Factory

Dinah WASHINGTON *US, female vocalist –*
Ruth Jones, b. 29 Aug 1924, d. 14 Dec 1963 (Singles: 8 Weeks)   pos/wks

			pos/wks
30 Nov 61	SEPTEMBER IN THE RAIN (re) Mercury AMT 1162		35 4
4 Apr 92	MAD ABOUT THE BOY Mercury DINAH 1		41 4

Geno WASHINGTON & The RAM JAM BAND
US, male vocalist and UK, male instrumental backing group (Singles: 20 Weeks, Albums: 51 Weeks)   pos/wks

			pos/wks
19 May 66	WATER Piccadilly 7N 35312		39 8
21 Jul 66	HI HI HAZEL (re) Piccadilly 7N 35329		45 4
6 Oct 66	QUE SERA SERA Piccadilly 7N 35346		43 3
2 Feb 67	MICHAEL (HE'S A LOVER) Piccadilly 7N 35359		39 5
10 Dec 66 ●	HAND CLAPPIN' FOOT STOMPIN' FUNKY-BUTT … LIVE!		
	Piccadilly NPL 38026 [1]		5 38
23 Sep 67 ●	HIPSTERS FLIPSTERS AND FINGER-POPPIN' DADDIES		
	Piccadilly NSPL 38032 [1]		8 13

[1] Geno Washington

Grover WASHINGTON Jr *US, male instrumentalist – saxophone,*
b. 12 Dec 1943, d. 17 Dec 1999 (Singles: 7 Weeks, Albums: 10 Weeks) pos/wks

			pos/wks
16 May 81	JUST THE TWO OF US Elektra K 12514		34 7
9 May 81	WINELIGHT Elektra K 52262		34 9
19 Dec 81	COME MORNING Elektra K 52337		98 1

Although uncredited, Bill Withers sings on 'Just the Two of Us'

Keith WASHINGTON See Kylie MINOGUE

Sarah WASHINGTON *UK, female vocalist (Singles: 13 Weeks)*   pos/wks

			pos/wks
14 Aug 93	I WILL ALWAYS LOVE YOU Almighty CDALMY 33		12 7
27 Nov 93	CARELESS WHISPER Almighty CDALMY 43		45 2
25 May 96	HEAVEN AM:PM 5815352		28 2
12 Oct 96	EVERYTHING AM:PM 5818872		30 2

W.A.S.P. *US, male vocal / instrumental*
group (Singles: 38 Weeks, Albums: 24 Weeks)   pos/wks

			pos/wks
31 May 86	WILD CHILD Capitol CL 388		71 2
11 Oct 86	95 – NASTY Capitol CL 432		70 1
29 Aug 87	SCREAM UNTIL YOU LIKE IT Capitol CL 458		32 5
31 Oct 87	I DON'T NEED NO DOCTOR (LIVE) Capitol CL 469		31 5
20 Feb 88	ANIMAL (F**K LIKE A BEAST) Music for Nations KUT 109		61 3
4 Mar 89	MEAN MAN Capitol CL 521		21 5
27 May 89	THE REAL ME Capitol CL 534		23 5
9 Sep 89	FOREVER FREE Capitol CL 546		25 5
4 Apr 92	CHAINSAW CHARLIE (MURDERS IN THE NEW MORGUE)		
	Parlophone RS 6308		17 2
6 Jun 92	THE IDOL Parlophone RPD 6314		41 2
31 Oct 92	I AM ONE Parlophone 10RG 6324		56 1
23 Oct 93	SUNSET AND BABYLON Capitol CDCL 698		38 2
8 Sep 84	W.A.S.P. Capitol EJ 2401951		51 2
9 Nov 85	THE LAST COMMAND Capitol WASP 2		48 1
8 Nov 86	INSIDE THE ELECTRIC CIRCUS Capitol EST 2025		53 3
26 Sep 87	LIVE … IN THE RAW Capitol EST 2040		23 4
15 Apr 89 ●	THE HEADLESS CHILDREN Capitol EST 2087		8 10
20 Jun 92	THE CRIMSON IDOL Parlophone CDPCSD 118		21 2
6 Nov 93	FIRST BLOOD … LAST CUTS Capitol CDESTFG 2217		69 1
1 Jul 95	STILL NOT BLACK ENOUGH Raw Power RAWCD 103		52 1

WASP STAR See XTC

The WATERBOYS *UK / Ireland, male vocal /*
instrumental group (Singles: 33 Weeks, Albums: 72 Weeks)   pos/wks

			pos/wks
2 Nov 85	THE WHOLE OF THE MOON Ensign ENY 520		26 7
14 Jan 89	FISHERMAN'S BLUES Ensign ENY 621		32 6
1 Jul 89	AND A BANG ON THE EAR Ensign ENY 624		51 4
6 Apr 91 ●	THE WHOLE OF THE MOON (re-issue) Ensign ENY 642		3 9
8 Jun 91	FISHERMAN'S BLUES (re-issue) Ensign ENY 645		75 1
15 May 93	THE RETURN OF PAN Geffen GFSTD 42		24 3
24 Jul 93	GLASTONBURY SONG Geffen GFSTD 49		29 3
16 Jun 84	A PAGAN PLACE Ensign ENCL 3		100 1
28 Sep 85	THIS IS THE SEA Ensign ENCL 5		37 18
29 Oct 88	FISHERMAN'S BLUES Ensign CHEN 5		13 19
22 Sep 90 ●	ROOM TO ROAM Ensign CHEN 16		5 6
11 May 91 ●	THE BEST OF THE WATERBOYS '81–'90 Ensign CHEN 19		2 16
5 Jun 93 ●	DREAM HARDER Geffen GED 24476		5 10
7 Oct 00	A ROCK IN THE WEARY LAND RCA 74321783052		47 1
21 Jun 03	UNIVERSAL HALL Puck PUCK 1		74 1

WATERFRONT *UK, male vocal / instrumental duo –*
Phil Cilia and Chris Duffy (Singles: 19 Weeks, Albums: 3 Weeks) pos/wks

			pos/wks
15 Apr 89	BROKEN ARROW Polydor WON 3		63 2
27 May 89	CRY Polydor WON 1		17 13

			pos/wks
9 Sep 89	● NATURE OF LOVE *Polydor WON 2*	**63**	4
12 Aug 89	WATERFRONT *Polydor 837970 1*	**45**	3

WATERGATE (see also DJ QUICKSILVER)
Turkey, male DJ / producer – Orhan Terzi (Singles: 10 Weeks) pos/wks

13 May 00	● HEART OF ASIA *Positiva CDTIV 129*	**3**	10

Dennis WATERMAN
UK, male actor / vocalist (Singles: 17 Weeks) pos/wks

25 Oct 80	● I COULD BE SO GOOD FOR YOU *EMI 5009* [1]	**3**	12
17 Dec 83	WHAT ARE WE GONNA GET 'ER INDOORS *EMI MIN 101* [2]	**21**	5

[1] Dennis Waterman with The Dennis Waterman Band [2] Dennis Waterman and George Cole

Crystal WATERS
US, female vocalist (Singles: 39 Weeks) pos/wks

18 May 91	● GYPSY WOMAN (LA DA DEE) *A&M AM 772*	**2**	10
7 Sep 91	MAKIN' HAPPY *A&M AM 790*	**18**	6
11 Jan 92	MEGAMIX *A&M AM 843*	**39**	3
3 Oct 92	GYPSY WOMAN (re-mix) *Epic 6584377*	**35**	2
23 Apr 94	100% PURE LOVE *A&M 8586692*	**15**	7
2 Jul 94	GHETTO DAY *A&M 8589592*	**40**	2
25 Nov 95	RELAX *Manifesto FESCD 4*	**37**	2
24 Aug 96	IN DE GHETTO *Manifesto FESCD 12* [1]	**35**	2
19 Apr 97	SAY … IF YOU FEEL ALRIGHT *Mercury 5742912*	**45**	1
20 Sep 03	MY TIME *Illustrious / Epic CDILL 018* [2]	**22**	4

[1] David Morales and the Bad Yard Club featuring Crystal Waters and Delta [2] Dutch featuring Crystal Waters

The flip side of 'Gypsy Woman' (re-mix) was 'Peace' (re-mix) by Sabrina Johnston

Latanza WATERS See E-SMOOVE featuring Latanza WATERS

Muddy WATERS *US, male vocalist / instrumentalist –*
guitar, b. 4 Apr 1915, d. 30 Apr 1983 (Singles: 6 Weeks) pos/wks

16 Jul 88	MANNISH BOY *Epic MUD 1*	**51**	6

Roger WATERS (see also PINK FLOYD) *UK, male vocalist /*
instrumentalist – bass (Singles: 8 Weeks, Albums: 25 Weeks) pos/wks

30 May 87	RADIO WAVES *Harvest EM 6*	**74**	1
26 Dec 87	THE TIDE IS TURNING (AFTER LIVE AID) *Harvest EM 37*	**54**	4
5 Sep 92	WHAT GOD WANTS PART 1 *Columbia 6581390*	**35**	3
12 May 84	THE PROS AND CONS OF HITCH HIKING *Harvest SHVL 240105*	**13**	11
27 Jun 87	RADIO K.A.O.S. *EMI KAOS 1*	**25**	7
22 Sep 90	THE WALL – LIVE IN BERLIN *Mercury 8466111*	**27**	3
19 Sep 92	● AMUSED TO DEATH *Columbia 4687612*	**8**	4

Lauren WATERWORTH
UK, female vocalist (Singles: 3 Weeks) pos/wks

1 Jun 02	BABY NOW THAT I'VE FOUND YOU *Jive 9253622*	**24**	3

Michael WATFORD *US, male vocalist (Singles: 2 Weeks)* pos/wks

26 Feb 94	SO INTO YOU *East West A 8309CD*	**53**	2

Adam WATKISS *UK, male vocalist (Albums: 3 Weeks)* pos/wks

15 Dec 01	THIS IS THE MOMENT *UMTV / Decca 166082*	**65**	3

Jody WATLEY (see also SHALAMAR)
US, female vocalist (Singles: 35 Weeks, Albums: 4 Weeks) pos/wks

9 May 87	LOOKING FOR A NEW LOVE *MCA MCA 1107*	**13**	11
17 Oct 87	DON'T YOU WANT ME *MCA MCA 1198*	**55**	3
8 Apr 89	REAL LOVE *MCA MCA 1324*	**31**	7
12 Aug 89	FRIENDS *MCA MCA 1352* [1]	**21**	6
10 Feb 90	EVERYTHING *MCA MCA 1395*	**74**	1
11 Apr 92	I'M THE ONE YOU NEED *MCA MCS 1608*	**50**	3
21 May 94	WHEN A MAN LOVES A WOMAN *MCA MCSTD 1964*	**33**	2
25 Apr 98	OFF THE HOOK *Atlantic AT 0024CD 1*	**51**	1
5 Sep 87	JODY WATLEY *MCA MCG 6024*	**62**	1
27 May 89	LARGER THAN LIFE *MCA MCG 6044*	**39**	2

[1] Jody Watley with Eric B and Rakim

Joe WATSON See RHYTHM MASTERS

Johnny 'Guitar' WATSON *US, male vocalist / instrumentalist –*
guitar, b. 3 Feb 1935, d. 17 May 1996 (Singles: 8 Weeks) pos/wks

28 Aug 76	I NEED IT *DJM DJS 10694*	**35**	5
23 Apr 77	A REAL MOTHER FOR YA *DJM DJS 10762*	**44**	3

Nigel WATSON See Peter GREEN

Russell WATSON (see also STEPS)
UK, male vocalist (Singles: 12 Weeks, Albums: 73 Weeks) pos/wks

30 Oct 99	SWING LOW '99 *Decca / Universal TV 4669502*	**38**	2
22 Jul 00	BARCELONA (FRIENDS UNTIL THE END) *Decca 4672772* [1]	**68**	1
18 May 02	SOMEONE LIKE YOU *Decca 4730002* [2]	**10**	4
21 Dec 02	NOTHING SACRED – A SONG FOR KIRSTY *Decca 4737402*	**17**	5
7 Oct 00	● THE VOICE *Decca 4672512*	**5**	36
10 Nov 01	● THE VOICE – ENCORE *Decca 4703002*	**6**	21
30 Nov 02	THE VOICE – REPRISE *Decca 4731002*	**13**	8
6 Nov 04	● AMORE MUSICA *Decca 4756294*	**10**	8+

[1] Russell Watson and Shaun Ryder [2] Russell Watson and Faye Tozer

Barratt WAUGH *UK, male vocalist (Singles: 1 Week)* pos/wks

26 Jul 03	SKIP A BEAT *White Elephant BNWCD 02*	**56**	1

WAVELENGTH *UK, male vocal group (Singles: 12 Weeks)* pos/wks

10 Jul 82	HURRY HOME *Ariola ARO 281*	**17**	12

WAVES See KATRINA and the WAVES

WAX *US / UK, male vocal / instrumental duo – Andrew Gold*
and Graham Gouldman (Singles: 16 Weeks, Albums: 3 Weeks) pos/wks

12 Apr 86	RIGHT BETWEEN THE EYES *RCA PB 40509*	**60**	5
1 Aug 87	BRIDGE TO YOUR HEART *RCA PB 41405*	**12**	11
12 Sep 87	AMERICAN ENGLISH *RCA PL 71430*	**59**	3

Anthony WAY
UK, male vocalist (Singles: 2 Weeks, Albums: 19 Weeks) pos/wks

15 Apr 95	PANIS ANGELICUS *Decca 4481642*	**55**	2
8 Apr 95	● THE CHOIR – MUSIC FROM THE BBC TV SERIES *Decca 4481652* [1]	**3**	12
9 Dec 95	THE CHOIRBOY *Permanent PERMCD 41*	**61**	3
14 Dec 96	THE CHOIRBOY'S CHRISTMAS *Decca 4550502*	**59**	3
15 Mar 97	WINGS OF A DOVE *Decca 4556452*	**69**	1

[1] Anthony Way and Stanislas Syrewicz

A WAY OF LIFE
US, male / female vocal / instrumental group (Singles: 3 Weeks) pos/wks

21 Apr 90	TRIPPIN' ON YOUR LOVE *Eternal YZ 464*	**55**	3

WAY OF THE WEST
UK, male vocal / instrumental group (Singles: 5 Weeks) pos/wks

25 Apr 81	DON'T SAY THAT'S JUST FOR WHITE BOYS *Mercury MER 66*	**54**	5

WAY OUT WEST
UK, male instrumental / production duo – Nick Warren and
Jody Wisternoff (Singles: 17 Weeks, Albums: 2 Weeks) pos/wks

3 Dec 94	AJARE *Deconstruction 74321243802*	**52**	1
2 Mar 96	DOMINATION *Deconstruction 74321342822*	**38**	2
14 Sep 96	THE GIFT *Deconstruction 74321401912* [1]	**15**	5
30 Aug 97	BLUE *Deconstruction 74321477512*	**41**	2
29 Nov 97	AJARE (re-mix) *Deconstruction 74321521352*	**36**	2
9 Dec 00	THE FALL *Wow WOW 005CD*	**61**	1
18 Aug 01	INTENSIFY *Distinctive Breaks DISNCD 74*	**46**	1
30 Mar 02	MINDCIRCUS *Distinctive Breaks DISNCD 80* [2]	**39**	2
21 Sep 02	STEALTH *Distinctive Breaks DISNCD 90* [3]	**67**	1
13 Sep 97	WAY OUT WEST *Deconstruction 74321501952*	**42**	1
1 Sep 01	INTENSIFY *Distinctive Breaks DISNCD 76*	**61**	1

[1] Way Out West featuring Miss Joanna Law [2] Way Out West featuring Tricia Lee Kelshall [3] Way Out West featuring Kirsty Hawkshaw

Bruce WAYNE *Germany, male DJ / producer (Singles: 2 Weeks)* pos/wks

13 Dec 97	READY *Logic 74321527012*	**44**	1
4 Jul 98	NO GOOD FOR ME *Logic 74321587052*	**70**	1

Jan WAYNE
Germany, male producer – Jan Christiansen (Singles: 8 Weeks) pos/wks

9 Nov 02	**BECAUSE THE NIGHT** *Product / Incentive PDT 02CDS* **14**	5
29 Mar 03	**TOTAL ECLIPSE OF THE HEART**	
	Product / Incentive PDT 10CDS **28**	3

Jeff WAYNE'S 'WAR OF THE WORLDS' 217 Top 500
Talented New York born producer / songwriter / arranger and keyboard player who was educated at the prestigious Julliard School of Music. Before unveiling his epic all-star concept album 'The War of the Worlds' (over four years on the chart) he produced a string of David Essex hits (Singles: 21 Weeks, Albums: 261 Weeks) pos/wks

9 Sep 78	**THE EVE OF THE WAR** *CBS 6496* **36**	8
10 Jul 82	**MATADOR** *CBS A 2493* [1] **57**	3
25 Nov 89 ●	**EVE OF THE WAR (re-mix)** *CBS 6551267* **3**	10
1 Jul 78 ●	**JEFF WAYNE'S MUSICAL VERSION OF THE WAR OF THE WORLDS** *CBS 96000* **5**	235
3 Oct 92	**JEFF WAYNE'S MUSICAL VERSION OF SPARTACUS** *Columbia 4720302* **36**	2
6 Jul 96	**JEFF WAYNE'S MUSICAL VERSION OF THE WAR OF THE WORLDS (re-issue)** *Columbia CDX 96000* **23**	21
19 Oct 96	**HIGHLIGHTS FROM JEFF WAYNE'S MUSICAL VERSION OF THE WAR OF THE WORLDS** *Columbia CD 32356* **64**	2
22 Apr 00	**JEFF WAYNE'S MUSICAL VERSION OF THE WAR OF THE WORLDS – ULLADUBULLA – THE REMIX ALBUM** *Columbia SONYTV 74CD* **64**	1

[1] Jeff Wayne

All albums feature various artists but are commonly credited to Jeff Wayne the creator and producer

WAYSTED *UK, male vocal / instrumental group (Albums: 5 Weeks)* pos/wks

8 Oct 83	**VICES** *Chrysalis CHR 1438* **78**	3
22 Sep 84	**WAYSTED** *Music for Nations MFN 31* **73**	2

The WEATHER GIRLS
US, female vocal duo – Martha Wash and Izora Rhodes Armstead, b 1942, d. 16 Sep 2004 (Singles: 14 Weeks) pos/wks

27 Aug 83 ●	**IT'S RAINING MEN (re)** *CBS A 2924* **2**	14

'It's Raining Men' first peaked at No.73 in 1983 and reached its peak position only on re-entry in Mar 1984

The WEATHER PROPHETS *UK, male vocal / instrumental group (Singles: 2 Weeks, Albums: 2 Weeks)* pos/wks

28 Mar 87	**SHE COMES FROM THE RAIN** *Elevation ACID 1* **62**	2
9 May 87	**MAYFLOWER** *Elevation ELV 1* **67**	2

WEATHER REPORT
US, male instrumental group (Albums: 12 Weeks) pos/wks

23 Apr 77	**HEAVY WEATHER** *CBS 81775* **43**	6
11 Nov 78	**MR. GONE** *CBS 82775* **47**	3
27 Feb 82	**WEATHER REPORT** *CBS 85326* **88**	2
24 Mar 84	**DOMINO THEORY** *CBS 25839* **54**	1

WEATHERMEN See Jonathan KING

J. WEAVE See CHINGY

Marti WEBB
UK, female vocalist (Singles: 42 Weeks, Albums: 33 Weeks) pos/wks

9 Feb 80 ●	**TAKE THAT LOOK OFF YOUR FACE** *Polydor POSP 100* **3**	12
19 Apr 80	**TELL ME ON A SUNDAY** *Polydor POSP 111* **67**	2
20 Sep 80	**YOUR EARS SHOULD BE BURNING NOW** *Polydor POSP 166* **61**	4
8 Jun 85 ●	**BEN** *Starblend STAR 6* **5**	11
20 Sep 86	**ALWAYS THERE** *BBC RESL 190* [1] **13**	12
6 Jun 87	**I CAN'T LET GO** *Rainbow RBR 12* **65**	1
16 Feb 80 ●	**TELL ME ON A SUNDAY** *Polydor POLD 5031* **2**	23
28 Sep 85	**ENCORE** *Starblend BLEND 1* **55**	4
6 Dec 86	**ALWAYS THERE** *BBC REB 619* **65**	5
10 Oct 92	**THE MAGIC OF THE MUSICALS** *Quality Television QTV 013* [1] ...**55**	1

[1] Marti Webb and the Simon May Orchestra [1] Marti Webb and Mark Rattray

WEBB BROTHERS
US, male vocal / instrumental duo (Singles: 1 Week) pos/wks

17 Feb 01	**I CAN'T BELIEVE YOU'RE GONE** *WEA WEA 320CD* **69**	1

Joan WEBER *US, female vocalist, b. 12 Dec 1935, d. 13 May 1981 (Singles: 1 Week)* pos/wks

18 Feb 55	**LET ME GO LOVER** *Philips PB 389* ▲ **16**	1

Ben WEBSTER See Gerry MULLIGAN and Ben WEBSTER

Nikki WEBSTER *Australia, female vocalist (Singles: 1 Week)* pos/wks

8 Jun 02	**STRAWBERRY KISSES** *Gotham 74321943642* **64**	1

The WEDDING PRESENT *UK, male vocal / instrumental group (Singles: 39 Weeks, Albums: 21 Weeks)* pos/wks

5 Mar 88	**NOBODY'S TWISTING YOUR ARM** *Reception REC 009* **46**	2
1 Oct 88	**WHY ARE YOU BEING SO REASONABLE NOW?** *Reception REC 011* **42**	2
7 Oct 89	**KENNEDY** *RCA PB 43117* **33**	3
17 Feb 90	**BRASSNECK** *RCA PB 43403* **24**	3
29 Sep 90	**3 SONGS (EP)** *RCA PB 44021* **25**	4
11 May 91	**DALLIANCE** *RCA PB 44495* **29**	3
27 Jul 91	**LOVENEST** *RCA PT 44750* **58**	1
18 Jan 92	**BLUE EYES** *RCA PB 45185* **26**	2
15 Feb 92	**GO-GO DANCER** *RCA PB 45183* **20**	1
14 Mar 92	**THREE** *RCA PB 45181* **14**	1
18 Apr 92	**SILVER SHORTS** *RCA PB 45311* **14**	1
16 May 92 ●	**COME PLAY WITH ME** *RCA PB 45313* **10**	2
13 Jun 92	**CALIFORNIA** *RCA PB 45315* **16**	1
18 Jul 92	**FLYING SAUCER** *RCA 74321101157* **22**	1
15 Aug 92	**BOING!** *RCA 74321101177* **19**	1
19 Sep 92	**LOVE SLAVE** *RCA 743211101167* **17**	1
17 Oct 92	**STICKY** *RCA 74321116917* **17**	1
14 Nov 92	**THE QUEEN OF OUTER SPACE** *RCA 74321116927* **23**	1
19 Dec 92	**NO CHRISTMAS** *RCA 74321116937* **25**	1
10 Sep 94	**YEAH YEAH YEAH YEAH YEAH** *Island CID 585* **51**	2
26 Nov 94	**IT'S A GAS** *Island CID 591* **71**	1
31 Aug 96	**2, 3, GO** *Cooking Vinyl FRYCD 048* **67**	1
25 Jan 97	**MONTREAL** *Cooking Vinyl FRYCD 053* **40**	1
27 Nov 04	**INTERSTATE 5** *Scopitones TONECD 18* **62**	1
24 Oct 87	**GEORGE BEST** *Reception LEEDS 001* **47**	2
23 Jul 88	**TOMMY** *Reception LEEDS 2* **42**	3
29 Apr 89	**UKRAINSKI VISTUIP V JOHNA PEELA** *RCA PL 74104* ...**22**	3
4 Nov 89	**BIZARRO** *RCA PL 74302* **22**	3
8 Jun 91	**SEA MONSTERS** *RCA PL 75012* **13**	3
20 Jun 92	**HIT PARADE 1** *RCA PD 75343* **22**	2
16 Jan 93	**HIT PARADE 2** *RCA 74321127752* **19**	2
24 Sep 94	**WATUSI** *Island CID 8014* **47**	1
3 Feb 96	**MINI** *Cooking Vinyl COOKCD 094* **40**	1
21 Sep 96	**SATURNALIA** *Cooking Vinyl COOKCD 099* **36**	1

Tracks on 3 Songs (EP): Corduroy / Crawl / Make Me Smile (Come Up and See Me)

Fred WEDLOCK *UK, male vocalist (Singles: 10 Weeks)* pos/wks

31 Jan 81 ●	**OLDEST SWINGER IN TOWN** *Rocket XPRES 46* **6**	10

WEE PAPA GIRL RAPPERS
UK, female rap / vocal duo – Samantha and Sandra Lawrence (Singles: 27 Weeks, Albums: 3 Weeks) pos/wks

12 Mar 88	**FAITH** *Jive JIVE 164* **60**	4
25 Jun 88	**HEAT IT UP** *Jive JIVE 174* [1] **21**	9
1 Oct 88 ●	**WEE RULE** *Jive JIVE 185* **6**	9
24 Dec 88	**SOULMATE** *Jive JIVE 193* **45**	4
25 Mar 89	**BLOW THE HOUSE DOWN** *Jive JIVE 197* **65**	1
5 Nov 88	**THE BEAT THE RHYME AND THE NOISE** *Jive HIP 67* **39**	3

[1] Wee Papa Girl Rappers featuring Two Men and a Drum Machine

Bert WEEDON *UK, male instrumentalist – guitar (Singles: 38 Weeks, Albums: 26 Weeks)* pos/wks

15 May 59 ●	**GUITAR BOOGIE SHUFFLE** *Top Rank JAR 117* **10**	9
20 Nov 59	**NASHVILLE BOOGIE** *Top Rank JAR 221* **29**	2
10 Mar 60	**BIG BEAT BOOGIE (re)** *Top Rank JAR 300* **37**	4
9 Jun 60	**TWELFTH STREET RAG** *Top Rank JAR 360* **47**	2
28 Jul 60	**APACHE (re)** *Top Rank JAR 415* **24**	4
27 Oct 60	**SORRY ROBBIE** *Top Rank JAR 517* **28**	11
2 Feb 61	**GINCHY** *Top Rank JAR 537* **35**	5
4 May 61	**MR GUITAR** *Top Rank JAR 559* **47**	1
16 Jul 60	**KING SIZE GUITAR** *Top Rank BUY 026* **18**	1
23 Oct 76 ★	**22 GOLDEN GUITAR GREATS** *Warwick WW 5019* **1**	25

WEEKEND *International, male /*
female vocal / instrumental group (Singles: 5 Weeks) pos/wks

14 Dec 85	**CHRISTMAS MEDLEY / AULD LANG SYNE** *Lifestyle XY 1* **47**	5

WEEKEND PLAYERS (see also GROOVE ARMADA)
UK, male / female production / vocal duo –
Rachel Foster and Andy Cato (Singles: 5 Weeks) pos/wks

8 Sep 01	**21ST CENTURY** *Multiply CDMULTY 78* **22**	4
16 Mar 02	**INTO THE SUN** *Multiply CDMULTY 84* **42**	1

Michelle WEEKS *US, female vocalist (Singles: 7 Weeks)* pos/wks

2 Aug 97	**MOMENT OF MY LIFE** *Ministry of Sound MOSCDS 1* [1] **23**	3
8 Nov 97	**DON'T GIVE UP** *Ministry of Sound MOSCDS 2* **28**	2
11 Jul 98	**GIVE HER LOVE** *VC Recordings VCRD 37* [2] **59**	1
3 May 03	**THE LIGHT** *Defected DFTD 064* **69**	1

[1] Bobby D'Ambrosio featuring Michelle Weeks [2] DJ Dado vs Michelle Weeks

WEEN *See FOO FIGHTERS*

WEEZER *US, male vocal / instrumental*
group (Singles: 19 Weeks, Albums: 19 Weeks) pos/wks

11 Feb 95	**UNDONE – THE SWEATER SONG** *Geffen GFSTD 85* **35**	2
6 May 95	**BUDDY HOLLY** *Geffen GFSTD 88* **12**	7
22 Jul 95	**SAY IT AIN'T SO** *Geffen GFSTD 95* **37**	2
5 Oct 96	**EL SCORCHO** *Geffen GFSTD 22167* **50**	1
14 Jul 01	**HASH PIPE** *Geffen 4975642* **21**	3
3 Nov 01	**ISLAND IN THE SUN** *Geffen 4976102* **31**	2
14 Sep 02	**KEEP FISHIN'** *Geffen 4977912* **29**	2
4 Mar 95	**WEEZER** *Geffen GED 24629* **23**	11
12 Oct 96	**PINKERTON** *Geffen GED 25007* **43**	1
26 May 01	**THE GREEN ALBUM** *Geffen 4930612* **31**	4
25 May 02	**MALADROIT** *Geffen 4933252* **16**	3

Frank WEIR and his Orchestra (see also Vera LYNN)
UK, orchestra – leader d. 12 May 1981 (Singles: 4 Weeks) pos/wks

15 Sep 60	**CARIBBEAN HONEYMOON** *Oriole CB 1559* **42**	4

WEIRD SCIENCE *UK, male DJ / production duo (Singles: 1 Week)* pos/wks

1 Jul 00	**FEEL THE NEED** *Nulife 74321751982* **62**	1

Eric WEISSBERG *See 'DELIVERANCE' SOUNDTRACK*

WELCH *See MARVIN, WELCH and FARRAR*

Denise WELCH *UK, female actor / vocalist (Singles: 3 Weeks)* pos/wks

4 Nov 95	**YOU DON'T HAVE TO SAY YOU LOVE ME / CRY ME A RIVER** *Virgin VSCDT 1569* **23**	3

Gillian WELCH
UK, female vocalist / instrumentalist – guitar (Albums: 1 Week) pos/wks

14 Jun 03	**SOUL JOURNEY** *WEA 5046668682* **65**	1

Paul WELLER (185 [Top 500]) (see also COUNCIL COLLECTIVE) *Angry young man reinvented as Britpop's elder statesman, b. John Weller, 25 May 1958, Surrey. Vocalist, guitarist and songwriter, 'The Modfather' achieved No.1 albums both solo and as leader of The Jam and Style Council. Won Best Male Solo Brit in 1995 and 1996 (Singles: 78 Weeks, Albums: 228 Weeks)* pos/wks

18 May 91	**INTO TOMORROW** *Freedom High FHP 1* [1] **36**	3
15 Aug 92	**UH HUH OH YEH** *Go Discs GOD 86* **18**	5
10 Oct 92	**ABOVE THE CLOUDS** *Go Discs GOD 91* **47**	2
17 Jul 93	**SUNFLOWER** *Go Discs GODCD 102* **16**	5
4 Sep 93	**WILD WOOD** *Go Discs GODCD 104* **14**	3
13 Nov 93	**THE WEAVER (EP)** *Go Discs GODCD 107* **18**	3
9 Apr 94	**HUNG UP** *Go Discs GODCD 111* **11**	3
5 Nov 94	**OUT OF THE SINKING** *Go Discs GODCD 121* **20**	3
6 May 95	● **THE CHANGINGMAN** *Go Discs GODCD 127* **7**	4
22 Jul 95	● **YOU DO SOMETHING TO ME** *Go Discs GODCD 130* **9**	6
30 Sep 95	**BROKEN STONES** *Go Discs GODCD 132* **20**	4
9 Mar 96	**OUT OF THE SINKING** (re-recording) *Go Discs GODCD 143* ...**16**	2
17 Aug 96	● **PEACOCK SUIT** *Go Discs GODCD 149* **5**	3
9 Aug 97	**BRUSHED** *Island CID 666* **14**	3
11 Oct 97	**FRIDAY STREET** *Island CID 676* **21**	2
6 Dec 97	**MERMAIDS** *Island CID 683* **30**	2

14 Nov 98	**BRAND NEW START** *Island CID 711* **16**	3
9 Jan 99	**WILD WOOD** (re-issue) *Island CID 734* **22**	3
2 Sep 00	**SWEET PEA, MY SWEET PEA** *Island CID 764* **44**	1
14 Sep 02	**IT'S WRITTEN IN THE STARS** *Independiente ISOM 63SMS* **7**	3
30 Nov 02	**LEAFY MYSTERIES** *Independiente ISOM 65MS* **23**	2
26 Jun 04	**THE BOTTLE** *V2 VVR 5026913* **13**	3
11 Sep 04	**WISHING ON A STAR** *V2 VVR 5026923* **11**	5
27 Nov 04	**THINKING OF YOU** *V2 VVR 5028463* **18**	3
12 Sep 92	● **PAUL WELLER** *Go Discs 8283432* **8**	7
18 Sep 93	● **WILD WOOD** *Go Discs 8284352* **2**	51
24 Sep 94	**LIVE WOOD** *Go Discs 8285612* **13**	5
27 May 95	★ **STANLEY ROAD** *Go Discs / Island 8286192* ■ **1**	87
5 Jul 97	● **HEAVY SOUL** *Go Discs / Island CID 8058* **2**	13
21 Nov 98	● **MODERN CLASSICS – THE GREATEST HITS** *Island CID 8080* ...**7**	19
22 Apr 00	● **HELIOCENTRIC** *Island CID 8093* **2**	8
20 Oct 01	● **DAYS OF SPEED** *Independiente ISOM 26CD* **3**	16
28 Sep 02	★ **ILLUMINATION** *Independiente ISOM 33CDL* ■ **1**	7
6 Sep 03	**FLY ON THE WALL – B SIDES & RARITIES** *Island 0635272*......**22**	3
25 Sep 04	● **STUDIO 150** *V2 VVR 1026908* **2**	12+

[1] Paul Weller Movement

Tracks on The Weaver (EP): The Weaver / This Is No Time / Another New Day / Ohio (live). Both versions of 'Out of the Sinking' feature uncredited vocals by Carleen Anderson

Brandi WELLS *US, female vocalist – Marguerite J Pinder, b. 13 May 1955, d. 25 Mar 2003 (Singles: 1 Week)* pos/wks

20 Feb 82	**WATCH OUT** *Virgin VS 479* **74**	1

Houston WELLS and the MARKSMEN *UK, male vocalist – Andrew Smith and instrumental group (Singles: 10 Weeks)* pos/wks

1 Aug 63	**ONLY THE HEARTACHES** *Parlophone R 5031* **22**	10

Mary WELLS *US, female vocalist, b. 13 May 1943, d. 26 Jul 1992 (Singles: 25 Weeks)* pos/wks

21 May 64	● **MY GUY** *Stateside SS 288* ▲ **5**	14
30 Jul 64	**ONCE UPON A TIME** *Stateside SS 316* [1] **50**	1
8 Jul 72	**MY GUY** (re-issue) *Tamla Motown TMG 820* **14**	10

[1] Marvin Gaye and Mary Wells

Terri WELLS *US, female vocalist (Singles: 9 Weeks)* pos/wks

2 Jul 83	**YOU MAKE IT HEAVEN** *Phillyworld PWS 111* **53**	2
5 May 84	**I'LL BE AROUND** *Phillyworld LON 48* **17**	7

Alex WELSH BAND *UK, male instrumentalist – trumpet, b. 9 Jul 1929, d. 25 Jun 1982 (Singles: 4 Weeks)* pos/wks

10 Aug 61	**TANSY** *Columbia DB 4686* **45**	4

Irvine WELSH *See PRIMAL SCREAM*

WENDY and LISA *US, female vocal duo – Wendy Melvoin and Lisa Coleman (Singles: 31 Weeks, Albums: 7 Weeks)* pos/wks

5 Sep 87	**WATERFALL** *Virgin VS 999* **66**	4
16 Jan 88	**SIDESHOW** *Virgin VS 1012* **49**	5
18 Feb 89	**ARE YOU MY BABY** *Virgin VS 1156* **70**	3
29 Apr 89	**LOLLY LOLLY** *Virgin VS 1175* **64**	3
8 Jul 89	**SATISFACTION** *Virgin VS 1194* **27**	8
18 Nov 89	**WATERFALL** (re-mix) *Virgin VS 1223* **69**	2
30 Jun 90	**STRUNG OUT** *Virgin VS 1272* **44**	5
10 Nov 90	**RAINBOW LAKE** *Virgin VS 1280* **70**	1
10 Oct 87	**WENDY AND LISA** *Virgin V 2444* **84**	2
28 Mar 89	**FRUIT AT THE BOTTOM** *Virgin V 2580* **45**	2
4 Aug 90	**EROICA** *Virgin V 2633* **33**	3

WES *France, male vocalist – Wes Madiko (Singles: 7 Weeks)* pos/wks

14 Feb 98	**ALANE** *Epic 6654682* **11**	6
27 Jun 98	**I LOVE FOOTBALL** *Epic 6660772* **75**	1

Dodie WEST *UK, female vocalist (Singles: 4 Weeks)* pos/wks

14 Jan 65	**GOING OUT OF MY HEAD** *Decca F 12046* **39**	4

Kanye WEST
US, male rapper / producer (Singles: 33 Weeks, Albums: 37 Weeks) pos/wks

3 Apr 04	● **THROUGH THE WIRE** *Roc-A-Fella / Def Jam 9862270* **9**	9
19 Jun 04	● **ALL FALLS DOWN** *Roc-A-Fella 9862670* [1] **10**	8

26 Jun 04 ●	TALK ABOUT OUR LOVE *Atlantic AT 017CD* [2]	6	10
11 Sep 04	JESUS WALKS *Roc-A-Fella 9863962*	16	6
28 Feb 04	THE COLLEGE DROPOUT *Roc-A-Fella / Def Jam 9861739*	12	37

[1] Kanye West featuring Syleena Johnson [2] Brandy featuring Kanye West

Keith WEST *UK, male vocalist – Keith Hopkins (Singles: 18 Weeks)* pos/wks

| 9 Aug 67 ● | EXCERPT FROM A TEENAGE OPERA *Parlophone R 5623* | 2 | 15 |
| 22 Nov 67 | SAM *Parlophone R 5651* | 38 | 3 |

Kit WEST See DEGREES OF MOTION featuring BITI

WEST END *UK, female vocal group (Singles: 2 Weeks)* pos/wks

| 19 Aug 95 | LOVE RULES *RCA 74321292702* | 44 | 2 |

WEST END featuring SYBIL
UK, male production duo and female vocalist (Singles: 13 Weeks) pos/wks

| 16 Jan 93 ● | THE LOVE I LOST *PWL Sanctuary PWCD 253* | 3 | 13 |

WEST HAM UNITED CUP SQUAD
UK, male football team vocalists (Singles: 2 Weeks) pos/wks

| 10 May 75 | I'M FOREVER BLOWING BUBBLES *Pye 7N 45470* | 31 | 2 |

WEST STREET MOB *US, male DJs / producers (Singles: 3 Weeks)* pos/wks

| 8 Oct 83 | BREAK DANCIN' - ELECTRIC BOOGIE (re) *Sugarhill SH 128* | 64 | 3 |

WESTBAM
Germany, male producer – Maximillian Lenz (Singles: 9 Weeks) pos/wks

9 Jul 94	CELEBRATION GENERATION *Low Spirit PQCD 5*	48	2
19 Nov 94	BAM BAM BAM *Low Spirit PZCD 329*	57	1
3 Jun 95	WIZARDS OF THE SONIC *Urban PZCD 344*	32	2
23 Mar 96	ALWAYS MUSIC *Low Spirit 5779152* [1]	51	1
13 Jun 98	WIZARDS OF THE SONIC (re-mix) *Wonderboy WBOYD 010* [2]	43	2
28 Nov 98	ROOF IS ON FIRE *Logic 74321633162*	58	1

[1] Westbam / Koon + Stephenson [2] Westbam vs Red Jerry

Hayley WESTENRA
New Zealand, female vocalist (Albums: 25 Weeks) pos/wks

| 27 Sep 03 ● | PURE *Decca 4753302* | 7 | 25+ |

'Pure' returned to the chart for Christmas 2004 with a bonus CD of new songs and a different catalogue number: Decca 4756538

WESTLIFE 119 Top 500
Record-shattering Irish boy band: Kian Egan, Mark Feehily, Nicky Byrne, Shane Filan and Bryan McFadden (left 2004). Only act to reach No.1 with their first seven releases or enter the chart at No.1 11 times out of their first 13 hits. They are also the first UK-based act to amass four No.1 singles in a year and they average over 1 million sales for each album release. On 1 Sep 2004, a live version of 'Flying Without Wings' enabled the group to become the first act to top the new Official UK Chart Company download chart (Singles: 205 Weeks, Albums: 190 Weeks) pos/wks

1 May 99 ★	SWEAR IT AGAIN (re) *RCA 74321662062* ■	1	13
21 Aug 99 ★	IF I LET YOU GO *RCA 74321692352* ■	1	11
30 Oct 99 ★	FLYING WITHOUT WINGS *RCA 74321709162* ■	1	13
25 Dec 99 ★	I HAVE A DREAM / SEASONS IN THE SUN *RCA 74321726012* ■	1	17
8 Apr 00 ★	FOOL AGAIN (re) *RCA 74321751562* ■	1	12
30 Sep 00 ★	AGAINST ALL ODDS (re) *Columbia 6698872* [1] ■	1	12
11 Nov 00 ★	MY LOVE *RCA 74321802792* ■	1	10
30 Dec 00 ●	WHAT MAKES A MAN *RCA 74321826252*	2	13
17 Mar 01 ★	UPTOWN GIRL *RCA 74321841682* ■	1	16
17 Nov 01 ★	QUEEN OF MY HEART *RCA 74321899132* ■	1	15
2 Mar 02 ★	WORLD OF OUR OWN *S 74321918802* ■	1	13
1 Jun 02 ●	BOP BOP BABY *S 74321940452*	5	10
16 Nov 02 ★	UNBREAKABLE (re) *S 74321975182* ■	1	16
5 Apr 03 ●	TONIGHT / MISS YOU NIGHTS *S 74321986792*	3	10
27 Sep 03 ●	HEY WHATEVER *S 82876560822*	4	7
29 Nov 03 ●	MANDY *S 82876570732* ■	1	9
6 Mar 04 ●	OBVIOUS *S 82876596322*	3	8
13 Nov 99 ●	WESTLIFE *RCA 74321713212*	2	69
18 Nov 00 ★	COAST TO COAST *RCA 74321808312* ■	1	28
24 Nov 01 ★	WORLD OF OUR OWN *RCA 74321903082* ■	1	35

23 Nov 02 ★	UNBREAKABLE – THE GREATEST HITS VOL.1 *S 74321975902* ■	1	34
6 Dec 03 ★	TURNAROUND *S 82876557412* ■	1	18
20 Nov 04 ★	... ALLOW US TO BE FRANK *S 82876651052*	3	6+

[1] Mariah Carey featuring Westlife

WESTMINSTER ABBEY CHOIR *UK, male / female*
choir – choirmaster Dr Martin Neary (Albums: 7 Weeks) pos/wks

| 20 Sep 97 | JOHN TAVERNER: INNOCENCE *Sony Classical SK 66613* | 34 | 4 |
| 12 Sep 98 | PERFECT PEACE *Sony Classical SONYTV 49CD* | 58 | 3 |

Kim WESTON See Marvin GAYE

WESTWORLD *UK / US, male / female vocal /*
instrumental group (Singles: 23 Weeks, Albums: 2 Weeks) pos/wks

21 Feb 87	SONIC BOOM BOY *RCA BOOM 1*	11	7
2 May 87	BA-NA-NA-BAM-BOO *RCA BOOM 2*	37	5
25 Jul 87	WHERE THE ACTION IS *RCA BOOM 3*	54	5
17 Oct 87	SILVERMAC *RCA BOOM 4*	42	5
15 Oct 88	EVERYTHING GOOD IS BAD *RCA PB 42243*	72	2
5 Sep 87	WHERE THE ACTION IS *RCA PL 71429*	49	2

WET WET WET 80 Top 500 *Glasgow quartet fronted by vocalist*
Marti Pellow, b. Mark McLoughlin, 23 Mar 1966. They were voted Best British Newcomers at the 1988 Brit Awards and they hold the record for most consecutive weeks at No.1 by a UK act – 15. Best-selling single: 'Love Is All Around' 1,783,827 (Singles: 212 Weeks, Albums: 284 Weeks) pos/wks

11 Apr 87 ●	WISHING I WAS LUCKY *Precious JEWEL 3*	6	14
25 Jul 87 ●	SWEET LITTLE MYSTERY *Precious JEWEL 4*	5	12
5 Dec 87 ●	ANGEL EYES (HOME AND AWAY) *Precious JEWEL 6*	5	12
19 Mar 88	TEMPTATION *Precious JEWEL 7*	12	8
14 May 88 ★	WITH A LITTLE HELP FROM MY FRIENDS *Childline CHILD 1*	1	11
30 Sep 89 ●	SWEET SURRENDER *Precious JEWEL 9*	6	8
9 Dec 89	BROKE AWAY *Precious JEWEL 10*	19	7
10 Mar 90	HOLD BACK THE RIVER *Precious JEWEL 11*	31	4
11 Aug 90	STAY WITH ME HEARTACHE / I FEEL FINE *Precious JEWEL 13*	30	4
14 Sep 91	MAKE IT TONIGHT *Precious JEWEL 15*	37	3
2 Nov 91	PUT THE LIGHT ON *Precious JEWEL 16*	56	2
4 Jan 92 ★	GOODNIGHT GIRL *Precious JEWEL 17*	1	11
21 Mar 92	MORE THAN LOVE *Precious JEWEL 18*	19	5
11 Jul 92	LIP SERVICE (EP) *Precious JEWEL 19*	15	5
8 May 93	BLUE FOR YOU / THIS TIME (LIVE) *Precious JWLCD 20*	38	2
6 Nov 93	SHED A TEAR *Precious JWLCD 21*	22	5
8 Jan 94	COLD COLD HEART *Precious JWLCD 22*	20	4
21 May 94 ★	LOVE IS ALL AROUND *Precious JWLCD 23* ◆	1	37
25 Mar 95 ●	JULIA SAYS *Precious JWLDD 24*	3	9
17 Jun 95 ●	DON'T WANT TO FORGIVE ME NOW *Precious JWLDD 25*	7	8
30 Sep 95 ●	SOMEWHERE SOMEHOW *Precious JWLDD 26*	7	7
2 Dec 95	SHE'S ALL ON MY MIND *Precious JWLDD 27*	17	7
30 Mar 96	MORNING *Precious JWLDD 28*	16	4
22 Mar 97 ●	IF I NEVER SEE YOU AGAIN (re) *Precious JWLCD 29*	3	9
14 Jun 97	STRANGE (re) *Precious JWLCD 30*	13	5
16 Aug 97 ●	YESTERDAY *Precious JWLCD 31*	4	6
13 Nov 04	ALL I WANT *Mercury 9868448*	14	3
3 Oct 87 ★	POPPED IN SOULED OUT *Precious JWWWL 1*	1	72
19 Nov 88 ●	THE MEMPHIS SESSIONS *Precious JWWWL 2*	3	13
11 Nov 89 ●	HOLDING BACK THE RIVER *Precious 842011 1*	2	26
8 Feb 92 ★	HIGH ON THE HAPPY SIDE *Precious 5104272* ■	1	25
29 May 93 ●	LIVE AT THE ROYAL ALBERT HALL *Precious 5147742* [1]	10	4
20 Nov 93 ★	END OF PART ONE (THEIR GREATEST HITS) *Precious 5184772*	1	67
22 Apr 95 ●	PICTURE THIS *Precious 5268512*	1	45
12 Apr 97 ●	10 *Precious Organisation 5345852*	2	26
20 Nov 04	THE GREATEST HITS *Mercury 9868751*	13	6+

[1] Wet Wet Wet with the Wren Orchestra

The listed A-side of 'With a Little Help from My Friends' was 'She's Leaving Home' by Billy Bragg with Cara Tivey. Tracks on Lip Service (EP): Lip Service / High on the Happy Side / Lip Service (Live) / More than Love (Live)

WE'VE GOT A FUZZBOX AND WE'RE GONNA USE IT *UK, female*
vocal / instrumental group (Singles: 39 Weeks, Albums: 6 Weeks) pos/wks

26 Apr 86	XX SEX / RULES AND REGULATIONS *Vindaloo UGH 11*	41	7
15 Nov 86	LOVE IS THE SLUG *Vindaloo UGH 14*	31	4
7 Feb 87	WHAT'S THE POINT *Vindaloo YZ 101* [1]	51	2
25 Feb 89	INTERNATIONAL RESCUE *WEA YZ 347*	11	10

		pos/wks
20 May 89	PINK SUNSHINE *WEA YZ 401* [1]	14 10
5 Aug 89	SELF! *WEA YZ 408* [1]	24 6
26 Aug 89 ●	BIG BANG *WEA WX 282*	5 6

[1] Fuzzbox

WHALE *Sweden, male / female vocal /*
instrumental group (Singles: 8 Weeks, Albums: 2 Weeks) pos/wks

		pos/wks
19 Mar 94	HOBO HUMPIN' SLOBO BABE *East West YZ 798CD*	46 2
15 Jul 95	I'LL DO YA *Hut HUTDG 51*	53 1
25 Nov 95	HOBO HUMPIN' SLOBO BABE (re-issue) *Hut HUTCD 64*	15 4
4 Jul 98	FOUR BIG SPEAKERS *Hut HUTCD 96* [1]	69 1
12 Aug 95	WE CARE *Hut DGHUT 25*	42 2

[1] Whale featuring Bus 75

WHALERS See Hal PAIGE and The WHALERS

WHAM! (118 Top 500) *Teen-dream duo with a feel-good, pure pop*
sound: George Michael (v), Andrew Ridgeley (g). They were the only British
act to have three chart-toppers in the UK and the US during the 1980s, a feat
George later equalled as a solo artist. Total UK single sales: 5,298,431. Best-
selling single: 'Last Christmas' / 'Everything She Wants' 1,420,000 (Singles:
137 Weeks, Albums: 259 Weeks) pos/wks

		pos/wks
16 Oct 82 ●	YOUNG GUNS (GO FOR IT) *Innervision IVL A2766*	3 17
15 Jan 83 ●	WHAM RAP! *Innervision IVL A2442*	8 11
14 May 83 ●	BAD BOYS *Innervision A 3143*	2 14
30 Jul 83 ●	CLUB TROPICANA *Innervision A 3613*	4 11
3 Dec 83	CLUB FANTASTIC MEGAMIX *Innervision A 3586*	15 8
26 May 84 ★	WAKE ME UP BEFORE YOU GO GO *Epic A 4440* ▲	1 16
13 Oct 84 ★	FREEDOM *Epic A 4743*	1 14
15 Dec 84 ●	LAST CHRISTMAS / EVERYTHING SHE WANTS *Epic GA / QA 4949* ◆ ▲	2 13
23 Nov 85 ★	I'M YOUR MAN *Epic A 6716*	1 12
14 Dec 85 ●	LAST CHRISTMAS (re-issue) *Epic WHAM 1*	6 7
21 Jun 86 ★	THE EDGE OF HEAVEN / WHERE DID YOUR HEART GO *Epic FIN 1*	1 10
20 Dec 86	LAST CHRISTMAS (2nd re-issue) *Epic 650269 7*	45 4
9 Jul 83 ●	FANTASTIC *Inner Vision IVL 25328* ■	1 116
17 Nov 84 ★	MAKE IT BIG *Epic EPC 86311* ■ ▲	1 72
19 Jul 86 ●	THE FINAL *Epic EPC 88681*	2 47
6 Dec 97 ●	THE BEST OF WHAM! *Epic 4890202*	4 24

Chart entry dated 21 June 1986 was a double record set with 'The Edge of Heaven
– Wham Rap 86 (re-mix)' on disc one and 'Battlestations' / 'Where Did Your Heart
Go' on disc two. Where Did Your Heart Go' listed only from 2 Aug 1986, peaking
at No.28. Chart entry dated 15 Dec 1984 was first catalogued as GA 4949, but
from 5 Jan 1985 the special re-mix of 'Everything She Wants' (QA 4949) was listed
as the A-side and this was the track that topped the US charts

Sarah WHATMORE *UK, female vocalist (Singles: 17 Weeks)* pos/wks

		pos/wks
21 Sep 02 ●	WHEN I LOST YOU *RCA 74321965952*	6 9
22 Feb 03	AUTOMATIC *RCA 82876504612*	11 8

WHATNAUTS See The MOMENTS

Rebecca WHEATLEY
UK, female actor / vocalist (Singles: 8 Weeks) pos/wks

		pos/wks
26 Feb 00 ●	STAY WITH ME (BABY) (re) *BBC Music WMSS 60222*	10 8

WHEATUS *US, male vocal /*
instrumental group (Singles: 37 Weeks, Albums: 30 Weeks) pos/wks

		pos/wks
17 Feb 01 ●	TEENAGE DIRTBAG *Columbia 6707962*	2 20
14 Jul 01 ●	A LITTLE RESPECT *Columbia 6714282*	3 12
26 Jan 02	WANNABE GANGSTAR / LEROY *Columbia 6721272*	22 5
3 Mar 01 ●	WHEATUS *Columbia 4996052*	7 30

Caron WHEELER
UK, female vocalist (Singles: 42 Weeks, Albums: 5 Weeks) pos/wks

		pos/wks
18 Mar 89 ●	KEEP ON MOVING *10 TEN 263* [1]	5 12
10 Jun 89 ★	BACK TO LIFE (HOWEVER DO YOU WANT ME) *10 TEN 265* [1]	1 14
8 Sep 90	LIVIN' IN THE LIGHT *RCA PB 43939*	14 6
10 Nov 90	UK BLAK *RCA PB 43719*	40 4
9 Feb 91	DON'T QUIT *RCA PB 44259*	53 3
7 Nov 92	I ADORE YOU *Perspective PERSS 7407*	59 2
11 Sep 93	BEACH OF THE WAR GODDESS *EMI CDEM 282*	75 1
13 Oct 90	UK BLAK *RCA PL 74751*	14 5

[1] Soul II Soul featuring Caron Wheeler

Bill WHELAN
Ireland, male composer (Singles: 16 Weeks, Albums: 38 Weeks) pos/wks

		pos/wks
17 Dec 94 ●	RIVERDANCE *Son RTEBUACD 1* [1]	9 16
25 Mar 95	MUSIC FROM RIVERDANCE – THE SHOW *Celtic Heartbeat 75678061112*	31 38

[1] Bill Whelan and Anuna featuring the RTE Concert Orchestra

WHEN IN ROME
UK, male vocal / instrumental group (Singles: 3 Weeks) pos/wks

		pos/wks
28 Jan 89	THE PROMISE *10 TEN 244*	58 3

WHIGFIELD *Denmark, female vocalist –*
Sannia Carlson (Singles: 52 Weeks, Albums: 7 Weeks) pos/wks

		pos/wks
17 Sep 94 ★	SATURDAY NIGHT *Systematic SYSCD 3* ◆ ■	1 18
10 Dec 94	ANOTHER DAY *Systematic SYSCD 4*	7 10
10 Jun 95	THINK OF YOU *Systematic SYSCDP 10*	7 11
9 Sep 95	CLOSE TO YOU *Systematic SYCDP 18*	13 7
16 Dec 95	LAST CHRISTMAS / BIG TIME *Systematic SYSCD 24*	21 5
10 Oct 98	SEXY EYES – REMIXES *ZYX ZYX 8085R 8*	68 1
1 Jul 95	WHIGFIELD *Systematic 8286512*	13 7

WHIPPING BOY
Ireland, male vocal / instrumental group (Singles: 4 Weeks) pos/wks

		pos/wks
14 Oct 95	WE DON'T NEED NOBODY ELSE *Columbia 6622205*	51 1
3 Feb 96	WHEN WE WERE YOUNG *Columbia 6628062*	46 2
25 May 96	TWINKLE *Columbia 6632272*	55 1

Nancy WHISKEY See Charles McDEVITT SKIFFLE GROUP featuring Nancy WHISKEY

The WHISPERS
US, male vocal group (Singles: 52 Weeks, Albums: 9 Weeks) pos/wks

		pos/wks
2 Feb 80 ●	AND THE BEAT GOES ON *Solar SO 1*	2 12
10 May 80	LADY *Solar SO 4*	55 3
12 Jul 80	MY GIRL *Solar SO 8*	26 6
14 Mar 81 ●	IT'S A LOVE THING *Solar SO 16*	9 11
13 Jun 81	I CAN MAKE IT BETTER *Solar SO 19*	44 5
19 Jan 85	CONTAGIOUS *MCA MCA 937*	56 3
28 Mar 87	AND THE BEAT GOES ON (re-issue) *Solar MCA 1126*	45 4
23 May 87	ROCK STEADY *Solar MCA 1152*	38 6
15 Aug 87	SPECIAL F/X *Solar MCA 1178*	69 2
14 Mar 81	IMAGINATION *Solar SOLA 7*	42 5
6 Jun 87	JUST GETS BETTER WITH TIME *Solar MCF 3381*	63 4

WHISTLE *US, male rap group (Singles: 8 Weeks)* pos/wks

		pos/wks
1 Mar 86 ●	(NOTHIN' SERIOUS) JUST BUGGIN' *Champion CHAMP 12*	7 8

Alex WHITCOMBE & BIG C *(see also QATTARA)*
UK, male production duo (Singles: 1 Week) pos/wks

		pos/wks
23 May 98	ICE RAIN *Xtravaganza 0091075 EXT*	44 1

Alan WHITE *(see also YES)*
UK, male instrumentalist – drums (Albums: 4 Weeks) pos/wks

		pos/wks
13 Mar 76	RAMSHACKLED *Atlantic K 50217*	41 4

Barry WHITE (128 Top 500)
Seventies soul and disco icon, b. 12 Sep 1944, Texas, US, d. 4 Jul 2003. This
singer / songwriter / pianist / producer / arranger was behind best-sellers by
Love Unlimited and Love Unlimited Orchestra. Lovingly named the "Walrus of
Love", his unmistakable deep voice has been heard in the charts for four
decades (Singles: 138 Weeks, Albums: 244 Weeks) pos/wks

		pos/wks
9 Jun 73	I'M GONNA LOVE YOU JUST A LITTLE MORE BABY *Pye International 7N 25610*	23 7
26 Jan 74	NEVER NEVER GONNA GIVE YA UP *Pye International 7N 25633*	14 11
17 Aug 74 ●	CAN'T GET ENOUGH OF YOUR LOVE, BABE *Pye International 7N 25661* ▲	8 12
2 Nov 74 ★	YOU'RE THE FIRST, THE LAST, MY EVERYTHING *20th Century BTC 2133*	1 14
8 Mar 75 ●	WHAT AM I GONNA DO WITH YOU *20th Century BTC 2177*	5 8
24 May 75	(FOR YOU) I'LL DO ANYTHING YOU WANT ME TO *20th Century BTC 2208*	20 6

		pos	wks
27 Dec 75 ●	LET THE MUSIC PLAY *20th Century BTC 2265*	9	8
6 Mar 76 ●	YOU SEE THE TROUBLE WITH ME *20th Century BTC 2277*	2	10
21 Aug 76	BABY, WE BETTER TRY TO GET IT TOGETHER *20th Century BTC 2298*	15	7
13 Nov 76	DON'T MAKE ME WAIT TOO LONG *20th Century BTC 2309*	17	8
5 Mar 77	I'M QUALIFIED TO SATISFY YOU *20th Century BTC 2328*	37	5
15 Oct 77	IT'S ECSTASY WHEN YOU LAY DOWN NEXT TO ME *20th Century BTC 2350*	40	3
16 Dec 78	JUST THE WAY YOU ARE *20th Century BTC 2380*	12	12
24 Mar 79	SHA LA LA MEANS I LOVE YOU *20th Century BTC 1041*	55	6
7 Nov 87	SHO' YOU RIGHT *Breakout USA 614*	14	7
16 Jan 88	NEVER NEVER GONNA GIVE YOU UP (re-mix) *Club JAB 59*	63	2
31 Mar 90	SECRET GARDEN *Qwest W 9992* [1]	67	1
21 Jan 95	PRACTICE WHAT YOU PREACH / LOVE IS THE ICON *A&M 5808992*	20	4
8 Apr 95	I ONLY WANT TO BE WITH YOU *A&M 5810252*	36	2
21 Dec 96	IN YOUR WILDEST DREAMS *Parlophone CDR 6451* [2]	32	3
4 Nov 00	LET THE MUSIC PLAY (re-mix) *Wonderboy WBOYD 020*	45	2
9 Mar 74	STONE GON' *Pye NSPL 28186*	18	17
6 Apr 74	RHAPSODY IN WHITE *Pye NSPL 28191*	50	1
2 Nov 74 ●	CAN'T GET ENOUGH *20th Century BT 444* ▲	4	34
26 Apr 75	JUST ANOTHER WAY TO SAY I LOVE YOU *20th Century BT 466*	12	15
22 Nov 75	GREATEST HITS *20th Century BTH 8000*	18	12
21 Feb 76	LET THE MUSIC PLAY *20th Century BT 502*	22	14
9 Apr 77	BARRY WHITE'S GREATEST HITS VOLUME 2 *20th Century BTH 8001*	17	7
10 Feb 79	THE MAN *20th Century BT 571*	46	4
21 Dec 85	HEART AND SOUL *K-Tel NE 1316*	34	10
17 Oct 87	THE RIGHT NIGHT AND BARRY WHITE *Breakout AMA 5154*	74	6
2 Jul 88 ●	THE COLLECTION *Mercury BWTV 1*	5	117
11 Feb 95	THE ICON IS LOVE *A&M 5402802*	44	3
15 Feb 03	LOVE SONGS *Universal TV 0686422*	21	4

[1] Quincy Jones featuring Al B Sure!, James Ingram, El DeBarge and Barry White
[2] Tina Turner featuring Barry White

Chris WHITE
UK, male vocalist (Singles: 4 Weeks)

		pos	wks
20 Mar 76	SPANISH WINE *Charisma CB 272*	37	4

Karyn WHITE
US, female vocalist (Singles: 38 Weeks, Albums: 30 Weeks)

		pos	wks
5 Nov 88	THE WAY YOU LOVE ME *Warner Bros. W 7773*	42	5
18 Feb 89	SECRET RENDEZVOUS *Warner Bros. W 7562*	52	3
10 Jun 89	SUPERWOMAN *Warner Bros. W 2920*	11	13
9 Sep 89	SECRET RENDEZVOUS (re-issue) *Warner Bros. W 2855*	22	9
17 Aug 91	ROMANTIC *Warner Bros. W 0028* ▲	23	5
18 Jan 92	THE WAY I FEEL ABOUT YOU *Warner Bros. W 0073*	65	2
24 Sep 94	HUNGAH *Warner Bros. W 0264CD*	69	1
11 Mar 89	KARYN WHITE *Warner Bros. WX 235*	20	27
21 Sep 91	RITUAL OF LOVE *Warner Bros. WX 411*	31	3

Keisha WHITE (see also OAKENFOLD)
UK, female vocalist (Singles: 4 Weeks)

		pos	wks
22 Feb 03	THE HARDER THEY COME *Perfecto PERF 49CDS* [1]	38	2
1 Mar 03	BIGGER BETTER DEAL *Echo ECSCD 129* [2]	67	1
27 Mar 04	WATCHA GONNA DO *Radar RAD 005CD*	53	1

[1] Vocals by Keisha White and Tricky [2] Desert Eagle Discs featuring Keisha White

Snowy WHITE (see also THIN LIZZY) *UK, male vocalist / instrumentalist – guitar (Singles: 12 Weeks, Albums: 5 Weeks)*

		pos	wks
24 Dec 83 ●	BIRD OF PARADISE *Towerbell TOW 42*	6	10
28 Dec 85	FOR YOU (re) *R4 FOR 3*	65	2
11 Feb 84	WHITE FLAMES *Towerbell TOWLP 3*	21	4
9 Feb 85	SNOWY WHITE *Towerbell TOWLP 8*	88	1

Tam WHITE
UK, male vocalist (Singles: 4 Weeks)

		pos	wks
15 Mar 75	WHAT IN THE WORLD'S COME OVER YOU *RAK 193*	36	4

Tony Joe WHITE *US, male vocalist / instrumentalist – guitar (Singles: 10 Weeks, Albums: 1 Week)*

		pos	wks
6 Jun 70	GROUPIE GIRL *Monument MON 1043*	22	10
26 Sep 70	TONY JOE *CBS 63800*	63	1

WHITE and TORCH
UK, male vocal / instrumental duo (Singles: 4 Weeks)

		pos	wks
2 Oct 82	PARADE *Chrysalis CHS 2641*	54	4

WHITE LION
US, male vocal / instrumental group (Albums: 3 Weeks)

		pos	wks
1 Jul 89	BIG GAME *Atlantic WX 277*	47	1
20 Apr 91	MANE ATTRACTION *Atlantic WX 415*	31	2

WHITE PLAINS *UK, male vocal / instrumental group – lead vocal Tony Burrows (Singles: 56 Weeks)*

		pos	wks
7 Feb 70 ●	MY BABY LOVES LOVIN' *Deram DM 280*	9	11
18 Apr 70	I'VE GOT YOU ON MY MIND *Deram DM 291*	17	11
24 Oct 70 ●	JULIE DO YA LOVE ME *Deram DM 315*	8	14
12 Jun 71	WHEN YOU ARE A KING *Deram DM 333*	13	11
17 Feb 73	STEP INTO A DREAM *Deram DM 371*	21	9

The WHITE STRIPES *US, male / female vocal / instrumental duo – Jack and Meg White (Singles: 22 Weeks, Albums: 63 Weeks)*

		pos	wks
24 Nov 01	HOTEL YORBA *XL Recordings XLS 139CD*	26	2
9 Mar 02	FELL IN LOVE WITH A GIRL *XL Recordings XLS 142CD*	21	2
14 Sep 02	DEAD LEAVES AND THE DIRTY GROUND *XL Recordings XLS 148CD*	25	2
3 May 03 ●	7 NATION ARMY *XL Recordings XLS 162CD*	7	4
13 Sep 03	I JUST DON'T KNOW WHAT TO DO WITH MYSELF *XL Recordings XLS 166CD*	13	5
29 Nov 03	THE HARDEST BUTTON TO BUTTON *XL Recordings XLS 173CD*	23	3
27 Nov 04	JOLENE (LIVE) *XL Recordings XLS 207CD*	16	4
18 Aug 01	WHITE BLOOD CELLS *Sympathy for the Record Industry SFTRI 660CD*	55	17
12 Apr 03 ★	ELEPHANT *XL XLCD 162* ■	1	46

'Jolene' was recorded 'Live under Blackpool lights'

WHITE TOWN
UK, male vocalist / producer – Jyoti Mishra (Singles: 10 Weeks)

		pos	wks
25 Jan 97 ★	YOUR WOMAN *Chrysalis CDCHS 5052* ■	1	9
24 May 97	UNDRESSED *Chrysalis CDCHS 5058*	57	1

WHITE ZOMBIE (see also Rob ZOMBIE) *US, male vocal / instrumental group (Singles: 4 Weeks, Albums: 6 Weeks)*

		pos	wks
20 May 95	MORE HUMAN THAN HUMAN *Geffen GFSTD 92*	51	2
18 May 96	ELECTRIC HEAD PART 2 (THE ECSTASY) *Geffen GFSXD 22140*	31	2
27 May 95	ASTRO CREEP 2000 / SUPERSEXY SWINGIN' SOUNDS *Geffen GED 24806*	25	6

'Supersexy Swingin' Sounds', a re-mix album, was listed with 'Astro Creep 2000' from 31 Aug 96 and sales were combined

WHITEHEAD BROS *US, male vocal duo – Kenny and Johnny Whitehead (Singles: 5 Weeks)*

		pos	wks
14 Jan 95	YOUR LOVE IS A 187 *Motown TMGCD 1434*	32	3
13 May 95	FORGET I WAS A G *Motown TMGCD 1441*	40	2

WHITEHOUSE *US / UK, male vocal / instrumental / production duo (Singles: 1 Week)*

		pos	wks
15 Aug 98	AIN'T NO MOUNTAIN HIGH ENOUGH *Beautiful Noise BNOISE 2CD*	60	1

WHITEOUT *UK, male vocal / instrumental group (Singles: 2 Weeks, Albums: 1 Week)*

		pos	wks
24 Sep 94	DETROIT *Silvertone ORECD 66*	73	1
18 Feb 95	JACKIE'S RACING *Silvertone ORECD 68*	72	1
1 Jul 95	BITE IT *Silvertone ORECD 536*	71	1

WHITESNAKE (222 Top 500) *Leading 1980s British rock group founded by ex-Deep Purple vocalist David Coverdale (b. 22 Sep 1949, North Yorkshire, UK), but with an ever-changing line-up. 'Whitesnake 1987', their most successful album, shifted more than 10 million copies worldwide (Singles: 112 Weeks, Albums: 162 Weeks)*

		pos	wks
24 Jun 78	SNAKE BITE (EP) *EMI International INEP 751* [1]	61	3
10 Nov 79	LONG WAY FROM HOME *United Artists BP 324*	55	2

		pos/wks
26 Apr 80	FOOL FOR YOUR LOVING *United Artists BP 352*	13 9
12 Jul 80	READY AN' WILLING (SWEET SATISFACTION)	
	United Artists BP 363	43 4
22 Nov 80	AIN'T NO LOVE IN THE HEART OF THE CITY	
	Sunburst / Liberty BP 381	51 4
11 Apr 81	DON'T BREAK MY HEART AGAIN *Liberty BP 395*	17 9
6 Jun 81	WOULD I LIE TO YOU *Liberty BP 399*	37 6
6 Nov 82	HERE I GO AGAIN / BLOODY LUXURY *Liberty BP 416* ▲	34 10
13 Aug 83	GUILTY OF LOVE *Liberty BP 420*	31 5
14 Jan 84	GIVE ME MORE TIME *Liberty BP 422*	29 4
28 Apr 84	STANDING IN THE SHADOW *Liberty BP 423*	62 4
9 Feb 85	LOVE AIN'T NO STRANGER *Liberty BP 424*	44 4
28 Mar 87	STILL OF THE NIGHT *EMI EMI 5606*	16 8
6 Jun 87 ●	IS THIS LOVE *EMI EM 3*	9 11
31 Oct 87 ●	HERE I GO AGAIN (re-mix) *EMI EM 35*	9 11
6 Feb 88	GIVE ME ALL YOUR LOVE *EMI EM 23*	18 6
2 Dec 89	FOOL FOR YOUR LOVING (re-recording) *EMI EM 123*	43 2
10 Mar 90	THE DEEPER THE LOVE *EMI EM 128*	35 3
25 Aug 90	NOW YOU'RE GONE *EMI EM 150*	31 4
6 Aug 94 ●	IS THIS LOVE / SWEET LADY LUCK (re-issue) *EMI CDEM 329*	25 4
7 Jun 97	TOO MANY TEARS *EMI CDEM 471* [2]	46 1
18 Nov 78	TROUBLE *EMI International INS 3022*	50 2
13 Oct 79	LOVE HUNTER *United Artists UAG 30264*	29 7
7 Jun 80 ●	READY AND WILLING *United Artists UAG 30302*	6 15
8 Nov 80 ●	LIVE IN THE HEART OF THE CITY *United Artists SNAKE 1*	5 15
18 Apr 81 ●	COME AND GET IT *Liberty LBG 30327*	2 23
27 Nov 82 ●	SAINTS 'N' SINNERS *Liberty LBG 30354*	9 9
11 Feb 84 ●	SLIDE IT IN *Liberty LBG 2400001*	9 7
11 Apr 87 ●	WHITESNAKE 1987 *EMI EMC 3528*	8 57
25 Nov 89 ●	SLIP OF THE TONGUE *EMI EMD 1013*	10 10
16 Jul 94 ●	GREATEST HITS *EMI CDEMD 1065*	4 12
21 Jun 97	RESTLESS HEART *EMI CDEMD 1104* [1]	34 2
5 Apr 03	BEST OF WHITESNAKE *EMI 5812452*	44 3

[1] David Coverdale's Whitesnake [2] David Coverdale and Whitesnake [1] David Coverdale and Whitesnake

Tracks on Snake Bite (EP): Bloody Mary / Steal Away / Ain't No Love in the Heart of the City / Come On

David WHITFIELD ⟨ 355 ⟩ Top 500

Most successful UK male singer in the US during the pre-rock years, b. 2 Feb 1925, Yorkshire, d. 16 Jan 1980. This operatic-style tenor had a formidable and predominantly female fan following in the 1950s (Singles: 190 Weeks) pos/wks

		pos/wks
2 Oct 53 ●	THE BRIDGE OF SIGHS *Decca F 10129*	9 1
16 Oct 53 ★	ANSWER ME (re) *Decca F 10192*	1 14
11 Dec 53 ●	RAGS TO RICHES (re) *Decca F 10207* [1]	3 11
19 Feb 54 ●	THE BOOK (re) *Decca F 10242*	5 15
18 Jun 54 ★	CARA MIA *Decca F 10327*	1 25
12 Nov 54 ●	SANTO NATALE (MERRY CHRISTMAS) *Decca F 10399*	2 10
11 Feb 55 ●	BEYOND THE STARS *Decca F 10458*	8 9
27 May 55	MAMA (2re) *Decca F 10515*	12 11
8 Jul 55 ●	EV'RYWHERE *Decca F 10515* [2]	3 20
25 Nov 55 ●	WHEN YOU LOSE THE ONE YOU LOVE *Decca F 10627* [3]	7 11
2 Mar 56 ●	MY SEPTEMBER LOVE (3re) *Decca F 10690*	3 24
24 Aug 56	MY SON JOHN *Decca F 10769*	22 4
31 Aug 56	MY UNFINISHED SYMPHONY *Decca F 10769*	29 1
25 Jan 57 ●	THE ADORATION WALTZ *Decca F 10833* [2]	9 11
5 Apr 57	I'LL FIND YOU (re) *Decca F 10864*	27 4
14 Feb 58	CRY MY HEART *Decca F 10978* [4]	22 3
16 May 58 ●	ON THE STREET WHERE YOU LIVE *Decca F 11018* [5]	16 14
8 Aug 58	THE RIGHT TO LOVE *Decca F 11039*	30 1
24 Nov 60	I BELIEVE *Decca F 11289*	49 1

[1] David Whitfield with Stanley Black and his Orchestra [2] David Whitfield with the Roland Shaw Orchestra [3] David Whitfield with Mantovani, his Orchestra and Chorus [4] David Whitfield with chorus and Mantovani and his Orchestra [5] David Whitfield with Cyril Stapleton and his Orchestra

Slim WHITMAN *US, male vocalist –*
Otis Whitman Jr (Singles: 77 Weeks, Albums: 61 Weeks) pos/wks

		pos/wks
15 Jul 55 ★	ROSE MARIE *London HL 8061*	1 19
29 Jul 55 ●	INDIAN LOVE CALL *London L 1149*	7 12
23 Sep 55	CHINA DOLL *London L 1149*	15 2
9 Mar 56	TUMBLING TUMBLEWEEDS *London HLU 8230*	19 2
13 Apr 56	I'M A FOOL (re) *London HLU 8252*	16 4
22 Jun 56 ●	SERENADE (re) *London HLU 8287*	8 15
12 Apr 57 ●	I'LL TAKE YOU HOME AGAIN KATHLEEN *London HLP 8403*	7 13
5 Oct 74	HAPPY ANNIVERSARY *United Artists UP 35728*	14 10

		pos/wks
14 Dec 74	HAPPY ANNIVERSARY *United Artists UAS 29670*	44 2
31 Jan 76 ★	THE VERY BEST OF SLIM WHITMAN *United Artists UAS 29898*	1 17
15 Jan 77 ★	RED RIVER VALLEY *United Artists UAS 29993*	1 14
15 Oct 77	HOME ON THE RANGE *United Artists UATV 30102*	2 13
13 Jan 79	GHOST RIDERS IN THE SKY *United Artists UATV 30202*	27 6
22 Dec 79	SLIM WHITMAN'S 20 GREATEST LOVE SONGS	
	United Artists UAG 30270	18 7
27 Sep 97	THE VERY BEST OF SLIM WHITMAN – 50TH ANNIVERSARY	
	COLLECTION *EMI CDEMC 3772*	54 2

Roger WHITTAKER ⟨ 336 ⟩ Top 500
World-renowned vocalist and whistler, b. 22 Mar 1936, Nairobi, Kenya. Easy-listening legend and popular live performer with more than 10 million albums sold in his home base of Germany (Singles: 85 Weeks, Albums: 116 Weeks) pos/wks

		pos/wks
8 Nov 69	DURHAM TOWN (THE LEAVIN') *Columbia DB 8613*	12 18
11 Apr 70 ●	I DON'T BELIEVE IN IF ANYMORE *Columbia DB 8664*	8 18
10 Oct 70	NEW WORLD IN THE MORNING *Columbia DB 8718*	17 14
3 Apr 71	WHY *Columbia DB 8752*	47 1
2 Oct 71	MAMMY BLUE *Columbia DB 8822*	31 10
26 Jul 75 ●	THE LAST FAREWELL *EMI 2294*	2 14
8 Nov 86 ●	THE SKYE BOAT SONG *Tembo TML 119* [1]	10 10
27 Jun 70	I DON'T BELIEVE IN IF ANYMORE *Columbia SCX 6404*	23 1
3 Apr 71	NEW WORLD IN THE MORNING *Columbia SCX 6456*	45 2
6 Sep 75 ●	THE VERY BEST OF ROGER WHITTAKER *Columbia SCX 6560*	5 42
15 May 76	THE SECOND ALBUM OF THE VERY BEST OF ROGER	
	WHITTAKER *EMI EMC 3117*	27 7
9 Dec 78	ROGER WHITTAKER SINGS THE HITS *Columbia SCX 6601*	52 5
4 Aug 79	20 ALL TIME GREATS *Polydor POLTV 8*	24 9
7 Feb 81	THE ROGER WHITTAKER ALBUM *K-Tel NE 1105*	18 14
27 Dec 86	SKYE BOAT SONG AND OTHER GREAT SONGS	
	Tembo TMB 113	89 1
23 May 87	HIS FINEST COLLECTION *Tembo RWTV 1*	15 19
23 Sep 89	HOME LOVIN' MAN *Tembo RWTV 2*	20 10
11 May 96	A PERFECT DAY – HIS GREATEST HITS & MORE	
	RCA 74321371562	74 1
7 Feb 04	NOW AND THEN – GREATEST HITS 1964–2004	
	BMG 82876588332	21 5

[1] Roger Whittaker and Des O'Connor

The WHO ⟨ 83 ⟩ Top 500 (see also The HIGH NUMBERS)
Legendary live band from London, whose 'Tommy' album (1969) popularised rock opera: Roger Daltrey CBE (v), Pete Townshend (g), John Entwistle, 'The Ox' (b) b. 9 Oct 1944, d. 27 Jun 2002, Keith Moon (d), b. 23 Aug 1947, d. 7 Sep 1978. These gold-record collectors have spent five decades breaking both guitars and box-office records (Singles: 247 Weeks, Albums: 233 Weeks) pos/wks

		pos/wks
18 Feb 65 ●	I CAN'T EXPLAIN *Brunswick 05926*	8 13
27 May 65 ●	ANYWAY ANYHOW ANYWHERE *Brunswick 05935*	10 12
4 Nov 65 ●	MY GENERATION *Brunswick 05944*	2 13
10 Mar 66 ●	SUBSTITUTE *Reaction 591 001*	5 13
24 Mar 66	A LEGAL MATTER *Brunswick 05956*	32 6
1 Sep 66 ●	I'M A BOY *Reaction 591 004*	2 13
1 Sep 66	THE KIDS ARE ALRIGHT (re) *Brunswick 05965*	41 4
15 Dec 66 ●	HAPPY JACK *Reaction 591 010*	3 11
27 Apr 67 ●	PICTURES OF LILY *Track 604 002*	4 10
26 Jul 67	THE LAST TIME / UNDER MY THUMB *Track 604 006*	44 3
18 Oct 67 ●	I CAN SEE FOR MILES *Track 604 011*	10 12
19 Jun 68	DOGS *Track 604 023*	25 5
23 Oct 68	MAGIC BUS *Track 604 024*	26 6
19 Mar 69 ●	PINBALL WIZARD *Track 604 027*	4 13
4 Apr 70	THE SEEKER *Track 604 036*	19 11
8 Aug 70	SUMMERTIME BLUES *Track 2094 002*	38 4
10 Jul 71 ●	WON'T GET FOOLED AGAIN *Track 2094 009*	9 12
23 Oct 71 ●	LET'S SEE ACTION *Track 2094 012*	16 12
24 Jun 72 ●	JOIN TOGETHER *Track 2094 102*	9 9
13 Jan 73	RELAY *Track 2094 106*	21 5
13 Oct 73	5.15 *Track 2094 115*	20 6
24 Jan 76 ●	SQUEEZE BOX *Polydor 2121 275*	10 9
30 Oct 76 ●	SUBSTITUTE (re-issue) *Polydor 2058 803*	7 7
22 Jul 78	WHO ARE YOU *Polydor WHO 1*	18 12
28 Apr 79	LONG LIVE ROCK *Polydor WHO 2*	48 5
7 Mar 81 ●	YOU BETTER YOU BET *Polydor WHO 004*	9 8
9 May 81	DON'T LET GO THE COAT *Polydor WHO 005*	47 4
2 Oct 82	ATHENA *Polydor WHO 6*	40 4
26 Nov 83	READY STEADY WHO (EP) *Polydor WHO 7*	58 4
20 Feb 88	MY GENERATION (re-issue) *Polydor POSP 907*	68 2
27 Jul 96	MY GENERATION (2nd re-issue) *Polydor 8546372*	31 2
25 Dec 65 ●	MY GENERATION *Brunswick LAT 8616*	5 11

		pos wks
17 Dec 66 ●	**A QUICK ONE** *Reaction 593002*	**4** 17
13 Jan 68	**THE WHO SELL-OUT** *Track 613002*	**13** 11
7 Jun 69 ●	**TOMMY** *Track 613013/4*	**2** 9
6 Jun 70 ●	**LIVE AT LEEDS** *Track 2406001*	**3** 21
11 Sep 71 ★	**WHO'S NEXT** *Track 2408102*	**1** 13
18 Dec 71 ●	**MEATY BEATY BIG AND BOUNCY** *Track 2406006*	**9** 8
17 Nov 73 ●	**QUADROPHENIA** *Track 2647013*	**2** 13
26 Oct 74 ●	**ODDS AND SODS** *Track 2406018*	**10** 4
23 Aug 75	**TOMMY (FILM SOUNDTRACK)** *Track 2657007*	**30** 2
18 Oct 75 ●	**THE WHO BY NUMBERS** *Polydor 2490129*	**7** 6
9 Oct 76 ●	**THE STORY OF THE WHO** *Polydor 2683069*	**2** 18
9 Sep 78 ●	**WHO ARE YOU** *Polydor WHOD 5004*	**6** 9
30 Jun 79	**THE KIDS ARE ALRIGHT** *Polydor 2675 174*	**26** 13
25 Oct 80	**MY GENERATION (re-issue)** *Virgin V 2179*	**20** 7
28 Mar 81 ●	**FACE DANCES** *Polydor WHOD 5037*	**2** 9
11 Sep 82	**IT'S HARD** *Polydor WHOD 5066*	**11** 6
17 Nov 84	**WHO'S LAST** *MCA WHO 1*	**48** 4
12 Oct 85	**THE WHO COLLECTION** *Impression IMDP 4*	**44** 6
19 Mar 88 ●	**WHO'S BETTER WHO'S BEST** *Polydor WTV 1*	**10** 11
19 Nov 88	**THE WHO COLLECTION** *Stylus SMR 570*	**71** 4
24 Mar 90	**JOIN TOGETHER** *Virgin VDT 102*	**59** 1
16 Jul 94	**30 YEARS OF MAXIMUM R&B** *Polydor 5217512*	**48** 1
4 Mar 95	**LIVE AT LEEDS (re-issue)** *Polydor 5271692*	**59** 1
6 Jul 96	**QUADROPHENIA (re-issue)** *Polydor 5319712*	**47** 2
24 Aug 96	**MY GENERATION – THE VERY BEST OF THE WHO** *Polydor 5331502*	**11** 6
26 Feb 00	**BBC SESSIONS** *BBC Music / Polydor 5477272*	**24** 2
21 Sep 02	**MY GENERATION (2nd re-issue)** *MCA / Uni-Island 1129262*	**47** 1
2 Nov 02	**THE ULTIMATE COLLECTION** *Polydor / Universal TV 0653002*	**17** 5
12 Jul 03	**LIVE AT THE ROYAL ALBERT HALL** *SPV Recordings SPV 09374882*	**72** 1
15 May 04 ●	**THEN AND NOW! – 1964-2004** *Polydor 9866577*	**5** 11

Tracks on Ready Steady Who (EP): Disguises / Circles / Batman / Bucket 'T' / Barbara Ann. The two albums titled 'The Who Collection' are different. The 2nd re-issue of 'My Generation' contains a bonus disc of out-takes and rarities. 'The Ultimate Collection' is a three-CD boxed set

WHO DA FUNK
US, male production duo and female vocalist (Singles: 8 Weeks) pos/wks

		pos wks
26 Oct 02	**SHINY DISCO BALLS (IMPORT)** *White Label SSA 03* [1]	**69** 1
2 Nov 02	**SHINY DISCO BALLS** *Cream CREAM 22CD* [1]	**15** 5
15 Feb 03	**STING ME RED (YOU THINK YOU'RE SO CLEVER)** *Cream CREAM 19CDS* [2]	**32** 2

[1] Who Da Funk featuring Jessica Eve [2] Who Da Funk featuring Terra Deva

WHODINI
US, male rap / DJ duo (Singles: 10 Weeks) pos/wks

		pos wks
25 Dec 82	**MAGIC'S WAND** *Jive JIVE 28*	**47** 6
17 Mar 84	**MAGIC'S WAND (THE WHODINI ELECTRIC EP)** *Jive JIVE 61*	**63** 4

Tracks on Magic's Wand (The Whodini Electric EP): Jive Magic Wand / Nasty Lady / Rap Machine / The Haunted House of Rock

WHOOLIGANZ
US, male rap duo (Singles: 2 Weeks) pos/wks

		pos wks
13 Aug 94	**PUT YOUR HANDZ UP** *Positiva CDTIV 17*	**53** 2

WHOOSH
UK, male production trio (Singles: 1 Week) pos/wks

		pos wks
13 Sep 97	**WHOOSH** *Wonderboy WBOYD 006*	**72** 1

WHYCLIFFE
UK, male vocalist – Bramwell Whycliffe (Singles: 2 Weeks) pos/wks

		pos wks
20 Nov 93	**HEAVEN** *MCA MCSTD 1944*	**56** 1
2 Apr 94	**ONE MORE TIME** *MCA MCSTD 1955*	**72** 1

WICKAMAN *See J MAJIK*

WIDEBOYS featuring Dennis G
UK, male production duo and male vocalist (Singles: 6 Weeks) pos/wks

		pos wks
27 Oct 01	**SAMBUCA** *Locked On / 679 Recordings 679L 002CD*	**15** 6

Gabrielle WIDMAN *See MONKEY BARS featuring Gabrielle WIDMAN*

Jane WIEDLIN (see also GO-GO's)
US, female vocalist (Singles: 14 Weeks, Albums: 3 Weeks) pos/wks

		pos wks
6 Aug 88	**RUSH HOUR** *Manhattan MT 36*	**12** 11
29 Oct 88	**INSIDE A DREAM** *Manhattan MT 55*	**64** 3
24 Sep 88	**FUR** *Manhattan MTL 1029*	**48** 3

WIGAN'S CHOSEN FEW
Canada, male vocal / instrumental group and UK, crowd chants (Singles: 11 Weeks) pos/wks

		pos wks
18 Jan 75 ●	**FOOTSEE** *Pye Disco Demand DDS 111*	**9** 11

WIGAN'S OVATION
UK, male vocal / instrumental group (Singles: 19 Weeks) pos/wks

		pos wks
15 Mar 75	**SKIING IN THE SNOW** *Spark SRL 1122*	**12** 10
28 Jun 75	**PER-SO-NAL-LY** *Spark SRL 1129*	**38** 6
29 Nov 75	**SUPER LOVE** *Spark SRL 1133*	**41** 3

WILCO
US, male vocal / instrumental group (Singles: 1 Week, Albums: 7 Weeks) pos/wks

		pos wks
17 Apr 99	**CAN'T STAND IT** *Reprise W 475CD1*	**67** 1
11 Jul 98	**MERMAID AVENUE** *Elektra 7559622042* [1]	**34** 2
20 Mar 99	**SUMMERTEETH** *Reprise 9362472822*	**38** 2
10 Jun 00	**MERMAID AVENUE – VOL. 2** *Elektra 7559625222* [1]	**61** 1
4 May 02	**YANKEE HOTEL FOXTROT** *Nonesuch 7559796692*	**40** 1
3 Jul 04	**A GHOST IS BORN** *Nonesuch 7559798092*	**50** 1

[1] Billy Bragg and Wilco

Jack WILD *UK, male actor / vocalist (Singles: 2 Weeks)* pos/wks

		pos wks
2 May 70	**SOME BEAUTIFUL** *Capitol CL 15635*	**46** 2

WILD CHERRY
US, male vocal / instrumental group (Singles: 11 Weeks) pos/wks

		pos wks
9 Oct 76 ●	**PLAY THAT FUNKY MUSIC** *Epic EPC 4593* ▲	**7** 11

WILD COLOUR
UK, male / female vocal / instrumental group (Singles: 2 Weeks) pos/wks

		pos wks
14 Oct 95	**DREAMS** *Perfecto PERF 105CD*	**25** 2

WILD HORSES
UK, male vocal / instrumental group (Albums: 4 Weeks) pos/wks

		pos wks
26 Apr 80	**WILD HORSES** *EMI EMC 3324*	**38** 4

WILD PAIR *See Paula ABDUL*

WILD WEEKEND
UK, male vocal / instrumental group (Singles: 2 Weeks) pos/wks

		pos wks
29 Apr 89	**BREAKIN' UP** *Parlophone R 6204*	**74** 1
5 May 90	**WHO'S AFRAID OF THE BIG BAD LOVE?** *Parlophone R 6249*	**70** 1

WILDCHILD
UK, male producer – Roger McKenzie (Singles: 20 Weeks) pos/wks

		pos wks
22 Apr 95	**LEGENDS OF THE DARK BLACK PART 2** *Hi-Life HICD 9*	**34** 3
21 Oct 95	**RENEGADE MASTER (re-issue)** *Hi-Life 5771312*	**11** 4
23 Nov 96	**JUMP TO MY BEAT** *Hi-Life 5757372*	**30** 2
17 Jan 98 ●	**RENEGADE MASTER '98** *Hi-Life 5692792*	**3** 10
25 Apr 98	**BAD BOY** *Polydor 5716072* [1]	**38** 1

[1] Wildchild featuring Jomalski

Although titled differently, first two hits are identical

Eugene WILDE
US, male vocalist – Ron Broomfield (Singles: 15 Weeks, Albums: 4 Weeks) pos/wks

		pos wks
13 Oct 84	**GOTTA GET YOU HOME TONIGHT** *Fourth & Broadway BRW 15*	**18** 9
2 Feb 85	**PERSONALITY** *Fourth & Broadway BRW 18*	**34** 6
8 Dec 84	**EUGENE WILDE** *Fourth & Broadway BRLP 502*	**67** 4

'Personality' was coupled with 'Let Her Feel It' by Simplicious

Kim WILDE ⟨216⟩ Top 500
Most charted British female vocalist in the 1980s, b. Kim Smith, 18 Nov 1960, London. Neither Kim nor her father, rock 'n' roll star Marty Wilde, managed a UK No.1, but Kim did top the US chart. Returned with major continental hit in Europe, dueting with Nena on 'Any Place, Any Time, Anywhere' in 2003 and is now a celebrity gardener (Singles: 194 Weeks, Albums: 88 Weeks) pos/wks

		pos wks
21 Feb 81 ●	**KIDS IN AMERICA** *RAK 327*	**2** 13
9 May 81 ●	**CHEQUERED LOVE** *RAK 330*	**4** 9
1 Aug 81	**WATER ON GLASS / BOYS** *RAK 334*	**11** 8
14 Nov 81	**CAMBODIA** *RAK 336*	**12** 12
17 Apr 82	**VIEW FROM A BRIDGE** *RAK 342*	**16** 7

16 Oct 82	CHILD COME AWAY *RAK 352*	.43	4
30 Jul 83	LOVE BLONDE *RAK 360*	.23	8
12 Nov 83	DANCING IN THE DARK *RAK 365*	.67	2
13 Oct 84	THE SECOND TIME *MCA KIM 1*	.29	6
8 Dec 84	THE TOUCH *MCA KIM 2*	.56	3
27 Apr 85	RAGE TO LOVE *MCA KIM 3*	.19	8
25 Oct 86 ●	YOU KEEP ME HANGIN' ON *MCA KIM 4* ▲	.2	14
4 Apr 87 ●	ANOTHER STEP (CLOSER TO YOU) *MCA KIM 5* 1	.6	11
8 Aug 87	SAY YOU REALLY WANT ME *MCA KIM 6*	.29	5
5 Dec 87 ●	ROCKIN' AROUND THE CHRISTMAS TREE *10 TEN 2* 2	.3	7
14 May 88	HEY MISTER HEARTACHE *MCA KIM 7*	.31	5
16 Jul 88 ●	YOU CAME *MCA KIM 8*	.3	11
1 Oct 88 ●	NEVER TRUST A STRANGER *MCA KIM 9*	.7	9
3 Dec 88 ●	FOUR LETTER WORD *MCA KIM 10*	.6	12
4 Mar 89	LOVE IN THE NATURAL WAY *MCA KIM 11*	.32	6
14 Apr 90	IT'S HERE *MCA KIM 12*	.42	4
16 Jun 90	TIME *MCA KIM 13*	.71	3
15 Dec 90	I CAN'T SAY GOODBYE *MCA KIM 14*	.51	3
2 May 92	LOVE IS HOLY *MCA KIM 15*	.16	6
27 Jun 92	HEART OVER MIND *MCA KIM 16*	.34	3
12 Sep 92	WHO DO YOU THINK YOU ARE *MCA KIM 17*	.49	3
10 Jul 93	IF I CAN'T HAVE YOU *MCA KIMTD 18*	.12	8
13 Nov 93	IN MY LIFE *MCA KIMTD 19*	.54	1
14 Oct 95	BREAKIN' AWAY *MCA KIMTD 21*	.43	2
10 Feb 96	THIS I SWEAR *MCA KIMTD 22*	.46	1
11 Jul 81 ●	KIM WILDE *RAK SRAK 544*	.3	14
22 May 82	SELECT *RAK SRAK 548*	.19	11
26 Nov 83	CATCH AS CATCH CAN *RAK SRAK 165408*	.90	1
17 Nov 84	TEASES AND DARES *MCA MCF 3250*	.66	2
18 May 85	THE VERY BEST OF KIM WILDE *RAK WILDE 1*	.78	4
15 Nov 86	ANOTHER STEP *MCA MCF 3339*	.73	5
25 Jun 88 ●	CLOSE *MCA MCG 6030*	.8	38
26 May 90	LOVE MOVES *MCA MCG 6088*	.37	3
30 May 92	LOVE IS *MCA 10625*	.21	3
25 Sep 93	THE SINGLES COLLECTION 1981-1993 *MCA MCD 10921*	.11	7

1 Kim Wilde and Junior 2 Mel [Mel Smith] and Kim

'Another Step' changed label number to MCA KIML 1 during its chart run

Marty WILDE
UK, male vocalist – Reginald Smith (Singles: 117 Weeks) pos/wks

11 Jul 58 ●	ENDLESS SLEEP *Philips PB 835*	.4	14
6 Mar 59 ●	DONNA (re) *Philips PB 902*	.3	18
5 Jun 59 ●	A TEENAGER IN LOVE *Philips PB 926*	.2	17
25 Sep 59 ●	SEA OF LOVE *Philips PB 959*	.3	12
11 Dec 59 ●	BAD BOY *Philips PB 972*	.7	8
10 Mar 60	JOHNNY ROCCO *Philips PB 1002*	.30	4
19 May 60	THE FIGHT *Philips PB 1022*	.47	1
22 Dec 60	LITTLE GIRL *Philips PB 1078*	.16	9
26 Jan 61 ●	RUBBER BALL *Philips PB 1101*	.9	9
27 Jul 61	HIDE AND SEEK *Philips PB 1161*	.47	2
9 Nov 61	TOMORROW'S CLOWN *Philips PB 1191*	.33	5
24 May 62	JEZEBEL *Philips PB 1240*	.19	11
25 Oct 62	EVER SINCE YOU SAID GOODBYE *Philips 326546 BF*	.31	7

Roxanne WILDE See DT8 PROJECT

Matthew WILDER *US, male vocalist (Singles: 11 Weeks)* pos/wks

21 Jan 84 ●	BREAK MY STRIDE *Epic A 3908*	.4	11

WILDFLOWER See APHRODITE featuring WILDFLOWER

The WILDHEARTS *UK, male vocal /*
instrumental group (Singles: 32 Weeks, Albums: 9 Weeks) pos/wks

20 Nov 93	TV TAN *Bronze YZ 784CD*	.53	2
19 Feb 94	CAFFEINE BOMB *Bronze YZ 794CD*	.31	3
9 Jul 94	SUCKERPUNCH *Bronze YZ 828CD*	.38	2
28 Jan 95	IF LIFE IS LIKE A LOVE BANK I WANT AN OVERDRAFT / GEORDIE IN WONDERLAND *East West YZ 874CD*	.31	3
6 May 95	I WANNA GO WHERE THE PEOPLE GO *East West YZ 923CD*	.16	3
29 Jul 95	JUST IN LUST *East West YZ 967CD*	.28	2
20 Apr 96	SICK OF DRUGS *Round WILD 1CD*	.14	3
29 Jun 96	RED LIGHT – GREEN LIGHT (EP) *Round WILD 2CD*	.30	2
16 Aug 97	ANTHEM *Mushroom MUSH 6CD*	.21	2
18 Oct 97	URGE *Mushroom MUSH 14CD*	.26	2
12 Oct 02	VANILLA RADIO *Round / Snapper SMACD 048S*	.26	2
1 Feb 03	STORMY IN THE NORTH – KARMA IN THE SOUTH *Round SMASCD 049*	.17	2

24 May 03	SO INTO YOU *Gut / Round CDGUT 49*	.22	2
15 Nov 03	TOP OF THE WORLD *Gut CDGUT 54*	.26	2
11 Sep 93	EARTH VS THE WILDHEARTS *East West 4509932871*	.46	1
3 Jun 95	P.H.U.Q. *East West 0630104372*	.6	4
1 Jun 96	FISHING FOR LUCKIES *Round 630148552*	.16	2
8 Nov 97	ENDLESS NAMELESS *Mushroom MUSH 13CD*	.41	1
6 Sep 03	THE WILDHEARTS *Gut GUTCD 25*	.54	1

Tracks on Red Light – Green Light (EP): Red Light – Green Light / Got It On Tuesday / Do Anything / The British All-American Homeboy Crowd

WILEY *US, male producer (Singles: 6 Weeks, Albums: 1 Week)* pos/wks

17 Apr 04	WOT DO U CALL IT? *XL Recordings XLS 179CD*	.31	4
21 Aug 04	PIES *XL Recordings XLS 188CD*	.45	2
8 May 04	TREDDIN' ON THIN ICE *XL Recordings XLCD 178*	.45	1

Jonathan WILKES *UK, male vocalist (Singles: 2 Weeks)* pos/wks

17 Mar 01	JUST ANOTHER DAY *Innocent SINCD 25*	.24	2

Colm WILKINSON *Ireland, male vocalist (Albums: 6 Weeks)* pos/wks

10 Jun 89	STAGE HEROES *RCA BL 74105*	.27	6

Sue WILKINSON *UK, female vocalist (Singles: 8 Weeks)* pos/wks

2 Aug 80	YOU GOTTA BE A HUSTLER IF YOU WANNA GET ON *Cheapskate CHEAP 2*	.25	8

WILL TO POWER *US, male / female vocal / instrumental*
duo – Bob Rosenberg and Suzi Carr (Singles: 18 Weeks) pos/wks

7 Jan 89 ●	BABY I LOVE YOUR WAY – FREEBIRD *Epic 6530947* ▲	.6	9
22 Dec 90	I'M NOT IN LOVE *Epic 6565377*	.29	9

Alyson WILLIAMS
US, female vocalist (Singles: 28 Weeks, Albums: 21 Weeks) pos/wks

4 Mar 89	SLEEP TALK *Def Jam 654656 7*	.17	9
6 May 89	MY LOVE IS SO RAW *Def Jam 654898 7* 1	.34	5
19 Aug 89 ●	I NEED YOUR LOVIN' *Def Jam 655143 7*	.8	11
18 Nov 89	I SECOND THAT EMOTION *Def Jam 655456 7* 2	.44	3
25 Mar 89	RAW *Def Jam 463293 1*	.29	21

1 Alyson Williams featuring Nikki D 2 Alyson Williams with Chuck Stanley

Andy WILLIAMS (41 *Top 500*) *Leading MOR vocalist who hosted a top-rated 1960s TV series, b. 3 Dec 1928, Iowa, US. He left the noted family act The Williams Brothers in 1951 and had an enviable portfolio of smooth UK and US hit singles and albums in the 1950s and 1960s. Had a surprise 1999 re-entry with 'Music to Watch Girls By' following its use in a TV car commercial (Singles: 238 Weeks, Albums: 447 Weeks)* pos/wks

19 Apr 57 ★	BUTTERFLY (re) *London HLA 8399*	.1	16
21 Jun 57	I LIKE YOUR KIND OF LOVE *London HLA 8437*	.16	10
14 Jun 62	STRANGER ON THE SHORE *CBS AAG 103*	.30	10
21 Mar 63 ●	CAN'T GET USED TO LOSING YOU *CBS AAG 138*	.2	18
27 Feb 64	A FOOL NEVER LEARNS *CBS AAG 182*	.40	4
16 Sep 65 ●	ALMOST THERE *CBS 201813*	.2	17
24 Feb 66	MAY EACH DAY *CBS 202042*	.19	8
22 Sep 66	IN THE ARMS OF LOVE *CBS 202300*	.33	7
4 May 67	MUSIC TO WATCH GIRLS BY *CBS 2675*	.33	6
2 Aug 67	MORE AND MORE *CBS 2886*	.45	1
13 Mar 68 ●	CAN'T TAKE MY EYES OFF YOU *CBS 3298*	.5	18
7 May 69	HAPPY HEART (re) *CBS 4062*	.19	10
14 Mar 70 ●	CAN'T HELP FALLING IN LOVE *CBS 4818*	.3	17
1 Aug 70	IT'S SO EASY (re) *CBS 5113*	.13	14
21 Nov 70	HOME LOVIN' MAN *CBS 5267*	.7	12
20 Mar 71 ●	(WHERE DO I BEGIN) LOVE STORY (re) *CBS 7020*	.4	18
5 Aug 72	LOVE THEME FROM 'THE GODFATHER' (SPEAK SOFTLY LOVE) (2re) *CBS 8166*	.42	9
8 Dec 73 ●	SOLITAIRE *CBS 1824*	.4	18
18 May 74	GETTING OVER YOU *CBS 2181*	.35	5
31 May 75	YOU LAY SO EASY ON MY MIND *CBS 3167*	.32	7
6 Mar 76	THE OTHER SIDE OF ME *CBS 3903*	.42	3
27 Mar 99 ●	MUSIC TO WATCH GIRLS BY (re-issue) *Columbia 6671322*	.9	6
29 Jun 02	CAN'T TAKE MY EYES OFF YOU *Columbia 6721052* 1	.23	4
26 Jun 65 ●	ALMOST THERE *CBS BPG 62533*	.4	46
7 Aug 65	CAN'T GET USED TO LOSING YOU *CBS BPG 62146*	.16	1
19 Mar 66	MAY EACH DAY *CBS BPG 62430*	.11	6
30 Apr 66	GREAT SONGS FROM MY FAIR LADY *CBS BPG 62430*	.30	1
23 Jul 66	SHADOW OF YOUR SMILE *CBS 62633*	.24	4
29 Jul 67	BORN FREE *CBS SBPG 63027*	.22	11

11 May 68 ★	LOVE ANDY *CBS 63167*	1	22
6 Jul 68 ●	HONEY *CBS 63311*	4	17
26 Jul 69	HAPPY HEART *CBS 63614*	22	9
27 Dec 69	GET TOGETHER WITH ANDY WILLIAMS *CBS 63800*	13	12
24 Jan 70	ANDY WILLIAMS' SOUND OF MUSIC *CBS 66214*	22	10
11 Apr 70 ★	GREATEST HITS *CBS 63920*	1	116
20 Jun 70 ●	CAN'T HELP FALLING IN LOVE *CBS 64067*	7	40
5 Dec 70 ●	ANDY WILLIAMS SHOW *CBS 64127*	10	6
27 Mar 71 ★	HOME LOVIN' MAN *CBS 64286*	1	26
31 Jul 71	LOVE STORY *CBS 64467*	11	11
29 Apr 72	THE IMPOSSIBLE DREAM *CBS 67236*	26	3
29 Jul 72	LOVE THEME FROM 'THE GODFATHER' *CBS 64869*	11	16
16 Dec 72	GREATEST HITS VOLUME 2 *CBS 65151*	23	10
22 Dec 73 ●	SOLITAIRE *CBS 65638*	3	26
15 Jun 74 ●	THE WAY WE WERE *CBS 80152*	7	11
11 Oct 75	THE OTHER SIDE OF ME *CBS 69152*	60	1
28 Jan 78 ●	REFLECTIONS *CBS 10006*	2	10
27 Oct 84	GREATEST LOVE CLASSICS *EMI ANDY 1* [1]	22	10
7 Nov 92	THE BEST OF ANDY WILLIAMS *Dino DINCD 50*	51	3
10 Apr 99	IN THE LOUNGE WITH ... ANDY WILLIAMS *Columbia 4916182*	39	4
19 Feb 00	THE VERY BEST OF ANDY WILLIAMS *Columbia SONYTV 78CD*	27	7
6 Jul 02	THE ESSENTIAL ANDY WILLIAMS *Columbia 5084142*	32	2

[1] Andy Williams and Denise Van Outen [1] Andy Williams and the Royal Philharmonic Orchestra

Andy and David WILLIAMS
US, male vocal duo (Singles: 5 Weeks) pos/wks

| 24 Mar 73 | I DON'T KNOW WHY (I JUST DO) *MCA MUS 1183* | 37 | 5 |

Do not see Andy Williams. This Andy is the nephew of the other Andy

Billy WILLIAMS
US, male vocalist, b. 28 Dec 1910, d. 17 Oct 1972 (Singles: 9 Weeks) pos/wks

| 2 Aug 57 | I'M GONNA SIT RIGHT DOWN AND WRITE MYSELF A LETTER (re) *Vogue Coral Q 72266* | 22 | 9 |

Danny WILLIAMS *South Africa, male vocalist (Singles: 74 Weeks)* pos/wks

25 May 61	WE WILL NEVER BE AS YOUNG AS THIS AGAIN *HMV POP 839*	44	3
6 Jul 61	THE MIRACLE OF YOU *HMV POP 885*	41	8
2 Nov 61 ★	MOON RIVER *HMV POP 932*	1	19
18 Jan 62	JEANNIE *HMV POP 968*	14	14
12 Apr 62 ●	THE WONDERFUL WORLD OF THE YOUNG *HMV POP 1002*	8	13
5 Jul 62	TEARS *HMV POP 1035*	22	7
28 Feb 63	MY OWN TRUE LOVE *HMV POP 1112*	45	3
30 Jul 77	DANCIN' EASY *Ensign ENY 3*	30	7

Deniece WILLIAMS *US, female vocalist –*
Deniece Chandler (Singles: 59 Weeks, Albums: 23 Weeks) pos/wks

2 Apr 77 ★	FREE *CBS 4978*	1	10
30 Jul 77 ●	THAT'S WHAT FRIENDS ARE FOR *CBS 5432*	8	11
12 Nov 77	BABY, BABY MY LOVE'S ALL FOR YOU *CBS 5779*	32	5
25 Mar 78 ●	TOO MUCH, TOO LITTLE, TOO LATE *CBS 6164* [1] ▲	3	14
29 Jul 78	YOU'RE ALL I NEED TO GET BY *CBS 6483* [1]	45	6
5 May 84 ●	LET'S HEAR IT FOR THE BOY (re) *CBS A 4319* ▲	2	13
21 May 77	THIS IS NIECEY *CBS 81869*	31	12
26 Aug 78	THAT'S WHAT FRIENDS ARE FOR *CBS 86068* [1]	16	11

[1] Johnny Mathis and Deniece Williams [1] Johnny Mathis and Deniece Williams

Diana WILLIAMS *US, female vocalist (Singles: 3 Weeks)* pos/wks

| 25 Jul 81 | TEDDY BEAR'S LAST RIDE *Capitol CL 207* | 54 | 3 |

Don WILLIAMS 476 Top 500 *Easy-on-the-ear country singer / songwriter and guitarist, b. 27 May 1939, Floyada, Texas. Member of Pozo-Seco Singers (1964-71), who amassed 17 US country No.1s between 1974 and 1986 and was named Country Music Association Vocalist of the Year in 1978 (Singles: 16 Weeks, Albums: 136 Weeks)* pos/wks

19 Jun 76	I RECALL A GYPSY WOMAN *ABC 4098*	13	10
23 Oct 76	YOU'RE MY BEST FRIEND *ABC 4144*	35	6
10 Jul 76	GREATEST HITS VOLUME 1 *ABC ABCL 5147*	29	15
19 Feb 77	VISIONS *ABC ABCL 5200*	13	20
15 Oct 77	COUNTRY BOY *ABC ABCL 5233*	27	5
5 Aug 78 ●	IMAGES *K-Tel NE 1033*	2	38
5 Aug 78	YOU'RE MY BEST FRIEND *ABC ABCD 5127*	58	1
4 Nov 78	EXPRESSIONS *ABC ABCL 5253*	28	8

22 Sep 79	NEW HORIZONS *K-Tel NE 1048*	29	12
15 Dec 79	PORTRAIT *MCA MCS 3045*	58	4
6 Sep 80	I BELIEVE IN YOU *MCA MCF 3077*	36	5
18 Jul 81	ESPECIALLY FOR YOU *MCA MCF 3114*	33	7
17 Apr 82	LISTEN TO THE RADIO *MCA MCF 3135*	69	3
23 Apr 83	YELLOW MOON *MCA MCF 3159*	52	1
15 Oct 83	LOVE STORIES *K-Tel NE 1252*	22	13
26 May 84	CAFE CAROLINA *MCA MCF 3225*	65	4

Eric WILLIAMS *See* QUEEN PEN; 2PAC

Freedom WILLIAMS
US, male rapper (Singles: 31 Weeks) pos/wks

15 Dec 90 ●	GONNA MAKE YOU SWEAT (EVERYBODY DANCE NOW) *CBS 6564540* [1] ▲	3	12
30 Mar 91	HERE WE GO *Columbia 6567537* [1]	20	7
6 Jul 91 ●	THINGS THAT MAKE YOU GO HMMM ... *Columbia 6566907* [1]	4	11
5 Jun 93	VOICE OF FREEDOM *Columbia 6593342*	62	1

[1] C & C Music Factory (featuring Freedom Williams)

Geoffrey WILLIAMS *UK, male vocalist (Singles: 8 Weeks)* pos/wks

11 Apr 92	IT'S NOT A LOVE THING *EMI EM 228*	63	2
22 Aug 92	SUMMER BREEZE *EMI EM 245*	56	3
18 Jan 97	DRIVE *Hands On CDHOR 11*	52	2
19 Apr 97	SEX LIFE *Hands On CDHOR 12*	71	1

Iris WILLIAMS
UK, female vocalist (Singles: 8 Weeks, Albums: 4 Weeks) pos/wks

| 27 Oct 79 | HE WAS BEAUTIFUL (CAVATINA) (THE THEME FROM 'THE DEER HUNTER') *Columbia DB 9070* | 18 | 8 |
| 22 Dec 79 | HE WAS BEAUTIFUL *Columbia SCX 6627* | 69 | 4 |

James WILLIAMS *See* D TRAIN; Bob SINCLAR

John WILLIAMS (see also Daniel BARENBOIM) *UK, male instrumentalist – guitar (Singles: 11 Weeks, Albums: 65 Weeks)* pos/wks

19 May 79	CAVATINA *Cube BUG 80*	13	11
3 Oct 70	PLAYS SPANISH MUSIC *CBS 72860*	46	1
8 Feb 76	RODRIGO: CONCERTO DE ARANJUEZ *CBS 79369* [1]	20	9
7 Jan 78	BEST OF FRIENDS *RCA RS 1094* [2]	18	22
17 Jun 78	TRAVELLING *Cube HIFLY 27*	23	5
30 Jun 79 ●	BRIDGES *Lotus WH 5015*	5	22
4 Aug 79	CAVATINA *Cube HIFLY 32*	64	3
26 Oct 96	JOHN WILLIAMS PLAYS THE MOVIES *Sony Classical S2K 62784*	54	3

[1] John Williams with the English Chamber Orchestra conducted by Daniel Barenboim [2] Cleo Laine and John Williams

John WILLIAMS
US, male orchestra leader (Singles: 12 Weeks, Albums: 46 Weeks) pos/wks

18 Dec 82	THEME FROM 'E.T.' (THE EXTRA-TERRESTRIAL) *MCA 800*	17	10
14 Aug 93	THEME FROM 'JURASSIC PARK' *MCA MCSTD 1927*	45	2
25 Dec 82	E.T. – THE EXTRATERRESTRIAL (FILM SOUNDTRACK) *MCA MCF 3160*	47	10
31 Jul 93	JURASSIC PARK (FILM SOUNDTRACK) *MCA MCD 10859*	42	5
2 Apr 94	SCHINDLER'S LIST (FILM SOUNDTRACK) *MCA MCD 10969*	59	2
15 May 99 ●	STAR WARS – THE PHANTOM MENACE (FILM SOUNDTRACK) *Sony Classical SK 61816*	8	17
10 Nov 01	HARRY POTTER AND THE PHILOSOPHER'S STONE (FILM SOUNDTRACK) *Atlantic 7567930865*	19	7
11 May 02	STAR WARS EPISODE II – ATTACK OF THE CLONES (FILM SOUNDTRACK) *Sony Classical SK 89932*	15	5

'Star Wars – The Phantom Menace' and 'Star Wars Episode II – Attack of the Clones' are performed by the London Symphony Orchestra

Kathryn WILLIAMS *UK, female vocalist / instrumentalist (Albums: 3 Weeks)* pos/wks

| 15 Sep 01 | LITTLE BLACK NUMBERS *East West 8573899242* | 70 | 1 |
| 12 Oct 02 | OLD LOW LIGHT *East West 0927475522* | 56 | 2 |

Kenny WILLIAMS
US, male vocalist (Singles: 7 Weeks) pos/wks

| 19 Nov 77 | (YOU'RE) FABULOUS BABE *Decca FR 13731* | 35 | 7 |

Larry WILLIAMS
US, male vocalist / instrumentalist – keyboards, b. 10 May 1935, d. 7 Jan 1980 (Singles: 18 Weeks) pos/wks

20 Sep 57	SHORT FAT FANNIE *London HLN 8472*	**21** 8
17 Jan 58	BONY MORONIE *London HLU 8532*	**11** 10

Lenny WILLIAMS
US, male vocalist (Singles: 7 Weeks) pos/wks

5 Nov 77	SHOO DOO FU FU OOH! *ABC 4194*	**38** 4
16 Sep 78	YOU GOT ME BURNING *ABC 4228*	**67** 3

Lucinda WILLIAMS
US, female vocalist / instrumentalist (Albums: 2 Weeks) pos/wks

16 Jun 01	ESSENCE *Lost Highway 1701972*	**63** 1
19 Apr 03	WORLD WITHOUT TEARS *Lost Highway 1703552*	**48** 1

Mark WILLIAMS See Karen BODDINGTON and Mark WILLIAMS

Mason WILLIAMS
US, male instrumentalist – guitar (Singles: 13 Weeks) pos/wks

28 Aug 68 ●	CLASSICAL GAS *Warner Bros. WB 7190*	**9** 13

Maurice WILLIAMS and The ZODIACS
US, male vocal group (Singles: 9 Weeks) pos/wks

5 Jan 61	STAY *Top Rank JAR 526* ▲	**14** 9

Melanie WILLIAMS
UK, female vocalist (Singles: 21 Weeks) pos/wks

10 Apr 93 ●	AIN'T NO LOVE (AIN'T NO USE) *Rob's CDROB 9* [1]	**3** 11
9 Apr 94	ALL CRIED OUT *Columbia 6601872*	**60** 2
11 Jun 94	EVERYDAY THANG *Columbia 6604712*	**38** 3
17 Sep 94	NOT ENOUGH? *Columbia 6607752*	**65** 1
18 Feb 95	YOU ARE EVERYTHING *Columbia 6611755* [2]	**28** 4

[1] Sub Sub featuring Melanie Williams [2] Melanie Williams and Joe Roberts

Pharrell WILLIAMS See PHARRELL; The NEPTUNES; N*E*R*D

Robbie WILLIAMS ⟨43⟩ `Top 500`
(see also 1 GIANT LEAP) *Ex-Take That teen idol who became a multi-award winning vocalist / songwriter and multi-millionaire after a UK record-breaking 2002 deal with EMI reportedly worth £80million, b. 13 Feb 1974, Stoke-on-Trent, UK. This energetic and humorous showman has won more Brit Awards (15) than any other artist, including one for the best song from 25 years of the Brits for 'Angels'. He has amassed 21 solo Top 20 hits (including six No.1s) and attracted record-breaking crowds of 375,000 to Knebworth in 2003. Robbie was inducted into the UK Music Hall of Fame in 2004, representing the 1990s. Best-selling single: 'Angels' 867,999 (Singles: 278 Weeks, Albums: 404 Weeks)* pos/wks

10 Aug 96 ●	FREEDOM (re) *Chrysalis CDFREE 1*	**2** 14
26 Apr 97 ●	OLD BEFORE I DIE (2re) *Chrysalis CDCHS 5055*	**2** 11
26 Jul 97 ●	LAZY DAYS *Chrysalis CDCHS 5063*	**8** 5
27 Sep 97	SOUTH OF THE BORDER *Chrysalis CDCHS 5068*	**14** 4
13 Dec 97 ●	ANGELS (4re) *Chrysalis CDCHS 5072*	**4** 27
28 Mar 98 ●	LET ME ENTERTAIN YOU *Chrysalis CDCHS 5080*	**3** 12
19 Sep 98 ★	MILLENNIUM (re) *Chrysalis CDCHS 5099* ■	**1** 21
12 Dec 98 ●	NO REGRETS *Chrysalis CDCHS 5100*	**4** 13
27 Mar 99 ●	STRONG *Chrysalis CDCHS 5107*	**4** 9
20 Nov 99 ★	IT'S ONLY US / SHE'S THE ONE (re) *Chrysalis CDCHS 5112* ■	**1** 20
12 Aug 00 ★	ROCK DJ (re) *Chrysalis CDCHS 5118* ■	**1** 20
21 Oct 00 ●	KIDS (2re) *Chrysalis CHCHS 5119* [1]	**2** 19
23 Dec 00 ●	SUPREME *Chrysalis CDCHS 5120*	**4** 10
21 Mar 01 ●	LET LOVE BE YOUR ENERGY (re) *Chrysalis CDCHS 5124*	**10** 11
21 Jul 01 ★	ETERNITY / THE ROAD TO MANDALAY *Chrysalis CDCHS 5126* ■	**1** 16
22 Dec 01 ★	SOMETHIN' STUPID *Chrysalis CDCHS 5132* [2] ■	**1** 12
14 Dec 02 ●	FEEL (re) *Chrysalis CDCHS 5150*	**4** 15
26 Apr 03 ●	COME UNDONE *Chrysalis CDCHS 5151*	**4** 11
9 Aug 03 ●	SOMETHING BEAUTIFUL *Chrysalis CDCHS 5152*	**3** 8
15 Nov 03 ●	SEXED UP (re) *Chrysalis CDCHS 5153*	**10** 10
16 Oct 04 ★	RADIO *Chrysalis CDCHSS 5156* ■	**1** 8
18 Dec 04 ●	MISUNDERSTOOD *Chrysalis CDCHSS 5157*	**8** 2+
11 Oct 97 ★	LIFE THRU A LENS *Chrysalis CDCHR 6127*	**1** 123
7 Nov 98 ★	I'VE BEEN EXPECTING YOU *Chrysalis 4978372*	**1** 98
9 Sep 00 ★	SING WHEN YOU'RE WINNING *Chrysalis 5281252* ■	**1** 62
1 Dec 01 ★	SWING WHEN YOU'RE WINNING *Chrysalis 5368262* ■	**1** 41
30 Nov 02 ★	ESCAPOLOGY *EMI 5439942* ■	**1** 50
11 Oct 03 ●	LIVE AT KNEBWORTH *Chrysalis 5946372*	**2** 21
30 Oct 04 ★	GREATEST HITS *Chrysalis 8668192* ■	**1** 9+

[1] Robbie Williams / Kylie Minogue [2] Robbie Williams and Nicole Kidman

'Angels' re-entered the chart in Jan, Feb and Mar 1999 and again in Jan 2000. 'Millennium' re-entered in Jan 2000

Saul WILLIAMS See KRUST

Vanessa WILLIAMS
US, female vocalist (Singles: 24 Weeks, Albums: 4 Weeks) pos/wks

20 Aug 88	THE RIGHT STUFF *Wing WING 3*	**71** 1
25 Mar 89	DREAMIN' *Wing WING 4*	**74** 2
19 Mar 89	THE RIGHT STUFF (re-mix) *Wing WINR 3*	**62** 2
21 Mar 92 ●	SAVE THE BEST FOR LAST *Polydor PO 192* ▲	**3** 11
8 Apr 95	THE SWEETEST DAYS *Mercury MERCD 422*	**41** 2
8 Jul 95	THE WAY THAT YOU LOVE *Mercury MERCD 439*	**52** 1
18 Sep 95	COLOURS OF THE WIND *Walt Disney WD 7677CD*	**21** 5
25 Apr 92	THE COMFORT ZONE *Polydor 5112672*	**24** 4

Vesta WILLIAMS
US, female vocalist (Singles: 13 Weeks) pos/wks

20 Dec 86	ONCE BITTEN TWICE SHY *A&M AM 362*	**14** 13

Wendell WILLIAMS
US, male rapper (Singles: 6 Weeks) pos/wks

6 Oct 90	EVERYBODY (RAP) *Deconstruction PB 44701* [1]	**30** 4
18 May 91	SO GROOVY *Deconstruction PB 44567*	**74** 2

[1] Criminal Element Orchestra and Wendell Williams

Wendy O WILLIAMS (see also The PLASMATICS)
US, female vocalist, b. 28 May 1949, d. 6 Apr 1998 (Albums: 1 Week) pos/wks

30 Jun 84	W.O.W. *Music for Nations MFN 24*	**100** 1

Ann WILLIAMSON
UK, female vocalist (Albums: 13 Weeks) pos/wks

15 Feb 86	PRECIOUS MEMORIES *Emerald Gem ERTV 1*	**16** 9
6 Feb 88	COUNT YOUR BLESSINGS *Emerald Gem ERTV 2*	**58** 4

Sonny Boy WILLIAMSON
US, male vocalist / instrumentalist – guitar – Rice Miller, b. 5 Dec 1899, d. 25 May 1965 (Albums: 1 Week) pos/wks

20 Jun 64	DOWN AND OUT BLUES *Pye NPL 28036*	**20** 1

WILLING SINNERS See Marc ALMOND

Bruce WILLIS
US, male actor / vocalist (Singles: 30 Weeks, Albums: 28 Weeks) pos/wks

7 Mar 87 ●	RESPECT YOURSELF *Motown ZB 41117*	**7** 10
30 May 87 ●	UNDER THE BOARDWALK *Motown ZB 41349*	**2** 15
12 Sep 87	SECRET AGENT MAN – JAMES BOND IS BACK *Motown ZB 41437*	**43** 4
23 Jan 88	COMIN' RIGHT UP *Motown ZB 41453*	**73** 1
18 Apr 87 ●	THE RETURN OF BRUNO *Motown ZL 72571*	**4** 28

Chris WILLIS See David GUETTA

Chill WILLS See LAUREL and HARDY with The AVALON BOYS featuring Chill WILLS

Viola WILLS
US, female vocalist (Singles: 16 Weeks) pos/wks

6 Oct 79 ●	GONNA GET ALONG WITHOUT YOU NOW *Ariola / Hansa AHA 546*	**8** 10
15 Mar 86	BOTH SIDES NOW / DARE TO DREAM *Streetwave KHAN 66*	**35** 6

Maria WILLSON
UK, female vocalist (Singles: 3 Weeks) pos/wks

9 Aug 03	CHOOZA LOOZA *Telstar CDSTAS 3343*	**29** 2
1 Nov 03	MR ALIBI *Telstar CDSTAS 3355*	**43** 1

Al WILSON
US, male vocalist (Singles: 5 Weeks) pos/wks

23 Aug 75	THE SNAKE *Bell 1436*	**41** 5

Brian WILSON (see also The BEACH BOYS)
US, male vocalist (Singles: 4 Weeks, Albums: 8 Weeks) pos/wks

2 Oct 04	WONDERFUL *Nonesuch / Must Destroy MDA 001X*	**29** 2
18 Dec 04	GOOD VIBRATIONS *Nonesuch NS 001CD*	**30** 2+
16 Sep 95	I JUST WASN'T MADE FOR THESE TIMES *MCA MCD 11270*	**59** 1

Singles re-entries are listed as (re), (2re), (3re).... which signifies that the hit re-entered the chart once, twice or three times...

			pos	wks
27 Jun 98	IMAGINATION *Giant 74321573032*		30	2
3 Jul 04	GETTIN IN OVER MY HEAD *Rhino 8122764712*		53	1
9 Oct 04 ●	SMILE *East West 7559798462*		7	4

Charlie WILSON *See The GAP BAND; SNOOP DOGG*

Dooley WILSON *US, male vocalist,*
b. Arthur Wilson, 3 Apr 1894, d. 30 May 1953 (Singles: 9 Weeks)   pos/wks

			pos	wks
3 Dec 77	AS TIME GOES BY *United Artists UP 36331*		15	9

Disc has credit: 'With the voices of Humphrey Bogart and Ingrid Bergman'

Gretchen WILSON
US, female vocalist (Singles: 2 Weeks, Albums: 1 Week)   pos/wks

			pos	wks
4 Sep 04	REDNECK WOMAN *Epic 6751732*		42	2
11 Sep 04	HERE FOR THE PARTY *Epic 5174312*		60	1

Jackie WILSON *US, male vocalist, b. 9 Jun 1934,*
Detroit, US, d. 21 Jan 1984 (Singles: 97 Weeks)   pos/wks

			pos	wks
15 Nov 57 ●	REET PETITE (THE SWEETEST GIRL IN TOWN) *Coral Q 72290*		6	14
14 Mar 58	TO BE LOVED (2re) *Coral Q 72306*		23	8
15 Sep 60	(YOU WERE MADE FOR) ALL MY LOVE (re) *Coral Q 72407*		33	7
22 Dec 60	ALONE AT LAST *Coral Q 72412*		50	1
14 May 69	(YOUR LOVE KEEPS LIFTING ME) HIGHER AND HIGHER *MCA BAG 2*		11	11
29 Jul 72 ●	I GET THE SWEETEST FEELING *MCA MU 1160*		9	13
3 May 75	I GET THE SWEETEST FEELING / (YOUR LOVE KEEPS LIFTING ME) HIGHER AND HIGHER (re-issue) *Brunswick BR 18*		25	8
29 Nov 86 ★	REET PETITE (THE SWEETEST GIRL IN TOWN) (re-issue) *SMP SKM 3*		1	17
28 Feb 87 ●	I GET THE SWEETEST FEELING (2nd re-issue) *SMP SKM 1*		3	11
4 Jul 87	(YOUR LOVE KEEPS LIFTING ME) HIGHER AND HIGHER (2nd re-issue) *SMP SKM 10*		15	7

(Your Love Keeps Lifting Me) 'Higher and Higher' was not listed with 'I Get the Sweetest Feeling' until 17 May 1975

Mari WILSON
UK, female vocalist (Singles: 34 Weeks, Albums: 9 Weeks)   pos/wks

			pos	wks
6 Mar 82	BEAT THE BEAT *Compact PINK 2*		59	3
8 May 82	BABY IT'S TRUE *Compact PINK 3*		42	6
11 Sep 82 ●	JUST WHAT I ALWAYS WANTED *Compact PINK 4*		8	10
13 Nov 82	(BEWARE) BOYFRIEND *Compact PINK 5*		51	4
19 Mar 83	CRY ME A RIVER *Compact PINK 6*		27	7
11 Jun 83	WONDERFUL *Compact PINK 7* [1]		47	4
26 Feb 83	SHOW PEOPLE *Compact COMP 2* [1]		24	9

[1] Mari Wilson and The Wilsations [1] Mari Wilson and The Wilsations

Meri WILSON
US, female vocalist, b. 15 Jun 1949, d. 28 Dec 2002 (Singles: 10 Weeks) pos/wks

			pos	wks
27 Aug 77 ●	TELEPHONE MAN *Pye International 7N 25747*		6	10

Mike 'Hitman' WILSON *US, male producer (Singles: 1 Week)*   pos/wks

			pos	wks
22 Sep 90	ANOTHER SLEEPLESS NIGHT *Arista 113506*		74	1

Precious WILSON *See ERUPTION; MESSIAH*

Ray WILSON *See Armin VAN BUUREN; STILTSKIN*

Tom WILSON *UK, male producer (Singles: 4 Weeks)*   pos/wks

			pos	wks
2 Dec 95	TECHNOCAT *Pukka CDPUKKA 4* [1]		33	3
16 Mar 96	LET YOUR BODY GO *Clubscene DCSRT 050*		60	1

[1] Technocat featuring Tom Wilson

Victoria WILSON JAMES *US, female vocalist (Singles: 1 Week)* pos/wks

			pos	wks
9 Aug 97	REACH 4 THE MELODY *Sony S3 VWJCD 1*		72	1

WILSON PHILLIPS
US, female vocal group (Singles: 33 Weeks, Albums: 38 Weeks)   pos/wks

			pos	wks
26 May 90 ●	HOLD ON *SBK SBK 6* ▲		6	12
18 Aug 90	RELEASE ME *SBK SBK 11* ▲		36	5
10 Nov 90	IMPULSIVE *SBK SBK 16*		42	3
11 May 91	YOU'RE IN LOVE *SBK SBK 25* ▲		29	5
23 May 92	YOU WON'T SEE ME CRY *SBK SBK 34*		18	5
22 Aug 92	GIVE IT UP *SBK SBK 36*		36	3

			pos	wks
30 Jun 90 ●	WILSON PHILLIPS *SBK SBKLP 5*		7	32
13 Jun 92 ●	SHADOWS AND LIGHT *SBK SBKCD 18*		6	6

WILT *Ireland, male vocal / instrumental group (Singles: 3 Weeks)*   pos/wks

			pos	wks
8 Apr 00	RADIO DISCO *Mushroom MUSH 71CDS*		56	1
8 Jul 00	OPEN ARMS *Mushroom MUSH 75CDS*		59	1
13 Jul 02	DISTORTION *Mushroom MUSH 103CDS*		66	1

Chris WILTSHIRE *See CLASS ACTION featuring Chris WILTSHIRE*

WIMBLEDON CHORAL SOCIETY
UK, choral group (Singles: 8 Weeks)   pos/wks

			pos	wks
4 Jul 98	WORLD CUP '98 – PAVANE *Telstar CDSTAS 2979*		20	5
12 Dec 98	IF – READ TO FAURE'S 'PAVANE' *BBC Worldwide WMSS 60062* [1]		45	3

[1] Des Lynam featuring Wimbledon Choral Society

WIN *UK, male vocal / instrumental*
group (Singles: 3 Weeks, Albums: 1 Week)   pos/wks

			pos	wks
4 Apr 87	SUPER POPOID GROOVE *Swamplands LON 128*		63	3
25 Apr 87	UH! TEARS BABY *Swamplands LONLP 31*		51	1

The WINANS *US, male vocal group (Singles: 1 Week)*   pos/wks

			pos	wks
30 Nov 85	LET MY PEOPLE GO (PART 1) *Qwest W 8874*		71	1

BeBe WINANS *See ETERNAL*

CeCe WINANS *See Whitney HOUSTON*

Mario WINANS (see also P DIDDY)
US, male vocalist (Singles: 21 Weeks, Albums: 20 Weeks)   pos/wks

			pos	wks
20 Nov 99	BEST FRIEND *Puff Daddy / Arista 74321712312* [1]		24	4
5 Jun 04	I DON'T WANNA KNOW (Import) *Universal 9862372 PMI* [2]		71	1
12 Jun 04 ★	I DON'T WANNA KNOW *Bad Boy MCSTD 40369* [2] ■		1	14
11 Sep 04	NEVER REALLY WAS *Bad Boy MCSTD 40372* [3]		44	2
1 May 04 ●	HURT NO MORE *Bad Boy 9862494*		3	20

[1] Puff Daddy featuring Mario Winans [2] Mario Winans featuring Enya & P Diddy [3] Mario Winans featuring Lil' Flip

WINDJAMMER *US, male vocal /*
instrumental group (Singles: 12 Weeks, Albums: 1 Week)   pos/wks

			pos	wks
30 Jun 84	TOSSING AND TURNING *MCA MCA 897*		18	12
25 Aug 84	WINDJAMMER II *MCA MCF 3231*		82	1

Rose WINDROSS *See SOUL II SOUL*

Barbara WINDSOR
UK, female actor / vocalist (Singles: 2 Weeks, Albums: 2 Weeks)   pos/wks

			pos	wks
3 Apr 99	YOU'VE GOT A FRIEND *Telstar TTVCD 3034*		45	2
24 Apr 99	THE MORE I SEE YOU *Telstar CDSTAS 3049* [1]		46	2

[1] Barbara Wilson and Mike Reid

Amy WINEHOUSE
UK, female vocalist (Singles: 4 Weeks, Albums: 21 Weeks)   pos/wks

			pos	wks
18 Oct 03	STRONGER THAN ME *Island CID 830*		71	1
24 Jan 04	TAKE THE BOX *Island CID 840*		57	1
17 Apr 04	IN MY BED / YOU SENT ME FLYING *Island CID 852*		60	1
4 Sep 04	PUMPS / HELP YOURSELF *Island CID 865*		65	1
1 Nov 03	FRANK *Island 9812918*		13	21

WING AND A PRAYER FIFE AND DRUM CORPS
US, male / female vocal / instrumental group (Singles: 7 Weeks)   pos/wks

			pos	wks
24 Jan 76	BABY FACE *Atlantic K 10705*		12	7

WINGER *US, male vocal / instrumental group (Singles: 3 Weeks)* pos/wks

			pos	wks
19 Jan 91	MILES AWAY *Atlantic A 7802*		56	3

Pete WINGFIELD
UK, male vocalist / instrumentalist – piano (Singles: 7 Weeks)   pos/wks

			pos	wks
28 Jun 75 ●	EIGHTEEN WITH A BULLET *Island WIP 6231*		7	7

WINGS *See Linda McCARTNEY; Paul McCARTNEY*

Josh WINK (see also SIZE 9) *US, male producer –*
Joshua Winkelman (Singles: 29 weeks, Albums: 1 week)   pos/wks

6 May 95	**DON'T LAUGH** *XL XLS 62CD* [1]	**38**	2
21 Oct 95 ●	**HIGHER STATE OF CONSCIOUSNESS (re)** *Manifesto FESCD 3*	**8**	12
2 Mar 96	**HYPNOTIZIN'** *XL XLS 71CD* [1]	**35**	2
27 Jul 96 ●	**HIGHER STATE OF CONSCIOUSNESS (re-mix)** *Manifesto FESCD 9* [2]	**7**	10
12 Aug 00	**HOW'S YOUR EVENING SO FAR** *ffrr FCD 384* [3]	**23**	3
21 Sep 96	**LEFT ABOVE THE CLOUDS** *XL Recordings XLCD 119*	**43**	1

[1] Winx [2] Wink [3] Josh Wink and Lil' Louis

Kate WINSLET *UK, female actor / vocalist (Singles: 14 Weeks)*   pos/wks

8 Dec 01 ●	**WHAT IF** *EMI / Liberty CDKATE 001*	**6**	14

Edgar WINTER GROUP
US, male instrumental group (Singles: 9 Weeks)   pos/wks

26 May 73	**FRANKENSTEIN** *Epic EPC 1440* ▲	**18**	9

Johnny WINTER
US, male vocal / instrumental group (Albums: 12 Weeks)   pos/wks

16 May 70	**SECOND WINTER** *CBS 66321*	**59**	2
31 Oct 70	**JOHNNY WINTER AND ...** *CBS 64117*	**29**	4
15 May 71	**JOHNNY WINTER AND LIVE** *CBS 64289*	**20**	6

Ruby WINTERS
US, female vocalist (Singles: 35 Weeks, Albums: 17 Weeks)   pos/wks

5 Nov 77 ●	**I WILL!** *Creole CR 141*	**4**	13
29 Apr 78	**COME TO ME!** *Creole CR 153*	**11**	12
26 Aug 78	**I WON'T MENTION IT AGAIN** *Creole CR 160*	**45**	5
16 Jun 79	**BABY LAY DOWN** *Creole CR 171*	**43**	5
10 Jun 78	**RUBY WINTERS** *Creole CRLP 512*	**27**	7
23 Jun 79	**SONGBIRD** *K-Tel NE 1045*	**31**	10

Steve WINWOOD   463   Top 500
R&B vocalist / instrumentalist – keyboards, b. 12 May 1948, Birmingham, UK, whose prodigious talent in the Spencer Davis Group led to supergroup Blind Faith in 1969 and the more enduring Traffic from 1967 to 1974. This Grammy winner became one of the most successful acts Stateside in the late 1980s (Singles: 33 Weeks, Albums: 122 Weeks)   pos/wks

17 Jan 81	**WHILE YOU SEE A CHANCE** *Island WIP 6655*	**45**	5
9 Oct 82	**VALERIE** *Island WIP 6818*	**51**	4
28 Jun 86	**HIGHER LOVE** *Island IS 288* ▲	**13**	9
13 Sep 86	**FREEDOM OVERSPILL** *Island IS 294*	**69**	1
24 Jan 87	**BACK IN THE HIGH LIFE AGAIN** *Island IS 303*	**53**	2
19 Sep 87	**VALERIE (re-mix)** *Island IS 336*	**19**	8
11 Jun 88	**ROLL WITH IT** *Virgin VS 1085* ▲	**53**	4
9 Jul 77	**STEVE WINWOOD** *Island ILPS 9494*	**12**	9
10 Jan 81	**ARC OF A DIVER** *Island ILPS 9576*	**13**	20
14 Aug 82 ●	**TALKING BACK TO THE NIGHT** *Island ILPS 9777*	**6**	13
12 Jul 86 ●	**BACK IN THE HIGH LIFE** *Island ILPS 9844*	**8**	42
7 Nov 87	**CHRONICLES** *Island SSW 1*	**12**	17
2 Jul 88 ●	**ROLL WITH IT** *Virgin V 2532* ▲	**4**	16
17 Nov 90	**REFUGEES OF THE HEART** *Virgin V 2650*	**26**	3
14 Jun 97	**JUNCTION SEVEN** *Virgin CDV 2832*	**32**	2

WIRE *UK, male vocal / instrumental*
group (Singles: 4 Weeks, Albums: 3 Weeks)   pos/wks

27 Jan 79	**OUTDOOR MINER** *Harvest HAR 5172*	**51**	3
13 May 89	**EARDRUM BUZZ** *Mute MUTE 87*	**68**	1
7 Oct 78	**CHAIRS MISSING** *Harvest SHSP 4093*	**48**	1
13 Oct 79	**154** *Harvest SHSP 4105*	**39**	1
9 May 87	**THE IDEAL COPY** *Mute STUMM 42*	**87**	1

WIRED *Holland / Finland, male*
production / instrumental duo (Singles: 1 Week)   pos/wks

20 Feb 99	**TRANSONIC** *Future Groove CDFGR 001*	**73**	1

WIRELESS
UK, male vocal / instrumental group (Singles: 2 Weeks)   pos/wks

28 Jun 97	**I NEED YOU** *Chrysalis CDCHS 5059*	**68**	1
7 Feb 98	**IN LOVE WITH THE FAMILIAR** *Chrysalis CDCHS 5075*	**69**	1

Norman WISDOM *UK, male actor / vocalist (Singles: 20 Weeks)*   pos/wks

19 Feb 54 ●	**DON'T LAUGH AT ME ('CAUSE I'M A FOOL)** *Columbia DB 3133*	**3**	15
15 Mar 57	**THE WISDOM OF A FOOL** *Columbia DB 3903*	**13**	5

WISDOME
Italy, male / female production / vocal group (Singles: 2 Weeks)   pos/wks

11 Mar 00	**OFF THE WALL** *Positiva CDTIV 125*	**33**	2

WISEGUYS (see also DJ TOUCHE)
UK, male DJ / producer – Theo Keating (Singles: 13 Weeks)   pos/wks

6 Jun 98	**OOH LA LA** *Wall of Sound WALLD 038*	**55**	1
12 Sep 98	**START THE COMMOTION** *Wall of Sound WALLD 044*	**66**	1
5 Jun 99 ●	**OOH LA LA (re-issue)** *Wall of Sound WALLD 038X*	**2**	10
11 Sep 99	**START THE COMMOTION (re-issue)** *Wall of Sound WALLD 059*	**47**	1

WISHBONE ASH
UK, male vocal / instrumental group (Albums: 76 Weeks)   pos/wks

23 Jan 71	**WISHBONE ASH** *MCA MKPS 2014*	**29**	3
9 Oct 71	**PILGRIMAGE** *MCA MDKS 8004*	**14**	9
20 May 72	**ARGUS** *MCA MDKS 8006*	**3**	20
26 May 73	**WISHBONE FOUR** *MCA MDKS 8011*	**12**	10
30 Nov 74	**THERE'S THE RUB** *MCA MCF 2585*	**16**	5
3 Apr 76	**LOCKED IN** *MCA MCF 2750*	**36**	2
27 Nov 76	**NEW ENGLAND** *MCA MCG 3523*	**22**	3
29 Oct 77	**FRONT PAGE NEWS** *MCA MCG 3524*	**31**	4
28 Oct 78	**NO SMOKE WITHOUT FIRE** *MCA MCG 3528*	**43**	1
2 Feb 80	**JUST TESTING** *MCA MCF 3052*	**41**	4
1 Nov 80	**LIVE DATES II** *MCA MCG 4012*	**40**	3
25 Apr 81	**NUMBER THE BRAVE** *MCA MCF 3103*	**61**	5
16 Oct 82	**BOTH BARRELS BURNING** *A&M ASH 1*	**22**	5

Bill WITHERS (see also Grover WASHINGTON Jr) *US, male vocalist / instrumentalist – guitar (Singles: 29 Weeks, Albums: 10 Weeks)*   pos/wks

12 Aug 72	**LEAN ON ME** *A&M AMS 7004* ▲	**18**	9
14 Jan 78 ●	**LOVELY DAY** *CBS 5773*	**7**	8
25 May 85	**OH YEAH!** *CBS A 6154*	**60**	3
10 Sep 88 ●	**LOVELY DAY (re-mix)** *CBS 6530017*	**4**	9
11 Feb 78	**MENAGERIE** *CBS 82265*	**27**	5
15 Jun 85	**WATCHING YOU WATCHING ME** *CBS 26200*	**60**	1
17 Sep 88	**GREATEST HITS** *CBS 32343*	**90**	4

WITNESS *UK, male vocal /*
instrumental group (Singles: 2 Weeks, Albums: 2 Weeks)   pos/wks

13 Mar 99	**SCARS** *Island CID 740*	**71**	1
19 Jun 99	**AUDITION** *Island CID 749*	**71**	1
24 Jul 99	**BEFORE THE CALM** *Island CID 8084*	**59**	1
4 Aug 01	**UNDER A SUN** *Island CID 8107*	**62**	1

WIX *See SPIRO and WIX*

WIZZARD *UK, male vocal / instrumental group – leader Roy Wood (Singles: 77 Weeks, Albums: 11 Weeks)*   pos/wks

9 Dec 72 ●	**BALL PARK INCIDENT** *Harvest HAR 5062*	**6**	12
21 Apr 73 ★	**SEE MY BABY JIVE** *Harvest HAR 5070* [1]	**1**	17
1 Sep 73 ★	**ANGEL FINGERS (A TEEN BALLAD)** *Harvest HAR 5076* [2]	**1**	10
8 Dec 73 ●	**I WISH IT COULD BE CHRISTMAS EVERYDAY** *Harvest HAR 5079* [3]	**4**	9
27 Apr 74 ●	**ROCK 'N' ROLL WINTER (LOONY'S TUNE)** *Warner Bros. K 16497*	**6**	7
10 Aug 74	**THIS IS THE STORY OF MY LOVE (BABY)** *Warner Bros. K 16434*	**34**	4
21 Dec 74 ●	**ARE YOU READY TO ROCK** *Warner Bros. K 16357*	**8**	10
19 Dec 81	**I WISH IT COULD BE CHRISTMAS EVERYDAY (re) (re-issue)** *Harvest HAR 5173* [3]	**23**	8
19 May 73	**WIZZARD BREW** *Harvest SHSP 4025*	**29**	7
17 Aug 74	**INTRODUCING EDDY AND THE FALCONS** *Warner Bros. K 52029*	**19**	4

[1] Vocal backing by The Suedettes [2] Vocal backing: The Suedettes and The Bleach Boys [3] Wizzard featuring vocal backing by The Suedettes plus The Stockland Green Bilateral School First Year Choir with additional noises by Miss Snob and Class 3C

The 'I Wish It Could Be Christmas Everyday' re-issue debuted and made No.41 in Dec 1981 before re-entering and peaking at No.23 in Dec 1984

Jah WOBBLE'S INVADERS OF THE HEART UK, male vocalist / multi-instrumentalist – John Wardle (Singles: 10 Weeks, Albums: 6 Weeks) pos/wks

1 Feb 92	**VISIONS OF YOU** Oval OVAL 103	35	5
30 Apr 94	**BECOMING MORE LIKE GOD** Island CID 571	36	2
25 Jun 94	**THE SUN DOES RISE** Island CIDX 587	41	3
28 May 94	**TAKE ME TO GOD** Island CID 8017	13	5
14 Oct 95	**SPINNER** All Saints ASCD 023 [1]	71	1

[1] Brian Eno and Jah Wobble

First hit features the uncredited vocals of Sinead O'Connor

Terry WOGAN
Ireland, male TV and radio presenter / vocalist (Singles: 5 Weeks) pos/wks

7 Jan 78	**THE FLORAL DANCE** Philips 6006 592	21	5

WOLF See The TROGGS

WOLFGANG PRESS
UK, male vocal / instrumental duo (Albums: 1 Week) pos/wks

4 Feb 95	**FUNKY LITTLE DEMONS** 4AD CADD 4016CD	75	1

WOLFMAN UK, male vocalist / instrumentalist – guitar – Peter Wolfe (Singles: 7 Weeks) pos/wks

24 Apr 04 ●	**FOR LOVERS** Rough Trade RTRADSCD 177 [1]	7	6
11 Dec 04	**NAPOLEON** Beyond Bedlam BEBAD 001CDS	44	1

[1] Wolfman featuring Pete Doherty

WOLFSBANE UK, male vocal / instrumental group (Singles: 1 Week, Albums: 3 Weeks) pos/wks

5 Oct 91	**EZY** Def American DEFA 11	68	1
5 Aug 89	**LIVE FAST DIE FAST** Def American 838486 1	48	1
20 Oct 90	**ALL HELL'S BREAKING LOOSE ...** Def American 8469671	48	1
19 Oct 91	**DOWN FALL THE GOOD GUYS** Def American 5104131	53	1

Bobby WOMACK (see also Wilton FELDER) US, male vocalist / instrumentalist – guitar (Singles: 22 Weeks, Albums: 15 Weeks) pos/wks

16 Jun 84	**TELL ME WHY** Motown TMG 1339	60	3
5 Oct 85	**I WISH HE DIDN'T TRUST ME SO MUCH** MCA MCA 994	64	2
26 Sep 87	**SO THE STORY GOES** Chrysalis LIB 3 [1]	34	8
7 Nov 87	**LIVING IN A BOX** MCA MCA 1210	70	2
3 Apr 93	**I'M BACK FOR MORE** Dome CDDOME 1002 [2]	27	5
13 May 95	**IT'S A MAN'S MAN'S MAN'S WORLD** Pulse 8 CDLOSE 89 [3]	73	1
19 Jun 04	**CALIFORNIA DREAMIN'** EMI WOMACK 001	59	1
28 Apr 84	**THE POET II** Motown ZL 72205	31	8
28 Sep 85	**SO MANY RIVERS** MCA MCF 3282	28	7

[1] Living in a Box featuring Bobby Womack [2] Lulu and Bobby Womack
[3] Jeanie Tracy and Bobby Womack

Lee Ann WOMACK US, female vocalist (Singles: 2 Weeks) pos/wks

9 Jun 01	**I HOPE YOU DANCE** MCA Nashville MCSTD 40254	40	2

WOMACK and WOMACK US, male / female vocal duo – Linda and Cecil Womack (Singles: 51 Weeks, Albums: 52 Weeks) pos/wks

28 Apr 84	**LOVE WARS** Elektra E 9799	14	10
30 Jun 84	**BABY I'M SCARED OF YOU** Elektra E 9733	72	2
6 Dec 86	**SOUL LOVE – SOUL MAN** Manhattan MT 16	58	6
6 Aug 88 ●	**TEARDROPS** Fourth & Broadway BRW 101	3	17
12 Nov 88	**LIFE'S JUST A BALLGAME** Fourth & Broadway BRW 116	32	5
25 Feb 89	**CELEBRATE THE WORLD** Fourth & Broadway BRW 125	19	8
5 Feb 94	**SECRET STAR** Warner Bros. W 0222CD [1]	46	3
21 Apr 84	**LOVE WARS** Elektra 960293	45	10
22 Jun 85	**RADIO M.U.S.I.C. MAN** Elektra EKT 6	56	2
27 Aug 88 ●	**CONSCIENCE** Fourth & Broadway BRLP 519	4	37

[1] House of Zekkariyas aka Womack and Womack

The WOMBLES (453 Top 500) Furriest (and possibly the tidiest) act in the Top 500 are natives of Wimbledon Common, London, and come under the musical guidance of songwriter and producer Mike Batt, b.Southampton, UK (Singles: 98 Weeks, Albums: 58 Weeks) pos/wks

26 Jan 74 ●	**THE WOMBLING SONG** CBS 1794	4	23
6 Apr 74 ●	**REMEMBER YOU'RE A WOMBLE** CBS 2241	3	16
22 Jun 74 ●	**BANANA ROCK** CBS 2465	9	13
12 Oct 74	**MINUETTO ALLEGRETTO** CBS 2710	16	9
7 Dec 74 ●	**WOMBLING MERRY CHRISTMAS** CBS 2842	2	8
10 May 75	**WOMBLING WHITE TIE AND TAILS (FOXTROT)** CBS 3266	22	7
9 Aug 75	**SUPER WOMBLE** CBS 3480	20	6
13 Dec 75	**LET'S WOMBLE TO THE PARTY TONIGHT** CBS 3794	34	5
21 Mar 98	**REMEMBER YOU'RE A WOMBLE (re-issue)** Columbia 6656202	13	5
13 Jun 98	**THE WOMBLING SONG (UNDERGROUND OVERGROUND) (re-issue)** Columbia 6660412	27	3
30 Dec 00	**I WISH IT COULD BE A WOMBLING MERRY CHRISTMAS EVERYDAY** Dramatico DRAMCDS 0001 [1]	22	3
2 Mar 74	**WOMBLING SONGS** CBS 65803	19	17
13 Jul 74	**REMEMBER YOU'RE A WOMBLE** CBS 80191	18	31
21 Dec 74	**KEEP ON WOMBLING** CBS 80526	17	6
8 Jan 77	**20 WOMBLING GREATS** Warwick PR 5022	29	1
18 Apr 98	**THE BEST WOMBLES ALBUM SO FAR – VOLUME 1** Columbia 4895622	26	3

[1] The Wombles with Roy Wood

Stevie WONDER (29 Top 500) Multi-award-winner, b. Steveland Judkins, 13 May 1950, Michigan, US, is one of the most successful singer / songwriters of all time. The youngest artist to top the US singles and albums charts (aged 13) also recorded Motown's biggest UK seller, 'I Just Called to Say I Love You'. This very popular live performer has recorded with many of the biggest names in music and has had his songs sung and sampled by countless acts. No one has amassed more No.1 US R&B hits than the blind entertainer who helped to turn Martin Luther King's birthday into a US holiday, and whose charitable work is legendary. Best-selling single: 'I Just Called to Say I Love You' 1,775,000 (Singles: 425 Weeks, Albums: 382 Weeks) pos/wks

3 Feb 66	**UPTIGHT (EVERYTHING'S ALRIGHT)** Tamla Motown TMG 545	14	10
18 Aug 66	**BLOWIN' IN THE WIND** Tamla Motown TMG 570	36	5
5 Jan 67	**A PLACE IN THE SUN** Tamla Motown TMG 588	20	5
26 Jul 67 ●	**I WAS MADE TO LOVE HER** Tamla Motown TMG 613	5	15
25 Oct 67	**I'M WONDERING** Tamla Motown TMG 626	22	8
8 May 68	**SHOO BE DOO BE DOO DA DAY** Tamla Motown TMG 653	46	4
18 Dec 68 ●	**FOR ONCE IN MY LIFE** Tamla Motown TMG 679	3	13
19 Mar 69	**I DON'T KNOW WHY I LOVE YOU (re)** Tamla Motown TMG 690	14	11
16 Jul 69 ●	**MY CHERIE AMOUR** Tamla Motown TMG 690	4	15
15 Nov 69	**YESTER-ME, YESTER-YOU, YESTERDAY** Tamla Motown TMG 717	2	13
28 Mar 70 ●	**NEVER HAD A DREAM COME TRUE** Tamla Motown TMG 731	6	12
18 Jul 70	**SIGNED SEALED DELIVERED I'M YOURS (re)** Tamla Motown TMG 744	15	10
21 Nov 70	**HEAVEN HELP US ALL** Tamla Motown TMG 757	29	11
15 May 71	**WE CAN WORK IT OUT** Tamla Motown TMG 772	27	7
22 Jan 72	**IF YOU REALLY LOVE ME** Tamla Motown TMG 798	20	7
3 Feb 73	**SUPERSTITION** Tamla Motown TMG 841 ▲	11	9
19 May 73	**YOU ARE THE SUNSHINE OF MY LIFE** Tamla Motown TMG 852 ▲	7	11
13 Oct 73	**HIGHER GROUND** Tamla Motown TMG 869	29	5
12 Jan 74	**LIVING FOR THE CITY** Tamla Motown TMG 881	15	9
13 Apr 74	**HE'S MISSTRA KNOW IT ALL** Tamla Motown TMG 892	10	9
19 Oct 74	**YOU HAVEN'T DONE NOTHIN'** Tamla Motown TMG 921 ▲	30	5
11 Jan 75	**BOOGIE ON REGGAE WOMAN** Tamla Motown TMG 928	12	8
18 Dec 76 ●	**I WISH** Motown TMG 1054 ▲	5	10
9 Apr 77 ●	**SIR DUKE** Motown TMG 1068 ▲	2	9
10 Sep 77	**ANOTHER STAR** Motown TMG 1083	29	5
24 Feb 79	**POPS, WE LOVE YOU** Motown TMG 1136 [1]	66	5
24 Nov 79	**SEND ONE YOUR LOVE** Motown TMG 1149	52	3
26 Jan 80	**BLACK ORCHID** Motown TMG 1173	63	3
29 Mar 80	**OUTSIDE MY WINDOW** Motown TMG 1179	52	4
13 Sep 80 ●	**MASTER BLASTER (JAMMIN')** Motown TMG 1204	2	10
27 Dec 80 ●	**I AIN'T GONNA STAND FOR IT** Motown TMG 1215	10	10
7 Mar 81 ●	**LATELY** Motown TMG 1226	3	13
25 Jul 81 ●	**HAPPY BIRTHDAY** Motown TMG 1235	2	11
23 Jan 82	**THAT GIRL** Motown TMG 1254	39	6
10 Apr 82 ★	**EBONY AND IVORY** Parlophone R 6054 [2] ▲	1	10
5 Jun 82 ●	**DO I DO** Motown TMG 1269	10	7
25 Sep 82	**RIBBON IN THE SKY** Motown TMG 1280	45	4
25 Aug 84 ★	**I JUST CALLED TO SAY I LOVE YOU (re)** Motown TMG 1349 ◆ ▲	1	26
1 Dec 84	**LOVE LIGHT IN FLIGHT** Motown TMG 1364	44	5
29 Dec 84	**DON'T DRIVE DRUNK (re)** Motown TMG 1372	62	3
7 Sep 85 ●	**PART-TIME LOVER** Motown ZB 40351 ▲	3	12
9 Nov 85	**THAT'S WHAT FRIENDS ARE FOR** Arista ARIST 638 [3] ▲	16	9
23 Nov 85	**GO HOME** Motown ZB 40501	67	2
8 Mar 86	**OVERJOYED** Motown ZB 40567	17	8

17 Jan 87	STRANGER ON THE SHORE OF LOVE *Motown WOND 2*	55	3
31 Oct 87	SKELETONS *Motown ZB 41439*	59	3
28 May 88	GET IT *Motown ZB 41883* [4]	37	4
6 Aug 88 ●	MY LOVE *CBS JULIO 2* [5]	5	11
20 May 89	FREE *Motown ZB 42855*	49	5
12 Oct 91	FUN DAY *Motown ZB 44957*	63	1
25 Feb 95	FOR YOUR LOVE *Motown TMGCD 1437*	23	4
22 Jul 95	TOMORROW ROBINS WILL SING *Motown 8603732*	71	1
19 Jul 97 ●	HOW COME, HOW LONG *Epic 6646202* [6]	10	5
31 Oct 98	TRUE TO YOUR HEART *Motown 8608832* [7]	51	1
27 Dec 03	SIGNED, SEALED, DELIVERED, I'M YOURS *Innocent SINCD 50* [8]	11	10
7 Sep 68	STEVIE WONDER'S GREATEST HITS *Tamla Motown STML 11075*	25	10
13 Dec 69	MY CHERIE AMOUR *Tamla Motown STML 11128*	17	2
12 Feb 72	GREATEST HITS VOLUME 2 *Tamla Motown STML 11196*	30	4
3 Feb 73	TALKING BOOK *Tamla Motown STMA 8007*	16	48
1 Sep 73	INNERVISIONS *Tamla Motown STMA 8011*	8	55
17 Aug 74	FULFILLINGNESS' FIRST FINALE *Tamla Motown STMA 8019*	5	16
16 Oct 76 ●	SONGS IN THE KEY OF LIFE *Tamla Motown TMSP 6002*	2	54
10 Nov 79 ●	JOURNEY THROUGH THE SECRET LIFE OF PLANTS *Motown TMSP 6009*	8	15
8 Nov 80 ●	HOTTER THAN JULY *Motown STMA 8035*	2	55
22 May 82 ●	ORIGINAL MUSIQUARIUM 1 *Motown TMSP 6012*	8	17
22 Sep 84 ●	THE WOMAN IN RED (FILM SOUNDTRACK) *Motown ZL 72285*	2	19
24 Nov 84	LOVE SONGS – 16 CLASSIC HITS *Telstar STAR 2251*	20	16
28 Sep 85 ●	IN SQUARE CIRCLE *Motown ZL 72005*	5	16
15 Nov 86	DIANA ROSS. MICHAEL JACKSON. GLADYS KNIGHT. STEVIE WONDER. THEIR VERY BEST BACK TO BACK *Priority PTVR 2* [1]	21	10
28 Nov 87	CHARACTERS *Motown ZL 72001*	33	4
8 Jun 91	JUNGLE FEVER (FILM SOUNDTRACK) *Motown ZL 71750*	56	1
25 Mar 95 ●	CONVERSATION PEACE *Motown 5302382*	8	4
23 Nov 96	SONG REVIEW – A GREATEST HITS COLLECTION *Motown 5307572*	19	12
23 Aug 97	SONGS IN THE KEY OF LIFE (RE-ISSUE) *Motown 5300342*	66	1
9 Nov 02	THE DEFINITIVE COLLECTION *Universal TV 0665022*	16	29

[1] Diana Ross, Marvin Gaye, Smokey Robinson and Stevie Wonder [2] Paul McCartney with Stevie Wonder [3] Dionne Warwick and Friends featuring Elton John, Stevie Wonder and Gladys Knight [4] Stevie Wonder and Michael Jackson [5] Julio Iglesias featuring Stevie Wonder [6] Babyface featuring Stevie Wonder [7] 98 Degrees featuring Stevie Wonder [8] Blue featuring Stevie Wonder and Angie Stone [1] Diana Ross / Michael Jackson / Gladys Knight / Stevie Wonder

'You Haven't Done Nothin'' included an additional credit on the label: 'Doo Doo Wopsssss by The Jackson 5'. 'I Just Called to Say I Loved You' re-entered in Dec 1985

Wayne WONDER *Jamaica, male vocalist – DeWayne Charles (Singles: 14 Weeks, Albums: 7 Weeks)*

			pos/wks
28 Jun 03 ●	NO LETTING GO *VP / Atlantic ATO 154CD*	3	8
8 Nov 03	BOUNCE ALONG *Atlantic ATO 165CD*	19	6
28 Jun 03	NO HOLDING BACK *VP / Atlantic 7567836282*	40	7

WONDER DOG *Germany, canine vocalist – Harry Thumann (Singles: 7 Weeks)*

			pos/wks
21 Aug 82	RUFF MIX *Flip FLIP 001*	31	7

The WONDER STUFF *UK, male vocal / instrumental group (Singles: 66 Weeks, Albums: 48 Weeks)*

			pos/wks
30 Apr 88	GIVE GIVE GIVE ME MORE MORE MORE *Polydor GONE 3*	72	2
16 Jul 88	A WISH AWAY *Polydor GONE 4*	43	5
24 Sep 88	IT'S YER MONEY I'M AFTER BABY *Polydor GONE 5*	40	4
11 Mar 89	WHO WANTS TO BE THE DISCO KING? *Polydor GONE 6*	28	3
23 Sep 89	DON'T LET ME DOWN GENTLY *Polydor GONE 7*	19	4
11 Nov 89	GOLDEN GREEN / GET TOGETHER *Polydor GONE 8*	33	3
12 May 90	CIRCLESQUARE *Polydor GONE 10*	20	4
13 Apr 91 ●	THE SIZE OF A COW *Polydor GONE 11*	5	7
25 May 91	CAUGHT IN MY SHADOW *Polydor GONE 12*	18	3
7 Sep 91	SLEEP ALONE *Polydor GONE 13*	43	2
26 Oct 91 ★	DIZZY *Sense SIGH 712* [1]	1	12
25 Jan 92 ●	WELCOME TO THE CHEAP SEATS (EP) *Polydor GONE 14*	8	5
25 Sep 93 ●	ON THE ROPES (EP) *Polydor GONCD 15*	10	4
27 Nov 93	FULL OF LIFE (HAPPY NOW) *Polydor GONCD 16*	28	3
26 Mar 94	HOT LOVE NOW! (EP) *Polydor GONCD 17*	19	3
10 Sep 94	UNBEARABLE *Polydor GONCD 18*	16	3
27 Aug 88	THE EIGHT LEGGED GROOVE MACHINE *Polydor GONLP 1*	18	7
14 Oct 89 ●	HUP *Polydor 8411871*	5	8

8 Jun 91 ●	NEVER LOVED ELVIS *Polydor 8472521*	3	23
16 Oct 93 ●	CONSTRUCTION FOR THE MODERN IDIOT *Polydor 5198942*	4	5
8 Oct 94 ●	IF THE BEATLES HAD READ HUNTER ... THE SINGLES *Polydor 5213972*	8	4
29 Jul 95	LIVE IN MANCHESTER *Windsong WINCD 074X*	74	1

[1] Vic Reeves and The Wonder Stuff

Tracks on Welcome to the Cheap Seats (EP): Welcome to the Cheap Seats / Me, My Mom, My Dad and My Brother / Will the Circle Be Unbroken / That's Entertainment. Tracks on On the Ropes (EP): On the Ropes / Professional Disturber of the Peace / Hank and John / Whites. Tracks on Hot Love Now (EP): Hot Love Now! / I Think I Must've Had Something Really Useful to Say / Room 512 / All the News That's Fit to Print

The WONDERS *US, male vocal / instrumental group (Singles: 3 Weeks)*

			pos/wks
22 Feb 97	THAT THING YOU DO! *Play-Tone 6640552*	22	3

WONDRESS See MANTRONIX

Brenton WOOD *US, male vocalist – Alfred Smith (Singles: 14 Weeks)*

			pos/wks
27 Dec 67 ●	GIMME LITTLE SIGN *Liberty LBF 15021*	8	14

Roy WOOD (see also ELECTRIC LIGHT ORCHESTRA; The MOVE; WIZZARD) *UK, male vocalist / multi-instrumentalist – Ulysses Adrian Wood (Singles: 44 Weeks, Albums: 14 Weeks)*

			pos/wks
11 Aug 73	DEAR ELAINE *Harvest HAR 5074*	18	8
1 Dec 73 ●	FOREVER *Harvest HAR 5078*	8	13
15 Jun 74	GOIN' DOWN THE ROAD *Harvest HAR 5083*	13	7
31 May 75	OH WHAT A SHAME *Jet 754*	13	7
22 Nov 86	WATERLOO *IRS IRM 125* [1]	45	4
23 Dec 95	I WISH IT COULD BE CHRISTMAS EVERYDAY *Woody WOODY 001CD* [2]	59	2
30 Dec 00	I WISH IT COULD BE A WOMBLING MERRY CHRISTMAS EVERYDAY *Dramatico DRAMCDS 0001* [3]	22	3
18 Aug 73	BOULDERS *Harvest SHVL 803*	15	8
24 Jul 82	THE SINGLES *Speed SPEED 1000*	37	6

[1] Doctor and the Medics featuring Roy Wood [2] Roy Wood Big Band
[3] The Wombles with Roy Wood

The WOODENTOPS *UK, male vocal / instrumental group (Singles: 1 Week, Albums: 6 Weeks)*

			pos/wks
11 Oct 86	EVERYDAY LIVING *Rough Trade RT 178*	72	1
12 Jul 86	GIANT *Rough Trade ROUGH 87*	35	4
5 Mar 88	WOODENFOOT COPS ON THE HIGHWAY *Rough Trade ROUGH 127*	48	2

Marcella WOODS See Matt DAREY; MELT featuring LITTLE MS MARCIE; LIQUID STATE featuring Marcella WOODS

Michael WOODS (see also M3; MI; WARRIOR) *UK, male producer (Singles: 2 Weeks)*

			pos/wks
21 Jun 03	IF YOU WANT ME *Incentive CENT 48CDS* [1]	46	1
29 Nov 03	SOLEX (CLOSE TO THE EDGE) *Free 2 Air 0150355 F2A*	52	1

[1] Michael Woods featuring Imogen Bailey

Edward WOODWARD *UK, male actor / vocalist (Singles: 2 Weeks, Albums: 12 Weeks)*

			pos/wks
16 Jan 71	THE WAY YOU LOOK TONIGHT (re) *DJM DJS 232*	42	2
6 Jun 70	THE MAN ALONE *DJM DJLPS 405*	53	2
19 Aug 72	THE EDWARD WOODWARD ALBUM *Jam JAL 103*	20	10

WOOKIE *UK, male producer / vocalist – Jason Chue (Singles: 11 Weeks)*

			pos/wks
3 Jun 00	WHAT'S GOING ON *Soul II Soul S2SCD 001*	45	1
12 Aug 00 ●	BATTLE *Soul II Soul / Pias S2SPCD 001* [1]	10	7
12 May 01	BACK UP (TO ME) *Soul II Soul S2SPCD 003* [1]	38	3

[1] Wookie featuring Lain

Sheb WOOLEY *US, male vocalist / actor. b. 10 Apr 1921, d. 16 Sep 2003 (Singles: 8 Weeks)*

			pos/wks
20 Jun 58	THE PURPLE PEOPLE EATER *MGM 981* ▲	12	8

The WOOLPACKERS
UK, male vocal group (Singles: 24 Weeks, Albums: 13 Weeks)   pos/wks

16 Nov 96 ●	HILLBILLY ROCK HILLBILLY ROLL RCA 74321425412	**5** 14
29 Nov 97	LINE DANCE PARTY RCA 74321512262	**25** 10
14 Dec 96	EMMERDANCE RCA 74321444052	**26** 10
29 Nov 97	THE GREATEST LINE DANCING PARTY ALBUM RCA 74321512272	**48** 3

WORKING WEEK UK, male / female vocal / instrumental group (Singles: 2 Weeks, Albums: 10 Weeks)   pos/wks

9 Jun 84	VENCEREMOS – WE WILL WIN Virgin VS 684	**64** 2
4 Jun 85	WORKING NIGHTS Virgin V 2343	**23** 9
27 Sep 86	COMPANEROS Virgin V 2397	**72** 1

WORLD See LIL' LOUIS

WORLD OF TWIST UK, male / female vocal / instrumental group (Singles: 12 Weeks, Albums: 1 Week)   pos/wks

24 Nov 90	THE STORM (re) Circa YR 55	**42** 5
23 Mar 91	SONS OF THE STAGE Circa YR 62	**47** 3
12 Oct 91	SWEETS Circa YR 72	**58** 2
22 Feb 92	SHE'S A RAINBOW Circa YR 82	**62** 2
9 Nov 91	QUALITY STREET Circa CIRCA 17	**50** 1

WORLD PARTY UK / Ireland, male vocal / instrumental group (Singles: 29 Weeks, Albums: 25 Weeks)   pos/wks

14 Feb 87	SHIP OF FOOLS Ensign ENY 606	**42** 6
16 Jun 90	MESSAGE IN THE BOX Ensign ENY 631	**39** 6
15 Sep 90	WAY DOWN NOW Ensign ENY 634	**66** 2
18 May 91	THANK YOU WORLD Ensign ENY 643	**68** 1
10 Apr 93	IS IT LIKE TODAY Ensign CDENY 658	**19** 6
10 Jul 93	GIVE IT ALL AWAY Ensign CDENY 659	**43** 3
2 Oct 93	ALL I GAVE Ensign CDENYS 660	**37** 3
7 Jun 97	BEAUTIFUL DREAM Chrysalis CDCHS 5053	**31** 2
21 Mar 87	PRIVATE REVOLUTION Chrysalis CHEN 4	**56** 4
19 May 90	GOODBYE JUMBO Ensign CHEN 10	**36** 10
8 May 93 ●	BANG! Ensign CDCHEN 33	**2** 8
28 Jun 97	EGYPTOLOGY Chrysalis CDCHR 6124	**34** 2
2 Sep 00	DUMBING UP Papillon BTFLYCD 0006	**64** 1

WORLD PREMIERE
US, male vocal / instrumental group (Singles: 4 Weeks)   pos/wks

28 Jan 84	SHARE THE NIGHT Epic A 4133	**64** 4

WORLD WARRIOR
UK, male producer – Simon Harris (Singles: 1 Week)   pos/wks

16 Apr 94	STREET FIGHTER II Living Beat LBECD 27	**70** 1

WORLDS APART UK, male vocal group (Singles: 17 Weeks)   pos/wks

27 Mar 93	HEAVEN MUST BE MISSING AN ANGEL Arista 74321139362	**29** 3
3 Jul 93	WONDERFUL WORLD Arista 74321153402	**51** 1
25 Sep 93	EVERLASTING LOVE Bell 74321164802	**20** 4
26 Mar 94	COULD IT BE I'M FALLING IN LOVE Bell 74321189952	**15** 6
4 Jun 94	BEGGIN' TO BE WRITTEN Bell 74321211982	**29** 3

WORLD'S FAMOUS SUPREME TEAM (see also Malcolm McLAREN)
US, male vocal / DJ group (Singles: 19 Weeks)   pos/wks

4 Dec 82 ●	BUFFALO GALS Charisma MALC 1 [1]	**9** 12
25 Feb 84	HEY DJ Charisma TEAM 1	**52** 5
8 Dec 90	OPERAA HOUSE Virgin VS 1273 [2]	**75** 1
3 Oct 98	BUFFALO GALS STAMPEDE (re-mix) Virgin VSCDT 1717 [3]	**65** 1

[1] Malcolm McLaren and the World's Famous Supreme Team [2] World Famous Supreme Team Show [3] Malcolm McLaren and the World's Famous Supreme Team plus Rakim and Roger Sanchez

WRECKLESS ERIC
UK, male vocalist – Eric Goulden (Albums: 5 Weeks)   pos/wks

1 Apr 78	WRECKLESS ERIC Stiff SEEZ 6	**46** 1
8 Mar 80	BIG SMASH Stiff SEEZ 21	**30** 4

WRECKX-N-EFFECT US, male vocal group (Singles: 18 Weeks)   pos/wks

13 Jan 90	JUICY Motown ZB 43295 [1]	**29** 7
5 Dec 92	RUMP SHAKER MCA MCS 1725	**24** 7
7 May 94	WRECKX SHOP MCA MCSTD 1969 [2]	**26** 2
13 Aug 94	RUMP SHAKER (re-issue) MCA MCSTD 1989	**40** 2

[1] Wrecks-N-Effect [2] Wreckx-N-Effect featuring Apache Indian

WREN ORCHESTRA See WET WET WET

Betty WRIGHT (see also Peter BROWN)
US, female vocalist (Singles: 23 Weeks)   pos/wks

25 Jan 75	SHOORAH! SHOORAH! RCA 2491	**27** 7
19 Apr 75	WHERE IS THE LOVE RCA 2548	**25** 7
8 Feb 86	PAIN Cooltempo COOL 117	**42** 6
9 Sep 89	KEEP LOVE NEW Sure Delight SD 11	**71** 3

Ian WRIGHT UK, male footballer / vocalist (Singles: 2 Weeks)   pos/wks

28 Aug 93	DO THE RIGHT THING M&G MAGCD 45	**43** 2

Linda WRIGHT See NEW ATLANTIC

Rick WRIGHT
UK, male vocalist / instrumentalist (Albums: 1 Week)   pos/wks

19 Oct 96	BROKEN CHINA EMI CDEMD 1098	**61** 1

Ruby WRIGHT
US, female vocalist, b. 8 Jan 1914, d. 14 Mar 2004 (Singles: 15 Weeks)   pos/wks

16 Apr 54 ●	BIMBO (re) Parlophone R 3816	**7** 5
22 May 59	THREE STARS Parlophone R 4556	**19** 10

'Three Stars' is narrated by Dick Pike

Steve WRIGHT UK, male DJ / vocalist (Singles: 10 Weeks)   pos/wks

27 Nov 82	I'M ALRIGHT RCA 296 [1]	**40** 6
15 Oct 83	GET SOME THERAPY RCA 362 [2]	**75** 1
1 Dec 84	THE GAY CAVALIEROS (THE STORY SO FAR) MCA 925	**61** 3

[1] Young Steve and The Afternoon Boys [2] Steve Wright and The Sisters of Soul

WUBBLE-U
UK, male production group (Singles: 1 Week)   pos/wks

7 Mar 98	PETAL Indolent DGOL 003CD1	**55** 1

Klaus WUNDERLICH Germany, male instrumentalist – organ, b. 18 Jun 1931, d. 28 Oct 1997 (Albums: 19 Weeks)   pos/wks

30 Aug 75	THE HIT WORLD OF KLAUS WUNDERLICH Decca SPA 434	**27** 8
20 May 78	THE UNIQUE KLAUS WUNDERLICH SOUND Decca DBC 5/5	**28** 4
26 May 79	THE FANTASTIC SOUND OF KLAUS WUNDERLICH Lotus LH 5013	**43** 5
17 Mar 84	ON THE SUNNY SIDE OF THE STREET Polydor POLD 5133	**81** 2

The WURZELS UK, male vocal / instrumental group (Singles: 31 Weeks, Albums: 29 Weeks)   pos/wks

2 Feb 67	DRINK UP THY ZIDER Columbia DB 8081 [1]	**45** 1
15 May 76 ★	THE COMBINE HARVESTER (BRAND NEW KEY) EMI 2450	**1** 13
11 Sep 76 ●	I AM A CIDER DRINKER (PALOMA BLANCA) EMI 2520	**3** 9
25 Jun 77	FARMER BILL'S COWMAN (I WAS KAISER BILL'S BATMAN) EMI 2637	**32** 5
11 Aug 01	COMBINE HARVESTER 2001 (re-mix) EMI Gold CDWURZ 001	**39** 2
12 Oct 02	DON'T LOOK BACK IN ANGER EMI Gold 5515082	**59** 1
11 Mar 67	ADGE CUTLER AND THE WURZELS Columbia SX 6126 [1]	**38** 4
3 Jul 76	COMBINE HARVESTER One Up OU 2138	**15** 20
2 Apr 77	GOLDEN DELICIOUS EMI Note NTS 122	**32** 5

[1] Adge Cutler and The Wurzels [1] Adge Cutler and The Wurzels

WU-TANG CLAN (see also CAPPADONNA; GZA / GENIUS; GHOSTFACE KILLAH; METHOD MAN; OL' DIRTY BASTARD; RAEKWON; The RZA) US, male rap / instrumental group (Singles: 21 Weeks, Albums: 23 Weeks)   pos/wks

16 Aug 97	TRIUMPH Loud 74321510212 [1]	**46** 1
21 Mar 98 ●	SAY WHAT YOU WANT / INSANE Mercury MERC 499 [2]	**4** 7
25 Nov 00	GRAVEL PIT Loud / Epic 67015182	**6** 13
14 Jun 97 ★	WU-TANG FOREVER Loud 74321457682 ■ ▲	**1** 10
2 Dec 00	THE W Epic 4995762	**19** 13

[1] Wu-Tang Clan featuring Cappadonna [2] Texas featuring Wu-Tang Clan (rap by Method Man and RZA)

Robert WYATT (see also SOFT MACHINE)
UK, male vocalist – Robert Wyatt-Ellidge (Singles: 11 Weeks)   pos/wks

28 Sep 74	I'M A BELIEVER *Virgin VS 114*	29	5
7 May 83	SHIPBUILDING *Rough Trade RT 115*	35	6

Michael WYCOFF *US, male vocalist (Singles: 2 Weeks)*   pos/wks

23 Jul 83	(DO YOU REALLY LOVE ME) TELL ME LOVE *RCA 348*	60	2

Pete WYLIE (see also WAH!)
UK, male vocalist (Singles: 18 Weeks)   pos/wks

3 May 86	SINFUL *Eternal MDM 7*	13	10
13 Sep 86	DIAMOND GIRL *Eternal MDM 12*	57	3
13 Apr 91	SINFUL! (SCARY JIGGIN' WITH DR LOVE) *Siren SRN 138* [1]	28	5

[1] Pete Wylie with The Farm

Bill WYMAN (see also THE ROLLING STONES)
UK, male vocalist / instrumentalist – bass –
William Perks (Singles: 13 Weeks, Albums: 8 Weeks)   pos/wks

25 Jul 81	(SI SI) JE SUIS UN ROCK STAR *A&M AMS 8144*	14	9
20 Mar 82	A NEW FASHION *A&M AMS 8209*	37	4
8 Jun 74	MONKEY GRIP *Rolling Stones COC 59102*	39	1
10 Apr 82	BILL WYMAN *A&M AMLH 68540*	55	6
27 May 00	GROOVIN' *Papillon BTFLYCD 003* [1]	52	1

[1] Bill Wyman's Rhythm Kings

Jane WYMAN See Bing CROSBY

Tammy WYNETTE *US, female vocalist – Virginia Wynette Pugh,*
b. 5 May 1942, d. 6 Apr 1998 (Singles: 35 Weeks, Albums: 49 Weeks)   pos/wks

26 Apr 75	★ STAND BY YOUR MAN *Epic EPC 7137*	1	12
28 Jun 75	D.I.V.O.R.C.E. *Epic EPC 3361*	12	7
12 Jun 76	I DON'T WANNA PLAY HOUSE *Epic EPC 4091*	37	4
7 Dec 91	● JUSTIFIED AND ANCIENT *KLF Communications KLF 099* [1]	2	12
17 May 75	● THE BEST OF TAMMY WYNETTE *Epic EPC 63578*	4	23
21 Jun 75	STAND BY YOUR MAN *Epic EPC 69141*	13	7
17 Dec 77	● 20 COUNTRY CLASSICS *CBS PR 5040*	3	11
4 Feb 78	COUNTRY GIRL MEETS COUNTRY BOY *Warwick PR 5039*	43	3
6 Jun 87	ANNIVERSARY – 20 YEARS OF HITS *Epic 450 3931*	45	5

[1] The KLF – guest vocals: Tammy Wynette

Mark WYNTER
UK, male vocalist – Terence Lewis (Singles: 80 Weeks)   pos/wks

25 Aug 60	IMAGE OF A GIRL *Decca F 11263*	11	10
10 Nov 60	KICKIN' UP THE LEAVES *Decca F 11279*	24	10
9 Mar 61	DREAM GIRL *Decca F 11323*	27	5
8 Jun 61	EXCLUSIVELY YOURS *Decca F 11354*	32	7
4 Oct 62	● VENUS IN BLUE JEANS *Pye 7N 15466*	4	15
13 Dec 62	● GO AWAY LITTLE GIRL *Pye 7N 15492*	6	11
6 Jun 63	SHY GIRL *Pye 7N 15525*	28	6
14 Nov 63	IT'S ALMOST TOMORROW *Pye 7N 15577*	12	12
9 Apr 64	ONLY YOU (AND YOU ALONE) *Pye 7N 15626*	38	4

Malcolm X *US, male orator, b. Malcolm Little,*
19 May 1925, d. 21 Feb 1965 (Singles: 4 Weeks)   pos/wks

7 Apr 84	NO SELL OUT *Tommy Boy IS 165*	60	4

Hit features credit: 'Music by Keith Le Blanc'

RICHARD X *UK, male producer – Richard Phillips*
(Singles: 16 Weeks, Albums: 2 Weeks)   pos/wks

29 Mar 03	● BEING NOBODY *Virgin RXCD 1* [1]	3	11
23 Aug 03	● FINEST DREAMS *Virgin RXCD 2* [2]	8	5
6 Sep 03	RICHARD X PRESENTS HIS X FACTOR *Virgin CDRICH 1*	31	2

[1] Richard X vs Liberty X [2] Richard X featuring Kelis

X-ECUTIONERS featuring Mike SHINODA
and Mr HAHN of LINKIN PARK *US, male DJ /*
production / rap group and male DJ / vocal duo (Singles: 9 Weeks)   pos/wks

13 Apr 02	● IT'S GOIN' DOWN *Epic 6725642*	7	9

X MAL DEUTSCHLAND *UK / Germany, male /*
female vocal / instrumental group (Albums: 1 Week)   pos/wks

7 Jul 84	TOCSIN *4AD CAD 407*	86	1

X MEN See SELENA vs X MEN

XAVIER See TJR featuring XAVIER

XAVIER
US, male / female vocal / instrumental group (Singles: 3 Weeks)   pos/wks

20 Mar 82	WORK THAT SUCKER TO DEATH / LOVE IS ON THE ONE *Liberty UP 651*	53	3

XPANSIONS
UK, male producer – Richie Malone (Singles: 21 Weeks)   pos/wks

6 Oct 90	ELEVATION *Optimism 113683*	49	5
23 Feb 91	● MOVE YOUR BODY (ELEVATION) *Arista 113 683*	7	9
15 Jun 91	WHAT YOU WANT *Arista 114 246* [1]	55	2
26 Aug 95	MOVE YOUR BODY (re-mix) *Arista 74321294982* [2]	14	4
30 Nov 02	ELEVATION (MOVE YOUR BODY) 2002 (re-mix) *RM RMRCD 10*	70	1

[1] Xpansions featuring Dale Joyner [2] Xpansions 95

'Move Your Body' is a re-mix of 'Elevation'

X-PRESS 2 *UK, male instrumental /*
production group (Singles: 24 Weeks, Albums: 3 Weeks)   pos/wks

5 Jun 93	LONDON X-PRESS *Junior Boy's Own JBO 12*	59	1
16 Oct 93	SAY WHAT! *Junior Boy's Own JBO 16CD*	32	2
30 Jul 94	ROCK 2 HOUSE / HIP HOUSIN' *Junior Boy's Own JBO 21CD* [1]	55	2
9 Mar 96	THE SOUND *Junior Boy's Own JBO 36*	38	1
12 Oct 96	TRANZ EURO XPRESS *Junior Boy's Own JBO 42CD*	45	1
30 Sep 00	AC / DC *Skint SKINT 57*	60	1
28 Apr 01	MUZIKIZUM *Skint SKINT 65*	52	1
20 Oct 01	SMOKE MACHINE *Skint SKINT 69*	43	1
20 Apr 02	● LAZY *Skint SKINT 74CD* [2]	2	13
21 Sep 02	I WANT YOU BACK *Skint SKINT 81CD*	50	1
4 May 02	MUZIKIZUM *Skint BRASSIC 23CD*	15	3

[1] X-Press 2 featuring Lo-Pro [2] X-Press 2 featuring David Byrne

'I Want You Back' features Dieter Meier

X-RAY SPEX *UK, male / female vocal /*
instrumental group (Singles: 33 Weeks, Albums: 14 Weeks)   pos/wks

29 Apr 78	THE DAY THE WORLD TURNED DAYGLO *EMI International INT 553*	23	8
22 Jul 78	IDENTITY *EMI International INT 563*	24	10
4 Nov 78	GERM FREE ADOLESCENCE *EMI International INT 573*	19	11
21 Apr 79	HIGHLY INFLAMMABLE *EMI International INT 583*	45	4
9 Dec 78	GERM FREE ADOLESCENTS *EMI International INS 3023*	30	14

XRS See DJ MARKY & XRS

XSCAPE *US, female vocal group (Singles: 15 Weeks)*   pos/wks

20 Nov 93	JUST KICKIN' IT *Columbia 6598622*	49	2
5 Nov 94	JUST KICKIN' IT (re-issue) *Columbia 6608642*	54	2
7 Oct 95	FEELS SO GOOD *Columbia 6625022*	34	2
27 Jan 96	WHO CAN I RUN TO *Columbia 6628112*	31	3
29 Jun 96	KEEP ON KEEPIN' ON *East West A 4287CD* [1]	39	2
19 Apr 97	KEEP ON KEEPIN' ON (re-issue) *East West A 3950CD 1* [1]	27	2
22 Aug 98	THE ARMS OF THE ONE WHO LOVES YOU *Columbia 6662522*	46	2

[1] MC Lyte featuring Xscape

XSTASIA
UK, male / female vocal / production duo (Singles: 1 Week) pos/wks

| 17 Mar 01 | SWEETNESS *Liquid Asset ASSETCD 005* | .65 | 1 |

X-STATIC
Italy, male / female vocal / instrumental group (Singles: 2 Weeks) pos/wks

| 4 Feb 95 | I'M STANDING (HIGHER) *Positiva CDTIV 25* | .41 | 2 |

XTC
UK, male vocal / instrumental group
(Singles: 70 Weeks, Albums: 51 Weeks) pos/wks

12 May 79	LIFE BEGINS AT THE HOP *Virgin VS 259*	.54	4
22 Sep 79	MAKING PLANS FOR NIGEL *Virgin VS 282*	.17	11
6 Sep 80	GENERALS AND MAJORS / DON'T LOSE YOUR TEMPER *Virgin VS 365*	.32	8
18 Oct 80	TOWERS OF LONDON *Virgin VS 372*	.31	5
24 Jan 81	SGT ROCK (IS GOING TO HELP ME) *Virgin VS 384*	.16	9
23 Jan 82 ●	SENSES WORKING OVERTIME *Virgin VS 462*	.10	9
27 Mar 82	BALL AND CHAIN *Virgin VS 482*	.58	4
15 Oct 83	LOVE ON A FARMBOY'S WAGES *Virgin VS 613*	.50	4
29 Sep 84	ALL YOU PRETTY GIRLS *Virgin VS 709*	.55	5
28 Jan 89	MAYOR OF SIMPLETON *Virgin VS 1158*	.46	5
4 Apr 92	THE DISAPPOINTED *Virgin VS 1404*	.33	5
13 Jun 92	THE BALLAD OF PETER PUMPKINHEAD *Virgin VS 1415*	.71	1
11 Feb 78	WHITE MUSIC *Virgin V 2095*	.38	4
28 Oct 78	GO 2 *Virgin V 2108*	.21	3
1 Sep 79	DRUMS AND WIRES *Virgin V 2129*	.34	7
20 Sep 80	BLACK SEA *Virgin V 2173*	.16	7
20 Feb 82 ●	ENGLISH SETTLEMENT *Virgin V 2223*	.5	11
13 Nov 82	WAXWORKS – SOME SINGLES (1977-1982) *Virgin V 2251*	.54	3
10 Sep 83	MUMMER *Virgin V 2264*	.51	4
27 Oct 84	THE BIG EXPRESS *Virgin V 2325*	.38	2
8 Nov 86	SKYLARKING *Virgin V 2399*	.90	1
11 Mar 89	ORANGES AND LEMONS *Virgin V 2581*	.28	3
9 May 92	NONSUCH *Virgin CDV 2699*	.28	2
28 Sep 96	FOSSIL FUEL – THE XTC SINGLES 1977-92 *Virgin CDVD 2811*	.33	2
6 Mar 99	APPLE VENUS – VOLUME 1 *Cooking Vinyl COOKCD 172*	.42	1
3 Jun 00	WASP STAR (APPLE VENUS VOLUME 2) *Cooking Vinyl COOKCD 194* [1]	.40	1

[1] XTC and Wasp Star

XTM & DJ CHUCKY presents ANNIA
Spain / Japan,
male DJ / production trio and female vocalist (Singles: 19 Weeks) pos/wks

| 7 Jun 03 ● | FLY ON THE WINGS OF LOVE *Serious SER 62CD* | .8 | 19 |

XZIBIT
US, male rapper – Alvin Joiner (Singles: 9 Weeks,
Albums: 13 Weeks) pos/wks

17 Mar 01	X *Epic 6709072* [1]	.14	7
16 Nov 02	MULTIPLY *Epic / Loud 6731552*	.39	2
10 Feb 01	RESTLESS *Epic 4989132*	.27	11
12 Oct 02	MAN VS MACHINE *Epic 5047539*	.43	2

[1] Xzibit featuring Snoop Dogg

Y?N-VEE
US, female vocal group (Singles: 1 Week) pos/wks

| 17 Dec 94 | CHOCOLATE *RAL RALCD 2* | .65 | 1 |

Y & T
US, male vocal / instrumental
group (Singles: 4 Weeks, Albums: 15 Weeks) pos/wks

| 13 Aug 83 | MEAN STREAK *A&M AM 135* | .41 | 4 |

11 Sep 82	BLACK TIGER *A&M AMLH 64910*	.53	8
10 Sep 83	MEAN STREAK *A&M AMLX 64960*	.35	4
18 Aug 84	IN ROCK WE TRUST *A&M AMLX 65007*	.33	3

Y-TRAXX
Belgium, male producer – Frederique de Backer
(Singles: 2 Weeks) pos/wks

| 24 May 97 | MYSTERY LAND (EP) *ffrr FCD 292* | .63 | 1 |
| 20 Sep 03 | MYSTERY LAND *Nebula NEBT 047* [1] | .70 | 1 |

[1] Y-Traxx featuring Neve

Tracks on Mystery Land (EP): Mystery Land (radio edit) / Trance Piano / Kiss the Sound / Mystery Land

Y-TRIBE featuring Elisabeth TROY
UK, male instrumental /
production duo and female vocalist (Singles: 3 Weeks) pos/wks

| 18 Dec 99 | ENOUGH IS ENOUGH (re) *Northwest 10 NORTHCD 002* | .49 | 3 |

YA KID K *See HI-TEK 3 featuring YA KID K; TECHNOTRONIC*

Weird Al YANKOVIC
US, male vocalist (Singles: 8 Weeks) pos/wks

| 7 Apr 84 | EAT IT *Scotti Bros. / Epic A 4257* | .36 | 7 |
| 4 Jul 92 | SMELLS LIKE NIRVANA *Scotti Bros. PO 219* | .58 | 1 |

YANNI
Greece, male instrumentalist –
keyboards – Yanni Chryssolmalis (Albums: 2 Weeks) pos/wks

| 4 Apr 98 | TRIBUTE *Virgin CDVUS 135* | .40 | 2 |

YANOU *See DJ SAMMY*

YARBROUGH and PEOPLES
US, male / female vocal / instrumental
duo – Calvin Yarbrough and Alisa Peoples (Singles: 20 Weeks) pos/wks

27 Dec 80 ●	DON'T STOP THE MUSIC *Mercury MER 53*	.7	12
5 May 84	DON'T WASTE YOUR TIME *Total Experience XE 501*	.60	3
11 Jan 86	GUILTY *Total Experience FB 49905*	.53	3
5 Jul 86	I WOULDN'T LIE *Total Experience FB 49841*	.61	2

The YARDBIRDS
(see also Jeff BECK; Eric CLAPTON; CREAM; Keith RELF) *UK, male vocal /*
instrumental group (Singles: 62 Weeks, Albums: 8 Weeks) pos/wks

12 Nov 64	GOOD MORNING LITTLE SCHOOLGIRL *Columbia DB 7391*	.44	4
18 Mar 65 ●	FOR YOUR LOVE *Columbia DB 7499*	.3	12
17 Jun 65 ●	HEART FULL OF SOUL *Columbia DB 7594*	.2	13
14 Oct 65 ●	EVIL HEARTED YOU / STILL I'M SAD *Columbia DB 7706*	.3	10
3 Mar 66 ●	SHAPES OF THINGS *Columbia DB 7848*	.3	9
2 Jun 66 ●	OVER UNDER SIDEWAYS DOWN *Columbia DB 7928*	.10	9
27 Oct 66	HAPPENINGS TEN YEARS TIME AGO *Columbia DB 8024*	.43	5
23 Jul 66	YARDBIRDS *Columbia SX 6063*	.20	8

YAVAHN *See RUFFNECK featuring YAVAHN*

YAZOO
(see also ASSEMBLY; ERASURE)
UK, female / male vocal / instrumental duo – Alison Moyet
and Vince Clarke (Singles: 55 Weeks, Albums: 86 Weeks) pos/wks

17 Apr 82 ●	ONLY YOU *Mute MUTE 020*	.2	14
17 Jul 82 ●	DON'T GO *Mute YAZ 001*	.3	11
20 Nov 82	THE OTHER SIDE OF LOVE *Mute YAZ 002*	.13	9
21 May 83	NOBODY'S DIARY *Mute YAZ 003*	.3	11
8 Dec 90	SITUATION *Mute YAZ 4*	.14	8
4 Sep 99	ONLY YOU (re-mix) *Mute CDYAZ 5*	.38	2
4 Sep 82 ●	UPSTAIRS AT ERIC'S *Mute STUMM 7*	.2	63
16 Jul 83 ★	YOU AND ME BOTH *Mute STUMM 12*	.1	20
18 Sep 99	ONLY YAZOO – THE BEST OF YAZOO *Mute CDMUTEL 6*	.22	3

YAZZ
UK, female vocalist – Yasmin Evans
(Singles: 69 Weeks, Albums: 32 Weeks) pos/wks

20 Feb 88 ●	DOCTORIN' THE HOUSE *Ahead of Our Time CCUT 27* [1]	.6	9
23 Jul 88 ★	THE ONLY WAY IS UP *Big Life BLR 4* [2]	.1	15
29 Oct 88 ●	STAND UP FOR YOUR LOVE RIGHTS *Big Life BLR 5*	.2	12
4 Feb 89 ●	FINE TIME *Big Life BLR 6*	.9	8
29 Apr 89	WHERE HAS ALL THE LOVE GONE *Big Life BLR 8*	.16	6
23 Jun 90	TREAT ME GOOD *Big Life BLR 24*	.20	5
28 Mar 92	ONE TRUE WOMAN *Polydor PO 198*	.60	2
31 Jul 93	HOW LONG *Polydor PZCD 252* [3]	.31	5
2 Apr 94	HAVE MERCY *Polydor PZCD 309*	.42	3
9 Jul 94	EVERYBODY'S GOT TO LEARN SOMETIME *Polydor PZCD 316*	.56	2

			pos/wks
28 Sep 96	GOOD THING GOING	East West EW 062CD	53 1
22 Mar 97	NEVER CAN SAY GOODBYE	East West EW 081CD	61 1
26 Nov 88 ●	WANTED	Big Life YAZZLP 1	3 32

[1] Coldcut featuring Yazz and the Plastic Population [2] Yazz and the Plastic Population [3] Yazz and Aswad

The YEAH YEAH YEAHS US, male / female vocal / instrumental group (Singles: 9 Weeks, Albums: 6 Weeks)

			pos/wks
16 Nov 02	MACHINE	Wichita WEBB 036SCD	37 2
26 Apr 03	DATE WITH THE NIGHT	Dress Up / Polydor 0657442	16 2
5 Jul 03	PIN	Dress Up / Polydor 9808085	26 2
4 Oct 03	MAPS	Dress Up / Polydor 9811413	26 2
13 Nov 04	Y CONTROL	Dress Up / Polydor 9868816	54 1
10 May 03	FEVER TO TELL	Dress Up / Polydor 0760612	13 6

Trisha YEARWOOD US, female vocalist (Singles: 1 Week, Albums: 2 Weeks)

			pos/wks
9 Aug 97	HOW DO I LIVE	MCA MCSTD 48064	66 1
25 Jul 98	WHERE YOUR ROAD LEADS	MCA Nashville UMD 80513	36 2

YELL! UK, male vocal duo – Paul Varney and Daniel James (Singles: 8 Weeks)

			pos/wks
20 Jan 90 ●	INSTANT REPLAY	Fanfare FAN 22	10 8

YELLO Switzerland, male vocal / instrumental duo – Dieter Meier and Boris Blank (Singles: 42 Weeks, Albums: 15 Weeks)

			pos/wks
25 Jun 83	I LOVE YOU	Stiff BUY 176	41 4
26 Nov 83	LOST AGAIN	Stiff BUY 191	73 1
9 Aug 86	GOLDRUSH	Mercury MER 218	54 3
22 Aug 87	THE RHYTHM DIVINE	Mercury MER 253 [1]	54 2
27 Aug 88 ●	THE RACE	Mercury YELLO 1	7 11
17 Dec 88	TIED UP	Mercury YELLO 2	60 5
25 Mar 89	OF COURSE I'M LYING	Mercury YELLO 3	23 8
22 Jul 89	BLAZING SADDLES	Mercury YELLO 4	47 2
8 Jun 91	RUBBERBANDMAN	Mercury YELLO 5	58 2
5 Sep 92	JUNGLE BILL	Mercury MER 376	61 2
7 Nov 92	THE RACE / BOSTICH (re-issue)	Mercury MER 382	55 1
15 Oct 94	HOW HOW	Mercury MERCD 414	59 1
21 May 83	YOU GOTTA SAY YES TO ANOTHER EXCESS	Stiff SEEZ 48	65 2
6 Apr 85	STELLA	Elektra EKT 1	92 1
4 Jul 87	ONE SECOND	Mercury MERH 100	48 3
10 Dec 88	FLAG	Mercury 8367781	56 7
29 Jun 91	BABY	Mercury 8487911	37 2

[1] Yello featuring Shirley Bassey

YELLOW DOG US / UK, male vocal / instrumental group (Singles: 13 Weeks)

			pos/wks
4 Feb 78 ●	JUST ONE MORE NIGHT	Virgin VS 195	8 9
22 Jul 78	WAIT UNTIL MIDNIGHT	Virgin VS 217	54 4

YELLOW MAGIC ORCHESTRA Japan, male instrumental group (Singles: 11 Weeks)

			pos/wks
14 Jun 80	COMPUTER GAME (THEME FROM 'THE INVADERS') A&M AMS 7502		17 11

The YELLOWCARD US, male vocal / instrumental group (Singles: 2 Weeks)

			pos/wks
12 Jun 04	WAY AWAY	Capitol CDCLS 855	63 1
18 Sep 04	OCEAN AVENUE	Capitol CDCLS 860	65 1

YELLOWCOATS See Paul SHANE and the YELLOWCOATS

Bryn YEMM UK, male vocalist (Albums: 14 Weeks)

			pos/wks
9 Jun 84	HOW DO I LOVE THEE	Lifestyle LEG 17	57 2
7 Jul 84	HOW GREAT THOU ART	Lifestyle LEG 15	67 8
22 Dec 84	THE BRYN YEMM CHRISTMAS COLLECTION	Bay BAY 104	95 2
26 Oct 85	MY TRIBUTE – BRYN YEMM INSPIRATIONAL ALBUM Word WSTR 9665 [1]		85 2

[1] Bryn Yemm and the Gwent Chorale

YEOVIL TOWN FC UK, male football team vocalists (Singles: 1 Week)

			pos/wks
28 Feb 04	YEOVIL TRUE	Yeovil Town FC 188	36 1

YES (242) Top 500 (see also ANDERSON BRUFORD WAKEMAN HOWE; Alan WHITE; CHRIS SQUIRE) 1970s progressive rock giants who later flirted successfully with AOR, formed London 1968. Noted Yes-men include Jon Anderson (v), Bill Bruford (d), Steve Howe (g), Rick Wakeman (k), Patrick Moraz (k) and ex-Buggle Trevor Horn (v/g), who masterminded their 1980s comeback (Singles: 31 Weeks, Albums: 226 Weeks)

			pos/wks
17 Sep 77 ●	WONDROUS STORIES	Atlantic K 10999	7 9
26 Nov 77	GOING FOR THE ONE	Atlantic K 11047	24 4
9 Sep 78	DON'T KILL THE WHALE	Atlantic K 11184	36 4
12 Nov 83	OWNER OF A LONELY HEART	Acto B 9817▲	28 9
31 Mar 84	LEAVE IT	Acto B 9787	56 4
3 Oct 87	LOVE WILL FIND A WAY	Atco A 9449	73 1
1 Aug 70	TIME AND A WORD	Atlantic 2400006	45 3
27 Feb 71 ●	THE YES ALBUM	Atlantic 2400101	4 34
4 Dec 71 ●	FRAGILE	Atlantic 2409019	7 17
23 Sep 72 ●	CLOSE TO THE EDGE	Atlantic K 50012	4 13
26 May 73 ●	YESSONGS	Atlantic K 60045	7 13
22 Dec 73 ★	TALES FROM TOPOGRAPHIC OCEANS	Atlantic K 80001	1 15
21 Dec 74 ●	RELAYER	Atlantic K 50096	4 11
29 Mar 75	YESTERDAYS	Atlantic K 50048	27 7
30 Jul 77 ★	GOING FOR THE ONE	Atlantic K 50379	1 28
7 Oct 78	TORMATO	Atlantic K 50518	8 11
30 Aug 80 ●	DRAMA	Atlantic K 50736	2 8
10 Jan 81	YESSHOWS	Atlantic K 60142	22 9
26 Nov 83	90125	Atco 790125	16 28
29 Mar 86	9012 LIVE: THE SOLOS	Atco 790 4741	44 3
10 Oct 87	BIG GENERATOR	Atco WEX 70	17 5
11 May 91 ●	UNION	Arista 211558	7 6
2 Apr 94	TALK	London 8284892	20 4
9 Nov 96	KEYS TO ASCENSION	Essential! EDFCD 417	48 1
15 Nov 97	KEYS TO ASCENSION 2	Essential! EDFCD 457	62 1
2 Oct 99	THE LADDER	Eagle EAGCD 088	36 1
22 Sep 01	MAGNIFICATION	Eagle EAGCD 189	71 1
9 Aug 03 ●	THE ULTIMATE YES – 35TH ANNIVERSARY	WSM 8122737022	10 7

Group was UK only up to 1978

Melissa YIANNAKOU See DESIYA featuring Melissa YIANNAKOU

YIN and YAN UK, male vocal duo – Chris Sanford and Bill Mitchell (Singles: 5 Weeks)

			pos/wks
29 Mar 75	IF	EMI 2282	25 5

Dwight YOAKAM US, male vocalist / instrumentalist – guitar (Singles: 2 Weeks, Albums: 4 Weeks)

			pos/wks
10 Jul 99	CRAZY LITTLE THING CALLED LOVE	Reprise W 497CD	43 2
9 May 87	HILLBILLY DELUXE	Reprise WX 106	51 3
13 Aug 88	BUENAS NOCHES FROM A LONELY ROOM	Reprise WX 193	87 1

YO-HANS See JODE featuring YO-HANS

YOMANDA (see also The CANDY GIRLS; DOROTHY; HI-GATE; CLERGY; Paul MASTERSON presents SUSHI) UK, male DJ / producer – Paul Masterson (Singles: 21 Weeks)

			pos/wks
24 Jul 99 ●	SYNTH & STRINGS	Manifesto FESCD 59	8 10
11 Mar 00	SUNSHINE	Manifesto FESCD 68	16 6
2 Sep 00	ON THE LEVEL	Manifesto FESCD 73	28 2
26 Jul 03	YOU'RE FREE	Incentive CENT 55CDS	22 3

Tukka YOOT See Us3

YORK Germany, male production / instrumental duo – Torsten and Jorg Stenzel (Singles: 21 Weeks)

			pos/wks
9 Oct 99	THE AWAKENING	Manifesto FESCD 60	11 5
10 Jun 00 ●	ON THE BEACH	Manifesto FESCD 70	4 10
18 Nov 00	FAREWELL TO THE MOON	Manifesto FESCD 76	37 2
27 Jan 01	THE FIELDS OF LOVE	Club Tools / Edel 0124095 CLU [1]	16 4

[1] ATB featuring York

YOSH presents LOVEDEEJAY AKEMI Holland, male producer – Yoshida Rosenboom (Singles: 5 Weeks)

			pos/wks
29 Jul 95	IT'S WHAT'S UPFRONT THAT COUNTS	Limbo LIMB 46CD	69 1
2 Dec 95	IT'S WHAT'S UPFRONT THAT COUNTS (re-mix) Limbo LIMB 50CD		31 2
20 Apr 96	THE SCREAMER	Limbo LIMB 54CD	38 2

YOSHIKI See Roger TAYLOR

Singles re-entries are listed as (re), (2re), (3re)…. which signifies that the hit re-entered the chart once, twice or three times…

YOTHU YINDI
Australia, male vocal / instrumental group (Singles: 1 Week) pos/wks

15 Feb 92	TREATY *Hollywood HWD 116*	72 1

Faron YOUNG
US, male vocalist, b. 25 Feb 1932, d. 10 Dec 1996 (Singles: 23 Weeks, Albums: 5 Weeks) pos/wks

15 Jul 72 ●	IT'S FOUR IN THE MORNING *Mercury 6052 140*	3 23
28 Oct 72	IT'S FOUR IN THE MORNING *Mercury 6338 095*	27 5

Jimmy YOUNG
UK, male vocalist (Singles: 88 Weeks) pos/wks

9 Jan 53	FAITH CAN MOVE MOUNTAINS *Decca F 9986*	11 1
21 Aug 53	ETERNALLY *Decca F 10130*	8 9
6 May 55 ★	UNCHAINED MELODY *Decca F 10502*	1 19
16 Sep 55 ★	THE MAN FROM LARAMIE *Decca F 10597*	1 12
23 Dec 55	SOMEONE ON YOUR MIND *Decca F 10640*	13 5
16 Mar 56 ●	CHAIN GANG *Decca F 10694*	9 6
8 Jun 56	WAYWARD WIND *Decca F 10736*	27 1
22 Jun 56	RICH MAN POOR MAN *Decca F 10736*	25 1
28 Sep 56 ●	MORE *Decca F 10774*	4 17
3 May 57	ROUND AND ROUND *Decca F 10875*	30 1
10 Oct 63	MISS YOU *Columbia DB 7119*	15 13
26 Mar 64	UNCHAINED MELODY (re-recording) *Columbia DB 7234*	43 3

'Round and Round' and 'Unchained Melody' on Columbia are with the Michael Sammes Singers

John Paul YOUNG
Australia, male vocalist (Singles: 19 Weeks) pos/wks

29 Apr 78 ●	LOVE IS IN THE AIR *Ariola ARO 117*	5 13
14 Nov 92	LOVE IS IN THE AIR (re-mix) *Columbia 6587697*	49 3
12 Jan 02	LOVE IS IN THE AIR (re-recording) *Positiva CDTIV 166* [1]	25 3

[1] Milk and Sugar vs John Paul Young

Karen YOUNG
UK, female vocalist (Singles: 21 Weeks) pos/wks

6 Sep 69 ●	NOBODY'S CHILD *Major Minor MM 625*	6 21

Karen YOUNG
US, female vocalist, b. 23 Mar 1951, d. 26 Jan 1991 (Singles: 9 Weeks) pos/wks

19 Aug 78	HOT SHOT *Atlantic K 11180*	34 7
24 Feb 79	HOT SHOT (re-issue) *Atlantic LV 8*	75 1
15 Nov 97	HOT SHOT '97 (re-recording) *Distinctive DISNCD 37*	68 1

Neil YOUNG 215 Top 500
(see also CROSBY STILLS NASH and YOUNG) *Single-minded vocalist, guitarist and singer-songwriter, b. 12 Nov 1945, Toronto, Ontario, Canada. Constantly changing musical direction, his roots were in country rock as a member of the Buffalo Springfield and CSN&Y. 'Shakey's' solo activity and work with support bands such as The International Harvesters, The Stray Gators and Crazy Horse has embraced country, punk, and rock and resulted in his oft-used title "The Godfather of Grunge" (Singles: 22 Weeks, Albums: 260 Weeks)* pos/wks

11 Mar 72 ●	HEART OF GOLD *Reprise K 14140* ▲	10 11
6 Jan 79	FOUR STRONG WINDS *Reprise K 14493*	57 4
27 Feb 93	HARVEST MOON *Reprise W 0139CD*	36 3
17 Jul 93	THE NEEDLE AND THE DAMAGE DONE *Reprise W 0191CD*	75 1
30 Oct 93	LONG MAY YOU RUN (LIVE) *Reprise W 0207CD*	71 1
9 Apr 94	PHILADELPHIA *Reprise W 0242CD*	62 2
31 Oct 70 ●	AFTER THE GOLD RUSH *Reprise RSLP 6383*	7 66
4 Mar 72 ★	HARVEST *Reprise K 54005* ▲	1 34
27 Oct 73	TIME FADES AWAY *Warner Bros. K 54010*	20 2
10 Aug 74	ON THE BEACH *Reprise K 54014*	42 2
5 Jul 75	TONIGHT'S THE NIGHT *Reprise K 54040*	48 1
27 Dec 75	ZUMA *Reprise K 54057*	44 2
9 Oct 76	LONG MAY YOU RUN *Reprise K 54081* [1]	12 5
9 Jul 77	AMERICAN STARS 'N BARS *Reprise K 54088*	17 8
17 Dec 77	DECADE *Reprise K 64037*	46 4
28 Oct 78	COMES A TIME *Reprise K 54099*	42 3
14 Jul 79	RUST NEVER SLEEPS *Reprise K 54105* [2]	13 13
1 Dec 79	LIVE RUST *Reprise K 64041* [2]	55 3
15 Nov 80	HAWKS & DOVES *Reprise K 54109*	34 3
14 Nov 81	RE-AC-TOR *Reprise K 54116* [2]	69 3
5 Feb 83	TRANS *Geffen GEF 25019*	29 5
3 Sep 83	EVERYBODY'S ROCKIN' *Geffen GEF 25590* [3]	50 3
14 Sep 85	OLD WAYS *Geffen GEF 26377*	39 3
2 Aug 86	LANDING ON WATER *Geffen 924 1091*	52 2
4 Jul 87	LIFE *Geffen WX 109* [2]	71 1
30 Apr 88	THIS NOTE'S FOR YOU *WEA WX 168* [4]	56 3
21 Oct 89	FREEDOM *Reprise WX 257*	17 5
22 Sep 90	RAGGED GLORY *Reprise WX 374*	15 5

2 Nov 91	WELD *Reprise 7599266711*	20 3
14 Nov 92 ●	HARVEST MOON *Reprise 9362450572*	9 18
23 Jan 93	LUCKY THIRTEEN *Geffen GED 24452*	69 1
26 Jun 93	UNPLUGGED *Reprise 9362453102*	4 13
27 Aug 94 ●	SLEEPS WITH ANGELS *Reprise 9362457492* [2]	2 7
8 Jul 95 ●	MIRROR BALL *Reprise 9362459342*	4 9
6 Jul 96	BROKEN ARROW *Reprise 9362462912* [2]	17 5
28 Jun 97	YEAR OF THE HORSE *Reprise 9362466522* [2]	36 2
6 May 00 ●	SILVER AND GOLD *Reprise 9362473052*	10 4
20 Apr 02	ARE YOU PASSIONATE? *Reprise 9362481112*	24 3
27 Jul 02	DECADE *Reprise 7599272332*	15 13
26 Jul 03	ON THE BEACH *Reprise 9362484972* [2]	42 1
30 Aug 03	GREENDALE *Reprise 9362485432*	24 3
27 Nov 04	GREATEST HITS *Reprise 9362489352*	45 2

[1] The Stills-Young Band [2] Neil Young & Crazy Horse [3] Neil and The Shocking Pinks [4] Neil Young and The Blue Notes

Paul YOUNG 137 Top 500
Soulful-sounding pop singer / songwriter (b. 17 Jan 1956, Bedfordshire, UK) who earlier fronted The Q-Tips and chart act Streetband. This multi-Brit Award winner sold seven million copies of his 'No Parlez' album (including more than one million in the UK) (Singles: 134 Weeks, Albums: 232 Weeks) pos/wks

18 Jun 83 ★	WHEREVER I LAY MY HAT (THAT'S MY HOME) *CBS A 3371* [1]	1 15
10 Sep 83 ●	COME BACK AND STAY *CBS A 3636*	4 9
19 Nov 83 ●	LOVE OF THE COMMON PEOPLE *CBS A 3585*	2 13
13 Oct 84 ●	I'M GONNA TEAR YOUR PLAYHOUSE DOWN *CBS A 4786*	9 7
8 Dec 84 ●	EVERYTHING MUST CHANGE *CBS A 4972*	9 11
9 Mar 85 ●	EVERYTIME YOU GO AWAY *CBS A 6300* ▲	4 11
22 Jun 85	TOMB OF MEMORIES (re) *CBS A 6321*	16 8
4 Oct 86	WONDERLAND *CBS YOUNG 1*	24 5
29 Nov 86	SOME PEOPLE *CBS YOUNG 2*	56 3
7 Feb 87	WHY DOES A MAN HAVE TO BE STRONG? *CBS YOUNG 3*	63 2
12 May 90	SOFTLY WHISPERING I LOVE YOU *CBS YOUNG 4*	21 6
7 Jul 90	OH GIRL *CBS YOUNG 5*	25 6
6 Oct 90	HEAVEN CAN WAIT *CBS YOUNG 6*	71 2
12 Jan 91	CALLING YOU *CBS YOUNG 7*	57 2
30 Mar 91 ●	SENZA UNA DONNA (WITHOUT A WOMAN) *London LON 294* [2]	4 12
10 Aug 91	BOTH SIDES NOW *MCA MCS 1546* [3]	74 1
26 Oct 91	DON'T DREAM IT'S OVER *Columbia 6574117*	20 5
25 Sep 93	NOW I KNOW WHAT MADE OTIS BLUE *Columbia 6596412*	14 7
27 Nov 93	HOPE IN A HOPELESS WORLD *Columbia 6598652*	42 3
23 Apr 94	IT WILL BE YOU *Columbia 6602812*	34 4
17 May 97	I WISH YOU LOVE *East West EW 100CD1*	33 2
30 Jul 83 ★	NO PARLEZ *CBS 25521*	1 119
6 Apr 85 ★	THE SECRET OF ASSOCIATION *CBS 26234* ■	1 49
1 Nov 86 ●	BETWEEN TWO FIRES *CBS 450 1501*	4 17
16 Jun 90 ●	OTHER VOICES *CBS 4669171*	4 11
14 Sep 91 ●	FROM TIME TO TIME – THE SINGLES COLLECTION *Columbia 4688251* ■	1 27
23 Oct 93	THE CROSSING *Columbia 4739282*	27 2
26 Nov 94	REFLECTIONS *Vision VISCD 1*	64 2
31 May 97	PAUL YOUNG *East West 630186192*	39 2
21 Jun 03	THE ESSENTIAL *Sony Music 5122992*	27 3

[1] Paul Young and The Family [2] Zucchero and Paul Young [3] Clannad and Paul Young

Retta YOUNG
US, female vocalist (Singles: 7 Weeks) pos/wks

24 May 75	SENDING OUT AN S.O.S. *All Platinum 6146 305*	28 7

Tracie YOUNG See TRACIE

Will YOUNG 416 Top 500
The first and biggest-selling reality pop TV show contestant in the UK, b. 20 Jan 1979, Berkshire, UK. Only Elton John's 'Candle in the Wind 1997' topped the 1,108,269 copies his debut single sold in its first week. He won a Brit award in 2003 for British Breakthrough Artist (Singles: 100 Weeks, Albums: 66 Weeks) pos/wks

9 Mar 02 ★	EVERGREEN / ANYTHING IS POSSIBLE *S 74321926142* ◆ ■	1 16
8 Jun 02 ★	LIGHT MY FIRE (re) *S 74321943002* ■	1 20
5 Oct 02 ★	THE LONG AND WINDING ROAD / SUSPICIOUS MINDS *S 74321965972* [1] ■	1 18
30 Nov 02 ●	DON'T LET ME DOWN / YOU AND I (re) *S 74321981262*	2 13
6 Dec 03 ★	LEAVE RIGHT NOW *S 82876578562* ■	1 18
27 Mar 04 ●	YOUR GAME *S 82876603622*	3 9
17 Jul 04 ●	FRIDAY'S CHILD *S 82876623932*	4 6
19 Oct 02 ★	FROM NOW ON *S 74321969592* ■	1 25
13 Dec 03 ★	FRIDAY'S CHILD *S 82876557462* ◆ ■	1 41

[1] Will Young and Gareth Gates / Gareth Gates

YOUNG and COMPANY
US, male / female vocal / instrumental group (Singles: 12 Weeks) pos/wks

1 Nov 80	I LIKE (WHAT YOU'RE DOING TO ME) *Excalibur EXC 501*	20	12

YOUNG AND MOODY BAND
UK, male vocal / instrumental group (Singles: 4 Weeks) pos/wks

10 Oct 81	DON'T DO THAT *Bronze BRO 130*	63	4

YOUNG BLACK TEENAGERS
US, male rap group (Singles: 3 Weeks) pos/wks

9 Apr 94	TAP THE BOTTLE *MCA MCSTD 1967*	39	3

YOUNG BUCK
US, male rapper – David Brown (Singles: 1 Week, Albums: 3 Weeks) pos/wks

23 Oct 04	LET ME IN *Interscope 9864517*	62	1
4 Sep 04	STRAIGHT OUTTA CA$HVILLE *Interscope 9863495*	22	3

YOUNG DISCIPLES
UK / US, male / female vocal / instrumental group (Singles: 17 Weeks, Albums: 5 Weeks) pos/wks

13 Oct 90	GET YOURSELF TOGETHER *Talkin Loud TLK 2*	68	1
23 Feb 91	APPARENTLY NOTHIN' (re) *Talkin Loud TLK 5*	13	11
5 Oct 91	GET YOURSELF TOGETHER (re-issue) *Talkin Loud TLK 15*	65	2
5 Sep 92	YOUNG DISCIPLES (EP) *Talkin Loud TLKX 18*	48	3
31 Aug 91	ROAD TO FREEDOM *Talkin Loud 5100971*	21	5

'Apparently Nothin' first peaked at No.46 in Feb 1991, making its peak position only on re-entry in Aug 1991. Tracks on Young Disciples (EP): Move On / Freedom / All I Have In Me / Move On (re-mix)

YOUNG GODS
Switzerland, male vocal / instrumental group (Albums: 1 Week) pos/wks

15 Feb 92	TV SKY *Play It Again Sam BIAS 201CD*	54	1

YOUNG HEART ATTACK
US, male / female vocal / instrumental group (Singles: 2 Weeks, Albums: 1 Week) pos/wks

10 Apr 04	TOMMY SHOTS *XL Recordings XLS 183CD*	54	1
17 Jul 04	STARLITE *XL Recordings XLS 191CD*	69	1
24 Apr 04	MOUTHFUL OF LOVE *XL Recordings XLCD 173*	71	1

YOUNG IDEA
UK, male vocal duo – Tony Cox and Douglas MacCrae-Brown (Singles: 6 Weeks) pos/wks

29 Jun 67	● WITH A LITTLE HELP FROM MY FRIENDS *Columbia DB 8205*	10	6

YOUNG MC
US, male rapper – Marvin Young (Singles: 7 Weeks) pos/wks

15 Jul 89	BUST A MOVE *Delicious Vinyl BRW 137*	73	2
17 Feb 90	PRINCIPAL'S OFFICE *Delicious Vinyl BRW 161*	54	3
17 Aug 91	THAT'S THE WAY LOVE GOES *Capitol CL 623*	65	2

YOUNG OFFENDERS
Ireland, male vocal / instrumental group (Singles: 1 Week) pos/wks

7 Mar 98	THAT'S WHY WE LOSE CONTROL *Columbia 6651942*	60	1

YOUNG ONES See Cliff RICHARD

YOUNG RASCALS
US, male vocal / instrumental group (Singles: 17 Weeks) pos/wks

25 May 67	● GROOVIN' *Atlantic 584 111* ▲	8	13
16 Aug 67	A GIRL LIKE YOU *Atlantic 584 128*	37	4

Leon YOUNG STRING CHORALE See Acker BILK

YOUNG VOICES CHOIR See DECLAN

Sydney YOUNGBLOOD
US, male vocalist – Sydney Ford (Singles: 31 Weeks, Albums: 17 Weeks) pos/wks

26 Aug 89	● IF ONLY I COULD *Circa YR 34*	3	14
9 Dec 89	SIT AND WAIT *Circa YR 40*	16	8
31 Mar 90	I'D RATHER GO BLIND *Circa YR 43*	44	5
29 Jun 91	HOOKED ON YOU *Circa YR 65*	72	2
20 Mar 93	ANYTHING *RCA 74321138672*	48	2
28 Oct 89	FEELING FREE *Circa CIRCA 9*	23	17

YOUNGER YOUNGER 28'S
UK, male / female vocal / instrumental group (Singles: 1 Week) pos/wks

5 Jun 99	WE'RE GOING OUT *V2 VVR 5006943*	61	1

YOURCODENAMEIS:MILO
UK, male vocal / instrumental group (Singles: 1 Week) pos/wks

16 Oct 04	SCHTEEVE *Fiction 9868526*	58	1

Z FACTOR
(see also HED BOYS; Li KWAN; Joey NEGRO; JAKATTA; AKABU featuring Linda CLIFFORD; PHASE II; IL PADRINOS featuring Jocelyn BROWN) *UK, male DJ / producer – Dave Lee (Singles: 2 Weeks)* pos/wks

21 Feb 98	GOTTA KEEP PUSHIN' *ffrr FCD 329*	47	1
17 Nov 01	RIDE THE RHYTHM *Direction 6718482*	52	1

Z2
UK, male production duo (Singles: 1 Week) pos/wks

26 Feb 00	I WANT YOU *Platipus PLATCD 67*	61	1

'I Want You' features vocalist Alison Rivers

Helmut ZACHARIAS ORCHESTRA
Germany, orchestra – leader b. 27 Jan 1920, d. 28 Feb 2002 (Singles: 11 Weeks) pos/wks

29 Oct 64	● TOKYO MELODY *Polydor NH 52341*	9	11

Pia ZADORA
US, female vocalist / actor – Pia Schipani (Singles: 6 Weeks) pos/wks

27 Oct 84	WHEN THE RAIN BEGINS TO FALL *Arista ARIST 584* [1]	68	2
12 Nov 88	DANCE OUT OF MY HEAD *Epic 6528867* [2]	65	4

[1] Jermaine Jackson and Pia Zadora [2] Pia

ZAGER and EVANS
US, male vocal duo – Denny Zager and Rick Evans (Singles: 13 Weeks) pos/wks

9 Aug 69	★ IN THE YEAR 2525 (EXORDIUM AND TERMINUS) *RCA 1860* ▲	1	13

Michael ZAGER BAND
US, male / female vocal / instrumental group (Singles: 12 Weeks) pos/wks

1 Apr 78	● LET'S ALL CHANT *Private Stock PVT 143*	8	12

Gheorghe ZAMFIR
Romania, male instrumentalist – pipes (Singles: 9 Weeks) pos/wks

21 Aug 76	● (LIGHT OF EXPERIENCE) DOINA DE JALE *Epic EPC 4310*	4	9

Tommy ZANG
US, male vocalist (Singles: 1 Week) pos/wks

16 Feb 61	HEY GOOD LOOKING *Polydor NH 66957*	45	1

ZAPP
US, male vocal / instrumental group (Singles: 6 Weeks) pos/wks

25 Jan 86	IT DOESN'T REALLY MATTER *Warner Bros. W 8879*	57	3
24 May 86	COMPUTER LOVE (PART 1) *Warner Bros. W 8805*	64	3

Frank ZAPPA
(see also MOTHERS OF INVENTION) *US, male vocalist / multi-instrumentalist, b. 21 Dec 1940, d. 4 Dec 1993 (Albums: 57 Weeks)* pos/wks

28 Feb 70	● HOT RATS *Reprise RSLP 6356*	9	27
19 Dec 70	CHUNGA'S REVENGE *Reprise RSLP 2030*	43	1
6 May 78	ZAPPA IN NEW YORK *Discreet K 69204*	55	1
10 Mar 79	SHEIK YERBOUTI *CBS 88339*	32	7

13 Oct 79	JOE'S GARAGE ACT I *CBS 86101*	62	3
19 Jan 80	JOE'S GARAGE ACTS II & III *CBS 88475*	75	1
16 May 81	TINSEL TOWN REBELLION *CBS 88516*	55	4
24 Oct 81	YOU ARE WHAT YOU IS *CBS 88560*	51	2
19 Jun 82	SHIP ARRIVING TOO LATE TO SAVE A DROWNING WITCH *CBS 85804*	61	4
18 Jun 83	THE MAN FROM UTOPIA *CBS 25251*	87	1
27 Oct 84	THEM OR US *EMI FZD 1*	53	2
30 Apr 88	GUITAR *Zappa ZAPPA 6*	82	2
2 Sep 95	STRICTLY COMMERCIAL – THE BEST OF FRANK ZAPPA *Rykodisc RCD 40600*	45	2

Francesco ZAPPALA
Italy, male producer (Singles: 3 Weeks) pos/wks

10 Aug 91	WE GOTTA DO IT *Fourth & Broadway BRW 225* [1]	57	2
2 May 92	NO WAY OUT *PWL Continental PWL 230*	69	1

[1] DJ Professor featuring Francesco Zappala

Lena ZAVARONI
UK, female vocalist, b. 4 Nov 1963, d. 1 Oct 1999 (Singles: 14 Weeks, Albums: 5 Weeks) pos/wks

9 Feb 74	● MA! (HE'S MAKING EYES AT ME) *Philips 6006 367*	10	11
1 Jun 74	(YOU'VE GOT) PERSONALITY *Philips 6006 391*	33	3
23 Mar 74	● MA *Philips 6308 201*	8	5

ZED BIAS
UK, male vocal / production group (Singles: 4 Weeks) pos/wks

15 Jul 00	NEIGHBOURHOOD *Locked On / XL Recordings LOX 122CD*	25	4

ZEE
UK, female vocalist – Lesley Cowling (Singles: 4 Weeks) pos/wks

6 Jul 96	DREAMTIME *Perfecto PERF 122CD*	31	2
22 Mar 97	SAY MY NAME *Perfecto PERF 135CD*	36	1
7 Feb 98	BUTTERFLY *Perfecto PERF 154CD 1* [1]	41	1

[1] Tilt featuring Zee

ZENA (see also MIS-TEEQ)
UK, female vocalist – Zena McNally (Singles: 2 Weeks) pos/wks

19 Jul 03	LET'S GET THIS PARTY STARTED *Serious SER 69CD*	69	1
14 Aug 04	BEEN AROUND THE WORLD *Mercury 9867104* [1]	44	1

[1] Zena featuring Vybz Kartel

The ZEPHYRS
UK, male vocal / instrumental group (Singles: 1 Week) pos/wks

18 Mar 65	SHE'S LOST YOU *Columbia DB 7481*	48	1

ZERO B
UK, male instrumentalist – keyboards – Peter Riding (Singles: 6 Weeks) pos/wks

22 Feb 92	THE EP (BRAND NEW MIXES) *Ffrreedom TAB 102*	32	4
24 Jul 93	RECONNECTION (EP) *Internal LIECD 6*	54	2

Tracks on The EP (Brand New Mixes): Lock Up / Spinning Wheel / Module / Tracks on Reconnection (EP): Love to Be in Love (2 mixes) / Lock Up (re-mix) / Ou Est Le Spoon

ZERO 7
UK, male production duo – Henry Binns and Sam Hardaker (Singles: 6 Weeks, Albums: 61 Weeks) pos/wks

18 Aug 01	DESTINY *Ultimate Dilemma UDRCDS 043* [1]	30	3
17 Nov 01	IN THE WAITING LINE *Ultimate Dilemma UDRCDS 045*	47	1
30 Mar 02	DISTRACTIONS *Ultimate Dilemma UDRCDS 046* [2]	45	1
29 May 04	SOMERSAULT *Ultimate Dilemma EW 290CD* [2]	56	1
5 May 01	SIMPLE THINGS *Ultimate Dilemma UDRCD 016*	28	43
13 Mar 04	● WHEN IT FALLS *Ultimate Dilemma 5046709875*	3	18

[1] Zero 7 featuring Sia and Sophie [2] Zero 7 featuring Sia

ZERO VU featuring Lorna B
UK, male / female vocal / production group (Singles: 1 Week) pos/wks

15 Mar 97	FEELS SO GOOD *Avex UK AVEXCD 53*	69	1

ZERO ZERO
UK, male instrumental / production duo (Singles: 1 Week) pos/wks

10 Aug 91	ZEROXED *Kickin KICK 9*	71	1

ZEUS *See GENERAL LEVY*

Warren ZEVON
US, male vocalist / instrumentalist – keyboards, b. 24 Jan 1947, d. 7 Sep 2003 (Albums: 1 Week) pos/wks

27 Sep 03	THE WIND *Rykodisc RCD 17001*	57	1

ZHANÉ
US, female vocal duo – Renee Neufville and Jean Norris (Singles: 18 Weeks, Albums: 1 Week) pos/wks

11 Sep 93	HEY MR DJ (re) *Epic 6596102*	26	5
19 Mar 94	GROOVE THANG *Motown TMGCD 1423*	34	3
20 Aug 94	VIBE *Motown TMGCD 1430*	67	1
25 Feb 95	SHAME *Jive JIVECD 372*	66	1
21 Sep 96	IT'S A PARTY *Elektra EKR 226CD* [1]	23	2
8 Mar 97	4 MORE *Tommy Boy TBCD 7779A* [2]	52	1
26 Apr 97	REQUEST LINE *Motown 8606452*	22	3
30 Aug 97	CRUSH *Motown 5716712*	44	1
11 Sep 99	JAMBOREE *Arista 74321692882* [3]	51	1
10 May 97	SATURDAY NIGHT *Motown 5305882*	52	1

[1] Busta Rhymes featuring Zhané [2] De La Soul featuring Zhané [3] Naughty By Nature featuring Zhané

ZIG and ZAG
Zog / Ireland, male puppet duo (Singles: 12 Weeks) pos/wks

24 Dec 94	● THEM GIRLS THEM GIRLS *RCA 74321251042*	5	9
1 Jul 95	HANDS UP! HANDS UP! *RCA 74321284392*	21	3

ZIGZAG JIVE FLUTES *See ELIAS and his ZIG-ZAG JIVE FLUTES*

Hans ZIMMER
Germany, male composer (Albums: 20 Weeks) pos/wks

27 May 00	GLADIATOR (FILM SOUNDTRACK) *Decca 4670942* [1]	17	16
3 Mar 01	HANNIBAL (FILM SOUNDTRACK) *Decca 4676962*	74	2
16 Jun 01	PEARL HARBOR (FILM SOUNDTRACK) *Hollywood / Warner Bros. 9362481132* [2]	50	2

[1] Hans Zimmer and Lisa Gerrard [2] Hans Zimmer with orchestra conducted by Gavin Greenaway

ZION TRAIN
UK, male / female vocal / instrumental group (Singles: 1 Week, Albums: 1 Week) pos/wks

27 Jul 96	RISE *China WOKCD 2085*	61	1
13 Jul 96	GROW TOGETHER *China WOLCD 1071*	56	1

ZODIAC MINDWARP and The LOVE REACTION
UK, male / female vocal / instrumental group (Singles: 11 Weeks, Albums: 5 Weeks) pos/wks

9 May 87	PRIME MOVER *Mercury ZOD 1*	18	6
14 Nov 87	BACKSEAT EDUCATION *Mercury ZOD 2*	49	3
2 Apr 88	PLANET GIRL *Mercury ZOD 3*	63	2
5 Mar 88	TATTOOED BEAT MESSIAH *Mercury ZODLP 1*	20	5

ZODIACS *See Maurice WILLIAMS and The ZODIACS*

ZOE
UK, female vocalist – Zoe Pollock (Singles: 22 Weeks, Albums: 1 Week) pos/wks

10 Nov 90	SUNSHINE ON A RAINY DAY *M&G MAGS 6*	53	5
24 Aug 91	● SUNSHINE ON A RAINY DAY (re-mix) *M&G MAGS 14*	4	11
2 Nov 91	LIGHTNING *M&G MAGS 18*	37	4
29 Feb 92	HOLY DAYS *M&G MAGS 21*	72	2
7 Dec 91	SCARLET RED AND BLUE *M&G 5114431*	67	1

Rob ZOMBIE (see also WHITE ZOMBIE)
US, male vocalist – Robert Cummings (Singles: 2 Weeks, Albums: 2 Weeks) pos/wks

26 Dec 98	DRAGULA *Geffen GFSTD 22367*	44	2
5 Sep 98	HELLBILLY DELUXE *Geffen GED 25212*	37	2

ZOMBIE NATION
Germany, male production duo – Florian 'Splank' Senfter and Emanuel 'Mooner' Günther (Singles: 16 Weeks) pos/wks

2 Sep 00	KERNKRAFT 400 (IMPORT) *TRANSK TRANSK 002*	61	1
30 Sep 00	● KERNKRAFT 400 *Data DATA 11CDS*	2	15

The ZOMBIES
UK, male vocal / instrumental group – includes Rod Argent and Colin Blunstone (Singles: 16 Weeks) pos/wks

13 Aug 64	SHE'S NOT THERE *Decca F 11940*	12	11
11 Feb 65	TELL HER NO *Decca F 12072*	42	5

ZOO EXPERIENCE featuring DESTRY
UK, male production group and US, male vocalist (Singles: 1 Week) pos/wks

22 Aug 92	LOVE'S GOTTA HOLD ON ME *Cooltempo COOL 261*	66	1

ZUCCHERO *Italy, male vocalist / instrumentalist – guitar –*
Adelmo Fornaciari (Singles: 24 Weeks, Albums: 4 Weeks) pos/wks

30 Mar 91 ●	SENZA UNA DONNA (WITHOUT A WOMAN) *London LON 294* [1]	4	12
18 Jan 92	DIAMANTE *London LON 313* [2]	44	7
24 Oct 92	MISERERE *London LON 329* [3]	15	5
18 May 91	ZUCCHERO *A&M EVERY 1*	29	4

[1] Zucchero and Paul Young [2] Zucchero with Randy Crawford [3] Zucchero with Luciano Pavarotti

The ZUTONS *UK, male vocal / instrumental*
group (Singles: 12 Weeks, Albums: 25 Weeks) pos/wks

31 Jan 04	PRESSURE POINT ... *Deltasonic DLTCDV 016*	19	3
17 Apr 04	YOU WILL YOU WON'T ... *Deltasonic DLTCD 020*	22	3
3 Jul 04	REMEMBER ME ... *Deltasonic DLTCD 2024*	39	2
30 Oct 04	DON'T EVER THINK (TOO MUCH) ... *Deltasonic DLTCD 2026*	15	3
25 Dec 04	CONFUSION ... *Deltasonic DLTCD 030*	37	1+
1 May 04	WHO KILLED ... THE ZUTONS? *Deltasonic DLTCD 019*	13	25+

ZWAN (see also The SMASHING PUMPKINS) *US, male vocal /*
instrumental group (Singles: 3 Weeks, Albums: 2 Weeks) pos/wks

8 Mar 03	HONESTLY *Reprise W 600CD*	28	2
14 Jun 03	LYRIC *Reprise W 607*	44	1
22 Feb 03	MARY STAR OF THE SEA *Reprise WB 484252*	33	2

ZZ TOP 187 Top 500
Low-slung, guitar-driven blues-rock trio formed in 1969 in Houston, Texas,
US: long-bearded duo Billy Gibbons (v/g), Dusty Hill (v/b) and clean-shaven
Frank Beard (d). Hugely popular stadium-packing festival headliners in the
1980s. Act, who joined the Rock and Roll Hall of Fame in 2004, were named
to ensure they would be the last act in record racks and hit books (Singles:
94 Weeks, Albums: 211 Weeks) pos/wks

3 Sep 83 ●	GIMME ALL YOUR LOVIN' (re) *Warner Bros. W 9693*	10	18
26 Nov 83	SHARP DRESSED MAN (re) *Warner Bros. W 9576*	22	13
31 Mar 84	TV DINNERS *Warner Bros. W 9334*	67	3
23 Feb 85	LEGS *Warner Bros. W 9272*	16	7
13 Jul 85	THE ZZ TOP SUMMER HOLIDAY (EP) *Warner Bros. W 8946*	51	5
19 Oct 85	SLEEPING BAG *Warner Bros. W 2001*	27	5
15 Feb 86	STAGES *Warner Bros. W 2002*	43	3
19 Apr 86	ROUGH BOY *Warner Bros. W 2003*	23	9
4 Oct 86	VELCRO FLY *Warner Bros. W 8650*	54	3
21 Jul 90	DOUBLEBACK *Warner Bros. W 9812*	29	6
13 Apr 91	MY HEAD'S IN MISSISSIPPI *Warner Bros. W 0009*	37	5
11 Apr 92 ●	VIVA LAS VEGAS *Warner Bros. W 0098*	10	7
20 Jun 92	ROUGH BOY (re-issue) *Warner Bros. W 0111*	49	3
29 Jan 94	PINCUSHION *RCA 74321184732*	15	3
7 May 94	BREAKAWAY *RCA 74321192282*	60	1
29 Jun 96	WHAT'S UP WITH THAT *RCA 74321394822*	58	1
16 Oct 99	GIMME ALL YOUR LOVIN' 2000 *Riverhorse RIVHCD 2* [1]	28	1
12 Jul 75	FANDANGO! *London SHU 8482*	60	1
8 Aug 81	EL LOCO *Warner Bros. K 56929*	88	2
30 Apr 83 ●	ELIMINATOR *Warner Bros. W 3774*	3	137
9 Nov 85 ●	AFTERBURNER *Warner Bros. WX 27*	2	40
27 Oct 90	RECYCLER *Warner Bros. WX 390*	8	7
25 Apr 92 ●	GREATEST HITS *Warner Bros. 7599268462*	5	17
5 Feb 94 ●	ANTENNA *RCA 74321152602*	3	5
21 Sep 96	RHYTHMEEN *RCA 74321394662*	32	2

[1] Martay featuring ZZ Top

'Gimme All Your Lovin' debuted at No.61 in 1983, only hitting its peak position
on re-entry in Oct 1984. 'Sharp Dressed Man' debuted at No.53 in Nov 1983,
only hitting its peak position in Dec 1984. Tracks on The ZZ Top Summer Holiday
(EP): Tush / Got Me Under Pressure / Beer Drinkers and Hell Raisers / I'm Bad,
I'm Nationwide

WHAT'S YOUR FAVOURITE ALBUM?

Sprinkled around the book are the favourite album lists from a variety of music celebrities. Now it's your turn. We want you, the reader, to choose your Top 10 albums from the hit LPs listed in these pages. Your votes will then contribute towards the ultimate Top 100 Albums chart.

By registering your votes you could win a gold disc of your own favourite album or 50 runner-up prizes of British Hit Singles & Albums t-shirts, mugs and badges. Your votes will help create a music expert's Top 100 Albums in celebration of the 50th anniversary of the UK albums chart in 2006.

Here's how to vote.

Choose your favourite Top 10 albums in one to ten order. Any album that has made the chart qualifies, although greatest hits and compilation LPs are ruled out.

Then, either post or email your list to the addresses below. Alternatively, you can enter your Top 10 by visiting our specially designated website page: www.bibleofpop.com/vote

The Editor
British Hit Singles & Albums
Guinness World Records
338 Euston Road
London NW1 3BD

Email editor@bibleofpop.com

TOP 100 ALBUMS / Voting Form

1. DÉJÀ VU – Crosby, Stills, Nash and Young
2. THE GOOD WILL OUT – Embrace
3. HOMEWORK – Daft Punk
4. EXILE ON MAIN STREET – The Rolling Stones
5. THE LOW END THEORY – A Tribe Called Quest
6. MCMXC A.D. – THE LIMITED EDITION – Enigma
7. SURF'S UP – The Beach Boys
8. BITCHES BREW – Miles Davis
9. THRILLER – Michael Jackson
10. HAVE A NICE DAY – Roxette

The complete list of every song that has ever made the singles chart. Use this section when you remember the song but can't recall which act or acts charted with it.

THE GROUP OF WINNERS AT THE 1978 DAILY MIRROR BRITISH ROCK AND POP AWARDS. THE BARRON KNIGHTS, ELECTRIC LIGHT ORCHESTRA, NICK LOWE, LEO SAYER, IAN DURY AND ROBIN GIBB ALL LOOK SUITABLY PLEASED WITH THEMSELVES, WHILE GERRY RAFFERTY (SECOND FROM LEFT) LOOKS GENUINELY STUNNED TO HAVE WON BEST SINGLE OF THE YEAR WITH 'BAKER STREET'

⬈ HOW TO USE THE SONG TITLE INDEX

This section of the book contains an alphabetical index of every hit song since 1952 in order. The song title is listed first, followed by the act name. Bold capital letters indicate where to look up act names alphabetically in the A-Z by artist section.

Songs with the same title but which are completely different in content are differentiated by a letter in brackets after the title: song [A], song [B], song [C], etc. A good example is the title 'AGAIN' as there are three different hits of that name, [A] by Jimmy Tarbuck, [B] by Janet Jackson and [C] by Juliet Roberts.

Cover versions of the same song share the same letter throughout. A good example of this is 'AIN'T NO SUNSHINE'. [A] Michael Jackson, [A] Sivuca and [A] Ladysmith Black Mambazo have all recorded the same song. Note that if the original version of a cover was never a chart hit, it will not be listed. In this case the original which failed to chart was recorded by Bill Withers and, therefore, finds no place in our book.

( ) — Sigur ROS
A-BA-NI-BI —
  Izhar COHEN and the ALPHA-BETA
'A' BOMB IN WARDOUR STREET — The JAM
THE A TEAM — Mike POST
AAAH D YAAA — GOATS
AARON'S PARTY (COME GET IT) —
  Aaron CARTER
ABACAB — GENESIS
ABACUS (WHEN I FALL IN LOVE) — AXUS
ABANDON [A] — DARE
ABANDON [B] — THAT PETROL EMOTION
ABANDON SHIP — BLAGGERS I.T.A.
ABBA-ESQUE (EP) — ERASURE
THE ABBEY ROAD EP — SPIRITUALIZED
ABC — The JACKSON FIVE
ABC AND D ... — BLUE BAMBOO
A.B.C. (FALLING IN LOVE'S NOT EASY) —
  DIRECT DRIVE
ABIDE WITH ME [A] — INSPIRATIONAL CHOIR
ABIDE WITH ME [A] — Vic REEVES
ABOUT LOVE — Roy DAVIS JR
ABOUT 3AM — DARK STAR
ABOVE THE CLOUDS — Paul WELLER
ABRACADABRA — Steve MILLER BAND
ABRAHAM, MARTIN AND JOHN — Marvin GAYE
ABSENT FRIENDS — The DIVINE COMEDY
ABSOLUTE [A] — SCRITTI POLITTI
ABSOLUT(E) [B] — Claudia BRÜCKEN
ABSOLUTE AFFIRMATION — RADIO 4
ABSOLUTE BEGINNERS [A] — The JAM
ABSOLUTE BEGINNERS [B] — David BOWIE
ABSOLUTE E-SENSUAL — Jaki GRAHAM
ABSOLUTE REALITY — The ALARM
ABSOLUTELY EVERYBODY —Vanessa AMOROSI
ABSOLUTELY FABULOUS —
  ABSOLUTELY FABULOUS
ABSTAIN — FIVE THIRTY
ABSURD — FLUKE
ABUSE ME — SILVERCHAIR
ACAPULCO 1922 —
  Kenny BALL and his JAZZMEN
ACCELERATE — SKIN UP
ACCELERATOR — PRIMAL SCREAM
ACCESS — DJ MISJAH and DJ TIM
ACCIDENT OF BIRTH — Bruce DICKINSON
ACCIDENT PRONE — STATUS QUO
ACCIDENT WAITING TO HAPPEN (EP) —
  Billy BRAGG
ACCIDENTALLY IN LOVE — COUNTING CROWS
ACCIDENTS — THUNDERCLAP NEWMAN
ACCIDENTS WILL HAPPEN —
  Elvis COSTELLO and the ATTRACTIONS
AC/DC — X-PRESS 2
ACE OF SPADES — MOTÖRHEAD
ACES HIGH — IRON MAIDEN
ACHILLES HEEL — TOPLOADER
ACHY BREAKY HEART [A] — Billy Ray CYRUS
ACHY BREAKY HEART [A] — Alvin and the CHIPMUNKS
  featuring Billy Ray CYRUS
ACID LAB — Alex REECE
ACID MAN — JOLLY ROGER
ACID TRAK — DILLINJA
ACKEE 1-2-3 — The BEAT
ACPERIENCE — HARDFLOOR
ACROBATS (LOOKING FOR BALANCE) — MOONY
ACT OF WAR — Elton JOHN and Millie JACKSON
ACTION [A] — The SWEET
ACTION [A] — DEF LEPPARD
ACTION [B] — SAINT ETIENNE
ACTION AND DRAMA — BIS

ACTIV 8 (COME WITH ME) — ALTERN 8
ACTIVATED — Gerald ALSTON
ACTUALLY IT'S DARKNESS — IDLEWILD
ADDAMS FAMILY (WHOOMP!) — TAG TEAM
ADDAMS GROOVE — HAMMER
ADDICTED [A] — SIMPLE PLAN
ADDICTED [B] — ENRIQUE IGLESIAS
ADDICTED TO BASS — PURETONE
ADDICTED TO LOVE [A] — Robert PALMER
ADDICTED TO LOVE (LIVE) [A] — Tina TURNER
ADDICTED TO LOVE [A] —
  SHAKE B4 USE vs Robert PALMER
ADDICTED TO YOU — Alec EMPIRE
ADDICTION — The ALMIGHTY
ADDICTIVE — TRUTH HURTS featuring RAKIM
ADELANTE — SASH!
ADIA — Sarah McLACHLAN
A.D.I.D.A.S. [A] — KORN
A.D.I.D.A.S. [B] —
  KILLER MIKE featuring BIG BOI
ADIDAS WORLD — Edwyn COLLINS
ADIEMUS — ADIEMUS
ADIOS AMIGO — Jim REEVES
THE ADORATION WALTZ — David WHITFIELD
  with the Roland SHAW ORCHESTRA
ADORATIONS — KILLING JOKE
ADORE — Joe ROBERTS
ADORED AND EXPLORED — Marc ALMOND
ADRENALIN (EP) — N-JOI
ADRIENNE — The CALLING
ADRIFT (CAST YOUR MIND) — ANTARCTICA
ADULT EDUCATION —
  Daryl HALL and John OATES
THE ADVENTURES OF THE LOVE CRUSADER —
  Sarah BRIGHTMAN and the STARSHIP TROOPERS
ADVICE FOR THE YOUNG AT HEART —
  TEARS FOR FEARS
AERIALS — SYSTEM OF A DOWN
AERODYNAMIK — KRAFTWERK
AEROPLANE — RED HOT CHILI PEPPERS
THE AEROPLANE SONG — STRAW
AFFAIR — CHERRELLE
AFFIRMATION — SAVAGE GARDEN
AFRAID — MÖTLEY CRÜE
AFRICA — TOTO
AFRICAN AND WHITE — CHINA CRISIS
AFRICAN DREAM —
  Wasis DIOP featuring Lena FIAGBE
AFRICAN HORIZON — MYSTICA
AFRICAN REIGN — DEEP C
AFRICAN WALTZ —
  Johnny DANKWORTH and his ORCHESTRA
AFRIKA — HISTORY featuring Q-TEE
AFRIKA SHOX — LEFTFIELD / BAMBAATAA
AFRO DIZZI ACT — CRY SISCO!
AFRO KING — EMF
AFRO PUFFS — LADY OF RAGE
AFRO SLEEZE — ROACH MOTEL
AFRODISIAC [A] — POWDER
AFRODISIAC [B] — BRANDY
THE AFRO-LEFT EP —
  LEFTFIELD featuring DJUM DJUM
AFTER A FASHION —Midge URE and Mick KARN
AFTER ALL [A] — FRANK AND WALTERS
AFTER ALL [A] — DELERIUM featuring JAEL
AFTER ALL THESE YEARS — FOSTER and ALLEN
AFTER HOURS — The BLUETONES
AFTER LOVE — BLANK & JONES
AFTER THE FIRE — Roger DALTREY
AFTER THE GOLDRUSH — PRELUDE
AFTER THE LOVE — JESUS LOVES YOU

AFTER THE LOVE HAS GONE [A] —
  EARTH WIND AND FIRE
AFTER THE LOVE HAS GONE [A] — DAMAGE
AFTER THE LOVE HAS GONE [B] — PRINCESS
AFTER THE LOVE HAS GONE [C] — STEPS
AFTER THE RAIN — TITIYO
AFTER THE RAIN HAS FALLEN — STING
AFTER THE WAR — Gary MOORE
AFTER THE WATERSHED — CARTER —
  THE UNSTOPPABLE SEX MACHINE
AFTER YOU'RE GONE (I'LL STILL BE LOVING YOU) —
  ONE TRUE VOICE
AFTER YOU'VE GONE — Alice BABS
AFTERGLOW — The MISSION
AFTERGLOW OF YOUR LOVE —
  The SMALL FACES
AFTERMATH [A] — NIGHTMARES ON WAX
AFTERMATH [B] — TRICKY
AFTERMATH [C] — R.E.M.
AFTERNOON DELIGHT —
  STARLAND VOCAL BAND
AFTERNOON OF THE RHINO —
  Mike POST COALITION
(AFTERNOON) SOAPS — ARAB STRAP
AFTERNOONS & COFFEESPOONS —
  CRASH TEST DUMMIES
AGADOO — BLACK LACE
AGAIN [A] — Jimmy TARBUCK
AGAIN [B] — Janet JACKSON
AGAIN [C] — Juliet ROBERTS
AGAIN AND AGAIN — STATUS QUO
AGAINST ALL ODDS [A] —
  Mariah CAREY featuring WESTLIFE
AGAINST ALL ODDS
  (TAKE A LOOK AT ME NOW) [A] — Phil COLLINS
AGAINST THE WIND — Maire BRENNAN
AGE AIN'T NOTHING BUT A NUMBER — AALIYAH
AGE OF LONELINESS — ENIGMA
AGE OF LOVE [A] — AGE OF LOVE
THE AGE OF LOVE — THE REMIXES [A] —
  AGE OF LOVE
AGE OF PANIC — SENSER
AGENT DAN — AGENT PROVOCATEUR
AGNES, QUEEN OF SORROW —
  BONNIE "PRINCE" BILLY
AHORA ES (NOW IS THE TIME) — 2 IN A ROOM
AI NO CORRIDA (I-NO-KO-REE-DA) —
  Quincy JONES featuring DUNE
AIKEA-GUINEA — COCTEAU TWINS
AIN'T COMPLAINING — STATUS QUO
AIN'T DOIN' NOTHIN' —
  Jet BRONX and the FORBIDDEN
AIN'T GOIN' TO GOA — ALABAMA 3
AIN'T GOING DOWN — Garth BROOKS
AIN'T GONNA BE THAT WAY — Marv JOHNSON
AIN'T GONNA BUMP NO MORE (WITH NO BIG FAT
  WOMAN) — Joe TEX
AIN'T GONNA CRY AGAIN — Peter COX
AIN'T GONNA WASH FOR A WEEK —
  BROOK BROTHERS
AIN'T GOT A CLUE — LURKERS
AIN'T GOT NO — I GOT LIFE — Nina SIMONE
AIN'T IT FUN — GUNS N' ROSES
AIN'T IT FUNNY — Jennifer LOPEZ
AIN'T LOVE A BITCH — Rod STEWART
AIN'T MISBEHAVIN' [A] — Johnnie RAY
AIN'T MISBEHAVIN' [A] —
  Tommy BRUCE and the BRUISERS
AIN'T MY BEATING HEART — TEN SHARP
AIN'T NO CASANOVA — SINCLAIR
AIN'T NO DOUBT — Jimmy NAIL

AIN'T NO LOVE (AIN'T NO USE) [A] —
  SUB SUB featuring Melanie WILLIAMS
AIN'T NO LOVE (AIN'T NO USE) [A] —
  SODA CLUB featuring Ashley JADE
AIN'T NO LOVE IN THE HEART OF THE CITY —
  WHITESNAKE
AIN'T NO MAN — Dina CARROLL
AIN'T NO MOUNTAIN HIGH ENOUGH [A] —
  Diana ROSS
AIN'T NO MOUNTAIN HIGH ENOUGH [A] —
  REMEMBER ME (MEDLEY) —
  BOYSTOWN GANG
AIN'T NO MOUNTAIN HIGH ENOUGH [A] —
  Jocelyn BROWN
AIN'T NO MOUNTAIN HIGH ENOUGH [A] —
  WHITEHOUSE
AIN'T NO NEED TO HIDE — Sandy B
AIN'T NO PLAYA — JAY-Z featuring Foxy BROWN
AIN'T NO PLEASING YOU — CHAS and DAVE
AIN'T NO STOPPIN' US —
  DJ LUCK & MC NEAT featuring JJ
AIN'T NO STOPPIN' US NOW [A] —
  McFADDEN and WHITEHEAD
AIN'T NO STOPPIN' US NOW [A] —
  BIG DADDY KANE
AIN'T NO STOPPING — ENIGMA
AIN'T NO STOPPING US NOW [A] —
  Luther VANDROSS
AIN'T NO STOPPING US NOW [A] —
  MOBO ALLSTARS
AIN'T NO STOPPING US NOW (PARTY
  FOR THE WORLD) — Steve WALSH
AIN'T NO SUNSHINE [A] — Michael JACKSON
AIN'T NO SUNSHINE [A] — SIVUCA
AIN'T NO SUNSHINE [A] — LADYSMITH
  BLACK MAMBAZO featuring DES'REE
AIN'T NOBODY [A] — RUFUS and Chaka KHAN
AIN'T NOBODY [A] — Jaki GRAHAM
AIN'T NOBODY [A] — Diana KING
AIN'T NOBODY [A] — LL COOL J
AIN'T NOBODY [A] — COURSE
AIN'T NOBODY BETTER — INNER CITY
AIN'T NOBODY (LOVES ME BETTER) —
  KWS and Gwen DICKEY
AIN'T NOTHIN' GOIN' ON BUT THE RENT —
  Gwen GUTHRIE
AIN'T NOTHIN' LIKE IT — Michael LOVESMITH
AIN'T NOTHIN' LIKE THE REAL THING [A] —
  Marvin GAYE and Tammi TERRELL
AIN'T NOTHING BUT A HOUSEPARTY [A] —
  SHOWSTOPPERS
AIN'T NOTHING BUT A HOUSEPARTY [A] —
  Phil FEARON
AIN'T NOTHING GONNA KEEP ME FROM YOU —
  Teri DE SARIO
AIN'T NOTHING LIKE THE REAL THING —
  Marcella DETROIT and Elton JOHN
AIN'T SHE SWEET — The BEATLES
AIN'T TALKIN' 'BOUT DUB —
  APOLLO FOUR FORTY
AIN'T THAT A LOT OF LOVE — SIMPLY RED
AIN'T THAT A SHAME [A] — Pat BOONE
AIN'T THAT A SHAME [A] — Fats DOMINO
AIN'T THAT A SHAME [A] —
  The FOUR SEASONS
AIN'T THAT ENOUGH — TEENAGE FANCLUB
AIN'T THAT ENOUGH FOR YOU —
  John DAVIS and the MONSTER ORCHESTRA
AIN'T THAT FUNNY — Jimmy JUSTICE
(AIN'T THAT) JUST LIKE ME — The HOLLIES
AIN'T THAT JUST THE WAY — Lutricia McNEAL

AIN'T THAT LOVING YOU BABY — Elvis PRESLEY
AIN'T THAT THE TRUTH — Frankie KELLY
AIN'T TOO PROUD TO BEG [A] — The TEMPTATIONS
AIN'T 2 PROUD 2 BEG [B] — TLC
AIN'T WE FUNKIN' NOW — BROTHERS JOHNSON
AIN'T WHAT YOU DO — BIG BROVAZ
AIR HOSTESS — BUSTED
THE AIR THAT I BREATHE [A] — The HOLLIES
THE AIR THAT I BREATHE [A] —SIMPLY RED
AIR TRAFFIC — THREE DRIVES
AIR 2000 — ALBION
AIR WE BREATHE — ALISHA'S ATTIC
THE AIR YOU BREATHE — BOMB THE BASS
AIRHEAD [A] — Thomas DOLBY
AIRHEAD [B] — GIRLS @ PLAY
AIRPLANE GARDENS — FAMILY CAT
AIRPORT — The MOTORS
AIRWAVE — RANK 1
AISHA — DEATH IN VEGAS
AISY WAISY — CARTOONS
AJARE — WAY OUT WEST
AL CAPONE — PRINCE BUSTER
AL DI LA — Emilio PERICOLI
ALA KABOO — SOUND 5
ALABAMA BLUES (REVISITED) — ST GERMAIN
ALABAMA JUBILEE — FERKO STRING BAND
ALABAMA SONG — David BOWIE
ALAN BEAN — HEFNER
ALANE — WES
ALARM CALL — BJÖRK
ALARMA — 666
ALBATROSS — FLEETWOOD MAC
ALBINONI VS STAR WARS — SIGUE SIGUE SPUTNIK
ALCOHOLIC — STARSAILOR
ALEXANDER GRAHAM BELL — The SWEET
ALFIE — Cilla BLACK
ALICE I WANT YOU JUST FOR ME — FULL FORCE
ALICE WHAT'S THE MATTER — TERRORVISION
ALICE (WHO THE X IS ALICE) (LIVING NEXT DOOR TO ALICE) — GOMPIE
ALISHA RULES THE WORLD — ALISHA'S ATTIC
ALISON — Linda RONSTADT
ALISON'S ROOM — 60FT DOLLS
ALIVE [A] — PEARL JAM
ALIVE [B] — HELIOTROPIC featuring Verna V
ALIVE [C] — BEASTIE BOYS
ALIVE [D] — P.O.D.
ALIVE [E] — ALIVE featuring D.D. KLEIN
ALIVE [F] — S CLUB
ALIVE [G] — SONIQUE
ALIVE AND KICKING [A] — SIMPLE MINDS
ALIVE AND KICKING [A] — EAST SIDE BEAT
ALKALINE — SCARFO
ALL ABOUT EVE — MARXMAN
ALL ABOUT LOVIN' YOU — BON JOVI
ALL ABOUT SOUL — Billy JOEL
ALL ABOUT US — Peter ANDRE
ALL ALONE AM I — Brenda LEE
ALL ALONE ON CHRISTMAS — Darlene LOVE
ALL ALONG THE WATCHTOWER — The Jimi HENDRIX EXPERIENCE
ALL ALONG THE WATCHTOWER (EP) — Jimi HENDRIX
THE ALL AMERICAN BOY — Bill PARSONS
ALL AMERICAN GIRLS — SISTER SLEDGE
ALL AND ALL — Joyce SIMS
ALL APOLOGIES — NIRVANA
ALL AROUND MY HAT [A] — STEELEYE SPAN
ALL AROUND MY HAT [A] — STATUS QUO with Maddy PRIOR from STEELEYE SPAN
ALL AROUND THE WORLD [A] — The JAM
ALL AROUND THE WORLD [B] — Lisa STANSFIELD
ALL AROUND THE WORLD [C] — Jason DONOVAN
ALL AROUND THE WORLD [D] — OASIS
ALL AROUND THE WORLD [E] — NORTHERN LINE
ALL BECAUSE OF YOU — GEORDIE
ALL 'BOUT THE MONEY — MEJA
ALL BY MYSELF [A] — Eric CARMEN
ALL BY MYSELF [A] — Celine DION
ALL CRIED OUT [A] — Alison MOYET
ALL CRIED OUT [B] — Melanie WILLIAMS
ALL CRIED OUT [C] — ALLURE featuring 112
ALL DAY ALL NIGHT — Stephanie MILLS
ALL DAY AND ALL OF THE NIGHT [A] — The KINKS
ALL DAY AND ALL OF THE NIGHT [A] — The STRANGLERS
ALL DOWNHILL FROM HERE — NEW FOUND GLORY
ALL EXHALE — Luke SLATER
ALL EYES — CHIKINKI
ALL FALL DOWN [A] — LINDISFARNE
ALL FALL DOWN [B] — FIVE STAR
ALL FALL DOWN [C] — ULTRAVOX
ALL FALL DOWN [D] — MIDGET
ALL FALLS DOWN — Kanye WEST featuring Syleena JOHNSON
ALL FIRED UP — Pat BENATAR
ALL FOR LEYNA — Billy JOEL
ALL FOR LOVE — Bryan ADAMS, Rod STEWART and STING
ALL FOR YOU — JANET
ALL 4 LOVE — COLOR ME BADD
ALL 4 LOVE (BREAK 4 LOVE 1990) — RAZE featuring LADY J and SECRETARY OF ENTERTAINMENT
ALL FUNKED UP — MOTHER
ALL GOD'S CHILDREN — Belinda CARLISLE
ALL GONE AWAY — JOYRIDER
ALL GOOD — DE LA SOUL featuring Chaka KHAN
ALL HOOKED UP — ALL SAINTS
ALL I AM (IS LOVING YOU) — The BLUEBELLS
ALL I ASK — RAE and CHRISTIAN featuring VEBA
ALL I ASK OF MYSELF IS THAT I HOLD TOGETHER — NED'S ATOMIC DUSTBIN
ALL I ASK OF YOU — Cliff RICHARD and Sarah BRIGHTMAN
ALL I DO — CLEPTOMANIACS featuring Bryan CHAMBERS
ALL I EVER NEED IS YOU — SONNY and CHER
ALL I EVER WANTED [A] — SANTANA
ALL I EVER WANTED [B] — HUMAN LEAGUE
ALL I EVER WANTED (DEVOTION) — MYSTERY
ALL I GAVE — WORLD PARTY
ALL I HAVE — Jennifer LOPEZ featuring LL COOL J
ALL I HAVE TO DO IS DREAM [A] — The EVERLY BROTHERS
ALL I HAVE TO DO IS DREAM [A] — Bobbie GENTRY and Glen CAMPBELL
ALL I HAVE TO DO IS DREAM [A] — Cliff RICHARD with Phil EVERLY
ALL I HAVE TO GIVE — BACKSTREET BOYS
(ALL I KNOW) FEELS LIKE FOREVER — Joe COCKER
ALL I NEED — AIR
ALL I NEED IS A MIRACLE — MIKE and the MECHANICS
ALL I NEED IS EVERYTHING — AZTEC CAMERA
ALL I NEED IS YOUR SWEET LOVIN' — Gloria GAYNOR
ALL I REALLY WANT — Alanis MORISSETTE
ALL I REALLY WANT TO DO [A] — The BYRDS
ALL I REALLY WANT TO DO [A] — CHER
ALL I SEE IS YOU — Dusty SPRINGFIELD
ALL I THINK ABOUT IS YOU — NILSSON
ALL I WANNA DO [A] — Sheryl CROW
ALL I WANNA DO [A] — Joanne FARRELL
ALL I WANNA DO [A] — Amy STUDT
ALL I WANNA DO [B] — TIN TIN OUT
ALL I WANNA DO [C] — DANNII
ALL I WANNA DO IS MAKE LOVE TO YOU — HEART
ALL I WANT [A] — Howard JONES
ALL I WANT [B] — THOSE 2 GIRLS
ALL I WANT [C] — SKUNK ANANSIE
ALL I WANT [D] — Susanna HOFFS
ALL I WANT [E] — The OFFSPRING
ALL I WANT [F] — PURESSENCE
ALL I WANT [G] — REEF
ALL I WANT [H] — MIS-TEEQ
ALL I WANT [I] — WET WET WET
ALL I WANT FOR CHRISTMAS IS A BEATLE — Dora BRYAN
ALL I WANT FOR CHRISTMAS IS YOU — Mariah CAREY
ALL I WANT FROM YOU — The TEMPTATIONS
ALL I WANT IS EVERYTHING — DEF LEPPARD
ALL I WANT IS YOU [A] — ROXY MUSIC
ALL I WANT IS YOU [B] — U2
ALL I WANT IS YOU [B] — BELLEFIRE
ALL I WANT IS YOU [C] — Bryan ADAMS
ALL I WANT IS YOU [D] — 911
ALL I WANT TO DO — UB40
ALL I WANT TO DO IS ROCK — TRAVIS
ALL I WANTED — IN TUA NUA
ALL IN MY HEAD — KOSHEEN
ALL IN YOUR HANDS — LAMB
ALL IS FULL OF LOVE — BJÖRK
ALL JOIN HANDS — SLADE
ALL KINDS OF EVERYTHING — DANA
ALL MAPPED OUT — The DEPARTURE
ALL MINE — PORTISHEAD
ALL MY BEST FRIENDS ARE METALHEADS — LESS THAN JAKE
ALL MY LIFE [A] — Major HARRIS
ALL MY LIFE [B] — K-CI & JOJO
ALL MY LIFE [C] — FOO FIGHTERS
ALL MY LOVE [A] — Cliff RICHARD
ALL MY LOVE [B] — HERNANDEZ
ALL MY LOVE [C] — QUEEN PEN featuring Eric WILLIAMS
ALL MY LOVE (ASK NOTHING) — SPEAR OF DESTINY
ALL MY LOVING — DOWLANDS
ALL MY TIME — Lauryn HILL
ALL MY TRIALS — Paul McCARTNEY
ALL 'N' ALL — 187 LOCKDOWN (featuring D'EMPRESS)
ALL N MY GRILL — Missy 'Misdemeanor' ELLIOTT featuring MC SOLAAR
ALL NIGHT ALL RIGHT — Peter ANDRE featuring Warren G
ALL NIGHT HOLIDAY — Russ ABBOT
ALL NIGHT LONG [A] — Dexter WANSELL
ALL NIGHT LONG [B] — RAINBOW
ALL NIGHT LONG [C] — CLOUD
ALL NIGHT LONG [D] — MARY JANE GIRLS
ALL NIGHT LONG [D] — Jay MONDI and the LIVING BASS
ALL NIGHT LONG [E] — GANT
ALL NIGHT LONG [F] — Faith EVANS featuring Puff DADDY
ALL NIGHT LONG (ALL NIGHT) — Lionel RICHIE
ALL NITE (DON'T STOP) — JANET
(ALL OF A SUDDEN) MY HEART SINGS — Paul ANKA
ALL OF ME — SABRINA
ALL OF ME FOR ALL OF YOU — 9.9
ALL OF ME LOVES ALL OF YOU — BAY CITY ROLLERS
ALL OF MY HEART — ABC
ALL OF MY LIFE — Diana ROSS
ALL OF THE GIRLS (ALL AI-DI GIRL DEM) — CARNIVAL featuring RIP vs RED RAT
ALL OF YOU [A] — Sammy DAVIS Jr
ALL OF YOU [A] — Julio IGLESIAS and Diana ROSS
ALL OF YOUR DAYS WILL BE BLESSED — Ed HARCOURT
ALL ON BLACK — ALKALINE TRIO
ALL OR NOTHING [A] — The SMALL FACES
ALL OR NOTHING [A] — DOGS D'AMOUR
ALL OR NOTHING [B] — MILLI VANILLI
ALL OR NOTHING [C] — JOE
ALL OR NOTHING [D] — CHER
ALL OR NOTHING [E] — O-TOWN
ALL OUT OF LOVE [A] — AIR SUPPLY
ALL OUT OF LOVE [A] — OTT
ALL OUT OF LOVE [A] — FOUNDATION featuring Natalie ROSSI
ALL OUT OF LOVE [B] — H & CLAIRE
ALL OUT TO GET YOU — The BEAT
ALL OVER — Lisa MAFFIA
ALL OVER ME [A] — Suzi CARR
ALL OVER ME [B] — Graham COXON
ALL OVER THE WORLD [A] — Françoise HARDY
ALL OVER THE WORLD [B] — ELECTRIC LIGHT ORCHESTRA
ALL OVER THE WORLD [C] — Junior GISCOMBE
ALL OVER YOU [A] — LEVEL 42
ALL OVER YOU [B] — LIVE
ALL POSSIBILITIES — BADLY DRAWN BOY
ALL RIGHT — Christopher CROSS
ALL RIGHT NOW [A] — FREE
ALL RIGHT NOW [A] — PEPSI and SHIRLIE
ALL RIGHT NOW [A] — LEMONESCENT
ALL RISE — BLUE
ALL SHE WANTS IS — DURAN DURAN
ALL SHOOK UP [A] — Elvis PRESLEY with the JORDANAIRES
ALL SHOOK UP [A] — Billy JOEL
ALL STAND UP (NEVER SAY NEVER) — STATUS QUO
ALL STAR — SMASH MOUTH
ALL STAR HIT PARADE — VARIOUS ARTISTS (EPs and LPs)
ALL STAR HIT PARADE NO.2 — VARIOUS ARTISTS (EPs and LPs)
ALL STOOD STILL — ULTRAVOX
ALL SUSSED OUT — The ALMIGHTY
ALL SYSTEMS GO — Donna SUMMER
ALL THAT GLITTERS — Gary GLITTER
ALL THAT I AM [A] — Elvis PRESLEY with the JORDANAIRES
ALL THAT I AM [B] — JOE
ALL THAT I CAN SAY — Mary J BLIGE
ALL THAT I GOT IS YOU — GHOSTFACE KILLAH
ALL THAT I NEED — BOYZONE
ALL THAT I'M ALLOWED (I'M THANKFUL) — Elton JOHN
ALL THAT MATTERED (LOVE YOU DOWN) — DE NUIT
ALL THAT MATTERS — LOUISE
ALL THAT MATTERS TO ME — Alexander O'NEAL
ALL THAT MONEY WANTS — PSYCHEDELIC FURS
ALL THAT SHE WANTS — ACE OF BASE
ALL THAT'S LEFT — THRICE
ALL THE LOVE IN THE WORLD [A] — CONSORTIUM
ALL THE LOVE IN THE WORLD [B] — Dionne WARWICK
ALL THE LOVER I NEED — Bianca KINANE
ALL THE MAN THAT I NEED [A] — Whitney HOUSTON
ALL THE MAN THAT I NEED [B] — Shernette MAY
ALL THE MONEY'S GONE — BABYLON ZOO
ALL THE MYTHS ON SUNDAY — DIESEL PARK WEST
ALL THE SMALL THINGS — BLINK-182
ALL THE THINGS — DILLINJA
ALL THE THINGS SHE SAID [A] — SIMPLE MINDS
ALL THE THINGS SHE SAID [B] — t.A.T.u.
ALL THE THINGS (YOUR MAN WON'T DO) — JOE
ALL THE TIME AND EVERYWHERE — Dickie VALENTINE
ALL THE WAY [A] — Frank SINATRA
ALL THE WAY [B] — ENGLAND FOOTBALL TEAM and the 'sound' of STOCK, AITKEN and WATERMAN
ALL THE WAY FROM AMERICA — Joan ARMATRADING
ALL THE WAY FROM MEMPHIS [A] — MOTT THE HOOPLE
ALL THE WAY FROM MEMPHIS [A] — CONTRABAND
ALL THE WAY TO RENO — R.E.M.
ALL THE WORLD LOVES LOVERS — PREFAB SPROUT
ALL THE YOUNG DUDES [A] — MOTT THE HOOPLE
ALL THE YOUNG DUDES [A] — Bruce DICKINSON
ALL THESE THINGS THAT I'VE DONE — The KILLERS
ALL THIS LOVE I'M GIVING [A] — MUSIC and MYSTERY featuring Gwen McCRAE
ALL THIS LOVE THAT I'M GIVING [A] — Gwen McCRAE
ALL THIS TIME [A] — TIFFANY
ALL THIS TIME [B] — STING
ALL THIS TIME [C] — MICHELLE
ALL THOSE YEARS AGO — George HARRISON
ALL THROUGH THE NIGHT — Cyndi LAUPER
ALL THRU THE NITE — P.O.V. featuring JADE
ALL TIME HIGH — Rita COOLIDGE
ALL TOGETHER NOW [A] — The FARM
ALL TOGETHER NOW [A] — EVERTON FOOTBALL CLUB
ALL TOGETHER NOW 2004 [A] — The FARM featuring S.F.X. BOYS' CHOIR, LIVERPOOL
ALL TOMORROW'S PARTIES — JAPAN
ALL TRUE MAN — Alexander O'NEAL
ALL WOMAN — Lisa STANSFIELD
ALL YOU EVER DO — VIOLENT DELIGHT
ALL YOU GOOD GOOD PEOPLE (EP) — EMBRACE
ALL YOU NEED IS HATE — The DELGADOS
ALL YOU NEED IS LOVE [A] — The BEATLES
ALL YOU NEED IS LOVE [A] — Tom JONES
ALL YOU PRETTY GIRLS — XTC
ALL YOU WANTED — Michelle BRANCH
THE ALLEY CAT SONG — David THORNE
ALLEY-OOP — HOLLYWOOD ARGYLES
ALLY'S TARTAN ARMY — Andy CAMERON
ALMA MATTERS — MORRISSEY
ALMAZ — Randy CRAWFORD
ALMOST DOESN'T COUNT — BRANDY
ALMOST GOLD — JESUS AND MARY CHAIN
ALMOST HEAR YOU SIGH — The ROLLING STONES
ALMOST SATURDAY NIGHT — Dave EDMUNDS
ALMOST SEE YOU (SOMEWHERE) — CHINA BLACK
ALMOST THERE — Andy WILLIAMS
ALMOST UNREAL — ROXETTE
ALONE [A] — Petula CLARK
ALONE [A] — SOUTHLANDERS
ALONE [A] — SHEPHERD SISTERS
ALONE [A] — KAYE SISTERS
ALONE [B] — HEART
ALONE [C] — BIG COUNTRY
ALONE [D] — The BEE GEES
ALONE [E] — LASGO
ALONE AGAIN IN THE LAP OF LUXURY — MARILLION
ALONE AGAIN (NATURALLY) — Gilbert O'SULLIVAN
ALONE AGAIN OR — The DAMNED
ALONE AT LAST — Jackie WILSON
ALONE WITH YOU — TEXAS
ALONE WITHOUT YOU [A] — KING
ALONE WITHOUT YOU [B] — Mark OWEN
ALONG CAME CAROLINE — Michael COX
ALPHA BETA GAGA — AIR
ALPHABET STREET — PRINCE
ALRIGHT [A] — Janet JACKSON
ALRIGHT [B] — URBAN SOUL
ALRIGHT [C] — KRIS KROSS
ALRIGHT [D] — SUPERGRASS
ALRIGHT [E] — CAST
ALRIGHT [F] — JAMIROQUAI
ALRIGHT [G] — CLUB 69 featuring Suzanne PALMER
ALRIGHT [H] — RED CARPET
ALRIGHT, ALRIGHT, ALRIGHT — MUNGO JERRY
ALRIGHT BABY — STEVENSON'S ROCKET
ALSO SPRACH ZARATHUSTRA (2001) — DEODATO
ALTERNATE TITLE — The MONKEES
ALWAYS [A] — Sammy TURNER
ALWAYS [B] — ATLANTIC STARR
ALWAYS [C] — URBAN SOUL
ALWAYS [D] — ERASURE
ALWAYS [E] — BON JOVI
ALWAYS [F] — MK featuring ALANA
ALWAYS [G] — SALIVA
ALWAYS [H] — BLINK-182
ALWAYS A PERMANENT STATE — David JAMES
ALWAYS AND EVER — Johnny KIDD and the PIRATES
ALWAYS AND FOREVER [A] — HEATWAVE
ALWAYS AND FOREVER [A] — Luther VANDROSS
ALWAYS AND FOREVER [B] — JJ72
ALWAYS BE MY BABY — Mariah CAREY
ALWAYS BREAKING MY HEART — Belinda CARLISLE

ALWAYS COME BACK TO YOUR LOVE — **Samantha MUMBA**
ALWAYS FIND A WAY — **NINE YARDS**
ALWAYS HAVE, ALWAYS WILL — **ACE OF BASE**
ALWAYS LOOK ON THE BRIGHT SIDE OF LIFE [A] — **MONTY PYTHON**
ALWAYS LOOK ON THE BRIGHT SIDE OF LIFE [A] — **CORONATION STREET CAST featuring Bill WADDINGTON**
ALWAYS MUSIC — **WESTBAM / KOON + STEPHENSON**
ALWAYS ON MY MIND [A] — **Elvis PRESLEY: Vocal acc. J.D. SUMNER & the STAMPS**
ALWAYS ON MY MIND [A] — **Willie NELSON**
ALWAYS ON MY MIND [A] — **PET SHOP BOYS**
ALWAYS ON THE RUN — **Lenny KRAVITZ**
ALWAYS ON TIME —**JA RULE featuring ASHANTI**
ALWAYS REMEMBER TO RESPECT AND HONOUR YOUR MOTHER PART ONE — **DUSTED**
ALWAYS SOMETHING THERE TO REMIND ME [A] — **NAKED EYES**
ALWAYS SOMETHING THERE TO REMIND ME [A] — **TIN TIN OUT featuring ESPIRITU**
ALWAYS THE LAST TO KNOW — **DEL AMITRI**
ALWAYS THE LONELY ONE — **Alan DREW**
ALWAYS THE SUN — **The STRANGLERS**
ALWAYS THERE [A] — **Marti WEBB and the Simon MAY ORCHESTRA**
ALWAYS THERE [B] — **INCOGNITO featuring Jocelyn BROWN**
ALWAYS THERE [B] — **INCOGNITO**
ALWAYS THERE [C] — **UB40**
ALWAYS TOMORROW — **Gloria ESTEFAN**
ALWAYS YOU AND ME — **Russ CONWAY**
ALWAYS: YOUR WAY — **MY VITRIOL**
ALWAYS YOURS — **Gary GLITTER**
ALWAYZ INTO SOMETHIN' — **N.W.A.**
AM I A TOY OR TREASURE — **Kay STARR**
AM I ON YOUR MIND — **OXYGEN featuring Andrea BRITTON**
AM I RIGHT? (EP) — **ERASURE**
AM I THAT EASY TO FORGET — **Engelbert HUMPERDINCK**
AM I THE SAME GIRL [A] — **Dusty SPRINGFIELD**
AM I THE SAME GIRL [A] — **SWING OUT SISTER**
AM I WASTING MY TIME ON YOU — **Frankie VAUGHAN**
AM I WRONG [A] — **Etienne DE CRECY**
AM I WRONG [B] — **MULL HISTORICAL SOCIETY**
AM I WRY? NO — **MEW**
AM TO PM — **Christina MILIAN**
AMANDA [A] — **Stuart GILLIES**
AMANDA [B] — **Craig McLACHLAN and CHECK 1-2**
AMATEUR HOUR — **SPARKS**
AMAZED — **LONESTAR**
AMAZING [A] — **AEROSMITH**
AMAZING [B] — **George MICHAEL**
AMAZING GRACE [A] — **Judy COLLINS**
AMAZING GRACE [A] — **Pipes and Drums and Military Band of the ROYAL SCOTS DRAGOON GUARDS**
THE AMAZING SPIDER-MAN — **MC SPY-D + FRIENDS**
AMAZON CHANT — **AIRSCAPE**
AMBUSH — **OUTLAWS**
AMEN (DON'T BE AFRAID) — **FLASH BROTHERS**
AMERICA [A] — **NICE**
AMERICA [A] — **KING KURT**
AMERICA [B] — **SIMON and GARFUNKEL**
AMERICA [C] — **David ESSEX**
AMERICA [E] — **Gary NUMAN**
AMERICA (I LOVE AMERICA) — **FULL INTENTION**
AMERICA THE BEAUTIFUL — **Elvis PRESLEY**
AMERICA: WHAT TIME IS LOVE? — **The KLF**
AMERICA — WORLD CUP THEME 1994 — **Leonard BERNSTEIN, Orchestra and Chorus**
THE AMERICAN — **SIMPLE MINDS**
AMERICAN BAD ASS — **KID ROCK**
AMERICAN DREAM [A] — **CROSBY, STILLS, NASH and YOUNG**
AMERICAN DREAM [B] — **POWER OF DREAMS**
AMERICAN DREAM [C] — **JAKATTA**
AMERICAN ENGLISH — **IDLEWILD**
AMERICAN GENERATION — **RITCHIE FAMILY**
AMERICAN GIRL — **Tom PETTY and the HEARTBREAKERS**
AMERICAN GIRLS — **COUNTING CROWS**
AMERICAN HEARTS — **Billy OCEAN**
AMERICAN IDIOT — **GREEN DAY**
AMERICAN IN AMSTERDAM — **WHEATUS**
AMERICAN LIFE — **MADONNA**
AMERICAN PIE [A] — **Don McLEAN**
AMERICAN PIE [A] — **CHUPITO**
AMERICAN PIE [A] — **JUST LUIS**
AMERICAN PIE [A] — **MADONNA**
AN AMERICAN TRILOGY [A] — **Elvis PRESLEY**
AMERICAN TRILOGY [A] — **Mickey NEWBURY**
AMERICAN TRILOGY [B] — **The DELGADOS**
AMERICAN TV — **TERRORVISION**
AMERICAN WOMAN — **The GUESS WHO**
AMERICANOS — **Holly JOHNSON**
AMERIKA — **RAMMSTEIN**
AMIGO — **BLACK SLATE**
AMIGOS PARA SIEMPRE (FRIENDS FOR LIFE) — **José CARRERAS and Sarah BRIGHTMAN**
AMITYVILLE (THE HOUSE ON THE HILL) — **LOVEBUG STARSKI**
AMNESIA [A] — **SHALAMAR**
AMNESIA [B] — **CHUMBAWAMBA**
AMONG MY SOUVENIRS — **Connie FRANCIS**
AMOR — **Julio IGLESIAS**
AMOR, AMOR — **Ben E KING**
AMOUR AMOUR — **The MOBILES**
AMOUR (C'MON) — **PORN KINGS**
AMOUREUSE — **Kiki DEE**
THE AMSTERDAM EP — **SIMPLE MINDS**
AN ACCIDENT IN PARADISE — **Sven VATH**
AN AFFAIR TO REMEMBER (OUR LOVE AFFAIR) — **Vic DAMONE**
AN ANGEL — **KELLY FAMILY**
AN EVERLASTING LOVE — **Andy GIBB**
AN INNOCENT MAN — **Billy JOEL**
AN OLYMPIC RECORD — **The BARRON KNIGHTS**
AN UBHAL AS AIRDE (THE HIGHEST APPLE) — **RUNRIG**
ANARCHY IN THE UK [A] — **The SEX PISTOLS**
ANARCHY IN THE UK [A] — **MEGADETH**
ANARCHY IN THE UK [A] — **GREEN JELLY**
ANA'S SONG — **SILVERCHAIR**
ANASTHASIA — **T99**
ANCHOR — **CAVE IN**
ANCHORAGE — **Michelle SHOCKED**
AND A BANG ON THE EAR — **WATERBOYS**
AND DA DRUM MACHINE — **PHATT B**
AND I LOVE YOU SO — **Perry COMO**
AND I WISH — **The DOOLEYS**
AND I'M TELLING YOU I'M NOT GOING [A] — **Jennifer HOLLIDAY**
AND I'M TELLING YOU I'M NOT GOING [A] — **Donna GILES**
AND IT HURTS — **DAYEENE**
AND IT WASN'T A DREAM — **RUTHLESS RAP ASSASSINS featuring Tracey CARMEN**
(AND NOW — THE WALTZ) C'EST LA VIE — **SLADE**
AND SHE WAS — **TALKING HEADS**
AND SO I WILL WAIT FOR YOU — **Dee FREDRIX**
AND SO IS LOVE — **Kate BUSH**
... AND STONES — **BLUE AEROPLANES**
... AND THAT'S BEFORE ME TEA! — **MR FOOD**
... (AND THAT'S NO LIE) — **HEAVEN 17**
AND THE BAND PLAYED ON (DOWN AMONG THE DEAD MEN) — **FLASH and the PAN**
AND THE BANDS PLAYED ON — **SAXON**
AND THE BEAT GOES ON — **WHISPERS**
AND THE HEAVENS CRIED — **Anthony NEWLEY**
AND THE LEADER ROCKS ON (MEGAMIX / MEDLEY) — **Gary GLITTER**
(AND THE) PICTURES IN THE SKY — **MEDICINE HEAD**
AND THE SUN WILL SHINE — **José FELICIANO**
AND THEN SHE KISSED ME — **Gary GLITTER**
AND THEN SHE SMILES — **MOCK TURTLES**
AND THEN THE RAIN FALLS — **BLUE AMAZON**
... AND THEY OBEY — **KINESIS**
AND YOU SMILED — **Matt MONRO**
ANDRES — **L7**
ANDROGYNY — **GARBAGE**
ANFIELD RAP (RED MACHINE IN FULL EFFECT) — **LIVERPOOL FC**
ANGEL [A] — **Rod STEWART**
ANGEL [B] — **Aretha FRANKLIN**
ANGEL [B] — **SIMPLY RED**
ANGEL [C] — **MADONNA**
ANGEL [D] — **AEROSMITH**
ANGEL [E] — **EURYTHMICS**
ANGEL [F] — **Jon SECADA**
ANGEL [G] — **A-HA**
ANGEL [H] — **GOLDIE**
ANGEL [I] — **MASSIVE ATTACK**
ANGEL [J] — **Tina COUSINS**
ANGEL [K] — **Ralph FRIDGE**
ANGEL [L] — **Lionel RICHIE**
ANGEL [M] — **SHAGGY featuring RAYVON**
ANGEL [N] — **Sarah McLACHLAN**
ANGEL [O] — **The CORRS**
THE ANGEL AND THE GAMBLER — **IRON MAIDEN**
ANGEL EYES — **ROXY MUSIC**
ANGEL EYES (HOME AND AWAY) — **WET WET WET**
ANGEL FACE — **GLITTER BAND**
ANGEL FINGERS (A TEEN BALLAD) — **WIZZARD: Vocal backing: the Suedettes and the Bleach Boys**
ANGEL IN BLUE — **J GEILS BAND**
ANGEL INTERCEPTOR — **ASH**
ANGEL (LADADI O-HEYO) — **JAM & SPOON featuring PLAVKA**
ANGEL LOOKING THROUGH — **STAGECOACH featuring Penny FOSTER**
ANGEL OF HARLEM — **U2**
ANGEL OF MINE [A] — **ETERNAL**
ANGEL OF MINE [A] — **MONICA**
ANGEL OF THE MORNING [A] — **PP ARNOLD**
ANGEL OF THE MORNING [A] — **Juice NEWTON**
ANGEL OF THE MORNING [A] — ANY WAY THAT YOU WANT ME (MEDLEY) — **Mary MASON**
ANGEL STREET — **M PEOPLE**
ANGELA JONES — **Michael COX**
ANGELEYES — **ABBA**
ANGELIA — **Richard MARX**
ANGELO — **BROTHERHOOD OF MAN**
ANGELS — **Robbie WILLIAMS**
THE ANGELS & SHADOWS PROJECT — **OMNI TRIO**
ANGELS DON'T LIE — **Jim REEVES**
ANGELS GO BALD: TOO — **Howie B**
ANGEL'S HEAP — **FINN**
ANGELS OF THE SILENCES — **COUNTING CROWS**
ANGEL'S SYMPHONY — **RAF**
ANGELS WITH DIRTY FACES [A] — **SHAM 69**
ANGELS WITH DIRTY FACES [B] — **SUGABABES**
ANGIE — **The ROLLING STONES**
ANGIE BABY — **Helen REDDY**
ANGRY AT THE BIG OAK TREE — **Frank IFIELD**
ANGRY CHAIR — **ALICE IN CHAINS**
ANGRY SKIES — **Maria NAYLER**
ANIMAL [A] — **DEF LEPPARD**
ANIMAL [B] — **LOST IT.COM**
ANIMAL [C] — **R.E.M.**
ANIMAL ARMY — **BABYLON ZOO**
ANIMAL CANNABUS — **MULL HISTORICAL SOCIETY**
ANIMAL INSTINCT [A] — **The COMMODORES**
ANIMAL INSTINCT [B] — **The CRANBERRIES**
ANIMAL NITRATE — **SUEDE**
THE ANIMAL SONG — **SAVAGE GARDEN**
ANIMATION — **The SKIDS**
A9 — **ARIEL**
ANITINA (THE FIRST TIME I SEE SHE DANCE) — **M/A/R/R/S**
ANNABELLA — **John WALKER**
ANNIE GET YOUR GUN — **SQUEEZE**
ANNIE I'M NOT YOUR DADDY — **Kid CREOLE and the COCONUTS**
ANNIE'S SONG [A] — **John DENVER**
ANNIE'S SONG [A] — **James GALWAY, flute, NATIONAL PHILHARMONIC ORCHESTRA; Charles Gerhart, conductor**
ANNIVERSARY WALTZ — **Anita HARRIS**
THE ANNIVERSARY WALTZ — PART ONE — **STATUS QUO**
THE ANNIVERSARY WALTZ — PART TWO — **STATUS QUO**
ANOMALY — CALLING YOUR NAME — **LIBRA presents TAYLOR**
ANOTHER BLOOMING CHRISTMAS — **Mel SMITH**
ANOTHER BODY MURDERED — **FAITH NO MORE and BOO-YAA T.R.I.B.E.**
ANOTHER BRICK IN THE WALL (PART 2) — **PINK FLOYD**
ANOTHER CHANCE — **Roger SANCHEZ**
ANOTHER CUP OF COFFEE — **MIKE and the MECHANICS**
ANOTHER DAY [A] — **Paul McCARTNEY**
ANOTHER DAY [B] — **WHIGFIELD**
ANOTHER DAY [C] — **BUCKSHOT LEFONQUE**
ANOTHER DAY [D] — **SKIP RAIDERS featuring JADA**
ANOTHER DAY [E] — **LEMAR**
ANOTHER DAY (ANOTHER GIRL) — **LAMBRETTAS**
ANOTHER DAY IN PARADISE [A] — **Phil COLLINS**
ANOTHER DAY IN PARADISE [A] — **JAM TRONIK**
ANOTHER DAY IN PARADISE [A] — **BRANDY and RAY J**
ANOTHER FUNNY HONEYMOON — **David DUNDAS**
ANOTHER GIRL — ANOTHER PLANET — **The ONLY ONES**
ANOTHER HEARTACHE — **Rod STEWART**
ANOTHER KIND OF LOVE — **Hugh CORNWELL**
ANOTHER LONELY NIGHT IN NEW YORK — **Robin GIBB**
ANOTHER LOVER — **DANE**
ANOTHER MAN — **Barbara MASON**
ANOTHER MONSTERJAM — **Simon HARRIS featuring EINSTEIN**
ANOTHER MORNING STONER — **... AND YOU WILL KNOW US BY THE TRAIL OF DEAD**
ANOTHER NAIL IN MY HEART — **SQUEEZE**
ANOTHER NIGHT [A] — **Aretha FRANKLIN**
ANOTHER NIGHT [B] — **Jason DONOVAN**
ANOTHER NIGHT [C] — **(MC SAR &) The REAL McCOY**
ANOTHER NIGHT IN — **STRANGELOVE**
ANOTHER ONE BITES THE DUST [A] — **QUEEN**
ANOTHER ONE BITES THE DUST [A] — **QUEEN with Wyclef JEAN featuring PRAS and FREE**
ANOTHER PART OF ME — **Michael JACKSON**
ANOTHER PEARL — **BADLY DRAWN BOY**
ANOTHER PIECE OF MEAT — **SCORPIONS**
ANOTHER PLANET — **PENDULUM**
ANOTHER ROCK AND ROLL CHRISTMAS — **Gary GLITTER**
ANOTHER SAD LOVE SONG — **Toni BRAXTON**
ANOTHER SATURDAY NIGHT [A] — **Sam COOKE**
ANOTHER SATURDAY NIGHT [A] — **Cat STEVENS**
ANOTHER SILENT DAY — **ADVENTURES**
ANOTHER SLEEPLESS NIGHT [A] — **Jimmy CLANTON**
ANOTHER SLEEPLESS NIGHT [B] — **Mike 'Hitman' WILSON**
ANOTHER SLEEPLESS NIGHT [B] — **Shawn CHRISTOPHER**
ANOTHER STAR [A] — **Stevie WONDER**
ANOTHER STAR [A] — **Kathy SLEDGE**
ANOTHER STEP (CLOSER TO YOU) — **Kim WILDE and JUNIOR**
ANOTHER SUITCASE IN ANOTHER HALL [A] — **Barbara DICKSON**
ANOTHER SUITCASE IN ANOTHER HALL [A] — **MADONNA**
ANOTHER TEAR FALLS — **The WALKER BROTHERS**
ANOTHER TIME, ANOTHER PLACE — **Engelbert HUMPERDINCK**
ANOTHER WAY — **Paul VAN DYK**
ANOTHER WEEKEND — **FIVE STAR**
ANOTHERLOVERHOLENYOHEAD — **PRINCE and the REVOLUTION**
ANSWER ME [A] — **David WHITFIELD**
ANSWER ME [A] — **Frankie LAINE**
ANSWER ME [A] — **Ray PETERSON**
ANSWER ME [A] — **Barbara DICKSON**
THE ANSWER TO WHY I HATE YOU — **SYMPOSIUM**
ANSWERING BELL — **Ryan ADAMS**
ANSWERS TO NOTHING — **Midge URE**
ANT RAP — **ADAM and the ANTS**
ANTE UP — **M.O.P. featuring Busta RHYMES**
ANTHEM [A] — **N-JOI**
ANTHEM [B] — **The WILDHEARTS**
THE ANTHEM — **GOOD CHARLOTTE**
ANTHEM (ONE DAY IN EVERY WEEK) — **The NEW SEEKERS**
ANTI-SOCIAL — **ANTHRAX**
ANTMUSIC — **ADAM and the ANTS**
THE ANTMUSIC EP (THE B-SIDES) — **ADAM and the ANTS**
ANY DREAM WILL DO — **Jason DONOVAN**
ANY MINUTE NOW — **SOULWAX**
ANY OLD IRON — **Peter SELLERS presents Mate's Skiffle Group featuring Fred Spoons E.P.N.S.**
ANY OLD TIME — **The FOUNDATIONS**
ANY ROAD — **George HARRISON**
ANY TIME ANY PLACE — **Janet JACKSON**
ANY WAY THAT YOU WANT ME — **The TROGGS**
ANY WAY YOU LOOK — **NORTHERN UPROAR**
ANYBODY SEEN MY BABY? — **The ROLLING STONES**
ANYMORE — **Sarah CRACKNELL**
ANYONE CAN FALL IN LOVE — **Anita DOBSON featuring the Simon MAY Orchestra**
ANYONE CAN PLAY GUITAR — **RADIOHEAD**
ANYONE FOR TENNIS (THE SAVAGE SEVEN THEME) — **CREAM**
ANYONE OF US (STUPID MISTAKE) — **GARETH GATES**
ANYONE WHO HAD A HEART [A] — **Cilla BLACK**
ANYONE WHO HAD A HEART [A] — **Dionne WARWICK**
ANYONE WHO HAD A HEART [A] — **Mary MAY**
ANYTHING? [A] — **DIRECT DRIVE**
ANYTHING [B] — **The DAMNED**
ANYTHING [C] — **Sydney YOUNGBLOOD**
ANYTHING [D] — **CULTURE BEAT**
ANYTHING [E] — **SWV**
ANYTHING [F] — **3T**
ANYTHING [G] — **DAMAGE**
ANYTHING [H] — **JAY-Z**
ANYTHING BUT DOWN — **Sheryl CROW**
ANYTHING CAN HAPPEN — **WAS (NOT WAS)**
ANYTHING FOR YOU [A] — **Gloria ESTEFAN and MIAMI SOUND MACHINE**
ANYTHING FOR YOU [B] — **STAMFORD AMP**
ANYTHING GOES — **HARPERS BIZARRE**
ANYTHING IS POSSIBLE [A] — **Debbie GIBSON**
ANYTHING IS POSSIBLE [B] — **Will YOUNG**
ANYTHING THAT'S ROCK 'N' ROLL — **Tom PETTY and the HEARTBREAKERS**
ANYTHING YOU WANT — **JODIE**
ANYTHING YOU WANT (I'VE GOT IT) — **ULTIMATE KAOS**
ANYTIME [A] — **NU-BIRTH**
ANYTIME [B] — **Brian McKNIGHT**
ANYTIME YOU NEED A FRIEND — **Mariah CAREY**
ANYWAY — **HONEYCRACK**
ANYWAY ANYHOW ANYWHERE — **The WHO**
ANYWAY THAT YOU WANT ME — **SPIRITUALIZED**
ANYWAY YOU DO IT — **LIQUID GOLD**
ANYWAY YOU WANT IT — **Dave CLARK FIVE**
ANYWHERE [A] — **DUBSTAR**
ANYWHERE [B] — **Beth ORTON**
ANYWHERE FOR YOU — **BACKSTREET BOYS**
ANYWHERE IS — **ENYA**
APACHE [A] — **The SHADOWS**
APACHE [A] — **Bert WEEDON**
APACHE [B] — **STARFIGHTER**
APACHE DROPOUT — **Edgar BROUGHTON BAND**
APEMAN — **The KINKS**
APHRODITE — **PARIS & SHARP**
APOLLO 9 — **Adam ANT**
APOLOGIES TO INSECT LIFE — **BRITISH SEA POWER**
APPARENTLY NOTHIN' [A] — **YOUNG DISCIPLES**
APPARENTLY NOTHING [A] — **The BRAND NEW HEAVIES**

THE APPLE EP — VARIOUS ARTISTS (EPs and LPs)
APPLE GREEN — MILLTOWN BROTHERS
APPLE OF MY EYE — Ed HARCOURT
THE APPLE STRETCHING — Grace JONES
APPLE TREE — Erykah BADU
APPLEJACK — Jet HARRIS and Tony MEEHAN
APPRENTICE OF THE UNIVERSE — PURE REASON REVOLUTION
APRIL LOVE — Pat BOONE
APRIL SKIES — JESUS AND MARY CHAIN
AQUARIUS [A] — Paul JONES
AQUARIUS [A] — LET THE SUNSHINE IN (MEDLEY) — 5TH DIMENSION
ARABIAN KNIGHTS — SIOUXSIE and the BANSHEES
ARE EVERYTHING — The BUZZCOCKS
ARE 'FRIENDS' ELECTRIC? — TUBEWAY ARMY
ARE WE HERE — ORBITAL
ARE YOU BEING SERVED — GRACE BROTHERS
ARE YOU BEING SERVED SIR? —John INMAN
ARE YOU BLUE OR ARE YOU BLIND — The BLUETONES
ARE YOU DREAMING — TWENTY 4 SEVEN featuring CAPTAIN HOLLYWOOD
ARE YOU GETTING ENOUGH OF WHAT MAKES YOU HAPPY — HOT CHOCOLATE
ARE YOU GONNA BE MY GIRL — JET
ARE YOU GONNA BE THERE — UP YER RONSON featuring Mary PEARCE
ARE YOU GONNA GO MY WAY — Lenny KRAVITZ
ARE YOU GROWING TIRED OF MY LOVE — STATUS QUO
ARE YOU HAPPY NOW? — Michelle BRANCH
ARE YOU HEARING (WHAT I HEAR)? — LEVEL 42
ARE YOU IN? — INCUBUS
ARE YOU JIMMY RAY? — Jimmy RAY
ARE YOU LONESOME TONIGHT? — Elvis PRESLEY with the JORDANAIRES
ARE YOU LOOKIN' AT ME? — Ricky TOMLINSON
ARE YOU MAN ENOUGH — UNO CLIO featuring Martine McCUTCHEON
ARE YOU MINE? — BROS
ARE YOU MY BABY — WENDY and LISA
ARE YOU OUT THERE — CRESCENDO
ARE YOU READY [A] — Billy OCEAN
ARE YOU READY? [B] — BREAK MACHINE
ARE YOU READY [C] — AC/DC
ARE YOU READY [D] — The GYRES
(ARE YOU READY) DO THE BUS STOP — FATBACK BAND
ARE YOU READY FOR LOVE [A] — Elton JOHN
ARE YOU READY FOR LOVE [B] — ULTRA HIGH
ARE YOU READY FOR SOME MORE — REEL 2 REAL
ARE YOU READY TO BE HEARTBROKEN? — Sandie SHAW
ARE YOU READY TO FLY — ROZALLA
ARE YOU READY TO PARTY — SHRINK
ARE YOU READY TO ROCK — WIZZARD
ARE YOU SATISFIED? (FUNKA NOVA) — RAH BAND
ARE YOU STILL HAVING FUN — Eagle-Eye CHERRY
ARE YOU SURE [A] — The ALLISONS
ARE YOU SURE [B] — SO
ARE YOU THAT SOMEBODY? — AALIYAH
(ARE YOU) THE ONE THAT I'VE BEEN ... — Nick CAVE and the BAD SEEDS
AREA CODES — LUDACRIS featuring Nate DOGG
ARGENTINA — Jeremy HEALY & AMOS
ARGENTINE MELODY (CANCION DE ARGENTINA) — SAN JOSE featuring Rodriguez ARGENTINA
ARIA — Acker BILK, his Clarinet and Strings
ARIANA — STARDUST
ARIENNE — Tasmin ARCHER
ARIZONA SKY — CHINA CRISIS
ARMAGEDDON DAYS ARE HERE (AGAIN) — The THE
ARMAGEDDON IT — DEF LEPPARD
ARMCHAIR ANARCHIST — KINGMAKER
ARMED AND EXTREMELY DANGEROUS — FIRST CHOICE
ARMED AND READY — Michael SCHENKER GROUP
ARMS ALOFT — Joe STRUMMER and the MESCALEROS
ARMS AROUND THE WORLD — LOUISE
ARMS OF LOREN — E'VOKE
ARMS OF MARY — SUTHERLAND BROTHERS and QUIVER
THE ARMS OF ORION — PRINCE with Sheena EASTON
ARMS OF SOLITUDE — OUI 3
THE ARMS OF THE ONE WHO LOVES YOU — XSCAPE
ARMY — Ben FOLDS FIVE
ARMY DREAMERS — Kate BUSH
ARMY OF ME — BJÖRK
ARMY OF TWO — DUM DUMS
ARNOLD LAYNE — PINK FLOYD
AROUND MY BRAIN — PROGRESS FUNK
AROUND THE WAY GIRL — LL COOL J
AROUND THE WORLD [A] — Ronnie HILTON
AROUND THE WORLD [A] — Bing CROSBY
AROUND THE WORLD [A] — Gracie FIELDS
AROUND THE WORLD [A] — MANTOVANI
AROUND THE WORLD [B] — EAST 17
AROUND THE WORLD [C] — DAFT PUNK
AROUND THE WORLD [D] — RED HOT CHILI PEPPERS
AROUND THE WORLD [E] — AQUA
AROUND THE WORLD (LA LA LA LA LA) — ATC
ARRANGED MARRIAGE — APACHE INDIAN
ARRESTED BY YOU — Dusty SPRINGFIELD
ARRIVEDERCI DARLING [A] — Anne SHELTON
ARRIVEDERCI DARLING [A] — Edna SAVAGE
ARSENAL NUMBER ONE — ARSENAL FC
ART FOR ART'S SAKE — 10cc
THE ART OF DRIVING — BLACK BOX RECORDER
THE ART OF LOSING — AMERICAN HI-FI
ART OF LOVE — ART OF NOISE
THE ART OF MOVING BUTTS — SHUT UP AND DANCE featuring ERIN
THE ART OF PARTIES — JAPAN
ARTHUR DALEY ('E'S ALRIGHT) — The FIRM
ARTHUR'S THEME (BEST THAT YOU CAN DO) — Christopher CROSS
AS — George MICHAEL and Mary J BLIGE
AS ALWAYS [A] — Farley 'Jackmaster' FUNK presents Ricky DILLARD
AS ALWAYS [A] — SECRET LIFE
AS GOOD AS IT GETS — GENE
AS I AM — SOUND OF ONE featuring GLADEZZ
AS I LAY ME DOWN — Sophie B HAWKINS
AS I LOVE YOU — Shirley BASSEY
AS IF WE NEVER SAID GOODBYE — Barbra STREISAND
AS LONG AS HE NEEDS ME — Shirley BASSEY
AS LONG AS THE PRICE IS RIGHT — DR FEELGOOD
AS LONG AS YOU FOLLOW — FLEETWOOD MAC
AS LONG AS YOU LOVE ME — BACKSTREET BOYS
AS LONG AS YOU'RE GOOD TO ME — Judy CHEEKS
AS TEARS GO BY — Marianne FAITHFULL
AS THE RUSH COMES — MOTORCYCLE
AS TIME GOES BY [A] — Richard ALLAN
AS TIME GOES BY [A] — Dooley WILSON
AS TIME GOES BY [A] — Jason DONOVAN
AS TIME GOES BY [B] — FUNKAPOLITAN
AS (UNTIL THE DAY) — KNOWLEDGE
AS USUAL — Brenda LEE
AS WE DO — DJ ZINC
AS YOU LIKE IT — Adam FAITH with John BARRY and his Orchestra
ASCEND — NITZER EBB
ASCENSION DON'T EVER WONDER [A] —MAXWELL
ASCENSION NO ONE'S GONNA LOVE YOU SO DON'T EVER WONDER [A] — MAXWELL
ASHES — EMBRACE
ASHES AND DIAMONDS — Zaine GRIFF
ASHES TO ASHES [A] — The MINDBENDERS
ASHES TO ASHES [B] — David BOWIE
ASHES TO ASHES [C] — FAITH NO MORE
ASIA MINOR — KOKOMO
ASK — The SMITHS
ASK THE LORD — HIPSWAY
ASLEEP IN THE BACK — ELBOW
ASSASSIN — The ORB
ASSASSINATOR 13 — CHIKINKI
ASSASSING — MARILLION
ASSESSMENT — The BETA BAND
ASSHOLE — Denis LEARY
ASSOCIATION — INTERNATIONAL AIRPORT / TEENAGE FANCLUB
ASTOUNDED — BRAN VAN 3000 featuring Curtis MAYFIELD
ASTRAL AMERICA — APOLLO 440
ASYLUM — The ORB
ASYLUMS IN JERUSALEM — SCRITTI POLITTI
AT HOME HE'S A TOURIST — GANG OF FOUR
AT MIDNIGHT — T-CONNECTION
AT MY MOST BEAUTIFUL — R.E.M.
AT NIGHT — SHAKEDOWN
AT THE CLUB — The DRIFTERS
AT THE EDGE — STIFF LITTLE FINGERS
AT THE END — IIO
AT THE HOP — DANNY and the JUNIORS
AT THE MOVIES — Roni SIZE
AT THE RIVER — GROOVE ARMADA
AT THE TOP OF THE STAIRS — FORMATIONS
AT THIS TIME OF YEAR — CRAIG
(AT YOUR BEST) YOU ARE LOVE — AALIYAH
ATHEAMA — NEBULA II
ATHENA — The WHO
ATLANTIS [A] — The SHADOWS
ATLANTIS [B] — DONOVAN
ATLANTIS [C] — SECTION-X
ATLANTIS IS CALLING (S.O.S. FOR LOVE) — MODERN TALKING
ATMOSPHERE [A] — Russ ABBOT
ATMOSPHERE [B] — JOY DIVISION
ATMOSPHERE [C] — KAYESTONE
ATMOSPHERIC ROAD — FAMILY CAT
ATOM BOMB — FLUKE
ATOM POWERED ACTION (EP) — BIS
ATOMIC — BLONDIE
ATOMIC CITY — Holly JOHNSON
ATTACK [A] — TOYS
ATTACK [B] — EXPLOITED
ATTACK ME WITH YOUR LOVE — CAMEO
ATTACK OF THE GHOSTRIDERS — The RAVEONETTES
ATTENTION TO ME — The NOLANS
ATTITUDE [A] — SEPULTURA
ATTITUDE [B] — ALIEN ANT FARM
ATTITUDE [C] — SUEDE
AUBERGE — Chris REA
AUDIO VIDEO — NEWS
AUDITION — WITNESS
AUF WIEDERSEH'N SWEETHEART — Vera LYNN
AUGUST OCTOBER — Robin GIBB
AULD LANG SYNE — WEEKEND
AUSLANDER — LIVING COLOUR
AUSTRALIA — MANIC STREET PREACHERS
AUTHORITY CONFRONTATION — SELFISH CUNT
AUTOBAHN — KRAFTWERK
AUTOBAHN 66 — PRIMAL SCREAM
AUTOBIOGRAPHY OF A CRACKHEAD — SHUT UP AND DANCE
AUTODRIVE — Herbie HANCOCK
AUTOMATIC [A] — POINTER SISTERS
AUTOMATIC [B] — Millie SCOTT
AUTOMATIC [C] — FLOORPLAY
AUTOMATIC [D] — Sarah WHATMORE
AUTOMATIC HIGH — S CLUB JUNIORS
AUTOMATIC LOVER [A] — VIBRATORS
AUTOMATIC LOVER [B] — Dee D JACKSON
AUTOMATIC LOVER (CALL FOR LOVE) — The REAL McCOY
AUTOMATICALLY SUNSHINE — The SUPREMES
AUTOMATIK — BEAT RENEGADES
AUTOPHILIA — The BLUETONES
AUTUMN — Roni SIZE and DIE
AUTUMN ALMANAC — The KINKS
AUTUMN CONCERTO — George MELACHRINO ORCHESTRA
AUTUMN LEAVES — COLDCUT
AUTUMN LOVE — ELECTRA
AUTUMN TACTICS — CHICANE
AVA ADORE — SMASHING PUMPKINS
AVALON — ROXY MUSIC
AVE MARIA [A] — Shirley BASSEY
AVE MARIA [A] — Lesley GARRETT and Amanda THOMPSON
AVE MARIA [A] — Andrea BOCELLI
AVENGING ANGELS — SPACE
AVENUE [A] — SAINT ETIENNE
AVENUE [B] — Paul VAN DYK
AVENUES AND ALLEYWAYS — Tony CHRISTIE
AVERAGE MAN [A] — SYMPOSIUM
AVERAGE MAN [B] — TURIN BRAKES
THE AVERAGE MAN [C] — SIMPLE KID
THE AWAKENING — YORK
AWAY FROM HOME — DR ALBAN
AWAY FROM ME — PUDDLE OF MUDD
AWFUL — HOLE
AXEL F [A] — Harold FALTERMEYER
AXEL F [A] — CLOCK
AXEL F [A] — SPACECORN
AY AY AY AY MOOSEY — MODERN ROMANCE
AYLA — AYLA
AZTEC GOLD — SILSOE
AZTEC LIGHTNING (THEME FROM BBC WORLD CUP GRANDSTAND) — HEADS
B-BOY HUMP — OLD SKOOL ORCHESTRA
B-BOY STANCE — FREESTYLERS featuring TENOR FLY
B GOOD 2 ME — Ronni SIMON
B LINE — LAMB
B O B BOMBS OVER BAGHDAD — OUTKAST
B 2 GETHER — ORIGINAL
B WITH ME — MIS-TEEQ
B WITH U — Junior SANCHEZ featuring DAJAE
BAA BAA BLACK SHEEP — SINGING SHEEP
BAAL'S HYMN (EP) — David BOWIE
BA-BA-BANKROBBERY (ENGLISH VERSION) — EAV
BABALON A.D. (SO GLAD FOR THE MADNESS) — CRADLE OF FILTH
BABARABATIRI — GYPSYMEN
BABE [A] — STYX
BABE [B] — TAKE THAT
BABES IN THE WOOD — MATCHBOX
BABETTE — Tommy BRUCE and the BRUISERS
BABIES — ASHFORD and SIMPSON
BABOOSHKA — Kate BUSH
B-A-B-Y — Rachel SWEET
BABY [A] — HALO JAMES
BABY [B] — ROZALLA
THE BABY — The HOLLIES
BABY, BABY [A] — Frankie LYMON and the TEENAGERS
BABY BABY [B] — EIGHTH WONDER
BABY BABY [C] — Amy GRANT
BABY BABY [D] — CORONA
BABY-BABY-BABY — TLC
BABY BABY BYE BYE — Jerry Lee LEWIS
BABY, BABY MY LOVE'S ALL FOR YOU — Deniece WILLIAMS
BABY BE MINE — BLACKSTREET featuring Teddy RILEY
BABY BLUE — Dusty SPRINGFIELD
BABY BOY [A] — BIG BROVAZ
BABY BOY [B] — BEYONCÉ featuring Sean PAUL
BABY BRITAIN — Elliott SMITH
BABY CAKES — 3 OF A KIND
BABY, CAN I GET YOUR NUMBER — OBI PROJECT featuring HARRY, ASHER D & DJ WHAT?
BABY CAN I HOLD YOU — BOYZONE
BABY COME BACK [A] — The EQUALS
BABY COME BACK [A] — Pato BANTON
BABY COME BACK [B] — PLAYER
BABY COME ON — SPACEMAID
BABY COME ON OVER — Samantha MUMBA
BABY COME TO ME [A] — Patti AUSTIN and James INGRAM
BABY COME TO ME [A] — Alexander O'NEAL featuring CHERELLE
BABY DID A BAD BAD THING — Chris ISAAK
BABY DON'T CHANGE YOUR MIND — Gladys KNIGHT and the PIPS
BABY DON'T CRY [A] — Lalah HATHAWAY
BABY DON'T CRY [B] — INXS
BABY DON'T FORGET MY NUMBER — MILLI VANILLI
BABY DON'T GET HOOKED ON ME — Mac DAVIS
BABY DON'T GO [A] — SONNY and CHER
BABY DON'T GO [B] — 4MANDU
BABY FACE [A] — LITTLE RICHARD
BABY FACE [A] — Bobby DARIN
BABY FACE [A] — WING AND A PRAYER FIFE AND DRUM CORPS
BABY GET HIGHER — David SNEDDON
BABY GOT BACK — SIR MIX-A-LOT
BABY I DON'T CARE [A] — Buddy HOLLY
BABY I DON'T CARE [A] — Elvis PRESLEY
BABY I DON'T CARE [B] — TRANSVISION VAMP
BABY I DON'T CARE [B] — Jennifer ELLISON
BABY I KNOW — The RUBETTES
BABY I LOVE U — Jennifer LOPEZ
BABY I LOVE YOU [A] — The RONETTES
BABY I LOVE YOU [A] — Dave EDMUNDS
BABY I LOVE YOU [A] — The RAMONES
BABY I LOVE YOU [A] — TSD
BABY I LOVE YOU [B] — Aretha FRANKLIN
BABY I LOVE YOU, OK! — KENNY
BABY I LOVE YOUR WAY [A] — Peter FRAMPTON
BABY I LOVE YOUR WAY [A] — BIG MOUNTAIN
BABY I LOVE YOUR WAY — FREEBIRD — WILL TO POWER
BABY I NEED YOUR LOVIN' — The FOURMOST
BABY I WON'T LET YOU DOWN — PICKETTYWITCH
BABY I'M-A WANT YOU — BREAD
BABY I'M SCARED OF YOU — WOMACK and WOMACK
BABY I'M YOURS [A] — PETER and GORDON
BABY I'M YOURS [A] — Linda LEWIS
BABY, IT'S COLD OUTSIDE — Tom JONES
BABY IT'S TRUE — Mari WILSON
BABY IT'S YOU [A] — Dave BERRY
BABY IT'S YOU [A] — The BEATLES
BABY IT'S YOU [B] — SILK
BABY IT'S YOU [C] — MN8
BABY IT'S YOU [D] — JOJO featuring BOW WOW
BABY JANE — Rod STEWART
BABY JUMP — MUNGO JERRY
BABY LAY DOWN — Ruby WINTERS
BABY LEE — John Lee HOOKER
BABY LET ME TAKE YOU HOME — The ANIMALS
BABY LOVE [A] — The SUPREMES
BABY LOVE [A] — Honey BANE
BABY LOVE [B] — REGINA
BABY LOVE [B] — Dannii MINOGUE
BABY LOVER — Petula CLARK
BABY MAKE IT SOON — MARMALADE
BABY MY HEART — The CRICKETS
BABY NEVER SAY GOODBYE — UNIT FOUR PLUS TWO
BABY NOW I — Dan REED NETWORK
BABY NOW THAT I'VE FOUND YOU [A] — The FOUNDATIONS
BABY NOW THAT I'VE FOUND YOU [A] — Lauren WATERWORTH
BABY OF MINE — Alan PRICE
BABY (OFF THE WALL) — SIRENS
... BABY ONE MORE TIME — Britney SPEARS
BABY PHAT — DE LA SOUL
BABY PLAYS AROUND (EP) — Elvis COSTELLO
BABY PLEASE DON'T GO — THEM
BABY ROO — Connie FRANCIS
BABY SITTIN' — Bobby ANGELO and the TUXEDOS
BABY SITTIN' BOOGIE — Buzz CLIFFORD
BABY STOP CRYING — Bob DYLAN
BABY TAKE A BOW — Adam FAITH
BABY TALK — ALISHA
BABY U LEFT ME (IN THE COLD) — MARILYN
BABY UNIVERSAL — TIN MACHINE
BABY WANTS TO RIDE — HANI
BABY, WE BETTER TRY TO GET IT TOGETHER — Barry WHITE
BABY WE CAN'T GO WRONG — Cilla BLACK
BABY, WHAT A BIG SURPRISE — CHICAGO
BABY WHAT I MEAN — The DRIFTERS
(BABY) YOU DON'T HAVE TO TELL ME — The WALKER BROTHERS
BABY YOU SHOULD KNOW — JOY ZIPPER

BABY YOU'RE DYNAMITE — Cliff RICHARD
BABYLON [A] —
    BLACK DOG featuring Ofra HAZA
BABYLON [B] — David GRAY
BABYLON'S BURNING — RUTS
BABY'S COMING BACK — JELLYFISH
BABY'S FIRST CHRISTMAS — Connie FRANCIS
BABY'S GOT A TEMPER — The PRODIGY
BABY'S REQUEST — Paul McCARTNEY
BABYSHAMBLES — Peter DOHERTY
BACHELOR BOY —
    Cliff RICHARD and The SHADOWS
BACHELORETTE — BJÖRK
BACK AND FORTH [A] — CAMEO
BACK AND FORTH [B] — AALIYAH
BACK AROUND — ELEVATOR SUITE
BACK BY DOPE DEMAND — KING BEE
BACK FOR GOOD [A] — TAKE THAT
BACK FOR GOOD [B] — REAL EMOTION
BACK FOR ME — Candee JAY
BACK FROM THE EDGE — Bruce DICKINSON
BACK HERE — BBMAK
BACK HOME — ENGLAND WORLD CUP SQUAD
BACK IN LOVE AGAIN — Donna SUMMER
BACK IN MY ARMS — Chris PAUL
BACK IN MY ARMS AGAIN — The SUPREMES
BACK IN MY ARMS (ONCE AGAIN) —
    Hazell DEAN
BACK IN MY LIFE [A] — Joe ROBERTS
BACK IN MY LIFE [B] — ALICE DEEJAY
BACK IN THE DAY [A] — AHMAD
BACK IN THE DAY [B] — ASHER D
BACK IN THE HIGH LIFE AGAIN —
    Steve WINWOOD
BACK IN THE UK — SCOOTER
BACK IN THE U.S.S.R. — The BEATLES
BACK IT UP — Robin S
THE BACK OF LOVE —
    ECHO and the BUNNYMEN
BACK OF MY HAND — JAGS
BACK OFF BOOGALOO — Ringo STARR
BACK ON MY FEET AGAIN —
    The FOUNDATIONS
BACK ON THE CHAIN GANG —
    The PRETENDERS
BACK ON THE ROAD [A] — The HISS
BACK ON THE ROAD [A] — MARMALADE
BACK ON THE ROAD [B] —
    EARTH WIND AND FIRE
BACK ON THE STREETS — SAXON
BACK ON TOP — Van MORRISON
BACK SEAT OF MY CAR — Linda McCARTNEY
BACK STABBERS — O'JAYS
BACK STREET LUV — CURVED AIR
BACK THEN — MORE FIRE CREW
BACK TO CALI — Mauro PICOTTO
BACK TO EARTH — Yves DERUYTER
BACK TO FRONT [A] — STIFF LITTLE FINGERS
BACK TO FRONT [B] — ADAMSKI
BACK TO LIFE (HOWEVER DO YOU WANT ME) —
    SOUL II SOUL featuring Caron WHEELER
BACK TO LOVE [A] —
    Evelyn 'Champagne' KING
BACK TO LOVE [B] — The BRAND NEW HEAVIES
BACK TO LOVE [C] — E-Z ROLLERS
BACK TO MY ROOTS — RuPAUL
BACK TO REALITY — INTELLIGENT HOODLUM
BACK TO SCHOOL AGAIN — The FOUR TOPS
BACK TO THE LIGHT — Brian MAY
BACK TO THE OLD SCHOOL — BASSHEADS
BACK TO THE SIXTIES — TIGHT FIT
BACK TO THE SIXTIES PART 2 — TIGHT FIT
BACK TO YOU — Bryan ADAMS
BACK TOGETHER — BABYBIRD
BACK TOGETHER AGAIN — Roberta FLACK
BACK TOGETHER AGAIN [A] — INNER CITY
BACK UP (TO ME) — WOOKIE featuring LAIN
BACK WHEN — ALLSTARS
BACK WITH THE BOYS AGAIN — Joe FAGIN
BACK WITH THE KILLER AGAIN —
    The AUTEURS
BACKCHAT — QUEEN
BACKFIELD IN MOTION — JB's ALL STARS
BACKFIRED [A] — Deborah HARRY
BACKFIRED [B] — MASTERS AT WORK
BACKS TO THE WALL — SAXON
BACKSEAT EDUCATION — ZODIAC
    MINDWARP and the LOVE REACTION
BACKSTABBERS — Mark MORRISON
BACKSTAGE — Gene PITNEY
BACKSTREET SYMPHONY — THUNDER
BACKSTROKIN' — FATBACK BAND
BACKTOGETHER —
    HARDSOUL featuring Ron CARROLL
BAD — Michael JACKSON
BAD ACTRESS — TERRORVISION
BAD AMBASSADOR — The DIVINE COMEDY
BAD ASS STRIPPA — JENTINA
BAD BABYSITTER — PRINCESS SUPERSTAR
BAD BAD BOY — NAZARETH
BAD BOY [A] — Marty WILDE
BAD BOY [B] — ADICTS
BAD BOY [C] — MIAMI SOUND MACHINE
BAD BOY [D] — WILDCHILD
BAD BOY FOR LIFE — P DIDDY featuring
    BLACK ROB and Mark CURRY
BAD BOYS [A] — WHAM!

BAD BOYS [B] — INNER CIRCLE
BAD BOYS HOLLER BOO — 5050
BAD CASE OF LOVIN' YOU (DOCTOR DOCTOR) —
    Robert PALMER
BAD COVER VERSION — PULP
BAD DAY [A] — CARMEL
BAD DAY [B] — R.E.M.
THE BAD DAYS (EP) — SPACE
BAD FEELING — The BEATINGS
BAD GIRL [A] — MADONNA
BAD GIRL [B] — SCARLET
BAD GIRL [C] — DJ RAP
BAD GIRLS [A] — Donna SUMMER
BAD GIRLS [B] — Juliet ROBERTS
BAD HABIT —
    A.T.F.C. presents ONEPHATDEEVA
BAD HABITS — Jenny BURTON
BAD INTENTIONS —
    DR DRE featuring KNOC-TURN'AL
BAD LIFE — PUBLIC IMAGE LTD
BAD LOVE — Eric CLAPTON
BAD LUCK — FM
BAD MAN — SISTER BLISS
BAD MEDICINE — BON JOVI
BAD MOON RISING —
    CREEDENCE CLEARWATER REVIVAL
A BAD NIGHT — Cat STEVENS
BAD OLD DAYS — CO-CO
BAD OLD MAN — BABYBIRD
BAD PENNY BLUES —
    Humphrey LYTTELTON BAND
THE BAD PHOTOGRAPHER — SAINT ETIENNE
BAD THING — CRY OF LOVE
BAD THINGS — N-JOI
BAD TIME — JAYHAWKS
BAD TO ME —
    Billy J KRAMER and the DAKOTAS
THE BAD TOUCH — BLOODHOUND GANG
A BAD TOWN — BIG SOUND AUTHORITY
BAD WEATHER — The SUPREMES
BAD YOUNG BROTHER — Derek B
BADABOOM — B2K featuring FABOLOUS
BADDER BADDER SCHWING —
    Freddy FRESH featuring FATBOY SLIM
BADDEST RUFFEST — BACKYARD DOG
BADGE — CREAM
BADMAN — COCKNEY REJECTS
THE BADMAN IS ROBBIN' — HIJACK
BAG IT UP — Geri HALLIWELL
BAGGY TROUSERS — MADNESS
THE BAGUIO TRACK — LUZON
BAILAMOS [A] — Enrique IGLESIAS
BAILAMOS [B] — M3
BAILANDO CON LOBOS — CABANA
BAKER STREET [A] — Gerry RAFFERTY
BAKER STREET [A] — UNDERCOVER
BAKERMAN — LAID BACK
BALL AND CHAIN — XTC
BALL OF CONFUSION — The TEMPTATIONS
BALL PARK INCIDENT — WIZZARD
BALLA BABY — CHINGY
THE BALLAD OF A LANDLORD — Terry HALL
THE BALLAD OF BONNIE AND CLYDE —
    Georgie FAME
THE BALLAD OF CHASEY LAIN —
    BLOODHOUND GANG
BALLAD OF DAVY CROCKETT [A] — Dick JAMES
THE BALLAD OF DAVY CROCKETT [A] —
    Bill HAYES
THE BALLAD OF DAVY CROCKETT [A] —
    Max BYGRAVES
THE BALLAD OF DAVY CROCKETT [A] —
    Tennessee Ernie FORD
THE BALLAD OF JAYNE — L.A. GUNS
THE BALLAD OF JOHN AND YOKO —
    The BEATLES
THE BALLAD OF LUCY JORDAN —
    Marianne FAITHFULL
BALLAD OF PALADIN —
    Duane EDDY and the REBELS
THE BALLAD OF PETER PUMPKINHEAD [A] —
    CRASH TEST DUMMIES
THE BALLAD OF PETER PUMPKINHEAD [A] —
    XTC
THE BALLAD OF SPOTTY MULDOON —
    Peter COOK
THE BALLAD OF THE GREEN BERETS —
    Staff Sergeant Barry SADLER
THE BALLAD OF TOM JONES —
    SPACE with Cerys of CATATONIA
BALLAD OF YOUTH — Richie SAMBORA
BALLERINA GIRL — Lionel RICHIE
BALLERINA (PRIMA DONNA) —
    Steve HARLEY and COCKNEY REBEL
BALLOON — CATHERINE WHEEL
THE BALLROOM BLITZ [A] — The SWEET
BALLROOM BLITZ [A] — Tia CARRERE
THE BALLROOM OF ROMANCE —
    Chris DE BURGH
BALMES — Ian POOLEY featuring ESTHERO
BAM BAM BAM — WESTBAM
BAMA BOOGIE WOOGIE — Cleveland EATON
BAMA LAMA BAMA LOO — LITTLE RICHARD
BAMBAATA 2012 — SHY FX
BAMBAKITA — Roni SIZE
BAMBINO — The SPRINGFIELDS
BAMBOO HOUSES — David SYLVIAN

BAMBOO MUSIC — David SYLVIAN
BAMBOOGIE — BAMBOO
BANANA BANANA — KING KURT
BANANA BOAT SONG [A] — Harry BELAFONTE
BANANA BOAT SONG [A] — TARRIERS
THE BANANA BOAT SONG [A] —
    Shirley BASSEY
BANANA REPUBLIC — The BOOMTOWN RATS
BANANA ROCK — The WOMBLES
THE BANANA SONG — GSP
BANANA SPLITS (THE TRA LA LA SONG) —
    The DICKIES
BA-NA-NA-BAM-BOO — WESTWORLD
BANANA-NA-NA (DUMB DI DUMB) —
    TECHNOHEAD
BAND OF GOLD [A] — Don CHERRY
BAND OF GOLD [B] — Freda PAYNE
BAND OF GOLD [B] — SYLVESTER
BAND ON THE RUN — Paul McCARTNEY
THE BAND PLAYED THE BOOGIE — CCS
BANDAGES — HOT HOT HEAT
BANDWAGON BLUES — TWISTED INDIVIDUAL
BANG [A] — BLUR
BANG [B] —
    Robbie RIVERA presents RHYTHM BANGERS
BANG AND BLAME — R.E.M.
BANG BANG [A] — SQUEEZE
BANG BANG [B] — B.A. ROBERTSON
BANG BANG (MY BABY SHOT ME DOWN) — CHER
BANG ON! — PROPELLERHEADS
BANG ZOOM (LET'S GO GO) — REAL ROXANNE
BANGERS AND MASH — Peter SELLERS
BANGIN' BASS — DA TECHNO BOHEMIAN
THE BANGIN' MAN — SLADE
BANGLA-DESH — George HARRISON
BANJO BOY [A] — JAN and KJELD
BANJO BOY [B] — George FORMBY
THE BANJO'S BACK IN TOWN — Alma COGAN
BANKROBBER [A] — AUDIOWEB
BANKROBBER [A] — The CLASH
BANKS OF THE OHIO — Olivia NEWTON-JOHN
BANNER MAN — BLUE MINK
BANQUET — BLOC PARTY
BARBADOS — TYPICALLY TROPICAL
BARBARA ANN — The BEACH BOYS
BARBARELLA — ALISHA'S ATTIC
BARBER'S ADAGIO FOR STRINGS —
    William ORBIT
BARBIE GIRL — AQUA
BARCELONA [A] — Freddie MERCURY
BARCELONA [B] — D KAY & EPSILON
    featuring STAMINA MC
BARCELONA (FRIENDS UNTIL THE END) —
    Russell WATSON
BARE NECESSITIES MEGAMIX —
    UK MIXMASTERS
BAREFOOT (EP) — ULTRAMARINE
BAREFOOT IN THE HEAD —
    A MAN CALLED ADAM
BAREFOOTIN' — Robert PARKER
BARK AT THE MOON — Ozzy OSBOURNE
BARMY LONDON ARMY — Charlie HARPER
BARNEY (... & ME) — BOO RADLEYS
BARREL OF A GUN — DEPECHE MODE
BARRIERS — SOFT CELL
THE BARTENDER AND THE THIEF —
    STEREOPHONICS
BASEMENT TRACK — HIGH CONTRAST
BASKET CASE — GREEN DAY
THE BASS EP — FERGIE
BASS (HOW LOW CAN YOU GO) —
    Simon HARRIS
BASS SHAKE — URBAN SHAKEDOWN
BASSCAD — AUTECHRE
BASSFLY — TILLMAN AND REIS
BASSLICK — SECOND PROTOCOL
BASSLINE — MANTRONIX
BAT OUT OF HELL — MEAT LOAF
BATTER UP — NELLY and ST LUNATICS
BATDANCE — PRINCE
BATHTIME — TINDERSTICKS
BATHWATER — NO DOUBT
BATMAN THEME — Neal HEFTI
BATTLE — WOOKIE
BATTLE OF NEW ORLEANS [A] —
    Johnny HORTON
BATTLE OF NEW ORLEANS [A] —
    Lonnie DONEGAN
BATTLE OF THE SEXES —
    FAITH, HOPE AND CHARITY
BATTLE OF WHO COULD CARE LESS —
    Ben FOLDS FIVE
BATTLEFLAG — LO FIDELITY ALLSTARS
THE BATTLE'S O'ER — Andy STEWART
BATTLESHIP CHAINS — GEORGIA SATELLITES
BAUBLES BANGLES AND BEADS —
    George SHEARING
BAUHAUS — CAPPELLA
BAWITABA — KID ROCK
BBC WORLD CUP GRANDSTAND —
    ROYAL PHILHARMONIC ORCHESTRA arranged and
    conducted by Louis CLARK
BE AGGRESSIVE — FAITH NO MORE
BE ALONE NO MORE — ANOTHER LEVEL
BE ANGELED — JAM & SPOON featuring REA
BE AS ONE — Maria NAYLER
BE-BOP-A-LULA — Gene VINCENT

BE CAREFUL — SPARKLE featuring R Kelly
BE COOL — PAFFENDORF
BE FAITHFUL — FATMAN SCOOP featuring
    the CROOKLYN CLAN
BE FREE — LIVE ELEMENT
BE FREE WITH YOUR LOVE — SPANDAU BALLET
BE GOOD TO YOURSELF — Frankie MILLER
BE HAPPY — Mary J BLIGE
BE MINE [A] — Lance FORTUNE
BE MINE [B] — The TREMELOES
BE MINE [C] — CHARLOTTE
BE MINE [D] — David GRAY
BE MINE TONIGHT — JAMMERS
BE MY BABY [A] — The RONETTES
BE MY BABY [B] — Vanessa PARADIS
BE MY BABY [C] — CAPPELLA
BE MY DOWNFALL — DEL AMITRI
BE MY ENEMY — The DEPARTURE
BE MY FRIEND — SOUL U*NIQUE
BE MY GIRL [A] — Jim DALE
BE MY GIRL [B] — DENNISONS
BE MY GUEST — Fats DOMINO
BE MY LIGHT BE MY GUIDE — GENE
BE MY LOVER — LA BOUCHE
BE MY NUMBER TWO — Joe JACKSON
BE MY TWIN — BROTHER BEYOND
BE NEAR ME — ABC
BE PROUD BE LOUD (BE HEARD) — TOYAH
BE QUICK OR BE DEAD — IRON MAIDEN
BE QUIET AND DRIVE (FAR AWAY) — DEFTONES
BE STIFF — DEVO
BE TENDER WITH ME BABY — Tina TURNER
BE THANKFUL FOR WHAT YOU'VE GOT —
    William DE VAUGHN
BE THE FIRST TO BELIEVE — a1
BE THERE [A] — TALL PAUL
BE THERE [B] — Ian BROWN
BE WITH ME ALWAYS — Cliff RICHARD
BE WITH YOU [A] — The BANGLES
BE WITH YOU [B] — ATOMIC KITTEN
BE YOUNG, BE FOOLISH, BE HAPPY — TAMS
BE YOUNG BE FOOLISH BE HAPPY — SONIA
BE YOURSELF — CELEDA
BEACH BABY — FIRST CLASS
BEACH BOY GOLD — GIDEA PARK
BEACH BOYS MEDLEY — The BEACH BOYS
BEACH BUMP — BABY FORD
BEACH OF THE WAR GODDESS —
    Caron WHEELER
BEACHBALL — NALIN & KANE
BEACHED — ORBITAL
BEACON LIGHT — WEEN
BEAR CAGE — The STRANGLERS
BEAT BOX — ART OF NOISE
A BEAT CALLED LOVE — GRID
BEAT DIS — BOMB THE BASS
BEAT FOR BEATNIKS —
    John BARRY ORCHESTRA
THE BEAT GOES ON [A] — SONNY and CHER
BEAT GOES ON [A] — The ALL SEEING I
THE BEAT GOES ON [B] — Bob SINCLAR
BEAT IT — Michael JACKSON
BEAT MAMA — CAST
BEAT STREET BREAKDOWN — GRANDMASTER FLASH,
    Melle MEL and the FURIOUS FIVE
BEAT SURRENDER — The JAM
BEAT THE BEAT — Mari WILSON
BEAT THE CLOCK — SPARKS
BEAT YOUR HEART OUT — The DISTILLERS
THE BEAT(EN) GENERATION — The THE
BEATIN' THE HEAT — JACK 'N' CHILL
BEATLES AND THE STONES —
    HOUSE OF LOVE
BEATLES MOVIE MEDLEY — The BEATLES
BEATNIK FLY — JOHNNY and the HURRICANES
BEATNIK GIRL — SNUG
BEATSTIME — SONIC SOLUTION
BEAUTIFUL [A] — MARILLION
BEAUTIFUL [B] — Matt DAREY
BEAUTIFUL [B] —
    Matt DAREY featuring Marcella WOODS
BEAUTIFUL [C] — ATHLETE
BEAUTIFUL [D] — LEMONESCENT
BEAUTIFUL [E] —
    BIGFELLA featuring Noel MCCALLA
BEAUTIFUL [F] — SNOOP DOGG featuring
    PHARRELL, uncle Charlie WILSON
BEAUTIFUL [G] — Christina AGUILERA
BEAUTIFUL ALONE — STRANGELOVE
BEAUTIFUL CHILD (A DEEPER LOVE) —
    MADELYNE
BEAUTIFUL DAY [A] — 3 COLOURS RED
BEAUTIFUL DAY [B] — U2
BEAUTIFUL DREAM — WORLD PARTY
THE BEAUTIFUL EXPERIENCE — PRINCE
BEAUTIFUL GIRL — INXS
BEAUTIFUL IMBALANCE — THRASHING DOVES
BEAUTIFUL IN MY EYES — Joshua KADISON
BEAUTIFUL INSIDE — LOUISE
BEAUTIFUL LIFE — ACE OF BASE
BEAUTIFUL LOVE [A] — ADEVA
BEAUTIFUL LOVE [B] — Julian COPE
BEAUTIFUL LOVER — BROTHERHOOD OF MAN
BEAUTIFUL NIGHT — Paul McCARTNEY
BEAUTIFUL NOISE — Neil DIAMOND
THE BEAUTIFUL OCCUPATION — TRAVIS
BEAUTIFUL ONES — SUEDE

BEAUTIFUL PEOPLE [A] — STRESS
BEAUTIFUL PEOPLE [B] — BIG COUNTRY
BEAUTIFUL PEOPLE [C] — Barbara TUCKER
THE BEAUTIFUL PEOPLE [d] —
	MARILYN MANSON
BEAUTIFUL SON — HOLE
BEAUTIFUL STRANGER — MADONNA
BEAUTIFUL SUNDAY — Daniel BOONE
BEAUTIFUL YOU — Neil SEDAKA
BEAUTY AND THE BEAST [A] — David BOWIE
BEAUTY AND THE BEAST [B] —
	Celine DION and Peabo BRYSON
BEAUTY DIES YOUNG — LOWGOLD
BEAUTY IS ONLY SKIN DEEP —
	The TEMPTATIONS
THE BEAUTY OF SILENCE —
	SVENSON and GIELEN
BEAUTY OF THE RIDE — SEBADOH
BEAUTY ON THE FIRE — Natalie IMBRUGLIA
BEAUTY'S ONLY SKIN DEEP — ASWAD
BECAUSE [A] — Demis ROUSSOS
BECAUSE [B] — Julian LENNON
BECAUSE I GOT HIGH — AFROMAN
BECAUSE I GOT IT LIKE THAT —
	The JUNGLE BROTHERS
BECAUSE I LOVE YOU [A] — Georgie FAME
BECAUSE I LOVE YOU [B] — Shakin' STEVENS
BECAUSE I LOVE YOU (THE POSTMAN SONG) —
	Stevie B
BECAUSE OF LOVE [A] — Billy FURY
BECAUSE OF LOVE [B] — Janet JACKSON
BECAUSE OF YOU [A] —
	DEXY'S MIDNIGHT RUNNERS
BECAUSE OF YOU [B] — GABRIELLE
BECAUSE OF YOU [C] — 98º
BECAUSE OF YOU [D] — SCANTY SANDWICH
BECAUSE OF YOU [E] — Marques HOUSTON
BECAUSE THE NIGHT [A] — Patti SMITH GROUP
BECAUSE THE NIGHT [A] —
	CO-RO featuring TARLISA
BECAUSE THE NIGHT [A] — 10,000 MANIACS
BECAUSE THE NIGHT [A] — Jan WAYNE
BECAUSE THEY'RE YOUNG [A] —
	Duane EDDY and the REBELS
BECAUSE THEY'RE YOUNG [A] — James DARREN
BECAUSE WE WANT TO — Billie PIPER
BECAUSE YOU — COSMIC ROUGH RIDERS
BECAUSE YOU LOVED ME (THEME FROM 'UP CLOSE
	AND PERSONAL') — Celine DION
BECAUSE YOU'RE MINE [A] — Mario LANZA
BECAUSE YOU'RE MINE [A] — Nat 'King' COLE
BECAUSE YOU'RE YOUNG —
	CLASSIX NOUVEAUX
BECOMING MORE LIKE ALFIE —
	The DIVINE COMEDY
BECOMING MORE LIKE GOD — Jah WOBBLE'S
	INVADERS OF THE HEART
BED OF NAILS — Alice COOPER
BED OF ROSES — BON JOVI
BEDS ARE BURNING — MIDNIGHT OIL
THE BED'S TOO BIG WITHOUT YOU —
	Sheila HYLTON
BEDSHAPED — KEANE
BEDSITTER — SOFT CELL
BEDTIME STORY — MADONNA
THE BEE — SCIENTIST
BEE BOM — Anthony NEWLEY
BEE STING — CAMOUFLAGE featuring MYSTI
BEEF — Gary CLAIL ON-U SOUND SYSTEM
BEEN A LONG TIME — FOG
BEEN AROUND THE WORLD [A] — PUFF DADDY
BEEN AROUND THE WORLD [B] —
	ZENA featuring Vybz KARTEL
BEEN CAUGHT STEALING — JANE'S ADDICTION
BEEN IT — The CARDIGANS
BEEN THINKING ABOUT YOU —
	Martine GIRAULT
BEEN THERE DONE THAT — SMOKE 2 SEVEN
BEEN TRAINING DOGS —
	The COOPER TEMPLE CLAUSE
BEEP ME 911 — Missy 'Misdemeanor' ELLIOTT
BEER DRINKERS AND HELL RAISERS —
	MOTÖRHEAD
BEETHOVEN (I LOVE TO LISTEN TO) —
	EURYTHMICS
BEETLEBUM — BLUR
BEFORE — PET SHOP BOYS
BEFORE TODAY — EVERYTHING BUT THE GIRL
BEFORE YOU LEAVE — PEPE DELUXÉ
BEFORE YOU LOVE ME — ALSOU
BEFORE YOU WALK OUT OF MY LIFE —
	MONICA
BEG, STEAL OR BORROW —
	The NEW SEEKERS
A BEGGAR ON A BEACH OF GOLD —
	MIKE and the MECHANICS
BEGGIN' — TIMEBOX
BEGGIN' TO BE WRITTEN — WORLDS APART
BEGGING YOU — The STONE ROSES
BEGIN AGAIN — SPACE
BEGIN THE BEGUINE (VOLVER A EMPEZAR) —
	Julio IGLESIAS
THE BEGINNING — SEAL
BEHIND A PAINTED SMILE — ISLEY BROTHERS
BEHIND BLUE EYES — LIMP BIZKIT
BEHIND CLOSED DOORS — Charlie RICH
BEHIND THE COUNTER — The FALL

BEHIND THE GROOVE — Teena MARIE
BEHIND THE MASK — Eric CLAPTON
BEHIND THE WHEEL — DEPECHE MODE
BEIN' AROUND — LEMONHEADS
BEING A GIRL (PART ONE) (EP) — MANSUN
BEING BOILED — HUMAN LEAGUE
BEING BORING — PET SHOP BOYS
BEING BRAVE — MENSWEAR
BEING NOBODY — RICHARD X vs LIBERTY X
BEING WITH YOU — Smokey ROBINSON
BEL AMOUR — BEL AMOUR
BELARUSE — LEVELLERS
BELFAST [A] — BONEY M
BELFAST [B] — BARNBRACK
BELFAST [C] — ENERGY ORCHARD
BELFAST [D] — ORBITAL
BELFAST BOY — Don FARDON
BELFAST CHILD — SIMPLE MINDS
BELFAST TRANCE —
	John 'OO' FLEMING vs SIMPLE MINDS
BELIEVE [A] — Lenny KRAVITZ
BELIEVE [B] — Q-TEX
BELIEVE [C] — Elton JOHN
BELIEVE [D] — GOLDIE
BELIEVE [E] — CHER
BELIEVE [F] — MINISTERS DA LA FUNK
	featuring Jocelyn BROWN
BELIEVE [G] — IAN VAN DAHL
BELIEVE IN ME [A] — UTAH SAINTS
BELIEVE IN ME [B] — QUIVVER
BELIEVE IN ME [C] — MANKEY
BELIEVE IN ME [D] — RAW STYLUS
BELIEVE IN THE BEAT — Carol Lynn TOWNES
BELIEVE WHAT YOU'RE SAYING — SUGAR
BELIEVER — REAL PEOPLE
BELIEVERS — BAZ
THE BELL — Mike OLDFIELD
BELL BOTTOM BLUES — Alma COGAN
BELL BOTTOMED TEAR —
	The BEAUTIFUL SOUTH
THE BELLE OF ST MARK — Sheila E
BELLISSIMA — DJ QUICKSILVER
BELLS OF AVIGNON — Max BYGRAVES
BELLS OF NY — SLO-MOSHUN
BELO HORIZONTI — HEARTISTS
BEN [A] — Marti WEBB
BEN [A] — Michael JACKSON
BEN [A] — Toni WARNE
BEND IT — Dave DEE, DOZY,
	BEAKY, MICK and TICH
BEND ME SHAPE ME [A] — AMEN CORNER
BEND ME SHAPE ME [A] — AMERICAN BREED
BENEDICTUS — BRAINBUG
BENJAMIN — VERUCA SALT
BENNIE AND THE JETS — Elton JOHN
BENNY'S THEME — Paul HENRY and
	the Mayson GLEN ORCHESTRA
BENTLEY'S GONNA SORT YOU OUT! —
	BENTLEY RHYTHM ACE
BERMUDA TRIANGLE — Barry MANILOW
BERNADETTE — The FOUR TOPS
BERRY — TC
BERSERKER — Gary NUMAN
BESAME MUCHO — Jet HARRIS
BESIDE YOU — Iggy POP
THE BEST — Tina TURNER
BEST BIT (EP) — Beth ORTON
	featuring Terry CALLIER
THE BEST CHRISTMAS OF THEM ALL —
	Shakin' STEVENS
BEST DAYS — JUICE
THE BEST DAYS OF OUR LIVES —
	LISBON LIONS featuring Martin
	O'NEIL & the CELTIC CHOIR
THE BEST DISCO IN TOWN —
	RITCHIE FAMILY
BEST FRIEND [A] — The BEAT
BEST FRIEND [B] —
	Mark MORRISON and Conner REEVES
BEST FRIEND [C] — PUFF DADDY
BEST FRIENDS [A] — TOY-BOX
BEST FRIENDS [B] — ALLSTARS
BEST FRIENDS FOREVER — TWEENIES
BEST FRIEND'S GIRL — ELECTRASY
BEST I CAN — QUEENSRYCHE
BEST IN ME — LET LOOSE
THE BEST IS YET TO COME — SCOOCH
BEST KEPT SECRET — CHINA CRISIS
BEST LOVE — COURSE
THE BEST OF EVERYTHING — Johnny MATHIS
THE BEST OF LOVE — Michael BOLTON
THE BEST OF ME [A] — Cliff RICHARD
THE BEST OF ME [B] — Bryan ADAMS
BEST OF MY LOVE [A] — The EMOTIONS
BEST OF MY LOVE [A] — Dee LEWIS
BEST OF MY LOVE [A] — LOVESTATION
BEST OF MY LOVE [A] — CJ LEWIS
BEST OF MY LOVE [A] — JAVINE
BEST OF ORDER — David SNEDDON
THE BEST OF TIMES — STYX
BEST OF YOU — Kenny THOMAS
(THE BEST PART OF) BREAKING UP [A] —
	The RONETTES
(THE BEST PART OF) BREAKING UP [A] —
	SYMBOLS
(THE BEST PART OF) BREAKING UP [A] —
	Roni GRIFFITH

BEST REGRETS — GENEVA
BEST THING — Adam RICKITT
THE BEST THING — SAVAGE GARDEN
BEST THING IN THE WORLD — OPTIMYSTIC
BEST THING THAT EVER HAPPENED TO ME —
	Gladys KNIGHT and the PIPS
THE BEST THINGS IN LIFE ARE FREE —
	Luther VANDROSS and Janet JACKSON
BEST WISHES — ULTRASOUND
THE BEST YEARS OF MY LIFE — Diana ROSS
BEST YEARS OF OUR LIVES —
	MODERN ROMANCE
BET YER LIFE I DO — HERMAN'S HERMITS
BETA — EMPIRION
BETCHA BY GOLLY WOW [A] — The STYLISTICS
BETCHA BY GOLLY WOW [A] — PRINCE
BETCHA CAN'T LOSE (WITH MY LOVE) —
	MAGIC LADY
BETCHA CAN'T WAIT — EAST 17
BETCHA' WOULDN'T HURT ME — Quincy JONES
BETTE DAVIS EYES — Kim CARNES
BETTER BE GOOD TO ME — Tina TURNER
BETTER BELIEVE IT (CHILDREN IN NEED) —
	Sid OWEN
BETTER BEST FORGOTTEN — STEPS
BETTER DAY — OCEAN COLOUR SCENE
BETTER DAYS [A] — GUN
BETTER DAYS [B] — Bruce SPRINGSTEEN
BETTER DAYS [C] — TQ
BETTER DAYS AHEAD — TYRREL CORPORATION
BETTER DO IT SALSA — GIBSON BROTHERS
BETTER GET READY — LULU
A BETTER LOVE — LONDONBEAT
BETTER LOVE NEXT TIME — DR HOOK
BETTER MADE — HEADSWIM
A BETTER MAN [A] — THUNDER
A BETTER MAN [B] — Brian KENNEDY
BETTER OFF ALONE —
	DJ JURGEN presents ALICE DEEJAY
BETTER OFF WITHOUT YOU — Hazell DEAN
BETTER TAKE TIME — SECOND IMAGE
BETTER THAN LIFE — ULTRABEAT
BETTER THAN THEM — NEW MODEL ARMY
BETTER THE DEVIL YOU KNOW [A] —
	Kylie MINOGUE
BETTER THE DEVIL YOU KNOW [A] — STEPS
BETTER THE DEVIL YOU KNOW [B] — SONIA
BETTER THINGS — The KINKS
BETTER USE YOUR HEAD —
	LITTLE ANTHONY and the IMPERIALS
BETTER WATCH OUT — ANT & DEC
BETTER WORLD — REBEL MC
BETTY BETTY BETTY — Lonnie DONEGAN
(BETWEEN A) ROCK AND A HARD PLACE —
	CUTTING CREW
BETWEEN ANGELS & INSECTS — PAPA ROACH
BETWEEN ME AND YOU —
	JA RULE featuring Christina MILIAN
BETWEEN THE SHEETS — ISLEY BROTHERS
BETWEEN THE WARS (EP) — Billy BRAGG
BEWARE OF THE BOYS —
	PANJABI MC featuring JAY-Z
BEWARE — Vivienne McKONE
(BEWARE) BOYFRIEND — Mari WILSON
BEYOND THE INVISIBLE — ENIGMA
BEYOND THE PALE — The MISSION
BEYOND THE REEF — Elvis PRESLEY
BEYOND THE SEA (LA MER) —
	George BENSON
BEYOND THE STARS —
	David WHITFIELD
BEYOND TIME — BLANK & JONES
BEYOND YOUR WILDEST DREAMS [A] —
	Lonnie GORDON
BEYOND YOUR WILDEST DREAMS [A] — SYBIL
THE BHOYS ARE BACK IN TOWN —
	DANCE TO TIPPERARY
BICYCLE RACE — QUEEN
BIG APPLE — KAJAGOOGOO
BIG AREA — THEN JERICO
BIG BAD EP — LITTLE ANGELS
BIG BAD JOHN — Jimmy DEAN
BIG BAD MAMMA —
	Foxy BROWN featuring DRU HILL
THE BIG BEAN — PIGBAG
BIG BEAT — CAPPELLA
THE BIG BEAT — Fats DOMINO
BIG BEAT BOOGIE — Bert WEEDON
BIG BIG WORLD — EMILIA
BIG BOSS GROOVE — STYLE COUNCIL
BIG BOY — MINUTEMAN
BIG BOYS DON'T CRY — LOLLY
BIG BROTHER UK TV THEME —
	ELEMENT FOUR
BIG BUBBLES, NO TROUBLES —
	ELLIS, BEGGS and HOWARD
BIG CITY — Dandy LIVINGSTONE
BIG DEAL — Bobby G
BIG DECISION —
	THAT PETROL EMOTION
BIG DICK MAN —
	SEX CLUB featuring BROWN SUGAR
BIG EIGHT — JUDGE DREAD
BIG FUN [A] — KOOL and the GANG
BIG FUN [B] — GAP BAND
BIG FUN [C] — INNER CITY
BIG GAY HEART — LEMONHEADS

BIG GIRL — PRECOCIOUS BRATS
	featuring KEVIN and PERRY
BIG GIRLS DON'T CRY — The FOUR SEASONS
BIG GREEN CAR — POLECATS
BIG GUN — AC/DC
A BIG HUNK O' LOVE — Elvis PRESLEY
THE BIG HURT [A] — Maureen EVANS
THE BIG HURT — Toni FISHER
BIG IN AMERICA — The STRANGLERS
BIG IN JAPAN — ALPHAVILLE
BIG IRON — Marty ROBBINS
THE BIG L — ROXETTE
BIG LOG — Robert PLANT
BIG LOVE [A] — FLEETWOOD MAC
BIG LOVE [B] — Pete HELLER
BIG LOVE [C] — FRESH BC
BIG MAN — FOUR PREPS
THE BIG MAN AND THE SCREAM TEAM MEET THE
	BARMY ARMY UPTOWN —
	PRIMAL SCREAM
BIG MAN IN A BIG HOUSE — Leroy VAN DYKE
BIG ME — FOO FIGHTERS
BIG MISTAKE — Natalie IMBRUGLIA
THE BIG MONEY — RUSH
BIG MOUTH STRIKES AGAIN — The SMITHS
BIG N BASHY — FALLACY featuring TUBBY T
BIG NEW PRINZ — The FALL
BIG NIGHT OUT — FUN LOVIN' CRIMINALS
THE BIG ONE — BLACK
THE BIG ONES GET AWAY —
	Buffy SAINTE-MARIE
BIG PANTY WOMAN — BAREFOOT MAN
BIG PIMPIN' — JAY-Z
BIG POPPA — NOTORIOUS B.I.G.
BIG PUNK — JUDGE DREAD
BIG RIVER — Jimmy NAIL
BIG SEVEN — JUDGE DREAD
BIG SHIP — Cliff RICHARD
BIG SIX — JUDGE DREAD
THE BIG SKY — Kate BUSH
BIG SKY NEW LIGHT — Martin
	STEPHENSON and the DAINTEES
BIG SPENDER — Shirley BASSEY
BIG SUR — The THRILLS
BIG TEASER — SAXON
BIG TEN — JUDGE DREAD
BIG THING COMING — The STRANGLERS
BIG TIME [A] — Rick JAMES
BIG TIME [B] — Peter GABRIEL
BIG TIME [C] — WHIGFIELD
BIG TIME OPERATOR —
	Zoot MONEY and the BIG ROLL BAND
BIG TIME SENSUALITY — BJÖRK
BIG WEDGE — FISH
BIG WHEELS — LLAMA FARMERS
BIG YELLOW TAXI [A] — Amy GRANT
BIG YELLOW TAXI [A] — Joni MITCHELL
BIG YELLOW TAXI [A] — COUNTING CROWS
	featuring Vanessa CARLTON
BIGAMY AT CHRISTMAS — Tony FERRINO
BIGGEST HORIZON — Clint BOON EXPERIENCE
BIGGER BETTER DEAL — DESERT EAGLE
	DISCS featuring Keisha WHITE
BIGGER THAN MY BODY — John MAYER
BIGSCARYANIMAL — Belinda CARLISLE
BIKINI GIRLS WITH MACHINE GUNS — CRAMPS
BIKO — Peter GABRIEL
BILJO — Clodagh RODGERS
BILL BAILEY — Bobby DARIN
BILL McCAI — The CORAL
BILLIE JEAN [A] — Michael JACKSON
BILLIE JEAN [A] — BATES
BILLIE JEAN [A] — SOUND BLUNTZ
BILLS, BILLS, BILLS — DESTINY'S CHILD
BILLS 2 PAY — GLAMMA KID
BILLY BOY —
	Dick CHARLESWORTH and his CITY GENTS
BILLY DON'T BE A HERO — PAPER LACE
BIMBO — Ruby WRIGHT
BINGO — CATCH
BINGO BANGO — BASEMENT JAXX
BIONIC — KING ADORA
BIONIC SANTA — Chris HILL
BIRD DOG — The EVERLY BROTHERS
BIRD OF PARADISE — Snowy WHITE
BIRD ON A WIRE — NEVILLE BROTHERS
BIRD SONG — Lene LOVICH
BIRDHOUSE IN YOUR SOUL —
	THEY MIGHT BE GIANTS
THE BIRDIE SONG (BIRDIE DANCE) — TWEETS
BIRDMAN — RIDE
BIRDS AND BEES — WARM SOUNDS
THE BIRDS AND THE BEES [A] — Alma COGAN
THE BIRDS AND THE BEES [A] — Jewel AKENS
BIRDS FLY (WHISPER TO A SCREAM) —
	ICICLE WORKS
BIRDS OF A FEATHER — KILLING JOKE
BIRTH — PEDDLERS
BIRTHDAY [A] — SUGARCUBES
BIRTHDAY [B] — Paul McCARTNEY
BIS VS THE DIY CORPS (EP) — BIS
THE BIT GOES ON — SNAKEBITE
A BIT OF U2 — KISS AMC
BITCH [A] — The ROLLING STONES
BITCH [B] — Meredith BROOKS
THE BITCH — OLYMPIC RUNNERS
THE BITCH IS BACK — Elton JOHN

BITCH SCHOOL — SPINAL TAP
BITCH WITH A PERM — Tim DOG
BITCHES BREW — INSPIRAL CARPETS
BITE YOUR LIP (GET UP AND DANCE) —
Elton JOHN
BITES DA DUST — PLANET PERFECTO
THE BITTER END — PLACEBO
BITS + PIECES — ARTEMESIA
BITS AND PIECES — Dave CLARK FIVE
BITS OF KIDS — STIFF LITTLE FINGERS
BITTER FRUIT — LITTLE STEVEN
BITTER SWEET — Marc ALMOND
BITTER SWEET SYMPHONY — The VERVE
BITTER TEARS — INXS
THE BITTEREST PILL
(I EVER HAD TO SWALLOW) — The JAM
BITTERSWEET — Billy OCEAN
BITTERSWEET BUNDLE OF MISERY —
Graham COXON
BITTERSWEET ME — R.E.M.
BIZARRE LOVE TRIANGLE — NEW ORDER
BIZZI'S PARTY — BIZZI
BJANGO — LUCKY MONKEYS
BLACK AND WHITE [A] — GREYHOUND
BLACK AND WHITE [B] — STATIC-X
BLACK & WHITE ARMY — BLACK & WHITE ARMY
BLACK ANGEL — Mica PARIS
BLACK BEAR — Frank CORDELL
BLACK BETTY [A] — RAM JAM
BLACK BETTY [A] — Tom JONES
BLACK BOOK — EYC
BLACK CAT — Janet JACKSON
BLACK CHERRY — GOLDFRAPP
BLACK COFFEE — ALL SAINTS
BLACK COFFEE IN BED — SQUEEZE
BLACK EYED BOY — TEXAS
THE BLACK EYED BOYS — PAPER LACE
BLACK GIRL — FOUR PENNIES
BLACK GOLD — SOUL ASYLUM
BLACK HEART — Marc ALMOND
THE BLACK HILLS OF DAKOTA — Doris DAY
BLACK HOLE SUN — SOUNDGARDEN
BLACK IS BLACK [A] — LOS BRAVOS
BLACK IS BLACK [A] — LA BELLE EPOQUE
BLACK IS BLACK [B] — The JUNGLE BROTHERS
BLACK JESUS — EVERLAST
BLACK LODGE — ANTHRAX
BLACK MAGIC WOMAN — FLEETWOOD MAC
BLACK MAN RAY — CHINA CRISIS
BLACK MEANING GOOD — REBEL MC
BLACK METALLIC (EP) — CATHERINE WHEEL
BLACK NIGHT — DEEP PURPLE
BLACK NITE CRASH — RIDE
BLACK OR WHITE — Michael JACKSON
BLACK ORCHID — Stevie WONDER
BLACK PEARL — Horace FAITH
BLACK PUDDING BERTHA (THE QUEEN OF NORTHERN
SOUL) — The GOODIES
BLACK SABBATH — MAGOO
BLACK SKIN BLUE EYED BOYS — The EQUALS
BLACK STATIONS WHITE STATIONS — M + M
BLACK STEEL — TRICKY
BLACK STOCKINGS — John BARRY ORCHESTRA
BLACK SUITS COMIN' (NOD YA HEAD) —
WILL SMITH
BLACK SUPERMAN (MUHAMMAD ALI) —
Johnny WAKELIN
BLACK TIE WHITE NOISE —
David BOWIE featuring Al B SURE!
BLACK VELVET — Alannah MYLES
BLACK VELVET BAND — DUBLINERS
BLACK WHITE — ASIAN DUB FOUNDATION
BLACKBERRY WAY — The MOVE
BLACKBIRD ON THE WIRE —
The BEAUTIFUL SOUTH
BLACKBOARD JUMBLE —
The BARRON KNIGHTS
BLACKEN MY THUMB — The DATSUNS
BLACKER THAN BLACK —
GOODBYE MR MACKENZIE
BLACKERTHREETRACKER (EP) — CURVE
BLACKWATER [A] — RAIN TREE CROW
BLACKWATER [B] — OCTAVE ONE
featuring Ann SAUNDERSON
BLAH — HELTAH SKELTAH and ORIGINOO GUNN
CLAPPAZ as the FABULOUS FIVE
BLAME IT ON ME — D:REAM
BLAME IT ON THE BASSLINE — Norman COOK
BLAME IT ON THE BOOGIE [A] —
The JACKSONS
BLAME IT ON THE BOOGIE [A] —
Mick JACKSON
BLAME IT ON THE BOOGIE [A] — BIG FU
BLAME IT ON THE BOOGIE [A] — CLOCK
BLAME IT ON THE BOSSA NOVA —
Eydie GORME
(BLAME IT ON THE) PONY EXPRESS —
Johnny JOHNSON and the BANDWAGON
BLAME IT ON THE RAIN — MILLI VANILLI
BLAME IT ON THE WEATHERMAN — B*WITCHED
BLANKET — URBAN SPECIES
BLANKET ON THE GROUND — Billie Jo SPEARS
BLASPHEMOUS RUMOURS — DEPECHE MODE
BLAST THE SPEAKERS — WARP BROTHERS
BLAZE OF GLORY — Jon BON JOVI
BLAZIN' — TALI
BLAZING SADDLES — YELLO

BLEACH — EASYWORLD
BLEED — CATATONIA
BLEED ME WHITE — EAT
BLESS YOU [A] — Tony ORLANDO
BLESS YOU [B] —
Martha REEVES and the VANDELLAS
BLIND — TALKING HEADS
BLIND [B] — BAD COMPANY
BLIND AMONG THE FLOWERS — TOURISTS
BLIND MAN — AEROSMITH
BLIND PILOTS —
The COOPER TEMPLE CLAUSE
BLIND VISION — BLANCMANGE
BLINDED BY THE LIGHT — MANFRED MANN
BLINDED BY THE LIGHTS — The STREETS
BLINDED BY THE SUN — The SEAHORSES
BLINDFOLD — MORCHEEBA
THE BLINDFOLD (EP) — CURVE
BLINK — Rosie RIBBONS
BLISS [A] — MUSE
BLISS [B] — SYNTAX
THE BLOCK PARTY — Lisa 'Left Eye' LOPES
BLOCK ROCKIN' BEATS —
The CHEMICAL BROTHERS
BLOCKBUSTER! — The SWEET
BLONDE HAIR BLUE JEANS — Chris DE BURGH
BLONDES (HAVE MORE FUN) — Rod STEWART
BLOOD IS PUMPIN' — VOODOO & SERANO
BLOOD MAKES NOISE — Suzanne VEGA
BLOOD MUSIC (EP) — EARTHLING
BLOOD OF EDEN — Peter GABRIEL
BLOOD ON THE DANCEFLOOR —
Michael JACKSON
BLOOD SWEAT AND TEARS — V
THE BLOOD THAT MOVES THE BODY — A-HA
BLOODNOK'S ROCK 'N' ROLL CALL —
The GOONS
BLOODSHOT EYES — MILLIE
BLOODSPORTS FOR ALL — CARTER —
THE UNSTOPPABLE SEX MACHINE
BLOODY LUXURY — WHITESNAKE
A BLOSSOM FELL [A] — Dickie VALENTINE
A BLOSSOM FELL [A] — Nat 'King' COLE
A BLOSSOM FELL [A] — Ronnie HILTON
BLOSSOMS FALLING — OOBERMAN
BLOW AWAY — George HARRISON
BLOW THE HOUSE DOWN [A] —
LIVING IN A BOX
BLOW THE HOUSE DOWN [B] —
WEE PAPA GIRL RAPPERS
BLOW UP THE OUTSIDE WORLD —
SOUNDGARDEN
BLOW YA MIND — LOCK 'N' LOAD
BLOW YOUR HORNY HORNS —
PERFECT PHASE
BLOW YOUR MIND — JAMIROQUAI
BLOW YOUR MIND (I AM THE WOMAN) —
Lisa PIN-UP
BLOW YOUR WHISTLE — DJ DUKE
THE BLOWERS DAUGHTER — Damien RICE
BLOWIN' IN THE WIND [A] — Stevie WONDER
BLOWING IN THE WIND [A] —
PETER, PAUL and MARY
BLOWIN' ME UP (WITH HER LOVE) —
JC CHASEZ
BLOWING WILD — Frankie LAINE
BLUE [A] — FINE YOUNG CANNIBALS
BLUE [B] — The VERVE
BLUE [C] — WAY OUT WEST
BLUE [D] — SYMPOSIUM
BLUE [E] — LeAnn RIMES
BLUE ANGEL [A] — Roy ORBISON
BLUE ANGEL [B] — Gene PITNEY
BLUE ANGELS — Pras MICHEL
BLUE BAYOU [A] — Roy ORBISON
BLUE BAYOU [A] — Linda RONSTADT
BLUE BLUE HEARTACHES — Johnny DUNCAN
and the BLUE GRASS BOYS
BLUE CHRISTMAS — Elvis PRESLEY
BLUE (DA BA DEE) — EIFFEL 65
BLUE DAY — CHELSEA FC
BLUE EMOTION — FIAT LUX
BLUE EYES [A] — Don PARTRIDGE
BLUE EYES [B] — Elton JOHN
BLUE EYES [C] — WEDDING PRESENT
BLUE FEAR [A] — ARMIN
BLUE FEAR 2004 [A] — Armin VAN BUUREN
BLUE FLOWERS — DR OCTAGON
BLUE FOR YOU — WET WET WET
BLUE GIRL — BRUISERS
BLUE GUITAR — Justin HAYWARD
BLUE HAT FOR A BLUE DAY — Nick HEYWARD
BLUE HOTEL — Chris ISAAK
BLUE IS THE COLOUR — CHELSEA FC
BLUE JEAN — David BOWIE
BLUE JEANS — LADYTRON
BLUE JEAN BOP — Gene VINCENT
BLUE LIGHT RED LIGHT (SOMEONE'S THERE) —
Harry CONNICK Jr
BLUE LOVE (CALL MY NAME) — DNA
BLUE MONDAY [A] — Fats DOMINO
BLUE MONDAY [B] — NEW ORDER
BLUE MOON [A] — Elvis PRESLEY
BLUE MOON [A] — MARCELS
BLUE MOON [A] — SHOWADDYWADDY
BLUE MOON [A] — John ALFORD
BLUE MORNING, BLUE DAY — FOREIGNER

BLUE PETER — Mike OLDFIELD
BLUE RIVER — Elvis PRESLEY
BLUE ROOM — The ORB
THE BLUE ROOM — T-EMPO
BLUE SAVANNAH — ERASURE
BLUE SKIES [A] —
John DUMMER and Helen APRIL
BLUE SKIES [B] — JETS
BLUE SKIES [C] — BT featuring Tori AMOS
BLUE SKIES [D] — LONGPIGS
BLUE SKY MINE — MIDNIGHT OIL
BLUE SONG — MINT ROYALE
BLUE STAR (THE MEDIC THEME) [A] —
Charlie APPLEWHITE
BLUE STAR (THE MEDIC THEME) [A] —
Cyril STAPLETON and his ORCHESTRA
BLUE STAR (THE MEDIC THEME) [A] —
Ron GOODWIN
BLUE SUEDE SHOES [A] — Carl PERKINS
BLUE SUEDE SHOES [A] — Elvis PRESLEY
BLUE TANGO — Ray MARTIN
BLUE TOMORROW — CHELSEA FC
BLUE TURNS TO GREY —
Cliff RICHARD and The SHADOWS
BLUE VELVET — Bobby VINTON
BLUE WATER — FIELDS OF THE NEPHILIM
BLUE WEEKEND — Karl DENVER
BLUE WORLD — The MOODY BLUES
BLUEBEARD — COCTEAU TWINS
BLUEBELL POLKA — Jimmy SHAND
BLUEBERRY HILL [A] — Fats DOMINO
BLUEBERRY HILL [A] —
John BARRY ORCHESTRA
BLUEBIRDS OVER THE MOUNTAIN —
The BEACH BOYS
BLUEBOTTLE — POB featuring DJ Patrick REID
BLUEBOTTLE BLUES — The GOONS
BLUE-EYED BOY — Al SAXON
BLUER THAN BLUE — Rolf HARRIS
BLUES BAND (EP) — BLUES BAND
BLUES FROM A GUN —
JESUS AND MARY CHAIN
BLUETONIC — The BLUETONES
BLURRED — PIANOMAN
BLURRY — PUDDLE OF MUDD
BO DIDDLEY — Buddy HOLLY
THE BOAT THAT I ROW — LULU
BOAT TO BOLIVIA —
Martin STEPHENSON and the DAINTEES
BOBBY TOMORROW — Bobby VEE
BOBBY'S GIRL — Susan MAUGHAN
BODIES — DROWNING POOL
BODY — FUNKY GREEN DOGS
BODY AND SOUL [A] — SISTERS OF MERCY
BODY AND SOUL [B] — MAI TAI
BODY AND SOUL [C] — Anita BAKER
BODY BUMPIN' (YIPPEE-YI-YO) —
PUBLIC ANNOUNCEMENT
THE BODY ELECTRIC — RUSH
BODY GROOVE — ARCHITECHS featuring NANA
BODY HEAT — James BROWN
BODY IN MOTION — ATLANTIC OCEAN
BODY LANGUAGE [A] — DETROIT SPINNERS
BODY LANGUAGE [B] — The DOOLEYS
BODY LANGUAGE [C] — QUEEN
BODY LANGUAGE [D] —
ADVENTURES OF STEVIE V
BODY MOVIN' [A] — BEASTIE BOYS
BODY MOVIN' [B] — DRUMSOUND /
Simon 'BASSLINE' SMITH
BODY MUSIC — STRIKERS
BODY ROCK [A] — Maria VIDAL
BODY ROCK [B] — SHIMON & Andy C
BODYROCK — TYMES 4
BODY ROCKIN' — Errol BROWN
THE BODY SHINE (EP) — Billy HENDRIX
BODY TALK — IMAGINATION
BODY II BODY — Samantha MUMBA
BODY WORK — HOT STREAK
BODYROCK — MOBY
BODYSHAKIN' — 911
BOG EYED JOG — Ray MOORE
BOHEMIAN LIKE YOU — The DANDY WARHOLS
BOHEMIAN RHAPSODY [A] — QUEEN
BOHEMIAN RHAPSODY [A] — BAD NEWS
BOHEMIAN RHAPSODY [A] — BRAIDS
BOHEMIAN RHAPSODY [A] — Rolf HARRIS
BOILER — LIMP BIZKIT
THE BOILER — RHODA with the SPECIAL AKA
BOING! — WEDDING PRESENT
BOLL WEEVIL SONG — Brook BENTON
BOM DIGI BOM (THINK ABOUT THE WAY) —
ICE MC
THE BOMB — LOVE CONNECTION
BOMB DIGGY — ANOTHER LEVEL
THE BOMB! (THESE SOUNDS FALL INTO
MY MIND) — BUCKETHEADS
BOMBADIN — 808 STATE
BOMBER — MOTÖRHEAD
BOMBSCARE — 2 BAD MICE
BOMBTRACK — RAGE AGAINST THE MACHINE
BON BON VIE — TS MONK
BOND — 808 STATE
BONE DRIVEN — BUSH
BONEY M MEGAMIX — BONEY M
BONEYARD — LITTLE ANGELS
BONITA APPLEBUM — A TRIBE CALLED QUEST

BONITA MANANA — ESPIRITU
'03 BONNIE & CLYDE —
JAY-Z featuring Beyoncé KNOWLES
BONNIE CAME BACK —
Duane EDDY and The REBELS
BONY MORONIE — Larry WILLIAMS
BOO! FOREVER — BOO RADLEYS
BOOGALOO PARTY — FLAMINGOS
BOOGIE [A] — DIVE
BOOGIE [B] — The BRAND NEW HEAVIES
featuring Nicole RUSSO
BOOGIE AT RUSSIAN HILL — John Lee HOOKER
BOOGIE DOWN [A] — Eddie KENDRICKS
BOOGIE DOWN [B] — Al JARREAU
BOOGIE DOWN (BRONX) — Man PARRISH
BOOGIE DOWN (GET FUNKY NOW) —
The REAL THING
BOOGIE MAN — MATCH
BOOGIE NIGHTS [A] — HEATWAVE
BOOGIE NIGHTS [A] — La FLEUR
BOOGIE NIGHTS [A] — SONIA
BOOGIE ON REGGAE WOMAN —
Stevie WONDER
BOOGIE ON UP — ROKOTTO
BOOGIE OOGIE OOGIE — A TASTE OF HONEY
BOOGIE SHOES —
KC and the SUNSHINE BAND
BOOGIE TOWN — FAT LARRY'S BAND
BOOGIE WONDERLAND — EARTH WIND
AND FIRE with The EMOTIONS
BOOGIE WOOGIE BUGLE BOY (DON'T STOP) —
2 IN A TENT
THE BOOK — David WHITFIELD
BOOK OF DAYS — ENYA
BOOK OF DREAMS — Suzanne VEGA
BOOK OF LOVE — MUDLARKS
BOOKS — BELLE & SEBASTIAN
BOOM BANG-A-BANG — LULU
BOOM BOOM [A] — BLACK SLATE
BOOM BOOM [B] — John Lee HOOKER
BOOM BOOM [C] — DEFINITION OF SOUND
BOOM BOOM [D] — N-TYCE
BOOM BOOM [E] —
Basil BRUSH featuring India BEAU
BOOM BOOM BOOM —
The OUTHERE BROTHERS
BOOM, BOOM, BOOM, BOOM!! —
The VENGABOYS
BOOM BOOM (LET'S GO BACK TO MY ROOM) —
Paul LEKAKIS
THE BOOM BOOM ROOM — NATASHA
BOOM, LIKE THAT — Mark KNOPFLER
BOOM ROCK SOUL — BENZ
BOOM SELECTION — GENIUS CRU
BOOM! SHAKE THE ROOM —
JAZZY JEFF and the FRESH PRINCE
BOOM! THERE SHE WAS — ROGER
BOOMBASTIC — SHAGGY
BOOO! — STICKY featuring MS DYNAMITE
BOOPS (HERE TO GO) — SLY and ROBBIE
BOOTI CALL — BLACKSTREET
BOOTIE CALL — ALL SAINTS
BOOTYLICIOUS — DESTINY'S CHILD
BOOTZILLA — BOOTSY'S RUBBER BAND
BOP BOP BABY — WESTLIFE
BOP GUN (ONE NATION) —
ICE CUBE featuring George CLINTON
BORA BORA — DA HOOL
BORDERLINE — MADONNA
BORN A WOMAN — Sandy POSEY
BORN AGAIN [A] — The CHRISTIANS
BORN AGAIN [B] — BADLY DRAWN BOY
BORN AGAIN [C] — STARSAILOR
BORN DEAD — BODY COUNT
BORN FREE — Vic REEVES
BORN IN ENGLAND — TWISTED X
BORN IN 69 —
ROCKET FROM THE CRYPT
BORN IN THE GHETTO — FUNKY POETS
BORN IN THE 70S — Ed HARCOURT
BORN IN THE USA — Bruce SPRINGSTEEN
BORN OF FRUSTRATION — JAMES
BORN ON THE 5TH OF NOVEMBER —
CARTER — THE UNSTOPPABLE SEX MACHINE
BORN SLIPPY — UNDERWORLD
BORN THIS WAY (LET'S DANCE) —
COOKIE CREW
BORN TO BE ALIVE [A] — Patrick HERNANDEZ
BORN TO BE ALIVE [B] —
ADAMSKI featuring SOHO
BORN TO BE MY BABY — BON JOVI
BORN TO BE SOLD — TRANSVISION VAMP
BORN TO BE WILD — STEPPENWOLF
BORN TO BE WITH YOU [A] —
The CHORDETTES
BORN TO BE WITH YOU [A] — Dave EDMUNDS
BORN TO LIVE AND BORN TO DIE —
The FOUNDATIONS
BORN TO LOSE — KING ADORA
BORN TO MAKE YOU HAPPY —
Britney SPEARS
BORN TO RAISE HELL —
MOTÖRHEAD / ICE-T / Whitfield CRANE
BORN TO RUN — Bruce SPRINGSTEEN
BORN TO TRY — Delta GOODREM
BORN TOO LATE — PONI-TAILS
BORN 2 B.R.E.E.D. — Monie LOVE

BORN WITH A SMILE ON MY FACE —
   Stephanie DE SYKES
BORNE ON THE WIND — Roy ORBISON
BORROWED LOVE — S.O.S. BAND
BORROWED TIME — John LENNON
BORSALINO — Bobby CRUSH
THE BOSS [A] — Diana ROSS
THE BOSS [A] — The BRAXTONS
BOSS DRUM — The SHAMEN
BOSS GUITAR — Duane EDDY and the REBELS
BOSS OF ME — THEY MIGHT BE GIANT
BOSSA NOVA BABY — Elvis PRESLEY
BOSTICH — YELLO
THE BOSTON TEA PARTY —
   The SENSATIONAL ALEX HARVEY BAND
BOTH ENDS BURNING — ROXY MUSIC
BOTH SIDES NOW [A] —
   CLANNAD and Paul YOUNG
BOTH SIDES NOW [A] — Judy COLLINS
BOTH SIDES NOW [A] — Viola WILLS
BOTH SIDES OF THE STORY — Phil COLLINS
BOTHER — STONE SOUR
THE BOTTLE [A] —
   TYRREL CORPORATION
THE BOTTLE [A] — Paul WELLER
THE BOTTLE [B] — The CHRISTIANS
BOTTLE LIVING — Dave GAHAN
BOULEVARD OF BROKEN DREAMS [A] —
   BEATMASTERS
BOULEVARD OF BROKEN DREAMS [B] —
   GREEN DAY
BOUNCE — Sarah CONNOR
BOUNCE ALONG — Wayne WONDER
BOUNCE, ROCK, SKATE, ROLL —
   BABY DC featuring IMAJIN
BOUNCE WITH THE MASSIVE — TZANT
THE BOUNCER — KICKS LIKE A MULE
BOUNCIN' BACK (BUMPIN' ME
   AGAINST THE WALL) — MYSTIKAL
BOUNCING FLOW — K2 FAMILY
BOUND 4 DA RELOAD (CASUALTY) —
   OXIDE & NEUTRINO
BOUNDARIES — Leena CONQUEST
   and HIP HOP FINGER
BOURGIE, BOURGIE —
   Gladys KNIGHT and the PIPS
BOUT — JAMELIA featuring Rah DIGGA
BOW DOWN MISTER — JESUS LOVES YOU
BOW WOW (THAT'S MY NAME) —
   LIL BOW WOW
BOW WOW WOW — FUNKDOOBIEST
THE BOX — ORBITAL
BOX SET GO — HIGH
THE BOXER — SIMON and GARFUNKEL
BOXER BEAT — JOBOXERS
BOXERS — MORRISSEY
BOY — LULU
THE BOY DONE GOOD — Billy BRAGG
BOY FROM NEW YORK CITY [A] —
   Alison JORDAN
THE BOY FROM NEW YORK CITY [A] — DARTS
A BOY FROM NOWHERE — Tom JONES
BOY I GOTTA HAVE YOU — RIO and MARS
BOY (I NEED YOU) —
   Mariah CAREY featuring CAM'RON
THE BOY IN THE BUBBLE — Paul SIMON
BOY IS CRYING — SAINT ETIENNE
THE BOY IS MINE —
   BRANDY and MONICA
A BOY NAMED SUE — Johnny CASH
BOY NEXT DOOR — JAMELIA
BOY OH BOY — RACEY
BOY ON TOP OF THE NEWS —
   DIESEL PARK WEST
BOY OR A GIRL — IMPERIAL DRAG
THE BOY RACER — MORRISSEY
THE BOY WHO CAME BACK — Marc ALMOND
THE BOY WITH THE THORN IN HIS SIDE —
   The SMITHS
THE BOY WITH THE X-RAY EYES —
   BABYLON ZOO
BOY WONDER — SPEEDY
BOY YOU KNOCK ME OUT —
   Tatyana ALI featuring Will SMITH
BOYS [A] — Kim WILDE
BOYS [B] — MARY JANE GIRLS
BOYS [C] — BON
BOYS [D] — Britney SPEARS
BOYS AND GIRLS [A] — HUMAN LEAGUE
BOYS AND GIRLS [B] —
   CHEEKY GIRLS with Andy NEWTON-LEE
THE BOYS ARE BACK IN TOWN [A] —
   THIN LIZZY
THE BOYS ARE BACK IN TOWN [A] —
   GLADIATORS
THE BOYS ARE BACK IN TOWN [A] —
   HAPPY MONDAYS
BOYS BETTER — The DANDY WARHOLS
BOYS CRY — Eden KANE
BOYS DON'T CRY — The CURE
THE BOYS IN THE OLD BRIGHTON BLUE —
   BRIGHTON AND HOVE ALBION FC
BOYS KEEP SWINGING — David BOWIE
THE BOYS OF SUMMER [A] — Don HENLEY
THE BOYS OF SUMMER [A] — DJ SAMMY
THE BOYS OF SUMMER [A] — The ATARIS
BOYS (SUMMERTIME LOVE) — SABRINA

BOYS WILL BE BOYS — OSMOND BOYS
BOZOS — LEVELLERS
BRACKISH — KITTIE
BRAIN — The JUNGLE BROTHERS
BRAIN STEW — GREEN DAY
BRAINS — NUT
BRAINWASHED (CALL YOU) — TOMCRAFT
BRAND NEW — FINITRIBE
BRAND NEW DAY [A] — DARKMAN
BRAND NEW DAY [B] — MINDS OF MEN
BRAND NEW DAY [C] — STING
BRAND NEW FRIEND — Lloyd COLE
BRAND NEW KEY — MELANIE
BRAND NEW LOVER — DEAD OR ALIVE
BRAND NEW START — Paul WELLER
BRANDY [A] — Scott ENGLISH
BRANDY [B] — O'JAYS
BRAS ON 45 (FAMILY VERSION) — Ivor BIGGUN
BRASS IN POCKET — The PRETENDERS
BRASS: LET THERE BE HOUSE —
   PARTY FAITHFUL
BRASSNECK — WEDDING PRESENT
BRAVE NEW WORLD [A] — David ESSEX
BRAVE NEW WORLD [B] — TOYAH
BRAVE NEW WORLD [C] — NEW MODEL ARMY
BRAZEN 'WEEP' — SKUNK ANANSIE
BRAZIL [A] — CRISPY AND COMPANY
BRAZIL [A] — RITCHIE FAMILY
BRAZILIAN DAWN — SHAKATAK
BRAZILIAN LOVE AFFAIR — George DUKE
BRAZILIAN LOVE SONG — Nat 'King' COLE
BREACH THE PEACE (EP) — SPIRAL TRIBE
BREAD AND BUTTER — NEWBEATS
BREAK AWAY — The BEACH BOYS
BREAK DANCIN' — ELECTRIC BOOGIE —
   WEST STREET MOB
BREAK DOWN THE DOORS —
   MORILLO featuring AUDIO BULLYS
BREAK EVERY RULE — Tina TURNER
BREAK 4 LOVE — RAZE
BREAK FROM THE OLD ROUTINE — OUI 3
BREAK IT DOWN AGAIN — TEARS FOR FEARS
BREAK IT TO ME GENTLY — Brenda LEE
BREAK MY STRIDE — Matthew WILDER
BREAK MY WORLD —
   DARK GLOBE featuring Amanda GHOST
BREAK OF DAWN — RHYTHM ON THE LOOSE
BREAK ON THROUGH — The DOORS
BREAK THE CHAIN [A] — Elkie BROOKS
BREAK THE CHAIN [B] — MOTIV 8
BREAK THE RULES — STATUS QUO
BREAK UP TO MAKE UP — The STYLISTICS
BREAK UPS 2 MAKE UPS —
   METHOD MAN featuring D'ANGELO
BREAK YA NECK — Busta RHYMES
BREAK YOU OFF — ROOTS featuring MUSIQ
BREAKADAWN — DE LA SOUL
BREAKAWAY [A] — The SPRINGFIELDS
BREAKAWAY [B] — GALLAGHER and LYLE
BREAKAWAY [C] — Tracey ULLMAN
BREAKAWAY [D] — Donna SUMMER
BREAKAWAY [E] — Kim APPLEBY
BREAKAWAY [F] — ZZ TOP
BREAKBEAT ERA — BREAKBEAT ERA
BREAK DANCE PARTY — BREAK MACHINE
BREAKDOWN [A] — ONE DOVE
BREAKDOWN [B] — DOUBLE SIX
BREAKFAST — ASSOCIATES
BREAKFAST AT TIFFANY'S —
   DEEP BLUE SOMETHING
BREAKFAST IN AMERICA — SUPERTRAMP
BREAKFAST IN BED [A] — Sheila HYLTON
BREAKFAST IN BED [A] —
   UB40 featuring Chrissie HYNDE
BREAKFAST ON PLUTO — Don PARTRIDGE
BREAKIN' AWAY — Kim WILDE
BREAKIN' DOWN — SKID ROW
BREAKIN' DOWN (SUGAR SAMBA) —
   JULIA and COMPANY
BREAKIN' DOWN THE WALLS OF HEARTACHE —
   Johnny JOHNSON and the BANDWAGON
BREAKIN' IN A BRAND NEW BROKEN HEART —
   Connie FRANCIS
BREAKIN' ... THERE'S NO STOPPING US —
   OLLIE and JERRY
BREAKIN' UP — WILD WEEKEND
BREAKIN' UP IS BREAKIN' MY HEART —
   Roy ORBISON
BREAKING AWAY — Jaki GRAHAM
BREAKING GLASS (EP) — David BOWIE
BREAKING HEARTS (AIN'T WHAT IT USED
   TO BE) — Elton JOHN
BREAKING POINT — BOURGIE BOURGIE
BREAKING THE GIRL —
   RED HOT CHILI PEPPERS
BREAKING THE HABIT — LINKIN PARK
BREAKING THE LAW — JUDAS PRIEST
BREAKING UP IS HARD TO DO [A] —
   Neil SEDAKA
BREAKING UP IS HARD TO DO [A] —
   PARTRIDGE FAMILY
BREAKING UP MY HEART — Shakin' STEVENS
BREAKING UP THE GIRL — GARBAGE
BREAKING US IN TWO — Joe JACKSON
BREAKOUT [A] — SWING OUT SISTER
BREAKOUT [B] — FOO FIGHTERS
THE BREAKS — Kurtis BLOW

BREAKTHRU' — QUEEN
BREATH OF LIFE — ERASURE
BREATH IN — FROU FROU
BREATHE [A] — Maria McKEE
BREATHE [B] — Midge URE
BREATHE [C] — The PRODIGY
BREATHE [D] — Kylie MINOGUE
BREATHE [E] — BLUE AMAZON
BREATHE [F] — Faith HILL
BREATHE [G] —
   SCIENCE DEPARTMENT featuring ERIRE
BREATHE [H] — TELEPOPMUSIK
BREATHE [I] —
   Blu CANTRELL featuring Sean PAUL
BREATHE [J] — FABOLOUS
BREATHE (A LITTLE DEEPER) —
   BLAMELESS
BREATHE A SIGH — DEF LEPPARD
BREATHE AGAIN — Toni BRAXTON
BREATHE AND STOP — Q-TIP
BREATHE, DON'T STOP —
   MR ON vs The JUNGLE BROTHERS
BREATHE EASY — BLUE
BREATHE IN — FROU FROU
BREATHE LIFE INTO ME — Mica PARIS
BREATHE ME — SIA
BREATHE, STRETCH, SHAKE — MA$E
BREATHING — Kate BUSH
BREATHING [B] — NORTH and SOUTH
BREATHING IS E-ZEE — E-ZEE POSSEE
BREATHLESS [A] — Jerry Lee LEWIS
BREATHLESS [B] — The CORRS
BREATHLESS [C] —
   Nick CAVE & The BAD SEEDS
THE BREEZE AND I [A] — Caterina VALENTE
THE BREEZE AND I [A] — FENTONES
BREEZE ON BY — Donny OSMOND
BRIAN WILSON — BARENAKED LADIES
BRICK — Ben FOLDS FIVE
BRICK HOUSE — The COMMODORES
THE BRICK TRACK VERSUS GITTY UP —
   SALT-N-PEPA
BRIDESHEAD THEME — Geoffrey BURGON
BRIDGE [A] — ORANGE JUICE
BRIDGE [B] — QUEENSRYCHE
THE BRIDGE — CACTUS WORLD NEWS
BRIDGE OF SIGHS — David WHITFIELD
BRIDGE OVER TROUBLED WATER [A] — SIMON and
   GARFUNKEL: Keyboard: Larry Knechtel
BRIDGE OVER TROUBLED WATER [A] —
   Linda CLIFFORD
BRIDGE OVER TROUBLED WATER [A] —
   Hannah JONES
BRIDGE TO YOUR HEART — WAX
BRIDGET THE MIDGET (THE QUEEN OF THE BLUES) —
   Ray STEVENS
BRIDGING THE GAP — NAS / Olu DARA
BRIGHT EYES [A] — Art GARFUNKEL
BRIGHT EYES [A] — Stephen GATELY
THE BRIGHT LIGHT — Tanya DONELLY
BRIGHT LIGHTS — The SPECIALS
BRIGHT SIDE OF LIFE — TENOR FLY
BRIGHT SIDE OF THE ROAD — Van MORRISON
BRIGHT YELLOW GUN — THROWING MUSES
BRIGHTER DAY — Kelly LLORENNA
BRIGHTER THAN SUNSHINE — AQUALUNG
BRIGHTEST STAR — DRIZABONE
BRILLIANT DISGUISE — Bruce SPRINGSTEEN
BRILLIANT FEELING — FULL MONTY
   ALLSTARS featuring TJ DAVIS
BRILLIANT MIND — FURNITURE
BRIMFUL OF ASHA — CORNERSHOP
BRING A LITTLE WATER SYLVIE —
   Lonnie DONEGAN
BRING 'EM ALL IN — Mike SCOTT
BRING FORTH THE GUILLOTINE —
   SILVER BULLET
BRING IT ALL BACK — S CLUB 7
BRING IT ALL HOME — Gerry RAFFERTY
BRING IT BACK — McALMONT & BUTLER
BRING IT BACK AGAIN — STRAY CATS
BRING IT BACK 2 LUV —
   PROJECT featuring GERIDEAU
BRING IT DOWN (THIS INSANE THING) —
   REDSKINS
BRING IT ON [A] — N'dea DAVENPORT
BRING IT ON [B] — GOMEZ
BRING IT ON [C] —
   Nick CAVE & the BAD SEEDS
BRING IT ON [D] — Alistair GRIFFIN
BRING IT ON ... BRING IT ON — James BROWN
BRING IT ON DOWN — JESUS JONES
BRING IT ON HOME —
   URBAN COOKIE COLLECTIVE
BRING IT ON HOME TO ME — The ANIMALS
BRING IT ON TO MY LOVE — DE NADA
BRING ME CLOSER — ALTERED IMAGES
BRING ME EDELWEISS — EDELWEISS
BRING ME LOVE — Andrea MENDEZ
BRING ME TO LIFE —
   EVANESCENCE featuring Paul McCoy
BRING ME YOUR CUP — UB40
BRING MY FAMILY BACK — FAITHLESS
BRING ON THE DANCING HORSES —
   ECHO and the BUNNYMEN
BRING THE FAMILY BACK — Billy PAUL
BRING THE NOISE [A] — PUBLIC ENEMY

BRING THE NOISE [A] —
   ANTHRAX featuring Chuck D
BRING UP THE MIC SOME MORE —
   RAGGA TWINS
BRING YOUR DAUGHTER ... TO THE SLAUGHTER —
   IRON MAIDEN
BRINGING BACK THOSE MEMORIES —
   Mark JOSEPH
BRINGING ON BACK THE GOOD TIMES —
   LOVE AFFAIR
BRISTOL STOMP — LATE SHOW
BRITANNIA RAG — Winifred ATWELL
BRITE SIDE — Deborah HARRY
BRITISH HUSTLE — HI TENSION
THE BRITISH WAY OF LIFE — CHORDS
THE BRITS 1990 —
   VARIOUS ARTISTS (MONTAGES)
BROKE — Cassius HENRY
BROKE AWAY — WET WET WET
BROKE — The BETA BAND
BROKEN ARROW [A] — WATERFRONT
BROKEN ARROW [B] — Rod STEWART
BROKEN BONES — LOVE INC.
BROKEN DOLL —
   Tommy BRUCE and the BRUISERS
BROKEN DOWN ANGEL — NAZARETH
BROKEN ENGLISH — SUNSCREEM
A BROKEN HEART CAN MEND —
   Alexander O'NEAL
BROKEN HEART (THIRTEEN VALLEYS) —
   BIG COUNTRY
BROKEN HEARTED — Ken DODD
BROKEN HEARTED MELODY — Sarah VAUGHAN
BROKEN HOMES — TRICKY
BROKEN LAND — ADVENTURES
BROKEN NOSE — CATHERINE WHEEL
BROKEN SILENCE — SO SOLID CREW
BROKEN STONES — Paul WELLER
BROKEN WINGS [A] — Art and Dotty TODD
BROKEN WINGS [A] — Dickie VALENTINE
BROKEN WINGS [A] — The STARGAZERS
BROKEN WINGS [B] — MR MISTER
BROKEN WINGS [B] — NETWORK
THE BROKEN YEARS — HIPSWAY
BRONTOSAURUS — The MOVE
BROOKLYN BEATS — Scotti DEEP
BROOKLYN-QUEENS — 3RD BASS
BROTHA PART II — Angie STONE
   featuring Alicia KEYS & EVE
BROTHER [A] — CCS
BROTHER [B] — URBAN SPECIES
BROTHER BRIGHT — ÇA VA ÇA VA
BROTHER LOUIE [A] — HOT CHOCOLATE
BROTHER LOUIE [A] — QUIREBOYS
BROTHER LOUIE [B] — MODERN TALKING
BROTHER OF MINE — ANDERSON
   BRUFORD WAKEMAN HOWE
BROTHERS AND SISTERS —
   2 FUNKY 2 starring Kathryn DION
BROTHERS GONNA WORK IT OUT —
   PUBLIC ENEMY
BROTHERS IN ARMS — DIRE STRAITS
BROWN-EYED HANDSOME MAN [A] —
   Buddy HOLLY
BROWN EYED HANDSOME MAN [A] —
   Paul McCARTNEY
BROWN GIRL IN THE RING — BONEY M
BROWN PAPER BAG — Roni SIZE / REPRAZENT
BROWN SKIN — india.arie
BROWN SUGAR [A] — The ROLLING STONES
BROWN SUGAR [B] — D'ANGELO
BRUISE PRISTINE — PLACEBO
BRUSHED — Paul WELLER
BRUTAL-8-E — ALTERN 8
BUBBLE — FLUKE
BUBBLING HOT — Pato BANTON
BUBBLIN' — BLUE
BUCCI BAG — Andrea DORIA
BUCK ROGERS — FEEDER
THE BUCKET — KINGS OF LEON
THE BUCKET OF WATER SONG —
   FOUR BUCKETEERS
BUDDHA OF SUBURBIA —
   David BOWIE featuring Lenny KRAVITZ
BUDDY — DE LA SOUL
BUDDY HOLLY — WEEZER
BUDDY X [A] — Neneh CHERRY
BUDDY X 99 [B] —
   DREEM TEEM vs Neneh CHERRY
BUFFALO BILL'S LAST SCRATCH —
   The BARRON KNIGHTS
BUFFALO GALS [A] — Malcolm McLAREN and the
   WORLD'S FAMOUS SUPREME TEAM
BUFFALO GALS STAMPEDE [A] —
   Malcolm McLAREN
BUFFALO SOLDIER —
   Bob MARLEY & the WAILERS
BUFFALO STANCE — Neneh CHERRY
THE BUG — DIRE STRAITS
BUG A BOO — DESTINY'S CHILD
BUG IN THE BASSBIN —
   INNERZONE ORCHESTRA
BUG POWDER DUST — BOMB THE BASS
BUGGIN — TRUE STEPPERS
BUGS — HEPBURN
BUILD [A] — The HOUSEMARTINS
BUILD [B] — INNOCENCE

BUILD ME UP BUTTERCUP [A] – The FOUNDATIONS
BUILD ME UP BUTTERCUP 2003 [A] – PARTY BOYS
BUILD YOUR LOVE – Johnnie RAY
BUILDING THE CITY OF LIGHT – Mike SCOTT
BULGARIAN – TRAVEL
BULL IN THE HEATHER – SONIC YOUTH
BULLDOG NATION – Kevin KENNEDY
BULLET – FLUKE
BULLET COMES – The CHARLATANS
BULLET IN THE GUN – PLANET PERFECTO
BULLET IN THE HEAD – RAGE AGAINST THE MACHINE
BULLET WITH BUTTERFLY WINGS – SMASHING PUMPKINS
BULLETPROOF! – POP WILL EAT ITSELF
BULLETS – CREED
BULLFROG – GTO
BULLITPROOF – BREAKBEAT ERA
BULLITT – Lalo SCHIFRIN
BULLS ON PARADE – RAGE AGAINST THE MACHINE
BULLY BOY – SHED SEVEN
BULLY FOR YOU – Tom ROBINSON
BUMP – FUN LOVIN' CRIMINALS
THE BUMP – KENNY
BUMP, BUMP, BUMP – B2K featuring P DIDDY
BUMP 'N' GRIND – R KELLY
BUMP N GRIND (I AM FEELING HOT TONIGHT) – M DUBS featuring LADY SAW
BUMPED – RIGHT SAID FRED
A BUNCH OF THYME – FOSTER and ALLEN
BUNSEN BURNER – John OTWAY
BUONA SERA [A] – Louis PRIMA
BUONA SERA [A] – Mr Acker BILK and his PARAMOUNT JAZZ BAND
BUONA SERA [A] – BAD MANNERS
BUOY – Mick KARN featuring David SYLVIAN
BURDEN IN MY HAND – SOUNDGARDEN
BURIAL – LEVITICUS
BURIED ALIVE BY LOVE – HIM
BURLESQUE – FAMILY
BURN [A] – DOCTOR and the MEDICS
BURN [B] – Tina ARENA
BURN [C] – USHER
BURN BABY BURN [A] – HUDSON-FORD
BURN BABY BURN [B] – ASH
BURN BURN – LOSTPROPHETS
BURN IT UP – BEATMASTERS with PP ARNOLD
BURN RUBBER ON ME (WHY YOU WANNA HURT ME) – GAP BAND
BURN YOUR YOUTH – JOHNNY PANIC
BURNED WITH DESIRE – Armin VAN BUUREN featuring Justine SUISSA
BURNIN' [A] – DAFT PUNK
BURNIN' [B] – K-KLASS
BURNIN' [C] – MIRRORBALL
BURNIN' HOT – Jermaine JACKSON
BURNIN' LOVE – CON FUNK SHUN
BURNING '95 [A] – MK featuring ALANA
BURNING [B] – BABY BUMPS
BURNING BRIDGES – Jack SCOTT
BURNING BRIDGES (ON AND OFF AND ON AGAIN) – STATUS QUO
BURNING CAR – John FOXX
BURNING DOWN ONE SIDE – Robert PLANT
BURNING DOWN THE HOUSE – Tom JONES and The CARDIGANS
BURNING HEART – SURVIVOR
BURNING LOVE – Elvis PRESLEY
BURNING OF THE MIDNIGHT LAMP – The Jimi HENDRIX EXPERIENCE
BURNING THE GROUND – DURAN DURAN
BURNING UP [A] – Tony DE VIT
BURNING UP [B] – BINI & MARTINI
BURNING WHEEL – PRIMAL SCREAM
BURST – DARLING BUDS
BURUCHACCA – MUKKAA
BURUNDI BLACK – BURUNDI STEIPHENSON BLACK
BURUNDI BLUES – BEATS INTERNATIONAL
BURY YOU – SYMPOSIUM
BUS STOP – The HOLLIES
BUSHEL AND A PECK – Vivian BLAINE
BUSHES – Markus NIKOLAI
BUSINESS – EMINEM
THE BUSINESS – Brian MAY
BUST A MOVE – YOUNG MC
BUST THIS HOUSE DOWN – PENTHOUSE 4
BUSTED – Ray CHARLES
BUSY BEE – UGLY KID JOE
BUSY DOING NOTHING – Dave STEWART
BUT I DO – Clarence 'Frogman' HENRY
BUT I DO LOVE YOU – LeAnn RIMES
BUT I FEEL GOOD – GROOVE ARMADA
BUT NOT FOR ME [A] – Ella FITZGERALD
BUT NOT FOR ME [A] – Ketty LESTER
BUT YOU LOVE ME DADDY – Jim REEVES
BUT YOU'RE MINE – SONNY and CHER
BUTCHER BABY – PLASMATICS
BUTTERCUP – Carl ANDERSON
BUTTERFINGERS – Tommy STEELE
BUTTERFLIES & HURRICANES – MUSE
BUTTERFLY [A] – Andy WILLIAMS
BUTTERFLY [A] – Charlie GRACIE
BUTTERFLY [B] – Danyel GERARD
BUTTERFLY [C] – Mariah CAREY
BUTTERFLY [D] – TILT featuring ZEE
BUTTERFLY [E] – CRAZY TOWN
BUTTERFLY KISSES – Bob CARLISLE
BUTTERFLY ON A WHEEL – The MISSION
BUY IT IN BOTTLES – Richard ASHCROFT
BUZZ BUZZ A DIDDLE IT – MATCHBOX
BUZZIN' – ASIAN DUB FOUNDATION
BY MY SIDE – INXS
BY THE DEVIL (I WAS TEMPTED) – BLUE MINK
BY THE FOUNTAINS OF ROME [A] – David HUGHES
BY THE FOUNTAINS OF ROME [A] – Edmund HOCKRIDGE
BY THE LIGHT OF THE SILVERY MOON – LITTLE RICHARD
BY THE TIME THIS NIGHT IS OVER – Kenny G with Peabo BRYSON
BY THE WAY [A] – BIG THREE
BY THE WAY [B] – The TREMELOES
BY THE WAY [C] – RED HOT CHILI PEPPERS
BY YOUR SIDE [A] – PETERS and LEE
BY YOUR SIDE [B] – Jimmy SOMERVILLE
BY YOUR SIDE [C] – SADE
BYE BABY – Ruby TURNER
BYE BYE BABY [A] – Johnny OTIS SHOW
BYE BYE BABY [B] – SYMBOLS
BYE BYE BABY [B] – BAY CITY ROLLERS
BYE BYE BABY [C] – Tony JACKSON and the VIBRATIONS
BYE BYE BABY [D] – TQ
BYE BYE BLUES – Bert KAEMPFERT
BYE BYE BOY – Jennifer ELLISON
BYE BYE BYE – 'N SYNC
BYE BYE LOVE – The EVERLY BROTHERS
B.Y.O.F. (BRING YOUR OWN FUNK) – FANTASTIC FOUR
BYRDS TURN TO STONE – SHACK
C MOON – Paul McCARTNEY
C U WHEN U GET THERE – COOLIO
C'MON PEOPLE (WE'RE MAKING IT NOW) – Richard ASHCROFT
ÇA PLANE POUR MOI [A] – PLASTIC BERTRAND
ÇA PLANE POUR MOI [A] – Leila K
CABARET – Louis ARMSTRONG Orchestra & Chorus
THE CABARET – TIME UK
CACHARPAYA (ANDES PUMPSA DAESI) – INCANTATION
CAFE DEL MAR – ENERGY 52
CAFFEINE BOMB – The WILDHEARTS
CALEDONIA – Frankie MILLER
CALENDAR GIRL – Neil SEDAKA
THE CALENDAR SONG (JANUARY, FEBRUARY, MARCH, APRIL, MAY) – TRINIDAD OIL COMPANY
CALIBRE CUTS – VARIOUS ARTISTS (MONTAGES)
CALIFORNIA [A] – WEDDING PRESENT
CALIFORNIA [B] – Belinda CARLISLE
CALIFORNIA [C] – Lenny KRAVITZ
CALIFORNIA DREAMIN' [A] – MAMAS and the PAPAS
CALIFORNIA DREAMING [A] – COLORADO
CALIFORNIA DREAMIN' [A] – RIVER CITY PEOPLE
CALIFORNIA DREAMIN' [A] – Bobby WOMACK
CALIFORNIA DREAMIN' [B]– ROYAL GIGOLOS
CALIFORNIA GIRLS [A] – The BEACH BOYS
CALIFORNIA GIRLS [A] – David Lee ROTH
CALIFORNIA HERE I COME [A] – Freddy CANNON
CALIFORNIA HERE I COME [B] – Sophie B HAWKINS
CALIFORNIA LOVE – 2PAC featuring Dr DRE
CALIFORNIA MAN – The MOVE
CALIFORNIA SAGA – CALIFORNIA – The BEACH BOYS
CALIFORNIA SCREAMIN' – CARRIE
CALIFORNIA WAITING – KINGS OF LEON
CALIFORNIA'S BLEEDING – AMEN
CALIFORNICATION – RED HOT CHILI PEPPERS
CALINDA – RITMO-DYNAMIC
THE CALL – BACKSTREET BOYS
CALL AND ANSWER – BARENAKED LADIES
CALL HER YOUR SWEETHEART – Frank IFIELD
CALL IT FATE – Richie DAN
CALL IT LOVE – DEUCE
CALL IT ROCK 'N' ROLL – GREAT WHITE
CALL IT WHAT YOU WANT [A] – NEW KIDS ON THE BLOCK
CALL IT WHAT YOU WANT [B] – CREDIT TO THE NATION
CALL ME [A] – BLONDIE
CALL ME [B] – GO WEST
CALL ME [C] – SPAGNA
CALL ME [D] – LE CLICK
CALL ME [E] – JAMELIA
CALL ME [F] – TWEET
(CALL ME) NUMBER ONE – The TREMELOES
CALL ME ROUND – PILOT
CALL MY NAME – ORCHESTRAL MANOEUVRES IN THE DARK
CALL OF THE WILD – Midge URE
CALL OFF THE SEARCH – Katie MELUA
CALL ON ME – Eric PRYDZ
CALL OUT THE DOGS – Gary NUMAN
CALL ROSIE ON THE PHONE – Guy MITCHELL
CALL THE MAN – Celine DION
CALL U SEXY – VS
THE CALL UP – The CLASH
CALL UP THE GROUPS – The BARRON KNIGHTS
CALLING – Geri HALLIWELL
CALLING ALL GIRLS – ATL
CALLING ALL THE HEROES – IT BITES
CALLING AMERICA – ELECTRIC LIGHT ORCHESTRA
CALLING ELVIS – DIRE STRAITS
CALLING OCCUPANTS OF INTERPLANETARY CRAFT (THE RECOGNISED ANTHEM OF WORLD CONTACT DAY) – The CARPENTERS
CALLING OUT YOUR NAME – Jimmy NAIL
CALLING YOU – Paul YOUNG
CALLING YOUR NAME – MARILYN
CALLS THE TUNE – Hazel O'CONNOR
CALM DOWN (BASS KEEPS PUMPIN') – CHRIS and JAMES
CALYPSO CRAZY – Billy OCEAN
CAMBODIA – Kim WILDE
CAMDEN TOWN – SUGGS
CAMEL BOBSLED RACE – DJ SHADOW
CAMELS – SANTOS
CAMOUFLAGE – Stan RIDGWAY
CAMPIONE 2000 – E-TYPE
CAN CAN 62 [A] – Peter JAY and the JAYWALKERS
CAN CAN [A] – BAD MANNERS
CAN CAN YOU PARTY – JIVE BUNNY and the MASTERMIXERS
CAN I – CASHMERE
CAN I GET A... – JAY-Z
CAN I GET A WITNESS – Sam BROWN
CAN I GET OVER – DEFINITION OF SOUND
CAN I KICK IT – A TRIBE CALLED QUEST
CAN I PLAY WITH MADNESS – IRON MAIDEN
CAN I TAKE YOU HOME LITTLE GIRL – The DRIFTERS
CAN I TOUCH YOU ...THERE – Michael BOLTON
CAN I TRUST YOU – The BACHELORS
CAN THE CAN – Suzi QUATRO
CAN THIS BE LOVE – Matt MONRO
CAN U DANCE – DJ 'FAST' EDDIE
CAN U DIG IT [A] – POP WILL EAT ITSELF
CAN U DIG IT [B] – JAMX & DELEON
CAN U FEEL IT [A] – ELEVATION
CAN U FEEL IT [B] – DEEP CREED '94
CAN WE – SWV
CAN WE FIX IT – BOB THE BUILDER
CAN WE START AGAIN? – TINDERSTICKS
CAN WE TALK ... – CODE RED
CAN YOU DIG IT? – MOCK TURTLES
CAN YOU DO IT – GEORDIE
CAN YOU FEEL IT [A] – The JACKSONS
CAN YOU FEEL IT? [A] – V
CAN YOU FEEL IT [B] – REEL 2 REAL
CAN YOU FEEL IT [C] – CLS
CAN YOU FEEL IT / CAN YOU FEEL IT – RAZE
CAN YOU FEEL IT (ROCK DA HOUSE) – NYCC
CAN YOU FEEL THE FORCE? – The REAL THING
CAN YOU FEEL THE LOVE TONIGHT – Elton JOHN
(CAN YOU) FEEL THE PASSION – BLUE PEARL
CAN YOU FEEL (WHAT I'M GOING THRU) – SHOLAN
CAN YOU FORGIVE HER – PET SHOP BOYS
CAN YOU FORGIVE ME – Karl DENVER
CAN YOU HANDLE IT [A] – DNA featuring Sharon REDD
CAN YOU HANDLE IT [A] – Sharon REDD
CAN YOU KEEP A SECRET – BROTHER BEYOND
CAN YOU PARTY – ROYAL HOUSE
CAN YOU PLEASE CRAWL OUT YOUR WINDOW – Bob DYLAN
CAN YOUR PUSSY DO THE DOG? – CRAMPS
CANCER FOR THE CURE – EELS
CANDIDA – DAWN
CANDIDATE FOR LOVE – TS MONK
CANDLE IN THE WIND [A] – Elton JOHN
CANDLE IN THE WIND 1997 [A] – Elton JOHN
CANDLEFIRE – DAWN OF THE REPLICANTS
CANDLELAND (THE SECOND COMING) – Ian McCULLOCH
CANDLELIGHT – SIX BY SEVEN
CANDLES – Alex REECE
CANDY [A] – CAMEO
CANDY [B] – Iggy POP
CANDY [C] – Mandy MOORE
CANDY [D] – ASH
CANDY EVERYBODY WANTS – 10,000 MANIACS
CANDY GIRL [A] – NEW EDITION
CANDY GIRL [B] – BABYBIRD
CANDY MAN – Brian POOLE and the TREMELOES
CANDY RAIN – SOUL FOR REAL
CANDYBAR EXPRESS – LOVE AND MONEY
CANDYMAN – SIOUXSIE and the BANSHEES
CANED AND UNABLE – HI-GATE
CANNED HEAT – JAMIROQUAI
CANNIBALS – Mark KNOPFLER
CANNONBALL [A] – Duane EDDY and the REBELS
CANNONBALL [B] – Damien RICE
CANNONBALL (EP) – The BREEDERS
CAN'T BE SURE – The SUNDAYS
CAN'T BE WITH YOU TONIGHT – Judy BOUCHER
CAN'T BUY ME LOVE [A] – The BEATLES
CAN'T BUY ME LOVE [A] – Ella FITZGERALD
CAN'T CHANGE ME – Chris CORNELL
CAN'T CONTAIN ME – TAZ
CAN'T CRY ANYMORE – Sheryl CROW
CAN'T DO A THING (TO STOP ME) – Chris ISAAK
CAN'T DO NUTTIN' FOR YA MAN – PUBLIC ENEMY
CAN'T DO RIGHT FOR DOING WRONG – Erin ROCHA
CAN'T EXPLAIN – LONGVIEW
CAN'T FAKE THE FEELING – Geraldine HUNT
CAN'T FIGHT THE MOONLIGHT – LeAnn RIMES
CAN'T FIGHT THIS FEELING – REO SPEEDWAGON
CAN'T FORGET YOU – SONIA
CAN'T GET ALONG WITHOUT YOU – Frankie VAUGHAN
CAN'T GET ANY HARDER – James BROWN
CAN'T GET AWAY – MOOD II SWING
CAN'T GET BY – SLAMM
CAN'T GET BY WITHOUT YOU [A] – The REAL THING
CAN'T GET BY WITHOUT YOU (THE SECOND DECADE REMIX) [A] – The REAL THING
CAN'T GET ENOUGH [A] – BAD COMPANY
CAN'T GET ENOUGH [B] – SUEDE
CAN'T GET ENOUGH [C] – SOULSEARCHER
CAN'T GET ENOUGH [D] – RAGHAV
CAN'T GET ENOUGH OF YOU – Eddy GRANT
CAN'T GET ENOUGH OF YOUR LOVE [A] – DARTS
CAN'T GET ENOUGH OF YOUR LOVE [B] – KWS
CAN'T GET ENOUGH OF YOUR LOVE [B] – Taylor DAYNE
CAN'T GET ENOUGH OF YOUR LOVE, BABE [B] – Barry WHITE
CAN'T GET IT BACK – MIS-TEEQ
(CAN'T GET MY) HEAD AROUND YOU – The OFFSPRING
CAN'T GET OUT OF BED – The CHARLATANS
CAN'T GET THE BEST OF ME – CYPRESS HILL
CAN'T GET USED TO LOSING YOU [A] – Andy WILLIAMS
CAN'T GET USED TO LOSING YOU [A] – The BEAT
CAN'T GET USED TO LOSING YOU [A] – COLOUR GIRL
CAN'T GET YOU OFF MY MIND – Lenny KRAVITZ
CAN'T GET YOU OUT OF MY HEAD – Kylie MINOGUE
CAN'T GET YOU OUT OF MY THOUGHTS – DUM DUMS
CAN'T GIVE ME LOVE – PEPSI and SHIRLIE
CAN'T GIVE YOU ANYTHING (BUT MY LOVE) – The STYLISTICS
CAN'T GIVE YOU MORE – STATUS QUO
CAN'T HAPPEN HERE – RAINBOW
CAN'T HAVE YOU – LYTE FUNKIE ONES
CAN'T HELP FALLING IN LOVE [A] – Elvis PRESLEY with the JORDANAIRES
CAN'T HELP FALLING IN LOVE [A] – Andy WILLIAMS
CAN'T HELP FALLING IN LOVE [A] – The STYLISTICS
CAN'T HELP FALLING IN LOVE [A] – LICK THE TINS
CAN'T HELP IT – HAPPY CLAPPERS
CAN'T HELP MYSELF – LINX
CAN'T HOLD US DOWN – Christina AGUILERA featuring LIL' KIM
CAN'T I – Nat 'King' COLE
CAN'T KEEP IT IN – Cat STEVENS
CAN'T KEEP LIVING THIS WAY – ROOTJOOSE
CAN'T KEEP ME SILENT – ANGELIC
CAN'T KEEP THIS FEELING IN – Cliff RICHARD
CAN'T KNOCK THE HUSTLE – JAY-Z featuring Mary J BLIGE
CAN'T LET GO [A] – EARTH WIND AND FIRE
CAN'T LET GO [B] – Mariah CAREY
CAN'T LET HER GO – BOYZ II MEN
CAN'T LET YOU GO [A] – Barry RYAN
CAN'T LET YOU GO [B] – RAINBOW
CAN'T LET YOU GO [C] – FABOLOUS featuring Mike SHOREY & LIL' MO
CAN'T LIVE WITH YOU (CAN'T LIVE WITHOUT YOU) – The MINDBENDERS
CAN'T LIVE WITHOUT YOU – SCORPIONS
(CAN'T LIVE WITHOUT YOUR) LOVE AND AFFECTION – NELSON
CAN'T MAKE UP MY MIND – SONIQUE
CAN'T NOBODY – Kelly ROWLAND
CAN'T NOBODY HOLD ME DOWN – PUFF DADDY featuring MA$E
CAN'T SAY 'BYE – STONEFREE
CAN'T SAY GOODBYE – POP!
CAN'T SAY HOW MUCH I LOVE YOU – Demis ROUSSOS
CAN'T SEE ME – Ian BROWN

CAN'T SET RULES ABOUT LOVE — Adam ANT
CAN'T SHAKE LOOSE — Agnetha FALTSKOG
CAN'T SHAKE THE FEELING — BIG FUN
CAN'T SMILE — VEX RED
CAN'T SMILE WITHOUT YOU [A] — Barry MANILOW
CAN'T SMILE WITHOUT YOU [A] — James BULLER
CAN'T STAND IT — WILCO
CAN'T STAND LOSING YOU [A] — The POLICE
CAN'T STAND LOSING YOU [A] — FEEDER
CAN'T STAND ME NOW — The LIBERTINES
CAN'T STAY AWAY FROM YOU — Gloria ESTEFAN and MIAMI SOUND MACHINE
CAN'T STOP [A] — AFTER 7
CAN'T STOP [B] — RED HOT CHILI PEPPERS
CAN'T STOP LOVIN' YOU — VAN HALEN
CAN'T STOP LOVING YOU — Phil COLLINS
CAN'T STOP RUNNING — SPACE MONKEY
CAN'T STOP THE MUSIC — VILLAGE PEOPLE
CAN'T STOP THESE THINGS — CHINA DRUM
CAN'T STOP THIS FEELING — RHYTHM-N-BASS
CAN'T STOP THIS THING WE STARTED — Bryan ADAMS
CAN'T TAKE MY EYES OFF YOU [A] — Andy WILLIAMS
CAN'T TAKE MY EYES OFF YOU [A] — BOYSTOWN GANG
CAN'T TAKE MY EYES OFF YOU [A] — Andy WILLIAMS and Denise VAN OUTEN
CAN'T TAKE NO MORE — SOUP DRAGONS
CAN'T TAKE YOUR LOVE — Pauline HENRY
CAN'T TRUSS IT — PUBLIC ENEMY
CAN'T TURN BACK — SPEEDWAY
CAN'T WAIT ANOTHER MINUTE — FIVE STAR
CAN'T WAIT TO BE WITH YOU — JAZZY JEFF & the FRESH PRINCE
CAN'T YOU HEAR MY HEART — Danny RIVERS
CAN'T YOU HEAR MY HEART BEAT? — GOLDIE and the GINGERBREADS
CAN'T YOU HEAR THE BEAT OF A BROKEN HEART — Iain GREGORY
CAN'T YOU SEE — TOTAL featuring the NOTORIOUS B.I.G.
CAN'T YOU SEE THAT SHE'S MINE — Dave CLARK FIVE
(CAN'T YOU) TRIP LIKE I DO — FILTER and the CRYSTAL METHOD
CANTALOOP — US3
CANTGETAMAN CANTGETAJOB (LIFE'S A BITCH) — SISTER BLISS
CANTO DELLA TERRA — Andrea BOCELLI
CANTON (LIVE) — JAPAN
CANTONESE BOY — JAPAN
CAPOIERA — INFRARED vs Gil FELIX
CAPSTICK COMES HOME — Tony CAPSTICK and the CARLTON MAIN / FRICKLEY COLLIERY BAND
CAPTAIN BEAKY — Keith MICHELL
CAPTAIN DREAD — DREADZONE
CAPTAIN KREMMEN (RETRIBUTION) — Kenny EVERETT
THE CAPTAIN OF HER HEART — DOUBLE
CAPTAIN OF YOUR SHIP — REPARATA and the DELRONS
CAPTAIN SCARLET THEME — Barry GRAY ORCHESTRA
CAPTURE THE FLAG — FRESH
CAPTURE THE HEART (EP) — RUNRIG
CAR BOOT SALE — BILL
CAR 67 — DRIVER 67
CAR SONG — MADDER ROSE
CAR WASH [A] — ROSE ROYCE
CAR WASH [A] — Gwen DICKEY
CAR WASH [A] — ROSE ROYCE featuring Gwen DICKEY
CAR WASH [A] — Christina AGUILERA featuring Missy ELLIOTT
CARA MIA — David WHITFIELD
CARAMEL — CITY HIGH featuring EVE
CARAVAN [A] — Duane EDDY and the REBELS
CARAVAN [B] — INSPIRAL CARPETS
CARAVAN OF LOVE [A] — ISLEY JASPER ISLEY
CARAVAN OF LOVE [A] — The HOUSEMARTINS
CARAVAN SONG — Barbara DICKSON
CARBON KID — ALPINESTARS featuring Brian MOLKO
CARDBOY KING — SALAD
CARDIAC ARREST — MADNESS
CAREFUL — HORSE
CARELESS HANDS — Des O'CONNOR
CARELESS LOVE — SWIMMING WITH SHARKS
CARELESS MEMORIES — DURAN DURAN
CARELESS WHISPER [A] — George MICHAEL
CARELESS WHISPER [A] — Sarah WASHINGTON
CARELESS WHISPER [A] — 2PLAY featuring Thomas JULES & JUCXI D
CARIBBEAN BLUE — ENYA
THE CARIBBEAN DISCO SHOW — LOBO
CARIBBEAN HONEYMOON — Frank WEIR
CARIBBEAN QUEEN (NO MORE LOVE ON THE RUN) — Billy OCEAN
CARMEN QUEASY — MAXIM
CARNATION — Liam GALLAGHER and Steve CRADOCK
CARNAVAL DE PARIS — DARIO G
CARNIVAL [A] — LIONROCK
CARNIVAL [B] — The CARDIGANS
CARNIVAL GIRL — TEXAS featuring Kardinal OFFISHALL
CARNIVAL IN HEAVEN — Malandra BURROWS
THE CARNIVAL IS OVER — The SEEKERS
CAROLINA MOON — Connie FRANCIS
CAROLINE [A] — STATUS QUO
CAROLINE [B] — Kirsty MacCOLL
CAROUSEL — ORIGINAL SOUNDTRACK (LP) — VARIOUS ARTISTS (EPs and LPs)
THE CAROUSEL WALTZ — Ray MARTIN
CARRERA 2 — THREE DRIVES
CARRIE [A] — Cliff RICHARD
CARRIE [B] — EUROPE
CARRIE-ANNE — The HOLLIES
CARRION — BRITISH SEA POWER
CARROT ROPE — PAVEMENT
CARRY ME HOME — GLOWORM
CARRY ON [A] — Martha WASH
CARRY ON [B] — SPACEHOG
CARRY ON [C] — Donna SUMMER and Giorgio MORODER
CARRY ON WAYWARD SON — KANSAS
CARRY THAT WEIGHT — TRASH
CARRY THE BLAME — RIVER CITY PEOPLE
CARRYING A TORCH — Tom JONES
CARS [A] — Gary NUMAN
CARS [A] — FEAR FACTORY
CARS (E REG MODEL) — Gary NUMAN
CARS AND GIRLS — PREFAB SPROUT
CARTE BLANCHE — VERACOCHA
CARTOON HEROES — AQUA
CARTROUBLE — ADAM and the ANTS
CASABLANCA — Kenny BALL and his JAZZMEN
CASANOVA [A] — Petula CLARK
CASANOVA [B] — COFFEE
CASANOVA [B] — BABY D
CASANOVA [C] — LEVERT
CASANOVA [C] — ULTIMATE KAOS
CASCADE — FUTURE SOUND OF LONDON
CASE OF THE EX — MYA
CASINO ROYALE — Herb ALPERT
CASINO ROYALE — DJ Zinc
CASSIUS 1999 — CASSIUS
CAST YOUR FATE TO THE WIND — SOUNDS ORCHESTRAL
CASTLE ROCK — The BLUETONES
CASTLES IN SPAIN — ARMOURY SHOW
CASTLES IN THE AIR [A] — Don McLEAN
CASTLES IN THE AIR [B] — COLOUR FIELD
CASTLES IN THE SAND — THUNDER
CASTLES IN THE SKY — IAN VAN DAHL
CASUAL SUB (BURNING SPEAR) — ETA
CAT AMONG THE PIGEONS — BROS
THE CAT CAME BACK — Sonny JAMES
THE CAT CREPT IN — MUD
CAT PEOPLE (PUTTING OUT FIRE) — David BOWIE
CATALAN — TOUR DE FORCE
CATALYST — OCEANSIZE
CATCH [A] — The CURE
CATCH [B] — SUNSCREEM
CATCH [C] — KOSHEEN
CATCH A FALLING STAR — Perry COMO
CATCH A FIRE — HADDAWAY
CATCH ME — ABSOLUTE
CATCH ME UP — GOMEZ
CATCH MY FALL — Billy IDOL
CATCH THE BREEZE — SLOWDIVE
CATCH THE FIRE — DRIZABONE
CATCH THE LIGHT — Martha WASH
CATCH THE SUN — DOVES
CATCH THE WIND — DONOVAN
CATCH UP TO MY STEP — JUNKIE XL featuring Solomon BURKE
CATCH US IF YOU CAN — Dave CLARK FIVE
CATERINA — Perry COMO
THE CATERPILLAR — The CURE
CATH — The BLUEBELLS
CATHEDRAL PARK — DUBSTAR
CATHEDRAL SONG — Tanita TIKARAM
CATHY'S CLOWN — The EVERLY BROTHERS
CATS IN THE CRADLE [A] — UGLY KID JOE
CATS IN THE CRADLE [A] — Jason DOWNS featuring MILK
CAUGHT A LITE SNEEZE — Tori AMOS
CAUGHT BY THE FUZZ — SUPERGRASS
CAUGHT BY THE RIVER — DOVES
CAUGHT IN A MOMENT — SUGABABES
CAUGHT IN MY SHADOW — The WONDER STUFF
CAUGHT IN THE MIDDLE [A] — Juliet ROBERTS
CAUGHT IN THE MIDDLE [B] — a1
CAUGHT IN THE MIDDLE [C] — Cerys MATTHEWS
CAUGHT OUT THERE — KELIS
CAUGHT UP IN MY HEART — OPTIMYSTIC
CAUGHT UP IN THE RAPTURE — Anita BAKER
CAUSING A COMMOTION — MADONNA
CAVATINA — John WILLIAMS
CAVE — MUSE
CCCAN'T YOU SEE — VICIOUS PINK
CECILIA — SUGGS featuring Louchie LOU and Michie ONE
THE CEDAR ROOM — DOVES
CELEBRATE [A] — AN EMOTIONAL FISH
CELEBRATE [B] — HORSE
CELEBRATE [C] — LEVELLERS
CELEBRATE OUR LOVE — ALICE DEEJAY
(CELEBRATE) THE DAY AFTER YOU — The BLOW MONKEYS with Curtis MAYFIELD
CELEBRATE THE WORLD — WOMACK and WOMACK
CELEBRATE YOUR MOTHER — The EIGHTIES MATCHBOX B-LINE DISASTER
CELEBRATION [A] — KOOL and the GANG
CELEBRATION [A] — Kylie MINOGUE
A CELEBRATION — U2
CELEBRATION GENERATION — WESTBAM
CELEBRATION OF LIFE — TRUCE
CELEBRITY HIT LIST — TERRORVISION
CELEBRITY SKIN — HOLE
CELL 151 — Steve HACKETT
THE CELTIC SOUL BROTHERS — DEXY'S MIDNIGHT RUNNERS
THE CELTS — ENYA
CEMENT — FEEDER
CEMENTED SHOES — MY VITRIOL
CENTER CITY — FAT LARRY'S BAND
CENTERFOLD [A] — J GEILS BAND
CENTERFOLD [A] — Adam AUSTIN
CENTRAL PARK ARREST — THUNDERTHIGHS
CENTRAL RESERVATION — Beth ORTON
CENTURY — INTASTELLA
CEREMONY — NEW ORDER
CERTAIN PEOPLE I KNOW — MORRISSEY
A CERTAIN SMILE — Johnny MATHIS
THE CERTAINTY OF CHANCE — The DIVINE COMEDY
C'EST LA VIE [A] — Robbie NEVIL
C'EST LA VIE [B] — UB40
C'EST LA VIE [C] — B*WITCHED
C'EST LA VIE [D] — Jean-Michel JARRE
C'EST SI BON — Conway TWITTY
CHA CHA CHA — FLIPMODE SQUAD
CHA CHA HEELS — Eartha KITT and BRONSKI BEAT
CHA CHA SLIDE [A] — MC JIG
CHA CHA SLIDE [A] — DJ CASPER
CHA CHA TWIST — DETROIT COBRAS
CHAIN GANG [A] — Jimmy YOUNG
CHAIN GANG [B] — Sam COOKE
CHAIN-GANG SMILE — BROTHER BEYOND
CHAIN OF FOOLS — Aretha FRANKLIN
CHAIN REACTION [A] — Diana ROSS
CHAIN REACTION [A] — STEPS
CHAIN REACTION [B] — HURRICANE #1
CHAINS [A] — COOKIES
CHAINS [B] — RIVER DETECTIVES
CHAINS [C] — Tina ARENA
CHAINS AROUND MY HEART — Richard MARX
CHAINS OF LOVE — ERASURE
CHAINSAW CHARLIE (MURDERS IN THE NEW MORGUE) — W.A.S.P.
CHAIRMAN OF THE BOARD — CHAIRMEN OF THE BOARD
CHALK DUST — THE UMPIRE STRIKES BACK — BRAT
THE CHAMP — MOHAWKS
CHAMPAGNE — SALT-N-PEPA
CHAMPAGNE DANCE — PAY AS U GO
CHAMPAGNE HIGHWAY — SKANDAL
THE CHAMPION — Willie MITCHELL
CHANCE — BIG COUNTRY
CHANCES — HOT CHOCOLATE
CHANGE [A] — TEARS FOR FEARS
CHANGE [B] — David GRANT
CHANGE [C] — Lisa STANSFIELD
CHANGE [D] — INCOGNITO
CHANGE [E] — BLIND MELON
CHANGE [F] — The LIGHTNING SEEDS
CHANGE [G] — DAPHNE
CHANGE [H] — PHATS & SMALL
CHANGE CLOTHES — JAY-Z
CHANGE HIS WAYS — Robert PALMER
CHANGE (IN THE HOUSE OF FLIES) — DEFTONES
CHANGE ME — JOCASTA
CHANGE MY MIND — The BLUESKINS
CHANGE OF HEART [A] — CHANGE
CHANGE OF HEART [B] — Cyndi LAUPER
A CHANGE OF HEART [C] — Bernard BUTLER
CHANGE THE WORLD [A] — Eric CLAPTON
CHANGE THE WORLD [B] — Dino LENNY vs The HOUSEMARTINS
CHANGE WITH THE TIMES — Van McCOY
A CHANGE WOULD DO YOU GOOD — Sheryl CROW
CHANGE YOUR MIND [A] — Gary NUMAN
CHANGE YOUR MIND [B] — UPSIDE DOWN
CHANGES [A] — Crispian ST PETERS
CHANGES [B] — IMAGINATION
CHANGES [C] — Alan PRICE
CHANGES [D] — 2PAC
CHANGES [E] — Sandy RIVERA featuring HAZE
CHANGES [F] — Kelly and Ozzy OSBOURNE
CHANGES ARE NO GOOD — The STILLS
CHANGING FOR YOU — CHI-LITES
CHANGING PARTNERS [A] — Bing CROSBY
CHANGING PARTNERS [A] — Kay STARR
THE CHANGINGMAN — Paul WELLER
CHANNEL Z — B-52's
CHANSON D'AMOUR — MANHATTAN TRANSFER
THE CHANT (WE R) / RIP PRODUCTIONS — RIP PRODUCTIONS
THE CHANT HAS BEGUN — LEVEL 42
THE CHANT HAS JUST BEGUN — The ALARM
CHANT NO.1 (I DON'T NEED THIS PRESSURE ON) — SPANDAU BALLET
CHANTILLY LACE [A] — BIG BOPPER
CHANTILLY LACE [A] — Jerry Lee LEWIS
CHAPEL OF LOVE [A] — DIXIE CUPS
CHAPEL OF LOVE [B] — LONDON BOYS
CHAPEL OF THE ROSES — Malcolm VAUGHAN
CHAPTER FOUR — RAM TRILOGY
CHAPTER 5 — RAM TRILOGY
CHAPTER 6 — RAM TRILOGY
CHARADE — The SKIDS
CHARIOT [A] — Rhet STOLLER
CHARIOT [B] — Petula CLARK
CHARIOTS OF FIRE — TITLES — VANGELIS
CHARITY — SKUNK ANANSIE
CHARLESTON — TEMPERANCE SEVEN
CHARLIE BIG POTATO — SKUNK ANANSIE
CHARLIE BROWN — The COASTERS
CHARLIE'S ANGELS 2000 — APOLLO FOUR FORTY
CHARLOTTE — KITTIE
CHARLOTTE ANNE — Julian COPE
CHARLOTTE SOMETIMES — The CURE
CHARLTON HESTON — STUMP
CHARLY — The PRODIGY
CHARMAINE — The BACHELORS
CHARMING BILLY — Johnny PRESTON
CHARMING DEMONS — SENSER
CHARMLESS MAN — BLUR
CHASE [A] — Giorgio MORODER
CHASE [A] — MIDI XPRESS
THE CHASE [A] — DJ EMPIRE presents Giorgio MORODER
CHASE THE SUN — PLANET FUNK
CHASING A RAINBOW — Terry HALL
CHASING FOR THE BREEZE — ASWAD
CHASING RAINBOWS — SHED SEVEN
CH-CHECK IT OUT — BEASTIE BOYS
CHEAP THRILLS — PLANET PATROL
CHEATED — PRAYING MANTIS
CHECK IT OUT (EVERYBODY) — BMR featuring FELICIA
CHECK OUT THE GROOVE — Bobby THURSTON
CHECK THE MEANING — Richard ASHCROFT
CHECK THIS OUT — LA MIX
CHECK YO SELF — ICE CUBE featuring DAS EFX
CHEEKAH BOW BOW (THAT COMPUTER SONG) — The VENGABOYS
CHEEKY — BONIFACE
CHEEKY ARMADA — ILLICIT featuring GRAM'MA FUNK
CHEEKY FLAMENCO — CHEEKY GIRLS
CHEEKY SONG (TOUCH MY BUM) — CHEEKY GIRLS
CHEERS THEN — BANANARAMA
CHELSEA — STAMFORD BRIDGE
CHEMICAL #1 — JESUS JONES
CHEMICAL WORLD — BLUR
THE CHEMICALS BETWEEN US — BUSH
CHEMISTRY [A] — The NOLANS
CHEMISTRY [B] — SEMISONIC
CHEQUE ONE-TWO — SUNSHIP featuring MCRB
CHEQUERED LOVE — Kim WILDE
CHERI BABE — HOT CHOCOLATE
CHERISH [A] — David CASSIDY
CHERISH [B] — KOOL and the GANG
CHERISH [B] — PAPPA BEAR featuring VAN DER TOORN
CHERISH [C] — MADONNA
CHERISH [D] — JODECI
CHERISH THE DAY [A] — SADE
CHERISH THE DAY [B] — PLUMMET
CHERISH WHAT IS DEAR TO YOU (WHILE IT'S NEAR TO YOU) — Freda PAYNE
CHERRY LIPS (DER ERDBEERMUND) — CULTURE BEAT
CHERRY LIPS (GO BABY GO!) — GARBAGE
CHERRY OH BABY — UB40
CHERRY PIE [A] — Jess CONRAD
CHERRY PIE [B] — WARRANT
CHERRY PINK AND APPLE BLOSSOM WHITE [A] — Perez 'Prez' PRADO and his Orchestra, the King of Mambo
CHERRY PINK AND APPLE BLOSSOM WHITE [A] — Eddie CALVERT
CHERRY PINK AND APPLE BLOSSOM WHITE [A] — MODERN ROMANCE
CHERUB ROCK — SMASHING PUMPKINS
CHERYL'S GOIN' HOME — Adam FAITH
CHESTNUT MARE — The BYRDS
CHEWING GUM — ANNIE
CHI MAI (THEME FROM THE TV SERIES 'THE LIFE AND TIMES OF DAVID LLOYD GEORGE') — Ennio MORRICONE
CHIC MYSTIQUE — CHIC
CHICAGO [A] — Frank SINATRA
CHICAGO [B] — Kiki DEE
CHICK CHICK CHICKEN — Natalie CASEY
CHICKA BOOM — Guy MITCHELL
CHICK-A-BOOM (DON'T YA JES LOVE IT) — Jonathan KING
CHICKEN — The EIGHTIES MATCHBOX B-LINE DISASTER

SONG TITLE INDEX 573

THE CHICKEN SONG — SPITTING IMAGE
THE CHIEF — Tony SCOTT
CHIEF INSPECTOR — Wally BADAROU
CHIHUAHUA [A] — BOW WOW WOW
CHIHUAHUA [B] — DARE
CHIHUAHUA [B] — DJ BOBO
CHIKKI CHIKKI AHH AHH — BABY FORD
CHILD [A] — DEFINITION OF SOUND
CHILD [B] — Mark OWEN
CHILD COME AWAY — Kim WILDE
CHILD OF LOVE — LEMON TREES
CHILD OF THE UNIVERSE — DJ TAUCHER
CHILD STAR — Marc ALMOND
CHILDREN [A] — EMF
CHILDREN [A] — Robert MILES
CHILDREN [B] — TILT
CHILDREN [C] — 4 CLUBBERS
CHILDREN OF PARADISE — BONEY M
CHILDREN OF THE NIGHT [A] — Richard MARX
CHILDREN OF THE NIGHT [B] — NAKATOMI
CHILDREN OF THE REVOLUTION [A] —
  BABY FORD
CHILDREN OF THE REVOLUTION [A] — T. REX
CHILDREN OF THE REVOLUTION [A] —
  UNITONE ROCKERS featuring STEEL
CHILDREN OF THE WORLD —
  Ana ANN & the LONDON COMMUNITY CHOIR
CHILDREN SAY — LEVEL 42
A CHILD'S PRAYER — HOT CHOCOLATE
CHILI BOM BOM — TEMPERANCE SEVEN
CHILL OUT (THINGS GONNA CHANGE) —
  John Lee HOOKER
CHILL TO THE PANIC — DEEP C
CHILLIN' — MODJO
CHILLIN' OUT — Curtis HAIRSTON
CHIME — ORBITAL
CHINA — Tori AMOS
CHINA DOLL [A] — Slim WHITMAN
CHINA DOLL [B] — Julian COPE
CHINA GIRL — David BOWIE
CHINA IN YOUR HAND — T'PAU
CHINA TEA — Russ CONWAY
CHINATOWN [A] — The MOVE
CHINATOWN [B] — THIN LIZZY
THE CHINESE WAY — LEVEL 42
CHING CHING (LOVIN' YOU STILL) —
  Terri WALKER
CHIQUITITA — ABBA
CHIRPY CHIRPY CHEEP CHEEP [A] —
  Mac and Katie KISSOON
CHIRPY CHIRPY CHEEP CHEEP [A] —
  MIDDLE OF THE ROAD
CHIRPY CHIRPY CHEEP CHEEP [A] —
  LINCOLN CITY FC featuring Michael COURTNEY
THE CHISELERS — The FALL
CHOC ICE — LONG AND THE SHORT
CHOCOLATE [A] — Y?N-VEE
CHOCOLATE [B] — SNOW PATROL
CHOCOLATE [C] — KYLIE
CHOCOLATE BOX — BROS
CHOCOLATE CAKE — CROWDED HOUSE
CHOCOLATE (CHOCO CHOCO) —
  SOUL CONTROL
CHOCOLATE GIRL — DEACON BLUE
CHOCOLATE SALTY BALLS (PS I LOVE YOU) —
  CHEF
CHOCOLATE SENSATION —
  Lenny FONTANA & DJ SHORTY
CHOICE? — The BLOW MONKEYS
CHOK THERE — APACHE INDIAN
CHOLI KE PEECHE — Bally SAGOO
CHOOSE — COLOR ME BADD
CHOOSE LIFE —
  PF PROJECT featuring Ewan McGREGOR
CHOOSE ME (RESCUE ME) — LOOSE ENDS
CHOOZA LOOZA — Maria WILLSON
CHOP SUEY! — SYSTEM OF A DOWN
CHORUS — ERASURE
THE CHOSEN FEW — The DOOLEYS
CHRISTIAN — CHINA CRISIS
CHRISTIANSANDS — TRICKY
CHRISTINE [A] — MISS X
CHRISTINE [B] — SIOUXSIE and the BANSHEES
CHRISTINE KEELER — SENSELESS THINGS
CHRISTMAS ALPHABET — Dickie VALENTINE
CHRISTMAS AND YOU — Dave KING
CHRISTMAS COUNTDOWN — Frank KELLY
CHRISTMAS IN BLOBBYLAND — MR BLOBBY
CHRISTMAS IN DREADLAND — JUDGE DREAD
CHRISTMAS IN HOLLIS — RUN-DMC
CHRISTMAS IN SMURFLAND — The SMURFS
CHRISTMAS IS ALL AROUND — Billy MACK
CHRISTMAS ISLAND — Dickie VALENTINE
A CHRISTMAS KISS — Daniel O'DONNELL
CHRISTMAS MEDLEY — WEEKEND
CHRISTMAS ON 45 — HOLLY and the IVYS
CHRISTMAS RAPPIN' — Kurtis BLOW
CHRISTMAS RAPPING — DIZZY HEIGHTS
CHRISTMAS SLIDE —
  Basil BRUSH featuring India BEAU
CHRISTMAS SONG — Gilbert O'SULLIVAN
CHRISTMAS SONG (CHESTNUTS ROASTING ON
  AN OPEN FIRE) [A] — Alexander O'NEAL
THE CHRISTMAS SONG [A] — Nat 'King' COLE
CHRISTMAS SPECTRE — JINGLE BELLES

CHRISTMAS THROUGH YOUR EYES —
  Gloria ESTEFAN
CHRISTMAS TIME — Bryan ADAMS
CHRISTMAS TIME (DON'T LET THE BELLS END) —
  The DARKNESS
CHRISTMAS WILL BE JUST ANOTHER
  LONELY DAY — Brenda LEE
CHRISTMAS WRAPPING — WAITRESSES
CHRONOLOGIE PART 4 — Jean-Michel JARRE
CHUCK E'S IN LOVE — Rickie Lee JONES
CHUNG KUO (REVISITED) — ADDAMS and GEE
CHURA LIYA — Bally SAGOO
CHURCH OF FREEDOM — AMOS
CHURCH OF NOISE — THERAPY?
THE CHURCH OF THE HOLY SPOOK —
  Shane MacGOWAN and the POPES
CHURCH OF THE POISON MIND —
  CULTURE CLUB
CHURCH OF YOUR HEART — ROXETTE
CIAO CIAO BAMBINA [A] —
  Domenico MODUGNO
CIAO CIAO BAMBINA [A] —
  Marino MARINI and his QUARTET
CIGARETTES AND ALCOHOL — OASIS
CINDERELLA — LEMONESCENT
CINDERELLA ROCKEFELLA —
  Esther and Abi OFARIM
CINDY INCIDENTALLY — The FACES
CINDY, OH CINDY [A] — Eddie FISHER
CINDY, OH CINDY [A] — Tony BRENT
CINDY, OH CINDY [A] — TARRIERS
CINDY'S BIRTHDAY —
  Shane FENTON and the FENTONES
CINNAMON GIRL — PRINCE
CIRCLE — Edie BRICKELL
  and the NEW BOHEMIANS
THE CIRCLE — OCEAN COLOUR SCENE
CIRCLE IN THE SAND — Belinda CARLISLE
CIRCLE OF LIFE — Elton JOHN
CIRCLE OF ONE — Oleta ADAMS
CIRCLES [A] — The NEW SEEKERS
CIRCLES [B] — SAFFRON
CIRCLES [C] — Adam F
CIRCLESQUARE — The WONDER STUFF
CIRCUS [A] — Lenny KRAVITZ
CIRCUS [B] — Eric CLAPTON
THE CIRCUS [C] — ERASURE
CIRCUS GAMES — The SKIDS
CITIES IN DUST —
  SIOUXSIE and the BANSHEES
THE CITY IS MINE —
  JAY-Z featuring BLACKSTREET
CITY LIGHTS — David ESSEX
CITYSONG — LUSCIOUS JACKSON
THE CIVIL WAR (EP) — GUNS N' ROSES
CLAIR — Gilbert O'SULLIVAN
CLAIRE — Paul and Barry RYAN
THE CLAIRVOYANT — IRON MAIDEN
CLAP BACK — JA RULE
THE CLAP CLAP SOUND — KLAXONS
CLAP YOUR HANDS [A] —
  Rocky SHARPE and the REPLAYS
CLAP YOUR HANDS [B] — CAMISRA
THE CLAPPING SONG (EP) [A] — Shirley ELLIS
THE CLAPPING SONG [A] — Shirley ELLIS
THE CLAPPING SONG [A] — BELLE STARS
CLARE — FAIRGROUND ATTRACTION
CLASH CITY ROCKERS — The CLASH
CLASSIC — Adrian GURVITZ
CLASSIC GIRL — JANE'S ADDICTION
CLASSICAL GAS [A] — Mason WILLIAMS
CLASSICAL GAS [A] — VANESSA-MAE
CLASSICAL MUDDLY —
  PORTSMOUTH SINFONIA
CLAUDETTE — The EVERLY BROTHERS
CLEAN CLEAN — BUGGLES
CLEAN UP YOUR OWN BACK YARD —
  Elvis PRESLEY
CLEANIN' OUT MY CLOSET — EMINEM
CLEAR BLUE WATER —
  OCEANLAB featuring Justine SUISSA
CLEMENTINE [A] — Bobby DARIN
CLEMENTINE [B] — Mark OWEN
CLEOPATRA'S CAT — SPIN DOCTORS
CLEOPATRA'S THEME — CLEOPATRA
CLEVER KICKS — The HISS
THE CLICHES ARE TRUE —
  MANCHILD featuring Kelly JONES
CLIMB EV'RY MOUNTAIN — Shirley BASSEY
CLINT EASTWOOD — GORILLAZ
CLIPPED — CURVE
CLOAKING — SEAFOOD
CLOCKS — COLDPLAY
CLOG DANCE — VIOLINSKI
CLOSE ... BUT — ECHOBELLY
CLOSE BUT NO CIGAR — Thomas DOLBY
CLOSE COVER — MINIMALISTIX
CLOSE EVERY DOOR — Phillip SCHOFIELD
CLOSE MY EYES — The OPEN
CLOSE MY EYES FOREVER —
  Lita FORD duet with Ozzy OSBOURNE
CLOSE THE DOOR [A] — The STARGAZERS
CLOSE THE DOOR [B] — Teddy PENDERGRASS
CLOSE TO ME — The CURE
CLOSE TO PERFECTION — Miquel BROWN
CLOSE (TO THE EDIT) — ART OF NOISE
CLOSE TO YOU [A] — Maxi PRIEST

CLOSE TO YOU [B] —
  The BRAND NEW HEAVIES
CLOSE TO YOU [C] — WHIGFIELD
CLOSE TO YOU [D] — Marti PELLOW
CLOSE TO YOUR HEART — JX
CLOSE YOUR EYES — Tony BENNETT
CLOSED FOR BUSINESS — MANSUN
CLOSER [A] — MR FINGERS
CLOSER [B] — NINE INCH NAILS
CLOSER [C] — LIQUID
THE CLOSER I GET TO YOU — Roberta FLACK
CLOSER THAN CLOSE — Rosie GAINES
CLOSER THAN MOST —
  The BEAUTIFUL SOUTH
CLOSER TO ALL YOUR DREAMS —
  RHYTHM QUEST
CLOSER TO ME — FIVE
CLOSER TO THE HEART — RUSH
THE CLOSEST THING TO CRAZY — Katie MELUA
CLOSEST THING TO HEAVEN [A] — KANE GANG
CLOSEST THING TO HEAVEN [B] —
  Lionel RICHIE
CLOSING TIME [A] — DEACON BLUE
CLOSING TIME [B] — SEMISONIC
CLOUD 8 — FRAZIER CHORUS
CLOUD LUCKY SEVEN — Guy MITCHELL
CLOUD NINE — The TEMPTATIONS
CLOUD 99 — ST ANDREWS CHORALE
CLOUD NUMBER 9 — Bryan ADAMS
CLOUDBURST [A] — Don LANG
CLOUDBURST [B] — NIAGRA
CLOUDBUSTING — Kate BUSH
CLOUDS — SOURCE
CLOUDS ACROSS THE MOON — RAH BAND
THE CLOUDS WILL SOON ROLL BY —
  Tony BRENT
CLOWN SHOES — Johnny BURNETTE
CLUB AT THE END OF THE STREET —
  Elton JOHN
CLUB BIZARRE — U96
CLUB COUNTRY — ASSOCIATES
CLUB FANTASTIC MEGAMIX — WHAM!
CLUB FOOT — KASABIAN
CLUB FOR LIFE '98 — CHRIS and JAMES
CLUB LONELY — GROOVE CONNEKTION 2
CLUB TROPICANA — WHAM!
CLUBBED TO DEATH — Rob DOUGAN
CLUBBIN' — Marques HOUSTON
  featuring Joe BUDDEN and PIED PIPER
CLUBLAND — Elvis COSTELLO
CLUNK CLINK — LAUREL and HARDY
CLUTCH — SHEA SEGER
C'MON [A] — MILLIONAIRE HIPPIES
C'MON [A] — MARIO
C'MON AND GET MY LOVE —
  D MOB with Cathy DENNIS
C'MON BILLY — P J HARVEY
C'MON CINCINNATI — DELAKOTA
C'MON C'MON — The VON BONDIES
C'MON EVERY BEATBOX —
  BIG AUDIO DYNAMITE
C'MON EVERYBODY [A] — Eddie COCHRAN
C'MON EVERYBODY [A] — The SEX PISTOLS
C'MON KIDS — BOO RADLEYS
C'MON LET'S GO — GIRLSCHOOL
C'MON MARIANNE — GRAPEFRUIT
C'MON PEOPLE — Paul McCARTNEY
C'MON PEOPLE (WE'RE MAKING IT NOW) —
  Richard ASHCROFT
COAST IS CLEAR — CURVE
COCHISE — AUDIOSLAVE
COCK A DOODLE DO IT — EGGS ON LEGS
COCKNEY TRANSLATION — Smiley CULTURE
CO-CO — The SWEET
COCO JAMBOO — MR PRESIDENT
COCOA — CLIPZ
COCOMOTION — EL COCO
COCONUT — NILSSON
COCOON — BJÖRK
CODE OF LOVE — Mike SARNE
CODE RED [A] — CONQUERING LION
CODE RED [B] — BOXER REBELLION
CODED LANGUAGE —
  KRUST featuring Saul WILLIAMS
COFFEE — SUPERSISTER
COFFEE + TV — BLUR
THE COFFEE SONG —
  Frank SINATRA
COGNOSCENTI VS INTELLIGENTSIA —
  CUBAN BOYS
COLD [A] — Annie LENNOX
COLD [B] — TEARS FOR FEARS
COLD AS CHRISTMAS — Elton JOHN
COLD AS ICE [A] — FOREIGNER
COLD AS ICE [A] — M.O.P.
COLD COLD HEART [A] — Midge URE
COLD COLD HEART [B] — WET WET WET
COLD DAY IN HELL — Gary MOORE
COLD HARD BITCH — JET
COLD HEARTED — Paula ABDUL
COLD LIGHT OF DAY — HALO
COLD LOVE — Donna SUMMER
COLD ROCK A PARTY — MC LYTE
COLD SHOULDER — CULTURE CLUB
COLD SWEAT [A] — THIN LIZZY
COLD SWEAT [B] — SUGARCUBES
COLD TURKEY — John LENNON

COLD WORLD —
  GENIUS / GZA featuring D'ANGELO
COLDCUT'S CHRISTMAS BREAK — COLDCUT
COLETTE — Billy FURY
COLOR OF MY SKIN — SWING 52
COLOSSUS — FRESH BC
THE COLOUR FIELD — COLOUR FIELD
COLOUR MY LIFE — M PEOPLE
THE COLOUR OF LOVE [A] — Billy OCEAN
THE COLOUR OF LOVE [B] — SNAP!
THE COLOUR OF LOVE [C] — REESE PROJECT
COLOUR OF MY LOVE — JEFFERSON
COLOUR THE WORLD — SASH!
COLOURBLIND — DARIUS
COLOURED KISSES — MARTIKA
COLOURS — DONOVAN
THE COLOURS — MEN THEY COULDN'T HANG
COLOURS FLY AWAY — TEARDROP EXPLODES
COLOURS IN WAVES — SOUTH
COLOURS OF THE WIND — Vanessa WILLIAMS
COMA AROMA — INAURA
COMA GIRL —
  Joe STRUMMER & the MESCALEROS
THE COMANCHEROS — Lonnie DONEGAN
THE COMBINE HARVESTER (BRAND NEW KEY) —
  WURZELS
COME — Martha WASH
COME AGAIN —
  TRUMAN & WOLFF featuring STEEL HORSES
COME ALONG PLEASE — Bob WALLIS
  and his STORYVILLE JAZZ BAND
COME AND GET IT — BADFINGER
COME AND GET ME — CLEOPATRA
COME AND GET SOME — COOKIE CREW
COME AND GET WITH ME — Keith SWEAT
COME AND GET YOUR LOVE —
  The REAL McCOY
COME AND STAY WITH ME —
  Marianne FAITHFULL
COME AS YOU ARE [A] — NIRVANA
COME AS YOU ARE [A] — Beverley KNIGHT
COME AWAY MELINDA — Barry ST JOHN
COME BABY COME — K7
COME BACK [A] — WAH!
COME BACK [B] — SPEAR OF DESTINY
COME BACK [C] — Luther VANDROSS
COME BACK [D] — LONDONBEAT
COME BACK [E] — Jessica GARLICK
COME BACK AND FINISH WHAT YOU STARTED —
  Gladys KNIGHT and the PIPS
COME BACK AND SHAKE ME —
  Clodagh RODGERS
COME BACK AND STAY — Paul YOUNG
COME BACK AROUND — FEEDER
COME BACK BABY — Dan READ NETWORK
COME BACK BRIGHTER — REEF
COME BACK DARLING — UB40
COME BACK (FOR REAL LOVE) —
  Alison LIMERICK
COME BACK JONEE — DEVO
COME BACK MY LOVE — DARTS
COME BACK TO ME [A] — Janet JACKSON
COME BACK TO ME [B] — ANGELHEART
COME BACK TO WHAT YOU KNOW — EMBRACE
COME BACK TOMORROW — INSPIRAL CARPETS
COME CLEAN — Hilary DUFF
COME DANCE WITH ME (LP) — Frank SINATRA
COME DANCING [A] — NO DICE
COME DANCING [B] — The KINKS
COME DIG IT — MACHEL
COME GET MY LOVIN' — DIONNE
COME GET SOME — ROOSTER
COME GIVE ME YOUR LOVE —
  Richie STEPHENS
COME HELL OR WATERS HIGH — DC LEE
COME HOME [A] — Dave CLARK FIVE
COME HOME [B] — JAMES
COME HOME [C] — LIL' DEVIOUS
COME HOME BILLY BIRD —
  The DIVINE COMEDY
COME HOME WITH ME BABY — DEAD OR ALIVE
COME IN OUT OF THE RAIN — Wendy MOTEN
COME INSIDE — THOMPSON TWINS
COME INTO MY LIFE [A] — Joyce SIMS
COME INTO MY LIFE [B] — GALA
COME INTO MY WORLD — Kylie MINOGUE
COME LIVE WITH ME — HEAVEN 17
COME NEXT SPRING — Tony BENNETT
COME ON [A] — The ROLLING STONES
COME ON [B] — DJ SEDUCTION
COME ON [C] — JESUS AND MARY CHAIN
COME ON [E] — NEW POWER GENERATION
COME ON [E] — LEVELLERS
COME ON! [A] — SOLO
COME ON! [B] — D4
COME ON (AND DO IT) — FPI PROJECT
COME ON AND GET SOME — COOKIE CREW
COME ON, COME ON — BRONSKI BEAT
COME ON DANCE DANCE —
  SATURDAY NIGHT BAND
COME ON EILEEN [A] — DEXY'S MIDNIGHT RUNNERS
  with the Emerald Express
COME ON ENGLAND! [A] —
  ENGLAND'S BARMY ARMY
COME ON ENGLAND [B] — 4-4-2
COME ON EVERYBODY (GET DOWN) — US3
COME ON HOME [A] — The SPRINGFIELDS

COME ON HOME [B] — Wayne FONTANA
COME ON HOME [C] —
  EVERYTHING BUT THE GIRL
COME ON HOME [D] — Cyndi LAUPER
COME ON LET'S GO [A] — LOS LOBOS
COME ON, LET'S GO [A] — Tommy STEELE
COME ON OVER [A] — Kym MARSH
COME ON OVER [B] — John SILVER
COME ON OVER BABY (ALL I WANT IS YOU) —
  Christina AGUILERA
COME ON OVER TO MY PLACE —
  The DRIFTERS
COME ON Y'ALL — RHYTHM MASTERS
COME ON YOU REDS —
  MANCHESTER UNITED FOOTBALL CLUB
COME OUTSIDE [A] —
  Mike SARNE with Wendy RICHARD
COME OUTSIDE [A] — JUDGE DREAD
COME PLAY WITH ME — WEDDING PRESENT
COME PRIMA —
  Marino MARINI and his QUARTET
(COME 'ROUND HERE) I'M THE ONE YOU NEED —
  MIRACLES
COME SEE ABOUT ME [A] — The SUPREMES
COME SEE ABOUT ME [A] — Shakin' STEVENS
COME SEE ME — PRETTY THINGS
COME SOFTLY TO ME — FLEETWOODS
COME SOFTLY TO ME [A] — Frankie
  VAUGHAN and the KAYE SISTERS
COME SOFTLY TO ME [A] —
  The NEW SEEKERS
COME TO DADDY — APHEX TWIN
COME TO ME [A] — Julie GRANT
COME TO ME [B] — Ruby WINTERS
COME TO ME [C] — ATEED
COME TO ME (I AM WOMAN) — Su POLLARD
COME TO MILTON KEYNES — STYLE COUNCIL
COME TO MY AID — SIMPLY RED
COME TO MY PARTY —
  Keith HARRIS and ORVILLE
COME TO THE DANCE —
  The BARRON KNIGHTS
COME TOGETHER [A] — The BEATLES
COME TOGETHER [A] — Michael JACKSON
COME TOGETHER (WAR CHILD) [A] —
  SMOKIN' MOJO FILTERS
COME TOGETHER [B] — PRIMAL SCREAM
COME TOGETHER [C] — M FACTOR
COME TOGETHER AS ONE — Will DOWNING
COME TOMORROW — MANFRED MANN
COME UNDONE [A] — DURAN DURAN
COME UNDONE [B] — Robbie WILLIAMS
COME WHAT MAY [A] — Vicky LEANDROS
COME WHAT MAY [A] —
  Nicole KIDMAN & Ewan McGREGOR
COME WITH ME [A] — Jesse GREEN
COME WITH ME [B] — Ronny JORDAN
COME WITH ME [C] — QATTARA
COME WITH ME [D] —
  PUFF DADDY featuring Jimmy PAGE
COME WITH ME [E] — SPECIAL D
COME WITH US — The CHEMICAL BROTHERS
COMEDY — SHACK
COMES A-LONG A-LOVE — Kay STARR
COMEUPPANCE — THOUSAND YARD STARE
COMFORTABLY NUMB — SCISSOR SISTERS
COMFORTING SOUNDS — MEW
COMIN' BACK — CRYSTAL METHOD
COMIN' HOME [A] — DELANEY and BONNIE
  and FRIENDS featuring Eric CLAPTON
COMIN' HOME [B] — DANGER DANGER
COMIN' IN AND OUT OF YOUR LIFE —
  Barbra STREISAND
COMIN' ON STRONG [A] — BROKEN ENGLISH
COMIN' ON STRONG [B] — DESIYA
  featuring Melissa YIANNAKOU
COMING ON STRONG —
  SIGNUM featuring Scott MAC
COMIN' RIGHT UP — Bruce WILLIS
COMING AROUND — TRAVIS
COMING AROUND AGAIN — Carly SIMON
COMING BACK — DJ DADO
COMING BACK FOR MORE [A] — LA MIX
COMING BACK FOR MORE [B] —
  JELLYBEAN featuring Richard DARBYSHIRE
COMING DOWN — The CULT
COMING HOME [A] — David ESSEX
COMING HOME [B] — MARSHALL HAIN
COMING HOME [C] —
  K-WARREN featuring LEE-O
COMING HOME BABY — Mel TORME
COMING HOME NOW — BOYZONE
COMING ON STRONG — SIGNUM
COMING OUT OF THE DARK —
  Gloria ESTEFAN
COMING SECOND — ELBOW
COMING UP — Paul McCARTNEY
COMING UP ROSES — CURVE
COMMENT TE DIRE ADIEU —
  Jimmy SOMERVILLE
COMMITMENT — LeAnn RIMES
COMMON PEOPLE — PULP
COMMUNICATION [A] — David McCALLUM
COMMUNICATION [B] — SPANDAU BALLET
COMMUNICATION [C] — POWER STATION
COMMUNICATION [D] — ARMIN
COMMUNICATION BREAKDOWN — JUNIOR

COMMUNICATION (SOMEBODY ANSWER
  THE PHONE) — Mario PIU
THE COMPASS — Dave CLARKE
COMPLETE — JAIMESON
COMPLETE CONTROL — The CLASH
THE COMPLETE DOMINATOR —
  HUMAN RESOURCE
THE COMPLETE STELLA —
  JAM & SPOON featuring PLAVKA
COMPLEX — Gary NUMAN
COMPLICATED — Avril LAVIGNE
COMPLIMENTS ON YOUR KISS — RED
  DRAGON with Brian and Tony GOLD
COMPUTER GAME (THEME FROM 'THE INVADERS') —
  YELLOW MAGIC ORCHESTRA
COMPUTER LOVE [A] — KRAFTWERK
COMPUTER LOVE (PART 1) [B] — ZAPP
COMPUTER LOVE [C] — SUPERCAR
CON LOS AÑOS QUE ME QUEDAN —
  Gloria ESTEFAN
THE CONCEPT — TEENAGE FANCLUB
CONCRETE AND CLAY [A] — Randy EDELMAN
CONCRETE AND CLAY [A] — UNIT FOUR PLUS TWO
CONCRETE SCHOOLYARD — JURASSIC 5
CONDEMNATION — DEPECHE MODE
CONFESSIN' (THAT I LOVE YOU) —
  Frank IFIELD
CONFESSIONS PART II — USHER
CONFETTI — LEMONHEADS
CONFIDE IN ME — Kylie MINOGUE
CONFUSION [A] — Lee DORSEY
CONFUSION [B] —
  ELECTRIC LIGHT ORCHESTRA
CONFUSION [C] — NEW ORDER
CONFUSION [C] —
  Arthur BAKER vs NEW ORDER
CONFUSION ... [D] — The ZUTONS
CONFUSION (HITS US EVERY TIME) — TRUTH
CONGO [A] — BOSS
CONGO [B] — GENESIS
CONGO SQUARE — GREAT WHITE
CONGRATULATIONS — Cliff RICHARD
CONNECTED [A] — STEREO MC's
CONNECTED [B] —
  Paul VAN DYK featuring VEGA 4
CONNECTION — ELASTICA
CONQUEST OF PARADISE — VANGELIS
CONQUISTADOR [A] — PROCOL HARUM
CONQUISTADOR [B] — ESPIRITU
CONSCIENCE — James DARREN
CONSCIOUS MAN — JOLLY BROTHERS
CONSIDER YOURSELF — Max BYGRAVES
CONSIDERATION — REEF
A CONSPIRACY — BLACK CROWES
CONSTANT CRAVING — kd lang
CONSTANTLY — Cliff RICHARD
CONSTANTLY WAITING — Pauline TAYLOR
CONTACT [A] — Edwin STARR
CONTACT ... [B] — EAT STATIC
CONTAGIOUS — WHISPERS
THE CONTINENTAL — Maureen McGOVERN
CONTRARY MARY — THEE UNSTRUNG
CONTRIBUTION — Mica PARIS
CONTROL [A] — Janet JACKSON
CONTROL [B] — TIME OF THE MUMPH
CONTROL [C] — PUDDLE OF MUDD
CONTROLLING ME — OCEANIC
CONTROVERSY — PRINCE
CONVERSATION INTERCOM — SOULWAX
CONVERSATIONS — Cilla BLACK
CONVOY — CW McCALL
CONVOY GB —
  Laurie LINGO and the DIPSTICKS
CONWAY — REEL 2 REAL
COOCHY COO — EN-CORE featuring
  Stephen EMMANUEL & ESKA
COOKIN' UP YAH BRAIN — 4 HERO
COOL BABY — Charlie GRACIE
COOL FOR CATS — SQUEEZE
COOL JERK — GO-GO's
COOL MEDITATION — THIRD WORLD
COOL OUT TONIGHT — David ESSEX
COOL RUNNING — TIK and TOK
COOL WATER — Frankie LAINE
COP THAT SH*T — TIMBALAND &
  MAGOO featuring Missy ELLIOTT
COPACABANA (AT THE COPA) —
  Barry MANILOW
COPPER GIRL — 3 COLOURS RED
COPPERHEAD ROAD — Steve EARLE
CORNER OF THE EARTH — JAMIROQUAI
CORNFLAKE GIRL — Tori AMOS
CORONATION RAG — Winifred ATWELL
CORPSES — Ian BROWN
CORRINE, CORRINA — Ray PETERSON
COSMIC GIRL — JAMIROQUAI
COSMONAUT NO.7 — SCARFO
THE COST OF LIVING (EP) — The CLASH
COSTAFINE TOWN — SPLINTER
COTTON EYE JOE — REDNEX
COTTONFIELDS — The BEACH BOYS
COULD HAVE TOLD YOU SO — HALO JAMES
COULD HEAVEN EVER BE LIKE THIS —
  Idris MUHAMMAD
COULD I HAVE THIS KISS FOREVER —
  Whitney HOUSTON and Enrique IGLESIAS
COULD IT BE — JAHEIM

COULD IT BE FOREVER [A] — David CASSIDY
COULD IT BE FOREVER [A] — GEMINI
COULD IT BE I'M FALLING IN LOVE [A] —
  DETROIT SPINNERS
COULD IT BE I'M FALLING IN LOVE (EP) [A] —
  DETROIT SPINNERS
COULD IT BE I'M FALLING IN LOVE [A] —
  David GRANT and Jaki GRAHAM
COULD IT BE I'M FALLING IN LOVE [A] —
  WORLDS APART
COULD IT BE MAGIC [A] — Donna SUMMER
COULD IT BE MAGIC [A] — Barry MANILOW
COULD IT BE MAGIC [A] — TAKE THAT
COULD WELL BE IN — The STREETS
COULD YOU BE LOVED —
  Bob MARLEY & the WAILERS
COULDN'T GET IT RIGHT —
  CLIMAX BLUES BAND
COULDN'T HAVE SAID IT BETTER —
  MEAT LOAF
COULDN'T SAY GOODBYE — Tom JONES
COULD'VE BEEN — TIFFANY
COULD'VE BEEN ME — Billy Ray CYRUS
COULD'VE BEEN YOU — CHER
COUNT ON ME [A] — Julie GRANT
COUNT ON ME [B] — Whitney HOUSTON
COUNT YOUR BLESSINGS — Bing CROSBY
COUNTDOWN — RUSH
COUNTERFEIT — LOWGOLD
COUNTING BACKWARDS — THROWING MUSES
COUNTING EVERY MINUTE — SONIA
COUNTING SHEEP — AIRHEAD
COUNTING TEARDROPS —
  Emile FORD and the CHECKMATES
COUNTING THE DAYS — ABI
COUNTRY BOY [A] — Fats DOMINO
COUNTRY BOY [B] — HEINZ
COUNTRY BOY [C] — Jimmy NAIL
COUNTRY HOUSE — BLUR
THE COUNTRY OF THE BLIND —
  FAITH BROTHERS
COUNTRY ROADS — HERMES HOUSE BAND
COURSE BRUV — GENIUS CRU
COUSIN NORMAN — MARMALADE
COVER FROM THE SKY — DEACON BLUE
COVER GIRL — NEW KIDS ON THE BLOCK
COVER ME — Bruce SPRINGSTEEN
COVER MY EYES (PAIN AND HEAVEN) —
  MARILLION
(COVER PLUS) WE'RE ALL GROWN UP —
  Hazel O'CONNOR
COVER UP — UB40
COVERED IN PUNK — PORTOBELLA
COVERS (EP) — EVERYTHING BUT THE GIRL
COWARD OF THE COUNTY — Kenny ROGERS
COWBOY — KID ROCK
COWBOY DREAMS — Jimmy NAIL
COWBOY JIMMY JOE — Alma COGAN
COWBOYS AND ANGELS — George MICHAEL
COWBOYS AND INDIANS — CROSS
COWBOYS & KISSES — ANASTACIA
COWGIRL — UNDERWORLD
COWPUNCHER'S CANTATA — Max BYGRAVES
COWPUNK MEDLUM —
  SPLODGENESSABOUNDS
COZ I LUV YOU — SLADE
CRACKERS INTERNATIONAL (EP) — ERASURE
CRACKIN' UP [A] — Tommy HUNT
CRACKING UP [B] — Nick LOWE
CRACKING UP — JESUS AND MARY CHAIN
CRACKLIN' ROSIE — Neil DIAMOND
CRADLE OF LOVE [A] — Johnny PRESTON
CRADLE OF LOVE [B] — Billy IDOL
CRANK — CATHERINE WHEEL
CRASH [A] — PRIMITIVES
CRASH [B] — FEEDER
CRASH AND BURN — SAVAGE GARDEN
CRASH! BOOM! BANG! — ROXETTE
CRASHED THE WEDDING — BUSTED
CRASHIN' A PARTY —
  LUMIDEE featuring N.O.R.E.
CRASHIN' IN — The CHARLATANS
CRAWL — HEADSWIM
CRAWL HOME — DESERT SESSIONS
CRAWLIN' BACK — Roy ORBISON
CRAWLING — LINKIN PARK
CRAWLING FROM THE WRECKAGE —
  Dave EDMUNDS
CRAWLING IN THE DARK — HOOBASTANK
CRAWLING UP A HILL — Katie MELUA
CRAYZY MAN — BLAST featuring VDC
CRAZIER — Gary NUMAN vs RICO
CRAZY [A] — MUD
CRAZY [B] — MANHATTANS
CRAZY [C] — ICEHOUSE
CRAZY [D] — The BOYS
CRAZY [E] — Patsy CLINE
CRAZY [E] — Julio IGLESIAS
CRAZY [E] — LeAnn RIMES
CRAZY [F] — SEAL
CRAZY [G] — Bob GELDOF
CRAZY [H] — AEROSMITH
CRAZY [I] — ETERNAL
CRAZY [J] — Mark MORRISON
CRAZY [K] — NUT
CRAZY [L] — AWESOME
CRAZY [M] — The MOFFATTS

CRAZY [N] — LUCID
CRAZY [O] — TOMCAT
CRAZY [P] — K-CI & JOJO
CRAZY BEAT — BLUR
CRAZY CHANCE — KAVANA
CRAZY CRAZY NIGHTS — KISS
CRAZY CUTS — GRANDMIXER DST
CRAZY DREAM — Jim DALE
CRAZY (FOR ME) — Freddie JACKSON
CRAZY FOR YOU [A] — MADONNA
CRAZY FOR YOU [B] — SYBIL
CRAZY FOR YOU [C] — INCOGNITO
CRAZY FOR YOU [D] — LET LOOSE
CRAZY HORSES — The OSMONDS
CRAZY IN LOVE — BEYONCÉ
CRAZY LITTLE PARTY GIRL — Aaron CARTER
CRAZY LITTLE THING CALLED LOVE [A] — QUEEN
CRAZY LITTLE THING CALLED LOVE [A] —
  Dwight YOAKAM
CRAZY LOVE [A] — Paul ANKA
CRAZY LOVE [B] — Maxi PRIEST
CRAZY LOVE [C] — Ce Ce PENISTON
CRAZY LOVE [D] — MJ COLE
CRAZY LOWDOWN WAYS —
  OCEAN COLOUR SCENE
THE CRAZY OTTO RAG — The STARGAZERS
THE CRAZY PARTY MIXES —
  JIVE BUNNY and the MASTERMIXERS
CRAZY RAP — AFROMAN
CRAZY SEXY MARVELLOUS — PAFFENDORF
CRAZY TRAIN — Ozzy OSBOURNE
CRAZY WATER — Elton JOHN
CRAZY WORDS CRAZY TUNE —
  Dorothy PROVINE
CRAZY YOU — GUN
CREAM [A] — PRINCE and the
  NEW POWER GENERATION
CREAM [B] — BLANK & JONES
CREAM (ALWAYS RISES TO THE TOP) —
  Gregg DIAMOND BIONIC BOOGIE
CREATION — STEREO MC's
CREATURES OF THE NIGHT — KISS
CREDO — FISH
THE CREEP [A] — Ken MACKINTOSH
CREEP [B] — RADIOHEAD
CREEP [C] — TLC
CREEQUE ALLEY — MAMAS and the PAPAS
CREOLE JAZZ — Mr Acker BILK and his
  PARAMOUNT JAZZ BAND
CRESCENT MOON — Lynden David HALL
CRICKETS SING FOR ANAMARIA — EMMA
CRIME OF PASSION — Mike OLDFIELD
CRIMINALLY INSANE — SLAYER
CRIMSON AND CLOVER —
  Joan JETT and the BLACKHEARTS
CRISPY BACON — Laurent GARNIER
CRITICAL (IF YOU ONLY KNEW) — WALL OF SOUND
  featuring Gerald LETHAN
CRITICIZE — Alexander O'NEAL
CROCKETT'S THEME — Jan HAMMER
CROCODILE ROCK — Elton JOHN
CROCODILE SHOES — Jimmy NAIL
CROCODILES — ECHO and the BUNNYMEN
CROSS MY BROKEN HEART — SINITTA
CROSS MY HEART — EIGHTH WONDER
CROSS THAT BRIDGE — WARD BROTHERS
CROSS THE TRACK (WE BETTER GO BACK) —
  MACEO & THE MACKS
CROSSROADS [A] — Tracy CHAPMAN
CROSSROADS [B] — BLAZIN' SQUAD
CROSSTOWN TRAFFIC [A] — Jimi HENDRIX
CROSSTOWN TRAFFIC [A] —
  The Jimi HENDRIX EXPERIENCE
THE CROWD — Roy ORBISON
THE CROWN —
  Gary BYRD and the GB EXPERIENCE
CROWS — MODEY LEMON
CRUCIAL — NEW EDITION
CRUCIFIED — ARMY OF LOVERS
CRUCIFY — Tori AMOS
CRUEL — PUBLIC IMAGE LTD
THE CRUEL SEA — DAKOTAS
CRUEL SUMMER [A] — BANANARAMA
CRUEL SUMMER [A] — ACE OF BASE
CRUEL TO BE KIND — Nick LOWE
CRUISE INTO CHRISTMAS MEDLEY —
  Jane McDONALD
CRUISIN' — D'ANGELO
CRUISING — SINITTA
THE CRUNCH — RAH BAND
CRUSH [A] — ZHANE
CRUSH [B] — Jennifer PAIGE
CRUSH [C] —
  Paul VAN DYK featuring SECOND SUN
CRUSH ME — HOUSE OF LOVE
CRUSH (1980 ME) [C] — Darren HAYES
CRUSH ON YOU [A] — JETS
CRUSH ON YOU [A] — Aaron CARTER
CRUSH ON YOU [B] — LIL' KIM
CRUSH TONIGHT —
  FAT JOE featuring GINUWINE
CRUSH WITH EYELINER — R.E.M.
CRUSHED BY THE WHEELS OF INDUSTRY —
  HEAVEN 17
CRUSHED LIKE FRUIT — INME
CRY [A] — Gerry MONROE
CRY [B] — GODLEY and CREME

CRY [C] – WATERFRONT
CRY [D] – The SUNDAYS
CRY [E] – SYSTEM F
CRY [F] – Michael JACKSON
CRY [G] – SIMPLE MINDS
CRY [H] – Faith HILL
CRY [I] – Kym MARSH
CRY [J] – Alex PARKS
CRY AND BE FREE – MARILYN
CRY BABY [A] – SPILLER
CRY BABY [B] – JEMINI
CRY BOY CRY – BLUE ZOO
CRY DIGNITY – DUB WAR
CRY FOR HELP [A] – Rick ASTLEY
CRY FOR HELP [B] – SHED SEVEN
CRY FOR ME – ROACHFORD
CRY FOR THE NATIONS – Michael SCHENKER GROUP
CRY FOR YOU – JODECI
CRY FREEDOM [A] – George FENTON and Jonas GWANGWA
CRY FREEDOM [B] – MOMBASSA
CRY INDIA – UMBOZA
CRY JUST A LITTLE BIT – Shakin' STEVENS
CRY LIKE A BABY – The BOX TOPS
CRY LITTLE SISTER (I NEED U NOW) – LOST BROTHERS featuring G Tom MAC
CRY ME A RIVER [A] – Julie LONDON
CRY ME A RIVER [A] – Mari WILSON
CRY ME A RIVER [A] – Denise WELCH
CRY ME A RIVER [B] – Justin TIMBERLAKE
CRY MY HEART – David WHITFIELD
CRY MYSELF TO SLEEP – Del SHANNON
CRY TO BE FOUND – DEL AMITRI
CRY TO HEAVEN – Elton JOHN
CRY TO ME – PRETTY THINGS
CRY WOLF – A-HA
CRYIN' [A] – Roy ORBISON
CRYING [A] – Don McLEAN
CRYING [A] – Roy ORBISON (duet with kd lang)
CRYIN' [B] – VIXEN
CRYIN' [C] – AEROSMITH
CRYIN' IN THE RAIN – The EVERLY BROTHERS
CRYIN' MY HEART OUT FOR YOU – Diana ROSS
CRYIN' TIME – Ray CHARLES
CRYING AT THE DISCOTHEQUE – ALCAZAR
THE CRYING GAME [A] – Dave BERRY
THE CRYING GAME [A] – BOY GEORGE
CRYING IN THE CHAPEL [A] – Lee LAWRENCE
CRYING IN THE CHAPEL [A] – Elvis PRESLEY with the JORDANAIRES
CRYING IN THE RAIN [A] – A-HA
CRYING IN THE RAIN [B] – CULTURE BEAT
CRYING LAUGHING LOVING LYING – Labi SIFFRE
CRYING OVER YOU – Ken BOOTHE
THE CRYING SCENE – AZTEC CAMERA
CRYPTIK SOULS CREW – LEN
CRYSTAL – NEW ORDER
CRYSTAL CLEAR – GRID
THE CRYSTAL LAKE – GRANDADDY
C'30, C'60, C'90 GO – BOW WOW WOW
CUBA [A] – GIBSON BROTHERS
CUBA [A] – EL MARIACHI
CUBAN PETE – Jim CARREY
CUBIK – 808 STATE
CUDDLY TOY – ROACHFORD
THE CUFF OF MY SHIRT – Guy MITCHELL
CULT OF PERSONALITY – LIVING COLOUR
CULT OF SNAP [A] – HI POWER
CULT OF SNAP! [A] – SNAP!
CUM ON FEEL THE NOIZE [A] – SLADE
CUM ON FEEL THE NOIZE [A] – QUIET RIOT
CUMBERLAND GAP [A] – Lonnie DONEGAN and his Skiffle Group
THE CUMBERLAND GAP [A] – VIPERS SKIFFLE GROUP
THE CUP OF LIFE – Ricky MARTIN
CUPBOARD LOVE – John LEYTON
CUPID [A] – Sam COOKE
CUPID [A] – Johnny NASH
CUPID [B] – JC 001
CUPID – I'VE LOVED YOU FOR A LONG TIME (MEDLEY) – DETROIT SPINNERS
CURIOSITY – JETS
CURIOUS – LEVERT SWEAT GILL
CURLY – The MOVE
THE CURSE OF VOODOO RAY – Lisa MAY
CURTAIN FALLS – BLUE
CUT CHEMIST SUITE – OZOMATLI
CUT HERE – The CURE
CUT ME DOWN – Lloyd COLE
CUT SOME RUG – The BLUETONES
CUT THE CAKE – AVERAGE WHITE BAND
CUT YOUR HAIR – PAVEMENT
A CUTE SWEET LOVE ADDICTION – Johnny GILL
CUTS ACROSS THE LAND – DUKE SPIRIT
CUTS BOTH WAYS – Gloria ESTEFAN
THE CUTTER – ECHO and the BUNNYMEN
CUTTY SARK – John BARRY ORCHESTRA
CYANIDE – LURKERS
CYBELE'S REVERIE – STEREOLAB
CYCLONE – DUB PISTOLS
THE CYPHER: PART 3 – Frankie CUTLASS
DA ANTIDOTE – STANTON WARRIORS
DA DA DA – TRIO
DA DOO RON RON – CRYSTALS
DA-FORCE – BEDLAM
DA FUNK – DAFT PUNK
DA GOODNESS – REDMAN
DA HYPE – JUNIOR JACK featuring Robert SMITH
DA YA THINK I'M SEXY? [A] – Rod STEWART
DA YA THINK I'M SEXY [A] – REVOLTING COCKS
DA YA THINK I'M SEXY [A] – N-TRANCE
DA YA THINK I'M SEXY? [A] – GIRLS OF FHM
D-A-A-ANCE – LAMBRETTAS
DADDY COOL [A] – BONEY M
DADDY COOL – THE GIRL CAN'T HELP IT [B] – DARTS
DADDY DON'T YOU WALK SO FAST – Daniel BOONE
DADDY'S HOME – Cliff RICHARD
DADDY'S LITTLE GIRL – Nikki D
DAGENHAM DAVE – MORRISSEY
DAILY – TQ
DALICKS – DJ FRESH
DALLIANCE – WEDDING PRESENT
DAMAGED – PLUMMET
THE DAMBUSTERS MARCH – The Central Band of the ROYAL AIR FORCE, Conductor W/Cdr AE SIMS OBE
DAMN GOOD – David Lee ROTH
DAMN I WISH I WAS YOUR LOVER – Sophie B HAWKINS
DAMNED DON'T CRY – VISAGE
DAMNED ON 45 – CAPTAIN SENSIBLE
DANCANDO LAMBADA – KAOMA
DANCE – THAT PETROL EMOTION
THE DANCE – Garth BROOKS
DANCE A LITTLE BIT CLOSER – CHARO and the SALSOUL ORCHESTRA
DANCE AND SHOUT – SHAGGY
DANCE AWAY – ROXY MUSIC
DANCE COMMANDER – ELECTRIC SIX
DANCE, DANCE – DESKEE
DANCE DANCE DANCE – The BEACH BOYS
DANCE, DANCE, DANCE (YOWSAH, YOWSAH, YOWSAH) – CHIC
DANCE (DISCO HEAT) – SYLVESTER
DANCE FOR ME [A] – SISQO
DANCE FOR ME [B] – Mary J. BLIGE featuring COMMON
DANCE, GET DOWN (FEEL THE GROOVE) – Al HUDSON
DANCE HALL DAYS – WANG CHUNG
DANCE HALL MOOD – ASWAD
DANCE INTO THE LIGHT – Phil COLLINS
DANCE LADY DANCE – CROWN HEIGHTS AFFAIR
DANCE LITTLE LADY DANCE – Tina CHARLES
DANCE LITTLE SISTER (PART ONE) – Terence Trent D'ARBY
DANCE ME UP – Gary GLITTER
DANCE NO MORE – E-LUSTRIOUS
DANCE OF THE CUCKOOS (THE 'LAUREL AND HARDY' THEME) – Band of the BLACK WATCH
DANCE OF THE MAD – POP WILL EAT ITSELF
DANCE ON! [A] – The SHADOWS
DANCE ON [A] – Kathy KIRBY
DANCE ON [B] – MOJO
DANCE OUT OF MY HEAD – Pia ZADORA
DANCE STANCE – DEXY'S MIDNIGHT RUNNERS
DANCE SUCKER – SET THE TONE
DANCE THE BODY MUSIC – OSIBISA
DANCE THE KUNG FU – Carl DOUGLAS
DANCE THE NIGHT AWAY – MAVERICKS
DANCE TO THE MUSIC [A] – SLY and the FAMILY STONE
DANCE TO THE MUSIC [A] – HUSTLERS CONVENTION featuring Dave LAUDAT and Ondrea DUVERNEY
DANCE TONIGHT – LUCY PEARL
DANCE WIT' ME – Rick JAMES
DANCE WITH ME [A] – The DRIFTERS
DANCE WITH ME [B] – Peter BROWN
DANCE WITH ME [C] – CONTROL
DANCE WITH ME [D] – TIN TIN OUT featuring Tony HADLEY
DANCE WITH ME [E] – Debelah MORGAN
DANCE WITH MY FATHER – Luther VANDROSS
DANCE WITH THE DEVIL – Cozy POWELL
(DANCE WITH THE) GUITAR MAN – Duane EDDY and the REBELS
DANCE (WITH U) – LEMAR
DANCE WITH YOU – Carrie LUCAS
DANCE WITH YOU (NACHNA TERE NAAL) – The RISHI RICH PROJECT featuring Jay SEAN & JUGGY D
DANCE YOURSELF DIZZY – LIQUID GOLD
DANCEHALL MOOD – ASWAD
DANCEHALL QUEEN – BEENIE MAN
DANCER [A] – Gino SOCCIO
DANCER [B] – Michael SCHENKER GROUP
DANCERAMA – SIGUE SIGUE SPUTNIK
DANCIN' EASY – Danny WILLIAMS
DANCIN' IN THE KEY OF LIFE – Steve ARRINGTON
DANCIN' IN THE MOONLIGHT (IT'S CAUGHT ME IN ITS SPOTLIGHT) – THIN LIZZY
DANCIN' ON A WIRE – SURFACE NOISE
DANCIN' PARTY [A] – Chubby CHECKER
DANCIN' PARTY [A] – SHOWADDYWADDY
DANCIN' THE NIGHT AWAY – VOGGUE
DANCIN' TONIGHT – STEREOPOL featuring NEVADA
DANCING BABY (OOGA-CHAKA) – TRUBBLE
DANCING GIRLS – Nik KERSHAW
DANCING IN OUTER SPACE – ATMOSFEAR
DANCING IN THE CITY – MARSHALL HAIN
DANCING IN THE DARK [A] – Kim WILDE
DANCING IN THE DARK [B] – Bruce SPRINGSTEEN
DANCING IN THE DARK [B] – BIG DADDY
DANCING IN THE DARK [C] – 4TUNE 500
DANCING IN THE MOONLIGHT – TOPLOADER
DANCING IN THE SHEETS – SHALAMAR
DANCING IN THE STREET [A] – Martha REEVES and the VANDELLAS
DANCING IN THE STREET [A] – David BOWIE and Mick JAGGER
DANCING IN THE STREET [B] – MATT BIANCO
DANCIN' (ON A SATURDAY NIGHT) – Barry BLUE
DANCING ON THE CEILING – Lionel RICHIE
DANCING ON THE FLOOR (HOOKED ON LOVE) – THIRD WORLD
DANCING ON THE JAGGED EDGE – SISTER SLEDGE
DANCING QUEEN [A] – ABBA
DANCING QUEEN [A] – ABBACADABRA
DANCING THE NIGHT AWAY – The MOTORS
DANCING TIGHT – Phil FEARON
DANCING WITH MYSELF – GENERATION X
DANCING WITH MYSELF (EP) – GENERATION X
DANCING WITH TEARS IN MY EYES – ULTRAVOX
DANCING WITH THE CAPTAIN – Paul NICHOLAS
DANDELION – The ROLLING STONES
DANGER [A] – AC/DC
DANGER [B] – BLAHZAY BLAHZAY
DANGER (BEEN SO LONG) – MYSTIKAL featuring NIVEA
DANGER GAMES – PINKEES
DANGER! HIGH VOLTAGE – ELECTRIC SIX
THE DANGER OF A STRANGER – Stella PARTON
DANGER ZONE – Kenny LOGGINS
DANGEROUS [A] – Penny FORD
DANGEROUS [B] – ROXETTE
DANGEROUS [C] – Busta RHYMES
DANGEROUS MINDS (EP) – VARIOUS ARTISTS (EPs and LPs)
DANGEROUS SEX – TACK HEAD
DANIEL – Elton JOHN
DARE ME – POINTER SISTERS
DARE TO DREAM – Viola WILLS
DARK ALAN (AILEIN DUINN) – CAPERCAILLIE
DARK AND LONG – UNDERWORLD
DARK CLOUDS – SPACE
DARK IS LIGHT ENOUGH – DUKE SPIRIT
THE DARK IS RISING – MERCURY REV
DARK IS THE NIGHT [A] – SHAKATAK
DARK IS THE NIGHT [B] – A-HA
DARK LADY – CHER
DARK MOON – Tony BRENT
DARK NIGHT – GORKY'S ZYGOTIC MYNCI
DARK SCIENCE (EP) – TILT
DARK SKY – Jimmy SOMERVILLE
DARK THERAPY – ECHOBELLY
DARKHEART – BOMB THE BASS
DARKLANDS – JESUS AND MARY CHAIN
DARKTOWN STRUTTERS BALL – Joe BROWN and the BRUVVERS
DARLIN' [A] – The BEACH BOYS
DARLIN' [A] – David CASSIDY
DARLIN' [B] – Frankie MILLER
DARLIN' [C] – Bob SINCLAIR featuring James WILLIAMS
DARLIN' DARLIN' BABY (SWEET, TENDER, LOVE) – O'JAYS
DARLING BE HOME SOON [A] – LET LOOSE
DARLING BE HOME SOON [A] – LOVIN' SPOONFUL
DARLING PRETTY – Mark KNOPFLER
DARTS OF PLEASURE – FRANZ FERDINAND
DAS BOOT – U96
DAS GLOCKENSPIEL – SCHILLER
DAT – Pluto SHERVINGTON
DATE WITH THE NIGHT – The YEAH YEAH YEAHS
DAUGHTER – PEARL JAM
DAUGHTER OF DARKNESS – Tom JONES
DAVID (I STILL HAVE LAST NIGHT IN MY BODY ...) – GUSGUS
DAVID WATTS – The JAM
DAVID'S SONG (MAIN THEME FROM 'KIDNAPPED') – Vladimir COSMA
DAVY'S ON THE ROAD AGAIN – MANFRED MANN
DAWN [A] – FLINTLOCK
DAWN [B] – Tony DE VIT
DAY AFTER DAY [A] – BADFINGER
DAY AFTER DAY [B] – The PRETENDERS
DAY AFTER DAY [C] – Julian LENNON
DAY & NIGHT – Billie PIPER
THE DAY BEFORE YESTERDAY'S MAN – SUPERNATURALS
THE DAY BEFORE YOU CAME [A] – ABBA
THE DAY BEFORE YOU CAME [A] – BLANCMANGE
DAY BY DAY [A] – Holly SHERWOOD
DAY BY DAY [B] – SHAKATAK featuring Al JARREAU
DAY BY DAY [C] – SERAFIN
THE DAY I FALL IN LOVE – Dolly PARTON and James INGRAM
THE DAY I MET MARIE – Cliff RICHARD
THE DAY I TRIED TO LIVE – SOUNDGARDEN
DAY IN DAY OUT – FEEDER
A DAY IN THE LIFE – BLACK RIOT
A DAY IN THE LIFE OF VINCE PRINCE – Russ ABBOT
THE DAY IS ENDED (THE DAY THOU GAVE US LORD, IS ENDED) – The Pipes and Drums and Military Band of the ROYAL SCOTS DRAGOON GUARDS
THE DAY IT RAINED FOREVER – AURORA
THE DAY THAT CURLY BILLY SHOT DOWN CRAZY SAM MCGHEE – The HOLLIES
THE DAY THE EARTH CAUGHT FIRE – CITY BOY
THE DAY THE RAINS CAME – Jane MORGAN
THE DAY THE WORLD TURNED DAY-GLO – X-RAY SPEX
DAY TIME – 4 STRINGS
DAY TRIPPER [A] – The BEATLES
DAY TRIPPER [A] – Otis REDDING
THE DAY WE CAUGHT THE TRAIN – OCEAN COLOUR SCENE
THE DAY WE FIND LOVE – 911
THE DAY WILL COME – QUAKE featuring Marcia RAE
A DAY WITHOUT LOVE – LOVE AFFAIR
DAYDREAM [A] – LOVIN' SPOONFUL
DAYDREAM [A] – RIGHT SAID FRED
DAYDREAM [B] – BACK TO THE PLANET
DAYDREAM BELIEVER [A] – The MONKEES
DAYDREAM BELIEVER [A] – Anne MURRAY
DAYDREAM BELIEVER (CHEER UP PETER REID) – SIMPLY RED AND WHITE
DAYDREAM IN BLUE – I MONSTER
DAYDREAMER [A] – David CASSIDY
DAYDREAMER [B] – MENSWEAR
DAYDREAMIN' – Tatyana ALI
DAYDREAMING – Penny FORD
DAY-IN DAY-OUT – David BOWIE
DAYLIGHT FADING – COUNTING CROWS
DAYLIGHT KATY – Gordon LIGHTFOOT
DAYS [A] – The KINKS
DAYS [A] – Kirsty MacCOLL
DAYS ARE OK – MOTELS
THE DAYS EP – The KINKS
DAYS GO BY – DIRTY VEGAS
DAYS LIKE THESE – Billy BRAGG
DAYS LIKE THIS [A] – Sheena EASTON
DAYS LIKE THIS [B] – Van MORRISON
DAYS LIKE THIS [C] – Shaun ESCOFFERY
DAYS OF NO TRUST – MAGNUM
DAYS OF OUR LIVEZ – BONE THUGS-N-HARMONY
THE DAYS OF PEARLY SPENCER – Marc ALMOND
DAYS OF YOUTH – LAURNEA
DAYSLEEPER – R.E.M.
DAYTIME FRIENDS – Kenny ROGERS
DAYTONA DEMON – Suzi QUATRO
DAYTRIP TO BANGOR (DIDN'T WE HAVE A LOVELY TIME) – FIDDLER'S DRAM
DAYZ LIKE THAT – FIERCE
DAZZ – BRICK
DAZZLE – SIOUXSIE and the BANSHEES
D-DARLING – Anthony NEWLEY
D-DAYS – Hazel O'CONNOR
DE DAH DAH (SPICE OF LIFE) – Keith MAC PROJECT
DE DO DO DO, DE DA DA DA – The POLICE
DE NIRO – DISCO EVANGELISTS
DEAD A'S – DJ Hype
DEAD BATTERY – PITCH SHIFTER
DEAD CITIES – EXPLOITED
DEAD END STREET – The KINKS
DEAD FROM THE WAIST DOWN – CATATONIA
DEAD GIVEAWAY – SHALAMAR
THE DEAD HEART – MIDNIGHT OIL
DEAD HUSBAND – DEEJAY PUNK-ROC
DEAD IN HOLLYWOOD – The MURDERDOLLS
DAYS LEAVES AND THE DIRTY GROUND – The WHITE STRIPES
DEAD MAN WALKING – David BOWIE
DEAD OR ALIVE – Lonnie DONEGAN
DEAD POP STARS – ALTERED IMAGES
DEAD RINGER FOR LOVE – MEAT LOAF
DEAD STAR – MUSE
DEADLIER THAN THE MALE – The WALKER BROTHERS
DEADLINE – DUTCH FORCE
DEADLINE USA – SHALAMAR
DEADWEIGHT – BECK
DEAF FOREVER – MOTORHEAD
THE DEAL – Pat CAMPBELL
THE DEAN AND I – 10cc
DEAR ADDY – Kid CREOLE and the COCONUTS
DEAR BOOPSIE – Pam HALL
DEAR DELILAH – GRAPEFRUIT
DEAR ELAINE – Roy WOOD

DEAR GOD — Midge URE
DEAR JESSIE [A] — MADONNA
DEAR JESSIE [A] — ROLLERGIRL
DEAR JOHN [A] — STATUS QUO
DEAR JOHN [B] — Eddi READER
DEAR LIE — TLC
DEAR LONELY HEARTS — Nat 'King' COLE
DEAR MAMA — 2PAC
DEAR MISS LONELY HEARTS — Philip LYNOTT
DEAR MRS APPLEBEE — David GARRICK
DEAR PRUDENCE —
  SIOUXSIE and the BANSHEES
DEATH DISCO — PUBLIC IMAGE LTD
DEATH OF A CLOWN — Dave DAVIES
DEBASER — PIXIES
DEBORA — T. REX
A DECADE UNDER THE INFLUENCE —
  TAKING BACK SUNDAY
DECADENCE DANCE — EXTREME
THE DECEIVER — The ALARM
DECEMBER — ALL ABOUT EVE
DECEMBER, 1963 (OH, WHAT A NIGHT) —
  The FOUR SEASONS
DECEMBER WILL BE MAGIC AGAIN — Kate BUSH
DECENT DAYS AND NIGHTS —
  The FUTUREHEADS
DECEPTION — FERGIE
DECK OF CARDS [A] — Max BYGRAVES
DECK OF CARDS [A] — Wink MARTINDALE
DEDICATED FOLLOWER OF FASHION —
  The KINKS
DEDICATED TO THE ONE I LOVE [A] —
  MAMAS and the PAPAS
DEDICATED TO THE ONE I LOVE [A] —
  Bitty McLEAN
DEDICATION — THIN LIZZY
DEEE-LITE THEME — DEEE-LITE
DEEP — EAST 17
THE DEEP — GLOBAL COMMUNICATION
DEEP AND WIDE AND TALL — AZTEC CAMERA
DEEP DEEP DOWN — HEPBURN
DEEP DEEP TROUBLE — The SIMPSONS
DEEP DOWN & DIRTY — STEREO MC's
DEEP FEELING — Mike SAGAR
DEEP FOREST — DEEP FOREST
DEEP HEAT '89 —
  VARIOUS ARTISTS (MONTAGES)
DEEP (I'M FALLING DEEPER) — ARIEL
DEEP IN MY HEART — CLUBHOUSE
DEEP IN THE HEART OF TEXAS —
  Duane EDDY and the REBELS
DEEP IN YOU — LIVIN' JOY
DEEP INSIDE — Mary J BLIGE
DEEP MENACE (SPANK) — D'MENACE
DEEP PURPLE [A] —
  Billy WARD and his DOMINOES
DEEP PURPLE [A] —
  Nino TEMPO and April STEVENS
DEEP PURPLE [A] —
  Donny and Marie OSMOND
DEEP RIVER WOMAN — Lionel RICHIE
DEEP SEA — AQUANAUTS
DEEP SHAG — LUSCIOUS JACKSON
DEEPER [A] — ESCRIMA
DEEPER [B] — DELIRIOUS?
DEEPER [C] — SERIOUS DANGER
DEEPER (EP) — DELIRIOUS?
DEEPER AND DEEPER [A] — Freda PAYNE
DEEPER AND DEEPER [B] — MADONNA
A DEEPER LOVE [A] — Aretha FRANKLIN
A DEEPER LOVE [A] —
  C & C MUSIC FACTORY / CLIVILLES & COLE
DEEPER LOVE (SYMPHONIC PARADISE) — BBE
DEEPER SHADE OF BLUE — STEPS
DEEPER THAN THE NIGHT —
  Olivia NEWTON-JOHN
THE DEEPER THE LOVE — WHITESNAKE
DEEPER UNDERGROUND — JAMIROQUAI
DEEPEST BLUE — DEEPEST BLUE
DEEPLY DIPPY — RIGHT SAID FRED
DEF CON ONE — POP WILL EAT ITSELF
DEFINITE DOOR — POSIES
DEFINITION OF HOUSE — MINIMAL FUNK
DEGREES — Ian POOLEY
DEJA VU —
  E-SMOOVE featuring Latanza WATERS
DEJA VU (UPTOWN BABY) —
  LORD TARIQ and Peter GUNZ
DELAWARE — Perry COMO
DELICATE — Terence Trent
  D'ARBY featuring DES'REE
DELICIOUS [A] — CATHERINE WHEEL
DELICIOUS [B] — KULAY
DELICIOUS [C] — Deni HINES featuring DON-E
DELICIOUS [D] — PURE SUGAR
DELICIOUS [E] — SLEEPER
DELICIOUS [F] — SHAMPOO
DELILAH [A] — Tom JONES
DELILAH [A] —
  The SENSATIONAL ALEX HARVEY BAND
DELILAH JONES — The McGUIRE SISTERS
DELIVER ME — SISTER BLISS
DELIVERANCE [A] — The MISSION
DELIVERANCE [B] — Bubba SPARXXX
DELIVERING THE GOODS — SKID ROW
DELLA AND THE DEALER — Hoyt AXTON

DELTA LADY — Joe COCKER
DELTA SUN BOTTLENECK STOMP —
  MERCURY REV
DEM GIRLS (I DON'T KNOW WHY) —
  OXIDE & NEUTRINO
DEMOCRACY — KILLING JOKE
DEMOLITION MAN — STING
DEMONS [A] — SUPER FURRY ANIMALS
DEMONS [B] —
  FATBOY SLIM featuring Macy GRAY
DENIS DENEE — BLONDIE
DENISE — FOUNTAINS OF WAYNE
DER KOMMISSAR — AFTER THE FIRE
DER SCHIEBER — Timo MAAS
DESAFINADO [A] — Ella FITZGERALD
DESAFINADO [A] — Stan GETZ
DESERT DROUGHT — CAST
DESERT SONG — STING
DESIDERATA — Les CRANE
A DESIGN FOR LIFE —
  MANIC STREET PREACHERS
DESIRE [A] — U2
DESIRE [B] — NU COLOURS
DESIRE [C] — BBE
DESIRE [C] — DJ ERIC
DESIRE [E] — Ultra NATE
DESIRE LINES — LUSH
DESIRE ME — DOLL
DESIREE — Neil DIAMOND
DESPERATE BUT NOT SERIOUS — Adam ANT
DESPERATE DAN — LIEUTENANT PIGEON
THE DESPERATE HOURS — Marc ALMOND
DESTINATION — DT8 featuring Roxanne WILDE
DESTINATION ESCHATON — The SHAMEN
DESTINATION SUNSHINE — BALEARIC BILL
DESTINATION VENUS — REZILLOS
DESTINATION ZULULAND — KING KURT
DESTINY [A] — Anne MURRAY
DESTINY [B] — Candi STATON
DESTINY [C] — The JACKSONS
DESTINY [D] — BABY D
DESTINY [E] — Kenny THOMAS
DESTINY [F] — DEM 2
DESTINY [G] —
  ZERO 7 featuring SIA and SOPHIE
DESTINY [G] — N-TRANCE
DESTINY CALLING — JAMES
DETROIT — WHITEOUT
DETROIT CITY — Tom JONES
DEUS — SUGARCUBES
DEUTSCHER GIRLS — ADAM and the ANTS
DEVIL — 666
DEVIL GATE DRIVE — Suzi QUATRO
DEVIL IN YOUR SHOES (WALKING ALL OVER) —
  SHED SEVEN
DEVIL INSIDE — INXS
DEVIL OR ANGEL — Billy FURY
THE DEVIL WENT DOWN TO GEORGIA —
  Charlie DANIELS BAND
DEVIL WOMAN [A] — Marty ROBBINS
DEVIL WOMAN [B] — Cliff RICHARD
THE DEVIL YOU KNOW — JESUS JONES
THE DEVIL'S ANSWER — ATOMIC ROOSTER
DEVIL'S BALL — DOUBLE
DEVIL'S GUN — CJ & CO
DEVIL'S HAIRCUT — BECK
DEVIL'S NIGHTMARE — OXIDE & NEUTRINO
DEVIL'S TOY — The ALMIGHTY
DEVIL'S TRILL — VANESSA-MAE
DEVOTED TO YOU — TEN CITY
DEVOTION [A] — KICKING BACK with TAXMAN
DEVOTION [B] — David HOLMES
D-FUNKTIONAL —
  MEKON featuring Afrika BAMBAATAA
DIABLO — GRID
DIAL MY HEART — The BOYS
DIABLA — FUNK D'VOID
DIAMANTE —
  ZUCCHERO with Randy CRAWFORD
DIAMOND BACK — MEKKA
DIAMOND DEW — GORKY'S ZYGOTIC MYNCI
DIAMOND DOGS — David BOWIE
DIAMOND GIRL — Pete WYLIE
DIAMOND LIFE — Louie VEGA & Jay
  'SINISTER' SEALEE featuring Julie MCKNIGHT
DIAMOND LIGHTS — GLENN and CHRIS
DIAMOND SMILES — The BOOMTOWN RATS
DIAMONDS [A] —
  Jet HARRIS and Tony MEEHAN
DIAMONDS [B] — Chris REA
DIAMONDS [C] — Herb ALPERT
DIAMONDS AND GUNS — TRANSPLANTS
DIAMONDS AND PEARLS —
  PRINCE and the NEW POWER GENERATION
DIAMONDS ARE FOREVER [A] — David McALMONT
DIAMONDS ARE FOREVER [A] — Shirley BASSEY
DIANA — Paul ANKA
DIANE [A] — The BACHELORS
DIANE [B] — THERAPY?
DIARY OF A WIMP — SPACE
THE DIARY OF HORACE WIMP —
  ELECTRIC LIGHT ORCHESTRA
DICK-A-DUM-DUM (KING'S ROAD) —
  Des O'CONNOR
DID I DREAM (SONG TO THE SIREN) —
  LOST WITNESS

DID IT AGAIN — Kylie MINOGUE
DID MY TIME — KORN
DID YOU EVER — Nancy SINATRA
DID YOU EVER REALLY LOVE ME —
  Nicki FRENCH
DID YOU EVER THINK — R KELLY
DID YOU HAVE TO LOVE ME LIKE YOU DID —
  COCONUTS
DIDDY — P DIDDY featuring The NEPTUNES
DIDN'T I (BLOW YOUR MIND THIS TIME) [A] —
  DELFONICS
DIDN'T I BLOW YOUR MIND [A] —
  NEW KIDS ON THE BLOCK
DIDN'T I TELL YOU TRUE —
  Thomas JULES-STOCK
DIDN'T WE ALMOST HAVE IT ALL —
  Whitney HOUSTON
DIE ANOTHER DAY — MADONNA
DIE LAUGHING — THERAPY?
DIE YOUNG — BLACK SABBATH
DIFFERENCES — GUYVER
DIFFERENT AIR — LIVING IN A BOX
A DIFFERENT BEAT — BOYZONE
A DIFFERENT CORNER — George MICHAEL
DIFFERENT STORY — BOWA featuring MALA
DIFFERENT STROKES — ISOTONIK
DIFFERENT TIME DIFFERENT PLACE —
  Julia FORDHAM
DIG FOR FIRE — PIXIES
DIGERIDOO — APHEX TWIN
DIGGI LOO-DIGGI LEY — HERREYS
DIGGIN' MY POTATOES — HEINZ
DIGGIN' ON YOU — TLC
DIGGING IN THE DIRT — Peter GABRIEL
DIGGING THE GRAVE — FAITH NO MORE
DIGGING YOUR SCENE — The BLOW MONKEYS
DIGITAL — GOLDIE featuring KRS ONE
DIGITAL LOVE — DAFT PUNK
DIGNITY [A] — DEACON BLUE
DIGNITY [B] — Bob DYLAN
DIL CHEEZ (MY HEART...) — Bally SAGOO
DILEMMA — NELLY featuring Kelly ROWLAND
DIM ALL THE LIGHTS — Donna SUMMER
A DIME AND A DOLLAR — Guy MITCHELL
DIMENSION — SALT TANK
DIMPLES — John Lee HOOKER
DIN DA DA — Kevin AVIANCE
DINAH — BLACKNUSS
DING DONG — George HARRISON
DING DONG SONG —
  GUNTHER & the SUNSHINE GIRLS
DING-A-DONG — TEACH-IN
DINNER WITH DELORES — PRINCE
DINNER WITH GERSHWIN — Donna SUMMER
DINOSAUR ADVENTURE 3D — UNDERWORLD
DIP IT LOW — Christina MILIAN
DIPPETY DAY — The SMURFS
DIRECT-ME — REESE PROJECT
DIRGE — DEATH IN VEGAS
DIRRTY —
  Christina AGUILERA featuring REDMAN
DIRT — DEATH IN VEGAS
DIRT OFF YOUR SHOULDER — JAY-Z
DIRTY BEATS — Roni SIZE / REPRAZENT
DIRTY CASH — ADVENTURES OF STEVIE V
DIRTY DAWG — NEW KIDS ON THE BLOCK
DIRTY DEEDS —
  Joan JETT and the BLACKHEARTS
DIRTY DEEDS DONE DIRT CHEAP — AC/DC
DIRTY DIANA — Michael JACKSON
DIRTY HARRY'S REVENGE —
  Adam F featuring BEENIE MAN
DIRTY LAUNDRY — Don HENLEY
DIRTY LOOKS — Diana ROSS
DIRTY LOVE — THUNDER
DIRTY MIND — SHAKESPEAR'S SISTER
DIRTY MONEY — Dee FREDRIX
DIRTY MOTHA —
  QWILO and FELIX DA HOUSECAT
DIRTY OLD TOWN — The POGUES
DIRTY OLD TOWN [A] — BHOYS FROM PARADISE
DIRTY STICKY FLOORS — Dave GAHAN
DIRTY WATER — MADE IN LONDON
DISAPPEAR — INXS
DISAPPEARING ACT — SHALAMAR
DISAPPOINTED [A] — PUBLIC IMAGE LTD
DISAPPOINTED [B] — ELECTRONIC
THE DISAPPOINTED — XTC
DISARM — SMASHING PUMPKINS
DISCIPLINE OF LOVE — Robert PALMER
D.I.S.C.O. [A] — OTTAWAN
D.I.S.C.O. [A] — N-TRANCE
DISCO BABES FROM OUTER SPACE —
  BABE INSTINCT
DISCO BEATLEMANIA — DBM
DISCO CONNECTION — Isaac HAYES
DISCO COP — BLUE ADONIS
  featuring LIL' MISS MAX
DISCO DOWN [A] — SHED SEVEN
DISCO DOWN [B] — HOUSE OF GLASS
DISCO DUCK (PART ONE) —
  Rick DEES and his CAST OF IDIOTS
DISCO INFERNO [A] — The TRAMMPS
DISCO INFERNO [A] — Tina TURNER
'DISCO' LA PASSIONE —
  Chris REA and Shirley BASSEY
DISCO LADY — Johnnie TAYLOR

DISCO MACHINE GUN —
  LO FIDELITY ALLSTARS
DISCO MUSIC — J.A.L.N. BAND
DISCO NIGHTS — (ROCK FREAK) — G.Q.
DISCO QUEEN — HOT CHOCOLATE
DISCO SCIENCE — MIRWAIS
DISCO STOMP — Hamilton BOHANNON
DISCO 2000 — PULP
DISCOBUG '97 — FREAKYMAN
DISCOHOPPING — KLUBBHEADS
DISCOLAND —
  FLIP & FILL featuring Karen PARRY
DISCONNECT — ROLLINS BAND
DISCO'S REVENGE — GUSTO
DISCOTHEQUE — U2
DISCRETION GLOVE — Stephen MALKMUS
DISEASE — MATCHBOX TWENTY
DISENCHANTED — COMMUNARDS
DISILLUSION — BADLY DRAWN BOY
DIS-INFECTED (EP) — The THE
DISPOSABLE TEENS — MARILYN MANSON
DISREMEMBRANCE — Dannii MINOGUE
DISSIDENT — PEARL JAM
THE DISTANCE — CAKE
DISTANT DRUMS — Jim REEVES
DISTANT STAR — Anthony HOPKINS
DISTANT SUN — CROWDED HOUSE
DISTORTION — WILT
DISTRACTIONS — ZERO 7 featuring SIA
DIVA — DANA INTERNATIONAL
DIVE! DIVE! DIVE! — Bruce DICKINSON
DIVE IN — CATCH
DIVE TO PARADISE — EUROGROOVE
DIVEBOMB — NUMBER ONE CUP
DIVINE EMOTIONS — Narada Michael WALDEN
DIVINE HAMMER — The BREEDERS
DIVINE THING — SOUP DRAGONS
DIVING — 4 STRINGS
DIVING FACES — LIQUID CHILD
D.I.V.O.R.C.E. [A] — Tammy WYNETTE
D.I.V.O.R.C.E. [A] — Billy CONNOLLY
DIXIE-NARCO (EP) — PRIMAL SCREAM
DIZZY [A] — Tommy ROE
DIZZY [A] —
  Vic REEVES and The WONDER STUFF
DJ [A] — David BOWIE
DJ [B] —
  RESONANCE featuring The BURRELLS
DJ [C] — H & CLAIRE
DJ [D] — JAMELIA
DJ CULTURE — PET SHOP BOYS
DJ, DJ — TRANSPLANTS
DJ NATION — NUKLEUZ DJS
DJ NATION - BOOTLEG EDITION —
  NUKLEUZ DJS
DJ NATION - HARDER EDITION —
  VARIOUS (NUKLEUZ DJS)
DJ SPINNIN' — PUNK CHIC
DJS FANS & FREAKS — BLANK & JONES
DJS TAKE CONTROL — SL2
DK 50-80 —
  John OTWAY and Wild Willy BARRETT
DO AND DON'T FOR LOVE — KIOKA
DO ANYTHING — NATURAL SELECTION
DO ANYTHING YOU WANNA DO —
  EDDIE and the HOT RODS
DO ANYTHING YOU WANT TO — THIN LIZZY
DO FOR LOVE — 2PAC
DO FRIES GO WITH THAT SHAKE —
  George CLINTON
DO I — GIFTED
DO I DO — Stevie WONDER
DO I HAVE TO SAY THE WORDS —
  Bryan ADAMS
DO I LOVE YOU — The RONETTES
DO I QUALIFY? — Lynden David HALL
DO IT — Tony DI BART
DO IT ALL OVER AGAIN — SPIRITUALIZED
DO IT AGAIN [A] — The BEACH BOYS
DO IT AGAIN [B] — STEELY DAN
DO IT AGAIN — BILLIE JEAN (MEDLEY) —
  CLUBHOUSE
DO IT ANY WAY YOU WANNA —
  PEOPLES CHOICE
DO IT, DO IT AGAIN — Raffaella CARRA
DO IT FOR LOVE [A] — Danni'elle GAHA
DO IT FOR LOVE [B] —
  SUBTERRANIA featuring Ann CONSUELO
DO IT FOR LOVE [C] — 4MANDU
DO IT NOW — BRAIN BASHERS
DO IT PROPERLY ('NO WAY BACK') —
  ADONIS featuring 2 PUERTO RICANS,
  A BLACK MAN AND A DOMINICAN
DO IT TO ME — Lionel RICHIE
DO IT TO ME AGAIN — SOULSEARCHER
DO IT TO THE CROWD — TWIN HYPE
DO IT TO THE MUSIC — RAW SILK
DO IT WITH MADONNA — The ANDROIDS
DO ME — BELL BIV DEVOE
DO ME RIGHT — INNER CITY
DO ME WRONG — Mel BLATT
DO MY THING — Busta RHYMES
DO NO WRONG — THIRTEEN SENSES
DO NOT DISTURB — BANANARAMA
DO NOT PASS ME BY — HAMMER
DO NOTHING — The SPECIALS
DO OR DIE — SUPER FURRY ANIMALS

DO RE ME SO FAR SO GOOD — CARTER — THE UNSTOPPABLE SEX MACHINE
DO SOMETHING — Macy GRAY
DO THAT THING — MASAI
DO THAT TO ME — LISA MARIE EXPERIENCE
DO THAT TO ME ONE MORE TIME — CAPTAIN and TENNILLE
DO THE BARTMAN — The SIMPSONS
DO THE BIRD [A] — Dee Dee SHARP
DO THE BIRD [A] — VERNONS GIRLS
DO THE CAN CAN — SKANDI GIRLS
DO THE CLAM — Elvis PRESLEY
DO THE CONGA — BLACK LACE
DO THE FUNKY CHICKEN — Rufus THOMAS
(DO) THE HUCKLEBUCK — COAST TO COAST
DO THE LOLLIPOP — TWEENIES
DO THE RIGHT THING [A] — REDHEAD KINGPIN and the FBI
DO THE RIGHT THING [B] — Ian WRIGHT
(DO THE) SPANISH HUSTLE — FATBACK BAND
DO THEY KNOW IT'S CHRISTMAS? [A] — BAND AID
DO THEY KNOW IT'S CHRISTMAS? [A] — BAND AID II
DO THEY KNOW IT'S CHRISTMAS? [A] — BAND AID 20
DO THIS MY WAY — KID 'N' PLAY
DO U FEEL 4 ME — EDEN
DO U KNOW WHERE YOU'RE COMING FROM — M-BEAT featuring JAMIROQUAI
DO U STILL — EAST 17
DO U WANNA FUNK — SPACE 2000
DO WAH DIDDY DIDDY [A] — MANFRED MANN
DO WAH DIDDY DIDDY [A] — BLUE MELONS
DO WAH DIDDY [A] — DJ OTZI
DO WATCHA DO — HYPER GO GO and ADEVA
DO WE ROCK — POINT BREAK
DO WHAT YOU DO [A] — Jermaine JACKSON
DO WHAT YOU DO [B] — Annabella LWIN
DO WHAT YOU DO DO WELL — Ned MILLER
DO WHAT YOU DO (EARWORM SONG) — Clint BOON EXPERIENCE
DO WHAT YOU FEEL [A] — Joey NEGRO
DO WHAT YOU FEEL [B] — JOHNNA
DO WHAT YOU GOTTA DO [A] — The FOUR TOPS
DO WHAT YOU GOTTA DO [A] — Nina SIMONE
DO WHAT YOU WANNA DO — T-CONNECTION
DO WHAT WE WOULD — ACZESS
DO WHAT'S GOOD FOR ME — 2 UNLIMITED
DO YA — INNER CITY
DO YA DO YA (WANNA PLEASE ME) — Samantha FOX
DO YA WANNA GET FUNKY WITH ME — Peter BROWN
DO YOU BELIEVE IN LOVE [A] — Huey LEWIS and the NEWS
DO YOU BELIEVE IN LOVE [B] — UNATION
DO YOU BELIEVE IN LOVE [C] — ULTRA-SONIC
DO YOU BELIEVE IN MIRACLES — SLADE
DO YOU BELIEVE IN SHAME — DURAN DURAN
DO YOU BELIEVE IN THE WESTWORLD — THEATRE OF HATE
DO YOU BELIEVE IN THE WONDER — Jeanie TRACY
DO YOU BELIEVE IN US — Jon SECADA
DO YOU DREAM IN COLOUR? — Bill NELSON
DO YOU FEEL LIKE I FEEL — Belinda CARLISLE
DO YOU FEEL LIKE WE DO — Peter FRAMPTON
DO YOU FEEL ME? (... FREAK YOU) — MEN OF VIZION
DO YOU FEEL MY LOVE? [A] — Eddy GRANT
DO YOU KNOW [A] — SECRET AFFAIR
DO YOU KNOW [B] — Michelle GAYLE
DO YOU KNOW (I GO CRAZY) — ANGEL CITY
DO YOU KNOW THE WAY TO SAN JOSE — Dionne WARWICK
DO YOU KNOW (WHAT IT TAKES) — ROBYN
DO YOU LIKE IT — KINGDOM COME
DO YOU LOVE ME [A] — Brian POOLE and the TREMELOES
DO YOU LOVE ME [A] — Dave CLARK FIVE
DO YOU LOVE ME [A] — DEEP FEELING
DO YOU LOVE ME [A] — DUKE BAYSEE
DO YOU LOVE ME [B] — MADEMOISELLE
DO YOU LOVE ME [C] — Nick CAVE and the BAD SEEDS
DO YOU LOVE ME BOY? — KERRI-ANN
DO YOU LOVE ME LIKE YOU SAY — Terence Trent D'ARBY
DO YOU LOVE WHAT YOU FEEL — INNER CITY
DO YOU MIND — Anthony NEWLEY
DO YOU REALIZE?? — The FLAMING LIPS
DO YOU REALLY LIKE IT — DJ PIED PIPER and the MASTERS OF CEREMONIES
(DO YOU REALLY LOVE ME) TELL ME LOVE — Michael WYCOFF
DO YOU REALLY LOVE ME TOO — Billy FURY
DO YOU REALLY WANT ME [A] — Jon SECADA
DO YOU REALLY WANT ME [B] — ROBYN
DO YOU REALLY (WANT MY LOVE) — JUNIOR
DO YOU REALLY WANT TO HURT ME — CULTURE CLUB
DO YOU REMEMBER — SCAFFOLD
DO YOU REMEMBER HOUSE — BLAZE
DO YOU REMEMBER (LIVE) — Phil COLLINS
DO YOU REMEMBER ROCK 'N' ROLL RADIO? — The RAMONES
DO YOU REMEMBER THE FIRST TIME — PULP
DO YOU SEE — Warren G
DO YOU SEE THE LIGHT (LOOKING FOR) — SNAP! featuring Niki HARIS
DO YOU SLEEP? — Lisa LOEB and NINE STORIES
DO YOU THINK ABOUT US — TOTAL
DO YOU THINK YOU'RE SPECIAL — NIO
DO YOU UNDERSTAND — The ALMIGHTY
DO YOU WANNA DANCE — Barry BLUE
DO YOU WANNA FUNK — SYLVESTER
DO YOU WANNA GET FUNKY — C&C MUSIC FACTORY / CLIVILLES & COLE
DO YOU WANNA GO OUR WAY??? — PUBLIC ENEMY
DO YOU WANNA HOLD ME — BOW WOW WOW
DO YOU WANNA PARTY — DJ SCOTT featuring Lorna B
DO YOU WANNA TOUCH ME? (OH YEAH) — Gary GLITTER
DO YOU WANT IT RIGHT NOW — DEGREES OF MOTION featuring BITI
DO YOU WANT ME [A] — SALT-N-PEPA
DO YOU WANT ME [B] — Q-TEX
DO YOU WANT ME? [C] — LEILANI
DO YOU WANT ME TO — FOUR PENNIES
DO YOU WANT TO DANCE — Cliff RICHARD and The SHADOWS
DO YOU WANT TO KNOW A SECRET? — Billy J KRAMER and the DAKOTAS
DO YOUR DANCE — ROSE ROYCE
THE DOCTOR — DOOBIE BROTHERS
DR BEAT — MIAMI SOUND MACHINE
DOCTOR DOCTOR [A] — UFO
DOCTOR DOCTOR [B] — THOMPSON TWINS
DR FEELGOOD — MÖTLEY CRÜE
DR FINLAY — Andy STEWART
DR GREENTHUMB — CYPRESS HILL
DR HECKYLL AND MR JIVE — MEN AT WORK
DOCTOR JACKYLL AND MISTER FUNK — Jackie McLEAN
DOCTOR JEEP — SISTERS OF MERCY
DOCTOR JONES — AQUA
DOCTOR KISS KISS — 5000 VOLTS
DR LOVE — Tina CHARLES
DR MABUSE — PROPAGANDA
DOCTOR MY EYES — The JACKSON FIVE
DR STEIN — HELLOWEEN
DR WHO — MANKIND
DOCTORIN' THE HOUSE — COLDCUT featuring YAZZ and the PLASTIC POPULATION
DOCTORIN' THE TARDIS — The TIMELORDS
DOCTOR'S ORDERS — SUNNY
DOES HE LOVE YOU — Reba McENTIRE
DOES IT FEEL GOOD — BT EXPRESS
DOES IT FEEL GOOD TO YOU — Carl COX
DOES SHE HAVE A FRIEND? — Gene CHANDLER
DOES THAT RING A BELL — DYNASTY
DOES THIS HURT — BOO RADLEYS
DOES YOUR CHEWING GUM LOSE ITS FLAVOUR — Lonnie DONEGAN
DOES YOUR HEART GO BOOM — Helen LOVE
DOES YOUR MOTHER KNOW — ABBA
DOESN'T ANYBODY KNOW MY NAME? — Vince HILL
DOESN'T REALLY MATTER — Janet JACKSON
DOG — DADA
DOG EAT DOG — ADAM and the ANTS
DOG ON WHEELS — BELLE & SEBASTIAN
DOG TRAIN — LEVELLERS
DOGGY DOGG WORLD — SNOOP DOGG
DOGMAN GO WOOF — UNDERWORLD
DOGMONAUT 2000 (IS THERE ANYONE OUT THERE?) — FRIGID VINEGAR
DOGS — The WHO
DOGS OF LUST — The THE
DOGS OF WAR — EXPLOITED
DOGS WITH NO TAILS — PALE
DOGZ N SLEDGEZ — MILLION DAN
DOIN' IT [A] — LL COOL J
DOIN' IT [B] — LIBERTY
DOIN' IT IN A HAUNTED HOUSE — Yvonne GAGE
DOIN' OUR OWN DANG — The JUNGLE BROTHERS
DOIN' OUR THING — PHOEBE ONE
DOIN' THE DO — Betty BOO
DOING ALRIGHT WITH THE BOYS — Gary GLITTER
DOLCE VITA — Ryan PARIS
DOLL HOUSE — KING BROTHERS
DOLL PARTS — HOLE
DOLLAR BILL — SCREAMING TREES
DOLLAR IN THE TEETH — UPSETTERS
DOLLARS — CJ LEWIS
DOLLARS IN THE HEAVENS — GENEVA
DOLLY MY LOVE — MOMENTS
DOLPHIN — SHED SEVEN
THE DOLPHIN'S CRY — LIVE
DOLPHINS MAKE ME CRY — Martyn JOSEPH
DOLPHINS WERE MONKEYS — Ian BROWN
DOMINATION — WAY OUT WEST
DOMINATOR — HUMAN RESOURCE
DOMINION — SISTERS OF MERCY
DOMINIQUE — SINGING NUN (Soeur Sourire)
DOMINO DANCING — PET SHOP BOYS
DOMINOES — Robbie NEVIL
DOMINOID — MOLOKO
THE DON — 187 LOCKDOWN
DON GARGON COMIN' — PROJECT 1
DON JUAN — Dave DEE, DOZY, BEAKY, MICK and TICH
DON QUIXOTE — Nik KERSHAW
DONALD WHERE'S YOUR TROOSERS — Andy STEWART
DONKEY CART — Frank CHACKSFIELD
DONNA [A] — Marty WILDE
DONNA [A] — Ritchie VALENS
DONNA [B] — 10cc
DON'T — Elvis PRESLEY
DON'T ANSWER ME [A] — Cilla BLACK
DON'T ANSWER ME [B] — Alan PARSONS PROJECT
DON'T ARGUE — CABARET VOLTAIRE
DON'T ASK ME — PUBLIC IMAGE LTD
DON'T ASK ME WHY — EURYTHMICS
DON'T BE A DUMMY — John DU CANN
DON'T BE A FOOL — LOOSE ENDS
DON'T BE A STRANGER — Dina CARROLL
DON'T BE AFRAID [A] — Aaron HALL
DON'T BE AFRAID [B] — MOONMAN
DON'T BE CRUEL [A] — Bill BLACK'S COMBO
DON'T BE CRUEL [A] — Billy SWAN
DON'T BE CRUEL [A] — Elvis PRESLEY
DON'T BE CRUEL [B] — Bobby BROWN
DON'T BE STUPID (YOU KNOW I LOVE YOU) — Shania TWAIN
DON'T BELIEVE A WORD — THIN LIZZY
DON'T BELIEVE THE HYPE [A] — MISTA E
DON'T BELIEVE THE HYPE [B] — PUBLIC ENEMY
DON'T BET MONEY HONEY — Linda SCOTT
DON'T BLAME IT ON LOVE — SHAKATAK
DON'T BLAME IT ON THAT GIRL — MATT BIANCO
DON'T BLAME ME [A] — The EVERLY BROTHERS
DON'T BLAME ME [A] — Frank IFIELD
DON'T BREAK MY HEART — UB40
DON'T BREAK MY HEART AGAIN — WHITESNAKE
DON'T BREAK THE HEART THAT LOVES YOU — Connie FRANCIS
DON'T BRING HARRY (EP) — The STRANGLERS
DON'T BRING LULU — Dorothy PROVINE
DON'T BRING ME DOWN [A] — PRETTY THINGS
DON'T BRING ME DOWN [B] — The ANIMALS
DON'T BRING ME DOWN [C] — ELECTRIC LIGHT ORCHESTRA
DON'T BRING ME DOWN [D] — SPIRITS
DON'T BRING ME YOUR HEARTACHES — Paul and Barry RYAN
DON'T CALL ME BABY [A] — VOICE OF THE BEEHIVE
DON'T CALL ME BABY [B] — MADISON AVENUE
DON'T CARE [A] — Klark KENT
DON'T CARE [B] — ANGEL'S REVERSE
DON'T COME AROUND HERE NO MORE — Tom PETTY and the HEARTBREAKERS
DON'T COME CLOSE — The RAMONES
DON'T COME HOME TOO SOON — DEL AMITRI
DON'T COME TO STAY — HOT HOUSE
DON'T CRY [A] — ASIA
DON'T CRY [B] — BOY GEORGE
DON'T CRY [C] — GUNS N' ROSES
DON'T CRY [D] — SEAL
DON'T CRY DADDY — Elvis PRESLEY
DON'T CRY FOR ME ARGENTINA [A] — Julie COVINGTON
DON'T CRY FOR ME ARGENTINA [A] — The SHADOWS
DON'T CRY FOR ME ARGENTINA [A] — MADONNA
DON'T CRY FOR ME ARGENTINA [A] — Mike FLOWERS POPS
DON'T CRY FOR ME ARGENTINA [A] — Sinead O'CONNOR
DON'T CRY OUT LOUD — Elkie BROOKS
DON'T DIE JUST YET — David HOLMES
DON'T DO IT BABY — Mac and Katie KISSOON
DON'T DO THAT [A] — GEORDIE
DON'T DO THAT [B] — YOUNG AND MOODY BAND
DON'T DON'T TELL ME NO — Sophie B HAWKINS
DON'T DREAM — DOVE
DON'T DREAM IT'S OVER [A] — CROWDED HOUSE
DON'T DREAM IT'S OVER [A] — Paul YOUN
DON'T DRIVE DRUNK — Stevie WONDER
DON'T DRIVE MY CAR — STATUS QUO
DON'T DROP BOMBS — Liza MINNELLI
DON'T EVER CHANGE — The CRICKETS
DON'T EVER THINK (TOO MUCH) ... — The ZUTONS
DON'T FALL IN LOVE (I SAID) — TOYAH
DON'T FALTER — MINT ROYALE
(DON'T FEAR) THE REAPER [A] — APOLLO FOUR FORTY
(DON'T FEAR) THE REAPER [A] — BLUE ÖYSTER CULT
DON'T FIGHT IT — Wilson PICKETT
DON'T FIGHT IT FEEL IT — PRIMAL SCREAM featuring Denise JOHNSON
DON'T FORBID ME — Pat BOONE
DON'T FORGET ME (WHEN I'M GONE) — GLASS TIGER
DON'T FORGET TO CATCH ME — Cliff RICHARD and The SHADOWS
DON'T FORGET TO DANCE — The KINKS
DON'T FORGET TO REMEMBER — The BEE GEES
DON'T GET ME WRONG — The PRETENDERS
DON'T GIVE IT UP — SONIC SURFERS
DON'T GIVE ME UP — Harold MELVIN and the BLUENOTES
DON'T GIVE ME YOUR LIFE — ALEX PARTY
DON'T GIVE UP [A] — Peter GABRIEL and Kate BUSH
DON'T GIVE UP [B] — Michelle WEEKS
DON'T GIVE UP [C] — CHICANE featuring Bryan ADAMS
DON'T GIVE UP 2004 [C] — CHICANE featuring Bryan ADAMS
DON'T GIVE UP [D] — LOUISE
DON'T GIVE UP ON US — David SOUL
DON'T GO [A] — JUDAS PRIEST
DON'T GO [B] — YAZOO
DON'T GO [B] — Lizzy MACK
DON'T GO [C] — HOTHOUSE FLOWERS
DON'T GO [D] — AWESOME 3
DON'T GO [D] — THIRD DIMENSION featuring Julie McDERMOTT
DON'T GO BREAKING MY HEART [A] — Elton JOHN and Kiki DEE
DON'T GO BREAKING MY HEART [A] — Elton JOHN with RuPAUL
DON'T GO MESSIN' WITH MY HEART — MANTRONIX
DON'T HANG UP — ORLONS
DON'T HOLD BACK — CHANSON
DON'T HURT YOURSELF — MARILLION
DON'T IT MAKE MY BROWN EYES BLUE — Crystal GAYLE
DON'T IT MAKE YOU FEEL GOOD — Stefan DENNIS
DON'T JUMP OFF THE ROOF DAD — Tommy COOPER
DON'T KILL IT CAROL — MANFRED MANN
DON'T KILL THE WHALE — YES
DON'T KNOCK IT (UNTIL YOU TRY IT) — Bobby NUNN
DON'T KNOCK THE ROCK — Bill HALEY and his COMETS
DON'T KNOW MUCH — Linda RONSTADT
DON'T KNOW WHAT TO TELL YA — AALIYAH
DON'T KNOW WHAT YOU GOT — CINDERELLA
DON'T KNOW WHY — Norah JONES
DON'T LAUGH — Josh WINK
DON'T LAUGH AT ME (CAUSE I'M A FOOL) — Norman WISDOM
DON'T LEAVE — FAITHLESS
DON'T LEAVE HOME — DIDO
DON'T LEAVE ME [A] — BLACKSTREET
DON'T LEAVE ME [B] — Malandra BURROWS
DON'T LEAVE ME BEHIND — EVERYTHING BUT THE GIRL
DON'T LEAVE ME THIS WAY [A] — COMMUNARDS with Sarah Jane MORRIS
DON'T LEAVE ME THIS WAY [A] — Harold MELVIN and the BLUENOTES
DON'T LEAVE ME THIS WAY [A] — Thelma HOUSTON
DON'T LET 'EM GRIND YOU DOWN — EXPLOITED
DON'T LET GO [A] — MANHATTAN TRANSFER
DON'T LET GO [B] — David SNEDDON
DON'T LET GO (LOVE) — EN VOGUE
DON'T LET GO THE COAT — The WHO
DON'T LET HIM STEAL YOUR HEART AWAY — Phil COLLINS
DON'T LET HIM TOUCH YOU — ANGELETTES
DON'T LET IT DIE — Hurricane SMITH
DON'T LET IT END — STYX
DON'T LET IT FADE AWAY — DARTS
DON'T LET IT GET YOU DOWN — ECHO and the BUNNYMEN
DON'T LET IT GO TO YOUR HEAD — The BRAND NEW HEAVIES
DON'T LET IT PASS YOU BY — UB40
DON'T LET IT SHOW ON YOUR FACE — ADEVA
DON'T LET LOVE GET YOU DOWN — Archie BELL and the DRELLS
DON'T LET ME BE MISUNDERSTOOD [A] — The ANIMALS
DON'T LET ME BE MISUNDERSTOOD [A] — SANTA ESMERALDA and Leroy GOMEZ
DON'T LET ME BE MISUNDERSTOOD [A] — Elvis COSTELLO
DON'T LET ME BE MISUNDERSTOOD [A] — Joe COCKER
DON'T LET ME BE THE LAST TO KNOW — Britney SPEARS
DON'T LET ME DOWN [A] — The FARM
DON'T LET ME DOWN [B] — Will YOUNG
DON'T LET ME DOWN GENTLY — The WONDER STUFF
DON'T LET ME GET ME — PINK
DON'T LET NOBODY HOLD YOU DOWN — LJ REYNOLDS

DON'T LET THE FEELING GO —
NIGHTCRAWLERS featuring John REID
DON'T LET THE RAIN COME DOWN —
Ronnie HILTON
DON'T LET THE STARS GET IN YOUR EYES —
Perry COMO with the RAMBLERS
DON'T LET THE SUN CATCH YOU CRYING —
GERRY and the PACEMAKERS
DON'T LET THE SUN GO DOWN ON ME [A] —
Elton JOHN
DON'T LET THE SUN GO DOWN ON ME [A] —
Oleta ADAMS
DON'T LET THE SUN GO DOWN ON ME [A] —
George MICHAEL and Elton JOHN
DON'T LET THIS MOMENT END —
Gloria ESTEFAN
DON'T LIE — SINCLAIR
DON'T LOOK ANY FURTHER [A] — Dennis EDWARDS
featuring Siedah GARRETT
DON'T LOOK ANY FURTHER [A] — KANE GANG
DON'T LOOK ANY FURTHER [A] — M PEOPLE
DON'T LOOK AT ME THAT WAY — Chaka KHAN
DON'T LOOK BACK [A] — BOSTON
DON'T LOOK BACK [B] —
FINE YOUNG CANNIBALS
DON'T LOOK BACK [C] — Lloyd COLE
DON'T LOOK BACK IN ANGER [A] — OASIS
DON'T LOOK BACK IN ANGER [A] — WURZELS
DON'T LOOK BACK INTO THE SUN —
The LIBERTINES
DON'T LOOK DOWN — PLANETS
DON'T LOOK DOWN [B] —
Mick RONSON with Joe ELLIOTT
DON'T LOOK DOWN — THE SEQUEL — GO WEST
DON'T LOSE THE MAGIC —
Shawn CHRISTOPHER
DON'T LOSE YOUR TEMPER — XTC
DON'T LOVE ME TOO HARD — The NOLANS
DON'T MAKE ME (FALL IN LOVE WITH YOU) —
Babbity BLUE
DON'T MAKE ME OVER [A] —
SWINGING BLUE JEANS
DON'T MAKE ME OVER [A] — SYBIL
DON'T MAKE ME WAIT [A] — PEECH BOYS
DON'T MAKE ME WAIT [B] — LOVELAND
featuring the voice of Rachel McFARLANE
DON'T MAKE ME WAIT [C] — 911
DON'T MAKE ME WAIT [A] — BOMB THE BASS
DON'T MAKE ME WAIT TOO LONG [A] —
Barry WHITE
DON'T MAKE ME WAIT TOO LONG [B] —
Roberta FLACK
DON'T MAKE MY BABY BLUE —
The SHADOWS
DON'T MAKE WAVES — The NOLANS
DON'T MARRY HER — The BEAUTIFUL SOUTH
DON'T MESS WITH DOCTOR DREAM —
THOMPSON TWINS
DON'T MESS WITH MY MAN [A] —
LUCY PEARL
DON'T MESS WITH MY MAN [B] — NIVEA
DON'T MESS WITH THE RADIO — NIVEA
DON'T MISS THE PARTYLINE — BIZZ NIZZ
DON'T MUG YOURSELF — The STREETS
DON'T NEED A GUN — Billy IDOL
DON'T NEED THE SUN TO SHINE
(TO MAKE ME SMILE) — GABRIELLE
DON'T PANIC [A] — LIQUID GOLD
DON'T PANIC [B] —
LOGO featuring Dawn JOSEPH
DON'T PAY THE FERRYMAN — Chris DE BURGH
DON'T PLAY THAT SONG — Aretha FRANKLIN
DON'T PLAY THAT SONG AGAIN —
Nicki FRENCH
DON'T PLAY WITH ME — ROZALLA
DON'T PLAY YOUR ROCK 'N ROLL TO ME —
SMOKIE
DON'T PULL YOUR LOVE — Sean MAGUIRE
DON'T PUSH IT — Ruth JOY
DON'T PUSH IT DON'T FORCE IT —
Leon HAYWOOD
DON'T PUT YOUR SPELL ON ME —
Ian McNABB
DON'T QUIT — Caron WHEELER
DON'T RUSH (TAKE LOVE SLOWLY) —
K-CI & JOJO
DON'T SAY GOODBYE — Paulina RUBIO
DON'T SAY I TOLD YOU SO — TOURISTS
DON'T SAY IT'S LOVE — JOHNNY HATES JAZZ
DON'T SAY IT'S OVER — GUN
DON'T SAY THAT'S JUST FOR WHITE BOYS —
WAY OF THE WEST
DON'T SAY YOU LOVE MEME — M2M
DON'T SAY YOUR LOVE IS KILLING ME —
ERASURE
DON'T SET ME FREE — Ray CHARLES
DON'T SHED A TEAR — Paul CARRACK
DON'T SING — PREFAB SPROUT
DON'T SLEEP IN THE SUBWAY — Petula CLARK
DON'T SLOW DOWN — UB40
DON'T SPEAK [A] — NO DOUBT
DON'T SPEAK [A] — CLUELESS
DON'T STAND SO CLOSE TO ME — The POLICE
DON'T STAY AWAY TOO LONG —
PETERS and LEE
DON'T STEAL OUR SUN — The THRILLS
DON'T STOP [A] — FLEETWOOD MAC

DON'T STOP [A] — STATUS QUO
DON'T STOP [B] — K.I.D.
DON'T STOP [C] — MOOD
DON'T STOP [D] — Jeffrey OSBORNE
DON'T STOP [E] — K-KLASS
DON'T STOP [F] — HAMMER
DON'T STOP [G] — RUFF DRIVERZ
DON'T STOP [H] — NO AUTHORITY
DON'T STOP [I] — ATB
DON'T STOP [J] — The ROLLING STONES
DON'T STOP BELIEVIN' — JOURNEY
DON'T STOP (FUNKIN' 4 JAMAICA) —
Mariah CAREY
DON'T STOP IT NOW — HOT CHOCOLATE
DON'T STOP (JAMMIN') — LA MIX
DON'T STOP LOVIN' ME BABY —
PINKERTON'S ASSORTED COLOURS
DON'T STOP ME NOW — QUEEN
DON'T STOP MOVIN' [A] — LIVIN' JOY
DON'T STOP MOVIN' [B] — S CLUB 7
DON'T STOP NOW —
Gene FARROW and GF BAND
DON'T STOP THAT CRAZY RHYTHM —
MODERN ROMANCE
DON'T STOP THE CARNIVAL — Alan PRICE
DON'T STOP THE DANCE — Bryan FERRY
DON'T STOP THE FEELING — Roy AYERS
DON'T STOP THE MUSIC [A] —
YARBROUGH and PEOPLES
DON'T STOP THE MUSIC [B] — Lionel RICHIE
DON'T STOP 'TIL YOU GET ENOUGH —
Michael JACKSON
DON'T STOP TWIST — Frankie VAUGHAN
DON'T STOP (WIGGLE WIGGLE) —
The OUTHERE BROTHERS
DON'T TAKE AWAY THE MUSIC — TAVARES
DON'T TAKE IT LYIN' DOWN — The DOOLEYS
DON'T TAKE IT PERSONAL — Jermaine JACKSON
DON'T TAKE IT PERSONAL (JUST ONE OF
DEM DAYS) — MONICA
DON'T TAKE MY KINDNESS FOR WEAKNESS —
HEADS with Shaun RYDER
DON'T TAKE MY MIND ON A TRIP —
BOY GEORGE
DON'T TAKE NO FOR AN ANSWER —
Tom ROBINSON
DON'T TALK [A] — Hank MARVIN
DON'T TALK [B] — Jon B
DON'T TALK ABOUT LOVE — BAD BOYS INC
DON'T TALK DIRTY TO ME —
Jermaine STEWART
DON'T TALK JUST KISS — RIGHT SAID FRED
Guest vocals: Jocelyn BROWN
DON'T TALK TO HIM —
Cliff RICHARD and The SHADOWS
DON'T TALK TO ME ABOUT LOVE —
ALTERED IMAGES
DON'T TELL ME [A] — CENTRAL LINE
DON'T TELL ME [B] — BLANCMANGE
DON'T TELL ME [C] — VAN HALEN
DON'T TELL ME [D] — MADONNA
DON'T TELL ME [E] — Avril LAVIGNE
DON'T TELL ME LIES — BREATHE
DON'T TELL ME YOU'RE SORRY — S CLUB 8
DON'T TEST — Junior TUCKER
DON'T THAT BEAT ALL — Adam FAITH
DON'T THINK I'M NOT — KANDI
DON'T THINK IT (FEEL IT) —
LANGE featuring LEAH
DON'T THINK THE WAY THEY DO — SPAN
DON'T THINK YOU'RE THE FIRST — The CORAL
DON'T THROW AWAY ALL THOSE TEARDROPS —
Frankie AVALON
DON'T THROW IT ALL AWAY — Gary BENSON
DON'T THROW YOUR LOVE AWAY —
The SEARCHERS
DON'T TREAT ME BAD — FIREHOUSE
DON'T TREAT ME LIKE A CHILD —
Helen SHAPIRO
DON'T TRY TO CHANGE ME — The CRICKETS
DON'T TRY TO STOP IT — ROMAN HOLLIDAY
DON'T TURN AROUND [A] —
The MERSEYBEATS
DON'T TURN AROUND [B] — ASWAD
DON'T TURN AROUND [B] — ACE OF BASE
DON'T WAIT UP — THUNDER
DON'T WALK [A] — MY LIFE STORY
DON'T WALK [B] — BIG SUPREME
DON'T WALK AWAY [A] —
ELECTRIC LIGHT ORCHESTRA
DON'T WALK AWAY [B] — The FOUR TOPS
DON'T WALK AWAY [C] — Pat BENATAR
DON'T WALK AWAY [D] — Toni CHILDS
DON'T WALK AWAY [E] — JADE
DON'T WALK AWAY [E] — JAVINE
DON'T WALK AWAY TILL I TOUCH YOU —
Elaine PAIGE
DON'T WANNA BE A PLAYER — JOE
DON'T WANNA BE ALONE — Tricia PENROSE
DON'T WANNA FALL IN LOVE — Jane CHILD
DON'T WANNA KNOW — SHY FX & T-POWER featuring
DI and MC SKIBADEE
DON'T WANNA LET YOU GO — FIVE
DON'T WANNA LOSE THIS FEELING —
Dannii MINOGUE
DON'T WANNA LOSE YOU [A] —
Gloria ESTEFAN

DON'T WANNA LOSE YOU [B] — Lionel RICHIE
DON'T WANNA SAY GOODNIGHT — KANDIDATE
DON'T WANT TO FORGIVE ME NOW —
WET WET WET
DON'T WANT TO WAIT ANYMORE — TUBES
DON'T WANT YOU BACK — Ellie CAMPBELL
DON'T WASTE MY TIME — Paul HARDCASTLE
DON'T WASTE YOUR TIME —
YARBROUGH and PEOPLES
DON'T WORRY [A] — Johnny BRANDON
DON'T WORRY [B] — Billy FURY
DON'T WORRY [C] — Kim APPLEBY
DON'T WORRY [D] — NEWTON
DON'T WORRY [E] — APPLETON
DON'T WORRY BABY — LOS LOBOS
DON'T WORRY BE HAPPY — Bobby McFERRIN
DON'T YOU — SECOND IMAGE
DON'T YOU (FORGET ABOUT ME) [A] —
SIMPLE MINDS
DON'T YOU FORGET ABOUT ME [A] —
BEST COMPANY
DON'T YOU GET SO MAD — Jeffrey OSBORNE
DON'T YOU JUST KNOW IT — AMAZULU
DON'T YOU KNOW — BUTTERSCOTCH
DON'T YOU KNOW IT — Adam FAITH
DON'T YOU LOVE ME [A] — 49ers
DON'T YOU LOVE ME [B] — ETERNAL
DON'T YOU ROCK ME DADDY-O [A] —
Lonnie DONEGAN
DON'T YOU ROCK ME DADDY-O [A] —
VIPERS SKIFFLE GROUP
DON'T YOU THINK IT'S TIME — Mike BERRY
DON'T YOU WANT ME [A] — HUMAN LEAGUE
DON'T YOU WANT ME BABY [A] —
Mandy SMITH
DON'T YOU WANT ME [A] — The FARM
DON'T YOU WANT ME [B] — Jody WATLEY
DON'T YOU WANT ME [C] — FELIX
DON'T YOU WORRY — MADASUN
DON'T YOU WORRY 'BOUT A THING —
INCOGNITO
DOO WOP (THAT THING) — Lauryn HILL
DOOBEDOOD'NDOOBE DOOBEDOOD'NDOOBE —
Diana ROSS
DOODAH! — CARTOONS
DOOMS NIGHT — Azzido DA BASS
DOOMSDAY — Evelyn THOMAS
DOOP — DOOP
THE DOOR — TURIN BRAKES
THE DOOR IS STILL OPEN TO MY HEART —
Dean MARTIN
DOOR #1 — LEVERT SWEAT GILL
DOORS OF YOUR HEART — The BEAT
DOOT DOOT — FREUR
THE DOPE SHOW — MARILYN MANSON
DOPES TO INFINITY — MONSTER MAGNET
DOUBLE BARREL — Dave and Ansil COLLINS
DOUBLE DOUBLE DUTCH — DOPE SMUGGLAZ
DOUBLE DROP — FIERCE GIRL
DOUBLE DUTCH [A] — FATBACK BAND
DOUBLE DUTCH [B] — Malcolm McLAREN
DOUBLEBACK — ZZ TOP
DOVE (I'LL BE LOVING YOU) — MOONY
DOVE L'AMORE — CHER
DOWN — BLINK-182
DOWN AND UNDER (TOGETHER) —
KID CRÈME featuring MC SHURAKANO
DOWN AT THE DOCTORS — DR FEELGOOD
DOWN BOY — Holly VALANCE
DOWN BY THE LAZY RIVER — The OSMONDS
DOWN BY THE WATER — P J HARVEY
DOWN DEEP INSIDE (THEME FROM 'THE
DEEP') — Donna SUMMER
DOWN DOWN — STATUS QUO
DOWN DOWN DOWN — GAMBAFREAKS
DOWN FOR THE ONE — Beverley KNIGHT
DOWN 4 U — Irv GOTTI presents JA RULE, ASHANTI,
Charli BALTIMORE & VITA
DOWN 4 WHATEVA — NUTTIN' NYCE
DOWN IN A HOLE — ALICE IN CHAINS
DOWN IN THE BOONDOCKS — Billy Joe ROYAL
DOWN IN THE SUBWAY — SOFT CELL
DOWN IN THE TUBE STATION AT MIDNIGHT — The JAM
DOWN LOW (NOBODY HAS TO KNOW) — R KELLY
DOWN ON THE BEACH TONIGHT — The DRIFTERS
DOWN ON THE CORNER —
CREEDENCE CLEARWATER REVIVAL
DOWN ON THE STREET — SHAKATAK
DOWN SO LONG — JEWEL
DOWN THAT ROAD — Shara NELSON
DOWN THE DRAIN — STAKKA BO
DOWN THE DUSTPIPE — STATUS QUO
DOWN THE HALL — The FOUR SEASONS
DOWN THE RIVER NILE — John LEYTON
DOWN THE WIRE — ASAP
DOWN TO EARTH [A] — CURIOSITY
DOWN TO EARTH [B] — Monie LOVE
DOWN TO EARTH [C] — GRACE
DOWN TO THE SEA — TIM BOOTH
DOWN TO THE WIRE — GHOST DANCE
DOWN UNDER — MEN AT WORK
DOWN WITH THE CLIQUE — AALIYAH
DOWN WITH THE KING — RUN-DMC
DOWN YONDER —
JOHNNY and the HURRICANES
DOWNHEARTED — Eddie FISHER
DOWNLOAD IT — CLEA

DOWNTOWN [A] — Petula CLARK
DOWNTOWN [B] — ONE 2 MANY
DOWNTOWN [C] — SWV
THE DOWNTOWN LIGHTS — BLUE NILE
DOWNTOWN TRAIN — Rod STEWART
DOWNTOWN VENUS — PM DAWN
DRACULA'S TANGO — TOTO COELO
DRAG ME DOWN — The BOOMTOWN RATS
DRAGGING ME DOWN — INSPIRAL CARPETS
DRAGNET [A] —
Ray ANTHONY and his ORCHESTRA
DRAGNET [A] — Ted HEATH
DRAGNET [A] — ART OF NOISE
DRAGON POWER — JKD BAND
DRAGONFLY — TORNADOS
DRAGOSTEA DIN TEI — O-ZONE
DRAGULA — Rob ZOMBIE
DRAIN THE BLOOD — The DISTILLERS
DRAMA! — ERASURE
DRAW OF THE CARDS — Kim CARNES
(DRAWING) RINGS AROUND THE WORLD —
SUPER FURRY ANIMALS
DRE DAY — DR DRE
DREADLOCK HOLIDAY — 10cc
DREAM — DIZZEE RASCAL
THE DREAM — DREAM FREQUENCY
DREAM A LIE — UB40
DREAM A LITTLE DREAM OF ME [A] —
Anita HARRIS
DREAM A LITTLE DREAM OF ME [A] —
MAMA CASS
DREAM ABOUT YOU — D'BORA
DREAM ANOTHER DREAM — RIALTO
DREAM BABY [A] — Roy ORBISON
DREAM BABY (HOW LONG MUST I DREAM) [A] —
Glen CAMPBELL
DREAM COME TRUE —
The BRAND NEW HEAVIES
DREAM GIRL — Mark WYNTER
DREAM KITCHEN — FRAZIER CHORUS
DREAM LOVER — Bobby DARIN
DREAM OF ME (BASED ON LOVE'S THEME) —
ORCHESTRAL MANOEUVRES IN THE DARK
DREAM OF OLWEN — SECOND CITY SOUND
DREAM ON — DEPECHE MODE
DREAM ON DREAMER —
The BRAND NEW HEAVIES
DREAM ON (IS THIS A DREAM) —
LOVE DECADE
DREAM SEQUENCE (ONE) — Pauline
MURRAY and the INVISIBLE GIRLS
DREAM SOME PARADISE — INTASTELLA
DREAM SWEET DREAMS — AZTEC CAMERA
DREAM TO ME — Dario G
DREAM TO SLEEP — H 20
DREAM UNIVERSE — DJ GARRY
DREAMBOAT [A] — Alma COGAN
DREAMBOAT [B] —
LIMMIE and the FAMILY COOKIN'
DREAMER [A] — SUPERTRAMP
DREAMER [A] — CK & SUPREME DREAM TEAM
DREAMER [B] — The JACKSONS
DREAMER [C] — COLDCUT
DREAMER [D] — LIVIN' JOY
DREAMER [E] — Ozzy OSBOURNE
THE DREAMER — ALL ABOUT EVE
DREAMIN' [A] — Johnny BURNETTE
DREAMIN' [B] — LIVERPOOL EXPRESS
DREAMIN' [C] — Cliff RICHARD
DREAMIN' [D] — STATUS QUO
DREAMIN' [E] — Vanessa WILLIAMS
DREAMIN' [F] — Loleatta HOLLOWAY
DREAMIN' [G] — AMP FIDDLER
DREAMING [A] — BLONDIE
DREAMING [B] — ORCHESTRAL
MANOEUVRES IN THE DARK
DREAMING [C] — Glen GOLDSMITH
DREAMING [D] — MN8
DREAMING [E] — RUFF DRIVERZ
DREAMING [F] — M PEOPLE
DREAMING [G] — BT
DREAMING [H] — AURORA
DREAMING [I] —
I DREAM featuring FRANKIE & CALVIN
THE DREAMING — Kate BUSH
DREAMING OF ME — DEPECHE MODE
DREAMING OF YOU [A] — THRILLSEEKERS
DREAMING OF YOU [B] — The CORAL
DREAMLOVER — Mariah CAREY
DREAMS [A] — FLEETWOOD MAC
DREAMS [A] — WILD COLOUR
DREAMS [A] — The CORRS
DREAMS [B] — Grace SLICK
DREAMS [C] — VAN HALEN
DREAMS [D] — GABRIELLE
DREAMS [E] — The CRANBERRIES
DREAMS [G] — QUENCH
DREAMS [F] —
SMOKIN BEATS featuring Lyn EDEN
DREAMS [H] — MISS SHIVA
DREAMS [I] — KINGS OF TOMORROW
A DREAM'S A DREAM — SOUL II SOUL
DREAMS CAN TELL A LIE — Nat 'King' COLE
THE DREAMS I DREAM — The SHADOWS
DREAMS OF CHILDREN — The JAM
DREAMS OF HEAVEN — GROUND LEVEL

DREAMS OF YOU — Ralph McTELL
DREAMS TO REMEMBER — Robert PALMER
DREAMSCAPE '94 — TIME FREQUENCY
DREAMTIME [A] — Daryl HALL
DREAMTIME [B] — ZEE
DREAMY DAYS — Roots MANUVA
DREAMY LADY — T. REX
DRED BASS — DEAD DRED
DRESS YOU UP — MADONNA
DRESSED FOR SUCCESS — ROXETTE
DRIFT AWAY — Michael BOLTON
DRIFTING [A] —
   Sheila WALSH and Cliff RICHARD
DRIFTING [B] —
   MOJOLATORS featuring CAMILLA
DRIFTING AWAY — LANGE featuring SKYE
DRIFTWOOD — TRAVIS
THE DRILL — DIRT DEVILS
DRINK THE ELIXIR — SALAD
DRINK UP THY ZIDER — WURZELS
DRINKING IN L.A. — BRAN VAN 3000
DRINKING SONG — Mario LANZA
DRIP FED FRED —
   Ian DURY and the BLOCKHEADS
DRIVE [A] — The CARS
DRIVE [B] — R.E.M.
DRIVE [C] — Geoffrey WILLIAMS
DRIVE [D] — INCUBUS
DRIVE-IN SATURDAY (SEATTLE — PHOENIX) —
   David BOWIE
DRIVE ME CRAZY — PARTIZAN
DRIVE ON — BROTHER BEYOND
DRIVE SAFELY DARLIN' — Tony CHRISTIE
DRIVEN BY YOU — Brian MAY
DRIVER'S SEAT — SNIFF 'N' THE TEARS
DRIVIN' HOME — Duane EDDY and the REBELS
DRIVING — EVERYTHING BUT THE GIRL
DRIVING AWAY FROM HOME (JIM'S TUNE) —
   IT'S IMMATERIAL
DRIVING HOME FOR CHRISTMAS (EP) —
   Chris REA
DRIVING IN MY CAR [A] — MADNESS
DRIVING IN MY CAR [A] — Maureen REES
DRIVING WITH THE BRAKES ON — DEL AMITRI
DROP DEAD GORGEOUS — REPUBLICA
DROP IT LIKE IT'S HOT —
   SNOOP DOGG featuring PHARRELL
DROP SOME DRUMS — [LOVE] TATTOO
DROP THE BOY — BROS
DROP THE PILOT — Joan ARMATRADING
DROP THE PRESSURE — MYLO
DROP THE ROCK (EP) — D-TEK
DROPS OF JUPITER (TELL ME) — TRAIN
DROWNED WORLD (SUBSTITUTE FOR LOVE) —
   MADONNA
THE DROWNERS — SUEDE
DROWNING [A] — The BEAT
DROWNING [B] — BACKSTREET BOYS
DROWNING [C] — CRAZY TOWN
DROWNING IN BERLIN — The MOBILES
DROWNING IN THE SEA OF LOVE —
   ADVENTURES
DROWSY WITH HOPE — SHAKEDOWN
THE DRUGS DON'T WORK — The VERVE
DRUMBEATS — SL2
DRUMMER MAN — TONIGHT
DRUMMIN' UP A STORM — Sandy NELSON
DRUMS ARE MY BEAT — Sandy NELSON
THE DRUMSTRUCK (EP) — N-JOI
DRUNK ON LOVE — BASIA
DRUNKARD LOGIC — FAT LADY SINGS
DRUNKEN FOOL — BURN
DRUNKEN STARS — Mampi SWIFT
DRY COUNTY [A] — BLACKFOOT
DRY COUNTY [B] — BON JOVI
DRY LAND — MARILLION
DRY RISER — KERBDOG
DRY YOUR EYES — The STREETS
DUALITY — SLIPKNOT
DUB BE GOOD TO ME — BEATS
   INTERNATIONAL featuring Lindy LAYTON
DUB WAR — DANCE CONSPIRACY
DUBPLATE CULTURE — SOUNDSCAPE
DUCHESS [A] — The STRANGLERS
DUCHESS [A] — MY LIFE STORY
DUCHESS [B] — GENESIS
DUCK FOR THE OYSTER — Malcolm McLAREN
DUCK TOY — HAMPENBERG
DUDE — BEENIE MAN featuring MS THING
DUDE DESCENDING A STAIRCASE — APOLLO FOUR
   FORTY featuring The BEATNUTS
DUDE (LOOKS LIKE A LADY) — AEROSMITH
DUEL [A] — PROPAGANDA
DUEL [B] — SWERVEDRIVER
DUELLING BANJOS —
   'DELIVERANCE' SOUNDTRACK
DUI — HAR MAR SUPERSTAR
DUKE OF EARL — DARTS
DUM DUM — Brenda LEE
DUM DUM GIRL — TALK TALK
DUMB [A] — The BEAUTIFUL SOUTH
DUMB [B] — The 411
DUMB WAITERS — PSYCHEDELIC FURS
DUMMY CRUSHER — KERBDOG
DUNE BUGGY — PRESIDENTS OF THE
   UNITED STATES OF AMERICA
DUNE SEA — UNBELIEVABLE TRUTH

DUNNO WHAT IT IS (ABOUT YOU) —
   BEATMASTERS
DURHAM TOWN (THE LEAVIN') —
   Roger WHITTAKER
DUSK TIL DAWN — Danny HOWELLS &
   Dick TREVOR featuring ERIRE
DUSTED — LEFTFIELD
DW WASHBURN — The MONKEES
D'YA WANNA GO FASTER — TERRORVISION
DYNAMITE [A] —
   Cliff RICHARD and The SHADOWS
DYNAMITE [B] — Stacy LATTISAW
DYNA-MITE [C] — MUD
DY-NA-MI-TEE — MS DYNAMITE
DYNOMITE (PART 1) —
   Tony CAMILLO'S BAZUKA
D'YOU KNOW WHAT I MEAN? — OASIS
E — DRUNKEN MUNKY
E=MC2 — BIG AUDIO DYNAMITE
E SAMBA — JUNIOR JACK
EACH AND EVERY ONE —
   EVERYTHING BUT THE GIRL
EACH TIME — EAST 17
EACH TIME YOU BREAK MY HEART —
   Nick KAMEN
EARDRUM BUZZ — WIRE
EARLY IN THE MORNING [A] — Buddy HOLLY
EARLY IN THE MORNING [B] — VANITY FARE
EARLY IN THE MORNING [C] — GAP BAND
EARLY TO BED — PONI-TAILS
EARTH ANGEL [A] — The CREW CUTS
EARTH ANGEL [B] — DREADZONE
THE EARTH DIES SCREAMING — UB40
EARTH SONG — Michael JACKSON
EARTHBOUND — Conner REEVES
EARTHSHAKER —
   Paul MASTERSON presents SUSHI
EASE MY MIND — ARRESTED DEVELOPMENT
EASE ON BY — BASS-O-MATIC
EASE ON DOWN THE ROAD —
   Diana ROSS and Michael JACKSON
EASE THE PRESSURE [A] — 2WO THIRD3
EASE THE PRESSURE [B] — The BELOVED
EASE YOUR MIND — GALLIANO
EASIER SAID THAN DONE [A] — ESSEX
EASIER SAID THAN DONE [B] — SHAKATAK
EASIER SAID THAN DONE [C] — STARGATE
EASIER TO LIE — AQUALUNG
EASIER TO WALK AWAY — Elton JOHN
EAST COAST / WEST COAST KILLAS —
   GROUP THERAPY
EAST EASY RIDER — Julian COPE
EAST OF EDEN — BIG COUNTRY
EAST RIVER — BRECKER BROTHERS
EAST WEST — HERMAN'S HERMITS
EASTER — MARILLION
EASY [A] — The COMMODORES
EASY [B] — LOUD
EASY [C] — TERRORVISION
EASY [D] — Emiliana TORRINI
EASY [E] — GROOVE ARMADA
EASY COME EASY GO —
   SUTHERLAND BROTHERS and QUIVER
EASY EASY — SCOTLAND WORLD CUP SQUAD
EASY GOING ME — Adam FAITH
EASY LADY — SPAGNA
EASY LIFE [A] — BODYSNATCHERS
EASY LIFE [B] — CABARET VOLTAIRE
EASY LIVIN' — FASTWAY
EASY LOVER —
   Philip BAILEY (duet with Phil COLLINS)
EASY RIDER — RAIN BAND
EASY TO SMILE — SENSELESS THINGS
EAT IT — Weird Al YANKOVIC
EAT ME DRINK ME LOVE ME —
   POP WILL EAT ITSELF
EAT MY GOAL — COLLAPSED LUNG
EAT THE RICH — AEROSMITH
EAT YOU ALIVE — LIMP BIZKIT
EAT YOUR HEART OUT — Paul HARDCASTLE
EAT YOURSELF WHOLE — KINGMAKER
EATEN ALIVE — Diana ROSS
EATING ME ALIVE —
   Diana BROWN and Barrie K SHARPE
EBB TIDE [A] — Frank CHACKSFIELD
EBB TIDE [A] — RIGHTEOUS BROTHERS
EBENEEZER GOODE — The SHAMEN
EBONY AND IVORY —
   Paul McCARTNEY with Stevie WONDER
EBONY EYES — The EVERLY BROTHERS
E-BOW THE LETTER — R.E.M.
ECHO BEACH [A] — MARTHA and the MUFFINS
ECHO BEACH [A] — TOYAH
ECHO CHAMBER — BEATS INTERNATIONAL
ECHO MY HEART — Lindy LAYTON
ECHO ON MY MIND PART II — EARTHLING
ECHOES IN A SHALLOW BAY (EP) —
   COCTEAU TWINS
ECUADOR — SASH!
ED'S FUNKY DINER (FRIDAY NIGHT, SATURDAY
   MORNING) — IT'S IMMATERIAL
EDDY VORTEX — Steve GIBBONS BAND
EDELWEISS — Vince HILL
EDEN — Sarah BRIGHTMAN
EDGE OF A BROKEN HEART — VIXEN
EDGE OF DARKNESS — Eric CLAPTON
THE EDGE OF HEAVEN — WHAM!

EDIE (CIAO BABY) — The CULT
EENY MEENY — SHOWSTOPPERS
EGG RUSH — FLOWERED UP
EGO — Elton JOHN
EGYPTIAN REGGAE — Jonathan
   RICHMAN and the MODERN LOVERS
EI — NELLY
EIGHT BY TEN — Ken DODD
8 DAYS A WEEK — SWEET FEMALE ATTITUDE
EIGHT MILES HIGH — The BYRDS
18 AND LIFE — SKID ROW
18 CARAT LOVE AFFAIR — ASSOCIATES
EIGHTEEN STRINGS — TINMAN
18 TIL I DIE — Bryan ADAMS
EIGHTEEN WITH A BULLET — Pete WINGFIELD
EIGHTEEN YELLOW ROSES — Bobby DARIN
EIGHTH DAY — Hazel O'CONNOR
8TH WORLD WONDER — Kimberley LOCKE
808 — BLAQUE IVORY
EIGHTIES — KILLING JOKE
80S ROMANCE — BELLE STARS
86'D — SUBCIRCUS
EINSTEIN A GO-GO — LANDSCAPE
EL BIMBO — BIMBO JET
EL CAMINOS IN THE WEST — GRANDADDY
EL CAPITAN — OPM
EL LUTE — BONEY M
EL NINO — AGNELLI & NELSON
EL PARAISO RICO — DEETAH
EL PASO — Marty ROBBINS
EL PRESIDENT — DRUGSTORE
EL SALVADOR — ATHLETE
EL SCORCHO — WEEZER
EL TRAGO (THE DRINK) — 2 IN A ROOM
EL VINO COLLAPSO — BLACK LACE
ELDORADO — DRUM THEATRE
ELEANOR RIGBY [A] — The BEATLES
ELEANOR RIGBY [A] — Ray CHARLES
ELECTED — Alice COOPER
ELECTION DAY — ARCADIA
ELECTRIC AVENUE — Eddy GRANT
ELECTRIC BARBARELLA — DURAN DURAN
ELECTRIC BLUE — ICEHOUSE
ELECTRIC BOOGALOO — OLLIE and JERRY
ELECTRIC GUITAR — FLUKE
ELECTRIC GUITARS — PREFAB SPROUT
ELECTRIC HEAD PART 2 (THE ECSTASY) —
   WHITE ZOMBIE
ELECTRIC LADY — GEORDIE
ELECTRIC MAINLINE — SPIRITUALIZED
ELECTRIC MAN — MANSUN
ELECTRIC TRAINS — SQUEEZE
ELECTRIC YOUTH — Debbie GIBSON
ELECTRICAL STORM — U2
ELECTRICITY [A] — SPIRITUALIZED
ELECTRICITY [B] — SUEDE
ELECTROLITE — R.E.M.
ELECTRONIC PLEASURE — N-TRANCE
ELEGANTLY AMERICAN: ONE NIGHT IN HEAVEN —
   M PEOPLE
ELEGANTLY WASTED — INXS
ELEKTROBANK — The CHEMICAL BROTHERS
ELEMENTS — NEO CORTEX
ELENI — TOL and TOL
ELENORE — The TURTLES
ELEPHANT PAW (GET DOWN TO THE FUNK) —
   PAN POSITION
ELEPHANT STONE — The STONE ROSES
ELEPHANT TANGO —
   Cyril STAPLETON and his ORCHESTRA
THE ELEPHANT'S GRAVEYARD (GUILTY) —
   The BOOMTOWN RATS
ELEVATE MY MIND — STEREO MC's
ELEVATION [A] — XPANSIONS
ELEVATION (MOVE YOUR BODY) 2002 [A] —
   XPANSIONS
ELEVATION [B] — GTO
ELEVATION [C] — U2
ELEVATION [D] — The OPEN
ELEVATOR SONG — DUBSTAR
ELEVEN TO FLY — TIN TIN OUT
ELISABETH SERENADE —
   Günter KALLMAN CHOIR
ELIZABETHAN REGGAE — Boris GARDINER
ELLE — DJ GREGORY
ELMO JAMES — CHAIRMEN OF THE BOARD
ELO (EP) — ELECTRIC LIGHT ORCHESTRA
ELOISE [A] — Barry RYAN
ELOISE [B] — The DAMNED
ELSTREE — BUGGLES
ELUSIVE BUTTERFLY [A] — Bob LIND
ELUSIVE BUTTERFLY [A] — Val DOONICAN
THE ELVIS MEDLEY — Elvis PRESLEY
EMBARRASSMENT — MADNESS
EMBRACE — AGNELLI & NELSON
EMBRACING THE SUNSHINE — BT
EMERALD CITY — The SEEKERS
EMERGE — FISCHERSPOONER
EMERGENCY — KOOL and the GANG
EMERGENCY (DIAL 999) — LOOSE ENDS
EMERGENCY ON PLANET EARTH —
   JAMIROQUAI
EMILY — BOWLING FOR SOUP
EMMA — HOT CHOCOLATE
EMOTIONAL CONTENT — FUNK D'VOID
EMOTIONAL RESCUE — The ROLLING STONES
EMOTIONAL TIME — HOTHOUSE FLOWERS

EMOTION [A] — Samantha SANG
EMOTION [A] — DESTINY'S CHILD
EMOTIONS [A] — Brenda LEE
EMOTIONS [B] — Mariah CAREY
THE EMPEROR'S NEW CLOTHES —
   Sinead O'CONNOR
EMPIRE — QUEENSRYCHE
EMPIRE LINE — MY LIFE STORY
EMPIRE SONG — KILLING JOKE
EMPIRE STATE HUMAN — HUMAN LEAGUE
EMPTY AT THE END —
   The ELECTRIC SOFT PARADE
EMPTY GARDEN — Elton JOHN
EMPTY ROOMS — Gary MOORE
EMPTY SKIES — KOSHEEN
EMPTY WORLD — DOGS D'AMOUR
ENCHANTED LADY — PASADENAS
ENCORE [A] — Cheryl LYNN
ENCORE [B] — TONGUE 'N' CHEEK
ENCORE UNE FOIS — SASH!
ENCORES (EP) — DIRE STRAITS
THE END HAS NO END — The STROKES
THE END IS THE BEGINNING IS THE END — SMASHING
   PUMPKINS
END OF A CENTURY — BLUR
THE END OF THE INNOCENCE — Don HENLEY
END OF THE LINE [A] — TRAVELING WILBURYS
END OF THE LINE [B] — HONEYZ
END OF THE ROAD — BOYZ II MEN
END OF THE WORLD [A] — Skeeter DAVIS
END OF THE WORLD [A] — SONIA
THE END OF THE WORLD [B] — The CURE
THE END ... OR THE BEGINNING —
   CLASSIX NOUVEAUX
ENDLESS — Dickie VALENTINE
ENDLESS ART — A HOUSE
ENDLESS LOVE [A] —
   Diana ROSS and Lionel RICHIE
ENDLESS LOVE [B] —
   Luther VANDROSS and Mariah CAREY
ENDLESS SLEEP [A] — Marty WILDE
ENDLESS SLEEP [B] — Jody REYNOLDS
ENDLESS SUMMER NIGHTS — Richard MARX
ENDLESSLY [A] — Brook BENTON
ENDLESSLY [B] — John FOXX
ENDS — EVERLAST
ENEMIES — HOPE OF THE STATES
ENEMY MAKER — DUB WAR
THE ENEMY WITHIN — THIRST
ENERGIZE — SLAMM
THE ENERGY (FEEL THE VIBE) — ASTRO TRAX
ENERGY FLASH (EP) — BELTRAM
ENERGY IS EUROBEAT — MAN TO MAN
ENERVATE — TRANSA
ENGINE ENGINE NO.9 — Roger MILLER
ENGINE NO.9 — MIDNIGHT STAR
ENGLAND CRAZY — RIDER & Terry VENABLES
ENGLAND SWINGS — Roger MILLER
ENGLAND, WE'LL FLY THE FLAG —
   ENGLAND WORLD CUP SQUAD
ENGLAND'S IRIE — BLACK GRAPE featuring
   Joe STRUMMER and Keith ALLEN
ENGLISH CIVIL WAR (JOHNNY COMES
   MARCHING HOME) — The CLASH
ENGLISH COUNTRY GARDEN [A] —
   Jimmie RODGERS
ENGLISH COUNTRY GARDEN [B] — DANDYS
ENGLISH SUMMER RAIN — PLACEBO
ENGLISHMAN IN NEW YORK — STING
ENJOY THE SILENCE — DEPECHE MODE
ENJOY THE SILENCE 04 [A] — DEPECHE MODE
ENJOY YOURSELF [A] — The JACKSONS
ENJOY YOURSELF [B] — A+
ENOLA GAY —
   ORCHESTRAL MANOEUVRES IN THE DARK
ENOUGH IS ENOUGH [A] — CHUMBAWAMBA
   and CREDIT TO THE NATION
ENOUGH IS ENOUGH [B] —
   Y-TRIBE featuring Elisabeth TROY
ENTER SANDMAN — METALLICA
ENTER THE SCENE —
   DJ SUPREME vs the RHYTHM MASTERS
ENTER YOUR FANTASY (EP) — Joey NEGRO
THE ENTERTAINER — Marvin HAMLISCH
ENTRY OF THE GLADIATORS —
   NERO and the GLADIATORS
ENVY — ASH
THE EP — ZERO B
EP THREE — HUNDRED REASONS
EP TWO — HUNDRED REASONS
EPIC — FAITH NO MORE
EPLE — RÖYKSOPP
EQUINOXE PART 5 — Jean-Michel JARRE
EQUINOXE PART V — The SHADOWS
ERASE / REWIND — The CARDIGANS
ERASURE-ISH (A LITTLE RESPECT / STOP!) —
   BJÖRN AGAIN
ERECTION (TAKE IT TO THE TOP) —
   CORTINA featuring BK & MADAM FRICTION
ERNIE (THE FASTEST MILKMAN IN THE WEST) —
   Benny HILL
EROTICA — MADONNA
ESCAPADE — Janet JACKSON
ESCAPE [A] — Gary CLAIL ON-U SOUND SYSTEM
ESCAPE [B] — ENRIQUE
ESCAPE ARTISTS NEVER DIE —
   FUNERAL FOR A FRIEND

ESCAPE (THE PINA COLADA SONG) — Rupert HOLMES
ESCAPING [A] — ASIA BLUE
ESCAPING [A] — Dina CARROLL
E.S.P. — The BEE GEES
ESPECIALLY FOR YOU [A] — Kylie MINOGUE and Jason DONOVAN
ESPECIALLY FOR YOU [A] — DENISE and JOHNNY
THE ESSENTIAL WALLY PARTY MEDLEY — GAY GORDON and the MINCE PIES
ET LES OISEAUX CHANTAIENT (AND THE BIRDS WERE SINGING) — SWEET PEOPLE
ET MÊME — Françoise HARDY
ETERNAL FLAME [A] — The BANGLES
ETERNAL FLAME [A] — ATOMIC KITTEN
ETERNAL LOVE — ANT & DEC
ETERNALLY — Jimmy YOUNG
ETERNITY [A] — ORION
ETERNITY [B] — Robbie WILLIAMS
ETHER RADIO — CHIKINKI
ETHNIC PRAYER — HAVANA
THE ETON RIFLES — The JAM
EUGINA — SALT TANK
EURODISCO — BIS
EUROPA AND THE PIRATE TWINS — Thomas DOLBY
EUROPE (AFTER THE RAIN) — John FOXX
EUROPEAN FEMALE — The STRANGLERS
EUROPEAN SON — JAPAN
EVANGELINE [A] — ICICLE WORKS
EVANGELINE [B] — COCTEAU TWINS
EVAPOR 8 — ALTERN 8
EVE OF DESTRUCTION — Barry McGUIRE
EVE OF THE WAR — Jeff WAYNE
EVE, THE APPLE OF MY EYE — BELL X1
EVEN AFTER ALL — Finley QUAYE
EVEN BETTER THAN THE REAL THING — U2
EVEN FLOW — PEARL JAM
EVEN MORE PARTY POPS — Russ CONWAY
EVEN NOW — Bob SEGER and the SILVER BULLET BAND
EVEN THE BAD TIMES ARE GOOD — The TREMELOES
EVEN THE NIGHTS ARE BETTER — AIR SUPPLY
EVEN THOUGH YOU BROKE MY HEART — GEMINI
EVEN THOUGH YOU'VE GONE — The JACKSONS
EVENING FALLS ... — ENYA
EVENING STAR — JUDAS PRIEST
EVER FALLEN IN LOVE [A] — FINE YOUNG CANNIBALS
EVER FALLEN IN LOVE (WITH SOMEONE YOU SHOULDN'T'VE) [A] — The BUZZCOCKS
EVER REST — MYSTICA
EVER SINCE YOU SAID GOODBYE — Marty WILDE
EVER SO LONELY — MONSOON
EVEREST — SUPERNATURALS
EVERGLADE — L7
EVERGREEN [A] — Hazell DEAN
EVERGREEN [A] — Belle LAWRENCE
EVERGREEN [B] — Will YOUNG
EVERLASTING — Natalie COLE
THE EVERLASTING — MANIC STREET PREACHERS
EVERLASTING LOVE [A] — LOVE AFFAIR
EVERLASTING LOVE [A] — Robert KNIGHT
EVERLASTING LOVE [A] — Rex SMITH and Rachel SWEET
EVERLASTING LOVE [A] — SANDRA
EVERLASTING LOVE [A] — WORLDS APART
EVERLASTING LOVE [A] — Gloria ESTEFAN
EVERLASTING LOVE [A] — CAST FROM CASUALTY
EVERLASTING LOVE [A] — Jamie CULLUM
EVERLASTING LOVE [B] — Howard JONES
EVERLONG — FOO FIGHTERS
EVERLOVIN' — Ricky NELSON
EVERMORE — Ruby MURRAY
EVERY ANGEL — ALL ABOUT EVE
EVERY BEAT OF MY HEART — Rod STEWART
EVERY BEAT OF THE HEART — RAILWAY CHILDREN
EVERY BREATH OF THE WAY — MELANIE
EVERY BREATH YOU TAKE — The POLICE
EVERY DAY — ANTICAPPELLA
EVERY DAY HURTS — SAD CAFE
EVERY DAY I FALL APART — SUPERSTAR
EVERY DAY I LOVE YOU — BOYZONE
EVERY DAY (I LOVE YOU MORE) — Jason DONOVAN
EVERY DAY OF MY LIFE — HOUSE TRAFFIC
EVERY DAY OF THE WEEK — JADE
EVERY DAY SHOULD BE A HOLIDAY — The DANDY WARHOLS
EVERY GIRL AND BOY — SPAGNA
EVERY HEARTBEAT — Amy GRANT
EVERY KINDA PEOPLE [A] — Robert PALMER
EVERY KINDA PEOPLE [A] — MINT JULEPS
EVERY KINDA PEOPLE [A] — Chaka DEMUS and PLIERS
EVERY LITTLE BIT HURTS — Spencer DAVIS GROUP
EVERY LITTLE STEP — Bobby BROWN
EVERY LITTLE TEARDROP — GALLAGHER and LYLE
EVERY LITTLE THING — Jeff LYNNE
EVERY LITTLE THING I DO — SOUL FOR REAL
EVERY LITTLE THING SHE DOES IS MAGIC [A] — The POLICE
EVERY LITTLE THING HE DOES IS MAGIC [A] — Shawn COLVIN
EVERY LITTLE THING SHE DOES IS MAGIC [A] — Chaka DEMUS and PLIERS
EVERY LITTLE TIME [A] — POPPERS presents AURA
EVERY LITTLE TIME [B] — ONYX featuring Gemma J
EVERY LOSER WINS — Nick BERRY
EVERY MAN MUST HAVE A DREAM — LIVERPOOL EXPRESS
EVERY MORNING — SUGAR RAY
EVERY NIGHT — Phoebe SNOW
EVERY NITE'S A SATURDAY NIGHT WITH YOU — The DRIFTERS
EVERY 1'S A WINNER — HOT CHOCOLATE
EVERY OTHER TIME — LYTE FUNKIE ONES
EVERY ROSE HAS ITS THORN — POISON
EVERY SINGLE DAY — DODGY
EVERY TIME — Janet JACKSON
EVERY TIME I FALL — Gina G
EVERY TIME I FALL IN LOVE — UPSIDE DOWN
EVERY TIME YOU TOUCH ME — MOBY
EVERY WHICH WAY BUT LOOSE — Eddie RABBITT
EVERY WOMAN KNOWS — LULU
EVERY WOMAN NEEDS LOVE — STELLA BROWNE
EVERY YEAR EVERY CHRISTMAS — Luther VANDROSS
EVERY YOU EVERY ME — PLACEBO
EVERYBODY [A] — Tommy ROE
EVERYBODY [B] — CAPPELLA
EVERYBODY [C] — ALTERN 8
EVERYBODY [D] — DJ BOBO
EVERYBODY [E] — CLOCK
EVERYBODY [F] — KINKY
EVERYBODY [G] — PROGRESS presents the BOY WUNDA
EVERYBODY [H] — HEAR'SAY
EVERYBODY (ALL OVER) — FPI PROJECT
EVERYBODY (ALL OVER THE WORLD) — FPI PROJECT
EVERYBO DY (BACKSTREET'S BACK) — BACKSTREET BOYS
EVERYBODY BE SOMEBODY — RUFFNECK featuring YAVAHN
EVERYBODY COME DOWN — The DELGADOS
EVERYBODY COME ON (CAN U FEEL IT) — MR REDS vs DJ SKRIBBLE
EVERYBODY CRIES — LIBERTY X
EVERYBODY DANCE [A] — CHIC
EVERYBODY DANCE [A] — EVOLUTION
EVERYBODY DANCE (THE HORN SONG) — Barbara TUCKER
EVERYBODY EVERYBODY — BLACK BOX
(EVERYBODY) GET DANCIN' — BOMBERS
EVERYBODY GET TOGETHER — Dave CLARK FIVE
EVERYBODY GET UP [A] — FIVE
EVERYBODY GET UP [B] — CAPRICCIO
EVERYBODY GETS A SECOND CHANCE — MIKE and the MECHANICS
EVERYBODY GO HOME THE PARTY'S OVER — Clodagh RODGERS
EVERYBODY GONFI-GON — TWO COWBOYS
EVERYBODY HAVE A GOOD TIME — Archie BELL and the DRELLS
EVERYBODY HERE WANTS YOU — Jeff BUCKLEY
EVERYBODY HURTS — R.E.M.
EVERYBODY IN THE PLACE (EP) — The PRODIGY
EVERYBODY IS A STAR — POINTER SISTERS
EVERYBODY KNOWS [A] — Dave CLARK FIVE
EVERYBODY KNOWS [B] — Dave CLARK FIVE
EVERYBODY KNOWS [C] — The FREE ASSOCIATION
EVERYBODY KNOWS (EXCEPT YOU) — The DIVINE COMEDY
EVERYBODY LET'S SOMEBODY LOVE — Frank K featuring Wiston OFFICE
EVERYBODY LOVES A LOVER — Doris DAY
EVERYBODY LOVES SOMEBODY — Dean MARTIN
EVERYBODY MOVE — Cathy DENNIS
EVERYBODY (MOVE YOUR BODY) — DIVA
EVERYBODY MUST PARTY — GEORGIE PORGIE
EVERYBODY NEEDS A 303 — FATBOY SLIM
EVERYBODY NEEDS SOMEBODY [A] — BIRDLAND
EVERYBODY NEEDS SOMEBODY [B] — Nick HOWARD
EVERYBODY NEEDS SOMEBODY TO LOVE — BLUES BROTHERS
EVERYBODY ON THE FLOOR (PUMP IT) — TOKYO GHETTO PUSSY
EVERYBODY PUMP — DJ POWER
EVERYBODY (RAP) — Wally JUMP Jr and the CRIMINAL ELEMENT
EVERYBODY SALSA — MODERN ROMANCE
EVERYBODY SAY EVERYBODY DO — LET LOOSE
EVERYBODY THINKS THAT THEY'RE GOING TO GET THEIRS — BIS
EVERYBODY UP! — GLAM METAL DETECTIVES
EVERYBODY WANTS HER — THUNDER
EVERYBODY WANTS TO RULE THE WORLD — TEARS FOR FEARS
EVERYBODY WANTS TO RUN THE WORLD — TEARS FOR FEARS
EVERYBODY'S A ROCKSTAR — TALL PAUL
EVERYBODY'S CHANGING — KEANE
EVERYBODY'S FOOL — EVANESCENCE
EVERYBODY'S FREE — ROZALLA
EVERYBODY'S FREE (TO WEAR SUNSCREEN) – THE SUNSCREEN SONG (CLASS OF '99) — Baz LUHRMANN
EVERYBODY'S GONE — SENSELESS THINGS
EVERYBODY'S GONNA BE HAPPY — The KINKS
EVERYBODY'S GOT SUMMER — ATLANTIC STARR
EVERYBODY'S GOT TO LEARN SOMETIME [A] — KORGIS
EVERYBODY'S GOT TO LEARN SOMETIME [A] — YAZZ
(EVERYBODY'S GOT TO LEARN SOMETIME) I NEED YOUR LOVING [A] — BABY D
EVERYBODY'S HAPPY NOWADAYS — The BUZZCOCKS
EVERYBODY'S LAUGHING — Phil FEARON
EVERYBODY'S SOMEBODY'S FOOL — Connie FRANCIS
EVERYBODY'S TALKIN' [A] — NILSSON
EVERYBODY'S TALKIN' [A] — The BEAUTIFUL SOUTH
EVERYBODY'S TALKIN' 'BOUT LOVE — SILVER CONVENTION
EVERYDAY [A] — The MOODY BLUES
EVERYDAY [B] — Don McLEAN
EVERYDAY [C] — SLADE
EVERYDAY [D] — JAM MACHINE
EVERYDAY [E] — ORCHESTRAL MANOEUVRES IN THE DARK
EVERYDAY [F] — Phil COLLINS
EVERYDAY [G] — INCOGNITO
EVERYDAY [H] — Craig McLACHLAN
EVERYDAY [I] — AGNELLI & NELSON
EVERYDAY [J] — BON JOVI
EVERYDAY GIRL — DJ RAP
EVERYDAY I WRITE THE BOOK — Elvis COSTELLO
EVERYDAY IS A WINDING ROAD — Sheryl CROW
EVERYDAY IS LIKE SUNDAY — MORRISSEY
EVERYDAY LIVING — WOODENTOPS
EVERYDAY NOW — TEXAS
EVERYDAY PEOPLE [A] — SLY and the FAMILY STONE
EVERYDAY PEOPLE [A] — Aretha FRANKLIN
EVERYDAY SUNSHINE — FISHBONE
EVERYDAY THANG — Melanie WILLIAMS
EVERYONE SAYS "HI" — David BOWIE
EVERYONE SAYS YOU'RE SO FRAGILE — IDLEWILD
EVERYONE'S GONE TO THE MOON — Jonathan KING
EVERYTHING [A] — Jody WATLEY
EVERYTHING [B] — KICKING BACK with TAXMAN
EVERYTHING [C] — UHF
EVERYTHING [D] — HYSTERIX
EVERYTHING [E] — Sarah WASHINGTON
EVERYTHING [F] — INXS
EVERYTHING [G] — Mary J BLIGE
EVERYTHING [H] — DUM DUMS
EVERYTHING [I] — Alanis MORISSETTE
EVERYTHING [J] — Fefe DOBSON
EVERYTHING A MAN COULD EVER NEED — Glen CAMPBELL
EVERYTHING ABOUT YOU — UGLY KID JOE
EVERYTHING CHANGES — TAKE THAT
EVERYTHING COUNTS — DEPECHE MODE
EVERYTHING EVENTUALLY — APPLETON
EVERYTHING GOOD IS BAD — WESTWORLD
EVERYTHING I AM — PLASTIC PENNY
(EVERYTHING I DO) I DO IT FOR YOU [A] — Bryan ADAMS
(EVERYTHING I DO) I DO IT FOR YOU [A] — FATIMA MANSIONS
(EVERYTHING I DO) I DO IT FOR YOU [A] — Q
EVERYTHING I HAVE IS YOURS — Eddie FISHER
EVERYTHING I OWN [A] — BREAD
EVERYTHING I OWN [A] — Ken BOOTHE
EVERYTHING I OWN [A] — BOY GEORGE
EVERYTHING I WANTED — Dannii MINOGUE
EVERYTHING IS ALRIGHT (UPTIGHT) — CJ LEWIS
EVERYTHING IS BEAUTIFUL — Ray STEVENS
EVERYTHING IS EVERYTHING [A] — Lauryn HILL
EVERYTHING IS EVERYTHING [A] — PHOENIX
EVERYTHING IS GONNA BE ALRIGHT — SOUNDS OF BLACKNESS
EVERYTHING IS GREAT — INNER CIRCLE
EVERYTHING I'VE GOT IN MY POCKET — Minnie DRIVER
EVERYTHING MUST CHANGE — Paul YOUNG
EVERYTHING MUST GO — MANIC STREET PREACHERS
EVERYTHING MY HEART DESIRES — Adam RICKITT
EVERYTHING SHE WANTS — WHAM!
EVERYTHING STARTS WITH AN 'E' — E-ZEE POSSEE
EVERYTHING TO EVERYONE — EVERCLEAR
EVERYTHING WILL FLOW — SUEDE
EVERYTHING YOU NEED — MADISON AVENUE
EVERYTHING YOU WANT — VERTICAL HORIZONS
EVERYTHING WILL TURN OUT FINE — STEALER'S WHEEL
EVERYTHING'S ALRIGHT — MOJOS
EVERYTHING'S COOL — POP WILL EAT ITSELF
EVERYTHING'S GONE GREEN — NEW ORDER
EVERYTHING'S GONNA BE ALRIGHT — SWEETBOX
EVERYTHING'S NOT YOU — STONEPROOF
EVERYTHING'S RUINED — FAITH NO MORE
EVERYTHING'S TUESDAY — CHAIRMEN OF THE BOARD
EVERYTIME [A] — LUSTRAL
EVERYTIME [B] — Tatyana ALI
EVERYTIME [C] — a1
EVERYTIME [D] — Britney SPEARS
EVERYTIME I CLOSE MY EYES — BABYFACE
EVERYTIME I THINK OF YOU — FM
EVERYTIME IT RAINS — ACE OF BASE
EVERYTIME YOU GO AWAY — Paul YOUNG
EVERYTIME YOU NEED ME — FRAGMA featuring Maria RUBIA
EVERYTIME YOU SLEEP — DEACON BLUE
EVERYTIME YOU TOUCH ME — QFX
EVERYWAY THAT I CAN — SERTAB
EVERYWHERE [A] — FLEETWOOD MAC
EVERYWHERE [B] — Michelle BRANCH
EVERYWHERE I GO [A] — ISOTONIK
EVERYWHERE I GO [B] — Jackson BROWNE
EVERYWHERE I LOOK — Daryl HALL and John OATES
EVE'S VOLCANO (COVERED IN SIN) — Julian COPE
EVIDENCE — FAITH NO MORE
EVIL — LADYTRON
EVIL HEARTED YOU — YARDBIRDS
EVIL MAN — FATIMA MANSIONS
THE EVIL THAT MEN DO — IRON MAIDEN
EVIL TWIN — LOVE / HATE
EVIL WOMAN — ELECTRIC LIGHT ORCHESTRA
EVOLUTIONDANCE PART ONE (EP) — EVOLUTION
EV'RY DAY OF MY LIFE — Malcolm VAUGHAN
EV'RY LITTLE BIT — Millie SCOTT
EV'RY TIME WE SAY GOODBYE — SIMPLY RED
EV'RYBODY'S TWISTIN' — Frank SINATRA
EV'RYWHERE — David WHITFIELD
THE EX — BILLY TALENT
EX-FACTOR — Lauryn HILL
EX-GIRLFRIEND — NO DOUBT
EXCERPT FROM A TEENAGE OPERA — Keith WEST
EXCITABLE — AMAZULU
EXCITED — M PEOPLE
EXCLUSIVE — APOLLO presents HOUSE OF VIRGINISM
EXCLUSIVELY YOURS — Mark WYNTER
EXCUSE ME BABY — MAGIC LANTERNS
EXCUSE ME MISS — JAY-Z
EXHALE (SHOOP SHOOP) —Whitney HOUSTON
EXODUS [A] — Bob MARLEY & the WAILERS
EXODUS [B] — SUNSCREEM
EXODUS LIVE [C] — LEVELLERS
EXODUS (THEME FROM 'EXODUS') — FERRANTE and TEICHER
THE EXORCIST [A] — SCIENTIST
EXORCIST [B] — SHADES OF RHYTHM
EXPANDER — FUTURE SOUND OF LONDON
EXPANSIONS '86 (EXPAND YOUR MIND) [A] — Chris PAUL featuring David JOSEPH
EXPANSIONS [A] — Scott GROOVES featuring Roy AYERS
EXPERIENCE — Diana ROSS
EXPERIMENT IV — Kate BUSH
EXPERIMENTS WITH MICE — Johnny DANKWORTH
EXPLAIN THE REASONS — FIRST LIGHT
EXPO 2000 — KRAFTWERK
EXPLORATION OF SPACE — COSMIC GATE
EXPRESS [A] — BT EXPRESS
EXPRESS [B] — Dina CARROLL
EXPRESS YOUR FREEDOM — ANTICAPPELLA
EXPRESS YOURSELF [A] — MADONNA
EXPRESS YOURSELF [B] — NWA
EXPRESS YOURSELF [C] — Jimi POLO
EXPRESSION — SALT-N-PEPA
EXPRESSLY (EP) — Edwyn COLLINS
EXPRESSO BONGO (EP) — Cliff RICHARD and The SHADOWS
EXTACY — SHADES OF RHYTHM
EXTENDED PLAY (EP) — Bryan FERRY
THE EXTENDED PLEASURE OF DANCE (EP) — 808 STATE
EXTERMINATE! — SNAP! featuring Niki HARIS
EXTREME WAYS — MOBY
EXTREMIS — HAL featuring Gillian ANDERSON
EYE BEE M — COMMANDER TOM
EYE FOR AN EYE — UNKLE
EYE HATE U — PRINCE
EYE KNOW — DE LA SOUL
EYE LEVEL (THEME FROM THE TV SERIES 'VAN DER VALK') — Simon PARK ORCHESTRA
EYE OF THE TIGER [A] — SURVIVOR
EYE OF THE TIGER [A] — Frank BRUNO

EYE TALK — FASHION
EYE TO EYE — Chaka KHAN
EYE WONDER — APPLES
EYEBALL (EYEBALL PAUL'S THEME) —
SUNBURST
EYES DON'T LIE — TRUCE
THE EYES HAVE IT — Karel FIALKA
EYES OF A STRANGER — QUEENSRYCHE
EYES OF BLUE — Paul CARRACK
EYES OF SORROW — A GUY CALLED GERALD
THE EYES OF TRUTH — ENIGMA
EYES ON YOU —
Jay SEAN featuring The RISHI RICH PROJECT
EYES THAT SEE IN THE DARK —
Kenny ROGERS
EYES WITHOUT A FACE — Billy IDOL
EZ PASS — HAR MAR SUPERSTAR
EZY — WOLFSBANE
THE F-WORD — BABYBIRD
FA FA FA FA FA (SAD SONG) — Otis REDDING
FABLE — Robert MILES
FABRICATED LUNACY — TERRIS
FABULOUS [A] — Charlie GRACIE
FABULOUS [B] — JAHEIM
THE FACE — AND WHY NOT?
FACE THE STRANGE EP — THERAPY?
FACE TO FACE — SIOUXSIE and the BANSHEES
FACES — 2 UNLIMITED
THE FACES (EP) — The FACES
FACT OF LIFE — OUI 3
FACTS + FIGURES — Hugh CORNWELL
THE FACTS OF LIFE [A] — Danny MADDEN
THE FACTS OF LIFE [B] —
BLACK BOX RECORDER
FACTS OF LOVE — CLIMIE FISHER
FADE — PARIS ANGELS
FADE INTO YOU — MAZZY STAR
FADE TO GREY — VISAGE
FADED — Ben HARPER
FADER — DRUGSTORE
FADING LIKE A FLOWER — ROXETTE
FAILING IN LOVE AGAIN — LONDONBEAT
FAILURE [A] — SKINNY
FAILURE [B] — KINGS OF CONVENIENCE
FAILURE'S NOT FLATTERING —
NEW FOUND GLORY
FAINT — LINKIN PARK
A FAIR AFFAIR (JE T'AIME) — Misty OLDLAND
FAIR BLOWS THE WIND FOR FRANCE — PELE
FAIR FIGHT — DJ ZINC
FAIRGROUND — SIMPLY RED
FAIRPLAY — SOUL II SOUL
FAIRWEATHER FRIEND — SYMPOSIUM
FAIRYTALE — DANA
FAIRYTALE OF NEW YORK —
The POGUES featuring Kirsty MacCOLL
FAIT ACCOMPLI — CURVE
FAITH [A] — George MICHAEL
FAITH [B] — WEE PAPA GIRL RAPPERS
FAITH CAN MOVE MOUNTAINS [A] —
Johnnie RAY and the FOUR LADS
FAITH CAN MOVE MOUNTAINS [A] —
Jimmy YOUNG
FAITH CAN MOVE MOUNTAINS [A] —
Nat 'King' COLE
FAITH HEALER — RECOIL
FAITH (IN THE POWER OF LOVE) — ROZALLA
FAITH OF THE HEART — Rod STEWART
FAITHFUL — GO WEST
THE FAITHFUL HUSSAR (DON'T CRY MY LOVE) [A] —
Vera LYNN
THE FAITHFUL HUSSAR [A] —
Louis ARMSTRONG
THE FAITHFUL HUSSAR [A] — Ted HEATH
FAITHFULNESS — SKIN
FAITHLESS — SCRITTI POLITTI
FAKE [A] — Alexander O'NEAL
FAKE [B] — SIMPLY RED
FAKE FUR — URUSEI YATSURA
FAKE PLASTIC TREES — RADIOHEAD
THE FAKE SOUND OF PROGRESS —
LOSTPROPHETS
FAKER — AUDIOWEB
FALCON — RAH BAND
FALL (EP) — RIDE
THE FALL [A] — MINISTRY
THE FALL [B] — WAY OUT WEST
FALL AT YOUR FEET [A] — CROWDED HOUSE
FALL AT YOUR FEET [A] —
CM2 featuring Lisa LAWS
FALL BACK DOWN — RANCID
FALL BEHIND ME — The DONNAS
FALL DOWN (SPIRIT OF LOVE) — TRAMAINE
FALL FROM GRACE — ESKIMOS & EGYPT
FALL IN LOVE WITH ME [A] —
EARTH WIND AND FIRE
FALL IN LOVE WITH ME [B] —
BOOTH and the BAD ANGEL
FALL IN LOVE WITH YOU —
Cliff RICHARD and The SHADOWS
FALL OUT — The POLICE
FALL TO LOVE — DIESEL PARK WEST
FALL TO PIECES — VELVET REVOLVER
FALL VS 2003 — The FALL
FALLEN — Sarah McLACHLAN
FALLEN ANGEL [A] — Frankie VALLI
FALLEN ANGEL [B] — POISON

FALLEN ANGEL [C] — Traci LORDS
FALLEN ANGEL [D] — ELBOW
FALLEN ANGELS — Buffy SAINTE-MARIE
FALLIN' [A] — Connie FRANCIS
FALLIN' [B] —
TEENAGE FANCLUB and DE LA SOUL
FALLIN' [C] — Alicia KEYS
FALLIN' [D] — UN-CUT
FALLIN' IN LOVE —
HAMILTON, Joe FRANK and REYNOLDS
FALLING [A] — Roy ORBISON
FALLING [B] — Julee CRUISE
FALLING [C] — Cathy DENNIS
FALLING [D] — Alison MOYET
FALLING [E] — ANT & DEC
FALLING [F] — BOOM!
FALLING [G] —
LIQUID STATE featuring Marcella WOODS
FALLING [H] — McALMONT & BUTLER
FALLING ANGELS RIDING — David ESSEX
FALLING APART AT THE SEAMS — MARMALADE
FALLING AWAY FROM ME — KORN
FALLING IN AND OUT OF LOVE —
FEMME FATALE
FALLING IN LOVE [A] — SURFACE
FALLING IN LOVE [B] — SYBIL
FALLING IN LOVE [C] — LA BOUCHE
FALLING IN LOVE AGAIN [A] — TECHNO TWINS
FALLING IN LOVE AGAIN [B] —
Eagle-Eye CHERRY
FALLING IN LOVE (IS HARD ON THE KNEES) —
AEROSMITH
FALLING INTO YOU — Celine DION
FALLING TO PIECES — FAITH NO MORE
FALSE ALARM — The BRONX
FALTER — HUNDRED REASONS
FAME [A] — David BOWIE
FAME [B] — Irene CARA
FAMILIAR FEELING — MOLOKO
FAMILIUS HORRIBILUS — POP WILL EAT ITSELF
FAMILY AFFAIR [A] —
SLY and the FAMILY STONE
FAMILY AFFAIR [A] —
BEF featuring Lalah HATHAWAY
FAMILY AFFAIR [A] — Shabba RANKS
featuring PATRA and TERRI & MONICA
FAMILY AFFAIR [B] — Mary J BLIGE
FAMILY MAN [A] — Mike OLDFIELD
FAMILY MAN [A] — Daryl HALL and John OATES
FAMILY MAN [B] — FLEETWOOD MAC
FAMILY MAN [C] — ROACHFORD
FAMILY OF MAN — The FARM
FAMILY PORTRAIT — PINK
FAMINE — Sinead O'CONNOR
FAN MAIL — The DICKIES
FAN THE FLAME — Barbara PENNINGTON
FANCY PANTS — KENNY
FAN'DABI'DOZI — KRANKIES
FANFARE FOR THE COMMON MAN —
EMERSON, LAKE and PALMER
FANLIGHT FANNY — Clinton FORD
FANTASTIC DAY — HAIRCUT 100
FANTASTIC VOYAGE — COOLIO
FANTASY [A] — EARTH WIND AND FIRE
FANTASY [A] — BLACK BOX
FANTASY [B] — Gerard KENNY
FANTASY [C] — FANTASY UFO
FANTASY [D] — TEN CITY
FANTASY [E] — Mariah CAREY
FANTASY [F] — LEVELLERS
FANTASY [G] — APPLETONS
FANTASY ISLAND [A] — TIGHT FIT
FANTASY ISLAND [B] — M PEOPLE
FANTASY REAL — Phil FEARON
FAR — LONGPIGS
FAR ABOVE THE CLOUDS — Mike OLDFIELD
FAR AND AWAY — AIDA
FAR AWAY — Shirley BASSEY
FAR FAR AWAY — SLADE
FAR FROM HOME — LEVELLERS
FAR FROM OVER — Frank STALLON
FAR GONE AND OUT —
JESUS AND MARY CHAIN
FAR OUT [A] —
SON'Z OF A LOOP DA LOOP ERA
FAR OUT [B] — DEEJAY PUNK-ROC
FAR-OUT SON OF LUNG AND THE
RAMBLINGS OF A MADMAN —
FUTURE SOUND OF LONDON
FARAWAY EYES — The ROLLING STONES
FARAWAY PLACES — The BACHELORS
FAREWELL — Rod STEWART
FAREWELL ANGELINA — Joan BAEZ
FAREWELL IS A LONELY SOUND —
Jimmy RUFFIN
FAREWELL MR SORROW — ALL ABOUT EVE
FAREWELL MY SUMMER LOVE [A] — CHAOS
FAREWELL MY SUMMER LOVE [A] —
Michael JACKSON
FAREWELL TO THE MOON — YORK
FAREWELL TO TWILIGHT — SYMPOSIUM
FARMER BILL'S COWMAN (I WAS KAISER
BILL'S BATMAN) — WURZELS
FARON YOUNG — PREFAB SPROUT
FASCINATED [A] — Lisa B
FASCINATED [B] — RAVEN MAIZE
FASCINATING RHYTHM — BASS-O-MATIC

FASHION — David BOWIE
FASHION CRISIS HITS NEW YORK —
FRANK AND WALTERS
FASHION '98 — GLAMMA KID
FASSY HOLE — Roni SIZE
FAST AS YOU CAN — Fiona APPLE
FAST BOY — The BLUETONES
FAST CAR [A] — Tracy CHAPMAN
FAST CAR [B] — DILLINJA
FAST FOOD SONG — FAST FOOD ROCKERS
FASTER — MANIC STREET PREACHERS
FASTER THAN THE SPEED OF NIGHT —
Bonnie TYLER
FASTER THE CHASE — INME
FASTLOVE — George MICHAEL
FAT BASTARD — MEDWAY
FAT BLACK HEART — PELE
FAT BOTTOMED GIRLS — QUEEN
FAT LIP — SUM 41
FAT NECK — BLACK GRAPE
FATAL HESITATION — Chris DE BURGH
FATHER [A] — The CHRISTIANS
FATHER [B] — LL COOL J
FATHER AND SON [A] — BOYZONE
FATHER AND SON [A] —
Ronan KEATING featuring YUSUF
FATHER CHRISTMAS DO NOT TOUCH ME —
The GOODIES
FATHER FIGURE — George MICHAEL
FATTIE BUM BUM [A] — Carl MALCOLM
FATTIE BUM BUM [A] — DIVERSIONS
FAVOURITE SHIRTS (BOY MEETS GIRL) —
HAIRCUT 100
FAVOURITE THINGS — BIG BROVAZ
FBI — The SHADOWS
FE' REAL —
Maxi PRIEST featuring APACHE INDIAN
F.E.A.R. — Ian BROWN
FEAR LOVES THIS PLACE — Julian COPE
FEAR OF THE DARK [A] — Gordon GILTRAP
FEAR OF THE DARK (LIVE) [B] — IRON MAIDEN
FEAR SATAN — MOGWAI
FEAR: THE MINDKILLER — EON
FED UP — HOUSE OF PAIN
FEDORA (I'LL BE YOUR DAWG) — CARAMBA
FEE FI FO FUM — CANDY GIRLS
FEED MY FRANKENSTEIN — Alice COOPER
FEED THE FEELING — PERCEPTION
FEED THE TREE — BELLY
FEED YOUR ADDICTION — EASTERN LANE
FEEDING TIME — LOOK
FEEL [A] — Ruth JOY
FEEL [B] — HOUSE OF LOVE
FEEL [C] — Robbie WILLIAMS
FEEL EVERY BEAT — ELECTRONIC
FEEL FREE — SOUL II SOUL
FEEL GOOD [A] — PHATS & SMALL
FEEL GOOD [B] — MADASUN
FEEL GOOD TIME —
PINK featuring William ORBIT
FEEL IT [A] — HI-LUX
FEEL IT [B] — Carol BAILEY
FEEL IT [C] — Neneh CHERRY
FEEL IT [D] — The TAMPERER featuring MAYA
FEEL IT [E] — Inaya DAY
FEEL IT BOY — BEENIE MAN
FEEL LIKE CALLING HOME — MR BIG
FEEL LIKE CHANGE — BLACK
FEEL LIKE MAKIN' LOVE [A] — Roberta FLACK
FEEL LIKE MAKIN' LOVE [A] — George BENSON
FEEL LIKE MAKIN' LOVE [B] — BAD COMPANY
FEEL LIKE MAKING LOVE [B] — Pauline HENRY
FEEL LIKE SINGIN' — Sandy B
FEEL LIKE SINGING — TAK TIX
FEEL ME — BLANCMANGE
FEEL ME FLOW — NAUGHTY BY NATURE
FEEL MY BODY —
Frank'o MOIRAGHI featuring AMNESIA
FEEL NO PAIN — SADE
FEEL SO FINE — Johnny PRESTON
FEEL SO GOOD [A] — MA$E
FEEL SO GOOD [B] —
JON THE DENTIST vs Ollie JAYE
FEEL SO HIGH — DES'REE
FEEL SO REAL [A] — Steve ARRINGTON
FEEL SO REAL [B] — DREAM FREQUENCY
FEEL SURREAL —
FREEFALL featuring PSYCHOTROPIC
FEEL THA VIBE — THAT KID CHRIS
FEEL THE BEAT [A] — CAMISRA
FEEL THE BEAT [B] — DARUDE
FEEL THE DRUM (EP) — PARKS & WILSON
FEEL THE DRUMS — NATIVE
FEEL THE HEAT — Roni SIZE
FEEL THE MUSIC — GURU
FEEL THE NEED [A] — Leif GARRETT
FEEL THE NEED [A] —
G NATION featuring ROSIE
FEEL THE NEED [B] — JT TAYLOR
FEEL THE NEED [C] — WEIRD SCIENCE
FEEL THE NEED IN ME [A] —
DETROIT EMERALDS
FEEL THE NEED IN ME [A] — FORREST
FEEL THE NEED IN ME [A] — Shakin' STEVENS
FEEL THE PAIN — DINOSAUR JR
FEEL THE RAINDROPS — ADVENTURES
FEEL THE REAL — David BENDETH

FEEL THE RHYTHM [A] — Jazzi P
FEEL THE RHYTHM [B] — TERRORIZE
FEEL THE RHYTHM [A] — JINNY
FEEL THE SAME — TRIPLE X
FEEL THE SUNSHINE — Alex REECE
FEEL TOO BUSY THINKING 'BOUT MY BABY —
STEPS
FEEL WHAT YOU WANT — Kristine W
FEELIN' — The LA's
FEELIN' ALRIGHT — EYC
THE FEELIN' (CLAP YOUR HANDS) —
RHYTHMATIC JUNKIES
FEELIN' FINE — ULTRABEAT
FEELIN' INSIDE — Bobby BROWN
FEELIN' SO GOOD — Jennifer LOPEZ
FEELIN' THE SAME WAY — Norah JONES
FEELIN' U —
SHY FX & T-POWER featuring Kele LE ROC
FEELIN' WAY TOO DAMN GOOD — NICKELBACK
FEELIN' YOU — ALI
THE FEELING [A] — URBAN HYPE
THE FEELING [B] —
TIN TIN OUT featuring SWEET TEE
FEELING FOR YOU — CASSIUS
FEELING GOOD [A] — Nina SIMONE
FEELING GOOD [A] — HUFF & HERB
FEELING GOOD [A] — MUSE
FEELING IT TOO — 3 JAYS
FEELING SO REAL — MOBY
FEELING THE LOVE — REACTOR
FEELING THIS — BLINK-182
FEELING THIS WAY —
CONDUCTOR & THE COWBOY
FEELINGS — Morris ALBERT
FEELINGS OF FOREVER — TIFFANY
FEELS GOOD (DON'T WORRY BOUT A THING) —
NAUGHTY BY NATURE featuring 3LW
(FEELS LIKE) HEAVEN — FICTION FACTORY
FEELS LIKE HEAVEN —
URBAN COOKIE COLLECTIVE
FEELS LIKE I'M IN LOVE — Kelly MARIE
FEELS LIKE THE FIRST TIME [A] — FOREIGNER
FEELS LIKE THE FIRST TIME [A] — SINITTA
FEELS LIKE THE RIGHT TIME — SHAKATAK
FEELS SO GOOD [A] — VAN HALEN
FEELS SO GOOD [B] — XSCAPE
FEELS SO GOOD [C] — Lorna B
FEELS SO GOOD [D] — Melanie B
FEELS SO REAL (WON'T LET GO) —
Patrice RUSHEN
FEELS SO RIGHT —
Victor SIMONELLI presents SOLUTION
FEENIN' — JODECI
FEET UP! — Guy MITCHELL
FELICITY — ORANGE JUICE
FELL IN LOVE WITH A BOY [A] — Joss Stone
FELL IN LOVE WITH A GIRL [A] —
The WHITE STRIPES
FELL ON BLACK DAYS — SOUNDGARDEN
FEMALE INTUITION — MAI TAI
FEMALE OF THE SPECIES — SPACE
FERGUS SINGS THE BLUES — DEACON BLUE
FERNANDO — ABBA
FERRIS WHEEL — The EVERLY BROTHERS
FERRY ACROSS THE MERSEY [A] —
GERRY and the PACEMAKERS
FERRY 'CROSS THE MERSEY [A] —
The CHRISTIANS, Holly JOHNSON,
Paul McCARTNEY, Gerry MARSDEN and
STOCK AITKEN WATERMAN
FESTIVAL TIME — SAN REMO STRINGS
FEUER FREI — RAMMSTEIN
FEVER [A] — Peggy LEE
FEVER [A] — Helen SHAPIRO
FEVER [A] — McCOYS
FEVER [A] — MADONNA
FEVER [B] — S-J
FEVER [C] — STARSAILOR
FEVER CALLED LOVE — R.H.C.
FEVER FOR THE FLAVA — HOT ACTION COP
FEVER PITCH THE EP — The PRETENDERS,
The LA'S, ORLANDO, Nick HORNBY
FICTION OF LIFE — CHINA DRUM
FIELD OF DREAMS —
FLIP & FILL featuring Jo JAMES
FIELDS OF FIRE (400 MILES) — BIG COUNTRY
FIELDS OF GOLD — STING
THE FIELDS OF LOVE — ATB featuring YORK
FIESTA [A] — The POGUES
FIESTA [B] — R KELLY featuring JAY-Z
!FIESTA FATAL! — B-TRIBE
FIFTEEN FEET OF PURE WHITE SNOW —
Nick CAVE and the BAD SEEDS
15 MINUTES OF FAME — SHEEP ON DRUGS
15 STEPS (EP) — MONKEY MAFIA
15 WAYS — The FALL
15 YEARS (EP) — LEVELLERS
5TH ANNIVERSARY EP — JUDGE DREAD
A FIFTH OF BEETHOVEN —
Walter MURPHY and the BIG APPLE BAND
50/50 — LEMAR
50 FT QUEENIE — P J HARVEY
FIFTY GRAND FOR CHRISTMAS — Paul HOLT
50 WAYS TO LEAVE YOUR LOVER —
Paul SIMON
51ST STATE — NEW MODEL ARMY
FIFTY-FOUR — SEA LEVEL

54-46 (WAS MY NUMBER) — ASWAD
59TH STREET BRIDGE SONG (FEELING GROOVY) —
    HARPERS BIZARRE
57 — Biffy CLYRO
57 CHANNELS (AND NOTHIN' ON) —
    Bruce SPRINGSTEEN
FIGARO — BROTHERHOOD OF MAN
FIGHT — McKOY
THE FIGHT — Marty WILDE
FIGHT FOR OURSELVES — SPANDAU BALLET
FIGHT FOR YOUR RIGHT (TO PARTY) — NYCC
FIGHT MUSIC — D12
THE FIGHT SONG — MARILYN MANSON
FIGHT TEST — The FLAMING LIPS
FIGHT THE POWER — PUBLIC ENEMY
FIGHT THE YOUTH — FISHBONE
FIGHTER — Christina AGUILERA
FIGHTING FIT — GENE
FIGURE OF EIGHT [A] — Paul McCARTNEY
FIGURE OF 8 [B] — GRID
FIJI — ATLANTIS vs AVATAR
FILL HER UP — GENE
FILL ME IN — Craig DAVID
FILLING UP WITH HEAVEN — HUMAN LEAGUE
A FILM FOR THE FUTURE — IDLEWILD
FILM MAKER — The COOPER TEMPLE CLAUSE
FILMSTAR — SUEDE
FILTHY — SAINT ETIENNE
THE FINAL ARREARS —
    MULL HISTORICAL SOCIETY
THE FINAL COUNTDOWN — EUROPE
FINALLY [A] — Ce Ce PENISTON
FINALLY [B] — KINGS OF TOMORROW
    featuring Julie McKNIGHT
FINALLY FOUND — HONEYZ
FINCHLEY CENTRAL — NEW VAUDEVILLE BAND
FIND A WAY [A] —
    COLDCUT featuring QUEEN LATIFAH
FIND A WAY [B] — A TRIBE CALLED QUEST
FIND 'EM, FOOL 'EM, FORGET 'EM — S EXPRESS
FIND ME (ODYSSEY TO ANYOONA) —
    JAM & SPOON featuring PLAVKA
FIND MY LOVE — FAIRGROUND ATTRACTION
FIND MY WAY BACK HOME —
    NASHVILLE TEENS
FIND THE ANSWER WITHIN — BOO RADLEYS
FIND THE COLOUR — FEEDER
FIND THE RIVER — R.E.M.
FIND THE TIME [A] — FIVE STAR
FIND THE TIME (PART ONE) [B] —
    QUADROPHENIA
FINDERS KEEPERS —
    CHAIRMEN OF THE BOARD
FINE DAY [A] — Rolf HARRIS
FINE DAY [B] — KIRSTY HAWKSHAW
FINE TIME [A] — NEW ORDER
FINE TIME [B] — YAZZ
FINER — NIGHTMARES ON WAX
FINER FEELINGS — Kylie MINOGUE
THE FINEST [A] — S.O.S. BAND
THE FINEST [A] — TRUCE
FINEST DREAMS — Richard X featuring KELIS
FINEST WORKSONG — R.E.M.
FINETIME — CAST
THE FINGER OF SUSPICION —
    Dickie VALENTINE with The STARGAZERS
FINGERS AND THUMBS (COLD SUMMER'S DAY) —
    ERASURE
FINGERS OF LOVE — CROWDED HOUSE
FINGS AIN'T WOT THEY USED T'BE [A] —
    Max BYGRAVES
FINGS AIN'T WOT THEY USED T'BE [A] —
    Russ CONWAY
FINISHED SYMPHONY — HYBRID
FIRE [A] — Crazy World of Arthur BROWN
FIRE [B] — POINTER SISTERS
FIRE [B] — Bruce SPRINGSTEEN
FIRE [C] — U2
FIRE [D] — SLY and ROBBIE
FIRE [E] — The PRODIGY
FIRE [F] — PRIZNA featuring DEMOLITION MAN
FIRE [G] — SCOOTER
FIRE [H] — Busta RHYMES
FIRE [I] — MOUSSE T
FIRE AND RAIN — James TAYLOR
FIRE BRIGADE — The MOVE
FIRE DOWN BELOW [A] — Jeri SOUTHERN
FIRE DOWN BELOW [A] — Shirley BASSEY
FIRE IN MY HEART — SUPER FURRY ANIMALS
FIRE ISLAND — FIRE ISLAND
FIRE IT UP — Busta RHYMES
FIRE OF LOVE —
    JUNGLE HIGH with BLUE PEARL
FIRE UP THE SHOESAW — LIONROCK
FIRE WIRE — COSMIC GATE
FIRE WOMAN — The CULT
FIRE WORKS — SIOUXSIE and the BANSHEES
FIREBALL [A] — Don SPENCER
FIREBALL [B] — DEEP PURPLE
FIREFLY — INME
FIRED UP — ELEVATORMAN
FIRED UP! — FUNKY GREEN DOGS
FIREPILE (EP) — THROWING MUSES
FIRES BURNING — RUN TINGS
FIRESTARTER — The PRODIGY
FIREWORKS — ROXETTE
FIREWORKS (EP) — EMBRACE

FIRM BIZ — FIRM featuring Dawn ROBINSON
FIRST ATHEIST TABERNACLE CHOIR —
    SPITTING IMAGE
FIRST BOY IN THIS TOWN (LOVE SICK) —
    SCRITTI POLITTI
THE FIRST CUT IS THE DEEPEST [A] —
    PP ARNOLD
FIRST CUT IS THE DEEPEST [A] —
    Rod STEWART
THE FIRST CUT IS THE DEEPEST [A] —
    Sheryl CROW
FIRST DATE — BLINK-182
FIRST DAY — The FUTUREHEADS
THE FIRST DAY (HORIZON) —
    MAN WITH NO NAME
FIRST DAY OF MY LIFE — The RASMUS
FIRST IMPRESSIONS — IMPRESSIONS
FIRST IT GIVETH —
    QUEENS OF THE STONE AGE
1ST MAN IN SPACE —
    The ALL SEEING I featuring Phil OAKEY
THE FIRST MAN YOU REMEMBER —
    Michael BALL
THE FIRST NIGHT — MONICA
FIRST OF MAY — The BEE GEES
1ST OF THA MONTH —
    BONE THUGS-N-HARMONY
FIRST OF THE GANG TO DIE — MORRISSEY
FIRST PICTURE OF YOU — LOTUS EATERS
FIRST TASTE OF LOVE — Ben E KING
THE FIRST THE LAST ETERNITY (TIL THE END) —
    SNAP! featuring SUMMER
FIRST THING IN THE MORNING — Kiki DEE
THE FIRST TIME [A] — Adam FAITH
THE FIRST TIME [B] — Robin BECK
THE FIRST TIME [C] — SURFACE
FIRST TIME EVER — Joanna LAW
THE FIRST TIME EVER I SAW YOUR FACE [A] —
    Roberta FLACK
THE FIRST TIME EVER I SAW YOUR FACE [A] —
    Celine DION
FIRST WE TAKE MANHATTAN —
    Jennifer WARNES
FISH OUT OF WATER — ONE MINUTE SILENCE
FISHERMAN'S BLUES — WATERBOYS
FIT BUT YOU KNOW IT — The STREETS
5 COLOURS IN HER HAIR — McFLY
FIVE FATHOMS — EVERYTHING BUT THE GIRL
5.15 — The WHO
555 — DELAKOTA
5-4-3-2-1 — MANFRED MANN
FIVE GET OVER EXCITED —
    The HOUSEMARTINS
500 (SHAKE BABY SHAKE) — LUSH
FIVE LITTLE FINGERS — Frankie McBRIDE
FIVE LIVE (EP) — George MICHAEL
    and QUEEN with Lisa STANSFIELD
5 MILE (THESE ARE THE DAYS) —
    TURIN BRAKES
FIVE MILES OUT — Mike OLDFIELD
5 MILES TO EMPTY — BROWNSTONE
FIVE MINUTES [A] — The STRANGLERS
5 MINUTES [B] — LIL' MO featuring
    Missy 'Misdemeanor' ELLIOTT
THE $5.98 EP — GARAGE DAYS RE-REVISITED —
    METALLICA
5 O'CLOCK — NONCHALANT
5 O'CLOCK WORLD — Julian COPE
5.7.0.5 — CITY BOY
5, 6, 7, 8 — STEPS
5 STEPS — DRU HILL
5000 MINUTES OF PAIN — MINUTEMAN
FIX — BLACKSTREET
FIX MY SINK —
    DJ SNEAK featuring BEAR WHO?
FIX UP LOOK SHARP — DIZZEE RASCAL
FIXATION — Andy LING
FIXER — VENT 414
FLAGPOLE SITTA — HARVEY DANGER
FLAMBOYANT — PET SHOP BOYS
FLAME — SEBADOH
THE FLAME [A] — ARCADIA
THE FLAME [B] — FINE YOUNG CANNIBALS
THE FLAME STILL BURNS — Jimmy NAIL
THE FLAME TREES OF THIKA —
    VIDEO SYMPHONIC
FLAMES OF PARADISE —
    Jennifer RUSH and Elton JOHN
FLAMING JUNE — BT
FLAMING SWORD — CARE
FLAP YOUR WINGS — NELLY
FLASH [A] — QUEEN
FLASH [A] — QUEEN + VANGUARD
FLASH [B] — BBE
FLASH [B] — BK and Nick SENTIENCE
FLASH [C] — GRIFTERS
FLASHBACK — IMAGINATION
FLASHBACK JACK — ADAMSKI
FLASHDANCE — DEEP DISH
FLASHDANCE ... WHAT A FEELING [A] —
    Irene CARA
FLASHDANCE ... WHAT A FEELING [A] —
    BJÖRN AGAIN
THE FLASHER —
    MISTURA featuring Lloyd MICHELS
FLAT BEAT — MR OIZO
FLATLINERS — NEBULA II

FLAVA [A] — Peter ANDRE
FLAVA [B] — IMAJIN
FLAVA IN YA EAR — Craig MACK
FLAVOUR OF THE OLD SCHOOL —
    Beverley KNIGHT
FLAVOR OF THE WEAK — AMERICAN HI-FI
FLAWLESS [A] — The ONES
FLAWLESS (GO TO THE CITY) [A] —
    George MICHAEL
FLEE FLY FLO — FE-M@IL
FLESH [A] — A SPLIT SECOND
FLESH [B] — Jan JOHNSTON
FLESH FOR FANTASY — Billy IDOL
FLESH OF MY FLESH — ORANGE JUICE
FLETCH THEME — Harold FALTERMEYER
FLIGHT OF ICARUS — IRON MAIDEN
FLIGHT 643 — DJ TIESTO
FLIP — Jesse GREEN
FLIP REVERSE — BLAZIN' SQUAD
THE FLIPSIDE — MOLOKO
FLIRT! — Jonathan KING
FLIRTATION WALTZ — Winifred ATWELL
F.L.M. — MEL and KIM
FLOAT ON [A] — FLOATERS
FLOAT ON [B] — MODEST MOUSE
FLOATATION — GRID
FLOATING — TERRA FIRMA
FLOATING IN THE WIND — HUDSON-FORD
FLOBBADANCE — BILL & BEN
FLOETIC — FLOETRY
FLOODLIT WORLD — ULTRASOUND
THE FLOOR — Johnny GILL
FLOOR-ESSENCE — MAN WITH NO NAME
FLOOR SPACE — OUR HOUSE
THE FLORAL DANCE [A] —
    BRIGHOUSE and RASTRICK BRASS BAND
FLORAL DANCE [A] — Terry WOGAN
FLORIBUNDA — MOTHER'S PRIDE
FLOWER DUET (FROM 'LAKMÉ') [A] —
    Mady MESPLE and Danielle MILLET with the
    PARIS OPÉRA-COMIQUE ORCHESTRA
    conducted by Alain LOMBARD
FLOWER DUET [A] — Jonathan
    PETERS presents LUMINAIRE
FLOWER OF SCOTLAND — SCOTTISH RUGBY
    TEAM with Ronnie BROWNE
FLOWER OF THE WEST — RUNRIG
FLOWERS [A] — TITIYO
FLOWERS [B] — SWEET FEMALE ATTITUDE
FLOWERS IN DECEMBER — MAZZY STAR
FLOWERS IN THE RAIN — The MOVE
FLOWERS IN THE WINDOW — TRAVIS
FLOWERS OF ROMANCE — PUBLIC IMAGE LTD
FLOWERS ON THE WALL —
    STATLER BROTHERS
FLOWERZ — Armand VAN HELDEN
FLOWTATION — Vincent DE MOOR
FLOY JOY — The SUPREMES
FLY [A] — SUGAR RAY
FLY [B] — POB featuring DJ Patrick REID
FLY [C] — Mark JOSEPH
FLY [D] — Matt GOSS
THE FLY — U2
FLY AWAY [A] — HADDAWAY
FLY AWAY [B] — Lenny KRAVITZ
FLY AWAY [C] — Vincent DE MOOR
FLY AWAY (BYE BYE) — EYES CREAM
FLY BI —
    TEEBONE featuring MC KIE and MC SPARKS
FLY BY II — BLUE
FLY GIRL — QUEEN LATIFAH
FLY LIFE — BASEMENT JAXX
FLY LIKE AN EAGLE — SEAL
FLY ON THE WINGS OF LOVE —
    XTM & DJ CHUCKY presents ANNIA
FLY ROBIN FLY — SILVER CONVENTION
FLY TO THE ANGELS — SLAUGHTER
FLY TOO HIGH — Janis IAN
FLY WITH ME — COLOURSOUND
FLYING [A] — CAST
FLYING [B] — Bryan ADAMS
FLYING ELVIS — LEILANI
FLYING HIGH [A] — The COMMODORES
FLYING HIGH [B] — FREEEZ
FLYING HIGH [C] —
    CAPTAIN HOLLYWOOD PROJECT
FLYING MACHINE — Cliff RICHARD
FLYING SAUCER — WEDDING PRESENT
THE FLYING SONG — PQM featuring CICA
FLYING WITHOUT WINGS — WESTLIFE
FLYSWATTER — EELS
FM (NO STATIC AT ALL) — STEELY DAN
FOE-DEE-O-DEE — The RUBETTES
FOG ON THE TYNE (REVISITED) —
    GAZZA and LINDISFARNE
FOGGY MOUNTAIN BREAKDOWN —
    Lester FLATT and Earl SCRUGGS
FOGHORN — A
THE FOLK SINGER — Tommy ROE
FOLLOW DA LEADER — NIGEL & MARVIN
FOLLOW ME [A] — JT TAYLOR
FOLLOW ME [B] — ALY-US
FOLLOW ME [C] — ATOMIC KITTEN
FOLLOW ME [D] — UNCLE KRACKER
FOLLOW THAT DREAM (EP) — Elvis PRESLEY
FOLLOW THE LEADER — Eric B and RAKIM
FOLLOW THE LEADERS — KILLING JOKE

FOLLOW THE RULES — LIVIN' JOY
FOLLOW YOU DOWN — GIN BLOSSOMS
FOLLOW YOU FOLLOW ME [A] — GENESIS
FOLLOW YOU FOLLOW ME [A] —
    Sonny JONES featuring Tara CHASE
FOLLOWED THE WAVES — AUF DER MAUR
FOLLOWING — The BANGLES
THE FOOD CHRISTMAS EP —
    VARIOUS ARTISTS (EPs and LPs)
FOOD FOR THOUGHT —
    The BARRON KNIGHTS
FOOD FOR THOUGHT [B] — UB40
FOOL [A] — Elvis PRESLEY
FOOL [B] — Al MATTHEWS
FOOL [C] — MANSUN
FOOL AGAIN — WESTLIFE
A FOOL AM I — Cilla BLACK
FOOL FOR LOVE — RUSSELL
FOOL FOR YOUR LOVING — WHITESNAKE
FOOL (IF YOU THINK IT'S OVER) [A] —
    Chris REA
FOOL IF YOU THINK IT'S OVER [A] —
    Elkie BROOKS
A FOOL NEVER LEARNS — Andy WILLIAMS
FOOL NO MORE — S CLUB 8
FOOL NUMBER ONE — Brenda LEE
THE FOOL ON THE HILL — Shirley BASSEY
A FOOL SUCH AS I —
    Elvis PRESLEY with the JORDANAIRES
FOOL TO CRY — The ROLLING STONES
FOOLED AROUND AND FELL IN LOVE —
    Elvin BISHOP
FOOLED BY A SMILE — SWING OUT SISTER
FOOLIN' YOURSELF — Paul HARDCASTLE
FOOLISH — ASHANTI
FOOLISH BEAT — Debbie GIBSON
FOOLISH LITTLE GIRL — SHIRELLES
FOOL'S GOLD — The STONE ROSES
FOOL'S PARADISE — Meli'sa MORGAN
FOOLS RUSH IN [A] — Brook BENTON
FOOLS RUSH IN [A] — Ricky NELSON
FOOT STOMPIN' MUSIC — Hamilton BOHANNON
FOOT TAPPER — The SHADOWS
FOOTLOOSE — Kenny LOGGINS
FOOTPRINT — DISCO CITIZENS
FOOTPRINTS IN THE SNOW —
    Johnny DUNCAN and the BLUE GRASS BOYS
FOOTSEE — WIGAN'S CHOSEN FEW
FOOTSTEPS [A] — Ronnie CARROLL
FOOTSTEPS [A] — Steve LAWRENCE
FOOTSTEPS [A] — SHOWADDYWADDY
FOOTSTEPS [B] — STILTSKIN
FOOTSTEPS [C] — Daniel O'DONNELL
FOOTSTEPS FOLLOWING ME — Frances NERO
FOR A FEW DOLLARS MORE — SMOKIE
FOR A FRIEND — COMMUNARDS
FOR A PENNY — Pat BOONE
FOR A LIFETIME —
    ASCENCION featuring Erin LORDAN
FOR ALL THAT YOU WANT — Gary BARLOW
FOR ALL THE COWS — FOO FIGHTERS
FOR ALL TIME — Catherine Zeta JONES
FOR ALL WE KNOW [A] — Nicki FRENCH
FOR ALL WE KNOW [A] — Shirley BASSEY
FOR ALL WE KNOW [A] — The CARPENTERS
FOR AMERICA — RED BOX
FOR AN ANGEL — Paul VAN DYK
FOR BRITAIN ONLY — Alice COOPER
(FOR GOD'S SAKE) GIVE MORE POWER
    TO THE PEOPLE — CHI-LITES
FOR HER LIGHT — FIELDS OF THE NEPHILIM
FOR LOVE (EP) — LUSH
FOR LOVERS —
    WOLFMAN featuring Peter DOHERTY
FOR MAMA — Matt MONRO
4 MY PEOPLE — Missy 'Misdemeanor' ELLIOTT
FOR OLD TIME'S SAKE —
    MILLICAN and NESBITT
FOR ONCE IN MY LIFE [A] — Stevie WONDER
FOR ONCE IN MY LIFE [A] — Dorothy SQUIRES
FOR REAL — TRICKY
FOR SPACIOUS LIES — Norman COOK
FOR SURE — SCOOCH
FOR THE DEAD — GENE
FOR THE GOOD TIMES — Perry COMO
FOR THOSE ABOUT TO ROCK (WE SALUTE YOU) —
    AC/DC
FOR TOMORROW — BLUR
FOR WHAT IT'S WORTH [A] — OUI 3
FOR WHAT IT'S WORTH [B] — The CARDIGANS
FOR WHAT YOU DREAM OF — BEDROCK
FOR WHOM THE BELL TOLLS [A] —
    Simon DUPREE and the BIG SOUND
FOR WHOM THE BELL TOLLS [B] —
    The BEE GEES
FOR YOU [A] — Ricky NELSON
FOR YOU [B] — FARMERS BOYS
FOR YOU [C] — Snowy WHITE
FOR YOU [D] — ELECTRONIC
FOR YOU [E] — STAIND
FOR YOU FOR LOVE — AVERAGE WHITE BAND
FOR YOU I WILL — MONICA
FOR YOU I'LL DO ANYTHING YOU WANT ME TO —
    Barry WHITE
FOR YOUR BABIES — SIMPLY RED
FOR YOUR BLUE EYES ONLY — Tony HADLEY
FOR YOUR EYES ONLY — Sheena EASTON

FOR YOUR LOVE [A] — **YARDBIRDS**
FOR YOUR LOVE [B] — **Stevie WONDER**
FORBIDDEN CITY — **ELECTRONIC**
FORBIDDEN COLOURS — **David SYLVIAN**
FORBIDDEN FRUIT — **Paul VAN DYK**
FORBIDDEN ZONE — **BEDROCK**
FORÇA — **Nelly FURTADO**
THE FORCE BEHIND THE POWER — **Diana ROSS**
FOREIGN SAND — **Roger TAYLOR**
FORERUNNER — **NATURAL BORN GROOVES**
A FOREST — **The CURE**
FOREST FIRE — **Lloyd COLE**
FOREVER [A] — **Roy WOOD**
FOREVER [B] — **KISS**
FOREVER [C] — **DAMAGE**
FOREVER [D] — **The CHARLATANS**
FOREVER [E] — **Tina COUSINS**
FOREVER [F] — **TRINITY-X**
FOREVER [G] — **N-TRANCE**
FOREVER [H] — **DEE DEE**
FOREVER AND A DAY [A] — **BROTHERS IN RHYTHM**
FOREVER AND A DAY [B] — **STATE ONE**
FOREVER AND EVER — **SLIK**
FOREVER AND EVER, AMEN — **Randy TRAVIS**
FOREVER AND FOR ALWAYS — **Shania TWAIN**
FOREVER AS ONE — **The VENGABOYS**
FOREVER AUTUMN — **Justin HAYWARD**
FOREVER CAME TODAY — **Diana ROSS and The SUPREMES**
FOREVER FAILURE — **PARADISE LOST**
FOREVER FREE — **W.A.S.P.**
FOREVER GIRL — **OTT**
FOREVER IN BLUE JEANS — **Neil DIAMOND**
FOREVER IN LOVE — **Kenny G**
FOREVER J — **Terry HALL**
A FOREVER KIND OF LOVE — **Bobby VEE**
(FOREVER) LIVE AND DIE — **ORCHESTRAL MANOEUVRES IN THE DARK**
FOREVER LOVE — **Gary BARLOW**
FOREVER MAN [A] — **Eric CLAPTON**
FOREVER MAN (HOW MANY TIMES) [A] — **BEATCHUGGERS featuring Eric CLAPTON**
FOREVER MORE [A] — **Puff JOHNSON**
FOREVER MORE [B] — **MOLOKO**
FOREVER NOW — **LEVEL 42**
FOREVER REELING — **KINESIS**
FOREVER TOGETHER — **Raven MAIZE**
FOREVER YOUNG [A] — **Rod STEWART**
FOREVER YOUNG [B] — **INTERACTIVE**
FOREVER YOUNG [C] — **4 VINI featuring Elisabeth TROY**
FOREVER YOUR GIRL — **Paula ABDUL**
FOREVERGREEN — **FINITRIBE**
FORGET ABOUT THE WORLD — **GABRIELLE**
FORGET ABOUT TOMORROW — **FEEDER**
FORGET ABOUT YOU — **The MOTORS**
FORGET HIM [A] — **Bobby RYDELL**
FORGET HIM [A] — **Billy FURY**
FORGET I WAS A G — **WHITEHEAD BROS**
FORGET ME KNOTS — **Roni SIZE**
FORGET ME NOT [A] — **Eden KANE**
FORGET ME NOT [B] — **Martha REEVES and the VANDELLAS**
FORGET-ME-NOT — **Vera LYNN**
FORGET ME NOTS [A] — **Patrice RUSHEN**
FORGET ME NOTS [A] — **TONGUE 'N' CHEEK**
FORGIVE ME — **Lynden David HALL**
FORGIVEN (I FEEL YOUR LOVE) — **SPACE BROTHERS**
FORGOT ABOUT DRE — **DR DRE featuring EMINEM**
FORGOTTEN DREAMS [A] — **Cyril STAPLETON and his ORCHESTRA**
FORGOTTEN DREAMS [A] — **Leroy ANDERSON and his POPS CONCERT ORCHESTRA**
FORGOTTEN TOWN — **The CHRISTIANS**
FORMED A BAND — **ART BRUT**
FORMULAE — **JJ72**
FORSAKEN DREAMS — **DILLINJA**
FORT WORTH JAIL — **Lonnie DONEGAN**
FORTRESS AROUND YOUR HEART — **STING**
FORTRESS EUROPE — **ASIAN DUB FOUNDATION**
FORTUNE FADED — **RED HOT CHILI PEPPERS**
FORTUNES OF WAR — **FISH**
40 MILES — **CONGRESS**
FORTY MILES OF BAD ROAD — **Duane EDDY and the REBELS**
40 YEARS — **Paul HARDCASTLE**
48 CRASH — **Suzi QUATRO**
45 R.P.M. — **POPPYFIELDS**
FORWARD THE REVOLUTION — **SPIRAL TRIBE**
FOUND A CURE — **Ultra NATÉ**
FOUND LOVE — **DOUBLE DEE featuring DANY**
FOUND OUT ABOUT YOU — **GIN BLOSSOMS**
FOUND OUT TOO LATE — **999**
FOUND THAT SOUL — **MANIC STREET PREACHERS**
FOUND YOU — **DODGY**
FOUNDATION — **BEENIE MAN**
FOUNTAIN O' YOUTH — **CANDYLAND**
FOUR BACHARACH AND DAVID SONGS (EP) — **DEACON BLUE**
FOUR BIG SPEAKERS — **WHALE**
FOUR FROM TOYAH (EP) — **TOYAH**
FOUR LETTER WORD — **Kim WILDE**
FOUR LITTLE HEELS [A] — **AVONS**
FOUR LITTLE HEELS [A] — **Brian HYLAND**
FOUR MINUTE WARNING — **Mark OWEN**
4 MORE — **DE LA SOUL**
FOUR MORE FROM TOYAH (EP) — **TOYAH**
4 MY PEOPLE — **Missy 'Misdemeanor' ELLIOTT**
4 PAGE LETTER — **AALIYAH**
THE 4 PLAY EPS — **R KELLY**
FOUR SEASONS IN ONE DAY — **CROWDED HOUSE**
4 SEASONS OF LONELINESS — **BOYZ II MEN**
FOUR STRONG WINDS — **Neil YOUNG**
FOUR TO THE FLOOR — **STARSAILOR**
FOURPLAY (EP) — **VARIOUS ARTISTS (EPs and LPs)**
14 HOURS TO SAVE THE EARTH — **TOMSKI**
FOURTH RENDEZ-VOUS — **Jean-Michel JARRE**
FOX FORCE FIVE — **CHRIS and JAMES**
FOX ON THE RUN [A] — **MANFRED MANN**
FOX ON THE RUN [B] — **The SWEET**
FOXHOLE — **TELEVISION**
FOXY, FOXY — **MOTT THE HOOPLE**
'FRAGGLE ROCK' THEME — **FRAGGLES**
FRAGILE [A] — **STING**
FRAGILE [A] — **Julio IGLESIAS**
FRAGILE THING — **BIG COUNTRY featuring Eddi READER**
FRANCESCA - THAT MADDENING GLARE — **SPECIAL NEEDS**
THE FRANK SONATA — **LONGPIGS**
FRANKENSTEIN — **Edgar WINTER GROUP**
FRANKIE — **SISTER SLEDGE**
FRANKIE AND JOHNNY [A] — **Elvis PRESLEY**
FRANKIE AND JOHNNY [A] — **Mr Acker BILK and his PARAMOUNT JAZZ BAND**
FRANKIE AND JOHNNY [A] — **Sam COOKE**
FRANTIC — **METALLICA**
FREAK [A] — **Bruce FOXTON**
FREAK [B] — **SILVERCHAIR**
FREAK [C] — **STRANGELOVE**
FREAK IT! — **STUDIO 45**
FREAK LIKE ME [A] — **Adina HOWARD**
FREAK LIKE ME [A] — **TRU FAITH & DUB CONSPIRACY**
FREAK LIKE ME [A] — **SUGABABES**
FREAK ME [A] — **SILK**
FREAK ME [A] — **ANOTHER LEVEL**
FREAK MODE — **The REELISTS**
FREAK ON A LEASH — **KORN**
FREAKIN' IT — **Will SMITH**
FREAKIN' OUT — **Graham COXON**
FREAKIN' YOU — **The JUNGLE BROTHERS**
FREAKS — **LIVE**
FREAKS (LIVE) — **MARILLION**
THE FREAKS COME OUT — **Cevin FISHER**
FREAKY BE BEAUTIFUL — **MOIST**
FREAKYTIME — **POINT BREAK**
THE FRED EP — **VARIOUS ARTISTS (EPs and LPs)**
FREDDY KREUGER — **REUBEN**
FREDERICK — **Patti SMITH GROUP**
FREE [A] — **Deniece WILLIAMS**
FREE [A] — **Will DOWNING**
FREE [A] — **Chanté MOORE**
FREE [B] — **CURIOSITY KILLED THE CAT**
FREE [C] — **Stevie WONDER**
FREE [D] — **Ultra NATÉ**
FREE [E] — **DJ QUICKSILVER**
FREE [F] — **VAST**
FREE [G] — **John 'OO' FLEMING**
FREE [H] — **Claire FREELAND**
FREE [I] — **MYA**
FREE [J] — **ESTELLE**
FREE (EP) — **FREE**
FREE AS A BIRD — **The BEATLES**
FREE AT LAST — **SIMON**
FREE (C'MON) — **CATCH**
FREE ELECTRIC BAND — **Albert HAMMOND**
FREE FALLIN' — **Tom PETTY and the HEARTBREAKERS**
FREE, GAY AND HAPPY — **COMING OUT CREW**
FREE HUEY — **BOO RADLEYS**
FREE (LET IT BE) — **STUART**
FREE LOVE — **Juliet ROBERTS**
FREE ME [A] — **Roger DALTREY**
FREE ME [B] — **CAST**
FREE ME [C] — **EMMA**
FREE 'N' EASY — **The ALMIGHTY**
FREE RANGE — **The FALL**
FREE SATPAL RAM — **ASIAN DUB FOUNDATION**
FREE SPIRIT — **Kim APPLEBY**
THE FREE STYLE MEGA-MIX — **Bobby BROWN**
FREE TO DECIDE — **The CRANBERRIES**
FREE TO FALL — **Deborah HARRY**
FREE TO LOVE AGAIN — **Suzette CHARLES**
FREE WORLD — **Kirsty MacCOLL**
FREE YOUR BODY — **Praga KHAN**
FREE YOUR MIND [A] — **EN VOGUE**
FREE YOUR MIND [B] — **SPACE BABY**
FREE YOURSELF — **UNTOUCHABLES**
FREEBASE — **TALL PAUL**
FREED FROM DESIRE — **GALA**
FREEDOM [A] — **WHAM!**
FREEDOM [B] — **Alice COOPER**
FREEDOM [C] — **George MICHAEL**
FREEDOM [C] — **Robbie WILLIAMS**
FREEDOM [D] — **A HOMEBOY, a HIPPIE and a FUNKI DREDD**
FREEDOM [E] — **LONDON BOYS**
FREEDOM [F] — **Michelle GAYLE**
FREEDOM [G] — **SHIVA**
FREEDOM [H] — **Robert MILES featuring Kathy SLEDGE**
FREEDOM [I] — **ERASURE**
FREEDOM (EP) — **QFX**
FREEDOM COME FREEDOM GO — **FORTUNES**
FREEDOM FIGHTERS — **The MUSIC**
FREEDOM GOT AN A.K. — **DA LENCH MOB**
FREEDOM (MAKE IT FUNKY) — **BLACK MAGIC**
FREEDOM OVERSPILL — **Steve WINWOOD**
FREEDOM'S PRISONER — **Steve HARLEY and COCKNEY REBEL**
FREEEK! — **George MICHAEL**
FREEFLOATING — **Gary CLARK**
FREEK 'N YOU — **JODECI**
FREELOADER — **DRIFTWOOD**
FREELOVE — **DEPECHE MODE**
FREESTYLER — **BOMFUNK MC'S**
FREET — **TATA BOX INHIBITORS**
FREEWAY OF LOVE — **Aretha FRANKLIN**
FREEWHEEL BURNIN' — **JUDAS PRIEST**
THE FREEZE — **SPANDAU BALLET**
FREEZE-FRAME — **J GEILS BAND**
FREEZE THE ATLANTIC — **CABLE**
FREIGHT TRAIN — **Charles McDEVITT SKIFFLE GROUP featuring Nancy WHISKEY**
FRENCH DISCO — **STEREOLAB**
FRENCH FOREIGN LEGION — **Frank SINATRA**
FRENCH KISS — **LIL' LOUIS**
FRENCH KISSES — **JENTINA**
FRENCH KISSIN' IN THE USA — **Deborah HARRY**
FREQUENCY [A] — **RHYTHMATIC**
FREQUENCY [B] — **ALTERN 8**
FRESH [A] — **KOOL and the GANG**
FRESH! [B] — **Gina G**
FRIDAY — **Daniel BEDINGFIELD**
FRIDAY I'M IN LOVE — **The CURE**
FRIDAY NIGHT (LIVE VERSION) — **KIDS FROM 'FAME'**
FRIDAY ON MY MIND [A] — **EASYBEATS**
FRIDAY ON MY MIND [A] — **Gary MOORE**
FRIDAY STREET — **Paul WELLER**
FRIDAY 13TH (EP) — **The DAMNED**
FRIDAY'S ANGELS — **GENERATION X**
FRIDAY'S CHILD — **Will YOUNG**
FRIED MY LITTLE BRAINS — **The KILLS**
A FRIEND — **KRS ONE**
FRIEND OF MINE — **Kelly PRICE**
FRIEND OR FOE — **Adam ANT**
FRIENDLY PERSUASION [A] — **FOUR ACES**
FRIENDLY PERSUASION [A] — **Pat BOONE**
FRIENDLY PRESSURE — **JHELISA**
FRIENDS [A] — **The BEACH BOYS**
FRIENDS [B] — **ARRIVAL**
FRIENDS [C] — **SHALAMAR**
FRIENDS [D] — **Amii STEWART**
FRIENDS [E] — **Jody WATLEY with Eric B and RAKIM**
FRIENDS [F] — **TIGER**
FRIENDS [G] — **HOPE OF THE STATES**
THE FRIENDS AGAIN EP — **FRIENDS AGAIN**
FRIENDS AND NEIGHBOURS — **Billy COTTON and his BAND**
FRIENDS FOREVER — **THUNDERBUGS**
FRIENDS IN LOW PLACES — **Garth BROOKS**
FRIENDS WILL BE FRIENDS — **QUEEN**
FRIENDSHIP — **Sabrina JOHNSTON**
FRIGGIN' IN THE RIGGIN' — **The SEX PISTOLS**
FRIGHTENED CITY — **The SHADOWS**
THE FROG PRINCESS — **The DIVINE COMEDY**
FROGGY MIX — **James BROWN**
FROGGY STYLE — **NUTTIN' NYCE**
FROM A DISTANCE [A] — **Bette MIDLER**
FROM A DISTANCE [A] — **Cliff RICHARD**
FROM A JACK TO A KING — **Ned MILLER**
FROM A LOVER TO A FRIEND — **Paul McCARTNEY**
FROM A TO H AND BACK AGAIN — **SHEEP ON DRUGS**
FROM A WINDOW [A] — **Billy J KRAMER and the DAKOTAS**
FROM A WINDOW [B] — **NORTHERN UPROAR**
FROM DESPAIR TO WHERE — **MANIC STREET PREACHERS**
FROM EAST TO WEST — **VOYAGE**
FROM HEAD TO TOE — **Elvis COSTELLO**
FROM HERE TO ETERNITY [A] — **Giorgio MORODER**
FROM HERE TO ETERNITY [B] — **IRON MAIDEN**
FROM HERE TO ETERNITY [C] — **Michael BALL**
FROM HERE TO THERE TO YOU — **Hank LOCKLIN**
FROM ME TO YOU — **The BEATLES**
FROM NEW YORK TO LA — **Patsy GALLANT**
FROM NOW ON — **Jaki GRAHAM**
FROM OUT OF NOWHERE — **FAITH NO MORE**
FROM RUSH HOUR WITH LOVE — **REPUBLICA**
FROM RUSSIA WITH LOVE [A] — **John BARRY ORCHESTRA**
FROM RUSSIA WITH LOVE [A] — **Matt MONRO**
FROM RUSSIA WITH LOVE [B] — **Matt DAREY**
FROM THA CHUUUCH TO DA PALACE — **SNOOP DOGG**
FROM THE BENCH AT BELVIDERE — **BOO RADLEYS**
FROM THE BOTTOM OF MY HEART — **The MOODY BLUES**
FROM THE FIRE — **FIELDS OF NEPHILIM**
FROM THE GHETTO — **Dread FLIMSTONE and the NEW TONE AGE FAMILY**
FROM THE HEART — **ANOTHER LEVEL**
FROM THE HIP (EP) — **Lloyd COLE**
FROM THE UNDERWORLD — **The HERD**
FROM THIS DAY — **MACHINE HEAD**
FROM THIS MOMENT ON — **Shania TWAIN**
FRONTIER PSYCHIATRIST — **The AVALANCHES**
FRONTIN' [A] — **PHARRELL WILLIAMS featuring JAY-Z**
FRONTIN' [A] — **Jamie CULLUM**
FROSTY THE SNOWMAN — **COCTEAU TWINS**
FROZEN — **MADONNA**
FROZEN HEART — **FM**
FROZEN METAL HEAD (EP) — **BEASTIE BOYS**
FROZEN ORANGE JUICE — **Peter SARSTEDT**
F**K IT (I DON'T WANT YOU BACK) — **EAMON**
***K THE MILLENNIUM — **2K**
FUEL — **METALLICA**
FU-GEE-LA — **The FUGEES**
FUGITIVE MOTEL — **ELBOW**
FULL METAL JACKET (I WANNA BE YOUR DRILL INSTRUCTOR) — **Abigail MEAD and Nigel GOULDING**
THE FULL MONTY-MONSTER MIX — **VARIOUS ARTISTS (EPs and LPs)**
FULL OF LIFE (HAPPY NOW) — **The WONDER STUFF**
FULL MOON — **BRANDY**
FULL TERM LOVE — **Monie LOVE**
FULL TIME JOB — **Doris DAY and Johnnie RAY**
FUN — **DA MOB featuring JOCELYN BROWN**
FUN DAY — **Stevie WONDER**
FUN FOR ME — **MOLOKO**
FUN FUN FUN — **STATUS QUO with The BEACH BOYS**
THE FUN LOVIN' CRIMINAL — **FUN LOVIN' CRIMINALS**
THE FUNERAL OF HEARTS — **HIM**
FUNERAL PYRE — **The JAM**
THE FUNERAL (SEPTEMBER 25, 1977) — **Thuli DUMAKUDE**
FUNGI MAMA (BEBOPAFUNKADISCOLYPSO) — **Tom BROWNE**
FUNK AND DRIVE — **ELEVATORMAN**
FUNK DAT — **SAGAT**
FUNK ON AH ROLL — **James BROWN**
THE FUNK PHENOMENA — **Armand VAN HELDEN**
FUNK THEORY — **ROKOTTO**
FUNKATARIUM — **JUMP**
FUNKDAFIED — **DA BRAT**
FUNKIN' FOR JAMAICA (N.Y.) — **Tom BROWN**
FUNKY BROADWAY — **Wilson PICKETT**
FUNKY COLD MEDINA — **Tone LOC**
FUNKY DORY — **Rachel STEVENS**
FUNKY GIBBON — **The GOODIES**
FUNKY GUITAR — **TC**
FUNKY JAM — **PRIMAL SCREAM**
FUNKY LOVE — **KAVANA**
FUNKY LOVE VIBRATIONS — **BASS-O-MATIC**
FUNKY MOPED — **Jasper CARROTT**
FUNKY MUSIC (SHO NUFF TURNS ME ON) — **UTAH SAINTS**
FUNKY NASSAU — **BEGINNING OF THE END**
FUNKY PLANET — **POWERS THAT BE**
FUNKY SENSATION — **LADIES CHOICE**
FUNKY STREET — **Arthur CONLEY**
FUNKY TOWN — **PSEUDO ECHO**
FUNKY WEEKEND — **The STYLISTICS**
FUNKYTOWN — **LIPPS INC**
FUNNY ALL OVER — **VERNONS GIRLS**
FUNNY BREAK (ONE IS ENOUGH) — **ORBITAL**
FUNNY FAMILIAR FORGOTTEN FEELINGS — **Tom JONES**
FUNNY FUNNY — **The SWEET**
FUNNY HOW — **AIRHEAD**
FUNNY HOW LOVE CAN BE — **IVY LEAGUE**
FUNNY HOW LOVE IS — **FINE YOUNG CANNIBALS**
FUNNY HOW TIME FLIES (WHEN YOU'RE HAVING FUN) — **Janet JACKSON**
FUNNY HOW TIME SLIPS AWAY — **Dorothy MOORE**
FUNNY WAY OF LAUGHIN' — **Burl IVES**
FUNTIME — **BOY GEORGE**
F.U.R.B. — F U RIGHT BACK — **FRANKEE**
FURIOUS ANGELS — **Rob DOUGAN**
FURNITURE — **FUGAZI**
FURNITURE MUSIC — **Bill NELSON**
FURTHER — **LONGVIEW**
THE FURTHER ADVENTURES OF NORTH (EP) — **VARIOUS ARTISTS (EPs and LPs)**
FUTURE — **Halo VARGAS**
FUTURE LOVE — **PRESENCE**
FUTURE LOVE (EP) — **SEAL**
FUTURE MANAGEMENT — **Roger TAYLOR**
THE FUTURE MUSIC (EP) — **LIQUID**
THE FUTURE OF THE FUTURE (STAY GOLD) — **DEEP DISH with EVERYTHING BUT THE GIRL**
FUTURE SHOCK — **Herbie HANCOCK**
FUTURE SOUND (EP) — **PHUTURE ASSASSINS**

THE FUTURE'S SO BRIGHT I GOTTA WEAR SHADES — TIMBUK 3
FUZION — PESHAY featuring CO-ORDINATE
FX — A GUY CALLED GERALD
G SPOT — Wayne MARSHALL
GABRIEL — Roy DAVIS Jr featuring Peven EVERETT
GAINESVILLE ROCK CITY — LESS THAN JAKE
GAL WINE — Chaka DEMUS and PLIERS
THE GAL WITH THE YALLER SHOES — Michael HOLLIDAY
GALAXIA — MOONMAN
GALAXIE — BLIND MELON
GALAXY — WAR
GALAXY OF LOVE — CROWN HEIGHTS AFFAIR
GALLOPING HOME — LONDON STRING CHORALE
GALLOWS POLE — Jimmy PAGE and Robert PLANT
GALVESTON — Glen CAMPBELL
GALVESTON BAY — Lonnie HILL
GAMBLER — MADONNA
GAMBLIN' BAR ROOM BLUES — The SENSATIONAL ALEX HARVEY BAND
GAMBLIN' MAN — Lonnie DONEGAN and his Skiffle Group
THE GAME [A] — ECHO and the BUNNYMEN
THE GAME [B] — Nichola HOLT
GAME BOY — KWS
GAME OF LOVE [A] — Wayne FONTANA and The MINDBENDERS
GAME OF LOVE [B] — Tony HADLEY
THE GAME OF LOVE [C] — SANTANA featuring Michelle BRANCH
GAME ON — CATATONIA
GAME OVER — SCARFACE
GAMEMASTER — LOST TRIBE
GAMES — NEW KIDS ON THE BLOCK
GAMES PEOPLE PLAY [A] — Joe SOUTH
GAMES PEOPLE PLAY [A] — INNER CIRCLE
THE GAMES WE PLAY — Andreas JOHNSON
GAMES WITHOUT FRONTIERS — Peter GABRIEL
GANDHARA — GODIEGO
(THE GANG THAT SANG) HEART OF MY HEART — Max BYGRAVES
GANGSTA, GANGSTA — NWA
GANGSTA'S PARADISE — COOLIO featuring LV
GANGSTA LOVIN' — EVE featuring Alicia KEYS
GANGSTER TRIPPIN' — FATBOY SLIM
GANGSTERS — The SPECIALS
GANGSTERS OF THE GROOVE — HEATWAVE
G.A.R.A.G.E. — CORRUPTED CRU featuring MC NEAT
GARAGE GIRLS — LONYO featuring MC ONYX STONE
GARDEN OF DELIGHT — The MISSION
GARDEN OF EDEN [A] — Dick JAMES
GARDEN OF EDEN [A] — Gary MILLER
GARDEN OF EDEN [A] — Joe VALINO
THE GARDEN OF EDEN [A] — Frankie VAUGHAN
GARDEN PARTY [A] — Ricky NELSON
GARDEN PARTY [B] — MARILLION
GARDEN PARTY [C] — MEZZOFORTE
GARY GILMORE'S EYES — ADVERTS
GARY GLITTER (EP) — Gary GLITTER
THE GAS FACE — 3RD BASS
GASOLINE ALLEY — Elkie BROOKS
GASOLINE ALLEY BRED — The HOLLIES
GATECRASHING — LIVING IN A BOX
GATHER IN THE MUSHROOMS — Benny HILL
GAUDETE — STEELEYE SPAN
GAY BAR — ELECTRIC SIX
GAY BOYFRIEND — HAZZARDS
THE GAY CAVALIEROS (THE STORY SO FAR) — Steve WRIGHT
GAYE — Clifford T WARD
GBI — Towa TEI featuring Kylie MINOGUE
GEE BABY — Peter SHELLEY
GEE BUT IT'S LONELY — Pat BOONE
GEE WHIZ IT'S YOU — Cliff RICHARD and The SHADOWS
GEEK STINK BREATH — GREEN DAY
GENERAL PUBLIC — GENERAL PUBLIC
GENERALS AND MAJORS — XTC
GENERATION SEX — The DIVINE COMEDY
GENERATIONS — INSPIRAL CARPETS
GENERATIONS OF LOVE — JESUS LOVES YOU
GENETIC ENGINEERING — ORCHESTRAL MANOEUVRES IN THE DARK
GENIE — B B and Q BAND
GENIE IN A BOTTLE [A] — Christina AGUILERA
GENIE IN A BOTTLE [A] — SPEEDWAY
GENIE WITH THE LIGHT BROWN LAMP — The SHADOWS
GENIUS — PITCH SHIFTER
GENIUS MOVE — THAT PETROL EMOTION
GENIUS OF LOVE — TOM TOM CLUB
GENO — DEXY'S MIDNIGHT RUNNERS
THE GENTLE ART OF CHOKING — MY VITRIOL
GENTLE ON MY MIND — Dean MARTIN
GENTLEMAN WHO FELL — MILLA
A GENTLEMAN'S EXCUSE ME — FISH
GENTLEMEN TAKE POLAROIDS — JAPAN
GEORDIE BOYS (GAZZA RAP) — GAZZA
GEORDIE IN WONDERLAND — The WILDHEARTS
GEORGIA ON MY MIND — Ray CHARLES
GEORGINA BAILEY — Noosha FOX
GEORGY GIRL — The SEEKERS
GEORGY PORGY [A] — CHARME
GEORGY PORGY [B] — Eric BENET featuring Faith EVANS
GEPETTO — BELLY
GERM FREE ADOLESCENCE — X-RAY SPEX
GERONIMO — The SHADOWS
GERTCHA — CHAS and DAVE
(GET A) GRIP (ON YOURSELF) — The STRANGLERS
GET A LIFE [A] — SOUL II SOUL
GET A LIFE [B] — Julian LENNON
GET A LIFE [C] — FREESTYLERS
GET A LITTLE FREAKY WITH ME — Aaron HALL
GET ALONG WITH YOU — KELIS
GET ANOTHER LOVE — Chantal CURTIS
GET AWAY — Georgie FAME and the BLUE FLAMES
GET BACK [A] — The BEATLES with Billy PRESTON
GET BACK [A] — Rod STEWART
GET BACK [B] — MOTHER
GET BUSY [A] — MR LEE
GET BUSY [B] — Sean PAUL
GET CARTER — Roy BUDD
GET DANCIN' — DISCO TEX and the SEX-O-LETTES
GET DOWN [A] — Gilbert O'SULLIVAN
GET DOWN [B] — Gene CHANDLER
GET DOWN [C] — M-D-EMM
GET DOWN [D] — Craig MACK
GET DOWN [E] — The JUNGLE BROTHERS
GET DOWN AND GET WITH IT — SLADE
GET DOWN ON IT [A] — KOOL and the GANG
GET DOWN ON IT [A] — Louchie LOU and Michie ONE
GET DOWN SATURDAY NIGHT — Oliver CHEATHAM
GET DOWN TONIGHT — KC and the SUNSHINE BAND
GET DOWN (YOU'RE THE ONE FOR ME) — BACKSTREET BOYS
GET 'EM OFF! — TOKYO DRAGONS
GET FREE — The VINES
GET GET DOWN — Paul JOHNSON
GET HERE [A] — Oleta ADAMS
GET HERE [A] — Q
GET HIGHER — BLACK GRAPE
GET IN THE SWING — SPARKS
GET INTO IT — Tony SCOTT
GET INTO THE MUSIC — DJ's RULE
GET INTO YOU — Dannii MINOGUE
GET INVOLVED — Raphael SAADIQ and Q-TIP
GET IT [A] — DARTS
GET IT [B] — Stevie WONDER and Michael JACKSON
GET IT ON [A] — T. REX
GET IT ON [A] — POWER STATION
GET IT ON [A] — BUS STOP
GET IT ON [B] — KINGDOM COME
GET IT ON [C] — INTENSO PROJECT featuring Lisa SCOTT-LEE
GET IT ON THE FLOOR — DMX featuring SWIZZ BEATZ
GET IT ON TONITE — Montell JORDAN
GET IT RIGHT [A] — Aretha FRANKLIN
GET IT RIGHT [B] — Joe FAGIN
GET IT RIGHT NEXT TIME — Gerry RAFFERTY
GET IT TOGETHER [A] — CRISPY AND COMPANY
GET IT TOGETHER [B] — BEASTIE BOYS
GET IT TOGETHER [C] — SEAL
GET IT UP — RM PROJECT
GET IT UP (THE FEELING) — Ultra NATÉ
GET IT UP FOR LOVE [A] — David CASSIDY
GET IT UP FOR LOVE [A] — Tata VEGA
GET IT UP FOR LOVE [A] — LUCIANA
GET IT WHILE IT'S HOT — NODESHA
GET IT WHILE YOU CAN — OLYMPIC RUNNERS
GET LOOSE [A] — Evelyn 'Champagne' KING
GET LOOSE [B] — LA MIX featuring Jazzi P
GET LOOSE [C] — The D4
GET LOST — Eden KANE
GET LUCKY — Jermaine STEWART
GET ME — DINOSAUR JR
GET ME HOME — Foxy BROWN featuring BLACKSTREET
GET ME OFF — BASEMENT JAXX
GET ME OUT — NEW MODEL ARMY
GET ME TO THE WORLD ON TIME — ELECTRIC PRUNES
GET MYSELF ARRESTED — GOMEZ
GET NO BETTER — CASSIDY featuring MASHONDA
GET OFF — The DANDY WARHOLS
GET OFF OF MY CLOUD — The ROLLING STONES
GET OFF THIS — CRACKER
GET OFF YOUR HIGH HORSE — ROLLO
GET ON IT — PHOEBE ONE
GET ON THE BUS — DESTINY'S CHILD featuring TIMBALAND
GET ON THE DANCE FLOOR — Rob BASE and DJ E-Z ROCK
GET ON THE FUNK TRAIN — MUNICH MACHINE
GET ON UP [A] — Jazzy DEE
GET ON UP [B] — JODECI
GET ON UP, GET ON DOWN — Roy AYERS
GET ON YOUR FEET — Gloria ESTEFAN
GET OUT [A] — Harold MELVIN and the BLUENOTES
GET OUT [B] — Busta RHYMES
GET OUT [C] — FELON
GET OUT OF MY LIFE WOMAN — Lee DORSEY
GET OUT OF MYSELF — REDD KROSS
GET OUT OF THIS HOUSE — Shawn COLVIN
GET OUT OF YOUR LAZY BED — MATT BIANCO
GET OUTTA MY DREAMS GET INTO MY CAR — Billy OCEAN
GET OVER IT — OK GO
GET OVER YOU [A] — The UNDERTONES
GET OVER YOU [B] — Sophie ELLIS-BEXTOR
GET READY [A] — The TEMPTATIONS
GET READY [A] — Carol HITCHCOCK
GET READY! [B] — ROACHFORD
GET READY [C] — MA$E featuring BLACKSTREET
GET READY FOR THIS — 2 UNLIMITED
GET REAL — Paul RUTHERFORD
GET SOME THERAPY — Steve WRIGHT
GET THAT LOVE — THOMPSON TWINS
GET THE BALANCE RIGHT — DEPECHE MODE
GET THE FUNK OUT — EXTREME
GET THE GIRL! KILL THE BADDIES! — POP WILL EAT ITSELF
GET THE KEYS AND GO — LLAMA FARMERS
GET THE MESSAGE — ELECTRONIC
GET THE PARTY STARTED — PINK
GET THROUGH — Mark JOSEPH
GET TOGETHER — The WONDER STUFF
GET TOUGH — KLEEER
GET UP [A] — Beverley KNIGHT
GET UP [B] — BLACKOUT
GET UP AND BOOGIE [A] — SILVER CONVENTION
GET UP AND BOOGIE [B] — Freddie JAMES
GET UP (AND LET YOURSELF GO) — J.A.L.N. BAND
GET UP AND MOVE — HARVEY
GET UP (BEFORE THE NIGHT IS OVER) — TECHNOTRONIC
GET UP (EVERYBODY) — Byron STINGILY
GET UP! GO INSANE! — STRETCH 'N' VERN present MADDOG
GET UP I FEEL LIKE BEING A SEX MACHINE — James BROWN
GET UP OFFA THAT THING — James BROWN
GET UP STAND UP [A] — PHUNKY PHANTOM
GET UP STAND UP [B] — STELLAR PROJECT featuring Brandi EMMA
GET UP SUNSHINE STREET — BIZARRE INC
GET UR FREAK ON — Missy 'Misdemeanor' ELLIOTT
GET WILD — NEW POWER GENERATION
GET YOUR BODY — ADAMSKI
GET YOUR FEET OUT OF MY SHOES — BOOTHILL FOOT-TAPPERS
GET YOUR HANDS OFF MY MAN! — Junior VASQUEZ
GET YOUR HANDS OFF MY WOMAN — The DARKNESS
GET YOUR LOVE BACK — The THREE DEGREES
GET YOURSELF TOGETHER — YOUNG DISCIPLES
GET-A-WAY — MAXX
GETAWAY — The MUSIC
GETO HEAVEN — COMMON featuring Macy GRAY
GETS ME THROUGH — Ozzy OSBOURNE
GETT OFF — PRINCE and the NEW POWER GENERATION
GETTIN' IN THE WAY — Jill SCOTT
GETTIN' INTO U — W.O.S.P.
GETTIN' IT RIGHT — Alison LIMERICK
GETTIN' JIGGY WIT IT — Will SMITH
GETTIN' MONEY — JUNIOR M.A.F.I.A.
GETTIN' READY FOR LOVE — Diana ROSS
GETTING A DRAG — Lynsey DE PAUL
GETTING AWAY WITH IT [A] — ELECTRONIC
GETTING AWAY WITH IT [B] — EGG
GETTING AWAY WITH IT (ALL MESSED UP) — JAMES
GETTING AWAY WITH MURDER — PAPA ROACH
GETTING BETTER — SHED SEVEN
GETTING CLOSER [A] — Paul McCARTNEY
GETTING CLOSER [B] — HAYWOODE
GETTING INTO SOMETHING — Alison MOYET
GETTING MIGHTY CROWDED — Betty EVERETT
GETTING OVER YOU — Andy WILLIAMS
GETTING UP — PIGBAG
GETTO JAM — DOMINO
GHETTO — RHYTHM MASTERS featuring Joe WATSON
GHETTO CHILD — DETROIT SPINNERS
GHETTO DAY — Crystal WATERS
GHETTO GIRL — SIMPLY RED
GHETTO HEAVEN — FAMILY STAND
GHETTO MUSICK — OUTKAST
GHETTO ROMANCE — DAMAGE
GHETTO SUPASTAR (THAT IS WHAT YOU ARE) — Pras MICHEL
G.H.E.T.T.O.U.T. — CHANGING FACES
THE GHOST AT NUMBER ONE — JELLYFISH
GHOST DANCER — ADDRISI BROTHERS
GHOST HOUSE — HOUSE ENGINEERS
GHOST IN YOU — PSYCHEDELIC FURS
THE GHOST OF LOVE [A] — TAVARES
GHOST OF LOVE [B] — FICTION FACTORY
THE GHOST OF TOM JOAD — Bruce SPRINGSTEEN
GHOST TOWN — The SPECIALS
GHOSTBUSTERS [A] — Ray PARKER Jr
GHOSTBUSTERS [A] — RUN-DMC
GHOSTDANCING — SIMPLE MINDS
GHOSTS [A] — JAPAN
GHOSTS [A] — TENTH PLANET
GHOSTS [B] — Michael JACKSON
GHOSTS [C] — DIRTY VEGAS
GIA — Despina VANDI
GIDDY-UP — 2 IN A ROOM
GIDDY-UP-A-DING-DONG — Freddie BELL and the BELLBOYS
THE GIFT [A] — INXS
THE GIFT [B] — Daniel O'DONNELL
THE GIFT [C] — WAY OUT WEST featuring Miss Joanna LAW
THE GIFT OF CHRISTMAS — CHILDLINERS
GIGANTOR — The DICKIES
GIGI — Billy ECKSTINE
GIGOLO — The DAMNED
GILLY GILLY OSSENFEFFER KATZENELLEN BOGEN BY THE SEA — Max BYGRAVES
GIMME ALL YOUR LOVIN' [A] — Jocelyn BROWN and Kym MAZELLE
GIMME ALL YOUR LOVIN' [A] — ZZ TOP
GIMME ALL YOUR LOVIN' 2000 [A] — MARTAY featuring ZZ TOP
GIMME DAT BANANA — BLACK GORILLA
GIMME DAT DING — PIPKINS
GIMME, GIMME, GIMME (A MAN AFTER MIDNIGHT) — ABBA
GIMME GIMME GOOD LOVIN' — CRAZY ELEPHANT
GIMME HOPE JO'ANNA — Eddy GRANT
GIMME LITTLE SIGN [A] — Brenton WOOD
GIMME LITTLE SIGN [A] — Danielle BRISEBOIS
GIMME LOVE — ALEXIA
GIMME LUV (EENIE MEENIE MINY MO) — David MORALES
GIMME SHELTER (EP) — VARIOUS ARTISTS (EPs and LPs)
GIMME SOME [A] — BRENDON
GIMME SOME [A] — PAT and MICK
GIMME SOME LOVE — Gina G
GIMME SOME LOVIN' — THUNDER
GIMME SOME LOVING — Spencer DAVIS GROUP
GIMME SOME MORE — Busta RHYMES
GIMME THE LIGHT — Sean PAUL
GIMME THAT BODY — HISTORY featuring Q-TEE
GIMME THE LIGHT — Sean PAUL
GIMME THE SUNSHINE — CURIOSITY
GIMME YOUR LUVIN' — ATLANTIC STARR
GIMMIX! PLAY LOUD — John Cooper CLARKE
GIN AND JUICE — SNOOP DOGGY DOGG
GIN GAN GOOLIE — SCAFFOLD
GIN HOUSE BLUES — AMEN CORNER
GIN SOAKED BOY — The DIVINE COMEDY
GINCHY — Bert WEEDON
GINGER — David DEVANT & his SPIRIT WIFE
GINGERBREAD — Frankie AVALON
GINNY COME LATELY — Brian HYLAND
GIRL [A] — ST LOUIS UNION
GIRL [A] — TRUTH
GIRL ALL THE BAD GUYS WANT — BOWLING FOR SOUP
GIRL / BOY (EP) — APHEX TWIN
THE GIRL CAN'T HELP IT — LITTLE RICHARD
GIRL CRAZY — HOT CHOCOLATE
GIRL DON'T COME — Sandie SHAW
THE GIRL FROM IPANEMA — Stan GETZ
GIRL FROM MARS — ASH
A GIRL I ONCE KNEW — NORTHERN UPROAR
THE GIRL I USED TO KNOW — BROTHER BEYOND
GIRL I'M GONNA MISS YOU — MILLI VANILLI
GIRL IN THE MOON — DARIUS
THE GIRL IN THE WOOD — Frankie LAINE
THE GIRL IS MINE — Michael JACKSON and Paul McCARTNEY
GIRL IS ON MY MIND — BLACK KEYS
GIRL (IT'S ALL I HAVE) — SHY
GIRL I'VE BEEN HURT — SNOW
A GIRL LIKE YOU [A] — Cliff RICHARD and The SHADOWS
A GIRL LIKE YOU [B] — YOUNG RASCALS
A GIRL LIKE YOU [C] — Edwyn COLLINS
THE GIRL OF MY BEST FRIEND [A] — Elvis PRESLEY
GIRL OF MY BEST FRIEND [A] — Bryan FERRY
GIRL OF MY DREAMS [A] — Tony BRENT
GIRL OF MY DREAMS [A] — Gerry MONROE
GIRL ON TV — LYTE FUNKIE ONES
GIRL POWER — SHAMPOO
THE GIRL SANG THE BLUES — The EVERLY BROTHERS
GIRL TALK — TLC
GIRL TO GIRL — 49ers
GIRL U FOR ME — SILK
GIRL U WANT — Robert PALMER
THE GIRL WITH THE LONELIEST EYES — HOUSE OF LOVE

GIRL YOU KNOW IT'S TRUE [A] — MILLI VANILLI
GIRL YOU KNOW IT'S TRUE [A] —
KEITH 'N' SHANE
GIRL YOU'LL BE A WOMAN SOON —
URGE OVERKILL
GIRL YOU'RE SO TOGETHER —
Michael JACKSON
GIRLFRIEND [A] — Michael JACKSON
GIRLFRIEND [A] — PEBBLES
GIRLFRIEND [C] — Billie PIPER
GIRLFRIEND [D] — 'N SYNC featuring NELLY
GIRLFRIEND [E] — Alicia KEYS
GIRLFRIEND [F] — B2K
GIRLFRIEND / BOYFRIEND — BLACKSTREET
GIRLFRIEND IN A COMA — The SMITHS
GIRLFRIEND'S STORY —
Gemma FOX featuring MC LYTE
GIRLIE — PEDDLERS
GIRLIE GIRLIE — Sophia GEORGE
GIRLS [A] — Johnny BURNETTE
GIRLS [B] — MOMENTS
GIRLS [C] —
POWERCUT featuring NUBIAN PRINZ
GIRLS [C] — BEASTIE BOYS
GIRLS [D] — The PRODIGY
THE GIRL'S A FREAK — DJ TOUCHE
GIRLS AIN'T NOTHING BUT TROUBLE —
JAZZY JEFF & the FRESH PRINCE
GIRLS AND BOYS [A] — PRINCE
GIRLS AND BOYS [B] — BLUR
GIRLS + BOYS [C] — HED BOYS
GIRLS AND BOYS [D] — GOOD CHARLOTTE
GIRLS ARE MORE FUN — Ray PARKER Jr
GIRLS ARE OUT TO GET YOU — FASCINATIONS
GIRLS BEST FRIEND — The DATSUNS
GIRLS CAN GET IT — DR HOOK
GIRLS DEM SUGAR —
BEENIE MAN featuring MYA
GIRLS GIRLS GIRLS [A] — Steve LAWRENCE
GIRLS GIRLS GIRLS [B] — The FOURMOST
GIRLS GIRLS GIRLS [C] — SAILOR
GIRLS GIRLS GIRLS [D] — KANDIDATE
GIRLS, GIRLS, GIRLS [E] — MÖTLEY CRÜE
GIRLS, GIRLS, GIRLS [F] — JAY-Z
GIRLS JUST WANT TO HAVE FUN [A] —
Cyndi LAUPER
GIRLS JUST WANNA HAVE FUN [A] — LOLLY
GIRL'S LIFE — GIRLFRIEND
GIRLS LIKE US —
B15 featuring Chrissy D & Lady G
(GIRLS GIRLS GIRLS) MADE TO LOVE —
Eddie HODGES
GIRLS NIGHT OUT — ALDA
GIRL'S NOT GREY — AFI
THE GIRLS OF SUMMER (EP) — ARAB STRAP
GIRLS ON FILM — DURAN DURAN
GIRLS ON MY MIND — FATBACK BAND
GIRLS ON TOP — GIRL THING
GIRLS TALK — Dave EDMUNDS
GIRLS' SCHOOL — Paul McCARTNEY
GIT DOWN (SHAKE YOUR THANG) —
GAYE BYKERS ON ACID
GIT DOWN — CENOGINERZ
GIT ON UP — DJ 'FAST' EDDIE
GITTIN' FUNKY — KID 'N' PLAY
GIV ME LUV — ALCATRAZ
GIVE A LITTLE BIT — SUPERTRAMP
GIVE A LITTLE LOVE [A] — BAY CITY ROLLERS
GIVE A LITTLE LOVE [B] — ASWAD
GIVE A LITTLE LOVE [C] — Daniel O'DONNELL
GIVE A LITTLE LOVE [D] — INVISIBLE MAN
GIVE A LITTLE LOVE BACK TO THE WORLD —
EMMA
GIVE AND TAKE [A] — PIONEERS
GIVE AND TAKE [B] — BRASS CONSTRUCTION
GIVE GIVE GIVE — Tommy STEELE
GIVE GIVE GIVE ME MORE MORE MORE —
The WONDER STUFF
GIVE HER MY LOVE — JOHNSTON BROTHERS
GIVE HER WHAT SHE WANTS —
Frankie OLIVER
GIVE IN TO ME — Michael JACKSON
GIVE IRELAND BACK TO THE IRISH —
Paul McCARTNEY
GIVE IT ALL AWAY — WORLD PARTY
GIVE IT AWAY [A] — RED HOT CHILI PEPPERS
GIVE IT AWAY [B] — DEEPEST BLUE
GIVE IT SOME EMOTION — TRACIE
GIVE IT TO ME [A] — The TROGGS
GIVE IT TO ME [B] — BAM BAM
GIVE IT TO ME BABY — Rick JAMES
GIVE IT TO ME NOW — KENNY
GIVE IT TO YOU [A] — Martha WASH
GIVE IT TO YOU [B] — Jordan KNIGHT
GIVE IT UP [A] — KC & the SUNSHINE BAND
GIVE IT UP [B] — CUT 'N' MOVE
GIVE IT UP [B] — TALK TALK
GIVE IT UP [C] — HOTHOUSE FLOWERS
GIVE IT UP [D] — WILSON PHILLIPS
GIVE IT UP [E] — GOODMEN
GIVE IT UP [F] — PUBLIC ENEMY
GIVE IT UP [G] — SELENA vs X.MEN
GIVE IT UP TURN IT LOOSE — EN VOGUE
GIVE ME A LITTLE MORE TIME — GABRIELLE
GIVE ME A REASON [A] — The CORRS
GIVE ME A REASON [B] —
Tony DE VIT featuring Niki MAK

GIVE ME A REASON [C] — TRIPLE EIGHT
GIVE ME ALL YOUR LOVE [A] — WHITESNAKE
GIVE ME ALL YOUR LOVE [B] — MAGIC AFFAIR
GIVE ME AN INCH — Hazel O'CONNOR
GIVE ME BACK ME BRAIN — DUFFO
GIVE ME BACK MY HEART — DOLLAR
GIVE ME BACK MY MAN — B-52's
GIVE ME FIRE — GBH
GIVE ME JUST A LITTLE MORE TIME [A] —
CHAIRMEN OF THE BOARD
GIVE ME JUST A LITTLE MORE TIME [A] —
Kylie MINOGUE
GIVE ME JUST ONE MORE NIGHT (UNA NOCHE) — 98°
GIVE ME LIFE — MR V
GIVE ME LOVE [A] — DIDDY
GIVE ME LOVE [B] —
DJ DADO vs Michelle WEEKS
GIVE ME LOVE (GIVE ME PEACE ON EARTH) —
George HARRISON
GIVE ME MORE TIME [A] — NICOLE
GIVE ME MORE TIME [A] — WHITESNAKE
GIVE ME ONE MORE CHANCE [A] —
Donald PEERS
GIVE ME ONE MORE CHANCE [B] —
Luke GOSS and the BAND OF THIEVES
GIVE ME RHYTHM — BLACK CONNECTION
GIVE ME SOME KINDA MAGIC — DOLLAR
GIVE ME SOME MORE — DJ GERT
GIVE ME STRENGTH —
JON OF THE PLEASED WIMMIN
GIVE ME THE NIGHT [A] — George BENSON
GIVE ME THE NIGHT [A] — MIRAGE
GIVE ME THE NIGHT [A] — Randy CRAWFORD
GIVE ME THE REASON — Luther VANDROSS
GIVE ME TIME — Dusty SPRINGFIELD
GIVE ME TONIGHT — SHANNON
GIVE ME YOU — Mary J BLIGE
GIVE ME YOUR BODY — CHIPPENDALES
GIVE ME YOUR HEART TONIGHT —
Shakin' STEVENS
GIVE ME YOUR LOVE — REEF
GIVE ME YOUR WORD [A] —
Tennessee Ernie FORD
GIVE ME YOUR WORD [A] — Billy FURY
GIVE MYSELF TO LOVE — Francis ROSSI
GIVE PEACE A CHANCE — John LENNON
GIVE U ONE 4 CHRISTMAS — HOT PANTZ
GIVE UP THE FUNK (LET'S DANCE) —
BT EXPRESS
GIVE YOU — DJAIMIN
GIVE YOU ALL THE LOVE — MISHKA
GIVEN TO FLY — PEARL JAM
GIVEN UP — MIRRORBALL
GIVIN' IT UP — INCOGNITO
GIVING HIM SOMETHING HE CAN FEEL —
EN VOGUE
GIVING IN — ADEMA
GIVING IT ALL AWAY — Roger DALTREY
GIVING IT BACK — Phil HURTT
GIVING UP, GIVING IN [A] —
The THREE DEGREES
GIVING UP GIVING IN [A] — Sheena EASTON
GIVING YOU THE BENEFIT — PEBBLES
GIVING YOU THE BEST THAT I GOT —
Anita BAKER
G.L.A.D. — Kim APPLEBY
GLAD ALL OVER [A] — Dave CLARK FIVE
GLAD ALL OVER [A] — CRYSTAL PALACE
GLAD IT'S ALL OVER — CAPTAIN SENSIBLE
GLAM — Lisa B
GLAM RAID — SPACE RAIDERS
GLAM ROCK COPS — CARTER —
THE UNSTOPPABLE SEX MACHINE
GLAM SLAM — PRINCE
GLASGOW RANGERS (NINE IN A ROW) —
RANGERS FC
GLASS OF CHAMPAGNE — SAILOR
GLASTONBURY SONG — WATERBOYS
GLENDORA [A] — Glen MASON
GLENDORA [A] — Perry COMO
GLENN MILLER MEDLEY —
John ANDERSON BIG BAND
GLITTER AND TRAUMA — BIFFY CLYRO
GLITTERBALL [A] — SIMPLE MINDS
GLITTERBALL [B] — FC KAHUNA
GLITTERING PRIZE — SIMPLE MINDS
GLOBAL LOVE — HIGH CONTRAST
GLOBETROTTER — TORNADOS
GLORIA [A] — Jonathan KING
GLORIA [B] — Laura BRANIGAN
GLORIA [B] — U2
GLORIA [C] —
Van MORRISON and John Lee HOOKER
GLORIOUS — Andreas JOHNSON
GLORY BOX — PORTISHEAD
GLORY DAYS — Bruce SPRINGSTEEN
GLORY GLORY MAN UNITED —
MANCHESTER UNITED FOOTBALL CLUB
GLORY OF LOVE — Peter CETERA
GLORY OF THE 80'S — Tori AMOS
GLORYLAND —
Daryl HALL and the SOUNDS OF BLACKNESS
GLOW — SPANDAU BALLET
THE GLOW OF LOVE — CHANGE
THE GLOW WORM — MILLS BROTHERS
GO [A] — Scott FITZGERALD
GO [B] — MOBY

GO [C] — JOCASTA
GO AWAY [A] — Gloria ESTEFAN
GO AWAY [B] — HONEYCRACK
GO AWAY LITTLE GIRL — Mark WYNTER
GO (BEFORE YOU BREAK MY HEART) —
Gigliola CINQUETTI
GO BUDDY GO — The STRANGLERS
GO CUT CREATOR GO — LL COOL J
GO DEEP — Janet JACKSON
GO DEH YAKA (GO TO THE TOP) — MONYAKA
GO ENGLAND — ENGLAND BOYS
GO FOR IT! —
COVENTRY CITY CUP FINAL SQUAD
GO FOR IT (HEART AND FIRE) — Joey B ELLIS
GO FOR THE HEART — SOX
GO GO GO — Chuck BERRY
GO HOME — Stevie WONDER
GO INTO THE LIGHT — Ian McNABB
GO LET IT OUT — OASIS
GO NORTH — Richard BARNES
GO NOW — The MOODY BLUES
GO ON BY — Alma COGAN
GO ON GIRL — Roxanne SHANTE
GO ON MOVE — REEL 2 REAL
GO TECHNO — 2 HOUSE
GO THE DISTANCE — Michael BOLTON
GO TO SLEEP — RADIOHEAD
GO WEST [A] — VILLAGE PEOPLE
GO WEST [A] — PET SHOP BOYS
GO WILD IN THE COUNTRY — BOW WOW WOW
GO WITH THE FLOW [A] — LOOP DA LOOP
GO WITH THE FLOW [B] —
QUEENS OF THE STONE AGE
GO YOUR OWN WAY — FLEETWOOD MAC
GOD — Tori AMOS
GOD GAVE ROCK AND ROLL TO YOU [A] —
ARGENT
GOD GAVE ROCK AND ROLL TO YOU II [A] — KISS
GOD IS A DJ [A] — FAITHLESS
GOD IS A DJ [B] — PINK
GOD OF ABRAHAM — MNO
GOD ONLY KNOWS [A] — The BEACH BOYS
GOD ONLY KNOWS [B] — DIESEL PARK WEST
GOD SAVE THE QUEEN — The SEX PISTOLS
GOD! SHOW ME MAGIC —
SUPER FURRY ANIMALS
GOD THANK YOU WOMAN — CULTURE CLUB
GODDESS ON A HIWAY — MERCURY REV
GODHEAD — NITZER EBB
GODHOPPING — DOGS DIE IN HOT CARS
GODLESS — The DANDY WARHOLS
GOD'S CHILD — BIG BANG THEORY
GOD'S GONNA PUNISH YOU — TYMES
GOD'S GREAT BANANA SKIN — Chris REA
GOD'S HOME MOVIE — HORSE
GOD'S KITCHEN — BLANCMANGE
GOD'S MISTAKE — TEARS FOR FEARS
GODSPEED — BT
GODSTAR — PSYCHIC TV
GODZILLA — CREATURES
GO-GO DANCER — WEDDING PRESENT
GOIN' DOWN — Melanie C
GOIN DOWN THE ROAD — Roy WOOD
GOIN' OUT OF MY HEAD — Dodie WEST
GOIN' PLACES — The JACKSONS
GOIN' TO THE BANK — The COMMODORES
GOIN' TO VEGAS — Jimmy RAY
GOING ALL THE WAY — ALLSTARS
GOING BACK — Dusty SPRINGFIELD
GOING BACK TO CALI — LL COOL J
GOING BACK TO MY HOME TOWN —
Hal PAIGE and the WHALERS
GOING BACK TO MY ROOTS [A] — ODYSSEY
GOING BACK TO MY ROOTS [A] — FPI PROJECT
GOING DOWN TO LIVERPOOL — The BANGLES
GOING DOWN TOWN TONIGHT — STATUS QUO
GOING FOR GOLD — SHED SEVEN
GOING FOR THE ONE — YES
GOIN' HOME [A] — The OSMONDS
GOING HOME [B] — TYRREL CORPORATION
GOING HOME (THEME OF 'LOCAL HERO') —
Mark KNOPFLER
GOING IN WITH MY EYES OPEN — David SOUL
GOING LEFT RIGHT — DEPARTMENT S
GOING NOWHERE — GABRIELLE
GOING OUT — SUPERGRASS
GOING OUT OF MY HEAD — FATBOY SLIM
GOING OUT WITH GOD — KINKY MACHINE
GOING ROUND — D'BORA
GOING THROUGH THE MOTIONS —
HOT CHOCOLATE
GOING TO A GO-GO [A] — MIRACLES
GOING TO A GO-GO [A] — SHARONETTES
GOING TO A GO GO [A] —
The ROLLING STONES
GOING UNDER — EVANESCENCE
GOING UNDERGROUND [A] — The JAM
GOING UNDERGROUND [A] — BUFFALO TOM
GOING UP THE COUNTRY — CANNED HEAT
GOLD [A] — John STEWART
GOLD [B] — SPANDAU BALLET
GOLD [C] — EAST 17
GOLD [D] — PRINCE
GOLD [E] — Beverley KNIGHT
GOLDEN — Jill SCOTT
GOLDEN AGE OF ROCK 'N' ROLL —
MOTT THE HOOPLE

GOLDEN BROWN [A] — The STRANGLERS
GOLDEN BROWN [A] — KALEEF
GOLDEN BROWN [B] — OMAR
GOLDEN DAYS — BUCKS FIZZ
GOLDEN GATE BRIDGE —
OCEAN COLOUR SCENE
GOLDEN GAZE — Ian BROWN
GOLDEN GREEN — The WONDER STUFF
GOLDEN GUN — SUEDE
THE GOLDEN LADY — The THREE DEGREES
GOLDEN LIGHTS — TWINKLE
THE GOLDEN PATH — The CHEMICAL
BROTHERS / THE FLAMING LIPS
GOLDEN RETRIEVER —
SUPER FURRY ANIMALS
GOLDEN SKIN — SILVER SUN
GOLDEN SLUMBERS — CARRY THAT WEIGHT — TRASH
GOLDEN TOUCH — RAZORLIGHT
GOLDEN YEARS [A] — David BOWIE
GOLDEN YEARS [A] — LOOSE ENDS
THE GOLDEN YEARS (EP) — MOTÖRHEAD
GOLDENBALLS (MR BECKHAM TO YOU) —
BELL & SPURLING
GOLDENHEAD — FAMILY CAT
GOLDENEYE — Tina TURNER
GOLDFINGER [A] — Shirley BASSEY
GOLDFINGER [B] — ASH
GOLDRUSH — YELLO
GONE [A] — Shirley BASSEY
GONE [B] — David HOLMES
GONE [C] — The CURE
GONE [D] — 'N SYNC
GONE AWAY — The OFFSPRING
GONE DEAD TRAIN — NAZARETH
GONE GONE GONE [A] —
The EVERLY BROTHERS
GONE, GONE, GONE [A] — Johnny MATHIS
GONE TILL NOVEMBER — Wyclef JEAN
GONE TOO SOON — Michael JACKSON
GONNA BUILD A MOUNTAIN [A] —]Matt MONRO
GONNA BUILD A MOUNTAIN [A] —
Sammy DAVIS Jr
GONNA CAPTURE YOUR HEART — BLUE
GONNA CATCH YOU [A] — Lonnie GORDON
GONNA CATCH YOU [A] — BARKIN
BROTHERS featuring Johnnie FIORI
GONNA GET ALONG WITHOUT YA NOW [A] —
PATIENCE and PRUDENCE
GONNA GET ALONG WITHOUT YA NOW [A] —
Trini LOPEZ
GONNA GET ALONG WITHOUT YOU NOW [A] —
Viola WILLS
GONNA GIVE HER ALL THE LOVE I'VE GOT —
Jimmy RUFFIN
GONNA MAKE YOU A STAR — David ESSEX
GONNA MAKE YOU AN OFFER YOU CAN'T REFUSE —
Jimmy HELMS
GONNA MAKE YOU BLUSH — PAPERDOLLS
GONNA MAKE YOU SWEAT
(EVERYBODY DANCE NOW) —
C & C MUSIC FACTORY / CLIVILLES & COLE
GONNA WORK IT OUT — HI-GATE
GOO GOO BARABAJAGAL (LOVE IS HOT) —
DONOVAN with the Jeff BECK GROUP
GOOD AS GOLD — The BEAUTIFUL SOUTH
GOOD BEAT — DEEE-LITE
GOOD BOYS — BLONDIE
GOOD DANCERS — SLEEPY JACKSON
GOOD DAY — Sean MAGUIRE
GOOD ENOUGH [A] — Bobby BROWN
GOOD ENOUGH [B] — DODGY
GOOD ENOUGH (LA VACHE) —
MILK INCORPORATED
GOOD EVENING FRIENDS —
Frankie LAINE and Johnnie RAY
GOOD EVENING PHILADELPHIA — Ricky ROSS
GOOD FEELING — REEF
GOOD FOR ME — Amy GRANT
GOOD FORTUNE — P J HARVEY
GOOD FRIEND — PARIS RED
GOOD FRUIT — HEFNER
GOOD GIRLS — JOE
GOOD GIRLS DON'T — KNACK
GOOD GOD [A] — KORN
GOOD GOD [B] — JFK
GOOD GOLLY MISS MOLLY [A] —
LITTLE RICHARD
GOOD GOLLY MISS MOLLY [A] —
Jerry Lee LEWIS
GOOD GOLLY MISS MOLLY [A] —
SWINGING BLUE JEANS
GOOD GOOD FEELING —
ERIC and the GOOD GOOD FEELING
GOOD GRIEF CHRISTINA — CHICORY TIP
A GOOD HEART — Feargal SHARKEY
A GOOD IDEA — SUGAR
GOOD LIFE [A] — INNER CITY
GOOD LIFE [B] — E.V.E.
THE GOOD LIFE [A] — Tony BENNETT
THE GOOD LIFE [B] —
NEW POWER GENERATION
GOOD LOVE — Meli'sa MORGAN
GOOD LOVE CAN NEVER DIE —
Alvin STARDUST
GOOD LOVE REAL LOVE — D'BORA
GOOD LOVER — D'INFLUENCE
GOOD LOVIN' — Regina BELLE

GOOD LOVIN' AIN'T EASY TO COME BY —
Marvin GAYE
GOOD LOVIN' GONE BAD — BAD COMPANY
GOOD LUCK —
BASEMENT JAXX featuring Lisa KEKAULA
GOOD LUCK CHARM —
Elvis PRESLEY with the JORDANAIRES
GOOD MORNING — Leapy LEE
GOOD MORNING BRITAIN — AZTEC CAMERA
GOOD MORNING FREEDOM — BLUE MINK
GOOD MORNING JUDGE — 10cc
GOOD MORNING LITTLE SCHOOLGIRL —
YARDBIRDS
GOOD MORNING STARSHINE — OLIVER
GOOD MORNING SUNSHINE — AQUA
GOOD OLD ARSENAL — ARSENAL FC
GOOD OLD ROCK 'N' ROLL — Dave CLARK FIVE
GOOD REASON — SEAFOOD
GOOD RHYMES — DA CLICK
GOOD SIGN — EMILIA
GOOD SONG — BLUR
GOOD SOULS — STARSAILOR
GOOD STUFF [A] — B-52's
GOOD STUFF [B] — KELIS
GOOD SWEET LOVIN' —
Louchie LOU and Michie ONE
THE GOOD, THE BAD AND THE UGLY — Hugo
MONTENEGRO, his Orchestra and Chorus
GOOD THING [A] — FINE YOUNG CANNIBALS
GOOD THING [B] — ETERNAL
GOOD THING GOING [A] — Sid OWEN
GOOD THING GOING (WE'VE GOT A GOOD
THING GOING) [A] — Sugar MINOTT
GOOD THING GOING [A] — YAZZ
GOOD THINGS — RIVAL SCHOOLS
GOOD TIME [A] — PERAN
GOOD TIME [B] — A
GOOD TIME BABY — Bobby RYDELL
GOOD TIMES [A] — The ANIMALS
GOOD TIMES [B] — CHIC
GOOD TIMES [C] — MATT BIANCO
GOOD TIMES [D] — REID
GOOD TIMES [E] — INXS
GOOD TIMES [F] —
Edie BRICKELL and the NEW BOHEMIANS
GOOD TIMES [G] — DREAM FREQUENCY
GOOD TIMES [H] — ED CASE
GOOD TIMES (BETTER TIMES) — Cliff RICHARD
GOOD TIMES GONNA COME — AQUALUNG
GOOD TIMIN' — Jimmy JONES
GOOD TO BE ALIVE — DJ RAP
GOOD TO GO LOVER — Gwen GUTHRIE
GOOD TRADITION — Tanita TIKARAM
GOOD VIBRATIONS [A] — The BEACH BOYS
GOOD VIBRATIONS [A] — PSYCHIC TV
GOOD VIBRATIONS [A] — Brian WILSON
GOOD VIBRATIONS [B] —
MARKY MARK and the FUNKY BUNCH
featuring Loleatta HOLLOWAY
GOOD VIBRATIONS [C] — BROTHERS
LIKE OUTLAW featuring Alison EVELYN
A GOOD YEAR FOR THE ROSES —
Elvis COSTELLO
GOODBYE [A] — Mary HOPKIN
GOODBYE [B] — The SUNDAYS
GOODBYE [C] — Air SUPPLY
GOODBYE [D] — SPICE GIRLS
GOODBYE [E] — DEF LEPPARD
GOODBYE [F] — The CORAL
A GOODBYE — CAMEO
GOODBYE BABY AND AMEN — LULU
GOODBYE BAD TIMES — Giorgio MORODER
GOODBYE BLUEBIRD — Wayne FONTANA
GOODBYE CIVILIAN — The SKIDS
GOODBYE CRUEL WORLD [A] — James DARREN
GOODBYE CRUEL WORLD [B] —
SHAKESPEAR'S SISTER
GOODBYE GIRL [A] — SQUEEZE
GOODBYE GIRL [B] — GO WEST
GOODBYE HEARTBREAK —
LIGHTHOUSE FAMILY
GOODBYE IS JUST ANOTHER WORD —
The NEW SEEKERS
GOODBYE JIMMY, GOODBYE — Ruby MURRAY
GOODBYE MR MACKENZIE —
GOODBYE MR MACKENZIE
GOODBYE MY LOVE [A] — The SEARCHERS
GOODBYE MY LOVE [B] — GLITTER BAND
GOODBYE NOTHING TO SAY —
JAVELLS featuring Nosmo KING
GOODBYE SAM HELLO SAMANTHA —
Cliff RICHARD
GOODBYE STRANGER [A] — SUPERTRAMP
GOODBYE STRANGER [B] — PEPSI and SHIRLIE
GOODBYE TO LOVE — The CARPENTERS
GOODBYE TO LOVE AGAIN — Maxi PRIEST
GOODBYE TONIGHT — LOSTPROPHETS
GOODBYE YELLOW BRICK ROAD — Elton JOHN
GOODBYE-EE [A] — Peter COOK
GOODBYE-EE [A] — 14-18
GOODBYE'S (THE SADDEST WORD) —
Celine DION
GOODGROOVE — Derek B
GOODNESS GRACIOUS ME — Peter SELLERS
GOODNIGHT [A] — Roy ORBISON
GOODNIGHT [B] — BABYBIRD

GOODNIGHT GIRL — WET WET WET
GOODNIGHT MIDNIGHT — Clodagh RODGERS
GOODNIGHT MOON — SHIVAREE
GOODNIGHT MRS FLINTSTONE —
PILTDOWN MEN
GOODNIGHT SAIGON — Billy JOEL
GOODNIGHT SWEET PRINCE — Mr Acker
BILK and his PARAMOUNT JAZZ BAND
GOODNIGHT TONIGHT — Paul McCARTNEY
GOODWILL CITY — GOODBYE MR MACKENZIE
GOODY GOODY —
Frankie LYMON and the TEENAGERS
GOODY TWO SHOES — Adam ANT
GOOGLE EYE — NASHVILLE TEENS
GORECKI — LAMB
GORGEOUS — GENE LOVES JEZEBEL
GOSP — LWS
GOSPEL OAK (EP) — Sinead O'CONNOR
GOSSIP CALYPSO — Bernard CRIBBINS
GOSSIP FOLKS —
Missy ELLIOTT featuring LUDACRIS
GOT A FEELING — Patrick JUVET
GOT A GIRL — FOUR PREPS
GOT A LITTLE HEARTACHE — Alvin STARDUST
GOT A LOT O' LIVIN' TO DO — Elvis PRESLEY
GOT A LOVE FOR YOU — JOMANDA
GOT A MATCH — Russ CONWAY
GOT FUNK — FUNK JUNKEEZ
GOT IT AT THE DELMAR — SENSELESS THINGS
GOT ME A FEELING — Misty OLDLAND
GOT MY MIND MADE UP — INSTANT FUNK
GOT MY MIND SET ON YOU —
George HARRISON
GOT MY MOJO WORKING — Jimmy SMITH
GOT MYSELF TOGETHER — BUCKETHEADS
GOT NO BRAINS — BAD MANNERS
GOT SOME TEETH — Obie TRICE
GOT THE FEELIN' — FIVE
GOT THE LIFE — KORN
GOT THE TIME — ANTHRAX
GOT 'TIL IT'S GONE — Janet JACKSON
GOT TO BE CERTAIN — Kylie MINOGUE
GOT TO BE FREE — 49ers
GOT TO BE REAL — ERIK
GOT TO BE THERE — Michael JACKSON
GOT TO GET — ROB 'n' RAZ featuring Leila K
GOT TO GET IT [A] — CULTURE BEAT
GOT TO GET IT [B] — SISQO
GOT TO GET UP — Afrika BAMBAATAA
GOT TO GET YOU BACK — Kym MAZELLE
GOT TO GET YOU INTO MY LIFE [A] —
Cliff BENNETT and the REBEL ROUSERS
GOT TO GET YOU INTO MY LIFE [A] —
EARTH WIND AND FIRE
GOT TO GIVE IT UP [A] — AALIYAH
GOT TO GIVE IT UP (PT.1) [A] — Marvin GAYE
GOT TO GIVE ME LOVE — Dana DAWSON
GOT TO HAVE YOUR LOVE [A] — MANTRONIX
GOT TO HAVE YOUR LOVE [A] — LIBERTY X
GOT TO KEEP ON — COOKIE CREW
GOT TO LOVE SOMEBODY — SISTER SLEDGE
GOT TO RELEASE —
SATURATED SOUL featuring MISS BUNTY
GOT UR SELF A ... — NAS
GOT YOU — Pharoahe MONCH
GOT YOU ON MY MIND — Tony BRENT
GOT YOUR MONEY —
OL' DIRTY BASTARD featuring KELIS
GOTHAM CITY — R KELLY
GOTTA BE A SIN — Adam ANT
GOTTA BE...MOVIN' ON UP — PM DAWN
GOTTA BE YOU — 3T
GOTTA CATCH 'EM ALL —
50 GRIND featuring POKEMON ALLSTARS
GOTTA GET A DATE — Frank IFIELD
GOTTA GET AWAY — The OFFSPRING
GOTTA GET IT RIGHT — Lena FIAGBE
GOTTA GET LOOSE — MR and MRS SMITH
GOTTA GET THRU THIS — Daniel BEDINGFIELD
GOTTA GET YOU HOME TONIGHT —
Eugene WILDE
GOTTA GO HOME — BONEY M
GOTTA HAVE HOPE — BLACKOUT
GOTTA HAVE RAIN — Max BYGRAVES
GOT-TA HAVE SOMETHING IN THE BANK, FRANK —
Frankie VAUGHAN and the KAYE SISTERS
GOTTA KEEP PUSHIN' — Z FACTOR
GOTTA KNOW (YOUR NAME) — MALAIKA
GOTTA LOTTA LOVE — ICE-T
GOTTA PULL MYSELF TOGETHER —
The NOLANS
GOTTA SEE BABY TONIGHT — Mr Acker
BILK and his PARAMOUNT JAZZ BAND
GOTTA SEE JANE — R Dean TAYLOR
GOTTA TELL YOU — Samantha MUMBA
GOURYELLA — GOURYELLA
GOVINDA [A] — RADHA KRISHNA TEMPLE
GOVINDA [B] — KULA SHAKER
GRACE [A] — BAND AKA
GRACE [B] — SUPERGRASS
GRACEADELICA — DARK STAR
GRACELAND — The BIBLE
GRANADA [A] — Frankie LAINE
GRANADA [A] — Frank SINATRA
GRAND COOLIE DAM — Lonnie DONEGAN
GRAND PIANO — MIXMASTER
GRANDAD — Clive DUNN

GRANDMA'S PARTY — Paul NICHOLAS
GRANDPA'S PARTY — Monie LOVE
GRANITE STATUE — SALAD
GRAPEVYNE — BROWNSTONE
GRATEFUL WHEN YOU'RE DEAD — JERRY
WAS THERE — KULA SHAKER
THE GRAVE AND THE CONSTANT —
FUN LOVIN' CRIMINALS
GRAVEL PIT — WU-TANG CLAN
GRAVITATE TO ME — The THE
GRAVITY [A] — James BROWN
GRAVITY [B] — EMBRACE
GREASE [A] — Frankie VALLI
GREASE [A] — Craig McLACHLAN
THE GREASE MEGAMIX —
John TRAVOLTA and Olivia NEWTON-JOHN
GREASE — THE DREAM MIX —
Frankie VALLI, John TRAVOLTA
and Olivia NEWTON-JOHN
GREASED LIGHTNIN' — John TRAVOLTA
GREAT BALLS OF FIRE [A] — Jerry Lee LEWIS
GREAT BALLS OF FIRE [A] — TINY TIM
THE GREAT BEYOND — R.E.M.
THE GREAT ESCAPE —
ENGLAND SUPPORTERS' BAND
THE GREAT ESCAPE 2000 —
ENGLAND SUPPORTERS' BAND
GREAT GOSH A'MIGHTY ! (IT'S A MATTER OF TIME) —
LITTLE RICHARD
THE GREAT PRETENDER [A] —
Jimmy PARKINSON
THE GREAT PRETENDER [A] —
Freddie MERCURY
THE GREAT PRETENDER [A] — The PLATTERS
THE GREAT ROCK 'N' ROLL SWINDLE —
The SEX PISTOLS
THE GREAT SNOWMAN — Bob LUMAN
THE GREAT SONG OF INDIFFERENCE —
Bob GELDOF
THE GREAT TEST — HUNDRED REASONS
GREAT THINGS — ECHOBELLY
THE GREAT TRAIN ROBBERY — BLACK UHURU
GREATER LOVE — SOUNDMAN and
Don LLOYDIE with Elisabeth TROY
THE GREATEST COCKNEY RIP-OFF —
COCKNEY REJECTS
GREATEST DAY — Beverley KNIGHT
THE GREATEST FLAME — RUNRIG
THE GREATEST HIGH — HURRICANE #1
THE GREATEST LOVE OF ALL [A] —
George BENSON
THE GREATEST LOVE OF ALL [A] —
Whitney HOUSTON
THE GREATEST LOVE YOU'LL NEVER KNOW —
Lutricia McNEAL
THE GREATEST ROMANCE EVER SOLD — PRINCE
THE GREATEST SHOW ON EARTH —
STRANGELOVE
THE GREATNESS AND PERFECTION OF LOVE —
Julian COPE
GREECE 2000 — THREE DRIVES
GREED — Laurent GARNIER
GREEDY FLY — BUSH
THE GREEDY UGLY PEOPLE — HEFNER
GREEN AND GREY — NEW MODEL ARMY
THE GREEN DOOR [A] — Frankie VAUGHAN
THE GREEN DOOR [A] — Jim LOWE
GREEN DOOR [A] — Glen MASON
GREEN DOOR [A] — Shakin' STEVENS
GREEN FIELDS — BEVERLEY SISTERS
GREEN FIELDS [A] — UNIT FOUR PLUS TWO
GREEN, GREEN GRASS OF HOME [A] —
Tom JONES
GREEN GREEN GRASS OF HOME [A] —
Elvis PRESLEY
GREEN JEANS — FLEE-REKKERS
THE GREEN LEAVES OF SUMMER —
Kenny BALL and his JAZZMEN
GREEN LIGHT — Cliff RICHARD
THE GREEN MAN — SHUT UP AND DANCE
THE GREEN MANALISHI (WITH THE TWO-PRONG
CROWN) — FLEETWOOD MAC
GREEN ONIONS — BOOKER T and the MG's
GREEN RIVER —
CREEDENCE CLEARWATER REVIVAL
GREEN SHIRT — Elvis COSTELLO
GREEN STREET GREEN —
NEW VAUDEVILLE BAND
GREEN TAMBOURINE [A] — LEMON PIPERS
GREEN TAMBOURINE [A] — SUNDRAGON
GREEN TINTED SIXTIES MIND — MR BIG
GREENBACK DOLLAR — Charles McDEVITT
SKIFFLE GROUP featuring Nancy WHISKEY
GREENBANK DRIVE — The CHRISTIANS
GREENFIELDS — BROTHERS FOUR
GREETINGS TO THE NEW BRUNETTE — Billy BRAGG
with Johnny MARR and Kirsty MacCOLL
GREY DAY — MADNESS
GRIMLY FIENDISH — The DAMNED
GRIND — ALICE IN CHAINS
GRIP '89 (GET A) GRIP (ON YOURSELF) —
The STRANGLERS
GRITTY SHAKER — David HOLMES
THE GROOVE — Rodney FRANKLIN
GROOVE BABY GROOVE (EP) — STARGAZERS
GROOVE IS IN THE HEART — DEEE-LITE
THE GROOVE LINE — HEATWAVE

GROOVE MACHINE — MARVIN and TAMARA
GROOVE OF LOVE — E.V.E.
GROOVE THANG — ZHANE
GROOVE TO MOVE — CHANNEL X
GROOVEBIRD — NATURAL BORN GROOVES
GROOVEJET (IF THIS AIN'T LOVE) — SPILLER,
lead vocals by Sophie ELLIS-BEXTOR
GROOVELINE — BLOCKSTER
THE GROOVER — T. REX
GROOVIN' [A] — YOUNG RASCALS
GROOVIN' [A] — WAR
GROOVIN' [A] — Pato BANTON
GROOVIN' IN THE MIDNIGHT — Maxi PRIEST
GROOVIN' (THAT'S WHAT WE'RE DOIN') —
S.O.S. BAND
GROOVIN' WITH MR BLOE — MR BLOE
GROOVY BABY — MICROBE
GROOVY BEAT — D.O.P.
GROOVY FEELING — FLUKE
A GROOVY KIND OF LOVE [A] —
The MINDBENDERS
A GROOVY KIND OF LOVE [A] — Les GRAY
A GROOVY KIND OF LOVE [A] — Phil COLLINS
THE GROOVY THANG — MINIMAL FUNK 2
GROOVY TRAIN — The FARM
THE GROUNDBREAKER — FALLACY & FUSION
GROUND LEVEL — STEREO MC's
GROUNDED — MY VITRIOL
GROUPIE GIRL — Tony Joe WHITE
GROWING ON ME — The DARKNESS
THE GRUDGE — MORTIIS
G.T.O. — SINITTA
GUAGLIONE — Perez PRADO
GUANTANAMERA [A] — SANDPIPERS
GUANTANAMERA [A] — The FUGEES
GUARANTEED — LEVEL 42
GUARDIAN ANGEL — Nino DE ANGELO
GUARDIANS OF THE LAND — George BOWYER
GUDBUY T'JANE — SLADE
GUDVIBE — TINMAN
GUERRILLA FUNK — PARIS
GUERRILLA RADIO —
RAGE AGAINST THE MACHINE
GUESS I WAS A FOOL — ANOTHER LEVEL
GUESS WHO'S BACK — RAKIM
GUESS YOU DIDN'T LOVE ME — Terri WALKER
GUIDING STAR — CAST
GUILTY [A] — Jim REEVES
GUILTY [B] — PEARLS
GUILTY [C] — Mike OLDFIELD
GUILTY [D] — Barbra STREISAND
GUILTY [E] — CLASSIX NOUVEAUX
GUILTY [F] — Paul HARDCASTLE
GUILTY [G] — YARBROUGH and PEOPLES
GUILTY [H] — BLUE
GUILTY [I] — The RASMUS
GUILTY CONSCIENCE —
EMINEM featuring DR. DRE
GUILTY OF LOVE — WHITESNAKE
GUITAR BOOGIE SHUFFLE — Bert WEEDON
GUITAR DATE — The 5.6.7.8'S
GUITAR MAN [A] — Elvis PRESLEY
THE GUITAR MAN [B] — BREAD
GUITAR TANGO — The SHADOWS
GUITARRA G — BANDA SONARA
GUN LAW — KANE GANG
GUNATANAMO — OUTLANDISH
GUNMAN — 187 LOCKDOWN
GUNS DON'T KILL PEOPLE, RAPPERS DO —
GOLDIE LOOKIN CHAIN
GUNS FOR HIRE — AC/DC
GUNS OF NAVARONE — SKATALITES
GUNSLINGER — Frankie LAINE
GUNZ AND PIANOZ — BASS BOYZ
GURNEY SLADE — Max HARRIS
THE GUSH — RAGING SPEEDHORN
GYM AND TONIC — SPACEDUST
GYPSY — FLEETWOOD MAC
GYPSY BEAT — PACKABEATS
GYPSY BOY, GYPSY GIRL —
SHARADA HOUSE GANG
GYPSY EYES — The Jimi HENDRIX EXPERIENCE
GYPSY ROAD — CINDERELLA
GYPSY ROADHOG — SLADE
GYPSY ROVER — HIGHWAYMEN
GYPSY WOMAN [A] — Brian HYLAND
GYPSY WOMAN [B] — Crystal WATERS
GYPSYS, TRAMPS AND THIEVES — CHER
HA CHA CHA (FUNKTION) —
BRASS CONSTRUCTION
HA HA SAID THE CLOWN — MANFRED MANN
HAD TO BE —
Cliff RICHARD and Olivia NEWTON-JOHN
HAIL CAESAR — AC/DC
HAIL HAIL ROCK 'N' ROLL — Garland JEFFREYS
HAIL MARY — MAKAVELI
HAITIAN DIVORCE — STEELY DAN
HALCYON — CHICANE
HALE BOPP — DER DRITTE RAUM
HALEY'S GOLDEN MEDLEY —
Bill HALEY and his COMETS
HALF A BOY AND HALF A MAN — Nick LOWE
HALF A HEART — H & CLAIRE
HALF A MINUTE — MATT BIANCO
HALF AS MUCH — Rosemary CLOONEY
HALF MAN HALF MACHINE —
GOLDIE LOOKIN CHAIN

HALF OF MY HEART — Emile FORD and the CHECKMATES
HALF ON A BABY — R KELLY
HALF THE DAY'S GONE AND WE HAVEN'T EARNT A PENNY — Kenny LYNCH
HALF THE MAN — JAMIROQUAI
HALF THE WORLD — Belinda CARLISLE
HALFWAY AROUND THE WORLD — A*TEENS
HALFWAY DOWN THE STAIRS — The MUPPETS
HALFWAY HOTEL — VOYAGER
HALFWAY TO HEAVEN — EUROPE
HALFWAY TO PARADISE — Billy FURY
HALFWAY UP HALFWAY DOWN — Dennis BROWN
HALLELUJAH — MILK AND HONEY featuring Gali ATARI
HALLELUJAH DAY — The JACKSON FIVE
HALLELUJAH FREEDOM — Junior CAMPBELL
HALLELUJAH I LOVE HER SO [A] — Dick JORDAN
HALLELUJAH I LOVE HER SO [A] — Eddie COCHRAN
HALLELUJAH MAN — LOVE AND MONEY
HALLELUJAH '92 — INNER CITY
HALLO SPACEBOY — David BOWIE
HALLOWED BE THY NAME (LIVE) — IRON MAIDEN
HALLS OF ILLUSION — INSANE CLOWN POSSE
HALO [A] — TEXAS
HALO [B] — SOIL
(HAMMER HAMMER) THEY PUT ME IN THE MIX — HAMMER
HAMMER HORROR — Kate BUSH
HAMMER TO FALL — QUEEN
HAMMER TO THE HEART — The TAMPERER featuring MAYA
HANDBAGS AND GLADRAGS — STEREOPHONICS
HAND A HANDKERCHIEF TO HELEN — Susan MAUGHAN
HAND HELD IN BLACK AND WHITE — DOLLAR
HAND IN GLOVE — Sandie SHAW
HAND IN HAND — GRACE
HAND IN MY POCKET — Alanis MORISSETTE
HAND IN YOUR HEAD — MONEY MARK
HAND OF THE DEAD BODY — SCARFACE featuring ICE CUBE
HAND ON MY HEART — SHRIEKBACK
HAND ON YOUR HEART — Kylie MINOGUE
HANDBAGS AND GLADRAGS [A] — Chris FARLOWE
HANDBAGS AND GLADRAGS [A] — STEREOPHONICS
HANDFUL OF PROMISES — BIG FUN
HANDFUL OF SONGS — Tommy STEELE
HANDLE WITH CARE — TRAVELING WILBURYS
HANDS — JEWEL
HANDS ACROSS THE OCEAN — The MISSION
HANDS AROUND MY THROAT — DEATH IN VEGAS
HANDS CLEAN — Alanis MORISSETTE
HANDS DOWN — ....DASHBOARD CONFESSIONAL
HANDS OFF — SHE'S MINE — The BEAT
HANDS TO HEAVEN — BREATHE
HANDS UP [A] — CLUBZONE
HANDS UP [B] — TREVOR & SIMON
HANDS UP (4 LOVERS) — RIGHT SAID FRED
HANDS UP (GIVE ME YOUR HEART) —OTTAWAN
HANDS UP! HANDS UP! — ZIG and ZAG
HANDY MAN [A] — Jimmy JONES
HANDY MAN [A] — Del SHANNON
HANG 'EM HIGH — Hugo MONTENEGRO
HANG IN LONG ENOUGH — Phil COLLINS
HANG MYSELF ON YOU — The CANDYSKINS
HANG ON IN THERE BABY [A] — Johnny BRISTOL
HANG ON IN THERE BABY [A] — CURIOSITY
HANG ON NOW — KAJAGOOGOO
HANG ON SLOOPY [A] — McCOYS
HANG ON SLOOPY [A] — SANDPIPERS
HANG ON TO A DREAM — Tim HARDIN
HANG ON TO YOUR LOVE — Jason DONOVAN
HANG TOGETHER — ODYSSEY
HANG YOUR HEAD — DEACON BLUE
HANGAR 18 — MEGADETH
HANGIN' — CHIC
HANGIN' ON A STRING — LOOSE ENDS
HANGIN' OUT — KOOL and the GANG
HANGIN' TOUGH — NEW KIDS ON THE BLOCK
HANGINAROUND — COUNTING CROWS
HANGING AROUND [A] — Hazel O'CONNOR
HANGING AROUND [B] — ME ME ME
HANGING AROUND [C] — The CARDIGANS
HANGING AROUND [D] — Gemma HAYES
HANGING AROUND [E] — The POLYPHONIC SPREE
HANGING AROUND WITH THE BIG BOYS — BLOOMSBURY SET
HANGING BY A MOMENT — LIFEHOUSE
HANGING GARDEN — The CURE
HANGING ON THE TELEPHONE — BLONDIE
HANGOVER — Betty BOO
HANKY PANKY [A] — Tommy JAMES and the SHONDELLS
HANKY PANKY [B] — MADONNA
HANNA HANNA — CHINA CRISIS
HAPPENIN' ALL OVER AGAIN [A] — Lonnie GORDON
HAPPENIN' ALL OVER AGAIN [A] — Tracy SHAW
THE HAPPENING — The SUPREMES
HAPPENINGS TEN YEARS TIME AGO — YARDBIRDS
HAPPINESS [A] — Ken DODD
HAPPINESS [B] — SERIOUS ROPE
HAPPINESS [C] — Roger TAYLOR
HAPPINESS [D] — PIZZAMAN
HAPPINESS [E] — KAMASUTRA featuring Jocelyn BROWN
HAPPINESS [F] — SOUND-DE-ZIGN
HAPPINESS HAPPENING — LOST WITNESS
HAPPINESS IS JUST AROUND THE BEND — Cuba GOODING
HAPPINESS IS ME AND YOU — Gilbert O'SULLIVAN
HAPPINESS (MY VISION IS CLEAR) — BINI & MARTINI
HAPPINESS — YOU MAKE ME HAPPY — SERIOUS ROPE
HAPPY [A] — SURFACE
HAPPY [A] — MN8
HAPPY [A] — Pauline HENRY
HAPPY [B] — NED'S ATOMIC DUSTBIN
HAPPY [C] — TRAVIS
HAPPY [D] — ASHANTI
HAPPY [E] — LIGHTHOUSE FAMILY
HAPPY [F] — Max SEDGLEY
HAPPY ANNIVERSARY [A] — Joan REGAN
HAPPY ANNIVERSARY [B] — Slim WHITMAN
HAPPY BIRTHDAY [A] — Stevie WONDER
HAPPY BIRTHDAY [B] — ALTERED IMAGES
HAPPY BIRTHDAY [C] — TECHNOHEAD
HAPPY BIRTHDAY REVOLUTION — LEVELLERS
HAPPY BIRTHDAY SWEET SIXTEEN — Neil SEDAKA
HAPPY BIZZNESS — ROACH MOTEL
HAPPY BUSMAN — FRANK AND WALTERS
HAPPY DAY — BLINK
HAPPY DAYS [A] — PRATT and McCLAIN with BROTHERLOVE
HAPPY DAYS [B] — SWEET MERCY featuring Joe ROBERTS
HAPPY DAYS [C] — PJ
HAPPY DAYS AND LONELY NIGHTS [A] — Frankie VAUGHAN
HAPPY DAYS AND LONELY NIGHTS [A] — JOHNSTON BROTHERS
HAPPY DAYS AND LONELY NIGHTS [A] — Ruby MURRAY
HAPPY ENDING — Joe JACKSON
HAPPY ENDINGS (GIVE YOURSELF A PINCH) — Lionel BART
HAPPY EVER AFTER — Julia FORDHAM
HAPPY FEELING — Hamilton BOHANNON
HAPPY GO LUCKY ME — George FORMBY
HAPPY GUITAR — Tommy STEELE
HAPPY HEART — Andy WILLIAMS
HAPPY HOME — 2PAC
HAPPY HOUR — The HOUSEMARTINS
HAPPY HOUSE — SIOUXSIE and the BANSHEES
HAPPY JACK — The WHO
HAPPY JUST TO BE WITH YOU — Michelle GAYLE
HAPPY (LOVE THEME FROM 'LADY SINGS THE BLUES') — Michael JACKSON
THE HAPPY MAN — Thomas LANG
HAPPY NATION — ACE OF BASE
HAPPY PEOPLE [A] — STATIC REVENGER
HAPPY PEOPLE [B] — R KELLY
H.A.P.P.Y. RADIO [A] — Edwin STARR
H-A-P-P-Y RADIO [A] — MICHAELA
HAPPY SHOPPER — 60FT DOLLS
HAPPY SONG — Otis REDDING
HAPPY TALK — CAPTAIN SENSIBLE
HAPPY TO BE ON AN ISLAND IN THE SUN — Demis ROUSSOS
HAPPY TO MAKE YOUR ACQUAINTANCE — Sammy DAVIS Jr
HAPPY TOGETHER [A] — The TURTLES
HAPPY TOGETHER [A] — Jason DONOVAN
THE HAPPY WANDERER [A] — OBERNKIRCHEN CHILDREN'S CHOIR
THE HAPPY WANDERER [A] — The STARGAZERS
HAPPY WHEN IT RAINS — JESUS AND MARY CHAIN
THE HAPPY WHISTLER [A] — Cyril STAPLETON and his ORCHESTRA
THE HAPPY WHISTLER [A] — Don ROBERTSON
HAPPY XMAS (WAR IS OVER) [A] — JOHN and YOKO and the PLASTIC ONO BAND with the HARLEM COMMUNITY CHOIR
HAPPY XMAS (WAR IS OVER) [A] — The IDOLS
HARBOUR LIGHTS — The PLATTERS
HARD AS A ROCK — AC/DC
HARD BEAT EP 19 — VARIOUS ARTISTS (EPs and LPs)
A HARD DAY'S NIGHT [A] — The BEATLES
A HARD DAY'S NIGHT [A] — Peter SELLERS
HARD HABIT TO BREAK — CHICAGO
HARD HEADED WOMAN — Elvis PRESLEY
HARD HEARTED HANNAH — TEMPERANCE SEVEN
HARD HOUSE MUSIC — MELT featuring LITTLE MS MARCIE
HARD KNOCK LIFE (GHETTO ANTHEM) — JAY-Z
A HARD RAIN'S A-GONNA FALL — Bryan FERRY
HARD ROAD — BLACK SABBATH
HARD TIMES COME EASY — Richie SAMBORA
HARD TO EXPLAIN — The STROKES
HARD TO HANDLE [A] — Otis REDDING
HARD TO HANDLE [A] — BLACK CROWES
HARD TO MAKE A STAND — Sheryl CROW
HARD TO SAY I'M SORRY [A] — CHICAGO
HARD TO SAY I'M SORRY [A] — AZ YET featuring Peter CETERA
HARD TO SAY I'M SORRY [A] — AQUAGEN
HARD UP — AWESOME 3
THE HARD WAY — NASHVILLE TEENS
THE HARDCORE EP — HYPNOTIST
HARDCORE HEAVEN — DJ SEDUCTION
HARDCORE HIP HOUSE — TYREE
HARDCORE — THE FINAL CONFLICT — HARDCORE RHYTHM TEAM
HARDCORE UPROAR — TOGETHER
HARDCORE WILL NEVER DIE — Q-BASS
HARDEN MY HEART — QUARTERFLASH
HARDER — KOSHEEN
HARDER BETTER FASTER STRONGER — DAFT PUNK
THE HARDER I TRY — BROTHER BEYOND
THE HARDER THEY COME [A] — ROCKER'S REVENGE featuring Donnie CALVIN
THE HARDER THEY COME [A] — MADNESS
THE HARDER THEY COME [B] — OAKENFOLD
HARDER TO BREATHE — MAROON5
THE HARDEST BUTTON TO BUTTON — The WHITE STRIPES
HARDEST PART IS THE NIGHT — BON JOVI
THE HARDEST THING — 98°
HARDROCK — Herbie HANCOCK
HARDTRANCE ACPERIENCE — HARDFLOOR
HARE KRISHNA MANTRA — RADHA KRISHNA TEMPLE
HARLEM DESIRE — LONDON BOYS
HARLEM SHUFFLE [A] — BOB and EARL
HARLEM SHUFFLE [A] — The ROLLING STONES
HARLEQUIN — THE BEAUTY AND THE BEAST — Sven VATH
HARMONIC GENERATOR — The DATSUNS
HARMONICA MAN — BRAVADO
HARMONY — TC
HARMONY IN MY HEAD — The BUZZCOCKS
HARMOUR LOVE — SYREETA
HARPER VALLEY P.T.A. — Jeannie C RILEY
HARVEST FOR THE WORLD [A] — ISLEY BROTHERS
HARVEST FOR THE WORLD [A] — The CHRISTIANS
HARVEST FOR THE WORLD [A] — Terry HUNTER
HARVEST MOON — Neil YOUNG
HARVEST OF LOVE — Benny HILL
HARVESTER OF SORROW — METALLICA
HAS IT COME TO THIS — The STREETS
HASH PIPE — WEEZER
HASTA LA VISTA — SYLVIA
HATE ME NOW — NAS featuring PUFF DADDY
THE HATE SONG — RAGING SPEEDHORN
HATE TO SAY I TOLD YOU SO — The HIVES
HATERS — SO SOLID CREW presents MR SHABZ featuring MBD & The REELISTS
HATS OFF TO LARRY — Del SHANNON
HAUNTED [A] — The POGUES
HAUNTED [A] — Shane MacGOWAN and Sinead O'CONNOR
HAUNTED BY YOU — GENE
HAVA NAGILA — SPOTNICKS
HAVE A CHEEKY CHRISTMAS — CHEEKY GIRLS
HAVE A DRINK ON ME — Lonnie DONEGAN
HAVE A GOOD FOREVER — COOLNOTES
HAVE A LITTLE FAITH — Joe COCKER
HAVE A NICE DAY [A] — Roxanne SHANTE
HAVE A NICE DAY [B] — STEREOPHONICS
HAVE FUN GO MAD [A] — BLAIR
HAVE FUN GO MAD [A] — TWEENIES
HAVE I STAYED TOO LONG — SONNY and CHER
HAVE I THE RIGHT [A] — HONEYCOMBS
HAVE I THE RIGHT [A] — DEAD END KIDS
HAVE I TOLD YOU LATELY [A] — Van MORRISON
HAVE I TOLD YOU LATELY [A] — Rod STEWART
HAVE I TOLD YOU LATELY THAT I LOVE YOU [A] — The CHIEFTAINS with Van MORRISON
HAVE IT ALL — FOO FIGHTERS
HAVE LOST IT (EP) — TEENAGE FANCLUB
HAVE LOVE, WILL TRAVEL (EP) — CRAZYHEAD
HAVE MERCY — YAZZ
HAVE PITY ON THE BOY — Paul and Barry RYAN
HAVE YOU EVER? — BRANDY
HAVE YOU EVER — S CLUB 7
HAVE YOU EVER BEEN IN LOVE — Leo SAYER
HAVE YOU EVER BEEN MELLOW — PARTY ANIMALS
HAVE YOU EVER BEEN MELLOW (EP) — PARTY ANIMALS
HAVE YOU EVER HAD IT BLUE — STYLE COUNCIL
HAVE YOU EVER LOVED SOMEBODY [A] — Paul and Barry RYAN
HAVE YOU EVER LOVED SOMEBODY [B] — The SEARCHERS
HAVE YOU EVER LOVED SOMEBODY [C] — Freddie JACKSON
HAVE YOU EVER NEEDED SOMEONE SO BAD — DEF LEPPARD
HAVE YOU EVER REALLY LOVED A WOMAN — Bryan ADAMS
HAVE YOU EVER SEEN THE RAIN [A] — CREEDENCE CLEARWATER REVIVAL
HAVE YOU EVER SEEN THE RAIN [A] — Bonnie TYLER
HAVE YOU EVER SEEN THE RAIN [A] — The JEEVAS
HAVE YOU SEEN HER [A] — CHI-LITES
HAVE YOU SEEN HER [A] — HAMMER
HAVE YOU SEEN YOUR MOTHER BABY STANDING IN THE SHADOW — The ROLLING STONES
HAVEN'T SEEN YOU — PERFUME
HAVEN'T STOPPED DANCING YET — GONZALEZ
HAVEN'T YOU HEARD — Patrice RUSHEN
HAVIN' A GOOD TIME — SOUVERNANCE
HAVING A PARTY — The OSMONDS
HAWAII TATTOO — WAIKIKIS
HAWAIIAN WEDDING SONG — Julie ROGERS
HAWKEYE — Frankie LAINE
HAYFEVER — TRASH CAN SINATRAS
HAYLING — FC KAHUNA
HAZARD — Richard MARX
HAZEL — LOOP DA LOOP
HAZELL — Maggie BELL
HAZIN' & PHAZIN' — CHOO CHOO PROJECT
HAZY SHADE OF WINTER [A] — The BANGLES
A HAZY SHADE OF WINTER [A] — SIMON and GARFUNKEL
HE AIN'T HEAVY, HE'S MY BROTHER [A] — The HOLLIES
HE AIN'T HEAVY, HE'S MY BROTHER [A] — Bill MEDLEY
HE AIN'T NO COMPETITION — BROTHER BEYOND
HE DOESN'T LOVE YOU LIKE I DO — Nick HEYWARD
HE DON'T LOVE YOU — HUMAN NATURE
HE GOT GAME — PUBLIC ENEMY featuring Stephen STILLS
HE GOT WHAT HE WANTED — LITTLE RICHARD
HE IS SAILING — JON and VANGELIS
HE KNOWS YOU KNOW — MARILLION
HE LOVES U NOT — DREAM
HE REMINDS ME — Randy CRAWFORD
HE THINKS HE'LL KEEP HER — Mary-Chapin CARPENTER
HE WAS BEAUTIFUL (CAVATINA) (THE THEME FROM 'THE DEER HUNTER') — Iris WILLIAMS
HE WASN'T MAN ENOUGH — Toni BRAXTON
HEAD — Julian COPE
HEAD ABOVE WATER — Clive GRIFFIN
HEAD LIKE A HOLE — NINE INCH NAILS
HEAD ON — JESUS AND MARY CHAIN
HEAD ON COLLISION — NEW FOUND GLORY
HEAD OVER FEET — Alanis MORISSETTE
HEAD OVER HEELS [A] — ABBA
HEAD OVER HEELS [B] — TEARS FOR FEARS
HEAD OVER HEELS [C] — Nic HAVERSON
HEAD OVER HEELS [D] — ALLURE featuring NAS
HEAD OVER HEELS IN LOVE — Kevin KEEGAN
HEAD TO TOE (EP) — The BREEDERS
HEADACHE — Frank BLACK
HEADING WEST — Cyndi LAUPER
HEADLESS CROSS — BLACK SABBATH
HEADLIGHTS ON THE PARADE — BLUE NILE
HEADLINE NEWS [A] — Edwin STARR
HEADLINE NEWS [B] — William BELL
HEADLINES — MIDNIGHT STAR
HEADLONG — QUEEN
HEADS DOWN NO NONSENSE MINDLESS BOOGIE — ALBERTO Y LOS TRIOS PARANOIAS
HEADS HIGH — MR VEGAS
HEADSPRUNG — LL COOL J
HEAL THE PAIN — George MICHAEL
HEAL (THE SEPARATION) — The SHAMEN
HEAL THE WORLD — Michael JACKSON
THE HEALING GAME — Van MORRISON
HEALING HANDS — Elton JOHN
HEALING LOVE — Cliff RICHARD
HEAR ME CALLING — 2WO THIRD3
HEAR MY CALL — Alison LIMERICK
HEAR MY NAME — Armand VAN HELDEN featuring Spalding ROCKWELL
HEAR THE DRUMMER (GET WICKED) — Chad JACKSON
HEAR YOU CALLING — AURORA
HEARD IT ALL BEFORE — Sunshine ANDERSON
HEARSAY '89 — Alexander O'NEAL
HEART [A] — JOHNSTON BROTHERS
HEART [A] — Max BYGRAVES
HEART [B] — Rita PAVONE
HEART [C] — PET SHOP BOYS
HEART [D] — Gary NUMAN
HEART [E] — SERAPHIM SUITE
HEART AND SOUL [A] — JAN and DEAN
HEART AND SOUL [B] — EXILE
HEART AND SOUL [C] — T'PAU
HEART AND SOUL [D] — NO SWEAT
HEART AND SOUL [E] — Cilla BLACK with Dusty SPRINGFIELD
HEART AND SOUL [F] — TSD
HEART AND SOUL (EP) — Huey LEWIS and the NEWS

THE HEART ASKS PLEASURE FIRST — Michael NYMAN
HEART ATTACK — Olivia NEWTON-JOHN
HEART ATTACK AND VINE — Screamin' Jay HAWKINS
HEART (DON'T CHANGE MY MIND) — Diana ROSS
HEART FAILED (IN THE BACK OF A TAXI) — SAINT ETIENNE
HEART FULL OF SOUL — YARDBIRDS
HEART GO BOOM — APOLLO FOUR FORTY
HEART LIKE A WHEEL — HUMAN LEAGUE
THE HEART OF A MAN — Frankie VAUGHAN
HEART OF A TEENAGE GIRL [A] — George CHAKIRIS
THE HEART OF A TEENAGE GIRL [A] — Craig DOUGLAS
HEART OF ASIA — WATERGATE
HEART OF GLASS [A] — BLONDIE
HEART OF GLASS [A] — ASSOCIATES
HEART OF GOLD [A] — Neil YOUNG
HEART OF GOLD [B] — JOHNNY HATES JAZZ
HEART OF GOLD [C] — FORCE & STYLES featuring Kelly LLORENNA
HEART OF GOLD [C] — Kelly LLORENNA
HEART OF LOTHIAN — MARILLION
THE HEART OF ROCK AND ROLL — Huey LEWIS and the NEWS
HEART OF SOUL — The CULT
HEART OF STONE [A] — KENNY
HEART OF STONE [B] — Suzi QUATRO
HEART OF STONE [C] — BUCKS FIZZ
HEART OF STONE [C] — CHER
HEART OF STONE [D] — Dave STEWART
HEART OF THE SUN — RED BOX
HEART OF THE WORLD — BIG COUNTRY
HEART ON MY SLEEVE — GALLAGHER and LYLE
HEART OVER MIND — Kim WILDE
HEART (STOP BEATING IN TIME) — Leo SAYER
HEART USER — Cliff RICHARD
HEARTACHE [A] — Roy ORBISON
HEARTACHE [B] — GENE LOVES JEZEBEL
HEARTACHE [C] — PEPSI and SHIRLIE
HEARTACHE ALL OVER THE WORLD — Elton JOHN
HEARTACHE AVENUE — MAISONETTES
HEARTACHE TONIGHT — The EAGLES
HEARTACHES [A] — Patsy CLINE
HEARTACHES [A] — Vince HILL
HEARTACHES BY THE NUMBER — Guy MITCHELL
HEARTBEAT [A] — Ruby MURRAY
HEARTBEAT [B] — Buddy HOLLY
HEARTBEAT [B] — ENGLAND SISTERS
HEARTBEAT [B] — SHOWADDYWADDY
HEARTBEAT [B] — Nick BERRY
HEARTBEAT [B] — HEARTBEAT COUNTRY
HEARTBEAT [C] — Sammy HAGAR
HEARTBEAT [D] — Tippa IRIE
HEARTBEAT [E] — Don JOHNSON
HEARTBEAT [F] — SEDUCTION
HEARTBEAT [G] — GRID
HEARTBEAT [H] — Jimmy SOMERVILLE
HEARTBEAT [I] — KRS ONE
HEARTBEAT [J] — STEPS
A HEARTBEAT AWAY — McGANNS
HEARTBEAT (TAINAI KAIKI II) RETURNING TO THE WOMB — David SYLVIAN
HEARTBREAK — MRS WOOD featuring Eve GALLAGHER
HEARTBREAK HOTEL [A] — Elvis PRESLEY
HEARTBREAK HOTEL [A] — Stan FREBERG
HEARTBREAK HOTEL [B] — The JACKSONS
HEARTBREAK HOTEL [C] — Whitney HOUSTON featuring Faith EVANS and Kelly PRICE
HEARTBREAK RADIO — Roy ORBISON
HEARTBREAK STATION — CINDERELLA
HEARTBREAK STROLL — The RAVEONETTES
HEARTBREAKER [A] — Dionne WARWICK
HEARTBREAKER [B] — MUSICAL YOUTH
HEARTBREAKER [C] — COLOR ME BADD
HEARTBREAKER [D] — Mariah CAREY featuring JAY-Z
HEARTBROKE AND BUSTED — MAGNUM
HEARTHAMMER (EP) — RUNRIG
HEARTLAND — The THE
THE HEARTLESS THEME AKA "THE SUPERGLUE RIDDIM" — HEARTLESS CREW
HEARTLIGHT — Neil DIAMOND
HEARTLINE — Robin GEORGE
THE HEART'S FILTHY LESSON — David BOWIE
THE HEART'S LONE DESIRE — Matthew MARSDEN
HEARTS ON FIRE [A] — Sam HARRIS
HEARTS ON FIRE [B] — Bryan ADAMS
HEART-SHAPED BOX — NIRVANA
HEARTSONG — Gordon GILTRAP
HEARTSPARK DOLLARSIGN — EVERCLEAR
THE HEAT IS ON [A] — Agnetha FALTSKOG
THE HEAT IS ON [B] — Glenn FREY
HEAT IT UP — TWO MEN, A DRUM MACHINE AND A TRUMPET
HEAT OF THE BEAT — Roy AYERS
HEAT OF THE MOMENT — ASIA
HEAT OF THE NIGHT — Bryan ADAMS
HEATHER HONEY — Tommy ROE
HEATSEEKER — AC/DC
HEAVEN [A] — Bryan ADAMS
HEAVEN [A] — DJ SAMMY and YANOU featuring DO
HEAVEN [B] — TWO PEOPLE
HEAVEN [C] — CHIMES
HEAVEN [D] — Chris REA
HEAVEN [E] — TIGERTAILZ
HEAVEN [F] — WHYCLIFFE
HEAVEN [G] — FITS OF GLOOM
HEAVEN [H] — Sarah WASHINGTON
HEAVEN [I] — KINANE
HEAVEN [J] — PSYCHEDELIC FURS
HEAVEN [K] — SOLO U.S.
HEAVEN & EARTH [A] — RED
HEAVEN AND EARTH [B] — POP!
HEAVEN AND HELL, THIRD MOVEMENT (THEME FROM THE BBC-TV SERIES 'THE COSMOS') — VANGELIS
HEAVEN BESIDE YOU — ALICE IN CHAINS
HEAVEN CAN WAIT — Paul YOUNG
HEAVEN FOR EVERYONE — QUEEN
HEAVEN GIVE ME WORDS — PROPAGANDA
HEAVEN HELP — Lenny KRAVITZ
HEAVEN HELP ME — Deon ESTUS
HEAVEN HELP MY HEART — Tina ARENA
HEAVEN HELP US ALL — Stevie WONDER
THE HEAVEN I NEED — The THREE DEGREES
HEAVEN IN MY HANDS — LEVEL 42
HEAVEN IS — DEF LEPPARD
HEAVEN IS A HALFPIPE — OPM
HEAVEN IS A PLACE ON EARTH [A] — Belinda CARLISLE
HEAVEN IS A PLACE ON EARTH [A] — SODA CLUB featuring Hannah ALETHEA
HEAVEN IS CLOSER (FEELS LIKE HEAVEN) — DARIO G
HEAVEN IS HERE — Julie FELIX
HEAVEN IS IN THE BACK SEAT OF MY CADILLAC — HOT CHOCOLATE
HEAVEN IS MY WOMAN'S LOVE — Val DOONICAN
HEAVEN IS WAITING — DANSE SOCIETY
HEAVEN KNOWS [A] — Donna SUMMER
HEAVEN KNOWS [B] — Jaki GRAHAM
HEAVEN KNOWS [B] — Lalah HATHAWAY
HEAVEN KNOWS [C] — Robert PLANT
HEAVEN KNOWS [D] — COOL DOWN ZONE
HEAVEN KNOWS [E] — Luther VANDROSS
HEAVEN KNOWS [F] — SQUEEZE
HEAVEN KNOWS — DEEP DEEP DOWN — Angel MORAES
HEAVEN KNOWS I'M MISERABLE NOW — The SMITHS
HEAVEN MUST BE MISSING AN ANGEL [A] — TAVARES
HEAVEN MUST BE MISSING AN ANGEL [A] — WORLDS APART
HEAVEN MUST HAVE SENT YOU — ELGINS
HEAVEN MUST HAVE SENT YOU BACK — CICERO
HEAVEN ON EARTH — SPELLBOUND
HEAVEN ON THE 7TH FLOOR — Paul NICHOLAS
HEAVEN OR HELL — The STRANGLERS
HEAVEN SCENT — BEDROCK
HEAVEN SENT [A] — Paul HAIG
HEAVEN SENT [B] — INXS
HEAVEN SENT [C] — M1
HEAVEN WILL COME — SPACE BROTHERS
HEAVENLY — SHOWADDYWADDY
HEAVEN'S EARTH — DELERIUM
HEAVEN'S HERE — Holly JOHNSON
HEAVEN'S ON FIRE — KISS
HEAVEN'S WHAT I FEEL — Gloria ESTEFAN
HEAVY FUEL — DIRE STRAITS
HEAVY MAKES YOU HAPPY — Bobby BLOOM
HEAVY VIBES — MONTANA SEXTET
HEDONISM (JUST BECAUSE YOU FEEL GOOD) — SKUNK ANANSIE
HELEN WHEELS — Paul McCARTNEY
HELICOPTER — BLOC PARTY
HELICOPTER TUNE — DEEP BLUE
HELIOPOLIS BY NIGHT — ABERFELDY
HELIUM — DALLAS SUPERSTARS
HELL HATH NO FURY — Frankie LAINE
HE'LL HAVE TO GO [A] — Jim REEVES
HE'LL HAVE TO GO [A] — Bryan FERRY
HE'LL HAVE TO STAY — Jeanne BLACK
HELL RAISER — The SWEET
HELL YEAH — GINUWINE
THE HELL EP — TRICKY vs the GRAVEDIGGAZ
THE HELL SONG — SUM 41
HELLA GOOD — NO DOUBT
HELLBOUND — TYGERS OF PAN TANG
HELLO [A] — Lionel RICHIE
HELLO [A] — Jhay PALMER featuring MC IMAGE
HELLO [B] — The BELOVED
HELLO AGAIN — Neil DIAMOND
HELLO AMERICA — DEF LEPPARD
HELLO BUDDY — The TREMELOES
HELLO DARLIN — Fuzz TOWNSHEND
HELLO DARLING — Tippa IRIE
HELLO DOLLY! [A] — The BACHELORS
HELLO DOLLY! [A] — Frank SINATRA
HELLO DOLLY! [A] — Frankie VAUGHAN
HELLO DOLLY! [A] — Kenny BALL and his JAZZMEN
HELLO DOLLY! [A] — Louis ARMSTRONG
HELLO, GOODBYE — The BEATLES
HELLO HAPPINESS — The DRIFTERS
HELLO HEARTACHE GOODBYE LOVE — Little Peggy MARCH
HELLO HELLO I'M BACK AGAIN — Gary GLITTER
HELLO HONKY TONKS (ROCK YOUR BODY) — PIZZAMAN
HELLO HOW ARE YOU — EASYBEATS
HELLO HURRAY — Alice COOPER
HELLO I AM YOUR HEART — Bette BRIGHT
HELLO I LOVE YOU — The DOORS
HELLO? IS THIS THING ON? — !!! (CHK CHK CHK)
HELLO JOSEPHINE — Wayne FONTANA and The MINDBENDERS
HELLO LITTLE GIRL — The FOURMOST
HELLO MARY LOU — Ricky NELSON
HELLO MUDDAH HELLO FADDAH — Allan SHERMAN
HELLO STRANGER — Yvonne ELLIMAN
HELLO SUMMERTIME — Bobby GOLDSBORO
HELLO SUNSHINE — SUPER FURRY ANIMALS
HELLO SUZIE — AMEN CORNER
HELLO, THIS IS JOANNIE (THE TELEPHONE ANSWERING MACHINE SONG) — Paul EVANS
HELLO TIGER — URUSEI YATSURA
HELLO (TURN YOUR RADIO ON) — SHAKESPEAR'S SISTER
HELLO WORLD [A] — The TREMELOES
HELLO WORLD [B] — SEA FRUIT
HELLO YOUNG LOVERS — Paul ANKA
HELLRAISER — Anne SAVAGE
HELL'S PARTY — GLAM
HELP! [A] — The BEATLES
HELP [A] — Tina TURNER
HELP [A] — BANANARAMA
HELP (EP) — VARIOUS ARTISTS (EPs and LPs)
HELP, GET ME SOME HELP! — OTTAWAN
HELP! I'M A FISH — LITTLE TREES
HELP IT ALONG — Cliff RICHARD
HELP ME [A] — Timo MAAS featuring KELIS
HELP ME [B] — Nick CARTER
HELP ME FIND A WAY TO YOUR HEART — Daryl HALL
HELP ME GIRL — The ANIMALS
HELP ME MAKE IT — HUFF AND PUFF
HELP ME MAKE IT THROUGH THE NIGHT [A] — Gladys KNIGHT and the PIPS
HELP ME MAKE IT THROUGH THE NIGHT [A] — John HOLT
HELP ME MAMA — LEMONESCENT
HELP ME RHONDA — The BEACH BOYS
HELP MY FRIEND — SLO-MOSHUN
HELP THE AGED — PULP
HELP YOURSELF [A] — Tom JONES
HELP YOURSELF [A] — Tony FERRINO
HELP YOURSELF [B] — Julian LENNON
HELP YOURSELF [C] — Amy WINEHOUSE
HELPLESS — Tracey ULLMAN
HELULE HELULE — The TREMELOES
HELYOM HALIB — CAPPELLA
HENRY LEE — Nick CAVE and the BAD SEEDS and P J HARVEY
HENRY VIII SUITE (EP) — EARLY MUSIC CONSORT directed by David MUNROW
HER — GUY
HER ROYAL MAJESTY — James DARREN
HERCULES — Frankie VAUGHAN
HERE — LUSCIOUS JACKSON
HERE AND NOW [A] — Luther VANDROSS
HERE AND NOW [B] — DEL AMITRI
HERE AND NOW [C] — STEPS
HERE COME THE GOOD TIMES — A HOUSE
HERE COMES MY BABY — The TREMELOES
HERE COMES SUMMER [A] — Jerry KELLER
HERE COMES SUMMER [A] — Dave CLARK FIVE
HERE COMES THAT FEELING — Brenda LEE
HERE COMES THAT SOUND — Simon HARRIS
HERE COMES THE BIG RUSH — ECHOBELLY
HERE COMES THE HAMMER — HAMMER
HERE COMES THE HOTSTEPPER — Ini KAMOZE
HERE COMES THE JUDGE [A] — Shorty LONG
HERE COMES THE JUDGE [B] — Pigmeat MARKHAM
HERE COMES THE MAN — BOOM BOOM ROOM
HERE COMES THE NICE — The SMALL FACES
HERE COMES THE NIGHT [A] — LULU
HERE COMES THE NIGHT [A] — THEM
HERE COMES THE NIGHT [B] — The BEACH BOYS
HERE COMES THE PAIN — Lee HASLAM
HERE COMES THE RAIN AGAIN — EURYTHMICS
HERE COMES THE STAR — HERMAN'S HERMITS
HERE COMES THE SUMMER — The UNDERTONES
HERE COMES THE SUN — Steve HARLEY and COCKNEY REBEL
HERE COMES THE WAR — NEW MODEL ARMY
HERE COMES YOUR MAN — PIXIES
HERE 4 ONE — BLAZIN' SQUAD
HERE I AM — Bryan ADAMS
HERE I AM (COME AND TAKE ME) — UB40
HERE I COME — Barrington LEVY
HERE I COME (SING DJ) — TALISMAN P featuring Barrington LEVY
HERE I GO — 2 UNLIMITED
HERE I GO AGAIN [A] — The HOLLIES
HERE I GO AGAIN [B] — Archie BELL and the DRELLS
HERE I GO AGAIN [C] — GUYS and DOLLS
HERE I GO AGAIN [D] — TWIGGY
HERE I GO AGAIN [E] — WHITESNAKE
HERE I GO AGAIN [E] — FRASH
HERE I STAND [A] — MILLTOWN BROTHERS
HERE I STAND [B] — Bitty McLEAN
HERE IN MY HEART — Al MARTINO
HERE IS THE NEWS — ELECTRIC LIGHT ORCHESTRA
HERE IT COMES — DOVES
HERE IT COMES AGAIN [A] — FORTUNES
HERE IT COMES AGAIN [B] — BLACK
HERE IT COMES AGAIN [C] — Melanie C
HERE SHE COMES AGAIN — The STANDS
HERE, THERE AND EVERYWHERE — Emmylou HARRIS
HERE TO STAY [A] — KORN
HERE TO STAY [B] — NEW ORDER
HERE WE ARE — Gloria ESTEFAN
HERE WE COME — Missy 'Misdemeanor' ELLIOTT
HERE WE GO [A] — EVERTON FOOTBALL CLUB
HERE WE GO [B] — C & C MUSIC FACTORY / CLIVILLES & COLE featuring Freedom WILLIAMS
HERE WE GO [C] — STAKKA BO
HERE WE GO [D] — ARAB STRAP
HERE WE GO [E] — FREESTYLERS
HERE WE GO AGAIN [A] — Ray CHARLES
HERE WE GO AGAIN [B] — PORTRAIT
HERE WE GO AGAIN [C] — A HOMEBOY, a HIPPIE and a FUNKI DREDD
HERE WE GO AGAIN [D] — Aretha FRANKLIN
HERE WE GO ROCK 'N' ROLL — SPIDER
HERE WE GO ROUND THE MULBERRY BUSH — TRAFFIC
HERE YOU COME AGAIN — Dolly PARTON
HERE'S MY A — RAPINATION
HERE'S TO LOVE (AULD LANG SYNE) — John CHRISTIE
HERE'S WHERE THE STORY ENDS — TIN TIN OUT
HERE WITH ME — DIDO
HERMANN LOVES PAULINE — SUPER FURRY ANIMALS
HERNANDO'S HIDEAWAY [A] — Johnnie RAY
HERNANDO'S HIDEAWAY [A] — JOHNSTON BROTHERS
HERO [A] — David CROSBY featuring Phil COLLINS
HERO [B] — Mariah CAREY
HERO [C] — Enrique IGLESIAS
HERO [D] — Chad KROEGER featuring Josey SCOTT
HERO OF THE DAY — METALLICA
HEROES [A] — David BOWIE
HEROES [B] — Roni SIZE / REPRAZENT
THE HEROES — SHED SEVEN
HEROES AND VILLAINS — The BEACH BOYS
HERSHAM BOYS — SHAM 69
HE'S A REBEL — CRYSTALS
HE'S A SAINT, HE'S A SINNER — Miquel BROWN
HE'S BACK (THE MAN BEHIND THE MASK) — Alice COOPER
HE'S GONNA STEP ON YOU AGAIN — John KONGOS
HE'S GOT NO LOVE — The SEARCHERS
HE'S GOT THE WHOLE WORLD IN HIS HANDS — Laurie LONDON
HE'S IN TOWN — ROCKIN' BERRIES
HE'S MINE — MOKENSTEF
HE'S MISSTRA KNOW IT ALL — Stevie WONDER
HE'S OLD ENOUGH TO KNOW BETTER — BROOK BROTHERS
HE'S ON THE PHONE — SAINT ETIENNE
HE'S SO FINE — CHIFFONS
HE'S THE GREATEST DANCER — SISTER SLEDGE
HE'S THE ONE — Billie DAVIS
HEWLETT'S DAUGHTER — GRANDADDY
HEXAGRAM — DEFTONES
HEY! — Julio IGLESIAS
HEY AMERICA — James BROWN
HEY! BABY [A] — Bruce CHANNEL
HEY BABY (UHH, AHH) [A] — DJ OTZI
HEY BABY (THE UNOFFICIAL WORLD CUP REMIX) [A] — DJ OTZI
HEY BABY [B] — NO DOUBT
HEY BOY HEY GIRL — The CHEMICAL BROTHERS
HEY CHILD — EAST 17
HEY DJ [A] — WORLD'S FAMOUS SUPREME TEAM
HEY DJ [A] — LIGHTER SHADE OF BROWN
HEY DJ – I CAN'T DANCE (TO THAT MUSIC YOU'RE PLAYING) — BEATMASTERS featuring BETTY BOO
HEY DJ! (PLAY THAT SONG) — N-TYCE
HEY DUDE — KULA SHAKER
HEY GIRL [A] — The SMALL FACES
HEY GIRL [B] — EXPRESSOS
HEY GIRL [C] — DELAYS
HEY GIRL DON'T BOTHER ME — TAMS

HEY GOD — BON JOVI
HEY GOOD LOOKIN' — Bo DIDDLEY
HEY GOOD LOOKING — Tommy ZANG
HEY JEALOUSY — GIN BLOSSOMS
HEY! JOE! [A] — Frankie LAINE
HEY JOE [B] — The Jimi HENDRIX EXPERIENCE
HEY JUDE [A] — The BEATLES
HEY JUDE [B] — Wilson PICKETT
HEY JULIE — FOUNTAINS OF WAYNE
HEY JUPITER — Tori AMOS
HEY LITTLE GIRL [A] — Del SHANNON
HEY LITTLE GIRL [B] — ICEHOUSE
HEY LITTLE GIRL [B] —
    Mathias WARE featuring Rob TAYLOR
HEY LORD, DON'T ASK ME QUESTIONS —
    Graham PARKER and the RUMOUR
HEY LOVE — KING SUN-D'MOET
HEY LOVER —
    LL COOL J featuring BOYZ II MEN
HEY! LUCIANI — The FALL
HEY MA — CAM'RON featuring Juelz SANTANA
HEY MAMA [A] — Frankie VAUGHAN
HEY MAMA [B] —
    Joe BROWN and the BRUVVERS
HEY MAMA [C] — BLACK EYED PEAS
HEY MANHATTAN! — PREFAB SPROUT
HEY MATTHEW — Karel FIALKA
HEY MISS PAYNE — CHEQUERS
HEY MR CHRISTMAS — SHOWADDYWADDY
HEY MR DJ [A] — ZHANE
HEY MR DJ [B] —
    OPEN ARMS featuring ROWETTA
HEY MR DJ [C] — Van MORRISON
HEY MR DREAM MAKER — Cliff RICHARD
HEY MISTER HEARTACHE — Kim WILDE
HEY MR MUSIC MAN — PETERS and LEE
HEY MUSIC LOVER — S EXPRESS
HEY NOW (GIRLS JUST WANT TO HAVE FUN) —
    Cyndi LAUPER
HEY NOW NOW — SWIRL 360
HEY PAPI — Alex CARTAÑA
HEY! PARADISE — FLICKMAN
HEY PAULA — PAUL and PAULA
HEY ROCK AND ROLL — SHOWADDYWADDY
HEY SENORITA — WAR
HEY SEXY LADY —
    SHAGGY featuring Brian & Tony GOLD
HEY STOOPID — Alice COOPER
HEY THERE [A] — Johnnie RAY
HEY THERE [A] — Lita ROZA
HEY THERE [A] — Rosemary CLOONEY
HEY THERE [A] — Sammy DAVIS Jr
(HEY THERE) LONELY GIRL [A] —
    Eddie HOLMAN
HEY THERE LONELY GIRL [A] — BIG FUN
HEY VENUS — THAT PETROL EMOTION
HEY WHATEVER — WESTLIFE
HEY! WHAT'S YOUR NAME — BABY JUNE
HEY WILLY — The HOLLIES
HEY YA! — OUTKAST
HEY YOU [A] — Tommy STEELE
HEY YOU [B] — QUIREBOYS
(HEY YOU) THE ROCKSTEADY CREW —
    ROCKSTEADY CREW
HEYKEN'S SERENADE (STANDCHEN) — The Pipes and
    Drums and Military Band of the ROYAL SCOTS
    DRAGOON GUARDS
HI DE HI, HI DE HO — KOOL and the GANG
HI DE HI (HOLIDAY ROCK) —
    Paul SHANE and the YELLOWCOATS
HI DE HO — K7
HI HI HAZEL [A] —
    Geno WASHINGTON and the RAM JAM BAND
HI HI HAZEL [A] — The TROGGS
HI, HI, HI — Paul McCARTNEY
HI HO SILVER — Jim DIAMOND
HI! HOW YA DOIN'? — Kenny G
HI-LILI, HI-LO [A] — Richard CHAMBERLAIN
HI LILI HI LO [A] — Alan PRICE
HI TENSION — HI TENSION
H! VLTG3 — LINKIN PARK
HIBERNACULUM — Mike OLDFIELD
HIDDEN AGENDA — Craig DAVID
HIDDEN PLACE — BJÖRK
HIDE — TWENTY 4 SEVEN
HIDE AND SEEK [A] — Marty WILDE
HIDE AND SEEK [B] — Howard JONES
HIDE U — KOSHEEN
HIDE YOUR HEART — KISS
HIDEAWAY [A] — Dave DEE, DOZY,
    BEAKY, MICK and TICH
HIDEAWAY [B] — DE'LACY
HIDE-A-WAY — NU SOUL featuring Kelli RICH
HI-FIDELITY — KIDS FROM 'FAME'
HIGH [A] — The CURE
HIGH [B] — HYPER GO GO
HIGH [C] — FEEDER
HIGH [D] — PROPHETS OF SOUND
HIGH [E] — LIGHTHOUSE FAMILY
HIGH AND DRY — RADIOHEAD
HIGH AS A KITE — OUR TRIBE / ONE TRIBE
HIGH CLASS BABY — Cliff RICHARD
HIGH ENERGY — Evelyn THOMAS
HIGH FIDELITY — Elvis COSTELLO
HIGH HEAD BLUES — BLACK CROWES
HIGH HOPES [A] — Frank SINATRA
HIGH HOPES [B] — PINK FLOYD

HIGH HORSE — Evelyn 'Champagne' KING
HIGH IN THE SKY — AMEN CORNER
HIGH LIFE — MODERN ROMANCE
HIGH NOON [A] — DJ SHADOW
HIGH NOON [B] — SERIOUS DANGER
HIGH NOON (DO NOT FORSAKE ME) —
    Frankie LAINE
HIGH ON A HAPPY VIBE —
    URBAN COOKIE COLLECTIVE
HIGH ON EMOTION — Chris DE BURGH
HIGH ROLLERS — ICE-T
HIGH SCHOOL CONFIDENTIAL —
    Jerry Lee LEWIS
HIGH TIME — Paul JONES
HIGH TIMES — JAMIROQUAI
HIGH VOLTAGE —
    JOHNNY and the HURRICANES
HIGH VOLTAGE (LIVE VERSION) [B] — AC/DC
HIGHER [A] — CREED
HIGHER [B] — David MORALES
HIGHER AND HIGHER — UNATION
HIGHER (FEEL IT) —
    Erick 'More' MORILLO presents RAW
HIGHER GROUND [A] — Stevie WONDER
HIGHER GROUND [A] —
    RED HOT CHILI PEPPERS
HIGHER GROUND [B] — GUN
HIGHER GROUND [C] — UB40
HIGHER GROUND [D] — SASHA
HIGHER LOVE — Steve WINWOOD
A HIGHER PLACE — PEYTON
HIGHER STATE OF CONSCIOUSNESS —
    Josh WINK
HIGHER THAN HEAVEN [A] — AGE OF CHANCE
HIGHER THAN HEAVEN [B] — Kéllé BRYAN
HIGHER THAN REASON —
    UNBELIEVABLE TRUTH
HIGHER THAN THE SUN — PRIMAL SCREAM
HIGHFLY — John MILES
HIGHLIFE — CYPRESS HILL
HIGHLY EVOLVED — The VINES
HIGHLY INFLAMMABLE — X-RAY SPEX
HIGHLY STRUNG — SPANDAU BALLET
HIGHRISE TOWN — The LANTERNS
HIGHWAY CODE — MASTER SINGERS
HIGHWAY 5 — BLESSING
HIGHWAY SONG — Nancy SINATRA
HIGHWAY TO HELL — AC/DC
HIGHWAYS OF MY LIFE — ISLEY BROTHERS
HIGHWIRE [A] — Linda CARR
HIGHWIRE [B] — The ROLLING STONES
HI-HEEL SNEAKERS — Tommy TUCKER
HI-HO SILVER LINING — Jeff BECK
HI-LILI HI-LO — Richard CHAMBERLAIN
HILLBILLY ROCK HILLBILLY ROLL —
    WOOLPACKERS
HIM [A] — Rupert HOLMES
HIM [B] — Sarah BRIGHTMAN
THE HINDU TIMES — OASIS
HIP HOP — DEAD PREZ
HIP HOP, BE BOP (DON'T STOP) —
    Man PARRISH
HIP HOP DON'T YA DROP — HONKY
HIP HOP HOORAY — NAUGHTY BY NATURE
HIP HOUSE — DJ 'FAST' EDDIE
HIP HOUSIN' — X-PRESS 2
HIP TO BE SQUARE —
    Huey LEWIS and the NEWS
HIP TO HIP — V
HIP TODAY — EXTREME
HIPPY CHICK — SOHO
HIPPY HIPPY SHAKE [A] —
    SWINGING BLUE JEANS
HIPPY HIPPY SHAKE [A] —
    GEORGIA SATELLITES
HIS GIRL — The GUESS WHO
HISTORY [A] — MAI TAI
HISTORY [B] — The VERVE
HISTORY [C] — Michael JACKSON
HISTORY NEVER REPEATS — SPLIT ENZ
HISTORY OF THE WORLD (PART 1) —
    The DAMNED
HISTORY REPEATING — PROPELLERHEADS
    featuring Miss Shirley BASSEY
HIT [A] — SUGARCUBES
HIT [B] — WANNADIES
HIT AND MISS — John BARRY ORCHESTRA
HIT AND RUN [A] — GIRLSCHOOL
HIT AND RUN [B] — TOTAL CONTRAST
HIT BY LOVE — Ce Ce PENISTON
HIT 'EM HIGH (MONSTARS' ANTHEM) —
    B REAL / BUSTA RHYMES / COOLIO /
    LL COOL J / METHOD MAN
HIT 'EM UP STYLE (OOPS!) — BLU CANTRELL
HIT 'EM WIT DA HEE — Missy 'Misdemeanor'
    ELLIOTT featuring LIL' KIM
HIT IT — The BEAT
HIT ME OFF — NEW EDITION
HIT ME WITH YOUR RHYTHM STICK —
    Ian and the BLOCKHEADS
HIT OR MISS (WAITED TOO LONG) —
    NEW FOUND GLORY
HIT THAT — The OFFSPRING
HIT THAT PERFECT BEAT — BRONSKI BEAT
HIT THE FREEWAY —
    Toni BRAXTON featuring LOON
HIT THE GROUND — DARLING BUDS

HIT THE GROUND RUNNING — Tim FINN
HIT THE NORTH — The FALL
HIT THE ROAD JACK — Ray CHARLES
HITCHIN' A RIDE [A] — VANITY FARE
HITCHIN' A RIDE [A] — SINITTA
HITCHIN' A RIDE [B] — GREEN DAY
HI-TEK — Mampi SWIFT
HITMIX (OFFICIAL BOOTLEG MEGA-MIX) —
    Alexander O'NEAL
HITS MEDLEY — GIPSY KINGS
HITSVILLE UK — The CLASH
HOBART PAVING — SAINT ETIENNE
HOBO HUMPIN' SLOBO BABE — WHALE
HOCUS POCUS — FOCUS
HOGWASH FARM (THE DIESEL HANDS EP) —
    DAWN OF THE REPLICANTS
HOKEY COKEY [A] — JUDGE DREAD
HOKEY COKEY [A] — SNOWMEN
HOKEY COKEY [A] — BLACK LACE
THE HOKEY COKEY [A] — CAPTAIN SENSIBLE
HOKOYO — ORANGE JUICE
HOKUS POKUS — INSANE CLOWN POSSE
HOLD BACK THE NIGHT [A] — The TRAMMPS
HOLD BACK THE NIGHT [A] — KWS
    features guest vocal from The TRAMMPS
HOLD BACK THE RIVER — WET WET WET
HOLD BACK TOMORROW — MIKI and GRIFF
HOLD IT — Stephen 'Tin Tin' DUFFY
HOLD IT DOWN [A] — SENSELESS THINGS
HOLD IT DOWN [B] — 2 BAD MICE
HOLD ME [A] — Teddy PENDERGRASS
    with Whitney HOUSTON
HOLD ME [B] — PJ PROBY
HOLD ME [B] — B.A. ROBERTSON
HOLD ME [C] — SAVAGE GARDEN
HOLD ME CLOSE — David ESSEX
HOLD ME IN YOUR ARMS — Rick ASTLEY
HOLD ME NOW [A] — THOMPSON TWINS
HOLD ME NOW [B] — Johnny LOGAN
HOLD ME NOW [C] — The POLYPHONIC SPREE
HOLD ME THRILL ME KISS ME [A] —
    Muriel SMITH
HOLD ME THRILL ME KISS ME [A] —
    Gloria ESTEFAN
HOLD ME THRILL ME KISS ME KILL ME — U2
HOLD ME TIGHT — Johnny NASH
HOLD ME TIGHTER IN THE RAIN — Billy GRIFFIN
HOLD MY BODY TIGHT — EAST 17
HOLD MY HAND [A] — Don CORNELL
HOLD MY HAND [B] — Ken DODD
HOLD MY HAND [C] —
    HOOTIE & THE BLOWFISH
HOLD ON [A] — STREETBAND
HOLD ON [B] — EN VOGUE
HOLD ON [C] — WILSON PHILLIPS
HOLD ON [D] — CB MILTON
HOLD ON [E] — HAPPY CLAPPERS
HOLD ON (EP) [F] — Ann NESBY
HOLD ON [G] —
    José NUNEZ featuring OCTAHVIA
HOLD ON [H] — GOOD CHARLOTTE
HOLD ON ME — PHIXX
HOLD ON MY HEART — GENESIS
HOLD ON TIGHT [A] —
    ELECTRIC LIGHT ORCHESTRA
HOLD ON TIGHT [B] — Samantha FOX
HOLD ON TO LOVE [A] — Peter SKELLERN
HOLD ON TO LOVE [B] — Gary MOORE
HOLD ON TO ME — MJ COLE
HOLD ON TO MY LOVE — Jimmy RUFFIN
HOLD ON TO THE NIGHTS — Richard MARX
HOLD ON TO WHAT YOU'VE GOT —
    Evelyn 'Champagne' KING
HOLD ON TO YOUR FRIENDS — MORRISSEY
HOLD ONTO OUR LOVE — James FOX
HOLD THAT SUCKER DOWN —
    OUR TRIBE / ONE TRIBE
HOLD THE HEART — BIG COUNTRY
HOLD THE LINE — TOTO
HOLD TIGHT [A] — Dave DEE,
    DOZY, BEAKY, MICK and TICH
HOLD TIGHT [B] — LIVERPOOL EXPRESS
HOLD YOU TIGHT — Tara KEMP
HOLD YOUR HEAD UP — ARGENT
HOLD YOUR HEAD UP HIGH —
    Boris DLUGOSCH presents BOOOM
HOLD YOUR HORSES, BABE —
    Celi BEE and the BUZZY BUNCH
HOLDIN' ON —
    Tony RALLO and the MIDNITE BAND
HOLDING BACK THE YEARS — SIMPLY RED
HOLDING ON [A] — Beverley CRAVEN
HOLDING ON [B] — CLOCK
HOLDING ON [C] — DJ MANTA
HOLDING ON [D] — Heather SMALL
HOLDING ON 4 U [A] — CLOCK
HOLDING ON FOR U [B] — LIBERTY X
HOLDING ON TO NOTHING —
    AGNELLI & NELSON featuring AUREUS
HOLDING ON TO YOU — Terence Trent D'ARBY
HOLDING ON (WHEN LOVE IS GONE) — L.T.D.
HOLDING OUT FOR A HERO — Bonnie TYLER
HOLE HEARTED — EXTREME
HOLE IN MY SHOE [A] — TRAFFIC
HOLE IN MY SHOE [A] — neil
HOLE IN MY SOUL — AEROSMITH
HOLE IN THE BUCKET [B] — SPEARHEAD

HOLE IN THE GROUND — Bernard CRIBBINS
HOLE IN THE HEAD — SUGABABES
HOLE IN THE ICE — Neil FINN
HOLE IN THE WORLD — The EAGLES
HOLIDAE IN —
    CHINGY featuring LUDACRIS & SNOOP DOGG
HOLIDAY [A] — MADONNA
HOLIDAY [A] — MAD'HOUSE
HOLIDAY 80 — HUMAN LEAGUE
HOLIDAY RAP —
    MC MIKER 'G' and Deejay SVEN
HOLIDAYS IN THE SUN — The SEX PISTOLS
HOLLER [A] — GINUWINE
HOLLER [B] — SPICE GIRLS
HOLLIEDAZE (MEDLEY) — The HOLLIES
THE HOLLOW — A PERFECT CIRCLE
HOLLOW HEART — BIRDLAND
THE HOLLOW MAN — MARILLION
HOLLY HOLY — UB40
HOLLYWOOD [A] — Boz SCAGGS
HOLLYWOOD [B] — MADONNA
HOLLYWOOD (DOWN ON YOUR LUCK) —
    THIN LIZZY
HOLLYWOOD NIGHTS —
    Bob SEGER and the SILVER BULLET BAND
HOLLYWOOD TEASE — GIRL
THE HOLY CITY — Moira ANDERSON
HOLY COW — Lee DORSEY
HOLY DAYS — ZOE
HOLY DIVER — DIO
HOLY JOE — HAYSI FANTAYZEE
THE HOLY RIVER — PRINCE
HOLY ROLLER — NAZARETH
HOLY ROLLER NOVOCAINE — KINGS OF LEON
HOLY SMOKE — IRON MAIDEN
HOLY WARS ... THE PUNISHMENT DUE —
    MEGADETH
HOMBURG — PROCOL HARUM
HOME [A] — PUBLIC IMAGE LTD
HOME [B] — GOD MACHINE
HOME [C] — DEPECHE MODE
HOME [D] — CHAKRA
HOME [E] — Sheryl CROW
HOME [F] —
    COAST 2 COAST featuring DISCOVERY
HOME [G] — Julie McKNIGHT
HOME [H] — BONE THUGS-N-HARMONY
    featuring Phil COLLINS
HOME [I] — SIMPLY RED
HOME ALONE —
    R KELLY featuring Keith MURRAY
HOME AND AWAY —
    Karen BODDINGTON and Mark WILLIAMS
HOME AND DRY — PET SHOP BOYS
HOME FOR CHRISTMAS DAY —
    RED CAR AND THE BLUE CAR
HOME IS WHERE THE HEART IS —
    Gladys KNIGHT and the PIPS
HOME LOVIN' MAN — Andy WILLIAMS
HOME OF THE BRAVE — Jody MILLER
HOME SWEET HOME — MÖTLEY CRÜE
HOMELY GIRL [A] — CHI-LITES
HOMELY GIRL [B] — UB40
HOMETOWN UNICORN —
    SUPER FURRY ANIMALS
HOMEWARD BOUND [A] —
    SIMON and GARFUNKEL
HOMEWARD BOUND [A] — QUIET FIVE
HOMICIDE [A] — 999
HOMICIDE [B] — SHADES OF RHYTHM
THE HOMING WALTZ — Vera LYNN
HOMOPHOBIC ASSHOLE — SENSELESS THINGS
HONALOOCHIE BOOGIE — MOTT THE HOOPLE
HONDY (NO ACCESS) — HONDY
HONEST I DO — Danny STORM
HONEST I DO LOVE YOU — Candi STATON
HONEST MEN PART TWO —
    ELECTRIC LIGHT ORCHESTRA
HONESTLY — ZWAN
HONEY [A] — Bobby GOLDSBORO
HONEY [B] — Mariah CAREY
HONEY [C] — MOBY
HONEY [D] — Billie Ray MARTIN
HONEY [E] — R KELLY and JAY-Z
HONEY BE GOOD — The BIBLE
HONEY CHILE [A] — Fats DOMINO
HONEY CHILE [B] —
    Martha REEVES and the VANDELLAS
HONEY COME BACK — Glen CAMPBELL
HONEY HONEY — SWEET DREAMS
HONEY I — George McCRAE
HONEY I NEED — PRETTY THINGS
HONEY I'M LOST — The DOOLEYS
HONEY TO THE BEE — Billie PIPER
HONEYCOMB — Jimmie RODGERS
THE HONEYDRIPPER — JETS
THE HONEYMOON SONG —
    MANUEL and his MUSIC OF THE MOUNTAINS
THE HONEYTHIEF — HIPSWAY
HONG KONG GARDEN —
    SIOUXSIE and the BANSHEES
HONKY CAT — Elton JOHN
THE HONKY DOODLE DAY EP — HONKY
HONKY TONK TRAIN BLUES — Keith EMERSON
HONKY TONK WOMEN —
    The ROLLING STONES
HONKY TONK WOMEN [A] — The POGUES

HOOCHIE BOOTY — ULTIMATE KAOS
HOODED — FRESH BC
HOOKED — 99TH FLOOR ELEVATORS
HOOKED ON A FEELING — Jonathan KING
HOOKED ON CAN-CAN —
ROYAL PHILHARMONIC ORCHESTRA arranged and conducted by Louis CLARK
HOOKED ON CLASSICS — ROYAL PHILHARMONIC ORCHESTRA arranged
and conducted by Louis CLARK
HOOKED ON LOVE — DEAD OR ALIVE
HOOKED ON YOU [A] — Sydney YOUNGBLOOD
HOOKED ON YOU [B] — VOLATILE
AGENTS featuring Simone BENN
HOOKS IN YOU — MARILLION
HOOLIGAN — EMBRACE
HOOLIGAN 69 — RAGGA TWINS
HOOLIGAN'S HOLIDAY — MÖTLEY CRÜE
HOORAY HOORAY, IT'S A HOLI-HOLIDAY [A] —
BONEY M
HOORAY HOORAY (IT'S A CHEEKY HOLIDAY)
[A] — CHEEKY GIRLS
HOOTIN' — Nigel GEE
HOOTS MON —
Jack Good presents LORD ROCKINGHAM'S XI
HOOVERS & HORNS — FERGIE
HOOVERVILLE (THEY PROMISED US THE WORLD) —
The CHRISTIANS
THE HOP — THEATRE OF HATE
HOPE — SHAGGY
HOPE AND WAIT — ORION TOO
HOPE (I WISH YOU'D BELIEVE ME) — WAH!
HOPE IN A HOPELESS WORLD — Paul YOUNG
HOPE (NEVER GIVE UP) — LOVELAND
featuring the voice of Rachel McFARLANE
HOPE OF DELIVERANCE — Paul McCARTNEY
HOPE ST — LEVELLERS
HOPELESS — Dionne FARRIS
HOPELESSLY — Rick ASTLEY
HOPELESSLY DEVOTED TO YOU [A] —
Olivia NEWTON-JOHN
HOPELESSLY DEVOTED TO YOU [A] — SONIA
THE HORN TRACK — EGYPTIAN EMPIRE
HORNY [A] — Mark MORRISON
HORNY [B] — MOUSSE T
HORNY AS FUNK — SOAPY
HORNY HORNS — PERFECT PHASE
HORROR HEAD (EP) — CURVE
HORSE — SPLODGENESSABOUNDS
HORSE AND CARRIAGE —
CAM'RON featuring MA$E
A HORSE WITH NO NAME — AMERICA
HORSEMEN — The BEES
HORSEPOWER — RAVESIGNAL III
HOSTAGE IN A FROCK — CECIL
HOT — IDEAL
HOT AND WET (BELIEVE IT) — TZANT
HOT BLOODED — FOREIGNER
HOT BOYZ — Missy 'Misdemeanour' ELLIOTT
HOT DIGGITY [A] — Perry COMO
HOT DIGGITY (DOG ZIGGITY BOOM) [A] —
The STARGAZERS
HOT DIGGITY (DOG ZIGGITY BOOM) [A] —
Michael HOLLIDAY
HOT DOG — Shakin' STEVENS
HOT FUN — 7TH HEAVEN
HOT HOT HOT [A] — ARROW
HOT HOT HOT [A] — PAT and MICK
HOT HOT HOT!!! [B] — The CURE
HOT IN HERRE [A] — NELLY
HOT IN HERRE [A] — TIGA
HOT IN THE CITY — Billy IDOL
HOT LEGS — Rod STEWART
HOT LIKE FIRE — AALIYAH
HOT LOVE [A] — T. REX
HOT LOVE [B] — David ESSEX
HOT LOVE [C] — Kelly MARIE
HOT LOVE [D] — FIVE STAR
HOT LOVE NOW — The WONDER STUFF
HOT PEPPER — Floyd CRAMER
HOT ROCKIN' — JUDAS PRIEST
(HOT S**T) COUNTRY GRAMMAR — NELLY
HOT SHOT [A] — Barry BLUE
HOT SHOT [B] — Karen YOUNG
HOT SHOT [C] — Cliff RICHARD
HOT SHOT TOTTENHAM! — TOTTENHAM
HOTSPUR FA CUP FINAL SQUAD
HOT SPOT — Foxy BROWN
HOT STUFF [A] — Donna SUMMER
HOT STUFF [A] — ARSENAL FC
HOT SUMMER SALSA —
JIVE BUNNY and the MASTERMIXERS
HOT TODDY — Ted HEATH
HOT TRACKS (EP) — NAZARETH
HOT VALVES (EP) — BE BOP DELUXE
HOT WATER — LEVEL 42
HOTEL — CASSIDY featuring R KELLY
HOTEL YORBA — The WHITE STRIPES
HOTEL CALIFORNIA [A] — The EAGLES
HOTEL CALIFORNIA [A] — JAM ON THE MUTHA
HOTEL ILLNESS — BLACK CROWES
HOTEL LOUNGE (BE THE DEATH OF ME) — dEUS
HOTLINE TO HEAVEN — BANANARAMA
HOTNESS —
DYNAMITE MC & ORIGIN UNKNOWN
HOUND DOG — Elvis PRESLEY
HOUND DOG MAN — FABIAN

HOUNDS OF LOVE — Kate BUSH
HOURGLASS — SQUEEZE
HOUSE ARREST — KRUSH
HOUSE ENERGY REVENGE — CAPPELLA
HOUSE FLY — TRICKY DISCO
A HOUSE IN THE COUNTRY — PRETTY THINGS
THE HOUSE IS HAUNTED (BY THE GHOST OF
YOUR LAST GOODBYE) — Marc ALMOND
THE HOUSE IS MINE — HYPNOTIST
HOUSE IS NOT A HOME —
CHARLES and EDDIE
HOUSE MUSIC — Eddie AMADOR
HOUSE NATION — HOUSEMASTER BOYZ
and the RUDE BOY OF HOUSE
HOUSE OF BROKEN LOVE — GREAT WHITE
HOUSE OF FIRE — Alice COOPER
HOUSE OF FUN — MADNESS
HOUSE OF GOD — D.H.S.
HOUSE OF JEALOUS LOVERS — The RAPTURE
HOUSE OF JOY — Vicki Sue ROBINSON
HOUSE OF LOVE [A] — EAST 17
HOUSE OF LOVE [B] — RuPAUL
HOUSE OF LOVE [C] — SKIN
HOUSE OF LOVE [D] — Amy GRANT
HOUSE OF LOVE (IN MY HOUSE) —
SMOOTH TOUCH
HOUSE OF THE BLUE DANUBE —
Malcolm McLAREN
THE HOUSE OF THE RISING SUN [A] —
The ANIMALS
THE HOUSE OF THE RISING SUN [A] —
FRIJID PINK
HOUSE OF THE RISING SUN [A] — RAGE
HOUSE ON FIRE [A] — The BOOMTOWN RATS
HOUSE ON FIRE [B] — ARKARNA
HOUSE SOME MORE — LOCK 'N' LOAD
THE HOUSE THAT JACK BUILT [A] — Alan PRICE
THE HOUSE THAT JACK BUILT [B] — TRACIE
A HOUSE WITH LOVE IN IT — Vera LYNN
HOUSECALL —
Shabba RANKS featuring Maxi PRIEST
HOUSES IN MOTION — TALKING HEADS
HOW ABOUT THAT — Adam FAITH
HOW AM I SUPPOSED TO LIVE WITHOUT YOU —
Michael BOLTON
HOW BIZARRE — OMC
HOW 'BOUT I LOVE YOU MORE —
MULL HISTORICAL SOCIETY
HOW 'BOUT US [A] — CHAMPAIGN
HOW 'BOUT US [A] — LULU
HOW CAN I BE SURE [A] — Dusty SPRINGFIELD
HOW CAN I BE SURE [A] — David CASSIDY
HOW CAN I BE SURE? [A] — Darren DAY
HOW CAN I FALL — BREATHE
HOW CAN I FORGET YOU — Elisa FIORILLO
HOW CAN I KEEP FROM SINGING — ENYA
HOW CAN I LOVE YOU MORE — M PEOPLE
HOW CAN I MEET HER —
The EVERLY BROTHERS
HOW CAN I TELL HER — The FOURMOST
HOW CAN THIS BE LOVE — Andrew GOLD
HOW CAN WE BE LOVERS — Michael BOLTON
HOW CAN WE EASE THE PAIN — Maxi PRIEST
HOW CAN YOU EXPECT TO BE TAKEN
SERIOUSLY — PET SHOP BOYS
HOW CAN YOU TELL — Sandie SHAW
HOW CAN YOU TELL ME IT'S OVER —
Lorraine CATO
HOW COME? [A] —
Ronnie LANE and SLIM CHANCE
HOW COME [B] —
Youssou N'DOUR and CANIBUS
HOW COME [C] — D12
HOW COME, HOW LONG —
BABYFACE featuring Stevie WONDER
HOW COME IT NEVER RAINS —
DOGS D'AMOUR
HOW COME YOU DON'T CALL ME —
Alicia KEYS
HOW COULD AN ANGEL BREAK MY HEART —
Toni BRAXTON with Kenny G
HOW COULD I? (INSECURITY) — ROACHFORD
HOW COULD THIS GO WRONG — EXILE
HOW COULD WE DARE TO BE WRONG —
Colin BLUNSTONE
HOW DEEP IS YOUR LOVE [A] — The BEE GEES
HOW DEEP IS YOUR LOVE [A] — PORTRAIT
HOW DEEP IS YOUR LOVE [A] — TAKE THAT
HOW DEEP IS YOUR LOVE [B] —
DRU HILL featuring REDMAN
HOW DID IT EVER COME TO THIS? —
EASYWORLD
HOW DID YOU KNOW —
Kurtis MANTRONIK presents CHAMONIX
HOW DO I KNOW? — MARLO
HOW DO I LIVE [A] — Trisha YEARWOOD
HOW DO I LIVE [A] — LeAnn RIMES
HOW DO YOU DO [A] — Al HUDSON
HOW DO YOU DO! [B] — ROXETTE
HOW DO YOU DO IT? —
GERRY and the PACEMAKERS
HOW DO YOU KNOW IT'S LOVE —
Teresa BREWER
HOW DO YOU LIKE IT — Keith SWEAT
HOW DO YOU SAY ... LOVE — DEEE-LITE
HOW DO YOU SPEAK TO AN ANGEL —
Dean MARTIN

HOW DO YOU WANT IT — 2PAC
HOW DO YOU WANT ME TO LOVE YOU? — 911
HOW DOES IT FEEL? [A] — SLADE
HOW DOES IT FEEL [B] — ELECTROSET
HOW DOES IT FEEL [C] — WANNADIES
(HOW DOES IT FEEL TO BE) ON TOP OF THE WORLD —
ENGLAND UNITED
HOW DOES IT FEEL TO FEEL — RIDE
HOW DOES THAT GRAB YOU DARLIN' —
Nancy SINATRA
HOW GEE — BLACK MACHINE
HOW HIGH — The CHARLATANS
HOW HIGH THE MOON [A] — Ella FITZGERALD
HOW HIGH THE MOON [A] — Gloria GAYNOR
HOW HOW — YELLO
HOW I WANNA BE LOVED — Dana DAWSON
HOW I'M COMIN' — LL COOL J
HOW IT IS — BIOHAZARD
HOW IT SHOULD BE — INSPIRAL CARPETS
HOW LONG [A] — ACE
HOW LONG [A] — Rod STEWART
HOW LONG [A] — YAZZ and ASWAD
HOW LONG [A] — Paul CARRACK
HOW LONG DO I GET — RAISSA
HOW LONG HAS IT BEEN — Jim REEVES
HOW LONG'S A TEAR TAKE TO DRY? —
The BEAUTIFUL SOUTH
HOW LUCKY YOU ARE — SKIN
HOW MANY LIES — SPANDAU BALLET
HOW MANY TEARS — Bobby VEE
HOW MANY TEARS CAN YOU HIDE —
Shakin' STEVENS
HOW MANY TIMES — BROTHER BEYOND
HOW MEN ARE — AZTEC CAMERA
HOW MUCH I FEEL — ALIBI
(HOW MUCH IS) THAT DOGGIE IN THE
WINDOW [A] — Lita ROZA
(HOW MUCH IS) THAT DOGGIE IN THE
WINDOW [A] — Patti PAGE
HOW MUCH LOVE [A] — Leo SAYER
HOW MUCH LOVE [B] — VIXEN
HOW MUSIC CAME ABOUT (BOP B
DA B DA DA) — GAP BAND
HOW SHE THREW IT ALL AWAY (EP) —
STYLE COUNCIL
HOW SOON — Henry MANCINI
HOW SOON IS NOW? [A] — The SMITHS
HOW SOON IS NOW — INNER SANCTUM
HOW SOON IS NOW? [A] —
HUNDRED REASONS
HOW SOON WE FORGET — Colonel ABRAMS
HOW SWEET IT IS [A] — Marvin GAYE
HOW SWEET IT IS [A] —
Junior WALKER and the ALL-STARS
HOW THE HEART BEHAVES — WAS (NOT WAS)
HOW TO BE A MILLIONAIRE — ABC
HOW TO BE DEAD — SNOW PATROL
HOW TO FALL IN LOVE PART 1 —
The BEE GEES
HOW TO WIN YOUR LOVE —
Engelbert HUMPERDINCK
HOW U LIKE BASS — Norman BASS
HOW WAS IT FOR YOU — JAMES
HOW WILL I KNOW — Whitney HOUSTON
HOW WILL I KNOW (WHO YOU ARE) — JESSICA
HOW WONDERFUL TO KNOW —
Pearl CARR and Teddy JOHNSON
HOW WONDERFUL YOU ARE —
Gordon HASKELL
HOW WOULD U FEEL —
David MORALES featuring Lea LORIEN
HOW YOU GONNA ACT LIKE THAT — TYRESE
HOW YOU GONNA SEE ME NOW —
Alice COOPER
HOW YOU REMIND ME — NICKELBACK
HOW'D I DO DAT — BENTLEY RHYTHM ACE
HOW'S IT GOING TO BE — THIRD EYE BLIND
HOW'S YOUR EVENING SO FAR —
Josh WINK and Lil' LOUIS
HOWARD'S WAY — Simon MAY
HOWZAT — SHERBET
HUBBLE BUBBLE TOIL AND TROUBLE —
MANFRED MANN
HUDSON STREET — AGNELLI & NELSON
HUG MY SOUL — SAINT ETIENNE
HUMAN [A] — HUMAN LEAGUE
HUMAN [B] — The PRETENDERS
HUMAN BEHAVIOUR — BJÖRK
HUMAN BEING — The BETA BAND
HUMAN BEINGS — SEAL
HUMAN NATURE [A] —
Gary CLAIL ON-U SOUND SYSTEM
HUMAN NATURE [A] — MADONNA
HUMAN RACING — Nik KERSHAW
HUMAN TOUCH [A] — Rick SPRINGFIELD
HUMAN TOUCH [B] — Bruce SPRINGSTEEN
HUMAN WORK OF ART [A] — Maxi PRIEST
HUMAN WORK OF ART [A] — Cliff RICHARD
HUMANISTIC — KAWALA
HUMANITY — REBEL MC
HUMMING BIRD — Frankie LAINE
HUMPIN' — GAP BAND
HUMPIN' AROUND — Bobby BROWN
HUNDRED MILE HIGH CITY —
OCEAN COLOUR SCENE
A HUNDRED POUNDS OF CLAY —
Craig DOUGLAS

HUNG UP — Paul WELLER
HUNGAH — Karyn WHITE
THE HUNGER — The DISTILLERS
HUNGER STRIKE — TEMPLE OF THE DOG
HUNGRY — KOSHEEN
HUNGRY EYES — EYEOPENER
HUNGRY FOR HEAVEN — DIO
HUNGRY FOR LOVE —
Johnny KIDD and the PIRATES
HUNGRY HEART — Bruce SPRINGSTEEN
HUNGRY LIKE THE WOLF — DURAN DURAN
HUNT — Barry RYAN
HUNTER [A] — BJÖRK
HUNTER [B] — DIDO
HUNTING HIGH AND LOW — A-HA
HURDY GURDY MAN — DONOVAN
HURRICANE [A] — Bob DYLAN
HURRICANE [B] — WARM JETS
HURRY HOME — WAVELENGTH
HURRY UP AND WAIT — STEREOPHONICS
HURRY UP HARRY — SHAM 69
HURT [A] — Elvis PRESLEY
HURT [A] — MANHATTANS
HURT [B] — Johnny CASH
HURT BY LOVE — Inez FOXX
HURT ME SO BAD — LULU
HURT SO GOOD [A] — Susan CADOGAN
HURT SO GOOD [A] — Jimmy SOMERVILLE
HURTING KIND (I'VE GOT MY EYES ON YOU) —
Robert PLANT
HUSAN — BHANGRA KNIGHTS vs HUSAN
HUSBAND — FLUFFY
HUSH [A] — DEEP PURPLE
HUSH [A] — KULA SHAKER
HUSH... NOT A WORD TO MARY —
John ROWLES
THE HUSTLE — Van McCOY
HUSTLE! (TO THE MUSIC ...) — FUNKY WORM
HYBRID — EAT STATIC
HYMN [A] — ULTRAVOX
HYMN [B] — MOBY
HYMN [C] —
ULTRAMARINE featuring David McALMONT
HYMN TO HER — The PRETENDERS
HYMNE À L'AMOUR (IF YOU LOVE ME) —
Elaine PAIGE
HYPER MUSIC — MUSE
HYPERACTIVE — Thomas DOLBY
HYPERBALLAD — BJÖRK
HYPERREAL — The SHAMEN
HYPNOSIS — MUD
HYPNOTIC ST-8 — ALTERN 8
HYPNOTIC TANGO — MASTER BLASTER
HYPNOTISED [A] — CABARET VOLTAIRE
HYPNOTISED [B] — SIMPLE MINDS
HYPNOTISED [C] — Paul OAKENFOLD
HYPNOTISING —
KID CREME featuring CHARLISE
HYPNOTIZE [A] — SCRITTI POLITTI
HYPNOTIZE [B] — D'INFLUENCE
HYPNOTIZE [C] — NOTORIOUS B.I.G.
HYPNOTIZIN' — Josh WINK
HYPOCRITE [A] — LUSH
HYPOCRITE [B] — The SPECIALS
HYSTERIA [A] — DEF LEPPARD
HYSTERIA [B] — MUSE
I — Petey PABLO
I ADORE MI AMOR — COLOR ME BADD
I ADORE YOU — Caron WHEELER
I AIN'T GOIN' OUT LIKE THAT — CYPRESS HILL
I AIN'T GONNA CRY — LITTLE ANGELS
I AIN'T GONNA STAND FOR IT —
Stevie WONDER
I AIN'T GOT TIME ANYMORE — Cliff RICHARD
I AIN'T LYIN' — George McCRAE
I AIN'T MAD AT CHA — 2PAC
I AIN'T MOVIN' — DES'REE
I AIN'T NEW TA THIS — ICE-T
I ALMOST FELT LIKE CRYING —
Craig McLACHLAN
I ALMOST LOST MY MIND — Pat BOONE
I ALONE — LIVE
I AM [A] — CHAKRA
I AM [B] — SUGGS
I AM A CIDER DRINKER (PALOMA BLANCA) — WURZELS
I AM A CLOWN — David CASSIDY
I AM A ROCK — SIMON and GARFUNKEL
I AM BLESSED — ETERNAL
I AM DOWN — SALT-N-PEPA
I AM I — QUEENSRYCHE
I AM I FEEL — ALISHA'S ATTIC
I AM ... I SAID — Neil DIAMOND
I AM (I'M ME) — TWISTED SISTER
I AM IN LOVE WITH THE WORLD —
CHICKEN SHED THEATRE
I AM MINE — PEARL JAM
I AM LV — LV
I AM ONE [A] — SMASHING PUMPKINS
I AM ONE [B] — W.A.S.P.
I AM THE BEAT — LOOK
I AM THE BLACK GOLD OF THE SUN — NUYORICAN
SOUL featuring Jocelyn BROWN
I AM THE LAW — ANTHRAX
I AM THE MOB — CATATONIA
I AM THE MUSIC HEAR ME! —
MILLIONAIRE HIPPIES
I AM THE MUSIC MAN — BLACK LACE

I AM THE NEWS – OCEAN COLOUR SCENE
I AM THE ONE – CRACKOUT
I AM THE RESURRECTION – The STONE ROSES
I AM THE SUN – DARK STAR
I AM WHAT I AM [A] – GREYHOUND
I AM WHAT I AM [B] – Mark OWEN
I AM WHAT I AM (FROM 'LA CAGE AUX FOLLES') – Gloria GAYNOR
I APOLOGISE – PJ PROBY
I BE THE PROPHET – STARVING SOULS
I BEG YOUR PARDON – KON KAN
I BEGIN TO WONDER – Dannii MINOGUE
I BELIEVE [A] – Frankie LAINE
I BELIEVE [A] – David WHITFIELD
I BELIEVE [A] – The BACHELORS
I BELIEVE [A] – ROBSON & JEROME
I BELIEVE [B] – EMF
I BELIEVE [C] – REESE PROJECT
I BELIEVE [D] – BON JOVI
I BELIEVE [E] – Robert PLANT
I BELIEVE [F] – Marcella DETROIT
I BELIEVE [G] – SOUNDS OF BLACKNESS
I BELIEVE [H] – BLESSID UNION OF SOULS
I BELIEVE [I] – HAPPY CLAPPERS
I BELIEVE [J] – BOOTH and the BAD ANGEL
I BELIEVE [K] – ABSOLUTE
I BELIEVE [L] – LANGE featuring SARAH DWYER
I BELIEVE [M] – JAMESTOWN featuring JOCELYN BROWN
I BELIEVE [N] – Stephen GATELY
I BELIEVE (A SOULFUL RERECORDING) – TEARS FOR FEARS
I BELIEVE I CAN FLY – R KELLY
I BELIEVE I'M GONNA LOVE YOU – Frank SINATRA
I BELIEVE IN A THING CALLED LOVE – The DARKNESS
I BELIEVE IN CHRISTMAS – TWEENIES
I BELIEVE IN FATHER CHRISTMAS – Greg LAKE
I BELIEVE (IN LOVE) – HOT CHOCOLATE
I BELIEVE IN LOVE – COOPER
I BELIEVE IN MIRACLES [A] – JACKSON SISTERS
I BELIEVE IN MIRACLES [A] – PASADENAS
I BELIEVE IN THE SPIRIT – Tim BURGESS
I BELIEVE IN YOU [A] – OUR TRIBE / ONE TRIBE
I BELIEVE IN YOU [B] – AMP FIDDLER
I BELIEVE IN YOU [C] – KYLIE
I BELIEVE IN YOU AND ME – Whitney HOUSTON
(I BELIEVE) LOVE'S A PRIMA DONNA – Steve HARLEY and COCKNEY REBEL
I BELIEVE MY HEART – Duncan JAMES & KEEDIE
I BELIEVE YOU – Dorothy MOORE
I BELONG – Kathy KIRBY
I BELONG TO YOU [A] – Whitney HOUSTON
I BELONG TO YOU [B] – Gina G
I BELONG TO YOU [C] – Lenny KRAVITZ
I BREATHE AGAIN – Adam RICKITT
I CALL YOUR NAME – A-HA
I CALLED U – LIL' LOUIS
I CAN – NAS
I CAN BUY YOU – A CAMP
I CAN CALL YOU – PORTRAIT
I CAN CAST A SPELL – DISCO TEX presents CLOUDBURST
I CAN CLIMB MOUNTAINS – HELL IS FOR HEROES
I CAN DANCE [A] – Brian POOLE and the TREMELOES
I CAN DANCE [B] – DJ 'FAST' EDDIE
I CAN DO IT – The RUBETTES
I CAN DO THIS – Monie LOVE
I CAN DREAM – SKUNK ANANSIE
I CAN DREAM ABOUT YOU – Dan HARTMAN
I CAN DRIVE – SHAKESPEAR'S SISTER
I CAN FEEL IT – The SILENCERS
I CAN HEAR MUSIC – The BEACH BOYS
I CAN HEAR THE GRASS GROW – The MOVE
I CAN HEAR VOICES – HI-GATE
I CAN HEAR YOUR HEARTBEAT – Chris REA
I CAN HELP [A] – Billy SWAN
I CAN HELP [A] – Elvis PRESLEY
I CAN LOVE YOU LIKE THAT – ALL-4-ONE
I CAN MAKE IT BETTER [A] – WHISPERS
I CAN MAKE IT BETTER [B] – Luther VANDROSS
I CAN MAKE YOU FEEL GOOD [A] – SHALAMAR
I CAN MAKE YOU FEEL GOOD [A] – KAVANA
I CAN MAKE YOU FEEL LIKE – MAXX
I CAN ONLY DISAPOINT U – MANSUN
I CAN PROVE IT [A] – Tony ETORIA
I CAN PROVE IT [A] – Phil FEARON
I CAN SEE CLEARLY NOW [A] – Johnny NASH
I CAN SEE CLEARLY NOW [A] – HOTHOUSE FLOWERS
I CAN SEE CLEARLY NOW [A] – Jimmy CLIFF
I CAN SEE CLEARLY NOW [B] – Deborah HARRY
I CAN SEE FOR MILES – The WHO
I CAN SEE HER NOW – DRAMATIS
I CAN SEE IT – BLANCMANGE
I CAN SING A RAINBOW – LOVE IS BLUE (MEDLEY) – DELLS
I CAN TAKE OR LEAVE YOUR LOVING – HERMAN'S HERMITS
I CANNOT GIVE YOU MY LOVE – Cliff RICHARD
I CAN'T ASK FOR ANYTHING MORE THAN YOU – Cliff RICHARD
I CAN'T BE WITH YOU – The CRANBERRIES
I CAN'T BELIEVE YOU'RE GONE – WEBB BROTHERS
I CAN'T BREAK DOWN – Sinead QUINN
I CAN'T CONTROL MYSELF – The TROGGS
I CAN'T DANCE – GENESIS
I CAN'T DENY IT – Rod STEWART
I CAN'T EXPLAIN – The WHO
I CAN'T FACE THE WORLD – LEMON TREES
I CAN'T GET NEXT TO YOU – The TEMPTATIONS
(I CAN'T GET NO) SATISFACTION [A] – The ROLLING STONES
(I CAN'T GET NO) SATISFACTION [A] – Jonathan KING
I CAN'T GET NO SLEEP – INDIA
I CAN'T GET YOU OUT OF MY MIND – Yvonne ELLIMAN
I CAN'T GO FOR THAT (NO CAN DO) – Daryl HALL and John OATES
(I CAN'T HELP) FALLING IN LOVE WITH YOU – UB40
I CAN'T HELP IT [A] – Johnny TILLOTSON
I CAN'T HELP IT [C] – JUNIOR
I CAN'T HELP IT [B] – BANANARAMA
I CAN'T HELP MYSELF [A] – The FOUR TOPS
I CAN'T HELP MYSELF [A] – Donnie ELBERT
I CAN'T HELP MYSELF [B] – ORANGE JUICE
I CAN'T HELP MYSELF [C] – Joey LAWRENCE
I CAN'T HELP MYSELF [D] – Julia FORDHAM
I CAN'T HELP MYSELF [E] – LUCID
I CAN'T IMAGINE THE WORLD WITHOUT ME – ECHOBELLY
I CAN'T LEAVE YOU ALONE [A] – George McCRAE
I CAN'T LEAVE YOU ALONE [A] – TRACIE
I CAN'T LET GO [A] – The HOLLIES
I CAN'T LET GO [B] – Marti WEBB
I CAN'T LET MAGGIE GO – HONEYBUS
I CAN'T LET YOU GO [A] – HAYWOODE
I CAN'T LET YOU GO [B] – 52ND STREET
I CAN'T LET YOU GO [C] – MACK VIBE featuring JACQUELINE
I CAN'T LET YOU GO [D] – IAN VAN DAHL
I CAN'T LIVE A DREAM – The OSMONDS
I CAN'T MAKE A MISTAKE – MC LYTE
I CAN'T MAKE IT – The SMALL FACES
I CAN'T MAKE IT ALONE [A] – PJ PROBY
I CAN'T MAKE IT ALONE [A] – Maria McKEE
I CAN'T MAKE YOU LOVE ME [A] – Bonnie RAITT
I CAN'T MAKE YOU LOVE ME [B] – George MICHAEL
(I CAN'T GET ME NO) SATISFACTION – DEVO
I CAN'T READ – David BOWIE
I CAN'T READ YOU – Daniel BEDINGFIELD
I CAN'T SAY GOODBYE – Kim WILDE
I CAN'T SAY GOODBYE TO YOU – Helen REDDY
I CAN'T SEE – Nicole RAY
I CAN'T STAND MY BABY – REZILLOS
I CAN'T STAND IT [A] – Spencer DAVIS GROUP
I CAN'T STAND IT [B] – CAPTAIN HOLLYWOOD PROJECT
I CAN'T STAND THE RAIN [A] – Ann PEEBLES
I CAN'T STAND THE RAIN [A] – ERUPTION
I CAN'T STAND THE RAIN [A] – Tina TURNER
I CAN'T STAND UP FOR FALLING DOWN – Elvis COSTELLO
I CAN'T STOP [A] – The OSMONDS
I CAN'T STOP [B] – Gary NUMAN
I CAN'T STOP [C] – Sandy RIVERA
I CAN'T STOP LOVIN' YOU (THOUGH I TRY) – Leo SAYER
I CAN'T STOP LOVING YOU – Ray CHARLES
I CAN'T TAKE THE POWER – OFF-SHORE
I CAN'T TELL A WALTZ FROM A TANGO – Alma COGAN
I CAN'T TELL THE BOTTOM FROM THE TOP – The HOLLIES
I CAN'T TELL YOU WHY – BROWNSTONE
I CAN'T TURN AROUND – JM SILK
I CAN'T TURN AWAY – SAVANNA
I CAN'T TURN YOU LOOSE – Otis REDDING
I CAN'T WAIT [A] – Stevie NICKS
I CAN'T WAIT [B] – NU SHOOZ
I CAN'T WAIT [B] – LADIES FIRST
I CAN'T WAIT ANYMORE – SAXON
I CARE (SOUL II SOUL) – SOUL II SOUL
I CAUGHT YOU OUT – Rebecca DE RUVO
I CLOSE MY EYES AND COUNT TO TEN – Dusty SPRINGFIELD
I COME FROM ANOTHER PLANET BABY – Julian COPE
I CONFESS – The BEAT
I COULD BE AN ANGLE – The EIGHTIES MATCHBOX B-LINE DISASTER
I COULD BE HAPPY – ALTERED IMAGES
I COULD BE SO GOOD FOR YOU – Dennis WATERMAN
I COULD BE THE ONE – Stacie ORRICO
I COULD EASILY FALL – Cliff RICHARD and The SHADOWS
I COULD HAVE BEEN A DREAMER – DIO
I COULD NEVER LOVE ANOTHER – The TEMPTATIONS
I COULD NEVER MISS YOU (MORE THAN I DO) – LULU
I COULD NEVER TAKE THE PLACE OF YOUR MAN – PRINCE
I COULD NOT LOVE YOU MORE – The BEE GEES
I COULD SING OF YOUR LOVE FOREVER – DELIRIOUS?
I COULDN'T LIVE WITHOUT YOUR LOVE – Petula CLARK
I COUNT THE TEARS – The DRIFTERS
I CRIED FOR YOU – Ricky STEVENS
I DID WHAT I DID FOR MARIA – Tony CHRISTIE
I DIDN'T KNOW I LOVED YOU (TILL I SAW YOU ROCK 'N' ROLL) [A] – Gary GLITTER
I DIDN'T KNOW I LOVED YOU (TILL I SAW YOU ROCK 'N' ROLL) [A] – ROCK GODDESS
I DIDN'T KNOW I WAS LOOKING FOR LOVE (EP) – EVERYTHING BUT THE GIRL
I DIDN'T MEAN IT – STATUS QUO
I DIDN'T MEAN TO HURT YOU – ROCKIN' BERRIES
I DIDN'T MEAN TO TURN YOU ON – Robert PALMER
I DIDN'T WANT TO NEED YOU – HEART
I DIE: YOU DIE – Gary NUMAN
I DIG YOU BABY – Marvin RAINWATER
I DISAPPEAR – METALLICA
I DO – JAMELIA
I DO, I DO, I DO, I DO, I DO – ABBA
I DO WHAT I DO ... THEME FOR '9 1/2 WEEKS' – John TAYLOR
I DON'T BELIEVE IN IF ANYMORE – Roger WHITTAKER
I DON'T BELIEVE IN MIRACLES [A] – Colin BLUNSTONE
I DON'T BELIEVE IN MIRACLES [B] – SINITTA
I DON'T BLAME YOU AT ALL – MIRACLES
I DON'T CARE [A] – LIBERACE
I DON'T CARE [B] – LOS BRAVOS
I DON'T CARE [C] – SHAKESPEAR'S SISTER
I DON'T CARE [D] – Tony De VIT
I DON'T CARE IF THE SUN DON'T SHINE – Elvis PRESLEY
I DON'T EVEN KNOW IF I SHOULD CALL YOU BABY – SOUL FAMILY SENSATION
I DON'T EVER WANT TO SEE YOU AGAIN – UNCLE SAM
I DON'T KNOW [A] – RUTH
I DON'T KNOW [B] – HONEYZ
I DON'T KNOW ANYBODY ELSE – BLACK BOX
I DON'T KNOW HOW TO LOVE HIM [A] – Petula CLARK
I DON'T KNOW HOW TO LOVE HIM [A] – Yvonne ELLIMAN
I DON'T KNOW IF IT'S RIGHT – Evelyn 'Champagne' KING
I DON'T KNOW WHAT IT IS – Rufus WAINWRIGHT
I DON'T KNOW WHAT IT IS BUT I LOVE IT – Chris REA
I DON'T KNOW WHAT YOU WANT BUT I CAN'T GIVE IT ANYMORE – PET SHOP BOYS
I DON'T KNOW WHERE IT COMES FROM – RIDE
I DON'T KNOW WHY [A] – Eden KANE
I DON'T KNOW WHY [B] – Shawn COLVIN
I DON'T KNOW WHY (I JUST DO) – Andy and David WILLIAMS
(I DON'T KNOW WHY) BUT I DO – Clarence 'Frogman' HENRY
I DON'T KNOW WHY I LOVE YOU – HOUSE OF LOVE
I DON'T KNOW WHY (I LOVE YOU) – Stevie WONDER
I DON'T LIKE MONDAYS – The BOOMTOWN RATS
I DON'T LOVE YOU ANYMORE – QUIREBOYS
I DON'T LOVE YOU BUT I THINK I LIKE YOU – Gilbert O'SULLIVAN
I DON'T MIND – The BUZZCOCKS
I DON'T MIND AT ALL – BOURGEOIS TAGG
I DON'T NEED ANYTHING – Sandie SHAW
I DON'T NEED NO DOCTOR (LIVE) – W.A.S.P.
I DON'T NEED TO TELL HER – LURKERS
I DON'T REALLY CARE – K-GEE
I DON'T REMEMBER – Peter GABRIEL
I DON'T SMOKE – DJ DEE KLINE
I DON'T THINK SO – DINOSAUR JR
I DON'T THINK THAT MAN SHOULD SLEEP ALONE – Ray PARKER Jr
I DON'T WANNA BE A STAR – CORONA
I DON'T WANNA DANCE – Eddy GRANT
I DON'T WANNA FIGHT – Tina TURNER
I DON'T WANNA GET HURT – Donna SUMMER
I DON'T WANNA GO ON WITH YOU LIKE THAT – Elton JOHN
I DON'T WANNA KNOW – Mario WINANS featuring ENYA & P DIDDY
I DON'T WANNA LOSE AT LOVE – Tanita TIKARAM
I DON'T WANNA LOSE MY WAY – DREAMCATCHER
I DON'T WANNA LOSE YOU [A] – KANDIDATE
I DON'T WANNA LOSE YOU [B] – Tina TURNER
I DON'T WANNA LOSE YOUR LOVE – The EMOTIONS
I DON'T WANNA PLAY HOUSE – Tammy WYNETTE
I DON'T WANNA TAKE THIS PAIN – Dannii MINOGUE
I DON'T WANT A LOVER – TEXAS
I DON'T WANT CONTROL OF YOU – TEENAGE FANCLUB
I DON'T WANT NOBODY (TELLIN' ME WHAT TO DO) – Cherie AMORE
I DON'T WANT OUR LOVING TO DIE – The HERD
I DON'T WANT TO – Toni BRAXTON
I DON'T WANT TO BE A FREAK (BUT I CAN'T HELP MYSELF) – DYNASTY
I DON'T WANT TO BE A HERO – JOHNNY HATES JAZZ
I DON'T WANT TO GO ON WITHOUT YOU – The MOODY BLUES
(I DON'T WANT TO GO TO) CHELSEA – Elvis COSTELLO
I DON'T WANT TO HURT YOU (EVERY SINGLE TIME) – Frank BLACK
I DON'T WANT TO MISS A THING – AEROSMITH
I DON'T WANT TO PUT A HOLD ON YOU – Berni FLINT
I DON'T WANT TO TALK ABOUT IT [A] – Rod STEWART
I DON'T WANT TO TALK ABOUT IT [A] – EVERYTHING BUT THE GIRL
I DON'T WANT TO WAIT – Paula COLE
I DON'T WANT YOUR LOVE – DURAN DURAN
I DREAM – TILT
I DREAMED – BEVERLEY SISTERS
I DROVE ALL NIGHT [A] – Cyndi LAUPER
I DROVE ALL NIGHT [A] – Roy ORBISON
I EAT CANNIBALS PART 1 – TOTO COELO
I ENJOY BEING A GIRL – Pat SUZUKI
I FEEL A CRY COMING ON – Hank LOCKLIN
I FEEL DIVINE – S-J
I FEEL FINE [A] – The BEATLES
I FEEL FINE [A] – WET WET WET
I FEEL FOR YOU [A] – Chaka KHAN
I FEEL FOR YOU [B] – Bob SINCLAR
I FEEL FREE – CREAM
I FEEL GOOD THINGS FOR YOU – DADDY'S FAVOURITE
I FEEL IT – MOBY
I FEEL LIKE BUDDY HOLLY – Alvin STARDUST
I FEEL LIKE WALKIN' IN THE RAIN – Millie JACKSON
I FEEL LOVE [A] – Donna SUMMER
I FEEL LOVE (MEDLEY) [A] – BRONSKI BEAT and Marc ALMOND
I FEEL LOVE [A] – MESSIAH
I FEEL LOVE [A] – VANESSA-MAE
I FEEL LOVE [B] – CRW
I FEEL LOVE COMIN' ON [A] – Felice TAYLOR
I FEEL LOVE COMIN' ON [A] – DANA
I FEEL LOVED – DEPECHE MODE
I FEEL SO – BOX CAR RACER
I FEEL SO BAD – Elvis PRESLEY
I FEEL SO FINE – KMC featuring DHANY
I FEEL SOMETHING IN THE AIR – CHER
I FEEL STEREO – Dino LENNY
I FEEL THE EARTH MOVE – MARTIKA
I FEEL YOU [A] – LOVE DECADE
I FEEL YOU [B] – DEPECHE MODE
I FEEL YOU [C] – Peter ANDRE
I FINALLY FOUND SOMEONE – Barbra STREISAND and Bryan ADAMS
I FORGOT [A] – COOLNOTES
I FORGOT [B] – Lionel RICHIE
I FOUGHT THE LAW [A] – Bobby FULLER FOUR
I FOUGHT THE LAW [A] – The CLASH
I FOUND HEAVEN – TAKE THAT
I FOUND LOVE [A] – Darlene DAVIS
I FOUND LOVE [B] – LONE JUSTICE
I FOUND LOVE [C] – C & C MUSIC FACTORY / CLIVILLES & COLE featuring Martha WASH
I FOUND LOVIN' [A] – FATBACK BAND
I FOUND LOVIN' [A] – Steve WALSH
I FOUND OUT – The CHRISTIANS
I FOUND OUT THE HARD WAY – FOUR PENNIES
I FOUND SOMEONE [A] – CHER
I FOUND SOMEONE [B] – Billy and Sarah GAINES
I FOUND SUNSHINE – CHI-LITES
I (FRIDAY NIGHT) – DUBSTAR
I GAVE IT UP (WHEN I FELL IN LOVE) – Luther VANDROSS
I GAVE MY EYES TO STEVIE WONDER – MILLION DEAD
I GAVE YOU EVERYTHING – CODE RED
I GAVE YOU MY HEART (DIDN'T I) – HOT CHOCOLATE
I GET A KICK OUT OF YOU – Gary SHEARSTON
I GET A LITTLE SENTIMENTAL OVER YOU – The NEW SEEKERS
I GET ALONG – PET SHOP BOYS
I GET AROUND – The BEACH BOYS
I GET LIFTED – Barbara TUCKER
I GET LONELY – Janet JACKSON
I GET SO EXCITED – The EQUALS

I STILL BELIEVE IN YOU — Cliff RICHARD
I STILL HAVEN'T FOUND WHAT I'M LOOKING FOR [A] — U2
I STILL HAVEN'T FOUND WHAT I'M LOOKING FOR [A] — CHIMES
I STILL LOVE YOU ALL — Kenny BALL and his JAZZMEN
I STILL REMEMBER — Gary NUMAN
I STILL THINK ABOUT YOU — DANGER DANGER
I STILL THINK OF YOU — UTAH SAINTS
I SURRENDER [A] — RAINBOW
I SURRENDER [B] — Rosie GAINES
I SURRENDER [C] — David SYLVIAN
I SURRENDER (TO THE SPIRIT OF THE NIGHT) — Samantha FOX
I SURRENDER TO YOUR LOVE — BY ALL MEANS
I SWEAR — ALL-4-ONE
I TALK TO THE TREES — Clint EASTWOOD
I TALK TO THE WIND — OPUS III
I THANK YOU [A] — SAM and DAVE
I THANK YOU [B] — ADEVA
I THINK I LOVE YOU [A] — PARTRIDGE FAMILY
I THINK I LOVE YOU [A] — VOICE OF THE BEEHIVE
I THINK I LOVE YOU [A] — KACI
I THINK I WANT TO DANCE WITH YOU — RUMPLE-STILTS-SKIN
I THINK I'M IN LOVE — SPIRITUALIZED
I THINK I'M IN LOVE WITH YOU — Jessica SIMPSON
I THINK I'M PARANOID — GARBAGE
I THINK IT'S GOING TO RAIN TODAY — UB40
I THINK OF YOU [A] — The MERSEYBEATS
I THINK OF YOU [B] — Perry COMO
I THINK OF YOU [C] — DETROIT EMERALDS
I THINK OF YOU [D] — Bryan POWELL
I THINK WE'RE ALONE NOW [A] — TIFFANY
I THINK WE'RE ALONE NOW [A] — PASCAL featuring Karen PARRY
I THOUGHT I MEANT THE WORLD TO YOU — Alysha WARREN
I THOUGHT IT TOOK A LITTLE TIME (BUT TODAY I FELL IN LOVE) — Diana ROSS
I THOUGHT IT WAS YOU [A] — Herbie HANCOCK
I THOUGHT IT WAS YOU [A] — SEX-O-SONIQUE
I THOUGHT IT WAS YOU [B] — Julia FORDHAM
I THREW IT ALL AWAY — Bob DYLAN
I TOLD YOU SO — Jimmy JONES
I TOUCH MYSELF — DIVINYLS
I TRY [A] — Macy GRAY
I TRY [B] — Talib KWELI featuring Mary J BLIGE
I TURN TO YOU [A] — Melanie C
I TURN TO YOU [B] — Christina AGUILERA
I UNDERSTAND [A] — G-CLEFS
I UNDERSTAND [A] — FREDDIE and the DREAMERS
I WALK THE EARTH — VOICE OF THE BEEHIVE
I WANNA BE A FLINTSTONE — SCREAMING BLUE MESSIAHS
I WANNA BE A HIPPY — TECHNOHEAD
I WANNA BE A WINNER — BROWN SAUCE
I WANNA BE ADORED — The STONE ROSES
I WANNA BE DOWN — BRANDY
I WANNA BE FREE — MINTY
I WANNA BE FREE (TO BE WITH HIM) — SCARLET
I WANNA BE IN LOVE AGAIN — BEIJING SPRING
I WANNA BE LOVED [A] — Ricky NELSON
I WANNA BE LOVED [B] — Elvis COSTELLO
I WANNA BE THE ONLY ONE — ETERNAL featuring BeBe WINANS
I WANNA BE WITH YOU [A] — COFFEE
I WANNA BE WITH YOU [B] — MAZE featuring Frankie BEVERLY
I WANNA BE WITH YOU [C] — Mandy MOORE
I WANNA BE U — CHOCOLATE PUMA
I WANNA BE YOUR LADY — Hinda HICKS
I WANNA BE YOUR LOVER — PRINCE
I WANNA BE YOUR MAN [A] — The ROLLING STONES
I WANNA BE YOUR MAN [A] — REZILLOS
I WANNA BE YOUR MAN [B] — Chaka DEMUS and PLIERS
I WANNA DANCE WIT' CHOO (DOO DAT DANCE) – PART 1 — DISCO TEX and the SEX-O-LETTES
I WANNA DANCE WITH SOMEBODY (WHO LOVES ME) [A] — Whitney HOUSTON
I WANNA DANCE WITH SOMEBODY [A] — FLIP & FILL
I WANNA DO IT WITH YOU — Barry MANILOW
I WANNA GET NEXT TO YOU — ROSE ROYCE
(I WANNA GIVE YOU) DEVOTION — NOMAD
I WANNA GO BACK — The NEW SEEKERS
I WANNA GO HOME — Lonnie DONEGAN
I WANNA GO WHERE THE PEOPLE GO — The WILDHEARTS
I WANNA HAVE SOME FUN — Samantha FOX
I WANNA HOLD ON TO YOU — Mica PARIS
I WANNA HOLD YOUR HAND — DOLLAR
I WANNA KNOW [A] — STACCATO
I WANNA KNOW [B] — JOE
I WANNA KNOW [C] — The BLUESKINS
(I WANNA KNOW) WHY — SINCLAIR
(I WANNA) LOVE MY LIFE AWAY — Gene PITNEY
I WANNA LOVE YOU [A] — JADE
I WANNA LOVE YOU [B] — SOLID HARMONIE
I WANNA LOVE YOU FOREVER — Jessica SIMPSON
I WANNA MAKE YOU FEEL GOOD — SYSTEM
I WANNA 1-2-1 WITH YOU — SOLID GOLD CHARTBUSTERS
I WANNA SEX YOU UP — COLOR ME BADD
I WANNA SING — Sabrina JOHNSTON
I WANNA STAY HOME — JELLYFISH
I WANNA STAY WITH YOU [A] — GALLAGHER and LYLE
I WANNA STAY WITH YOU [A] — UNDERCOVER
I WANNA THANK YA — Angie STONE featuring SNOOP DOGG
I WANT AN ALIEN FOR CHRISTMAS — FOUNTAINS OF WAYNE
I WANT CANDY [A] — Brian POOLE and the TREMELOES
I WANT CANDY [A] — BOW WOW WOW
I WANT CANDY [A] — CANDY GIRLS
I WANT CANDY [A] — Aaron CARTER
I WANT HER — Keith SWEAT
I WANT IT ALL — QUEEN
I WANT IT THAT WAY — BACKSTREET BOYS
I WANT LOVE — Elton JOHN
I WANT MORE [A] — CAN
I WANT MORE [B] — FAITHLESS
I WANT OUT — HELLOWEEN
I WANT OUT (I CAN'T BELIEVE) — Harry 'Choo-Choo' ROMERO
I WANT THAT MAN — Deborah HARRY
I WANT THE WORLD — 2WO THIRD3
I WANT TO BE ALONE — 2WO THIRD3
(I WANT TO BE) ELECTED — Bruce DICKINSON
I WANT TO BE FREE — TOYAH
I WANT TO BE STRAIGHT — Ian DURY and the BLOCKHEADS
I WANT TO BE THERE WHEN YOU COME — ECHO and the BUNNYMEN
I WANT TO BE WANTED — Brenda LEE
I WANT TO BE YOUR MAN — ROGER
I WANT TO BE YOUR PROPERTY — BLUE MERCEDES
I WANT TO BREAK FREE — QUEEN
I WANT TO GIVE — Perry COMO
I WANT TO GO WITH YOU — Eddy ARNOLD
I WANT TO HEAR IT FROM YOU — GO WEST
I WANT TO HOLD YOUR HAND — The BEATLES
(I WANT TO) KILL SOMEBODY — S*M*A*S*H
I WANT TO KNOW WHAT LOVE IS [A] — FOREIGNER
I WANT TO KNOW WHAT LOVE IS [A] — Terri SYMON
I WANT TO LIVE — GRACE
I WANT TO STAY HERE [A] — Eydie GORME
I WANT TO STAY HERE [A] — MIKI and GRIFF
I WANT TO THANK YOU — Robin S
I WANT TO TOUCH YOU — CATHERINE WHEEL
I WANT TO WAKE UP WITH YOU — Boris GARDINER
I WANT TO WALK YOU HOME — Fats DOMINO
I WANT U — Rosie GAINES
I WANT YOU [A] — Bob DYLAN
I WANT YOU [A] — Sophie B HAWKINS
I WANT YOU [B] — Gary LOW
I WANT YOU [C] — UTAH SAINTS
I WANT YOU [D] — Juliet ROBERTS
I WANT YOU [E] — SECRET LIFE
I WANT YOU [F] — SALAD
I WANT YOU [G] — INSPIRAL CARPETS
I WANT YOU [H] — SAVAGE GARDEN
I WANT YOU [I] — Z2
I WANT YOU [J] — CZR featuring DELANO
I WANT YOU [K] — JANET
I WANT YOU (ALL TONIGHT) — Curtis HAIRSTON
I WANT YOU BACK [A] — The JACKSON FIVE
I WANT YOU BACK [A] — Michael JACKSON with The JACKSON FIVE
I WANT YOU BACK [A] — CLEOPATRA
I WANT YOU BACK [B] — BANANARAMA
I WANT YOU BACK [C] — 'N SYNC
I WANT YOU BACK [D] — Melanie B featuring Missy 'Misdemeanor' ELLIOTT
I WANT YOU BACK [E] — XPRESS-2
I WANT YOU FOR MYSELF — ANOTHER LEVEL / GHOSTFACE KILLAH
I WANT YOU (FOREVER) — Carl COX
I WANT YOU I NEED YOU I LOVE YOU — Elvis PRESLEY
I WANT YOU NEAR ME — Tina TURNER
I WANT YOU TO BE MY BABY — Billie DAVIS
I WANT YOU TO WANT ME [A] — CHEAP TRICK
I WANT YOU TO WANT ME [B] — SOLID HARMONIE
I WANT YOUR LOVE [A] — CHIC
I WANT YOUR LOVE [A] — Roger SANCHEZ
I WANT YOUR LOVE [B] — TRANSVISION VAMP
I WANT YOUR LOVE [C] — ATOMIC KITTEN
I WANT YOUR LOVIN' (JUST A LITTLE BIT) — Curtis HAIRSTON
I WANT YOUR SEX — George MICHAEL
I WAS A KING — Shabba RANKS
I WAS BORN ON CHRISTMAS DAY — SAINT ETIENNE
I WAS BORN TO BE ME — Tom JONES
I WAS BORN TO LOVE YOU — Freddie MERCURY
I WAS BROUGHT TO MY SENSES — STING
I WAS KAISER BILL'S BATMAN — Whistling Jack SMITH
I WAS MADE FOR DANCIN' — Leif GARRETT
I WAS MADE FOR LOVIN' YOU — KISS
I WAS MADE TO LOVE HER — Stevie WONDER
I WAS MADE TO LOVE YOU — Lorraine CATO
I WAS ONLY JOKING — Rod STEWART
I WAS RIGHT AND YOU WERE WRONG — DEACON BLUE
I WAS THE ONE — Elvis PRESLEY
I WAS TIRED OF BEING ALONE — Patrice RUSHEN
I WASN'T BUILT TO GET UP — SUPERNATURALS
I WEAR MY SKIN — ONE MINUTE SILENCE
I (WHO HAVE NOTHING) [A] — Shirley BASSEY
I (WHO HAVE NOTHING) [A] — Tom JONES
I (WHO HAVE NOTHING) [A] — SYLVESTER
I WILL [A] — Billy FURY
I WILL [A] — Ruby WINTERS
I WILL ALWAYS LOVE YOU [A] — Whitney HOUSTON
I WILL ALWAYS LOVE YOU [A] — Sarah WASHINGTON
I WILL ALWAYS LOVE YOU [A] — Rik WALLER
I WILL BE RELEASED — UP YER RONSON featuring Mary PEARCE
I WILL BE WITH YOU — T'PAU
I WILL BE YOUR GIRLFRIEND — DUBSTAR
I WILL COME TO YOU — HANSON
I WILL DRINK THE WINE — Frank SINATRA
I WILL FOLLOW — UNA MAS
I WILL GO WITH YOU (CON TE PARTIRO) — Donna SUMMER
I WILL LOVE AGAIN — LARA FABIAN
I WILL LOVE YOU ALL MY LIFE — FOSTER and ALLEN
I WILL LOVE YOU (EV'RY TIME WHEN WE ARE GONE) — FUREYS
I WILL REMEMBER — TOTO
I WILL RETURN — SPRINGWATER
I WILL SURVIVE [A] — ARRIVAL
I WILL SURVIVE [B] — Gloria GAYNOR
I WILL SURVIVE [B] — Billie Jo SPEARS
I WILL SURVIVE [B] — Chantay SAVAGE
I WILL SURVIVE [B] — Diana ROSS
I WILL SURVIVE [B] — CAKE
I WILL WAIT — HOOTIE & THE BLOWFISH
I WISH [A] — Stevie WONDER
I WISH [B] — GABRIELLE
I WISH [C] — SKEE-LO
I WISH [D] — R KELLY
I WISH HE DIDN'T TRUST ME SO MUCH — Bobby WOMACK
I WISH I COULD SHIMMY LIKE MY SISTER KATE — OLYMPICS
(I WISH I KNEW HOW IT WOULD FEEL TO BE) FREE [A] — LIGHTHOUSE FAMILY
I WISH I KNEW HOW IT WOULD FEEL TO BE FREE [A] — Sharlene HECTOR with the NEW INSPIRATIONAL CHOIR
I WISH I WAS A GIRL — VIOLENT DELIGHT
I WISH I WAS YOU — NEW RHODES
I WISH IT COULD BE CHRISTMAS EVERYDAY [A] — WIZZARD
I WISH IT COULD BE CHRISTMAS EVERYDAY [A] — Roy WOOD
I WISH IT COULD BE A WOMBLING MERRY CHRISTMAS EVERYDAY [A] — The WOMBLES with Roy WOOD
I WISH IT WASN'T TRUE — SUPATONIC
I WISH IT WOULD RAIN [A] — The TEMPTATIONS
I WISH IT WOULD RAIN [A] — The FACES
I WISH IT WOULD RAIN DOWN — Phil COLLINS
I WISH U HEAVEN — PRINCE
I WISH YOU LOVE — Paul YOUNG
I WISH YOU WOULD — Jocelyn BROWN
I WONDER [A] — Dickie VALENTINE
I WONDER [A] — Jane FROMAN
I WONDER [B] — Brenda LEE
I WONDER [C] — CRYSTALS
I WONDER HOW — SHINING
I WONDER IF HEAVEN GOT A GHETTO — 2PAC
I WONDER IF I TAKE YOU HOME — LISA LISA and CULT JAM with FULL FORCE
I WONDER WHO'S KISSING HER NOW — Emile FORD and the CHECKMATES
I WONDER WHY [A] — SHOWADDYWADDY
I WONDER WHY [B] — Curtis STIGERS
I WONDER WHY HE'S THE GREATEST DJ — TONY TOUCH featuring TOTAL
I WON'T BACK DOWN — Tom PETTY and the HEARTBREAKERS
I WON'T BLEED FOR YOU — CLIMIE FISHER
I WON'T CHANGE YOU — Sophie ELLIS-BEXTOR
I WON'T CLOSE MY EYES — UB40
I WON'T COME IN WHILE HE'S THERE — Jim REEVES
I WON'T CRY — Glen GOLDSMITH
I WON'T FEEL BAD — SIMPLY RED
I WON'T FORGET YOU — Jim REEVES
I WON'T HOLD YOU BACK — TOTO
I WON'T LAST A DAY WITHOUT YOU — The CARPENTERS
I WON'T LET THE SUN GO DOWN ON ME — Nik KERSHAW
I WON'T LET YOU DOWN [A] — PhD
I WON'T LET YOU DOWN [A] — W.I.P. featuring EMMIE
I WON'T MENTION IT AGAIN — Ruby WINTERS
I WON'T RUN AWAY — Alvin STARDUST
I WOULD DIE 4 U [A] — PRINCE
I WOULD DIE 4 U [A] — SPACE COWBOY
I WOULD DO FOR YOU — UB40
I WOULD FIX YOU — KENICKIE
I WOULD NEVER — BLUE NILE
I WOULDN'T BELIEVE YOUR RADIO — STEREOPHONICS
I WOULDN'T LIE — YARBROUGH and PEOPLES
I WOULDN'T NORMALLY DO THIS KIND OF THING — PET SHOP BOYS
I WOULDN'T TRADE YOU FOR THE WORLD — The BACHELORS
I WOULDN'T WANNA HAPPEN TO YOU — EMBRACE
I WRITE THE SONGS — David CASSIDY
I WROTE YOU A SONG — Misty OLDLAND
IBIZA — MAXIMA featuring LILY
THE ICE CREAM MAN — TORNADOS
ICE HOCKEY HAIR — SUPER FURRY ANIMALS
ICE ICE BABY — VANILLA ICE
ICE IN THE SUN — STATUS QUO
ICE RAIN — Alex WHITCOMBE & BIG C
ICEBLINK LUCK — COCTEAU TWINS
ICH BIN EIN AUSLANDER — POP WILL EAT ITSELF
ICH WILL — RAMMSTEIN
ICING ON THE CAKE — Stephen 'Tin Tin' DUFFY
I'D BE SURPRISINGLY GOOD FOR YOU — Linda LEWIS
I'D DIE WITHOUT YOU — PM DAWN
I'D DO ANYTHING — Mike PRESTON
I'D DO ANYTHING FOR LOVE (BUT I WON'T DO THAT) — MEAT LOAF
I'D LIE FOR YOU (AND THAT'S THE TRUTH) — MEAT LOAF
I'D LIKE TO TEACH THE WORLD TO SING (IN PERFECT HARMONY) [A] — The NEW SEEKERS
I'D LIKE TO TEACH THE WORLD TO SING [A] — NO WAY SIS
I'D LIKE TO TEACH THE WORLD TO SING [A] — Demi HOLBORN
I'D LOVE YOU TO WANT ME — LOBO
I'D NEVER FIND ANOTHER YOU — Billy FURY
I'D RATHER DANCE WITH YOU — KINGS OF CONVENIENCE
I'D RATHER GO BLIND [A] — CHICKEN SHACK
I'D RATHER GO BLIND [A] — Ruby TURNER
I'D RATHER GO BLIND [A] — Sydney YOUNGBLOOD
I'D RATHER JACK — REYNOLDS GIRLS
I'D REALLY LOVE TO SEE YOU TONIGHT — ENGLAND DAN and John Ford COLEY
THE IDEAL HEIGHT — BIFFY CLYRO
IDEAL WORLD — The CHRISTIANS
IDENTITY — X-RAY SPEX
IDIOTS AT THE WHEEL (EP) — KINGMAKER
IDLE GOSSIP — Perry COMO
IDLE ON PARADE (EP) — Anthony NEWLEY
IDOL — Amanda GHOST
THE IDOL [A] — W.A.S.P.
THE IDOL [B] — Marc ALMOND
IEYA — TOYAH
IF [A] — Telly SAVALAS
IF [A] — Dolly PARTON
IF [A] — YIN and YAN
IF [A] — John ALFORD
IF [B] — Janet JACKSON
IF ... [C] — The BLUETONES
IF — READ TO FAURÉ'S 'PAVANE' [D] — WIMBLEDON CHORAL SOCIETY
IF A MAN ANSWERS — Bobby DARIN
IF ANYONE FINDS THIS, I LOVE YOU — Ruby MURRAY
IF DREAMS CAME TRUE — Pat BOONE
IF EVER — 3RD STOREE
IF EVERY DAY WAS LIKE CHRISTMAS — Elvis PRESLEY
IF EVERYBODY LOOKED THE SAME — GROOVE ARMADA
IF EYE LOVE U 2 NIGHT — MAYTE
IF GOD WILL SEND HIS ANGELS — U2
IF HE TELLS YOU — Adam FAITH
IF I AIN'T GOT YOU — Alicia KEYS
IF I CAN DREAM — Elvis PRESLEY
IF I CAN DREAM (EP) — Michael BALL
IF I CAN'T — 50 CENT & G-UNIT
IF I CAN'T CHANGE YOUR MIND — SUGAR
IF I CAN'T HAVE YOU [A] — Yvonne ELLIMAN
IF I CAN'T HAVE YOU [A] — Kim WILDE
IF I COULD [A] — David ESSEX

IF I COULD [B] — HUNDRED REASONS
IF I COULD BUILD MY WHOLE WORLD AROUND YOU — Marvin GAYE
IF I COULD (EL CONDOR PASA) — Julie FELIX
IF I COULD FLY — GRACE
IF I COULD GIVE ALL MY LOVE — COUNTING CROWS
IF I COULD GO! — Angie MARTINEZ featuring LIL' MO & SACARIO
IF I COULD ONLY MAKE YOU CARE — Mike BERRY
IF I COULD ONLY SAY GOODBYE — David HASSELHOFF
IF I COULD TALK I'D TELL YOU — LEMONHEADS
IF I COULD TURN BACK THE HANDS OF TIME — R KELLY
IF I COULD TURN BACK TIME — CHER
IF I DIDN'T CARE — David CASSIDY
IF I EVER FALL IN LOVE — SHAI
IF I EVER LOSE MY FAITH IN YOU — STING
IF I FALL — Alice MARTINEAU
IF I GIVE MY HEART TO YOU [A] — Doris DAY
IF I GIVE MY HEART TO YOU [A] — Joan REGAN
IF I GIVE YOU MY NUMBER — ANT & DEC
IF I HAD A HAMMER — Trini LOPEZ
IF I HAD NO LOOT — TONY TONI TONÉ
IF I HAD WORDS — Scott FITZGERALD
IF I HAD YOU — KORGIS
IF I HAVE TO GO AWAY — JIGSAW
IF I HAVE TO STAND ALONE — Lonnie GORDON
IF I KNEW THEN WHAT I KNOW NOW — Val DOONICAN
IF I LET YOU GO — WESTLIFE
IF I LOVE U 2 NITE — Mica PARIS
IF I LOVE YA THEN I NEED YA IF I NEED YA THEN I WANT YOU AROUND — Eartha KITT
IF I LOVED YOU — Richard ANTHONY
IF I NEEDED SOMEONE — The HOLLIES
IF I NEVER FEEL BETTER — PHOENIX
IF I NEVER KNEW YOU (LOVE THEME FROM 'POCAHONTAS') — Jon SECADA and SHANICE
IF I NEVER SEE YOU AGAIN — WET WET WET
IF I ONLY HAD TIME — John ROWLES
IF I ONLY KNEW — Tom JONES
IF I REMEMBER — BENZ
IF I RULED THE WORLD [A] — Harry SECOMBE
IF I RULED THE WORLD [A] — Tony BENNETT
IF I RULED THE WORLD [B] — Kurtis BLOW
IF I RULED THE WORLD [B] — NAS
IF I SAID YOU HAVE A BEAUTIFUL BODY WOULD YOU HOLD IT AGAINST ME — BELLAMY BROTHERS
IF I SAY YES — FIVE STAR
IF I SHOULD FALL FROM GRACE WITH GOD — The POGUES
IF I SHOULD LOVE AGAIN — Barry MANILOW
IF I SURVIVE — HYBRID featuring Julee CRUISE
IF I THOUGHT YOU'D EVER CHANGE YOUR MIND [A] — Cilla BLACK
IF I THOUGHT YOU'D EVER CHANGE YOUR MIND [A] — Agnetha FALTSKOG
IF I TOLD YOU THAT — Whitney HOUSTON / George MICHAEL
IF I WAS [A] — Midge URE
IF I WAS [B] — ASWAD
IF I WAS A RIVER — Tina ARENA
IF I WAS YOUR GIRLFRIEND — PRINCE
IF I WERE A CARPENTER [A] — Bobby DARIN
IF I WERE A CARPENTER [A] — The FOUR TOPS
IF I WERE A CARPENTER [A] — Robert PLANT
IF I WERE A RICH MAN — TOPOL
IF I WERE YOU [A] — kd lang
IF I WERE YOU [B] — Candee JAY
IF I'M NOT YOUR LOVER — Al B SURE!
IF IT DON'T FIT DON'T FORCE IT — Kellee PATTERSON
IF IT HAPPENS AGAIN — UB40
IF IT MAKES YOU HAPPY — Sheryl CROW
IF IT WASN'T FOR THE REASON THAT I LOVE YOU — Miki ANTHONY
IF IT'S ALRIGHT WITH YOU BABY — KORGIS
IF IT'S LOVE THAT YOU WANT — Donny OSMOND
IF LEAVING ME IS EASY — Phil COLLINS
IF LIFE IS LIKE A LOVE BANK I WANT AN OVERDRAFT — The WILDHEARTS
IF LOOKS COULD KILL — TRANSVISION VAMP
IF LOVE WAS A TRAIN — Michelle SHOCKED
IF LOVE WAS LIKE GUITARS — Ian McNABB
IF LOVING YOU IS WRONG (I DON'T WANT TO BE RIGHT) — Rod STEWART
IF MADONNA CALLS — Junior VASQUEZ
IF MY FRIENDS COULD SEE ME NOW — Linda CLIFFORD
IF NOT FOR YOU — Olivia NEWTON-JOHN
IF NOT YOU — DR HOOK
IF ONLY — HANSON
IF ONLY I COULD — Sydney YOUNGBLOOD
IF ONLY I COULD LIVE MY LIFE AGAIN — Jane MORGAN
IF ONLY TOMORROW — Ronnie CARROLL
(IF PARADISE IS) HALF AS NICE — AMEN CORNER
IF SHE KNEW WHAT SHE WANTS — The BANGLES
IF SHE SHOULD COME TO YOU — Anthony NEWLEY
IF 60S WERE 90S — BEAUTIFUL PEOPLE
IF THAT WERE ME — Melanie C
IF THAT'S YOUR BOYFRIEND (HE WASN'T LAST NIGHT) — Me'Shell NDEGEOCELLO
IF THE KIDS ARE UNITED — SHAM 69
IF THE RIVER CAN BEND — Elton JOHN
IF THE WHOLE WORLD STOPPED LOVING — Val DOONICAN
IF THERE WAS A MAN — The PRETENDERS
IF THERE'S ANY JUSTICE — LEMAR
IF THIS IS IT — Huey LEWIS and the NEWS
IF THIS IS LOVE [A] — JJ
IF THIS IS LOVE [B] — Jeanie TRACY
IF TOMORROW NEVER COMES — Ronan KEATING
IF U WANT ME — Michael WOODS featuring Imogen BAILEY
IF WE FALL IN LOVE TONIGHT — Rod STEWART
IF WE HOLD ON TOGETHER — Diana ROSS
IF WE TRY — Karen RAMIREZ
IF WE WERE LOVERS — Gloria ESTEFAN
IF YA GETTIN' DOWN — FIVE
IF YOU ASKED ME TO — Celine DION
IF YOU BELIEVE — Johnnie RAY
IF YOU BUY THIS RECORD YOUR LIFE WILL BE BETTER — The TAMPERER featuring MAYA
IF YOU C JORDAN — SOMETHING CORPORATE
IF YOU CAN WANT — Smokey ROBINSON and the MIRACLES
IF YOU CAN'T DO IT WHEN YOU'RE YOUNG, WHEN CAN YOU DO IT? — THEAUDIENCE
IF YOU CAN'T GIVE ME LOVE — Suzi QUATRO
IF YOU CAN'T SAY NO — Lenny KRAVITZ
IF YOU CAN'T STAND THE HEAT — BUCKS FIZZ
IF YOU CARED — Kim APPLEBY
IF YOU COME BACK — BLUE
IF YOU COME TO ME — ATOMIC KITTEN
IF YOU COULD READ MY MIND [A] — Gordon LIGHTFOOT
IF YOU COULD READ MY MIND [A] — STARS ON 54
IF YOU COULD SEE ME NOW — SHAKATAK
IF YOU DON'T KNOW ME BY NOW [A] — Harold MELVIN and the BLUENOTES
IF YOU DON'T KNOW ME BY NOW [A] — SIMPLY RED
IF YOU DON'T LOVE ME — PREFAB SPROUT
IF YOU DON'T WANT ME TO DESTROY YOU — SUPER FURRY ANIMALS
IF YOU DON'T WANT MY LOVE — Robert JOHN
IF YOU EVER — EAST 17 featuring GABRIELLE
IF YOU EVER LEAVE ME — Barbra STREISAND
IF YOU FEEL IT — Thelma HOUSTON
IF YOU GO — Jon SECADA
IF YOU GO AWAY [A] — Terry JACKS
IF YOU GO AWAY [B] — NEW KIDS ON THE BLOCK
IF YOU GOTTA GO GO NOW — MANFRED MANN
IF YOU GOTTA MAKE A FOOL OF SOMEBODY — FREDDIE and the DREAMERS
IF YOU HAD MY LOVE — Jennifer LOPEZ
IF YOU HAVE TO GO — GENEVA
IF YOU KNEW SOUSA (AND FRIENDS) — ROYAL PHILHARMONIC ORCHESTRA arranged and conducted by Louis CLARK
IF YOU KNOW WHAT I MEAN — Neil DIAMOND
IF YOU LEAVE — ORCHESTRAL MANOEUVRES IN THE DARK
IF YOU LEAVE ME NOW [A] — CHICAGO
IF YOU LEAVE ME NOW [A] — UPSIDE DOWN
IF YOU LEAVE ME NOW [A] — SYSTEM presents KERRI B
IF YOU LET ME STAY — Terence Trent D'ARBY
IF YOU LOVE HER — Dick EMERY
IF YOU LOVE ME (I WON'T CARE) — Mary HOPKIN
IF YOU LOVE ME — BROWNSTONE
IF YOU LOVE SOMEBODY SET THEM FREE — STING
IF YOU ONLY LET ME IN — MN8
IF YOU REALLY CARED — GABRIELLE
IF YOU REALLY LOVE ME — Stevie WONDER
IF YOU REALLY WANNA KNOW — Marc DORSEY
IF YOU REALLY WANT TO — MEAT LOAF
IF YOU REMEMBER ME — Chris THOMPSON
IF YOU SHOULD NEED A FRIEND — FIRE ISLAND
IF YOU TALK IN YOUR SLEEP — Elvis PRESLEY
IF YOU THINK YOU KNOW HOW TO LOVE ME — SMOKIE
(IF YOU THINK YOU'RE) GROOVY — PP ARNOLD
IF YOU TOLERATE THIS YOUR CHILDREN WILL BE NEXT — MANIC STREET PREACHERS
IF YOU WALK AWAY — Peter COX
IF YOU WANNA BE HAPPY [A] — Jimmy SOUL
IF YOU WANNA BE HAPPY [A] — Rocky SHARPE and the REPLAYS
IF YOU WANNA PARTY — MOLELLA featuring The OUTHERE BROTHERS
IF YOU WANT — LUCIANA
IF YOU WANT ME — Hinda HICKS
IF YOU WANT MY LOVE — CHEAP TRICK
IF YOU WANT MY LOVIN' — Evelyn 'Champagne' KING
IF YOU WERE HERE TONIGHT [A] — Alexander O'NEAL
IF YOU WERE HERE TONIGHT [A] — Matt GOSS
IF YOU WERE MINE MARY — Eddy ARNOLD
IF YOU WERE THE ONLY BOY IN THE WORLD — Stevie MARSH
IF YOU WERE WITH ME NOW — Kylie MINOGUE and Keith WASHINGTON
IF YOU'LL BE MINE — BABYBIRD
IF YOUR GIRL ONLY KNEW — AALIYAH
IF YOUR HEART ISN'T IN IT — ATLANTIC STARR
IF YOU'RE GONE — MATCHBOX 20
IF YOU'RE LOOKIN' FOR A WAY OUT — ODYSSEY
IF YOU'RE NOT THE ONE — Daniel BEDINGFIELD
IF YOU'RE READY (COME GO WITH ME) [A] — STAPLE SINGERS
IF YOU'RE READY (COME GO WITH ME) [A] — Ruby TURNER featuring Jonathan BUTLER
IF YOU'RE THINKING OF ME — DODGY
IGGIN' ME — Chico DeBARGE
IGNITION — R KELLY
IGNORANCE — OCEANIC
IGUANA — Mauro PICOTTO
IKO IKO [A] — DIXIE CUPS
IKO IKO [A] — BELLE STARS
IKO IKO [A] — NATASHA
IL ADORE — BOY GEORGE
IL EST NÉ LE DIVIN ENFANT — SIOUXSIE and the BANSHEES
IL NOSTRO CONCERTO — Umberto BINDI
IL SILENZIO — Nini ROSSO
I'LL ALWAYS BE AROUND — C & C MUSIC FACTORY / CLIVILLES & COLE
I'LL ALWAYS BE IN LOVE WITH YOU — Michael HOLLIDAY
I'LL ALWAYS LOVE MY MAMA — INTRUDERS
I'LL ALWAYS LOVE YOU — Taylor DAYNE
I'LL BE — Foxy BROWN featuring JAY-Z
(I'LL BE A) FREAK FOR YOU — ROYALLE DELITE
I'LL BE AROUND [A] — Terri WELLS
I'LL BE AROUND [A] — DETROIT SPINNERS
I'LL BE BACK — ARNEE and the TERMINATERS
I'LL BE GOOD — RENE and ANGELA
I'LL BE GOOD TO YOU — Quincy JONES featuring Ray CHARLES and Chaka KHAN
I'LL BE HOME — Pat BOONE
I'LL BE HOME THIS CHRISTMAS — Shakin' STEVENS
I'LL BE LOVING YOU (FOREVER) — NEW KIDS ON THE BLOCK
I'LL BE MISSING YOU — PUFF DADDY and Faith EVANS featuring 112
I'LL BE SATISFIED — Shakin' STEVENS
I'LL BE THERE [A] — GERRY and the PACEMAKERS
I'LL BE THERE [B] — Jackie TRENT
I'LL BE THERE [C] — The JACKSON FIVE
I'LL BE THERE [C] — Mariah CAREY
I'LL BE THERE [D] — INNOCENCE
I'LL BE THERE [E] — 99TH FLOOR ELEVATORS featuring Tony DE VIT
I'LL BE THERE [F] — EMMA
I'LL BE THERE FOR YOU [A] — BON JOVI
I'LL BE THERE FOR YOU [B] — SOLID HARMONIE
I'LL BE THERE FOR YOU (DOYA DODODO DOYA) — HOUSE OF VIRGINISM
I'LL BE THERE FOR YOU (THEME FROM 'FRIENDS') — REMBRANDTS
I'LL BE THERE FOR YOU — YOU'RE ALL I NEED TO GET BY — METHOD MAN featuring Mary J BLIGE
I'LL BE WAITING [A] — Clive GRIFFIN
I'LL BE WAITING [B] — FULL INTENTION presents SHENA
(I'LL BE WITH YOU) IN APPLE BLOSSOM TIME — Rosemary JUNE
I'LL BE YOUR ANGEL — KIRA
I'LL BE YOUR BABY TONIGHT [A] — Robert PALMER and UB40
I'LL BE YOUR BABY TONIGHT [A] — Norah JONES
I'LL BE YOUR EVERYTHING — Tommy PAGE
I'LL BE YOUR FRIEND — Robert OWENS
I'LL BE YOUR SHELTER — Taylor DAYNE
I'LL COME RUNNIN' — JUICE
I'LL COME RUNNING — Cliff RICHARD
I'LL COME WHEN YOU CALL — Ruby MURRAY
I'LL CRY FOR YOU — EUROPE
I'LL CUT YOUR TAIL OFF — John LEYTON
I'LL DO ANYTHING — TO MAKE YOU MINE — HOLLOWAY & CO.
I'LL DO YA — WHALE
I'LL FIND MY WAY HOME — JON and VANGELIS
I'LL FIND YOU [A] — David WHITFIELD
I'LL FIND YOU [B] — Michelle GAYLE
I'LL FLY FOR YOU — SPANDAU BALLET
I'LL GET BY [A] — Connie FRANCIS
I'LL GET BY [A] — Shirley BASSEY
I'LL GIVE YOU THE EARTH (TOUS LES BATEAUX, TOUS LES OISEAUX) — Keith MICHELL
I'LL GO ON HOPING — Des O'CONNOR
I'LL GO WHERE YOUR MUSIC TAKES ME [A] — Jimmy JAMES and the VAGABONDS
I'LL GO WHERE YOUR MUSIC TAKES ME [A] — Tina CHARLES
I'LL HOUSE YOU — Richie RICH meets The JUNGLE BROTHERS
I'LL KEEP ON LOVING YOU — PRINCESS
I'LL KEEP YOU SATISFIED — Billy J KRAMER and the DAKOTAS
I'LL KEEP YOUR DREAMS ALIVE — George BENSON and Patti AUSTIN
I'LL LOVE YOU FOREVER TODAY — Cliff RICHARD
I'LL MAKE LOVE TO YOU — BOYZ II MEN
I'LL MANAGE SOMEHOW — MENSWEAR
I'LL MEET YOU AT MIDNIGHT — SMOKIE
I'LL NEVER BREAK YOUR HEART — BACKSTREET BOYS
I'LL NEVER FALL IN LOVE AGAIN [A] — Johnnie RAY
I'LL NEVER FALL IN LOVE AGAIN [B] — Tom JONES
I'LL NEVER FALL IN LOVE AGAIN [C] — Bobbie GENTRY
I'LL NEVER FIND ANOTHER YOU — The SEEKERS
I'LL NEVER GET OVER YOU [A] — Johnny KIDD and the PIRATES
I'LL NEVER GET OVER YOU [B] — The EVERLY BROTHERS
I'LL NEVER GET OVER YOU (GETTING OVER ME) — EXPOSÉ
I'LL NEVER LOVE THIS WAY AGAIN — Dionne WARWICK
I'LL NEVER QUITE GET OVER YOU — Billy FURY
I'LL NEVER STOP — 'N SYNC
I'LL NEVER STOP LOVING YOU — Doris DAY
I'LL PICK A ROSE FOR MY ROSE — Marv JOHNSON
I'LL PUT YOU TOGETHER AGAIN (FROM DEAR ANYONE) — HOT CHOCOLATE
I'LL REMEMBER — MADONNA
I'LL REMEMBER TONIGHT — Pat BOONE
I'LL SAIL THIS SHIP ALONE — The BEAUTIFUL SOUTH
I'LL SAY FOREVER MY LOVE — Jimmy RUFFIN
I'LL SEE IT THROUGH — TEXAS
I'LL SEE YOU ALONG THE WAY — Rick CLARKE
I'LL SEE YOU AROUND — SILVER SUN
I'LL SEE YOU IN MY DREAMS — Pat BOONE
I'LL SET YOU FREE — The BANGLES
I'LL SLEEP WHEN I'M DEAD — BON JOVI
I'LL STAND BY YOU [A] — The PRETENDERS
I'LL STAND BY YOU [A] — GIRLS ALOUD
I'LL STAY BY YOU — Kenny LYNCH
I'LL STAY SINGLE — Jerry LORDAN
I'LL STEP DOWN — Garry MILLS
I'LL STICK AROUND — FOO FIGHTERS
I'LL STOP AT NOTHING — Sandie SHAW
I'LL TAKE THE RAIN — R.E.M.
I'LL TAKE YOU HOME [A] — The DRIFTERS
I'LL TAKE YOU HOME [A] — Cliff BENNETT and the REBEL ROUSERS
I'LL TAKE YOU HOME AGAIN KATHLEEN — Slim WHITMAN
I'LL TAKE YOU THERE [A] — STAPLE SINGERS
I'LL TAKE YOU THERE [A] — GENERAL PUBLIC
I'LL TRY ANYTHING — Dusty SPRINGFIELD
I'LL WAIT — Taylor DAYNE
I'LL WALK WITH GOD — Mario LANZA
ILLEGAL ALIEN — GENESIS
ILLEGAL GUNSHOT — RAGGA TWINS
ILLUMINATIONS — SWANS WAY
ILLUSIONS — CYPRESS HILL
ILOVEROCKNROLL — JESUS AND MARY CHAIN
I'M A BELIEVER [A] — The MONKEES
I'M A BELIEVER [A] — Robert WYATT
I'M A BELIEVER [A] — EMF
I'M A BETTER MAN (FOR HAVING LOVED YOU) — Engelbert HUMPERDINCK
I'M A BITCH — OLGA
I'M A BOY — The WHO
I'M A CUCKOO — BELLE & SEBASTIAN
I'M A DISCO DANCER — Christopher JUST
I'M A DOUN FOR LACK O' JOHNNIE (A LITTLE SCOTTISH FANTASY) — VANESSA-MAE
(I'M A) DREAMER — B B and Q BAND
I'M A FOOL — Slim WHITMAN
I'M A FOOL TO CARE — Joe BARRY
I'M A GOOD MAN — Martin SOLVEIG
I'M A LITTLE CHRISTMAS CRACKER — BOUNCING CZECKS
I'M A MAN [A] — Spencer DAVIS GROUP
I'M A MAN [A] — CHICAGO
I'M A MAN NOT A BOY [A] — Chesney HAWKES
I'M A MAN NOT A BOY [B] — NORTH AND SOUTH
I'M A MAN — YE KE YE KE (MEDLEY) — CLUBHOUSE
I'M A MESSAGE — IDLEWILD
I'M A MIDNIGHT MOVER — Wilson PICKETT
I'M A MOODY GUY — Shane FENTON and the FENTONES
I'M A SLAVE 4 U — Britney SPEARS
I'M A SUCKER FOR YOUR LOVE — Teena MARIE, co-lead vocals Rick JAMES

I'M A TIGER – LULU
I'M A WONDERFUL THING, BABY – Kid CREOLE and the COCONUTS
I'M ALIVE [A] – The HOLLIES
I'M ALIVE [B] – ELECTRIC LIGHT ORCHESTRA
I'M ALIVE [C] – CUT 'N' MOVE
I'M ALIVE [D] – SEAL
I'M ALIVE [E] – STRETCH 'N' VERN present MADDOG
I'M ALIVE [F] – Celine DION
I'M ALL ABOUT YOU – DJ LUCK & MC NEAT featuirng Ari GOLD
I'M ALL YOU NEED – Samantha FOX
I'M ALRIGHT [A] – Steve WRIGHT
I'M ALRIGHT [B] – Katherine E
(I'M ALWAYS HEARING) WEDDING BELLS – Eddie FISHER
(I'M ALWAYS TOUCHED BY YOUR) PRESENCE DEAR – BLONDIE
I'M AN UPSTART – ANGELIC UPSTARTS
I'M BACK FOR MORE – LULU and Bobby WOMACK
I'M BAD – LL COOL J
I'M BLUE – The 5.6.7.8'S
I'M BORN AGAIN – BONEY M
I'M BROKEN – PANTERA
I'M CHILLIN' – Kurtis BLOW
I'M COMIN' HARDCORE – M.A.N.I.C.
I'M COMING HOME – Tom JONES
I'M COMING HOME CINDY – Trini LOPEZ
I'M COMING OUT – Diana ROSS
I'M COMING WITH YA – Matt GOSS
I'M COUNTING ON YOU – Petula CLARK
I'M CRYING – The ANIMALS
I'M DOIN' FINE – DAY ONE
I'M DOING FINE – Jason DONOVAN
I'M DOIN' FINE NOW [A] – NEW YORK CITY
I'M DOING FINE NOW [A] – PASADENAS
I'M EASY – FAITH NO MORE
I'M EVERY WOMAN [A] – Chaka KHAN
I'M EVERY WOMAN [A] – Whitney HOUSTON
I'M FALLING – The BLUEBELLS
I'M FOR REAL – NIGHTMARES ON WAX
I'M FOREVER BLOWING BUBBLES [A] – WEST HAM UNITED CUP SQUAD
I'M FOREVER BLOWING BUBBLES [A] – COCKNEY REJECTS
I'M FREE [A] – Roger DALTREY
I'M FREE [B] – SOUP DRAGONS
I'M FREE [C] – Jon SECADA
I'M GLAD – Jennifer LOPEZ
I'M GOIN' DOWN – Mary J BLIGE
I'M GOING ALL THE WAY – SOUNDS OF BLACKNESS
I'M GOING HOME – Gene VINCENT
I'M GOING SLIGHTLY MAD – QUEEN
I'M GONE – Diana ROSS
I'M GONNA BE A COUNTRY GIRL AGAIN – Buffy SAINTE-MARIE
I'M GONNA BE ALRIGHT – Jennifer LOPEZ
I'M GONNA BE (500 MILES) – The PROCLAIMERS
I'M GONNA BE STRONG [A] – Gene PITNEY
I'M GONNA BE STRONG [A] – Cyndi LAUPER
I'M GONNA BE WARM THIS WINTER – Connie FRANCIS
I'M GONNA CHANGE EVERYTHING – Jim REEVES
(I'M GONNA) CRY MYSELF BLIND – PRIMAL SCREAM
I'M GONNA GET MARRIED – Lloyd PRICE
I'M GONNA GET ME A GUN – Cat STEVENS
I'M GONNA GET THERE SOMEHOW – Val DOONICAN
I'M GONNA GET YA BABY – BLACK CONNECTION
I'M GONNA GET YOU – BIZARRE INC
I'M GONNA GETCHA GOOD! – Shania TWAIN
I'M GONNA GIT YOU SUCKA – GAP BAND
I'M GONNA KNOCK ON YOUR DOOR [A] – Eddie HODGES
I'M GONNA KNOCK ON YOUR DOOR [A] – Little Jimmy OSMOND
I'M GONNA LOVE HER FOR BOTH OF US – MEAT LOAF
I'M GONNA LOVE YOU FOREVER – CROWN HEIGHTS AFFAIR
I'M GONNA LOVE YOU A LITTLE BIT MORE BABY – Barry WHITE
I'M GONNA MAKE YOU LOVE ME – Diana ROSS and The SUPREMES and The TEMPTATIONS
I'M GONNA MAKE YOU MINE [A] – Lou CHRISTIE
I'M GONNA MAKE YOU MINE [B] – Tanya BLOUNT
I'M GONNA MISS YOU FOREVER – Aaron CARTER
I'M GONNA RUN AWAY FROM YOU – Tami LYNN
I'M GONNA SIT RIGHT DOWN AND WRITE MYSELF A LETTER [A] – Billy WILLIAMS
I'M GONNA SIT RIGHT DOWN AND WRITE MYSELF A LETTER [A] – Barry MANILOW
I'M GONNA SOOTHE YOU – Maria McKEE
I'M GONNA TEAR YOUR PLAYHOUSE DOWN – Paul YOUNG
I'M IN A DIFFERENT WORLD – The FOUR TOPS
I'M IN A PHILLY MOOD – Daryl HALL
I'M IN FAVOUR OF FRIENDSHIP – FIVE SMITH BROTHERS
I'M IN HEAVEN [A] – Jason NEVINS presents UKNY / Holly JAMES
I'M IN HEAVEN [B] – N-TRANCE
I'M IN IT FOR LOVE – Donny OSMOND
I'M IN LOVE [A] – The FOURMOST
I'M IN LOVE [B] – Evelyn 'Champagne' KING
I'M IN LOVE [C] – Ruby TURNER
I'M IN LOVE [D] – Lillo THOMAS
I'M IN LOVE [E] – STARPARTY
I'M IN LOVE AGAIN [A] – Fats DOMINO
I'M IN LOVE AGAIN [B] – SAD CAFE
I'M IN LOVE (AND I LOVE THE FEELING) – ROSE ROYCE
I'M IN LOVE WITH A GERMAN FILM STAR – PASSIONS
I'M IN LOVE WITH THE GIRL ON A CERTAIN MANCHESTER MEGASTORE CHECKOUT DESK – FRESHIES
I'M IN LUV – JOE
I'M IN THE MOOD – Ce Ce PENISTON
I'M IN THE MOOD FOR DANCING – The NOLANS
I'M IN THE MOOD FOR LOVE [A] – LORD TANAMO
I'M IN THE MOOD FOR LOVE [A] – Jools HOLLAND and JAMIROQUAI
I'M IN YOU – Peter FRAMPTON
I'M INTO SOMETHING GOOD – HERMAN'S HERMITS
I'M JUST A BABY – Louise CORDET
I'M JUST A SINGER (IN A ROCK & ROLL BAND) – The MOODY BLUES
I'M JUST YOUR PUPPET ON A ... (STRING) – LONDONBEAT
I'M LEAVIN' – Elvis PRESLEY
I'M LEAVIN' – OUTSIDAZ featuring Rah DIGGA & Melanie BLATT
I'M LEAVING – LODGER
I'M LEAVING IT UP TO YOU [A] – DALE and GRACE
I'M LEAVING IT (ALL) UP TO YOU [A] – Donny and Marie OSMOND
I'M LEFT, YOU'RE RIGHT, SHE'S GONE – Elvis PRESLEY
I'M LIKE A BIRD – Nelly FURTADO
I'M LIVING IN SHAME – Diana ROSS and The SUPREMES
I'M LONELY – Hollis P MONROE
I'M LOOKING FOR THE ONE (TO BE WITH ME) – JAZZY JEFF & the FRESH PRINCE
I'M LOOKING OUT THE WINDOW – Cliff RICHARD
I'M LOST WITHOUT YOU – Billy FURY
I'M LUCKY – Joan ARMATRADING
I'M MANDY FLY ME – 10cc
I'M NEVER GIVING UP – SWEET DREAMS
IM NIN'ALU – Ofra HAZA
I'M NO ANGEL – Marcella DETROIT
I'M NO REBEL – VIEW FROM THE HILL
I'M NOT A FOOL – COCKNEY REJECTS
I'M NOT A JUVENILE DELINQUENT – Frankie LYMON and the TEENAGERS
I'M NOT ANYBODY'S GIRL – KACI
I'M NOT ASHAMED – BIG COUNTRY
I'M NOT FEELING YOU – Yvette MICHELLE
I'M NOT GIVING YOU UP – Gloria ESTEFAN
I'M NOT GONNA LET YOU (GET THE BEST OF ME) – Colonel ABRAMS
I'M NOT IN LOVE [A] – 10cc
I'M NOT IN LOVE [A] – Johnny LOGAN
I'M NOT IN LOVE [A] – WILL TO POWER
I'M NOT IN LOVE [A] – FUN LOVIN' CRIMINALS
I'M NOT PERFECT (BUT I'M PERFECT FOR YOU) – Grace JONES
I'M NOT READY – Keith SWEAT
I'M NOT SATISFIED – FINE YOUNG CANNIBALS
I'M NOT SCARED – EIGHTH WONDER
I'M NOT THE MAN I USED TO BE – FINE YOUNG CANNIBALS
I'M NOT TO BLAME – ALIBI
I'M NOT A GIRL, NOT YET A WOMAN – Britney SPEARS
(I'M NOT YOUR) STEPPING STONE – The SEX PISTOLS
I'M ON AUTOMATIC – Gary NUMAN
I'M ON FIRE [A] – 5000 VOLTS
I'M ON FIRE [B] – Bruce SPRINGSTEEN
I'M ON MY WAY [A] – Dean PARRISH
I'M ON MY WAY [B] – The PROCLAIMERS
I'M ON MY WAY [C] – Betty BOO
I'M ON MY WAY TO A BETTER PLACE – CHAIRMEN OF THE BOARD
I'M ONLY SLEEPING – SUGGS
I'M OUT OF YOUR LIFE – ARNIE'S LOVE
I'M OUTSTANDING – Shaquille O'NEAL
I'M OUTTA LOVE – ANASTACIA
I'M OVER YOU – Martine McCUTCHEON
I'M QUALIFIED TO SATISFY YOU – Barry WHITE
I'M RAVING – SCOOTER
I'M READY [A] – CAVEMAN
I'M READY [B] – SIZE 9
I'M READY [C] – Bryan ADAMS
I'M READY FOR LOVE – Martha REEVES and the VANDELLAS
I'M REAL [A] – James BROWN featuring FULL FORCE
I'M REAL [B] – Jennifer LOPEZ featuring JA RULE
I'M REALLY HOT – Missy ELLIOTT
I'M RIFFIN (ENGLISH RASTA) – MC DUKE
I'M RIGHT HERE – Samantha MUMBA
I'M RUSHING – BUMP
I'M SHAKIN' – ROONEY
I'M SHY MARY ELLEN I'M SHY – Bob WALLIS and his STORYVILLE JAZZ BAND
I'M SICK OF YOU – GOODBYE MR MACKENZIE
I'M SO BEAUTIFUL – DIVINE
I'M SO CRAZY ('BOUT YOU) – KC and the SUNSHINE BAND
I'M SO CRAZY – PAR-T-ONE vs INXS
I'M SO EXCITED – POINTER SISTERS
I'M SO GLAD I'M STANDING HERE TODAY – CRUSADERS, featured vocalist Joe COCKER
I'M SO HAPPY [A] – LIGHT OF THE WORLD
I'M SO HAPPY [B] – JULIA and COMPANY
I'M SO HAPPY [C] – Walter BEASLEY
I'M SO HAPPY I CAN'T STOP CRYING – STING
I'M SO IN LOVE – Alysha WARREN
I'M SO INTO YOU – SWV
I'M SO LONELY – CAST
I'M SORRY [A] – The PLATTERS
I'M SORRY [B] – Brenda LEE
I'M SORRY [C] – HOTHOUSE FLOWERS
I'M SORRY I MADE YOU CRY – Connie FRANCIS
I'M STANDING (HIGHER) – X-STATIC
I'M STARTING TO GO STEADY – Johnny PRESTON
I'M STILL GONNA NEED YOU – The OSMONDS
I'M STILL IN LOVE WITH YOU [A] – Al GREEN
I'M STILL IN LOVE WITH YOU [B] – Sean PAUL featuring SASHA
I'M STILL STANDING – Elton JOHN
I'M STILL WAITING [A] – Diana ROSS
I'M STILL WAITING [A] – Courtney PINE
I'M STILL WAITING [B] – ANGELHEART
I'M STONE IN LOVE WITH YOU [A] – The STYLISTICS
I'M STONE IN LOVE WITH YOU [A] – Johnny MATHIS
I'M TELLIN YOU – Chubby CHUNKS
I'M TELLING YOU NOW – FREDDIE and the DREAMERS
I'M THAT TYPE OF GUY – LL COOL J
I'M THE FACE – The HIGH NUMBERS
I'M THE LEADER OF THE GANG (I AM!) [A] – Gary GLITTER
I'M THE LEADER OF THE GANG [A] – Hulk HOGAN with GREEN JELLY
I'M THE LONELY ONE – Cliff RICHARD and The SHADOWS
I'M THE MAN – ANTHRAX
I'M THE ONE – GERRY and the PACEMAKERS
I'M THE ONE FOR YOU – ADEVA
I'M THE ONE YOU NEED – Jody WATLEY
I'M THE URBAN SPACEMAN – BONZO DOG DOO-DAH BAND
I'M TIRED OF GETTING PUSHED AROUND – TWO MEN, A DRUM MACHINE AND A TRUMPET
I'M TOO SCARED – Steven DANTE
I'M TOO SEXY – RIGHT SAID FRED
I'M WAKING UP TO US – BELLE & SEBASTIAN
I'M WALKIN' – Fats DOMINO
I'M WALKING BACKWARDS FOR CHRISTMAS – The GOONS
I'M WALKING BEHIND YOU [A] – Eddie FISHER with Sally SWEETLAND (soprano)
I'M WALKING BEHIND YOU [A] – Dorothy SQUIRES
I'M WITH YOU – Avril LAVIGNE
I'M WONDERING – Stevie WONDER
I'M YOUR ANGEL – Celine DION and R KELLY
I'M YOUR BABY TONIGHT – Whitney HOUSTON
I'M YOUR BOOGIE MAN – KC and the SUNSHINE BAND
I'M YOUR MAN [A] – BLUE ZOO
I'M YOUR MAN [B] – WHAM!
I'M YOUR MAN [B] – Lisa MOORISH
I'M YOUR MAN [B] – Shane RICHIE
I'M YOUR PUPPET – James and Bobby PURIFY
I'M YOUR TOY – Elvis COSTELLO
IMAGE – Hank LEVINE
IMAGE OF A GIRL [A] – Nelson KEENE
IMAGE OF A GIRL [A] – Mark WYNTER
IMAGE OF YOU – RED SNAPPER
IMAGINATION [A] – Rocky SHARPE and the REPLAYS
IMAGINATION [B] – BELOUIS SOME
IMAGINATION [C] – JON THE DENTIST vs Ollie JAYE
IMAGINE [A] – John LENNON
IMAGINE [A] – Randy CRAWFORD
IMAGINE [B] – Shola AMA
IMAGINE ME IMAGINE YOU – FOX
IMITATION OF LIFE [A] – Billie Ray MARTIN
IMITATION OF LIFE [B] – R.E.M.
IMMACULATE FOOLS – IMMACULATE FOOLS
IMMORTALITY – Celine DION with special guests The BEE GEES
IMPERIAL WIZARD – David ESSEX
IMPORTANCE OF YOUR LOVE – Vince HILL
IMPOSSIBLE [A] – CAPTAIN HOLLYWOOD PROJECT
IMPOSSIBLE [B] – The CHARLATANS
THE IMPOSSIBLE DREAM – CARTER – THE UNSTOPPABLE SEX MACHINE
IMPOSSIBLE LOVE – UB40
THE IMPRESSION THAT I GET – MIGHTY MIGHTY BOSSTONES
THE IMPRESSIONS EP – SOLAR STONE
IMPULSIVE – WILSON PHILLIPS
IN A BIG COUNTRY – BIG COUNTRY
IN A BROKEN DREAM [A] – PYTHON LEE JACKSON
IN A BROKEN DREAM [A] – THUNDER
IN A CAGE (ON PROZAC) – MY RED CELL
IN A DREAM – LONGVIEW
IN A GOLDEN COACH (THERE'S A HEART OF GOLD) [A] – Billy COTTON and his BAND
IN A GOLDEN COACH (THERE'S A HEART OF GOLD) [A] – Dickie VALENTINE
IN A LIFETIME – CLANNAD featuring BONO
IN A LITTLE SPANISH TOWN – Bing CROSBY
IN A PERSIAN MARKET – Sammy DAVIS Jr
IN A ROOM – DODGY
IN A STATE [A] – 2 FOR JOY
IN A STATE [B] – UNKLE
IN A WORD OR 2 – Monie LOVE
IN ALL THE RIGHT PLACES – Lisa STANSFIELD
IN AND OUT [A] – Willie HUTCH
IN AND OUT [B] – 3RD EDGE
IN & OUT [C] – SPEEDWAY
IN AND OUT OF LOVE [A] – Diana ROSS and The SUPREMES
IN AND OUT OF LOVE [B] – IMAGINATION
IN AND OUT OF MY LIFE [A] – Tonja DANTZLER
IN AND OUT OF MY LIFE [B] – A.T.F.C. presents ONEPHATDEEVA
IN BETWEEN DAYS – The CURE
IN BLOOM – NIRVANA
THE IN CROWD [A] – Dobie GRAY
THE 'IN' CROWD [A] – Bryan FERRY
IN DA CLUB – 50 CENT
IN DE GHETTO – David MORALES and the BAD YARD CLUB featuring Crystal WATERS and DELTA
IN DEMAND – TEXAS
IN DREAMS – Roy ORBISON
IN DULCE DECORUM – The DAMNED
IN DULCI JUBILO – Mike OLDFIELD
IN FOR A PENNY – SLADE
IN 4 CHOONS LATER – ROZALLA
IN GOD'S COUNTRY (IMPORT) – U2
IN IT FOR LOVE – Richie SAMBORA
IN IT FOR THE MONEY – CLIENT
IN LIVERPOOL – Suzanne VEGA
IN LOVE [A] – Michael HOLLIDAY
IN LOVE [B] – The DATSUNS
IN LOVE [C] – Lisa MAFFIA
IN LOVE WITH LOVE – Deborah HARRY
IN LOVE WITH THE FAMILIAR – WIRELESS
IN MY ARMS – ERASURE
IN MY BED [A] – DRU HILL
IN MY BED [B] – Amy WINEHOUSE
IN MY CHAIR – STATUS QUO
IN MY DEFENCE – Freddie MERCURY
IN MY DREAMS [A] – Will DOWNING
IN MY DREAMS [B] – JOHNNA
IN MY EYES – MILK INC.
IN MY HEART – TEXAS
IN MY LIFE [A] – SOULED OUT
IN MY LIFE [B] – Kim WILDE
IN MY LIFE [C] – José NUNEZ featuring OCTAHVIA
IN MY LIFE [D] – RYZE
IN MY MIND – MILKY
IN MY OWN TIME – FAMILY
IN MY PLACE – COLDPLAY
IN MY STREET – CHORDS
IN MY WORLD – ANTHRAX
IN OLD LISBON – Frank CHACKSFIELD
IN OUR LIFETIME – TEXAS
IN PRIVATE – Dusty SPRINGFIELD
IN PURSUIT – BOXER REBELLION
IN SPIRIT – DILEMMA
IN SUMMER – Billy FURY
IN THE AIR TONIGHT [A] – Phil COLLINS
IN THE AIR TONITE [A] – LIL' KIM featuring Phil COLLINS
IN THE ARMS OF LOVE [A] – Andy WILLIAMS
IN THE ARMS OF LOVE [B] – Catherine Zeta JONES
IN THE ARMY NOW – STATUS QUO
IN THE BACK OF MY MIND – FLEETWOOD MAC
IN THE BAD BAD OLD DAYS – The FOUNDATIONS
IN THE BEGINNING [A] – Frankie LAINE
IN THE BEGINNING [B] – EYC
IN THE BEGINNING [C] – Roger GOODE featuring Tasha BAXTER
IN THE BEST POSSIBLE TASTE (PART 2) – KINGMAKER
IN THE BLEAK MID WINTER – NEVADA

IT ONLY TAKES A MINUTE [A] – Jonathan KING
IT ONLY TAKES A MINUTE [A] – TAVARES
IT ONLY TAKES A MINUTE [A] – TAKE THAT
IT ONLY TOOK A MINUTE – Joe BROWN and the BRUVVERS
IT OUGHTA SELL A MILLION – Lyn PAUL
IT SEEMS TO HANG ON [A] – ASHFORD and SIMPSON
IT SEEMS TO HANG ON [A] – KWS
IT SHOULD HAVE BEEN ME [A] – Yvonne FAIR
IT SHOULD'VE BEEN ME [A] – ADEVA
IT STARTED ALL OVER AGAIN – Brenda LEE
IT STARTED WITH A KISS – HOT CHOCOLATE / Errol BROWN
IT SURE BRINGS OUT THE LOVE IN YOUR EYES – David SOUL
IT TAKES ALL NIGHT LONG – Gary GLITTER
IT TAKES MORE – MS DYNAMITE
IT TAKES SCOOP – FATMAN SCOOP featuring The CROOKLYN CLAN
IT TAKES TWO [A] – Marvin GAYE
IT TAKES TWO BABY [A] – Liz KERSHAW and Bruno BROOKES
IT TAKES TWO [A] – Rod STEWART and Tina TURNER
IT TAKES TWO [B] – Rob BASE and DJ E-Z ROCK
IT TAKES TWO TO TANGO – Richard MYHILL
IT WAS A GOOD DAY – ICE CUBE
IT WAS EASIER TO HURT HER – Wayne FONTANA
IT WASN'T ME – SHAGGY featuring Ricardo 'Rikrok' DUCENT
IT WILL BE ALRIGHT – ODYSSEY
IT WILL BE YOU – Paul YOUNG
IT WILL COME IN TIME – Billy PRESTON and SYREETA
IT WILL MAKE ME CRAZY – FELIX
IT WON'T BE LONG – Alison MOYET
IT WON'T SEEM LIKE CHRISTMAS (WITHOUT YOU) – Elvis PRESLEY
THE ITALIAN THEME – Cyril STAPLETON and his ORCHESTRA
ITALO HOUSE MIX – ROCOCO
ITCHYCOO PARK [A] – The SMALL FACES
ITCHYCOO PARK [A] – M PEOPLE
IT'LL BE ME – Cliff RICHARD and The SHADOWS
IT'S A BEAUTIFUL THING – OCEAN COLOUR SCENE
IT'S A BETTER THAN GOOD TIME – Gladys KNIGHT and the PIPS
IT'S A DISCO NIGHT (ROCK DON'T STOP) – ISLEY BROTHERS
IT'S A FINE DAY [A] – OPUS III
IT'S A FINE DAY [A] – MISS JANE
IT'S A GAME – BAY CITY ROLLERS
IT'S A GAS – WEDDING PRESENT
IT'S A GIRL THING – MY LIFE STORY
IT'S A GOOD LIFE – Cevin FISHER featuring Romona KELLY
IT'S A HARD LIFE – QUEEN
IT'S A HEARTACHE – Bonnie TYLER
IT'S A LONG WAY TO THE TOP (IF YOU WANNA ROCK 'N' ROLL) – AC/DC
IT'S A LOVE THING – WHISPERS
IT'S A LOVING THING – CB MILTON
IT'S A MAN'S MAN'S MAN'S WORLD [A] – James BROWN
IT'S A MAN'S MAN'S MAN'S WORLD [A] – BRILLIANT
IT'S A MAN'S MAN'S MAN'S WORLD [A] – Jeanie TRACY and Bobby WOMACK
IT'S A MIRACLE – CULTURE CLUB
IT'S A MISTAKE – MEN AT WORK
IT'S A PARTY [A] – Busta RHYMES featuring ZHANE
IT'S A PARTY [B] – BOUNTY KILLER
IT'S A RAGGY WALTZ – Dave BRUBECK QUARTET
IT'S A RAINBOW – RAINBOW
IT'S A RAINY DAY – ICE MC
IT'S A SHAME [A] – DETROIT SPINNERS
IT'S A SHAME [B] – KRIS KROSS
IT'S A SHAME ABOUT RAY – LEMONHEADS
IT'S A SHAME (MY SISTER) – Monie LOVE
IT'S A SIN – PET SHOP BOYS
IT'S A SIN TO TELL A LIE – Gerry MONROE
IT'S A TRIP (TUNE IN, TURN ON, DROP OUT) – CHILDREN OF THE NIGHT
IT'S ABOUT TIME – LEMONHEADS
IT'S ABOUT TIME YOU WERE MINE – THUNDERBUGS
IT'S ALL ABOUT THE BENJAMINS – PUFF DADDY
IT'S ALL ABOUT U – SWV
IT'S ALL ABOUT YOU – JUSTIN
IT'S ALL ABOUT YOU (NOT ABOUT ME) – Tracie SPENCER
IT'S ALL BEEN DONE – BARENAKED LADIES
IT'S ALL COMING BACK TO ME NOW [A] – PANDORA'S BOX
IT'S ALL COMING BACK TO ME NOW [A] – Celine DION
IT'S ALL GONE – Chris REA
IT'S ALL GOOD [A] – HAMMER
IT'S ALL GOOD [B] – DA MOB featuring JOCELYN BROWN
IT'S ALL GRAVY – ROMEO featuring Christina MILIAN
IT'S ALL IN THE GAME [A] – Tommy EDWARDS
IT'S ALL IN THE GAME [A] – Cliff RICHARD
IT'S ALL IN THE GAME [A] – The FOUR TOPS
IT'S ALL OVER – Cliff RICHARD
IT'S ALL OVER NOW [A] – Shane FENTON and the FENTONES
IT'S ALL OVER NOW [B] – The ROLLING STONES
IT'S ALL OVER NOW BABY BLUE [A] – Joan BAEZ
IT'S ALL OVER NOW BABY BLUE [A] – MILLTOWN BROTHERS
IT'S ALL THE WAY LIVE (NOW) – COOLIO
IT'S ALL RIGHT – Sterling VOID
IT'S ALL TRUE – LEMONHEADS
IT'S ALL UP TO YOU – Jim CAPALDI
IT'S ALL VAIN – MAGNOLIA
IT'S ALL YOURS – MC LYTE
IT'S ALMOST TOMORROW [A] – DREAMWEAVERS
IT'S ALMOST TOMORROW [A] – Mark WYNTER
IT'S ALRIGHT [A] – SHO NUFF
IT'S ALRIGHT [B] – PET SHOP BOYS
IT'S ALRIGHT [B] – HYPER GO GO
IT'S ALRIGHT [C] – EAST 17
IT'S ALRIGHT [D] – Bryan POWELL
IT'S ALRIGHT [E] – Deni HINES
IT'S ALRIGHT [F] – ECHO and the BUNNYMEN
IT'S ALRIGHT (BABY'S COMING BACK) – EURYTHMICS
IT'S ALRIGHT, I FEEL IT! – NUYORICAN SOUL featuring Jocelyn BROWN
IT'S ALRIGHT NOW – The BELOVED
IT'S AN OPEN SECRET – JOY STRINGS
IT'S BEEN AWHILE – STAIND
IT'S BEEN NICE – The EVERLY BROTHERS
IT'S BEEN SO LONG – George McCRAE
IT'S BETTER TO HAVE (AND DON'T NEED) – Don COVAY
IT'S CALLED A HEART – DEPECHE MODE
IT'S DIFFERENT FOR GIRLS – Joe JACKSON
IT'S ECSTASY WHEN YOU LAY DOWN NEXT TO ME – Barry WHITE
IT'S FOR YOU – Cilla BLACK
IT'S FOUR IN THE MORNING – Faron YOUNG
IT'S GETTING BETTER – MAMA CASS
IT'S GOIN DOWN – X-ECUTIONERS featuring Mike SHINODA & Mr HAHN of LINKIN PARK
IT'S GOING TO HAPPEN! – The UNDERTONES
IT'S GONNA BE A COLD COLD CHRISTMAS – DANA
IT'S GONNA BE A LOVELY DAY – S.O.U.L. S.Y.S.T.E.M. introducing Michelle VISAGE
IT'S GONNA BE ... (A LOVELY DAY) – BRANCACCIO & AISHER
IT'S GONNA BE ALL RIGHT – GERRY and the PACEMAKERS
IT'S GONNA BE ALRIGHT [A] – Ruby TURNER
IT'S GONNA BE ALRIGHT [B] – PUSSY 2000
IT'S GONNA BE ME – 'N SYNC
IT'S GONNA BE MY WAY – PRECIOUS
IT'S GOOD NEWS WEEK – HEDGEHOPPERS ANONYMOUS
IT'S GREAT WHEN WE'RE TOGETHER – Finley QUAYE
IT'S GRIM UP NORTH – JUSTIFIED ANCIENTS OF MU MU
IT'S GROWING – The TEMPTATIONS
IT'S HAPPENIN' – PLUS ONE featuring SIRRON
IT'S HARD SOMETIMES – Frankie KNUCKLES
IT'S HARD TO BE HUMBLE – Mac DAVIS
IT'S HERE – Kim WILDE
IT'S IMPOSSIBLE – Perry COMO
IT'S IN EVERY ONE OF US – Cliff RICHARD
IT'S IN HIS KISS (THE SHOOP SHOOP SONG) [A] – Betty EVERETT
IT'S IN HIS KISS [A] – Linda LEWIS
IT'S IN OUR HANDS – BJÖRK
IT'S IN YOUR EYES – Phil COLLINS
IT'S ... IT'S ... THE SWEET MIX – The SWEET
IT'S JURASSIC – SOUL CITY ORCHESTRA
IT'S JUST A FEELING – TERRORIZE
IT'S JUST PORN MUM – TRUCKS
(IT'S JUST) THE WAY THAT YOU LOVE ME – Paula ABDUL
IT'S LATE [A] – Ricky NELSON
IT'S LATE [A] – Shakin' STEVENS
(IT'S LIKE A) SAD OLD KINDA MOVIE – PICKETTYWITCH
IT'S LIKE THAT – RUN-DMC vs Jason NEVINS
IT'S LIKE THAT Y'ALL – SWEET TEE
IT'S LOVE – Ken DODD
IT'S LOVE THAT REALLY COUNTS – The MERSEYBEATS
IT'S LOVE (TRIPPIN') – GOLDTRIX presents Andrea BROWN
IT'S LULU – BOO RADLEYS
IT'S ME – Alice COOPER
IT'S MY HOUSE [A] – Diana ROSS
IT'S MY HOUSE [A] – STORM
IT'S MY LIFE [A] – The ANIMALS
IT'S MY LIFE [B] – TALK TALK
IT'S MY LIFE [B] – LIQUID PEOPLE vs TALK TALK
IT'S MY LIFE [B] – NO DOUBT
IT'S MY LIFE [C] – DR ALBAN
IT'S MY LIFE [D] – BON JOVI
IT'S MY PARTY [A] – Lesley GORE
IT'S MY PARTY [A] – Dave STEWART with Barbara GASKIN
IT'S MY PARTY [B] – Chaka KHAN
IT'S MY TIME – The EVERLY BROTHERS
IT'S MY TURN [A] – Diana ROSS
IT'S MY TURN [B] – ANGELIC
IT'S NATURE'S WAY (NO PROBLEM) – DOLLAR
IT'S NEVER TOO LATE – Diana ROSS
IT'S NICE TO GO TRAV'LING – Frank SINATRA
IT'S NO GOOD – DEPECHE MODE
IT'S NOT A LOVE THING – Geoffrey WILLIAMS
IT'S NOT RIGHT BUT (IT'S OK) – Whitney HOUSTON
IT'S NOT THE END OF THE WORLD? – SUPER FURRY ANIMALS
IT'S NOT UNUSUAL – Tom JONES
IT'S NOW OR NEVER – Elvis PRESLEY
IT'S OH SO QUIET – BJÖRK
IT'S OK [A] – DELIRIOUS?
IT'S OK [B] – ATOMIC KITTEN
IT'S OKAY – DES'REE
IT'S ON [A] – FLOWERED UP
IT'S ON [B] – NAUGHTY BY NATURE
IT'S ON YOU (SCAN ME) – EUROGROOVE
IT'S ONE OF THOSE NIGHTS (YES LOVE) – PARTRIDGE FAMILY
IT'S ONLY LOVE [A] – Tony BLACKBURN
IT'S ONLY LOVE [A] – Elvis PRESLEY
IT'S ONLY LOVE [B] – Gary 'US' BONDS
IT'S ONLY LOVE [C] – Bryan ADAMS
IT'S ONLY LOVE [C] – Tina TURNER
IT'S ONLY LOVE [D] – SIMPLY RED
IT'S ONLY MAKE BELIEVE [A] – Billy FURY
IT'S ONLY MAKE BELIEVE [A] – CHILD
IT'S ONLY MAKE BELIEVE [A] – Conway TWITTY
IT'S ONLY MAKE BELIEVE [A] – Glen CAMPBELL
IT'S ONLY NATURAL – CROWDED HOUSE
IT'S ONLY ROCK AND ROLL [A] – The ROLLING STONES
IT'S ONLY ROCK 'N' ROLL [A] – VARIOUS ARTISTS (EPs and LPs)
IT'S ONLY US – Robbie WILLIAMS
IT'S 'ORRIBLE BEING IN LOVE (WHEN YOU'RE 8 1/2) – CLAIRE and FRIENDS
IT'S OVER [A] – Roy ORBISON
IT'S OVER [B] – FUNK MASTER
IT'S OVER [C] – LEVEL 42
IT'S OVER [B] – CLOCK
IT'S OVER [D] – RIMES featuring Shaila PROSPERE
IT'S OVER [E] – KURUPT
IT'S OVER (DISTORTION) – PIANOHEADZ
IT'S OVER LOVE – Todd TERRY PROJECT presents SHANNON
IT'S OVER NOW [A] – Ultra NATÉ
IT'S OVER NOW [B] – Deborah COX
IT'S OVER NOW [C] – 112
IT'S PARTY TIME AGAIN – George VAN DUSEN
IT'S PROBABLY ME – STING with Eric CLAPTON
IT'S RAINING [A] – DARTS
IT'S RAINING [B] – Shakin' STEVENS
IT'S RAINING AGAIN – SUPERTRAMP
IT'S RAINING MEN [A] – WEATHER GIRLS
IT'S RAINING MEN [A] – Martha WASH
IT'S RAINING MEN [A] – Geri HALLIWELL
IT'S SO EASY – Andy WILLIAMS
IT'S SO HIGH – Matt FRETTON
IT'S SO NICE (TO HAVE YOU HOME) – The NEW SEEKERS
IT'S STILL ROCK AND ROLL TO ME – Billy JOEL
IT'S STILL YOU – Michael BALL
IT'S SUMMERTIME (LET IT GET INTO YOU) – SMOOTH
IT'S TEMPTATION – SHEER ELEGANCE
IT'S THE END OF THE WORLD AS WE KNOW IT – R.E.M.
IT'S THE SAME OLD SONG [A] – The FOUR TOPS
IT'S THE SAME OLD SONG [A] – Jonathan KING
IT'S THE SAME OLD SONG [A] – KC and the SUNSHINE BAND
IT'S THE WAY YOU MAKE ME FEEL – STEPS
IT'S TIME [A] – Elvis COSTELLO
IT'S TIME [B] – Ferry CORSTEN
IT'S TIME FOR LOVE – CHI-LITES
IT'S TIME TO CRY – Paul ANKA
IT'S TOO LATE [A] – Carole KING
IT'S TOO LATE [A] – QUARTZ introducing Dina CARROLL
IT'S TOO LATE [B] – Luci SILVAS
IT'S TOO LATE NOW [A] – SWINGING BLUE JEANS
IT'S TOO LATE NOW [B] – Long John BALDRY
IT'S TOO SOON TO KNOW – Pat BOONE
IT'S TRICKY [A] – RUN-DMC
IT'S TRICKY 2003 [A] – RUN-DMC featuring Jacknife LEE
IT'S TRUE – QUEEN PEN
IT'S UP TO YOU – Ricky NELSON
IT'S UP TO YOU PETULA – EDISON LIGHTHOUSE
IT'S UP TO YOU (SHINING THROUGH) – LAYO & BUSHWACKA!
IT'S WHAT'S UPFRONT THAT COUNTS – YOSH presents LOVEDEEJAY AKEMI
IT'S WHAT WE'RE ALL ABOUT – SUM 41
IT'S WONDERFUL (TO BE LOVED BY YOU) – Jimmy RUFFIN
IT'S WRITTEN IN THE STARS – Paul WELLER
IT'S WRITTEN ON YOUR BODY – Ronnie BOND
IT'S YER MONEY I'M AFTER BABY – The WONDER STUFF
IT'S YOU [A] – Freddie STARR
IT'S YOU [B] – MANHATTANS
IT'S YOU [C] – EMF
IT'S YOU ONLY YOU (MEIN SCHMERZ) – Lene LOVICH
IT'S YOUR DAY TODAY – PJ PROBY
IT'S YOUR DESTINY – ELECTRA
IT'S YOUR LIFE – SMOKIE
IT'S YOUR THING – ISLEY BROTHERS
IT'S YOUR TIME – Arthur BAKER
IT'S YOURS – Jon CUTLER featuring E-MAN
ITSY BITSY TEENIE WEENIE YELLOW POLKA DOT BIKINI [A] – Brian HYLAND
ITSY BITSY TEENY WEENY YELLOW POLKA DOT BIKINI [A] – BOMBALURINA
ITZA TRUMPET THING – MONTANO vs THE TRUMPET MAN
I'VE BEEN A BAD BAD BOY – Paul JONES
I'VE BEEN AROUND THE WORLD – Marti PELLOW
I'VE BEEN DRINKING – Jeff BECK and Rod STEWART
I'VE BEEN HURT – Guy DARRELL
I'VE BEEN IN LOVE BEFORE – CUTTING CREW
I'VE BEEN LONELY SO LONG – Frederick KNIGHT
I'VE BEEN LOSING YOU – A-HA
I'VE BEEN THINKING ABOUT YOU – LONDONBEAT
I'VE BEEN TO A MARVELLOUS PARTY – The DIVINE COMEDY
I'VE BEEN WAITING – STEREO NATION
I'VE BEEN WATCHIN' – JOE PUBLIC
I'VE BEEN WRONG BEFORE – Cilla BLACK
I'VE DONE EVERYTHING FOR YOU – Sammy HAGAR
I'VE FOUND LOVE AGAIN – Richard CARTRIDGE
I'VE GOT A LITTLE PUPPY – The SMURFS
I'VE GOT A LITTLE SOMETHING FOR YOU – MN8
I'VE GOT A THING ABOUT YOU BABY – Elvis PRESLEY
I'VE GOT MINE – UB40
I'VE GOT NEWS FOR YOU – Feargal SHARKEY
I'VE GOT SOMETHING TO SAY – REEF
I'VE GOT THE MUSIC IN ME – Kiki DEE
I'VE GOT THIS FEELING – MAVERICKS
I'VE GOT TO LEARN TO SAY NO – Richard 'Dimples' FIELDS
I'VE GOT TO MOVE – Calvin RICHARDSON
I'VE GOT YOU – Martine McCUTCHEON
I'VE GOT YOU ON MY MIND [A] – Dorian GRAY
I'VE GOT YOU ON MY MIND [A] – WHITE PLAINS
I'VE GOT YOU UNDER MY SKIN [A] – The FOUR SEASONS
I'VE GOT YOU UNDER MY SKIN [A] – Neneh CHERRY
I'VE GOT YOU UNDER MY SKIN [A] – Frank SINATRA with BONO
(I'VE GOT YOUR) PLEASURE CONTROL – Simon HARRIS featuring Lonnie GORDON
I'VE GOTTA GET A MESSAGE TO YOU – The BEE GEES
I'VE HAD ENOUGH [A] – Paul McCARTNEY
I'VE HAD ENOUGH [B] – EARTH WIND AND FIRE
I'VE HAD ENOUGH [C] – Ivan MATIAS
I'VE HAD ENOUGH [D] – HILLMAN MINX
(I'VE HAD) THE TIME OF MY LIFE – Bill MEDLEY and Jennifer WARNES
I'VE JUST BEGUN TO LOVE YOU – DYNASTY
I'VE LOST YOU – Elvis PRESLEY
I'VE NEVER BEEN IN LOVE – Suzi QUATRO
I'VE NEVER BEEN TO ME – CHARLENE
I'VE PASSED THIS WAY BEFORE – Jimmy RUFFIN
I'VE SEEN THE WORD – BLANCMANGE
I'VE TOLD EVERY LITTLE STAR – Linda SCOTT
I'VE WAITED SO LONG – Anthony NEWLEY
IVORY – SKIN UP
IVORY TOWER – KAYE SISTERS
IZ U – NELLY
IZZO (H.O.V.A.) – JAY-Z
JACK AND DIANE – John Cougar MELLENCAMP
JACK AND JILL – RAYDIO
JACK AND JILL PARTY – Pete BURNS
JACK IN THE BOX [A] – Clodagh RODGERS
JACK IN THE BOX [B] – MOMENTS
JACK LE FREAK – CHIC
JACK MIX II/III – MIRAGE
JACK MIX IV – MIRAGE
JACK MIX VII – MIRAGE
JACK O' DIAMONDS – Lonnie DONEGAN
JACK TALKING – Dave STEWART
THE JACK THAT HOUSE BUILT – JACK 'N' CHILL

JACK THE GROOVE — RAZE
JACK THE RIPPER [A] — LL COOL J
JACK THE RIPPER [B] —
　Nick CAVE and the BAD SEEDS
JACK TO THE SOUND OF THE UNDERGROUND —
　HITHOUSE
JACK YOUR BODY — Steve 'Silk' HURLEY
JACK'S HEROES —
　The POGUES and The DUBLINERS
JACKET HANGS — BLUE AEROPLANES
JACKIE — Scott WALKER
JACKIE WILSON SAID (I'M IN HEAVEN WHEN YOU SMILE)
　— DEXY'S MIDNIGHT RUNNERS
JACKIE'S RACING — WHITEOUT
JACKSON — Nancy SINATRA
JACKY — Marc ALMOND
JACQUELINE — Bobby HELMS
JACQUES DERRIDA — SCRITTI POLITTI
JACQUES YOUR BODY (MAKE ME SWEAT) —
　LES RYTHMES DIGITALES
JA-DA — JOHNNY and the HURRICANES
JADED [A] — GREEN DAY
JADED [B] — AEROSMITH
JAGGED END — LINCOLN CITY FC
　featuring Michael COURTNEY
JAGUAR — DJ ROLANDO AKA AZTEC MYSTIC
JAIL HOUSE RAP — FAT BOYS
JAILBIRD — PRIMAL SCREAM
JAILBREAK [A] — THIN LIZZY
JAILBREAK [B] — PARADOX
JAILHOUSE ROCK — Elvis PRESLEY
JAILHOUSE ROCK (EP) — Elvis PRESLEY
JAM — Michael JACKSON
THE JAM EP — A TRIBE CALLED QUEST
JAM IT JAM — SHE ROCKERS
JAM J — JAMES
JAM, JAM, JAM (ALL NIGHT LONG) —
　PEOPLES CHOICE
JAM ON REVENGE (THE WIKKI WIKKI SONG) —
　NEWCLEUS
JAM SIDE DOWN — STATUS QUO
JAMAICAN IN NEW YORK — SHINEHEAD
JAMBALAYA [A] — Jo STAFFORD
JAMBALAYA [A] — Fats DOMINO
JAMBALAYA (ON THE BAYOU) [A] —
　The CARPENTERS
JAMBOREE — NAUGHTY BY
　NATURE featuring ZHANÉ
JAMES BOND THEME [A] —
　John BARRY ORCHESTRA
JAMES BOND THEME [A] — MOBY
JAMES DEAN (I WANNA KNOW) —
　Daniel BEDINGFIELD
JAMES HAS KITTENS — BLU PETER
JAMMIN' IN AMERICA — GAP BAND
JAMMING — Bob MARLEY & the WAILERS
JANA — KILLING JOKE
JANE [A] — STARSHIP
JANE [B] — PERFECT DAY
JANEIRO — SOLID SESSIONS
JANIE, DON'T TAKE YOUR LOVE TO TOWN —
　Jon BON JOVI
JANUARY — PILOT
JANUARY FEBRUARY — Barbara DICKSON
JAPANESE BOY — ANEKA
JARROW SONG — Alan PRICE
JAWS — Lalo SCHIFRIN
JAYOU — JURASSIC 5
JAZZ CARNIVAL — AZYMUTH
JAZZ IT UP — REEL 2 REAL
JAZZ RAP — Kim CARNEGIE
JAZZ THING — GANG STARR
JAZZIN' THE WAY YOU KNOW — JAZZY M
JE NE SAIS PAS POURQUOI — Kylie MINOGUE
JE SUIS MUSIC — CERRONE
JE T'AIME ... MOI NON PLUS [A] —
　Jane BIRKIN and Serge GAINSBOURG
JE T'AIME (MOI NON PLUS) [A] — JUDGE DREAD
JE T'AIME (ALLO ALLO) [A] —
　RENÉ and YVETTE
JE VOULAIS (TE DIRE QUE JE T'ATTENDS) —
　MANHATTAN TRANSFER
JEALOUS AGAIN — BLACK CROWES
JEALOUS GUY [A] — ROXY MUSIC
JEALOUS GUY [A] — John LENNON
JEALOUS HEART [A] —
　CADETS with Eileen READ
JEALOUS HEART [A] — Connie FRANCIS
JEALOUS LOVE [A] — JOBOXERS
JEALOUS LOVE [B] — Hazell DEAN
JEALOUS MIND — Alvin STARDUST
JEALOUSY — Billy FURY
JEALOUSY [B] — Amii STEWART
JEALOUSY [C] — ADVENTURES OF STEVIE V
JEALOUSY [D] — PET SHOP BOYS
JEALOUSY [E] — OCTOPUS
THE JEAN GENIE — David BOWIE
JEAN THE BIRDMAN — David SYLVIAN
JEANETTE — The BEAT
JEANNIE — Danny WILLIAMS
JEANNIE, JEANNIE, JEANNIE — Eddie COCHRAN
JEANNY — FALCO
JEANS ON — David DUNDAS
JEDI WANNABE — BELLATRIX
JEEPSTER [A] — T. REX
JEEPSTER [A] — POLECATS
JELLYHEAD — CRUSH

JENNIFER ECCLES — The HOLLIES
JENNIFER JUNIPER [A] — DONOVAN
JENNIFER JUNIPER [A] —
　SINGING CORNER meets DONOVAN
JENNIFER SHE SAID — Lloyd COLE
JENNY — STELLASTARR*
JENNY FROM THE BLOCK — Jennifer LOPEZ
JENNY JENNY — LITTLE RICHARD
JENNY ONDIOLINE — STEREOLAB
JENNY TAKE A RIDE —
　Mitch RYDER and the DETROIT WHEELS
JEOPARDY — Greg KIHN BAND
JEREMY — PEARL JAM
JERICHO [A] — SIMPLY RED
JERICHO [B] — The PRODIGY
JERK IT OUT — CAESARS
JERUSALEM [A] — The FALL
JERUSALEM [A] — FAT LES
JERUSALEM [A] — Herb ALPERT
JESAMINE — CASUALS
JESSE HOLD ON — B*WITCHED
JESSICA — Adam GREEN
JESSIE — Joshua KADISON
JESSIE'S GIRL — Rick SPRINGFIELD
JESUS — Cliff RICHARD
JESUS CHRIST — LONGPIGS
JESUS CHRIST POSE — SOUNDGARDEN
JESUS HAIRDO — The CHARLATANS
JESUS HE KNOWS ME — GENESIS
JESUS SAYS — ASH
JESUS TO A CHILD — George MICHAEL
JESUS WALKS — Kanye WEST
JET — Paul McCARTNEY
JET CITY WOMAN — QUEENSRŸCHE
JET-STAR — TEKNO TOO
JEWEL — CRANES
JEZEBEL [A] — Marty WILDE
JEZEBEL [A] — Shakin' STEVENS
JIBARO — ELECTRA
JIG-A-JIG — EAST OF EDEN
JIGGA JIGGA! — SCOOTER
JIGGY — CLIPZ
JILTED JOHN — JILTED JOHN
JIMMIE JONES — VAPORS
JIMMY — PURPLE HEARTS
JIMMY JIMMY — The UNDERTONES
JIMMY LEE — Aretha FRANKLIN
JIMMY MACK —
　Martha REEVES and the VANDELLAS
JIMMY OLSEN'S BLUES — SPIN DOCTORS
JIMMY UNKNOWN — Lita ROZA
JIMMY'S GIRL — Johnny TILLOTSON
JINGLE BELL ROCK [A] — Max BYGRAVES
JINGLE BELL ROCK [A] —
　Chubby CHECKER and Bobby RYDELL
JINGLE BELLS — JUDGE DREAD
JINGLE BELLS LAUGHING ALL THE WAY —
　HYSTERICS
JINGO [A] — CANDIDO
JINGO [A] — JELLYBEAN
JINGO [A] — FKW
JITTERBUGGIN' — HEATWAVE
JIVE TALKIN' [A] — The BEE GEES
JIVE TALKIN' [A] — BOOGIE BOX HIGH
JJ TRIBUTE — ASHA
JOAN OF ARC — ORCHESTRAL
　MANOEUVRES IN THE DARK
JOANNA [A] — Scott WALKER
JOANNA [B] — KOOL and the GANG
JOANNA [C] — MRS WOOD
JOCELYN SQUARE — LOVE AND MONEY
JOCK MIX 1 —
　MAD JOCKS featuring JOCKMASTER B.A.
JOCKO HOMO — DEVO
JODY — Jermaine STEWART
JOE — INSPIRAL CARPETS
JOE LE TAXI — Vanessa PARADIS
JOE LOUIS — John SQUIRE
JOE 90 (THEME) — Barry GRAY ORCHESTRA
JOGI — PANJABI MC featuring JAY-Z
JOHN AND JULIE — Eddie CALVERT
JOHN, I'M ONLY DANCING [A] — David BOWIE
JOHN I'M ONLY DANCING [A] — POLECATS
JOHN KETTLEY (IS A WEATHERMAN) —
　TRIBE OF TOFFS
JOHN WAYNE IS BIG LEGGY —
　HAYSI FANTAYZEE
JOHNNY AND MARY — Robert PALMER
JOHNNY ANGEL [A] — Shelley FABARES
JOHNNY ANGEL [A] — Patti LYNN
JOHNNY B GOODE [A] — Jimi HENDRIX
JOHNNY B GOODE [A] — Peter TOSH
JOHNNY B GOODE [A] — JUDAS PRIEST
JOHNNY CASH — SONS AND DAUGHTERS
JOHNNY COME HOME —
　FINE YOUNG CANNIBALS
JOHNNY COME LATELY — Steve EARLE
JOHNNY DAY — Rolf HARRIS
JOHNNY FRIENDLY — JOBOXERS
JOHNNY GET ANGRY — Carol DEENE
JOHNNY JOHNNY — PREFAB SPROUT
JOHNNY MATHIS' FEET —
　AMERICAN MUSIC CLUB
JOHNNY PANIC AND THE BIBLE OF DREAMS —
　Johnny PANIC and the BIBLE OF DREAMS
JOHNNY REGGAE — PIGLETS
JOHNNY REMEMBER ME [A] — John LEYTON

JOHNNY REMEMBER ME [A] — METEORS
JOHNNY ROCCO — Marty WILDE
JOHNNY THE HORSE — MADNESS
JOHNNY WILL — Pat BOONE
JOIN IN AND SING AGAIN —
　JOHNSTON BROTHERS
JOIN IN AND SING (NO.3) —
　JOHNSTON BROTHERS
JOIN ME — LIGHTFORCE
JOIN OUR CLUB — SAINT ETIENNE
JOIN THE PARTY — HONKY
JOIN TOGETHER — The WHO
JOINING YOU — Alanis MORISSETTE
JOINTS & JAMS — BLACK EYED PEAS
JOJO ACTION — MR PRESIDENT
JOKE (I'M LAUGHING) — Eddi READER
THE JOKER — Steve MILLER BAND
THE JOKER (THE WIGAN JOKER) —
　ALLNIGHT BAND
JOLE BLON — Gary 'US' BONDS
JOLENE [A] — Dolly PARTON
JOLENE [A] — STRAWBERRY SWITCHBLADE
JOLENE (LIVE) [A] — The WHITE STRIPES
JONAH — BREATHE
JONATHAN DAVID — BELLE & SEBASTIAN
THE JONES' — The TEMPTATIONS
JONES VS JONES — KOOL and the GANG
JONESTOWN MIND — The ALMIGHTY
JOOK GAL — ELEPHANT MAN
JORDAN: THE EP — PREFAB SPROUT
JOSEPH MEGA REMIX — Jason DONOVAN
JOSEPHINE [A] — Chris REA
JOSEPHINE [B] — TERRORVISION
JOSEY — DEEP BLUE SOMETHING
JOURNEY — Duncan BROWNE
THE JOURNEY [A] — 911
THE JOURNEY [B] — CITIZEN CANED
JOURNEY TO THE MOON — BIDDU
JOURNEY TO THE PAST — AALIYAH
JOY [A] — BAND AKA
JOY [B] — Teddy PENDERGRASS
JOY [C] — SOUL II SOUL
JOY [D] — STAXX featuring Carol LEEMING
JOY [E] — 7669
JOY [F] — BLACKSTREET
JOY [G] — Deni HINES
JOY [H] — Kathy BROWN
JOY! [I] — GAY DAD
JOY [J] — Mark RYDER
JOY AND HAPPINESS — STABBS
JOY AND HEARTBREAK —
　MOVEMENT 98 featuring Carroll THOMPSON
JOY AND PAIN [A] — Donna ALLEN
JOY AND PAIN [[B] —
　MAZE featuring Frankie BEVERLY
JOY AND PAIN [A] —
　Rob BASE and DJ E-Z ROCK
JOY AND PAIN [C] — ANGELLE
(JOY) I KNOW IT — ODYSSEY
JOY OF LIVING [A] — Cliff RICHARD
JOY OF LIVING [B] — OUI 3
JOY TO THE WORLD —
　THREE DOG NIGHT
JOYBRINGER — MANFRED MANN
JOYENERGIZER — Joy KITIKONTI
JOYRIDE — ROXETTE
JOYRIDER (YOU'RE PLAYING WITH FIRE) —
　COLOUR GIRL
JOYS OF CHRISTMAS — Chris REA
JOYS OF LIFE — David JOSEPH
JUDGE FUDGE — HAPPY MONDAYS
THE JUDGEMENT IS THE MIRROR —
　DALI'S CAR
JUDY IN DISGUISE (WITH GLASSES) —
　John FRED and the PLAYBOY BAND
JUDY OVER THE RAINBOW — ORANGE
JUDY SAYS (KNOCK YOU IN THE HEAD) —
　VIBRATORS
JUDY TEEN —
　Steve HARLEY and COCKNEY REBEL
JUGGLING — RAGGA TWINS
JUICY [A] — WRECKX-N-EFFECT
JUICY [A] — NOTORIOUS B.I.G.
JUICY FRUIT — MTUME
A JUICY RED APPLE — SKIN UP
JUKE BOX BABY — Perry COMO
JUKE BOX GYPSY — LINDISFARNE
JUKE BOX HERO — FOREIGNER
JUKE BOX JIVE — The RUBETTES
JULIA [A] — EURYTHMICS
JULIA [B] — Chris REA
JULIA [C] — SILVER SUN
JULIA SAYS — WET WET WET
JULIE ANNE — KENNY
JULIE DO YA LOVE ME [A] — Bobby SHERMAN
JULIE DO YA LOVE ME [A] — WHITE PLAINS
JULIE (EP) — LEVELLERS
JULIE OCEAN — The UNDERTONES
JULIET — FOUR PENNIES
JULIET (KEEP THAT IN MIND) — Thea GILMORE
JULY — OCEAN COLOUR SCENE
JUMBO [A] — The BEE GEES
JUMBO [B] — UNDERWORLD
JUMP [A] — VAN HALEN
JUMP [A] — AZTEC CAMERA
JUMP [A] — BUS STOP
JUMP [B] — KRIS KROSS

JUMP! [C] — MOVEMENT
JUMP [D] — GIRLS ALOUD
JUMP AROUND — HOUSE OF PAIN
JUMP BACK (SET ME FREE) — Dhar BRAXTON
JUMP DOWN — B*WITCHED
JUMP (FOR MY LOVE) —
　POINTER SISTERS
JUMP JIVE AN' WAIL —
　Brian SETZER ORCHESTRA
JUMP 'N SHOUT — BASEMENT JAXX
THE JUMP OFF —
　LIL' KIM featuring MR. CHEEKS
JUMP ON DEMAND — [SPUNGE]
JUMP START — Natalie COLE
JUMP THE GUN — The THREE DEGREES
JUMP THEY SAY — David BOWIE
JUMP TO IT — Aretha FRANKLIN
JUMP TO MY BEAT — WILDCHILD
JUMP TO MY LOVE — INCOGNITO
JUMP TO THE BEAT [A] — Stacy LATTISAW
JUMP TO THE BEAT [A] — Dannii MINOGUE
JUMP UP — JUST 4 JOKES featuring MC RB
JUMPIN' — LIBERTY X
JUMPIN' JACK FLASH [A] —
　The ROLLING STONES
JUMPIN' JACK FLASH [A] — Aretha FRANKLIN
JUMPIN' JIVE — Joe JACKSON
JUMPIN' JUMPIN' — DESTINY'S CHILD
JUNE AFTERNOON — ROXETTE
JUNEAU — FUNERAL FOR A FRIEND
THE JUNGLE BOOK GROOVE — JUNGLE BOOK
JUNGLE BROTHER — The JUNGLE BROTHERS
JUNGLE FEVER — CHAKACHAS
JUNGLE HIGH — JUNO REACTOR
JUNGLE ROCK [A] — Hank MIZELL
JUNGLE ROCK [A] — JUNGLE BOYS
JUNGLIST —
　DRUMSOUND & Simon 'BASSLINE' SMITH
JUNIOR'S FARM — Paul McCARTNEY
JUNKIES — EASYWORLD
JUPITER — EARTH WIND AND FIRE
JUS' A RASCAL — DIZZEE RASCAL
JUS' COME — COOL JACK
JUS 1 KISS — BASEMENT JAXX
JUS' REACH (RECYCLED) — GALLIANO
JUST [A] — RADIOHEAD
JUST [B] — Jamie SCOTT
JUST A DAY — FEEDER
JUST A DAY AWAY —
　BARCLAY JAMES HARVEST
JUST A DREAM [A] — NENA
JUST A DREAM [B] — Donna DE LORY
JUST A FEELING — BAD MANNERS
JUST A FEW THINGS THAT I AIN'T —
　The BEAUTIFUL SOUTH
JUST A FRIEND [A] — Biz MARKIE
JUST A FRIEND [B] — MARIO
JUST A GIRL — NO DOUBT
JUST A GROOVE — NOMAD
JUST A LITTLE — LIBERTY X
JUST A LITTLE BIT — UNDERTAKERS
JUST A LITTLE BIT BETTER —
　HERMAN'S HERMITS
JUST A LITTLE BIT LONGER (EP) —
　Maxi PRIEST
JUST A LITTLE BIT OF LOVE — Rebekah RYAN
JUST A LITTLE BIT TOO LATE —
　Wayne FONTANA and The MINDBENDERS
JUST A LITTLE MISUNDERSTANDING —
　CONTOURS
JUST A LITTLE GIRL — Amy STUDT
JUST A LITTLE MORE — DELUXE
JUST A LITTLE MORE LOVE —
　David GUETTA featuring Chris WILLIS
JUST A LITTLE TOO MUCH — Ricky NELSON
JUST A LITTLE WHILE — JANET
JUST A MAN — Mark MORRISON
JUST A MIRAGE — JELLYBEAN
JUST A SHADOW — BIG COUNTRY
JUST A SMILE — PILOT
JUST A STEP FROM HEAVEN — ETERNAL
JUST A TOUCH — Keith SWEAT
JUST A TOUCH OF LOVE — SLAVE
JUST A TOUCH OF LOVE (EVERYDAY) — C & C MUSIC
　FACTORY / CLIVILLES & COLE
JUST AN ILLUSION — IMAGINATION
JUST ANOTHER BROKEN HEART —
　Sheena EASTON
JUST ANOTHER DAY [A] — Jon SECADA
JUST ANOTHER DAY [B] — Jonathan WILKES
JUST ANOTHER DREAM — Cathy DENNIS
JUST ANOTHER GROOVE — MIGHTY DUB KATZ
JUST ANOTHER ILLUSION — HURRICANE #1
JUST ANOTHER NIGHT — Mick JAGGER
JUST AROUND THE HILL — SASH!
JUST AS LONG AS YOU ARE THERE —
　Vanessa PARADIS
JUST AS MUCH AS EVER — Nat 'King' COLE
JUST BE —
　TIESTO featuring Kirsty HAWKSHAW
JUST BE DUB TO ME [A] — REVELATION
JUST BE GOOD TO ME [A] — S.O.S. BAND
JUST BE TONIGHT — BBG
JUST BECAUSE — JANE'S ADDICTION
JUST BEFORE YOU LEAVE — DEL AMITRI
JUST BETWEEN YOU AND ME — APRIL WINE

JUST BORN — Jim DALE
JUST CALL — SHERRICK
JUST CALL ME — GOOD GIRLS
JUST CAN'T GET ENOUGH [A] —
DEPECHE MODE
JUST CAN'T GET ENOUGH [B] —
TRANSFORMER 2
JUST CAN'T GET ENOUGH [C] — Harry 'Choo
Choo' ROMERO presents Inaya DAY
JUST CAN'T GET ENOUGH (NO NO NO NO) —
EYE TO EYE featuring Taka BOOM
JUST CAN'T GIVE YOU UP — MYSTIC MERLIN
JUST CAN'T STAND IT — MATT BIANCO
JUST CAN'T WAIT (SATURDAY) —
ONEHUNDREDPERCENT featuring
Jennifer JOHN
JUST CHECKIN' — The BEAUTIFUL SOUTH
JUST CRUISIN' — Will SMITH
JUST DON'T WANT TO BE LONELY [A] —
MAIN INGREDIENT
JUST DON'T WANT TO BE LONELY [A] —
Freddie McGREGOR
JUST FADE AWAY — STIFF LITTLE FINGERS
JUST FOR KICKS — Mike SARNE
JUST FOR MONEY — Paul HARDCASTLE
JUST FOR OLD TIME'S SAKE —
FOSTER and ALLEN
JUST FOR ONE DAY (HEROES) —
David GUETTA vs BOWIE
JUST FOR YOU [A] —
FREDDIE and the DREAMERS
JUST FOR YOU [B] — GLITTER BAND
JUST FOR YOU [C] — Alan PRICE
JUST FOR YOU [D] — M PEOPLE
JUST FOR YOU [E] — Lionel RICHIE
JUST FUCK — Tom NEVILLE
JUST GET UP AND DANCE —
Afrika BAMBAATAA
JUST GETS BETTER — TJR featuring XAVIER
JUST GIVE THE DJ A BREAK —
DYNAMIX II featuring TOO TOUGH TEE
JUST GOOD FRIENDS —
FISH featuring Sam BROWN
JUST GOT LUCKY — JOBOXERS
JUST GOT PAID — Johnny KEMP
JUST HOLD ON — TOPLOADER
JUST IN CASE — JAHEIM
JUST IN LUST — The WILDHEARTS
JUST IN TIME — RAW SILK
JUST KEEP IT UP — Dee CLARK
JUST KEEP ME MOVING — kd LANG
JUST KEEP ROCKIN' —
DOUBLE TROUBLE and the REBEL MC
JUST KICK — COHEN vs DELUXE
JUST KICKIN' IT — XSCAPE
JUST LET ME DO MY THING — SINE
JUST LIKE A MAN — DEL AMITRI
JUST LIKE A PILL — PINK
JUST LIKE A WOMAN — MANFRED MANN
JUST LIKE ANYONE — SOUL ASYLUM
JUST LIKE BRUCE LEE — KILL CITY
JUST LIKE EDDIE — HEINZ
JUST LIKE FRED ASTAIRE — JAMES
JUST LIKE HEAVEN — The CURE
JUST LIKE HONEY — JESUS AND MARY CHAIN
JUST LIKE JESSE JAMES — CHER
JUST LIKE PARADISE — David Lee ROTH
(JUST LIKE) STARTING OVER — John LENNON
JUST LISTEN TO MY HEART — SPOTNICKS
JUST LOOKIN' — The CHARLATANS
JUST LOOKING — STEREOPHONICS
JUST LOSE IT — EMINEM
JUST LOVING YOU — Anita HARRIS
JUST MELLOW — RUTHLESS RAP ASSASSINS
JUST MY IMAGINATION (RUNNING AWAY
WITH ME) — The TEMPTATIONS
JUST MY IMAGINATION [A] — McGANNS
JUST MY SOUL RESPONDING —
Smokey ROBINSON
JUST ONE LOOK [A] — The HOLLIES
JUST ONE LOOK [A] —
FAITH, HOPE AND CHARITY
JUST ONE MORE KISS — RENÉE and RENATO
JUST ONE MORE NIGHT — YELLOW DOG
JUST ONE SMILE — Gene PITNEY
JUST OUT OF REACH (OF MY TWO EMPTY ARMS) —
Ken DODD
JUST OUTSIDE OF HEAVEN — H 20
JUST PLAY MUSIC — BIG AUDIO DYNAMITE
JUST PLAYIN' — JT PLAYAZ
JUST PUT YOUR HAND IN MINE —
SPACE COWBOY
JUST RIGHT — SOUL II SOUL
JUST ROUND —
A VERY GOOD FRIEND OF MINE
JUST SAY NO — GRANGE HILL CAST
JUST SAY YOU LOVE ME — MALACHI
JUST SEVEN NUMBERS (CAN STRAIGHTEN OUT
MY LIFE) — The FOUR TOPS
JUST SHOW ME HOW TO LOVE YOU —
Sarah BRIGHTMAN & the LONDON
SYMPHONY ORCHESTRA featuring José CURA
JUST SO YOU KNOW — AMERICAN HEAD CHARGE
JUST TAH LET YOU KNOW — EAZY-E
JUST TAKE MY HEART — MR BIG
JUST THE ONE —
LEVELLERS, special guest Joe STRUMMER

JUST THE TWO OF US [A] —
Grover WASHINGTON Jr
JUST THE TWO OF US [A] — Will SMITH
JUST THE WAY — Alfonzo HUNTER
JUST THE WAY I'M FEELING — FEEDER
JUST THE WAY IT IS — Lisa MOORISH
JUST THE WAY YOU ARE [A] — Billy JOEL
JUST THE WAY YOU ARE [A] — Barry WHITE
JUST THE WAY YOU ARE [B] — MILKY
JUST THE WAY YOU LIKE IT — S.O.S. BANDJUST
THIRTEEN — LURKERS
JUST THIS SIDE OF LOVE —
Malandra BURROWS
JUST TO BE CLOSE TO YOU —
The COMMODORES
JUST TO SEE HER — Smokey ROBINSON
JUST WALK IN MY SHOES —
Gladys KNIGHT and the PIPS
JUST WALKING IN THE RAIN — Johnnie RAY
JUST WANNA KNOW — Maxi PRIEST
JUST WANNA TOUCH ME —
FIDELFATTI featuring RONNETTE
JUST WANT TO LIVE — The OPEN
JUST WAVE HELLO — Charlotte CHURCH
JUST WHAT I ALWAYS WANTED — Mari WILSON
JUST WHAT I NEEDED — The CARS
JUST WHEN I NEEDED YOU MOST [A] —
Randy VANWARMER
JUST WHEN I NEEDED YOU MOST [A] —
Barbara JONES
JUST WHEN YOU'RE THINKIN' THINGS OVER —
The CHARLATANS
JUST WHO IS THE FIVE O'CLOCK HERO —
The JAM
(JUST) YOU AND ME — NEW VISION
JUSTIFIED AND ANCIENT —
The KLF guest vocals: Tammy WYNETTE
JUSTIFY MY LOVE — MADONNA
JUSTIFY THE RAIN — COSMIC ROUGH RIDERS
JUXTAPOZED WITH U —
SUPER FURRY ANIMALS
KA-CHING! — Shania TWAIN
KALEIDOSCOPE SKIES —
JAM & SPOON featuring PLAVKA
KAMICHI — HELL IS FOR HEROES
KAMIKAZE — KING ADORA
KANSAS CITY [A] — LITTLE RICHARD
KANSAS CITY [A] — Trini LOPEZ
KANSAS CITY STAR — Roger MILLER
KARA-KARA — NEW WORLD
KARAOKE QUEEN — CATATONIA
KARAOKE SOUL — Tom McRAE
KARMA CHAMELEON — CULTURE CLUB
KARMA HOTEL — SPOOKS
KARMA POLICE — RADIOHEAD
KARMACOMA — MASSIVE ATTACK
KARMADROME — POP WILL EAT ITSELF
KATE — Ben FOLDS FIVE
KATHLEEN — ROACHFORD
KATHLEEN (EP) — TINDERSTICKS
KAYLEIGH — MARILLION
KEEEP YOUR BODY WORKIN' — KLEEER
KEEP A KNOCKIN' — LITTLE RICHARD
KEEP AWAY FROM OTHER GIRLS —
Helen SHAPIRO
KEEP COMING BACK — Richard MARX
KEEP CONTROL — SONO
KEEP DOIN' IT — SHOWDOWN
KEEP EACH OTHER WARM — BUCKS FIZZ
(KEEP FEELING) FASCINATION —
HUMAN LEAGUE
KEEP FISHIN' — WEEZER
KEEP GIVIN' ME YOUR LOVE —
Ce Ce PENISTON
KEEP GIVING ME LOVE [A] — D TRAIN
KEEP GIVING ME LOVE [B] — BOMB THE BASS
KEEP HOPE ALIVE [A] — SERIAL DIVA
KEEP HOPE ALIVE [B] — CRYSTAL METHOD
KEEP IN TOUCH — FREEEZ
KEEP IN TOUCH (BODY TO BODY) —
SHADES OF LOVE
KEEP IT CLEAR — DTI
KEEP IT COMIN' (DANCE TILL YOU CAN'T DANCE NO
MORE) — C & C MUSIC
FACTORY / CLIVILLES & COLE
KEEP IT COMIN' LOVE —
KC and the SUNSHINE BAND
KEEP IT DARK — GENESIS
KEEP IT ON — Hannah JONES
KEEP IT OUT OF SIGHT —
Paul and Barry RYAN
KEEP IT TOGETHER — David GRANT
KEEP IT UP — SHARADA HOUSE GANG
KEEP LOVE NEW — Betty WRIGHT
KEEP LOVE TOGETHER [A] — LOVE TO INFINITY
KEEP LOVE TOGETHER [B] —
SODA CLUB featuring Andrea ANATOLA
KEEP ME A SECRET — Ainslie HENDERSON
KEEP ME FROM THE COLD — Curtis STIGERS
KEEP ME IN MIND — BOY GEORGE
KEEP ON [A] — Bruce CHANNEL
KEEP ON [B] — CABARET VOLTAIRE
KEEP ON BELIEVING — GRAND PRIX
KEEP ON BURNING — Edwyn COLLINS
KEEP ON DANCIN' — GARY'S GANG
KEEP ON DANCIN' (LET'S GO) —
PERPETUAL MOTION

KEEP ON DANCING — BAY CITY ROLLERS
KEEP ON JAMMIN' — Willie HUTCH
KEEP ON JUMPIN' [A] —
LISA MARIE EXPERIENCE
KEEP ON JUMPIN' [A] — Todd TERRY featuring
Martha WASH and Jocelyn BROWN
KEEPIN' ON [A] — REDSKINS
KEEP ON KEEPIN' ON [B] —
MC LYTE featuring XSCAPE
KEEP ON LOVING YOU — REO SPEEDWAGON
KEEP ON MOVIN' [A] — SOUL II SOUL
KEEP ON MOVIN' [B] — FIVE
KEEP ON MOVING [C] —
Bob MARLEY & the WAILERS
KEEP ON PUMPIN' IT — VISIONMASTERS
with Tony KING and Kylie MINOGUE
KEEP ON PUSHING OUR LOVE —
NIGHTCRAWLERS featuring John
REID and Alysha WARREN
KEEP ON RUNNIN' (TILL YOU BURN) —
UK SUBS
KEEP ON RUNNING [A] —
Spencer DAVIS GROUP
KEEP ON RUNNING [A] — John ALFORD
(KEEP ON) SHINING — LOVELAND featuring
the voice of Rachel McFARLANE
KEEP ON TRUCKIN' — Eddie KENDRICKS
KEEP ON WALKIN' — Ce Ce PENISTON
KEEP PUSHIN' [A] — CLOCK
KEEP PUSHIN' [B] —
Boris DLUGOSCH presents BOOOM
KEEP REACHING OUT FOR LOVE — LINER
KEEP SEARCHIN' (WE'LL FOLLOW THE SUN) —
Del SHANNON
KEEP STEPPIN' — OMAR
KEEP TALKING — PINK FLOYD
KEEP THE CUSTOMER SATISFIED —
Marsha HUNT
KEEP THE FAITH — BON JOVI
KEEP THE FIRE BURNIN' —
Dan HARTMAN starring Loleatta HOLLOWAY
KEEP THE FIRES BURNING — CLOCK
KEEP THE HOME FIRES BURNING —
The BLUETONES
KEEP THE MUSIC STRONG — BIZARRE INC
KEEP THEIR HEADS RINGIN' — DR DRE
KEEP THIS FREQUENCY CLEAR — DTI
KEEP WARM — JINNY
KEEP WHAT YA GOT — Ian BROWN
KEEP YOUR EYE ON ME — Herb ALPERT
KEEP YOUR HANDS OFF MY BABY —
LITTLE EVA
KEEP YOUR HANDS TO YOURSELF —
GEORGIA SATELLITES
KEEP YOUR LOVE — PARTIZAN
KEEP YOUR WORRIES — GURU'S
JAZZMATAZZ featuring Angie STONE
KEEPER OF THE CASTLE — The FOUR TOPS
KEEPIN' LOVE NEW — Howard JOHNSON
KEEPIN' THE FAITH — DE LA SOUL
KEEPING A RENDEZVOUS — BUDGIE
KEEPING SECRETS — SWITCH
KEEPING THE DREAM ALIVE — FREIHEIT
KEEPS ME WONDERING WHY —
Steve Miller BAND
KELLY — Wayne GIBSON
KELLY WATCH THE STARS — AIR
KELLY'S HEROES — BLACK GRAPE
KENNEDY — WEDDING PRESENT
KENTUCKY RAIN — Elvis PRESLEY
KERNKRAFT 400 — ZOMBIE NATION
KERRY KERRY — CINERAMA
THE KETCHUP SONG (ASEREJE) —
LAS KETCHUP
KEVIN CARTER — MANIC STREET PREACHERS
KEWPIE DOLL [A] — Frankie VAUGHAN
KEWPIE DOLL [A] — Perry COMO
THE KEY [A] — SENSER
THE KEY [B] — Matt GOSS
KEY LARGO — Bertie HIGGINS
THE KEY THE SECRET —
URBAN COOKIE COLLECTIVE
KEY TO MY LIFE — BOYZONE
KICK IN THE EYE — BAUHAUS
KICK IN THE EYE (EP) — BAUHAUS
KICK IT [A] — NITZER EBB
KICK IT [B] — REGGAE BOYZ
KICK IT [C] —
PEACHES featuring Iggy POP
KICK IT IN — SIMPLE MINDS
KICKIN' HARD — KLUBBHEADS
KICKIN' IN THE BEAT — Pamela FERNANDEZ
KICKIN' UP DUST — LITTLE ANGELS
KICKING MY HEART AROUND —
BLACK CROWES
KICKIN' UP THE LEAVES — Mark WYNTER
KICKS (EP) — UK SUBS
KID [A] — The PRETENDERS
KID 2000 [A] —
HYBRID featuring Chrissie HYNDE
KIDDIO — Brook BENTON
KIDS — Robbie WILLIAMS / Kylie MINOGUE
THE KIDS ARE ALRIGHT — The WHO
THE KIDS ARE BACK — TWISTED SISTER
THE KIDS AREN'T ALRIGHT — The OFFSPRING
KIDS IN AMERICA — Kim WILDE
THE KID'S LAST FIGHT — Frankie LAINE

KIDS OF THE CENTURY — HELLOWEEN
KIDS ON THE STREET — ANGELIC UPSTARTS
KIKI RIRI BOOM — SHAFT
KILLAMANGIRO — BABY SHAMBLES
KILL ALL HIPPIES — PRIMAL SCREAM
KILL THE KING — RAINBOW
KILL THE POOR — DEAD KENNEDYS
KILL YOUR TELEVISION —
NED'S ATOMIC DUSTBIN
KILLED BY DEATH — MOTÖRHEAD
KILLER [A] — ADAMSKI
KILLER (EP) [A] — SEAL
KILLER [A] — ATB
KILLER ON THE LOOSE — THIN LIZZY
KILLER QUEEN — QUEEN
KILLERS LIVE (EP) — THIN LIZZY
KILLIN' TIME — Tina COUSINS
KILLING IN THE NAME —
RAGE AGAINST THE MACHINE
THE KILLING JAR —
SIOUXSIE and the BANSHEES
KILLING ME SOFTLY WITH HIS SONG [A] —
Roberta FLACK
KILLING ME SOFTLY [A] — The FUGEES
THE KILLING MOON —
ECHO and the BUNNYMEN
THE KILLING OF GEORGIE — Rod STEWART
A KIND OF CHRISTMAS CARD —
Morten HARKET
A KIND OF MAGIC — QUEEN
KINDA LOVE — DARIUS
KINDA NEW — SPEKTRUM
KINETIC — GOLDEN GIRLS
KINETIC '99 — GOLDEN GIRLS
KING — UB40
THE KING AND QUEEN OF AMERICA —
EURYTHMICS
KING CREOLE — Elvis PRESLEY
KING FOR A DAY [A] — THOMPSON TWINS
KING FOR A DAY [B] — JAMIROQUAI
KING IN A CATHOLIC STYLE (WAKE UP) —
CHINA CRISIS
THE KING IS DEAD — GO WEST
THE KING IS HALF UNDRESSED — JELLYFISH
THE KING IS HERE — 45 KING
KING KONG — Terry LIGHTFOOT
and his NEW ORLEANS JAZZMEN
KING MIDAS IN REVERSE — The HOLLIES
KING OF CLOWNS — Neil SEDAKA
KING OF DREAMS — DEEP PURPLE
KING OF EMOTION — BIG COUNTRY
KING OF KINGS — Ezz RECO and
the LAUNCHERS with Boysie GRANT
THE KING OF KISSINGDOM — MY LIFE STORY
KING OF LOVE — Dave EDMUNDS
KING OF MISERY — HONEYCRACK
KING OF MY CASTLE — WAMDUE PROJECT
KING OF NEW YORK — FUN LOVIN' CRIMINALS
KING OF PAIN — The POLICE
THE KING OF ROCK 'N' ROLL —
PREFAB SPROUT
KING OF SNAKE — UNDERWORLD
KING OF SORROW — SADE
KING OF THE COPS — Billy HOWARD
KING OF THE DANCEHALL — BEENIE MAN
KING OF THE KERB — ECHOBELLY
KING OF THE NEW YORK STREET — DION
KING OF THE ROAD — Roger MILLER
KING OF THE ROAD (EP) — The PROCLAIMERS
KING OF THE RUMBLING SPIRES — T. REX
THE KING OF WISHFUL THINKING — GO WEST
KING ROCKER — GENERATION X
KING WITHOUT A CROWN — ABC
KINGDOM — ULTRAMARINE
KINGS AND QUEENS — KILLING JOKE
KING'S CALL — Philip LYNOTT
KINGS OF THE WILD FRONTIER —
ADAM and the ANTS
KINGSTON TOWN — UB40
KINKY AFRO — HAPPY MONDAYS
KINKY BOOTS —
Patrick MacNEE and Honor BLACKMAN
KINKY LOVE — PALE SAINTS
KIKI RIRI BOOM — SHAFT
KISS [A] — Dean MARTIN
KISS [B] — PRINCE
KISS [A] — AGE OF CHANCE
KISS [B] — ART OF NOISE featuring Tom JONES
KISS AND SAY GOODBYE — MANHATTANS
KISS AND TELL [A] — Bryan FERRY
KISS AND TELL [B] — BROWNSTONE
KISS FROM A ROSE — SEAL
KISS KISS — Holly VALANCE
KISS LIKE ETHER — Claudia BRÜCKEN
KISS ME [A] — Stephen 'Tin Tin' DUFFY
KISS ME [B] — SIXPENCE NONE THE RICHER
KISS ME ANOTHER — Georgia GIBBS
KISS ME DEADLY — Lita FORD
KISS ME GOODBYE — Petula CLARK
KISS ME HONEY HONEY, KISS ME —
Shirley BASSEY
KISS ME QUICK — Elvis PRESLEY
KISS MY EYES — Bob SINCLAR
KISS OF LIFE [A] — SADE
KISS OF LIFE [B] — SUPERGRASS
KISS ON MY LIST —
Daryl HALL and John OATES

KISS ON THE LIPS — The DUALERS
KISS THAT FROG — Peter GABRIEL
KISS THE BRIDE — Elton JOHN
KISS THE DIRT (FALLING DOWN THE
MOUNTAIN) — INXS
KISS THE GIRL — Peter ANDRE
KISS THE RAIN — Billie MYERS
KISS THEM FOR ME —
SIOUXSIE and the BANSHEES
KISS THIS THING GOODBYE —
DEL AMITRI
KISS (WHEN THE SUN DON'T SHINE) —
The VENGABOYS
KISS YOU ALL OVER [A] — EXILE
KISS YOU ALL OVER [A] — NO MERCY
KISSES IN THE MOONLIGHT —
George BENSON
KISSES ON THE WIND —
Neneh CHERRY
KISSES SWEETER THAN WINE [A] —
Jimmie RODGERS
KISSES SWEETER THAN WINE [A] —
Frankie VAUGHAN
KISSIN' COUSINS — Elvis PRESLEY
KISSIN' IN THE BACK ROW OF THE MOVIES —
The DRIFTERS
KISSIN' YOU — TOTAL
KISSING A FOOL — George MICHAEL
KISSING GATE — Sam BROWN
KISSING WITH CONFIDENCE — Will POWERS
KITE —
Simon DUPREE and the BIG SOUND
KITSCH — Barry RYAN
KITTY — Cat STEVENS
KLACTOVEESEDSTEIN —
BLUE RONDO A LA TURK
KLUB KOLLABORATIONS — BK
KLUBBHOPPING — KLUBBHEADS
KNEE DEEP AND DOWN — RAIN BAND
KNEE DEEP IN THE BLUES — Guy MITCHELL
KNEE DEEP IN THE BLUES [A] —
Tommy STEELE
KNIFE EDGE — The ALARM
KNIVES OUT — RADIOHEAD
KNOCK KNOCK WHO'S THERE — Mary HOPKIN
KNOCK ME OUT — GARY'S GANG
KNOCK ON WOOD [A] — Eddie FLOYD
KNOCK ON WOOD [A] — Otis REDDING
KNOCK ON WOOD [A] — David BOWIE
KNOCK ON WOOD [A] — Amii STEWART
KNOCK OUT — TRIPLE 8
KNOCK THREE TIMES — DAWN
KNOCKED IT OFF — B.A. ROBERTSON
KNOCKED OUT — Paula ABDUL
KNOCKIN' ON HEAVEN'S DOOR [A] —
Bob DYLAN
KNOCKIN' ON HEAVEN'S DOOR [A] —
Eric CLAPTON
KNOCKIN' ON HEAVEN'S DOOR [A] —
GUNS N' ROSES
KNOCKIN' ON HEAVEN'S DOOR [A] —
DUNBLANE
KNOCKING AT YOUR BACK DOOR —
DEEP PURPLE
KNOCKS ME OFF MY FEET — Donell JONES
KNOW BY NOW — Robert PALMER
KNOW YOU WANNA — 3RD EDGE
KNOW YOUR RIGHTS — The CLASH
KNOWING ME, KNOWING YOU — ABBA
K.O. — SMUJJI
KOKOMO [A] — The BEACH BOYS
KOKOMO [A] — Adam GREEN
KOMMOTION — Duane EDDY and the REBELS
KON-TIKI — The SHADOWS
KOOCHIE RYDER — FREAKY REALISTIC
KOOCHY — Armand VAN HELDEN
KOOKIE KOOKIE (LEND ME YOUR COMB) —
Connie STEVENS
KOOKIE LITTLE PARADISE — Frankie VAUGHAN
KOOL IN THE KAFTAN — B.A. ROBERTSON
KOOTCHI — Neneh CHERRY
KOREAN BODEGA — FUN LOVIN' CRIMINALS
KOWALSKI — PRIMAL SCREAM
KRUPA — APOLLO FOUR FORTY
KU KLUX KLAN — STEEL PULSE
KUMBAYA — SANDPIPERS
KUNG FU — ASH
KUNG FU FIGHTING [A] — Carl DOUGLAS
KUNG FU FIGHTING [A] —
BUS STOP featuring Carl DOUGLAS
KUNG-FU — 187 LOCKDOWN
KUT IT — RED EYE
KYRIE — MR MISTER
KYRILA (EP) — Demis ROUSSOS
LA — MARC et CLAUDE
LA BAMBA [A] — Ritchie VALENS
LA BAMBA [A] — LOS LOBOS
LA BOOGA ROOGA — SURPRISE SISTERS
LA BREEZE — SIMIAN
L.A. CONNECTION — RAINBOW
LA DEE DAH — Jackie DENNIS
LA DERNIÈRE VALSE — Mireille MATHIEU
LA-DI-DA — SAD CAFE
LA DONNA E MOBILE — José CARRERAS
featuring Plácido DOMINGO and
Luciano PAVAROTTI with MEHTA

LA FEMME ACCIDENT —
ORCHESTRAL MANOEUVRES IN THE DARK
LA FOLIE — The STRANGLERS
LA ISLA BONITA — MADONNA
LA LA LA [A] — MASSIEL
LA LA LA [B] — Naila BOSS
LA LA LA HEY HEY —
The OUTHERE BROTHERS
LA LA LAND — GREEN VELVET
LA-LA MEANS I LOVE YOU [A] — DELFONICS
LA LA (MEANS I LOVE YOU) [A] —
SWING OUT SISTER
LA LUNA [A] — Belinda CARLISLE
LA LUNA [B] — MOVIN' MELODIES
LA MER (BEYOND THE SEA) — Bobby DARIN
LA MOUCHE — CASSIUS
LA MUSICA — RUFF DRIVERZ
LA PLUME DE MA TANTE — HUGO and LUIGI
LA PRIMAVERA — SASH!
THE L.A. RUN — CARVELLS
LA SERENISSIMA (THEME FROM 'VENICE
IN PERIL') [A] — RONDO VENEZIANO
LA SERENISSIMA [A] — DNA
L.A. TODAY —
Alex GOLD featuring Philip OAKEY
LA TRISTESSE DURERA (SCREAM TO A SIGH) —
MANIC STREET PREACHERS
À LA VIE, À L'AMOUR — Jakie QUARTZ
LA VIE EN ROSE — Grace JONES
L.A. WOMAN — Billy IDOL
LA YENKA — JOHNNY and CHARLEY
LABELLED WITH LOVE — SQUEEZE
LABOUR OF LOVE — HUE and CRY
THE LABRYINTH — MOOGWAI
LADIES [A] — MANTRONIX
LADIES MAN — The D4
LADIES NIGHT [A] — KOOL and the GANG
LADIES NIGHT [A] — ATOMIC KITTEN
featuring KOOL and the GANG
LADY [A] — WHISPERS
LADY [B] — Kenny ROGERS
LADY [C] — D'ANGELO
LADY BARBARA — HERMAN'S HERMITS
LADY D'ARBANVILLE — Cat STEVENS
LADY ELEANOR — LINDISFARNE
LADY GODIVA — PETER and GORDON
LADY (HEAR ME TONIGHT) — MODJO
THE LADY IN RED — Chris DE BURGH
LADY IS A TRAMP — Buddy GRECO
LADY JANE [A] — David GARRICK
LADY JANE [A] — Tony MERRICK
LADY LET IT LIE — FISH
LADY LOVE BUG — Clodagh RODGERS
LADY LOVE (ONE MORE TIME) —
George BENSON
LADY LUCK [A] — Lloyd PRICE
LADY LUCK [B] — Rod STEWART
LADY LYNDA — The BEACH BOYS
LADY MADONNA — The BEATLES
LADY MARMALADE (VOULEZ-VOUS COUCHER
AVEC MOI CE SOIR?) [A] — LaBELLE
LADY MARMALADE [A] — ALL SAINTS
LADY MARMALADE [A] —
Christina AGUILERA, LIL' KIM, MYA and PINK
LADY ROSE — MUNGO JERRY
LADY SHINE (SHINE ON) —
THS — THE HORN SECTION
LADY WILLPOWER —
UNION GAP featuring Gary PUCKETT
LADY WRITER — DIRE STRAITS
LADY (YOU BRING ME UP) [A] —
The COMMODORES
LADY (YOU BRING ME UP) [A] —
SIMPLY SMOOTH
LADYBIRD — Nancy SINATRA
THE LADYBOY IS MINE — STUNTMASTERZ
LADYFINGERS — LUSCIOUS JACKSON
LADYFLASH — The GO! TEAM
LADYKILLERS — LUSH
LADYSHAVE — GUS GUS
LAGARTIJA NICK — BAUHAUS
LAID — JAMES
LAID SO LOW (TEARS ROLL DOWN) —
TEARS FOR FEARS
LAILA — TAZ and STEREO NATION
LAKINI'S JUICE — LIVE
LAMBADA — KAOMA
LAMBORGHINI — SHUT UP AND DANCE
LAMENT — ULTRAVOX
LAMPLIGHT — David ESSEX
LANA — Roy ORBISON
LAND OF A MILLION DRUMS — OUTKAST
LAND OF CONFUSION — GENESIS
LAND OF HOPE AND GLORY — EX PISTOLS
THE LAND OF MAKE BELIEVE [A] —
BUCKS FIZZ
THE LAND OF MAKE BELIEVE [A] — ALLSTARS
LAND OF 1000 DANCES — Wilson PICKETT
THE LAND OF RING DANG DO — KING KURT

LAND OF THE LIVING [A] — Kristine W
LAND OF THE LIVING [B] — MILK INC
LANDSLIDE [A] — Olivia NEWTON-JOHN
LANDSLIDE [B] — HARMONIX
LANDSLIDE [C] — SPIN CITY
LANDSLIDE [D] — DIXIE CHICKS
LANDSLIDE OF LOVE — TRANSVISION VAMP

THE LANE — ICE-T
THE LANGUAGE OF LOVE —
John D LOUDERMILK
LANGUAGE OF VIOLENCE —
DISPOSABLE HEROES OF HIPHOPRISY
LAP OF LUXURY — JETHRO TULL
LAPDANCE —
N*E*R*D featuring Lee HARVEY and VITA
LARGER THAN LIFE — BACKSTREET BOYS
LAS PALABRAS DE AMOR — QUEEN
LAS VEGAS — Tony CHRISTIE
LASER LOVE [A] — T. REX
LASER LOVE [B] — AFTER THE FIRE
THE LAST BEAT OF MY HEART —
SIOUXSIE and the BANSHEES
LAST CHANCE — CHINA DRUM
LAST CHRISTMAS [A] — WHAM!
LAST CHRISTMAS [A] — WHIGFIELD
LAST CHRISTMAS [A] — ALIEN VOICES
featuring The THREE DEGREES
LAST CUP OF SORROW — FAITH NO MORE
LAST DANCE — Donna SUMMER
LAST DAY — SILVER SUN
LAST DROP — Kevin LYTTLE
THE LAST FAREWELL [A] — Roger WHITTAKER
THE LAST FAREWELL [A] — Ship's Company and Royal
Marine Band of HMS ARK ROYAL
THE LAST FAREWELL [A] — Elvis PRESLEY
LAST FILM — KISSING THE PINK
LAST GOODBYE [A] — Jeff BUCKLEY
LAST GOODBYE [B] — ATOMIC KITTEN
LAST HORIZON — Brian MAY
LAST KISS — PEARL JAM
THE LAST KISS — David CASSIDY
LAST NIGHT [A] — The MERSEYBEATS
LAST NIGHT [B] — KID 'N' PLAY
LAST NIGHT [C] — AZ YET
LAST NIGHT [D] — Gloria GAYNOR
LAST NIGHT A DJ BLEW MY MIND —
FAB FOR featuring Robert OWENS
LAST NIGHT A DJ SAVED MY LIFE [A] — INDEEP
LAST NIGHT A DJ SAVED MY LIFE [A] —
COLD JAM featuring GRACE
LAST NIGHT A DJ SAVED MY LIFE [A] —
SYLK 130
LAST NIGHT A DJ SAVED MY LIFE [A] —
Seamus HAJI
LAST NIGHT ANOTHER SOLDIER —
ANGELIC UPSTARTS
LAST NIGHT AT DANCELAND —
Randy CRAWFORD
LAST NIGHT I DREAMT THAT SOMEBODY
LOVED ME — The SMITHS
LAST NIGHT IN SOHO — Dave DEE,
DOZY, BEAKY, MICK and TICH
LAST NIGHT ON EARTH — U2
LAST NIGHT ON THE BACK PORCH —
Alma COGAN
LAST NIGHT WAS MADE FOR LOVE —
Billy FURY
LAST NITE [A] — The STROKES
LAST NITE [A] — VITAMIN C
LAST OF THE FAMOUS INTERNATIONAL PLAYBOYS —
MORRISSEY
LAST ONE STANDING — GIRL THING
LAST PLANE (ONE WAY TICKET) —
Clint EASTWOOD and General SAINT
LAST RESORT — PAPA ROACH
LAST RHYTHM — LAST RHYTHM
THE LAST SONG [A] — Elton JOHN
THE LAST SONG [B] — ALL-AMERICAN REJECTS
LAST STOP: THIS TOWN — EELS
LAST SUMMER — LOSTPROPHETS
LAST THING ON MY MIND [A] — BANANARAMA
LAST THING ON MY MIND [A] — STEPS
LAST THING ON MY MIND [A] —
Ronan KEATING & LeAnn RIMES
THE LAST TIME [A] — The ROLLING STONES
THE LAST TIME [A] — The WHO
THE LAST TIME [B] — PARADISE LOST
LAST TIME FOREVER — SQUEEZE
LAST TIME I SAW HIM — Diana ROSS
LAST TO KNOW — PINK
LAST TRAIN HOME — LOSTPROPHETS
LAST TRAIN TO CLARKSVILLE — The MONKEES
LAST TRAIN TO LONDON —
ELECTRIC LIGHT ORCHESTRA
LAST TRAIN TO SAN FERNANDO — Johnny
DUNCAN and the BLUE GRASS BOYS
LAST TRAIN TO TRANCENTRAL — The KLF
THE LAST WALTZ — Engelbert HUMPERDINCK
LATE AT NIGHT — FUTURESHOCK
LATE IN THE DAY — SUPERGRASS
LATE IN THE EVENING — Paul SIMON
LATELY [A] — Rudy GRANT
LATELY [A] — Stevie WONDER
LATELY [B] — SKUNK ANANSIE
LATELY [C] — DIVINE
LATELY [C] — Samantha MUMBA
LATELY [D] — Lisa SCOTT-LEE
THE LATIN THEME — Carl COX
LATIN THING — LATIN THING
LATINO HOUSE — MIRAGE
LAUGH AT ME — SONNY
THE LAUGHING GNOME — David BOWIE
LAUGHTER IN THE RAIN — Neil SEDAKA
THE LAUNCH — DJ JEAN

LAUNDROMAT — NIVEA
LAURA [A] — Nick HEYWARD
LAURA [B] — Jimmy NAIL
LAURA [C] — NEK
LAURA [D] — SCISSOR SISTERS
LAUREL AND HARDY — The EQUALS
LAVA — SILVER SUN
LAVENDER — MARILLION
LAW OF THE LAND — The TEMPTATIONS
LAW UNTO MYSELF — KONKRETE
LAWDY MISS CLAWDY — Elvis PRESLEY
LAWNCHAIRS — OUR DAUGHTER'S WEDDING
LAY ALL YOUR LOVE ON ME — ABBA
LAY BACK IN THE ARMS OF SOMEONE — SMOKIE
LAY DOWN — STRAWBS
LAY DOWN SALLY — Eric CLAPTON
LAY DOWN YOUR ARMS [A] — Anne SHELTON
LAY DOWN YOUR ARMS [B] —
Belinda CARLISLE
LAY LADY LAY — Bob DYLAN
LAY LOVE ON YOU — Luisa FERNANDEZ
LAY YOUR HANDS ON ME [A] —
THOMPSON TWINS
LAY YOUR HANDS ON ME [B] — BON JOVI
LAY YOUR LOVE ON ME [A] — RACEY
LAY YOUR LOVE ON ME [B] — ROACHFORD
LAYLA — Eric CLAPTON
LAZARUS — BOO RADLEYS
LAZY [A] — SUEDE
LAZY [B] — X-PRESS 2 featuring David BYRNE
LAZY BONES — Jonathan KING
LAZY DAYS — Robbie WILLIAMS
LAZY LINE PAINTER JANE —
BELLE & SEBASTIAN
LAZY LOVER — SUPERNATURALS
LAZY RIVER — Bobby DARIN
LAZY SUNDAY — The SMALL FACES
LAZYITIS — ONE ARMED BOXER —
HAPPY MONDAYS and Karl DENVER
LE DISC JOCKEY — ENCORE
LE FREAK — CHIC
LE VOIE LE SOLEIL — SUBLIMINAL CUTS
LEADER OF THE PACK [A] — SHANGRI-LAS
LEADER OF THE PACK [A] — TWISTED SISTER
LEADER OF THE PACK [A] —
JOAN COLLINS FAN CLUB
LEAFY MYSTERIES — Paul WELLER
LEAN BACK — TERROR SQUAD featuring
FAT JOE (aka Joey Crack) & REMY
LEAN ON ME [A] — Bill WITHERS
LEAN ON ME [A] — MUD
LEAN ON ME [A] — CLUB NOUVEAU
LEAN ON ME [A] — Michael BOLTON
LEAN ON ME (WITH THE FAMILY) —
2-4 FAMILY
LEAN ON ME (AH-LI-AYO) — RED BOX
LEAN ON ME I WON'T FALL OVER — CARTER —
THE UNSTOPPABLE SEX MACHINE
LEAN ON YOU — Cliff RICHARD
LEAN PERIOD — ORANGE JUICE
LEAP OF FAITH — Bruce SPRINGSTEEN
LEAP UP AND DOWN (WAVE YOUR KNICKERS
IN THE AIR) — ST CECILIA
LEARN TO FLY — FOO FIGHTERS
LEARNIN' THE BLUES — Frank SINATRA
LEARNIN' THE GAME — Buddy HOLLY
LEARNING TO FLY [A] —
Tom PETTY and the HEARTBREAKERS
LEARNING TO FLY [B] — MOTHER'S PRIDE
LEAVE A LIGHT ON — Belinda CARLISLE
LEAVE A LITTLE LOVE — LULU
LEAVE A TENDER MOMENT ALONE — Billy JOEL
LEAVE 'EM SOMETHING TO DESIRE — SPRINKLER
LEAVE (GET OUT) — JOJO
LEAVE HOME — The CHEMICAL BROTHERS
LEAVE IN SILENCE — DEPECHE MODE
LEAVE IT [A] — Mike McGEAR
LEAVE IT [B] — YES
LEAVE IT ALONE — LIVING COLOUR
LEAVE IT UP TO ME — Aaron CARTER
LEAVE ME ALONE — Michael JACKSON
LEAVE RIGHT NOW — Will YOUNG
LEAVE THEM ALL BEHIND — RIDE
LEAVIN' [A] — Tony RICH PROJECT
LEAVIN' [B] — Shelby LYNNE
LEAVIN' ON A JET PLANE —
PETER, PAUL and MARY
LEAVING HERE — BIRDS
LEAVING LAS VEGAS — Sheryl CROW
LEAVING ME NOW — LEVEL 42
LEAVING NEW YORK — R.E.M.
LEAVING ON A JET PLANE —
Chantal KREVIAZUK
LEAVING ON THE MIDNIGHT TRAIN —
Nick STRAKER BAND
THE LEAVING SONG PT.2 — AFI
THE LEBANON — HUMAN LEAGUE
LEEDS, LEEDS, LEEDS — LEEDS UNITED FC
LEEDS UNITED — LEEDS UNITED FC
LEFT BANK — Winifred ATWELL
LEFT BEHIND — SLIPKNOT
LEFT OF CENTER —
Suzanne VEGA featuring Joe JACKSON
LEFT OUTSIDE ALONE — ANASTACIA
LEFT TO MY OWN DEVICES — PET SHOP BOYS
LEGACY — Mad COBRA featuring Richie STEPHENS
THE LEGACY — PUSH

LEGACY (EP) – MANSUN
LEGACY (SHOW ME LOVE) – SPACE BROTHERS
LEGAL MAN – BELLE & SEBASTIAN
A LEGAL MATTER – The WHO
LEGEND OF A COWGIRL – Imani COPPOLA
LEGEND OF THE GOLDEN SNAKE – DEPTH CHARGE
THE LEGEND OF XANADU – Dave DEE, DOZY, BEAKY, MICK and TICH
LEGENDS OF THE DARK BLACK PART 2 – WILDCHILD
LEGO SKANGA – Rupie EDWARDS
LEGS [A] – ART OF NOISE
LEGS [B] – ZZ TOP
LEMMINGS – SFX
LEMON TREE – FOOL'S GARDEN
LENINGRAD – Billy JOEL
LENNY – SUPERGRASS
LENNY AND TERENCE – CARTER – THE UNSTOPPABLE SEX MACHINE
LENNY VALENTINO – The AUTEURS
LEONARD NIMOY – FREAKY REALISTIC
LEROY – WHEATUS
LES BICYCLETTES DE BELSIZE – Engelbert HUMPERDINCK
LES FLEUR – 4 HERO
L'ESPERANZA [A] – Sven VATH
L'ESPERANZA [B] – AIRSCAPE
LESS TALK MORE ACTION – Tim DELUXE
LESSON ONE – Russ CONWAY
LESSONS IN LOVE [A] – ALLISONS
LESSONS IN LOVE [B] – LEVEL 42
LESSONS LEARNED FROM ROCKY I TO ROCKY III – CORNERSHOP
LET A BOY CRY – GALA
LET A GOOD THING GO – Gemma HAYES
LET 'EM IN [A] – Paul McCARTNEY
LET 'EM IN [A] – Billy PAUL
LET 'EM IN [A] – SHINEHEAD
LET FOREVER BE – The CHEMICAL BROTHERS
LET GO WITH THE FLOW – The BEAUTIFUL SOUTH
LET HER CRY – HOOTIE & THE BLOWFISH
LET HER DOWN EASY – Terence Trent D'ARBY
LET HER FALL – THEN JERICO
LET HER FEEL IT – SIMPLICIOUS
LET HER GO – STRAWBERRY SWITCHBLADE
LET IT ALL BLOW – DAZZ BAND
LET IT ALL HANG OUT – Jonathan KING
LET IT BE [A] – The BEATLES
LET IT BE [A] – FERRY AID
LET IT BE ME [A] – The EVERLY BROTHERS
LET IT BE ME [A] – JUSTIN
LET IT BE WITH YOU – BELOUIS SOME
LET IT FLOW – SPIRITUALIZED
LET IT LAST – Carleen ANDERSON
LET IT LIVE – HAVEN
LET IT LOOSE – LEMON TREES
LET IT RAIN [A] – UFO
LET IT RAIN [B] – EAST 17
LET IT RAIN [C] – 4 STRINGS
LET IT REIGN – INNER CITY
LET IT RIDE – Todd TERRY PROJECT
LET IT ROCK [A] – Chuck BERRY
LET IT ROCK [A] – The ROLLING STONES
LET IT ROLL – RAZE presents Doug LAZY
LET IT SLIDE [A] – MUDHONEY
LET IT SLIDE [B] – ARIEL
LET IT SWING – BOBBYSOCKS
LET LOVE BE THE LEADER – FM
LET LOVE BE YOUR ENERGY – Robbie WILLIAMS
LET LOVE LEAD THE WAY – SPICE GIRLS
LET LOVE RULE – Lenny KRAVITZ
LET LOVE SHINE – AMOS
LET LOVE SPEAK UP ITSELF – The BEAUTIFUL SOUTH
LET ME BE – BLACK DIAMOND
LET ME BE THE NUMBER 1 (LOVE OF YOUR LIFE) – Dooley SILVERSPOON
LET ME BE THE ONE [A] – The SHADOWS
LET ME BE THE ONE [B] – FIVE STAR
LET ME BE THE ONE [C] – BLESSID UNION OF SOULS
LET ME BE THE ONE [D] – MINT CONDITION
LET ME BE THE ONE [E] – Cliff RICHARD
LET ME BE YOUR FANTASY – BABY D
(LET ME BE YOUR) TEDDY BEAR – Elvis PRESLEY
LET ME BE YOUR UNDERWEAR – CLUB 69
LET ME BE YOUR WINGS – Barry MANILOW
LET ME BE YOURS – FIVE STAR
LET ME BLOW YA MIND – EVE featuring Gwen STEFANI
LET ME CLEAR MY THROAT [A] – DJ KOOL
LET ME CLEAR MY THROAT [B] – PUBLIC DOMAIN
LET ME COME ON HOME – Otis REDDING
LET ME CRY ON YOUR SHOULDER – Ken DODD
LET ME DOWN EASY – The STRANGLERS
LET ME ENTERTAIN YOU – Robbie WILLIAMS
LET ME FLY – Darren STYLES & Mark BREEZE present INFEXTIOUS
LET ME GO – HEAVEN 17
LET ME GO HOME – ALL ABOUT EVE
LET ME GO LOVER [A] – Teresa BREWER
LET ME GO LOVER [A] – Dean MARTIN
LET ME GO LOVER [A] – Ruby MURRAY
LET ME GO LOVER [A] – Joan WEBER
LET ME GO LOVER [A] – Kathy KIRBY
LET ME HEAR YOU SAY 'OLE OLE' – The OUTHERE BROTHERS
LET ME IN [A] – The OSMONDS
LET ME IN [A] – OTT
LET ME IN [B] – YOUNG BUCK
LET ME INTRODUCE YOU TO THE FAMILY – The STRANGLERS
LET ME KISS YOU [A] – MORRISSEY
LET ME KISS YOU [A] – Nancy SINATRA
LET ME KNOW [A] – JUNIOR
LET ME KNOW [B] – Maxi PRIEST
LET ME KNOW (I HAVE A RIGHT) – Gloria GAYNOR
LET ME LET GO – Faith HILL
LET ME LIVE – QUEEN
LET ME LOVE YOU FOR TONIGHT – KARIYA
LET ME MOVE ON – GENE
LET ME RIDE – DR DRE
LET ME ROCK YOU – KANDIDATE
LET ME SEE – MORCHEEBA
LET ME SHOW YOU [A] – K-KLASS
LET ME SHOW YOU [B] – CAMISRA
LET ME SHOW YOU [C] – Tony MOMRELLE
LET ME TAKE YOU THERE – Betty BOO
LET ME TALK – EARTH WIND AND FIRE
LET ME TRY AGAIN – Tammy JONES
LET ME WAKE UP IN YOUR ARMS – LULU
LET MY LOVE OPEN YOUR DOOR – Pete TOWNSHEND
LET MY NAME BE SORROW – Mary HOPKIN
LET MY PEOPLE GO (PART 1) – WINANS
LET MY PEOPLE GO-GO – RAINMAKERS
LET ROBESON SING – MANIC STREET PREACHERS
LET SOMEBODY LOVE YOU – Keni BURKE
LET THE BASS KICK – 2 FOR JOY
LET THE BEAT CONTROL YOUR BODY – 2 UNLIMITED
LET THE BEAT HIT 'EM [A] – LISA LISA
LET THE BEAT HIT 'EM [A] – SHENA
LET THE DAY BEGIN – CALL
LET THE DRUMS SPEAK – MIGHTY DUB KATS
LET THE FLAME BURN BRIGHTER – Graham KENDRICK
LET THE FREAK – BIG RON
LET THE GOOD TIMES ROLL – SHEEP ON DRUGS
LET THE HAPPINESS IN – David SYLVIAN
LET THE HEALING BEGIN – Joe COCKER
LET THE HEARTACHES BEGIN – Long John BALDRY
LET THE LITTLE GIRL DANCE – Billy BLAND
LET THE LOVE – Q-TEX
LET THE MUSIC HEAL YOUR SOUL – BRAVO ALL STARS
LET THE MUSIC (LIFT YOU UP) – Darlene LEWIS
LET THE MUSIC MOVE U – RAZE
LET THE MUSIC PLAY [A] – Barry WHITE
LET THE MUSIC PLAY [B] – Charles EARLAND
LET THE MUSIC PLAY [C] – SHANNON
LET THE MUSIC PLAY [C] – BBG
LET THE MUSIC PLAY [C] – Mary KIANI
LET THE MUSIC TAKE CONTROL – JM SILK
LET THE MUSIC USE YOU – NIGHTWRITERS
LET THE PEOPLE KNOW – TOPLOADER
LET THE RHYTHM MOVE YOU – SHARADA HOUSE GANG
LET THE RHYTHM PUMP – Doug LAZY
LET THE SUNSHINE IN [A] – PEDDLERS
LET THE SUNSHINE IN [A] – MILK & SUGAR featuring Lizzy PATTINSON
LET THE WATER RUN DOWN – PJ PROBY
LET THEM ALL TALK – Elvis COSTELLO
LET THERE BE DRUMS – Sandy NELSON
LET THERE BE HOUSE – DESKEE
LET THERE BE LIGHT – Mike OLDFIELD
LET THERE BE LOVE [A] – Nat 'King' COLE with George SHEARING
LET THERE BE LOVE [B] – SIMPLE MINDS
LET THERE BE PEACE ON EARTH (LET IT BEGIN WITH ME) – Michael WARD
LET THERE BE ROCK – ONSLAUGHT
LET THIS BE A PRAYER – ROLLO GOES SPIRITUAL with Pauline TAYLOR
LET THIS FEELING – Simone ANGEL
LET TRUE LOVE BEGIN – Nat 'King' COLE
LET U GO – ATB
LET YOUR BODY GO – Tom WILSON
LET YOUR BODY GO DOWNTOWN – Martyn FORD ORCHESTRA
LET YOUR HEAD GO – Victoria BECKHAM
LET YOUR HEART DANCE – SECRET AFFAIR
LET YOUR LOVE FLOW – BELLAMY BROTHERS
LET YOUR SOUL BE YOUR PILOT – STING
LET YOUR YEAH BE YEAH [A] – PIONEERS
LET YOUR YEAH BE YEAH [A] – Ali CAMPBELL
LET YOURSELF GO [A] – T-CONNECTION
LET YOURSELF GO [B] – SYBIL
LETHAL INDUSTRY – DJ TIESTO
LETITGO – PRINCE
LETS – Sarah VAUGHAN
LET'S ALL CHANT [A] – Michael ZAGER BAND
LET'S ALL CHANT [A] – PAT and MICK
LET'S ALL CHANT [A] – GUSTO
(LET'S ALL GO BACK) DISCO NIGHTS – JAZZ and the BROTHERS GRIMM
LET'S ALL (GO TO THE FIRE DANCES) – KILLING JOKE
LET'S ALL GO TOGETHER – MARION
LET'S ALL SING LIKE THE BIRDIES SING – TWEETS
LET'S BE FRIENDS – Johnny NASH
LET'S BE LOVERS TONIGHT – SHERRICK
LET'S CALL IT QUITS – SLADE
LET'S CELEBRATE – NEW YORK SKYY
LET'S CLEAN UP THE GHETTO – PHILADELPHIA INTERNATIONAL ALL-STARS
LET'S DANCE [A] – Chris MONTEZ
LET'S DANCE [A] – Liz KERSHAW and Bruno BROOKES
LET'S DANCE [B] – BOMBERS
LET'S DANCE [C] – David BOWIE
LET'S DANCE [D] – MIDDLESBROUGH FC
LET'S DANCE [D] – Chris REA
LET'S DANCE [E] – FIVE
LET'S DO IT AGAIN [A] – George BENSON
LET'S DO IT AGAIN [B] – Lynden David HALL
LET'S DO ROCK STEADY – BODYSNATCHERS
LET'S DO THE LATIN HUSTLE [A] – Eddie DRENNON and B.B.S. UNLIMITED
LET'S DO THE LATIN HUSTLE [A] – M and O BAND
LET'S FACE THE MUSIC AND DANCE – Nat 'King' COLE
LET'S FLY AWAY – VOYAGE
LET'S FUNK TONIGHT – BLUE FEATHER
LET'S GET BACK TO BED ... BOY – Sarah CONNOR featuring TQ
LET'S GET BRUTAL – NITRO DELUXE
LET'S GET DOWN [A] – ISOTONIK
LET'S GET DOWN [B] – Mark MORRISON
LET'S GET DOWN [C] – TONY TONI TONÉ
LET'S GET DOWN [D] – JT PLAYAZ
LET'S GET DOWN [E] – SPACEDUST
LET'S GET FUNKTIFIED – BOILING POINT
LET'S GET HAPPY – MASS ORDER
LET'S GET ILL – P DIDDY featuring KELIS
LET'S GET IT ON [A] – Marvin GAYE
LET'S GET IT ON [B] – Shabba RANKS
LET'S GET IT ON [C] – BIG BOSS STYLUS presents RED VENOM
LET'S GET IT STARTED – BLACK EYED PEAS
LET'S GET IT UP – AC/DC
LET'S GET MARRIED – The PROCLAIMERS
LET'S GET READY TO RHUMBLE – ANT & DEC
LET'S GET ROCKED – DEF LEPPARD
LET'S GET SERIOUS – Jermaine JACKSON
LET'S GET TATTOOS – CARTER – THE UNSTOPPABLE SEX MACHINE
LET'S GET THIS PARTY STARTED – ZENA
LET'S GET THIS STRAIGHT (FROM THE START) – DEXY'S MIDNIGHT RUNNERS
LET'S GET TOGETHER [A] – Hayley MILLS
LET'S GET TOGETHER [B] – Alexander O'NEAL
LET'S GET TOGETHER AGAIN [A] – BIG BEN BANJO BAND
LET'S GET TOGETHER AGAIN [B] – GLITTER BAND
LET'S GET TOGETHER (IN OUR MINDS) – GORKY'S ZYGOTIC MYNCI
LET'S GET TOGETHER NO.1 – BIG BEN BANJO BAND
LET'S GET TOGETHER (SO GROOVY NOW) – KRUSH PERSPECTIVE
LET'S GET TOGETHER TONITE – Steve WALSH
LET'S GO [A] – ROUTERS
LET'S GO [B] – The CARS
LET'S GO [C] – VARDIS
LET'S GO ALL THE WAY – SLY FOX
LET'S GO CRAZY – PRINCE
LET'S GO DISCO – The REAL THING
LET'S GO ROUND AGAIN [A] – AVERAGE WHITE BAND
LET'S GO ROUND AGAIN [A] – LOUISE
LET'S GO ROUND THERE – DARLING BUDS
LET'S GO STEADY AGAIN – Neil SEDAKA
LET'S GO TO BED – The CURE
LET'S GO TO SAN FRANCISCO – FLOWERPOT MEN
LET'S GO TOGETHER – CHANGE
LET'S GROOVE [A] – EARTH WIND AND FIRE
LET'S GROOVE [A] – PHAT 'N' PHUNKY
LET'S GROOVE [B] – George MOREL featuring Heather WILDMAN
LET'S HANG ON [A] – The FOUR SEASONS
LET'S HANG ON [A] – Johnny JOHNSON and the BANDWAGON
LET'S HANG ON [A] – DARTS
LET'S HANG ON [A] – Barry MANILOW
LET'S HANG ON [A] – SHOOTING PARTY
LET'S HAVE A BALL – Winifred ATWELL
LET'S HAVE A DING DONG – Winifred ATWELL
LET'S HAVE A PARTY [A] – Winifred ATWELL
LET'S HAVE A PARTY [B] – Wanda JACKSON
LET'S HAVE A QUIET NIGHT IN – David SOUL
LET'S HAVE ANOTHER PARTY – Winifred ATWELL
LET'S HEAR IT FOR THE BOY – Deniece WILLIAMS
LET'S JUMP THE BROOMSTICK [A] – Brenda LEE
LET'S JUMP THE BROOMSTICK [A] – COAST TO COAST
LET'S JUST CALL IT LOVE – Lisa STANSFIELD
LET'S KILL MUSIC – The COOPER TEMPLE CLAUSE
LET'S LIVE IT UP (NITE PEOPLE) – David JOSEPH
LET'S LOVEDANCE TONIGHT – GARY'S GANG
LET'S MAKE A BABY – Billy PAUL
LET'S MAKE A NIGHT TO REMEMBER – Bryan ADAMS
LET'S PARTY – JIVE BUNNY and the MASTERMIXERS
LET'S PLAY HOUSE – KRAZE
LET'S PRETEND – LULU
LET'S PUSH IT [A] – INNOCENCE
LET'S PUSH IT [B] – NIGHTCRAWLERS featuring John REID
LET'S PUSH THINGS FORWARD – The STREETS
LET'S PUT IT ALL TOGETHER – The STYLISTICS
LET'S RIDE – Montell JORDAN
LET'S ROCK – E-TRAX
LET'S ROCK 'N' ROLL – Winifred ATWELL
LET'S SEE ACTION – The WHO
LET'S SLIP AWAY – Cleo LAINE
LET'S SPEND THE NIGHT TOGETHER [A] – The ROLLING STONES
LET'S SPEND THE NIGHT TOGETHER [A] – MASH!
LET'S START OVER – Pamela FERNANDEZ
LET'S START THE DANCE – Hamilton BOHANNON
LET'S START TO DANCE AGAIN – Hamilton BOHANNON
LET'S STAY HOME TONIGHT – JOE
LET'S STAY TOGETHER [A] – Al GREEN
LET'S STAY TOGETHER [A] – Bobby M featuring Jean CARN
LET'S STAY TOGETHER [A] – Tina TURNER
LET'S STAY TOGETHER [A] – PASADENAS
LET'S STICK TOGETHER – Bryan FERRY
LET'S SWING AGAIN – JIVE BUNNY and the MASTERMIXERS
LET'S TALK ABOUT SHHH – ONE WAY
LET'S TALK ABOUT LOVE – Helen SHAPIRO
LET'S TALK ABOUT SEX – SALT-N-PEPA
LET'S THINK ABOUT LIVING – Bob LUMAN
LET'S TRY AGAIN – NEW KIDS ON THE BLOCK
LET'S TURKEY TROT – LITTLE EVA
LET'S TWIST AGAIN [A] – Chubby CHECKER
LET'S TWIST AGAIN [A] – John ASHER
LET'S WAIT AWHILE – Janet JACKSON
LET'S WALK THAT-A-WAY – Doris DAY and Johnnie RAY
LET'S WHIP IT UP (YOU GO GIRL) – SLEAZESISTERS
LET'S WOMBLE TO THE PARTY TONIGHT – The WOMBLES
LET'S WORK – Mick JAGGER
LET'S WORK IT OUT – RAGHAV featuring JAHAZIEL
LET'S WORK TOGETHER – CANNED HEAT
THE LETTER [A] – LONG AND THE SHORT
THE LETTER [B] – The BOX TOPS
THE LETTER [B] – The MINDBENDERS
THE LETTER [B] – Joe COCKER
THE LETTER [B] – Amii STEWART
THE LETTER [C] – PJ HARVEY
LETTER FROM AMERICA – The PROCLAIMERS
LETTER FULL OF TEARS – Billy FURY
LETTER TO A SOLDIER – Barbara LYON
A LETTER TO ELISE – The CURE
LETTER TO LUCILLE – Tom JONES
LETTER 2 MY UNBORN – 2PAC
A LETTER TO YOU – Shakin' STEVENS
LETTERS TO YOU – FINCH
LETTIN' YA MIND GO – DESERT
LETTING GO – Paul McCARTNEY
LETTING THE CABLES SLEEP – BUSH
LEVI STUBBS' TEARS – Billy BRAGG
LFO – LFO
LIAR [A] – Graham BONNET
LIAR [B] – ROLLINS BAND
LIAR LIAR – CREDIT TO THE NATION
LIARS' BAR – The BEAUTIFUL SOUTH
LIBERATE – Lee HASLAM
LIBERATION [A] – LIBERATION
LIBERATION [B] – PET SHOP BOYS
LIBERATION [C] – Lippy LOU
LIBERATION (TEMPTATION – FLY LIKE AN EAGLE) – Matt DAREY
LIBERATOR – SPEAR OF DESTINY
LIBERIAN GIRL – Michael JACKSON
LIBERTY TOWN – PERFECT DAY
LIBIAMO – José CARRERAS featuring Placido DOMINGO and Luciano PAVAROTTI with MEHTA
LICENCE TO KILL – Gladys KNIGHT and the PIPS
LICK A SHOT – CYPRESS HILL
LICK A SMURP FOR CHRISTMAS (ALL FALL DOWN) – Jonathan KING
LICK IT – 20 FINGERS
LICK IT UP – KISS
LIDO SHUFFLE – Boz SCAGGS
LIE TO ME – BON JOVI
LIES [A] – STATUS QUO

LIES [B] — THOMPSON TWINS
LIES [C] — Jonathan BUTLER
LIES [D] — EN VOGUE
LIES [E] — EMF
THE LIES IN YOUR EYES — The SWEET
LIFE [A] — HADDAWAY
LIFE [B] — BLAIR
LIFE [C] — DES'REE
THE LIFE [D] — STYLES & Pharoahe MONCH
LIFE AIN'T EASY — CLEOPATRA
LIFE AT A TOP PEOPLE'S HEALTH FARM — STYLE COUNCIL
LIFE BECOMING A LANDSLIDE — MANIC STREET PREACHERS
LIFE BEGINS AT THE HOP — XTC
LIFE FOR RENT — DIDO
LIFE GOES ON — GEORGIE PORGIE
LIFE GOES ON — LeAnn RIMES
LIFE GOT COLD — GIRLS ALOUD
LIFE IN A DAY [A] — SIMPLE MINDS
LIFE IN A DAY [B] — I AM KLOOT
LIFE IN A NORTHERN TOWN — DREAM ACADEMY
LIFE IN MONO — MONO
LIFE IN ONE DAY — Howard JONES
LIFE IN TOKYO — JAPAN
LIFE IS A FLOWER — ACE OF BASE
LIFE IS A HIGHWAY — Tom COCHRANE
LIFE IS A LONG SONG — JETHRO TULL
LIFE IS A MINESTRONE — 10cc
LIFE IS A ROCK (BUT THE RADIO ROLLED ME) — REUNION
LIFE IS A ROLLERCOASTER — Ronan KEATING
LIFE IS FOR LIVING — BARCLAY JAMES HARVEST
LIFE IS SWEET — The CHEMICAL BROTHERS
LIFE IS TOO SHORT GIRL — SHEER ELEGANCE
A LIFE LESS ORDINARY — ASH
LIFE, LOVE AND HAPPINESS — Brian KENNEDY
LIFE LOVE AND UNITY — DREADZONE
THE LIFE OF RILEY — The LIGHTNING SEEDS
LIFE OF SURPRISES — PREFAB SPROUT
LIFE ON MARS? — David BOWIE
LIFE ON YOUR OWN — HUMAN LEAGUE
LIFE STORY — Angie STONE
LIFE SUPPORT MACHINE — THESE ANIMAL MEN
LIFEBOAT — Terry NEASON
THE LIFEBOAT PARTY — Kid CREOLE and the COCONUTS
LIFEFORMS — FUTURE SOUND OF LONDON
LIFELINE — SPANDAU BALLET
LIFE'S A CINCH — MUNDY
LIFE'S BEEN GOOD — Joe WALSH
LIFE'S JUST A BALLGAME — WOMACK and WOMACK
LIFE'S TOO SHORT [A] — HOLE IN ONE
LIFE'S TOO SHORT [B] — The LIGHTNING SEEDS
LIFE'S WHAT YOU MAKE IT — TALK TALK
LIFESAVER — GURU
LIFESTYLES OF THE RICH AND FAMOUS — GOOD CHARLOTTE
LIFETIME LOVE — Joyce SIMS
LIFETIME PILING UP — TALKING HEADS
LIFETIMES — SLAM featuring Tyrone PALMER
LIFT — 808 STATE
LIFT EVERY VOICE (TAKE ME AWAY) — MASS ORDER
LIFT IT HIGH (ALL ABOUT BELIEF) — MANCHESTER UNITED FOOTBALL CLUB
LIFT ME UP [A] — Howard JONES
LIFT ME UP [B] — RED 5
LIFT ME UP [C] — Geri HALLIWELL
LIFT ME UP [D] — REEL
LIFTED — LIGHTHOUSE FAMILY
LIFTING ME HIGHER — GEMS FOR JEM
LIGHT — Pharoahe MONCH
THE LIGHT [A] — COMMON
THE LIGHT [B] — Michelle WEEKS
LIGHT A CANDLE — Daniel O'DONNELL
LIGHT A RAINBOW — TUKAN
LIGHT AIRCRAFT ON FIRE — The AUTEURS
LIGHT AND DAY — The POLYPHONIC SPREE
THE LIGHT COMES FROM WITHIN — Linda McCARTNEY
LIGHT EMITTING ELECTRICAL WAVE — THESE ANIMAL MEN
LIGHT FLIGHT — PENTANGLE
LIGHT IN YOUR EYES — Sheryl CROW
LIGHT MY FIRE [A] — The DOORS
LIGHT MY FIRE [A] — José FELICIANO
LIGHT MY FIRE [A] — Mike FLOWERS POPS
LIGHT MY FIRE [A] — UB40
LIGHT MY FIRE [A] — Will YOUNG
LIGHT MY FIRE [B] — CLUBHOUSE
LIGHT MY FIRE — 137 DISCO HEAVEN (MEDLEY) — Amii STEWART
(LIGHT OF EXPERIENCE) DOINA DE JALE — Gheorghe ZAMFIR
LIGHT OF LOVE — T. REX
LIGHT OF MY LIFE — LOUISE
LIGHT OF THE WORLD — Kim APPLEBY
LIGHT UP THE FIRE — PARCHMENT
LIGHT UP THE NIGHT — BROTHERS JOHNSON
LIGHT UP THE WORLD FOR CHRISTMAS — LAMPIES
LIGHT YEARS — PEARL JAM
LIGHT YOUR ASS ON FIRE — Busta RHYMES featuring PHARRELL
LIGHTER — DJ SS
LIGHTNIN' STRIKES — Lou CHRISTIE
LIGHTNING — ZOE
LIGHTNING CRASHES — LIVE
LIGHTNING FLASH — BROTHERHOOD OF MAN
LIGHTNING STRIKES — Ozzy OSBOURNE
THE LIGHTNING TREE — SETTLERS
LIGHTS OF CINCINNATI — Scott WALKER
LIGHTS OUT — Lisa Marie PRESLEY
LIKE A BABY — Len BARRY
LIKE A BUTTERFLY — Mac and Katie KISSOON
LIKE A CAT — CRW featuring VERONIKA
LIKE A CHILD — Julie ROGERS
LIKE A CHILD AGAIN — The MISSION
LIKE A FEATHER — Nikka COSTA
LIKE A HURRICANE — The MISSION
LIKE A MOTORWAY — SAINT ETIENNE
LIKE A PLAYA — LA GANZ
LIKE A PRAYER [A] — MADONNA
LIKE A PRAYER [A] — MAD'HOUSE
LIKE A ROLLING STONE [A] — Bob DYLAN
LIKE A ROLLING STONE [A] — The ROLLING STONES
LIKE A ROSE — a1
LIKE A SATELLITE (EP) — THUNDER
LIKE A VIRGIN — MADONNA
LIKE A WOMAN — Tony RICH PROJECT
LIKE A YO-YO — SABRINA
LIKE AN ANIMAL — GLOVE
LIKE AN OLD TIME MOVIE — Scott McKENZIE
LIKE CLOCKWORK — The BOOMTOWN RATS
LIKE DREAMERS DO [A] — APPLEJACKS
LIKE DREAMERS DO [B] — Mica PARIS featuring Courtney PINE
LIKE FLAMES — BERLIN
LIKE GLUE — Sean PAUL
LIKE I DO [A] — Maureen EVANS
LIKE I DO [B] — FOR REAL
LIKE I LIKE IT — AURRA
LIKE I LOVE YOU — Justin TIMBERLAKE
LIKE IT OR LEAVE IT — CHIKINKI
LIKE I'VE NEVER BEEN GONE — Billy FURY
LIKE LOVERS DO — Lloyd COLE
LIKE MARVIN GAYE SAID (WHAT'S GOING ON) — SPEECH
LIKE PRINCES DO — DIESEL PARK WEST
LIKE SISTER AND BROTHER — The DRIFTERS
LIKE STRANGERS — The EVERLY BROTHERS
LIKE THIS AND LIKE THAT [A] — MONICA
LIKE THIS AND LIKE THAT [B] — LaKiesha BERRI
LIKE THIS LIKE THAT — Mauro PICOTTO
LIKE TO GET TO KNOW YOU WELL — Howard JONES
LIKE WE USED TO BE — Georgie FAME
A LIL' AIN'T ENOUGH — David Lee ROTH
LIL' BIG MAN — Omera MUMBA
LIL' DEVIL — The CULT
LIL' DUB — SPACE MONKEYZ vs GORILLAZ
LIL' RED RIDING HOOD [A] — SAM THE SHAM and the PHARAOHS
LIL RED RIDING HOOD [A] — 999
LILAC WINE — Elkie BROOKS
LILY THE PINK — SCAFFOLD
LILY WAS HERE — Candy DULFER
LIMBO ROCK — Chubby CHECKER
LINDA LU — Johnny KIDD and the PIRATES
THE LINE — Lisa STANSFIELD
LINE DANCE PARTY — WOOLPACKERS
LINE UP — ELASTICA
LINES — PLANETS
LINGER — The CRANBERRIES
THE LION SLEEPS TONIGHT (WIMOWEH) [A] — TOKENS
THE LION SLEEPS TONIGHT [A] — Dave NEWMAN
THE LION SLEEPS TONIGHT [A] — TIGHT FIT
LIONROCK — LIONROCK
THE LION'S MOUTH — KAJAGOOGOO
LIP GLOSS — PULP
LIP SERVICE (EP) — WET WET WET
LIP UP FATTY — BAD MANNERS
LIPS LIKE SUGAR — ECHO and the BUNNYMEN
LIPSMACKIN' ROCK 'N' ROLLIN' — Peter BLAKE
LIPSTICK — ROCKET FROM THE CRYPT
LIPSTICK ON YOUR COLLAR — Connie FRANCIS
LIPSTICK POWDER AND PAINT — Shakin' STEVENS
LIQUID COOL — APOLLO FOUR FORTY
LIQUID DREAMS — O-TOWN
LIQUID LIPS — The BLUETONES
LIQUIDATOR — HARRY J ALL STARS
LISTEN — URBAN SPECIES
LISTEN (EP) — STIFF LITTLE FINGERS
LISTEN LIKE THIEVES [A] — INXS
LISTEN LIKE THIEVES [A] — WAS (NOT WAS)
LISTEN LITTLE GIRL — Keith KELLY
LISTEN TO ME [A] — Buddy HOLLY
LISTEN TO ME [B] — The HOLLIES
LISTEN TO THE MUSIC — DOOBIE BROTHERS
LISTEN TO THE OCEAN — NINA and FREDERICK
LISTEN TO THE RADIO: ATMOSPHERICS — Tom ROBINSON
LISTEN TO THE RHYTHM — K3M
LISTEN TO THE RHYTHM FLOW — GTO
LISTEN TO WHAT THE MAN SAID — Paul McCARTNEY
LISTEN TO YOUR FATHER — Feargal SHARKEY
LISTEN TO YOUR HEART [A] — ROXETTE
LISTEN TO YOUR HEART [B] — SONIA
LITHIUM — NIRVANA
LITTLE ARITHMETICS — dEUS
LITTLE ARROWS — Leapy LEE
LITTLE BABY NOTHING — MANIC STREET PREACHERS
LITTLE BAND OF GOLD — James GILREATH
LITTLE BERNADETTE — Harry BELAFONTE
LITTLE BIRD — Annie LENNOX
A LITTLE BIT — Rosie RIBBONS
A LITTLE BIT FURTHER AWAY — KOKOMO
A LITTLE BIT ME A LITTLE BIT YOU — The MONKEES
A LITTLE BIT MORE [A] — DR HOOK
A LITTLE BIT MORE [A] — 911
A LITTLE BIT MORE [B] — Kym SIMS
A LITTLE BIT OF ACTION — NADIA
LITTLE BIT OF HEAVEN — Lisa STANSFIELD
LITTLE BIT OF LOVE — FREE
LITTLE BIT OF LOVIN' — Kele LE ROC
A LITTLE BIT OF LUCK — DJ LUCK & MC NEAT
A LITTLE BIT OF SNOW — Howard JONES
A LITTLE BIT OF SOAP — SHOWADDYWADDY
A LITTLE BITTY TEAR [A] — Burl IVES
LITTLE BITTY TEAR [A] — MIKI and GRIFF
LITTLE BLACK BOOK [A] — Jimmy DEAN
LITTLE BLACK BOOK [B] — Belinda CARLISLE
LITTLE BLUE BIRD — Vince HILL
A LITTLE BOOGIE WOOGIE IN THE BACK OF MY MIND [A] — Gary GLITTER
A LITTLE BOOGIE WOOGIE (IN THE BACK OF MY MIND) [A] — Shakin' STEVENS
LITTLE BOY LOST — Michael HOLLIDAY
LITTLE BOY SAD — Johnny BURNETTE
LITTLE BRITAIN — DREADZONE
LITTLE BROTHER — BLUE PEARL
LITTLE BROWN JUG — Glenn MILLER
LITTLE BY LITTLE [A] — Dusty SPRINGFIELD
LITTLE BY LITTLE [B] — OASIS
LITTLE CHILD — DES'REE
LITTLE CHILDREN — Billy J KRAMER and the DAKOTAS
LITTLE CHRISTINE — Dick JORDAN
LITTLE DARLIN' [A] — DIAMONDS
LITTLE DARLIN' [B] — Marvin GAYE
LITTLE DARLING — The RUBETTES
LITTLE DEVIL — Neil SEDAKA
LITTLE DISCOURAGE — IDLEWILD
LITTLE DOES SHE KNOW — KURSAAL FLYERS
LITTLE DONKEY [A] — BEVERLEY SISTERS
LITTLE DONKEY [A] — Gracie FIELDS
LITTLE DONKEY [A] — NINA and FREDERICK
LITTLE DROPS OF SILVER — Gerry MONROE
LITTLE DRUMMER BOY [A] — BEVERLEY SISTERS
LITTLE DRUMMER BOY [A] — Harry SIMEONE CHORALE
LITTLE DRUMMER BOY [A] — Michael FLANDERS
LITTLE DRUMMER BOY [A] — PIPES and DRUMS and MILITARY BAND of the ROYAL SCOTS DRAGOON GUARDS
LITTLE DRUMMER BOY [A] — RuPAUL
LITTLE 15 — DEPECHE MODE
LITTLE FLUFFY CLOUDS — The ORB
LITTLE GIRL [A] — Marty WILDE
LITTLE GIRL [B] — The TROGGS
LITTLE GIRL [C] — BANNED
LITTLE GIRL LOST — ICICLE WORKS
LITTLE GREEN APPLES — Roger MILLER
LITTLE HOUSE OF SAVAGES — The WALKMEN
A LITTLE IN LOVE — Cliff RICHARD
LITTLE JEANNIE — Elton JOHN
LITTLE L — JAMIROQUAI
LITTLE LADY — ANEKA
A LITTLE LESS CONVERSATION — ELVIS vs JXL
LITTLE LIES — FLEETWOOD MAC
LITTLE LOST SOMETIMES — The ALMIGHTY
A LITTLE LOVE A LITTLE KISS — Karl DENVER
A LITTLE LOVE AND UNDERSTANDING — Gilbert BECAUD
A LITTLE LOVIN' — Neil SEDAKA
A LITTLE LOVING — The FOURMOST
LITTLE MAN — SONNY and CHER
LITTLE MIRACLES (HAPPEN EVERY DAY) — Luther VANDROSS
LITTLE MISS CAN'T BE WRONG — SPIN DOCTORS
LITTLE MISS LONELY — Helen SHAPIRO
LITTLE MISS PERFECT — Summer MATTHEWS
A LITTLE MORE LOVE — Olivia NEWTON-JOHN
A LITTLE PEACE — NICOLE
A LITTLE PIECE OF LEATHER — Donnie ELBERT
LITTLE PINK STARS — RADISH
LITTLE RED CORVETTE — PRINCE
LITTLE RED MONKEY — Frank CHACKSFIELD
LITTLE RED ROOSTER — The ROLLING STONES
A LITTLE RESPECT [A] — ERASURE
A LITTLE RESPECT [A] — WHEATUS
LITTLE RHYMES — MERCURY REV
A LITTLE SAMBA — UGLY DUCKLING
LITTLE SERENADE — Eddie CALVERT
THE LITTLE SHOEMAKER — Petula CLARK
LITTLE SISTER — Elvis PRESLEY
A LITTLE SOUL — PULP
LITTLE STAR [A] — ELEGANTS
LITTLE STAR [B] — MADONNA
LITTLE THINGS [A] — Dave BERRY
LITTLE THINGS [B] — india.arie
LITTLE THINGS MEAN A LOT [A] — Alma COGAN
LITTLE THINGS MEAN A LOT [A] — Kitty KALLEN
LITTLE THOUGHTS — BLOC PARTY
A LITTLE TIME — The BEAUTIFUL SOUTH
LITTLE TOWN — Cliff RICHARD
LITTLE TOWN FLIRT — Del SHANNON
LITTLE TRAIN — Max BYGRAVES
LITTLE WHITE BERRY — Roy CASTLE
LITTLE WHITE BULL — Tommy STEELE
LITTLE WHITE LIES — STATUS QUO
LITTLE WILLY — The SWEET
LITTLE WONDER — David BOWIE
A LITTLE YOU — FREDDIE and the DREAMERS
LIVE AND LEARN — JOE PUBLIC
LIVE AND LET DIE [A] — Paul McCARTNEY
LIVE AND LET DIE [A] — GUNS N' ROSES
LIVE ANIMAL (F**K LIKE A BEAST) — W.A.S.P.
LIVE ANOTHER LIFE — PLASTIC BOY featuring ROZALLA
LIVE AT TFI FRIDAY (EP) — STING
LIVE AT THE MARQUEE (EP) — EDDIE and the HOTRODS
LIVE EP — BARCLAY JAMES HARVEST
THE LIVE EP — Gary NUMAN
LIVE FOR LOVING YOU — Gloria ESTEFAN
LIVE FOR THE ONE I LOVE — Tina ARENA
LIVE FOREVER — OASIS
LIVE IN A HIDING PLACE — IDLEWILD
LIVE IN MANCHESTER (PARTS 1 + 2) — N-JOI
LIVE IN THE SKY — Dave CLARK FIVE
LIVE IN TROUBLE — The BARRON KNIGHTS
LIVE IS LIFE [A] — OPUS
LIVE IS LIFE [B] — HERMES HOUSE BAND & DJ OTZI
LIVE IT UP — MENTAL AS ANYTHING
LIVE LIKE HORSES — Elton JOHN and Luciano PAVAROTTI
LIVE MY LIFE — BOY GEORGE
LIVE OR DIE — DILLINJA
LIVE TO TELL — MADONNA
LIVE TOGETHER — Lisa STANSFIELD
LIVE YOUR LIFE BE FREE — Belinda CARLISLE
LIVELY — Lonnie DONEGAN
LIVERPOOL (ANTHEM) — LIVERPOOL FC
LIVERPOOL LOU — SCAFFOLD
LIVERPOOL (WE'RE NEVER GONNA ...) — LIVERPOOL FC
LIVIN' IN THE LIGHT — Caron WHEELER
LIVIN' IT UP [A] — NORTHERN UPROAR
LIVIN' IT UP [B] — JA RULE featuring CASE
LIVIN' IT UP (FRIDAY NIGHT) — BELL and JAMES
LIVIN' LA VIDA LOCA — Ricky MARTIN
LIVIN' LOVIN' DOLL — Cliff RICHARD
LIVIN' ON A PRAYER — BON JOVI
LIVIN' ON THE EDGE — AEROSMITH
LIVIN' ON THE EDGE OF THE NIGHT — Iggy POP
LIVIN' THING [A] — ELECTRIC LIGHT ORCHESTRA
LIVIN' THING [A] — The BEAUTIFUL SOUTH
LIVIN' IN THIS WORLD — GURU
LIVING AFTER MIDNIGHT — JUDAS PRIEST
LIVING BY NUMBERS — NEW MUSIK
THE LIVING DAYLIGHTS — A-HA
LIVING DOLL [A] — Cliff RICHARD and The DRIFTERS
LIVING DOLL [A] — Cliff RICHARD and the YOUNG ONES featuring Hank B MARVIN
THE LIVING DREAM — SUNDANCE
LIVING FOR THE CITY [A] — Stevie WONDER
LIVING FOR THE CITY [A] — GILLAN
LIVING FOR YOU — SONNY and CHER
LIVING IN A BOX [A] — LIVING IN A BOX
LIVING IN A BOX [A] — Bobby WOMACK
LIVING IN A FANTASY — URBAN HYPE
LIVING IN A WORLD (TURNED UPSIDE DOWN) — PRIVATE LIVES
LIVING IN AMERICA — James BROWN
LIVING IN ANOTHER WORLD — TALK TALK
LIVING IN DANGER — ACE OF BASE
LIVING IN HARMONY — Cliff RICHARD
LIVING IN SIN — BON JOVI
LIVING IN THE PAST [A] — JETHRO TULL
LIVING IN THE PAST [B] — DRUM THEATRE
LIVING IN THE ROSE (THE BALLADS EP) — NEW MODEL ARMY
LIVING IN THE (SLIGHTLY MORE RECENT) PAST — JETHRO TULL
LIVING IN THE SUNSHINE — CLUBHOUSE
LIVING IN THE UK — SHAKATAK
LIVING NEXT DOOR TO ALICE — SMOKIE featuring Roy 'Chubby' BROWN
LIVING ON AN ISLAND — STATUS QUO
LIVING ON MY OWN — Freddie MERCURY
LIVING ON THE CEILING — BLANCMANGE
LIVING ON THE FRONT LINE — Eddy GRANT
LIVING ON VIDEO — TRANS-X

LIVING WITH THE HUMAN MACHINES — STRANGELOVE
THE LIVING YEARS — MIKE and the MECHANICS
LIZARD (GONNA GET YOU) — Mauro PICOTTO
LK (CAROLINA CAROL BELA) — DJ MARKY & XRS featuring STAMINA MC
L'L'LUCY — MUD
LO MISMO QUE YO (IF ONLY) — Alex CUBA BAND featuring Ron SEXSMITH
LOADED [A] — PRIMAL SCREAM
LOADED [B] — Ricky MARTIN
LOADSAMONEY (DOIN' UP THE HOUSE) — Harry ENFIELD
LOBSTER & SCRIMP — TIMBALAND featuring JAY-Z
LOC'ED AFTER DARK — Tone LOC
LOCAL BOY IN THE PHOTOGRAPH — STEREOPHONICS
LOCK AND LOAD — Bob SEGER and the SILVER BULLET BAND
LOCK UP YA DAUGHTERS — The NOISE NEXT DOOR
LOCK UP YOUR DAUGHTERS — SLADE
LOCKED OUT — CROWDED HOUSE
LOCKED UP — AKON featuring STYLES P
LOCO — FUN LOVIN' CRIMINALS
LOCO IN ACAPULCO — The FOUR TOPS
LOCOMOTION — ORCHESTRAL MANOEUVRES IN THE DARK
LOCO-MOTION [A] — VERNONS GIRLS
THE LOCO-MOTION [A] — LITTLE EVA
THE LOCOMOTION [A] — Dave STEWART
THE LOCO-MOTION [A] — Kylie MINOGUE
L.O.D. (LOVE ON DELIVERY) — Billy OCEAN
THE LODGERS — STYLE COUNCIL
THE LOGICAL SONG [A] — SUPERTRAMP
THE LOGICAL SONG [A] — SCOOTER
L'OISEAU ET L'ENFANT — Marie MYRIAM
LOLA [A] — The KINKS
LOLA [A] — Andy TAYLOR
LOLA STARS AND STRIPES — The STILLS
LOLA'S THEME [A] — SHAPESHIFTERS
LOLLIPOP [A] — The CHORDETTES
LOLLIPOP [A] — MUDLARKS
LOLLY LOLLY — WENDY and LISA
LONDINIUM — CATATONIA
LONDON BOYS — T. REX
LONDON CALLING — The CLASH
LONDON GIRLS — CHAS and DAVE
LONDON KID — Jean-Michel JARRE featuring Hank MARVIN
LONDON NIGHTS — LONDON BOYS
A LONDON THING — Scott GARCIA featuring MC STYLES
LONDON TIMES — RADIO HEART featuring Gary NUMAN
LONDON TONIGHT — COLLAPSED LUNG
LONDON TOWN [A] — Paul McCARTNEY
LONDON TOWN [B] — LIGHT OF THE WORLD
LONDON TOWN [C] — BUCKS FIZZ
LONDON TOWN [D] — JDS
LONDON X-PRESS — X-PRESS 2
LONDON'S BRILLIANT — Wendy JAMES
LONDON'S BRILLIANT PARADE — Elvis COSTELLO
LONDRES STRUTT — SMELLS LIKE HEAVEN
THE LONE RANGER — QUANTUM JUMP
LONE RIDER — John LEYTON
THE LONELIEST MAN IN THE WORLD — TOURISTS
LONELINESS [A] — Des O'CONNOR
LONELINESS [B] — TOMCRAFT
LONELINESS IS GONE — NINE YARDS
LONELY [A] — Eddie COCHRAN
LONELY [B] — Mr Acker BILK and his PARAMOUNT JAZZ BAND
LONELY [C] — Peter ANDRE
LONELY BALLERINA — MANTOVANI
LONELY BOY [A] — Paul ANKA
LONELY BOY [B] — Andrew GOLD
LONELY BOY LONELY GUITAR — Duane EDDY and the REBELS
THE LONELY BULL — Herb ALPERT
LONELY CITY — John LEYTON
LONELY, CRYIN' ONLY — THERAPY?
LONELY DAYS — The BEE GEES
LONELY DAYS, LONELY NIGHTS — Don DOWNING
LONELY (HAVE WE LOST OUR LOVE) — Lance ELLINGTON
LONELY HEART — UFO
THE LONELY MAN THEME — Cliff ADAMS ORCHESTRA
LONELY NIGHT — MAGNUM
THE LONELY ONE — ALICE DEEJAY
LONELY PUP (IN A CHRISTMAS SHOP) — Adam FAITH
LONELY STREET — Clarence 'Frogman' HENRY
LONELY SYMPHONY — Frances RUFFELLE
LONELY TEENAGER — DION
LONELY THIS CHRISTMAS — MUD
LONELY TOGETHER — Barry MANILOW
THE LONER — Gary MOORE
LONESOME — Adam FAITH
LONESOME DAY — Bruce SPRINGSTEEN
LONESOME NUMBER ONE — Don GIBSON
LONESOME (SI TU VOIS MA MÈRE) — Chris BARBER'S JAZZ BAND
LONESOME TRAVELLER — Lonnie DONEGAN
LONG AFTER TONIGHT IS ALL OVER — Jimmy RADCLIFFE
LONG AND LASTING LOVE (ONCE IN A LIFETIME) — Glenn MEDEIROS
THE LONG AND WINDING ROAD [A] — Ray MORGAN
THE LONG AND WINDING ROAD [A] — Will YOUNG and Gareth GATES
LONG AS I CAN SEE THE LIGHT [A] — CREEDENCE CLEARWATER REVIVAL
LONG AS I CAN SEE THE LIGHT [A] — MONKEY MAFIA
LONG BLACK VEIL — The STRANGLERS
LONG COOL WOMAN IN A BLACK DRESS — The HOLLIES
A LONG DECEMBER — COUNTING CROWS
LONG DISTANCE — TURIN BRAKES
THE LONG GOODBYE — Ronan KEATING
LONG HAIRED LOVER FROM LIVERPOOL — Little Jimmy OSMOND with the Mike CURB CONGREGATION
LONG HOT SUMMER — STYLE COUNCIL
LONG HOT SUMMER NIGHT — JT TAYLOR
LONG LEGGED GIRL (WITH THE SHORT DRESS ON) — Elvis PRESLEY
LONG LEGGED WOMAN DRESSED IN BLACK — MUNGO JERRY
LONG LIVE LOVE [A] — Sandie SHAW
LONG LIVE LOVE [A] — Nick BERRY
LONG LIVE LOVE [B] — Olivia NEWTON-JOHN
LONG LIVE ROCK — The WHO
LONG LIVE ROCK 'N' ROLL — RAINBOW
LONG LIVE THE UK MUSIC SCENE — Helen LOVE
LONG LONG WAY TO GO — DEF LEPPARD
LONG LOST LOVER — The THREE DEGREES
LONG MAY YOU RUN (LIVE) — Neil YOUNG
LONG NIGHT — The CORRS
THE LONG RUN — The EAGLES
LONG SHOT KICK DE BUCKET — PIONEERS
LONG TALL GLASSES — Leo SAYER
LONG TALL SALLY [A] — Pat BOONE
LONG TALL SALLY [A] — LITTLE RICHARD
LONG TERM LOVERS OF PAIN (EP) — HUE AND CRY
LONG TIME — ARROW
LONG TIME COMING [A] — BUMP & FLEX
LONG TIME COMING [B] — DELAYS
LONG TIME GONE — GALLIANO
LONG TRAIN RUNNING [A] — BANANARAMA
LONG TRAIN RUNNIN' [A] — DOOBIE BROTHERS
A LONG WALK — Jill SCOTT
LONG WAY — ROOTJOOSE
LONG WAY AROUND — Eagle-Eye CHERRY featuring Neneh CHERRY
LONG WAY FROM HOME — WHITESNAKE
LONG WAY SOUTH — JJ72
LONG WAY TO GO — Stevie NICKS
LONG WHITE CAR — HIPSWAY
LONGER — Dan FOGELBERG
THE LONGEST TIME — Billy JOEL
LONGTIME BOY — NINA and FREDERICK
LONGVIEW — GREEN DAY
LONNIE DONEGAN SHOWCASE (LP) — Lonnie DONEGAN
LONNIE'S SKIFFLE PARTY — Lonnie DONEGAN
LOO-BE-LOO — CHUCKS
THE LOOK — ROXETTE
LOOK AROUND — Vince HILL
LOOK AT ME — Geri HALLIWELL
LOOK AT ME (I'M IN LOVE) — MOMENTS
LOOK AT ME NOW — JESSY
LOOK AT THAT GIRL — Guy MITCHELL
LOOK AT US — NORTHERN HEIGHTZ
LOOK AT YOURSELF — David McALMONT
LOOK AWAY — BIG COUNTRY
LOOK BEFORE YOU LEAP — Dave CLARK FIVE
LOOK BUT DON'T TOUCH (EP) — SKIN
LOOK FOR A STAR — Garry MILLS
LOOK HOMEWARD ANGEL — Johnnie RAY
LOOK INTO MY EYES — BONE THUGS-N-HARMONY
LOOK MAMA — Howard JONES
LOOK ME IN THE HEART — Tina TURNER
THE LOOK OF LOVE [A] — Gladys KNIGHT and the PIPS
THE LOOK OF LOVE [A] — T-EMPO
THE LOOK OF LOVE [B] — ABC
THE LOOK OF LOVE [C] — MADONNA
LOOK THROUGH ANY WINDOW — The HOLLIES
LOOK THROUGH MY EYES — Phil COLLINS
LOOK UP TO THE LIGHT — EVOLUTION
LOOK WHAT YOU DONE FOR ME — Al GREEN
LOOK WHAT YOU STARTED — The TEMPTATIONS
LOOK WHAT YOU'VE DONE — JET
LOOK WHO IT IS — Helen SHAPIRO
LOOK WHO'S DANCING — Ziggy MARLEY and the MELODY MAKERS
LOOK WHO'S PERFECT NOW — TRANSISTER
LOOK WHO'S TALKING — DR ALBAN
LOOK WOT YOU DUN — SLADE
LOOKIN' AT YOU — Warren G featuring TOI
LOOKIN' THROUGH THE WINDOWS — The JACKSON FIVE
LOOKING AFTER NO.1 — The BOOMTOWN RATS
LOOKING AT MIDNIGHT — IMAGINATION
LOOKING FOR A LOVE — Joyce SIMS
LOOKING FOR A NEW LOVE — Jody WATLEY
LOOKING FOR A PLACE — MANIA
LOOKING FOR A SONG — BIG AUDIO DYNAMITE
LOOKING FOR ATLANTIS — PREFAB SPROUT
LOOKING FOR CLUES — Robert PALMER
LOOKING FOR LEWIS AND CLARK — LONG RYDERS
LOOKING FOR LINDA — HUE AND CRY
LOOKING FOR LOVE — Karen RAMIREZ
LOOKING FOR LOVE TONIGHT — FAT LARRY'S BAND
LOOKING FOR THE SUMMER — Chris REA
LOOKING HIGH HIGH HIGH — Bryan JOHNSON
LOOKING THROUGH PATIENT EYES — PM DAWN
LOOKING THROUGH THE EYES OF LOVE [A] — Gene PITNEY
LOOKING THRU THE EYES OF LOVE [A] — PARTRIDGE FAMILY
LOOKING THROUGH YOUR EYES — LeAnn RIMES
LOOKING UP — Michelle GAYLE
LOOKS LIKE I'M IN LOVE AGAIN — ERIK
LOOKS, LOOKS, LOOKS — SPARKS
LOOP-DE-LOOP — Frankie VAUGHAN
LOOP DI LOVE — Jonathan KING
LOOPS OF FURY (EP) — The CHEMICAL BROTHERS
LOOPS OF INFINITY — COSMIC BABY
LOOPZILLA — George CLINTON
LOOSE — THERAPY?
LOOSE CANNON — KILLING JOKE
LOOSE FIT — HAPPY MONDAYS
LOOSEN YOUR HOLD — SOUTH
LOPEZ — 808 STATE
LORDS OF THE NEW CHURCH — Tasmin ARCHER
LORELEI — Lonnie DONEGAN
LORRAINE — BAD MANNERS
LOS ANGELES IS BURNING — BAD RELIGION
LOS AMERICANOS — ESPIRITU
LOSE CONTROL — JAMES
LOSE IT — SUPERGRASS
LOSE MY BREATH — DESTINY'S CHILD
LOSE YOURSELF — EMINEM
LOSER [A] — BECK
LOSER [B] — THUNDER
LOSING GRIP — Avril LAVIGNE
LOSING MY GRIP — SAMSON
LOSING MY MIND — Liza MINNELLI
LOSING MY RELIGION — R.E.M.
LOSING YOU [A] — Brenda LEE
LOSING YOU [B] — Dusty SPRINGFIELD
LOST AGAIN — YELLO
LOST AND FOUND — D*NOTE
THE LOST ART OF KEEPING A SECRET — QUEENS OF THE STONE AGE
LOST CAT — CATATONIA
LOST FOR WORDS — Ronan KEATING
LOST IN A MELODY — DELAYS
LOST IN AMERICA — Alice COOPER
LOST IN EMOTION [A] — LISA LISA
LOST IN EMOTION [B] — John 'OO' FLEMING
LOST IN FRANCE — Bonnie TYLER
LOST IN LOVE [A] — UP YER RONSON featuring Mary PEARCE
LOST IN LOVE [B] — LEGEND B
LOST IN MUSIC [A] — SISTER SLEDGE
LOST IN MUSIC [B] — STEREO MC's
LOST IN SPACE [A] — APOLLO FOUR FORTY
LOST IN SPACE [B] — ELECTRASY
LOST IN SPACE [C] — LIGHTHOUSE FAMILY
LOST IN THE PLOT — The DEARS
LOST IN THE TRANSLATION — PACIFICA
LOST IN YOU [A] — Rod STEWART
LOST IN YOU [B] — Garth BROOKS as Chris GAINES
LOST IN YOUR EYES — Debbie GIBSON
LOST IN YOUR LOVE — Tony HADLEY
LOST JOHN — Lonnie DONEGAN
LOST MYSELF — LONGPIGS
LOST WEEKEND — Lloyd COLE
LOST WITHOUT YOU [A] — Jayn HANNA
LOST WITHOUT YOU [B] — Delta GOODREM
LOST WITHOUT YOUR LOVE — BREAD
LOST YOU SOMEWHERE — CHICANE
A LOT OF LOVE — Marti PELLOW
LOTUS — R.E.M.
LOUIE LOUIE [A] — KINGSMEN
LOUIE LOUIE [A] — MOTÖRHEAD
LOUIE LOUIE [A] — FAT BOYS
LOUIE LOUIE [A] — THREE AMIGOS
LOUIS QUATORZE — BOW WOW WOW
LOUISE [A] — Phil EVERLY
LOUISE [B] — HUMAN LEAGUE
LOUNGER — DOGS DIE IN HOT CARS
LOUNGIN' — LL COOL J
L.O.V.E. — Al GREEN
LOVE [A] — John LENNON
LOVE [A] — Jimmy NAIL
LOVE ACTION (I BELIEVE IN LOVE) — HUMAN LEAGUE
LOVE AIN'T GONNA WAIT FOR YOU — S CLUB
LOVE AIN'T HERE ANYMORE — TAKE THAT
LOVE AIN'T NO STRANGER — WHITESNAKE
LOVE ALL DAY — Nick HEYWARD
LOVE ALL THE HURT AWAY — Aretha FRANKLIN and George BENSON
LOVE AND AFFECTION [A] — Joan ARMATRADING
LOVE AND AFFECTION [A] — SINITTA
LOVE & AFFECTION [A] — MR PINK presents the PROGRAM
LOVE AND ANGER — Kate BUSH
LOVE AND DESIRE (PART 1) — ARPEGGIO
LOVE AND DEVOTION — (MC SAR &) The REAL McCOY
LOVE AND HAPPINESS (YEMAYA Y OCHUN) — RIVER OCEAN featuring INDIA
LOVE AND KISSES — Dannii MINOGUE
LOVE AND LONELINESS — The MOTORS
LOVE AND MARRIAGE — Frank SINATRA
LOVE AND MONEY — LOVE AND MONEY
LOVE AND PAIN — CARLTON
LOVE AND PRIDE — KING
LOVE AND REGRET — DEACON BLUE
LOVE AND TEARS — Naomi CAMPBELL
LOVE AND UNDERSTANDING — CHER
LOVE ANYWAY — Mike SCOTT
LOVE AT FIRST SIGHT [A] — Kylie MINOGUE
LOVE @ 1ST SIGHT [B] — Mary J BLIGE featuring METHOD MAN
LOVE AT FIRST SIGHT (JE T'AIME ... MOI NON PLUS) — SOUNDS NICE featuring Tim MYCROFT
LOVE ATTACK — Shakin' STEVENS
LOVE BALLAD — George BENSON
LOVE BE MY LOVER (PLAYA SOL) — NOVOCANE vs NO ONE DRIVING
LOVE BITES — DEF LEPPARD
LOVE BLONDE — Kim WILDE
LOVE BOMB BABY — TIGERTAILZ
LOVE BREAKDOWN — ROZALLA
LOVE BUG — RAMSEY and FEN featuring Lynsey MOORE
LOVE BUG — SWEETS FOR MY SWEET (MEDLEY) — Tina CHARLES
LOVE BURNS — BLACK REBEL MOTORCYCLE CLUB
LOVE CAN BUILD A BRIDGE [A] — CHILDREN FOR RWANDA
LOVE CAN BUILD A BRIDGE [A] — CHER, Chrissie HYNDE & Neneh CHERRY with Eric CLAPTON
LOVE CAN MOVE MOUNTAINS — Celine DION
LOVE CAN'T TURN AROUND [A] — Farley 'Jackmaster' FUNK with Darryl PANDY
LOVE CAN'T TURN AROUND [A] — HEAVY WEATHER
THE LOVE CATS — The CURE
LOVE CHANGES (EVERYTHING) [A] — CLIMIE FISHER
LOVE CHANGES EVERYTHING [B] — Michael BALL
LOVE CHILD [A] — Diana ROSS and The SUPREMES
LOVE CHILD [B] — GOODBYE MR MACKENZIE
LOVE CITY GROOVE — LOVE CITY GROOVE
LOVE COME DOWN [A] — Evelyn 'Champagne' KING
LOVE COME DOWN [A] — Alison LIMERICK
LOVE COME DOWN [B] — Eve GALLAGHER
LOVE COME HOME — OUR TRIBE with Franke PHARAOH and Kristine W
LOVE COME RESCUE ME — LOVESTATION
LOVE COMES AGAIN — TIESTO featuring BT
LOVE COMES QUICKLY — PET SHOP BOYS
LOVE COMES TO MIND — CHIMES
LOVE COMMANDMENTS — Gisele JACKSON
LOVE CONQUERS ALL [A] — DEEP PURPLE
LOVE CONQUERS ALL [B] — ABC
LOVE DANCE — VISION
LOVE DETECTIVE — ARAB STRAP
LOVE DISCO STYLE — EROTIC DRUM BAND
LOVE DOESN'T HAVE TO HURT — ATOMIC KITTEN
LOVE DON'T COME EASY — The ALARM
LOVE DON'T COST A THING — Jennifer LOPEZ
LOVE DON'T LET ME GO — David GUETTA featuring Chris WILLIS
LOVE DON'T LIVE — URBAN BLUES PROJECT presents Michael PROCTER
LOVE DON'T LIVE HERE ANYMORE [A] — ROSE ROYCE
LOVE DON'T LIVE HERE ANYMORE [A] — Jimmy NAIL
LOVE DON'T LIVE HERE ANYMORE [A] — DOUBLE TROUBLE
LOVE DON'T LOVE YOU — EN VOGUE
LOVE ENOUGH FOR TWO — PRIMA DONNA
LOVE ENUFF — SOUL II SOUL
LOVE EVICTION — Lonnie GORDON
LOVE FOOLOSOPHY — JAMIROQUAI
LOVE FOR LIFE — Lisa MOORISH
THE LOVE GAME — MUDLARKS
LOVE GAMES [A] — The DRIFTERS
LOVE GAMES [B] — LEVEL 42
LOVE GAMES [C] — BELLE and the DEVOTIONS
LOVE GLOVE — VISAGE
LOVE GROOVE (GROOVE WITH YOU) — SMOOTH
LOVE GROWS (WHERE MY ROSEMARY GOES) — EDISON LIGHTHOUSE

LOVE GUARANTEED — DAMAGE
LOVE HANGOVER [A] — Diana ROSS
LOVE HANGOVER [A] — ASSOCIATES
LOVE HANGOVER [A] — Pauline HENRY
LOVE HANGOVER [B] — SCARLET
LOVE HAS COME AGAIN — HUMAN MOVEMENT featuring Sophie MOLETA
LOVE HAS COME AROUND — Donald BYRD
LOVE HAS FOUND ITS WAY — Dennis BROWN
LOVE HAS PASSED AWAY — SUPERNATURALS
LOVE HER — The WALKER BROTHERS
LOVE HERE I COME — BAD BOYS INC
LOVE HIT ME — Maxine NIGHTINGALE
LOVE HOUSE — Samantha FOX
LOVE HOW YOU FEEL — Sharon REDD
LOVE HURTS [A] — Jim CAPALDI
LOVE HURTS [A] — CHER
LOVE HURTS [B] — Peter POLYCARPOU
THE LOVE I LOST [A] — Harold MELVIN and the BLUENOTES
THE LOVE I LOST [A] — WEST END featuring SYBIL
LOVE IN A PEACEFUL WORLD — LEVEL 42
LOVE IN AN ELEVATOR — AEROSMITH
LOVE IN ANGER — ARMOURY SHOW
LOVE IN C MINOR — CERRONE
LOVE IN ITSELF — DEPECHE MODE
LOVE IN THE FIRST DEGREE — BANANARAMA
LOVE IN THE KEY OF C — Belinda CARLISLE
LOVE IN THE NATURAL WAY — Kim WILDE
LOVE IN THE SUN — GLITTER BAND
THE LOVE IN YOUR EYES [A] — Vicky LEANDROS
THE LOVE IN YOUR EYES [A] — Daniel O'DONNELL
LOVE INFINITY — SILVER CITY
LOVE INJECTION — TRUSSEL
LOVE INSIDE — Sharon FORRESTER
LOVE IS ... [A] — VIKKI
LOVE IS [B] — Alannah MYLES
LOVE IS A BATTLEFIELD — Pat BENATAR
LOVE IS A BEAUTIFUL THING — Al GREEN
LOVE IS A GOLDEN RING — Frankie LAINE
LOVE IS A KILLER — VIXEN
LOVE IS A MANY SPLENDORED THING — FOUR ACES
LOVE IS A STRANGER — EURYTHMICS
LOVE IS A WONDERFUL COLOUR — ICICLE WORKS
LOVE IS A WONDERFUL THING — Michael BOLTON
LOVE IS ALL [A] — Malcolm ROBERTS
LOVE IS ALL [A] — Engelbert HUMPERDINCK
LOVE IS ALL [B] — The RAPTURE
LOVE IS ALL AROUND [A] — The TROGGS
LOVE IS ALL AROUND [A] — WET WET WET
LOVE IS ALL AROUND [B] — DJ BOBO
LOVE IS ALL IS ALRIGHT — UB40
LOVE IS ALL THAT MATTERS — HUMAN LEAGUE
LOVE IS ALL WE NEED — Mary J BLIGE
LOVE IS BLUE [A] — Jeff BECK
LOVE IS BLUE (L'AMOUR EST BLEU) [A] — Paul MAURIAT
LOVE IS BLUE [B] — Edward BALL
LOVE IS CONTAGIOUS — Taja SEVELLE
LOVE IS EVERYWHERE — CICERO
LOVE IS FOREVER — Billy OCEAN
LOVE IS HERE AND NOW YOU'RE GONE — The SUPREMES
LOVE IS HOLY — Kim WILDE
LOVE IS IN CONTROL (FINGER ON THE TRIGGER) — Donna SUMMER
LOVE IS IN THE AIR [A] — John Paul YOUNG
LOVE IS IN THE AIR [A] — MILK & SUGAR vs John Paul YOUNG
LOVE IS IN YOUR EYES — LEMON TREES
LOVE IS JUST THE GREAT PRETENDER — ANIMAL NIGHTLIFE
LOVE IS LIFE — HOT CHOCOLATE
LOVE IS LIKE A VIOLIN — Ken DODD
LOVE IS LIKE OXYGEN — The SWEET
LOVE IS LOVE — Barry RYAN
LOVE IS NOT A GAME — J MAJIK featuring Kathy BROWN
LOVE IS ON THE ONE — XAVIER
LOVE IS ON THE WAY — Luther VANDROSS
LOVE IS ONLY A FEELING — The DARKNESS
LOVE IS SO EASY — STARGARD
LOVE IS SO NICE — URBAN SOUL
LOVE IS STRANGE — The EVERLY BROTHERS
LOVE IS STRONG — The ROLLING STONES
LOVE IS STRONGER THAN DEATH — The THE
LOVE IS STRONGER THAN PRIDE — SADE
LOVE IS THE ANSWER — ENGLAND DAN and John Ford COLEY
LOVE IS THE ART — LIVING IN A BOX
LOVE IS THE DRUG [A] — ROXY MUSIC
LOVE IS THE DRUG [A] — Grace JONES
LOVE IS THE GOD — Maria NAYLER
LOVE IS THE GUN — BLUE MERCEDES
LOVE IS THE ICON — Barry WHITE
LOVE IS THE KEY — The CHARLATANS
LOVE IS THE LAW — The SEAHORSES
LOVE IS THE MESSAGE — LOVE INCORPORATED featuring MC NOISE
LOVE IS THE SEVENTH WAVE — STING
LOVE IS THE SLUG — WE'VE GOT A FUZZBOX AND WE'RE GONNA USE IT
LOVE IS THE SWEETEST THING — Peter SKELLERN
(LOVE IS) THE TENDER TRAP — Frank SINATRA
LOVE IS WAR — BRILLIANT
LOVE IZ — Erick SERMON
LOVE KILLS [A] — Freddie MERCURY
LOVE KILLS [B] — Joe STRUMMER
LOVE KISSES AND HEARTACHES — Maureen EVANS
LOVE LADY — DAMAGE
LOVE LETTER — Marc ALMOND
LOVE LETTERS [A] — Ketty LESTER
LOVE LETTERS [A] — Elvis PRESLEY
LOVE LETTERS [A] — Alison MOYET
LOVE LETTERS [B] — ALI
LOVE LETTERS IN THE SAND [A] — Pat BOONE
LOVE LETTERS IN THE SAND [A] — Vince HILL
LOVE LIES LOST — Helen TERRY
LOVE LIGHT IN FLIGHT — Stevie WONDER
LOVE LIKE A FOUNTAIN — Ian BROWN
LOVE LIKE A MAN — TEN YEARS AFTER
LOVE LIKE A RIVER — CLIMIE FISHER
LOVE LIKE A ROCKET — Bob GELDOF
LOVE LIKE BLOOD — KILLING JOKE
LOVE LIKE THIS — Faith EVANS
LOVE LIKE YOU AND ME — Gary GLITTER
A LOVE LIKE YOURS — Ike and Tina TURNER
L.O.V.E. ... LOVE — ORANGE JUICE
LOVE LOVE LOVE — Bobby HEBB
LOVE LOVE LOVE — HERE I COME — ROLLO
LOVE LOVES TO LOVE LOVE — LULU
LOVE MACHINE [A] — Elvis PRESLEY
LOVE MACHINE [B] — MIRACLES
LOVE MACHINE [C] — GIRLS ALOUD
LOVE MADE ME — VIXEN
LOVE MAKES NO SENSE — Alexander O'NEAL
LOVE MAKES THE WORLD GO ROUND [A] — Perry COMO
LOVE MAKES THE WORLD GO ROUND [A] — JETS
LOVE MAKES THE WORLD GO ROUND [B] — DON-E
LOVE MAN — Otis REDDING
LOVE ME [A] — Yvonne ELLIMAN
LOVE ME [A] — Martine McCUTCHEON
LOVE ME [B] — Diana ROSS
LOVE ME [C] — PATRIC
LOVE ME AND LEAVE ME — The SEAHORSES
LOVE ME AS THOUGH THERE WERE NO TOMORROW — Nat 'King' COLE
LOVE ME BABY — Susan CADOGAN
LOVE ME DO — The BEATLES
LOVE ME FOR A REASON [A] — The OSMONDS
LOVE ME FOR A REASON [A] — BOYZONE
LOVE ME FOREVER [A] — FOUR ESQUIRES
LOVE ME FOREVER [A] — Eydie GORME
LOVE ME FOREVER [A] — Marion RYAN
LOVE ME LIKE A LOVER — Tina CHARLES
LOVE ME LIKE I LOVE YOU — BAY CITY ROLLERS
LOVE ME LIKE THIS — REAL TO REEL
LOVE ME LOVE MY DOG — Peter SHELLEY
LOVE ME NOW [A] — Briana CORRIGAN
LOVE ME NOW [B] — SECRET KNOWLEDGE
LOVE ME OR LEAVE ME [A] — Sammy DAVIS Jr
LOVE ME OR LEAVE ME [A] — Doris DAY
LOVE ME RIGHT NOW — ROSE ROYCE
LOVE ME RIGHT (OH SHEILA) — ANGEL CITY
LOVE ME TENDER [A] — Elvis PRESLEY
LOVE ME TENDER [A] — Richard CHAMBERLAIN
LOVE ME TENDER [A] — Roland RAT SUPERSTAR
LOVE ME THE RIGHT WAY — RAPINATION featuring Kym MAZELLE
LOVE ME TO SLEEP — HOT CHOCOLATE
LOVE ME TONIGHT [A] — Tom JONES
LOVE ME TONIGHT [B] — Trevor WALTERS
LOVE ME WARM AND TENDER — Paul ANKA
LOVE ME WITH ALL YOUR HEART — Karl DENVER
LOVE MEETING LOVE — LEVEL 42
LOVE MISSILE F1-11 — SIGUE SIGUE SPUTNIK
LOVE MOVES (IN MYSTERIOUS WAYS) — Julia FORDHAM
LOVE MY WAY — PSYCHEDELIC FURS
LOVE NEEDS NO DISGUISE — Gary NUMAN and DRAMATIS
LOVE NEVER DIES ... — Belinda CARLISLE
LOVE OF A LIFETIME [A] — Chaka KHAN
LOVE OF A LIFETIME [B] — HONEYZ
LOVE OF MY LIFE [A] — The DOOLEYS
LOVE OF MY LIFE [B] — QUEEN
THE LOVE OF RICHARD NIXON — MANIC STREET PREACHERS
LOVE OF THE COMMON PEOPLE [A] — Nicky THOMAS
LOVE OF THE COMMON PEOPLE [A] — Paul YOUNG
LOVE OF THE LOVED — Cilla BLACK
LOVE OH LOVE — Lionel RICHIE
LOVE ON A FARMBOY'S WAGES — XTC
LOVE ON A MOUNTAIN TOP [A] — Robert KNIGHT
LOVE ON A MOUNTAIN TOP [A] — SINITTA
LOVE ON A SUMMER NIGHT — McCRARYS
LOVE ON LOVE [A] — E-ZEE POSSEE
LOVE ON LOVE [A] — Candi STATON
LOVE ON THE LINE [A] — BARCLAY JAMES HARVEST
LOVE ON THE LINE [B] — BLAZIN' SQUAD
LOVE ON THE NORTHERN LINE — NORTHERN LINE
LOVE ON THE ROCKS — Neil DIAMOND
LOVE ON THE RUN — CHICANE featuring Peter CUNNAH
LOVE ON THE SIDE — BROKEN ENGLISH
LOVE ON YOUR SIDE — THOMPSON TWINS
LOVE OR MONEY [A] — BLACKWELLS
LOVE OR MONEY [A] — Jimmy CRAWFORD
LOVE OR MONEY [A] — Billy FURY
LOVE OR MONEY [B] — Sammy HAGAR
LOVE OR NOTHING — Diana BROWN and Barrie K SHARPE
LOVE OVER GOLD (LIVE) — DIRE STRAITS
LOVE OVERBOARD — Gladys KNIGHT and the PIPS
LOVE PAINS [A] — Hazell DEAN
LOVE PAINS [A] — Liza MINNELLI
THE LOVE PARADE — DREAM ACADEMY
LOVE PATROL — The DOOLEYS
LOVE, PEACE & GREASE — BT
LOVE PEACE AND HARMONY — DREAM FREQUENCY
LOVE, PEACE & NAPPINESS — LOST BOYZ
LOVE PLUS ONE — HAIRCUT 100
LOVE POTION NO.9 — TYGERS OF PAN TANG
LOVE POWER — Dionne WARWICK and Jeffrey OSBORNE
LOVE PROFUSION — MADONNA
LOVE REACTION — DIVINE
LOVE REALLY HURTS WITHOUT YOU — Billy OCEAN
LOVE REARS ITS UGLY HEAD — LIVING COLOUR
LOVE REMOVAL MACHINE — The CULT
LOVE RENDEZVOUS — M PEOPLE
LOVE RESURRECTION [A] — Alison MOYET
LOVE RESURRECTION [A] — D'LUX
LOVE REVOLUTION — PHIXX
LOVE ROLLERCOASTER — RED HOT CHILI PEPPERS
LOVE RULES — WEST END
THE LOVE SCENE — JOE
LOVE SCENES — Beverley CRAVEN
LOVE SEE NO COLOUR — The FARM
LOVE SENSATION — 911
LOVE SHACK — B-52's
LOVE SHADOW — FASHION
LOVE SHINE — RHYTHM SOURCE
LOVE SHINE A LIGHT — KATRINA and the WAVES
LOVE SHINES THROUGH — CHAKRA
LOVE SHOULD BE A CRIME — O-TOWN
LOVE SHOULDA BROUGHT YOU HOME — Toni BRAXTON
LOVE SHY — Kristine BLOND
LOVE SICK — Bob DYLAN
LOVE SITUATION — Mark FISHER featuring Dotty GREEN
LOVE SLAVE — WEDDING PRESENT
LOVE SNEAKIN' UP ON YOU — Bonnie RAITT
A LOVE SO BEAUTIFUL — Michael BOLTON
LOVE SO BRIGHT — Mark SHAW
LOVE SO RIGHT — The BEE GEES
LOVE SO STRONG — SECRET LIFE
LOVE SONG [A] — The DAMNED
LOVE SONG [B] — SIMPLE MINDS
LOVE SONG [C] — UTAH SAINTS
LOVE SONG FOR A VAMPIRE — Annie LENNOX
LOVE SONGS ARE BACK AGAIN (MEDLEY) — BAND OF GOLD
THE LOVE SONGS EP — Daniel O'DONNELL
LOVE SPREADS — The STONE ROSES
LOVE STIMULATION — HUMATE
LOVE STORY [A] — JETHRO TULL
LOVE STORY [B] — LAYO & BUSHWACKA!
LOVE STORY (VS FINALLY) [B] — LAYO & BUSHWACKA!
LOVE STRAIN — Kym MAZELLE
A LOVE SUPREME — Will DOWNING
LOVE TAKE OVER — FIVE STAR
LOVE TAKES TIME — Mariah CAREY
LOVE THE LIFE — JTQ
LOVE THE ONE YOU'RE WITH [A] — Stephen STILLS
LOVE THE ONE YOU'RE WITH [A] — BUCKS FIZZ
LOVE THE ONE YOU'RE WITH [A] — Luther VANDROSS
LOVE THEM — EAMON featuring GHOSTFACE
LOVE THEME FROM 'A STAR IS BORN' (EVERGREEN) — Barbra STREISAND
LOVE THEME FROM SPARTACUS — Terry CALLIER
LOVE THEME FROM 'THE GODFATHER' (SPEAK SOFTLY LOVE) — Andy WILLIAMS
LOVE THEME FROM 'THE THORN BIRDS' — Juan MARTIN
LOVE THING [A] — PASADENAS
LOVE THING [B] — Tina TURNER
LOVE THING [C] — EVOLUTION
LOVE ... THY WILL BE DONE — MARTIKA
LOVE TIMES LOVE — HEAVY PETTIN'
LOVE X LOVE — George BENSON
LOVE TO HATE YOU — ERASURE
LOVE II LOVE — DAMAGE
LOVE TO LOVE YOU — The CORRS
LOVE TO LOVE YOU BABY — Donna SUMMER
LOVE TO SEE YOU CRY — Enrique IGLESIAS
LOVE TO STAY — ALTERED IMAGES
LOVE TOGETHER — LA MIX
LOVE TOUCH — Rod STEWART
LOVE TOWN — Booker NEWBERRY III
LOVE TRAIN [A] — O'JAYS
LOVE TRAIN [B] — Holly JOHNSON
LOVE TRIAL — Kelly MARIE
LOVE, TRUTH AND HONESTY — BANANARAMA
LOVE U 4 LIFE — JODECI
LOVE U MORE — SUNSCREEM
LOVE UNLIMITED — FUN LOVIN' CRIMINALS
LOVE WALKED IN — THUNDER
LOVE WARS — WOMACK AND WOMACK
LOVE WASHES OVER — ART OF TRANCE
LOVE WHAT YOU DO — The DIVINE COMEDY
LOVE WILL COME — TOMSKI
LOVE WILL COME THROUGH — TRAVIS
LOVE WILL CONQUER ALL — Lionel RICHIE
LOVE WILL FIND A WAY [A] — David GRANT
LOVE WILL FIND A WAY [B] — YES
LOVE WILL KEEP US ALIVE — The EAGLES
LOVE WILL KEEP US TOGETHER [A] — CAPTAIN and TENNILLE
LOVE WILL KEEP US TOGETHER [B] — JTQ featuring Alison LIMERICK
LOVE WILL LEAD YOU BACK — Taylor DAYNE
LOVE WILL MAKE YOU FAIL IN SCHOOL — Rocky SHARPE and the REPLAYS
LOVE WILL NEVER DO (WITHOUT YOU) — Janet JACKSON
LOVE WILL SAVE THE DAY — Whitney HOUSTON
LOVE WILL SET YOU FREE (JAMBE MYTH) — STARCHASER
LOVE WILL TEAR US APART — JOY DIVISION
LOVE WON'T LET ME WAIT — Major HARRIS
LOVE WON'T WAIT — Gary BARLOW
LOVE WORTH DYING FOR — THUNDER
A LOVE WORTH WAITING FOR — Shakin' STEVENS
LOVE YOU ALL MY LIFETIME — Chaka KHAN
LOVE YOU ANYWAY — DE NADA
LOVE YOU DOWN — READY FOR THE WORLD
LOVE YOU INSIDE OUT — The BEE GEES
LOVE YOU LIKE MAD — VS
LOVE YOU MORE — The BUZZCOCKS
LOVE YOU SOME MORE — Cevin FISHER featuirng Sheila SMITH
THE LOVE YOU SAVE — The JACKSON FIVE
LOVE YOUR MONEY — DAISY CHAINSAW
LOVE YOUR SEXY ... !! — BYKER GROOOVE!
LOVE ZONE — Billy OCEAN
LOVEBIRDS — DODGY
LOVEDRIVE — SCORPIONS
LOVEFOOL — The CARDIGANS
LOVELIGHT (RIDE ON A LOVE TRAIN) — Jayn HANNA
LOVELY — Bubba SPARXXX
LOVELY DAUGHTER — MERZ
LOVELY DAY — Bill WITHERS
LOVELY DAZE — JAZZY JEFF & the FRESH PRINCE
LOVELY MONEY — The DAMNED
LOVELY ONE — The JACKSONS
LOVELY THING — REGGAE PHILHARMONIC ORCHESTRA
LOVENEST — WEDDING PRESENT
LOVER [A] — Dan REED NETWORK
LOVER [B] — Joe ROBERTS
LOVER [C] — Rachel McFARLANE
LOVER COME BACK TO ME — DEAD OR ALIVE
THE LOVER IN ME — Sheena EASTON
THE LOVER IN YOU — SUGARHILL GANG
LOVER LOVER LOVER — Ian McCULLOCH
LOVER PLEASE — VERNONS GIRLS
A LOVER SPURNED — Marc ALMOND
THE LOVER THAT YOU ARE — PULSE featuring Antoinette ROBERSON
LOVERBOY [A] — Billy OCEAN
LOVER BOY [B] — CHAIRMEN OF THE BOARD
LOVERBOY [C] — MARIAH featuring CAMEO
LOVERIDE — NUANCE featuring Vikki LOVE
A LOVER'S CONCERTO — TOYS
A LOVER'S HOLIDAY — CHANGE
LOVER'S LANE — GEORGIO
THE LOVERS — Alexander O'NEAL
LOVERS OF THE WORLD UNITE — DAVID and JONATHAN
THE LOVERS WE WERE — Michael BALL
LOVE'S A LOADED GUN — Alice COOPER
LOVE'S ABOUT TO CHANGE MY HEART — Donna SUMMER
LOVE'S BEEN GOOD TO ME — Frank SINATRA
LOVE'S COMIN' AT YA — Melba MOORE
LOVE'S CRASHING WAVES — DIFFORD and TILBROOK
LOVE'S DIVINE — SEAL
LOVE'S EASY TEARS — COCTEAU TWINS
LOVE'S GONNA GET YOU [A] — UK PLAYERS
LOVE'S GONNA GET YOU [B] — Jocelyn BROWN

LOVE'S GOT A HOLD ON MY HEART — STEPS
LOVE'S GOT ME — LOOSE ENDS
LOVE'S GOT ME ON A TRIP SO HIGH —
Loni CLARK
LOVE'S GOTTA HOLD ON ME [A] — DOLLAR
LOVE'S GOTTA HOLD ON ME [B] —
ZOO EXPERIENCE featuring DESTRY
LOVE'S GREAT ADVENTURE — ULTRAVOX
LOVE'S JUST A BROKEN HEART — Cilla BLACK
LOVE'S MADE A FOOL OF YOU [A] —
The CRICKETS
LOVE'S MADE A FOOL OF YOU [A] —
Buddy HOLLY
LOVE'S MADE A FOOL OF YOU [A] —
MATCHBOX
LOVES ME LIKE A ROCK — Paul SIMON
LOVE'S ON EVERY CORNER —
Dannii MINOGUE
LOVE'S SUCH A WONDERFUL THING —
The REAL THING
LOVE'S SWEET EXILE —
MANIC STREET PREACHERS
LOVE'S TAKEN OVER — Chanté MOORE
LOVE'S THEME —
LOVE UNLIMITED ORCHESTRA
LOVE'S UNKIND [A] — Donna SUMMER
LOVE'S UNKIND [A] — Sophie LAWRENCE
LOVESICK [A] — GANG STARR
LOVESICK [B] — UNDERCOVER
LOVESICK BLUES — Frank IFIELD
LOVESONG — The CURE
LOVESTRUCK — MADNESS
LOVETOWN — Peter GABRIEL
LOVEY DOVEY — Tony TERRY
LOVIN' — CRW
LOVIN' EACH DAY — Ronan KEATING
LOVIN' IS EASY — HEAR'SAY
LOVIN' (LET ME LOVE YOU) — APACHE INDIAN
LOVIN', LIVIN' AND GIVIN' — Diana ROSS
LOVIN' ON THE SIDE — REID
LOVIN' THINGS — MARMALADE
LOVIN' UP A STORM — Jerry Lee LEWIS
LOVIN' YOU [A] — SHANICE
LOVIN' YOU [A] — UBM
LOVIN' YOU [A] — SPARKLE
LOVING AND FREE — Kiki DEE
LOVING ARMS — Elvis PRESLEY
LOVING EVERY MINUTE — LIGHTHOUSE FAMILY
LOVING JUST FOR FUN — Kelly MARIE
LOVING ON THE LOSING SIDE — Tommy HUNT
LOVING THE ALIEN — David BOWIE
LOVING YOU [A] — Elvis PRESLEY
LOVIN' YOU [B] — Minnie RIPERTON
LOVING YOU '03 [B] — MARC et CLAUDE
LOVING YOU [C] — MASSIVO featuring TRACY
LOVING YOU [C] — Donald BYRD
LOVING YOU [D] — Chris REA
LOVING YOU [E] — Feargal SHARKEY
LOVING YOU AGAIN — Chris REA
LOVIN' YOU AIN'T EASY — PAGLIARO
LOVING YOU HAS MADE ME BANANAS —
Guy MARKS
LOVING YOU IS SWEETER THAN EVER [A] —
The FOUR TOPS
LOVING YOU IS SWEETER THAN EVER [A] —
Nick KAMEN
LOVING YOU MORE — BT
Brian HARVEY and the REFUGEE CREW
LOVING YOU (OLE OLE OLE) —
LOVING YOU'S A DIRTY JOB BUT SOMEBODY'S GOTTA
DO IT — Bonnie TYLER, guest vocals Todd
RUNDGREN
LOW [A] — CRACKER
LOW [B] — FOO FIGHTERS
LOW [C] — Kelly CLARKSON
LOW FIVE — SNEAKER PIMPS
LOW LIFE IN HIGH PLACES — THUNDER
LOW RIDER — WAR
LOWDOWN [A] — Boz SCAGGS
LOWDOWN [A] — HINDSIGHT
LOWDOWN [B] — ELECTRAFIXION
LOWRIDER — CYPRESS HILL
THE LOYALISER — FATIMA MANSIONS
LSD (EP) — KAOTIC CHEMISTRY
L.S.F. — KASABIAN
LSI — The SHAMEN
LUCAS WITH THE LID OFF — LUCAS
LUCHINI AKA (THIS IS IT) — CAMP LO
LUCILLE [A] — LITTLE RICHARD
LUCILLE [A] — The EVERLY BROTHERS
LUCILLE [B] — Kenny ROGERS
LUCKY — Britney SPEARS
LUCKY DEVIL [A] — Carl DOBKINS Jr
LUCKY DEVIL [A] — Frank IFIELD
LUCKY FIVE — Russ CONWAY
LUCKY LIPS —
Cliff RICHARD and The SHADOWS
LUCKY LOVE — ACE OF BASE
LUCKY LUCKY ME — Marvin GAYE
LUCKY MAN — The VERVE
LUCKY NUMBER — Lene LOVICH
LUCKY ONE — Amy GRANT
THE LUCKY ONE — Laura BRANIGAN
LUCKY PRESSURE — Roni SIZE / REPRAZENT
LUCKY 7 MEGAMIX — UK MIXMASTERS
LUCKY STAR [A] — MADONNA
LUCKY STAR [B] — SUPERFUNK

LUCKY STAR [C] —
BASEMENT JAXX featuring DIZZEE RASCAL
LUCKY STARS — Dean FRIEDMAN
LUCKY TOWN (LIVE) — Bruce SPRINGSTEEN
LUCKY YOU — The LIGHTNING SEEDS
LUCRETIA MY REFLECTION —
SISTERS OF MERCY
LUCY — HABIT
LUCY IN THE SKY WITH DIAMONDS —
Elton JOHN
LUDI — DREAM WARRIORS
LUKA — Suzanne VEGA
LULLABY [A] — The CURE
LULLABY [B] — Shawn MULLINS
LULLABY [C] — Melanie B
LULLABY [D] — STARSAILOR
LULLABY [E] — LEMAR
LULLABY OF BROADWAY — Winifred SHAW
LULLABY OF THE LEAVES — VENTURES
LUMBERED — Lonnie DONEGAN
LUMP — PRESIDENTS OF THE UNITED STATES OF
AMERICA
THE LUNATICS (HAVE TAKEN OVER THE
ASYLUM) — FUN BOY THREE
LUNCH OR DINNER —
Sunshine ANDERSON
LUSH — ORBITAL
LUST FOR LIFE — Iggy POP
LUTON AIRPORT — CATS UK
LUV DA SUNSHINE — INTENSO PROJECT
LUV DUP — HIGH FIDELITY
LUV 4 LUV — Robin S
LUV IS COOL — SYSTEM OF LIFE
LUV ME LUV ME — SHAGGY
LUV U BETTER — LL COOL J
LUV'D UP — CRUSH
LUVSTRUCK — SOUTHSIDE SPINNERS
LUVSTUFF — SAGAT
LYDIA — Dean FRIEDMAN
LYIN' EYES — The EAGLES
LYRIC — ZWAN
LYRIC ON MY LIP — TALI
MA BAKER — BONEY M
MA BAKER — SOMEBODY SCREAM — BONEY M
MA! (HE'S MAKING EYES AT ME) [A] —
Johnny OTIS SHOW
MA HE'S MAKING EYES AT ME [A] —
Lena ZAVARONI
MA, I DON'T LOVE HER —
CLIPSE featuring Faith EVANS
MA SAYS, PA SAYS —
Doris DAY and Johnnie RAY
MA SOLITUDA — CATHERINE WHEEL
MACARENA [A] —
LOS DEL MAR featuring Wil VELOZ
MACARENA [A] — LOS DEL RIO
MACARENA [A] — CHIPMUNKS
MACARTHUR PARK [A] — Richard HARRIS
MACARTHUR PARK [A] — Donna SUMMER
MACH 5 — PRESIDENTS OF THE
UNITED STATES OF AMERICA
MACHINE — The YEAH YEAH YEAHS
MACHINE + SOUL — Gary NUMAN
MACHINE GUN — The COMMODORES
MACHINE SAYS YES — FC KAHUNA
MACHINEHEAD — BUSH
MACHINERY — Sheena EASTON
MACK THE KNIFE [A] — Louis ARMSTRONG
MACK THE KNIFE [A] — Bobby DARIN
MACK THE KNIFE [A] — Ella FITZGERALD
MACK THE KNIFE [A] — KING KURT
MACUSHLA — Bernie NOLAN
MAD ABOUT THE BOY — Dinah WASHINGTON
MAD ABOUT YOU [A] — Bruce RUFFIN
MAD ABOUT YOU [B] — Belinda CARLISLE
MAD ABOUT YOU [C] — STING
MAD DOG — ELASTICA
MAD EYED SCREAMER — CREATURES
MAD IF YA DON'T — GAYLE & GILLIAN
MAD LOVE (EP) — LUSH
MAD PASSIONATE LOVE — Bernard BRESSLAW
MAD WORLD [A] — TEARS FOR FEARS
MAD WORLD [A] —
Michael ANDREWS featuring Gary JULES
MADAGASCAR — ART OF TRANCE
MADAM BUTTERFLY (UN BEL DI VEDREMO) —
Malcolm McLAREN
MADAME HELGA — STEREOPHONICS
MADCHESTER RAVE ON (EP) —
HAPPY MONDAYS
MADE FOR LOVIN' YOU — ANASTACIA
MADE IN ENGLAND — Elton JOHN
MADE IN HEAVEN — Freddie MERCURY
MADE IN 2 MINUTES —
BUG KANN and the PLASTIC JAM
MADE IT BACK —
Beverley KNIGHT featuring REDMAN
MADE IT BACK 99 — Beverley KNIGHT
MADE IT LAST — HIGH CONTRAST
MADE OF STONE — The STONE ROSES
MADE YOU — Adam FAITH
MADE YOU LOOK — NAS
THE MADISON — Ray ELLINGTON
MADLY IN LOVE — BROS
MADNESS (IS ALL IN THE MIND) — MADNESS
MADNESS THING — LEILANI
MAGGIE — FOSTER and ALLEN

MAGGIE MAY — Rod STEWART
MAGGIE'S FARM [A] — Bob DYLAN
MAGGIE'S FARM [A] — The SPECIALS
MAGGIE'S FARM (LIVE) [A] — TIN MACHINE
MAGGIE'S LAST PARTY — V.I.M.
MAGIC [A] — PILOT
MAGIC [B] — Olivia NEWTON-JOHN
MAGIC [C] — SASHA
MAGIC [D] — D'INFLUENCE
MAGIC [E] — Nick DRAKE
MAGIC BUS — The WHO
MAGIC CARPET RIDE — MIGHTY DUB KATZ
MAGIC FLY [A] — SPACE
MAGIC FLY [A] — MINIMALISTIX
THE MAGIC FRIEND — 2 UNLIMITED
MAGIC HOUR [A] — HALO JAMES
MAGIC HOUR [B] — CAST
THE MAGIC IS THERE — Daniel O'DONNELL
MAGIC MANDRAKE — SARR BAND
MAGIC MIND — EARTH WIND AND FIRE
MAGIC MOMENTS [A] — Perry COMO
MAGIC MOMENTS [A] — Ronnie HILTON
THE MAGIC NUMBER — DE LA SOUL
THE MAGIC PIPER (OF LOVE) — Edwyn COLLINS
MAGIC ROUNDABOUT — Jasper CARROTT
MAGIC SMILE — Rosie VELA
MAGIC STYLE — BADMAN
MAGIC TOUCH [A] — ODYSSEY
MAGIC TOUCH [B] — ROSE ROYCE
MAGIC TOUCH [C] — LOOSE ENDS
MAGICAL — BUCKS FIZZ
MAGICAL MYSTERY TOUR (DOUBLE EP) —
The BEATLES
MAGICAL SPIEL — Barry RYAN
MAGIC'S BACK (THEME FROM 'THE GHOSTS
OF OXFORD STREET') —
Malcolm McLAREN featuring Alison LIMERICK
MAGIC'S WAND — WHODINI
THE MAGNIFICENT — AGENT oo
THE MAGNIFICENT SEVEN [A] —
John BARRY ORCHESTRA
THE MAGNIFICENT SEVEN [A] — Al CAIOLA
THE MAGNIFICENT 7 [A] — SCOOBIE
THE MAGNIFICENT SEVEN [B] — The CLASH
MAGNUM — MAGNUM
MAH-NA, MAH-NA — Piero UMILIANI
MAID OF ORLEANS (THE WALTZ JOAN OF ARC) —
ORCHESTRAL MANOEUVRES IN THE DARK
MAIDEN JAPAN (EP) — IRON MAIDEN
MAIDS, WHEN YOU'RE YOUNG NEVER WED AN
OLD MAN — DUBLINERS
THE MAIGRET THEME — Joe LOSS
THE MAIN ATTRACTION — Pat BOONE
MAIN OFFENDER — The HIVES
MAIN THEME FROM 'EXODUS' — SEMPRINI
MAIN THEME FROM 'THE THORN BIRDS' —
Henry MANCINI
MAIN TITLE THEME FROM 'MAN WITH THE
GOLDEN ARM' [A] — Billy MAY
MAIN TITLE THEME FROM 'MAN WITH THE
GOLDEN ARM' [A] — Jet HARRIS
MAINSTREAM — Thea GILMORE
MAIS OUI — KING BROTHERS
THE MAJESTY OF ROCK — SPINAL TAP
MAJOR TOM (COMING HOME) —
Peter SCHILLING
MAJORCA — Petula CLARK
MAKE A DAFT NOISE FOR CHRISTMAS —
The GOODIES
MAKE A FAMILY — Gary CLARK
MAKE A MOVE ON ME — Olivia NEWTON-JOHN
MAKE BELIEVE IT'S YOUR FIRST TIME —
The CARPENTERS
MAKE HER MINE — Nat 'King' COLE
MAKE IT A PARTY — Winifred ATWELL
MAKE IT CLAP —
Busta RHYMES featuring SPLIFF STAR
MAKE IT EASY — SHYSTIE
MAKE IT EASY ON YOURSELF —
The WALKER BROTHERS
MAKE IT GOOD — a1
MAKE IT HAPPEN — Mariah CAREY
MAKE IT HOT [A] — Nicole RAY featuring
Missy 'Misdemeanor' ELLIOTT
MAKE IT HOT [B] — VS
MAKE IT LAST [A] — SKIPWORTH and TURNER
MAKE IT LAST [B] — EMBRACE
MAKE IT MINE — The SHAMEN
MAKE IT ON MY OWN — Alison LIMERICK
MAKE IT REAL — SCORPIONS
MAKE IT RIGHT —
Christian FALK featuring DEMETREUS
MAKE IT SOON — Tony BRENT
MAKE IT TONIGHT — WET WET WET
MAKE IT UP WITH LOVE — ATL
MAKE IT WITH YOU [A] — BREAD
MAKE IT WITH YOU [A] — PASADENAS
MAKE IT WITH YOU [A] — LET LOOSE
MAKE IT WITH YOU [B] — UNIVERSAL
MAKE LOVE EASY — Freddie JACKSON
MAKE LOVE LIKE A MAN — DEF LEPPARD
MAKE LOVE TO ME! — Jo STAFFORD
MAKE LOVE TO ME [A] — John LEYTON
MAKE LOVE TO ME [B] — Jill FRANCIS
MAKE LUV —
ROOM 5 featuring Oliver CHEATHAM
MAKE ME AN ISLAND — Joe DOLAN

MAKE ME BAD — KORN
MAKE ME LAUGH — ANTHRAX
MAKE ME SMILE (COME UP AND SEE ME) [A] —
Steve HARLEY and COCKNEY REBEL
MAKE ME SMILE (COME UP AND SEE ME) [A] —
ERASURE
MAKE ME WANNA SCREAM — Blu CANTRELL
MAKE MY BODY ROCK — JOMANDA
MAKE MY DAY — Buju BANTON
MAKE MY HEART FLY — The PROCLAIMERS
MAKE MY LOVE — Shawn CHRISTOPHER
MAKE SOMEONE HAPPY — Jimmy DURANTE
MAKE THAT MOVE — SHALAMAR
MAKE THE DEAL — OCEAN COLOUR SCENE
MAKE THE WORLD GO AWAY [A] —
Eddy ARNOLD
MAKE THE WORLD GO AWAY [A] —
Donny and Marie OSMOND
MAKE THE WORLD GO ROUND [A] — Sandy B
MAKE THE WORLD GO ROUND 2004 [A] — Sandy B
MAKE UP YOUR MIND — BASS JUMPERS
MAKE WAY FOR NODDY — NODDY
MAKE WAY FOR THE INDIAN —
APACHE INDIAN and TIM DOG
MAKE YOURS A HAPPY HOME —
Gladys KNIGHT and the PIPS
MAKES ME LOVE YOU — ECLIPSE
MAKES ME WANNA DIE — TRICKY
MAKIN' HAPPY — Crystal WATERS
MAKIN' IT — David NAUGHTON
MAKIN' LOVE — Floyd ROBINSON
MAKIN' OUT — Mark OWEN
MAKIN' WHOOPEE — Ray CHARLES
MAKING LOVE (OUT OF NOTHING AT ALL) —
Bonnie TYLER
MAKING PLANS FOR NIGEL — XTC
MAKING THE MOST OF — DODGY
MAKING TIME — CREATION
MAKING UP AGAIN — GOLDIE
MAKING YOUR MIND UP — BUCKS FIZZ
MALE STRIPPER — Man PARRISH
MALIBU — HOLE
MALT AND BARLEY BLUES —
McGUINNESS FLINT
MAMA [A] — David WHITFIELD
MAMA [A] — Connie FRANCIS
MAMA [B] — Dave BERRY
MAMA [C] — GENESIS
MAMA [D] — Kim APPLEBY
MAMA [E] — SPICE GIRLS
MAMA GAVE BIRTH TO THE SOUL CHILDREN — QUEEN
LATIFAH + DE LA SOUL
MAMA I'M COMING HOME — Ozzy OSBOURNE
MA-MA-MA-BELLE —
ELECTRIC LIGHT ORCHESTRA
MAMA NEVER TOLD ME — SISTER SLEDGE
MAMA SAID [A] — Carleen ANDERSON
MAMA SAID [B] — METALLICA
MAMA SAID KNOCK YOU OUT — LL COOL J
MAMA TOLD ME NOT TO COME [A] —
THREE DOG NIGHT
MAMA TOLD ME NOT TO COME [A] —
Tom JONES and STEREOPHONICS
MAMA USED TO SAY [A] — JUNIOR
MAMA USED TO SAY [A] — AZURE
MAMA WEER ALL CRAZEE NOW — SLADE
MAMA — WHO DA MAN? —
Richard BLACKWOOD
MAMA'S BOY — Suzi QUATRO
MAMA'S PEARL — The JACKSON FIVE
MAMBO ITALIANO [A] —
Rosemary CLOONEY and the MELLOMEN
MAMBO ITALIANO [A] — Dean MARTIN
MAMBO ITALIANO [A] — SHAFT
MAMBO NO.5 (A LITTLE BIT OF ...) [A] —
Lou BEGA
MAMBO NO.5 [A] — BOB THE BUILDER
MAMBO ROCK — Bill HALEY and his COMETS
MAMMA GAVE BIRTH TO THE SOUL CHILDREN —
QUEEN LATIFAH + DE LA SOUL
MAMMA MIA [A] — ABBA
MAMMA MIA [A] — A*TEENS
MAMOUNA — Bryan FERRY
MAMY BLUE [A] — LOS POP TOPS
MAMY BLUE [A] — Roger WHITTAKER
MAN — Rosemary CLOONEY
THE MAN DON'T GIVE A FUCK —
SUPER FURRY ANIMALS
THE MAN FROM LARAMIE [A] — Al MARTINO
THE MAN FROM LARAMIE [A] — Jimmy YOUNG
MAN FROM MADRID — Tony OSBORNE SOUND
THE MAN FROM NAZARETH — John Paul JOANS
MAN! I FEEL LIKE A WOMAN! — Shania TWAIN
THE MAN I LOVE — Kate BUSH
THE MAN IN BLACK — Cozy POWELL
MAN IN THE MIRROR — Michael JACKSON
MAN IN THE MOON — CSILLA
MAN LIKE ME — NO REASON
A MAN NEEDS TO BE TOLD —
The CHARLATANS
MAN OF MYSTERY — The SHADOWS
MAN OF STEEL — MEAT LOAF
MAN OF THE WORLD — FLEETWOOD MAC
MAN ON FIRE [A] — Frankie VAUGHAN
MAN ON FIRE [B] — Roger TAYLOR
MAN ON THE CORNER — GENESIS

MAN ON THE EDGE — IRON MAIDEN
MAN ON THE MOON — R.E.M.
MAN OUT OF TIME — Elvis COSTELLO
MAN SHORTAGE — LOVINDEER
THE MAN THAT GOT AWAY — Judy GARLAND
MAN TO MAN — HOT CHOCOLATE
THE MAN WHO PLAYS THE MANDOLINO —
Dean MARTIN
THE MAN WHO SOLD THE WORLD [A] — LULU
THE MAN WHO SOLD THE WORLD (LIVE) [A] —
David BOWIE
THE MAN WHO TOLD EVERYTHING — DOVES
THE MAN WITH THE CHILD IN HIS EYES —
Kate BUSH
MAN WITH THE RED FACE — Laurent GARNIER
A MAN WITHOUT LOVE [A] —
Kenneth McKELLAR
A MAN WITHOUT LOVE [A] —
Engelbert HUMPERDINCK
MANCHESTER UNITED —
MANCHESTER UNITED FOOTBALL CLUB
MANCHILD — Neneh CHERRY
MANDINKA — Sinead O'CONNOR
MANDOLIN RAIN —
Bruce HORNSBY and the RANGE
MANDOLINS IN THE MOONLIGHT —
Perry COMO
MANDY [A] — Barry MANILOW
MANDY [A] — WESTLIFE
MANDY (LA PANSE) — Eddie CALVERT
MANEATER — Daryl HALL and John OATES
MANGOS — Rosemary CLOONEY
MANHATTAN SKYLINE — A-HA
MANHATTAN SPIRITUAL — Reg OWEN
MANIAC — Michael SEMBELLO
MANIC MINDS — MANIX
MANIC MONDAY — The BANGLES
MANILA —
SEELENLUFT featuring Michael SMITH
MANNEQUIN — KIDS FROM 'FAME'
MANNISH BOY — Muddy WATERS
MAN-SIZE — P J HARVEY
MANSIZE ROOSTER — SUPERGRASS
MANTRA FOR A STATE OF MIND — S EXPRESS
MANY RIVERS TO CROSS [A] — UB40
MANY RIVERS TO CROSS [A] — CHER
MANY TEARS AGO — Connie FRANCIS
MANY TOO MANY — GENESIS
MANY WEATHERS APART — MERZ
MAPS — The YEAH YEAH YEAHS
MARBLE BREAKS IRON BENDS — Peter FENTON
MARBLEHEAD JOHNSON — The BLUETONES
MARBLES — BLACK GRAPE
MARCH OF THE MODS — Joe LOSS
MARCH OF THE PIGS — NINE INCH NAILS
MARCH OF THE SIAMESE CHILDREN —
Kenny BALL and his JAZZMEN
MARCHETA — Karl DENVER
MARGATE — CHAS and DAVE
MARGIE — Fats DOMINO
MARGO — Billy FURY
MARGUERITA TIME — STATUS QUO
MARIA [A] — PJ PROBY
MARIA [B] — BLONDIE
MARIA ELENA [A] — LOS INDIOS TABAJARAS
MARIA ELENA [B] — Gene PITNEY
MARIA (I LIKE IT LOUD) — SCOOTER vs
Marc ACARDIPANE & Dick RULES
MARIA MARIA — SANTANA
MARIANA — GIBSON BROTHERS
MARIANNE [A] — HILLTOPPERS
MARIANNE [B] — Cliff RICHARD
MARIE — The BACHELORS
MARIE CELESTE — POLECATS
MARIE MARIE — Shakin' STEVENS
(MARIE'S THE NAME) HIS LATEST FLAME —
Elvis PRESLEY
MARJORINE — Joe COCKER
MARKET SQUARE HEROES — MARILLION
MARLENE ON THE WALL — Suzanne VEGA
MAROC 7 — The SHADOWS
MARQUEE MOON — TELEVISION
MARQUIS — LINOLEUM
MARRAKESH EXPRESS —
CROSBY, STILLS, NASH and YOUNG
MARRIED MEN — Bonnie TYLER
MARRY ME — Mike PRESTON
MARTA — The BACHELORS
MARTA'S SONG — DEEP FOREST
MARTHA'S HARBOUR — ALL ABOUT EVE
MARTIAN HOP —
Rocky SHARPE and the REPLAYS
MARTIKA'S KITCHEN — MARTIKA
MARVELLOUS — The LIGHTNING SEEDS
MARVIN — MARVIN THE PARANOID ANDROID
MARY [A] — SUPERGRASS
MARY [B] — SCISSOR SISTERS
MARY ANN — BLACK LACE
MARY ANNE — The SHADOWS
MARY HAD A LITTLE BOY — SNAP!
MARY HAD A LITTLE LAMB — Paul McCARTNEY
MARY JANE [A] — Del SHANNON
MARY JANE [B] — MEGADETH
MARY JANE [C] — SPIN DOCTORS
MARY JANE (ALL NIGHT LONG) — Mary J BLIGE
MARY JANE'S LAST DANCE —
Tom PETTY and the HEARTBREAKERS

MARY OF THE 4TH FORM —
The BOOMTOWN RATS
MARY'S BOY CHILD [A] — Harry BELAFONTE
MARY'S BOY CHILD [A] — NINA and FREDERICK
MARY'S BOY CHILD - OH MY LORD [A] — BONEY M
MARY'S PRAYER — DANNY WILSON
MAS QUE MANCADA — RONALDO'S REVENGE
MAS QUE NADA [A] — ECHOBEATZ
MAS QUE NADA [A] — TAMBA TRIO
MAS QUE NADA [B] —
COLOUR GIRL featuring PSG
MASH IT UP — MDM
MASQUERADE [A] — The SKIDS
MASQUERADE [B] — Evelyn THOMAS
MASQUERADE [C] — The FALL
MASQUERADE [D] — GERIDEAU
MASS DESTRUCTION — FAITHLESS
THE MASSES AGAINST THE CLASSES —
MANIC STREET PREACHERS
MASSIVE ATTACK (EP) — MASSIVE ATTACK
MASTER AND SERVANT — DEPECHE MODE
MASTER BLASTER (JAMMIN') [A] —
Stevie WONDER
MASTERBLASTER 2000 [A] —
DJ LUCK & MC NEAT
THE MASTERPLAN —
Diana BROWN and Barrie K SHARPE
MATADOR — Jeff WAYNE
MATCHSTALK MEN AND MATCHSTALK CATS AND DOGS
(LOWRY'S SONG) —
BRIAN and MICHAEL
MATED — David GRANT and Jaki GRAHAM
MATERIAL GIRL — MADONNA
MATHAR — INDIAN VIBES
MATINÉE — FRANZ FERDINAND
A MATTER OF FACT — INNOCENCE
MATTER OF TIME — NINE YARDS
A MATTER OF TRUST — Billy JOEL
MATTHEW AND SON — Cat STEVENS
MATT'S MOOD [A] — MATT BIANCO
MATT'S MOOD [B] — BREEKOUT KREW
MAX DON'T HAVE SEX WITH YOUR EX —
E-ROTIC
THE MAXI PRIEST EP — Maxi PRIEST
MAXIMUM (EP) — DREADZONE
MAXIMUM OVERDRIVE — 2 UNLIMITED
MAY EACH DAY — Andy WILLIAMS
MAY I HAVE THE NEXT DREAM WITH YOU —
Malcolm ROBERTS
MAY IT BE — ENYA
MAY THE SUNSHINE — NAZARETH
MAY YOU ALWAYS [A] —
The McGUIRE SISTERS
MAY YOU ALWAYS [A] — Joan REGAN
MAYBE [A] — Thom PACE
MAYBE [B] — ENRIQUE
MAYBE [C] — EMMA
MAYBE [D] — N*E*R*D
MAYBE I KNOW [A] — Lesley GORE
MAYBE I KNOW [A] — SEASHELLS
MAYBE I'M AMAZED [A] — Paul McCARTNEY
MAYBE I'M AMAZED [A] — Carleen ANDERSON
MAYBE I'M DEAD — MONEY MARK
MAYBE LOVE — Stevie NICKS
MAYBE THAT'S WHAT IT TAKES — Alex PARKS
MAYBE TOMORROW [A] — Billy FURY
MAYBE TOMORROW [B] — CHORDS
MAYBE TOMORROW [C] — UB40
MAYBE TOMORROW [D] — STEREOPHONICS
MAYBE (WE SHOULD CALL IT A DAY) —
Hazell DEAN
MAYOR OF SIMPLETON — XTC
McDONALD'S CAVE — PILTDOWN MEN
ME AGAINST THE MUSIC —
Britney SPEARS featuring MADONNA
ME AND BABY BROTHER — WAR
ME AND JULIO DOWN BY THE SCHOOLYARD —
Paul SIMON
ME AND MR SANCHEZ —
BLUE RONDO A LA TURK
ME AND MRS JONES [A] — Billy PAUL
ME AND MRS JONES [A] — Freddie JACKSON
ME AND MY GIRL (NIGHT-CLUBBING) —
David ESSEX
ME AND MY LIFE — The TREMELOES
ME AND MY SHADOW —
Frank SINATRA and Sammy DAVIS Jr
ME AND THE FARMER — The HOUSEMARTINS
ME AND YOU AND A DOG NAMED BOO — LOBO
ME AND YOU VERSUS THE WORLD — SPACE
ME, IN TIME — The CHARLATANS
ME' ISRAELITES — CHOPS-EMC + EXTENSIVE
ME JULIE — Ali G & SHAGGY
ME MYSELF AND I [A] — DE LA SOUL
ME, MYSELF AND I [B] — BEYONCÉ
ME MYSELF I — Joan ARMATRADING
ME NO POP I —
Kid CREOLE and the COCONUTS
ME OR YOU? — KILLING JOKE
ME THE PEACEFUL HEART — LULU
MEA CULPA PART II — ENIGMA
MEAN GIRL — STATUS QUO
MEAN MAN — W.A.S.P.
MEAN MEAN MAN — Wanda JACKSON
MEAN STREAK [A] — Cliff RICHARD
MEAN STREAK [B] — Y & T

MEAN TO ME — Shaye COGAN
MEAN WOMAN BLUES — Roy ORBISON
THE MEANING OF CHRISTMAS —
Boris GARDINER
THE MEANING OF LOVE [A] — DEPECHE MODE
THE MEANING OF LOVE [B] — MICHELLE
MEANT TO LIVE — SWITCHFOOT
MEANTIME — The FUTUREHEADS
MEASURE OF A MAN — SAM & MARK
MEAT PIE SAUSAGE ROLL —
GRANDAD ROBERTS AND HIS SON ELVIS
MECCA — CHEETAHS
MECHANICAL WONDER —
OCEAN COLOUR SCENE
THE MEDAL SONG — CULTURE CLUB
MEDICATION — SPIRITUALIZED
MEDICINE SHOW — BIG AUDIO DYNAMITE
THE MEDICINE SONG — Stephanie MILLS
MEET EL PRESIDENTE — DURAN DURAN
MEET HER AT THE LOVE PARADE — DA HOOL
MEET ME ON THE CORNER [A] —
Max BYGRAVES
MEET ME ON THE CORNER [B] — LINDISFARNE
(MEET) THE FLINTSTONES — B-52's
MEGABLAST — BOMB THE BASS
MEGACHIC — CHIC MEDLEY — CHIC
MEGALOMANIA — PELE
MEGALOMANIAC — INCUBUS
MEGAMIX [A] — TECHNOTRONIC
MEGAMIX [B] — Crystal WATERS
MEGAMIX [C] — CORONA
MEGAMIX [D] — BONEY M
MEGAREX — T. REX
MEIN TEIL — RAMMSTEIN
MEISO — DJ KRUSH
MELANCHOLY ROSE — Marc ALMOND
MELLOW DOUBT — TEENAGE FANCLUB
MELLOW MELLOW RIGHT ON — LOWRELL
MELLOW YELLOW — DONOVAN
THE MELOD-EP — DODGY
MELODY OF LOVE — INK SPOTS
MELODY OF LOVE (WANNA BE LOVED) —
Donna SUMMER
MELT [A] — SIOUXSIE and the BANSHEES
MELT [B] — MELANIE C
MELTING POT — BLUE MINK
MEMO FROM TURNER — Mick JAGGER
MEMORIES [A] — PUBLIC IMAGE LTD
MEMORIES [B] — Mike BERRY
MEMORIES [C] — Beverley CRAVEN
MEMORIES ARE MADE OF THIS [A] —
Dave KING
MEMORIES ARE MADE OF THIS [A] —
Dean MARTIN
MEMORIES ARE MADE OF THIS [A] —
Val DOONICAN
MEMORY [A] — Elaine PAIGE
MEMORY [A] — Barbra STREISAND
MEMORY [A] — Aled JONES
THE MEMORY REMAINS — METALLICA
MEMPHIS — Lonnie MACK
MEMPHIS TENNESSEE [A] — Chuck BERRY
MEMPHIS TENNESSEE [A] — Dave BERRY
MEN IN BLACK [A] — Frank BLACK
MEN IN BLACK [A] — Will SMITH
MENTAL — MANIC MCs featuring Sara CARLSON
MENTAL PICTURE — Jon SECADA
MENTASM — SECOND PHASE
MERCEDES BOY — PEBBLES
MERCI CHERI — Vince HILL
MERCURY — LOWGOLD
MERCURY AND SOLACE — BT
MERCY MERCY ME — I WANT YOU —
Robert PALMER
MERMAIDS — Paul WELLER
MERRY CHRISTMAS DARLING —
The CARPENTERS
MERRY CHRISTMAS EVERYONE —
Shakin' STEVENS
MERRY GENTLE POPS —
The BARRON KNIGHTS
A MERRY JINGLE — GREEDIES
THE MERRY PLOUGHBOY — Dermot O'BRIEN
MERRY XMAS EVERYBODY [A] — SLADE
MERRY XMAS EVERYBODY [A] —
METAL GURUS
MERRY X-MESS —
ROTTERDAM TERMINATION SOURCE
MERSEYBEAST — Ian McNABB
MESCALITO — SOURMASH
MESMERISE — CHAPTERHOUSE
MESMERIZE — JA RULE featuring ASHANTI
A MESS OF BLUES [A] — Elvis PRESLEY
A MESS OF BLUES [A] — STATUS QUO
THE MESSAGE [A] — GRANDMASTER FLASH,
Melle MEL and the FURIOUS FIVE
THE MESSAGE [B] — 49ers
MESSAGE IN A BOTTLE [A] — The POLICE
MESSAGE IN A BOTTLE [A] —
DANCE FLOOR VIRUS
MESSAGE IN A BOTTLE [A] — T-FACTORY
MESSAGE IN THE BOX — WORLD PARTY
THE MESSAGE IS LOVE — Arthur BAKER
and the BACKBEAT DISCIPLES featuring
Al GREEN
MESSAGE OF LOVE [A] — The PRETENDERS
MESSAGE OF LOVE [B] — LOVEHAPPY

MESSAGE TO MARTHA (KENTUCKY BLUEBIRD) [A] —
Adam FAITH
MESSAGE TO MARTHA [A] — Lou JOHNSON
A MESSAGE TO YOU RUDY — The SPECIALS
A MESSAGE TO YOUR HEART —
Samantha JANUS
MESSAGE II (SURVIVAL) — GRANDMASTER FLASH,
Melle MEL and the FURIOUS FIVE
MESSAGE UNDERSTOOD — Sandie SHAW
MESSAGES —
ORCHESTRAL MANOEUVRES IN THE DARK
MESSAGES FROM THE STARS — RAH BAND
MESSED UP — The BEAT UP
MESSIN' — LADIES FIRST
METAFORCE — ART OF NOISE
METAL GURU — T. REX
METAL HEALTH — QUIET RIOT
METAL MICKEY — SUEDE
METEOR MAN — Dee D JACKSON
METHOD OF MODERN LOVE —
Daryl HALL and John OATES
METROSOUND — Adam F & J MAJIK
METROPOLIS — Oliver LIEB presents SMOKED
MEXICALI ROSE — Karl DENVER
THE MEXICAN — FENTONES
MEXICAN GIRL — SMOKIE
MEXICAN RADIO — WALL OF VOODOO
MEXICAN WAVE — KERBDOG
MEXICO — Long John BALDRY
MF FROM HELL — The DATSUNS
MFEO — KAVANA
MI CHICO LATINO — Geri HALLIWELL
MI TIERRA — Gloria ESTEFAN
MIAMI — Will SMITH
MIAMI HIT MIX — Gloria ESTEFAN
MIAMI VICE THEME — Jan HAMMER
MICHAEL [A] — HIGHWAYMEN
MICHAEL [B] —
Geno WASHINGTON and the RAM JAM BAND
MICHAEL [C] — FRANZ FERDINAND
MICHAEL AND THE SLIPPER TREE —
The EQUALS
MICHAEL CAINE — MADNESS
MICHAEL JACKSON MEDLEY — ASHAYE
MICHAEL ROW THE BOAT — Lonnie DONEGAN
MICHELLE [A] — DAVID and JONATHAN
MICHELLE [A] — OVERLANDERS
MICHIKO — SULTANS OF PING
MICKEY [A] — Toni BASIL
MICKEY [A] — LOLLY
MICRO KID — LEVEL 42
THE MICROPHONE FIEND — Eric B and RAKIM
MICROWAVED — PITCHSHIFTER
MIDAS TOUCH — MIDNIGHT STAR
THE MIDDLE — JIMMY EAT WORLD
MIDDLE OF THE NIGHT —
BROTHERHOOD OF MAN
MIDDLEMAN — TERRORVISION
MIDLIFE CRISIS — FAITH NO MORE
MIDNIGHT [A] — Paul ANKA
MIDNIGHT [B] — UN-CUT
MIDNIGHT AT THE LOST AND FOUND —
MEAT LOAF
MIDNIGHT AT THE OASIS [A] — Maria MULDAUR
MIDNIGHT AT THE OASIS [A] —
The BRAND NEW HEAVIES
MIDNIGHT BLUE — Louise TUCKER
MIDNIGHT COWBOY —
MIDNIGHT COWBOY SOUNDTRACK
MIDNIGHT FLYER — Nat 'King' COLE
MIDNIGHT GROOVIN' — LIGHT OF THE WORLD
MIDNIGHT IN A PERFECT WORLD —
DJ SHADOW
MIDNIGHT IN CHELSEA — Jon BON JOVI
MIDNIGHT IN MOSCOW —
Kenny BALL and his JAZZMEN
MIDNIGHT RIDER — Paul DAVIDSON
MIDNIGHT SHIFT — Buddy HOLLY
MIDNIGHT SUMMER DREAM —
The STRANGLERS
MIDNIGHT TO SIX MAN — PRETTY THINGS
MIDNIGHT TRAIN TO GEORGIA —
Gladys KNIGHT and the PIPS
MIDNITE — D'INFLUENCE
MIDNITE DYNAMOS — MATCHBOX
MIDNITE SPECIAL — Paul EVANS
MIDSUMMER MADNESS (EP) —
RHYTHM SECTION
MIGHT BE STARS — WANNADIES
THE MIGHTY HIGH — REVIVAL 3000
MIGHTY JOE — SHOCKING BLUE
THE MIGHTY POWER OF LOVE — TAVARES
MIGHTY QUINN — MANFRED MANN
MIG29 — MIG29
MIKE OLDFIELD'S SINGLE (THEME FROM
TUBULAR BELLS) — Mike OLDFIELD
MILES AWAY [A] — John FOXX
MILES AWAY [B] — WINGER
MILES FROM HOME — PESHAY
MILK — GARBAGE featuring TRICKY
MILK AND ALCOHOL — DR FEELGOOD
MILKMAN'S SON — UGLY KID JOE
MILKSHAKE — KELIS
MILKY WAY — SHEER ELEGANCE
THE MILL HILL SELF HATE CLUB —
Edward BALL
MILLENNIUM [A] — KILLING JOKE

MILLENNIUM [B] — Robbie WILLIAMS
MILLENNIUM CHIMES — BIG BEN
THE MILLENNIUM PRAYER — Cliff RICHARD
MILLION DOLLAR LOVE — DUB WAR
MILLION DRUMS — Tony SHEVETON
A MILLION LOVE SONGS — TAKE THAT
MILLION MILES AWAY — The OFFSPRING
MILLION SUNS — OOBERMAN
MILLIONAIRE — KELIS featuring ANDRE 3000
MILLIONAIRE SWEEPER — KENICKIE
MILLIONS LIKE US — PURPLE HEARTS
MILLY MOLLY MANDY — Glyn POOLE
MILORD [A] — Edith PIAF
MILORD [A] — Frankie VAUGHAN
MIND — The FARM
MIND ADVENTURES — DES'REE
MIND BLOWIN' — SMOOTH
MIND BLOWING DECISIONS — HEATWAVE
MIND BODY SOUL — FANTASY UFO
MIND GAMES — John LENNON
MIND OF A TOY — VISAGE
A MIND OF ITS OWN — Victoria BECKHAM
THE MIND OF LOVE (WHERE IS YOUR HEAD, KATHRYN?) — kd LANG
THE MIND OF THE MACHINE — N-TRANCE
MIND OVER MONEY — TURIN BRAKES
MIND UP TONIGHT — Melba MOORE
MINDCIRCUS — WAY OUT WEST featuring Tricia LEE
MINDLESS BOOGIE — HOT CHOCOLATE
MINDSTREAM — MEAT BEAT MANIFESTO
MINE — EVERYTHING BUT THE GIRL
MINE ALL MINE — CA$HFLOW
MINE TO GIVE — PHOTEK featuring Robert J OWENS
MINEFIELD — I-LEVEL
MINERVA — DEFTONES
MINISTRY OF LOVE — HYSTERIC EGO
MINISTRY OF MAYHEM — The NOISE NEXT DOOR
MINNIE THE MOOCHER — REGGAE PHILHARMONIC ORCHESTRA
MINORITY — GREEN DAY
MINT CAR — The CURE
MINUETTO ALLEGRETTO — The WOMBLES
MINUTE BY MINUTE — DOOBIE BROTHERS
A MINUTE OF YOUR TIME — Tom JONES
THE MINUTE YOU'RE GONE — Cliff RICHARD
MIRACLE [A] — Jon BON JOVI
MIRACLE [B] — OLIVE
A MIRACLE — HIDDEN CAMERAS
THE MIRACLE [A]— QUEEN
THE MIRACLE [B]— Cliff RICHARD
MIRACLE GOODNIGHT — David BOWIE
THE MIRACLE OF LOVE — EURYTHMICS
THE MIRACLE OF YOU — Danny WILLIAMS
MIRACLES [A] — Gary NUMAN
MIRACLES [B] — PET SHOP BOYS
MIRROR IN THE BATHROOM — The BEAT
MIRROR MAN — HUMAN LEAGUE
MIRROR MIRROR [A] — PINKERTON'S ASSORTED COLOURS
MIRROR MIRROR [B] — Diana ROSS
MIRROR MIRROR (MON AMOUR) — DOLLAR
MIRRORS — Sally OLDFIELD
MIS-SHAPES — PULP
MISERERE — ZUCCHERO with Luciano PAVAROTTI
MISERY [A] — SOUL ASYLUM
MISERY [B] — The MOFFATTS
MISFIT [A] — CURIOSITY KILLED THE CAT
MISFIT [B] — Amy STUDT
MISGUIDED — DYVERSE
MISIRLOU (THE THEME TO THE MOTION PICTURE 'PULP FICTION') — SPAGHETTI SURFERS
MISLED [A] — KOOL and the GANG
MISLED [B] — QUIREBOYS
MISLED [C] — Celine DION
MISS AMERICA — BIG DISH
MISS CALIFORNIA — Dante THOMAS featuring PRAS
MISS CHATELAINE — kd LANG
MISS FAT BOOTY — PART II — MOS DEF featuring GHOSTFACE KILLAH
MISS HIT AND RUN — Barry BLUE
MISS INDEPENDENT — Kelly CLARKSON
MISS LUCIFER — PRIMAL SCREAM
MISS MODULAR — STEREOLAB
MISS PARKER [A] — BENZ
MISS PARKER [B] — MORGAN
MISS PERFECT — ABS featuring NODESHA
MISS SARAJEVO — PASSENGERS
MISS THE GIRL — CREATURES
MISS WORLD — HOLE
MISS YOU [A] — Jimmy YOUNG
MISS YOU [B] — The ROLLING STONES
MISS YOU LIKE CRAZY — Natalie COLE
MISS YOU MUCH — Janet JACKSON
MISS YOU NIGHTS [A] — Cliff RICHARD
MISS YOU NIGHTS [A] — WESTLIFE
MISSING [A] — Terry HALL
MISSING [B] — EVERYTHING BUT THE GIRL
MISSING WORDS — SELECTER
MISSING YOU [A] — Chris DE BURGH
MISSING YOU [B] — John WAITE
MISSING YOU [B] — Tina TURNER
MISSING YOU [C] — Mary J BLIGE
MISSING YOU [C] — SOUL II SOUL featuring Kym MAZELLE
MISSING YOU [D] — Lucy CARR
MISSING YOU NOW — Michael BOLTON featuring Kenny G
MISSION OF LOVE — Jason DONOVAN
MISSIONARY MAN — EURYTHMICS
MISSISSIPPI — PUSSYCAT
MISSY MISSY — Paul and Barry RYAN
MISTI BLU — AMILLIONSONS
MISTAKES AND REGRETS — ... AND YOU WILL KNOW US BY THE TRAIL OF DEAD
MR ALIBI — Maria WILLSON
MR BACHELOR — LOOSE ENDS
MR BASS MAN — Johnny CYMBAL
MR BIG STUFF [A] — HEAVY D and the BOYZ
MR BIG STUFF [A] — QUEEN LATIFAH, SHADES and FREE
MR BLOBBY — MR BLOBBY
MR BLUE [A] — David MacBETH
MR BLUE [A] — Mike PRESTON
MR BLUE SKY — ELECTRIC LIGHT ORCHESTRA
MR BRIGHTSIDE — The KILLERS
MR CABDRIVER — Lenny KRAVITZ
MR CROWLEY — Ozzy OSBOURNE
MR CUSTER — Charlie DRAKE
MR DEVIL — BIG TIME CHARLIE
MR DJ [A] — CONCEPT
MR DJ [B] — BLACKOUT
MR E'S BEAUTIFUL BLUES — EELS
MR FIXIT — ROOTJOOSE
MR FRIDAY NIGHT — Lisa MOORISH
MR GUDER — The CARPENTERS
MR GUITAR — Bert WEEDON
MR HANKEY THE CHRISTMAS POO — MR HANKEY
MISTER JONES — OUT OF MY HAIR
MR JONES — COUNTING CROWS
MR KIRK'S NIGHTMARE — 4 HERO
MR LEE — Diana ROSS
MR LOVERMAN — Shabba RANKS
MR MANIC AND SISTER COOL — SHAKATAK
MISTER MENTAL — The EIGHTIES MATCHBOX B-LINE DISASTER
MR PHARMACIST — The FALL
MR PORTER — Mickie MOST
MR PRESIDENT — D, B, M and T
MR RAFFLES (MAN, IT WAS MEAN) — Steve HARLEY and COCKNEY REBEL
MR SANDMAN [A] — The CHORDETTES
MR SANDMAN [A] — Dickie VALENTINE
MISTER SANDMAN [A] — Max BYGRAVES
MISTER SANDMAN [A] — FOUR ACES
MR SECOND CLASS — Spencer DAVIS GROUP
MR SLEAZE — STOCK AITKEN WATERMAN
MR SOFT — Steve HARLEY and COCKNEY REBEL
MR SOLITAIRE — ANIMAL NIGHTLIFE
MR SUCCESS — Frank SINATRA
MR TAMBOURINE MAN — The BYRDS
MR TELEPHONE MAN — NEW EDITION
MR VAIN — CULTURE BEAT
MR WENDAL — ARRESTED DEVELOPMENT
MR WONDERFUL — Peggy LEE
MR WRITER — STEREOPHONICS
MR ZERO — Keith RELF
MISTLETOE AND WINE — Cliff RICHARD
MISTY [A] — Johnny MATHIS
MISTY [A] — Ray STEVENS
MISTY BLUE — Dorothy MOORE
MISTY MORNING, ALBERT BRIDGE — The POGUES
MISUNDERSTANDING — GENESIS
MISUNDERSTOOD [A] — BON JOVI
MISUNDERSTOOD [B] — Robbie WILLIAMS
MISUNDERSTOOD MAN — Cliff RICHARD
MITCH — BISCUIT BOY
MITTAGEISEN (METAL POSTCARD) — SIOUXSIE and the BANSHEES
MIX IT UP — Dan REED NETWORK
MIXED BIZNESS — BECK
MIXED EMOTIONS — The ROLLING STONES
MIXED TRUTH — RAGGA TWINS
MIXED UP WORLD — Sophie ELLIS-BEXTOR
MIYAKO HIDEAWAY — MARION
M'LADY — SLY and the FAMILY STONE
MMM MMM MMM MMM — CRASH TEST DUMMIES
MMMBOP — HANSON
MO' FIRE — BAD COMPANY
MO MONEY MO PROBLEMS — NOTORIOUS B.I.G. featuring PUFF DADDY and MA$E
MOAN & GROAN — Mark MORRISON
MOANIN' — Chris FARLOWE
MOB RULES — BLACK SABBATH
MOBILE — Ray BURNS
MOBSCENE — MARILYN MANSON
MOCKINGBIRD [A] — Inez FOXX
MOCKINGBIRD [A] — Carly SIMON
MOCKINGBIRD [A] — BELLE STARS
MOCKINGBIRD HILL — MIGIL FIVE
THE MODEL — KRAFTWERK
MODERN AGE — The STROKES
MODERN ART — ART BRUT
MODERN FEELING — IKARA COLT
MODERN GIRL [A] — Sheena EASTON
MODERN GIRL [B] — MEAT LOAF
MODERN LOVE — David BOWIE
MODERN ROMANCE (I WANT TO FALL IN LOVE AGAIN) — Francis ROSSI
A MODERN WAY OF LETTING GO — IDLEWILD
THE MODERN WORLD — The JAM
MODUS OPERANDI — PHOTEK
MOI ... LOLITA — ALIZÉE
MOIRA JANE'S CAFE — DEFINITION OF SOUND
MOLLIE'S SONG — Beverley CRAVEN
MOLLY — CARRIE
MOLLY'S CHAMBERS — KINGS OF LEON
MOMENT OF MY LIFE — Bobby D'AMBROSIO featuring Michelle WEEKS
MOMENTS IN LOVE — ART OF NOISE
MOMENTS IN SOUL — JT and the BIG FAMILY
MOMENTS OF PLEASURE — Kate BUSH
MON AMI — GIRESSE
MON AMOUR TOKYO — PIZZICATO FIVE
MONA — Craig McLACHLAN
MONA LISA — Conway TWITTY
MONDAY MONDAY — MAMAS and the PAPAS
MONDAY MORNING — The CANDYSKINS
MONDAY MORNING 5:19 — RIALTO
MONEY [A] — Bern ELLIOTT and the FENMEN
MONEY [A] — FLYING LIZARDS
MONEY [A] — BACKBEAT BAND
MONEY [B] — Dan REED NETWORK
MONEY [C] — SKIN
MONEY [D] — Charli BALTIMORE
MONEY [E] — JAMELIA
(MONEY CAN'T) BUY ME LOVE — BLACKSTREET
MONEY DON'T MATTER 2 NIGHT — PRINCE and the NEW POWER GENERATION
MONEY (EVERYBODY LOVES HER) — GUN
MONEY FOR NOTHING — DIRE STRAITS
MONEY GO ROUND (PART 1) — STYLE COUNCIL
MONEY GREEDY — TRICKY
MONEY HONEY — BAY CITY ROLLERS
MONEY IN MY POCKET — Dennis BROWN
MONEY LOVE — Neneh CHERRY
MONEY, MONEY, MONEY — ABBA
MONEY THAT'S YOUR PROBLEM — TONIGHT
MONEY TO BURN — Richard ASHCROFT
MONEY'S TOO TIGHT (TO MENTION) [A] — VALENTINE BROTHERS
MONEY'S TOO TIGHT (TO MENTION) [A] — SIMPLY RED
MONEYTALKS — AC/DC
MONIE IN THE MIDDLE — Monie LOVE
THE MONKEES — RAMPAGE
THE MONKEES EP — The MONKEES
MONKEY [A] — George MICHAEL
MONKEY [B] — SHAFT
MONKEY BUSINESS [A] — SKID ROW
MONKEY BUSINESS [B] — DANGER DANGER
MONKEY CHOP — DAN-I
MONKEY GONE TO HEAVEN — PIXIES
MONKEY MAN [A] — MAYTALS
MONKEY MAN [A] — GENERAL LEVY
MONKEY SPANNER — Dave and Ansil COLLINS
MONKEY WAH — RADICAL ROB
MONKEY WRENCH — FOO FIGHTERS
MONO — Courtney LOVE
MONOCULTURE — SOFT CELL
MONSIEUR DUPONT — Sandie SHAW
MONSTER — L7
MONSTER — LIQUID PEOPLE vs SIMPLE MINDS
MONSTER MASH — Bobby 'Boris' PICKETT and the CRYPT-KICKERS
MONSTERS AND ANGELS — VOICE OF THE BEEHIVE
MONTEGO BAY [A] — Freddie NOTES and the RUDIES
MONTEGO BAY [A] — Bobby BLOOM
MONTEGO BAY [A] — SUGAR CANE
MONTEGO BAY [A] — AMAZULU
MONTREAL — WEDDING PRESENT
MONTREUX (EP) — SIMPLY RED
MONTUNO — Gloria ESTEFAN
MONY MONY [A] — Tommy JAMES and the SHONDELLS
MONY MONY [A] — AMAZULU
MONY MONY [A] — Billy IDOL
MONY MONY [A] — STATUS QUO
THE MOOD CLUB — FIRSTBORN
MOODSWINGS — MY VITRIOL
MOODY BLUE — Elvis PRESLEY
MOODY PLACES — NORTHSIDE
MOODY RIVER — Pat BOONE
MOOG ERUPTION — DIGITAL ORGASM
MOON — VIRUS
MOON HOP — Derrick MORGAN
MOON OVER BOURBON STREET — STING
MOON RIVER [A] — Henry MANCINI
MOON RIVER [A] — Danny WILLIAMS
MOON RIVER [A] — GREYHOUND
MOON SHADOW — Cat STEVENS
MOON TALK — Perry COMO
MOONCHILD — FIELDS OF THE NEPHILIM
MOONGLOW [A] — Morris STOLOFF
MOONGLOW [A] — SOUNDS ORCHESTRAL
MOONLIGHT AND MUZAK — M
MOONLIGHT & ROSES — Jim REEVES
MOONLIGHT GAMBLER — Frankie LAINE
MOONLIGHT SERENADE — Glenn MILLER
MOONLIGHT SHADOW — Mike OLDFIELD
MOONLIGHTING — Leo SAYER
'MOONLIGHTING' THEME — Al JARREAU
MOONSHINE SALLY — MUD
MOR — BLUR
MORE [A] — Jimmy YOUNG
MORE [A] — Perry COMO
MORE [B] — SISTERS OF MERCY
MORE ... [C] — HIGH
MORE & MORE — SPOILED & ZIGO
MORE AND MORE [A] — Andy WILLIAMS
MORE AND MORE [B] — CAPTAIN HOLLYWOOD PROJECT
MORE & MORE [C] — JOE featuring G-UNIT
MORE AND MORE PARTY POPS — Russ CONWAY
MORE BEATS & PIECES — COLDCUT
MORE GOOD OLD ROCK 'N' ROLL — Dave CLARK FIVE
MORE HUMAN THAN HUMAN — WHITE ZOMBIE
THE MORE I GET THE MORE I WANT — KWS featuring Teddy PENDERGRASS
THE MORE I SEE (THE LESS I BELIEVE) — FUN BOY THREE
THE MORE I SEE YOU [A] — Joy MARSHALL
THE MORE I SEE YOU [A] — Chris MONTEZ
THE MORE I SEE YOU [A] — Barbara WINDSOR and Mike REID
MORE LIFE IN A TRAMP'S VEST — STEREOPHONICS
MORE LIKE THE MOVIES — DR HOOK
MORE LOVE [A] — Feargal SHARKEY
MORE LOVE [B] — NEXT OF KIN
MORE MONEY FOR YOU AND ME (MEDLEY) — FOUR PREPS
MORE, MORE, MORE [A] — Andrea TRUE CONNECTION
MORE MORE MORE [A] — BANANARAMA
MORE MORE MORE [A] — Rachel STEVENS
MORE, MORE, MORE [B] — CARMEL
MORE PARTY POPS — Russ CONWAY
MORE THAN A FEELING — BOSTON
MORE THAN A LOVER — Bonnie TYLER
MORE THAN A WOMAN [A] — TAVARES
MORE THAN A WOMAN [A] — 911
MORE THAN A WOMAN [B] — AALIYAH
MORE THAN EVER (COME PRIMA) [A] — Malcolm VAUGHAN
MORE THAN EVER (COME PRIMA) [A] — Robert EARL
MORE THAN I CAN BEAR — MATT BIANCO
MORE THAN I CAN SAY [A] — The CRICKETS
MORE THAN I CAN SAY [A] — Bobby VEE
MORE THAN I CAN SAY [A] — Leo SAYER
MORE THAN I NEEDED TO KNOW — SCOOCH
MORE THAN IN LOVE — Kate ROBBINS and BEYOND
MORE THAN LIKELY — PM DAWN featuring BOY GEORGE
MORE THAN LOVE [A] — Ken DODD
MORE THAN LOVE [B] — WET WET WET
MORE THAN ONE KIND OF LOVE — Joan ARMATRADING
MORE THAN PHYSICAL — BANANARAMA
MORE THAN THAT — BACKSTREET BOYS
MORE THAN THIS [A] — ROXY MUSIC
MORE THAN THIS [A] — EMMIE
MORE THAN THIS [B] — Peter GABRIEL
MORE THAN US (EP) — TRAVIS
MORE THAN WORDS — EXTREME
MORE THAN YOU KNOW — MARTIKA
THE MORE THEY KNOCK, THE MORE I LOVE YOU — Gloria D BROWN
MORE TO LIFE — Cliff RICHARD
MORE TO LOVE — VOLCANO
MORE TO THIS WORLD — BAD BOYS INC
THE MORE YOU IGNORE ME THE CLOSER I GET — MORRISSEY
THE MORE YOU LIVE, THE MORE YOU LOVE — A FLOCK OF SEAGULLS
MORGEN — Ivo ROBIC
MORNIN' — Al JARREAU
MORNING [A] — Val DOONICAN
MORNING [B] — WET WET WET
THE MORNING AFTER (FREE AT LAST) —STRIKE
MORNING AFTERGLOW — ELECTRASY
MORNING ALWAYS COMES TOO SOON — Brad CARTER
MORNING DANCE — SPYRO GYRA
MORNING GLORY — James and Bobby PURIFY
MORNING HAS BROKEN [A] — Cat STEVENS
MORNING HAS BROKEN [A] — Neil DIAMOND
MORNING HAS BROKEN [A] — Daniel O'DONNELL
THE MORNING OF OUR LIVES — Jonathan RICHMAN and the MODERN LOVERS
THE MORNING PAPERS — PRINCE and the NEW POWER GENERATION
MORNING SIDE OF THE MOUNTAIN — Donny and Marie OSMOND
MORNING WONDER — The EARLIES
MORNINGLIGHT — TEAM DEEP
MORNINGTOWN RIDE — The SEEKERS
THE MOST BEAUTIFUL GIRL — Charlie RICH
THE MOST BEAUTIFUL GIRL IN THE WORLD — PRINCE (SYMBOL)
MOST GIRLS — PINK

MOST HIGH — Jimmy PAGE
THE MOST TIRING DAY — CECIL
MOTHER — DANZIG
MOTHER — M FACTOR
MOTHER AND CHILD REUNION — Paul SIMON
MOTHER DAWN — BLUE PEARL
MOTHER FIXATION — MINUTEMAN
MOTHER NATURE AND FATHER TIME —
Nat 'King' COLE
MOTHER OF MINE — Neil REID
MOTHER UNIVERSE — SOUP DRAGONS
MOTHER-IN-LAW — Ernie K-DOE
MOTHERLAND-A-FRI-CA — TRIBAL HOUSE
MOTHERLESS CHILD — Eric CLAPTON
MOTHER'S TALK — TEARS FOR FEARS
MOTHERSHIP RECONNECTION —
Scott GROOVES featuring PARLIAMENT /
FUNKADELIC
THE MOTION OF LOVE — GENE LOVES JEZEBEL
THE MOTIVE (LIVING WITHOUT YOU) —
THEN JERICO
MOTIVELESS CRIME — SOUTH
MOTIVATION — SUM 41
MOTOR BIKIN' — Chris SPEDDING
MOTORBIKE BEAT — REZILLOS
MOTORBIKE TO HEAVEN — SALAD
MOTORCYCLE EMPTINESS —
MANIC STREET PREACHERS
MOTORCYCLE MICHAEL — Jo Ann CAMPBELL
MOTORCYCLE RIDER — ICICLE WORKS
MOTÖRHEAD LIVE — MOTÖRHEAD
MOTORMANIA — ROMAN HOLLIDAY
MOTORTOWN — KANE GANG
THE MOTOWN SONG — Rod STEWART
MOTOWNPHILLY — BOYZ II MEN
MOULDY OLD DOUGH — LIEUTENANT PIGEON
MOUNTAIN GREENERY — Mel TORME
MOUNTAIN OF LOVE — Kenny LYNCH
MOUNTAINS — PRINCE
THE MOUNTAIN'S HIGH — DICK and DEEDEE
MOUSE IN A HOLE — HEAVY STEREO
MOUTH — Merril BAINBRIDGE
MOUTH FOR WAR — PANTERA
MOVE [A] — INSPIRAL CARPETS
MOVE [B] — MOBY
MOVE ANY MOUNTAIN — The SHAMEN
MOVE AWAY — CULTURE CLUB
MOVE AWAY JIMMY BLUE — DEL AMITRI
MOVE BABY MOVE — SARTORELLO
MOVE CLOSER [A] — Phyllis NELSON
MOVE CLOSER [A] — Tom JONES
MOVE IN A LITTLE CLOSER —
HARMONY GRASS
MOVE IT — Cliff RICHARD
MOVE IT BABY — Simon SCOTT
MOVE IT LIKE THIS — BAHA MEN
MOVE IT UP — CAPPELLA
MOVE MANIA — SASH! featuring SHANNON
MOVE ME NO MOUNTAIN — SOUL II SOUL
MOVE MOVE MOVE (THE RED TRIBE) —
MANCHESTER UNITED FOOTBALL CLUB
MOVE NOW —
Mark B featuring Tommy EVANS
MOVE ON BABY — CAPPELLA
MOVE ON UP [A] — Curtis MAYFIELD
MOVE ON UP [A] — Sue CHALONER
MOVE ON UP [A] — TRICKSTER
MOVE OVER DARLING [A] — Doris DAY
MOVE OVER DARLING [A] — Tracey ULLMAN
MOVE RIGHT OUT — Rick ASTLEY
MOVE THAT BODY [A] — TECHNOTRONIC
MOVE THAT BODY [B] — NUSH
MOVE THE CROWD — Eric B and RAKIM
MOVE THIS MOUNTAIN —
Sophie ELLIS-BEXTOR
MOVE TO MEMPHIS — A-HA
MOVE YA BODY — NINA SKY
MOVE YOUR ASS — SCOOTER
MOVE YOUR BODY [A] —
Gene FARROW and GF BAND
MOVE YOUR BODY [B] — TYREE
MOVE YOUR BODY [C] — XPANSIONS
MOVE YOUR BODY [D] — ANTICAPPELLA
MOVE YOUR BODY [E] — EUROGROOVE
MOVE YOUR BODY [F] —
RUFFNECK featuring YAVAHN
MOVE YOUR BODY [G] — EIFFEL 65
MOVE YOUR FEET [A] — M-D-EMM
MOVE YOUR FEET [B] — JUNIOR SENIOR
MOVE YOUR FEET TO THE RHYTHM OF THE BEAT —
HITHOUSE
MOVE YOUR LOVE — DJH featuring STEFY
MOVEMENT — LCD SOUNDSYSTEM
MOVIE STAR [A] — HARPO
MOVIES [A] — HOTHOUSE FLOWERS
MOVIES [B] — ALIEN ANT FARM
MOVIESTAR — STEREOPHONICS
MOVIN' [A] — BRASS CONSTRUCTION
MOVIN' [A] — 400 BLOWS
MOVIN' [B] — MARATHON
MOVIN' [C] — MONE
MOVIN' ON [A] — BANANARAMA
MOVIN' ON [B] — APACHE INDIAN
MOVIN' ON [C] — Debbie PENDER
MOVIN' ON [D] —
PROSPECT PARK / Carolyn HARDING
MOVIN' OUT (ANTHONY'S SONG) — Billy JOEL

MOVIN' THRU YOUR SYSTEM — JARK PRONGO
MOVIN TOO FAST —
ARTFUL DODGER and Romina JOHNSON
MOVING — SUPERGRASS
MOVING IN THE RIGHT DIRECTION —
PASADENAS
MOVING ON — DREADZONE
MOVING ON UP — M PEOPLE
MOVING ON UP (ON THE RIGHT SIDE) —
Beverley KNIGHT
MOVING TO BLACKWATER — REUBEN
MOVING TO CALIFORNIA — STRAW
MOVING UP MOVING ON — MOZAIC
MOZART 40 — SOVEREIGN COLLECTION
MOZART SYMPHONY NO.40 IN G MINOR
K550 1ST MOVEMENT (ALLEGRO MOLTO) —
Waldo de los RIOS
MRS HOOVER — The CANDYSKINS
MRS MILLS' MEDLEY — MRS MILLS
MRS ROBINSON [A] — SIMON and GARFUNKEL
MRS ROBINSON (EP) [A] —
SIMON and GARFUNKEL
MRS ROBINSON [A] — LEMONHEADS
MRS WASHINGTON — GIGOLO AUNTS
MS GRACE — TYMES
MS JACKSON — OUTKAST
MUCH AGAINST EVERYONE'S ADVICE —
SOULWAX
MUCH LOVE — Shola AMA
MUCHO MACHO — TOTO COELO
(MUCHO MAMBO) SWAY — SHAFT
MUCK IT OUT! — FARMERS BOYS
MUDDY WATER BLUES — Paul RODGERS
MUHAMMAD ALI — FAITHLESS
MULDER AND SCULLY — CATATONIA
MULE (CHANT NO.2) — BEGGAR and CO
MULE SKINNER BLUES [A] — Rusty DRAPER
MULE SKINNER BLUES [A] — FENDERMEN
MULE TRAIN — Frank IFIELD
MULL OF KINTYRE — Paul McCARTNEY
MULTIPLY — XZIBIT
MULTIPLICATION [A] — Bobby DARIN
MULTIPLICATION [A] — SHOWADDYWADDY
MUM'S GONE TO ICELAND — BENNET
MUNDAYA (THE BOY) —
Tim DELUXE featuring Shahin BADAR
MUNDIAN TO BACH KE — PANJABI MC
THE MUPPET SHOW MUSIC HALL EP —
The MUPPETS
MURDER ON THE DANCEFLOOR —
Sophie ELLIS-BEXTOR
MURDER SHE WROTE [A] — Tairrie B
MURDER SHE WROTE [B] —
Chaka DEMUS and PLIERS
MURDERATION — EBONY DUBSTERS
MURPHY AND THE BRICKS — Noel MURPHY
MURPHY'S LAW — CHERI
MUSAK — TRISCO
MUSCLE DEEP — THEN JERICO
MUSCLE MUSEUM — MUSE
MUSCLEBOUND — SPANDAU BALLET
MUSCLES — Diana ROSS
MUSIC [A] — John MILES
MUSIC [A] — FARGETTA
MUSIC [B] — ONE WAY featuring Al HUDSON
MUSIC [C] — FR DAVID
MUSIC [D] — D TRAIN
MUSIC [E] — OMAR
MUSIC [F] — MADONNA
MUSIC [G] —
Erick SERMON featuring Marvin GAYE
MUSIC AND DANCE — IMAGINATION
MUSIC AND YOU [A] — Sal SOLO
MUSIC & YOU [B] —
ROOM 5 featuring Oliver CHEATHAM
MUSIC FOR CHAMELEONS — Gary NUMAN
MUSIC GETS THE BEST OF ME —
Sophie ELLIS-BEXTOR
THE MUSIC I LIKE — ALEXIA
MUSIC IN MY MIND — Adam F
THE MUSIC IN YOU —
MONOBOY featuring DELORES
MUSIC IS A PASSION — ATLANTIC OCEAN
MUSIC IS LIFE — DIRT DEVILS
THE MUSIC IS MOVING [B] — FARGETTA
MUSIC IS MOVING [B] — CORTINA
MUSIC IS MY RADAR — BLUR
MUSIC IS THE ANSWER —
Danny TENAGLIA and CELEDA
MUSIC MAKES ME HIGH — LOST BOYZ
MUSIC MAKES YOU FEEL LIKE DANCING —
BRASS CONSTRUCTION
MUSIC MAKES YOU LOSE CONTROL —
LES RYTHMES DIGITALES
THE MUSIC OF GOODBYE (LOVE THEME FROM
'OUT OF AFRICA') — Al JARREAU
MUSIC OF MY HEART —
'N SYNC / Gloria ESTEFAN
THE MUSIC OF THE NIGHT [A] —
Michael CRAWFORD
THE MUSIC OF THE NIGHT [A] —
Barbra STREISAND (duet
with Michael CRAWFORD)
THE MUSIC OF TORVILL AND DEAN (EP) —
Richard HARTLEY / Michael REED ORCHESTRA
MUSIC REVOLUTION — SCUMFROG
MUSIC SAVED MY LIFE — Cevin FISHER

MUSIC SOUNDS BETTER WITH YOU —
STARDUST
MUSIC STOP — RAILWAY CHILDREN
MUSIC TAKES YOU — BLAME
THE MUSIC THAT WE HEAR (MOOG ISLAND) —
MORCHEEBA
MUSIC TO WATCH GIRLS BY — Andy WILLIAMS
MUSICAL FREEDOM (MOVING ON UP) —
Paul SIMPSON featuring ADEVA
MUSICAL MELODY — UNIQUE 3
THE MUSIC'S GOT ME [A] — BASS BUMPERS
THE MUSIC'S GOT ME [A] —
BROOKLYN BOUNCE
THE MUSIC'S NO GOOD WITHOUT YOU —
CHER
MUSIQUE — DAFT PUNK
MUSKRAT — The EVERLY BROTHERS
MUSKRAT RAMBLE — Freddy CANNON
MUST BE LOVE — FYA featuring SMUJJI
MUST BE MADISON — Joe LOSS
MUST BE SANTA — Tommy STEELE
MUST BE THE MUSIC [A] — HYSTERIX
MUST BE THE MUSIC [B] — Joey NEGRO
MUST BEE THE MUSIC — KING BEE
A MUST TO AVOID — HERMAN'S HERMITS
(MUST YOU ALWAYS) TEASE ME — Keith KELLY
MUSTAFA CHA CHA CHA —
STAIFFI and his MUSTAFAS
MUSTANG SALLY [A] — Wilson PICKETT
MUSTANG SALLY [A] — COMMITMENTS
MUSTAPHA — Bob AZZAM and his ORCHESTRA
MUTANTS IN MEGA CITY ONE —
FINK BROTHERS
MUTATIONS (EP) — ORBITAL
MUTUAL ATTRACTION — CHANGE
MUTUALLY ASSURED DESTRUCTION — GILLAN
MUZIKIZUM — X-PRESS 2
MY ADIDAS — RUN-DMC
MY AFFAIR — Kirsty MacCOLL
MY ALL — Mariah CAREY
MY ANGEL — ROCK GODDESS
MY ARMS KEEP MISSING YOU — Rick ASTLEY
MY BABY — LIL' ROMEO
MY BABY JUST CARES FOR ME — Nina SIMONE
MY BABY LEFT ME [A] — Dave BERRY
MY BABY LEFT ME — THAT'S ALL RIGHT
(MEDLEY) [A] — SLADE
MY BABY LOVES LOVIN' — WHITE PLAINS
MY BAG — Lloyd COLE
MY BAND — D12
MY BEAT — BLAZE featuring Palmer BROWN
MY BEATBOX — DEEJAY PUNK-ROC
MY BEAUTIFUL FRIEND — The CHARLATANS
MY BEST FRIEND'S GIRL — The CARS
MY BLUE HEAVEN — Frank SINATRA
MY BODY — LEVERT SWEAT GILL
MY BONNIE —
Tony SHERIDAN and The BEATLES
MY BOO — USHER featuring Alicia KEYS
MY BOOK — The BEAUTIFUL SOUTH
MY BOOMERANG WON'T COME BACK —
Charlie DRAKE
MY BOY — Elvis PRESLEY
MY BOY FLAT TOP — Frankie VAUGHAN
MY BOY LOLLIPOP — MILLIE
MY BOYFRIEND'S BACK — ANGELS
MY BRAVE FACE — Paul McCARTNEY
MY BROTHER JAKE — FREE
MY CAMERA NEVER LIES — BUCKS FIZZ
MY CHERIE AMOUR — Stevie WONDER
MY CHILD — Connie FRANCIS
MY COCO — STELLASTARR*
MY COO-CA-CHOO — Alvin STARDUST
MY COUNTRY — MIDNIGHT OIL
MY CULTURE — 1 GIANT LEAP
MY CUTIE CUTIE — Shakin' STEVENS
MY DEFINITION OF A BOOMBASTIC JAZZ STYLE —
DREAM WARRIORS
MY DESIRE — AMIRA
MY DESTINY — Lionel RICHIE
MY DING-A-LING — Chuck BERRY
MY DIXIE DARLING — Lonnie DONEGAN
MY DJ (PUMP IT UP SOME) — Richie RICH
MY DOCS — KISS AMC
MY DRUG BUDDY — LEMONHEADS
MY DYING MACHINE — Gary NUMAN
MY EVER CHANGING MOODS — STYLE COUNCIL
MY EYES ADORED YOU — Frankie VALLI
MY FAMILY DEPENDS ON ME — SIMONE
MY FATHER'S EYES — Eric CLAPTON
MY FATHER'S SHOES — LEVEL 42
MY FATHER'S SON — Conner REEVES
MY FAVORITE MISTAKE — Sheryl CROW
MY FAVOURITE GAME — The CARDIGANS
MY FAVOURITE WASTE OF TIME — Owen PAUL
MY FEELING — JUNIOR JACK
MY FEET KEEP DANCING — CHIC
MY FIRST NIGHT WITHOUT YOU —
Cyndi LAUPER
MY FOOLISH FRIEND — TALK TALK
MY FORBIDDEN LOVER [A] — CHIC
MY FORBIDDEN LOVER [A] —
Romina JOHNSON
MY FRIEND [A] — Frankie LAINE
MY FRIEND [B] — Roy ORBISON
MY FRIEND [C] — GROOVE ARMADA
MY FRIEND JACK [A] — SMOKE

MY FRIEND JACK [A] — BONEY M
MY FRIEND STAN — SLADE
MY FRIEND THE SEA — Petula CLARK
MY FRIENDS — RED HOT CHILI PEPPERS
MY FRIENDS OVER YOU —
NEW FOUND GLORY
MY GENERATION [A] — The WHO
MY GENERATION [B] — LIMP BIZKIT
MY GETAWAY — T-BOZ
MY GIRL [A] — Otis REDDING
MY GIRL [A] — The TEMPTATIONS
MY GIRL [A] — WHISPERS
MY GIRL [B] — MADNESS
MY GIRL [C] — Rod STEWART
MY GIRL BILL — Jim STAFFORD
MY GIRL JOSEPHINE [A] — Fats DOMINO
MY GIRL JOSEPHINE [A] — SUPERCAT
MY GIRL LOLLIPOP (MY BOY LOLLIPOP) —
BAD MANNERS
MY GIRL LOVES ME — SHALAMAR
MY GIRL MY GIRL — Warren STACEY
MY GUY [A] — Mary WELLS
MY GUY [B] — Tracey ULLMAN
MY GUY — MY GIRL (MEDLEY) [A] —
Amii STEWART and Johnny BRISTOL
MY GUY — MY GIRL (MEDLEY) [A] —
Amii STEWART and Deon ESTUS
MY HAND OVER MY HEART — Marc ALMOND
MY HAPPINESS — Connie FRANCIS
MY HAPPY ENDING — Avril LAVIGNE
MY HEAD'S IN MISSISSIPPI — ZZ TOP
MY HEART — Gene VINCENT
MY HEART CAN'T TELL YOU NO —
Rod STEWART
MY HEART GOES BANG (GET ME TO THE
DOCTOR) — DEAD OR ALIVE
MY HEART GOES BOOM — FRENCH AFFAIR
MY HEART HAS A MIND OF ITS OWN —
Connie FRANCIS
MY HEART THE BEAT — D-SHAKE
MY HEART WILL GO ON — Celine DION
MY HEART'S BEATING WILD (TIC TAC TIC TAC) —
GIBSON BROTHERS
MY HEART'S SYMPHONY —
Gary LEWIS and the PLAYBOYS
MY HERO — FOO FIGHTERS
MY HOMETOWN — Bruce SPRINGSTEEN
MY HOUSE — TERRORVISION
MY HOUSE IS YOUR HOUSE — MAXTREME
MY IRON LUNG — RADIOHEAD
MY JAMAICAN GUY — Grace JONES
MY KIND OF GIRL [A] — Matt MONRO
MY KIND OF GIRL [A] — Frank SINATRA
MY KINDA LIFE — Cliff RICHARD
MY KINGDOM — FUTURE SOUND OF LONDON
MY LAST NIGHT WITH YOU — ARROWS
MY LIFE — Billy JOEL
MY LIFE IS IN YOUR HANDS — MELTDOWN
MY LITTLE BABY — Mike BERRY
MY LITTLE BROTHER — ART BRUT
MY LITTLE CORNER OF THE WORLD —
Anita BRYANT
MY LITTLE GIRL [A] — The CRICKETS
MY LITTLE GIRL [B] — AUTUMN
MY LITTLE LADY — The TREMELOES
MY LITTLE ONE — MARMALADE
MY LOVE [A] — Petula CLARK
MY LOVE [B] — Paul McCARTNEY
MY LOVE [C] — Lionel RICHIE
MY LOVE [D] —
Julio IGLESIAS featuring Stevie WONDER
MY LOVE [E] — LONDON BOYS
MY LOVE [F] — Mary J BLIGE
MY LOVE [G] — Kele LE ROC
MY LOVE [H] — WESTLIFE
MY LOVE [I] —
KLUSTER featuring Ron CARROLL
MY LOVE AND DEVOTION [A] — Doris DAY
MY LOVE AND DEVOTION [A] — Matt MONRO
MY LOVE FOR YOU — Johnny MATHIS
MY LOVE IS A FIRE — Donny OSMOND
MY LOVE IS ALWAYS —
SAFFRON HILL featuring Ben ONONO
MY LOVE IS DEEP — Sara PARKER
MY LOVE IS FOR REAL [A] —
Paula ABDUL featuring Ofra HAZA
MY LOVE IS FOR REAL [A] — STRIKE
MY LOVE IS GUARANTEED — SYBIL
MY LOVE IS LIKE ... WO — MYA
MY LOVE IS MAGIC — BAS NOIR
MY LOVE IS SO RAW —
Alyson WILLIAMS featuring Nikki D
MY LOVE IS THE SHHH! — SOMETHIN' FOR THE
PEOPLE featuring TRINA and TAMARA
MY LOVE IS WAITING — Marvin GAYE
MY LOVE IS YOUR LOVE — Whitney HOUSTON
MY LOVE LIFE — MORRISSEY
MY LOVER'S PRAYER [A] — Otis REDDING
MY LOVER'S PRAYER [B] — Alistair GRIFFIN
MY LOVIN' — EN VOGUE
MY MAGIC MAN — ROCHELLE
MY MAMMY — HAPPENINGS
MY MAN, A SWEET MAN — Millie JACKSON
MY MAN AND ME — Lynsey DE PAUL
MY MARIE — Engelbert HUMPERDINCK
MY MATE PAUL — David HOLMES
MY MELANCHOLY BABY — Tommy EDWARDS

MY MELANCHOLY BABY [A] — CHAS and DAVE
MY MIND'S EYE — The SMALL FACES
MY MUM IS ONE IN A MILLION — Children of TANSLEY SCHOOL
MY MY MY — Armand VAN HELDEN
MY NAME IS — EMINEM
MY NAME IS JACK — MANFRED MANN
MY NAME IS NOT SUSAN — Whitney HOUSTON
MY NAME IS PRINCE — PRINCE and the NEW POWER GENERATION
MY NECK, MY BACK (LICK IT) — KHIA
MY OH MY [A] — SAD CAFE
MY OH MY [B] — SLADE
MY OH MY [C] — AQUA
MY OLD MAN'S A DUSTMAN — Lonnie DONEGAN and his Group
MY OLD PIANO — Diana ROSS
MY ONE SIN — Nat 'King' COLE
MY ONE TEMPTATION — Mica PARIS
MY ONE TRUE FRIEND — Bette MIDLER
MY ONLY LOVE — Bob SINCLAR
MY OWN SUMMER (SHOVE IT) — DEFTONES
MY OWN TRUE LOVE — Danny WILLIAMS
MY OWN WAY — DURAN DURAN
MY OWN WORST ENEMY — LIT
MY PEACE OF HEAVEN — TEN CITY
MY PERFECT COUSIN — The UNDERTONES
MY PERSONAL POSSESSION — Nat 'King' COLE
MY PHILOSOPHY — BOOGIE DOWN PRODUCTIONS
MY PLACE — NELLY
MY PLAGUE — SLIPKNOT
MY PRAYER [A] — The PLATTERS
MY PRAYER [A] — Gerry MONROE
MY PREROGATIVE [A] — Bobby BROWN
MY PREROGATIVE [A] — Britney SPEARS
MY PRETTY ONE — Cliff RICHARD
MY PUPPET PAL — TIGER
MY RECOVERY INJECTION — BIFFY CLYRO
MY REMEDY — Hinda HICKS
MY RESISTANCE IS LOW — Robin SARSTEDT
MY RISING STAR — NORTHSIDE
MY SACRIFICE — CREED
MY SALT HEART — HUE AND CRY
MY SENTIMENTAL FRIEND — HERMAN'S HERMITS
MY SEPTEMBER LOVE — David WHITFIELD
MY SHARONA — KNACK
MY SHIP IS COMING IN — The WALKER BROTHERS
MY SIDE OF THE BED — Susanna HOFFS
MY SIMPLE HEART — The THREE DEGREES
MY SISTER — Juliana HATFIELD
MY 16TH APOLOGY (EP) — SHAKESPEAR'S SISTER
MY SON JOHN — David WHITFIELD
MY SON, MY SON — Vera LYNN with Frank WEIR, his Saxophone, his Orchestra and Chorus
MY SPECIAL ANGEL [A] — Bobby HELMS
MY SPECIAL ANGEL [A] — Malcolm VAUGHAN
MY SPECIAL CHILD — Sinead O'CONNOR
MY SPECIAL DREAM — Shirley BASSEY
MY SPIRIT — TILT
MY STAR — Ian BROWN
MY SUNDAY BABY — DALE SISTERS
MY SUPERSTAR — DIMESTARS
MY SWEET JANE — GUN
MY SWEET LORD — George HARRISON
MY SWEET ROSALIE — BROTHERHOOD OF MAN
MY TELEPHONE — COLDCUT
MY TIME — SOUVLAKI
MY TOOT TOOT — Denise LA SALLE
MY TOWN — GLASS TIGER
MY TRUE LOVE — Jack SCOTT
MY UKULELE — Max BYGRAVES
MY UNFINISHED SYMPHONY — David WHITFIELD
MY UNKNOWN LOVE — COUNT INDIGO
MY VISION — JAKATTA featuring SEAL
MY WAY [A] — Eddie COCHRAN
MY WAY [B] — Frank SINATRA
MY WAY [B] — Dorothy SQUIRES
MY WAY [B] — Elvis PRESLEY
MY WAY [B] — The SEX PISTOLS
MY WAY [B] — Shane MacGOWAN
MY WAY [C] — LIMP BIZKIT
MY WAY OF GIVING IN — Chris FARLOWE
MY WAY OF THINKING — UB40
MY WEAKNESS IS NONE OF YOUR BUSINESS — EMBRACE
MY WHITE BICYCLE — NAZARETH
MY WOMAN'S MAN — Dave DEE
MY WORLD [A] — CUPID'S INSPIRATION
MY WORLD [B] — The BEE GEES
MY WORLD [C] — SECRET AFFAIR
MY WORLD OF BLUE — Karl DENVER
MYFANWY — David ESSEX
MYSTERIES OF LOVE — LA MIX
MYSTERIES OF THE WORLD — MFSB
MYSTERIOUS GIRL — Peter ANDRE
MYSTERIOUS TIMES — SASH! featuring Tina COUSINS
MYSTERIOUS WAYS — U2
MYSTERY [A] — DIO
MYSTERY [B] — MYSTERY
MYSTERY GIRL [A] — Jess CONRAD
MYSTERY GIRL [B] — DUKES
MYSTERY LADY — Billy OCEAN
MYSTERY LAND (EP) [A] — Y-TRAXX
MYSTERY LAND [B] — Y-TRAXX featuring NEVE
MYSTERY SONG — STATUS QUO
MYSTERY TRAIN — Elvis PRESLEY
MYSTICAL MACHINE GUN — KULA SHAKER
MYSTIFY — INXS
MYZSTERIOUS MIZSTER JONES — SLADE
NA NA HEY HEY KISS HIM GOODBYE [A] — STEAM
NA NA HEY HEY KISS HIM GOODBYE [A] — BANANARAMA
NA NA IS THE SADDEST WORD — The STYLISTICS
NA NA NA — Cozy POWELL
NADINE (IS IT YOU) — Chuck BERRY
NAGASAKI BADGER — DISCO CITIZENS
NAILS IN MY FEET — CROWDED HOUSE
NAIROBI — Tommy STEELE
NAIVE SONG — MIRWAIS
NAKASAKI EP (I NEED A LOVER TONIGHT) — Ken DOH
NAKED [A] — REEF
NAKED [B] — LOUISE
NAKED AND SACRED [A] — Chynna PHILLIPS
NAKED AND SACRED [A] — Maria NAYLER
NAKED EYE — LUSCIOUS JACKSON
NAKED IN THE RAIN — BLUE PEARL
NAKED LOVE (JUST SAY YOU WANT ME) — QUARTZ and Dina CARROLL
NAKED WITHOUT YOU — ROACHFORD
NAME AND NUMBER — CURIOSITY
THE NAME OF THE GAME — ABBA
THE NAMELESS ONE — Wendy JAMES
NANCY BOY — PLACEBO
A NANNY IN MANHATTAN — LILYS
NAPOLEON — WOLFMAN
NAPPY LOVE — The GOODIES
NARCO TOURISTS — SLAM vs UNKLE
NARCOTIC INFLUENCE — EMPIRION
NASHVILLE BOOGIE — Bert WEEDON
NASHVILLE CATS — LOVIN' SPOONFUL
NASTRADAMUS — NAS
NASTY — Janet JACKSON
NASTY GIRLS — TWA
NATALIE'S PARTY — SHACK
NATHAN JONES [A] — The SUPREMES
NATHAN JONES [A] — BANANARAMA
NATIONAL EXPRESS — The DIVINE COMEDY
NATIVE BOY (UPTOWN) — ANIMAL NIGHTLIFE
NATIVE LAND — EVERYTHING BUT THE GIRL
NATIVE NEW YORKER [A] — ODYSSEY
NATIVE NEW YORKER [A] — BLACK BOX
NATURAL [A] — Bryan POWELL
NATURAL [B] — Peter ANDRE
NATURAL [C] — S CLUB 7
NATURAL BLUES — MOBY
NATURAL BORN BUGIE — HUMBLE PIE
NATURAL BORN KILLAZ — DR DRE and ICE CUBE
NATURAL HIGH [A] — BLOODSTONE
NATURAL HIGH [B] — Bitty McLEAN
NATURAL LIFE — NATURAL LIFE
NATURAL ONE — FOLK IMPLOSION
NATURAL SINNER — FAIR WEATHER
NATURAL THING — INNOCENCE
NATURAL WORLD — RODEO JONES
NATURE BOY [A] — Bobby DARIN
NATURE BOY [A] — George BENSON
NATURE BOY [A] — CENTRAL LINE
NATURE BOY [B] — Nick CAVE & The BAD SEEDS
NATURE OF LOVE — WATERFRONT
NATURE'S TIME FOR LOVE — Joe BROWN and the BRUVVERS
NAUGHTY CHRISTMAS (GOBLIN IN THE OFFICE) — FAT LES
NAUGHTY GIRL [A] — Holly VALANCE
NAUGHTY GIRL [B] — BEYONCÉ
NAUGHTY GIRLS (NEED LOVE TOO) — Samantha FOX featuring FULL FORCE
THE NAUGHTY LADY OF SHADY LANE [A] — AMES BROTHERS
THE NAUGHTY LADY OF SHADY LANE [A] — Dean MARTIN
NAUGHTY NAUGHTY — John PARR
NAUGHTY NAUGHTY NAUGHTY — Joy SARNEY
THE NAUGHTY NORTH AND THE SEXY SOUTH — E-MOTION
NAZIS — Roger TAYLOR
NEANDERTHAL MAN — HOTLEGS
NEAR TO YOU — TEENAGE FANCLUB and JAD FAIR
NEAR WILD HEAVEN — R.E.M.
NEAR YOU — MIGIL FIVE
NEARER THAN HEAVEN — DELAYS
NEARLY LOST YOU — SCREAMING TREES
NECESSARY EVIL — BODY COUNT
NEED GOOD LOVE — TUFF JAM
NEED YOU TONIGHT — INXS
NEED YOUR LOVE SO BAD [A] — FLEETWOOD MAC
NEED YOUR LOVE SO BAD [A] — Gary MOORE
NEEDIN' U [A] — David MORALES
NEEDIN' U II [A] — David MORALES presents the FACE featuring Juliet ROBERTS
THE NEEDLE AND THE DAMAGE DONE — Neil YOUNG
NEEDLES AND PINS [A] — The SEARCHERS
NEEDLES AND PINS [A] — SMOKIE
NEGASONIC TEENAGE WARHEAD — MONSTER MAGNET
NEGATIVE — MANSUN
NEHEMIAH — HOPE OF THE STATES
NEIGHBOR — UGLY KID JOE
NEIGHBOURHOOD [A] — SPACE
NEIGHBOURHOOD [B] — ZED BIAS
NEIL JUNG — TEENAGE FANCLUB
NEITHER ONE OF US (WANTS TO BE THE FIRST TO SAY GOODBYE) — Gladys KNIGHT and the PIPS
NELLIE THE ELEPHANT — TOY DOLLS
NELSON MANDELA — The SPECIALS
NE-NE NA-NA NA-NA NU-NU — BAD MANNERS
NEON KNIGHTS — BLACK SABBATH
NEON LIGHTS — KRAFTWERK
NEPTUNE — INME
NERVOUS — MATT BIANCO
NERVOUS BREAKDOWN [A] — Carleen ANDERSON
NERVOUS BREAKDOWN [B] — SHRINK
NERVOUS SHAKEDOWN — AC/DC
NERVOUS WRECK — RADIO STARS
NESSAJA — SCOOTER
NESSUN DORMA [A] — Luciano PAVAROTTI
NESSUN DORMA FROM 'TURANDOT' [A] — Luis COBOS featuring Placido DOMINGO
NETHERWORLD — LSG
NEUROTICA — CUD
NEUTRON DANCE — POINTER SISTERS
NEVER [A] — HEART
NEVER [B] — HOUSE OF LOVE
NEVER [C] — JOMANDA
NEVER [D] — ELECTRAFIXION
NEVER 'AD NOTHIN' — ANGELIC UPSTARTS
NEVER AGAIN [A] — DISCHARGE
NEVER AGAIN [B] — The MISSION
NEVER AGAIN [C] — JC 001
NEVER AGAIN [D] — HAPPY CLAPPERS
NEVER AGAIN [E] — NICKELBACK
NEVER AGAIN (THE DAYS TIME ERASED) — CLASSIX NOUVEAUX
NEVER BE ANYONE ELSE BUT YOU — Ricky NELSON
NEVER BE THE SAME AGAIN — Melanie C / Lisa 'Left-Eye' LOPES
NEVER BEFORE — DEEP PURPLE
NEVER CAN SAY GOODBYE [A] — The JACKSON FIVE
NEVER CAN SAY GOODBYE [A] — Gloria GAYNOR
NEVER CAN SAY GOODBYE [A] — COMMUNARDS
NEVER CAN SAY GOODBYE [A] — YAZZ
NEVER CAN TELL — I KAMANCHI
NEVER DO A TANGO WITH AN ESKIMO — Alma COGAN
NEVER DO YOU WRONG — Stephanie MILLS
NEVER DONE NOTHING LIKE THAT BEFORE — SUPERGRASS
NEVER ENDING SONG OF LOVE — The NEW SEEKERS
NEVER ENDING STORY — LIMAHL
NEVER ENOUGH [A] — JESUS JONES
NEVER ENOUGH [B] — The CURE
NEVER ENOUGH [C] — Boris DLUGOSCH featuring Roisin MURPHY
NEVER ENOUGH [D] — The OPEN
NEVER EVER — ALL SAINTS
NEVER FELT LIKE THIS BEFORE — Shaznay LEWIS
NEVER FELT THIS WAY — HI-LUX
NEVER FORGET — TAKE THAT
NEVER FOUND A LOVE LIKE THIS BEFORE — UPSIDE DOWN
NEVER GIVE UP — Monie LOVE
NEVER GIVE UP ON A GOOD THING — George BENSON
NEVER GIVE YOU UP — Sharon REDD
NEVER GOIN' DOWN — ADAMSKI and Jimi POLO
NEVER GOING NOWHERE — The BLUETONES
NEVER GONNA BE THE SAME — DANNY WILSON
NEVER GONNA CHANGE MY MIND — Joey LAWRENCE
NEVER GONNA COME BACK DOWN — BT
NEVER GONNA CRY AGAIN — EURYTHMICS
NEVER GONNA FALL IN LOVE AGAIN — DANA
NEVER GONNA GIVE YOU UP [A] — MUSICAL YOUTH
NEVER GONNA GIVE YOU UP [B] — Rick ASTLEY
NEVER GONNA (GIVE YOU UP) [B] — FKW
NEVER GONNA GIVE YOU UP (WON'T LET YOU BE) — Patrice RUSHEN
NEVER GONNA LEAVE YOUR SIDE — Daniel BEDINGFIELD
NEVER GONNA LET YOU GO [A] — Sergio MENDES
NEVER GONNA LET YOU GO [B] — Tina MOORE
NEVER GOODBYE — Karl DENVER
NEVER HAD A DREAM COME TRUE [A] — Stevie WONDER
NEVER HAD A DREAM COME TRUE [B] — S CLUB 7
NEVER HAD IT SO GOOD — TAKE 5
NEVER IN A MILLION YEARS — The BOOMTOWN RATS
NEVER KNEW LOVE [A] — Rick ASTLEY
NEVER KNEW LOVE [B] — Oleta ADAMS
NEVER KNEW LOVE [C] — NIGHTCRAWLERS featuring John REID
NEVER KNEW LOVE [D] — Stella BROWNE
NEVER KNEW LOVE LIKE THIS [A] — Alexander O'NEAL and CHERRELLE
NEVER KNEW LOVE LIKE THIS [A] — Pauline HENRY featuring Wayne MARSHALL
NEVER KNEW LOVE LIKE THIS BEFORE — Stephanie MILLS
NEVER LEAVE YOU - UH OOH, UH OOOH! — LUMIDEE
NEVER LEFT HIS HARDCORE — NRG
NEVER LET GO [A] — John BARRY ORCHESTRA
NEVER LET GO [B] — HYPER GO GO
NEVER LET GO [C] — Cliff RICHARD
NEVER LET HER SLIP AWAY [A] — Andrew GOLD
NEVER LET HER SLIP AWAY [A] — Trevor WALTERS
NEVER LET HER SLIP AWAY [A] — UNDERCOVER
NEVER LET ME DOWN — David BOWIE
NEVER LET ME DOWN AGAIN — DEPECHE MODE
NEVER LET YOU DOWN — HONEYZ
NEVER LET YOU GO — NEW KIDS ON THE BLOCK
NEVER LOOK BACK — DUMONDE
NEVER LOSE THAT FEELING — SWERVEDRIVER
NEVER LOST HIS HARDCORE — NRG
NEVER MIND — Cliff RICHARD
NEVER MIND THE PRESENTS — The BARRON KNIGHTS
NEVER MISS THE WATER — Chaka KHAN and Me'Shell NDEGEOCELLO
NEVER MY LOVE — Sugar MINOTT
NEVER NEVER [A] — The ASSEMBLY
NEVER NEVER [B] — WARM JETS
NEVER NEVER GONNA GIVE YA UP [A] — Barry WHITE
NEVER, NEVER GONNA GIVE YOU UP [A] — Lisa STANSFIELD
NEVER NEVER LOVE — SIMPLY RED
NEVER, NEVER, NEVER (GRANDE, GRANDE, GRANDE) — Shirley BASSEY
NEVER ON SUNDAY [A] — CHAQUITO
NEVER ON SUNDAY [A] — Lynn CORNELL
NEVER ON SUNDAY [A] — Don COSTA
NEVER ON SUNDAY [A] — MAKADOPOULOS and his GREEK SERENADERS
NEVER ON SUNDAY [A] — MANUEL and his MUSIC OF THE MOUNTAINS
NEVER (PAST TENSE) — ROC PROJECT featuring Tina ARENA
NEVER REALLY WAS — Mario WINANS featuring LIL' FLIP
NEVER SAW A MIRACLE — Curtis STIGERS
NEVER SAY DIE — BLACK SABBATH
NEVER SAY DIE (GIVE A LITTLE BIT MORE) — Cliff RICHARD
NEVER SAY GOODBYE — BON JOVI
NEVER STOP [A] — ECHO and the BUNNYMEN
NEVER STOP [B] — The BRAND NEW HEAVIES
NEVER SURRENDER — SAXON
NEVER TAKE ME ALIVE — SPEAR OF DESTINY
NEVER TEAR US APART — INXS
NEVER THERE — CAKE
NEVER TOO FAR — Mariah CAREY
NEVER TOO LATE — Kylie MINOGUE
NEVER TOO MUCH — Luther VANDROSS
NEVER TRUST A STRANGER — Kim WILDE
NEVER TURN AWAY — ORCHESTRAL MANOEUVRES IN THE DARK
NEVER TURN YOUR BACK ON MOTHER EARTH — SPARKS
NEVER UNDERSTAND — JESUS AND MARY CHAIN
NEVERENDING — HALO
NEVERTHELESS — Frankie VAUGHAN
NEVERTHELESS (I'M IN LOVE WITH YOU) — The NEW SEEKERS
NEW — NO DOUBT
NEW AMSTERDAM — Elvis COSTELLO
NEW ANGER — Gary NUMAN
NEW BEGINNING [A] — Stephen GATELY
NEW BEGINNING [B] — PRECIOUS
NEW BEGINNING (MAMBA SEYRA) — BUCKS FIZZ
NEW BIRD — REEF
NEW BORN — MUSE
NEW DAWN — PROPHETS OF SOUND
NEW DAY [A] — Wyclef JEAN featuring BONO
A NEW DAY [B] — KILLING JOKE
A NEW DAY HAS COME — Celine DION
NEW DIMENSION — IMAGINATION
NEW DIRECTION — FREAKPOWER
NEW DIRECTION — S CLUB JUNIORS
NEW EMOTION — TIME FREQUENCY
A NEW ENGLAND — Kirsty MacCOLL
A NEW FASHION — Bill WYMAN

A NEW FLAME — SIMPLY RED
NEW GENERATION — SUEDE
NEW GRANGE — CLANNAD
NEW GUITAR IN TOWN — LURKERS
NEW HOME NEW LIFE — The ALARM
NEW KICKS — JOHANN
NEW KID IN TOWN — The EAGLES
NEW KIND OF MEDICINE — Ultra NATÉ
NEW LIFE — DEPECHE MODE
NEW LIVE AND RARE (EP) — DEEP PURPLE
NEW LIVE AND RARE II (EP) — DEEP PURPLE
NEW LIVE AND RARE III (EP) — DEEP PURPLE
NEW MISTAKE — JELLYFISH
NEW MOON ON MONDAY — DURAN DURAN
NEW ORLEANS [A] — Gary 'US' BONDS
NEW ORLEANS [A] —
  Bern ELLIOTT and the FENMEN
NEW ORLEANS [A] — HARLEY QUINNE
NEW ORLEANS [A] — GILLAN
NEW POLICY ONE — TERRORVISION
THE NEW POLLUTION — BECK
NEW POWER GENERATION — PRINCE
NEW SENSATION — INXS
NEW SONG — Howard JONES
A NEW SOUTH WALES — The ALARM
NEW THING FROM LONDON TOWN —
  Gary NUMAN
NEW TOY — Lene LOVICH
NEW WAY, NEW LIFE —
  ASIAN DUB FOUNDATION
NEW WORLD IN THE MORNING —
  Roger WHITTAKER
NEW WORLD MAN — RUSH
NEW WORLD MAN (LIVE) — RUSH
NEW YEAR — SUGABABES
NEW YEAR'S DAY [A] — U2
NEW YEAR'S DUB [A] — MUSIQUE vs U2
NEW YORK AFTERNOON — MONDO KANE
NEW YORK CITY — T. REX
NEW YORK CITY BOY — PET SHOP BOYS
NEW YORK CITY COPS — The STROKES
NEW YORK EYES —
  NICOLE with Timmy THOMAS
NEW YORK GROOVE — HELLO
NEW YORK MINING DISASTER 1941 —
  The BEE GEES
NEW YORK, NEW YORK [A] — Gerard KENNY
NEW YORK NEW YORK [B] — Ryan ADAMS
NEW YORK UNDERCOVER (EP) —
  VARIOUS ARTISTS (EPs and LPs)
NEWBORN — ELBOW
NEWBORN FRIEND — SEAL
NEWS AT TEN — VAPORS
NEWS OF THE WORLD — The JAM
THE NEXT BIG THING — JESUS JONES
NEXT DOOR TO AN ANGEL — Neil SEDAKA
THE NEXT EPISODE —
  DR DRE featuring SNOOP DOGG
NEXT LEVEL — ILS
NEXT LIFETIME — Erykah BADU
THE NEXT TIME —
  Cliff RICHARD and The SHADOWS
NEXT TIME YOU FALL IN LOVE —
  Reva RICE and Greg ELLIS
NEXT TO YOU — ASWAD
NEXT YEAR — FOO FIGHTERS
NHS (EP) — DJ Doc SCOTT
NIALL QUINN'S DISCO PANTS —
  A LOVE SUPREME
NICE GUY EDDIE — SLEEPER
NICE IN NICE — The STRANGLERS
NICE LEGS SHAME ABOUT HER FACE —MONKS
NICE 'N' EASY — Frank SINATRA
NICE 'N SLEAZY — The STRANGLERS
NICE 'N' SLOW — Freddie JACKSON
NICE ONE CYRIL — COCKEREL CHORUS
NICE AND SLOW [A] — Jesse GREEN
NICE & SLOW [B] — USHER
NICE WEATHER FOR DUCKS — LEMON JELLY
NIGHT [A] — The FOUR SEASONS
THE NIGHT [A] — INTASTELLA
THE NIGHT [B] — SCOOTER
THE NIGHT [C] — SOFT CELL
A NIGHT AT DADDY GEE'S —
  SHOWADDYWADDY
A NIGHT AT THE APOLLO LIVE! —
  Daryl HALL and John OATES featuring
  David RUFFIN and Eddie KENDRICK
NIGHT BIRDS — SHAKATAK
NIGHT BOAT TO CAIRO — MADNESS
THE NIGHT CHICAGO DIED — PAPER LACE
NIGHT CRAWLER — JUDAS PRIEST
NIGHT DANCING — Joe FARRELL
NIGHT FEVER [A] — FATBACK BAND
NIGHT FEVER [B] — The BEE GEES
NIGHT FEVER [B] — Carol DOUGLAS
NIGHT FEVER [B] — Adam GARCIA
THE NIGHT FEVER MEGAMIX —
  UK MIXMASTERS
THE NIGHTFLY — BLANK & JONES
NIGHT GAMES — Graham BONNET
THE NIGHT HAS A THOUSAND EYES —
  Bobby VEE
NIGHT IN MOTION — CUBIC 22
NIGHT IN MY VEINS — The PRETENDERS
A NIGHT IN NEW YORK —
  Elbow BONES and the RACKETEERS

THE NIGHT IS YOUNG — Gary MILLER
NIGHT LADIES — CRUSADERS
NIGHT LIFE — David Lee ROTH
NIGHT LINE — Randy CRAWFORD
NIGHT MOVES —
  Bob SEGER and the SILVER BULLET BAND
NIGHT NURSE —
  SLY and ROBBIE featuring SIMPLY RED
NIGHT OF FEAR — The MOVE
NIGHT OF THE LIVING BASEHEADS —
  PUBLIC ENEMY
NIGHT OF THE LONG GRASS — The TROGGS
NIGHT OF THE VAMPIRE — MOONTREKKERS
NIGHT OWL — Gerry RAFFERTY
NIGHT PORTER — JAPAN
THE NIGHT THE EARTH CRIED — GRAVEDIGGAZ
(THE NIGHT THE LIGHTS WENT OUT IN)
  MASSACHUSETTS — The BEE GEES
THE NIGHT THE WINE AND THE ROSES —
  LIQUID GOLD
THE NIGHT THEY DROVE OLD DIXIE DOWN —
  Joan BAEZ
A NIGHT TO REMEMBER [A] — SHALAMAR
NIGHT TO REMEMBER [A] — 911
NIGHT TRAIN [A] — Buddy MORROW
NIGHT TRAIN [B] — VISAGE
NIGHT VISION — HELL IS FOR HEROES
THE NIGHT YOU MURDERED LOVE — ABC
NIGHTBIRD — CONVERT
NIGHTLIFE — KENICKIE
NIGHTMARE [A] — GILLAN
NIGHTMARE [B] — SAXON
NIGHTMARE [C] — KID UNKNOWN
NIGHTMARE [D] — BRAINBUG
NIGHTMARES — A FLOCK OF SEAGULLS
NIGHTRAIN — GUNS N' ROSES
NIGHTS IN WHITE SATIN [A] —
  The MOODY BLUES
NIGHTS IN WHITE SATIN [A] — The DICKIES
NIGHTS IN WHITE SATIN [A] — Elkie BROOKS
NIGHTS OF PLEASURE — LOOSE ENDS
NIGHTS ON BROADWAY — Candi STATON
NIGHTS OVER EGYPT — INCOGNITO
NIGHTSHIFT — The COMMODORES
NIGHTSWIMMING — R.E.M.
NIGHTTRAIN — PUBLIC ENEMY
THE NIGHTTRAIN — KADOC
NIKITA — Elton JOHN
NIKKE DOES IT BETTER —
  NIKKE! NICOLE!
NIMBUS — 808 STATE
9 AM (THE COMFORT ZONE) — LONDONBEAT
9PM (TILL I COME) — ATB
NINE TIMES OUT OF TEN —
  Cliff RICHARD and The SHADOWS
9 TO 5 [A] — Sheena EASTON
9 TO 5 [B] — Dolly PARTON
NINE WAYS — JDS
900 NUMBER — 45 KING
911 — Wyclef JEAN featuring Mary J BLIGE
911 IS A JOKE — PUBLIC ENEMY
977 — The PRETENDERS
19 — Paul HARDCASTLE
1980 — ESTELLE
1985 — BOWLING FOR SOUP
1998 — BINARY FINARY
1999 [A] — PRINCE
1999 [B] — BINARY FINARY
1979 — SMASHING PUMPKINS
NINETEEN63 — NEW ORDER
1962 — GRASS-SHOW
NINETEENTH NERVOUS BREAKDOWN —
  The ROLLING STONES
19/2000 — GORILLAZ
90S GIRL — BLACKGIRL
98.6 [A] — BYSTANDERS
98.6 [B] — KEITH
95 — NASTY — W.A.S.P.
99 1/2 — Carol Lynn TOWNES
99.9°F — Suzanne VEGA
99 PROBLEMS — JAY-Z
99 RED BALLOONS — NENA
NINETY-NINE WAYS — Tab HUNTER
96 TEARS [A] —
  ? (QUESTION MARK) and the MYSTERIANS
96 TEARS [A] — The STRANGLERS
92°F — POP WILL EAT ITSELF
'92 TOUR (EP) — MOTÖRHEAD
NIPPLE TO THE BOTTLE — Grace JONES
NITE AND DAY — Al B SURE!
NITE AND FOG — MERCURY REV
NITE KLUB — The SPECIALS
NITE LIFE — Kim ENGLISH
NI-TEN-ICHI-RYU (TWO SWORDS TECHNIQUE) —
  PHOTEK
NITRO — PALE X
N-N-NINETEEN NOT OUT — COMMENTATORS
NO — Chuck D
NO ALIBIS — Eric CLAPTON
NO ARMS CAN EVER HOLD YOU —
  The BACHELORS
NO BLUE SKIES — Lloyd COLE
NO CHARGE [A] — JJ BARRIE
NO CHANCE (NO CHARGE) [A] —
  Billy CONNOLLY
NO CHEAP THRILL — Suzanne VEGA
NO CHRISTMAS — WEDDING PRESENT

NO CLASS — MOTÖRHEAD
NO CLAUSE 28 — BOY GEORGE
NO CONVERSATION — VIEW FROM THE HILL
NO DIGGITY — BLACKSTREET featuring DR DRE
NO DISTANCE LEFT TO RUN — BLUR
NO DOUBT [A] — 702
NO DOUBT [B] — IMAJIN
NO DOUBT ABOUT IT — HOT CHOCOLATE
NO DREAM IMPOSSIBLE — LINDSAY
NO EDUCATION NO FUTURE (F**K THE
  CURFEW) — MOGWAI
NO ESCAPIN' THIS — The BEATNUTS
NO FACE, NO NAME, NO NUMBER — TRAFFIC
NO FLOW — Lisa ROXANNE
NO FOOL (FOR LOVE) — Hazell DEAN
NO FRONTS — DOG EAT DOG
NO GETTING OVER YOU — PARIS
NO GOOD — DA FOOL
NO GOOD ADVICE — GIRLS ALOUD
NO GOOD FOR ME — Bruce WAYNE
NO GOOD 4 ME — OXIDE & NEUTRINO
NO GOOD (START THE DANCE) — The PRODIGY
NO GOODBYES — Curtis MAYFIELD
NO GOVERNMENT — NICOLETTE
NO HIDING PLACE — Ken MACKINTOSH
NO HONESTLY — Lynsey DE PAUL
NO LAUGHING IN HEAVEN — GILLAN
NO LETTING GO — Wayne WONDER
NO LIES — S.O.S. BAND
NO LIMIT [A] — 2 UNLIMITED
NO LIMITS [A] — BAKSHELF DOG
NO LOVE — Joan ARMATRADING
NO MAN'S LAND [A] — Gerard KENNY
NO MAN'S LAND [B] — Billy JOEL
(NO MATTER HOW HIGH I GET) I'LL STILL BE LOOKIN'
  UP TO YOU — Wilton FELDER
NO MATTER HOW I TRY — Gilbert O'SULLIVAN
NO MATTER WHAT [A] — BADFINGER
NO MATTER WHAT [B] — BOYZONE
NO MATTER WHAT I DO — Will MELLOR
NO MATTER WHAT SIGN YOU ARE —
  Diana ROSS and The SUPREMES
NO MATTER WHAT THEY SAY — LIL' KIM
NO MATTER WHAT YOU DO —
  Benny BENASSI presents The BIZ
NO MEMORY — SCARLET FANTASTIC
NO MERCY — The STRANGLERS
NO MILK TODAY — HERMAN'S HERMITS
NO ME — The McGUIRE SISTERS
NO MORE [B] — UNIQUE 3
NO MORE [C] — RUFF ENDZ
NO MORE [D] — a1
NO MORE AFFAIRS — TINDERSTICKS
NO MORE ALCOHOL — SUGGS featuring Louchie LOU
  and Michie ONE
NO MORE (BABY I'MA DO RIGHT) — 3LW
NO MORE DRAMA — Mary J BLIGE
NO MORE HEROES — The STRANGLERS
NO MORE (I CAN'T STAND IT) — MAXX
NO MORE 'I LOVE YOU'S' [A] — LOVER SPEAKS
NO MORE 'I LOVE YOU'S' [A] — Annie LENNOX
NO MORE LIES — Gary NUMAN
NO MORE LONELY NIGHTS (BALLAD) —
  Paul McCARTNEY
(NO MORE) LOVE AT YOUR CONVENIENCE —
  Alice COOPER
NO MORE MR NICE GUY [A] — Alice COOPER
NO MORE MR NICE GUY [A] — MEGADETH
NO MORE RAINY DAYS — FREE SPIRIT
NO MORE TALK — DUBSTAR
NO MORE TEARS [A] — HOLLYWOOD BEYOND
NO MORE TEARS [B] — Jaki GRAHAM
NO MORE TEARS [C] — Ozzy OSBOURNE
NO MORE TEARS (ENOUGH IS ENOUGH) [A] —
  Barbra STREISAND and Donna SUMMER
NO MORE TEARS (ENOUGH IS ENOUGH) [A] —
  Jocelyn BROWN and Kym MAZELLE
NO MORE THE FOOL — Elkie BROOKS
NO MORE TOMORROWS — Paul JOHNSON
NO MORE TURNING BACK — GITTA
NO MULE'S FOOL — FAMILY
NO NEED — ALFIE
NO NO JOE — SILVER CONVENTION
NO, NO, NO [A] — Nancy NOVA
NO, NO, NO [B] — DESTINY'S CHILD
NO NO NO [C] —
  MANIJAMA featuring MUKUPA & L'IL T
NO, NOT NOW — HOT HOT HEAT
NO ONE [A] — Ray CHARLES
NO ONE [B] — 2 UNLIMITED
NO ONE BUT YOU [A] — Billy ECKSTINE
NO-ONE BUT YOU [B] — QUEEN
NO ONE CAN — MARILLION
NO ONE CAN BREAK A HEART LIKE YOU —
  Dave CLARK FIVE
NO ONE CAN LOVE YOU MORE THAN ME —
  Kym MAZELLE
NO ONE CAN MAKE MY SUNSHINE SMILE —
  The EVERLY BROTHERS
NO ONE CAN STOP US NOW — CHELSEA FC
NO ONE DRIVING — John FOXX
NO ONE ELSE COMES CLOSE — JOE
NO ONE GETS THE PRIZE — Diana ROSS
NO ONE IS INNOCENT — The SEX PISTOLS
NO ONE IS TO BLAME — Howard JONES
NO ONE KNOWS —
  QUEENS OF THE STONE AGE

NO ONE LIKE YOU — SCORPIONS
NO ONE SPEAKS — GENEVA
NO ONE TO CRY TO — Ray CHARLES
NO ONE WILL EVER KNOW — Frank IFIELD
NO ONE'S DRIVING — Dave CLARKE
NO ORDINARY LOVE — SADE
NO ORDINARY MORNING — CHICANE
NO OTHER BABY [A] — Bobby HELMS
NO OTHER BABY [A] — Paul McCARTNEY
NO OTHER LOVE [A] — Ronnie HILTON
NO OTHER LOVE [A] — Edmund HOCKRIDGE
NO OTHER LOVE [A] — JOHNSTON BROTHERS
NO PANTIES — TRINA
NO PARTICULAR PLACE TO GO — Chuck BERRY
NO PIGEONS — SPORTY THIEVZ
NO PLACE TO HIDE — KORN
NO PROMISES — ICEHOUSE
NO RAIN — BLIND MELON
NO REGRETS [A] — Shirley BASSEY
NO REGRETS [B] — The WALKER BROTHERS
NO REGRETS [B] — Midge URE
NO REGRETS [C] — Robbie WILLIAMS
NO RELIGION — Van MORRISON
NO REST — NEW MODEL ARMY
NO SCRUBS — TLC
NO SELF CONTROL — Peter GABRIEL
NO SELL OUT — Malcolm X
NO SENSE — NEW MODEL ARMY
NO SLEEP NO NEED (EP) — VAULTS
NO SLEEP TILL BROOKLYN — BEASTIE BOYS
NO SON OF MINE — GENESIS
NO STONE UNTURNED — TRUTH
NO STRESS — CYCLEFLY
NO SUCH THING — John MAYER
NO SURPRISES — RADIOHEAD
NO SURRENDER — DEUCE
NO SURVIVORS — GBH
NO SWEAT '98 — NORTH AND SOUTH
NO TENGO DINERO — LOS UMBRELLOS
NO TIME — LIL' KIM featuring PUFF DADDY
NO TIME TO BE 21 — ADVERTS
NO TIME TO CRY — SISTERS OF MERCY
NO TIME TO PLAY — GURU featuring DC LEE
NO WAY — FREAKPOWER
NO WAY BACK — ADONIS featuring 2 PUERTO RICANS,
  A BLACK MAN AND A DOMINICAN
NO WAY NO WAY — VANILLA
NO WAY OUT — Francesco ZAPPALA
NO WOMAN NO CRY [A] —
  Bob MARLEY & the WAILERS
NO WOMAN NO CRY [A] — LONDONBEAT
NO WOMAN, NO CRY [A] — The FUGEES
THE NOBODIES — MARILYN MANSON
NOBODY [A] — Toni BASIL
NOBODY [B] — TONGUE 'N' CHEEK
NOBODY [C] — Shara NELSON
NOBODY [D] — Keith SWEAT
NOBODY BETTER — Tina MOORE
NOBODY BUT YOU —
  Gladys KNIGHT and the PIPS
NOBODY DOES IT BETTER — Carly SIMON
NOBODY ELSE [A] — Nick KAMEN
NOBODY ELSE [B] — TYRESE
NOBODY I KNOW — PETER and GORDON
NOBODY KNOWS [A] — Nik KERSHAW
NOBODY KNOWS [B] — Tony RICH PROJECT
NOBODY MADE ME — Randy EDELMAN
NOBODY NEEDS YOUR LOVE — Gene PITNEY
NOBODY TOLD ME — John LENNON
NOBODY WANTS TO BE LONELY —
  Ricky MARTIN and Christina AGUILERA
NOBODY WINS — Elton JOHN
NOBODY'S BUSINESS — H2o
NOBODY'S BUSINESS [B] — PEACE BY PIECE
NOBODY'S CHILD [A] — Karen YOUNG
NOBODY'S CHILD [A] — TRAVELING WILBURYS
NOBODY'S DIARY' BUT MINE — Frank IFIELD
NOBODY'S DIARY — YAZOO
NOBODY'S FOOL [A] — Jim REEVES
NOBODY'S FOOL [B] — HAIRCUT 100
NOBODY'S HERO — STIFF LITTLE FINGERS
NOBODY'S HOME — Avril LAVIGNE
NOBODY'S SUPPOSED TO BE HERE —
  Deborah COX
NOBODY'S TWISTING YOUR ARM —
  WEDDING PRESENT
NOCTURNE — T99
NOMANSLAND (DAVID'S SONG) —
  DJ SAKIN & FRIENDS
NOMZAMO (ONE PEOPLE ONE CAUSE) —
  LATIN QUARTER
NON HO L'ETA PER AMARTI —
  Gigliola CINQUETTI
NONE OF YOUR BUSINESS — SALT-N-PEPA
(NONSTOPOPERATION) — DUST JUNKYS
NORA MALONE — Teresa BREWER
NORMAN — Carol DEENE
NORMAN BATES — LANDSCAPE
NORMAN 3 — TEENAGE FANCLUB
NORTH COUNTRY BOY — The CHARLATANS
NORTH, SOUTH, EAST, WEST —
  MARVIN and TAMARA
NORTH TO ALASKA — Johnny HORTON
NORTHERN LIGHTS — RENAISSANCE
NORTHERN LITES — SUPER FURRY ANIMALS
NORTHERN STAR — Melanie C
NOT A DRY EYE IN THE HOUSE — MEAT LOAF

NOT A JOB — ELBOW
NOT A MINUTE TOO SOON — VIXEN
NOT ABOUT US — GENESIS
NOT ALONE — Bernard BUTLER
NOT ANYONE — BLACK BOX
NOT AS A STRANGER — Frank SINATRA
NOT AT ALL — STATUS QUO
NOT ENOUGH? — Melanie WILLIAMS
NOT ENOUGH LOVE IN THE WORLD — CHER
NOT EVEN GONNA TRIP — HONEYZ
NOT FADE AWAY — The ROLLING STONES
NOT FOR ALL THE LOVE IN THE WORLD —
    The THRILLS
NOT FOR YOU — PEARL JAM
NOT GON' CRY — Mary J BLIGE
NOT GONNA GET US — t.A.T.u.
NOT IF YOU WERE THE LAST JUNKIE ON EARTH —
    The DANDY WARHOLS
NOT IN LOVE — ENRIQUE featuring KELIS
NOT ME, NOT I — Delta GOODREM
NOT NOW JOHN — PINK FLOYD
NOT OVER YET [A] — GRACE
NOT OVER YET 99 [A] —
    Planet PERFECTO featuring GRACE
NOT OVER YOU YET — Diana ROSS
NOT RESPONSIBLE — Tom JONES
NOT SLEEPING AROUND —
    NED'S ATOMIC DUSTBIN
NOT SO MANIC NOW — DUBSTAR
NOT SUCH AN INNOCENT GIRL —
    Victoria BECKHAM
NOT THAT KIND — ANASTACIA
NOT THE GIRL YOU THINK YOU ARE —
    CROWDED HOUSE
(NOT THE) GREATEST RAPPER —
    1000 CLOWNS
NOT TODAY — Mary J. BLIGE featuring EVE
NOT TONIGHT — LIL' KIM
NOT TOO LATE FOR LOVE — Beverley KNIGHT
NOT TOO LITTLE NOT TOO MUCH —
    Chris SANDFORD
NOT UNTIL THE NEXT TIME — Jim REEVES
NOT WHERE IT'S AT — DEL AMITRI
NOTGONNACHANGE — SWING OUT SISTER
NOTHIN' — N.O.R.E.
NOTHIN' AT ALL — HEART
NOTHIN' BUT A GOOD TIME — POISON
NOTHIN' BUT A PARTY — TRUCE
NOTHIN' MY LOVE CAN'T FIX —
    Joey LAWRENCE
NOTHIN' PERSONAL — DUST JUNKYS
(NOTHIN' SERIOUS) JUST BUGGIN' — WHISTLE
NOTHIN' (THAT COMPARES 2 U) —
    The JACKSONS
NOTHIN' TO DO — Michael HOLLIDAY
NOTHING [A] — FRAZIER CHORUS
NOTHING [B] — FLUFFY
NOTHING [C] — A
NOTHING [D] — HOLDEN & THOMPSON
NOTHING AS IT SEEMS — PEARL JAM
NOTHING AT ALL — Luke SLATER
NOTHING 'BOUT ME — STING
NOTHING BUT LOVE — OPTIMYSTIC
NOTHING CAN CHANGE THIS LOVE —
    Bitty McLEAN
NOTHING CAN DIVIDE US — Jason DONOVAN
NOTHING CAN STOP ME — Gene CHANDLER
NOTHING CAN STOP US — SAINT ETIENNE
NOTHING COMES EASY — Sandie SHAW
NOTHING COMPARES 2 U [A] —
    Sinead O'CONNOR
NOTHING COMPARES 2 U [A] — MXM
NOTHING ELSE MATTERS — METALLICA
NOTHING EVER HAPPENS — DEL AMITRI
NOTHING HAS BEEN PROVED [A] —
    Dusty SPRINGFIELD
NOTHING HAS BEEN PROVED [A] —
    STRINGS OF LOVE
NOTHING HURTS LIKE LOVE —
    Daniel BEDINGFIELD
NOTHING IN PARTICULAR —
    The BROTHERHOOD
NOTHING IS FOREVER — ULTRACYNIC
NOTHING IS REAL BUT THE GIRL — BLONDIE
NOTHING LASTS FOREVER —
    ECHO and the BUNNYMEN
NOTHING LEFT — ORBITAL
NOTHING LEFT TOULOUSE — SAD CAFE
NOTHING LESS THAN BRILLIANT —
    Sandie SHAW
NOTHING NATURAL — LUSH
NOTHING REALLY MATTERS — MADONNA
NOTHING RHYMED — Gilbert O'SULLIVAN
NOTHING SACRED – A SONG FOR KIRSTY —
    RUSSELL WATSON
NOTHING TO DECLARE — LAPTOP
NOTHING TO FEAR — Chris REA
NOTHING TO LOSE [A] — UK
NOTHING TO LOSE [B] — S EXPRESS
NOTHING WITHOUT ME — MANCHILD
NOTHING WRONG WITH YOU —
    FINN BROTHERS
NOTHING'S GONNA CHANGE MY LOVE FOR YOU —
    Glenn MEDEIROS
NOTHING'S GONNA STOP ME NOW — Samantha FOX
NOTHING'S GONNA STOP US NOW — STARSHIP
NOTHIN'S GONNA CHANGE — Labi SIFFRE

NOTORIOUS — DURAN DURAN
NOTORIOUS B.I.G. — NOTORIOUS B.I.G.
NOVELTY WAVES — BIOSPHERE
NOVEMBER RAIN — GUNS N' ROSES
NOVEMBER SPAWNED A MONSTER —
    MORRISSEY
NOVOCAINE FOR THE SOUL — EELS
NOW [A] — Al MARTINO
NOW [B] — Val DOONICAN
NOW [C] — DEF LEPPARD
NOW ALWAYS AND FOREVER — GAY DAD
NOW AND FOREVER — Richard MARX
NOW I KNOW WHAT MADE OTIS BLUE —
    Paul YOUNG
NOW I'M HERE — QUEEN
NOW IS THE TIME —
    Jimmy JAMES and the VAGABONDS
NOW IS TOMORROW — DEFINITION OF SOUND
NOW IT'S GONE — CHORDS
NOW IT'S ON — GRANDADDY
NOW I'VE FOUND YOU — Sean MAGUIRE
NOW OR NEVER — Tom NOVY featuring LIMA
NOW THAT I OWN THE BBC — SPARKS
NOW THAT THE MAGIC HAS GONE —
    Joe COCKER
NOW THAT WE'VE FOUND LOVE [A] —
    THIRD WORLD
NOW THAT WE FOUND LOVE [A] —
    HEAVY D and the BOYZ
NOW THAT YOU LOVE ME — The ALICE BAND
NOW THAT YOU'VE GONE —
    MIKE and the MECHANICS
NOW THEY'LL SLEEP — BELLY
NOW THOSE DAYS ARE GONE — BUCKS FIZZ
NOW WE ARE FREE —
    GLADIATOR featuring IZZY
NOW WE'RE THRU — POETS
NOW YOU'RE GONE [A] — BLACK
NOW YOU'RE GONE [B] — WHITESNAKE
NOW YOU'RE IN HEAVEN — Julian LENNON
NOWHERE [A] — THERAPY?
NOWHERE [B] — LONGVIEW
NOWHERE AGAIN — SECRET MACHINES
NOWHERE FAST — MEAT LOAF
NOWHERE GIRL — B-MOVIE
NOWHERE LAND — CLUBHOUSE
NOWHERE MAN — THREE GOOD REASONS
NOWHERE TO RUN [A] —
    Martha REEVES and the VANDELLAS
NOWHERE TO RUN 2000 [A] —
    NU GENERATION
N-R-G — ADAMSKI
NU FLOW — BIG BROVAZ
NUCLEAR — Ryan ADAMS
NUCLEAR DEVICE (THE WIZARD OF AUS) —
    The STRANGLERS
NUCLEAR HOLIDAY — 3 COLOURS RED
NUFF VIBES EP — APACHE INDIAN
NUMB [A] — LINKIN PARK
NUMB [A] / ENCORE — JAY-Z / LINKIN PARK
#9 DREAM — John LENNON
THE NUMBER OF THE BEAST — IRON MAIDEN
NUMBER ONE [A] — EYC
NUMBER ONE [B] — A
NUMBER ONE [C] — PLAYGROUP
NUMBER 1 [D] — TWEENIES
NUMBER 1 [E] — EBONY DUBSTERS
NUMBER ONE BLIND — VERUCA SALT
NUMBER ONE DEE JAY — GOODY GOODY
NUMBER ONE DOMINATOR — TOP
NUMBER ONE RAT FAN —
    Roland RAT SUPERSTAR
THE NUMBER ONE SONG IN HEAVEN —
    SPARKS
NUMBERS — SOFT CELL
NUMERO UNO — STARLIGHT
NUNC DIMITTIS — Paul PHOENIX
NURSERY RHYMES — ICEBERG SLIMM
NURTURE — LFO
NUT ROCKER —
    B BUMBLE and the STINGERS
NUTBUSH CITY LIMITS [A] —
    Ike and Tina TURNER
NUTBUSH CITY LIMITS [A] — Tina TURNER
NUTHIN' BUT A 'G' THANG — DR DRE
NWO — MINISTRY
NYC — INTERPOL
N.Y.C. (CAN YOU BELIEVE THIS CITY) —
    CHARLES and EDDIE
O BABY — SIOUXSIE and the BANSHEES
O L'AMOUR [A] — DOLLAR
OH L'AMOUR [A] — ERASURE
O' MY FATHER HAD A RABBIT — Ray MOORE
O-O-O — ADRENALIN M.O.D.
O SUPERMAN — Laurie ANDERSON
OAKLAND STROKE — TONY TONI TONÉ
OBJECTION (TANGO) — SHAKIRA
OBJECTS IN THE REAR VIEW MIRROR
    MAY APPEAR CLOSER THAN THEY ARE —
    MEAT LOAF
OB-LA-DI OB-LA-DA [A] — BEDROCKS
OB-LA-DI, OB-LA-DA [A] — MARMALADE
OBLIVION — TERRORVISION
OBLIVION (HEAD IN THE CLOUDS) (EP) — MANIX
OBLIVIOUS — AZTEC CAMERA
THE OBOE SONG — CLERGY
OBSESION (SI ES AMOR) — 3RD WISH

OBSESSED — 999
OBSESSION [A] — Reg OWEN
OBSESSION [B] — ANIMOTION
OBSESSION [C] — ARMY OF LOVERS
OBSESSION [D] — ULTRA-SONIC
OBSESSION [E] — TIESTO & JUNKIE XL
OBSESSIONS — SUEDE
OBSTACLE 1 — INTERPOL
OBVIOUS — WESTLIFE
THE OBVIOUS CHILD — Paul SIMON
OBVIOUSLY — McFLY
OCEAN AVENUE — YELLOWCARD
OCEAN BLUE — ABC
OCEAN DEEP — Cliff RICHARD
OCEAN DRIVE — LIGHTHOUSE FAMILY
OCEAN OF ETERNITY — FUTURE BREEZE
OCEAN PIE — SHED SEVEN
OCEAN SPRAY — MANIC STREET PREACHERS
OCTOBER SWIMMER — JJ72
ODE TO BILLY JOE — Bobbie GENTRY
ODE TO BOY — Alison MOYET
ODE TO JOY (FROM BEETHOVEN'S SYMPHONY NO.9) —
    BBC CONCERT ORCHESTRA, BBC SYMPHONY CHORUS
    cond. Stephen JACKSON
ODE TO MY FAMILY — The CRANBERRIES
THE ODYSSEY — DRUMSOUND / Simon 'BASSLINE'
    SMITH
OF COURSE I'M LYING — YELLO
OF COURSE YOU CAN — SPEARHEAD
OFF ON HOLIDAY — SUGGS
OFF ON YOUR OWN (GIRL) — Al B SURE!
OFF THE HOOK — Jody WATLEY
OFF THE WALL [A] — Michael JACKSON
OFF THE WALL [A] — WISDOME
OFFICIAL SECRETS — M
OFFSHORE — CHICANE
OFFSHORE BANKING BUSINESS — MEMBERS
OH BABE, WHAT WOULD YOU SAY? —
    Hurricane SMITH
OH BABY — RHIANNA
OH BABY I ... — ETERNAL
(OH BABY MINE) I GET SO LONELY —
    FOUR KNIGHTS
OH BOY [A] — The CRICKETS
OH BOY [A] — MUD
OH BOY [B] — FABULOUS BAKER BOYS
OH BOY [C] — CAM'RON
OH BOY (THE MOOD I'M IN) —
    BROTHERHOOD OF MAN
OH CAROL [A] — Neil SEDAKA
OH CAROL! [A] —
    Clint EASTWOOD and General SAINT
OH CAROL [B] — SMOKIE
OH CAROLINA — SHAGGY
OH DIANE — FLEETWOOD MAC
OH FATHER — MADONNA
OH GIRL [A] — CHI-LITES
OH GIRL [A] — Paul YOUNG
OH, HAPPY DAY .[A] — JOHNSTON BROTHERS
OH HAPPY DAY [B] —
    Edwin HAWKINS SINGERS
OH HOW I MISS YOU — The BACHELORS
OH JIM — GAY DAD
OH JULIE — Shakin' STEVENS
OH LA LA LA — 2 EIVISSA
OH LONESOME ME — Craig DOUGLAS
OH, LORI — ALESSI
OH LOUISE — JUNIOR
OH ME OH MY (I'M A FOOL FOR YOU BABY)
    — LULU
OH, MEIN PAPA — Eddie CALVERT
OH MILLWALL — MILLWALL FC
OH MY GOD [A] — A TRIBE CALLED QUEST
OH MY GOD [B] — KAISER CHIEFS
OH MY PAPA (OH, MEIN PAPA) —
    Eddie FISHER
OH NO [A] — The COMMODORES
OH NO [B] — MOS DEF and Nate
    DOGG featuring Pharoahe MONCH
OH NO NOT MY BABY [A] — MANFRED MANN
OH! NO NOT MY BABY [A] — Rod STEWART
OH NO NOT MY BABY [A] — CHER
OH NO WON'T DO (EP) — CUD
OH-OH, I'M FALLING IN LOVE AGAIN —
    Jimmie RODGERS
OH PATTI (DON'T FEEL SORRY FOR LOVERBOY) —
    SCRITTI POLITTI
OH, PEOPLE — Patti LaBELLE
OH, PRETTY WOMAN [A] — Roy ORBISON
OH PRETTY WOMAN [B] — Gary MOORE
OH ROMEO — Mindy McCREADY
OH SHEILA — READY FOR THE WORLD
OH THE GUILT — NIRVANA
OH U WANT MORE? —
    TY featuring Roots MANUVA
OH WELL [A] — FLEETWOOD MAC
OH WELL [A] — OH WELL
OH WHAT A CIRCUS — David ESSEX
OH! WHAT A DAY — Craig DOUGLAS
OH WHAT A FEELING — CHANGE
OH WHAT A NIGHT — CLOCK
OH WHAT A SHAME — Roy WOOD
OH! WHAT A WORLD — SISTER BLISS
OH WORLD — Paul RUTHERFORD
OH YEAH! [A] — Bill WITHERS
OH YEAH [B] — ASH
OH YEAH [C] — CAPRICE

OH YEAH [D] — Foxy BROWN
OH YEAH, BABY — DWEEB
OH YEAH (ON THE RADIO) — ROXY MUSIC
OH YES! YOU'RE BEAUTIFUL — Gary GLITTER
OH YOU PRETTY THING — Peter NOONE
OHIO — UTAH SAINTS
OI! —
    PLATINUM 45 featuring MORE FIRE CREW
OK — BIG BROVAZ
OK? — Julie COVINGTON, Rula LENSKA, Charlotte
    CORNWELL and Sue JONES-DAVIES
OK FRED — Errol DUNKLEY
OKAY! —
    Dave DEE, DOZY, BEAKY, MICK and TICH
OL' MACDONALD — Frank SINATRA
OL' RAG BLUES — STATUS QUO
OLD [A] — DEXY'S MIDNIGHT RUNNERS
OLD [B] — MACHINE HEAD
OLD AND WISE — Alan PARSONS PROJECT
OLD BEFORE I DIE — Robbie WILLIAMS
THE OLD FASHIONED WAY (LES PLAISIRS DÉMODÉS) —
    Charles AZNAVOUR
OLD FLAMES — FOSTER and ALLEN
OLD FOLKS — A
OLD HABITS DIE HARD —
    Mick JAGGER and Dave STEWART
OLD MAN AND ME (WHEN I GET TO HEAVEN) —
    HOOTIE & THE BLOWFISH
THE OLD MAN AND THE ANGEL — IT BITES
OLD OAKEN BUCKET — Tommy SANDS
THE OLD PAYOLA ROLL BLUES —
    Stan FREBERG
OLD PI-ANNA RAG — Dickie VALENTINE
OLD POP IN AN OAK — REDNEX
OLD RED EYES IS BACK —
    The BEAUTIFUL SOUTH
OLD RIVERS — Walter BRENNAN
THE OLD RUGGED CROSS — Ethna CAMPBELL
OLD SHEP — Clinton FORD
OLD SIAM SIR — Paul McCARTNEY
OLD SMOKEY — JOHNNY and the HURRICANES
THE OLD SONGS — Barry MANILOW
OLDER — George MICHAEL
OLDEST SWINGER IN TOWN — Fred WEDLOCK
OLE OLA (MULHER BRASILEIRA) —
    Rod STEWART
OLIVE TREE — Judith DURHAM
OLIVER'S ARMY — Elvis COSTELLO
OLYMPIAN — GENE
OLYMPIC — 808 STATE
THE OMD REMIXES EP —
    ORCHESTRAL MANOEUVRES IN THE DARK
OMEN — ORBITAL
THE OMEN — BELTRAM
OMEN III — MAGIC AFFAIR
ON — APHEX TWIN
ON A CAROUSEL — The HOLLIES
ON A CROWDED STREET —
    Barbara PENNINGTON
ON A DAY LIKE TODAY — Bryan ADAMS
ON A LITTLE STREET IN SINGAPORE —
    MANHATTAN TRANSFER
ON A MISSION — ALOOF
ON A NIGHT LIKE THIS — Kylie MINOGUE
ON A RAGGA TIP — SL2
ON A ROPE — ROCKET FROM THE CRYPT
ON A SATURDAY NIGHT —
    Terry DACTYL and the DINOSAURS
ON A SLOW BOAT TO CHINA —
    Emile FORD and the CHECKMATES
ON A SUNDAY — Nick HEYWARD
ON A SUN-DAY — BENZ
ON AND ON [A] — ASWAD
ON AND ON [B] — LONGPIGS
ON & ON [C] — Erykah BADU
ON BENDED KNEE — BOYZ II MEN
ON EVERY STREET — DIRE STRAITS
ON FIRE [A] — T-CONNECTION
ON FIRE [B] — Tone LOC
ON FIRE [C] — Lloyd BANK$
ON HER MAJESTY'S SECRET SERVICE —
    PROPELLERHEADS
ON HORSEBACK — Mike OLDFIELD
ON MOTHER KELLY'S DOORSTEP —
    Danny LA RUE
ON MY KNEES —
    The 411 featuring GHOSTFACE KILLAH
ON MY MIND —
    FUTURESHOCK featuring Ben ONONO
ON MY OWN [A] —
    Patti LaBELLE and Michael McDONALD
ON MY OWN [B] — Craig McLACHLAN
ON MY OWN [C] — PEACH
ON MY RADIO — SELECTER
ON MY WAY [A] — MR FINGERS
ON MY WAY [B] — Mike KOGLIN
ON MY WAY HOME — ENYA
ON MY WORD — Cliff RICHARD
ON OUR OWN (FROM GHOSTBUSTERS II) —
    Bobby BROWN
ON POINT — HOUSE OF PAIN
ON SILENT WINGS — Tina TURNER
ON STAGE (EP) — Kate BUSH
ON STANDBY — SHED SEVEN
ON THE BEACH [A] —
    Cliff RICHARD and The SHADOWS
ON THE BEACH [B] — Chris REA

ON THE BEACH [B] — YORK
ON THE BEAT — B B and Q BAND
ON THE BIBLE — DEUCE
ON THE DANCEFLOOR — DJ DISCIPLE
ON THE HORIZON — Melanie C
ON THE INSIDE (THEME FROM 'PRISONER CELL BLOCK H') — Lynne HAMILTON
ON THE LEVEL — YOMANDA
ON THE MOVE — BARTHEZZ
ON THE NIGHT — PAT and MICK
ON THE ONE — LUKK featuring Felicia COLLINS
ON THE RADIO [A] — Donna SUMMER
ON THE RADIO [A] — Martine McCUTCHEON
ON THE RADIO (REMEMBER THE DAYS) — Nelly FURTADO
ON THE REBOUND — Floyd CRAMER
ON THE ROAD AGAIN — CANNED HEAT
ON THE ROPES (EP) — The WONDER STUFF
ON THE ROSE — TIGER
ON THE RUN [A] — DE BOS
ON THE RUN [B] — OMC
ON THE RUN [C] — BIG TIME CHARLIE
ON THE RUN [D] — The CRESCENT
ON THE RUN [E] — Tillman UHRMACHER
ON THE STREET WHERE YOU LIVE [A] — Vic DAMONE
ON THE STREET WHERE YOU LIVE [A] — David WHITFIELD
ON THE TOP OF THE WORLD — DIVA SURPRISE featuring Georgia JONES
ON THE TRAIL — PRIME MOVERS
ON THE TURNING AWAY — PINK FLOYD
ON THE WINGS OF A NIGHTINGALE — The EVERLY BROTHERS
ON THE WINGS OF LOVE — Jeffrey OSBORNE
ON WITH THE MOTLEY — Harry SECOMBE
ON YA WAY — HELICOPTER
ON YOUR OWN [A] — The VERVE
ON YOUR OWN [B] — BLUR
ONCE — GENEVIEVE
ONCE AGAIN [A] — CUD
1NCE AGAIN [A] — A TRIBE CALLED QUEST
ONCE AROUND THE BLOCK — BADLY DRAWN BOY
ONCE AROUND THE SUN — CAPRICE
ONCE BITTEN TWICE SHY [A] — Ian HUNTER
ONCE BITTEN TWICE SHY [B] — Vesta WILLIAMS
ONCE I HAD A SWEETHEART — PENTANGLE
ONCE IN A LIFETIME — TALKING HEADS
ONCE IN EVERY LIFETIME — Ken DODD
ONCE MORE — The ORB
ONCE THERE WAS A TIME — Tom JONES
ONCE UPON A DREAM — Billy FURY
ONCE UPON A LONG AGO — Paul McCARTNEY
ONCE UPON A TIME [A] — Marvin GAYE and Mary WELLS
ONCE UPON A TIME [B] — Tom JONES
ONCE UPON A TIME [C] — The POGUES
ONCE UPON A TIME IN AMERICA — The JEEVAS
ONCE YOU'VE TASTED LOVE — TAKE THAT
ONE [A] — METALLICA
ONE [B] — The BEE GEES
ONE [C] — U2
ONE [C] — Mica PARIS
ONE [C] — LIGHTHOUSE FAMILY
ONE [D] — Busta RHYMES featuring Erykah BADU
ONE (EP) — MANSUN
THE ONE [A] — Elton JOHN
THE ONE [B] — BACKSTREET BOYS
THE ONE [C] — DEE DEE
THE ONE [D] — Cassius HENRY featuring FREEWAY
ONE & ONE — Robert MILES featuring Maria NAYLER
ONE AND ONE IS ONE — MEDICINE HEAD
THE ONE AND ONLY [A] — Gladys KNIGHT and the PIPS
THE ONE AND ONLY [B] — Chesney HAWKES
ONE ARMED SCISSOR — AT THE DRIVE-IN
ONE BETTER DAY — MADNESS
ONE BETTER WORLD — ABC
ONE BIG FAMILY E.P. — EMBRACE
ONE BROKEN HEART FOR SALE — Elvis PRESLEY
ONE BY ONE — CHER
ONE CALL AWAY — CHINGY featuring J WEAV
ONE COOL REMOVE — Shawn COLVIN with Mary-Chapin CARPENTER
ONE DANCE WON'T DO — Audrey HALL
ONE DAY [A] — TYRREL CORPORATION
ONE DAY [B] — D MOB
ONE DAY AT A TIME [A] — Lena MARTELL
ONE DAY AT A TIME [B] — The ALICE BAND
ONE DAY I'LL FLY AWAY — Randy CRAWFORD
ONE DAY IN YOUR LIFE [A] — Michael JACKSON
ONE DAY IN YOUR LIFE [B] — ANASTACIA
ONE DRINK TOO MANY — SAILOR
ONE FINE DAY [A] — CHIFFONS
ONE FINE DAY [B] — OPERA BABES
ONE FINE DAY [C] — JAKATTA
ONE FINE MORNING — Tommy HUNT
ONE FOOT IN THE GRAVE — Eric IDLE featuring Richard WILSON

THE ONE FOR ME — JOE
ONE FOR SORROW — STEPS
ONE FOR THE MOCKINGBIRD — CUTTING CREW
ONE FOR THE MONEY — Horace BROWN
ONE FOR YOU, ONE FOR ME [A] — Jonathan KING
ONE FOR YOU ONE FOR ME [A] — La BIONDA
ONE GIANT LOVE — CUD
ONE GIFT OF LOVE — DEAR JON
ONE GOODBYE IN TEN — Shara NELSON
ONE GREAT THING — BIG COUNTRY
ONE HEADLIGHT — WALLFLOWERS
ONE HEART — Celine DION
ONE HEART BETWEEN TWO — Dave BERRY
ONE HELLO — Randy CRAWFORD
ONE HORSE TOWN — The THRILLS
100 MILES AND RUNNIN' — NWA
101 — Sheena EASTON
101 DAM-NATIONS — SCARLET PARTY
138 TREK — DJ ZINC
100% — Mary KIANI
100% PURE LOVE — Crystal WATERS
THE ONE I GAVE MY HEART TO — AALIYAH
THE ONE I LOVE — R.E.M.
ONE IN A MILLION — AALIYAH
ONE IN TEN [A] — UB40
ONE IN TEN [A] — 808 STATE vs UB40
ONE INCH ROCK — T. REX
ONE KISS FROM HEAVEN — LOUISE
ONE LAST BREATH — CREED
ONE LAST KISS — J GEILS BAND
ONE LAST LOVE SONG — The BEAUTIFUL SOUTH
ONE LOVE [A] — ATLANTIC STARR
ONE LOVE [B] — Pat BENATAR
ONE LOVE [C] — The STONE ROSES
ONE LOVE [D] — DR ALBAN
ONE LOVE [E] — The PRODIGY
ONE LOVE [F] — BLUE
ONE LOVE FAMILY — LIQUID
ONE LOVE IN MY LIFETIME — INNOCENCE
ONE LOVE — PEOPLE GET READY — Bob MARLEY & the WAILERS
ONE LOVER AT A TIME — ATLANTIC STARR
ONE LOVER (DON'T STOP THE SHOW) — FORREST
ONE MAN — CHANELLE
ONE MAN ARMY — OUR LADY PEACE
ONE MAN BAND — Leo SAYER
ONE MAN IN MY HEART — HUMAN LEAGUE
ONE MAN WOMAN — Sheena EASTON
ONE MAN'S BITCH — PHOEBE ONE
ONE MIND, TWO HEARTS — PARADISE
ONE MINUTE MAN — Missy 'Misdemeanor' ELLIOTT featuring LUDACRIS
ONE MIRROR TOO MANY — BLACK CROWES
ONE MOMENT IN TIME — Whitney HOUSTON
ONE MORE — HAZIZA
ONE MORE CHANCE [A] — Diana ROSS
ONE MORE CHANCE [B] — Maxi PRIEST
ONE MORE CHANCE [C] — EYC
ONE MORE CHANCE [D] — MADONNA
ONE MORE CHANCE [E] — The ONE
ONE MORE CHANCE [F] — Michael JACKSON
ONE MORE CHANCE - STAY WITH ME — NOTORIOUS B.I.G.
ONE MORE DANCE — Esther and Abi OFARIM
ONE MORE GOOD NIGHT WITH THE BOYS — Tasmin ARCHER
ONE MORE NIGHT — Phil COLLINS
ONE MORE RIVER — LUCIANA
ONE MORE SATURDAY NIGHT — MATCHBOX
ONE MORE SUNRISE (MORGEN) — Dickie VALENTINE
ONE MORE TIME [A] — WHYCLIFFE
ONE MORE TIME [B] — DAFT PUNK
ONE MORE TRY [A] — George MICHAEL
ONE MORE TRY [B] — Kristine W
ONE NATION — MASQUERADE
ONE NATION UNDER A GROOVE (PART 1) — FUNKADELIC
ONE NIGHT [A] — Elvis PRESLEY
ONE NIGHT [A] — MUD
ONE NIGHT IN BANGKOK — Murray HEAD
ONE NIGHT IN HEAVEN — M PEOPLE
ONE NIGHT STAND [A] — LET LOOSE
ONE NIGHT STAND [B] — ALOOF
ONE NINE FOR SANTA — Fogwell FLAX and the ANKLEBITERS from FREEHOLD JUNIOR SCHOOL
ONE OF THE LIVING — Tina TURNER
ONE OF THE LUCKY ONES — Joan REGAN
ONE OF THE PEOPLE — ADAMSKI
ONE OF THESE DAYS — AMBASSADOR
ONE OF THESE NIGHTS — The EAGLES
ONE OF THOSE NIGHTS — BUCKS FIZZ
ONE OF US [A] — ABBA
ONE OF US [B] — Joan OSBORNE
ONE OF US [C] — HELL IS FOR HEROES
ONE OF US MUST KNOW (SOONER OR LATER) — Bob DYLAN
ONE ON ONE — Daryl HALL and John OATES
ONE PERFECT SUNRISE — ORBITAL
ONE PIECE AT A TIME — Johnny CASH
ONE REASON WHY — Craig McLACHLAN
ONE ROAD — LOVE AFFAIR
ONE RULE FOR YOU — AFTER THE FIRE

ONE SHINING MOMENT — Diana ROSS
ONE SHOT — The BROTHERHOOD
ONE SLIP — PINK FLOYD
ONE SMALL DAY — ULTRAVOX
ONE STEP — KILLAH PRIEST
ONE STEP AHEAD — Nik KERSHAW
ONE STEP AWAY — TAVARES
ONE STEP BEYOND... — MADNESS
ONE STEP CLOSER [A] — LINKIN PARK
ONE STEP CLOSER [B] — S CLUB JUNIORS
ONE STEP CLOSER (TO LOVE) — George McCRAE
ONE STEP FURTHER — BARDO
ONE STEP OUT OF TIME — Michael BALL
ONE STEP TOO FAR — FAITHLESS featuring DIDO
ONE SWEET DAY — Mariah CAREY and BOYZ II MEN
1000 % — FATIMA MANSIONS
ONE TO ANOTHER — The CHARLATANS
THE ONE TO CRY — ESCORTS
1 TO 1 RELIGION — BOMB THE BASS featuring CARLTON
THE ONE TO SING THE BLUES — MOTÖRHEAD
ONE TONGUE — HOTHOUSE FLOWERS
ONE TRUE WOMAN — YAZZ
1-2-3 [A] — Len BARRY
1-2-3 [B] — PROFESSIONALS
1-2-3 [C] — Gloria ESTEFAN and MIAMI SOUND MACHINE
1-2-3 [D] — CHIMES
ONE, TWO, THREE [E] — Dina CARROLL
1-2-3 O'LEARY — Des O'CONNOR
1234 — MRS WOOD
1234 (SUMPIN' NEW) — COOLIO
ONE VISION — QUEEN
ONE VOICE — Bill TARMEY
ONE WAY — LEVELLERS
ONE WAY LOVE — Cliff BENNETT and the REBEL ROUSERS
ONE WAY MIRROR — KINESIS
ONE WAY OUT — REID
ONE WAY TICKET — ERUPTION
ONE WEEK — BARENAKED LADIES
ONE WILD NIGHT — BON JOVI
ONE WISH — SHYSTIE
ONE WOMAN — JADE
THE ONES YOU LOVE — Rick ASTLEY
ONION SONG — Marvin GAYE
ONLY — ANTHRAX
ONLY A BOY — Tim BURGESS
ONLY CRYING — Keith MARSHALL
THE ONLY FLAME IN TOWN — Elvis COSTELLO
ONLY FOOLS (NEVER FALL IN LOVE) — SONIA
ONLY FOR A WHILE — TOPLOADER
ONLY FOR LOVE — LIMAHL
ONLY HAPPY WHEN IT RAINS — GARBAGE
ONLY HUMAN — Dina CARROLL
ONLY IF ... — ENYA
ONLY IN MY DREAMS — Debbie GIBSON
THE ONLY LIVING BOY IN NEW CROSS — CARTER — THE UNSTOPPABLE SEX MACHINE
THE ONLY LIVING BOY IN NEW YORK (EP) — EVERYTHING BUT THE GIRL
ONLY LOVE — Nana MOUSKOURI
ONLY LOVE CAN BREAK YOUR HEART [A] — Elkie BROOKS
ONLY LOVE CAN BREAK YOUR HEART [A] — MINT JULEPS
ONLY LOVE CAN BREAK YOUR HEART [A] — SAINT ETIENNE
ONLY LOVE REMAINS — Paul McCARTNEY
ONLY LOVING DOES IT — GUYS and DOLLS
THE ONLY MAN ON THE ISLAND [A] — Vic DAMONE
THE ONLY MAN ON THE ISLAND [A] — Tommy STEELE
ONLY ME — HYPERLOGIC
ONLY ONE — Peter ANDRE
THE ONLY ONE [A] — TRANSVISION VAMP
THE ONLY ONE [B] — GUN
THE ONLY ONE [C] — THUNDER
THE ONLY ONE I KNOW — The CHARLATANS
ONLY ONE ROAD — Celine DION
ONLY ONE WOMAN — MARBLES
ONLY ONE WORD — PROPAGANDA
THE ONLY RHYME THAT BITES — MC TUNES versus 808 STATE
ONLY SAW TODAY - INSTANT KARMA — AMOS
ONLY SIXTEEN [A] — Sam COOKE
ONLY SIXTEEN [A] — Craig DOUGLAS
ONLY SIXTEEN [A] — Al SAXON
ONLY TENDER LOVE — DEACON BLUE
ONLY THE HEARTACHES — Houston WELLS
ONLY THE LONELY (KNOW HOW I FEEL) [A] — Roy ORBISON
ONLY THE LONELY [A] — PRELUDE
ONLY THE LONELY [B] — T'PAU
ONLY THE LOOT CAN MAKE ME HAPPY — R KELLY
ONLY THE MOMENT — Marc ALMOND
ONLY THE ONES WE LOVE — Tanita TIKARAM
ONLY THE STRONG SURVIVE [A] — Billy PAUL
ONLY THE STRONG SURVIVE [B] — DJ KRUSH
ONLY THE STRONGEST WILL SURVIVE — HURRICANE #1
ONLY THE WOMEN KNOW — SIX CHIX

THE ONLY THING THAT LOOKS GOOD ON ME IS YOU — Bryan ADAMS
ONLY TIME — ENYA
ONLY TIME WILL TELL [A] — ASIA
ONLY TIME WILL TELL [B] — TEN CITY
ONLY TO BE WITH YOU — ROACHFORD
ONLY WANNA KNOW U COS URE FAMOUS — OXIDE & NEUTRINO
THE ONLY WAY IS UP — YAZZ and the PLASTIC POPULATION
THE ONLY WAY OUT — Cliff RICHARD
ONLY WHEN I LOSE MYSELF — DEPECHE MODE
ONLY WHEN I SLEEP — The CORRS
ONLY WHEN YOU LEAVE — SPANDAU BALLET
ONLY WITH YOU — CAPTAIN HOLLYWOOD PROJECT
ONLY WOMEN BLEED — Julie COVINGTON
ONLY YESTERDAY — The CARPENTERS
ONLY YOU [A] — HILLTOPPERS
ONLY YOU [A] — The PLATTERS
ONLY YOU [A] — Mark WYNTER
ONLY YOU [A] — Jeff COLLINS
ONLY YOU [A] — Ringo STARR
ONLY YOU [A] — John ALFORD
ONLY YOU (AND YOU ALONE) [A] — CHILD
ONLY YOU [B] — Teddy PENDERGRASS
ONLY YOU [C] — YAZOO
ONLY YOU [C] — FLYING PICKETS
ONLY YOU [D] — PRAISE
ONLY YOU [E] — PORTISHEAD
ONLY YOU [F] — CASINO
ONLY YOU CAN — FOX
ONLY YOU CAN ROCK ME — UFO
ONLY YOUR LOVE — BANANARAMA
ONWARD CHRISTIAN SOLDIERS — Harry SIMEONE CHORALE
OO ... AH ... CANTONA — OO LA LA
OOCHIE WALLY — QB FINEST featuring NAS and BRAVEHEARTS
OOCHY KOOCHY (F.U. BABY, YEAH YEAH) — BABY FORD
OO-EEH BABY — STONEBRIDGE McGUINNESS
OOH! AAH! CANTONA — 1300 DRUMS featuring the UNJUSTIFIED ANCIENTS OF MU
OOH AAH (G-SPOT) — Wayne MARSHALL
OOH-AH-AA (I FEEL IT) — EYC
OOH AAH ... JUST A LITTLE BIT — Gina G
OOH BABY — Gilbert O'SULLIVAN
OOH BOY — ROSE ROYCE
OOH I DO — Lynsey DE PAUL
OOH I LIKE IT — Jonny L
OOH! LA! LA! [A] — Joe 'Mr Piano' HENDERSON
OOH LA LA [B] — COOLIO
OOH LA LA [C] — Rod STEWART
OOH LA LA [D] — WISEGUYS
OOH LA LA LA — RED RAW featuring 007
OOH LA LA LA (LET'S GO DANCIN') — KOOL and the GANG
OOH! MY SOUL — LITTLE RICHARD
OOH STICK YOU! — DAPHNE & CELESTE
OOH TO BE AH — KAJAGOOGOO
OOHHH BABY — Vida SIMPSON
OOH-WAKKA-DOO-WAKKA-DAY — Gilbert O'SULLIVAN
OOH WEE — Mark RONSON featuring GHOSTFACE KILLAH & Nate DOGG
OOH! WHAT A LIFE — GIBSON BROTHERS
OOO LA LA LA — Teena MARIE
OOOH — DE LA SOUL featuring REDMAN
OOOIE, OOOIE, OOOIE — PRICKLY HEAT
OOOPS — 808 STATE featuring BJÖRK
OOOPS UP — SNAP!
OOPS!... I DID IT AGAIN — Britney SPEARS
OOPS (OH MY) — TWEET
OOPS UP SIDE YOUR HEAD [A] — The GAP BAND
OOPS UPSIDE YOUR HEAD [A] — DJ CASPER featuring The GAP BAND
007 [A] — Desmond DEKKER and the ACES
007 [A] — MUSICAL YOUTH
OPAL MANTRA — THERAPY?
OPEN ARMS [A] — Mariah CAREY
OPEN ARMS [B] — WILT
OPEN ARMS [C] — TINA
OPEN HEART ZOO — Martin GRECH
AN OPEN LETTER TO NYC — BEASTIE BOYS
OPEN ROAD [A] — Gary BARLOW
OPEN ROAD [B] — Bryan ADAMS
OPEN SESAME — Leila K
OPEN UP [A] — MUNGO JERRY
OPEN UP [B] — LEFTFIELD
OPEN UP THE RED BOX — SIMPLY RED
OPEN UP YOUR HEART — Joan REGAN
OPEN UP YOUR MIND (LET ME IN) — REAL PEOPLE
OPEN YOUR EYES [A] — BLACK BOX
OPEN YOUR EYES [B] — GOLDFINGER
OPEN YOUR HEART [A] — HUMAN LEAGUE
OPEN YOUR HEART [B] — MADONNA
OPEN YOUR HEART [C] — M PEOPLE
OPEN YOUR MIND [A] — 808 STATE
OPEN YOUR MIND [B] — USURA
THE OPERA HOUSE — Jack E MAKOSSA
THE OPERA SONG (BRAVE NEW WORLD) — Jurgen VRIES featuring CMC

OPERAA HOUSE —
  WORLD'S FAMOUS SUPREME TEAM
OPERATION BLADE (BASS IN THE PLACE) —
  PUBLIC DOMAIN
OPERATOR [A] — MIDNIGHT STAR
OPERATOR [B] — LITTLE RICHARD
OPIUM SCUMBAGZ — Olav BASOSKI
O.P.P. — NAUGHTY BY NATURE
OPPORTUNITIES (LET'S MAKE LOTS OF MONEY) —
  PET SHOP BOYS
OPPOSITES ATTRACT — Paula ABDUL
OPTIMISTIC — SOUNDS OF BLACKNESS
OPUS 40 — MERCURY REV
OPUS 17 (DON'T YOU WORRY 'BOUT ME) —
  The FOUR SEASONS
ORANGE BLOSSOM SPECIAL — SPOTNICKS
ORANGE CRUSH — R.E.M.
THE ORANGE THEME — CYGNUS X
ORCHARD ROAD — Leo SAYER
ORCHESTRAL MANOEUVRES IN THE
  DARKNESS — DIFF'RENT DARKNESS
ORDINARY ANGEL — HUE AND CRY
ORDINARY DAY [A] — CURIOSITY
ORDINARY DAY [B] — Vanessa CARLTON
ORDINARY GIRL — Alison MOYET
ORDINARY LIVES — The BEE GEES
ORDINARY WORLD [A] — DURAN DURAN
ORDINARY WORLD [A] — AURORA
ORIGINAL — LEFTFIELD
ORIGINAL BIRD DANCE — ELECTRONICAS
ORIGINAL NUTTAH — UK APACHI with SHY FX
ORIGINAL PRANKSTER — The OFFSPRING
ORIGINAL SIN — Elton JOHN
ORIGINAL SIN (THEME FROM 'THE SHADOW') —
  Taylor DAYNE
ORINOCO FLOW — ENYA
ORLANDO DAWN — LIQUID
ORPHEUS — ASH
ORVILLE'S SONG — Keith HARRIS and ORVILLE
OSCAR — SHACK
OSSIE'S DREAM (SPURS ARE ON THEIR WAY TO
  WEMBLEY) — TOTTENHAM HOTSPUR FA CUP FINAL
  SQUAD
THE OTHER MAN'S GRASS (IS ALWAYS GREENER) —
  Petula CLARK
THE OTHER SIDE [A] — AEROSMITH
THE OTHER SIDE [B] — David GRAY
THE OTHER SIDE OF LOVE — YAZOO
THE OTHER SIDE OF ME — Andy WILLIAMS
THE OTHER SIDE OF SUMMER —
  Elvis COSTELLO
THE OTHER SIDE OF THE SUN — Janis IAN
THE OTHER SIDE OF YOU —
  MIGHTY LEMON DROPS
THE OTHER WOMAN, THE OTHER MAN —
  Gerard KENNY
OTHERNESS (EP) — COCTEAU TWINS
OTHERSIDE — RED HOT CHILI PEPPERS
OTHERWISE — MORCHEEBA
OUIJA BOARD OUIJA BOARD — MORRISSEY
OUR DAY WILL COME —
  RUBY and the ROMANTICS
OUR FAVOURITE MELODIES — Craig DOUGLAS
OUR FRANK — MORRISSEY
OUR GOAL — ARSENAL FC
OUR HOUSE — MADNESS
OUR KIND OF LOVE — HANNAH
OUR LAST SONG TOGETHER — Neil SEDAKA
OUR LIPS ARE SEALED [A] — GO-GO's
OUR LIPS ARE SEALED [A] — FUN BOY THREE
OUR LIVES — The CALLING
OUR LOVE — Elkie BROOKS
(OUR LOVE) DON'T THROW IT ALL AWAY —
  Andy GIBB
OUR RADIO ROCKS — ANT & DEC
OUR WORLD — BLUE MINK
OUT COME THE FREAKS — WAS (NOT WAS)
OUT COME THE FREAKS (AGAIN) —
  WAS (NOT WAS)
OUT DEMONS OUT —
  Edgar BROUGHTON BAND
OUT HERE ON MY OWN — Irene CARA
OUT IN THE DARK — LURKERS
OUT IN THE FIELDS —
  Gary MOORE and Phil LYNOTT
OUT IS THROUGH — Alanis MORISSETTE
OUT OF BREATH —
  Roni SIZE featuring RAHZEL
OUT OF CONTROL [A] — ANGELIC UPSTARTS
OUT OF CONTROL [B] — The ROLLING STONES
OUT OF CONTROL [C] —
  The CHEMICAL BROTHERS
OUT OF CONTROL (BACK FOR MORE) —
  DARUDE
OUT OF HAND — MIGHTY LEMON DROPS
OUT OF MY HEAD — MARRADONA
OUT OF MY HEART — BBMAK
OUT OF MY MIND [A] — Johnny TILLOTSON
OUT OF MY MIND [B] — DURAN DURAN
OUT OF OUR MINDS — CRACKOUT
OUT OF REACH [A] — VICE SQUAD
OUT OF REACH [B] — PRIMITIVES
OUT OF REACH [C] — GABRIELLE
OUT OF SEASON — The ALMIGHTY
OUT OF SIGHT [A] — BABYBIRD
OUT OF SIGHT [B] — SPIRITUALIZED
OUT OF SIGHT, OUT OF MIND — LEVEL 42

OUT OF SPACE — The PRODIGY
OUT OF TEARS — The ROLLING STONES
OUT OF THE BLUE [A] — Debbie GIBSON
OUT OF THE BLUE [B] — SYSTEM F
OUT OF THE BLUE [C] — Delta GOODREM
OUT OF THE SILENT PLANET — IRON MAIDEN
OUT OF THE SINKING — Paul WELLER
OUT OF THE STORM — INCOGNITO
OUT OF THE VOID — GRASS-SHOW
OUT OF THIS WORLD — Tony HATCH
OUT OF TIME [A] —
  Chris FARLOWE and the THUNDERBIRDS
OUT OF TIME [A] — Dan McCAFFERTY
OUT OF TIME [A] — The ROLLING STONES
OUT OF TIME [B] — BLUR
OUT OF TOUCH [A] —
  Daryl HALL and John OATES
OUT OF TOUCH [A] — UNITING NATIONS
OUT OF TOWN — Max BYGRAVES
OUT OF MY MIND — TRUE STEPPERS and Dane
  BOWERS featuring Victoria BECKHAM
OUT ON THE FLOOR — Dobie GRAY
OUT THERE [A] — DINOSAUR JR
OUT THERE [B] — FRIENDS OF MATTHEW
OUT WITH HER — The BLOW MONKEYS
OUTA SPACE — Billy PRESTON
OUTTATHAWAY — The VINES
OUTDOOR MINER — WIRE
OUTERSPACE GIRL — The BELOVED
OUTLAW — OLIVE
OUTRAGEOUS — STIX 'N' STONED
OUTSHINED — SOUNDGARDEN
OUTSIDE [A] — OMAR
OUTSIDE [B] — George MICHAEL
OUTSIDE [C] — STAIND
OUT-SIDE [D] — The BETA BAND
OUTSIDE IN THE RAIN — Gwen GUTHRIE
OUTSIDE MY WINDOW — Stevie WONDER
OUTSIDE OF HEAVEN — Eddie FISHER
OUTSIDE YOUR DOOR — The STANDS
OUTSIDE YOUR ROOM (EP) — SLOWDIVE
OUTSTANDING [A] — GAP BAND
OUTSTANDING [A] — Kenny THOMAS
OUTSTANDING [A] — Andy COLE
OUTTA SPACE — MELLOW TRAX
OVER — PORTISHEAD
OVER AND OVER [A] — Dave CLARK FIVE
OVER AND OVER [B] — JAMES BOYS
OVER AND OVER [C] — SHALAMAR
OVER AND OVER [D] —
  PLUX featuring Georgia JONES
OVER AND OVER [E] — Puff JOHNSON
OVER MY HEAD — LIT
OVER MY SHOULDER —
  MIKE and the MECHANICS
OVER RISING — The CHARLATANS
OVER THE EDGE — The ALMIGHTY
OVER THE HILLS AND FAR AWAY —
  Gary MOORE
OVER THE RAINBOW [A] —
  YOU BELONG TO ME — MATCHBOX
OVER THE RAINBOW [A] — Sam HARRIS
OVER THE RAINBOW [A] — Eva CASSIDY
OVER THE RIVER — Bitty McLEAN
OVER THE SEA — Jesse RAE
OVER THE WEEKEND — Nick HEYWARD
OVER THERE — BABE TEAM
OVER THERE (I DON'T CARE) —
  HOUSE OF PAIN
OVER TO YOU JOHN (HERE WE GO AGAIN) —
  JIVE BUNNY and the MASTERMIXERS
OVER UNDER SIDEWAYS DOWN — YARDBIRDS
OVER YOU [A] — FREDDIE and the DREAMERS
OVER YOU [B] — ROXY MUSIC
OVER YOU [C] — Ray PARKER Jr
OVER YOU [D] — JUSTIN
OVER YOU [E] —
  Warren CLARKE featuring Kathy BROWN
OVERCOME — TRICKY
OVERDRIVE — DJ SANDY vs HOUSETRAP
OVERJOYED — Stevie WONDER
OVERKILL [A] — MOTÖRHEAD
OVERKILL [B] — MEN AT WORK
OVERLOAD [A] — SUGABABES
OVERLOAD [B] — VOODOO & SERANO
OVERNIGHT CELEBRITY — TWISTA
OVERPROTECTED — Britney SPEARS
OVERRATED — Siobhan DONAGHY
OVERTHROWN — LIBIDO
OVERTIME — LEVEL 42
OWNER OF A LONELY HEART — YES
OXBOW LAKES — The ORB
OXYGEN [A] — BLAGGERS I.T.A.
OXYGEN [B] — JJ72
OXYGENE 8 — Jean-Michel JARRE
OXYGENE PART IV — Jean-Michel JARRE
OXYGENE 10 — Jean-Michel JARRE
OYE — Gloria ESTEFAN
OYE COMA VA — Tito PUENTE Jr and the LATIN
  RHYTHM featuring Tito PUENTE,
  INDIA and Cali ALEMAN
OYE MI CANTO (HEAR MY VOICE) —
  Gloria ESTEFAN
P MACHINERY — PROPAGANDA
PABLO — Russ CONWAY
PACIFIC — 808 STATE
PACIFIC MELODY — AIRSCAPE

PACK OF WOLVES — NIGHTBREED
PACK UP YOUR SORROWS — Joan BAEZ
PACKET OF PEACE — LIONROCK
PACKJAMMED (WITH THE PARTY POSSE) —
  STOCK AITKEN WATERMAN
PAC-MAN — POWERPILL
PACMAN — Ed RUSH & OPTICAL
THE PADDLE — DJ TOUCHE
PAGAN POETRY — BJÖRK
PAID IN FULL — Eric B and RAKIM
PAID MY DUES — ANASTACIA
PAIN [A] — Betty WRIGHT
PAIN [B] — JIMMY EAT WORLD
THE PAIN INSIDE — COSMIC ROUGH RIDERS
PAIN KILLER — TURIN BRAKES
PAINKILLER [B] — JUDAS PRIEST
PAINT A PICTURE — MAN WITH NO NAME
PAINT IT BLACK [A] — The ROLLING STONES
PAINT IT BLACK [A] — MODETTES
PAINT ME DOWN — SPANDAU BALLET
PAINT THE SILENCE — SOUTH
PAINTED MOON — The SILENCERS
PAINTER MAN [A] — CREATION
PAINTER MAN [A] — BONEY M
A PAIR OF BROWN EYES — The POGUES
PAISLEY PARK — PRINCE
PAL OF MY CRADLE DAYS — Ann BREEN
PALE BLUE EYES —
  Paul QUINN and Edwyn COLLINS
PALE MOVIE — SAINT ETIENNE
PALE RED — Jerry BURNS
PALE SHELTER — TEARS FOR FEARS
PALISADES PARK — Freddy CANNON
PALOMA BLANCA — George BAKER SELECTION
PAMELA PAMELA — Wayne FONTANA
PANAMA — VAN HALEN
THE PANDEMONIUM SINGLE — KILLING JOKE
PANDORA'S BOX [A] — PROCOL HARUM
PANDORA'S BOX [B] —
  ORCHESTRAL MANOEUVRES IN THE DARK
PANDORA'S KISS — LOUISE
PANIC — The SMITHS
PANIC ON — MADDER ROSE
PANINARO — PET SHOP BOYS
PANIS ANGELICUS — Anthony WAY
PANTHER PARTY — MAD MOSES
PAPA DON'T PREACH [A] — MADONNA
PAPA DON'T PREACH [A] — Kelly OSBOURNE
PAPA LOVES MAMA — Joan REGAN
PAPA LOVES MAMBO — Perry COMO
PAPA OOM MOW MOW [A] — Gary GLITTER
PAPA OOM MOW MOW [A] — SHARONETTES
PAPA WAS A ROLLIN' STONE [A] —
  The TEMPTATIONS
PAPA WAS A ROLLING STONE [A] —
  WAS (NOT WAS)
PAPA'S GOT A BRAND NEW BAG —
  James BROWN
PAPA'S GOT A BRAND NEW PIGBAG [A] —
  PIGBAG
PAPA'S GOT A BRAND NEW PIGBAG [A] —
  SILENT UNDERDOG
PAPER DOLL [A] —
  Windsor DAVIES and Don ESTELLE
PAPER DOLL [B] — PM DAWN
PAPER HOUSE — FOOLPROOF
PAPER PLANE — STATUS QUO
PAPER ROSES [A] — Anita BRYANT
PAPER ROSES [A] — Maureen EVANS
PAPER ROSES [A] — KAYE SISTERS
PAPER ROSES [A] — Marie OSMOND
PAPER SUN — TRAFFIC
PAPER TIGER — Sue THOMPSON
PAPERBACK WRITER — The BEATLES
PAPERCUT — LINKIN PARK
PAPERFACES — FEEDER
PAPILLON — N-JOI
PAPUA NEW GUINEA —
  FUTURE SOUND OF LONDON
PARA MI — MOTIVATION
PARADE — WHITE and TORCH
PARADISE [A] — Frank IFIELD
PARADISE [B] — The STRANGLERS
PARADISE [C] — BLACK
PARADISE [D] — SADE
PARADISE [E] — BIRDLAND
PARADISE [F] — Diana ROSS
PARADISE [G] — Ralph FRIDGE
PARADISE [H] — KACI
PARADISE [I] — LL COOL J featuring AMERIE
PARADISE BIRD — Amii STEWART
PARADISE CITY [A] — GUNS N' ROSES
PARADISE CITY [A] — N-TRANCE
PARADISE LOST — The HERD
PARADISE SKIES — MAX WEBSTER
PARALYZED — Elvis PRESLEY
PARANOID [A] — BLACK SABBATH
PARANOID [A] — The DICKIES
PARANOID ANDROID — RADIOHEAD
PARANOIMIA — ART OF NOISE
PARDON ME — INCUBUS
PARIS BY AIR — TYGERS OF PAN TANG
PARIS IS ONE DAY AWAY — MOOD
PARIS MATCH — STYLE COUNCIL
PARISIENNE GIRL — INCOGNITO
PARISIENNE WALKWAYS — Gary MOORE
PARKLIFE — BLUR

PART OF THE PROCESS — MORCHEEBA
PART OF THE UNION — STRAWBS
PART TIME LOVE [A] —
  Gladys KNIGHT and the PIPS
PART TIME LOVE [B] — Elton JOHN
PART-TIME LOVER — Stevie WONDER
PARTAY FEELING — B-CREW
PARTY — Elvis PRESLEY
THE PARTY — KRAZE
PARTY ALL NIGHT [A] — KREUZ
PARTY ALL NIGHT [B] — MYTOWN
PARTY CRASHERS — RADIO 4
PARTY DOLL [A] — Buddy KNOX
PARTY DOLL [A] — JETS
PARTY FEARS TWO — ASSOCIATES
PARTY FOR TWO —
  Shania TWAIN with Mark McGRATH
PARTY FOUR (EP) —
  MAD JOCKS featuring JOCKMASTER B.A.
PARTY FREAK — CA$HFLOW
PARTY HARD [A] — PULP
PARTY HARD [B] — Andrew W.K.
PARTY IN PARIS — UK SUBS
PARTY LIGHTS — GAP BAND
PARTY PARTY — Elvis COSTELLO
PARTY PEOPLE (LIVE YOUR LIFE FREE) —
  PIANOMAN
PARTY PEOPLE...FRIDAY NIGHT — 911
PARTY POPS — Russ CONWAY
PARTY TIME — FATBACK BAND
PARTY TIME (THE GO-GO EDIT) — Kurtis BLOW
PARTY UP THE WORLD — D:REAM
PARTY ZONE —
  DAFFY DUCK featuring the GROOVE GANG
PARTYLINE — BRASS CONSTRUCTION
PARTYMAN — PRINCE
THE PARTY'S OVER — Lonnie DONEGAN
PASADENA — TEMPERANCE SEVEN
PASILDA — AFRO MEDUSA
PASS AND MOVE (IT'S THE LIVERPOOL GROOVE) —
  LIVERPOOL FC
PASS IT ON [A] — Bitty McLEAN
PASS IT ON [B] — The CORAL
PASS THAT DUTCH — Missy ELLIOTT
PASS THE COURVOISIER – PART II — Busta RHYMES
  featuring P DIDDY & PHARRELL
PASS THE DUTCHIE — MUSICAL YOUTH
PASS THE MIC — BEASTIE BOYS
PASS THE VIBES — DEFINITION OF SOUND
A PASSAGE TO BANGKOK — RUSH
THE PASSENGER [A] —
  SIOUXSIE and the BANSHEES
THE PASSENGER [A] — Iggy POP
PASSENGERS — Elton JOHN
PASSIN' ME BY — The PHARCYDE
PASSING BREEZE — Russ CONWAY
PASSING STRANGERS [A] —
  Billy ECKSTINE and Sarah VAUGHAN
PASSING STRANGERS [A] — Joe LONGTHORNE
PASSING STRANGERS [B] — ULTRAVOX
PASSION [A] — Rod STEWART
PASSION [B] — GAT DECOR
PASSION [C] — JON OF THE PLEASED WIMMIN
PASSION [D] — AMEN! UK
P.A.S.S.I.O.N. — RYTHM SYNDICATE
PASSION IN DARK ROOMS — MOOD
PASSION KILLER — ONE THE JUGGLER
THE PASSION OF LOVERS — BAUHAUS
PASSION RULES THE GAME — SCORPIONS
PASSIONATE FRIEND — TEARDROP EXPLODES
PAST, PRESENT AND FUTURE —
  CINDY and the SAFFRONS
PAST THE MISSION — Tori AMOS
PATCHES — Clarence CARTER
PATHS —
  Robert MILES featuring Nina MIRANDA
PATHS OF PARADISE — Johnnie RAY
PATHWAY TO THE MOON — MN8
PATIENCE [A] — GUNS N' ROSES
PATIENCE [B] — Nerina PALLOT
PATIENCE OF ANGELS — Eddi READER
PATIO SONG — GORKY'S ZYGOTIC MYNCI
PATRICIA — Perez PRADO
THE PAY OFF — Kenny BALL and his JAZZMEN
PAY TO THE PIPER —
  CHAIRMEN OF THE BOARD
PAYBACK TIME —
  DYSFUNCTIONAL PSYCHEDELIC WALTONS
THE PAYBACK MIX — James BROWN
PAYING THE PRICE OF LOVE — The BEE GEES
PCP — MANIC STREET PREACHERS
P.E. 2000 — PUFF DADDY
PEACE — Sabrina JOHNSTON
PEACE AND JOY — SOUNDSATION
PEACE + LOVEISM —
  SON'Z OF A LOOP DA LOOP ERA
PEACE IN OUR TIME [A] — Elvis COSTELLO
PEACE IN OUR TIME [B] — BIG COUNTRY
PEACE IN OUR TIME [C] — Cliff RICHARD
PEACE IN THE WORLD — DON-E
PEACE ON EARTH — HI TENSION
PEACE ON EARTH — LITTLE DRUMMER BOY —
  David BOWIE and Bing CROSBY
PEACE THROUGHOUT THE WORLD —
  Maxi PRIEST
PEACEFUL — Georgie FAME
PEACH — PRINCE

PEACHES [A] — The STRANGLERS
PEACHES [B] — DARTS
PEACHES [C] — PRESIDENTS OF THE UNITED STATES OF AMERICA
PEACHES & CREAM — 112
PEACOCK SUIT — Paul WELLER
PEAKIN' — BLEACHIN'
PEARL — CHAPTERHOUSE
PEARL IN THE SHELL — Howard JONES
PEARL RIVER — THREE 'N ONE presents JOHNNY SHAKER featuring SERIAL DIVA
PEARL'S A SINGER — Elkie BROOKS
PEARL'S GIRL — UNDERWORLD
PEARLY-DEWDROPS' DROPS — COCTEAU TWINS
PEEK-A-BOO [A] — NEW VAUDEVILLE BAND
PEEK-A-BOO [B] — The STYLISTICS
PEEK-A-BOO [C] — SIOUXSIE and the BANSHEES
THE PEEL SESSIONS (1ST JUNE 1982) — NEW ORDER
PEGGY SUE — Buddy HOLLY
PEGGY SUE GOT MARRIED — Buddy HOLLY
PENNIES FROM HEAVEN — INNER CITY
PENNY ARCADE — Roy ORBISON
PENNY LANE — The BEATLES
PENNY LOVER — Lionel RICHIE
PENTHOUSE AND PAVEMENT — HEAVEN 17
PEOPLE [A] — TYMES
PEOPLE [B] — INTASTELLA
PEOPLE [C] — ALFIE
PEOPLE ARE PEOPLE — DEPECHE MODE
PEOPLE ARE STILL HAVING SEX — LATOUR
PEOPLE ARE STRANGE — ECHO and the BUNNYMEN
PEOPLE EVERYDAY — ARRESTED DEVELOPMENT
PEOPLE GET READY [A] — Jeff BECK and Rod STEWART
PEOPLE GET READY [A] — Rod STEWART
PEOPLE GET REAL — SAINT ETIENNE
PEOPLE HOLD ON — COLDCUT featuring Lisa STANSFIELD
PEOPLE IN THA MIDDLE — SPEARHEAD
PEOPLE LIKE YOU AND PEOPLE LIKE ME — GLITTER BAND
PEOPLE OF LOVE — AMEN UK
PEOPLE OF THE SUN — RAGE AGAINST THE MACHINE
PEPE [A] — Duane EDDY and the REBELS
PEPE [A] — Russ CONWAY
PEPPER — BUTTHOLE SURFERS
PEPPER BOX — PEPPERS
PEPPERMINT TWIST [A] — Joey DEE and the STARLITERS
PEPPERMINT TWIST [B] — Danny PEPPERMINT and the JUMPING JACKS
PER SEMPRE AMORE (FOREVER IN LOVE) — LOLLY
PERFECT [A] — FAIRGROUND ATTRACTION
PERFECT [B] — The LIGHTNING SEEDS
PERFECT [C] — ANT & DEC
PERFECT [D] — SMASHING PUMPKINS
PERFECT BLISS — BELLEFIRE
PERFECT DAY [A] — EMF
PERFECT DAY [B] — DURAN DURAN
PERFECT DAY [B] — Kirsty MacCOLL
PERFECT DAY [B] — VARIOUS ARTISTS (EPs and LPs)
PERFECT DAY [C] — SKIN
A PERFECT DAY ELISE — P J HARVEY
THE PERFECT DRUG — NINE INCH NAILS
PERFECT GENTLEMEN — Wyclef JEAN
THE PERFECT KISS — NEW ORDER
PERFECT LOVESONG — The DIVINE COMEDY
PERFECT MOMENT — Martine McCUTCHEON
PERFECT MOTION — SUNSCREEM
PERFECT PLACE — VOICE OF THE BEEHIVE
PERFECT SKIN — Lloyd COLE
PERFECT STRANGERS — DEEP PURPLE
PERFECT 10 — The BEAUTIFUL SOUTH
PERFECT TIMING — Kiki DEE
PERFECT WAY — SCRITTI POLITTI
PERFECT WORLD — Huey LEWIS and the NEWS
THE PERFECT YEAR — Dina CARROLL
PERFIDIA — VENTURES
PERFUME — PARIS ANGELS
PERFUMED GARDEN — RAH BAND
PERHAPS LOVE — Placido DOMINGO with John DENVER
PERMANENT TEARS — Eagle-Eye CHERRY
PERPETUAL DAWN — The ORB
PERRY MASON — Ozzy OSBOURNE
PERSEVERANCE — TERRORVISION
PERSONAL FEELING — AUDIOWEB
PERSONAL JESUS [A] — DEPECHE MODE
PERSONAL JESUS [A] — Johnny CASH
PERSONAL JESUS [A] — MARILYN MANSON
PERSONAL TOUCH — Errol BROWN
PERSONALITY [A] — Anthony NEWLEY
PERSONALITY [A] — Lloyd PRICE
(YOU'VE GOT) PERSONALITY [A] — Lena ZAVARONI
PERSONALITY [B] — Eugene WILDE
PER-SO-NAL-LY — WIGAN'S OVATION
PERSUASION — Tim FINN
A PESSIMIST IS NEVER DISAPPOINTED — THEAUDIENCE
PETAL — WUBBLE-U
PETER AND THE WOLF — CLYDE VALLEY STOMPERS
PETER GUNN [A] — Duane EDDY and the REBELS
PETER GUNN [A] — ART OF NOISE
PETER PIPER — RUN-DMC
PETITE FLEUR — Chris BARBER'S JAZZ BAND
PETS — PORNO FOR PYROS
THE PHANTOM OF THE OPERA — Sarah BRIGHTMAN
PHASED (EP) — ALL ABOUT EVE
PHAT GIRLS — IGNORANTS
PHATT BASS — WARP BROTHERS
PHENOMENON — LL COOL J
PHEW WOW — FARMERS BOYS
PHILADELPHIA — Neil YOUNG
PHILADELPHIA FREEDOM — Elton JOHN
PHOBIA — FLOWERED UP
PHONE HOME — Jonny CHINGAS
PHOREVER PEOPLE — The SHAMEN
PHOTOGRAPH [A] — Ringo STARR
PHOTOGRAPH [B] — DEF LEPPARD
PHOTOGRAPH OF MARY — Trey LORENZ
PHUTURE 2000 — Carl COX
PHYSICAL — Olivia NEWTON-JOHN
PIANISSIMO — Ken DODD
PIANO IN THE DARK — Brenda RUSSELL
PIANO LOCO — DJ LUCK & MC NEAT
PIANO MEDLEY NO. 114 — Charlie KUNZ
PIANO PARTY — Winifred ATWELL
PICCADILLY PALARE — MORRISSEY
PICK A BALE OF COTTON — Lonnie DONEGAN
PICK A PART THAT'S NEW — STEREOPHONICS
PICK ME UP, I'LL DANCE — Melba MOORE
PICK UP THE PIECES [A] — HUDSON-FORD
PICK UP THE PIECES [B] — AVERAGE WHITE BAND
PICKIN' A CHICKEN — Eve BOSWELL
PICKNEY GAL — Desmond DEKKER and the ACES
PICNIC IN THE SUMMERTIME — DEEE-LITE
PICTURE OF YOU — BOYZONE
A PICTURE OF YOU — Joe BROWN and the BRUVVERS
PICTURE THIS — BLONDIE
PICTURES IN THE DARK — Mike OLDFIELD featuring Aled JONES, Anita HEGERLAND and Barry PALMER
PICTURES OF LILY — The WHO
PICTURES OF MATCHSTICK MEN — STATUS QUO
PICTURES OF YOU — The CURE
PIE JESU — Sarah BRIGHTMAN
PIECE BY PIECE [A] — Kenny THOMAS
PIECE BY PIECE [B] — FEEDER
PIECE OF MY HEART [A] — Sammy HAGAR
PIECE OF MY HEART [A] — SHAGGY
PIECE OF THE ACTION [A] — BUCKS FIZZ
PIECE OF THE ACTION [B] — MEAT LOAF
PIECES — MY VITRIOL
PIECES OF A DREAM — INCOGNITO
PIECES OF ICE — Diana ROSS
PIECES OF ME — Ashlee SIMPSON
PIED PIPER [A] — Crispian ST PETERS
PIED PIPER [A] — BOB and MARCIA
PIED PIPER (THE BEEJE) — Steve RACE
PIES — WILEY
PIHA — Ian POOLEY & MAGIK J
PILGRIMAGE — SOURMASH
PILLOW TALK — SYLVIA
PILLS AND SOAP — Elvis COSTELLO
PILOT OF THE AIRWAVES — Charlie DORE
PILOTS — GOLDFRAPP
PILTDOWN RIDES AGAIN — PILTDOWN MEN
P.I.M.P. — 50 CENT
PIN — The YEAH YEAH YEAHS
PINBALL — Brian PROTHEROE
PINBALL WIZARD [A] — The WHO
PINBALL WIZARD [A] — Elton JOHN
PINBALL WIZARD [A] — SEE ME, FEEL ME (MEDLEY) — The NEW SEEKERS
PINCUSHION — ZZ TOP
PINEAPPLE HEAD — CROWDED HOUSE
PING ONE DOWN — GOMEZ
PING PONG — STEREOLAB
PINK — AEROSMITH
PINK CADILLAC — Natalie COLE
PINK CHAMPAGNE [A] — Shakin' STEVENS
PINK CHAMPAGNE [B] — RHYTHM ETERNITY
PINK FLOWER — DAISY CHAINSAW
THE PINK G.R.EASE — PINK GREASE
THE PINK PARKER EP — Graham PARKER and the RUMOUR
PINK SUNSHINE — WE'VE GOT A FUZZBOX AND WE'RE GONNA USE IT
PINKY BLUE — ALTERED IMAGES
PIPELINE [A] — CHANTAYS
PIPELINE [A] — Bruce JOHNSTON
PIPES OF PEACE — Paul McCARTNEY
PIRANHA — TRIPPING DAISY
PISSING IN THE WIND — BADLY DRAWN BOY
PISTOL PACKIN' MAMA — Gene VINCENT
PISTOL WHIP — Joshua RYAN
PITCHIN' (IN EVERY DIRECTION) — HI-GATE
A PLACE CALLED HOME — PJ HARVEY
A PLACE IN THE SUN [A] — The SHADOWS
A PLACE IN THE SUN [B] — Stevie WONDER
PLACE IN YOUR HEART — NAZARETH
PLACE YOUR HANDS — REEF
PLACES — TILT
PLACES THAT BELONG TO YOU — Barbra STREISAND
PLAN A — The DANDY WARHOLS
PLAN B — DEXY'S MIDNIGHT RUNNERS
PLAN 9 — 808 STATE
PLANET CARAVAN — PANTERA
PLANET CLAIRE — B-52's
THE PLANET DANCE (MOVE YA BODY) — LIQUID OXYGEN
PLANET E — KC FLIGHTT
PLANET EARTH — DURAN DURAN
PLANET GIRL — ZODIAC MINDWARP and the LOVE REACTION
PLANET LOVE — DJ QUICKSILVER
THE PLANET OF LOVE — Carl COX
PLANET OF SOUND — PIXIES
PLANET ROCK [A] — Afrika BAMBAATAA
PLANET ROCK [A] — Paul OAKENFOLD presents Afrika BAMBAATAA
PLANET ROCK [A] — POWERS THAT BE
PLANET TELEX — RADIOHEAD
PLANET VIOLET — NALIN I.N.C.
PLANETARY SIT-IN (EVERY GIRL HAS YOUR NAME) — Julian COPE
THE PLASTIC AGE — BUGGLES
PLASTIC DREAMS — JAYDEE
PLASTIC MAN — The KINKS
PLATINUM BLONDE — PRELUDE
PLATINUM POP — THIS YEAR'S BLONDE
PLAY — Jennifer LOPEZ
PLAY (EP) — RIDE
PLAY DEAD — BJÖRK
PLAY IT COOL — SUPER FURRY ANIMALS
PLAY ME LIKE YOU PLAY YOUR GUITAR — Duane EDDY and the REBELS
PLAY THAT FUNKY MUSIC [A] — WILD CHERRY
PLAY THAT FUNKY MUSIC [A] — VANILLA ICE
PLAY THAT FUNKY MUSIC [A] — THUNDER
PLAY THE GAME — QUEEN
PLAY TO WIN — HEAVEN 17
PLAYA HATA — LUNIZ
PLAYA NO MO' — LINA
PLAYAS GON' PLAY — 3LW
PLAYAZ CLUB — RAPPIN' 4-TAY
PLAYED-A-LIVE (THE BONGO SONG) — SAFRI DUO
THE PLAYER — Carl COX
PLAYGROUND — Anita HARRIS
PLAYGROUND LOVE — AIR
PLAYGROUND TWIST — SIOUXSIE and the BANSHEES
PLAYING WITH KNIVES — BIZARRE INC
PLAYING WITH THE BOY — TECHNICIAN 2
PLAYTHING — LINX
PLAYTIME — Roni SIZE
PLEASANT VALLEY SUNDAY — The MONKEES
PLEASE [A] — Elton JOHN
PLEASE [B] — U2
PLEASE [C] — Robin GIBB
PLEASE BE CRUEL — INSPIRAL CARPETS
PLEASE COME HOME FOR CHRISTMAS [A] — The EAGLES
PLEASE COME HOME FOR CHRISTMAS [A] — BON JOVI
PLEASE DON'T ASK ABOUT BARBARA — Bobby VEE
PLEASE DON'T BE SCARED — Barry MANILOW
PLEASE DON'T FALL IN LOVE — Cliff RICHARD
PLEASE DON'T GO [A] — Donald PEERS
PLEASE DON'T GO [B] — DOUBLE YOU?
PLEASE DON'T GO [B] — KC and the SUNSHINE BAND
PLEASE DON'T GO [B] — KWS
PLEASE DON'T GO [C] — NO MERCY
PLEASE DON'T MAKE ME CRY — UB40
PLEASE DON'T TEASE — Cliff RICHARD and the SHADOWS
PLEASE DON'T TOUCH — Johnny KIDD
PLEASE DON'T TURN ME ON — ARTFUL DODGER
PLEASE FORGIVE ME [A] — Bryan ADAMS
PLEASE FORGIVE ME [B] — David GRAY
PLEASE HELP ME, I'M FALLING — Hank LOCKLIN
PLEASE MR POSTMAN [A] — BACKBEAT BAND
PLEASE MR POSTMAN [A] — The CARPENTERS
PLEASE PLEASE ME [A] — The BEATLES
PLEASE PLEASE ME [A] — David CASSIDY
PLEASE RELEASE ME — Mike FLOWERS POPS
PLEASE SAVE ME — SUNSCREEM vs PUSH
PLEASE SIR — Martyn JOSEPH
PLEASE STAY [A] — CRYIN' SHAMES
PLEASE STAY [B] — Kylie MINOGUE
PLEASE TELL HIM THAT I SAID HELLO — DANA
PLEASE (YOU GOT THAT ...) — INXS
PLEASE YOURSELF — BIG SUPREME
PLEASURE BOYS — VISAGE
PLEASURE DOME — SOUL II SOUL
PLEASURE FROM THE BASS — TIGA
PLEASURE LOVE — DE FUNK featuring F45
PLEASURE PRINCIPLE — Janet JACKSON
PLENTY GOOD LOVIN' — Connie FRANCIS
PLOWED — SPONGE
PLUG ME IN (TO THE CENTRAL LOVE LINE) — SCARLET FANTASTIC
PLUG IN BABY — MUSE
PLUG IT IN — BASEMENT JAXX featuring JC CHASEZ
PLUS — ECHELON
PLUSH — STONE TEMPLE PILOTS
THE POACHER — Ronnie LANE and SLIM CHANCE
POCKET CALCULATOR — KRAFTWERK
POEMS — NEARLY GOD
POETRY IN MOTION — Johnny TILLOTSON
POGUETRY IN MOTION (EP) — The POGUES
POING — ROTTERDAM TERMINATION SOURCE
POINT OF NO RETURN [A] — NU SHOOZ
POINT OF NO RETURN [B] — CENTORY
POINT OF VIEW (SQUEEZE A LITTLE LOVIN) — MATUMBI
POINT OF VIEW — DB BOULEVARD
POISON [A] — Alice COOPER
POISON [B] — BELL BIV DEVOE
POISON [C] — The PRODIGY
POISON [D] — BARDOT
POISON ARROW — ABC
POISON HEART — The RAMONES
POISON IVY [A] — The COASTERS
POISON IVY [A] — PARAMOUNTS
POISON IVY [A] — LAMBRETTAS
POISON STREET — NEW MODEL ARMY
POLICE AND THIEVES — Junior MURVIN
POLICE OFFICER — Smiley CULTURE
POLICE STATE — T-POWER
POLICEMAN SKANK ... (THE STORY OF MY LIFE) — AUDIOWEB
POLICY OF TRUTH — DEPECHE MODE
THE POLITICS OF DANCING — RE-FLEX
POLK SALAD ANNIE — Elvis PRESLEY
POLYESTERDAY — GUS GUS
PON DE RIVER, PON DE BANK — ELEPHANT MAN
PONY — GINUWINE
PONY TIME — Chubby CHECKER
POODLE ROCKIN' — GORKY'S ZYGOTIC MYNCI
POOL HALL RICHARD — The FACES
POOR JENNY — The EVERLY BROTHERS
POOR LENO — RÖYKSOPP
POOR LITTLE FOOL — Ricky NELSON
POOR MAN'S SON — ROCKIN' BERRIES
POOR ME — Adam FAITH
POOR MISGUIDED FOOL — STARSAILOR
POOR PEOPLE OF PARIS — Winifred ATWELL
POP — 'N SYNC
POP COP — The GYRES
POP GO THE WORKERS — The BARRON KNIGHTS
POP GOES MY LOVE — FREEEZ
POP GOES THE WEASEL [A] — Anthony NEWLEY
POP GOES THE WEASEL [B] — 3RD BASS
POP IS DEAD — RADIOHEAD
POP LIFE — PRINCE
POP MUZIK [A] — M
POP MUZIK [A] — ALL SYSTEMS GO
THE POP SINGER'S FEAR OF THE POLLEN COUNT — The DIVINE COMEDY
POP THAT BOOTY — Marques HOUSTON featuring Jermaine "JD" DUPRI
POP YA COLLAR — USHER
POPCORN — HOT BUTTER
POPCORN LOVE — NEW EDITION
POPPA JOE — The SWEET
POPPA PICCOLINO — Diana DECKER
POPPED!! — FOOL BOONA
POPS WE LOVE YOU — Diana ROSS, Marvin GAYE, Smokey ROBINSON and Stevie WONDER
POPSCENE — BLUR
POP!ULAR — Darren HAYES
PORCELAIN — MOBY
PORT-AU-PRINCE — Winifred ATWELL and Frank CHACKSFIELD
PORTRAIT OF MY LOVE — Matt MONRO
PORTSMOUTH — Mike OLDFIELD
PORTUGUESE WASHERWOMAN — Joe 'Fingers' CARR
POSITIVE BLEEDING — URGE OVERKILL
POSITIVE EDUCATION — SLAM
A POSITIVE VIBRATION — BLACK BOX
POSITIVELY FOURTH STREET — Bob DYLAN
POSITIVITY — SUEDE
POSSEE (I NEED YOU ON THE FLOOR) — SCOOTER
POSSESSED — VEGAS
POSSESSION — TRANSFER
POSSIBLY MAYBE — BJÖRK
POST MODERN SLEAZE — SNEAKER PIMPS
POSTCARD FROM HEAVEN — LIGHTHOUSE FAMILY
POSTMAN PAT — Ken BARRIE
POUNDCAKE — VAN HALEN
POUNDING — DOVES
POUR SOME SUGAR ON ME — DEF LEPPARD
POW POW POW — FONTANA featuring Darryl D'BONNEAU
POWDER BLUE — ELBOW
THE POWER [A] — SNAP!
THE POWER 96 [A] — SNAP! featuring EINSTEIN
THE POWER (OF BHANGRA) [A] — SNAP! vs MOTIVO

POWER [B] — **NU COLOURS**
THE POWER [B] — **Monie LOVE**
POWER AND THE GLORY — **SAXON**
THE POWER IS YOURS — **REDSKINS**
POWER OF A WOMAN — **ETERNAL**
THE POWER (OF ALL THE LOVE IN THE WORLD) — **D:REAM**
P.OWER OF A.MERICAN N.ATIVES — **DANCE 2 TRANCE**
THE POWER OF GOODBYE — **MADONNA**
POWER OF LOVE [A] — **DEEE-LITE**
POWER OF LOVE [B] — **Q-TEX**
POWER OF LOVE - LOVE POWER — **Luther VANDROSS**
THE POWER OF LOVE [A] — **FRANKIE GOES TO HOLLYWOOD**
THE POWER OF LOVE [A] — **Holly JOHNSON**
THE POWER OF LOVE [B] — **Celine DION**
THE POWER OF LOVE [B] — **FITS OF GLOOM featuring Lizzy MACK**
THE POWER OF LOVE [B] — **Jennifer RUSH**
THE POWER OF LOVE [C] — **Huey LEWIS and the NEWS**
POWER RANGERS — **MIGHTY MORPH'N POWER RANGERS**
POWER TO ALL OUR FRIENDS — **Cliff RICHARD**
POWER TO THE PEOPLE — **John LENNON**
POWERGEN (ONLY YOUR LOVE) — **PKA**
POWERLESS (SAY WHAT YOU WANT) — **Nelly FURTADO**
POWERTRIP — **MONSTER MAGNET**
THE POWER ZONE — **TIME FREQUENCY**
PRACTICE WHAT YOU PREACH — **Barry WHITE**
PRAISE — **INNER CITY**
PRAISE YOU — **FATBOY SLIM**
PRANCE ON — **Eddie HENDERSON**
PRAY [A] — **HAMMER**
PRAY [B] — **TAKE THAT**
PRAY [C] — **Tina COUSINS**
PRAY [D] — **LASGO**
PRAY [E] — **SYNTAX**
PRAY FOR LOVE — **LOVE TO INFINITY**
PRAYER — **DISTURBED**
PRAYER FOR THE DYING — **SEAL**
PRAYER FOR YOU — **TEXAS**
A PRAYER TO THE MUSIC — **MARCO POLO**
PRAYER TOWER — **PARADISE ORGANISATION**
PRAYING FOR TIME — **George MICHAEL**
PREACHER MAN — **BANANARAMA**
PREACHER, PREACHER — **ANIMAL NIGHTLIFE**
PRECIOUS [A] — **The JAM**
PRECIOUS [B] — **Annie LENNOX**
PRECIOUS HEART — **TALL PAUL vs INXS**
PRECIOUS ILLUSIONS — **Alanis MORISSETTE**
PRECIOUS LIFE — **CRW presents VERONIKA**
PRECIOUS TIME — **Van MORRISON**
PREDICTABLE — **GOOD CHARLOTTE**
PREGNANT FOR THE LAST TIME — **MORRISSEY**
PREPARE TO LAND — **SUPERNATURALS**
PRESENCE OF LOVE (LAUGHERNE) — **The ALARM**
PRESS — **Paul McCARTNEY**
PRESSURE [A] — **SUNSCREEM**
PRESSURE [B] — **Billy OCEAN**
PRESSURE [C] — **DRIZABONE**
THE PRESSURE — **SOUNDS OF BLACKNESS**
PRESSURE COOKER — **G CLUB presents BANDA SONORA**
PRESSURE DROP — **Izzy STRADLIN'**
PRESSURE ON — **Roger TAYLOR**
PRESSURE POINT ... — **The ZUTONS**
PRESSURE US — **SUNSCREEM**
PRETEND [A] — **Nat 'King' COLE**
PRETEND [A] — **Alvin STARDUST**
PRETEND BEST FRIEND — **TERRORVISION**
PRETEND WE'RE DEAD — **L7**
PRETENDER GOT MY HEART — **ALISHA'S ATTIC**
PRETENDER TO THE THRONE — **The BEAUTIFUL SOUTH**
PRETTIEST EYES — **The BEAUTIFUL SOUTH**
PRETTY BLUE EYES — **Craig DOUGLAS**
PRETTY BROWN EYES — **Jim REEVES**
PRETTY DEEP — **Tanya DONELLY**
PRETTY FLAMINGO — **MANFRED MANN**
PRETTY FLY (FOR A WHITE GUY) — **The OFFSPRING**
PRETTY GOOD YEAR — **Tori AMOS**
PRETTY GREEN EYES — **ULTRABEAT**
PRETTY IN PINK — **PSYCHEDELIC FURS**
PRETTY JENNY — **Jess CONRAD**
PRETTY LADY — **SAVANA**
PRETTY LITTLE ANGEL EYES [A] — **Curtis LEE**
PRETTY LITTLE ANGEL EYES [A] — **SHOWADDYWADDY**
PRETTY LITTLE BLACK-EYED SUSIE — **Guy MITCHELL**
PRETTY NOOSE — **SOUNDGARDEN**
PRETTY PAPER — **Roy ORBISON**
PRETTY THING — **Bo DIDDLEY**
PRETTY VACANT — **The SEX PISTOLS**
PRETTY WOMAN — **JUICY LUCY**
THE PRICE OF LOVE [A] — **The EVERLY BROTHERS**
THE PRICE OF LOVE [A] — **Bryan FERRY**
PRICE TO PLAY — **STAIND**
PRICE YOU PAY — **QUESTIONS**
PRIDE (IN THE NAME OF LOVE) [A] — **U2**
PRIDE (IN THE NAME OF LOVE) [A] — **C & C MUSIC FACTORY / CLIVILLES & COLE**
PRIDE'S PARANOIA — **FUTURESHOCK**
PRIMAL SCREAM — **MÖTLEY CRÜE**
PRIMARY — **The CURE**
PRIMARY INSTINCT — **SENSELESS THINGS**
PRIMARY RHYMING — **MC TUNES**
PRIME MOVER [A] — **RUSH**
PRIME MOVER [B] — **ZODIAC MINDWARP and the LOVE REACTION**
PRIME TIME [A] — **TUBES**
PRIME TIME [B] — **HAIRCUT 100**
PRIME TIME [C] — **MTUME**
PRIMROSE LANE — **Dickie PRIDE**
THE PRINCE — **MADNESS**
A PRINCE AMONG ISLANDS (EP) — **CAPERCAILLIE**
PRINCE CHARMING — **ADAM and the ANTS**
PRINCE HARRY — **SOHO DOLLS**
PRINCE IGOR — **Warren G**
PRINCE OF DARKNESS — **BOW WOW WOW**
PRINCE OF PEACE — **GALLIANO**
PRINCES OF THE NIGHT — **BLAST featuring VDC**
PRINCESS IN RAGS — **Gene PITNEY**
PRINCESS OF THE NIGHT — **SAXON**
PRINCIPAL'S OFFICE — **YOUNG MC**
PRINCIPLES OF LUST — **ENIGMA**
PRISONER — **ALL BLUE**
THE PRISONER — **FAB**
PRISONER OF LOVE [A] — **SPEAR OF DESTINY**
PRISONER OF LOVE [B] — **Millie SCOTT**
A PRISONER OF THE PAST — **PREFAB SPROUT**
PRIVATE DANCER — **Tina TURNER**
PRIVATE EMOTION — **Ricky MARTIN featuring MEJA**
PRIVATE EYE — **ALKALINE TRIO**
PRIVATE EYES — **Daryl HALL and John OATES**
PRIVATE INVESTIGATIONS — **DIRE STRAITS**
PRIVATE LIFE — **Grace JONES**
PRIVATE NUMBER [A] — **William BELL**
PRIVATE NUMBER [A] — **911**
PRIVATE PARTY — **Wally JUMP Jr and the CRIMINAL ELEMENT**
PRIVILEGE (SET ME FREE) — **Patti SMITH GROUP**
PRIX CHOC REMIXES — **Etienne DE CRECY**
PRIZE OF GOLD — **Joan REGAN**
PROBABLY A ROBBERY — **RENEGADE SOUNDWAVE**
PROBLEM IS — **DUB PISTOLS featuring Terry HALL**
PROBLEMS — **The EVERLY BROTHERS**
PROCESS OF ELIMINATION — **Eric GABLE**
PROCESSED BEATS — **KASABIAN**
PROCESSION — **NEW ORDER**
PRODIGAL BLUES — **Billy IDOL**
PRODIGAL SON — **STEEL PULSE**
PRODUCT OF THE WORKING CLASS — **LITTLE ANGELS**
PROFESSIONAL WIDOW (IT'S GOT TO BE BIG) — **Tori AMOS**
PROFIT IN PEACE — **OCEAN COLOUR SCENE**
PROFOUNDLY IN LOVE WITH PANDORA — **Ian DURY and the BLOCKHEADS**
PROFOUNDLY YOURS — **HUE AND CRY**
PRO-GEN — **The SHAMEN**
THE PROGRAM — **David MORALES**
PROMISE — **DELIRIOUS?**
A PROMISE — **ECHO and the BUNNYMEN**
THE PROMISE [A] — **ARCADIA**
THE PROMISE [B] — **WHEN IN ROME**
THE PROMISE [C] — **Michael NYMAN**
THE PROMISE [D] — **ESSENCE**
PROMISE ME — **Beverley CRAVEN**
THE PROMISE OF A NEW DAY — **Paula ABDUL**
THE PROMISE YOU MADE — **COCK ROBIN**
PROMISED LAND [A] — **Chuck BERRY**
PROMISED LAND [A] — **Elvis PRESLEY**
PROMISED LAND [B] — **Joe SMOOTH**
PROMISED LAND [B] — **STYLE COUNCIL**
PROMISED YOU A MIRACLE — **SIMPLE MINDS**
PROMISES [A] — **Ken DODD**
PROMISES [B] — **Eric CLAPTON**
PROMISES [C] — **The BUZZCOCKS**
PROMISES [D] — **BASIA**
PROMISES [E] — **TAKE THAT**
PROMISES [F] — **PARIS RED**
PROMISES [G] — **The CRANBERRIES**
PROMISES [H] — **DEF LEPPARD**
PROMISES PROMISES — **The COOPER TEMPLE CLAUSE**
PROPER CRIMBO — **BO SELECTA**
PROPHASE — **TRANSA**
THE PROPHET — **CJ BOLLAND**
PROTECT YOUR MIND (FOR THE LOVE OF A PRINCESS) — **DJ SAKIN & FRIENDS**
PROTECTION — **MASSIVE ATTACK**
PROUD — **Heather SMALL**
PROUD MARY [A] — **CHECKMATES LTD**
PROUD MARY [A] — **CREEDENCE CLEARWATER REVIVAL**
THE PROUD ONE — **The OSMONDS**
PROUD TO FALL — **Ian McCULLOCH**
PROVE IT — **TELEVISION**
PROVE YOUR LOVE — **Taylor DAYNE**
PROVIDER — **N*E*R*D**
PSYCHE ROCK — **Pierre HENRY**
PSYCHEDELIC SHACK — **The TEMPTATIONS**
PSYCHO BASE — **SHADES OF RHYTHM**
PSYCHONAUT — **FIELDS OF THE NEPHILIM**
PSYCHOSIS SAFARI — **The EIGHTIES MATCHBOX B-LINE DISASTER**
PSYKO FUNK — **BOO-YAA T.R.I.B.E.**
PTS.OF.ATHRTY — **LINKIN PARK**
A PUB WITH NO BEER — **Slim DUSTY**
PUBLIC ENEMY NO:1 — **HYPO PSYCHO**
PUBLIC IMAGE — **PUBLIC IMAGE LTD**
PUCKWUDGIE — **Charlie DRAKE**
PUFF — **Kenny LYNCH**
PULL THE WIRES FROM THE WALL — **The DELGADOS**
PULL UP TO THE BUMPER [A] — **Grace JONES**
PULL UP TO THE BUMPER [A] — **PATRA**
PULLING MUSSELS (FROM THE SHELL) — **SQUEEZE**
PULLING PUNCHES — **David SYLVIAN**
PULSAR 2002 — **Mauro PICOTTO**
PULS(T)AR — **Ben LIEBRAND**
PULVERTURM — **Niels VAN GOGH**
PUMP IT UP [A] — **Elvis COSTELLO**
PUMP IT UP [B] — **Joe BUDDEN**
PUMP IT UP [C] — **DANZEL**
PUMP ME UP — **GRANDMASTER FLASH, Melle MEL and the FURIOUS FIVE**
PUMP UP LONDON — **MR LEE**
PUMP UP THE BITTER — **STARTURN ON 45 (PINTS)**
PUMP UP THE JAM — **TECHNOTRONIC**
PUMP UP THE VOLUME [A] — **GREED featuring Ricardo Da FORCE**
PUMP UP THE VOLUME [A] — **M/A/R/R/S**
PUMPIN — **Tom NOVY**
PUMPING ON YOUR STEREO — **SUPERGRASS**
PUMPKIN — **TRICKY**
PUMPS — **Amy WINEHOUSE**
PUNCH AND JUDY — **MARILLION**
PUNK — **Ferry CORSTEN**
PUNK ROCK 101 — **BOWLING FOR SOUP**
PUNK ROCK PRINCESS — **SOMETHING CORPORATE**
PUNKA — **KENICKIE**
PUNKY REGGAE PARTY — **Bob MARLEY & the WAILERS**
PUPPET MAN — **Tom JONES**
PUPPET ON A STRING — **Sandie SHAW**
PUPPY LOVE [A] — **Paul ANKA**
PUPPY LOVE [A] — **Donny OSMOND**
PUPPY LOVE [A] — **S CLUB JUNIORS**
THE PUPPY SONG — **David CASSIDY**
PURE [A] — **The LIGHTNING SEEDS**
PURE [B] — **GTO**
PURE [C] — **3 COLOURS RED**
PURE AND SIMPLE — **HEAR'SAY**
PURE MASSACRE — **SILVERCHAIR**
PURE MORNING — **PLACEBO**
PURE PLEASURE — **DIGITAL EXCITATION**
PURE PLEASURE SEEKER — **MOLOKO**
PURE SHORES — **ALL SAINTS**
PURELY BY COINCIDENCE — **SWEET SENSATION**
PURGATORY — **IRON MAIDEN**
PURITY — **NEW MODEL ARMY**
PURPLE HAZE [A] — **The Jimi HENDRIX EXPERIENCE**
PURPLE HAZE [B] — **GROOVE ARMADA**
PURPLE HEATHER — **Rod STEWART**
PURPLE LOVE BALLOON — **CUD**
PURPLE MEDLEY — **PRINCE**
PURPLE PEOPLE EATER [A] — **Jackie DENNIS**
THE PURPLE PEOPLE EATER [A] — **Sheb WOOLEY**
PURPLE PILLS — **D12**
PURPLE RAIN — **PRINCE**
PUSH [A] — **MOIST**
PUSH [B] — **MATCHBOX 20**
PUSH [C] — **GHOSTFACE featuring Missy ELLIOTT**
THE PUSH (FAR FROM HERE) — **Paul JACKSON / Steve SMITH**
PUSH IT [A] — **SALT-N-PEPA**
PUSH IT [B] — **GARBAGE**
PUSH IT ALL ASIDE — **ALISHA'S ATTIC**
PUSH THE BEAT [A] — **CAPPELLA**
PUSH THE BEAT [A] — **MIRAGE**
PUSH THE FEELING ON — **NIGHTCRAWLERS featuring John REID**
PUSH UP — **FREESTYLERS**
PUSH UPSTAIRS — **UNDERWORLD**
THE PUSHBIKE SONG — **MIXTURES**
PUSHIN' ME OUT — **D-SIDE**
PUSS — **JESUS LIZARD**
PUSS 'N BOOTS — **Adam ANT**
PUSSYCAT — **MULU**
PUT A LIGHT IN THE WINDOW — **KING BROTHERS**
PUT A LITTLE LOVE IN YOUR HEART [A] — **Dave CLARK FIVE**
PUT A LITTLE LOVE IN YOUR HEART [A] — **Annie LENNOX and Al GREEN**
PUT 'EM HIGH — **STONEBRIDGE featuring THERESE**
PUT HIM OUT — **MS DYNAMITE**
PUT HIM OUT OF YOUR MIND — **DR FEELGOOD**
PUT IT THERE — **Paul McCARTNEY**
PUT MY ARMS AROUND YOU — **Kevin KITCHEN**
PUT OUR HEADS TOGETHER — **O'JAYS**
PUT THE LIGHT ON — **WET WET WET**
PUT THE MESSAGE IN THE BOX — **Brian KENNEDY**
PUT THE NEEDLE ON IT — **Dannii MINOGUE**
PUT THE NEEDLE TO THE RECORD — **Wally JUMP Jr and the CRIMINAL ELEMENT**
PUT YOUR ARMS AROUND ME [A] — **TEXAS**
PUT YOUR ARMS AROUND ME [B] — **NATURAL**
PUT YOUR FAITH IN ME — **Alison LIMERICK**
PUT YOUR HANDS TOGETHER — **D MOB**
PUT YOUR HANDS WHERE MY EYES COULD SEE — **Busta RHYMES**
PUT YOUR HANDS UP — **REFLEX featuring MC VIPER**
PUT YOUR HANDZ UP — **WHOOLIGANZ**
PUT YOUR HEAD ON MY SHOULDER — **Paul ANKA**
PUT YOUR LOVE IN ME — **HOT CHOCOLATE**
PUT YOUR MONEY WHERE YOUR MOUTH IS — **ROSE ROYCE**
PUT YOURSELF IN MY PLACE [A] — **ISLEY BROTHERS**
PUT YOURSELF IN MY PLACE [A] — **ELGINS**
PUT YOURSELF IN MY PLACE [B] — **Kylie MINOGUE**
PUTTIN' ON THE STYLE — **Lonnie DONEGAN and his Skiffle Group**
PYJAMARAMA — **ROXY MUSIC**
PYRAMID SONG — **RADIOHEAD**
P.Y.T. (PRETTY YOUNG THING) — **Michael JACKSON**
QUADROPHONIA — **QUADROPHONIA**
QUANDO M'INNAMORO (A MAN WITHOUT LOVE) — **SANDPIPERS**
QUANDO QUANDO QUANDO [A] — **Pat BOONE**
QUANDO QUANDO QUANDO [A] — **Engelbert HUMPERDINCK**
THE QUARTER MOON — **VIPs**
QUARTER TO THREE — **Gary 'US' BONDS**
QUE SERA — **Chris REA**
QUE SERA MI VIDA (IF YOU SHOULD GO) — **GIBSON BROTHERS**
QUE SERA SERA [A] — **Doris DAY**
QUE SERA SERA [A] — **Geno WASHINGTON and the RAM JAM BAND**
QUE SERA SERA [A] — **HERMES HOUSE BAND**
QUE TAL AMERICA — **TWO MAN SOUND**
QUEEN FOR TONIGHT — **Helen SHAPIRO**
QUEEN JANE — **KINGMAKER**
QUEEN OF CLUBS — **KC and the SUNSHINE BAND**
QUEEN OF HEARTS [A] — **Dave EDMUNDS**
QUEEN OF HEARTS [B] — **CHARLOTTE**
QUEEN OF MY HEART — **WESTLIFE**
QUEEN OF MY SOUL — **AVERAGE WHITE BAND**
QUEEN OF NEW ORLEANS — **Jon BON JOVI**
THE QUEEN OF 1964 — **Neil SEDAKA**
THE QUEEN OF OUTER SPACE — **WEDDING PRESENT**
QUEEN OF RAIN — **ROXETTE**
QUEEN OF THE HOP — **Bobby DARIN**
QUEEN OF THE NEW YEAR — **DEACON BLUE**
QUEEN OF THE NIGHT — **Whitney HOUSTON**
QUEEN OF THE RAPPING SCENE (NOTHING EVER GOES THE WAY YOU PLAN) — **MODERN ROMANCE**
THE QUEEN'S BIRTHDAY SONG — **ST JOHN'S COLLEGE SCHOOL CHOIR and the Band of the GRENADIER GUARDS**
QUEEN'S FIRST EP — **QUEEN**
QUEER — **GARBAGE**
QUEST — **SYSTEM 7**
QUESTION — **The MOODY BLUES**
THE QUESTION — **SEVEN GRAND HOUSING AUTHORITY**
QUESTION OF FAITH — **LIGHTHOUSE FAMILY**
A QUESTION OF LUST — **DEPECHE MODE**
A QUESTION OF TIME — **DEPECHE MODE**
QUESTIONS AND ANSWERS [A] — **SHAM 69**
QUESTIONS & ANSWERS [B] — **BIFFY CLYRO**
QUESTIONS I CAN'T ANSWER — **HEINZ**
QUESTIONS (MUST BE ASKED) — **David FORBES**
QUICK JOEY SMALL (RUN JOEY RUN) — **KASENETZ-KATZ SINGING ORCHESTRAL CIRCUS**
QUIEREME MUCHO (YOURS) — **Julio IGLESIAS**
QUIET LIFE — **JAPAN**
THE QUIET THINGS THAT NO ONE EVER KNOWS — **BRAND NEW**
QUIT PLAYING GAMES (WITH MY HEART) — **BACKSTREET BOYS**
QUIT THIS TOWN — **EDDIE and the HOT RODS**
QUITE A PARTY — **FIREBALLS**
QUITE RIGHTLY SO — **PROCOL HARUM**
QUOTE GOODBYE QUOTE — **Carolyne MAS**
QUOTH — **POLYGON WINDOW**
R.R. EXPRESS — **ROSE ROYCE**
R TO THE A — **CJ LEWIS**
R U READY — **SALT-N-PEPA**
R U SLEEPING — **INDO**
RABBIT — **CHAS and DAVE**
THE RACE [A] — **YELLO**
RACE [B] — **TIGER**

RACE [C] — The LEAVES
RACE FOR THE PRIZE — The FLAMING LIPS
THE RACE IS ON [A] — Suzi QUATRO
THE RACE IS ON [B] —
    Dave EDMUNDS and the STRAY CATS
RACE WITH THE DEVIL [A] — Gene VINCENT
RACE WITH THE DEVIL [B] — GIRLSCHOOL
RACE WITH THE DEVIL [B] — GUN
RACHEL — Al MARTINO
RACHMANINOFF'S 18TH VARIATION ON A THEME BY
    PAGANINI (THE STORY OF THREE LOVES) —
    Winifred ATWELL
RACING GREEN — HIGH CONTRAST
RACIST FRIEND — The SPECIALS
RADANCER — MARMALADE
RADAR LOVE [A] — GOLDEN EARRING
RADAR LOVE [A] — OH WELL
RADIATION VIBE — FOUNTAINS OF WAYNE
RADICAL YOUR LOVER — LITTLE ANGELS
RADICCIO (EP) — ORBITAL
RADIO [A] — Roger TAYLOR
RADIO [B] — TEENAGE FANCLUB
RADIO [C] — The CORRS
RADIO [D] — CLIENT
RADIO [E] — Robbie WILLIAMS
RADIO [F] — LUDES
RADIO AFRICA — LATIN QUARTER
RADIO DISCO — WILT
RADIO GAGA [A] — QUEEN
RADIO GAGA [A] — ELECTRIC SIX
RADIO HEAD — TALKING HEADS
RADIO HEART —
    RADIO HEART featuring Gary NUMAN
RADIO MUSICOLA — Nik KERSHAW
RADIO #1 — AIR
RADIO ON — Ricky ROSS
RADIO RADIO — Elvis COSTELLO
RADIO ROMANCE — TIFFANY
RADIO SONG — R.E.M.
RADIO WALL OF SOUND — SLADE
RADIO WAVES — Roger WATERS
RADIOACTIVE — Gene SIMMONS
RADIOACTIVITY — KRAFTWERK
RAG DOLL [A] — The FOUR SEASONS
RAG DOLL [B] — AEROSMITH
RAG MAMA RAG — The BAND
RAGAMUFFIN MAN — MANFRED MANN
RAGE HARD —
    FRANKIE GOES TO HOLLYWOOD
RAGE TO LOVE — Kim WILDE
RAGGA HOUSE (ALL NIGHT LONG) —
    Simon HARRIS
RAGGAMUFFIN GIRL — APACHE INDIAN
RAGING (EP) [A] — BEYOND
RAGING [B] — COSMIC GATE
RAGS TO RICHES [A] — David WHITFIELD
RAGS TO RICHES [A] — Elvis PRESLEY
RAGTIME COWBOY JOE — CHIPMUNKS
RAIN [A] — Bruce RUFFIN
RAIN [B] — STATUS QUO
RAIN [C] — The CULT
RAIN [D] — MADONNA
RAIN [E] — GROOVE CORPORATION
THE RAIN — Oran 'Juice' JONES
THE RAIN (SUPA DUPA FLY) —
    Missy 'Misdemeanor' ELLIOTT
RAIN AND TEARS — APHRODITE'S CHILD
RAIN DOWN ON ME — KANE
RAIN FALLS — Frankie KNUCKLES
RAIN FOREST [A] — BIDDU
RAIN FOREST [B] — Paul HARDCASTLE
RAIN IN THE SUMMERTIME — The ALARM
RAIN KING — COUNTING CROWS
RAIN ON ME — ASHANTI
RAIN OR SHINE — FIVE STAR
RAIN RAIN RAIN —
    Frankie LAINE and the FOUR LADS
RAIN SHOWERS — SIZZLA
RAINBOW [A] — MARMALADE
RAINBOW [B] — PETERS and LEE
RAINBOW CHASER — NIRVANA
RAINBOW CHILD — Dan REED NETWORK
RAINBOW COUNTRY —
    Bob MARLEY & the WAILERS
RAINBOW IN THE DARK — DIO
RAINBOW LAKE — WENDY and LISA
RAINBOW PEOPLE — MANIX
RAINBOW (SAMPLE FREE) — SOLO
RAINBOW THEME - FROZEN RAINBOW — SAXON
RAINBOW VALLEY — LOVE AFFAIR
RAINBOWS OF COLOUR — GROOVERIDER
RAINCLOUD — LIGHTHOUSE FAMILY
THE RAINDANCE — DARE
RAINDROPS KEEP FALLIN' ON MY HEAD [A] —
    Bobbie GENTRY
RAINDROPS KEEP FALLIN' ON MY HEAD [A] —
    BJ THOMAS
RAINDROPS KEEP FALLING ON MY HEAD [A] —
    Sacha DISTEL
RAININ' THROUGH MY SUNSHINE —
    The REAL THING
RAINING ALL OVER THE WORLD — ADVENTURES
RAINING IN MY HEART — Leo SAYER
RAINMAKER [A] — SPARKLEHORSE
RAINMAKER [B] — IRON MAIDEN
RAINY DAY WOMEN NOS. 12 & 35 —
    Bob DYLAN

RAINY DAYS AND MONDAYS —
    The CARPENTERS
RAINY DAYZ — Mary J. BLIGE
RAINY NIGHT IN GEORGIA — Randy CRAWFORD
A RAINY NIGHT IN SOHO — The POGUES
RAISE — HYPER GO GO
RAISE YOUR HAND — Eddie FLOYD
RAISE YOUR HANDS [A] — REEL 2 REAL
RAISE YOUR HANDS [B] —
    BIG ROOM GIRL featuring Darryl PANDY
RAISED ON ROCK — Elvis PRESLEY
RAM GOAT LIVER — Pluto SHERVINGTON
RAMA LAMA DING DONG —
    Rocky SHARPE and the REPLAYS
RAMBLIN' ROSE — Nat 'King' COLE
RAM-BUNK-SHUSH — VENTURES
RAME — SNAP! featuring RUKMANI
RAMONA — The BACHELORS
RANDY — BLUE MINK
RANKING FULL STOP — The BEAT
RAOUL AND THE KINGS OF SPAIN —
    TEARS FOR FEARS
RAP DIS (U DON'T KNOW THIS SHIT) —
    OXIDE & NEUTRINO
RAP SCHOLAR — DAS EFX featuring REDMAN
RAP SUMMARY — BIG DADDY KANE
(RAP) SUPERSTAR — CYPRESS HILL
RAP YOUR LOVE — SET THE TONE
RAPE ME — NIRVANA
RAPID HOPE LOSS —
    DASHBOARD CONFESSIONAL
RAPP PAYBACK (WHERE IZ MOSES?) —
    James BROWN
RAPPAZ R N DAINJA — KRS ONE
RAPPER'S DELIGHT — SUGARHILL GANG
RAPTURE [A] — BLONDIE
RAPTURE [B] — IIO
RARE, PRECIOUS AND GONE — Mike SCOTT
THE RASCAL KING —
    MIGHTY MIGHTY BOSSTONES
RASPBERRY BERET — PRINCE
RASPUTIN — BONEY M
THE RAT — The WALKMEN
RAT IN MI KITCHEN — UB40
RAT RACE — The SPECIALS
RAT RAPPING — Roland RAT SUPERSTAR
RAT TRAP — The BOOMTOWN RATS
RATAMAHATTA — SEPULTURA
THE RATTLER — GOODBYE MR MACKENZIE
RATTLESNAKES — Lloyd COLE
RAUNCHY [A] — Bill JUSTIS
RAUNCHY [A] — Ken MACKINTOSH
RAVE ALERT — Praga KHAN
THE RAVE DIGGER — MC LETHAL
RAVE GENERATOR — TOXIC TWO
RAVE ON — Buddy HOLLY
RAVEL'S PAVANE POUR UNE INFANTE DEFUNTE —
    William ORBIT
RAVING I'M RAVING — SHUT UP AND DANCE
RAW [A] — SPANDAU BALLET
RAW [B] — The ALARM
RAW [C] — MELKY SEDECK
RAW POWER — APOLLO FOUR FORTY
RAWHIDE — Frankie LAINE
RAY OF LIGHT — MADONNA
RAYS OF THE RISING SUN [A] —
    Denise JOHNSON
RAYS OF THE RISING SUN [A] — MOZAIC
RAZOR'S EDGE — MEAT LOAF
RAZZAMATAZZ — Quincy JONES
RAZZLE DAZZLE [A] —
    Bill HALEY and his COMETS
RAZZLE DAZZLE [B] — HEATWAVE
RE: EVOLUTION — The SHAMEN
RE-REWIND THE CROWD SAY BO SELECTA —
    ARTFUL DODGER featuring Craig DAVID
REACH [A] — Judy CHEEKS
REACH [B] — LIL' MO' YIN YANG
REACH [C] — Gloria ESTEFAN
REACH [D] — S CLUB 7
REACH 4 THE MELODY —
    Victoria WILSON JAMES
REACH FOR THE STARS — Shirley BASSEY
REACH OUT —
    MIDFIELD GENERAL featuring LINDA LEWIS
REACH OUT AND TOUCH — Diana ROSS
REACH OUT FOR ME — Dionne WARWICK
REACH OUT I'LL BE THERE [A] —
    The FOUR TOPS
REACH OUT I'LL BE THERE [A] —
    Gloria GAYNOR
REACH OUT I'LL BE THERE [A] —
    Michael BOLTON
REACH UP — Toney LEE
(REACH UP FOR THE) SUNRISE —
    DURAN DURAN
REACH UP (PAPA'S GOT A BRAND NEW
    PIG BAG) — PERFECTO ALLSTARZ
REACHIN' [A] — PHASE II
REACHIN' [A] — Joey NEGRO
REACHIN [A] — HOUSE OF VIRGINISM
REACHING FOR THE BEST — EXCITERS
REACHING FOR THE WORLD —
    Harold MELVIN and the BLUENOTES
REACHOUT — DJ ZINC
REACT — Erick SERMON featuring REDMAN
READ 'EM AND WEEP — Barry MANILOW

READ MY LIPS [A] — DSK
READ MY LIPS [B] — ALEX PARTY
READ MY LIPS (ENOUGH IS ENOUGH) —
    Jimmy SOMERVILLE
READ MY MIND — Conner REEVES
READY — Bruce WAYNE
READY AN' WILLING (SWEET SATISFACTION) —
    WHITESNAKE
READY FOR A NEW DAY — Martha WASH
READY FOR LOVE [A] — Jimmy JONES
READY FOR LOVE [B] — Gary MOORE
READY OR NOT [A] — The LIGHTNING SEEDS
READY OR NOT [B] — DJ DADO
READY OR NOT [C] — The FUGEES
READY OR NOT [C] — COURSE
READY OR NOT [D] — a1
READY OR NOT HERE I COME (CAN'T HIDE
    FROM YOUR LOVE) — DELFONICS
READY STEADY GO [A] — GENERATION X
READY STEADY GO [B] — OAKENFOLD
READY STEADY WHO (EP) — The WHO
READY TO GO — REPUBLICA
READY TO RECEIVE — ANIMALHOUSE
READY TO RUN — DIXIE CHICKS
READY, WILLING AND ABLE — Doris DAY
REAL [A] — Donna ALLEN
REAL [B] — PLUMB
REAL A LIE — AUF DER MAUR
REAL COOL WORLD — David BOWIE
REAL EMOTION — REID
REAL FASHION REGGAE STYLE —
    Carey JOHNSON
REAL GONE KID — DEACON BLUE
REAL GOOD — DOUBLE SIX
REAL GOOD TIME — ALDA
REAL GREAT BRITAIN —
    ASIAN DUB FOUNDATION
REAL LIFE [A] — SIMPLE MINDS
REAL LIFE [B] — BON JOVI
THE REAL LIFE — RAVEN MAIZE
REAL LOVE [A] — Ruby MURRAY
REAL LOVE [B] — Jody WATLEY
REAL LOVE [C] — DRIZABONE
REAL LOVE [D] — DARE
REAL LOVE [D] — TIME FREQUENCY
REAL LOVE [E] — Mary J BLIGE
REAL LOVE [F] — The BEATLES
THE REAL ME — W.A.S.P.
A REAL MOTHER FOR YA —
    Johnny 'Guitar' WATSON
REAL PEOPLE — APACHE INDIAN
REAL REAL REAL — JESUS JONES
THE REAL SLIM SHADY — EMINEM
THE REAL THING [A] —
    JELLYBEAN featuring Steven DANTE
THE REAL THING [B] — BROTHERS JOHNSON
THE REAL THING [C] — ABC
THE REAL THING [D] — Tony DI BART
THE REAL THING [E] — Lisa STANSFIELD
THE REAL THING [F] — 2 UNLIMITED
REAL THINGS — JAVINE
REAL TO ME — Brian McFADDEN
REAL VIBRATION (WANT LOVE) —
    EXPRESS OF SOUND
REAL WILD CHILD (WILD ONE) — Iggy POP
THE REAL WILD HOUSE — Raul ORELLANA
REAL WORLD — D-SIDE
REALITY USED TO BE A FRIEND OF MINE —
    PM DAWN
REALLY DOE — ICE CUBE
REALLY FREE —
    John OTWAY and Wild Willy BARRETT
REALLY SAYING SOMETHING —
    BANANARAMA with FUN BOY THREE
REAP THE WILD WIND — ULTRAVOX
REASON — IAN VAN DAHL
THE REASON [A] — Celine DION
THE REASON [B] — HOOBASTANK
REASON FOR LIVING — Roddy FRAME
REASON TO BELIEVE — Rod STEWART
REASON TO LIVE — KISS
REASONS — KLESHAY
REASONS TO BE CHEERFUL (PT. 3) —
    Ian DURY and the BLOCKHEADS
REBEL MUSIC — REBEL MC
REBEL NEVER GETS OLD — David BOWIE
REBEL REBEL — David BOWIE
REBEL ROUSER —
    Duane EDDY and the REBELS
REBEL RUN — TOYAH
REBEL WITHOUT A PAUSE — PUBLIC ENEMY
REBEL WOMAN — DNA featuring Jazzi P
REBEL YELL [A] — Billy IDOL
REBEL YELL [B] — SCOOTER
REBIRTH OF SLICK (COOL LIKE DAT) —
    DIGABLE PLANETS
RECIPE FOR LOVE — Harry CONNICK Jr
RECKLESS — AFRIKA BAMBAATAA
    and FAMILY featuring UB40
RECKLESS GIRL — BEGINERZ
RECONNECTION (EP) — ZERO B
RECOVER YOUR SOUL — Elton JOHN
RECOVERY — Fontella BASS
RED — ELBOW
RED ALERT — BASEMENT JAXX
RED BALLOON — Dave CLARK FIVE
RED BLOODED WOMAN — Kylie MINOGUE

RED DRESS — Alvin STARDUST
RED FRAME WHITE LIGHT —
    ORCHESTRAL MANOEUVRES IN THE DARK
RED GUITAR — David SYLVIAN
RED HOT [A] — PRINCESS
RED HOT [B] — VANESSA-MAE
A RED LETTER DAY — PET SHOP BOYS
RED LIGHT GREEN, LIGHT — Mitchell TOROK
RED LIGHT — GREEN LIGHT (EP) —
    The WILDHEARTS
RED LIGHT SPECIAL — TLC
RED LIGHT SPELLS DANGER — Billy OCEAN
RED RAIN — Peter GABRIEL
RED RED WINE [A] —
    Jimmy JAMES and the VAGABONDS
RED RED WINE [A] — Tony TRIBE
RED RED WINE [A] — UB40
RED RIVER ROCK —
    JOHNNY and the HURRICANES
RED SAILS IN THE SUNSET — Fats DOMINO
THE RED SHOES — Kate BUSH
RED SKIES [A] — FIXX
RED SKIES [B] — SAMSON
RED SKY — STATUS QUO
THE RED STROKES — Garth BROOKS
RED SUN RISING — LOST WITNESS
THE RED THE WHITE THE BLACK THE BLUE —
    HOPE OF THE STATES
RED THREE: THUNDER — Dave CLARKE
REDEFINE — SOIL
REDEMPTION SONG —
    Joe STRUMMER and the MESCALEROS
REDHEAD — BARON
REDNECK WOMAN — Gretchen WILSON
REDUNDANT — GREEN DAY
REELIN' AND ROCKIN' [A] — Dave CLARK FIVE
REELIN' AND ROCKIN' [A] — Chuck BERRY
REELING — PASADENAS
REET PETITE (THE SWEETEST GIRL IN
    TOWN) [A] — Jackie WILSON
REET PETITE [A] — DARTS
REET PETITE [A] — PINKY and PERKY
REFLECT — THREE 'N ONE
REFLECTION — VANESSA-MAE
REFLECTIONS —
    Diana ROSS and The SUPREMES
REFLECTIONS OF MY LIFE — MARMALADE
THE REFLEX — DURAN DURAN
REFUSE-RESIST — SEPULTURA
REGGAE FOR IT NOW — Bill LOVELADY
REGGAE LIKE IT USED TO BE —
    Paul NICHOLAS
REGGAE MUSIC — UB40
REGGAE TUNE — Andy FAIRWEATHER-LOW
REGINA — SUGARCUBES
REGRET — NEW ORDER
REGULATE — Warren G
REIGN — UNKLE featuring Ian BROWN
REIGNS — JA RULE
REILLY — OLYMPIC ORCHESTRA
RELAX [A] — FRANKIE GOES TO HOLLYWOOD
RELAX [B] — Crystal WATERS
RELAX [C] — DEETAH
RELAY — The WHO
RELEASE [A] — AFRO CELT SOUND SYSTEM
RELEASE [B] — MEDWAY
RELEASE ME [A] — Engelbert HUMPERDINCK
RELEASE ME [B] — WILSON PHILLIPS
RELEASE THE PRESSURE — LEFTFIELD
RELEASE YO' SELF [A] — METHOD MAN
RELEASE YO SELF [B] — TRANSATLANTIC SOUL
RELIGHT MY FIRE —
    TAKE THAT featuring LULU
RELIGION — FRONT 242
RELOAD — PPK
REMEDY — BLACK CROWES
REMEMBER [A] —
    The Jimi HENDRIX EXPERIENCE
REMEMBER [B] — ROCK CANDY
REMEMBER [C] — BT
REMEMBER [D] — DISTURBED
REMEMBER I LOVE YOU — Jim DIAMOND
REMEMBER ME [A] — Diana ROSS
REMEMBER ME [B] — Cliff RICHARD
REMEMBER ME [C] — BLUE BOY
REMEMBER ME [D] — JORIO
REMEMBER ME [E] — BRITISH SEA POWER
REMEMBER ME ... [F] — The ZUTONS
REMEMBER ME THIS WAY — Gary GLITTER
REMEMBER ME WITH LOVE — Gloria ESTEFAN
REMEMBER (SHA-LA-LA) — BAY CITY ROLLERS
REMEMBER THE DAY — INNOCENCE
(REMEMBER THE DAYS OF THE) OLD SCHOOL YARD —
    Cat STEVENS
REMEMBER THE RAIN — Bob LIND
REMEMBER THE TIME — Michael JACKSON
REMEMBER THEN — SHOWADDYWADDY
REMEMBER (WALKIN' IN THE SAND) —
    SHANGRI-LAS
REMEMBER WHEN — The PLATTERS
REMEMBER YESTERDAY — John MILES
REMEMBER YOU'RE A WOMBLE —
    The WOMBLES
REMEMBER YOU'RE MINE — Pat BOONE
REMEMBERESE — The STILLS
REMEMBERING CHRISTMAS —
    EXETER BRAMDEAN BOYS' CHOIR

REMEMBERING THE FIRST TIME – SIMPLY RED
REMEMBRANCE DAY – B-MOVIE
REMIND ME – RÖYKSOPP
REMINDING ME (OF SEF) – COMMON featuring Chantay SAVAGE
REMINISCE [A] – Mary J BLIGE
REMINISCE [B] – BLAZIN' SQUAD
REMINISCING – Buddy HOLLY
REMIXES - VOL.2 – Ed RUSH & OPTICAL
REMOTE CONTROL – BEASTIE BOYS
RENAISSANCE – M PEOPLE
RENDEZVOUS [A] – Tina CHARLES
RENDEZVOUS [B] – TYGERS OF PAN TANG
RENDEZVOUS [C] – Craig DAVID
RENDEZ-VOUS '98 – APOLLO FOUR FORTY
RENDEZ-VU – BASEMENT JAXX
RENÉ DMC (DEVASTATING MACHO CHARISMA) – RENÉ and YVETTE
RENEGADE CAVALCADE – ASH
RENEGADE MASTER – WILDCHILD
RENEGADE SNARES – OMNI TRIO
RENEGADE SOUNDWAVE – RENEGADE SOUNDWAVE
RENEGADES OF FUNK – Afrika BAMBAATAA
RENT – PET SHOP BOYS
RENTA SANTA – Chris HILL
RENTED ROOMS – TINDERSTICKS
RE-OFFENDER – TRAVIS
REPEAT – MANIC STREET PREACHERS
REPEATED LOVE – ATGOC
REPORT TO THE DANCEFLOOR – ENERGISE
REPRESENT – SOUL II SOUL
REPTILIA – The STROKES
REPUBLICAN PARTY REPTILE (EP) – BIG COUNTRY
REPUTATION – Dusty SPRINGFIELD
REPUTATIONS (JUST BE GOOD TO ME) – Andrea GRANT
REQUEST LINE [A] – ZHANE
REQUEST LINE [B] – BLACK EYED PEAS featuring Macy GRAY
REQUIEM [A] – SLIK
REQUIEM [B] – LONDON BOYS
RESCUE – ECHO and the BUNNYMEN
RESCUE ME [A] – Fontella BASS
RESCUE ME [B] – The ALARM
RESCUE ME [C] – MADONNA
RESCUE ME [D] – BELL BOOK & CANDLE
RESCUE ME [E] – ULTRA
RESCUE ME [F] – SUNKIDS featuring CHANCE
RESPECT [A] – Aretha FRANKLIN
RESPECT [A] – REAL ROXANNE
RESPECT [A] – ADEVA
RESPECT [B] – SUB SUB
RESPECT [C] – Judy CHEEKS
RESPECT YOURSELF [A] – KANE GANG
RESPECT YOURSELF [A] – Bruce WILLIS
RESPECT YOURSELF [A] – Robert PALMER
RESPECTABLE [A] – The ROLLING STONES
RESPECTABLE [B] – MEL and KIM
RESPECTABLE [B] – GIRLS @ PLAY
REST & PLAY EP – ORBITAL
REST IN PEACE – EXTREME
REST OF MY LOVE – URBAN COOKIE COLLECTIVE
REST OF THE NIGHT – Natalie COLE
RESTLESS [A] – Johnny KIDD and the PIRATES
RESTLESS [B] – GILLAN
RESTLESS [C] – STATUS QUO
RESTLESS [D] – JX
RESTLESS DAYS (SHE CRIES OUT LOUD) – AND WHY NOT?
RESTLESS (I KNOW YOU KNOW) – NEJA
RESURECTION – PPK
RESURRECTION – Brian MAY with Cozy POWELL
RESURRECTION JOE – The CULT
THE RESURRECTION SHUFFLE – ASHTON, GARDNER AND DYKE
RETOX – FATBOY SLIM
RETREAT – HELL IS FOR HEROES
RETURN OF DJANGO – UPSETTERS
THE RETURN OF EVIL BILL – CLINIC
THE RETURN OF NOTHING – SANDSTORM
THE RETURN OF PAN – WATERBOYS
RETURN OF THE ELECTRIC WARRIOR (EP) – T. REX
THE RETURN OF THE LOS PALMAS SEVEN – MADNESS
RETURN OF THE MACK – Mark MORRISON
RETURN OF THE RED BARON – ROYAL GUARDSMEN
THE RETURN (TIME TO SAY GOODBYE) – DJ VISAGE featuring CLARISSA
RETURN TO BRIXTON – The CLASH
RETURN TO INNOCENCE – ENIGMA
RETURN TO ME – Dean MARTIN
RETURN TO REALITY – ANTARTICA
RETURN TO SENDER – Elvis PRESLEY with the JORDANAIRES
REUNITED – PEACHES and HERB
REVEILLE ROCK – JOHNNY and the HURRICANES
REVELATION – ELECTRIQUE BOUTIQUE
REVERENCE [A] – JESUS AND MARY CHAIN
REVERENCE [B] – FAITHLESS
REVEREND BLACK GRAPE – BLACK GRAPE
REVIVAL [A] – Chris BARBER'S JAZZ BAND
REVIVAL [B] – EURYTHMICS
REVIVAL [C] – Martine GIRAULT
REVOL – MANIC STREET PREACHERS
REVOLT INTO STYLE – Bill NELSON
REVOLUTION [A] – The CULT
REVOLUTION [B] – THOMPSON TWINS
REVOLUTION [C] – ARRESTED DEVELOPMENT
REVOLUTION [D] – COLDCUT
REVOLUTION [E] – BK
REVOLUTION (IN THE SUMMERTIME) – COSMIC ROUGH RIDERS
REVOLUTION BABY – TRANSVISION VAMP
REVOLUTION 909 – DAFT PUNK
REVOLUTIONS – Jean-Michel JARRE
REVOLUTIONS (EP) – SHARKEY
REVOLVING DOOR – CRAZY TOWN
REWARD – TEARDROP EXPLODES
REWIND [A] – CELETIA
REWIND [B] – PRECIOUS
REWIND (FIND A WAY) – Beverley KNIGHT
RHAPSODY – The FOUR SEASONS
RHAPSODY IN THE RAIN – Lou CHRISTIE
RHIANNON – FLEETWOOD MAC
RHINESTONE COWBOY – Glen CAMPBELL
RHINESTONE COWBOY (GIDDY UP GIDDY UP) – RIKKI & DAZ featuring Glen CAMPBELL
THE RHYME – Keith MURRAY
THE RHYTHM – CLOCK
RHYTHM & BLUES ALIBI – GOMEZ
RHYTHM AND GREENS – The SHADOWS
RHYTHM BANDITS – JUNIOR SENIOR
RHYTHM DIVINE – Enrique IGLESIAS
THE RHYTHM DIVINE – YELLO featuring Shirley BASSEY
RHYTHM IS A DANCER – SNAP!
RHYTHM IS A MYSTERY – K-KLASS
RHYTHM IS GONNA GET YOU – Gloria ESTEFAN and MIAMI SOUND MACHINE
RHYTHM NATION – Janet JACKSON
RHYTHM OF LIFE – Oleta ADAMS
RHYTHM OF LOVE – SCORPIONS
RHYTHM OF MY HEART [A] – Rod STEWART
RHYTHM OF MY HEART [A] – RUNRIG
RHYTHM OF THE BEAST – Nicko McBRAIN
RHYTHM OF THE JUNGLE – QUICK
RHYTHM OF THE NIGHT [A] – DeBARGE
RHYTHM OF THE NIGHT [A] – POWERHOUSE
THE RHYTHM OF THE NIGHT [C] – CORONA
RHYTHM OF THE RAIN [A] – CASCADES
RHYTHM OF THE RAIN [A] – Jason DONOVAN
RHYTHM TAKES CONTROL – UNIQUE 3
RHYTHM TALK – JOCKO
RIBBON IN THE SKY – Stevie WONDER
RICE IS NICE – LEMON PIPERS
RICH AH GETTING RICHER – REBEL MC
RICH AND STRANGE – CUD
RICH IN PARADISE – FPI PROJECT
RICH KIDS – RICH KIDS
RICH MAN POOR MAN – Jimmy YOUNG
RICHARD III – SUPERGRASS
RICOCHET [A] – Joan REGAN
RICOCHET [B] – B B and Q BAND
RICOCHET [C] – FAITH NO MORE
RIDDIM – US3
RIDDLE – EN VOGUE
THE RIDDLE – Nik KERSHAW
RIDDLE ME – UB40
RIDE [A] – Ana ANN
RIDE [B] – The VINES
RIDE [C] – DYNAMITE MC
RIDE (EP) – RIDE
RIDE A ROCKET – LITHIAM and Sonya MADAN
RIDE A WHITE SWAN – T. REX
RIDE A WILD HORSE – Dee CLARK
RIDE AWAY – Roy ORBISON
RIDE IT – GERI
RIDE LIKE THE WIND [A] – Christopher CROSS
RIDE LIKE THE WIND [A] – EAST SIDE BEAT
RIDE LIKE THE WIND [A] – SAXON
RIDE MY SEE-SAW – The MOODY BLUES
RIDE ON BABY – Chris FARLOWE
RIDE ON THE RHYTHM The – Louie VEGA and Marc ANTHONY
RIDE ON TIME – BLACK BOX
RIDE THE BULLET – ARMY OF LOVERS
RIDE THE GROOVE – PLAYERS ASSOCIATION
RIDE THE LOVE TRAIN – LIGHT OF THE WORLD
RIDE THE RHYTHM – Z FACTOR
RIDE THE STORM – AKABU featuring Linda CLIFFORD
RIDE THE TIGER – BOO RADLEYS
RIDE-O-ROCKET – BROTHERS JOHNSON
RIDE WID US – SO SOLID CREW
RIDE WIT ME – NELLY featuring CITY SPUD
RIDE WIT U – JOE featuring G-UNIT
RIDERS IN THE SKY [A] – RAMRODS
RIDERS IN THE SKY [A] – The SHADOWS
RIDERS ON THE STORM [A] – The DOORS
RIDERS ON THE STORM [A] – Annabel LAMB
RIDICULOUS THOUGHTS – The CRANBERRIES
RIDING ON A TRAIN – PASADENAS
RIDING ON THROUGH – DEEE-LITE
RIDING WITH THE ANGELS – SAMSON
RIGHT ABOUT NOW – MOUSSE T featuring Emma LANFORD
RIGHT AND EXACT – Chrissy WARD
RIGHT BACK WHERE WE STARTED FROM [A] – Maxine NIGHTINGALE
RIGHT BACK WHERE WE STARTED FROM [A] – SINITTA
RIGHT BEFORE MY EYES [A] – Patti DAY
RIGHT BEFORE MY EYES [A] – N'N'G featuring KALLAGHAN
RIGHT BESIDE YOU – Sophie B HAWKINS
RIGHT BETWEEN THE EYES – WAX
RIGHT BY YOUR SIDE – EURYTHMICS
THE RIGHT COMBINATION – SEIKO and Donnie WAHLBERG
THE RIGHT DECISION – JESUS JONES
RIGHT HERE [A] – SWV
RIGHT HERE [B] – ULTIMATE KAOS
RIGHT HERE RIGHT NOW [A] – JESUS JONES
RIGHT HERE RIGHT NOW [B] – DISCO CITIZENS
RIGHT HERE RIGHT NOW [C] – FIERCE
RIGHT HERE RIGHT NOW [D] – FATBOY SLIM
RIGHT HERE WAITING – Richard MARX
RIGHT IN THE NIGHT (FALL IN LOVE WITH MUSIC) – JAM & SPOON featuring PLAVKA
RIGHT IN THE SOCKET – SHALAMAR
THE RIGHT KINDA LOVER – Patti LaBELLE
RIGHT NEXT DOOR (BECAUSE OF ME) – Robert CRAY BAND
RIGHT NOW [A] – CREATURES
RIGHT NOW [B] – AIRHEAD
RIGHT NOW [C] – ATOMIC KITTEN
RIGHT NOW 2004 [C] – ATOMIC KITTEN
RIGHT ON! – SILICONE SOUL featuring Louise Clare MARSHALL
RIGHT ON TRACK – BREAKFAST CLUB
RIGHT SAID FRED – Bernard CRIBBINS
RIGHT STUFF – LC ANDERSON vs PSYCHO RADIO
THE RIGHT STUFF [A] – Bryan FERRY
THE RIGHT STUFF [B] – Vanessa WILLIAMS
THE RIGHT THING – SIMPLY RED
THE RIGHT THING TO DO – Carly SIMON
THE RIGHT THING TO SAY – Nat 'King' COLE
RIGHT THURR – CHINGY
THE RIGHT TIME – ULTRA
RIGHT TO BE WRONG – Joss STONE
THE RIGHT TO LOVE – David WHITFIELD
THE RIGHT WAY – Peter ANDRE
RIKKI DON'T LOSE THAT NUMBER [A] – STEELY DAN
RIKKI DON'T LOSE THAT NUMBER [A] – Tom ROBINSON
RING – ALEXIA
RING A DING GIRL – Ronnie CARROLL
RING MY BELL [A] – Anita WARD
RING MY BELL [A] – JAZZY JEFF & the FRESH PRINCE
RING MY BELL [B] – Monie LOVE vs ADEVA
RING OF BRIGHT WATER – Val DOONICAN
RING OF FIRE [A] – Duane EDDY and the REBELS
RING OF FIRE [B] – The ANIMALS
RING OF ICE – Jennifer RUSH
RING OUT SOLSTICE BELLS (EP) – JETHRO TULL
RING RING [A] – ABBA
RING RING [B] – DOLLAR
RING RING RING – Aaron SOUL
RING RING RING (HA HA HEY) – DE LA SOUL
RING THE BELLS – JAMES
RINGO – Lorne GREENE
RIO [A] – Michael NESMITH
RIO [B] – DURAN DURAN
RIOT RADIO – DEAD 60S
RIP – Gary NUMAN
RIP IT UP [A] – LITTLE RICHARD
RIP IT UP [A] – Bill HALEY and his COMETS
RIP IT UP [A] – Elvis PRESLEY
RIP IT UP [B] – ORANGE JUICE
RIP IT UP [C] – RAZORLIGHT
RIP PRODUCTIONS – RIP PRODUCTIONS
RIPGROOVE – DOUBLE 99
RIPPED IN 2 MINUTES – A vs B
RIPPIN KITTIN – GOLDEN BOY with MISS KITTIN
RISE [A] – Herb ALPERT
RISE [B] – PUBLIC IMAGE LTD
RISE [C] – ZION TRAIN
RISE [D] – Eddie AMADOR
RISE [E] – GABRIELLE
RISE [F] – SOUL PROVIDERS featuring Michelle SHELLERS
THE RISE AND FALL OF FLINGEL BUNT – The SHADOWS
RISE & FALL – Craig DAVID featuring STING
RISE AND SHINE – The CARDIGANS
RISE 'IN – Steve LAWLER
RISE OF THE EAGLES – The EIGHTIES MATCHBOX B-LINE DISASTER
RISE TO THE OCCASION – CLIMIE FISHER
RISE UP – JAMAICA UNITED
RISIN' TO THE TOP – Keni BURKE
RISING FREE (EP) – Tom ROBINSON BAND
RISING SIGN – HURRICANE #1
RISING SUN [A] – MEDICINE HEAD
RISING SUN [B] – The FARM
RISINGSON – MASSIVE ATTACK
THE RITUAL – EBONY DUBSTERS
THE RIVER [A] – Bruce SPRINGSTEEN
THE RIVER [B] – KING TRIGGER
THE RIVER [C] – TOTAL CONTRAST
THE RIVER [D] – The BEAUTIFUL SOUTH
THE RIVER [E] – BREED 77
RIVER BELOW – BILLY TALENT
RIVER DEEP MOUNTAIN HIGH [A] – Ike and Tina TURNER
RIVER DEEP MOUNTAIN HIGH [A] – The SUPREMES and The FOUR TOPS
THE RIVER (LE COLLINE SONO IN FIORE) – Ken DODD
RIVER MAN – Nick DRAKE
THE RIVER OF DREAMS – Billy JOEL
RIVER OF PAIN – THUNDER
RIVER STAY 'WAY FROM MY DOOR – Frank SINATRA
THE RIVERBOAT SONG – OCEAN COLOUR SCENE
RIVERDANCE – Bill WHELAN featuring ANUNA and the RTE CONCERT ORCHESTRA
RIVERS OF BABYLON – BONEY M
THE RIVERS OF BELIEF – ENIGMA
THE RIVER'S RUN DRY – Vince HILL
ROACHES – TRANCESETTERS
ROAD RAGE – CATATONIA
ROAD RUNNER – Junior WALKER and the ALL-STARS
THE ROAD TO HELL (PART 2) – Chris REA
THE ROAD TO MANDALAY – Robbie WILLIAMS
ROAD TO NOWHERE – TALKING HEADS
ROAD TO OUR DREAM – T'PAU
THE ROAD TO PARADISE – BHOYS FROM PARADISE
ROAD TO YOUR SOUL – ALL ABOUT EVE
ROAD TRIPPIN' – RED HOT CHILI PEPPERS
ROADBLOCK – STOCK AITKEN WATERMAN
ROADHOUSE MEDLEY (ANNIVERSARY WALTZ PART 25) – STATUS QUO
ROADRUNNER – Jonathan RICHMAN and the MODERN LOVERS
ROAM – B-52's
ROBERT DE NIRO'S WAITING – BANANARAMA
ROBIN HOOD [A] – Dick JAMES
ROBIN HOOD [A] – Gary MILLER
ROBIN (THE HOODED MAN) – CLANNAD
ROBIN'S RETURN – Neville DICKIE
ROBOT – TORNADOS
ROBOT MAN – Connie FRANCIS
ROBOT WARS (ANDROID LOVE) – SIR KILLALOT vs ROBO BABE
THE ROBOTS – KRAFTWERK
ROCCO – DEATH IN VEGAS
ROCHDALE COWBOY – Mike HARDING
ROC-IN-IT – Deejay PUNK-ROC vs ONYX
THE ROCK [A] – DELAKOTA
THE ROCK [B] – The ALARM
THE ROCK [C] – PUNX
ROCK AND A HARD PLACE – The ROLLING STONES
ROCK AND ROLL DREAMS COME THROUGH – MEAT LOAF
ROCK AND ROLL IS DEAD – Lenny KRAVITZ
ROCK AND ROLL (IS GONNA SET THE NIGHT ON FIRE) – PRETTY BOY FLOYD
ROCK AND ROLL MUSIC – The BEACH BOYS
ROCK AND ROLL (PARTS 1 & 2) – Gary GLITTER
ROCK AND ROLL WALTZ – Kay STARR
ROCK AROUND THE CLOCK [A] – Bill HALEY and his COMETS
ROCK AROUND THE CLOCK [A] – TELEX
ROCK AROUND THE CLOCK [A] – TEN POLE TUDOR
ROCK BOTTOM [A] – Lynsey DE PAUL
ROCK BOTTOM [B] – BABYFACE
ROCK DA FUNKY BEATS – PUBLIC DOMAIN featuring Chuck D
ROCK DA HOUSE – TALL PAUL
ROCK DJ – Robbie WILLIAMS
ROCK HARD – Suzi QUATRO
R.O.C.K. IN THE USA – John Cougar MELLENCAMP
ROCK IS DEAD – MARILYN MANSON
ROCK ISLAND LINE [A] – Lonnie DONEGAN
ROCK ISLAND LINE [A] – Stan FREBERG
ROCK LOBSTER – B-52's
ROCK ME AMADEUS – FALCO
ROCK ME BABY [A] – David CASSIDY
ROCK ME BABY [B] – Johnny NASH
ROCK ME BABY [C] – BABY ROOTS
ROCK ME GENTLY – Andy KIM
ROCK ME GOOD – UNIVERSAL
ROCK ME STEADY – DJ PROFESSOR
ROCK ME TONIGHT (FOR OLD TIME'S SAKE) – Freddie JACKSON
ROCK MY HEART – HADDAWAY
ROCK MY WORLD – FIVE STAR
ROCK 'N' ME – Steve MILLER BAND
ROCK 'N' ROLL [A] – John McENROE and Pat CASH with the FULL METAL RACKETS
ROCK 'N' ROLL [B] – STATUS QUO
ROCK 'N' ROLL AIN'T NOISE POLLUTION – AC/DC
ROCK 'N' ROLL CHILDREN – DIO
ROCK 'N' ROLL DAMNATION – AC/DC

ROCK 'N' ROLL DANCE PARTY —
JIVE BUNNY and the MASTERMIXERS
ROCK 'N' ROLL (DOLE) — J PAC
ROCK 'N' ROLL DREAMS COME THROUGH —
Jim STEINMAN
ROCK 'N' ROLL GYPSY — SAXON
ROCK 'N' ROLL HIGH SCHOOL —
The RAMONES
ROCK 'N' ROLL (I GAVE YOU THE BEST YEARS
OF MY LIFE) — Kevin JOHNSON
ROCK 'N' ROLL IS KING —
ELECTRIC LIGHT ORCHESTRA
ROCK 'N' ROLL LADY — SHOWADDYWADDY
ROCK 'N' ROLL LIES — RAZORLIGHT
ROCK 'N' ROLL MERCENARIES —
MEAT LOAF featuring John PARR
ROCK 'N' ROLL NIGGER — BIRDLAND
ROCK 'N' ROLL OUTLAW — ROSE TATTOO
ROCK 'N ROLL STAGE SHOW (LP) —
Bill HALEY and his COMETS
ROCK 'N' ROLL SUICIDE — David BOWIE
ROCK 'N' ROLL WINTER (LOONY'S TUNE) —
WIZZARD
ROCK OF AGES — DEF LEPPARD
ROCK ON — David ESSEX
ROCK ON BROTHER — CHEQUERS
THE ROCK SHOW — BLINK-182
ROCK STAR — N*E*R*D
ROCK STEADY [A] — WHISPERS
ROCK STEADY [B] —
Bonnie RAITT and Bryan ADAMS
(ROCK) SUPERSTAR — CYPRESS HILL
ROCK THE BELLS — KADOC
ROCK THE BOAT [A] — HUES CORPORATION
ROCK THE BOAT [A] — FORREST
ROCK THE BOAT [A] — DELAGE
ROCK THE BOAT [B] — AALIYAH
ROCK THE CASBAH — The CLASH
ROCK THE DISCOTEK — RAMP
ROCK THE FUNKY BEATS —
NATURAL BORN CHILLERS
ROCK THE HOUSE [A] —
SOURCE featuring NICOLE
ROCK THE HOUSE [B] — GORILLAZ
ROCK THE JOINT — Bill HALEY and his COMETS
ROCK THE MIDNIGHT — David GRANT
ROCK THE NIGHT — EUROPE
ROCK THIS TOWN — STRAY CATS
ROCK 'TIL YOU DROP — STATUS QUO
ROCK 2 HOUSE — X-PRESS 2
ROCK WIT U (AWWW BABY) — ASHANTI
ROCK WIT'CHA — Bobby BROWN
ROCK WITH THE CAVEMAN — Tommy STEELE
ROCK WITH YOU — D'INFLUENCE
ROCK WITH YOU [A] — Michael JACKSON
ROCK YOUR BABY [A] — George McCRAE
ROCK YOUR BABY [B] — KWS
ROCK YOUR BODY [A] — CLOCK
ROCK YOUR BODY [B] — Justin TIMBERLAKE
ROCK YOUR BODY ROCK — Ferry CORSTEN
ROCK-A-BEATIN' BOOGIE —
Bill HALEY and his COMETS
ROCK-A-BILLY — Guy MITCHELL
ROCKABILLY BOB — COLUMBO featuring OOE
ROCKABILLY GUY — POLECATS
ROCKABILLY REBEL — MATCHBOX
ROCK-A-BYE YOUR BABY (WITH A DIXIE MELODY) —
Jerry LEWIS
ROCK-A-DOODLE-DOO — Linda LEWIS
THE ROCKAFELLER SKANK — FATBOY SLIM
ROCK-A-HULA BABY —
Elvis PRESLEY with the JORDANAIRES
ROCKALL — MEZZOFORTE
ROCKARIA! — ELECTRIC LIGHT ORCHESTRA
ROCKER — ALTER EGO
ROCKET [A] — MUD
ROCKET [B] — DEF LEPPARD
ROCKET MAN — SPOTNICKS
ROCKET MAN (I THINK IT'S GOING TO BE A LONG LONG
TIME) [A] — Elton JOHN
ROCKET MAN (I THINK IT'S GOING TO BE A LONG LONG
TIME) [A] — Kate BUSH
ROCKET RIDE — FELIX DA HOUSECAT
ROCKET 2 U — JETS
ROCKIN' ALL OVER THE WORLD — STATUS QUO
ROCKIN' ALONE — MIKI and GRIFF
ROCKIN' AROUND THE CHRISTMAS TREE [A] —
Brenda LEE
ROCKIN' AROUND THE CHRISTMAS TREE [A] —
JETS
ROCKIN' AROUND THE CHRISTMAS TREE [A] —
Kim WILDE
ROCKIN' BACK INSIDE MY HEART —
Julee CRUISE
ROCKIN' CHAIR — MAGNUM
ROCKIN' FOR MYSELF — MOTIV 8
ROCKIN' GOOD CHRISTMAS —
Roy 'Chubby' BROWN
A ROCKIN' GOOD WAY — Bonnie TYLER
ROCKIN' ME — DJ PROFESSOR
ROCKIN' MY BODY —
49ers featuring Ann-Marie SMITH
ROCKIN' OVER THE BEAT — TECHNOTRONIC
ROCKIN' RED WING — Sammy MASTERS
ROCKIN' ROBIN [A] — Bobby DAY
ROCKIN' ROBIN [A] — Michael JACKSON
ROCKIN' ROBIN [A] — LOLLY

ROCKIN' ROLL BABY — The STYLISTICS
ROCKIN' SOUL — HUES CORPORATION
ROCKIN' THE SUBURBS — Ben FOLDS
ROCKIN' THROUGH THE RYE —
Bill HALEY and his COMETS
ROCKIN' TO THE MUSIC — BLACK BOX
ROCKIN' TO THE RHYTHM — CONVERT
ROCKIN' WITH RITA (HEAD TO TOE) —
VINDALOO SUMMER SPECIAL
ROCKING GOOSE —
JOHNNY and the HURRICANES
ROCKING MUSIC — Martin SOLVEIG
ROCKIT — Herbie HANCOCK
ROCKS [A] — PRIMAL SCREAM
ROCKS [A] — Rod STEWART
ROCKS ON THE ROAD — JETHRO TULL
ROCKY — Austin ROBERTS
ROCKY MOUNTAIN WAY (EP) — Joe WALSH
THE RODEO SONG —
Garry LEE and SHOWDOWN
RODRIGO'S GUITAR CONCERTO DE ARANJUEZ (THEME
FROM 2ND MOVEMENT) —
MANUEL and his MUSIC OF THE MOUNTAINS
ROFO'S THEME — ROFO
ROK DA HOUSE [A] —
BEATMASTERS featuring the COOKIE CREW
ROK DA HOUSE [B] —
VINYLGROOVER and The RED HED
ROK THE NATION —
ROB 'N' RAZ featuring Leila K
ROLL AWAY — Dusty SPRINGFIELD
ROLL AWAY THE STONE — MOTT THE HOOPLE
ROLL ON — MIS-TEEQ
ROLL ON DOWN THE HIGHWAY —
BACHMAN-TURNER OVERDRIVE
ROLL OVER BEETHOVEN —
ELECTRIC LIGHT ORCHESTRA
ROLL OVER LAY DOWN — STATUS QUO
ROLL TO THE BONES — RUSH
ROLL TO ME — DEL AMITRI
ROLL WITH IT [A] — Steve WINWOOD
ROLL WITH IT [B] — OASIS
A ROLLER SKATING JAM NAMED 'SATURDAYS' —
DE LA SOUL
ROLLERBLADE [A] — Nick HEYWARD
ROLLERBLADE [B] — MOVIN' MELODIES
ROLLERCOASTER (EP) [A] —
JESUS AND MARY CHAIN
ROLLERCOASTER (EP) [B] —
EVERYTHING BUT THE GIRL
ROLLERCOASTER [C] — GRID
ROLLERCOASTER [D] — NORTHERN UPROAR
ROLLERCOASTER [E] — B*WITCHED
ROLLIN' — LIMP BIZKIT
ROLLIN' HOME — STATUS QUO
ROLLIN' IN MY 5.0 — VANILLA ICE
ROLLIN' ON — CIRRUS
ROLLING STONE — David ESSEX
ROLLOUT (MY BUSINESS) — LUDACRIS
ROLLOVER DJ — JET
ROLODEX PROPAGANDA — AT THE DRIVE-IN
ROMAN P — PSYCHIC TV
ROMANCE (LET YOUR HEART GO) —
David CASSIDY
ROMANCING THE STONE — Eddy GRANT
ROMANTIC — Karyn WHITE
ROMANTIC RIGHTS —
DEATH FROM ABOVE 1979
ROMANTICA — Jane MORGAN
ROME WASN'T BUILT IN A DAY — MORCHEEBA
ROMEO [A] — Petula CLARK
ROMEO [B] — MR BIG
ROMEO [C] — BASEMENT JAXX
ROMEO AND JULIET — DIRE STRAITS
ROMEO DUNN — ROMEO
ROMEO ME — SLEEPER
ROMEO WHERE'S JULIET? — COLLAGE
RONDO — Kenny BALL and his JAZZMEN
RONI — Bobby BROWN
ROOBARB AND CUSTARD — SHAFT
ROOF IS ON FIRE — WESTBAM
ROOFTOP SINGING — NEW WORLD
ROOM AT THE TOP — Adam ANT
ROOM ELEVEN — DAISY CHAINSAW
ROOM IN BROOKLYN — John SQUIRE
ROOM IN YOUR HEART — LIVING IN A BOX
ROOMS ON FIRE — Stevie NICKS
ROOM ON THE 3RD FLOOR — McFLY
ROOTS — [SPUNGE]
ROOTS BLOODY ROOTS — SEPULTURA
ROSALIE – COWGIRLS' SONG (MEDLEY) —
THIN LIZZY
ROSALYN — PRETTY THINGS
ROSANNA — TOTO
THE ROSE [A] — Heather PEACE
THE ROSE [A] — Michael BALL
ROSE GARDEN [A] — Lynn ANDERSON
ROSE GARDEN [B] — NEW WORLD
A ROSE HAS TO DIE — The DOOLEYS
A ROSE IS STILL A ROSE — Aretha FRANKLIN
ROSE MARIE — Slim WHITMAN
ROSE ROUGE — ST GERMAIN
ROSEABILITY — IDLEWILD
ROSES [A] — HAYWOODE
ROSES [B] — RHYTHM-N-BASS
ROSES [C] — dEUS
ROSES [D] — OUTKAST

ROSES ARE RED [A] — Ronnie CARROLL
ROSES ARE RED [A] — Bobby VINTON
ROSES ARE RED [B] — MAC BAND
featuring the McCAMPBELL BROTHERS
ROSES IN THE HOSPITAL —
MANIC STREET PREACHERS
ROSES OF PICARDY — Vince HILL
ROSETTA — Alan PRICE
ROSIE [A] — Don PARTRIDGE
ROSIE [B] — Joan ARMATRADING
ROTATION — Herb ALPERT
ROTTERDAM — The BEAUTIFUL SOUTH
ROUGH BOY — ZZ TOP
ROUGH BOYS [A] — Pete TOWNSHEND
ROUGH BOYS [B] — NORTHERN UPROAR
ROUGH JUSTICE — BANANARAMA
ROUGH WITH THE SMOOTH — Shara NELSON
ROUGH NECK (EP) — PROJECT 1
ROULETTE — Russ CONWAY
ROUND AND ROUND [A] — Jimmy YOUNG
ROUND AND ROUND [B] — SPANDAU BALLET
ROUND AND ROUND [C] — Jaki GRAHAM
ROUND AND ROUND [D] — NEW ORDER
ROUND & ROUND [E] —
HI-TEK featuring JONELL
ROUND EVERY CORNER — Petula CLARK
ROUND HERE [A] — COUNTING CROWS
ROUND HERE [B] — George MICHAEL
ROUND ROUND — SUGABABES
THE ROUSSOS PHENOMENON (EP) —
Demis ROUSSOS
ROXANNE — The POLICE
ROYAL EVENT — Russ CONWAY
ROYAL MILE — Gerry RAFFERTY
ROY'S KEEN — MORRISSEY
RSVP [A] — FIVE STAR
RSVP [B] — Jason DONOVAN
RSVP [C] — POP WILL EAT ITSELF
RUB A DUB DUB — The EQUALS
RUB-A-DUB — DOUBLE TROUBLE
RUBBER BALL [A] — AVONS
RUBBER BALL [A] — Bobby VEE
RUBBER BALL [A] — Marty WILDE
RUBBER BULLETS — 10cc
RUBBERBAND [A] — Kate BUSH
THE RUBBERBAND MAN — DETROIT SPINNERS
RUBBERBANDMAN — YELLO
RUBBERNECKIN' — Elvis PRESLEY
RUBBISH —
CARTER — THE UNSTOPPABLE SEX MACHINE
THE RUBETTES — The AUTEURS
RUBY ANN — Marty ROBBINS
RUBY DON'T TAKE YOUR LOVE TO TOWN —
Kenny ROGERS
RUBY RED [A] — SLADE
RUBY RED [B] — Marc ALMOND
RUBY TUESDAY [A] — MELANIE
RUBY TUESDAY [A] — Rod STEWART
RUBY TUESDAY [A] — The ROLLING STONES
RUDD — IKARA COLT
RUDE BOY ROCK — LIONROCK
RUDE BUOYS OUTA JAIL — The SPECIALS
RUDI GOT MARRIED —
Laurel AITKEN and the UNITONE
RUDI'S IN LOVE — LOCOMOTIVE
RUDY'S ROCK — Bill HALEY and his COMETS
RUFF IN THE JUNGLE BIZNESS — The PRODIGY
RUFF MIX — WONDER DOG
RUFFNECK — MC LYTE
RUGGED AND MEAN, BUTCH AND ON SCREEN —
PEE BEE SQUAD
RUINED IN A DAY — NEW ORDER
RULES AND REGULATIONS — WE'VE GOT
A FUZZBOX AND WE'RE GONNA USE IT
RULES OF THE GAME — BUCKS FIZZ
RUMBLE IN THE JUNGLE — The FUGEES
RUMORS — TIMEX SOCIAL CLUB
RUMOUR HAS IT — Donna SUMMER
RUMOURS [A] — HOT CHOCOLATE
RUMOURS [B] — AWESOME
RUMOURS [C] — DAMAGE
RUMP SHAKER — WRECKX-N-EFFECT
RUN [A] — Sandie SHAW
RUN [B] — SPIRITUALIZED
RUN [C] — LIGHTHOUSE FAMILY
RUN [D] — SNOW PATROL
RUN AWAY [A] — 10cc
RUN AWAY [B] —
(MC SAR &) The REAL McCOY
RUN AWAY (I WANNA BE WITH YOU) — NIVEA
RUN BABY RUN [A] — NEWBEATS
RUN BABY RUN [B] — Sheryl CROW
RUN BACK — Carl DOUGLAS
RUN DADDY RUN — FUN LOVIN' CRIMINALS
RUN FOR COVER — SUGABABES
RUN FOR HOME — LINDISFARNE
RUN FOR YOUR LIFE [A] — BUCKS FIZZ
RUN FOR YOUR LIFE [B] — NORTHERN LINE
RUN FROM LOVE — Jimmy SOMERVILLE
RUN ON — MOBY
RUN RUDOLPH RUN — Chuck BERRY
RUN RUN RUN [A] — JO JO GUNNE
RUN RUN RUN [B] — PHOENIX
RUN RUNAWAY — SLADE
RUN SILENT — SHAKESPEAR'S SISTER
RUN TO HIM — Bobby VEE
RUN TO ME — The BEE GEES

RUN TO MY LOVIN' ARMS — Billy FURY
RUN TO THE DOOR — Clinton FORD
RUN TO THE HILLS — IRON MAIDEN
RUN TO THE SUN — ERASURE
RUN TO YOU [A] — Bryan ADAMS
RUN TO YOU [A] — RAGE
RUN TO YOU [B] — Whitney HOUSTON
RUN TO YOU [C] — ROXETTE
RUN 2 — NEW ORDER
RUNAROUND — JAMES
RUNAROUND — Martha WASH
RUNAROUND SUE [A] — DION
RUNAROUND SUE [A] — Doug SHELDON
RUNAROUND SUE [A] — RACEY
RUNAWAY [A] — Del SHANNON
RUNAWAY [B] — DEEE-LITE
RUNAWAY [C] — Janet JACKSON
RUNAWAY [D] — E'VOKE
RUNAWAY [E] — The CORRS
RUNAWAY [F] —
NUYORICAN SOUL featuring INDIA
THE RUNAWAY — Elkie BROOKS
RUNAWAY BOYS — STRAY CATS
RUNAWAY GIRL — Sterling VOID
RUNAWAY HORSES — Belinda CARLISLE
RUNAWAY LOVE — EN VOGUE
RUNAWAY SKIES — CELETIA
RUNAWAY TRAIN [A] —
Elton JOHN and Eric CLAPTON
RUNAWAY TRAIN [B] — SOUL ASYLUM
THE RUNNER — The THREE DEGREES
RUNNIN [A] — BASSTOY
RUNNIN' [A] — Mark PICCHIOTTI
presents BASSTOY featuring DANA
RUNNIN' [B] — BASS BUMPERS
RUNNIN' [C] — 2PAC and NOTORIOUS B.I.G.
RUNNIN' [D] — The PHARCYDE
RUNNIN' AWAY [A] —
SLY and the FAMILY STONE
RUNNIN' AWAY [A] — NICOLE
RUNNIN' DOWN A DREAM —
Tom PETTY and the HEARTBREAKERS
RUNNIN' (DYING TO LIVE) —
TUPAC featuring NOTORIOUS B.I.G.
RUNNIN' FOR THE RED LIGHT (I GOTTA LIFE) —
MEAT LOAF
RUNNIN' WITH THE DEVIL — VAN HALEN
RUNNING ALL OVER THE WORLD —
STATUS QUO
RUNNING AROUND TOWN — Billie Ray MARTIN
RUNNING BEAR — Johnny PRESTON
RUNNING FREE — IRON MAIDEN
RUNNING FROM PARADISE —
Daryl HALL and John OATES
RUNNING IN THE FAMILY — LEVEL 42
RUNNING OUT OF TIME — DIGITAL ORGASM
RUNNING SCARED — Roy ORBISON
RUNNING UP THAT HILL — Kate BUSH
RUNNING WITH THE NIGHT — Lionel RICHIE
RUN'S HOUSE — RUN-DMC
RUPERT — Jackie LEE
RUSH [A] — FREAKPOWER
RUSH [B] — KLESHAY
THE RUSH — Luther VANDROSS
RUSH HOUR [A] — Jane WIEDLIN
RUSH HOUR [A] — JOYRIDER
RUSH HOUR [B] — BAD COMPANY
RUSH RUSH — Paula ABDUL
RUSHES — DARIUS
RUSHING — Loni CLARK
RUSSIANS — STING
RUST — ECHO and the BUNNYMEN
RUSTY CAGE — SOUNDGARDEN
S CLUB PARTY — S CLUB 7
SABOTAGE — BEASTIE BOYS
SABRE DANCE — LOVE SCULPTURE
SACRAMENTO (A WONDERFUL TOWN) —
MIDDLE OF THE ROAD
SACRED CYCLES — Peter LAZONBY
SACRED TRUST — ONE TRUE VOICE
SACRIFICE — Elton JOHN
SAD BUT TRUE — METALLICA
SAD EYES — Robert JOHN
SAD MOVIES (MAKE ME CRY) —
Carol DEENE
SAD MOVIES MAKE ME CRY [A] —
Sue THOMPSON
SAD SONGS (SAY SO MUCH) — Elton JOHN
SAD SWEET DREAMER — SWEET SENSATION
SADDLE UP — David CHRISTIE
SADIE'S SHAWL — Frank CORDELL
SADNESS PART 1 — ENIGMA
SAFARI (EP) — The BREEDERS
SAFE FROM HARM [A] — MASSIVE ATTACK
SAFE FROM HARM [A] — NARCOTIC THRUST
THE SAFETY DANCE — MEN WITHOUT HATS
SAFFRON — EASTERN LANE
SAID I LOVED YOU BUT I LIED — Michael BOLTON
SAID SHE WAS A DANCER — JETHRO TULL
SAIL AWAY [A] — LITTLE ANGELS
SAIL AWAY [B] — URBAN COOKIE COLLECTIVE
SAIL AWAY [C] — David GRAY
SAIL ON — The COMMODORES
SAILING [A] — Rod STEWART
SAILING [B] — Christopher CROSS
SAILING OFF THE EDGE OF THE WORLD —
STRAW

SAILING ON THE SEVEN SEAS —
ORCHESTRAL MANOEUVRES IN THE DARK
SAILOR [A] — Anne SHELTON
SAILOR [A] — Petula CLARK
SAILORTOWN — ENERGY ORCHARD
THE SAINT [A] — THOMPSON TWINS
THE SAINT [B] — ORBITAL
ST ANGER — METALLICA
ST ELMO'S FIRE (MAN IN MOTION) —
John PARR
SAINT OF ME — The ROLLING STONES
ST TERESA — Joan OSBORNE
ST THERESE OF THE ROSES —
Malcolm VAUGHAN
ST VALENTINE'S DAY MASSACRE (EP) —
MOTÖRHEAD and GIRLSCHOOL
(also known as HEADGIRL)
THE SAINTS ARE COMING — The SKIDS
THE SAINTS ROCK 'N ROLL —
Bill HALEY and his COMETS
SALE OF THE CENTURY — SLEEPER
SALLY [A] — Gerry MONROE
SALLY [B] — CARMEL
SALLY [C] — KERBDOG
SALLY ANN — Joe BROWN and the BRUVVERS
SALLY CINNAMON — The STONE ROSES
SALLY DON'T YOU GRIEVE — Lonnie DONEGAN
SALLY MACLENNANE — The POGUES
SAL'S GOT A SUGAR LIP — Lonnie DONEGAN
SALSA HOUSE — Richie RICH
SALSOUL NUGGET (IF U WANNA) —
M&S presents GIRL NEXT DOOR
SALT IN THE WOUND —
CARPET BOMBERS FOR PEACE
SALT SWEAT SUGAR — JIMMY EAT WORLD
SALTWATER [A] — Julian LENNON
SALTWATER [B] — CHICANE featuring
Maire BRENNAN of CLANNAD
SALTY DOG — PROCOL HARUM
SALVA MEA — FAITHLESS
SALVATION — The CRANBERRIES
SAM [A] — Keith WEST
SAM [B] — Olivia NEWTON-JOHN
SAMANTHA — Kenny BALL and his JAZZMEN
SAMBA DE JANEIRO — BELLINI
SAMBA MAGIC — SUMMER DAZE
SAMBA PA TI — SANTANA
SAMBUCA — WIDEBOYS featuring Dennis G
SAME OLD BRAND NEW YOU — a1
THE SAME OLD SCENE — ROXY MUSIC
SAME OLD STORY — ULTRAVOX
SAME PICTURE — GOLDRUSH
SAME SONG — DIGITAL UNDERGROUND
SAME TEMPO — CHANGING FACES
SAME THING IN REVERSE —
BOY GEORGE
SAMSON AND DELILAH [A] —
MIDDLE OF THE ROAD
SAMSON AND DELILAH [B] — BAD MANNERS
SAN ANTONIO ROSE — Floyd CRAMER
SAN BERNADINO — CHRISTIE
SAN DAMIANO (HEART AND SOUL) —
Sal SOLO
SAN FRANCISCAN NIGHTS — The ANIMALS
SAN FRANCISCO (BE SURE TO WEAR
SOME FLOWERS IN YOUR HAIR) —
Scott McKENZIE
SAN FRANCISCO DAYS — Chris ISAAK
SAN FRANCISCO (YOU'VE GOT ME) —
VILLAGE PEOPLE
SAN MIGUEL [A] — KINGSTON TRIO
SAN MIGUEL [A] — Lonnie DONEGAN
SANCTIFIED LADY — Marvin GAYE
SANCTIFY YOURSELF — SIMPLE MINDS
SANCTIMONIOUS — HALO
SANCTUARY [A] — IRON MAIDEN
SANCTUARY [B] — NEW MUSIK
SANCTUARY [C] — DEJURE
SANCTUS (MISSA LUBA) —
TROUBADOURS DU ROI BAUDOUIN
SAND IN MY SHOES — DIDO
SANDBLASTED (EP) — SWERVEDRIVER
SANDCASTLES — BOMB THE BASS
SANDMAN — BLUE BOY
SANDS OF TIME — KALEEF
SANDSTORM [A] — CAST
SANDSTORM [B] — DARUDE
SANDWICHES — DETROIT GRAND PU BAHS
SANDY — John TRAVOLTA
SANITY — KILLING JOKE
SANTA BRING MY BABY BACK (TO ME) —
Elvis PRESLEY
SANTA CLAUS IS BACK IN TOWN —
Elvis PRESLEY
SANTA CLAUS IS COMING TO TOWN [A] —
The JACKSON FIVE
SANTA CLAUS IS COMIN' TO TOWN [A] —
The CARPENTERS
SANTA CLAUS IS COMIN' TO TOWN [A] —
Bruce SPRINGSTEEN
SANTA CLAUS IS COMING TO TOWN [A] —
BJÖRN AGAIN
SANTA CLAUS IS ON THE DOLE —
SPITTING IMAGE
SANTA CRUZ (YOU'RE NOT THAT FAR) —
The THRILLS
SANTA MARIA [A] — TATJANA

SANTA MARIA [A] —
DJ MILANO featuring SAMANTHA FOX
SANTA MONICA (WATCH THE WORLD DIE) —
EVERCLEAR
SANTA'S LIST — Cliff RICHARD
SANTO NATALE (MERRY CHRISTMAS) —
David WHITFIELD
SARA [A] — FLEETWOOD MAC
SARA [A] — STARSHIP
SARAH — THIN LIZZY
SARTORIAL ELOQUENCE — Elton JOHN
SAT IN YOUR LAP — Kate BUSH
SATAN — ORBITAL
SATAN REJECTED MY SOUL — MORRISSEY
THE SATCH EP — Joe SATRIANI
SATELLITE [A] — HOOTERS
SATELLITE [B] — The BELOVED
SATELLITE [C] — OCEANLAB
SATELLITE KID — DOGS D'AMOUR
SATELLITE OF LOVE '04 — Lou REED
SATIN SHEETS — BELLAMY BROTHERS
SATISFACTION [A] — Aretha FRANKLIN
SATISFACTION [A] — Otis REDDING
SATISFACTION [A] — VANILLA ICE
SATISFACTION [B] — WENDY and LISA
SATISFACTION [C] — EVE
SATISFACTION [D] —
Benny BENASSI presents the BIZ
SATISFACTION GUARANTEED
(OR TAKE YOUR LOVE BACK) —
Harold MELVIN and the BLUENOTES
SATISFIED — Richard MARX
SATISFIED (TAKE ME HIGHER) — H2o
SATISFY MY LOVE [A] — EXOTERIX
SATISFY MY LOVE [B] — Sabrina JOHNSTON
SATISFY MY LOVE [C] — PESHAY
SATISFY MY SOUL —
Bob MARLEY & the WAILERS
SATISFY YOU — PUFF DADDY
SATURDAY [A] — Joey NEGRO
SATURDAY [A] — EAST 57th
STREET featuring Donna ALLEN
SATURDAY [B] — OMAR
SATURDAY GIG — MOTT THE HOOPLE
SATURDAY LOVE [A] —
CHERELLE with Alexander O'NEAL
SATURDAY LOVE [A] —ILLEGAL MOTION
featuring Simone CHAPMAN
SATURDAY NIGHT [A] — T-CONNECTION
SATURDAY NIGHT [B] — BLUE NILE
SATURDAY NIGHT [C] — SINDY
SATURDAY NIGHT [C] — WHIGFIELD
SATURDAY NIGHT [D] — SUEDE
SATURDAY NIGHT [E] — UD PROJECT
SATURDAY NIGHT AT THE MOVIES [A] —
The DRIFTERS
SATURDAY NIGHT AT THE MOVIES [A] —
ROBSON & JEROME
SATURDAY NIGHT (BENEATH THE PLASTIC PALM TREES)
— LEYTON BUZZARDS
SATURDAY NIGHT PARTY (READ MY LIPS) —
ALEX PARTY
SATURDAY NIGHT SUNDAY MORNING —
T-EMPO
SATURDAY NIGHT'S ALRIGHT FOR FIGHTING —
Elton JOHN
SATURDAY NITE [A] — EARTH WIND AND FIRE
SATURDAY NITE [B] —
The BRAND NEW HEAVIES
SATURDAY NITE AT THE DUCK-POND —
COUGARS
SATURDAY (OOOH OOOH) — LUDACRIS
SATURDAY'S NOT WHAT IT USED TO BE —
KINGMAKER
SATURN 5 — INSPIRAL CARPETS
THE SAVAGE — The SHADOWS
SAVANNA DANCE — DEEP FOREST
SAVE A LITTLE BIT — Glen GOLDSMITH
SAVE A PRAYER — DURAN DURAN
SAVE A PRAYER [A] — 56K featuring BEJAY
SAVE IT FOR LATER — The BEAT
SAVE IT 'TIL THE MOURNING AFTER —
SHUT UP AND DANCE
SAVE ME [A] —
Dave DEE, DOZY, BEAKY, MICK and TICH
SAVE ME [B] — SILVER CONVENTION
SAVE ME [C] — QUEEN
SAVE ME [D] — FLEETWOOD MAC
SAVE ME [E] — BIG COUNTRY
SAVE ME [F] — EMBRACE
SAVE ME [G] — MEEKER
SAVE ME [H] — REMY ZERO
SAVE OUR LOVE — ETERNAL
SAVE THE BEST FOR LAST —
Vanessa WILLIAMS
SAVE THE CHILDREN — Marvin GAYE
SAVE THE LAST DANCE FOR ME [A] —
The DRIFTERS
SAVE THE LAST DANCE FOR ME [A] —
Ben E KING
SAVE THE LAST DANCE FOR ME [A] —
GENERAL SAINT
SAVE TONIGHT — Eagle-Eye CHERRY
SAVE UP ALL YOUR TEARS — CHER
SAVE US — Philip JAP
SAVE YOUR KISSES FOR ME —
BROTHERHOOD OF MAN

SAVE YOUR LOVE — RENÉE and RENATO
SAVE YOUR LOVE (FOR NUMBER 1) —
RENÉ and ANGELA
SAVE YOURSELF — SPEEDWAY
SAVED [A] — MR ROY
SAVED [B] — OCTOPUS
SAVED BY THE BELL — Robin GIBB
SAVED MY LIFE — LIL' LOUIS
SAVING ALL MY LOVE FOR YOU —
Whitney HOUSTON
SAVING FOREVER FOR YOU — SHANICE
SAVIOUR'S DAY — Cliff RICHARD
SAXUALITY — Candy DULFER
SAXY LADY — QUIVVER
SAY — CREATURES
SAY A LITTLE PRAYER —
BOMB THE BASS featuring MAUREEN
SAY A PRAYER — Taylor DAYNE
SAY CHEESE (SMILE PLEASE) —
FAST FOOD ROCKERS
SAY GOODBYE — S CLUB
SAY ... IF YOU FEEL ALRIGHT — Crystal WATERS
SAY, HAS ANYBODY SEEN MY
SWEET GYPSY ROSE — DAWN
SAY HELLO TO THE ANGELS — INTERPOL
SAY HELLO WAVE GOODBYE [A] — SOFT CELL
SAY HELLO WAVE GOODBYE [A] — David GRAY
SAY HOW I FEEL — Rhian BENSON
SAY I WON'T BE THERE — The SPRINGFIELDS
SAY I'M YOUR NUMBER ONE — PRINCESS
SAY IT [A] — ABC
SAY IT [B] — Maria RUBIA
SAY IT AGAIN [A] — Jermaine STEWART
SAY IT AGAIN [B] — PRECIOUS
SAY IT AIN'T SO — WEEZER
SAY IT ISN'T SO [A] —
Daryl HALL and John OATES
SAY IT ISN'T SO [B] — BON JOVI
SAY IT ISN'T SO [C] — Gareth GATES
SAY IT ONCE — ULTRA
SAY IT WITH FLOWERS —
Dorothy SQUIRES and Russ CONWAY
SAY IT WITH PRIDE —
SCOTLAND WORLD CUP SQUAD
SAY JUST WORDS — PARADISE LOST
SAY MY NAME [A] — ZEE
SAY MY NAME [B] — DESTINY'S CHILD
SAY NO GO — DE LA SOUL
SAY NOTHIN' — OMAR
SAY SAY SAY —
Paul McCARTNEY and Michael JACKSON
SAY SOMETHING [A] — JAMES
SAY SOMETHING [B] — HAVEN
SAY SOMETHING ANYWAY — BELLEFIRE
SAY THAT YOU'RE HERE — FRAGMA
SAY WHAT! — X-PRESS 2
SAY WHAT YOU WANT — TEXAS
SAY WHEN — Lene LOVICH
SAY WONDERFUL THINGS — Ronnie CARROLL
SAY YEAH [A] — LIMIT
SAY YEAH [B] — BULLETPROOF
SAY YOU DO — ULTRA
SAY YOU DON'T MIND — Colin BLUNSTONE
SAY YOU LOVE ME [A] — FLEETWOOD MAC
SAY YOU LOVE ME [B] — SIMPLY RED
SAY YOU LOVE ME [C] — JOHNSON
SAY YOU REALLY WANT ME — Kim WILDE
SAY YOU, SAY ME — Lionel RICHIE
SAY YOU WILL — FOREIGNER
SAY YOU'LL BE MINE [A] — Amy GRANT
SAY YOU'LL BE MINE [B] — STEPS
SAY YOU'LL BE MINE [C] — QFX
SAY YOU'LL BE THERE — SPICE GIRLS
SAY YOU'LL STAY UNTIL TOMORROW —
Tom JONES
SAY YOU'RE MINE AGAIN — June HUTTON
(SAY) YOU'RE MY GIRL — Roy ORBISON
SAY YOU'RE WRONG — Julian LENNON
SCALES OF JUSTICE — LIVING IN A BOX
SCANDAL — QUEEN
SCANDALOUS [A] — CLICK
SCANDALOUS [B] — MIS-TEEQ
SCAR TISSUE — RED HOT CHILI PEPPERS
SCARED — SLACKER
SCARLET — ALL ABOUT EVE
SCARLET RIBBONS — Harry BELAFONTE
SCARLETT O'HARA —
Jet HARRIS and Tony MEEHAN
SCARS — WITNESS
SCARY MONSTERS (AND SUPER CREEPS) —
David BOWIE
SCARY MOVIES — BAD MEETS EVIL
featuring EMINEM and ROYCE DA 5'9
THE SCARY-GO-ROUND EP — JELLYFISH
SCATMAN (SKI-BA-BOP-BA-DOP-BOP) —
SCATMAN JOHN
SCATMAN'S WORLD — SCATMAN JOHN
SCATTER & SWING — LIONROCK
SCATTERLINGS OF AFRICA [A] — JULUKA
SCATTERLINGS OF AFRICA [A] —
Johnny CLEGG and SAVUKA
SCHEMING — MAXIM
SCHMOO — SPOOKY
SCHONEBERG — MARMION
SCHOOL DAY [A] — Chuck BERRY
SCHOOL DAY [B] — Don LANG
SCHOOL LOVE — Barry BLUE

SCHOOL OF ROCK — SCHOOL OF ROCK
SCHOOL'S OUT [A] — Alice COOPER
SCHOOL'S OUT [B] — DAPHNE & CELESTE
SCHOOLTIME CHRONICLE — Smiley CULTURE
SCHTEEVE — YOURCODENAMEIS:MILO
SCIENCE OF SILENCE — Richard ASHCROFT
THE SCIENTIST — COLDPLAY
SCOOBY DOO [A] — DWEEB
SCOOBY DOO [B] — J MAJIK and WICKAMAN
SCOOBY SNACKS — FUN LOVIN' CRIMINALS
SCOPE — PARIS ANGELS
SCORCHIO — SASHA
SCORPIO RISING —
DEATH IN VEGAS with Liam GALLAGHER
SCOTCH ON THE ROCKS —
Band of the BLACK WATCH
SCOTLAND BE GOOD — TARTAN ARMY
SCOTLAND FOR EVER (EP) — Sidney DEVINE
SCOTS MACHINE — VOYAGE
SCOTTISH RAIN — The SILENCERS
A SCOTTISH SOLDIER — Andy STEWART
SCRAMBLED EGGS — Roni SIZE
THE SCRATCH — SURFACE NOISE
SCREAM [A] — DISCO ANTHEM
SCREAM [B] —
Michael JACKSON and Janet JACKSON
SCREAM [C] — NUT
SCREAM IF YOU WANNA GO FASTER —
Geri HALLIWELL
SCREAM (PRIMAL SCREAM) — MANTRONIX
SCREAM UNTIL YOU LIKE IT — W.A.S.P.
THE SCREAMER —
YOSH presents LOVEDEEJAY AKEMI
SCULLERY — Clifford T WARD
SE A VIDE É (THAT'S THE WAY LIFE IS) —
PET SHOP BOYS
SEA OF BLUE — TECHNATION
SEA OF HEARTBREAK — Don GIBSON
SEA OF LOVE [A] — Marty WILDE
SEA OF LOVE [A] — HONEYDRIPPERS
SEAGULL — RAINBOW COTTAGE
THE SEAGULL'S NAME WAS NELSON — Peter E
BENNETT with the CO-OPERATION CHOIR
SEAL MY FATE — BELLY
SEAL OUR FATE — Gloria ESTEFAN
SEALED WITH A KISS [A] — Brian HYLAND
SEALED WITH A KISS [A] — Jason DONOVAN
SEANCE — NEBULA II
SEARCH AND DESTROY — DICTATORS
SEARCH FOR THE HERO — M PEOPLE
SEARCHIN' [A] — The COASTERS
SEARCHIN' [A] — The HOLLIES
SEARCHIN' FOR MY RIZLA — RATPACK
SEARCHIN' (I GOTTA FIND A MAN) —
Hazell DEAN
SEARCHIN' MY SOUL — Vonda SHEPARD
SEARCHING [A] — CHANGE
SEARCHING [B] — CHINA BLACK
SEARCHING FOR A SOUL — Conner REEVES
SEARCHING FOR THE GOLDEN EYE —
MOTIV 8 and Kym MAZELLE
SEASIDE — The ORDINARY BOYS
SEASIDE SHUFFLE —
Terry DACTYL and the DINOSAURS
SEASON NO.5 — BEDLAM AGO GO
SEASONS IN THE ABYSS — SLAYER
SEASONS IN THE SUN [A] — Terry JACKS
SEASONS IN THE SUN [A] — WESTLIFE
SEASONS OF GOLD — GIDEA PARK
SEASONSTREAM (EP) —
THOUSAND YARD STARE
SEATTLE — PUBLIC IMAGE LTD
2ND AMENDMENT — EASYWORLD
SECOND CHANCE — Phillip LEO
SECOND HAND ROSE — Barbra STREISAND
SECOND NATURE [A] — Dan HARTMAN
SECOND NATURE [B] — ELECTRONIC
SECOND ROUND KO — CANIBUS
THE SECOND SUMMER OF LOVE —
DANNY WILSON
THE SECOND TIME — Kim WILDE
THE SECOND TIME AROUND — SHALAMAR
THE SECOND TIME (THEME FROM 'BILITIS') —
Elaine PAIGE
SECRET [A] —
ORCHESTRAL MANOEUVRES IN THE DARK
SECRET [B] — MADONNA
SECRET AGENT MAN — JAMES BOND
IS BACK — Bruce WILLIS
SECRET COMBINATION — Randy CRAWFORD
SECRET GARDEN [A] — T'PAU
SECRET GARDEN [B] — Quincy JONES
featuring Al B SUREl, James INGRAM,
El DeBARGE and Barry WHITE
SECRET GARDEN [C] — Bruce SPRINGSTEEN
SECRET HEART — TIGHT FIT
SECRET KISS — The CORAL
SECRET LOVE [A] — Doris DAY
SECRET LOVE [A] — Kathy KIRBY
SECRET LOVE [A] — Daniel O'DONNELL
SECRET LOVE [B] — The BEE GEES
SECRET LOVE [C] — Danni'elle GAHA
SECRET LOVE [D] — SHAH
SECRET LOVE [E] — Kelly PRICE
SECRET LOVERS — ATLANTIC STARR
SECRET MESSAGES —
ELECTRIC LIGHT ORCHESTRA

SECRET RENDEZVOUS [A] —
  RENÉ and ANGELA
SECRET RENDEZVOUS [B] — Karyn WHITE
SECRET SMILE — SEMISONIC
SECRET STAR — WOMACK and WOMACK
THE SECRET VAMPIRE SOUNDTRACK (EP) — BIS
SECRETLY — SKUNK ANANSIE
SECRETS [A] —
  SUTHERLAND BROTHERS and QUIVER
SECRETS [B] — FIAT LUX
SECRETS [C] — PRIMITIVES
SECRETS [D] — SUNSCREEM
SECRETS [E] — ETERNAL
SECRETS [F] — MUTINY UK
SECRETS IN THE STREET — Nils LOFGREN
SECRETS (OF SUCCESS) — COOKIE CREW
SECRETS OF THE HEART — Chesney HAWKES
THE SECOND LINE — CLINIC
THE SECRETS THAT YOU KEEP — MUD
THE SEDUCTION (LOVE THEME) —
  James LAST BAND
SEE A BRIGHTER DAY — JTQ
SEE EMILY PLAY — PINK FLOYD
SEE IT IN A BOY'S EYES — JAMELIA
SEE JUNGLE (JUNGLE BOY) — BOW WOW WOW
SEE LINE WOMAN' '99 — SONGSTRESS
SEE ME — Luther VANDROSS
SEE MY BABY JIVE —
  WIZZARD: Vocal backing by the Suedettes
SEE MY FRIEND — The KINKS
SEE THAT GLOW — THIS ISLAND EARTH
SEE THE DAY — DC LEE
SEE THE LIGHTS — SIMPLE MINDS
SEE THE STAR — DELIRIOUS?
SEE THOSE EYES — ALTERED IMAGES
SEE THRU IT —
  APHRODITE featuring WILDFLOWER
SEE WANT MUST HAVE — BLUE MERCEDES
SEE YA — ATOMIC KITTEN
SEE YOU — DEPECHE MODE
SEE YOU LATER — REGENTS
SEE YOU LATER ALLIGATOR —
  Bill HALEY and his COMETS
THE SEED (2.0) —
  ROOTS featuring Cody CHESNUTT
SEEING THINGS — BLACK CROWES
THE SEEKER — The WHO
SEEMS FINE — The CONCRETES
SEEN THE LIGHT — SUPERGRASS
SEETHER — VERUCA SALT
SEIZE THE DAY — FKW
SELA — Lionel RICHIE
SELECTA (URBAN HEROES) —
  JAMESON & VIPER
SELF! — WE'VE GOT A FUZZBOX
  AND WE'RE GONNA USE IT
SELF CONtROL — Laura BRANIGAN
SELF DESTRUCTION —
  STOP THE VIOLENCE MOVEMENT
SELF ESTEEM — The OFFSPRING
SELF SUICIDE — GOLDIE LOOKIN CHAIN
SELFISH — The OTHER TWO
SELLING JESUS — SKUNK ANANSIE
SELLING THE DRAMA — LIVE
SEMI-CHARMED LIFE — THIRD EYE BLIND
SEMI-DETACHED SUBURBAN MR JAMES —
  MANFRED MANN
SEND HIS LOVE TO ME — P J HARVEY
SEND IN THE CLOWNS — Judy COLLINS
SEND ME AN ANGEL [A] — BLACKFOOT
SEND ME AN ANGEL [B] — SCORPIONS
SEND ME THE PILLOW YOU DREAM ON —
  Johnny TILLOTSON
SEND MY HEART — ADVENTURES
SEND ONE YOUR LOVE — Stevie WONDER
SEND YOUR LOVE — STING
SENDING OUT AN S.O.S. — Retta YOUNG
SEÑORITA — Justin TIMBERLAKE
SENSATION — ELECTROSET
SENSATIONAL — Michelle GAYLE
SENSE [A] — The LIGHTNING SEEDS
SENSE [B] — Terry HALL
SENSE OF DANGER —
  PRESENCE featuring Shara NELSON
SENSES WORKING OVERTIME — XTC
SENSITIVITY — Ralph TRESVANT
SENSITIZE — THAT PETROL EMOTION
SENSUAL SOPHIS-TI-CAT — Carl COX
THE SENSUAL WORLD — Kate BUSH
SENSUALITY — LOVESTATION
SENTIMENTAL [A] — Alexander O'NEAL
SENTIMENTAL [B] — Deborah COX
SENTIMENTAL [C] — Kym MARSH
SENTIMENTAL FOOL — Lloyd COLE
SENTINEL — Mike OLDFIELD
SENZA UNA DONNA (WITHOUT A WOMAN) —
  ZUCCHERO and Paul YOUNG
SEPARATE LIVES — Phil COLLINS
SEPARATE TABLES — Chris DE BURGH
SEPARATE WAYS — Gary MOORE
SEPTEMBER — EARTH WIND AND FIRE
SEPTEMBER IN THE RAIN —
  Dinah WASHINGTON
SEPTEMBER SONG — Ian McCULLOCH
SERENADE [A] — Mario LANZA
SERENADE [B] — Mario LANZA
SERENADE [B] — Slim WHITMAN

SERENADE [C] — SHADES
SERENATA — Sarah VAUGHAN
SERENITY IN MURDER — SLAYER
SERIOUS [A] — Billy GRIFFIN
SERIOUS [B] — SERIOUS INTENTION
SERIOUS [C] — Donna ALLEN
SERIOUS [D] — DEJA
SERIOUS [E] — DURAN DURAN
SERIOUS [F] — Maxwell D
SERIOUS MIX — MIRAGE
SERPENTS KISS — The MISSION
SESAME'S TREET — SMART E'S
SET ADRIFT ON MEMORY BLISS — PM DAWN
SET FIRE TO ME — Willie COLON
SET IN STONE — BEDROCK
SET IT OFF [A] —
  HARLEQUIN 4s / BUNKER KRU
SET IT OFF [B] — PEACHES
SET ME FREE [A] — KINKS
SET ME FREE [B] — Jaki GRAHAM
SET ME FREE [C] — BRIT PACK
SET THE RECORD STRAIGHT — REEF
SET THEM FREE — ASWAD
THE SET UP (YOU DON'T KNOW) —
  Obie TRICE featuring NATE DOGG
SET YOU FREE — N-TRANCE
SET YOUR LOVING FREE — Lisa STANSFIELD
SETTING SUN — THE CHEMICAL BROTHERS
SETTLE DOWN [A] — Lillo THOMAS
SETTLE DOWN [B] — UNBELIEVABLE TRUTH
7 [A] —
  PRINCE and the NEW POWER GENERATION
SEVEN [B] — David BOWIE
SEVEN (EP) — JAMES
SEVEN AND SEVEN IS (LIVE VERSION) —
  Alice COOPER
SEVEN CITIES — SOLAR STONE
7 COLOURS — LOST WITNESS
SEVEN DAFFODILS [A] — CHEROKEES
SEVEN DAFFODILS [A] — MOJOS
SEVEN DAYS [A] — Anne SHELTON
SEVEN DAYS [B] — STING
SEVEN DAYS [C] —
  Mary J BLIGE featuring George BENSON
7 DAYS [D] — Craig DAVID
SEVEN DAYS AND ONE WEEK — BBE
SEVEN DAYS IN THE SUN — FEEDER
SEVEN DRUNKEN NIGHTS — DUBLINERS
747 — KENT
747 (STRANGERS IN THE NIGHT) — SAXON
SEVEN LITTLE GIRLS SITTING IN THE BACK SEAT [A] —
  AVONS
SEVEN LITTLE GIRLS SITTING IN THE BACK SEAT [A] —
  Paul EVANS
SEVEN LITTLE GIRLS SITTING IN THE BACKSEAT [A] —
  BOMBALURINA
SEVEN LONELY DAYS — Gisele MacKENZIE
7 NATION ARMY — The WHITE STRIPES
7 O'CLOCK — QUIREBOYS
SEVEN ROOMS OF GLOOM — The FOUR TOPS
SEVEN SEAS — ECHO and the BUNNYMEN
SEVEN SEAS OF RHYE — QUEEN
7 SECONDS —
  Youssou N'DOUR (featuring Neneh CHERRY)
7:7 EXPANSION — SYSTEM 7
7-6-5-4-3-2-1 (BLOW YOUR WHISTLE) — RIMSHOTS
SEVEN TEARS — GOOMBAY DANCE BAND
7 TEEN — REGENTS
$7000 AND YOU — The STYLISTICS
7 WAYS TO LOVE — COLA BOY
SEVEN WONDERS — FLEETWOOD MAC
7 YEAR BITCH — SLADE
SEVEN YEARS IN TIBET — David BOWIE
SEVENTEEN [A] —
  Boyd BENNETT and his ROCKETS
SEVENTEEN [A] — Frankie VAUGHAN
SEVENTEEN [B] — LET LOOSE
SEVENTEEN [C] — LADYTRON
17 AGAIN — EURYTHMICS
SEVENTH SON — Georgie FAME
78 STONE WOBBLE — GOMEZ
74-75 — CONNELLS
77 STRINGS —
  Kurtis MANTRONIK presents CHAMONIX
SEVENTY-SIX TROMBONES — KING BROTHERS
72 — TURIN BRAKES
SEVERINA — The MISSION
SEX [A] — SLEAZESISTERS
SEX [B] —
  Robbie RIVERA featuring Billy Paul W
SEX AND CANDY — MARCY PLAYGROUND
SEX AS A WEAPON — Pat BENATAR
SEX BOMB — Tom JONES & Mousse T
SEX, DRUGS AND ROCKS THROUGH YOUR
  WINDOW — AGENT BLUE
SEX LIFE — Geoffrey WILLIAMS
SEX ME —
  R KELLY and Public ANNOUNCEMENT
THE SEX OF IT —
  Kid CREOLE and the COCONUTS
SEX ON THE BEACH — T-SPOON
SEX ON THE STREETS — PIZZAMAN
SEX OVER THE PHONE — VILLAGE PEOPLE
SEX TALK (LIVE) — T'PAU
SEX TYPE THING — STONE TEMPLE PILOTS
SEXCRIME (NINETEEN EIGHTY FOUR) —
  EURYTHMICS

SEXED UP — Robbie WILLIAMS
SEXOMATIC — BAR-KAYS
SEXIEST MAN IN JAMAICA — MINT ROYALE
SEXUAL [A] — Maria ROWE
SEXUAL [B] — AMBER
SEXUAL GUARANTEE — ALCAZAR
(SEXUAL) HEALING — Marvin GAYE
SEXUAL REVOLUTION — Macy GRAY
SEXUALITY — Billy BRAGG
SEXX LAWS — BECK
SEXY — MFSB
SEXY BOY — AIR
SEXY CINDERELLA — Lynden David HALL
SEXY CREAM — SLICK
SEXY EYES — DR HOOK
SEXY EYES – REMIXES — WHIGFIELD
SEXY GIRL — Lillo THOMAS
SEXY MF —
  PRINCE and the NEW POWER GENERATION
SGT. PEPPER'S LONELY HEARTS CLUB BAND – WITH A
  LITTLE HELP FROM MY FRIENDS — The BEATLES
SGT ROCK (IS GOING TO HELP ME) — XTC
SHA LA LA LA LEE [A] — PLASTIC BERTRAND
SHA LA LA LA LEE [A] — The SMALL FACES
SHA LA LA — MANFRED MANN
SHA LA LA MEANS I LOVE YOU — Barry WHITE
SHACKLES (PRAISE YOU) — MARY MARY
SHADDAP YOU FACE —
  Joe DOLCE MUSIC THEATRE
SHADES OF BLUE (EP) — The THE
SHADES OF GREEN — The MISSION
SHADES OF PARANOIMIA — ART OF NOISE
SHADES OF SUMMER — RODEO JONES
SHADES (THEME FROM THE CROWN PAINT TELEVISION
  COMMERCIAL) —
  UNITED KINGDOM SYMPHONY
SHADOW DANCING — Andy GIBB
THE SHADOW OF LOVE — The DAMNED
SHADOWS OF THE NIGHT — Pat BENATAR
SHADOWTIME — SIOUXSIE and the BANSHEES
SHADY LADY — Gene PITNEY
SHADY LANE — PAVEMENT
SHAFT — VAN TWIST
SHAKE [A] — Otis REDDING
SHAKE [B] — Andrew RIDGELEY
SHAKE! (HOW ABOUT A SAMPLING, GENE?) —
  GENE AND JIM ARE INTO SHAKES
SHAKE IT BABY —
  DJD presents HYDRAULIC DOGS
SHAKE IT DOWN — MUD
SHAKE IT (NO TE MUEVAS TANTO) [A] —
  LEE-CABRERA
SHAKE IT (MOVE A LITTLE CLOSER) [A] —
  LEE-CABRERA featuring Alex CARTAÑA
SHAKE ME I RATTLE — KAYE SISTERS
SHAKE RATTLE AND ROLL —
  Bill HALEY and his COMETS
(SHAKE, SHAKE, SHAKE) SHAKE YOUR BOOTY —
  KC and the SUNSHINE BAND
SHAKE THE DISEASE — DEPECHE MODE
SHAKE THIS MOUNTAIN — HORSE
SHAKE UR BODY —
  SHY FX and T-POWER featuring DI
SHAKE (WHAT YA MAMA GAVE YA) — GENERAL LEVY
  vs ZEUS featuring Bally JAGPAL
SHAKE YA ASS — MYSTIKAL
SHAKE YA BODY — N-TRANCE
SHAKE YA SHIMMY — PORN KINGS vs
  FLIP & FILL featuring 740 BOYZ
SHAKE YA TAILFEATHER —
  NELLY, P DIDDY and Murphy LEE
SHAKE YOU DOWN — Gregory ABBOTT
SHAKE YOUR BODY (DOWN TO THE GROUND) [A] —
  FULL INTENTION
SHAKE YOUR BODY (DOWN TO THE GROUND) [A] —
  The JACKSONS
SHAKE YOUR BON-BON — Ricky MARTIN
SHAKE YOUR FOUNDATIONS — AC/DC
SHAKE YOUR GROOVE THING —
  PEACHES and HERB
SHAKE YOUR HEAD — WAS (NOT WAS)
SHAKE YOUR LOVE — Debbie GIBSON
SHAKE YOUR RUMP TO THE FUNK —
  BAR-KAYS
SHAKE YOUR THANG (IT'S YOUR THING) —
  SALT-N-PEPA
SHAKERMAKER — OASIS
SHAKESPEARE'S SISTER — The SMITHS
SHAKESPEARE'S (WAY WITH) WORDS —
  ONE TRUE VOICE
SHAKIN' ALL OVER —
  Johnny KIDD and the PIRATES
SHAKIN' LIKE A LEAF — The STRANGLERS
THE SHAKIN' STEVENS EP — Shakin' STEVENS
SHAKING THE TREE —
  Youssou N'DOUR and Peter GABRIEL
SHAKTI (THE MEANING OF WITHIN) —
  MONSOON
SHAKALAKA BABY — Preeya KALIDAS
SHALALA LALA — The VENGABOYS
SHA-LA-LA (MAKE ME HAPPY) — Al GREEN
SHALL WE TAKE A TRIP — NORTHSIDE
SHAME [A] — Alan PRICE
SHAME [B] — Evelyn 'Champagne' KING
SHAME [B] — ALTERN 8
SHAME [B] — ZHANÉ
SHAME [B] — RUFF DRIVERZ

SHAME [C] —
  ORCHESTRAL MANOEUVRES IN THE DARK
SHAME [D] — EURYTHMICS
SHAME [E] — PJ HARVEY
SHAME AND SCANDAL IN THE FAMILY —
  Lance PERCIVAL
SHAME ON ME — Alexander O'NEAL
SHAME ON YOU — GUN
SHAME SHAME SHAME [A] — Jimmy REED
SHAME SHAME SHAME [B] —
  SHIRLEY and COMPANY
SHAME SHAME SHAME [B] — SINITTA
SHAMELESS — Garth BROOKS
SHAMROCKS AND SHENANIGANS —
  HOUSE OF PAIN
SHANG-A-LANG — BAY CITY ROLLERS
SHANGHAI'D IN SHANGHAI — NAZARETH
SHANGRI-LA — The RUTLES
SHANNON — Henry GROSS
SHANTE — MASS PRODUCTION
SHAPE — SUGABABES
SHAPE OF MY HEART [A] — STING
SHAPE OF MY HEART [B] — BACKSTREET BOYS
THE SHAPE OF THINGS TO COME —
  HEADBOYS
THE SHAPE YOU'RE IN — Eric CLAPTON
SHAPES OF THINGS — YARDBIRDS
SHAPES THAT GO TOGETHER — A-HA
SHARE MY LIFE — INNER CITY
SHARE THE FALL — Roni SIZE / REPRAZENT
SHARE THE NIGHT — WORLD PREMIERE
SHARE YOUR LOVE (NO DIGGITY) — PASSION
SHARING YOU — Bobby VEE
SHARK — THROWING MUSES
SHARP AS A KNIFE — Brandon COOKE
  featuring Roxanne SHANTE
SHARP DRESSED MAN — ZZ TOP
SHATTERED DREAMS — JOHNNY HATES JAZZ
SHATTERED GLASS — DTOX
SHAZAM! — Duane EDDY and the REBELS
SH-BOOM [A] — The CREW CUTS
SH-BOOM [A] — Stan FREBERG
SH-BOOM (LIFE COULD BE A DREAM) [A] —
  DARTS
SHE [A] — Charles AZNAVOUR
SHE [A] — Elvis COSTELLO
SHE [B] — VEGAS
SHE AIN'T WORTH IT — Glenn MEDEIROS
  featuring Bobby BROWN
SHE BANGS — Ricky MARTIN
SHE BANGS THE DRUMS — The STONE ROSES
SHE BELIEVES IN ME [A] — Kenny ROGERS
SHE BELIEVES (IN ME) [A] — Ronan KEATING
SHE BLINDED ME WITH SCIENCE —
  Thomas DOLBY
SHE BOP — Cyndi LAUPER
SHE CAME HOME FOR CHRISTMAS — MEW
SHE CAN ROCK IT — POWER STATION
SHE COMES FROM THE RAIN —
  WEATHER PROPHETS
SHE COMES IN THE FALL —
  INSPIRAL CARPETS
SHE CRIES YOUR NAME — Beth ORTON
SHE DON'T FOOL ME — STATUS QUO
SHE DON'T LET NOBODY —
  Chaka DEMUS and PLIERS
SHE DRIVES ME CRAZY —
  FINE YOUNG CANNIBALS
SHE DROVE ME TO DAYTIME TELEVISION —
  FUNERAL FOR A FRIEND
SHE GOT GAME — TYMES 4
SHE GOT SOUL — Jocelyn BROWN
SHE HATES ME — PUDDLE OF MUDD
SHE HITS ME — 4 OF US
SHE HOLDS THE KEY — SECRET LIFE
SHE IS BEAUTIFUL — Andrew W.K.
SHE IS LOVE — OASIS
SHE IS SUFFERING —
  MANIC STREET PREACHERS
SHE KISSED ME — Terence Trent D'ARBY
SHE KISSED ME (IT FELT LIKE A HIT) —
  SPIRITUALIZED
SHE KNOWS — BALAAM AND THE ANGEL
SHE LEFT ME ON FRIDAY — SHED SEVEN
SHE LOVED LIKE DIAMOND — SPANDAU BALLET
SHE LOVES ME NOT — PAPA ROACH
SHE LOVES YOU — The BEATLES
SHE MAKES MY DAY — Robert PALMER
SHE MAKES MY NOSE BLEED — MANSUN
SHE MEANS NOTHING TO ME —
  Phil EVERLY and Cliff RICHARD
SHE MOVES (LA LA LA) — KARAJA
SHE NEEDS LOVE —
  Wayne FONTANA and The MINDBENDERS
SHE SAID [A] — LONGPIGS
SHE SAID [B] — The PHARCYDE
SHE SAID [C] —
  Jon SPENCER BLUES EXPLOSION
SHE SELLS — BANDERAS
SHE SELLS SANCTUARY — The CULT
SHE SHE LITTLE SHEILA — Gene VINCENT
SHE SOLD ME MAGIC — Lou CHRISTIE
SHE TALKS TO ANGELS — BLACK CROWES
SHE TAUGHT ME HOW TO YODEL —
  FRANK IFIELD featuring the
  BACKROOM BOYS

SHE USED TO BE MINE — **SPIN DOCTORS**
SHE WANTS TO DANCE WITH ME — **Rick ASTLEY**
SHE WANTS TO MOVE — **N*E*R*D**
SHE WANTS YOU — **Billie PIPER**
SHE WAS HOT — **The ROLLING STONES**
SHE WEARS MY RING — **Solomon KING**
SHE WEARS RED FEATHERS — **Guy MITCHELL**
SHE WILL BE LOVED — **MAROON5**
SHE WILL HAVE HER WAY — **Neil FINN**
SHE WON'T TALK TO ME — **Luther VANDROSS**
SHE WORKS HARD FOR THE MONEY — **Donna SUMMER**
SHED A TEAR — **WET WET WET**
SHED MY SKIN — **D*NOTE**
SHE'D RATHER BE WITH ME — **The TURTLES**
SHEELA-NA-GIG — **P J HARVEY**
SHEENA IS A PUNK ROCKER — **The RAMONES**
SHEEP — **The HOUSEMARTINS**
THE SHEFFIELD GRINDER — **Tony CAPSTICK and the CARLTON MAIN / FRICKLEY COLLIERY BAND**
SHEFFIELD SONG — **SUPERNATURALS**
SHEILA — **Tommy ROE**
SHEILA TAKE A BOW — **The SMITHS**
SHELLSHOCK — **NEW ORDER**
SHELTER — **The BRAND NEW HEAVIES**
SHELTER ME [A] — **CINDERELLA**
SHELTER ME [B] — **CIRCUIT**
THE SHEPHERD'S SONG — **Tony OSBORNE SOUND**
SHERIFF FATMAN — **CARTER — THE UNSTOPPABLE SEX MACHINE**
SHERRI DON'T FAIL ME NOW — **STATUS QUO**
SHERRY [A] — **The FOUR SEASONS**
SHERRY [A] — **Adrian BAKER**
SHE'S A BAD MAMA JAMA (SHE'S BUILT, SHE'S STACKED) — **Carl CARLTON**
SHE'S A GIRL AND I'M A MAN — **Lloyd COLE**
SHE'S A GOOD GIRL — **SLEEPER**
SHE'S A GROOVY FREAK — **The REAL THING**
SHE'S A LADY — **Tom JONES**
SHE'S A LITTLE ANGEL — **LITTLE ANGELS**
SHE'S A MYSTERY TO ME — **Roy ORBISON**
SHE'S A RAINBOW — **WORLD OF TWIST**
SHE'S A RIVER — **SIMPLE MINDS**
SHE'S A STAR — **JAMES**
SHE'S A SUPERSTAR — **The VERVE**
SHE'S A VISION — **ALL EYES**
SHE'S A WIND UP — **DR FEELGOOD**
SHE'S A WOMAN — **SCRITTI POLITTI featuring Shabba RANKS**
SHE'S ABOUT A MOVER — **SIR DOUGLAS QUINTET**
SHE'S ALL ON MY MIND — **WET WET WET**
SHE'S ALRIGHT — **Bitty McLEAN**
SHE'S ALWAYS A WOMAN — **Billy JOEL**
SHE'S CRAFTY — **BEASTIE BOYS**
SHE'S EVERY WOMAN — **Garth BROOKS**
SHE'S GONE [A] — **Buddy KNOX**
SHE'S GONE [B] — **Daryl HALL and John OATES**
SHE'S GONE [B] — **Matthew MARSDEN featuring DESTINY'S CHILD**
SHE'S GONNA BREAK SOON — **LESS THAN JAKE**
SHE'S GONNA WIN — **BILBO**
SHE'S GOT CLAWS — **Gary NUMAN**
SHE'S GOT ISSUES — **The OFFSPRING**
SHE'S GOT IT — **LITTLE RICHARD**
SHE'S GOT ME GOING CRAZY — **2 IN A ROOM**
SHE'S GOT THAT VIBE — **R KELLY**
SHE'S GOT YOU — **Patsy CLINE**
SHE'S IN FASHION — **SUEDE**
SHE'S IN LOVE WITH YOU — **Suzi QUATRO**
SHE'S IN PARTIES — **BAUHAUS**
SHE'S LEAVING HOME — **Billy BRAGG with Cara TIVEY**
SHE'S LIKE THE WIND — **Patrick SWAYZE featuring Wendy FRASER**
SHE'S LOST YOU — **ZEPHYRS**
SHE'S MINE — **CAMEO**
SHE'S MY MACHINE — **David Lee ROTH**
SHE'S NEW TO YOU — **Susan MAUGHAN**
SHE'S NOT LEAVING — **The RESEARCH**
SHE'S NOT THERE [A] — **ZOMBIES**
SHE'S NOT THERE [A] — **Neil MacARTHUR**
SHE'S NOT THERE [A] — **SANTANA**
SHE'S NOT YOU — **Elvis PRESLEY with the JORDANAIRES**
SHE'S ON FIRE — **TRAIN**
SHE'S ON IT — **BEASTIE BOYS**
SHE'S OUT OF MY LIFE — **Michael JACKSON**
SHE'S PLAYING HARD TO GET — **HI-FIVE**
(SHE'S) SEXY AND 17 — **STRAY CATS**
SHE'S SO BEAUTIFUL — **Cliff RICHARD**
SHE'S SO COLD — **The ROLLING STONES**
SHE'S SO FINE — **THUNDER**
SHE'S SO HIGH [A] — **BLUR**
SHE'S SO HIGH [B] — **Tal BACHMAN**
SHE'S SO HIGH [B] — **Kurt NILSEN**
SHE'S SO MODERN — **The BOOMTOWN RATS**
SHE'S STRANGE — **CAMEO**
SHE'S THE MASTER OF THE GAME — **Richard Jon SMITH**
SHE'S THE ONE [A] — **James BROWN**
SHE'S THE ONE [B] — **Robbie WILLIAMS**

SHIFTING WHISPERING SANDS [A] — **Billy VAUGHN**
THE SHIFTING WHISPERING SANDS (PARTS 1 & 2) [A] — **Eamonn ANDREWS**
SHIMMY SHAKE — **740 BOYZ**
SHINDIG — **The SHADOWS**
SHINE [A] — **Joe BROWN and the BRUVVERS**
SHINE [B] — **MOTÖRHEAD**
SHINE [C] — **ASWAD**
SHINE [D] — **MOLLY HALF HEAD**
SHINE [E] — **SPACE BROTHERS**
SHINE [F] — **MONTROSE AVENUE**
SHINE [G] — **SLOWDIVE**
SHINE A LITTLE LOVE — **ELECTRIC LIGHT ORCHESTRA**
SHINE EYE — **RAGGA TWINS**
SHINE EYE GAL — **Shabba RANKS**
SHINE LIKE A STAR — **BERRI**
SHINE ON [A] — **HOUSE OF LOVE**
SHINE ON [B] — **DEGREES OF MOTION featuring BITI**
SHINE ON ME — **LOVESTATION**
SHINE ON SILVER SUN — **STRAWBS**
SHINE SO HARD (EP) — **ECHO and the BUNNYMEN**
SHINE (SOMEONE WHO NEEDS ME) — **MONACO**
SHINED ON ME — **PRAISE CATS**
SHINEON — **SCOTT & LEON**
SHINING [A] — **DOUBLE DEE**
SHINING [B] — **Kristian LEONTIOU**
SHINING LIGHT — **ASH**
SHINING ROAD — **CRANES**
SHINING STAR — **MANHATTANS**
SHINING STAR (EP) — **INXS**
SHINOBI VS DRAGON NINJA — **LOSTPROPHETS**
SHINY DISCO BALLS — **WHO DA FUNK featuring Jessica EVE**
SHINY HAPPY PEOPLE — **R.E.M.**
SHINY SHINY — **HAYSI FANTAYZEE**
SHIP AHOY — **MARXMAN**
SHIP OF FOOLS [A] — **WORLD PARTY**
SHIP OF FOOLS [B] — **ERASURE**
SHIPBUILDING [A] — **Robert WYATT**
SHIPBUILDING [A] — **Tasmin ARCHER**
SHIPS IN THE NIGHT — **BE BOP DELUXE**
SHIPS (WHERE WERE YOU) — **BIG COUNTRY**
SHIPWRECKED — **GENESIS**
SHIRALEE — **Tommy STEELE**
SHIRLEY — **Shakin' STEVENS**
SH!T ON YOU — **D12**
SHIVER [A] — **George BENSON**
SHIVER [B] — **S-J**
SHIVER [C] — **COLDPLAY**
SHIVERING SAND — **MEGA CITY FOUR**
SHO' YOU RIGHT — **Barry WHITE**
SHOCK THE MONKEY — **Peter GABRIEL**
SHOCK TO THE SYSTEM — **Billy IDOL**
SHOCK YOUR MAMA — **Debbie GIBSON**
SHOCKAHOLIC — **KINKY MACHINE**
SHOCKED — **Kylie MINOGUE**
SHOES — **REPARATA and the DELRONS**
SHOO BE DOO BE DOO DA DAY — **Stevie WONDER**
SHOO DOO FU FU OOH! — **Lenny WILLIAMS**
SHOOP — **SALT-N-PEPA**
THE SHOOP SHOOP SONG (IT'S IN HIS KISS) — **CHER**
SHOORAH! SHOORAH! — **Betty WRIGHT**
SHOOT ALL THE CLOWNS — **Bruce DICKINSON**
SHOOT ME (WITH YOUR LOVE) — **Tasha THOMAS**
SHOOT ME WITH YOUR LOVE — **D:REAM**
SHOOT SHOOT — **UFO**
SHOOT THE DOG — **George MICHAEL**
SHOOT YOUR GUN — **22-20S**
SHOOTING FROM MY HEART — **BIG BAM BOO**
SHOOTING FROM THE HEART — **Cliff RICHARD**
SHOOTING STAR [A] — **BOYZONE**
SHOOTING STAR [B] — **DOLLAR**
SHOOTING STAR [C] — **FLIP & FILL**
SHOOTING STAR [D] — **DEEPEST BLUE**
SHOPLIFTERS OF THE WORLD UNITE — **The SMITHS**
SHOPPING — **SUPERSISTER**
SHORLEY WALL — **OOBERMAN**
SHORT CUT TO SOMEWHERE — **FISH**
SHORT DICK MAN — **20 FINGERS**
SHORT FAT FANNIE — **Larry WILLIAMS**
SHORT SHORT MAN — **20 FINGERS**
SHORT SKIRT LONG JACKET — **CAKE**
SHORT'NIN' BREAD — **VISCOUNTS**
SHORT'NIN' BREAD ROCK — **Tony CROMBIE and his ROCKETS**
SHORTSHARPSHOCK (EP) — **THERAPY?**
SHORTY — **WANNADIES**
SHORTY (GOT HER EYES ON ME) — **Donell JONES**
SHORTY (YOU KEEP PLAYING WITH MY MIND) — **IMAJIN featuring Keith MURRAY**
SHOT BY BOTH SIDES — **MAGAZINE**
SHOT DOWN IN THE NIGHT — **HAWKWIND**
SHOT IN THE DARK [A] — **Ozzy OSBOURNE**
SHOT IN THE DARK [B] — **DJ HYPE**
SHOT OF POISON — **Lita FORD**
SHOT OF RHYTHM AND BLUES — **Johnny KIDD and the PIRATES**
SHOT SHOT — **GOMEZ**

SHOTGUN WEDDING [A] — **Roy C**
SHOTGUN WEDDING [A] — **Rod STEWART**
SHOULD I DO IT? — **POINTER SISTERS**
SHOULD I EVER (FALL IN LOVE) — **NIGHTCRAWLERS featuring John REID**
SHOULD I STAY — **GABRIELLE**
SHOULD I STAY OR SHOULD I GO — **The CLASH**
SHOULDER HOLSTER — **MORCHEEBA**
SHOULDN'T DO THAT — **KAJAGOOGOO**
SHOULD'VE KNOWN BETTER — **Richard MARX**
SHOUT [A] — **LULU**
SHOUT [A] — **Louchie LOU and Michie ONE**
SHOUT [B] — **TEARS FOR FEARS**
SHOUT [C] — **ANT & DEC**
SHOUT SHOUT (KNOCK YOURSELF OUT) — **Rocky SHARPE and the REPLAYS**
SHOUT TO THE TOP [A] — **STYLE COUNCIL**
SHOUT TO THE TOP [A] — **Fire ISLAND featuring Loleatta HOLLOWAY**
SHOUTING FOR THE GUNNERS — **ARSENAL FC**
THE SHOW [A] — **Doug E FRESH and the GET FRESH CREW**
THE SHOW [B] — **GIRLS ALOUD**
SHOW A LITTLE LOVE — **ULTIMATE KAOS**
SHOW ME [A] — **DEXY'S MIDNIGHT RUNNERS**
SHOW ME [B] — **Lindy LAYTON**
SHOW ME [C] — **Ultra NATÉ**
SHOW ME [D] — **Dana DAWSON**
SHOW ME A SIGN — **KONTAKT**
SHOW ME GIRL — **HERMAN'S HERMITS**
SHOW ME HEAVEN [A] — **Maria McKEE**
SHOW ME HEAVEN [A] — **Tina ARENA**
SHOW ME HEAVEN [A] — **CHIMIRA**
SHOW ME HEAVEN [A] — **SAINT featuring Suzanna DEE**
SHOW ME LOVE [A] — **Robin S**
SHOW ME LOVE [B] — **ROBYN**
SHOW ME LOVE [C] — **INDIEN**
SHOW ME MARY — **CATHERINE WHEEL**
SHOW ME THE MEANING OF BEING LONELY — **BACKSTREET BOYS**
SHOW ME THE MONEY — **ARCHITECHS**
SHOW ME THE WAY [A] — **Peter FRAMPTON**
SHOW ME THE WAY [B] — **OSMOND BOYS**
SHOW ME YOUR MONKEY — **PERCY FILTH**
SHOW ME YOUR SOUL — **Lenny KRAVITZ / P DIDDY / LOON / Pharrell WILLIAMS**
SHOW ME YOU'RE A WOMAN — **MUD**
THE SHOW MUST GO ON [A] — **Leo SAYER**
THE SHOW MUST GO ON [B] — **QUEEN**
THE SHOW (THEME FROM 'CONNIE') — **Rebecca STORM**
SHOW YOU THE WAY TO GO [A] — **The JACKSONS**
SHOW YOU THE WAY TO GO [A] — **Dannii MINOGUE**
SHOWDOWN [A] — **ELECTRIC LIGHT ORCHESTRA**
SHOWDOWN [B] — **Jody LEI**
SHOWER YOUR LOVE — **KULA SHAKER**
SHOWING OUT (GET FRESH AT THE WEEKEND) — **MEL and KIM**
SHOWROOM DUMMIES — **KRAFTWERK**
THE SHUFFLE — **Van McCOY**
SHUGGIE LOVE — **MONKEY BARS featuring Gabrielle WIDMAN**
SHUT 'EM DOWN — **PUBLIC ENEMY**
SHUT UP [A] — **MADNESS**
SHUT UP [B] — **Kelly OSBOURNE**
SHUT UP [C] — **BLACK EYED PEAS**
SHUT UP AND DANCE — **AEROSMITH**
SHUT UP AND FORGET ABOUT IT — **DANE**
SHUT UP AND KISS ME — **Mary-Chapin CARPENTER**
SHUT UP (AND SLEEP WITH ME) — **SIN WITH SEBASTIAN**
SHUT YOUR MOUTH [A] — **MADE IN LONDON**
SHUT YOUR MOUTH [B] — **GARBAGE**
SHUTDOWN — **PITCHSHIFTER**
SHY BOY — **BANANARAMA**
SHY GIRL — **Mark WYNTER**
SHY GUY [A] — **Diana KING**
SHY GUY [A] — **ASWAD**
(SI SI) JE SUIS UN ROCK STAR — **Bill WYMAN**
SI TU DOIS PARTIR — **FAIRPORT CONVENTION**
SIC TRANSIT GLORIA GLORY FADES — **BRAND NEW**
SICK AND TIRED [A] — **Fats DOMINO**
SICK AND TIRED [B] — **The CARDIGANS**
SICK AND TIRED [C] — **ANASTACIA**
SICK MAN BLUES — **The GOODIES**
SICK OF DRUGS — **The WILDHEARTS**
SICK OF GOODBYES — **SPARKLEHORSE**
SICK OF IT — **PRIMITIVES**
SIDE — **TRAVIS**
SIDE BY SIDE — **Kay STARR**
SIDE SADDLE — **Russ CONWAY**
THE SIDEBOARD SONG (GOT MY BEER IN THE SIDEBOARD HERE) — **CHAS and DAVE**
SIDESHOW [A] — **CHANTER SISTERS**
SIDESHOW [A] — **Barry BIGGS**
SIDEWALK TALK — **JELLYBEAN**
SIDEWALKING — **JESUS AND MARY CHAIN**
THE SIDEWINDER SLEEPS TONITE — **R.E.M.**
SIGHT FOR SORE EYES — **M PEOPLE**
THE SIGN — **ACE OF BASE**

SIGN 'O' THE TIMES — **PRINCE**
SIGN OF THE TIMES [A] — **Bryan FERRY**
SIGN OF THE TIMES [B] — **BELLE STARS**
SIGN OF THE TIMES [C] — **GRANDMASTER FLASH, Melle MEL and the FURIOUS FIVE**
A SIGN OF THE TIMES — **Petula CLARK**
SIGN YOUR NAME — **Terence Trent D'ARBY**
SIGNAL [A] — **JD aka 'DREADY'**
SIGNAL [B] — **FRESH BC**
SIGNALS OVER THE AIR — **THURSDAY**
THE SIGNATURE TUNE OF 'THE ARMY GAME' — **Michael MEDWIN, Bernard BRESSLAW, Alfie BASS and Leslie FYSON**
SIGNED SEALED DELIVERED I'M YOURS [A] — **Stevie WONDER**
SIGNED SEALED DELIVERED (I'M YOURS) [A] — **BOYSTOWN GANG**
SIGNED, SEALED, DELIVERED, I'M YOURS [A] — **BLUE featuring Stevie WONDER and Angie STONE**
SIGNS ... — **BLAMELESS**
SIGNS [A] — **TESLA**
SIGNS [B] — **DJ BADMARSH & SHRI featuring UK APACHE**
SILENCE [A] — **DELERIUM**
SILENCE 2004 [A] — **DELERIUM featuring Sarah McLACHLAN**
SILENCE [B] — **TAIKO**
SILENCE [C] — **GOMEZ**
THE SILENCE — **Mike KOGLIN**
SILENCE IS EASY — **STARSAILOR**
SILENCE IS GOLDEN — **The TREMELOES**
SILENCE WHEN YOU'RE BURNING — **HAPPYLIFE**
SILENT ALL THESE YEARS — **Tori AMOS**
SILENT LUCIDITY — **QUEENSRŸCHE**
SILENT NIGHT [A] — **Bing CROSBY**
SILENT NIGHT [A] — **The DICKIES**
SILENT NIGHT [A] — **BROS**
SILENT NIGHT [A] — **Sinead O'CONNOR**
SILENT NIGHT — SEVEN O'CLOCK NEWS [A] — **SIMON and GARFUNKEL**
SILENT RUNNING — **MIKE and the MECHANICS**
SILENT SCREAM — **Richard MARX**
SILENT SIGH — **BADLY DRAWN BOY**
SILENT TO THE DARK II — **The ELECTRIC SOFT PARADE**
SILENT VOICE — **INNOCENCE**
SILENT WORDS — **Jan JOHNSTON**
SILENTLY BAD MINDED — **PRESSURE DROP**
SILHOUETTES [A] — **HERMAN'S HERMITS**
SILHOUETTES [A] — **Cliff RICHARD**
SILK PYJAMAS — **Thomas DOLBY**
SILLY GAMES [A] — **Janet KAY**
SILLY GAMES [A] — **Lindy LAYTON featuring Janet KAY**
SILLY LOVE — **10cc**
SILLY LOVE SONGS — **Paul McCARTNEY**
SILLY THING — **The SEX PISTOLS**
SILVER [A] — **ECHO and the BUNNYMEN**
SILVER [B] — **MOIST**
SILVER [C] — **HUNDRED REASONS**
SILVER AND GOLD — **ASAP**
SILVER DREAM MACHINE (PART 1) — **David ESSEX**
SILVER LADY — **David SOUL**
SILVER LINING — **STIFF LITTLE FINGERS**
SILVER MACHINE — **HAWKWIND**
SILVER SCREEN SHOWER SCENE — **FELIX DA HOUSECAT**
SILVER SHADOW — **ATLANTIC STARR**
SILVER SHORTS — **WEDDING PRESENT**
SILVER STAR — **The FOUR SEASONS**
SILVER THUNDERBIRD — **Marc COHN**
SILVERMAC — **WESTWORLD**
SILVERY RAIN — **Cliff RICHARD**
SIMBA GROOVE — **HI POWER**
SIMON SAYS [A] — **Pharoahe MONCH**
SIMON SAYS [B] — **1910 FRUITGUM CO**
SIMON SMITH AND HIS AMAZING DANCING BEAR — **Alan PRICE**
SIMON TEMPLER — **SPLODGENESSABOUNDS**
SIMPLE AS THAT — **Huey LEWIS and the NEWS**
SIMPLE GAME — **The FOUR TOPS**
SIMPLE KIND OF LIFE — **NO DOUBT**
SIMPLE LIFE — **Elton JOHN**
SIMPLE SIMON (YOU GOTTA REGARD) — **MANTRONIX**
SIMPLE SINCERITY — **RADISH**
SIMPLE THINGS — **SAW DOCTORS**
THE SIMPLE THINGS — **Joe COCKER**
THE SIMPLE TRUTH (A CHILD IS BORN) — **Chris DE BURGH**
SIMPLY IRRESISTABLE — **Robert PALMER**
SIN — **NINE INCH NAILS**
SINBAD — **SYSTEM 7**
SINCE DAY ONE — **Teena MARIE**
SINCE I DON'T HAVE YOU [A] — **Art GARFUNKEL**
SINCE I DON'T HAVE YOU [A] — **GUNS N' ROSES**
SINCE I LEFT YOU — **The AVALANCHES**
SINCE I MET YOU BABY [A] — **Gary MOORE and BB KING**
SINCE I MET YOU BABY [B] — **UB40 and LADY SAW**

SINCE I TOLD YOU IT'S OVER —
STEREOPHONICS
SINCE YESTERDAY —
STRAWBERRY SWITCHBLADE
SINCE YOU'RE GONE — The CARS
SINCE YOU'VE BEEN GONE [A] —
Aretha FRANKLIN
SINCE YOU'VE BEEN GONE [B] — RAINBOW
SINCERE — MJ COLE
SINCERELY — The McGUIRE SISTERS
SINFUL — Pete WYLIE
SING — TRAVIS
SING A HAPPY SONG [A] — George McCRAE
SING A HAPPY SONG [B] — O'JAYS
SING A LITTLE SONG —
Desmond DEKKER and the ACES
SING-A-LONG [A] — A
SING-A-LONG [B] — SHANKS & BIGFOOT
SING A SONG — Byron STINGILY
SING A SONG (BREAK IT DOWN) —
MANTRONIX
SING A SONG OF FREEDOM — Cliff RICHARD
SING AND SHOUT — SECOND IMAGE
SING BABY SING — The STYLISTICS
SING DON'T SPEAK — BLACKFOOT SUE
SING FOR ABSOLUTION — MUSE
SING FOR EVER — ST PHILIPS CHOIR
SING FOR THE MOMENT — EMINEM
SING HALLELUJAH! — DR ALBAN
SING IT AGAIN WITH JOE —
Joe 'Mr Piano' HENDERSON
SING IT BACK — MOLOKO
SING IT (THE HALLELUJAH SONG) — MOZAIC
SING IT TO YOU (DEE-DOOB-DEE-DOO) —
Lavinia JONES
SING IT WITH JOE —
Joe 'Mr Piano' HENDERSON
SING LIKE AN ANGEL — Jerry LORDAN
SING LITTLE BIRDIE —
Pearl CARR and Teddy JOHNSON
SING ME — BROTHERS
SING ME AN OLD FASHIONED SONG —
Billie Jo SPEARS
SING (OOH-EE-OOH) — Vivienne McKONE
SING OUR OWN SONG — UB40
SING SING — GAZ
SING UP FOR THE CHAMPIONS —
REDS UNITED
SING YOUR LIFE — MORRISSEY
SINGALONG-A-SANTA — SANTA CLAUS
and the CHRISTMAS TREES
SINGALONG-A-SANTA AGAIN —
SANTA CLAUS and the CHRISTMAS TREES
THE SINGER SANG HIS SONG —
The BEE GEES
SINGIN' IN THE RAIN PART 1 —
Sheila B DEVOTION
THE SINGING DOGS (MEDLEY) —
SINGING DOGS
SINGING IN MY SLEEP — SEMISONIC
SINGING THE BLUES [A] — Guy MITCHELL
SINGING THE BLUES [A] —
Tommy STEELE and the STEELMEN
SINGING THE BLUES [A] — Dave EDMUNDS
SINGING THE BLUES [A] — Daniel O'DONNELL
SINGLE [A] — EVERYTHING BUT THE GIRL
SINGLE [B] — PET SHOP BOYS
SINGLE [C] — Natasha BEDINGFIELD
THE SINGLE — RISE
SINGLE AGAIN — FIERY FURNACES
SINGLE GIRL [A] — Sandy POSEY
SINGLE GIRL [B] — LUSH
SINGLE LIFE — CAMEO
THE SINGLES 1981-83 — BAUHAUS
SINK THE BISMARCK — Don LANG
SINK TO THE BOTTOM —
FOUNTAINS OF WAYNE
SINNER — Neil FINN
SINS OF THE FAMILY — PF SLOAN
SIPPIN' SODA — Guy MITCHELL
SIR DANCEALOT — OLYMPIC RUNNERS
SIR DUKE — Stevie WONDER
SIREN SOUNDS — Roni SIZE
SISSYNECK — BECK
SISTA SISTA — Beverley KNIGHT
SISTER [A] — BROS
SISTER [B] — SISTER 2 SISTER
SISTER DEW — dEUS
SISTER FRICTION — HAYSI FANTAYZEE
SISTER HAVANA — URGE OVERKILL
SISTER JANE — NEW WORLD
SISTER MOON — TRANSVISION VAMP
SISTER OF MERCY — THOMPSON TWINS
SISTER PAIN — ELECTRAFIXION
SISTER SAVIOUR — RAPTURE
SISTER SISTER — SISTER BLISS
SISTER SURPRISE — Gary NUMAN
THE SISTERS (EP) — PULP
SISTERS ARE DOIN' IT FOR THEMSELVES —
EURYTHMICS and Aretha FRANKLIN
SIT AND WAIT — Sydney YOUNGBLOOD
SIT DOWN — JAMES
SIT DOWN AND CRY — Errol DUNKLEY
THE SIT SONG — The BARRON KNIGHTS
SITTIN' ON A FENCE — TWICE AS MUCH
(SITTIN' ON) THE DOCK OF THE BAY —
Otis REDDING

SITTIN' UP IN MY ROOM — BRANDY
SITTING AT HOME — HONEYCRACK
SITTING DOWN HERE — Lene MARLIN
SITTING IN THE PARK — Georgie FAME
SITTING ON THE TOP OF THE WORLD —
LIVERPOOL FC
SITUATION — YAZOO
SIX — MANSUN
SIX DAYS — DJ SHADOW
SIX FEET DEEP (EP) — GRAVEDIGGAZ
643 (LOVE'S ON FIRE) —
DJ TIESTO featuring Suzanne PALMER
SIX MILLION STEPS (WEST RUNS SOUTH) —
Rahni HARRIS and F.L.O.
SIX PACK — The POLICE
THE SIX TEENS — The SWEET
634-5789 — Wilson PICKETT
SIXTEEN — MUSICAL YOUTH
SIXTEEN BARS — The STYLISTICS
SIXTEEN REASONS — Connie STEVENS
SIXTEEN TONS [A] — Frankie LAINE
SIXTEEN TONS [A] — Tennessee Ernie FORD
THE 6TH SENSE — COMMON
THE SIXTH SENSE —
VARIOUS ARTISTS (MONTAGES)
68 GUNS — The ALARM
SIXTY MILE SMILE — 3 COLOURS RED
60 MILES AN HOUR — NEW ORDER
SIXTY MINUTE MAN — The TRAMMPS
69 POLICE — David HOLMES
THE SIZE OF A COW — The WONDER STUFF
SKA — DJ ZINC
SKA TRAIN —
BEATMASTERS featuring Betty BOO
SKAT STRUT —
MC SKAT KAT and the STRAY MOB
SKATEAWAY — DIRE STRAITS
SK8ER BOI — Avril LAVIGNE
SKELETONS — Stevie WONDER
SKIFFLE SESSION (EP) — Lonnie DONEGAN
SKIING IN THE SNOW — WIGAN'S OVATION
SKIN — CHARLOTTE
SKIN DEEP [A] — Duke ELLINGTON
SKIN DEEP [A] — Ted HEATH
SKIN DEEP [B] — The STRANGLERS
THE SKIN GAME — Gary NUMAN
SKIN O' MY TEETH — MEGADETH
SKIN ON SKIN — GRACE
SKIN TRADE — DURAN DURAN
THE SKIN UP EP — SKIN
SKINHEAD MOONSTOMP — SYMARIP
SKIP A BEAT — Barrett WAUGH
SKIP TO MY LU — LISA LISA
SKUNK FUNK — GALLIANO
SKWEEZE ME PLEEZE ME — SLADE
SKY — SONIQUE
A SKY BLUE SHIRT AND A RAINBOW TIE —
Norman BROOKS
SKY HIGH [A] — JIGSAW
SKY HIGH [A] — NEWTON
SKY PILOT — The ANIMALS
SKY PLUS — NYLON MOON
SKYDIVE — FREEFALL featuring Jan JOHNSTON
THE SKYE BOAT SONG —
Roger WHITTAKER and Des O'CONNOR
SKYLARK — Michael HOLLIDAY
SKY'S THE LIMIT — NOTORIOUS B.I.G.
SKYWRITER — The JACKSON FIVE
SLADE — ALIVE AT READING (EP) — SLADE
SLAIN BY ELF — URUSEI YATSURA
SLAIN THE TRUTH (AT THE ROADHOUSE) —
The BASEMENT
SLAM [A] — HUMANOID
SLAM [B] — ONYX
SLAM DUNK (DA FUNK) — FIVE
SLAM JAM — WWF SUPERSTARS
SLANG — DEF LEPPARD
SLAP AND TICKLE — SQUEEZE
SLASH 'N' BURN —
MANIC STREET PREACHERS
SLASHDOTDASH — FATBOY SLIM
SLAVE NEW WORLD — SEPULTURA
SLAVE TO LOVE — Bryan FERRY
SLAVE TO THE GRIND — SKID ROW
SLAVE TO THE RHYTHM — Grace JONES
SLAVE TO THE VIBE — AFTERSHOCK
SLAVE TO THE WAGE — PLACEBO
SLAVES NO MORE — The BLOW MONKEYS
SLEAZY BED TRACK — The BLUETONES
SLEDGEHAMMER — Peter GABRIEL
SLEDGER — PORN KINGS
SLEEP [A] — MARION
SLEEP [B] — CONJURE ONE
SLEEP ALONE — The WONDER STUFF
SLEEP FREAK — HEAVY STEREO
SLEEP NOW IN THE FIRE —
RAGE AGAINST THE MACHINE
SLEEP ON THE LEFT SIDE — CORNERSHOP
SLEEP TALK — Alyson WILLIAMS
SLEEP TALK — A.T.F.C. featuring Lisa Millett
SLEEP WALK — SANTO and JOHNNY
SLEEP WELL TONIGHT — GENE
SLEEP WITH ME — BIRDLAND
SLEEPER — AUDIOWEB
SLEEPING AWAKE — P.O.D.
SLEEPING BAG — ZZ TOP

SLEEPING IN — MENSWEAR
SLEEPING IN MY CAR — ROXETTE
SLEEPING ON THE JOB — GILLAN
SLEEPING SATELLITE — Tasmin ARCHER
SLEEPING WITH THE LIGHT — BUSTED
SLEEPING WITH THE LIGHTS ON —
Curtis STIGERS
SLEEPING WITH VICTOR — Lynden David HALL
SLEEPWALK — ULTRAVOX
SLEEPY JOE — HERMAN'S HERMITS
SLEEPY SHORES — Johnny PEARSON
SLEIGH RIDE — S CLUB JUNIORS
SLICE OF DA PIE — Monie LOVE
SLID — FLUKE
SLIDE [A] — RAH BAND
SLIDE [B] — GOO GOO DOLLS
SLIDE ALONG SIDE — SHIFTY
SLIDING — Ian McCULLOCH
SLIGHT RETURN — The BLUETONES
THE SLIGHTEST TOUCH — FIVE STAR
SLIP AND DIP — COFFEE
SLIP AND SLIDE — MEDICINE HEAD
(SLIP & SLIDE) SUICIDE — KOSHEEN
SLIP SLIDIN' AWAY — Paul SIMON
SLIP YOUR DISC TO THIS — HEATWAVE
SLIPPERY PEOPLE — TALKING HEADS
SLIPPIN' — DMX
SLIPPING AWAY [A] — Dave EDMUNDS
SLIPPING AWAY [B] — MANSUN
SLITHER — VELVET REVOLVER
SLOOP JOHN B — The BEACH BOYS
SLOPPY HEART — FRAZIER CHORUS
SLOW — KYLIE
SLOW AND SEXY —
Shabba RANKS featuring Johnny GILL
SLOW DOWN [A] — John MILES
SLOW DOWN [B] — LOOSE ENDS
SLOW EMOTION REPLAY — The THE
SLOW FLOW — The BRAXTONS
SLOW HANDS — INTERPOL
SLOW IT DOWN — EAST 17
SLOW JAMZ — TWISTA
SLOW MOTION — ULTRAVOX
SLOW RIVERS —
Elton JOHN and Cliff RICHARD
SLOW TRAIN TO DAWN — The THE
SLOW TRAIN TO PARADISE — TAVARES
SLOW TWISTIN' — Chubby CHECKER
SLOWDIVE — SIOUXSIE and the BANSHEES
SLOWHAND — POINTER SISTERS
SLY — MASSIVE ATTACK
SMACK MY BITCH UP — The PRODIGY
SMALL ADS — SMALL ADS
SMALL BIT OF LOVE — SAW DOCTORS
SMALL BLUE THING — Suzanne VEGA
SMALL SAD SAM — Phil McLEAN
SMALL TOWN — John Cougar MELLENCAMP
SMALL TOWN BOY — UK
A SMALL VICTORY — FAITH NO MORE
SMALLTOWN BOY — BRONSKI BEAT
SMALLTOWN CREED — KANE GANG
SMARTY PANTS — FIRST CHOICE
SMASH IT UP — The DAMNED
SMASH SUMTHIN' —
REDMAN featuring Adam F
S.M.D.U. — BROCK LANDARS
SMELLS LIKE NIRVANA — Weird Al YANKOVIC
SMELLS LIKE TEEN SPIRIT [A] — NIRVANA
SMELLS LIKE TEEN SPIRIT [A] — ABIGAIL
SMILE [A] — Nat 'King' COLE
SMILE [A] — Robert DOWNEY Jr
SMILE [B] — PUSSYCAT
SMILE [C] — Audrey HALL
SMILE [D] — ASWAD
SMILE [E] — SUPERNATURALS
SMILE [F] — LONESTAR
SMILE [G] — FUTURE BREEZE
SMILE [H] — MONROE
THE SMILE — David ESSEX
A SMILE IN A WHISPER —
FAIRGROUND ATTRACTION
SMILER — HEAVY STEREO
SMOKE — Natalie IMBRUGLIA
SMOKE GETS IN YOUR EYES [A] —
The PLATTERS
SMOKE GETS IN YOUR EYES [A] — BLUE HAZE
SMOKE GETS IN YOUR EYES [A] —
Bryan FERRY
SMOKE GETS IN YOUR EYES [A] —
John ALFORD
SMOKE MACHINE — X-PRESS 2
SMOKE ON THE WATER [A] — DEEP PURPLE
SMOKE ON THE WATER [A] —
ROCK AID ARMENIA
SMOKEBELCH II — SABRES OF PARADISE
SMOKESTACK LIGHTNIN' — HOWLIN' WOLF
SMOKEY BLUE'S AWAY —
A NEW GENERATION
SMOKIN' IN THE BOYS' ROOM [A] —
BROWNSVILLE STATION
SMOKIN' IN THE BOYS ROOM [A] —
MÖTLEY CRÜE
SMOKIN' ME OUT — Warren G
SMOOTH — SANTANA
SMOOTH CRIMINAL [A] — Michael JACKSON
SMOOTH CRIMINAL [A] — ALIEN ANT FARM
SMOOTH OPERATOR [A] — SADE

SMOOTH OPERATOR [B] — BIG DADDY KANE
SMOOTHIN' GROOVIN' — INGRAM
SMOULDER — KING ADORA
SMUGGLER'S BLUES — Glenn FREY
THE SMURF — Tyrone BRUNSON
THE SMURF SONG — The SMURFS
SNAKE — R KELLY featuring BIG TIGGER
THE SNAKE — Al WILSON
SNAKE BITE [P] — WHITESNAKE
SNAKE IN THE GRASS —
Dave DEE, DOZY, BEAKY, MICK and TICH
SNAP! MEGAMIX — SNAP!
SNAP YOUR FINGAZ — KUMARA
SNAPPED IT — KRUST
SNAPPINESS — BBG
SNAPSHOT 3 — Roni SIZE
SNEAKIN' SUSPICION — DR FEELGOOD
SNEAKING OUT THE BACK DOOR —
MATT BIANCO
SNOBBERY AND DECAY — ACT
SNOOKER LOOPY — CHAS and DAVE
SNOOP DOGG — SNOOP DOGGY DOGG
SNOOP'S UPSIDE YA HEAD —
SNOOP DOGGY DOGG featuring
Charlie WILSON
SNOOPY VS THE RED BARON [A] — HOTSHOTS
SNOOPY VS THE RED BARON [A] —
ROYAL GUARDSMEN
SNOT RAP — Kenny EVERETT
SNOW [A] — ORN
SNOW [B] — JJ72
SNOW COACH — Russ CONWAY
SNOWBIRD — Anne MURRAY
SNOWBOUND FOR CHRISTMAS —
Dickie VALENTINE
THE SNOWS OF NEW YORK — Chris DE BURGH
SO ALIVE — Ryan ADAMS
SO AMAZING — Luther VANDROSS
SO BEAUTIFUL [A] —
URBAN COOKIE COLLECTIVE
SO BEAUTIFUL [B] — Chris DE BURGH
SO BEAUTIFUL [C] —
DJ INNOCENCE featuring ALEX CHARLES
SO CALLED FRIEND — TEXAS
SO CLOSE [A] — Diana ROSS
SO CLOSE [B] — Daryl HALL and John OATES
SO CLOSE [C] — Dina CARROLL
SO CLOSE TO LOVE — Wendy MOTEN
SO COLD THE NIGHT — COMMUNARDS
SO CONFUSED —
2PLAY featuring RAGHAV & JUCXI
SO DAMN BEAUTIFUL — POLOROID
SO DAMN COOL — UGLY KID JOE
SO DEEP — REESE PROJECT
SO DEEP IS THE NIGHT — Ken DODD
SO DO I — Kenny BALL and his JAZZMEN
SO EASY — RÖYKSOPP
SO EMOTIONAL — Whitney HOUSTON
SO FAR AWAY — DIRE STRAITS
SO FINE [A] — Howard JOHNSON
SO FINE [B] — KINANE
SO FRESH, SO CLEAN — OUTKAST
SO GOOD [A] — Roy ORBISON
SO GOOD [B] — ETERNAL
SO GOOD [C] — BOYZONE
SO GOOD [D] — Juliet ROBERTS
SO GOOD SO RIGHT — Brenda RUSSELL
SO GOOD TO BE BACK HOME AGAIN —
TOURISTS
SO GOOD (TO COME HOME TO) —
Ivan MATIAS
SO GRIMEY — SO SOLID CREW
SO GROOVY — Wendell WILLIAMS
SO HARD — PET SHOP BOYS
SO HELP ME GIRL — Gary BARLOW
SO HERE I AM — UB40
SO HOT — JC
SO I BEGIN — GALLEON
SO IN LOVE —
ORCHESTRAL MANOEUVRES IN THE DARK
SO IN LOVE (THE REAL DEAL) — Judy CHEEKS
SO IN LOVE WITH YOU [A] — Freddy BRECK
SO IN LOVE WITH YOU [B] —
SPEAR OF DESTINY
SO IN LOVE WITH YOU [C] — TEXAS
SO IN LOVE WITH YOU [D] — DUKE
SO INTO YOU [A] — Michael WATFORD
SO INTO YOU [B] — The WILDHEARTS
SO IT WILL ALWAYS BE — The EVERLY BROTHERS
SO LET ME GO FAR — DODGY
SO LITTLE TIME — ARKARNA
SO LONELY [A] — The POLICE
SO LONELY [B] — JAKATTA
SO LONG [A] — FISCHER-Z
SO LONG [B] — FIERCE
SO LONG BABY — Del SHANNON
SO LOW — OCEAN COLOUR SCENE
SO MACHO — SINITTA
SO MANY WAYS [A] — The BRAXTONS
SO MANY WAYS [B] — Ellie CAMPBELL
SO MUCH IN LOVE [A] — TYMES
SO MUCH IN LOVE [A] — ALL-4-ONE
SO MUCH IN LOVE [B] — MIGHTY AVENGERS
SO MUCH LOVE — Tony BLACKBURN
SO MUCH LOVE TO GIVE — TOGETHER
SO MUCH TROUBLE IN THE WORLD —
Bob MARLEY & the WAILERS

SO NATURAL – Lisa STANSFIELD
SO NEAR TO CHRISTMAS – Alvin STARDUST
SO PURE [A] – BABY D
SO PURE [B] – Alanis MORISSETTE
SO REAL [A] – LOVE DECADE
SO REAL [B] – HARRY
SO RIGHT [A] – RAILWAY CHILDREN
SO RIGHT [B] – K-KLASS
SO ROTTEN – BLAK TWANG featuring JAHMALI
SO SAD THE SONG – Gladys KNIGHT and the PIPS
SO SAD (TO WATCH GOOD LOVE GO BAD) – The EVERLY BROTHERS
SO SAYS I – The SHINS
SO SEXY – TWISTA featuring R KELLY
SO SORRY I SAID – Liza MINNELLI
SO STRONG – Ben SHAW featuring Adele HOLNESS
SO TELL ME WHY – POISON
SO THE STORY GOES – LIVING IN A BOX featuring Bobby WOMACK
SO THIS IS ROMANCE – LINX
SO TIRED [A] – Frankie VAUGHAN
SO TIRED [B] – Ozzy OSBOURNE
SO TIRED OF BEING ALONE – SYBIL
SO WHATCHA GONNA DO NOW – PUBLIC ENEMY
SO WHAT – Gilbert O'SULLIVAN
SO WHAT! – Ronny JORDAN
SO WHAT IF I – DAMAGE
SO WHY SO SAD – MANIC STREET PREACHERS
SO YESTERDAY – Hilary DUFF
SO YOU WIN AGAIN – HOT CHOCOLATE
SO YOU'D LIKE TO SAVE THE WORLD – Lloyd COLE
SO YOUNG [A] – SUEDE
SO YOUNG [B] – The CORRS
SOAK UP THE SUN – Sheryl CROW
SOAPBOX – LITTLE ANGELS
SOBER [A] – DRUGSTORE
SOBER [B] – Jennifer PAIGE
SOC IT TO ME – BADFELLAS featuring CK
SOCKIT2ME – Missy 'Misdemeanor' ELLIOTT featuring DA BRAT
SODA POP – MERRION, McCALL & KENSIT
SOFT AS YOUR FACE – SOUP DRAGONS
SOFT LIKE ME – SAINT ETIENNE
SOFT TOP HARD SHOULDER – Chris REA
SOFTLY AS I LEAVE YOU – Matt MONRO
SOFTLY, SOFTLY [A] – Ruby MURRAY
SOFTLY SOFTLY [B] – The EQUALS
SOFTLY WHISPERING I LOVE YOU [A] – CONGREGATION
SOFTLY WHISPERING I LOVE YOU [A] – Paul YOUNG
SOLACE OF YOU – LIVING COLOUR
SOLD – BOY GEORGE
SOLD ME DOWN THE RIVER – The ALARM
SOLD MY ROCK 'N' ROLL (GAVE IT FOR FUNKY SOUL) – Linda CARR
SOLD OUT (EP) – REEL BIG FISH
SOLDIER BLUE – Buffy SAINTE-MARIE
SOLDIER BOY [A] – SHIRELLES
SOLDIER BOY [A] – CHEETAHS
SOLDIER GIRL – The POLYPHONIC SPREE
SOLDIER OF LOVE – Donny OSMOND
SOLDIER'S SONG – The HOLLIES
SOLEX (CLOSE TO THE EDGE) – Michael WOODS
SOLEY SOLEY – MIDDLE OF THE ROAD
SOLID – ASHFORD and SIMPSON
SOLID BOND IN YOUR HEART – STYLE COUNCIL
SOLID GOLD EASY ACTION – T. REX
SOLID ROCK (LIVE) – DIRE STRAITS
SOLID WOOD – Alison MOYET
SOLITAIRE [A] – Andy WILLIAMS
SOLITAIRE [A] – The CARPENTERS
SOLITARY MAN – HIM
SOLOMON BITES THE WORM – The BLUETONES
SOLSBURY HILL [A] – Peter GABRIEL
SOLSBURY HILL [A] – ERASURE
(SOLUTION TO) THE PROBLEM – MASQUERADE
SOLVED – UNBELIEVABLE TRUTH
SOME BEAUTIFUL – Jack WILD
SOME CANDY TALKING – JESUS AND MARY CHAIN
SOME FANTASTIC PLACE – SQUEEZE
SOME FINER DAY – ALL ABOUT EVE
SOME GIRLS [A] – RACEY
SOME GIRLS [B] – ULTIMATE KAOS
SOME GIRLS [C] – Rachel STEVENS
SOME GIRLS (DANCE WITH WOMEN) – JC CHASEZ
SOME GUYS HAVE ALL THE LUCK [A] – Robert PALMER
SOME GUYS HAVE ALL THE LUCK [A] – Rod STEWART
SOME GUYS HAVE ALL THE LUCK [A] – Maxi PRIEST
SOME JUSTICE – URBAN SHAKEDOWN
SOME KIND OF A SUMMER – David CASSIDY
SOME KIND OF BLISS – Kylie MINOGUE
SOME KIND OF FRIEND – Barry MANILOW
SOME KIND OF HEAVEN – BBG
SOME KIND OF WONDERFUL – The BLOW MONKEYS
SOME KINDA EARTHQUAKE – Duane EDDY and the REBELS
SOME KINDA FUN – Chris MONTEZ
SOME LIE 4 LOVE – L.A. GUNS
SOME LIKE IT HOT – POWER STATION
SOME MIGHT SAY [A] – OASIS
SOME MIGHT SAY [A] – DE-CODE featuring Beverli SKEETE
SOME MIGHT SAY [A] – SUPERNOVA
SOME OF YOUR LOVIN' – Dusty SPRINGFIELD
SOME OLD GIRL – PADDINGTONS
SOME OTHER GUY – BIG THREE
SOME OTHER SUCKER'S PARADE – DEL AMITRI
SOME PEOPLE [A] – Carol DEENE
SOME PEOPLE [B] – BELOUIS SOME
SOME PEOPLE [C] – Paul YOUNG
SOME PEOPLE [D] – Cliff RICHARD
SOME PEOPLE SAY – TERRORVISION
SOME SAY – Kristian LEONTIOU
SOME THINGS YOU NEVER GET USED TO – Diana ROSS and The SUPREMES
SOME VELVET MORNING – PRIMAL SCREAM & Kate MOSS
SOMEBODY [A] – The STARGAZERS
SOMEBODY [B] – JUNIOR
SOMEBODY [C] – DEPECHE MODE
SOMEBODY [D] – Bryan ADAMS
SOMEBODY [E] – BRILLIANT
SOMEBODY [F] – SHORTIE vs BLACK LEGEND
SOMEBODY ELSE'S GIRL – Billy FURY
SOMEBODY ELSE'S GUY [A] – Ce Ce PENISTON
SOMEBODY ELSE'S GUY [A] – Jocelyn BROWN
SOMEBODY ELSE'S GUY [A] – Louchie LOU and Michie ONE
SOMEBODY HELP ME – Spencer DAVIS GROUP
(SOMEBODY) HELP ME OUT – BEGGAR and CO
SOMEBODY IN THE HOUSE SAY YEAH! – 2 IN A ROOM
SOMEBODY LIKE YOU – ELATE
SOMEBODY LOVES YOU – Nik KERSHAW
SOMEBODY PUT SOMETHING IN MY DRINK – The RAMONES
SOMEBODY STOLE MY GAL – Johnnie RAY
SOMEBODY TO LOVE [A] – Brad NEWMAN
SOMEBODY TO LOVE [A] – JETS
SOMEBODY TO LOVE [B] – QUEEN
SOMEBODY TO LOVE [C] – BOOGIE PIMPS
SOMEBODY TO SHOVE – SOUL ASYLUM
SOMEBODY TOLD ME – The KILLERS
SOMEBODY'S BABY – Pat BENATAR
SOMEBODY'S WATCHING ME – ROCKWELL
SOMEDAY [A] – Ricky NELSON
SOMEDAY [B] – GAP BAND
SOMEDAY [C] – GLASS TIGER
SOMEDAY [D] – Mariah CAREY
SOMEDAY [D] – REZONANCE Q
SOMEDAY [E] – M PEOPLE
SOMEDAY [F] – EDDY
SOMEDAY [G] – LOVE TO INFINITY
SOMEDAY [H] – ETERNAL
SOMEDAY [I] – CHARLOTTE
SOMEDAY [J] – The STROKES
SOMEDAY [K] – NICKELBACK
SOMEDAY I'LL BE SATURDAY NIGHT – BON JOVI
SOMEDAY I'LL FIND YOU – Shola AMA and Craig ARMSTRONG / The DIVINE COMEDY
SOMEDAY (I'M COMING BACK) – Lisa STANSFIELD
SOMEDAY MAN – The MONKEES
SOMEDAY ONE DAY – The SEEKERS
SOMEDAY WE'LL BE TOGETHER – Diana ROSS and The SUPREMES
SOMEDAY WE'LL KNOW – NEW RADICALS
SOMEDAY WE'RE GONNA LOVE AGAIN – The SEARCHERS
SOMEDAY (YOU'LL BE SORRY) – Kenny BALL and his JAZZMEN
SOMEDAY (YOU'LL COME RUNNING) – FM
SOMEDAY (YOU'LL WANT ME TO WANT YOU) – Jodie SANDS
SOMEHOW SOMEWHERE – DEEP SENSATION
SOMEONE [A] – Johnny MATHIS
SOMEONE [B] – ASCENSION
SOMEONE [C] – SWV featuring Puff DADDY
SOMEONE ALWAYS GETS THERE FIRST – BENNET
SOMEONE BELONGING TO SOMEONE – The BEE GEES
SOMEONE ELSE NOT ME – DURAN DURAN
SOMEONE ELSE'S BABY – Adam FAITH
SOMEONE ELSE'S ROSES – Joan REGAN
SOMEONE LIKE ME – ATOMIC KITTEN
SOMEONE LIKE YOU [A] – Dina CARROLL
SOMEONE LIKE YOU [B] – Russell WATSON and Faye TOZER
SOMEONE LOVES YOU HONEY – Lutricia McNEAL
SOMEONE MUST HAVE HURT YOU A LOT – Frankie VAUGHAN
SOMEONE ON YOUR MIND – Jimmy YOUNG
SOMEONE SAVED MY LIFE TONIGHT – Elton JOHN
SOMEONE SHOULD TELL HER – MAVERICKS
SOMEONE SOMEONE – Brian POOLE and the TREMELOES
SOMEONE SOMEWHERE – WANNADIES
SOMEONE SOMEWHERE (IN SUMMERTIME) – SIMPLE MINDS
SOMEONE THERE FOR ME – Richard BLACKWOOD
SOMEONE TO CALL MY LOVER – JANET
SOMEONE TO HOLD – Trey LORENZ
SOMEONE TO LOVE [A] – Sean MAGUIRE
SOMEONE TO LOVE [B] – EAST 17
SOMEONE TO SOMEBODY – Feargal SHARKEY
SOMEONE'S DAUGHTER – Beth ORTON
SOMEONE'S LOOKING AT YOU – The BOOMTOWN RATS
SOMEONE'S TAKEN MARIA AWAY – Adam FAITH
SOMERSAULT – ZERO 7 featuring SIA
SOMETHIN' ELSE – Eddie COCHRAN
SOMETHIN' 4 DA HONEYZ – Montell JORDAN
SOMETHIN' IS GOIN' ON – Cliff RICHARD
SOMETHIN' STUPID [A] – Nancy SINATRA and Frank SINATRA
SOMETHIN' STUPID [A] – Ali CAMPBELL
SOMETHING STUPID [A] – Amanda BARRIE and Johnny BRIGGS
SOMETHIN' STUPID [A] – Robbie WILLIAMS and Nicole KIDMAN
SOMETHING [A] – Georgie FAME
SOMETHING [B] – The BEATLES
SOMETHING [B] – Shirley BASSEY
SOMETHING [C] – LASGO
SOMETHING ABOUT THE MUSIC – DA SLAMMIN' PHROGZ
SOMETHING ABOUT THE WAY YOU LOOK TONIGHT – Elton JOHN
SOMETHING ABOUT U (CAN'T BE BEAT) – MR ROY
SOMETHING ABOUT YOU [A] – LEVEL 42
SOMETHING ABOUT YOU [B] – MR ROY
SOMETHING ABOUT YOU [C] – NEW EDITION
SOMETHING BEAUTIFUL – Robbie WILLIAMS
SOMETHING BEAUTIFUL REMAINS – Tina TURNER
SOMETHING BETTER BEGINNING – HONEYCOMBS
SOMETHING BETTER CHANGE – The STRANGLERS
SOMETHING 'BOUT YOU BABY I LIKE [A] – Tom JONES
SOMETHING 'BOUT YOU BABY I LIKE [A] – STATUS QUO
SOMETHING CHANGED – PULP
SOMETHING DEEP INSIDE – Billie PIPER
SOMETHING DIFFERENT – SHAGGY
SOMETHING ELSE [A] – The SEX PISTOLS
SOMETHING ELSE [B] – AGENT BLUE
SOMETHING FOR THE GIRL WITH EVERYTHING – SPARKS
SOMETHING FOR THE PAIN – BON JOVI
SOMETHING FOR THE WEEKEND [A] – The DIVINE COMEDY
SOMETHING FOR THE WEEKEND [B] – FRED & ROXY
SOMETHING 4 THE WEEKEND [C] – SUPER FURRY ANIMALS
SOMETHING GOIN' ON – Todd TERRY featuring Martha WASH and Jocelyn BROWN
SOMETHING GOOD – UTAH SAINTS
SOMETHING GOT ME STARTED – SIMPLY RED
SOMETHING HAPPENED ON THE WAY TO HEAVEN – Phil COLLINS
SOMETHING HERE IN MY HEART (KEEPS A-TELLIN' ME NO) – PAPER DOLLS
SOMETHING IN COMMON – Bobby BROWN and Whitney HOUSTON
SOMETHING IN MY HOUSE – DEAD OR ALIVE
SOMETHING IN THE AIR [A] – THUNDERCLAP NEWMAN
SOMETHING IN THE AIR [A] – FISH
SOMETHING IN THE AIR [A] – Tom PETTY and the HEARTBREAKERS
SOMETHING IN YOUR EYES [A] – BELL BIV DEVOE
SOMETHING IN YOUR EYES [B] – Ed CASE
(SOMETHING INSIDE) SO STRONG [A] – Labi SIFFRE
(SOMETHING INSIDE) SO STRONG [A] – Michael BALL
(SOMETHING INSIDE) SO STRONG [A] – Rik WALLER
SOMETHING JUST AIN'T RIGHT – Keith SWEAT
SOMETHING MISSING – Petula CLARK
SOMETHING OLD, SOMETHING NEW – FANTASTICS
SOMETHING ON MY MIND – Chris ANDREWS
SOMETHING OUTA NOTHING – Letitia DEAN and Paul MEDFORD
SOMETHING SO GOOD – RAILWAY CHILDREN
SOMETHING SO REAL (CHINHEADS THEME) – LOVE DECREE
SOMETHING SO RIGHT – Annie LENNOX featuring Paul SIMON
SOMETHING SPECIAL [A] – Steve HARVEY
SOMETHING SPECIAL [B] – NOMAD
SOMETHING TELLS ME (SOMETHING IS GONNA HAPPEN TONIGHT) – Cilla BLACK
SOMETHING THAT I SAID – RUTS
SOMETHING THAT YOU SAID – The BANGLES
SOMETHING TO BELIEVE IN [A] – POISON
SOMETHING TO BELIEVE IN [B] – The RAMONES
SOMETHING TO DO – DEPECHE MODE
SOMETHING TO MISS – SENSELESS THINGS
SOMETHING WILD – RARE
SOMETHING WORTHWHILE – GUN
SOMETHING YOU GOT – AND WHY NOT?
SOMETHING'S BEEN MAKING ME BLUE – SMOKIE
SOMETHING'S BURNING – Kenny ROGERS
SOMETHING'S COOKIN' IN THE KITCHEN – DANA
SOMETHING'S GOIN' ON [A] – MYSTIC 3
SOMETHING'S GOING ON [B] – A
SOMETHING'S GOTTA GIVE – Sammy DAVIS Jr
SOMETHING'S GOTTEN HOLD OF MY HEART [A] – Gene PITNEY
SOMETHING'S GOTTEN HOLD OF MY HEART [A] – Marc ALMOND featuring special guest star Gene PITNEY
SOMETHING'S HAPPENING – HERMAN'S HERMITS
SOMETHING'S JUMPIN' IN YOUR SHIRT – Malcolm McLAREN
SOMETHING'S MISSING – CHORDS
SOMETIMES [A] – ERASURE
SOMETIMES [B] – MAX Q
SOMETIMES [C] – JAMES
SOMETIMES [D] – The BRAND NEW HEAVIES
SOMETIMES [E] – TIN TIN OUT
SOMETIMES [F] – LES RYTHMES DIGITALES featuring Nik KERSHAW
SOMETIMES [G] – Britney SPEARS
SOMETIMES [H] – ASH
SOMETIMES ALWAYS – JESUS AND MARY CHAIN
SOMETIMES I MISS YOU SO MUCH – PM DAWN
SOMETIMES IT HURTS – TINDERSTICKS
SOMETIMES IT SNOWS IN APRIL – AMAR
SOMETIMES IT'S A BITCH – Stevie NICKS
SOMETIMES LOVE JUST AIN'T ENOUGH – Don HENLEY
SOMETIMES (THEME FROM 'CHAMPIONS') – Elaine PAIGE
SOMETIMES WHEN WE TOUCH [A] – Dan HILL
SOMETIMES WHEN WE TOUCH [A] – NEWTON
SOMEWHERE [A] – PJ PROBY
SOMEWHERE [A] – PET SHOP BOYS
SOMEWHERE [B] – EFUA
SOMEWHERE ACROSS FOREVER – STELLASTARR*
SOMEWHERE ALONG THE WAY – Nat 'King' COLE
SOMEWHERE DOWN THE CRAZY RIVER – Robbie ROBERTSON
SOMEWHERE ELSE – CHINA DRUM
SOMEWHERE I BELONG – LINKIN PARK
SOMEWHERE IN AMERICA (THERE'S A STREET NAMED AFTER MY DAD) – WAS (NOT WAS)
SOMEWHERE IN MY HEART – AZTEC CAMERA
SOMEWHERE IN THE COUNTRY – Gene PITNEY
SOMEWHERE IN THE NIGHT – Barry MANILOW
SOMEWHERE MY LOVE [A] – MANUEL and his MUSIC OF THE MOUNTAINS
SOMEWHERE MY LOVE [A] – Mike SAMMES SINGERS
SOMEWHERE ONLY WE KNOW – KEANE
SOMEWHERE OUT THERE – Linda RONSTADT and James INGRAM
SOMEWHERE OVER THE RAINBOW – Cliff RICHARD
SOMEWHERE SOMEBODY – FIVE STAR
SOMEWHERE SOMEHOW – WET WET WET
SON OF A GUN – JX
SON OF A GUN (I BET YOU THINK THIS SONG IS ABOUT YOU) – Janet JACKSON with Carly SIMON featuring Missy ELLIOTT
SON-OF-A PREACHER MAN – Dusty SPRINGFIELD
SON OF HICKORY HOLLER'S TRAMP – OC SMITH
SON OF MARY – Harry BELAFONTE
SON OF MY FATHER – CHICORY TIP
SON OF SAM – Elliott SMITH
SON OF THREE – The BREEDERS
SON THIS IS SHE – John LEYTON
(SONG FOR A) FUTURE GENERATION – B-52's
SONG FOR GUY – Elton JOHN
SONG FOR LOVE – EXTREME
A SONG FOR MAMA – BOYZ II MEN
SONG FOR SHELTER – FATBOY SLIM
A SONG FOR THE LOVERS – Richard ASHCROFT
SONG FOR WHOEVER – The BEAUTIFUL SOUTH
SONG FROM THE EDGE OF THE WORLD – SIOUXSIE and the BANSHEES
THE SONG FROM THE MOULIN ROUGE – MANTOVANI
SONG OF DREAMS – Becky TAYLOR
SONG OF JOY – Miguel RIOS
SONG OF LIFE – LEFTFIELD

SONG OF MEXICO — Tony MEEHAN COMBO
THE SONG OF MY LIFE — Petula CLARK
SONG OF THE DREAMER — Johnnie RAY
SONG SUNG BLUE — Neil DIAMOND
THE SONG THAT I SING (THEME FROM
  'WE'LL MEET AGAIN') — STUTZ BEARCATS
  and the Denis KING ORCHESTRA
SONG TO THE SIREN — THIS MORTAL COIL
SONG 2 — BLUR
SONGBIRD [A] — Kenny G
SONGBIRD [B] — OASIS
SONGS FOR CHRISTMAS '87 (EP) —
  MINI POPS
SONGS FOR SWINGING LOVERS (LP) —
  Frank SINATRA
SONIC BOOM BOY — WESTWORLD
SONIC BOOM (LIFE'S TOO SHORT) —
  QUO VADIS
SONIC EMPIRE — MEMBERS OF MAYDAY
SONNET — The VERVE
'SONS AND DAUGHTERS' THEME —
  KERRI and MICK
SONS OF THE STAGE — WORLD OF TWIST
SOON — MY BLOODY VALENTINE
SOON BE DONE — SHAGGY
SOONER OR LATER — Larry GRAHAM
SOOPA HOOPZ —
  SOOPA HOOPZ featuring QPR MASSIVE
SOOTHE ME — SAM and DAVE
SORRENTO MOON (I REMEMBER) —
  Tina ARENA
SORROW [A] — MERSEYS
SORROW [A] — David BOWIE
SORRY BUT I'M GONNA HAVE TO PASS —
  The COASTERS
SORRY DOESN'T ALWAYS MAKE IT RIGHT —
  Diana ROSS
SORRY FOR YOU — Roni SIZE
SORRY (I DIDN'T KNOW) —
  MONSTA BOY featuring DENZIE
SORRY (I RAN ALL THE WAY HOME) —
  IMPALAS
SORRY I'M A LADY — BACCARA
SORRY ROBBIE — Bert WEEDON
SORRY SEEMS TO BE THE HARDEST WORD [A] —
  Elton JOHN
SORRY SEEMS TO BE THE HARDEST WORD [A] —
  BLUE featuring Elton JOHN
SORRY SUZANNE — The HOLLIES
A SORTA FAIRYTALE — Tori AMOS
SORTED FOR E'S AND WIZZ — PULP
S.O.S. [A] — ABBA
S.O.S. [B] — ABC
THE SOS EP — The SHAMEN
SOUL BEAT CALLING — I KAMANCHI
SOUL BOSSA NOVA — COOL, the FAB, and the
  GROOVY present Quincy JONES
THE SOUL CAGES — STING
SOUL CHA CHA — Van McCOY
THE SOUL CITY WALK —
  Archie BELL and the DRELLS
SOUL CLAP '69 — BOOKER T and the MG's
SOUL COAXING — Raymond LEFEVRE
SOUL DEEP [A] — The BOX TOPS
SOUL DEEP [A] — Gary 'US' BONDS
SOUL DEEP (PART 1) — COUNCIL COLLECTIVE
SOUL DRACULA — HOT BLOOD
SOUL FINGER — BAR-KAYS
SOUL FREEDOM — FREE YOUR SOUL —
  DEGREES OF MOTION featuring BITI
SOUL HEAVEN —
  GOODFELLAS featuring Lisa MILLETT
SOUL INSIDE — SOFT CELL
SOUL INSPIRATION — Simon CLIMIE
SOUL LIMBO — BOOKER T and the MG's
SOUL LOVE — BLESSING
SOUL LOVE — SOUL MAN —
  WOMACK and WOMACK
SOUL MAN [A] — SAM and DAVE
SOUL MAN [A] — Sam MOORE and Lou REED
SOUL OF MY SOUL — Michael BOLTON
THE SOUL OF MY SUIT — T. REX
SOUL PASSING THROUGH SOUL — TOYAH
SOUL PROVIDER — Michael BOLTON
SOUL SEARCHIN' TIME — The TRAMMPS
SOUL SERENADE — Willie MITCHELL
SOUL SISTER, BROWN SUGAR —
  SAM and DAVE
SOUL SOUND — SUGABABES
SOUL TRAIN — SWANS WAY
SOULJACKER PART 1 — EELS
SOULMATE — WEE PAPA GIRL RAPPERS
SOULS — Rick SPRINGFIELD
THE SOULSHAKER — MAX LINEN
SOUL'S ON FIRE — TRACIE
SOUND — JAMES
THE SOUND — X-PRESS 2
SOUND ADVICE — Roni SIZE
SOUND AND VISION — David BOWIE
SOUND BWOY BURIAL — GANT
SOUND CLASH (CHAMPION SOUND) —
  KICK SQUAD
THE SOUND OF BAMBOO — FLICKMAN
THE SOUND OF BLUE — JFK
THE SOUND OF CONFUSION — SECRET AFFAIR
THE SOUND OF CRYING — PREFAB SPROUT
SOUND OF DRUMS — KULA SHAKER

SOUND OF EDEN [A] — SHADES OF RHYTHM
SOUND OF EDEN [A] — CASINO
THE SOUND OF MUSIC — DAYTON
THE SOUND OF MUSIK — FALCO
THE SOUND OF: OH YEAH — TOMBA VIRA
THE SOUND OF SILENCE — The BACHELORS
SOUND OF SOUNDS — GOMEZ
SOUND OF SPEED (EP) —
  JESUS AND MARY CHAIN
THE SOUND OF THE CROWD — HUMAN LEAGUE
THE SOUND OF THE SUBURBS — MEMBERS
SOUND OF THE UNDERGROUND —
  GIRLS ALOUD
THE SOUND OF VIOLENCE — CASSIUS
THE SOUND OF YOUR CRY — Elvis PRESLEY
SOUND SYSTEM [A] — STEEL PULSE
SOUND SYSTEM [B] — DRUM CLUB
SOUND YOUR FUNKY HORN —
  KC and the SUNSHINE BAND
SOUNDS OF EDEN (EVERYTIME I SEE THE GIRL) —
  DEEP COVER
SOUNDS OF WICKEDNESS — TZANT
SOUR TIMES — PORTISHEAD
SOUTH AFRICAN MAN — Hamilton BOHANNON
SOUTH MANZ — DILLINJA
SOUTH OF THE BORDER — Robbie WILLIAMS
SOUTH OF THE RIVER — Mica PARIS
SOUTH PACIFIC — DJ ZINC
SOUTHAMPTON BOYS —
  RED 'N' WHITE MACHINES
SOUTHERN COMFORT — Berni FLINT
SOUTHERN FREEEZ — FREEEZ
SOUTHERN NIGHTS — Glen CAMPBELL
SOUTHERN SUN — OAKENFOLD
SOUTHSIDE — Dave CLARKE
SOUVENIR —
  ORCHESTRAL MANOEUVRES IN THE DARK
SOUVENIRS — VOYAGE
SOWETO [A] — Malcolm McLAREN
SOWETO [B] — Jeffrey OSBORNE
SOWING THE SEEDS OF HATRED —
  CREDIT TO THE NATION
SOWING THE SEEDS OF LOVE —
  TEARS FOR FEARS
SPACE [A] — NEW MODEL ARMY
SPACE [B] — SLIPMATT
SPACE AGE LOVE SONG —
  A FLOCK OF SEAGULLS
SPACE BASS — SLICK
THE SPACE BETWEEN —
  Dave MATTHEWS BAND
SPACE COWBOY — JAMIROQUAI
SPACE JAM — QUAD CITY DJs
THE SPACE JUNGLE — ADAMSKI
SPACE LORD — MONSTER MAGNET
SPACE OASIS — Billie Ray MARTIN
SPACE ODDITY — David BOWIE
SPACE RIDER — Shaun ESCOFFERY
SPACE STATION NO.5 [A] — Sammy HAGAR
SPACE STATION NUMBER 5 [A] — MONTROSE
SPACE WALK — LEMON JELLY
SPACED INVADER —
  HATIRAS featuring SLARTA JOHN
SPACEHOPPER — BAD COMPANY
SPACEMAN [A] — 4 NON BLONDES
SPACEMAN [B] — BABYLON ZOO
A SPACEMAN CAME TRAVELLING —
  Chris DE BURGH
SPACER — Sheila B DEVOTION
SPANISH — Craig DAVID
SPANISH DANCE TROUPE —
  GORKY'S ZYGOTIC MYNCI
SPANISH EYES — Al MARTINO
SPANISH FLEA — Herb ALPERT
SPANISH HARLEM [A] — Jimmy JUSTICE
SPANISH HARLEM [A] —
  SOUNDS INCORPORATED
SPANISH HARLEM [A] — Aretha FRANKLIN
SPANISH HORSES — AZTEC CAMERA
SPANISH STROLL — MINK DeVILLE
SPANISH WINE — Chris WHITE
SPARE PARTS — Bruce SPRINGSTEEN
SPARK — Tori AMOS
SPARKLE — MY LIFE STORY
SPARKLE OF MY EYES — UB40 and LADY SAW
SPARKS — RÖYKSOPP
SPARKY'S DREAM — TEENAGE FANCLUB
THE SPARROW — RAMBLERS
  (from the Abbey Hey Junior School)
THE SPARTANS — SOUNDS INCORPORATED
SPEAK LIKE A CHILD — STYLE COUNCIL
SPEAK TO ME PRETTY — Brenda LEE
SPEAK TO ME SOMEONE — GENE
SPEAKEASY — SHED SEVEN
SPECIAL [A] — GARBAGE
SPECIAL 2003 [B] — LEE-CABRERA
THE SPECIAL A.K.A. LIVE! EP — The SPECIALS
SPECIAL BREW — BAD MANNERS
SPECIAL CASES — MASSIVE ATTACK
SPECIAL F/X — WHISPERS
SPECIAL KIND OF LOVE — Dina CARROLL
SPECIAL KIND OF LOVER — NU COLOURS
SPECIAL KIND OF SOMETHING — KAVANA
SPECIAL NEEDS — PLACEBO
SPECIAL WAY — RIVER CITY PEOPLE
THE SPECIAL YEARS — Val DOONICAN
SPECTACULAR — Graham COXON

SPEECHLESS — D-SIDE
SPEED — Billy IDOL
SPEED (CAN YOU FEEL IT) —
  Azzido DA BASS featuring Roland CLARK
SPEED AT THE SOUND OF LONELINESS —
  ALABAMA 3
SPEED YOUR LOVE TO ME — SIMPLE MINDS
SPEEDWELL — SAINT ETIENNE
SPEEDY GONZALES — Pat BOONE
THE SPELL! — FUNKY WORM
SPELLBOUND — SIOUXSIE and the BANSHEES
SPEND SOME TIME —
  The BRAND NEW HEAVIES
SPEND THE DAY —
  URBAN COOKIE COLLECTIVE
SPEND THE NIGHT [A] — COOLNOTES
SPEND THE NIGHT [B] — Danny J LEWIS
SPENDING MY TIME — ROXETTE
SPICE OF LIFE — MANHATTAN TRANSFER
SPICE UP YOUR LIFE — SPICE GIRLS
SPIDERS & SNAKES — Jim STAFFORD
SPIDERWEBS — NO DOUBT
SPIES LIKE US — Paul McCARTNEY
SPIKEE — UNDERWORLD
SPILLER FROM RIO (DO IT EASY) — LAGUNA
SPIN SPIN SUGAR — SNEAKER PIMPS
SPIN THAT WHEEL (TURTLES GET REAL) —
  HI-TEK 3 featuring YA KID K
SPIN THE BLACK CIRCLE — PEARL JAM
SPIN THE WHEEL — BELLEFIRE
SPINDRIFT (EP) — THOUSAND YARD STARE
SPINNIN' AND SPINNIN' — SYREETA
SPINNING — CLARKESVILLE
SPINNING AROUND — Kylie MINOGUE
SPINNING ROCK BOOGIE — Hank C BURNETTE
SPINNING THE WHEEL — George MICHAEL
SPINNIN' WHEELS — The CRESCENT
SPIRAL SCRATCH (EP) — The BUZZCOCKS
SPIRAL SYMPHONY — SCIENTIST
SPIRIT [A] — BAUHAUS
SPIRIT [B] — Wayne MARSHALL
SPIRIT [C] — SOUNDS OF BLACKNESS
SPIRIT [D] — Craig MACK
SPIRIT BODY AND SOUL — The NOLANS
SPIRIT IN THE SKY [A] — Norman GREENBAUM
SPIRIT IN THE SKY [A] —
  DOCTOR and the MEDICS
SPIRIT IN THE SKY [A] —
  Gareth GATES featuring the KUMARS
SPIRIT INSIDE — SPIRITS
THE SPIRIT IS WILLING — Peter STRAKER and the
  HANDS OF DR TELENY
SPIRIT OF RADIO — RUSH
SPIRIT OF '76 — The ALARM
SPIRITS (HAVING FLOWN) — The BEE GEES
SPIRITS IN THE MATERIAL WORLD [A] — The POLICE
SPIRITS IN THE MATERIAL WORLD [A] —
  Pato BANTON with STING
SPIRITUAL HIGH (STATE OF INDEPENDENCE) —
  MOODSWINGS / CHRISSIE HYNDE
SPIRITUAL LOVE — URBAN SPECIES
SPIRITUAL THANG — Eric BENET
SPIRITUALIZED — Finley QUAYE
SPIT IN THE RAIN — DEL AMITRI
SPIT IT OUT — SLIPKNOT
SPITTING GAMES — SNOW PATROL
SPLIFFHEAD — RAGGA TWINS
SPLISH SPLASH [A] — Bobby DARIN
SPLISH SPLASH [A] — Charlie DRAKE
SPOOKY [A] — CLASSICS IV
SPOOKY [A] — ATLANTA RHYTHM SECTION
SPOOKY [B] — NEW ORDER
SPOONMAN — SOUNDGARDEN
SPOT THE PIGEON (EP) — GENESIS
SPREAD A LITTLE HAPPINESS — STING
SPREAD LOVE —
  FIGHT CLUB featuring Laurent KONRAD
SPREAD YOUR WINGS — QUEEN
SPRING IN MY STEP — NU-MATIC
SPRINGTIME FOR THE WORLD —
  The BLOW MONKEYS
SPUTNIK — STYLUS TROUBLE
SPY IN THE HOUSE OF LOVE —
  WAS (NOT WAS)
SPYBREAK! — PROPELLERHEADS
SPYCATCHER — J MAJIK and WICKAMAN
(SQUARE ROOT OF) 231 — ANTICAPPELLA
SQUARES — The BETA BAND
SQUEEZE BOX — The WHO
SQUIRT — FLUKE
SS PAPARAZZI — STOCK AITKEN WATERMAN
S-S-S-SINGLE BED — FOX
SSSST (LISTEN) — JONAH
STABBED IN THE BACK — MIND OF KANE
STACCATO'S THEME — Elmer BERNSTEIN
STACY'S MOM — FOUNTAINS OF WAYNE
STAGE ONE — SPACE MANOEVRES
STAGES — ZZ TOP
STAGGER LEE — Lloyd PRICE
STAINSBY GIRLS — Chris REA
THE STAIRCASE (MYSTERY) —
  SIOUXSIE and the BANSHEES
STAIRWAY OF LOVE [A] — Michael HOLLIDAY
STAIRWAY OF LOVE [A] — Terry DENE
STAIRWAY TO HEAVEN [A] — Neil SEDAKA
STAIRWAY TO HEAVEN [B] —
  FAR CORPORATION

STAIRWAY TO HEAVEN [B] — DREAD ZEPPELIN
STAIRWAY TO HEAVEN [B] — Rolf HARRIS
STAKES IS HIGH — DE LA SOUL
STAKKER HUMANOID — HUMANOID
STALEMATE — MAC BAND featuring
  the McCAMPBELL BROTHERS
STAMP! — AMOS
STAN — EMINEM
STAN BOWLES — The OTHERS
STAND [A] — R.E.M.
STAND [B] — POISON
STAND ABOVE ME —
  ORCHESTRAL MANOEUVRES IN THE DARK
STAND AND DELIVER — ADAM and the ANTS
STAND AND FIGHT —
  PACK featuring Nigel BENN
STAND BACK —
  LINUS LOVES featuring Sam OBERNIK
STAND BY — ROMAN HOLLIDAY
STAND BY LOVE — SIMPLE MINDS
STAND BY ME [A] — Ben E KING
STAND BY ME [A] — John LENNON
STAND BY ME [A] — Kenny LYNCH
STAND BY ME [A] — 4 THE CAUSE
STAND BY ME [B] — OASIS
STAND BY MY WOMAN — Lenny KRAVITZ
STAND BY YOUR MAN — Tammy WYNETTE
STAND CLEAR — ADAM F featuring M.O.P.
STAND DOWN MARGARET (DUB) — The BEAT
STAND INSIDE YOUR LOVE —
  SMASHING PUMPKINS
STAND OR FALL — FIXX
STAND TOUGH — POINT BREAK
STAND UP [A] — David Lee ROTH
STAND UP [B] — Loleatta HOLLOWAY
STAND UP [C] — THUNDER
STAND UP [D] — LOVE TRIBE
STAND UP [E] — LUDACRIS
STAND UP FOR YOUR LOVE RIGHTS — YAZZ
STAND UP TALL — DIZZEE RASCAL
STANDING — Silvio ECOMO
STANDING HERE ALL ALONE — MICHELLE
STANDING IN THE NEED OF LOVE —
  RIVER CITY PEOPLE
STANDING IN THE ROAD — BLACKFOOT SUE
STANDING IN THE SHADOW — WHITESNAKE
STANDING IN THE SHADOWS OF LOVE —
  The FOUR TOPS
STANDING ON THE CORNER [A] — FOUR LADS
STANDING ON THE CORNER [A] —
  KING BROTHERS
STANDING ON THE INSIDE — Neil SEDAKA
STANDING ON THE TOP (PART 1) —
  The TEMPTATIONS featuring Rick JAMES
STANDING ON THE VERGE (OF GETTING IT ON) —
  PLATINUM HOOK
STANDING OUTSIDE A BROKEN PHONE
  BOOTH WITH MONEY IN MY HAND —
  PRIMITIVE RADIO GODS
STANDING OUTSIDE THE FIRE —
  Garth BROOKS
STANDING THERE — CREATURES
STANDING WATCHING — CHERRYFALLS
STANLEY (HERE I AM) — AIRHEADZ
STAR [A] — STEALER'S WHEEL
STAR [B] — EARTH WIND AND FIRE
STAR [C] — NAZARETH
STAR [D] — Kiki DEE
STAR [E] — SECOND IMAGE
STAR [F] — ERASURE
STAR [G] — D:REAM
STAR [H] — The CULT
STAR [I] — Bryan ADAMS
STAR [J] — PRIMAL SCREAM
THE STAR AND THE WISEMAN —
  LADYSMITH BLACK MAMBAZO
STAR CATCHING GIRL —
  BROTHER BROWN featuring FRANK'EE
STAR CHASERS — 4 HERO
STAR FLEET — Brian MAY
STAR GUITAR — The CHEMICAL BROTHERS
STAR ON A TV SHOW — The STYLISTICS
STAR PEOPLE '97 — George MICHAEL
STAR SIGN — TEENAGE FANCLUB
STAR 69 — FATBOY SLIM
STAR TREKKIN' — The FIRM
STAR WARS THEME — CANTINA BAND —
  MECO
STARBRIGHT — Johnny MATHIS
STARCHILD — LEVEL 42
STARCROSSED — ASH
STARDATE 1990 — Dan REED NETWORK
STARDUST [A] —
  Billy WARD and HIS DOMINOES
STARDUST [A] — Nat 'King' COLE
STARDUST [B] — David ESSEX
STARDUST [B] — Martin L. GORE
STARDUST [C] — MENSWEAR
STARGAZER — SIOUXSIE and the BANSHEES
STARING AT THE RUDE BOYS — RUTS
STARING AT THE SUN — U2
STARLIGHT [A] — DESIDERIO
STARLIGHT [B] — SUPERMEN LOVERS
STARLITE — YOUNG HEART ATTACK
STARLOVERS — GUS GUS
STARMAKER — KIDS FROM 'FAME'
STARMAN [A] — David BOWIE

STARMAN [A] – CULTURE CLUB
STARRY EYED – Michael HOLLIDAY with the Michael SAMMES SINGERS
STARRY EYED SURPRISE – OAKENFOLD
A STARRY NIGHT – JOY STRINGS
STARS [A] – SYLVESTER
STARS [B] – FELIX
STARS [C] – HEAR 'N' AID
STARS [D] – SIMPLY RED
STARS [E] – CHINA BLACK
STARS [F] – DUBSTAR
STARS [G] – ROXETTE
STARS [H] – MORJAC featuring Raz CONWAY
STARS AND STRIPES FOREVER – Mr Acker BILK and his PARAMOUNT JAZZ BAND
STARS ON 45 – STARSOUND
STARS ON 45 VOL.3 – STARSOUND
STARS ON 45 VOL.2 – STARSOUND
STARS ON STEVIE – STARSOUND
STARS OVER 45 – CHAS and DAVE
STARS SHINE IN YOUR EYES – Ronnie HILTON
STARSHIP – ICEBERG SLIMM featuring COREE
STARSHIP TROOPERS – Sarah BRIGHTMAN
STARSKY & HUTCH – THE THEME – Andy G's STARSKY & HUTCH ALL STARS
START – The JAM
START A BRAND NEW LIFE (SAVE ME) – BASSHEADS
START AGAIN [A] – TEENAGE FANCLUB
START AGAIN [B] – MONTROSE AVENUE
START CHOPPIN' – DINOSAUR JR
START ME UP [A] – The ROLLING STONES
START ME UP [B] – SALT-N-PEPA
START MOVIN' [A] – Sal MINEO
START MOVIN' [A] – Terry DENE
START TALKING LOVE – MAGNUM
START THE COMMOTION – WISEGUYS
STARTING AGAIN – SECOND IMAGE
STARTING OVER AGAIN – Natalie COLE
STARTING TOGETHER – Su POLLARD
STARTOUCHERS – DIGITAL ORGASM
STARTRAX CLUB DISCO – STARTRAX
STARTURN ON 45 (PINTS) – STAR TURN ON 45 (PINTS)
STARVATION – STARVATION
STATE OF INDEPENDENCE [A] – Donna SUMMER
STATE OF INDEPENDENCE [A] – JON and VANGELIS
STATE OF LOVE – IMAGINATION
STATE OF MIND [A] – FISH
STATE OF MIND [B] – Holly VALANCE
STATE OF SHOCK – The JACKSONS, lead vocals Mick JAGGER and Michael JACKSON
STATE OF THE NATION – NEW ORDER
STATUESQUE – SLEEPER
STATUS ROCK – HEADBANGERS
STAY [A] – Maurice WILLIAMS and the ZODIACS
STAY [A] – The HOLLIES
STAY [A] – Jackson BROWNE
STAY [A] – DREAMHOUSE
STAY [B] – Barry MANILOW
STAY [C] – SHAKESPEAR'S SISTER
STAY [D] – Kenny THOMAS
STAY [E] – ETERNAL
STAY [F] – 60FT DOLLS
STAY [G] – 18 WHEELER
STAY [H] – SASH!
STAY [I] – Bernard BUTLER
STAY [J] – Mica PARIS
STAY [K] – Stephen GATELY
STAY [L] – Rob TISSERA, VINYLGROOVER & The RED HED
STAY A LITTLE WHILE, CHILD – LOOSE ENDS
STAY A WHILE – RAKIM
STAY ANOTHER DAY – EAST 17
STAY AWAY FROM ME – STAR SPANGLES
STAY AWHILE – Dusty SPRINGFIELD
STAY BEAUTIFUL – MANIC STREET PREACHERS
STAY (FARAWAY, SO CLOSE) – U2
STAY FOREVER – Joey LAWRENCE
STAY GOLD – DEEP DISH
STAY (I MISSED YOU) – Lisa LOEB and NINE STORIES
STAY IN THE SUN – KENICKIE
STAY ON THESE ROADS – A-HA
STAY OUT OF MY LIFE – FIVE STAR
STAY RIGHT HERE – AKIN
STAY THE SAME [A] – BENT
STAY THE SAME [B] – GABRIELLE
STAY THIS WAY – The BRAND NEW HEAVIES
STAY TOGETHER [A] – SUEDE
STAY TOGETHER [B] – Barbara TUCKER
STAY (TONIGHT) – ISHA-D
STAY WITH ME [A] – The FACES
STAY WITH ME [B] – BLUE MINK
STAY WITH ME [C] – EIGHTH WONDER
STAY WITH ME [D] – The MISSION
STAY WITH ME [E] – John O'KANE
STAY WITH ME [F] – ERASURE
STAY WITH ME [G] – ULTRA HIGH
STAY WITH ME [H] – Richie RICH
STAY WITH ME [I] – ANGELIC
STAY WITH ME BABY [A] – The WALKER BROTHERS
STAY WITH ME BABY [A] – David ESSEX
STAY WITH ME BABY [A] – Ruby TURNER
STAY WITH ME (BABY) [A] – Rebecca WHEATLEY
STAY WITH ME HEARTACHE – WET WET WET
STAY WITH ME TILL DAWN [A] – Judie TZUKE
STAY WITH ME TILL DAWN [A] – LUCID
STAY WITH ME TONIGHT [A] – Jeffrey OSBORNE
STAY WITH ME TONIGHT [B] – HUMAN LEAGUE
STAY WITH YOU – LEMON JELLY
STAY YOUNG – ULTRASOUND
STAYIN' ALIVE [A] – The BEE GEES
STAYIN' ALIVE [A] – Richard ACE
STAYIN' ALIVE [A] – N-TRANCE featuring Ricardo DA FORCE
STAYING ALIVE 95 [A] – FEVER featuring Tippa IRIE
STAYING FAT – BLOC PARTY
STAYING IN – Bobby VEE
STAYING OUT FOR THE SUMMER – DODGY
STAYING TOGETHER – Debbie GIBSON
STEAL MY SUNSHINE – LEN
STEAL YOUR FIRE – GUN
STEAL YOUR LOVE AWAY – GEMINI
STEALTH – WAY OUT WEST
STEAM [A] – Peter GABRIEL
STEAM [B] – EAST 17
STEAMY WINDOWS – Tina TURNER
STEEL BARS – Michael BOLTON
A STEEL GUITAR AND A GLASS OF WINE – Paul ANKA
STEELO – 702
STEM – DJ SHADOW
STEP BACK IN TIME – Kylie MINOGUE
STEP BY STEP [A] – Steve PERRY
STEP BY STEP [B] – Joe SIMON
STEP BY STEP [C] – TAFFY
STEP BY STEP [D] – NEW KIDS ON THE BLOCK
STEP BY STEP [E] – Whitney HOUSTON
STEP IN THE NAME OF LOVE – R KELLY
A STEP IN THE RIGHT DIRECTION – TRUTH
STEP INSIDE LOVE – Cilla BLACK
STEP INTO A DREAM – WHITE PLAINS
STEP INTO A WORLD (RAPTURE'S DELIGHT) – KRS ONE
STEP INTO CHRISTMAS – Elton JOHN
STEP INTO MY OFFICE BABY – BELLE & SEBASTIAN
STEP INTO MY WORLD – HURRICANE #1
STEP INTO THE BREEZE – SPIRITUALIZED
STEP IT UP – STEREO MC's
STEP OFF – JUNIOR
STEP OFF (PART 1) – GRANDMASTER FLASH, Melle MEL and the FURIOUS FIVE
STEP ON – HAPPY MONDAYS
STEP ON MY OLD SIZE NINES – STEREOPHONICS
STEP RIGHT UP – Jaki GRAHAM
STEP TO ME (DO ME) – MANTRONIX
STEPPIN' OUT [A] – KOOL and the GANG
STEPPIN' OUT [B] – Joe JACKSON
STEPPIN STONES – DJ ZINC
STEPPING STONE [A] – The FARM
STEPPING STONE [A] – ANT & DEC
STEPTOE AND SON AT BUCKINGHAM PALACE – Wilfrid BRAMBELL and Harry H CORBETT
STEP-TWO-THREE-FOUR – STRICT INSTRUCTOR
STEREO – PAVEMENT
STEREOTYPE – The SPECIALS
STEREOTYPES – BLUR
STEVE MCQUEEN – Sheryl CROW
STEWBALL – Lonnie DONEGAN
STICK IT OUT – RIGHT SAID FRED
STICKS AND STONES – CUD
STICKY – WEDDING PRESENT
STIFF UPPER LIP – AC/DC
STILL [A] – Karl DENVER
STILL [A] – Ken DODD
STILL [B] – The COMMODORES
STILL [C] – Macy GRAY
STILL A FRIEND OF MINE – INCOGNITO
STILL A THRILL – SYBIL
STILL BE LOVIN' YOU – DAMAGE
STILL BELIEVE – Shola AMA
STILL D.R.E. – DR DRE
STILL FEEL THE RAIN – STEX
STILL GOT THE BLUES (FOR YOU) – Gary MOORE
STILL I'M SAD – YARDBIRDS
STILL IN LOVE [A] – GO WEST
STILL IN LOVE [B] – Lionel RICHIE
STILL IN LOVE SONG – The STILLS
STILL OF THE NIGHT – WHITESNAKE
STILL ON YOUR SIDE – BBMAK
STILL THE SAME – SLADE
STILL TOO YOUNG TO REMEMBER – IT BITES
STILL WAITING – SUM 41
STILL WATER (LOVE) – The FOUR TOPS
STILL WATERS (RUN DEEP) – The BEE GEES
STILLNESS IN TIME – JAMIROQUAI
THE STING – RAGTIMERS
STING ME – BLACK CROWES
STING ME RED (YOU THINK YOU'RE SO CLEVER) – WHO DA FUNK featuring TERRA DEVA
STINGRAY – The SHADOWS
THE STINGRAY MEGAMIX – FAB
STINKIN THINKIN – HAPPY MONDAYS
STIR IT UP – Johnny NASH
STOLE – Kelly ROWLAND
STOLEN – Jay SEAN
STOLEN CAR – Beth ORTON
STOLEN CAR (TAKE ME DANCING) – STING
STOMP [A] – BROTHERS JOHNSON
STOMP [A] – Quincy JONES
STOMP [B] – GOD'S PROPERTY
STOMP [C] – STEPS
STONE BY STONE – CATATONIA
STONE COLD – RAINBOW
STONE LOVE – KOOL and the GANG
STONED LOVE – The SUPREMES
STONEY END – Barbra STREISAND
STONEY GROUND – GUYS and DOLLS
THE STONK – HALE and PACE and the STONKERS
STOOD ON GOLD – GORKY'S ZYGOTIC MYNCI
STOOD UP – Ricky NELSON
STOOL PIGEON – Kid CREOLE and the COCONUTS
STOP [A] – Sam BROWN
STOP [A] – JAMELIA
STOP [B] – SPICE GIRLS
STOP [C] – BLACK REBEL MOTORCYCLE CLUB
STOP (EP) – MEGA CITY FOUR
STOP AND GO – David GRANT
STOP BAJON ... PRIMAVERA – Tullio DE PISCOPO
STOP BREAKING MY HEART – INNER CIRCLE
STOP BY – Rahsaan PATTERSON
STOP DRAGGIN' MY HEART AROUND – Stevie NICKS with Tom PETTY and the HEARTBREAKERS
STOP FEELING SORRY FOR YOURSELF – Adam FAITH
STOP HER ON SIGHT (SOS) – Edwin STARR
STOP! IN THE NAME OF LOVE – Diana ROSS and The SUPREMES
STOP LISTENING – Tanita TIKARAM
STOP LIVING THE LIE – David SNEDDON
STOP LOOK AND LISTEN [A] – Wayne FONTANA and The MINDBENDERS
STOP LOOK AND LISTEN [B] – Donna SUMMER
STOP LOOK LISTEN (TO YOUR HEART) – Diana ROSS and Marvin GAYE
STOP LOVING ME STOP LOVING YOU – Daryl HALL
STOP ME (IF YOU'VE HEARD IT ALL BEFORE) – Billy OCEAN
STOP MY HEAD – Evan DANDO
STOP PLAYING WITH MY MIND – Barbara TUCKER
STOP SIGN – ABS
STOP STARTING TO START STOPPING (EP) – D.O.P.
STOP STOP STOP – The HOLLIES
STOP THAT GIRL – Chris ANDREWS
STOP THE CAVALRY – Jona LEWIE
STOP THE ROCK – APOLLO FOUR FORTY
STOP THE VIOLENCE – BOOGIE DOWN PRODUCTIONS
STOP THE WAR NOW – Edwin STARR
STOP THE WORLD – EXTREME
STOP THIS CRAZY THING – COLDCUT
STOP TO LOVE – Luther VANDROSS
STOP YOUR CRYING – SPIRITUALIZED
STOP YOUR SOBBING – The PRETENDERS
STORIES [A] – IZIT
STORIES [B] – THERAPY?
STORIES [C] – HOLIDAY PLAN
STORIES OF JOHNNY – Marc ALMOND
STORM [A] – Dave CLARKE
STORM [B] – SPACE KITTENS
STORM [C] – VANESSA-MAE
STORM [D] – STORM
THE STORM – WORLD OF TWIST
STORM ANIMAL – STORM
STORM IN A TEACUP – FORTUNES
THE STORM IS OVER NOW – R KELLY
STORMS IN AFRICA (PART II) – ENYA
STORMTROOPER IN DRAG – Paul GARDINER
STORMY IN THE NORTH – KARMA IN THE SOUTH – The WILDHEARTS
THE STORY OF LOVE – OTT
STORY OF MY LIFE [A] – Kristian LEONTIOU
THE STORY OF MY LIFE [B] – Alma COGAN
THE STORY OF MY LIFE [B] – Dave KING
THE STORY OF MY LIFE [B] – Gary MILLER
THE STORY OF MY LIFE [B] – Michael HOLLIDAY
STORY OF MY LOVE – Conway TWITTY
STORY OF THE BLUES – Gary MOORE
THE STORY OF THE BLUES – WAH!
THE STORY OF TINA [A] – Al MARTINO
THE STORY OF TINA [A] – Ronnie HARRIS
STOWAWAY – Barbara LYON
STRAIGHT AHEAD [A] – KOOL and the GANG
STRAIGHT AHEAD [B] – TUBE & BERGER featuring Chrissie HYNDE
STRAIGHT AT YER HEAD – LIONROCK
STRAIGHT FROM THE HEART [A] – Bryan ADAMS
STRAIGHT FROM THE HEART [B] – DOOLALLY
STRAIGHT LINES – NEW MUSIK
STRAIGHT OUT OF THE JUNGLE – The JUNGLE BROTHERS
STRAIGHT TO HELL – The CLASH
STRAIGHT TO MY FEET – HAMMER
STRAIGHT TO THE HEART – The REAL THING
STRAIGHT TO YOU – Nick CAVE and the BAD SEEDS
STRAIGHT UP [A] – Paula ABDUL
STRAIGHT UP [B] – Chanté MOORE
STRAIGHT UP NO BENDS – Brian HARVEY
STRAIGHTEN OUT – The STRANGLERS
STRANDED [A] – HEART
STRANDED [B] – DEEP DISH
STRANDED [C] – Lutricia McNEAL
STRANGE – WET WET WET
STRANGE AND BEAUTIFUL (I'LL PUT A SPELL ON YOU) – AQUALUNG
STRANGE BAND – FAMILY
STRANGE BREW – CREAM
STRANGE CURRENCIES – R.E.M.
STRANGE GLUE – CATATONIA
STRANGE KIND OF LOVE – LOVE AND MONEY
STRANGE KIND OF WOMAN – DEEP PURPLE
STRANGE LADY IN TOWN – Frankie LAINE
STRANGE LITTLE GIRL [A] – SAD CAFE
STRANGE LITTLE GIRL [B] – The STRANGLERS
STRANGE MAGIC – ELECTRIC LIGHT ORCHESTRA
STRANGE RELATIONSHIP – Darren HAYES
STRANGE TOWN – The JAM
STRANGE WAY – ALL ABOUT EVE
STRANGE WORLD [A] – KÉ
STRANGE WORLD [B] – PUSH
STRANGELOVE – DEPECHE MODE
STRANGER – SHAKATAK
THE STRANGER – The SHADOWS
STRANGER IN A STRANGE LAND – IRON MAIDEN
STRANGER IN MOSCOW – Michael JACKSON
STRANGER IN PARADISE [A] – Bing CROSBY
STRANGER IN PARADISE [A] – Don CORNELL
STRANGER IN PARADISE [A] – Eddie CALVERT
STRANGER IN PARADISE [A] – FOUR ACES
STRANGER IN PARADISE [A] – Tony BENNETT
STRANGER IN PARADISE [A] – Tony MARTIN
STRANGER IN TOWN – Del SHANNON
A STRANGER ON HOME GROUND – FAITH BROTHERS
STRANGER ON THE SHORE [A] – Mr Acker BILK and his PARAMOUNT JAZZ BAND
STRANGER ON THE SHORE [A] – Andy WILLIAMS
STRANGER ON THE SHORE OF LOVE – Stevie WONDER
STRANGER THINGS – ABC
STRANGERS IN OUR TOWN – SPEAR OF DESTINY
STRANGERS IN THE NIGHT – Frank SINATRA
STRANGERS WHEN WE MEET – David BOWIE
THE STRANGEST PARTY (THESE ARE THE TIMES) – INXS
THE STRANGEST THING '97 – George MICHAEL
STRANGLEHOLD – UK SUBS
STRASBOURG – The RAKES
STRATEGIC HAMLETS – URUSEI YATSURA
STRAW DOGS – STIFF LITTLE FINGERS
STRAWBERRY – Nicole RENEE
STRAWBERRY BLONDE – Frank D'RONE
STRAWBERRY FAIR – Anthony NEWLEY
STRAWBERRY FIELDS FOREVER [A] – The BEATLES
STRAWBERRY FIELDS FOREVER [A] – CANDY FLIP
STRAWBERRY KISSES – Nikki WEBSTER
STRAWBERRY LETTER 23 – BROTHERS JOHNSON
STRAY CAT STRUT – STRAY CATS
THE STREAK – Ray STEVENS
STREAMLINE TRAIN – VIPERS SKIFFLE GROUP
STREET CAFE – ICEHOUSE
A STREET CALLED HOPE – Gene PITNEY
STREET DANCE – BREAK MACHINE
STREET DREAMS – NAS
STREET FIGHTER II – WORLD WARRIOR
STREET FIGHTING MAN – The ROLLING STONES
STREET GANG – A.R.E. WEAPONS
STREET LIFE [A] – ROXY MUSIC
STREET LIFE [B] – CRUSADERS
STREET LIFE [C] – BEENIE MAN
STREET OF DREAMS – RAINBOW
STREET SPIRIT (FADE OUT) – RADIOHEAD
STREET TUFF – REBEL MC and DOUBLE TROUBLE
STREETPLAYER (MECHANIK) – FASHION
THE STREETS – WC featuring SNOOP DOGG & Nate DOGG
STREETS OF LONDON [A] – Ralph McTELL
STREETS OF LONDON [A] – ANTI-NOWHERE LEAGUE
STREETS OF PHILADELPHIA – Bruce SPRINGSTEEN
STREETWALKIN' – SHAKATAK
STRENGTH – The ALARM
STRENGTH TO STRENGTH – HUE AND CRY
STRESSED OUT – A TRIBE CALLED QUEST featuring Faith EVANS and Raphael SAADIQ

SURRENDER [D] — Roger TAYLOR
SURRENDER [E] — LASGO
SURRENDER YOUR LOVE [A] — NIGHTCRAWLERS featuring John REID
SURRENDER (YOUR LOVE) [B] — JAVINE
SURROUND YOURSELF WITH SORROW — Cilla BLACK
SURVIVAL CAR — FOUNTAINS OF WAYNE
SURVIVE — David BOWIE
SURVIVOR — DESTINY'S CHILD
SUSANNA — ART COMPANY
SUSANNAH'S STILL ALIVE — Dave DAVIES
SUSAN'S HOUSE — EELS
SUSIE DARLIN' [A] — Robin LUKE
SUSIE DARLIN' [A] — Tommy ROE
SUSPICION [A] — Terry STAFFORD
SUSPICION [A] — Elvis PRESLEY
SUSPICIOUS MINDS [A] — Elvis PRESLEY
SUSPICIOUS MINDS [A] — Candi STATON
SUSPICIOUS MINDS [A] — FINE YOUNG CANNIBALS
SUSPICIOUS MINDS [A] — Gareth GATES
SUSSUDIO — Phil COLLINS
SUZANNE BEWARE OF THE DEVIL — Dandy LIVINGSTONE
SVEN SVEN SVEN — BELL & SPURLING
SW LIVE (EP) — Peter GABRIEL
SWALLOW MY PRIDE — The RAMONES
SWALLOWED — BUSH
SWAMP THING — GRID
SWAN LAKE — CATS
SWASTIKA EYES — PRIMAL SCREAM
SWAY [A] — Dean MARTIN
SWAY [A] — Bobby RYDELL
SWAY [B] — STRANGELOVE
SWEAR IT AGAIN — WESTLIFE
SWEARIN' TO GOD — Frankie VALLI
SWEAT — USURA
SWEAT (A LA LA LA LA LONG) — INNER CIRCLE
SWEAT IN BULLET — SIMPLE MINDS
SWEATING BULLETS — MEGADETH
SWEDISH RHAPSODY [A] — MANTOVANI
SWEDISH RHAPSODY [A] — Ray MARTIN
SWEET AND LOW — Deborah HARRY
SWEET BABY — Macy GRAY featuring Erykah BADU
SWEET BIRD OF TRUTH — The THE
SWEET CAROLINE — Neil DIAMOND
SWEET CATATONIA — CATATONIA
SWEET CHEATIN' RITA — Alvin STARDUST
SWEET CHILD O' MINE [A] — GUNS N' ROSES
SWEET CHILD O' MINE [A] — Sheryl CROW
SWEET DANGER — ANGELWITCH
SWEET DREAM — JETHRO TULL
SWEET DREAMS [A] — Dave SAMPSON
SWEET DREAMS (ARE MADE OF THIS) [B] — EURYTHMICS
SWEET DREAMS [B] — DJ SCOTT featuring Lorna B
SWEET DREAMS [B] — SWING featuring Dr ALBAN
SWEET DREAMS [C] — Tommy McLAIN
SWEET DREAMS [C] — Roy BUCHANAN
SWEET DREAMS [C] — Elvis COSTELLO
SWEET DREAMS [D] — LA BOUCHE
SWEET DREAMS MY L.A. EX — Rachel STEVENS
SWEET EMOTION — AEROSMITH
SWEET FREEDOM [A] — Michael McDONALD
SWEET FREEDOM [A] — SAFRI DUO featuring Michael McDONALD
SWEET FREEDOM [B] — POSITIVE GANG
SWEET FREEDOM PART 2 — POSITIVE GANG
SWEET HARMONY [A] — LIQUID
SWEET HARMONY [B] — The BELOVED
SWEET HEART CONTRACT — MAGAZINE
SWEET HITCH-HIKER — CREEDENCE CLEARWATER REVIVAL
SWEET HOME ALABAMA — LYNYRD SKYNYRD
SWEET ILLUSION — Junior CAMPBELL
SWEET IMPOSSIBLE YOU — Brenda LEE
SWEET INSPIRATION — Johnny JOHNSON and the BANDWAGON
SWEET INVISIBILITY — HUE AND CRY
SWEET JOHNNY — GORKY'S ZYGOTIC MYNCI
SWEET LADY — TYRESE
SWEET LADY LUCK — WHITESNAKE
SWEET LEAF — MOGWAI
SWEET LIES [A] — Robert PALMER
SWEET LIES [B] — Ellie CAMPBELL
SWEET LIKE CHOCOLATE — SHANKS & BIGFOOT
SWEET LIPS — MONACO
SWEET LITTLE MYSTERY — WET WET WET
SWEET LITTLE ROCK 'N' ROLLER — SHOWADDYWADDY
SWEET LITTLE SIXTEEN [A] — Chuck BERRY
SWEET LITTLE SIXTEEN [A] — Jerry Lee LEWIS
SWEET LOVE [A] — The COMMODORES
SWEET LOVE [B] — Anita BAKER
SWEET LOVE [B] — M-BEAT
SWEET LOVE 2K [B] — FIERCE
SWEET LUI-LOUISE — IRONHORSE
SWEET LULLABY — DEEP FOREST
SWEET MEMORY — BELLE STARS
SWEET MUSIC — SHOWADDYWADDY
SWEET 'N' SOUR — Jon SPENCER BLUES EXPLOSION
SWEET NOTHIN'S [A] — Brenda LEE
SWEET NOTHINS [A] — The SEARCHERS
A SWEET OLD FASHIONED GIRL — Teresa BREWER
SWEET PEA — MANFRED MANN
SWEET PEA, MY SWEET PEA — Paul WELLER
SWEET POTATOE PIE — DOMINO
SWEET REVENGE — SPOOKS
SWEET REVIVAL (KEEP IT COMIN') — SHADES OF RHYTHM
SWEET SENSATION [A] — MELODIANS
SWEET SENSATION [B] — SHADES OF RHYTHM
SWEET SENSATION [C] — SHABOOM
SWEET SENSUAL LOVE — BIG MOUNTAIN
SWEET SHOP AVENGERZ — BIS
SWEET SISTER — PEACE BY PIECE
SWEET SIXTEEN — Billy IDOL
SWEET SMELL OF SUCCESS — The STRANGLERS
SWEET SOMEBODY — SHANNON
SWEET SOUL MUSIC — Arthur CONLEY
SWEET SOUL SISTER — The CULT
SWEET STUFF — Guy MITCHELL
SWEET SUBURBIA — The SKIDS
SWEET SURRENDER [A] — Rod STEWART
SWEET SURRENDER [B] — WET WET WET
SWEET, SWEET SMILE — The CARPENTERS
SWEET TALKIN' GUY — CHIFFONS
SWEET TALKIN' WOMAN — ELECTRIC LIGHT ORCHESTRA
SWEET THANG — JONESTOWN
SWEET THING — Mick JAGGER
SWEET TOXIC LOVE — JESUS LOVES YOU
SWEET UNDERSTANDING LOVE — The FOUR TOPS
SWEET WILLIAM — MILLIE
SWEETER THAN THE MIDNIGHT RAIN — Luke GOSS and the BAND OF THIEVES
SWEETER THAN WINE — Dionne RAKEEM
SWEETER THAN YOU — Ricky NELSON
SWEETEST CHILD — Maria McKEE
SWEETEST DAY OF MAY — Joe T VANNELLI PROJECT
THE SWEETEST DAYS — Vanessa WILLIAMS
THE SWEETEST GIRL [A] — SCRITTI POLITTI
SWEETEST GIRL [A] — MADNESS
SWEETEST SMILE — BLACK
SWEETEST SOUL SENSATIONS — The LIGHTNING SEEDS
THE SWEETEST SURRENDER — FACTORY OF UNLIMITED RHYTHM
SWEETEST SWEETEST — Jermaine JACKSON
THE SWEETEST TABOO — SADE
SWEETEST THING [A] — GENE LOVES JEZEBEL
SWEETEST THING [B] — U2
THE SWEETEST THING [C] — The FUGEES
SWEETHEART — Engelbert HUMPERDINCK
SWEETIE PIE — Eddie COCHRAN
SWEETNESS [A] — Michelle GAYLE
SWEETNESS [B] — XSATSIA
SWEETNESS [C] — JIMMY EAT WORLD
SWEETNESS AND LIGHT — LUSH
SWEETS — WORLD OF TWIST
SWEETS FOR MY SWEET [A] — The SEARCHERS
SWEETS FOR MY SWEET [A] — CJ LEWIS
SWEETSMOKE — MR SCRUFF
SWEETY — REEF
SWIM — FISHBONE
SWIMMING HORSES — SIOUXSIE and the BANSHEES
SWING LOW [A] — UB40 featuring UNITED COLOURS OF SOUND
SWING LOW '99 [A] — Russell WATSON
SWING LOW (RUN WITH THE BALL) [A] — UNION featuring the ENGLAND WORLD CUP SQUAD
SWING LOW SWEET CHARIOT [A] — Eric CLAPTON
SWING LOW SWEET CHARIOT [A] — LADYSMITH BLACK MAMBAZO featuring CHINA BLACK
SWING MY WAY — KP & ENVYI
SWING MY HIPS (SEX DANCE) — LEMONESCENT
SWING, SWING — ALL-AMERICAN REJECTS
SWING THAT HAMMER — Mike COTTON'S JAZZMEN
SWING THE MOOD — JIVE BUNNY and the MASTERMIXERS
SWING YOUR DADDY — Jim GILSTRAP
SWINGIN' — LIGHT OF THE WORLD
SWINGIN' LOW — OUTLAWS
SWINGIN' SHEPHERD BLUES [A] — Ella FITZGERALD
SWINGIN' SHEPHERD BLUES [A] — Moe KOFFMAN QUARTETTE
SWINGIN' SHEPHERD BLUES [A] — Ted HEATH
SWINGING IN THE RAIN — Norman VAUGHAN
SWINGING ON A STAR — Big Dee IRWIN
SWINGING SCHOOL — Bobby RYDELL
SWINGS AND ROUNDABOUTS — Roni SIZE
SWISS MAID — Del SHANNON
SWITCH [A] — BENELUX and Nancy DEE
SWITCH [B] — SENSER
SWITCH [C] — Howie B
SWITCH [D] — PESHAY
THE SWITCH — PLANET FUNK
SWITCHED ON SWING — KINGS OF SWING ORCHESTRA
SWOON — The MISSION
SWORDS OF A THOUSAND MEN — TEN POLE TUDOR
SYLVIA — FOCUS
SYLVIA'S MOTHER — DR HOOK
SYLVIE — SAINT ETIENNE
SYMMETRY C — BRAINCHILD
SYMPATHY [A] — RARE BIRD
SYMPATHY [B] — MARILLION
SYMPATHY FOR THE DEVIL [A] — GUNS N' ROSES
SYMPATHY FOR THE DEVIL [A] — The ROLLING STONES
SYMPHONY — Donell RUSH
SYMPHONY OF DESTRUCTION — MEGADETH
SYNAESTHESIA (FLY AWAY) — THRILLSEEKERS featuring SHERYL DEANE
SYNCHRONICITY II — The POLICE
SYNERGY — TRANCESETTERS
SYNTH & STRINGS — YOMANDA
SYSTEM ADDICT — FIVE STAR
SYSTEM CHECK — BROCKIE & Ed SOLO
SYSTEM OF SURVIVAL — EARTH WIND AND FIRE
THE TABLE — The BEAUTIFUL SOUTH
TABOO — GLAMMA KID featuring Shola AMA
TACKY LOVE SONG — CREDIT TO THE NATION
TAHITI (FROM 'MUTINY ON THE BOUNTY') — David ESSEX
TAINTED LOVE [A] — SOFT CELL
TAINTED LOVE [A] — IMPEDANCE
TAINTED LOVE [A] — ICON
TAINTED LOVE [A] — MARILYN MANSON
TAKE — COLOUR FIELD
TAKE A BOW — MADONNA
TAKE A CHANCE ON ME — ABBA
TAKE A CHANCE WITH ME — ROXY MUSIC
TAKE A FREE FALL — DANCE 2 TRANCE
TAKE A HEART — SORROWS
(TAKE A LITTLE) PIECE OF MY HEART — Erma FRANKLIN
TAKE A LITTLE TIME — Gary MOORE
TAKE A LOOK — LEVEL 42
TAKE A LOOK AROUND — The TEMPTATIONS
TAKE A LOOK AROUND (THEME FROM 'MI:2') — LIMP BIZKIT
TAKE A LOOK AT YOURSELF — COVERDALE PAGE
TAKE A MESSAGE TO MARY — The EVERLY BROTHERS
TAKE A PICTURE — FILTER
TAKE A REST — GANG STARR
TAKE A RUN AT THE SUN — DINOSAUR JR
TAKE A TOKE — C & C MUSIC FACTORY / CLIVILLES & COLE
TAKE CALIFORNIA — PROPELLERHEADS
TAKE CARE OF YOURSELF — LEVEL 42
TAKE CONTROL [A] — STATE OF MIND
TAKE CONTROL [B] — John B
TAKE CONTROL [C] — JAIMESON featuring Angel BLU and CK
TAKE CONTROL OF THE PARTY — BG THE PRINCE OF RAP
TAKE DOWN THE UNION JACK — Billy BRAGG and the BLOKES
TAKE FIVE [A] — Dave BRUBECK QUARTET
TAKE 5 [B] — NORTHSIDE
TAKE 4 (EP) — Mike OLDFIELD
TAKE GOOD CARE OF HER — Adam WADE
TAKE GOOD CARE OF MY BABY [A] — Bobby VEE
TAKE GOOD CARE OF MY BABY [A] — SMOKIE
TAKE GOOD CARE OF MY HEART — MICHAELA
TAKE GOOD CARE OF YOURSELF — The THREE DEGREES
TAKE IT — FLOWERED UP
TAKE IT AND RUN — The BANDITS
TAKE IT AWAY — Paul McCARTNEY
TAKE IT BACK — PINK FLOYD
TAKE IT EASY [A] — LET LOOSE
TAKE IT EASY [B] — MINT ROYALE
TAKE IT EASY [C] — 3SL
TAKE IT EASY ON ME — A HOUSE
TAKE IT FROM ME [A] — Roger CHRISTIAN
TAKE IT FROM ME [B] — GIRLFRIEND
TAKE IT OFF — The DONNAS
TAKE IT ON THE RUN — REO SPEEDWAGON
TAKE IT OR LEAVE IT — The SEARCHERS
TAKE IT SATCH (EP) — Louis ARMSTRONG
TAKE IT TO THE LIMIT — The EAGLES
TAKE IT TO THE STREETS — RAMPAGE featuring Billy LAWRENCE
TAKE IT TO THE TOP [A] — KOOL and the GANG
TAKE IT TO THE TOP [B] — CLOUD
TAKE ME — DREAM FREQUENCY
TAKE ME AWAY [A] — TRUE FAITH with FINAL CUT
TAKE ME AWAY [A] — CAPPELLA featuring Loleatta HOLLOWAY
TAKE ME AWAY [B] — D:REAM
TAKE ME AWAY [C] — CULTURE BEAT
TAKE ME AWAY (I'LL FOLLOW YOU) — BAD BOYS INC
TAKE ME AWAY (INTO THE NIGHT) — 4 STRINGS
TAKE ME AWAY (PARADISE) — MIX FACTORY
TAKE ME BACK — RHYTHMATIC
TAKE ME BACK TO LOVE AGAIN — Kathy SLEDGE
TAKE ME BAK 'OME — SLADE
TAKE ME BY THE HAND — SUBMERGE featuring Jan JOHNSTON
TAKE ME DOWN TO THE RIVER — SKIN
TAKE ME FOR A LITTLE WHILE — COVERDALE PAGE
TAKE ME FOR WHAT I'M WORTH — The SEARCHERS
TAKE ME GIRL I'M READY — Junior WALKER and the ALL-STARS
TAKE ME HIGH — Cliff RICHARD
TAKE ME HIGHER [A] — R.A.F.
TAKE ME HIGHER [B] — Diana ROSS
TAKE ME HIGHER [C] — GEORGIE PORGIE
TAKE ME HOME [A] — Phil COLLINS
TAKE ME HOME [B] — Joe COCKER
TAKE ME HOME (A GIRL LIKE ME) — Sophie ELLIS-BEXTOR
TAKE ME HOME COUNTRY ROADS — Olivia NEWTON-JOHN
TAKE ME I'M YOURS — SQUEEZE
TAKE ME IN YOUR ARMS (ROCK ME A LITTLE WHILE) — DOOBIE BROTHERS
TAKE ME IN YOUR ARMS AND LOVE ME [A] — Gladys KNIGHT and the PIPS
TAKE ME IN YOUR ARMS AND LOVE ME [A] — SCRITTI POLITTI
TAKE ME NOW — Tammy PAYNE
TAKE ME OUT — FRANZ FERDINAND
TAKE ME OVER — McKAY
TAKE ME THERE — BLACKSTREET and MYA featuring MA$E and BLINKY BLIN
TAKE ME TO HEAVEN — BABY D
TAKE ME TO THE CLOUDS ABOVE — LMC vs U2
TAKE ME TO THE MARDI GRAS — Paul SIMON
TAKE ME TO THE NEXT PHASE — ISLEY BROTHERS
TAKE ME TO YOUR HEART — Rick ASTLEY
TAKE ME TO YOUR HEART AGAIN — Vince HILL
TAKE ME TO YOUR HEAVEN — Charlotte NILSSON
TAKE ME UP [A] — SOUNDSOURCE
TAKE ME UP [B] — SONIC SURFERS featuring Jocelyn BROWN
TAKE ME WITH U [A] — PRINCE
TAKE ME WITH YOU [B] — COSMOS
TAKE MY ADVICE — Kym SIMS
TAKE MY BREATH AWAY (LOVE THEME FROM 'TOP GUN') [A] — BERLIN
TAKE MY BREATH AWAY [A] — SODA CLUB featuring Hannah ALETHEA
TAKE MY BREATH AWAY [B] — Emma BUNTON
TAKE MY HAND — Jurgen VRIES featuring Andrea BRITTON
TAKE MY HEART — Al MARTINO
TAKE MY HEART (YOU CAN HAVE IT IF YOU WANT IT) — KOOL and the GANG
TAKE MY SCARS — MACHINE HEAD
TAKE MY TIME — Sheena EASTON
TAKE OFF SOME TIME — NEW ATLANTIC
TAKE ON ME [A] — A-HA
TAKE ON ME [A] — a1
TAKE ON THE WORLD — JUDAS PRIEST
TAKE THAT LOOK OFF YOUR FACE — Marti WEBB
TAKE THAT SITUATION — Nick HEYWARD
TAKE THAT TO THE BANK — SHALAMAR
TAKE THE BOX — Amy WINEHOUSE
TAKE THE LONG ROAD AND WALK IT — The MUSIC
TAKE THE LONG WAY HOME — FAITHLESS
TAKE THESE CHAINS FROM MY HEART — Ray CHARLES
TAKE THIS HEART — Richard MARX
TAKE THIS TIME — Sean MAGUIRE
TAKE TO THE MOUNTAINS — Richard BARNES
TAKE YOU OUT — Luther VANDROSS
TAKE YOU THERE — Ronni SIMON
TAKE YOUR MAMA — SCISSOR SISTERS
TAKE YOUR MAMA FOR A RIDE — LULU
TAKE YOUR PARTNER BY THE HAND — Howie B featuring Robbie ROBERTSON
TAKE YOUR SHOES OFF — CHEEKY GIRLS
TAKE YOUR TIME [A] — HIGH
TAKE YOUR TIME [B] — MANTRONIX
TAKE YOUR TIME [C] — LOVE BITE
TAKE YOUR TIME (DO IT RIGHT) PART 1 — S.O.S. BAND
TAKEN FOR GRANTED — SIA
TAKES A LITTLE TIME — TOTAL CONTRAST
TAKES TWO TO TANGO — Louis ARMSTRONG
TAKIN' A CHANCE ON YOU — DOLLAR
TAKIN' HOLD — Sam LA MORE
TAKING OFF — The CURE
TAKING ON THE WORLD — GUN
TAKING THE VEIL — David SYLVIAN
TALES FROM A DANCEOGRAPHIC OCEAN EP — JAM & SPOON featuring PLAVKA
TALES FROM THE HARD SIDE — BIOHAZARD
TALES OF THE HOOD — TUBBY T
TALK ABOUT IT IN THE MORNING — Martyn JOSEPH

TALK ABOUT OUR LOVE — BRANDY featuring Kanye WEST
TALK BACK — DOUBLE TROUBLE
TALK DIRTY TO ME — POISON
TALK OF THE TOWN — The PRETENDERS
TALK SHOWS ON MUTE — INCUBUS
TALK TALK [A] — TALK TALK
TALK TALK TALK — The ORDINARY BOYS
TALK TO ME [A] — THIRD WORLD
TALK TO ME [B] — Stevie NICKS
TALK TO ME [C] — Anita BAKER
TALK TO ME [D] — 60FT DOLLS
TALKIN' ALL THAT JAZZ — STETSASONIC
TALKING IN YOUR SLEEP [A] — Crystal GAYLE
TALKING IN YOUR SLEEP [A] — Martine McCUTCHEON
TALKING IN YOUR SLEEP [B] — BUCKS FIZZ
TALKING LOUD AND CLEAR — ORCHESTRAL MANOEUVRES IN THE DARK
TALKING OF LOVE — Anita DOBSON
TALKING WITH MYSELF — ELECTRIBE 101
TALL DARK STRANGER — Rose BRENNAN
TALL 'N' HANDSOME — OUTRAGE
TALLAHASSEE LASSIE [A] — Freddy CANNON
TALLAHASSEE LASSIE [A] — Tommy STEELE
TALLYMAN — Jeff BECK
TALULA — Tori AMOS
TAM-TAM POUR L'ÉTHIOPIE — STARVATION
TAMMY — Debbie REYNOLDS
TANGERINE — FEEDER
TANGO IN MONO — EXPRESSOS
TANSY — Alex WELSH
TANTALISE (WO WO EE YEH YEH) — JIMMY THE HOOVER
TAP THE BOTTLE — YOUNG BLACK TEENAGERS
TAP TURNS ON THE WATER — CCS
TAPE LOOP — MORCHEEBA
TARANTINO'S NEW STAR — NORTH AND SOUTH
TARANTULA — FAITHLESS
TARA'S THEME [A] — SPIRO and WIX
TARA'S THEME FROM 'GONE WITH THE WIND' [A] — ROSE OF ROMANCE ORCHESTRA
TARZAN BOY — BALTIMORA
TASTE IN MEN — PLACEBO
TASTE IT — INXS
A TASTE OF AGGRO — The BARRON KNIGHTS
TASTE OF BITTER LOVE — Gladys KNIGHT and the PIPS
A TASTE OF HONEY — Acker BILK and his PARAMOUNT JAZZ BAND
THE TASTE OF INK — The USED
THE TASTE OF YOUR TEARS — KING
TASTE THE PAIN — RED HOT CHILI PEPPERS
TASTE YOU — AUF DER MAUR
TASTE YOUR LOVE — Horace BROWN
TASTY FISH — The OTHER TWO
TASTY LOVE — Freddie JACKSON
TATTOO — Mike OLDFIELD
TATTOOED MILLIONAIRE — Bruce DICKINSON
TATTVA — KULA SHAKER
TAVERN IN THE TOWN — Terry LIGHTFOOT and his NEW ORLEANS JAZZMEN
TAXI — J BLACKFOOT
TAXLOSS — MANSUN
TCHAIKOVSKY ONE — SECOND CITY SOUND
TE AMO — SULTANA
TEA FOR TWO CHA CHA — Tommy DORSEY ORCHESTRA starring Warren COVINGTON
TEACH ME TO TWIST — Chubby CHECKER and Bobby RYDELL
TEACH ME TONIGHT — DE CASTRO SISTERS
TEACH YOU TO ROCK — Tony CROMBIE and his ROCKETS
TEACHER [A] — JETHRO TULL
TEACHER [B] — I-LEVEL
THE TEACHER — BIG COUNTRY
TEACHER, TEACHER — Johnny MATHIS
TEAR AWAY — DROWNING POOL
TEAR DOWN THE WALLS — NO SWEAT
A TEAR FELL — Teresa BREWER
TEAR ME APART — Suzi QUATRO
TEAR OFF YOUR OWN HEAD (IT'S A DOLL REVOLUTION) — Elvis COSTELLO
TEAR SOUP — QUESTIONS
TEARDROP [A] — SANTO and JOHNNY
TEARDROP [B] — MASSIVE ATTACK
TEARDROP CITY — The MONKEES
TEARDROPS [A] — Shakin' STEVENS
TEARDROPS [B] — WOMACK and WOMACK
TEARDROPS [B] — LOVESTATION
TEARDROPS [C] — The 411
TEARIN' UP MY HEART — 'N SYNC
TEARING — ROLLINS BAND
TEARING US APART — Eric CLAPTON and Tina TURNER
TEARS [A] — Danny WILLIAMS
TEARS [B] — Ken DODD
TEARS [C] — Frankie KNUCKLES
TEARS [C] — NU COLOURS
TEARS ARE FALLING — KISS
TEARS ARE NOT ENOUGH — ABC
TEARS DON'T LIE — MARK 'OH
TEARS FROM A WILLOW — OOBERMAN
TEARS FROM HEAVEN — HEARTBEAT
TEARS FROM THE MOON — CONJURE ONE
THE TEARS I CRIED — GLITTER BAND
TEARS IN HEAVEN — Eric CLAPTON
TEARS IN THE RAIN — N-TRANCE
TEARS IN THE WIND — CHICKEN SHACK
THE TEARS OF A CLOWN [A] — Smokey ROBINSON and the MIRACLES
TEARS OF A CLOWN [A] — The BEAT
TEARS OF THE DRAGON — Bruce DICKINSON
TEARS ON MY PILLOW [A] — Johnny NASH
TEARS ON MY PILLOW [B] — Kylie MINOGUE
TEARS ON THE TELEPHONE [A] — Claude FRANÇOIS
TEARS ON THE TELEPHONE [B] — HOT CHOCOLATE
TEARS RUN RINGS — Marc ALMOND
TEARS WON'T WASH AWAY THESE HEARTACHES — Ken DODD
TEASE ME — Chaka DEMUS and PLIERS
TEASER — George BENSON
TECHNARCHY — CYBERSONIK
TECHNO FUNK — LOST
TECHNO TRANCE — D-SHAKE
TECHNOCAT — Tom WILSON
TEDDY BEAR [A] — Red SOVINE
TEDDY BEAR [B] — Booker NEWBURY III
TEDDY BEAR'S LAST RIDE — Diana WILLIAMS
TEEN ANGEL — Mark DINNING
TEEN BEAT — Sandy NELSON
TEENAGE — UK SUBS
TEENAGE ANGST — PLACEBO
TEENAGE DEPRESSION — EDDIE and the HOT RODS
TEENAGE DIRTBAG — WHEATUS
TEENAGE DREAM — T. REX
TEENAGE IDOL — Ricky NELSON
TEENAGE KICKS — The UNDERTONES
TEENAGE LAMENT '74 — Alice COOPER
TEENAGE PUNKS — SULTANS OF PING
TEENAGE RAMPAGE — The SWEET
TEENAGE SCREAMERS — TOKYO DRAGONS
TEENAGE SENSATION — CREDIT TO THE NATION
TEENAGE TURTLES — BACK TO THE PLANET
TEENAGE WARNING — ANGELIC UPSTARTS
A TEENAGER IN LOVE [A] — Craig DOUGLAS
A TEENAGER IN LOVE [A] — DION
A TEENAGER IN LOVE [A] — Marty WILDE
TEENSVILLE — Chet ATKINS
TEETHGRINDER — THERAPY?
TELEFUNKIN' — N-TYCE
TELEGRAM SAM — T. REX
TELEGRAPH — ORCHESTRAL MANOEUVRES IN THE DARK
THE TELEPHONE ALWAYS RINGS — FUN BOY THREE
TELEPHONE LINE — ELECTRIC LIGHT ORCHESTRA
TELEPHONE MAN — Meri WILSON
TELEPHONE OPERATOR — Pete SHELLEY
TELEPHONE THING — The FALL
TELEPORT — MAN WITH NO NAME
TELETUBBIES SAY EH-OH! — TELETUBBIES
TELEVATORS — The MARS VOLTA
TELEVISION THE DRUG OF THE NATION — DISPOSABLE HEROES OF HIPHOPRISY
TELL HER ABOUT IT — Billy JOEL
TELL HER I'M NOT HOME — Ike and Tina TURNER
TELL HER NO — ZOMBIES
TELL HER THIS — DEL AMITRI
TELL HIM [A] — Billie DAVIS
TELL HIM [A] — EXCITERS
TELL HIM [A] — HELLO
TELL HIM [A] — QUENTIN and ASH
TELL HIM [B] — Barbra STREISAND and Celine DION
TELL IT LIKE IT T-I-IS — B-52's
TELL IT ON THE MOUNTAIN — PETER, PAUL and MARY
TELL IT TO MY HEART [A] — Taylor DAYNE
TELL IT TO MY HEART [A] — Q-CLUB
TELL IT TO MY HEART [A] — Kelly LLORENNA
TELL IT TO THE RAIN — The FOUR SEASONS
TELL LAURA I LOVE HER — Ricky VALANCE
TELL ME [A] — Nick KAMEN
TELL ME [B] — GROOVE THEORY
TELL ME [C] — DRU HILL
TELL ME [D] — Billie MYERS
TELL ME [E] — Melanie B
TELL ME A STORY — Jimmy BOYD and Frankie LAINE
TELL ME DO U WANNA — GINUWINE
TELL ME (HOW IT FEELS) — 52ND STREET
TELL ME I'M NOT DREAMING — TITIYO
TELL ME IT IS TRUE — UB40
TELL ME IT'S REAL — K-CI & JOJO
TELL ME MA — SHAM ROCK
TELL ME ON A SUNDAY — Marti WEBB
TELL ME THAT YOU LOVE ME — Paul ANKA
TELL ME THE WAY — CAPPELLA
TELL ME THERE'S A HEAVEN — Chris REA
TELL ME TO MY FACE — KEITH
TELL ME TOMORROW [A] — Smokey ROBINSON
TELL ME TOMORROW [B] — PRINCESS
TELL ME WHAT HE SAID — Helen SHAPIRO
TELL ME WHAT YOU SEE — The VON BONDIES
TELL ME WHAT YOU WANT [A] — Jimmy RUFFIN
TELL ME WHAT YOU WANT [B] — LOOSE ENDS
TELL ME WHAT YOU WANT [C] — BLU PETER
TELL ME WHAT YOU WANT ME TO DO — Tevin CAMPBELL
TELL ME WHEN [A] — APPLEJACKS
TELL ME WHEN [B] — HUMAN LEAGUE
TELL ME WHEN THE FEVER ENDED — ELECTRIBE 101
TELL ME WHERE YOU'RE GOING — SILJE
TELL ME WHY [A] — Elvis PRESLEY
TELL ME WHY [B] — Alvin STARDUST
TELL ME WHY [C] — MUSICAL YOUTH
TELL ME WHY [D] — Bobby WOMACK
TELL ME WHY [E] — THIS WAY UP
TELL ME WHY [F] — GENESIS
TELL ME WHY [G] — DECLAN featuring YOUNG VOICES CHOIR
TELL ME WHY (THE RIDDLE) — Paul VAN DYK featuring SAINT ETIENNE
TELL THAT GIRL TO SHUT UP — TRANSVISION VAMP
TELL THE CHILDREN — SHAM 69
TELLIN' STORIES — The CHARLATANS
TELSTAR — TORNADOS
TEMMA HARBOUR — Mary HOPKIN
TEMPERAMENTAL — EVERYTHING BUT THE GIRL
TEMPERATURE RISING — PKA
TEMPERTEMPER — GOLDIE
TEMPLE OF DOOM — DJ FRESH
TEMPLE OF DREAMS [A] — MESSIAH
TEMPLE OF DREAMS [B] — FUTURE BREEZE
TEMPLE OF LOVE — SISTERS OF MERCY
TEMPO FIESTA (PARTY TIME) — ITTY BITTY BOOZY WOOZY
TEMPORARY BEAUTY — Graham PARKER and the RUMOUR
TEMPTATION [A] — The EVERLY BROTHERS
TEMPTATION [B] — NEW ORDER
TEMPTATION [C] — HEAVEN 17
TEMPTATION [D] — Joan ARMATRADING
TEMPTATION [E] — WET WET WET
TEMPTED — SQUEEZE
TEMPTED TO TOUCH — RUPEE
10AM AUTOMATIC — BLACK KEYS
10538 OVERTURE — ELECTRIC LIGHT ORCHESTRA
10 IN 01 — MEMBERS OF MAYDAY
TEN MILES HIGH — LITTLE ANGELS
10 SECOND BIONIC MAN — KINKY MACHINE
TEN STOREY LOVE SONG — The STONE ROSES
TEN THOUSAND MILES — Michael HOLLIDAY
10 X 10 — 808 STATE
TEN TO TWENTY — SNEAKER PIMPS
10 YEARS ASLEEP — KINGMAKER
TEN YEARS TIME — GABRIELLE
TENDER — BLUR
TENDER HANDS — Chris DE BURGH
TENDER HEART — Lionel RICHIE
TENDER LOVE [A] — FORCE M.D.s
TENDER LOVE [A] — Kenny THOMAS
TENDERLY — Nat 'King' COLE
TENDERNESS — Diana ROSS
TENNESSEE — ARRESTED DEVELOPMENT
TENNESSEE WIG WALK — Bonnie LOU
TENSHI — GOURYELLA
THE TENTH PLANET — DISTORTED MINDS
TEQUILA [A] — CHAMPS
TEQUILA [A] — Ted HEATH
TEQUILA [A] — NO WAY JOSÉ
TEQUILA [B] — TERRORVISION
TEQUILA SUNRISE — CYPRESS HILL
TERESA — Joe DOLAN
TERRITORY — SEPULTURA
TERRY — TWINKLE
TERRY'S THEME FROM 'LIMELIGHT' [A] — Frank CHACKSFIELD
TERRY'S THEME FROM 'LIMELIGHT' [A] — Ron GOODWIN
TESLA GIRLS — ORCHESTRAL MANOEUVRES IN THE DARK
THE TEST — The CHEMICAL BROTHERS
TEST OF TIME [A] — Will DOWNING
TEST OF TIME [A] — The CRESCENT
TEST THE THEORY — AUDIOWEB
TESTAMENT 4 — Chubby CHUNKS
TESTIFY [A] — M PEOPLE
TESTIFY [B] — Byron STINGILY
TETRIS — DOCTOR SPIN
TEXAS — Chris REA
TEXAS COWBOYS — GRID
THA CROSSROADS — BONE THUGS-N-HARMONY
THA DOGGFATHER — SNOOP DOGG
THA HORNS OF JERICHO — DJ SUPREME
THA WILD STYLE — DJ SUPREME
THANK ABBA FOR THE MUSIC — VARIOUS ARTISTS (EPs and LPs)
THANK GOD I FOUND YOU — 98°
THANK GOD IT'S CHRISTMAS — QUEEN
THANK GOD IT'S FRIDAY — R KELLY
THANK U — Alanis MORISSETTE
THANK U VERY MUCH — SCAFFOLD
THANK YOU [A] — PALE FOUNTAINS
THANK YOU [B] — BOYZ II MEN
THANK YOU [C] — DIDO
THANK YOU [D] — JAMELIA
THANK YOU BABY (FOR MAKIN' SOMEDAY COME SO SOON) — Shania TWAIN
THANK YOU FOR A GOOD YEAR — Alexander O'NEAL
THANK YOU FOR BEING A FRIEND — Andrew GOLD
THANK YOU FOR HEARING ME — Sinead O'CONNOR
THANK YOU FOR LOVING ME — BON JOVI
THANK YOU FOR THE MUSIC — ABBA
THANK YOU FOR THE PARTY — DUKES
THANK YOU FOR THE VENOM — MY CHEMICAL ROMANCE
THANK YOU MY LOVE — IMAGINATION
THANK YOU WORLD — WORLD PARTY
THANKS A LOT — Brenda LEE
THANKS FOR MY CHILD — Cheryl Pepsii RILEY
THANKS FOR SAVING MY LIFE — Billy PAUL
THANKS FOR THE MEMORY (WHAM BAM THANK YOU MAM) — SLADE
THANKS FOR THE NIGHT — The DAMNED
THAT CERTAIN SMILE — Midge URE
THAT DAY — Natalie IMBRUGLIA
THAT DON'T IMPRESS ME MUCH — Shania TWAIN
THAT EXTRA MILE — RICKY
THAT FEELING — DJ CHUS presents GROOVE FOUNDATION
THAT GIRL [A] — Stevie WONDER
THAT GIRL [B] — Maxi PRIEST featuring SHAGGY
THAT GIRL [C] — McFLY
THAT GIRL BELONGS TO YESTERDAY — Gene PITNEY
THAT GIRL (GROOVY SITUATION) — Freddie McGREGOR
THAT GREAT LOVE SOUND — The RAVEONETTES
THAT JOKE ISN'T FUNNY ANYMORE — The SMITHS
THAT LADY — ISLEY BROTHERS
THAT LOOK — DE'LACY
THAT LOOK IN YOUR EYE — Ali CAMPBELL
THAT LOVING FEELING — CICERO
THAT LUCKY OLD SUN — VELVETS
THAT MAN (HE'S ALL MINE) — INNER CITY
THAT MAN WILL NOT HANG — McLUSKEY
THAT MEANS A LOT — PJ PROBY
THAT NOISE — Anthony NEWLEY
THAT OLD BLACK MAGIC — Sammy DAVIS Jr
THAT OLE DEVIL CALLED LOVE — Alison MOYET
THAT SAME OLD FEELING — PICKETTYWITCH
THAT SOUND — Michael MOOG
THAT SOUNDS GOOD TO ME — JIVE BUNNY and the MASTERMIXERS
THAT THING YOU DO! — The WONDERS
THAT WAS MY VEIL — John PARISH and Polly Jean HARVEY
THAT WAS THEN THIS IS NOW [A] — ABC
THAT WAS THEN, THIS IS NOW [B] — The MONKEES
THAT WAS YESTERDAY — FOREIGNER
THAT WOMAN'S GOT ME DRINKING — Shane MacGOWAN and the POPES
THAT ZIPPER TRACK — DJ DAN presents NEEDLE DAMAGE
THAT'LL BE THE DAY [A] — The CRICKETS
THAT'LL BE THE DAY [A] — The EVERLY BROTHERS
THAT'LL DO NICELY — BAD MANNERS
THAT'S ALL — GENESIS
THAT'S ALL RIGHT — Elvis PRESLEY
THAT'S AMORE — Dean MARTIN
THAT'S ENTERTAINMENT — The JAM
THAT'S HOW A LOVE SONG WAS BORN — Ray BURNS with the CORONETS
THAT'S HOW GOOD YOUR LOVE IS — IL PADRINOS featuring JOCELYN BROWN
THAT'S HOW I FEEL ABOUT YOU — LONDONBEAT
THAT'S HOW I'M LIVING [A] — Tony SCOTT
THAT'S HOW I'M LIVIN' [B] — ICE-T
THAT'S HOW STRONG MY LOVE IS — IN CROWD
THAT'S JUST THE WAY IT IS — Phil COLLINS
THAT'S LIFE — Frank SINATRA
THAT'S LIVIN' ALRIGHT — Joe FAGIN
THAT'S LOVE — Billy FURY
THAT'S LOVE, THAT IT IS — BLANCMANGE
THAT'S MORE LIKE IT — SKYLARK
THAT'S MY DOLL — Frankie VAUGHAN
THAT'S MY HOME — Mr Acker BILK and his PARAMOUNT JAZZ BAND
THAT'S NICE — Neil CHRISTIAN
THAT'S RIGHT — DEEP RIVER BOYS
THAT'S THE WAY — HONEYCOMBS
THAT'S THE WAY GOD PLANNED IT — Billy PRESTON
THAT'S THE WAY I LIKE IT [A] — KC and the SUNSHINE BAND
THAT'S THE WAY (I LIKE IT) [A] — DEAD OR ALIVE
THAT'S THE WAY (I LIKE IT) [A] — CLOCK
THAT'S THE WAY I WANNA ROCK 'N' ROLL — AC/DC
THAT'S THE WAY IT FEELS — TWO NATIONS
THAT'S THE WAY IT IS [A] — MEL and KIM

THAT'S THE WAY IT IS [B] — Celine DION
THAT'S THE WAY LOVE GOES [A] — Charles DICKENS
THAT'S THE WAY LOVE GOES [B] — YOUNG MC
THAT'S THE WAY LOVE GOES [C] — Janet JACKSON
THAT'S THE WAY LOVE IS [A] — TEN CITY
THAT'S THE WAY LOVE IS [A] — VOLCANO
THAT'S THE WAY LOVE IS [A] — Byron STINGILY
THAT'S THE WAY LOVE IS [B] — Bobby BROWN
THAT'S THE WAY OF THE WORLD — D MOB with Cathy DENNIS
THAT'S THE WAY THE MONEY GOES — M
THAT'S THE WAY YOU DO IT — PURPLE KINGS
THAT'S WHAT FRIENDS ARE FOR [A] — Deniece WILLIAMS
THAT'S WHAT FRIENDS ARE FOR [B] — Dionne WARWICK and FRIENDS featuring Elton JOHN, Stevie WONDER and Gladys KNIGHT
THAT'S WHAT I LIKE — JIVE BUNNY and the MASTERMIXERS
THAT'S WHAT I THINK — Cyndi LAUPER
THAT'S WHAT I WANT — MARAUDERS
THAT'S WHAT I WANT TO BE — Neil REID
THAT'S WHAT LIFE IS ALL ABOUT — Bing CROSBY
THAT'S WHAT LOVE CAN DO — TOUTES LES FILLES
THAT'S WHAT LOVE IS FOR — Amy GRANT
THAT'S WHAT LOVE WILL DO — Joe BROWN and the BRUVVERS
THAT'S WHEN I REACH FOR MY REVOLVER — MOBY
THAT'S WHEN I THINK OF YOU — 1927
THAT'S WHEN THE MUSIC TAKES ME — Neil SEDAKA
THAT'S WHERE MY MIND GOES — SLAMM
THAT'S WHERE THE HAPPY PEOPLE GO — The TRAMMPS
THAT'S WHY I LIE — Ray J
THAT'S WHY I'M CRYING — IVY LEAGUE
THAT'S WHY WE LOSE CONTROL — YOUNG OFFENDERS
THAT'S YOU — Nat 'King' COLE
THEM BONES — ALICE IN CHAINS
THEM GIRLS THEM GIRLS — ZIG and ZAG
... THEM THANGS — 50 CENT & G-UNIT
THEM THERE EYES — Emile FORD and the CHECKMATES
THEME — SABRES OF PARADISE
THE THEME [A] — UNIQUE 3
THE THEME [B] — Tracey LEE
THE THEME [C] — DREEM TEEM
THE THEME [D] — Jurgen VRIES
THEME FOR A DREAM — Cliff RICHARD and The SHADOWS
THEME FOR YOUNG LOVERS — The SHADOWS
THEME FROM 'A SUMMER PLACE' [A] — Norrie PARAMOR
THE THEME FROM 'A SUMMER PLACE' [A] — Percy FAITH
THEME FROM 'CADE'S COUNTY' — Henry MANCINI
THEME FROM 'CHEERS' — Gary PORTNOY
THEME FROM 'COME SEPTEMBER' — Bobby DARIN
THEME FROM DIXIE — Duane EDDY and the REBELS
THEME FROM 'DR KILDARE' [A] — Johnnie SPENCE
THEME FROM 'DR KILDARE' (THREE STARS WILL SHINE TONIGHT) [A] — Richard CHAMBERLAIN
THEME FROM 'E.T.' (THE EXTRA-TERRESTRIAL) — John WILLIAMS
THEME FROM GUTBUSTER — BENTLEY RHYTHM ACE
THEME FROM 'HARRY'S GAME' — CLANNAD
THEME FROM 'HILL STREET BLUES' — Mike POST
THEME FROM 'JURASSIC PARK' — John WILLIAMS
THEME FROM 'MAHOGANY' (DO YOU KNOW WHERE YOU'RE GOING TO) — Diana ROSS
THEME FROM M*A*S*H (SUICIDE IS PAINLESS) [A] — MASH
THEME FROM M.A.S.H. (SUICIDE IS PAINLESS) [A] — MANIC STREET PREACHERS
THEME FROM 'MISSION: IMPOSSIBLE' — Adam CLAYTON and Larry MULLEN
THEME FROM 'NEW YORK, NEW YORK' — Frank SINATRA
THEME FROM PICNIC — Morris STOLOFF
THEME FROM P.O.P. — PERFECTLY ORDINARY PEOPLE
THEME FROM 'RANDALL & HOPKIRK (DECEASED)' — Nina PERSSON and David ARNOLD
THEME FROM S-EXPRESS — S EXPRESS
THEME FROM 'SHAFT' [A] — Isaac HAYES
THEME FROM 'SHAFT' [A] — EDDY and the SOUL BAND
THEME FROM SPARTA FC #2 — The FALL
THEME FROM 'SUPERMAN' (MAIN TITLE) — LONDON SYMPHONY ORCHESTRA
THEME FROM 'THE APARTMENT' — FERRANTE and TEICHER
THEME FROM 'THE DEER HUNTER' (CAVATINA) — The SHADOWS
THEME FROM THE FILM 'THE LEGION'S LAST PATROL' — Ken THORNE
THEME FROM 'HONG KONG BEAT' — Richard DENTON and Martin COOK
THEME FROM 'THE ONEDIN LINE' — VIENNA PHILHARMONIC ORCHESTRA
THEME FROM 'THE PERSUADERS' — John BARRY ORCHESTRA
THEME FROM 'THE PROFESSIONALS' — Laurie JOHNSON
THEME FROM 'THE THREEPENNY OPERA' [A] — Louis ARMSTRONG
THEME FROM 'THE THREEPENNY OPERA' [A] — Dick HYMAN TRIO
THEME FROM 'THE THREEPENNY OPERA' [A] — Billy VAUGHN
THEME FROM 'THE TRAVELLING MAN' — Duncan BROWNE
THEME FROM 'THE VALLEY OF THE DOLLS' [A] — Dionne WARWICK
THEME FROM TURNPIKE (EP) — dEUS
THEME FROM 'VIETNAM' (CANON IN D) — Orchestre de Chambre Jean-François PAILLARD
THEME FROM 'WHICH WAY IS UP' — STARGARD
THEME FROM 'Z CARS' [A] — Norrie PARAMOR
THEME FROM 'Z CARS' JOHNNY TODD [A] — Johnny KEATING
THEME ONE — Cozy POWELL
THEN — The CHARLATANS
THEN CAME YOU [A] — Dionne WARWICK and the DETRIOT SPINNERS
THEN CAME YOU [A] — JUNIOR
THEN HE KISSED ME — CRYSTALS
THEN I FEEL GOOD — Katherine E
THEN I KISSED HER — The BEACH BOYS
THEN YOU CAN TELL ME GOODBYE — CASINOS
THEN YOU TURN AWAY — ORCHESTRAL MANOEUVRES IN THE DARK
THERE AIN'T NOTHIN' LIKE THE LOVE — MONTAGE
THERE AIN'T NOTHING LIKE SHAGGIN' — TAMS
THERE ARE MORE QUESTIONS THAN ANSWERS — Johnny NASH
THERE ARE MORE SNAKES THAN LADDERS — CAPTAIN SENSIBLE
THERE BUT FOR FORTUNE — Joan BAEZ
THERE BUT FOR THE GRACE OF GOD — FIRE ISLAND
THERE BY THE GRACE OF GOD — MANIC STREET PREACHERS
THERE GOES MY EVERYTHING [A] — Engelbert HUMPERDINCK
THERE GOES MY EVERYTHING [A] — Elvis PRESLEY
THERE GOES MY FIRST LOVE — The DRIFTERS
THERE GOES THAT SONG AGAIN — Gary MILLER
THERE GOES THE FEAR — DOVES
THERE GOES THE NEIGHBORHOOD — Sheryl CROW
THERE I GO — Vikki CARR
THERE I GO AGAIN — POWER OF DREAMS
THERE IS A LIGHT THAT NEVER GOES OUT — The SMITHS
THERE IS A MOUNTAIN — DONOVAN
THERE IS A STAR — PHARAO
THERE IS ALWAYS SOMETHING THERE TO REMIND ME — The HOUSEMARTINS
THERE IS NO LOVE BETWEEN US ANYMORE — POP WILL EAT ITSELF
THERE IT IS — SHALAMAR
THERE I'VE SAID IT AGAIN [A] — Al SAXON
THERE I'VE SAID IT AGAIN [A] — Bobby VINTON
THERE MUST BE A REASON — Frankie LAINE
THERE MUST BE A WAY [A] — Joni JAMES
THERE MUST BE A WAY [A] — Frankie VAUGHAN
THERE MUST BE AN ANGEL (PLAYING WITH MY HEART) — EURYTHMICS
THERE MUST BE THOUSANDS — QUADS
THERE SHE GOES [A] — The LA's
THERE SHE GOES [A] — SIXPENCE NONE THE RICHER
THERE SHE GOES AGAIN — QUIREBOYS
THERE SHE GOES, MY BEAUTIFUL WORLD — Nick CAVE & The BAD SEEDS
THERE THERE — RADIOHEAD
THERE THERE MY DEAR — DEXY'S MIDNIGHT RUNNERS
THERE WILL NEVER BE ANOTHER TONIGHT — Bryan ADAMS
THERE WILL NEVER BE ANOTHER YOU [A] — Chris MONTEZ
THERE WILL NEVER BE ANOTHER YOU [B] — Jimmy RUFFIN
THERE WON'T BE MANY COMING HOME — Roy ORBISON
THERE YOU GO — PINK
THERE YOU'LL BE — Faith HILL
(THERE'LL BE BLUEBIRDS OVER) THE WHITE CLIFFS OF DOVER — Robson GREEN and Jerome FLYNN
THERE'LL BE SAD SONGS (TO MAKE YOU CRY) — Billy OCEAN
THERE'S A BRAND NEW WORLD — FIVE STAR
THERE'S A GHOST IN MY HOUSE [A] — R Dean TAYLOR
THERE'S A GHOST IN MY HOUSE [A] — The FALL
THERE'S A GOLDMINE IN THE SKY — Pat BOONE
THERE'S A GUY WORKS DOWN THE CHIPSHOP SWEARS HE'S ELVIS — Kirsty MacCOLL
THERE'S A HEARTACHE FOLLOWING ME — Jim REEVES
THERE'S A HOLE IN MY BUCKET — Harry BELAFONTE
THERE'S A KIND OF HUSH [A] — HERMAN'S HERMITS
THERE'S A KIND OF HUSH (ALL OVER THE WORLD) [A] — The CARPENTERS
THERE'S A SILENCE — The ELECTRIC SOFT PARADE
THERE'S A STAR — ASH
THERE'S A WHOLE LOT OF LOVING — GUYS & DOLLS
THERE'S ALWAYS ROOM ON THE BROOM —The LIARS
(THERE'S) ALWAYS SOMETHING THERE TO REMIND ME — Sandie SHAW
(THERE'S GONNA BE A) SHOWDOWN — Archie BELL and the DRELLS
THERE'S GOT TO BE A WAY — Mariah CAREY
(THERE'S GOTTA BE) MORE TO LIFE — Stacie ORRICO
THERE'S MORE TO LOVE — COMMUNARDS
THERE'S NO LIVING WITHOUT YOU — Will DOWNING
THERE'S NO ONE QUITE LIKE GRANDMA — ST WINIFRED'S SCHOOL CHOIR
THERE'S NO OTHER WAY — BLUR
THERE'S NOTHING BETTER THAN LOVE — Luther VANDROSS
THERE'S NOTHING I WON'T DO — JX
THERE'S NOTHING LIKE THIS — OMAR
THERE'S SOMETHING WRONG IN PARADISE — Kid CREOLE and the COCONUTS
THERE'S THE GIRL — HEART
THERE'S YOUR TROUBLE — DIXIE CHICKS
THESE ARE DAYS — 10,000 MANIACS
THESE ARE THE DAYS [A] — O-TOWN
THESE ARE THE DAYS [B] — Jamie CULLUM
THESE ARE THE DAYS OF OUR LIVES — QUEEN
THESE ARE THE TIMES — DRU HILL
THESE ARMS OF MINE — The PROCLAIMERS
THESE BOOTS ARE MADE FOR WALKIN' [A] — Nancy SINATRA
THESE BOOTS ARE MADE FOR WALKIN' [A] — Billy Ray CYRUS
THESE DAYS — BON JOVI
THESE DREAMS — HEART
THESE EARLY DAYS — EVERYTHING BUT THE GIRL
THESE THINGS ARE WORTH FIGHTING FOR — Gary CLAIL ON-U SOUND SYSTEM
THESE THINGS WILL KEEP ME LOVING YOU — VELVELETTES
THESE WOODEN IDEAS — IDLEWILD
THESE WORDS — Natasha BEDINGFIELD
THEY ALL LAUGHED — Frank SINATRA
(THEY CALL HER) LA BAMBA — The CRICKETS
THEY DON'T CARE ABOUT US — Michael JACKSON
THEY DON'T KNOW [A] — Tracey ULLMAN
THEY DON'T KNOW [B] — Jon B
THEY DON'T KNOW [C] — SO SOLID CREW
THEY GLUED YOUR HEAD ON UPSIDE DOWN — The BELLRAYS
(THEY LONG TO BE) CLOSE TO YOU [A] — The CARPENTERS
(THEY LONG TO BE) CLOSE TO YOU [A] — Gwen GUTHRIE
THEY SAY IT'S GONNA RAIN — Hazell DEAN
THEY SHOOT HORSES DON'T THEY? — RACING CARS
THEY WILL KILL US ALL — The BRONX
THEY'RE COMING TO TAKE ME AWAY HA-HAAA! — NAPOLEON XIV
THEY'RE HERE — EMF
THIEVES IN THE TEMPLE — PRINCE
THIEVES LIKE US — NEW ORDER
THIGHS HIGH (GRIP YOUR HIPS AND MOVE) — Tom BROWNE
THIN LINE BETWEEN LOVE AND HATE — The PRETENDERS
THE THIN WALL — ULTRAVOX
A THING CALLED LOVE — Johnny CASH
THE THING I LIKE — AALIYAH
THINGS — Bobby DARIN
THE THINGS — AUDIO BULLYS
THINGS CAN ONLY GET BETTER [A] — Howard JONES
THINGS CAN ONLY GET BETTER [B] — D:REAM
THINGS FALL APART — SERAFIN
THINGS GET BETTER — Eddie FLOYD
THINGS HAVE CHANGED — Bob DYLAN
THINGS I'VE SEEN — SPOOKS
THINGS THAT ARE — RUNRIG
THINGS THAT MAKE YOU GO HMMM ... — C & C MUSIC FACTORY / CLIVILLES & COLE
THE THINGS THE LONELY DO — AMAZULU
THINGS THAT GO BUMP IN THE NIGHT — ALLSTARS
THE THINGS WE DO FOR LOVE [A] — 10cc
THINGS WILL GO MY WAY — The CALLING
THINGS WE DO FOR LOVE [B] — Horace BROWN
THINK [A] — Brenda LEE
THINK [B] — Chris FARLOWE
THINK [C] — Aretha FRANKLIN
THINK ABOUT ... — DJH featuring STEFY
THINK ABOUT ME — ARTFUL DODGER featuring Michelle ESCOFFERY
THINK ABOUT THAT — Dandy LIVINGSTONE
THINK ABOUT THE WAY (BOM DIGI DIGI BOM ...) — ICE MC
THINK ABOUT YOUR CHILDREN — Mary HOPKIN
THINK FOR A MINUTE — The HOUSEMARTINS
THINK I'M GONNA FALL IN LOVE WITH YOU — The DOOLEYS
THINK IT ALL OVER — Sandie SHAW
THINK IT OVER — The CRICKETS
THINK OF ME (WHEREVER YOU ARE) — Ken DODD
THINK OF YOU [A] — USHER
THINK OF YOU [B] — WHIGFIELD
THINK SOMETIMES ABOUT ME — Sandie SHAW
THINK TWICE — Celine DION
THINKIN' ABOUT YOUR BODY — Bobby McFERRIN
THINKIN' AIN'T FOR ME — Paul JONES
THINKING ABOUT TOMORROW — Beth ORTON
THINKING ABOUT YOUR BODY — 2 MAD
THINKING ABOUT YOUR LOVE [A] — SKIPWORTH and TURNER
THINKING ABOUT YOUR LOVE [A] — Phillip LEO
THINKING ABOUT YOUR LOVE [B] — Kenny THOMAS
THINKING IT OVER — LIBERTY
THINKING OF YOU [A] — SISTER SLEDGE
THINKING OF YOU [A] — MAUREEN
THINKING OF YOU [A] — Curtis LYNCH Jr featuring Kele LE ROC and RED RAT
THINKING OF YOU [A] — Paul WELLER
THINKING OF YOU [B] — COLOUR FIELD
THINKING OF YOU [C] — HANSON
THINKING OF YOU [D] — STATUS QUO
THINKING OF YOU BABY — Dave CLARK FIVE
THINKING OVER — Dana GLOVER
THIRD FINGER, LEFT HAND — PEARLS
THE THIRD MAN — The SHADOWS
THIRD RAIL — SQUEEZE
13 STEPS LEAD DOWN — Elvis COSTELLO
THE 13TH — The CURE
13TH DISCIPLE — FIVE THIRTY
30 CENTURY MAN — CATHERINE WHEEL
36D — The BEAUTIFUL SOUTH
THIRTY THREE — SMASHING PUMPKINS
THIS AIN'T A LOVE SONG — BON JOVI
THIS AND THAT — Tom JONES
THIS BEAT IS MINE — Vicky D
THIS BEAT IS TECHNOTRONIC — TECHNOTRONIC
THIS BOY [A] — JUSTIN
THIS BOY [A] — Tom BAXTER
THIS BRUTAL HOUSE — NITRO DELUXE
THIS CAN BE REAL — CANDY FLIP
THIS CHARMING MAN — The SMITHS
THIS CORROSION — SISTERS OF MERCY
THIS COWBOY SONG — STING featuring Pato BANTON
THIS DJ — Warren G
THIS DOOR SWINGS BOTH WAYS — HERMAN'S HERMITS
THIS FEELIN' — Frank HOOKER and POSITIVE PEOPLE
THIS FEELING — PURESSENCE
THIS FLIGHT TONIGHT — NAZARETH
THIS GARDEN — LEVELLERS
THIS GENERATION — ROACHFORD
THIS GIVEN LINE — The ELECTRIC SOFT PARADE
THIS GOLDEN RING — FORTUNES
THIS GROOVE — Victoria BECKHAM
THIS GUY'S IN LOVE WITH YOU — Herb ALPERT
THIS HERE GIRAFFE — The FLAMING LIPS
THIS HOUSE [A] — Tracie SPENCER
THIS HOUSE [B] — Alison MOYET
THIS HOUSE IS NOT A HOME — REMBRANDTS
THIS HOUSE (IS WHERE YOUR LOVE STANDS) — BIG SOUND AUTHORITY
THIS I PROMISE YOU — 'N SYNC
THIS I SWEAR [A] — Richard DARBYSHIRE
THIS I SWEAR [B] — Kim WILDE
THIS IS A CALL — FOO FIGHTERS
THIS IS A REBEL SONG — Sinead O'CONNOR
THIS IS A WARNING — DILLINJA
THIS IS ENGLAND — The CLASH
THIS IS FOR REAL — David DEVANT & HIS SPIRIT WIFE
THIS IS FOR THE LOVER IN YOU — BABYFACE
THIS IS FOR THE POOR — The OTHERS
THIS IS GOODBYE — Lucy CARR
THIS IS HARDCORE — PULP
THIS IS HOW IT FEELS — INSPIRAL CARPETS
THIS IS HOW WE DO IT [A] — Montell JORDAN
THIS IS HOW WE DO IT [A] — MIS-TEEQ
THIS IS HOW WE PARTY — S.O.A.P.
THIS IS IT! [A] — Adam FAITH
THIS IS IT [B] — Melba MOORE
THIS IS IT [B] — Dannii MINOGUE

TO WIN JUST ONCE — SAW DOCTORS
TO YOU I BELONG — B*WITCHED
TO YOU I BESTOW — MUNDY
TOAST — STREETBAND
TOAST OF LOVE — The THREE DEGREES
TOBACCO ROAD — NASHVILLE TEENS
TOCA ME — FRAGMA
TOCA'S MIRACLE — FRAGMA: Vocals by Co Co
TOCCATA — SKY
TOCCATA AND FUGUE — VANESSA-MAE
TODAY [A] — Sandie SHAW
TODAY [B] — TALK TALK
TODAY [C] — SMASHING PUMPKINS
TODAY FOREVER — RIDE
TODAY'S THE DAY — Sean MAGUIRE
TODAY'S YOUR LUCKY DAY —
   Harold MELVIN and the BLUENOTES
TOGETHER [A] — Connie FRANCIS
TOGETHER [A] — PJ PROBY
TOGETHER [B] — OC SMITH
TOGETHER [C] — Danny CAMPBELL and SASHA
TOGETHER [D] —
   ARTIFICIAL FUNK featuring Nellie ETTISON
TOGETHER AGAIN [A] — Ray CHARLES
TOGETHER AGAIN [B] — Janet JACKSON
TOGETHER FOREVER — Rick ASTLEY
TOGETHER IN ELECTRIC DREAMS —
   Giorgio MORODER
TOGETHER WE ARE BEAUTIFUL [A] —
   Steve ALLAN
TOGETHER WE ARE BEAUTIFUL [A] —
   Fern KINNEY
TOGETHERNESS — Mike PRESTON
TOKOLOSHE MAN — John KONGOS
TOKYO — CLASSIX NOUVEAUX
TOKYO JOE — Bryan FERRY
TOKYO MELODY — Helmut ZACHARIAS
TOKYO STEALTH FIGHTER — Dave ANGEL
TOKYO STORM WARNING — Elvis COSTELLO
TOLEDO — Elvis COSTELLO / Burt BACHARACH
TOM DOOLEY — KINGSTON TRIO
TOM DOOLEY [A] — Lonnie DONEGAN
TOM HARK [A] —
   ELIAS and his ZIGZAG JIVE FLUTES
TOM HARK [A] — Ted HEATH
TOM HARK [A] — PIRANHAS
TOM JONES INTERNATIONAL — Tom JONES
TOM PILLIBI — Jacqueline BOYER
TOM SAWYER — RUSH
TOM THE MODEL —
   Beth GIBBONS & RUSTIN MAN
TOM THE PEEPER — ACT ONE
TOM-TOM TURNAROUND — NEW WORLD
TOM TRAUBERT'S BLUES (WALTZING MATILDA) —
   Rod STEWART
TOMB OF MEMORIES — Paul YOUNG
TOMBOY — Perry COMO
TOMMY GUN — The CLASH
TOMMY SHOTS — YOUNG HEART ATTACK
TOMORROW [A] — Johnny BRANDON
TOMORROW [B] — Sandie SHAW
TOMORROW [C] — COMMUNARDS
TOMORROW [D] — TONGUE 'N' CHEEK
TOMORROW [E] — SILVERCHAIR
TOMORROW [F] — JAMES
TOMORROW [G] — DUMONDE
TOMORROW COMES TODAY — GORILLAZ
TOMORROW NEVER DIES — Sheryl CROW
TOMORROW NIGHT — ATOMIC ROOSTER
TOMORROW PEOPLE —
   Ziggy MARLEY and the MELODY MAKERS
TOMORROW RISING — Cliff RICHARD
TOMORROW ROBINS WILL SING —
   Stevie WONDER
TOMORROW TOMORROW — The BEE GEES
TOMORROW'S CLOWN — Marty WILDE
TOMORROW'S GIRLS [A] — UK SUBS
TOMORROW'S GIRLS [B] — Donald FAGEN
TOMORROW'S (JUST ANOTHER DAY) —
   MADNESS
TOM'S DINER [A] — Suzanne VEGA
TOM'S DINER [A] —
   DNA featuring Suzanne VEGA
TOM'S PARTY — T-SPOON
TONES OF HOME — BLIND MELON
TONGUE — R.E.M.
TONGUE TIED — The CAT
TONIGHT [A] — Shirley BASSEY
TONIGHT [B] — The MOVE
TONIGHT [C] — The RUBETTES
TONIGHT [D] — Zaine GRIFF
TONIGHT [E] — MODETTES
TONIGHT [F] — Steve HARVEY
TONIGHT [G] — KOOL and the GANG
TONIGHT [H] — The BOOMTOWN RATS
TONIGHT [I] — David BOWIE
TONIGHT [J] — NEW KIDS ON THE BLOCK
TONIGHT [K] — DEF LEPPARD
TONIGHT [L] — BAD COMPANY
TONIGHT [M] — WESTLIFE
TONIGHT (COULD BE THE NIGHT) — VELVETS
TONIGHT I CELEBRATE MY LOVE —
   Peabo BRYSON and Roberta FLACK
TONIGHT I'M ALRIGHT —
   Narada Michael WALDEN
TONIGHT I'M FREE — ANT & DEC
TONIGHT I'M GONNA LET GO — Syleena JOHNSON

TONIGHT I'M GONNA LOVE YOU ALL OVER —
   The FOUR TOPS
TONIGHT I'M YOURS (DON'T HURT ME) —
   Rod STEWART
TONIGHT IN TOKYO — Sandie SHAW
TONIGHT IS WHAT IT MEANS TO BE YOUNG —
   Jim STEINMAN
TONIGHT TONIGHT — SMASHING PUMPKINS
TONIGHT TONIGHT TONIGHT — GENESIS
TONIGHT YOU BELONG TO ME —
   PATIENCE and PRUDENCE
TONITE [A] — PHATS & SMALL
TONITE [B] — SUPERCAR
TOO BEAUTIFUL TO LAST —
   Engelbert HUMPERDINCK
TOO BAD — NICKELBACK
TOO BIG — Suzi QUATRO
TOO BLIND TO SEE IT — Kym SIMS
TOO BUSY THINKING 'BOUT MY BABY [A] —
   Marvin GAYE
TOO BUSY THINKING ABOUT MY BABY [A] —
   MARDI GRAS
TOO BUSY THINKING 'BOUT MY BABY [A] —
   STEPS
TOO CLOSE [A] — NEXT
TOO CLOSE [A] — BLUE
TOO DRUNK TO FUCK — DEAD KENNEDYS
TOO FAR GONE — Lisa SCOTT-LEE
TOO FUNKY — George MICHAEL
TOO GONE, TOO LONG — EN VOGUE
TOO GOOD — LITTLE TONY
TOO GOOD TO BE FORGOTTEN [A] — CHI-LITES
TOO GOOD TO BE FORGOTTEN [A] — AMAZULU
TOO GOOD TO BE TRUE —
   Tom PETTY and the HEARTBREAKERS
TOO HARD TO BE FREE — AMEN
TOO HOT [A] — KOOL and the GANG
TOO HOT [B] — COOLIO
TOO HOT [C] — FUN LOVIN' CRIMINALS
TOO HOT [D] — FYA
TOO HOT TA TROT — The COMMODORES
TOO HOT TO HANDLE — HEATWAVE
TOO LATE — JUNIOR
TOO LATE FOR GOODBYES — Julian LENNON
TOO LATE TO SAY GOODBYE — Richard MARX
TOO LATE, TOO SOON — Jon SECADA
TOO LOST IN YOU — SUGABABES
TOO MANY BEAUTIFUL GIRLS — Clinton FORD
TOO MANY BROKEN HEARTS —
   Jason DONOVAN
TOO MANY DJ'S — SOULWAX
TOO MANY FISH —
   Frankie KNUCKLES featuring ADEVA
TOO MANY GAMES —
   MAZE featuring Frankie BEVERLY
TOO MANY MC'S — PUBLIC DOMAIN
TOO MANY PEOPLE — Pauline HENRY
TOO MANY RIVERS — Brenda LEE
TOO MANY TEARS —
   David COVERDALE and WHITESNAKE
TOO MANY WALLS — Cathy DENNIS
TOO MUCH [A] — Elvis PRESLEY
TOO MUCH [B] — BROS
TOO MUCH [C] — SPICE GIRLS
TOO MUCH FOR ONE HEART —
   Michael BARRYMORE
TOO MUCH HEAVEN — The BEE GEES
TOO MUCH INFORMATION — DURAN DURAN
TOO MUCH KISSING — SENSELESS THINGS
TOO MUCH LOVE WILL KILL YOU [A] —
   Brian MAY
TOO MUCH LOVE WILL KILL YOU [A] — QUEEN
TOO MUCH TEQUILA — CHAMPS
TOO MUCH TOO LITTLE TOO LATE [A] —
   Johnny MATHIS and Deniece WILLIAMS
TOO MUCH, TOO LITTLE, TOO LATE [A] —
   SILVER SUN
TOO MUCH TOO YOUNG — LITTLE ANGELS
TOO MUCH TROUBLE — LIMAHL
TOO NICE TO TALK TO — The BEAT
TOO REAL — LEVELLERS
TOO RIGHT TO BE WRONG — CARTER TWINS
TOO RISKY — Jim DAVIDSON
TOO SHY — KAJAGOOGOO
TOO SOON TO KNOW — Roy ORBISON
TOO TIRED — Gary MOORE
TOO WICKED (EP) — ASWAD
TOO YOUNG [A] — Bill FORBES
TOO YOUNG [A] — Donny OSMOND
TOO YOUNG TO DIE — JAMIROQUAI
TOO YOUNG TO GO STEADY — Nat 'King' COLE
TOOK MY LOVE — BIZARRE INC
TOOK THE LAST TRAIN — David GATES
TOP O' THE MORNING TO YA —
   HOUSE OF PAIN
TOP OF THE POPS — REZILLOS
TOP OF THE STAIRS — SKEE-LO
TOP OF THE WORLD [A] — The CARPENTERS
TOP OF THE WORLD [B] — VAN HALEN
TOP OF THE WORLD [C] —
   BRANDY featuring MA$E
TOP OF THE WORLD [D] —
   The WILDHEARTS
TOP OF THE WORLD (OLE, OLE, OLE) —
   CHUMBAWAMBA
TOP TEEN BABY — Garry MILLS

TOPKNOT —
   CORNERSHOP presents Bubbley KAUR
TOPSY (PARTS 1 AND 2) — Cozy COLE
TORCH — SOFT CELL
TORERO — Julius LAROSA
TORERO — CHA CHA CHA [A] —
   Renato CAROSONE and his SEXTET
TORN — Natalie IMBRUGLIA
TORN BETWEEN TWO LOVERS —
   Mary MacGREGOR
TORTURE [A] — The JACKSONS
TORTURE [B] — KING
TOSH — FLUKE
TOSS IT UP — MAKAVELI
TOSSING AND TURNING [A] — IVY LEAGUE
TOSSING AND TURNING [B] — WINDJAMMER
TOSSING AND TURNING [C] —
   CHAKKA BOOM BANG
TOTAL CONFUSION —
   A HOMEBOY, a HIPPIE and a FUNKI DREDD
TOTAL ECLIPSE OF THE HEART [A] —
   Bonnie TYLER
TOTAL ECLIPSE OF THE HEART [A] —
   Nicki FRENCH
TOTAL ECLIPSE OF THE HEART [A] —
   Jan WAYNE
TOTAL ERASURE — Philip JAP
THE TOTAL MIX — BLACK BOX
TOTTENHAM TOTTENHAM — TOTTENHAM
   HOTSPUR FA CUP FINAL SQUAD
TOUCH — LORI and the CHAMELEONS
THE TOUCH — Kim WILDE
TOUCH BY TOUCH — Diana ROSS
TOUCH IT — MONIFAH
TOUCH ME [A] — 49ers
TOUCH ME [B] —
   Rui DA SILVA featuring CASSANDRA
TOUCH ME (ALL NIGHT LONG) — Cathy DENNIS
TOUCH ME — ANGEL CITY
TOUCH ME (I WANT YOUR BODY) —
   Samantha FOX
TOUCH ME IN THE MORNING — Diana ROSS
TOUCH ME TEASE ME [A] —
   CASE featuring Foxxy BROWN
TOUCH ME TEASE ME [A] — 3SL
TOUCH ME TOUCH ME —
   Dave DEE, DOZY, BEAKY, MICK and TICH
TOUCH ME WITH YOUR LOVE — Beth ORTON
TOUCH MYSELF — T-BOZ
A TOUCH OF EVIL — JUDAS PRIEST
A TOUCH OF LOVE — CLEOPATRA
A TOUCH OF VELVET – A STING OF BRASS —
   Ron GRAINER ORCHESTRA
TOUCH THE SKY — 29 PALMS
TOUCH TOO MUCH — AC/DC
A TOUCH TOO MUCH — ARROWS
TOUCH YOU — KATOI
TOUCHED BY GOD — KATCHA
TOUCHED BY THE HAND OF CICCIOLINA —
   POP WILL EAT ITSELF
TOUCHED BY THE HAND OF GOD —
   NEW ORDER
TOUCHY! — A-HA
TOUGHER THAN THE REST —
   Bruce SPRINGSTEEN
TOUR DE FRANCE — KRAFTWERK
TOURNIQUET [A] — MARILYN MANSON
TOURNIQUET [B] — HEADSWIM
TOUS LES GARÇONS ET LES FILLES —
   Françoise HARDY
TOWER OF STRENGTH [A] —
   Frankie VAUGHAN
TOWER OF STRENGTH [A] — Gene McDANIELS
TOWER OF STRENGTH [B] — The MISSION
TOWER OF STRENGTH [C] — SKIN
TOWERS OF LONDON — XTC
TOWN — NORTHERN UPROAR
TOWN CALLED MALICE — The JAM
TOWN CLOWNS — BLAMELESS
TOWN CRIER — Craig DOUGLAS
TOWN OF PLENTY — Elton JOHN
TOWN TO TOWN — MICRODISNEY
TOWN WITHOUT PITY [A] — Gene PITNEY
TOWN WITHOUT PITY [A] — Eddi READER
TOXIC — Britney SPEARS
TOXIC GIRL — KINGS OF CONVENIENCE
TOXICITY — SYSTEM OF A DOWN
TOXYGENE — The ORB
TOY — CASUALS
TOY BALLOONS — Russ CONWAY
TOY BOY — SINITTA
TOY SOLDIERS — Martika
TOYS FOR BOYS — MARION
TRACEY IN MY ROOM — EBTG vs SOUL VISION
TRACIE — LEVEL 42
TRACKIN' — Billy CRAWFORD
TRACKS OF MY TEARS [A] — MIRACLES
TRACKS OF MY TEARS [A] — Linda RONSTADT
TRACKS OF MY TEARS [A] — Colin BLUNSTONE
TRACKS OF MY TEARS [A] — GO WEST
TRACY — CUFFLINKS
TRADE (EP) (DISC 2) —
   VARIOUS ARTISTS (EPs and LPs)
TRAFFIC [A] — STEREOPHONICS
TRAFFIC [B] — TIESTO
TRAGEDY [A] — ARGENT
TRAGEDY [B] — The BEE GEES

TRAGEDY [B] — STEPS
TRAGEDY AND MYSTERY — CHINA CRISIS
TRAGIC COMIC — EXTREME
TRAIL OF TEARS — DOGS D'AMOUR
THE TRAIL OF THE LONESOME PINE —
   LAUREL and HARDY with the AVALON BOYS
   featuring Chill WILLS
TRAILER LOAD A GIRLS — Shabba RANKS
TRAIN [A] — SISTERS OF MERCY
TRAIN [B] — GOLDFRAPP
THE TRAIN IS COMING [A] — SHAGGY
THE TRAIN IS COMING [A] — UB40
TRAIN OF CONSEQUENCES — MEGADETH
TRAIN OF LOVE — Alma COGAN
TRAIN OF THOUGHT [A] — A-HA
TRAIN OF THOUGHT [B] — ESCRIMA
TRAIN ON A TRACK — Kelly ROWLAND
TRAIN TO SKAVILLE — ETHIOPIANS
TRAIN TOUR TO RAINBOW CITY — PYRAMIDS
TRAINS AND BOATS AND PLANES [A] —
   Billy J KRAMER and the DAKOTAS
TRAINS AND BOATS AND PLANES [A] —
   Burt BACHARACH
TRAMBONE — KREW-KATS
TRAMP [A] — Otis REDDING
TRAMP [B] — SALT-N-PEPA
TRAMPOLENE — Julian COPE
TRAMPS AND THIEVES — QUIREBOYS
TRANCESCRIPT — HARDFLOOR
TRANQUILLIZER — GENEVA
TRANSAMAZONIA — The SHAMEN
TRANSATLANTIC — ROACH MOTEL
TRANSFER AFFECTION — A FLOCK OF SEAGULLS
TRANSISTOR RADIO — Benny HILL
TRANSMISSION [A] — GAY DAD
TRANSMISSION [B] — VIOLENT DELIGHT
TRANSONIC — WIRED
TRANZ EURO XPRESS — X-PRESS 2
TRANZY STATE OF MIND — PUSH
TRAPPED [A] — Colonel ABRAMS
TRAPPED [B] — GUYVER
TRASH [A] — ROXY MUSIC
TRASH [B] — SUEDE
TRASHED — SKIN
TRAVELIN' BAND —
   CREEDENCE CLEARWATER REVIVAL
TRAVELIN' HOME — Vera LYNN
TRAVELIN' MAN — Ricky NELSON
THE TRAVELLER — SPEAR OF DESTINY
TRAVELLERS TUNE — OCEAN COLOUR SCENE
TRAVELLIN' LIGHT —
   Cliff RICHARD and The SHADOWS
TRAVELLING LIGHT — TINDERSTICKS
TRAVELLING MAN — STUDIO 2
TREASON (JUST A STORY) —
   TEARDROP EXPLODES
TREASURE OF LOVE — Clyde McPHATTER
TREAT 'EM RIGHT — Chubb ROCK
TREAT HER LIKE A LADY [A] —
   The TEMPTATIONS
TREAT HER LIKE A LADY [B] — Celine DION
TREAT HER LIKE A LADY [C] — JOE
TREAT HER RIGHT — Roy HEAD
TREAT INFAMY — REST ASSURED
TREAT ME GOOD — YAZZ
TREAT ME LIKE A LADY [A] — FIVE STAR
TREAT ME LIKE A LADY [B] — Zoe BIRKETT
TREAT ME RIGHT — ADEVA
TREATY — YOTHU YINDI
TREBLE CHANCE — Joe 'Mr Piano' HENDERSON
TREE FROG — HOPE A.D.
TREES — PULP
TREMBLE — MARC et CLAUDE
TREMELO SONG (EP) — The CHARLATANS
THE TRIAL OF HISSING SID — Keith MICHELL
TRIALS OF LIFE — KALEEF
TRIBAL BASE — REBEL MC featuring
   TENOR FLY and Barrington LEVY
TRIBAL DANCE — 2 UNLIMITED
TRIBUTE (RIGHT ON) — PASADENAS
TRIBUTE TO A KING — William BELL
TRIBUTE TO BUDDY HOLLY — Mike BERRY
TRIBUTE TO JIM REEVES — LARRY
   CUNNINGHAM and the MIGHTY AVONS
TRIBUTE TO OUR ANCESTORS — RUBBADUBB
TRICK ME — KELIS
A TRICK OF THE LIGHT — TRIFFIDS
TRICK OF THE NIGHT — BANANARAMA
TRICKY DISCO — TRICKY DISCO
TRICKY KID — TRICKY
TRIGGER HIPPIE — MORCHEEBA
TRIGGER INSIDE — THERAPY?
TRINI TRAX — Trini LOPEZ
TRIP II THE MOON — ACEN
A TRIP TO TRUMPTON — URBAN HYPE
TRIPLE TROUBLE — BEASTIE BOYS
TRIPPIN' [A] — Mark MORRISON
TRIPPIN' [B] — Oris JAY presents DELSENA
TRIPPIN' ON SUNSHINE — PIZZAMAN
TRIPPIN' ON YOUR LOVE [A] — A WAY OF LIFE
TRIPPIN' ON YOUR LOVE [A] — Kenny THOMAS
TRIPPY — ARAB STRAP
TRIPWIRE — LIONROCK
TRIUMPH [A] — WU-TANG CLAN
TRIUMPH [B] — The HISS
TRIXSTAR — BLAK TWANG featuring EST'ELLE
TROCADERO — SHOWADDYWADDY

THE TROOPER — **IRON MAIDEN**
TROPIC ISLAND HUM — **Paul McCARTNEY**
TROPICAL ICE-LAND — **FIERY FURNACES**
TROPICAL SOUNDCLASH — **DJ GREGORY**
TROPICALIA — **BECK**
T.R.O.U.B.L.E. — **Elvis PRESLEY**
TROUBLE [A] — **GILLAN**
TROUBLE [B] — **Lindsey BUCKINGHAM**
TROUBLE [C] — **HEAVEN 17**
TROUBLE [D] — **SHAMPOO**
TROUBLE [E] — **COLDPLAY**
TROUBLE [F] — **CYPRESS HILL**
TROUBLE [G] — **PINK**
TROUBLE BOYS — **THIN LIZZY**
TROUBLE IN PARADISE — **Al JARREAU**
TROUBLE IS MY MIDDLE NAME [A] — **BROOK BROTHERS**
TROUBLE IS MY MIDDLE NAME [A] — **FOUR PENNIES**
TROUBLE TOWN — **Martin STEPHENSON and the DAINTEES**
TROUBLE WITH HARRY — **ALFI and HARRY**
THE TROUBLE WITH LOVE IS — **Kelly CLARKSON**
TROUBLED GIRL — **Karen RAMIREZ**
TROY (THE PHOENIX FROM THE FLAME) — **Sinead O'CONNOR**
TRUCK ON — **SIMPLE KID**
TRUCK ON (TYKE) — **T. REX**
TRUDIE — **Joe 'Mr Piano' HENDERSON**
TRUE [A] — **SPANDAU BALLET**
TRUE [B] — **JAIMESON featuring Angel BLU**
TRUE BLUE — **MADONNA**
TRUE COLORS [A] — **Cyndi LAUPER**
TRUE COLORS [A] — **Phil COLLINS**
TRUE COLOURS [B] — **GO WEST**
TRUE DEVOTION — **Samantha FOX**
TRUE FAITH — **NEW ORDER**
TRUE LOVE [A] — **Bing CROSBY**
TRUE LOVE [A] — **Terry LIGHTFOOT and his NEW ORLEANS JAZZMEN**
TRUE LOVE [A] — **Richard CHAMBERLAIN**
TRUE LOVE [A] — **Shakin' STEVENS**
TRUE LOVE [A] — **Elton JOHN and Kiki DEE**
TRUE LOVE [B] — **CHIMES**
TRUE LOVE FOR EVER MORE — **The BACHELORS**
TRUE LOVE NEVER DIES — **FLIP & FILL featuring Kelly LLORENNA**
TRUE LOVE WAYS [A] — **Buddy HOLLY**
TRUE LOVE WAYS [A] — **PETER and GORDON**
TRUE LOVE WAYS [A] — **Cliff RICHARD**
TRUE LOVE WAYS [A] — **David ESSEX and Catherine Zeta JONES**
TRUE LOVE WILL FIND YOU IN THE END — **SPECTRUM**
TRUE NATURE — **JANE'S ADDICTION**
TRUE SPIRIT — **Carleen ANDERSON**
TRUE STEP TONIGHT — **TRUE STEPPERS featuring Brian HARVEY and Donell JONES**
TRUE (THE FAGGOT IS YOU) — **MOREL**
TRUE TO FORM — **HYBRID featuring Peter HOOK**
TRUE TO US — **VANILLA**
TRUE TO YOUR HEART — **98°**
TRUGANINI — **MIDNIGHT OIL**
TRULY [A] — **Lionel RICHIE**
TRULY [A] — **Steven HOUGHTON**
TRULY [B] — **Hinda HICKS**
TRULY [C] — **PESHAY featuring Kym MAZELLE**
TRULY [D] — **DELERIUM featuring Nerina PALLOT**
TRULY MADLY DEEPLY — **SAVAGE GARDEN**
TRULY ONE — **ORIGIN UNKNOWN**
TRUST [A] — **BROTHER BEYOND**
TRUST [B] — **NED'S ATOMIC DUSTBIN**
TRUST ME — **GURU featuring N'Dea DAVENPORT**
TRUST ME TO OPEN MY MOUTH — **SQUEEZE**
THE TRUTH [A] — **Colonel ABRAMS**
THE TRUTH [B] — **REAL PEOPLE**
THE TRUTH IS NO WORDS — **The MUSIC**
TRUTH OR DARE — **Shirley MURDOCK**
TRY [A] — **BROS**
TRY [B] — **IAN VAN DAHL**
TRY [C] — **Nelly FURTADO**
TRY A LITTLE KINDNESS — **Glen CAMPBELL**
TRY A LITTLE TENDERNESS — **Otis REDDING**
TRY AGAIN — **AALIYAH**
TRY AGAIN TODAY — **The CHARLATANS**
TRY HONESTLY — **Billy TALENT**
TRY JAH LOVE — **THIRD WORLD**
TRY ME OUT — **CORONA**
TRY MY WORLD — **Georgie FAME**
TRY TO UNDERSTAND — **LULU**
TRY TRY TRY [A] — **Julian COPE**
TRY TRY TRY [B] — **SMASHING PUMPKINS**
TRYIN' — **HILLTOPPERS**
TRYIN' TO GET THE FEELING AGAIN — **The CARPENTERS**
TRYING TO FORGET — **Jim REEVES**
TRYING TO GET TO YOU — **Elvis PRESLEY**
TRYOUTS FOR THE HUMAN RACE — **SPARKS**
TSOP THE SOUND OF PHILADELPHIA — **MFSB featuring The THREE DEGREES**
TSUNAMI — **MANIC STREET PREACHERS**
T-10 — **DISTORTED MINDS**
TU AMOR — **KACI**
TU M'AIMES ENCORE (TO LOVE ME AGAIN) — **Celine DION**
TUBTHUMPING — **CHUMBAWAMBA**
TUBULAR BELLS — **CHAMPS BOYS**
TUCH ME — **Fonda RAE**
TUESDAY AFTERNOON — **Jennifer BROWN**
TUESDAY MORNING — **The POGUES**
TUESDAY SUNSHINE — **QUESTIONS**
TUFF ACT TO FOLLOW — **MN8**
TUG OF WAR — **Paul McCARTNEY**
TULANE — **Steve GIBBONS BAND**
TULIPS — **BLOC PARTY**
TULIPS FROM AMSTERDAM — **Max BYGRAVES**
TUM BIN JIYA — **Bally SAGOO**
TUMBLING DICE — **The ROLLING STONES**
TUMBLING TUMBLEWEEDS — **Slim WHITMAN**
THE TUNE — **SUGGS**
TUNES SPLITS THE ATOM — **MC TUNES versus 808 STATE**
TUNNEL OF LOVE [A] — **DIRE STRAITS**
TUNNEL OF LOVE [B] — **FUN BOY THREE**
TUNNEL OF LOVE [C] — **Bruce SPRINGSTEEN**
TURN [A] — **TRAVIS**
TURN [B] — **FEEDER**
TURN OFF THE LIGHT — **Nelly FURTADO**
TURN AROUND [A] — **FAB!**
TURN AROUND [B] — **PHATS & SMALL**
TURN AROUND AND COUNT 2 TEN — **DEAD OR ALIVE**
TURN BACK THE CLOCK — **JOHNNY HATES JAZZ**
TURN BACK TIME — **AQUA**
TURN IT AROUND [A] — **ALENA**
TURN IT AROUND [B] — **4 STRINGS**
TURN IT DOWN — **The SWEET**
TURN IT INTO LOVE — **Hazell DEAN**
TURN IT ON — **LEVEL 42**
TURN IT ON AGAIN — **GENESIS**
TURN IT UP [A] — **CONWAY BROTHERS**
TURN IT UP [B] — **Richie RICH**
TURN IT UP [C] — **TECHNOTRONIC featuring MELISSA and EINSTEIN**
TURN IT UP [D] — **Peter ANDRE**
TURN IT UP [E] — **RAJA NEE**
TURN IT UP — **Busta RHYMES**
TURN IT UP (SAY YEAH) — **DJ DUKE**
TURN ME LOOSE — **Wally JUMP Jr and the CRIMINAL ELEMENT**
TURN ME ON [A] — **Danny TENAGLIA**
TURN ME ON [B] — **Kevin LYTTLE**
TURN ME ON [C] — **RMXCRW featuring EBON-E plus AMBUSH**
TURN ME ON TURN ME OFF — **Honey BANE**
TURN ME OUT — **PRAXIS**
TURN ME OUT (TURN TO SUGAR) — **PRAXIS**
TURN OFF — **MILLTOWN BROTHERS**
TURN ON THE NIGHT — **KISS**
TURN ON TUNE IN COP OUT — **FREAKPOWER**
TURN THE BEAT AROUND — **Gloria ESTEFAN**
TURN THE MUSIC UP! [A] — **PLAYERS ASSOCIATION**
TURN THE MUSIC UP [A] — **Chris PAUL**
TURN THE TIDE — **SYLVER**
TURN TO GOLD — **David AUSTIN**
TURN TO STONE — **ELECTRIC LIGHT ORCHESTRA**
TURN! TURN! TURN! — **The BYRDS**
TURN UP THE BASS — **TYREE**
TURN UP THE NIGHT — **BLACK SABBATH**
TURN UP THE POWER — **N-TRANCE**
TURN UP THE SOUND — **Lisa PIN-UP**
TURN YOUR BACK ON ME — **KAJAGOOGOO**
TURN YOUR LIGHTS DOWN LOW — **Bob MARLEY & the WAILERS**
TURN YOUR LOVE AROUND [A] — **George BENSON**
TURN YOUR LOVE AROUND [A] — **Tony DI BART**
TURN YOUR RADIO ON — **Ray STEVENS**
TURNED AWAY — **AUDIO BULLYS**
TURNING AWAY — **Shakin' STEVENS**
TURNING JAPANESE — **VAPORS**
TURNING THE TOWN RED — **Elvis COSTELLO**
TURQUOISE [A] — **DONOVAN**
TURQUOISE [B] — **CIRCULATION**
TURTLE POWER — **PARTNERS IN KRYME**
TURTLE RHAPSODY — **ORCHESTRA ON THE HALF SHELL**
TUSK — **FLEETWOOD MAC**
TUTTI FRUTTI — **LITTLE RICHARD**
TUXEDO JUNCTION — **MANHATTAN TRANSFER**
TV — **FLYING LIZARDS**
TV CRIMES — **BLACK SABBATH**
TV DINNERS — **ZZ TOP**
TV SAVAGE — **BOW WOW WOW**
TV TAN — **The WILDHEARTS**
TVC 15 — **David BOWIE**
TWANGLING THREE FINGERS IN A BOX — **MIKE**
TWEEDLE DEE [A] — **Frankie VAUGHAN**
TWEEDLE DEE [A] — **Georgia GIBBS**
TWEEDLE DEE [A] — **Little Jimmy OSMOND**
TWEEDLEE DEE, TWEEDLE DUM — **MIDDLE OF THE ROAD**
THE TWELFTH OF NEVER [A] — **Cliff RICHARD**
THE TWELFTH OF NEVER [A] — **Donny OSMOND**
THE TWELFTH OF NEVER [A] — **Elvis PRESLEY**
THE TWELFTH OF NEVER [A] — **CARTER TWINS**
TWELFTH STREET RAG — **Bert WEEDON**
12:51 — **The STROKES**
12 REASONS WHY I LOVE HER — **MY LIFE STORY**
TWELVE STEPS TO LOVE — **Brian POOLE and the TREMELOES**
20TH CENTURY — **BRAD**
20TH CENTURY BOY — **T. REX**
20 DEGREES — **Jonny L**
TWENTY FOREPLAY — **Janet JACKSON**
TWENTY FOUR HOURS FROM TULSA — **Gene PITNEY**
20 HZ (NEW FREQUENCIES) — **CAPRICORN**
£20 TO GET IN — **SHUT UP AND DANCE**
20 SECONDS TO COMPLY — **SILVER BULLET**
TWENTY TINY FINGERS [A] — **Alma COGAN**
TWENTY TINY FINGERS [A] — **CORONETS**
TWENTY TINY FINGERS [A] — **The STARGAZERS**
20/20 — **George BENSON**
TWENTY WILD HORSES — **STATUS QUO**
TWENTY YEARS — **PLACEBO**
21ST CENTURY — **WEEKEND PLAYERS**
TWENTY-FIRST CENTURY BOY — **SIGUE SIGUE SPUTNIK**
21ST CENTURY (DIGITAL BOY) — **BAD RELIGION**
21ST CENTURY GIRLS — **21ST CENTURY GIRLS**
24 HOURS FROM YOU — **NEXT OF KIN**
24 HOURS [A] — **Betty BOO**
24 HOURS [B] — **AGENT SUMO**
24 HOURS A DAY — **NOMAD**
24/7 [A] — **3T**
24/7 [B] — **FIXATE**
TWENTYFOURSEVEN — **ARTFUL DODGER featuring Melanie BLATT**
24-7-365 — **CHARLES and EDDIE**
25 MILES [A] — **Edwin STARR**
25 MILES 2001 [A] — **THREE AMIGOS**
25 OR 6 TO 4 — **CHICAGO**
24 SYCAMORE — **Gene PITNEY**
29 PALMS — **Robert PLANT**
21 — **PADDINGTONS**
21 QUESTIONS — **50 CENT featuring Nate DOGG**
21 SECONDS — **SO SOLID CREW**
22 DAYS — **22-20S**
TWICE AS HARD — **BLACK CROWES**
TWILIGHT — **ELECTRIC LIGHT ORCHESTRA**
TWILIGHT CAFE — **Susan FASSBENDER**
TWILIGHT TIME — **The PLATTERS**
TWILIGHT WORLD — **SWING OUT SISTER**
TWILIGHT ZONE [A] — **IRON MAIDEN**
TWILIGHT ZONE [B] — **2 UNLIMITED**
TWILIGHT ZONE — TWILIGHT TONE (MEDLEY) — **MANHATTAN TRANSFER**
TWILIGHTS LAST GLEAMING — **HIGH CONTRAST**
TWIN EARTH — **MONSTER MAGNET**
TWINKIE LEE — **Gary WALKER**
TWINKLE — **WHIPPING BOY**
TWINKLE TOES — **Roy ORBISON**
TWINKLE TWINKLE (I'M NOT A STAR) — **JAZZY JEFF & the FRESH PRINCE**
TWINLIGHTS (EP) — **COCTEAU TWINS**
THE TWIST [A] — **Chubby CHECKER**
TWIST [B] — **GOLDFRAPP**
TWIST 'EM OUT — **DILLINJA featuring SKIBADEE**
TWIST (ROUND 'N' ROUND) — **CHILL FAC-TORR**
TWIST TWIST — **CHAKACHAS**
THE TWIST (YO, TWIST) — **FAT BOYS and Chubby CHECKER**
TWIST AND SHOUT [A] — **Brian POOLE and the TREMELOES**
TWIST AND SHOUT [A] — **ISLEY BROTHERS**
TWIST AND SHOUT [A] — **SALT-N-PEPA**
TWIST AND SHOUT [A] — **Chaka DEMUS and PLIERS featuring Jack RADICS and TAXI GANG**
TWIST AND SHOUT [B] — **DEACON BLUE**
TWIST 'EM OUT — **DILLINJA**
TWIST IN MY SOBRIETY — **Tanita TIKARAM**
TWIST OF FATE [A] — **Olivia NEWTON-JOHN**
TWIST OF FATE [B] — **Siobhan DONAGHY**
TWISTED — **Keith SWEAT**
TWISTED (EVERYDAY HURTS) — **SKUNK ANANSIE**
THE TWISTER — **VIPER**
TWISTERELLA — **RIDE**
TWISTIN' THE NIGHT AWAY [A] — **Sam COOKE**
TWISTIN' THE NIGHT AWAY [A] — **DIVINE**
TWISTING BY THE POOL — **DIRE STRAITS**
'TWIXT TWELVE AND TWENTY — **Pat BOONE**
TWO (EP) — **MANSUN**
2 BECOME 1 — **SPICE GIRLS**
TWO CAN PLAY THAT GAME — **Bobby BROWN**
2 DEEP — **GANG STARR**
TWO DIFFERENT WORLDS — **Ronnie HILTON**
2 FACED — **LOUISE**
TWO FATT GUITARS (REVISITED) — **DIRECKT**
2-4-6-8 MOTORWAY — **Tom ROBINSON**
TWO HEARTS [A] — **Stephanie MILLS featuring Teddy PENDERGRASS**
TWO HEARTS [B] — **Phil COLLINS**
TWO HEARTS [C] — **Cliff RICHARD**
TWO HEARTS BEAT AS ONE — **U2**
TWO HEARTS TOGETHER — **ORANGE JUICE**
TWO IN A MILLION [A] — **Mica PARIS**
TWO IN A MILLION [B] — **S CLUB 7**
TWO KINDS OF TEARDROPS — **Del SHANNON**
2 LEGIT 2 QUIT — **HAMMER**
TWO LITTLE BOYS [A] — **Rolf HARRIS**
TWO LITTLE BOYS [A] — **SPLODGENESSABOUNDS**
2 MINUTES TO MIDNIGHT — **IRON MAIDEN**
TWO MONTHS OFF — **UNDERWORLD**
THE TWO OF US — **Mac and Katie KISSOON**
TWO OUT OF THREE AIN'T BAD — **MEAT LOAF**
TWO PAINTINGS AND A DRUM (EP) — **Carl COX**
TWO PEOPLE [A] — **Tina TURNER**
2 PEOPLE [B] — **Jean Jacques SMOOTHIE**
TWO PINTS OF LAGER AND A PACKET OF CRISPS PLEASE — **SPLODGENESSABOUNDS**
2 + 2 = 5 — **RADIOHEAD**
TWO PRINCES — **SPIN DOCTORS**
2 REMIXES BY AFX — **AFX**
TWO SILHOUETTES — **Del SHANNON**
2 STEP ROCK — **The BANDITS**
TWO STEPS BEHIND — **DEF LEPPARD**
TWO STREETS — **Val DOONICAN**
2 THE RHYTHM — **SOUND FACTORY**
2000 MILES — **The PRETENDERS**
2, 3, GO — **WEDDING PRESENT**
2 TIMES — **Ann LEE**
TWO-TIMING TOUCH AND BROKEN BONES — **The HIVES**
THE TWO TONE EP — **VARIOUS ARTISTS (EPs and LPs)**
TWO TRIBES — **FRANKIE GOES TO HOLLYWOOD**
2-WAY — **RAYVON**
2 WAY STREET — **MISSJONES**
TWO WORLDS COLLIDE — **INSPIRAL CARPETS**
TWO WRONGS (DON'T MAKE A RIGHT) — **Wyclef JEAN**
TWYFORD DOWN — **GALLIANO**
TYPE — **LIVING COLOUR**
TYPICAL! — **FRAZIER CHORUS**
TYPICAL AMERICAN — **GOATS**
TYPICAL GIRLS — **The SLITS**
TYPICAL MALE — **Tina TURNER**
U — **Loni CLARK**
U & ME — **CAPPELLA**
U + ME = LOVE — **FUNKY WORM**
U BLOW MY MIND — **BLACKSTREET**
U CAN'T TOUCH THIS — **HAMMER**
U DON'T HAVE TO SAY U LOVE ME — **MASH!**
U FOUND OUT — **HANDBAGGERS**
U GIRLS — **NUSH**
U GOT IT BAD — **USHER**
U GOT THE LOOK — **PRINCE**
U GOT 2 KNOW — **CAPPELLA**
U GOT 2 LET THE MUSIC — **CAPPELLA**
U (I GOT THE FEELING) — **DJ SCOT PROJECT**
U KNOW WHAT'S UP — **Donell JONES**
U KNOW Y — **MOGUAI**
U KRAZY KATZ — **ANT & DEC**
U MAKE ME WANNA — **BLUE**
U R THE BEST THING — **D:REAM**
U REMIND ME — **USHER**
U SAVED ME — **R KELLY**
U SEXY THING — **CLOCK**
U SHINE ON — **Matt DAREY and Marcella WOODS**
U SURE DO — **STRIKE**
U-TURN — **USHER**
U WILL KNOW — **BMU**
UBIK — **Timo MAAS**
UGLY [A] — **DAPHNE & CELESTE**
UGLY [B] — **Bubba SPARXXX**
THE UGLY DUCKLING — **Mike REID**
UH HUH OH YEH — **Paul WELLER**
UH LA LA LA — **ALEXIA**
UH UH NO NO CASUAL SEX — **Carrie McDOWELL**
UHF — **UHF**
UHH IN YOU — **SNOW**
UH HUH — **B2K**
UH-UH OOH OOH LOOK OUT (HERE IT COMES) — **Roberta FLACK**
UK BLAK — **Caron WHEELER**
UK-USA — **ESKIMOS & EGYPT**
'ULLO JOHN GOT A NEW MOTOR? — **Alexei SAYLE**
THE ULTIMATE — **FUNKY CHOAD featuring Nick SKITZ**
THE ULTIMATE HIGH — **TIME FREQUENCY**
THE ULTIMATE SIN — **Ozzy OSBOURNE**
ULTIMATE TRUNK FUNK (EP) — **The BRAND NEW HEAVIES**
ULTRA FLAVA — **HELLER & FARLEY PROJECT**
ULTRA — OBSCENE — **BREAKBEAT ERA**
ULTRA STIMULATION — **Finley QUAYE**
ULTRAFUNKULA — **Armand VAN HELDEN**
UM, UM, UM, UM, UM, UM [A] — **Major LANCE**
UM, UM, UM, UM, UM, UM [A] — **Wayne FONTANA and The MINDBENDERS**
UMI SAYS — **MOS DEF**
UN BANC, UN ARBRE, UNE RUE — **SÉVÉRINE**
(UN, DOS, TRES) MARIA — **Ricky MARTIN**
UNA PALOMA BLANCA (WHITE DOVE) — **Jonathan KING**
UNBEARABLE — **The WONDER STUFF**
UNBELIEVABLE [A] — **EMF**
UNBELIEVABLE [A] — **SKIN**

UNBELIEVABLE [B] — Lisa LASHES
UN-BREAK MY HEART — Toni BRAXTON
UNBREAKABLE — WESTLIFE
UNCERTAIN SMILE — The THE
UNCHAIN MY HEART — Joe COCKER
UNCHAINED MELODY [A] — Al HIBBLER
UNCHAINED MELODY [A] — Jimmy YOUNG
UNCHAINED MELODY [A] — Les BAXTER
UNCHAINED MELODY [A] — LIBERACE
UNCHAINED MELODY [A] —
   RIGHTEOUS BROTHERS
UNCHAINED MELODY [A] — Leo SAYER
UNCHAINED MELODY [A] —
   Robson GREEN and Jerome FLYNN
UNCHAINED MELODY [A] — Gareth GATES
UNCLE JOHN FROM JAMAICA —
   The VENGABOYS
UNCLE SAM — MADNESS
UNCONDITIONAL LOVE [A] — Donna SUMMER
UNCONDITIONAL LOVE [B] — Susanna HOFFS
UNDECIDED — Youssou N'DOUR
UNDER A RAGING MOON — Roger DALTREY
UNDER ATTACK — ABBA
UNDER MY THUMB [A] — The WHO
UNDER MY THUMB [A] — Wayne GIBSON
UNDER MY WHEELS — Alice COOPER
UNDER NEW MANAGEMENT —
   The BARRON KNIGHTS
UNDER ONE ROOF — The RUBETTES
UNDER PRESSURE —
   QUEEN and David BOWIE
UNDER THE BOARDWALK [A] — The DRIFTERS
UNDER THE BOARDWALK [A] — TOM TOM CLUB
UNDER THE BOARDWALK [A] — Bruce WILLIS
UNDER THE BRIDGE [A] —
   RED HOT CHILI PEPPERS
UNDER THE BRIDGE [A] — ALL SAINTS
UNDER THE BRIDGES OF PARIS [A] —
   Dean MARTIN
UNDER THE BRIDGES OF PARIS [A] —
   Eartha KITT
UNDER THE COVERS EP — HARRY
UNDER THE GOD — TIN MACHINE
UNDER THE GUN — SISTERS OF MERCY
UNDER THE MOON OF LOVE —
   SHOWADDYWADDY
UNDER THE THUMB — Amy STUDT
UNDER THE WATER —
   BROTHER BROWN featuring FRANK'EE
UNDER YOUR SPELL — Ronny JORDAN
UNDER YOUR THUMB — GODLEY and CREME
UNDERCOVER ANARCHIST — SILVER BULLET
UNDERCOVER ANGEL — Alan O'DAY
UNDERCOVER LOVER — SMOOTH
UNDERCOVER OF THE NIGHT —
   The ROLLING STONES
UNDERDOG (SAVE ME) — TURIN BRAKES
UNDERDOSE — INME
UNDERGROUND [A] — David BOWIE
UNDERGROUND [B] — Ben FOLDS FIVE
UNDERGROUND [C] — RHYTHM MASTERS
UNDERLOVE — Melba MOORE
UNDERNEATH IT ALL — NO DOUBT
UNDERNEATH THE BLANKET GO —
   Gilbert O'SULLIVAN
UNDERNEATH YOUR CLOTHES — SHAKIRA
UNDERPASS — John FOXX
UNDERSTAND THIS GROOVE — FRANKE
UNDERSTANDING JANE — ICICLE WORKS
UNDERWATER [A] — Harry THUMANN
UNDERWATER [B] — DELERIUM featuring RANI
UNDERWATER LOVE — SMOKE CITY
UNDIVIDED LOVE — LOUISE
UNDONE — THE SWEATER SONG — WEEZER
UNDRESSED — WHITE TOWN
UNEMPLOYED IN SUMMERTIME —
   Emiliana TORRINI
UNEXPLAINED — GRAVEDIGGAZ
UNEXPLAINED (EP) — EMF
UNFINISHED SYMPATHY — MASSIVE ATTACK
UNFORGETTABLE — Natalie COLE
THE UNFORGETTABLE FIRE — U2
UNFORGIVABLE SINNER — Lene MARLIN
UNFORGIVEN — D:REAM
THE UNFORGIVEN — METALLICA
THE UNFORGIVEN II — METALLICA
UNHOLY — KISS
UNIFORM — INSPIRAL CARPETS
UNIFORMS (CORPS D'ESPRIT) —
   Pete TOWNSHEND
UNINTENDED — MUSE
UNINVITED GUEST — MARILLION
UNION CITY BLUE — BLONDIE
UNION OF THE SNAKE — DURAN DURAN
UNITED — JUDAS PRIEST
UNITED CALYPSO '98 — REDS UNITED
UNITED COLOURS — BEST SHOT
UNITED STATES OF WHATEVER — Liam LYNCH
UNITED (WE LOVE YOU) —
   MANCHESTER UNITED FOOTBALL CLUB
UNITED WE STAND —
   BROTHERHOOD OF MAN
UNITY — UNITY
U.N.I.T.Y. — QUEEN LATIFAH
UNITY (PART 1 — THE THIRD COMING) —
   Afrika BAMBAATAA and James BROWN
UNIVERSAL [A] — The SMALL FACES

UNIVERSAL [B] —
   ORCHESTRAL MANOEUVRES IN THE DARK
THE UNIVERSAL [C] — BLUR
UNIVERSAL HEART-BEAT — Juliana HATFIELD
UNIVERSAL MUSIC — METEOR SEVEN
UNIVERSAL NATION — PUSH
UNIVERSALLY SPEAKING —
   RED HOT CHILI PEPPERS
THE UNKNOWN — Mark B & BLADE
UNLEASH THE DRAGON — SISQO
UNLOCK THE FUNK — LOCKSMITH
THE UNNAMED FEELING — METALLICA
UNO — MUSE
UNO MAS — Daniel O'DONNELL
UNPRETTY — TLC
UNSAFE BUILDING 1990 — The ALARM
UNSKINNY BOP — POISON
UNSQUARE DANCE — Dave BRUBECK QUARTET
UNSTABLE — ADEMA
THE UNSUNG HEROES OF HIP HOP —
   SUBSONIC 2
UNTIL IT SLEEPS — METALLICA
UNTIL IT'S TIME FOR YOU TO GO [A] —
   FOUR PENNIES
UNTIL IT'S TIME FOR YOU TO GO [A] —
   Elvis PRESLEY
UNTIL MY DYING DAY — UB40
UNTIL THE DAY — FUNKY GREEN DOGS
UNTIL THE DAY I DIE — STORY OF THE YEAR
UNTIL THE END OF TIME — 2PAC
UNTIL THE NIGHT — Billy JOEL
UNTIL THE TIME IS THROUGH — FIVE
UNTIL YOU COME BACK TO ME — ADEVA
UNTIL YOU COME BACK TO ME (THAT'S WHAT I'M
   GONNA DO) — Aretha FRANKLIN
UNTIL YOU COME BACK TO ME (THAT'S WHAT I'M
   GONNA DO) [A] — Miki HOWARD
UNTIL YOU FIND OUT —
   NED'S ATOMIC DUSTBIN
UNTIL YOU LOVED ME — The MOFFATTS
UNTIL YOU SUFFER SOME (FIRE AND ICE) —
   POISON
UNTOUCHABLE — RIALTO
UNWRITTEN — Natasha BEDINGFIELD
UP! — Shania TWAIN
UP ABOVE MY HEAD I HEAR MUSIC IN THE AIR —
   Frankie LAINE and Johnnie RAY
UP AGAINST THE WALL — Tom ROBINSON
UP ALL NIGHT [A] — SLAUGHTER
UP ALL NIGHT [B] — John B
UP AND DOWN [A] — HIGH
UP AND DOWN [B] — The VENGABOYS
UP & DOWN [C] — BOYSTEROUS
UP & DOWN [D] — SCENT
UP AROUND THE BEND [A] —
   CREEDENCE CLEARWATER REVIVAL
UP AROUND THE BEND [A] — HANOI ROCKS
UP AT THE LAKE — The CHARLATANS
UP IN A PUFF OF SMOKE — Polly BROWN
UP MIDDLE FINGER — OXIDE & NEUTRINO
UP ON THE CATWALK — SIMPLE MINDS
UP ON THE DOWN SIDE —
   OCEAN COLOUR SCENE
UP ON THE ROOF [A] — Kenny LYNCH
UP ON THE ROOF [A] — Julie GRANT
UP ON THE ROOF [A] — ROBSON & JEROME
UP ROCKING BEATS — BOMFUNK MC'S
UP TEMPO — TRONIKHOUSE
UP THE BRACKET — The LIBERTINES
UP THE HILL BACKWARDS — David BOWIE
UP THE JUNCTION — SQUEEZE
UP THE LADDER TO THE ROOF —
   The SUPREMES
UP THE POOL — JETHRO TULL
UP TO NO GOOD — PORN KINGS
UP TO THE WILDSTYLE —
   PORN KINGS vs DJ SUPREME
UP, UP AND AWAY — Johnny MANN SINGERS
UP WHERE WE BELONG —
   Joe COCKER and Jennifer WARNES
UP WITH PEOPLE — LAMBCHOP
UP WITH THE COCK — JUDGE DREAD
UPFIELD — Billy BRAGG
UPRISING — ARTIFICIAL INTELLIGENCE
UPROCK — ROCKSTEADY CREW
UPSIDE DOWN [A] — Diana ROSS
UPSIDE DOWN [B] — A*TEENS
UPTIGHT — Shara NELSON
UPTIGHT (EVERYTHING'S ALRIGHT) —
   Stevie WONDER
UPTOWN DOWNTOWN — FULL INTENTION
UPTOWN FESTIVAL — SHALAMAR
UPTOWN GIRL [A] — Billy JOEL
UPTOWN GIRL [A] — WESTLIFE
UPTOWN TOP RANKING [A] —
   ALTHIA and DONNA
UPTOWN TOP RANKING [A] — ALI and FRAZIER
UPTOWN UPTEMPO WOMAN —
   Randy EDELMAN
URBAN CITY GIRL — BENZ
URBAN GUERRILLA — HAWKWIND
URBAN PRESSURE — GRIM NORTHERN SOCIAL
URBAN TRAIN —
   DJ TIESTO featuring Kirsty HAWKSHAW
URGE — The WILDHEARTS
THE URGE — Freddy CANNON
URGENT — FOREIGNER

URGENTLY IN LOVE — Billy CRAWFORD
US MALE — Elvis PRESLEY
USA — WWF SUPERSTARS
USE IT UP AND WEAR IT OUT [A] — ODYSSEY
USE IT UP AND WEAR IT OUT [A] —
   PAT and MICK
USED FOR GLUE — RIVAL SCHOOLS
USED TA BE MY GIRL — O'JAYS
USELESS — DEPECHE MODE
USELESS (I DON'T NEED YOU NOW) —
   Kym MAZELLE
U16 GIRLS — TRAVIS
UTOPIA — GOLDFRAPP
V THIRTEEN — BIG AUDIO DYNAMITE
VACATION — Connie FRANCIS
VADO VIA — DRUPI
VAGABONDS — NEW MODEL ARMY
VALENTINE — T'PAU
VALENTINO — Connie FRANCIS
VALERIE — Steve WINWOOD
VALLERI — The MONKEES
VALLEY OF TEARS [A] — Fats DOMINO
VALLEY OF TEARS [A] — Buddy HOLLY
VALLEY OF THE DOLLS — GENERATION X
VALLEY OF THE SHADOWS —
   ORIGIN UNKNOWN
THE VALLEY ROAD —
   Bruce HORNSBY and the RANGE
VALOTTE — Julian LENNON
VAMOS A LA PLAYA — RIGHEIRA
VAMP — OUTLANDER
VAMPIRE RACECOURSE — SLEEPY JACKSON
VANESSA — Ted HEATH
VANILLA RADIO — The WILDHEARTS
VANITY KILLS — ABC
VAPORIZER — LUPINE HOWL
VAPORS — SNOOP DOGG
VASOLINE — STONE TEMPLE PILOTS
VAVOOM! — MAN WITH NO NAME
VAYA CON DIOS (MAY GOD BE WITH YOU) [A] —
   Les PAUL and Mary FORD
VAYA CON DIOS (MAY GOD BE WITH YOU) [A] —
   MILLICAN and NESBITT
VEGAS [A] — SLEEPER
VEGAS [B] — AGNELLI & NELSON
VEGAS TWO TIMES — STEREOPHONICS
VEHICLE — IDES OF MARCH
VELCRO FLY — ZZ TOP
VELOURIA — PIXIES
VELVET MOODS —
   Johan GIELEN presents ABNEA
VENCEREMOS — WE WILL WIN —
   WORKING WEEK
VENI VIDI VICI — Ronnie HILTON
VENTOLIN — APHEX TWIN
VENTURA HIGHWAY — AMERICA
VENUS [A] — Dickie VALENTINE
VENUS [A] — Frankie AVALON
VENUS [B] — SHOCKING BLUE
VENUS [B] — BANANARAMA
VENUS [B] — DON PABLO'S ANIMALS
VENUS AND MARS — Jo BREEZER
VENUS AS A BOY — BJÖRK
VENUS IN BLUE JEANS — Mark WYNTER
VENUS IN FURS — VELVET UNDERGROUND
VERMILION — SLIPKNOT
VERNON'S WONDERLAND —
   VERNON'S WONDERLAND
VERONICA [A] — Elvis COSTELLO
VERONICA [B] — SULTANS OF PING
VERDI — Mauro PICOTTO
VERSION OF ME — THOUSAND YARD STARE
VERTIGO — U2
VERY BEST FRIEND — PROUD MARY
VERY METAL NOISE POLLUTION (EP) —
   POP WILL EAT ITSELF
A VERY PRECIOUS LOVE — Doris DAY
THE VERY THOUGHT OF YOU [A] —
   Tony BENNETT
THE VERY THOUGHT OF YOU [A] —
   Natalie COLE
VESSEL —
   Ed RUSH & OPTICAL / UNIVERSAL PROJECT
VIBE — ZHANÉ
VIBEOLOGY — Paula ABDUL
VIBRATOR — Terence Trent D'ARBY
VICE — RAZORLIGHT
VICIOUS CIRCLES [A] — POLTERGEIST
VICIOUS CIRCLES [A] — VICIOUS CIRCLES
VICTIM OF LOVE [A] — ERASURE
VICTIM OF LOVE [B] — Bryan ADAMS
VICTIMS — CULTURE CLUB
VICTIMS OF SUCCESS — DOGS D'AMOUR
VICTORIA [A] — The KINKS
VICTORIA [A] — The FALL
VICTORY — KOOL and the GANG
VIDEO — india.arie
VIDEO KILLED THE RADIO STAR [A] — BUGGLES
VIDEO KILLED THE RADIO STAR [A] —
   PRESIDENTS OF THE UNITED STATES OF AMERICA
VIDEO KILLED THE RADIO STAR [A] —
   DRAGONHEART
VIDEOTHEQUE — DOLLAR
VIENNA — ULTRAVOX
VIENNA CALLING — FALCO
VIETNAM — Jimmy CLIFF
VIEW FROM A BRIDGE — Kim WILDE

A VIEW TO A KILL — DURAN DURAN
VILLAGE OF ST BERNADETTE — Anne SHELTON
VINCENT — Don McLEAN
VINDALOO — FAT LES
VIOLA — MOOGWAI
VIOLAINE — COCTEAU TWINS
VIOLENCE OF SUMMER (LOVE'S TAKING OVER) —
   DURAN DURAN
VIOLENTLY (EP) — HUE AND CRY
VIOLENTLY HAPPY — BJÖRK
VIOLET [A] — SEAL
VIOLET [B] — HOLE
V.I.P. — The JUNGLE BROTHERS
VIRGIN MARY — Lonnie DONEGAN
VIRGINIA PLAIN [A] — ROXY MUSIC
VIRGINIA PLAIN [A] — SLAMM
VIRTUAL INSANITY — JAMIROQUAI
VIRTUALITY — VBIRDS
VIRUS [A] — IRON MAIDEN
VIRUS [B] — MUTINY UK
VISAGE — VISAGE
THE VISION —
   Mario PIU presents DJ ARABESQUE
VISION INCISION — LO FIDELITY ALLSTARS
VISION OF LOVE — Mariah CAREY
VISION OF YOU — Belinda CARLISLE
VISIONARY — REDD KROSS
VISIONS [A] — Cliff RICHARD
VISIONS [B] — Lena FIAGBE
VISIONS IN BLUE — ULTRAVOX
VISIONS OF CHINA — JAPAN
VISIONS OF PARADISE — Mick JAGGER
VISIONS OF YOU —
   Jah WOBBLE'S INVADERS of the HEART
VITAL SIGNS — RUSH
VITO SATAN — CAMPAG VELOCET
VIVA BOBBY JOE — The EQUALS
VIVA EL FULHAM —
   Tony REES and the COTTAGERS
VIVA ENGLAND — UNDERCOVER
VIVA FOREVER — SPICE GIRLS
VIVA LA MEGABABES — SHAMPOO
VIVA LA RADIO — LOLLY
VIVA LAS VEGAS [A] — Elvis PRESLEY
VIVA LAS VEGAS [A] — ZZ TOP
VIVE LE ROCK — Adam ANT
VIVID — ELECTRONIC
VIVRANT THING — Q-TIP
THE VOICE [A] — ULTRAVOX
THE VOICE [B] — Eimear QUINN
VOICE IN THE WILDERNESS —
   Cliff RICHARD and The SHADOWS
VOICE OF FREEDOM — Freedom WILLIAMS
THE VOICE WITHIN — Christina AGUILERA
VOICES [A] — DARIO G
VOICES [B] — BEDROCK
VOICES [C] — Ann LEE
VOICES [D] — DISTURBED
VOICES [E] — KC FLIGHTT vs FUNKY JUNCTION
VOICES IN THE SKY — The MOODY BLUES
VOID — EXOTERIX
VOLARE [A] — Charlie DRAKE
VOLARE [A] — Dean MARTIN
VOLARE [A] — Domenico MODUGNO
VOLARE [A] — Marino MARINI and his QUARTET
VOLARE [A] — Bobby RYDELL
VOLCANO GIRLS — VERUCA SALT
VOLUME 1 (WHAT YOU WANT WHAT YOU NEED) —
   INDUSTRY STANDARD
VOODOO — WARRIOR
VOODOO CHILE —
   The Jimi HENDRIX EXPERIENCE
VOODOO LOVE —
   LEE-CABRERA presents PHASE 2
VOODOO PEOPLE — The PRODIGY
VOODOO RAY — A GUY CALLED GERALD
VOODOO VOODOO — Den HEGARTY
VOULEZ-VOUS — ABBA
THE VOW — TOYAH 3
VOYAGE VOYAGE — DESIRELESS
VOYAGER — PENDULUM
VOYEUR — Kim CARNES
VULNERABLE — ROXETTE
WACK ASS MF — RHYTHMKILLAZ
WADE IN THE WATER — Ramsey LEWIS
WAGES DAY — DEACON BLUE
THE WAGON — DINOSAUR JR
WAIL — Jon SPENCER BLUES EXPLOSION
WAIT — Kym MAZELLE
WAIT A MINUTE — Ray J featuring LIL' KIM
WAIT AND BLEED — SLIPKNOT
WAIT FOR ME — Malcolm VAUGHAN
WAIT FOR ME, DARLING —
   Joan REGAN with the JOHNSTON BROTHERS
WAIT FOR ME MARY-ANNE — MARMALADE
WAIT UNTIL MIDNIGHT — YELLOW DOG
WAIT UNTIL TONIGHT (MY LOVE) — Phil FEARON
WAITING [A] — STYLE COUNCIL
WAITING [B] — GREEN DAY
THE WAITING 18 — AMEN
WAITING FOR A GIRL LIKE YOU — FOREIGNER
WAITING FOR A STAR TO FALL —
   BOY MEETS GIRL
WAITIN' FOR A SUPERMAN —
   The FLAMING LIPS
WAITING FOR A TRAIN — FLASH and the PAN

WAITING FOR AN ALIBI — THIN LIZZY
WAITING FOR SUMMER — DELIRIOUS?
WAITING FOR THAT DAY — George MICHAEL
(WAITING FOR) THE GHOST TRAIN —
MADNESS
WAITING FOR THE GREAT LEAP FORWARDS —
Billy BRAGG
WAITING FOR THE LOVEBOAT — ASSOCIATES
WAITING FOR THE NIGHT — SAXON
WAITING FOR THE SUN — RUFF DRIVERZ
WAITING FOR TONIGHT — Jennifer LOPEZ
WAITING HOPEFULLY — D*NOTE
WAITING IN VAIN [A] —
Bob MARLEY & the WAILERS
WAITING IN VAIN [A] —
Lee RITENOUR and Maxi PRIEST
WAITING IN VAIN [A] — Annie LENNOX
WAITING ON A FRIEND —
The ROLLING STONES
WAKE IN THE CITY — IKARA COLT
WAKE ME UP BEFORE YOU GO GO — WHAM!
WAKE UP — DANSE SOCIETY
WAKE UP AND SCRATCH ME —
SULTANS OF PING
WAKE UP BOO! — BOO RADLEYS
WAKE UP DEAD — MEGADETH
WAKE UP EVERYBODY —
Harold MELVIN and the BLUENOTES
WAKE UP LITTLE SUSIE [A] —
The EVERLY BROTHERS
WAKE UP LITTLE SUSIE [A] — KING BROTHERS
WAKE UP (MAKE A MOVE) — LOSTPROPHETS
WAKE UP SUSAN — DETROIT SPINNERS
WAKING UP — ELASTICA
WAKING WITH A STRANGER —
TYRREL CORPORATION
WALHALLA — GOURYELLA
WALK — PANTERA
THE WALK [A] — INMATES
THE WALK [B] — The CURE
WALK AWAY [A] —
Shane FENTON and the FENTONES
WALK AWAY [B] — Matt MONRO
WALK AWAY [C] — SISTERS OF MERCY
WALK AWAY [D] — Joyce SIMS
WALK AWAY FROM LOVE — David RUFFIN
WALK AWAY RENEE — The FOUR TOPS
WALK DON'T RUN [A] —
John BARRY ORCHESTRA
WALK DON'T RUN [A] — VENTURES
WALK — MY LIFE STORY
WALK HAND IN HAND [A] — Jimmy PARKINSON
WALK HAND IN HAND [A] — Ronnie CARROLL
WALK HAND IN HAND [A] — Tony MARTIN
WALK HAND IN HAND [A] —
GERRY and the PACEMAKERS
WALK IDIOT WALK — The HIVES
WALK IN LOVE — MANHATTAN TRANSFER
A WALK IN THE BLACK FOREST —
Horst JANKOWSKI
WALK IN THE NIGHT [A] —
Junior WALKER and the ALL-STARS
WALK IN THE NIGHT [A] — Paul HARDCASTLE
A WALK IN THE PARK — Nick STRAKER BAND
WALK INTO THE SUN — DIRTY VEGAS
WALK INTO THE WIND — VEGAS
WALK LIKE A CHAMPION — KALEEF
WALK LIKE A MAN [A] — The FOUR SEASONS
WALK LIKE A MAN [A] — DIVINE
WALK LIKE A PANTHER '98 —
The ALL SEEING I featuring Tony CHRISTIE
WALK LIKE AN EGYPTIAN — The BANGLES
WALK OF LIFE [A] — DIRE STRAITS
WALK OF LIFE [B] — Billie PIPER
WALK ON [A] — Roy ORBISON
WALK ON [B] — U2
WALK ON AIR — T'PAU
WALK ON BY [A] — Leroy VAN DYKE
WALK ON BY [B] — Dionne WARWICK
WALK ON BY [B] — The STRANGLERS
WALK ON BY [B] — AVERAGE WHITE BAND
WALK ON BY [B] — D TRAIN
WALK ON BY [B] — SYBIL
WALK ON BY [B] — GABRIELLE
WALK ON GILDED SPLINTERS — Marsha HUNT
WALK ON THE WILD SIDE [A] — Lou REED
WALK ON THE WILD SIDE [A] — BEAT SYSTEM
WALK ON THE WILD SIDE [A] —
Jamie J MORGAN
WALK ON WATER — MILK INC
WALK OUT TO WINTER — AZTEC CAMERA
WALK RIGHT BACK [A] —
The EVERLY BROTHERS
WALK RIGHT BACK [A] — Perry COMO
WALK RIGHT IN — ROOFTOP SINGERS
WALK RIGHT NOW — The JACKSONS
WALK TALL — Val DOONICAN
WALK THE DINOSAUR — WAS (NOT WAS)
WALK ... (THE DOG) LIKE AN EGYPTIAN —
JODE featuring YO-HANS
WALK THIS LAND — E-Z ROLLERS
WALK THIS WAY — RUN-DMC
WALK THIS WORLD — Heather NOVA
WALK THROUGH THE FIRE — Peter GABRIEL
WALK THROUGH THE WORLD — Marc COHN
WALK WITH FAITH IN YOUR HEART —
The BACHELORS

WALK WITH ME — The SEEKERS
WALK WITH ME MY ANGEL — Don CHARLES
WALK WITH ME TALK WITH ME DARLING —
The FOUR TOPS
WALKAWAY — CAST
WALKED OUTTA HEAVEN — JAGGED EDGE
WALKIE TALKIE MAN — STERIOGRAM
WALKIN' — CCS
WALKIN' BACK TO HAPPINESS —
Helen SHAPIRO
WALKIN IN THE NAME — FUNKSTAR DE LUXE
WALKIN' IN THE RAIN WITH THE ONE I LOVE — LOVE
UNLIMITED
A WALKIN' MIRACLE —
LIMMIE and the FAMILY COOKIN'
WALKIN' ON — SHEER BRONZE featuring
Lisa MILLETT
WALKIN' ON THE SUN — SMASH MOUTH
WALKIN' ON UP — DJ PROFESSOR
WALKIN' TALL [A] — Frankie VAUGHAN
WALKIN' TALL [B] — Adam FAITH
WALKIN' THE DOG — DENNISONS
WALKIN' THE LINE —
BRASS CONSTRUCTION
WALKIN' TO MISSOURI — Tony BRENT
WALKING AFTER YOU: BEACON LIGHT —
FOO FIGHTERS
WALKING ALONE — Richard ANTHONY
WALKING AWAY — Craig DAVID
WALKING BY MYSELF — Gary MOORE
WALKING DEAD — PURESSENCE
WALKING DOWN MADISON — Kirsty MacCOL
WALKING DOWN YOUR STREET —
The BANGLES
WALKING IN MEMPHIS [A] — Marc COHN
WALKING IN MEMPHIS [B] — CHER
WALKING IN MY SHOES — DEPECHE MODE
WALKING IN MY SLEEP — Roger DALTREY
WALKING IN RHYTHM — BLACKBYRDS
WALKING IN THE AIR [A] — Aled JONES
WALKING IN THE AIR [A] —
Peter AUTY and the SINFONIA OF LONDON
conducted by Howard BLAKE
WALKING IN THE AIR [A] —
DIGITAL DREAM BABY
WALKING IN THE RAIN [A] —
The WALKER BROTHERS
WALKING IN THE RAIN [B] —
PARTRIDGE FAMILY
WALKING IN THE RAIN [B] —
MODERN ROMANCE
WALKING IN THE SUN — TRAVIS
WALKING INTO SUNSHINE — BAD MANNERS
WALKING INTO SUNSHINE — CENTRAL LINE
WALKING MY BABY BACK HOME — Johnnie RAY
WALKING MY CAT NAMED DOG —
Norma TANEGA
WALKING ON AIR [A] — FRAZIER CHORUS
WALKING ON AIR [B] — BAD BOYS INC
WALKING ON BROKEN GLASS — Annie LENNOX
WALKING ON ICE — RIVER CITY PEOPLE
WALKING ON SUNSHINE [A] —
ROCKER'S REVENGE featuring Donnie CALVIN
WALKING ON SUNSHINE [A] — Eddy GRANT
WALKING ON SUNSHINE [A] — KRUSH
WALKING ON SUNSHINE [B] —
KATRINA and the WAVES
WALKING ON THE CHINESE WALL —
Philip BAILEY
WALKING ON THE MILKY WAY —
ORCHESTRAL MANOEUVRES IN THE DARK
WALKING ON THE MOON — The POLICE
WALKING ON THIN ICE — Yoko ONO
WALKING ON WATER — MADASUN
WALKING THE FLOOR OVER YOU — Pat BOONE
WALKING TO NEW ORLEANS — Fats DOMINO
WALKING WITH THEE — CLINIC
WALKING WOUNDED —
EVERYTHING BUT THE GIRL
THE WALL STREET SHUFFLE — 10cc
WALLFLOWER — MEGA CITY FOUR
WALLS COME TUMBLING DOWN! —
STYLE COUNCIL
THE WALLS FELL DOWN — MARBLES
WALTZ AWAY DREAMING — George MICHAEL
WALTZ DARLING — Malcolm McLAREN
WALTZ #2 (XO) — Elliott SMITH
WALTZING ALONG — JAMES
WAM BAM [A] — HANDLEY FAMILY
WAM BAM [B] — NT GANG
THE WANDERER [A] — DION
THE WANDERER [A] — STATUS QUO
THE WANDERER [B] — Donna SUMMER
WANDERIN' EYES [A] — Charlie GRACIE
WANDERIN' EYES [A] — Frankie VAUGHAN
THE WANDERING DRAGON —
SHADES OF RHYTHM
WANDERLUST — DELAYS
WAND'RIN' STAR — Lee MARVIN
WANNA BE STARTIN' SOMETHIN' —
Michael JACKSON
WANNA BE THAT WAY — IKARA COLT
WANNA BE WITH YOU — JINNY
WANNA BE YOUR LOVER — GAYLE & GILLIAN
WANNA DROP A HOUSE (ON THAT BITCH) —
URBAN DISCHARGE featuring SHE
WANNA GET TO KNOW YOU — G-UNIT

WANNA GET UP — 2 UNLIMITED
WANNA MAKE YOU GO ... UUH! —
THOSE 2 GIRLS
WANNABE — SPICE GIRLS
WANNABE GANGSTAR — WHEATUS
WANT LOVE — HYSTERIC EGO
WANT YOU BAD — The OFFSPRING
WANTED [A] — Perry COMO
WANTED [A] — Al MARTINO
WANTED [B] — The DOOLEYS
WANTED [C] — STYLE COUNCIL
WANTED [D] — HALO JAMES
WANTED [E] — PRINCESS IVORI
WANTED DEAD OR ALIVE [A] — BON JOVI
WANTED DEAD OR ALIVE [B] —
2PAC and SNOOP DOGG
WANTED IT ALL — CLAYTOWN TROUPE
WAP-BAM-BOOGIE — MATT BIANCO
WAR [A] — Edwin STARR
WAR [A] — Bruce SPRINGSTEEN
WAR BABIES — SIMPLE MINDS
WAR BABY — Tom ROBINSON
WAR CHILD — BLONDIE
WAR LORD — The SHADOWS
WAR OF NERVES — ALL SAINTS
WAR PARTY — Eddy GRANT
THE WAR SONG — CULTURE CLUB
WAR STORIES — STARJETS
WARFAIR — CLAWFINGER
WARHEAD — UK SUBS
WARLOCK — BLACK RIOT
WARM AND TENDER LOVE — Percy SLEDGE
WARM IT UP — KRIS KROSS
WARM LOVE — BEATMASTERS
WARM MACHINE — BUSH
WARM SUMMER DAZE — VYBE
WARM WET CIRCLES — MARILLION
WARMED OVER KISSES — Brian HYLAND
WARNING [A] — ADEVA
WARNING [B] — AKA
WARNING [C] — FREESTYLERS
WARNING [D] — GREEN DAY
WARNING SIGN — Nick HEYWARD
WARPAINT — BROOK BROTHERS
WARPED — RED HOT CHILI PEPPERS
WARRIOR — MC WILDSKI
WARRIOR [B] — DANCE 2 TRANCE
WARRIOR [C] — WARRIOR
WARRIOR GROOVE — DSM
WARRIOR SOUND — PRESSURE DROP
WARRIORS [A] — Gary NUMAN
WARRIORS [B] — ASWAD
WARRIORS (OF THE WASTELAND) —
FRANKIE GOES TO HOLLYWOOD
WAS IT WORTH IT? — PET SHOP BOYS
WAS THAT ALL IT WAS — Kym MAZELLE
WAS THAT YOU — SPEAR OF DESTINY
WASH IN THE RAIN — The BEES
WASH YOUR FACE IN MY SINK —
DREAM WARRIORS
WASSUUP — DA MUTTZ
WASTED [A] — DEF LEPPARD
WASTED [B] — SMALLER
WASTED IN AMERICA — LOVE / HATE
WASTED TIME [A] — SKID ROW
WASTED TIME [B] — KINGS OF LEON
WASTED YEARS — IRON MAIDEN
WASTELAND — The MISSION
WASTELANDS — Midge URE
WASTER — REEF
WASTING MY TIME [A] — DEFAULT
WASTING MY TIME [B] — KOSHEEN
WATCH ME — Labi SIFFRE
WATCH OUT — Brandi WELLS
WATCH THE MIRACLE START — Pauline HENRY
WATCH WHAT YOU SAY —
GURU featuring Chaka KHAN
WATCHA GONNA DO — Keisha WHITE
WATCHDOGS — UB40
A WATCHER'S POINT OF VIEW — PM DAWN
WATCHING — THOMPSON TWINS
WATCHING CARS GO BY — FELIX DA HOUSECAT vs
SASHA and Armand VAN HELDEN
WATCHING THE DETECTIVES — Elvis COSTELLO
WATCHING THE RIVER FLOW — Bob DYLAN
WATCHING THE WHEELS — John LENNON
WATCHING THE WILDLIFE —
FRANKIE GOES TO HOLLYWOOD
WATCHING THE WORLD GO BY — Maxi PRIEST
WATCHING WINDOWS —
Roni SIZE / REPRAZENT
WATCHING XANADU —
MULL HISTORICAL SOCIETY
WATCHING YOU — ETHER
WATCHING YOU WATCHING ME — David GRANT
WATER [A] —
Geno WASHINGTON and the RAM JAM BAND
WATER [B] — MARTIKA
WATER FROM A VINE LEAF — William ORBIT
THE WATER IS OVER MY HEAD —
ROCKIN' BERRIES
THE WATER MARGIN — GODIEGO
WATER ON GLASS — Kim WILDE
WATER RUNS DRY — BOYZ II MEN
WATER WATER — Tommy STEELE
WATER WAVE — Mark VAN DALE with ENRICO
WATERFALL [A] — WENDY and LISA

WATERFALL [B] — The STONE ROSES
WATERFALL [C] — ATLANTIC OCEAN
WATERFALLS [A] — Paul McCARTNEY
WATERFALLS [B] — TLC
WATERFRONT — SIMPLE MINDS
WATERLOO [A] — Stonewall JACKSON
WATERLOO [B] — ABBA
WATERLOO [B] — DOCTOR and the MEDICS
featuring Roy WOOD
WATERLOO SUNSET [A] — The KINKS
WATERLOO SUNSET [A] — Cathy DENNIS
WATERY, DOMESTIC (EP) — PAVEMENT
THE WAVE — COSMIC GATE
THE WAVE OF THE FUTURE — QUADROPHONIA
WAVES — BLANCMANGE
WAVY GRAVY — SASHA
WAX THE VAN — LOLA
THE WAY [A] — FUNKY GREEN DOGS
THE WAY [B] — GLOBAL COMMUNICATION
THE WAY [C] — FASTBALL
WAY AWAY — YELLOWCARD
WAY BACK HOME —
Junior WALKER and the ALL-STARS
WAY BEHIND ME — PRIMITIVES
WAY DOWN — Elvis PRESLEY: Vocal acc. J.D. Sumner
& the Stamps Qt. K. Westmoreland, S. Neilson & M.
Smith
WAY DOWN NOW — WORLD PARTY
WAY DOWN YONDER IN NEW ORLEANS —
Freddy CANNON
THE WAY DREAMS ARE — Daniel O'DONNELL
THE WAY I AM — EMINEM
THE WAY I FEEL [A] — LEMON TREES
THE WAY I FEEL [B] — ROACHFORD
THE WAY I FEEL ABOUT YOU — Karyn WHITE
THE WAY I WALK — Jack SCOTT
THE WAY I WANT TO TOUCH YOU —
CAPTAIN and TENNILLE
WAY IN MY BRAIN — SL2
THE WAY IT GOES — STATUS QUO
THE WAY IT IS [A] —
Bruce HORNSBY and the RANGE
THE WAY IT IS [A] — CHAMELEON
THE WAY IT USED TO BE —
Engelbert HUMPERDINCK
THE WAY IT WAS — BARON
THE WAY IT'S GOIN' DOWN (T.W.I.S.M. FOR LIFE) —
Shaquille O'NEAL
WAY OF LIFE [A] — FAMILY DOGG
WAY OF LIFE [B] — Dave CLARKE
WAY OF THE WORLD [A] — CHEAP TRICK
WAY OF THE WORLD [B] — Tina TURNER
THE WAY (PUT YOUR HAND IN MY HAND) —
DIVINE INSPIRATION
THE WAY SHE LOVES ME — Richard MARX
THE WAY THAT YOU FEEL — ADEVA
THE WAY THAT YOU LOVE — Vanessa WILLIAMS
THE WAY TO YOUR LOVE — HEAR'SAY
THE WAY WE WERE — Barbra STREISAND
THE WAY WE WERE — TRY TO REMEMBER —
Gladys KNIGHT and the PIPS
THE WAY YOU ARE — TEARS FOR FEARS
THE WAY YOU DO THE THINGS YOU DO —
UB40
THE WAY YOU LIKE IT — ADEMA
THE WAY YOU LOOK TONIGHT [A] —
LETTERMEN
THE WAY YOU LOOK TONIGHT [A] —
Denny SEYTON and the SABRES
THE WAY YOU LOOK TONIGHT [A] —
Edward WOODWARD
THE WAY YOU LOVE ME [A] — Karyn WHITE
THE WAY YOU LOVE ME [B] — Faith HILL
THE WAY YOU MAKE ME FEEL [A] —
Michael JACKSON
THE WAY YOU MAKE ME FEEL [B] —
Ronan KEATING
THE WAY YOU MOVE —
OUTKAST featuring SLEEPY BROWN
THE WAY YOU WORK IT — EYC
WAYDOWN — CATHERINE WHEEL
WAYS OF LOVE — CLAYTOWN TROUPE
WAYWARD WIND [A] — Jimmy YOUNG
WAYWARD WIND [A] — Tex RITTER
THE WAYWARD WIND [A] — Gogi GRANT
THE WAYWARD WIND [A] — Frank IFIELD
WE ALL FOLLOW MAN UNITED —
MANCHESTER UNITED FOOTBALL CLUB
WE ALL SLEEP ALONE — CHER
WE ALL STAND TOGETHER — Paul McCARTNEY
WE ALMOST GOT IT TOGETHER —
Tanita TIKARAM
WE ARE — Ana JOHNSSON
WE ARE ALIVE — Paul VAN DYK
WE ARE ALL MADE OF STARS — MOBY
WE ARE BACK — LFO
WE ARE DA CLICK — DA CLICK
WE ARE DETECTIVE — THOMPSON TWINS
WE ARE EACH OTHER —
The BEAUTIFUL SOUTH
WE ARE E-MALE — E-MALE
WE ARE FAMILY — SISTER SLEDGE
WE ARE GLASS — Gary NUMAN
WE ARE GOING ON DOWN — DEADLY SINS
WE ARE I. E. — Lennie DE ICE
WE ARE IN LOVE [A] — Adam FAITH
WE ARE IN LOVE [B] — Harry CONNICK Jr

WE ARE LOVE — DJ ERIC
WE ARE NOT ALONE — Frankie VAUGHAN
WE ARE RAVING — THE ANTHEM — SLIPSTREEM
WE ARE THE BAND — MORE
WE ARE THE CHAMPIONS [A] — QUEEN
WE ARE THE CHAMPIONS [A] — Hank MARVIN featuring Brian MAY
WE ARE THE FIRM — COCKNEY REJECTS
WE ARE THE PIGS — SUEDE
WE ARE THE WORLD — USA FOR AFRICA
WE BELONG — Pat BENATAR
WE BELONG IN THIS WORLD TOGETHER — STEREO MC's
WE BUILT THIS CITY — STARSHIP
WE CALL IT ACIEED — D MOB
WE CAME TO DANCE — ULTRAVOX
WE CAN — LeAnn RIMES
WE CAN BE BRAVE AGAIN — ARMOURY SHOW
WE CAN DO ANYTHING — COCKNEY REJECTS
WE CAN DO IT (EP) — LIVERPOOL FC
WE CAN GET DOWN — MYRON
WE CAN MAKE IT — MONE
WE CAN MAKE IT HAPPEN — PRINCE CHARLES and the CITY BEAT BAND
WE CAN WORK IT OUT [A] — The BEATLES
WE CAN WORK IT OUT [A] — Stevie WONDER
WE CAN WORK IT OUT [A] — The FOUR SEASONS
WE CAN WORK IT OUT [B] — BRASS CONSTRUCTION
WE CARE A LOT — FAITH NO MORE
WE CLOSE OUR EYES — GO WEST
WE COME 1 — FAITHLESS
WE COME TO PARTY — N-TYCE
WE COULD BE KINGS — GENE
WE COULD BE TOGETHER — Debbie GIBSON
WE DIDN'T START THE FIRE — Billy JOEL
WE DO IT — R & J STONE
WE DON'T CARE — AUDIO BULLYS
WE DON'T HAVE TO ... TAKE OUR CLOTHES OFF TO HAVE A GOOD TIME — Jermaine STEWART
WE DON'T NEED A REASON — DARE
WE DON'T NEED ANOTHER HERO (THUNDERDOME) — Tina TURNER
WE DON'T NEED NOBODY ELSE — WHIPPING BOY
(WE DON'T NEED THIS) FASCIST GROOVE THANG — HEAVEN 17
WE DON'T TALK ANYMORE — Cliff RICHARD
WE DON'T WORK FOR FREE — GRANDMASTER FLASH, Melle MEL and the FURIOUS FIVE
WE FIT TOGETHER — O-TOWN
WE GOT A LOVE THANG — Ce Ce PENISTON
WE GOT IT — IMMATURE featuring SMOOTH
WE GOT LOVE — Alma COGAN
WE GOT OUR OWN THANG — HEAVY D and the BOYZ
WE GOT THE FUNK — POSITIVE FORCE
WE GOT THE GROOVE — PLAYERS ASSOCIATION
WE GOT THE LOVE [A] — TOUCH OF SOUL
WE GOT THE LOVE [B] — Lindy LAYTON
WE GOT THE LOVE [B] — ERIK
WE GOT THE LOVE [C] — TRI
WE GOTTA DO IT — DJ PROFESSOR featuring Francesco ZAPPALA
WE GOTTA GET OUT OF THIS PLACE [A] — The ANIMALS
WE GOTTA GET OUT OF THIS PLACE [A] — ANGELIC UPSTARTS
WE GOTTA LOVE — Kym SIMS
WE HATE IT WHEN OUR FRIENDS BECOME SUCCESSFUL — MORRISSEY
WE HAVE A DREAM — SCOTLAND WORLD CUP SQUAD
WE HAVE ALL THE TIME IN THE WORLD — Louis ARMSTRONG
WE HAVE EXPLOSIVE — FUTURE SOUND OF LONDON
WE HAVEN'T TURNED AROUND — GOMEZ
WE JUST BE DREAMIN' — BLAZIN' SQUAD
WE JUST WANNA PARTY WITH YOU — SNOOP DOGG
WE KILL THE WORLD (DON'T KILL THE WORLD) — BONEY M
WE KNOW SOMETHING YOU DON'T KNOW — DJ FORMAT featuring CHALI 2NA & AKIL
WE LET THE STARS GO — PREFAB SPROUT
WE LIKE TO PARTY! (THE VENGABUS) — The VENGABOYS
WE LOVE EACH OTHER — Charlie RICH
WE LOVE YOU [A] — The ROLLING STONES
WE LOVE YOU [B] — ORCHESTRAL MANOEUVRES IN THE DARK
WE LOVE YOU [C] — MENSWEAR
WE LUV U — GRAND THEFT AUDIO
WE NEED A RESOLUTION — AALIYAH featuring TIMBALAND
WE NEED LOVE — CASHMERE
WE ROCK — DIO
WE SAIL ON THE STORMY WATERS — Gary CLARK
WE SHALL OVERCOME — Joan BAEZ
WE SHOULD BE TOGETHER — Cliff RICHARD
WE SHOULDN'T HOLD HANDS IN THE DARK — LA MIX

WE TAKE MYSTERY (TO BED) — Gary NUMAN
WE THUGGIN' — FAT JOE
WE TRYING TO STAY ALIVE — The FUGEES
WE USED TO BE FRIENDS — The DANDY WARHOLS
WE WAIT AND WE WONDER — Phil COLLINS
WE WALKED IN LOVE — DOLLAR
WE WANNA THANK YOU (THE THINGS YOU DO) — BIG BROVAZ
(WE WANT) THE SAME THING — Belinda CARLISLE
WE WANT YOUR SOUL — FREELAND
WE WILL — Gilbert O'SULLIVAN
WE WILL MAKE LOVE — Russ HAMILTON
WE WILL MEET AGAIN — Oleta ADAMS
WE WILL NEVER BE AS YOUNG AS THIS AGAIN — Danny WILLIAMS
WE WILL ROCK YOU — FIVE and QUEEN
WE WILL SURVIVE — WARP BROTHERS
WEAK [A] — SWV
WEAK [B] — SKUNK ANANSIE
WEAK BECOME HEROES — The STREETS
WEAK IN THE PRESENCE OF BEAUTY — Alison MOYET
WEAK SPOT — Evelyn THOMAS
WEAR MY HAT — Phil COLLINS
WEAR MY RING AROUND YOUR NECK — Elvis PRESLEY
WEAR YOU TO THE BALL — UB40
WEAR YOUR LOVE LIKE HEAVEN — DEFINITION OF SOUND
WEATHER FORECAST — MASTER SINGERS
WEATHER WITH YOU — CROWDED HOUSE
WEAVE YOUR SPELL — LEVEL 42
THE WEAVER (EP) — Paul WELLER
THE WEDDING — Julie ROGERS
THE WEDDING [B] — Cliff RICHARD
WEDDING BELL BLUES — 5TH DIMENSION
WEDDING BELLS — GODLEY and CREME
WEDDING RING — Russ HAMILTON
WEDNESDAY WEEK — The UNDERTONES
WEE RULE — WEE PAPA GIRL RAPPERS
WEE TOM — LORD ROCKINGHAM'S XI
WEEK IN WEEK OUT — The ORDINARY BOYS
WEEKEND [A] — Eddie COCHRAN
WEEKEND [A] — Mick JACKSON
WEEKEND [C] — CLASS ACTION featuring Chris WILTSHIRE
WEEKEND [C] — Todd TERRY Project
WEEKEND [D] — BAD HABIT BOYS
WEEKEND! [E] — SCOOTER
THE WEEKEND — Michael GRAY
WEEKEND GIRL — S.O.S. BAND
THE WEEKEND HAS LANDED — MINKY
WEEKENDER — FLOWERED UP
THE WEIGHT — The BAND
WEIGHT FOR THE BASS — UNIQUE 3
WEIGHT OF THE WORLD — Ringo STARR
WEIRD [A] — REEF
WEIRD [B] — HANSON
WEIRDO — The CHARLATANS
WELCOME — Gino LATINO
WELCOME BACK — MA$E
WELCOME HOME — PETERS and LEE
WELCOME HOME BABY — BROOK BROTHERS
WELCOME TO CHICAGO EP — Gene FARRIS
WELCOME TO MY TRUTH — ANASTACIA
WELCOME TO MY WORLD — Jim REEVES
WELCOME TO OUR WORLD (OF MERRY MUSIC) — MASS PRODUCTION
WELCOME TO PARADISE — GREEN DAY
WELCOME TO THE CHEAP SEATS (EP) — The WONDER STUFF
WELCOME TO THE FUTURE — SHIMMON & WOOLFSON
WELCOME TO THE JUNGLE — GUNS N' ROSES
WELCOME TO THE PLEASURE DOME — FRANKIE GOES TO HOLLYWOOD
WELCOME TO THE REAL WORLD — GUN
WELCOME TO THE TERRORDOME — PUBLIC ENEMY
WELCOME TO TOMORROW — SNAP! featuring SUMMER
WELL ALL RIGHT — SANTANA
WE'LL BE RIGHT BACK — STEINSKI and MASS MEDIA
WE'LL BE TOGETHER — STING
WE'LL BE WITH YOU — POTTERS
WE'LL BRING THE HOUSE DOWN — SLADE
WELL DID YOU EVAH! — Deborah HARRY and Iggy POP
WE'LL FIND OUR DAY — Stephanie DE SYKES
WE'LL GATHER LILACS — ALL MY LOVING (MEDLEY) — Simon MAY
WELL I ASK YOU — Eden KANE
WE'LL SING IN THE SUNSHINE — LANCASTRIANS
WE'RE ALL ALONE — Rita COOLIDGE
WE'RE ALL IN LOVE — BLACK REBEL MOTORCYCLE CLUB
WE'RE ALMOST THERE — Michael JACKSON
WE'RE COMIN' AT YA — QUARTZ
WE'RE COMING HOME — MR SMASH & FRIENDS
WE'RE GOING OUT — YOUNGER YOUNGER 28'S
WE'RE GOING TO IBIZA! — The VENGABOYS

WE'RE GOING TO MISS YOU — JAMES
WE'RE GONNA DO IT AGAIN — MANCHESTER UNITED FOOTBALL CLUB
WE'RE GONNA GO FISHIN' — Hank LOCKLIN
WE'RE IN THIS LOVE TOGETHER — Al JARREAU
WE'RE IN THIS TOGETHER [A] — SIMPLY RED
WE'RE IN THIS TOGETHER [B] — NINE INCH NAILS
WE'RE NOT ALONE — HHC
WE'RE NOT GONNA SLEEP TONIGHT — Emma BUNTON
WE'RE NOT GONNA TAKE IT — TWISTED SISTER
WE'RE ON THE BALL — ANT & DEC
WE'RE ONLY YOUNG ONCE — AVONS
WE'RE REALLY SAYING SOMETHING — BUFFALO G
WE'RE THROUGH — The HOLLIES
WEST END GIRLS [A] — PET SHOP BOYS
WEST END GIRLS [A] — EAST 17
WEST END PAD — Cathy DENNIS
WEST OF ZANZIBAR — Anthony STEEL and the RADIO REVELLERS
WEST ONE (SHINE ON ME) — RUTS
WESTERN MOVIES — OLYMPICS
WESTSIDE [A] — TQ
WESTSIDE [B] — ATHLETE
WET DREAM — Max ROMEO
WET MY WHISTLE — MIDNIGHT STAR
WE'VE GOT IT GOIN' ON — BACKSTREET BOYS
WE'VE GOT THE JUICE — Derek B
WE'VE GOT THE WHOLE WORLD AT OUR FEET — ENGLAND WORLD CUP SQUAD
WE GOT THE WHOLE WORLD IN OUR HANDS — NOTTINGHAM FOREST FC with PAPER LACE
WE'VE GOT TO LIVE TOGETHER — R.A.F.
WE'VE GOT TO WORK IT OUT — BEL CANTO
WE'VE GOT TONITE [A] — Bob SEGER and the SILVER BULLET BAND
WE'VE GOT TONIGHT [A] — Kenny ROGERS and Sheena EASTON
WE'VE GOT TONIGHT [A] — Elkie BROOKS
WE'VE GOT TONIGHT [A] — Bob SEGER and the SILVER BULLET BAND
WE'VE GOT TONIGHT [A] — Ronan KEATING featuring LULU
WE'VE HAD ENOUGH — ALKALINE TRIO
WE'VE ONLY JUST BEGUN [A] — The CARPENTERS
WE'VE ONLY JUST BEGUN [A] — Bitty McLEAN
WFL — HAPPY MONDAYS
WHADDA U WANT (FROM ME) — Frankie KNUCKLES featuring ADEVA
WHADDA WE LIKE? — ROUND SOUND presents ONYX STONE & MC MALIBU
WHAM BAM — CANDY GIRLS
WHAM RAP! — WHAM!
WHAT — SOFT CELL
WHAT A BEAUTIFUL DAY — LEVELLERS
WHAT A CRAZY WORLD WE'RE LIVING IN — Joe BROWN and the BRUVVERS
WHAT A DIFFERENCE A DAY MADE — Esther PHILLIPS
WHAT A FOOL BELIEVES [A] — DOOBIE BROTHERS
WHAT A FOOL BELIEVES [A] — Aretha FRANKLIN
WHAT A FOOL BELIEVES [A] — Peter COX
WHAT A GIRL WANTS — Christina AGUILERA
WHAT A MOUTH — Tommy STEELE
WHAT A NIGHT — CITY BOY
WHAT A PARTY — Fats DOMINO
WHAT A WASTE! — Ian DURY and the BLOCKHEADS
WHAT A WASTER — The LIBERTINES
WHAT A WOMAN IN LOVE WON'T DO — Sandy POSEY
WHAT A WONDERFUL WORLD [A] — Louis ARMSTRONG Orchestra & Chorus
WHAT A WONDERFUL WORLD [A] — Nick CAVE and Shane MacGOWAN
WHAT A WONDERFUL WORLD [A] — Cliff RICHARD
(WHAT A) WONDERFUL WORLD — Johnny NASH
WHAT ABOUT LOVE — HEART
WHAT ABOUT ME — The CRIBS
WHAT ABOUT THIS LOVE — MR FINGERS
WHAT ABOUT US [A] — POINT BREAK
WHAT ABOUT US? [B] — BRANDY
WHAT ABOUT YOUR FRIENDS — TLC
WHAT AM I GONNA DO — Emile FORD and the CHECKMATES
WHAT AM I GONNA DO (I'M SO IN LOVE WITH YOU) — Rod STEWART
WHAT AM I GONNA DO WITH YOU — Barry WHITE
WHAT AM I TO YOU — Kenny LYNCH
WHAT ARE WE GONNA DO ABOUT IT? — MERCY MERCY
WHAT ARE WE GONNA GET 'ER INDOORS — Dennis WATERMAN
WHAT ARE YOU DOING SUNDAY — DAWN
WHAT BECAME OF THE LIKELY LADS — The LIBERTINES
WHAT BECOMES OF THE BROKENHEARTED [A] — Jimmy RUFFIN

WHAT BECOMES OF THE BROKEN HEARTED [A] — Dave STEWART; Guest vocals: Colin BLUNSTONE
WHAT BECOMES OF THE BROKENHEARTED [A] — ROBSON & JEROME
WHAT CAN I DO — The CORRS
WHAT CAN I SAY — Boz SCAGGS
(WHAT CAN I SAY) TO MAKE YOU LOVE ME — Alexander O'NEAL
WHAT CAN YOU DO FOR ME [A] — UTAH SAINTS
WHAT CAN YOU DO 4 ME? [B] — Lisa LASHES
WHAT 'CHA GONNA DO — ETERNAL
WHAT DID (I DO TO YOU) (EP) — Lisa STANSFIELD
WHAT DIFFERENCE DOES IT MAKE — The SMITHS
WHAT DO I DO — Phil FEARON
WHAT DO I DO NOW — SLEEPER
WHAT DO I GET? — The BUZZCOCKS
WHAT DO I HAVE TO DO — Kylie MINOGUE
WHAT DO YA SAY — Chubby CHECKER
WHAT DO YOU WANT? — Adam FAITH
WHAT DO YOU WANT FROM ME? — MONACO
WHAT DO YOU WANT TO MAKE THOSE EYES AT ME FOR? [A] — Emile FORD and the CHECKMATES
WHAT DO YOU WANT TO MAKE THOSE EYES AT ME FOR [A] — Shakin' STEVENS
WHAT DOES IT FEEL LIKE? — FELIX DA HOUSECAT
WHAT DOES IT TAKE — THEN JERICO
WHAT DOES IT TAKE (TO WIN YOUR LOVE) [A] — Junior WALKER and the ALL-STARS
WHAT DOES IT TAKE (TO WIN YOUR LOVE) [A] — Kenny G
WHAT DOES YOUR SOUL LOOK LIKE — DJ SHADOW
WHAT EVER HAPPENED TO OLD FASHIONED LOVE — Daniel O'DONNELL
WHAT GOD WANTS PART 1 — Roger WATERS
WHAT GOES AROUND [A] — Bitty McLEAN
WHAT GOES AROUND [B] — LUCIANA
WHAT GOES AROUND COMES AROUND — Bob MARLEY & the WAILERS
WHAT GOES ON — Bryan FERRY
WHAT GOOD AM I — Cilla BLACK
WHAT HAPPENED TO THE MUSIC — Joey NEGRO
WHAT HAVE I DONE TO DESERVE THIS — PET SHOP BOYS and Dusty SPRINGFIELD
WHAT HAVE THEY DONE TO MY SONG MA [A] — The NEW SEEKERS
WHAT HAVE THEY DONE TO MY SONG MA [A] — MELANIE
WHAT HAVE THEY DONE TO THE RAIN — The SEARCHERS
WHAT HAVE YOU DONE FOR ME LATELY — Janet JACKSON
WHAT HAVE YOU DONE (IS THIS ALL) — OUR TRIBE / ONE TRIBE
WHAT HOPE HAVE I — SPHINX
WHAT I AM [A] — Edie BRICKELL and the NEW BOHEMIANS
WHAT I AM [A] — TIN TIN OUT featuring Emma BUNTON
WHAT I CAN DO FOR YOU — Sheryl CROW
WHAT I DO BEST — Robin S
WHAT I GO TO SCHOOL FOR — BUSTED
WHAT I GOT — SUBLIME
WHAT I LIKE MOST ABOUT YOU IS YOUR GIRLFRIEND — The SPECIALS
WHAT I MEAN — MODJO
WHAT I MISS THE MOST — ALOOF
WHAT I SAW — KINGS OF LEON
WHAT IF ... — The LIGHTNING SEEDS
WHAT IF — Kate WINSLET
WHAT IF A WOMAN — JOE
WHAT IN THE WORLD — NU COLOURS
WHAT IN THE WORLD'S COME OVER YOU [A] — Jack SCOTT
WHAT IN THE WORLD'S COME OVER YOU [A] — ROCKIN' BERRIES
WHAT IN THE WORLD'S COME OVER YOU [A] — Tam WHITE
WHAT IS A MAN — The FOUR TOPS
WHAT IS HOUSE (EP) — LFO
WHAT IS LIFE [A] — Olivia NEWTON-JOHN
WHAT IS LIFE [A] — Shawn MULLINS
WHAT IS LIFE? [B] — BLACK UHURU
WHAT IS LOVE [A] — Howard JONES
WHAT IS LOVE [B] — DEEE-LITE
WHAT IS LOVE [C] — HADDAWAY
WHAT IS THE PROBLEM? — GRAFITI
WHAT IS THIS THING CALLED LOVE — Alexander O'NEAL
WHAT IS TRUTH — Johnny CASH
WHAT IT FEELS LIKE FOR A GIRL — MADONNA
WHAT IT IS [A] — Garnet MIMMS and TRUCKIN' CO
WHAT IT IS [B] — Freddy FRESH
WHAT IT'S LIKE — EVERLAST
WHAT I'VE GOT IN MIND — Billie Jo SPEARS
WHAT KIND OF FOOL — ALL ABOUT EVE
WHAT KIND OF FOOL AM I? [A] — Anthony NEWLEY
WHAT KIND OF FOOL AM I? [A] — Sammy DAVIS Jr

WHERE ARE YOU NOW [A] — Jackie TRENT
WHERE ARE YOU NOW? [B] — GENERATOR
WHERE CAN I FIND LOVE — LIVIN' JOY
WHERE DID ALL THE GOOD TIMES GO — Donny OSMOND
WHERE DID I GO WRONG — UB40
WHERE DID OUR LOVE GO [A] — The SUPREMES
WHERE DID OUR LOVE GO? [A] — Donnie ELBERT
WHERE DID OUR LOVE GO [A] — MANHATTAN TRANSFER
WHERE DID OUR LOVE GO [A] — Tricia PENROSE
WHERE DID WE GO WRONG — LIQUID GOLD
WHERE DID YOUR HEART GO — WHAM!
WHERE DO BROKEN HEARTS GO — Whitney HOUSTON
(WHERE DO I BEGIN) LOVE STORY [A] — Andy WILLIAMS
(WHERE DO I BEGIN) LOVE STORY [A] — Shirley BASSEY
WHERE DO I STAND? — MONTROSE AVENUE
WHERE DO U WANT ME TO PUT IT — SOLO U.S.
WHERE DO WE GO — TEN CITY
WHERE DO WE GO FROM HERE — Cliff RICHARD
WHERE DO YOU GO — NO MERCY
WHERE DO YOU GO TO (MY LOVELY) — Peter SARSTEDT
WHERE DOES MY HEART BEAT NOW — Celine DION
WHERE DOES THE TIME GO — Julia FORDHAM
WHERE EAGLES FLY — CRYSTAL PALACE
WHERE HAS ALL THE LOVE GONE [A] — YAZZ
WHERE HAS ALL THE LOVE GONE [B] — MAUREEN
WHERE HAS LOVE GONE — Holly JOHNSON
WHERE HAVE ALL THE COWBOYS GONE? — Paula COLE
WHERE HAVE YOU BEEN TONIGHT — SHED SEVEN
WHERE I FIND MY HEAVEN — GIGOLO AUNTS
WHERE I WANNA BE — Shade SHEIST featuring Nate DOGG and KURUPT
WHERE I'M HEADED — Lene MARLIN
WHERE IN THE WORLD [A] — SWING OUT SISTER
WHERE IN THE WORLD [B] — BBM
WHERE IS MY MAN — Eartha KITT
WHERE IS THE FEELING — Kylie MINOGUE
WHERE IS THE LOVE [A] — Roberta FLACK
WHERE IS THE LOVE [A] — Betty WRIGHT
WHERE IS THE LOVE [A] — Mica PARIS and Will DOWNING
WHERE IS THE LOVE? [B] — ADEVA
WHERE IS THE LOVE? [C] — BLACK EYED PEAS
WHERE IS THE LOVE (WE USED TO KNOW) — DELEGATION
WHERE IS TOMORROW — Cilla BLACK
WHERE IT'S AT — BECK
WHERE LOVE LIVES — Alison LIMERICK
WHERE MY GIRLS AT? — 702
WHERE THE ACTION IS — WESTWORLD
WHERE THE BOYS ARE — Connie FRANCIS
WHERE THE HEART IS — SOFT CELL
WHERE THE HOOD AT — DMX
WHERE THE PARTY AT? — JAGGED EDGE featuring NELLY
WHERE THE POOR BOYS DANCE — LULU
WHERE THE ROSE IS SOWN — BIG COUNTRY
WHERE THE STORY ENDS — BLAZIN' SQUAD
WHERE THE STREETS HAVE NO NAME — U2
WHERE THE STREETS HAVE NO NAME — CAN'T TAKE MY EYES OFF YOU — PET SHOP BOYS
WHERE THE WILD ROSES GROW — Nick CAVE and Kylie MINOGUE
WHERE THE WINDS BLOW — Frankie LAINE
WHERE WERE YOU — ADULT NET
WHERE WERE YOU HIDING WHEN THE STORM BROKE — The ALARM
WHERE WERE YOU (ON OUR WEDDING DAY)? — Lloyd PRICE
WHERE WILL THE DIMPLE BE? — Rosemary CLOONEY
WHERE WILL YOU BE — Sue NICHOLLS
WHERE YOU ARE — Rahsaan PATTERSON
WHERE YOU GONNA BE TONIGHT? — Willie COLLINS
WHERE'S JACK THE RIPPER — GROOVERIDER
WHERE'S ME JUMPER — SULTANS OF PING FC
WHERE'S MY ...? — Adam F featuring LIL' MO
WHERE'S ROMEO — ÇA VA ÇA VA
WHERE'S THE LOVE — HANSON
WHERE'S YOUR HEAD AT? — BASEMENT JAXX
WHERE'S YOUR LOVE BEEN — HELIOCENTRIC WORLD
WHEREVER I LAY MY HAT (THAT'S MY HOME) — Paul YOUNG
WHEREVER I MAY ROAM — METALLICA
WHEREVER WOULD I BE — Dusty SPRINGFIELD and Daryl HALL
WHEREVER YOU ARE — Neil FINN
WHEREVER YOU WILL GO — The CALLING
WHICH WAY SHOULD I JUMP — MILLTOWN BROTHERS
WHICH WAY YOU GOIN' BILLY? — POPPY FAMILY
WHIGGLE IN LINE — BLACK DUCK
WHILE I LIVE — Kenny DAMON
WHILE YOU SEE A CHANCE — Steve WINWOOD
WHINE AND GRINE — PRINCE BUSTER
WHIP IT — DEVO
WHIPLASH — JFK
WHIPPIN' PICCADILLY — GOMEZ
WHISKEY IN THE JAR [A] — THIN LIZZY
WHISKEY IN THE JAR [A] — DUBLINERS
WHISKEY IN THE JAR [A] — The POGUES
WHISKEY IN THE JAR [A] — METALLICA
THE WHISPER — SELECTER
WHISPER A PRAYER — Mica PARIS
WHISPER YOUR NAME — HUMAN NATURE
WHISPERING [A] — The BACHELORS
WHISPERING [A] — Nino TEMPO and April STEVENS
WHISPERING GRASS — Windsor DAVIES as BSM Williams and Don ESTELLE as Gunner Sugden (Lofty)
WHISPERING HOPE — Jim REEVES
WHISPERING YOUR NAME — Alison MOYET
WHISPERS — Elton JOHN
WHISPERS — Ian BROWN
WHISTLE DOWN THE WIND [A] — Nick HEYWARD
WHISTLE DOWN THE WIND [B] — Tina ARENA
THE WHISTLE SONG [A] — Frankie KNUCKLES
THE WHISTLE SONG (BLOW MY WHISTLE BITCH) [B] — DJ ALIGATOR PROJECT
THE WHISTLER — HONKY
WHITE BIRD — VANESSA-MAE
WHITE BOY WITH A FEATHER — Jason DOWNS featuring MILK
WHITE BOYS AND HEROES — Gary NUMAN
WHITE CHRISTMAS [A] — MANTOVANI
WHITE CHRISTMAS [A] — Pat BOONE
WHITE CHRISTMAS [A] — Freddie STARR
WHITE CHRISTMAS [A] — Bing CROSBY
WHITE CHRISTMAS [A] — DARTS
WHITE CHRISTMAS [A] — Jim DAVIDSON
WHITE CHRISTMAS [A] — Keith HARRIS and ORVILLE
WHITE CHRISTMAS [A] — Max BYGRAVES
WHITE CLIFFS OF DOVER [A] — Mr Acker BILK and his PARAMOUNT JAZZ BAND
WHITE CLIFFS OF DOVER [A] — RIGHTEOUS BROTHERS
WHITE COATS (EP) — NEW MODEL ARMY
WHITE FLAG — DIDO
WHITE HORSES — Jackie LEE
WHITE LIE — FOREIGNER
WHITE LIGHT, WHITE HEAT — David BOWIE
WHITE LIGHTNING — The FALL
WHITE LINES (DON'T DON'T DO IT) [A] — GRANDMASTER FLASH, Melle MEL and the FURIOUS FIVE
WHITE LINES (DON'T DO IT) [A] — DURAN DURAN
WHITE LOVE — ONE DOVE
(WHITE MAN) IN HAMMERSMITH PALAIS — The CLASH
WHITE NO SUGAR — Clint BOON EXPERIENCE
WHITE PUNKS ON DOPE — TUBES
WHITE RIBBON DAY — DELIRIOUS?
WHITE RIOT — The CLASH
WHITE ROOM — CREAM
WHITE SILVER SANDS — Bill BLACK'S COMBO
WHITE SKIES — SUNSCREEM
A WHITE SPORT COAT [A] — KING BROTHERS
A WHITE SPORT COAT [A] — Terry DENE
WHITE WEDDING [A] — Billy IDOL
WHITE WEDDING [A] — The MURDERDOLLS
A WHITER SHADE OF PALE [A] — PROCOL HARUM
A WHITER SHADE OF PALE [A] — MUNICH MACHINE
A WHITER SHADE OF PALE [A] — Annie LENNOX
WHO? — Ed CASE and SWEETIE IRIE
WHO AM I [A] — Adam FAITH
WHO AM I [B] — BEENIE MAN
WHO ARE WE [A] — Ronnie HILTON
WHO ARE WE [A] — Vera LYNN
WHO ARE YOU — The WHO
WHO CAN I RUN TO — XSCAPE
WHO CAN IT BE NOW? — MEN AT WORK
WHO CAN MAKE ME FEEL GOOD — BASSHEADS
WHO COMES TO BOOGIE — LITTLE BENNY and the MASTERS
WHO COULD BE BLUER — Jerry LORDAN
WHO DO U LOVE — Deborah COX
WHO DO YOU LOVE [A] — JUICY LUCY
WHO DO YOU LOVE? [B] — INTRUDERS
WHO DO YOU LOVE [C] — José PADILLA featuring Angela JOHN
WHO DO YOU LOVE NOW (STRINGER) — RIVA featuring Dannii MINOGUE
WHO DO YOU THINK YOU ARE [A] — CANDLEWICK GREEN
WHO DO YOU THINK YOU ARE [A] — SAINT ETIENNE
WHO DO YOU THINK YOU ARE [B] — Kim WILDE
WHO DO YOU THINK YOU ARE [C] — SPICE GIRLS
WHO DO YOU WANT FOR YOUR LOVE — ICICLE WORKS
WHO FEELS LOVE? — OASIS
WHO FOUND WHO — JELLYBEAN featuring Elisa FIORILLO
WHO GETS THE LOVE — STATUS QUO
WHO INVITED YOU? — The DONNAS
WHO IS IT [A] — MANTRONIX
WHO IS IT [B] — Michael JACKSON
WHO IS IT [C] — BJÖRK
WHO KEEPS CHANGING YOUR MIND — SOUTH ST PLAYER
WHO KILLED BAMBI — TEN POLE TUDOR
WHO LET IN THE RAIN — Cyndi LAUPER
WHO LET THE DOGS OUT — BAHA MEN
WHO LOVES YOU — The FOUR SEASONS
WHO MADE WHO — AC/DC
WHO NEEDS ENEMIES — The COOPER TEMPLE CLAUSE
WHO NEEDS LOVE (LIKE THAT) — ERASURE
WHO PAYS THE FERRYMAN? — Yannis MARKOPOULOS
WHO PAYS THE PIPER — Gary CLAIL ON-U SOUND SYSTEM
WHO PUT THE BOMP (IN THE BOMP, BOMP, BOMP) [A] — VISCOUNTS
WHO PUT THE BOMP (IN THE BOMP-A-BOMP-A-BOMP) [A] — SHOWADDYWADDY
WHO PUT THE LIGHTS OUT — DANA
WHO SAID (STUCK IN THE UK) — PLANET FUNK
WHO THE HELL ARE YOU — MADISON AVENUE
WHO TOLD YOU — Roni SIZE / REPRAZENT
WHO WANTS THE WORLD — The STRANGLERS
WHO WANTS TO BE THE DISCO KING? — The WONDER STUFF
WHO WANTS TO LIVE FOREVER [A] — QUEEN
WHO WANTS TO LIVE FOREVER [A] — Sarah BRIGHTMAN
WHO WAS IT — Hurricane SMITH
WHO WE BE — DMX
WHO WEARS THESE SHOES — Elton JOHN
WHO WERE YOU WITH IN THE MOONLIGHT — DOLLAR
WHO, WHAT, WHEN, WHERE, WHY — MANHATTAN TRANSFER
WHO WHERE WHY — JESUS JONES
WHO WILL SAVE YOUR SOUL — JEWEL
WHO WILL YOU RUN TO — HEART
WHO YOU ARE — PEARL JAM
WHO YOU LOOKING AT — SALFORD JETS
WHO YOU WIT — JAY-Z
WHOA — BLACK ROB
WHO'D SEE COO — OHIO PLAYERS
WHODUNIT — TAVARES
WHOLE AGAIN — ATOMIC KITTEN
WHOLE LOTTA LOVE [A] — CCS
WHOLE LOTTA LOVE [A] — GOLDBUG
WHOLE LOTTA LOVE [A] — LED ZEPPELIN
WHOLE LOTTA ROSIE — AC/DC
WHOLE LOTTA SHAKIN' GOIN' ON — Jerry Lee LEWIS
WHOLE LOTTA TROUBLE — Stevie NICKS
WHOLE LOTTA WOMAN — Marvin RAINWATER
WHOLE NEW WORLD — IT BITES
A WHOLE NEW WORLD (ALADDIN'S THEME) — Regina BELLE and Peabo BRYSON
THE WHOLE OF THE MOON [A] — WATERBOYS
THE WHOLE OF THE MOON [A] — LITTLE CAESAR
THE WHOLE TOWN'S LAUGHING AT ME — Teddy PENDERGRASS
THE WHOLE WORLD — OUTKAST featuring KILLER MIKE
THE WHOLE WORLD LOST ITS HEAD — GO-GO's
WHOOMP! (THERE IT IS) [A] — TAG TEAM
WHOOMPH! (THERE IT IS) [A] — CLOCK
WHOOMP THERE IT IS [A] — BM DUBS present MR RUMBLE
WHOOPS NOW — Janet JACKSON
WHOOSH — WHOOSH
WHO'S AFRAID OF THE BIG BAD LOVE — WILD WEEKEND
WHO'S AFRAID OF THE BIG BAD NOISE! — AGE OF CHANCE
WHO'S COMING ROUND — 5050
WHO'S CRYING NOW — JOURNEY
WHO'S DAVID — BUSTED
WHO'S GONNA LOVE ME — IMPERIALS
WHO'S GONNA RIDE YOUR WILD HORSES — U2
WHO'S GONNA ROCK YOU — The NOLANS
WHO'S IN THE HOUSE — BEATMASTERS
WHO'S IN THE STRAWBERRY PATCH WITH SALLY — DAWN
WHO'S JOHNNY ('SHORT CIRCUIT' THEME) — El DeBARGE
WHO'S LEAVING WHO — Hazell DEAN
WHO'S LOVING MY BABY — Shola AMA
WHO'S SORRY NOW [A] — Johnnie RAY
WHO'S SORRY NOW [A] — Connie FRANCIS
WHO'S THAT GIRL? [A] — EURYTHMICS
WHO'S THAT GIRL [A] — FLYING PICKETS
WHO'S THAT GIRL [B] — MADONNA
WHO'S THAT GIRL [C] — EVE
WHO'S THAT GIRL (SHE'S GOT IT) — A FLOCK OF SEAGULLS
WHO'S THAT MIX — THIS YEAR'S BLONDE
WHO'S THE BAD MAN? — Dee PATTEN
WHO'S THE DADDY — LOVEBUG
WHO'S THE DARKMAN — DARKMAN
WHO'S THE MACK! — Mark MORRISON
WHO'S THE MAN — HOUSE OF PAIN
WHO'S ZOOMIN' WHO — Aretha FRANKLIN
WHOSE FIST IS THIS ANYWAY (EP) — PRONG
WHOSE LAW (IS IT ANYWAY) — GURU JOSH
WHOSE PROBLEM? — MOTELS
WHY [A] — Anthony NEWLEY
WHY [A] — Frankie AVALON
WHY [A] — Donny OSMOND
WHY [B] — Roger WHITTAKER
WHY [C] — Carly SIMON
WHY [C] — GLAMMA KID
WHY? [D] — BRONSKI BEAT
WHY [E] — Annie LENNOX
WHY [F] — D MOB with Cathy DENNIS
WHY [G] — Ricardo DA FORCE
WHY [H] — 3T
WHY [I] — MIS-TEEQ
WHY? [J] — AGENT SUMO
WHY ARE PEOPLE GRUDGEFUL — The FALL
WHY ARE YOU BEING SO REASONABLE NOW — WEDDING PRESENT
WHY BABY WHY — Pat BOONE
WHY BELIEVE IN YOU — TEXAS
WHY CAN'T YOU — Clarence 'Frogman' HENRY
WHY CAN'T I BE YOU [A] — The CURE
WHY CAN'T I BE YOU? [B] — SHED SEVEN
WHY CAN'T I WAKE UP WITH YOU — TAKE THAT
WHY CAN'T THIS BE LOVE — VAN HALEN
WHY CAN'T WE BE LOVERS — HOLLAND-DOZIER featuring Lamont DOZIER
WHY CAN'T WE LIVE TOGETHER — Timmy THOMAS
WHY CAN'T YOU FREE SOME TIME — Armand VAN HELDEN
WHY DID YA — Tony DI BART
WHY DID YOU DO IT — STRETCH
WHY DIDN'T YOU CALL ME — Macy GRAY
WHY DO FOOLS FALL IN LOVE [A] — Alma COGAN
WHY DO FOOLS FALL IN LOVE [A] — TEENAGERS featuring Frankie LYMON
WHY DO FOOLS FALL IN LOVE [A] — Diana ROSS
WHY DO I ALWAYS GET IT WRONG — LIVE REPORT
WHY DO I DO? — Tyler JAMES
WHY DO LOVERS BREAK EACH OTHER'S HEARTS — SHOWADDYWADDY
WHY DO YOU KEEP ON RUNNING — STINX
WHY DOES A MAN HAVE TO BE STRONG — Paul YOUNG
WHY DOES IT ALWAYS RAIN ON ME? — TRAVIS
WHY DOES MY HEART FEEL SO BAD? — MOBY
WHY DON'T THEY UNDERSTAND — George HAMILTON IV
WHY DON'T WE FALL IN LOVE — AMERIE featuring LUDACRIS
WHY DON'T WE TRY AGAIN — Brian MAY
WHY DON'T YOU — RAGE
WHY DON'T YOU BELIEVE ME — Joni JAMES
WHY DON'T YOU DANCE WITH ME — FUTURE BREEZE
WHY DON'T YOU DO IT FOR ME? — 22-20S
WHY DON'T YOU GET A JOB? — The OFFSPRING
WHY DON'T YOU TAKE ME — ONE DOVE
WHY D'YA LIE TO ME — SPIDER
WHY (LOOKING BACK) — HEARTLESS CREW
WHY ME [A] — Linda MARTIN
WHY ME [B] — A HOUSE
WHY ME [C] — ANT & DEC
WHY ME [D] — ASHER D
WHY (MUST WE FALL IN LOVE) — Diana ROSS and The SUPREMES and The TEMPTATIONS
WHY MUST WE WAIT UNTIL TONIGHT — Tina TURNER
WHY NOT NOW — Matt MONRO
WHY NOT TONIGHT — MOJOS
WHY OH WHY — SPEARHEAD
WHY, OH WHY, OH WHY — Gilbert O'SULLIVAN
WHY SHE'S A GIRL FROM THE CHAINSTORE — The BUZZCOCKS
WHY SHOULD I — Bob MARLEY & the WAILERS
WHY SHOULD I BE LONELY — Tony BRENT
WHY SHOULD I CRY — Nona HENDRYX
WHY SHOULD I LOVE YOU — DES'REE
WHY WHY BYE BYE — Bob LUMAN
WHY WHY WHY — DEJA VU
WHY YOU FOLLOW ME — Eric BENET
WHY YOU TREAT ME SO BAD — SHAGGY featuring GRAND PUBA
WHY'D YOU LIE TO ME — ANASTACIA
WHY'S EVERYBODY ALWAYS PICKIN' ON ME? — BLOODHOUND GANG
WIBBLING RIVALRY (INTERVIEWS WITH NOEL AND LIAM GALLAGHER) — OASIS
WICHITA LINEMAN — Glen CAMPBELL
WICKED — ICE CUBE

WICKED GAME — Chris ISAAK
WICKED LOVE — OCEANIC
WICKED WAYS — The BLOW MONKEYS
WICKEDEST SOUND — REBEL MC featuring TENOR FLY
THE WICKER MAN — IRON MAIDEN
WICKI WACKY HOUSE PARTY — TEAM
WIDE AWAKE IN A DREAM — Barry BIGGS
WIDE BOY — Nik KERSHAW
WIDE EYED AND LEGLESS — Andy FAIRWEATHER-LOW
WIDE EYED ANGEL — ORIGIN
WIDE OPEN SKY — GOLDRUSH
WIDE OPEN SPACE — MANSUN
WIDE PRAIRIE — Linda McCARTNEY
WIFEY — NEXT
WIG WAM BAM [A] — BLACK LACE
WIG WAM BAM [A] — DAMIAN
WIGGLE IT — 2 IN A ROOM
WIGGLY WORLD — MR JACK
WIG-WAM BAM — The SWEET
WIKKA WRAP — EVASIONS
THE WILD AMERICA (EP) — Iggy POP
WILD AND WONDERFUL — The ALMIGHTY
WILD AS ANGELS EP — LEVELLERS
WILD BOYS [A] — PHIXX
THE WILD BOYS [A] — DURAN DURAN
WILD CAT — Gene VINCENT
WILD CHILD [A] — W.A.S.P.
WILD CHILD [B] — ENYA
WILD DANCES — RUSLANA
WILD FLOWER — The CULT
WILD FRONTIER — Gary MOORE
WILD HEARTED SON — The CULT
WILD HEARTED WOMAN — ALL ABOUT EVE
WILD HONEY — The BEACH BOYS
WILD IN THE COUNTRY — Elvis PRESLEY
WILD IS THE WIND — David BOWIE
WILD LOVE — MUNGO JERRY
WILD LUV — ROACH MOTEL
WILD 'N FREE — REDNEX
WILD NIGHT — John Cougar MELLENCAMP
WILD ONE — Bobby RYDELL
THE WILD ONE — Suzi QUATRO
THE WILD ONES — SUEDE
WILD SIDE — MÖTLEY CRÜE
WILD SIDE OF LIFE [A] — Tommy QUICKLY
WILD SIDE OF LIFE [A] — STATUS QUO
THE WILD SON — The VEILS
WILD SURF — ASH
WILD THING [A] — The TROGGS
WILD THING [A] — The GOODIES
WILD THING [B] — Tone LOC
WILD WEST HERO — ELECTRIC LIGHT ORCHESTRA
WILD WILD LIFE — TALKING HEADS
WILD WILD WEST [A] — GET READY
WILD WILD WEST [B] — Will SMITH featuring DRU HILL – additional vocals Kool Moe DEE
WILD WIND — John LEYTON
WILD WOMEN DO — Natalie COLE
WILD WOOD — Paul WELLER
WILD WORLD [A] — Jimmy CLIFF
WILD WORLD [A] — Maxi PRIEST
WILD WORLD [A] — MR BIG
WILDERNESS — Jurgen VRIES featuring SHENA
WILDEST DREAMS — IRON MAIDEN
WILDLIFE (EP) — GIRLSCHOOL
WILDSIDE — MARKY MARK and the FUNKY BUNCH
WILDWOOD — Paul WELLER
WILFRED THE WEASEL — Keith MICHELL
WILL I — IAN VAN DAHL
WILL I EVER — ALICE DEEJAY
WILL I WHAT — Mike SARNE with Billie DAVIS
WILL THE WOLF SURVIVE — LOS LOBOS
WILL 2K — Will SMITH
WILL WE BE LOVERS — DEACON BLUE
WILL YOU [A] — Hazel O'CONNOR
WILL YOU [B] — P.O.D.
WILL YOU BE MY BABY — GRAND PUBA
WILL YOU BE THERE — Michael JACKSON
WILL YOU BE THERE (IN THE MORNING) — HEART
WILL YOU BE WITH ME — Maria NAYLER
WILL YOU LOVE ME TOMORROW [A] — SHIRELLES
WILL YOU LOVE ME TOMORROW [A] — MELANIE
WILL YOU LOVE ME TOMORROW [A] — Bryan FERRY
WILL YOU MARRY ME — Paula ABDUL
WILL YOU SATISFY? — CHERRELLE
WILL YOU WAIT FOR ME — KAVANA
WILLIAM, IT WAS REALLY NOTHING — The SMITHS
WILLIE CAN [A] — Alma COGAN
WILLIE CAN [A] — BEVERLEY SISTERS
WILLING TO FORGIVE — Aretha FRANKLIN
WILLINGLY — Malcolm VAUGHAN
WILLOW TREE — IVY LEAGUE
WILMOT — SABRES OF PARADISE
WIMMIN' — Ashley HAMILTON
WIMOWEH — Karl DENVER
WIN PLACE OR SHOW (SHE'S A WINNER) — INTRUDERS
WINCHESTER CATHEDRAL — NEW VAUDEVILLE BAND
THE WIND — P J HARVEY
THE WIND BENEATH MY WINGS [A] — Lee GREENWOOD
WIND BENEATH MY WINGS [A] — Bette MIDLER
WIND BENEATH MY WINGS [A] — Bill TARMEY
WIND BENEATH MY WINGS [A] — Steven HOUGHTON
THE WIND CRIES MARY — The Jimi HENDRIX EXPERIENCE
WIND IT UP (REWOUND) — The PRODIGY
WIND ME UP (LET ME GO) — Cliff RICHARD
WIND OF CHANGE — SCORPIONS
WIND THE BOBBIN UP! — Jo JINGLES
WINDINGS — SUGARCOMA
A WINDMILL IN OLD AMSTERDAM — Ronnie HILTON
WINDMILLS OF YOUR MIND — Noel HARRISON
WINDOW PANE (EP) — REAL PEOPLE
WINDOW SHOPPING — R Dean TAYLOR
WINDOWLICKER — APHEX TWIN
WINDOWS '98 — SIL
WINDPOWER — Thomas DOLBY
THE WINDSOR WALTZ — Vera LYNN
WINDSWEPT — Bryan FERRY
WINGS OF A DOVE — MADNESS
WINGS OF LOVE — BONE
THE WINKER'S SONG (MISPRINT) — Ivor BIGGUN
THE WINKLE MAN — JUDGE DREAD
THE WINNER [A] — HEARTBEAT
THE WINNER [B] — COOLIO
THE WINNER TAKES IT ALL — ABBA
WINNING DAYS — The VINES
WINTER [A] — LOVE AND MONEY
WINTER [B] — Tori AMOS
WINTER CEREMONY (TOR-CHENEY-NAHANA) — SACRED SPIRIT
THE WINTER GARDENS — SPECIAL NEEDS
WINTER IN JULY — BOMB THE BASS
WINTER MELODY — Donna SUMMER
WINTER SONG — Chris REA
A WINTER STORY — Aled JONES
WINTER WONDERLAND [A] — Johnny MATHIS
WINTER WONDERLAND [A] — COCTEAU TWINS
WINTER WORLD OF LOVE — Engelbert HUMPERDINCK
A WINTER'S TALE [A] — David ESSEX
A WINTER'S TALE [B] — QUEEN
WIPE OUT [A] — SURFARIS
WIPE OUT [A] — ANIMAL
WIPE THE NEEDLE — RAGGA TWINS
WIPEOUT — FAT BOYS and The BEACH BOYS
WIRED FOR SOUND — Cliff RICHARD
THE WISDOM OF A FOOL [A] — Norman WISDOM
THE WISDOM OF A FOOL [A] — Ronnie CARROLL
WISE UP! SUCKER — POP WILL EAT ITSELF
WISER TIME — BLACK CROWES
WISH — SOUL II SOUL
A WISH AWAY — The WONDER STUFF
WISH I COULD FLY — ROXETTE
WISH I DIDN'T MISS YOU — Angie STONE
WISH I HAD AN ANGEL — NIGHTWISH
WISH I WAS SKINNY — BOO RADLEYS
WISH I WERE YOU — ALISHA'S ATTIC
WISH THE WORLD AWAY — AMERICAN MUSIC CLUB
WISH YOU WERE HERE [A] — Eddie FISHER
WISH YOU WERE HERE [B] — FIRST LIGHT
WISH YOU WERE HERE ... [C] — ALOOF
WISH YOU WERE HERE [D] — Wyclef JEAN
WISH YOU WERE HERE [E] — INCUBUS
WISHES — HUMAN NATURE
WISHES OF HAPPINESS AND PROSPERITY (YEHA-NOHA) — SACRED SPIRIT
WISHFUL THINKING — CHINA CRISIS
WISHIN' AND HOPIN' — The MERSEYBEATS
WISHING — Buddy HOLLY
WISHING I WAS LUCKY — WET WET WET
WISHING I WAS THERE — Natalie IMBRUGLIA
WISHING (IF I HAD A PHOTOGRAPH OF YOU) — A FLOCK OF SEAGULLS
WISHING ON A STAR [A] — ROSE ROYCE
WISHING ON A STAR [A] — FRESH 4 featuring Lizz E
WISHING ON A STAR [A] — COVER GIRLS
WISHING ON A STAR [A] — Lisa MAY
WISHING ON A STAR [A] — JAY-Z featuring Gwen DICKEY
WISHING ON A STAR [A] — Paul WELLER
WISHING WELL [A] — FREE
WISHING WELL [B] — Terence Trent D'ARBY
THE WISHING WELL — G.O.S.H.
WISHING YOU WERE HERE — Alison MOYET
WISHING YOU WERE SOMEHOW HERE AGAIN — Sarah BRIGHTMAN
WISHLIST — PEARL JAM
THE WITCH — RATTLES
WITCH DOCTOR [A] — David SEVILLE
WITCH DOCTOR [A] — Don LANG
WITCH DOCTOR [A] — CARTOONS
THE WITCH QUEEN OF NEW ORLEANS — REDBONE
THE WITCH'S PROMISE — JETHRO TULL
WITCHCRAFT [A] — Frank SINATRA
WITCHCRAFT [A] — Robert PALMER
WITCHES' BREW — Janie JONES
WITH A GIRL LIKE YOU — The TROGGS
WITH A LITTLE HELP FROM MY FRIENDS [A] — Joe BROWN and the BRUVVERS
WITH A LITTLE HELP FROM MY FRIENDS [A] — YOUNG IDEA
WITH A LITTLE HELP FROM MY FRIENDS [A] — Joe COCKER
WITH A LITTLE HELP FROM MY FRIENDS [A] — WET WET WET
WITH A LITTLE HELP FROM MY FRIENDS [A] — SAM & MARK
WITH A LITTLE LOVE — Sam BROWN
WITH A LITTLE LUCK — Paul McCARTNEY
WITH ALL MY HEART — Petula CLARK
WITH ARMS WIDE OPEN — CREED
WITH EVERY BEAT OF MY HEART — Taylor DAYNE
WITH EVERY HEARTBEAT — FIVE STAR
WITH GOD ON OUR SIDE — NEVILLE BROTHERS
WITH ME — DESTINY'S CHILD
WITH MY OWN EYES — SASH!
WITH ONE LOOK — Barbra STREISAND
WITH OR WITHOUT YOU [A] — U2
WITH OR WITHOUT YOU [A] — Mary KIANI
WITH PEN IN HAND — Vikki CARR
WITH THE EYES OF A CHILD — Cliff RICHARD
WITH THE WIND AND THE RAIN IN YOUR HAIR — Pat BOONE
WITH THESE HANDS [A] — Shirley BASSEY
WITH THESE HANDS [A] — Tom JONES
WITH YOU — Jessica SIMPSON
WITH YOU I'M BORN AGAIN — Billy PRESTON and SYREETA
WITH YOUR LOVE — Malcolm VAUGHAN
WITHOUT A DOUBT — BLACK SHEEP
WITHOUT HER — Herb ALPERT
WITHOUT LOVE [A] — Tom JONES
WITHOUT LOVE [B] — Donna LEWIS
WITHOUT LOVE [C] — Dina CARROLL
WITHOUT ME — EMINEM
WITHOUT YOU [A] — Matt MONRO
WITHOUT YOU [B] — NILSSON
WITHOUT YOU [B] — Mariah CAREY
WITHOUT YOU [C] — MÖTLEY CRÜE
WITHOUT YOU [D] — LUCY PEARL
WITHOUT YOU (ONE AND ONE) — Lindy LAYTON
WITHOUT YOUR LOVE — Roger DALTREY
WITNESS (EP) — Ann NESBY
WITNESS FOR THE WORLD — CRY BEFORE DAWN
WITNESS (1 HOPE) — ROOTS MANUVA
THE WIZARD — Paul HARDCASTLE
WIZARDS OF THE SONIC [A] — WESTBAM
WIZZY WOW — BLACKSTREET
WOE IS ME — Helen SHAPIRO
W.O.L.D. — Harry CHAPIN
WOLF — SHY FX
WOMAN (UH-HUH) [A] — Jose FERRER
WOMAN [B] — PETER and GORDON
WOMAN [C] — John LENNON
WOMAN [D] — ANTI-NOWHERE LEAGUE
WOMAN [E] — Neneh CHERRY
WOMAN FROM LIBERIA — Jimmie RODGERS
THE WOMAN I LOVE — The HOLLIES
WOMAN IN CHAINS [A] — TEARS FOR FEARS
A WOMAN IN LOVE [A] — FOUR ACES
A WOMAN IN LOVE [A] — Ronnie HILTON
A WOMAN IN LOVE [A] — Frankie LAINE
WOMAN IN LOVE [A] — The THREE DEGREES
WOMAN IN LOVE [B] — Barbra STREISAND
WOMAN IN LOVE [B] — Rebekah RYAN
WOMAN IN ME — Carleen ANDERSON
THE WOMAN IN ME [A] — Donna SUMMER
THE WOMAN IN ME [B] — KINANE
WOMAN IN WINTER — The SKIDS
WOMAN OF MINE — Dean FRIEDMAN
WOMAN OF PRINCIPLE — TROUBLE FUNK
WOMAN TO WOMAN — Beverley CRAVEN
WOMAN TROUBLE — ARTFUL DODGER and Robbie CRAIG featuring Craig DAVID
WOMAN, WOMAN — Gary PUCKETT and the UNION GAP
WOMANKIND — LITTLE ANGELS
A WOMAN'S PLACE — Gilbert O'SULLIVAN
A WOMAN'S STORY — Marc ALMOND
WOMAN'S WORLD — JAGS
A WOMAN'S WORTH — Alicia KEYS
WOMBLING MERRY CHRISTMAS — The WOMBLES
THE WOMBLING SONG — The WOMBLES
WOMBLING WHITE TIE AND TAILS (FOX TROT) — The WOMBLES
WOMEN BEAT THEIR MEN — Junior CARTIER
WOMEN IN UNIFORM [A] — SKYHOOKS
WOMEN IN UNIFORM [A] — IRON MAIDEN
WOMEN OF IRELAND — Mike OLDFIELD
WON — The BETA BAND
WONDER — EMBRACE
WONDERBOY — TENACIOUS D
THE WONDER OF LOVE — LOVELAND featuring the voice of Rachel McFARLANE
THE WONDER OF YOU [A] — Ronnie HILTON
THE WONDER OF YOU [A] — Ray PETERSON
THE WONDER OF YOU [A] — Elvis PRESLEY
WONDERBOY — The KINKS
WONDERFUL [A] — Mari WILSON
WONDERFUL [B] — RUNRIG
WONDERFUL [C] — Adam ANT
WONDERFUL [D] — EVERCLEAR
WONDERFUL [E] — Brian WILSON
WONDERFUL [F] — JA RULE featuring R KELLY & ASHANTI
WONDERFUL CHRISTMASTIME — Paul McCARTNEY
WONDERFUL COPENHAGEN — Danny KAYE
WONDERFUL DREAM — Anne-Marie DAVID
WONDERFUL EXCUSE — FAMILY CAT
WONDERFUL LAND — The SHADOWS
WONDERFUL LIFE [A] — BLACK
WONDERFUL LIFE [A] — TJ DAVIS
A WONDERFUL NIGHT — FATBOY SLIM
THE WONDERFUL SECRET OF LOVE — Robert EARL
WONDERFUL THINGS — Frankie VAUGHAN
A WONDERFUL TIME UP THERE [A] — Pat BOONE
A WONDERFUL TIME UP THERE [A] — Alvin STARDUST
WONDERFUL TONIGHT [A] — DAMAGE
WONDERFUL TONIGHT (LIVE) [A] — Eric CLAPTON
WONDERFUL! WONDERFUL! [A] — Ronnie HILTON
WONDERFUL, WONDERFUL [A] — Gary MILLER
WONDERFUL WORLD [A] — Sam COOKE
WONDERFUL WORLD [A] — HERMAN'S HERMITS
WONDERFUL WORLD [B] — WORLDS APART
WONDERFUL WORLD BEAUTIFUL PEOPLE — Jimmy CLIFF
WONDERFUL WORLD OF THE YOUNG — Danny WILLIAMS
WONDERING WHY — MJ COLE
WONDERLAND [A] — The COMMODORES
WONDERLAND [B] — BIG COUNTRY
WONDERLAND [C] — Paul YOUNG
WONDERLAND [D] — 911
WONDERLAND [E] — PSYCHEDELIC WALTONS featuring Roisin MURPHY
WONDERMAN — RIGHT SAID FRED
WONDERWALL [A] — OASIS
WONDERWALL [A] — Mike FLOWERS POPS
WONDERWALL [A] — DE-CODE featuring Beverli SKEETE
WONDERWALL [A] — Ryan ADAMS
WONDROUS PLACE — Billy FURY
WONDROUS STORIES — YES
WON'T GET FOOLED AGAIN — The WHO
WON'T GIVE IN — FINN BROTHERS
WON'T LET THIS FEELING GO — SUNDANCE
WON'T SOMEBODY DANCE WITH ME — Lynsey DE PAUL
WON'T STOP LOVING YOU — A CERTAIN RATIO
WON'T TALK ABOUT IT [A] — Billy BRAGG
WON'T TALK ABOUT IT [A] — Norman COOK
WON'T TALK ABOUT IT [A] — BEATS INTERNATIONAL
WON'T YOU HOLD MY HAND NOW — KING
WON'T YOU SAY — Christian FRY
WOO HOO — The 5.6.7.8'S
WOOD BEEZ (PRAY LIKE ARETHA FRANKLIN) — SCRITTI POLITTI
WOODEN HEART — Elvis PRESLEY
WOODPECKERS FROM SPACE — VIDEO KIDS
WOODSTOCK — MATTHEWS' SOUTHERN COMFORT
WOO-HAH!! GOT YOU ALL IN CHECK — Busta RHYMES
WOOLY BULLY — SAM THE SHAM and the PHARAOHS
WOPBABALUBOP — FUNKDOOBIEST
THE WORD — DOPE SMUGGLAZ
THE WORD GIRL — SCRITTI POLITTI
A WORD IN YOUR EAR — ALFIE
THE WORD IS LOVE (SAY THE WORD) — VOICES OF LIFE
WORD IS OUT — Kylie MINOGUE
WORD LOVE — RHIANNA
WORD OF MOUTH — MIKE and the MECHANICS
WORD PERFECT — KRS ONE
WORD UP [A] — CAMEO
WORD UP [A] — GUN
WORD UP [A] — Melanie B
WORDS [A] — ALLISONS
WORDS [B] — The BEE GEES
WORDS [B] — Rita COOLIDGE
WORDS [B] — BOYZONE
WORDS [C] — FR DAVID
WORDS [D] — The CHRISTIANS
WORDS [E] — Paul VAN DYK
WORDS ARE NOT ENOUGH — STEPS
WORDS OF LOVE — MAMAS and the PAPAS
WORDS THAT SAY — MEGA CITY FOUR
WORDS WITH THE SHAMAN — David SYLVIAN
WORDY RAPPINGHOOD [A] — TOM TOM CLUB
WORDY RAPPINGHOOD [A] — CHICKS ON SPEED
WORK [A] — TECHNOTRONIC
WORK [B] — Barrington LEVY
WORK ALL DAY — Barry BIGGS
WORK IT [A] — Missy ELLIOTT
WORK IT [B] — NELLY featuring Justin TIMBERLAKE

WORK IT OUT [A] — SHIVA
WORK IT OUT [B] — DEF LEPPARD
WORK IT OUT [C] — BEYONCÉ
WORK IT TO THE BONE — LNR
WORK IT UP — SLEAZESISTERS
WORK MI BODY —
  MONKEY MAFIA featuring PATRA
W.O.R.K. (N.O. NAH NO NO MY DADDY DON'T) —
  BOW WOW WOW
WORK REST AND PLAY (EP) — MADNESS
WORK THAT BODY — Diana ROSS
WORK THAT MAGIC — Donna SUMMER
WORK THAT SUCKER TO DEATH — XAVIER
WORKAHOLIC — 2 UNLIMITED
THE WORKER — FISCHER-Z
WORKIN' FOR THE MAN — Roy ORBISON
WORKIN' MY WAY BACK TO YOU —
  The FOUR SEASONS
WORKIN' OVERTIME — Diana ROSS
WORKIN' UP A SWEAT — FULL CIRCLE
WORKING FOR THE YANKEE DOLLAR —
  The SKIDS
WORKING IN A GOLDMINE — AZTEC CAMERA
WORKING IN THE COALMINE — Lee DORSEY
WORKING MAN — Rita MacNEIL
WORKING MOTHER — Martyn JOSEPH
WORKING MY WAY BACK TO YOU — FORGIVE ME GIRL
  (MEDLEY) — DETROIT SPINNERS
WORKING ON A BUILDING OF LOVE —
  CHAIRMEN OF THE BOARD
WORKING ON IT — Chris REA
WORKING WITH FIRE AND STEEL —
  CHINA CRISIS
WORLD — The BEE GEES
THE WORLD — Nick HEYWARD
WORLD CUP '98 — PAVANE —
  WIMBLEDON CHORAL SOCIETY
WORLD DESTRUCTION — TIME ZONE
WORLD FILLED WITH LOVE — Craig DAVID
WORLD IN MOTION ... — ENGLANDNEWORDER
THE WORLD IN MY ARMS — Nat 'King' COLE
WORLD IN MY EYES — DEPECHE MODE
THE WORLD IN MY HANDS — SNAP! featuring
  SUMMER
WORLD IN UNION [A] — Kiri TE KANAWA
WORLD IN UNION [A] — Shirley BASSEY
WORLD IN UNION '95 —
  LADYSMITH BLACK MAMBAZO
WORLD IN YOUR HANDS — CULTURE BEAT
THE WORLD IS A GHETTO —
  GETO BOYS featuring FLAJ
THE WORLD IS FLAT — ECHOBELLY
THE WORLD IS MINE [A] — Malcolm VAUGHAN
THE WORLD IS MINE [B] — ICE CUBE
THE WORLD IS NOT ENOUGH — GARBAGE
THE WORLD IS STONE — Cyndi LAUPER
THE WORLD IS WHAT YOU MAKE IT —
  Paul BRADY
WORLD LOOKING AWAY — MORCHEEBA
WORLD OF BROKEN HEARTS — AMEN CORNER
WORLD OF GOOD — SAW DOCTORS
A WORLD OF OUR OWN [A] — The SEEKERS
WORLD OF OUR OWN [B] — WESTLIFE
WORLD ON FIRE — Sarah McLACHLAN
THE WORLD OUTSIDE [A] — Russ CONWAY
THE WORLD OUTSIDE [A] — Ronnie HILTON
THE WORLD OUTSIDE [A] — FOUR ACES
WORLD OUTSIDE YOUR WINDOW —
  Tanita TIKARAM
THE WORLD SHE KNOWS — DMAC
WORLD SHUT YOUR MOUTH — Julian COPE
WORLD (THE PRICE OF LOVE) — NEW ORDER
THE WORLD TONIGHT — Paul McCartney
THE WORLD WE KNEW (OVER AND OVER) —
  Frank SINATRA
A WORLD WITHOUT HEROES — KISS
A WORLD WITHOUT LOVE —
  PETER and GORDON
WORLD WITHOUT YOU — Belinda CARLISLE
WORLDS APART — CACTUS WORLD NEWS
THE WORLD'S GREATEST — R KELLY
WORLD'S ON FIRE — BREED 77
WORRY ABOUT THE WIND — HAL
WORST COMES TO WORST —
  DILATED PEOPLES
WORZEL'S SONG — Jon PERTWEE
WOT! — CAPTAIN SENSIBLE
WOT DO U CALL IT? — WILEY
WOT'S IT TO YA — Robbie NEVIL
WOULD — ALICE IN CHAINS
WOULD I LIE TO YOU [A] — WHITESNAKE
WOULD I LIE TO YOU? [B] — EURYTHMICS
WOULD I LIE TO YOU [C] —
  CHARLES and EDDIE
WOULD YOU ...? — TOUCH & GO
WOULD YOU BE HAPPIER? — The CORRS
WOULDN'T CHANGE A THING [A] —
  Kylie MINOGUE
WOULDN'T CHANGE A THING [B] —
  HAVEN
WOULDN'T IT BE GOOD — Nik KERSHAW
WOULDN'T IT BE NICE — The BEACH BOYS
WOULDN'T YOU LOVE TO LOVE ME —
  Taja SEVELLE
WOW — Kate BUSH
WOW AND FLUTTER — STEREOLAB
WOW WOW — NA NA — GRAND PLAZ

WOZ NOT WOZ —
  Eric PRYDZ & Steve ANGELLO
WRAP HER UP — Elton JOHN
WRAP ME UP — ALEX PARTY
WRAP MY BODY TIGHT — Johnny GILL
WRAP YOUR ARMS AROUND ME —
  Agnetha FALTSKOG
WRAPPED AROUND HER —
  Joan ARMATRADING
WRAPPED AROUND YOUR FINGER —
  The POLICE
WRAPPING PAPER — CREAM
WRATH CHILD — IRON MAIDEN
WRATH OF KANE — BIG DADDY KANE
WRECK OF THE ANTOINETTE —
  Dave DEE, DOZY, BEAKY, MICK and TICH
THE WRECK OF THE EDMUND FITZGERALD —
  Gordon LIGHTFOOT
THE WRECKONING — BOOMKAT
WRECKX SHOP —
  WRECKZ-N-EFFECT featuring APACHE INDIAN
WRENCH — The ALMIGHTY
WRESTLEMANIA — WWF SUPERSTARS
WRITING ON THE WALL — Tommy STEELE
WRITING TO REACH YOU — TRAVIS
WRITTEN IN THE STARS —
  Elton JOHN and LeAnn RIMES
WRITTEN ON THE WIND — Roger DALTREY
WRONG — EVERYTHING BUT THE GIRL
WRONG IMPRESSION — Natalie IMBRUGLIA
WRONG NUMBER — The CURE
WRONG OR RIGHT —
  SABRE featuring PRESIDENT BROWN
WUNDERBAR — TEN POLE TUDOR
WUTHERING HEIGHTS — Kate BUSH
X [A] — SNOOP DOGG
X [B] — WARRIOR
X GON' GIVE IT TO YA — DMX
X RAY FOLLOW ME — SPACE FROG
X Y & ZEE — POP WILL EAT ITSELF
XANADU — Olivia NEWTON-JOHN and
  ELECTRIC LIGHT ORCHESTRA
X-FILES [A] — DJ DADO
THE X-FILES [A] — Mark SNOW
XMAS PARTY — SNOWMEN
X-MAS TIME — DJ OTZI
XPAND YA MIND (EXPANSIONS) —
  WAG YA TAIL
XPRESS YOURSELF — FAMILY FOUNDATION
X-RATED — DJ NATION
XX SEX — WE'VE GOT A FUZZBOX AND WE'RE
  GONNA USE IT
Y CONTROL — The YEAH YEAH YEAHS
Y (HOW DEEP IS YOUR LOVE) —
  DJ SCOT PROJECT
Y VIVA ESPAÑA — SYLVIA
Y VIVA SUSPENDERS — JUDGE DREAD
YA DON'T SEE THE SIGNS — Mark B & BLADE
YA MAMA — FATBOY SLIM
YA PLAYIN YASELF — JERU THE DAMAJA
YA YA TWIST — Petula CLARK
YAAAH — D-SHAKE
YABBA DABBA DOO — DARKMAN
YAH MO B THERE —
  James INGRAM with Michael MCDONALD
YAKETY YAK — The COASTERS
YEAH [A] — AUDIOWEB
YEAH [B] — WANNADIES
YEAH! [C] —
  USHER featuring LIL' JON & LUDACRIS
YEAH! BUDDY — ROYAL HOUSE
YEAH, YEAH, YEAH, YEAH, YEAH [A] —
  The POGUES
YEAH YEAH YEAH YEAH YEAH [B] —
  WEDDING PRESENT
YEAR OF DECISION — The THREE DEGREES
YEAR OF THE CAT — Al STEWART
YEAR OF THE RAT — BADLY DRAWN BOY
YEAR 3000 — BUSTED
YEARNING FOR YOUR LOVE — GAP BAND
YEARS FROM NOW — DR HOOK
YEARS GO BY — Stan CAMPBELL
YEARS LATER — CACTUS WORLD NEWS
YEARS MAY COME, YEARS MAY GO —
  HERMAN'S HERMITS
YEBO — ART OF NOISE
YEH, YEH [A] — Georgie FAME
YEH YEH [A] — MATT BIANCO
YEH YEH YEH — MELANIE C
YEHA-NOHA (WISHES OF HAPPINESS
  AND PROSPERITY) — SACRED SPIRIT
YEKE YEKE — Mory KANTE
YELLOW — COLDPLAY
YELLOW PEARL — Philip LYNOTT
YELLOW RIVER — CHRISTIE
THE YELLOW ROSE OF TEXAS [A] —
  Ronnie HILTON
THE YELLOW ROSE OF TEXAS [A] —
  Gary MILLER
THE YELLOW ROSE OF TEXAS [A] —
  Mitch MILLER
YELLOW SUBMARINE — The BEATLES
YEOVIL TRUE — YEOVIL TOWN FC
YEP — Duane EDDY and the REBELS
YER OLD — REEF
YES [A] — Merry CLAYTON
YES [B] — Bernard BUTLER

YES I DO — Shakin' STEVENS
YES I WILL — The HOLLIES
YES MY DARLING DAUGHTER — Eydie GORME
YES SIR, I CAN BOOGIE — BACCARA
YES TONIGHT JOSEPHINE [A] — Johnnie RAY
YES TONIGHT JOSEPHINE [A] — JETS
YESTERDAY [A] — The BEATLES
YESTERDAY [A] — Ray CHARLES
YESTERDAY [A] — Marianne FAITHFULL
YESTERDAY [A] — Matt MONRO
YESTERDAY [A] — WET WET WET
YESTERDAY HAS GONE —
  CUPID'S INSPIRATION
YESTERDAY HAS GONE [A] —
  PJ PROBY and Marc ALMOND featuring
  the MY LIFE STORY ORCHESTRA
YESTERDAY MAN — Chris ANDREWS
YESTERDAY ONCE MORE [A] —
  The CARPENTERS
YESTERDAY ONCE MORE [A] — REDD KROSS
YESTERDAY TODAY — OCEAN COLOUR SCENE
YESTERDAY WENT TOO SOON — FEEDER
YESTERDAY WHEN I WAS MAD —
  PET SHOP BOYS
YESTERDAYS — GUNS N' ROSES
YESTERDAY'S DREAMS — The FOUR TOPS
YESTERDAY'S GONE —
  Chad STUART and Jeremy CLYDE
YESTERDAY'S MEN — MADNESS
YESTER-ME, YESTER-YOU, YESTERDAY —
  Stevie WONDER
YET ANOTHER DAY —
  Armin VAN BUUREN featuring Ray WILSON
YIM — JEZ & CHOOPIE
YING TONG SONG [A] — The GOONS
YIPPIE-I-OH — BARNDANCE BOYS
Y.M.C.A. — VILLAGE PEOPLE
YO!! SWEETNESS — HAMMER
YO YO GET FUNKY — DJ 'FAST' EDDIE
THE YODELLING SONG — Frank IFIELD
YOSHIMI BATTLES THE PINK ROBOTS PT.1 —
  The FLAMING LIPS
YOU [A] —
  Johnny JOHNSON and the BANDWAGON
YOU [B] — George HARRISON
YOU [C] — Randy EDELMAN
YOU [D] — TEN SHARP
YOU [E] — Bonnie RAITT
YOU [F] — STAXX featuring Carol LEEMING
YOU [G] — POINT BREAK
YOU [H] — S CLUB 7
YOU [I] — Shaznay LEWIS
YOU [J] — THEE UNSTRUNG
YOU (EP) — FIVE THIRTY
YOU AIN'T GOING NOWHERE — The BYRDS
YOU AIN'T LIVIN' TILL YOU'RE LOVIN' —
  Marvin GAYE
YOU AIN'T REALLY DOWN — STATUS IV
YOU AIN'T SEEN NOTHIN' YET [A] — BUS STOP
YOU AIN'T SEEN NOTHING YET [A] —
  BACHMAN-TURNER OVERDRIVE
YOU ALL DAT — BAHA MEN
YOU ALWAYS HURT THE ONE YOU LOVE [A] —
  Connie FRANCIS
YOU ALWAYS HURT THE ONE YOU LOVE [A] —
  Clarence 'Frogman' HENRY
YOU AND I [A] — Rick JAMES
YOU AND I [B] — Will YOUNG
YOU AND I WILL NEVER SEE THINGS EYE TO EYE —
  KINGMAKER
YOU AND ME [A] — LINER
YOU AND ME [B] — DJ SEDUCTION
YOU AND ME [C] — Lisa B
YOU AND ME [C] — EASYWORLD
YOU + ME — TECHNIQUE
YOU AND ME SONG — WANNADIES
YOU AND ME TONIGHT [A] — AURRA
YOU AND ME (TONIGHT) [B] — Alistair GRIFFIN
YOU AND YOUR HEART SO BLUE —
  BUCKS FIZZ
YOU ANGEL YOU — MANFRED MANN
YOU ARE — Lionel RICHIE
YOU ARE ALIVE — FRAGMA
YOU ARE AWFUL — Dick EMERY
YOU ARE BEAUTIFUL — Johnny MATHIS
YOU ARE EVERYTHING [A] — PEARLS
YOU ARE EVERYTHING [A] —
  Diana ROSS and Marvin GAYE
YOU ARE EVERYTHING [A] —
  Melanie WILLIAMS and Joe ROBERTS
YOU ARE IN MY SYSTEM — Robert PALMER
YOU ARE MY DESTINY — Paul ANKA
YOU ARE MY FIRST LOVE — Ruby MURRAY
YOU ARE MY HIGH —
  DEMON vs HEARTBREAKER
YOU ARE MY LADY — Freddie JACKSON
YOU ARE MY LOVE — LIVERPOOL EXPRESS
YOU ARE MY MELODY — CHANGE
YOU ARE MY WORLD — COMMUNARDS
YOU ARE NOT ALONE — Michael JACKSON
YOU ARE SOMEBODY — FULL INTENTION
YOU ARE THE GENERATION THAT BOUGHT MORE
  SHOES AND YOU GET WHAT YOU DESERVE —
  JOHNNY BOY
YOU ARE THE ONE — A-HA
YOU ARE THE SUNSHINE OF MY LIFE —
  Stevie WONDER

YOU ARE THE UNIVERSE —
  The BRAND NEW HEAVIES
YOU ARE THE WAY — PRIMITIVES
YOU ARE THE WEAKEST LINK — ECHOBASS
YOU BE ILLIN' — RUN-DMC
YOU BELONG IN ROCK 'N' ROLL —
  TIN MACHINE
YOU BELONG TO ME [A] — Jo STAFFORD
YOU BELONG TO ME [B] — Gary GLITTER
YOU BELONG TO ME [C] — JX
YOU BELONG TO ME [D] — Michael MOOG
YOU BET YOUR LOVE — Herbie HANCOCK
YOU BETTER —
  MOUNT RUSHMORE presents the KNACK
YOU BETTER COME HOME — Petula CLARK
YOU BETTER YOU BET — The WHO
YOU BLOW ME AWAY — Robert PALMER
YOU BRING ME JOY [A] — MEECHIE
YOU BRING ME JOY [B] — RHYTHM FACTOR
YOU BRING ME UP — K-CI & JOJO
YOU BRING ON THE SUN — LONDONBEAT
YOU CAME — Kim WILDE
YOU CAME, YOU SAW, YOU CONQUERED —
  PEARLS
YOU CAN CALL ME AL — Paul SIMON
YOU CAN COUNT ON ME — Jaki GRAHAM
YOU CAN DANCE (IF YOU WANT TO) — GO GO
  LORENZO and the DAVIS PINCKNEY PROJECT
YOU CAN DO IT [A] — Al HUDSON
YOU CAN DO IT [B] —
  ICE CUBE featuring MACK 10 + MS TOI
YOU CAN DO MAGIC [A] —
  LIMMIE and the FAMILY COOKIN'
YOU CAN DO MAGIC [B] — AMERICA
YOU CAN GET IT — MAXX
YOU CAN GET IT IF YOU REALLY WANT —
  Desmond DEKKER and the ACES
YOU CAN GO YOUR OWN WAY — Chris REA
YOU CAN HAVE HIM — Dionne WARWICK
YOU CAN HAVE IT ALL [A] — George McCRAE
YOU CAN HAVE IT ALL [B] — Eve GALLAGHER
YOU CAN HAVE IT (TAKE MY HEART) —
  Robert PALMER
YOU CAN LOVE ME NOW —
  HOTHOUSE FLOWERS
YOU CAN MAKE ME DANCE SING OR
  ANYTHING (EVEN TAKE THE DOG FOR A WALK, MEND
  A FUSE, FOLD AWAY THE
  IRONING BOARD, OR ANY OTHER DOMESTIC SHORT
  COMINGS) —
  The FACES / Rod STEWART
YOU CAN NEVER STOP ME LOVING YOU —
  Kenny LYNCH
YOU CAN TALK TO ME — The SEAHORSES
YOU CAN WIN IF YOU WANT —
  MODERN TALKING
YOU CAN'T BE TRUE TO TWO — Dave KING
YOU CAN'T BLAME LOVE —
  THOMAS and TAYLOR
YOU CAN'T CHANGE ME — Roger SANCHEZ
  featuring Armand VAN HELDEN and
  N'Dea DAVENPORT
YOU CAN'T GO HOME AGAIN — DJ SHADOW
YOU CAN'T HIDE (YOUR LOVE FROM ME) —
  David JOSEPH
YOU CAN'T HURRY LOVE [A] — The SUPREMES
YOU CAN'T HURRY LOVE [A] — Phil COLLINS
YOU CAN'T HURRY LOVE [B] —
  The CONCRETES
YOU CAN'T RUN FROM LOVE —
  Maxine SINGLETON
YOU CAN'T SIT DOWN —
  Phil UPCHURCH COMBO
YOU CAN'T STOP ROCK 'N' ROLL —
  TWISTED SISTER
YOU CAN'T STOP THE REIGN —
  Shaquille O'NEAL
YOU CAUGHT MY EYE — Judy BOUCHER
YOU COME FROM EARTH — Lena FIAGBE
YOU COME THROUGH — PJ HARVEY
YOU COULD BE MINE — GUNS N' ROSES
YOU COULD BE MY EVERYTHING —
  Mikey GRAHAM
YOU COULD HAVE BEEN A LADY —
  HOT CHOCOLATE
YOU COULD HAVE BEEN WITH ME —
  Sheena EASTON
YOU DID CUT ME — CHINA CRISIS
YOU DIDN'T EXPECT THAT — Billy CRAWFORD
YOU DISAPPEAR FROM VIEW —
  TEARDROP EXPLODES
YOU DO — Bernard BUTLER
YOU DO SOMETHING TO ME [A] —
  Paul WELLER
YOU DO SOMETHING TO ME [B] — DUM DUMS
YOU DON'T BELIEVE ME — STRAY CATS
YOU DON'T BRING ME FLOWERS —
  Barbra STREISAND
YOU DON'T CARE ABOUT US — PLACEBO
YOU DON'T FOOL ME — QUEEN
YOU DON'T HAVE TO BE A BABY TO CRY —
  CARAVELLES
YOU DON'T HAVE TO BE A STAR (TO BE IN MY SHOW)
  — Marilyn McCOO and Billy DAVIS Jr
YOU DON'T HAVE TO BE IN THE ARMY TO FIGHT IN THE
  WAR — MUNGO JERRY
YOU DON'T HAVE TO GO — CHI-LITES

YOUR HURTIN' KIND OF LOVE —
Dusty SPRINGFIELD
YOUR KISS IS SWEET — SYREETA
YOUR KISSES ARE CHARITY — CULTURE CLUB
YOUR LATEST TRICK — DIRE STRAITS
YOUR LOSS MY GAIN — OMAR
YOUR LOVE [A] — HIPSWAY
YOUR LOVE [C] — Frankie KNUCKLES
YOUR LOVE [C] — Diana ROSS
YOUR LOVE [D] — INNER CITY
YOUR LOVE GETS SWEETER — Finley QUAYE
(YOUR LOVE HAS LIFTED ME) HIGHER AND HIGHER —
Rita COOLIDGE
YOUR LOVE IS A 187 — WHITEHEAD BROS
YOUR LOVE IS CALLING — EVOLUTION
YOUR LOVE IS KING — SADE
YOUR LOVE IS LIFTING ME — NOMAD
(YOUR LOVE KEEPS LIFTING ME) HIGHER AND HIGHER
— Jackie WILSON
YOUR LOVE TAKES ME HIGHER —
The BELOVED
YOUR LOVING ARMS — Billie Ray MARTIN
YOUR LUCKY DAY IN HELL — EELS
YOUR MA SAID YOU CRIED IN YOUR SLEEP
LAST NIGHT — Doug SHELDON
YOUR MAGIC PUT A SPELL ON ME —
LJ JOHNSON
YOUR MAMA DON'T DANCE — POISON
YOUR MAMMA WON'T LIKE ME — Suzi QUATRO
YOUR MIRROR — SIMPLY RED
YOUR MOTHER'S GOT A PENIS —
GOLDIE LOOKIN CHAIN
YOUR MUSIC —
INTENSO PROJECT featuring Laura JAYE
YOUR NEW CUCKOO — The CARDIGANS
YOUR OWN SPECIAL WAY — GENESIS
YOUR PAINTED SMILE — Bryan FERRY
YOUR PERSONAL TOUCH —
Evelyn 'Champagne' KING
YOUR SECRET LOVE — Luther VANDROSS
YOUR SMILE — OCTOPUS
YOUR SONG [A] — Elton JOHN
YOUR SONG [A] — Billy PAUL
YOUR SONG [A] — Rod STEWART
YOUR SWAYING ARMS — DEACON BLUE
YOUR TENDER LOOK —
Joe BROWN and the BRUVVERS
YOUR TIME HASN'T COME YET BABY —
Elvis PRESLEY
YOUR TIME IS GONNA COME —
DREAD ZEPPELIN
YOUR TOWN — DEACON BLUE
YOUR WOMAN — WHITE TOWN
YOU'RE A BETTER MAN THAN I — SHAM 69
YOU'RE A LADY — Peter SKELLERN
YOU'RE A STAR — AQUARIAN DREAM
YOU'RE A SUPERSTAR — LOVE INC.
YOU'RE ALL I NEED — MÖTLEY CRÜE
YOU'RE ALL I NEED TO GET BY [A] —
Marvin GAYE
YOU'RE ALL I NEED TO GET BY [A] —
Johnny MATHIS and Deniece WILLIAMS
YOU'RE ALL THAT MATTERS TO ME —
Curtis STIGERS
YOU'RE BREAKIN' MY HEART — Keely SMITH
YOU'RE DRIVING ME CRAZY — TEMPERANCE SEVEN

YOU'RE EVERYTHING TO ME — Boris GARDINER
(YOU'RE) FABULOUS BABE — Kenny WILLIAMS
YOU'RE FREE — YOMANDA
YOU'RE FREE TO GO — Jim REEVES
YOU'RE GONE — MARILLION
YOU'RE GONNA GET NEXT TO ME —
Bo KIRKLAND and Ruth DAVIS
YOU'RE GONNA MISS ME —
TURNTABLE ORCHESTRA
YOU'RE GORGEOUS — BABYBIRD
(YOU'RE) HAVING MY BABY — Paul ANKA
YOU'RE HISTORY — SHAKESPEAR'S SISTER
YOU'RE IN A BAD WAY — SAINT ETIENNE
YOU'RE IN LOVE — WILSON PHILLIPS
YOU'RE IN MY HEART [A] — Rod STEWART
YOU'RE IN MY HEART [B] — David ESSEX
YOU'RE INVITED (BUT YOUR FRIEND CAN'T COME) —
Vince NEIL
YOU'RE LOOKING HOT TONIGHT —
Barry MANILOW
YOU'RE LYING — LINX
YOU'RE MAKIN' ME HIGH — Toni BRAXTON
YOU'RE MORE THAN A NUMBER IN MY LITTLE RED
BOOK — The DRIFTERS
YOU'RE MOVING OUT TODAY —
Carole Bayer SAGER
YOU'RE MY ANGEL — Mikey GRAHAM
YOU'RE MY BEST FRIEND [A] — QUEEN
YOU'RE MY BEST FRIEND [B] —
Don WILLIAMS
YOU'RE MY EVERYTHING [A] —
The TEMPTATIONS
YOU'RE MY EVERYTHING [B] —
Max BYGRAVES
YOU'RE MY EVERYTHING [C] — EAST SIDE BEAT
YOU'RE MY EVERYTHING [C] — Lee GARRETT
YOU'RE MY GIRL — ROCKIN' BERRIES
YOU'RE MY HEART, YOU'RE MY SOUL —
MODERN TALKING
YOU'RE MY LAST CHANCE — 52ND STREET
YOU'RE MY LIFE — Barry BIGGS
YOU'RE MY MATE — RIGHT SAID FRED
YOU'RE MY NUMBER ONE — S CLUB 7
(YOU'RE MY ONE AND ONLY) TRUE LOVE —
Ann-Marie SMITH
(YOU'RE MY) SOUL AND INSPIRATION —
RIGHTEOUS BROTHERS
YOU'RE MY WORLD [A] — Cilla BLACK
YOU'RE MY WORLD [B] — Nick HEYWARD
YOU'RE NEVER TOO YOUNG — COOLNOTES
YOU'RE NO GOOD [A] — SWINGING BLUE JEANS
YOU'RE NO GOOD [B] — ASWAD
YOU'RE NOT ALONE [A] — OLIVE
YOU'RE NOT ALONE [B] — EMBRACE
YOU'RE NOT HERE — TYRREL CORPORATION
YOU'RE OK [A] — OTTAWAN
YOU'RE OK [B] — kd LANG
YOU'RE ONE — IMPERIAL TEEN
(YOU'RE PUTTIN') A RUSH ON ME —
Stephanie MILLS
YOU'RE READY NOW — Frankie VALLI
YOU'RE SHINING — STYLES & BREEZE
YOU'RE SINGING OUR LOVE SONG TO
SOMEBODY ELSE — Jerry WALLACE
YOU'RE SIXTEEN [A] — Johnny BURNETTE
YOU'RE SIXTEEN [A] — Ringo STARR

YOU'RE SO RIGHT FOR ME —
EASTSIDE CONNECTION
YOU'RE SO VAIN — Carly SIMON
YOU'RE STILL THE ONE — Shania TWAIN
YOU'RE SUCH A GOOD LOOKING WOMAN —
Joe DOLAN
YOU'RE THE BEST THING — STYLE COUNCIL
(YOU'RE THE) DEVIL IN DISGUISE —
Elvis PRESLEY with the JORDANAIRES
YOU'RE THE FIRST, THE LAST, MY EVERYTHING —
Barry WHITE
YOU'RE THE GREATEST LOVER —
Jonathan KING
YOU'RE THE INSPIRATION — CHICAGO
YOU'RE THE ONE [A] — Kathy KIRBY
YOU'RE THE ONE [B] — Petula CLARK
YOU'RE THE ONE [C] — BANG
YOU'RE THE ONE [D] — SWV
YOU'RE THE ONE FOR ME — D TRAIN
YOU'RE THE ONE FOR ME — DAYBREAK
— AM — Paul HARDCASTLE
YOU'RE THE ONE FOR ME, FATTY —
MORRISSEY
YOU'RE THE ONE I LOVE — Shola AMA
YOU'RE THE ONE THAT I WANT [A] —
John TRAVOLTA and Olivia NEWTON-JOHN
YOU'RE THE ONE THAT I WANT [A] —
Hylda BAKER and Arthur MULLARD
YOU'RE THE ONE THAT I WANT [A] —
Craig McLACHLAN and Debbie GIBSON
YOU'RE THE ONLY GOOD THING — Jim REEVES
YOU'RE THE ONLY ONE — Val DOONICAN
YOU'RE THE REASON — WAMDUE PROJECT
YOU'RE THE REASON WHY — The RUBETTES
YOU'RE THE STAR — Rod STEWART
YOU'RE THE STORM — The CARDIGANS
YOU'RE THE STORY OF MY LIFE —
Judy CHEEKS
YOU'RE THE TOP CHA — Al SAXON
YOU'RE THE VOICE [A] — John FARNHAM
YOU'RE THE VOICE [A] — HEART
YOU'RE WALKING — ELECTRIBE 101
YOURS — Dionne WARWICK
YOURS FATALLY — BIG BROVAZ
YOURS UNTIL TOMORROW — Gene PITNEY
YOUTH AGAINST FASCISM — SONIC YOUTH
YOUTH GONE WILD — SKID ROW
YOUTH OF NATION ON FIRE — Bill NELSON
YOUTH OF THE NATION — P.O.D.
YOUTH OF TODAY — MUSICAL YOUTH
YOU'VE BEEN DOING ME WRONG —
DELEGATION
YOU'VE BEEN GONE —
CROWN HEIGHTS AFFAIR
YOU'VE COME BACK — PJ PROBY
YOU'VE GOT A FRIEND [A] — James TAYLOR
YOU'VE GOT A FRIEND [A] —
The BRAND NEW HEAVIES
YOU'VE GOT A FRIEND [B] —
Big FUN and SONIA featuring Gary BARNACLE
YOU'VE GOT A LOT TO ANSWER FOR —
CATATONIA
YOU'VE GOT ANOTHER THING COMIN' —
JUDAS PRIEST
YOU'VE GOT IT — SIMPLY RED
YOU'VE GOT IT BAD — OCEAN COLOUR SCENE

YOU'VE GOT LOVE — Buddy HOLLY and The CRICKETS
YOU'VE GOT ME DANGLING ON A STRING —
CHAIRMEN OF THE BOARD
YOU'VE GOT ME THINKING — The BELOVED
YOU'VE GOT MY NUMBER (WHY DON'T
YOU USE IT?) — The UNDERTONES
YOU'VE GOT THAT SOMETHIN' — ROBYN
YOU'VE GOT TO CHOOSE — DARLING BUDS
YOU'VE GOT TO GIVE ME ROOM —
Oleta ADAMS
YOU'VE GOT TO HIDE YOUR LOVE AWAY —
SILKIE
YOU'VE GOT YOUR TROUBLES — FORTUNES
YOU'VE LOST THAT LOVIN' FEELIN' [A] —
Cilla BLACK
YOU'VE LOST THAT LOVIN' FEELIN' [A] —
RIGHTEOUS BROTHERS
YOU'VE LOST THAT LOVIN' FEELIN' [A] —
Telly SAVALAS
YOU'VE LOST THAT LOVIN' FEELIN' [A] —
Daryl HALL and John OATES
YOU'VE MADE ME SO VERY HAPPY —
BLOOD SWEAT AND TEARS
(YOU'VE) NEVER BEEN IN LOVE LIKE THIS BEFORE —
UNIT FOUR PLUS TWO
YOU'VE NOT CHANGED — Sandie SHAW
YOU'VE SAID ENOUGH — CENTRAL LINE
YOYO BOY — ALBERTA
YUM, YUM (GIMME SOME) — FATBACK BAND
YUMMY YUMMY YUMMY — OHIO EXPRESS
ZABADAK! —
Dave DEE, DOZY, BEAKY, MICK and TICH
ZAMBESI [A] — Lou BUSCH and His Orchestra
ZAMBESI [A] — Eddie CALVERT
ZAMBESI [A] —
PIRANHAS featuring Boring Bob GROVER
ZEPHYR — ELECTRAFIXION
THE ZEPHYR SONG —
RED HOT CHILI PEPPERS
ZEROES & ONES — JESUS JONES
ZEROTONINE — JUNKIE XL
ZEROX — ADAM and the ANTS
ZEROXED — ZERO ZERO
ZIGGY STARDUST — BAUHAUS
ZING A LITTLE ZONG — Bing CROSBY and Jane WYMAN
ZING WENT THE STRINGS OF MY HEART —
The TRAMMPS
ZION YOUTH — DREADZONE
ZIP — LOCK — LIT
ZIP GUN BOOGIE — T. REX
ZIP-A-DEE-DOO-DAH —
Bob B SOXX and the BLUE JEANS
ZODIACS — Roberta KELLY
ZOE — PAGANINI TRAXX
ZOMBIE [A] — The CRANBERRIES
ZOMBIE [A] — A.D.A.M. featuring AMY
THE ZOO — SCORPIONS
THE ZOO (THE HUMAN ZOO) —
The COMMODORES
ZOOM [A] — The COMMODORES
ZOOM [B] — Scott BRADLEY
ZOOM [C] — DR DRE and LL COOL J
ZORBA'S DANCE [A] — Marcello MINERBI
ZORBA'S DANCE [A] — LCD
ZUNGA ZENG — K7 and The SWING KIDS

1000 NUMBER ONE SINGLES

1952 - 2005

Sunday 16 January 2005 became a milestone date in pop history when the double A-side single 'One Night' / 'I Got Stung' became the 1,000th single to top the UK chart. In the next 73 pages we take you on a chart-topping journey which starts on this page in November 1952 with Al Martino and ends in January 2005 with Elvis Presley.

Before immersing yourself in our 1,000 No.1s rundown, take note of these useful tips about the way in which we compiled the list. Along with the track times, factual trivia, writers and US peak positions, we have included the relevant flip side to each chart-topper. However, no B-side is listed where the single comprised a double A-side or the release contained only a virtually identical version of the same song – something that happened frequently from the start of the CD era. US chart peak positions are from the best-sellers chart prior to August 1958 and then the Billboard Hot 100 which was launched at that time. Readers wishing to pinpoint what was No.1 on a particular day should note that the dates listed in this chronological rundown of chart-toppers are for the end of a song's first week at the top spot, as chart tradition decrees. Therefore, if the date which interests you is, say, 20 Jan 1953, 'Comes a-Long a-Love' by Kay Starr would have been No.1. For more help with dates of No.1s, visit our website: **www.bibleofpop.com**.

Finally, for the answer to the frequently asked question "How do I find out what was a Christmas No.1 and what wasn't?", the answer is simple. This is always the last single we list in each year, except for 'Mr Blobby' in 1993 which returned to No.1 in time for Christmas, having previously been No.1 earlier in December.

Special thanks to Ray Spiller and Tony Upton for their contributions to this section of the book.

1952

↗ NO.1
14 NOV ●●●●●●●●●
HERE IN MY HEART (3.13)
Al Martino (Pat Genero, Lou Levinson, Bill Borrelli). Martino, who would later act opposite Marlon Brando in The Godfather, was backed by 52 musicians on his transatlantic chart-topping debut disc. (B-side: I Cried Myself to Sleep) **US 1**

1953

↗ NO.2
16 JAN ●
YOU BELONG TO ME (3.05)
Jo Stafford (Pee Wee King, Redd Stewart, Chilton Price). The first No.1 by a female and the first song composed by a country and western artist to top the chart. (B-side: Pretty Boy (Pretty Girl)) **US 1**

↗ NO.3
23 JAN ●
COMES A-LONG A-LOVE (2.10)
Kay Starr (Al Sherman). Written by the Russian-born father of Richard and Robert Sherman, composers of Mary Poppins. (B-side: Three Letters) **US 22**

↗ NO.4
30 JAN ●
OUTSIDE OF HEAVEN (2.36)
Eddie Fisher
(Sammy Gallop, Chester Conn). Heart-throb Fisher recorded this while serving in the army. (B-side: Lady of Spain) **US 10**

↗ NO.5
6 FEB ●●●●●
DON'T LET THE STARS GET IN YOUR EYES (2.39)
Perry Como with The Ramblers (Slim Willet). Como hated this song, which was originally a US country and western hit for Slim Willet and The Bush Cutters. (B-side: To Know You (Is to Love You) **US 1**

↗ NO.6
13 MAR ●●●●
SHE WEARS RED FEATHERS (3.09)
Guy Mitchell (Bob Merrill). The only hit about a love affair between an English banker and a hula-hula girl. (B-side: Why Should I Go Home?)

↗ NO.7
10 APR ●
BROKEN WINGS (2.52)
The Stargazers (John Jerome, Bernard Gunn). First No.1 by a British group. This US song was originally recorded in the UK by Dickie Valentine. (B-side: Make It Soon)

↗ NO.8
17 APR ●
(HOW MUCH IS) THAT DOGGIE IN THE WINDOW (2.13)
Lita Roza (Bob Merrill). Patti Page's original recording topped the US chart. Lita Roza disliked the song and refused to sing it on stage. (B-side: Tell Me We'll Meet Again)

↘ **CHART-TOPPER NO.4:** Eddie Fisher in the Candid TV series studio with his first wife Debbie Reynolds. Actress Debbie had a US No.1 hit with 'Tammy' and later gave birth to daughter Carrie Fisher, who won acclaim for her performances in the Star Wars movies

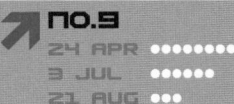

NO.9
24 APR •••••••••
3 JUL ••••••
21 AUG •••

I BELIEVE (2.07)
Frankie Laine (Erwin Drake, Irvin Graham, Jimmy Shirl, Al Stillman). Composed for Jane Froman, who didn't believe it was commercial enough to record, until Frankie Laine proved her wrong. (B-side: Your Cheatin' Heart) **US 2**

NO.10
26 JUN •

I'M WALKING BEHIND YOU (3.06)
Eddie Fisher with Sally Sweetland (Billy Reid). This you-married-the-wrong-guy ode was composed by Reid for his ex-wife Dorothy Squires, who married Roger Moore at the time of the hit. (B-side: Hold Me) **US 1**

NO.11
14 AUG •

THE SONG FROM THE MOULIN ROUGE (2.33)
Mantovani (Georges Auric). The first movie theme No.1, which had been a 10-week chart-topper stateside for Percy Faith's Orchestra. (B-side: Vola Columba) **US 13**

NO.12
11 SEP ••••••

LOOK AT THAT GIRL (2.50)
Guy Mitchell (Bob Merrill). The first No.1 by an American artist that failed to chart in the US. (B-side: Wise Man or Fool)

NO.13
23 OCT ••

HEY JOE! (2.19)
Frankie Laine (Boudleaux Bryant). Penned by the writer of many Everly Brothers hits and originally a country and western No.1 by Carl Smith. (B-side: Sittin' in the Sun (Countin' My Money)) **US 11**

NO.14
6 NOV •
11 DEC (EQUAL TOP) •

ANSWER ME (2.36) **David Whitfield** (Gerhard Winkler, Fred Rauch, Carl Sigman). Whitfield released two versions – one religion free – to dodge a similar BBC ban imposed on Frankie Laine's recording of this German song. (B-side: Dance, Gypsy, Dance)

NO.15
13 NOV ••••
11 DEC (EQUAL TOP) •
18 DEC •••

ANSWER ME (2.37)
Frankie Laine (Gerhard Winkler, Fred Rauch,

Carl Sigman). First song to top the chart twice, it allegedly may have subconsciously influenced Paul McCartney's 'Yesterday'. (B-side: Ramblin' Man)

1954

NO.16
8 JAN •••••••••

OH, MEIN PAPA (2.45)
Eddie Calvert (Paul Burkhard). This Swiss song was the first No.1 to be recorded at Abbey Road and holds the record for the most weeks at No.1 by an instrumental. (B-side: Mystery Street) **US 9**

NO.17
12 MAR •••••
23 APR •

I SEE THE MOON (2.38)
The Stargazers (Meredith Wilson). Produced by Dick Rowe (the man who famously turned down The Beatles), this was a cover of a US hit by The Mariners. (B-side: Eh Cumpari!)

NO.18
16 APR •
7 MAY ••••••••

SECRET LOVE (3.40)
Doris Day (Paul Francis Webster, Sammy Fain). An Academy Award-winning song from Doris Day's western movie Calamity Jane. (B-side: The Deadwood Stage) **US 1**

NO.19
30 APR •

SUCH A NIGHT (2.13)
Johnnie Ray (Lincoln Chase). A cover version of the suggestive Clyde McPhatter and The Drifters US R&B hit which ran into problems with the censors. (B-side: An Orchid for the Lady)

NO.20
2 JUL ••••••••••

CARA MIA (3.08)
David Whitfield (Lee Lange, Tulio Trapani, aka producer Bunny Lewis and Mantovani). Arranged by Mantovani, this was the first British male vocal record to make the US Top 10 and the first to earn a gold disc. (B-side: Love, Tears and Kisses) **US 10**

NO.21
10 SEP •

LITTLE THINGS MEAN A LOT (2.58)
Kitty Kallen (Carl Shultz, Edith Lindermann). The first one-hit wonder was recorded by this one-time 1940s big-band singer. (B-side: I Don't Think You Love Me Anymore) **US 1**

NO.22
17 SEP •••

THREE COINS IN THE FOUNTAIN (3.04) **Frank Sinatra** (Sammy Cahn, Julie Styne). The original soundtrack version of the 1954 Academy Award-winning film theme. (B-side: I Could Have Told You) **US 7**

NO.23
8 OCT ••••
19 NOV •

HOLD MY HAND (2.45)
Don Cornell (Jack Lawrence, Richard Myers). The song from the movie Susan Slept Here was banned by the BBC for mentioning "the kingdom of heaven". (B-side: I'm Blessed) **US 5**

NO.24
5 NOV ••

MY SON, MY SON (2.41)
Vera Lynn with Frank Weir, his saxophone, his Orchestra and Chorus (Bob Howard, Melville Farley, Eddie Calvert). Vera Lynn's biggest hit, Calvert wrote this 'son' song as a follow-up to 'Oh, Mein Papa'. (B-side: Our Heaven on Earth)

NO.25
26 NOV •

THIS OLE HOUSE (2.22)
Rosemary Clooney (Stuart Hamblen). Hamblen composed the song on a wilderness hunting trip after discovering the body of an old man in a remote shack. (B-side: Hey There) **US 1**

NO.26
3 DEC •••••

LET'S HAVE ANOTHER PARTY (5.23) **Winifred Atwell** (Nat D Ayer, Clifford Grey, James W Tate, Ray Henderson, Mort Dixon, Albert Fitz, William Penn, Gus Cahn, Walter Donaldson, Leslie Stuart, Harry Armstrong, Ted Snyder, Leo Wood, Harry Wood). The only female instrumentalist to top the chart. (B-side: Let's Have Another Party (Part 2))

1955

NO.27
7 JAN •
21 JAN ••

THE FINGER OF SUSPICION (2.50)
Dickie Valentine with The Stargazers (Al Lewis, Paul Mann). The original recording of an American song that failed to chart in the US. (B-side: Who's Afraid)

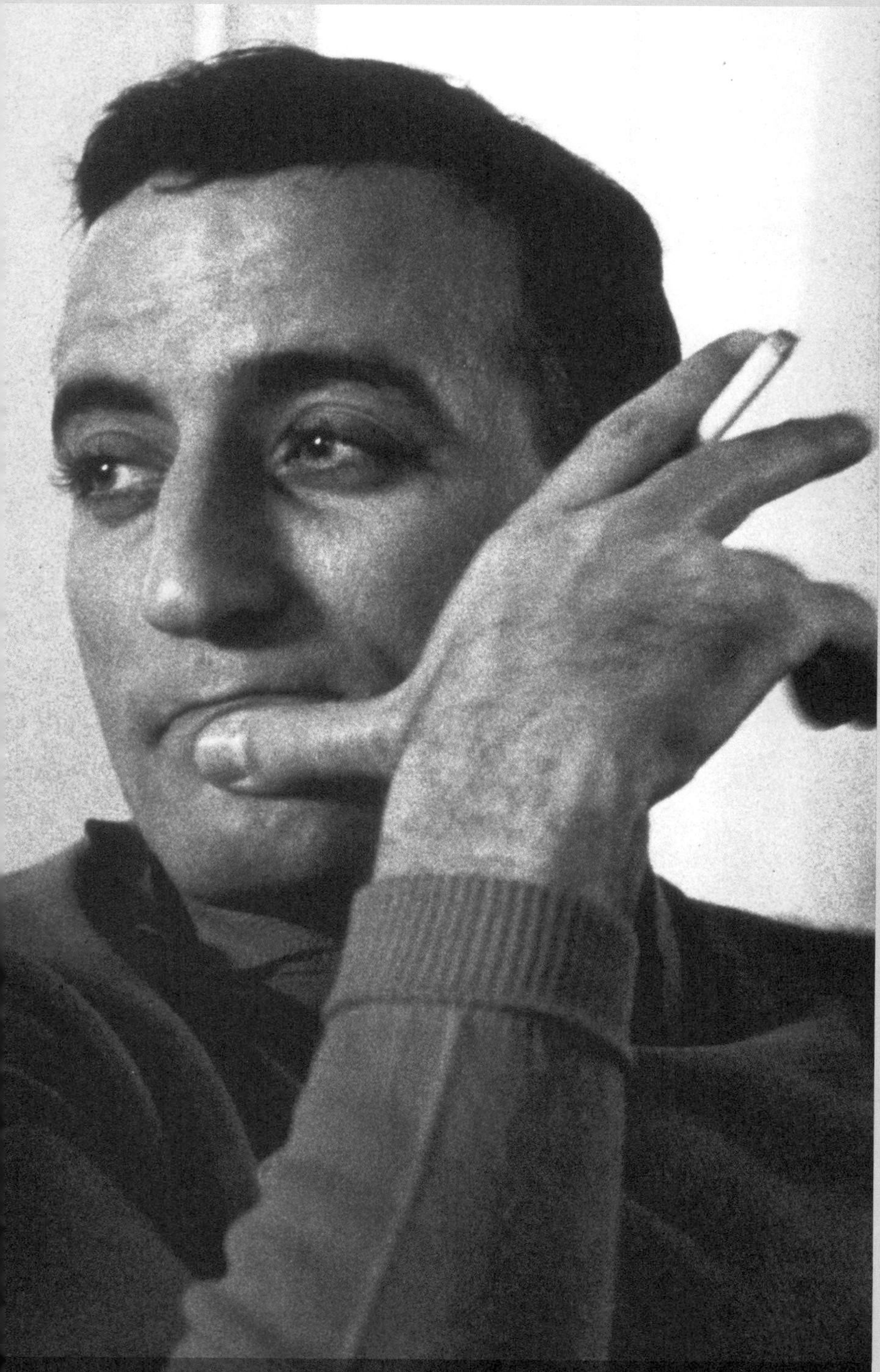

↗ NO.28
14 JAN •
4 FEB ••

MAMBO ITALIANO (2.30)
Rosemary Clooney and The Mellomen
(Bob Merrill). The sole mambo No.1 before
1999 was banned in the US because lyrically
"it did not reach standards of good taste".
(B-side: We'll Be Together Again) **US 10**

↗ NO.29
18 FEB •••

SOFTLY, SOFTLY (2.26)
Ruby Murray (Mark Paul, Pierre Dudan,
Paddy Roberts). The only chart-topper from
the singing sensation of 1955, who had five
singles simultaneously in the Top 20. (B-side:
What Could Be More Beautiful)

↗ NO.30
11 MAR •••••••

GIVE ME YOUR WORD (3.09)
Tennessee Ernie Ford (George Wyle, Irving
Taylor). This cowboy ballad was overlooked in
Ford's homeland. (B-side: River of No Return)

↗ NO.31
29 APR ••

**CHERRY PINK AND APPLE
BLOSSOM WHITE** (3.01)
Perez 'Prez' Prado and His Orchestra
(Louis Guilielmi Louiguy). The mambo king's
re-recording (for the movie Underwater!) of a
French song he first cut in 1951. It topped the US
chart for 10 weeks. (B-side: Maria Elena) **US 1**

↗ NO.32
13 MAY ••

STRANGER IN PARADISE (3.04)
Tony Bennett (Robert Wright, George Forrest).
The biggest version of six UK hits from the
musical Kismet, which was based on
Borodin's composition Polotsvian Dances.
(B-side: Take Me Back Again) **US 2**

↗ NO.33
27 MAY ••••

**CHERRY PINK AND APPLE
BLOSSOM WHITE** (2.23)
Eddie Calvert (Louis Guilielmi Louiguy). "The
Man with the Golden Trumpet" was backed
by the poll-winning Ted Heath Orchestra on
his version of the previous month's No.1.
(B-side: Roses of Picardy)

↗ NO.34
24 JUN •••

UNCHAINED MELODY (2.34)
Jimmy Young (Alex North, Hy Zaret). The
most successful chart song of all time was
originally sung by Todd Duncan in the movie
Unchained. (B-side: Help Me Forget)

↘ **CHART-TOPPER NO.32:** Tony Bennett was given his big break by Bob Hope
when the comedian spotted him as a Greenwich Village singer and MC performing under
the name Joe Bari

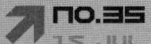
NO.35
15 JUL ●●
DREAMBOAT (1.45)
Alma Cogan (Al Hoffman). Alma's only No.1 was earlier recorded by American groups the Paulette Sisters and Five DeMarco Sisters. (B-side: ((The Diddle-Ee-I) Irish Mambo)

NO.36
29 JUL ●●●●●●●●●●●
ROSE MARIE (2.18)
Slim Whitman (Rudolf Friml, Otto Harbach, Oscar Hammerstein II). For 36 years this recording of a 1924 song held the record for the most successive weeks at No.1. It sold more than 750,000 in the UK alone. (B-side: We Stood at the Altar)

NO.37
14 OCT ●●●●
THE MAN FROM LARAMIE (2.21)
Jimmy Young (Lester Lee, Ned Washington). This James Stewart western movie theme, first recorded unsuccessfully by Al Martino, made JY the first UK act to score No.1s with successive singles. (B-side: No Arms Can Ever Hold You)

NO.38
11 NOV ●●
HERNANDO'S HIDEAWAY (2.30)
Johnston Brothers (Richard Adler, Jerry Ross). A castanet-clicking song from The Pajama Game whose 29-year-old composer Ross died of leukaemia on the day it reached No.1. (B-Side: Hey There)

NO.39
25 NOV ●●●
6 JAN 1956 ●●
ROCK AROUND THE CLOCK (2.10)
Bill Haley and His Comets (Jimmy de Knight, Max C Freedman). Britain's first million-seller (1,392,000) and the record that launched rock 'n' roll around the world. The Sonny Dae & His Knights' original was a relative flop. 'Rock Around the Clock' was originally recorded by Haley as a favour to his manager James Myers. The song took off only when featured in the Glenn Ford movie Blackboard Jungle. (B-side: Thirteen Women) **US 1**

NO.40
16 DEC ●●●
CHRISTMAS ALPHABET (2.07)
Dickie Valentine (Buddy Kaye, Jules Loman). The first chart-topper to name-check "Christmas" was originally recorded in the US the previous year by The McGuire Sisters. (B-side: Where Are You Tonight?)

1956

NO.41
20 JAN ●●●●
SIXTEEN TONS (2.35)
Tennessee Ernie Ford (Merle Travis). This mining song written and recorded in 1947 by Travis was a transatlantic No.1 despite a BBC ban for mentioning "St Peter". (B-side: You Don't Have to Be a Baby to Cry) **US 1**

NO.42
17 FEB ●●●●
MEMORIES ARE MADE OF THIS (2.16) **Dean Martin** (Terry Gilkyson, Richard Dehr, Frank Miller). Folk group The Easy Riders composed and sang backing vocals on Dino's biggest hit. (B-side: Change of Heart) **US 1**

NO.43
16 MAR ●●
6 APR ●●
IT'S ALMOST TOMORROW (2.46)
Dreamweavers
(Wade Buff, Eugene Adkinson). The US septet, which included the composers, financed the session that produced this allegedly "cheap sounding" million-seller. (B-Side: You've Got Me Wondering) **US 8**

NO.44
30 MAR ●
ROCK AND ROLL WALTZ (2.45)
Kay Starr
(Dick Ware, Shorty Allen). Starr did not want to record this "Rock and Roll" song, which sold 350,000 in its first four days in the US. (B-side: I've Changed My Mind a Thousand Times) **US 1**

NO.45
13 APR ●●●
THE POOR PEOPLE OF PARIS (1.57) **Winifred Atwell** (Marguerite Monnot, René Rouzaud). The pianist who inspired Elton John clicked with a song first recorded by Edith Piaf as 'La Goulante du Pauvre Jean'. (B-side: Piano Tuner's Boogie)

NO.46
4 MAY ●●●●●●
NO OTHER LOVE (3.06)
Ronnie Hilton
(Richard Rodgers, Oscar Hammerstein II). The song from the musical Me and Juliet hit the top three years after Perry Como scored a US No.1 with it. (B-side: It's All Been Done Before)

NO.47
15 JUN ●●●●●
I'LL BE HOME (2.59)
Pat Boone
(Ferdinand Washington, Stan Lewis). Elvis's No.1 rival stopped the King's 'Heartbreak Hotel' from reaching the top with this cover of an R&B hit by The Flamingos. (B-side: Tutti Frutti) **US 6**

NO.48
20 JUL ●●●
WHY DO FOOLS FALL IN LOVE? (2.19)
Teenagers featuring Frankie Lymon (Frankie Lymon, Jimmy Merchant, Herman Santiago). Thirteen-year-old Lymon was the first teenage chart-topper, and this was the first R&B disc to reach No.1. (B-side: Please Be Mine) **US 6**

NO.49
10 AUG ●●●●●●
WHATEVER WILL BE, WILL BE (QUE SERA, SERA) (2.03)
Doris Day
(Ray Evans, Jay Livingston). Soon after signing a $1m deal with Columbia, Day scored with this Oscar winner from Hitchcock's film The Man Who Knew Too Much. (B-side: We'll Love Again) **US 3**

NO.50
21 SEP ●●●●
LAY DOWN YOUR ARMS (2.55)
Anne Shelton (Leon Land, Ake Gerhard, Paddy Roberts). Originally titled 'Ann-Caroline', this Swedish song, which some thought encouraged cowardice in the services, gave the other Forces' Sweetheart her biggest hit. (B-side: Daydreams) **US 59**

NO.51
19 OCT ●●●●
A WOMAN IN LOVE (2.19)
Frankie Laine (Frank Loesser). Laine's fourth and final No.1 was written especially for Marlon Brando to sing in the film version of Guys and Dolls. (B-side: Make Me a Child Again) **US 19**

NO.52
16 NOV ●●●●●●●
JUST WALKING IN THE RAIN (2.37)
Johnnie Ray
(Johnny Bragg, Robert S Riley). Ray's 15th Top 20 hit in four years was written and first recorded by inmates of the Tennessee State Prison under the name The Prisonaires. (B-side: In the Candlelight) **US 3**

▾ **CHART-TOPPER NO.54**: Tommy Steele, who secured his only No.1 when backed by The Steelmen, was a Bermondsey-born teen idol discovered performing in Soho's legendary 2i's coffee bar

1957

↗ NO.53
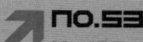
4 JAN •
18 JAN •
1 FEB (EQUAL TOP) •
SINGING THE BLUES (2.25)
Guy Mitchell (Melvin Endsley). Producer Mitch Miller's third successive No.1 had been a C&W topper by Marty Robbins. (B-side: Crazy with Love) **US 1**

↗ NO.54
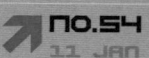
11 JAN •
SINGING THE BLUES (2.22)
Tommy Steele and The Steelmen (Melvin Endsley). "Britain's answer to Elvis" topped the chart before Presley and was the only one of manager Larry Parnes' stable of acts to reach No.1. (B-side: Rebel Rock)

↗ NO.55
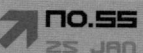
25 JAN •
1 FEB (EQUAL TOP) •
8 FEB ••
THE GARDEN OF EDEN (2.31)
Frankie Vaughan (Denise Norwood). This cover of Joe Valino's US hit was penned by the first solo female songwriter to compose a UK No.1. The song encountered airplay problems due to its semi-religious lyric. (B-side: Priscilla)

↗ NO.56
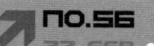
22 FEB •••••••
YOUNG LOVE (2.25)
Tab Hunter
(Carol Joyner, Ric Cartey).
A cover of Sonny James' US hit gave the film star the summer's big hit. It had originally been recorded by composer Cartey. (B-side: Red Sails in the Sunset) **US 1**

↗ NO.57

12 APR •••••
CUMBERLAND GAP (1.56)
Lonnie Donegan and His Skiffle Group (Traditional: arranged by Lonnie Donegan). The King of Skiffle scored the first of his three No.1s thanks to his high-powered rendition of this old US folk song. (B-side: Love Is Strange)

↗ NO.58
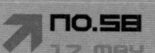
17 MAY •
ROCK-A-BILLY (2.12)
Guy Mitchell (Woody Harris, Eddie V Deane). The one-time country singer scored his fourth No.1 with this tribute to the C&W-meets-R&B musical style that Elvis introduced to the world. (B-side: Got a Feeling) **US 10**

↗ NO.59
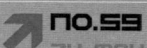
24 MAY ••
BUTTERFLY (2.19)
Andy Williams (Anthony September). His cover of Charlie Gracie's US hit gave balladeer Williams a brief ride on the rock 'n' roll bandwagon. (B-side: It Doesn't Take Very Long) **US 4**

↗ NO.60
7 JUN •••
YES TONIGHT, JOSEPHINE (2.28)
Johnnie Ray (Winfield Scott, Dorothy Goodman). "The Cry Guy" had his last No.1 with a song penned by Winfield Scott of R&B group The Cues. (B-side: No Wedding Today)

↗ NO.61
28 JUN ••
GAMBLIN' MAN (3.14) /
PUTTIN' ON THE STYLE (3.34)
Lonnie Donegan and His Skiffle Group (Woody Guthrie, Lonnie Donegan / traditional: arranged by Norman Cazden). The first live No.1 and first double-sided topper was available on a revolutionary "unbreakable" 78rpm single.

↗ NO.62

12 JUL •••••••
ALL SHOOK UP (1.56)
Elvis Presley with The Jordanaires (Otis Blackwell, Elvis Presley). The King's first No.1 had been released earlier by David Hill. It became the first record by a white act to top the US R&B chart. (B-side: That's When Your Heartaches Begin) **US 1**

↗ NO.63

30 AUG •••••••••
DIANA (2.23) **Paul Anka**
(Paul Anka). Recorded in just one take, 'Diana' earned Anka a gold record on

both sides of the Atlantic, with world sales of more than 10 million copies, including 1,240,000 in the UK. (B-side: Don't Gamble with Love) **US 1**

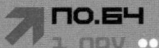

NO.64
1 NOV •••

THAT'LL BE THE DAY (2.15)
The Crickets (Buddy Holly, Jerry Allison, Norman Petty). Lead singer Buddy Holly first recorded this song as a solo artist. It was the first song the Quarry Men (Beatles) ever recorded. (B-side: I'm Lookin' for Someone to Love) **US 1**

NO.65
22 NOV •••••••

MARY'S BOY CHILD (4.17)
Harry Belafonte (Jester Hairston). The US Top 20 hit in 1956 sold a million copies in the UK in a (then) record six weeks. (B-side: Eden Was Just Like This) **US 12**

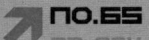

1958

NO.66
10 JAN ••

GREAT BALLS OF FIRE (1.50)
Jerry Lee Lewis (Otis Blackwell, Jack Hammer). Written for the film Juke Box Jamboree, this classic rock 'n' roll song was initially offered to Carl Perkins, who rejected it. (B-side: Mean Woman Blues) **US 2**

NO.67
24 JAN •••

JAILHOUSE ROCK (2.24) **Elvis Presley** (Jerry Leiber, Mike Stoller). The first record to enter at No.1 and rack up 250,000 advance orders was the title song from Elvis's third film. (B-side: Treat Me Nice) **US 1**

NO.68
14 FEB ••

THE STORY OF MY LIFE (2.12)
Michael Holliday (Burt Bacharach, Hal David). This Norrie Paramor-produced classic was Burt Bacharach's first No.1 and became the second chart-topper that had first been recorded by C&W star Marty Robbins. (B-side: Keep Your Heart)

NO.69
28 FEB ••••••••

MAGIC MOMENTS (2.37)
Perry Como (Burt Bacharach, Hal David). Bacharach and David's second successive No.1 was America's first official gold record and a winner at the first Grammy Awards. (B-side: Catch a Falling Star) **US 3**

NO.70
25 APR •••

WHOLE LOTTA WOMAN (2.35)
Marvin Rainwater (Marvin Rainwater). Only a minor US hit for the "Singing Cherokee", who, like many including Al Martino, was discovered on Arthur Godfrey's Talent Scouts television show. (B-side: Baby, Don't Go) **US 60**

NO.71
16 MAY ••••••

WHO'S SORRY NOW? (2.17)
Connie Francis (Ted Snyder, Bert Kalmar, Herman Ruby). After nine US flops, Connie topped the chart with a 1923 song suggested by her father, which she considered "too square". (B-side: You Were Only Fooling) **US 5**

NO.72
27 JUN •
4 JUL (EQUAL TOP) •

ON THE STREET WHERE YOU LIVE (2.42) **Vic Damone** (Alan Jay Lerner, Frederick Loewe). John Michael King first sang this show-stopping song in the award-winning My Fair Lady. It was the last of Mitch Miller's 16 No.1s. (B-side: Arrivederci Roma) **US 8**

NO.73
4 JUL (EQUAL TOP) •
11 JUL ••••••

ALL I HAVE TO DO IS DREAM (2.18) / **CLAUDETTE** (2.08)
The Everly Brothers (Felice and Boudleaux Bryant / Roy Orbison). The duo's first UK No.1 also topped the US pop, C&W and R&B charts. **US 1 / 30**

NO.74
22 AUG •••••

WHEN (2.25)
The Kalin Twins (Jack Reardon, Paul Evans). For the only time, one pair of brothers replaced another at the top. Newcomer Cliff Richard supported the twins on their UK tour. (B-side: Three O'Clock Thrill) **US 5**

NO.75
26 SEP ••••••

CAROLINA MOON (2.33) / **STUPID CUPID** (2.11)
Connie Francis (Benny Davis, Joe Burke / Neil Sedaka, Howard Greenfield). The song that stopped Cliff's debut disc, 'Move It', from reaching No.1 had been a US chart-topper in 1929 by Gene Austin. **US 14 / 8**

NO.76
7 NOV •••

IT'S ALL IN THE GAME (2.39)
Tommy Edwards (Charles Gates Dawes, Carl

Sigman). A re-recording of a song written in 1912 by a US vice-president, which Tommy first took into the US Top 20 in 1951. (B-side: Please Love Me Forever) **US 1**

NO.77
28 NOV •••

HOOTS MON (2.14)
Jack Good presents Lord Rockingham's XI (Harry Robinson). The first British penned and played rock 'n' roll chart-topper, from the Oh, Boy! TV show house band, sold more than 500,000. (B-side: Blue Train)

NO.78
19 DEC •••••

IT'S ONLY MAKE BELIEVE (2.12)
Conway Twitty (Conway Twitty, Jack Nance). Originally intended as the B-side. The song which took 10 minutes to write was a Top 10 hit for four different artists. (B-side: I'll Try) **US 1**

1959

NO.79
23 JAN •

THE DAY THE RAINS CAME (2.57)
Jane Morgan (Gilbert Becaud, Carl Sigman). Originally recorded by Gilbert Becaud as 'Le Jour Où la Pluie Viendra'. The B-side was Jane's French-language version. (B-side: Le Jour Où la Pluie Viendra) **US 21**

NO.80
30 JAN •••

ONE NIGHT (2.30) / **I GOT STUNG** (1.50)
Elvis Presley (Dave Bartholomew, Pearl King / Aaron Schroeder, David Hill). The record racked up 250,000 advance orders, and the A-side was originally an X-rated R&B song ('One Night of Sin') by Smiley Lewis. **US 4 / 8**

NO.81
20 FEB ••••

AS I LOVE YOU (2.52)
Shirley Bassey (Jay Livingston, Ray Evans). Jo Stafford recorded this song without success in 1955 and Carmen McRae sang it in the 1957 rock 'n' roll film The Big Beat. (B-side: Hands Across the Sea)

NO.82
20 MAR •

SMOKE GETS IN YOUR EYES (2.37)
The Platters (Jerome Kern, Otto Harbach). The late 1950s vocal group's only UK topper was first sung by Tamara in the 1933 musical Roberta. (B-side: No Matter What You Are) **US 1**

⤴ NO.83
27 MAR ••••
SIDE SADDLE (1.54)
Russ Conway (Russ Conway, aka Trevor Stanford). Originally written for the 1956 musical Beauty and the Beast, and first titled 'Come and Dance', it spent 30 weeks in the Top 30. (B-side: Pixilated Penguin)

⤴ NO.84
24 APR •••
IT DOESN'T MATTER ANYMORE (2.04) **Buddy Holly**
(Paul Anka). Holly's first posthumous release was his biggest hit. His friend Paul Anka donated his royalties to Buddy's widow. (B-side: Raining in My Heart) **US 13**

⤴ NO.85
15 MAY •••••
A FOOL SUCH AS I (2.30) /
I NEED YOUR LOVE TONIGHT (2.04)
Elvis Presley with The Jordanaires
(William Trader / Sid Wayne, Bix Reichner). The A-side was first recorded by another Colonel Tom Parker artist, Hank Snow. The single had a million-plus advance orders in the US. **US 2 / 4**

⤴ NO.86
19 JUN ••
ROULETTE (1.52)
Russ Conway (Russ Conway, aka Trevor Stanford). The year's top-selling artist earned his second silver disc for 250,000 sales of this second successive self-penned No.1. (B-side: Trampolina)

⤴ NO.87
3 JUL ••••
DREAM LOVER (2.29)
Bobby Darin (Bobby Darin). On his last and most successful teen-targeted hit, Darin was joined by R&B vocal group The Cues and pianist Neil Sedaka. (B-side: Bullmoose) **US 2**

⤴ NO.88
31 JUL ••••••
LIVING DOLL (2.36)
Cliff Richard and The Drifters
(Lionel Bart). Cliff's first No.1 was also a rare UK visitor to the US Top 40. It was a re-recording of a song he sang in the film Serious Charge. (B-side: Apron Strings) **US 30**

⤴ NO.89
11 SEP ••••
ONLY SIXTEEN
(2.10) **Craig Douglas**
(Barbara Campbell [aka Lou Adler, Herb Alpert, Sam Cooke]). Craig was only 18 when he topped the chart with this teen tune co-written and originally recorded by Sam Cooke. (B-side: My First Love Affair)

⤴ NO.90
9 OCT •
HERE COMES SUMMER (2.07)
Jerry Keller (Jerry Keller). Oddly, this self-penned No.1, which started out as the B-side, hit the top after summer had gone. (B-side: Time Has a Way) **US 14**

⤴ NO.91
16 OCT ••
MACK THE KNIFE (3.05)
Bobby Darin (Bertolt Brecht, Kurt Weill, Marc Blitzstein). The first Grammy Record of the Year was originally performed by Weill's wife, Lotte Lenya – whom Darin names-checks on his version. (B-side: Was There a Call for Me) **US 1**

⤴ NO.92
30 OCT •••••
TRAVELLIN' LIGHT (2.37)
Cliff Richard and The Shadows (Sid Tepper, Roy C Bennett). Written especially for Cliff by two of America's top songsmiths, it was one of his eight Top 20 entries in just 12 months. (B-side: Dynamite)

⤴ NO.93
4 DEC ••
18 DEC (EQUAL TOP) •
WHAT DO YOU WANT? (1.35)
Adam Faith (Les Vandyke). The shortest No.1 single, which was released by its composer on Woolworth's cheap cover version label, Embassy. (B-side: From Now Until Forever)

⤴ NO.94
18 DEC (EQUAL TOP) •
25 DEC •••••
WHAT DO YOU WANT TO MAKE THOSE EYES AT ME FOR? (2.06)
Emile Ford and The Checkmates (Joseph McCarthy, Howard Johnson, Jimmy Monaco). A million-selling revival of a 1916 song first performed by Henry Lewis in the show Follow Me. (B-side: Don't Tell Me Your Troubles)

1960

⤴ NO.95
29 JAN •
STARRY EYED (2.21)
Michael Holliday (Earl Shuman, Mort Garson). With vocal backing from the Mike Sammes Singers, Liverpool's first No.1 act of the 1960s hit with a song originally cut by US teen idol, and later property millionaire, Gary Stites. (B-side: The Steady Game)

⤴ NO.96
5 FEB ••••
WHY (2.27)
Anthony Newley (Bob Marcucci, Peter de Angelis). This multi-talented performer first hit the top with a cover of Frankie Avalon's US No.1. He re-recorded it with daughter Tara in 1992. (B-side: Anything You Wanna Do)

⤴ NO.97
18 MAR •
POOR ME (1.45)
Adam Faith (Les Vandyke). 'Poor Me' was also the title of the first autobiography from the first British act to reach the top five with his first seven hits. (B-side: The Reason)

⤴ NO.98
17 MAR ••
RUNNING BEAR (2.39)
Johnny Preston (J P Richardson). Composer Richardson (The Big Bopper), who also helped out on backing vocals, did not live to see his song chart. (B-side: My Heart Knows) **US 1**

⤴ NO.99
31 MAR ••••
MY OLD MAN'S A DUSTMAN (3.18)
Lonnie Donegan and His Group (Traditional: new lyrics by Lonnie Donegan, Peter Buchanan, Beverley Thorn). Skiffle music's sole survivor in the 1960s recorded his third chart-topper live at the Gaumont Cinema, Doncaster. (B-side: The Golden Vanity)

⤴ NO.100
28 APR •
DO YOU MIND (2.18)
Anthony Newley (Lionel Bart). The actor turned singer turned songwriter turned Vegas entertainer also charted in the US, despite being covered by Andy Williams. (B-side: Girls Were Made to Love and Kiss) **US 91**

⤴ NO.101
5 MAY •••••••
CATHY'S CLOWN (2.22)
The Everly Brothers (Don and Phil Everly). The first Warner Brothers release was a transatlantic topper. It's a true story about Don's old high school sweetheart. (B-side: Always It's You) **US 1**

⤴ NO.102
23 JUN ••
THREE STEPS TO HEAVEN (2.23)
Eddie Cochran (Eddie and Bob Cochran). Like Buddy Holly, Eddie's first posthumous release was his biggest hit. He was backed on the track by Buddy's band The Crickets. (B-side: Cut Across Shorty)

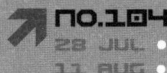

NO.103
7 JUL •••

GOOD TIMIN' (2.05)
Jimmy Jones (Fred Tobias, Clint Ballard Jr). What's the connection between chart-toppers Jimmy and Chrissie Hynde? They both fronted a group called The Pretenders before going solo. (B-side: Too Long Will Be Too Late) **US 3**

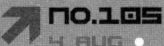

NO.104
28 JUL •
11 AUG ••

PLEASE DON'T TEASE (2.58)
Cliff Richard and The Shadows (Pete Chester, Bruce Welch). The first Cliff No.1 penned by a Shadow. Co-writer Chester is the son of 1940s / 50s comic and DJ "Cheerful" Charlie Chester. (B-side: Where Is My Heart)

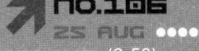

NO.105
4 AUG •

SHAKIN' ALL OVER (2.20)
Johnny Kidd and The Pirates (Frederick Heath, Gus Robinson). Regarded by many as the best early British rock 'n' roll record, it was written in 10 minutes just before the session as a B-side. (B-side: Yes Sir, That's My Baby)

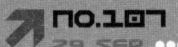

NO.106
25 AUG •••••

APACHE (2.53)
The Shadows (Jerry Lordan). The group's fourth single and first hit featured Cliff on bongos. It sold more than a million in Europe and was first recorded by Bert Weedon. (B-side: Quartermasters Stores)

NO.107
29 SEP •••

TELL LAURA I LOVE HER (2.41)
Ricky Valance (Jeff Barry, Ben Raleigh). The Welsh one-hit wonder scored with a cover of a death ditty originally recorded by Ray Peterson. As expected, it was banned by the BBC. (B-side: Once Upon a Time)

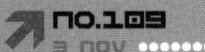

NO.108
20 OCT •

ONLY THE LONELY (KNOW HOW I FEEL) (2.23)
Roy Orbison (Roy Orbison, Joe Melson). The writer of earlier No.1 'Claudette' (Everly Brothers) hit the top with a song previously rejected by both Elvis and the Everlys. (B-side: Here Comes That Song Again) **US 2**

NO.109
3 NOV ••••••••

IT'S NOW OR NEVER (3.25)
Elvis Presley (Eduardo di Capua, Aaron Shroeder, Wally Gold). This adaptation of the 1901 operatic ode 'O Sole Mio' entered at No.1

and sold 1,210,000 in the UK in a record 45 days. (B-side: Make Me Know It) **US 1**

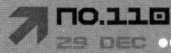

NO.110
29 DEC ••

I LOVE YOU (2.03)
Cliff Richard and The Shadows (Bruce Welch). This was the seventh British penned and performed No.1 in 1960 – equalling the complete total for the whole of the 1950s. (B-side: D in Love)

1961

NO.111
12 JAN ••

POETRY IN MOTION (2.30)
Johnny Tillotson (Paul Kauffman, Mike Anthony). Several acts rejected this song, which Johnny had to record twice, firstly in New York and then Nashville, before he got it perfect. (B-side: Princess, Princess) **US 2**

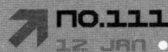

NO.112
26 JAN ••••

ARE YOU LONESOME TONIGHT? (3.05)
Elvis Presley with The Jordanaires (Ray Turk, Lou Handman). Many acts, including Al Jolson, earlier recorded this 1926 song. Elvis's "monologue" version was based on Blue Barron's 1950 rendition. (B-side: I Gotta Know) **US 1**

NO.113
23 FEB •

SAILOR (2.57)
Petula Clark (Fini Busch, Werner Scharfenburger). An Austrian song originally recorded by Lolita as 'Seemann' gave the one-time child star her first No.1. (B-side: My Heart)

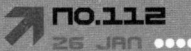

NO.114
2 MAR •••

WALK RIGHT BACK (2.16) / **EBONY EYES** (2.15)
The Everly Brothers (Sonny Curtis / John D Loudermilk). The A-side was composed by a member of The Crickets, who backed the brothers on the track. The flip side was the only No.1 about a plane crash. **US 7 / 8**

NO.115
23 MAR ••••••

WOODEN HEART (1.58)
Elvis Presley (Burt Kaempfert, Kay Twomey, Fred Wise, Ben Weisman). This G.I. Blues track was not deemed strong enough for a US release. A chart-topping cover there by Joe Dowell proved RCA wrong. (B-side: Tonight Is So Right for Love)

NO.116
4 MAY ••

BLUE MOON (2.17)
The Marcels (Richard Rodgers, Lorenz Hart). Producer Stu Philips combined the group's rendition of doo-wop song 'Zoom' with this standard, and came up with a transatlantic No.1. (B-side: Goodbye to Love) **US 1**

NO.117
18 MAY •

ON THE REBOUND (2.07)
Floyd Cramer (Floyd Cramer). This noted session man (Elvis, Jim Reeves, etc) allegedly based this song on fellow Nashville session pianist Don Robertson's 'Instrumental in A'. (B-side: Mood Indigo) **US 4**

NO.118
25 MAY •

YOU'RE DRIVING ME CRAZY (3.57)
The Temperance Seven (Walter Donaldson). The first of many No.1s for producer George Martin had first been heard sung by Eddie Foy Jr and Adele Astaire in the 1930 show Smiles. (B-side: Charley My Boy)

NO.119
1 JUN ••••

SURRENDER (1.51)
Elvis Presley with The Jordanaires (Ernesto, B G de Curtis; English lyrics by Doc Pomus, Mort Shuman). Elvis's eighth No.1 was written in Italy in 1911 as 'Torna a Sorrento'. It coincided with his last live appearance for eight years. (B-side: Lonely Man) **US 1**

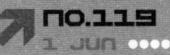

NO.120
29 JUN •••

RUNAWAY (2.20)
Del Shannon (Del Shannon, Max Crook). This self-penned debut disc, which featured the Musitron – a forerunner of the synthesizer – was a transatlantic topper. (B-side: Jody) **US 1**

NO.121
20 JUL ••

TEMPTATION (2.09)
The Everly Brothers (Nacio Herb Brown, Arthur Freed). Despite missing the US Top 20, the brothers made it two UK No.1s in a row with a song written for Bing Crosby's 1933 film Going Hollywood. (B-side: Stick with Me) **US 27**

NO.122
3 AUG •

WELL I ASK YOU (2.14)
Eden Kane (Les Vandyke). An original UK chart song that was covered stateside by past US chart-topper Kay Starr and future

American No.1 act Bobby Vinton. (B-side: Before I Lose My Mind)

↗ **NO.123**
10 AUG ●●●
YOU DON'T KNOW (2.40)
Helen Shapiro (John Schroeder, Mike Hawker). Helen became the youngest female ever to top the chart, which she did aged 14 years, 316 days. Helen's producer was Norri Paramor whose assistant John Schroeder had been introduced to the Bethnal Green girl by singing coach Maurice Burman (B-side: Marvellous Lie)

↗ **NO.124**
31 AUG ●●●
28 SEP ●●●
JOHNNY REMEMBER ME (2.37)
John Leyton (Geoff Goddard). After actor Leyton sang this death ditty on TV's Harper's West One (he played a pop singer), it amassed an impressive 40,000 advance orders. (B-side: There Must Be)

↗ **NO.125**
21 SEP ●
REACH FOR THE STARS (2.55) /
CLIMB EV'RY MOUNTAIN (3.09)
Shirley Bassey (Udo Jurgens: English lyrics by David West / Richard Rodgers, Oscar Hammerstein II). The A-side started in Germany as 'Woner Ich Auch Komm, Wohin Ich Auch Geh' and the flip side was from the Austria-set The Sound of Music.

↗ **NO.126**
5 OCT ●
KON-TIKI (1.53)
The Shadows (Michael Carr). Veteran songsmith Carr was inspired to write this about the balsawood raft that sailed 4,300 miles from Peru to Polynesia. (B-side: 36-24-36)

↗ **NO.127**
12 OCT ●
MICHAEL (2.46)
The Highwaymen (Traditional: arranged by Dave Fisher). A major US DJ poll named this adaptation of a Georgia slave song by five Connecticut University students Record of the Year. (B-side: Santiano) **US 1**

↗ **NO.128**
19 OCT ●●●
WALKIN' BACK TO HAPPINESS (2.29) **Helen Shapiro** (John Schroeder, Mike Hawker). Helen now became the only act to notch up two No.1 singles while still at school. It sold a million worldwide. (B-side: Kiss 'n Run) **US 100**

↗ **NO.129**
9 NOV ●●●●
(MARIE'S THE NAME) HIS LATEST FLAME (2.07) /
LITTLE SISTER (2.31)
Elvis Presley (Doc Pomus, Mort Shuman). Elvis's record-breaking fifth No.1 in 12 months. The A-side was previously rejected by Bobby Vee and Bobby Darin, but recorded by Del Shannon. **US 4 / 5**

↗ **NO.130**
7 DEC ●●●
TOWER OF STRENGTH (2.07)
Frankie Vaughan (Burt Bacharach, Bob Hilliard). A cover of Gene McDaniels' US hit, which was also recorded at the time by newcomer Paul Raven (Gary Glitter). (B-side: Rachel)

↗ **NO.131**
28 DEC ●●
MOON RIVER (2.35)
Danny Williams (Henry Mancini, Johnny Mercer). This Oscar-winning song was first an instrumental American hit for composer Mancini and a vocal hit for R&B artist Jerry Butler. (B-side: A Weaver of Dreams)

1962

↗ **NO.132**
11 JAN ●●●●●●
THE YOUNG ONES (3.10)
Cliff Richard and The Shadows (Sid Tepper, Roy C Bennett). This million-seller (which had advance orders of 524,000) was the first UK disc to enter at No.1. It stopped 'Let's Twist Again' from reaching the top. (B-side: We Say Yeah)

↗ **NO.133**
22 FEB ●●●●
ROCK-A-HULA BABY (1.59) /
CAN'T HELP FALLING IN LOVE (3.04)
Elvis Presley with The Jordanaires (Fred Wise, Ben Weisman, Dolores Fuller / George David Weiss, Hugo Peretti, Luigi Creatore). Both tracks come from the soundtrack to Elvis's most successful film Blue Hawaii. The second track was based on French song 'Plaisir d'Amour'. **US 23 / 2**

↗ **NO.134**
22 MAR ●●●●●●●●
WONDERLAND LAND (2.01)
The Shadows
(Jerry Lordan). The group's biggest UK hit

stopped Bruce Channel from hitting the top with the timeless 'Hey Baby'. (B-side: Stars Fell on Stockton)

↗ **NO.135**
17 MAY ●
NUT ROCKER (1.59)
B Bumble and The Stingers (Pyotr Ilyich Tchaikovsky). This LA session group covered the equally quirkily named Jack B Nimble & the Quicks' rockin' treatment of Tchaikovsky's 'Nutcracker'. The producer was Kim Fowley. Fowley was the American equivalent of the UK's Jonathan King. (B-side: Nautilus) **US 23**

↗ **NO.136**
24 MAY ●●●●●
GOOD LUCK CHARM (2.24)
Elvis Presley with The Jordanaires (Aaron Schroeder, Wally Gold). His 16th US No.1 was also his sixth and final transatlantic No.1. It came from the pen of the 'It's Now or Never' writers. (B-side: Anything That's Part of You) **US 1**

↗ **NO.137**
28 JUN ●●
COME OUTSIDE (2.50)
Mike Sarne with Wendy Richard (Charles Blackwell). A dancehall novelty featured EastEnder Richard (Pauline Fowler). It was the first record by a male / female duo to reach the top. (B-side: Fountain of Love)

↗ **NO.138**
12 JUL ●●
I CAN'T STOP LOVING YOU (4.11)
Ray Charles (Don Gibson). Composer Gibson's original C&W version of Ray's biggest hit had been a million-selling US Top 10 entry in 1958. (B-side: Born to Lose) **US 1**

↗ **NO.139**
26 JUL ●●●●●●●
I REMEMBER YOU (2.03)
Frank Ifield (Johnny Mercer, Victor Scherzinger). This rare UK visitor to the US top five sold 1,096,000 in Britain. The song was first sung by Dorothy Lamour in the 1942 film The Fleet's In. (B-side: I Listen to My Heart) **US 5**

↗ **NO.140**
13 SEP ●●●
SHE'S NOT YOU (2.10)
Elvis Presley with The Jordanaires (Doc Pomus, Jerry Leiber, Mike Stoller). This single completed Elvis' second run of four No.1 hits in a row. It was a rare collaboration by these three famous songwriters. (B-side: Just Tell Her Jim Said Hello) **US 5**

↘ **CHART-TOPPER No.141:** The Tornados were the first British group to go to No.1 in America. The group was Billy Fury's backing band and featured German bass player Heinz Burt, ex-Pirates lead guitarist Alan Caddy, rhythm guitarist George Bellamy, organist Roger La Verne and drummer Clem Cattini

↗ **No.141**
4 OCT ●●●●●
TELSTAR (3.15)
The Tornados (Joe Meek).
The first record by a British group to head the US chart. It was inspired by the launch of the first communications satellite and sold 967,000 copies in the UK. (B-side: Jungle Fever) **US 1**

↗ **No.142**
8 NOV ●●●●●
LOVESICK BLUES (2.16)
Frank Ifield (Irving Mills, Cliff Friend). Frank's version of this 1922 song that Hank Williams made famous in 1949 had 200,000 advance orders in the UK. (B-side: She Taught Me How to Yodel) **US 44**

↗ **No.143**
13 DEC ●●●
RETURN TO SENDER (2.08)
Elvis Presley with **The Jordanaires** (Otis Blackwell, Winfield Scott). For the second year in a row, Elvis clocked up four No.1s. It was the last US record to reach No.1 for 18 months. (B-side: Where Do You Come From) **US 2**

↗ **No.144**
3 JAN ●●●
THE NEXT TIME (2.56) /
BACHELOR BOY (2.01)
Cliff Richard and The Shadows

(The second track listed from 10 Jan only) (Buddy Kane, Philip Springer / Bruce Welch, Cliff Richard). Both tracks were featured in Cliff's film Summer Holiday and the prophetic B-side was the first chart-topping song that he had a hand in writing. **US 0 / 99**

↗ **No.145**
24 JAN ●
DANCE ON! (2.22)
The Shadows
(Valerie and Elaine Murtagh, Ray Adams). The group dethroned their vocalist Cliff with a song penned for them by Columbia Records label-mates The Avons. Kathy Kirby reached No.11 with her vocal version of this song in 1963 later in the summer. (B-side: All Day)

↗ **NO.146**
31 JAN ●●●
DIAMONDS (2.24)
Jet Harris and Tony Meehan
(Jerry Lordan). The first instrumental duo to reach No.1 replaced their former group, The Shadows. Like the latter's first No.1 without Cliff, 'Apache', it was written by Lordan. (B-side: Footstomp)

↗ **NO.147**
21 FEB ●●●
THE WAYWARD WIND (2.44)
Frank Ifield (Stan Labowsky, Herb Newman). Gogi Grant's 1956 US chart-topper made Frank the first UK act to score three No.1s in a row. (B-side: I'm Smiling Now)

↗ **NO.148**
14 MAR ●●
4 APR ●
SUMMER HOLIDAY (2.05)
Cliff Richard and The Shadows
(Bruce Welch, Brian Bennett). The Shadows penned this film theme, which gave them their last No.1 with Cliff, and stopped The Beatles' 'Please Please Me' from reaching No.1. (B-side: Dancing Shoes)

↗ **NO.149**
28 MAR ●
FOOT TAPPER (2.33)
The Shadows
(Hank B Marvin, Bruce Welch). This instrumental completed a trio of No.1s for producer Norrie Paramor and it gave composer Welch his second in a row. (B-side: The Breeze and I)

↗ **NO.150**
11 APR ●●●
HOW DO YOU DO IT? (1.54)
Gerry and The Pacemakers
(Mitch Murray). The first Beat Boom No.1 was originally written for Adam Faith and previously recorded by The Beatles. (B-side: Away from You) **US 9**

↗ **NO.151**
2 MAY ●●●●●●●
FROM ME TO YOU (1.56)
The Beatles (John Lennon, Paul McCartney). The first of 17 No.1s by the world's most successful group. In the US, a cover by Del Shannon grabbed more sales at the time. (B-side: Thank You Girl) **US 41**

↗ **NO.152**
20 JUN ●●●●
I LIKE IT (2.14)
Gerry and The Pacemakers (Mitch Murray). A song first recorded by The Dave Clark Five made the Merseybeat band the first act to reach the top with their first two releases. (B-side: It's Happened to Me) **US 17**

↗ **NO.153**
18 JUL ●●
CONFESSIN' (THAT I LOVE YOU) (2.04) **Frank Ifield**
(Al J Neiburg, Doc Daugherty, Ellis Reynolds). Ifield's fourth No.1 in 12 months had first been a US hit for Louis Armstrong, Guy Lombardo and Rudy Vallee in 1930. (B-side: Waltzing Matilda) **US 58**

↗ **NO.154**
1 AUG ●
(YOU'RE THE) DEVIL IN DISGUISE (2.19) **Elvis Presley with The Jordanaires** (Bill Giant, Bernie Baum, Florence Kaye). The only American recording to reach the top that year was also Elvis's last newly recorded No.1 of the decade. (B-side: Please Don't Drag That String Around) **US 3**

↗ **NO.155**
8 AUG ●●
SWEETS FOR MY SWEET (2.29)
The Searchers
(Doc Pomus, Mort Shuman). The Drifters originally recorded the song that was the fourth No.1 in four months by Liverpool groups. (B-side: It's All Been a Dream)

↗ **NO.156**
22 AUG ●●●
BAD TO ME (2.18)
Billy J Kramer and The Dakotas
(John Lennon, Paul McCartney). John Lennon composed this song while he was on holiday in Spain with his and Kramer's manager Brian Epstein. (B-side: I Call Your Name) **US 9**

↗ **NO.157**
12 SEP ●●●●
28 NOV ●●
SHE LOVES YOU (2.20)
The Beatles
(John Lennon, Paul McCartney). Its 300,000 advance orders broke the UK record. It went on to sell 1,890,000 copies, making it the Fab Four's most commercially successful single. (B-side: I'll Get You) **US 1**

↗ **NO.158**
10 OCT ●●●
DO YOU LOVE ME (2.22)
Brian Poole and The Tremeloes
(Berry Gordy Jr). The first southern band to top the chart in the Beat Boom era did so with a cover of a Motown song first recorded by The Contours. (B-side: Why Can't You Love Me?)

↗ **NO.159**
31 OCT ●●●●
YOU'LL NEVER WALK ALONE
(2.39) **Gerry and The Pacemakers**
(Richard Rodgers, Oscar Hammerstein II). Marsden's men made it three out of three with their update of a song first performed by Jan Clayton in the 1945 musical Carousel. (B-side: It's All Right) **US 48**

↗ **NO.160**
12 DEC ●●●●●
I WANT TO HOLD YOUR HAND
(2.25) **The Beatles**
(John Lennon, Paul McCartney). The single that started the "British Invasion" sold more than a million in its first three days in the UK and eventually 10 million worldwide. (B-side: This Boy) **US 1**

1964

↗ **NO.161**
16 JAN ●●
GLAD ALL OVER (2.42)
Dave Clark Five
(Dave Clark, Mike Smith). Their third single on their third label launched the only British group that really challenged The Beatles worldwide in 1964. (B-side: I Know You) **US 6**

↗ **NO.162**
30 JAN ●●●
NEEDLES AND PINS (2.12)
The Searchers
(Sonny Bono, Jack Nitzsche). The group's biggest transatlantic hit was co-written by Cher's first husband, Sonny Bono, and first recorded by Jackie De Shannon. (B-side: Saturday Night Out) **US 13**

↗ **NO.163**
20 FEB ●
DIANE (2.31)
The Bachelors
(Erno Rapee, Lew Pollack). The song that made the trio the earliest Irish chart-toppers was first heard in cinemas in 1927 during the silent movie Seventh Heaven. (B-side: The Stars Will Remember) **US 10**

↗ **NO.164**
27 FEB ●●●
ANYONE WHO HAD A HEART (2.51)
Cilla Black
(Burt Bacharach, Hal David). Dionne Warwick originally recorded the song that sold a lorra lorra records for Cilla – almost passing the million sales mark. (B-side: Just for You)

↘ **CHART-TOPPER NO.156, 165:** Liverpudlian Billy J Kramer (born William Howard Ashton) was backed by Manchester group The Dakotas on both No.1s. It was John Lennon who had the idea of a fab middle initial 'J' for Kramer, which stood for precisely nothing

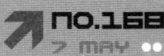

NO.168
7 MAY ●●

DON'T THROW YOUR LOVE AWAY
(2.17) **The Searchers**
(Jimmy Wisner, Billy Jackson). The Liverpool act's third No.1 in nine months had first been recorded as a throwaway B-side by US R&B group The Orlons. (B-side: I Pretend I'm with You) **US 16**

NO.169
21 MAY ●

JULIET (2.22)
The Four Pennies (Mike Wilsh, Fritz Fryer, Lionel Morton). This self-penned ballad was originally intended to be the B-side. It was the only UK No.1 of 1964 not to chart in America. (B-side: Tell Me Girl)

NO.170
28 MAY ●●●●

YOU'RE MY WORLD (2.59) **Cilla Black**
(Umberto Bindi, Gino Paoli, Carl Sigman). Cilla's second successive chart-topper was the fourth UK No.1 with lyrics by Carl Sigman. (B-side: Suffer Now I Must) **US 26**

NO.171
25 JUN ●●

IT'S OVER (2.48)
Roy Orbison (Roy Orbison, Bill Dees). The first US recorded No.1 for 11 months also appeared on two chart-topping greatest hits albums in 1975 and 1978. (B-side: Indian Wedding) **US 9**

NO.172
9 JUL ●

THE HOUSE OF THE RISING SUN (4.29)
The Animals (Traditional: arranged by Alan Price). The group knew this traditional blues song from Josh White's version, although they based their rendition on Bob Dylan's recording of it. (B-side: Talkin' 'Bout You) **US 1**

NO.173
16 JUL ●

IT'S ALL OVER NOW (3.27)
The Rolling Stones (Bobby and Shirley Womack). Recorded in Chicago's Chess studios, the Stones' first No.1 was penned and originally recorded by Bobby Womack's act The Valentinos. (B-side: Good Times, Bad Times) **US 26**

NO.174
23 JUL ●●●

A HARD DAY'S NIGHT (2.28)
The Beatles (John Lennon, Paul McCartney). The title song from the group's first film, the soundtrack of which sold a million in the US in a record four days. (B-side: Things We Said Today) **US 1**

NO.165
19 MAR ●●

LITTLE CHILDREN (2.46)
Billy J Kramer and The Dakotas
(Mort Shuman, John Leslie McFarland). The first non Lennon and McCartney-penned Kramer single was their biggest US hit. Manager Brian Epstein did not want it released but Kramer insisted. (B-side: They Remind Me of You) **US 7**

NO.166
2 APR ●●●

CAN'T BUY ME LOVE (2.12)
The Beatles (John Lennon, Paul McCartney).

This single broke advance orders records on both sides of the Atlantic (one million in the UK and two million in the US) and headed an all-Beatles US top five. (B-side: You Can't Do That) **US 1**

NO.167
23 APR ●●

A WORLD WITHOUT LOVE (2.39)
Peter and Gordon
(John Lennon, Paul McCartney). Lennon and McCartney's eighth No.1 as composers in just 14 months and fifth in the US in 22 weeks. This was a song rejected by Billy J Kramer which the two former Westminister School boys snapped up. (B-side: If I Were You) **US 1**

NO.175
13 AUG ••
DO WAH DIDDY DIDDY (2.23)
Manfred Mann (Jeff Barry, Ellie Greenwich).
The seventh UK record to top the US charts in just eight months was a cover of a song first recorded by US R&B group The Exciters.
(B-side: What You Gonna Do) **US 1**

NO.176
27 AUG ••
HAVE I THE RIGHT (2.57)
The Honeycombs
(Ken Howard, Alan Blaikley). The last No.1 for legendary producer Joe Meek was penned by the group's managers, who later wrote many hits for Dave Dee and The Herd.
(B-side: Please Don't Pretend Again) **US 5**

NO.177
10 SEP ••
YOU REALLY GOT ME (2.12)
The Kinks (Ray Davies).
This timeless rock classic followed two flops for the group that had earlier supported The Beatles, Dave Clark Five and The Hollies on tour. (B-side: It's All Right) **US 7**

NO.178
24 SEP ••
I'M INTO SOMETHING GOOD (2.33)
Herman's Hermits (Carole King, Gerry Goffin). The youthful Manchester combo started their enviable run of transatlantic hits with a cover of an Earl Jean R&B record.
(B-side: Your Hand in Mine) **US 13**

NO.179
8 OCT ••
12 NOV •
OH, PRETTY WOMAN (2.59)
Roy Orbison (Roy Orbison, Bill Dees).
The Big O scored his only transatlantic topper with the second No.1 he had written about his wife, Claudette (see No.73).
(B-side: Yo Te Amo Maria) **US 1**

NO.180
22 OCT •••
(THERE'S) ALWAYS SOMETHING THERE TO REMIND ME (2.36)
Sandie Shaw (Burt Bacharach, Hal David).
Adam Faith discovered the 17-year-old barefoot pop princess who hit the top with a ballad earlier recorded by R&B artist Lou Johnson. (B-side: Don't You Know) **US 52**

NO.181
19 NOV ••
BABY LOVE (2.36)
The Supremes
(Brian Holland, Lamont Dozier, Eddie Holland).

The first single by a female group to top the chart was also Motown Records' first UK No.1. (B-side: Ask Any Girl) **US 1**

NO.182
3 DEC •
LITTLE RED ROOSTER (3.04)
The Rolling Stones (Willie Dixon).
Blues legend Dixon wrote this song for Chess R&B artist Howlin' Wolf. Perhaps surprisingly, this Stones single was not released stateside.
(B-side: Off the Hook)

NO.183
18 DEC •••••
I FEEL FINE (2.18)
The Beatles (John Lennon, Paul McCartney).
The Christmas No.1 in the UK and US claimed to include the first use of feedback guitar and amassed record UK advance orders of 750,000. (B-side: She's a Woman) **US 1**

1965

NO.184
14 JAN ••
YEH, YEH (2.46)
Georgie Fame and The Blue Flames (Rogers Grant, Pat Patrick, Jon Hendricks). The song originally recorded by Hendricks' jazz trio – Hendricks, Lambert and Ross – had been a US instrumental hit for Mongo Santamaria.
(B-side: Preach and Teach) **US 21**

NO.185
28 JAN •
GO NOW (3.11)
The Moody Blues (Larry Banks, Milton Bennett). The Midlands band's transatlantic Top 10 hit was earlier recorded by R&B artist Bessie Banks, whose husband Larry composed it for her. (B-side: It's Easy Child) **US 10**

NO.186
4 FEB ••
YOU'VE LOST THAT LOVIN' FEELIN' (3.41)
The Righteous Brothers (Phil Spector, Barry Mann, Cynthia Weil). This classic Phil Spector-produced pop record reached the UK Top 20 on three separate occasions. It's the most played song ever on US radio. (B-side: There's a Woman) **US 1**

NO.187
18 FEB •
TIRED OF WAITING FOR YOU (2.30)
The Kinks (Ray Davies). The group's third successive self-penned transatlantic Top 10 entry in just six months. (B-side: Come on Now) **US 6**

NO.188
25 FEB ••
I'LL NEVER FIND ANOTHER YOU (2.41)
The Seekers (Tom Springfield). The first Australian act to top the UK charts, and the first to reach the US top five, did so with a song written and produced by Dusty' Springfield's brother Tom. (B-side: Open Up Them Pearly Gates) **US 4**

NO.189
11 MAR •
IT'S NOT UNUSUAL (2.00)
Tom Jones (Les Reed, Gordon Mills). The song was composed for Sandie Shaw. The record, which featured noted session guitarist Jimmy Page, returned to the Top 20 in 1987.
(B-side: To Wait for Love) **US 10**

NO.190
18 MAR •••
THE LAST TIME (3.40)
The Rolling Stones (Mick Jagger, Keith Richard). For the first time, the group both hit with a self-penned song and scored a transatlantic Top 20 entry. (B-side: Play with Fire) **US 9**

NO.191
8 APR •
CONCRETE AND CLAY (2.16)
Unit Four Plus Two (Brian Parker, Tommy Moeller). The only chart-topper to mention either 'concrete' or 'clay' lost a US chart battle to a sound-alike cover by Eddie Rambeau.
(B-side: When I Fall in Love) **US 28**

NO.192
15 APR •
THE MINUTE YOU'RE GONE (2.19)
Cliff Richard (Jimmy Gately). Recorded in Nashville with producer Billy 'Stand By Your Man' Sherrill. The song had been a US country No.1 by Sonny James. (B-side: Just Another Guy)

NO.193
22 APR •••
TICKET TO RIDE (3.09)
The Beatles (John Lennon, Paul McCartney).
Actually written by John alone, the first single from the group's second film Help! was voted the top single of 1965 in the Melody Maker poll. (B-side: Yes It Is) **US 1**

NO.194
13 MAY •
KING OF THE ROAD (2.27)
Roger Miller (Roger Miller). Oddly, among the Grammy awards earned by this country track were ones for Best Contemporary Rock & Roll

Recording and Performance. (B-side: Atta Boy Girl) **US 4**

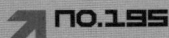

NO.195
20 MAY ●

WHERE ARE YOU NOW (2.45)
Jackie Trent (Jackie Trent, Tony Hatch). The UK's top female British songwriter of the 1960s scored with a song that gave future husband Tony Hatch his fifth No.1 in just two years. (B-side: On the Other Side of the Tracks)

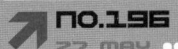

NO.196
27 MAY ●●●

LONG LIVE LOVE (2.39)
Sandie Shaw (Chris Andrews). Prolific hit writer Andrews' only No.1. Despite Sandie singing it on The Ed Sullivan Show, this big European hit failed to chart in the US. (B-side: I've Heard About Him)

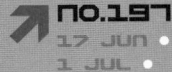

NO.197
17 JUN ●
1 JUL ●

CRYING IN THE CHAPEL (2.24)
Elvis Presley with The Jordanaires (Artie Glenn). Cut at the same session as 1960 No.1 'Surrender'. The song was written by Glenn for his teenage son, Artie Jr, who had a US hit with it in 1953. (B-side: I Believe in the Man in the Sky) **US 3**

NO.198
24 JUN ●
8 JUL ●●

I'M ALIVE (2.24)
The Hollies (Clint Ballard Jr). The group's first No.1 (and their last for 23 years) had been written by Ballard for Wayne Fontana and the Mindbenders. (B-side: You Know He Did)

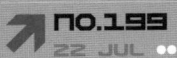

NO.199
22 JUL ●●

MR TAMBOURINE MAN (2.19)
The Byrds (Bob Dylan). The first Dylan-penned topper was also the first No.1 by a US group for four years. Jim McGuinn was the only Byrd who actually played an instrument on the track: the legendary 12-string Rickenbacker (B-side: I Knew I'd Want You) **US 1**

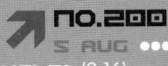

NO.200
5 AUG ●●●

HELP! (2.16)
The Beatles (John Lennon, Paul McCartney). Lennon wrote this movie title song alone. It hit as the group made their ground-breaking appearance at New York's Shea Stadium. (B-side: I'm Down) **US 1**

NO.201
26 AUG ●●

I GOT YOU BABE (3.07)
Sonny and Cher (Sonny Bono). These hippie-styled former Phil Spector session singers were the most talked about new act of 1965. This No.1 started out as a B-side. (B-side: It's Gonna Rain) **US 1**

NO.202
9 SEP ●●

(I CAN'T GET NO) SATISFACTION (3.45) **The Rolling Stones** (Mick Jagger, Keith Richard). This legendary rock track was recorded in the US and gave the Stones their first American No.1 before being released in the UK. (B-side: Spider and the Fly) **US 1**

NO.203
23 SEP ●

MAKE IT EASY ON YOURSELF (3.12) **The Walker Brothers** (Burt Bacharach, Hal David). The American trio relocated to the UK and hit the top with an update of an earlier Jerry Butler US hit. It was Bacharach's sixth No.1. (B-side: But I Do) **US 16**

NO.204
30 SEP ●●●●●

TEARS (2.48)
Ken Dodd (Billy Uhr, Frank Capano). The man voted Top Show Business Personality of 1965 had the year's biggest seller with 1,521,000 copies sold in total. Rudy Vallee had made the song popular in 1931. (B-side: You and I)

NO.205
4 NOV ●●●

GET OFF OF MY CLOUD (2.54) **The Rolling Stones** (Mick Jagger, Keith Richard). Their fifth No.1 in a row was also their second successive self-composed transatlantic chart-topper. (B-side: The Singer Not the Song) **US 1**

NO.206
25 NOV ●●●

THE CARNIVAL IS OVER (3.09) **The Seekers** (Tom Springfield). This single, which sold 1,400,000 in the UK, stopped The Who's anthemic classic 'My Generation' from reaching No.1. (B-side: We Shall Not Be Moved)

NO.207
16 DEC ●●●●●

DAY TRIPPER (2.48) / **WE CAN WORK IT OUT** (2.47)
The Beatles (John Lennon, Paul McCartney). Their third successive Christmas No.1. In the US, both sides independently reached the top five. **US 5 / 1**

1966

NO.208
20 JAN ●

KEEP ON RUNNING (2.42)
Spencer Davis Group (Jackie Edwards). After four covers of US R&B songs failed to break them, the Steve Winwood-fronted group scored with a song penned by ska star Edwards. (B-side: High Time Baby) **US 76**

NO.209
27 JAN ●●●

MICHELLE (2.22)
The Overlanders (John Lennon, Paul McCartney). Three days after it was cut, the group's version of the Grammy-winning bilingual Beatles ballad was on sale, and three weeks later it was top. (B-side: Cradle of Love)

NO.210
17 FEB ●●●●

THESE BOOTS ARE MADE FOR WALKIN' (2.41)
Nancy Sinatra (Lee Hazlewood). With more than a dozen moderate sellers behind her, Nancy had a hit big enough to stop the Stones' '19th Nervous Breakdown' from making No.1. (B-side: The City Never Sleeps at Night) **US 1**

NO.211
17 MAR ●●●●

THE SUN AIN'T GONNA SHINE ANYMORE (3.02) **The Walker Brothers** (Bob Crewe, Bob Gaudio). For the second time in six months, the trio hit No.1 with a cover of a lost love lament. This time Frankie Valli recorded the song first. (B-side: After the Lights Go Out) **US 13**

NO.212
14 APR ●●

SOMEBODY HELP ME (2.00)
Spencer Davis Group (Jackie Edwards). Four months after their debut No.1, the group returned to the top with another Chris Blackwell-produced, Jackie Edwards-penned song. (B-side: Stevie's Blues) **US 47**

NO.213
28 APR ●

YOU DON'T HAVE TO SAY YOU LOVE ME (2.47)
Dusty Springfield (Pino Donaggio, Vito Pallavicini, Vicki Wickham, Simon Napier-Bell). Dusty appeared in the 1965 San Remo Song Festival in Italy, and had an international hit with her English rendition of the winning song. (B-side: Every Ounce of Strength) **US 4**

↗ NO.214
5 MAY •••

PRETTY FLAMINGO (2.30)
Manfred Mann (Mark Barkan). Tommy Vann first recorded the song that gave the group their last hit with singer Paul Jones, and their only hit featuring bassist Jack Bruce. (B-side: You're Standing Up) **US 29**

↗ NO.215
26 MAY •

PAINT IT BLACK (3.45)
The Rolling Stones (Mick Jagger, Keith Richard). Brian Jones's sitar playing featured on this transatlantic No.1, which prevented the Troggs' 'Wild Thing' from reaching the top. (B-side: Long Long While) **US 1**

↗ NO.216
2 JUN •••

STRANGERS IN THE NIGHT (2.36)
Frank Sinatra (Bert Kaempfert, Charlie Singleton, Eddie Snyder). German composer Kaempfert's second transatlantic topper gave Ol' Blue Eyes his only one. From the movie A Man Could Get Killed. (B-side: My Kind of Town) **US 1**

↗ NO.217
23 JUN ••

PAPERBACK WRITER (2.17)
The Beatles (John Lennon, Paul McCartney). Soon after their last live show, the group made it 10 toppers in a row with this Paul-penned paean to a different kind of writer. (B-side: Rain) **US 1**

↗ NO.218
7 JUL ••

SUNNY AFTERNOON (3.32)
The Kinks (Ray Davies).
The group's third UK No.1 was also a hit in many other territories and was their last major US Top 40 entry of the 1960s. (B-side: I'm Not Like Everybody Else) **US 14**

↗ NO.219
21 JUL •

GET AWAY (2.32)
Georgie Fame and The Blue Flames (Clive Powell). Fame's only self-penned topper was written as a TV jingle to advertise Esso petrol. (B-side: El Bandido) **US 70**

↗ NO.220
28 JUL •

OUT OF TIME (3.35)
Chris Farlowe and The Thunderbirds (Mick Jagger, Keith Richard). The No.1 single when England won the football World Cup – a feat neither Farlowe nor the team has repeated. (B-side: Baby Make It Soon)

↗ NO.221
4 AUG ••

WITH A GIRL LIKE YOU (2.06)
The Troggs (Reg Presley).
The charismatic group's only UK No.1 had been on the B-side of their earlier US chart-topper 'Wild Thing'. (B-side: I Want You) **US 29**

↗ NO.222
18 AUG ••••

YELLOW SUBMARINE (2.37) /
ELEANOR RIGBY (2.05)
The Beatles (John Lennon, Paul McCartney). 'Yellow Submarine', sung by Ringo, completed the group's record run of 11 successive chart-toppers and stopped 'God Only Knows' (The Beach Boys) from reaching No.1. **US 2 / 11**

↗ NO.223
15 SEP •

ALL OR NOTHING (3.01)
The Small Faces (Steve Marriott, Ronnie Lane). This self-produced track, the group's only No.1, achieved nothing in the US – unlike their later singles 'Itchycoo Park' and 'Tin Soldier'. (B-side: Understanding)

↗ NO.224
22 SEP •••••

DISTANT DRUMS (2.52) **Jim Reeves** (Cindy Walker). Two years after his death, Reeves scored his only No.1 with a war song that stopped The Who from scoring a No.1 with 'I'm a Boy'. (B-side: Old Tige) **US 45**

↗ NO.225
27 OCT •••

REACH OUT I'LL BE THERE (2.55)
The Four Tops (Brian Holland, Lamont Dozier, Eddie Holland). The legendary Motown quartet's only No.1 on both sides of the Atlantic returned to the Top 20 when remixed by Stock Aitken Waterman in 1988. (B-side: Until You Love Someone) **US 1**

↗ NO.226
17 NOV ••

GOOD VIBRATIONS (3.35)
The Beach Boys (Brian Wilson, Mike Love). Seventeen recording sessions in four different studios over a six-month period produced one of the greatest pop records of all time. (B-side: Wendy) **US 1**

↗ NO.227
1 DEC •••••••

GREEN, GREEN GRASS OF HOME (3.02) **Tom Jones** (Claude 'Curly' Putnam Jr). A country-penned death ditty that had first been recorded by Johnny Darrell sold 1,205,000 copies in the UK by the Welsh wizard. (B-side: Promise Her Anything) **US 11**

1967

↗ NO.228
19 JAN ••••

I'M A BELIEVER (2.44)
The Monkees (Neil Diamond). Thanks to The Monkees' TV series, this single amassed advance orders of more than one million in the US and gave Diamond his first No.1. (B-side: [I'm Not Your] Stepping Stone) **US 1**

↗ NO.229
16 FEB ••

THIS IS MY SONG (3.14)
Petula Clark (Charlie Chaplin).
Seventy-seven-year-old silent movie superstar Chaplin wrote this theme for his film A Countess in Hong Kong. (B-side: The Show Is Over) **US 3**

↗ NO.230
2 MAR ••••••

RELEASE ME (3.18)
Engelbert Humperdinck
(Eddie Miller, Robert Yount, Dub Williams, Robert Harris). It sold 1,365,000 copies and thereby stopped The Beatles' 'Penny Lane' / 'Strawberry Fields Forever' from reaching No.1. The song was first recorded by composer Miller as a B-side in 1950. (B-side: Ten Guitars) **US 4**

↗ NO.231
13 APR ••

SOMETHIN' STUPID (2.40)
Nancy and Frank Sinatra (C Carson Parks). After both achieving solo No.1s in 1966, the duo hit the top together – the only dad and daughter to achieve this feat before the Osbournes. (B-side: Call Me) **US 1**

↗ NO.232
27 APR •••

PUPPET ON A STRING (2.21)
Sandie Shaw (Bill Martin, Phil Coulter). The UK's first Eurovision winner made Sandie the first female to amass three No.1s. Worldwide sales exceeded four million. (B-side: Tell the Boys)

↗ NO.233
18 MAY •••

SILENCE IS GOLDEN (3.07)
The Tremeloes (Bob Gaudio, Bob Crewe). The song that started as a B-side of The Four Seasons' 'Rag Doll' gave the Essex group their biggest transatlantic hit. (B-side: Let Your Hair Hang Down) **US 11**

↗ NO.234
8 JUN ••••••

A WHITER SHADE OF PALE (4.04)
Procol Harum (Keith Reid, Gary Brooker). A surreal, self-penned, Bach-based song which sold six million copies around the globe. This classic track returned to the Top 20 in 1972. (B-side: Lime Street Blues) **US 5**

↗ NO.235
19 JUL •••

ALL YOU NEED IS LOVE (3.48)
The Beatles (John Lennon, Paul McCartney). An estimated 400 million people in two dozen countries saw the group launch this single live on the global TV show Our World. (B-side: Baby You're a Rich Man) **US 1**

↗ NO.236
9 AUG ••••

SAN FRANCISCO (BE SURE TO WEAR SOME FLOWERS IN YOUR HAIR) (2.56)
Scott McKenzie (John Phillips). The Summer of Love hippie anthem sold seven million copies worldwide. However, Scott's fame faded like the flowers that he sang about. (B-side: What's the Difference) **US 4**

↗ NO.237
6 SEP •••••

THE LAST WALTZ (2.58)
Engelbert Humperdinck (Les Reed, Barry Mason). Engelbert achieved his second UK million-seller of the year with one of the most performed British songs of all time. (B-side: That Promise) **US 25**

↗ NO.238
11 OCT ••••

(THE NIGHT THE LIGHTS WENT OUT IN) MASSACHUSETTS (2.25)
The Bee Gees (Barry, Robin and Maurice Gibb). The Gibb brothers' first chart-topper as artists, or composers, was about a US state that (at the time) they had never even visited. (B-side: Barker of the UFO) **US 11**

↗ NO.239
8 NOV ••

BABY NOW THAT I FOUND YOU (2.35)
The Foundations (Tony Macaulay, John McLeod). This London-based band hit the top with their debut single, which gave the composers the first of two successive No.1s. (B-side: Come Back to Me) **US 11**

↗ NO.240
22 NOV ••

LET THE HEARTACHES BEGIN (3.12)
Long John Baldry (Tony Macaulay, John McLeod). The biggest hit from the legendary

↘ **CHART-TOPPER NO.240:** Blues singer Long John Baldry is the tallest pop star to top the charts. The 6' 7" Londoner hit the top with a less than bluesy ballad before returning to more familiar music territory and a move to Canada in the 1980s

UK R&B performer, whose earlier groups had included Rod Stewart and Elton John. (B-side: Annabella) **US 88**

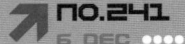

NO.241
6 DEC ●●●●●●●
HELLO, GOODBYE (3.28)
The Beatles (John Lennon, Paul McCartney). Another transatlantic Christmas No.1 which stopped their 'Magical Mystery Tour (Double EP)' from topping the chart. (B-side: I Am the Walrus) **US 1**

1968

NO.242
24 JAN ●
THE BALLAD OF BONNIE AND CLYDE (3.08)
Georgie Fame (Mitch Murray, Peter Callender). Inspired by the film Bonnie and Clyde, Fame's third and last No.1 gave the UK R&B legend a major European hit and his biggest US seller. (B-side: Beware of the Dog) **US 7**

NO.243
31 JAN ●●
EVERLASTING LOVE (2.58)
Love Affair (Buzz Cason, Mac Gayden). Like the previous chart-topper, this cover of Robert Knight's US hit was produced by Mike Smith. (B-side: Gone Are the Songs of Yesterday)

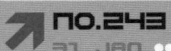

NO.244
14 FEB ●●
MIGHTY QUINN (2.50)
Manfred Mann (Bob Dylan). UK actor Anthony Quinn's performance in the movie The Savage Innocents inspired Dylan to write the Manfreds' third No.1. (B-side: By Request, Edwin Garvey) **US 10**

NO.245
28 FEB ●●●
CINDERELLA ROCKEFELLA (2.28)
Esther and Abi Ofarim (Mason Williams). Composer Williams was joined by Nancy Ames on the first version of the retro-sounding novelty song that took this Israeli couple to the top. (B-side: Lonesome Road) **US 68**

NO.246
20 MAR ●
THE LEGEND OF XANADU (3.34)
Dave Dee, Dozy, Beaky, Mick and Tich (Ken Howard, Alan Blaikley). The group's managers wrote the Latin-laced, whip-cracking, mini epic that gave one

of the decade's top acts their only No.1. (B-side: Please)

NO.247
27 MAR ●●
LADY MADONNA (2.15)
The Beatles (John Lennon, Paul McCartney). In truth, McCartney wrote and performed this track alone. It halted the progress of Tom Jones and 'Delilah' to the top. (B-side: The Inner Light) **US 4**

NO.248
10 APR ●●
CONGRATULATIONS (2.30)
Cliff Richard (Bill Martin, Phil Coulter). Cliff earned his biggest European seller to date with the song that finished as runner-up in the Eurovision Song Contest. (B-side: High 'N' Dry) **US 99**

NO.249
24 APR ●●●●
WHAT A WONDERFUL WORLD (2.15) **/ CABARET** (2.47)
Louis Armstrong Orchestra and Chorus (George David Weiss, George Douglas / John Kander, Fred Ebb). Forty-five years after his first recording, 66-year-old Satchmo became the oldest chart-topper. **US 32 / 0**

NO.250
22 MAY ●●●●
YOUNG GIRL (3.09)
Union Gap featuring Gary Puckett (Jerry Fuller). Hibbing, Minnesota's second favourite son (after Bob Dylan), also returned to the UK Top 20 with this underage anthem in 1974. (B-side: I'm Losing You) **US 2**

NO.251
19 JUN ●●
JUMPIN' JACK FLASH (3.39)
The Rolling Stones (Mick Jagger, Keith Richards). The Stones' return to their earlier and earthier sound was voted Top Single of the Year by Melody Maker readers. (B-side: Child of the Moon) **US 3**

NO.252
3 JUL ●●●
BABY COME BACK (2.26)
The Equals (Eddy Grant). This two-year-old track finally took off after it hit in Germany and the Netherlands. The song came back to the top with Pato Banton in 1994. (B-side: Hold Me Closer) **US 32**

NO.253
24 JUL ●
I PRETEND (2.47)
Des O'Connor (Les Reed, Barry Mason). The ever-popular entertainer's only No.1

came from the writers of previous toppers for Engelbert and Tom Jones. (B-side: Thinking of You)

NO.254
31 JUL ●●
21 AUG ●●
MONY MONY (2.51)
Tommy James and The Shondells (Bobby Bloom, Richie Cordell, Bo Gentry, Tommy James). The only No.1 that owes its existence to an insurance company, Mutual of New York, whose flashing neon sign inspired the writers. (B-side: One Two Three and I Fell) **US 3**

NO.255
14 AUG ●
FIRE (2.55)
The Crazy World of Arthur Brown (Vincent Crane, Arthur Brown, Peter Ker, Michael Finesilver). 'Fire' made this British band hot internationally. They may have been one-hit wonders, but Alice Cooper and his clones owe them something. (B-side: Rest Cure) **US 2**

NO.256
28 AUG ●
DO IT AGAIN (2.13)
The Beach Boys (Brian Wilson, Mike Love). Their earlier surfin' singles may have sold only stateside, but this musical return to the beach was a far bigger hit in the UK. (B-side: Wake the World) **US 20**

NO.257
4 SEP ●
I'VE GOTTA GET A MESSAGE TO YOU (3.06)
The Bee Gees (Barry, Robin and Maurice Gibb). This self-penned death row message gave the brothers their first US Top 10 entry and their last UK No.1 for 10 years. (B-side: Kitty Can) **US 8**

NO.258
11 SEP ●●
HEY JUDE (7.06)
The Beatles (John Lennon, Paul McCartney). Written by Paul about John's son Julian, it was the longest No.1 to date and spent (a 1960s record) nine weeks at the top in the US. (B-side: Revolution) **US 1**

NO.259
25 SEP ●●●●●●
THOSE WERE THE DAYS (4.59)
Mary Hopkin (Gene Raskin, Alexander Vertinski). The second release on The Beatles' own Apple label replaced the first at No.1. The song was first recorded by The Limeliters in 1962. (B-side: Turn Turn Turn) **US 2**

KEY ● = 1 week at No.1 (2.52) = minutes and seconds of track (Guy Chambers) = songwriter **US 32** = US peak position

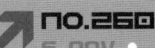

NO.260
6 NOV ●

WITH A LITTLE HELP FROM MY FRIENDS (5.06)
Joe Cocker (John Lennon, Paul McCartney). A third Beatles-involved chart-topper in a row. The song returned to the top by both Wet Wet Wet (1988) and Sam & Mark (2004). (B-side: Something's Coming On) **US 68**

NO.261
13 NOV ●●●●

THE GOOD, THE BAD AND THE UGLY (2.46)
Hugo Montenegro, His Orchestra and Chorus (Ennio Morricone). The spaghetti western theme was the first instrumental No.1 for more than five years. Montenegro conducted the orchestra and provided the grunts. (B-side: There's Got to Be a Better Way) **US 2**

NO.262
11 DEC ●●●
8 JAN 1969 ●

LILY THE PINK (4.20)
Scaffold (John Gorman, Mike McGear (aka McCartney), Roger McGough). The last of producer Norrie Paramor's 27 No.1s. Yet again a McCartney had the Christmas No.1 – this time Paul's brother Mike. (B-side: Buttons on Your Mind)

1969

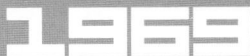

NO.263
1 JAN ●
15 JAN ●●

OB-LA-DI, OB-LA-DA (2.59)
Marmalade (John Lennon, Paul McCartney). A song from The Beatles' 'White Album' made Marmalade the toast of Scotland: they were the first north of the border band to hit the top. (B-side: Chains)

NO.264
29 JAN ●

ALBATROSS (3.08)
Fleetwood Mac (Peter Green). America's favourite AOR band of the 1970s had their biggest UK hit with a Peter Green-penned instrumental which failed to chart in the US. (B-side: Jigsaw Puzzle Blues)

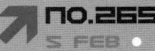

NO.265
5 FEB ●

BLACKBERRY WAY (3.40)
The Move (Roy Wood). The ground-breaking Midlands band had nine Top 20 entries and scored their only No.1 with this psychedelic sing-along. (B-side: Something)

NO.266
12 FEB ●●

(IF PARADISE IS) HALF AS NICE (2.49) **Amen Corner** (Lucio Battisti, Jack Fishman). The late 1960s teen idols jumped from 19 to No.1 with this English-language version of an Italian song first recorded by composer Battisti. (B-side: Hey Hey Girl)

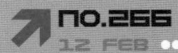

NO.267
26 FEB ●●●●

WHERE DO YOU GO TO (MY LOVELY) (5.16)
Peter Sarstedt (Peter Sarstedt). Eden Kane's brother (and one-time roadie) equalled Eden's earlier feat when he topped the chart with this 'poor little rich girl' ode. (B-side: Morning Mountains) **US 70**

CHART-TOPPER NO.266: Amen Corner were fronted by Welshman Andy Fairweather-Low, who is currently in demand as an extremely skilled session musician, and most recently has been assisting Eric Clapton

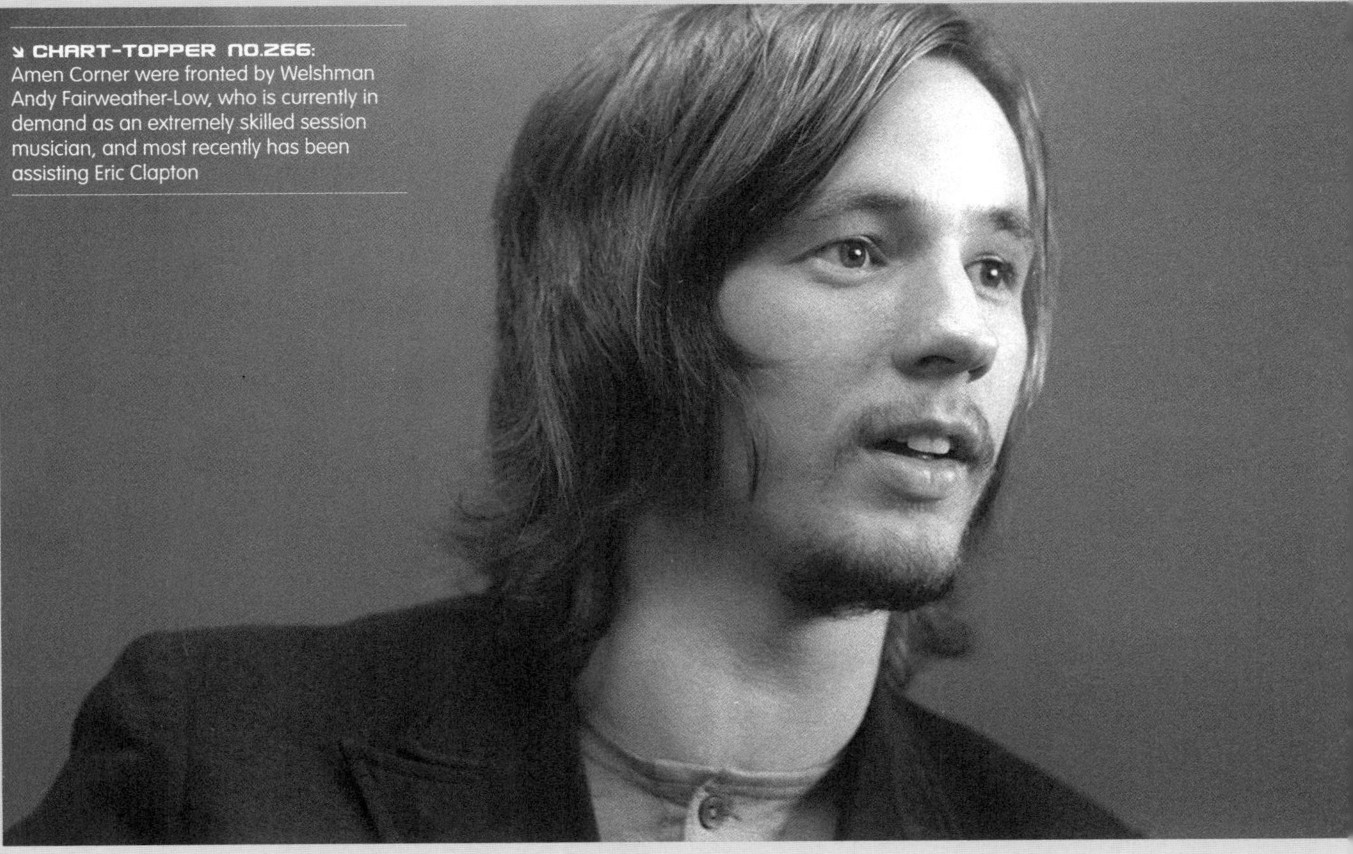

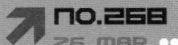

NO.268
26 MAR •••
I HEARD IT THROUGH THE GRAPEVINE (3.12)
Marvin Gaye (Norman Whitfield, Barrett Strong). This Motown classic revived a 1967 million-seller by labelmate Gladys Knight. It was Gaye's 18th US Top 40 entry and first in the UK. (B-side: Chained) **US 1**

NO.269
16 APR •
ISRAELITES (2.33)
Desmond Dekker and The Aces (Desmond Dekker, Leslie Kong). The first reggae record to reach the top (and the US Top 10) returned to the Top 10 six years later. (B-side: The Man) **US 9**

NO.270
23 APR ••••••
GET BACK (3.10)
The Beatles with Billy Preston (John Lennon, Paul McCartney). The only Beatles record to enter the chart at No.1 was sung up on the roof at Apple Records in that famous video. (B-side: Don't Let Me Down) **US 1**

NO.271
4 JUN •
DIZZY (2.52)
Tommy Roe (Tommy Roe, Freddy Weller). Roe co-wrote 'Dizzy' (which Vic Reeves also took to the top in 1991) with Weller, who later had a string of US hits as a country singer. (B-side: The You I Need) **US 1**

NO.272
11 JUN •••
THE BALLAD OF JOHN AND YOKO (2.57) **The Beatles** (John Lennon, Paul McCartney). The group's last UK No.1 was a "blasphemous" true-life tale about John and his wife, which had a lot of US DJs wanting to crucify him. (B-side: Old Brown Shoe) **US 8**

NO.273
2 JUL •••
SOMETHING IN THE AIR (3.53)
Thunderclap Newman (Speedy Keen). Who would have thought that Pete Townshend's only No.1 would have been as a producer and bass player on this single? (B-side: Wilhelmina) **US 37**

NO.274
23 JUL •••••
HONKY TONK WOMEN (2.59)
The Rolling Stones (Mick Jagger, Keith Richard). The group's last

No.1 stopped ex-Beatle John Lennon's Plastic Ono Band's first disc, 'Give Peace a Chance', from reaching the top. (B-side: You Can't Always Get What You Want) **US 1**

NO.275
30 AUG •••
IN THE YEAR 2525 (EXORDIUM AND TERMINUS) (3.16)
Zager and Evans (Rick Evans). This pessimistic peek into the future was written in 1964. These Nebraska natives are among the few transatlantic No.1 one-hit wonders. (B-side: Little Kids) **US 1**

NO.276
20 SEP •••
BAD MOON RISING (2.18)
Creedence Clearwater Revival (John Fogerty). One of the era's most popular live bands never managed a No.1 in the US, where they had to be happy with five No.2 hits. (B-side: Lodi) **US 2**

NO.277
11 OCT •
JE T'AIME ... MOI NON PLUS (4.21)
Jane Birkin and Serge Gainsbourg (Serge Gainsbourg). This controversial sex-simulating single was the first foreign-language No.1 and Gainsbourg was the first French act to reach No.1. (B-side: Jane B) **US 58**

NO.278
18 OCT •
I'LL NEVER FALL IN LOVE AGAIN (2.50) **Bobbie Gentry** (Burt Bacharach, Hal David). A song first sung by Jill O'Hara in the musical Promises, Promises gave the composers their fifth topper of the decade. (B-side: Ace Insurance Man)

NO.279
25 OCT ••••••••
SUGAR, SUGAR (2.44)
The Archies (Jeff Barry, Andy Kim). A song The Monkees rejected became the world's top hit of 1969. It was also the first UK No.1 by a non-human act, selling 979,000 in the process. (B-side: Melody Hill) **US 1**

NO.280
20 DEC ••••••
TWO LITTLE BOYS (3.16)
Rolf Harris (Theodore Morse, Edward Madden). What better way to end the musically ground-breaking decade of love and peace than with a 66-year-old war song? (B-side: I Love My Love)

1970

NO.281
31 JAN •••••
LOVE GROWS (WHERE MY ROSEMARY GOES) (2.46)
Edison Lighthouse (Barry Mason, Tony Macaulay). The first chart debutants to top the chart in just two weeks featured "The voice that launched 1,000 groups", Tony Burrows. (B-side: Every Lonely Day) **US 5**

NO.282
7 MAR •••
WAND'RIN' STAR (4.26)
Lee Marvin (Alan Jay Lerner, Frederick Loewe). The song that stopped The Beatles' 'Let It Be' from being No.1 was first recorded by James Barton in the 1951 musical Paint You Wagon. (B-side: I Talk to the Trees (by Clint Eastwood))

NO.283
28 MAR •••
BRIDGE OVER TROUBLED WATER (4.49) **Simon and Garfunkel:** Keyboard: Larry Knechtel (Paul Simon). A multi-Grammy winner that was voted the Best International Pop Single of the last 25 years at the first Brit awards in 1977. (B-side: Keep the Customer Satisfied) **US 1**

NO.284
18 APR ••
ALL KINDS OF EVERYTHING (3.00)
Dana (Denny Lindsay, Jackie Smith). The year's Eurovision Song Contest winner made teenager Dana the only (future) Member of the European Parliament to chart. (B-side: Channel Breeze)

NO.285
2 MAY ••
SPIRIT IN THE SKY (3.57)
Norman Greenbaum (Norman Greenbaum). The original version of the semi-religious song also topped the chart with versions by Doctor and the Medics (1986) and Gareth Gates (2003). (B-side: Milk Cow) **US 3**

NO.286
16 MAY •••
BACK HOME (2.02)
England World Cup Squad (Bill Martin, Phil Coulter). The first football record to top the table was released to coincide with England's ultimately unsuccessful attempt to retain the World Cup. (B-side: Cinnamon Stick)

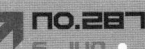

KEY   ● = 1 week at No.1   (2.52) = minutes and seconds of track   (Guy Chambers) = songwriter   **US 32** = US peak position

NO.287
6 JUN ●

YELLOW RIVER (2.44)
Christie (Jeff Christie). Q: What do you do when The Tremeloes reject a song you have written for them? A: Record it yourself and sell two million copies. (B-side: Down the Mississippi Line) **US 23**

NO.288
13 JUN ●●●●●●●

IN THE SUMMERTIME (3.28)
Mungo Jerry (Ray Dorset).
The first three-track chart-topper leapt from 13-1 in the UK, and stopped Free's 'All Right Now' from making No.1. (B-sides: Mighty Man / The Dust Pneumonia Blues) **US 3**

NO.289
1 AUG ●●●●●●

THE WONDER OF YOU (2.34)
Elvis Presley (Baker Knight).
A song that Ray Peterson and Ronnie Hilton had clicked with in 1959 returned the King to the top after six years away. (B-side: Mama Liked the Roses) **US 9**

NO.290
12 SEP ●

THE TEARS OF A CLOWN (2.58)
Smokey Robinson and The Miracles
(Henry Cosby, William Robinson, Stevie Wonder). Recorded as a throwaway album track in 1967, which turned into a transatlantic topper after being unearthed by Motown's UK company. (B-side: Who's Gonna Take the Blame) **US 1**

NO.291
19 SEP ●●●●●●

BAND OF GOLD (2.54)
Freda Payne (Ron Dunbar, Edith Wayne).
The former wife of Gregory 'Shake You Down' Abbott sang the only No.1 about an unconsummated marriage.
(B-side: The Easiest Way to Fall) **US 3**

NO.292
31 OCT ●●●

WOODSTOCK (4.24)
Matthews' Southern Comfort
(Joni Mitchell). A song written by Joni Mitchell for Crosby, Stills, Nash and Young about the rock festival she did not appear at but they did. The CSN&Y version made No.11 in the US. (B-side: Scion) **US 23**

NO.293
21 NOV

VOODOO CHILE (5.11)
The Jimi Hendrix Experience (Jimi Hendrix).
The legendary performer's only chart-topper

↘ CHART-TOPPER NO.288: Mungo Jerry were named after one of the cats in the T S Eliot verses. Lead singer Ray Dorset, who sported the thickest sideburns in pop, was working as a laboratory assistant at the time of their chart-topping performance on Top of the Pops and had to ask for time off work to perform

was a three-track single that hit shortly after his death. (B-sides: Hey Joe / All Along the Watchtower)

↗ **NO.294**
28 NOV ●●●●●●

I HEAR YOU KNOCKING (2.41)
Dave Edmunds' Rockpile
(Dave Bartholomew, Pearl King).
Oddly, Dave didn't update the line "I told you way back in 52" on his revival of a 1955 million-seller, which Smiley Lewis cut first. (B-side: Black Bill) **US 4**

1971

↗ **NO.295**
9 JAN ●●●

GRANDAD (3.22)
Clive Dunn (Herbie Flowers, Kenny Pickett).
Noted rock musician and Blue Mink member Flowers composed this festive favourite that took TV's Lance Corporal Jones to the top. (B-side: I Play the Spoons)

↗ **NO.296**
30 JAN ●●●●●

MY SWEET LORD (4.36)
George Harrison (George Harrison).
The first solo No.1 by an ex-Beatle returned to the top after George's death in 2001 – a feat equalled only by Queen with 'Bohemian Rhapsody'. (B-side: What Is Life) **US 1**

↗ **NO.297**
6 MAR ●●

BABY JUMP (4.07)
Mungo Jerry (Ray Dorset). The first act since Gerry and The Pacemakers to reach the top with their first two releases. (B-sides: Maggie / Midnight Special / Mighty Man)

↗ **NO.298**
20 MAR ●●●●●●

HOT LOVE (4.55)
T. Rex (Marc Bolan).
Only Clive Dunn had prevented 'Ride a White Swan' from topping the chart, but nothing could stop the follow-up from the glam rock gods. (B-sides: Woodland Rock / The King of the Mountain Cometh) **US 72**

↗ **NO.299**
1 MAY ●●

DOUBLE BARREL (2.24)
Dave and Ansil Collins (Winston Riley).
A rare internationally successful reggae single from the first toasting topper. All together now: "I, am the magnificent…" (B-side: Double Barrel [Version 2]) **US 22**

↗ **NO.300**
15 MAY ●●●●●

KNOCK THREE TIMES (2.56)
Dawn (Irwin Levine, L Russell Brown).
The girls in this popular 70s act did not actually sing on the track that prevented 'Brown Sugar' by the Stones from reaching No.1. (B-side: Home) **US 1**

↗ **NO.301**
19 JUN ●●●●●

CHIRPY CHIRPY CHEEP CHEEP (2.57) **Middle of the Road**
(Lally Scott). According to the group, their cover of the song, first recorded by its composer, sold 10 million around the globe. (B-side: Rainin' 'N' Painin')

↗ **NO.302**
24 JUL ●●●●

GET IT ON (4.24)
T. Rex (Marc Bolan).
After a name change to 'Bang a Gong', so it was not confused with Chase's 'Get It On', this became the duo's only major US hit. (B-side: Raw Ramp) **US 10**

↗ **NO.303**
21 AUG ●●●●

I'M STILL WAITING (3.43)
Diana Ross (Deke Richards).
This US flop gave Diana her only UK chart-topper of the decade. She had to wait 15 years to return to N o.1. (B-side: Reach Out I'll Be There) **US 63**

↗ **NO.304**
18 SEP ●●●

HEY GIRL DON'T BOTHER ME (2.23) **The Tams**
(Ray Whitley). A seven-year-old US R&B single that charted thanks to Northern Soul interest. The act didn't bother Top 20 collectors again. (B-side: Take Away) **US 41**

↗ **NO.305**
9 OCT ●●●●●

MAGGIE MAY (5.13)
Rod Stewart
(Rod Stewart, Martin Quittenton). The track and its parent album, 'Every Picture Tells a Story', were simultaneous UK and US toppers – a record-breaking feat. (B-side: Reason to Believe) **US 1**

↗ **NO.306**
13 NOV ●●●●

COZ I LUV YOU (3.22)
Slade (Noddy Holder, Jim Lea).
The first of their seven phonetically spelt hits was composed in just 20 minutes. (B-side: My Life Is Natural)

↗ **NO.307**
11 DEC ●●●●

ERNIE (THE FASTEST MILKMAN IN THE WEST) (3.50)
Benny Hill (Benny Hill).
The internationally acclaimed comic's dramatic dairy ditty also topped the chart down under. (B-side: Ting a Ling a Loo)

1972

↗ **NO.308**
8 JAN ●●●●

I'D LIKE TO TEACH THE WORLD TO SING (IN PERFECT HARMONY) (2.21) **The New Seekers**
(Roger Cook, Roger Greenaway, William Backer, Billy Davis). The re-worded Coca-Cola advert that taught the world to sing TV commercials if they wanted to get hits sold 990,000 copies. (B-side: Boom Town) **US 7**

↗ **NO.309**
5 FEB ●●

TELEGRAM SAM (3.44)
T. Rex (Marc Bolan).
This one-time acoustic duo's third No.1 introduced us to characters such as Golden Nose Slim, Purple Pie Pete and Jungle Faced Jake. (B-sides: Cadillac / Baby Strange) **US 67**

↗ **NO.310**
19 FEB ●●●

SON OF MY FATHER (3.11)
Chicory Tip
(Giorgio Moroder, Peter Belotte, Michael Holm). The single that stopped Don McLean's 'American Pie' from making No.1 had been recorded earlier by its (soon to be famous) composer. (B-side: Pride Comes Before a Fall) **US 91**

↗ **NO.311**
11 MAR ●●●●●

WITHOUT YOU (3.15)
Nilsson (Peter Ham, Tom Evans).
Penned and first performed by the composers' group Badfinger, this classic lost love song also topped the chart by Mariah Carey in 1994. (B-side: Gotta Get Up) **US 1**

↗ **NO.312**
15 APR ●●●●●

AMAZING GRACE (2.39)
Pipes and Drums and Military Band of the Royal Scots Dragoon Guards (Traditional).
Selling 962,000 in the process, this Scottish army bagpipe band scored an international hit with this melody that was composed in 1779. (B-side: Cornet Carillon) **US 11**

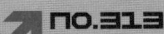 NO.313
28 MAY ●●●●
METAL GURU (2.24)
T. Rex (Marc Bolan).
The act's fourth visit to the top in just 14 months prevented Elton John from getting his first No.1 with 'Rocket Man'.
(B-sides: Thunderwing / Lady)

NO.314
17 JUN ●●
VINCENT (3.58)
Don McLean (Don McLean).
Don followed a million-seller about legendary artist Buddy Holly with another about legendary artist Vincent 'Starry, Starry Night' Van Gogh. (B-side: Castles in the Air) **US 12**

NO.315
1 JUL ●
TAKE ME BAK 'OME (3.11)
Slade (Noddy Holder, Jim Lea). The English teachers' worst nightmares made it back to the top with a self-penned stomper about a girl called Sidney. (B-side: Wonderin') **US 97**

NO.316
8 JUL ●●●●●
PUPPY LOVE (3.03)
Donny Osmond (Paul Anka).
The 14-year-old teeny bop idol's first No.1 came with a song written by 18-year-old Paul Anka in 1959. (B-side: Let My People Go) **US 3**

NO.317
12 AUG ●●●
SCHOOL'S OUT (3.27)
Alice Cooper (Alice Cooper, Michael Bruce). The early 1970s most outrageous rocker was inspired to write this by the 1940s comedy movies of those rebellious teens the Bowery Boys. (B-side: Gutter Cat) **US 7**

NO.318
2 SEP ●
YOU WEAR IT WELL (4.21)
Rod Stewart
(Rod Stewart, Martin Quittenton).
For the only time in his career, Stewart scored two successive No.1s. Both were penned with guitarist Quittenton, who also played on this track. (B-side: Lost Paraguayos) **US 13**

NO.319
9 SEP ●●●
MAMA WEER ALL CRAZEE NOW (3.42) **Slade**
(Noddy Holder, Jim Lea). The first non-Beatles single to enter in the first week at the No.2 spot made it three No.1s in a year for the Wolverhampton outfit. (B-side: Man Who Speaks Evil) **US 76**

NO.320
30 SEP ●●
HOW CAN I BE SURE (3.06)
David Cassidy (Felix Cavaliere, Eddie Brigati).
Five years before the pin-up of The Partridge Family topped the chart with this song it had been a US top five entry for The Young Rascals. (B-side: Ricky's Tune) **US 25**

NO.321
14 OCT ●●●●
MOULDY OLD DOUGH (2.42)
Lieutenant Pigeon (Nigel Fletcher, Robert Woodward). Group members, mother and son Hilda and Rob Woodward, recorded this No.1 in their front room. (B-side: The Villain)

NO.322
11 NOV ●●
CLAIR (2.57)
Gilbert O'Sullivan
(Gilbert O'Sullivan). In the UK, this ode to his manager's young daughter followed the No.2 hit 'Alone Again (Naturally)'. In the US, the peak positions were reversed. (B-side: What Could Be Nicer) **US 2**

↘ **CHART-TOPPER NO.317:** Alice Cooper, whose leader's real name is Vincent Furnier, were the subject of attempted banning orders by a group of UK mothers and MPs when the band tried to bring their outrageous stage act to Britain. The publicity helped to boost sales of the rebellious 'School's Out' and sent it to the top of the chart

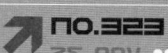
NO.323
25 NOV ●●●●
MY DING-A-LING (4.17)
Chuck Berry (Chuck Berry).
The legendary 1950s rocker had a transatlantic topper with a double entendre ditty first recorded in 1952 by Dave Bartholomew. (B-side: Let's Boogie) **US 1**

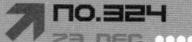
NO.324
23 DEC ●●●●●
LONG HAIRED LOVER FROM LIVERPOOL (2.12)
Little Jimmy Osmond with The Mike Curb Congregation (Christopher Kingsley).
The youngest No.1 act ever (nine years and 251 days) stopped David Bowie's 'The Jean Genie' from reaching the peak, selling 998,000 copies. (B-side: Mother of Mine) **US 38**

1973

NO.325
27 JAN ●●●●●
BLOCKBUSTER! (3.12)
The Sweet (Nicky Chinn, Mike Chapman).
One of their eight chart-toppers in Germany, this gave the British glam rockers their only UK No.1. (B-side: Need a Lot of Lovin') **US 73**

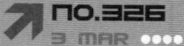
NO.326
3 MAR ●●●●
CUM ON FEEL THE NOIZE (4.27) **Slade**
(Noddy Holder, Jim Lea).
In the US, Slade sold few records. However, Quiet Riot's carefully cloned cover was a top five hit there 10 years later. (B-side: I'm Mee, I'm Now, An' That's Orl) **US 98**

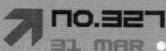
NO.327
31 MAR ●
THE TWELFTH OF NEVER (2.41) **Donny Osmond**
(Jay Livingston, Paul Francis Webster).
The song, which was adapted from the old folk tune 'I Gave My Love a Cherry', was initially a US Top 10 hit for Johnny Mathis in 1957. (B-side: Life Is Just What You Make It) **US 8**

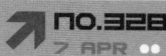
NO.328
7 APR ●●
GET DOWN
(2.39) **Gilbert O'Sullivan**
(Gilbert O'Sullivan). This was the third transatlantic Top 10 hit in a year for the first Irish solo act to top the UK chart. (B-side: Very Extraordinary Sort of Girl) **US 7**

NO.329
21 APR ●●●●
TIE A YELLOW RIBBON ROUND THE OLE OAK TREE (3.23)
Dawn (Irwin Levine, L Russell Brown).
This 988,000-selling single was the true tale of a convict who returned home after a three-year sentence for fraud on a southbound bus in Georgia. (B-side: I Can't Believe How Much I Love You) **US 1**

NO.330
19 MAY ●●●●
SEE MY BABY JIVE (4.58)
Wizzard: Vocal backing by The Suedettes (Roy Wood). Wood spent a small fortune recording this track, which gave the group a major hit in many countries. (B-side: Bend Over Beethoven)

NO.331
16 JUN ●
CAN THE CAN (3.34)
Suzi Quatro (Nicky Chinn, Mike Chapman).
One of the 1970s' most successful teams – Quatro, Chinn and Chapman – had a No.1 with their first recording together. (B-side: Ain't Ya Somethin' Honey) **US 56**

NO.332
23 JUN ●
RUBBER BULLETS (4.40)
10cc (Kevin Godley, Lol Creme, Graham Gouldman). 10cc's Eric Stewart's first No.1 after four No.2s stopped Fleetwood Mac's 'Albatross' from reaching the top for the second time. (B-side: Waterfall) **US 73**

NO.333
30 JUN ●●●
SKWEEZE ME PLEEZE ME (4.29)
Slade (Noddy Holder, Jim Lea).
This single made Slade the first British act to have two of their singles enter at No.1. (B-side: Kill 'Em at the Hot Club Tonite)

NO.334
21 JUL ●
WELCOME HOME (3.30)
Peters and Lee (Jean-Alphonse Dupré, Stanislas Beldone: English lyrics by Bryan Blackburn). The song that started life in France as 'Vivre' gave the Opportunity Knocks winners a No.1 with their first single. (B-side: Can't Keep My Mind on the Game)

NO.335
28 JUL ●●●●
I'M THE LEADER OF THE GANG (I AM!) (3.28)
Gary Glitter (Gary Glitter, Mike Leander).
Thirteen years after his first release, as Paul

Raven, Glitter grabbed the first of his three chart-toppers. (B-side: Just Fancy That)

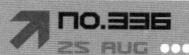
NO.336
25 AUG ●●●●
YOUNG LOVE (2.32)
Donny Osmond (Carole Joyner, Ric Cartey).
The song that jumped from No.16 to No.1 was first cut by composer Cartey and sold a million in 1957 by both Tab Hunter and Sonny James. (B-side: A Million to One) **US 25**

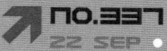
NO.337
22 SEP ●
ANGEL FINGERS (A TEEN BALLAD) (4.31)
Wizzard: Vocal backing: The Suedettes and The Bleach Boys (Roy Wood).
Multi-talented ex-Move man Wood was one of the few artists to head the chart with two different groups. (B-side: You Got the Jump on Me)

NO.338
29 SEP ●●●●
EYE LEVEL (THEME FROM THE TV SERIES 'VAN DER VALK') (2.22)
Simon Park Orchestra
(Simon Park, Jack Trombey). Ten months after it first charted, Park's only claim to chart fame became the first TV theme to reach No.1 with total sales of 1,001,400. (B-side: Distant Hills)

NO.339
27 OCT ●●●
DAYDREAMER (2.49) /
THE PUPPY SONG (2.46)
David Cassidy
(Terry Dempsey / Harry Nilsson). In his homeland, this TV-launched teeny bop idol managed only one Top 10 hit, and this double A-side failed to reach even the US Hot 100.

NO.340
17 NOV ●●●●
I LOVE YOU LOVE ME LOVE (3.11)
Gary Glitter
(Gary Glitter, Mike Leander).
The biggest-selling single by the glam rock giant entered at No.1. In the US, it was covered by Tommy James. (B-side: Hands Up! It's a Stick Up)

NO.341
15 DEC ●●●●●
MERRY XMAS EVERYBODY (3.26)
Slade (Noddy Holder, Jim Lea).
The most-charted Christmas record of all time was recorded on a hot July day in New York. (B-side: Don't Blame Me)

1974

↗ NO.342
19 JAN ●
YOU WON'T FIND ANOTHER FOOL LIKE ME (3.17)
The New Seekers featuring Lyn Paul
(Tony Macaulay, Geoff Stephens). The group equalled their predecessors, The Seekers, by amassing eight Top 20 entries and two No.1s. (B-side: Song for Me and You)

↗ NO.343
26 JAN ●●●●
TIGER FEET (3.51)
Mud (Nicky Chinn, Mike Chapman). The group's fourth Top 20 entry achieved the rare feat of leaping from No.10 to No.1. (B-side: Mr Bagatelle)

↗ NO.344
23 FEB ●●
DEVIL GATE DRIVE (3.46)
Suzi Quatro (Nicky Chinn, Mike Chapman). The second successive No.1 for the Chinn and Chapman writer-production duo. It was also covered in the US by Tommy James (see No.340). (B-side: In the Morning)

↗ NO.345
9 MAR ●
JEALOUS MIND (2.41)
Alvin Stardust (Peter Shelley). The only No.1 recorded by one of the decade's most popular performers was penned by his successful label mate, Peter Shelley. (B-side: Guitar Star)

↗ NO.346
16 MAR ●●●
BILLY DON'T BE A HERO (4.01)
Paper Lace (Mitch Murray, Peter Callander). These Opportunity Knocks winners' biggest UK hit prevented The Hollies from hitting the No.1 spot with 'The Air That I Breathe'. (B-side: Celia) **US 96**

↗ NO.347
6 APR ●●●●
SEASONS IN THE SUN (3.27)
Terry Jacks (Jacques Brel: English lyrics by Rod McKuen). This song was first recorded in French by its composer and in English by The Kingston Trio (1964). Westlife took it back to the top in 1999. (B-side: Put the Bone In) **US 1**

↗ NO.348
4 MAY ●●
WATERLOO (2.45)
Abba (Björn Ulvaeus, Benny Andersson, Stig Anderson). The first Scandinavian act to top

↘ **CHART-TOPPER NO.331, 344:** Bass-playing, leather-suited, Suzi Quatro was far more popular in the UK than in her native America. The Detroit-born rocker's double top was a product of the Chinn, Chapman and Most team

the chart did so with the year's Eurovision Song Contest winner. It returned to the Top 20 in 2004. (B-side: Watch Out) **US 6**

↗ NO.349
18 MAY ●●●●
SUGAR BABY LOVE (3.30)
The Rubettes (Wayne Bickerton, Tony Waddington). One of Europe's most popular groups in the 1970s had their biggest UK hit

with their only single featuring Paul DaVinci. (B-side: You Could Have Told Me) **US 37**

↗ NO.350
15 JUN ●
THE STREAK (3.13)
Ray Stevens (Ray Stevens). A couple of dozen streaking singles were released stateside. This "Don't look" warning to Ethel out-ran the rest. (B-side: You've Got the Music Inside) **US 1**

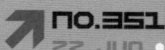

NO.351
22 JUN ●

ALWAYS YOURS (3.23)
Gary Glitter (Mike Leander, Gary Glitter).
Glitter clocked up his third chart-topper in a
year – all were co-written with his producer
Mike Leander. (B-side: I'm Right, You're
Wrong, I Win)

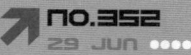

NO.352
29 JUN ●●●●

SHE (2.33)
Charles Aznavour (Charles Aznavour,
Herbert Kretzmer). The only French male solo
singer to top the chart did so with the theme
music from the TV series The Seven Faces of
Woman. (B-side: La Barraka)

NO.353
27 JUL ●●●

ROCK YOUR BABY (3.17)
George McCrae
(Harry W Casey, Richard Finch). The first disco
chart-topper was a major hit worldwide,
selling more than 10 million copies.
(B-side: Rock Your Baby [Part 2]) **US 1**

NO.354
17 AUG ●●

WHEN WILL I SEE YOU AGAIN (2.46)
The Three Degrees
(Kenny Gamble, Leon Huff). The only No.1 on
the successful Philadelphia International label
was by the only US girl group to top the chart
in the 1970s. (B-side: I Didn't Know) **US 2**

NO.355
31 AUG ●●●

LOVE ME FOR A REASON (3.59)
The Osmonds
(Johnny Bristol). The song originally recorded
by its composer became The Osmonds'
biggest seller and the first hit for Boyzone.
(B-side: Fever) **US 10**

NO.356
21 SEP ●●●

KUNG FU FIGHTING (3.12)
Carl Douglas (Carl Douglas).
This worldwide, 10-million-selling,
transatlantic chart-topper was quickly
recorded at the end of a session as a
proposed B-side. (B-side: Gamblin' Man) **US 1**

NO.357
12 OCT ●

ANNIE'S SONG (2.59)
John Denver (John Denver). Few acts sold as
many singles and albums in the US during
the 1970s as Denver. However, in the UK this
ode to his wife was one of just two hit singles.
(B-side: Cool an' Green an' Shady) **US 1**

NO.358
19 OCT ●

SAD SWEET DREAMER (3.25)
Sweet Sensation (D E S Parton). Tony Hatch
produced these New Faces winners. The
outspoken TV talent show judge produced
the winning act and got a No.1. Ring any
bells? (B-side: Sure Thing, Yes, I Do) **US 14**

NO.359
26 OCT ●●●

EVERYTHING I OWN (3.45)
Ken Boothe (David Gates).
The song that also reached No.1 by Boy
George in 1987 was first recorded by the
composer's group, Bread, and was a US Top
5 hit in 1972. (B-side: Drum Song)

↘ **CHART-TOPPER NO.366:** For their two-week stay at the top in 1975, Steve Harley and Cockney Rebel comprised Harley on vocals, Stuart Elliott on drums, Jim Cregan on guitar, Duncan Mackay on keyboards and George Ford on bass

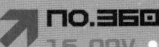
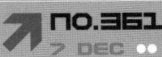 **NO.360**
16 NOV ●●●

GONNA MAKE YOU A STAR (3.36)
David Essex (David Essex).
The first No.1 from the act voted Top British Male Vocalist of 1974 prevented Queen from getting their first chart-topper with 'Killer Queen'. (B-side: Window)

NO.361
7 DEC ●●

YOU'RE THE FIRST, THE LAST, MY EVERYTHING (3.25)
Barry White (Barry White, Tony Sepe, Peter Radcliffe). The legendary 'Walrus of Love' had his first and last No.1 with the first UK release on the 20th Century label. (B-side: More Than Anything, You're My Everything) **US 2**

NO.362
21 DEC ●●●●

LONELY THIS CHRISTMAS (3.33)
Mud (Nicky Chinn, Mike Chapman).
This epic, Elvis-inspired Christmas cracker stopped the progress of Bachman Turner Overdrive's 'You Ain't Seen Nothin' Yet' to the top. (B-side: I Can't Stand It)

1975

NO.363
18 JAN ●

DOWN DOWN (3.48)
Status Quo (Francis Rossi, Robert Young).
Since no other group can match Quo's number of chart entries, it's amazing they have spent only one week on top.
(B-side: Nightride).

NO.364
25 JAN ●

MS GRACE (3.36)
The Tymes (John Hall, Johanna Hall).
The first of six No.1s from US acts in 1975, none of which reached the Top 10 in their homeland. (B-side: The Crutch) **US 91**

NO.365
1 FEB ●●●

JANUARY (3.28)
Pilot (David Paton). Pilot were the first of two successive groups to fly from No.9 to the top spot, and both were produced by Alan Parsons. (B-side: Never Give Up) **US 87**

NO.366
22 FEB ●●

MAKE ME SMILE (COME UP AND SEE ME) (3.57)
Steve Harley and Cockney Rebel (Steve Harley). The original version of their biggest hit returned to the chart in both 1992 and 1995, and Erasure's rendition was a Top 20 hit in 2003. (B-side: Another Journey) **US 96**

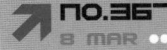 **NO.367**
8 MAR ●●

IF (3.07)
Telly Savalas
(David Gates). His unique version of this Bread 1971 US top five hit made the 51-year-old TV cop the oldest person to top the chart with their debut hit. (B-side: You and Me Against the World)

NO.368
22 MAR ●●●●●●

BYE BYE BABY (2.46)
Bay City Rollers
(Bob Gaudio, Bob Crewe).
The tartan-clad teeny bop idols said hello to the top spot with a song that reached the US Top 20 in 1965 by The Four Seasons.
(B-side: It's for You)

NO.369
3 MAY ●●

OH BOY (2.52)
Mud (Sonny West, Norman Petty, Bill Tilghman). Co-writer West first recorded this song as "Alla My Love" in 1957, and Buddy Holly and The Crickets hit with it a year later.
(B-side: Moonshine Sally)

NO.370
17 MAY ●●●

STAND BY YOUR MAN (2.39)
Tammy Wynette
(Billy Sherrill, Tammy Wynette).
The first female country singer to top the chart did so with a song that had been a country No.1 in the US seven years earlier.
(B-side: Your Good Girl's Gonna Go Bad) **US 19**

NO.371
7 JUN ●●●

WHISPERING GRASS (2.57)
Windsor Davies as BSM Williams and Don Estelle as Gunner Sugden (Lofty)
(Fred and Doris Fisher).
The stars of TVs It Ain't Half Hot Mum had an unusual No.1 with a retro Ink Spots-cloned cover of that distinctive group's 1940 hit.
(B-side: I Should Have Known)

NO.372
28 JUN ●●

I'M NOT IN LOVE (6.01)
10cc
(Graham Gouldman, Eric Stewart).
In 1977, in one of the earliest 'Top 100 Singles of All Time' polls, this classic single was voted No.1. (B-side: Good News) **US 2**

NO.373
12 JUL ●

TEARS ON MY PILLOW (3.15)
Johnny Nash (Ernie Smith).
Eighteen years after he started recording, this Texas-born reggae singer scored his only UK No.1. (B-side: Beautiful Baby)

NO.374
19 JUL ●●●

GIVE A LITTLE LOVE (3.11)
Bay City Rollers (Johnny Goodison, Phil Wainman). Rollermania was at its height when the group scored their second successive No.1 with a song penned by ex-Brotherhood of Man member Goodison.
(B-side: She'll Be Crying over You)

NO.375
9 AUG ●

BARBADOS (3.30)
Typically Tropical (Jeffrey Calvert, Max West).
Two studio engineers came up with this catchy novelty, which The Vengaboys rejigged as 'We're Going to Ibiza!' in 1999.
(B-side: Sandy)

NO.376
16 AUG ●●●

CAN'T GIVE YOU ANYTHING (BUT MY LOVE) (3.11)
The Stylistics (Hugo Peretti, Luigi Creatore, George David Weiss). One of the 1970s' top-selling US R&B groups in Britain had two No.1 albums, but this was their only chart-topping single. (B-side: I'd Rather Be Hurt by You [Than Be Loved by Somebody Else]) **US 51**

NO.377
6 SEP ●●●●

SAILING (4.35)
Rod Stewart (Gavin Sutherland).
Originally recorded by The Sutherland Brothers in 1972. Rod's anthemic rendition also reached the top three in 1976.
(B-side: Stone Cold Sober) **US 58**

NO.378
4 OCT ●●●

HOLD ME CLOSE (3.50)
David Essex (David Essex). Essex clocked up his second and last No.1 as he concluded a very successful world tour that took in four continents. (B-side: Good Ol' Rock 'n' Roll)

NO.379
25 OCT ●●

I ONLY HAVE EYES FOR YOU (3.38)
Art Garfunkel
(Harry Warren, Al Dubin). Art's first solo hit was a cloned version of The Flamingos' 1959 revival of a song sung by Dick Powell and

Ruby Keeler in the 1934 film Dames.
(B-side: Looking for the Right One) **US 18**

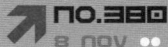

NO.380
8 NOV ••
SPACE ODDITY (5.14)
David Bowie (David Bowie).
Bowie's timeless debut hit from 1969 returned
to top the chart. This time it was released as
a three-track maxi single. (B-sides: Changes /
Velvet Goldmine) **US 15**

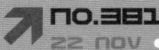

NO.381
22 NOV •
D.I.V.O.R.C.E. (2.54)
Billy Connolly
(Billy Connolly, Claude Putnam Jr, Bobby
Braddock). The only No.1 song about a dog
that dislikes visiting the vet? Unusually, this
parody outsold the hit it was based on.
(B-side: Cuckoo)

NO.382
29 NOV •••••••••
BOHEMIAN RHAPSODY (5.50)
Queen (Freddie Mercury).
The winning song in the British Hit Singles
readers' poll in 2003 was the first record to
spend nine weeks at the top since 1957.
(B-side: I'm in Love with My Car) **US 9**

1976

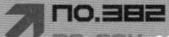

NO.383
31 JAN ••
MAMMA MIA (3.27)
Abba
(Stig Anderson, Björn Ulvaeus, Benny
Andersson). This Abba song became the title
of their very successful musical and finally
opened the UK's door to acts from mainland
Europe. (B-side: Intermezzo No.1) **US 32**

NO.384
14 FEB •
FOREVER AND EVER (3.38)
Slik (Bill Martin, Phil Coulter).
The Bay City Rollers' writer and production
team was also behind this heavily hyped
Scottish band, which featured Midge Ure.
(B-side: Again My Love)

NO.385
21 FEB ••
**DECEMBER, 1963 (OH, WHAT
A NIGHT)** (3.28)
The Four Seasons (Bob Gaudio, Judy Parker).
After the Bay City Rollers, Detroit Spinners and
Tremeloes had made the top with covers of
their songs, the group finally had their own
No.1. (B-side: Slip Away) **US 1**

NO.386
6 MAR •••
**I LOVE TO LOVE (BUT MY
BABY LOVES TO DANCE)** (3.03)
Tina Charles
(Jack Robinson, James Bolden). The noted
session singer (she was lead vocalist of 5000
Volts and sang on Steve Harley's No.1)
became the UK's disco queen of 1976.
(B-side: Disco Fever)

NO.387
27 MAR ••••••
SAVE YOUR KISSES FOR ME (3.03)
Brotherhood of Man
(Tony Hiller, Martin Lee, Lee Sheridan).
This self-composed Eurovision Song Contest
winner sold 1,006,200 in the UK and was a
smash all round Europe.
(B-side: Let's Love Together) **US 27**

NO.388
8 MAY ••••
FERNANDO (4.09)
Abba
(Stig Anderson, Björn Ulvaeus, Benny
Andersson). A song that member Frida first
recorded as a soloist in Swedish. It was
Australia's top single of the year and sold a
million in Germany. (B-side: Hey Hey Helen)
US 13

NO.389
5 JUN •
NO CHARGE (3.42)
JJ Barrie
(Harlan Howard). A Mother's Day-targeted
tear-jerker that had topped the US country
chart by Melba Montgomery gave JJ his ticket
to one-hit wonderland. (B-side: Till You're
Loving Me Again)

NO.390
12 JUN ••
**THE COMBINE HARVESTER
(BRAND NEW KEY)** (3.01)
The Wurzels
(Melanie Safka). A country No.1 was replaced
by a West Country No.1. This parochial
parody stopped Paul McCartney's 'Silly Love
Songs' from making the top.
(B-side: The Blackbird)

NO.391
26 JUN •••
YOU TO ME ARE EVERYTHING (3.21)
The Real Thing
(Ken Gold, Micky Denne). This track, by the
top UK R&B group of the 1970s, was the first
to make the Top 10 in its original form and as
a remix, which it did in 1986. (B-side: Keep an
Eye [On Your Best Friend) **US 64**

NO.392
17 JUL •
THE ROUSSOS PHENOMENON (EP)
(3.35) **Demis Roussos**
(Tracks 1-3: Stylianos Valviano, Robert
Costandinos / Track 4: Stylianos Valviano,
Charalampie Chalkitis, Robert Costandinos).
The first official EP to top the chart came from
the first Egyptian artist to reach No.1.
(EP tracks: Forever and Ever / Sing an Ode to
Love / So Dreamy / My Friend the Wind)

NO.393
24 JUL ••••••
DON'T GO BREAKING MY HEART
(4.31) **Elton John and Kiki Dee**
(Ann Orson, Carte Blanche [Elton
John, Bernie Taupin]). Elton's 14th
Top 20 entry gave him his first No.1.
Fourteen years and another 14 Top 20
hits later, he scored his first solo topper.
(B-side: Snow Queen) **US 1**

NO.394
4 SEP ••••••
DANCING QUEEN (3.51)
Abba
(Stig Anderson, Benny Andersson, Björn
Ulvaeus). Abba's only transatlantic No.1
leapt to the top slot in the UK from No.16.
In 1992, this club classic returned to the Top
20. (B-side: That's Me) **US 1**

NO.395
16 OCT ••••
MISSISSIPPI (4.34)
Pussycat
(Werner Theunissen). The first Dutch chart-
toppers did so with an ode to an American
state, which was a huge hit everywhere but
in America. It sold 947,000 in the UK.
(B-side: Do It)

NO.396
13 NOV •••
IF YOU LEAVE ME NOW (3.56)
Chicago
(Peter Cetera). The biggest worldwide chart
smash by one of America's most consistent
hit-makers of the 1960s and 1970s.
(B-side: Together Again) **US 1**

NO.397
4 DEC •••
UNDER THE MOON OF LOVE (3.16)
Showaddywaddy
(Tommy Boyce, Curtis Lee).
These rock 'n' roll revivalists' rendition of
a song first cut by Curtis Lee stopped the
progress of Queen's 'Somebody to Love'
to No.1 and sold 985,000 in the process.
(B-side: Lookin' Back)

↘ **CHART-TOPPER NO.390:** The Wurzels' single visit to No.1 was courtesy of a reworded West Country version of US singer / songwriter Melanie's 'Brand New Key'. Melanie harvested the royalty cheques

↗ NO.398
25 DEC •••

WHEN A CHILD IS BORN (SOLEADO) (3.41)
Johnny Mathis
(Fred Jay, Di Damicco Ciro). A sentimental seasonal release that was first recorded by German singer Michael Holm gave the song stylist his only solo No.1. (B-side: Every Time You Touch Me [I Get High])

1977

↗ NO.399
15 JAN ••••

DON'T GIVE UP ON US (3.35) **David Soul**
(Tony Macaulay). This UK-written song and production gave the singer turned actor turned singer (and later British citizen) a transatlantic No.1 with 1,145,000 UK sales. (B-side: Black Bean Soup) **US 1**

↗ NO.400
12 FEB •

DON'T CRY FOR ME ARGENTINA (5.24) **Julie Covington**
(Tim Rice, Andrew Lloyd Webber). The song, originally performed by Elaine Paige in the Lloyd Webber musical Evita, was the biggest-selling single by a female vocalist at the time, shifting more than 993,000 copies. (B-side: Rainbow High)

↗ NO.401
19 FEB •••

WHEN I NEED YOU (4.08)
Leo Sayer
(Albert Hammond, Carole Bayer Sager). Sayer's first UK No.1 after three No.2 hits was produced by American Richard Perry, who also produced the single that replaced it. 'When I Need You' prevented Heatwave's disco classic 'Boogie Nights' from topping the chart. (B-side: I Think We Fell in Love Too Fast) **US 1**

↗ NO.402
12 MAR •••

CHANSON D'AMOUR (2.51)
Manhattan Transfer
(Wayne Shanklin). Oddly, the US group's rendition of this 1958 US million-seller by Art and Dotty Todd failed to chart in their homeland. (B-side: Popsicle Toes)

↗ NO.403
2 APR •••••

KNOWING ME, KNOWING YOU (3.59)
Abba (Stig Anderson, Benny Andersson, Björn Ulvaeus). No single spent longer at No.1 in 1977 than Abba's fifth self-penned chart-topper. (B-side: Happy Hawaii) **US 14**

↗ NO.404
7 MAY ••

FREE (2.51)
Deniece Williams (Deniece Williams, Hank Redd, Nathan Watts, Susaye Green). Maurice White of Earth Wind and Fire produced the ex-Stevie Wonder backing

singer's chart-topping debut hit.
(B-side: Cause You Love Me Baby) **US 25**

↗ NO.405
21. MAY ●●●●
I DON'T WANT TO TALK ABOUT IT (4.21) / **FIRST CUT IS THE DEEPEST** (4.48) **Rod Stewart** (Danny Whitten / Cat Stevens). The A-side had first been recorded by Neil Young's group Crazy Horse, while its flip side was initially cut by composer Stevens. **US 46 / 21**

↗ NO.406
18 JUN ●
LUCILLE (3.30)
Kenny Rogers (Roger Bowling, Hal Bynum). The only country singer to top the UK chart twice did so with a song he learned and

recorded in just 15 minutes and one take.
(B-side: Till I Get It Right) **US 5**

↗ NO.407
25 JUN ●
SHOW YOU THE WAY TO GO (3.27)
The Jacksons (Kenny Gamble, Leon Huff). These Motown discoveries clocked up their only UK No.1 after they had left the label with a song written and produced by Gamble and Huff. (B-side: Blues Away) **US 28**

↗ NO.408
2 JUL ●●●
SO YOU WIN AGAIN (4.29)
Hot Chocolate (Russ Ballard). Group leader Errol Brown wrote most of the chart regulars' hits, but oddly did not pen their only No.1. (B-side: A Part of Being with You) **US 31**

↗ NO.409
23 JUL ●●●●
I FEEL LOVE (3.45)
Donna Summer (Giorgio Moroder, Pete Bellotte, Donna Summer). This classic club song was Summer's sole No.1. The song returned to the Top 10 by Bronski Beat in 1985 and Summer herself in 1995. (B-side: Can't We Just Sit Down [And Talk About It]) **US 6**

↗ NO.410
20 AUG ●
ANGELO (3.16)
Brotherhood of Man (Tony Hiller, Martin Lee, Lee Sheridan). This sad saga made the quartet the first UK Eurovision Song Contest winners to return to the top. (B-side: All Night)

↗ NO.411
27 AUG ●
FLOAT ON (4.09)
The Floaters (Arnold Ingram, James Mitchell Jr, Marvin Willis). Despite introducing themselves individually on their No.1 record, The Floaters – Ralph, Charles, Paul and Larry – sank without trace shortly afterwards. (B-side: Everything Happens for a Reason) **US 2**

↗ NO.412
3 SEP ●●●●●
WAY DOWN (2.35)
Elvis Presley: Vocal acc JD Sumner & The Stamps Qt, K Westmoreland, S Neilson and M Smith (Layng Martine Jr). This single had dropped way down before Elvis's death sent it shooting up to the top. It was the King's last No.1 for 25 years. (B-side: Pledging My Love) **US 18**

↗ NO.413
8 OCT ●●●
SILVER LADY (3.40)
David Soul (Tony Macaulay, Geoff Stephens). TV cop Hutch, who was the year's top-selling artist, followed his million-selling debut hit with another 'Made in Britain' global hit. (B-side: Rider) **US 52**

↗ NO.414
29 OCT ●
YES SIR, I CAN BOOGIE (4.32)
Baccara (Frank Dostal, Rolf Soja). Spain's first UK chart-topping act just pipped France's La Belle Epoque at the post to become the first female duo to reach the top. (B-side: Cara Mia)

↗ NO.415
5 NOV ●●●●
THE NAME OF THE GAME (3.55)
Abba (Stig Anderson, Benny Andersson, Björn Ulvaeus). The battle for No.1 on the

↘ **CHART-TOPPER NO.399, 413:** Born in Chicago, but raised in Germany, David Soul (TV's Hutch in Starsky and Hutch) spent seven weeks at No.1 in the UK in 1977 and a further week atop the Billboard chart

chart's 25th anniversary was won by Abba, who stopped Queen from saying 'We Are the Champions'.
(B-side: I Wonder [Departure]) **US 12**

⬈ NO.416
3 DEC ●●●●●●●●●
MULL OF KINTYRE (4.41) /
GIRLS' SCHOOL (4.35)
Wings (Paul McCartney, Denny Laine)
The first UK two-million-seller with total sales of 2,050,000 was a major hit in most countries, but only 'Girls' School' made it in the US. **US 0 / 32**

⬈ NO.417
4 FEB ●
UPTOWN TOP RANKING (3.53)
Althia and Donna (Althia Forest, Donna Reid).
The youngest female duo to reach No.1 could not manage another chart entry, never mind a top ranking one. (B-side: Calico Suit)

⬈ NO.418
11 FEB ●
FIGARO (2.53)
Brotherhood of Man (Tony Hiller, Martin Lee, Lee Sheridan). Q: A foreign male's name, ending with 'o', that was a Brotherhood of Man No.1? A: Take your pick, 'Angelo' or 'Figaro'. (B-side: You Can Say That Again)

⬈ NO.419
18 FEB ●●●
TAKE A CHANCE ON ME (4.00)
Abba (Benny Andersson, Björn Ulvaeus).
The group's second transatlantic top three entry was their sixth UK No.1 in just over two years. (B-side: I'm a Marionette) **US 3**

⬈ NO.420
11 MAR ●●●●
WUTHERING HEIGHTS (4.27)
Kate Bush (Kate Bush).
This unique teenage singer / songwriter shares her birthday with Emily Brontë, who had also scored with her self-penned debut 'Wuthering Heights'. (B-side: Kite)

⬈ NO.421
8 APR ●●●
MATCHSTALK MEN AND MATCHSTALK CATS AND DOGS (LOWRY'S SONG) (4.32)
Brian and Michael (Michael Coleman).
This catchy L S Lowry-inspired one-hit wonder stopped Blondie from reaching No.1 with their debut hit 'Denis'. (B-side: The Old Rocking Chair)

⬈ NO.422
29 APR ●●
NIGHT FEVER (3.30)
The Bee Gees (Barry, Robin and Maurice Gibb). This disco classic, taken from the 30-million-selling 'Saturday Night Fever' soundtrack, gave the three brothers their third No.1. (B-side: Down the Road) **US 1**

⬈ NO.423
13 MAY ●●●●●
RIVERS OF BABYLON (4.15) /
BROWN GIRL IN THE RING (3.05)
Boney M
(Traditional: arranged by Frank Farian, Hans-Georg Mayer). Both sides made independent trips into the top three and helped to make this a 1,985,000-selling single. **US 30 / 0**

⬈ NO.424
17 JUN ●●●●●●●●●
YOU'RE THE ONE THAT I WANT (2.48) **John Travolta and Olivia Newton-John** (John Farrar). This 1,975,000 seller came from the duo's movie Grease. It returned to the top five in both 1990 (as part of the 'Grease Megamix') and 1998. (B-side: Alone at a Drive In Movie [inst] – Ernie Watts) **US 1**

⬈ NO.425
19 AUG ●●●●●
THREE TIMES A LADY (3.36)
The Commodores (Lionel Richie Jr).
Motown's top UK seller at the time, with sales of more than 975,000. Richie's mother was the inspiration for the song.
(B-side: Can't Let You Tease Me) **US 1**

⬈ NO.426
23 SEP ●
DREADLOCK HOLIDAY (4.59)
10cc (Eric Stewart, Graham Gouldman).
This international hit was inspired by the holiday stories that Justin Hayward of The Moody Blues told to the composers.
(B-side: Nothing Can Move Me) US 44

⬈ NO.427
30 SEP ●●●●●●●
SUMMER NIGHTS (3.35)
John Travolta, Olivia Newton-John and cast (Warren Casey, Jim Jacobs).
They released only two singles together, but both topped the UK charts (with a combined 16 weeks at No.1). (B-side: Rock 'n' Roll Party Queen [Louis St Louis]) **US 5**

⬈ NO.428
18 NOV ●●
RAT TRAP (4.56)
The Boomtown Rats (Bob Geldof).
The first new wave No.1 was also the first

No.1 for both Bob Geldof and the future Mr Shania Twain, producer Robert 'Mutt' Lange.
(B-side: So Strange)

⬈ NO.429
2 DEC ●
DA YA THINK I'M SEXY? (5.29)
Rod Stewart (Rod Stewart, Carmen Appice).
Disco was at its height when Rod the rocker climbed on the bandwagon and took this dancehall favourite to the top around the globe. (B-side: Dirty Weekend) **US 1**

⬈ NO.430
9 DEC ●●●●
MARY'S BOY CHILD – OH MY LORD (4.04) **Boney M**
(Jester Harrison, Frank Farian, Fred Jay).
The group scored their second UK million-seller (1,790,000) with a song that was a Christmas No.1 for Harry Belafonte in 1957.
(B-side: Dancing in the Street) **US 85**

⬈ NO.431
6 JAN ●●●
Y.M.C.A. (3.44)
Village People
(Jacques Morali, Henri Belolo, Victor Willis).
This classic club anthem passed the million sales mark in Germany, the US and the UK, where it sold more than 150,000 copies in just one day. Total UK sales were 1,380,000.
(B-side: The Women) **US 2**

⬈ NO.432
27 JAN ●
HIT ME WITH YOUR RHYTHM STICK (3.41) **Ian and The Blockheads** (Ian Dury, Chas Jankel). This clever combination of new wave and disco sold 978,000 in the UK and charted again in 1985 and 1991. (B-side: There Ain't Half Been Some Clever Bastards)

⬈ NO.433
3 FEB ●●●●
HEART OF GLASS (4.00)
Blondie (Chris Stein, Deborah Harry).
Rak Records' ace producer Mike Chapman helped Debbie Harry and her group to score the first of their three No.1s.
(B-side: Rifle Range) **US 1**

⬈ NO.434
3 MAR ●●
TRAGEDY (5.04)
The Bee Gees
(Barry, Maurice and Robin Gibb).
The world's top group of the late 1970s scored their fifth successive US No.1 with

this song, which in 1998 topped the UK chart by Steps. (B-side: Until) **US 1**

↗ NO.435
17 MAR ••••
I WILL SURVIVE (3.17)
Gloria Gaynor (Dino Fekaris, Freddie Perren).
This karaoke classic started life as the B-side of Gloria's cover version of Clout's 'Substitute'. A remix reached the top five in 1993.
(B-side: Anybody Wanna Party?) **US 1**

↗ NO.436
14 APR ••••••
BRIGHT EYES (3.56)
Art Garfunkel (Mike Batt).
More than 1,155,000 people in the UK brought Art's interpretation of Womble man Mike Batt's theme from the animated film Watership Down. (B-side: Kehaar's Theme)

↗ NO.437
26 MAY •••
SUNDAY GIRL (3.04)
Blondie (Chris Stein).
Blondie spent longer in the Top 75 than anyone else in 1979, and no single reached the top quicker than the two weeks it took 'Sunday Girl' to get there.
(B-side: I Know But I Don't Know)

↗ NO.438
16 JUN ••
RING MY BELL (3.18)
Anita Ward (Frederick Knight).
Composer / producer Knight played all the instruments on this disco classic that made US schoolteacher Miss Ward a one-hit wonder. (B-side: If I Could Feel That Old Feeling Again) **US 1**

↗ NO.439
30 JUN ••••
ARE 'FRIENDS' ELECTRIC? (5.22)
Tubeway Army (Gary Numan).
The track that introduced the world to Gary Numan topped the chart at the same time as the group's first album 'Replicas'.
(B-side: We Are So Fragile)

↗ NO.440
28 JUL ••••
I DON'T LIKE MONDAYS (4.16)
The Boomtown Rats (Bob Geldof).
An international hit about 16-year-old Brenda Spencer, who shot and killed two teachers and injured nine children at a Cleveland elementary school.
(B-side: It's All the Rage) **US 73**

↗ NO.441
25 AUG ••••
WE DON'T TALK ANY MORE (4.13)
Cliff Richard (Alan Tarney).
Cliff's biggest UK hit of the 1970s was one of only three US Top 10 entries he has ever achieved. (B-side: Count Me Out) **US 7**

↗ NO.442
22 SEP •
CARS (3.55)
Gary Numan (Gary Numan).
Both Numan and the previous chart-topper were born with the surname Webb. This classic car song re-charted in 1987, 1993 and 1996. (B-side: Asylum) **US 9**

↗ NO.443
29 SEP •••
MESSAGE IN A BOTTLE (4.52)
The Police (Sting). The first of the trio's four No.1 singles was also the first No.1 in the UK for the Herb Alpert-owned A&M label.
(B-side: Landlord) **US 74**

↗ NO.444
28 OCT •
VIDEO KILLED THE RADIO STAR (3.27) **Buggles**
(Bruce Woolley, Trevor Horn, Geoff Downes).
This prophetic song, which introduced the music world to Trevor Horn, was the first video to be seen on MTV.
(B-side: Kid Dynamo) **US 40**

↗ NO.445
27 OCT •••
ONE DAY AT A TIME (3.14)
Lena Martell (Kris Kristofferson).
In America, the song that turned Lena into a one-hit wonder (after 18 years of recording) was used as a theme tune by Alcoholics Anonymous. (B-side: Hello Misty Morning)

↘ **CHART-TOPPER NO.446:** : Dr Hook, another US act that topped the UK chart without the same success in their native America. Their only No.1, 'When You're In Love With A Beautiful Woman', was written by Even Stevens and produced by Ron Haffkine

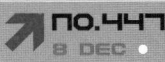

NO.446
17 NOV ●●●

WHEN YOU'RE IN LOVE WITH A BEAUTIFUL WOMAN (2.53)
Dr Hook (Even Stevens). The group's Ray Sawyer was one of three eye-patch-wearing chart-toppers. The others? Johnny Kidd and Gabrielle. (B-side: Dooley Jones) **US 6**

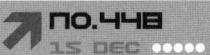

NO.447
8 DEC ●

WALKING ON THE MOON (5.03)
The Police (Sting). No singles in 1979 entered at No.1, but, like the previous Police record, this track took just two weeks to make the journey. (B-side: Visions of the Night)

NO.448
15 DEC ●●●●●

ANOTHER BRICK IN THE WALL (PART 2) (3.09)
Pink Floyd (Roger Waters).
One of the year's biggest global hits sold 995,000 in the UK and a similar figure in the US for the group that never returned to the singles Top 20, despite massive success with their albums. (B-side: One of My Turns) **US 1**

1980

NO.449
19 JAN ●●

BRASS IN POCKET (3.04)
The Pretenders
(Chrissie Hynde, James Honeyman-Scott). The group's biggest hit reached the top in the same week they became the first group to have their debut album go straight in at No.1. (B-sides: Swinging London / Nervous But Shy) **US 14**

NO.450
2 FEB ●●

THE SPECIAL A.K.A. LIVE! EP (2.06) **The Specials**
(Jerry Dammers, Lloyd Chalmers, Dimitri Tiomkin, Paul Francis Webster / Sydney Roy Crooks, Jackie Robinson, George Agard / Harry Johnson / Morty Naismith, Roy Ellis). The lead track, 'Too Much Too Young', was a truncated, speeded-up version of a live track from their first album.
(EP Tracks: Too Much Too Young / Guns of Navarone / Longshot Kick De Bucket / The Liquidator / Skinhead Moonstomp)

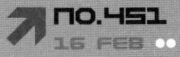

NO.451
16 FEB ●●

COWARD OF THE COUNTY (4.17)
Kenny Rogers (Roger Bowling, B E Wheeler).

The only country artist to have two No.1s in the UK starred in a movie the following year based on this story of a worm that turned. (B-side: I Want to Make You Smile) **US 3**

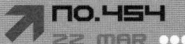

NO.452
1 MAR ●●

ATOMIC (3.46)
Blondie (Chris Stein, Debbie Harry).
This track made Blondie the first, and only, US-formed group to top the UK chart in both the 1970s and 1980s.
(B-side: Die Young, Stay Pretty) **US 39**

NO.453
15 MAR ●

TOGETHER WE ARE BEAUTIFUL (4.11) **Fern Kinney**
(Ken Leray). A song which the composer recorded unsuccessfully in 1977 took Kinney to the top, although she never bothered the chart compilers again.
(B-side: Baby Let Me Kiss You)

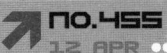

NO.454
22 MAR ●●●

GOING UNDERGROUND (2.53) /
DREAMS OF CHILDREN (3.06)
The Jam (Paul Weller).
The first double A-side to debut at No.1 was helped by the fact that initial copies came with an additional three-track single, featuring 'Away from the Numbers' and 'The Modern World' on the A-side and 'Down in the Tube Station at Midnight' on the B-side.

NO.455
12 APR ●●

WORKING MY WAY BACK TO YOU – FORGIVE ME GIRL (MEDLEY) (4.00)
The Detroit Spinners
(Sandy Linzer, Denny Randell, Michael Zager). The medley's first song completed a trio of Four Seasons covers to reach No.1, following 'Silence Is Golden' (1967) and 'Bye Bye Baby' (1975). (B-side: Disco Ride) **US 2**

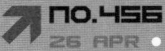

NO.456
26 APR ●

CALL ME (3.26)
Blondie (Giorgio Moroder, Debbie Harry).
This was 1980's biggest US seller thanks, in part, to Giorgio Moroder's production and its inclusion in the movie American Gigolo.
(B-side: Call Me (instrumental)) **US 1**

NO.457
3 MAY ●●

GENO (3.27)
Dexy's Midnight Runners
(Kevin Rowland, Al Archer).

The Birmingham band's tribute to the US-born and UK-based soul singer Geno Washington, who never had a major UK or US hit of his own. (B-side: Breaking Down the Walls of Heartache)

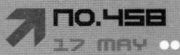

NO.458
17 MAY ●●

WHAT'S ANOTHER YEAR (2.56)
Johnny Logan
(Shay Healy). This was only the third foreign Eurovision winner to top the UK chart. Logan went on to win the contest again in 1987.
(B-side: One Night Stand)

NO.459
31 MAY ●●●

THEME FROM M*A*S*H (SUICIDE IS PAINLESS) (2.53)
Mash (Mike Altman, Johnny Mandel).
The theme from the film and long-running TV series was recorded 10 years before hitting No.1. No follow-up was ever released. (B-side: The M.A.S.H. March)

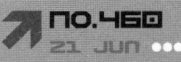

NO.460
21 JUN ●●●

CRYING (3.40)
Don McLean (Roy Orbison, Joe Melson).
Exactly eight years after his previous No.1, McLean hit the top again with a revival of a minor Roy Orbison UK hit from 1961.
(B-side: Genesis (In the Beginning)) **US 5**

NO.461
12 JUL ●●

XANADU (3.29)
Olivia Newton-John and Electric Light Orchestra (Jeff Lynne).
Olivia's only No.1s came with duets from films in which she starred. This movie theme gave ELO their only No.1 from 27 Top 40 hits.
(B-side: Fool Country) **US 8**

NO.462
26 JUL ●●

USE IT UP AND WEAR IT OUT (3.49) **Odyssey**
(Sandy Linzer, L Russell Brown).
The third US single to reach the top in the UK in 1980 without making the American Top 100 (joining Fern Kinney and M*A*S*H). (B-side: Don't Tell Me Tell Her)

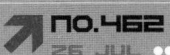

NO.463
9 AUG ●●

THE WINNER TAKES IT ALL (4.52) **Abba**
(Benny Andersson, Björn Ulvaeus).
Group members Benny and Agnetha (who sang lead on this track) thought this was "the best song Abba ever did". It was their eighth No.1. (B-side: Elaine) **US 8**

↗ NO.464
23 AUG ●●
ASHES TO ASHES (3.39)
David Bowie (David Bowie).
Bowie's second No.1 provided an update on the character from his first one, 'Space Oddity', revealing Major Tom as a junkie this time. (B-side: Move On)

↗ NO.465
6 SEP ●
START (2.16)
The Jam (Paul Weller).
The band's ninth hit of the year, thanks to a slew of re-issues charting in April, provided the highest tally for any act in 1980. (B-side: Liza Radley)

↗ NO.466
13 SEP ●●
FEELS LIKE I'M IN LOVE (3.15)
Kelly Marie (Ray Dorset).
This syndrum-punctuated hit was composed by Mungo Jerry's leader and had flopped when Kelly first released it 18 months earlier. (B-side: I Can't Get Enough)

↗ NO.467
27 SEP ●●●●
DON'T STAND SO CLOSE TO ME (3.52) **The Police**
(Sting). Making the band only the seventh act ever to debut in pole position, this was the trio's third chart-topper within a year. (B-side: Friends) **US 10**

↗ NO.468
25 OCT ●●●
WOMAN IN LOVE (3.47)
Barbra Streisand (Barry and Robin Gibb). From the album 'Guilty', Streisand's only UK No.1 made her the first female to top the singles and albums charts simultaneously . (B-side: Run Wild) **US 1**

↗ NO.469
15 NOV ●●
THE TIDE IS HIGH (4.32)
Blondie (John Holt).
Originally sung by the composer's group The Paragons, this reggae cover made Blondie the first US-based group to have three No.1s in a row. (B-side: Susie and Jeffrey) **US 1**

↗ NO.470
29 NOV ●●●
SUPER TROUPER (4.08)
Abba (Benny Andersson, Björn Ulvaeus). The ninth, and final, chart-topper for the Superswedes brought their tally of weeks at No.1 to 31 – the highest for any overseas group. (B-side: The Piper) **US 45**

↗ NO.471
20 DEC ●
(JUST LIKE) STARTING OVER (3.55)
John Lennon (John Lennon).
The song initially peaked at No.8, but news of Lennon's murder catapulted this modest hit from No.21 to the top – the first disc to jump to No.1 from outside the Top 20 since 'Hey Jude' in 1968.
(B-side: Kiss Kiss Kiss) **US 1**

↗ NO.472
27 DEC ●●
THERE'S NO ONE QUITE LIKE GRANDMA (2.59)
St Winifred's School Choir (Gordon Lorenz). The first choir to top the chart in its own right had previously backed fellow one-hit wonders Brian and Michael on their No.1. (B-side: Pinocchio)

1981

↗ NO.473
10 JAN ●●●●
IMAGINE (3.01)
John Lennon (John Lennon).
During this 1,486,000-selling 1975 release's run at the top, Lennon featured on three of the top five singles – the first act to do so since Frankie Laine in 1953.
(B-side: Working Class Hero) **US 3**

↗ NO.474
7 FEB ●●
WOMAN (3.25)
John Lennon (John Lennon).
Three No.1s in seven weeks is the fastest ever hat-trick. Lennon also duplicated a feat previously achieved only by The Beatles by replacing himself at No.1 (B-side: Beautiful Boy – Yoko Ono) **US 2**

↗ NO.475
21 FEB ●●●
SHADDAP YOU FACE (3.11)
Joe Dolce Music Theatre (Joe Dolce).
This US vocalist, in character as the Italian Guiseppe, famously kept Ultravox's 'Vienna' at No.2 for all three weeks of his chart reign. (B-side: Ain't No Hurry) **US 53**

↗ NO.476
14 MAR ●●
JEALOUS GUY (4.51)
Roxy Music (John Lennon).
Recorded as a tribute, this cover gave Lennon the distinction of being the sole writer of four of the six No.1s since his death.
(B-side: To Turn You On)

↗ NO.477
28 MAR ●●●
THIS OLE HOUSE (3.04)
Shakin' Stevens (Stuart Hamblen). It was originally recorded by its composer in 1954, and Rosemary Clooney and Shaky became the first soloists of different sexes to take the same song to No.1. (B-side: Let Me Show You How)

↗ NO.478
18 APR ●●●
MAKING YOUR MIND UP (2.37)
Bucks Fizz (Andy Hill, John Danter).
This was the UK's fourth Eurovision winner. The act included Cheryl Baker from 1978 Euro-flop group Co-Co. (B-side: Don't Stop)

↗ NO.479
9 MAY ●●●●●
STAND AND DELIVER (3.07)
Adam and The Ants
(Adam Ant, Marco Pirroni). The eighth act to debut at No.1 since the UK chart began did so in a year when they spent 91 weeks on the chart. (B-side: Beat My Guest)

↗ NO.480
13 JUN ●●
BEING WITH YOU (3.56)
Smokey Robinson (William "Smokey" Robinson). More than 10 years after vacating the top spot with The Miracles, Smokey claimed his only solo No.1 with a song he had penned for Kim Carnes. (B-side: What's in Your Life for Me) **US 2**

↗ NO.481
27 JUN ●●
ONE DAY IN YOUR LIFE (4.12)
Michael Jackson (Sam Brown III, Renee Armand). This 1975 album track was Jackson's first solo chart-topper and provided the only instance of consecutive Motown No.1s. (B-side: Take Me Back) **US 55**

↗ NO.482
11 JUL ●●●
GHOST TOWN (3.40)
The Specials (Jerry Dammers). The group's last single featuring three of their mainstays, Terry Hall, Neville Staples and Lynval Golding, who had left to form Fun Boy Three. (B-sides: Why? / Friday Night, Saturday Morning)

↗ NO.483
1 AUG ●●●●
GREEN DOOR (3.13)
Shakin' Stevens (Bob Davie, Marvin Moore). A quarter of a century after the song charted by Jim Lowe and Frankie Vaughan, Shaky's rockin' update jumped from No.22 to No.1. (B-side: Don't Turn Your Back)

↗ **NO.484**
29 AUG •

JAPANESE BOY (3.55)
Aneka (Bobby Heatlie).
Scottish folk singer Mary Sandeman donned a kimono and wig for this No.1 novelty, which was considered "too Chinese" by her Japanese label. (B-side: A Fond Kiss)

↗ **NO.485**
5 SEP ••

TAINTED LOVE (2.39)
Soft Cell (Ed Cobb).
This update of Gloria Jones's 1964 northern soul classic sold 1,135,000 and was penned by a member of earlier chart acts The Four Preps and Piltdown Men. (B-side: Where Did Our Love Go) **US 8**

↗ **NO.486**
19 SEP ••••

PRINCE CHARMING (3.16)
Adam and The Ants
(Marco Pirroni, Adam Ant).
Sales of their second No.1 were helped by a video where Adam went to the ball thanks to his fairy godmother Diana Dors. (B-side: Christian D'Or)

↗ **NO.487**
17 OCT ••••

IT'S MY PARTY (3.46)
Dave Stewart with Barbara Gaskin
(Herb Weiner, Wally Gold, John Gluck Jr).
This cover of Lesley Gore's 1963 US topper made a surprise leap from No.8 to deny The Tweets a No.1 hit with 'The Birdie Song' (B-side: Waiting in the Wings) **US 72**

↗ **NO.488**
14 NOV •

EVERY LITTLE THING SHE DOES IS MAGIC (4.20)
The Police (Sting).
The song was rush released and charted only a month after The Police's last hit. The light-hearted video that accompanied the single was shot at George Martin's recording studio in Montserrat. (B-side: Flexible Strategy) **US 3**

↗ **NO.489**
21 NOV ••

UNDER PRESSURE (3.55)
Queen and David Bowie
(Queen, David Bowie).
The first instance of two chart-topping UK acts combining to create another No.1. Sampled by Vanilla Ice on his 1990 topper 'Ice Ice Baby'. (B-side: Soul Brother – Queen) **US 29**

↘ **CHART-TOPPER NO.479, 486, 502:** Adam and the Ants and Adam Ant were responsible for the audio-visual movement Antmusic. Extravagant videos for their singles featured pantomime imagery and included guest stars Diana Dors and Lulu

↗ **NO.490**
5 DEC ●

BEGIN THE BEGUINE
(VOLVER A EMPEZAR) (4.43)
Julio Iglesias
(Cole Porter: Spanish lyrics by Julio Iglesias).
This song, from the flop 1935 musical Jubilee,
became the first Spanish-language No.1 after
the 1970 Eurovision entrant's own lyrics were
added. (B-side: De Niña A Mujer)

↗ **NO.491**
12 DEC ●●●●

DON'T YOU WANT ME
(3.57) **Human League**
(Jo Callis, Phil Oakey, Philip Adrian Wright).
The fourth single from their album 'Dare' was
the group's biggest hit, selling more than a
million copies in both the UK and US.
(B-side: Seconds) **US 1**

1982

↗ **NO.492**
16 JAN ●●

THE LAND OF MAKE BELIEVE (3.46)
Bucks Fizz (Andy Hill, Peter Sinfield).
The Eurovision winners' second No.1 ended
with a poem read by 11-year-old Abby
Kimber from fellow chart act Minipops.
(B-side: Now You're Gone)

↗ **NO.493**
30 JAN ●

OH JULIE (2.32)
Shakin' Stevens (Shakin' Stevens).
Shaky's first self-penned hit was his third No.1
within a year and was a US Top 40 hit for
Barry Manilow later the same year.
(B-side: I'm Knockin')

↗ **NO.494**
6 FEB ●

COMPUTER LOVE (3.49) /
THE MODEL (3.39)
Kraftwerk
(Ralf Hutter, Karl Bartos, Emil Schulz).
A 1981 Top 40 entrant which hit the top when
emphasis was put on the original B-side
'The Model', from the band's 1978 album
The Man-Machine.

↗ **NO.495**
13 FEB ●●●

TOWN CALLED MALICE (2.55) /
PRECIOUS (2.51)
The Jam (Paul Weller).
By debuting at No.1, the second successive
double-sided topper stopped The Stranglers'
controversial 'Golden Brown' from reaching
the peak.

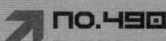

↘ **CHART-TOPPER NO.454, 465, 495, 511:** All three members of The Jam were from Woking in Surrey. The trio, Paul Weller (left), Rick Buckler (centre) and Bruce Foxton (right), are pictured on their extensive farewell tour in 1983

↗ **NO.496**
6 MAR ●●●

THE LION SLEEPS TONIGHT (3.15)
Tight Fit (Hugo Peretti, Luigi Creatore, George David Weiss, Solomon Linda, Paul Campbell). Selling 978,000 this time around, this song was first recorded by Zulu group Solomon Linda & The Evening Birds as 'Mbube' in 1939. The song hit in the 1960s under this title and also as 'Wimoweh'. (B-sides: Rhythm, Movement and Throbbing / Beep Beep)

↗ **NO.497**
27 MAR ●●●

SEVEN TEARS (3.48)
Goombay Dance Band (Wolff-Ekkehardt Stein, Wolfgang Jass). The second German-based group to top the UK chart, after Kraftwerk the previous month, is the only No.1 act to include a fire-eater. (B-side: Mama Coco)

↗ **NO.498**
17 APR ●

MY CAMERA NEVER LIES (3.46)
Bucks Fizz (Andy Hill, Nicola Martin). The group emulated fellow Eurovision winners Sandie Shaw and Brotherhood of Man by having three No.1 singles. (B-side: What Am I Gonna Do)

↗ **NO.499**
24 APR ●●●

EBONY AND IVORY (3.40)
Paul McCartney with Stevie Wonder (Paul McCartney). Although they had clocked up more than 900 chart weeks between them at this stage, neither man had achieved a solo No.1. (B-side: Rainclouds – Paul McCartney) US 1

↗ **NO.500**
15 MAY ●●

A LITTLE PEACE (3.01)
Nicole (Ralph Siegel, Bernd Meinunger). This Eurovision winner was the third German No.1 of 1982. It stopped Yazoo's 'Only You' from claiming the prestigious 500th No.1. (B-side: Thank You, Merci)

↗ **NO.501**
29 MAY ●●

HOUSE OF FUN (2.55)
Madness (Mike Barson, Lee Thompson). No group spent longer on the chart in the 1980s than Madness, whose only No.1 was the only chart-topper for Stiff Records in the 1980s. (B-side: Don't Look Back)

↗ **NO.502**
12 JUN ●●

GOODY TWO SHOES (3.29)
Adam Ant (Adam Ant, Marco Pirroni).

With his first solo release, Adam joined an elite group of individuals to top the UK chart both solo and as part of a group. (B-side: Red Scab) US 12

↗ **NO.503**
26 JUN ●

I'VE NEVER BEEN TO ME (3.53)
Charlene (Ron Miller, Ken Hirsch). Originally recorded by Nancy Wilson, this version was a minor US hit in 1977 before being rediscovered thanks initially to a Florida DJ. (B-side: Somewhere in My Life) US 3

↗ **NO.504**
3 JUL ●●

HAPPY TALK (3.26)
Captain Sensible (Richard Rodgers, Oscar Hammerstein II). This song, which was first sung by Juanita Hall in the 1949 musical South Pacific, made the jump from No.33 to the top. (B-side: I Can't Stand It)

↗ **NO.505**
17 JUL ●●●

FAME (3.47)
Irene Cara (Michael Gore, Dean Pitchford). Selling 975,000 copies in the process, this two-year-old film theme and soundtrack LP simultaneously headed the charts thanks to the popularity of the Fame TV series. (B-side: Never Alone). US 4

↗ **NO.506**
7 AUG ●●●●

COME ON EILEEN (4.12)
Dexy's Midnight Runners with The Emerald Express (Kevin Rowland, Jimmy Patterson, Kevin Adams). The only 1982 release to sell a million copies also topped the US chart eight months later. (B-side: Dubious) US 1

↗ **NO.507**
4 SEP ●●●●

EYE OF THE TIGER (4.01)
Survivor (Frankie Sullivan, Jim Peterik). Rocky star Sylvester Stallone personally asked Survivor to write and record the theme to Rocky III, and this gave them a transatlantic No.1 and UK sales of 990,000. (B-side: Take Me on a Saturday) US 1

↗ **NO.508**
2 OCT ●●●

PASS THE DUTCHIE (3.21)
Musical Youth (Jackie Mittoo, Fitzroy Simpson, Lloyd Ferguson). First recorded by The Mighty Diamonds as 'Pass the Kutchie', this version jumped from No.26 to No.1 – the biggest jump by any UK group. (B-side: Give Love a Chance) US 10

↗ **NO.509**
23 OCT ●●●

DO YOU REALLY WANT TO HURT ME (4.23)
Culture Club (Culture Club). Their controversial leader Boy George refused to sing it more than once in the studio and did not want this track released as a single. (B-side: Culture Club featuring Papa Weasel – Dub Version) US 2

↗ **NO.510**
13 NOV ●●●

I DON'T WANNA DANCE (3.39)
Eddy Grant (Eddy Grant). A 1968 chart-topper as a member of The Equals, Grant had the longest wait of any individual between a No.1 in a group and as a soloist. (B-side: I Don't Wanna Dance (a capella)) US 53

↗ **NO.511**
4 DEC ●●

BEAT SURRENDER (3.24)
The Jam (Paul Weller). The Jam equalled a record set by Slade in 1973 when this, their final single, became their third one to debut at No.1. (B-side: Shopping)

↗ **NO.512**
18 DEC ●●●●

SAVE YOUR LOVE (3.07)
Renée and Renato (John and Sue Edward). Hilary Lester (the voice of Renée) left the act before this hit, so the video featured a wig-wearing stand-in who had no facial close-ups. (B-side: If Love Is Not the Reason)

1983

↗ **NO.513**
15 JAN ●●

YOU CAN'T HURRY LOVE (2.52)
Phil Collins (Brian Holland, Lamont Dozier, Eddie Holland). The first of Collins' two solo No.1s, both with covers of 1966 UK hits, was the third chart-topper for its legendary writing trio. (B-side: I Cannot Believe It's True) US 10

↗ **NO.514**
29 JAN ●●●

DOWN UNDER (3.43)
Men at Work (Colin Hay, Ron Strykert). This single and its parent album, Business as Usual, simultaneously topped both the UK and US singles and albums charts. (B-side: Crazy) US 10

⬎ CHART-TOPPER NO.529: The 1983 Christmas No.1 by The Flying Pickets stayed at the top for five weeks. The Pickets were Ken Gregson, Gareth Williams, Red Stripe, Rick Lloyd, David Brett and singer / actor Brian Hibbard, who appeared in Coronation Street

↗ NO.515
19 FEB ••
TOO SHY (3.44)
Kajagoogoo (Kajagoogoo: Lyrics by Limahl, Nick Beggs). This international smash was co-produced by Duran Duran's Nick Rhodes before his own band had scored a UK No.1 of its own. **US 5**

↗ NO.516
5 MAR •
BILLIE JEAN (4.53)
Michael Jackson (Michael Jackson). The six Top 20 singles from Thriller, the world's best-selling album, managed only this one week in pole position between them. (B-side: It's the Falling in Love) **US 1**

↗ NO.517
12 MAR ••
TOTAL ECLIPSE OF THE HEART (4.30)
Bonnie Tyler (Jim Steinman). The only single by a British woman to top the UK and US charts. Tyler was also the first UK female to have a No.1 single from a No.1 album. (B-side: Take Me Back) **US 1**

↗ NO.518
26 MAR ••
IS THERE SOMETHING I SHOULD KNOW? (4.09)
Duran Duran (Duran Duran). Emulating The Jam and Adam and The Ants by debuting at No.1 with their first chart-topper was no mean feat – "about as easy as a nuclear war". (B-side: Faith in This Colour) **US 4**

↗ NO.519
9 APR •••
LET'S DANCE (4.08)
David Bowie (David Bowie). Bowie's 23rd transatlantic hit was his only No.1 in both the UK and US. It was also Chic's Nile Rodgers' first No.1 as a producer. (B-side: Cat People (Putting Out the Fire)) **US 4**

↗ NO.520
30 APR ••••
TRUE (5.31)
Spandau Ballet (Gary Kemp). Uniquely, the title track from a chart-topping album replaced another at No.1. The albums did the same thing during this single's run at the top. (B-side: Lifeline) **US 4**

↗ NO.521
28 MAY •
CANDY GIRL (3.36)
New Edition (Maurice Starr, Michael Jonzun). This teen quintet's component parts (Ralph Tresvant, Bobby Brown and Bell Biv Devoe) all returned to the Top 10, but the group never did. **US 46**

↗ NO.522
4 JUN ••••
EVERY BREATH YOU TAKE (4.14)
The Police (Sting). This single made ex-Policeman Sting the first person to compose single-handedly five UK No.1s. It was also the basis of Puff Daddy's 1997 topper. (B-side: Murder by Numbers) **US 1**

↗ NO.523
2 JUL •••
BABY JANE (4.43)
Rod Stewart (Rod Stewart, Jay Davis). With this release, Rod became the first UK male to have six entirely solo No.1s – a total never bettered. (B-side: Ready Now) **US 14**

↗ NO.524
23 JUL •••
WHEREVER I LAY MY HAT (THAT'S MY HOME) (4.10)
Paul Young (Marvin Gaye, Norman Whitfield, Barrett Strong). This cover of a 1963 Marvin Gaye recording gave Gaye his only No.1 as a composer in his lifetime. (B-side: Broken Man) **US 70**

↗ NO.525
13 AUG •••
GIVE IT UP (4.04)
KC and The Sunshine Band (Harry Casey, Debra Carter). After five No.1s in their US homeland, the act finally had a UK chart-topper exactly nine years after opening their UK chart account. (B-side: It's Too Hard to Say Goodbye) **US 18**

↗ NO.526
3 SEP •
RED RED WINE (3.01)
UB40 (Neil Diamond). Inspired by Tony Tribe's recording of the composer's original, the act's first UK No.1 didn't top the US chart until five years later. (B-side: Sufferin') **US 1**

↗ NO.527
24 SEP ••••••
KARMA CHAMELEON (4.00)
Culture Club (Culture Club). The year's top seller at 1,405,000 came during a chart run that made the act the first British group to reach the top five with their first seven hits. (B-side: That's the Way) **US 1**

↗ NO.528
5 NOV •••••
UPTOWN GIRL (3.15)
Billy Joel (Billy Joel). The runner-up in the year-end chart was dedicated to Joel's then girlfriend, Christie Brinkley, who appeared in the video. (B-side: Careless Talk) **US 3**

↗ NO.529
18 DEC •••••
ONLY YOU (3.19)
The Flying Pickets (Vince Clarke). The first a cappella No.1 tumbled straight to No.10, a drop outdone only by Harry Belafonte's 1957 Christmas topper's drop to No.12. (B-side: Disco Down)

1984

↗ NO.530
14 JAN ●●
PIPES OF PEACE (3.23)
Paul McCartney (Paul McCartney).
This single made Paul the only act to top the chart solo, in a duo (Stevie Wonder), a trio (Wings), a quartet (The Beatles) and quintet (The Beatles with Billy Preston). (B-side: So Bad)

↗ NO.531
28 JAN ●●●●●
RELAX (3.55)
Frankie Goes to Hollywood
(Peter Gill, Holly Johnson, Mark O'Toole).
This controversial, Trevor Horn-produced million seller (1,910,000) spent more weeks on the UK chart (59 in total) than any other No.1 hit. (B-side: One September Monday) **US 10**

↗ NO.532
3 MAR ●●●
99 RED BALLOONS (3.50)
Nena ·
(Jörn-Uwe Fahrenkrog-Petersen, Carlo Karges). This song uniquely made the UK and US top three by the same act in different languages – in America the original German '99 Luftballons' charted. (B-side: Ich Bleib' Im Bett) **US 2**

↗ NO.533
24 MAR ●●●●●●
HELLO (4.08)
Lionel Richie (Lionel Richie).
With this single, Richie emulated Diana Ross and Donny Osmond by topping the UK and US charts both solo and as part of a group (The Commodores). (B-side: All Night Long (All Night) (Instrumental) **US 1**

↗ NO.534
5 MAY ●●●●
THE REFLEX (4.24)
Duran Duran (Duran Duran).
Remixed by Chic's Nile Rodgers, this was the band's only transatlantic chart-topper during a run of 10 consecutive UK Top 10s. (B-side: Make Me Smile [Come Up and See Me]) **US 1**

↗ NO.535
2 JUN ●●
WAKE ME UP BEFORE YOU GO GO (3.50)
Wham! (George Michael).
The first of 11 UK No.1s featuring George Michael's vocals ironically contained the line: "I'm not planning on going solo" (see No.537). (B-side: Wake Me Up Before You Go Go [instrumental]) **US 1**

↘ CHART-TOPPER NO.518, 534: Duran Duran's lead singer Simon Le Bon was the last member to join the group. A barmaid at the Rum Runner Disco recommended her ex-boyfriend, who was a Birmingham University drama student, and Le Bon was evidently what the band was looking for

↗ NO.536
16 JUN ●●●●●●●●●
TWO TRIBES (3.55)
Frankie Goes to Hollywood
(Peter Gill, Holly Johnson, Mark O'Toole).
During this single's run at the top, the act became the first to sell a million copies of both of their first two releases. (B-side: One February Friday) **US 43**

↗ NO.537
18 AUG ●●●
CARELESS WHISPER (5.01)
George Michael (George Michael, Andrew Ridgeley). The second in an unprecedented trio of consecutive million-selling UK No.1s prevented Black Lace's 'Agadoo' from topping the chart. (B-side: [instrumental]) **US 1**

↗ NO.538
8 SEP ●●●●●●
I JUST CALLED TO SAY I LOVE YOU (4.23)
Stevie Wonder (Stevie Wonder).
On his 315th week of chart action over an 18-year period, Wonder finally scored a solo No.1 with Motown's only UK million-seller (1,775,000). (B-side: [instrumental]) **US 1**

↗ NO.539
20 OCT ●●●
FREEDOM (5.20)
Wham! (George Michael). With this release, three of the last five chart-toppers had writer credits for George Michael. Unusually, the track was not supported by a video. (B-side: Freedom [instrumental]) **US 3**

↗ NO.540
10 NOV ●●●
I FEEL FOR YOU (4.04)
Chaka Khan (Prince).
This cover of a 1979 Prince album track featured Stevie Wonder on harmonica and samples his live US No.1 debut hit 'Fingertips'. (B-side: China Town) **US 3**

↗ NO.541
1 DEC ●
I SHOULD HAVE KNOWN BETTER (4.06)
Jim Diamond (Jim Diamond, Graham Lyle).
This plea for forgiveness made the former PhD vocalist the first solo Scotsman to top the chart since Billy Connolly in 1975. Diamond famously declared that he didn't want to be No.1 for more than one week, as a release incorporating a very good cause was about to follow. As it turned out, the Band Aid release date was delayed a week. (B-side: Impossible Dream)

↗ NO.542
8 DEC ●
THE POWER OF LOVE (5.28)
Frankie Goes to Hollywood
(Peter Gill, Holly Johnson, Brian Nash, Mark O'Toole). Frankie equalled the 21-year-old record set by fellow Liverpudlians Gerry and The Pacemakers by topping the chart with their first three hits. (B-side: The World Is My Oyster)

↗ NO.543
15 DEC •••••

DO THEY KNOW IT'S CHRISTMAS?
(3.45) **Band Aid**
(Bob Geldof, Midge Ure). This all-star single for famine relief was (then) the biggest seller in UK history, shifting 3,550,000 copies and leaving the No.2, Wham!'s 'Last Christmas', as the biggest seller never to top the chart. (B-side: Feed the World) **US 13**

1985

↗ NO.544
19 JAN •••

I WANT TO KNOW WHAT LOVE IS
(4.59) **Foreigner**
(Mick Jones). This track featured the New Jersey Mass Choir, US diva Jennifer Holliday, Motown's Jr Walker and Thompson Twins' Tom Bailey. (B-side: Street Thunder) **US 1**

↗ NO.545
9 FEB ••••

I KNOW HIM SO WELL (4.13)
Elaine Paige and Barbara Dickson
(Tim Rice, Björn Ulvaeus, Benny Andersson). This version of the show-stopping song from the musical Chess sold more than 900,000 copies, making it the best-selling single by a female duo. (B-side: Chess – London Symphony Orchestra)

↗ NO.546
9 MAR ••

YOU SPIN ME ROUND
(LIKE A RECORD) (3.12)
Dead or Alive (Dead or Alive).
The first of Stock Aitken Waterman's No.1 productions reached the top in its 14th chart week – the slowest climb at the time. (B-side: Misty Circles) **US 11**

↗ NO.547
23 MAR ••••

EASY LOVER (5.04)
Philip Bailey (duet with Phil Collins)
(Philip Bailey, Phil Collins, Nathan East). The first instance of two soloists who first charted in groups (Earth Wind and Fire and Genesis, respectively) combining to have a No.1 duet. (B-side: Woman – Philip Bailey) **US 2**

↗ NO.548
20 APR ••

WE ARE THE WORLD (7.05)
USA for Africa
(Michael Jackson, Lionel Richie). Following on from Band Aid, this all-star US cast had the world's biggest seller of the 1980s. Only Bob Geldof contributed to both charity singles. (B-side: Grace – Quincy Jones) **US 1**

↗ NO.549
4 MAY •

MOVE CLOSER (4.10)
Phyllis Nelson (Phyllis Nelson).
The first female one-hit wonder to compose her own hit and the first woman from overseas to write her own No.1. (B-side: Somewhere in the City)

↗ NO.550
11 MAY •••••

19 (3.36)
Paul Hardcastle (Paul Hardcastle, William Coutourie, Jonas McCord, Mike Oldfield). It was based on samples from a Vietnam War documentary, and Oldfield was added to the writer credits due to the alleged infringement of 'Tubular Bells'. (B-side: Fly by Night) **US 15**

↘ **CHART-TOPPER NO.552:** Produced by Nile Rodgers, Sister Sledge's 'Frankie' was a song inspired by ol' blue eyes, Sinatra. The Philadelphia girls never topped the chart with 'Frankie' or anything else in their homeland

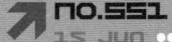 **NO.551**
15 JUN ●●

YOU'LL NEVER WALK ALONE (2.37)
The Crowd
(Richard Rodgers, Oscar Hammerstein II).
This charity disc made former Pacemakers
leader Gerry Marsden the first vocalist to
appear on different No.1 recordings of the
same song. (B-side: Messages)

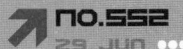 **NO.552**
29 JUN ●●●●

FRANKIE (3.53)
Sister Sledge
(Joy Denny). The first sister act to top the
chart did so with an uncharacteristic pop
ditty whose lyric was claimed to be inspired
by Frank Sinatra. (B-side: Hold Out Poppy)
US 75

NO.553
27 JUL ●

**THERE MUST BE AN ANGEL
(PLAYING WITH MY HEART)** (4.28)
Eurythmics
(Dave Stewart, Annie Lennox).
The only week at the top for the UK chart's
most successful male / female duo and the
fifth No.1 since 1982 to feature Stevie Wonder.
(B-side: Grown Up Girls) **US 22**

NO.554
3 AUG ●●●●

INTO THE GROOVE (4.33)
Madonna
(Madonna, Steve Bray).
During this disc's run at No.1, a reactivated
'Holiday' reached No.2, making Madonna
the only woman to "do the double". (B-side:
Shoo-Bee-Doo)

NO.555
31 AUG ●

I GOT YOU BABE (3.08)
UB40 featuring Chrissie Hynde
(Sonny Bono). The only time two previous
chart-toppers (Hynde as a Pretender)
collaborated on a former No.1 song
and took it back to the top. (B-side:
Theme from Labour of Love – UB40) **US 28**

NO.556
7 SEP ●●●●

DANCING IN THE STREET (3.09)
David Bowie and Mick Jagger
(Ivy Hunter, William Stevenson, Marvin
Gaye). This Martha and The Vandellas
revival, previewed on video at Live Aid,
was the first pairing of previously
charted solo males to create a No.1.
(B-side: Dancing in the Street [instrumental])
US 7

NO.557
5 OCT ●

IF I WAS (5.18)
Midge Ure
(Midge Ure, Danny Mitchell).
Having already topped the chart as Slik's
vocalist in 1976, and as a member of Band
Aid, whose hit he co-wrote, Ure achieved
a solo No.1. (B-side: Piano)

NO.558
12 OCT ●●●●●

THE POWER OF LOVE (4.22)
Jennifer Rush
(Candy de Rouge, Günther Mende,
Jennifer Rush, Mary Susan Applegate).
The first million-selling single (1,321,500) by a
female artist also established a new longevity
record for climbing to No.1 – it did so in its
16th week. (B-side: I See a Shadow (Not a
Fantasy)) **US 57**

NO.559
16 NOV ●●

A GOOD HEART (4.33)
Feargal Sharkey
(Maria McKee).
The former Undertones member's
chart-topper was written by a Lone
Justice member and produced by
Eurythmics member David A Stewart.
(B-side: Anger Is Holy) **US 67**

NO.560
30 NOV ●●

I'M YOUR MAN (4.04)
Wham! (George Michael).
The duo's third No.1, combined with a
re-issued 'Last Christmas', made Wham!
the first UK duo to have simultaneous
Top 10 hits. (B-side: Do It Right
[instrumental]) **US 3**

NO.561
14 DEC ●●

SAVING ALL MY LOVE FOR YOU
(3.51) **Whitney Houston**
(Michael Masser, Gerry Goffin).
This cover of a 1978 Marilyn McCoo and Billy
Davis Jr album track was the first of Whitney's
three transatlantic chart-toppers.
(B-side: All at Once) **US 1**

NO.562
28 DEC ●●

MERRY CHRISTMAS EVERYONE
(3.39) **Shakin' Stevens**
(Bob Heatlie).
The fourth and final No.1 for the act with
the most 1980s hits (30) was the second
Christmas No.1 produced by Dave Edmunds.
(B-side: With My Heart)

1986

NO.563
11 JAN ●●

WEST END GIRLS (3.57)
Pet Shop Boys (Neil Tennant, Chris Lowe).
Having flopped on its first release in 1994, this
re-recording was their first of more than 20
Top 10 hits – a record for a duo. (B-side: A
Man Could Get Arrested) **US 1**

NO.564
25 JAN ●●

THE SUN ALWAYS SHINES ON TV
(5.02) **A-Ha**
(Pal Waaktaar). The first Norwegian group to
top the chart was voted Top Group of 1986 by
Smash Hits readers. (B-side: Driftwood)
US 20

NO.565
8 FEB ●●●●

**WHEN THE GOING GETS TOUGH,
THE TOUGH GET GOING** (4.07)
Billy Ocean
(Wayne Braithwaite, Barry J Eastmond, R J
"Mutt" Lange, Billy Ocean). From the movie
Jewel of the Nile, the song's video featured its
stars (Michael Douglas, Kathleen Turner and
Danny DeVito) as backing vocalists.
(B-side: When the Going Gets Tough,
the Tough Get Going [instrumental]) **US 2**

NO.566
8 MAR ●●●

CHAIN REACTION (3.46)
Diana Ross (Barry, Robin and Maurice Gibb).
Ross's first solo visit to No.1 since 1971
remains the longest gap between newly
recorded chart-toppers by a solo female.
(B-side: More and More) **US 66**

NO.567
29 MAR ●●●

LIVING DOLL (4.17)
**Cliff Richard and the Young Ones featuring
Hank B Marvin** (Lionel Bart).
The first Comic Relief charity single paired
Cliff and Hank (re-creating their roles from the
original 1959 No.1) with TVs worst students.
(B-side: All the Little Flowers Are Happy –
Cliff Richard and the Young Ones)

NO.568
19 APR ●●●

A DIFFERENT CORNER (3.58)
George Michael (George Michael).
The first solo artist to reach the top spot
with his first two releases, Michael already
had a hat-trick of No.1s with Wham! (B-side:
A Different Corner [instrumental]) **US 7**

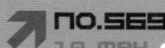

NO.569
18 MAY ●

ROCK ME AMADEUS (3.10)
Falco (Rob Bolland, Ferdi Bolland, Falco). The first Austrian act to top the UK chart did so with a celebration of fellow countryman and composer Wolfgang Amadeus Mozart. (B-side: Urban Tropical) **US 1**

NO.570
17 MAY ●●●

THE CHICKEN SONG (2.38)
Spitting Image (Philip Pope, Robert Grant, Doug Naylor). Named after the political satire TV show in which they appeared, these latex puppets were the first non-human British act to reach No.1. (B-side: I've Never Met a Nice South African)

NO.571
7 JUN ●●●

SPIRIT IN THE SKY (3.23)
Doctor and the Medics

(Norman Greenbaum). The first song to be No.1 for two different chart debutants was also the first 1970s chart-topper to repeat the trick in the 1980s. (B-side: Laughing at the Pieces – studio version) **US 69**

NO.572
28 JUN ●●

THE EDGE OF HEAVEN (4.37) /
WHERE DID YOUR HEART GO (4.31)
Wham! (George Michael).
With the seven-inch format available only as a double pack, the duo's fourth No.1 was the first double single to top the chart. It featured an additional C and D-side single in the same sleeve (B-sides: Wham RAP 86; Battlestations) **US 10 / 0**

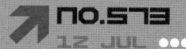

NO.573
12 JUL ●●●

PAPA DON'T PREACH (4.30)
Madonna (Brian Elliott: additional lyrics by Madonna). The song written for Madonna's label-mate Christina Dent gave Madge her

first transatlantic No.1 and was also a chart-topper around Europe. (B-side: Ain't No Big Deal) **US 1**

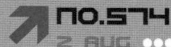

NO.574
2 AUG ●●●

THE LADY IN RED (4.08)
Chris De Burgh (Chris De Burgh).
The first No.1 by an act born in Argentina was De Burgh's first UK Top 40 single after 23 releases and 10 million album sales worldwide. (B-side: Say Goodbye to It All) **US 3**

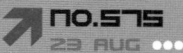

NO.575
23 AUG ●●●

I WANT TO WAKE UP WITH YOU
(4.00) **Boris Gardiner**
(Ben Peters). The song was originally recorded by Mac Davis in 1980. Boris waited 16 years from his instrumental debut hit for a No.1 with this vocal follow-up. (B-side: You're Good for Me)

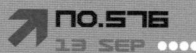

NO.576
13 SEP ●●●●

DON'T LEAVE ME THIS WAY (4.30)
Communards with Sarah Jane Morris
(Kenny Gamble, Leon Huff, Cary Gilbert). In the UK, this revival outperformed both Harold Melvin's original and Thelma Houston's US No.1 cover version, both of which charted in 1977. (B-side: Sanctified) **US 40**

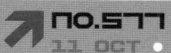

NO.577
11 OCT ●

TRUE BLUE (4.16)
Madonna (Madonna, Stephen Bray).
The title track from the year's best-selling album helped Madonna to become the first American female to score three solo No.1s. (B-side: Holiday) **US 3**

NO.578
18 OCT ●●●

EVERY LOSER WINS (3.11)
Nick Berry
(Simon May, Stewart James, Bradley James). Simon Wicks from the TV soap EastEnders achieved the biggest chart climb for a single on its way to the top, going from No.66 to No.4. (B-side: Every Loser Wins [instrumental] – Stewart James and Bradley James)

NO.579
8 NOV ●●●●

TAKE MY BREATH AWAY [LOVE THEME FROM 'TOP GUN'] (4.08)
Berlin
(Giorgio Moroder, Tom Whitlock).
The Oscar-winning theme from Top Gun reached the top three again four years later and spent a total of 30 weeks on the chart. (B-side: Radar Radio – Giorgio Moroder) **US 1**

↘ CHART-TOPPER NO.574: Chris De Burgh's romantic ballad 'The Lady in Red' reigned at the top for three weeks in the summer of 1986. The 'lady' in question was thought to be his lady wife Diane

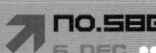
⬈ NO.580
6 DEC ●●
THE FINAL COUNTDOWN (3.57)
Europe (Joey Tempest). The first all Swedish group to top the chart had competed, unsuccessfully, in the 1982 Eurovision heats as The Force. (B-side: On Broken Wings) **US 8**

⬈ NO.581
20 DEC ●
CARAVAN OF LOVE (3.28)
The Housemartins (Ernie Isley, Chris Jasper, Marvin Isley). An a capella cover of Isley Jasper Isley's 1985 hit. Members Paul Heaton and Norman Cook would return to the summit in different guises. (B-side: When I First Met Jesus)

⬈ NO.582
27 DEC ●●●●
REET PETITE (THE SWEETEST GIRL IN TOWN) (2.39)
Jackie Wilson (Berry Gordy, Tyran Carlo). This recording had the slowest journey to No.1 of any track, with the re-issue reaching No.1 29 years and 42 days after the original charted. (B-sides: You Brought About a Change in Me / I'm the One to Do It) **US 62**

1987

⬈ NO.583
24 JAN ●●
JACK YOUR BODY (3.15)
Steve 'Silk' Hurley (Steve 'Silk' Hurley). The first house music No.1 actually broke chart rules because the 12-inch format exceeded the 25-minute maximum length allowed at the time. (B-side: Dub Your Body)

⬈ NO.584
7 FEB ●●
I KNEW YOU WERE WAITING (FOR ME) (3.58)
Aretha Franklin and George Michael (Simon Climie, Denis Morgan). Making Michael the first person to reach No.1 as half of two different duos, this single held former Wham! backing singers Pepsi and Shirlie at No.2 with 'Heartache'. (B-side: I Knew You Were Waiting for Me [instrumental]) **US 1**

⬈ NO.585
21 FEB ●●●
STAND BY ME (2.55)
Ben E King (Jerry Leiber, Mike Stoller, Ben E King). With Percy Sledge's 'When a Man Loves a Woman' at No.2, this was the only instance of recordings more than 20 years old occupying the top two places. (B-side: Yakety Yak – Coasters) **US 9**

⬈ NO.586
14 MAR ●●
EVERYTHING I OWN (3.55)
Boy George (David Gates). Although the 1972 Bread original missed the Top 30, this became the 11th song to be No.1 for two different acts (see No.359). (B-side: Use Me)

⬈ NO.587
28 MAR ●
RESPECTABLE (3.19)
Mel and Kim (Mike Stock, Matt Aitken, Pete Waterman). The first British sisters to top the chart provided Stock Aitken Waterman with their first No.1 as writers. (B-side: Respectable [instrumental])

⬈ NO.588
4 APR ●●●
LET IT BE (4.34)
Ferry Aid
(John Lennon, Paul McCartney). This charity single featured about 120 performers, including the previous week's No.1 act and original vocalist Paul McCartney. (B-side: Let It Be [gospel jam mix])

⬈ NO.589
25 APR ●●
LA ISLA BONITA (4.00)
Madonna
(Madonna, Patrick Leonard). With this single, Madonna clinched the record for most No.1s by a female artist (four), all of which she co-produced and co-wrote. (B-side: La Isla Bonita [instrumental]) **US 4**

⬈ NO.590
9 MAY ●●●●
NOTHING'S GONNA STOP US NOW (4.23) **Starship**
(Diane Warren, Albert Hammond). From the movie Mannequin, this was the first UK Top 10 hit for the band formed more than 20 years previously as Jefferson Airplane. (B-side: Layin' It on the Line) **US 1**

⬂ CHART-TOPPER NO.585: Ben E King got a long overdue UK chart-topper courtesy of his song 'Stand By Me' featuring in the movie of the same name, starring a young River Phoenix. King's classic hit twice entered the lower reaches of the charts in 1961 before its cinema boost in the 1980s and its use in a Levi's jeans commercial

↗ NO.591
6 JUN ••

I WANNA DANCE WITH SOMEBODY (WHO LOVES ME) (4.52)
Whitney Houston (George Merrill, Shannon Rubicam). The first No.1 single to be available on CD was Houston's second topper and the third 1987 No.1 produced by Narada Michael Walden. (B-side: Moment of Truth) **US 1**

↗ NO.592
20 JUN ••

STAR TREKKIN' (3.33)
The Firm (Grahame Lister, John O'Connor). This novelty hit had the lowest start position for a future No.1, entering at No.74 two weeks before beaming up to the summit. (B-side: Dub Trek)

↗ NO.593
4 JUL •••

IT'S A SIN (4.59)
Pet Shop Boys (Neil Tennant, Chris Lowe). This Hi-NRG stomper had a lyric inspired by Tennant's strict Catholic upbringing and a video directed by Derek Jarman. (B-side: You Know Where You Went Wrong) **US 9**

↗ NO.594
25 JUL •

WHO'S THAT GIRL (3.56)
Madonna (Madonna, Patrick Leonard). The title song from her film comedy was the first in an unprecedented sequence of consecutive movie title song chart-toppers. (B-side: White Heat) **US 1**

↗ NO.595
1 AUG ••

LA BAMBA (2.46)
Los Lobos
(Traditional: arranged by Ritchie Valens). A song from the Ritchie Valens biopic, which closely followed Valens' own 1958 arrangement, was the first No.1 sung entirely in Spanish. (B-side: Charlena) **US 1**

↗ NO.596
15 AUG ••

I JUST CAN'T STOP LOVING YOU
(4.21) **Michael Jackson**
(Michael Jackson). After reaching No.1 as a soloist, with his brothers and in USA for Africa, Jacko had a chart-topping duet – although partner Siedah Garrett received no label credit. (B-side: Baby Be Mine) **US 1**

↗ NO.597
29 AUG •••••

NEVER GONNA GIVE YOU UP (3.30)
Rick Astley (Mike Stock, Matt Aitken, Pete Waterman). The year's biggest seller was the longest run at the top of the chart by any British male in the 1980s and the first of his two US No.1s. (B-side: Never Gonna Give You Up [instrumental]) **US 1**

↗ NO.598
3 OCT ••

PUMP UP THE VOLUME (5.07) /
ANITINA (THE FIRST TIME I SEE SHE DANCE) (4.06)
M/A/R/R/S (Steven and Martin Young, A R Kane, C J Mackintosh, John Fryer, Dave Darrell / A R Kane, Colourbox). The more popular side was a Colourbox and A R Kane collaboration and was the first of many independently distributed, sample-laden, UK club tracks to cross over. **US 13 / 0**

↗ NO.599
17 OCT ••••

YOU WIN AGAIN (3.52)
The Bee Gees (Barry, Robin and Maurice Gibb). With this, their fifth No.1, the brothers Gibb became the only group to top the chart in the 60s, 70s and 80s. (B-side: Backtafunk) **US 75**

↗ NO.600
14 NOV •••••

CHINA IN YOUR HAND (4.02)
T'Pau (Carol Decker, Ron Rogers). After their first hit, 'Heart and Soul', unusually broke first in the US, this follow-up never bothered chart compilers across the pond. (B-side: No Sense of Pride)

↗ NO.601
19 DEC ••••

ALWAYS ON MY MIND (3.54)
Pet Shop Boys (Mark James, Johnny Christopher, Wayne Thompson). Originally sung by Brenda Lee in 1971, the duo's third No.1 had been a 1973 UK Top 10 hit for Elvis and was recorded for a TV tribute to him. (B-side: Do I Have To) **US 4**

1988

↗ NO.602
16 JAN ••

HEAVEN IS A PLACE ON EARTH
(4.03) **Belinda Carlisle**
(Rick Nowels, Ellen Shipley). Carlisle spearheaded the first occurrence of three successive female chart-toppers with this follow-up to her non-charting debut solo release. (B-side: We Can Change) **US 1**

↗ NO.603
30 JAN •••

I THINK WE'RE ALONE NOW (3.47)
Tiffany (Ritchie Cordell). This cover of a 1967 US hit for Tommy James and the Shondells was No.1 in the UK, while her follow-up, 'Could've Been', hit No.1 stateside. (B-side: No Rules) **US 1**

↗ NO.604
20 FEB •••••

I SHOULD BE SO LUCKY (3.23)
Kylie Minogue (Mike Stock, Matt Aitken, Pete Waterman). The first of a female record-breaking 13 Top 10 hits from her first 13 releases for the first Australian woman to top the chart. (B-side: I Should Be So Lucky [instrumental]) **US 28**

↗ NO.605
26 MAR ••

DON'T TURN AROUND (3.40)
Aswad (Diane Warren, Albert Hammond). Previously recorded by Kim Goody, Tina Turner and Luther Ingram, this cover gave Aswad overdue pop success after 12 years of reggae chart hits. (B-side: Woman)

↗ NO.606
9 APR •••

HEART (4.16)
Pet Shop Boys (Neil Tennant, Chris Lowe). The fourth Top 10 hit from their album 'Actually' was the duo's fourth chart-topper and brought their total weeks at No.1 to 12. (B-side: I Get Excited [You Get Excited Too])

↗ NO.607
30 APR ••

THEME FROM S-EXPRESS (3.54)
S-Express
(Mark Moore, Pascal Gabriel).
Featuring samples from Rose Royce's 1979 'Is It Love You're After', this disco-house track was allegedly recorded by DJ Mark Moore for only £250. (B-side: The Trip) **US 91**

↗ NO.608
14 MAY •

PERFECT (3.35)
Fairground Attraction
(Mark E Nevin). This skiffle-flavoured Brit Best Single winner, taken from their Brit-winning album, was written by the band's guitarist. (B-side: Mythology) **US 80**

↗ NO.609
21 MAY ••••

WITH A LITTLE HELP FROM MY FRIENDS (2.37) /
SHE'S LEAVING HOME (2.59)
Wet Wet Wet / Billy Bragg with Cara Tivey (John Lennon, Paul McCartney). Taken from a Childline charity album of Beatles covers, 'With a Little Help… ' was the first Beatles original to be No.1 in two different versions.

↘ **CHART-TOPPER NO.563, 593, 601, 606:** The four Pet Shop Boys' No.1s all occurred within the first three years of their chart career. They almost bagged a fifth in 1996 when 'Go West' stalled in the runner-up spot behind 'Mr Vain' (Culture Beat) and 'Boom! Shake the Room' (Jazzy Jeff & The Fresh Prince)

↗ **NO.610**
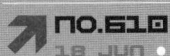
18 JUN ●
DOCTORIN' THE TARDIS (3.35)
Timelords
(Mike Chapman, Nicky Chinn, Roy Grainer, Gary Glitter, Mike Leander, Timelords). This chart-topper by a disguised KLF included snatches of The Sweet's 'Blockbuster', Gary Glitter's debut hit and the Doctor Who theme. (B-side: Communications – KLF) **US 66**

↗ **NO.611**

25 JUN ●●
I OWE YOU NOTHING (3.41)
Bros (The Brothers – Nicky Graham, Tom Watkins). Having failed to chart with its debut single, the act got its only No.1 from this re-issue during a run of eight consecutive Top 10 hits. (B-side: I Owe You Nothing [The Voice])

↗ **NO.612**
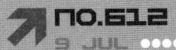
9 JUL ●●●●
NOTHING'S GONNA CHANGE MY LOVE FOR YOU (3.48)
Glenn Medeiros (Michael Masser, Gerry Goffin). This cover of a 1985 George Benson album track, by the Hawaiian radio talent contest winner, stiffed on its original UK release in 1987. (B-side: You Left the Loneliest Heart) **US 12**

↗ **NO.613**
6 AUG ●●●●●
THE ONLY WAY IS UP (4.00)
Yazz and the Plastic Population
(George Jackson, Johnny Henderson). After Yazz sang on Coldcut's first hit, Coldcut returned the favour by producing Yazz's cover of a 1983 Otis Clay recording. (B-side: Bad House Music) **US 96**

↗ **NO.614**
10 SEP ●●
A GROOVY KIND OF LOVE
(3.29) **Phil Collins**
(Toni Wine, Carole Bayer Sager). From his movie Buster, it bettered the transatlantic No.2 placing of The Mindbenders' 1966 version of a song first recorded by the composers as Diane and Anita. (B-side: Big Noise [instrumental]) **US 1**

↗ **NO.615**
24 SEP ●●
HE AIN'T HEAVY, HE'S MY BROTHER (4.14)
The Hollies
(Bob Russell, Bobby Scott). Originally recorded by Kelly Gordon, this track finally hit No.1 almost 19 years after first charting thanks to a Miller Lite TV ad. (B-side: Carrie Anne) **US 7**

↗ **NO.616**
8 OCT ●
DESIRE (2.59)
U2
(U2: lyrics by Bono). U2 had been chart regulars for seven years before topping the chart with this taster from their fourth No.1 album Rattle and Hum. (B-side: Hallelujah Here She Comes) **US 3**

↗ **NO.617**
15 OCT ●●
ONE MOMENT IN TIME (4.00)
Whitney Houston
(Albert Hammond, John Bettis). Recorded for a Seoul Olympics tie-in album, the single earned Houston silver for sales, completing a hat-trick of UK No.1s. (B-side: Olympic Joy [instrumental] – Kashif) **US 5**

↗ **NO.618**
29 OCT ●●●
ORINOCO FLOW (3.45)
Enya (Enya Brennan, Roma Ryan). The former Clannad vocalist, and first Irish female to hit No.1 since Dana in 1970, produced, played and sang on this international hit. (B-side: Out of the Blue) **US 24**

↗ **NO.619**
19 NOV ●●●
THE FIRST TIME (3.18)
Robin Beck
(Gavin Spencer, Tom Anthony, Terry Boyle). After waiting 35 years for three consecutive female chart-toppers, the chart saw this feat occur twice in one year, with Robin Beck's Coke ad song completing the second trio of female hits. (B-side: The First Time [instrumental])

↗ **NO.620**
10 DEC ●●●●
MISTLETOE AND WINE (3.53)
Cliff Richard (Leslie Stewart, Jeremy Paul, Keith Strachan). This adaptation of a song originally performed by Twiggy in a TV production of The Little Match Girl was the year's best seller and Cliff's first self-produced hit. (B-side: Marmaduke)

1989

↗ NO.621
7 JAN •••

ESPECIALLY FOR YOU (3.58)
Kylie Minogue and Jason Donovan
(Mike Stock, Matt Aitken, Pete Waterman).
The Neighbours couple celebrated a joint
chart-topper, while Angry Anderson sat at
No.3 with their soap characters' wedding
song 'Suddenly'. (B-side: All I Wanna Do)

↗ NO.622
28 JAN ••••

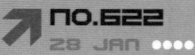

SOMETHING'S GOTTEN HOLD OF
MY HEART (4.40)
**Marc Almond featuring special guest star
Gene Pitney**
(Roger Cook, Roger Greenaway).
Recorded solo for Almond's 'The Stars We
Are' album, new vocals by the original 1967
hit-maker were added, giving Pitney his first
No.1 almost 28 years after his chart debut.
(B-side: Something's Gotten Hold of My Heart
– Marc Almond)

↗ NO.623
25 FEB ••

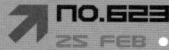

BELFAST CHILD (6.38)
Simple Minds (Traditional: lyrics by Simple
Minds). The sleeves bore the title 'Ballad of
the Streets EP', but the seven-inch had only
two tracks. This was the longest No.1 since
'We are the World'. (B-side: Mandela Day)

↗ NO.624
11 MAR ••

TOO MANY BROKEN HEARTS (3.26)
Jason Donovan (Mike Stock, Matt Aitken,
Pete Waterman). This single, from the year's
best-selling album 'Ten Good Reasons',
made Kylie and Jason (both 20) the youngest
chart-topping duo both to have solo No.1s
(B-side: Wrap My Arms Around You)

↗ NO.625
25 MAR •••

LIKE A PRAYER (5.40)
Madonna (Madonna, Patrick Leonard).
This single, from the album of the same
name, made Madonna the first woman
simultaneously to top the UK singles and

albums charts twice – the first time being
in July 1986. (B-side: Act of Contrition) **US 1**

↗ NO.626
15 APR ••••

ETERNAL FLAME (3.55)
The Bangles
(Susanna Hoffs, Billy Steinberg, Tom Kelly).
After The Supremes and Sister Sledge, this was
the third all-female group to top the UK chart,
but the first to play their own instruments too.
(B-side: What I Mean to Say) **US 1**

↗ NO.627
13 MAY •

HAND ON YOUR HEART (3.49)
Kylie Minogue (Mike Stock, Matt Aitken, Pete
Waterman). The first of three consecutive
No.1s produced by Stock Aitken Waterman –
the first producers to put together such a run
since George Martin in 1964.
(B-side: Just Wanna Love You)

↗ NO.628
20 MAY •••

FERRY 'CROSS THE MERSEY (3.59)
The Christians, Holly Johnson, Paul

↘ **CHART-TOPPER NO.635:**
Ex-Razzmatazz TV presenter Lisa Stansfield
hit big all around the world in 1989. Her
biggest hit made her the first white British
female to achieve a Black Music No.1 in the US

McCartney, Gerry Marsden and Stock Aitken Waterman
(Gerry Marsden). The second charity cover of a Gerry and the Pacemakers hit to reach No.1 with new vocals by Marsden. This version benefited the Hillsborough Disaster Fund. (B-side: Abide With Me)

↗ **NO.629**
18 JUN ●●
SEALED WITH A KISS (2.31)
Jason Donovan (Gary Geld, Peter Udell). This cover of a song Brian Hyland took to the Top 10 in both 1962 and 1975 prevented Cliff's '100th single' (according to EMI) from topping the chart.(B-side: Just Call Me Up)

↗ **NO.630**
24 JUN ●●●●
BACK TO LIFE (HOWEVER DO YOU WANT ME) (3.48)
Soul II Soul featuring Caron Wheeler (Beresford Romeo, Caron Wheeler, Simon Law, Nellee Hooper). Originally an a capella track on their debut album, 'Club Classics Vol. One', this US million-seller was the first No.1 by a UK act also to top the US R&B chart. (B-side: Back to Life (However Do You Want Me) [instrumental]) US 4

↗ **NO.631**
22 JUL ●●
YOU'LL NEVER STOP ME LOVING YOU (3.23)
Sonia
(Mike Stock, Matt Aitken, Pete Waterman). The ninth different act to have a Stock Aitken Waterman-produced chart-topper also had the honour of performing their seventh and final No.1 composition. (B-side: You'll Never Stop Me Loving You [instrumental])

↗ **NO.632**
5 AUG ●●●●●
SWING THE MOOD (4.03)
Jive Bunny and the Mastermixers (Composers: Various)
With the help of a cartoon rabbit, the guys from the Music Factory DJ mixing service created a phenomenon by sampling a host of 1950s and 1960s hits. (B-side: Glenn Miller Medley) US 11

↗ **NO.633**
9 SEP ●●●●●●
RIDE ON TIME (4.33)
Black Box (Dan Hartman, Daniele Davoli, Mirko Limoni, Valerio Semplici). The first Italian No.1 act used French model Katrin Quinol to mime to Loleatta Holloway's vocals, selling 973,850 copies in the process. The act's original recording sampled Holloway's 'Love Sensation'. US 33

↗ **NO.634**
21 OCT ●●●
THAT'S WHAT I LIKE (4.02)
Jive Bunny and the Mastermixers (Composers: Various) Another medley of old hits, this time sandwiched between The Ventures' 'Hawaii 5-0', was the third sample-based No.1 in a row. (B-side: Pretty Blue Eyes) US 69

↗ **NO.635**
11 NOV ●●
ALL AROUND THE WORLD (4.22)
Lisa Stansfield (Lisa Stansfield, Ian Devaney, Andy Morris). This US million-seller, penned with Stansfield's former Blue Zone bandmates, was the first single by a white British female to top the US R&B singles chart. (B-side: Wake Up Baby) US 3

↗ **NO.636**
25 NOV ●●●
YOU GOT IT (THE RIGHT STUFF) (4.10) **New Kids on the Block** (Maurice Starr). This 1988 US hit kick-started a sequence of eight consecutive UK Top 10 hits in just 13 months and brought the next generation of boy bands to the UK. (B-side: You Got It (The Right Stuff) [instrumental]) US 3

↗ **NO.637**
16 DEC ●
LET'S PARTY (4.24)
Jive Bunny and the Mastermixers (Composers: Various)
The first single to debut at No.1 and be replaced by another single debuting at the top the following week. Jive Bunny completed the fastest hat-trick of No.1s from only three releases. (B-side: Auld Lang Syne)

↗ **NO.638**
23 DEC ●●●
DO THEY KNOW IT'S CHRISTMAS? (4.23) **Band Aid II**
(Bob Geldof, Midge Ure).
The year's seventh Stock Aitken Waterman-produced No.1. The only act to appear on both this and the original Band Aid single was Bananarama. (B-side: Do They Know It's Christmas? [instrumental])

1990

↗ **NO.639**
13 JAN ●●
HANGIN' TOUGH (RE-ISSUE) (4.18) **New Kids on the Block** (Maurice Starr). The new kids on the block (literally) returned to the top with a re-issue of their debut single

just 35 days after 'You Got it (The Right Stuff)' vacated No.1. (B-side: Didn't I [Blow Your Mind]) US 1

↗ **NO.640**
27 JAN ●●●
TEARS ON MY PILLOW (2.29)
Kylie Minogue (Sylvester Bradford, Al Lewis). Produced by Stock Aitken Waterman and originally recorded by Little Anthony and The Imperials, Kylie's ninth successive top four hit was the second 'Tears on My Pillow' to reach the top. (B-side: We Know the Meaning of Love)

↗ **NO.641**
3 FEB ●●●●
NOTHING COMPARES 2 U (5.09)
Sinead O'Connor (Prince). The video for this poignant love song, written by Prince for the group The Family, was shot in one take and memorably moved O'Connor to tears. (B-side: Jump in the River) US 1

↗ **NO.642**
3 MAR ●●●●
DUB BE GOOD TO ME (3.59)
Beats International featuring Lindy Layton (Norman Cook, Jimmy Jam, Terry Lewis). Group leader Cook (aka Fatboy Slim) tweaked the title of the S.O.S. Band's 'Just Be Good to Me' for this cover, which was written by producers Jam and Lewis. (B-side: Invasion of the Estate Agents – Beats International) US 76

↗ **NO.643**
31 MAR ●●●●
THE POWER (3.46)
Snap! (Benito Benites, John "Virgo" Garrett III). Guest vocalist Penny Ford (a replacement for Chaka Khan) sang on a track that charted on another three occasions: as part of the Snap! Megamix (1991), a remix in 1996 and a bhangra remix in 2003. US 2

↗ **NO.644**
14 APR ●●●●
VOGUE (4.49)
Madonna
(Madonna, Shep Pettibone). Madonna's 20th consecutive Top 10 hit was the only song on the I'm Breathless album not taken from the Dick Tracey soundtrack. She sang the rest of the LP in character as Dick's love interest, Breathless Mahoney. (B-side: Keep It Together) US 1

↗ **NO.645**
12 MAY ●●●●
KILLER (4.12)
Adamski
(Adam Tinley, Sealhenry Samuel). 'Killer' featured co-writer Seal's uncredited vocals. Eighteen months later he released his own

version and took it back into the Top 10.
(B-side: Bassline Changed My Life)

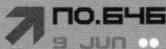

NO.646
9 JUN ●●

WORLD IN MOTION ... (4.28)
Englandneworder (New Order, Keith Allen).
New Order, Keith Allen and some members
of the England squad (including a rapping
John Barnes) joined forces for this World Cup
anthem. (B-side: The B Side)

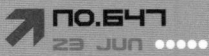

NO.647
23 JUN ●●●●●

SACRIFICE (5.09) /
HEALING HANDS (4.24)
Elton John (Elton John, Bernie Taupin).
Both sides of this double-A were released
separately as singles in 1989 before a
re-issue brought them together to raise
money for Aids charities. This became Elton's
first solo No.1. **US 18 / 13**

NO.648
28 JUL ●●●●

TURTLE POWER (4.12)
Partners in Kryme
(James P Alpern, Richard A Usher Jr). Q: Who
scored the UK's first rap No.1? A: Not Vanilla
Ice, not MC Hammer, but the Teenage Mutant
Ninja Turtle-promoting Partners in Kryme
(Keeping Rhythm Your Motivating Energy).
(B-sides: Splinters Tale 1 / Splinters Tale 2 –
Orchestra on the Half Shell) **US 13**

NO.649
25 AUG ●●●

**ITSY BITSY TEENY WEENY
YELLOW POLKA DOT BIKINI** (3.39)
Bombalurina (Lee Pockriss, Paul Vance).
Brian Hyland's debut disc was given a title
change and makeover by children's TV
presenter Timmy Mallett. It is the longest
non-bracketed title of any No.1.
(B-side: Clap Yo Hands Stomp Yo Feet)

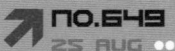

NO.650
15 SEP ●●

THE JOKER (3.35)
Steve Miller Band (Steve Miller).
The single that famously kept 'Groove Is in
the Heart' off No.1 after a sales tie found a
new lease of life, thanks to a Levi's ad, almost
17 years after its original release. (B-side:
Don't Let Nobody Turn You Around) **US 1**

NO.651
29 SEP ●●●●

SHOW ME HEAVEN (3.49)
Maria McKee (Joshua Rifkin, Eric Rackin,
Maria McKee). The Lone Justice singer waited
five years for a No.1 in her own right after
co-writing 'A Good Heart' for Feargal Sharkey.

This much-covered ballad – taken from the
Tom Cruise movie Days of Thunder – was her
only Top 30 single. (B-side: Car Building –
Hans Zimmer)

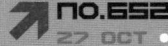

NO.652
27 OCT ●

A LITTLE TIME (2.58)
The Beautiful South
(Paul Heaton, Dave Rotheray). The group's
original female vocalist, Briana Corrigan,
shared the mic with Dave Hemingway as
Hull's finest spent a little time at No.1. The
track won Best Video at the Brits in 1991.
(B-side: In Other Words I Hate You)

NO.653
3 NOV ●●●●

UNCHAINED MELODY (3.34)
The Righteous Brothers
(Hy Zaret, Alex North). The eighth (and by no
means final) chart run for Zaret and North's
classic. A steamy pottery scene in the film
Ghost propelled this timeless ballad to No.1
25 years after its original release, setting a
record for the longest gap between two No.1
versions of the same song (see No.34). (B-
side: (You're My) Soul and Inspiration) **US 13**

NO.654
1 DEC ●●●●

ICE ICE BABY (4.30)
Vanilla Ice
(Vanilla Ice, Earthquake, David Bowie,
Queen). The short-lived career of this white
rapper, amusingly christened Robert Van
Winkle, was built around an unmistakable
'Under Pressure' sample. (B-side: It's a Party)
US 1

NO.655
29 DEC ●

SAVIOUR'S DAY (4.52)
Cliff Richard (Chris Eaton).
"The Peter Pan of Pop" became the first act
to top the chart in five decades with his third
Christmas No.1. (B-side: Six Song Rock'n'Roll
Medley)

1991

NO.656
5 JAN ●●

**BRING YOUR DAUGHTER ...
TO THE SLAUGHTER** (4.42)
Iron Maiden (Bruce Dickinson).
Unusually, this single had two tracks on one
side (A and B together) and nothing (except
the band's signatures) on the flip side. It had
the lowest first-week sale for a No.1 at the
time – 29,918. (B-side: I'm a Mover)

NO.657
19 JAN ●

SADNESS PART 1 (4.15)
Enigma
(Michael Cretu, Franz Gregorian,
David Fairstein).
Cretu, the first Romanian to conquer the
chart, weaved his magic with the help of
Gregorian chant-reciting monks, his wife's
vocals and a seductive beat. The song's
original title refers to French novelist Marquis
de Sade. **US 5**

NO.658
26 JAN ●

INNUENDO (6.33)
Queen
(Queen). The band's first No.1 since
'Under Pressure' and their last before
the death of their charismatic front man.
(B-side: Bijou).

NO.659
2 FEB ●

3:A.M. ETERNAL (3.37)
**The KLF featuring Children of the
Revolution**
(Jim Cauty, Bill Drummond, Ricardo Lyte).
The controversial Kopyright Liberation Front
went to No.1 as The Timelords before they
repeated the trick here. (B-side: Guns of Mu
Mu). **US 5**

NO.660
16 FEB ●●●

DO THE BARTMAN (3.58)
The Simpsons
(Bryan Loren). Performed by Nancy Cartwright
as Bart Simpson, the child star of the popular
cartoon series, this track – or so the story
goes – was produced by Michael Jackson.

NO.661
9 MAR ●●

SHOULD I STAY OR SHOULD I GO
(3.07) **The Clash**
(The Clash). The second No.1 in six months to
be resurrected thanks to a jeans commercial
provided The Clash with their first Top 10
entry. The original peaked at No.17 in 1982.
(B-side: Rush – Big Audio Dynamite 2) **US 45**

NO.662
23 MAR ●

THE STONK (3.45)
Hale and Pace and the Stonkers
(Joe Griffiths, Gareth Hale, Norman Pace).
Queen's Brian May produced this Comic
Relief single and also joined the TV comedy
duo as a performer, along with honourable
Stonker Roger Taylor.(B-side: The Smile Song
– Victoria Wood)

KEY • = 1 week at No.1 (2.52) = minutes and seconds of track (Guy Chambers) = song writer US 32 = US peak position

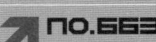

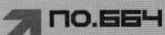

NO.663
30 MAR •••••

THE ONE AND ONLY (3.40)
Chesney Hawkes
(Nik Kershaw). Heart-throb Hawkes's one and only Top 20 hit, penned by a 1980s teen idol, made him the first chart-topping son of a chart-topping father Len 'Chip' Hawkes of The Tremeloes. (B-side: It's Gonna Be Tough) **US 10**

NO.664
4 MAY •••••

THE SHOOP SHOOP SONG (IT'S IN HIS KISS) (2.48)
Cher (Rudy Clark). The title of Betty Everett's 1968 hit was inverted and gave Cher her first No.1 since 1965. It was the second successive chart-topper by an artist who starred in the film in which his / her song appeared. (B-side: Baby I'm Yours) **US 33**

NO.665
8 JUN •••

I WANNA SEX YOU UP (4.05)
Color Me Badd (Dr Freeze). The New York quartet's No.1, from the film New Jack City, was the first to mention sex in the title. **US 2**

NO.666
29 JUN ••

ANY DREAM WILL DO (3.55)
Jason Donovan
(Tim Rice, Andrew Lloyd Webber). The former soap star was still a fixture in the writers' Joseph and His Amazing Technicolor Dreamcoat show when he staged a career comeback after two relative chart flops. (B-side: Close Every Door)

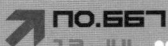

NO.667
13 JUL ••••••••••••••••

(EVERYTHING I DO) I DO IT FOR YOU (4.07)
Bryan Adams (Bryan Adams, Michael Kamen, Robert John 'Mutt' Lange). The theme from Robin Hood: Prince of Thieves stayed at No.1 for 16 consecutive weeks, beating Slim Whitman's record and falling just two weeks short of Frankie Laine's non-consecutive total (see No.9). The single, which sold 1,527,800 copies, was turned down by Lisa Stansfield, Kate Bush and Annie Lennox. (B-side: She's Only Happy When She's Dancing (live)) **US 1**

NO.668
2 NOV •

THE FLY (4.29)
U2 (U2). Heavy D and the Boyz, Extreme,

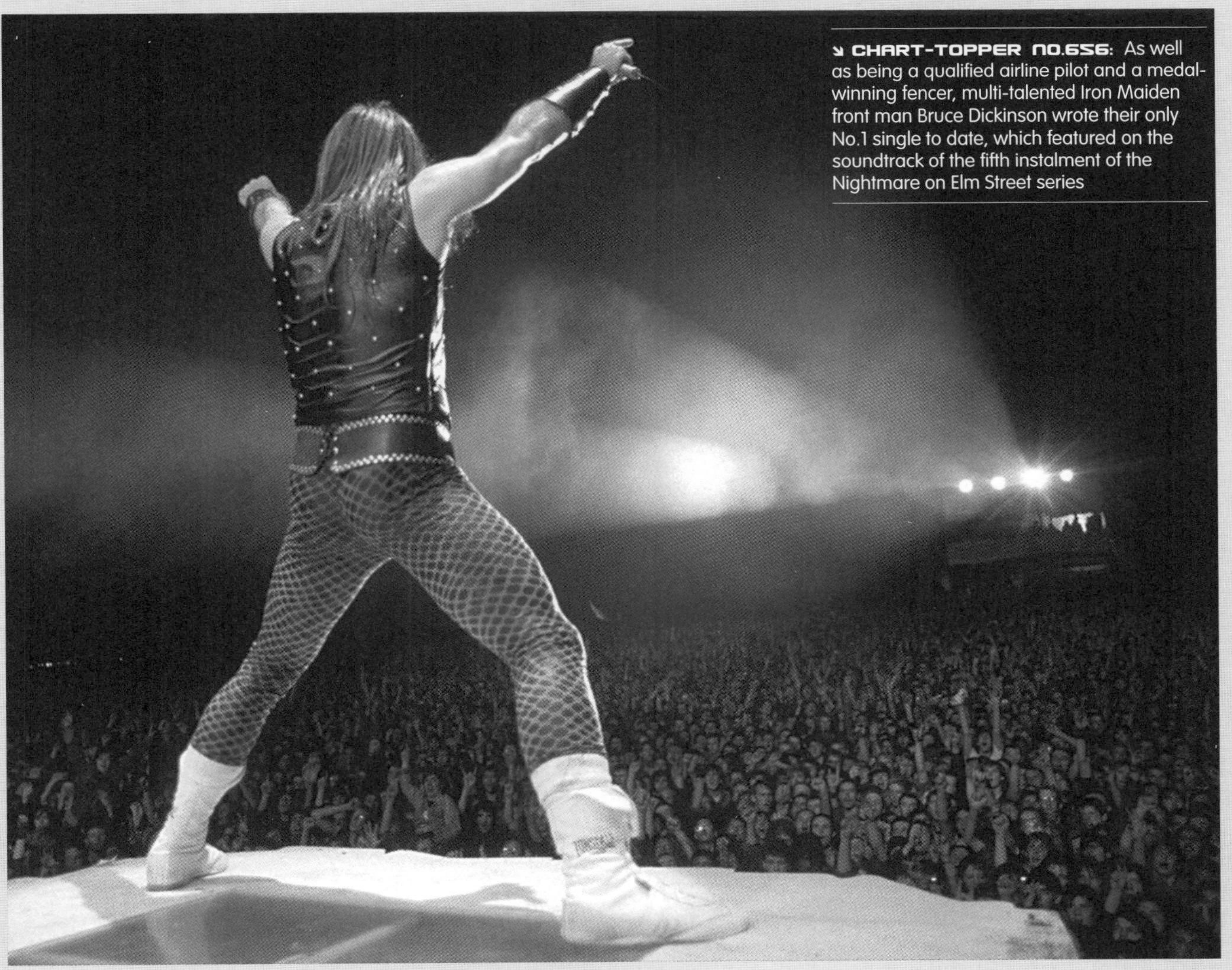

CHART-TOPPER NO.656: As well as being a qualified airline pilot and a medal-winning fencer, multi-talented Iron Maiden front man Bruce Dickinson wrote their only No.1 single to date, which featured on the soundtrack of the fifth instalment of the Nightmare on Elm Street series

↘ **CHART-TOPPER NO.675:** Right Said Fred brothers Richard and Fred spent years working in the background for various groups, the most unlikely of all being Fred's stint in Bob Dylan's backing band

Right Said Fred, Salt-n-Pepa, The Scorpions and 2 Unlimited couldn't dethrone Bryan Adams but U2 could, partly due to the fact that their record company said this single would be available for only three weeks. (B-side: Alex Descends into Hell for a Bottle of Milk / Korova 1) **US 58**

↗ **NO.669**
9 NOV ••
DIZZY (3.19)
Vic Reeves and The Wonder Stuff (Tommy Roe, Freddy Weller). Shooting Star Reeves followed fellow comedians Hale and Pace to the summit with Roe's 22-year-old No.1. (B-side: Oh Mr Hairdresser)

↗ **NO.670**
23 NOV ••
BLACK OR WHITE (3.22)
Michael Jackson (Michael Jackson). This ironically titled hit handed the self-proclaimed 'King of Pop' his fourth No.1. Unusually, a re-mix of the track climbed to No.14 as the original made its way down the chart. **US 1**

↗ **NO.671**
7 DEC ••
DON'T LET THE SUN GO DOWN ON ME (5.47)
George Michael and Elton John (Elton John, Bernie Taupin). The duo teamed up to release

a new version of Elton's hit from 1974 just two months after Oleta Adams took her cover into the Top 40. It was also the first of Michael's 14 consecutive Top 10s. (B-side: I Believe [When I Fall in Love It Will Be Forever]) **US 1**

↗ **NO.672**
21 DEC •••••
BOHEMIAN RHAPSODY (RE-ISSUE) (5.57) / **THESE ARE THE DAYS OF OUR LIVES** (4.15)
Queen (Freddie Mercury / Queen). Following Mercury's death, this was the only single to top the chart on two separate occasions for the same act (until 'My Sweet Lord' in 2002) and the first single to be No.1 in four calendar years. It sold 2,130,000 copies in 1975-76 and 1991-92 combined. **US 2 / 0**

1992

↗ **NO.673**
25 JAN ••••
GOODNIGHT GIRL (3.40)
Wet Wet Wet (Graeme Clark, Tommy Cunningham, Neil Mitchell, Marti Pellow). This self-penned heart-warmer ended a two-year barren spell in the charts for the Glasgow quartet. (B-sides: Ambrose Wykes / Put the Light On [uncredited])

↗ **NO.674**
22 FEB ••••••••
STAY (3.51)
Shakespear's Sister (Siobhan Fahey, Marcella Detroit, Guiot (Dave Stewart)). American Detroit and Bananarama's Brit Fahey, whose deep, sinister voice shattered the peace halfway through this single, were the first transatlantic female duo to have a UK No.1. (B-side: The Trouble with Andre) **US 4**

↗ **NO.675**
18 APR •••
DEEPLY DIPPY (3.16)
Right Said Fred (Richard Fairbrass, Fred Fairbrass, Rob Manzoli). The bald Fairbrass brothers duly achieved that elusive No.1 – after 'I'm Too Sexy's six-week vigil stalled at No.2 behind Bryan Adams. (B-side: Deeply Dubby)

↗ **NO.676**
9 MAY •••••
PLEASE DON'T GO (3.35) / **GAME BOY** (5.37)
KWS (Harry W Casey, Richard Finch / Chris King, Winston Williams). A dance version of the KC and The Sunshine Band favourite, released one week before the European hit version by Double You? (aka Italian Willie Morales). **US 6**

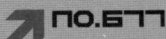

NO.677
13 JUN ●●●●●
ABBA-ESQUE [EP] (3.45)
Erasure (Tracks 1, 3 and 4: Benny Andersson, Björn Ulvaeus; Track 2: Benny Andersson, Björn Ulvaeus, Stig Anderson). This EP, a tribute to the Swedish superstars, provided Erasure with their only No.1. It featured 'Lay All Your Love on Me', 'S.O.S.', 'Take a Chance on Me' (the only previous No.1) and 'Voulez-Vous'.

NO.678
18 JUL ●●●
AIN'T NO DOUBT (3.57)
Jimmy Nail (Guy Pratt, Danny Schogger, Jimmy Nail, Charlie Dore). The Geordie actor turned singer penned this with actress turned singer Dore, whose career was over after one single. Nail nailed three top five hits. (B-side: What Can I Say)

NO.679
8 AUG ●●●●●●
RHYTHM IS A DANCER (3.41)
Snap! (Benito Benitez, John "Virgo" Garrett III, Thea Austin, Durron Butler). Despite a tasteless line ("I'm as serious as cancer when I say rhythm is a dancer"), only Whitney Houston and Shakespear's Sister had longer stays at No.1 in 1992. US 5

NO.680
19 SEP ●●●●
EBENEEZER GOODE (3.39)
Shamen (Colin Angus, Richard West). Banned by the BBC for its blatantly obvious drug references and shelved after four weeks of release, Pulp's Jarvis Cocker was not a fan: "I thought it was a despicable record," he said.

NO.681
17 OCT ●●
SLEEPING SATELLITE (4.42)
Tasmin Archer (Tasmin Archer, John Beck, John Hughes). This distinctive space-themed track made the Yorkshire lass a star across Europe. US 32

NO.682
31 OCT ●●●
END OF THE ROAD (3.35)
Boyz II Men (L A Reid, Babyface, Daryl Simmons). The quartet renowned for their pitch-perfect a capella harmonies won a Grammy for this R&B ballad, a 13-week chart-topper in the US that took nine weeks to reach No.1 in the UK. US 1

NO.683
21 NOV ●●
WOULD I LIE TO YOU (3.40)
Charles and Eddie (Mick Leeson, Peter Vale).

The first black and white male duo to reach the top since Paul McCartney and Stevie Wonder. (B-side: Unconditional) US 13

NO.684
5 DEC ●●●●●●●●●●
I WILL ALWAYS LOVE YOU (4.32)
Whitney Houston (Dolly Parton). Parton's ode to Porter Wagoner provided Houston with the longest stay at No.1 by a female. The funeral favourite sold 1,355,055 copies and returned to the Top 40 for Christmas 1993. (B-side: Jesus Loves Me) US 1

NO.685
13 FEB ●●●●●
NO LIMIT (3.17)
2 Unlimited (Anita Dels, Ray Slijngaard, Phil Wilde, Jean Paul de Coster). There appeared to be "No no, no no no no, no no no no, no no limit" to the success of the first Dutch act to reach No.1 since Pussycat.

NO.686
28 MAR ●●
OH CAROLINA (3.11)
Shaggy (John Folkes). This little-known Folkes Brothers song arrived at the height of the 1990s reggae revolution. Snow and Shabba Ranks completed a reggae 1,2,3. US 59

NO.687
3 APR ●●●●
YOUNG AT HEART (RE-ISSUE) (3.24)
The Bluebells (Bobby Hodgens, Siobhan Fahey). The power of TV advertising revived this Bananarama track long after The Bluebells had gone their separate ways. Their only Top 10 hit – twice. (B-side: I'm Falling)

NO.688
1 MAY ●●●
FIVE LIVE [EP] (5.16)
George Michael and Queen with Lisa Stansfield (Track 1: 'Somebody to Love' - Freddie Mercury; Track 2: 'Killer / Papa Was a Rolling Stone' - Seal, Adam Tinley / Norman Whitfield, Barrett Strong; Track 3: 'These Are the Days Of Our Lives' - Queen; Track 4: 'Calling You' - Bob Telson; Track 5: 'Dear Friends' - Queen). 1 and 3 were from the Freddie Mercury tribute concert at Wembley, 2 and 4 were from the George Michael Cover To Cover tour and 5 was from the album Sheer Heart Attack.

NO.689
22 MAY ●●●
ALL THAT SHE WANTS (3.31)
Ace of Base (Joker, Buddha).

The third Swedish act to have a UK No.1 just wanted another baby but ended up with a UK smash. US 2

NO.690
12 JUN ●●●●●
(I CAN'T HELP) FALLING IN LOVE WITH YOU (3.21)
UB40 (Hugo Peretti, Luigi Creatore, George David Weiss). The Brummie collective reached No.1 three times with covers, here extending the title of the Elvis chart-topper. Their version of Elvis's flip side to this, 'Rock-a-Hula Baby', failed to materialise. (B-side: Jungle Love) US 1

NO.691
26 JUN ●●●
DREAMS (3.40)
Gabrielle (Gabrielle, Tim Laws). Dreams can and did come true for the eyepatch-wearing soul diva, even though she was refused permission to sample Tracy Chapman's 'Fast Car'. US 26

NO.692
17 JUL ●●●●
PRAY (3.42)
Take That (Gary Barlow). Britain's biggest boy band until the emergence of Boyzone and Westlife kicked off an amazing run of eight No.1s from nine releases with this summer sizzler.

NO.693
14 AUG ●●
LIVING ON MY OWN (RE-MIX) (3.37)
Freddie Mercury (Freddie Mercury). Originally a minor hit in 1985, this No More Brothers re-mix of 'Living on My Own' gave Queen's lead vocalist his only solo chart-topper 20 months after his death.

NO.694
28 AUG ●●●●
MR VAIN (4.17)
Culture Beat (Steven Lewis, Noise Katzmann, Jay Supreme). Europe's monster summer smash, from this multinational dance troupe, was the first No.1 not available on seven-inch vinyl. (B-sides: (Cherry Lips) Der Erdbeermund / I Like You). US 17

NO.695
25 SEP ●●
BOOM! SHAKE THE ROOM (3.46)
Jazzy Jeff & The Fresh Prince (Will Smith, Lee Haggard, Walter Williams, Ken Mayberry, Leroy Bonner, Clarence Satchell, Marshall Jones, Jimmy 'Diamond' Williams, Merv Pierce, Billy Beck, Ralph Middlebrook). After ditching 'DJ' from his name, Jazzy Jeff scored his biggest UK hit with Fresh Prince, who had further success as

an actor and rapper under his real name, Will Smith. (B-side: Summertime) **US 13**

↗ NO.696
9 OCT ●●
RELIGHT MY FIRE (4.08)
Take That featuring Lulu (Dan Hartman). Take an old Hartman song, replace Loleatta Holloway with Lulu (who had waited 29 years for her first No.1), add an unstoppable boy band into the mix, stir and serve flaming hot. (B-side: Why Can't I Wake Up with You [live])

↗ NO.697
23 OCT ●●●●●●●
I'D DO ANYTHING FOR LOVE (BUT I WON'T DO THAT) (5.23)
Meat Loaf (Jim Steinman). The year's best-seller (761,200 copies sold) featured vocalist Lorraine Crosby. We never did find out what it was that he wouldn't do for love. (B-side: Back into Hell) **US 1**

↗ NO.698
11 DEC ●
25 DEC ●●
MR BLOBBY (3.35)
Mr Blobby (Paul Shaw, David Rogers). The incoherent, clumsy, made-for-TV blob, star of Noel Edmonds' House Party, toyed with Take That and then ruined their plans for a Christmas No.1. (B-side: Mr Blobby's Theme)

↗ NO.699
18 DEC ●
BABE (3.54)
Take That (Gary Barlow). The only group to be deposed by a pink and yellow-coloured non-human was the first act to have three consecutive singles enter at No.1, Mark Owen took lead vocals on this ballad. (B-side: All I Want Is You).

1994

↗ NO.700
8 JAN ●●
TWIST AND SHOUT (3.58)
Chaka Demus and Pliers featuring Jack Radics and Taxi Gang (Bert Berns, Phil Medley). Jamaican duo Chaka Demus and Pliers' reggae twist on a song enjoying its fourth chart run turned it into a first-time UK No.1. (B-side: Rhythm Killer)

↗ NO.701
22 JAN ●●●●
THINGS CAN ONLY GET BETTER (RE-ISSUE) (3.58)
D:Ream (Peter Cunnah, Jamie Petrie). An uplifting dance track optimistically

adopted by the Labour Party made three trips to the Top 30 in four years.

↗ NO.702
19 FEB ●●●●
WITHOUT YOU (3.34)
Mariah Carey (Pete Ham, Tom Evans). The tragic Badfinger song written about Pete Ham's lover and covered by Nilsson was the first single by a solo female to debut at No.1. Its subject, Beverley Tucker, was reportedly horrified by Mariah's version. (B-side: Never Forget You) **US 3**

↗ NO.703
19 MAR ●●●
DOOP (3.31)
Doop (Frederick Ridderhof). The Dutch instrumental duo resurrected the Charleston dance craze, memorably filling the Top of the Pops studio with a myriad of movers and shakers.

↗ NO.704
9 APR ●●
EVERYTHING CHANGES (3.33)
Take That (Gary Barlow, Mike Ward, Eliot Kennedy, Cary Baylis). Another No.1 debut, their fourth straight in succession, found the boys in an uptempo mood with Robbie Williams on lead vocals. (B-side: Beatles Medley)

↗ NO.705
23 APR ●●
THE MOST BEAUTIFUL GIRL IN THE WORLD (4.38)
Symbol (Prince) (Symbol (Prince)) The artist formerly known as Prince and later known as The Artist and TAFKAP turned into a symbol to bag his first chart-topper after 40 previous hits. (B-side: Beautiful) **US 3**

↗ NO.706
7 MAY ●
THE REAL THING (3.48)
Tony Di Bart (Lucinda Drayton, Tony Di Bart, Andy Blissett). One of two Top 10 songs called 'The Real Thing' vying for supremacy in May initially failed to chart in 1993. A Joy Brothers re-mix did the trick second time round.

↗ NO.707
14 MAY ●
INSIDE (4.40)
Stiltskin (Peter Lawlor). This rock band followed 'The Joker' and 'Should I Stay or Should I Go' to the top off the back of a Levi's ad. Ray Wilson's tortured vocals were never heard again in the Top 30. (B-side: America)

↗ NO.708
21 MAY ●●
COME ON YOU REDS (3.27)
Manchester United Football Club (Francis Rossi, Andy Brown, John Edwards). This song, by the first English football club to net a No.1, charted the day after the Reds beat Chelsea 4-0 in the FA Cup Final.

↗ NO.709
4 JUN ●●●●●●●●●●●●●●●
LOVE IS ALL AROUND (4.03)
Wet Wet Wet (Reg Presley). The album 'Picture This' received a huge boost in sales when this Troggs cover, from Four Weddings and a Funeral, shifted 1,783,827 copies, but Phonogram deleted the single a week shy of Bryan Adams' record stay at No.1. The unlucky All-For-One were kept at No.2 for seven of its 15 weeks on top. (B-side: I Can Give You Everything) **US 45**

↗ NO.710
17 SEP ●●●●
SATURDAY NIGHT (4.05)
Whigfield (Larry Pignagnoli, Davide Riva). The second successive No.1 million-seller (1,092,300) set another chart milestone when it became the first song by a new act to debut at No.1.

↗ NO.711
15 OCT ●●
SURE (3.40)
Take That (Gary Barlow, Robbie Williams, Mark Owen). Their previous single peaked at No.3 to deny them a fifth straight No.1 debut, but the boys soon returned to form with a self-penned single that triggered another sequence of four successive No.1 entries.

↗ NO.712
29 OCT ●●●●
BABY COME BACK (3.51)
Pato Banton (Eddy Grant). The reggae revival continued as uncredited UB40 duo Ali and Robin Campbell joined Banton to equal The Equals' chart-topping feat with this song. (B-side: Gwarn)

↗ NO.713
26 NOV ●●
LET ME BE YOUR FANTASY (3.50)
Baby D (Floyd Dyce). This track filled dance floors up and down the country for two years before it found commercial success. A re-mix returned to the Top 20 in 2000.

↗ NO.714
18 DEC ●●●●●
STAY ANOTHER DAY (4.26)
East 17 (Tony Mortimer, Rob Kean, Dominic

KEY ● = 1 week at No.1 (2.52) = minutes and seconds of track (Guy Chambers) = songwriter **US 32** = US peak position

Hawken). A slushy boy band ballad complete with bells and snow gave the Walthamstow lads their only No.1 single, despite the seasonal competition from Mariah Carey at No.2.

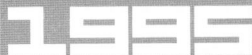

1995

NO.715
14 JAN ●●●

COTTON EYE JOE (3.10)
Rednex
(Jan Ericsson, Oban, Pat Reiniz).
Despite the stereotypical hillbilly video being banned on some TV stations, the record clocked up 500,000 US sales and sold 2.5 million in Europe. Rednex became the third Swedish act to top the UK chart following the successes of Abba and Ace of Base. **US 25**

NO.716
4 FEB ●●●●●●●

THINK TWICE (4.48)
Celine Dion (Andy Hill, Pete Sinfield).
The first of two million-selling singles for the Canadian chanteuse reached No.1 12 weeks after its No.30 debut in November 1994. (B-sides: Le Monde Est Stone / If Love Is Out of the Question / If You Ask Me To) **US 95**

NO.717
25 MAR ●

LOVE CAN BUILD A BRIDGE (4.14)
Cher, Chrissie Hynde and Neneh Cherry with Eric Clapton
(Naomi Judd, John Jarvis, Paul Overstreet). This superstar line-up's take on the Judds' country No.1 gave Cherry and Clapton their only UK chart-toppers. It raised money for Comic Relief. (B-sides: Help / Can't Get Enough of Your Love)

NO.718
1 APR ●

DON'T STOP (WIGGLE WIGGLE) (3.06) **Outhere Brothers**
(Hula Mahone, Craig Simpkins, Keith Mayberry, Aladino). Success eluded US rappers Mahone and Simpkins in their homeland, but they quickly notched up two UK No.1s – this being the first.

NO.719
8 APR ●●●●

BACK FOR GOOD (4.01)
Take That (Gary Barlow). Widely regarded as the finest moment of their four-year career, 'Back for Good' was Robbie Williams's last single while still a member of the group before he embarked on a solo career.
(B-sides: Sure [live] / Beatles Tribute [live]) **US 7**

NO.720
6 MAY ●

SOME MIGHT SAY (5.29)
Oasis (Noel Gallagher).
The first No.1 for the feuding, swaggering Liam and Noel. The song re-entered the Top 75 six times up to the end of 1996 and a 12-inch version charted separately. (B-sides: Talk Tonight / Acquiesce / Headshrinker).

NO.721
13 MAY ●

DREAMER (RE-MIX) (3.41)
Livin' Joy (Paolo Visnadi, Janice Robinson).
This infectious club anthem, a re-mix of their

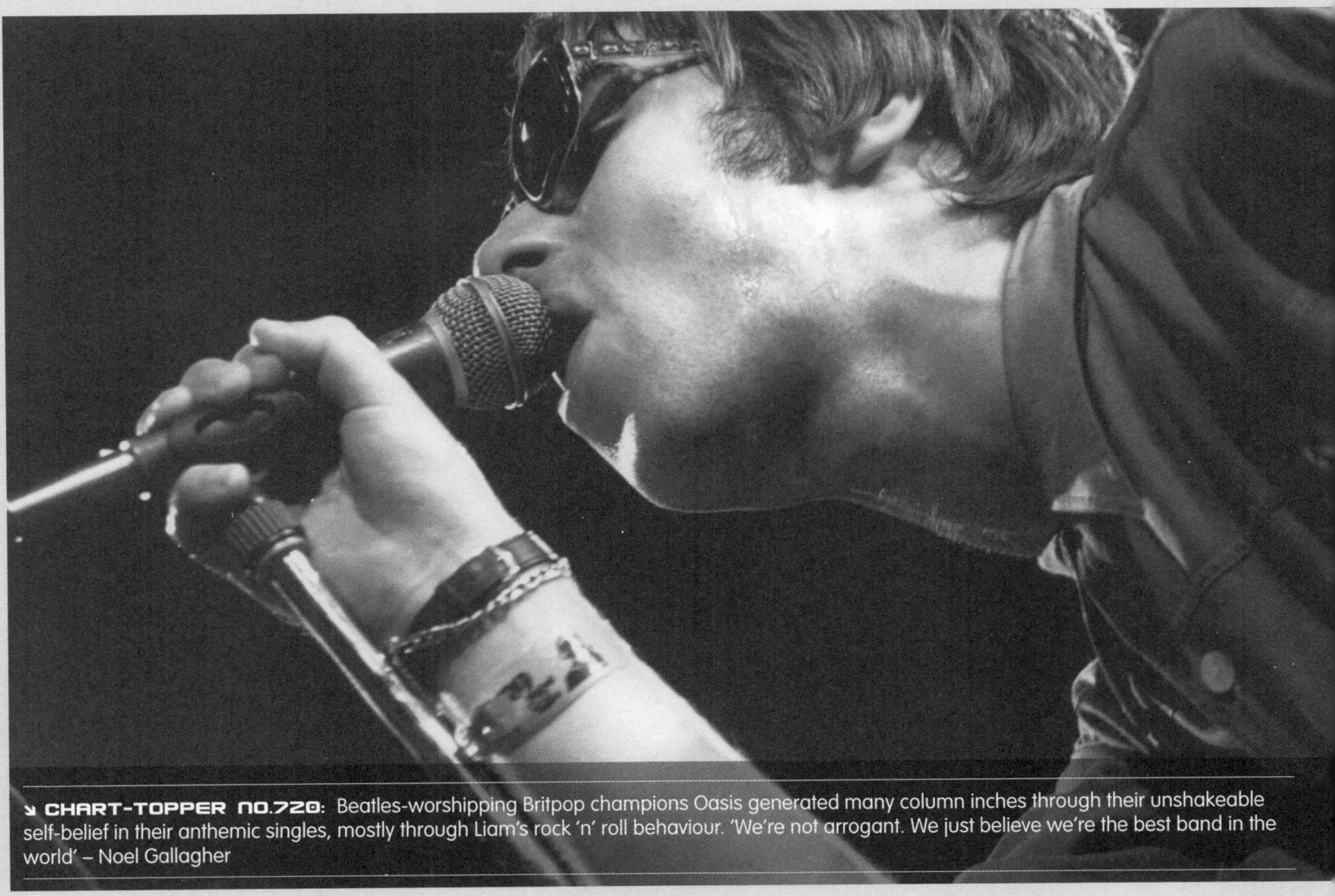

CHART-TOPPER NO.720: Beatles-worshipping Britpop champions Oasis generated many column inches through their unshakeable self-belief in their anthemic singles, mostly through Liam's rock 'n' roll behaviour. 'We're not arrogant. We just believe we're the best band in the world' – Noel Gallagher

Top 20 hit from 1994, featured vocalist Tameka Starr. **US 72**

↗ NO.722
20 MAY ●●●●●●●
UNCHAINED MELODY (3.20) /
(THERE'LL BE BLUEBIRDS OVER)
THE WHITE CLIFFS OF DOVER
(3.18) **Robson Green and Jerome Flynn** (Hy Zaret, Alex North / Walter Kent, Nat Burton). The stars of TV's Soldier, Soldier, the first UK act to make their chart debut at No.1, were paid £50,000 by Simon Cowell to record 'Unchained Melody' after unprecedented public demand. It sold 1,843,700 copies in 17 weeks.

↗ NO.723
8 JUL ●●●●
BOOM BOOM BOOM (3.21)
Outhere Brothers
(Hula Mahone, Keith Mayberry). The first US act to top the UK chart with its first two singles. Despite the song's repetitive chorus and X-rated verses, it sold 651,000 copies. **US 65**

↗ NO.724
5 AUG ●●●
NEVER FORGET (5.30)
Take That (Gary Barlow). The gospel-tinged 'Never Forget' charted at a time when Robbie had already left the group, although his vocals were still evident on their seventh No.1. (B-side: Interview with Take That)

↗ NO.725
26 AUG ●●
COUNTRY HOUSE (3.56)
Blur (Damon Albarn, Blur).
Blur's much-hyped battle for chart supremacy with Britpop arch-rivals Oasis (the story made the national news) saw 'Country House' beat 'Roll with it' to No.1. Blur have since disowned the song. (B-sides: One Born Every Minute / To the End – Blur and Françoise Hardy)

↗ NO.726
9 SEP ●●
YOU ARE NOT ALONE (4.32)
Michael Jackson (R Kelly).
This ballad, written and produced by Kelly, was Jackson's fifth solo chart-topper and the first single to enter the US Billboard Hot 100 at No.1. (B-side: Rock with You [remix]) **US 1**

↗ NO.727
23 SEP ●
BOOMBASTIC (3.53)
Shaggy
(Orville Burrell, Robert Livingstone, King Floyd). The fifth No.1 to owe its success to a Levi's ad was by the first Jamaican to bag two No.1s. **US 3**

↗ NO.728
30 SEP ●●●●
FAIRGROUND (4.25)
Simply Red (Mick Hucknall).
This single sold 783,000 copies to become the group's biggest hit and only No.1. (B-sides: Stars [live] / The Right Thing [live])

↗ NO.729
28 OCT ●●
GANGSTA'S PARADISE (4.02)
Coolio featuring LV (Artis Ivey Jr, Stevie Wonder, Larry Sanders, Doug Rasheed). Coolio and Large Variety's Grammy-winning worldwide smash, based on Wonder's 'Pastime Paradise', shifted 1,246,300 copies. It appeared in the film Dangerous Minds. (B-sides: Fantastic Voyage / Mama I'm in Love wit a Gangsta [clean radio mix]) **US 1**

↗ NO.730
11 NOV ●●●●
I BELIEVE (2.07) /
UP ON THE ROOF (2.38)
Robson & Jerome (Ervin Drake, Irvin Graham, Jimmy Shirl, Al Stillman / Gerry Goffin, Carole King). Discarding their surnames for their second chart-topping double-A, the actors took 'I Believe' back to No.1 22 years after its initial run and made it third time lucky for the Goffin / King classic.

↗ NO.731
9 DEC ●●●●●●
EARTH SONG (5.04)
Michael Jackson (Michael Jackson).
Jackson's heartfelt plea to save the world, written and produced by the man himself, denied The Beatles their first No.1 in 26 years (B-side: 'Wanna Be Startin' Somethin')

1996

↗ NO.732
20 JAN ●
JESUS TO A CHILD (6.50)
George Michael (George Michael). His first single on the Virgin label (after his contractual difficulties with Sony) raised money for the Help a London Child charity. (B-sides: One More Try [live gospel version] / Older [inst]) **US 7**

↗ NO.733
27 JAN ●●●●●
SPACEMAN (4.01)
Babylon Zoo (Jas Mann).
Another Levi's ad launched this futuristic track into orbit. It sold 400,000 copies in its first week (a record for a debut act) and 1,098,900 copies in total. (B-sides: Metal Vision / Blue Nude)

↘ **CHART-TOPPER NO.692, 696, 699, 704, 711, 719, 724, 735:**
Post-New Kids on the Block and pre-Spice Girls, Take That were the biggest thing in pop. Their fans were so distressed when they split in February 1996 that Childline and the Samaritans set up helplines to counsel the grieving, a story that even made the BBC national news

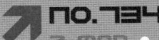

NO.734
2 MAR ●
DON'T LOOK BACK IN ANGER (4.49)
Oasis
(Noel Gallagher).
This melodic Britpop anthem featured
Noel on vocals and continued their Beatles
worship with the line "I'm gonna start a
revolution from my bed". (B-sides: Step Out /
Underneath the Sky / Cum on Feel the Noize)
US 55

NO.735
9 MAR ●●●
HOW DEEP IS YOUR LOVE (3.42)
Take That
(Robin, Barry and Maurice Gibb).
An emotional press conference on 13 February
announced the split, and several weeks later
they bowed out with their eighth No.1. The
video showed the quartet tied to chairs,
drenched and defeated. (B-sides: Every Guy /
Lady Tonight / Sunday to Saturday)

NO.736
30 MAR ●●●
FIRESTARTER (3.47)
The Prodigy
(Liam Howlett, Keith Flint, Trevor Horn, Art of
Noise). "Twisted firestarter" Flint snarled his
way to the top with a sample of the Art of
Noise's 'Close to the Edit'. Three weeks later,
seven of their previous hits re-charted.
(B-side: Molotov Bitch) **US 30**

NO.737
28 APR ●●
RETURN OF THE MACK (3.28)
Mark Morrison
(Mark Morrison).
It took six weeks for this law-breaking R&B
singer, who later re-christened himself as
Abdul Rahman, to climb to No.1. **US 2**

NO.738
4 MAY ●●●
FASTLOVE (5.23)
George Michael
(George Michael, Patrice Rushen, Fred
Washington). The first of two chart-toppers
to sample Rushen's 'Forget Me Nots'
(see No.772). (B-sides: I'm Your Man /
Fastlove [Part 2]) **US 8**

NO.739
25 MAY ●
OOH AAH … JUST A LITTLE BIT
(3.24) **Gina G**
(Simon Tauber, Steve Rodway).
This cheeky song went to No.1 the day after
the Aussie songstress came eighth for the UK
at the Eurovision Song Contest in Oslo. **US 12**

NO.740
1 JUN ●
6 JUL ●
**THREE LIONS (THE OFFICIAL
SONG OF THE ENGLAND
FOOTBALL TEAM)** (3.45)
**Baddiel and Skinner and The Lightning
Seeds** (Ian Broudie, Frank Skinner, David
Baddiel). This patriotic football anthem,
written for Euro 96 and enthusiastically
adopted by England fans ever since, was
replaced at No.1 by the Fugees – twice.

NO.741
8 JUN ●●●●
13 JUL ●
KILLING ME SOFTLY (4.54)
Fugees (Norman Gimbel, Charles Fox).
The biggest-selling single of 1996 (1,268,200)
shifted more copies than 'Wannabe' by the
end of the year (although 'Wannabe' outsold
it in total sales [see No.743]). Roberta Flack
took the song (with its full title) into the Top 10
in 1973. (B-sides: Fu-Gee-La / Vocab).

NO.742
20 JUL ●
FOREVER LOVE (3.36)
Gary Barlow (Gary Barlow).
Barlow's poignant solo debut was his seventh
No.1 as a songwriter and, along with The
Fugees, prevented the Spice Girls from making
their chart bow at No.1. (B-side: I Miss It All)

NO.743
27 JUL ●●●●●●●
WANNABE (2.52)
Spice Girls (Richard Stannard, Matthew
Rowe, Spice Girls). The million-selling single
(1,269,841) that introduced us to Baby, Ginger,
Posh, Scary and Sporty was the only one of
their nine chart-toppers not to enter at No.1.
The first all-girl British group to have a UK
No.1 gave birth to girl power. (B-side: Bumper
to Bumper) **US 1**

NO.744
14 SEP ●
FLAVA (4.01)
Peter Andre
(Peter Andre, Andy Whitmore, Wayne Hector,
Cee). 'Flava' went one rung higher than
'Mysterious Girl' to hand the British-born,
Australian-raised, well-honed Andre his first
UK No.1 as performer and songwriter.

NO.745
21 SEP ●●
READY OR NOT (3.58)
Fugees (Wyclef Jean, Pras Michel, Lauryn Hill,
William Hart, Thomas Bell). The opposition
knew the score when Lauryn, Wyclef and

Pras collected their second successive No.1
with a sample of The Delfonics' 'Ready or Not
Here I Come (Can't Hide from Love)'.
(B-side: The Score)

NO.746
5 OCT ●
**BREAKFAST AT TIFFANY'S
(RE-ENTRY)** (4.16)
Deep Blue Something (Todd David Pipes).
Just two months after stalling at No.55, the
melodic US rockers rose to No.1 with a song
inspired by Audrey Hepburn's performance in
the film Roman Holiday. Pipes thought one of
Hepburn's other films would make a better
song title. (B-sides: A Water Prayer / Sun) **US 5**

NO.747
12 OCT ●
SETTING SUN (4.00)
The Chemical Brothers
(Ed Simons, Tom Rowlands, Noel Gallagher).
Gallagher joined the "brothers" on a dance
track that spent just two weeks in the Top 10.
They teamed up again in 1999 with 'Let
Forever Be'. (B-side: Buzz Tracks)

NO.748
19 OCT ●
WORDS (3.55)
Boyzone (Robin, Barry and Maurice Gibb).
The record-shattering boy band scored
their first No.1 at their sixth attempt and
gave The Bee Gees their second chart-topper
of the year as songwriters. (B-side: The
Price of Love)

NO.749
26 OCT ●●
SAY YOU'LL BE THERE (3.56)
Spice Girls (Spice Girls, Eliot Kennedy).
More than 350,000 fans were there to snap
up a copy in the first week to ensure the girls
became the first female group to score two
consecutive No.1s. (B-side: Take Me Home)
US 3

NO.750
9 NOV ●●
**WHAT BECOMES OF THE
BROKENHEARTED** (3.21) /
**SATURDAY NIGHT AT THE
MOVIES** (2.30) /
YOU'LL NEVER WALK ALONE (3.23)
Robson & Jerome
(James Dean, Paul Riser, William
Weatherspoon / Barry Mann, Cynthia Weil /
Richard Rodgers, Oscar Hammerstein II).
The first triple-A to reach No.1 featured past
hits by Jimmy Ruffin, The Drifters and Gerry
and the Pacemakers. Robson & Jerome were
the first act to enter the chart at No.1 with
their first three hits.

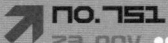

↗ NO.751
23 NOV ••

BREATHE (3.59)
The Prodigy
(Liam Howlett, Keith Flint, Maxim). The band's best-selling single with sales of 722,554. This frenetic, mind-blowing rave anthem gave the lads from Essex their 11th successive Top 15 hit and denied The Fugees their third consecutive No.1 with 'No Woman, No Cry'. (B-sides: Their Law [live] with Pop Will Eat Itself / Poison [Live] / The Trick)

↗ NO.752
7 DEC •

I FEEL YOU (3.57)
Peter Andre
(Peter Andre, Glen Goldsmith, Terry Jones, Oliver Jacobs). Like The Chemical Brothers (see No.747), the lowest-selling No.1 of the year spent just two weeks in the Top 10 for the top male vocalist of 1996. (B-side: You Are [Part 1])

↗ NO.753
14 DEC •

A DIFFERENT BEAT (3.24)
Boyzone
(Ronan Keating, Stephen Gately, Shane Lynch, Keith Duffy, Ray Hedges, Martin Brannigan). The Irish quintet had co-written their three previous original hits but claimed their first No.1 credit with 'A Different Beat', which featured tribal chants. (B-side: Angel)

↗ NO.754
21 DEC •

KNOCKIN' ON HEAVEN'S DOOR (4.07) /
THROW THESE GUNS AWAY (4.08)
Dunblane
(Bob Dylan / Edward Christopher, Thomas Millar). The Dylan classic was re-recorded with a new verse, local musicians and Mark Knopfler on guitar after 16 children and a teacher were killed by a gunman at a school in Dunblane, Scotland, in March 1996. (B-sides: Bairns of Dunblane / Only Love to Give).

↗ NO.755
28 DEC •••

2 BECOME 1 (4.04)
Spice Girls
(Spice Girls, Richard Stannard, Matt Rowe). Their second and final million-seller was a heart-warming Christmas smoocher that sold enough copies in two weeks to make it the 10th best-selling single of the year. (B-sides: One of These Girls / Wannabe [remix]) **US 4**

1997

↗ NO.756
18 JAN •

PROFESSIONAL WIDOW (IT'S GOT TO BE BIG) (RE-MIX) (3.48)
Tori Amos (Tori Amos). Five months after peaking at No.20, Armand Van Helden's radically reworked track turned this thought-provoking pianist into a dance diva.

↗ NO.757
25 JAN •

YOUR WOMAN (4.20)
White Town (Jyoti Mishra).
The Indian-born Mishra had no need to "abort, retry (or) fail?" as the track he produced in his bedroom was an instant success. He was the first solo male to make his chart debut at No.1. (B-sides: Give Me Some Pain / Theme for a Mid Afternoon Game Show / Theme for a Late Documentary about the Dangers of Drug Abuse) **US 23**

↗ NO.758
1 FEB •

BEETLEBUM (5.04)
Blur
(Damon Albarn, Graham Coxon, Alex James, Dave Rowntree). The single fell from No.1 to No.7 and then No.29 but gave its writers their second No.1. It was recorded in Iceland. (B-sides: All Your Life / A Spell for Money)

↗ NO.759
8 FEB •

AIN'T NOBODY (4.49)
LL Cool J (David Wolinski).
Jaki Graham, Diana King, Course and even Chaka Khan's original version could not match the chart success achieved by this rap pioneer (B-side: Come to Butt Head) **US 46**

↗ NO.760
15 FEB •

DISCOTHEQUE (5.06)
U2 (Bono, The Edge, Adam Clayton, Larry Mullen, Simon Pyke). The fifth No.1 in five weeks was the 20th consecutive Top 20 single for these rock giants and their first chart-topper since 1991. (B-sides: Holy Joe [garage mix] / Holy Joe [guilty mix]) **US 10**

↗ NO.761
22 FEB •••

DON'T SPEAK (4.20)
No Doubt (Gwen and Eric Stefani).
This single was never released in the US but did make No Doubt the first US act to debut at No.1 in the UK. (B-sides: Hey You [acoustic] / Greener Pastures)

↗ NO.762
15 MAR •••

MAMA (3.39) /
WHO DO YOU THINK YOU ARE (3.41)
Spice Girls
(Spice Girls, Richard Stannard, Matt Rowe / Spice Girls, Andy Watson, Paul Wilson). Comic Relief and Mother's Day (the girls' mothers appeared in the 'Mama' video) fuelled sales of their record-breaking fourth successive No.1. The second A-side was performed at the Brits, where Geri's Union Jack dress stole the show.

↗ NO.763
5 APR •

BLOCK ROCKIN' BEATS (3.25)
The Chemical Brothers (Tom Rowlands, Ed Simons, Jesse Weaver). An uncredited Schoolly D vocal filled the void left by Noel Gallagher but the result was still the same – another No.1 for Rowlands and Simons. (B-sides: Prescription Beats / Morning Lemon)

↗ NO.764
12 APR •••

I BELIEVE I CAN FLY (4.43)
R Kelly (R Kelly). Kelly's inspirational ballad, from the film Space Jam, climbed to No.1 after falling to No.5 from its No.2 debut. It was one of seven Top 20 hits from the album 'R'. (B-side: Religious Love [inst]) **US 2**

↗ NO.765
3 MAY •

BLOOD ON THE DANCEFLOOR (4.14)
Michael Jackson
(Michael Jackson, Teddy Riley).
Jacko put his ongoing personal problems aside to score his seventh – and most recent – solo No.1 with this uptempo jam. (B-side: Dangerous [club mix]) **US 42**

↗ NO.766
10 MAY •

LOVE WON'T WAIT (4.16)
Gary Barlow (Madonna, Shep Pettibone). This Madonna-penned single (her only No.1 written for another act) took Barlow's tally of chart-toppers in the 1990s to a record 10. It led the first ever top three of new entries. (B-sides: Meaning of a Love Song / Always)

↗ NO.767
17 MAY ••

YOU'RE NOT ALONE (RE-ISSUE) (4.11) **Olive**
(Tim Kellett, Robin Taylor-Firth). This single peaked at No.42 in 1996 before a re-issue sent it to No.1. Vocalist Ruth Ann Boyle went on to work with Enigma, but Olive's days were all but numbered. **US 56**

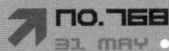
NO.768
31 MAY •

I WANNA BE THE ONLY ONE (3.37)
Eternal featuring BeBe Winans
(BeBe Winans, James Lawrence).
After 12 consecutive Top 15 singles, Eternal
managed that elusive No.1 with BeBe
Winans, who, despite a rich musical
heritage, enjoyed his one and only UK hit.
(B-sides: All tracks, Eternal only: A Friend Is
a Friend / Show Me / Don't You Leave Me)

NO.769
7 JUN •••

MMMBOP (3.58)
Hanson
(Isaac, Taylor and Zach Hanson).
These young brothers, who wrote this sing-
along smash of the summer (selling 715,369
copies in the process), were the first family
group to reach No.1 with their debut single.
(B-Side: The Man from Milwaukee) **US 1**

NO.770
28 JUN •••
26 JUL •••

I'LL BE MISSING YOU (5.10)
Puff Daddy and Faith Evans featuring 112
(Sting). The single that saw off The Verve's
'Bitter Sweet Symphony' to debut at No.1
was a moving tribute to slain rapper
Notorious B.I.G. and was based on The
Police's 'Every Breath You Take'. It sold
seven million copies worldwide and
1,409,688 in the UK. (B-sides: We'll
Always Love Big Poppa / Cry On) **US 1**

NO.771
19 JUL •

D'YOU KNOW WHAT I MEAN? (7.23)
Oasis (Noel Gallagher).
Sandwiched between the No.1 runs of 'I'll Be
Missing You', D'You Know What I Mean?' was
the longest ever No.1 single. It surpassed the
previous record-holder, 'Hey Jude' (see
No.258), by 17 seconds but was quickly
overshadowed by the band's next chart-
topper (see No.781). (B-sides: Stay Young /
Angel Child [demo] / Heroes)

NO.772
16 AUG ••••

MEN IN BLACK (3.46)
Will Smith
(Will Smith, Patrice Rushen, Terry McFadden,
Fred Washington). The second No.1 in 15
months to sample Rushen's 'Forget Me Nots'
(see No.738) gave the artist formerly known
as the Fresh Prince his second No.1. It
was used in the film of the same name.
(B-sides: Escobar '97 – Nas / Dah Dee
Dah – Alicia Keys)

↘ CHART-TOPPER NO.769: Super-young supergroup Hanson explain the thinking
behind the unusual spelling of the title of their No.1 hit song: 'It wasn't quite MMMMMMbop,
and it wasn't quite MMbop, it was MMMbop … just looked good, three Ms and a bop'

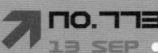

NO.773
13 SEP ●

THE DRUGS DON'T WORK (4.47)
The Verve (Richard Ashcroft).
Ashcroft's mournful masterpiece, the band's only No.1, captured the mood of the nation after the death of Diana, Princess of Wales. (B-side: Three Steps)

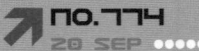

NO.774
20 SEP ●●●●●

CANDLE IN THE WIND 1997 (4.00)
/ SOMETHING ABOUT THE WAY YOU LOOK TONIGHT (5.08)
Elton John (Elton John, Bernie Taupin).
Elton re-wrote his ode to Marilyn Monroe as a tribute to Diana, performing it at her funeral. It became the fastest-selling (658,000 copies in the UK on the first day) and biggest-selling (more than 33 million copies worldwide and 4,864,611 in the UK) single of all time amid the outpouring of grief. (B-side: You Can Make History) **US 1 / 0**

↘ CHART-TOPPER NO.785: Cornershop had a very special guest star on their I Was Born for the 7th Time album. It featured a spoken word contribution from beat poet Allen Ginsberg, who died months before the record was released

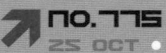

NO.775
25 OCT ●

SPICE UP YOUR LIFE (2.53)
Spice Girls (Spice Girls, Richard Stannard, Matt Rowe). The unstoppable quintet's "power to the world" anthem gave them a fifth successive No.1 and another platinum disc. (B-side: Spice Invaders) **US 18**

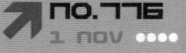

NO.776
1 NOV ●●●●

BARBIE GIRL (3.14)
Aqua (Soren Rasted, Claus Noreen, Rene Dif, Lene Nykstrom). The group's colourful brand of bubblegum pop conjured up a massive seller (1,722,400) in 'Barbie Girl'. The first of their three successive chart-toppers kept Natalie Imbruglia's 'Torn' off No.1. **US 7**

NO.777
29 NOV ●●
10 JAN ●

PERFECT DAY (3.46)
Various (Lou Reed). This track was released off the back of a BBC TV ad in support of live music. Bono, Tom Jones, Tammy Wynette, David Bowie, Elton John, writer Reed and many other stars each sang a line of the million-plus seller (1,548,500), which became a fundraiser for Children in Need.

NO.778
13 DEC ●●

TELETUBBIES SAY EH-OH! (3.30)
Teletubbies
(Andrew McCrorie-Shand, Andrew Davenport). Toddlers' favourites Tinky Winky (the purle one), Dipsy (the green one), Laa-

Laa (the yellow one) and Po (the red one) sold more than a million by simply reciting their names and shouting "Teletubbies say eh-oh!". (B-sides: Bumps a Daisy / Tip Toe Dance)

NO.779
27 DEC ●●

TOO MUCH (3.52)
Spice Girls (Spice Girls, Andy Watkins, Paul Wilson). The Spice Girls stole the Christmas No.1 (their second in a row) from the Teletubbies and became the first act since The Beatles to have six No.1s in a row. (B-side: Walk of Life) **US 9**

1998

NO.780
17 JAN ●

NEVER EVER (5.12)
All Saints (Rickidy Raw, Shaznay Lewis). The first of All Saints' five No.1 singles, sold 770,000 copies in the eight weeks before it reached No.1 (a record achievement) and 1,254,604 copies in total. (B-side: I Remember) **US 4**

NO.781
24 JAN ●

ALL AROUND THE WORLD (9.38)
Oasis (Noel Gallagher). The longest No.1 single of all time extended the band's own record, set in July 1997, by a staggering two

minutes and 15 seconds. (B-sides: The Fame / Flashbox / Street Fighting Man)

NO.782
31 JAN ●

YOU MAKE ME WANNA ... (3.39)
Usher (Jermaine Dupri, Seal, Usher Raymond). Usher became the youngest individual credited writer of a No.1 since Paul Anka (who wrote his 1957 hit 'Diana') when this sultry smash topped the chart three months after his 19th birthday.

NO.783
7 FEB ●●

DOCTOR JONES (3.24)
Aqua (Soren Rasted, Claus Noreen, Rene Dif, Lene Nykstrom). 'Doctor Jones' succeeded where Abba's 'Ring Ring' failed, making Aqua the first Scandinavian act to reach No.1 with its first two chart entries.

NO.784
21 FEB ●
14 MAR ●

MY HEART WILL GO ON (5.09)
Celine Dion (James Horner, Will Jennings). Her first million-seller took 12 weeks to reach No.1, but her soaring ballad from the box-office smash Titanic broke the ice immediately and sold 1,312,551. (B-sides: Because You Loved Me / When I Fall In Love – with Clive Griffin / Beauty and the Beast – with Peabo Bryson) **US 1**

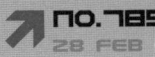

↗ **NO.785**
28 FEB •

BRIMFUL OF ASHA (RE-MIX) (4.03)
Cornershop (Tjinder Singh). The ubiquitous Norman Cook twiddled the knobs on this re-mix of the band's 1997 chart flop. After huge radio support, it sold more than 200,000 copies in its first week. (B-side: U47s)

↗ **NO.786**
7 MAR •

FROZEN (6.09)
Madonna (Madonna, Patrick Leonard). Madonna's first chart-topper since 'Vogue' in 1990 was her eighth No.1. Producer William Orbit stamped his signature sound all over this atmospheric track. **US 2**

↗ **NO.787**
21 MAR ••••••

IT'S LIKE THAT (4.12)
Run-DMC vs Jason Nevins
(Joseph Simmons, Darryl McDaniels, Lawrence Smith). These rap pioneers kept 'Stop' – the only Spice Girls single not to reach No.1 – at bay and sold 1,119,900 copies in the process. It was the longest unbroken run at No.1 since 1996.

↗ **NO.788**
2 MAY •

ALL THAT I NEED (3.38)
Boyzone (Carl Sturken, Evan Rogers). Shortly after fallen idol Gary Glitter had been charged and later sentenced to prison, Boyzone equalled his male chart record of 11 Top 10 hits from the start of a career. (B-sides: Never Easy / Paradise / Working My Way Back to You)

↗ **NO.789**
9 MAY •
23 MAY •

UNDER THE BRIDGE (5.02) /
LADY MARMALADE (4.01)
All Saints
(Anthony Kiedis, Michael Balzary, John Frusciante, Chad Smith / Bob Crewe, Kenny Nolan). The girls put their own stamp on these Top 20 hits by The Red Hot Chili Peppers and LaBelle. (B-side: No More Lies)

↗ **NO.790**
16 MAY •

TURN BACK TIME (4.07)
Aqua
(Soren Rasted, Claus Noreen, Rene Dif, Lene Nykstrom). The wacky Scandinavians targeted a more mature audience with this ballad, a third self-penned No.1 that made them the first overseas act to have their first three hits enter at No.1.

↗ **NO.791**
30 MAY •

FEEL IT (3.16)
The Tamperer featuring Maya
(Michael and Jackie Jackson). A club classic that sampled The Jacksons' 'Can You Feel it'. It was Michael's seventh No.1 as a composer. (B-side: Feel in the House)

↗ **NO.792**
6 JUN ••

C'EST LA VIE (2.52)
B*Witched
(B*Witched, Ray Hedges, Tracey Ackerman, Martin Brannigan). The youngest girl group to reach No.1 was also the first Irish act to enter the chart at No.1 with a debut single. (B-sides: We Four Girls / B*Witched Quiz Show) **US 9**

↗ **NO.793**
20 JUN •••

THREE LIONS '98 (3.58)
Baddiel and Skinner
and The Lightning Seeds
(Ian Broudie, David Baddiel, Frank Skinner). With lyrics amended from the Euro 96 version, 'Three Lions '98' was knocked off the top spot the week England were knocked out of the World Cup in France. The year's unofficial football anthem, 'Vindaloo', was at No.2 during the song's chart-topping run. (B-sides: Tout Est Possible / Three Lions [original version])

↗ **NO.794**
11 JUL •

BECAUSE WE WANT TO (3.48)
Billie (Dion Rambo, Jacques Richmond, Wendy Page, Jim Marr). The future Mrs Chris Evans was, at 15, the youngest female to debut at No.1. (B-side: G.h.e.t.t.o.u.t.)

↗ **NO.795**
18 JUL •

FREAK ME (3.35)
Another Level (Roy Murray, Keith Sweat). The year's biggest-selling new UK group took this Silk song to another level – 45 places higher than the original. (B-side: Whatever You Want)

↗ **NO.796**
25 JUL •

DEEPER UNDERGROUND (3.21)
Jamiroquai (Jason Kay, Toby Smith). This monster hit from the Godzilla soundtrack gave hat-lover Kay and his band their first No.1. The video cost $1m.

↗ **NO.797**
1 AUG ••

VIVA FOREVER (4.12)
Spice Girls (Spice Girls, Richard Stannard,

Matt Rowe). Another Godzilla track, 'Come with Me', had to settle for second place when the Spice Girls returned to winning ways with this fairytale ballad.

↗ **NO.798**
15 AUG •••

NO MATTER WHAT (4.33)
Boyzone (Andrew Lloyd Webber, Jim Steinman). Boyzone's inspirational ballad, from the Lloyd Webber musical Whistle Down the Wind, became the biggest-selling single by an Irish act (1,074,192). It won the first Record of the Year show on ITV. (B-sides: Where Have You Been / All That I Need)

↗ **NO.799**
5 SEP •

IF YOU TOLERATE THIS YOUR CHILDREN WILL BE NEXT (4.48)
Manic Street Preachers
(James Dean Bradfield, Sean Moore, Nick Jones). Q: Before the Manics, who were the last Welsh group to have a UK No.1? A: Amen Corner, in 1969. Both this single, and its parent album, 'This Is My Truth Tell Me Yours', kept Steps releases off No.1. (B-sides: Prologue to History / Montana-Autumn-78)

↗ **NO.800**
12 SEP •

BOOTIE CALL (3.35)
All Saints (Shaznay Lewis, Karl Gordon). The 800th No.1, the group's third No.1 of 1998, fell from No.1 to No.7, a feat last achieved by Blur (see No.758). (B-side: Get Down)

↗ **NO.801**
19 SEP •

MILLENNIUM (4.05)
Robbie Williams (Robbie Williams, Guy Chambers, John Barry, Leslie Bricusse). A sample of 'You Only Live Twice' helped Robbie to achieve his first No.1 since leaving Take That. Parents everywhere breathed a huge sigh of relief when it kept 'Sex on the Beach' at No.2. (B-sides: Lazy Days / Angels [live])

↗ **NO.802**
26 SEP •

I WANT YOU BACK (3.27)
Melanie B featuring Missy 'Misdemeanor' Elliott (Missy Elliott, Gerard, Thomas, Donald Holmes). The first of eight 'solo' No.1s for members of the Spice Girls gave Scary an eighth No.1, equalling Madonna's female record.

↗ **NO.803**
3 OCT ••

ROLLERCOASTER (3.19)
B*Witched (B*Witched, Ray Hedges, Tracey Ackerman, Martin Brannigan). Ireland's most

successful female group was the first female act to enter at No.1 with its first two hits. They kept both Brandy singles off the top. (B-side: Get Happy / B*Witched Go to the Moon)

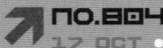

NO.804
17 OCT ●

GIRLFRIEND (3.55)
Billie (Dion Rambo, Jacques Richmond). Miss Piper's second chart-topper set another record for the young starlet – the first female solo act to reach No.1 with her first two singles. (B-side: Love Groove)

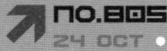

NO.805
24 OCT ●

GYM AND TONIC (3.22)
Spacedust (Spacedust). A precursor to Eric Prydz's 'Call on Me', perhaps? This dance workout whipped people into shape using Bob Sinclar's Jane Fonda-sampling 'Gymtonic'. (B-side: Spacegroove)

NO.806
31 OCT ●●●●●●●

BELIEVE (3.56)
Cher (Brian Higgins, Paul Barry, Steve Torch, Matt Gray, Stuart McLennen, Timothy Powell). The year's biggest-seller (1,672,108) brought the vocoder back into fashion. At 52, Cher was the oldest female solo chart-topper and her seven-week spell at No.1 has not been matched since. **US 1**

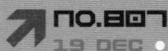

NO.807
19 DEC ●

TO YOU I BELONG (3.04)
B*Witched (B*Witched, Ray Hedges, Tracey Ackerman, Martin Brannigan). A third No.1 for the only female act to debut at No.1 with their first three singles. This one was a Christmassy ballad. (B-sides: Fly Away / B*Witched's Message to Santa).

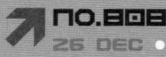

NO.808
26 DEC ●

GOODBYE (4.45)
Spice Girls (Spice Girls, Richard Stannard, Matt Rowe). The Spice Girls snared their third consecutive seasonal chart-topper. The title of the song led many to believe this was their chart swansong. (B-side: Christmas Wrapping) **US 11**

1999

NO.809
2 JAN ●

CHOCOLATE SALTY BALLS (PS I LOVE YOU) (4.55)
Chef (Trey Parker).

The naughty novelty comeback of Isaac Hayes, the voice of Chef in the animated cartoon series South Park, who made his previous chart appearance in 1976. (B-sides: Come Sail Away – Eric Cartman / Mentally Dull – Vitro and Cast of South Park)

NO.810
9 JAN ●

HEARTBEAT (4.24) /
TRAGEDY (4.30)
Steps
(Jackie James / Barry, Maurice and Robin Gibb). This double-A made its debut at No.2 in November 1998 and fell as low as No.8 before rising to the top seven weeks later. It sold 1,150,285 copies, despite some disapproving voices about the group's rendition of the Bee Gees' classic.

NO.811
16 JAN ●

PRAISE YOU (5.23)
Fatboy Slim
(Norman Cook, Camille Yarborough). Cook's third No.1 under a third guise (see Nos.581 and 642) will be remembered for its interesting video featuring a group of dancers. (B-sides: Sho Nuff / The Rockafeller Skank) **US 36**

NO.812
23 JAN ●

A LITTLE BIT MORE (3.47)
911 (Bobby Gosh).
Dr Hook's heart-warming love song gave this boy band their ninth consecutive Top 10 hit and only No.1. 911's Lee Brennan later co-wrote Blue's second No.1 of 2001. (B-sides: Don't Walk Away / Nothing Stops the Rain [French version])

NO.813
30 JAN ●

PRETTY FLY (FOR A WHITE GUY) (3.08) **The Offspring**
(Dexter Holland, Robert John 'Mutt' Lange, Joe Elliott, Steve Clark). This Def Leppard-sampling head-nodder led the first rock 1-2 since No Doubt and Kula Shaker in 1997 when 'Tequila' by Terrorvision came in at No.2. (B-side: All I Want [live]) **US 53**

NO.814
6 FEB ●

YOU DON'T KNOW ME (4.01)
Armand Van Helden
featuring Duane Harden
(Armand Van Helden, Duane Harden). Prolific re-mixer Helden, the man behind Tori Amos' No.1, had only two minor hits to his name before he hit the top. (B-side: Rock Da Spot)

NO.815
13 FEB ●

MARIA (4.07)
Blondie (Jimmy Destri). The comeback kings of 1999 scored their sixth No.1 18 years after their fifth. At 53, Debbie Harry was one year older than Cher when she topped the chart with 'Believe'. **US 82**

NO.816
20 FEB ●

FLY AWAY (3.41)
Lenny Kravitz (Lenny Kravitz).
The 10th different No.1 in 10 weeks won Kravitz a Grammy for Best Male Rock Vocal Performance. It flew to No.1 after its use in a Peugeot TV commercial. (B-side: Believe [live acoustic]) **US 12**

NO.817
27 FEB ●●

...BABY ONE MORE TIME (3.30)
Britney Spears (Max Martin).
The youngest female member of the million club (1,450,154) achieved the fastest-selling debut single ever (464,000 copies in the first week) with her saucy debut. The video showed a 17-year-old, school uniform-clad Britney and was an instant hit with her male fans. (B-Side Autumn Goodbye) **US 1**

NO.818
13 MAR ●●

WHEN THE GOING GETS TOUGH (3.37) **Boyzone**
(Wayne Braithwaite, Barry J Eastmond, R J 'Mutt' Lange, Billy Ocean). This abbreviated Ocean cover, which raised money for Comic Relief, was Boyzone's fifth and penultimate No.1. (B-sides: What a Wonderful World – Alison Moyet and LSO / Love Can Build a Bridge [documentary])

NO.819
27 MAR ●

BLAME IT ON THE WEATHERMAN (3.33) **B*Witched**
(Ray Hedges, Tracey Ackerman, Martin Brannigan, Andy Caine). B*Witched broke another record with their fourth No.1: no act had made its debut at No.1 with its first four releases. Uniquely, this single also saw group members Edele and Keavy replace their brother, Boyzone's Shane, at No.1.

NO.820
3 APR ●●

FLAT BEAT (3.56)
Mr Oizo (Quentin Dupieux). Eminem had this head-banging yellow puppet, christened Flat Eric, to thank for the No.2 chart placing of his debut single. Dupieux, the man behind the

instrumental from a Levi's ad, gave France its first UK No.1 since Charles Aznavour in 1974. (B-side: Monday Massacre)

↗ **NO.821**
17 APR ●●

PERFECT MOMENT (3.49)
Martine McCutcheon
(Wendy Page, Jim Marr). The third star of TV soap EastEnders to score a UK No.1. The others? Wendy Richard and Nick Berry.
(B-sides: You, Me & Us / Gettin' Ready for Love)

↗ **NO.822**
1 MAY ●●

SWEAR IT AGAIN (4.09)
Westlife (Steve Mac, Wayne Hector).
The first boy band to debut at No.1 achieved the first of their 12 chart-toppers with a ballad written by Mac and Hector, talented vocalists in their own right. Mac also produced the group's only single to chart in the US.
(B-side: Forever) **US 20**

↗ **NO.823**
15 MAY ●

I WANT IT THAT WAY (3.33)
Backstreet Boys
(Max Martin, Andreas Carlsson). The world-conquering boy band's only UK No.1, after seven Top 10 hits, was co-written by the top pop Swede Andreas Carlsson, who penned Britney's debut. (B-sides: My Heart Stays with You / I'll Be There for You) **US 6**

↗ **NO.824**
22 MAY ●

YOU NEEDED ME (3.27)
Boyzone (Randy Goodrum).
Nine weeks after they were last at No.1, Anne Murray's ballad became the boys' sixth and final No.1 and 15th successive top five entry. It kept Geri Halliwell's debut disc at No.2.
(B-sides: Words Can't Describe / Megamix)

↗ **NO.825**
29 MAY ●●

SWEET LIKE CHOCOLATE (3.29)
Shanks & Bigfoot (Stephen Meade, Daniel Langsman). The Doolally DJs created such a buzz for their club smash that one London DJ was threatened with GBH by a group of knife-wielding girls disappointed that they couldn't hear the track because his promo copy hadn't arrived.

↗ **NO.826**
12 JUN ●

EVERYBODY'S FREE (TO WEAR SUNSCREEN) - THE SUNSCREEN SONG (CLASS OF '99) (5.05)
Baz Luhrmann (Tim Cox, Nigel Swanston, Mary Schmich). This thought-provoking yet

↘ CHART-TOPPER NO.816: Lenny Kravitz's mother was good friends with Miles Davis's wife, Cicely Tyson. When the jazz great threw a party for his 60th birthday, Lenny found himself jamming alongside three legends: Chick Corea, Herbie Hancock and Carlos Santana

humorous spoken-word No.1, a modern-day 'Desiderata', formed part of Schmich's graduation speech. (B-side: Love Is in the Air)

↗ **NO.827**
19 JUN ●

BRING IT ALL BACK (3.30)
S Club 7 (Eliot Kennedy, Mike Percy, Tim Lever, S Club 7). The stars of the TV series Miami 7, including future solo star and pin-up Rachel Stevens, were the biggest vocal group to reach No.1. (B-side: So Right)

↗ **NO.828**
26 JUN ●

BOOM, BOOM, BOOM, BOOM!! (3.24)
The Vengaboys (Dennis Van Den Driessen, Wessel Van Diepen). The fourth chart-topper in six years to have the word 'boom' in the

title was Positiva Records' first UK No.1 after more than 70 releases. **US 84**

↗ **NO.829**
3 JUL ●●

(9PM) TILL I COME (2.41)
ATB (Andre Tanneberger, Arcos Ferrerons, Gilabert Posadas, Garrido Rivera). Australian and German imports and a vinyl-only version stoked the interest in German Tanneberger's club classic several months before its full release.

↗ **NO.830**
17 JUL ●●●

LIVIN' LA VIDA LOCA (4.01)
Ricky Martin (Robi Rosa, Desmond Child). A hip-swivelling, booty-shaking transatlantic party anthem that added Puerto Rico to the

list of countries with a UK No.1. It gave songwriter Child (Bon Jovi, Aerosmith, Kiss) his first chart-topper after 27 previous hits. (B-side: La Copa De La Vida) **US 1**

NO.831
7 AUG ••

WHEN YOU SAY NOTHING AT ALL (4.18) **Ronan Keating**
(Paul Overstreet, Don Schlitz). The ballad that won bluegrass babe Alison Krauss a Grammy and Keith Whitley a place at the top of the US country chart enjoyed its UK chart run four months before Keating's Boyzone released their final single. (B-side: This Is Your Song)

NO.832
21 AUG •

IF I LET YOU GO (3.38)
Westlife (Jörgen Elofsson, Per Magnusson, David Kreuger). Co-managed by the man they knocked off No.1, Westlife claimed their second chart-topper with another ballad, this time written by the prolific Swedes. (B-side: Try Again)

NO.833
28 AUG •

MI CHICO LATINO (3.14)
Geri Halliwell (Geri Halliwell, Paul Wilson, Andy Watkins). The former Spice Girl collected the first of her four consecutive chart-toppers with a Latin-tinged summer hit.

NO.834
4 SEP ••

MAMBO NO.5 (A LITTLE BIT OF ...) (3.42) **Lou Bega**
(Perez Prado, David LuBega, Christian Pletschacher). Germany's Bega and his harem of name-checked lovelies sparked off an international dance craze with Prado's 50s favourite. Two years later, Bob the Builder cranked up another mambo revival.

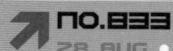

NO.835
18 SEP •

WE'RE GOING TO IBIZA! (3.38)
The Vengaboys (Jeff Calvert, Geraint Hughes). The multinational collective's take on Typically Tropical's 'Barbados'. (B-side: Paradise)

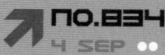

NO.836
25 SEP •••

BLUE (DA BA DEE) (4.45)
Eiffel 65 (Massimo Gabutti, Maurizio Lobina, Gianfranco Randone). Europe's dominance of the UK chart continued as these Italians sold 1,023,500 copies of a single that topped 10 European charts simultaneously. The word 'blue' appeared 41 times in the song's colourful lyrics. **US 6**

NO.837
16 OCT ••

GENIE IN A BOTTLE (3.37)
Christina Aguilera (Steve Kipner, David Frank, Pam Sheyne). The lyrics to this racy transatlantic smash rubbed some people up the wrong way in the US and had to be amended. She followed Britney, her fellow former Mickey Mouse Club Mouseketeer, to the top of the chart. (B-side: Blessed) **US 1**

NO.838
30 OCT •

FLYING WITHOUT WINGS (3.35)
Westlife (Steve Mac, Wayne Hector). The second fastest hat-trick of No.1s (from chart debut) took six months to achieve. This single snared the second ITV Record of the Year prize. (B-side: Everybody Knows)

NO.839
6 NOV •

KEEP ON MOVIN' (3.18)
Five (Richard Stannard, Julian Gallagher, Jay Brown, Abs Breen, Sean Conlon). After six Top 10 hits and three consecutive No.2s, the funky boy band celebrated their first chart-topper. Three members of Five co-wrote the track. (B-sides: How Do You Feel [remix] / Reminiscing)

NO.840
13 NOV •

LIFT ME UP (3.15)
Geri Halliwell (Geri Halliwell, Tracey Ackerman, Andy Watkins, Paul Wilson). Geri won the much-publicised battle of solo Spice Girls past and present when this single sold more copies than 'What I Am', Emma's duet with Tin Tin Out. (B-sides: Live and Let Die / Very Slowly)

NO.841
20 NOV •

IT'S ONLY US (2.50) /
SHE'S THE ONE (4.19)
Robbie Williams (Guy Chambers, Steve Power / Karl Wallinger). World Party original 'She's the One' was the most played track of this double-A. The ballad's video showed Robbie (in truth his body double) as an Olympic ice-skating champion. (B-side: Millennium [live])

NO.842
27 NOV •

KING OF MY CASTLE (3.27)
Wamdue Project (Chris Brann). Brann, the producer behind the Wamdue Project, was indifferent to the remix that sent his dance single to the top after the original missed the Top 75 altogether in 1998. It was the sixth No.1 of the year to chart first as an import.

NO.843
4 DEC •••

THE MILLENNIUM PRAYER (4.40)
Cliff Richard
(Traditional: arranged by Paul Field, Stephen Deal). Sir Cliff pulled off a millennium masterstroke by singing the Lord's Prayer to the tune of Auld Lang Syne, backed by an orchestra and choir. (B-side: Two Worlds)

NO.844
25 DEC ••••

I HAVE A DREAM (4.06) /
SEASONS IN THE SUN (4.04)
Westlife (Benny Andersson, Björn Ulvaeus / Jacques Brel, Rod McKuen). Hope (Abba) and despair (Terry Jacks) in equal measure as Westlife kept up their impressive run of best-sellers. This one equalled Elvis's record of four No.1s in a year. (B-side: On the Wings of Love)

NO.845
22 JAN •

THE MASSES AGAINST THE CLASSES (3.24)
Manic Street Preachers
(James Dean Bradfield, Sean Moore, Nick Jones). The political Welsh rockers' 30th Top 75 entry, but only their second chart-topper. (B-sides: Close My Eyes / Rock & Roll Music)

NO.846
29 JAN •

BORN TO MAKE YOU HAPPY (3.36)
Britney Spears
(Kristian Lundin, Andreas Carlsson). The youngest million-selling female in chart history (see No.817) returned to the top with the second No.1 from her ... Baby One More Time album. (B-side: [You Drive Me] Crazy)

NO.847
5 FEB ••

RISE (3.36)
Gabrielle
(Bob Dylan, Louise Bobb, Ferdy Under-Hamilton, Ollie Dagois). The soul balladeer, who co-wrote this track, used a sample of 'Knockin' on Heaven's Door' to 'rise' to No.1 – and this time she had no trouble getting permission (see No.691). (B-side: Dreams)

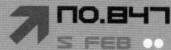

NO.848
19 FEB •

GO LET IT OUT (4.38)
Oasis (Noel Gallagher). The first single released on their Big Brother label, from the album Standing on the Shoulder of Giants,

featured new guitarist Gem Archer (Heavy Stereo) and bass player Andy Bell (Ride, Hurricane #1). (B-sides: Let's All Make Believe / [As Long As They've Got] Cigarettes in Hell)

↗ **no.849**
26 FEB ●●
PURE SHORES (4.30) **All Saints**
(Shaznay Lewis, William Orbit). The first of two successive film soundtrack No.1s produced by Orbit was featured in The Beach.
(B-side: If You Don't Know What I Know)

↗ **no.850**
11 MAR ●
AMERICAN PIE (4.33)
Madonna
(Don McLean).
The Queen of Pop racked up her 52nd hit with a much shortened, chart-friendly version of Don McLean's eight-minute, 36-second Buddy Holly tribute from 1972 which only No.2 in its original version. **US 29**

↗ **no.851**
18 MAR ●
DON'T GIVE UP (3.40)
Chicane featuring Bryan Adams
(Nick Bracegirdle, Bryan Adams, Ray Hedges). Producer Bracegirdle (aka Chicane) collaborated with Power Circle, Mason and Maire Brennan on previous singles, but none were as well received as this dance smash with the Canadian rocker.

↗ **no.852**
25 MAR ●
BAG IT UP (3.43)
Geri Halliwell
(Geri Halliwell, Paul Wilson, Andy Watkins). Geri's record-breaking (for a female soloist) third consecutive No.1 and her 10th No.1 in total – another record for a female performer.
(B-sides: These Boots Are Made for Walking / Perhaps, Perhaps, Perhaps)

↗ **no.853**
1 APR ●
NEVER BE THE SAME AGAIN (4.13)
Melanie C / Lisa 'Left Eye' Lopes
(Melanie Chisholm, Rhett Lawrence, Lisa Lopes, Paul Cruz). TLC's Lopes, who bagged her only chart-topper, was killed in a car crash two years after this reached No.1.
(B-side: I Wonder What It Would Be Like)

↗ **no.854**
8 APR ●
FOOL AGAIN (3.54)
Westlife (Jörgen Elofsson, Per Magnusson, David Kreuger).
The first act to have five No.1s with their first five singles returned with another Swedish-penned ballad. (B-side: Tunnel of Love)

↗ **no.855**
15 APR ●
FILL ME IN (3.51)
Craig David
(Craig David, Mark Hill).
This 'born to do it' south coast superstar was the youngest British male to write and record a No.1. He is one of the few British acts to reach the US Top 20 in the 21st century.
(B-side: Apartment) **US 15**

↗ **no.856**
22 APR ●●
TOCA'S MIRACLE (3.22)
Fragma: Vocals by Co Co
(Ramon Zenker, Dirk and Marco Duderstadt, Victor Imbres, Rob Davis).
This dancefloor smash fused the German / Spanish group's 'Toca Me', a hit six months previously, with 'Co Co's 'I Need a Miracle'.
(B-side: Everybody Knows) **US 99**

↘ **CHART-TOPPER no.799, 845:** The Manic Street Preachers were the first Western rock band to play Cuba in 2001, when they played to an audience including an appreciative Fidel Castro, in Havana's Karl Marx Theatre

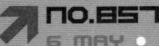

NO.857
6 MAY •

BOUND 4 DA RELOAD (CASUALTY) (3.48)
Oxide & Neutrino (Alex Rivers, Kenneth Freeman, Mark Oseitutu). The part-time So Solid Crew teenage duo "garaged up" the theme tune from hospital drama Casualty. The 12-inch vinyl format, too long for the singles chart, appeared on the albums list. (B-side: Express Dr Funk)

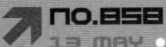

NO.858
13 MAY •

OOPS! ... I DID IT AGAIN (3.32)
Britney Spears
(Max Martin, Rami Yacoub). Oops! Britney "I'm not that innocent" Spears needed four stitches in a head wound when a camera fell on her while shooting the raunchy video for this song. She was briefly the youngest female to claim three No.1s. (B-sides: Deep in My Heart / From the Bottom of My Broken Heart) **US 9**

NO.859
20 MAY •

DON'T CALL ME BABY (RE-ISSUE) (3.47)
Madison Avenue (Cheyne Coates, Andy Van Dorsselaer, Duane Morrison, Guiseppe Chierchia). This re-issued, Australian-produced dance track peaked 29 places higher than it did in November 1999. **US 88**

NO.860
27 MAY •

DAY AND NIGHT (3.15)
Billie Piper (Eliot Kennedy, Tim Lever, Billie Piper, Mark Cawley). The teeny-bopper was four months shy of her 18th birthday when she became the youngest female to have three No.1s. It was her first single to be released under her full name.

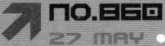

NO.861
3 JUN •••

IT FEELS SO GOOD (3.48)
Sonique (Sonia Clarke, Simon Belofsky, Graeme Pleeth, Linus Burdick). Kate Bush's 'Wuthering Heights' was the last single by a UK female to spend longer at No.1. DJ Clarke (aka Sonique) co-wrote the track. **US 8**

NO.862
24 JUN •

YOU SEE THE TROUBLE WITH ME (4.54) **Black Legend**
(Barry White, Ray Parker Jr).
White refused to lend his sizeable talents to this club monster, which originally sampled his voice, so Elroy 'Spoonface' Powell

re-recorded the track for the Italian production duo. (B-side: Across the Ocean)

NO.863
1 JUL •

SPINNING AROUND (3.28)
Kylie Minogue
(Ira Shickman, Dinky Bingham, Kara DioGuardi, Paula Abdul). After a gap of almost six years, Kylie returned to the Top 10 and claimed her first No.1 since 1990. Songwriter Abdul intended to record it as her comeback single, but instead decided to revive her career as a judge on American Idol.

NO.864
8 JUL •

THE REAL SLIM SHADY (4.47)
Eminem (Marshall Mathers, Andre Young, Melvin Bradfield). The first of Slim Shady's five chart-toppers, which came together from a drum track programmed by Dr Dre, angered Christina Aguilera with a tasteless line about her alleged encounters with Carson Daly and Fred Durst. (B-side: Guilty Conscience – Eminem featuring Dr Dre) **US 4**

NO.865
15 JUL •

BREATHLESS (3.32)
The Corrs (Robert John 'Mutt' Lange, The Corrs). The only mixed family group to have a UK No.1. The song was written with Shania Twain's husband in Switzerland. (B-sides: Head in the Air / Judy) **US 34**

NO.866
22 JUL •

LIFE IS A ROLLERCOASTER (3.54)
Ronan Keating (Rick Nowels, Gregg Alexander). This song, co-written by New Radicals singer Alexander, became Keating's 18th consecutive top five hit – a record that was broken when his next single peaked at No.6. (B-sides: Life Is a Rollercoaster [karaoke] / Thank God I Kissed You)

NO.867
29 JUL •

WE WILL ROCK YOU (2.58)
Five and Queen
(Brian May, Richard Breen, Jason Brown). The only time this rock classic appeared on the singles chart (it was originally the B-side of Queen's 'We Are the Champions') was when, uniquely, two groups joined forces on a No.1 record. (B-side: Keep On Movin')

NO.868
5 AUG •

7 DAYS (3.54)
Craig David (Craig David, Mark Hill, Darren Hill). The youngest British male to reach No.1

twice (until Gareth Gates in 2002) stayed at the top for seven days – during which time he had met a girl, taken her for a drink, made love to her and "chilled". (B-sides: Stop Messing Around / Fill Me In [acoustic]) **US 33**

NO.869
12 AUG •

ROCK DJ (4.17)
Robbie Williams (Robbie Williams, Guy Chambers, Kelvin Andrews, Nelson Pigford, Ekundayo Paris). The second chart-topper of 2000 with a Barry White link (see No.862) sampled 'It's Ecstasy When You Lay Down Next to Me' and gave Robbie his 10th No.1, his third post-Take That. (B-side: Talk to Me)

NO.870
19 AUG •

I TURN TO YOU (4.13)
Melanie C (Melanie Chisholm, Rick Nowels, Billy Steinberg). The first woman to top the chart as a soloist, in a duo (Lisa 'Left Eye' Lopes) and in a group (Spice Girls). Her 15th consecutive top five hit. (B-side: Never Be the Same Again [live])

NO.871
26 AUG •

GROOVEJET (IF THIS AIN'T LOVE) (4.48) **Spiller**
(Cristiano Spiller, Sophie Ellis-Bextor, Robert Davis, Vince Montana Jr, Ron Walker). A chart battle not seen since the Blur vs Oasis showdown saw Spiller (with guest vocalist Ellis-Bextor) fend off Victoria Beckham's 'Out of Your Mind' to become the year's fastest seller – 202,591 copies in the first week.

NO.872
2 SEP •

MUSIC (3.48)
Madonna (Madonna Ciccone, Mirwais Ahmadzai). Madonna's 10th No.1 spent more time in the Top 75 (23 weeks) than any of her previous 52 chart entries. The video featured comedian Ali G as her limo driver. **US 1**

NO.873
9 SEP •

TAKE ON ME (3.33)
a1 (Pal Waaktaar, Mags Furuholmen, Morten Harket). The band's sole Norwegian, Christian Ingebrigtsen, did his fellow countrymen A-ha proud with this faithful cover, accompanied by a futuristic video. It was the 12th successive No.1 to spend one week at the top. (B-sides: Beatles Medley / I Got Sunshine)

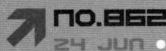

NO.874
16 SEP ••

LADY (HEAR ME TONIGHT) (3.42)
Modjo (Yann Destagnol, Romain Tranchart,

Nile Rodgers, Bernard Edwards). The first French group to have a UK No.1 borrowed a guitar loop from Chic's 'Soup for One' for their tale of boy meets girl. (B-side: Rollercoaster) US 81

NO.875
30 SEP ●●
AGAINST ALL ODDS (3.21)
Mariah Carey featuring Westlife
(Phil Collins). Carey originally recorded this Collins classic alone for her album 'Rainbow', but Westlife added their vocals for the single version. It was Carey's second No.1 – both covers.

NO.876
14 OCT ●
BLACK COFFEE (4.50)
All Saints (Tom Nichols, Alexander Soos, Kirsty Elizabeth Roper). Complete with freshly ground vocal and espresso mixes, Melanie, Natalie and Nicole and Shaznay brewed up their fifth chart-topper from seven attempts. (B-side: I Don't Wanna Be Alone)

NO.877
21 OCT ●
BEAUTIFUL DAY (4.07)
U2 (Adam Clayton, David Evans, Paul Hewson, Larry Mullen).
The sixth Irish-made No.1 of 2000 was transformed into a football anthem when it was used by ITV as the theme tune to its Premiership football highlights show. (B-sides: Summer Rain / Always) US 21

NO.878
28 OCT ●
STOMP (3.18)
Steps (Mark Topham, Karl Twigg, Rita Campbell). Another Step-tastic dance routine to master from the first girl / boy combo to hit the top twice since Bucks Fizz in 1982. (B-side: Tragedy)

NO.879
4 NOV ●
HOLLER (3.56) /
LET LOVE LEAD THE WAY (4.16)
Spice Girls (Rodney Jerkins, LeShawn Daniels, Fred Jerkins III, Spice Girls / Rodney Jerkins, LeShawn Daniels, Fred Jerkins III, Spice Girls, Harvey Mason Jr). Two years after waving 'Goodbye' with an eighth No.1, the Ginger-less Spice Girls surpassed Take That and the Stones and tied Abba's total of UK No.1s.

NO.880
11 NOV ●
MY LOVE (3.52)
Westlife (Pelle Nylen, Per Magnusson, David Kreuger, Jörgen Elofsson). The quintet's

seventh single, seventh No.1 and seventh ballad deposed Elvis as the act to accumulate seven No.1s in the shortest time. It took them 18 months. (B-side: If I Let You Go)

NO.881
18 NOV ●
SAME OLD BRAND NEW YOU (3.46)
a1 (Eric Foster White, Ben Adams, Mark Read, Christian Ingebrigtsen).
The first boy band quartet to have two chart-toppers (separated by just nine weeks) co-wrote and played on this track. (B-sides: One in Love / Funkin' Up / Funkin' Up [remix])

NO.882
25 NOV ●
CAN'T FIGHT THE MOONLIGHT (3.35)
LeAnn Rimes (Diane Warren). The fourth teenager and 11th solo female singer to have a No.1 record in 2000. The song, produced by Trevor Horn, was used in the film Coyote Ugly. (B-side: But I Do Love You) US 71

NO.883
2 DEC ●
INDEPENDENT WOMEN PART 1 (3.43)
Destiny's Child (Samuel Barnes, Jean Olivier, Cory Rooney, Beyoncé Knowles).
The first of two chart-topping girl power anthems for Charlie's Angels. They were the first US female trio to top the chart since The Three Degrees in 1974. US 1

NO.884
9 DEC ●
NEVER HAD A DREAM COME TRUE (3.59)
S Club 7 (Cathy Dennis, Simon Ellis).
A Christmas ballad, performed by the group of the moment, with all proceeds going to charity. How could it fail? (B-sides: Perfect Christmas / Reach [remix]) US 10

NO.885
16 DEC ●
STAN (5.33)
Eminem (Marshall Mathers, Dido Armstrong, Paul Herman).
The haunting track that launched the career of Dido by sampling 'Thank You' tells the dark tale of an obsessed fan who drives off a bridge with his pregnant wife in the boot when Eminem doesn't reply to his letters. (B-sides: Get You Mad / My Name Is) US 51

NO.886
23 DEC ●●●
CAN WE FIX IT? (3.07)
Bob the Builder (Paul K Joyce).
The biggest-selling single of 2000 (853,151 in three weeks) was the 42nd No.1 of the year. It featured the voice of actor Neil Morrissey and

denied Westlife their eighth consecutive No.1. (B-side: Bob's Line Dance)

NO.887
13 JAN ●
TOUCH ME (3.30)
Rui Da Silva featuring Cassandra
(Rui Da Silva, Cassandra Fox).
The first Portuguese act to have a UK hit single, let alone a No.1, brought the total number of countries with chart-topping success in the UK to 20.

NO.888
20 JAN ●
LOVE DON'T COST A THING (3.43)
Jennifer Lopez (Damon Sharpe, Greg Lawson, Georgette Franklin, Jeremy Monroe, Amille Harris). Produced by Birmingham's Ric Wake, the demanding, materialistic J-Lo was not fooling anyone with this ironically titled single, which played over the closing credits of her film The Wedding Planner. (B-side: On the 6 Megamix) US 3

NO.889
27 JAN ●●
ROLLIN' (3.35)
Limp Bizkit (Wes Borland, Sam Rivers, John Otto, Fred Durst).
Subtitled 'Air Raid Vehicle' and censored for its X-rated language, this self-penned rock anthem was taken from the album Chocolate Starfish and the Hot Dog Flavored Water. (B-side: Take a Look Around [live]) US 65

NO.890
10 FEB ●●●●
WHOLE AGAIN (3.05)
Atomic Kitten (Stuart Kershaw, Andy McCluskey, Bill Padleey, Jeremy Godfrey). The pregnant Kerry Katona sang on the single, only to be replaced by Precious girl Jenny Frost, who reaped the rewards of the Kittens' success. (B-side: Holiday)

NO.891
10 MAR ●
IT WASN'T ME (3.49)
Shaggy featuring Ricardo 'Rikrok' Ducent
(Orville Burrell, Ricardo Ducent, Shaun Pizzonia, Brian Thompson).
This cheeky transatlantic smash, in which Shaggy denied all knowledge of a sexual encounter with the girl next door, was inspired by an Eddie Murphy comedy routine in the film Raw. It sold a total of 1,180,700 copies in the UK. (B-side: Dance and Shout [remix]) US 1

NO.892
17 MAR ●

UPTOWN GIRL (3.08)
Westlife (Billy Joel). The group's eighth No.1 broke their string of eight consecutive ballads. Model Claudia Schiffer appeared in the video, in place of Joel's original 'uptown girl', Christie Brinkley. (B-side: Angels Wings)

NO.893
24 MAR ●●●

PURE AND SIMPLE (3.46)
Hear'Say
(Peter Kirtley, Tim Hawes, Alison Clarkson).
A 25-week stay in the Top 75 netted sales of 1,078,400 for the Popstars winners and signalled the birth of reality TV's assault on the charts. It was co-written by rapper Betty Boo (Clarkson). (B-sides: Bridge over Troubled Water / Can't Stop Thinkin' about You)

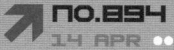

NO.894
14 APR ●●

WHAT TOOK YOU SO LONG (3.44)
Emma Bunton (Martin Harrington, Richard Stannard, Julian Gallagher, Emma Bunton, John Themis, David Morgan). The Spice Girls became the only group with four chart-topping solo members when this single went to No.1. It also left Victoria as the only Spice Girl without a solo No.1. (B-sides: [Hey You] Free Up Your Mind / Merry-Go Round)

NO.895
28 APR ●

SURVIVOR (4.00)
Destiny's Child (Beyoncé Knowles, Anthony Dent, Mathew Knowles). The sassy trio stormed into the record books as the first American female group to have two No.1 singles in the UK. Co-written by father and daughter, the song was inspired by the US reality TV show of the same name. (B-sides: Independent Women [live] / So Good) **US 2**

NO.896
5 MAY ●
26 MAY ●

DON'T STOP MOVIN' (3.54)
S Club 7
(Simon Ellis, Sheppard Solomon, S Club 7).

The first single since All Saints in 1998 to return to the top and their second consecutive No.1 to knock a Destiny's Child single off the top. (B-side: Right Guy)

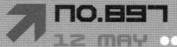

NO.897
12 MAY ●●

IT'S RAINING MEN (3.47)
Geri Halliwell (Paul Jabara, Paul Shaffer). Hallelujah! Geri's record-breaking fourth consecutive No.1 is a feat achieved by no other female solo artist. The song, a favourite in the gay clubs, was made famous by The Weather Girls. (B-sides: I Was Made That Way / Brave New World)

NO.898
2 JUN ●

DO YOU REALLY LIKE IT (3.22)
**DJ Pied Piper
and The Masters of Ceremonies**
(Eugene Nwohia, Ronald Nwohia, Steve Wickham, Paul Newman, Ashley Livingstone). More than 148,500 people liked this garage track enough in its first seven days of release to ensure a No.1.

↘ **CHART-TOPPER NO.893, 902:** TV's Popstars Hear'Say spent a total of four weeks at the top in 2001. Of the original line-up, only Kym Marsh went on to grab a solo hit single, just missing out on the top spot with 'Cry' in 2003. And yes, that is Louis Walsh behind Kim in the picture!

NO.899
9 JUN •••
ANGEL (3.32)
Shaggy featuring Rayvon (Orville Burrell, Ahmet Ertegun, Eddie Curtis, Chip Taylor, Ricardo Ducent, Nigel Staff, Shaun Pizzonia, Dave Kelly, Steve Miller). The 13th different charting 'Angel' featured excerpts from Merrilee Rush's 'Angel of the Morning' and Steve Miller Band's 'The Joker'. **US 1**

NO.900
30 JUN •
LADY MARMALADE (4.26)
Christina Aguilera, Lil' Kim, Mya and Pink (Bob Crewe, Kenny Nolan). The feisty foursome enquired "Voulez-vous coucher avec moi ce soir?" just three years after All Saints took the LaBelle classic – originally recorded by The Eleventh Hour – to No.1. **US 1**

NO.901
7 JUL •
THE WAY TO YOUR LOVE (3.15)
Hear'Say
(Mikkel S Eriksen, Hallgeir Rustan, Tor Erik Hermansen). The Popstars found their way back to No.1, selling nearly half a million fewer copies in seven days than 'Pure and Simple' did in its first week in the shops. (B-sides: Look Inside Yourself / Pure and Simple [remix])

NO.902
14 JUL •
ANOTHER CHANCE (3.27)
Roger Sanchez (Roger Sanchez, Steve Lukather). The renowned DJ, producer and record label owner sampled Toto's 'I Won't Hold You Back' on this track.

NO.903
21 JUL ••
ETERNITY (5.01) /
THE ROAD TO MANDALAY (3.57)
Robbie Williams
(Robbie Williams, Guy Chambers). The flamboyant showman offered up another reflective 'Angels' and 'She's the One'-styled tear-jerker ('Eternity'), which secured the 10th No.1 of his career. (B-side: Toxic)

NO.904
4 AUG ••
ETERNAL FLAME (3.12)
Atomic Kitten
(Susanna Hoffs, Billy Steinberg, Tom Kelly). This Bangles favourite became the first single to top the chart twice by two different female-fronted acts and, for the first time, it led an all-female group top two with runners-up Destiny's Child. (B-side: Album Medley)

NO.905
18 AUG •
21 SECONDS (2.42)
So Solid Crew
(Dwayne Vincent, Ashley Walters, Jermaine Williams, Shane Neil, Lisa Maffia, Michael Harvey, Marvin Dawkins, Jason Moore, Darren Weir, Jason Phillips, Mahtari Aminu). Nine Crew members had just 21 seconds to impress with a rap on the mic on this frenetic track. Several members, notably Maffia and Romeo, diced with solo careers.

NO.906
25 AUG ••
LET'S DANCE (3.34)
Five (Martin Harrington, Ash Howes, Julian Gallagher, Richard Stannard, Richard Breen, Sean Conlon, Jason Brown). The funky 'Let's Dance', not to be confused with Bowie's 'Let's Dance', gave the group their third and final No.1. (B-side: Sometimes)

NO.907
8 SEP •
TOO CLOSE (3.46)
Blue (Keir Gist, Darren Lighty, Robert Huggar, Raphael Brown, Robert Ford, Denzil Miller, James Moore, Kurt Walker, Lawrence Smith). The original version, by American R&B group Next, stalled at No.24 in 1998 but gave boy band Blue their first taste of No.1.

NO.908
15 SEP •
MAMBO NO.5 (3.17)
Bob the Builder (Perez Prado, Lou Bega, Christian Pletschacher). The animated handyman's second No.1 repeated the success of Lou Bega's 1999 version of a song written by Prado in 1950. (B-side: Super Spud)

NO.909
22 SEP ••
HEY BABY (UHH, AHH) (3.36)
DJ Otzi (Bruce Channel, Margaret Cobb). The year's cheesy summer anthem arrived courtesy of Austrian DJ Gerry Friedle and his take on Bruce Channel's 1962 original. (B-side: Uh! Ah!)

NO.910
29 SEP ••••
CAN'T GET YOU OUT OF MY HEAD (3.47)
Kylie Minogue (Cathy Dennis, Rob Davis). Kylie's unforgettable white dress propelled this single past the million sales barrier (1,037,235) in the UK, and it sold more than three million worldwide. Sophie Ellis-Bextor turned down the chance to record it. (B-sides: Boy / Rendezvous at Sunset) **US 7**

NO.911
27 OCT •••
BECAUSE I GOT HIGH (3.17)
Afroman
(Joseph Foreman). The American rapper wrote this controversial ditty – the most popular mobile phone ring tone of 2002 – about the joys of smoking pot when he was still at junior high school. (B-sides: Let's All Get Drunk / Back on the Bus) **US 13**

NO.912
17 NOV •
QUEEN OF MY HEART (4.22)
Westlife (Steve McCutcheon, Wayne Hector, Steve Robson, John McLaughlin). The group's ninth No.1 equalled the chart-topping feats of Abba and the Spice Girls and took them clear of Take That's total of eight No.1s. (B-sides: When You're Looking Like That / Reason for Living)

NO.913
24 NOV •
IF YOU COME BACK (3.23)
Blue (Ray Ruffin, Nicole Formescu, Ian Hope, Lee Brennan). Duncan, Anthony, Lee and Simon returned to No.1 just 12 weeks after their first visit with a song co-written by Brennan, formerly of boy band 911.

NO.914
1 DEC •
HAVE YOU EVER (3.20)
S Club 7 (Cathy Dennis, Andrew Frampton, Christopher Braide). This charity smoocher was the group's fourth and final No.1. No mixed boy / girl group has had more UK No.1s. (B-side: Dangerous)

NO.915
8 DEC ••
12 JAN 2002 •
GOTTA GET THRU THIS (2.44)
Daniel Bedingfield
(Daniel Bedingfield).
The versatile New Zealander recorded this track in his bedroom. Unusually, it returned to the top in the quiet early sales period in 2002 with what was then the lowest weekly sale for a No.1 – 25,354.

NO.916
22 DEC •••
SOMETHIN' STUPID (2.50)
Robbie Williams and Nicole Kidman (Carson C Parks). Originally a No.1 for Frank and Nancy Sinatra in 1967, 'Somethin' Stupid' was the 27th song to reach the top in two different versions. (B-sides: Eternity [orchestral version] / My Way [live])

2002

↗ NO.917
19 JAN •

MORE THAN A WOMAN (3.10)
Aaliyah (Tim Mosley, Stephen Garrett). The first of two consecutive posthumous No.1s. Aaliyah had 15 hits under her belt but no chart-topper before her tragic death made her recordings more popular than ever. **US 25**

↗ NO.918
26 JAN •

MY SWEET LORD (RE-ISSUE) (4.38)
George Harrison (George Harrison). The writer of the 10th posthumous chart-topper was, in 1976, successfully sued for "subconsciously plagiarising" The Chiffons' 'He's So Fine' on this track. It emulated 'Bohemian Rhapsody' as the only single to top the chart on two separate occasions. (B-side: Let It Down)

↗ NO.919
2 FEB ••••

HERO (4.11)
Enrique (Paul Barry, Enrique Iglesias, Mark Taylor). Julio's son took our breath away with a romantic ballad that became a post-11 September salute to America's fallen heroes. (B-side: Bailamos) **US 3**

↗ NO.920
2 MAR •

WORLD OF OUR OWN (3.30)
Westlife (Steve Mac, Wayne Hector). Another uptempo track from the boy band balladeers, who achieved the lowest first-week sales of their career to date – 75,000 – but still notched up a 10th No.1. (B-sides: Crying Girl / Angel)

↗ NO.921
9 MAR •••

EVERGREEN (4.10) /
ANYTHING IS POSSIBLE (3.40)
Will Young (Jörgen Elofsson, Per Magnusson, David Kreuger / Cathy Dennis, Christopher Braide). The best-selling single of 2002 (1,779,919) and 11th best-seller of all time sold more than 385,000 copies on the first day of release for the Pop Idol winner.

↗ NO.922
30 MAR ••••

UNCHAINED MELODY (3.52)
Gareth Gates (Alex North, Hy Zaret). The fourth version of this timeless classic to reach No.1 sold 1,318,700 in total as Pop Idol runner-up dethroned the Pop Idol winner. Gates was also the youngest British male solo star to have a No.1, wiping Craig

Douglas' name from the record books. (B-sides: Evergreen / Anything Is Possible)

↗ NO.923
27 APR •

THE HINDU TIMES (3.52)
Oasis (Noel Gallagher). Eight years, 16 Top 40 hits and six No.1s into their career, the Britpop survivors returned with a swaggering rock 'n' roll anthem that also went to No.1 in Italy and Canada. (B-sides: Just Getting Older / Idler's Dream)

↗ NO.924
4 MAY •

FREAK LIKE ME (3.36)
Sugababes (Mark Valentine, Eugene Hanes, Loren Hill, William Collins, George Clinton, Gary Cooper, Gary Numan). Keisha, Mutya and new babe Heidi's first No.1 was based on a bootleg that gave the Adina Howard original and Numan's sampled 'Are 'Friends' Electric?' a new audience. (B-side: Breathe Easy)

↗ NO.925
11 MAY •

KISS KISS (3.26)
Holly Valance (Juliette Jaimes, Steve Welton-Jaimes, Aksu Sezen). The third Neighbours actor turned singer to have a UK No.1 covered Turkish heart-throb Tarkan's saucy ditty 'Simarik'.

↗ NO.926
18 MAY •

IF TOMORROW NEVER COMES (3.35)
Ronan Keating (Garth Brooks, Kent Blazy). This poignant yet lyrically depressing ballad, originally on country giant Garth Brooks' self-titled debut album, called for lovers everywhere to live for the moment. (B-side: Sea of Love)

↗ NO.927
25 MAY •

JUST A LITTLE (3.46)
Liberty X (Michelle Escoffery, George Hammond Hagan, John Hammond Hagan). The Popstars finalists who failed to make it into Hear'Say had to wait just a little over six months for their first No.1. (B-sides: Breathe / Thinking It Over)

↗ NO.928
1 JUN •

WITHOUT ME (4.16)
Eminem (Marshall Mathers, Jeff Bass, Anne Dudley, Kevin Bell, Trevor Horn, Malcolm McLaren). With a little help from 'Buffalo Gals', Eminem was the first rapper to become a three-time chart-topper with a song that name-checked Elvis, Moby, Prince and Limp Bizkit. (B-side: The Way I Am) **US 2**

↗ NO.929
8 JUN ••

LIGHT MY FIRE (3.31)
Will Young (Jim Morrison, John Densmore, Robby Krieger, Ray Manzarek). More José Feliciano than The Doors, the Pop Idol winner's cover version sold 177,000 in its first week – a far cry from the 1,108,269 copies 'Evergreen' / 'Anything Is Possible' shifted in seven days. (B-sides: Ain't No Sunshine / Beyond the Sea)

↗ NO.930
22 JUN ••••

A LITTLE LESS CONVERSATION (3.33) **Elvis vs JXL** (Billy Strange, Mac Davis). The King's record-breaking 18th No.1 and his first since 'Way Down' in 1977. Elvis's 114th hit, a chart flop when it was first released in 1968, was given a new lease of life by a TV advert and JXL, aka Dutch producer Tom Holkenborg. **US 50**

↗ NO.931
20 JUL •••

ANYONE OF US (STUPID MISTAKE) (3.48)
Gareth Gates (Per Magnusson, David Kreuger, Jörgen Elofsson). The first male solo artist since Shakin' Stevens in 1981 to register two No.1 singles that spent three or more weeks at the top. (B-side: Forever Blue)

↗ NO.932
10 AUG ••

COLOURBLIND (3.36)
Darius (Pete Glenister, Darius Danesh, Deni Lew). After his publicity-grabbing Pop Idol version of Britney's ' … Baby One More Time' came one of pop's great ironies: the 21-year-old Glaswegian saw off Britney's 'Boys' to land the No.1. (B-side: It's Not Unusual [live])

↗ NO.933
24 AUG •

ROUND ROUND (3.55)
Sugababes (Brian Higgins, Miranda Cooper, Lisa Cowling, Tim Powell, Nick Coler, Sugababes, Florian Pflüger, Felix Stecher, Robin Hoffman, Rino Spadavecchia). Twelve writers had a hand in the girls' second No.1, including the members of Germany's Dublex Inc, who penned the sampled 'Tango Forte'. (B-sides: Groove Is Going On / Freak Like Me [remix])

↗ NO.934
31 AUG •

CROSSROADS (3.12)
Blazin' Squad (Blazin' Squad, Bone DJ, Uneek). The 10-member Walthamstow collective,

10 the week she claimed her first solo No.1. (B-side: Get the Party Started [live]) **US 8**

THE LONG AND WINDING ROAD
(3.28) / **SUSPICIOUS MINDS** (3.57)
Will Young and Gareth Gates / Gareth Gates (John Lennon, Paul McCartney / Francis Zambon). These two classics by The Beatles and Elvis were given a Pop Idol makeover, handing Lennon and McCartney their 29th and 28th No.1s respectively as songwriters. (B-side: I Get the Sweetest Feeling)

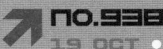

THE KETCHUP SONG (ASEREJE)
(3.33) **Las Ketchup**
(Manuel Ruiz, Manny Benito). Pilar, Lola and Lucia Munoz (daughters of Spanish flamenco guitarist Antonio 'el Tomate' Fernandez) brought their catchy European summer smash, loosely based on 'Rapper's Delight', to the UK and baffled everybody with its nonsensical lyrics. **US 54**

DILEMMA (3.54)
Nelly featuring Kelly Rowland
(Kenny Gamble, Bunny Sigler, Cornell Haynes, Antoine Macon). Based on a sample of Patti LaBelle's 'Love, Need and Want You'. Blue, U2 and even Justin Timberlake's debut solo single failed to loosen the pair's grip on No.1. (B-side: Kings Highway) **US 1**

NO.940
9 NOV •
HEAVEN (3.37)
DJ Sammy and Yanou featuring Do
(Bryan Adams, Jim Vallance). Samuel Bouriah (aka DJ Sammy) became the fifth Spanish act to top the chart with a cover of the Bryan Adams classic from 1985. **US 8**

NO.941
16 NOV •
UNBREAKABLE (4.31)
Westlife (Jörgen Elofsson, John Reid). Spurred on by the title, some people tested the theory on the group's CDs, but Westlife remained unbreakable – and unstoppable – with an 11th No.1. (B-side: Never Knew I Was Losing You)

NO.942
23 NOV ••
DIRRTY (4.01)
Christina Aguilera featuring Redman (Dana Stinson, Christina Aguilera, Balewa

↘ **CHART-TOPPER NO.939:** Rhyming duo Nelly and Kelly's 'Dilemma' was related to infidelity, and caused confusion in the UK with Kelly's mention of her 'Boo'. This is US slang for boyfriend, derived from the French 'beau'

touted as a "poppier So Solid Crew", rapped their way to the summit with a cover of Bone Thugs-N-Harmony's 'Tha Crossroads'. (B-side: Uproar)

NO.935
7 SEP •••
THE TIDE IS HIGH (GET THE FEELING) (3.27)
Atomic Kitten (John Holt, Howard Barrett, Tyrone Evans). The first female trio to have

three No.1 singles. One of only two songs to top the chart twice by two different female-fronted acts. The other? 'Eternal Flame'. (B-sides: Album Medley / Dancing in the Street)

NO.936
28 SEP •
JUST LIKE A PILL (3.54)
Pink (Pink, Dallas Austin).
The colourful Alecia Moore was one of a record-equalling seven new entries in the Top

Muhammad, Jasper Cameron, Reggie Noble). This song's raunchy video depicted a scantily clad Aguilera as a fighter and was banned in Thailand because, unbeknown to director David LaChapelle, posters surrounding the boxing ring promoted the country's sex industry. (B-side: I Will Be) **US 48**

↗ NO.943
7 DEC ●

IF YOU'RE NOT THE ONE (4.20)
Daniel Bedingfield (Daniel Bedingfield). This heartfelt ballad, which claimed pole position exactly one year after 'Gotta Get Thru This' did the same, was labelled as a modern classic by acid-tongued Pop Idol judge Simon Cowell. (B-side: James Dean [I Wanna Know] [acoustic]) **US 15**

↗ NO.944
14 DEC ●

LOSE YOURSELF (5.25)
Eminem
(Marshall Mathers, Jeff Bass, Luis Resto). This Oscar and Grammy-winning single was taken from the soundtrack of 8 Mile, the foul-

mouthed rapper's movie debut, and topped the US Billboard Hot 100 for 11 weeks. (B-side: Renegade – Eminem featuring Jay-Z) **US 1**

↗ NO.945
21 DEC ●

SORRY SEEMS TO BE THE HARDEST WORD (3.29)
Blue featuring Elton John
(Elton John, Bernie Taupin). A fifth No.1 for Elton and a third for Blue. It was the former's fifth original track to be re-recorded – either solo or as a duet – since 1991.
(B-side: Lonely This Christmas – Blue)

↗ NO.946
28 DEC ●●●●

SOUND OF THE UNDERGROUND (3.40) **Girls Aloud**
(Miranda Cooper, Niara Scarlett, Brian Higgins, Xenomania). This single led a Christmas top three of acts who appeared on Popstars: The Rivals, shutting out boy band winners One True Voice and The Cheeky Girls with first-week sales of more than 213,000. (B-side: Stay Another Day)

2003

↗ NO.947
25 JAN ●●

STOP LIVING THE LIE (3.51)
David Sneddon (David Sneddon). The Fame Academy winner sold 108,000 copies for his first week at No.1, but he was living a lie and called time on his career before the end of the year.
(B-sides: Goodnight Girl / Don't Let the Sun Go Down on Me [acoustic])

↗ NO.948
8 FEB ●●●●

ALL THE THINGS SHE SAID (3.28)
t.A.T.u. (Sergei Galoyan, Trevor Horn, Martin Kierszenbaum, Elena Kiper, Valerij Polienko). Surpassing the achievements of PPK and Alsou, the only other charting Russians, Julia and Lena stoked the tabloid rumour mill about their sexuality and then disappeared without trace after performing at the Eurovision Song Contest. (B-side: Stars) **US 20**

↘ **CHART-TOPPER NO.837, 900, 942, 949:** With four No.1s in four years from 1999, 2004 was a relatively quiet chart year for Christina Aguilera, although she did still set pulses racing in that bouncy TV commercial for a well-known mobile phone company

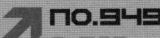

NO.949
8 MAR ●●

BEAUTIFUL (3.58)
Christina Aguilera (Linda Perry). Perry's first No.1 after stalling at No.2 with both Pink's 'Get the Party Started' and 'What's Up', her biggest hit as a member of the group 4 Non Blondes. She intended to release this ballad as her own comeback single. (B-side: Dirrty (remix) – Christina Aguilera featuring Redman) **US 2**

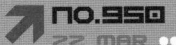

NO.950
22 MAR ●●

SPIRIT IN THE SKY (3.27)
Gareth Gates featuring The Kumars (Norman Greenbaum). A chart-topper for composer Greenbaum (1970) and Doctor and the Medics (1986), Gates's version featured TV family The Kumars and was a fundraiser for Comic Relief. (B-side: Dance Again)

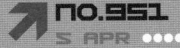

NO.951
5 APR ●●●●

MAKE LUV (3.30)
Room 5 featuring Oliver Cheatham (Oliver Cheatham, Kevin McCord). The work of Belgian-based Italian DJ and producer Vito Lucente (Junior Jack), with 55-year-old Cheatham's re-recorded vocals from his minor 1983 hit 'Get Down Saturday Night'.

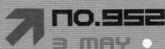

NO.952
3 MAY ●

YOU SAID NO (2.46)
Busted (James Bourne, Matt Jay, Charlie Simpson, Steve Robson, John McLaughlin). 'You Said No' made the step to No.1 after the band's first two hits peaked at No.3 and No.2 respectively. (B-side: Mrs Robinson)

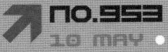

NO.953
10 MAY ●

LONELINESS (2.42)
Tomcraft (Eniac, Andrea Martin, Ivan Matias, Edmund Clement). Tomcraft is German DJ Thomas Bruckner. 'Loneliness' started out as an instrumental, on to which was placed the vocals of British singer Vivian.

NO.954
17 MAY ●●●●

IGNITION (3.05)
R Kelly (R Kelly). The first record to enjoy an increase in sales while at No.1 (by just 3 per cent) since Enrique's 'Hero'. (B-sides: Apologies of a Thug / Who's That – R Kelly & Fat Joe) **US 2**

NO.955
14 JUN ●●●●

BRING ME TO LIFE (3.56)
Evanescence featuring Paul McCoy (David Hodges, Amy Lee, Ben Moody). This "piano ballad turned riff-driven barnburner", from the Daredevil soundtrack, featured the lead singer from US rock band 12 Stones. (B-side: Farther Away) **US 6**

NO.956
12 JUL ●●●

CRAZY IN LOVE (3.56)
Beyoncé (Beyoncé Knowles, Rich Hamilton, Shawn Carter, Eugene Record). This booty-shaking transatlantic smash, the only UK and US chart-topper of 2003, featured Beyoncé's boyfriend, Jay-Z, and sampled the horn section from The Chi-Lites' 'Are You My Woman (Tell Me So)'. (B-side: Summertime) **US 1**

NO.957
2 AUG ●

NEVER GONNA LEAVE YOUR SIDE (3.55) **Daniel Bedingfield** (Daniel Bedingfield). The fifth single from the album 'Gotta Get Thru This' was his last chart smash before a car crash in his native New Zealand put his career on hold. (B-side: Right Girl (live))

NO.958
9 AUG ●●●●

BREATHE (3.47)
Blu Cantrell featuring Sean Paul (Andrea Martin, Ivan Matias, Richard Bembery, Melvin Bradford, Stefan Harris, Alvin Joyner, Marshall Mathers, Charles Aznavour). The 12th song since Cher's 'Believe' to enjoy four weeks at the top, 'Breathe' sampled Eminem ('What's the Difference') and Aznavour ('Parce Que (Tu Crois)'. **US 99**

NO.959
6 SEP ●

ARE YOU READY FOR LOVE (3.30)
Elton John (Thom Bell, Leroy M Bell, Casey Jones). Originally a No.42 hit for the Rocket Man in 1979, DJs finally tapped the song's dancefloor potential 24 years later and blasted it into orbit. (B-side: Three Way Love Affair)

NO.960
13 SEP ●●●●●●

WHERE IS THE LOVE? (3.49)
Black Eyed Peas (Will Adams, Allan Pineda, Jaime Gomez, Justin Timberlake, Michael Fratantuno, George Pajon Jr, Printz Board). It took seven songwriters, a 40-piece orchestra and Justin Timberlake's guest vocals to produce the biggest seller of 2003. It shifted 625,198 copies during its 19 weeks on the chart. (B-side: Sumthin' for That Ass)

NO.961
25 OCT ●

HOLE IN THE HEAD (3.37)
Sugababes (Brian Higgins, Miranda Cooper, Tim Powell, Nick Coler, Mutya Buena, Heidi Range, Keisha Buchanan, Niara Scarlett). As they did with 'Round Round', the three girls co-wrote their third chart-topper, taken from their third album, 'Three'. (B-side: Who) **US 96**

NO.962
1 NOV ●●

BE FAITHFUL (2.44)
Fatman Scoop featuring The Crooklyn Clan (Edmund Bini, Joseph Rizzo, Isaac Freeman, Sean Combs, Faith Evans, Ronald Lawrence, Shondrae Crawford, Clarence Emery, Bernard Edwards, Nile Rodgers, Andres Titus, William McLean, Johnny Hammond Smith, Allen Jones, James Elxander, Ben Cauley). The New York-based hip hop DJ (Isaac Freeman III) finally struck gold five years after this track was recorded. It sampled 'Love Like This' by Faith Evans, who is one of 16 credited co-writers.

NO.963
15 NOV ●

SLOW (3.13)
Kylie Minogue (Emiliana Torrini, Dan Carey, Kylie Minogue). The Aussie songstress's first No.1 as a co-writer came from her third consecutive album to spawn a first single No.1. (B-side: Soul on Fire)

NO.964
22 NOV ●

CRASHED THE WEDDING (2.39)
Busted (James Bourne, Tom Fletcher). Britney Spears and Madonna's much-publicised duet had to settle for No.2 when this single became the band's second chart-topper. (B-sides: Build Me Up Buttercup / That's Entertainment)

NO.965
29 NOV ●

MANDY (3.16)
Westlife (Scott English, Richard Kerr). The all-conquering Irish boy band returned to familiar territory (a Shadows-equalling 12th No.1) with a cover of a ballad made famous by Barry Manilow in 1975. (B-side: Flying without Wings)

NO.966
6 DEC ●●

LEAVE RIGHT NOW (3.33)
Will Young (Francis Eg White). The original Pop Idol's fourth chart-topper from five attempts nearly lost out to Shane Richie when record store stocks ran low midweek. (B-sides: Ticket to Love / Cry)

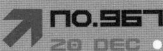

NO.967
20 DEC ●

CHANGES (4.08)
Kelly and Ozzy Osbourne (Tommy Iommi,

Terry Butler, Bill Ward, Ozzy Osbourne).
The second father-and-daughter
collaboration, after Frank and Nancy Sinatra,
to reach No.1. The ballad originally appeared
on Black Sabbath's 1972 LP 'Black Sabbath
Vol 4'. (B-side: Dig Me Out [live])

↗ NO.968
27 DEC ●●●

MAD WORLD (3.03)
Michael Andrews featuring Gary Jules
(Roland Orzabal). Fifty dollars and 90 minutes
was all it took to rework the Tears for Fears
classic. It only just pipped the much-fancied
Darkness to become the Christmas No.1.
(B-side: No Poetry)

↗ NO.969
17 JAN ●●●

ALL THIS TIME (4.22)
Michelle
(Steve Mac, Wayne Hector, Neil Tennant).
Pop Idol winner Michelle McManus equalled
Lena Martell's 25-year record for the most
consecutive weeks at No.1 by a Scottish
female when she spent a third week at the
top. (B-side: On the Radio)

↗ NO.970
7 FEB ●●

**TAKE ME TO THE CLOUDS
ABOVE** (2.49)
LMC vs U2 (George Merrill, Shannon
Rubicam, Narada Michael Walden, U2).
A dance track that fused U2's 'With or Without
You' with the opening lines of Whitney
Houston's 'How Will I Know'. Rachel
McFarlane is the uncredited vocalist.

↗ NO.971
21 FEB ●

**WITH A LITTLE HELP
FROM MY FRIENDS** (3.06) /
MEASURE OF A MAN (2.19)
Sam & Mark (John Lennon, Paul McCartney /
Cathy Dennis, Steve Morales, David Siegel).
The fifth Pop Idol act to register a UK No.1 and
the third act to take the Lennon and
McCartney composition to the top after Joe
Cocker (1968) and Wet Wet Wet (1988).

↗ NO.972
28 FEB ●

WHO'S DAVID (3.31)
Busted (James Bourne, Tom Fletcher).
So who was David? Nobody in particular.
"I just chose David because it rhymed with
the word invaded!" confirmed band member
Bourne. (B-side: Teenage Kicks)

↗ NO.973
6 MAR ●

MYSTERIOUS GIRL (3.36)
Peter Andre
(Peter Andre, Peter Jacobs, Oliver Jacobs,
Glen Goldsmith, Bubbler Ranx).
An appearance on TV's I'm a Celebrity …
fuelled the re-release of a song that originally
peaked at No.53 in 1995 and reached No.2
when it was re-issued in 1996.

↗ NO.974
13 MAR ●

TOXIC (3.20)
Britney Spears
(Cathy Dennis, Christian Karlsson, Pontus
Winnberg, Henrick Jonback). Britney's fourth
No.1 – her first since 2000 – sold 102,576
copies in the first week. It was accompanied
by another provocative video. **US 9**

↗ NO.975
28 MAR ●

CHA CHA SLIDE (3.41)
DJ Casper
(Marvel Thompson). The step-tastic 'Cha Cha
Slide', which, unusually, climbed to No.1 from
its No.2 chart debut, was first released in the
US in 2000. **US 83**

↗ NO.976
27 MAR ●●

YEAH! (4.13)
Usher featuring Lil' Jon & Ludacris
(Patrick Smith, Garrett Hamler (aka Sean
Garrett), James Phillips, La Marquis Jefferson,
Jonathan Smith, Chris Bridges, Robert
McDowell). Six years after his first No.1, this
transatlantic "crunk'n'B" smash became the
first track simultaneously to top the UK and
US singles charts since Beyoncé's 'Crazy in
Love'. (B-side: Red Light) **US 1**

↗ NO.977
10 APR ●●

5 COLOURS IN HER HAIR (2.58)
McFly (Tom Fletcher, Danny Jones, James
Bourne). Busted's best mates stormed the
chart with a catchy 60s-flavoured song. It
paid homage to the rainbow-locked Emily
Corrie from TV's As If. (B-side: Lola)

↗ NO.978
24 APR ●●●●

FK IT (I DON'T WANT YOU BACK)**
(3.48) **Eamon**
(Eamon Doyle, Kirk Robinson, Mark Passey).
The year's biggest seller until the penultimate
week of 2004 contained 33 expletives and
prompted its subject matter, (alleged)
ex-girlfriend Frankee, to record her scathing
reply … **US 16**

↗ NO.979
22 MAY ●●●

F.U.R.B. - F U RIGHT BACK (3.20)
Frankee
(Eamon Doyle, Frankee, Jennifer Graziano,
Mark Passey, Kirk Robinson). Released in
response to Eamon's 'F**k It (I Don't Want You
Back)', this X-rated track proved once and for
all that hell hath no fury like a 20-year-old
female vocalist scorned. **US 63**

↗ NO.980
12 JUN ●●

I DON'T WANNA KNOW (3.37)
Mario Winans featuring Enya & P Diddy
(Mario Winans, Enya, Rona Ryan, Nicky Ryan,
Lo Down, Chauncey Hawkins).
This unusual collaboration married Winans'
sultry vocals to the bad boy of rap, helped
along by Enya's soothing 'Boadicea' sample.
(B-side: Pretty Girl Bullshit – Mario Winans
and Foxy Brown) **US 2**

↗ NO.981
26 JUN ●

EVERYTIME (3.56)
Britney Spears
(Britney Spears, Annette Stamatelatos).
A controversial video that showed Britney
apparently drowning in a bath propelled
this ballad to No.1. It was written about her
ex-boyfriend, Justin Timberlake.

↗ NO.982
3 JUL ●

OBVIOUSLY (3.19)
McFly (Tom Fletcher, Danny Jones, James
Bourne). Danny, Tom, Dougie and Harry's
second 60s-flavoured single, like their first,
was co-written by Bourne from mentors
Busted. (B-side: Help / Interview with McFly)

↗ NO.983
10 JUL ●●

BURN (4.16)
Usher (Brian Cox, Jermaine Dupri, Usher
Raymond). This ballad followed in the
footsteps of 'Yeah!' to become Usher's
second consecutive transatlantic No.1. He
spent a record-breaking 28 weeks at the top
of the US Billboard Hot 100 in 2004.

↗ NO.984
24 JUL ●

LOLA'S THEME (3.20)
Shapeshifters
(Simon Marlin, Max Reich, Karen Poole,
Gianni Bini, Fulvio Perniola, Patrick Moten).
This euphoric club classic contained elements
of two songs – Anthony White's 'Love Me
Tonight' and Johnnie Taylor's 'What About My
Love'. Lola was Shapeshifter Marlin's wife.

↗ NO.985
31 JUL •

DRY YOUR EYES (4.32)
The Streets (Mike Skinner). Skinner was the first UK rapper to reach No.1. This tear-jerking ballad about love, loss and longing topped the singles chart the week his album returned to No.1. (B-side: It's Too Late [live])

↗ NO.986
7 AUG ••

THUNDERBIRDS (3.15) / **3AM** (3.16)
Busted (Lauren Christy, Scott Spock, Graham Edwards, James Bourne, Charlie Simpson, Matthew Sargeant, Barry Gray).
The seventh ITV Record of the Year ('Thunderbirds') gave the Suffolk outfit their fourth No.1, eighth successive top three hit and best first-week sale (70,665) to date.

↗ NO.987
21 AUG •

BABY CAKES (4.12)
3 of a Kind (Liana Caruana, Nicholas Gallante, Marc Portelli). This trio of DJs initially found an audience for the song on east London's underground pirate radio station Rinse FM before releasing it commercially.

↗ NO.988
28 AUG ••

THESE WORDS (3.36)
Natasha Bedingfield
(Natasha Bedingfield, Steve Kipner, Andrew Frampton, Wayne Wilkins). One half of the only chart-topping siblings (Daniel is her big brother) became the first No.1 to name-check poets Byron, Shelley and Keats in the same song. (B-side: Single [live])

↗ NO.989
11 SEP •

MY PLACE (3.45) /
FLAP YOUR WINGS (3.51)
Nelly (Nelly, Dorian Moore, Randy Edelman, Eddie DeBarge, William DeBarge, Etterlene Jordan, Kenny Gamble, Leon Huff / Nelly, Chad Hugo, Pharrell Williams). The Texan rapper's double A-side featured tracks from each of his simultaneously released albums, 'Suit' and 'Sweat'. (B-side: Hot in Herre) **US 4 / 52**

↗ NO.990
18 SEP •

REAL TO ME (3.42)
Brian McFadden (Guy Chambers, Brian McFadden). The former Westlifer notched up his 13th No.1, penned with Robbie Williams's former songwriting partner Chambers, and made a pledge to enjoy life's simple pleasures – picnics in the garden and English tea. (B-side: Uncomplicated)

↘ CHART-TOPPER NO.985: Mike Skinner (The Streets) recorded his debut album *Original Pirate Material* in his bedroom studio at home. If you listen closely to 'Turn the Page', you can hear his mother in the background telling him to 'turn the music down, it's dinner time'

↗ NO.991
25 SEP •••
23 OCT ••

CALL ON ME (3.03)
Eric Prydz (Eric Prydz, Steve Winwood, Will Jennings). The first Swedish chart-topper since Rednex in 1994 sampled the chorus of Steve Winwood's 'Valerie' and sold just 21,749 copies to secure a fifth, non-consecutive week at No.1 – a record low, at the time.

↗ NO.992
16 OCT •

RADIO (3.52)
Robbie Williams
(Robbie Williams, Stephen 'Tin Tin' Duffy). 'Radio', a product of his new songwriting partnership with 80s hit-maker Duffy, took his tally of No.1s to 13 – seven with Take That, five solo and his Christmas smash with Nicole Kidman. (B-side: Northern Town)

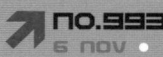

NO.993
6 NOV ●

WONDERFUL (4.32)
Ja Rule featuring R Kelly & Ashanti
(Jeffrey Atkins, Irving Lorenzo, Kendred Smith, Robert Kelly). The fourth and most successful collaborative hit for Ja Rule and Ashanti and a third No.1 for R Kelly.
(B-sides: Livin' It Up / Always on Time) **US 5**

NO.994
13 NOV ●

JUST LOSE IT (4.09)
Eminem (Marshall Mathers, Andre Young, Mike Elizondo, Mark Batson, Christopher

Pope). Complete with a video that poked fun at Michael Jackson, 'Just Lose It' featured the same "Guess who's back" intro as his 2002 No.1 'Without Me'. **US 6**

NO.995
28 NOV ●

VERTIGO (3.11)
U2
(Adam Clayton, David Evans, Paul Hewson, Larry Mullen). The Irish icons' sixth chart-topper and, for the first time, their second No.1 in succession. It had already topped the download chart, where it managed eight weeks at No.1. (B-side: Are You Gonna Wait Forever?) **US 31**

NO.996
27 NOV ●●

I'LL STAND BY YOU (3.39)
Girls Aloud
(Chrissie Hynde, Tom Kelly, Billy Steinberg). This 10-year-old Pretenders ballad took the "gift-wrapped kitty cats" back to No.1 for the first time since their debut single. It was chosen as the theme for the 25th anniversary of Children in Need. (B-side: Real Life)

NO.997
11 DEC ●●●●

DO THEY KNOW IT'S CHRISTMAS? (5.02) **Band Aid 20**
(Bob Geldof, Midge Ure). Bono, Paul McCartney, Dido, The Darkness and a rapping Dizzee Rascal were some of the performers on the third No.1 version of this song, with all proceeds aiding the disaster in Sudan. It sold 292,594 copies in its first week, ousted Eamon as the year's best-seller after two weeks and sold 1,065,749 copies by the end of the year.

2005

NO.998
8 JAN ●

AGAINST ALL ODDS (3:16)
Steve Brookstein (Phil Collins).
TV's X Factor winner took Collins's 1984 No.2 hit to the top for the second time this century. (See No.875). Unusually, it did not enter at No.1. (B-sides: Smile / Help Me Make It Through the Night)

NO.999
15 JAN ●

JAILHOUSE ROCK (RE-ISSUE) (2:10) **Elvis Presley**
(Jerry Leiber, Mike Stoller). The third single to return to the top (with a record 47-year gap) was the first of 17 re-issued No.1 hits for the King in less than four months.
(B-side: Treat Me Nice)

NO.1000
22 JAN ●

ONE NIGHT (RE-ISSUE) (2.32) /
I GOT STUNG (RE-ISSUE) (1.50)
Elvis Presley
(Dave Bartholomew, Pearl King / Aaron Schroeder, David Hill). This 46-year-old No.1 returned to the top with the lowest weekly sale ever for a chart-topper at 20,463. Side one was a "cleaned-up" version of a 1956 R&B hit by Smiley Lewis, and Elvis thought so little of the flip side that he refused to sing it on stage.

↘ **CHART-TOPPER NO.997:** 'Do They Know It's Christmas?' was easily the biggest-selling single of 2004. Here, participating Band Aid 20 vocalist Lemar receives the British Hit Singles special No.1 Award on ITV's CD:UK show, presented by Cat Deeley

No prizes for guessing who's top of this Top 20 of the most successful chart-topping acts. Stretching his lead over his closest rivals, The Beatles, Elvis has increased his lead at the top of this list with more chart-topping action in the 21st century.

Those pop legends with the longest chart careers obviously have an advantage in this rundown. However, acts that have lasted the course less successfully are still well represented. In this respect, a special mention should be reserved for the Spice Girls, whose ratio of nine UK No.1 singles from 10 hits is exceptional.

MOST NO.1 HITS

In the event of a tie the ratio of No.1s from the smallest number of hits is taken into account.

1.	ELVIS PRESLEY	20 No.1s	(138 hits)
2.	THE BEATLES	17 No.1s	(32 hits)
3.	CLIFF RICHARD	14 No.1s	(129 hits)
4.	WESTLIFE	12 No.1s	(17 hits)
5.	THE SHADOWS	12 No.1s	(63 hits)
6.	MADONNA	10 No.1s	(61 hits)
7.	SPICE GIRLS	9 No.1s	(10 hits)
8.	ABBA	9 No.1s	(27 hits)
9.	TAKE THAT	8 No.1s	(16 hits)
10.	THE ROLLING STONES	8 No.1s	(50 hits)
11.	GEORGE MICHAEL	7 No.1s	(32 hits)
12.	KYLIE MINOGUE	7 No.1s	(40 hits)
13.	MICHAEL JACKSON	7 No.1s	(55 hits)
14.	BOYZONE	6 No.1s	(16 hits)
15.	OASIS	6 No.1s	(21 hits)
= 16.	BLONDIE	6 No.1s	(22 hits)
= 16.	ROBBIE WILLIAMS	6 No.1s	(22 hits)
18.	SLADE	6 No.1s	(36 hits)
19.	U2	6 No.1s	(37 hits)
20.	QUEEN	6 No.1s	(52 hits)

All figures include re-issues and relate to the 1,000 No.1s from 14 November 1952 to 22 January 2005.

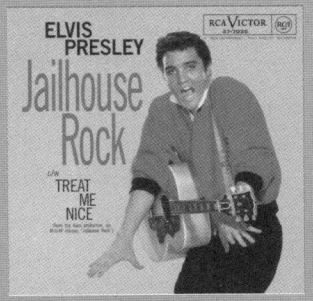

ELVIS PRESLEY
Jailhouse Rock
c/w TREAT ME NICE

⬏ THE ELVIS COLLECTOR'S BOX OF DELIGHTS: SONY BMG BEGAN RELEASING ALL ELVIS' UK NO.1 SINGLES, WEEK BY WEEK, FOLLOWING THE ANNIVERSARY OF HIS 70TH BIRTHDAY IN JANUARY 2005. 'JAILHOUSE ROCK' WAS THE FIRST SINGLE IN CHART HISTORY TO ENTER AT NO.1 WHEN ORIGINALLY RELEASED IN 1958. IT DID IT AGAIN IN 2005, BECOMING THE 999TH UK NO.1. A CONTROLLING INTEREST IN ELVIS' ESTATE HAD TAKEN PLACE JUST A MONTH BEFORE THE KING RETURNED TO THE TOP OF THE SINGLES CHART, WHEN LISA MARIE PRESLEY SOLD 85 PER CENT OF ELVIS PRESLEY ENTERPRISES TO NEW YORK BUSINESSMAN ROBERT FX SILLERMAN. THE PRICE? A REPORTED 100 MILLION DOLLARS.

↗ PICTURE CREDITS

THE TOP 100 SINGLES OF ALL TIME

085429

NOW AVAILABLE FOR KARAOKE

Exercise your vocal cords on the 100 greatest songs, as voted for by the readers of British Hit Singles.

Choose either the full seven disc CD+G set with an SRRP of £49.99 or the three disc Top 40 (40-song) version with an SRRP of £24.99. The discs will play audio on all CD/DVD players and display the lyrics of each hit on a CDG karaoke player. You can purchase CDG karaoke players from as little as £29.99 from www.easykaraoke.com Toys R Us and all good record and karaoke stores.

GOLD DISCS TO MARK THAT SPECIAL OCCASION

Maybe it's the No.1 for the day you were born or another key date in your life or that of a friend or loved one.

The Gold Disc.com has just the thing to create that perfect gift by matching your key dates to any of the 1,000 No.1 singles. The jukebox calculator at www.thegolddisc.com/jukebox.htm will give you the information you need, or you can search through the 1,000 No.1s section in this book.

The Gold Disc.com specialises in a selection of superb replica discs in three sizes (7", 10" and 12") and CD presentations to celebrate great singles and albums for great occasions. For further details visit www.thegolddisc.com/bhs.htm

Or write to:
GOLD DISC INFORMATION
British Hit Singles & Albums
Guinness World Records
338 Euston Road
London NW1 3BD

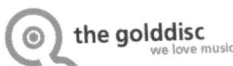